ARCTIC OCEAN

SVALBARD
(NORWAY)

Barents Sea

FINLAND
Helsinki

Tallinn
ESTONIA
Riga
LATVIA
LITHUANIA
Minsk
Vilnius
BELARUS

RUSSIAN FEDERATION

Laptev Sea

East
Siberian
Sea

Moscow

Sea of
Okhotsk

Bering Sea

LAND
UKRAINE
Kyiv

SLOVAKIA
Bratislava
UNGARY
ROMANIA
Budapest
Chișinău
MOLDOVA
Bucharest
SERBIA
NEGRO
Sofia
BULGARIA
FYRM
GREECE
Athens

Astana

KAZAKHSTAN

Ulan Bator

MONGOLIA

DEMOCRATIC
PEOPLE'S
REPUBLIC
OF KOREA

Black Sea
GEORGIA
Tbilisi
ARMENIA
Ankara
Yerevan
AZERBAIJAN
TURKEY
Nicosia
CYPRUS
Baku

UZBEKISTAN
Tashkent
Almaty
Bishkek
KYRGYZSTAN
TURKMENISTAN
Asgabat
TAJIKISTAN
Dushanbe

Beijing

PEOPLE'S REPUBLIC
OF CHINA

Pyongyang
Seoul
REPUBLIC
OF KOREA

Sea
of
Japan

JAPAN

Tokyo

SYRIA
Beirut
Damascus
LEBANON
ISRAEL
Baghdad
Amman
JORDAN
IRAQ

Tehran

IRAN

AFGHANISTAN
Kabul

Islamabad

East
China Sea

rranean Sea
Cairo
PALESTINIAN
AUTONOMOUS
AREAS
Kuwait City
KUWAIT
BAHRAIN
Manama
Riyadh
Doha
QATAR
UAE
Abu Dhabi
Muscat

PAKISTAN

New
Delhi

NEPAL
Kathmandu
Thimphu
BHUTAN
BANGLADESH
Dhaka

MACAO
(CHINA)
HONG KONG
(CHINA)

Taipei
TAIWAN

EGYPT

YA

HAD

SAUDI
ARABIA

OMAN

INDIA

MYANMAR
Hanoi
Vientiane

South
China
Sea

NORTHERN MARIANA
ISLANDS
(USA)

PACIFIC

Khartoum
ERITREA
Asmara
YEMEN
San'a
DJIBOUTI

Yangon
THAILAND
LAOS
VIET NAM

Manila

GUAM
(USA)

OCEAN

SUDAN
'Djamena

Addis
Ababa

ETHIOPIA

SOMALIA

Bay of
Bengal

Bangkok
CAMBODIA
Phnom-
Penh

PHILIPPINES

Philippine

MARSHALL
ISLANDS

Sea

PALAU

NAURU

CENTRAL
AFRICAN
REPUBLIC

Colombo
SRI
LANKA
Sri
Jayawardenepura

BRUNEI
Bandar
Seri Begawan

FEDERATED STATES
OF MICRONESIA

DEMOCRATIC
REPUBLIC
OF THE
CONGO
UGANDA
Kampala
KENYA
Nairobi

MALDIVES

Kuala Lumpur
Putrajaya
MALAYSIA
SINGAPORE

KIRIBATI

RWANDA
Kigali
BURUNDI
Bujumbura

Victoria
SEYCHELLES

BRITISH INDIAN
OCEAN TERRITORY
(UNITED KINGDOM)

nshasa
TANZANIA
Dodoma
Dar es Salaam

INDIAN

Jakarta

INDONESIA

PAPUA
NEW
GUINEA

SOLOMON
ISLANDS
Honiara

TUVALU

TOKELAU
(NEW ZEALAND)

GOLA
Lubumbashi
COMOROS
Moroni
MAYOTTE
(FRANCE)

CHRISTMAS
ISLAND
(AUSTRALIA)

COCOS ISLANDS
(AUSTRALIA)

OCEAN

Dili
TIMOR-LESTE
Port Moresby

Coral Sea

WALLIS AND FUTUNA
ISLANDS
(FRANCE)

SAMOA

ZAMBIA
Lusaka
Lilongwe

Antananarivo
MAURITIUS
Port Louis
RÉUNION
(FRANCE)

VANUATU
Port Vila

FIJI
Suva

AMERICAN
SAMOA
(USA)

Harare
ZIMBABWE

MADAGASCAR

NIUE
(NZ)

BIA
BOTSWANA
Gaborone
Pretoria
Maputo
MOZAMBIQUE

NEW
CALEDONIA
(FRANCE)

TONGA

Mbabane
SWAZILAND

LESOTHO
Maseru

AUSTRALIA

NORFOLK ISLAND
(AUSTRALIA)

SOUTH
AFRICA

Canberra

Tasman
Sea

NEW
ZEALAND

Wellington

Mozambique
Channel

Lilongwe

ANTARCTICA

© Routledge, supplied by the Cartographic Unit, University of Southampton

THE EUROPA
WORLD
YEAR BOOK
2005

THE EUROPA
WORLD
YEAR BOOK
2005

VOLUME I

PART ONE: INTERNATIONAL ORGANIZATIONS
PART TWO: AFGHANISTAN–JORDAN

Routledge
Taylor & Francis Group

LONDON AND NEW YORK

First published 1926

© Routledge 2005
Haines House, 21 John Street, London, WC1N 2BP, United Kingdom
(A member of the Taylor & Francis Group)

ISBN 1-85743-306-8 (The Set)
1-85743-304-1 (Vol. I)
ISSN 0071-2302
Library of Congress Catalog Card Number 59-2942

Senior Editor: Joanne Maher

Statistics Editor: Philip McIntyre

Regional Editors: Lynn Daniel, Lucy Dean, Iain Frame, Imogen Gladman,
Dominic Heaney, Juliet Love, Jillian O'Brien, Jacqueline West

International Organizations Editors: Catriona Appeatu Holman, Helen Canton

Associate Regional Editor: Elizabeth Kerr

Technology Editor: Ian Preston

Assistant Editors: Eleanor Baynes, Mary Bispham, Camilla Chew, Katie Dawson,
Anthony Gladman, Nicola Gollan, Michael Grayer, Kirstie Macdonald,
Catriona Marcham, James Middleton, Frances Mussellwhite, Patrick Raleigh,
Christopher Tooke, Edward Tyerman, Daniel Ward

Production Co-ordinator: Andreas Gosling

Editorial Clerical Assistant: Charley McCartney

Editorial Director: Paul Kelly

Typeset in New Century Schoolbook

Typeset by Unwin Brothers Limited, The Gresham Press, Old Woking, Surrey

Printed and bound by Polestar Wheatons, Exeter

FOREWORD

THE EUROPA WORLD YEAR BOOK was first published in 1926. Since 1960 it has appeared in annual two-volume editions, and has become established as an authoritative reference work, providing a wealth of detailed information on the political, economic and commercial institutions of the world.

Volume I contains a comprehensive listing of some 1,700 international organizations and the first part of the alphabetical survey of countries of the world, from Afghanistan to Jordan. Volume II contains countries from Kazakhstan to Zimbabwe.

The International Organizations section gives extensive coverage to the United Nations and its related agencies and bodies. There are also detailed articles concerning more than 60 other major international and regional organizations; entries for many affiliated organizations appear within these articles. In addition, briefer details of some 1,500 other international organizations appear in a separate section which starts on page 364. A comprehensive Index of International Organizations can be found at the end of Volume I.

Each country is covered by an individual chapter, containing: an introductory survey including recent history, economic affairs, government, defence, education, and public holidays; an economic and demographic survey using the latest available statistics on area and population, health and welfare, agriculture, forestry, fishing, industry, finance, trade, transport, tourism, the media, and education; and a directory section listing names, addresses and other useful facts about organizations in the fields of government, political parties, diplomatic representation, judiciary, religions, the media, telecommunications, banking, insurance, trade and industry, development organizations, chambers of commerce, industrial and trade associations, utilities, trade unions, transport, and tourism.

The entire content of the print edition of THE EUROPA WORLD YEAR BOOK is now available online at www.europaworld.com. This prestigious resource incorporates sophisticated search and browse functions as well as specially commissioned visual and statistical content. An ongoing programme of updates of key areas of information ensures currency of content, and enhances the richness of the coverage for which THE EUROPA WORLD YEAR BOOK is renowned.

Readers are referred to the nine titles in the Europa Regional Surveys of the World series: AFRICA SOUTH OF THE SAHARA, CENTRAL AND SOUTH-EASTERN EUROPE, EASTERN EUROPE, RUSSIA AND CENTRAL ASIA, THE FAR EAST AND AUSTRALASIA, THE MIDDLE EAST AND NORTH AFRICA, SOUTH AMERICA, CENTRAL AMERICA AND THE CARIBBEAN, SOUTH ASIA, THE USA AND CANADA and WESTERN EUROPE, available in print as well as online, offer comprehensive analysis at regional, sub-regional and country level. More detailed coverage of international organizations may be found in THE EUROPA DIRECTORY OF INTERNATIONAL ORGANIZATIONS.

The content of THE EUROPA WORLD YEAR BOOK is extensively revised and updated by a variety of methods, including direct mailing to all the institutions listed. Many other sources are used, such as national statistical offices, government departments and diplomatic missions. The editors thank the innumerable individuals and organizations world-wide whose generous co-operation in providing current information for this edition is invaluable in presenting the most accurate and up-to-date material available.

May 2005

ACKNOWLEDGEMENTS

The editors gratefully acknowledge particular indebtedness for permission to reproduce material from the following publications: the United Nations' *Demographic Yearbook, Statistical Yearbook, Monthly Bulletin of Statistics, Industrial Commodity Statistics Yearbook* and *International Trade Statistics Yearbook*; the United Nations Educational, Scientific and Cultural Organization's *Statistical Yearbook*; the Food and Agriculture Organization of the United Nations' statistical database; the International Labour Office's statistical database and *Yearbook of Labour Statistics*; the World Bank's *World Bank Atlas, Global Development Finance, World Development Report* and *World Development Indicators*; the International Monetary Fund's statistical database, *International Financial Statistics* and *Government Finance Statistics Yearbook*; the World Tourism Organization's *Yearbook of Tourism Statistics*; and *The Military Balance 2004–2005*, a publication of the International Institute for Strategic Studies, Arundel House, 13–15 Arundel Street, London WC2R 3DX.

HEALTH AND WELFARE STATISTICS: SOURCES AND DEFINITIONS

Total fertility rate Source: WHO, *The World Health Report* (2003). The number of children that would be born per woman, assuming no female mortality at child-bearing ages and the age-specific fertility rates of a specified country and reference period.

Under-5 mortality rate Source: UNICEF, *The State of the World's Children* (2004). The ratio of registered deaths of children under 5 years to the total number of registered live births over the same period.

HIV/AIDS Source: UNAIDS. Estimated percentage of adults aged 15 to 49 years living with HIV/AIDS. < indicates 'fewer than'.

Health expenditure Source: WHO, *The World Health Report* (2003).
US $ per head (PPP)
International dollar estimates, derived by dividing local currency units by an estimate of their purchasing-power parity (PPP) compared with the US dollar. PPPs are the rates of currency conversion that equalize the purchasing power of different currencies by eliminating the differences in price levels between countries.
% of GDP
GDP levels for OECD countries follow the most recent UN System of National Accounts. For non-OECD countries a value was estimated by utilizing existing UN, IMF and World Bank data.
Public expenditure
Government health-related outlays plus expenditure by social schemes compulsorily affiliated with a sizeable share of the population, and extrabudgetary funds allocated to health services. Figures include grants or loans provided by international agencies, other national authorities, and sometimes commercial banks.

Access to water and sanitation Source: WHO/UNICEF Joint Monitoring Programme on Water Supply and Sanitation (JMP) (Mid-Term Assessment, 2004). Defined in terms of the percentage of the population using improved facilities in terms of the type of technology and levels of service afforded. For water, this includes house connections, public standpipes, boreholes with handpumps, protected dug wells, protected spring and rainwater collection; allowance is also made for other locally defined technologies. Sanitation is defined to include connection to a sewer or septic tank system, pour-flush latrine, simple pit or ventilated improved pit latrine, again with allowance for acceptable local technologies. Access to water and sanitation does not imply that the level of service or quality of water is 'adequate' or 'safe'.

Human Development Index (HDI) Source: UNDP, *Human Development Report* (2004). A summary of human development measured by three basic dimensions: prospects for a long and healthy life, measured by life expectancy at birth; knowledge, measured by adult literacy rate (two-thirds' weight) and the combined gross enrolment ratio in primary, secondary and tertiary education (one-third weight); and standard of living, measured by GDP per head (PPP US $). The index value obtained lies between zero and one. A value above 0.8 indicates high human development, between 0.5 and 0.8 medium human development, and below 0.5 low human development. A centralized data source for all three dimensions was not available for all countries. In some such cases other data sources were used to calculate a substitute value; however, this was excluded from the ranking. Other countries, including non-UNDP members, were excluded from the HDI altogether. In total, 177 countries were ranked for 2002.

CONTENTS

* A complete Index of International Organizations is to be found
on p. 2451.

CONTENTS

PART TWO
Afghanistan–Jordan

An Index of Territories is to be found at the end of Volume II.

ABBREVIATIONS

AB	Aktiebolag (Joint-Stock Company); Alberta
Abog.	Abogado (Lawyer)
Acad.	Academician; Academy
ACP	African, Caribbean and Pacific (countries)
ACT	Australian Capital Territory
AD	anno Domini
ADB	African Development Bank; Asian Development Bank
ADC	aide-de-camp
Adm.	Admiral
admin.	administration
AfDB	African Development Bank
AG	Aktiengesellschaft (Joint-Stock Company)
AH	anno Hegirae
a.i.	ad interim
AID	(US) Agency for International Development
AIDS	acquired immunodeficiency syndrome
AK	Alaska
Al.	Aleja (Alley, Avenue)
AL	Alabama
ALADI	Asociación Latinoamericana de Integración
Alt.	Alternate
AM	Amplitude Modulation
a.m.	ante meridiem (before noon)
amalg.	amalgamated
Apdo	Apartado (Post Box)
APEC	Asia-Pacific Economic Co-operation
approx.	approximately
Apt	Apartment
AR	Arkansas
ARV	advanced retroviral
AŞ	Anonim Şirketi (Joint-Stock Company)
A/S	Aktieselskab (Joint-Stock Company)
ASEAN	Association of South East Asian Nations
asscn	association
assoc.	associate
ASSR	Autonomous Soviet Socialist Republic
asst	assistant
AU	African Union
Aug.	August
auth.	authorized
av., Ave	Avenija, Avenue
Avda	Avenida (Avenue)
Avv.	Avvocato (Lawyer)
AZ	Arizona
b.b.	bez broja (without number)
BC	British Columbia
BC	before Christ
Bd	Board
Bd, Bld, Blv., Blvd	Boulevard
b/d	barrels per day
BFPO	British Forces' Post Office
Bhd	Berhad (Public Limited Company)
Bldg	Building
blk	block
Blvr	Bulevar
BP	Boîte postale (Post Box)
br.(s)	branch(es)
Brig.	Brigadier
BSE	bovine spongiform encephalopathy
BSEC	(Organization of the) Black Sea Economic Co-operation

bte	boîte (box)
BTN	Brussels Tariff Nomenclature
Bul.	Bulvar (boulevard)
bulv.	bulvarīs (boulevard)
C	Centigrade
c.	circa; cuadra(s) (block(s))
CA	California
CACM	Central American Common Market
Cad.	Caddesi (Street)
CAP	Common Agricultural Policy
cap.	capital
Capt.	Captain
CARICOM	Caribbean Community and Common Market
CBSS	Council of Baltic Sea States
CCL	Caribbean Congress of Labour
Cdre	Commodore
CEMAC	Communauté économique et monétaire de l'Afrique centrale
Cen.	Central
CEO	Chief Executive Officer
CFA	Communauté Financière Africaine; Coopération Financière en Afrique centrale
CFP	Common Fisheries Policy; Communauté française du Pacifique; Comptoirs français du Pacifique
Chair.	Chairman/person/woman
Chih.	Chihuahua
CI	Channel Islands
Cia	Companhia
Cía	Compañía
Cie	Compagnie
c.i.f.	cost, insurance and freight
C-in-C	Commander-in-Chief
circ.	circulation
CIS	Commonwealth of Independent States
CJD	Creutzfeldt-Jakob disease
cm	centimetre(s)
cnr	corner
CO	Colorado
Co	Company; County
c/o	care of
Coah.	Coahuila
Col	Colonel
Col.	Colima; Colonia
COMESA	Common Market for Eastern and Southern Africa
Comm.	Commission; Commendatore
Commdr	Commander
Commdt	Commandant
Commr	Commissioner
Cond.	Condiminio
Confed.	Confederation
Cont.	Contador (Accountant)
COO	Chief Operating Officer
Corp.	Corporate
Corpn	Corporation
CP	Case Postale, Caixa Postal, Casella Postale (Post Box); Communist Party
CPSU	Communist Party of the Soviet Union
Cres.	Crescent
CSCE	Conference on Security and Co-operation in Europe
CSTAL	Confederación Sindical de los Trabajadores de América Latina
CT	Connecticut
CTCA	Confederación de Trabajadores Centro-americanos
Cttee	Committee

cu	cubic
cwt	hundredweight
DC	District of Columbia; Distrito Capital; Distrito Central
d.d.	delniška družba, dioničko društvo (joint stock company)
DE	Departamento Estatal; Delaware
Dec.	December
Del.	Delegación
Dem.	Democratic; Democrat
Dep.	Deputy
dep.	deposits
Dept	Department
devt	development
DF	Distrito Federal
Dgo	Durango
Diag.	Diagonal
Dir	Director
Div.	Division(al)
DM	Deutsche Mark
DMZ	demilitarized zone
DNA	deoxyribonucleic acid
DN	Distrito Nacional
Doc.	Docent
Dott.	Dottore/essa
Dr	Doctor
Dr.	Drive
Dra	Doctora
Dr Hab.	Doktor Habilitowany (Assistant Professor)
dr.(e)	drachma(e)
Drs	Doctorandus
DU	depleted uranium
dwt	dead weight tons
E	East; Eastern
EBRD	European Bank for Reconstruction and Development
EC	European Community
ECA	(United Nations) Economic Commission for Africa
ECE	(United Nations) Economic Commission for Europe
ECLAC	(United Nations) Economic Commission for Latin America and the Caribbean
ECO	Economic Co-operation Organization
Econ.	Economist; Economics
ECOSOC	(United Nations) Economic and Social Council
ECOWAS	Economic Community of West African States
ECU	European Currency Unit
Edif.	Edificio (Building)
edn	edition
EEA	European Economic Area
EFTA	European Free Trade Association
e.g.	exempli gratia (for example)
EIB	European Investment Bank
eKv	electron kilovolt
EMS	European Monetary System
EMU	Economic and Monetary Union
eMv	electron megavolt
Eng.	Engineer; Engineering
EP	Empresa Pública
ERM	exchange rate mechanism
ESACA	Emisora de Capital Abierto Sociedad Anónima
Esc.	Escuela; Escudos; Escritorio

ESCAP	(United Nations) Economic and Social Commission for Asia and the Pacific
ESCWA	(United Nations) Economic and Social Commission for Western Asia
esq.	esquina (corner)
est.	established; estimate; estimated
etc.	et cetera
EU	European Union
eV	eingetragener Verein
excl.	excluding
exec.	executive
Ext.	Extension
F	Fahrenheit
f.	founded
FAO	Food and Agriculture Organization
f.a.s.	free alongside ship
Feb.	February
Fed.	Federation; Federal
FL	Florida
FM	frequency modulation
fmr(ly)	former(ly)
f.o.b.	free on board
Fr	Father
Fr.	Franc
Fri.	Friday
FRY	Federal Republic of Yugoslavia
ft	foot (feet)
FYRM	former Yugoslav republic of Macedonia
g	gram(s)
g.	gatve (street)
GA	Georgia
GATT	General Agreement on Tariffs and Trade
GCC	Gulf Co-operation Council
Gdns	Gardens
GDP	gross domestic product
Gen.	General
GeV	giga electron volts
GM	genetically modified
GmbH	Gesellschaft mit beschränkter Haftung (Limited Liability Company)
GMO(s)	genetically modified organism(s)
GMT	Greenwich Mean Time
GNI	gross national income
GNP	gross national product
Gov.	Governor
Govt	Government
Gro	Guerrero
grt	gross registered tons
GSM	Global System for Mobile Communications
Gto	Guanajuato
GWh	gigawatt hours
ha	hectares
HE	His/Her Eminence; His/Her Excellency
hf	hlutafelag (Limited Company)
HI	Hawaii
HIPC	heavily indebted poor country
HIV	human immunodeficiency virus
hl	hectolitre(s)
HM	His/Her Majesty
Hon.	Honorary, Honourable
hp	horsepower
HQ	Headquarters
HRH	His/Her Royal Highness
HSH	His/Her Serene Highness
IA	Iowa
IBRD	International Bank for Reconstruction and Development (World Bank)
ICC	International Chamber of Commerce; International Criminal Court
ICFTU	International Confederation of Free Trade Unions
ICRC	International Committee of the Red Cross
ICTR	International Criminal Tribunal for Rwanda
ICTY	International Criminal Tribunal for the former Yugoslavia
ID	Idaho
IDA	International Development Association
IDB	Inter-American Development Bank
IDPs	Internally Displaced Persons
i.e.	id est (that is to say)
IFC	International Finance Corporation
IGAD	Intergovernmental Authority on Development
IL	Illinois
ILO	International Labour Organization/Office
IMF	International Monetary Fund
in (ins)	inch (inches)
IN	Indiana
Inc, Incorp.	
Incd	Incorporated
incl.	including
Ind.	Independent
INF	Intermediate-Range Nuclear Forces
Ing.	Engineer
Insp.	Inspector
Int.	International
Inzå.	Engineer
IPU	Inter-Parliamentary Union
Ir	Engineer
IRF	International Road Federation
irreg.	irregular
Is	Islands
ISIC	International Standard Industrial Classification
IT	information technology
ITU	International Telecommunication Union
Iur.	Lawyer
Jal.	Jalisco
Jan.	January
Jnr	Junior
Jr	Jonkheer (Esquire); Junior
Jt	Joint
kg	kilogram(s)
KG	Kommandit Gesellschaft (Limited Partnership)
kHz	kilohertz
KK	Kaien Kaisha (Limited Company)
km	kilometre(s)
kom.	komnata (room)
kor.	korpus (block)
k'och.	k'ochasi (street)
KS	Kansas
küç	küçasi (street)
kv.	kvartal (apartment block); kvartira (apartment)
kW	kilowatt(s)
kWh	kilowatt hours
KY	Kentucky
LA	Louisiana
lauk	laukums (square)
lb	pound(s)
LDCs	Least Developed Countries
Lic.	Licenciado
Licda	Licenciada
LNG	liquefied natural gas
LPG	liquefied petroleum gas
Lt, Lieut	Lieutenant
Ltd	Limited
m	metre(s)
m.	million
MA	Massachusetts
Maj.	Major
Man.	Manager; managing
MB	Manitoba
mbH	mit beschränkter Haftung (with limited liability)
MD	Maryland
MDG	Millennium Development Goal
ME	Maine
Me	Maître
mem.(s)	member(s)
MEP	Member of the European Parliament
Mercosul	Mercado Comum do Sul (Southern Common Market)
Mercosur	Mercado Común del Sur (Southern Common Market)
Méx.	México
MFN	most favoured nation
mfrs	manufacturers
Mgr	Monseigneur; Monsignor
MHz	megahertz
MI	Michigan
MIA	missing in action
Mich.	Michoacán
MIGA	Multilateral Investment Guarantee Agency
Mil.	Military
Mlle	Mademoiselle
mm	millimetre(s)
Mme	Madame
MN	Minnesota
mnt.	mante (road)
MO	Missouri
Mon.	Monday
Mor.	Morelos
MOU	memorandum of understanding
MP	Member of Parliament
MS	Mississippi
MSS	Manuscripts
MT	Montana
MW	megawatt(s); medium wave
MWh	megawatt hour(s)
N	North; Northern
n.a.	not available
nab.	naberezhnaya (embankment, quai)
NAFTA	North American Free Trade Agreement
nám.	náměstí (square)
Nat.	National
NATO	North Atlantic Treaty Organization
Nay.	Nayarit
NB	New Brunswick
NC	North Carolina
NCD	National Capital District
NCO	non-commissioned officer
ND	North Dakota
NE	Nebraska; North-East
NEPAD	New Partnership for Africa's Development
NGO	non-governmental organization
NH	New Hampshire
NJ	New Jersey
NL	Newfoundland and Labrador, Nuevo León
NM	New Mexico
NMP	net material product
no	numéro, número (number)
no.	number
Nov.	November
nr	near
nrt	net registered tons

NS	Nova Scotia
NSW	New South Wales
NT	Northwest Territories
NU	Nunavut Territory
NV	Naamloze Vennootschap (Limited Company); Nevada
NW	North-West
NY	New York
NZ	New Zealand
OAPEC	Organization of Arab Petroleum Exporting Countries
OAS	Organization of American States
OAU	Organization of African Unity
Oax.	Oaxaca
Oct.	October
OECD	Organisation for Economic Co-operation and Development
OECS	Organisation of Eastern Caribbean States
Of.	Oficina (Office)
OH	Ohio
OIC	Organization of the Islamic Conference
OK	Oklahoma
ON	Ontario
OPEC	Organization of the Petroleum Exporting Countries
opp.	opposite
OR	Oregon
Org.	Organization
ORIT	Organización Regional Interamericana de Trabajadores
OSCE	Organization for Security and Co-operation in Europe
p.	page
p.a.	per annum
PA	Palestinian Authority; Pennsylvania
Parl.	Parliament(ary)
per.	pereulok (lane, alley)
PE	Prince Edward Island
Perm. Rep.	Permanent Representative
PF	Postfach (Post Box)
PK	Post Box (Turkish)
Pl.	Plac, Plads (square)
pl.	platz; place; ploshchad (square)
PLC	Public Limited Company
PLO	Palestine Liberation Organization
p.m.	post meridiem (after noon)
PMB	Private Mail Bag
PNA	Palestinian National Authority
POB	Post Office Box
pp.	pages
PPP	purchasing-power parity
PQ	Québec
PR	Puerto Rico
pr.	prospekt, prospekti (avenue)
Pres.	President
PRGF	Poverty Reduction and Growth Facility
Prin.	Principal
Prof.	Professor
Propr	Proprietor
Prov.	Province; Provincial; Provinciale (Dutch)
prov.	provulok (lane)
pst.	puistotie (avenue)
PT	Perseroan Terbatas (Limited Company)
Pte	Private; Puente (Bridge)
Pty	Proprietary
p.u.	paid up
publ.	publication; published
Publr	Publisher
Pue.	Puebla
Pvt.	Private

QC	Québec
QIP	Quick Impact Project
Qld	Queensland
Qro	Querétaro
Q. Roo	Quintana Roo
q.v.	quod vide (to which refer)
Rag.	Ragioniere (Accountant)
Rd	Road
R(s)	rand; rupee(s)
reg., regd	register; registered
reorg.	reorganized
Rep.	Republic; Republican; Representative
Repub.	Republic
res	reserve(s)
retd	retired
Rev.	Reverend
RI	Rhode Island
RJ	Rio de Janeiro
Rm	Room
RN	Royal Navy
ro-ro	roll-on roll-off
RP	Recette principale
Rp.(s)	rupiah(s)
RSFSR	Russian Soviet Federative Socialist Republic
Rt	Right
S	South; Southern; San
SA	Société Anonyme, Sociedad Anónima (Limited Company); South Australia
SAARC	South Asian Association for Regional Co-operation
SAECA	Sociedad Anónima Emisora de Capital Abierto
SADC	Southern African Development Community
SAR	Special Administrative Region
SARL	Sociedade Anônima de Responsabilidade Limitada (Joint-Stock Company of Limited Liability)
SARS	Severe Acute Respiratory Syndrome
Sat.	Saturday
SC	South Carolina
SD	South Dakota
Sdn Bhd	Sendirian Berhad (Private Limited Company)
SDR(s)	Special Drawing Right(s)
SE	South-East
Sec.	Secretary
Secr.	Secretariat
Sen.	Senior; Senator
Sept.	September
SER	Sua Eccellenza Reverendissima (His Eminence)
SFRY	Socialist Federal Republic of Yugoslavia
Sin.	Sinaloa
SITC	Standard International Trade Classification
SJ	Society of Jesus
SK	Saskatchewan
SLP	San Luis Potosí
SMEs	small and medium-sized enterprises
s/n	sin número (without number)
Soc.	Society
Sok.	Sokak (Street)
Son.	Sonora
Şos.	Şosea (Road)
SP	São Paulo
SpA	Società per Azioni (Joint-Stock Company)
Sq.	Square
sq	square (in measurements)
Sr	Senior; Señor
Sra	Señora
Srl	Società a Responsabilità Limitata (Limited Company)

SSR	Soviet Socialist Republic
St	Saint, Sint; Street
Sta	Santa
Ste	Sainte
STI(s)	sexually transmitted infection(s)
str.	strada, stradă (street)
str-la	stradelă (street)
subs.	subscriptions; subscribed
Sun.	Sunday
Supt	Superintendent
SUV	sports utility vehicle
sv.	Saint
SW	South-West
Tab.	Tabasco
Tamps	Tamaulipas
TAŞ	Turkiye Anonim Şirketi (Turkish Joint-Stock Company)
Tas	Tasmania
TD	Teachta Dàla (Member of Parliament)
tech., techn.	technical
tel.	telephone
TEU	20-ft equivalent unit
Thur.	Thursday
TN	Tennessee
tř	třída (avenue)
Treas.	Treasurer
Tue.	Tuesday
TV	television
TX	Texas
u.	utca (street)
u/a	unit of account
UAE	United Arab Emirates
UEE	Unidade Económica Estatal
UEMOA	Union économique et monetaire ouest-africaine
UK	United Kingdom
ul.	ulica, ulitsa (street)
UM	ouguiya
UN	United Nations
UNAIDS	United Nations Joint Programme on HIV/AIDS
UNCTAD	United Nations Conference on Trade and Development
UNDP	United Nations Development Programme
UNEP	United Nations Environment Programme
UNESCO	United Nations Educational, Scientific and Cultural Organization
UNHCHR	UN High Commissioner for Human Rights
UNHCR	United Nations High Commissioner for Refugees
UNICEF	United Nations Children's Fund
Univ.	University
UNODC	United Nations Office on Drugs and Crime
UNRWA	United Nations Relief and Works Agency for Palestine Refugees in the Near East
Urb.	Urbanización (District)
USA	United States of America
USAID	United States Agency for International Development
USSR	Union of Soviet Socialist Republics
UT	Utah
VA	Virginia
VAT	value-added tax
VEB	Volkseigener Betrieb (Public Company)
v-CJD	new variant Creutzfeldt-Jakob disease
Ven.	Venerable
Ver.	Veracruz
VHF	Very High Frequency

ABBREVIATIONS

VI	(US) Virgin Islands	WCL	World Confederation of Labour	WTO	World Tourism Organization; World Trade Organization
Vic	Victoria	Wed.	Wednesday		
Vn	Veien (Street)	WEU	Western European Union	WV	West Virginia
vol.(s)	volume(s)	WFP	World Food Programme	WY	Wyoming
VT	Vermont	WFTU	World Federation of Trade Unions		
vul.	vulitsa, vulytsa (street)			yr	year
		WHO	World Health Organization	YT	Yukon Territory
W	West; Western	WI	Wisconsin	Yuc.	Yucatán
WA	Western Australia; Washington (State)	WSSD	World Summit on Sustainable Development		

INTERNATIONAL TELEPHONE CODES

To make international calls to telephone and fax numbers listed in *The Europa World Year Book*, dial the international code of the country from which you are calling, followed by the appropriate country code for the organization you wish to call (listed below), followed by the area code (if applicable) and telephone or fax number listed in the entry.

	Country code	+ or − GMT*		Country code	+ or − GMT*
Afghanistan	93	+4½	Djibouti	253	+3
Albania	355	+1	Dominica	1 767	−4
Algeria	213	+1	Dominican Republic	1 809	−4
Andorra	376	+1	Ecuador	593	−5
Angola	244	+1	Egypt	20	+2
Antigua and Barbuda	1 268	−4	El Salvador	503	−6
Argentina	54	−3	Equatorial Guinea	240	+1
Armenia	374	+4	Eritrea	291	+3
Australia	61	+8 to +10	Estonia	372	+2
Australian External Territories:			Ethiopia	251	+3
Australian Antarctic Territory	672	+3 to +10	Fiji	679	+12
Christmas Island	61	+7	Finland	358	+2
Cocos (Keeling) Islands	61	+6½	Finnish External Territory:		
Norfolk Island	672	+11½	Åland Islands	358	+2
Austria	43	+1	France	33	+1
Azerbaijan	994	+5	French Overseas Departments:		
Bahamas	1 242	−5	French Guiana	594	−3
Bahrain	973	+3	Guadeloupe	590	−4
Bangladesh	880	+6	Martinique	596	−4
Barbados	1 246	−4	Réunion	262	+4
Belarus	375	+2	French Overseas Collectivité Territoriale:		
Belgium	32	+1	Saint Pierre and Miquelon	508	−3
Belize	501	−6	French Overseas Collectivité Départementale:		
Benin	229	+1	Mayotte	269	+3
Bhutan	975	+6	French Overseas Territory:		
Bolivia	591	−4	Wallis and Futuna Islands	681	+12
Bosnia and Herzegovina	387	+1	French Overseas Countries:		
Botswana	267	+2	French Polynesia	689	−9 to −10
Brazil	55	−3 to −4	New Caledonia	687	+11
Brunei	673	+8	Gabon	241	+1
Bulgaria	359	+2	Gambia	220	0
Burkina Faso	226	0	Georgia	995	+4
Burundi	257	+2	Germany	49	+1
Cambodia	855	+7	Ghana	233	0
Cameroon	237	+1	Greece	30	+2
Canada	1	−3 to −8	Grenada	1 473	−4
Cape Verde	238	−1	Guatemala	502	−6
Central African Republic	236	+1	Guinea	224	0
Chad	235	+1	Guinea-Bissau	245	0
Chile	56	−4	Guyana	592	−4
China, People's Republic	86	+8	Haiti	509	−5
Special Administrative Regions:			Honduras	504	−6
Hong Kong	852	+8	Hungary	36	+1
Macao	853	+8	Iceland	354	0
China (Taiwan)	886	+8	India	91	+5½
Colombia	57	−5	Indonesia	62	+7 to +9
Comoros	269	+3	Iran	98	+3½
Congo, Democratic Republic	243	+1	Iraq	964	+3
Congo, Republic	242	+1	Ireland	353	0
Costa Rica	506	−6	Israel	972	+2
Côte d'Ivoire	225	0	Italy	39	+1
Croatia	385	+1	Jamaica	1 876	−5
Cuba	53	−5	Japan	81	+9
Cyprus	357	+2	Jordan	962	+2
'Turkish Republic of Northern			Kazakhstan	7	+6
Cyprus'	90 392	+2	Kenya	254	+3
Czech Republic	420	+1	Kiribati	686	+12 to +13
Denmark	45	+1	Korea, Democratic People's		
Danish External Territories:			Republic (North Korea)	850	+9
Faroe Islands	298	0	Korea, Republic (South Korea)	82	+9
Greenland	299	−1 to −4	Kuwait	965	+3

	Country code	+ or − GMT*
Kyrgyzstan	996	+5
Laos	856	+7
Latvia	371	+2
Lebanon	961	+2
Lesotho	266	+2
Liberia	231	0
Libya	218	+1
Liechtenstein	423	+1
Lithuania	370	+2
Luxembourg	352	+1
Macedonia, former Yugoslav republic	389	+1
Madagascar	261	+3
Malawi	265	+2
Malaysia	60	+8
Maldives	960	+5
Mali	223	0
Malta	356	+1
Marshall Islands	692	+12
Mauritania	222	0
Mauritius	230	+4
Mexico	52	−6 to −7
Micronesia, Federated States	691	+10 to +11
Moldova	373	+2
Monaco	377	+1
Mongolia	976	+7 to +9
Morocco	212	0
Mozambique	258	+2
Myanmar	95	+6½
Namibia	264	+2
Nauru	674	+12
Nepal	977	+5¾
Netherlands	31	+1
Netherlands Dependencies:		
Aruba	297	−4
Netherlands Antilles	599	−4
New Zealand	64	+12
New Zealand's Dependent and Associated Territories:		
Tokelau	690	−10
Cook Islands	682	−10
Niue	683	−11
Nicaragua	505	−6
Niger	227	+1
Nigeria	234	+1
Norway	47	+1
Norwegian External Territory:		
Svalbard	47	+1
Oman	968	+4
Pakistan	92	+5
Palau	680	+9
Palestinian Autonomous Areas	970	+2
Panama	507	−5
Papua New Guinea	675	+10
Paraguay	595	−4
Peru	51	−5
The Philippines	63	+8
Poland	48	+1
Portugal	351	0
Qatar	974	+3
Romania	40	+2
Russian Federation	7	+2 to +12
Rwanda	250	+2
Saint Christopher and Nevis	1 869	−4
Saint Lucia	1 758	−4
Saint Vincent and the Grenadines	1 784	−4
Samoa	685	−11
San Marino	378	+1
São Tomé and Príncipe	239	0
Saudi Arabia	966	+3
Senegal	221	0
Serbia and Montenegro	381	+1

	Country code	+ or − GMT*
Seychelles	248	+4
Sierra Leone	232	0
Singapore	65	+8
Slovakia	421	+1
Slovenia	386	+1
Solomon Islands	677	+11
Somalia	252	+3
South Africa	27	+2
Spain	34	+1
Sri Lanka	94	+6
Sudan	249	+2
Suriname	597	−3
Swaziland	268	+2
Sweden	46	+1
Switzerland	41	+1
Syria	963	+2
Tajikistan	992	+5
Tanzania	255	+3
Thailand	66	+7
Timor-Leste	670	+9
Togo	228	0
Tonga	676	+13
Trinidad and Tobago	1 868	−4
Tunisia	216	+1
Turkey	90	+2
Turkmenistan	993	+5
Tuvalu	688	+12
Uganda	256	+3
Ukraine	380	+2
United Arab Emirates	971	+4
United Kingdom	44	0
United Kingdom Crown Dependencies	44	0
United Kingdom Overseas Territories:		
Anguilla	1 264	−4
Ascension Island	247	0
Bermuda	1 441	−4
British Virgin Islands	1 284	−4
Cayman Islands	1 345	−5
Diego Garcia (British Indian Ocean Territory)	246	+5
Falkland Islands	500	−4
Gibraltar	350	+1
Montserrat	1 664	−4
Pitcairn Islands	872	−8
Saint Helena	290	0
Tristan da Cunha	2 897	0
Turks and Caicos Islands	1 649	−5
United States of America	1	−5 to −10
United States Commonwealth Territories:		
Northern Mariana Islands	1 670	+10
Puerto Rico	1 787	−4
United States External Territories:		
American Samoa	1 684	−11
Guam	1 671	+10
United States Virgin Islands	1 340	−4
Uruguay	598	−3
Uzbekistan	998	+5
Vanuatu	678	+11
Vatican City	39	+1
Venezuela	58	−4
Viet Nam	84	+7
Yemen	967	+3
Zambia	260	+2
Zimbabwe	263	+2

* Time difference in hours + or − Greenwich Mean Time (GMT). The times listed compare the standard (winter) times. Some countries adopt Summer (Daylight Saving) Time — i.e. + 1 hour — for part of the year.

PART ONE
International Organizations

THE UNITED NATIONS

Address: United Nations, New York, NY 10017, USA.

Telephone: (212) 963-1234; **fax:** (212) 963-4879; **internet:** www.un .org.

The United Nations was founded in 1945 to maintain international peace and security and to develop international co-operation in addressing economic, social, cultural and humanitarian problems.

The United Nations was a name devised by President Franklin D. Roosevelt of the USA. It was first used in the Declaration by United Nations of 1 January 1942, when representatives of 26 nations pledged their governments to continue fighting together against the Axis powers.

The United Nations Charter (see p. 21) was drawn up by the representatives of 50 countries at the United Nations Conference on International Organization, which met at San Francisco from 25 April to 26 June 1945. The representatives deliberated on the basis of proposals put forward by representatives of China, the USSR, the United Kingdom and the USA at Dumbarton Oaks in August–October 1944. The Charter was signed on 26 June 1945. Poland, not represented at the Conference, signed it later but nevertheless became one of the original 51 members.

The United Nations officially came into existence on 24 October 1945, when the Charter had been ratified by China, France, the USSR, the United Kingdom and the USA, and by a majority of other signatories. United Nations Day is celebrated annually on 24 October.

The UN's chief administrative officer is the Secretary-General, elected for a five-year term by the General Assembly on the recommendation of the Security Council. He acts in that capacity at all meetings of the General Assembly, the Security Council, the Economic and Social Council, and the Trusteeship Council, and performs such other functions as are entrusted to him by those organs. He is required to submit an annual report to the General Assembly and may bring to the attention of the Security Council any matter which, in his opinion, may threaten international peace.

In March 2005 the Secretary-General announced a series of proposals for extensive reforms of the UN (see General Assembly).

Secretary-General: KOFI ANNAN (Ghana) (1997–2006).

Membership

MEMBERS OF THE UNITED NATIONS

(with assessments for percentage contributions to the UN budget for 2004–06, and year of admission)

Afghanistan	0.002	1946
Albania	0.005	1955
Algeria	0.076	1962
Andorra	0.005	1993
Angola	0.001	1976
Antigua and Barbuda	0.003	1981
Argentina	0.956	1945
Armenia	0.002	1992
Australia	1.592	1945
Austria	0.859	1955
Azerbaijan	0.005	1992
Bahamas	0.013	1973
Bahrain	0.030	1971
Bangladesh	0.010	1974
Barbados	0.010	1966
Belarus[1]	0.018	1945
Belgium	1.069	1945
Belize	0.001	1981
Benin	0.002	1960
Bhutan	0.001	1971
Bolivia	0.009	1945
Bosnia and Herzegovina	0.003	1992
Botswana	0.012	1966
Brazil	1.523	1945
Brunei	0.034	1984
Bulgaria	0.017	1955
Burkina Faso	0.002	1960
Burundi	0.001	1962
Cambodia	0.002	1955
Cameroon	0.008	1960
Canada	2.813	1945
Cape Verde	0.001	1975
Central African Republic	0.001	1960
Chad	0.001	1960
Chile	0.223	1945

China, People's Republic	2.053	1945
Colombia	0.155	1945
Comoros	0.001	1975
Congo, Democratic Republic	0.003	1960
Congo, Republic	0.001	1960
Costa Rica	0.030	1945
Côte d'Ivoire	0.010	1960
Croatia	0.037	1992
Cuba	0.043	1945
Cyprus	0.039	1960
Czech Republic[2]	0.183	1993
Denmark	0.718	1945
Djibouti	0.001	1977
Dominica	0.001	1978
Dominican Republic	0.035	1945
Ecuador	0.019	1945
Egypt	0.120	1945
El Salvador	0.022	1945
Equatorial Guinea	0.002	1968
Eritrea	0.001	1993
Estonia	0.012	1991
Ethiopia	0.004	1945
Fiji	0.004	1970
Finland	0.533	1955
France	6.030	1945
Gabon	0.009	1960
The Gambia	0.001	1965
Georgia	0.003	1992
Germany	8.662	1973
Ghana	0.004	1957
Greece	0.530	1945
Grenada	0.001	1974
Guatemala	0.030	1945
Guinea	0.003	1958
Guinea-Bissau	0.001	1974
Guyana	0.001	1966
Haiti	0.003	1945
Honduras	0.005	1945
Hungary	0.126	1955
Iceland	0.034	1946
India	0.421	1945
Indonesia	0.142	1950
Iran	0.157	1945
Iraq	0.016	1945
Ireland	0.350	1955
Israel	0.467	1949
Italy	4.885	1955
Jamaica	0.008	1962
Japan	19.468	1956
Jordan	0.011	1955
Kazakhstan	0.025	1992
Kenya	0.009	1963
Kiribati	0.001	1999
Korea, Democratic People's Republic	0.010	1991
Korea, Republic	1.796	1991
Kuwait	0.162	1963
Kyrgyzstan	0.001	1992
Laos	0.001	1955
Latvia	0.015	1991
Lebanon	0.024	1945
Lesotho	0.001	1966
Liberia	0.001	1945
Libya	0.132	1955
Liechtenstein	0.005	1990
Lithuania	0.024	1991
Luxembourg	0.077	1945
Macedonia, former Yugoslav republic	0.006	1993
Madagascar	0.003	1960
Malawi	0.001	1964
Malaysia	0.203	1957
Maldives	0.001	1965
Mali	0.002	1960
Malta	0.014	1964
Marshall Islands	0.001	1991
Mauritania	0.001	1961
Mauritius	0.011	1968
Mexico	1.883	1945
Micronesia, Federated States	0.001	1991
Moldova	0.001	1992
Monaco	0.003	1993
Mongolia	0.001	1961
Morocco	0.047	1956

Mozambique	0.001	1975
Myanmar	0.010	1948
Namibia	0.006	1990
Nauru	0.001	1999
Nepal	0.004	1955
Netherlands	1.690	1945
New Zealand	0.221	1945
Nicaragua	0.001	1945
Niger	0.001	1960
Nigeria	0.042	1960
Norway	0.679	1945
Oman	0.070	1971
Pakistan	0.055	1947
Palau	0.001	1994
Panama	0.019	1945
Papua New Guinea	0.003	1975
Paraguay	0.012	1945
Peru	0.092	1945
Philippines	0.095	1945
Poland	0.461	1945
Portugal	0.470	1955
Qatar	0.064	1971
Romania	0.060	1955
Russia[3]	1.100	1945
Rwanda	0.001	1962
Saint Christopher and Nevis	0.001	1983
Saint Lucia	0.002	1979
Saint Vincent and the Grenadines	0.001	1980
Samoa (formerly Western Samoa)	0.001	1976
San Marino	0.003	1992
São Tomé and Príncipe	0.001	1975
Saudi Arabia	0.713	1945
Senegal	0.005	1960
Serbia and Montenegro[4]	0.019	2000
Seychelles	0.002	1976
Sierra Leone	0.001	1961
Singapore	0.388	1965
Slovakia[2]	0.051	1993
Slovenia	0.082	1992
Solomon Islands	0.001	1978
Somalia	0.001	1960
South Africa	0.292	1945
Spain	2.520	1955
Sri Lanka	0.017	1955
Sudan	0.008	1956
Suriname	0.001	1975
Swaziland	0.002	1968
Sweden	0.998	1946
Switzerland	1.197	2002
Syria	0.038	1945
Tajikistan	0.001	1992
Tanzania	0.006	1961
Thailand	0.209	1946
Timor-Leste	0.001	2002
Togo	0.001	1960
Tonga	0.001	1999
Trinidad and Tobago	0.022	1962
Tunisia	0.032	1956
Turkey	0.372	1945
Turkmenistan	0.005	1992
Tuvalu	0.001	2000
Uganda	0.006	1962
Ukraine[1]	0.039	1945
United Arab Emirates	0.235	1971
United Kingdom	6.127	1945
USA	22.000	1945
Uruguay	0.048	1945
Uzbekistan	0.014	1992
Vanuatu	0.001	1981
Venezuela	0.171	1945
Viet Nam	0.021	1977
Yemen[5]	0.006	1947/67
Zambia	0.002	1964
Zimbabwe	0.007	1980

Total Membership: 191 (April 2005)

[1] Until December 1991 both Belarus and Ukraine were integral parts of the USSR and not independent countries, but had separate UN membership.

[2] Czechoslovakia, which had been a member of the UN since 1945, ceased to exist as a single state on 31 December 1992. In January 1993, as Czechoslovakia's legal successors, the Czech Republic and Slovakia were granted UN membership, and seats on subsidiary bodies that had previously been held by Czechoslovakia were divided between the two successor states.

[3] Russia assumed the USSR's seat in the General Assembly and its permanent seat on the Security Council in December 1991, following the USSR's dissolution.

[4] Admitted as the Federal Republic of Yugoslavia. Present name was adopted in February 2003.

[5] The Yemen Arab Republic (admitted to the UN as Yemen in 1947) and the People's Democratic Republic of Yemen (admitted as Southern Yemen in 1967) merged to form the Republic of Yemen in May 1990.

SOVEREIGN STATES NOT IN THE UNITED NATIONS
(April 2005)

China (Taiwan)   Vatican City (Holy See)

Diplomatic Representation

PERMANENT MISSIONS TO THE UNITED NATIONS
(April 2005)

Afghanistan: 360 Lexington Ave, 11th Floor, New York, NY 10017; tel. (212) 972-1212; fax (212) 972-1216; e-mail afgwatan@aol.com; Permanent Representative Dr RAVAN A. G. FARHÂDI.

Albania: 320 East 79th St, New York, NY 10021; tel. (212) 249-2059; fax (212) 535-2917; e-mail albania@un.int; Permanent Representative ZEF MAZI.

Algeria: 326 East 48th St, New York, NY 10017; tel. (212) 750-1960; fax (212) 759-5274; e-mail mission@algeria-un.org; internet www.algeria-un.org; Permanent Representative ABDALLAH BAALI.

Andorra: 2 United Nations Plaza, 25th Floor, New York, NY 10017; tel. (212) 750-8064; fax (212) 750-6630; e-mail andorra@un.int; Permanent Representative JULIÀ VILA COMA.

Angola: 125 East 73rd St, New York, NY 10021; tel. (212) 861-5656; fax (212) 861-9295; e-mail ang-un@angolamissionun.org; internet www.angolamissionun.org; Permanent Representative ISMAEL ABRÃO GASPAR MARTINS.

Antigua and Barbuda: 610 Fifth Ave, Suite 311, New York, NY 10020; tel. (212) 541-4117; fax (212) 757-1607; e-mail antigua@un.int; internet www.un.int/antigua; Permanent Representative JOHN W. ASHE.

Argentina: 1 United Nations Plaza, 25th Floor, New York, NY 10017; tel. (212) 688-6300; fax (212) 980-8395; e-mail argentina@un.int; internet www.un.int/argentina; Permanent Representative CÉSAR MAYORAL.

Armenia: 119 East 36th St, New York, NY 10016; tel. (212) 686-9079; fax (212) 686-3934; e-mail armenia@un.int; internet www.un.int/armenia; Permanent Representative ARMEN MARTIROSIAN.

Australia: 150 East 42nd St, 33rd Floor, New York, NY 10017; tel. (212) 351-6600; fax (212) 351-6610; e-mail australia@un.int; internet www.australiaun.org; Permanent Representative JOHN DAUTH.

Austria: 823 United Nations Plaza, 8th Floor, New York, NY 10017; tel. (212) 949-1840; fax (212) 953-1302; e-mail austria@un.int; internet www.un.int/austria; Permanent Representative GERHARD PFANZELTER.

Azerbaijan: 866 United Nations Plaza, Suite 560, New York, NY 10017; tel. (212) 371-2559; fax (212) 371-2784; e-mail azerbaijan@un.int; Permanent Representative YASHAR ALIYEV.

Bahamas: 231 East 46th St, New York, NY 10017; tel. (212) 421-6925; fax (212) 759-2135; e-mail bahamas@un.int; Permanent Representative PAULETTE A. BETHEL.

Bahrain: 866 Second Ave, 14th/15th Floor, New York, NY 10017; tel. (212) 223-6200; fax (212) 319-0687; e-mail bahrain@un.int; internet www.un.int/bahrain; Permanent Representative TAWFEEQ AHMED KHALIL ALMANSOOR.

Bangladesh: 821 United Nations Plaza, 8th Floor, New York, NY 10017; tel. (212) 867-3434; fax (212) 972-4038; e-mail bangladesh@un.int; internet www.un.int/bangladesh; Permanent Representative Dr IFTEKHAR AHMED CHOWDHURY.

Barbados: 800 Second Ave, 2nd Floor, New York, NY 10017; tel. (212) 867-8431; fax (212) 986-1030; e-mail barbados@un.int; Permanent Representative CHRISTOPHER F. HACKETT.

Belarus: 136 East 67th St, New York, NY 10021; tel. (212) 535-3420; fax (212) 734-4810; e-mail belarus@un.int; internet www.un.int/belarus; Permanent Representative ANDREI DAPKIUNAS.

Belgium: 823 United Nations Plaza, 4th Floor, New York, NY 10017; tel. (212) 378-6300; fax (212) 681-7618; e-mail belgium@un.int; internet www.un.int/belgium; Permanent Representative JOHAN C. VERBEKE.

Belize: 800 Second Ave, Suite 400G, New York, NY 10017; tel. (212) 593-0999; fax (212) 593-0932; e-mail blzun@undp.org; Permanent Representative STUART LESLIE.

Benin: 4 East 73rd St, New York, NY 10021; tel. (212) 249-6014; fax (212) 988-3714; e-mail benin@un.int; internet www.un.int/benin; Permanent Representative JOEL WASSI ADECHI.

Bhutan: 2 United Nations Plaza, 27th Floor, New York, NY 10017; tel. (212) 826-1919; fax (212) 826-2998; e-mail pmbnewyork@aol .com; Permanent Representative DAW PENJO.

Bolivia: 211 East 43rd St, 8th Floor, Room 802, New York, NY 10017; tel. (212) 682-8132; fax (212) 682-8133; e-mail bolivia@un.int; Permanent Representative ERNESTO ARANÍBAR QUIROGA.

Bosnia and Herzegovina: 866 United Nations Plaza, Suite 580, New York, NY 10017; tel. (212) 751-9015; fax (212) 751-9019; e-mail bosnia@un.int; internet www.un.int/bosnia; Permanent Representative MIRZA KUSLJUGIC.

Botswana: 103 East 37th St, New York, NY 10016; tel. (212) 889-2277; fax (212) 725-5061; e-mail botswana@un.int; Permanent Representative LEGWAILA JOSEPH LEGWAILA.

Brazil: 747 Third Ave, 9th Floor, New York, NY 10017; tel. (212) 372-2600; fax (212) 371-5716; e-mail braun@delbrasonu.org; internet www.un.int/brazil; Permanent Representative RONALDO MOTA SARDENBERG.

Brunei: 771 First Ave, New York, NY 10017; tel. (212) 697-3465; fax (212) 697-9889; e-mail info@bruneimission-ny.org; Permanent Representative ABDUL GHAFOR SHOFRY.

Bulgaria: 11 East 84th St, New York, NY 10028; tel. (212) 737-4790; fax (212) 472-9865; e-mail bulgaria@un.int; internet www.un .int/bulgaria; Permanent Representative STEFAN TAFROV.

Burkina Faso: 115 East 73rd St, New York, NY 10021; tel. (212) 288-7515; fax (212) 772-3562; e-mail burkinafaso@un.int; Permanent Representative MICHEL KAFANDO.

Burundi: 336 East 45th St, 12th Floor, New York, NY 10017; tel. (212) 499-0001; fax (212) 499-0006; e-mail burundi@un.int; Permanent Representative MARC NTETURUYE.

Cambodia: 866 United Nations Plaza, Suite 420, New York, NY 10017; tel. (212) 223-0676; fax (212) 223-0425; e-mail cambodia@un .int; internet www.un.int/cambodia; Permanent Representative CHEM WIDHYA.

Cameroon: 22 East 73rd St, New York, NY 10021; tel. (212) 794-2296; fax (212) 249-0533; e-mail info@cameroonmission.org; internet www.cameroonmission.org; Permanent Representative MARTIN BELINGA EBOUTOU.

Canada: 1 Dag Hammarskjöld Plaza, 885 Second Ave, 14th Floor, New York, NY 10017; tel. (212) 848-1100; fax (212) 848-1195; e-mail canada@un.int; internet www.un.int/canada; Permanent Representative ALLAN ROCK.

Cape Verde: 27 East 69th St, New York, NY 10021; tel. (212) 472-0333; fax (212) 794-1398; e-mail capeverde@un.int; Permanent Representative MARIAS DE FATIMA LIMA DA VEIGA.

Central African Republic: 386 Park Ave South, Room 1114, New York, NY 10016; tel. (212) 679-8089; fax (212) 545-8326; e-mail caf@ un.int; Permanent Representative FERNAND POUKRE-KONO.

Chad: 211 East 43rd St, Suite 1703, New York, NY 10017; tel. (212) 986-0980; fax (212) 986-0152; e-mail chad@un.int; Permanent Representative MAHAMAT ALI ADOUM.

Chile: 3 Dag Hammarskjöld Plaza, 305 East 47th St, 10th/11th Floor, New York, NY 10017; tel. (212) 832-3323; fax (212) 832-0236; e-mail chile@un.int; internet www.un.int/chile; Permanent Representative JUAN GABRIEL VALDES.

China, People's Republic: 350 East 35th St, New York, NY 10016; tel. (212) 655-6100; fax (212) 634-7626; e-mail chinamission_un@ fmprc.gov.cn; internet www.china-un.org; Permanent Representative WANG GUANGYA.

Colombia: 140 East 57th St, 5th Floor, New York, NY 10022; tel. (212) 355-7776; fax (212) 371-2813; e-mail colombia@colombiaun .org; internet www.colombiaun.org; Permanent Representative MARIA ANGELA HOLGUÍN.

Comoros: 420 East 50th St, New York, NY 10022; tel. (212) 972-8010; fax (212) 983-4712; e-mail comoros@un.int; internet www.un .int/comoros; Chargé d'affaires a.i. MAHMOUD MOHAMED ABOUD.

Congo, Democratic Republic: 866 United Nations Plaza, Suite 511, New York, NY 10017; tel. (212) 319-8061; fax (212) 319-8232; e-mail drcongo@un.int; internet www.un.int/drcongo; Permanent Representative CHRISTIAN ILEKA ATOKI.

Congo, Republic: 14 East 65th St, New York, NY 10021; tel. (212) 744-7840; fax (212) 744-7975; e-mail congo@un.int; Permanent Representative BASILE IKOUEBE.

Costa Rica: 211 East 43rd St, Room 903, New York, NY 10017; tel. (212) 986-6373; fax (212) 986-6842; e-mail pmnu@rree.go.cr; internet www.un.int/costarica; Permanent Representative BERND H. NIEHAUS.

Côte d'Ivoire: 46 East 74th St, New York, NY 10021; tel. (212) 717-5555; fax (212) 717-4492; e-mail ivorycoast@un.int; internet www .un.int/cotedivoire; Chargé d'affaires AHIPEAUD GUEBO NOËL EMMANUEL.

Croatia: 820 Second Ave, 19th Floor, New York, NY 10017; tel. (212) 986-1585; fax (212) 986-2011; e-mail croatia@un.int; internet www.un.int/croatia; Permanent Representative Dr VLADIMIR DROBNJAK.

Cuba: 315 Lexington Ave and 38th St, New York, NY 10016; tel. (212) 689-7215; fax (212) 779-1697; e-mail cuba@un.int; internet www.un.int/cuba; Permanent Representative ORLANDO REQUEIJO GUAL.

Cyprus: 13 East 40th St, New York, NY 10016; tel. (212) 481-6023; fax (212) 685-7316; e-mail cyprus@un.int; internet www.un.int/ cyprus; Permanent Representative SOTIRIOS ZACKHEOS.

Czech Republic: 1109-1111 Madison Ave, New York, NY 10028; tel. (212) 535-8814; fax (212) 772-0586; e-mail un.newyork@embassy .mzv.cz; internet www.czechembassy.org; Permanent Representative HYNEK KMONICEK.

Denmark: 1 Dag Hammarskjöld Plaza, 885 Second Ave, 18th Floor, New York, NY 10017; tel. (212) 308-7009; fax (212) 308-3384; e-mail nycmis@um.dk; internet www.un.int/denmark; Permanent Representative ELLEN MARGRETHE LØJ.

Djibouti: 866 United Nations Plaza, Suite 4011, New York, NY 10017; tel. (212) 753-3163; fax (212) 223-1276; e-mail djibouti@nyct .net; Permanent Representative ROBLE OLHAYE.

Dominica: 800 Second Ave, Suite 400H, New York, NY 10017; tel. (212) 949-0853; fax (212) 808-4975; e-mail dominica@un.int; Permanent Representative SIMON PAUL RICHARDS.

Dominican Republic: 144 East 44th St, 4th Floor, New York, NY 10017; tel. (212) 867-0833; fax (212) 986-4694; e-mail undomrep@aol .com; internet www.un.int/dr; Permanent Representative MARINO DE JESÚS VILLANUEVA CALLOT.

Ecuador: 866 United Nations Plaza, Room 516, New York, NY 10017; tel. (212) 935-1680; fax (212) 935-1835; e-mail ecuador@un .int; internet www.un.int/ecuador; Permanent Representative JAIME MONCAYO.

Egypt: 304 East 44th St, New York, NY 10017; tel. (212) 503-0300; fax (212) 949-5999; e-mail egypt@un.int; Permanent Representative MAGED ABDELFATTAH ABDELAZIZ.

El Salvador: 46 Park Ave, New York, NY 10016; tel. (212) 679-1616; fax (212) 725-7831; e-mail elsalvador@un.int; Permanent Representative CARMEN MARÍA GALLARDO HERNÁNDEZ.

Equatorial Guinea: 57 Magnolia Ave, Mount Vernon, NY 10553; tel. (914) 667-8999; fax (914) 667-8778; e-mail eqguinea@un.int; Permanent Representative LINO SIMA EKUA AVOMO.

Eritrea: 800 Second Ave, 18th Floor, New York, NY 10017; tel. (212) 687-3390; fax (212) 687-3138; e-mail eritrea@un.int; internet www .un.int/eritrea; Permanent Representative AHMED TAHIR BADURI.

Estonia: 600 Third Ave, 26th Floor, New York, NY 10016; tel. (212) 883-0640; fax (212) 883-0648; e-mail mission.newyork@mfa.ee; Permanent Representative TINA INTELMANN.

Ethiopia: 866 Second Ave, 3rd Floor, New York, NY 10017; tel. (212) 421-1830; fax (212) 754-0360; e-mail ethiopia@un.int; internet www.un.int/ethiopia; Permanent Representative Dr ABDULMEJID HUSSEIN.

Fiji: 630 Third Ave, 7th Floor, New York, NY 10017; tel. (212) 687-4130; fax (212) 687-3963; e-mail fiji@un.int; Permanent Representative ISIKIA RABICI SAVUA.

Finland: 866 United Nations Plaza, Suite 222, New York, NY 10017; tel. (212) 355-2100; fax (212) 759-6156; e-mail sanomat.yke@ formin.fi; internet www.un.int/finland; Permanent Representative KIRSTI EEVA HELENA LINTONEN.

France: 1 Dag Hammarskjöld Plaza, 245 East 47th St, 44th Floor, New York, NY 10017; tel. (212) 308-5700; fax (212) 421-6889; e-mail france@un.int; internet www.un.int/france; Permanent Representative JEAN-MARC ROCHEREAU DE LA SABLIERE.

Gabon: 18 East 41st St, 9th Floor, New York, NY 10017; tel. (212) 686-9720; fax (212) 689-5769; e-mail gabon@un.int; Permanent Representative DENIS DANGUE RÉWAKA.

The Gambia: 800 Second Ave, Suite 400F, New York, NY 10017; tel. (212) 949-6640; fax (212) 808-4975; e-mail gambia@un.int; Permanent Representative CRISPIN GREY-JOHNSON.

Georgia: 1 United Nations Plaza, 26th Floor, New York, NY 10021; tel. (212) 759-1949; fax (212) 759-1832; e-mail georgia@un.int; internet www.un.int/georgia; Permanent Representative REVAZ ADAMIA.

Germany: 871 United Nations Plaza, New York, NY 10017; tel. (212) 940-0400; fax (212) 940-0402; e-mail germany@un.int; internet www.germany-info.org/un; Permanent Representative Dr GUNTER PLEUGER.

Ghana: 19 East 47th St, New York, NY 10017; tel. (212) 832-1300; fax (212) 751-6743; e-mail ghanaperm@aol.com; Permanent Representative NANA EFFAH-APENTENG.

Greece: 866 Second Ave, 13th Floor, New York, NY 10017; tel. (212) 888-6900; fax (212) 888-4440; e-mail mission@greeceun.org; internet www.greeceun.org; Permanent Representative ADAMANTIOS VASSILAKIS.

Grenada: 800 Second Ave, Suite 400K, New York, NY 10017; tel. (212) 599-0301; fax (212) 599-1540; e-mail grenada@un.int; Permanent Representative Dr RUTH ELIZABETH ROUSE.

Guatemala: 57 Park Ave, New York, NY 10016; tel. (212) 679-4760; fax (212) 685-8741; e-mail guatemala@un.int; internet www.un.int/guatemala; Permanent Representative JORGE SKINNER-KLÉE ARENALES.

Guinea: 140 East 39th St, New York, NY 10016; tel. (212) 687-8115; fax (212) 687-8248; e-mail guinea@un.int; Permanent Representative MAMADY TRAORÉ.

Guinea-Bissau: 211 East 43rd St, Room 704, New York, NY 10017; tel. (212) 338-9394; fax (212) 293-0264; e-mail guinea-bissau@un.int; Chargé d'affaires a.i. ALFREDO LOPES CABRAL.

Guyana: 866 United Nations Plaza, Suite 555, New York, NY 10017; tel. (212) 527-3232; fax (212) 935-7548; e-mail guyana@un.int; Permanent Representative SAMUEL R. INSANALLY.

Haiti: 801 Second Ave, Room 600, New York, NY 10017; tel. (212) 370-4840; fax (212) 661-8698; e-mail haiti@un.int; Permanent Representative LÉO MÉRORÈS.

Honduras: 866 United Nations Plaza, Suite 417, New York, NY 10017; tel. (212) 752-3370; fax (212) 223-0498; e-mail m.suazo@worldnet.att.net; internet www.un.int/honduras; Permanent Representative MANUEL ACOSTA BONILLA.

Hungary: 227 East 52nd St, New York, NY 10022; tel. (212) 752-0209; fax (212) 755-5395; e-mail hungary@un.int; internet www.un.int/hungary; Permanent Representative LÁSZLÓ MOLNÁR.

Iceland: 800 Third Ave, 36th Floor, New York, NY 10022; tel. (212) 593-2700; fax (212) 593-6269; e-mail icecon.ny@utn.stjr.is; internet brunnur.stjr.is/embassy/newyork.nsf/pages/index.html; Permanent Representative HJALMAR W. HANNESSON.

India: 235 East 43rd St, New York, NY 10017; tel. (212) 490-9660; fax (212) 490-9656; e-mail india@un.int; internet www.un.int/india; Permanent Representative NIRUPAM SEN.

Indonesia: 325 East 38th St, New York, NY 10016; tel. (212) 972-8333; fax (212) 972-9780; e-mail ptri@indonesiamission-ny.org; internet www.indonesiamission-ny.org; Permanent Representative REZLAN ISHAR JENIE.

Iran: 622 Third Ave, 34th Floor, New York, NY 10017; tel. (212) 687-2020; fax (212) 867-7086; e-mail iran@un.int; internet www.un.int/iran; Permanent Representative Dr MOHAMMAD JAVAD ZARIF.

Iraq: 14 East 79th St, New York, NY 10021; tel. (212) 737-4433; fax (212) 772-1794; e-mail missionofiraq@nyc.rr.com; internet www.iraqi-mission.org; Permanent Representative SAMIR SHAKIR MAHMOOD SUMAIDAIE.

Ireland: 1 Dag Hammarskjöld Plaza, 885 Second Ave, 19th Floor, New York, NY 10017; tel. (212) 421-6934; fax (212) 752-4726; e-mail ireland@un.int; internet www.un.int/ireland; Permanent Representative DAVID COONEY.

Israel: 800 Second Ave, New York, NY 10017; tel. (212) 499-5510; fax (212) 499-5516; e-mail israel@un.int; internet www.israel-un.org; Permanent Representative DAN GILLERMAN.

Italy: 2 United Nations Plaza, 24th Floor, New York, NY 10017; tel. (212) 486-9191; fax (212) 486-1036; e-mail italy@un.int; internet www.italyun.org; Permanent Representative MARCELLO SPATAFORA.

Jamaica: 767 Third Ave, 9th Floor, New York, NY 10017; tel. (212) 935-7509; fax (212) 935-7607; e-mail jamaica@un.int; internet www.un.int/jamaica; Permanent Representative STAFFORD OLIVER NEIL.

Japan: 866 United Nations Plaza, 2nd Floor, New York, NY 10017; tel. (212) 223-4300; fax (212) 751-1966; e-mail mission@un-japan.org; internet www.un.int/japan; Permanent Representative KENZO OSHIMA.

Jordan: 866 United Nations Plaza, Suite 552, New York, NY 10017; tel. (212) 832-9553; fax (212) 832-5346; e-mail jordan@un.int; Permanent Representative Prince ZEID RA'AD ZEID AL-HUSSEIN.

Kazakhstan: 866 United Nations Plaza, Suite 586, New York, NY 10017; tel. (212) 230-1900; fax (212) 230-1172; e-mail kazakhstan@un.int; internet www.un.int/kazakhstan; Permanent Representative YERZHAN KAZYKHANOV.

Kenya: 866 United Nations Plaza, Room 486, New York, NY 10017; tel. (212) 421-4740; fax (212) 486-1985; e-mail kenya@un.int; internet www.un.int/kenya/; Permanent Representative JUDITH MBULA BAHEMUKA.

Korea, Democratic People's Republic: 820 Second Ave, 13th Floor, New York, NY 10017; tel. (212) 972-3105; fax (212) 972-3154; e-mail dprk@un.int; Permanent Representative PAK GIL YON.

Korea, Republic: 335 East 45th St, New York, NY 10017; tel. (212) 439-4000; fax (212) 986-1083; e-mail korea@un.int; internet www.un.int/korea; Permanent Representative KIM SAM-HOON.

Kuwait: 321 East 44th St, New York, NY 10017; tel. (212) 973-4300; fax (212) 370-1733; e-mail kuwait@kuwaitmission.com; internet www.kuwaitmission.com; Permanent Representative NABEELA ABDULLA AL-MULLA.

Kyrgyzstan: 866 United Nations Plaza, Suite 477, New York, NY 10017; tel. (212) 486-4214; fax (212) 486-5259; e-mail kyrgyzstan@un.int; Permanent Representative NURBEK JEENBAEV.

Laos: 317 East 51st St, New York, NY 10022; tel. (212) 832-2734; fax (212) 750-0039; e-mail lao@un.int; internet www.un.int/lao; Permanent Representative ALOUNKÈO KITTIKHOUN.

Latvia: 333 East 50th St, New York, NY 10022; tel. (212) 838-8877; fax (212) 838-8920; e-mail irppanony@aol.com; Permanent Representative GINTS JEGERMANIS.

Lebanon: 866 United Nations Plaza, Room 531–533, New York, NY 10017; tel. (212) 355-5460; fax (212) 838-2819; e-mail lebanon@un.int; Chargé d'affaires a.i. SAMI KRONFOL.

Lesotho: 204 East 39th St, New York, NY 10016; tel. (212) 661-1690; fax (212) 682-4388; e-mail lesotho@un.int; internet www.un.int/lesotho; Permanent Representative PERCY M. MANGOAELA.

Liberia: 820 Second Ave, 13th Floor, New York, NY 10017; tel. (212) 687-1033; fax (212) 687-1035; e-mail liberia@un.int; Permanent Representative LAMI KAWAH.

Libya: 309–315 East 48th St, New York, NY 10017; tel. (212) 752-5775; fax (212) 593-4787; e-mail info@libya-un.org; internet www.libya-un.org; Permanent Representative ÀLI ABDUSSALAM TREKY.

Liechtenstein: 633 Third Ave, 27th Floor, New York, NY 10017; tel. (212) 599-0220; fax (212) 599-0064; e-mail liechtenstein@un.int; internet www.un.int/liechtenstein; Permanent Representative CHRISTIAN WENAWESER.

Lithuania: 420 Fifth Ave, 3rd Floor, New York, NY 10018; tel. (212) 354-7820; fax (212) 354-7833; e-mail lithuania@un.int; internet www.un.int/lithuania; Permanent Representative GEDIMINAS SERKSNYS.

Luxembourg: 17 Beekman Pl., New York, NY 10022; tel. (212) 935-3589; fax (212) 935-5896; e-mail luxun@undp.org; internet www.un.int/luxembourg; Permanent Representative JEAN-MARC HOSCHEIT.

Macedonia, former Yugoslav republic: 866 United Nations Plaza, Suite 517, New York, NY 10017; tel. (212) 308-8504; fax (212) 308-8724; e-mail macedonia@un.int; internet www.un.int/macedonia; Permanent Representative Dr IGOR DZUNDEV.

Madagascar: 820 Second Ave, Suite 800, New York, NY 10017; tel. (212) 986-9491; fax (212) 986-6271; e-mail repermad@ren.com; internet www.un.int/madagascar; Permanent Representative ZINA ANDRIANARIVELO-RAZAFY.

Malawi: 600 Third Ave, 21st Floor, New York, NY 10016; tel. (212) 949-0180; fax (212) 599-5021; e-mail malawiun@aol.com; Permanent Representative Prof. BROWN B. CHIMPHAMBA.

Malaysia: 313 East 43rd St, New York, NY 10017; tel. (212) 986-6310; fax (212) 490-8576; e-mail malaysia@un.int; internet www.un.int/malaysia; Permanent Representative RASTAM MOHAMAD ISA.

Maldives: 820 Second Ave, Suite 800C, New York, NY 10017; tel. (212) 599-6195; fax (212) 661-6405; e-mail mdv@undp.org; internet www.un.int/maldives; Permanent Representative Dr MOHAMED LATHEEF.

Mali: 111 East 69th St, New York, NY 10021; tel. (212) 737-4150; fax (212) 472-6778; e-mail malionu@aol.com; Permanent Representative CHEICK SIDI DIARRA.

Malta: 249 East 35th St, New York, NY 10016; tel. (212) 725-2345; fax (212) 779-7097; e-mail mltun@un.int; Permanent Representative VICTOR CAMILLERI.

Marshall Islands: 800 Second Ave, 18th Floor, New York, NY 10017; tel. (212) 983-3040; fax (212) 983-3202; e-mail marshallislands@un.int; Permanent Representative ALFRED CAPELLE.

Mauritania: 211 East 43rd St, Suite 2000, New York, NY 10017; tel. (212) 986-7963; fax (212) 986-8419; e-mail mauritania@un.int; Permanent Representative MOHAMED MAHMOUD OULD EL GHAOUTH.

Mauritius: 211 East 43rd St, 15th Floor, New York, NY 10017; tel. (212) 949-0190; fax (212) 697-3829; e-mail mauritius@un.int; Permanent Representative JAGDISH KOONJUL.

Mexico: 2 United Nations Plaza, 28th Floor, New York, NY 10017; tel. (212) 752-0220; fax (212) 688-8862; e-mail mexico@un.int; internet www.un.int/mexico; Permanent Representative ENRIQUE BERRUGA FILLOY.

Micronesia, Federated States: 820 Second Ave, Suite 17A, New York, NY 10017; tel. (212) 697-8370; fax (212) 697-8295; e-mail fsmun@fsmgov.org; internet www.fsmgov.org/fsmun; Permanent Representative MASAO NAKAYAMA.

Moldova: 35 East 29th St, New York, NY 10016; tel. (212) 447-1867; fax (212) 447-4067; e-mail unmoldova@aol.com; internet www.un .int/moldova; Permanent Representative VSEVOLOD GRIGORE.

Monaco: 866 United Nations Plaza, Suite 520, New York, NY 10017; tel. (212) 832-0721; fax (212) 832-5358; e-mail monaco@un .int; internet www.un.int/monaco; Permanent Representative GILLE NOGHES.

Mongolia: 6 East 77th St, New York, NY 10021; tel. (212) 737-3874; fax (212) 861-9460; e-mail mongolia@un.int; internet www.un.int/ mongolia; Permanent Representative BAATAR CHOISUREN.

Morocco: 866 Second Ave, 6th and 7th Floors, New York, NY 10017; tel. (212) 421-1580; fax (212) 980-1512; e-mail morocco@un.int; internet www.un.int/morocco; Permanent Representative MOHAMED BENNOUNA.

Mozambique: 420 East 50th St, New York, NY 10022; tel. (212) 644-5965; fax (212) 644-5972; e-mail mozambique@un.int; internet www.un.int/mozambique; Permanent Representative FILIPE CHI-DUMO.

Myanmar: 10 East 77th St, New York, NY 10021; tel. (212) 535-1310; fax (212) 737-2421; e-mail myanmar@un.int; Permanent Representative KYAW TINT SWE.

Namibia: 135 East 36th St, New York, NY 10016; tel. (212) 685-2003; fax (212) 685-1561; e-mail namibia@un.int; internet www.un .int/namibia; Permanent Representative MARTIN ANDJABA.

Nauru: 800 Second Ave, Suite 400D, New York, NY 10017; tel. (212) 937-0074; fax (212) 937-0079; Permanent Representative MARLENE INEMWIN MOSES.

Nepal: 820 Second Ave, Suite 17B, New York, NY 10017; tel. (212) 370-3988; fax (212) 953-2038; e-mail nepal@un.int; internet www.un .int/nepal; Permanent Representative MURARI RAJ SHARMA.

Netherlands: 235 East 45th St, 16th Floor, New York, NY 10017; tel. (212) 697-5547; fax (212) 370-1954; e-mail netherlands@un.int; internet www.pvnewyork.org; Permanent Representative DIRK JAN VAN DEN BERG.

New Zealand: 1 United Nations Plaza, 25th Floor, New York, NY 10017; tel. (212) 826-1960; fax (212) 758-0827; e-mail nz@un.int; internet www.nzmissionny.org; Permanent Representative DON MACKAY.

Nicaragua: 820 Second Ave, Suite 801, New York, NY 10017; tel. (212) 490-7997; fax (212) 286-0815; e-mail nicaragua@un.int; internet www.un.int/nicaragua; Permanent Representative EDUARDO J. SEVILLA SOMOZA.

Niger: 417 East 50th St, New York, NY 10022; tel. (212) 421-3260; fax (212) 753-6931; e-mail nigerun@aol.com; internet www.un.int/ niger; Permanent Representative OUSMANE MOUTARI.

Nigeria: 828 Second Ave, New York, NY 10017; tel. (212) 953-9130; fax (212) 697-1970; e-mail nigeria@un.int; Permanent Representative AMINU BASHIR WALI.

Norway: 825 Third Ave, 39th Floor, New York, NY 10022; tel. (212) 421-0280; fax (212) 688-0554; e-mail delun@mfa.no; internet www.un.norway-un.org; Permanent Representative JOHAN LUDVIK LOVALD.

Oman: 866 United Nations Plaza, Suite 540, New York, NY 10017; tel. (212) 355-3505; fax (212) 644-0070; e-mail oman@un.int; Permanent Representative FUAD MUBARAK AL-HINAI.

Pakistan: 8 East 65th St, New York, NY 10021; tel. (212) 879-8600; fax (212) 744-7348; e-mail pakistan@un.int; internet www.un.int/ pakistan; Permanent Representative MUNIR AKRAM.

Palau: 767 Third Ave, 34th Floor, New York, NY 10017; tel. (212) 546-0410; fax (212) 826-2858; e-mail palau@un.int; Permanent Representative STUART BECK.

Panama: 866 United Nations Plaza, Suite 4030, New York, NY 10017; tel. (212) 421-5420; fax (212) 421-2694; e-mail emb@ panama_msun.org; Permanent Representative RICARDO ALBERTO ARIAS.

Papua New Guinea: 201 East 42nd St, Suite 405, New York, NY 10017; tel. (212) 557-5001; fax (212) 557-5009; e-mail png@un.int; Permanent Representative ROBERT GUBA AISI.

Paraguay: 211 East 43rd St, Suite 400, New York, NY 10017; tel. (212) 687-3490; fax (212) 818-1282; e-mail paraguay@un.int; Permanent Representative ELADIO LOIZAGA.

Peru: 820 Second Ave, Suite 1600, New York, NY 10017; tel. (212) 687-3336; fax (212) 972-6975; e-mail peru@un.int; Permanent Representative OSWALDO DE RIVERO.

Philippines: 556 Fifth Ave, 5th Floor, New York, NY 10036; tel. (212) 764-1300; fax (212) 840-8602; e-mail misunphil@idt.net; internet www.un.int/phillipines; Chargé d'affaires a.i. LAURO L. BAJA.

Poland: 9 East 66th St, New York, NY 10021; tel. (212) 744-2506; fax (212) 517-6771; internet www.un.int/ poland; Permanent Representative ANDRZEJ TOWPIK.

Portugal: 866 Second Ave, 9th Floor, New York, NY 10017; tel. (212) 759-9444; fax (212) 355-1124; e-mail portugal@un.int; internet www.un.int/portugal; Permanent Representative JOÃO MANUEL GUERRA SALGUEIRO.

Qatar: 809 United Nations Plaza, 4th Floor, New York, NY 10017; tel. (212) 486-9335; fax (212) 758-4952; e-mail newyork@mofa.gov .qa; Permanent Representative NASSIR BIN ABDULAZIZ AL-NASSER.

Romania: 573–577 Third Ave, New York, NY 10016; tel. (212) 682-3273; fax (212) 682-9746; e-mail romania@un.int; internet www.un .int/romania; Permanent Representative MIHNEA IOAN MOTOC.

Russia: 136 East 67th St, New York, NY 10021; tel. (212) 861-4900; fax (212) 628-0252; e-mail rusun@un.int; internet www.un.int/ russia; Permanent Representative ANDREY V. DENISOV.

Rwanda: 124 East 39th St, New York, NY 10016; tel. (212) 679-9010; fax (212) 679-9133; e-mail rwanda@un.int; Permanent Representative STANISLAS KAMANZI.

Saint Christopher and Nevis: 414 East 75th St, 5th Floor, New York, NY 10021; tel. (212) 535-1235; fax (212) 535-6858; e-mail sknmission@aol.com; Permanent Representative Dr JOSEPH R. CHRISTMAS.

Saint Lucia: 800 Second Ave, 9th Floor, New York, NY 10017; tel. (212) 697-9360; fax (212) 697-4993; e-mail stlucia@un.int; internet www.un.int/stlucia; Permanent Representative JULIAN ROBERT HUNTE.

Saint Vincent and the Grenadines: 801 Second Ave, 21st Floor, New York, NY 10017; tel. (212) 687-4490; fax (212) 949-5946; e-mail stvg@un.int; Permanent Representative MARGARET HUGHES FERRARI.

Samoa: 800 Second Ave, Suite 400J, New York, NY 10017; tel. (212) 599-6196; fax (212) 599-0797; e-mail samoa@un.int; Permanent Representative ALI'IOAIGA FETURI ELISAIA.

San Marino: 327 East 50th St, New York, NY 10022; tel. (212) 751-1234; fax (212) 751-1436; e-mail sanmarinoun@hotmail.com; Permanent Representative GIAN NICOLA FILIPPI BALESTRA.

São Tomé and Príncipe: 400 Park Ave, 7th Floor, New York, NY 10022; tel. (212) 317-0533; fax (212) 317-0580; e-mail stp@un.int; Chargé d'affaires a.i. DOMINGOS AUGUSTO FERREIRA.

Saudi Arabia: 405 Lexington Ave, 56th Floor, New York, NY 10017; tel. (212) 697-4830; fax (212) 983-4895; e-mail saudi-mission@un.int; internet www.saudi-un-ny.org; Permanent Representative FAWZI BIN ABD AL-MAJEED SHOBOKSHI.

Senegal: 238 East 68th St, New York, NY 10021; tel. (212) 517-9030; fax (212) 517-3032; e-mail senegal@un.int; internet www.un .int/senegal; Permanent Representative PAUL BADJI.

Serbia and Montenegro: 854 Fifth Ave, New York, NY 10021; tel. (212) 879-8700; fax (212) 879-8705; e-mail yugoslavia@un.int; internet www.un.int/serbia-montenegro; Permanent Representative NEBOYŠA KALUDJEROVIĆ.

Seychelles: 800 Second Ave, Room 400C, New York, NY 10017; tel. (212) 972-1785; fax (212) 972-1786; e-mail seychelles@un.int; Permanent Representative JEREMIE BONNELAME (designate).

Sierra Leone: 245 East 49th St, New York, NY 10017; tel. (212) 688-1656; fax (212) 688-4924; e-mail sierraleone@un.int; Permanent Representative JOE ROBERT PEMAGBI.

Singapore: 231 East 51st St, New York, NY 10022; tel. (212) 826-0840; fax (212) 826-2964; e-mail sgpun@prodigy.net; internet www

.mfa.gov.sg/newyork; Permanent Representative KISHORE MAHBU-BANI.

Slovakia: 866 United Nations Plaza, Suite 494, New York, NY 10017; tel. (212) 980-1558; fax (212) 980-3295; e-mail slovakia@un.int; Permanent Representative PETER BURIAN.

Slovenia: 600 Third Ave, 24th Floor, New York, NY 10016; tel. (212) 370-3007; fax (212) 370-1824; e-mail mny@mzz-dkp.gov.si; internet www.un.int/slovenia; Permanent Representative ROMAN KIRN.

Solomon Islands: 800 Second Ave, Suite 400L, New York, NY 10017; tel. (212) 599-6193; fax (212) 661-8925; e-mail solomonislands@un.int; Permanent Representative COLIN D. BECK.

Somalia: 425 East 61st St, Suite 702, New York, NY 10021; tel. (212) 688-9410; fax (212) 759-0651; e-mail somalianet@hotmail.com; internet www.iaed.org/somalia; Permanent Representative AHMED ABDI HASHI.

South Africa: 333 East 38th St, 9th Floor, New York, NY 10016; tel. (212) 213-5583; fax (212) 692-2498; e-mail soafun@worldnet.att.net; internet www.southafrica-newyork.net/pmun; Permanent Representative DUMISANI SHADRACK KUMALO.

Spain: 823 United Nations Plaza, 9th Floor, New York, NY 10017; tel. (212) 661-1050; fax (212) 949-7247; e-mail spain@spainum.org; internet www.spainun.org; Permanent Representative JUAN ANTONIO YÁÑEZ-BARNUEVO.

Sri Lanka: 630 Third Ave, 20th Floor, New York, NY 10017; tel. (212) 986-7040; fax (212) 986-1838; e-mail srilanka@un.int; Permanent Representative PRASAD KARIYAWASAM.

Sudan: 655 Third Ave, Suite 500-510, New York, NY 10017; tel. (212) 573-6033; fax (212) 573-6160; e-mail sudan@un.int; Permanent Representative ELFATIH MOHAMED AHMED ERWA.

Suriname: 866 United Nations Plaza, Suite 320, New York, NY 10017; tel. (212) 826-0660; fax (212) 980-7029; e-mail suriname@un.int; internet www.un.int/suriname; Permanent Representative EWALD WENSLEY LIMON.

Swaziland: 408 East 50th St, New York, NY 10022; tel. (212) 371-8910; fax (212) 754-2755; e-mail swaziland@un.int; Permanent Representative CLIFFORD SIBUSIO MAMBA.

Sweden: 1 Dag Hammarskjöld Plaza, 885 Second Ave, 46th Floor, New York, NY 10017; tel. (212) 583-2500; fax (212) 832-0389; e-mail sweden@un.int; internet www.un.int/sweden; Permanent Representative ANDERS LIDÉN.

Switzerland: 633 Third Ave, 29th floor, New York, NY 10017; tel. (212) 286-1540; fax (212) 286-1555; e-mail vertretung-un@nyc.rep.admin.ch; internet www.uno.admin.ch/sub_uno/e/uno.html; Permanent Representative PETER MAURER.

Syria: 820 Second Ave, 15th Floor, New York, NY 10017; tel. (212) 661-1313; fax (212) 867-3985; e-mail syria@un.int; internet www.syria-un.org; Permanent Representative FAYSSAL MEKDAD.

Tajikistan: 136 East 67th St, New York, NY 10021; tel. (212) 744-2196; fax (212) 472-7645; e-mail tajikistan@un.int; Permanent Representative RASHID ALIMOV.

Tanzania: 201 East 42nd St, 17th Floor, New York, NY 10017; tel. (212) 972-9160; fax (212) 682-5232; e-mail tzrepny@aol.com; Permanent Representative AUGUSTINE PHILIP MAHIGA.

Thailand: 351 East 52nd St, New York, NY 10022; tel. (212) 754-2230; fax (212) 754-2535; e-mail thailand@un.int; Permanent Representative LAXANACHANTORN LAOHAPHAN.

Timor-Leste: 866 Second Ave, 9th floor, New York, NY 10017; tel. (212) 759-3675; fax (212) 759-4196; e-mail timor-leste@un.int; internet www.un.int/timor-leste; Permanent Representative JOSÉ LUÍS GUTERRES.

Togo: 112 East 40th St, New York, NY 10016; tel. (212) 490-3455; fax (212) 983-6684; e-mail togo@un.int; e-mail onu@republicoftogo.com; Permanent Representative ROLAND YAO KPOTSRA.

Tonga: 800 Second Ave, Suite 400J, New York, NY 10017; tel. (212) 599-6190; fax (212) 808-4975; e-mail tongaunmission@aol.com; Permanent Representative FEKITAMOELOA 'UTOIKAMANU.

Trinidad and Tobago: 820 Second Ave, 5th Floor, New York, NY 10017; tel. (212) 697-7620; fax (212) 682-3580; e-mail tto@un.int; Permanent Representative PHILIP R.A. SEALY.

Tunisia: 31 Beekman Pl., New York, NY 10022; tel. (212) 751-7503; fax (212) 751-0569; e-mail tunisia@un.int; internet www.tunisiaonline.com/tunisia-un/index.html; Permanent Representative ALI HACHANI.

Turkey: 821 United Nations Plaza, 10th Floor, New York, NY 10017; tel. (212) 949-0150; fax (212) 949-0086; e-mail turkey@un.int; internet www.un.int/turkey; Permanent Representative BAKI ILKIN.

Turkmenistan: 866 United Nations Plaza, Suite 424, New York, NY 10021; tel. (212) 486-8908; fax (212) 486-2521; e-mail turkmenistan@un.int; Permanent Representative AKSOLTAN T. ATAEVA.

Tuvalu: 800 Second Ave, Suite 400B, New York, N.Y. 10017; tel. (212) 490-0534; fax (212) 808-4975; Permanent Representative ENELE SOSENE SOPOAGA.

Uganda: 336 East 45th St, New York, NY 10017; tel. (212) 949-0110; fax (212) 687-4517; e-mail ugandaamb@aol.com; internet www.un.int/uganda; Permanent Representative FRANCIS BUTAGIRA.

Ukraine: 220 East 51st St, New York, NY 10022; tel. (212) 759-7003; fax (212) 355-9455; e-mail mail@uamission.org; internet www.uamission.org; Permanent Representative VALERIY P. KUCHINSKY.

United Arab Emirates: 747 Third Ave, 36th Floor, New York, NY 10017; tel. (212) 371-0480; fax (212) 371-4923; e-mail uae@un.int; Permanent Representative ABDULAZIZ NASSER R. ASH-SHAMSI.

United Kingdom: 1 Dag Hammarskjöld Plaza, 885 Second Ave, New York, NY 10017; tel. (212) 745-9200; fax (212) 745-9316; e-mail uk@un.int; internet www.ukun.org; Permanent Representative Sir EMYR JONES PARRY.

USA: 799 United Nations Plaza, New York, NY 10017; tel. (212) 415-4000; fax (212) 415-4443; e-mail usa@un.int; internet www.un.int/usa; Permanent Representative JOHN BOLTON (designate).

Uruguay: 866 United Nations Plaza, Suite 322, New York, NY 10017; tel. (212) 752-8240; fax (212) 593-0935; e-mail uruguay@un.int; internet www.un.int/uruguay; Permanent Representative FELIPE H. PAOLILLO.

Uzbekistan: 866 United Nations Plaza, Suite 326, New York, NY 10017; tel. (212) 486-4242; fax (212) 486-7998; e-mail uzbekistan@un.int; Permanent Representative ALISHER VOHIDOV.

Vanuatu: 866 United Nations Plaza, 3rd Floor, New York, NY 10017; tel. (212) 425-9600; fax (212) 425-9653; e-mail vanuatu@un.int; Chargé d'affaires a.i. SELWYN ARUTANGAI.

Venezuela: 335 East 46th St, New York, NY 10017; tel. (212) 557-2055; fax (212) 557-3528; e-mail venezuela@un.int; internet www.un.int/venezuela; Permanent Representative FERMIN TORO JIMENEZ.

Viet Nam: 866 United Nations Plaza, Suite 435, New York, NY 10017; tel. (212) 644-0594; fax (212) 644-5732; e-mail vietnamun@aol.com; internet www.un.int/vietnam; Permanent Representative LE LUONG MINH.

Yemen: 413 East 51st St, New York, NY 10022; tel. (212) 355-1730; fax (212) 750-9613; e-mail yemen@un.int; internet www.un.int/yemen; Permanent Representative ABDULLAH M. AS-SAIDI.

Zambia: 237 East 52nd St, New York, NY 10022; tel. (212) 888-5770; fax (212) 888-5213; e-mail zambia@un.int; internet www.un.int/zambia; Permanent Representative MWELWA CHAMBIKABALENSHI CHIBOTWE CHUSHI MUSAMBACHI.

Zimbabwe: 128 East 56th St, New York, NY 10022; tel. (212) 980-9511; fax (212) 308-6705; e-mail zimbabwe@un.int; Permanent Representative T. J. B. BONIFACE GUWA CHIDYAUSIKU.

OBSERVERS

Non-member states, inter-governmental organizations, etc., which have received an invitation to participate in the sessions and the work of the General Assembly as Observers, maintaining permanent offices at the UN.

Holy See: 25 East 39th St, New York, NY 10016; tel. (212) 370-7885; fax (212) 370-9622; e-mail vatobservny@qwest.net; internet www.holyseemission.org; Permanent Representative Most Rev. CELESTINO MIGLIORE (Titular Archbishop of Canosa).

International Federation of Red Cross and Red Crescent Societies: 630 Third Ave, Suite 2104, New York, NY 10017; tel. (212) 338-0161; fax (212) 338-9832; e-mail redcross@un.int; Permanent Representative ENCHO GOSPODINOV.

Sovereign Military Order of Malta: 216 East 47th St, 8th Floor, New York, NY 10017; tel. (212) 355-6213; fax (212) 355-4014; e-mail sm-malta@un.int; Permanent Representative JOSÉ ANTONIO LINATI-BOSCH.

The following inter-governmental organizations have a standing invitation to participate as Observers, but do not maintain permanent offices at the United Nations:

African, Caribbean and Pacific Group of States;

African Development Bank;

Agency for the Prohibition of Nuclear Weapons in Latin America and the Caribbean;

Andean Community;

Association of Caribbean States;

Central American Integration System;

Commonwealth of Independent States;

Council of Europe;

East African Community;
Economic Co-operation Organization;
Eurasian Economic Community;
GUAAM;
International Criminal Police Organization (Interpol);
International Institute for Democracy and Electoral Assistance;
Inter-Parliamentary Union;
Latin American Economic System;
Latin American Parliament;
Organisation for Economic Co-operation and Development;
Organization for Security and Co-operation in Europe;
Organization of American States;
Organization of the Black Sea Economic Co-operation;
Permanent Court of Arbitration;
Pacific Islands Forum.

United Nations Information Centres/Services

Algeria: 9A rue Emile Payen, Hydra, Algiers; tel. (2) 691212; fax (2) 692315; e-mail unic.dz@undp.org; internet www.unic.org.dz.

Argentina: Junín 1940, 1°, 1113 Buenos Aires; tel. (1) 4803-7671; fax (1) 4804-7545; e-mail buenosaires@unic.org.ar; internet www.unic.org.ar; also covers Uruguay.

Armenia: 375001 Yerevan, 14 Karl Libknekht St, 1st Floor; tel. (3741) 560-212; fax (3741) 561-406; e-mail dpi@undpi.am; internet www.undpi.am.

Australia: POB 4045, 46–48 York St, 5th Floor, Sydney, NSW 2001; tel. (2) 9262-5111; fax (2) 9262-5886; e-mail unic@un.org.au; internet www.un.org.au; also covers Fiji, Kiribati, Nauru, New Zealand, Samoa, Tonga, Tuvalu and Vanuatu.

Austria: POB 500, Vienna International Centre, 1400 Vienna; tel. (1) 26060-4666; fax (1) 26060-5899; e-mail unis@unis.unvienna.org; internet www.unis.unvienna.org; also covers Hungary, Slovakia and Slovenia.

Azerbaijan: 1001 Baku, UMSO Anniversary St; tel. (12) 498-98-88; fax (12) 492-24-21; e-mail dpi@un.azeri.com; internet www.un-az.org.

Bahrain: POB 26004, Bldg 69, Rd 1901, Manama 319; tel. (973) 311-676; fax (973) 311-692; e-mail unic.bahrain@undp.org; also covers Qatar and the United Arab Emirates.

Bangladesh: POB 3658, House 60, Rd 11A, Dhanmondi, Dhaka 1209; tel. (2) 8118600; fax (2) 8112343; e-mail unic.dhaka@undp.org; internet www.unicdhaka.org.

Belarus: 220050 Minsk, 17 Kirov St, 6th Floor; tel. 2278149; fax 22260340; e-mail dpi_by@un.dp.org; internet www.un.minsk.by.

Bolivia: Apdo 9072, Calle 14 esq. S. Bustamante, Ed. Metrobol II, Calacoto, La Paz; tel. (2) 2795544; fax (2) 2795963; e-mail unicbol@nu.org.bo; internet www.no.org.bo/cinu.

Brazil: Palacio Itamaraty, Avda Marechal Floriano 196, 20080-002 Rio de Janeiro; tel. (21) 253-2211; fax (21) 233-5753; e-mail infounic@unicrio.org.br; internet www.unicrio.org.br.

Burkina Faso: BP 135, ave Georges Konseiga, Secteur no 4, Ouagadougou; tel. 30-60-76; fax 31-13-22; e-mail cinu.oui@fasonet.bf; internet www.cinu-burkina.org; also covers Chad, Mali and Niger.

Burundi: BP 2160, ave de la Révolution 117, Bujumbura; tel. (2) 225018; fax (2) 241798; e-mail unicbuj@cbinf.com.

Cameroon: PB 836, Immeuble Kamdem, rue Joseph Clère, Yaoundé; tel. 22-50-43; fax 23-51-73; e-mail unic@un.cm; internet www.un.cm/cinu; also covers the Central African Republic and Gabon.

Chile: Edif. Naciones Unidas, Avda Dag Hammarskjöld, Casilla 179-D, Santiago; tel. (2) 210-2000; fax (2) 208-1946; e-mail dpisantiago@eclac.cl.

Colombia: Apdo Aéreo 058964 Calle 100, No. 8A-55, 10°, Santafé de Bogotá 2; tel. (1) 257-6044; fax (1) 257-6244; e-mail uniccol@mbox.unicc.org; internet www.onucolombia.org; also covers Ecuador and Venezuela.

Congo, Democratic Republic: PB 7248, blvd du 30 juin, Kinshasa; tel. 884-5537; fax 884-3675; e-mail unic.kinshasa@undp.org.

Congo, Republic: POB 13210, ave Foch, Case ORTF 15, Brazzaville; tel. 814447; fax 812744; e-mail prosper.mihindou@undp.org.

Czech Republic: nam. Kinských 6, 150 00 Prague 5; tel. (2) 57199831; fax (2) 47316761; e-mail unicprg@terminal.cz; internet www.unicprague.cz.

Egypt: POB 982, World Trade Centre, 1191 Corniche El Nil, Boulak, Cairo; tel. (2) 5315593; fax (2) 3553705; e-mail info@unic-eg.org; internet www.unic-eg.org; also covers Saudi Arabia.

Eritrea: POB 5366, Andinet St, Zone 4 Admin. 07, Airport Rd, Asmara; tel. (1) 182166; fax (1) 1801081; e-mail fo.eri@undp.org.

Ethiopia: POB 3001, Africa Hall, Addis Ababa; tel. (1) 515826; fax (1) 510365; e-mail ecainfo@un.org.

Ghana: POB 2339, Gamel Abdul Nassar/Liberia Roads, Accra; tel. (21) 665511; fax (21) 7010930; e-mail info@unicar.org.gh; also covers Sierra Leone.

Georgia: 380079 Tbilisi, Eristavi St 9; tel. (32) 998558; fax (32) 250271; e-mail registry.ge@undp.org; internet www.undp.org.ge.

India: 55 Lodi Estate, New Delhi 110 003; tel. (11) 462-8877; fax (11) 462-0293; internet www.unic.org.in; also covers Bhutan.

Indonesia: Gedung Surya, 14th Floor, 9 Jalan M. H. Thamrin Kavling, Jakarta 10350; tel. (21) 3983-1011; fax (21) 3983-1010; e-mail unicjak@cbn.net.id.

Iran: POB 15875-4557; 185 Ghaem Magham Farahani Ave, Tehran 15868; tel. (21) 873-1534; fax (21) 204-4523; e-mail unic@unic.un.or.ir; internet www.unic-ir.org.

Japan: UNU Bldg, 8th Floor, 53–70 Jingumae S-chome, Shibuya-ku, Tokyo 150 0001; tel. (3) 5467-4451; fax (3) 5467-4455; e-mail unic@untokyo.jp; internet www.unic.or.jp; also covers Palau.

Kazakhstan: 480100 Almaty, Tole bi 67; tel. (3272) 69-53-27; fax (3272) 58-26-54; e-mail registry.kz@undp.org.

Kenya: POB 30552, United Nations Office, Gigiri, Nairobi; tel. (20) 623292; fax (20) 624349; e-mail unic@unep.org; internet www.unicnairobi.org; also covers Seychelles and Uganda.

Lebanon: Riad es-Solh Sq., POB 11-8575-4956, Chouran, Beirut; tel. (1) 981301; fax (1) 981516; e-mail unic-beirut@un.org; also covers Jordan, Kuwait and Syria.

Lesotho: POB 301, Maseru 100; tel. (22) 312496; fax (22) 310042; e-mail unic.maseru@undp.org.

Liberia: Dubar Bldg, Virginia, Monrovia; tel. 2260195; fax 205407; e-mail registry.1r@undp.org.

Libya: POB 286, Shara Muzzafar al-Aftas, Hay al-Andalous, Tripoli; tel. (21) 4777885; fax (21) 4777343; e-mail fo.lby@undp.org.

Madagascar: PB 1348, 22 rue Rainitovo, Antasahavola, Antananarivo; tel. (20) 2224115; fax (20) 33315; e-mail unic.ant@dts.mg; internet www.onu.dts.mg.

Mexico: Presidente Masaryk 29, 6°, México 11 570, DF; tel. (55) 5263-9724; fax (55) 5203-8238; e-mail unicmex@un.org.mx; internet www.cinu.org.mx; also covers Cuba and the Dominican Republic.

Morocco: BP 601, Angle Charia Ibnouzaid 6, Rabat; tel. (7) 7686-33; fax (7) 7683-77; e-mail unicmor@unicmor.ma; internet www.cinu.org.ma.

Myanmar: POB 230, 6 Natmauk Rd, Yangon; tel. (1) 292619; fax (1) 292911; e-mail unic.myanmar@undp.org.

Namibia: Private Bag 13351, Paratus Bldg, 372 Independence Ave, Windhoek; tel. (61) 233034; fax (61) 233036; e-mail unic@un.na; internet www.un.na/unic.htm.

Nepal: POB 107, UN House, Kathmandu; tel. (1) 524366; fax (1) 523991; e-mail registry.np@undp.org.

Nicaragua: Apdo 3260, Palacio de la Cultura, Managua; tel. (2) 664253; fax (2) 222362; e-mail cedoc@sdnnic.org.ni.

Nigeria: POB 1068, 17 Kingsway Rd, Ikoyi, Lagos; tel. (1) 269-4886; fax (1) 269-1934; e-mail uniclag@unicnig.org; internet www.unicnig.org.

Pakistan: POB 1107, House No. 26, 88th St, G-6/3, Islamabad; tel. (51) 270610; fax (51) 271856; e-mail unic@isb.paknet.com.pk; internet www.un.org.pk/unic.

Panama: POB 6-9083, El Dorado; Banco Central Hispano Edif., 1°, Calle Gerardo Ortega y Av. Samuel Lewis, Panama City; tel. (7) 233-0557; fax (7) 223-2198; e-mail cinup@cciglobal.net.pa; internet www.cinup.org.

Paraguay: Casilla de Correo 1107, Edif. City, 3°, Asunción; tel. (21) 614443; fax (21) 449611; e-mail unic.py@undp.org.

Peru: POB 14-0199, Lord Cochrane 130, San Isidro, Lima 27; tel. (1) 441-8745; fax (1) 441-8735; e-mail informes@uniclima.org.pe; internet www.uniclima.org.pe.

Philippines: NEDA Bldg, Ground Floor, 106 Amorsolo St, Legaspi Village, Makati City, Manila; tel. (2) 8920611; fax (2) 8163011;

e-mail infocentre@unicmanila.org; also covers Papua New Guinea and Solomon Islands.

Poland: 00-608 Warsaw, Al. Niepodległości 186; 02-514 Warsaw, POB 1; tel. (22) 8259245; fax (22) 8255785; e-mail unic.pl@undp.org; internet www.unic.un.org.pl.

Romania: POB 1-701, 16 Aurel Vlaicu St, Bucharest; tel. (1) 2113242; fax (1) 2113506; e-mail unic@undp.ro.

Russia: 4/16 Glazovsky Per., Moscow; tel. (095) 241-2894; fax (095) 230-2138; e-mail dpi-moscow@unic.ru; internet www.unic.ru.

Senegal: BP 154, Immeuble UNESCO, 12 ave Roume, Dakar; tel. 823-30-70; fax 822-26-79; e-mail cinu.dakar@sentoo.sn; internet www.cinu-dakar.org; also covers Cape Verde, Côte d'Ivoire, The Gambia, Guinea, Guinea-Bissau and Mauritania.

South Africa: Metro Park Bldg, 351 Schoeman St, POB 12677, Pretoria 0126; tel. (12) 338-5077; fax (12) 320-1122; e-mail unic@un.org.za.

Sri Lanka: POB 1505, 202-204 Bauddhaloka Mawatha, Colombo 7; tel. (1) 580691; fax (1) 581116; e-mail anusha.atukorale@undp.org.

Sudan: POB 1992, UN Compound, Gamma'a Ave, Khartoum; tel. (11) 773121; fax (11) 773128; e-mail unic.sd@undp.org; also covers Somalia.

Switzerland: Palais des Nations, 1211 Geneva 10; tel. (22) 9172300; fax (22) 9170030; e-mail press_geneva@unog.ch; internet www.unog.ch/unis/unis1.htm; also covers Bulgaria.

Tanzania: POB 9224, Old Boma Bldg, Morogoro Rd/Sokoine Drive, Dar es Salaam; tel. (22) 2119510; fax (22) 2112923; e-mail fo.tza@undp.org.

Thailand: ESCAP, United Nations Bldg, Rajadamnern Nok Ave, Bangkok 10200; tel. (2) 288-1234; fax (2) 288-1000; e-mail unisbkk.unescap@un.org; internet www.unescap.org/unic; also covers Cambodia, Hong Kong, Laos, Malaysia, Singapore and Viet Nam.

Togo: BP 911, 107 blvd du 13 janvier, Lomé; tel. and fax 2212306; e-mail cinutogo@laposte.tg; also covers Benin.

Trinidad and Tobago: POB 130, Bretton Hall, 16 Victoria Ave, Port of Spain; tel. 623-4813; fax 623-4332; e-mail unicpos@unicpos.org.tt; also covers Antigua and Barbuda, the Bahamas, Barbados, Belize, Dominica, Grenada, Guyana, Jamaica, the Netherlands Antilles, Saint Christopher and Nevis, Saint Lucia, Saint Vincent and the Grenadines and Suriname.

Tunisia: BP 863, 61 blvd Bab-Benat, Tunis; tel. (71) 560-203; fax (71) 568-811; e-mail onu.tunis@planet.tn; internet www.onu.org.tn.

Turkey: PK 407, Birlik Mahallesi, 2 Cad. No. 11, 06610 Cankaya, Ankara; tel. (312) 4541051; fax (312) 4961499; e-mail unic@un.org.tr; internet www.un.org.tr/unic.html.

Ukraine: 01021 Kyiv-21, Klovsky Uzviz, 1; tel. (44) 253-55-59; fax (44) 253-26-07; e-mail registry@unkiev.ua; internet www.un.kiev.ua.

USA: 1775 K St, NW, Suite 400, Washington, DC 20006; tel. (202) 331-8670; fax (202) 331-9191; e-mail unicwash@unicwash.org; internet www.unicwash.org.

Uzbekistan: 700029 Tashkent, 4 Taras Shevchenko St; tel. (371) 139-09-77; fax (371) 133-69-65; e-mail registry.uz@undp.org; internet www.undp.uz.

Western Europe: Regional United Nations Information Centre, The Residence Palace, Bloc C, 155 rue de la Loi/Wetstraat, 1040 Brussels, Belgium; tel. (2) 289-28-90; fax (2) 502-40-61; e-mail info@runic-europe.org; internet www.runic-europe.org; serves Belgium, Cyprus, Denmark, Finland, France, Germany, Greece, The Holy See, Iceland, Ireland, Italy, Luxembourg, Malta, the Netherlands, Norway, Portugal, San Marino, Spain, Sweden, United Kingdom; also provides liaison with the institutions of the European Union.

Yemen: POB 237, Handhal St, 4 Al-Boniya Arca, San'a; tel. (1) 274000; fax (1) 274043; e-mail unicyem@ynet.ye.

Zambia: POB 32905, Lusaka 10101; tel. (1) 228487; fax (1) 222958; e-mail unic@zamnet.zam; also covers Botswana, Malawi and Swaziland.

Zimbabwe: POB 4408, Sanders House, 2nd Floor, First St/Jason Moyo Ave, Harare; tel. (4) 777060; fax (4) 750476; e-mail unic@samara.co.uk; internet www.samara.co.zw/unic.

Conferences

Global conferences are convened regularly by the United Nations. Special sessions of the General Assembly assess progress achieved in the implementation of conference action plans. The following conferences and special sessions were scheduled for 2005:

International Meeting to Review Implementation of the Barbados Programme of Action for the Sustainable Development of Small Island Developing States (Jan.: Port-Louis, Mauritius);

World Conference on Disaster Reduction (Jan.: Kobe, Japan);

Review Conference of the Parties to the Treaty on the Non-Proliferation of Nuclear Weapons (May: New York);

Special Solemn Meeting of the General Assembly to Commemorate the 60th Anniversary of the End of the Second World War (May: New York);

Second High-Level Dialogue on Financing for Development (June: New York);

Review Conference to Review Progress made in Implementing the Programme of Action to Prevent, Combat and Eradicate the Illicit Trade in Small Arms and Light Weapons in All its Aspects (June–July: New York);

Civil Society Forging Partnerships to Prevent Violent Conflicts and Build Peace (July: New York);

Meeting to Review Implementation of the UN Millennium Declaration of September 2000 (Sept.: New York);

World Summit on the Information Society, phase II (Nov.: Tunis, Tunisia).

Co-ordinating Bodies

The 28-member United Nations System Chief Executives Board for Co-ordination—CEB, founded in 1946 as the Administrative Committee on Co-ordination and renamed in 2001, convenes at least twice a year under the chairmanship of the Secretary General to co-ordinate UN system-wide policies, activities and management issues. In 1997 the United Nations Development Group (UNDG) was established, under the chairmanship of the Administrator of UNDP, uniting the heads of some 20 UN funds, programmes and departments concerned with sustainable development, in order to promote coherent policy at country level. Project management services are provided throughout the UN system of entities and organizations, as well as to certain bilateral donors, international financial institutions and governments, by the United Nations Office for Project Services—UNOPS. UNOPS, founded in 1995 and a member of the UNDG, is self-financing, funded by fees earned from the services that it provides. The Inter-Agency Standing Committee—IASC, founded in 1992, comprises the executive heads of 17 leading UN and other agencies and NGO consortia, who convene at least twice a year under the leadership of the Emergency Relief Co-ordinator (see OCHA, see p. 41). It co-ordinates and administers the international response to complex and major humanitarian disasters, and the development of relevant policies.

Finance

The majority of the UN's peace-keeping operations (see p. 69) are financed separately from the UN's regular budget by assessed contributions from member states.

In recent years the UN has suffered financial difficulties, owing to an expansion of the organization's political and humanitarian activities and delay on the part of member states in paying their contributions. In 1993 the UN Secretary-General formulated a series of economy measures to be applied throughout the organization, in order to avert a financial crisis. However, the fragility of the UN's financial situation has persisted, partly owing to delays in the process between approval of a peace-keeping operation and receipt of contributions for that budget. In December 2000 the General Assembly approved a restructuring of scale of assessment calculations, the methodology and accuracy of which had been contested in recent years, particularly by the USA. From 2001 the level of US contributions to the regular annual budget was reduced from 25% to 22%, while annual contributions were raised for several nations with rapidly developing economies. At December 2004 119 member states had paid their regular budget assessments in full, while the remaining members owed some US $357m. Of the total amount of unpaid assessments the USA owed $241m. In addition, many member states owed outstanding assessment contributions to the peace-keeping and international tribunal budgets at that time. The scale of assessment calculations was to be reviewed again in 2006.

In 1997 a US business executive, Ted Turner, announced a donation of US $1,000m., which was to be paid in regular instalments over a 10-year period through his 'UN Foundation', and was to finance humanitarian and environmental programmes. A UN Fund for International Partnerships (UNFIP) was established to administer the donation. In the same year the UN Secretary-General pledged to implement administrative reforms of the UN and proposed a reduction in the organization's budget. A Development Account was established in December under the Secretary-General's reform programme; administrative savings were to be channelled through this to finance development projects. In late 1999 the Secretary-General stated that a further reduction in the UN budget would compromise the organization's capacity to implement mandated activities. The budget for 2004–05 amounted to $3,160.9m.

TWO-YEAR BUDGET OF THE UNITED NATIONS
(US $'000)

	2004–05
Overall policy-making, direction and co-ordination	593,884.9
Political affairs	349,252.2
International justice and law	70,245.4
International co-operation for development	336,495.3
Regional co-operation for development	388,613.7
Human rights and humanitarian affairs	170,670.5
Public information	155,869.9
Common support services	516,168.9
Internal oversight	23,227.2
Jointly-financed activities and special expenses	102,445.3
Capital expenditures	58,651.3
Staff assessment	382,270.7
Development Account	13,065.0
Total	3,160,860.3

United Nations Publications

Africa Recovery (quarterly).

Basic Facts About the United Nations.

Demographic Yearbook.

Index to Proceedings (of the General Assembly; the Security Council; the Economic and Social Council; the Trusteeship Council).

International Law Catalogue.

Monthly Bulletin of Statistics.

Population and Vital Statistics Report (quarterly).

Statistical Yearbook (also on CD-Rom).

The UN Chronicle (quarterly).

United Nations Disarmament Yearbook.

United Nations Juridical Yearbook.

World Economic and Social Survey.

World Situation and Prospects.

World Statistics Pocketbook.

Yearbook of the United Nations (also on CD-Rom).

Other UN publications are listed in the chapters dealing with the agencies concerned.

Secretariat

According to the UN Charter the Secretary-General is the chief administrative officer of the organization, and he may appoint further Secretariat staff as required. The principal departments and officers of the Secretariat are listed below. The chief administrative staff of the UN Regional Commissions and of all the subsidiary organs of the UN are also members of the Secretariat staff and are listed in the appropriate chapters. The Secretariat staff also includes a number of special missions and special appointments, including some of senior rank.

In June 2003 the total number of staff of the Secretariat holding appointments continuing for a year or more was approximately 15,082, including those serving away from the headquarters, but excluding staff working for the UN specialized agencies and subsidiary organs.

In July 1997 the Secretary-General initiated a comprehensive reform of the administration of the UN and abolished some 1,000 Secretariat posts. The reforms aimed to restructure the Secretariat's substantive work programme around the UN's five core missions, i.e. peace and security, economic and social affairs, development co-operation, humanitarian affairs and human rights. During 1997 the Centre for Human Rights and the Office of the High Commissioner for Human Rights were consolidated into a single office under the reform process, while a new Office for Drug Control and Crime Prevention was established, within the framework of the UN Office in Vienna, to integrate efforts to combat crime, drug abuse and terrorism; this was subsequently renamed the UN Office on Drugs and Crime. In December a new post of Deputy Secretary-General was created to assist in the management of Secretariat operations, in particular the ongoing reform process, and represent the Secretary-General as required. In 1999 the Secretary-General proposed the 'Global Compact', a new initiative bringing together UN agencies, governments, labour and non-governmental organizations and private corporations to advance nine universally recognized principles in the areas of human rights, labour and environment.

In April 2001 the Secretary-General issued a 'Call to Action' to address the HIV/AIDS pandemic and proposed the establishment of a fund to help developing countries manage the crisis and other health emergencies; the ensuing Global Fund to Fight AIDS, TB and Malaria became operational in 2002 (see World Health Organization). In December 2001, on the recommendation of the Secretary-General, the General Assembly established the Office of the High Representative for the Least Developed Countries, Landlocked Developing Countries and Small Island Developing States. In May 2002 the Secretary-General appointed the first United Nations Security Co-ordinator. A new Department for Safety and Security, headed by an Under-Secretary-General for Safety and Security and replacing the Office of the United Nations Security Co-ordinator, was established in February 2005, taking over responsibility for the safety of UN personnel.

In June 2004 a Panel of Eminent Persons on Civil Society and UN Relationships—appointed by the Secretary-General in February 2003, as part of the ongoing UN reform process, with a mandate to explore and make recommendations on the interaction between civil society, private-sector enterprise, parliaments and the UN—issued its final report. A High-Level Panel on Threats, Challenges and Change, appointed by the Secretary-General in November 2003 (in the aftermath of the deaths in August of 21 UN staff members, including Sergio Vieira de Mello, UN High Commissioner for Human Rights, in a terrorist attack in Baghdad, Iraq) to evaluate the ability of the UN to address threats to the peace and security of the international community and to recommend relevant policy and institutional changes, including reforms to the Security Council, published its findings in December 2004. The report of the Secretary-General entitled 'In Larger Freedom: Towards Development, Security and Human Rights for All', issued in March 2005 after consideration of the High-Level Panel's report, proposed a realignment of the Secretariat's structure, entailing the establishment of a peace-building support office and strengthening support within the body for mediation by the Secretary-General (his 'good offices'), democracy, and the rule of law. He also determined to establish a cabinet-style decision-making executive within the Secretariat, supported by a small subsidiary cabinet secretariat, and proposed a higher level of managerial authority for the role of Secretary-General. Further proposals included the appointment of a Scientific Adviser to the Secretary-General, mandated to supply strategic scientific advice on policy matters, and a comprehensive review of the functioning of the Office of Internal Oversight Services. The Secretary-General's reform proposals were to be presented at the September 2005 five-year review conference of the Millennium Declaration (see General Assembly).

Secretary-General: Kofi Annan (Ghana).

Deputy Secretary-General: Louise Fréchette (Canada).

EXECUTIVE OFFICE OF THE SECRETARY-GENERAL

Under-Secretary-General, Chief of Staff: Mark Malloch Brown (United Kingdom).

Assistant Secretary-General: (vacant).

Assistant Secretary-General, External Relations: Gillian Sorensen (USA).

DEPARTMENT FOR DISARMAMENT AFFAIRS

Under-Secretary-General: Nobuyasu Abe (Japan).

DEPARTMENT FOR SAFETY AND SECURITY

Under-Secretary-General: David Veness (United Kingdom).

DEPARTMENT OF ECONOMIC AND SOCIAL AFFAIRS

Under-Secretary-General: José Antonio Ocampo (Colombia).

Assistant Secretary-General, Special Adviser on Gender Issues and the Advancement of Women: Angela King (Jamaica).

Assistant Secretary-General, Policy Co-ordination and Inter-Agency Affairs: Patrizio Civili (Italy).

DEPARTMENT OF GENERAL ASSEMBLY AND CONFERENCE MANAGEMENT

Under-Secretary-General: CHEN JIAN (People's Republic of China).

Assistant Secretary-General: ANGELA KANE (Germany).

DEPARTMENT OF MANAGEMENT

Under-Secretary-General: CATHERINE BERTINI (USA).

Assistant Secretary-General, Controller: JEAN-PIERRE HALBWACHS (Mauritius).

Assistant Secretary-General, Human Resources: ROSEMARY MCCREERY (Ireland).

Assistant Secretary-General, Central Support: ANDREW TOH (Singapore).

DEPARTMENT OF PEACE-KEEPING OPERATIONS

Under-Secretary-General: JEAN-MARIE GUÉHENNO (France).

Assistant Secretary-General: HÉDI ANNABI (Tunisia).

Assistant Secretary-General: JANE HOLL LUTE (USA).

DEPARTMENT OF POLITICAL AFFAIRS

Under-Secretary-General: Sir KIERAN PRENDERGAST (United Kingdom).

Assistant Secretary-General: DANILO TÜRK (Slovenia).

Assistant Secretary-General: TULIAMENI KALOMOH (Namibia).

DEPARTMENT OF PUBLIC INFORMATION

Under-Secretary-General: SHASHI THAROOR (India).

OFFICE FOR THE CO-ORDINATION OF HUMANITARIAN AFFAIRS

Under-Secretary-General for Humanitarian Affairs and Emergency Relief Co-ordinator: JAN EGELAND (Norway).

Assistant Secretary-General for Humanitarian Affairs and Deputy Emergency Relief Co-ordinator: MARGARETA WAHLSTROM (Sweden).

OFFICE ON DRUGS AND CRIME

Under-Secretary-General: ANTONIO MARIA COSTA (Italy).

OFFICE OF INTERNAL OVERSIGHT SERVICES

Under-Secretary-General: DILEEP NAIR (Singapore).

OFFICE OF THE HIGH REPRESENTATIVE FOR THE LEAST DEVELOPED COUNTRIES, LANDLOCKED DEVELOPING COUNTRIES AND SMALL ISLAND DEVELOPING STATES

Under-Secretary-General and High Representative: ANWARUL KARIM CHOWDHURY (Bangladesh).

OFFICE OF LEGAL AFFAIRS

Under-Secretary-General, The Legal Counsel: NICOLAS MICHEL (Switzerland).

Assistant Secretary-General: RALPH ZACKLIN (United Kingdom).

OFFICE OF THE SPECIAL REPRESENTATIVE OF THE SECRETARY-GENERAL FOR CHILDREN AND ARMED CONFLICT

Under-Secretary-General: OLARA OTUNNU (Uganda).

OFFICE OF THE UNITED NATIONS HIGH COMMISSIONER FOR HUMAN RIGHTS

Palais des Nations, 1211 Geneva 10, Switzerland; tel. (22) 9179000; fax (22) 9179010; internet www.unhchr.ch.

High Commissioner: LOUISE ARBOUR (Canada).

Deputy High Commissioner: MEHR KHAN WILLIAMS (Pakistan).

GENEVA OFFICE

Palais des Nations, 1211 Geneva 10, Switzerland; tel. (22) 9071234; fax (22) 9179010; internet www.unog.ch.

Director-General: SERGEI ORDZONIKIDZE (Russia).

NAIROBI OFFICE

POB 30552, Nairobi, Kenya; tel. and fax (22) 62-4266.

Director-General: Dr KLAUS TÖPFER (Germany).

VIENNA OFFICE

Vienna International Centre, POB 500, 1400 Vienna, Austria; tel. (1) 26060-0; fax (1) 26333-89; internet www.un.or.at.

Director-General: ANTONIO MARIA COSTA (Italy).

General Assembly

The General Assembly was established as a principal organ of the United Nations under the UN Charter (see p. 21). It first met on 10 January 1946. It is the main deliberative organ of the United Nations, and the only one composed of representatives of all the UN member states. Each delegation consists of not more than five representatives and five alternates, with as many advisers as may be required. The Assembly meets regularly for three months each year, and special sessions may also be held. It has specific responsibility for electing the Secretary-General and members of other UN councils and organs, and for approving the UN budget and the assessments for financial contributions by member states. It is also empowered to make recommendations (but not binding decisions) on questions of international security and co-operation.

The regular session of the General Assembly commences in mid-September. After the election of its President and other officers, the Assembly opens its general debate, a two-week period during which the head of each delegation makes a formal statement of his or her government's views on major world issues. Since 1997 the Secretary-General has presented his report on the work of the UN at the start of the general debate. The Assembly then begins examination of the principal items on its agenda: it acts directly on some agenda items, but most business is handled by the six Main Committees (listed below), which study and debate each item and present draft resolutions to the Assembly. After a review of the report of each Main Committee, the Assembly formally approves or rejects the Committee's recommendations. On designated 'important questions', such as recommendations on international peace and security, the admission of new members to the United Nations, or budgetary questions, a two-thirds majority is needed for adoption of a resolution. Other questions may be decided by a simple majority. In the Assembly, each member has one vote. Voting in the Assembly is sometimes replaced by an effort to find consensus among member states, in order to strengthen support for the Assembly's decisions: the President consults delegations in private to find out whether they are

willing to agree to adoption of a resolution without a vote; if they are, the President can declare that a resolution has been so adopted.

Special sessions of the Assembly may be held to discuss issues which require particular attention (e.g. illicit drugs) and 'emergency special sessions' may also be convened to discuss situations on which the UN Security Council has been unable to reach a decision. The Assembly's 10th emergency special session, concerning Illegal Israeli Actions in Occupied East Jerusalem and the rest of the Occupied Palestinian Territory, commenced in April 1997 and has been subsequently reconvened intermittently. The 23rd meeting of the session, called in December 2003 by Arab and non-aligned countries, requested that the International Court of Justice (ICJ) render an advisory opinion on the legal consequences arising from the construction of a wall by Israel in the Occupied Palestinian Territory including in and around East Jerusalem; this action was taken by the General Assembly following two failures by the Security Council to adopt resolutions on the matter. The 24th meeting of the session was convened in July 2004 to discuss the ICJ's ruling on this matter, which had been delivered earlier in that month. A special session on children, reviewing progress made since the World Summit for Children, held in 1990, and the adoption in 1989 of the Convention on the Rights of the Child, was convened in May 2002. In January 2005 a special session took place to commemorate the 60th anniversary of the liberation of the Nazi concentration camps.

The Assembly's 55th session (from September 2000) was designated as the Millennium Assembly. In early September a Millennium Summit of UN heads of state or government was convened to debate 'The Role of the United Nations in the 21st Century'. The Millennium Summit issued the UN Millennium Declaration, identifying the values and principles that should guide the organization in key areas including peace, development, environment, human rights, protection of the vulnerable, and the special needs of the African continent; and specified six fundamental values underlying international relations: freedom; equality; solidarity; tolerance;

respect for nature; and a sense of shared responsibility for the global economy and social development. The summit adopted the following so-called Millennium Development Goals (MDGs), each incorporating specific targets to be attained by 2015: the eradication of extreme poverty and hunger; attainment of universal primary education; promotion of gender equality and empowerment of women; reduction of child mortality rates; improvement in maternal health rates; combating HIV/AIDS, malaria and other diseases; ensuring environmental sustainability; and the development of a global partnership for development. Reform of the Security Council and the need for increased UN co-operation with the private sector, non-governmental organizations and civil society in pursuing its goals were also addressed by the summit. Progress in attaining the MDGs was to be reviewed on a regular basis. A five-year review conference of the Millennium Declaration was scheduled to be convened in September 2005 at the level of heads of state and of government.

In October 2003 the President of the Assembly appointed six facilitators to oversee discussions on means of revitalizing the Assembly, and in mid-December the Assembly adopted a landmark resolution that, while reaffirming relevant provisions of the UN Charter and the UN Millennium Declaration, outlined a number of reforms to the Assembly's operations. The changes, aimed at enhancing the Assembly's authority, role, efficiency and impact, were to take effect following broad consultations over the next two years. The resolution provided for a regular meeting of the Presidents of the Assembly, Security Council and ECOSOC, with a view to strengthening co-operation and complementarity in the respective work programmes of the three bodies. In July 2004 the Assembly adopted a resolution on further revitalization of its work, with provisions for streamlining its agenda, sharpening the focus of the six Main Committees, and reducing paperwork.

In March 2005 the Secretary-General presented to the General Assembly a report entitled 'In Larger Freedom: Towards Development, Security and Human Rights for All'. Building on the September 2000 Millennium Declaration, the report focused on three main pillars, defined as: 'Freedom from Want', urging developing countries to improve governance and combat corruption, and industrialized nations to increase funds for development assistance and debt relief and to provide immediate free market access to all exports from least developed countries; 'Freedom from Fear', urging states to agree a new consensus on security matters and adopting a definition of an act of terrorism as one 'intended to cause death or serious bodily harm to civilians or non-combatants with the purpose of intimidating a population or compelling a government or an international organization to do or abstain from doing any act'; and 'Freedom to Live in Dignity', urging the international community to support the principle of 'responsibility to protect'. The report also detailed a number of recommendations for strengthening the UN, which were to be considered by the September 2005 review conference of the Millennium Declaration. These included: rationalizing the work of the Assembly (see above) and focusing its agenda on substantive topical issues, such as international migration and the conclusion of a new comprehensive international strategy against terrorism; restructuring the Secretariat; expanding the membership of the Security Council; and establishing a new UN Human Rights Council to replace the Commission on Human Rights (see ECOSOC).

President of 59th Session: (from September 2004) JEAN PING (Gabon).

MAIN COMMITTEES

There are six Main Committees, on which all members have a right to be represented. Each Committee includes an elected Chairperson and two Vice-Chairs.

First Committee: Disarmament and International Security.

Second Committee: Economic and Financial.

Third Committee: Social, Humanitarian and Cultural.

Fourth Committee: Special Political and Decolonization.

Fifth Committee: Administrative and Budgetary.

Sixth Committee: Legal.

OTHER SESSIONAL COMMITTEES

General Committee: f. 1946; composed of 28 members, including the Assembly President, the 21 Vice-Presidents of the Assembly and the Chairs of the six Main Committees.

Credentials Committee: f. 1946; composed of nine members appointed at each Assembly session.

POLITICAL AND SECURITY MATTERS

Special Committee on Peace-keeping Operations: f. 1965; 34 appointed members.

Disarmament Commission: f. 1978 (replacing body f. 1952); 61 members.

UN Scientific Committee on the Effects of Atomic Radiation: f. 1955; 21 members.

Committee on the Peaceful Uses of Outer Space: f. 1959; 61 members; has a Legal Sub-Committee and a Scientific and Technical Sub-Committee.

Ad Hoc Committee on the Indian Ocean: f. 1972; 44 members.

Committee on the Exercise of the Inalienable Rights of the Palestinian People: f. 1975; 25 members.

Special Committee on the Implementation of the Declaration on Decolonization: f. 1961; 24 members.

Ad Hoc Committee on Terrorism: f. 1996.

DEVELOPMENT

Commission on Science and Technology for Development: f. 1992; 33 members.

Committee on Energy and Natural Resources Development: f. 1998; 24 members.

United Nations Environment Programme (UNEP) Governing Council: f. 1972; 58 members.

LEGAL QUESTIONS

International Law Commission: f. 1947; 34 members elected for a five-year term; originally established in 1946 as the Committee on the Progressive Development of International Law and its Codification.

Advisory Committee on the UN Programme of Assistance in Teaching, Study, Dissemination and Wider Appreciation of International Law: f. 1965; 25 members.

UN Commission on International Trade Law: f. 1966; 36 members.

Special Committee on the Charter of the United Nations and on the Strengthening of the Role of the Organization: f. 1975; composed of all UN members.

There is also a UN Administrative Tribunal and a Committee on Applications for Review of Administrative Tribunal Judgments.

ADMINISTRATIVE AND FINANCIAL QUESTIONS

Advisory Committee on Administrative and Budgetary Questions: f. 1946; 16 members appointed for three-year terms.

Committee on Contributions: f. 1946; 18 members appointed for three-year terms.

International Civil Service Commission: f. 1972; 15 members appointed for four-year terms.

Committee on Information: f. 1978, formerly the Committee to review UN Policies and Activities; 95 members.

There is also a Board of Auditors, Investments Committee, UN Joint Staff Pension Board, Joint Inspection Unit, UN Staff Pension Committee, Committee on Conferences, and Committee for Programme and Co-ordination.

Security Council

The Security Council was established as a principal organ under the United Nations Charter (see p. 21); its first meeting was held on 17 January 1946. Its task is to promote international peace and security in all parts of the world.

MEMBERS

Permanent members:

People's Republic of China, France, Russia, United Kingdom, USA. The remaining 10 members are normally elected (five each year) by the General Assembly for two-year periods (five countries from Africa and Asia, two from Latin America, one from eastern Europe, and two from western Europe and others).

Non-permanent members in 2005:

Algeria, Benin, Brazil, Philippines, Romania (term expires 31 December 2005).

Argentina, Denmark, Greece, Japan, Tanzania (term expires 31 December 2006).

Rotation of the Presidency in 2005:

Argentina (January); Benin (February); Brazil (March); People's Republic of China (April); Denmark (May); France (June); Greece (July); Japan (August); Philippines (September); Romania (October); Russia (November); United Kingdom (December).

Organization

The Security Council has the right to investigate any dispute or situation which might lead to friction between two or more countries, and such disputes or situations may be brought to the Council's attention either by one of its members, by any member state, by the General Assembly, by the Secretary-General or even, under certain conditions, by a state which is not a member of the United Nations.

The Council has the right to recommend ways and means of peaceful settlement and, in certain circumstances, the actual terms of settlement. In the event of a threat to or breach of international peace or an act of aggression, the Council has powers to take 'enforcement' measures in order to restore international peace and security. These include severance of communications and of economic and diplomatic relations and, if required, action by air, land and sea forces.

All members of the United Nations are pledged by the Charter to make available to the Security Council, on its call and in accordance with special agreements, the armed forces, assistance and facilities necessary to maintain international peace and security. These agreements, however, have not yet been concluded.

The Council is organized to be able to function continuously. The Presidency of the Council is held monthly in turn by the member states in English alphabetical order. Each member of the Council has one vote. On procedural matters decisions are made by the affirmative vote of any nine members. For decisions on other matters the required nine affirmative votes must include the votes of the five permanent members. This is the rule of 'great power unanimity' popularly known as the 'veto' privilege. In practice, an abstention by one of the permanent members is not regarded as a veto. Any member, whether permanent or non-permanent, must abstain from voting in any decision concerning the pacific settlement of a dispute to which it is a party. Any member of the UN that is party to a dispute under consideration by the Council may participate in the Council's discussions without a vote.

The allocation of the Security Council's permanent seats reflects the post-Second World War international situation. It is envisaged that reforms to the Council should be implemented aimed at establishing a more equitable regional representation and recognizing the current global balance of power. Consideration of such reform commenced in 1993 at the 48th Session of the General Assembly, which established a Working Group to assess the issue. In October 1994 a general debate of the General Assembly revealed widespread support for expanding the Security Council to 20 seats and awarding permanent membership to Japan and Germany. In March 1997 the President of the General Assembly formally introduced a proposal for reform, which envisaged a Council consisting of 24 members, including five new permanent members and four new non-permanent members. In September 2000 the UN Millennium Summit declared support for continued discussions on reform of the Council. A summit meeting of the Council convened during the Millennium Summit issued a declaration on ensuring an effective role for the Council in maintaining international peace and security, with particular reference to Africa. The report of the High-Level Panel on Threats, Challenges and Change (see Secretariat), issued in December 2004, stated that the role of the developed countries that contribute most to the UN financially (in terms of contributions to assessed budgets), militarily (through participation in peace-keeping operations), and diplomatically should be reflected in the Council's decision making processes, as well as the interests of the broader membership (particularly those of developing countries). The report proposed two models for the expansion of the Council. The first entailed the provision of six new permanent seats (broadening the current regional representation on the Council), with no veto, and of three non-permanent seats with a two-year term; while the second entailed the establishment of a new category of eight 'semi-permanent' seats to be occupied for periods of four years. In his report entitled 'In Larger Freedom: Towards Development, Security and Human Rights for All', issued in March 2005 (see General Assembly), the Secretary-General supported the High-Level Panel's proposals on Security Council reform.

Activities

As the UN organ primarily responsible for maintaining peace and security, the Security Council is empowered to deploy UN forces in the event that a dispute leads to fighting. It may also authorize the use of military force by a coalition of member states or a regional organization. During 2004–05 the Security Council continued to monitor closely all existing peace-keeping missions and the situations in countries where missions were being undertaken, and to authorize extensions of their mandates accordingly. In February 2004 the Council authorized the establishment (in April) of the UN Operation in Côte d'Ivoire (UNOCI) with a mandate to support the implementation of the Linas-Marcoussis cease-fire agreement concluded in Côte d'Ivoire in January 2003. In April 2004 the Council authorized the deployment of the UN Stabilization Mission in Haiti (MINUSTAH) to help to restore a secure environment in that country and to support the efforts of the transitional government. In the following month the Council approved a UN Operation in Burundi (ONUB) which was to incorporate the existing mission of the African Union in that country and work to create conditions conducive to implementation of the Arusha peace agreement.

On 12 September 2001 the Security Council expressed its unequivocal condemnation of the terrorist attacks against targets in the USA, which had occurred on the previous day. It expressed its readiness to combat terrorism and reiterated the right to individual or collective self-defence in accordance with the UN Charter. At the end of September the Council adopted Resolution 1373 establishing a Counter-Terrorism Committee (CTC) to monitor a range of measures to combat international terrorism, including greater international co-operation and information exchange and suppressing the financing of terrorist groups. A special session of the Council at ministerial level was convened on the issue of terrorism in November. The Council continued to review the work of the CTC and to urge all states to submit reports on efforts to implement Resolution 1373, as well as to ratify relevant international conventions and protocols. In January 2003 the Council met at ministerial level to discuss international terrorism, including the issue of particular states maintaining stocks of weapons of mass destruction. The meeting adopted a resolution urging intensified efforts to combat terrorism and full co-operation with the CTC. The CTC has made efforts to strengthen contacts with international, regional and sub-regional organizations, and in March 2003 it convened a meeting of 57 such groupings and agreed on a co-ordinated approach to the suppression of terrorism. A follow-up meeting was convened in March 2004. In that month the Council adopted a resolution to strengthen the CTC by classifying it as a special subsidiary body of the Council, headed by a Bureau and assisted by an Executive Directorate (the Counter-Terrorism Committee Executive Directorate—CTED). In the following month the Council established the '1540 Committee', to monitor the implementation of Resolution 1540, adopted in April, which considered the threat posed by the possible acquisition and use by non-state actors, particularly terrorists, of weapons of mass destruction, and urged all states to establish controls to prevent the proliferation of such weapons. The Committee was to function for a period of no longer than two years. The December 2004 report of the High-Level Panel on Threats, Challenges and Change stated that, confronted by a terrorism 'nightmare scenario', the Council would need to take earlier, more pro-active and more decisive action than hitherto.

The imposition of sanctions by the Security Council as a means of targeting regimes and groupings that are deemed to threaten international peace and security has increased significantly in recent years and has been subjected to widespread scrutiny regarding enforceability and the potential adverse humanitarian consequences for general populations. In the latter respect the Council has, since

1999, incorporated clauses on humanitarian assessment in its resolutions; the sanctions that took effect against the Taliban regime in Afghanistan and al-Qa'ida in January 2001 were the first to entail mandatory monitoring of the humanitarian impact. In 2000 a proposal was submitted to the Council regarding the establishment of a permanent body to monitor sanctions violations. The UN Secretary-General established a working group in April 2000 to evaluate sanctions policy. Draft versions of the group's final report, most recently issued in February 2002, have recommended that future Security Council resolutions enforcing sanctions should clearly specify intended goals and targets, include incentives to reward partial compliance, and focus in particular on the finances and movements of leaders (so-called 'smart sanctions'). The group's work was ongoing in 2005. In April 2000 the Council authorized the establishment of a temporary monitoring mechanism to investigate alleged violations of the sanctions imposed against the UNITA rebels in Angola, owing to their failure to implement earlier Council resolutions demanding compliance with the obligations of the peace process in that country. In July 2000 the Council voted to prohibit the exportation of all rough diamonds from Sierra Leone that had not been officially certified by that country's Government. (It had become evident that the ongoing conflicts in Sierra Leone and Angola were fuelled by rebel groups' illegal exploitation of diamond resources and use of the proceeds derived therefrom to purchase armaments.) In December a panel of experts appointed by the Council issued a report on the connections between the illicit exportation of diamonds from Sierra Leone and the international trade in armaments. In March 2001 the Council banned the purchase of diamonds exported from Liberia, and demanded that the Liberian authorities refrain from purchasing so-called 'conflict diamonds' from illegal sources and cease providing support to rebel organizations, with particular reference to the main rebel grouping active in Sierra Leone. The Council also re-imposed an embargo on the sale or supply of armaments to Liberia and imposed diplomatic restrictions on high-level Liberian government officials, with effect from May. In January 2003 the Council endorsed a new diamond certification scheme, known as the Kimberley Process, which had entered into effect on 1 January following an agreement reached by some 30 governments to regulate the trade in rough diamonds and eliminate the illegal sale of diamonds to fund conflicts. In May the Council imposed, additionally, a ban on the sale of timber products originating in Liberia. In December the Council endorsed the imposition against Liberia of a revised sanctions regime, to complement developments in the peace process there. The sale or supply of arms and related materials to Liberia (except for use by UNMIL) and the purchase of rough diamonds and timber products from that country remained prohibited, and restrictions remained in force on travel by designated Liberian individuals. In May 2002 the Council suspended the travel restrictions on senior officials of the UNITA movement in Angola, following the signing of a cease-fire agreement ending hostilities in that country. All sanctions against UNITA were removed in December and the relevant Sanctions Committee, established pursuant to a resolution adopted in 1993, was dissolved. In September 2003 the Council voted to end punitive measures imposed against Libya in 1992 and 1993 relating to the destruction of a commercial airline flight over Lockerbie, United Kingdom, in December 1988. In July 2003 the Council banned the sale or supply of armaments and other military assistance to militias in the Democratic Republic of the Congo (DRC), and in November an arms embargo, travel restrictions and an assets freeze were imposed on designated individuals and entities in Côte d'Ivoire.

In June 2004 the Security Council authorized the deployment of a special political mission (the UN Advance Mission in Sudan—UNAMIS) to undertake preparatory work towards the possible future establishment of a full peace operation in Darfur, Sudan. In the following month the Council imposed an arms embargo against non-governmental entities and individuals—including the Janjaweed militias—in Darfur, and demanded that the Sudanese Government disarm the militias.

In December 1996 the Security Council approved the implementation of Resolution 986, which was adopted in April 1995, to provide for the limited export of Iraqi petroleum to enable the purchase of humanitarian supplies and the provision of contributions to the UN Compensation Committee (which had been established to settle claims against Iraq resulting from the 1990 Gulf War). The Council was responsible for renewing the mandate of the agreement and for approving contracts for the sale of petroleum and the purchase of food and medical goods. In October 1999 the Council adopted Resolution 1284, establishing a new policy towards Iraq. The resolution provided for an unlimited ceiling on petroleum exports under the agreed humanitarian programme, and for a suspension of sanctions dependent upon Iraq's co-operation with a new arms inspection body, the UN Monitoring, Verification and Inspection Commission (UNMOVIC) that was to replace the UN Special Commission (UNSCOM, established in 1991 to monitor the disposal of weapons), whose inspectors had withdrawn from Iraq in December 1998. At the end of March 2000 the Council doubled the maximum permitted

revenue that Iraq might use to purchase petroleum industry spare parts and other equipment under the ongoing programme. A new sanctions regime was discussed during 2001. This envisaged facilitating the transfer of civilian and humanitarian goods to Iraq, while tightening border checks for military or other illegal trading. Disagreements among Council members concerned the extra responsibility placed on Iraq's neighbouring countries and the compilation of a list of 'controlled' items requiring special approval to be imported into Iraq. The existing oil-for-food scheme was extended in July, after Russia confirmed that it would veto the new proposals, and again in November. At that time, however, the Council approved a draft Goods for Review List (GRL), which it intended to enter into effect in the following year, subject to further negotiations. In May 2002 the Council adopted Resolution 1409 to implement the new sanctions regime. The programme was extended for a further 180 days in December, although negotiations continued regarding adjustments to the GRL, advocated by the USA to tighten the restrictions on military-related items. Further goods to be subject to approval were agreed by the Council at the end of that month.

In September 2002 the US President, George W. Bush, expressed concern that Iraq was challenging international security owing to its non-compliance with previous UN resolutions relating to the elimination of weapons of mass destruction. Subsequently, diplomatic discussions intensified regarding the need for a new UN resolution on Iraq, amidst increasing pressure from the US administration to initiate military action. An open debate was held in the Security Council in October, at the request of the Non-aligned Movement. On 8 November the Council adopted Resolution 1441 providing for an enhanced inspection mission and a detailed timetable according to which Iraq would have a final opportunity to comply with its disarmament obligations. Following Iraq's acceptance of the resolution, inspectors from UNMOVIC and the IAEA arrived in Iraq in late November, with Council authorization to have unrestricted access to all areas and the right to interview Iraqi scientists and weapons experts. In early December Iraq submitted a declaration of all aspects of its weapons programmes, as required under Resolution 1441. In early January 2003 UNMOVIC's then Executive Chairman, Dr Hans Blix, briefed the Council on Iraq's declaration and the inspection activities. A full update was presented to the Council on 27 January, as required by Resolution 1441 60 days after the resumption of inspections. The Director-General of the IAEA, Dr Mohammad el-Baradei, called for an ongoing mandate for his inspectors to clarify the situation regarding nuclear weapons. However, Blix declared that Iraq had potentially misled the UN on aspects of its chemical and biological weapons programmes and urged more active and substantive co-operation on the part of the Iraqi authorities to determine the existence or otherwise of proscribed items and activities. On 14 February Blix reported to the Council that the Iraqi authorities had recently become more active in proposing and undertaking measures to co-operate with UNMOVIC, and on 7 March he noted that Iraq had started to destroy, under UNMOVIC supervision, its Al Samoud 2 missiles and associated items, having accepted the conclusion of an international panel that these exceeded the permissable range decreed by the Council. Blix declared that the destruction to date of 34 Al Samoud 2 missiles and other items represented a 'substantial measure of disarmament', and that a significant Iraqi effort was under way to clarify a major source of uncertainty regarding quantities of biological and chemical weapons that had been unilaterally destroyed in 1991. Blix stated that UNMOVIC inspectors would require a number of further months in which to verify sites and items, analyse documents, interview relevant persons and draw conclusions, with a view to verifying Iraq's compliance with Resolution 1441. Meanwhile, extensive debate was conducted in the Council regarding Iraq's acceptance of its disarmament obligations and appropriate consequent measures, including the need for a new Council resolution to enforce Resolution 1441. On 24 February the USA, United Kingdom and Spain submitted a draft resolution to the Council stating that Iraq had failed to co-operate 'immediately, unconditionally and actively' with UNMOVIC, as required by Resolution 1441, and insisting upon immediate full co-operation, failing which military force should be used to remove the incumbent regime; France, Germany and Russia, however, demanded that UNMOVIC should be given more time to fulfil its mandate. On 18 March UNMOVIC personnel were withdrawn from Iraq in view of the abandonment by the USA, United Kingdom and Spain of efforts to win the Council's support for their draft resolution and consequent ultimatum by the USA that the Iraqi leadership should leave the country immediately or face a military invasion. Unilateral military action by US, British and allied forces commenced on 19 March. On that day, presenting to the Council UNMOVIC's draft work programme (required under Resolution 1284 to be formulated within a fixed period after the commencement of inspection activities), Blix stated that the Commission's experts had found that the Iraqi authorities had hitherto supplied only limited new information that would be of substantial assistance in resolving outstanding issues of concern. Upon the initiation of military action Iraq's petroleum exports under the oil-for-food programme were suspended immediately. On 28 March the Security Council adopted a resolution enabling technical adjustments to the oil-for-food programme and authorizing the UN Secretary-General to facilitate the delivery and receipt of goods contracted by the Iraqi Government for the humanitarian needs of its people.

On 22 May 2003, following the overthrow of Saddam Hussain in April, the Security Council adopted Resolution 1483, withdrawing economic sanctions against Iraq, and providing for the resumption of petroleum exports and the phasing-out, by November, of the oil-for-food programme. The resolution also supported the formation by the Iraqi people, assisted by the 'Coalition Provisional Authority' (the occupying powers under unified command) and a new Special Representative of the Secretary-General, of an Iraqi-run interim administration, pending the establishment by the Iraqi people of an internationally recognized, representative government that would assume the responsibilities of the Authority. On the same day an open meeting of the Council was briefed on the post-conflict situation in Iraq by several UN agencies conducting humanitarian operations there and also by the International Committee of the Red Cross. The Council reaffirmed in Resolution 1483 that Iraq must meet its disarmament obligations and declared that the Council would revisit the mandates of UNMOVIC and the IAEA in this regard. Reporting on UNMOVIC's activities in June, shortly before retiring as the Commission's Executive Chairman, Blix stated that, although responsibility for weapons inspections in Iraq had been taken over by a US-led Iraq Survey Group, UNMOVIC remained available to continue its work in the field. Blix declared that while significant quantities of proscribed items remained unaccounted for in Iraq and might exist, it was not justifiable to assume that they must exist. He also suggested that the Commission could eventually be transformed into an agency for verifying or monitoring biological weapons and missiles world-wide. In mid-August the Council authorized the establishment of the UN Assistance Mission for Iraq (UNAMI), which was mandated to support the Secretary-General in fulfilling his responsibilities under Resolution 1483. Shortly afterwards the newly-appointed Special Representative of the Secretary-General for Iraq (and UN High Commissioner for Human Rights), Sergio Vieira de Mello, and 21 other UN staff were killed in a terrorist attack on the UNAMI headquarters in Baghdad. In response the Council adopted a resolution strongly condemning all forms of violence against participants in humanitarian operations and urging that perpetrators thereof should be brought to justice. Subsequently, until the formation of the Iraqi Interim Government at the end of June 2004 (see below), UNAMI operated primarily from outside Iraq (from Cyprus, Jordan and Kuwait). In mid-October 2003 the Council authorized a multinational peace-keeping force, under unified command, to help maintain security in Iraq and to support UNAMI and the institutions of the Iraqi interim administration. In the following month the Council adopted a resolution that stressed the importance of continuing to enforce the ban on trade in armaments with Iraq and authorized the establishment of a sanctions committee to identify those individuals and entities holding the outstanding financial assets of the former Saddam Hussain regime. In April 2004 the Council adopted a resolution welcoming the decision of the Secretary-General in the previous month to appoint a high-level panel to investigate allegations of fraud and corruption in the administration of the oil-for-food programme; the panel released interim reports in February and March 2005. Resolution 1546, adopted by the Council in June 2004, endorsed the newly-formed Iraq Interim Government and outlined a timetable for Iraq's transition to democratic government. The resolution was approved after several weeks of discussions mainly concerned with the extent of Iraqi sovereignty and the continued presence of multinational forces in that country. In August the Council renewed UNAMI's mandate for one year. The Council welcomed the elections held in January 2005 to the new Iraq Transitional National Assembly, while reaffirming the role of the Special Representative of the Secretary-General and UNAMI in support of Iraqi efforts to promote national dialogue, and urging the international community to continue to provide advisers and technical support towards UN activities in Iraq. The Council has reiterated demands for the repatriation of all Kuwaiti and third-country nationals who had been missing since the 1990 Gulf War and for the return of their property.

During 2004–05 the Council continued to provide a forum for discussion of the situation in the Middle East and violence in the West Bank and Gaza and in Israel and to support a comprehensive and just settlement to the situation based on relevant Council resolutions, the outcome (including the principle of 'land for peace') of the Madrid Conference held in October–November 1991, agreements previously reached by the parties, and the peace initiative of Saudi Crown Prince Abdullah that was endorsed by the Arab League summit in March 2002. In that month the Council adopted Resolution 1397 which envisaged two separate states of Israel and Palestine existing within secure and recognized borders. In April the Council called for Israel to withdraw its troops from Palestinian cities, following a massive military incursion, and expressed grave concern at the humanitarian situation in Jenin refugee camp, which had been a particular target of Israel's efforts to repress Palestinian extremists, resulting in more than one hundred deaths and widespread destruction of the camp's infrastructure. In September the Council demanded that Israel refrain from any further military action in the city of Ramallah and withdraw all forces to positions held prior to September 2000. The resolution also called upon the Palestinian (National) Authority to bring to justice those responsible for acts of terrorism against Israel. In November 2003 the Council endorsed the adoption in April by the so-called 'Quartet' comprising envoys from the UN, European Union, Russia and USA of a 'performance-based roadmap to a permanent two-state solution to the Israeli-Palestinian conflict'. In May 2004 the Council condemned the killing of Palestinian civilians during incursions by the Israeli military into the area of Rafah. The Council welcomed the summit meeting held in February 2005, in Sharm el-Sheikh, Egypt, between the Palestinian and Israeli leaders, at which they reaffirmed commitment to the stalled roadmap peace plan, and the Council also welcomed conciliatory actions subsequently taken by both sides.

In 2004 the Council held several meetings to consider the situation in Africa, with a special focus on conflict prevention and resolution. The Council conducted a mission to West Africa in June, which focused on the link between security and development, good governance and respect for human rights as the foundation for peace and prosperity. The mission emphasized the necessity of an active approach to conflict prevention.

The Security Council addressed the situation in Afghanistan at regular intervals during 2004. In March 2005 the Council extended the mandate of the UN Assistance Mission in Afghanistan for 12 months. It has also successively extended the mandate of the International Security Assistance Force in Afghanistan.

In November 2001 the Council adopted as a resolution specific commitments and measures to protect children from the effects of armed conflict and to meet their humanitarian needs. The abuse of children in armed conflicts was the subject of a further presidential statement issued in May 2002 and an open debate in January 2004. A new resolution on children and armed conflict was adopted in April of that year. A presidential statement issued in October 2002 proposed that countries formulate national registers of arms brokers to counter illicit brokering of small arms and impose stricter penalties for illicit trading activities. In March 2003 the Council adopted a declaration on the threat to peace and security in West Africa caused by the proliferation of small arms and light weapons and by mercenary activities; an open debate on small arms was held in January 2004. A Council presidential statement issued in March 2002 identified core objectives for the protection of civilians in conflict situations. An open debate on the subject was held in December. In July 2004 the Council held an open debate on the relationship between the Security Council and regional organizations. Other ongoing themes considered by the Council in recent years have included women, the role of the UN in supporting justice and the rule of law, and the role of the UN in post-conflict national reconciliation.

In August 2000 the Security Council requested the Secretary-General to negotiate an agreement with the Government of Sierra Leone to establish an independent Special Court with a mandate to prosecute those with greatest responsibility for crimes against humanity and other serious violations of international humanitarian law committed in Sierra Leone since November 1996. An agreement was signed between the UN and Sierra Leonean Government in January 2002. Trial proceedings commenced in June 2004. At March 2005 a total of 13 people had been indicted by the Special Court, although two indictments were withdrawn in December 2003 following the deaths of two of the accused.

SPECIAL SUBSIDIARY BODY

The Counter-Terrorism Committee (CTC), established pursuant to Security Council Resolution 1373 (2001) and, in March 2004, in accordance with Resolution 1535 (2004), elevated to a special subsidiary body, comprises a Plenary (composed of the Council member states) and a Bureau, and is assisted by an Executive Directorate (the Counter-Terrorism Committee Executive Directorate—CTED).

COMMITTEES

In March 2005 there were two **Standing Committees**, each composed of representatives of all Council member states:

Committee of Experts on Rules of Procedure (studies and advises on rules of procedure and other technical matters);

Committee on the Admission of New Members.

Ad hoc Committees, which are established as needed, comprise all Council members and meet in closed session:

Governing Council of the UN Compensation Commission established by Security Council Resolution 692 (1991);

Security Council Committee on Council Meetings away from Headquarters;

1540 Committee established pursuant to Security Council Resolution 1540 (2004).

Within this category are the Sanctions Committees, which may be established to oversee economic or political enforcement measures, imposed by the Security Council to maintain or restore international peace and security. At March 2005 the following committees were operational:

Security Council Committee established pursuant to Resolution 1572 (2004) concerning Côte d'Ivoire;

Security Council Committee established pursuant to Resolution 1533 (2004) concerning the Democratic Republic of the Congo;

Security Council Committee established pursuant to Resolution 1521 (2003) concerning Liberia;

Security Council Committee established pursuant to Resolution 1518 (2003) concerning the financial assets of the former Iraqi regime;

Security Council Committee established pursuant to Resolution 1267 (1999) concerning al-Qa'ida and the Taliban and associated individuals and entities;

Security Council Committee established pursuant to Resolution 1132 (1997) concerning Sierra Leone;

Security Council Committee established pursuant to Resolution 918 (1994) concerning Rwanda;

Security Council Committee established pursuant to Resolution 751 (1992) concerning Somalia.

A Working Group on General Issues on Sanctions was established in 2000, on a temporary basis, to consider ways of improving the effectiveness of UN sanctions. A Working Group established pursuant to Resolution 1566 (2004) is mandated to consider practical measures to be imposed upon individuals, groups or entities involved in or associated with terrorist activities, other than those designated by the Committee on al-Qa'ida and the Taliban; and the possibility of establishing an international fund to compensate victims of terrorist acts and their families.

AD HOC INTERNATIONAL TRIBUNALS

In May 1993 the Security Council, acting under Article VII of the UN Charter, adopted Resolution 827, which established an *ad hoc* 'war crimes' tribunal. The so-called International Tribunal for the Prosecution of Persons Responsible for Serious Violations of International Humanitarian Law Committed in the Territory of the Former Yugoslavia (also referred to as the International Criminal Tribunal for the former Yugoslavia—ICTY) was inaugurated in The Hague, Netherlands, in November. The ICTY consists of a Chief Prosecutor's office, and 16 permanent judges, of whom 11 sit in three trial chambers and five sit in a seven-member appeals chamber (with the remaining two appeals chamber members representing the ICTR, see below). In addition, a maximum at any one time of nine *ad litem* judges, drawn from a pool of 27, serve as required. Public hearings were initiated in November 1994. The first trial proceedings commenced in May 1996, and the first sentence was imposed by the Tribunal in November. In July and November 1995 the Tribunal formally charged the Bosnian Serb political and military leaders Radovan Karadžić and Gen. Ratko Mladić, on two separate indictments, with genocide, crimes against humanity, violation of the laws and customs of war and serious breaches of the Geneva Conventions. In July 1996 the Tribunal issued international warrants for their arrest. Amended indictments, confirmed in May 2000, and announced in October and November, respectively, included the withdrawal of the fourth charge against Mladić. Karadžić and Mladić remained at large in early 2005. In April 2000 Momčilo Krajišnik, a senior associate of Karadžić, was detained by the ICTY, charged with genocide, war crimes and crimes against humanity. Biljana Plavšić, a further former Bosnian Serb political leader, surrendered to the Tribunal in January 2001, also indicted on charges of genocide, war crimes and crimes against humanity. In the following month three Bosnian Serb former soldiers were convicted by the ICTY of utilizing mass rape and the sexual enslavement of women as instruments of terror in wartime. In February 2003 Plavšić was sentenced to eleven years' imprisonment, having pleaded guilty in October 2002 to one of the charges against her (persecutions: a crime against humanity). (Under a plea agreement reached with the Tribunal the remaining charges had been withdrawn.) In mid-1998 the ICTY began investigating reported acts of violence against civilians committed by both sides in the conflict in the southern Serbian province of Kosovo and Metohija. In early 1999 there were reports of large-scale organized killings, rape and expulsion of the local Albanian population by Serbian forces. In April ICTY personnel visited refugee camps in neighbouring countries in order to compile evidence of the atrocities, and obtained intelligence information from NATO members regarding those responsible for the incidents. In May the then President of the then Federal Republic of Yugoslavia (FRY, renamed Serbia and Montenegro in February 2003), Slobodan Milošević, was indicted, along with three senior government ministers and the chief-of-staff of the army, charged with crimes against humanity and violations of the customs of war committed in Kosovo since 1 January 1999; international warrants were issued for their arrests. In June, following the establishment of an international force to secure peace in Kosovo, the ICTY established teams of experts to investigate alleged atrocities at 529 identified grave sites. The new FRY administration, which had assumed power following legislative and presidential elections in late 2000, contested the impartiality of the ICTY, proposing that Milošević and other members of the former regime should be tried before a national court. In April 2001 Milošević was arrested by the local authorities in Belgrade. Under increasing international pressure, the Federal Government approved his extradition in June, and he was immediately transferred to the ICTY, where he was formally charged with crimes against humanity committed in Kosovo in 1999. A further indictment of crimes against humanity committed in Croatia during 1991–92 was confirmed in October 2001, and a third indictment, which included charges of genocide committed in Bosnia and Herzegovina in 1991–95, was confirmed in November 2001. In February 2002 the Appeals Chamber ordered that the three indictments be considered in a single trial. The trial commenced later in that month. Milošević, however, continued to protest at the alleged illegality of his arrest and refused to recognize the jurisdiction of the Court. The case has been delayed repeatedly owing to the ill health of the defendant. In August 2001 the ICTY passed its first sentence of genocide, convicting a former Bosnian Serb military commander, Gen. Radislav Kristić, for his role in the deaths of up to 8,000 Bosnian Muslim men and boys in Srebreniča in July 1995. In January 2003 Fatmir Limaj, an ethnic Albanian deputy in the Kosovo parliament and former commander of the Kosovo Liberation Army (KLA), was indicted by the ICTY on several counts of crimes against humanity and war crimes that were allegedly committed in mid-1998 against Serb and Albanian detainees at the KLA's Lapusnik prison camp. Limaj was arrested in Slovenia in February 2003 and transferred to ICTY custody in early March. At March 2005 62 people were in custody at the Tribunal's detention unit and one person was in custody in Croatia under Tribunal authority, while 15 arrest warrants remained outstanding. Of those who had appeared in proceedings before the Tribunal, 13 were awaiting appeal, 37 had received their final sentence and five had been acquitted. Five indictments had been withdrawn following the transfer of the accused to the Tribunal. Some 13 people had completed their sentences. It was envisaged that the Tribunal's trial activities would be terminated by 2008. During 2004 the Tribunal assisted with the establishment of a planned new special chamber for war crimes prosecutions in the Bosnia and Herzegovina state court, and also helped Croatia to strengthen its national judicial capacity in preparation for future war crimes prosecutions within that country.

President of the ICTY: THEODOR MERON (USA).

ICTY Prosecutor: CARLA DEL PONTE (Switzerland).

Registrar: HANS HOLTHUIS (Netherlands), Public Information Unit, POB 13888, 2501 EW The Hague, Netherlands; tel. (70) 512-5233; fax (70) 512-5355; internet www.un.org/icty.

In November 1994 the Security Council adopted Resolution 955, establishing an International Criminal Tribunal for Rwanda (ICTR) to prosecute persons responsible for genocide and other serious violations of humanitarian law that had been committed in Rwanda and by Rwandans in neighbouring states. Its temporal jurisdiction was limited to the period 1 January to 31 December 1994. The Tribunal consists of 11 permanent judges, of whom nine sit in four trial chambers (based in Arusha, Tanzania) and two sit in the seven-member appeals chamber that is shared with the ICTY and based at The Hague. In August 2002 the UN Security Council endorsed a proposal by the ICTR President to elect a pool of 18 *ad litem* judges to the Tribunal with a view to accelerating its activities and bringing them to a conclusion by 2008–10. In October 2003 the Security Council increased the number of *ad litem* judges who may serve on the Tribunal at any one time from four to nine. A high security detention facility had been built within the compound of the prison in Arusha. The first plenary session of the Tribunal was held in The Hague in June 1995; formal proceedings at its permanent headquarters in Arusha were initiated in November. The first trial of persons charged by the Tribunal commenced in January 1997, and sentences were imposed in July. In September 1998 the former Rwandan Prime Minister, Jean Kambanda, and a former mayor of Taba, Jean-Paul Akayesu, both Hutu extremists, were found guilty of genocide and crimes against humanity; Kambanda subsequently became the first person ever to be sentenced under the 1948 Convention on the Prevention and Punishment of the Crime of Genocide. In October 2000 the Tribunal rejected an appeal by Kambanda. In November 1999 the Rwandan Government temporarily suspended co-operation with the Tribunal in protest at a decision of the appeals chamber to release an indicted former government official owing to procedural delays. (The appeals chamber subsequently reversed this decision.) In 2001 two ICTR investigators employed on defence teams were arrested and charged with genocide, having been found to be working at the Tribunal under assumed identities. Relations between the Rwandan Government and the ICTR deteriorated again in 2002, with the then Chief Prosecutor accusing the Rwandan authorities of failing to facilitate the travel of witnesses to the Tribunal and withholding access to documentary materials, and counter accusations by the Rwandan Government that the Tribunal's progress was too slow, that further suspected perpetrators of genocide had been inadvertently employed by the Tribunal and that Rwandan witnesses attending the Tribunal had not received sufficient protection. Reporting to the UN Security Council in July, the then Chief Prosecutor alleged that the Rwandan non-co-operation ensued from her recent decision to indict former members of the Tutsi-dominated Rwanda Patriotic Army for human rights violations committed against Hutus in 1994. In September 2003 the trial of Théoneste Bagosora, a former military commander accused of masterminding the genocide, commenced, after considerable procedural delays. In January 2004 a former minister of culture and education, Jean de Dieu Kamuhanda, was found guilty on two counts of genocide and extermination as a crime against humanity. In the following month Samuel Imanishimwe, a former military

commander, was convicted on seven counts of genocide, crimes against humanity and serious violations of the Geneva Conventions. Two others were acquitted of similar charges. In early May 2004 Yussufu Munyakazi, accused of directing mass killings by the Interahamwe militia in Cyangugu and Kibuye Provinces, was arrested in the Democratic Republic of the Congo. By March 2005 the Tribunal had delivered judgments against 23 accused, of whom 20 were found guilty and three acquitted. A further 26 people were on trial at that time, while 16 indictees were awaiting trial. Nine people remained at large.

President of the ICTR: ERIK MØSE (Norway).

ICTR Prosecutor: HASSAN BUBACAR JALLOW (The Gambia).

Registrar: ADAMA DIENG (Senegal), Arusha International Conference Centre, POB 6016, Arusha, Tanzania; tel. (212) 963 2850; fax (212) 963 2848; e-mail ictr-press@un.org; internet www.ictr.org.

Both Tribunals are supported by teams of investigators and human rights experts working in the field to collect forensic and other evidence in order to uphold indictments. Evidence of mass graves resulting from large-scale unlawful killings has been uncovered in both regions.

Trusteeship Council

The Trusteeship Council (comprising the People's Republic of China—a non-active member until May 1989, France, Russia, the United Kingdom and the USA) was established to supervise United Nations Trust Territories through their administering authorities and to promote the political, economic, social and educational advancement of their inhabitants towards self-government or independence (see Charter, see p. 21). On 1 October 1994 the last territory remaining under UN trusteeship, the Republic of Palau (part of the archipelago of the Caroline Islands), declared its independence under a compact of free association with the USA, its

administering authority. The Security Council terminated the Trusteeship Agreement on 10 November, having determined that the objectives of the agreement had been fully attained. On 1 November the Trusteeship Council formally suspended its operations; thereafter it was to be convened on an extraordinary basis as required. The report of the UN Secretary-General entitled 'In Larger Freedom: Towards Development, Security and Human Rights for All', issued in March 2005, proposed that the Trusteeship Council should be terminated.

Economic and Social Council—ECOSOC

ECOSOC promotes world co-operation on economic, social, cultural and humanitarian problems. (See Charter of the United Nations.)

MEMBERS
Fifty-four members are elected by the General Assembly for three-year terms: 18 are elected each year. Membership is allotted by regions as follows: Africa 14 members, western Europe and others 13, Asia 11, Latin America 10, eastern Europe 6.

President: MUNIR AKRAM (Pakistan) (2005).

ORGANIZATION
The Council, which meets annually for four weeks in July, alternately in New York and Geneva, is mainly a central policy-making and co-ordinating organ. It has a co-ordinating function between the UN and the specialized agencies, and also makes consultative arrangements with approved voluntary or non-governmental organizations which work within the sphere of its activities. The Council has functional and regional commissions to carry out much of its detailed work. ECOSOC's purview extends to more than 70% of the human and financial resources of the UN system.

The report of the UN Secretary-General entitled 'In Larger Freedom: Towards Development, Security and Human Rights for All', issued in March 2005, outlined a number of proposed changes to ECOSOC aimed at improving its effectiveness. These included: the organization by the Council of annual ministerial-level progress reviews of agreed development goals, in particular the Millennium Development Goals pledged by UN heads of state and government in September 2000; the Council's serving as a regular high-level forum on international development co-operation; the organization by the Council, whenever required, of meetings to assess and promote co-ordinated responses to threats to development, such as famines, epidemics and major natural disasters; and the development of a permanent structure within the Council for monitoring the economic and social dimensions of conflicts, with the aim of improving prospects for long-term recovery, reconstruction and reconciliation, and working in co-operation with a proposed new Peace-building Commission.

Every April ECOSOC holds consultations with the IMF and World Bank. The Council was given a leading role in following up the implementation of the Monterrey Consensus, adopted by the March 2002 International Conference on Financing for Development. In April 2005 ECOSOC, the IMF, World Bank and WTO were scheduled to discuss 'coherence, co-ordination and co-operation in the context of the implementation of the Monterrey Consensus'.

SESSIONAL COMMITTEES
Each sessional committee comprises the 54 members of the Council: there is a First (Economic) Committee, a Second (Social) Committee and a Third (Programme and Co-ordination) Committee.

FUNCTIONAL COMMISSIONS
Commission on Crime Prevention and Criminal Justice: f. 1992; aims to formulate an international convention on crime prevention and criminal justice; 40 members.

Commission on Human Rights: f. 1946; seeks greater respect for the basic rights of man, the prevention of discrimination and the protection of minorities; reviews specific instances of human rights violation and dispatches rapporteurs to investigate allegations of abuses in particular countries; provides policy guidance; works on declarations, conventions and other instruments of international law; meets annually for six weeks; 53 members; there is a Sub-Commission on the Promotion and Protection of Human Rights, comprising working groups on issues such as slavery, indigenous populations, detention and communications; in March 2005 the UN Secretary-General proposed that the Commission should be replaced by a new Human Rights Council.

Commission on Narcotic Drugs: f. 1946; mainly concerned in combating illicit traffic; 53 members; there is a Sub-Commission on Illicit Drug Traffic and Related Matters in the Near and Middle East.

Commission on Population and Development: f. 1946; advises the Council on population matters and their relation to socio-economic conditions; 47 members.

Commission on Science and Technology for Development: f. 1992; works on the restructuring of the UN in the economic, social and related fields; 33 members.

Commission for Social Development: f. 1946 as the Social Commission; advises ECOSOC on issues of social and community development; 46 members.

Commission on the Status of Women: f. 1946; aims at equality of political, economic and social rights for women, and supports the right of women to live free of violence; 45 members.

Commission on Sustainable Development: f. 1993 to oversee integration into the UN's work of the objectives set out in 'Agenda 21', the programme of action agreed by the UN Conference on Environment and Development in June 1992; 53 members.

Statistical Commission: Standardizes terminology and procedure in statistics and promotes the development of national statistics; 24 members.

United Nations Forum on Forests: f. 2000.

COMMITTEES AND SUBSIDIARY BODIES

Commission on Human Settlements: f. 1977.

Committee for Development Policy: f. 1965.

Committee on Energy and Natural Resources for Development: f. 1998.

Committee on Negotiations with Intergovernmental Agencies: f. 1946.

Committee on Non-Governmental Organizations: f. 1946.

Committee for Programme and Co-ordination: f. 1962.

Permanent Forum on Indigenous Issues: f. 2000.

In addition there is an *ad hoc* open-ended working group on informatics and there are expert bodies on: the transport of dangerous goods and the globally harmonized system of classification and labelling of chemicals; geographical names; public administration and finance; international co-operation in tax matters; and economic, social and cultural rights.

REGIONAL COMMISSIONS
(see United Nations Regional Commissions)

Economic Commission for Africa (ECA).

Economic Commission for Europe (ECE).

Economic Commission for Latin America and the Caribbean (ECLAC).

Economic and Social Commission for Asia and the Pacific (ESCAP).

Economic and Social Commission for Western Asia (ESCWA).

RELATED BODIES

Board of Trustees of the International Research and Training Institute for the Advancement of Women (INSTRAW): 11 members.

International Narcotics Control Board: f. 1964; 13 members.

Programme Co-ordination Board for the Joint UN Programme on HIV/AIDS (UNAIDS): f. 1995; 22 members.

UNDP/UNFPA Executive Board: 36 members, elected by ECOSOC.

UNHCR Executive Committee: 53 members, elected by ECOSOC.

UNICEF Executive Board: 36 members, elected by ECOSOC.

WFP Executive Board: one-half of the 36 members are elected by ECOSOC, one-half by FAO; governing body of the World Food Programme.

International Court of Justice

Address: Peace Palace, Carnegieplein 2, 2517 KJ The Hague, Netherlands.
Telephone: (70) 302-23-23; **fax:** (70) 364-99-28; **e-mail:** information@icj-cij.org; **internet:** www.icj-cij.org.

Established in 1945, the Court is the principal judicial organ of the UN. All members of the UN are parties to the Statute of the Court. (See Charter, see p. 21)

THE JUDGES
(March 2005; in order of precedence)

	Term Ends*
President: SHI JIUYONG (People's Republic of China)	2012
Vice-President: RAYMOND RANJEVA (Madagascar)	2009
Judges:	
ABDUL G. KOROMA (Sierra Leone)	2012
VLADLEN S. VERESHCHETIN (Russia)	2006
ROSALYN HIGGINS (United Kingdom)	2009
GONZALO PARRA-ARANGUREN (Venezuela)	2009
PIETER H. KOOIJMANS (Netherlands)	2006
JOSÉ FRANCISCO REZEK (Brazil)	2006
AWN SHAWKAT AL-KHASAWNEH (Jordan)	2009
THOMAS BUERGENTHAL (USA)	2009
NABIL ELARABY (Egypt)	2006
HISASHI OWADA (Japan)	2012
BRUNO SIMMA (Germany)	2012
PETER TOMKA (Slovakia)	2012
RONNY ABRAHAM (France)	2014

Registrar: PHILIPPE COUVREUR (Belgium).
*Each term ends on 5 February of the year indicated.

The Court is composed of 15 judges, each of a different nationality, elected with an absolute majority by both the General Assembly and the Security Council. Representation of the main forms of civilization and the different legal systems of the world are borne in mind in their election. Candidates are nominated by national panels of jurists.

The judges are elected for nine years and may be re-elected; elections for five seats are held every three years. The Court elects its President and Vice-President for each three-year period. Members may not have any political, administrative, or other professional occupation, and may not sit in any case with which they have been otherwise connected than as a judge of the Court. For the purposes of a case, each side—consisting of one or more States—may, unless the Bench already includes a judge with a corresponding nationality, choose a person from outside the Court to sit as a judge on terms of equality with the Members. Judicial decisions are taken by a majority of the judges present, subject to a quorum of nine Members. The President has a casting vote.

FUNCTIONS

The International Court of Justice operates in accordance with a Statute which is an integral part of the UN Charter. Only States may be parties in cases before the Court; those not parties to the Statute may have access in certain circumstances and under conditions laid down by the Security Council.

The Jurisdiction of the Court comprises:

1. All cases which the parties refer to it jointly by special agreement (indicated in the list below by a stroke between the names of the parties);

2. All matters concerning which a treaty or convention in force provides for reference to the Court. About 700 bilateral or multilateral agreements make such provision. Among the more noteworthy: Treaty of Peace with Japan (1951), European Convention for Peaceful Settlement of Disputes (1957), Single Convention on Narcotic Drugs (1961), Protocol relating to the Status of Refugees (1967), Hague Convention on the Suppression of the Unlawful Seizure of Aircraft (1970);

3. Legal disputes between States which have recognized the jurisdiction of the Court as compulsory for specified classes of dispute. Declarations by the following 64 States accepting the compulsory jurisdiction of the Court are in force (although many with reservations): Australia, Austria, Barbados, Belgium, Botswana, Bulgaria, Cambodia, Cameroon, Canada, the Democratic Republic of the Congo, Costa Rica, Côte d'Ivoire, Cyprus, Denmark, the Dominican Republic, Egypt, Estonia, Finland, The Gambia, Georgia, Greece, Guinea, Guinea-Bissau, Haiti, Honduras, Hungary, India, Japan, Kenya, Lesotho, Liberia, Liechtenstein, Luxembourg, Madagascar, Malawi, Malta, Mauritius, Mexico, Nauru, the Netherlands, New Zealand, Nicaragua, Nigeria, Norway, Pakistan, Panama, Paraguay, Peru, the Philippines, Poland, Portugal, Senegal, Serbia and Montenegro, Somalia, Spain, Sudan, Suriname, Swaziland, Sweden, Switzerland, Togo, Uganda, the United Kingdom and Uruguay.

Disputes as to whether the Court has jurisdiction are settled by the Court.

Judgments are without appeal, but are binding only for the particular case and between the parties. States appearing before the Court undertake to comply with its Judgment. If a party to a case fails to do so, the other party may apply to the Security Council, which may make recommendations or decide upon measures to give effect to the Judgment.

Advisory opinions on legal questions may be requested by the General Assembly, the Security Council or, if so authorized by the Assembly, other United Nations organs or specialized agencies.

Rules of Court governing procedure are made by the Court under a power conferred by the Statute.

In July 1993 the Court established a seven-member Chamber for Environmental Matters, in view of the world-wide expansion of environmental law and protection.

CONSIDERED CASES

Judgments

Since 1946 more than 80 contentious cases have been referred to the Court by States. Some were removed from the list as a result of settlement or discontinuance, or on the grounds of a lack of basis for jurisdiction. Cases which have been the subject of a Judgment by the Court include: Monetary Gold Removed from Rome in 1943 (Italy *v.* France, United Kingdom and USA); Sovereignty over Certain Frontier Land (Belgium/Netherlands); Arbitral Award made by the King of Spain on 23 December 1906 (Honduras *v.* Nicaragua); Temple of Preah Vihear (Cambodia *v.* Thailand); South West Africa (Ethiopia and Liberia *v.* South Africa); Northern Cameroons (Cameroon *v.* United Kingdom); North Sea Continental Shelf (Federal Republic of Germany/Denmark and Netherlands); Appeal relating to the Jurisdiction of the ICAO Council (India *v.* Pakistan); Fisheries Jurisdiction (United Kingdom *v.* Iceland; Federal Republic of Germany *v.* Iceland); Nuclear Tests (Australia *v.* France; New Zealand *v.* France); Aegean Sea Continental Shelf (Greece *v.* Turkey); United States of America Diplomatic and Consular Staff in Tehran (USA *v.* Iran); Continental Shelf (Tunisia/Libya); Delimitation of the Maritime Boundary in the Gulf of Maine Area (Canada/USA); Continental Shelf (Libya/Malta); Application for revision and interpretation of the Judgment of 24 February 1982 in the case concerning the Continental Shelf (Tunisia *v.* Libya); Military and Paramilitary Activities in and against Nicaragua (Nicaragua *v.* USA); Frontier Dispute (Burkina Faso/Mali); Delimitation of Maritime Boundary (Denmark *v.* Norway); Maritime Boundaries (Guinea-Bissau *v.* Senegal); Elettronica Sicula SpA (USA *v.* Italy); Land, Island and Maritime Frontier Dispute (El Salvador/Honduras) (in one aspect of which Nicaragua was permitted to intervene) (also, in 2003, Application for Revision of the 1992 Judgment in the Case concerning the Land, Island and Maritime Frontier Dispute, requested by El Salvador); Delimitation of Maritime Boundary in the area between Greenland and Jan Mayen island (Denmark *v.* Norway); Maritime Delimitation and Territorial Questions between Qatar and Bahrain (Qatar *v.* Bahrain); Territorial Dispute (Libya/Chad); East Timor (Portugal *v.* Australia); the Gabčíkovo–Nagymaros Hydroelectric Project (Hungary *v.* Slovakia), aspects of which were still under consideration in 2005; Fisheries Jurisdiction (Spain *v.* Canada); Delimitation of the Boundary around Kasikili Sedudu Island (Botswana *v.* Namibia); La Grand case (Germany *v.* USA); Arrest Warrant of 11 April 2000 (Democratic Republic of the Congo *v.* Belgium); Land and Maritime Boundary between Cameroon and Nigeria (Cameroon *v.* Nigeria, with Equatorial Guinea intervening); Sovereignty over Pulau Ligatan and Pulau Sipadan (Indonesia/Malaysia); Destruction of Oil Platforms (Iran *v.* USA); Avena and other Mexican Nationals (Mexico *v.* USA); Legality of Use of Force (Serbia and Montenegro *v.* Belgium; Canada; France; Germany; Italy; the Netherlands; Portugal; and the United Kingdom); and Certain Property (Liechtenstein *v.* Germany).

Other cases under consideration, or pending before the Court, in 2005 were: cases brought by Bosnia and Herzegovina and Croatia against the Federal Republic of Yugoslavia (FRY, now Serbia and Montenegro) concerning the application of the 1948 Convention on the Prevention and Punishment of the Crime of Genocide (a related application brought by the FRY for revision of a judgment in 1996 was ruled inadmissable in February 2003); a case brought by Guinea against the Democratic Republic of the Congo (DRC) concerning the treatment of a Guinean business executive, Ahmadou Sadio Diallo;

cases concerning the legality of the use of force brought by the FRY against Spain and the USA; cases brought by the DRC against Uganda and against Rwanda, regarding armed activities on the territory of the DRC; dispute between Nicaragua and Honduras concerning maritime delimitation in the Caribbean Sea; a case brought by Nicaragua against Colombia concerning territory and maritime delimitation in the western Caribbean; a case regarding a frontier dispute brought by Benin and Niger; a case brought by the Republic of the Congo against France seeking an annulment of investigations and criminal proceedings under way in France concerning the alleged involvement of several high-ranking Congolese officials in crimes against humanity reportedly perpetrated in the Republic of the Congo; a case brought by Malaysia and Singapore concerning the sovereignty of Pedra Branca/Pulau Batu Puteh, Middle Rocks and South Ledge; and a case brought by Romania against Ukraine concerning Maritime Delimitation in the Black Sea. In September 2003 two cases brought by Libya against the United Kingdom and the USA (Questions of Interpretation and Application of the 1971 Montreal Convention arising from the Aerial Incident at Lockerbie) were withdrawn at the request of the three parties.

Advisory Opinions

Matters on which the Court has delivered an Advisory Opinion at the request of the United Nations General Assembly include the following: Condition of Admission of a State to Membership in the United Nations; Competence of the General Assembly for the Admission of a State to the United Nations; Interpretation of the Peace Treaties with Bulgaria, Hungary and Romania; International Status of South West Africa; Reservations to the Convention on the Prevention and Punishment of the Crime of Genocide; Effect of Awards of Compensation Made by the United Nations Administrative Tribunal (UNAT); Western Sahara; Application for Review of UNAT Judgment No. 333; Applicability of the Obligation to Arbitrate under Section 21 of the United Nations Headquarters Agreement of 26 June 1947 (relating to the closure of the Observer Mission to the United Nations maintained by the Palestine Liberation Organization); Legalitiy of the Use or Threat of Nuclear Weapons; and Legal Consequences of the Construction of a Wall by Israel in the Occupied Palestinian Territory.

An Advisory Opinion has been given at the request of the Security Council: Legal Consequences for States of the continued presence of South Africa in Namibia (South West Africa) notwithstanding Security Council resolution 276 (1970).

In 1989 (at the request of the UN Economic and Social Council—ECOSOC) the Court gave an Advisory Opinion on the Applicability of Article 6, Section 22, of the Convention on the Privileges and Immunities of the United Nations. The Court has also, at the request of UNESCO, given an Advisory Opinion on Judgments of the Administrative Tribunal of the ILO upon Complaints made against UNESCO, and on the Constitution of the Maritime Safety Committee of the Inter-Governmental Maritime Consultative Organization, at the request of IMCO. In July 1996 the Court delivered an Advisory Opinion on the Legality of the Use by a State of Nuclear Weapons in Armed Conflict, requested by WHO. In April 1999 the Court delivered an Advisory Opinion, requested by ECOSOC, on the Difference Relating to Immunity from Legal Process of a Special Rapporteur of the Commission on Human Rights.

Finance

The UN budget appropriation for the Court for the two year period 2004–05 amounted to US $31.5m.

Publications

Acts and Documents, No. 5 (contains Statute and Rules of the Court, the Resolution concerning its internal judicial practice and other documents).

Bibliography (annually).

Pleadings ((Written Pleadings and Statements, Oral Proceedings, Correspondence): series).

Reports ((Judgments, Opinions and Orders): series).

Yearbook.

Charter of the United Nations

Signed 26 June 1945

(Note: The report of the UN Secretary-General entitled 'In Larger Freedom: Towards Development, Security and Human Rights for All', issued in March 2005, proposed the following amendments to the Charter: the elimination of the 'enemy' clauses in Articles 53 and 107; the deletion of Chapter XIII, 'The Trusteeship Council'; and the deletion of Article 47 on The Military Staff Committee and related references.)

We the peoples of the United Nations determined

to save succeeding generations from the scourge of war, which twice in our lifetime has brought untold sorrow to mankind, and to reaffirm faith in fundamental human rights, in the dignity and worth of the human person, in the equal rights of men and women and of nations large and small, and

to establish conditions under which justice and respect for the obligations arising from treaties and other sources of international law can be maintained, and

to promote social progress and better standards of life in larger freedom,

And for these ends

to practise tolerance and live together in peace with one another as good neighbours, and

to unite our strength to maintain international peace and security, and

to ensure, by the acceptance of principles and the institution of methods, that armed force shall not be used, save in the common interest, and

to employ international machinery for the promotion of the economic and social advancement of all peoples,

Have resolved to combine our efforts to accomplish these aims.

Accordingly, our respective Governments, through representatives assembled in the city of San Francisco, who have exhibited their full powers found to be in good and due form, have agreed to the present Charter of the United Nations and do hereby establish an international organization to be known as the United Nations.

I. PURPOSES AND PRINCIPLES

Article 1

The Purposes of the United Nations are:

1. To maintain international peace and security, and to that end: to take effective collective measures for the prevention and removal of threats to the peace, and for the suppression of acts of aggression or other breaches of the peace, and to bring about by peaceful means, and in conformity with the principles of justice and international law, adjustment or settlement of international disputes or situations which might lead to a breach of the peace;

2. To develop friendly relations among nations based on respect for the principle of equal rights and self-determination of peoples, and to take other appropriate measures to strengthen universal peace;

3. To achieve international co-operation in solving international problems of an economic, social, cultural, or humanitarian character, and in promoting and encouraging respect for human rights and for fundamental freedoms for all without distinction as to race, sex, language, or religion; and

4. To be a centre for harmonizing the accusations of nations in the attainment of these common ends.

Article 2

The Organization and its Members, in pursuit of the Purposes stated in Article 1, shall act in accordance with the following Principles.

1. The Organization is based on the principle of the sovereign equality of all its Members;

2. All Members, in order to ensure to all of them the rights and benefits resulting from membership, shall fulfil in good faith the obligations assumed by them in accordance with the present Charter;

3. All Members shall settle their international disputes by peaceful means in such a manner that international peace and security, and justice, are not endangered;

4. All Members shall refrain in their international relations from the threat or use of force against the territorial integrity or political independence of any state, or in any manner inconsistent with the Purposes of the United Nations;

5. All Members shall give the United Nations every assistance in any action it takes in accordance with the present Charter, and shall refrain from giving assistance to any state against which the United Nations is taking preventive or enforcement action;

6. The Organization shall ensure that states which are not Members of the United Nations act in accordance with these Principles so far as may be necessary for the maintenance of international peace and security;

7. Nothing contained in the present Charter shall authorize the United Nations to intervene in matters which are essentially within the domestic jurisdiction of any state or shall require the Members to submit such matters to settlement under the present Charter; but this principle shall not prejudice the application of enforcement measures under Chapter VII.

II. MEMBERSHIP

Article 3

The original Members of the United Nations shall be the states which, having participated in the United Nations Conference on International Organization at San Francisco, or having previously signed the Declaration by United Nations of January 1, 1942, sign the present Charter and ratify it in accordance with Article 110.

Article 4

1. Membership in the United Nations is open to all other peace-loving states which accept the obligations contained in the present Charter and, in the judgement of the Organization, are able and willing to carry out these obligations.

2. The admission of any such state to membership in the United Nations will be effected by a decision of the General Assembly upon the recommendation of the Security Council.

Article 5

A member of the United Nations against which preventive or enforcement action has been taken by the Security Council may be suspended from the exercise of the rights and privileges of membership by the General Assembly upon the recommendation of the Security Council. The exercise of these rights and privileges may be restored by the Security Council.

Article 6

A Member of the United Nations which has persistently violated the Principles contained in the present Charter may be expelled from the Organization by the General Assembly upon the recommendation of the Security Council.

III. ORGANS

Article 7

1. There are established as the principal organs of the United Nations: a General Assembly, a Security Council, an Economic and Social Council, a Trusteeship Council, an International Court of Justice, and a Secretariat.

2. Such subsidiary organs as may be found necessary may be established in accordance with the present Charter.

Article 8

The United Nations shall place no restrictions on the eligibility of men and women to participate in any capacity and under conditions of equality in its principal and subsidiary organs.

IV. THE GENERAL ASSEMBLY

Composition

Article 9

1. The General Assembly shall consist of all the Members of the United Nations.

2. Each Member shall have not more than five representatives in the General Assembly.

Functions and Powers

Article 10

The General Assembly may discuss any questions or any matters within the scope of the present Charter or relating to the powers and functions of any organs provided for in the present Charter, and, except as provided in Article 12, may make recommendations to the Members of the United Nations or to the Security Council or to both on any such questions or matters.

Article 11

1. The General Assembly may consider the general principles of co-operation in the maintenance of international peace and security, including the principles governing disarmament and the regulation of armaments, and may make recommendations with regard to such principles to the Members or to the Security Council or to both.

2. The General Assembly may discuss any questions relating to the maintenance of international peace and security brought before it by any Member of the United Nations, or by the Security Council, or by a state which is not a Member of the United Nations in accordance with Article 35, paragraph 2, and, except as provided in Article 12, may make recommendations with regard to any such question to the state or states concerned or to the Security Council or both. Any such question on which action is necessary shall be referred to the Security Council by the General Assembly either before or after discussion.

3. The General Assembly may call the attention of the Security Council to situations which are likely to endanger international peace and security.

4. The powers of the General Assembly set forth in this Article shall not limit the general scope of Article 10.

Article 12

1. While the Security Council is exercising in respect of any dispute or situation the functions assigned to it in the present Charter, the General Assembly shall not make any recommendations with regard to that dispute or situation unless the Security Council so requests.

2. The Secretary-General, with the consent of the Security Council, shall notify the General Assembly at each session of any matters relative to the maintenance of international peace and security which are being dealt with by the Security Council and shall similarly notify the General Assembly, or the Members of the United Nations if the General Assembly is not in session, immediately the Security Council ceases to deal with such matters.

Article 13

1. The General Assembly shall initiate studies and make recommendations for the purpose of:

(a) promoting international co-operation in the political field and encouraging the progressive development of international law and its codification;

(b) promoting international co-operation in the economic, social, cultural, educational, and health fields, and assisting in the realization of human rights and fundamental freedoms for all without distinction as to race, sex, language, or religion.

2. The further responsibilities, functions and powers of the General Assembly with respect to matters mentioned in paragraph 1(b) above are set forth in Chapters IX and X.

Article 14

Subject to the provision of Article 12, the General Assembly may recommend measures for the peaceful adjustment of any situation, regardless of origin, which it deems likely to impair the general welfare or friendly relations among nations, including situations resulting from a violation of the provisions of the present Charter setting forth the Purposes and Principles of the United Nations.

Article 15

1. The General Assembly shall receive and consider annual and special reports from the Security Council; these reports shall include an account of the measures that the Security Council has decided upon or taken to maintain international peace and security.

2. The General Assembly shall receive and consider reports from the other organs of the United Nations.

Article 16

The General Assembly shall perform such functions with respect to the international trusteeship system as are assigned to it under Chapters XII and XIII, including the approval of the trusteeship agreements for areas not designated as strategic.

Article 17

1. The General Assembly shall consider and approve the budget of the Organization.

2. The expenses of the Organization shall be borne by the Members as apportioned by the General Assembly

3. The General Assembly shall consider and approve any financial and budgetary arrangements with specialized agencies referred to in Article 57 and shall examine the administrative budgets of such specialized agencies with a view to making recommendations to the agencies concerned.

Voting

Article 18

1. Each Member of the General Assembly shall have one vote.

2. Decisions of the General Assembly on important questions shall be made by a two-thirds majority of the members present and voting. These questions shall include: recommendations with respect to the maintenance of international peace and security, the election of the non-permanent Members of the Security Council, the election of the Members of the Economic and Social Council, the election of Members of the Trusteeship Council in accordance with paragraph 1(c) of Article 86, the admission of new Members to the United Nations, the suspension of the rights and privileges of membership, the expulsion of Members, questions relating to the operation of the trusteeship system, and budgetary questions.

3. Decisions on other questions, including the determination of additional categories of questions to be decided by a two-thirds majority, shall be made by a majority of the members present and voting.

Article 19

A Member of the United Nations which is in arrears in the payment of its financial contributions to the Organization shall have no vote in the General Assembly if the amount of its arrears equals or exceeds the amount of the contributions due from it for the preceding two full years. The General Assembly may, nevertheless, permit such a Member to vote if it is satisfied that the failure to pay is due to conditions beyond the control of the Member.

Procedure

Article 20

The General Assembly shall meet in regular annual sessions and in such special sessions as occasion may require. Special sessions shall be convoked by the Secretary-General at the request of the Security Council or of a majority of the members of the United Nations.

Article 21

The General Assembly shall adopt its own rules of procedure. It shall elect its President for each session.

Article 22

The General Assembly may establish such subsidiary organs as it deems necessary for the performance of its functions.

V. THE SECURITY COUNCIL

Composition

Article 23

1. The Security Council shall consist of 11 Members of the United Nations. The Republic of China, France, the Union of Soviet Socialist Republics, the United Kingdom of Great Britain and Northern Ireland, and the United States of America shall be permanent members of the Security Council. The General Assembly shall elect six other Members of the United Nations to be non-permanent members of the Security Council, due regard being specially paid, in the first instance to the contribution of Members of the United Nations to the maintenance of international peace and security and to the other purposes of the Organization, and also to equitable geographical distribution.

2. The non-permanent members of the Security Council shall be elected for a term of two years. In the first election of the non-permanent members, however, three shall be chosen for a term of one year. A retiring member shall not be eligible for immediate re-election.

3. Each member of the Security Council shall have one representative.

Note: From 1971 the Chinese seat in the UN General Assembly and its permanent seat in the Security Council were occupied by the People's Republic of China. In December 1991 Russia assumed the former USSR's seat in the UN General Assembly and its permanent seat in the Security Council.

Functions and Powers

Article 24

1. In order to ensure prompt and effective action by the United Nations, its Members confer on the Security Council primary responsibility for the maintenance of international peace and security, and agree that in carrying out its duties under this responsibility the Security Council acts on their behalf.

2. In discharging these duties the Security Council shall act in accordance with the Purposes and Principles of the United Nations. The specific powers granted to the Security Council for the discharge of these duties are laid down in Chapters VI, VII, VIII and XII.

3. The Security Council shall submit annual and, when necessary, special reports to the General Assembly for its consideration.

Article 25

The Members of the United Nations agree to accept and carry out the decisions of the Security Council in accordance with the present Charter.

Article 26

In order to promote the establishment and maintenance of international peace and security with the least diversion for armaments of the world's human and economic resources, the Security Council shall be responsible for formulating, with the assistance of the Military Staff Committee referred to in Article 47, plans to be submitted to the Members of the United Nations for the establishment of a system for the regulation of armaments.

Voting

Article 27

1. Each member of the Security Council shall have one vote.

2. Decisions of the Security Council on procedural matters shall be made by an affirmative vote of seven members.

3. Decisions of the Security Council on all other matters shall be made by an affirmative vote of seven members including the concurring votes of the permanent members; provided that, in decisions under Chapter VI, and under paragraph 3 of Article 52, a party to a dispute shall abstain from voting.

Procedure

Article 28

1. The Security Council shall be so organized as to be able to function continuously. Each member of the Security Council shall for this purpose be represented at all times at the seat of the Organization.

2. The Security Council shall hold periodic meetings at which each of its members may, if it so desires, be represented by a member of the government or by some other specially designated representative.

3. The Security Council may hold meetings at such places other than the seat of the Organization as in its judgment will best facilitate its work.

Article 29

The Security Council may establish such subsidiary organs as it deems necessary for the performance of its functions.

Article 30

The Security Council shall adopt its own rules of procedure, including the method of selecting its President.

Article 31

Any Member of the United Nations which is not a member of the Security Council may participate, without vote, in the discussion of any question brought before the Security Council whenever the latter considers that the interests of that Member are specially affected.

Article 32

Any Member of the United Nations which is not a member of the Security Council or any state which is not a Member of the United Nations, if it is a party to a dispute under consideration by the Security Council, shall be invited to participate, without vote, in the discussion relating to the dispute. The Security Council shall lay down such conditions as it deems just for the participation of a state which is not a Member of the United Nations.

VI. PACIFIC SETTLEMENT OF DISPUTES

Article 33

1. The parties to any dispute, the continuance of which is likely to endanger the maintenance of international peace and security, shall, first of all, seek a solution by negotiation, enquiry, mediation, conciliation, arbitration, judicial settlement, resort to regional agencies or arrangements, or other peaceful means of their own choice.

2. The Security Council shall, when it deems necessary, call upon the parties to settle their disputes by such means.

Article 34

The Security Council may investigate any dispute, or any situation which might lead to international friction or give rise to a dispute, in order to determine whether the continuance of the dispute or situation is likely to endanger the maintenance of international peace and security.

Article 35

1. Any Member of the United Nations may bring any dispute, or any situation of the nature referred to in Article 34, to the attention of the Security Council or of the General Assembly.

2. A state which is not a Member of the United Nations may bring to the attention of the Security Council or of the General Assembly any dispute to which it is a party if it accepts in advance, for the purposes of the dispute, the obligations of pacific settlement provided in the present Charter.

3. The proceedings of the General Assembly in respect of matters brought to its attention under this Article will be subject to the provisions of Articles 11 and 12.

Article 36

1. The Security Council may, at any stage of a dispute of the nature referred to in Article 33 or of a situation of like nature, recommend appropriate procedures or methods of adjustment.

2. The Security Council should take into consideration any procedures for the settlement of the dispute which have already been adopted by the parties.

3. In making recommendations under this Article the Security Council should also take into consideration that legal disputes should as a general rule be referred by the parties to the International Court of Justice in accordance with the provisions of the statute of the Court.

Article 37

1. Should the parties to a dispute of the nature referred to in Article 33, fail to settle it by the means indicated in that Article, they shall refer it to the Security Council.

2. If the Security Council deems that the continuance of the dispute is in fact likely to endanger the maintenance of international peace and security, it shall decide whether to take action under Article 36 or to recommend such terms of settlement as it may consider appropriate.

Article 38

Without prejudice to the provisions of Articles 33 to 37, the Security Council may, if all the parties to any dispute so request, make recommendations to the parties with a view to a pacific settlement of the dispute.

VII. ACTION WITH RESPECT TO THREATS TO THE PEACE, BREACHES OF THE PEACE, AND ACTS OF AGGRESSION

Article 39

The Security Council shall determine the existence of any threat to the peace, breach of the peace, or act of aggression and shall make recommendations, or decide what measures shall be taken in accordance with Articles 41 and 42, to maintain or restore international peace and security.

Article 40

In order to prevent an aggravation of the situation, the Security Council may, before making the recommendations or deciding upon the measures provided for in Article 39, call upon the parties concerned to comply with such provisional measures as it deems necessary or desirable. Such provisional measures shall be without prejudice to the rights, claims, or position of the parties concerned. The Security Council shall duly take account of failure to comply with such provisional measures.

Article 41

The Security Council may decide what measures not involving the use of armed force are to be employed to give effect to its decisions, and it may call upon the Members of the United Nations to apply such measures. These may include complete or partial interruption of economic relations and of rail, sea, air, postal, telegraphic, radio, and other means of communication, and the severance of diplomatic relations.

Article 42

Should the Security Council consider that measures provided for in Article 41 would be inadequate or have proved to be inadequate, it may take such action by air, sea, or land forces as may be necessary to maintain or restore international peace and security. Such action may include demonstrations, blockade, and other operations by air, sea, or land forces of Members of the United Nations.

Article 43

1. All Members of the United Nations, in order to contribute to the maintenance of international peace and security, undertake to make available to the Security Council, on its call and in accordance with a special agreement or agreements, armed forces, assistance, and facilities, including rights of passage, necessary for the purpose of maintaining international peace and security.

2. Such agreement or agreements shall govern the numbers and types of forces, their degree of readiness and general location, and the nature of the facilities and assistance to be provided.

3. The agreement or agreements shall be negotiated as soon as possible on the initiative of the Security Council. They shall be concluded between the Security Council and Members or between the Security Council and groups of Members and shall be subject to ratification by the signatory states in accordance with their respective constitutional processes.

Article 44

When the Security Council has decided to use force it shall, before calling upon a Member not represented on it to provide armed forces in fulfilment of the obligations assumed under Article 43, invite that Member, if the Member so desires, to participate in the decisions of the Security Council concerning the employment of contingents of that Member's armed forces.

Article 45

In order to enable the United Nations to take urgent military measures, Members shall hold immediately available national air-force contingents for combined international enforcement action. The strength and degree of readiness of these contingents and plans for their combined action shall be determined, within the limits laid down in the special agreement and agreements referred to in Article 43, by the Security Council with the assistance of the Military Staff Committee.

Article 46

Plans for the application of armed force shall be made by the Security Council with the assistance of the Military Staff Committee.

Article 47

1. There shall be established a Military Staff Committee to advise and assist the Security Council on all questions relating to the Security Council's military requirements for the maintenance of international peace and security, the employment and command of forces placed at its disposal, the regulation of armaments, and possible disarmament.

2. The Military Staff Committee shall consist of the Chiefs of Staff of the permanent members of the Security Council or their representatives. Any Member of the United Nations not permanently represented on the Committee shall be invited by the Committee to be associated with it when the efficient discharge of the Committee's responsibilities requires the participation of that Member in its work.

3. The Military Staff Committee shall be responsible under the Security Council for the strategic direction of any armed forces placed at the disposal of the Security Council. Questions relating to the command of such forces shall be worked out subsequently.

4. The Military Staff Committee, with the authorization of the Security Council and after consultation with appropriate regional agencies, may establish regional sub-committees.

Article 48

1. The action required to carry out the decisions of the Security Council for the maintenance of international peace and security shall be taken by all the Members of the United Nations or by some of them, as the Security Council may determine.

2. Such decisions shall be carried out by the Members of the United Nations directly and through their action in the appropriate international agencies of which they are members.

Article 49

The Members of the United Nations shall join in affording mutual assistance in carrying out the measures decided upon by the Security Council.

Article 50

If preventive or enforcement measures against any state are taken by the Security Council, any other state, whether a Member of the United Nations or not, which finds itself confronted with special economic problems arising from the carrying out of those measures shall have the right to consult the Security Council with regard to a solution of those problems.

Article 51

Nothing in the present Charter shall impair the inherent right of individual or collective self-defence if an armed attack occurs against a Member of the United Nations, until the Security Council has taken measures necessary to maintain international peace and security. Measures taken by Members in the exercise of this right of self-defence shall be immediately reported to the Security Council and shall not in any way affect the authority and responsibility of the Security Council under the present Charter to take at any time such action as it deems necessary in order to maintain or restore international peace and security.

VIII. REGIONAL ARRANGEMENTS

Article 52

1. Nothing in the present Charter precludes the existence of regional arrangements or agencies for dealing with such matters relating to the maintenance of international peace and security as are appropriate for regional action, provided that such arrangements or agencies and their activities are consistent with the Purposes and Principles of the United Nations.

2. The Members of the United Nations entering into such arrangements or constituting such agencies shall make every effort to achieve pacific settlement of local disputes through such regional agencies before referring them to the Security Council.

3. The Security Council shall encourage the development of pacific settlement of local disputes through such regional arrangements or by such regional agencies either on the initiative of the states concerned or by reference from the Security Council.

4. This Article in no way impairs the application of Articles 34 and 35.

Article 53

1. The Security Council shall, where appropriate, utilize such regional arrangements or agencies for enforcement action under its authority. But no enforcement action shall be taken under regional arrangements or by regional agencies without the authorization of the Security Council, with the exception of measures against any enemy state, as defined in paragraph 2 of this Article, provided for pursuant to Article 107 or in regional arrangements directed against renewal of aggressive policy on the part of any such state, until such time as the Organization may, on request of the Governments concerned, be charged with the responsibility for preventing further aggression by such a state.

The term enemy state as used in paragraph I of this Article applies to any state which during the Second World War has been an enemy of any signatory of the present Charter.

Article 54

The Security Council shall at all times be kept fully informed of activities undertaken or in contemplation under regional arrangements or by regional agencies for the maintenance of international peace and security.

IX. INTERNATIONAL ECONOMIC AND SOCIAL CO-OPERATION

Article 55

With a view to the creation of conditions of stability and well-being which are necessary for peaceful and friendly relations among nations based on respect for the principle of equal rights and self-determination of peoples, the United Nations shall promote:

   (a) higher standards of living, full employment, and conditions of economic and social progress and development;

   (b) solutions of international economic, social, health, and related problems; and international cultural and educational co-operation; and

   (c) universal respect for, and observance of, human rights and fundamental freedoms for all without distinction as to race, sex, language, or religion.

Article 56

All Members pledge themselves to take joint and separate action in co-operation with the Organization for the achievement of the purposes set forth in Article 55.

Article 57

1. The various specialized agencies, established by intergovernmental agreement and having wide international responsibilities, as defined in their basic instruments, in economic, social, cultural, educational, health, and related fields, shall be brought into relationship with the United Nations in accordance with the provisions of Article 63.

2. Such agencies thus brought into relationship with the United Nations are hereinafter referred to as specialized agencies.

Article 58

The Organization shall make recommendations for the co-ordination of the policies and activities of the specialized agencies.

Article 59

The Organization shall, where appropriate, initiate negotiations among the states concerned for the creation of any new specialized agencies required for the accomplishment of the purposes set forth in Article 55.

Article 60

Responsibility for the discharge of the functions of the Organization set forth in this Chapter shall be vested in the General Assembly and, under the authority of the General Assembly, in the Economic and Social Council, which shall have for this purpose the powers set forth in Chapter X.

X. THE ECONOMIC AND SOCIAL COUNCIL

Composition

Article 61

1. The Economic and Social Council shall consist of 18 Members of the United Nations elected by the General Assembly.

2. Subject to the provisions of paragraph 3, six members of the Economic and Social Council shall be elected each year for a term of three years. A retiring member shall be eligible for immediate re-election.

3. At the first election, 18 members of the Economic and Social Council shall be chosen. The term of office of six members so chosen shall expire at the end of one year, and of six other members at the end of two years, in accordance with arrangements made by the General Assembly.

4. Each member of the Economic and Social Council shall have one representative.

Functions and Powers

Article 62

1. The Economic and Social Council may make or initiate studies and reports with respect to international economic, social, cultural, educational, health, and related matters and may make recommendations with respect to any such matters to the General Assembly, to the Members of the United Nations, and to the specialized agencies concerned.

2. It may make recommendations for the purpose of promoting respect for, and observance of, human rights and fundamental freedoms for all.

3. It may prepare draft conventions for submission to the General Assembly, with respect to matters falling within its competence.

4. It may call, in accordance with the rules prescribed by the United Nations, international conferences on matters falling within its competence.

Article 63

1. The Economic and Social Council may enter into agreements with any of the agencies referred to in Article 57, defining the terms on which the agency concerned shall be brought into relationship with the United Nations. Such agreements shall be subject to approval by the General Assembly.

2. It may co-ordinate the activities of the specialized agencies through consultation with and recommendations to such agencies and through recommendations to the General Assembly and to the Members of the United Nations.

Article 64

1. The Economic and Social Council may take appropriate steps to obtain regular reports from the specialized agencies. It may make arrangements with the Members of the United Nations and with specialized agencies to obtain reports on the steps taken to give effect to its own recommendations and to recommendations on matters falling within its competence made by the General Assembly.

2. It may communicate its observations on these reports to the General Assembly.

Article 65

The Economic and Social Council may furnish information to the Security Council and shall assist the Security Council upon its request.

Article 66

1. The Economic and Social Council shall perform such functions as fall within its competence in connection with the carrying out of the recommendations of the General Assembly.

2. It may, with the approval of the General Assembly, perform services at the request of Members of the United Nations and at the request of specialized agencies.

3. It shall perform such other functions as are specified elsewhere in the present Charter or as may be assigned to it by the General Assembly.

Voting

Article 67

1. Each member of the Economic and Social Council shall have one vote.

2. Decisions of the Economic and Social Council shall be made by a majority of the members present and voting.

Procedure

Article 68

The Economic and Social Council shall set up commissions in economic and social fields and for the promotion of human rights, and such other commissions as may be required for the performance of its functions.

Article 69

The Economic and Social Council shall invite any Member of the United Nations to participate, without vote, in its deliberations on any matter of particular concern to that Member.

Article 70

The Economic and Social Council may make arrangements for representatives of the specialized agencies to participate, without vote, in its deliberations and in those of the commissions established by it, and for its representatives to participate in the deliberations of the specialized agencies.

Article 71

The Economic and Social Council may make suitable arrangements for consultation with non-governmental organizations which are concerned with matters within its competence. Such arrangements may be made with international organizations and, where appropriate, with national organizations after consultation with the Member of the United Nations concerned.

Article 72

1. The Economic and Social Council shall adopt its own rules of procedure, including the method of selecting its President.

2. The Economic and Social Council shall meet as required in accordance with its rules, which shall include provision for the convening of meetings on the request of a majority of its members.

XI. NON-SELF-GOVERNING TERRITORIES

Article 73

Members of the United Nations which have or assume responsibilities for the administration of territories whose peoples have not yet attained a full measure of self-government recognize the principle that the interests of the inhabitants of these territories are paramount, and accept as a sacred trust the obligation to promote to the utmost, within the system of international peace and security established by the present Charter, the well-being of the inhabitants of these territories, and, to this end:

(a) to ensure, with due respect for the culture of the peoples concerned, their political, economic, social, and educational advancement, their just treatment, and their protection against abuses;

(b) to develop self-government, to take due account of the political aspirations of the peoples, and to assist them in the progressive development of their free political institutions, according to the particular circumstances of each territory and its peoples and their varying stages of advancement;

(c) to further international peace and security;

(d) to promote constructive measures of development, to encourage research, and to co-operate with one another and, when and where appropriate, with specialized international bodies with a view to the practical achievement of the social, economic, and scientific purposes set forth in this Article; and

(e) to transmit regularly to the Secretary-General for information purposes, subject to such limitations as security and constitutional considerations may require, statistical and other information of a technical nature relating to economic, social, and educational conditions in the territories for which they are respectively responsible other than those territories to which Chapters XII and XIII apply.

Article 74

Members of the United Nations also agree that their policy in respect of the territories to which this Chapter applies, no less than in respect of their metropolitan areas, must be based on the general principles of good-neighbourliness, due account being taken of the interests and well-being of the rest of the world, in social, economic, and commercial matters.

XII. INTERNATIONAL TRUSTEESHIP SYSTEM

Article 75

The United Nations shall establish under its authority an international trusteeship system for the administration and supervision of such territories as may be placed thereunder by subsequent individual agreements. These territories are hereinafter referred to as trust territories.

Article 76

The basic objectives of the trusteeship system, in accordance with the Purposes of the United Nations laid down in Article 1 of the present Charter, shall be:

(a) to further international peace and security;

(b) to promote the political, economic, social, and educational advancement of the inhabitants of the trust territories, and their progressive development towards self-government or independence as may be appropriate to the particular circumstances of each territory and its peoples and the freely expressed wishes of the peoples concerned, and as may be provided by the terms of each trusteeship agreement;

(c) to encourage respect for human rights and for fundamental freedoms for all without distinction as to race, sex, language, or religion, and to encourage recognition of the interdependence of the peoples of the world; and

(d) to ensure equal treatment in social, economic, and commercial matters for all Members of the United Nations and their nationals, and also equal treatment for the latter in the administration of justice, without prejudice to the attainment of the foregoing objectives and subject to the provisions of Article 80.

Article 77

1. The trusteeship system shall apply to such territories in the following categories as may be placed thereunder by means of trusteeship agreements.

(a) territories now held under mandate;

(b) territories which may be detached from enemy states as a result of the Second World War; and

(c) territories voluntarily placed under the system by states responsible for their administration.

2. It will be a matter for subsequent agreement as to which territories in the foregoing categories will be brought under the trusteeship system and upon what terms.

Article 78

The trusteeship system shall not apply to territories which have become Members of the United Nations, relationship among which shall be based on respect for the principle of sovereign equality.

Article 79

The terms of trusteeship for each territory to be placed under the trusteeship system, including any alteration or amendment, shall be agreed upon by the states directly concerned, including the mandatory power in the case of territories held under mandate by a Member of the United Nations, and shall be approved as provided for in Articles 83 and 85.

Article 80

1. Except as may be agreed upon in individual trusteeship agreements, made under Articles 77, 79, and 81, placing each territory under the trusteeship system, and until such agreements have been concluded, nothing in this Chapter shall be construed in or of itself to alter in any manner the rights whatsoever of any states or any peoples or the terms of existing international instruments to which Members of the United Nations may respectively be parties.

2. Paragraph 1 of this Article shall not be interpreted as giving grounds for delay or postponement of the negotiation and conclusion of agreements for placing mandated and other territories under the trusteeship system as provided for in Article 77.

Article 81

The trusteeship agreement shall in each case include the terms under which the trust territory will be administered and designate the authority which will exercise the administration of the trust territory. Such authority, hereinafter called the administering authority, may be one or more states or the Organization itself.

Article 82

There may be designated, in any trusteeship agreement, a strategic area or areas which may include part or all of the trust territory to which the agreement applies, without prejudice to any special agreement or agreements made under Article 43.

Article 83

1. All functions of the United Nations relating to strategic areas, including the approval of the terms of the trusteeship agreements and of their alteration or amendment, shall be exercised by the Security Council.

2. The basic objectives set forth in Article 76 shall be applicable to the people of each strategic area.

3. The Security Council shall, subject to the provisions of the trusteeship agreements and without prejudice to security considerations, avail itself of the assistance of the Trusteeship Council to perform those functions of the United Nations under the trusteeship system relating to political, economic, social, and educational matters in the strategic areas.

Article 84

It shall be the duty of the administering authority to ensure that the trust territory shall play its part in the maintenance of international peace and security. To this end the administering authority may make use of volunteer forces, facilities, and assistance from the trust territory in carrying out the obligations towards the Security Council undertaken in this regard by the administering authority, as well as for local defence and the maintenance of law and order within the trust territory.

Article 85

1. The functions of the United Nations with regard to trusteeship agreements for all areas not designated as strategic, including the approval of the terms of the trusteeship agreements and of their alteration or amendment, shall be exercised by the General Assembly.

2. The Trusteeship Council, operating under the authority of the General Assembly, shall assist the General Assembly in carrying out these functions.

XIII. THE TRUSTEESHIP COUNCIL

Composition

Article 86

1. The Trusteeship Council shall consist of the following Members of the United Nations:

(a) those Members administering trust territories;

(b) such of those Members mentioned by name in Article 23 as are not administering trust territories; and

(c) as many other Members elected for three-year terms by the General Assembly as may be necessary to ensure that the total number of members of the Trusteeship Council is equally divided between those Members of the United Nations which administer trust territories and those which do not.

2. Each member of the Trusteeship Council shall designate one specially qualified person to represent it therein.

Note: On 1 October 1994 the Republic of Palau, the last remaining territory under UN trusteeship, became independent. The Trusteeship Council formally suspended operations on 1 November; subsequently it was to be convened, as required, on an extraordinary basis.

Functions and Powers

Article 87

The General Assembly and, under its authority, the Trusteeship Council, in carrying out their functions, may:

(a) consider reports submitted by the administering authority;

(b) accept petitions and examine them in consultation with the administering authority;

(c) provide for periodic visits to the respective trust territories at times agreed upon with the administering authority; and

(d) take these and other actions in conformity with the terms of the trusteeship agreements.

Article 88

The Trusteeship Council shall formulate a questionnaire on the political, economic, social, and educational advancement of the inhabitants of each trust territory, and the administering authority for each trust territory within the competence of the General Assembly shall make an annual report to the General Assembly upon the basis of such questionnaire.

Voting

Article 89

1. Each member of the Trusteeship Council shall have one vote.

2. Decisions of the Trusteeship Council shall be made by a majority of the members present and voting.

Procedure

Article 90

1. The Trusteeship Council shall adopt its own rules of procedure, including the method of selecting its President.

2. The Trusteeship Council shall meet as required in accordance with its rules, which shall include provision for the convening of meetings on the request of a majority of its members.

Article 91

The Trusteeship Council shall, when appropriate, avail itself of the assistance of the Economic and Social Council and of the specialized agencies in regard to matters with which they are respectively concerned.

XIV. THE INTERNATIONAL COURT OF JUSTICE

Article 92

The International Court of Justice shall be the principal judicial organ of the United Nations. It shall function in accordance with the annexed Statute, which is based upon the Statute of the Permanent Court of International Justice and forms an integral part of the present Charter.

Article 93

1. All Members of the United Nations are *ipso facto* parties to the Statute of the International Court of Justice.

2. A state which is not a Member of the United Nations may become a party to the Statute of the International Court of Justice on condition to be determined in each case by the General Assembly upon the recommendation of the Security Council.

Article 94

1. Each Member of the United Nations undertakes to comply with the decision of the International Court of Justice in any case to which it is a party.

2. If any party to a case fails to perform the obligations incumbent upon it under a judgment rendered by the Court, the other party may have recourse to the Security Council, which may, if it deems necessary, make recommendations or decide upon measures to be taken to give effect to the judgment.

Article 95

Nothing in the present Charter shall prevent Members of the United Nations from entrusting the solution of their differences to other tribunals by virtue of agreements already in existence or which may be concluded in the future.

Article 96

1. The General Assembly or the Security Council may request the International Court of Justice to give an advisory opinion on any legal question.

2. Other organs of the United Nations and specialized agencies, which may at any time be so authorized by the General Assembly, may also request advisory opinions of the Court on legal questions arising within the scope of their activities.

XV. THE SECRETARIAT

Article 97

The Secretariat shall comprise a Secretary-General and such staff as the Organization may require. The Secretary-General shall be appointed by the General Assembly upon the recommendation of the Security Council. He shall be the chief administrative officer of the Organization.

Article 98

The Secretary-General shall act in that capacity in all meetings of the General Assembly, of the Security Council, of the Economic and Social Council, and of the Trusteeship Council, and shall perform such other functions as are entrusted to him by these organs. The Secretary-General shall make an annual report to the General Assembly on the work of the Organization.

Article 99

The Secretary-General may bring to the attention of the Security Council any matter which in his opinion may threaten the maintenance of international peace and security.

Article 100

1. In the performance of their duties the Secretary-General and the staff shall not seek or receive instructions from any government or from any other authority external to the Organization. They shall refrain from any action which might reflect on their position as international officials responsible only to the Organization.

2. Each Member of the United Nations undertakes to respect the exclusively international character of the responsibilities of the Secretary-General and the staff and not to seek to influence them in the discharge of their responsibilities.

Article 101

1. The staff shall be appointed by the Secretary-General under regulations established by the General Assembly.

2. Appropriate staffs shall be permanently assigned to the Economic and Social Council, the Trusteeship Council, and, as required, to other organs of the United Nations. These staffs shall form a part of the Secretariat.

3. The paramount consideration in the employment of the staff and in the determination of the conditions of service shall be the necessity of securing the highest standards of efficiency, competence, and integrity. Due regard shall be paid to the importance of recruiting the staff on as wide a geographical basis as possible.

XVI. MISCELLANEOUS PROVISIONS

Article 102

1. Every treaty and every international agreement entered into by any Member of the United Nations after the present Charter comes into force shall as soon as possible be registered with the Secretariat and published by it.

2. No party to any such treaty or international agreement which has not been registered in accordance with the provisions of paragraph 1 of this Article may invoke that treaty or agreement before any organ of the United Nations.

Article 103

In the event of a conflict between the obligations of the Members of the United Nations under the present Charter and their obligations under any other international agreement, their obligations under the present Charter shall prevail.

Article 104

The Organization shall enjoy in the territory of each of its Members such legal capacity as may be necessary for the exercise of its functions and the fulfilment of its purposes.

Article 105

1. The Organization shall enjoy in the territory of each of its Members such privileges and immunities as are necessary for the fulfilment of its purposes.

2. Representatives of the Members of the United Nations and officials of the Organization shall similarly enjoy such privileges and immunities as are necessary for the independent exercise of their functions in connection with the Organization.

3. The General Assembly may make recommendations with a view to determining the details of the application of paragraphs 1 and 2 of this Article or may propose conventions to the Members of the United Nations for this purpose.

XVII. TRANSITIONAL SECURITY ARRANGEMENTS

Article 106

Pending the coming into force of such special agreements referred to in Article 43 as in the opinion of the Security Council enable it to begin the exercise of its responsibilities under Article 42, the parties to the Four-Nation Declaration signed at Moscow, October 30, 1943, and France, shall, in accordance with the provisions of paragraph 5 of that Declaration, consult with one another and as occasion requires with other Members of the United Nations with a view to such joint action on behalf of the Organization as may be necessary for the purpose of maintaining international peace and security.

Article 107

Nothing in the present Charter shall invalidate or preclude action, in relation to any state which during the Second World War has been an enemy of any signatory to the present Charter, taken or authorized as a result of that war by the Governments having responsibility for such action.

XVIII. AMENDMENTS

Article 108

Amendments to the present Charter shall come into force for all Members of the United Nations when they have been adopted by a vote of two-thirds of the members of the General Assembly and ratified in accordance with their respective constitutional processes by two-thirds of the Members of the United Nations, including all the permanent members of the Security Council.

Article 109

1. A General Conference of the Members of the United Nations for the purpose of reviewing the present Charter may be held at a date and place to be fixed by a two-thirds vote of the members of the General Assembly and by a vote of any seven members of the Security Council. Each Member of the United Nations shall have one vote in the conference.

2. Any alteration of the present Charter recommended by a two-thirds vote of the conference shall take effect when ratified in accordance with their respective constitutional processes by two-thirds of the Members of the United Nations including all the permanent members of the Security Council.

3. If such a conference has not been held before the tenth annual session of the General Assembly following the coming into force of the present Charter, the proposal to call such a conference shall be placed on the agenda of that session of the General Assembly, and the conference shall be held if so decided by a majority vote of the members of the General Assembly and by a vote of any seven members of the Security Council.

XIX. RATIFICATION AND SIGNATURE

Article 110

1. The present Charter shall be ratified by the signatory states in accordance with their respective constitutional processes.

2. The ratifications shall be deposited with the Government of the United States of America, which shall notify all the signatory states of each deposit as well as the Secretary-General of the Organization when he has been appointed.

3. The present Charter shall come into force upon the deposit of ratifications by the Republic of China, France, the Union of Soviet Socialist Republics, the United Kingdom of Great Britain and Northern Ireland, and the United States of America, and by a majority of the other signatory states. A protocol of the ratifications deposited shall thereupon be drawn up by the Government of the United States of America which shall communicate copies thereof to all the signatory states.

4. The states signatory to the present Charter which ratify it after it has come into force will become original Members of the United Nations on the date of the deposit of their respective ratifications.

Article 111

The present Charter, of which the Chinese, French, Russian, English, and Spanish texts are equally authentic, shall remain deposited in the archives of the Government of the United States of America. Duly certified copies thereof shall be transmitted by that Government to the Governments of the other signatory states.

IN FAITH WHEREOF the representatives of the Governments of the United Nations have signed the present Charter.

Done at the city of San Francisco the twenty-sixth day of June, one thousand nine hundred and forty-five.

AMENDMENTS

The following amendments to Articles 23 and 27 of the Charter came into force in August 1965.

Article 23

1. The Security Council shall consist of 15 Members of the United Nations. The Republic of China, France, the Union of Soviet Socialist Republics, the United Kingdom of Great Britain and Northern Ireland, and the United States of America shall be permanent members of the Security Council. The General Assembly shall elect 10 other Members of the United Nations to be non-permanent members of the Security Council, due regard being specially paid, in the first instance to the contribution of Members of the United Nations to the maintenance of international peace and security and to the other purposes of the Organization, and also to equitable geographical distribution.

2. The non-permanent members of the Security Council shall be elected for a term of two years. In the first election of the non-permanent members after the increase of the membership of the Security Council from 11 to 15, two of the four additional members shall be chosen for a term of one year. A retiring member shall not be eligible for immediate re-election.

3. Each member of the Security Council shall have one representative.

Article 27

1. Each member of the Security Council shall have one vote.

2. Decisions of the Security Council on procedural matters shall be made by an affirmative vote of nine members.

3. Decisions of the Security Council on all other matters shall be made by an affirmative vote of nine members including the concurring votes of the permanent members; provided that, in decisions under Chapter VI and under paragraph 3 of Article 52, a party to a dispute shall abstain from voting.

The following amendments to Article 61 of the Charter came into force in September 1973.

Article 61

1. The Economic and Social Council shall consist of 54 Members of the United Nations elected by the General Assembly.

2. Subject to the provisions of paragraph 3, 18 members of the Economic and Social Council shall be elected each year for a term of three years. A retiring member shall be eligible for immediate re-election.

3. At the first election after the increase in the membership of the Economic and Social Council from 27 to 54 members, in addition to the members elected in place of the nine members whose term of office expires at the end of that year, 27 additional members shall be elected. Of these 27 additional members, the term of office of nine members so elected shall expire at the end of one year, and of nine other members at the end of two years, in accordance with arrangements made by the General Assembly.

4. Each member of the Economic and Social Council shall have one representative.

The following amendment to Paragraph 1 of Article 109 of the Charter came into force in June 1968.

Article 109

1. A General Conference of the Members of the United Nations for the purpose of reviewing the present Charter may be held at a date and place to be fixed by a two-thirds vote of the members of the General Assembly and by a vote of any nine members of the Security Council. Each Member of the United Nations shall have one vote in the conference.

UNITED NATIONS REGIONAL COMMISSIONS

Economic Commission for Europe—ECE

Address: Palais des Nations, 1211 Geneva 10, Switzerland.
Telephone: (22) 9171234; **fax:** (22) 9170505; **e-mail:** info.ece@unece.org; **internet:** www.unece.org.

The UN Economic Commission for Europe (ECE) was established in 1947. It provides a regional forum for governments from European countries, the USA, Canada, Israel and central Asian republics to study the economic, environmental and technological problems of the region and to recommend courses of action. ECE is also active in the formulation of international legal instruments and the setting of international norms and standards.

MEMBERS

Albania	Liechtenstein
Andorra	Lithuania
Armenia	Luxembourg
Austria	Macedonia, former Yugoslav
Azerbaijan	republic
Belarus	Malta
Belgium	Moldova
Bosnia and Herzegovina	Monaco
Bulgaria	Netherlands
Canada	Norway
Croatia	Poland
Cyprus	Portugal
Czech Republic	Romania
Denmark	Russia
Estonia	San Marino
Finland	Serbia and Montenegro
France	Slovakia
Georgia	Slovenia
Germany	Spain
Greece	Sweden
Hungary	Switzerland
Iceland	Tajikistan
Ireland	Turkey
Israel	Turkmenistan
Italy	Ukraine
Kazakhstan	United Kingdom
Kyrgyzstan	Uzbekistan
Latvia	

Organization

(March 2005)

COMMISSION

ECE, with ECAFE (now ESCAP), was the earliest of the five regional economic commissions set up by the UN Economic and Social Council (ECOSOC). The Commission holds an annual plenary session and several informal sessions, and meetings of subsidiary bodies are convened throughout the year.

SECRETARIAT

The secretariat services the meetings of the Commission and its subsidiary bodies and publishes periodic surveys and reviews, including a number of specialized statistical bulletins on timber, housing, building, and transport (see list of publications below). The Executive Secretary carries out secretarial functions for the Executive Bodies of several regional conventions and their protocols (see below). The ECE and UN Secretariats also service the ECOSOC Committee of Experts on the Transport of Dangerous Goods.

Executive Secretary: Brigita Schmögnerová (Slovakia).

Activities

The guiding principle of ECE activities is the promotion of sustainable development. Within this framework, ECE's main objectives are to provide assistance to countries of central and eastern Europe in their transition from centrally-planned to market economies and to achieve the integration of all members into the European and global economies. Environmental protection, transport, statistics, trade facilitation and economic analysis are all principal topics in the ECE work programme, which also includes activities in the fields of timber, energy, trade, industry, and human settlements.

The 52nd plenary session of the ECE, held in April 1997, introduced a programme of reform, reducing the number of principal subsidiary bodies from 14 to seven, in order to concentrate resources on the core areas of work listed below, assisted by sub-committees and groups of experts. The Commission also determined to strengthen economic co-operation within Europe and to enhance co-operation and dialogue with other sub-regional organizations.

ECE's principal subsidiary bodies were to assess any implications that the enlargement of the European Union in May 2004 might have on their activities.

Economic Analysis: An Economic Analysis Division conducts regular analyses of economic developments and prospects in the region, as well as in-depth studies of specific topics, including structural change, European integration, economic transition. A population activities unit undertakes relevant analysis and research into population issues in Europe and North America. Through its work the Division aims to contribute to the monitoring and implementation of the UN Millennium Development Goals in the region. Organizes seminars, workshops, and expert meetings. Works with the Organisation for Security and Co-operation in Europe to develop conflict prevention strategies based on addressing risks in the economic and environmental situation (to this end the two organizations signed a Memorandum of Understanding in December 2004). Actively involved in preparations for the International Conference on Financing for Development, held in Mexico, in March 2002, and in adopting and implementing the resulting Monterrey Consesus.

Environment: ECE aims to facilitate and promote co-operation among member governments in developing and implementing policies for environmental protection, the rational use of natural resources, and sustainable development. It supports the integration of environmental policy into sectoral policies, seeks solutions to environmental problems, particularly those of a transboundary nature and assists in strengthening environmental management capabilities, particularly in countries in transition. A programme of Environmental Performance Reviews helps to improve the effectiveness of environmental management and policies. The Committee on Environmental Policy brings governments together to formulate policy and provides a forum for the exchange of experience and good practices. It prepares the Environment for Europe ministerial-level conferences (normally held every four years—2007: Belgrade, Serbia and Montenegro) and supports a Pan-European Programme on the environment, transport and health. ECE promotes the implementation of international agreements on the environment and assesses national policies and legislation. In addition, it has negotiated the following conventions relating to the environment and serves as their secretariat: the Convention on Long-range Transboundary Air Pollution (which entered into force in 1983 and has been extended by eight protocols); the Convention on Environmental Impact Assessment in a Transboundary Context ('Espoo Convention', entered into force in 1997, one protocol); the Convention on the Transboundary Effects of Industrial Accidents (entered into force in 2000, one protocol); the Convention on Access to Information, Public Participation in Decision-making and Access to Justice in Environmental Matters ('Aarhus Convention', entered into force in 2001, one protocol); and the Convention of the Protection and Use of Transboundary Watercourses and International Lakes ('Water Convention', entered into force in 1996, two protocols).

Human Settlements: ECE's Committee on Human Settlements reviews trends and policies in the field of human settlements; undertakes studies and organizes seminars; promotes international co-operation in the field of housing and urban and regional research, as well as partnerships between the public, non-governmental and private sector; assists the countries of central and eastern Europe, which are currently in the process of economic transition, in reformulating their policies relating to housing, land management, sustainable human settlements, and planning and development. Issues relating to land administration are considered by a specialized Working Party, which convenes every two years.

Industrial Restructuring, Energy and Enterprise Development: ECE aims to assist member states to restructure uncompetitive industrial sectors and enterprises, to promote new enterprises and to develop a knowledge-based economy. It provides a forum for exchange of information and for greater co-operation between the private and public sector. ECE administers a programme on Women's Entrepreneurship. Working groups on legal and commercial practices promote public-private partnerships, real estate and land reform, and the enforcement of intellectual property rights. A sub-programme of ECE's Industrial Restructuring, Energy and Enterprise Development Division is concerned with promoting a sustainable energy development strategy for the region. Activitie include labelling classification systems and related legal and policy frameworks; liberalization of energy markets, pricing policies and supply security; harmonization of energy policies and practices; rational use of energy, efficiency and conservation; energy infrastructure including interconnection of electric power and gas networks; coal and thermal power generation in the context of sustainable energy development; Energy Efficiency 21 Project; promotion and development of a market-based Gas Industry in Economies in Transition—Gas Centre programme; and technical assistance and operational activities in energy for the benefit of countries with economies in transition.

Trade Development: ECE acts as a forum for studying means of expanding and diversifying trade among European countries, as well as with countries in other regions, and for drawing up recommendations on how to achieve these ends. It aims to analyse trends, problems and prospects in intra-European trade, to explore means of encouraging the flow of international direct investment into the newly opening economies of central and eastern Europe, and to promote new or improved methods of trading by means of marketing, industrial co-operation, contractual guides, and the facilitation of international trade procedures. An Agricultural Standards Unit aims to establish quality standards for use by governments, producers, importers and exporters. In 2002 the UN Centre for Trade Facilitation and Electronic Business (UN/CEFACT) was established, under ECE auspices, to contribute to the growth of international commerce by harmonizing trade processes and procedures. It has developed international standards (notably through the Electronic Data Interchange for Administration, Commerce and Transport—UN/EDIFACT), trade facilitation recommendations, and technical specifications. In September 2004 a UN Trust Fund was established to support and accelerate the work of the Centre. At that time it was formulating a policy on intellectual property rights and had released the first Aggregate Core Components library.

Statistics: ECE's Statistical Division makes available economic indicators and other data and analyses conducted by the Commission. It services a Conference of European Statisticians which promotes improvement of national statistics and their international comparability in economic, social, demographic and environmental fields, the co-ordination of statistical activities of international organizations active in Europe and North America, and responds to the increasing need for international statistical co-operation both within the ECE region and between the region and other regions.

Transport: ECE aims to promote a coherent, efficient, safe and sustainable transport system through the development of international agreements, conventions and other instruments covering a wide range of questions relating to road, rail, inland water and combined transport. Working parties of the Transport Division are concerned with inland water transport, border-crossings and customs, road traffic safety, limitation of aircraft noise, requirements for the construction of road vehicles, transport regulations in the fields of transport of dangerous goods and perishable foodstuffs and monitoring scrap metal radiation. Specialized groups consider transport trends and economics and compile transport statistics. It assists central and eastern European countries, as well as ECE member states from central Asia, to develop their transport systems and infrastructures.

Timber: ECE's Timber Committee works closely, through an integrated programme, with the European Forestry Commission of the FAO to promote sustainable forest management in Europe, the CIS and North America. It regularly reviews markets for forest products; analyses long-term trends and prospects for forestry and timber; keeps under review developments in the forest industries, including environmental and energy-related aspects. The Committee meets annually to review the programme, as well as to discuss policy and market trends and outlook.

SUB-REGIONAL PROGRAMMES

Southeast European Co-operative Initiative (SECI): initiated in December 1996, in order to encourage co-operation among countries of the sub-region and to facilitate their access to the process of European integration. Nine *ad hoc* Project Groups have been established to undertake preparations for the following selected projects: trade facilitation; transport infrastructure, in particular road and rail networks; financial policies to promote small and medium-sized enterprises; co-operation to combat crime and corruption; energy efficiency demonstration zone networks; interconnection of natural gas networks; co-operation among securities markets; and the recovery programme for rivers, lakes and adjacent seas (with particular emphasis on the Danube River Basin). Activities are overseen by a SECI Agenda Committee and a SECI Business Advisory Council. Participating countries: Albania, Bosnia and Herzegovina, Bulgaria, Croatia, Greece, Hungary, the former Yugoslav republic of Macedonia, Moldova, Romania, Serbia and Montenegro, Slovenia and Turkey.

Special Programme for the Economies of Central Asia (SPECA): initiated in March 1998 as a joint programme of ECE and ESCAP. Aims to strengthen sub-regional co-operation, in particular in the following areas: the development of transport infrastructure and facilitation of cross-border activities; the rational use of energy and water; regional development and attraction of foreign investment; and development of multiple routes for pipeline transportation of hydrocarbons to global markets. In February 2002 SPECA's Regional Advisory Committee endorsed the terms of reference for the establishment of a Business Advisory Council of SPECA, which aimed to bring together business representatives from participating countries and from their major trading and economic partners. The inaugural session of the Council was held in June, in Almaty, Kazakhstan. Participating countries: Kazakhstan, Kyrgyzstan, Tajikistan, Turkmenistan and Uzbekistan. In 2004 SPECA published a report concerned with the rational and efficient use of water and energy resources in Central Asia.

Finance

ECE's proposed programme budget for the two years 2004–05 was US $46.9m.

Publications

ECE Annual Report.
Annual Bulletin of Housing and Building Statistics for Europe and North America.
Annual Bulletin of Transport Statistics for Europe and North America.
ECE Highlights (3 a year).
The ECE in the Age of Change.
Economic Survey of Europe (2 a year).
Statistical Journal of the UNECE (quarterly).
Non-Observed Economy in National Accounts.
Statistical Standards and Studies.
Statistics of Road Traffic Accidents in Europe and North America.
Timber Bulletin (6 a year).
Timber Committee Yearbook (annually).
Trends in Europe and North America: Statistical Yearbook of the ECE (annually).
UN Manual of Tests and Criteria of Dangerous Goods.
UN Recommendations on the Transport of Dangerous Goods.
UNECE International Legal Instruments, Norms and Standards.
The UNECE Works for Quality and Safety: Norms and Standards.
Women and Men in Europe and North America.
World Robotics (annually).
Studies on air pollution, forestry and timber, water, gas, energy; environmental performance reviews; country profiles on the housing sector; transport agreements; customs conventions; maps; trade and investment briefings and guides; reports on fertility and family, gender, migration and population ageing; statistical bulletins; sectoral studies; discussion papers. Reports, proceedings of meetings, technical documents, codes of conduct, codes of practice, guide-lines to governments, etc.

Economic and Social Commission for Asia and the Pacific—ESCAP

Address: United Nations Bldg, Rajadamnern Nok Ave, Bangkok 10200, Thailand.

Telephone: (2) 288-1234; **fax:** (2) 288-1000; **e-mail:** unisbkk .unescap@un.org; **internet:** www.unescap.org.

The Commission was founded in 1947 to encourage the economic and social development of Asia and the Far East; it was originally known as the Economic Commission for Asia and the Far East (ECAFE). The title ESCAP, which replaced ECAFE, was adopted after a reorganization in 1974. From 2002 ESCAP's administrative structures and programme activities underwent a process of intensive restructuring.

MEMBERS

Afghanistan	Korea, Democratic	Philippines
Armenia	People's Republic	Russia
Australia	Korea, Republic	Samoa
Azerbaijan	Kyrgyzstan	Singapore
Bangladesh	Laos	Solomon Islands
Bhutan	Malaysia	Sri Lanka
Brunei	The Maldives	Tajikistan
Cambodia	Marshall Islands	Thailand
China, People's	Micronesia,	Timor-Leste
Republic	Federated States	Tonga
Fiji	Mongolia	Turkey
France	Myanmar	Turkmenistan
Georgia	Nauru	Tuvalu
India	Nepal	United Kingdom
Indonesia	Netherlands	USA
Iran	New Zealand	Uzbekistan
Japan	Pakistan	Vanuatu
Kazakhstan	Palau	Viet Nam
Kiribati	Papua New Guinea	

ASSOCIATE MEMBERS

American Samoa	Hong Kong	Northern Mariana
Cook Islands	Macao	Islands
French Polynesia	New Caledonia	
Guam	Niue	

Organization

(March 2005)

COMMISSION

The Commission meets annually at ministerial level to examine the region's problems, to review progress, to establish priorities and to decide upon the recommendations of the Executive Secretary or the subsidiary bodies of the Commission.

Ministerial and intergovernmental conferences on specific issues may be held on an *ad hoc* basis with the approval of the Commission, although no more than one ministerial conference and five intergovernmental conferences may be held during one year.

COMMITTEES AND SPECIAL BODIES

The following advise the Commission and help to oversee the work of the Secretariat:

Committee on Poverty Reduction: has sub-committees on Poverty Reduction Practices; and Statistics.

Committee on Managing Globalization: has sub-committees on International Trade and Investment; Transport Infrastructure and Facilitation and Tourism; Environment and Sustainable Development; and Information, Communications and Space Technology.

Committee on Emerging Social Issues: has sub-committees on Socially Vulnerable Groups; and Health and Development.

Special Body on Least-Developed and Land-locked Developing Countries: meets every two years.

Special Body on Pacific Island Developing Countries: meets every two years.

In addition, an Advisory Committee of permanent representatives and other representatives designated by members of the Commission functions as an advisory body.

SECRETARIAT

The Secretariat operates under the guidance of the Commission and its subsidiary bodies. It consists of the Office of the Executive Secretary and two servicing divisions, covering administration and programme management, in addition to the following substantive divisions: Emerging Social Issues; Environment and Sustainable Development; Information, Communication and Space Technology; Poverty and Development; Statistics; Trade and Investment; and Transport and Tourism.

The Secretariat also includes a Poverty Centre, a Least Developed Countries Co-ordination Unit, and the UN information service/Bangkok.

Executive Secretary: KIM HAK-SU (Republic of Korea).

SUB-REGIONAL OFFICE

United Nations ESCAP Pacific Operations Centre—UN-EPOC: Private Mail Bag 9004, Port Vila, Vanuatu; tel. 23458; fax 23921; e-mail escap@vanuatu.com.vu; f. 1984, to provide effective advisory and technical assistance at a sub-regional level and to identify the needs of island countries; under the Commission-wide reform process implemented in the early 2000s responsibility for UN-EPOC's work programme was to be placed under ESCAP'S Poverty and Development sub-programme; it was also agreed that the Centre would be relocated to Suva, Fiji; Dir NIKENIKE VUROBARAVU.

Activities

ESCAP acts as a UN regional centre, providing the only intergovernmental forum for the whole of Asia and the Pacific, and executing a wide range of development programmes through technical assistance, advisory services to governments, research, training and information. Following the massive earthquake and consequent devastating sea movements, or tsunamis, that occurred in late December 2004 in the Indian Ocean, ESCAP assisted other UN and international agencies with an initial emergency response and undertook early reviews of the impact of the event and of related disaster management and disaster reduction issues.

In 1992 ESCAP began to reorganize its programme activities and conference structures in order to reflect and serve the region's evolving development needs. The approach that was adopted focused on regional economic co-operation, poverty alleviation through economic growth and social development, and environmental and sustainable development. In May 2002, having considered the recommendations of an intergovernmental review meeting held in March, ESCAP determined to implement a further restructuring of its conference structures and thematic priorities. Three main thematic programmes were identified: poverty reduction (comprising sub-programmes on poverty and development; and statistics), managing globalization (with sub-programmes on trade and investment; environment; and space technology); and emerging social issues (with sub-programmes on health and development, gender and development, and population and social integration).

Emerging Social Issues: The sub-programme has three sections: Health and development, Gender and development, and Population and social integration. The sub-programme's main objective is to assess and respond to regional trends and challenges in social policy and human resources development, with particular emphasis on the planning and delivery of social services and training programmes for disadvantaged groups, including the poor, youths, women, the disabled, and the elderly. Aims to strengthen the capacity of public and non-government institutions to address the problems of such marginalized social groups and to foster partnerships between governments, the private sector, community organizations and all other involved bodies. Undertakes work through the health and development section on controlling the spread of HIV/AIDS, drug abuse and combating sexual exploitation. Implements global and regional mandates, such as the Programme of Action of the World Summit for Social Development and the Jakarta Plan of Action on Human Resources Development. The Biwako Millennium Framework for Action towards an Inclusive, Barrier-free and Rights-based Society for Persons with Disabilities in Asia and the Pacific was adopted by ESCAP as a regional guide-line underpinning the Asian and Pacific Decade of Disabled Persons (2003–12). In 1998 ESCAP initiated a programme of assistance in establishing a regional network of Social Development Management Information Systems (SOMIS). ESCAP collaborated with other agencies towards the adoption, in November

2001, of a Regional Platform on Sustainable Development for Asia and the Pacific. The Commission undertook regional preparations for the World Summit on Sustainable Development, which was held in Johannesburg, South Africa, in August–September 2002. In following-up the summit ESCAP undertook to develop a bio-diversity park, which was officially inaugurated in Rawalpindi, Pakistan, in January 2005. The Commission also prepares specific publications relating to population and implements global and regional mandates, such as the Programme of Action of the International Conference on Population and Development. The Secretariat co-ordinates the Asia-Pacific Population Information Network (POPIN). The fifth Asia and Pacific Population Conference, sponsored by ESCAP, was held in Bangkok, Thailand, in December 2002.

Environment and Sustainable Development: Concerned with strengthening national capabilities to achieve environmentally-sound and sustainable development by integrating economic concerns, such as the sustainable management of natural resources, into economic planning and policies. The sub-programme is responsible for implementation of the Regional Action Programme for Environmentally Sound and Sustainable Development for the period 2001–05. Other activities have included the promotion of integrated water resources development and management, including water quality and conservation and a reduction in water-related natural disasters; strengthening the formulation of policies in the sustainable development of land and mineral resources; the consideration of energy resource options, such as rural energy supply, energy conservation and the planning of power networks; and promotion of the use of space technology applications for environmental management, natural disaster monitoring and sustainable development.

Information, Communications and Space Technology: The work of the sub-programme is undertaken by the following sections: ICT Policy, ICT Applications, and Space Technology Applications. Aims to strengthen capacity for access to and the application of ICT and space technology. The sub-programme supports the development of cross-sectoral policies and strategies, and also supports regional co-operation aimed at sharing knowledge between advanced and developing economies and in areas such as cyber-crime and information security.

Poverty and Development: The work of the sub-programme is undertaken by the following sections: Development Policy, Socio-economic Anaylsis and Poverty Reduction. The sub-programme aims to increase the understanding of the economic and social development situation in the region, with particular attention given to the attainment of the UN Millennium Development Goals, sustainable economic growth, poverty alleviation, the integration of environmental concerns into macroeconomic decisions and policy-making processes, and enhancing the position of the region's disadvantaged economies. The sub-programme is responsible for the provision of technical assistance, and the production of relevant documents and publications.

Statistics: Provides training and advice in priority areas, including national accounts statistics, poverty indicators, gender statistics, population censuses and surveys, and the strengthening and management of statistical systems. Supports co-ordination throughout the region of the development, implementation and revision of selected international statistical standards. Disseminates comparable socio-economic statistics, with increased use of the electronic media, promotes the use of modern information and communications technology (ICT) in the public sector and trains senior-level officials in the effective management of ICT.

Trade and Investment: Provides technical assistance and advisory services. Aims to enhance institutional capacity-building; gives special emphasis to the needs of least-developed, land-locked and island developing countries, and to economies in transition in accelerating their industrial and technological advancement, promoting their exports, and furthering their integration into the region's economy; supports the development of electronic commerce and other information technologies in the region; and promotes the intra-regional and inter-subregional exchange of trade, investment and technology through the strengthening of institutional support services such as regional information networks.

Transport and Tourism: Aims to develop inter- and intra-regional transport links to enhance trade and tourism, mainly through implementation of an Asian Land Transport Infrastructure Development (ALTID) programme. ALTID projects include the development of the Trans-Asian Railway and of the Asian Highway road network. Other activities are aimed at improving the planning process in developing infrastructure facilities and services, in accordance with the Regional Action Programme (Phase II, 2002–06) of the New Delhi Action Plan on Infrastructure Development in Asia and the Pacific, which was adopted at a ministerial conference held in October 1996, and at enhancing private sector involvement in national infrastructure development through financing, management, operations and risk-sharing. A Ministerial Conference on Infrastructure Development was organized by ESCAP in November 2001. The meeting concluded a memorandum of understanding, initially signed by ESCAP, Kazakhstan, the Republic of Korea, Mongolia and Russia, to facilitate the transport of container goods along the Trans-Asian Railway. The sub-programme aims to reduce the adverse environmental impact of the provision of infrastructure facilities and to promote more equitable and easier access to social amenities. Tourism concerns include the development of human resources, improved policy planning for tourism development, greater investment in the industry, and minimizing the environmental impact of tourism. In November 2003 ESCAP approved a new initiative, the Asia-Pacific Network for Transport and Logistics Education and Research (ANTLER), to comprise education, training and research centres throughout the region.

Throughout all the sub-programmes, ESCAP aims to focus particular attention on the needs and concerns of least-developed, land-locked and island developing nations, and economies in transition in the region.

CO-OPERATION WITH THE ASIAN DEVELOPMENT BANK

In July 1993 a memorandum of understanding was signed by ESCAP and the Asian Development Bank, outlining priority areas of co-operation between the two organizations. These were: regional and sub-regional co-operation; issues concerning the least-developed, land-locked and island developing member countries; poverty alleviation; women in development; population; human resource development; the environment and natural resource management; statistics and data bases; economic analysis; transport and communications; and industrial restructuring and privatization. The two organizations were to co-operate in organizing workshops, seminars and conferences, in implementing joint projects, and in exchanging information and data on a regular basis. A new memorandum of understanding between the two organizations was signed in May 2004 with an emphasis on achieving poverty reduction throughout the region. In late 2004 ESCAP, with the Bank and UNDP, undertook to conduct a regional report on implementation of the UN Millennium Development Goals, which was scheduled to be presented in September 2005.

ASSOCIATED BODIES

Asian and Pacific Centre for Transfer of Technology: APCTT Bldg, POB 4575, Qutab Institutional Area, New Delhi 110 016, India; tel. (11) 26966509; fax (11) 26856274; e-mail infocentre@apctt .org; internet www.apctt.org; f. 1977 to assist countries of the ESCAP region by strengthening their capacity to develop, transfer and adopt technologies relevant to the region, and to identify and to promote regional technology development and transfer; Dir SE-JUN MOON; publs *Asia Pacific Tech Monitor*, *VATIS Updates on Biotechnology*, *Food Processing*, *Ozone Layer Protection*, *Non-Conventional Energy*, and *Waste Technology* (each every 2 months), *International Technology and Business Opportunities: Catalogue* (quarterly).

ESCAP/WMO Typhoon Committee: PAGASA, 4th Floor, Science Garden, Agham Rd, Diliman, Quezon City, Philippines; tel. and fax (632) 4349026; e-mail tcs@tcsphilippines.org; f. 1968; an intergovernmental body sponsored by ESCAP and the World Meteorological Organization for mitigation of typhoon damage. It aims at establishing efficient typhoon and flood warning systems through improved meteorological and telecommunication facilities. Other activities include promotion of disaster preparedness, training of personnel and co-ordination of research. The committee's programme is supported from national resources and also by UNDP and other international and bilateral assistance. Mems: Cambodia, People's Republic of China, Hong Kong, Japan, Democratic People's Republic of Korea, Republic of Korea, Laos, Macao, Malaysia, Philippines, Singapore, Thailand, USA, Viet Nam; Co-ordinator of Secretariat Dr ROMAN L. KINTANAR.

Statistical Institute for Asia and the Pacific: JETRO-IDE Building, 2–2 Wakaba 3-chome, Mihama-ku, Chiba-shi, Chiba 2618787, Japan; tel. (43) 2999782; fax (43) 2999780; e-mail staff@ unsiap.or.jp; internet www.unsiap.or.jp; f. 1970; trains government statisticians at the Institute and in various co-operating countries in Asia and the Pacific; prepares teaching materials, assists in the development of training on official statistics in national and sub-regional centres; Dir TOMAS P. AFRICA (Philippines).

UN Asian and Pacific Centre for Agricultural Engineering and Machinery—UNAPCAEM: A7F, China International Science & Technology Convention Centre, 12 Yumin Rd, Chaoyang District, Beijing 100029, People's Republic of China; tel. (10) 8225-3581; fax (10) 8225-3584; e-mail apcaem@un.org; internet www.apcaem.org; f. 1977 as Regional Network for Agricultural Engineering and Machinery, elevated to regional centre in 2002; aims to reduce poverty by enhancing technical co-operation throughout the region, and promotes agricultural engineering and machinery, agro-based industry, small and medium-sized enterprises development and biotechnologies. Mems: Bangladesh, People's Republic of China, Democratic People's Republic of Korea, Fiji, India, Indonesia, Iran, Mongolia, Nepal, Pakistan, Philippines, Republic of Korea, Sri Lanka, Thailand, Viet Nam; Dir Dr ADRIANUS G. RIJK.

UNESCAP Centre for Alleviation of Poverty through Secondary Crops' Development in Asia and the Pacific: Jalan Merdeka 145, Bogor 16111, Indonesia; tel. (251) 343277; fax (251) 336290; e-mail capsa@uncapsa.org; internet www.uncapsa.org; f. 1981 as CGPRT Centre, current name adopted April 2004; initiates and promotes socio-economic and policy research, training, dissemination of information and advisory services to enhance the living conditions of rural poor populations reliant on secondary crop agriculture; Dir Dr TACO BOTTEMA (Netherlands); publs *CGPRT Flash*(monthly), *Palawija News* (quarterly), working paper series, monograph series and statistical profiles.

WMO/ESCAP Panel on Tropical Cyclones: Technical Support Unit (TSU), c/o Headquarters, Pakistan Meteorological Dept, POB 1214, H-8/2, Islamabad, Pakistan; tel. (51) 9257314; fax (51) 4432588; e-mail tsupmd@hotmail.com; internet www.tsuptc-wmo.org; f. 1972 to mitigate damage caused by tropical cyclones in the Bay of Bengal and the Arabian Sea. Mems: Bangladesh, India, the Maldives, Myanmar, Oman, Pakistan, Sri Lanka, Thailand; TSU Co-ordinator Dr QAMAR-UZ-ZAMAN CHAUDHRY.

Finance

For the two-year period 2004–05 ESCAP's proposed programme budget, an appropriation from the UN budget, was US $64.7m. The regular budget is supplemented annually by funds from various sources for technical assistance.

Publications

Annual Report.

Agro-chemicals News in Brief (quarterly).

Asia-Pacific Development Journal (2 a year).

Asia-Pacific in Figures (annually).

Asia-Pacific Population Journal (quarterly).

Asia-Pacific Remote Sensing and GIS Journal (2 a year).

Atlas of Mineral Resources of the ESCAP Region.

Bulletin on Asia-Pacific Perspectives (annually).

Confluence (water resources newsletter, 2 a year).

Economic and Social Survey of Asia and the Pacific (annually).

Environmental News Briefing (every 2 months).

ESCAP Energy News (2 a year).

ESCAP Human Resources Development Newsletter (2 a year).

ESCAP Population Data Sheet (annually).

ESCAP Tourism Newsletter (2 a year).

Fertilizer Trade Information Monthly Bulletin.

Foreign Trade Statistics of Asia and the Pacific (every 2 years).

Government Computerization Newsletter (irregular).

Industry and Technology Development News for Asia and the Pacific (annually).

Poverty Alleviation Initiatives (quarterly).

Regional Network for Agricultural Machinery Newsletter (3 a year).

Small Industry Bulletin for Asia and the Pacific (annually).

Social Development Newsletter (2 a year).

Space Technology Applications Newsletter (quarterly).

Statistical Indicators for Asia and the Pacific (quarterly).

Statistical Newsletter (quarterly).

Statistical Yearbook for Asia and the Pacific.

Trade and Investment Information Bulletin (monthly).

Transport and Communications Bulletin for Asia and the Pacific (annually).

Water Resources Journal (quarterly).

Bibliographies; country and trade profiles; commodity prices; statistics.

Economic Commission for Latin America and the Caribbean—ECLAC

Address: Edif. Naciones Unidas, Avda Dag Hammarskjöld, Casilla 179D, Santiago, Chile.

Telephone: (2) 2102000; **fax:** (2) 2080252; **e-mail:** dpisantiago@eclac.cl; **internet:** www.eclac.org.

The UN Economic Commission for Latin America was founded in 1948 to co-ordinate policies for the promotion of economic development in the Latin American region. The current name of the Commission was adopted in 1984.

MEMBERS

Antigua and Barbuda	Ecuador	Peru
Argentina	El Salvador	Portugal
Bahamas	France	Saint Christopher and Nevis
Barbados	Germany	Saint Lucia
Belize	Grenada	Saint Vincent and the Grenadines
Bolivia	Guatemala	Spain
Brazil	Guyana	Trinidad and Tobago
Canada	Haiti	United Kingdom
Chile	Honduras	USA
Colombia	Italy	Uruguay
Costa Rica	Jamaica	Venezuela
Cuba	Mexico	
Dominica	Netherlands	
Dominican Republic	Nicaragua	
	Panama	
	Paraguay	

ASSOCIATE MEMBERS

Anguilla	Montserrat	Puerto Rico
Aruba	Netherlands Antilles	United States Virgin Islands
British Virgin Islands		

Organization

(March 2005)

COMMISSION

The Commission normally meets every two years in one of the Latin American capitals. The 30th session was held in San Juan, Puerto Rico, in June–July 2004 and the 31st session was to be held in Uruguay in 2006. The Commission has established the following permanent bodies:

Caribbean Development and Co-operation Committee.

Central American Development and Co-operation Committee.

Committee of High-Level Government Experts.

Committee of the Whole.

Regional Conference on the Integration of Women into the Economic and Social Development of Latin America and the Caribbean.

Regional Council for Planning.

SECRETARIAT

The Secretariat employs more than 500 staff and is headed by the Offices of the Executive Secretary and of the Secretary of the Commission. ECLAC's work programme is carried out by the following divisions: Economic Development; Social Development; International Trade; Production, Productivity and Management; Statistics and Economic Projections; Sustainable Development and Human Settlements; Natural Resources and Infrastructure; Documents and Publications; and Population. There are also units for information and conference services, women and development and special studies, an electronic information section, and a support division of administration.

Executive Secretary: José Luis Machinea.

Deputy Executive Secretary (and Head of the Office of the Secretary of the Commission): Alicia Bárcena.

SUB-REGIONAL OFFICES

Caribbean: 1 Chancery Lane, POB 1113, Port of Spain, Trinidad and Tobago; tel. 623-5595; fax 623-8485; e-mail registry@eclacpos .org; internet www.eclacpos.org; f. 1956; covers non-Spanish-speaking Caribbean countries; functions as the Caribbean Development and Co-operation Committee and as the secretariat for the Programme of Action for the Sustainable Development of Small Island Developing States; Dir Neil Pierre.

Central America and Spanish-speaking Caribbean: Avda Presidente Masaryk 29, 11570 México, DF; tel. (55) 5263-9600; fax (55) 5531-1151; e-mail cepal@un.org.mx; internet www.eclac.org .mx; f. 1951; covers Central America and Spanish-speaking Caribbean countries; Dir Rebeca Grynspan.

There are also national offices, in Santafé de Bogotá, Brasília, Buenos Aires and Montevideo and a liaison office in Washington, DC.

Activities

ECLAC collaborates with regional governments in the investigation and analysis of regional and national economic problems, and provides guidance in the formulation of development plans. Its activities include research; analysis; publication of information; provision of technical assistance; participation in seminars and conferences; training courses; and co-operation with national, regional and international organizations.

The 26th session of the Commission, which was held in San José, Costa Rica, in April 1996, considered means of strengthening the economic and social development of the region, within the framework of a document prepared by ECLAC's Secretariat, and adopted a resolution which defined ECLAC as a centre of excellence, charged with undertaking an analysis of specific aspects of the development process, in collaboration with member governments. In May 1998 the 27th session of the Commission, held in Oranjestad, Aruba, approved the ongoing reform programme, and in particular efforts to enhance the effectiveness and transparency of ECLAC's activities. The main topics of debate at the meeting were public finances, fiscal management and social and economic development. The Commission adopted a Fiscal Covenant, incorporating measures to consolidate fiscal adjustment and to strengthen public management, democracy and social equity, which was to be implemented throughout the region and provide the framework for further debate at national and regional level. ECLAC's 28th session, convened in Mexico City in April 2000, debated a document prepared by the Secretariat which proposed that the pursuit of social equity, sustainable development and 'active citizenship' (with emphasis on the roles of education and employment) should form the basis of future policy-making in the region.

ECLAC's 29th session, which was held in Brasília, Brazil, in May 2002, focused on the process of globalization. The meeting adopted the Brasilia Resolution, which outlined a strategic agenda to meet the challenges of globalization. Proposed action included the consolidation of democracy, strengthening social protection, the formulation of policies to reduce macroeconomic and financial vulnerability, and the development of sustainable and systemic competitiveness. The objectives of the agenda were to achieve a guaranteed supply of general public goods, to overcome, steadily, the imbalances in the world order, and to build, gradually, an international social agenda based on rights. The Resolution requested that ECLAC strengthen its work in the relevant areas. The 30th session was held in June–July 2004 in San Juan, Puerto Rico. Among the issues discussed were proposals in a new ECLAC study entitled *Productive Development in Open Economies*, activities to be undertaken, with UNESCO, to promote education in the region, and other areas of activity in 2006–07.

ECLAC works closely with other agencies within the UN system and with other regional and multinational organizations. ECLAC is co-operating with the OAS and the Inter-American Development Bank in the servicing of intergovernmental groups undertaking preparatory work for the establishment of a Free Trade Area of the Americas (FTAA). In May 2001 ECLAC hosted the first meeting of the Americas Statistics Conference. In January 2002 ECLAC hosted an Interregional Conference on Financing for Development, held in Mexico City, which it had organized as part of the negotiating process prior to the World Summit on Financing for Development, held in March. In June senior representatives of ECLAC, UNDP, the

World Bank and the Inter-American Development Bank signed a Protocol of Intentions with a commitment to co-ordinate activities in pursuit of the development goals proclaimed by the so-called Millennium Summit meeting of the General Assembly in September 2000. ECLAC was to adapt the objectives of the goals to the reality of countries in the region. In July 2004 the 30th session of the Commission approved the establishment of an intergovernmental forum to monitor the implementation of decisions emerging from the World Summit on Sustainable Development, held in Johannesburg, South Africa, in September 2002. ECLAC provides regional support to the UN Information and Communication Technologies Task Force, which was established in November 2001. A working meeting on the establishment of a regional network under the Task Force, in order to plan and monitor the development of digital technology in the region, was held in June 2002. In January 2003 a regional conference was convened, in the Dominican Republic, in preparation for the World Summit on the Information Society, the first phase of which was held in December, in Geneva, Switzerland. In July 2004 delegates to the 30th session of the Commission requested that ECLAC co-ordinate a regional preparatory meeting to define objectives and proposals for the second phase of the Summit, scheduled to be convened in November 2005 in Tunis, Tunisia. In November 2003 ECLAC launched 'Redesa', a web-based network of institutions and experts in social and environmental statistics.

Latin American and Caribbean Institute for Economic and Social Planning (ILPES): Edif. Naciones Unidas, Avda Dag Hammarskjöld 3477, Vitacura, Santiago, Chile; tel. (2) 2102506; fax (2) 2066104; e-mail paul.dekock@cepal.org; internet www.ilpes.org; f. 1962; supports regional governments through the provision of training, advisory services and research in the field of public planning policy and co-ordination; Dir José Luis Machinea.

Latin American Demographic Centre (CELADE): Edif. Naciones Unidas, Avda Dag Hammarskjöld, Casilla 179D, Santiago, Chile; tel. (2) 2102002; fax (2) 2080252; e-mail mvilla@eclac.cl; internet www.eclac.org/celade; f. 1957, became an integral part of ECLAC in 1975; provides technical assistance to governments, universities and research centres in demographic analysis, population policies, integration of population factors in development planning, and data processing; conducts three-month courses on demographic analysis for development and various national and regional seminars; provides demographic estimates and projections, documentation, data processing, computer packages and training; Dir Dirk Jaspers-Faijer.

Finance

For the two-year period 2004–05 ECLAC's proposed regular budget, an appropriation from the UN, amounted to US $81.2m. In addition, extra-budgetary activities are financed by governments, other organizations, and UN agencies, including UNDP, UNFPA and UNICEF.

Publications

Boletín del Banco de Datos del CELADE (annually).

Boletín demográfico (2 a year).

Boletín de Facilitación del Comercio y el Transporte (monthly).

CEPAL News (digital, monthly).

CEPAL Review (Spanish and English, 3 a year).

CEPALINDEX (annually).

Co-operation and Development (Spanish and English, quarterly).

DOCPAL Resúmenes (population studies, 2 a year).

ECLAC Notes/Notas de la CEPAL (every 2 months).

Economic Survey of Latin America and the Caribbean (Spanish and English, annually).

Foreign Investment in Latin America and the Caribbean (annually).

Latin America and the Caribbean in the World Economy (annually).

Latin American Projections 2001–02.

Notas de Población (2 a year).

PLANINDEX (2 a year).

Preliminary Overview of the Economies of Latin America and the Caribbean (annually).

Social Panorama of Latin America (annually).

Statistical Yearbook for Latin America and the Caribbean (Spanish and English).

Studies, reports, bibliographical bulletins.

Economic Commission for Africa—ECA

Address: Africa Hall, POB 3001, Addis Ababa, Ethiopia.
Telephone: (1) 517200; **fax:** (1) 514416; **e-mail:** ecainfo@uneca.org;
internet: www.uneca.org.

The UN Economic Commission for Africa (ECA) was founded in 1958 by a resolution of the UN Economic and Social Council (ECOSOC) to initiate and take part in measures for facilitating Africa's economic development.

MEMBERS

Algeria	Eritrea	Niger
Angola	Ethiopia	Nigeria
Benin	Gabon	Rwanda
Botswana	The Gambia	São Tomé and
Burkina Faso	Ghana	Príncipe
Burundi	Guinea	Senegal
Cameroon	Guinea-Bissau	Seychelles
Cape Verde	Kenya	Sierra Leone
Central African	Lesotho	Somalia
Republic	Liberia	South Africa
Chad	Libya	Sudan
Comoros	Madagascar	Swaziland
Congo, Democratic	Malawi	Tanzania
Republic	Mali	Togo
Congo, Republic	Mauritania	Tunisia
Côte d'Ivoire	Mauritius	Uganda
Djibouti	Morocco	Zambia
Egypt	Mozambique	Zimbabwe
Equatorial Guinea	Namibia	

Organization

(March 2005)

COMMISSION

The Commission may only act with the agreement of the government of the country concerned. It is also empowered to make recommendations on any matter within its competence directly to the government of the member or associate member concerned, to governments admitted in a consultative capacity, and to the UN Specialized Agencies. The Commission is required to submit for prior consideration by ECOSOC any of its proposals for actions that would be likely to have important effects on the international economy.

CONFERENCE OF MINISTERS

The Conference, which meets every two years, is attended by ministers responsible for economic or financial affairs, planning and development of governments of member states, and is the main deliberative body of the Commission.

The Commission's responsibility to promote concerted action for the economic and social development of Africa is vested primarily in the Conference, which considers matters of general policy and the priorities to be assigned to the Commission's programmes, considers inter-African and international economic policy, and makes recommendations to member states in connection with such matters.

OTHER POLICY-MAKING BODIES

A Conference of Ministers of Finance and a Conference of Ministers Responsible for Economic and Social Development and Planning meet in alternate years to formulate policy recommendations. Each is served by a committee of experts. Five intergovernmental committees of experts attached to the Sub-regional Development Centres (see below) meet annually and report to the Commission through a Technical Preparatory Committee of the Whole, which was established in 1979 to deal with matters submitted for the consideration of the Conference.

Seven other committees meet regularly to consider issues relating to the following policy areas: women and development; development information; sustainable development; human development and civil society; industry and private sector development; natural resources and science and technology; and regional co-operation and integration.

SECRETARIAT

The Secretariat provides the services necessary for the meeting of the Conference of Ministers and the meetings of the Commission's subsidiary bodies, carries out the resolutions and implements the programmes adopted there. It comprises an Office of the Executive Secretary and the following divisions: Development Information Services; Development Policy and Management; Economic and Social Policy; Gender and Development; Sustainable Development; and Trade and Regional Integration.

Executive Secretary: KINGSLEY Y. AMOAKO (Ghana).

SUB-REGIONAL DEVELOPMENT CENTRES

Multinational Programming and Operational Centres (MULPOCs) were established, in 1977, to implement regional development programmes. In May 1997 the Commission decided to transform the MULPOCs into Sub-regional Development Centres (SRDCs) in order to enable member states to play a more effective role in the process of African integration and to facilitate the integration efforts of the other UN agencies active in the sub-regions. In addition, the SRDCs were to act as the operational arms of ECA at national and sub-regional levels: to ensure harmony between the objectives of sub-regional and regional programmes and those defined by the Commission; to provide advisory services; to facilitate sub-regional economic co-operation, integration and development; to collect and disseminate information; to stimulate policy dialogue; and to promote gender issues.

Central Africa: POB 14935, Yaoundé, Cameroon; tel. 23-14-61; fax 23-31-85; e-mail casrdrc@un.cm; Officer-in-Charge HACHIM KOUMARÉ.

East Africa: POB 4654, Kigali, Rwanda; tel. 586549; fax 586546; e-mail mdiouf@uneca.org; Dir MBAYE DIOUF.

North Africa: blvd Mohammed V, POB 316, Tangier, Morocco; tel. (39) 322346; fax (39) 340357; e-mail srdc-na@uneca.org; internet www.uneca-na.org; Dir KARIMA BOUNEMRA BEN SOLTANE.

Southern Africa: POB 30647, Lusaka, Zambia; tel. (1) 228503; fax (1) 236949; e-mail uneca@zamnet.zm; internet www.uneca-org.zm; Officer-in-Charge DICKSON MZUMARA.

West Africa: POB 744, Niamey, Niger; tel. 72-29-61; fax 72-28-94; e-mail srdcwest@eca.ne; Dir HALIDOU OUEDRAOGO.

Activities

The Commission's activities are designed to encourage sustainable socio-economic development in Africa and to increase economic co-operation among African countries and between Africa and other parts of the world. The Secretariat has been guided in its efforts by major regional strategies including the Abuja Treaty establishing the African Economic Community signed under the aegis of the Organization of African Unity (OAU, now African Union—AU) in 1991, the UN System-wide Special Initiative on Africa (launched in 1996, see below), and the UN New Agenda for the Development of Africa covering the period 1991–2000. ECA was designated as the main body responsible for identifying and preparing programmes on economic and corporate governance under the New Partnership for Africa's Development (NEPAD), launched in October 2001. Under ECA's proposed programme of work for the period 2002–05 greater emphasis was to be given to: improving indicators for monitoring progress towards achievement of the UN's Millennium Development Goals; examining the environmental implications of sustainable development; promoting measures for conflict resolution; supporting improvements in economic management; promoting information and communication technology; strengthening support to the Regional Economic Communities (RECs); and promoting gender equality.

In 1996 the ECA launched a major programme of reform aimed at rationalizing and strengthening its capacity. A new phase initiated in 2003 focused on improving management and administrative systems, with a view to creating a more results-based organization.

In November 2000 an informal 'Big Table' meeting convened between ministers of finance from African countries and OECD ministers of development co-operation focused on transforming Africa's relationship with its development partners; a second Big Table meeting in October 2001 addressed means of establishing a new African co-operation framework. The third Big Table meeting, held in January 2003, considered the role played by the IMF in low-income countries. A special session was convened in October 2003, and in October 2004 the fourth Big Table meeting was held to discuss stimulating private investment in Africa.

In April 2003 ECA and the African Development Bank synchronized their annual legislative meetings in an effort to find a common position on addressing the principal challenges confronting the continent. They concluded that development was constrained by national debt, a persistent decline in exports, and weak economic growth rates. They also urged a thorough review of development strategies to determine whether poor outcomes were the result of bad policy, poor implementation or external factors. ECA's Executive Secretary proposed the establishment of a mechanism to monitor both the use of donor funds and the honouring of donor commitments; he also emphasized the need to focus on domestic resource mobilization and good economic management. ECA and OECD proposed that a joint review should be conducted every two years with a view to advancing policy coherence and mutual accountability between African countries and their external partners.

A Commission on HIV/AIDS and Governance in Africa, with its secretariat based at ECA headquarters, was launched in mid-September 2003. The Commission, an initiative of the UN Secretary-General, was mandated to assess the impact of the HIV/AIDS pandemic on national structures and African economic development and to incorporate its findings in a Final Report to be issued in June 2005.

DEVELOPMENT INFORMATION SERVICES

The Development Information Services Division (DISD) has responsibility for co-ordinating the implementation of the Harnessing Information Technology for Africa project (in the context of the UN System-wide Special Initiative on Africa) and for implementing the African Information Society Initiative (AISI), a framework for creating an information and communications infrastructure; for overseeing quality enhancement and dissemination of statistical databases; for improving access to information by means of enhanced library and documentation services and output; and for strengthening geo-information systems for sustainable development. In addition, ECA encourages member governments to liberalize the telecommunications sector and stimulate imports of computers in order to enable the expansion of information technology throughout Africa. ECA manages the Information Technology Centre for Africa (see below). The Commission administers the Partnership for Information and Communication Technologies in Africa (PICTA), which was established in 1999 as an informal grouping of donors and agencies concerning with developing an information society in Africa. ECA provides institutional and logistical support to an African Ministerial Committee which was established in April 2004 to consider proposals of the first phase of the World Summit on Information Society (WSIS), convened in December 2003. ECA's DISD co-ordinated preparations for the African Regional Preparatory Conference for the second phase of the WSIS (scheduled to be convened in Tunis, Tunisia, in November 2005), which was held in Accra, Ghana, in February 2005. The conference considered an action plan to expand access and use of ICTs throughout Africa.

Regional statistical development activities are managed through the Co-ordinating Committee on African Statistical Development (CASD, established in 1992). The CASD facilitates the harmonization of statistical systems and methodologies at regional and national level; establishes mechanisms for the continuous exchange of information between governments, national agencies and regional and sub-regional bodies, and all bilateral and multilateral agencies; identifies and proposes new lines of action; and informs the Conference of African Planners, Statisticians and Population and Information Specialists on the progress of the Addis Ababa Plan of Action for Statistical Development in the 1990s (adopted in 1992). In May 1997 five task forces were established to undertake the CASD's activities; these covered the following areas: improving e-mail connectivity; monitoring the implementation of the Addis Ababa Plan of Action; strengthening statistical training programme for Africa (STPA) centres; assisting with the formation of census and household survey data service centres in up to five pilot countries, and with the establishment of a similar regional ECA service centre; and establishing live databases, comprising core macro and sectoral statistical indicators, initially as a pilot project, with eventual links to a regional database facility.

ECA assists its member states in population data collection and data processing; analysis of demographic data obtained from censuses or surveys; training demographers at the Regional Institute for Population Studies (RIPS) in Accra, Ghana, and at the Institut de formation et de recherche démographiques (IFORD) in Yaoundé, Cameroon; formulation of population policies and integrating population variables in development planning, through advisory missions and through the organization of national seminars on population and development; and dissemination of demographic information.

In 1999 ECA's Committee on Development Information established the African Virtual Library and Information Network (AVLIN) as a hub for the exchange of data among African researchers and policy-makers. In August 2000 ECA launched the Africa Knowledge Networks Forum (AKNF). The Forum, to be convened on an annual basis under ECA auspices, was to facilitate co-operation in information-sharing and research between professional research and development networks, and also between these and policy-makers, educators, civil society organizations and the private sector. It was to provide technical support to the ADF process (see below). In May 2003 the Committee on Development Information, convened to address the theme 'Information for Governance', urged governments to make consistent use of information systems in decision-making and in the decentralization of services and resources. During that month ECA launched the e-Policy Resource Network for Africa, under the Global e-Policy Resource Network initiative aimed at expanding the use and benefits of information and communication technologies.

DEVELOPMENT POLICY AND MANAGEMENT

ECA aims to assist governments, public corporations, universities and the private sector in improving their financial management; strengthening policy-making and analytical capacities; adopting measures to redress skill shortages; enhancing human resources development and utilization; and promoting social development through programmes focusing on youth, people with disabilities and the elderly. The Secretariat organizes training workshops, seminars and conferences at national, sub-regional and regional levels for ministers, public administrators and senior policy-makers, as well as for private and non-governmental organizations.

Following the failure to implement many of the proposals under the UN Industrial Development Decade for Africa (IDDA, 1980–90) and the UN Programme of Action for African Economic Recovery and Development (1986–90), a second IDDA was adopted by the Conference of African Ministers of Industry in July 1991. The main objectives of IDDA II (1993–2003) included the consolidation and rehabilitation of existing industries, the expansion of new investments, and the promotion of small-scale industries and technological capabilities. In June 1996 a conference, organized by ECA, was held in Accra, Ghana, with the aim of reviving private investment in Africa in order to stimulate the private sector and promote future economic development. In October 1999 the first African Development Forum (ADF) was held in Addis Ababa, Ethiopia. The ADF process was initiated by ECA to formulate an agenda for effective, sustainable development in African countries through dialogue and partnership between governments, academics, the private sector, donor agencies etc. It was intended that the process would focus towards an annual meeting concerned with a specific development issue. The first Forum was convened on the theme 'The Challenge to Africa of Globalization and the Information Age'. It reviewed the AISI (see above) and formulated country action plans and work programmes. The four issues addressed were: strengthening Africa's information infrastructure; Africa and the information economy; information and communication technologies for improved governance; and democratizing access to the information society. The second ADF, convened in October 2000 on the theme 'AIDS: the Greatest Leadership Challenge', addressed the impact on Africa of the HIV/AIDS epidemic and issued a Consensus and Plan of Action. The third ADF, held in March 2002, addressed the theme 'Defining Priorities for Regional Integration'. ADF IV took place in October 2004 with the theme of 'Governance for a Progressing Africa'.

In 1997 ECA hosted the first of a series of meetings on good governance, in the context of the UN System-wide Special Initiative on Africa. The second African Governance Forum (AGF II) was held in Accra, Ghana, in June 1998. The Forum focused on accountability and transparency, which participants agreed were essential elements in promoting development in Africa and should involve commitment from both governments and civil organizations. AGF III was convened in June 1999 in Bamako, Mali, to consider issues relating to conflict prevention, management and governance. The fourth AGF, which took place in Kampala, Uganda, in September 2000, focused on parliamentary processes and their role in consolidating good governance on the continent. AGF V, addressing the role of local government in reducing poverty in Africa, was held in Maputo, Mozambique, in May 2002. In 2003 28 countries participated in a study to assess and monitor progress towards good governance in Africa. A synopsis of the ensuing report, the *Africa Governance Report*, was presented at ADF IV in October 2004.

ECONOMIC AND SOCIAL POLICY

The Economic and Social Policy division concentrates on the following areas: economic policy analysis, trade and debt, social policy and poverty analysis, and the co-ordination and monitoring of special issues and programmes. Monitoring economic and social trends in the African region and studying the development problems concerning it are among the fundamental tasks of the Commission, while the special issues programme updates legislative bodies regarding the progress made in the implementation of initiatives affecting the continent. Every year the Commission publishes the *Survey of Economic and Social Conditions in Africa* and the *Economic Report on Africa*. In May 2004 the first annual meeting was held of a new Advisory Board on Statistics in Africa, comprising 15 experts from national statistical offices, sub-regional bodies and training institutes, which aimed to advise ECA on statistical developments in Africa and guide the Commission in future statistical activities.

The Commission gives assistance to governments in general economic analysis, fiscal, financial and monetary management, trade liberalization, regional integration and planning. ECA's work on economic planning has been broadened in recent years, in order to give more emphasis to macro-economic management in a mixed economy approach: a project is being undertaken to develop short-term forecasting and policy models to support economic management. The Commission has also undertaken a major study of the informal sector in African countries. Special assistance is given to least-developed, land-locked and island countries which have a much lower income level than other countries and which are faced with heavier constraints. Studies are also undertaken to assist longer-term planning.

ECA assists member states by undertaking studies on domestic trade, expansion of intra-African trade, transnational corporations, integration of women in trade and development, and strengthening the capacities of state-trading organizations. Studies have been prepared on problems and prospects likely to arise for the African region from the implementation of the Common Fund for Commodities and the Generalized System of Trade Preferences (both supervised by UNCTAD); the impacts of exchange-rate fluctuations on the economies of African countries; and on the long-term implications of different debt arrangements for African economies. ECA encourages the diversification of production, the liberalization of cross-border trade and the expansion of domestic trade structures, within regional economic groupings, in order to promote intra-African trade. ECA also helps to organize regional and 'All-Africa' trade fairs.

In March–April 1997 the Conference of African Ministers of Finance, meeting in Addis Ababa, reviewed a new initiative of the World Bank and IMF to assist the world's most heavily indebted poor countries (of which about three-quarters are in sub-Saharan Africa). While the Conference recognized the importance of the involvement of multilateral institutions in assisting African economies to achieve a sustainable level of development, it criticized aspects of the structural adjustment programmes imposed by the institutions and advocated more flexible criteria to determine eligibility for the new scheme. In November 2003 ECA convened an expert group meeting on international debt, held in Dakar, Senegal. The meeting determined to establish an *ad hoc* Technical Committee to formulate recommendations on debt relief and financing for development.

GENDER AND DEVELOPMENT

ECA aims to improve the socio-economic prospects of women through the promotion of equal access to resources and opportunities, and equal participation decision-making. An African Centre for Gender and Development was established in 1975 to service all national, sub-regional and regional bodies involved in development issues relating to related to gender and the advancement of women. The Centre manages the African Women's Development Fund, which was established in June 2000. The preliminary results of a new African Gender and Development Index were presented in January 2005.

SUSTAINABLE DEVELOPMENT

ECA aims to strengthen the capacity of member countries to design institutional structures and implement policies and programmes, in areas such as food production, population, environment and human settlements, to achieve sustainable development. It also actively promotes the use of science and technology in achieving sustainable development. In 1995 ECA published its first comprehensive report and statistical survey of human development issues in African countries. The *Human Development in Africa Report*, which was to be published every two years, aimed to demonstrate levels of development attained, particularly in the education and child health sectors, to identify areas of concern and to encourage further action by policy-makers and development experts. A *Bulletin on Sustainable Development* aims to monitor, review and disseminate information regarding development research and activities, in particular in respect of implementation of recommendations ensuring from the World Summit on Sustainable Development, held in August–September 2002 in Johannesburg, South Africa.

ECA is actively involved in the promotion of food security in African countries through raising awareness of the relationship between population, food security, the environment and sustainable development; encouraging the advancement of science and technology in member states; and providing policy analysis support and technical advisory services. The strengthening of national population policies was an important element of ECA's objective of ensuring food security in African countries.

ECA provides guidance in the formulation of policies towards the achievement of Africa's development objectives to the policy-making organs of the UN and the AU. It contributes to the work of the General Assembly and other specialized agencies by providing an African perspective in the preparation of development strategies. In March 1996 the UN announced its System-wide Special Initiative on Africa to mobilize resources and to implement a series of political and economic development objectives over a 10-year period. ECA's

Executive Secretary is the Co-Chairperson, with the Administrator of the UNDP, of the Steering Committee for the Initiative.

TRADE AND REGIONAL INTEGRATION

The Trade and Regional Integration Division (TRID) is concerned with the Sub-regional Development Centres (SRDCs—see above), the integrated development of transboundary water resources, and facilitating and enhancing the process of regional economic integration. It also administers activities the transport and communications and mineral and energy sectors. In June 2002 ECA issued its first *Annual Report on Regional Integration*. A report entitled *Assessing Regional Integration in Africa* was published in July 2004. The division hosts the African Trade Policy Centre.

ECA was appointed lead agency for the second United Nations Transport and Communications Decade in Africa (UNTACDA II), covering the period 1991–2000. The principal aim of UNTACDA II was the establishment of an efficient, integrated transport and communications system in Africa. ECA and the World Bank jointly co-ordinate the sub-Saharan Africa Transport Programme (SSATP), established in 1987, which aims to facilitate policy development and related capacity-building in the continent's transport sector. A meeting of all participants in the programme is held annually. In September 2004 the SSATP conference, hosted by ECA, recognized the importance of the transport sector in achieving the Millennium Development Goals (MDGs) and proposed a ministerial review to ensure the integration of transport issues in MDG strategies. The regional Road Management Initiative (RMI) under the SSATP seeks to encourage a partnership between the public and private sectors to manage and maintain road infrastructure more efficiently and thus to improve country-wide communications and transportation activities. An Urban Mobility component of the SSATP aims to improve sub-Saharan African urban transport services, while a Trade and Transport component aims to enhance the international competitiveness of regional economies through the establishment of more cost-effective services for shippers. The Railway Restructuring element focuses on the provision of financially sustainable railway enterprises. In December 2003 the first Central African Forum on Transport Infrastructure and Regional Integration, organized by TRID, was convened in Yaounde, Cameroon. The third African road safety congress was held in April 1997, in Pretoria, South Africa. The congress, which was jointly organized by ECA and OECD, aimed to increase awareness of the need to adopt an integrated approach to road safety problems. Other transport priorities have included consideration of a new African air transport policy, workshops on port restructuring, and regional and country analyses of transport trends and reforms.

The Fourth Regional Conference on the Development and Utilization of Mineral Resources in Africa, held in March 1991, adopted an action plan that included the formulation of national mineral exploitation policies; and the promotion of the gemstone industry, small-scale mining and the iron and steel industry. ECA supports the Southern African Mineral Resources Development Centre in Dar-es-Salaam, Tanzania, and the Central African Mineral Development Centre in Brazzaville, Republic of the Congo, which provide advisory and laboratory services to their respective member states.

ECA's Energy Programme provides assistance to member states in the development of indigenous energy resources and the formulation of energy policies to extricate member states from continued energy crises. In 1997 ECA strengthened co-operation with the World Energy Council and agreed to help implement the Council's African Energy Programme. In May 2004 ECA was appointed as the secretariat of a new UN-Energy/Africa initiative which aimed to facilitate the exchange of information, good practices and knowledge-sharing among UN organizations and with private sector companies, non-governmental organizations, power utilities and other research and academic institutions.

ECA assists member states in the assessment and use of water resources and the development of river and lake basins common to more than one country. ECA encourages co-operation between countries with regard to water issues and collaborates with other UN agencies and regional organizations to promote technical and economic co-operation in this area. In 1992, on the initiative of ECA, the Interagency Group for Water in Africa (IGWA) was established to co-ordinate and harmonize the water-related activities of the UN and other organizations on the continent. ECA has been particularly active in efforts to promote the integrated development of the water resources of the Zambezi river basin and of Lake Victoria. In December 2003 ECA hosted the Pan-African Implementation and Partnership Conference on Water (PANAFCON).

In all of its activities ECA aims to strengthen institutional capacities in order to support the process of regional integration, and aims to assist countries to implement existing co-operative agreements, for example by promoting the harmonization of macroeconomic and taxation policies and the removal of non-tariff barriers to trade. ECA aims to strengthen African participation in international negotiations. To this end, assistance has been provided to member states in the ongoing multilateral trade negotiations under the World Trade Organization; in the annual conferences of the IMF and the World Bank; in negotiations with the EU; and in meetings related to economic co-operation among developing countries.

ASSOCIATED BODY

Information Technology Centre for Africa (ITCA): POB 3001, Addis Ababa, Ethiopia; tel. (1) 514520; fax (1) 510512; e-mail mfaye@uneca.org; internet www.uneca.org/itca; aims to strengthen the continent's communications infrastructure and promote the use of information and communications technologies in planning and policy-making; stages exhibitions and provides training facilities.

Finance

For the two-year period 2004–05 ECA's regular budget, an appropriation from the UN budget, was an estimated US $88.1m.

Publications

Africa in Figures.

African Statistical Yearbook.

African Trade Bulletin (2 a year).

African Women's Report (annually).

Africa's Population and Development Bulletin.

Annual Report on Regional Integration.

ECA Development Policy Review.

ECA Environment Newsletter (3 a year).

ECANews (monthly).

Economic Report on Africa (annually).

Focus on African Industry (2 a year).

GenderNet (annually).

Human Development in Africa Report (every 2 years).

Human Rights Education.

Report of the Executive Secretary (every 2 years).

Survey of Economic and Social Conditions in Africa (annually).

TRIDNews (monthly).

Country reports, policy and discussion papers, reports of conferences and meetings, training series, working paper series.

Economic and Social Commission for Western Asia— ESCWA

Address: Riad es-Solh Sq., POB 11-8575, Beirut, Lebanon.

Telephone: (1) 981301; **fax:** (1) 981510; **e-mail:** webmaster-escwa@un.org; **internet:** www.escwa.org.lb.

The UN Economic Commission for Western Asia was established in 1974 by a resolution of the UN Economic and Social Council (ECOSOC), to provide facilities of a wider scope for those countries previously served by the UN Economic and Social Office in Beirut (UNESOB). The name 'Economic and Social Commission for Western Asia' (ESCWA) was adopted in 1985.

MEMBERS

Bahrain	Palestine
Egypt	Qatar
Iraq	Saudi Arabia
Jordan	Syria
Kuwait	United Arab Emirates
Lebanon	Yemen
Oman	

Organization

(March 2005)

COMMISSION

The Commission meets every two years in ministerial session to determine policy and establish work directives. Representatives of UN bodies and specialized agencies, regional organizations, other UN member states, and non-governmental organizations having consultative status with ECOSOC may attend as observers. The 22nd ministerial session of the Commission was held in April 2003; the 23rd session was scheduled to be convened in May 2005.

PREPARATORY COMMITTEE

The Committee has the task of reviewing programming issues and presenting recommendations in that regard to the sessions of the Commission. It is the principal subsidiary body of the Commission and functions as its policy-making structure. Six specialized intergovernmental committees have been established to consider specific areas of activity, to report on these to the Preparatory Committee and to assist the Committee in formulating ESCWA's medium-term work programmes.

Statistics Committee: established in 1992; meets every two years.

Committee on Social Development: established in 1994; meets every two years.

Committee on Energy: established in 1995; meets every two years.

Committee on Water Resources: established in 1995; meets every two years.

Committee on Transport: established in 1997; meets annually.

Committee on Liberalization of Foreign Trade and Economic Globalization: established in 1997; meets every two years.

Committee on the Status of Women: established in 2003; meets every two years.

In addition, a Consultative Committee on Scientific Technological Development and Technological Innovation was established in 2001, and was to meet every two years, comprising experts from public institutions, the private sector, civil society and research centres; the first meeting of the Committee was convened in July 2002.

SECRETARIAT

The Secretariat comprises an Executive Secretary, a Deputy Executive Secretary, a Senior Adviser and Secretary of the Commission, an Information Services Unit and divisions for administrative services and programme planning and technical co-operation. ESCWA's technical and substantive activities are undertaken by the following divisions: globalization and regional integration; social development; sustainable development and productivity; information and communication technology; economic analysis; and the ESCWA Centre for Women. The Secretariat administers the UN Regional Co-ordination Group for the ESCWA region, which was established in March 1999.

Executive Secretary: MERVAT M. TALLAWY (Egypt).

Activities

ESCWA is responsible for proposing policies and actions to support development and to further economic co-operation and integration in western Asia. ESCWA undertakes or sponsors studies of economic, social and development issues of the region, collects and disseminates information, and provides advisory services to member states in various fields of economic and social development. It also organizes conferences and intergovernmental and expert group meetings and sponsors training workshops and seminars.

Much of ESCWA's work is carried out in co-operation with other UN bodies, as well as with other international and regional organizations, for example the League of Arab States, the Co-operation Council for the Arab States of the Gulf (GCC) and the Organization of the Islamic Conference (OIC). In April 2001 ESCWA convened an inaugural consultative meeting with representatives of more than 100 non-governmental organizations, in order to strengthen co-operation with civil society. In April 2003 the Commission endorsed the establishment of an Arab language centre, to be based at the Commission's headquarters, in order to advance the use of Arabic in United Nations documents.

In late 2001 ESCWA initiated a pilot scheme to support the socio-economic development of local communities in southern Lebanon. A project to upgrade skills and the capacities of small businesses commenced in April 2002, within the framework of the so-called ESCWA Assistance for Southern Lebanon (EASL) programme, while two vocational training centres became operational in mid-2002. The April 2003 ministerial session of the Commission emphasized ESCWA's increased involvement in post-war reconstruction and rehabilitation, and recommended the staging of a forum of representatives from Arab and other countries to address the social and economic rehabilitation of Palestine. An ESCWA Iraq Task Force was established to design and implement development projects in Iraq in order to facilitate the rehabilitation of Iraqi economy and society. The Task Force organizes training workshops and management courses and administers a database of professionals and other experts willing to contribute to Iraq's reconstruction.

ESCWA works within the framework of medium-term plans, which are divided into two-year programmes of action and priorities. The plan for the period 2002–05 was approved at a special session of the Commission in March 2002. Amendments to the plan and programme budget were incorporated during 2003 in accordance with new priority areas of activity concerned with greater regional integration, in particular in water management, globalization, integrated social policies and technology. In April 2003 the 22nd ministerial session of the Commission addressed the following as issues of importance for the future of the region: the strengthening of Arab regional co-operation; and the impact of the lack of stability in the region on its economic and social development.

MANAGEMENT OF RESOURCES FOR SUSTAINABLE DEVELOPMENT

ESCWA's Division of Sustainable Development and Productivity administers the sub-programme of work entitled Integrated Policies for the Management of Regional Resources for Sustainable Development. The main objective of the sub-programme is to promote regional co-ordination and co-operation in the management of natural resources, in particular water resources and energy, and the protection of the environment. Work in this area aims to counter the problem of an increasing shortage of freshwater resources and deterioration in water quality resulting from population growth, agricultural land use and socio-economic development, by supporting measures for more rational use and conservation of water resources, and by promoting public awareness of and community participation in water and environmental protection projects. In addition, ESCWA assists governments in the formulation and implementation of capacity-building programmes and the development of surface and groundwater resources. ESCWA aimed to promote greater co-operation among member and non-member countries in the management and use of shared water resources.

ESCWA supports co-operation in the establishment of electricity distribution and supply networks throughout the region and promotes the use of alternative sources of energy and the development of new and renewable energy technologies. Similarly, ESCWA promotes the application of environmentally sound technologies in order to achieve sustainable development, as well as measures to recycle resources, minimize waste and reduce the environmental impact of transport operations and energy use. Under the sub-programme ESCWA collaborates with national, regional and international organizations in monitoring and reporting on emerging environmental issues and to pursue implementation of Agenda 21, which was adopted at the June 1992 UN Conference on Environment and Development, with particular regard to land and water resource management and conservation.

INTEGRATED SOCIAL POLICIES

ESCWA's key areas of activity in this sub-programme, administered by the Social Development Division, aim to achieve regional co-operation in promoting comprehensive and integrated social policies, for example regarding population, sustainable human development, the advancement of women and gender equality, and human settlements. Technical co-operation activities included post-conflict reconstruction in south Lebanon and Palestine, the promotion of information technology and electronic braille for the disabled, local community development in rural areas and the development of sub-regional social policy reports.

ESCWA's objectives with regard to population are to increase awareness and understanding of links between population factors and poverty, human rights and the environment, and to strengthen the capacities of member states to analyse and assess demographic trends and migration. In the area of human development ESCWA aims to further the alleviation of poverty and to generate a sustainable approach to development through, for example, greater involvement of community groups in decision-making and projects to strengthen production and income-generating capabilities. The sub-programme incorporates activities to ensure all gender-related recommendations of the four world conferences could be pursued in the region, including support for the role of the family and assistance to organizations for monitoring and promoting the advancement of women. An ESCWA Committee on the Status of Women and a Centre for Women were established in October 2003. In December ESCWA issued its first *Status of Arab Women Report*; this was to assess the situation of Arab women at two-yearly intervals. With regard to human settlements, the objectives of the sub-programme are to monitor and identify problems resulting from rapid urbanization and social change, to promote understanding and awareness of the problems and needs of human settlements, and to strengthen the capacity of governments in the region in formulating appropriate policies and strategies for sustainable human settlement development.

The sub-programme was serve as a forum for preparatory and follow-up meetings to global conferences. In February 2002 ESCWA organized a ministerial preparatory meeting for the World Assembly on Ageing, which was convened, in Madrid, Spain, in April. The meeting adopted an Arab Plan on the Elderly up to the Year 2012. In July 2004 a regional forum was held, in Beirut, to prepare for a 10-year review of the UN Fourth World Conference on Women, held in Beijing, People's Republic of China, in September 1995.

COMPARABLE STATISTICS

In the medium-term ESCWA intended to develop the statistical systems of member states in order to improve the relevance and accuracy of economic and social data, and to implement measures to make the information more accessible to planners and researchers. This sub-programme, entitled Comparable Statistics for Improved Planning and Decision-making, aims to improve human and institutional capacities, in particular in the use of statistical tools for data analysis, to expand the adoption and implementation of international statistical methods, and to promote co-operation to further the regional harmonization of statistics.

ECONOMIC ANALYSIS AND FORECASTING

This sub-programme, administered by the Economic Analysis Division, aims to increase the capacity of member countries to co-ordinate economic policies and achieve sustainable economic development. The overall objective is to improve economic management by enhancing the coverage, availability and use of indicators, statistics, and other financial data and trends. The Division was to conduct studies, hold expert group meetings and provide training and technical assistance in support of these objectives.

REGIONAL INTEGRATION AND GLOBALIZATION

ESCWA aims to assist member states to achieve sustainable economic development in the region and to integrate more fully into the world economy. Under the sub-programme Regional Integration and Responding to Globalization ESCWA aims to assist member countries to identify the challenges and opportunities created by the World Trade Organization (WTO) and other regional groupings, in particular with regard to free trade areas, the liberalization and management of financial markets, and the promotion of foreign direct investment. It also intended to to provide guidance on alternative development strategies to reduce the dominance of the petroleum sector. The sub-programme was to work closely with other UN agencies and regional and international organizations, in particular the League of Arab States and WTO. ESCWA aims to promote co-operation among member states in transport and infrastructure policies and greater uniformity of safety and legal standards, the latter with a view to facilitating border crossings between countries in the region. ESCWA, similarly, aims to assist local industries to meet regional and international standards and regulations, as well as to improve the competitiveness of industries through the development of skills and policies and greater co-operation with other national and regional support institutions. The sub-programme was to co-ordinate efforts to achieve the adoption and ratification of regional transport agreements, for example the Agreement on International Roads in the Arab Mashreq as part of a framework agreement to develop an Integrated Transport System, which was concluded in May 2001 and the Agreement on International Railways, which was adopted in April 2003.

INFORMATION AND COMMUNICATION TECHNOLOGY

The aim of this sub-programme is to increase the capabilities of ESCWA member countries to benefit from information and communication technology (ICT) in support of sustainable development and regional integration. It aims to narrow the so-called digital gap between Arab countries and other regions, and, consequently, improve the competitiveness of local industries and the effectiveness of local services. During 2004–05 ESCWA planned to undertake pilot projects on new technologies for poverty reduction in selected member countries. The sub-programme was responsible for advising member countries on the implementation of recommendations issued by the World Summit on the Information Society, held in December 2003, and on preparations for the second phase of the

Summit, scheduled to be held in Tunis, Tunisia, in 2005. The Arab Regional Preparatory Conference for the second phase of the WSIS was convened in Damascus, Syria, in November 2004. An expert group meeting on legal and regulatory frameworks for e-business in member countries was scheduled to be convened in 2005.

Finance

ESCWA's projected share of the UN budget for the two years 2004–05 was US $51.1m.

Publications

All publications are annual, unless otherwise indicated.

Annual Report.
Agriculture and Development in Western Asia.
ESCWA Update (monthly).
External Trade Bulletin of the ESCWA Region.
National Accounts Studies of the ESCWA Region.
Population Bulletin of the ESCWA Region.
Prices and Financial Statistics in the ESCWA Region.
Socio-economic Data Sheet (every 2 years).
Statistical Abstract of the ESCWA Region.
Status of Arab Women Report (every 2 years).
Survey of Economic and Social Developments in the ESCWA Region.
Transport Bulletin.
Weekly News.

OTHER UNITED NATIONS BODIES

Office for the Co-ordination of Humanitarian Affairs— OCHA

Address: United Nations Plaza, New York, NY 10017, USA.
Telephone: (212) 963-1234; **fax:** (212) 963-1312; **e-mail:** ochany@un.org; **internet:** ochaonline.un.org.

OCHA was established in January 1998 as part of the UN Secretariat, with a mandate to co-ordinate international humanitarian assistance and to provide policy and other advice on humanitarian issues. It replaced the Department of Humanitarian Affairs, established in 1992.

Organization

(March 2005)

OCHA has headquarters in New York, and in Geneva, Switzerland. It maintains regional support offices in Dakar, Senegal (for west Africa), Johannesburg, South Africa (southern Africa) and Nairobi, Kenya (central and east Africa); and deploys regional disaster response advisers in Panama (for Latin America and the Caribbean), Kobe, Japan (Asia), and Suva, Fiji (the Pacific). OCHA also maintains field presences in Africa, Europe, Asia and Latin America. In 2004 there were 733 staff posts, one-third of which were based at the headquarters.

Under Secretary-General for Humanitarian Affairs and Emergency Relief Co-ordinator: JAN EGELAND (Norway).

Activities

OCHA's mandate is to work with UN agencies, governments, inter-governmental humanitarian organizations and non-governmental organizations to ensure that a prompt, co-ordinated and effective response is provided to complex emergencies and natural disasters. OCHA monitors developments throughout the world and undertakes contingency planning. It liaises with UN Resident Co-ordinators, Humanitarian Co-ordinators and country teams, and reaches agreement with other UN bodies regarding the division of responsibilities, which may include field missions to assess requirements, organizing Consolidated Inter-agency Appeals for financial assistance (see below), and mobilizing other resources. The Emergency Relief Co-ordinator is the principal adviser to the UN Secretary-General on humanitarian issues. He chairs the Inter-Agency Standing Committee (IASC), which co-ordinates and administers the international response to humanitarian disasters and the development of relevant policies. The Co-ordinator also acts as Convener of the Executive Committee for Humanitarian Affairs, which provides a forum for humanitarian agencies, as well as the political and peace-keeping departments of the UN Secretariat, to exchange information on emergency situations and humanitarian issues. From 2001 OCHA implemented the recommendations of an internal review process aimed at strengthening its three core functions of co-ordination, advocacy and policy development. In 2001 a new strategic planning process was also initiated. OCHA's medium-term strategic plan for 2003–05 incorporated the following three objectives: effective and accountable leadership for humanitarian co-ordination in support of humanitarian partners; effective and proactive advocacy for vulnerable populations affected by disasters and emergencies; and transparent management and adequate, sustainable financial support. Biennial planning and budgeting were to be introduced from 2006–07.

OCHA's Early Warning Unit identifies and monitors potentially emerging humanitarian crises, as well as humanitarian emergencies at risk of deterioration and potentially resurgent humanitarian emergencies. Analysis by the Unit determines the at-risk areas to which inter-agency contingency planning missions should be directed.

OCHA maintains internet-based Integrated Regional Information Networks (IRINs). The first IRIN was created in 1995 in Nairobi, Kenya, to disseminate information on the humanitarian situation in central and east Africa. Additional IRINs have since been established in Abidjan, Côte d'Ivoire (covering west Africa), Johannesburg, South Africa (for southern Africa) and Islamabad, Pakistan (for central Asia). The IRINs provide new coverage of a total of 46 countries in sub-Saharan Africa and eight countries in central Asia. A complementary service, ReliefWeb, launched in 1996, monitors crises and publishes information on the internet.

OCHA's Humanitarian Emergency and Response Co-ordination branches (based, respectively, at the New York and Geneva headquarters) co-operate in mobilizing and co-ordinating international emergency assistance. The Response Co-ordination branch facilitates and participates in situation assessment missions; prepares briefings and issues Situation Reports to inform the international community on ongoing humanitarian crises, the type and level of assistance required and action being undertaken; and provides administrative support to OCHA field offices. The Emergency Services branch, based at the Geneva headquarters, undertakes disaster-preparedness activities and manages international rapid response missions in the field. UN Disaster Assessment and Co-ordination (UNDAC) teams, established by OCHA with the aid of donor governments, are available for immediate deployment to help to determine requirements and to co-ordinate assistance in those countries affected by disasters, for example by establishing reliable telecommunications and securing other logistical support. OCHA maintains a Central Register of Disaster Management Capacities, which may be available for international assistance. In addition, a stockpile of emergency equipment and supplies is maintained at the UN Humanitarian Response Depot in Brindisi, Italy, ready for immediate dispatch. The Field Co-ordination Support Section of the Emergency Services Branch acts as the secretariat of INSARAG, an inter-governmental network dealing with urban search and rescue (USAR) issues. INSARAG facilitates information exchange, defines standards for international USAR assistance, and develops methodology for international co-ordination in earthquake response. A joint OCHA/UNEP Environment Unit mobilizes and co-ordinates international assistance in environmental emergency situations. In January 2002 a Unit on Internal Displacement was established within OCHA with the aim of strengthening international assistance for people displaced from their homes by civil conflict and natural disasters.

The focal point within the UN system for co-ordinating disaster reduction activities in the socio-economic, humanitarian and development fields is the International Strategy for Disaster Reduction (ISDR), which has an Inter-Agency Secretariat (UN/ISDR) based in in Geneva. The UN Under-Secretary-General for Humanitarian Affairs presides over the ISDR's Inter-Agency Task Force on Disaster Reduction (IATF/DR), which comprises 25 UN, international, regional and civil society organizations and is the principal body within the UN system responsible for developing disaster reduction policy. In January 2005 the UN/ISDR organized a World Conference on Disaster Reduction, held in Kobe, Japan, which launched the International Early Warning Programme (IEWP), comprising UN bodies and agencies including the ISDR, UNEP, WFP and the WMO. The IEWP was to improve global resilience to natural disasters (such as droughts, wildland fires, volcanic eruptions, earthquakes, tsunamis—tidal waves, floods and hurricanes) by improving the exchange of observational data, promoting education on disaster preparedness, and ensuring an effective response mechanism to be activated on the issue of warnings.

OCHA facilitates the Consolidated Inter-agency Appeal Process (CAP), which aims to organize a co-ordinated response to resource mobilization following humanitarian crises. Participants in the process include UN bodies and agencies and other international governmental and non-governmental organizations (including the International Red Cross and Red Crescent Movement). Under guidelines adopted by the IASC in 1994, the CAP was clearly defined as a programming mechanism rather than simply an appeal process. Technical guide-lines adopted in 1999 established a framework for developing a Common Humanitarian Action Plan (CHAP) to address a crisis, co-ordinating the relevant inter-agency appeal (on the basis of the CHAP), and preparing strategic monitoring reports. CAP appeals for 2005, seeking an estimated US $1,700m., were issued in

November 2004; they concerned complex humanitarian crises affecting some 26m. people in 14 countries and regions. A Central Emergency Revolving Fund (CERF), under the authority of the Emergency Relief Co-ordinator, enables humanitarian agencies to provide an immediate response to emergencies, before donor contributions become available. Agencies borrowing from the fund are required to reimburse the amount loaned within a certain period of time, which is not to exceed one year.

Following a massive earthquake in the Indian Ocean in late December 2004, which caused a series of tsunamis that devastated coastal regions in 12 countries in South and South-East Asia and East Africa (directly causing at least 160,000 confirmed deaths, rendering a further 1m. people homeless and depriving 5m. people of basic services, as assessed at January 2005), OCHA was to co-ordinate an initial six-month programme of emergency and recovery assistance covering the period January–June 2005. In early January the UN Secretary-General, Kofi Annan, appealed for US \$977m. in immediate funding.

Finance

OCHA's budgetary requirements for 2005 were an estimated US \$99.4m.

Publications

Annual Report.
OCHA News (weekly).

United Nations Office on Drugs and Crime—UNODC

Address: Vienna International Centre, POB 500, 1400 Vienna, Austria.
Telephone: (1) 26060-0; **fax:** (1) 26060-5866; **e-mail:** unodc@unodc .org; **internet:** www.unodc.org.

The UN Office on Drugs and Crime (UNODC) was established in November 1997 (as the Office for Drug Control and Crime Prevention—ODCCP) to strengthen the UN's integrated approach to issues relating to drug control, crime prevention and international terrorism. A reform programme was launched in 2002 aimed at integrating further the Office's areas of activity. The Office was renamed in October of that year. It comprises two principal components: the United Nations Drug Programme and the United Nations Crime Programme. In 2003 UNODC was restructured into the following four divisions: Operations; Treaty Affairs; Research and Public Affairs; and Management. There is a UNODC liaison office in New York and there are 22 field offices world-wide.

Executive Director: ANTONIO MARIA COSTA (Italy).

United Nations Drug Programme

The UN Drug Programme was established in 1991 as the UN International Drug Control Programme—UNDCP and was renamed in 2002. It is responsible for co-ordinating the activities of all UN specialized agencies and programmes in matters of international drug control. The structures of the former Division of Narcotic Drugs, the UN Fund for Drug Abuse Control and the secretariat of the International Narcotics Control Board (see below) were integrated into the Programme. Accordingly, it became the focal point for promoting the UN Decade Against Drug Abuse (1991–2000) and for assisting member states to implement the Global Programme of Action that was adopted by the UN General Assembly in 1990 with the objective of achieving an international society free of illicit drugs and drug abuse. At a special summit meeting of the General Assembly, held in June 1998, heads of state and representatives of some 150 countries adopted a global strategy, formulated on the basis of UNDCP proposals, to reduce significantly the production of and demand for illicit substances by 2008. UNDCP subsequently launched the Global Assessment Programme on Drug Abuse (GAP), which aimed to establish one global and nine regional drug abuse data systems to collect and evaluate data on the extent of and patterns of illegal substance abuse. In the context of drug supply reduction the Illicit Crop Monitoring Programme (ICMP) supports the development of comprehensive monitoring systems in the six countries believed to account for some 90% of illicit opium and coca production (Afghanistan, Bolivia, Colombia, Laos, Myanmar and Peru); a global monitoring component of the ICMP provides technical assistance to the national monitoring systems. The ICMP is facilitated by a combination of satellite sensing (with the assistance of the European Space Agency), aerial surveillance and ground-level surveys, which provide a reliable collection and analysis mechanism for data on the production of illicit substances. The Alternative Development Programme supports projects to create alternative sources of income for farmers economically dependent on the production of illicit narcotic crops. The Drug Programme aims to suppress trafficking in these substances and supports efforts to enhance regional and cross-border co-operation in implementing law enforcement initiatives. The Drug Programme serves as an international centre of expertise and information on drug abuse control, with the capacity to provide legal and technical assistance in relevant areas of concern. It supports governments in efforts to strengthen their institutional capacities for drug control (for example, drug identification and drug law enforcement training) and to prepare and implement national drug control 'action plans'.

The Drug Programme's approach to reducing demand for illicit drugs combines strategies in the areas of prevention, treatment and rehabilitation. It sponsors activities to generate public awareness of the harmful effects of drug abuse, for example through its Global Youth Network project, which was established in 1998 with the aim of involving young people in prevention activities, and through the system of goodwill ambassadors associated with its 'Sports Against Drugs' campaign. The Drug Programme works with governments, as well as non-governmental and private organizations and local community partners, in the detection, treatment, rehabilitation and social reintegration of drug addicts. It also undertakes research to monitor the drugs problem: for example, assessing the characteristics of drug-takers and the substances being used in order to help identify people at risk of becoming drug-takers and to enhance the effectiveness of national programmes to address the issue the (see also GAP, above).

The Drug Programme promotes implementation of the following major treaties which govern the international drug control system: the Single Convention on Narcotic Drugs (1961) and a Protocol amending the Convention (1972); the Convention on Psychotropic Substances (1971); and the UN Convention against Illicit Traffic in Narcotic Drugs and Psychotropic Substances (1988). Among other important provisions, these treaties aim to restrict severely the production of narcotic drugs, while ensuring an adequate supply for medical and scientific purposes, to prevent profits obtained from the illegal sale of drugs being diverted into legal usage and to secure the extradition of drug-traffickers and the transfer of proceedings for criminal prosecution. The Drug Programme assists countries to adapt their national legislation and drug policies to facilitate their compliance with these conventions and to enhance co-ordinated inter-governmental efforts to control the movement of narcotic drugs. The Drug Programme services meetings of the International Narcotics Control Board (INCB), an independent body responsible for promoting and monitoring government compliance with the provisions of the drug control treaties, and of the Commission on Narcotic Drugs, which, as a functional committee of ECOSOC (see p. 18), is the main policy-making organ within the UN system on issues relating to international drug abuse control. The INCB is promoting co-ordinated global action to prevent illicit internet sales of internationally-controlled prescription drugs by so-called 'online pharmacies'.

UNODC co-operates closely with other international, regional and non-governmental organizations and maintains dialogue with agencies advocating drug abuse control. It is a co-sponsor, with ILO, UNDP, UNESCO, UNFPA, UNICEF, WHO, the World Bank and UNHCR of the Joint Programme on HIV/AIDS (UNAIDS), which was established on 1 January 1996. UNODC's participation is in recognition of the importance of international drug control efforts in preventing the spread of HIV/AIDS.

In October 2004 UNODC and the World Customs Organization launched a joint Container Control Programme aimed at improving port control measures in developing countries.

United Nations Crime Programme

Through the United Nations Crime Programme, which is implemented by the Centre for International Crime Prevention—CICP, established in 1997, UNODC is responsible for crime prevention, criminal justice and criminal law reform. The Programme oversees the application of international standards and norms relating to these areas, for example the Minimum Rules for the Treatment of Prisoners, Conventions against Torture, and Other Cruel, Inhuman or Degrading Treatment or Punishment, and Safeguards Guaranteeing the Protection of the Rights of Those Facing the Death Penalty. The Programme provides member states with technical assistance to strengthen national capacities to establish appropriate legal and criminal justice systems and to combat transnational organized crime (see below). The Programme supports the Commission on Crime Prevention and Criminal Justice, a functional committee of ECOSOC, which provides guidance in developing global anti-crime policies. The Programme manages the Global Programme against Corruption, a Global Programme against Trafficking in Human Beings (trafficking in human beings for sexual exploitation or forced labour is regarded as the fastest-growing area of international organized crime), and a Global Programme on Organized Crime, which aimed to analyse emerging transnational criminal organizations and assist countries to formulate strategies to combat the problem. The CICP supported member states in the preparation of the UN Convention against Transnational Organized Crime; the so-called Palermo Convention, with two additional Protocols on trafficking in human beings and the smuggling of migrants, was opened for signature in December 2000 at a UN conference on combating organized crime held in Sicily, Italy, and entered into force in September 2003. The Programme assisted with the formulation of the UN Convention against Corruption, which was opened for signature in December 2003 in Merida, Mexico; by February 2005 the Convention had been signed by 118 countries and ratified by 15.

The Crime Programme promotes research and undertakes studies of new forms of crime prevention, in collaboration with the UN Interregional Crime and Justice Research Institute (UNICRI). It also maintains a UN Crime and Justice Information Network database (UNCJIN), which provides information on national crime statistics, publications and links to other relevant intergovernmental agencies and research and academic institutes.

The UNODC's Terrorism Prevention Branch, established in 1999, researches trends in terrorist activity and assists countries with improving their capabilities to investigate and prevent acts of terrorism. The Branch promotes international co-operation in combating the problem, is compiling a database on global terrorism, and has initiated a study into the connections between terrorist activity and other forms of crime.

The UN Global Programme against Money Laundering (GPML), established in March 1999, assists governments with formulating legislation against money laundering and establishing and maintaining appropriate frameworks to counter the problem. GPML activities include the provision of technical assistance, training, and the collection, research and analysis of crime data. The Programme, in collaboration with other governmental organizations, law enforcement agencies and academic institutions, co-ordinates the International Money Laundering Information Network (IMoLIN), an internet-based information resource (accessible at www.imolin.org). IMoLIN incorporates the Anti-Money Laundering International Database (a comprehensive database on money-laundering legislation throughout the world that constituted a key element in the Office's activities in support of the elaboration of the International Convention against Transnational Organized Crime—see above). At the first GPML Forum, held in the Cayman Islands in March 2000, the governments of 31 participating 'offshore' financial centres agreed in principle to adopt internationally-accepted standards of financial regulation and measures against money laundering.

UNODC organized several regional preparatory meetings prior to the 11th UN Congress on Crime Prevention and Criminal Justice, which was scheduled to be held in Bangkok, Thailand, in April 2005.

Finance

UNODC receives an allocation from the regular budget of the UN, although voluntary contributions from member states and private organizations represent the majority (about 90%) of its resources. The proposed consolidated budget for the two-year period 2004–05 amounted to some US $224.8m., including programme expenditure of $191.1m., of which $91.2m. was to be allocated to meeting global challenges, $54.2m. to anti-trafficking activities, $9.6m. to core programmes on research and analysis, advocacy, etc., $8.6m. to activities relating to the rule of law, and $1.9m. to anti-terrorism activities.

Publications

Bulletin on Narcotics.

Forum on Crime and Society.

Global Illicit Drug Trends.

Global Report on Crime and Justice.

Technical Series.

The United Nations and Juvenile Justice: A Guide to International Standards and Best Practices.

UNODC Update (quarterly).

World Drug Report.

Office of the United Nations High Commissioner for Human Rights—OHCHR

Address: Palais des Nations, 1211 Geneva 10, Switzerland.

Telephone: (22) 9179000; **fax:** (22) 9179022; **e-mail:** infodesk@ohchr.org; **internet:** www.ohchr.org.

The Office is a body of the UN Secretariat and is the focal point for UN human rights activities. Since September 1997 it has incorporated the Centre for Human Rights.

Organization

(March 2005)

HIGH COMMISSIONER

In December 1993 the UN General Assembly decided to establish the position of a United Nations High Commissioner for Human Rights (UNHCHR) following a recommendation of the World Conference on Human Rights, held in Vienna, Austria, in June of that year. The High Commissioner, who is the UN official with principal responsibility for UN human rights activities, is appointed by the UN Secretary-General, with the approval of the General Assembly, for a four-year term in office, renewable for one term.

High Commissioner: LOUISE ARBOUR (Canada).

ADMINISTRATION

The Office was restructured in 2003 to comprise the Executive Office of the High Commissioner, the Administrative Service, and the following five branches: Research and Right to Development, responsible for human rights policy development, undertaking research and providing information to the High Commissioner and other human rights experts, working groups, etc.; Treaties and Commission, which provides administrative support to UN human rights treaties bodies (such as the Human Rights Committee, which monitors the implementation of the 1976 International Covenant on Civil and Political Rights, and the Committee on Torture), and to bodies established under the UN Charter, including the Commission on Human Rights and its working groups, and the Sub-commission on the Promotion and Protection of Human Rights and its working groups; Special Procedures, which provides enhanced support to fact-finding and investigatory mechanisms of the Commission on Human Rights; Capacity Building and Field Operations, which develops and manages advisory services and other technical assistance projects at the request of governments and supports fact-finding and investigatory mechanisms addressing specific country situations; and External Relations, responsible for communications and media relations. There is also a branch office in New York, USA, and a Policy Planning and Methodology Unit.

FIELD PRESENCES

As the Office's involvement in field work has expanded, in support of UN peace-making, peace-keeping and peace-building activities, a substantial structure of field presences has developed. In 2005 OHCHR was engaged operationally in 40 countries. There were regional offices in Addis Ababa, Ethiopia; Almaty, Kazakhstan; Bangkok, Thailand; Beirut, Lebanon; Pretoria, South Africa; Santiago, Chile; Tashkent, Uzbekistan; and Yaoundé, Cameroon; and country offices with human rights promotion and protection mandates were maintained in Afghanistan, Bosnia and Herzegovina, Burundi, Cambodia, Colombia, the Democratic Republic of the Congo, and Serbia and Montenegro. The Office also supplied human rights advisers to UN country teams in Angola, Guyana, Nepal, Sri Lanka and Uganda; was responsible for the human rights components of 15 UN peace missions; and was undertaking a number of technical co-operation projects.

Activities

The mandate of the OHCHR incorporates the following functions and responsibilities: the promotion and protection of human rights throughout the world; the reinforcement of international co-operation in the field of human rights; the promotion of universal ratification and implementation of international standards; the establishment of a dialogue with governments to ensure respect for human rights; and co-ordination of efforts by other UN programmes and organs to promote respect for human rights. Upon request OHCHR undertakes assessments of national human rights needs, in consultation with governments. Through the provision of guidance and training it supports the establishment of independent national human rights institutions. The Office may also study and react to cases of serious violations of human rights, and may undertake diplomatic efforts to prevent violations. It also produces educational and other information material to enhance understanding of human rights. The High Commissioner was designated as the co-ordinator of the UN Decade for Human Rights Education (1995–2004). OHCHR co-operates with academic bodies and non-governmental organizations working the area of human rights.

OHCHR was the lead agency in undertaking preparations for the World Conference against Racism, Racial Discrimination, Xenophobia and Related Intolerance, convened in Durban, South Africa, in August–September 2001 and attended by representatives of 168 governments. The following five core themes were addressed at Durban: sources, causes, forms and contemporary manifestations of racism; victims; prevention, education and protection measures; provision of remedies and redress (i.e. compensation); and future strategies to achieve full and effective equality. The Conference adopted the 'Durban Declaration' and a Programme of Action, in accordance with which national plans of action were to be implemented by participating states: universal ratification of the International Convention on the Elimination of all Forms of Racism (ICERD) was to be prioritized, with the broadest possible ratification of other human rights instruments, and national legislation was to be improved in line with the ICERD. OHCHR was to play a leading role in following up the implementation of the Programme of Action; on the recommendation of the Conference an interim Anti-discrimination Unit was established within the Office for this purpose.

The Office provides secretariat services to the UN Voluntary Fund for Victims of Torture, which was established in 1981.

OHCHR field offices and operations ('field presences'—see above) undertake a variety of activities, such as training and other technical assistance, support for Special Rapporteurs (usually appointed by the Commission on Human Rights to investigate human rights emergencies), monitoring and fact-finding. Increasingly they provide support to conflict prevention, peace-making, peace-keeping and peace-building activities. OHCHR co-operates with the UN Department of Peace-keeping Operations and Department of Political Affairs in developing the human rights component of peace-keeping and peace-building missions.

The OHCHR quick response desk co-ordinates urgent appeals for assistance in addressing human rights emergencies. The High Commissioner issues reports on human rights emergencies to the Commission on Human Rights.

TECHNICAL CO-OPERATION PROGRAMME

The UN Technical Co-operation Programme in the Field of Human Rights was established in 1955 to assist states, at their request, to strengthen their capacities in the observance of democracy, human rights, and the rule of law. Examples of work undertaken within the framework of the programme include training courses and workshops on good governance and the observance of human rights, expert advisory services on the incorporation of international human rights standards into national legislation and policies and on the formulation of national plans of action for the promotion and protection of human rights, fellowships, the provision of information and documentation, and consideration of promoting a human rights culture. In recent years the Programme, one of the key components of OHCHR's activities, has expanded to undertake UN system-wide human rights support activities, for example in the area of peace-keeping (see above). A project management and technical co-operation unit was established in 2002. A global review of the programme, undertaken in 2003, recommended that technical co-operation activities should become more results-based.

Finance

The Office is financed from the regular budget of the UN, as well as by a number of voluntary and trust funds. For the two years 2004–05 the approved regular budget appropriation for OHCHR amounted to US $60.6m. Under its 2005 annual appeal to the international community for voluntary contributions the Office requested $59.8m.

Publications

Annual Report.
Fact sheet series.
Human Rights Quarterly.
Human rights study series.
Professional training series.
Other reference material, reports, proceedings of conferences, workshops, etc.

United Nations Human Settlements Programme—UN-Habitat

Address: POB 30030, 00100 Nairobi, Kenya.
Telephone: (20) 623120; **fax:** (20) 623477; **e-mail:** infohabitat@unhabitat.org; **internet:** www.unhabitat.org.

UN-Habitat (formerly the United Nations Centre for Human Settlements, UNCHS-Habitat, established in October 1978 to service the intergovernmental Commission on Human Settlements) became a full UN programme in January 2002. UN-Habitat serves as a focus for human settlements and sustainable urban development activities in the UN system.

Organization

(March 2005)

GOVERNING COUNCIL

The Governing Council (formerly the Commission on Human Settlements) meets once every two years and has 58 members, serving for four years. Sixteen members are from Africa, 13 from Asia, 10 from Latin America and the Caribbean, six from eastern European countries, and 13 from western European and other countries. The Committee of Permanent Representatives to UN-Habitat, which meets at least four times a year, functions as an inter-sessional subsidiary body of the Governing Council. The Governing Council reports to the UN General Assembly through ECOSOC.

SECRETARIAT

The Secretariat services the Governing Council, implements its resolutions and ensures the integration and co-ordination of technical co-operation, research and policy advice. Its Work Programme incorporates the following priority areas, as defined by the Governing Council: adequate shelter for all and sustainable human settlements development; monitoring the Habitat Agenda; regional and technical co-operation; and human settlements financing. The Secretariat is responsible for monitoring the implementation of the objectives of the Second UN Conference on Human Settlements, Habitat II, which was held in Istanbul, Turkey, in June 1996.

Executive Director: ANNA KAJUMULO TIBAIJUKA (Tanzania).

Activities

Nearly one-half of the world's population lives in towns and cities and about one-third of the world's urban population (nearly 1,000m. people) lives in slums without access to basic sanitation. UN-Habitat supports the UN Millennium development target of improving significantly the lives of at least 100m. slum dwellers by 2020. It supports and conducts capacity-building and operational research, provides technical co-operation and policy advice, and disseminates information with the aim of strengthening the development and management of human settlements. In October 2003 the Programme predicted that, owing to unprecedented urban growth accompanied by poverty and social inequalities, the number of slum dwellers world-wide would double to about 2,000m. by 2030, rendering the above UN Millennium development target a minimum objective.

In June 1996 representatives of 171 national governments and of more than 500 municipal authorities attending Habitat II adopted a Global Plan of Action (the 'Habitat Agenda'), which incorporated detailed programmes of action to realize economic and social development and environmental sustainability, and endorsed the conference's objectives of ensuring 'adequate shelter for all' and 'sustainable human settlements development in an urbanizing world'. UN-Habitat provides the leadership and serves as a focal point for the implementation of the Agenda. In 1999 UNCHS (Habitat) approved a set of 23 resolutions to reduce poverty, improve shelter and environmental conditions, promote good governance, and improve the status of women. In 1999 UNCHS (Habitat) and the World Bank jointly launched the Cities Alliance, which also comprised G-7 and other governments, UNEP, the Asian Development Bank, and local authorities, and aimed to increase resources reaching the urban poor by improving ongoing urban programmes, and by strengthening links between grant-funded urban development co-operation and investment follow-up. A special session of the UN General Assembly, entitled Istanbul + 5, was held in June 2001 to report on the implementation of the recommendations of the Habitat II conference. The special session adopted a Declaration on Cities and Other Human Settlements in the New Millennium that reaffirmed commitment to the objectives of the Habitat Agenda and urged an intensification of efforts towards eradicating widespread poverty, which was identified as the main impediment to achieving these, and towards promoting good governance. The special session also resolved to increase international co-operation in several other areas, including addressing HIV/AIDS, urban crime and violence, environmental issues, and the problems posed by conflicts and refugees; and recommended the enhancement of the status and role of UNCHS (Habitat). Consequently, in December 2001 the General Assembly authorized the elevation of the body to a full UN programme with a strengthened mandate to address and implement the Habitat Agenda and, in January 2002, UN-Habitat was inaugurated.

UN-Habitat maintains a Global Urban Observatory to monitor implementation of the Habitat Agenda and to report on local and national plans of action, international and regional support programmes and ongoing research and development. The Observatory, which works closely with the Best Practices and Local Leadership Programme and the Urban Indicators Programme, operates through an international network of regional and national institutions, all of which provide local training in appropriate data collection methods and in the development, adoption and maintenance of reliable information systems.

Through its Women in Human Settlements Development Programme, which was established in 1990, the Programme—then UNCHS (Habitat)—ensured that the issue of human settlements was included in the agenda of the UN Fourth World Conference on Women, which was held in Beijing, People's Republic of China, in September 1995, and successfully incorporated the right of women to ownership of land and property into the Global Platform for Action which resulted from the conference. An advisory board, the Huairou Commission, comprising women from 'grass-roots' groups, non-governmental organizations, the UN and research and political institutions, has since been established to ensure a link between the Beijing and Habitat Agendas and the inclusion of gender issues in the follow-up to Habitat II.

UN-Habitat participates in implementing the human settlements component of Agenda 21, which was adopted at the UN Conference on Environment and Development in June 1992, and is also responsible for the chapter of Agenda 21 that refers to solid waste management and sewage-related issues. The Programme implements a programme entitled 'Localizing Agenda 21', to assist local authorities in developing countries to address local environmental and infrastructure-related problems. It also collaborates with national governments, private-sector and non-governmental institutions and UN bodies to achieve the objectives of Agenda 21. The Settlement Infrastructure and Environment Programme was initiated in 1992 to support developing countries in improving the environment of human settlements through policy advice and planning, infrastructure management and enhancing awareness of environmental and health concerns in areas such as water, sanitation, waste management and transport. In October 2002 UN-Habitat launched a Water and Sanitation Trust Fund aimed at supporting the goal of halving the proportion of the world's population lacking access to basic sanitation or clean water by 2015, that was set by the World Summit on Sustainable Development (WSSD), held in Johannesburg, South Africa, during August–September to assess strategies for strengthening the implementation of Agenda 21. In March 2003 UN-Habitat issued a report entitled *Water and Sanitation in the World's Cities: Local Action for Global Goals* in which it recommended a major review of the global urban sanitation situation. UN-Habitat and UNEP jointly co-ordinate the Managing Water for African Cities programme, which promotes efficient water demand management, capacity-building to alleviate the environmental impact of urbanization on freshwater resources, information exchange on water management and conservation issues, and the exchange of best practices in urban water management. The programme is being implemented in Abidjan, Cote d'Ivoire; Accra, Ghana; Addis Ababa, Ethiopia; Dakar, Senegal; Johannesburg, South Africa; Lusaka, Zambia; and Nairobi, Kenya. In March 2003 UN-Habitat and the Asian Development Bank (ADB) signed an agreement on the establishment of a new Water for Asian Cities Programme. The ADB was to provide US $10m. in grants and $500m. in loans in support of the programme over a five-year period. A global Urban Management Programme aims to strengthen the contribution of cities and towns in developing countries towards human development, including economic growth, social advancements, the reduction of poverty and the improvement of the environment. The Programme, which is active in 120 cities, is an international technical co-operation project, of which UN-Habitat is the executing agency, the World Bank is an associated agency, while UNDP provides core funding and monitoring. The Programme is operated through regional offices, in collaboration with bilateral and multilateral support agencies, and brings together national and local authorities, community leaders and representatives of the private sector to consider specific issues and solutions to urban problems. The related Safer Cities Programme was initiated in 1996. A Sustainable Cities Programme, operated jointly with UNEP, is concerned with incorporating environmental issues into urban planning and management, in order to ensure sustainable and equitable development. The Programme is active in some 20 cities world-wide, although a prepared series of policy guide-lines is used in many others. Some 95% of the Programme's resources are spent at city level to strengthen the capacities of municipal authorities and their public-, private- and community-sector partners in the field of environmental planning and management, with the objective that the concepts and approaches of the Programme are replicated throughout the region. UN-Habitat provided the secretariat of the inaugural World Urban Forum, held in April–May 2002 with participation by national governments and Habitat Agenda partners. The Forum, which represents a merger of the former Urban Environment Forum and International Forum on Urban Poverty, aims to promote international co-operation in shelter and urban development issues. The second World Urban Forum was convened in Barcelona, Spain, in September 2004. In addition, UN-Habitat supports training and other activities designed to strengthen management development (in particular in the provision and maintenance of services and facilities) at local and community level. UN-Habitat's Global Campaign for Secure Tenure and Global Campaign on Urban Governance both emphasize urban poverty reduction. UN-Habitat focused on the theme of 'Sustainable Urbanization' as its main contribution to the WSSD held in August–September 2002 (see above).

In November 2004 UN-Habitat hosted the first meeting of a new initiative, the Global Research Network on Human Settlements (HS-Net). HS-Net was to act as a forum for human settlements researchers, research institutions and networks, and was to advised the UN-Habitat Secretariat on the preparation of its two 'flagship reports', the *Global Report on Human Settlements* and *State of the World's Cities*.

Increasingly the Programme is being called upon to contribute to the relief, rehabilitation and development activities undertaken by the UN in areas affected by regional and civil conflict. It has been actively involved in the reconstruction of human settlements and other development activities in Afghanistan, as well as contributing to reconstruction programmes in Timor-Leste, Iraq, Myanmar, Rwanda and Somalia. From January 2000–November 2002 it administered a Housing and Property Directorate that was established in post-conflict Kosovo and Metohija, within the framework of the UN's interim administration in the province. In May 2003 the Governing Council determined to establish a Human Settlements Programme in the Palestinian Occupied Territories. In February 2004 UN-Habitat announced the development of an Urban and

Housing Rehabilitation Programme aimed at promoting sustainable post-war reconstruction in Iraq. UN-Habitat also provides assessment and technical support in the aftermath of natural disasters. Reconstruction and recovery activities are co-ordinated by the Risk and Disaster Management Unit. In January 2005, following a massive earthquake under the Indian Ocean in December 2004, which caused a series of tidal waves (tsunami) that devastated coastal regions in 12 countries, UN-Habitat established a Tsunami Human Settlements Recovery Facility, with initial seed capital of US $1m. that was to be allocated for rapid response activities mainly in Indonesia, Somalia, Sri Lanka and Thailand. There was to be a particular focus on the following five areas: emergency environmental clean-up; critical infrastructure rehabilitation (especially of clean water and sanitation); emergency shelter provision; and restoration of livelihoods. In December 2003 UN-Habitat signed a Memorandum of Understanding with UNHCR that covered several areas of co-operation including sheltering refugees and returnees, settlement and infrastructure planning, and property rights.

Finance

UN-Habitat's work programme is financed from the UN regular budget, the Habitat and Human Settlements Foundation and from extra-budgetary resources. The approved budget for the two-year period 2004–05 amounted to US $44.4m.

Publications

Global Report on Human Settlements (annually).
State of the World's Cities (every 2 years).
Habitat Debate (quarterly).
Water for Cities (quarterly).
UMP e-Newsletter (quarterly).
Technical reports and studies, occasional papers, bibliographies, directories.

United Nations Children's Fund—UNICEF

Address: 3 United Nations Plaza, New York, NY 10017, USA.
Telephone: (212) 326-7000; **fax:** (212) 887-7465; **e-mail:** info@unicef.org; **internet:** www.unicef.org.
UNICEF was established in 1946 by the UN General Assembly as the UN International Children's Emergency Fund, to meet the emergency needs of children in post-war Europe. In 1950 its mandate was expanded to respond to the needs of children in developing countries. In 1953 the General Assembly decided that UNICEF should continue its work, as a permanent arm of the UN system, with an emphasis on programmes giving long-term benefits to children everywhere, particularly those in developing countries. In 1965 UNICEF was awarded the Nobel Peace Prize.

Organization

(March 2005)

EXECUTIVE BOARD

The Executive Board, as the governing body of UNICEF, comprises 36 member governments from all regions, elected in rotation for a three-year term by ECOSOC. The Board establishes policy, reviews programmes and approves expenditure. It reports to the General Assembly through ECOSOC.

SECRETARIAT

The Executive Director of UNICEF is appointed by the UN Secretary-General in consultation with the Executive Board. The administration of UNICEF and the appointment and direction of staff are the responsibility of the Executive Director, under policy directives laid down by the Executive Board, and under a broad authority delegated to the Executive Director by the Secretary-General. In December 2003 there were more than 7,000 UNICEF staff positions, of which about 85% were in the field.
Executive Director: ANN VENEMAN (USA) (from 1 May 2005).

UNICEF OFFICES

UNICEF has a network of eight regional and 126 field offices serving 157 countries and territories. Its offices in Tokyo, Japan, and Brussels, Belgium, support fund-raising activities; UNICEF's supply division is administered from the office in Copenhagen, Denmark. A research centre concerned with child development is based in Florence, Italy.

Belgium: rue Montoyer 14, 1000 Brussels; tel. (2) 513-22-51; fax (2) 513-22-90; e-mail brussels@unicef.be; internet unicef.be.

Japan: UNU Headquarters Bldg, 8th Floor, 53–70, Jingumae 5-chome, Shibuya-ku, Tokyo 150-0001, Japan; tel. (3) 5467-4431; fax (3) 5467-4437; e-mail tokyo@unicef.org; internet www.unicef.or.jp.

Regional Office for the Americas and the Caribbean: Apdo 3667, Balboa Ancón, Panamá, Panama; tel. (507) 315-7400; fax (507) 317-0258; e-mail webtacro@unicef.org; internet www.uniceflac.org.

Regional Office for Central and Eastern Europe, the Commonwealth of Independent States and the Baltic States: Palais des Nations, 1211 Geneva 10, Switzerland; tel. (22) 9095111; fax (22) 9095909.

Regional Office for East Asia and the Pacific: POB 2-154, Bangkok 10200, Thailand; tel. (2) 2805931; fax (2) 2803563; e-mail eapro@unicef.org.

Regional Office for Eastern and Southern Africa: POB 44145, Nairobi, Kenya 00100; tel. (20) 621234; fax (20) 622678; e-mail unicefesaro@unicef.org.

Regional Office for the Middle East and North Africa: POB 1551, UNICEF House, Tla'a al-Ali al Dahak Bin Soufian St, 11821 Amman, Jordan; tel. (6) 5539977; fax (6) 5538880; e-mail menaro@unicef.org.jo.

Regional Office for South Asia: POB 5815, Leknath Marg, Kathmandu, Nepal; tel. 4419471; fax 4419479; e-mail rosa@unicef.org.

Regional Office for West and Central Africa: POB 29720, Dakar-Yoff, Senegal; tel. 869-58-58; fax 820-89-65; e-mail wcaro@unicef.org.

UNICEF Innocenti Research Centre: Piazza SS. Annunziata 12, 50122 Florence, Italy; tel. (055) 20330; fax (055) 2033220; e-mail florence@unicef.org; internet www.unicef-icc.org; f. 1988 as International Child Development Centre; aims to strengthen UNICEF's research capability and to support the Fund's advocacy for children world-wide.

UNICEF Supply Division: UNICEF Plads, Freeport 2100, Copenhagen; tel. (45) 35273527; fax (45) 35269421; e-mail supply@unicef.org; internet www.unicef.org/supply.

NATIONAL COMMITTEES

UNICEF is supported by 37 National Committees, mostly in industrialized countries, whose volunteer members, numbering more than 100,000, raise money through various activities, including the sale of greetings cards. The Committees also undertake advocacy and awareness campaigns on a number of issues and provide an important link with the general public.

Activities

UNICEF is dedicated to the well-being of children, adolescents and women and works for the realization and protection of their rights within the frameworks of the Convention on the Rights of the Child, which was adopted by the UN General Assembly in 1989 and by 2005 was almost universally ratified, and of the Convention on the Elimination of All Forms of Discrimination Against Women, adopted by the UN General Assembly in 1979. Promoting the full implementation of the Conventions, UNICEF aims to ensure that children world-wide are given the best possible start in life and attain a good level of basic education, and that adolescents are given every opportunity to develop their capabilities and participate successfully in society. The Fund also continues to provide relief and rehabilitation assistance in emergencies. Through its extensive field network in some 157 developing countries and territories, UNICEF undertakes, in co-ordination with governments, local communities and other aid organizations, programmes in health, nutrition, education, water and sanitation, the environment, gender issues and development, and other fields of importance to children. Emphasis is placed on low-cost, community-based programmes. UNICEF programmes are increasingly focused on supporting children and women during critical periods of their life, when intervention can make a lasting difference, i.e. early childhood, the primary school years, adolescence and the reproductive years. Priorities include early years development, immunization strategies, girls' education, combating the spread and impact of HIV/AIDS, and strengthening the protection of children against violence, exploitation and abuse. These priorities are guided by the relevant UN Millennium Development Goals adopted by world leaders in 2000, and by the 'A World Fit for Children' declaration and plan of action endorsed by the UN General Assembly special session on Children in 2002 (see below).

UNICEF was instrumental in organizing the World Summit for Children, held in September 1990 and attended by representatives from more than 150 countries, including 71 heads of state or government. The Summit produced a Plan of Action which recognized the rights of the young to 'first call' on their countries' resources and formulated objectives for the year 2000, including: (i) a reduction of the 1990 mortality rates for infants and children under five years by one-third, or to 50–70 per 1,000 live births, whichever is lower; (ii) a reduction of the 1990 maternal mortality rate by one-half; (iii) a reduction by one-half of the 1990 rate of severe malnutrition among children under the age of five; (iv) universal access to safe drinking water and to sanitary means of excreta disposal; and (v) universal access to basic education and completion of primary education by at least 80% of children. UNICEF supported the efforts of governments to achieve progress towards these objectives. The Fund served as the substantive secretariat for, and played a leading role in helping governments and other partners prepare for, the UN General Assembly special session on Children, which was held in May 2002 to assess the outcome of the 1990 summit and to determine a set of actions and objectives for the next 10 years. At the session the General Assembly adopted a declaration entitled 'A World Fit for Children', reaffirming its commitment to the agenda of the 1990 summit, and outlining a plan of action that resolved to achieve as yet unmet World Summit goals by 2010 and to work towards the attainment by 2015 of 21 new goals and targets supporting UN Millennium Development Goals in the areas of education, health and the protection of children. The latter included: a reduction of mortality rates for infants and children under five by two-thirds; a reduction of maternal mortality rates by three-quarters; a reduction by one-third in the rate for severe malnutrition among children under the age of five; and enrolment in primary education by 90% of children. UNICEF's medium-term strategic plan for 2002–05 incorporated the following aims: 80% immunization coverage for children in 80% of countries globally; a reduction by one-half in the number of deaths caused by measles; and the certified global eradication of poliomyelitis. A database of economic and social indicators is available at www.unicef.org/information/databases.

In 2000 UNICEF launched a new initiative, the Global Movement for Children—comprising governments, private- and public-sector bodies, and individuals—which aimed to rally world-wide support to improve the lives of all children and adolescents. In April 2001 a 'Say Yes for Children' campaign was adopted by the Global Movement, identifying 10 critical actions required to further its objectives. These were: eliminating all forms of discrimination and exclusion; putting children first; ensuring a caring environment for every child; fighting HIV/AIDS; eradicating violence against and abuse and exploitation of children; listening to children's views; universal education; protecting children from war; safeguarding the earth for children; and combating poverty. In 2003 UNICEF, WHO, the World Bank and other partners established a new Child Survival Partnership, which was to act as a forum for the promotion of co-ordinated action in support of efforts to reduce the level of child mortality in 42 targeted developing countries.

UNICEF, in co-operation with other UN agencies, promotes universal access to and completion of basic and good quality education. The Fund, with UNESCO, UNDP, UNFPA and the World Bank, co-sponsored the World Conference on Education for All, held in Thailand in March 1990, and undertook efforts to achieve the objectives formulated by the conference, which included the elimination of disparities in education between boys and girls. UNICEF participated in and fully supports the objectives and framework for action adopted by the follow-up World Education Forum in Dakar, Senegal, in April 2000. The Fund supports education projects in sub-Saharan Africa, South Asia and countries in the Middle East and North Africa, and implements a Girls' Education Programme in more than 100 countries, which aims to increase the enrolment of girls in primary schools. More than 120m. children world-wide, of whom nearly 53% are girls, remain deprived of basic education. In 2002 UNICEF initiated the '25 by 2005' initiative, which aimed to eliminate gender disparities in education in 25, mainly African and Asian, countries by 2005. A UNICEF-led initiative facilitated the return to school of around 1.3m. Afghan girls during 2002–04. Some 19% of the Fund's direct programme assistance was allocated to girls' education in 2003.

Through UNICEF's efforts the needs and interests of children were incorporated into Agenda 21, which was adopted as a plan of action for sustainable development at the UN Conference on Environment and Development, held in June 1992. In mid-1997, at the UN General Assembly's Special Session on Sustainable Development, UNICEF highlighted the need to improve safe water supply, sanitation and hygiene, and thereby reduce the risk of diarrhoea and other water-borne diseases, as fundamental to fulfilment of child rights. The Fund supports initiatives to provide the benefits of safe water, sanitation and hygiene education to communities in some 90 developing countries; and participates in the inter-agency initiative Focusing Resources on Effective School Health (FRESH). UNICEF also works with UNEP to promote environment issues of common concern and with the World Wide Fund for Nature to support the conservation of local ecosystems.

UNICEF aims to break the cycle of poverty by advocating for the provision of increased development aid to developing countries, and aims to help poor countries obtain debt relief and to ensure access to basic social services. To this end it supports NetAid, an internet-based strategy to promote sustainable development and combat extreme poverty. UNICEF is the leading agency in promoting the 20/20 initiative, which was endorsed at the World Summit for Social Development, held in Copenhagen, Denmark, in March 1995. The initiative encourages the governments of developing and donor countries to allocate at least 20% of their domestic budgets and official development aid respectively, to healthcare, primary education and low-cost safe water and sanitation.

UNICEF estimates that the births of some 50m. children annually are not officially registered, and promotes universal registration in order to prevent the abuse of children without proof of age and nationality, for example through trafficking, forced labour, early marriage and military recruitment. It estimates that some 246m. children are involved in exploitative labour and that annually around 1.2m. children are trafficked. The Fund, which vigorously opposes the exploitation of children as a violation of their basic human rights, works with ILO and other partners to promote an end to exploitative and hazardous child labour, and supports special projects to provide education, counselling and care for the estimated 250m. children between the ages of five and 14 years working in developing countries. UNICEF played a major role at the World Congress against Commercial Sexual Exploitation of Children, held in Stockholm, Sweden, in 1996, which adopted a Declaration and Agenda for Action to end the sexual exploitation of children. UNICEF also actively participated in the International Conference on Child Labour held in Oslo, Norway, in November 1997. The Conference adopted an Agenda for Action to eliminate the worst forms of child labour, including slavery-like practices, forced labour, commercial sexual exploitation and the use of children in drugs-trafficking and other hazardous forms of work. UNICEF supports the 1999 ILO Worst Forms of Child Labour Convention, which aims at the prohibition and elimination of the worst forms of child labour. In 1999 UNICEF launched a global initiative, Education as a Preventive Strategy Against Child Labour, with the aim of providing education to children forced to miss school because of work. The Fund helped to draft and promotes full ratification and implementation of an Optional Protocol to the Convention of the Rights of the Child concerning the sale of children, child prostitution and pornography, which was adopted in May 2000 and entered into force in January 2002. UNICEF co-sponsored and actively participated in the Second Congress Against Commercial Sexual Exploitation of Children held in Yokohama, Japan, in December 2001. Some 10% of the Fund's direct programme assistance was allocated to the improved protection of children in 2003.

In 2003 UNICEF allocated 36% of its direct programme assistance to early childhood development and 21% to its Immunization Plus activities (focusing on the promotion of improved child-care practices, the strengthening of local health systems, and the delivery of other life-saving services—such as the provision of vitamin A supplements—during immunization campaigns). The Fund estimates that around 11m. children under five years of age die each year, mainly in developing countries, and the majority from largely preventable causes. UNICEF has worked with WHO and other partners to increase global immunization coverage against the following six diseases: measles, poliomyelitis, tuberculosis, diphtheria, whooping cough and tetanus. In 2002 UNICEF, in partnership with WHO, governments and other partners, helped to immunize more than 500m. children under five years of age in 53 countries against polio. In 1999 UNICEF, WHO, the World Bank and a number of public- and private-sector partners launched the Global Alliance for Vaccines and Immunization (GAVI), which aimed to protect children of all nationalities and socio-economic groups against vaccine-preventable diseases. GAVI's strategy included improving access to sustainable immunization services, expanding the use of existing vaccines, accelerating the development and introduction of new vaccines and technologies and promoting immunization coverage as a focus of international development efforts. Between 2001–04 GAVI helped to protect around 35m. children in developing countries against hepatitis B. UNICEF and WHO also work in conjunction on the Integrated Management of Childhood Illness programme to control diarrhoeal dehydration, a major cause of death among children under five years of age in the developing world. UNICEF-assisted programmes for the control of diarrhoeal diseases promote the low-cost manufacture and distribution of prepackaged salts or home-made solutions. The use of 'oral rehydration therapy' has risen significantly in recent years, and is believed to prevent more than 1m. child deaths annually. During 1990–2000 diarrhoea-related deaths were reduced by one-half. UNICEF also promotes the need to improve sanitation and access to safe water supplies in developing nations in order to reduce the risk of diarrhoea and other waterborne diseases (see 20/20 initiative, above). To control acute respiratory infections, another leading cause of death in children under five in developing countries, UNICEF works with WHO in training health workers to diagnose and treat the associated diseases. As a result, the level of child deaths from pneumonia and other respiratory infections has been reduced by one-half since 1990. Around 1m. children die from malaria every year, mainly in sub-Saharan Africa. In October 1998 UNICEF, together with WHO, UNDP and the World Bank, inaugurated a new global campaign, Roll Back Malaria, to fight the disease. UNICEF supports control programmes in more than 30 countries. In 2002 UNICEF provided more than 4m. insecticide-treated nets as protection against malarial mosquitoes. The Fund also provides vitamin A supplements in support of its immunization programmes.

According to UNICEF estimates, around 27% of children under five years of age are underweight, while each year malnutrition contributes to about one-half of the child deaths in that age group and leaves millions of others with physical and mental disabilities. More than 2,000m. people world-wide (mainly women and children in developing countries) are estimated to be deficient in one or more essential vitamins and minerals, such as vitamin A, iodine and iron. UNICEF supports national efforts to reduce malnutrition, for example, fortifying staple foods with micronutrients, widening women's access to education, improving household food security and basic health services, and promoting sound child-care and feeding practices. Since 1991 more than 15,000 hospitals in at least 136 countries have been designated 'baby-friendly', having implemented a set of UNICEF and WHO recommendations entitled '10 steps to successful breast-feeding'. In 1996 UNICEF expressed its concern at the impact of international economic embargoes on child health, citing as an example the extensive levels of child malnutrition recorded in Iraq. UNICEF remains actively concerned at the levels of child malnutrition and accompanying diseases in Iraq and in the Democratic People's Republic of Korea, which has also suffered severe food shortages.

UNICEF estimates that more than 500,000 women die every year during pregnancy or childbirth, largely because of inadequate maternal healthcare. For every maternal death, approximately 30 further women suffer permanent injuries or chronic disabilities as a result of complications during pregnancy or childbirth. With its partners in the Safe Motherhood Initiative—UNFPA, WHO, the World Bank, the International Planned Parenthood Federation, the Population Council, and Family Care International—UNICEF promotes measures to reduce maternal mortality and morbidity, including improving access to quality reproductive health services, educating communities about safe motherhood and the rights of women, training midwives, and expanding access to family planning services.

UNICEF is concerned at the danger posed by HIV/AIDS to the realization of children's rights and in 2003 allocated 9% of its programme expenditure to this area. At the end of 2004 it was estimated that 2.2m. children under 15 were living with HIV/AIDS world-wide. Some 640,000 children under 15 were estimated to have been newly infected during that year, while 510,000 died as a result of AIDS. It was estimated that more than one-half of all new HIV infections during 2003 occurred in young people, aged below 25. It is believed that more than 14m. children world-wide have lost one or both parents to AIDS since the start of the epidemic. UNICEF's priorities in this area include prevention of infection among young people (through, for example, support for education programmes and dissemination of information through the media), reduction in mother-to-child transmission, care and protection of orphans and other vulnerable children, and care and support for children, young people and parents living with HIV/AIDS. UNICEF works closely in this field with governments and co-operates with other UN agencies in the Joint UN Programme on HIV/AIDS (UNAIDS), which became operational on 1 January 1996. In July 2002 UNICEF, UNAIDS and WHO jointly produced a study entitled *Young People and HIV/AIDS: Opportunity in Crisis*, examining young people's sexual behaviour patterns and knowledge of HIV/AIDS. UNICEF advocates Life Skills-Based Education as a means of empowering young people to cope with challenging situations and encouraging them to adopt healthy patterns of behaviour.

UNICEF provides emergency relief assistance, supports education, health, mine-awareness and psychosocial activities and helps to demobilize and rehabilitate child soldiers in countries and territories affected by violence and social disintegration. It assists children orphaned or separated from their parents and made homeless through armed conflict. In recent years several such emergency operations have been undertaken, including in Afghanistan, Angola, Burundi, Democratic Republic of the Congo, Iran, Iraq, Kosovo, Liberia, Sierra Leone and Sudan. In 2004 UNICEF provided emergency assistance to children in 55 countries. In 1999 UNICEF adopted a Peace and Security Agenda to help guide international efforts in this field. Emergency education assistance includes the provision of 'Edukits' in refugee camps and the reconstruction of school buildings. In the area of health the Fund co-operates with WHO to arrange 'days of tranquility' in order to facilitate the immunization of children in conflict zones. Psychosocial assistance activities include special programmes to assist traumatized children and help unaccompanied children to be reunited with parents or extended families.

In January 2005, following a massive earthquake in the Indian Ocean in December 2004, which caused a series of tidal waves, or tsunamis, that devastated coastal regions in 12 countries in South and South-East Asia and East Africa, UNICEF requested emergency funding of US $144.5m. in assistance over an initial six-month period for an estimated 1.5m. children and young people who had been displaced from their homes. UNICEF was to support the provision of emergency immunization to prevent an increase in the prevalence of fatal childhood diseases; the provision of basic medicines; supply of safe water and provision of basic sanitation; care for traumatized children; identification and protection of the large numbers of orphans and children who had been separated from their families; and the rehabilitation of schools and provision of education kits for children whose schooling had been disrupted by the natural disaster. In order to prevent the onset of acute malnutrition among vulnerable groups, the Fund was to assist with the establishment of supplementary feeding centres and to provide fortified blended food to displaced children under the age of five suffering malnutrition and to pregnant and lactating women.

An estimated 300,000 children are involved in armed conflicts as soldiers, porters and forced labourers. UNICEF encourages ratification of the Optional Protocol to the Convention on the Rights of the Child on the involvement of children in armed conflict, which was adopted by the General Assembly in May 2000 and entered into force in February 2002, and bans the compulsory recruitment of combatants below 18 years. The Fund also urges states to make unequivocal statements endorsing 18 as the minimum age of voluntary recruitment to the armed forces. UNICEF was an active participant in the so-called 'Ottawa' process (supported by the Canadian Government) to negotiate an international ban on anti-personnel land-mines which, it was estimated, killed and maimed between 8,000 and 10,000 children every year. The Convention on the Prohibition of the Use, Stockpiling, Production and Transfer of Anti-Personnel Mines and on their Destruction was adopted in December 1997 and entered into force in March 1999. By January 2005 the Convention had been ratified by 144 countries. UNICEF is committed to campaigning for its universal ratification and full implementation, and also supports mine-awareness campaigns.

Finance

UNICEF is funded by voluntary contributions from governments and non-governmental and private-sector sources. UNICEF's income is divided into contributions for 'regular resources' (used for country programmes of co-operation approved by the Executive Board, programme support, and management and administration costs) and contributions for 'other resources' (for special purposes, including expanding the outreach of country programmes of co-operation and ensuring capacity to deliver critical assistance to women and children, for example during humanitarian crises). Total income in 2003 amounted to US $1,688m., of which 67% was from governments and intergovernmental organizations. The total projected income for 2004 and 2005 amounted to $1,685m. and $1,708m., respectively.

UNICEF's total expenditure in 2003 amounted to US $1,480m. The total projected expenditure for 2004 and 2005 totalled, respectively, $1,649m. and $1,682m.

Publications

Facts and Figures (in English, French and Spanish).

The State of the World's Children (annually, in Arabic, English, French, Russian and Spanish and about 30 other national languages).

UNICEF Annual Report (in English, French and Spanish).

UNICEF at a Glance (in English, French and Spanish).

World Malaria Report (with WHO).

Reports and studies; series on children and women; nutrition; education; children's rights; children in wars and disasters; working children; water, sanitation and the environment; analyses of the situation of children and women in individual developing countries.

United Nations Conference on Trade and Development—UNCTAD

Address: Palais des Nations, 1211 Geneva 10, Switzerland.
Telephone: (22) 917-5809; **fax:** (22) 917-0051; **e-mail:** info@unctad.org; **internet:** www.unctad.org.

UNCTAD was established in December 1964. It is the principal instrument of the UN General Assembly concerned with trade and development, and is the focal point within the UN system for integrated activities relating to trade, finance, technology, investment and sustainable development. It aims to maximize the trade and development opportunities of developing countries, in particular least-developed countries, and to assist them to adapt to the increasing globalization and liberalization of the world economy.

Organization

(March 2005)

CONFERENCE

The Conference is the organization's highest policy-making body and normally meets every four years at ministerial level in order to formulate major policy guide-lines and to decide on UNCTAD's forthcoming programme of work. The 11th session was held in São Paulo, Brazil, in June 2004. As well as its 191 members, many intergovernmental and non-governmental organizations (NGOs) participate in UNCTAD's work as observers.

TRADE AND DEVELOPMENT BOARD

The Trade and Development Board is the executive body of UNCTAD. It comprises elected representatives from 146 UNCTAD member states and is responsible for ensuring the overall consistency of UNCTAD's activities, as well as those of its subsidiary bodies. The Board meets for a regular annual session lasting about 10 days, at which it examines global economic issues. It may also meet a further three times a year in order to address management or institutional matters.

COMMISSIONS

The Trade and Development Board has three Commissions: the Commission on Trade in Goods and Services and Commodities; the Commission on Investment, Technology and Related Financial Issues; and the Commission on Enterprise, Business Facilitation and Development. The Commissions meet once a year in regular session and may convene up to 10 Expert Meetings a year on specific issues.

SECRETARIAT

The secretariat comprises the following Divisions: Globalization and Development Strategies; International Trade in Goods and Services and Commodities; Investment, Technology and Enterprise Development; Services Infrastructure for Development and Trade Efficiency. It also incorporates the Office of the Special Co-ordinator for Least Developed, Land-locked, and Small Island Developing States.

The UNCTAD secretariat, comprising some 400 staff, undertakes policy analysis; monitoring, implementation and follow-up of decisions of intergovernmental bodies; technical co-operation in support of UNCTAD's policy objectives; and information exchanges and consultations of various types.

Officer-in-Charge: CARLOS FORTIN (Chile).

Activities

In February 2000 the 10th session of the Conference, held in Bangkok, Thailand, adopted the Bangkok Declaration, which stated the importance of promoting equitable and sustainable development in view of increasing global interdependence, trade liberalization and advances in technology. The Declaration emphasized UNCTAD's commitment to a fair, non-discriminatory and fully-integrated multilateral trading system that would not tolerate the marginalization of the world's least developed economies, and urged that the next round of multilateral trade negotiations address development issues. The Declaration noted the need for increased policy coherence at national and international level, and for more effective co-operation and co-ordination among multilateral institutions. It recommended open debate on global development issues by all development partners, including the private sector, NGOs, academics and politicians. The Conference also adopted a Plan of Action which assessed the consequences of globalization for development, recommended measures to be implemented by the international community, and provided a strategic framework for UNCTAD's future work programme. The 11th session of the Conference was convened in São Paulo, Brazil, in June 2004, on the theme of 'Enhancing coherence between national development strategies and global economic processes towards economic growth and development'.

INTERNATIONAL TRADE

During the 1980s UNCTAD focused on its role of providing a forum for the negotiation of international agreements on commodities, including cocoa, jute, rubber and tropical timber. (Such agreements are designed to ensure the stabilization of conditions in the trade of the commodities concerned.) UNCTAD's monitoring and facilitation of international commodity agreements has subsequently continued. The establishment of the Common Fund for Commodities (see p. 370) was agreed by UNCTAD in 1980, and the Fund came into operation in September 1989. More recently UNCTAD has been concerned to assist countries to adopt risk management and financial strategies against commodity dependence and price fluctuation, and to encourage diversification to reduce dependence on single commodities. Under the Bangkok agreements, UNCTAD was committed to improve market transparency and the availability of information, in particular through the improved use of technology.

Since the 1970s UNCTAD has been actively involved in work relating to restrictive business practices. In 1980 the UN General Assembly adopted a set of mutually agreed equitable principles and rules for the control of restrictive business practices, which had been negotiated under UNCTAD auspices. An Intergovernmental Group of Experts monitors and reviews its implementation. UNCTAD provides technical assistance to developing countries in the formulation and enforcement of competition legislation and consumer protection law and policies. It is also responsible for reviewing the developmental impact of international agreements on competition law. Through its Programme on Dispute Settlements UNCTAD provides training on aspects of settlement in international trade, investment and intellectual property disputes. UNCTAD has established a Commercial Diplomacy Programme to provide training and capacity-building to strengthen the participation and effectiveness of developing member countries in international and regional trade negotiations.

During the 1990s UNCTAD undertook research into the design and implementation of a multilateral system to trade emissions of so-called greenhouse gases. UNCTAD's Carbon Market Programme analyses the impact of measures to address climate change through the reduction of greenhouse gas emissions and works to promote a fair and effective global carbon market. In June 1997, in co-operation with the Earth Council, UNCTAD established a Greenhouse Gas Emissions Trading Policy Forum to support the development of a plurilateral emissions market. In June 1999 the International Emissions Trading Association (IETA) was established, sponsored by UNCTAD and the Earth Council. The IETA, which was envisaged as a successor to the Forum, comprised commercial companies, business organizations and regional and national trading associations, as well as invited international organizations, research institutes and NGOs. It was to serve as a forum for the exchange of information and ideas relating to international emissions trading and as a means of developing the market in emission permit trading, which was scheduled to be launched in 2008. During the initial phase of the IETA's operations UNCTAD provided temporary secretariat support.

UNCTAD is responsible for the Generalized System of Preferences (GSP), initiated in 1971, whereby a proportion of both agricultural and manufactured goods that are exported by developing countries receive preferential tariff treatment by certain developed countries, Russia and several central European countries. UNCTAD monitors changes in and amendments to national GSP schemes and reviews the use of these schemes by beneficiary developing countries. In addition, the Commission on Trade in Goods and Services and Commodities (see above) is responsible for providing a forum to examine the operation of schemes, the benefits they offer and the future role of the GSP. In March 2001 the European Union introduced a new initiative, the so-called Everything but Arms scheme, to amend the GSP regime in member countries to provide free market access to all products from LDCs (see below), except arms and munitions, and with special provisions for rice, sugar and bananas. UNCTAD's database of trade control measures has been made available through a Trade Analysis and Information System (TRAINS). A Trade Analysis Branch was established in 1999 to improve the understanding of current and emerging issues in international trade of concern to developing countries.

In 1996 UNCTAD launched a BIOTRADE Initiative to stimulate trade and investment in biological resources, as a basis for equitable, sustainable development. Under the Initiative UNCTAD has established partnerships with national and regional organizations, using their local knowledge and expertise to develop and implement biodiversity programmes. The Initiative also supports the development of appropriate policies and legislation to support the sustainable trade and investment in biodiversity, i.e. to address issues such as benefit sharing, intellectual property rights and poverty alleviation. In 2002 UNCTAD and the International Trade Centre jointly launched a BioTrade Facilitation Programme, which aimed to promote the trade in biodiversity products and services through arrangements that would enhance sustainable bio-resources management, product development, value-adding processing and marketing.

INVESTMENT, TECHNOLOGY AND ENTERPRISE DEVELOPMENT

UNCTAD has been mandated as the organ within the UN system responsible for negotiating a multilateral framework governing direct foreign investment that would protect the interests of the poorest countries, taking account of the work already undertaken by OECD in this area. In UNCTAD's revised approach, encouragement of foreign direct investment and of domestic private enterprise in developing countries and countries in transition have become central to the agency's work. UNCTAD is increasingly seeking the input and participation of non-governmental groups, such as academics, NGOs and business representatives, in its intergovernmental machinery, where appropriate. UNCTAD's Division of Investment, Technology and Enterprise Development organizes regional meetings, technical symposia and training courses in aspects of international investment agreements. It also conducts Investment Policy Reviews to assess and promote a country's investment potential. Within the Division the Advisory Service on Investment and Training (ASIT) executes the technical assistance programme for investment promotion strategies. UNCTAD'S Commission on Investment, Technology and Related Financial Issues undertakes the functions of the former ECOSOC Commission on International Investment and Transnational Corporations, which aimed to provide an understanding of the nature of foreign direct investment and transnational corporations, to secure effective international agreements and to strengthen the capacity of developing countries in their dealings with transnational corporations through an integrated approach, including research, information and technical assistance. A subsidiary body—the Intergovernmental Group of Experts on International Standards of Accounting and Reporting—aimed to improve the availability of information disclosed by transnational corporations. In November 1997 the UN General Assembly endorsed a proposal of the UN Secretary-General that the Group report directly through the UNCTAD Commission on Investment, Technology and Related Financial Issues.

The Commission on Enterprise, Business Facilitation and Development advises countries on policy-related issues and training activities concerning the development of entrepreneurship. It facilitates the exchange of experiences on the formulation and implementation of enterprise development strategies, including privatization, public-sector co-operation and the special problems relating to enterprise development in countries in economic transition. Since 1996 UNCTAD has administered Empretec, initially started as a pilot programme in 1988, which undertakes capacity-building activities to develop institutional structures supportive of enterprise and small business ventures. The programme also aims to foster business links with other transnational corporations.

Since May 1993 UNCTAD has serviced the ECOSOC Commission on Science and Technology for Development, which provides a forum for discussion of the following issues relating to science and technology for development: technology for small-scale economic activities to address the basic needs of low-income countries; gender implications of science and technology for developing countries; science and technology and the environment; the contribution of technologies to industrialization in developing countries; and the role of information technologies, in particular in relation to developing countries. The Commission meets every two years.

SERVICES INFRASTRUCTURE

Activities to enhance transport and trade logistics constitute an important component of UNCTAD's efforts to improve the participation of developing countries in international trade. It convenes expert meetings, extends technical support and organizes specialized training activities. In March 1999, at a diplomatic conference held under the auspices of UNCTAD and the International Maritime Organization (IMO), an International Convention on the Arrest of Ships was adopted. Other initiatives have resulted in the adoption of the UN Convention on the Carriage of Goods by Sea (Hamburg Rules—1978), the UN Convention on International Multimodal Transport (1980), the UN Convention on a Code of Conduct for Liner Conferences (effective from 1983), the UN Convention on Conditions for Registration of Ships (1986), and the International Convention on Maritime Liens and Mortgages. UNCTAD administers a Port Training Programme, as part of its TrainforTrade initiative, which emphasizes the need for human resources and capacity-building activities to support trading efforts by developing countries. UNCTAD promotes the use of e-commerce as a means of development. It publishes an annual *E-Commerce and Development Report* which analyses issues that influence the expansion of e-commerce in developing countries and identifies means of promoting its use in order to support economic and social development. UNCTAD organized a meeting on e-finance at the UN International Conference on Financing for Development, which was held in Monterrey, Mexico, in March 2002. During the 1980s UNCTAD developed an Automated System for Customs Data (ASYCUDA), which by early 2005 was operational in more than 80 countries and regions. It serves as a customs management system, using international standards, covering essential trade procedures, such as customs declarations, accounting procedures and transit documentation. In March 2002 UNCTAD inaugurated a fully electronic version of ASYCUDA to enable transactions to be undertaken using the internet. A software package, Advance Cargo Information System (ACIS), enables shipping lines and railway companies to track the movement of cargo. Through the use of ACIS and ASYCUDA UNCTAD aims to enhance the effective exchange of information in order to counter customs fraud.

In November 2002 the Global Trade Point Network (GTPNet), which was launched by UNCTAD in 1994 as an electronic source of trade-related information for use by small and medium-sized enterprises, was transferred to the World Trade Point Federation, an organization established by UNCTAD in 2000 to represent the programme's beneficiaries and to maintain the network of trade points.

LEAST DEVELOPED COUNTRIES

UNCTAD aims to give particular attention to the needs of the world's 49 least developed countries (LDCs—as defined by the UN). The eighth session of the Conference requested that detailed analyses of the socio-economic situations and domestic policies of the LDCs, their resource needs, and external factors affecting their economies be undertaken as part of UNCTAD's work programme. The ninth session determined that particular attention be given to the problems of the LDCs in all areas of UNCTAD's work. The 10th session focused on the impact of globalization on developing economies and on means of improving trade opportunities for the LDCs. UNCTAD served as the secretariat for the Third UN Conference on the Least Developed Countries, which took place in Brussels, Belgium, in May 2001. The Conference, which was attended by more than 6,500 participants from governments, NGOs and other elements of civil society, considered issues including governance, peace and social stability, enhancing productive capacities, intellectual property and development, infrastructure development, and financing growth and development. A Programme of Action for 2001–10, which had been elaborated by LDCs and their development partners, was adopted by the Conference. UNCTAD was to support its implementation, with particular emphasis on the needs of landlocked and small island developing states.

GLOBALIZATION AND DEVELOPMENT

UNCTAD works to promote policies and strategies at national and international level in support of development, and analyses issues, such as financial crises, to support sustainable economic management. It contributed to the implementation and review of the UN New Agenda for the Development of Africa in the 1990s (UNNADF). UNCTAD provides assistance to developing countries in the area of debt-management, and in seeking debt relief from their creditors.

UNCTAD is responsible for the software component of a joint programme with the World Bank to extend technical co-operation to developing countries in the field of debt management. The assistance is based on the development and distribution of software (the Debt Management and Financial Analysis System—DMFAS) designed to enable debtor countries to analyse data, make projections, and to plan strategies for debt repayment and reorganization. In early 2005 the programme was operational in 62 countries. UNCTAD provides training for operators in the use of the software, and for senior officials, to increase their awareness of institutional reforms which might be necessary for effective debt management. In 1995 UNCTAD initiated a programme of technical assistance to support the Palestinian people, within the context of involvement with Palestinian economy which had begun in 1979 with a study of the economic situation in the occupied territories.

The Secretariat provided technical assistance to developing countries in connection with the Uruguay Round of multilateral trade negotiations (see World Trade Organization—WTO). The International Trade Centre in Geneva is operated jointly by WTO and UNCTAD. In February 2002 UNCTAD initiated a new capacity-building and technical assistance programme to help developing countries in trade negotiations resulting from the WTO meeting held in Doha, Qatar, in November 2001.

Finance

The operational expenses of UNCTAD are borne by the regular budget of the UN, and amount to approximately US $50m. annually. Technical co-operation activities, financed from extra-budgetary resources, amount to some $25m. annually.

Publications

E-commerce and Development Report (annually).
Least Developed Countries Report (annually).
Monthly Commodity Price Bulletin.
Review of Maritime Transport (annually).
Trade and Development Report (annually).
Transnational Corporations (3 a year).
UNCTAD Commodity Yearbook.
UNCTAD Handbook of Statistics (annually, also available on CD-Rom).
UNCTAD News (3 a year).
World Commodity Survey.
World Investment Report (annually).

United Nations Development Programme—UNDP

Address: One United Nations Plaza, New York, NY 10017, USA.
Telephone: (212) 906-5295; **fax:** (212) 906-5364; **e-mail:** hq@undp.org; **internet:** www.undp.org.

The Programme was established in 1965 by the UN General Assembly. Its central mission is to help countries to eradicate poverty and achieve a sustainable level of human development, an approach to economic growth that encompasses individual well-being and choice, equitable distribution of the benefits of development, and conservation of the environment. UNDP advocates for a more inclusive global economy. UNDP is the focus of UN efforts to achieve the Millennium Development Goals (see below).

Organization

(March 2005)

UNDP is responsible to the UN General Assembly, to which it reports through ECOSOC.

EXECUTIVE BOARD

The Executive Board is responsible for providing intergovernmental support to, and supervision of, the activities of UNDP and the UN Population Fund (UNFPA). It comprises 36 members: eight from Africa, seven from Asia and the Pacific, four from eastern Europe, five from Latin America and the Caribbean and 12 from western Europe and other countries. Members serve a three-year term.

SECRETARIAT

Offices and divisions at the Secretariat include: an Operations Support Group; Offices of the United Nations Development Group, the Human Development Report, Development Studies, Audit and Performance Review, Evaluation, and Communications; and Bureaux for Crisis Prevention and Recovery, Resources and Strategic Partnerships, Development Policy, and Management. Five regional bureaux, all headed by an assistant administrator, cover: Africa; Asia and the Pacific; the Arab states; Latin America and the Caribbean; and Europe and the Commonwealth of Independent States.

Administrator: KEMAL DERVIŞ (Turkey) (designate).
Associate Administrator: Dr ZÉPHIRIN DIABRÉ (Burkina Faso).

COUNTRY OFFICES

In almost every country receiving UNDP assistance there is an office, headed by the UNDP Resident Representative, who usually also serves as UN Resident Co-ordinator, responsible for the co-ordination of all UN technical assistance and operational development activities, advising the Government on formulating the country programme, ensuring that field activities are undertaken, and acting as the leader of the UN team of experts working in the country. The offices function as the primary presence of the UN in most developing countries.

Activities

UNDP provides advisory and support services to governments and UN teams with the aim of advancing sustainable human development and building national development capabilities. Assistance is mostly non-monetary, comprising the provision of experts' services, consultancies, equipment and training for local workers. Developing countries themselves contribute significantly to the total project costs in terms of personnel, facilities, equipment and supplies. UNDP also supports programme countries in attracting aid and utilizing it efficiently. A network of nine Sub-regional Resource Facilities (SURFs) has been established to strengthen and co-ordinate UNDP's role as a global knowledge provider and channel for sharing knowledge and experience.

During the late 1990s UNDP undertook an extensive internal process of reform, 'UNDP 2001', which placed increased emphasis on its activities in the field and on performance and accountability. In 2001 UNDP established a series of Thematic Trust Funds to enable increased support of priority programme activities. In accordance with the more results-oriented approach developed under the 'UNDP 2001' process UNDP introduced a new Multi-Year Funding Framework (MYFF), which outlined the country-driven goals around which funding was to be mobilized, integrating programme objectives, resources, budget and outcomes. The MYFF was to provide the basis for the Administrator's Business Plans for the same duration and enables policy coherence in the implementation of programmes at country, regional and global levels. A Results-Oriented Annual Report (ROAR) was produced for the first time in 2000 from data compiled by country offices and regional programmes. In September 2000 the first ever Ministerial Meeting of ministers of development co-operation and foreign affairs and other senior officials from donor and programme countries, convened in New York, USA, endorsed UNDP's shift to a results-based orientation.

In accordance with the second phase of the MYFF, covering 2004–07, UNDP was to focus on the following five practice areas: democratic governance; poverty reduction; energy and the environment; crisis prevention and recovery; and combating HIV/AIDS. Other important 'cross-cutting' themes, to be incorporated throughout the programme areas, included gender equality, information and communication technologies, and human rights.

From the mid-1990s UNDP also assumed a more active and integrative role within the UN system-wide development framework. UNDP Resident Representatives—usually also serving as UN Resident Co-ordinators, with responsibility for managing inter-agency co-operation on sustainable human development initiatives at country level—were to play a focal role in implementing this approach. In order to promote its co-ordinating function UNDP allocated increased resources to training and skill-sharing programmes. In 1997 the UNDP Administrator was appointed to chair the UN Development Group (UNDG), which was established as part of a series of structural reform measures initiated by the UN Secretary-General, with the aim of strengthening collaboration between all UN funds, programmes and bodies concerned with development. The UNDG promotes coherent policy at country level through the system of UN Resident Co-ordinators (see above), the Common Country Assessment mechanism (CCA, a country-based process for evaluating national development situations), and the UN Development Assistance Framework (UNDAF, the foundation for planning and co-ordinating development operations at country level, based on the CCA). Within the framework of the Administrator's Business Plans for 2000–03 a new Bureau for Resources and Strategic Partnerships was established to build and strengthen working partnerships with other UN bodies, donor and programme countries, international financial institutions and development banks, civil society organizations and the private sector. The Bureau was also to serve UNDP's regional bureaux and country offices through the exchange of information and promotion of partnership strategies.

MILLENNIUM DEVELOPMENT GOALS

UNDP, through its leadership of the UNDG and management of the Resident Co-ordinator system, has a co-ordinating function as the focus of UN system-wide efforts to achieve the so-called Millennium Development Goals (MDGs), pledged by 189 governments attending a summit meeting of the UN General Assembly in September 2000. The objectives were to establish a defined agenda to reduce poverty and improve the quality of lives of millions of people and to serve as a framework for measuring development. There are eight MDGs, as follows, for which one or more specific targets have been identified:

i) to eradicate extreme poverty and hunger, with the aim of reducing by 50% the number of people with an income of less than US \$1 a day and those suffering from hunger by 2015;

ii) to achieve universal primary education by 2015;

iii) to promote gender equality and empower women, in particular to eliminate gender disparities in primary and secondary education by 2005 and at all levels by 2015;

iv) to reduce child mortality, with a target reduction of two-thirds in the mortality rate among children under five by 2015;

v) to improve maternal health, and specifically to reduce by 75% the numbers of women dying in childbirth;

vi) to combat HIV/AIDS, malaria and other diseases;

vii) to ensure environmental sustainability, including targets to integrate the principles of sustainable development into country policies and programmes, to reduce by 50% the number of people without access to safe drinking water by 2015, to achieve significant improvement in the lives of at least 100m. slum dwellers by 2020;

viii) to develop a global partnership for development, including efforts to deal with international debt, to address the needs of least developed countries and landlocked and small island developing states, to develop decent and productive youth employment, to provide access to affordable, essential drugs in developing countries, and to make available the benefits of new technologies.

UNDP plays a leading role in efforts to integrate the MDGs into all aspects of UN activities at country level and to ensure the MDGs are incorporated into national development strategies. The Programme supports reporting by countries, as well as regions and sub-regions, on progress towards achievement of the goals, and on specific social, economic and environmental indicators, through the formulation of MDG reports. These form the basis of a global report, issued annually by the UN Secretary-General since mid-2002. UNDP provides administrative and technical support to the Millennium Project, an independent advisory body established by the UN Secretary-General in 2002 to develop a practical action plan to achieve the MDGs. Financial support of the Project is channelled through a Millennium Trust Fund, administered by UNDP. In January 2005 the Millennium Project presented its report, based on extensive research conducted by teams of experts, which included recommendations for the international system to support country level development efforts and identified a series of Quick Wins to bring conclusive benefit to millions of people in the short-term. UNDP also works to raise awareness of the MDGs and to support advocacy efforts at all levels, for example through regional publicity campaigns, target-specific publications and support for the Millennium Campaign to generate support for the goals in developing and developed countries.

DEMOCRATIC GOVERNANCE

UNDP supports national efforts to ensure efficient and accountable governance, improve the quality of democratic processes, and to build effective relations between the state, the private sector and civil society, which are essential to achieving sustainable development. As in other practice areas, UNDP assistance includes policy advice and technical support, capacity-building of institutions and individuals, advocacy and public information and communication, the promotion and brokering of dialogue, and knowledge networking and sharing of good practices. In March 2002 a UNDP Governance Centre was inaugurated in Oslo, Norway, to enhance the role of UNDP in support of democratic governance and to assist countries to implement democratic reforms in order to achieve the MDGs.

UNDP works to strengthen parliaments and other legislative bodies as institutions of democratic participation. It assists with constitutional reviews and reform, training of parliamentary staff, and capacity-building of political parties and civil organizations as part of this objective. UNDP undertakes missions to help prepare for and ensure the conduct of free and fair elections. Increasingly, UNDP is also focused on building the long-term capacity of electoral institutions and practices within a country, for example voter registration, election observation, the establishment of electoral commissions, and voter and civic education projects. Similarly, UNDP aims to ensure an efficient, independent and fair judicial system is available to all, in particular the poor and disadvantaged. Within its justice sector programme UNDP undertakes a variety of projects to improve access to justice. UNDP also works to promote access to information, the integration of human rights issues into activities concerned with sustainable human development, as well as support for the international human rights system.

Since 1997 UNDP has been mandated to assist developing countries to fight corruption and improve accountability, transparency and integrity (ATI). It has worked to establish national and international partnerships in support of its anti-corruption efforts and used its role as a broker of knowledge and experience to uphold ATI principles at all levels of public financial management and governance. UNDP publishes case studies of its anti-corruption efforts and assists governments to conduct self-assessments of their public financial management systems.

Within the democratic governance practice area UNDP supports more than 300 projects at international, country and city levels designed to improve conditions for the urban poor, in particular through improvement in urban governance. The Local Initiative Facility for Urban Environment (LIFE) undertakes small-scale projects in low-income communities, in collaboration with local authorities, the private sector and community-based groups, and promotes a participatory approach to local governance. UNDP also works closely with the UN Capital Development Fund to implement projects in support of decentralized governance, which it has recognized as a key element to achieving sustainable development goals.

UNDP aims to ensure that, rather than creating an ever-widening 'digital divide', ongoing rapid advancements in information technology are harnessed by poorer countries to accelerate progress in achieving sustainable human development. UNDP advises governments on technology policy, promotes digital entrepreneurship in programme countries and works with private-sector partners to provide reliable and affordable communications networks. The Bureau for Development Policy operates the Information and Communication Technologies for Development Programme, which aims to promote sustainable human development through increased utilization of information and communications technologies globally. The Programme aims to establish technology access centres in developing countries. A Sustainable Development Networking Programme focuses on expanding internet connectivity in poorer countries through building national capacities and supporting local internet sites. UNDP has used mobile internet units to train people even in isolated rural areas. In 1999 UNDP, in collaboration with an international communications company, Cisco Systems, and other partners, launched NetAid, an internet-based forum (accessible at www.netaid.org) for mobilizing and co-ordinating fundraising and other activities aimed at alleviating poverty and promoting sustainable human development in the developing world. With Cisco Systems and other partners, UNDP has worked to establish academies of information technology to support training and capacity-building in developing countries. By September 2003 88 academies had been established. UNDP and the World Bank jointly host the secretariat of the Digital Opportunity Task Force, a partnership between industrialized and developing countries, business and non-governmental organizations that was established in 2000. UNDP is a partner in the Global Digital Technology Initiative, launched in 2002 to strengthen the role of information and communications technologies in achieving the development goals of developing countries. In January 2004 UNDP and Microsoft Corporation announced an agreement to develop jointly information and communication technology (ICT) projects aimed at assisting developing countries to achieve the MDGs.

POVERTY REDUCTION

UNDP's activities to facilitate poverty eradication include support for capacity-building programmes and initiatives to generate sustainable livelihoods, for example by improving access to credit, land and technologies, and the promotion of strategies to improve education and health provision for the poorest elements of populations (with a focus on women and girls). UNDP aims to help governments to reassess their development priorities and to design initiatives for sustainable human development. In 1996, following the World Summit for Social Development, which was held in Copenhagen, Denmark, in March 1995, UNDP launched the Poverty Strategies Initiative (PSI) to strengthen national capacities to assess and monitor the extent of poverty and to combat the problem. All PSI projects were to involve representatives of governments, the private sector, social organizations and research institutions in policy debate and formulation. Following the introduction, in 1999, by the World Bank and IMF of Poverty Reduction Strategy Papers (PRSPs), UNDP has tended to direct its efforts to helping governments draft these documents, and, since 2001, has focused on linking the papers to efforts to achieve and monitoring progress towards the MDGs. In early 2004 UNDP inaugurated the International Poverty Centre, in Brasilia, Brazil, which aimed to foster the capacity of countries to formulate and implement poverty reduction strategies and to encourage South-South co-operation in all relevant areas of research and decision-making. In particular, the Centre aimed to assist countries to meet Millennium goals and targets through the research and implementation of pro-poor growth policies and social protection and human development strategies, and the monitoring of poverty and inequality.

UNDP country offices support the formulation of national human development reports (NHDRs), which aim to facilitate activities such as policy-making, the allocation of resources and monitoring progress towards poverty eradication and sustainable development. In addition, the preparation of Advisory Notes and Country Co-operation Frameworks by UNDP officials helps to highlight country-specific aspects of poverty eradication and national strategic priorities. In January 1998 the Executive Board adopted eight guiding principles relating to sustainable human development that were to be implemented by all country offices, in order to ensure a focus to UNDP activities. Since 1990 UNDP has published an annual *Human Development Report*, incorporating a Human Development Index, which ranks countries in terms of human development, using three key indicators: life expectancy, adult literacy and basic income required for a decent standard of living. In 1997 a Human Poverty Index and a Gender-related Development Index, which assesses gender equality on the basis of life expectancy, education and income, were introduced into the Report for the first time. In 1997 a UNDP scheme to support private-sector and community-based initiatives to generate employment opportunities, MicroStart, became operational.

In 1996 UNDP initiated a process of collaboration between city authorities world-wide to promote implementation of the commitments made at the 1995 Copenhagen summit for social development and to help to combat aspects of poverty and other urban problems, such as poor housing, transport, the management of waste disposal, water supply and sanitation. The so-called World Alliance of Cities Against Poverty was formally launched in October 1997, in the context of the International Decade for the Eradication of Poverty. The first Forum of the Alliance was convened in October 1998, in Lyon, France; it has subsequently been held every two years.

UNDP sponsors the International Day for the Eradication of Poverty, held annually on 17 October.

ENERGY AND THE ENVIRONMENT

UNDP plays a role in developing the agenda for international co-operation on environmental and energy issues, focusing on the relationship between energy policies, environmental protection, poverty and development. UNDP promotes the development of national capacities and other strategies that support sustainable development practices, for example through the formulation and implementation of Poverty Reduction Strategies and National Strategies for Sustainable Development. UNDP works to ensure the effective governance of freshwater and aquatic resources, and promotes co-operation in transboundary water management. It works closely with other agencies to promote safe sanitation, ocean and coastal management, and community water supplies. Another priority area of UNDP's Energy and Environment Practice is to promote clean energy technologies (through the Clean Development Mechanism) and to extend access to sustainable energy services, including the introduction of renewable alternatives to conventional fuels, as well as access to investment financing for sustainable energy.

UNDP recognizes that desertification and land degradation is a major cause of rural poverty and promotes sustainable land management, drought preparedness and reform of land tenure as means of addressing the problem. It also aims to reduce poverty caused by land degradation through implementation of environmental conventions at a national and international level. In 2002 UNDP inaugurated an Integrated Drylands Development Programme which aimed to ensure that the needs of people living in drylands are met and considered at a local and national level. By 2004 the programme was being implemented, by the Drylands Development

Centre, in 19 African and West Asian countries. UNDP is also concerned with sustainable management of forestries, fisheries and agriculture. Its Biodiversity Global Programme assists developing countries and communities to integrate issues relating to sustainable practices and biodiversity into national and global practices. Since 1992 UNDP has administered a Small Grants Programme, funded by the Global Environment Facility, to support community-based initiatives concerned with biodiversity conservation, prevention of land degradation and the elimination of persistent organic pollutants. The Equator Initiative was inaugurated in 2002 as a partnership between UNDP, representatives of governments, civil society and businesses, with the aim of reducing poverty in communities along the equatorial belt by fostering local partnerships, harnessing local knowledge and promoting conservation and sustainable practices.

CRISIS PREVENTION AND RECOVERY

UNDP collaborates with other UN agencies in countries in crisis and with special circumstances to promote relief and development efforts, in order to secure the foundations for sustainable human development and thereby increase national capabilities to prevent or pre-empt future crises. In particular, UNDP is concerned to achieve reconciliation, reintegration and reconstruction in affected countries, as well as to support emergency interventions and management and delivery of programme aid. Special development initiatives include the demobilization of former combatants and destruction of illicit small armaments, rehabilitation of communities for the sustainable reintegration of returning populations and the restoration and strengthening of democratic institutions. UNDP is seeking to incorporate conflict prevention into its development strategies. The Conflict-related Development Analysis (CDA), building upon conflict assessment activities undertaken during 2001–02 in countries including Guatemala, Guinea-Bissau, Nepal, Nigeria and Tajikistan, is being developed as a tool for country offices to use in formulating and analyzing programmes in conflict zones. UNDP has established a mine action unit within its Bureau for Crisis Prevention and Recovery in order to strengthen national de-mining capabilities including surveying, mapping and clearance of anti-personnel landmines. UNDP also works closely with UNICEF to raise mine awareness and implement risk reduction education programmes.

UNDP is the focal point within the UN system for strengthening national capacities for natural disaster reduction (prevention, preparedness and mitigation relating to natural, environmental and technological hazards). UNDP's Bureau of Crisis Prevention and Recovery oversees the system-wide Disaster Management Training Programme, which was established in 1991. By the end of 2004 the Programme had conducted more than 70 workshops benefiting some 6,000 participants. In February 2004 UNDP introduced a Disaster Risk Index that enabled vulnerability and risk to be measured and compared between countries and demonstrated the correspondence between human development and death rates following natural disasters. UNDP was actively involved in preparations for the second World Conference on Disaster Reduction which was held in Kobe, Japan, in January 2005.

In late December 2004 UNDP's Disaster Reduction Unit responded immediately to the earthquake and subsequent large waves (tsunamis) that devastated many coastal regions in the Indian Ocean by contacting country officers, gathering information and dispatching emergency funds and teams of technical staff. The Unit aimed to ensure a smooth transition from relief activities to rehabilitation, and that risk reduction measures were integrated into all reconstruction and development plans. In January 2005 the UN Secretary-General launched a Flash Appeal for US $977m. to finance recovery and rehabilitation measures. Under the Appeal UNDP requested $22m. to establish an Emergency Capacity Building for Recovery and Reconstruction Planning Facility, specifically for countries in the South and South-East Asia region. UNDP was, additionally, to be allocated $60m. to provide shelter and basic services to some 40,000 displaced households in Aceh Province, Indonesia, $3m. to strengthen the capacity of local organizations in Indonesia to implement disaster recovery projects, and $2.5m. to create short-term income generation schemes for more than 2,000 families of fishermen.

In 2004 UNDP assisted mine action efforts in Azerbaijan, Tajikistan and Ukraine.

HIV/AIDS

UNDP regards the HIV/AIDS pandemic as a major challenge to development, and advocates for making HIV/AIDS a focus of national planning; supports decentralized action against HIV/AIDS at community level; helps to strengthen national capacities at all levels to combat the disease; and aims to link support for prevention activities, education and treatment with broader development planning and responses. UNDP places a particular focus on combating the spread of HIV/AIDS through the promotion of women's rights.

UNDP is a co-sponsor, jointly with WHO, the World Bank, UNICEF, UNESCO, UNODC, ILO, UNFPA, WFP and UNHCR, of the Joint UN Programme on HIV/AIDS (UNAIDS), which became operational on 1 January 1996. UNAIDS co-ordinates UNDP's HIV and Development Programme.

Finance

UNDP and its various funds and programmes are financed by the voluntary contributions of members of the United Nations and the Programme's participating agencies, as well as through cost-sharing by recipient governments and third-party donors. In 2004–05 total voluntary contributions were projected at US $3,500m., of which a projected $1,700m. constituted regular (core) resources and $1,807m. third-party co-financing and thematic trust fund income. Cost-sharing by programme country governments was projected at $2,100m., bringing total resources (both donor and local) to a projected $5,600m.

Publications

Annual Report of the Administrator.
Choices (quarterly).
Global Public Goods: International Co-operation in the 21st Century.
Human Development Report (annually, also available on CD-ROM).
Poverty Report (annually).
Results-Oriented Annual Report.

Associated Funds and Programmes

UNDP is the central funding, planning and co-ordinating body for technical co-operation within the UN system. A number of associated funds and programmes, financed separately by means of voluntary contributions, provide specific services through the UNDP network. UNDP manages a trust fund to promote economic and technical co-operation among developing countries.

CAPACITY 2015

UNDP initiated Capacity 2015 at the World Summit for Sustainable Development, which was held in August–September 2002. Capacity 2015 aims to support developing countries in expanding their capabilities to meet the Millennium Development Goals pledged by governments at a summit meeting of the UN General Assembly in September 2000.

GLOBAL ENVIRONMENT FACILITY (GEF)

The GEF, which is managed jointly by UNDP, the World Bank and UNEP, began operations in 1991 and was restructured in 1994. Its aim is to support projects concerning climate change, the conservation of biological diversity, the protection of international waters, reducing the depletion of the ozone layer in the atmosphere, and (since October 2002) arresting land degradation and addressing the issue of persistent organic pollutants. The GEF acts as the financial mechanism for the Convention on Biological Diversity and the UN Framework Convention on Climate Change. UNDP is responsible for capacity-building, targeted research, pre-investment activities and technical assistance. UNDP also administers the Small Grants Programme of the GEF, which supports community-based activities by local non-governmental organizations, and the Country Dialogue Workshop Programme, which promotes dialogue on national priorities with regard to the GEF. Some 32 donor countries pledged US $2,920m. for the third periodic replenishment of GEF funds (GEF-3), covering the period 2002–06. During 1991–2003 the GEF allocated $4,500m. in grants and raised $14,474m. in co-financing from other sources in support of more than 1,400 projects.

Chair. and CEO: Dr Leonard Good (Canada).

MONTREAL PROTOCOL

Through its Montreal Protocol Unit UNDP collaborates with public and private partners in developing countries to assist them in eliminating the use of ozone-depleting substances (ODS), in accordance with the Montreal Protocol to the Vienna Convention for the Protection of the Ozone Layer, through the design, monitoring and evaluation of ODS phase-out projects and programmes. In particular, UNDP provides technical assistance and training, national capacity-building and demonstration projects and technology transfer investment projects. By mid-2003, through the Executive Committee of the Montreal Protocol, UNDP had implemented pro-

jects and activities resulting in the elimination of 33,529 metric tons of ODS.

UNDP DRYLANDS DEVELOPMENT CENTRE (DDC)

The Centre, based in Nairobi, Kenya, was established in February 2002, superseding the former UN Office to Combat Desertification and Drought (UNSO). (UNSO had been established following the conclusion, in October 1994, of the UN Convention to Combat Desertification in Those Countries Experiencing Serious Drought and/or Desertification, Particularly in Africa; in turn, UNSO had replaced the former UN Sudano-Sahelian Office.) The DDC was to focus on the following areas: ensuring that national development planning takes account of the needs of dryland communities, particularly in poverty reduction strategies; helping countries to cope with the effects of climate variability, especially drought, and to prepare for future climate change; and addressing local issues affecting the utilization of resources.

Director: Philip Dobie (United Kingdom).

PROGRAMME OF ASSISTANCE TO THE PALESTINIAN PEOPLE (PAPP)

PAPP, established in 1978, is committed to strengthening newly-created institutions in the Israeli-occupied Territories and emerging Palestinian autonomous areas, to creating employment opportunities and to stimulating private and public investment in the area to enhance trade and export potential. Examples of PAPP activities include the following: construction of sewage collection networks and systems in the northern Gaza Strip; provision of water to 500,000 people in rural and urban areas of the West Bank and Gaza; construction of schools, youth and health centres; support to vegetable and fish traders through the construction of cold storage and packing facilities; and provision of loans to strengthen industry and commerce. In 2004 PAPP marked its 25th anniversary on the theme 'Partnership for the future'.

UNITED NATIONS CAPITAL DEVELOPMENT FUND (UNCDF)

The Fund was established in 1966 and became fully operational in 1974. It invests in poor communities in least-developed countries through local governance projects and microfinance operations, with the aim of increasing such communities' access to essential local infrastructure and services and thereby improving their productive capacities and self-reliance. UNDCF encourages participation by local people and local governments in the planning, implementation and monitoring of projects. The Fund aims to promote the interests of women in community projects and to enhance their earning capacities. In 1998 the Fund nominated 15 less-developed countries in which to concentrate subsequent programmes. A Special Unit for Microfinance (SUM), established in 1997 as a joint UNDP/UNCDF operation, was fully integrated into UNCDF in 1999. UNDCF/SUM helps to develop financial services for poor communities and supports UNDP's MicroStart initiative. In 2003 the UN Secretary-General designated UNCDF, with the UN Department of Economic and Social Affairs, as a co-ordinator of the International Year of Microcredit in 2005. UNCDF's annual programming budget amounts to some US $40m.

Officer-in-Charge: Henriette Keijzers.

UNITED NATIONS DEVELOPMENT FUND FOR WOMEN (UNIFEM)

UNIFEM is the UN's lead agency in addressing the issues relating to women in development and promoting the rights of women worldwide. The Fund provides direct financial and technical support to enable low-income women in developing countries to increase earnings, gain access to labour-saving technologies and otherwise improve the quality of their lives. It also funds activities that include women in decision-making related to mainstream development projects. In 2001 UNIFEM's Trust Fund in Support of Actions to Eliminate Violence Against Women (established in 1996) provided grants to 21 national and regional programmes. During 1996–2004 the Trust Fund awarded grants totalling US $8.3m. in support of 175 initiatives in 96 countries. UNIFEM has supported the preparation of national reports in 30 countries and used the priorities identified in these reports and in other regional initiatives to formulate a Women's Development Agenda for the 21st century. Through these efforts, UNIFEM played an active role in the preparation for the UN Fourth World Conference on Women, which was held in Beijing, People's Republic of China, in September 1995. UNIFEM participated at a special session of the General Assembly convened in June 2000 to review the conference, entitled Women 2000: Gender Equality, Development and Peace for the 21st Century (Beijing + 5). In March 2001 UNIFEM, in collaboration with International Alert, launched a Millennium Peace Prize for Women. UNIFEM maintains that the empowerment of women is a key to combating the HIV/AIDS pandemic, in view of the fact that women and adolescent girls are often culturally, biologically and economically more vulnerable to infection and more likely to bear responsibility for caring for the sick. In March 2002 UNIFEM launched a three-year programme aimed at making the gender and human rights dimensions of the pandemic central to policy-making in ten countries. A new online resource (www.genderandaids.org) on the gender dimensions of HIV/AIDS was launched in February 2003. UNIFEM was a co-founder of WomenWatch (accessible online at www.un.org/womenwatch), a UN system-wide resource for the advancement of gender equality. Following the massive earthquake and tsunamis that struck parts of the Indian Ocean in late December 2004, UNIFEM undertook to promote the needs and rights of women and girls in all emergency relief and reconstruction efforts, in particular in Indonesia, Sri Lanka and Somalia, and supported capacity-building of grass-roots organizations. Programme expenditure in 2003 totalled $27.0m.

Director: NOELEEN HEYZER (Singapore), Headquarters: 304 East 45th St, 15th Floor, New York, NY 10017, USA; tel. (212) 906-6400; fax (212) 906-6705; e-mail unifem@undp.org; internet www.unifem .org.

UNITED NATIONS VOLUNTEERS (UNV)

The United Nations Volunteers is an important source of middle-level skills for the UN development system supplied at modest cost, particularly in the least-developed countries. Volunteers expand the scope of UNDP project activities by supplementing the work of international and host-country experts and by extending the influence of projects to local community levels. UNV also supports technical co-operation within and among the developing countries by encouraging volunteers from the countries themselves and by forming regional exchange teams comprising such volunteers. UNV is involved in areas such as peace-building, elections, human rights, humanitarian relief and community-based environmental programmes, in addition to development activities.

The UN International Short-term Advisory (UNISTAR) Programme, which is the private-sector development arm of UNV, has increasingly focused its attention on countries in the process of economic transition. Since 1994 UNV has administered UNDP's Transfer of Knowledge Through Expatriate Nationals (TOKTEN) programme, which was initiated in 1977 to enable specialists and professionals from developing countries to contribute to development efforts in their countries of origin through short-term technical assignments.

At the end of March 2005 4,884 UNVs were serving in 135 countries. At that time the total number of people who had served under the initiative amounted to more than 30,000 in some 140 countries.

Executive Co-ordinator: AD DE RAAD (Netherlands), Headquarters: POB 260111, 53153 Bonn, Germany; tel. (228) 8152000; fax (228) 8152001; e-mail information@unvolunteers.org; internet www .unv.org.

United Nations Environment Programme—UNEP

Address: POB 30552, Nairobi, Kenya.

Telephone: (20) 621234; **fax:** (20) 624489; **e-mail:** cpiinfo@unep .org; **internet:** www.unep.org.

The United Nations Environment Programme was established in 1972 by the UN General Assembly, following recommendations of the 1972 UN Conference on the Human Environment, in Stockholm, Sweden, to encourage international co-operation in matters relating to the human environment.

Organization

(March 2005)

GOVERNING COUNCIL

The main functions of the Governing Council, which meets every two years, are to promote international co-operation in the field of the environment and to provide general policy guidance for the direction and co-ordination of environmental programmes within the UN system. It comprises representatives of 58 states, elected by the UN General Assembly, for four-year terms, on a regional basis. The Council is assisted in its work by a Committee of Permanent Representatives.

HIGH-LEVEL COMMITTEE OF MINISTERS AND OFFICIALS IN CHARGE OF THE ENVIRONMENT

The Committee was established by the Governing Council in 1997, with a mandate to consider the international environmental agenda and to make recommendations to the Council on reform and policy issues. In addition, the Committee, comprising 36 elected members, was to provide guidance and advice to the Executive Director, to enhance UNEP's collaboration and co-operation with other multilateral bodies and to help to mobilize financial resources for UNEP.

SECRETARIAT

Offices and divisions at UNEP headquarters include the Office of the Executive Director; the Secretariat for Governing Bodies: Offices for Evaluation and Oversight, Programme Co-ordination and Management, and Resource Mobilization; and divisions of communications and public information, early warning and assessment, policy development and law, policy implementation, technology and industry and economics, regional co-operation and representation, environmental conventions, and Global Environment Facility co-ordination.

Executive Director: Dr KLAUS TÖPFER (Germany).

REGIONAL OFFICES

Africa: POB 30552, Nairobi, Kenya; tel. (20) 624292; fax (20) 623928; internet www.unep.org/roa.

Asia and the Pacific: UN Bldg, 10th Floor, Rajdamnern Ave, Bangkok 10200, Thailand; tel. (2) 288-1870; fax (2) 280-3829; e-mail uneproap@un.org; internet www.roap.unep.org.

Europe: 11–13 chemin des Anémones, 1219 Châtelaine, Geneva, Switzerland; tel. (22) 9178279; fax (22) 9178024; e-mail roe@unep .ch; internet www.unep.ch/roe.

Latin America and the Caribbean: Blvd de los Virreyes 155, Lomas Virreyes, 11000 México, DF, Mexico; tel. (55) 52024841; fax (55) 52020950; e-mail registro@pnuma.org; internet www.pnuma .org.

North America: 1707 H St NW, Washington, DC 20006, USA; tel. (202) 785-0465; fax (202) 785-2096; e-mail uneprona@un.org; internet www.rona.unep.org.

West Asia: POB 10880, Manama, Bahrain; tel. 276072; fax 276075; e-mail uneprowa@unep.org.bh; internet www.unep.org.bh.

OTHER OFFICES

Convention on International Trade in Endangered Species of Wild Fauna and Flora—CITES: 15 chemin des Anémones, 1219 Châtelaine, Geneva, Switzerland; tel. (22) 9178139; fax (22) 7973417; e-mail cites@unep.ch; internet www.cites.org; Sec.-Gen. WILLEM WOUTER WIJNSTEKERS (Netherlands).

Global Programme of Action for the Protection of the Marine Environment from Land-based Activities: POB 16227, 2500 BE The Hague, Netherlands; tel. (70) 3114460; fax (70) 3456648; e-mail gpa@unep.nl; internet www.gpa.unep.org; Co-ordinator Dr VEERLE VANDEWEERD.

New York Office: DC-2 Bldg, Room 0803, 2 United Nations Plaza, New York, NY 10017, USA; tel. (212) 963-8210; fax (212) 963-7341; e-mail info@nyo.unep.org; internet www.nyo.unep.org.

Regional Co-ordinating Unit for East Asian Seas: UN Bldg, 10th Floor, Rajdamnern Ave, Bangkok 10200, Thailand; tel. (2) 288-1234; fax (2) 267-0808; e-mail kirkman.unescap@un.org; internet www.unep.org/water/regseas/easian/htm; Co-ordinator HUGH KIRKMAN.

Regional Co-ordinating Unit for the Caribbean Environment Programme: 14–20 Port Royal St, Kingston, Jamaica; tel. 9229267; fax 9229292; e-mail uneprcuja@cwjamaica.com; internet www.cep .unep.org; Co-ordinator NELSON ANDRADE COLMENARES.

Secretariat of the Basel Convention: CP 356, 13–15 chemin des Anémones, 1219 Châtelaine, Geneva, Switzerland; tel. (22) 9178218; fax (22) 7973454; e-mail sbc@unep.ch; internet www.basel.int; Exec. Sec. SACHIKO KUWABARA-YAMAMOTO.

Secretariat of the Multilateral Fund for the Implementation of the Montreal Protocol: 1800 McGill College Ave, 27th Floor, Montréal, QC, Canada H3A 3J6; tel. (514) 282-1122; fax (514) 282-

0068; e-mail secretariat@unmfs.org; internet www.multilateralfund
.org; Chief MARIA NOLAN (United Kingdom).

UNEP Addis Ababa Liaison Office: ECA New Building, 4th
Floor, No. 4NC4-4N13, POB 3001, Addis Ababa, Ethiopia; tel. (1)
443431; fax (1) 521633; e-mail unepoffice@uneca.org.

UNEP Arab League Liaison Office: POB 212, Cairo, Egypt; tel.
(2) 3361349; fax (2) 3370658.

**UNEP/CMS (Convention on the Conservation of Migratory
Species of Wild Animals) Secretariat:** Martin-Luther-King-Str.
8, 53175 Bonn, Germany; tel. (228) 8152402; fax (228) 8152449;
e-mail secretariat@cms.int; internet www.cms.int; Exec. Sec. ROBERT
HEPWORTH.

UNEP Chemicals: International Environment House, 11–13
chemin des Anémones, 1219 Châtelaine, Geneva, Switzerland; tel.
(22) 9178192; fax (22) 7973460; e-mail chemicals@unep.ch; internet
www.chem.unep.ch; Dir JAMES B. WILLIS.

**UNEP Co-ordinating Unit for the Mediterranean Action
Plan—MEDU:** Leoforos Vassileos Konstantinou 48, POB 18019,
11610 Athens, Greece; tel. (210) 7273100; fax (210) 7253196; e-mail
unepmedu@unepmap.gr; internet www.unepmap.org; Co-ordinator
PAUL MIFSUD.

UNEP Division of Technology, Industry and Economics: Tour
Mirabeau, 39–43, Quai André Citroën, 75739 Paris Cédex 15,
France; tel. 1-44-37-14-41; fax 1-44-37-14-74; e-mail unep.tie@unep
.fr; internet www.uneptie.org/; Dir MONIQUE BARBUT (France).

**UNEP International Environmental Technology Centre—
IETC:** 2–110 Ryokuchi koen, Tsurumi-ku, Osaka 538-0036, Japan;
tel. (6) 6915-4581; fax (6) 6915-0304; e-mail ietc@unep.or.jp; internet
www.unep.or.jp.

UNEP Ozone Secretariat: POB 30552, Nairobi, Kenya; tel. (20)
624691; fax (20) 623913; e-mail ozoneinfo@unep.org; internet www
.unep.org/ozone/; Exec. Sec. MARCO GONZALEZ (Costa Rica).

**UNEP-SCBD (Convention on Biological Diversity—
Secretariat):** 413 St Jacques St, Office 800, Montréal, QC, Canada
H2Y 1N9; tel. (514) 288-2220; fax (514) 288-6588; e-mail
secretariat@biodiv.org; internet www.biodiv.org; Exec. Sec. HAM-
DALLAH ZEDAN.

**UNEP Secretariat for the UN Scientific Committee on the
Effects of Atomic Radiation:** Vienna International Centre,
Wagramerstrasse 5, POB 500, 1400 Vienna, Austria; tel. (1) 26060-
4330; fax (1) 26060-5902; e-mail norman.gentner@unvienna.org;
internet www.unscear.org; Sec. Dr NORMAN GENTNER.

Activities

UNEP serves as a focal point for environmental action within the
UN system. It aims to maintain a constant watch on the changing
state of the environment; to analyse the trends; to assess the
problems using a wide range of data and techniques; and to promote
projects leading to environmentally sound development. It plays a
catalytic and co-ordinating role within and beyond the UN system.
Many UNEP projects are implemented in co-operation with other
UN agencies, particularly UNDP, the World Bank group, FAO,
UNESCO and WHO. About 45 intergovernmental organizations
outside the UN system and 60 international non-governmental
organizations have official observer status on UNEP's Governing
Council, and, through the Environment Liaison Centre in Nairobi,
UNEP is linked to more than 6,000 non-governmental bodies concerned with the environment. UNEP also sponsors international
conferences, programmes, plans and agreements regarding all
aspects of the environment.

In February 1997 the Governing Council, at its 19th session,
adopted a ministerial declaration (the Nairobi Declaration) on
UNEP's future role and mandate, which recognized the organization
as the principal UN body working in the field of the environment and
as the leading global environmental authority, setting and overseeing the international environmental agenda. In June a special
session of the UN General Assembly, referred to as 'Rio + 5', was
convened to review the state of the environment and progress
achieved in implementing the objectives of the UN Conference on
Environment and Development (UNCED), held in Rio de Janeiro,
Brazil, in June 1992. The meeting adopted a Programme for Further
Implementation of Agenda 21 (a programme of activities to promote
sustainable development, adopted by UNCED) in order to intensify
efforts in areas such as energy, freshwater resources and technology
transfer. The meeting confirmed UNEP's essential role in advancing
the Programme and as a global authority promoting a coherent legal
and political approach to the environmental challenges of sustainable development. An extensive process of restructuring and realignment of functions was subsequently initiated by UNEP, and a new
organizational structure reflecting the decisions of the Nairobi Dec-

laration was implemented during 1999. UNEP played a leading role
in preparing for the World Summit on Sustainable Development
(WSSD), held in August–September 2002 in Johannesburg, South
Africa, to assess strategies for strengthening the implementation of
Agenda 21. Governments participating in the conference adopted
the Johannesburg Declaration and WSSD Plan of Implementation,
in which they strongly reaffirmed commitment to the principles
underlying Agenda 21 and also pledged support to all internationally-agreed development goals, including the UN Millennium Development Goals adopted by governments attending a summit meeting
of the UN General Assembly in September 2000. Participating
governments made concrete commitments to attaining several specific objectives in the areas of water, energy, health, agriculture and
fisheries, and biodiversity. These included a reduction by one-half in
the proportion of people world-wide lacking access to clean water or
good sanitation by 2015, the restocking of depleted fisheries by 2015,
a reduction in the ongoing loss in biodiversity by 2010, and the
production and utilization of chemicals without causing harm to
human beings and the environment by 2020. Participants determined to increase usage of renewable energy sources and to develop
by 2005 integrated water resources management and water efficiency plans. A large number of partnerships between governments,
private sector interests and civil society groups were announced at
the conference.

In May 2000 UNEP sponsored the first annual Global Ministerial
Environment Forum (GMEF), held in Malmö, Sweden, and attended
by environment ministers and other government delegates from
more than 130 countries. Participants reviewed policy issues in the
field of the environment and addressed issues such as the impact on
the environment of population growth, the depletion of earth's
natural resources, climate change and the need for fresh water
supplies. The Forum issued the Malmö Declaration, which identified
the effective implementation of international agreements on environmental matters at national level as the most pressing challenge
for policy-makers. The Declaration emphasized the importance of
mobilizing domestic and international resources and urged
increased co-operation from civil society and the private sector in
achieving sustainable development. The second GMEF, held in
Nairobi in February 2001, addressed means of strengthening international environmental governance, establishing an Open-Ended
Intergovernmental Group of Ministers or Their Representatives
(IGM) to prepare a report on possible reforms. GMEF-6, scheduled to
be held in February 2006 in Dubai, United Arab Emirates, was to
consider energy and the environment and chemicals management.

ENVIRONMENTAL ASSESMENT AND EARLY WARNING
The Nairobi Declaration resolved that the strengthening of UNEP's
information, monitoring and assessment capabilities was a crucial
element of the organization's restructuring, in order to help establish priorities for international, national and regional action, and to
ensure the efficient and accurate dissemination of emerging environmental trends and emergencies.

In 1995 UNEP launched the Global Environment Outlook (GEO)
process of environmental assessment. UNEP is assisted in its analysis of the state of the global environment by an extensive network
of collaborating centres. The first *Global Environment Outlook,
GEO-I*, was published in January 1997, the second, *GEO 2000*, in
September 1999, and *GEO-3* in May 2002. From 2003 reports on the
process were to be issued annually. The following regional and
national *GEO* reports have been produced: *Africa Environment
Outlook* (2002), *Brazil Environment Outlook* (2002), *Latin America
and the Caribbean—Environment Outlook 2000*, *Caucasus Environment Outlook* (2002), *North America's Environment* (2002), *Pacific
Islands Environment Outlook* (1999), and *Western Indian Ocean
Environment Outlook* (1999). UNEP is leading a major Global International Waters Assessment (GIWA) to consider all aspects of the
world's water-related issues, in particular problems of shared transboundary waters, and of future sustainable management of water
resources. UNEP is also a sponsoring agency of the Joint Group of
Experts on the Scientific Aspects of Marine Environmental Pollution
and contributes to the preparation of reports on the state of the
marine environment and on the impact of land-based activities on
that environment. In November 1995 UNEP published a Global
Biodiversity Assessment, which was the first comprehensive study
of biological resources throughout the world. The UNEP—World
Conservation Monitoring Centre (UNEP—WCMC), established in
June 2000, provides biodiversity-related assessment. UNEP is a
partner in the International Coral Reef Action Network—ICRAN,
which was established in 2000 to manage and protect coral reefs
world-wide. In June 2001 UNEP launched the Millennium Ecosystems Assessment, which was expected to be completed in 2004.
Other major assessments under way in 2002 included GIWA (see
above); the Assessment of Impact and Adaptation to Climate
Change; the Solar and Wind Energy Resource Assessment; the
Regionally-Based Assessment of Persistent Toxic Substances; the
Land Degradation Assessment in Drylands; and the Global Method-

ology for Mapping Human Impacts on the Biosphere (GLOBIO) project.

UNEP's environmental information network includes the Global Resource Information Database (GRID), which converts collected data into information usable by decision-makers. The UNEP-IN-FOTERRA programme facilitates the exchange of environmental information through an extensive network of national 'focal points'. By March 2005 177 countries were participating in the network. Through UNEP-INFOTERRA UNEP promotes public access to environmental information, as well as participation in environmental concerns. UNEP aims to establish in every developing region an Environment and Natural Resource Information Network (ENRIN) in order to make available technical advice and manage environmental information and data for improved decision-making and action-planning in countries most in need of assistance. UNEP aims to integrate its information resources in order to improve access to information and to promote its international exchange. This has been pursued through UNEPnet, an internet-based interactive environmental information- and data-sharing facility, and Mercure, a telecommunications service using satellite technology to link a network of 16 earth stations throughout the world.

UNEP's information, monitoring and assessment structures also serve to enhance early-warning capabilities and to provide accurate information during an environmental emergency.

POLICY DEVELOPMENT AND LAW

UNEP aims to promote the development of policy tools and guide-lines in order to achieve the sustainable management of the world environment. At a national level it assists governments to develop and implement appropriate environmental instruments and aims to co-ordinate policy initiatives. Training workshops in various aspects of environmental law and its applications are conducted. UNEP supports the development of new legal, economic and other policy instruments to improve the effectiveness of existing environmental agreements.

UNEP was instrumental in the drafting of a Convention on Biological Diversity (CBD) to preserve the immense variety of plant and animal species, in particular those threatened with extinction. The Convention entered into force at the end of 1993; by April 2005 187 countries and the European Community were parties to the CBD. The CBD's Cartagena Protocol on Biosafety (so called as it had been addressed at an extraordinary session of parties to the CBD convened in Cartagena, Colombia, in February 1999) was adopted at a meeting of parties to the CBD held in Montréal, Canada, in January 2000, and entered into force in September 2003; by April 2005 the Protocol had been ratified by 118 countries and the European Community. The Protocol regulates the transboundary movement and use of living modified organisms resulting from biotechnology in order to reduce any potential adverse effects on biodiversity and human health. It establishes an Advanced Informed Agreement procedure to govern the import of such organisms. In January 2002 UNEP launched a major project aimed at supporting developing countries with assessing the potential health and environmental risks and benefits of genetically-modified (GM) crops, in preparation for the Protocol's entry into force. In February the parties to the CBD and other partners convened a conference, in Montréal, to address ways in which the traditional knowledge and practices of local communities could be preserved and used to conserve highly-threatened species and ecosystems. The sixth conference of parties to the CBD, held in April 2002, adopted detailed voluntary guide-lines concerning access to genetic resources and sharing the benefits attained from such resources with the countries and local communities where they originate; a global work programme on forests; and a set of guiding principles for combating alien invasive species. UNEP supports co-operation for biodiversity assessment and management in selected developing regions and for the development of strategies for the conservation and sustainable exploitation of individual threatened species (e.g. the Global Tiger Action Plan). It also provides assistance for the preparation of individual country studies and strategies to strengthen national biodiversity management and research. UNEP administers the Convention on International Trade in Endangered Species of Wild Flora and Fauna (CITES), which entered into force in 1975.

In October 1994 87 countries, meeting under UN auspices, signed a Convention to Combat Desertification (see UNDP Drylands Development Centre), which aimed to provide a legal framework to counter the degradation of drylands. An estimated 75% of all drylands have suffered some land degradation, affecting approximately 1,000m. people in 110 countries. UNEP continues to support the implementation of the Convention, as part of its efforts to protect land resources. UNEP also aims to improve the assessment of dryland degradation and desertification in co-operation with governments and other international bodies, as well as identifying the causes of degradation and measures to overcome these.

UNEP is the lead UN agency for promoting environmentally sustainable water management. It regards the unsustainable use of water as the most urgent environmental and sustainable development issue, and estimates that two-thirds of the world's population will suffer chronic water shortages by 2025, owing to rising demand for drinking water as a result of growing populations, decreasing quality of water because of pollution, and increasing requirements of industries and agriculture. In 2000 UNEP adopted a new water policy and strategy, comprising assessment, management and co-ordination components. The Global International Waters Assessment (see above) is the primary framework for the assessment component. The management component includes the Global Programme of Action (GPA) for the Protection of the Marine Environment from Land-based Activities (adopted in November 1995), and UNEP's freshwater programme and regional seas programme. The GPA for the Protection of the Marine Environment for Land-based Activities focuses on the effects of activities such as pollution on freshwater resources, marine biodiversity and the coastal ecosystems of small-island developing states. UNEP aims to develop a similar global instrument to ensure the integrated management of freshwater resources. It promotes international co-operation in the management of river basins and coastal areas and for the development of tools and guide-lines to achieve the sustainable management of freshwater and coastal resources. UNEP provides scientific, technical and administrative support to facilitate the implementation and co-ordination of 14 regional seas conventions and 13 regional plans of action, and is developing a strategy to strengthen collaboration in their implementation. The new water policy and strategy emphasizes the need for improved co-ordination of existing activities. UNEP aims to play an enhanced role within relevant co-ordination mechanisms, such as the UN open-ended informal consultation process on oceans and the law of the sea.

In 1996 UNEP, in collaboration with FAO, began to work towards promoting and formulating a legally binding international convention on prior informed consent (PIC) for hazardous chemicals and pesticides in international trade, extending a voluntary PIC procedure of information exchange undertaken by more than 100 governments since 1991. The Convention was adopted at a conference held in Rotterdam, Netherlands, in September 1998, and entered into force in February 2004. It aims to reduce risks to human health and the environment by restricting the production, export and use of hazardous substances and enhancing information exchange procedures.

In conjunction with UN-Habitat, UNDP, the World Bank and other organizations and institutions, UNEP promotes environmental concerns in urban planning and management through the Sustainable Cities Programme, as well as regional workshops concerned with urban pollution and the impact of transportation systems. In 1994 UNEP inaugurated an International Environmental Technology Centre (IETC), with offices in Osaka and Shiga, Japan, in order to strengthen the capabilities of developing countries and countries with economies in transition to promote environmentally-sound management of cities and freshwater reservoirs through technology co-operation and partnerships.

UNEP has played a key role in global efforts to combat risks to the ozone layer, resultant climatic changes and atmospheric pollution. UNEP worked in collaboration with the World Meteorological Organization to formulate the UN Framework Convention on Climate Change (UNFCCC), with the aim of reducing the emission of gases that have a warming effect on the atmosphere, and has remained an active participant in the ongoing process to review and enforce the implementation of the Convention and of its Kyoto Protocol. UNEP was the lead agency in formulating the 1987 Montreal Protocol to the Vienna Convention for the Protection of the Ozone Layer (1985), which provided for a 50% reduction in the production of chlorofluorocarbons (CFCs) by 2000. An amendment to the Protocol was adopted in 1990, which required complete cessation of the production of CFCs by 2000 in industrialized countries and by 2010 in developing countries; these deadlines were advanced to 1996 and 2006, respectively, in November 1992. In 1997 the ninth Conference of the Parties (COP) to the Vienna Convention adopted a further amendment which aimed to introduce a licensing system for all controlled substances. The eleventh COP, meeting in Beijing, People's Republic of China, in November–December 1999, adopted the Beijing Amendment, which imposed tighter controls on the import and export of hydrochlorofluorocarbons, and on the production and consumption of bromochloromethane (Halon-1011, an industrial solvent and fire extinguisher). The Beijing Amendment entered into force in December 2001. A Multilateral Fund for the Implementation of the Montreal Protocol was established in June 1990 to promote the use of suitable technologies and the transfer of technologies to developing countries. UNEP, UNDP, the World Bank and UNIDO are the sponsors of the Fund, which by 30 June 2004 had approved financing for more than 4,300 projects in 134 developing countries at a cost of US $1,631m. Commitments of $474m. were made to the fifth replenishment of the Fund, covering the three-year period 2003–05.

POLICY IMPLEMENTATION

UNEP's Division of Environmental Policy Implementation incorporates two main functions: technical co-operation and response to environmental emergencies.

With the UN Office for the Co-ordination of Humanitarian Assistance (OCHA), UNEP has established a joint Environment Unit to mobilize and co-ordinate international assistance and expertise for countries facing environmental emergencies and natural disasters. In mid-1999 UNEP and UN-Habitat jointly established a Balkan Task Force (subsequently renamed UNEP Balkans Unit) to assess the environmental impact of NATO's aerial offensive against the Federal Republic of Yugoslavia (now Serbia and Montenegro). In November 2000 the Unit led a field assessment to evaluate reports of environmental contamination by debris from NATO ammunition containing depleted uranium. A final report, issued by UNEP in March 2001, concluded that there was no evidence of widespread contamination of the ground surface by depleted uranium and that the radiological and toxicological risk to the local population was negligible. It stated, however, that considerable scientific uncertainties remained, for example as to the safety of groundwater and the longer-term behaviour of depleted uranium in the environment, and recommended precautionary action. In December 2001 UNEP established a new Post-conflict Assessment Unit, which replaced, and extended the scope of, the Balkans Unit. In 2005 the Post-conflict Assessment Unit was undertaking activities in Afghanistan, and was compiling desk assessments of the state of the environment in Iraq, Liberia and the Palestinian territories.

UNEP, together with UNDP and the World Bank, is an implementing agency of the Global Environment Facility (GEF), which was established in 1991 as a mechanism for international co-operation in projects concerned with biological diversity, climate change, international waters and depletion of the ozone layer. UNEP services the Scientific and Technical Advisory Panel, which provides expert advice on GEF programmes and operational strategies.

TECHNOLOGY, INDUSTRY AND ECONOMICS

The use of inappropriate industrial technologies and the widespread adoption of unsustainable production and consumption patterns have been identified as being inefficient in the use of renewable resources and wasteful, in particular in the use of energy and water. UNEP aims to encourage governments and the private sector to develop and adopt policies and practices that are cleaner and safer, make efficient use of natural resources, incorporate environmental costs, ensure the environmentally sound management of chemicals, and reduce pollution and risks to human health and the environment. In collaboration with other organizations and agencies UNEP works to define and formulate international guide-lines and agreements to address these issues. UNEP also promotes the transfer of appropriate technologies and organizes conferences and training workshops to provide sustainable production practices. Relevant information is disseminated through the International Cleaner Production Information Clearing House. UNEP, together with UNIDO, has established 27 National Cleaner Production Centres to promote a preventive approach to industrial pollution control. In October 1998 UNEP adopted an International Declaration on Cleaner Production, with a commitment to implement cleaner and more sustainable production methods and to monitor results; the Declaration had 529 signatories at January 2005, including representatives of 54 national governments. In 1997 UNEP and the Coalition for Environmentally Responsible Economies initiated the Global Reporting Initiative, which, with participation by corporations, business associations and other organizations and stakeholders, develops guidelines for voluntary reporting by companies on their economic, environmental and social performance. In April 2002 UNEP launched the 'Life-Cycle Initiative', which aims to assist governments, businesses and other consumers with adopting environmentally-sound policies and practice, in view the upward trend in global consumption patterns.

UNEP provides institutional servicing to the Basel Convention on the Control of Transboundary Movements of Hazardous Wastes and their Disposal, which was adopted in 1989 with the aim of preventing the disposal of wastes from industrialized countries in countries that have no processing facilities. In March 1994 the second meeting of parties to the Convention determined to ban the exportation of hazardous wastes between industrialized and developing countries. The third meeting of parties to the Convention, held in 1995, proposed that the ban should be incorporated into the Convention as an amendment. The resulting so-called Ban Amendment (prohibiting exports of hazardous wastes for final disposal and recycling from states and/or parties also belonging to OECD and, or, the European Union, and from Liechtenstein, to any other state party to the Convention) required ratification by three-quarters of the 62 signatory states present at the time of adoption before it could enter into effect; by April 2005 the Ban Amendment had been ratified by 56 parties. In 1998 the technical working group of the Convention agreed a new procedure for clarifying the classification and characterization of specific hazardous wastes. The fifth full meeting of parties to the Convention, held in December 1999, adopted the Basel Declaration outlining an agenda for the period 2000–10, with a particular focus on minimizing the production of hazardous wastes. At April 2005 the number of parties to the Convention totalled 165. In December 1999 132 states adopted a Protocol to the Convention to address issues relating to liability and compensation for damages from waste exports. The governments also agreed to establish a multilateral fund to finance immediate clean-up operations following any environmental accident.

The UNEP Chemicals office was established to promote the sound management of hazardous substances, central to which has been the International Register of Potentially Toxic Chemicals (IRPTC). UNEP aims to facilitate access to data on chemicals and hazardous wastes, in order to assess and control health and environmental risks, by using the IRPTC as a clearing house facility of relevant information and by publishing information and technical reports on the impact of the use of chemicals.

UNEP's OzonAction Programme works to promote information exchange, training and technological awareness. Its objective is to strengthen the capacity of governments and industry in developing countries to undertake measures towards the cost-effective phasing-out of ozone-depleting substances. UNEP also encourages the development of alternative and renewable sources of energy. To achieve this, UNEP is supporting the establishment of a network of centres to research and exchange information of environmentally-sound energy technology resources.

REGIONAL CO-OPERATION AND REPRESENTATION

UNEP maintains six regional offices. These work to initiate and promote UNEP objectives and to ensure that all programme formulation and delivery meets the specific needs of countries and regions. They also provide a focal point for building national, subregional and regional partnership and enhancing local participation in UNEP initiatives. Following UNEP's reorganization a co-ordination office was established at headquarters to promote regional policy integration, to co-ordinate programme planning, and to provide necessary services to the regional offices.

UNEP provides administrative support to several regional conventions, for example the Lusaka Agreement on Co-operative Enforcement Operations Directed at Illegal Trade in Wild Flora and Fauna, which entered into force in December 1996 having been concluded under UNEP auspices in order to strengthen the implementation of the CBD and CITES in Eastern and Central Africa. UNEP also organizes conferences, workshops and seminars at national and regional levels, and may extend advisory services or technical assistance to individual governments.

CONVENTIONS

UNEP aims to develop and promote international environmental legislation in order to pursue an integrated response to global environmental issues, to enhance collaboration among existing convention secretariats, and to co-ordinate support to implement the work programmes of international instruments.

UNEP has been an active participant in the formulation of several major conventions (see above). The Division of Environmental Conventions is mandated to assist the Division of Policy Development and Law in the formulation of new agreements or protocols to existing conventions. Following the successful adoption of the Rotterdam Convention in September 1998, UNEP played a leading role in formulating a multilateral agreement to reduce and ultimately eliminate the manufacture and use of Persistent Organic Pollutants (POPs), which are considered to be a major global environmental hazard. The agreement on POPs, concluded in December 2000 at a conference sponsored by UNEP in Johannesburg, South Africa, was adopted by 127 countries in May 2001; it entered into force in May 2004, three months after its ratification by the requisite 50 states in February of that year.

UNEP has been designated to provide secretariat functions to a number of global and regional environmental conventions (see above for list of offices).

COMMUNICATIONS AND PUBLIC INFORMATION

UNEP's public education campaigns and outreach programmes promote community involvement in environmental issues. Further communication of environmental concerns is undertaken through the media, an information centre service and special promotional events, including World Environment Day, photography competitions, and the awarding of the Sasakawa Prize (to recognize distinguished service to the environment by individuals and groups) and of the Global 500 Award for Environmental Achievement. In 1996 UNEP initiated a Global Environment Citizenship Programme to promote acknowledgment of the environmental responsibilities of all sectors of society.

Finance

UNEP derives its finances from the regular budget of the United Nations and from voluntary contributions to the Environment Fund. A budget of US $144m. was proposed for the two-year period 2006–07, of which $122m. was for programme activities, $5.8m. for programme support, $10.2m. for management and administration, and $6m. for fund programme reserves.

Publications

Annual Report.
APELL Newsletter (2 a year).
Cleaner Production Newsletter (2 a year).
Climate Change Bulletin (quarterly).
Connect (UNESCO-UNEP newsletter on environmental degradation, quarterly).
Earth Views (quarterly).
Environment Forum (quarterly).
Environmental Law Bulletin (2 a year).

Financial Services Initiative (2 a year).
GEF News (quarterly).
Global Environment Outlook (every 2–3 years).
Global Water Review.
GPA Newsletter.
IETC Insight (3 a year).
Industry and Environment Review (quarterly).
Leave it to Us (children's magazine, 2 a year).
Managing Hazardous Waste (2 a year).
Our Planet (quarterly).
OzonAction Newsletter (quarterly).
Tierramerica (weekly).
Tourism Focus (2 a year).
UNEP Chemicals Newsletter (2 a year).
UNEP Update (monthly).
World Atlas of Biodiversity.
World Atlas of Coral Reefs.
World Atlas of Desertification.
Studies, reports, legal texts, technical guide-lines, etc.

United Nations High Commissioner for Refugees—UNHCR

Address: CP 2500, 1211 Geneva 2 dépôt, Switzerland.

Telephone: (22) 7398111; **fax:** (22) 7397312; **e-mail:** unhcr@unhcr.ch; **internet:** www.unhcr.ch.

The Office of the High Commissioner was established in 1951 to provide international protection for refugees and to seek durable solutions to their problems.

Organization

(March 2005)

HIGH COMMISSIONER

The High Commissioner is elected by the United Nations General Assembly on the nomination of the Secretary-General, and is responsible to the General Assembly and to the UN Economic and Social Council (ECOSOC).

Acting High Commissioner: WENDY CHAMBERLAIN (USA).

EXECUTIVE COMMITTEE

The Executive Committee of the High Commissioner's Programme (ExCom), established by ECOSOC, gives the High Commissioner policy directives in respect of material assistance programmes and advice in the field of international protection. In addition, it oversees UNHCR's general policies and use of funds. ExCom, which comprises representatives of 66 states, both members and non-members of the UN, meets once a year.

ADMINISTRATION

Headquarters include the Executive Office, comprising the offices of the High Commissioner, the Deputy High Commissioner and the Assistant High Commissioner. The Inspector General, the Director of the UNHCR liaison office in New York, and the Director of the Department of International Protection report directly to the High Commissioner. The other principal administrative units are the Division of Financial and Supply Management, the Division of Human Resources Management, the Division of External Relations, the Division of Information Systems and Telecommunications, the Emergency and Security Service, and the Department of Operations, which is responsible for the five regional bureaux covering Africa; Asia and the Pacific; Europe; the Americas and the Caribbean; and Central Asia, South-West Asia, North Africa and the Middle East. At July 2004 there were 252 UNHCR offices in 116 countries worldwide. At that time UNHCR employed 6,143 people, including short-term staff, of whom 5,109 (or 83%) were working in the field.

Activities

The competence of the High Commissioner extends to any person who, owing to well-founded fear of being persecuted for reasons of race, religion, nationality or political opinion, is outside the country of his or her nationality and is unable or, owing to such fear or for reasons other than personal convenience, remains unwilling to accept the protection of that country; or who, not having a nationality and being outside the country of his or her former habitual residence, is unable or, owing to such fear or for reasons other than personal convenience, is unwilling to return to it. This competence may be extended, by resolutions of the UN General Assembly and decisions of ExCom, to cover certain other 'persons of concern', in addition to refugees meeting these criteria. Refugees who are assisted by other UN agencies, or who have the same rights or obligations as nationals of their country of residence, are outside the mandate of UNHCR.

In recent years there has been a significant shift in UNHCR's focus of activities. Increasingly UNHCR has been called upon to support people who have been displaced within their own country (i.e. with similar needs to those of refugees but who have not crossed an international border) or those threatened with displacement as a result of armed conflict. In addition, greater support has been given to refugees who have returned to their country of origin, to assist their reintegration, and UNHCR is working to enable local communities to support the returnees, frequently through the implementation of Quick Impact Projects (QIPs). In 2004 UNHCR led the formulation of a UN system-wide Strategic Plan for IDPs.

UNHCR has been increasingly concerned with the problem of statelessness and promotes new accessions to the 1954 Convention Relating to the Status of Stateless Persons and the 1964 Convention on the Reduction of Statelessness. It is estimated that as many as 9m. people world-wide may have no legal nationality.

At December 2003 the refugee population world-wide provisionally totalled 9.7m. UNHCR was also concerned with 1.1m. recently returned refugees, 4.2m. internally displaced persons (IDPs), 995,000 asylum seekers, 233,000 returned IDPs and 912,000 others.

World Refugee Day, sponsored by UNHCR, is held annually on 20 June.

INTERNATIONAL PROTECTION

As laid down in the Statute of the Office, UNHCR's primary function is to extend international protection to refugees and its second function is to seek durable solutions to their problems. In the exercise of its mandate UNHCR seeks to ensure that refugees and asylum-seekers are protected against *refoulement* (forcible return), that they receive asylum, and that they are treated according to internationally recognized standards. UNHCR pursues these objectives by a variety of means that include promoting the conclusion and ratification by states of international conventions for the protection of refugees. UNHCR promotes the adoption of liberal practices of asylum by states, so that refugees and asylum-seekers are granted admission, at least on a temporary basis.

The most comprehensive instrument concerning refugees that has been elaborated at the international level is the 1951 United Nations Convention relating to the Status of Refugees. This Convention, the scope of which was extended by a Protocol adopted in 1967, defines the rights and duties of refugees and contains provisions dealing with a variety of matters which affect the day-to-day lives of refugees. The application of the Convention and its Protocol is supervised by UNHCR. Important provisions for the treatment of refugees are also contained in a number of instruments adopted at the regional level. These include the 1969 Convention Governing the Specific Aspects of Refugee Problems adopted by OAU (now AU) member states in 1969, the European Agreement on the Abolition of Visas for Refugees, and the 1969 American Convention on Human Rights.

UNHCR has actively encouraged states to accede to the 1951 United Nations Refugee Convention and the 1967 Protocol: 145 states had acceded to either or both of these basic refugee instruments by February 2005. An increasing number of states have also adopted domestic legislation and/or administrative measures to implement the international instruments, particularly in the field of procedures for the determination of refugee status. UNHCR has sought to address the specific needs of refugee women and children, and has also attempted to deal with the problem of military attacks on refugee camps, by adopting and encouraging the acceptance of a set of principles to ensure the safety of refugees. In recent years it has formulated a strategy designed to address the fundamental causes of refugee flows. In 2001, in response to widespread concern about perceived high numbers of asylum-seekers and large-scale international economic migration and human trafficking, UNHCR initiated a series of Global Consultations on International Protection with the signatories to the 1951 Convention and 1967 Protocol, and other interested parties, with a view to strengthening both the application and scope of international refugee legislation. A consultation of 156 Governments, convened in Geneva, in December, reaffirmed commitment to the central role played by the Convention and Protocol. The final consultation, held in May 2002, focused on durable solutions and the protection of refugee women and children. Subsequently, based on the findings of the Global Consultations process, UNHCR developed an Agenda on Protection with six main objectives: strengthening the implementation of the 1951 Convention and 1967 Protocol; the protection of refugees within broader migration movements; more equitable sharing of burdens and responsibilities and building of capacities to receive and protect refugees; addressing more effectively security-related concerns; increasing efforts to find durable solutions; and meeting the protection needs of refugee women and children. The Agenda was endorsed by the Executive Council in October 2002. In September of that year the High Commissioner for Refugees launched the *Convention Plus* initiative, which aims to address contemporary global asylum issues by developing, on the basis of the Agenda on Protection, international agreements and measures to supplement the 1951 Convention and 1967 Protocol.

In June 2004 UNHCR became the tenth co-sponsor of UNAIDS.

ASSISTANCE ACTIVITIES

The first phase of an assistance operation uses UNHCR's capacity of emergency response. This enables UNHCR to address the immediate needs of refugees at short notice, for example, by employing specially trained emergency teams and maintaining stockpiles of basic equipment, medical aid and materials. A significant proportion of UNHCR expenditure is allocated to the next phase of an operation, providing 'care and maintenance' in stable refugee circumstances. This assistance can take various forms, including the provision of food, shelter, medical care and essential supplies. Also covered in many instances are basic services, including education and counselling.

As far as possible, assistance is geared towards the identification and implementation of durable solutions to refugee problems—this being the second statutory responsibility of UNHCR. Such solutions generally take one of three forms: voluntary repatriation, local integration or resettlement in another country. Where voluntary repatriation, increasingly the preferred solution, is feasible, the Office assists refugees to overcome obstacles preventing their return to their country of origin. This may be done through negotiations with governments involved, or by providing funds either for the physical movement of refugees or for the rehabilitation of returnees once back in their own country. In 2005 UNHCR was supporting the implementation of the Guidance Note on Durable Solutions for Displaced Persons, adopted in 2004 by the UN Development Group.

When voluntary repatriation is not an option, efforts are made to assist refugees to integrate locally and to become self-supporting in their countries of asylum. This may be done either by granting loans to refugees, or by assisting them, through vocational training or in other ways, to learn a skill and to establish themselves in gainful

occupations. One major form of assistance to help refugees re-establish themselves outside camps is the provision of housing. In cases where resettlement through emigration is the only viable solution to a refugee problem, UNHCR negotiates with governments in an endeavour to obtain suitable resettlement opportunities, to encourage liberalization of admission criteria and to draw up special immigration schemes. During 2003 an estimated 26,000 refugees were resettled under UNHCR auspices.

In the early 1990s UNHCR aimed to consolidate efforts to integrate certain priorities into its programme planning and implementation, as a standard discipline in all phases of assistance. The considerations include awareness of specific problems confronting refugee women, the needs of refugee children, the environmental impact of refugee programmes and long-term development objectives. In an effort to improve the effectiveness of its programmes, UNHCR has initiated a process of delegating authority, as well as responsibility for operational budgets, to its regional and field representatives, increasing flexibility and accountability. An Evaluation and Policy Analysis Unit reviews systematically UNHCR's operational effectiveness.

All UNHCR personnel are required to sign, and all interns, contracted staff and staff from partner organizations are required to acknowledge, a Code of Conduct, to which is appended the UN Secretary-General's bulletin on special measures for protection from sexual exploitation and sexual abuse (issued in October 2003). The post of Senior Adviser to the High Commissioner on Gender Issues, within the Executive Office, was established in 2004.

INDIAN OCEAN TSUNAMI RESPONSE

In January 2005, following a massive earthquake in the Indian Ocean in December 2004, which caused a series of tidal waves, or tsunamis, that devastated coastal regions in 12 countries in South and South-East Asia and East Africa, UNHCR requested emergency funding of US $75m. to support an initial six-month relief operation to provide shelter, non-food relief supplies and logistical support for survivors in Aceh, Indonesia (close to the epicentre of the earthquake), Sri Lanka and Somalia. UNHCR widened its scope in this case from its mandate to protect and assist people fleeing persecution and violence in view of the enormous impact of the natural disaster.

EAST ASIA AND THE PACIFIC

In early 1998 the Hong Kong authorities formally terminated the policy of granting a port of first asylum to Vietnamese 'boat people'. In February 2000 UNHCR welcomed a decision by the Hong Kong authorities to offer permanent residency status to the occupants of the last remaining Vietnamese detention camp (totalling 973 refugees and 435 'non-refugees'). By the end of May, when the camp was closed, more than 200 Vietnamese had failed to apply for residency. At 31 December 2003 UNHCR was providing assistance to an estimated further 297,219 Vietnamese refugees in mainland People's Republic of China (PRC). In 1995, in accordance with an agreement concluded with the Chinese Government, UNHCR initiated a programme to redirect its local assistance to promote long-term self-sufficiency in the poorest settlements, including support for revolving-fund rural credit schemes. UNHCR favours the local integration of the majority of the Vietnamese refugee population in the PRC as a durable solution to the situation.

From April 1991 increasing numbers of Rohingya Muslims in Myanmar fled into Bangladesh to escape brutality and killings perpetrated by the Myanma armed forces. UNHCR launched an international appeal for financial aid for the refugees, at the request of Bangladesh, and collaborated with other UN agencies in providing humanitarian assistance. UNHCR refused to participate in a programme of repatriation of the Myanma refugees agreed by Myanmar and Bangladesh, on the grounds that no safe environment existed for them to return to. In May 1993 a memorandum of understanding between UNHCR and Bangladesh was signed, whereby UNHCR would be able to monitor the repatriation process and ensure that people were returning of their own free will. In November a memorandum of understanding, signed with the Myanma Government, secured UNHCR access to the returnees. The first refugees returned to Myanmar with UNHCR assistance at the end of April 1994. They and all subsequent returnees were provided with a small amount of cash, housing grants and two months' food rations, and were supported by several small-scale reintegration projects. Attempts by UNHCR to find a local solution for those unwilling to return to Myanmar have been met with resistance by the Bangladeshi Government. By the end of December 2003 an estimated 19,743 Myanma refugees still remained in camps in Bangladesh and were receiving basic care from UNHCR.

In the early 1990s members of ethnic minorities in Myanmar attempted to flee attacks by government troops into Thailand; however, the Thai Government refused to recognize them as refugees or to offer them humanitarian assistance. In December 1997 Thailand and Myanmar agreed to commence 'screening' the refugees to determine those who had fled persecution and those who were economic migrants. Screening activities were suspended during 2001–04. In February 2004 the Myanmar Government granted UNHCR access to areas along the Myanmar-Thailand border, thereby potentially enabling the large-scale voluntary repatriation of some 140,500 Myanma (mainly Karen/Kayin) refugees remaining in camps there. The Myanmar Government requested that UNHCR should plan for the return and reintegration of IDPs as well as refugees. UNHCR, however, decided to postpone repatriation and reintegration operations pending the conclusion of an internationally acceptable peace agreement between the Myanmar authorities and militants that would secure the safety of returnees.

In April 1999, following the announcement by the Indonesian Government, in January, that it would consider a form of autonomy or independence for East Timor, some 26,000 Indonesian settlers left their homes as a result of clashes between opposing groups and uncertainty regarding the future of the territory. The popular referendum on the issue, conducted at the end of August, and the resulting victory for the independence movement, provoked a violent reaction by pro-integration militia. UNHCR, along with other international personnel, was forced to evacuate the territory in early September. At that time there were reports of forced mass deportations of East Timorese to West Timor, while a large number of others fled their homes into remote mountainous areas of East Timor. In mid-September UNHCR staff visited West Timor to review the state of refugee camps, allegedly under the control of militia, and to persuade the authorities to permit access for humanitarian personnel. It was estimated that 250,000–260,000 East Timorese had fled to West Timor, of whom some 230,000 were registered in 28 camps at the end of September. At that time there were also an estimated 190,000–300,000 people displaced within East Timor, although the International Committee of the Red Cross estimated that a total of 800,000 people, or some 94% of the population, had been displaced, or deported, during the crisis. The arrival of multinational troops, from 20 September, helped to stabilize the region and enable the safe receipt and distribution of food supplies, prompting several thousands to return from hiding. Most homes, however, along with almost all other buildings in the capital, Dili, had been destroyed. In early October UNHCR, together with the International Organization for Migration, initiated a repatriation programme for the refugees in West Timor. However, despite an undertaking by the Indonesian Government in mid-October that it would ensure the safety of all refugees and international personnel, persistent intimidation by anti-independence militia impeded the registration and repatriation processes. UNHCR initially aimed to complete the repatriation programme by mid-2001, prior to the staging of elections to a Constituent Assembly by the UN Transitional Administration in East Timor (UNTAET, which assumed full authority over the territory in February 2000). However, in September 2000 UNHCR suspended its activities in West Timor, following the murder by militiamen there of three of its personnel. A UN Security Council resolution, adopted soon afterwards, deplored this incident and strongly urged the Indonesian authorities to disable the militia and to guarantee the future security of all refugees and humanitarian personnel. In mid-September UNTAET and the Indonesian Government signed a Memorandum of Understanding on co-operation in resolving the refugee crisis. However, despite a subsequent operation by the Indonesian security forces to disarm the militia, intimidation of East Timorese refugees reportedly persisted, and UNHCR did not redeploy personnel to West Timor. The Office did, however, liaise with other humanitarian organizations to facilitate continuing voluntary repatriations, which have been encouraged by the Indonesian authorities. UNHCR's operation in East Timor aimed to promote the safe voluntary repatriation of refugees, monitor returnees, support their reintegration through the implementation of QIPs, pursue efforts towards sustainable development and the rehabilitation of communities, and to promote reconciliation and respect for human rights. In mid-May East Timor (now Timor-Leste) achieved independence. At that time almost 205,000 East Timorese refugees were reported to have returned since October 1999. UNHCR and the newly-elected administration were co-operating to encourage further repatriation, as well as to assist with Timor-Leste's accession to the international instruments of protection and with the development of new national refugee protection legislation. On 31 December 2002 UNHCR terminated the refugee status of people who fled East Timor in 1999. Some 16,000 former East Timorese refugees remained in West Timor in early 2005; UNHCR was assisting them in areas including food security and health and education provision, and was working to ensure durable solutions to their situation.

SOUTH ASIA

From 1979, as a result of civil strife in Afghanistan, there was a massive movement of refugees from that country into Pakistan and Iran creating the world's largest refugee population, which reached a peak of almost 6.3m. people in 1990. In 1988 UNHCR agreed to

provide assistance for the voluntary repatriation of refugees, both in ensuring the rights of the returning population and in providing material assistance such as transport, immunization, and supplies of food and other essentials. In April 1992, following the establishment of a new Government in Afghanistan, refugees began to repatriate in substantial numbers, although, meanwhile, large numbers of people continued to flee into Pakistan as a result of persisting insecurity. From October 1996 an escalation of hostilities in northern and western regions of Afghanistan resulted in further massive population displacement. By the end of 1998 the total number of returnees from Iran and Pakistan since 1988 amounted to more than 4.2m. In recent years UNHCR, with other UN agencies, attempted to meet the immediate needs of IDPs and recent returnees in Afghanistan through systematic monitoring and, for example, by initiating small-scale multi-sectoral QIPs to improve shelter, rural water supply and local infrastructure; organizing income-generating and capacity-building activities; and providing food and tools. However, the ongoing civil conflict, as well as successive severe droughts and harsh winter conditions, caused renewed population displacement, precluding a settlement of the refugee situation and entailing immense difficulties in undertaking comprehensive relief efforts. Activities were disrupted by periodic withdrawals of UN international personnel owing to security concerns. The humanitarian crisis worsened considerably during 2000. In mid-2001 UNHCR warned that the food insecurity in the country was continuing to deteriorate and that population movements were ongoing. In September, prompted by the threat of impending military action directed by a US-led global coalition against targets in the Taliban-administered areas of Afghanistan, UNHCR launched a US $252m. appeal to finance an emergency relief operation to cope with a potentially large further movement of Afghan refugees and IDPs. Although all surrounding countries imposed 'closed border' policies (with Pakistan reportedly permitting limited entry to Afghans in possession of correct travel documentation), it was envisaged that, were the security situation to deteriorate significantly, large numbers of Afghans might attempt to cross into the surrounding countries (mainly Iran and Pakistan) at unsecured points of entry. UNHCR urged the adoption of more liberal border policies and began substantially to reinforce its presence in Iran and Pakistan. Activities undertaken included the supply of basic relief items such as tents and health and hygiene kits and assistance with the provision of community services such as education for school-age children. The construction and maintenance of new camps near the Pakistan-Afghanistan border was initiated in co-operation with the Pakistan Government and other agencies, and it was also planned to construct new refugee shelters in Iran. Emergency contingency plans were also formulated for a relief initiative to assist a projected further 500,000 IDPs (in addition to the large numbers of people already displaced) inside Afghanistan. Large population movements out of cities were reported from the start of the international political crisis. An estimated 6m. Afghans (about one-quarter of the total population) were believed to be extremely vulnerable, requiring urgent food aid and other relief supplies. In mid-September all foreign UN field staff were withdrawn from Afghanistan for security reasons; meanwhile, in order to address the humanitarian situation, a Crisis Group was established by several UN agencies, including UNHCR, and a crisis management structure came into operation at UNHCR headquarters. In October (when air-strikes were initiated against Afghanistan) UNHCR opened a staging camp at a major crossing point on the Afghanistan-Pakistan border, and put in place a system for monitoring new refugee arrivals (implemented by local people rather than by UNHCR personnel). It was estimated that from October 2001–January 2002 about 50,000 Afghan refugees entered Pakistan officially, while about 150,000 crossed into the country at unofficial border points; many reportedly sought refuge with friends and relatives. Much smaller movements into Iran were reported. Spontaneous repatriations also occurred during that period (reportedly partly owing to the poor conditions at many camps in Pakistan), and UNHCR-assisted IDP returns were also undertaken. UNHCR resumed operations within Afghanistan in mid-November 2001, distributing supplies and implementing QIPs, for example the provision of warm winter clothing. From that month some 130,000 Afghan refugees in Pakistan were relocated from inadequate accommodation to new camps. On 1 March 2002 UNHCR initiated, jointly with the new interim Afghan administration, an assisted repatriation programme. UNHCR also concluded tripartite accords on repatriation with the Afghan authorities and with Iran and Pakistan. In that month UNHCR signed a new agreement with the Iranian Government to grant access to Afghans in detention centres throughout that country and to undertake a screening programme for asylum-seekers, in order to deal with the problem of undocumented refugees. At 31 December 2003 1.1m. Afghan refugees remained in Pakistan, 834,699 in Iran, and 10,283 in India, all of whom were UNHCR-assisted. By the end of 2004 more than 3.5m. refugees had returned from Pakistan and Iran since early 2002; of these, 838,000 returned during 2004 (760,000 with UNHCR assistance). In addition, an estimated 400,000 IDPs had resettled within Afghanistan by late 2004. During 2005 UNHCR planned to facilitate a further 305,000 voluntary refugee repatriations, as well as assisting some 55,000 IDP returns, and helping around 30,000 IDPs to integrate into their site of displacement. UNHCR provides returning refugees with transport and an initial reintegration package, including a cash grant and food and basic household items, and monitors their situation. Particular focus is placed upon the situation of returnee women and prevention of gender-based violence, and on encouraging the return of professional workers, especially doctors and teachers. The Office also works to improve local infrastructure and water supply facilities, and by the end of 2004 had completed the construction of 115,000 shelter units. UNHCR aims to strengthen the capacity of the Afghan Government to manage the return and sustainable reintegration of refugees and IDPs.

In 1991–92 thousands of people of Nepalese ethnic origin living in Bhutan sought refuge from alleged persecution by fleeing to Nepal. In December 2000 Bhutan and Nepal reached agreement on a joint verification mechanism for the repatriation of the refugees, which had been hitherto the principal issue precluding a resolution of the situation. The first verification of Bhutanese refugees was undertaken in March 2001. Some 12,000 refugees had undergone the verification process by early 2005, by which time, however, voluntary repatriations had not commenced. At the end of 2003 there were an estimated 103,650 Bhutanese refugees in Nepal, the majority of whom were receiving UNHCR assistance in the form of food, shelter, medical care and water.

During 1983–2001 hostilities between the Sri Lankan Government and Tamil separatists resulted in the displacement of more than 1m. Sri Lankan Tamil refugees (who sought shelter in India) and IDPs. Ongoing efforts by UNHCR to repatriate the Sri Lankan refugees were disrupted in late 1995 by an offensive by Sri Lankan government troops against the northern Jaffna peninsula, which caused a massive displacement of the local Tamil population. Increasing insecurity from late 1999 prompted further population movements. However, following the conclusion of a cease-fire agreement between the Sri Lankan Government and Tamil separatists in February 2002, the number of spontaneous returns accelerated. At 31 December 2003 there were 386,104 Sri Lankan IDPs of concern to UNHCR and 76,722 recently returned IDPs, as well as an estimated 60,922 Sri Lankan refugees remaining in camps in southern India (compared with some 84,000 at February 2002). At end-December 2003 India's total refugee population of some 164,757 also included 92,349 refugees from the People's Republic of China (mainly Tibetans).

CENTRAL ASIA

In late 1992 people began to flee civil conflict in Tajikistan and to seek refuge in Afghanistan. During 1993 an emergency UNHCR operation established a reception camp to provide the 60,000 Tajik refugees with basic assistance, and began to move them away from the border area to safety. In December a tripartite agreement was concluded by UNHCR and the Tajik and Afghan Governments regarding the security of refugees returning to Tajikistan. UNHCR monitored the repatriation process and provided materials for the construction of almost 20,000 homes. The operation was concluded by the end of 1997. Nevertheless, at the end of 2000, there were still nearly 60,000 Tajik refugees remaining in other countries of the former USSR. In the early 2000s an initiative was being implemented to integrate locally some 10,000 Tajik refugees of Kyrgyz ethnic origin in Kyrgyzstan and 12,500 Tajik refugees of Turkmen origin in Turkmenistan; by mid-2004 more than 4,000 of the former had received Kyrgyz citizenship; it was envisaged that a Kyrgyz-Tajik agreement on a simplified procedure for citizenship acquisition, concluded in mid-2003, would accelerate this process. At 31 December 2003 some 51,344 Tajik refugees were being hosted by Turkmenistan and Uzbekistan. From late 2001 about 9,000 Afghan refugees repatriated from Tajikistan under the auspices of UNHCR and the International Organization for Migration. UNHCR expressed concern following the adoption by the Tajikistan authorities in May 2002 of refugee legislation that reportedly contravened the 1951 Convention relating to the Status of Refugees and its 1967 Protocol. In 2003 UNHCR agreed to participate in an EU border management programme in Central Asia; initially it was to rehabilitate two border posts in Uzbekistan and provide training in refugee law for border officials in that country.

NORTH AFRICA AND THE MIDDLE EAST

UNHCR co-ordinates humanitarian assistance for the estimated 165,000 Sahrawis registered as refugees in four camps in the Tindouf area of Algeria. In September 1997 an agreement was reached on implementing the 1991 Settlement Plan for the Western Sahara. Accordingly, UNHCR was to help organize the registration and safe return of some 120,000 Sahrawi refugees provisionally identified as eligible to vote in the planned referendum on the future of the territory. In addition, UNHCR was to facilitate the reintegration of

the returnees and monitor their rehabilitation. By 2005, however, little progress had been achieved towards the implementation of the Settlement Plan and subsequent alternative settlement proposals.

In June 1992 people fleeing the civil war and famine in Somalia began arriving in Yemen in large numbers. UNHCR set up camps to accommodate some 50,000 refugees, providing them with shelter, food, water and sanitation. As a result of civil conflict in Yemen in mid-1994, a large camp in the south of the country was demolished and other refugees had to be relocated, while the Yemen authorities initiated a campaign of forcible repatriation. During 1998–mid-2000 the refugee population in Yemen expanded, owing to an influx of Somalis fleeing civil conflict and, to a lesser extent, people displaced by the 1998–2000 Eritrea–Ethiopia border conflict. The relocation of refugees to a newly-constructed camp at al-Kharaz, central Yemen, was undertaken during 2000–01. At December 2003 Yemen was hosting an estimated 61,881, mostly Somali, refugees.

In April 1994 UNHCR initiated a programme to provide food and relief assistance to Turkish Kurds who had fled into northern Iraq. In September 1996 fighting escalated among the Kurdish factions in northern Iraq. By the time a cease-fire agreement was concluded in November some 65,000 Iraqi Kurds had fled across the border into Iran. UNHCR, together with the Iranian Government, provided these new refugees with basic humanitarian supplies. By the end of the year, however, the majority of refugees had returned to Iraq, owing to poor conditions in the temporary settlements, security concerns at being located in the border region and pressure from the Iranian authorities. In December UNHCR announced its intention to withdraw from the Atroush camp in northern Iraq, which housed an estimated 15,000 Turkish Kurds, following several breaches of security in the camp. UNHCR proceeded to transfer 3,500 people to other local settlements, and continued to provide humanitarian assistance to those refugees who had settled closer to Iraqi-controlled territory but who had been refused asylum. During 1997–2000 some 2,200 Turkish Kurds repatriated from Iraq with assistance from UNHCR. In January 2004 UNHCR reached a preliminary agreement with Turkey and the USA on the voluntary repatriation of 13,000 Turkish Kurds remaining as refugees in Iraq.

In March–May 1991, following the war against Iraq by a multinational force, and the subsequent Iraqi suppression of resistance in Kurdish areas in the north of the country, there was massive movement of some 1.5m., mainly Kurdish, Iraqi refugees into Iran and Turkey. UNHCR was designated the principal UN agency to attempt to alleviate the crisis. In May the refugees began to return to Iraq in huge numbers and UNHCR assisted in their repatriation, establishing relief stations along their routes from Iran and Turkey. Following the war to liberate Kuwait UNHCR gave protection and assistance to Iraqis, Bidoon (stateless people) and Palestinians who were forced to leave that country. In May 2000 the Kuwaiti authorities determined that all Bidoon still resident in the country should register officially with the national authorities by 27 June; while it was agreed that citizenship requirement restrictions would be eased for some 36,000 Bidoon who had been enumerated at a population census in 1965, the remaining stateless residents (numbering an estimated 75,000) were to be required to apply for short-term residency permits. At 31 December 2003 there were, provisionally, 1,518 registered refugees in Kuwait, however, it was estimated that an additional 101,000 people in Kuwait were of concern to UNHCR, mainly Bidoons, Iraqis and Palestinians.

In March 2001 the Governments of Iran and Iraq concluded a bilateral accord on the voluntary repatriation of some 5,000 Iranians and 5,000 Iraqis; UNHCR was to assist with the implementation of the agreement and subsequently provided counselling to those refugee families to enable them to make a decision on repatriation. At the end of 2002 the total refugee population in Iraq amounted to an estimated 134,190, the majority of whom were Palestinians. At that time there was still a substantial Iraqi refugee population in the region, mainly comprising the 201,671 Iraqis then sheltering in Iran. In March 2003, in view of the initiation of US-led military action against the Saddam Hussain regime in Iraq, UNHCR and the International Federation of Red Cross and Red Crescent Societies signed an agreement on co-operation in providing humanitarian relief in Iraq and neighbouring countries. From mid-2003, following the overthrow of the Saddam Hussain Government, UNHCR developed plans for the eventual phased repatriation of more than 500,000 of the then estimated 4m. Iraqis exiled world-wide, and for the return to their homes of some 800,000 IDPs, contingent upon the stabilization of the political and security situation in the country. The Office also provided assistance to several thousand refugees from other countries (including Iranians, Palestinians and Syrians) who had been supported by the previous Iraqi administration but were now suffering harassment; many had abandoned their homes in Iraq owing to insufficient security and inadequate supplies. In June tents, blankets and stoves were provided to more than 800 Palestinian families who had been rendered homeless in Baghdad. Some 400 Palestinians fled from Iraq to Jordan, where they were accommodated in a tented camp near the border with Iraq. Negotiations with Iran were initiated to enable Iranian refugees to repatriate across the Iraq–Iran border. From March–May 2003 and following the bomb attack in August on the UN headquarters in Baghdad all international UN humanitarian personnel were withdrawn from Iraq, leaving national staff to conduct operations on the ground. By 31 December 2003 some 150,196 Iraqi refugees remained in Iran. By the end of 2004 UNHCR had facilitated voluntary returns by 19,300 Iraqi refugees from Iran, Lebanon and Saudi Arabia. In addition, more than 270,000 spontaneous returns by Iraqi refugees were reported from mid-2003–late 2004. However, owing to the ongoing unstable security situation, UNHCR and the Iraqi Interim Government (inaugurated in June 2004) have discouraged Iraqi refugees from returning home, and UNHCR has issued a warning against repatriation to governments hosting Iraqi refugees, as well as advising continued protection of Iraqi asylum-seekers. In early 2005 UNHCR was undertaking reintegration activities for returned refugees and IDPs, including the provision of technical support for the rebuilding of homes, and assistance with the reconstruction of local infrastructures and also in the areas of education, training and income-generation. In addition, at that time, UNHCR was providing advice and support to the Iraqi Interim Goverment's Ministry of Displacement and Migration. UNHCR and the International Organization for Migration were jointly supporting the Iraqi Property Claims Commission, established by the Iraqi authorities in January 2004. UNHCR appealed for US $42m. to fund its operations in Iraq during 2005.

In December 2003 UNHCR provided tents, mattresses and blankets to people rendered homeless by a devastating earthquake in and around Bam, Iran.

SUB-SAHARAN AFRICA

UNHCR has provided assistance to refugee and internally displaced populations in many parts of the continent where civil conflict, violations of human rights, drought, famine or environmental degradation have forced people to flee their home regions. The majority of African refugees and returnees are located in countries that are themselves suffering major economic problems and are thus unable to provide the basic requirements of the uprooted people. Furthermore, UNHCR has often failed to receive adequate international financial support to implement effective relief programmes. In March 2004 a UNHCR-sponsored Dialogue on Voluntary Repatriation and Sustainable Reintegration in Africa endorsed the creation of an international working group—comprising African governments, UN agencies, the African Union and other partners—to support the return and sustainable reintegration of refugees in several African countries, including Angola, Burundi, the Democratic Republic of the Congo, Eritrea, Liberia, Rwanda, Sierra Leone, Somalia and Sudan. At 31 December 2003 there were an estimated 4.0m. people of concern to UNHCR in sub-Saharan Africa.

The Horn of Africa, afflicted by famine, separatist violence and ethnic conflict, has experienced large-scale population movements in recent years. Following the overthrow of the regime of former Somali president Siad Barre in January 1991 hundreds of thousands of Somalis fled to neighbouring countries. In 1992 UNHCR initiated a repatriation programme for the massive Somali and Ethiopian refugee populations in Kenya, which included assistance with reconstruction projects and the provision of food to returnees and displaced persons. However, continuing instability in many areas of Somalia impeded the completion of the repatriation process to that country and resulted in further population displacement. Repatriations accelerated in the early 2000s owing to advances in the peace process. During 1992–mid-2004 more than 1m. Somali refugees returned to their country, of whom 476,000 received UNHCR assistance. However, many areas of the country have remained unstable, drought-affected and lacking in basic services. The Office, with other partners, has implemented community-based QIPs, aimed at facilitating long-term self-reliance by improving local education and health provision, water supply and productive capacity. It was hoped that the inauguration of a new Somali parliament in August 2004 might lead to improved stability and an eventual increase in voluntary repatriations. At the end of 2003 there remained an estimated total Somali refugee population of 402,152, of whom 154,272 were in Kenya, 59,246 in Yemen and 28,276 in Ethiopia. There were also 370,000 Somali IDPs. By November 1997 UNHCR estimated that some 600,000 Ethiopians had repatriated from neighbouring countries, either by spontaneous or organized movements. The voluntary repatriation operation of Ethiopian refugees from Sudan (which commenced in 1993) was concluded in mid-1998. With effect from 1 March 2000 UNHCR withdrew the automatic refugee status of Ethiopians who left their country before 1991. Transportation and rehabilitation assistance were provided for 9,321 of these, who wished to repatriate. The new Kenyan Government inaugurated in January 2003 aimed to adopt new refugee legislation, with a view to revitalizing the management of refugee structures and promoting refugee self-sufficiency activities. At 31 December there remained an estimated total Ethiopian refugee population of 62,601; some 15,251 Ethiopians remained in

Sudan (with 806 assisted by UNHCR) and 11,139 were in Kenya (all assisted by UNHCR). At that time Ethiopia itself was hosting a total of 130,274 refugees (of whom the majority were Sudanese), while Kenya was sheltering 237,512 (mainly Somalis).

From 1992 some 500,000 Eritreans took refuge in Sudan as a result of separatist conflicts; however, by 1995 an estimated 125,000 had returned spontaneously, in particular following Eritrea's accession to independence in May 1993. A UNHCR repatriation programme to assist the remaining refugees, which had been delayed for various political, security and funding considerations, was initiated in November 1994. Its implementation, however, was hindered by a shortfall in donor funding and by differences between the Eritrean and Sudanese Governments, and Sudan continued to host substantial numbers of Eritrean refugees. Renewed conflict between Eritrea and Ethiopia, which commenced in 1998, had, by mid-1999, resulted in the displacement of some 350,000 Eritreans and 300,000 Ethiopians. In mid-2000, following an escalation of the conflict in May, UNHCR reported that some 95,000 Eritreans had sought refuge in Sudan, while smaller numbers had fled to Djibouti and Yemen. Following the conclusion of a cease-fire agreement between Eritrea and Ethiopia in June, UNHCR initiated an operation to repatriate the most recent wave of Eritrean refugees from Sudan, and also inaugurated a scheme to repatriate 147,000 long-term refugees. UNHCR and other agencies collaborated to rehabilitate areas of Eritrea that were receiving returnees. During 2001 UNHCR withdrew assistance to Eritrean IDPs, whose numbers had declined from a peak of 300,000 to about 45,000 by May. At the end of 2002 UNHCR terminated the refugee status of Eritreans who fled their country since 1993. At 31 December 2003 the total number of Eritreans sheltering in Sudan was estimated at 108,251, of whom 72,906 were receiving UNHCR assistance. During mid-2000–end-2003 UNHCR assisted 54,000 voluntary repatriations of Eritrean refugees from Sudan. Thereafter UNHCR aimed to support the repatriation of a further 35,000 Eritrean refugees and to close 16 of the 18 camps for Eritreans in Sudan, maintaining the two remaining camps to shelter Eritreans with continuing eligibility for international protection. The initial deadline of end-2004 for achieving this was not met owing to inadequate funding.

At 31 December 2003 an estimated 606,179 Sudanese were exiled as refugees, mainly in Uganda, Chad, Ethiopia, Kenya, the Democratic Republic of the Congo (DRC) and the Central African Republic, owing to continuing civil unrest in southern Sudan and the emergence in early 2003 of a new conflict zone in the western Sudanese province of Darfur (see below). Some 454,660 Sudanese refugees were receiving assistance from UNHCR. The Ugandan Government, hosting an estimated 198,281 Sudanese refugees at that time (178,281 UNHCR-assisted), has provided new resettlement sites and, jointly with UNHCR and other partners, has developed a Self-Reliance Strategy, which envisages achieving self-sufficiency for the long-term refugee population through integrating services for refugees into existing local structures. It was reported that about three-fifths of refugees in Uganda achieved self-sufficiency in food in 2003. In view of the conclusion of a peace agreement between the Sudanese Government and rebels in July 2002, and the consolidation of the peace process during 2003–04, UNHCR, in collaboration with other humanitarian agencies, planned to support the voluntary repatriation and reintegration of some 150,000 refugees to southern Sudan in 2004–05, and, also, to facilitate the return of around 80,000 IDPs.

During April 2003–end-2004 around 200,000 refugees from Sudan's western Darfur region sought shelter across the Sudan-Chad border, having fled an alleged campaign of killing, rapes and destruction of property conducted by pro-government militias against the indigenous population. In addition, an estimated 1.5m. people were displaced within Darfur at the end of 2004. UNHCR's activities in Chad in 2004–early 2005 included registering the incoming Sudanese refugees and conducting an urgent operation to relocate them from the insecure and arid border region to camps in the interior of Chad. The Office has also organized airlifts of relief items, including tents, blankets and plastic sheeting, and has supplied the refugees with stoves and firewood. During 2005 UNHCR aimed to improve and expand access to water, healthcare and education in the camps, to continue to manage supplementary and therapeutic feeding facilities in order to combat widespread malnutrition among the refugees, and to provide psychosocial support to traumatized refugees. The eventual introduction of income-generating activities was also planned. UNHCR established a presence within Darfur in June 2004, when it opened offices at Nyala and El Geneina. It was envisaged that a further office at El-Fasher would be opened during 2005. UNCHR teams have undertaken efforts to train Sudanese managers of camps in Darfur in the areas of protection and human rights. In September 2004 UNHCR appealed for US $104.8m. for its operations in eastern Chad, including preparation for a possible additional influx of up to 100,000 new refugees. Some $9.1m. was requested for UNHCR's activities within Darfur.

Following an outbreak of civil conflict in the Central African Republic (CAR) in early 2003, resulting in a *coup d'état* in March, some 41,000 CAR refugees fled to southern Chad. By early 2005 some 33,000 CAR refugees reportedly remained in Chad, of whom around 27,000 were accommodated by UNHCR in two camps.

Significant population displacements have occurred in West Africa in recent years, particularly since the outbreak in 1989 of enduring violent conflict in Liberia. Rebel insurgencies, fuelled by the illegal trade in 'conflict diamonds' and a proliferation of small arms, subsequently spread to Sierra Leone, Guinea and, latterly, Côte d'Ivoire (see below). During 1992 and the first half of 1993 refugees fleeing unrest in Senegal and Togo, as well as Liberia, increased the regional refugee population substantially. In accordance with a Liberian peace agreement, signed in July 1993, UNHCR was responsible for the repatriation of Liberian refugees who had fled to Guinea, Côte d'Ivoire and Sierra Leone. UNHCR also began to provide emergency relief to the displaced population within the country. Persisting political insecurity prevented any solution to the refugee problem, and in mid-1996 UNHCR suspended its preparatory activities for a large-scale repatriation and reintegration operation of Liberian refugees, owing to an escalation in hostilities. In early 1997 the prospect of a peaceful settlement in Liberia prompted a spontaneous movement of refugees returning home, and in April UNHCR initiated an organized repatriation of Liberian refugees from Ghana. The establishment of a democratically-elected Liberian government in August and the consolidation of the peace settlement were expected to accelerate the return of refugees and other displaced persons. However, the process was hindered by logistical difficulties, the persisting volatility particularly of some border regions, and alleged atrocities perpetrated by Liberian troops. During 1998 and 1999 an estimated 15,000 Liberians fled to Guinea from insecurity in the Lofa area of northern Liberia; meanwhile, UNHCR was forced to suspend its operations in Lofa. By the end of 2000 nearly 400,000 Liberians were reported to have repatriated, more than one-third with UNHCR assistance. UNHCR has organized QIPs to facilitate the reintegration of the returnees. Mounting insecurity in southern Guinea from September 2000 (see below) accelerated the return of Liberian refugees from camps there. However, during 2001 some 80,000 Liberians were displaced from their homes, and refugee camps for Sierra Leoneans were disrupted, owing to an escalation of violence particularly in the Lofa and Gbarpolu areas. At 31 December 2003 there were still an estimated 353,314 Liberian refugees (272,348 UNHCR-assisted), of whom 149,639 were in Guinea (only 89,408 UNHCR-assisted). At that time there were 531,616 Liberian IDPs of concern to UNHCR. In mid-2003 a further 147,000 Liberian refugees fled to neighbouring countries following an escalation in hostilities. However, owing to progress subsequently achieved in the Liberian peace process, including, in August, the deployment of an ECOWAS peace-keeping force (ECOMIL) to the country, exile of President Charles Taylor and conclusion of a peace agreement by the parties to the conflict, and the deployment in October of a UN peace-keeping force (replacing ECOMIL), mass voluntary spontaneous returns by Liberian refugees were reported in 2004. The Office remained, nevertheless, concerned over continuing instability in eastern and western areas of the country and inadequate provision for the disarmament and rehabilitation of former Liberian combatants.

Further large-scale population displacement in West Africa followed an escalation of violence in Sierra Leone in early 1995. By December 1996 there were nearly 370,000 Sierra Leonean refugees in Liberia and Guinea, while a further 654,600 internally displaced Sierra Leoneans were of concern to UNHCR. The repatriation of Sierra Leonean refugees from Liberia was initiated in February 1997. However, the programme was suspended in May, owing to renewed political violence, which forced UNHCR staff to evacuate the country, and the seizure of power by military forces. Thousands of people fled to other parts of the country, as well as to neighbouring countries to escape the hostilities. Following the intervention of the ECOMOG multinational force (authorized by ECOWAS) and the conclusion of a peace agreement in October, residents of the Sierra Leone capital, Freetown, who had been displaced by the conflict, began to return. In February 1998 ECOMOG troops took control of Freetown from the rebel military forces, and in the following month the elected President, Ahmed Tejan Kabbah, was reinstated as Head of State. None the less, large numbers of Sierra Leoneans continued to cross the borders into neighbouring countries, owing to ongoing violence in the northern and eastern regions of the country and severe food shortages. In early 1999 anti-government forces again advanced on Freetown, prompting heavy fighting with ECOMOG troops and the displacement of thousands more civilians. In February a reported 200,000 people fled the town of Kenema in southeastern Sierra Leone following attacks by rebel militia. In May a cease-fire agreement was concluded between the Government and opposition forces, and a formal peace accord was signed in early July, under which the rebels were to be disarmed and demobilized; however, the agreement broke down in May 2000. The resumption of hostilities delayed a planned repatriation operation and displaced an estimated 50,000 people from their homes. A new cease-fire agreement was signed by the Sierra Leone Government and the

principal rebel group in early November. Meanwhile, persistent insecurity in northeastern and some border areas of Sierra Leone prompted further movements of Sierra Leonean refugees to Guinea during 2000. From September, however, unrest in southern Guinea (see below) caused some Sierra Leonean refugees who had been sheltering in camps there to repatriate. In 2001 UNHCR, while assisting, with the International Organization for Migration, returns by sea from the Guinean capital Conakry to Freetown, organized radio broadcasts to southern Guinea warning Sierra Leoneans against attempting to escape the unrest there by returning over the land border into volatile northeastern and other border areas of Sierra Leone. By 31 December 2003 there were an estimated 25,000 Sierra Leonean refugees in Guinea and 13,941 in Liberia. Some 15,002 of the Sierra Leonean refugees in Guinea and reportedly all of those remaining in Liberia were being assisted by UNHCR. There were also 33,255 recently returned refugees in Sierra Leone of concern to UNHCR. The successful staging of legislative and presidential elections in May of that year and the consolidation of the peace process accelerated refugee returns. UNHCR terminated voluntary repatriation operations for Sierra Leonean refugees at 31 July 2004, by which time the Office had assisted about 180,000 of a total 280,000 returns since 2000, as well as implementing emergency and community development projects. Thereafter, refugee status was to be determined on an individual basis for those who had not yet returned. UNHCR's activities in assisting refugees in the region have included a focus on the prevention of sexual and gender-based violence in refugee camps—a regional action plan to combat such violence was initiated in 2002—and collaboration with other agencies to ensure continuity between initial humanitarian assistance and long-term development support.

In August 2000 the security situation in southern border areas of Guinea deteriorated owing to increasing insurgencies by rebels from Liberia and Sierra Leone, which displaced a large number of Guineans from their homes and also endangered an estimated 460,000 mainly Liberian and Sierra Leonean refugees (see above) accommodated in Guinean camps. In mid-September UNHCR and other aid organizations withdrew their international personnel and suspended food distribution in these areas following the murder by armed rebels of a member of UNHCR staff. Insecurity, hunger and mounting hostility from elements of the local population subsequently led significant numbers of refugees to flee the unprotected camps. Many sought to reach northern Guinea, while some returned spontaneously to their countries of origin. Following an escalation in fighting between Guinean government forces and insurgent rebels in early December refugee movements intensified; however, it was reported that an estimated 180,000 refugees and 70,000 IDPs remained stranded without humanitarian assistance in the southwestern Bec de Perroquet area. Later in December UNHCR dispatched emergency teams to assist with the relocation of refugees who had escaped the conflict zone. In February 2001 the High Commissioner negotiated with the parties to the conflict for the establishment of a humanitarian 'lifeline' to enable the delivery of assistance to and possible evacuation of the refugees and IDPs trapped at Bec de Perroquet: conveys of food aid began to reach the area at the end of that month. Meanwhile, UNHCR opened five new refugee settlements in central Guinea and, supported by the Guinean authorities, dispatched search teams into Bec de Perroquet in an attempt to find and evacuate refugees still stranded there. UNHCR withdrew from Beq de Perroquet at the end of May. During 2001 a total of 63,662 mainly Sierra Leonean refugees were relocated.

UNHCR provided assistance to 120,000 people displaced by the extreme insecurity that developed in Côte d'Ivoire from September 2002. About 25,000 Côte d'Ivoire refugees fled to southern Liberia, and others sought shelter in Ghana, Guinea and Mali. In addition, during November–January 2003 an estimated 40,000 Liberian refugees in Côte d'Ivoire repatriated, in both spontaneous and partly UNHCR-assisted movements, having suffered harassment since the onset of the conflict. UNHCR initiated a number of QIPs aimed at rehabilitating the infrastructure of communities that were to receive returned Côte d'Ivoire refugees (of whom there were more than 15,000 by late 2004).

Since 1993 the Great Lakes region of central Africa has experienced massive population displacement, causing immense operational challenges and demands on the resources of international humanitarian and relief agencies. In October of that year a military coup in Burundi prompted some 580,000 people to flee into Rwanda and Tanzania, although many had returned by early 1994. By May 1994, however, an estimated 860,000 people from Burundi and Rwanda had fled to neighbouring states (following a resurgence of ethnic violence in both countries), including 250,000 mainly Rwandan Tutsi refugees who entered Tanzania over a 24-hour period in late April in the most rapid mass exodus ever witnessed by UNHCR. In May UNHCR began an immediate operation to airlift emergency supplies to the refugees. For the first time in an emergency operation UNHCR organized support to be rendered in the form of eight defined 'service packages', for example, to provide domestic fuel, road servicing and security or sanitation facilities. Despite overcrowding in camps and a high incidence of cholera and dysentery (particularly in camps in eastern Zaire, where many thousands of Rwandan Hutus had sought refuge following the establishment of a new Government in July) large numbers of refugees refused to accept UNHCR-assisted repatriation, owing to fears of reprisal ethnic killings. In September reports of mass ethnic violence in Rwanda, which were disputed by some UN agencies, continued to disrupt UNHCR's policy of repatriation and to prompt returnees to cross the border back into Zaire. Security in the refugee camps, which was undermined by the presence of military and political elements of the former Rwandan regime, remained an outstanding concern for UNHCR. A resurgence of violence in Burundi, in February 1995, provoked further mass population movements. However, in March the Tanzanian authorities, reportedly frustrated at the lack of international assistance for the refugees and the environmental degradation resulting from the camps, closed Tanzania's border with Burundi, thus preventing the admission into the country of some 100,000 Rwandan Hutu refugees who were fleeing camps in Burundi. While persisting disturbances in Rwanda disrupted UNHCR's repatriation programme, in April Rwandan government troops employed intimidation tactics to force some 90,000 internally displaced Hutus to leave a heavily-populated camp in the south-west of the country; other small camps were closed. In August the Zairean Government initiated a short-lived programme of forcible repatriation of the estimated 1m. Rwandan and 70,000 Burundian Hutu refugees remaining in the country, which prompted as many as 100,000 refugees to flee the camps into the surrounding countryside. In September Rwanda agreed to strengthen its reception facilities and to provide greater security and protection for returnees, in collaboration with UNHCR, in order to prepare for any large-scale repatriation. UNHCR, meanwhile, expanded its information campaign, to promote the return of refugees, and enhanced its facilities at official border entry points. In December UNHCR negotiated an agreement between the Rwandan and Tanzanian authorities concerning the repatriation of the estimated 500,000 Rwandans remaining in camps in Tanzania. UNHCR agreed to establish a separate camp in north-west Tanzania in order to accommodate elements of the refugee population that might disrupt the repatriation programme. The repatriation of Rwandan refugees from all host countries was affected by reports of reprisals against Hutu returnees by the Tutsi-dominated Government in Rwanda. In February 1996 the Zairean Government renewed its efforts to accelerate the repatriation process, owing to concerns that the camps were becoming permanent settlements and that they were being used to train and rearm a Hutu militia. In July the Burundian Government forcibly repatriated 15,000 Rwandan refugees, having announced the closure of all remaining refugee camps. The repatriation programme was condemned by UNHCR and was suspended by the country's new military authorities, but only after many more thousands of refugees had been obliged to return to Rwanda and up to 30,000 had fled to Tanzania.

In October 1996 an escalation of hostilities between Zairean government forces, accused by Rwanda of arming the Hutu *Interahamwe* militia, and Zairean (Banyamulenge) Tutsis, who had been the focus of increasingly violent assaults, resulted in an extreme humanitarian crisis. Some 250,000 refugees fled 12 camps in the east of the country, including 90,000 Burundians who returned home. An estimated 500,000 refugees regrouped in Muganga camp, west of Goma, with insufficient relief assistance, following the temporary evacuation of international aid workers. UNHCR appealed to all Rwandan Hutu refugees to return home, and issued assurances of the presence of human rights observers in Rwanda to enhance their security. In November, with the apparent withdrawal of *Interahamwe* forces and the advance of the Tutsi-dominated Alliance des forces démocratiques pour la libération du Congo-Zaïre (AFDL), an estimated 600,000 refugees unexpectedly returned to Rwanda; however, concern remained on the part of the international community for the substantial number of Rwandan Hutu refugees at large in eastern Zaire. Further mass movement of Rwandan refugee populations occurred in December, owing to the threat of forcible repatriation by the Tanzanian Government, which had announced its intention of closing all camps by the end of the year. UNHCR initiated a repatriation programme; however, 200,000 refugees, unwilling to return to Rwanda, fled their camps. The majority of the refugees were later identified by the Tanzanian national army and escorted to the Rwandan border. By the end of December some 483,000 refugees had returned to Rwanda from Tanzania.

In February 1997 violence in Zaire intensified, which prompted some 56,000 Zaireans to flee into Tanzania and disrupted the distribution of essential humanitarian supplies to refugees remaining in Zaire. An estimated 170,000 refugees abandoned their temporary encampment at Tingi-Tingi, fearing attacks by the advancing AFDL forces. About 75,000 reassembled at Ubundu, south of Kisangani, while the fate of the other refugees remained uncertain. In March and April continued reports of attacks on refugee camps by AFDL forces and local Zaireans, resulted in large numbers of people fleeing into the surrounding countryside, with the consequent deaths of many of the most vulnerable members of the refugee population from disease and starvation. At the end of April the leader of the AFDL, Laurent-Désiré Kabila, ordered the repatriation of all Rwandan Hutu refugees by the UN within 60 days. Emergency air and land operations to evacuate some 185,000 refugees who had regrouped into temporary settlements were initiated a few days later. The repatriation process, however, was hindered by administrative and logistical difficulties and lack of co-operation on the part of the AFDL forces. By June an estimated 215,000 Rwandans were still missing or dispersed throughout the former Zaire (renamed the Democratic Republic of the Congo—DRC—by the AFDL in May). In the following months relations between the Kabila Government and UNHCR deteriorated as a result of several incidences of forcible repatriations of refugees to Rwanda and reports that the authorities were hindering a UN investigation into alleged abuses of human rights, committed against the Rwandan Hutu refugees by AFDL forces. In August an agreement was concluded to provide for the voluntary repatriation of some 75,000 refugees from the DRC remaining in Tanzania, under UNHCR supervision. However, the conflict that erupted in the DRC in August 1998 (see below) led to further large population movements. The repatriation of the estimated 260,000 Burundians remaining in Tanzania was also impeded, from early 1998, by an escalation of violence, which destabilized areas of return for both refugees and IDPs. In December 1997 a tripartite agreement was signed to provide for the organized repatriation of the remaining former Zairean refugees in Rwanda, with both Governments agreeing to observe strict conditions of security for the refugees on both sides of the border.

During the late 1990s UNHCR resolved to work, in co-operation with UNDP and WFP, to rehabilitate areas previously inhabited by refugees in central African countries of asylum and undertook to repair roads, bridges and other essential transport infrastructure, improve water and sanitation facilities, and strengthen the education sector. However, the political stability of the region remained extremely uncertain, and, from August 1998, DRC government forces and rebels became involved in a civil war in which the militaries of several regional governments were also implicated. From late 1998 substantial numbers of DRC nationals fled to neighbouring countries (mainly Tanzania and Zambia) or were displaced within the DRC. Meanwhile, the DRC, in turn, was hosting a significant refugee population. Although a cease-fire agreement was signed by all parties to the conflict in July 1999, this did not begin to be implemented until early 2001, when Kabila was assassinated and succeeded as President by his son, Maj.-Gen. Joseph Kabila. Following the DRC Government's adoption of peace agreements, in July and August 2002, with, respectively, the Rwandan and Ugandan Governments, nearly all Rwandan and Ugandan forces were withdrawn before the end of that year. Meanwhile, troop withdrawals were also initiated by Angola, Burundi, Namibia and Zimbabwe. In view of the conclusion, in December, of a peace agreement providing for the staging of elections in the DRC after a transition period of 24 months, UNHCR planned for eventual mass refugee returns. The Office, in co-operation with UNDP, the UN Mission in the DRC (MONUC) and the World Bank, was to assist efforts to demobilize, disarm and repatriate former combatants. Insecurity continued to prevail, however, during 2003–early 2005, in northeastern areas of the DRC, resulting in continuing population displacements. In 2003 UNHCR provided assistance to 35,000 refugees from north-eastern DRC sheltering in Burundi. During that year the Office assisted about 37,000 refugee returns to Burundi (where largely favourable progress had been achieved in the ongoing peace process), while a further 45,000 Burundian refugees returned spontaneously. A tripartite agreement on assistance was concluded by the Burundian and Tanzanian Governments and UNHCR in August 2003. UNHCR concluded similar accords during that year with the Rwandan Government and other states hosting Rwandan refugees, paving the way for significant voluntary refugee returns to Rwanda during 2004–05. The major populations of concern to UNHCR in the Great Lakes region at 31 December 2003 were, provisionally, as follows: 234,033 refugees in the DRC; 82,049 returned refugees in Burundi; and a refugee population of 649,770 in Tanzania, the largest concentration of refugees on the continent. UNHCR has provided education, environmental protection and healthcare programmes at camps in Tanzania, with a focus on the empowerment of women, eliminating gender-based violence and controlling the spread of HIV/AIDS. UNHCR also provides support to those refugees permitted by the Tanzanian Government to resettle permanently in that country. The security of international aid personnel in the Great Lakes region has been of concern and UNHCR assists the Tanzanian authorities with ensuring that camps retain a humanitarian, civilian ethos and exclude infiltrators without entitlement to humanitarian protection.

In mid-1997 an estimated 40,000 refugees from the Republic of the Congo fled to the DRC, following a short-lived outbreak of civil conflict. In December a memorandum of understanding was signed by representatives of the two Governments and of UNHCR, providing for their immediate repatriation. From late 1998 the resumption of conflict in the Republic of the Congo disrupted UNHCR humanitarian efforts in that country and caused significant numbers of Congolese to seek refuge in the DRC and Gabon, and the internal displacement of as many as 500,000 people. Following the agreement of a cease-fire in December the majority of IDPs returned home. More than 60,000 Congolese refugees had repatriated by the end of 2000. A tripartite accord on the voluntary repatriation of Congolese refugees from Gabon was concluded by UNHCR and the Congolese and Gabon Governments during 2001. At December 2003 Congolese refugees remaining in Gabon numbered 12,122, and some 6,626 Congolese refugees remained in the DRC (of whom 1,215 were being assisted by UNHCR). The Office was continuing to assist with their repatriation and reintegration in 2004–05, following the conclusion of a peace accord between the Congolese Government and rebels in March 2003. During 2000 more than 80,000 refugees from the DRC sought protection in the Republic of the Congo, which was hosting 81,004 refugees from the DRC at end-2003 (of whom 79,555 were UNHCR-assisted).

In 1994 continuing civil conflict in Angola caused some 370,000 people to leave their home areas. Prior to the signing of a peace settlement in November, UNHCR provided assistance to 112,000 internally displaced Angolans and returnees, although military activities, which hindered accessibility, undermined the effectiveness of the assistance programme. In mid-1995, following a consolidation of the peace process in Angola, UNHCR appealed for US $44m. to support the voluntary repatriation of some 300,000 Angolan refugees through a two-and-a-half-year operation. By June 1996 implementation of the repatriation programme was delayed, reportedly owing to poor accommodation and other facilities for returnees, limited progress in confining and disarming opposition troops and the continued hazard of land-mines throughout the country. During 1997 an estimated 53,000 Angolans voluntarily returned from the DRC and Zambia, bringing the total returnees to some 130,000 since mid-1995. In November 1997 UNHCR resolved to implement an operation to provide for the repatriation and reintegration of the remaining Angolan refugees by June 1999. UNHCR allocated $15.7m. to support the repatriation process and other activities in Angola, including strengthening the country's road infrastructure, monitoring areas of return, the implementation of reintegration projects and promoting links with other development programmes. In May 1998, however, the security situation in Angola deteriorated, and at the end of June UNHCR declared a temporary suspension of the repatriation operation. The renewed violence also resulted in further population displacement, with refugee movements into the DRC continuing during 1998–2001. In July 2000 UNHCR expanded its operations in Angola to support IDPs by providing emergency humanitarian assistance and helping IDP communities and local administrations with the provision of basic services, demining and the rehabilitation of local infrastructures. Following the signing of the Luanda Peace Agreement in April 2002 between the Angolan Government and rebels of the União National para a Independência Total de Angola, UNHCR made preparations for the voluntary repatriation of a projected 400,000 Angolan refugees sheltering elsewhere in southern Africa. At the end of 2003 UNHCR was providing assistance to some 132,977 Angolan returned refugees. Meanwhile, an estimated 323,575 Angolans were still sheltering in neighbouring countries at that time, including 158,894 in Zambia and 123,714 in the DRC. It was estimated that in all more than 4.3m. Angolans were displaced from their homes during the 1980s and 1990s, and by the end of 2003 a total of about 4.1m. IDPs, refugees and demobilized fighters had reportedly returned home. By the end of 2004 the Office had rehabilitated the nine main repatriation corridors into Angola. Some 33,000 UNHCR-assisted and 30,000 spontaneous refugee returns to Angola were envisaged in 2005. UNHCR was working to consolidate the reintegration of returnees. HIV/AIDS- and mine-awareness training were being offered at refugee reception centres.

THE AMERICAS AND THE CARIBBEAN

In May 1989, when an International Conference on Central American Refugees (CIREFCA) was held in Guatemala, there were some 146,400 refugees receiving UNHCR assistance (both for emergency relief and for longer-term self-sufficiency programmes) in the region, as well as an estimated 1.8m. other refugees and displaced persons. UNHCR and UNDP were designated as the principal UN organizations to implement the CIREFCA plan of action for the repatriation or resettlement of refugees, alongside national co-ordinating committees. UNHCR QIPs were implemented in the transport, health, agricultural production and other sectors to support returnee reintegration (of both refugees and internally displaced persons) into local communities, and to promote the self-sufficiency of the returning populations. Implementation of UNHCR's programme for the repatriation of some 45,000 Guatemalan refugees in Mexico began in January 1993 with a convoy of 2,400 people.

UNHCR initiated projects to support the reintegration of Guatemalan returnees, and in 1994–95 undertook a campaign to clear undetonated explosives in forest areas where they had resettled. The CIREFCA process was formally concluded in June 1994, by which time some 118,000 refugees had voluntarily returned to their countries of origin under the auspices of the programme, while thousands of others had integrated into their host countries. In December a meeting was held, in San José, Costa Rica, to commemorate the 10th anniversary of the Cartagena Declaration, which had provided a comprehensive framework for refugee protection in the region. The meeting adopted the San José Declaration on Refugees and Displaced Persons, which aimed to harmonize legal criteria and procedures to consolidate actions for durable solutions of voluntary repatriation and local integration in the region. UNHCR's efforts in the region subsequently emphasized legal issues and refugee protection, while assisting governments to formulate national legislation on asylum and refugees. Since 1996 several thousand Guatemalan refugees have received Mexican citizenship under a fast-track naturalization programme. At December 2003 6,075 refugees remained in Mexico. During 2005 UNHCR was to assist the Mexican authorities with completing the naturalization of some 2,000 Guatemalan refugees, and also with the naturalization of 2,800 refugees of other nationalities sheltering in urban areas. In December 2004 regional leaders met in Mexico City to commemorate the 20th anniversary of the Cartagena Declaration, and launched a new plan of action aimed at addressing current refugee problems in Central America, with a particular focus on the humanitarian crisis in Colombia and the border areas of its neighbouring countries (see below), and the increasing numbers of refugees concentrated in urban centres in the region.

In 1999 the Colombian Government approved an operational plan proposed by UNHCR to address a massive population displacement that has arisen in that country in recent years (escalating from 1997), as a consequence of ongoing internal conflict and alleged human rights abuses committed by armed groups. Significant cross-border movements of Colombian refugees into neighbouring countries prompted UNHCR to intensify its border-monitoring activities during the early 2000s to enhance its capacity to forecast and react to new population movements. UNHCR has assisted with the implementation of an IDP registration plan, provided training in emergency response to displacements, and supported ongoing changes in Colombia's legislative framework for IDPs. UNHCR has also co-operated with UNICEF to improve the provision of education to displaced children. During 2005 UNHCR aimed to support compliance with national legislation and policies on IDPs and to promote durable solutions for IDPs such as return, relocation and integration into local communities. The Office has focused on building up stockpiles of relief items in neighbouring countries and has developed contingency plans with other partners to enable the rapid deployment of personnel to border areas should the exodus of refugees from Colombia intensify further. At the end of 2003 Costa Rica was hosting 8,266 Colombian refugees (from a total refugee population of 13,508). Ecuador was accommodating 6,381 refugees and 2,565 asylum-seekers, mainly from Colombia. At that time there were some 1.2m. IDPs within Colombia of concern to UNHCR.

Canada and the USA are major countries of resettlement for refugees. UNHCR provides counselling and legal services for asylum-seekers in these countries. At 31 December 2003 the estimated refugee populations totalled 133,094 in Canada and 452,548 in the USA, while asylum-seekers numbered 41,575 and 334,862 respectively.

CENTRAL AND SOUTH-EASTERN EUROPE

The political changes in Central and Eastern Europe during the early 1990s resulted in a dramatic increase in the number of asylum-seekers and displaced people in the region. UNHCR was the agency designated by the UN Secretary-General to lead the UN relief operation to assist those affected by the conflict in the former Yugoslavia. It was responsible for the supply of food and other humanitarian aid to the besieged capital of Bosnia and Herzegovina, Sarajevo, and to Muslim and Croatian enclaves in the country, under the armed escort of the UN Protection Force. Assistance was provided not only to Bosnian refugees in Croatia and displaced people within Bosnia and Herzegovina's borders, but also, in order to forestall further movements of people, to civilians whose survival was threatened. The operation was often seriously hampered by armed attacks (resulting, in some cases, in fatalities), distribution difficulties and underfunding from international donors. The Dayton peace agreement, which was signed in December 1995 bringing an end to the conflict, secured the right for all refugees and displaced persons freely to choose their place of residence within the new territorial arrangements of Bosnia and Herzegovina. Thus, the immediate effect of the peace accord was further population displacement, including a mass exodus of almost the entire Serb population of Sarajevo. Under the peace accord, UNHCR was responsible for planning and implementing the repatriation of all

Bosnian refugees and displaced persons, then estimated at 2m.; however, there were still immense obstacles to freedom of movement, in particular for minorities wishing to return to an area dominated by a different politico-ethnic faction. Returns by refugees and IDPs (including significant numbers of refugees returning to areas where they represented minority ethnic communities) accelerated from 2000, owing to an improvement in security conditions. In 2001 so-called 'minority returns' totalled 92,061, bringing the total number of minority returns since 1998 to 287,000; minority returns continued during 2002–04. In July 2002 the heads of state of Bosnia and Herzogovina, Croatia and the FRY met in Sarajevo with a view to resolving a number of outstanding issues including the return of remaining refugees. The repossession by their rightful owners and reconstruction of illegally appropriated properties have been key issues for returned refugees to the region. By the end of 2003 most claims on properties in Bosnia and Herzegovina had been settled. By that time there was still an estimated total Bosnian refugee population of some 300,006, of whom some 105,973 were receiving assistance from UNHCR. The majority of the Bosnian refugee population were in the Federal Republic of Yugoslavia (FRY, now Serbia and Montenegro). In addition, there were 14,012 recently returned refugees and 40,303 returned IDPs of concern to UNHCR in Bosnia and Herzegovina and 327,188 IDPs who had yet to return home.

From March 1998 attacks by Serbian forces against members of a separatist movement in the southern Serbian province of Kosovo and Metohija resulted in large-scale population displacement. Of particular concern were some 50,000 people who had fled to the surrounding mountains, close to the Albanian border, without shelter or adequate provisions. In October the withdrawal of Serbian troops and the involvement of the international community in the provision of aid and monitoring of the situation in Kosovo was thought to have prompted substantial numbers to have returned home. However, in December there were reports of renewed attacks by Serbian forces on the local Albanian population, which persisted into 1999. The failure of peace negotiations prompted further displacement, and in late March an estimated 95,000 people fled their homes following the withdrawal of international observers of the OSCE and the commencement of a NATO operation, which aimed to halt the Serbian attacks and compel the FRY to agree to a peace settlement. By mid-April UNHCR estimated that up to 1.3m. Kosovar Albanians had been displaced since the fighting began in 1998, with reports that thousands had been forcibly expelled by Serbian troops in recent weeks. UNHCR attempted to provide emergency relief to the thousands of refugees who fled to neighbouring countries, and expressed concern for those remaining in the province, of whom up to 400,000 were thought to be living without shelter. In early April 1999 UNHCR condemned the decision of the authorities in the former Yugoslav republic of Macedonia (FYRM) forcibly to evacuate some 30,000 refugees from camps in Blace, near the FRY border, and subsequently to close the border to further refugees. At that time UNHCR helped to co-ordinate an international effort to evacuate substantial numbers of the refugees to third countries, and issued essential identity and travel documents. In Albania UNHCR funded transport to relocate an estimated 250,000 people from the border town of Kukës, where resources and the local infrastructure were strained by the massive population influx, to other sites throughout the country. At the start of June the Kosovar refugee population totalled some 443,300 people in Albania, 247,800 in the FYRM, 69,300 in Montenegro, and 21,700 in Bosnia and Herzegovina, while under a joint Humanitarian Evacuation Programme with the International Organization for Migration, more than 90,000 refugees had been evacuated to 29 countries. UNHCR organized host families to receive a large proportion of the refugees, while additional shelter was provided in the form of tented camps and collective centres. In mid-June, following a cease-fire accord and an agreement by the FRY to withdraw all forces and paramilitary units, UNHCR initiated a large-scale registration operation of Kosovar refugees and began to deliver emergency provisions to assist the displaced population within Kosovo. Despite warnings of anti-personnel devices and lack of shelter, UNHCR estimated that some 477,000 refugees had returned in a spontaneous repatriation movement by the end of June. Meanwhile, it was reported that a total of 170,000 Serbs left Kosovo, fearing reprisal attacks by returning ethnic Albanians; in addition, some 50,000 members of the Roma minority moved out of the province. In September UNHCR estimated that one-third of all homes in Kosovo had been destroyed or seriously damaged during the conflict, prompting concerns regarding the welfare of returning refugees and IDPs in the coming winter months. UNHCR distributed 'shelter kits' to assist the process of reconstruction of homes, and proceeded to accelerate the distribution of blankets and winter clothing, as well as of fuel, food, water, and the provision of medical care throughout Serbia and Montenegro. In mid-2000 UNHCR scaled down its emergency

humanitarian activities in Kosovo and provided a UN Humanitarian Co-ordinator to oversee the transition to long-term reconstruction and development, in co-operation with the UN Interim Administration Mission in Kosovo (UNMIK). UNHCR and OSCE have periodically jointly assessed the situation of minority communities in Kosovo; in May 2002 the two organizations reported that discrimination against and intimidation of minorities in the province was prevalent, hindering minority returns and integration. An outbreak of inter-ethnic conflict in March 2004 was expected to further impede the process. At end of 2003 there were still 256,891 IDPs in Serbia and Montenegro, the majority of whom were from Kosovo. In addition, Serbia and Montenegro was hosting 291,403 refugees, of whom 99,785 were from Bosnia and Herzegovina and 189,746 from Croatia.

In response to the mounting insecurity in the FYRM from early 2001, as conflict escalated between ethnic Albanian rebels and government troops, 81,000 Macedonian refugees fled to Kosovo (of whom several thousand repatriated promptly) and 12,000 to southern Serbia during February–August, while over that period more than 50,000 people became displaced within the FYRM. In June UNHCR appealed for funds to finance the provision of emergency humanitarian assistance to the Macedonian refugees, and opened a registration centre in Kosovo. Repatriations accelerated following the conclusion in August of a framework peace agreement between the opposing parties, however many people remained displaced owing to fears they would return to communities in which they would belong to an ethnic minority. At the end of 2003 there were 2,201 returned refugees and 6,764 returned IDPs of concern to UNHCR in the FYRM.

EASTERN EUROPE

In December 1992 UNHCR dispatched teams to establish offices in both Armenia and Azerbaijan to assist people displaced as a result of the war between the two countries and to provide immediate relief. A cease-fire agreement was signed between the two sides in May 1994, although violations of the accord were subsequently reported and relations between the two countries remained tense. At the end of 2003 the region was still supporting a massive displaced population, including 239,250 Azerbaijani refugees in Armenia and 575,609 IDPs of concern to UNHCR in Azerbaijan. UNHCR's humanitarian activities have focused on improving shelter, in particular for the most vulnerable among the refugee population, and promoting economic self-sufficiency and stability.

In Georgia, where almost 300,000 people left their homes as a result of civil conflict from 1991, UNHCR has attempted to encourage income-generating activities among the displaced population, to increase the Georgian Government's capacity to support those people and to assist the rehabilitation of people returning to their areas of origin. At 31 December 2003 there were 260,215 Georgian IDPs, affected by the ongoing conflicts in Abkhazia and South Ossetia. In late 1999 an estimated 7,000 refugees fleeing insecurity in Chechnya (see below) entered Georgia. By August 2004 about 2,650 Chechen refugees reportedly remained in Georgia. UNHCR has delivered food to the Chechen refugees and the host families with whom the majority are staying, and has also assisted the refugees through shelter renovation, psychosocial support and the provision of child-care facilities and health and community development support, as well as monitoring refugee-host family relations. From 1994 UNHCR pursued a process to establish a comprehensive approach to the problems of refugees, returnees, IDPs and migrants in the Commonwealth of Independent States (CIS). A regional conference convened in Geneva, Switzerland, in May 1996, endorsed a framework of activities aimed at managing migratory flows and at developing institutional capacities to prevent mass population displacements. At that time it was estimated that more than 9m. former citizens of the USSR had relocated since its disintegration as a result of conflict, economic pressures and ecological disasters. By early 2005 all CIS member states excepting Uzbekistan had acceded to the 1951 Convention.

In March 1995 UNHCR initiated an assistance programme for people displaced as a result of conflict in the separatist republic of Chechnya (the Chechen Republic of Ichkeriya, the Russian Federation), as part of a UN inter-agency relief effort, in collaboration with the International Committee of the Red Cross (ICRC). UNHCR continued its activities in 1996, at the request of the Russian Government, at which time the displaced population within Chechnya and in the surrounding republics totalled 490,000. During 1997 UNHCR provided reintegration assistance to 25,000 people who returned to Chechnya, despite reports of sporadic violence. The security situation in the region deteriorated sharply in mid-1999, following a series of border clashes and incursions by Chechen separatist forces into the neighbouring republic of Dagestan. In September Russian military aircraft began an aerial offensive against suspected rebel targets in Chechnya, and at the end of the month ground troops moved into the republic. By November an estimated 225,000 Chechens had fled to neighbouring Ingushetiya. UNHCR dispatched food supplies to assist the IDPs and, from February 2000, periodically sent relief convoys into Chechnya, where there was still a substantial displaced population; the poor security situation, however, prevented other UNHCR deployment within Chechnya. In late 2000 UNHCR assisted with the construction of the first tented camp to provide adequate winter shelter for Chechens in Ingushetiya; many others were being sheltered in local homes. During 2004, however, the Russian authorities closed the three tented refugee camps that had been operational in Ingushetiya at December 2003; the final camp closure was completed in June 2004. Temporary lodging (consisting of rooms in accommodation centres or in private homes) was to be provided for those refugees who did not wish to return home. At 31 May an estimated 54,000 Chechen refugees remained in Ingushetiya, including 24,366 registered in 186 temporary settlements.

CO-OPERATION WITH OTHER ORGANIZATIONS

UNHCR works closely with other UN agencies, intergovernmental organizations and non-governmental organizations (NGOs) to increase the scope and effectiveness of its operations. Within the UN system UNHCR co-operates, principally, with the World Food Programme in the distribution of food aid, UNICEF and the World Health Organization in the provision of family welfare and child immunization programmes, OCHA in the delivery of emergency humanitarian relief, UNDP in development-related activities and the preparation of guide-lines for the continuum of emergency assistance to development programmes, and the Office of the UN High Commissioner for Human Rights. UNHCR also has close working relationships with the International Committee of the Red Cross and the International Organization for Migration. In 2004 UNHCR worked with 565 NGOs as 'implementing partners', enabling UNHCR to broaden the use of its resources while maintaining a co-ordinating role in the provision of assistance.

TRAINING

UNHCR organizes training programmes and workshops to enhance the capabilities of field workers and non-UNHCR staff, in the following areas: the identification and registration of refugees; people-orientated planning; resettlement procedures and policies; emergency response and management; security awareness; stress management; and the dissemination of information through the electronic media.

Finance

The United Nations' regular budget finances a proportion of UNHCR's administrative expenditure. The majority of UNHCR's programme expenditure (about 98%) is funded by voluntary contributions, mainly from governments. The Private Sector and Public Affairs Service aims to increase funding from non-governmental donor sources, for example by developing partnerships with foundations and corporations. Following approval of the Unified Annual Programme Budget any subsequently-identified requirements are managed in the form of Supplementary Programmes, financed by separate appeals. The total Unified Annual Programme Budget for 2005 was projected at US $982m.

Publications

Refugees (quarterly, in English, French, German, Italian, Japanese and Spanish).

Refugee Resettlement: An International Handbook to Guide Reception and Integration.

Refugee Survey Quarterly.

Sexual and Gender-based Violence Against Refugees, Returnees and Displaced Persons: Guide-lines for Prevention and Response.

The State of the World's Refugees (every 2 years).

UNHCR Handbook for Emergencies.

Press releases, reports.

Statistics

POPULATIONS OF CONCERN TO UNHCR BY REGION*
('000 persons, at 31 December 2003, provisional figures)

	Refugees†	Asylum-seekers	Returned refugees‡	Others of concern§	Total
Africa	2,863	160	345	610	3,977
CASWANAME	2,915	24	705	421	4,064
Asia and the Pacific	816	18	8	562	1,405
Europe	2,453	410	36	2,470	5,368
Latin America	38	7	0	1,271	1,316
North America	586	376	—	—	962
Total	9,672	995	1,095	5,332	17,093

*UNHCR's Africa region covers the countries of sub-Saharan Africa. 'CASWANAME' denotes Central Asia, South West Asia, North Africa and the Middle East. Latin America covers Central and South America and the Caribbean.
† Includes persons recognized as refugees under international law, and also people receiving temporary protection and assistance outside their country but who have not been formally recognized as refugees.
‡ Refugees who returned to their place of origin during 2003.
§ Mainly internally displaced persons (IDPs) and former IDPs who returned to their place of origin during 2003.

POPULATIONS OF CONCERN TO UNHCR BY COUNTRY*
('000 persons, at 31 December 2003, provisional figures)

	Refugees†	Asylum-seekers	Returned refugees†	Others of concern†
Africa				
Angola	13.4	1.0	133.0	—
Burundi	41.0	10.6	82.4	2.0
Chad	146.4	0.2	0.6	—
Democratic Republic of the Congo	234.0	0.4	3.2	—
Côte d'Ivoire	76.1	1.3	16.6	38.0
Ethiopia	130.3	0.0	0.2	—
Guinea	184.3	2.5	—	—
Kenya	237.5	4.0	0.1	—
Liberia	34.0	—	21.0	546.6
South Africa	26.6	84.1	—	—
Sudan	138.2	0.5	0.1	22.0
Tanzania	649.8	0.2	0.0	—
Uganda	230.9	0.7	4.4	—
Zambia	226.7	0.2	0.0	—
CASWANAME				
Afghanistan	0.0	0.0	645.9	266.3
Algeria	169.0	0.0	0.0	—
Iran	984.9	0.0	3.9	—
Iraq‡	134.2	0.4	55.2	—
Kuwait	1.5	0.2	—	101.0
Pakistan§	1,124.3	5.4	0.0	—
Saudi Arabia	240.8	0.1	—	—
Asia and the Pacific				
China, People's Republic‖	299.4	0.0	—	—
India	164.8	0.5	—	—
Nepal	123.7	0.2	—	10.7
Sri Lanka	0.0	0.0	0.5	462.8
Thailand	119.1	2.7	—	0.0
Europe				
Armenia	239.3	0.0	—	—
Azerbaijan	0.3	8.8	—	576.0
Bosnia and Herzegovina	22.5	0.7	14.0	367.5
France	130.8	22.9	—	—
Germany	960.4	153.7	—	—
Georgia	3.9	—	0.1	260.6
Netherlands	140.9	44.7	—	—
Russia	9.9	0.3	0.0	795.4
Serbia and Montenegro	291.4	0.0	9.4	344.3
Sweden	112.2	35.3	—	—
United Kingdom	276.5	24.5		

— continued	Refugees†	Asylum-seekers	Returned refugees†	Others of concern†
Latin America				
Colombia . .	0.2	0.0	0.1	1,244
North America				
Canada . . .	133.1	41.6	—	—
USA	452.5	334.9	—	—

*The list includes only those countries having 100,000 or more persons of concern to UNHCR.
† See table above for definitions.
‡ 2002 figures.
§ Excluding Afghans sheltering in urban areas.
‖ Excluding Hong Kong Special Administrative Region.

ORIGIN OF MAJOR REFUGEE POPULATIONS AND PERSONS IN REFUGEE-LIKE SITUATIONS*

('000 persons, 31 December 2003, provisional figures)

Origin	Refugees
Afghanistan	2,136.0
Sudan	606.2
Burundi	531.6
Democratic Republic of the Congo	453.4
Palestinian Territories†	427.8
Somalia	402.2
Iraq	368.4
Viet Nam	363.2

* Information on the origin of refugees is not available for a number of, mainly industrialized, countries.
† Data exclude some 4.1m. Palestinian refugees who come under the mandate of UNRWA. Palestinians who are outside the UNRWA area of operation, for example those in Iraq and Libya, are considered to be of concern to UNHCR.

United Nations Peace-keeping

Address: Department of Peace-keeping Operations, Room S-3727-B, United Nations, New York, NY 10017, USA.

Telephone: (212) 963-8077; **fax:** (212) 963-9222; **internet:** www.un.org/Depts/dpko/.

United Nations peace-keeping operations have been conceived as instruments of conflict control. The UN has used these operations in various conflicts, with the consent of the parties involved, to maintain international peace and security, without prejudice to the positions or claims of parties, in order to facilitate the search for political settlements through peaceful means such as mediation and the good offices of the UN Secretary-General. Each operation is established with a specific mandate, which requires periodic review by the UN Security Council. United Nations peace-keeping operations fall into two categories: peace-keeping forces and observer missions.

Peace-keeping forces are composed of contingents of military and civilian personnel, made available by member states. These forces assist in preventing the recurrence of fighting, restoring and maintaining peace, and promoting a return to normal conditions. To this end, peace-keeping forces are authorized as necessary to undertake negotiations, persuasion, observation and fact-finding. They conduct patrols and interpose physically between the opposing parties. Peace-keeping forces are permitted to use their weapons only in self-defence.

Military observer missions are composed of officers (usually unarmed), who are made available, on the Secretary-General's request, by member states. A mission's function is to observe and report to the Secretary-General (who, in turn, informs the Security Council) on the maintenance of a cease-fire, to investigate violations and to do what it can to improve the situation.

Peace-keeping forces and observer missions must at all times maintain complete impartiality and avoid any action that might affect the claims or positions of the parties. A UN Stand-by Arrangements System (UNSAS) became operational in 1994; at July 2003 some 77 countries were participating in the system by making available specialized civilian and military personnel, as well as other services and equipment. In January 1995 the UN Secretary-General presented a report to the Security Council, reassessing the UN's role in peace-keeping. The document stipulated that UN forces in conflict areas should not be responsible for peace-enforcement duties, and included a proposal for the establishment of a 'rapid reaction' force which would be ready for deployment within a month of being authorized by the Security Council. In September 1997 the UN Secretary-General established a staff to plan and organize the formation of the so-called UN Stand-by Forces High Readiness Brigade (SHIRBRIG). SHIRBRIG, based in Denmark, was declared available to the UN in January 2000 and became fully operational later in that year with the deployment of troops to the newly-authorized UN Mission in Ethiopia and Eritrea (UNMEE) for a duration of six months. In September 2003 SHIRBRIG deployed some 20 personnel to the newly-established UN Mission in Liberia (UNMIL). In July 2004 a SHIRBRIG team assisted the preparation of a UN Advance Mission in Sudan and in January 2005 a reconnaissance team visited Sudan to consider the deployment of SHIRBRIG troops. By 2004 Argentina, Austria, Canada, Denmark, Finland, Italy, Ireland, Lithuania, the Netherlands, Norway, Poland, Portugal, Romania, Slovenia, Spain and Sweden had formally committed troops to the force. A further five countries were participating as observers.

In August 2000 a report on UN peace-keeping activities prepared by a team of experts appointed by the Secretary-General assessed the aims and requirements of peace-keeping operations and recommended several measures to improve the performance of the Department of Peace-Keeping Operations (DPKO), focusing on its planning and management capacity from the inception of an operation through to post-conflict peace-building activities, and on its rapid response capability. Proposed reforms included the establishment of a body to improve co-ordination of information and strategic analysis requirements; the promotion of partnership arrangements between member states (within the context of UNSAS) enabling the formation of several coherent multinational brigades, and improved monitoring of the preparedness of potential troop contributor nations, with a view to facilitating the effective deployment of most operations within 30 days of their authorization in a Security Council resolution; the adoption of 'on-call' reserve lists to ensure the prompt deployment of civilian police and specialists; the preparation of a global logistics support strategy; and a restructuring of the DPKO to improve administrative efficiency. The study also urged an increase in resources for funding peace-keeping operations and the adoption of a more flexible financing mechanism, and emphasized the importance of the UN's conflict prevention activities. In November the Security Council, having welcomed the report, adopted guide-lines aimed at improving its management of peace-keeping operations, including providing missions with clear and achievable mandates. In June 2001 the Council adopted a resolution incorporating a Statement of principles on co-operation with troop-contributing countries, which aimed to strengthen the relationship between those countries and the UN and to enhance the effectiveness of peace-keeping operations. A new Rapid Deployment Level within UNSAS was inaugurated in July 2002. In 2004 the Department established a Special Investigation Team, at the request of the UN Secretary-General, which, in November, visited the Democratic Republic of the Congo to examine allegations of sexual exploitation and abuse committed by peace-keeping personnel.

The UN's peace-keeping forces and observer missions are financed in most cases by assessed contributions from member states of the organization. In recent years a significant expansion in the UN's peace-keeping activities has been accompanied by a perpetual financial crisis within the organization, as a result of the increased financial burden and some member states' delaying payment. At 31 January 2005 outstanding assessed contributions to the peace-keeping budget amounted to some US $2,320m.

By early 2005 the UN had deployed a total of 59 peace-keeping operations, of which 13 were authorized in the period 1948–88 and 46 since 1988, reaching a peak in 1993 with a total deployment of more than 80,000 troops from 77 countries. At 31 January 2005 103 countries were contributing some 65,050 personnel to the ongoing operations, of whom 56,197 were peace-keeping troops, 6,765 civilian police and 2,088 military observers.

In 2005 the UN was maintaining a number of political and peace-building missions; of these, the UN Assistance Mission in Afghanistan (UNAMA, established by a resolution of the Security Council in March 2002) and the UN Advance Mission in Sudan (UNAMIS, endorsed by the Council in June 2004) were directly supported by the DPKO.

The report of the Secretary-General entitled 'In Larger Freedom: Towards Development, Security and Human Rights for All', issued in March 2005, proposed the creation of an intergovernmental Peace-building Commission, as well as a Peace-building Support Office within the Secretariat, with a view to ensuring the 'sustained and sustainable' implementation of peace agreements.

UNITED NATIONS DISENGAGEMENT OBSERVER FORCE—UNDOF

Address: Camp Faouar, Syria.

Force Commander: Maj.-Gen. BALA NANDA SHARMA (Nepal).

UNDOF was established for an initial period of six months by a UN Security Council resolution in May 1974, following the signature in Geneva of a disengagement agreement between Syrian and Israeli forces. The mandate has since been extended by successive resolutions. The initial task of the Force was to take over territory evacuated in stages by the Israeli troops, in accordance with the disengagement agreement, to hand over territory to Syrian troops, and to establish an area of separation on the Golan Heights.

UNDOF continues to monitor the area of separation; it carries out inspections of the areas of limited armaments and forces; uses its best efforts to maintain the cease-fire; and undertakes activities of a humanitarian nature, such as arranging the transfer of prisoners and war-dead between Syria and Israel. The Force operates exclusively on Syrian territory.

At 31 January 2005 the Force comprised 1,023 troops; it is assisted by approximately 80 military observers of UNTSO's Observer Group Golan, and supported by 143 international and local civilian personnel. Further UNTSO military observers help UNDOF in the performance of its tasks, as required. The General Assembly appropriated US $43.03m. to cover the cost of the operation for the period 1 July 2004–30 June 2005.

UNITED NATIONS INTERIM ADMINISTRATION MISSION IN KOSOVO— UNMIK

Address: Priština, Kosovo.

Special Representative of the UN Secretary-General and Head of Mission: SØREN JESSEN-PETERSEN (Denmark).

Principal Deputy Special Representative of the UN Secretary-General: LAURENCE (LARRY) G. ROSSIN (USA).

Deputy Special Representative for Police and Justice: JEAN DOUSSARD (France).

Deputy Special Representative for Civil Administration: FRANCESCO BASTAGLI (Italy).

Deputy Special Representative for (OSCE) Institution Building in Kosovo: PASCAL FIESCHI (France).

Deputy Special Representative for (EU) Reconstruction in Kosovo: JOACHIM RÜCKER (Germany).

In June 1999 NATO suspended a 10-week aerial offensive against the then Federal Republic of Yugoslavia (now Serbia and Montenegro), following an agreement by the Serbian authorities to withdraw all security and paramilitary forces from the southern province of Kosovo and Metohija, where Serbian repression of a separatist movement had prompted a humanitarian crisis and co-ordinated international action to resolve the conflict. On 10 June the UN Security Council adopted Resolution 1244, which outlined the terms of a political settlement for Kosovo and provided for the deployment of international civilian and security personnel. The security presence, termed the Kosovo Peace Implementation Force (KFOR), was to be led by NATO, while the UN was to oversee all civilian operations. UNMIK was established under the terms of Resolution 1244 as the supreme legal and executive authority in Kosovo, with responsibility for all civil administration and for facilitating the reconstruction and rehabilitation of the province as an autonomous region. For the first time in a UN operation other organizations were mandated to co-ordinate aspects of the mission in Kosovo, under the UN's overall jurisdiction. The four key elements, or Pillars, of UNMIK were (I) humanitarian affairs (led by UNHCR); (II) civil administration; (III) democratization and institution-building (OSCE); and (IV) economic reconstruction (EU). At the end of the first year of UNMIK's presence the element of humanitarian assistance was phased out. A new Pillar (I), concerned with police and justice, was established in May 2001, under the direct leadership of the UN. On arriving in the province at the end of June 1999 UNMIK and KFOR established a Joint Implementation Commission to co-ordinate and supervise the demilitarization of the Kosovo Liberation Army. UNMIK initiated a mass information campaign (and later administered new radio stations in Kosovo) to urge co-operation with the international personnel in the province and tolerance for all ethnic communities. A Mine Co-ordinating Centre supervised efforts to deactivate anti-personnel devices and to ensure the safety of the returning ethnic Albanian population. In July the UN Secretary-General's permanent Special Representative took office, and chaired the first meeting of the Kosovo Transitional Council (KTC), which had been established by the UN as a multi-ethnic consultative organ, the highest political body under UNMIK, to help to restore law and order in the province and to reintegrate the local administrative infrastructure. In August a Joint Advisory Council on Legislative Matters was constituted, with representatives of UNMIK and the local judiciary, in order to consider measures to eliminate discrimination from the province's legal framework. At the end of July UNMIK personnel began to supervise customs controls at Kosovo's international borders. Other developments in the first few months of UNMIK's deployment included the establishment of joint commissions on energy and public utilities, education, and health, a Technical Advisory Commission on establishing a judiciary and prosecution service, and, in October, the establishment of a Fuel Supervisory Board to administer the import, sale and distribution of petroleum. Central financial institutions for the province were inaugurated in November. In the same month UNMIK established a Housing and Property Directorate and Claims Commission in order to resolve residential property disputes. In September the KTC agreed to establish a Joint Security Committee, in response to concerns at the escalation of violence in the province, in particular attacks on remaining Serbian civilians. In mid-December the leaders of the three main political groupings in Kosovo agreed on provisional power-sharing arrangements with UNMIK. The so-called Kosovo-UNMIK Joint Interim Administrative Structure established an eight-member executive Interim Administrative Council and a framework of administrative departments. The KTC was to maintain its consultative role. In January 2000 UNMIK oversaw the inauguration of the Kosovo Protection Corps, a civilian agency comprising mainly former members of the newly-demilitarized Kosovo Liberation Army, which was to provide an emergency response service and a humanitarian assistance capacity, to assist in de-mining operations and contribute to rebuilding local infrastructure. In August UNMIK, in view of its mandate to assist with the regeneration of the local economy, concluded an agreement with a multinational consortium to rehabilitate the important Trepca non-ferrous mining complex. During mid-2000 UNMIK organized the voter registration process for the forthcoming territory-wide municipal elections. These were held in late October with a strong voter turnout, although participation by minority communities was low. In mid-December the Supreme Court of Kosovo was inaugurated, comprising 16 judges appointed by the Special Representative. During 2000 UNMIK police and KFOR co-operated in conducting joint security operations; the establishment of a special security task force to combat ethnically-motivated political violence, comprising senior UNMIK police and KFOR members, was agreed in June. From January 2001 UNMIK international travel documents were distributed to Kosovars without Yugoslav passports. From early June, in response to ongoing concern at violence between ethnic Albanians and security forces in the former Yugoslav republic of Macedonia (FYRM), UNMIK designated 19 authorized crossing points at Kosovo's international borders with Albania and the FYRM, and its boundaries with Montenegro and Serbia. In mid-May the Special Representative of the Secretary-General signed the Constitutional Framework on Interim Self-Government, providing for the establishment of a Constitutional Assembly. UNMIK undertook efforts to register voters, in particular those from minority ethnic groups, and to continue to facilitate the return of displaced persons to their home communities. The last session of the KTC was held in October, and a general election was conducted, as scheduled, on 17 November. In December the Special Representative of the Secretary-General inaugurated the new 120-member Assembly. However, disagreements ensued among the three main political parties represented in the Assembly concerning the appointment of the positions of President and Prime Minister. In February 2002 the Special Representative of the Secretary-General negotiated an agreement with the leaders of the main political parties that resolved the deadlock in establishing the Interim Government. Accordingly, in March the new President, Prime Minister and Interim Government were inaugurated, enabling the commencement of the process of developing self-governing institutions. In November the mission established the UNMIK Administration—Mitrovica, superseding parallel institutions that had operated hitherto in Serb-dominated northern Mitrovica, and thereby extending UNMIK's authority over all Kosovo. During that month a second series of municipal elections took place.

In March 2003 a Transfer Council was established with responsibility for transferring competencies from UNMIK to the provisional institutions of self-government (PISG). In June UNMIK, with UNDP, launched a Rapid Response Returns Facility (RRRF) to assist returnees from inside and outside Kosovo through the provision of housing and socio-economic support; by July more than 7,000 returns had been reported. In October the Special Representative of the Secretary-General invited Kosovan and Serb leaders, as well as representatives of the Contact Group, to participate in direct talks. The outcome of the meeting, held in Vienna, Austria, was an agreement to pursue a process of direct dialogue. In March 2004 two working groups, concerned with energy and with missing persons, were established within the framework of direct dialogue; however, the process was suspended following serious ethnic violence which occurred during that month (see below). Also in October 2003 UNMIK established a task force to combat corruption, and concluded with Montenegro a Memorandum of Understanding on Police Co-operation, with the aim of jointly targeting organized crime. In the following month a Memorandum of Understanding was signed with the International Commission on Missing Persons, formalizing co-operation in using DNA technology to identify missing persons. In December the Special Representative of the Secretary-General and the Kosovan Prime Minister jointly launched *Standards for Kosovo*, drafted by the UN and partners and detailing eight fundamental democratic standards to be applied in the territory. Leaders of the Serb community declined to participate in the process. At the end of March 2004 the Special Representative and Prime Minister Rexhapi launched the Kosovo Standards Implementation Plan as a mechanism for reviewing the standards and assessing the progress of the PISG. In mid-March rioting erupted in Kosovska Mitrovica and violent clashes between Serb and Albanian communities occurred throughout the province. After two days of serious incident 19 civilians were reported to have been killed, some 1,000 injured and an estimated 4,100 people from the Kosovan Serb, Roma and Ashkali communities had been displaced. In addition, 730 houses and 36 sites of cultural or religious importance had been damaged or destroyed. UNMIK undertook to restore the confidence of the affected communities, to assist with the reconstruction of damaged infrastructure and to investigate the organizers and main perpetrators of the violence. It also initiated a review of its own operational procedures as well as the conduct of local politicians. The priority areas for the mission were identified as providing a secure environment, including the protection of minorities, and ensuring the success of the Implementation Plan. In August a newly-appointed Special Representative of the UN Secretary-General also re-emphasized the need to stimulate the local economy. In that month UNMIK, with UNDP and the local authorities, launched a youth employment creation project. In September UNMIK established a Financial Information Centre to help to deter money-laundering and other related offences. UNMIK assisted in preparations for legislative elections, to be held in October, and supported efforts to ensure a large and representative voter turn-out. In November the Special Representative of the Secretary-General met the newly-elected political leaders and agreed on the establishment of new ministries for energy and mining, local government, and returns and communities. The inaugural session of the new Assembly was convened in December. In that month the Special Representative and the new Prime Minister, Ramush Haradinaj, concluded an agreement on making the Standards a priority for the Kosovan Government and on action for their implementation. In January 2005 a new UNMIK Senior Adviser on Minority Issues was appointed in order to assist the government's efforts to integrate fully minorities into Kosovan society. In March Haradinaj resigned following his indictment by the International Criminal Tribunal for the former Yugoslavia.

At 31 January 2005 UNMIK comprised 3,509 civilian police, 738 international civilian personnel, 2,699 local civilian personnel, and 37 military personnel. The General Assembly apportioned US $278.41m. to the Special Account for UNMIK to finance the operation during the period 1 July 2004–30 June 2005.

UNITED NATIONS INTERIM FORCE IN LEBANON—UNIFIL

Address: Naqoura, Lebanon.

Personal Representative of the UN Secretary-General for Southern Lebanon: STAFFAN DE MISTURA (Sweden).

Force Commander: Maj.-Gen. ALAIN PELLEGRINI (France).

UNIFIL was established by UN Security Council Resolution 425 in March 1978, following an invasion of Lebanon by Israeli forces. The force was mandated to confirm the withdrawal of Israeli forces, to restore international peace and security, and to assist the Government of Lebanon in ensuring the return of its effective authority in southern Lebanon. UNIFIL also extended humanitarian assistance

to the population of the area, particularly following the second Israeli invasion of Lebanon in 1982. UNIFIL has provided civilians with food, water, fuel; medical and dental services; and some veterinary assistance. In April 1992, in accordance with its mandate, UNIFIL completed the transfer of part of its zone of operations to the control of the Lebanese army.

In March 1998 the Israeli Government announced that it recognized Security Council Resolution 425, requiring the unconditional withdrawal of its forces from southern Lebanon. It stipulated, however, that any withdrawal of its troops must be conditional on receiving security guarantees from the Lebanese authorities. A formal decision to this effect, adopted on 1 April, was rejected by the Lebanese and Syrian Governments. In mid-April 2000 the Israeli Government formally notified the UN Secretary-General of its intention to comply forthwith and in full with Resolution 425. Later in that month the UN Secretary-General dispatched a team of experts to study the technical aspects of the impending implementation of Resolution 425, and sent a delegation, led by both his Special Co-ordinator for the Middle East Peace Process, Terje Roed-Larsen, and the Commander of UNIFIL, to consult with regional governments and groupings. The withdrawal of Israeli troops commenced in mid-May. Meanwhile, the Security Council endorsed an operational plan to enable UNIFIL to verify the withdrawal. All concerned parties were urged to co-operate with UNIFIL in order to ensure the full implementation of the resolution. In accordance with its mandate, UNIFIL was to be disbanded following the resumption by the Lebanese Government of effective authority and the normal responsibilities of a state throughout the area, including the re-establishment of law and order structures. In mid-June the UN Secretary-General confirmed that Israeli forces had been fully evacuated from southern Lebanon. Soon afterwards UNIFIL reported several Israeli violations of the line of withdrawal, the so-called Blue Line. The Israeli Government agreed to rectify these by the end of July, and on 24 July the UN Secretary-General confirmed that no serious violations remained. UNIFIL, reinforced with additional troops, patrolled the area vacated by the Israeli forces, monitored the line of withdrawal, undertook demining activities, and continued to provide humanitarian assistance. From August the Lebanese Government deployed a Joint Security Force to the area and began re-establishing local administrative structures and reintegrating basic services into the rest of the country. However, the authorities declined to deploy military personnel along the border zone, on the grounds that a comprehensive peace agreement with Israel would first need to be achieved. In November, following two serious violations of the Blue Line in the previous month by both Israeli troops and Hezbollah militia, the Security Council urged the Lebanese Government to take effective control of the whole area vacated by Israel and to assume international responsibilities. In January 2001 the UN Secretary-General reported that UNIFIL no longer exercised control over the area of operation, which remained relatively stable. The Security Council endorsed his proposals to reconfigure the Force in order to focus on its remaining mandate of maintaining and observing the cease-fire along the line of withdrawal; this was completed by the end of 2002. In response to an increase from early 2002 in incidents generating tension in the area of UNIFIL's operation, reportedly perpetrated by Hezbollah and other militants, and continuous Israeli air violations of the Blue Line, the Secretary-General's Personal Representative for Southern Lebanon and Terje Roed-Larsen undertook diplomatic efforts aimed at restoring stability, and, despite restrictions on its movements, UNIFIL increased its patrols. In January 2003 the UN Secretary-General reported that the number of ground violations of the Blue Line had decreased significantly. During the first half of 2003 the situation in the area of UNIFIL's operation remained relatively calm. From August, however, the number of reported violent incidents increased. In January 2004 the Secretary-General observed that continuing Israeli air violations of the Blue Line and incidences of Hezbollah anti-aircraft fire directed at Israeli villages had exacerbated tensions in the area, particularly during the latter half of 2003. Nonetheless, UNIFIL continued to work to clear areas of land of anti-personnel devices and to assist the integration of the formerly occupied zone into the rest of the country. In July 2004 UNIFIL representatives, with other UN officials, worked to defuse tensions following an alleged Hezbollah sniper attack against Israeli forces and subsequent Israeli violations of Lebanese airspace. At the end of that year the UN expressed concern at further repeated violations of the Blue Line from both sides.

At 31 January 2005 the Force comprised 1,994 troops, assisted by some 50 military observers of UNTSO's Observer Group Lebanon, and also by some 404 international and local civilian staff. The General Assembly appropriation for the operation for the period 1 July 2004–30 June 2005 amounted to US $97.8m.

UNITED NATIONS MILITARY OBSERVER GROUP IN INDIA AND PAKISTAN— UNMOGIP

Address: Rawalpindi, Pakistan (November–April), Srinagar, India (May–October).

Chief Military Observer: Maj.-Gen. GUIDO PALMIERI (Italy).

The Group was established in 1948 by UN Security Council resolutions aiming to restore peace in the region of Jammu and Kashmir, the status of which has become a matter of dispute between the Governments of India and Pakistan. Following a cease-fire which came into effect in January 1949, the military observers of UNMOGIP were deployed to assist in its observance. There is no periodic review of UNMOGIP's mandate. In 1971, following the signature of a new cease-fire agreement, India claimed that UNMOGIP's mandate had lapsed, since it was originally intended to monitor the agreement reached in 1949. Pakistan, however, regarded UNMOGIP's mission as unchanged, and the Group's activities have continued, although they have been somewhat restricted on the Indian side of the 'line of control', which was agreed by India and Pakistan in 1972.

At 31 January 2005 there were 44 military observers deployed on both sides of the 'line of control', supported by 68 international and local civilian personnel. The operation was allocated US $16.8m. from the regular budget of the UN for 2004–05.

UNITED NATIONS MISSION FOR THE REFERENDUM IN WESTERN SAHARA— MINURSO

Address: el-Aaiún, Western Sahara.

Special Representative of the UN Secretary-General and Chief of Mission: ALVARO DE SOTO (Peru).

Force Commander: Maj.-Gen. GYORGY SZARAZ (Hungary).

In April 1991 the UN Security Council endorsed the establishment of MINURSO to verify a cease-fire in the disputed territory of Western Sahara, which came into effect in September 1991, and to implement a settlement plan, involving the repatriation of Western Saharan refugees (in co-ordination with UNHCR), the release of all Sahrawi political prisoners, and the organization of a referendum on the future of the territory. Western Sahara is claimed by Morocco, the administering power since 1975, and by the Algerian-supported Frente Popular para la Liberación de Saguia el Hamra y Río de Oro—Frente Polisario. Although originally envisaged for January 1992, the referendum was postponed indefinitely. In 1992 and 1993 the UN Secretary-General's Special Representative organized negotiations between the Frente Polisario and the Moroccan Government, who were in serious disagreement regarding criteria for eligibility to vote in the plebiscite (in particular, the Moroccan Government insisted that more than 100,000 members of ethnic groups who had been forced to leave the territory under Spanish rule prior to the last official census in 1974, the results of which were to be used as a basis for voter registration, should be allowed to participate in the referendum). In March 1993 the Security Council advocated that further efforts should be made to compile a satisfactory electoral list and to resolve the outstanding differences on procedural issues. An Identification Commission was consequently established to begin the process of voter registration, although this was obstructed by the failure of the Moroccan Government and the Frente Polisario to pursue political dialogue. The identification and registration operation was formally initiated in August 1994; however, the process was complicated by the dispersed nature of the Western Saharan population. In December 1995 the UN Secretary-General reported that the identification of voters had stalled, owing to persistent obstruction of the process on the part of the Moroccan and Frente Polisario authorities. In May 1996 the Security Council endorsed a recommendation of the Secretary-General to suspend the identification process until all sides demonstrate their willingness to co-operate with the mission. The Council decided that MINURSO's operational capacity should be reduced by 20%, with sufficient troops retained to monitor and verify the cease-fire.

In early 1997 the new Secretary-General of the UN, Kofi Annan, attempted to revive the possibility of an imminent resolution of the dispute, amid increasing concerns that the opposing authorities were preparing for a resumption of hostilities in the event of a collapse of the existing cease-fire, and appointed James Baker, a former US Secretary of State, as his Personal Envoy to the region. In June Baker obtained the support of Morocco and the Frente Polisario, as well as Algeria and Mauritania (which border the disputed territory), to conduct further negotiations in order to advance the referendum process. Direct talks between senior representatives of the Moroccan Government and the Frente Polisario authorities were initiated later in that month, in Lisbon, Portugal, under the auspices of the UN, and attended by Algeria and Mauritania in an observer capacity. In September the two sides concluded an agreement which aimed to resolve the outstanding issues of contention and enable the referendum to be conducted in late 1998. The agreement included a commitment by both parties to identify eligible Sahrawi voters on an individual basis, in accordance with the results of the 1974 census, and a code of conduct to ensure the impartiality of the poll. In October 1997 the Security Council endorsed a recommendation of the Secretary-General to increase the strength of the mission, to enable it to supervise nine identification centres. The process of voter identification resumed in December. The agenda for the settlement plan envisaged that the identification process would be followed by a process of appeal, the publication of a final list of voters, and then by a transitional period, under UN authority, during which all Sahrawi refugees would be repatriated. The referendum was scheduled to be conducted in December 1998.

In January 1998 the Security Council approved the deployment of an engineering unit to support MINURSO's demining activities. By early September of that year the initial identification process had been completed, with a total of 147,350 voters identified, including 87,238 since December 1997. However, the controversial issue of the eligibility of 65,000 members of three Saharan tribal groups remained unresolved. In October the Security Council endorsed a series of measures proposed by the Secretary-General to advance the referendum, including a strengthened Identification Commission to consider requests from any applicant from the three disputed tribal groups on an individual basis. The proposals also incorporated the need for an agreement by both sides with UNHCR with regard to arrangements for the repatriation of refugees. In November, following a visit to the region by the Secretary-General, the Frente Polisario accepted the proposals, and in March 1999 the Moroccan Government signed an agreement with the UN to secure the legal basis of the MINURSO operation. In May the Moroccan Government and the Frente Polisario agreed in principle to a draft plan of action for cross-border confidence measures. A new timetable envisaged the referendum being held in July 2000. In July 1999 the UN published the first part of a provisional list of 84,251 qualified voters. The appeals process then commenced. In late November almost 200 Moroccan prisoners of war were released by the Frente Polisario, following a series of negotiations led by the Special Representative of the UN Secretary-General. The identification of applicants from the three disputed Saharan tribal groups was completed at the end of December. In January 2000 the second, final part of the provisional list of qualified voters was issued, and a six-week appeals process ensued. In December 1999 the Security Council acknowledged that persisting disagreements obstructing the implementation of the settlement plan (mainly concerning the processing and analysis of appeals, the release of remaining prisoners and the repatriation of refugees) precluded any possibility of conducting the planned referendum before 2002.

In June 2001 the Personal Envoy of the UN Secretary-General elaborated a draft Framework Agreement on the Status of Western Sahara as an alternative to the settlement plan. The draft Agreement envisaged the disputed area remaining part of Morocco, but with substantial devolution of authority. Any referendum would be postponed. The Security Council authorized Baker to discuss the proposals with all concerned parties. However, the Frente Polisario and Algeria rejected the draft Agreement. In November the Security Council, at the insistence of the Frente Polisario, requested the opinion of the UN Legal Counsel regarding the legality of two short-term reconnaissance licences granted by Morocco to international petroleum companies for operation in Western Sahara. In January 2002 the Secretary-General's Personal Envoy visited the region and met with leaders of both sides. He welcomed the release by the Frente Polisario of a further 115 Moroccan prisoners, but urged both sides to release all long-term detainees. In July the Frente Polisario released a further 101 Moroccan prisoners, leaving a total of 1,260 long-term detainees, of whom 816 had been held for more than 20 years. During February–November 2003 the Frente Polisario released 643 more prisoners; meanwhile, Morocco continued to detain 150 Saharawi prisoners. In January the Secretary-General's Personal Envoy presented to both sides and to the Governments of neighbouring states a new arrangement for a political settlement, providing for self-determination, that had been requested by Resolution 1429 of the Security Council. Throughout 2003 MINURSO representatives pursued further consultation with regard to the proposals. In July the Frente Polisario accepted the so-called Peace Plan for Self-Determination of the People of Western Sahara. In April 2004, however, it was rejected by the Moroccan Government.

In March 2004 MINURSO co-operated with UNHCR to implement a family visits programme, providing for exchange of contacts of relatives divided by the dispute. MINURSO provided transport and other logistical support for the scheme, which was intended to be part of a series of confidence-building measures. In June James Baker resigned as Personal Envoy of the Secretary-General. It was announced that the Special Representative of the UN Secretary-General was to assume responsibility for pursuing 'a just, lasting and mutually acceptable political solution'. In September the Special Representative held his first series of formal meetings with all parties to the dispute. In October and in January 2005, however, the UN Secretary-General reported that no further progress had been achieved, and determined to review the concept and structure of the mission.

The mission has headquarters in the north and south of the disputed territory, and there is a liaison office in Tindouf, Algeria, which was established in order to maintain contact with the Frente Polisario (which is based in Algeria) and the Algerian Government.

At 31 January 2005 MINURSO comprised 198 military observers, 27 troops and four civilian police, supported by 236 international and local civilian personnel. The General Assembly appropriation to cover the cost of the mission for the period 1 July 2004–30 June 2005 amounted to US \$44.04m.

UNITED NATIONS MISSION IN ETHIOPIA AND ERITREA—UNMEE

Address: Asmara, Eritrea; Addis Ababa, Ethiopia.

Special Representative of the Secretary-General and Head of Mission: LEGWAILA JOSEPH LEGWAILA (Botswana).

Force Commander: Maj.-Gen. RAJENDER SINGH (India).

At the end of July 2000 the Security Council authorized the establishment of UNMEE to facilitate compliance with and verify a cease-fire agreement that had been signed by the Governments of Eritrea and Ethiopia in mid-June (having been mediated by the Organization of African Unity—OAU, now African Union—AU), with a view to settling a two-year border conflict between the two countries. In mid-September the Security Council authorized the deployment of up to 4,200 military personnel (including 220 military observers) to the operation, which was given an initial six-month mandate. The Security Council emphasized that UNMEE's mandate would be terminated on completion of the process to delimit and demarcate the Eritrea–Ethiopia border. In December the Eritrean and Ethiopian authorities concluded a full peace accord, providing for the establishment of a Boundary Commission mandated to delimit the border on the basis of relevant colonial treaties and international law. The eventual decision of the Commission was to be accepted by both parties as 'final and binding'. In February 2001 the Military Co-ordination Commission (which had been established jointly by the UN and the OAU in accordance with the cease-fire accord to address military and technical aspects of the peace process, and had met for the first time in December 2000) agreed a timetable to enable Eritrean and Ethiopian forces, monitored by UNMEE, to redeploy in order to establish a 25-km temporary security zone in the border area; the security zone was declared operational in mid-April 2001. UNMEE was subsequently to continue to monitor both forces, to co-ordinate and provide technical assistance for demining activities in the vacated and adjacent areas, and to co-ordinate local humanitarian and human rights activities by UN and other agencies. From mid-2001 UNMEE repeatedly protested against alleged restrictions placed on its freedom of movement by the Eritrean authorities in areas adjoining the security zone, as these impeded the mission's capability to monitor the redeployment of that country's forces. In January 2002 the Security Council, noting that Eritrea had started to permit UNMEE delegates to visit certain parts of the adjacent areas on submission of 24 hours' notice, urged that the mission be allowed full freedom of movement. The Council also requested that the Eritrean Government disclose details of an alleged continuing military and police presence within the temporary security zone, and that it conclude a status of forces agreement with the Secretary-General. (This remained to be signed in 2005.) In mid-April 2002 the Eritrea–Ethiopia Boundary Commission published its decision on the delimitation of the two countries' common border. The Secretary-General urged Eritrea and Ethiopia to implement the decision without delay. UNMEE was to monitor the next phase of the peace process, involving the border's physical demarcation. In addition, the mission was to undertake demining activities in the area, in order to facilitate the demarcation; to determine with both sides technical modalities for the transfer of territory; and to provide logistical and administrative support for the Boundary Commission's field office. In August the Security Council adjusted the mission's mandate to support the implementation of decisions adopted by the Boundary Commission. During late April and early May the Ethiopian Government temporarily closed the Ethiopian border to UNMEE personnel, claiming that UNMEE had not consulted sufficiently with it regarding the mission's logistical support for, and the transfer of personnel to, the Boundary Commission's field office; that the Commission had not established its field presence on the Ethiopian side of the border; and that UNMEE had inappropriately permitted journalists to visit a border village. In

2003 and early 2004 the Secretary-General noted that the movements of UNMEE personnel were being restricted by both the Eritrean and Ethiopian authorities. In early 2004 the Ethiopian Government contested aspects of the decision of the Boundary Commission, thereby delaying its implementation. In January the Secretary-General appointed a new Special Envoy on Ethiopia and Eritrea, Lloyd Axworthy, who was mandated to consult with the Eritrean and Ethiopian authorities with a view to accelerating the implementation of the December 2000 peace accord. The Special Envoy held consultations with the Ethiopian authorities in February 2004; the Eritrean leadership, however, refused to receive him. In May the Security Council urged both sides to co-operate more fully with UNMEE and expressed concern at ongoing restrictions on the movement of UN troops. Little political progress was achieved during the year; in November, however, the Ethiopian Government presented a new five-point peace plan.

During 2002–03 UNMEE personnel undertook various humanitarian projects including the provision of medical assistance, rebuilding and extending water supplies, constructing shelters for the internally displaced population, and rehabilitating roads. In July 2002 two outreach centres were opened in Addis Ababa (Ethiopia) and Asmara (Eritrea) to provide information to the public about the peace process. In 2004 UNMEE undertook to conduct awareness and training programmes in aspects of demining, HIV/AIDS and human rights.

At 31 January 2005 UNMEE comprised 3,147 troops, 217 military observers, and 768 international and local civilian personnel. The General Assembly appropriation to cover the cost of the mission for the period 1 July 2004–30 June 2005 amounted to US \$216.03m., to be financed by a Special Account.

UNITED NATIONS MISSION IN LIBERIA— UNMIL

Address: Monrovia, Liberia.

Special Representative of the Secretary-General and Head of Mission: JACQUES PAUL KLEIN (USA).

Force Commander: Maj.-Gen. JOSEPH OWONIBI (Nigeria).

UNMIL was authorized by the UN Security Council in September 2003 to support the implementation of the cease-fire accord agreed in June and the Comprehensive Peace Agreement concluded in August by the parties to the conflict in Liberia. UNMIL was mandated to assist with the development of an action plan for the disarmament, demobilization, reintegration and, where appropriate, repatriation of all armed groups and to undertake a programme of voluntary disarmament; to protect civilians and UN personnel, equipment and facilities; to support humanitarian and human rights activities; to support the implementation of national security reforms; and, in co-operation with ECOWAS and other partners, to assist the National Transitional Government (inaugurated in mid-October) with the training of a national police force and the restructuring of the military. Troops were also to assist with the rehabilitation of damaged physical infrastructure, in particular the road network. On 1 October UNMIL assumed authority from an ECOWAS-led multinational force in Liberia (the ECOWAS Mission in Liberia—ECOMIL) which had been endorsed by the Security Council in August; ECOMIL's 3,600 troops were reassigned to UNMIL, which had an authorized maximum strength of 15,000 military personnel. In 2004 UNMIL's civil affairs component was conducting an assessment of the functional capacities of public administration structures, including government ministries, to assist the National Transitional Government in re-establishing authority throughout Liberia. UNMIL was to support the National Transitional Government in preparing the country for national elections, which were expected to be held in October 2005. In December 2003 the programme for disarmament, demobilization, rehabilitation and reintegration (DDRR) officially commenced when the first cantonment site was opened. However, the process was disrupted by an unexpectedly large influx of former combatants and a few days later the process was temporarily suspended. In mid-January 2004 an agreement was concluded by all parties on necessary prerequisites to proceeding with the programme, including the launch of an information campaign, which was to be co-ordinated and organized by UNMIL, and the construction of new reception centres and cantonment sites. The DDRR process resumed, under UNMIL command, in mid-April. A training programme for the country's new police service, which aimed to complete the training of some 3,500 officers within two years, was inaugurated in July and the first UN-trained police officers were deployed at the end of the year. In August UNMIL launched a further vocational training scheme for some 640 former combatants to learn building skills. At that time more than 6,800 demobilized soldiers had received reintegration support, although UNMIL expressed concern at the lack of international funding for reintegration efforts. In view of increased security for civilians and humanitarian agencies large-scale programmes for the repatriation and resettlement of refugees and internally displaced persons were initiated. By the end of October, when the disarmament phase of the DDRR programme was officially terminated, more than 96,000 former combatants, including 10,000 child soldiers, had handed over their weapons. At the same time, however, UNMIL troops were deployed throughout the country to restore order, after an outbreak of sectarian hostilities prompted widespread looting and destruction of property and businesses. In early December the Special Representative of the UN Secretary-General hosted a meeting of the heads of all West African peace-keeping and political missions, in order to initiate a more integrated approach to achieving stability and peace throughout the region.

At 31 January 2005 UNMIL comprised 14,472 troops, 205 military observers, 1,098 civilian police, and 1,150 international and local civilian personnel. The General Assembly appropriation to the Special Account for UNMIL amounted to US $864.82m. for the period 1 July 2004–30 June 2005.

UNITED NATIONS MISSION IN SIERRA LEONE—UNAMSIL

Address: Freetown, Sierra Leone.

Special Representative of the Secretary-General and Chief of Mission: DAUDI NGELAUTWA MWAKAWAGO (Tanzania).

Force Commander and Chief Military Observer: Maj.-Gen. SAJJAD AKRAM (Pakistan).

In July 1998 the Security Council established a UN observer mission in Sierra Leone (UNOMSIL) to monitor the military and security situation in that country following the restoration of a democratically-elected government. UNOMSIL was authorized to oversee the disarmament and demobilization of former combatants, as well as the voluntary disarmament of members of the civilian defence force, and to assist in monitoring respect for international humanitarian law. The Special Representative, with the civilian component of the mission, was authorized to advise the Sierra Leone authorities on police practice, training and reform, and to help to address the country's human rights needs. UNOMSIL was to work closely with forces of the Economic Community for West African States (ECOWAS) in promoting peace and national reconciliation. In January 1999, following a sudden escalation of hostilities, the UN Security Council extended the mandate of UNOMSIL for a further two months, although it acknowledged that several UNOMSIL military observers, together with civilian support staff, would withdraw to Conakry, Guinea, until the security situation improved. In March the Security Council condemned the ongoing violation of human rights in Sierra Leone and urged all neighbouring countries to prevent the cross-border supply of armaments to anti-government forces. None the less, the Council extended the mission's mandate until mid-June and, subsequently, until mid-December. In August the Security Council authorized a provisional expansion of UNOMSIL of up to 210 military observers, in order to support the implementation of a peace agreement that had been signed by the parties to the Sierra Leone conflict in July, in Lomé, Togo. In October the Council authorized the establishment of the UN Mission in Sierra Leone (UNAMSIL), comprising up to 6,000 military personnel, to help to consolidate peace in that country. UNAMSIL was mandated to co-operate with the Sierra Leone Government and all other parties to enforce the cease-fire accord and Lomé peace agreement, to implement a plan for the disarmament, demobilization and reintegration of all former combatants, and to facilitate the delivery of humanitarian assistance. The mission was to assume responsibility for all civilian, political and military components of UNOMSIL, the mandate of which was terminated with immediate effect. In February 2000 the Council expanded UNAMSIL's mandate to include the provision of security at key locations and government installations, assistance to the Sierra Leone law enforcement authorities, and the safe keeping and subsequent disposal of military equipment collected from former combatants. The Council also enlarged the mission's authorized strength from 6,000 to 11,100 military personnel.

During early 2000, in contravention of the Lomé accord, Sierra Leone rebels repeatedly obstructed the implementation of the disarmament and demobilization programme. In May, following an attack on a contingent of UNAMSIL troops in the previous month, rebels killed several mission personnel and captured and detained around 500 others; these were all released later in the month. In response to the breakdown in security the United Kingdom deployed a force in Sierra Leone in early May, with a mandate to evacuate British nationals; the presence of the British troops was also regarded, however, as a deterrent to any escalation in rebel activities pending the arrival of UNAMSIL reinforcements. In mid-May the Security Council approved a further increase in the mission's authorized strength, providing for a total of 13,000 military personnel. The United Kingdom withdrew most of its force in the following month, leaving a small contingent to train Sierra Leone government troops and undertake security duties. In mid-July UNAMSIL mounted a successful operation to release 233 of its personnel, who had been surrounded by rebels in eastern Sierra Leone since the end of May. The Security Council adopted a resolution in July banning the direct and indirect importation of rough diamonds from rebel-controlled areas of Sierra Leone, following mounting concern at the role played by illicit diamond exploitation in motivating and funding anti-government activities. In August the Security Council recommended that UNAMSIL should be strengthened to enable it to secure approach routes to the Lungi and Freetown peninsulas and to counter continuing attacks by armed rebels. The Security Council asked the Secretary-General to assess the number of additional troops that would be required to achieve this. UNAMSIL was also mandated to provide security to the Special Court for Sierra Leone, whose establishment jointly by the UN and the Sierra Leone Government was authorized by a resolution adopted by the Security Council in August. The Court, which was to try those accused of perpetrating crimes against humanity and war crimes in Sierra Leone since November 1996, was inaugurated in March 2004 and trial proceedings commenced in June.

A new cease-fire agreement, entailing the recommencement of the disarmament, demobilization and reintegration plan, was signed by the Sierra Leone Government and the principal rebel group in early November 2000. In March 2001 the Council expanded the mission's authorized maximum strength to 17,500 military personnel and also approved a revised concept of operations that envisaged the deployment of UNAMSIL troops, government representatives, and international humanitarian personnel into rebel-controlled areas, with a view to re-establishing basic services and the authority of the state. In December the Security Council noted that the Sierra Leone Government, assisted by UNAMSIL, had yet to establish full authority over the rebel-dominated diamond-producing areas of the country. In January 2002 the Security Council welcomed the significant progress that had been achieved in the implementation of the disarmament, demobilization and reintegration plan, including the official completion of the disarmament element during that month. In support of legislative and presidential elections that were staged in Sierra Leone in mid-May, UNAMSIL temporarily redeployed some 11,000 troops to high-risk areas of the country, and provided practical assistance to the Sierra Leone police, to the country's National Electoral Commission, and to electoral observer teams. At this time UNAMSIL intensified patrols of border areas with Liberia in response to increasing incursions by Liberian rebels into Sierra Leone. Following the elections, UNAMSIL was to continue to support the Sierra Leone Government in restoring the nation-wide authority of the state; in consolidating peace, security and national reconciliation; promoting the rehabilitation of the judicial system and respect for human rights; undertaking humanitarian projects; and by addressing outstanding issues such as the reintegration of former combatants.

From September 2002, in view of the prevailing generally stable security situation in much of Sierra Leone, responsibility for patrolling a number of strategic areas began to be transferred from UNAMSIL to the Sierra Leone military, although UNAMSIL military observers, as well as civilian police and human rights officials, remained deployed throughout the country. From February 2003 UNAMSIL forces conducted joint border patrols with Sierra Leone government troops. In April, in conjunction with local police, UNAMSIL instigated a programme to eradicate illegal mining activities. In March the UN Special Representative for Children and Armed Conflict praised UNAMSIL for integrating child protection into its operations. UNAMSIL provided technical and logistical support to the Sierra Leone authorities in preparing for local elections that were conducted in May 2004. In March the Security Council reaffirmed plans to scale-down the force to some 5,000 troops by December and determined that a residual force, consisting of up to 3,250 troops, was to remain in the country for an initial six-month period, from 1 January 2005, in order to assist the transition of authority for security enforcement to the Sierra Leone Government. In August 2004 UNAMSIL transferred security primacy for the country's eastern province to the Government. Authority for security in the last area, including the capital, Freetown, was handed over in September. In that month the Security Council extended the mission's mandate until 30 June 2005, in accordance with the previous reduction plan, and outlined the main military, civilian police and civilian tasks of the residual force. These included strengthening the capacity of the armed forces and police to maintain security and stability throughout the country, support for local police monitoring of border and diamond-mining areas, assistance with police recruitment and training, monitoring the repatriation and reintegration of former combatants from abroad, and monitoring the progress towards the consolidation of state authority.

At 31 January 2005 UNAMSIL comprised 3,958 troops and 134 military observers, assisted by 75 civilian police and 767 international and local civilian personnel. The budget for the mission amounted to US $301.87m. for the period 1 July 2004–30 June 2005, funded from a Special Account comprising assessed contributions from UN member states.

UNITED NATIONS MISSION IN THE DEMOCRATIC REPUBLIC OF THE CONGO—MONUC

Address: Kinshasa, Democratic Republic of the Congo.

Liaison offices are situated in Bujumbura (Burundi); Addis Ababa (Ethiopia); Windhoek (Namibia); Kigali (Rwanda); Kampala (Uganda); Lusaka (Zambia); and Harare (Zimbabwe).

Special Representative of the UN Secretary-General and Chief of Mission: WILLIAM LACY SWING (USA).

Force Commander: Maj.-Gen. SAMAILA ILIYA (Nigeria).

Deputy Force Commander and Chief Military Observer: Maj.-Gen. PATRICK CAMMAERT (Netherlands).

In August 1999 the UN Security Council authorized the deployment of up to 90 military liaison personnel to support implementation of a cease-fire agreement for the Democratic Republic of the Congo (DRC) which had been signed in Lusaka, Zambia, in July, by the heads of state of the DRC, Angola, Namibia, Rwanda, Uganda and Zimbabwe. The Council approved the establishment of MONUC in late November. With an initial mandate until 1 March 2000, the mission was, in co-operation with a Joint Military Commission comprising representatives of the parties to the conflict, to oversee the implementation of the agreement, including monitoring the cease-fire and the disengagement of forces. The mission was also mandated to facilitate the delivery of humanitarian assistance and to develop a mine action plan and undertake emergency demining activities. The first phase of MONUC's operations entailed the deployment of unarmed liaison and technical assessment officers, as well as other multi-disciplinary personnel, previously authorized by the Council, to the capitals of the states party to the Lusaka accord and, where possible, to rebel group headquarters. In February 2000 the Security Council authorized the expansion of the mission to comprise up to 5,537 military personnel, including up to 500 observers, thereby enabling the commencement of the second phase of the operation, under which military observers were to be dispatched to the DRC to monitor and verify the cease-fire and disengagement of forces. In April a sub-plan on military disengagement and redeployment was agreed in Kampala, Uganda, by the parties to the conflict and, in December, a revised sub-plan was adopted in Harare, Zimbabwe. However, by early 2001 the Lusaka cease-fire accord and Kampala and Harare sub-plans remained to be implemented and only a small contingent of MONUC observers had been deployed in the DRC. In mid-February the Security Council adopted a resolution demanding that the parties to the conflict commence the phased disengagement and redeployment of their forces by mid-March and stipulating that plans for the full withdrawal of foreign troops and the disarmament, demobilization and resettlement of militia must be prepared and adopted by mid-May. The resolution raised the maximum number of military observers to 550, to be stationed around four regional headquarters; the deployment of up to 1,900 armed security personnel to protect these bases was also authorized. River boat units were to be deployed to assist with the transportation of observers and supplies and to reinforce the mission's presence; it was hoped that commercial activity along river routes would thus also be supported. Small contingents of MONUC troops were deployed in the DRC from March, including, in the following month, to the strategic rebel-occupied north-eastern town of Kisangani. In June the Security Council approved a revised concept of operations for MONUC, entailing the establishment of a civilian police element, enhancing the mission's presence in Kisangani and strengthening its logistic support capabilities. In October 2002 the UN Secretary-General reported that 90 teams of military observers were stationed at 50 sites in the DRC. Preparations were under way for the implementation of the mission's third phase of operations (authorized at the end of 2001), which was to entail the deployment of a full peace-keeping force to oversee the complete withdrawal of foreign troops from DRC territory and the disarmament, demobilization and reintegration of rebel forces. In December 2002 the UN Security Council authorized the expansion of the mission to co-ordinate this process.

Some progress towards the implementation of the Lusaka cease-fire accord was achieved at the Inter-Congolese Dialogue held in Sun City, South Africa, from mid-February–mid-April 2002, when a bilateral power-sharing agreement was concluded between the DRC Government and Mouvement de libération du Congo—MLC rebels supported by the Ugandan Government. In mid-May a failed mutiny attempt by dissident rebels in Kisangani led to an outbreak of violence that resulted in at least 50 civilian fatalities. MONUC conducted patrols of the city and provided protection to a number of individuals who considered their lives to be at risk. Subsequently the Rwandan-backed Rassemblement congolais pour la démocratie (RCD)-Goma rebels controlling Kisangani accused the Special Representative of the Secretary-General of displaying a pro-Government bias and announced that he and several mission personnel were 'banned' from the area occupied by the grouping. A resolution of the Security Council in early June demanded that the RCD-Goma rebels cease their obstruction of the mission's activities in Kisangani immediately.

Following the adoption in July and August 2002, respectively, of the so-called Pretoria agreement between the DRC and Rwandan Governments, and Luanda agreement between the DRC and Ugandan Governments, nearly all Rwandan and Ugandan forces were withdrawn before the end of that year. Meanwhile, troop withdrawals, under MONUC observation, were also initiated by Angola, Burundi, Namibia and Zimbabwe. In December the Security Council adopted a resolution expanding the mission's authorized military strength to 8,700, to consist mainly of two intervention forces, which were to be deployed gradually. During that month the All-Inclusive Agreement on the Transition in the DRC, providing for the staging of elections in the DRC after a transition period of 24 months, was signed by the participants in the Inter-Congolese Dialogue, in Pretoria, South Africa.

In response to continuing armed conflict and human rights violations in Bunia, north-eastern DRC, resulting in the deaths of more than 400 civilians in May 2003, a UN-backed temporary Interim Emergency Multinational Force (IEMF) was deployed to stabilize the situation there from June. In July the Security Council adopted a resolution increasing MONUC's authorized strength to 10,800 troops and extending the mission's mandate. The resolution authorized MONUC to take necessary measures to protect civilians and humanitarian workers under imminent threat of physical violence and to protect UN personnel and facilities, and imposed an arms embargo against all DRC and foreign armed groups in the east of the country. MONUC supported the IEMF during mid-2003, prior to resuming full responsibility for maintaining security in Bunia and thus replacing the Force in mid-September. At the end of June a DRC Transitional Government was established, in accordance with the December 2002 All-Inclusive Agreement on the Transition in the DRC. MONUC retained a presence in Kinshasa to provide security for the new administration. An electoral assistance unit was created within the Mission to support the preparations for the national elections scheduled under the Agreement to take place within a two-year timeframe. In July 2003 the Security Council adopted a resolution imposing an arms embargo on rebel groups and foreign troops operating in the Kivu and Ituri regions of eastern DRC and mandating MONUC to monitor the flow of arms there.

In late May 2004 MONUC attempted to negotiate a cease-fire after fighting occurred in Bukavu, eastern DRC, between troops of the transitional government and forces loyal to the dissident military leaders Gen. Laurent Nkunda and Col Jules Mutebutsi. At the start of June, however, the dissident forces seized control of Bukavu, in order, it was claimed, to prevent further alleged killings of the minority Congolese Tutsi (Banyamulenge) population. Many properties, including UN warehouses, were looted. In other areas of the country there were violent protests against MONUC for failing to intervene in the situation. A few days later the dissident troops withdrew. In mid-June a MONUC team of human rights investigators determined that there was no evidence of any atrocities having been perpetrated against the Banyamulenge. In July thousands more people living in the eastern Lake Kivu district were displaced as a result of further clashes between government and dissident troops. In August a Burundian Hutu rebel group, the National Liberation Forces (FNL), claimed responsibility for the deaths of more than 160 Banyamulenge at a UN refugee camp in Gatumba, Burundi, close to the DRC border. The UN Security Council met in emergency session following the incident, amid concern at the escalation of tensions in the region. MONUC and UN forces in Burundi determined to reinforce security along the border. A Joint Verification Commission was established, in September, by the DRC and Rwandan authorities to address border security issues and to improve bilateral relations, for which MONUC was to serve as its secretariat. In October the Security Council agreed to expand MONUC to some 16,700 troops (although less than the force strength recommended by the UN Secretary-General) in order to reinforce its operational capabilities and avert further deterioration in the stability of the country. The Council also identified new responsibilities for the mission, including the protection of civilians 'under immediate threat of violence', inspection of air cargo in eastern regions to ensure that the ban on arms trading is upheld, and reporting on the presence of foreign troops and relevant troop movements, as well as tasks in support of the consolidation of the Transitional Government. In November MONUC undertook a joint operation with the Congolese army to protect the eastern Walungu area from rebel troops and deployed an additional brigade to North Kivu to provide additional security in the region. At the same time it established a new operations centre to monitor the disarmament of combatants and the retreat of foreign forces. Efforts to stabilize those parts of the country, however, were undermined from late November by reports from the Rwandan Government that it was prepared to attack former rebels living in the DRC who were perceived to be an ongoing threat to Rwandan security. The Security Council urged all states to refrain from any action that affected regional security or contravened international law, and, specifically, demanded the withdrawal of any Rwandan forces from the DRC and the disarmament of any rebel militia. An escalation of inter-factional hostilities in North Kivu province prompted an estimated 30,000 to leave their homes. MONUC troops established a temporary buffer zone in the worst affected areas in order to facilitate the delivery of humanitarian aid. Reports of factional violence continued in early 2005. In late February nine MONUC peace-keeping soldiers were killed during a patrol of a suspected militia camp in the Ituri district.

MONUC works closely with the Multi-Country Demobilization and Reintegration Programme, administered by the World Bank, and with UNDP, the lead agency for reintegration in the DRC.

In July 2001 MONUC launched a Quick Impact Projects programme; by mid-2004 some 78 projects had been undertaken in areas including education; health; environment; agriculture; public infrastructure rehabilitation; income generating activities; and support for vulnerable groups.

At 31 January 2005 MONUC comprised 13,206 troops, 569 military observers and 175 civilian police, assisted by 1,875 international and local civilian personnel. The budget for the mission amounted to US $746.1m. for the period 1 July 2004–30 June 2005, funded from a Special Account comprising assessed contributions from UN member states.

UNITED NATIONS MISSION OF SUPPORT IN EAST TIMOR—UNMISET

Address: Dili, Timor-Leste.

Special Representative of the UN Secretary-General and Head of Mission: SUKEHIRO HASEGAWA (Japan).

Force Commander: Lt-Gen. KHAIRUDDIN MAT YUSOF (Malaysia).

UNMISET was established on 20 May 2002, initially with a mandate for one year, when Timor-Leste (previously known as East Timor) attained its independence. It succeeded the UN Transitional Administration in East Timor (UNTAET), which had been established in October 1999 to govern the territory on an interim basis following the outcome of a popular referendum in favour of independence from Indonesia. UNMISET was to provide assistance to core administrative structures, to extend interim law enforcement and public security services, to assist the development of a national police force, and to contribute to the maintenance of external and internal security. The civilian component of UNMISET was to include a Serious Crimes Unit and a Human Rights Unit, as well as focal points for gender and HIV/AIDS. The Mission was mandated to devolve all operational responsibilities to the Timor-Leste authorities within two years. In March 2003 the UN Secretary-General reported that, owing to an escalation in insecurity (including riots and attacks by armed groups) in Timor-Leste from November 2002, and the current early stage in the development of the national police force, original plans swiftly to downsize the mission should be revised. He proposed adjustments to the configuration and military strategy of UNMISET, aimed at facilitating the restoration of stability. In December 2003 the Timor-Leste National Police Force assumed responsibility for routine policing throughout the country. In February 2004 the UN Secretary-General recommended that UNMISET's mandate should be extended for one year after its scheduled expiry in May. In May responsibility for policing and external security was transferred from UNMISET to the Timor-Leste Government. In that month the Security Council extended the mission, with a modified mandate, for a six-month period, and determined to reduce the mission's authorized strength to 58 civilian advisers, 157 civilian police advisers, 42 military liaison officers, 310 troops and a 125-person International Response Unit. During the year the mission continued to provide assistance to the country's judicial system, establishment of core administrative structures and the development of a national police force. The Serious Crimes Unit completed its investigations at the end of November. In that month the UN Security Council authorized the final extension of the mission's mandate until 20 May 2005. It determined to maintain UNMISET's existing mandate and force strength in order to enable the mission to complete its mandated tasks and to consolidate its achievements.

At 31 January 2005 UNMISET comprised 429 troops, 147 civilian police officers and 43 military observers, supported by 812 international and local civilian personnel. The General Assembly budget appropriation to the Special Account for the mission amounted to US $85.15m. for the period 1 July 2004–30 June 2005.

UNITED NATIONS OBSERVER MISSION IN GEORGIA—UNOMIG

Address: Sukhumi, Georgia.

Special Representative of the UN Secretary-General and Head of Mission: HEIDI TAGLIAVINI (Switzerland).

Chief Military Observer: Maj.-Gen. HUSSEIN AHMED GHOBASHI (Egypt).

UNOMIG was established in August 1993 to verify compliance with a cease-fire agreement, signed in July between the Government of Georgia and the Abkhazian separatist movement. The mission was the UN's first undertaking in the former USSR. In October the UN Secretary-General stated that a breakdown in the cease-fire agreement had invalidated UNOMIG's mandate. He proposed, however, to maintain, for information purposes, the eight-strong UNOMIG team in the city of Sukhumi, which had been seized by Abkhazian forces in late September. In December the Security Council authorized the deployment of additional military observers in response to the signing of a memorandum of understanding by the conflicting parties earlier that month. Further peace negotiations, which were conducted in January–March 1994 under the authority of the UN Secretary-General's Special Envoy, achieved no political consensus. In July the Security Council endorsed the establishment of a Commonwealth of Independent States (CIS) peace-keeping force to verify a cease-fire agreement that had been signed in May. At the same time the Security Council increased UNOMIG's authorized strength and expanded the mission's mandate to incorporate the following tasks: to monitor and verify the implementation of the agreement and to investigate reported violations; to observe the operation of the CIS peace-keeping force; to verify that troops and heavy military equipment remain outside the security zone and the restricted weapons zone; to monitor the storage of the military equipment withdrawn from the restricted zones; to monitor the withdrawal of Georgian troops from the Kodori Gorge region to locations beyond the Abkhazian frontiers; and to patrol regularly the Kodori Gorge. Peace negotiations were pursued in 1995, despite periodic outbreaks of violence in Abkhazia. In July 1996 the Security Council urged the Abkhazian side to accelerate significantly the process of voluntary return of Georgian refugees and displaced persons to Abkhazia. In October the Council decided to establish a human rights office as part of UNOMIG. In May 1997 the Security Council issued a Presidential Statement urging greater efforts towards achieving a peaceful solution to the dispute. The Statement endorsed a proposal of the UN Secretary-General to strengthen the political element of UNOMIG to enable the mission to assume a more active role in furthering a negotiated settlement. In July direct discussions between representatives of the Georgian and Abkhazian authorities, the first in more than two years, were held under UN auspices. In early 1998 the security situation in Abkhazia deteriorated. Following an outbreak of violence in May the conflicting parties signed a cease-fire accord, which incorporated an agreement that UNOMIG and CIS forces would continue to work to create a secure environment to allow for the return of displaced persons to the Gali region of Abkhazia. In addition, the UN Security Council urged both parties to establish a protection unit to ensure the safety of UN military observers. In December 2000, following a series of detentions and hostage-takings of Mission personnel in the Kodori Gorge during late 1999 and 2000, UNOMIG suspended patrols of that area. Reviewing the operation in January 2001 the UN Secretary-General expressed concern at the recent recurrent abductions and urged the Abkhazian side to cease imposing restrictions on the mission's freedom of movement. A Programme of Action on confidence-building measures was concluded in March; however, the negotiation process was interrupted from April, owing to increasing insecurity in the conflict zone and the ongoing activities of illegal armed groups. In October a UNOMIG helicopter was shot down in the Kodori Gorge, resulting in the deaths of nine people. UNOMIG suspended its patrols of the area. In January 2002 a protocol was signed between the conflicting parties providing for the withdrawal of Georgian troops from the upper Kodori valley and the resumption of UN ground patrols. Further discussion on implementation of the protocol resulted in the first joint patrol being conducted in late March. In April a protocol was concluded by both sides for a final withdrawal of Georgian troops and the resumption of regular UNOMIG/CIS patrols. Renewed diplomatic efforts to secure a political agreement on the future status of Abkhazia initially focused on a paper of Basic Principles for the Distribution of Competences between Tbilisi and Sukhumi, which had been prepared by the Special Representative of the UN Secretary-General. The document was rejected as a basis for negotiations by the Abkhazian leadership; however, discussions were held between the leadership of the two sides to consider measures to stabilize further the situation in the Kodori Gorge. Both sides agreed to resolve all outstanding issues by peaceful means. Meeting in Geneva, Switzerland, in February and

July 2003 the UN Secretary General's so-called 'Group of Friends on Georgia', comprising France, Germany, Russia, the United Kingdom and the USA, identified co-operation in economic, political and security matters and the return of refugees and internally-displaced persons as being of key importance for the advancement of the peace process and therefore also priority focus areas for UNOMIG. From November a new civilian police component of UNOMIG became operational, although objections by certain Abkhaz groups prevented their deployment in the Gali sector. UNOMIG's Engineering Section continued to undertake small-scale reconstruction projects, in particular of roads and bridges, in order to facilitate communications. UNOMIG co-operates closely with the CIS peace-keeping force, and a joint UNOMIG-CIS fact-finding team undertakes investigations of violent incidents. In October 2003 UNOMIG and the CIS peace-keeping force signed a protocol entailing closer co-operation in combating crime and improving security. During 2004 the Secretary-General's Special Representative attempted to maintain a dialogue with all sides and interested parties to the dispute, which, in the absence of negotiations on the central political issues, focused on security guarantees. In May the Special Representative chaired a meeting with regard to security guarantees, held in accordance with recommendations of the Group of Friends on Georgia and with agreements reached at a previous meeting convened in February. No further substantive dialogue was held during the year, although in December the UN hosted a high-level meeting of the Group of Friends which reviewed the main challenges and determined to meet both sides in early 2005 in order to consider the resumption of negotiations.

At 31 January 2005 UNOMIG comprised 122 military observers and 11 civilian police, supported by 279 international and local civilian personnel. The General Assembly budget appropriation to the Special Account for the mission amounted to US $33.59m. for the period 1 July 2004–30 June 2005.

UNITED NATIONS OPERATIONS IN BURUNDI—ONUB

Address: Bujumbura, Burundi.

Special Representative of the Secretary-General and Head of Mission: CAROLYN MCASKIE (Canada).

Force Commander: Maj.-Gen. DERRICK MBUYISELO MGWEBI (South Africa).

ONUB was established by Security Council Resolution 1545 of May 2004, which authorized a UN force to help to implement the terms of the Arusha Agreement, signed in August 2000 to secure peace and national reconciliation in Burundi. Included in its mandate was to monitor cease-fire agreements and investigate any violations, to undertake the disarmament and demobilization of combatants, to attempt to monitor the illegal flow of arms across national borders, to help to create secure conditions for the distribution of humanitarian assistance and the return of refugees and displaced persons, and to ensure a secure environment for free, transparent and peaceful elections to take place. ONUB was to assume authority of the existing African Mission in Burundi (AMIB), sent by African Union nations. ONUB commenced operations, for an initial six-month period, on 1 June, when command of some 2,612 troops from Ethiopia, Mozambique and South Africa was officially transferred from AMIB. In August ONUB's Head of Mission participated in talks on post-transitional power-sharing arrangements which were held in Pretoria, South Africa. In mid-August ONUB initiated a preliminary investigation into the killing of more than 160 Congolese Tutsi refugees in a camp at Gatumba, close to the border with the Democratic Republic of the Congo (DRC), allegedly by Burundian Hutu rebels of the National Liberation Forces (FNL). ONUB, with UN forces in the DRC, determined to strengthen security along the border between the two countries. In October ONUB announced the establishment of three demobilization centres and guaranteed their security. The programme to disarm, demobilize and reintegrate former combatants was officially initiated in December. An estimated 2,750 former soldiers demobilized in the first month. At the same time the World Food Programme launched a scheme to distribute food rations to those participating in the programme prior to their reintegration into civilian life. From November ONUB began radio broadcasts to generate support for the peace process, including voter registration and national reconciliation.

At 31 January 2005 ONUB comprised 5,188 troops, 190 military observers and 524 international and local civilian staff. The mission was to be financed by assessments in respect of a Special Account. The approved budget for the period 1 July 2004–30 June 2005 amounted to US $329.71m.

UNITED NATIONS OPERATION IN CÔTE D'IVOIRE—UNOCI

Address: Abidjan, Côte d'Ivoire.

Special Representative of the Secretary-General and Head of Mission: PIERRE SCHORI (Sweden).

Force Commander: Maj.-Gen. ABDOULAYE FALL (Senegal).

UNOCI was authorized by the UN Security Council in February 2004 and began operations in early April. UNOCI was mandated to observe and monitor the implementation of the Linas-Marcoussis Agreement, signed by the parties to the conflict in Côte d'Ivoire in January 2003, and hitherto supported by the UN Mission in Côte d'Ivoire (MINUCI), forces of the Economic Community of West African States—ECOWAS and French peace-keeping troops. UNOCI was authorized also to assist with the disarmament, demobilization and reintegration of rebel groups, to protect civilians and UN personnel, institutions and equipment, and to support ongoing humanitarian and human rights activities. With a contingent of the French *'Licorne'* peace-keeping force, UNOCI was to monitor a so-called Zone of Confidence separating the two areas of the country under government and rebel control. In early June the Special Representative of the Secretary-General held talks with the President and leader of the opposition, following the withdrawal of opposition representatives from the coalition government. At the end of July all parties, attending a meeting of West African heads of state that had been convened by the UN Secretary-General and the President of Ghana, endorsed the Accra III Agreement identifying means of implementing the Linas-Marcoussis Accord. UNOCI was to participate in a tripartite monitoring group, together with ECOWAS and the African Union, to oversee progress in implementing the agreement. In mid-August UNOCI launched a radio station, in accordance with its mandate, to assist the process of national reunification and in the following month established some secure transit routes between the areas under government and rebel control in order to facilitate travel and enable family reunions None the less, by October UNOCI officials expressed concern at ongoing violations of human rights and a deterioration in security, as well as a lack of progress in implementing provisions of the peace accords.

In early November 2004 government troops violated the cease-fire and the Zone of Confidence by launching attacks against rebel Forces Nouvelles in the north of the country. An emergency session of the UN Security Council, convened following an escalation of the hostilities and a fatal air strike on a French peace-keeping unit, urged both sides to refrain from further violence. Security further deteriorated in the south of the country when French troops destroyed the government air force prompting rioting in Abidjan and violence directed towards foreign nationals. UNOCI assisted with the evacuation of foreign workers and their families and provided secure refuge for other personnel. In mid-November the Security Council imposed an immediate embargo on the sale or supply of armaments to Côte d'Ivoire and determined that additional sanctions would enter into effect in one month unless both sides respect the terms of the peace agreement. The Council's resolution also demanded a cessation of hostilities and of the use of media broadcasts to incite hatred and violence against foreigners. UNOCI was to monitor the terms of the resolution and to broadcast its own messages of support for the peace process. By the end of that month reports indicated that the security situation had improved and that some of the estimated 19,000 who fled the country to Liberia had started to return. In addition, conditions in the northern city of Bouaké were improving as water and electricity supplies were restored. In December UNOCI funded three quick-impact social projects, in order to highlight the humanitarian aspect of the mission, and commenced joint patrols with government forces to uphold security in Abidjan. In February 2005 the UN Security Council demanded that all parties co-operate with UNOCI in compiling a comprehensive list of armaments under their control as preparation for implementing a programme of disarmament, demobilization and reintegration.

At 31 January 2005 UNOCI had an operational strength of 5,843 troops, 166 military observers and 215 civilian police officers, supported by 404 international and local civilian personnel. The General Assembly appropriated US $96.4m. to cover the cost of establishing the mission in the period 4 April–30 June 2004, and $378.48m. for maintenance of the mission during the period 1 July 2004–30 June 2005.

UNITED NATIONS PEACE-KEEPING FORCE IN CYPRUS—UNFICYP

Address: Nicosia, Cyprus.

Special Representative of the UN Secretary-General and Chief of Mission: ZBIGNIEW WLOSOWICZ (Poland).

Force Commander: Maj.-Gen. HERBERT JOAQUIN FIGOLI ALMANDOS (Uruguay).

UNFICYP was established in March 1964 by a UN Security Council resolution (initially for a three-month duration, subsequently periodically extended) to prevent a recurrence of fighting between the Greek and Turkish Cypriot communities, and to contribute to the maintenance of law and order and a return to normal conditions. The Force controls a 180-km buffer zone, established (following the Turkish intervention in 1974) between the cease-fire lines of the Turkish forces and the Cyprus National Guard. It is mandated to investigate and act upon all violations of the cease-fire and buffer zone. The Force also performs humanitarian functions, such as facilitating the supply of electricity and water across the cease-fire lines, and offering emergency medical services. In August 1996 serious hostilities between elements of the two communities in the UN-controlled buffer zone resulted in the deaths of two people and injuries to many others, including 12 UN personnel. Following further intercommunal violence, UNFICYP advocated the prohibition of all weapons and military posts along the length of the buffer zone. The Force also proposed additional humanitarian measures to improve the conditions of minority groups living in the two parts of the island. In July 1997 a series of direct negotiations between the leaders of the two communities was initiated, in the presence of the UN Secretary-General's Special Adviser; however, the talks were suspended at the end of that year. In November 1999 the Greek Cypriot and Turkish Cypriot leaders agreed to participate in proximity negotiations, to be mediated by the UN. Consequently, five rounds of these took place during the period December 1999–November 2000. In January 2002 a new series of direct talks between the leaders of the two communities commenced, under the auspices of the Secretary-General's Special Adviser. In May the Secretary-General visited Cyprus and met the two leaders. Further meetings between the Secretary-General and the two leaders took place in September (in Paris) and October (New York). In November he submitted to them for consideration a document providing the basis for a comprehensive settlement agreement; a revised version of the document was released in the following month. A further revised version of the draft settlement plan document was presented to the leaders of the two communities during a visit by the Secretary-General to Cyprus in late February 2003. He urged that both sides put this to separate simultaneous referendums at the end of March, in the hope that, were the settlement plan approved, Cyprus would be able to accede to the European Union in a reunited state on 1 May 2004. Progress stalled, however, at a meeting between the two sides held in early March 2003 in The Hague, Netherlands. In April the Security Council adopted a resolution calling upon both parties to continue to work towards a settlement using the Secretary-General's plan as the unique basis for future negotiations. In reports to the Security Council the UN Secretary-General has consistently recognized UNFICYP as being indispensable to maintaining calm on the island and to creating the best conditions for his good offices. In November 2003 he noted that a number of restrictions placed on UNFICYP's activities during 2000 by the Turkish Cypriot authorities and Turkish forces remained in place. In February 2004 the Greek Cypriot and Turkish Cypriot leaders committed themselves to the Secretary-General's settlement plan. Negotiations on settling outstanding differences were chaired by the Secretary-General's Special Adviser for Cyprus throughout March. Despite a lack of agreement when the two sides met with the Secretary-General in late March, a finalized text was presented at the end of that month. The proposed Foundation Agreement was subsequently put to referendums in both sectors in April when it was approved by two-thirds of Turkish Cypriot voters, but rejected by some 75% of Greek Cypriot voters. In June the Secretary-General determined to undertake a comprehensive review of UNFICYP's mandate and force levels, in view of the political developments on the island, and announced his decision not to resume his good offices. In October the Security Council endorsed the recommendations of the Secretary-General's review team, which included a reduction in the mission's authorized strength from 1,230 to 860 military personnel, to include 40 military observers and liaison officers, and an increase in the deployment of civilian police officers from 44 to 69. In November UNFICYP troops initiated an EU-funded project to remove anti-personnel landmines from the buffer zone separating the two communities.

At 31 January 2005 UNFICYP had an operational strength of 916 troops and 43 civilian police-officers, supported by 153 international and local civilian staff. The General Assembly appropriated US $51.99m. to the Special Account for UNFICYP to finance the period 1 July 2004–30 June 2005, of which one-third was to be funded by voluntary contributions from the Government of Cyprus and $6.5m. to be donated by the Government of Greece.

UNITED NATIONS STABILIZATION MISSION IN HAITI—MINUSTAH

Address: Port-au-Prince, Haiti.

Special Representative of the UN Secretary-General: JUAN GABRIEL VALDÉS (Chile).

Force Commander: Lt-Gen. AUGUSTO HELENO RIBEIRO PEREIRA (Brazil).

In early 2004 political tensions within Haiti escalated as opposition groups demanded political reforms and the resignation of President Jean-Bertrand Aristide. Increasingly violent public demonstrations took place throughout the country, in spite of diplomatic efforts by regional organizations to resolve the crisis, and in February armed opposition forces seized control of several northern cities. At the end of that month, with opposition troops poised to march on the capital and growing pressure from the international community, President Aristide tendered his resignation and fled the country. On that same day the UN Security Council, acting upon a request by the interim President, authorized the establishment of a Multinational Interim Force (MIF) to help to secure law and order in Haiti. The Council also declared its readiness to establish a follow-on UN mission. In late April the Security Council agreed to establish MINUSTAH, which was to assume authority from the MIF with effect from 1 June. MINUSTAH was mandated to create a stable and secure environment, to support the transitional government in institutional development and organizing and monitoring elections, and to monitor the human rights situation. Among its declared objectives was the improvement of living conditions of the population through security measures, humanitarian actions and economic development. In September MINUSTAH worked closely with other UN agencies and non-governmental organizations to distribute food and other essential services to thousands of people affected by a severe tropical storm. By the end of 2004 MINUSTAH's priority continued to be the security situation in the country. However, the following civil units were fully operational: electoral assistance; child protection; gender; civil affairs; human rights; and HIV/AIDS. In January 2005 MINUSTAH, with the UN Development Programme, the Haitian Government and the Provisional Electoral Council, signed an agreement on the organization of a general election, which was scheduled to be held later in that year.

At 31 January 2005 MINUSTAH comprised 5,994 troops, 1,398 civilian police and 616 international and local civilian staff. The mission is financed by assessments in respect of a Special Account. The approved budget for the period 1 July 2004–30 June 2005 amounted to US $379.1m.

UNITED NATIONS TRUCE SUPERVISION ORGANIZATION—UNTSO

Address: Government House, Jerusalem.

Chief-of-Staff: Brig.-Gen. CLIVE LILLEY (New Zealand).

UNTSO was established initially to supervise the truce called by the UN Security Council in Palestine in May 1948 and has assisted in the application of the 1949 Armistice Agreements. Its activities have evolved over the years, in response to developments in the Middle East and in accordance with the relevant resolutions of the Security Council. There is no periodic renewal procedure for UNTSO's mandate.

UNTSO observers assist UN peace-keeping forces in the Middle East, at present UNIFIL and UNDOF. The mission maintains offices in Beirut, Lebanon and Damascus, Syria. In addition, UNTSO operates a number of outposts in the Sinai region of Egypt to maintain a UN presence there. UNTSO observers have been available at short notice to form the nucleus of new peace-keeping operations.

The operational strength of UNTSO at 31 January 2005 was 152 military observers, supported by 216 international and local civilian staff. UNTSO expenditures are covered by the regular budget of the United Nations. The cost of the operation in 2004–05 was estimated to be US $58.8m.

United Nations Population Fund—UNFPA

Address: 220 East 42nd St, New York, NY 10017, USA.
Telephone: (212) 297-5000; **fax:** (212) 297-4911; **internet:** www
.unfpa.org.

Created in 1967 as the Trust Fund for Population Activities, the UN
Fund for Population Activities (UNFPA) was established as a Fund
of the UN General Assembly in 1972 and was made a subsidiary
organ of the UN General Assembly in 1979, with the UNDP Governing Council (now the Executive Board) designated as its governing body. In 1987 UNFPA's name was changed to the United
Nations Population Fund (retaining the same acronym).

Organization

(March 2005)

EXECUTIVE DIRECTOR

The Executive Director, who has the rank of Under-Secretary-
General of the UN, is responsible for the overall direction of the
Fund, working closely with governments, other United Nations
bodies and agencies, and non-governmental and international
organizations to ensure the most effective programming and use of
resources in population activities.
Executive Director: THORAYA A. OBAID (Saudi Arabia).

EXECUTING AGENCIES

UNFPA provides financial and technical assistance to developing
countries and countries with economies in transition, at their
request. In many projects assistance is extended through member
organizations of the UN system (in particular, FAO, ILO, UNESCO,
WHO), although projects are executed increasingly by national
governments themselves. The Fund may also call on the services of
international, regional and national non-governmental and training
organizations, as well as research institutions. In addition, eight
UNFPA regional technical support teams, composed of experts from
the UN, its specialized agencies and non-governmental organizations, assist countries at all stages of project/programme development and implementation.

FIELD ORGANIZATION

UNFPA operates field offices, each headed by an UNFPA Representative, in more than 100 countries. In other countries UNFPA
uses UNDP's field structure of Resident Representatives as the
main mechanism for performing its work. The field offices assist
governments in formulating requests for aid and co-ordinate the
work of the executing agencies in any given country or area. UNFPA
has eight regional technical support teams (see above).

Activities

The major functions of UNFPA, according to its mandate, are: to
advance the knowledge and capacity to respond to needs in population and family planning; to promote awareness of population
problems in developed and developing countries and possible strategies to deal with them; to assist countries, at their request, in
dealing with their population problems, in the forms and means best
suited to the individual countries' requirements; and to play a
leading role in the UN system in promoting population programmes
and support and co-ordinate projects.

In co-operation with the UN Population Division, UNFPA played
an important role in preparing for and conducting the International
Conference on Population and Development (ICPD), held in Cairo,
Egypt, in September 1994. UNFPA's then Executive Director, Dr
Nafis Sadik, acted as Secretary-General of the Conference, which
was attended by representatives of 182 countries. The Fund was
appointed as the lead body within the UN system responsible for
following up and implementing the Programme of Action adopted by
the ICPD. This outlined the objectives to be pursued for the next 20
years (despite reservations recorded by the representatives of some
predominantly Roman Catholic and Islamic countries, concerning
sections which they regarded as endorsing abortion and sexual
promiscuity). The Programme's objectives envisaged universal
access to reproductive health and family planning services, a reduction in infant, child and maternal mortality, a life expectancy at
birth of 75 years or more, and universal access to primary education
for all children by 2015. The Programme emphasized the necessity of
empowering and educating women, in order to achieve successful
sustainable human development. Annual expenditure required for
the implementation of the objectives was estimated to amount to

US \$17,000m. in 2000, increasing to \$21,700m. in 2015: of these
amounts, the international community or donor countries would
need to contribute about one-third. During 1995 UNFPA undertook
to redefine its programme directions, resource allocations and policy
guide-lines in order to implement effectively the recommendations of
the ICPD Programme of Action. The Executive Board subsequently
endorsed the following as core programme areas: Reproductive
Health, including family planning and sexual health; Population
and Development Strategies; and Advocacy (for example, human
rights, education, basic health services and the empowerment of
women) (see below). A special session of the UN General Assembly
(entitled ICPD + 5, and attended by delegates from 177 countries)
was held in June–July 1999 to assess progress in achieving the
objectives of the Cairo Conference and to identify priorities for future
action. ICPD + 5 adopted several key actions for further implementation of the Programme of Action. These included advancing
understanding of the connections between poverty, gender inequalities, health, education, the environment, financial and human
resources, and development; focusing on the economic and social
implications of demographic change; greater incorporation of gender
issues into social and development policies and greater involvement
of women in decision-making processes; greater support for
HIV/AIDS prevention activities; and strengthened political commitment to the reproductive health of adolescents. Several new objectives were adopted by the special session, including the achievement
of 60% availability of contraceptives and reproductive health care
services by 2005, 80% by 2010, with universal availability by 2015.
UNFPA prioritizes the role of reproductive health in attaining the
Millennium Development Goals, agreed in September 2000 by a
summit of UN heads of state or government.

UNFPA is participating in the UN System-wide Special Initiative
on Africa that was initiated by the UN Secretary-General in March
1996. UNFPA's principal involvement is to assist countries to implement efforts for reproductive health and to promote the integration
of population considerations into development planning. UNFPA
collaborates with other UN agencies and international experts to
develop a reliable, multidisciplinary set of indicators to measure
progress towards achieving the objectives of different global conferences and to help formulate reproductive health programmes and
monitor their success. UNFPA is a co-sponsor of the Joint UN
Programme on HIV/AIDS (UNAIDS), and is the UNAIDS convening
agency with responsibility for young people and for condom programming, as well as taking a leading role in the UNAIDS inter-
agency task team on gender and HIV/AIDS. The Fund organized a
high-level panel discussion on the theme 'Gender and HIV/AIDS' at
the UN General Assembly special session on HIV/AIDS held in June
2001.

REPRODUCTIVE HEALTH AND SAFE MOTHERHOOD

UNFPA recognizes that improving reproductive health is an essential requirement for improving the general welfare of the population
and the basis for empowering women and achieving sustainable
social and economic development. The ICPD succeeded in raising the
political prominence of reproductive health issues and stimulating
consideration by governments of measures to strengthen and
restructure their health services and policies. UNFPA encourages
the integration of family planning into all maternal, child and other
reproductive health care. Its efforts to improve the quality of these
services include support for the training of health-care personnel
and promoting greater accessibility. Many reproductive health projects focus on the reduction of maternal mortality (i.e. those related
to pregnancy), which was included as a central objective of the ICPD
Programme, and recognized as a legitimate element of international
human rights instruments concerning the right to life/survival.
UNFPA supports projects in 89 countries to reduce maternal deaths,
which amount to about 500,000 each year. Efforts have focused on
improving accessibility to essential obstetric care and ensuring the
provision of skilled attendance to women in labour. UNFPA participates with UNICEF and other partners in the Averting Maternal
Death and Disability programme, which aims to increase the availability of emergency obstetric care in developing countries. In 2003
the Fund launched a Global Campaign to End Fistula, which aims to
improve the prevention and treatment of this serious obstetric
condition in 30 countries in Africa and Asia. An initiative is also
under way to map the occurrence of fistula in certain developing
countries. The ICPD reported that a major cause of maternal deaths
was unsafe abortions, and urged governments to confront the issue
as a major public health concern. UNFPA is concerned with reducing
the use of abortion (i.e. its use as a means of family planning). The
Fund, in co-operation with the other participants in UNAIDS (see
above), aims to strengthen the global response to the HIV/AIDS
epidemic, and is also concerned to reduce levels of other sexually-

transmitted infections (STIs) and reproductive tract infections (RTIs), and of infertility. UNFPA gives special attention to the specific needs of adolescents, for example through education and counselling initiatives, and to women in emergency situations. The Fund maintains that meeting the reproductive health needs of adolescents is an urgent priority in combating poverty and HIV/AIDS. Through the joint Adolescent Girls Initiative, UNFPA, UNICEF and WHO promote policy dialogues in 11 countries. UNFPA distributes emergency reproductive health supplies (including home delivery kits), with a focus on HIV-prevention, to regions affected by conflict or natural disaster and supports counselling, education and training activities, and the construction of clinics and other health facilities, following humanitarian crises. UNFPA also supports research into contraceptives and training in contraceptive technology. UNFPA organizes in-depth studies on national contraceptive requirements and aims to ensure an adequate supply of contraceptives and reproductive health supplies to developing countries. In the early 2000s the Fund and other partners developed a Reproductive Health Commodity Strategy (RHCS), which aimed to improve developing countries' self-sufficiency in the management and provision of reproductive health commodities. A series of regional workshops on the RHCS were completed in 2003. UNFPA encourages partnerships between private-sector interests and the governments of developing nations, with a view to making affordable commercial contraceptive products more easily available to consumers and thereby enabling governments to direct subsidies at the poorest sectors of society.

POPULATION AND DEVELOPMENT STRATEGIES

UNFPA helps countries to formulate and implement comprehensive population policies as a central part of any strategies to achieve sustainable development. The Fund aims to ensure that the needs and concerns of women are incorporated into development and population policies. Under this programme area UNFPA provides assistance and training for national statistical offices in undertaking basic data collection, for example censuses and demographic surveys. UNFPA also provides assistance for analysis of demographic and socio-economic data, for research on population trends and for the formulation of government policies. It supports a programme of fellowships in demographic analysis, data processing and cartography. In October 2001 UNFPA organized a meeting of experts on population ageing in preparation for the Second World Assembly on Ageing, which was held in April 2002.

ADVOCACY

UNFPA's advocacy role is incorporated into all its programming activities in support of the objectives of the ICPD. Consequently, the Fund aims to encourage the participation of women at all levels of decision- and policy-making and supports programmes that improve the access of all girls and women to education and grant women equal access to land, credit and employment opportunities. UNFPA's annual *State of World Population Report* has consistently focused on the improved welfare of women as an issue of basic human rights; this includes the eradication of all forms of gender discrimination,

entitlement to reproductive choice and a zero-tolerance approach to the protection of women from sexual and domestic violence and coercion. UNFPA helps to promote awareness of these objectives and to incorporate them into national programmes. In 1997 UNFPA appointed a special ambassador to generate international awareness of the dangers of female genital mutilation. UNFPA emphasizes the role of knowledge and prevention in combating the spread of HIV/AIDS. There are special programmes on youth, on ageing and on migration, and the Fund is currently increasing educational and research activities in the area of population and the environment. UNFPA works with the military in a number of countries to provide information to men on areas such as family planning and STI and HIV prevention. UNFPA attempts to increase awareness of population issues through regional and national seminars, publications (see below) and audio-visual aids (such as webfilms and CD-Roms), participation in conferences (including video conferences), and through a pro-active relationship with the mass media.

Finance

UNFPA is supported entirely by voluntary contributions from donor countries. In 2003 UNFPA's income totalled US $397.9m., of which $292.3m. was regular income and $105.6m. derived from trust funds, other restricted funds and cost-sharing arrangements. The Fund's provisional regular income totalled $326m., contributed by a record 166 countries, in 2004. Country programme expenditure in 2003 totalled some $140.5m., and a further $35.9m. was spent on regional and interregional projects. Of total programme expenditure in 2003 about 61% was allocated to reproductive health care and family planning, and about 20% to population and development stategies. In that year the regional distribution of the Fund's assistance was as follows: sub-Saharan Africa 36%, Asia and the Pacific 30%, the Arab States and Europe 13%, and Latin America and the Caribbean 8%, while interregional and global programmes received 13% of total assistance.

Publications

Adding it Up: The Benefits of Investing in Sexual and Reproductive Health Care (in English, published jointly with the Alan Guttmacher Institute).

Annual Report.

Dispatches (every two months, in Arabic, English, French and Spanish).

Frontlines: News from the Field (electronic newsletter).

Preventing HIV Infection, Promoting Reproductive Health: UNFPA Response (annually, in English, French and Spanish).

State of World Population (annually, in Arabic, English, French, Russian and Spanish).

Reports, technical publications, guide-lines and manuals.

United Nations Relief and Works Agency for Palestine Refugees in the Near East—UNRWA

Address: Gamal Abd an-Nasser St, Gaza City.
Address: Bayader Wadi Seer, POB 140157, Amman 11814, Jordan.
Telephone: (7) 6777333; **fax:** (7) 6777555; **Telephone:** (6) 5826171; **fax:** (6) 5826177; **e-mail:** unrwa-pio@unrwa.org; **internet:** www.un.org/unrwa/.

UNRWA was established by the UN General Assembly to provide relief, health, education and welfare services for Palestine refugees in the Near East, initially on a short-term basis. UNRWA began operations in May 1950 and, in the absence of a solution to the refugee problem, its mandate has subsequently been extended by the General Assembly.

Organization

(March 2005)

UNRWA employs an international staff of about 120 and more than 24,200 local staff, mainly Palestine refugees. In 1996 the agency's headquarters were relocated, from Vienna, Austria, to Gaza and

Jordan. The Commissioner-General is the head of all UNRWA operations and reports directly to the UN General Assembly. UNRWA has no governing body, but its activities are reviewed annually by a 10-member Advisory Commission comprising representatives of the governments of:

Belgium	Jordan	Turkey
Egypt	Lebanon	United Kingdom
France	Syria	USA
Japan		

Acting Commissioner-General: KAREN KONING ABU ZAYD (USA).

FIELD OFFICES

Each field office is headed by a director and has departments responsible for education, health and relief and social services programmes, finance, administration, supply and transport, legal affairs and public information.

Gaza: POB 61; Al Azhar Rd, Rimal Quarter, Gaza City; tel. (7) 2824508; fax (7) 6777444.

Jordan: POB 484, 11118 Amman; Al Zubeidi Bldg No. 16, Mustafa Bin Abdullah St, Barakeh, Tla'a Al-Ali, Amman; tel. (6) 5609100; fax (6) 5609112.

Lebanon: POB 11-0947, Beirut 1107 2060; Bir Hassan, Ghobeiri, Beirut; tel. (1) 840490; fax (1) 840466.

Syria: POB 4313; UN Compound, Mezzah Highway/Beirut Rd, Damascus; tel. (11) 6133035; fax (11) 6133047.

West Bank: POB 19149, Jerusalem; Sheik Jarrah Qtr, East Jerusalem; tel. (2) 5890400; fax (2) 5890744.

LIAISON OFFICES

Egypt: 2 Dar-el-Shifa St, Garden City, POB 227, Cairo; tel. (2) 794-8502; fax (2) 794-8504.

Switzerland: Rm 92–93 Annexe Le Bocage, Palais des Nations, 1211 Geneva; tel. (22) 9171166; fax (22) 9170956.

USA: 1 United Nations Plaza, Room DC1–1265, New York, NY 10017; tel. (212) 963-2255; fax (212) 935-7899.

Activities

ASSISTANCE ACTIVITIES

Since 1950 UNRWA has been the main provider of relief, health, education and social services for Palestine refugees in Lebanon, Syria, Jordan, the West Bank and the Gaza Strip. For UNRWA's purposes, a Palestine refugee is one whose normal residence was in Palestine for a minimum of two years before the 1948 conflict and who, as a result of the Arab–Israeli hostilities, lost his or her home and means of livelihood. To be eligible for assistance, a refugee must reside in one of the five areas in which UNRWA operates and be in need. A refugee's descendants who fulfil certain criteria are also eligible for UNRWA assistance. At 30 June 2004 UNRWA was providing essential services to 4,186,711 registered refugees. Of these, an estimated 1,226,213 (29%) were living in 59 camps serviced by the Agency, while the remaining refugees had settled in the towns and villages already existing. In that month UNRWA and the Swiss Government hosted an international conference to address the humanitarian needs of the Palestinian refugees. The conference, which was convened in Geneva, was attended by representatives of 67 countries and 34 international organizations. The recommendations of the conference contributed to a new medium-term plan, covering 2005–09, which was presented in February 2005. The plan focused on the following four main objectives for the agency: to ensure parity of UNRWA's services with the host authority and international standards; to address the needs of vulnerable refugees; to maximize the economic potential of refugees; and to build capacity within UNRWA.

UNRWA's three principal areas of activity are education, health, and relief and social services. Some 81% of the Agency's 2004 general fund budget was devoted to these three operational programmes.

Education accounted for 54% of UNRWA's 2004 budget. In the 2003/04 school year there were 491,978 pupils enrolled in 663 UNRWA schools, and 15,814 educational staff. UNRWA also operated eight vocational and teacher-training centres, which provided a total of 5,131 training places. UNRWA awarded 56 scholarships for study at Arab universities in 2002/03. Technical co-operation for the Agency's education programme is provided by UNESCO.

Health services accounted for 18% of UNRWA's 2004 general fund budget. At mid-2004 there were 122 primary health care units providing outpatient medical care, disease prevention and control, maternal and child health care and family planning services, of which 89 also offered dental care. At that time the number of health staff totalled 3,642. During 2004 patient visits to UNRWA medical units numbered 8.83m. UNRWA also operates a hospital in the West Bank and offers assistance towards emergency and other secondary treatment, mainly through contractual agreements with non-governmental and private hospitals. Technical assistance for the health programme is provided by WHO. At the end of 2003 UNRWA employed 75 school counsellors and 41 mental health counsellors in schools, clinics and community centres under its Pyscho-Social Support programme aimed at assisting refugees experiencing acute psychological stress.

Relief and social services accounted for 10% of UNRWA's general fund budget for 2004. These services comprise the distribution of food rations, the provision of emergency shelter and the organization of welfare programmes for the poorest refugees (at 30 June 2004 246,907 refugees, or 6% of the total registered refugee population, were eligible to receive special hardship assistance). In 2004 UNRWA provided technical and financial support to 64 women's programme centres and 37 community-based rehabilitation centres.

In order to encourage Palestinian self-reliance the Agency issues grants to ailing businesses and loans to families who qualify as special hardship cases. In 1991 UNRWA launched an income gen-

eration programme, which provides capital loans to small businesses and micro-enterprises with the objective of creating sustainable employment and eliminating poverty, particularly in the Occupied Territories. The programme was extended to Palestinian refugees in Syria in June 2003. By 30 June 2004 76,668 loans, with a total estimated value of US \$85.4m., had been issued to new and existing Palestinian-owned enterprises.

SPECIAL PROGRAMMES

Following the signing of the Declaration of Principles by the Palestine Liberation Organization and the Israeli Government in September 1993, UNRWA initiated a Peace Implementation Programme (PIP) to improve services and infrastructure for Palestinian refugees. In September 1994 the first phase of the scheme (PIP I) was concluded after the receipt of US \$93.2m. in pledged donations. PIP I projects included the construction of 33 schools and 24 classrooms and specialized education rooms, the rehabilitation of 4,700 shelters, the upgrading of solid waste disposal facilities throughout the Gaza Strip and feasibility studies for two sewerage systems. It was estimated that these projects created more than 5,500 jobs in the Gaza Strip for an average period of four months each. PIP II, the second phase of the scheme, was concluded in December 1999. By June 2004 the total number of UNRWA projects, including those implemented under the PIP scheme, amounted to 746, while funds received or pledged by that time totalled \$331.8m.

Since 1993 UNRWA has been engaged in the construction, equipping and commissioning of a 232-bed hospital in the Gaza Strip, with funds from the European Union and its member states. The outpatient facilities opened in mid-2000. The hospital and an affiliated nursing college were to be integrated into the health care system of the Palestinian (National) Authority (PA), once the process of commissioning had been completed.

AID TO DISPLACED PERSONS

After the renewal of Arab–Israeli hostilities in the Middle East in June 1967, hundreds of thousands of people fled from the fighting and from Israeli-occupied areas to east Jordan, Syria and Egypt. UNRWA provided emergency relief for displaced refugees and was additionally empowered by a UN General Assembly resolution to provide 'humanitarian assistance, as far as practicable, on an emergency basis and as a temporary measure' for those persons other than Palestine refugees who were newly displaced and in urgent need. In practice, UNRWA lacked the funds to aid the other displaced persons and the main burden of supporting them devolved on the Arab governments concerned. The Agency, as requested by the Government of Jordan in 1967 and on that Government's behalf, distributes rations to displaced persons in Jordan who are not registered refugees of 1948.

RECENT EMERGENCIES

UNRWA's emergency humanitarian support activities for Palestinian refugees include the provision of basic food and medical supplies; the implementation of a programme of emergency workdays, which aims to provide employment and income for labourers with dependents, while improving the local infrastructure; the provision of extra schooling days to make up for those missed because of the conflict, trauma counselling for children, and post-injury rehabilitation; and the reconstruction of shelters. In November 2000 UNRWA launched an emergency humanitarian appeal for US \$39m. in additional funds to assist Palestinian refugees affected by the most recent escalation of violence in the region and the Israeli-imposed blockade on PA-controlled territory. UNRWA became the lead agency with responsibility for the co-ordination and delivery of emergency assistance, as well as for monitoring the immediate needs of the local populations. A second appeal was made by the Agency in April 2001, for some \$37m., and a third emergency appeal, for \$77m., was issued in June. In mid-January 2002 UNRWA reacted immediately to assess the needs of refugees following the demolition of 54 shelters by Israeli forces, and provided emergency supplies, including tents, blankets, mats and food. A fourth emergency appeal, for some \$117m., was launched at the end of January to provide food aid, medical care, shelter reconstruction and emergency work programmes for refugees in the affected areas. In February the Commissioner-General protested at the Israeli bombing of Gaza City and at the damage caused by Israeli security forces in the Palestinian towns of Jenin and Nablus. In March the Commissioner-General expressed deep concern at the worsening humanitarian situation in the Palestinian territories, as well as his outrage at the death of an UNRWA staff member during an Israeli incursion into Tulkarem camp. Later in that month UNRWA assessed that the damage inflicted against UNRWA infrastructure during March amounted to \$3.8m. In early April UNRWA efforts to deliver emergency food and medical supplies to Ramallah hospital and other areas in the West Bank were hindered by attacks and threats by Israeli troops. The Commissioner-General expressed concern at the deteriorating security and humanitarian situation and for the welfare of detained and besieged UN workers. In mid-April UNRWA was permitted limited access to Jenin refugee camp, which had experienced extensive fighting during a two-week period of occupation by Israeli forces. UNRWA delivered food and water and attempted to co-ordinate international efforts to send search and rescue teams into the camp. It also undertook to reintroduce essential services and to initiate the reconstruction of refugee homes. At the same time UNRWA noted with concern the entry restrictions imposed by Israel against the Gaza Strip, which were causing extreme food shortages. In May UNRWA organized a conference of 28 countries to highlight the need for an additional $70m. to meet the humanitarian requirements resulting from the Israeli incursions. Some $56m. in additional aid was requested in July. During that month the United Arab Emirates Red Crescent Society agreed to provide UNRWA with $27m. in funding towards a two-year programme to rehabilitate the Jenin camp. Under Phase I of the programme preparatory assessments were to be undertaken and improvements were to be made to 70 shelters belonging to the most vulnerable camp residents; some 400 shelters and the camp's water supply, sewage system, electricity network and roads were to be reconstructed under Phase II; while the final Phase III was to involve repairs to communal facilities such as schools and health centres.

In December 2002 UNRWA launched an appeal for US $93.7m. to fund emergency relief efforts in the first six months of 2003; by February 2003, however, only a small proportion of the requested funds had been pledged and none received, necessitating a retrenchment of the Agency's assistance activities. Following a renewed appeal by UNRWA's Commissioner-General in that month, a total of US $41.3m. had been pledged by the termination of the appeal period at 30 June. In May UNRWA protested strongly at the imposition by the Israeli authorities of a ban on movement by UN international staff within Gaza that was severely impeding the Agency's activities. In June the Agency announced its sixth emergency appeal, requesting $102.9m. to cover its emergency relief efforts during the period 1 July–31 December. During 2003 the demolition of homes in Gaza and the West Bank by Israeli military forces escalated significantly; it was reported that during the period November 2000–December 2003 more than 15,000 people had thus been rendered homeless, and that more than 16,000 temporary shelters had been damaged. Throughout 2003 UNRWA expressed concern at the construction by Israel of the West Bank 'security fence', or 'barrier', which was estimated to affect some 200,000 people through loss of land, water, agricultural resources and education, and hindered UNRWA's ability to provide and distribute humanitarian assistance. A seventh Emergency Appeal, amounting to $195.6m., was issued in December to finance UNRWA's emergency relief activities in 2004, of which some $62m. was to be allocated to the emergency workdays programme and some $55m. to the provision of basic food commodities for 222,000 severely impoverished refugee families. In May 2004 a Supplementary Appeal, for $15.8m., was launched following large-scale incursions by Israeli forces into densely populated areas of Rafah, Gaza Strip, as a result of which some 60 people were reported to have died and 298 buildings, housing more than 700 people, had been destroyed or irreparably damaged. The additional funds requested were to meet the immediate needs of those affected, the majority of whom were UNRWA registered refugees, including the provision of food, financial support and emergency housing. In mid-July UNRWA organized a supply convoy to deliver some 370 metric tons of food to an estimated 20,000 people in the northern town of Beit Hanoun, which had been besieged by the Israeli military since the end of June. A further incursion by the Israeli Defence Force into northern Gaza Strip was initiated at the end of September, isolating some 36,000 people. UNRWA delivered emergency food aid to 1,000 families affected by the operation, and undertook an assessment of its impact when Israeli troops withdrew in mid-October. In December UNRWA launched an appeal for $185.8m. to fund emergency relief operations in 2005, including the reconstruction of homes, emergency employment schemes, food aid, and emergency health provision.

Statistics

Refugees Registered with UNRWA
(31 December 2004)

Country	Number	% of total
Jordan	1,776,669	42
Gaza Strip	952,295	23
West Bank	682,657	16
Syria	421,737	10
Lebanon	399,152	9
Total	4,232,510	100

Finance

UNRWA is financed almost entirely by voluntary contributions from governments and the European Union, the remainder being provided by UN bodies, non-governmental organizations, business corporations and private sources, which also contribute to extra-budgetary activities. UNRWA's general fund budget for 2004 amounted to US $350.97m.

Publication

Annual Report of the Commissioner-General of UNRWA.

United Nations Training and Research Institutes

UNITED NATIONS INSTITUTE FOR DISARMAMENT RESEARCH—UNIDIR

Address: Palais des Nations, 1211 Geneva 10, Switzerland.

Telephone: (22) 9173186; **fax:** (22) 9170176; **e-mail:** unidir@unog.ch; **internet:** www.unidir.org.

UNIDIR is an autonomous institution within the United Nations. It was established by the General Assembly in 1980 for the purpose of undertaking independent research on disarmament and related problems, particularly international security issues. UNIDIR's statute became effective on 1 January 1985.

The work of the Institute is based on the following objectives: to provide the international community with more diversified and complete data on problems relating to international security, the armaments race and disarmament in all fields, so as to facilitate progress towards greater global security and towards economic and social development for all peoples; to promote informed participation by all states in disarmament efforts; to assist ongoing negotiations on disarmament, and continuing efforts to ensure greater international security at a progressively lower level of armaments, in particular nuclear weapons, by means of objective studies and analyses; and to conduct long-term research on disarmament in order to provide a general insight into the problems involved and to stimulate new initiatives for negotiations. UNIDIR's activities are divided into the following three areas: global security and disarmament, regional security and disarmament, and human security and disarmament.

The work programme of UNIDIR is reviewed annually and is subject to approval by its Board of Trustees. During 2004 UNIDIR organized conferences and seminars on a range of issues, including: the safeguarding of space for all: security and peaceful uses; the launch of open skies, a co-operative approach to military transparency and confidence-building; and an electronic conference on a new agenda for security and disarmament. Examples of ongoing research projects in 2004 included weapons for development; missiles and missile defences; and preventing biological weapons proliferation. Research projects are conducted within the Institute, or commissioned to individual experts or research organizations. For some major studies, multinational groups of experts are established. The Institute offers a research fellowship programme focusing on topics relating to regional security. UNIDIR maintains a database on research institutes (DATARIs) in the field of international security (accessible at dataris.sipri.org). The Institute organizes an ongoing discussion series, the so-called Geneva Forum, as a means of sharing expertise on a broad range of issues among government and non-governmental officials, UN personnel, media representatives and academics. The Geneva Forum publishes the *Media Guide to Disarmament and Arms Control.*

The Institute is financed mainly by voluntary contributions from governments and public or private organizations. A contribution to the costs of the Director and staff may be provided from the UN regular budget.

The Director of UNIDIR reports annually to the General Assembly on the activities of the Institute. The UN Secretary-General's Advisory Board on Disarmament Studies functions as UNIDIR's Board of Trustees.

Director: PATRICIA LEWIS (United Kingdom).

Publications: *Disarmament Forum* (quarterly), *UNIDIR Newsletter* (quarterly), research reports (6 a year), research papers (irregular).

UNITED NATIONS INSTITUTE FOR TRAINING AND RESEARCH—UNITAR

Address: Palais des Nations, 1211 Geneva 10, Switzerland.

Telephone: (22) 9171234; **fax:** (22) 9178047; **e-mail:** info@unitar.org; **internet:** www.unitar.org.

UNITAR was established in 1963, as an autonomous body within the United Nations, in order to enhance the effectiveness of the latter body in achieving its major objectives. In recent years the main focus of the Institute has shifted to training and capacity-building, with basic research being conducted only if extra-budgetary funds are made available. Training is provided at various levels for personnel on assignments under the United Nations and its specialized agencies or under organizations operating in related fields. It is focused on two main areas of concern: diplomacy and international affairs; and economic and social development. In 2005 UNITAR programmes included courses on the management of international affairs; peace-keeping and preventive diplomacy; the application of environmental law; the legal aspects of debt and financial management; foreign economic relations; chemicals and waste management; climate change; the information society; the special needs of women and children affected by conflict; AIDS competence; and international migration policy. Most training programmes are designed and conducted in Geneva. The New York office, established in 1996, organizes the training of delegates at United Nations headquarters. In October 2001 UNITAR, in collaboration with the authorities in Hiroshima, Japan, initiated the Hiroshima Programmes, which aimed to organize training activities in the Asia and Pacific region to promote peace and security and economic and social development. Also in 2001, in partnership with UNOPS, the International Training Center for Local Actors (CIFAL) was inaugurated in Divonne-les-Bains, France, to assist with UN crisis situation management activities and focus on the role of local communities in emergency humanitarian responses.

UNITAR offers a fellowship programme in peace-making and preventive diplomacy to provide advanced training for international and national civil servants in conflict analysis and mediation. It also organizes, jointly with the UN Office for Legal Affairs, an annual fellowship programme in international law.

UNITAR is financed by voluntary contributions from UN member states, by donations from foundations and other non-governmental sources, and by income generated by its Reserve Fund.

Executive Director: MARCEL A. BOISARD (Switzerland).

UNITED NATIONS INTERNATIONAL RESEARCH AND TRAINING INSTITUTE FOR THE ADVANCEMENT OF WOMEN— INSTRAW

Address: Calle César Nicolás Pensón 102-A, POB 21747, Santo Domingo, Dominican Republic.

Telephone: (809) 685-2111; **fax:** (809) 685-2117; **e-mail:** comments@un-instraw.org; **internet:** www.un-instraw.org.

The Institute was established by ECOSOC, and endorsed by the General Assembly, in 1976, following a recommendation of the World Conference on the International Women's Year (1975). INSTRAW provides training, conducts research and collects and disseminates relevant information in order to stimulate and to assist the advancement of women and their integration in the development process, both as participants and beneficiaries. In June 2000 INSTRAW inaugurated the Gender Awareness Information and Networking System (GAINS), an internet-based database on research and training materials.Research areas in 2005 focused on financing for development, and remittances and gender. In early 2005 INSTRAW published a series of reports on progress achieved in 12 critical areas of the Beijing Platform for Action, referring to the final document of the fourth World Conference on Women, held in Beijing, People's Republic of China, in 1995.

INSTRAW was created as an autonomous body of the UN, funded by voluntary contributions. However, in December 2002 the UN General Assembly endorsed a number of recommendations on the future operation of the Institute presented by a working party appointed in December 2001; these included: abolishing the auton-omous status of the Institute; abolishing its Board of Trustees; linking the Institute to the UN Secretariat's Department of Political and Social Affairs, under the direct authority of the Department's Under-Secretary-General; and allocating INSTRAW US $500,000 annually from the UN regular budget. Accordingly, in August 2003 ECOSOC adopted a resolution that amended INSTRAW's statute to replace the Board of Trustees with a 10–member Executive Board (comprising two representatives from each of the UN's five regional groupings elected by ECOSOC for a three-year term of office). INSTRAW's core budget for 2005 amounted to $1.13m.

Director: CARMEN MORENO (Mexico).

Publications: *INSTRAW News*, training materials, research studies.

UNITED NATIONS INTERREGIONAL CRIME AND JUSTICE RESEARCH INSTITUTE— UNICRI

Address: Viale Maestri del Lavoro 10, 10127 Turin, Italy.

Telephone: (011) 6537111; **fax:** (011) 6313368; **e-mail:** unicri@unicri.it; **internet:** www.unicri.it.

The Institute was established in 1968 as the United Nations Social Defence Research Institute. Its present name was adopted by a resolution of ECOSOC in 1989. The Institute undertakes research, training and information activities in the fields of crime prevention and criminal justice, at international, regional and national levels.

In collaboration with national governments, UNICRI aims to establish a reliable base of knowledge and information on organized crime; to identify strategies for the prevention and control of crime, within the framework of contributing to socio-economic development and protecting human rights; and to design systems to support policy formulation, implementation and evaluation. UNICRI organizes workshops and conferences, and promotes the exchange of information through its international documentation centre on criminology. Main areas of activity during 2004 included global programmes against trafficking in human beings, corruption, and organized crime. The UNICRI Terrorism Prevention Unit, mandated to combat international terrorism through technical co-operation activities, works closely with law enforcement agencies worldwide.

UNICRI is funded by the United Nations Crime Prevention and Criminal Justice Fund, which is financed by voluntary contributions from UN member states, non-governmental organizations, academic institutions and other concerned bodies.

Director: GIOACCHINO POLIMENI (Italy).

Publications: *UNICRI Journal* (2 a year), training materials, research studies.

UNITED NATIONS RESEARCH INSTITUTE FOR SOCIAL DEVELOPMENT—UNRISD

Address: Palais des Nations, 1211 Geneva 10, Switzerland.

Telephone: (22) 9173020; **fax:** (22) 9170650; **e-mail:** info@unrisd.org; **internet:** www.unrisd.org.

UNRISD was established in 1963 as an autonomous body within the United Nations, to conduct multi-disciplinary research into the social dimensions of contemporary problems affecting development.

The Institute aims to provide governments, development agencies, grass-roots organizations and scholars with a better understanding of how development policies and processes of economic, social and environmental change affect different social groups.

UNRISD research is undertaken in collaboration with a network of national research teams drawn from local universities and research institutions. UNRISD aims to promote and strengthen research capacities in developing countries. Its main focus areas are the eradication of poverty; the promotion of democracy and human rights; environmental sustainability; gender equality; and the effects of globalization. During the period 2000–05 UNRISD's main programme areas and areas of research were: civil society and social movements; democracy, governance and human rights; identities, conflict and cohesion; social policy development; and technology and society. In March 2005 UNRISD presented a major policy report on gender and development in the 10 years since the Beijing fourth World Conference on Women.

The Institute is supported by voluntary grants from governments, and also receives financing from other UN organizations, and from various other national and international agencies.

Director: THANDIKA MKANDAWIRE (Sweden).

Publications: *UNRISD Social Development News* (1–2 a year), discussion papers and monographs, special reports, programme and occasional papers.

UNITED NATIONS SYSTEM STAFF COLLEGE

Address: Viale Maestri del Lavoro 10, 10127 Turin, Italy.

Telephone: (011) 6535906; **fax:** (011) 6535901; **e-mail:** unscp@itcilo.it; **internet:** www.unssc.org/unscp.

In July 2001 the UN General Assembly approved a statute for the UN System Staff College (UNSSC), which, it envisaged, would provide knowledge management, training and continuous learning opportunities for all UN personnel, with a view to developing UN system-wide co-operation and operational effectiveness. The inaugural meeting of the Board of Governors was held in November, and the College formally began operations on 1 January 2002. It aims to promote the exchange of knowledge and shared learning, to administer learning and training workshops, as well as distance learning opportunities, to provide support and expert advice, and to act as a clearing house for learning activities. The College organizes its activities on the following programme clusters: Learning advisory services; Learning resources; Management and leadership development (which co-ordinates the Senior Management System Leadership Development project); Induction training and support; Institutional capacity building; Strengthening the resident co-ordinator system and UN country teams; Human rights-based approaches and the implementation of the Millennium Development Goals; Peace and security; and Partnerships and the global compact.

The UNSSC is financed by a combination of course fees, voluntary grants from governments and contributions in kind from various UN organizations in the form of staff secondments.

Director: TIMOTHY CARTWRIGHT (Canada).

UNITED NATIONS UNIVERSITY—UNU

Address: 53–70, Jingumae 5-chome, Shibuya-ku, Tokyo 150-8925, Japan.

Telephone: (3) 3499-2811; **fax:** (3) 3499-2828; **e-mail:** mbox@hq.unu.edu; **internet:** www.unu.edu.

The University is sponsored jointly by the United Nations and UNESCO. It is an autonomous institution within the United Nations, guaranteed academic freedom by a charter approved by the General Assembly in 1973. It is governed by a 28-member University Council of scholars and scientists, of whom 24 are appointed by the Secretary-General of the UN and the Director-General of UNESCO (who, together with the Executive Director of UNITAR, are *ex-officio* members of the Council; the Rector is also on the Council). The University is not traditional in the sense of having students or awarding degrees, but works through networks of collaborating institutions and individuals. These include Associated Institutions (universities and research institutes linked with the UNU under general agreements of co-operation). The UNU undertakes multidisciplinary research on problems that are the concern of the United Nations and its agencies, and works to strengthen research and training capabilities in developing countries. It provides post-graduate fellowships for scientists and scholars from developing countries, and conducts various training activities in association with its programme. Its main thematic programme areas are peace; governance; development; science, technology and society; and environment.

The UNU's research and training centres and programmes include the World Institute for Development Economics Research (UNU/WIDER) in Helsinki, Finland; the Institute for New Technologies (UNU/INTECH) in Maastricht, Netherlands; the International Institute for Software Technology (UNU/IIST) in Macao; the UNU Institute for Natural Resources in Africa (UNU-INRA) in Accra, Ghana (with a mineral resources unit in Lusaka, Zambia); the UNU Programme for Biotechnology in Latin America and the Caribbean (UNU/BIOLAC), based in Caracas, Venezuela; the International Leadership Institute (UNU/ILI) in Amman, Jordan; the Institute of Advanced Studies (UNU/IAS), based in Yokohama, Japan; the UNU International Network on Water, Environment and Health (UNU/INWEH) in Hamilton, Canada; the UNU Programme on Comparative Regional Integration Studies (UNU/CRIS), in Bruges, Belgium; the UNU Food and Nutrition Programme for Human and Social Development, based at Cornell University, USA; the UNU Geothermal Training Programme (UNU/GTP) and UNU Fisheries Training Programme (UNU/FTP), both based in Iceland; and the Institute for Environment and Health Security, based in Bonn, Germany. An Initiative on Conflict Resolution and Ethnicity (INCORE), is jointly managed by UNU and the University of Ulster.

The UNU is financed by voluntary contributions from UN member states. The budget for 2005 amounted to US $40.7m.

Rector: Prof. HANS J. A. VAN GINKEL (Netherlands).

Publications: *UNU Nexions* (2 a year), *Work In Progress* (1–2 a year), *WIDERAngle* (2 a year), *Africa Research* (irregular), regular journals, abstracts, research papers.

UNIVERSITY FOR PEACE

Address: POB 138-6100, San José, Costa Rica.

Telephone: 205-9000; **fax:** 249-1929; **e-mail:** info@upeace.org; **internet:** www.upeace.org.

The University for Peace was established by the United Nations in 1980 to conduct research on, *inter alia,* disarmament, mediation, the resolution of conflicts, the preservation of the environment, international relations, peace education and human rights. The Council of the University (the governing body, comprising 17 members) was reconstituted in March 1999, meeting for the first time since 1994. In May 1999 the Council initiated a programme of extensive reforms and expansion. A programme of short courses for advanced international training was reintroduced in 2001. In 2000 a University for Peace Centre and Policy Institute was established in Geneva, Switzerland, and an Institute for Media, Peace and Security was inaugurated, with administrative headquarters in Paris, France. In 2001 the World Centre for Research and Training in Conflict Resolution was established in Bogotá, Colombia. By 2004 Masters degrees were available in International Law and the Settlement of Disputes, International Law and Human Rights, Natural Resources and Sustainable Development, Gender and Peace-Building, International Peace Studies, Environmental Security and Peace, and Peace Education. The University aims to develop a global network of partner institutions. In January 2002 the University launched its Africa Programme, which aims to build African capacity for education, training and research on matters related to peace and security. A Central Asia Programme, concerned with education in peace-building and conflict prevention in the former Soviet Central Asia, was initiated in late 2000. A University for Peace Academic Advisory Council, mandated to improve the organization of the University's academic programme and build partnerships and networks with other academic institutions for collaboration in the areas of both teaching and research, was inaugurated in May 2003.

Rector and Chief Executive Officer: JULIA MARTON-LEFÈVRE (from May 2005).

World Food Programme—WFP

Address: Via Cesare Giulio Viola 68, Parco dei Medici, 00148 Rome, Italy.

Telephone: (06) 6513-1; **fax:** (06) 6513-2840; **e-mail:** wfpinfo@wfp.org; **internet:** www.wfp.org.

WFP, the principal food aid organization of the United Nations, became operational in 1963. It aims to alleviate acute hunger by providing emergency relief following natural or man-made humanitarian disasters, and supplies food aid to people in developing countries to eradicate chronic undernourishment, to support social development and to promote self-reliant communities.

Organization

(March 2005)

EXECUTIVE BOARD

The governing body of WFP is the Executive Board, comprising 36 members, 18 of whom are elected by the UN Economic and Social Council (ECOSOC) and 18 by the Council of the Food and Agriculture Organization (FAO). The Board meets four times each year at WFP headquarters.

SECRETARIAT

WFP's Executive Director is appointed jointly by the UN Secretary-General and the Director-General of FAO and is responsible for the management and administration of the Programme. At December 2003 there were 8,770 staff members, more than 90% of whom were working in the field. WFP administers some 87 country offices, in order to provide operational, financial and management support at a more local level, and has established seven regional bureaux, located in Bangkok, Thailand (for Asia), Cairo, Egypt (for the Middle East, Central Asia and the Mediterranean), Rome, Italy (for Eastern Europe), Managua, Nicaragua (for Latin America and the Caribbean), Yaoundé, Cameroon (for Central Africa), Kampala, Uganda (for Eastern and Southern Africa), and Dakar, Senegal (for West Africa).

Executive Director: JAMES T. MORRIS (USA).

Activities

WFP is the only multilateral organization with a mandate to use food aid as a resource. It is the second largest source of assistance in the UN, after the World Bank group, in terms of actual transfers of resources, and the largest source of grant aid in the UN system. WFP handles more than one-third of the world's food aid. WFP is also the largest contributor to South–South trade within the UN system, through the purchase of food and services from developing countries. WFP's mission is to provide food aid to save lives in refugee and other emergency situations, to improve the nutrition and quality of life of vulnerable groups and to help to develop assets and promote the self-reliance of poor families and communities. WFP aims to focus its efforts on the world's poorest countries and to provide at least 90% of its total assistance to those designated as 'low-income food-deficit'. At the World Food Summit, held in November 1996, WFP endorsed the commitment to reduce by 50% the number of undernourished people, no later than 2015. During 2003 WFP food assistance benefited some 104.2m. people world-wide (compared with 72m. in 2002), of whom 16.2m. received aid through development projects, 61.2m. through emergency operations, and 26.8m. through Protracted Relief and Recovery Operations (see below). Total food deliveries in 2003 amounted to 4.6m. metric tons, compared with 3.7m. metric tons in 2002.

WFP aims to address the causes of chronic malnourishment, which it identifies as poverty and lack of opportunity. It emphasizes the role played by women in combating hunger, and endeavours to address the specific nutritional needs of women, to increase their access to food and development resources, and to promote girls' education. It also focuses resources on supporting the food security of households and communities affected by HIV/AIDS and on promoting food security as a means of mitigating extreme poverty and vulnerability and thereby combating the spread and impact of HIV/AIDS. In February 2003 WFP and the Joint UN Programme on HIV/AIDS (UNAIDS) concluded an agreement to address jointly the relationship between HIV/AIDS, regional food shortages and chronic hunger, with a particular focus on Africa, South-East Asia and the Caribbean. In October of that year WFP became a co-sponsor of UNAIDS. WFP urges the development of new food aid strategies as a means of redressing global inequalities and thereby combating the threat of conflict and international terrorism.

WFP food donations must meet internationally-agreed standards applicable to trade in food products. In May 2003 WFP's Executive Board approved a new policy on donations of genetically-modified (GM) foods and other foods derived from biotechnology, determining that the Programme would continue to accept donations of GM/biotech food and that, when distributing it, relevant national standards would be respected.

In the early 1990s there was a substantial shift in the balance between emergency relief ('food-for-life') and development assistance ('food-for-growth') provided by WFP, owing to the growing needs of victims of drought and other natural disasters, refugees and displaced persons. By 1994 two-thirds of all food aid was for relief assistance and one-third for development, representing a direct reversal of the allocations five years previously. In addition, there was a noticeable increase in aid given to those in need as a result of civil war, compared with commitments for victims of natural disasters. Accordingly, WFP has developed a range of mechanisms to enhance its preparedness for emergency situations and to improve its capacity for responding effectively to situations as they arise. A new programme of emergency response training was inaugurated in 2000, while security concerns for personnel was incorporated as a new element into all general planning and training activities. Through its Vulnerability Analysis and Mapping (VAM) project, WFP aims to identify potentially vulnerable groups by providing information on food security and the capacity of different groups for coping with shortages, and to enhance emergency contingency-planning and long-term assistance objectives. In 2003 VAM field

units were operational in more than 50 countries. WFP also co-operates with other UN agencies including FAO (collaborating on 77 projects in 41 countries in 2003), IFAD (collaborating on 21 projects in that year), UNHCR and UNICEF. The key elements of WFP's emergency response capacity are its strategic stores of food and logistics equipment, stand-by arrangements to enable the rapid deployment of personnel, communications and other essential equipment, and the Augmented Logistics Intervention Team for Emergencies (ALITE), which undertakes capacity assessments and contingency-planning. During 2000 WFP led efforts, undertaken with other UN humanitarian agencies, for the design and application of local UN Joint Logistics Centre facilities, which aimed to co-ordinate resources in an emergency situation. In 2001 a new UN Humanitarian Response Depot was opened in Brindisi, Italy, under the direction of WFP experts, for the storage of essential rapid response equipment. In that year the Programme published a set of guidelines on contingency planning.

Through its development activities, WFP aims to alleviate poverty in developing countries by promoting self-reliant families and communities. Food is supplied, for example, as an incentive in development self-help schemes and as part-wages in labour-intensive projects of many kinds. In all its projects WFP aims to assist the most vulnerable groups and to ensure that beneficiaries have an adequate and balanced diet. Activities supported by the Programme include the settlement and resettlement of groups and communities; land reclamation and improvement; irrigation; the development of forestry and dairy farming; road construction; training of hospital staff; community development; and human resources development such as feeding expectant or nursing mothers and schoolchildren, and support for education, training and health programmes. No individual country is permitted to receive more than 10% of the Programme's available development resources. During 2001 WFP initiated a new Global School Feeding Campaign to strengthen international co-operation to expand educational opportunities for poor children and to improve the quality of the teaching environment. In December 2003 WFP launched a *19-Cents-a-day* campaign to encourage donors to support its school feeding activities (19 US cents being the estimated cost of one school lunch). During that year school feeding projects benefited 15.2m. children in 69 countries.

Following a comprehensive evaluation of its activities, WFP is increasingly focused on linking its relief and development activities to provide a continuum between short-term relief and longer-term rehabilitation and development. In order to achieve this objective, WFP aims to integrate elements that strengthen disaster mitigation into development projects, including soil conservation, reafforestation, irrigation infrastructure, and transport construction and rehabilitation; and to promote capacity-building elements within relief operations, e.g. training, income-generating activities and environmental protection measures. In 1999 WFP adopted a new Food Aid and Development policy, which aims to use food assistance both to cover immediate requirements and to create conditions conducive to enhancing the long-term food security of vulnerable populations. During that year WFP began implementing Protracted Relief and Recovery Operations (PRROs), where the emphasis is on fostering stability, rehabilitation and long-term development for victims of natural disasters, displaced persons and refugees. PRROs are introduced no later than 18 months after the initial emergency operation and last no more than three years. When undertaken in collaboration with UNHCR and other international agencies, WFP has responsibility for mobilizing basic food commodities and for related transport, handling and storage costs. The 14 PRROs undertaken in 2003 involved the provision of 1.68m. metric tons of food, at a cost of some US $946.5m.

By March 2005 donors had pledged commitments of US $702.1m. towards total requested funding of $2,071.5m. for WFP's Africa Hunger Alert campaign, launched in December 2002. In early 2005 WFP was undertaking operations to feed some 22m. people suffering severe food insecurity in 22 sub-Saharan African countries. A PRRO was to be implemented during 2005–07 in Lesotho, Malawi, Mozambique, Swaziland and Zambia, following on from emergency feeding activities initiated in those countries and Zimbabwe in 2001. The WFP Executive Director was appointed by the UN Secretary-General in July 2002 as his Special Envoy on the ongoing humanitarian crisis in that sub-region, which was attributed to the combined effects of drought, flooding and, in some cases, alleged economic mismanagement, aggravated by the effects of the regional epidemic of HIV/AIDS. (It is estimated that one-half of all HIV/AIDS sufferers in southern Africa are employed in farming.) A PRRO was also being implemented in Angola to assist with the resettlement of IDPs and former combatants. In April 2004 WFP estimated that 1.2m. people were in urgent need of food aid in Darfur, western Sudan, owing to ongoing ethnic conflict. By June WFP revised the number of beneficiaries to 2m. given the long-term effects of mass population displacement on food supply and harvests. At that time WFP appealed for $200m. to finance the food aid operation and for a further $30.5m. to distribute food to an estimated 192,500 people who had fled the violence into Chad. The Democratic Republic of the Congo, Côte d'Ivoire, Eritrea and Liberia were also a particular focus of WFP activities in sub-Saharan Africa in 2005. The food situation in the Democratic People's Republic of Korea (DPRK) has required substantial levels of emergency food supplies in recent years, owing to natural disasters and consistently poor harvests. During 1995–99 an estimated 1.5m.–3.5m. people died of starvation in the DPRK. WFP's 10th emergency operation in the DPRK, for 2005, aimed to provide food aid to 6.5m. people (including 2.7m. children), at a cost of $202m. In January of that year WFP reported that nearly 70% of the DPRK's population remained dependent on cereal distributions, and that existing cereal stocks and commitments were sufficient to cover the next six months. WFP's DPRK operation has been adversely affected by periodic gaps in funding, resulting intermittently in the suspension of the distribution of cereal rations. The Programme has urged continuing international support for humanitarian activities in the DPRK in order to maintain progress achieved since 1999 in reducing the rate of malnutrition. WFP has also been active in Afghanistan, where severe drought and conflict have caused massive food insecurity and population displacement. A PRRO covering the period 1 April 2003–31 March 2005 and extending to an estimated 9.2m. Afghans followed on from a number of emergency operations undertaken in Afghanistan in recent years and aimed to provide family rations through food-for-work activities, to assist schoolchildren and teachers through food-for-education and training schemes, and to support adolescent girls, vulnerable women and ex-combatants through non-formal education projects. In March 2003 WFP appealed for donations totalling $1,300m. to finance its food aid operations in Iraq, as part of a larger United Nations 'flash appeal' for $2,218m. in humanitarian support for that country during April–October. WFP undertook a massive logistics operation to distribute food aid throughout Iraq with an intended total of 26m. beneficiaries; some 2m. metric tons of food aid were delivered to the country over that period, representing WFP's largest ever single emergency assistance operation. WFP was subsequently to remain engaged in preventing hunger in Iraq, undertaking activities including surveying food security, strengthening national capacity, assisting a newly-established distribution system, and supporting a government-administered school-feeding programme. A WFP one-year emergency operation to assist children and other vulnerable groups in Iraq was launched in September 2004. In January of that year WFP launched an emergency operation in response to a devastating earthquake in Bam, Iran, which occurred at the end of the previous month. WFP estimates that some 46% of Haiti's population is malnourished and, in early 2005, was supporting vulnerable people in that country through education, nutrition and health, and disaster mitigation activities.

In January 2005, following a massive earthquake in the Indian Ocean in December 2004, which caused a series of tidal waves, or tsunamis, that devastated coastal regions in 12 countries in South and South-East Asia and East Africa, WFP requested emergency funding of US $256m. to support an initial six-month programme to feed 2m. people affected by the natural disaster. By mid-January

2005 about one-third of the required funding had been mobilized and food aid was being provided for 1.1m. people in the region, including 300,000 in Aceh, Indonesia (close to the epicentre of the earthquake). WFP was also participating in efforts to establish a viable logistical infrastructure for humanitarian operations in the region.

Finance

The Programme is funded by voluntary contributions from donor countries, intergovernmental bodies such as the European Commission, and the private sector. Contributions are made in the form of commodities, finance and services (particularly shipping). Commitments to the International Emergency Food Reserve (IEFR), from which WFP provides the majority of its food supplies, and to the Immediate Response Account of the IEFR (IRA), are also made on a voluntary basis by donors. WFP's operational expenditures in 2003 amounted to US $3,275.3m. Contributions by donors in that year totalled $2,600.0m, of which $1,389.1m. was for the IEFR.

Publications

Annual Report.
Food and Nutrition Handbook.
School Feeding Handbook.

Statistics

OPERATIONAL EXPENDITURE IN 2003, BY REGION AND TYPE*
(US $ '000)

Region	Development	Relief	Special operations	Total (incl. others†)
Sub-Saharan Africa	125,391	1,358,993	20,992	1,514,000
Asia	68,382	304,898	20,868	399,157
Latin America and the Caribbean	34,122	17,597	—	51,719
North Africa and the Middle East	16,279	1,112,907	40,610	1,232,874
Europe and the CIS	—	68,538	—	69,101
Total	228,678	2,811,441	82,769	3,275,319

* Excludes programme support and administrative costs.
† Includes trust fund expenditures and operational expenditures that cannot be apportioned by project/operation.

SPECIALIZED AGENCIES WITHIN THE UN SYSTEM

Food and Agriculture Organization of the United Nations—FAO

Address: Viale delle Terme di Caracalla, 00100 Rome, Italy.
Telephone: (06) 5705-1; **fax:** (06) 5705-3152; **e-mail:** fao-hq@fao
.org; **internet:** www.fao.org.
FAO, the first specialized agency of the UN to be founded after the
Second World War, aims to alleviate malnutrition and hunger, and
serves as a co-ordinating agency for development programmes in the
whole range of food and agriculture, including forestry and fisheries.
It helps developing countries to promote educational and training
facilities and the creation of appropriate institutions.

MEMBERS

FAO has 188 members (including the European Union as a member
organization).

Organization

(March 2005)

CONFERENCE

The governing body is the FAO Conference of member nations. It
meets every two years, formulates policy, determines the Organization's programme and budget on a biennial basis, and elects new
members. It also elects the Director-General of the Secretariat and
the Independent Chairman of the Council. Every other year, FAO
also holds conferences in each of its five regions (Africa, Asia and the
Pacific, Europe, Latin America and the Caribbean, and the Near
East).

COUNCIL

The FAO Council is composed of representatives of 49 member
nations, elected by the Conference for staggered three-year terms. It
is the interim governing body of FAO between sessions of the
Conference. The most important standing Committees of the
Council are: the Finance and Programme Committees, the Committee on Commodity Problems, the Committee on Fisheries, the
Committee on Agriculture and the Committee on Forestry.

SECRETARIAT

The number of FAO staff in 2005 was around 3,450, of whom 1,450
were professional staff and 2,000 general service staff. About one-
half of the Organization's staff were based at headquarters. Work is
supervised by the following Departments: Administration and
Finance; General Affairs and Information; Economic and Social
Policy; Agriculture; Forestry; Fisheries; Sustainable Development;
and Technical Co-operation.

Director-General: JACQUES DIOUF (Senegal).

REGIONAL OFFICES

Africa: POB 1628, Accra, Ghana; tel. (21) 675000; fax (21) 668427;
e-mail fao-raf@fao.org; Regional Rep. JOSEPH TCHICAYA.

Asia and the Pacific: Maliwan Mansion, Phra Atit Rd, Bangkok
10200, Thailand; tel. (662) 697-4000; fax (662) 697-4445; e-mail
fao-rap@fao.org; internet www.fao.or.th; Regional Rep. HE CHANG-
CHUI.

Europe: Viale delle Terme di Caracalla, Room A-304, 00100 Rome,
Italy; tel. (06) 57051; fax (06) 57053152; internet www.fao.org/
regional/europe; Regional Rep. CLAUDE FORTHOMME.

Latin America and the Caribbean: Avda Dag Hammarskjöld
3241, Casilla 10095, Vitacura, Santiago, Chile; tel. (2) 337-2102; fax
(2) 337-2101; e-mail fao-rlc@field.fao.org; internet www.fao.org/
regional/lamerica/default.htm; Regional Rep. GUSTAVO GORDILLO DE
ANDA.

Near East: 11 El-Eslah el-Zerai St, Dokki, POB 2223, Cairo, Egypt;
tel. (2) 3316000; fax (2) 7495981; e-mail fao-rne@fao.org; Regional
Rep. MOHAMED ALBRAITHEN.

In addition, the following Sub-regional Offices are operational: in
Harare, Zimbabwe (for Southern and Eastern Africa); in Bridgetown, Barbados (for the Caribbean); in Tunis, Tunisia (for North
Africa); in Budapest, Hungary (for Central and Eastern Europe);
and in Apia, Samoa (for the Pacific Islands).

JOINT DIVISION AND LIAISON OFFICES

**Joint FAO/IAEA Division of Nuclear Techniques in Food and
Agriculture:** Wagramerstrasse 5, 1400 Vienna, Austria; tel. (1)
2600-0; fax (1) 2600-7; e-mail official.mail@iaea.org; Dir JAMES D.
DARGIE.

European Union and Belgium: 30 blvd Simon Bolivar, 1000
Brussels, Belgium; tel. (2) 203-85-87; fax (2) 203-85-89; e-mail
fao-lobr@fao.org; Dir JOERGEN MAERSK PEDERSEN.

Japan: 6F Yokohama International Organizations Centre, Pacifico-
Yokohama, 1-1-1, Minato Mirai, Nishi-ku, Yokohama 220-0012; tel.
(45) 222-1101; fax (45) 222-1103.

North America: Suite 300, 2175 K St, NW, Washington, DC 20437,
USA; tel. (202) 653-2400; fax (202) 653-5760; e-mail fao-lowa@fao
.org; Dir C. H. RIEMENSCHNEIDER.

United Nations: Suite DC1-1125, 1 United Nations Plaza, New
York, NY 10017, USA; tel. (212) 963-6036; fax (212) 963-5425; e-mail
fao-lony@field.fao.org; Dir HOWARD W. HJORT.

Activities

FAO aims to raise levels of nutrition and standards of living by
improving the production and distribution of food and other commodities derived from farms, fisheries and forests. FAO's ultimate
objective is the achievement of world food security, 'Food for All'. The
organization provides technical information, advice and assistance
by disseminating information; acting as a neutral forum for discussion of food and agricultural issues; advising governments on
policy and planning; and developing capacity directly in the field.

In November 1996 FAO hosted the World Food Summit, which
was held in Rome and was attended by heads of state and senior
government representatives of 186 countries. Participants approved
the Rome Declaration on World Food Security and the World Food
Summit Plan of Action, with the aim of halving the number of people
afflicted by undernutrition, at that time estimated to total 828m.
world-wide, by no later than 2015. A review conference to assess
progress in achieving the goals of the summit, entitled World Food
Summit: Five Years Later, held in June 2002, reaffirmed commitment to this objective, which is also incorporated into the UN
Millennium Development Goal of eradicating extreme poverty and
hunger. During that month FAO announced the formulation of a
global 'Anti-Hunger Programme', which aimed to promote investment in the agricultural sector and rural development, with a
particular focus on small farmers, and to enhance food access for
those most in need, for example through the provision of school
meals, schemes to feed pregnant and nursing mothers and food-for-
work programmes. In late 2003 FAO reported that an estimated
842m. people world-wide were undernourished; of these 798m.
resided in developing countries.

In November 1999 the FAO Conference approved a long-term
Strategic Framework for the period 2000–15, which emphasized
national and international co-operation in pursuing the goals of the
1996 World Food Summit. The Framework promoted interdisciplin-
arity and partnership, and defined three main global objectives:
constant access by all people to sufficient nutritionally adequate and
safe food to ensure that levels of undernourishment were reduced by
50% by 2015 (see above); the continued contribution of sustainable
agriculture and rural development to economic and social progress
and well-being; and the conservation, improvement and sustainable
use of natural resources. It identified five corporate strategies (each
supported by several strategic objectives), covering the following
areas: reducing food insecurity and rural poverty; ensuring enabling
policy and regulatory frameworks for food, agriculture, fisheries and

forestry; creating sustainable increases in the supply and availability of agricultural, fisheries and forestry products; conserving and enhancing sustainable use of the natural resource base; and generating knowledge. In November 2001 the FAO Conference adopted a medium-term plan covering 2002–07, based on the Strategic Framework. In November 2004 the FAO Council adopted a set of voluntary Right to Food Guide-lines that aimed to 'support the progressive realization of the right to adequate food in the context of national food security' by providing practical guidance to countries in support of their efforts to achieve the 1996 World Food Summit commitment and UN Millennium Development Goal relating to hunger reduction.

FAO organizes an annual series of fund-raising events, 'TeleFood', some of which are broadcast on television and the internet, in order to raise public awareness of the problems of hunger and malnutrition. Since its inception in 1997 public donations to TeleFood have reached almost US \$14m., financing more than 1,750 'grass-roots' projects in 124 countries. The projects have provided tools, seeds and other essential supplies directly to small-scale farmers, and have been especially aimed at helping women.

In 1999 FAO signed a memorandum of understanding with UNAIDS on strengthening co-operation. In December 2001 FAO, IFAD and WFP determined to strengthen inter-agency collaboration in developing strategies to combat the threat posed by the HIV/AIDS epidemic to food security, nutrition and rural livelihoods. During that month experts from those organizations and UNAIDS held a technical consultation on means of mitigating the impact of HIV/AIDS on agriculture and rural communities in affected areas.

In September 2004 FAO published *Recommendations for the Prevention, Control and Eradication of Highly Pathogenic Avian Influenza (HPAI) in Asia*. In the same month, following new outbreaks of the disease in the People's Republic of China, Cambodia, Viet Nam, Malaysia and Thailand, FAO and the World Health Organization declared the avian influenza epidemic to be a 'crisis of global importance'. FAO was working closely with the World Organisation for Animal Health to study and help to contain the disease.

The Technical Co-operation Department has responsibility for FAO's operational activities, including policy development assistance to member countries; investment support; and the management of activities associated with the development and implementation of country, sub-regional and regional programmes. The Department manages the technical co-operation programme (TCP, which funds 13% of FAO's field programme expenditures), and mobilizes resources.

AGRICULTURE

FAO's most important area of activity is crop production, accounting annually for about one-quarter of total field programme expenditure. FAO assists developing countries in increasing agricultural production, by means of a number of methods, including improved seeds and fertilizer use, soil conservation and reforestation, better water resource management techniques, upgrading storage facilities, and improvements in processing and marketing. FAO places special emphasis on the cultivation of under-exploited traditional food crops, such as cassava, sweet potato and plantains.

In 1985 the FAO Conference approved an International Code of Conduct on the Distribution and Use of Pesticides, and in 1989 the Conference adopted an additional clause concerning 'Prior Informed Consent' (PIC), whereby international shipments of newly banned or restricted pesticides should not proceed without the agreement of importing countries. Under the clause, FAO aims to inform governments about the hazards of toxic chemicals and to urge them to take proper measures to curb trade in highly toxic agrochemicals while keeping the pesticides industry informed of control actions. In 1996 FAO, in collaboration with UNEP, publicized a new initiative which aimed to increase awareness of, and to promote international action on, obsolete and hazardous stocks of pesticides remaining throughout the world (estimated in 2001 to total some 500,000 metric tons). In September 1998 a new legally-binding treaty on trade in hazardous chemicals and pesticides was adopted at an international conference held in Rotterdam, Netherlands. The so-called Rotterdam Convention required that hazardous chemicals and pesticides banned or severely restricted in at least two countries should not be exported unless explicitly agreed by the importing country. It also identified certain pesticide formulations as too dangerous to be used by farmers in developing countries, and incorporated an obligation that countries halt national production of those hazardous compounds. The treaty entered into force in February 2004. FAO was co-operating with UNEP to provide an interim secretariat for the Convention. In July 1999 a conference on the Rotterdam Convention, held in Rome, established an Interim Chemical Review Committee with responsibility for recommending the inclusion of chemicals or pesticide formulations in the PIC procedure. As part of its continued efforts to reduce the environmental risks posed by over-reliance on pesticides, FAO has extended to other regions its Integrated Pest Management (IPM) programme in

Asia and the Pacific on the use of safer and more effective methods of pest control, such as biological control methods and natural predators (including spiders and wasps), to avert pests. In February 2001 FAO warned that some 30% of pesticides sold in developing countries did not meet internationally accepted quality standards. A revised International Code of Conduct on the Distribution and Use of Pesticides, adopted in November 2002, aimed to reduce the inappropriate distribution and use of pesticides and other toxic compounds, particularly in developing countries.

FAO's Joint Division with the International Atomic Energy Agency (IAEA) tests controlled-release formulas of pesticides and herbicides that gradually free their substances and can limit the amount of agrochemicals needed to protect crops. The Joint FAO/IAEA Division is engaged in exploring biotechnologies and in developing non-toxic fertilizers (especially those that are locally available) and improved strains of food crops (especially from indigenous varieties). In the area of animal production and health, the Joint Division has developed progesterone-measuring and disease diagnostic kits, of which thousands have been delivered to developing countries. FAO's plant nutrition activities aim to promote nutrient management, such as the Integrated Plant Nutritions Systems (IPNS), which are based on the recycling of nutrients through crop production and the efficient use of mineral fertilizers.

The conservation and sustainable use of plant and animal genetic resources are promoted by FAO's Global System for Plant Genetic Resources, which includes five databases, and the Global Strategy on the Management of Farm Animal Genetic Resources. An FAO programme supports the establishment of gene banks, designed to maintain the world's biological diversity by preserving animal and plant species threatened with extinction. FAO, jointly with UNEP, has published a document listing the current state of global livestock genetic diversity. In June 1996 representatives of more than 150 governments convened in Leipzig, Germany, at a meeting organized by FAO (and hosted by the German Government) to consider the use and conservation of plant genetic resources as an essential means of enhancing food security. The meeting adopted a Global Plan of Action, which included measures to strengthen the development of plant varieties and to promote the use and availability of local varieties and locally-adapted crops to farmers, in particular following a natural disaster, war or civil conflict. In November 2001 the FAO Conference adopted the International Treaty on Plant Genetic Resources for Food and Agriculture, which was to provide a framework to ensure access to plant genetic resources and to related knowledge, technologies and funding. The Treaty entered into force on 29 June 2004, having received the required number of ratifications (40) by signatory states.

The Emergency Prevention System for Transboundary Animal and Plant Pests and Diseases (EMPRES) was established in 1994 to strengthen FAO's activities in the prevention, early warning of, control and, where possible, eradication of pests and highly contagious livestock diseases (which the system categorizes as epidemic diseases of strategic importance, such as rinderpest or foot-and-mouth; diseases requiring tactical attention at international or regional level, e.g. Rift Valley fever; and emerging diseases, e.g. bovine spongiform encephalopathy—BSE). EMPRES has a desert locust component, and has published guide-lines on all aspects of desert locust monitoring. FAO has assumed responsibility for technical leadership and co-ordination of the Global Rinderpest Eradication Programme (GREP), which has the objective of eliminating the disease by 2010. Following technical consultations in late 1998, an Intensified GREP was launched. In November 1997 FAO initiated a Programme Against African Trypanosomiasis, which aimed to counter the disease affecting cattle in almost one-third of Africa. EMPRES promotes Good Emergency Management Practices (GEMP) in animal health. The system is guided by the annual meeting of the EMPRES Expert Consultation. In May 2004 FAO and the World Organisation for Animal Health signed an agreement in which they clarified their respective areas of competence and paved the way for improved co-operation, in response to an increase in contagious transboundary animal diseases (such as foot-and-mouth disease and avian influenza, see below). The two bodies agreed to establish a global framework on the control of transboundary animal diseases, entailing improved international collaboration and circulation of information. FAO advises countries on good agricultural practices, disease control and eradication methods and co-operates with the World Organisation for Animal Health in building national surveillance and early warning systems. In September FAO issued a set of recommendations on the prevention, control and eradication of highly pathogenic avian influenza, which had spread to humans in south-east Asia in late 2003. During 2004 FAO provided technical co-operation assistance to Cambodia, Indonesia, Laos, Thailand and Viet Nam aimed at preparing a post-avian influenza rehabilitation programme.

FAO's organic agriculture programme provides technical assistance and policy advice on the production, certification and trade of organic produce. In July 2001 the FAO/WHO Codex Alimentarius Commission adopted guide-lines on organic livestock production, covering organic breeding methods, the elimination of growth hormones and certain chemicals in veterinary medicines, and the use of good quality organic feed with no meat or bone meal content.

ENVIRONMENT

At the UN Conference on Environment and Development (UNCED), held in Rio de Janeiro, Brazil, in June 1992, FAO participated in several working parties and supported the adoption of Agenda 21, a programme of activities to promote sustainable development. FAO is responsible for the chapters of Agenda 21 concerning water resources, forests, fragile mountain ecosystems and sustainable agriculture and rural development. FAO was designated by the UN General Assembly as the lead agency for co-ordinating the International Year of Mountains (2002), which aimed to raise awareness of mountain ecosystems and to promote the conservation and sustainable development of mountainous regions.

FISHERIES

FAO's Fisheries Department consists of a multi-disciplinary body of experts who are involved in every aspect of fisheries development from coastal surveys, conservation management and use of aquatic genetic resources, improvement of production, processing and storage, to the compilation and analysis of statistics, development of computer databases, improvement of fishing gear, institution-building and training. In November 1993 the FAO Conference adopted an agreement to improve the monitoring and control of fishing vessels operating on the high seas that are registered under 'flags of convenience', in order to ensure their compliance with internationally accepted marine conservation and management measures. In March 1995 a ministerial meeting of fisheries adopted the Rome Consensus on World Fisheries, which identified a need for immediate action to eliminate overfishing and to rebuild and enhance depleting fish stocks. In November the FAO Conference adopted a Code of Conduct for Responsible Fishing, which incorporated many global fisheries and aquaculture issues (including fisheries resource conservation and development, fish catches, seafood and fish processing, commercialization, trade and research) to promote the sustainable development of the sector. In February 1999 the FAO Committee on Fisheries adopted new international measures, within the framework of the Code of Conduct, in order to reduce over-exploitation of the world's fish resources, as well as plans of action for the conservation and management of sharks and the reduction in the incidental catch of seabirds in longline fisheries. The voluntary measures were endorsed at a ministerial meeting, held in March and attended by representatives of some 126 countries, which issued a declaration to promote the implementation of the Code of Conduct and to achieve sustainable management of fisheries and aquaculture. In March 2001 FAO adopted an international plan of action to address the continuing problem of so-called illegal, unreported and unregulated fishing (IUU). In that year FAO estimated that about one-half of major marine fish stocks were fully exploited, one-quarter under-exploited, at least 15% over-exploited, and 10% depleted or recovering from depletion. IUU was estimated to account for up to 30% of total catches in certain fisheries. In October FAO and the Icelandic Government jointly organized the Reykjavik Conference on Responsible Fisheries in the Marine Ecosystem, which adopted a declaration on pursuing responsible and sustainable fishing activities in the context of ecosystem-based fisheries management (EBFM). EBFM involves determining the boundaries of individual marine ecosystems, and maintaining or rebuilding the habitats and biodiversity of each of these so that all species will be supported at levels of maximum production. FAO promotes aquaculture (which contributes almost one-third of annual global fish landings) as a valuable source of animal protein and income-generating activity for rural communities. In February 2000 FAO and the Network of Aquaculture Centres in Asia and the Pacific (NACA) jointly convened a Conference on Aquaculture in the Third Millennium, which was held in Bangkok, Thailand, and attended by participants representing more than 200 governmental and non-governmental organizations. The Conference debated global trends in aquaculture and future policy measures to ensure the sustainable development of the sector. It adopted the Bangkok Declaration and Strategy for Aquaculture Beyond 2000.

FORESTRY

FAO focuses on the contribution of forestry to food security, on effective and responsible forest management and on maintaining a balance between the economic, ecological and social benefits of forest resources. The Organization has helped to develop national forestry programmes and to promote the sustainable development of all types of forest. FAO administers the global Forests, Trees and People Programme, which promotes the sustainable management of tree and forest resources, based on local knowledge and management practices, in order to improve the livelihoods of rural people in developing countries. FAO's Strategic Plan for Forestry was approved in March 1999; its main objectives were to maintain the environmental diversity of forests, to realize the economic potential of forests and trees within a sustainable framework, and to expand access to information on forestry.

NUTRITION

The International Conference on Nutrition, sponsored by FAO and WHO, took place in Rome in December 1992. It approved a World Declaration on Nutrition and a Plan of Action, aimed at promoting efforts to combat malnutrition as a development priority. Since the conference, more than 100 countries have formulated national plans of action for nutrition, many of which were based on existing development plans such as comprehensive food security initiatives, national poverty alleviation programmes and action plans to attain the targets set by the World Summit for Children in September 1990. In October 1996 FAO, WHO and other partners jointly organized the first World Congress on Calcium and Vitamin D in Human Life, held in Rome. In January 2001 a joint team of FAO and WHO experts issued a report concerning the allergenicity of foods derived from biotechnology (i.e. genetically modified—GM—foods). In July the Codex Alimentarius Commission agreed the first global principles for assessing the safety of GM foods, and approved a series of maximum levels of environmental contaminants in food. FAO and WHO jointly convened a Global Forum of Food Safety Regulators in Marrakesh, Morocco, in January 2002. In April the two organizations announced a joint review of their food standards operations, including the activities of the Codex Alimentarius Commission. In July 2004 the Codex Alimentarius Commission adopted a definition of product tracing, increasingly regarded as an important component of national and international food regulatory systems. In October FAO and WHO jointly launched the International Food Safety Authorities Network (INFOSAN), which aimed to promote the exchange of food safety information and to advance co-operation among food safety authorities.

PROCESSING AND MARKETING

An estimated 20% of all food harvested is lost before it can be consumed, and in some developing countries the proportion is much higher. FAO helps reduce immediate post-harvest losses, with the introduction of improved processing methods and storage systems. It also advises on the distribution and marketing of agricultural produce and on the selection and preparation of foods for optimum nutrition. Many of these activities form part of wider rural development projects. Many developing countries rely on agricultural products as their main source of foreign earnings, but the terms under which they are traded are usually more favourable to the industrialized countries. FAO continues to favour the elimination of export subsidies and related discriminatory practices, such as protectionist measures that hamper international trade in agricultural commodities. FAO has organized regional workshops and national projects in order to help member states to implement World Trade Organization regulations, in particular with regard to agricultural policy, intellectual property rights, sanitary and phytosanitary measures, technical barriers to trade and the international standards of the Codex Alimentarius. FAO evaluates new market trends and helps to develop improved plant and animal quarantine procedures. In November 1997 the FAO Conference adopted new guide-lines on surveillance and on export certification systems in order to harmonize plant quarantine standards. FAO participates in PhAction, a forum of 12 agencies that was established in 1999 to promote post-harvest research and the development of effective post-harvest services and infrastructure.

FOOD SECURITY

FAO's policy on food security aims to encourage the production of adequate food supplies, to maximize stability in the flow of supplies, and to ensure access on the part of those who need them. In 1994 FAO initiated the Special Programme for Food Security (SPFS), designed to assist low-income countries with a food deficit to increase food production and productivity as rapidly as possible, primarily through the widespread adoption by farmers of improved production technologies, with emphasis on areas of high potential. FAO was actively involved in the formulation of the Plan of Action on food security that was adopted at the World Food Summit in November 1996, and was to be responsible for monitoring and promoting its implementation. In March 1999 FAO signed agreements with IFAD and WFP that aimed to increase co-operation within the framework of the SPFS. A budget of US $10.5m. was allocated to the SPFS for the two-year period 2004–05. In 2004 the SPFS was operational in 100 countries, of which 42 were in Africa. About 70 of these countries were categorized as 'low-income food-deficit'. The Programme promotes South-South co-operation to improve food security and the exchange of knowledge and experience. By September 2003 28 bilateral co-operation agreements were in force, for example, between Egypt and Cameroon, and Viet Nam and Benin.

FAO's Global Information and Early Warning System (GIEWS), which become operational in 1975, maintains a database on and monitors the crop and food outlook at global, regional, national and sub-national levels in order to detect emerging food supply difficulties and disasters and to ensure rapid intervention in countries experiencing food supply shortages. It publishes regular reports on the weather conditions and crop prospects in sub-Saharan Africa and in the Sahel region, issues special alerts which describe the situation in countries or sub-regions experiencing food difficulties, and recommends an appropriate international response. FAO's annual publication *State of Food Insecurity in the World* is based on data compiled by the Organization's Food Insecurity and Vulnerability Information and Mapping Systems programme.

An Inter-Agency Task Force on the UN Response to Long-Term Food Security, Agricultural Development and Related Aspects in the Horn of Africa, appointed by the UN Secretary-General in April 2000, is chaired by the Director-General of FAO.

FAO INVESTMENT CENTRE

The Investment Centre was established in 1964 to help countries to prepare viable investment projects that will attract external financing. The Centre focuses its evaluation of projects on two fundamental concerns: the promotion of sustainable activities for land management, forestry development and environmental protection, and the alleviation of rural poverty. By December 2004 the Centre had approved a total of 1,400 projects for 140 developing countries, representing a total investment of around US $76,000m.

EMERGENCY RELIEF

FAO works to rehabilitate agricultural production following natural and man-made disasters by providing emergency seed, tools, and technical and other assistance. Jointly with the United Nations, FAO is responsible for WFP, which provides emergency food supplies and food aid in support of development projects. FAO's Division for Emergency Operations and Rehabilitation was responsible for preparing the emergency agricultural relief component of the 2005 UN inter-agency appeals for 14 countries and regions.

In January 2005, following a massive earthquake in the Indian Ocean in December 2004, which caused a series of tidal waves, or tsunamis, that devastated coastal regions in 11 countries in South and South-East Asia and East Africa, FAO requested emergency funding of US $26m. to support an initial six-month rehabilitation operation to restore the livelihoods of fishermen and farmers affected by the natural disaster.

INFORMATION

FAO collects, analyses, interprets and disseminates information through various media, including an extensive internet site. It issues regular statistical reports, commodity studies, and technical manuals in local languages (see list of publications below). Other materials produced by the FAO include information booklets, reference papers, reports of meetings, training manuals and audio-visuals.

FAO's internet-based interactive World Agricultural Information Centre (WAICENT) offers access to agricultural publications, technical documentation, codes of conduct, data, statistics and multimedia resources. FAO compiles and co-ordinates an extensive range of international databases on agriculture, fisheries, forestry, food and statistics, the most important of these being AGRIS (the International Information System for the Agricultural Sciences and Technology) and CARIS (the Current Agricultural Research Information System). Statistical databases include the GLOBEFISH databank and electronic library, FISHDAB (the Fisheries Statistical Database), FORIS (Forest Resources Information System), and GIS (the Geographic Information System). In addition, FAOSTAT provides access to updated figures in 10 agriculture-related topics. The AGORA (Access to Global Online Research in Agriculture) initiative, launched in November 2003 by FAO and other partners, aims to provide free or low-cost access to more than 400 scientific journals in agriculture, nutrition and related fields for researchers from developing countries.

In June 2000 FAO organized a high-level Consultation on Agricultural Information Management (COAIM), which aimed to increase access to and use of agricultural information by policy-makers and others. The second COAIM was held in September 2002; a third meeting, scheduled to be held in June 2004, was postponed.

World Food Day, commemorating the foundation of FAO, is held annually on 16 October.

FAO Councils and Commissions

(Based at the Rome headquarters unless otherwise indicated)

African Commission on Agricultural Statistics: c/o FAO Regional Office for Africa, POB 1628, Accra, Ghana; f. 1961 to advise member countries on the development and standardization of food and agricultural statistics; 37 member states.

African Forestry and Wildlife Commission: f. 1959 to advise on the formulation of forest policy and to review and co-ordinate its implementation on a regional level to exchange information and advise on technical problems; 42 member states.

Asia and Pacific Commission on Agricultural Statistics: c/o FAO Regional Office, Maliwan Mansion, Phra Atit Rd, Bangkok 10200, Thailand; f. 1962 to review the state of food and agricultural statistics in the region and to advise member countries on the development and standardization of agricultural statistics; 25 member states.

Asia and Pacific Plant Protection Commission: c/o FAO Regional Office, Maliwan Mansion, Phra Atit Rd, Bangkok 10200, Thailand; f. 1956 (new title 1983) to strengthen international co-operation in plant protection to prevent the introduction and spread of destructive plant diseases and pests; 25 member states.

Asia-Pacific Fishery Commission: c/o FAO Regional Office, Maliwan Mansion, Phra Atit Rd, Bangkok 10200, Thailand; f. 1948 to develop fisheries, encourage and co-ordinate research, disseminate information, recommend projects to governments, propose standards in technique and management measures; 20 member states.

Asia-Pacific Forestry Commission: internet www.apfcweb.org; f. 1949 to advise on the formulation of forest policy, and review and co-ordinate its implementation throughout the region to exchange information and advise on technical problems; 29 member states.

Caribbean Plant Protection Commission: f. 1967 to preserve the existing plant resources of the area; 13 member states.

Commission for Controlling the Desert Locust in the Eastern Region of its Distribution Area in South West Asia: f. 1964 to carry out all possible measures to control plagues of the desert locust in Afghanistan, India, Iran and Pakistan.

Commission for Controlling the Desert Locust in the Near East: c/o FAO Regional Office for the Near East, POB 2223, Cairo, Egypt; f. 1967 to promote national and international research and action with respect to the control of the desert locust in the Near East.

Commission for Controlling the Desert Locust in North-West Africa: f. 1971 to promote research on control of the desert locust in NW Africa.

Commission for Inland Fisheries of Latin America: f. 1976 to promote, co-ordinate and assist national and regional fishery and limnological surveys and programmes of research and development leading to the rational utilization of inland fishery resources; 21 member states.

Commission on Genetic Resources for Food and Agriculture: internet www.fao.org/ag/cgrfa/default.htm; f. 1983 as the Commission on Plant Genetic Resources, renamed in 1995; provides a forum for negotiation on the conservation and sustainable utilization of genetic resources for food and agriculture, and the equitable sharing of benefits derived from their use; 164 mems.

European Commission on Agriculture: f. 1949 to encourage and facilitate action and co-operation in technological agricultural problems among member states and between international organizations concerned with agricultural technology in Europe.

European Commission for the Control of Foot-and-Mouth Disease: internet www.fao.org/ag/againfo/commissions/en/eufmd/eufmd.html; f. 1953 to promote national and international action for the control of the disease in Europe and its final eradication.

European Forestry Commission: f. 1947 to advise on the formulation of forest policy and to review and co-ordinate its implementation on a regional level to exchange information and to make recommendations; 27 member states.

European Inland Fisheries Advisory Commission: internet www.fao.org/fi/body/eifac/eifac.asp; f. 1957 to promote improvements in inland fisheries and to advise member governments and FAO on inland fishery matters; 34 mems.

FAO/WHO Codex Alimentarius Commission: internet www.codexalimentarius.net; f. 1962 to make proposals for the co-ordination of all international food standards work and to publish a code of international food standards; established Intergovernmental Task Force on Foods Derived from Biotechnology in 1999; Trust Fund to support participation by least-developed countries was inaugurated in February 2003; 165 member states.

General Fisheries Council for the Mediterranean—GFCM: internet www.fao.org/fi/body/rfb/index.htm; f. 1952 to develop aquatic resources, to encourage and co-ordinate research in the fishing and allied industries, to assemble and publish information, and to recommend the standardization of equipment, techniques and nomenclature.

Indian Ocean Fishery Commission: f. 1967 to promote national programmes, research and development activities, and to examine management problems; 41 member states.

International Poplar Commission: f. 1947 to study scientific, technical, social and economic aspects of poplar and willow cultivation to promote the exchange of ideas and material between research workers, producers and users; to arrange joint research programmes, congresses, study tours; to make recommendations to the FAO Conference and to National Poplar Commissions.

International Rice Commission: internet www.fao.org/ag/AGP/AGPC/doc/field/commrice/welcome.htm; f. 1949 to promote national and international action on production, conservation, distribution and consumption of rice, except matters relating to international trade; 60 member states.

Latin American and Caribbean Forestry Commission: f. 1948 to advise on formulation of forest policy and review and co-ordinate its implementation throughout the region to exchange information and advise on technical problems; meets every two years; 31 member states.

Near East Forestry Commission: f. 1953 to advise on formulation of forest policy and review and co-ordinate its implementation throughout the region to exchange information and advise on technical problems; 20 member states.

Near East Regional Commission on Agriculture: c/o FAO Regional Office, POB 2223, Cairo, Egypt; f. 1983 to conduct periodic reviews of agricultural problems in the region to promote the formulation and implementation of regional and national policies and programmes for improving production of crops and livestock; to strengthen the management of crops, livestock and supporting services and research; to promote the transfer of technology and regional technical co-operation; and to provide guidance on training and human resources development.

North American Forestry Commission: f. 1959 to advise on the formulation and co-ordination of national forest policies in Canada, Mexico and the USA to exchange information and to advise on technical problems; three member states.

Regional Animal Production and Health Commission for Asia and the Pacific: c/o FAO Regional Office, Maliwan Mansion, Phra Atit Rd, Bangkok 10200, Thailand; internet www.aphca.org; f. 1973 to promote livestock development in general, and national and international research and action with respect to animal health and husbandry problems in the region; 15 member states.

Regional Commission on Land and Water Use in the Near East: f. 1967 to review the current situation with regard to land and water use in the region to identify the main problems concerning the development of land and water resources which require research and study and to consider other related matters.

Western Central Atlantic Fishery Commission: f. 1973 to assist international co-operation for the conservation, development and utilization of the living resources, especially shrimps, of the Western Central Atlantic.

Finance

FAO's Regular Programme, which is financed by contributions from member governments, covers the cost of FAO's Secretariat, its Technical Co-operation Programme (TCP) and part of the cost of several special action programmes. The proposed budget for the two-year period 2004–05 totalled US $749m. Much of FAO's technical assistance programme is funded from extra-budgetary sources, predominantly by trust funds that come mainly from donor countries and international financing institutions. The single largest contributor is the United Nations Development Programme (UNDP).

Publications

Animal Health Yearbook.
Commodity Review and Outlook (annually).
Environment and Energy Bulletin.
Ethical Issues in Food and Agriculture.
Fertilizer Yearbook.
Food Crops and Shortages (6 a year).
Food Outlook (5 a year).
Food Safety and Quality Update (monthly; electronic bulletin).
Forest Resources Assessment.
Plant Protection Bulletin (quarterly).
Production Yearbook.
Quarterly Bulletin of Statistics.
The State of Food and Agriculture (annually).
The State of Food Insecurity in the World (annually).
The State of World Fisheries and Aquaculture (every two years).
The State of the World's Forests (every 2 years).
Trade Yearbook.
Unasylva (quarterly).
Yearbook of Fishery Statistics.
Yearbook of Forest Products.
World Animal Review (quarterly).
World Watch List for Domestic Animal Diversity.
Commodity reviews; studies, manuals.

International Atomic Energy Agency—IAEA

Address: POB 100, Wagramerstrasse 5, 1400 Vienna, Austria.

Telephone: (1) 26000; **fax:** (1) 26007; **e-mail:** official.mail@iaea.org; **internet:** www.iaea.org.

The International Atomic Energy Agency (IAEA) is an intergovernmental organization, established in 1957 in accordance with a decision of the General Assembly of the United Nations. Although it is autonomous, the IAEA is administratively a member of the United Nations, and reports on its activities once a year to the UN General Assembly. Its main objectives are to enlarge the contribution of atomic energy to peace, health and prosperity throughout the world and to ensure, so far as it is able, that assistance provided by it or at its request or under its supervision or control is not used in such a way as to further any military purpose.

MEMBERS

IAEA has 137 members.

Organization

(March 2005)

GENERAL CONFERENCE

The Conference, comprising representatives of all member states, convenes each year for general debate on the Agency's policy, budget and programme. It elects members to the Board of Governors, and approves the appointment of the Director-General; it admits new member states.

BOARD OF GOVERNORS

The Board of Governors consists of 35 member states: 22 elected by the General Conference for two-year periods and 13 designated by the Board from among member states which are advanced in nuclear technology. It is the principal policy-making body of the Agency and is responsible to the General Conference. Under its own authority, the Board approves all safeguards agreements, important projects and safety standards. In 1999 the General Conference adopted a resolution on expanding the Board's membership to 43, to include 18 states designated as the most advanced in nuclear technology. The resolution required ratification by two-thirds of member states to come into effect.

SECRETARIAT

The Secretariat, comprising about 2,250 staff, is headed by the Director-General, who is assisted by six Deputy Directors-General. The Secretariat is divided into six departments: Technical Co-operation; Nuclear Energy; Nuclear Safety and Security; Nuclear Sciences and Applications; Safeguards; and Management. A Standing Advisory Group on Safeguards Implementation advises the Director-General on technical aspects of safeguards.

Director-General: Dr MOHAMMAD EL-BARADEI (Egypt).

Activities

In recent years the IAEA has implemented several reforms of its management structure and operations. The three pillars supporting the Agency's activities are: safety and security, science and technology (assisting research on and practical application of atomic energy for peaceful uses), and safeguards and verification (ensuring that special fissionable and other materials, services, equipment and information made available by the Agency or at its request or under its supervision are not used for any non-peaceful purpose).

TECHNICAL CO-OPERATION AND TRAINING

The IAEA provides assistance in the form of experts, training and equipment to technical co-operation projects and applications world-wide, with an emphasis on radiation protection and safety-related activities. Training is provided to scientists, and experts and lecturers are assigned to provide specialized help on specific nuclear applications. The IAEA supported the foundation in September 2003 of the World Nuclear University, comprising a world-wide network of institutions that aim to strengthen international co-operation in promoting the safe use of nuclear power in energy production, and in the application of nuclear science and technology in areas including sustainable agriculture and nutrition, medicine, fresh water resources management and environmental protection.

FOOD AND AGRICULTURE

In co-operation with FAO, the Agency conducts programmes of applied research on the use of radiation and isotopes in fields including: efficiency in the use of water and fertilizers; improvement of food crops by induced mutations; eradication or control of destructive insects by the introduction of sterilized insects (radiation-based Sterile Insect Technique); improvement of livestock nutrition and health; studies on improving efficacy and reducing residues of pesticides, and increasing utilization of agricultural wastes; and food preservation by irradiation. The programmes are implemented by the Joint FAO/IAEA Division of Nuclear Techniques in Food and Agriculture and by the FAO/IAEA Agriculture and Biotechnology Laboratory, based at IAEA's laboratory complex in Seibersdorf, Austria. A Training and Reference Centre for Food and Pesticide Control, based at Seibersdorf, supports the implementation of national legislation and trade agreements ensuring the quality and safety of food products in international trade.

LIFE SCIENCES

In co-operation with the World Health Organization (WHO), the IAEA promotes the use of nuclear techniques in medicine, biology and health-related environmental research, provides training, and conducts research on techniques for improving the accuracy of radiation dosimetry.

The IAEA/WHO Network of Secondary Standard Dosimetry Laboratories (SSDLs) comprises 81 laboratories in 62 member states. The Agency's Dosimetry Laboratory in Seibersdorf performs dose intercomparisons for both SSDLs and radiotherapy centres. The IAEA undertakes maintenance plans for nuclear laboratories; national programmes of quality control for nuclear medicine instruments; quality control of radioimmunoassay techniques; radiation sterilization of medical supplies; and improvement of cancer therapy.

PHYSICAL AND CHEMICAL SCIENCES

The Agency's programme in physical sciences includes industrial applications of isotopes and radiation technology; application of nuclear techniques to mineral exploration and exploitation; radiopharmaceuticals; and hydrology, involving the use of isotope techniques for assessment of water resources. Nuclear data services are provided, and training is given for nuclear scientists from developing countries. The Physics, Chemistry and Instrumentation Laboratory

at Seibersdorf supports the Agency's research in human health, industry, water resources and environment.

NUCLEAR POWER

At December 2003 there were 439 nuclear power plants in operation and 31 reactors under construction throughout the world (of which 20 were located in Asia). Nuclear power accounted for about 16% of total electrical energy generated during 2003. The IAEA helps developing member states to introduce nuclear-powered electricity-generating plants through assistance with planning, feasibility studies, surveys of manpower and infrastructure, and safety measures. The Agency also assesses life extension and decommissioning strategies for ageing nuclear power plants. It publishes books on numerous aspects of nuclear power, and provides training courses on safety in nuclear power plants and other topics. An energy data bank collects and disseminates information on nuclear technology, and a power-reactor information system monitors the technical performance of nuclear power plants. There is increasing interest in the use of nuclear reactors for seawater desalination and radiation hydrology techniques to provide potable water. In July 1992 the EC, Japan, Russia and the USA signed an agreement to co-operate in the engineering design of an International Thermonuclear Experimental Reactor (ITER). The project aimed to demonstrate the scientific and technological feasibility of fusion energy, with the aim of providing a source of clean, abundant energy in the 21st century. An Extension Agreement, signed in 1998, provided for the continuation of the project. Negotiations on the Joint Implementation of ITER commenced in June 2001. The People's Republic of China and the Republic of Korea also participate in the process. In May 2001 the International Project on Innovative Nuclear Reactors and Fuel Cycles (INPRO) was inaugurated. INPRO aimed to promote nuclear energy as a means of meeting future sustainable energy requirements and to facilitate the exchange of information by member states to advance innovations in nuclear technology. The IAEA is a permanent observer at the Generation IV International Forum (GIF), which was inaugurated in 2000 and aims to establish a number of international collaborative nuclear research and development agreements.

RADIOACTIVE WASTE MANAGEMENT

The Agency provides practical help to member states in the management of radioactive waste. The Waste Management Advisory Programme (WAMAP) was established in 1987, and undertakes advisory missions in member states. A code of practice to prevent the illegal dumping of radioactive waste was drafted in 1989, and another on the international trans-boundary movement of waste was drafted in 1990. A ban on the dumping of radioactive waste at sea came into effect in 1994, under the Convention on the Prevention of Marine Pollution by Dumping of Wastes and Other Matters. The IAEA was to determine radioactive levels, for purposes of the Convention, and provide assistance to countries for the safe disposal of radioactive wastes. The Agency has issued modal regulations for the air, sea and land transportation of all radioactive materials.

In September 1997 the IAEA adopted a Joint Convention on the Safety of Spent Fuel Management and on the Safety of Radioactive Waste Management. The first internationally-binding legal device to address such issues, the Convention was to ensure the safe storage and disposal of nuclear and radioactive waste, during both the construction and operation of a nuclear power plant, as well as following its closure. The Convention entered into force in June 2001, and had been ratified by 34 parties at December 2004.

NUCLEAR SAFETY

The IAEA's nuclear safety programme encourages international co-operation in the exchange of information, promoting implementation of its safety standards and providing advisory safety services. It includes the IAEA International Nuclear Event Scale (INES), which measures the severity of nuclear events, incidents and accidents; the Incident Reporting System; an emergency preparedness programme (which maintains an Emergency Response Centre); operational safety review teams; the 15-member International Nuclear Safety Advisory Group (INSAG); the Radiation Protection Advisory Team; and a safety research co-ordination programme. The safety review teams provide member states with advice on achieving and maintaining a high level of safety in the operation of nuclear power plants, while research programmes establish risk criteria for the nuclear fuel cycle and identify cost-effective means to reduce risks in energy systems. In May 1998 the Director-General initiated a review of the Agency's nuclear strategy, proposing the development of national safety profiles, more active promotion of safety services and improved co-operation at governmental and non-governmental levels. By the end of 2002 60 member states had agreed to report nuclear events under the INES.

The revised edition of the Basic Safety Standards for Radiation Protection (IAEA Safety Series No. 9) was approved in 1994. The Nuclear Safety Standards programme, initiated in 1974 with five codes of practice and more than 60 safety guides, was revised in 1987 and again in 1995.

Following a serious accident at the Chornobyl (Chernobyl) nuclear power plant in Ukraine (then part of the USSR) in April 1986, two conventions were formulated by the IAEA and entered into force in October. The first, the Convention on Early Notification of a Nuclear Accident, commits parties to provide information about nuclear accidents with possible trans-boundary effects at the earliest opportunity (it had 92 parties by December 2004); and the second commits parties to endeavour to provide assistance in the event of a nuclear accident or radiological emergency (this had 90 parties by December 2004). During 1990 the IAEA organized an assessment of the consequences of the Chernobyl accident, undertaken by an international team of experts, who reported to an international conference on the effects of the accident, convened at the IAEA headquarters in Vienna in May 1991. In February 1993 INSAG published an updated report on the Chernobyl incident, which emphasized the role of design factors in the accident, and the need to implement safety measures in the RBMK-type reactor. In March 1994 an IAEA expert mission visited Chernobyl and reported continuing serious deficiencies in safety at the defunct reactor and the units remaining in operation. An international conference reviewing the radiological consequences of the accident, 10 years after the event, was held in April 1996, co-sponsored by the IAEA, WHO and the European Commission. The last of the Chernobyl plant's three operating units was officially closed in December 2000. The IAEA was to offer a wide range of assistance during Chernobyl's decommissioning period, the first stage of which was expected to have a duration of five years.

In September 1999 the IAEA activated its Emergency Response Centre, following a serious incident at a fuel conversion facility in Tokaimura, Japan. The Centre was used to process information from the Japanese authorities and to ensure accurate reporting of the event. In October a three-member IAEA team of experts visited the site to undertake a preliminary investigation into the causes and consequences of the accident.

An International Convention on Nuclear Safety was adopted at an IAEA conference in June 1994. The Convention applies to land-based civil nuclear power plants: adherents commit themselves to fundamental principles of safety, and maintain legislative frameworks governing nuclear safety. The Convention entered into force in October 1996 and had been ratified by 55 states by December 2004.

In September 1997 more than 80 member states adopted a protocol to revise the 1963 Vienna Convention on Civil Liability for Nuclear Damage, fixing the minimum limit of liability for the operator of a nuclear reactor at 300m. Special Drawing Rights (SDRs, the accounting units of the IMF) in the event of an accident. The amended protocol also extended the length of time during which claims may be brought for loss of life or injury. It entered into force in October 2003. A Convention on Supplementary Compensation for Nuclear Damage established a further compensatory fund to provide for the payment of damages following an accident; contributions to the Fund were to be calculated on the basis of the nuclear capacity of each member state. The Convention had 15 signatories and five contracting states by December 2004.

In July 1996 the IAEA co-ordinated a study on the radiological situation at the Mururoa and Fangatauta atolls, following the French nuclear test programmes in the South Pacific. Results published in May 1998 concluded there was no radiological health risk and that neither remedial action nor continued environmental monitoring was necessary.

The IAEA is developing a training course on measurement methods and risk analysis relating to the presence of depleted uranium (which can be used in ammunition) in post-conflict areas. In November 2000 IAEA specialists participated in a fact-finding mission organized by UNEP in Kosovo and Metohija, which aimed to assess the environmental and health consequences of the use of depleted uranium in ammunition by NATO during its aerial offensive against the Federal Republic of Yugoslavia (now Serbia and Montenegro) in 1999. (A report on the situation was published by UNEP in March 2001.) In June 2003 the Agency published the results of an assessment undertaken in 2002 of the possible long-term radiological impact of depleted uranium residues, derived from the 1991 Gulf War, at several locations in Kuwait; it determined that the residues did not pose a health threat to local populations.

In May 2001 the IAEA convened an international conference to address the protection of nuclear material and radioactive sources from illegal trafficking. In September, in view of the perpetration of major terrorist attacks against targets in the USA during that month, the IAEA General Conference addressed the potential for nuclear-related terrorism. It adopted a resolution that emphasized the importance of the physical protection of nuclear material in preventing its illicit use or the sabotage of nuclear facilities and nuclear materials. Three main potential threats were identified: the acquisition by a terrorist group of a nuclear weapon; acquisition of nuclear material to construct a nuclear weapon or cause a radiological hazard; and violent acts against nuclear facilities to cause a

radiological hazard. In March 2002 the Board of Governors approved in principle an action plan to improve global protection against acts of terrorism involving nuclear and other radioactive materials. The plan addressed the physical protection of nuclear materials and facilities; the detection of malicious activities involving radioactive materials; strengthening national control systems; the security of radioactive sources; evaluation of security and safety at nuclear facilities; emergency response to malicious acts or threats involving radioactive materials; ensuring adherence to international guidelines and agreements; and improvement of programme co-ordination and information management. It was estimated that the Agency's upgraded nuclear security activities would require significant additional annual funding. In March 2003 the IAEA organized an International Conference on Security of Radioactive Sources, held in Vienna.

DISSEMINATION OF INFORMATION

The International Nuclear Information System (INIS), which was established in 1970, provides a computerized indexing and abstracting service. Information on the peaceful uses of atomic energy is collected by member states and international organizations and sent to the IAEA for processing and dissemination (see list of publications below). The IAEA also co-operates with FAO in an information system for agriculture (AGRIS) and with the World Federation of Nuclear Medicine and Biology, and the non-profit Cochrane Collaboration, in maintaining an electronic database of best practice in nuclear medicine. The IAEA Nuclear Data Section provides cost-free data centre services and co-operates with other national and regional nuclear and atomic data centres in the systematic world-wide collection, compilation, dissemination and exchange of nuclear reaction data, nuclear structure and decay data, and atomic and molecular data for fusion.

SAFEGUARDS

The Treaty on the Non-Proliferation of Nuclear Weapons (known also as the Non-Proliferation Treaty or NPT), which entered into force in 1970, requires each 'non-nuclear-weapon state' (one which had not manufactured and exploded a nuclear weapon or other nuclear explosive device prior to 1 January 1967) which is a party to the Treaty to conclude a safeguards agreement with the IAEA. Under such an agreement, the state undertakes to accept IAEA safeguards on all nuclear material in all its peaceful nuclear activities for the purpose of verifying that such material is not diverted to nuclear weapons or other nuclear explosive devices. In May 1995 the Review and Extension Conference of parties to the NPT agreed to extend the NPT indefinitely, and reaffirmed support for the IAEA's role in verification and the transfer of peaceful nuclear technologies. At the next review conference, held in April–May 2000, the five 'nuclear-weapon states'— the People's Republic of China, France, Russia, the United Kingdom and the USA—issued a joint statement pledging their commitment to the ultimate goal of complete nuclear disarmament under effective international controls. By December 2004 183 non-nuclear-weapon states and the five nuclear-weapon states were parties to the Treaty, but a number of non-nuclear-weapon states had not complied, within the prescribed time-limit, with their obligations under the Treaty regarding the conclusion of the relevant safeguards agreement with the Agency. The Democratic Republic of Korea (DPRK), which had acceded to the NPT in December 1985, announced its withdrawal from the Treaty in January 2003 (see below).

The five nuclear-weapon states have concluded safeguards agreements with the Agency that permit the application of IAEA safeguards to all their nuclear activities, excluding those with 'direct national significance'. A Comprehensive Nuclear Test Ban Treaty (CTBT) was opened for signature in September 1996, having been adopted by the UN General Assembly. The Treaty was to enter into international law upon ratification by all 44 nations with known nuclear capabilities. A separate verification organization was to be established, based in Vienna. A Preparatory Commission for the treaty organization became operational in 1997. By December 2004 174 countries had signed the CTBT and 120 had ratified it, including 33 of the 44 states with known nuclear capabilities. However, the US Senate rejected ratification of the CTBT in October 1999.

Several regional nuclear weapons treaties require their member states to conclude comprehensive safeguards agreements with the IAEA, including the Treaty for the prohibition of Nuclear Weapons in Latin America (Tlatelolco Treaty, with 33 states party at December 2004); the South Pacific Nuclear-Free Zone Treaty (Rarotonga Treaty, 13 states party at December 2004); the Treaty in the South-East Asia Nuclear-Weapon Free Zone (Treaty of Bangkok, adopted in 1995, 10 states party at December 2004); and the African Nuclear-Weapon Free Zone Treaty (Pelindaba Treaty, adopted in 1996, with 19 states party at December 2004). In September 2002 experts from Kazakhstan, Kyrgyzstan, Tajikistan, Turkmenistan and Uzbekistan, meeting in Samarkand, Uzbekistan, approved the draft text of a treaty on establishing a Central Asian Nuclear

Weapon Free Zone. At the end of 2003 a total of 229 IAEA safeguards agreements were in force with 146 states. Of these, 70 states had declared significant nuclear activities and were under inspection. Approximately 2,363 inspections were conducted in 2003 at 644 locations. There were 908 nuclear installations and locations containing nuclear material subject to IAEA safeguards at the end of 2001. Expenditure on the Safeguards Regular Budget for 2002 was US $78.5m, and extra-budgetary programme expenditure amounted to $19.7m. The IAEA has established an imagery database of nuclear sites; some 293 digital image surveillance systems were in operation at the end of 2002.

In June 1995 the Board of Governors approved measures to strengthen the safeguards system, including allowing inspection teams greater access to suspected nuclear sites and to information on nuclear activities in member states, reducing the notice time for inspections by removing visa requirements for inspectors and using environmental monitoring (i.e. soil, water and air samples) to test for signs of radioactivity. In April 1996 the IAEA initiated a programme to prevent and combat illicit trafficking of nuclear weapons, and in May 1998 the IAEA and the World Customs Organization signed a Memorandum of Understanding to enhance co-operation in the prevention of illicit nuclear trafficking. In May 1997 the Board of Governors adopted a model additional protocol approving measures to strengthen safeguards further, in order to ensure the compliance of non-nuclear-weapon states with IAEA commitments. The new protocol compelled member states to provide inspection teams with improved access to information concerning existing and planned nuclear activities, and to allow access to locations other than known nuclear sites within that country's territory. By March 2005 65 states had ratified additional protocols to their safeguards agreements.

IAEA's Safeguards Analytical Laboratory analyses nuclear fuel-cycle samples collected by IAEA safeguards inspectors. The Agency's Marine Environment Laboratory, in Monaco, studies radionuclides and other ocean pollutants.

In April 1992 the DPRK ratified a safeguards agreement with the IAEA. In late 1992 and early 1993, however, the IAEA unsuccessfully requested access to two non-declared sites in the DPRK, where it was suspected that material capable of being used for the manufacture of nuclear weapons was stored. In March 1993 the DPRK announced its intention of withdrawing from the NPT: it suspended its withdrawal in June, but continued to refuse full access to its nuclear facilities for IAEA inspectors. In May 1994 the DPRK began to refuel an experimental nuclear power reactor at Yongbyon, but refused to allow the IAEA to analyse the spent fuel rods in order to ascertain whether plutonium had been obtained from the reactor for possible military use. In June the IAEA Board of Governors halted IAEA technical assistance to the DPRK (except medical assistance) because of continuous violation of the NPT safeguards agreements. In the same month the DPRK withdrew from the IAEA (though not from the NPT); however, it allowed IAEA inspectors to remain at the Yongbyon site to conduct safeguards activities. In October the Governments of the DPRK and the USA concluded an agreement whereby the former agreed to halt construction of two new nuclear reactors, on condition that it received international aid for the construction of two 'light water' reactors (which could not produce materials for the manufacture of nuclear weapons). The DPRK also agreed to allow IAEA inspections of all its nuclear sites, but only after the installation of one of the 'light water' reactors had been completed (entailing a significant time lapse). In November IAEA inspectors visited the DPRK to initiate verification of the suspension of the country's nuclear programme, in accordance with the agreement concluded in the previous month. From 1995 the IAEA pursued technical discussions with the DPRK authorities as part of the Agency's efforts to achieve the full compliance of the DPRK with the IAEA safeguards agreement. By the end of 1999 the canning of spent fuel rods from the Yongbyon nuclear power reactor was completed. However, little overall progress had been achieved, owing to the obstruction of inspectors by the authorities in that country, including their refusal to provide samples for analysis. The IAEA was unable to verify the suspension of the nuclear programme and declared that the DPRK continued to be in non-compliance with its NPT safeguards agreement. In accordance with a decision of the General Conference in September 2001, IAEA inspectors subsequently resumed a continuous presence in the DPRK. The DPRK authorities permitted low-level inspections of the Yongbyon site by an IAEA technical team in January and May 2002. It was envisaged at that time that the new 'light water' reactors would become operational by 2008. However, in December 2002, following repeated requests by the IAEA that the DPRK verify the accuracy of reports that it was implementing an undeclared uranium enrichment programme, the DPRK authorities disabled IAEA safeguards surveillance equipment placed at three facilities in Yongbyon and took measures to restart reprocessing capabilities at the site, requesting the immediate withdrawal of the Agency's inspectors. (The inspectors were withdrawn at the end of the month.) In early January 2003 the IAEA Board of Governors adopted a resolution deploring the

DPRK's non-co-operation and urging its immediate and full compliance with the Agency. Shortly afterwards, however, the DPRK announced its withdrawal from the NPT, stating that it would limit its nuclear activities to peaceful purposes. In February the IAEA found the DPRK to be in further non-compliance with its safeguards agreement, and condemned the reported successful reactivation of the Yongbyon reactor. In August a series of six-party talks on the situation was launched, involving the DPRK, the People's Republic of China (PRC), Japan, the Republic of Korea, Russia and the USA, under the auspices of the PRC Government. In September 2004 the General Conference adopted a resolution that urged the DPRK to dismantle promptly and completely any nuclear weapons programme and to recognize the verification role of the Agency, while strongly encouraging the ongoing diplomatic efforts to achieve a peaceful outcome. In February 2005 the DPRK suspended its participation in the six-party talks, and asserted that it had developed nuclear weapons as a measure of self-defence.

In April 1991 the UN Security Council requested the IAEA to conduct investigations into Iraq's capacity to produce nuclear weapons, following the end of the war between Iraq and the UN-authorized, US-led multinational force. The IAEA was to work closely with a UN Special Commission of experts (UNSCOM), established by the Security Council, whose task was to inspect and dismantle Iraq's weapons of mass destruction (including chemical and biological weapons). In July the IAEA declared that Iraq had violated its safeguards agreement with the IAEA by not submitting nuclear material and relevant facilities in its uranium-enrichment programme to the Agency's inspection. This was the first time that a state party to the NPT had been condemned for concealing a programme of this nature. In October the sixth inspection team, composed of UNSCOM and representatives of the IAEA, was reported to have obtained conclusive documentary evidence that Iraq had a programme for developing nuclear weapons. By February 1994 all declared stocks of nuclear-weapons-grade material had been removed from Iraq. Subsequently, the IAEA pursued a programme of long-term surveillance of nuclear activity in Iraq, under a mandate issued by the UN Security Council. In September 1996 Iraq submitted to the IAEA a 'full, final and complete' declaration of its nuclear activities. However, in September-October 1997 the IAEA recommended that Iraq disclose further equipment, materials and information relating to its nuclear programme. In April 1998 IAEA technical experts were part of a special group that entered eight presidential sites in Iraq to collect baseline data, in accordance with a Memorandum of Understanding concluded between the UN Secretary-General and the Iraqi authorities in February. The accord aimed to ensure full Iraqi co-operation with UNSCOM and IAEA personnel. In August, however, Iraq suspended co-operation with UN inspectors, which prevented IAEA from implementing its programme of ongoing monitoring and verification (OMV) activities. Iraq's action was condemned by the IAEA General Conference in September. In October IAEA reported that while there was no evidence of Iraq having produced nuclear weapons or having retained or obtained a capability for the production of nuclear weapons, the Agency was unable to guarantee that all items had been found. All IAEA inspectors were temporarily relocated from Iraq to Bahrain in November, in accordance with a decision to withdraw UNSCOM personnel owing to Iraq's failure to agree to resume co-operation. In March 2000 UNSCOM was replaced by a new arms inspection body, the UN Monitoring, Verification and Inspection Commission (UNMOVIC). Although the IAEA carried out inventory verifications of nuclear material in Iraq in January 2000, January 2001 and January 2002, pursuant to Iraq's NPT safeguards agreement, full inspection activities in conjunction with UNMOVIC remained suspended. In September 2002 the US President expressed concern that Iraq was challenging international security owing to its non-compliance with successive UN resolutions relating to the elimination of weapons of mass destruction. In November the UN Security Council adopted Resolution 1441 providing for an enhanced inspection mission and a detailed timetable according to which Iraq would have a final opportunity to comply with its disarmament obligations. Following Iraq's acceptance of the resolution, experts from the IAEA's so-called Iraq Nuclear Verification Office and UNMOVIC resumed inspections on 27 November, with Council authorization to have unrestricted access to all areas and the right to interview Iraqi scientists and weapons experts. In early December Iraq submitted a declaration of all aspects of its weapons programmes, as required under Resolution 1441. In January 2003 Dr Mohammad el-Baradei, the IAEA Director-General, requested an ongoing mandate for his inspectors to clarify the situation regarding nuclear weapons. In mid-March el-Baradei reported that no evidence had been found of nuclear weapons programme activities in Iraq, while also stating that the Agency had not had sufficient time to complete its investigations. Shortly before the initiation of unilateral military action against Iraq by US and allied forces on 19 March IAEA and UNMOVIC personnel were withdrawn from the country. Their field activities were suspended and, following the overthrow in April of the Saddam

Hussain regime, responsibility for weapons inspections in Iraq were assumed by a US-led Iraq Survey Group. In late April el-Baradei emphasized the necessity of securing the sites of Iraq's declared nuclear materials from looting and damage and declared that, as the sole organization legally empowered by the NPT and successive Security Council resolutions to verify Iraq's nuclear disarmament, the Agency should resume its inspection activities in Iraq forthwith; this request was subsequently reiterated.

In September 2003 the IAEA adopted a resolution demanding that the Iranian Government sign, ratify and fully implement an additional protocol to its safeguards agreement promptly and unconditionally. The Agency also urged Iran to suspend its uranium enrichment and reprocessing activities, pending satisfactory application of the provisions of the additional protocol. Iran issued a declaration of its nuclear activities in October, and, in December, concluded an additional protocol and agreed to suspend uranium enrichment processing, as requested. The Agency dispatched inspectors to Iran from October to conduct an intensive verification process. In April 2004 the IAEA Director-General visited Iran and concluded an agreement on a joint action plan to address the outstanding issues of the verification process. Iran provided an initial declaration under the addition protocol in May. In June, however, the Director-General expressed his continued concern at the extent of Iranian co-operation with IAEA inspectors. In September Board of Governors adopted a resolution in which it strongly regretted continuing enrichment-related and reprocessing activities by Iran and requested their immediate suspension. The Director-General announced in late November that the suspension had been verified. Following the announcement by Libya in mid-December 2003 that it would conclude an additional protocol to its safeguards agreement with the IAEA, the Agency worked closely with that country to verify the extent of its past undeclared and present nuclear materials and activities. The Libyan authorities signed an additional protocol in March 2004. While assessing nuclear activities in Iran and Libya from late 2003 the Agency also undertook investigations into the supply routes and sources of the technology and materials used in their past undeclared nuclear programmes, demonstrating evidence of a complex black market. The Agency demanded full co-operation from the source countries involved.

In late 1997 the IAEA began inspections in the USA to verify the conversion for peaceful uses of nuclear material released from the military sector. In 1998 the United Kingdom announced that substantial quantities of nuclear material previously in its military programme would become available for verification under its voluntary offer safeguards agreement.

NUCLEAR FUEL CYCLE
The Agency promotes the exchange of information between member states on technical, safety, environmental, and economic aspects of nuclear fuel cycle technology, including uranium prospecting and the treatment and disposal of radioactive waste; it provides assistance to member states in the planning, implementation and operation of nuclear fuel cycle facilities and assists in the development of advanced nuclear fuel cycle technology. Every two years, in collaboration with OECD, the Agency prepares estimates of world uranium resources, demand and production.

Finance
The Agency is financed by regular and voluntary contributions from member states. Expenditure approved under the regular budget for 2005 amounted to some US $272.9m., and the target for voluntary contributions to finance the IAEA technical assistance and co-operation programme in that year was $77.5m.

Publications
Annual Report.
IAEA Bulletin (quarterly).
IAEA Newsbriefs (every 2 months).
IAEA Yearbook.
INIS Atomindex (bibliography, 2 a month).
INIS Reference Series.
INSAG Series.
Legal Series.
Meetings on Atomic Energy (quarterly).
The Nuclear Fuel Cycle Information System: A Directory of Nuclear Fuel Cycle Facilities.
Nuclear Fusion (monthly).
Nuclear Safety Review (annually).
Nuclear Technology Review (annually).
Panel Proceedings Series.
Publications Catalogue (annually).
Safety Series.
Technical Directories.
Technical Reports Series.

International Bank for Reconstruction and Development—IBRD (World Bank)

Address: 1818 H St, NW, Washington, DC 20433, USA.

Telephone: (202) 473-1000; **fax:** (202) 477-6391; **e-mail:** pic@worldbank.org; **internet:** www.worldbank.org.

The IBRD was established in December 1945. Initially it was concerned with post-war reconstruction in Europe; since then its aim has been to assist the economic development of member nations by making loans where private capital is not available on reasonable terms to finance productive investments. Loans are made either directly to governments, or to private enterprises with the guarantee of their governments. The World Bank, as it is commonly known, comprises the IBRD and the International Development Association (IDA). The affiliated group of institutions, comprising the IBRD, the IDA, the International Finance Corporation (IFC), the Multilateral Investment Guarantee Agency (MIGA) and the International Centre for Settlement of Investment Disputes (ICSID, see below), is now referred to as the World Bank Group.

MEMBERS
There are 184 members. Only members of the International Monetary Fund (IMF) may be considered for membership in the World Bank. Subscriptions to the capital stock of the Bank are based on each member's quota in the IMF, which is designed to reflect the country's relative economic strength. Voting rights are related to shareholdings.

Organization
(March 2005)

Officers and staff of the IBRD serve concurrently as officers and staff in the IDA. The World Bank has offices in New York, Brussels, Paris (for Europe), Frankfurt, London, Geneva and Tokyo, as well as in more than 100 countries of operation. Country Directors are located in some 30 country offices.

BOARD OF GOVERNORS
The Board of Governors consists of one Governor appointed by each member nation. Typically, a Governor is the country's finance minister, central bank governor, or a minister or an official of comparable rank. The Board normally meets once a year.

EXECUTIVE DIRECTORS
With the exception of certain powers specifically reserved to them by the Articles of Agreement, the Governors of the Bank have delegated their powers for the conduct of the general operations of the World Bank to a Board of Executive Directors which performs its duties on a full-time basis at the Bank's headquarters. There are 24 Executive Directors (see table below); each Director selects an Alternate. Five Directors are appointed by the five members having the largest number of shares of capital stock, and the rest are elected by the Governors representing the other members. The President of the Bank is Chairman of the Board.

The Executive Directors fulfil dual responsibilities. First, they represent the interests of their country or groups of countries. Second, they exercise their authority as delegated by the Governors in overseeing the policies of the Bank and evaluating completed projects. Since the Bank operates on the basis of consensus (formal votes are rare), this dual role involves frequent communication and consultations with governments so as to reflect accurately their views in Board discussions.

The Directors consider and decide on Bank policy and on all loan and credit proposals. They are also responsible for presentation to the Board of Governors at its Annual Meetings of an audit of accounts, an administrative budget, the *Annual Report* on the operations and policies of the World Bank, and any other matter that, in their judgement, requires submission to the Board of Governors. Matters may be submitted to the Governors at the Annual Meetings or at any time between Annual Meetings.

EXECUTIVE DIRECTORS

The general operations of the Bank are conducted by a Board of 24 Executive Directors. Five Directors are appointed by the five members having the largest number of shares of capital stock, and the rest are elected by the Governors representing the other members. The President of the Bank is Chairman of the Board.

PRINCIPAL OFFICERS

The principal officers of the Bank are the President of the Bank, two Managing Directors, three Senior Vice-Presidents and 24 Vice-Presidents.

President and Chairman of Executive Directors: PAUL WOLFOWITZ (USA) (from 1 June 2005).

Managing Director: SHENGMAN ZHANG (People's Republic of China).

Vice-President and Corporate Secretary: W. PAATII OFOSU-AMAAH (Ghana).

Activities

FINANCIAL OPERATIONS

IBRD capital is derived from members' subscriptions to capital shares, the calculation of which is based on their quotas in the International Monetary Fund. At 30 June 2004 the total subscribed capital of the IBRD was US \$189,718m., of which the paid-in portion was \$11,483m. (6.1%); the remainder is subject to call if required. Most of the IBRD's lendable funds come from its borrowing, on commercial terms, in world capital markets, and also from its retained earnings and the flow of repayments on its loans. IBRD loans carry a variable interest rate, rather than a rate fixed at the time of borrowing.

IBRD loans usually have a 'grace period' of five years and are repayable over 15 years or fewer. Loans are made to governments, or must be guaranteed by the government concerned, and are normally made for projects likely to offer a commercially viable rate of return. In 1980 the World Bank introduced structural adjustment lending, which (instead of financing specific projects) supports programmes and changes necessary to modify the structure of an economy so that it can restore or maintain its growth and viability in its balance-of-payments over the medium-term.

The IBRD and IDA together made 245 new lending and investment commitments totalling US \$20,080.1m. during the year ending 30 June 2004, compared with 240 (amounting to \$18,513.2m.) in the previous year. During 2003/04 the IBRD alone approved commitments totalling \$11,045.4m. (compared with \$11,230.7m. in the previous year), of which \$4,981.6m. (45%) was allocated to Latin America and the Caribbean and \$3,012.9m. (27%) to Europe and Central Asia. Disbursements by the IBRD in the year ending 30 June 2004 amounted to \$10,109m. (For details of IDA operations, see separate chapter on IDA.)

IBRD operations are supported by medium- and long-term borrowings in international capital markets. During the year ending 30 June 2004 the IBRD's net income amounted to US \$4,328m.

The World Bank's primary objectives are the achievement of sustainable economic growth and the reduction of poverty in developing countries. In the context of stimulating economic growth the Bank promotes both private-sector development and human resource development and has attempted to respond to the growing demands by developing countries for assistance in these areas. In March 1997 the Board of Executive Directors endorsed a 'Strategic Compact' to increase the effectiveness of the Bank in achieving its central objective of poverty reduction. The reforms included greater decentralization of decision-making, and investment in front-line operations, enhancing the administration of loans, and improving access to information and co-ordination of Bank activities through a knowledge management system comprising four thematic networks: the Human Development Network; the Environmentally and

Socially Sustainable Development Network; the Finance, Private Sector and Infrastructure Development Network; and the Poverty Reduction and Economic Management Network. In 2000/01 the Bank adopted a new Strategic Framework which emphasized two essential approaches for Bank support: strengthening the investment climate and prospects for sustainable development in a country, and supporting investment in the poor. In September 2001 the Bank announced that it was to join the UN as a full partner in implementing the so-called Millennium Development Goals (MDGs), and was to make them central to its development agenda. The objectives, which were approved by governments attending a special session of the UN General Assembly in September 2000, represented a new international consensus to achieve determined poverty reduction targets. These included reducing by 50% the number of people with an income of less than US \$1 a day and those suffering from hunger and lack of safe drinking water by 2015, achieving education for all, reducing maternal mortality, and combating HIV/AIDS, malaria and other major diseases. The Bank was closely involved in preparations for the International Conference on Financing for Development, which was held in Monterrey, Mexico, in March 2002. The meeting adopted the Monterrey Consensus, which outlined measures to support national development efforts and to achieve the MDGs. During 2002/03 the Bank, with the IMF, undertook to develop a monitoring framework to review progress in the MDG agenda. The first *Global Monitoring Report* was issued by the Bank and IMF in April 2004. Other efforts to support a greater emphasis on development results were also undertaken by the Bank during 2003/04 as part of a new strategic action plan.

The Bank's efforts to reduce poverty include the compilation of country-specific assessments and the formulation of country assistance strategies (CASs) to review and guide the Bank's country programmes. Since August 1998 the Bank has published CASs, with the approval of the government concerned. A new results-based CAS initiative was piloted in 2003/04. In 1998/99 the Bank's Executive Directors endorsed a Comprehensive Development Framework (CDF) to effect a new approach to development assistance based on partnerships and country responsibility, with an emphasis on the interdependence of the social, structural, human, governmental, economic and environmental elements of development. The Framework, which aimed to enhance the overall effectiveness of development assistance, was formulated after a series of consultative meetings organized by the Bank and attended by representatives of governments, donor agencies, financial institutions, non-governmental organizations, the private sector and academics.

In December 1999 the Bank introduced a new approach to implement the principles of the CDF, as part of its strategy to enhance the debt relief scheme for heavily indebted poor countries (see below). Applicant countries were requested to formulate, in consultation with external partners and other stakeholders, a results-oriented national strategy to reduce poverty, to be presented in the form of a Poverty Reduction Strategy Paper (PRSP). In cases where there might be some delay in issuing a full PRSP, it was permissible for a country to submit a less detailed 'interim' PRSP (I-PRSP) in order to secure the preliminary qualification for debt relief. By June 2004 42 countries had finalized full PRSPs. The approach also requires the publication of annual progress reports. In 2000/01 the Bank introduced a new Poverty Reduction Support Credit to help low-income countries to implement the policy and institutional reforms outlined in their PRSP. The first credits were approved for Uganda and Viet Nam in May and June respectively. In January 2002 a PRSP public review conference, attended by more than 200 representatives of donor agencies, civil society groups, and developing country organizations was held as part of an ongoing review of the scheme by the Bank and the IMF. Increasingly, PRSPs have been considered by the international community to be the appropriate country-level framework to assess progress towards achieving the MDGs.

In September 1996 the World Bank/IMF Development Committee endorsed a joint initiative to assist heavily indebted poor countries (HIPCs) to reduce their debt burden to a sustainable level, in order to make more resources available for poverty reduction and economic growth. A new Trust Fund was established by the World Bank in November to finance the initiative. The Fund, consisting of an initial allocation of US \$500m. from the IBRD surplus and other contributions from multilateral creditors, was to be administered by IDA. Of the 41 HIPCs identified by the Bank, 33 were in sub-Saharan Africa. In April 1997 the World Bank and the IMF announced that Uganda was to be the first beneficiary of the initiative, enabling the Ugandan Government to reduce its external debt by some 20%, or an estimated \$338m. In early 1999 the World Bank and IMF initiated a comprehensive review of the HIPC initiative. By April meetings of the Group of Seven industrialized nations (G-7) and of the governing bodies of the Bank and IMF indicated a consensus that the scheme needed to be amended and strengthened, in order to allow more countries to benefit from the initiative, to accelerate the process by which a country may qualify for assistance, and to enhance the effectiveness of debt relief. In June the G-7 and Russia, meeting in Cologne, Germany, agreed to increase contributions to the HIPC Trust Fund and to cancel substantial amounts of outstanding debt, and proposed more flexible terms for eligibility. In September the Bank and IMF reached an agreement on an enhanced HIPC scheme, with further revenue to be generated through the revaluation of a percentage of IMF gold reserves. Under the enhanced initiative it was agreed that, during the initial phase of the process to ensure suitability for debt relief, each applicant country should formulate a PRSP, and should demonstrate prudent financial management in the implementation of the strategy for at least one year, with support from the IDA and IMF. At the pivotal 'decision point' of the process, having thus developed and successfully applied the poverty reduction strategy, applicant countries still deemed to have an unsustainable level of debt were to qualify for interim debt relief from the IMF and IDA, as well as relief on highly concessional terms from other official bilateral creditors and multilateral institutions. During the ensuing 'interim period' countries were required successfully to implement further economic and social development reforms, as a final demonstration of suitability for securing full debt relief at the 'completion point' of the scheme. Data produced at the decision point was to form the base for calculating the final debt relief (in contrast to the original initiative, which based its calculations on projections of a country's debt stock at the completion point). In the majority of cases a sustainable level of debt was targeted at 150% of the net present value (NPV) of the debt in relation to total annual exports (compared with 200%–250% under the original initiative). Other countries with a lower debt-to-export ratio were to be eligible for assistance under the scheme, providing that their export earnings were at least 30% of GDP (lowered from 40% under the original initiative) and government revenue at least 15% of GDP (reduced from 20%). By the end of 2004 15 countries (Benin, Bolivia, Burkina Faso, Ethiopia, Ghana, Guyana, Madagascar, Mali, Mauritania, Mozambique, Nicaragua, Niger, Senegal, Tanzania and Uganda) had reached completion point under the enhanced HIPC initiative, while a further 12 countries had reached their decision point. At July total assistance committed under the HIPC initiative amounted to US $31,981m., or $53,692m. in total estimated nominal debt service relief, of which the Bank had committed $12,922m.

During 2000/01 the World Bank strengthened its efforts to counter the problem of HIV and AIDS in developing countries. In November 2001 the Bank appointed its first Global HIV/AIDS Adviser. In September 2000 a new Multi-Country HIV/AIDS Programme for Africa (MAP) was launched, in collaboration with UNAIDS and other major donor agencies and non-governmental organizations. Some US $500m. was allocated to the initiative and was used to support efforts in seven countries. In February 2002 the Bank approved an additional $500m. for a second phase of MAP, which was envisaged to assist HIV/AIDS schemes in a further 12 countries, as well as regional activities. A MAP initiative for the Caribbean, with a budget of $155m., was launched in 2001. The Bank has undertaken research into the long-term effects of HIV/AIDS, and hosts the Global HIV/AIDS Monitoring and Evaluation Support Team of UNAIDS.

In addition to providing financial services, the Bank also undertakes analytical and advisory services, and supports learning and capacity-building, in particular through the World Bank Institute (see below), the Staff Exchange Programme and knowledge-sharing initiatives. The Bank has supported efforts, such as the Global Development Gateway, to disseminate information on development issues and programmes, and, since 1988, has organized the Annual Bank Conference on Development Economics (ABCDE) to provide a forum for the exchange and discussion of development-related ideas and research. In September 1995 the Bank initiated the Information for Development Programme (InfoDev) with the aim of fostering partnerships between governments, multilateral institutions and private-sector experts in order to promote reform and investment in developing countries through improved access to information technology.

TECHNICAL ASSISTANCE

The provision of technical assistance to member countries has become a major component of World Bank activities. The economic and sector work (ESW) undertaken by the Bank is the vehicle for considerable technical assistance and often forms the basis of CASs and other strategic or advisory reports. In addition, project loans and credits may include funds earmarked specifically for feasibility studies, resource surveys, management or planning advice, and training. The Economic Development Institute has become one of the most important of the Bank's activities in technical assistance. It provides training in national economic management and project analysis for government officials at the middle and upper levels of responsibility. It also runs overseas courses aiming to build up local training capability, and administers a graduate scholarship programme.

The Bank serves as an executing agency for projects financed by the UN Development Programme. It also administers projects financed by various trust funds.

Technical assistance (usually reimbursable) is also extended to countries that do not need Bank financial support, e.g. for training and transfer of technology. The Bank encourages the use of local consultants to assist with projects and stimulate institutional capability.

The Project Preparation Facility (PPF) was established in 1975 to provide cash advances to prepare projects that may be financed by the Bank. In December 1994 the PPF's commitment authority was increased from US $220m. to $250m. In 1992 the Bank established an Institutional Development Fund (IDF), which became operational on 1 July; the purpose of the Fund was to provide rapid, small-scale financial assistance, to a maximum value of $500,000, for capacity-building proposals. In 2002 the IDF was reoriented to focus on good governance, in particular financial accountability and system reforms.

In March 1996 a new programme to co-ordinate development efforts in Africa was announced by the UN Secretary-General. The World Bank was to facilitate the mobilization of the estimated US $25,000m. required to achieve the objectives of the Special Initiative over a 10-year period. In addition, the Bank was to provide technical assistance to enable countries to devise economic plans (in particular following a period of civil conflict), agricultural development programmes and a common strategy for African countries to strengthen the management capacities of the public sector.

ECONOMIC RESEARCH AND STUDIES

In the 1990s the World Bank's research, conducted by its own research staff, was increasingly concerned with providing information to reinforce the Bank's expanding advisory role to developing countries and to improve policy in the Bank's borrowing countries. The principal areas of current research focus on issues such as maintaining sustainable growth while protecting the environment and the poorest sectors of society, encouraging the development of the private sector, and reducing and decentralizing government activities.

Consultative Group on International Agricultural Research (CGIAR): founded in 1971 under the sponsorship of the World Bank, FAO and UNDP. (In 1995 UNEP was invited to become the fourth sponsoring member, and in 2001/02 IFAD became a co-sponsor.) The Bank is chairman of the Group (which includes governments, private foundations and multilateral development agencies) and provides its secretariat. The Group was formed to raise financial support for international agricultural research work for improving crops and animal production in the developing countries; it supports 16 research centres. Its work is focused on the following five research areas: increasing productivity; protecting the environment; saving biodiversity; improving policies; and strengthening national research; Dir Francisco Reifschneider (Brazil).

CO-OPERATION WITH OTHER ORGANIZATIONS

The World Bank co-operates with other international partners with the aim of improving the impact of development efforts. It collaborates with the IMF in implementing the HIPC scheme and the two agencies work closely to achieve a common approach to development initiatives. The Bank has established strong working relationships with many other UN bodies, in particular through a mutual commitment to poverty reduction objectives. In May 2000 the Bank signed a joint statement of co-operation with the OECD. The Bank holds regular consultations with other multilateral development banks and with the European Union with respect to development issues. The Bank-NGO Committee provides an annual forum for discussion with non-governmental organizations (NGOs). Strengthening co-operation with external partners was a fundamental element of the Comprehensive Development Framework, which was adopted in 1998/99 (see above). In 2001/02 a Partnership Approval and Tracking System was implemented to provide information on the Bank's regional and global partnerships.

In 1997 a Partnerships Group was established to strengthen the Bank's work with development institutions, representatives of civil society and the private sector. The Group established a new Development Grant Facility, which became operational in October, to support partnership initiatives and to co-ordinate all of the Bank's grant-making activities. In 2003/04 the Facility had funds of US $178.2m. Also in 1997 the Bank, in partnership with the IMF, UNCTAD, UNDP, the World Trade Organization (WTO) and International Trade Commission, established an Integrated Framework for Trade-related Assistance to Least Developed Countries, at the request of the WTO, to assist those countries to integrate into the global trading system and improve basic trading capabilities.

In June 1995 the World Bank joined other international donors (including regional development banks, other UN bodies, Canada, France, the Netherlands and the USA) in establishing a Consultative Group to Assist the Poorest (CGAP), which was to channel funds to the most needy through grass-roots agencies. An initial credit of approximately US $200m. was committed by the donors. The Bank manages the CGAP Secretariat, which is responsible for the administration of external funding and for the evaluation and approval of project financing. The CGAP provides technical assistance, training and strategic advice to microfinance institutions and other relevant bodies. As an implementing agency of the Global Environment Facility (GEF) the Bank assists countries to prepare and supervise GEF projects relating to biological diversity, climate change and other environmental protection measures. It is an example of a partnership in action which addresses a global agenda, complementing Bank country assistance activities. Other Trust Funds administered by the Bank include the Global Program to Eradicate Poliomyelitis, launched during the financial year 2002/03, the Least Developed Countries Fund for Climate Change, established in September 2002, and an Education for All Fast-Track Initiative Catalytic Trust Fund, established in 2003/04.

The Bank is a lead organization in providing reconstruction assistance following natural disasters or conflicts, usually in collaboration with other UN agencies or international organizations, and through special trust funds. In November 2001 the Bank worked with UNDP and the Asian Development Bank to assess the needs of Afghanistan following the removal of the Taliban authorities in that country. At an International Conference on Reconstruction Assistance to Afghanistan, held in Tokyo, Japan, in January 2002, the Bank's President proposed extending US $500m. in assistance over a 30-month period, and providing an immediate amount of $50m.–$70m. in grants. In May an Afghanistan Reconstruction Trust Fund was established to provide a co-ordinated financing mechanism to support the interim administration in that country. The Bank is the Administrator of the Trust, which is managed jointly by the Bank, Asian Development Bank, Islamic Development Bank and the UNDP. In May 2003 a Bank representative participated in an international advisory and monitoring board to assess reconstruction and development needs following international conflict in Iraq and removal of its governing regime. In October the Bank, with the UN Development Group, published a report identifying 14 priority areas for reconstruction, with funding requirements of $36,000m. over the period 2004–07, which was presented to an international donor conference held later in that month. The conference, held in Madrid, Spain, approved the establishment of an International Reconstruction Fund Facility for Iraq to channel international donations and to co-ordinate reconstruction activities. In January 2004 the Bank's Board of Executive Directors authorized the Bank to administer an integral part of the facility, the Iraq Trust Fund, to finance a programme of emergency projects and technical assistance. By the end of that year international donors had contributed some $400m. to the Fund. In early 2005 the Bank responded immediately to assist countries affected by a massive earthquake and subsequent tsunamis which devastated many coastal areas of some 11 countries in the Indian Ocean at the end of December 2004. Bank staff undertook assessments and other efforts to accelerate recovery planning, mobilize financial support and help to co-ordinate relief and recovery efforts in affected regions. Some $672m. was allocated by the Bank, mainly in grants to be directed to Indonesia, Sri Lanka and the Maldives, for the first phase of reconstruction efforts.

The Bank conducts co-financing and aid co-ordination projects with official aid agencies, export credit institutions, and commercial banks to leverage additional concessional funds for recipient countries. During the year ending 30 June 2004 the Bank's main partners were the Inter-American Development Bank (which provided US $3,700m.) and the European Commission ($640m.).

EVALUATION

The Operations Evaluation Department is an independent unit within the World Bank. It conducts Country Assistance Evaluations to assess the development effectiveness of a Bank country programme, and studies and publishes the results of projects after a loan has been fully disbursed, so as to identify problems and possible improvements in future activities. In addition, the department reviews the Bank's global programmes and produces the *Annual Review of Development Effectiveness*. In 1996 a Quality Assurance Group was established to monitor the effectiveness of the Bank's operations and performance.

In September 1993 the Bank established an independent Inspection Panel, consistent with the Bank's objective of improving project implementation and accountability. The Panel, which became operational in September 1994, was to conduct independent investigations and report on complaints from local people concerning the design, appraisal and implementation of development projects supported by the Bank. By mid-2004 the Panel had received 33 formal requests for inspection and had recommended investigations in 14 of those cases.

During 2003/04 the Inspection Panel received six new requests for inspections, relating to a petroleum and pipeline project in Came-

roon, a sewerage project in the Philippines, an indigenous and community biodiversity project in Mexico, sewerage and environmental management in Colombia, and urban transport in Mumbai, India (two requests).

IBRD INSTITUTIONS

World Bank Institute (WBI): founded in March 1999 by merger of the Bank's Learning and Leadership Centre, previously responsible for internal staff training, and the Economic Development Institute (EDI), which had been established in 1955 to train government officials concerned with development programmes and policies. The new Institute aimed to emphasize the Bank's priority areas through the provision of training courses and seminars relating to poverty, crisis response, good governance and anti-corruption strategies. From 2004 the Institute was to place greater emphasis on individual country needs and on long-term institutional capacity-building. During 2003/04 WBI activities reached some 78,000 participants in 124 countries. The Institute has continued to support a Global Knowledge Partnership, which was established in 1997 to promote alliances between governments, companies, other agencies and organizations committed to applying information and communication technologies for development purposes. Under the EDI a World Links for Development programme was also initiated to connect schools in developing countries with partner establishments in industrialized nations via the internet. In 1999 the WBI expanded its programmes through distance learning, a Global Development Network, and use of new technologies. A new initiative, Global Development Learning Network (GDLN), aimed to expand access to information and learning opportunities through the internet, video-conferences and organized exchanges. At late-2004 there were 70 GDLN centres, or affiliates. At mid-2004 formal partnership arrangements were in place between WBI and some 125 learning centres and public, private and non-governmental organizations; Vice-Pres. FRANNIE LÉAUTIER (Tanzania/France).

International Centre for Settlement of Investment Disputes (ICSID): founded in 1966 under the Convention of the Settlement of Investment Disputes between States and Nationals of Other States. The Convention was designed to encourage the growth of private foreign investment for economic development, by creating the possibility, always subject to the consent of both parties, for a Contracting State and a foreign investor who is a national of another Contracting State to settle any legal dispute that might arise out of such an investment by conciliation and/or arbitration before an impartial, international forum. The governing body of the Centre is its Administrative Council, composed of one representative of each Contracting State, all of whom have equal voting power. The President of the World Bank is (*ex officio*) the non-voting Chairman of the Administrative Council. At the end of 2004 142 countries had signed and ratified the Convention to become ICSID Contracting States. By mid-2004 the Centre had concluded 83 cases, while 78 were pending; Sec.-Gen. ROBERTO DAÑINO (Peru).

Publications

Abstracts of Current Studies: The World Bank Research Program (annually).

Annual Report on Operations Evaluation.

Annual Report on Portfolio Performance.

Annual Review of Development Effectiveness.

Doing Business (annually).

EDI Annual Report.

Global Commodity Markets (quarterly).

Global Development Finance (annually, also on CD-Rom and online).

Global Economic Prospects (annually).

ICSID Annual Report.

ICSID Review—Foreign Investment Law Journal (2 a year).

Joint BIS-IMF-OECD-World Bank Statistics on External Debt (quarterly, also available online at www.worldbank.org/data/jointdebt.html).

New Products and Outreach (EDI, annually).

News from ICSID (2 a year).

Poverty Reduction and the World Bank (annually).

Poverty Reduction Strategies Newsletter (quarterly).

Research News (quarterly).

Staff Working Papers.

Transition (every 2 months).

World Bank Annual Report.

World Bank Atlas (annually).

World Bank Economic Review (3 a year).

The World Bank and the Environment (annually).

World Bank Research Observer.

World Development Indicators (annually, also on CD-Rom and online).

World Development Report (annually, also on CD-Rom).

Statistics

LENDING OPERATIONS, BY SECTOR
(projects approved, year ending 30 June; US $ million)

	2003	2004
Agriculture, fishing and forestry . . .	1,213.2	1,386.1
Education	2,348.7	1,684.5
Energy and mining	1,088.4	966.5
Finance	1,446.3	1,808.9
Health and other social services . . .	3,442.6	2,997.1
Industry and trade	796.7	797.9
Information and communication . . .	115.3	90.9
Law, justice and public administration .	3,956.5	4,978.7
Transportation	2,727.3	3,777.8
Water, sanitation and flood protection .	1,378.3	1,591.6
Total	18,513.2	20,080.1

IBRD INCOME AND EXPENDITURE
(US $ million, year ending 30 June)

Revenue	2003	2004
Income from loans:		
Interest	5,659	4,328
Commitment charges	83	75
Income from investments and securities	418	304
Other income	202	235
Total income	6,362	4,942

Expenditure	2003	2004
Interest on borrowings	3,509	2,708
Amortization of issuance and		
prepayment costs	85	81
Administrative expenses	882	934
Contributions to special programmes .	156	179
Provision for loan losses	−1,300	−665
Other financial expenses	9	9
Total	3,341	3,246
Operating income	3,021	1,696
Effects of adjustment and accounting		
charge	2,323	−4,100
Net income	5,344	−2,404

IBRD LOANS AND IDA CREDITS APPROVED, BY SECTOR AND REGION
(1 July 2003–30 June 2004; US $ million)

Sector	Africa	East Asia and Pacific	South Asia	Europe and Central Asia	Latin America and the Caribbean	Middle East and North Africa	Total
Agriculture, fishing and forestry	268.5	290.4	251.9	168.6	379.6	27.2	1,386.1
Education	362.9	118.6	665.8	164.0	218.3	154.9	1,684.5
Energy and mining	365.8	67.2	130.8	352.2	50.5	0.0	966.5
Finance	165.8	49.0	331.4	836.9	405.1	20.8	1,808.9
Health and other social services	723.1	84.3	334.6	244.3	1,558.9	52.0	2,997.1
Industry and trade	95.4	78.7	46.1	126.3	428.0	23.4	797.9
Information and communication	52.9	0.0	16.9	7.0	14.0	0.0	90.9
Law, justice and public administration . . .	1,004.1	257.5	925.5	1,176.8	1,521.3	93.6	4,978.7
Transportation	716.6	1,209.9	444.8	321.2	675.7	409.6	3,777.8
Water, sanitation and flood protection . . .	360.8	417.1	273.7	162.0	68.4	309.5	1,591.6
Total	4,115.9	2,572.7	3,421.6	3,559.1	5,319.8	1,091.0	20,080.1
of which: IBRD	0.0	1,665.5	439.5	3,012.9	4,981.6	946.0	11,045.4
IDA	4,115.9	907.2	2,982.1	546.2	338.2	145.0	9,034.6
Number of operations	68	30	34	52	50	11	245

IBRD OPERATIONS AND RESOURCES, 2000–2004
(US $ million, years ending 30 June)

	1999/2000	2000/01	2001/02	2002/03	2003/04
Loans approved	10,919	10,487	11,452	11,231	11,045
Gross disbursements	13,332	11,784	11,256	11,921	10,109
New medium- to long-term borrowings	15,206	17,223	22,803	19,305	12,535
Net income	1,991	1,489	2,778	5,344	−2,404
Subscribed capital	188,606	189,505	189,505	189,567	189,718
Loans outstanding	120,104	118,866	121,589	116,240	109,610

Source: *World Bank Annual Report 2004.*

EXECUTIVE DIRECTORS AND THEIR VOTING POWER
(November 2004)

Executive Director	Casting votes of	IBRD Total votes	IBRD % of total	IDA Total votes	IDA % of total
Appointed:					
CAROLE BROOKINS	USA	265,219	16.39	2,019,309	14.15
YOSHIO OKUBO	Japan	127,250	7.87	1,541,960	10.81
ECKHARD DEUTSCHER	Germany	72,649	4.49	989,929	6.94
PIERRE DUQUESNE	France	69,647	4.30	611,024	4.28
TOM SCHOLAR	United Kingdom	69,647	4.30	715,264	5.01
Elected:					
GINO ALZETTA (Belgium)	Austria, Belarus*, Belgium, Czech Republic, Hungary, Kazakhstan, Luxembourg, Slovakia, Slovenia, Turkey	77,669	4.80	642,918	4.51
LUIS MARTI (Spain)	Costa Rica, El Salvador, Guatemala, Honduras, Mexico, Nicaragua, Spain, Venezuela*	72,786	4.50	305,544	2.14
AD MELKERT (Netherlands) . . .	Armenia, Bosnia and Herzegovina, Bulgaria*, Croatia, Cyprus, Georgia, Israel, the former Yugoslav republic of Macedonia, Moldova, Netherlands, Romania*, Ukraine	72,208	4.46	522,439	3.66
MARCEL MASSE (Canada)	Antigua and Barbuda*, The Bahamas*, Barbados, Belize, Canada, Dominica, Grenada, Guyana, Ireland, Jamaica*, Saint Christopher and Nevis, Saint Lucia, Saint Vincent and the Grenadines	62,217	3.85	623,359	4.37
OTAVIANO CANUTO DOS SANTOS FILHO (Brazil)	Brazil, Colombia, Dominican Republic, Ecuador, Haiti, Panama, Philippines, Suriname*, Trinidad and Tobago	58,124	3.59	439,683	3.08
BIAGIO BOSSONE (Italy)	Albania, Greece, Italy, Malta*, Portugal, San Marino*, Timor-Leste	56,705	3.50	504,788	3.54
JOHN AUSTIN (New Zealand) . . .	Australia, Cambodia, Kiribati, Republic of Korea, Marshall Islands, Federated States of Micronesia, Mongolia, New Zealand, Palau, Papua New Guinea, Samoa, Solomon Islands,Vanuatu	55,800	3.45	428,234	3.00
MATHIAS SINAMENYE (Burundi) . . .	Angola, Botswana, Burundi, Eritrea, Ethiopia, The Gambia, Kenya, Lesotho, Liberia, Malawi, Mozambique, Namibia*, Nigeria, Seychelles*, Sierra Leone, South Africa, Sudan, Swaziland, Tanzania, Uganda, Zambia, Zimbabwe	55,190	3.41	609,238	4.27
C. M. VASUDEV (India)	Bangladesh, Bhutan, India, Sri Lanka	54,945	3.40	598,568	4.19
THORSTEINN INGOLFSSON (Iceland) . .	Denmark, Estonia*, Finland, Iceland, Latvia, Lithuania*, Norway, Sweden	54,039	3.34	698,470	4.89
SID AHMED DIB (Algeria)	Afghanistan, Algeria, Ghana, Iran, Morocco, Pakistan, Tunisia	51,544	3.19	275,381	1.93
PIETRO VEGLIO (Switzerland) . . .	Azerbaijan, Kyrgyzstan, Poland, Serbia and Montenegro, Switzerland, Tajikistan, Turkmenistan*, Uzbekistan	49,192	3.04	534,032	3.74
MAHDY ISMAIL ALJAZZAF (Kuwait) . .	Bahrain*, Egypt, Iraq, Jordan, Kuwait, Lebanon, Libya, Maldives, Oman, Qatar*, Syria, United Arab Emirates, Yemen	47,042	2.91	306,304	2.15
ZHU GUANGYAO	People's Republic of China	45,049	2.78	273,252	1.91
YAHYA ABDULLAH M. ALYAHYA . . .	Saudi Arabia	45,045	2.78	502,122	3.52
ALEXY G. KVASOV	Russia	45,045	2.78	39,573	0.28
HERWIDAYATMO (Indonesia)	Brunei*, Fiji, Indonesia, Laos, Malaysia, Myanmar, Nepal, Singapore, Thailand, Tonga, Viet Nam	41,096	2.54	389,830	2.73
JAIME QUIJANDRIA SALMON (Peru) . .	Argentina, Bolivia, Chile, Paraguay, Peru, Uruguay*	37,499	2.32	248,510	1.74
PAULO F. GOMES (Guinea-Bissau) . .	Benin, Burkina Faso, Cameroon, Cape Verde, Central African Republic, Chad, Comoros, Democratic Republic of the Congo, Republic of the Congo, Côte d'Ivoire, Djibouti, Equatorial Guinea, Gabon, Guinea, Guinea-Bissau, Madagascar, Mali, Mauritania, Mauritius, Niger, Rwanda, São Tomé and Príncipe, Senegal, Togo	32,252	1.99	449,724	3.15

Note: Somalia (802 votes in IBRD and 10,506 in IDA) did not participate in the 2004 regular election of Executive Directors.
* Member of IBRD only (not IDA).

International Development Association—IDA

Address: 1818 H Street, NW, Washington, DC 20433, USA.
Telephone: (202) 473-1000; **fax:** (202) 477-6391; **internet:** www
.worldbank.org/ida.

The International Development Association began operations in
November 1960. Affiliated to the IBRD, IDA advances capital to the
poorer developing member countries on more flexible terms than
those offered by the IBRD.

MEMBERS

IDA has 165 members.

Organization

(March 2005)

Officers and staff of the IBRD serve concurrently as officers and staff
of IDA.

President and Chairman of Executive Directors: PAUL WOLF-
OWITZ (*ex officio*) (from 1 June 2005).

Activities

IDA assistance is aimed at the poorer developing countries (i.e. those
with an annual GNP per capita of less than US $865 in 2002 dollars
were to qualify for assistance in 2003/04) and support their poverty
reduction strategies. Under IDA lending conditions, credits can be
extended to countries whose balance of payments could not sustain
the burden of repayment required for IBRD loans. Terms are more
favourable than those provided by the IBRD; credits are for a period
of 35 or 40 years, with a 'grace period' of 10 years, and carry no
interest charges. At mid-2004 81 countries were eligible for IDA
assistance, including several small-island economies with a GNP per
head greater than $865, but which would otherwise have little or no
access to Bank funds, and 15 so-called 'blend borrowers' which are
entitled to borrow from both the IDA and IBRD. IDA administers a
Trust Fund, which was established in November 1996 as part of a
World Bank/IMF initiative to assist heavily indebted poor countries
(HIPCs).

IDA's total development resources, consisting of members' subscriptions and supplementary resources (additional subscriptions
and contributions), are replenished periodically by contributions
from the more affluent member countries. Discussions on the 13th
replenishment of IDA funds commenced in February 2001, and for
the first time involved representatives of borrowing countries, civil
society and other public groups. A final commitment, providing for
some US $23,000m. in resources for the period 1 July 2002–30 June
2005, was concluded in July 2002 by 38 donor countries. The IDA-13
lending framework emphasized the following objectives: promoting
sound policies for growth and poverty reduction; ensuring effective
assistance and measurable results; improving co-ordination, transparency, and consultation; and providing for substantial replenishment of resources. The replenishment programme also provided for
greater use of grants to address the problems of the poorest recipient
countries, for example those most vulnerable to debt, those in post-
conflict situations, as well as reconstruction projects after a natural
disaster and HIV/AIDS programmes. Negotiations on the 14th
replenishment of IDA funds commenced in February 2004. An
agreement to provide a substantial replenishment of funds was
concluded in February 2005, when 40 donor countries committed
$34,000m. for the period 1 July 2005–30 June 2008.

During the year ending 30 June 2004 IDA credits totalling
US $9,034.6m. were approved, compared with $7,282.5m. in the
previous year. Of total IDA assistance during 2003/04 $4,115.9m.
(46%) was for Africa and $2,982.1m. (33%) for South Asia. The
largest borrowers of IDA credits were India ($1,033.0m. for six
projects), the Democratic Republic of the Congo ($749.3m. for six
projects), Pakistan ($731.2m. for seven projects) and Viet Nam
($705.6m. for four projects),. Of the total new lending in 2003/04
some $1,712m. (or 19%) was in the form of grants for the poorest or
most vulnerable countries.

Publication

Annual Report.

Statistics

IDA OPERATIONS AND RESOURCES, 2000–2004
(US $ million, years ending 30 June)

	1999/2000	2000/01	2001/02	2002/03	2003/04
Commitments*	4,358	6,764	8,068	7,282	9,035
Disbursements	5,177	5,492	6,612	7,019	6,936

*Excluding HIPC development grants.
Source: *World Bank Annual Report 2004.*

International Finance Corporation—IFC

Address: 2121 Pennsylvania Ave, NW, Washington, DC 20433,
USA.
Telephone: (202) 473-3800; **fax:** (202) 974-4384; **e-mail:**
information@ifc.org; **internet:** www.ifc.org.

IFC was founded in 1956 as a member of the World Bank Group to
stimulate economic growth in developing countries by financing
private-sector investments, mobilizing capital in international
financial markets, and providing technical assistance and advice to
governments and businesses.

MEMBERS

IFC has 177 members.

Organization

(March 2005)

IFC is a separate legal entity in the World Bank Group. Executive
Directors of the World Bank also serve as Directors of IFC. The
President of the World Bank is *ex officio* Chairman of the IFC Board
of Directors, which has appointed him President of IFC. Subject to
his overall supervision, the day-to-day operations of IFC are conducted by its staff under the direction of the Executive Vice-President.

PRINCIPAL OFFICERS

President: PAUL WOLFOWITZ (USA) (from 1 June 2005).

Executive Vice-President: ASSAAD JABRE (acting).

REGIONAL AND INDUSTRY DEPARTMENTS

Seven Regional Departments cover: sub-Saharan Africa; East Asia and the Pacific; South Asia; Central and Eastern Europe; Southern Europe and Central Asia; Latin America and the Caribbean; and the Middle East and North Africa. These aim to develop strategies for member countries, promote businesses, and strengthen relations with governments and the private sector. The Industry Departments include Agribusiness; Global Financial Markets; Global Information and Communications Technologies (jointly managed with the World Bank); Global Manufacturing and Services; Health and Education; Infrastructure; Oil, Gas, Mining and Chemicals (jointly managed with the World Bank); Private Equity and Investment Funds; Small and Medium Enterprises (jointly managed with the World Bank); and Trust Funds.

REGIONAL AND RESIDENT MISSIONS

There are Regional and Resident Missions in Australia, Brazil, Cambodia, Cameroon, People's Republic of China, Côte d'Ivoire, Dominican Republic, Egypt, Ghana, India, Japan, Kazakhstan, Kenya, Laos, Mauritius, Nepal, Russia, South Africa, Trinidad and Tobago, Turkey, Viet Nam and Zimbabwe. There are also Special Representatives in France, Germany and the United Kingdom (for Europe), and other programme co-ordinators, managers and investment officers in more than 30 additional countries.

Activities

IFC aims to promote economic development in developing member countries by assisting the growth of private enterprise and effective capital markets. It finances private sector projects, through loans, the purchase of equity, quasi-equity products, and risk management services, and assists governments to create conditions that stimulate the flow of domestic and foreign private savings and investment. IFC may provide finance for a project that is partly state-owned, provided that there is participation by the private sector and that the project is operated on a commercial basis. IFC also mobilizes additional resources from other financial institutions, in particular through syndicated loans, thus providing access to international capital markets. IFC provides a range of advisory services to help to improve the investment climate in developing countries and offers technical assistance to private enterprises and governments.

To be eligible for financing, projects must be profitable for investors, as well as financially and economically viable; must benefit the economy of the country concerned; and must comply with IFC's environmental and social guide-lines. IFC aims to promote best corporate governance and management methods and sustainable business practices, and encourages partnerships between governments, non-governmental organizations and community groups. In 2001/02 IFC developed a Sustainability Framework to help to assess the longer-term economic, environmental and social impact of projects. The first Sustainability Review was published in mid-2002. In 2002/03 IFC assisted 10 international banks to draft a voluntary set of guide-lines (the Equator Principles), based on IFC's environmental, social and safeguard monitoring policies, to be applied to their global project finance activities. By 30 June 2004 24 financial institutions had signed up to the Equator Principles.

IFC's authorized capital is US $2,450m. At 30 June 2004 paid-in capital was $2,362m. The World Bank was originally the principal source of borrowed funds, but IFC also borrows from private capital markets. IFC's net income amounted to $993m. in 2003/04, compared with $487m. in the previous year.

In the year ending 30 June 2004 project financing approved by IFC amounted to US $5,633m. for 217 projects (compared with $5,033m. for 204 projects in the previous year). Of the total approved, $4,753m. was for IFC's own account, while $880m. was in the form of loan syndications and underwriting of securities issues and investment funds by more than 100 participant banks and institutional investors. Generally, the IFC limits its financing to less than 25% of the total cost of a project, but may take up to a 35% stake in a venture (although never as a majority shareholder). Disbursements for IFC's account amounted to $3,152m. in 2003/04 (compared with $2,959m. in the previous year).

The largest proportion of investment commitments in 2003/04 was allocated to Europe and Central Asia (36%). Latin America and the Caribbean received 28%, East Asia and the Pacific 14%, South Asia

9%, sub-Saharan Africa 7% and Middle East and North Africa 4%. In that year almost one-third of total financing committed (30%) was for financial services. Other commitments included warehousing and utilities (13%), oil, gas, mining (11%) and information (6%).

Since 1990 IFC has undertaken risk-management services, in order to assist institutions to avoid financial risks that arise from changes in interest rates, in exchange rates or in commodity prices. In 2003/04 IFC committed 10 risk-management transactions for companies and banks.

IFC's Private Sector Advisory Services (PSAS), jointly managed with the World Bank, advises governments and private enterprises on policy, transaction implementation and foreign direct investment. The Foreign Investment Advisory Service (FIAS), also jointly operated and financed with the World Bank, provides advice on promoting foreign investment and strengthening the country's investment framework at the request of governments. During 2003/04 FIAS completed 60 advisory projects. At the end of that year the service had assisted more than 130 countries since it commenced operations in 1986. Under the Technical Assistance Trust Funds Program (TATF), established in 1988, IFC manages resources contributed by various governments and agencies to provide finance for feasibility studies, project identification studies and other types of technical assistance relating to project preparation. By mid-2004 contributions to the TATF programme totalled US $188m. and more than 1,380 technical assistance projects had been approved.

IFC support for private sector development includes technical assistance and advisory services for small-scale entrepreneurs to assist the development of business proposals and efforts to generate funding for their projects. IFC has established, with the support of external donors, a network of Small and Medium Enterprise (SME) facilities and programmes which aim to provide support services at enterprise level; to assist the development of local private sector support institutions; and to advocate ways to improve the business-enabling environment. The Africa Project Development Facility (APDF) was established in 1986 by IFC, UNDP and the African Development Bank, and has headquarters in Johannesburg, South Africa, with other offices in Cape Town (South Africa), Cameroon, Ghana, Kenya, and Nigeria. The Facility also promotes capacity-building for SMEs, local business associations and financial institutions. It works closely with the African Management Services Company (AMSCo, established in 1989, with headquarters in Amsterdam, the Netherlands) which helps to find qualified senior executives and technical personnel to work with African companies, assist in the training of local managers, and provide management support. The South Pacific Project Facility, based in Sydney, Australia, was established in 1991, mainly to assist local businesses in the IFC Pacific Island member countries. A separate office in Port Moresby, Papua New Guinea, was opened in 1997. The Facility was renamed as the Pacific Enterprise Development Facility from August 2003. The Mekong Private Sector Development Facility (MPDF) became operational in 1997 (initially as a five-year technical assistance programme, the Mekong Project Development Facility), specifically to support the development of SMEs in Cambodia, Laos and Viet Nam. In September 2000 the Southeast Europe Enterprise Development (SEED) initiative was formally launched at its headquarters in Sarajevo, Bosnia and Herzegovina, as a five-year scheme to support the development of the private-sector in Albania, Bosnia and Herzegovina, Kosovo, the former Yugoslav republic of Macedonia, and the Federal Republic of Yugoslavia (now Serbia and Montenegro). In May 2002 a China Project Development Facility, with headquarters in Chengdu, Sichuan Province, became operational. During 2002/03 the North Africa Enterprise Development facility was inaugurated, with offices in Algeria, Egypt and Morocco. In October 2002 the SouthAsia Enterprise Development Facility, based in Dhaka, Bangladesh, became operational. A Program for Eastern Indonesian SME Development, based in Bali, Indonesia, was established in September 2003.

Publications

Annual Report.

Emerging Stock Markets Factbook (annually).

Impact (quarterly).

Lessons of Experience (series).

Results on the Ground (series).

Review of Small Businesses (annually).

Discussion papers and technical documents.

Statistics

IFC OPERATIONS AND RESOURCES, 1995–2004
(fiscal years ending 30 June)

	1995	1996	1997	1998	1999	2000	2001	2002	2003	2004
Approved investments										
Number of new projects	213	264	276	304	255	259	239	223	186	217
Total financing (US $ million) . . .	5,467	8,118	6,722	5,905	5,280	5,846	5,357	5,835	5,449	5,633
Total project costs* (US $ million) . .	19,352	19,633	17,945	15,726	15,578	21,136	16,747	15,514	13,006	17,938
Disbursements (IFC's own account, US $ million)	1,808	2,053	2,003	2,054	2,102	2,210	1,535	1,498	2,959	3,152
Resources and income (US $ million)										
Borrowings	7,993	8,956	10,123	11,162	12,429	14,919	15,457	16,581	17,315	16,254
Paid-in capital	1,875	2,076	2,229	2,337	2,350	2,358	2,360	2,360	2,360	2,361
Retained earnings	1,726	2,071	2,503	2,749	2,998	3,378	3,723	3,938	4,425	5,418
Net income	188	346	432	246	249	380	345	215	487	993

* Including investment mobilized from other sources.

Source: *IFC Annual Report 2004.*

Multilateral Investment Guarantee Agency—MIGA

Address: 1818 H Street, NW, Washington, DC 20433, USA.
Telephone: (202) 473-6163; **fax:** (202) 522-2630; **internet:** www.miga.org.

MIGA was founded in 1988 as an affiliate of the World Bank. Its mandate is to encourage the flow of foreign direct investment to, and among, developing member countries, through the provision of political risk insurance and investment marketing services to foreign investors and host governments, respectively.

MEMBERS

MIGA has 164 member countries. Membership is open to all countries that are members of the World Bank.

Organization

(March 2005)

MIGA is legally and financially separate from the World Bank. It is supervised by a Council of Governors (comprising one Governor and one Alternate of each member country) and an elected Board of Directors (of no less than 12 members).

President: PAUL WOLFOWITZ (USA) (from 1 June 2005).

Executive Vice-President: YUKIKO OMURA (Japan).

Activities

The convention establishing MIGA took effect in April 1988. Authorized capital was US $1,082m. In April 1998 the Board of Directors approved an increase in MIGA's capital base. A grant of $150m. was transferred from the IBRD as part of the package, while the capital increase (totalling $700m. callable capital and $150m. paid-in capital) was approved by MIGA's Council of Governors in April 1999. A three-year subscription period then commenced, covering the period April 1999–March 2002 (later extended to March 2003). At 30 June 2004 102 countries had subscribed $682.6m. of the new capital increase. At that time total subscriptions to the capital stock amounted to $1,818.0m., of which $347.6m. was paid-in.

MIGA guarantees eligible investments against losses resulting from non-commercial risks, under four main categories:

(i) transfer risk resulting from host government restrictions on currency conversion and transfer;

(ii) risk of loss resulting from legislative or administrative actions of the host government;

(iii) repudiation by the host government of contracts with investors in cases in which the investor has no access to a competent forum;

(iv) the risk of armed conflict and civil unrest.

Before guaranteeing any investment, MIGA must ensure that it is commercially viable, contributes to the development process and is not harmful to the environment. During the fiscal year 1998/99

MIGA and IFC appointed the first Compliance Advisor and Ombudsman to consider the concerns of local communities directly affected by MIGA or IFC sponsored projects. In February 1999 the Board of Directors approved an increase in the amount of political risk insurance available for each project, from US $75m. to $200m.

During the year ending 30 June 2004 MIGA issued 55 investment insurance contracts for 35 projects with a value of US $1,076m., compared with 59 contracts valued at $1,372m. in the previous financial year. The amount of direct investment associated with the contracts in 2003/04 totalled approximately $5,200m. (compared with $3,900m. in 2002/03). Since 1988 the total investment facilitated amounted to some $49,700m. in 85 countries, through 656 contracts.

MIGA works with local insurers, export credit agencies, development finance institutions and other organizations to promote insurance in a country, to ensure a level of consistency among insurers and to support capacity-building within the insurance industry. By mid-2004 MIGA had signed memoranda of understanding with 37 partners.

MIGA also offers technical assistance and investment marketing services to help to promote foreign investment in developing countries and in transitional economies, and to disseminate information on investment opportunities. In October 1995 MIGA established a new network on investment opportunities, which connected investment promotion agencies (IPAs) throughout the world on an electronic information network. The so-called IPA*net* aimed to encourage further investments among developing countries, to provide access to comprehensive information on investment laws and conditions and to strengthen links between governmental, business and financial associations and investors. A new version of IPA*net* was launched in 1997 (and can be accessed at www.ipanet.net). In June 1998 MIGA initiated a new internet-based facility, 'PrivatizationLink', to provide information on investment opportunities resulting from the privatization of industries in developing economies. In October 2000 a specialized facility within the service was established to facilitate investment in Russia (russia.privatizationlink.com). During 2000/01 an office was established in Paris, France, to promote and co-ordinate European investment in developing countries, in particular in Africa and Eastern Europe. In March 2002 MIGA opened a regional office, based in Johannesburg, South Africa. In September a new regional office was inaugurated in Singapore, in order to facilitate foreign investment in Asia.

In April 2002 MIGA launched a new service, 'FDIXchange', to provide potential investors, advisors and financial institutions with up-to-date market analysis and information on foreign direct investment opportunities in emerging economies (accessible at www.fdixchange.com). An FDIXchange Investor Information Development Programme was launched in January 2003. In January 2004 a new FDI Promotion Centre became available on the internet (www.fdipromotion.com) to facilitate information exchange and knowledge-sharing among investment promotion professionals, in particular in developing countries. During 2003/04 MIGA established a new fund, the Invest-in-Development Facility, to enhance the role of foreign investment in attaining the Millennium Development Goals.

In October 2003 MIGA, jointly with Austria, established a European Investor Outreach Facility for Southeastern Europe, to strengthen the capacity of the five western Balkan countries to attract other European investment. The Facility was established as a two-and-a-half year pilot project.

Publications

Annual Report.

Investment Promotion Quarterly.

MIGA News (quarterly).

International Civil Aviation Organization—ICAO

Address: 999 University St, Montréal, QC H3C 5H7, Canada.
Telephone: (514) 954-8219; **fax:** (514) 954-6077; **e-mail:** icaohq@icao.int; **internet:** www.icao.int.

The Convention on International Civil Aviation was signed in Chicago in 1944. As a result, ICAO was founded in 1947 to develop the techniques of international air navigation and to help in the planning and improvement of international air transport.

MEMBERS

ICAO has 188 contracting states.

Organization

(March 2005)

ASSEMBLY

Composed of representatives of all member states, the Assembly is the organization's legislative body and meets at least once every three years. It reviews the work of the organization, sets out the work programme for the next three years, approves the budget and determines members' contributions. The 35th Assembly was held in September–October 2004.

COUNCIL

Composed of representatives of 36 member states, elected by the Assembly. It is the executive body, and establishes and supervises subsidiary technical committees and makes recommendations to member governments; meets in virtually continuous session; elects the President, appoints the Secretary-General, and administers the finances of the organization. The Council is assisted by the Air Navigation Commission (on technical matters), the Air Transport Committee (on economic matters), the Committee on Joint Support of Air Navigation Services and the Finance Committee. The functions of the Council are:

(i) to adopt international standards and recommended practices and incorporate them as annexes to the Convention on International Civil Aviation;

(ii) to arbitrate between member states on matters concerning aviation and implementation of the Convention;

(iii) to investigate any situation which presents avoidable obstacles to development of international air navigation;

(iv) to take whatever steps are necessary to maintain safety and regularity of operation of international air transport;

(v) to provide technical assistance to the developing countries under the UN Development Programme and other assistance programmes.

President of the Council: Dr ASSAD KOTAITE (Lebanon).

SECRETARIAT

The Secretariat, headed by a Secretary-General, is divided into five main divisions: the Air Navigation Bureau, the Air Transport Bureau, the Technical Co-operation Bureau, the Legal Bureau, and the Bureau of Administration and Services.

Secretary-General: TAÏEB CHÉRIF (Algeria).

REGIONAL OFFICES

Asia and Pacific: 252/1 Vipavadee Rangsit Rd, Ladyao, Chatuchak, POB 11, Bangkok 10900, Thailand; tel. (2) 537-8189; fax (2) 537-8199; e-mail icao_apac@bangkok.icao.int; internet www.icao.int/apac; Regional Dir LALIT B. SHAH.

Eastern and Southern Africa: Limuru Rd, Gigiri, POB 46294, Nairobi, Kenya; tel. (20) 622395; fax (20) 623028; e-mail icao@icao.unon.org; internet www.icao.int/esaf; Regional Dir LOT MOLLEL.

European and North Atlantic: 3 bis, Villa Émile-Bergerat, 92522 Neuilly-sur-Seine Cédex, France; tel. 1- 46-41-85-85; fax 1-46-41-85-00; e-mail icaoeurnat@paris.icao.int; internet www.icao.int/eurnat; Regional Dir KARSTEN THEIL.

Middle East: POB 85, Cairo Airport Post Office Terminal One, Cairo 11776, Egypt; tel. (2) 267-4840; fax (2) 2674843; e-mail icaomid@cairo.icao.int; internet www.icao.int/mid; Regional Dir MOHAMED R. M. KHONJI.

North America, Central America and the Caribbean: Apdo Postal 5-377, CP 06500, México, DF, Mexico; tel. (55) 5250-3211; fax (55) 5203-2757; e-mail icao_nacc@mexico.icao.int; internet www.icao.int/nacc; Regional Dir RAYMOND YBARRA.

South America: Apdo 4127, Lima 100, Peru; tel. (1) 575-1646; fax (1) 575-0974; e-mail mail@lima.icao.int; internet www.lima.icao.int; Regional Dir JOSÉ MIGUEL CEPPI.

Western and Central Africa: 15 blvd de la République, BP 2356, Dakar, Senegal; tel. 839-9393; fax 823-6926; e-mail icaodkr@icao.sn; internet www.icao.int/wacaf; Regional Dir AMADOU CHEIFFOU.

Activities

ICAO aims to ensure the safe and orderly growth of civil aviation; to encourage skills in aircraft design and operation; to improve airways, airports and air navigation; to prevent the waste of resources in unreasonable competition; to safeguard the rights of each contracting party to operate international air transport; and to prevent discriminatory practices. ICAO collects and publishes statistics relating to civil aviation.

SAFETY AND SECURITY

ICAO aims to ensure and enhance all aspects of air safety and security. A Global Aviation Safety Plan (GASP) was initiated in 1998 to promote new safety measures. ICAO assists member countries to develop appropriate educational and training activities. It also supports programmes to assist the victims of aircraft accidents. The 32nd Assembly, held in September–October 1998, endorsed the establishment of a Universal Safety Oversight Audit Programme (USOAP), to provide for mandatory, systematic and harmonized safety audits regularly to be undertaken in member states in fields including the airworthiness of aircraft, flight operations and personnel licensing. The Programme became operational on 1 January 1999 with the aim of auditing all member states and compiling an Audit Findings and Differences Database over an initial three-year period. The Programme was subsequently extended, and from 1 January 2005 was expanded to incorporate all safety-related provisions of the Annexes to the Chicago Convention. In June 2002 a Universal Security Audit Programme was launched, as part of the Aviation Security Plan of Action (see below), to help to identify and correct deficiencies in the implementation of security-related standards. The first mandatory security audit was conducted in November; an initial audit of all contracting states was scheduled to have been completed by the end of 2007.

In October 1998 a protocol to the Chicago Convention, prohibiting the use of weapons against civil aircraft in flight, entered into effect, having been adopted in 1984 following an attack on a Korean Airlines passenger flight. During the late 1990s ICAO implemented a programme to address potential malfunctions, resulting from the date change at the start of the new century, of systems affecting the safety, regularity and efficiency of international civil aviation operations; this entailed the harmonization of regional contingency plans and the development of an extensive inventory of air traffic systems and aviation facilities. In 2000 ICAO developed model legislation to cover offences committed on board aircraft by unruly passengers (other than hijacking, sabotage etc., which are already governed by international legislation). Following the major terrorist attacks perpetrated against targets in the USA in September 2001, involving the use of hijacked aircraft as weapons, the 33rd Assembly—held in September–October—adopted a Declaration on the Misuse of Civil

Aircraft as Weapons of Destruction and Other Terrorist Acts involving Civil Aviation. The Declaration urged a review of the Organization's aviation security programme and consideration of the initiation of a programme to audit airport security arrangements and member states civil aviation security programmes. The Assembly also approved the concept of an International Financial Facility for Aviation Safety (IFFAS). In October the Council established a Special Group on Aviation War Risk Insurance to make recommendations on the development of a co-ordinated and long-term approach in this area. A proposal by the Special Group concerning the establishment of a Global Scheme on Aviation War Risk Insurance (Globaltime), to be provided by a non-profit entity with initial multilateral government support, was approved in principle by the Council in May 2002. A high-level ministerial conference, convened under ICAO auspices in February of that year to discuss preventing, combating and eradicating acts of terrorism involving civil aviation, and strengthening the Organization's role in overseeing the adoption and national implementation of security-related standards and procedures, endorsed a global Aviation Security Plan of Action and reaffirmed the responsibility of states to ensure aviation security on their territories. The Plan provided for continued implementation of the USOAP until the end of 2004; development of an effective global response to emerging threats; strengthened security-related provisions of the Convention on International Civil Aviation; and enhanced co-ordination of regional and subregional audit programmes. In June 2003 ICAO published measures for preventing the spread by air travel of Severe Acute Respiratory Syndrome (SARS) and other contagious diseases, based on guide-lines issued by the World Health Organization. ICAO is developing a globally inter-operable system of Machine Readable Travel Documents (MRTDs), incorporating biometric identification data, in order to enhance airport and international security.

NAVIGATION

ICAO's Air Navigation Bureau develops technical studies for the Air Navigation Commission, as well as recommendations for standards and recommended practices relating to the safety, regularity and efficiency of international air navigation. Areas of activity include meteorology, automated data interchange systems, accident investigation and prevention, aviation medicine and air traffic management. In March 1998 the ICAO Council adopted a Global Air Navigation Plan for Communications, Navigation, Surveillance, and Air Traffic Management (CNS/ATM) Systems. In May an international conference was held in Rio de Janeiro, Brazil, to consider implementation of the CNS/ATM systems. The conference urged greater financing and co-operation between states to ensure that the CNS/ATM becomes the basis of a global ATM system. An Air Traffic Management Operational Concept Panel, which was to develop standards and recommend procedures for the development of an integrated ATM system, was convened for the first time in March–April 1999. In October 1998 the Assembly adopted a Charter on the Rights and Obligations of States relating to Global Navigation Satellite Systems (GNSS) to serve as an interim framework on the GNSS. A long-term legal framework on principles governing the GNSS, including a new international convention, remains under consideration. The 11th Air Navigation Conference, convened by ICAO in September–October 2003, in Montréal, endorsed an operational concept for a globally harmonized air navigation system that aimed to enhance safety and reduce airspace and airport congestion.

ENVIRONMENT

ICAO activities with respect to the environment are primarily focused on areas that require a co-ordinated international approach, i.e. aircraft noise and engine emissions. International standards and guide-lines for noise certification of aircraft and international provisions for the regulation of aircraft engine emissions have been adopted and published in Annex 16 to the Chicago Convention. ICAO was recognized in the 1997 Kyoto Protocol to the Framework Convention on Climate Change as the global body through which industrialized nations were to pursue the limitation or reduction of so-called greenhouse gas emissions from international aviation. In 1998 ICAO's Committee on Aviation Environmental Protection recommended a reduction of 16% in the permissible levels of nitrogen oxides emitted by aircraft engines. The new limits, to be applicable

to new engine designs from 2003, were adopted by the ICAO Council in early 1999. In June 2001 the Council adopted a stricter noise standard (applicable from 1 January 2006) for jet and large propeller-driven aircraft, as well as new noise limits for helicopters and new provisions concerning re-certification. In October the Assembly approved a series of measures developed by the Committee concerning a balanced approach to aircraft noise and based on the following elements: quieter aircraft; land-use planning and management in the vicinity of airports; operational procedures for noise abatement; and operating restrictions.

ICAO SPECIFICATIONS

These are contained in annexes to the Chicago Convention, and in three sets of Procedures for Air Navigation Services (PANS Documents). The specifications are periodically revised in keeping with developments in technology and changing requirements. The 18 annexes to the Convention include personnel licensing, rules relating to the conduct of flights, meteorological services, aeronautical charts, air–ground communications, safety specifications, identification, air-traffic control, rescue services, environmental protection, security and the transporting of dangerous goods. Technical Manuals and Circulars are issued to facilitate implementation.

ICAO REGIONAL PLANS

These set out the technical requirements for air navigation facilities in the nine ICAO regions; Regional Offices offer assistance (see addresses above). Because of growth in air traffic and changes in the pattern of air routes, the Plans are periodically amended. ICAO maintains a structure of Planning and Implementation Regional Groups.

TECHNICAL CO-OPERATION

ICAO's Technical Co-operation Bureau promotes the implementation of ICAO Standards and Recommended Practices, including the CNS/ATM and safety oversight measures, and assists developing countries in the execution of various projects, financed by UNDP and other sources. The TRAINAIR programme helps relevant institutions to develop a standard aviation training package, and promotes international co-operation in training and course development.

ICAO works in close co-operation with other UN bodies, such as the World Meteorological Organization, the International Telecommunication Union, the Universal Postal Union, the World Health Organization and the International Maritime Organization. Non-governmental organizations which also participate in ICAO's work include the International Air Transport Association (see p. 428), the Airports Council International (see p. 427), the International Federation of Air Line Pilots' Associations (see p. 387), and the International Council of Aircraft Owner and Pilot Associations.

Finance

ICAO is financed mainly by contributions from member states. The 34th Session of the Assembly, held in September–October 2004, approved a budget allocation of US $64.7m. for the following year, and $65.8m. for 2006.

Publications

Aircraft Accident Digest.

Air Navigation Plans.

Annual Civil Aviation Report.

Civil Aviation Statistics of the World (annually).

ICAO Journal (10 a year, in English, French and Spanish; quarterly digest in Russian).

Lexicon of Terms.

Transition (CNS/ATM newsletter, quarterly).

World of Civil Aviation (annually).

Conventions, agreements, rules of procedures, regulations, technical publications and manuals.

International Fund for Agricultural Development—IFAD

Address: Via del Serafico 107, 00142 Rome, Italy.
Telephone: (06) 54591; **fax:** (06) 5043463; **e-mail:** ifad@ifad.org;
internet: www.ifad.org.

IFAD was established in 1977, following a decision by the 1974 UN World Food Conference, with a mandate to combat hunger and eradicate poverty on a sustainable basis in the low-income, food-deficit regions of the world. Funding operations began in January 1978.

MEMBERS

IFAD has 163 members.

Organization

(March 2005)

GOVERNING COUNCIL

Each member state is represented in the Governing Council (the Fund's highest authority) by a Governor and an Alternate. Sessions are held annually with special sessions as required. The Governing Council elects the President of the Fund (who also chairs the Executive Board) by a two-thirds majority for a four-year term. The President is eligible for re-election.

EXECUTIVE BOARD

Consists of 18 members and 18 alternates, elected by the Governing Council, who serve for three years. The Executive Board is responsible for the conduct and general operation of IFAD and approves loans and grants for projects; it holds three regular sessions each year. An independent Office of Evaluation reports directly to the Board.

The governance structure of the Fund is based on the classification of members. Membership of the Executive Board is distributed as follows: eight List A countries (i.e. industrialized donor countries), four List B (petroleum-exporting developing donor countries), and six List C (recipient developing countries), divided equally among the three Sub-List C categories (i.e. for Africa, Europe, Asia and the Pacific, and Latin America and the Caribbean).

President and Chairman of Executive Board: LENNART BÅGE (Sweden).

Vice-President: CYRIL ENWEZE (Nigeria).

DEPARTMENTS

IFAD has three main administrative departments, each headed by an Assistant President: Finance and Administration; Programme Management (with five regional Divisions and a Technical Advisory Division); and External Affairs (including a Policy Division, Communication Division and a Resource Mobilization Unit). Offices of the General Counsel and of Internal Audit report to the Office of the President and Vice-President. At November 2003 IFAD had 295.5 filled staff positions.

Activities

IFAD provides financing primarily for projects designed to improve food production systems in developing member states and to strengthen related policies, services and institutions. In allocating resources IFAD is guided by: the need to increase food production in the poorest food-deficit countries; the potential for increasing food production in other developing countries; and the importance of improving the nutrition, health and education of the poorest people in developing countries, i.e. small-scale farmers, artisanal fishermen, nomadic pastoralists, indigenous populations, rural women, and the rural landless. All projects emphasize the participation of beneficiaries in development initiatives, both at the local and national level. Issues relating to gender and household food security are incorporated into all aspects of its activities. IFAD is committed to achieving the so-called Millennium Development Goals, pledged by governments attending a special session of the UN General Assembly in September 2000, and, in particular, the objective to reduce by 50% the proportion of people living in extreme poverty by 2015. In 2001 the Fund introduced new measures to improve monitoring and impact evaluation, in particular to assess its contribution to achieving the Millennium Goals. IFAD's Strategic Framework for 2002–06 reiterates its commitment to enabling the rural poor to overcome their poverty. Accordingly, the Fund's efforts were to focus on the following objectives: strengthening the capacity of the rural poor and their organizations; improving equitable access to productive natural resources and technology; and increasing access to financial services and markets. Within this Framework the Fund has also formulated regional strategies for rural poverty reduction, based on a series of regional poverty assessments. In 2003 a new Policy Division was established under the External Affairs Department. The new Division was to co-ordinate policy work at the corporate level and aimed to launch a Policy Forum in 2004, comprising IFAD senior management and staff.

IFAD is a leading repository in the world of knowledge, resources and expertise in the field of rural hunger and poverty alleviation. In 2001 it renewed its commitment to becoming a global knowledge institution for rural poverty-related issues. Through its technical assistance grants, IFAD aims to promote research and capacity-building in the agricultural sector, as well as the development of technologies to increase production and alleviate rural poverty. In recent years IFAD has been increasingly involved in promoting the use of communication technology to facilitate the exchange of information and experience among rural communities, specialized institutions and organizations, and IFAD-sponsored projects. Within the strategic context of knowledge management, IFAD has supported initiatives to support regional electronic networks, such as ENRAP (see below) in Asia and the Pacific and FIDAMERICA in Latin America and the Caribbean, as well as to develop other lines of communication between organizations, local agents and the rural poor.

IFAD is empowered to make both grants and loans. Grants are limited to 7.5% of the resources committed in any one financial year. Loans are available on highly concessionary, intermediate and ordinary terms. Highly concessionary loans carry no interest but have an annual service charge of 0.75% and a repayment period of 40 years, including a 10-year grace period. Intermediate term loans are subject to a variable interest charge, equivalent to 50% of the interest rate charged on World Bank loans, and are repaid over 20 years. Ordinary loans carry a variable interest charge equal to that charged by the World Bank, and are repaid over 15–18 years. In 2003 highly concessionary loans represented some 76% of total lending in that year. In order to increase the impact of its lending resources on food production, the Fund seeks as much as possible to attract other external donors and beneficiary governments as co-financiers of its projects. In 2003 external cofinancing accounted for some 17.5% of all project funding, while domestic contributions, i.e. from recipient governments and other local sources, accounted for almost 25.8%.

At the end of 2003 total IFAD loans approved since 1978 amounted to US $8,072.7m. for 653 projects. During the same period the Fund approved 1,718 research and technical assistance grants, at a cost of $463.0m. In 2003 total IFAD project loans approved amounted to $403.6m. for 25 projects, as follows: $93.5m. for four operations in Asia and the Pacific (or 23.2% of the total committed in that year), $76.8m. for five projects in the Near East and North Africa (19.0%), $84.9m. for seven projects in Western and Central Africa (21.0%), $74.5m. for five projects in Eastern and Southern Africa (18.5%), and $74.0m. for four projects in Latin America and the Caribbean (18.3%). Technical assistance grants amounting to $20.3m. (for research, training and project preparation and development) were awarded, bringing the total financial assistance approved in 2003 to $424.0m., compared with $389.8m. in 2002.

IFAD's development projects usually include a number of components, such as infrastructure (e.g. improvement of water supplies, small-scale irrigation and road construction); input supply (e.g. improved seeds, fertilizers and pesticides); institutional support (e.g. research, training and extension services); and producer incentives (e.g. pricing and marketing improvements). IFAD also attempts to enable the landless to acquire income-generating assets: by increasing the provision of credit for the rural poor, it seeks to free them from dependence on the capital market and to generate productive activities.

In addition to its regular efforts to identify projects and programmes, IFAD organizes special programming missions to certain selected countries to undertake a comprehensive review of the constraints affecting the rural poor, and to help countries to design strategies for the removal of these constraints. In general, projects based on the recommendations of these missions tend to focus on institutional improvements at the national and local level to direct inputs and services to small farmers and the landless rural poor. Monitoring and evaluation missions are also sent to check the progress of projects and to assess the impact of poverty reduction efforts.

The Fund supports projects that are concerned with environmental conservation, in an effort to alleviate poverty that results from the deterioration of natural resources. In addition, it extends environmental assessment grants to review the environmental consequences of projects under preparation. In October 1997 IFAD was appointed to administer the Global Mechanism of the Convention to Combat Desertification in those Countries Experiencing Drought and Desertification, particularly in Africa, which entered into force in December 1996. The Mechanism was envisaged as a means of mobilizing and channelling resources for implementation of the Convention. A series of collaborative institutional arrangements were to be concluded between IFAD, UNDP and the World Bank in order to facilitate the effective functioning of the Mechanism. In May 2001 the Global Environmental Facility approved IFAD as an executing agency.

In February 1998 IFAD inaugurated a new Trust Fund to complement the multilateral debt initiative for Heavily Indebted Poor Countries (HIPCs). The Fund was intended to assist IFAD's poorest members deemed to be eligible under the initiative to channel resources from debt repayments to communities in need. In February 2000 the Governing Council approved full participation by IFAD in the enhanced HIPC debt initiative agreed by the World Bank and IMF in September 1999.

During 1998 the Executive Board endorsed a policy framework for the Fund's provision of assistance in post-conflict situations, with the aim of achieving a continuum from emergency relief to a secure basis from which to pursue sustainable development. In July 2001 IFAD and UNAIDS signed a memorandum of understanding on developing a co-operation agreement. A meeting of technical experts from IFAD, FAO, WFP and UNAIDS, held in December, addressed means of mitigating the impact of HIV/AIDS on food security and rural livelihoods in affected regions. In January 2005 IFAD announced that it aimed to mobilize some US $100m. to assist countries affected by the devastating tsunamis which had struck coastal regions in 11 countries in the Indian Ocean in late December 2004. IFAD was also participating in needs assessments in Indonesia, Sri Lanka and the Maldives, which were to provide the basis for longer-term resource allocation and mobilization.

During the late 1990s IFAD established several partnerships within the agribusiness sector, with a view to improving performance at project level, broadening access to capital markets, and encouraging the advancement of new technologies. Since 1996 it has chaired the Support Group of the Global Forum on Agricultural Research (GFAR), which facilitates dialogue between research centres and institutions, farmers' organizations, non-governmental bodies, the private sector and donors. In October 2001 IFAD became a co-sponsor of the Consultative Group on International Agricultural Research (CGIAR).

Finance

In accordance with the Articles of Agreement establishing IFAD, the Governing Council periodically undertakes a review of the adequacy of resources available to the Fund and may request members to make additional contributions. The sixth replenishment of IFAD funds, covering the period 2003–04 and amounting to US $560m., was approved in February 2003 and became effective in December. The provisional budget for administrative expenses for 2004 amounted to $57m.

Publications

Annual Report.
IFAD Update (2 a year).
Rural Poverty Report 2001.
Staff Working Papers (series).

International Labour Organization—ILO

Address: 4 route des Morillons, 1211 Geneva 22, Switzerland.
Telephone: (22) 7996111; **fax:** (22) 7988685; **e-mail:** ilo@ilo.org; **internet:** www.ilo.org.

ILO was founded in 1919 to work for social justice as a basis for lasting peace. It carries out this mandate by promoting decent living standards, satisfactory conditions of work and pay and adequate employment opportunities. Methods of action include the creation of international labour standards; the provision of technical co-operation services; and research and publications on social and labour matters. In 1946 ILO became a specialized agency associated with the UN. It was awarded the Nobel Peace Prize in 1969. ILO's tripartite structure gives representation to employers' and workers' organizations alongside governments.

MEMBERS

ILO has 177 members.

Organization

(March 2005)

INTERNATIONAL LABOUR CONFERENCE

The supreme deliberative body of ILO, the Conference meets annually in Geneva, with a session devoted to maritime questions when necessary; it is attended by about 2,000 delegates, advisers and observers. National delegations are composed of two government delegates, one employers' delegate and one workers' delegate. Non-governmental delegates can speak and vote independently of the views of their national government. The conference elects the Governing Body and adopts International Labour Conventions and Recommendations. Every two years the Conference adopts the ILO Budget.

The President and Vice-Presidents hold office for the term of the Conference only.

GOVERNING BODY

ILO's executive council meets three times a year in Geneva to decide policy and programmes. It is composed of 28 government members, 14 employers' members and 14 workers' members. Ten of the titular government seats are held permanently by 'states of chief industrial importance': Brazil, the People's Republic of China, France, Germany, India, Italy, Japan, Russia, the United Kingdom and the USA. The remaining 18 are elected from other countries every three years. Employers' and workers' members are elected as individuals, not as national candidates.

Among the Committees formed by the Governing Body are: the Committee on Freedom of Association; the Programme, Financial and Administrative Committee; the Building Sub-Committee; the Committee on Legal Issues and International Labour Standards; the Sub-Committee on Multinational Enterprises; the Working Party on Policy regarding the Revision of Standards; the Committee on Employment and Social Policy; the Committee on Sectoral and Technical Meetings and Related Issues; the Committee on Technical Co-operation; and the Working Party on the Social Dimension of Globalization.

Chairperson: (2004–05) PHILIPPE SÉGUIN (France).

Employers' Vice-Chairperson: DANIEL FUNES DE RIOJA (Argentina).

Workers' Vice-Chairperson: Sir ROY TROTMAN (Barbados).

INTERNATIONAL LABOUR OFFICE

The International Labour Office is ILO's secretariat, operational headquarters and publishing house. It is staffed in Geneva and in the field by about 2,250 people of some 120 nationalities. Operations are decentralized to regional, area and branch offices in nearly 40 countries.

Director-General: JUAN O. SOMAVÍA (Chile).

REGIONAL OFFICES

Africa: BP 3960, Abidjan 01, Côte d'Ivoire; tel. 20-21-26-39; fax 22-21-28-80; e-mail abidjan@ilo.org.

Latin America and the Caribbean: Apdo Postal 14–124, Lima, Peru; tel. (1) 6150300; fax (1); tel. 6150400; e-mail oit@oit.org.pe.

Arab States: POB 11-4088, Beirut, Lebanon; tel. (1) 752400; fax (1) 752405; e-mail beirut@ilo.org.

Asia and the Pacific: POB 2-349, Bangkok 10200, Thailand; tel. 2881234; fax 2881735; e-mail bangkok@ilo.org.

Europe and Central Asia: 4 route des Morillons, 1211 Geneva 22, Switzerland; tel. (22) 7996666; fax (22) 7996061; e-mail europe@ilo.org.

Activities

ILO has identified the following four areas of activity as strategic objectives: to promote and realize standards and fundamental principles and rights at work; to create greater opportunities for women and men to secure decent employment and income; to enhance the coverage and effectiveness of social protection for all; and to strengthen tripartism and social dialogue.

STANDARDS AND FUNDAMENTAL PRINCIPLES AND RIGHTS AT WORK

One of ILO's primary functions is the adoption by the International Labour Conference of conventions and recommendations setting minimum labour standards. Through ratification by member states, conventions create binding obligations to put their provisions into effect. Recommendations provide guidance as to policy and practice. By November 2004 a total of 185 conventions and 195 recommendations had been adopted, ranging over a wide field of social and labour matters, based on the following principles: freedom of association, the abolition of forced and child labour, and the elimination of discrimination in employment promotion, training and the protection of workers. Together they form the International Labour Code. By late 2004 7,243 ratifications of the conventions had been registered by member states. The Committee of Experts on the Application of Conventions and Recommendations and the Conference Committee on the Application of Standards monitor the adoption of international labour standards. In June 1998 a Declaration on Fundamental Principles and Rights at Work, establishing eight fundamental labour standards, was adopted by the Conference. All member states were obliged to observe the four principles upon which these standards were based (see above), whether or not they had ratified the corresponding international conventions.

From 1996 ILO resolved to strengthen its efforts, working closely with UNICEF, to encourage member states to ratify and to implement relevant international standards on child labour. In June 1999 the International Labour Conference adopted the Worst Forms of Child Labour Convention (No. 182); the convention entered into force in November 2000. By November 2004 it had been ratified by 150 states. The Organization helped to organize an International Conference on Child Labour, convened in The Hague, Netherlands, in February 2002. In May ILO issued a global study entitled *A Future without Child Labour*, in which it estimated that one-eighth of the world's children were exposed to the worst forms of child labour. The first World Day against Child Labour, sponsored by ILO, was held on 12 June; it has subsequently been held annually. By 2004 more than 90 countries were taking part in ILO's International Programme for the Elimination of Child Labour (IPEC, established in 1992), with emphasis placed on the elimination of the most severe forms of labour such as hazardous working conditions and occupations, child prostitution and trafficking of children. In addition, IPEC gives special attention to children who are particularly vulnerable, for example those under 12 years of age.

In May 2003 ILO issued the first global report on discrimination at work, *Time for Equality at Work*, compiled as a follow-up to the 1998 Declaration on Fundamental Principles and Rights at Work.

EMPLOYMENT AND INCOME

ILO aims to monitor, examine and report on the situation and trends in employment throughout the world, and considers the effects on employment and social justice of economic trade, investment and related phenomena. In 2003 ILO estimated that some 185.9m. workers world-wide (6.2% of the global labour force) were unemployed, and in 2004 estimated that 550m. people, or 20% of people employed world-wide, were living on less than US $1 a day. In February 2002 ILO established a World Commission on the Social Dimension of Globalization to consider means of utilizing economic globalization to stimulate economic growth and reduce poverty. The Commission issued its final report, entitled *A Fair Globalization*, in February 2004. It was endorsed by the 92nd International Labour Conference, held in June. In March 2003 ILO adopted the Global Employment Agenda, a comprehensive framework for managing changes to employment derived from the developing global economy, through investment in knowledge and skills, maintaining a healthy labour market and ensuring adequate social safety nets.

ILO's programme sector on skills, knowledge and employability supports governments in structuring policies for improved investment in learning and training for enhanced employability, productivity and social inclusion. The programme focuses on promoting access to training and decent work for specific groups, such as youths, the disabled, and workers in the informal economy, and on protecting the rights of the elderly. The Job Creation and Enterprise Development Programme aims to assist governments, employers, workers and other related groups with fostering a successful business environment, for example through the identification and implementation of appropriate policies, legal frameworks and management strategies, the promotion of access to business development

and training services, and the promotion of local economic development programmes. It also incorporates a specific programme to promote the development of micro and small enterprises, in co-operation with governments, communities and other social partners. ILO's Gender Promotion Programme aims to promote effective gender mainstreaming and is responsible for a global programme for the creation of more and better jobs for women and men. The programme assists countries to develop and implement National Action Plans to achieve this objective. A programme on crisis response and reconstruction addresses the effect on employment of armed conflicts, natural disasters, social movements or political transitions, and financial and economic disruptions. The impact of current global financial and economic trends on employment creation, poverty alleviation and social exclusion are addressed by ILO's Social Finance Programme. The programme works to reduce vulnerability, to create jobs through enterprise development, and to make financial policies more employment-sensitive, for example by providing information on microfinance and promoting microfinance institutions, and by conducting research on the impact of financial sector liberalization on the poor.

The Multinational Enterprise Programme is responsible for the promotion of and follow-up to the Tripartite Declaration of Principles concerning Multinational Enterprises and Social Policy, which was adopted in 1977 and amended in 2000. The Declaration provides international guide-lines, agreed by governments and employers' and workers' organizations, on investment policy and practice. The programme is also responsible for co-ordinating work on corporate social responsibility, as well as for ILO's participation in the Global Compact, an initiative of the UN Secretary-General, which was inaugurated in 2000 comprising leaders in the fields of business, labour and civil society who undertook to promote human rights, the fundamental principles of ILO, and protection of the environment.

ILO maintains technical relations with the IMF, the World Bank, OECD, the WTO and other international organizations on global economic issues, international and national strategies for employment, structural adjustment, and labour market and training policies. A number of employment policy reviews have been carried out by ILO within the framework of the UN Administrative Committee on Co-ordination Task Force on Full Employment and Sustainable Livelihoods.

SOCIAL PROTECTION

Access to an adequate level of social protection is recognized in ILO's 1944 Declaration of Philadelphia, as well as in a number of international labour standards, as a basic right of all individuals. ILO aims to enable countries to extend social protection to all groups in society and to improve working conditions and safety at work. The fundamental premise of ILO's programme sector on socio-economic security is that basic security for all is essential for productive work and human dignity in the future global economy. The achievement of basic security is deemed to entail the attainment of basic humanitarian needs, including universal access to health services and a decent level of education. The programme aims to address the following concerns: what constitutes socio-economic security and insecurity in member countries; identifying the sources of such insecurity; and identifying economic, labour and social policies that could improve socio-economic security while promoting sustainable economic growth. The programme focuses on the following dimensions of work-based security: the labour market (the provision of adequate employment opportunities); employment (for example, protection against dismissal); occupational security (the opportunity to develop a career); work (protection against accidents, illness and stress at work); skills; income ; and representation (the right to collective representation in the labour market, through independent trade unions and employers associations, etc.). ILO's Social Security Policy and Development Branch assists member states and constituents in the design, reform and implementation of social security policies based on the principles embodied in international labour standards, with a special focus on developing strategies to extend social security coverage. The Branch provides general research and analysis of social security issues; extends technical assistance to member states for designing, reforming and expanding social security schemes; provides services to enable community-based organizations to develop their own social security systems; promotes and oversees the implementation of ILO standards on social security; develops training programmes and materials; and disseminates information. The Financial, Actuarial and Statistical Services Branch aims to improve the financial planning, management and governance of national social security schemes and social protection systems. In June 2003 ILO inaugurated a Global Campaign on Social Security and Coverage for All, with a particular focus on the informal economy. ILO estimates that only one-fifth of the world's population has sufficient social security coverage. The key operational tool of the Campaign is ILO's STEP (Strategies and Tools against Social Exclusion and Poverty) Programme which undertakes field work, research, training and the dissemination of knowledge to help to extend social protection and combat social exclusion.

ILO's Programme on Safety and Health at Work and the Environment aims to protect workers in hazardous occupations; to provide protection to vulnerable groups of workers outside the scope of normal protection measures; to improve the capacity of governments and employers' and workers' organizations to address workers' well-being, extend the scope of occupational health care etc.; and to ensure that policy-makers recognize and document the social and economic impact of implementing measures that enhance workers' protection. ILO Guidelines on Occupational Safety and Health Management Systems (ILO-OSH 2001) provides a framework of action at an international, national and organizational level. ILO's Conditions of Work Branch conducts research and provides advocacy, training and technical co-operation to governments and employers' and workers' organizations in areas such as wages, working time, maternity protection and life outside of work. The International Migration Branch focuses on protecting the rights, and promoting the integration, of migrant workers, forging international consensus on the management of migration, and furthering knowledge of international migration. In June 2004 the 92nd International Labour Conference adopted a plan of action providing for the development of a multilateral framework to extend labour protection standards to migrant workers. The framework was to include international guide-lines on labour inspection, the promotion of decent work, recruitment, and hazardous employment. ILO's Global Programme on HIV/AIDS and the World of Work, formally established in November 2000, issued a code of practice in May 2001, focusing on prevention, management and mitigation of the impact of HIV/AIDS on the world of work, support for HIV/AIDS-affected workers, and eliminating discrimination on the basis of perceived HIV status. ILO is a co-sponsor (with UNICEF, UNDP, UNFPA, UNESCO, WHO, the World Bank, WFP, UNODC and UNHCR) of the Joint UN Programme on HIV/AIDS (UNAIDS), which was established on 1 January 1996 to co-ordinate and strengthen world-wide action against HIV/AIDS. In July 2004 an ILO report assessed the financial cost of HIV/AIDS in terms of loss of output and estimated the impact of the epidemic on the global labour force.

SOCIAL DIALOGUE

This area was identified as one of the four strategic objectives in order to concentrate and reinforce ILO's support for strengthening the process of tripartism, the role and activities of its tripartite constituents (i.e. governments, employers and workers' organizations), and, in particular, their capacity to engage in and to promote the use of social dialogue. ILO recognizes that the enactment of labour laws, and ensuring their effective enforcement, collective bargaining and other forms of co-operation are important means of promoting social justice. It aims to assist governments and employers' and workers' organizations to establish sound labour relations, to adapt labour laws to meet changing economic and social needs, and to improve labour administration.

The Social Dialogue, Labour Law and Labour Administration Department maintains an International Observatory of Labour Law which provides information concerning national labour legislation and facilitates the dissemination of information regarding development in labour law throughout the world. The Department also supports the training and professional development of labour court judges and publishes the proceedings of meetings of European labour court judges.

The 91st International Labour Conference, held in June 2003, focused special attention on reports of ongoing infringements of, and continued failure over several years to implement, the Freedom of Association and Protection of the Right to Organize Convention, 1948 (No. 87) in Belarus and Myanmar. The Conference urged the Belarus Government not to interfere in the internal affairs of trade unions. A commission to examine alleged abuses of trade union rights in that country was established in November. In November 2004 ILO's Governing Body resolved to send a high level mission to Myanmar to resolve outstanding issues relating to allegations of forced labour. A Committee on Freedom of Association examines allegations of abuses committed against trade union organizations and reports to the Governing Body.

INSTITUTES

International Institute for Labour Studies (IILS): 4 route des Morillons, 1211 Geneva 22, Switzerland; tel. (22) 7996128; fax (22) 7998542; e-mail inst@ilo.org; established in 1960 and based at ILO's Geneva headquarters, the Institute promotes the study and discussion of policy issues of concern to ILO and its constituents, i.e. government, employers and workers. The core theme of the Institute's activities is the interaction between labour institutions, development and civil society in a global economy. It identifies emerging social and labour issues by developing new areas for research and action, and encourages dialogue on social policy between the tripartite constituency of ILO and the international academic community and other experts. The Institute maintains research networks, conducts courses, seminars and social policy forums, and supports internships and visiting scholar and internship programmes. The ILO Director-General is Chairman of the Board of the Institute.

International Training Centre of ILO: Corso Unità d'Italia 125, 10127 Turin, Italy; tel. (011) 693-6372; fax (011) 693-6350; internet www.itcilo.it; the Centre became operational in 1965. It provides programmes for directors in charge of technical and vocational institutions, training officers, senior and middle-level managers in private and public enterprises, trade union leaders, and technicians, primarily from the developing regions of the world. Since 1991 the Centre has been increasingly used by UN agencies to provide training for improving the management of development and for building national capacities to sustain development programmes. The ILO Director-General is Chairman of the Board of the Centre.

Finance

The proposed regular budget for the two years 2004–05 was US $448.0m.

Publications

(in English, French and Spanish unless otherwise indicated)

Bulletin of Labour Statistics (quarterly).

Global Employment Trends.

International Labour Review (quarterly).

International studies, surveys, works of practical guidance or reference (on questions of social policy, manpower, industrial relations, working conditions, social security, training, management development, etc.)).

Key Indicators of the Labour Market.

Labour Law Documents (selected labour and social security laws and regulations; 3 a year).

Official Bulletin (3 a year).

Reports (for the annual sessions of the International Labour Conference, etc. (also in Arabic, Chinese and Russian).

World Employment Report (every 2–3 years).

World Labour Report (every 2 years).

World of Work (magazine issued in several languages; 5 a year).

Yearbook of Labour Statistics.

Also maintains a database on international labour standards, ILOLEX, and a database on national labour law, NATLEX, in electronic form.

International Maritime Organization—IMO

Address: 4 Albert Embankment, London, SE1 7SR, United Kingdom.

Telephone: (20) 7735-7611; **fax:** (20) 7587-3210; **e-mail:** info@imo.org; **internet:** www.imo.org.

The Inter-Governmental Maritime Consultative Organization (IMCO) began operations in 1959, as a specialized agency of the UN to facilitate co-operation among governments on technical matters affecting international shipping. Its main functions are the achievement of safe and efficient navigation, and the control of pollution caused by ships and craft operating in the marine environment. IMCO became IMO in 1982.

MEMBERS

IMO has 164 members and three associate members.

Organization

(March 2005)

ASSEMBLY

The Assembly consists of delegates from all member countries, who each have one vote. Associate members and observers from other governments and the international agencies are also present. Regular sessions are held every two years. The Assembly is responsible for the election of members to the Council and approves the appointment of the Secretary-General of the Secretariat. It considers reports from all subsidiary bodies and decides the action to be taken on them; it votes the agency's budget and determines the work programme and financial policy. The 23rd regular session of the Assembly, held in London in November–December 2003, endorsed the establishment of a Member State Audit Scheme and also adopted: guide-lines on places of refuge for ships in need of assistance and a related resolution on maritime assistance; guide-lines on ship recycling; a resolution on the development and improvement of partnership arrangements for technical co-operation; and a strategic plan for the Organization covering the six-year period 2004–10.

The Assembly also recommends to members measures to promote maritime safety and and security; and to prevent and control maritime pollution from ships.

COUNCIL

The Council is the governing body of the Organization between the biennial sessions of the Assembly. Its members, representatives of 40 states, are elected by the Assembly for a term of two years. The Council appoints the Secretary-General; transmits reports by the subsidiary bodies, including the Maritime Safety Committee, to the Assembly, and reports on the work of the Organization generally; submits budget estimates and financial statements with comments and recommendations to the Assembly. The Council normally meets twice a year.

Facilitation Committee: Constituted by the Council in May 1972 as a subsidiary body, this Committee deals with measures to facilitate maritime travel and transport and matters arising from the 1965 Facilitation Convention. Membership is open to all IMO member states.

MARITIME SAFETY COMMITTEE

The Maritime Safety Committee is open to all IMO members. The Committee meets at least once a year and submits proposals to the Assembly on technical matters affecting the safety of shipping. In December 2002 a conference of contracting states to the 1974 International Convention on Safety of Life at Sea (see below) adopted a series of security measures relating to the international maritime and port industries that had been formulated by the Safety Committee in view of the major terrorist attacks perpetrated against targets in the USA in September 2001.

Sub-Committees:

Bulk Liquids and Gases*
Carriage of Dangerous Goods,
  Solid Cargoes and Containers
Fire Protection
Flag State Implementation*
Radiocommunications and
  Search and Rescue

Safety of Navigation
Ship Design and
  Equipment
Stability and Load Lines and
  Fishing Vessel Safety
Standards of Training and
  Watchkeeping

*Also sub-committees of the Marine Environment Protection Committee.

LEGAL COMMITTEE

Established by the Council in June 1967 to deal initially with problems connected with the loss of the tanker *Torrey Canyon,* and subsequently with any legal problems laid before IMO. Membership open to all IMO member states.

MARINE ENVIRONMENT PROTECTION COMMITTEE

Established by the eighth Assembly (1973) to co-ordinate IMO's work on the prevention and control of marine pollution from ships, and to assist IMO in its consultations with other UN bodies, and with international organizations and expert bodies in the field of marine pollution. Membership is open to all IMO members.

TECHNICAL CO-OPERATION COMMITTEE

Evaluates the implementation of projects for which IMO is the executing agency, and generally reviews IMO's technical assistance programmes. Established in 1965 as a subsidiary body of the Council, and formally institutionalized by means of an amendment to the IMO constitution in 1984. Its membership is open to all IMO member states.

SECRETARIAT

The Secretariat consists of the Secretary-General and a staff appointed by the Secretary-General and recruited on as wide a geographical basis as possible.

Secretary-General: EFTHIMIOS MITROPOULOS (Greece).

Divisions of the Secretariat:

Administrative
Conference
Legal Affairs and External
  Relations

Marine Environment
Maritime Safety
Technical Co-operation

Activities

In addition to the work of its committees and sub-committees, the organization works in connection with the following Conventions, of which it is the depository:

Convention on Facilitation of International Maritime Traffic, 1965. Came into force in March 1967.

International Convention on Load Lines, 1966. Came into force in July 1968. Revised protocol came into force in January 2005.

International Convention on Tonnage Measurement of Ships, 1969. Convention embodies a universal system for measuring ships' tonnage. Came into force in 1982.

International Convention relating to Intervention on the High Seas in Cases of Oil Pollution Casualties, 1969. Came into force in May 1975. A Protocol adopted in 1973 came into force in 1983.

International Convention on Civil Liability for Oil Pollution Damage, 1969. Came into force in June 1975. Protocol of 1992 came into force in May 1996.

International Convention on the Establishment of an International Fund for Compensation for Oil Pollution Damage, 1971. Came into force in October 1978. Protocol of 1992 came into force in May 1996.

Convention relating to Civil Liability in the Field of Maritime Carriage of Nuclear Material, 1971. Came into force in 1975.

Special Trade Passenger Ships Agreement, 1971. Came into force in 1974.

Convention on the International Regulations for Preventing Collisions at Sea, 1972. Came into force in July 1977.

Convention on the Prevention of Marine Pollution by Dumping of Wastes and Other Matter, 1972. Came into force in August 1975. Extended to include a ban on low-level nuclear waste in November 1993; came into force in February 1994.

International Convention for Safe Containers, 1972. Came into force in September 1977.

International Convention for the Prevention of Pollution from Ships, 1973 (as modified by the Protocol of 1978, known as MARPOL 73/78). Came into force in October 1983. Extended to include regulations to prevent air pollution in September 1997; amendments will come into force 12 months after 15 countries whose combined fishing fleets constitute 50% of the world's merchant fleet have become parties thereto.

International Convention on Safety of Life at Sea (SOLAS), 1974. Came into force in May 1980. A Protocol drawn up in 1978 came into force in May 1981. Numerous extensions and amendments.

Athens Convention relating to the Carriage of Passengers and their Luggage by Sea, 1974. Came into force in April 1987.

Convention on the International Maritime Satellite Organization, 1976. Came into force in July 1979.

Convention on Limitation of Liability for Maritime Claims, 1976. Came into force in December 1986. A Protocol came into force in May 2004.

International Convention for the Safety of Fishing Vessels, Torremolinos, 1977. Will come into force 12 months after 15 countries whose combined fishing fleets constitute 50% of world fishing fleets of 24 metres in length and over have become parties thereto.

International Convention on Standards of Training, Certification and Watchkeeping for Seafarers, 1978. Came into force in April 1984; restructured by amendments that entered into force in February 1997.

International Convention on Maritime Search and Rescue, 1979. Came into force in June 1985.

International Convention for the Suppression of Unlawful Acts against the Safety of International Shipping, 1988. Came into force in March 1992.

Protocol for the Suppression of Unlawful Acts against the Safety of Fixed Platform located on the Continental Shelf, 1988. Came into force in March 1992.

International Convention on Salvage, 1989. Came into force in July 1996.

International Convention on Oil Pollution, Preparedness, Response and Co-operation, 1990. Came into force on 13 May 1995.

International Convention on Liability and Compensation for Damage in Connection with the Carriage of Hazardous and Noxious Substances by Sea, 1996. Will come into force 18 months after 12 states of which four have not less than 2m. units of gross tonnage have become parties thereto.

International Convention on Civil Liability for Bunker Oil Pollution Damage, 2001.

Convention on Control of Harmful Anti-fouling Systems on Ships, 2001. Will enter into force 12 months after 25 states representing 25% of the world's merchant shipping tonnage have become parties thereto.

International Convention for the Control and Management of Ships' Ballast Water and Sediments, 2004. Will come into force 12 months after 30 states representing not less than 35% of the world's merchant shipping tonnage have become parties thereto.

Port State Control Agreements: Paris Memorandum of Understanding (MOU) on Port State Control, 1982; Viña del Mar Agreement, 1992; Tokyo MOU, 1993; Caribbean MOU, 1996; Mediterranean MOU, 1997; Indian Ocean MOU, 1998; Abuja MOU, 1999; Black Sea, MOU, 2000.

TRAINING INSTITUTES

IMO Maritime Law Institute—IMLI: POB 31, Msida, MSD 01, Malta; tel. 319343; fax 343092; e-mail info@imli.org; internet www.imli.org; provides degree courses, other training courses, study and research facilities for specialists in maritime law; promotes the development and dissemination of knowledge and expertise in the international legal regime of merchant shipping and related areas; Dir Prof. DAVID ATTARD.

International Maritime Academy—IMA: via E. Weiss 15, 34127 Trieste, Italy; tel. (040) 350829; fax (040) 350322; e-mail imoima@ imoima.org; internet www.imoima.org; f. 1988; provides postgraduate training for seafarers and onshore staff employed in maritime-related fields; Dir Adm. FRANCESCO SPANIO.

World Maritime University—WMU: POB 500, Citadellsvägen 29, 201 24 Malmö, Sweden; tel. (40) 356300; fax (40) 128442; e-mail info@wmu.se; internet www.wmu.se; f. by IMO in 1983; offers postgraduate courses in maritime disciplines, a doctoral programme and professional development courses; undertakes various research projects; Pres. Dr KARL LAUBSTEIN (Canada); Registrar B. P. BROWNE (USA); publs *WMU Newsletter*, *WMU Handbook*, *WMU Journal of Maritime Affairs*, several books on maritime issues.

OTHER AFFILIATED BODIES

Regional Marine Pollution Emergency Response Centre for the Mediterranean Sea—REMPEC: Manoel Island, Gzira GZR 03, Malta; tel. 21337296; fax 21339951; e-mail rempec@rempec.org; internet www.rempec.org; f. 1976 as the Regional Oil Combating Centre for the Mediterranean Sea; administered by IMO in conjunction with the Regional Seas Programme of the UN Environment Programme ; aims to develop measures to combat pollution in the Mediterranean; Dir ROBERTO PATRUNO.

Regional Marine Pollution Emergency Information and Training Center for the Wider Caribbean Region: Fokkerweg 26, Willemstad Curacao, Netherlands Antilles; tel. 461-4012; fax 461-1996; e-mail uneprcuja@cwjamaica.com; internet www .rempeeitic.org; f. 1995; aims to help prevent and respond to major pollution incidents in the region's marine environment; administered by IMO in conjunction with the Regional Seas Programme of the UN Environment Programme .

Finance

Contributions are received from the member states. The budget appropriation for the two years 2004–05 amounted to £46.2m.

Publications

IMO News (quarterly).

Numerous specialized publications, including international conventions of which IMO is depositary.

International Monetary Fund—IMF

Address: 700 19th St, NW, Washington, DC 20431, USA.
Telephone: (202) 623-7300; **fax:** (202) 623-6278; **e-mail:** publicaffairs@imf.org; **internet:** www.imf.org.

The IMF was established at the same time as the World Bank in December 1945, to promote international monetary co-operation, to facilitate the expansion and balanced growth of international trade and to promote stability in foreign exchange.

MEMBERS

The IMF has 184 members.

Organization

(March 2005)

Managing Director: RODRIGO DE RATO Y FIGAREDO (Spain).

First Deputy Managing Director: ANNE KRUEGER (USA).

Deputy Managing Directors: TAKATOSHI KATO (Japan), AGUSTÍN CARSTENS (Mexico).

BOARD OF GOVERNORS

The highest authority of the Fund is exercised by the Board of Governors, on which each member country is represented by a Governor and an Alternate Governor. The Board normally meets once a year. The Board of Governors has delegated many of its powers to the Executive Directors. However, the conditions governing the admission of new members, adjustment of quotas and the election of Executive Directors, as well as certain other important powers, remain the sole responsibility of the Board of Governors. The voting power of each member on the Board of Governors is related to its quota in the Fund (see table below).

In September 1999 the Board of Governors adopted a resolution to transform the Interim Committee of the Board of Governors (established 1974) into the International Monetary and Financial Committee (IMFC). The IMFC, which held its inaugural meeting in April 2000, comprises 24 members, representing the same countries or groups of countries as those on the Board of Executive Directors (see below). It advises and reports to the Board on matters relating to the management and adaptation of the international monetary and financial system, sudden disturbances that might threaten the system and proposals to amend the Articles of Agreement, but has no decision-making authority.

The Development Committee (the Joint Ministerial Committee of the Boards of Governors of the World Bank and the IMF on the Transfer of Real Resources to Developing Countries, created in 1974, with a structure similar to that of the IMFC) reviews development policy issues and financing requirements.

BOARD OF EXECUTIVE DIRECTORS

The 24-member Board of Executive Directors, responsible for the day-to-day operations of the Fund, is in continuous session in Washington, under the chairmanship of the Fund's Managing Director or Deputy Managing Directors. The USA, the United Kingdom, Germany, France and Japan each appoint one Executive Director. There is also one Executive Director each from the People's Republic of China, Russia and Saudi Arabia, while the remainder are elected by groups of the remaining countries. As in the Board of Governors, the voting power of each member is related to its quota in the Fund, but in practice the Executive Directors normally operate by consensus.

The Managing Director of the Fund serves as head of its staff, which is organized into departments by function and area. At 31 December 2003 the Fund staff employed about 2,700 staff members from 141 countries.

Activities

The purposes of the IMF, as defined in the Articles of Agreement, are:

(i) To promote international monetary co-operation through a permanent institution which provides the machinery for consultation and collaboration on monetary problems;

(ii) To facilitate the expansion and balanced growth of international trade, and to contribute thereby to the promotion and maintenance of high levels of employment and real income and to the development of members' productive resources;

(iii) To promote exchange stability, to maintain orderly exchange arrangements among members, and to avoid competitive exchange depreciation;

(iv) To assist in the establishment of a multilateral system of payments in respect of current transactions between members and in the elimination of foreign exchange restrictions which hamper the growth of trade;

(v) To give confidence to members by making the general resources of the Fund temporarily available to them, under adequate safeguards, thus providing them with the opportunity to correct maladjustments in their balance of payments, without resorting to measures destructive of national or international prosperity;

(vi) In accordance with the above, to shorten the duration of and lessen the degree of disequilibrium in the international balances of payments of members.

In joining the Fund, each country agrees to co-operate with the above objectives. In accordance with its objective of facilitating the expansion of international trade, the IMF encourages its members to accept the obligations of Article VIII, Sections two, three and four, of the Articles of Agreement. Members that accept Article VIII undertake to refrain from imposing restrictions on the making of payments and transfers for current international transactions and from engaging in discriminatory currency arrangements or multiple currency practices without IMF approval. By January 2005 161 members had accepted Article VIII status.

The financial crises of the late 1990s, notably in several Asian countries, Brazil and Russia, contributed to widespread discussions concerning the strengthening of the international monetary system. In April 1998 the Executive Board identified the following fundamental aspects of the debate: reinforcing international and domestic financial systems; strengthening IMF surveillance; promoting greater availability and transparency of information regarding member countries' economic data and policies; emphasizing the central role of the IMF in crisis management; and establishing effective procedures to involve the private sector in forestalling or resolving financial crises. During 1999/2000 the Fund implemented several measures in connection with its ongoing efforts to appraise and reinforce the global financial architecture, including, in March 2000, the adoption by the Executive Board of a strengthened framework to safeguard the use of IMF resources. During 2000 the Fund established the IMF Center, in Washington, DC, which aimed to promote awareness and understanding of its activities. In September the Fund's new Managing Director announced his intention to focus and streamline the principles of conditionality (which links Fund financing with the implementation of specific economic policies by the recipient countries) as part of the wider reform of the international financial system. A comprehensive review was undertaken, during which the issue was considered by public forums and representatives of civil society. New guide-lines on conditionality, which,*inter alia*, aimed to promote national ownership of policy reforms and to introduce specific criteria for the implementation of conditions given different states' circumstances, were approved by the Executive Board in September 2002. In 2000/01 the Fund established an International Capital Markets Department to improve its understanding of financial markets and a separate Consultative Group on capital markets to serve as a forum for regular dialogue between the Fund and representatives of the private sector.

In 2002 a position of Director for Special Operations was created to enhance the Fund's ability to respond to critical situations affecting member countries. In February the newly-appointed Director immediately assumed leadership of the staff team working with the authorities in Argentina to help that country to overcome its extreme economic and social difficulties. In September the IMFC approved further detailed consideration of a sovereign debt restructuring mechanism (SDRM), which aimed to establish a procedure to enable countries with an unsustainable level of debt to renegotiate loans more effectively. In January 2003 the IMF hosted a conference for representatives from the financial sector and civil society and other public officials and academics to discuss aspects of the SDRM. In April, after further discussion of the issue by the Board of Directors, the IMFC stated that the SDRM would not be implemented, although other means of orderly resolution of financial crises were to remain under consideration. In their meeting the Directors determined that the Fund promote more actively the use of Collective Action Clauses in international bond contracts, as a voluntary measure to facilitate debt restructuring should the need arise.

SURVEILLANCE

Under its Articles of Agreement, the Fund is mandated to oversee the effective functioning of the international monetary system. Accordingly, the Fund aims to exercise firm surveillance over the exchange rate policies of member states and to assess whether a country's economic situation and policies are consistent with the objectives of sustainable development and domestic and external stability. The Fund's main tools of surveillance are regular, bilateral consultations with member countries conducted in accordance with Article IV of the Articles of Agreement, which cover fiscal and monetary policies, balance of payments and external debt developments, as well as policies that affect the economic performance of a country, such as the labour market, social and environmental issues and good governance, and aspects of the country's capital accounts, and finance and banking sectors. In April 1997, in an effort to improve the value of surveillance by means of increased transparency, the Executive Board agreed to the voluntary issue of Press Information Notices (PINs) (on the internet and in *IMF Economic Reviews),* following each member's Article IV consultation with the Board, to those member countries wishing to make public the Fund's views. Other background papers providing information on and analysis of economic developments in individual countries continued to be made available. In addition, World Economic Outlook discussions are held, normally twice a year, by the Executive Board to assess policy implications from a multilateral perspective and to monitor global developments.

The rapid decline in the value of the Mexican peso in late 1994 and the financial crisis in Asia, which became apparent in mid-1997, focused attention on the importance of IMF surveillance of the economies and financial policies of member states and prompted the Fund to enhance the effectiveness of its surveillance and to encourage the full and timely provision of data by member countries in order to maintain fiscal transparency. In April 1996 the IMF established the Special Data Dissemination Standard (SDDS), which was intended to improve access to reliable economic statistical information for member countries that have, or are seeking, access to international capital markets. In March 1999 the IMF undertook to strengthen the Standard by the introduction of a new reserves data template. By January 2005 58 countries had subscribed to the Standard. In December 1997 the Executive Board approved a new General Data Dissemination System (GDDS), to encourage all member countries to improve the production and dissemination of core economic data. The operational phase of the GDDS commenced in May 2000. By July 2004 78 countries had participated in the GDDS. The Fund maintains a Dissemination Standards Bulletin Board (accessible at dsbb.imf.org), which aims to ensure that information on SDDS subscribing countries is widely available.

In April 1998 the then Interim Committee adopted a voluntary Code of Good Practices on Fiscal Transparency: Declaration of Principles, which aimed to increase the quality and promptness of official reports on economic indicators, and in September 1999 it adopted a Code of Good Practices on Transparency in Monetary and Financial Policies: Declaration of Principles. The IMF and World Bank jointly established a Financial Sector Assessment Programme (FSAP) in May 1999, initially as a pilot project, which aimed to promote greater global financial security through the preparation of confidential detailed evaluations of the financial sectors of individual countries. It remained under regular review by the Boards of Governors of the Fund and World Bank. As part of the FSAP, Fund staff may conclude a Financial System Stability Assessment (FSSA), addressing issues relating to macroeconomic stability and the strength of a country's financial system. A separate component of the FSAP are Reports on the Observance of Standards and Codes (ROSCs), which are compiled after an assessment of a country's implementation and observance of internationally recognized financial standards. By March 2005 524 ROSCs had been completed for 106 economies.

In March 2000 the IMF Executive Board adopted a strengthened framework to safeguard the use of IMF resources. All member countries making use of Fund resources were to be required to publish annual central bank statements audited in accordance with internationally accepted standards. It was also agreed that any instance of intentional misreporting of information by a member country should be publicized. In the following month the Executive Board approved the establishment of an Independent Evaluation Office (IEO) to conduct objective evaluations of IMF policy and operations. The Office commenced activities in July 2001. In 2003/04 the Office issued reports on the role of the IMF in the capital account crises in Brazil, Indonesia and the Republic of Korea, and on fiscal adjustment in IMF-supported programmes.

In April 2001 the Executive Board agreed on measures to enhance international efforts to counter money-laundering, in particular through the Fund's ongoing financial supervision activities and its programme of assessment of offshore financial centres (OFCs). By mid-2004 41 initial OFC assessments had been concluded. In November 2001 the IMFC, in response to the terrorist attacks against targets in the USA, which had occurred in September, resolved, *inter alia*, to strengthen the Fund's focus on surveillance, and, in particular, to extend measures to counter money-laundering to include the funds of terrorist organizations. It determined to accelerate efforts to assess offshore centres and to provide technical support to enable poorer countries to meet international financial standards. In March 2004 the Board of Directors resolved that an anti-money laundering and countering the financing of terrorism (AML/CFT) component be introduced into regular OFC and FSAP assessments conducted by the Fund and the World Bank, following a pilot programme undertaken from November 2002 with the World Bank, the Financial Action Task Force and other regional supervisory bodies.

SPECIAL DRAWING RIGHTS

The special drawing right (SDR) was introduced in 1970 as a substitute for gold in international payments, and was intended eventually to become the principal reserve asset in the international monetary system. SDRs are allocated to members in proportion to their quotas. In October 1996 the Executive Board agreed to a new allocation of SDRs in order to achieve their equitable distribution among member states (i.e. all members would have an equal number of SDRs relative to the size of their quotas). In particular, this was deemed necessary since 38 countries that had joined the Fund since the last allocation of SDRs in 1981 had not yet received any of the units of account. In September 1997 at the annual meeting of the Executive Board, a resolution approving a special allocation of SDR 21,400m. was passed, in order to ensure an SDR to quota ratio of 29.32%, for all member countries. The resolution was to come into effect following its acceptance by 60% of member countries, having 85% of the total voting power. (At September 2004 131 members, holding 77% of the voting power, had agreed to the proposal.)

From 1974 to 1980 the SDR was valued on the basis of the market exchange rate for a basket of 16 currencies, belonging to the members with the largest exports of goods and services; since 1981 it has been based on the currencies of the five largest exporters (France, Germany, Japan, the United Kingdom and the USA), although the list of currencies and the weight of each in the SDR valuation basket is revised every five years. In January 1999 the IMF incorporated the new currency of the European Economic and Monetary Union, the euro, into the valuation basket; it replaced the French and German currencies, on the basis of their conversion rates with the euro as agreed by the EU. From 1 January 2001 the relative weights assigned to the currencies in the valuation basket were redistributed. The value of the SDR averaged US $1.39883 during 2003, and at 11 January 2005 stood at $1.52484.

The Second Amendment to the Articles of Agreement (1978) altered and expanded the possible uses of the SDR in transactions with other participants. These 'prescribed holders' of the SDRs have the same degree of freedom as Fund members to buy and sell SDRs and to receive or use them in loans, pledges, swaps, donations or settlement of financial obligations. At January 2004 there were 15 'prescribed holders': the African Development Bank and the African Development Fund, the Arab Monetary Fund, the Asian Development Bank, the Bank of Central African States, the Bank for International Settlements, the Central Bank of West African States, the Eastern Caribbean Central Bank, the European Central Bank, the International Bank for Reconstruction and Development, the International Development Association, the International Fund for Agricultural Development, the Islamic Development Bank, the Latin American Reserve Fund and the Nordic Investment Bank.

QUOTAS

Each member is assigned a quota related to its national income, monetary reserves, trade balance and other economic indicators. A member's subscription is equal to its quota and is payable partly in SDRs and partly in its own currency. The quota determines a member's voting power, which is based on one vote for each SDR 100,000 of its quota *plus* the 250 votes to which each member is entitled. A member's quota also determines its access to the financial resources of the IMF, and its allocation of SDRs.

Quotas are reviewed at intervals of not more than five years, to take into account the state of the world economy and members' different rates of development. Special increases, separate to the general review, may be made in exceptional circumstances. These have been approved by the Fund for the People's Republic of China in 1980 and 2001, for Saudi Arabia in 1981, and for Cambodia in 1984. In June 1990 the Board of Governors authorized proposals for a Ninth General Review of quotas. Total quotas were to be increased by roughly 50% (depending on various factors). At the same time the Board of Governors stipulated that the quota increase could occur only after the Third Amendment of the IMF's Articles of Agreement had come into effect. The amendment provides for the suspension of voting and other related rights of members that do not fulfil their obligations under the Articles. By September 1992 the necessary proportion of IMF members had accepted the amendment, and it

entered into force in November. The Tenth General Review of quotas was concluded in December 1994, with the Board recommending no further increase in quotas. However, the Board resolved to monitor closely the Fund's liquidity. In October 1996 the Fund's Managing Director advocated an increase in quotas under the latest review of at least two-thirds in the light of the IMF's reduced liquidity position. (The IMF had extended unprecedentedly large amounts in stand-by arrangements during the period 1995–96, notably to Mexico and Russia.) In January 1998 the Board of Governors adopted a resolution in support of an increase in quotas of 45%, subject to approval by member states constituting 85% of total quotas (as at December 1997). Sufficient consent had been granted by January 1999 to enable the Eleventh General Review of Quotas to enter into effect. The Twelfth General Review was initiated in December 2001, and was concluded at the end of January 2003 without an increase in quotas. At January 2005 total quotas in the Fund amounted to SDR 213,478.4m.

RESOURCES

Members' subscriptions form the basic resource of the IMF. They are supplemented by borrowing. Under the General Arrangements to Borrow (GAB), established in 1962, the 'Group of Ten' industrialized nations (G-10—Belgium, Canada, France, Germany, Italy, Japan, the Netherlands, Sweden, the United Kingdom and the USA) and Switzerland (which became a member of the IMF in May 1992 but which had been a full participant in the GAB from April 1984) undertake to lend the Fund as much as SDR 17,000m. in their own currencies, to assist in fulfilling the balance-of-payments requirements of any member of the group, or in response to requests to the Fund from countries with balance-of-payments problems that could threaten the stability of the international monetary system. In 1983 the Fund entered into an agreement with Saudi Arabia, in association with the GAB, making available SDR 1,500m., and other borrowing arrangements were completed in 1984 with the Bank for International Settlements, the Saudi Arabian Monetary Agency, Belgium and Japan, making available a further SDR 6,000m. In 1986 another borrowing arrangement with Japan made available SDR 3,000m. In May 1996 GAB participants concluded an agreement in principle to expand the resources available for borrowing to SDR 34,000m., by securing the support of 25 countries with the financial capacity to support the international monetary system. The so-called New Arrangements to Borrow (NAB) was approved by the Executive Board in January 1997. It was to enter into force, for an initial five-year period, as soon as the five largest potential creditors participating in NAB had approved the initiative and the total credit arrangement of participants endorsing the scheme had reached at least SDR 28,900m. While the GAB credit arrangement was to remain in effect, the NAB was expected to be the first facility to be activated in the event of the Fund's requiring supplementary resources. In July 1998 the GAB was activated for the first time in more than 20 years in order to provide funds of up to US $6,300m. in support of an IMF emergency assistance package for Russia (the first time the GAB had been used for a non-participant). The NAB became effective in November, and was used for the first time as part of an extensive programme of support for Brazil, which was adopted by the IMF in early December. (In March 1999, however, the activation was cancelled.) In November 2002 NAB participants agreed to renew the arrangement for a further five-year period from November 2003, and approved Chile's Central Bank as the 26th participant.

DRAWING ARRANGEMENTS

Exchange transactions within the Fund take the form of members' purchases (i.e. drawings) from the Fund of the currencies of other members for the equivalent amounts of their own currencies. Fund resources are available to eligible members on an essentially short-term and revolving basis to provide members with temporary assistance to contribute to the solution of their payments problems. Before making a purchase, a member must show that its balance of payments or reserve position makes the purchase necessary. Apart from this requirement, reserve tranche purchases (i.e. purchases that do not bring the Fund's holdings of the member's currency to a level above its quota) are permitted unconditionally.

With further purchases, however, the Fund's policy of 'conditionality' means that a member requesting assistance must agree to adjust its economic policies, as stipulated by the IMF. All requests other than for use of the reserve tranche are examined by the Executive Board to determine whether the proposed use would be consistent with the Fund's policies, and a member must discuss its proposed adjustment programme (including fiscal, monetary, exchange and trade policies) with IMF staff. Purchases outside the reserve tranche are made in four credit tranches, each equivalent to 25% of the member's quota; a member must reverse the transaction by repurchasing its own currency (with SDRs or currencies specified by the Fund) within a specified time. A credit tranche purchase is usually made under a 'Stand-by Arrangement' with the Fund, or under the

Extended Fund Facility. A Stand-by Arrangement is normally of one or two years' duration, and the amount is made available in instalments, subject to the member's observance of 'performance criteria'; repurchases must be made within three-and-a-quarter to five years. An Extended Arrangement is normally of three years' duration, and the member must submit detailed economic programmes and progress reports for each year; repurchases must be made within four-and-a-half to 10 years. A member whose payments imbalance is large in relation to its quota may make use of temporary facilities established by the Fund using borrowed resources, namely the 'enlarged access policy' established in 1981, which helps to finance Stand-by and Extended Arrangements for such a member, up to a limit of between 90% and 110% of the member's quota annually. Repurchases are made within three-and-a-half to seven years. In October 1994 the Executive Board approved a temporary increase in members' access to IMF resources, on the basis of a recommendation by the then Interim Committee. The annual access limit under IMF regular tranche drawings, Stand-by Arrangements and Extended Fund Facility credits was increased from 68% to 100% of a member's quota, with the cumulative access limit remaining at 300% of quota. The arrangements were extended, on a temporary basis, in November 1997.

In addition, special-purpose arrangements have been introduced, all of which are subject to the member's co-operation with the Fund to find an appropriate solution to its difficulties. The Compensatory Financing Facility (CCF) provides compensation to members whose export earnings are reduced as a result of circumstances beyond their control, or which are affected by excess costs of cereal imports. In December 1997 the Executive Board established a new Supplemental Reserve Facility (SRF) to provide short-term assistance to members experiencing exceptional balance-of-payments difficulties resulting from a sudden loss of market confidence. The SRF was activated immediately to provide SDR 9,950m. to the Republic of Korea, as part of a Stand-by Arrangement amounting to SDR 15,550m. (at that time the largest amount ever committed by the Fund). In July 1998 SDR 4,000m. was made available to Russia under the SRF and, in December, some SDR 9,100m. was extended to Brazil under the SRF as part of a new Stand-by Arrangement. In January 2001 some SDR 2,100m. in SRF resources were approved for Argentina as part of an SDR 5,187m. Stand-by Arrangement augmentation. (In January 2002 the Executive Board approved an extension of one year for Argentina's SRF repayments.) The SDR 22,821m. Stand-by credit approved for Brazil in September 2002 included some SDR 7,600m. committed under the SRF. In April 1999 an additional facility, the Contingent Credit Lines (CCL), was established to provide short-term financing on similar terms to the SRF in order to prevent more stable economies being affected by adverse international financial developments and to maintain investor confidence. No funds were ever committed under the CCL, however, and in November 2003 the Executive Board resolved to allow the facility to terminate, as scheduled, at the end of that month. The Board requested further consideration of other precautionary arrangements to limit the risk of financial crises. In April 2004 the Board approved a new financing policy, the Trade Integration Mechanism, to assist countries experiencing short-term balance-of-payments shortfalls as a result of trade liberalization by other countries.

In October 1995 the Interim Committee of the Board of Governors endorsed recent decisions of the Executive Board to strengthen IMF financial support to members requiring exceptional assistance. An Emergency Financing Mechanism was established to enable the IMF to respond swiftly to potential or actual financial crises, while additional funds were made available for short-term currency stabilization. (The Mechanism was activated for the first time in July 1997, in response to a request by the Philippines Government to reinforce the country's international reserves, and was subsequently used during that year to assist Thailand, Indonesia and the Republic of Korea, and, in July 1998, Russia.) Emergency assistance was also to be available to countries in a post-conflict situation, extending the existing arrangements for countries having been affected by natural disasters, to facilitate the rehabilitation of their economies and to improve their eligibility for further IMF concessionary arrangements. Assistance, typically, was to be limited to 25% of a member's quota, although up to 50% would be permitted in certain circumstances. In May 2001 a post-conflict emergency assistance account was established to administer contributions from bilateral donors. During 2003/04 one country, Burundi, drew SDR 9.6m. from the account.

In November 1999 the Fund's existing facility to provide balance-of-payments assistance on concessionary terms to low-income member countries, the Enhanced Structural Adjustment Facility, was reformulated as the Poverty Reduction and Growth Facility (PRGF), with greater emphasis on poverty reduction and sustainable development as key elements of growth-orientated economic strategies. Assistance under the PRGF (for which 77 countries were deemed eligible) was to be carefully matched to specific national requirements. Prior to drawing on the facility each recipient country

was, in collaboration with representatives of civil society, non-governmental organizations and bilateral and multilateral institutions, to develop a national poverty reduction strategy, which was to be presented in a Poverty Reduction Strategy Paper (PRSP). PRGF loans carry an interest rate of 0.5% per year and are repayable over 10 years, with a five-and-a-half-year grace period; each eligible country is normally permitted to borrow up to 140% of its quota (in exceptional circumstances the maximum access can be raised to 185%). A PGRF Trust replaced the former ESAF Trust.

The PRGF supports, through long-maturity loans and grants, IMF participation in a joint initiative, with the World Bank, to provide exceptional assistance to heavily indebted poor countries (HIPCs), in order to help them to achieve a sustainable level of debt management. The initiative was formally approved at the September 1996 meeting of the Interim Committee, having received the support of the 'Paris Club' of official creditors, which agreed to increase the relief on official debt from 67% to 80%. In all, 41 HIPCs were identified, of which 33 were in sub-Saharan Africa. In April 1997 Uganda was approved as the first beneficiary of the initiative (see World Bank). Resources for the HIPC initiative are channelled through the PRGF Trust. In early 1999 the IMF and World Bank initiated a comprehensive review of the HIPC scheme, in order to consider modifications of the initiative and to strengthen the link between debt relief and poverty reduction. A consensus emerged among the financial institutions and leading industrialized nations to enhance the scheme, in order to make it available to more countries, and to accelerate the process of providing debt relief. In September the IMF Board of Governors expressed its commitment to undertaking an off-market transaction of a percentage of the Fund's gold reserves (i.e. a sale, at market prices, to central banks of member countries with repayment obligations to the Fund, which were then to be made in gold), as part of the funding arrangements of the enhanced HIPC scheme; this was undertaken during the period December 1999–April 2000. Under the enhanced initiative it was agreed that countries seeking debt relief should first formulate, and successfully implement for at least one year, a national poverty reduction strategy (see above). In May 2000 Uganda became the first country to qualify for full debt relief under the enhanced scheme. By January 2005 15 countries had reached completion point under the enhanced HIPC initiative, while a further 12 eligible countries had reached their decision point. At that time the Fund had committed an estimated SDR 1,789m. to the initiative.

During 2003/04 the IMF approved funding commitments for new arrangements amounting to SDR 15,486m., compared with SDR 30,571m. in the previous year. Of the total amount, SDR 14,518.4m. was committed under five new Stand-by Arrangements and the augmentation of one already in place for Brazil. The arrangement approved in September 2002, in support of the Brazilian Government's efforts to secure economic and financial stability, was the largest ever stand-by credit agreed by the Fund, amounting to SDR 22,821m. Ten new PRGF arrangements were approved in 2003/04, and an existing commitment (for Madagascar) was augmented, amounting to SDR 966.9m. During 2003/04 members' purchases from the general resources account amounted to SDR 17,830m., compared with SDR 21,784m. in the previous year, with the main users of IMF resources being Brazil (SDR 9,594m.) and Argentina (SDR 5,372m.). Outstanding IMF credit at 30 April 2004 totalled SDR 69,031m., compared with SDR 72,879m. as at the previous year.

TECHNICAL ASSISTANCE

Technical assistance is provided by special missions or resident representatives who advise members on every aspect of economic management, while more specialized assistance is provided by the IMF's various departments. In 2000/01 the IMFC determined that technical assistance should be central to IMF's work in crisis prevention and management, in capacity-building for low-income countries, and in restoring macroeconomic stability in countries following a financial crisis. Technical assistance activities subsequently underwent a process of review and reorganization to align them more closely with IMF policy priorities and other initiatives, for example the Financial Stability Assessment Programme. During 2003/04 the largest area of technical assistance involvement was sub-Saharan Africa, with other post-conflict assistance extended to Cambodia and Timor-Leste. Several countries in central and eastern Europe received technical assistance related to preparations for joining the European Union on 1 May 2004. In January 2005 the IMF Managing Director announced the Fund's commitment to providing expert advice and assistance to countries affected by tsunamis that had devastated coastal regions throughout the Indian Ocean in the previous month, in particular to assess the macroeconomic impact of the disaster and immediate budgetary and balance-of-payments needs.

The majority of technical assistance is provided by the Departments of Monetary and Exchange Affairs, of Fiscal Affairs and of Statistics, and by the IMF Institute. The Institute, founded in 1964, trains officials from member countries in financial analysis and policy, balance-of-payments methodology and public finance; it also gives assistance to national and regional training centres.

In May 1998 an IMF—Singapore Regional Training Institute (an affiliate of the IMF Institute) was inaugurated, in collaboration with the Singaporean Government, in order to provide training for officials from the Asia-Pacific region. The IMF is a co-sponsor, with UNDP and the Japan administered account, of the Joint Vienna Institute, which was opened in the Austrian capital in October 1992 and which trains officials from former centrally-planned economies in various aspects of economic management and public administration. In January 1999 the IMF, in co-operation with the African Development Bank and the World Bank, announced the establishment of a Joint Africa Institute, in Abidjan, Côte d'Ivoire, which was to offer training to officials from African countries from the second half of the year. The IMF Institute also co-operates with other established regional training centres and institutes in order to refine its delivery of technical assistance and training services. During 2000/01 the Institute established a new training programme with government officials in the People's Republic of China and agreed to establish a regional training centre for Latin America in Brazil. A Caribbean Regional Technical Assistance Centre (CARTAC), located in Barbados, began operations in November 2001. In October 2002 an East African Regional Technical Assistance Centre (East AFRITAC), based in Dar es Salaam, Tanzania, was inaugurated as the first of a planned series of sub-regional centres in Africa with the objective of developing local capacity in economic and financial management. A second AFRITAC was opened in Bamako, Mali in May 2003, to cover the West African region. In September 2002 the IMF signed a memorandum of understanding with the African Capacity Building Foundation to strengthen collaboration, in particular within the context of a new IMF Africa Capacity-Building Initiative.

Publications

Annual Report.

Balance of Payments Statistics Yearbook.

Direction of Trade Statistics (quarterly and annually).

Emerging Markets Financing (quarterly).

Finance and Development (quarterly).

Financial Statements of the IMF (quarterly).

Global Financial Stability Report (2 a year).

Government Finance Statistics Yearbook.

IMF Commodity Prices (monthly).

IMF Research Bulletin (quarterly).

IMF Survey (2 a month).

International Financial Statistics (monthly and annually, also on CD-ROM).

Joint BIS-IMF-OECD-World Bank Statistics on External Debt (quarterly).

Quarterly Report on the Assessments of Standards and Codes.

Staff Papers (3 a year).

World Economic Outlook (2 a year).

Other country reports, economic and financial surveys, occasional papers, pamphlets, books.

Statistics

QUOTAS
(SDR million)

	5 January 2005
Afghanistan	161.9
Albania	48.7
Algeria	1,254.7
Angola	286.3
Antigua and Barbuda	13.5
Argentina	2,117.1
Armenia	92.0
Australia	3,236.4
Austria	1,872.3
Azerbaijan	160.9
Bahamas	130.3
Bahrain	135.0
Bangladesh	533.3
Barbados	67.5
Belarus	386.4
Belgium	4,605.2

— *continued*	5 January 2005
Belize	18.8
Benin	61.9
Bhutan	6.3
Bolivia	171.5
Bosnia and Herzegovina	169.1
Botswana	63.0
Brazil	3,036.1
Brunei	215.2
Bulgaria	640.2
Burkina Faso	60.2
Burundi	77.0
Cambodia	87.5
Cameroon	185.7
Canada	6,369.2
Cape Verde	9.6
Central African Republic	55.7
Chad	56.0
Chile	856.1
China, People's Republic	6,369.2
Colombia	774.0
Comoros	8.9
Congo, Democratic Republic	533.0
Congo, Republic	84.6
Costa Rica	164.1
Côte d'Ivoire	325.2
Croatia	365.1
Cyprus	139.6
Czech Republic	819.3
Denmark	1,642.8
Djibouti	15.9
Dominica	8.2
Dominican Republic	218.9
Ecuador	302.3
Egypt	943.7
El Salvador	171.3
Equatorial Guinea	32.6
Eritrea	15.9
Estonia	65.2
Ethiopia	133.7
Fiji	70.3
Finland	1,263.8
France	10,738.5
Gabon	154.3
The Gambia	31.1
Georgia	150.3
Germany	13,008.2
Ghana	369.0
Greece	823.0
Grenada	11.7
Guatemala	210.2
Guinea	107.1
Guinea-Bissau	14.2
Guyana	90.9
Haiti	81.9
Honduras	129.5
Hungary	1,038.4
Iceland	117.6
India	4,158.2
Indonesia	2,079.3
Iran	1,497.2
Iraq	1,188.4
Ireland	838.4
Israel	928.2
Italy	7,055.5
Jamaica	273.5
Japan	13,312.8
Jordan	170.5
Kazakhstan	365.7
Kenya	271.4
Kiribati	5.6
Korea, Republic	1,633.6
Kuwait	1,381.1
Kyrgyzstan	88.8
Laos	52.9
Latvia	126.8
Lebanon	203.0
Lesotho	34.9
Liberia*	(129.2) 71.3
Libya	1,123.7
Lithuania	144.2
Luxembourg	279.1
Macedonia, former Yugoslav republic	68.9
Madagascar	122.2
Malawi	69.4

— *continued*	5 January 2005
Malaysia	1,486.6
Maldives	8.2
Mali	93.3
Malta	102.0
Marshall Islands	3.5
Mauritania	64.4
Mauritius	101.6
Mexico	2,585.8
Micronesia, Federated States	5.1
Moldova	123.2
Mongolia	51.1
Morocco	588.2
Mozambique	113.6
Myanmar	258.4
Namibia	136.5
Nepal	71.3
Netherlands	5,162.4
New Zealand	894.6
Nicaragua	130.0
Niger	65.8
Nigeria	1,753.2
Norway	1,671.7
Oman	194.0
Pakistan	1,033.7
Palau	3.1
Panama	206.6
Papua New Guinea	131.6
Paraguay	99.9
Peru	638.4
Philippines	879.9
Poland	1,369.0
Portugal	867.4
Qatar	263.8
Romania	1,030.2
Russia	5,945.4
Rwanda	80.1
Saint Christopher and Nevis	8.9
Saint Lucia	15.3
Saint Vincent and the Grenadines	8.3
Samoa	11.6
San Marino	17.0
São Tomé and Príncipe	7.4
Saudi Arabia	6,985.5
Senegal	161.8
Serbia and Montenegro	467.7
Seychelles	8.8

— *continued*	5 January 2005
Sierra Leone	103.7
Singapore	862.5
Slovakia	357.5
Slovenia	231.7
Solomon Islands	10.4
Somalia*	(81.7) 44.2
South Africa	1,868.5
Spain	3,048.9
Sri Lanka	413.4
Sudan*	(315.1) 169.7
Suriname	92.1
Swaziland	50.7
Sweden	2,395.5
Switzerland	3,458.5
Syria	293.6
Tajikistan	87.0
Tanzania	198.9
Thailand	1,081.9
Timor-Leste	8.2
Togo	73.4
Tonga	6.9
Trinidad and Tobago	335.6
Tunisia	286.5
Turkey	964.0
Turkmenistan	75.2
Uganda	180.5
Ukraine	1,372.0
United Arab Emirates	611.7
United Kingdom	10,738.5
USA	37,149.3
Uruguay	306.5
Uzbekistan	275.6
Vanuatu	17.0
Venezuela	2,659.1
Viet Nam	329.1
Yemen	243.5
Zambia	489.1
Zimbabwe	353.4

* At 5 January 2005 these members had overdue obligations and were therefore ineligible to consent to the increase in quotas under the Eleventh General Review (which came into effect in January 1999). The figures listed are those determined under previous reviews, while the figures in parentheses are the proposed Eleventh General Review quotas. The proposed quotas are those in parentheses. The Twelfth General Review was concluded at the end of January 2003 without an increase in quotas.

FINANCIAL ACTIVITIES
(SDR million, year ending 30 April)

Type of Transaction	1999	2000	2001	2002	2003	2004
Total disbursements	24,897	6,890	10,229	30,146	23,002	18,695
Purchases by facility (General Resources Account)*	24,071	6,377	9,599	29,194	21,784	17,830†
Loans under SAF/PRGF arrangements	826	513	630	952	1,218	865
Repurchases and repayments	11,092	23,627	11,831	19,976	8,712	22,528
Repurchases	10,465	22,993	11,243	19,207	7,784	21,638
Trust Fund and SAF/PRGF loan repayments	627	634	588	769	928	890
Total outstanding credit provided by Fund (end of year)	67,175	50,370	48,691	58,699	72,879	69,031
Of which:						
General Resources Account	60,651	43,968	42,219	52,081	65,978	62,153
SAF Arrangements	565	456	432	341	137	86
PRGF Arrangements‡	5,870	5,857	5,951	6,188	6,676	6,703
Trust Fund	89	89	89	89	89	89

* Including reserve tranche purchases.
† Comprising (in SDR million): 16 in reserve tranche purchases, 10 in emergency assistance, 12,865 in Stand-by Arrangements and credit tranche purchases, 1,132 under the Extended Fund Facility, and 3,807 under the Supplemental Reserve Facility.
‡ Including Saudi Fund for Development associated loans.

Source: *International Monetary Fund Annual Report 2004.*

BOARD OF EXECUTIVE DIRECTORS
(January 2005)

Director	Casting Votes of	Total Votes	%
Appointed:			
NANCY P. JACKLIN	USA	371,743	17.14
SHIGEO KASHIWAGI	Japan	133,378	6.15
KARLHEINZ BISCHOFBERGER	Germany	130,332	6.01
PIERRE DUQUESNE	France	107,635	4.96
TOM SCHOLAR	United Kingdom	107,635	4.96
Elected:			
WILLY KIEKENS (Belgium)	Austria, Belarus, Belgium, Czech Republic, Hungary, Kazakhstan, Luxembourg, Slovakia, Slovenia, Turkey	111,696	5.15
JEROEN KREMERS (Netherlands)	Armenia, Bosnia and Herzegovina, Bulgaria, Croatia, Cyprus, Georgia, Israel, the former Yugoslav republic of Macedonia, Moldova, Netherlands, Romania, Ukraine	105,412	4.86
MOISÉS J. SCHWARTZ (Mexico)	Costa Rica, El Salvador, Guatemala, Honduras, Mexico, Nicaragua, Spain, Venezuela	92,989	4.29
PIER CARLO PADOAN (Italy)	Albania, Greece, Italy, Malta, Portugal, San Marino, Timor-Leste	90,968	4.19
KEVIN G. LYNCH (Canada)	Antigua and Barbuda, Bahamas, Barbados, Belize, Canada, Dominica, Grenada, Ireland, Jamaica, Saint Christopher and Nevis, Saint Lucia, Saint Vincent and the Grenadines	80,636	3.72
JON A. SOLHEIM (Norway)	Denmark, Estonia, Finland, Iceland, Latvia, Lithuania, Norway, Sweden	76,276	3.52
JONG NAM OH (Republic of Korea)	Australia, Kiribati, Republic of Korea, Marshall Islands, Federated States of Micronesia, Mongolia, New Zealand, Palau, Papua New Guinea, Philippines, Samoa, Seychelles, Solomon Islands, Vanuatu	72,423	3.34
A. SHAKOUR SHAALAN (Egypt)	Bahrain, Egypt, Iraq, Jordan, Kuwait, Lebanon, Libya, Maldives, Oman, Qatar, Syria, United Arab Emirates, Yemen	70,852	3.26
SULAIMAN M. AL-TURKI	Saudi Arabia	70,105	3.23
HOOI ENG PHANG (Malaysia)	Brunei, Cambodia, Fiji, Indonesia, Laos, Malaysia, Myanmar, Nepal, Singapore, Thailand, Tonga, Viet Nam	69,019	3.18
PETER J. NGUMBULLU (Tanzania)	Angola, Botswana, Burundi, Eritrea, Ethiopia, The Gambia, Kenya, Lesotho, Malawi, Mozambique, Namibia, Nigeria, Sierra Leone, South Africa, Sudan, Swaziland, Tanzania, Uganda, Zambia	65,221	3.01
WANG XIAOYI	People's Republic of China	63,942	2.95
FRITZ ZURBRÜGG (Switzerland)	Azerbaijan, Kyrgyzstan, Poland, Serbia and Montenegro, Switzerland, Tajikistan, Turkmenistan, Uzbekistan	61,827	2.85
ALEKSEI V. MOZHIN	Russia	59,704	2.75
ABBAS MIRAKHOR (Iran)	Afghanistan, Algeria, Ghana, Iran, Morocco, Pakistan, Tunisia	53,662	2.47
MURILO PORTUGAL (Brazil)	Brazil, Colombia, Dominican Republic, Ecuador, Guyana, Haiti, Panama, Suriname, Trinidad and Tobago	53,634	2.47
B. P. MISRA (India)	Bangladesh, Bhutan, India, Sri Lanka	52,112	2.40
HÉCTOR R. TORRES (Argentina)	Argentina, Bolivia, Chile, Paraguay, Peru, Uruguay	43,395	2.00
DAMIAN ONDO MAÑE (Equatorial Guinea)	Benin, Burkina Faso, Cameroon, Cape Verde, Central African Republic, Chad, Comoros, Democratic Republic of the Congo, Republic of the Congo, Côte d'Ivoire, Djibouti, Equatorial Guinea, Gabon, Guinea, Guinea-Bissau, Madagascar, Mali, Mauritania, Mauritius, Niger, Rwanda, São Tomé and Príncipe, Senegal, Togo	30,749	1.42

Note: The total number of votes does not include the votes of Somalia (0.03% of the total of votes in the General Department and the Special Drawing Rights Department), which did not participate in the 2002 election of Executive Directors. Liberia's voting rights (0.04%) were suspended on 5 March 2003 and Zimbabwe's voting rights (0.17%) were suspended effective 6 June 2003.

International Telecommunication Union—ITU

Address: Place des Nations, 1211 Geneva 20, Switzerland.

Telephone: (22)7305111; **fax:** (22)7337256; **e-mail:** itumail@itu.int; **internet:** www.itu.int.

Founded in 1865, ITU became a specialized agency of the UN in 1947. It acts *inter alia* to encourage world co-operation for the improvement and national use of telecommunications to promote technical development, to harmonize national policies in the field, and to promote the extension of telecommunications throughout the world.

MEMBERS

ITU has 189 member states. More than 650 scientific and technical companies, public and private operators, broadcasters and other organizations are also ITU members.

Organization

(March 2005)

PLENIPOTENTIARY CONFERENCE

The supreme organ of ITU; normally meets every four years. The main tasks of the Conference are to elect ITU's leadership, establish policies, revise the Constitution and Convention (see below) and approve limits on budgetary spending. The 2002 Conference was held in Marrakesh, Morocco, in September–October. The next Conference was scheduled to be convened in Doha, Qatar, in March 2006.

WORLD CONFERENCES ON INTERNATIONAL TELECOMMUNICATIONS

The World Conferences on International Telecommunications are held at the request of members and after approval by the Plenipotentiary Conference. The World Conferences are authorized to review and revise the regulations applying to the provision and operation of international telecommunications services. As part of the 1993 restructuring of ITU, separate Conferences were to be held by three sectors (see below): Radiocommunication Conferences (to be held every two or three years); Telecommunication Standardization Assemblies (to be held every four years or at the request of one-quarter of ITU members); and Telecommunication Development Conferences (to be held every four years).

ITU COUNCIL

The Council meets annually in Geneva and is composed of 46 members elected by the Plenipotentiary Conference.

The Council ensures the efficient co-ordination and implementation of the work of the Union in all matters of policy, administration and finance, in the interval between Plenipotentiary Conferences, and approves the annual budget.

GENERAL SECRETARIAT

The Secretary-General is elected by the Plenipotentiary Conference, and is responsible to it for the Secretariat's work, and for the Union's administrative and financial services. The Secretariat's staff totals some 800, representing more than 80 nationalities; the official and working languages are Arabic, Chinese, English, French, Russian and Spanish.

Secretary-General: Yoshio Utsumi (Japan).

Deputy Secretary-General: Roberto Blois Montes de Souza (Brazil).

Constitution and Convention

Between 1865 and 1992 each Plenipotentiary Conference adopted a new Convention of ITU. At the Additional Plenipotentiary Conference held in December 1992, in Geneva, Switzerland, a new Constitution and Convention were signed. They were partially amended by the following two Plenipotentiary Conferences held in Kyoto, Japan, in 1994, and Minneapolis, USA, in 1998. The Constitution contains the fundamental provisions of ITU, whereas the Convention contains other provisions which complement those of the Constitution and which, by their nature, require periodic revision.

The Constitution establishes the purposes and structure of the Union, contains the general provisions relating to telecommunications and special provisions for radio, and deals with relations with the UN and other organizations. The Convention establishes the functioning of the Union and the three sectors, and contains the general provisions regarding conferences and assemblies. Both instruments are further complemented by the administrative regulations listed below.

INTERNATIONAL TELECOMMUNICATIONS REGULATIONS

The International Telecommunications Regulations were adopted in 1988 and entered into force in 1990. They establish the general principles relating to the provision and operation of international telecommunication services offered to the public. They also establish rules applicable to administrations and recognized private operating agencies. Their provisions are applied to both wire and wireless telegraph and telephone communications in so far as the Radio Regulations do not provide otherwise. The 2002 Plenipotentiary Conference determined to initiate a review process of the International Telecommunications Regulations and agreed to convene a World Conference on International Telecommunications within four to five years, on the basis of recommendations arising from the review.

RADIO REGULATIONS

The Radio Regulations, which first appeared in 1906, include general rules for the assignment and use of frequencies and the associated orbital positions for space stations. They include a Table of Frequency Allocations (governing the use of radio frequency bands between 9 kHz and 400 GHz) for the various radio services (*inter alia* radio broadcasting, television, radio astronomy, navigation aids, point-to-point service, maritime mobile, amateur).

The 1979 World Administrative Radio Conference undertook a complete revision of the radio spectrum allocation. Partial revisions were also made by subsequent world and regional administrative radio conferences, particularly with reference to space radiocommunications, using satellites. The last revision of the Radio Regulations was signed in Istanbul, Turkey, in 2000.

Activities

In December 1992 an Additional Plenipotentiary Conference was held in Geneva, Switzerland, which agreed on reforms to the structure and functioning of ITU. As a result, ITU comprised three sectors corresponding to its main functions: standardization; radiocommunication; and development. Separate sector conferences were to be held. In October 1994 the ordinary Plenipotentiary Conference, held in Kyoto, Japan, adopted ITU's first strategic plan. A second strategic plan, for the period 1999–2003, was adopted by the conference, convened in Minneapolis, USA, in October–November 1998. The plan recognized new trends and developments in the world telecommunication environment, such as globalization, liberalization, and greater competition, assessed their implications for ITU, and proposed new strategies and priorities to enable ITU to function effectively. The conference approved the active involvement of ITU in governance issues relating to the internet, and recommended that a World Summit on the Information Society be convened, given the rapid developments in that field. Accordingly, the Union is undertaking a lead role in organizing the summit, under the auspices of the UN Secretary-General, which is being held in two phases: the first took place in Geneva in December 2003, and the second was scheduled to be held in Tunis, Tunisia in November 2005. The Geneva meeting, attended by representatives of 175 countries, approved a Declaration of Principles and Plan of Action, and recognized the central role of ITU in building an information society. In October 2002 the Plenipotentiary Conference, convened in Marrakesh, Morocco, adopted a strategic plan for the period 2004–07 which emphasized ITU's role in facilitating universal access to the global information economy and society. ITU was to take a lead role in UN initiatives concerning information and communication technologies and support all efforts to bridge the international digital divide.

RADIOCOMMUNICATION SECTOR

The role of the sector is to ensure an equitable and efficient use of the radio-frequency spectrum by all radiocommunication services, to conduct studies, and to adopt recommendations on sector issues. The Radio Regulations are reviewed and revised by the World Radiocommunication Conferences. The technical work on issues to be considered by the conferences is conducted by Radiocommunication Assemblies, on the basis of recommendations made by Study Groups. These groups of experts study technical questions relating to radiocommunications, according to a study programme formulated by the Assemblies. The Assemblies may approve, modify or reject any recommendations of the Study Groups, and are authorized to establish new groups and to abolish others. The procedural rules used in the application of the Radio Regulations were to be considered by a Radio Regulations Board, which may also perform duties relating to the allocation and use of frequencies and consider cases of interference. The sector administers ITU's 'International Mobile Telecommunication-2000' initiative relating to third generation (3G) mobile communication systems, which aims to provide wireless access to the global telecommunication infrastructure through satellite and terrestrial systems.

The administrative work of the sector is the responsibility of the Radiocommunication Bureau, which is headed by an elected Director. The Bureau co-ordinates the work of Study Groups, provides administrative support for the Radio Regulations Board, and works alongside the General Secretariat to prepare conferences and to provide relevant assistance to developing countries. The Director is assisted by an Advisory Group.

Director: Valery Timofeev (Russia).

TELECOMMUNICATION STANDARDIZATION SECTOR

The sector was established to study technical, operational and tariff issues in order to standardize telecommunications throughout the world. The sector's conferences consider draft standards, referred to as Recommendations, which, if approved, establish ITU guidelines to guarantee the effective provision of telecommunication services. According to the priority given to different issues concerning draft standards, the conferences may maintain, establish or abolish Study Groups. Recommendations may be approved outside of the four-year interval between conferences if a Study Group concludes such action to be urgent. According to the 1999–2003 strategic plan, one of the priorities for the sector was to be the formulation of recommendations relating to Internet Protocol-based networks, as well as more general recommendations to keep pace with the rapid technological developments and expansion of market demand. A World Telecommunication Standardization Assembly (WTSA) held in Montréal, Canada, in September–October 2000, approved settlement rates for international connections. The meeting also approved the establishment of a management board to oversee the implementation of 3G mobile services. The 2004–07 strategic plan emphasized the need for the sector to take a more effective role in drafting standards relating to the information society, and to co-ordinate work undertaken by other relevant bodies. In October 2004 the WTSA, convened in Florianópolis, Brazil, highlighted the importance of next-general networks, and established a new study group to consider the issue. Other resolutions approved by the Assembly were concerned with cybersecurity, countering unsolicited electronic mail, and bridging the standardization gap between developed and developing countries.

Preparations for conferences and other meetings of the sector are made by the Telecommunication Standardization Bureau (ITU-T). It administers the application of conference decisions, as well as relevant provisions of the International Telecommunications Regulations. ITU-T is headed by an elected Director, who is assisted by an Advisory Group. The Director reports to conferences and to the ITU Council on the activities of the sector.

Director: HOULIN ZHAO (People's Republic of China).

TELECOMMUNICATION DEVELOPMENT SECTOR

The sector's objectives are to facilitate and enhance telecommunications development by offering, organizing and co-ordinating technical co-operation and assistance activities, to promote the development of telecommunication networks and services in developing countries, to facilitate the transfer of appropriate technologies and the use of resources, and to provide advice on issues specific to telecommunications. The sector implements projects under the UN development system or other funding arrangements. The 2004–07 strategic plan emphasized the need for the sector to assist developing countries gain access to and realize the benefits of information and communication technologies (ICTs). In January 2005 ITU launched an initiative to establish a network of some 100 Multipurpose Community Telecentres in 20 African countries, with the aim of providing broader access to ICTs.

The sector holds conferences regularly to encourage international co-operation in the development of telecommunications, and to determine strategies for development. Conferences consider the result of work undertaken by Study Groups on issues of benefit to developing countries, including development policy, finance, network planning and operation of services.

The administrative work of the sector is conducted by the Telecommunication Development Bureau, which may also study specific problems presented by a member state. The Director of the Bureau reports to conferences and the ITU Council, and is assisted by an Advisory Board.

Director: HAMEDOUN I. TOURÉ (Mali).

INFORMATION

ITU issues numerous technical and statistical publications (see below) and maintains a library and archives. It also offers the use of an on-line computer-based telecom information exchange service (TIES), which provides access to ITU databases, document exchange, and other telecommunication information.

Finance

The 2002 Plenipotentiary Conference approved a budget of 328.87m. Swiss francs for the two-year period 2004–05.

Publications

ITU Internet Reports.
ITU News (10 a year, in English, French and Spanish).
World Telecommunication Development Report.

Conventions, statistics, regulations, technical documents and manuals, conference documents.

United Nations Educational, Scientific and Cultural Organization—UNESCO

Address: 7 place de Fontenoy, 75352 Paris 07 SP, France.

Telephone: 1-45-68-10-00; **fax:** 1-45-67-16-90; **e-mail:** scg@unesco .org; **internet:** www.unesco.org.

UNESCO was established in 1946 'for the purpose of advancing, through the educational, scientific and cultural relations of the peoples of the world, the objectives of international peace and the common welfare of mankind'.

MEMBERS

UNESCO has 191 members and six associate members.

Organization

(March 2005)

GENERAL CONFERENCE

The supreme governing body of the Organization, the Conference meets in ordinary session once in two years and is composed of representatives of the member states.

EXECUTIVE BOARD

The Board, comprising 58 members, prepares the programme to be submitted to the Conference and supervises its execution; it meets twice or sometimes three times a year.

SECRETARIAT

Director-General: KOÏCHIRO MATSUURA (Japan).

CO-OPERATING BODIES

In accordance with UNESCO's constitution, national Commissions have been set up in most member states. These help to integrate work within the member states and the work of UNESCO.

PRINCIPAL REGIONAL OFFICES

Africa

Regional Bureau for Education: BP 3311, Dakar, Senegal; tel. 823-83-93; fax 849-23-23; e-mail dakar@unesco.org; Dir A. PARSURAMEN.

Regional Bureau for Science: POB 30592, Nairobi, Kenya; tel. (20) 21-59-91; fax (20) 62-12-34; e-mail nairobi@unesco.org; f. 1965 to execute UNESCO's regional science programme, and to assist in the planning and execution of national programmes; Dir PAUL B. VITTA.

UNESCO International Institute for Capacity Building in Africa—UNESCO–IICBA: POB 2305, Addis Ababa, Ethiopia; tel. (1) 55-75-86; fax (1) 55-75-85; e-mail info@unesco-iicba.org; internet www.unesco-iicba.org; f. 1999 to promote capacity building in the following areas: teacher education, curriculum development; educational policy, planning and management, and distance education; Dir (vacant).

Arab States

Regional Office for Education in the Arab States: POB 5244, ave Cité Sportive, Beirut, Lebanon; tel. (1) 850013; fax (1) 824854; e-mail beirut@unesco.org; internet www.unesco.org; Dir V. BILLEH.

Regional Office for Science and Technology in the Arab States—ROSTAS: 8 Abdel Rahman Fahmy St, Garden City, Cairo 11511, Egypt; tel. (2) 7945599; fax (2) 78945296; e-mail cairo@ unesco.org; internet www.unesco-cairo.org; also covers informatics; Dir Dr MOHAMED EL-DEEK.

Regional Office for Social and Human Sciences in the Arab Region: POB 363, 12 rue de Rhodes-Notre Dame, 1002 Tunis, Tunisia; tel. (1) 790947; fax (1) 791588; e-mail tunis@unesco.org; liaison office with the Arab League Educational, Cultural and Scientific Organization; Dir FRANCISCO CARRILLO-MONTESINOS.

Asia and the Pacific

Regional Office for Science and Technology for South-East Asia: UN Bldg (2nd Floor), Jalan M. H. Thamrin 14, Tromol Pos 1273/JKT, Jakarta 10002, Indonesia; tel. (21) 3141308; fax (21)

3150382; e-mail uhjak@unesco.org; internet www.unesco.or.id; Dir Prof. STEPHEN HILL.

UNESCO Asia and Pacific Regional Bureau for Communication and Information: B-5/29, Safdarjung Enclave, New Delhi 110057, India; tel. (11) 671-3000; fax (11) 671-3001; e-mail newdelhi@unesco.org; internet unescodelhi.nic.in; f. 1948 as UNESCO New Delhi Office; aims to widen access to information and knowledge resources, with a special focus on reaching poor/illiterate people and other marginalized groups; Dir Prof. MOSHEN TAWFIK; publs *Annual Report*, *Library Accessions List* (monthly), *Quarterly Newsletter*.

UNESCO Asia and Pacific Regional Bureau for Education: 920 Sukhumvit Rd, POB 967, Bangkok 10110, Thailand; tel. (2) 391-0577; fax (2) 391-0866; e-mail bangkok@unescobkk.org; internet www.unescobkk.org; Dir SHELDON SCHAEFFER.

Europe and North America

European Centre for Higher Education—CEPES: Str. Stirbei Vodà 39, 010102 Bucharest, Romania; tel. (1) 313-0839; fax (1) 312-3567; e-mail info@cepes.ro; internet www.cepes.ro; Dir JAN SADLAK.

Regional Bureau for Science in Europe: Palazzo Zorzi, 4930 castello, 30122 Venice, Italy; tel. (041) 260-1511; fax (041) 528-9995; e-mail roste@unesco.org; internet www.unesco.org/venice; Dir Dr HOWARD MOORE.

Latin America and the Caribbean

Caribbean Network of Educational Innovation for Development: The Towers, 3rd Floor, 25 Dominica Drive, Kingston, Jamaica; tel. 929-7087; fax 929-8468; e-mail kingston@unesco.org; internet www.unesco.org/ext/field/carneid; Dir of Caribbean Office HÉLÈNE-MARIE GOSSELIN.

International Institute for Higher Education in Latin America and the Caribbean—IESALC: Avda Los Chorros con Calle Acueducto, Edif. Asovincar, Altos de Sebucán, Apdo 68394, Caracas 1062 A, Venezuela; tel. (2) 283-1411; fax (2) 283-1454; e-mail caracas@unesco.org; internet www.iesalc.unesco.org.ve; Dir CLAUDIO RAMA VITALE.

Regional Office for Culture in Latin America and the Caribbean—ORCALC: Apdo 4158, Havana 4, Cuba; tel. (7) 832-7741; fax (7) 833-3144; e-mail havana@unesco.org.cu; internet www .unesco.org.cu; f. 1950; activities include research and programmes of cultural development and cultural tourism; maintains a documentation centre and a library of 14,500 vols; Dir FRANCISCO JOSÉ LACAYO PARAJÓN; Publs *Oralidad* (annually), *Boletín Electrónico* (quarterly).

Regional Office for Education in Latin America and the Caribbean—OREALC: Calle Enrique Delpiano 2058, Providencia, Santiago, Chile; Casilla 127, Correo 29, Providencia, Santiago, Chile; tel. (2) 472-4600; fax (2) 655-1046; e-mail unesco@unesco.cl; internet www.unesco.cl; Dir ANA LUIZA MACHADO PINHEIRO.

Regional Office for Science for Latin America and the Caribbean: Calle Dr Luis Piera 1992, 2°, Casilla 859, 11000 Montevideo, Uruguay; tel. (2)413-2075; fax (2) 413-2094; e-mail orcyt@ unesco.org.uy; internet www.unesco.org.uy; Dir JORGE GRANDI.

Activities

In November 2001 the General Conference approved a medium-term strategy to guide UNESCO during the period 2002–07. The Conference adopted a new unifying theme for the organization: 'UNESCO contributing to peace and human development in an era of globalization through education, the sciences, culture and communication'. UNESCO's central mission as defined under the strategy was to contribute to peace and human development in the globalized world through its four programme domains (Education, Natural and Social and Human Sciences, Culture, and Communication and Information), incorporating the following three principal dimensions: developing universal principles and norms to meet emerging challenges and protect the 'common public good'; promoting pluralism and diversity; and promoting empowerment and participation in the emerging knowledge society through equitable access, capacity-building and knowledge-sharing. Programme activities were to be focused particularly on supporting disadvantaged and excluded groups or geographic regions. The organization aimed to decentralize its operations in order to ensure more country-driven programming. The UN General Assembly designated UNESCO as the lead agency for co-ordinating the International Decade for a Culture of Peace and Non-Violence for the Children of the World (2001–10), with a focus on education, and the UN Literacy Decade (2003–12). In 2004 UNESCO was the lead agency in promoting the International Year to Commemorate the Struggle Against Slavery and its Abolition. In the implementation of all its activities UNESCO aims to contribute to achieving the UN Millennium Development Goal (MDG) of halving levels of extreme poverty by 2015, as well as other MDGs concerned with education and sustainable development (see below).

Since the 1990s Africa has been a priority focus of UNESCO's activities. In November 2001 UNESCO organized an international seminar entitled *Forward-looking approaches and innovative strategies to promote the development of Africa in the 21st century*, which aimed to review UNESCO's strategy on Africa in the light of the recently launched New Partnership on Africa's Development (see under African Union).

EDUCATION

Since its establishment UNESCO has devoted itself to promoting education in accordance with principles based on democracy and respect for human rights. The Associated Schools Project (ASPnet—comprising some 7,509 institutions in 175 countries in early 2005) has, since 1953, promoted the principles of peace, human rights, democracy and international co-operation through education.

In March 1990 UNESCO, with other UN agencies, sponsored the World Conference on Education for All. 'Education for All' was subsequently adopted as a guiding principle of UNESCO's contribution to development. In April 2000 several UN agencies, including UNESCO and UNICEF, and other partners sponsored the World Education Forum, held in Dakar, Senegal, to assess international progress in achieving the goal of 'Education for All' and to adopt a strategy for further action (the 'Dakar Framework'), with the aim of ensuring universal basic education by 2015. The Forum launched the Global Initiative for Education for All. The Dakar Framework emphasized the role of improved access to education in the reduction of poverty and in diminishing inequalities within and between societies. UNESCO was appointed as the lead agency in the implementation of the Framework. UNESCO's role in pursuing the goals of the Dakar Forum was to focus on co-ordination, advocacy, mobilization of resources, and information-sharing at international, regional and national levels. It was to oversee national policy reforms, with a particular focus on the integration of 'Education for All' objectives into national education plans. UNESCO's work programme on Education aims to promote an effective follow-up to the Forum and comprises the following two main components: Basic education for all: meeting the commitments of the Dakar World Education Forum; and Building knowledge societies through quality education and a renewal of education systems. 'Basic Education for All', signifying the promotion of access to learning opportunities throughout the lives of all individuals, including the most disadvantaged, is the principal theme of the programme, and deemed to require urgent action. The second part of the strategy aims to improve the quality of educational provision and renew and diversify education systems, with a view to ensuring that educational needs at all levels were met. This component includes updating curricular programmes in secondary education, strengthening science and technology activities and ensuring equal access to education for girls and women. (UNESCO supports the UN Girls' Education Initiative, established following the Dakar Forum.) A particular focus is placed on the importance of knowledge, information and communication in the increasingly globalized world, and the significance of education as a means of empowerment for the poor and of enhancing basic quality of life.

UNESCO advocates 'Literacy for All' as a key component of 'Education for All', regarding literacy as essential to basic education and to social and human development. In December 2001 the UN General Assembly appointed UNESCO to be the co-ordinating agency of the UN Literacy Decade (2003–12), which aimed to formulate an international plan of action to raise literacy standards throughout the world.

In December 1993 the heads of government of nine highly-populated developing countries (Bangladesh, Brazil, the People's Republic of China, Egypt, India, Indonesia, Mexico, Nigeria and Pakistan), meeting in New Delhi, India, agreed to co-operate, with the objective of achieving comprehensive primary education for all children and of expanding further learning opportunities for children and adults. By September 1999 all of the so-called 'E-9' (or Education-9) countries had officially signed the 'Delhi Declaration' issued by the meeting. UNESCO is working towards the UN MDGs of eliminating gender disparity in primary and secondary education by 2005 and attaining universal primary education in all countries by 2015.

Within the UN system, UNESCO is responsible for providing technical assistance and educational services in the context of emergency situations. This includes providing education to refugees and displaced persons, as well as assistance for the rehabilitation of national education systems.

In Palestine, UNESCO collaborates with UNRWA to assist with the training of teachers, educational planning and rehabilitation of schools.

UNESCO is concerned with improving the quality, relevance and efficiency of higher education. It assists member states in reforming their national systems, organizes high-level conferences for Ministers of Education and other decision-makers, and disseminates research papers. A World Conference on Higher Education was convened in October 1998 in Paris, France. The Conference adopted a World Declaration on Higher Education for the 21st Century, incorporating proposals to reform higher education, with emphasis on access to education, and educating for individual development and active participation in society. The Conference also approved a framework for Priority Action for Change and Development of Higher Education, which comprised guide-lines for governments and institutions to meet the objectives of greater accessibility, as well as improved standards and relevancy of higher education.

The International Institute for Educational Planning and the International Bureau of Education (see below) undertake training, research and the exchange of information on aspects of education. A UNESCO Institute for Education, based in Hamburg, Germany, researches literacy activities and the evolution of adult learning systems. UNESCO aims to promote the use of new information and communication technologies in the expansion of learning opportunities. A joint UNESCO/ILO committee of experts has been established to consider strategies for enhancing the status of the teaching profession. The UNESCO International Institute for Capacity Building in Africa, based in Addis Ababa, Ethiopia, promotes capacity building in teacher education, curriculum development, educational policy, planning and management, and distance education.

The April 2000 World Education Forum recognized the global HIV/AIDS pandemic to be a significant challenge to the attainment of 'Education for All'. UNESCO, as a co-sponsor of UNAIDS, takes an active role in promoting formal and non-formal preventive health education.

NATURAL SCIENCES

In November 1999 the General Conference endorsed a Declaration on Science and the Use of Scientific Knowledge and an agenda for action, which had been adopted at the World Conference on Science, held in June–July 1999, in Budapest, Hungary. UNESCO was to co-ordinate the follow-up to the conference and, in conjunction with the International Council for Science, to promote initiatives in international scientific partnership. The following are priority areas of UNESCO's work programme on Natural Sciences: Science and technology: capacity-building and management; and Sciences, environment and sustainable development. Water Security in the 21st Century is the principal theme, involving addressing threats to water resources and their associated ecosystems. UNESCO was the lead UN agency involved in the preparation of the first *World Water Development Report*, issued in March 2003. In that year the UNESCO Institute for Water Education was inaugurated in Delft, the Netherlands. UNESCO was a joint co-ordinator of the International Year of Freshwater (2003), which aimed to raise global awareness of the importance of improving the protection and management of freshwater resources. The Science and technology component of the programme focuses on the follow-up of the World Conference on Science, involving the elaboration of national policies on science and technology; strengthening science education; improving university teaching and enhancing national research capacities; and reinforcing international co-operation in mathematics, physics, chemistry, biology, biotechnology and the engineering sciences. UNESCO aims to contribute to bridging the divide between community-held traditional knowledge and scientific knowledge. UNESCO supports the UN MDG concerning the implementation, by 2005, of national strategies for sustainable development with a view to achieving by 2015 the reversal of current trends in the loss of environmental resources.

UNESCO aims to improve the level of university teaching of the basic sciences through training courses, establishing national and regional networks and centres of excellence, and fostering co-operative research. In carrying out its mission, UNESCO relies on partnerships with non-governmental organizations and the world scientific communities. With the International Council of Scientific Unions and the Third World Academy of Sciences, UNESCO operates a short-term fellowship programme in the basic sciences and an exchange programme of visiting lecturers. In September 1996 UNESCO initiated a 10-year World Solar Programme, which aimed to promote the application of solar energy and to increase research, development and public awareness of all forms of ecologically-sustainable energy use.

UNESCO has over the years established various forms of intergovernmental co-operation concerned with the environmental sciences and research on natural resources, in order to support the recommendations of the June 1992 UN Conference on Environment and Development and, in particular, the implementation of 'Agenda 21' to promote sustainable development. The International Geological Correlation Programme, undertaken jointly with the International Union of Geological Sciences, aims to improve and facilitate global research of geological processes. In the context of the International Decade for Natural Disaster Reduction (declared in 1990), UNESCO conducted scientific studies of natural hazards and means of mitigating their effects and organized several disaster-related workshops. The International Hydrological Programme considers scientific aspects of water resources assessment and management; and the Intergovernmental Oceanographic Commission focuses on issues relating to oceans, shorelines and marine resources, in particular the role of the ocean in climate and global systems. The IOC has been actively involved in the establishment of a Global Coral Reef Monitoring Network and is developing a Global Ocean Observing System. An initiative on Environment and Development in Coastal Regions and in Small Islands is concerned with ensuring environmentally-sound and sustainable development by strengthening management of the following key areas: freshwater resources; the mitigation of coastline instability; biological diversity; and coastal ecosystem productivity. UNESCO hosts the secretariat of the World Water Assessment Programme on freshwater resources.

UNESCO's Man and the Biosphere Programme supports a world-wide network of biosphere reserves (comprising 459 sites in 97 countries in November 2004), which aim to promote environmental conservation and research, education and training in biodiversity and problems of land use (including the fertility of tropical soils and the cultivation of sacred sites). In October 2002 UNESCO announced that the 138 biospheres in mountainous areas would play a leading role in a new Global Change Monitoring Programme aimed at assessing the impact of global climate changes. Following the signing of the Convention to Combat Desertification in October 1994, UNESCO initiated an International Programme for Arid Land Crops, based on a network of existing institutions, to assist implementation of the Convention.

Abdus Salam International Centre for Theoretical Physics: based in Trieste, Italy, the Centre brings together scientists from the developed and developing countries. With support from the Italian Government, the Centre has been operated jointly by the IAEA and UNESCO since 1970. At the end of 1995 administrative responsibility for the Centre was transferred to UNESCO, although IAEA remained a partner in the operations of the Centre. Each year it offers seminars followed by a research workshop, as well as short topical seminars, training courses, symposia and panels. Independent research is also carried out. The programme concentrates on condensed matter physics, high-energy physics, mathematics, physics of weather and climate, structure and nonlinear dynamics of the earth, and microprocessors; Dir KATEPALLI R. SREENIVASEN.

SOCIAL AND HUMAN SCIENCES

UNESCO is mandated to contribute to the world-wide development of the social and human sciences and philosophy, which it regards as of great importance in policy-making and maintaining ethical vigilance. The structure of UNESCO's Social and Human Sciences programme takes into account both an ethical and standard-setting dimension, and research, policy-making, action in the field and future-oriented activities. UNESCO's work programme on Social and Human Sciences comprises three main components: Ethics of science and technology; Promotion of human rights, peace and democratic principles; and Improvement of policies relating to social transformations and promotion of anticipation and prospective studies. The priority Ethics of science and technology element aims to reinforce UNESCO's role as an intellectual forum for ethical reflection on challenges related to the advance of science and technology; oversee the follow-up of the Universal Declaration on the Human Genome and Human Rights (see below); promote education in science and technology; ensure UNESCO's role in promoting good practices through encouraging the inclusion of ethical guiding principles in policy formulation and reinforcing international networks; and to promote international co-operation in human sciences and philosophy. The Social and Human Sciences programme has the main intellectual and conceptual responsibility for the transdisciplinary theme 'eradication of poverty, especially extreme poverty'.

UNESCO aims to promote and protect human rights and acts as an interdisciplinary, multicultural and pluralistic forum for reflection on issues relating to the ethical dimension of scientific advances, for example in biogenetics, new technology, and medicine. In May 1997 the International Bioethics Committee, a group of 36 specialists who meet under UNESCO auspices, approved a draft version of a Universal Declaration on the Human Genome and Human Rights, in an attempt to provide ethical guide-lines for developments in human genetics. The Declaration, which identified some 100,000 hereditary genes as 'common heritage', was adopted by the UNESCO General Conference in November and committed states to promoting the dissemination of relevant scientific knowledge and co-operating in genome research. In October 2003 the General Conference adopted an International Declaration on Human Genetic Data, establishing standards for scientists working in that field. UNESCO hosts the secretariat of the 18-member World

Commission on the Ethics of Scientific Knowledge and Technology (COMEST), which aims to serve as a forum for the exchange of information and ideas and to promote dialogue between scientific communities, decision-makers and the public. COMEST met for the first time in April 1999 in Oslo, Norway. Its second meeting, which took place in December 2001 in Berlin, Germany, focused on the ethics of energy, fresh water and outer space. The third meeting of COMEST, held in Rio de Janeiro, Brazil, in December 2003, inaugurated a new regional-focused approach. An extraordinary meeting of COMEST was held in May 2004, and the fourth regular session was convened in Bangkok, Thailand, in March 2005.

In 1994 UNESCO initiated an international social science research programme, the Management of Social Transformations (MOST), to promote capacity-building in social planning at all levels of decision-making. UNESCO sponsors several research fellowships in the social sciences. In other activities UNESCO promotes the rehabilitation of underprivileged urban areas, the research of socio-cultural factors affecting demographic change, and the study of family issues.

UNESCO aims to assist the building and consolidation of peaceful and democratic societies. An international network of institutions and centres involved in research on conflict resolution is being established to support the promotion of peace. Other training, workshop and research activities have been undertaken in countries that have suffered conflict. An International Youth Clearing House and Information Service (INFOYOUTH) aims to increase and consolidate the information available on the situation of young people in society, and to heighten awareness of their needs, aspirations and potential among public and private decision-makers. UNESCO also focuses on the educational and cultural dimensions of physical education and sport and their capacity to preserve and improve health. Fundamental to UNESCO's mission is the rejection of all forms of discrimination. It disseminates scientific information aimed at combating racial prejudice, works to improve the status of women and their access to education, and promotes equality between men and women.

CULTURE

In undertaking efforts to preserve the world's cultural and natural heritage UNESCO has attempted to emphasize the link between culture and development. In November 2001 the General Conference adopted the UNESCO Universal Declaration on Cultural Diversity, which affirmed the importance of intercultural dialogue in establishing a climate of peace. The work programme on Culture includes the following interrelated components: Reinforcing normative action in the field of culture; Protecting cultural diversity and promoting cultural pluralism and intercultural dialogue; and Strengthening links between culture and development. A particluar focus is placed on all aspects of cultural heritage, and on the encouragement of cultural diversity and dialogue between cultures and civilizations. UNESCO was designated as the lead agency for co-ordinating the UN Year for Cultural Heritage, celebrated in 2002. In January 2002 UNESCO inaugurated a six-year initiative, the Global Alliance on Cultural Diversity, to promote partnerships between governments, non-governmental bodies and the private sector with a view to supporting cultural diversity through the strengthening of cultural industries and the prevention of cultural piracy. UNESCO is formulating a draft International Convention on the Protection of the Diversity of Cultural Contents and Artistic Expressions.

UNESCO's World Heritage Programme, inaugurated in 1978, aims to protect historic sites and natural landmarks of outstanding universal significance, in accordance with the 1972 UNESCO Convention Concerning the Protection of the World Cultural and Natural Heritage, by providing financial aid for restoration, technical assistance, training and management planning. At March 2005 the 'World Heritage List' comprised 788 sites in 134 countries, of which 611 had cultural significance, 154 were natural landmarks, and 23 were of 'mixed' importance. Examples included: the Great Barrier Reef in Australia, the Galapagos Islands (Ecuador), Chartres Cathedral (France), the Taj Mahal at Agra (India), Auschwitz concentration camp (Poland), the historic sanctuary of Machu Picchu (Peru), Robben Island (South Africa), the Serengeti National Park (Tanzania), and the archaeological site of Troy (Turkey). UNESCO also maintains a 'List of World Heritage in Danger', comprising 35 sites at March 2005, in order to attract international attention to sites particularly at risk from the environment or human activities. In October 2002 UNESCO's Executive Board approved the establishment of an International Co-ordination Committee for the Safeguarding of Afghanistan's Cultural Heritage, to be administered by UNESCO with participation by other agencies and organizations, donor nations and experts. In May–July 2003, owing to the overthrow of the Saddam Hussain regime in March–April and ongoing insecurity, UNESCO sent two assessment missions to Iraq to compile an inventory of cultural property and record the condition of major institutions and archaeological sites. In early July UNESCO and Interpol signed an agreement on the compilation of a database

of objects of cultural importance looted in Iraq during the period of unrest.

The formulation of a Declaration against the Intentional Destruction of Cultural Heritage was authorized by the General Conference in November 2001. In addition, the November General Conference adopted the Convention on the Protection of the Underwater Cultural Heritage, covering the protection from commercial exploitation of shipwrecks, submerged historical sites, etc., situated in the territorial waters of signatory states. UNESCO also administers the 1954 Hague Convention on the Protection of Cultural Property in the Event of Armed Conflict and the 1970 Convention on the Means of Prohibiting and Preventing the Illicit Import, Export and Transfer of Ownership of Cultural Property. In 1992 a World Heritage Centre was established to enable rapid mobilization of international technical assistance for the preservation of cultural sites. Through the World Heritage Information Network (WHIN), a world-wide network of more than 800 information providers, UNESCO promotes global awareness and information exchange.

UNESCO supports efforts for the collection and safeguarding of humanity's non-material 'intangible' heritage, including oral traditions, music, dance and medicine. In May 2001 UNESCO awarded the title of 'Masterpieces of the Oral and Intangible Heritage of Humanity' to 19 cultural spaces (i.e. physical or temporal spaces hosting recurrent cultural events) and popular forms of expression deemed to be of outstanding value. UNESCO produces an *Atlas of the World's Languages in Danger of Disappearing*. The most recent edition, issued in February 2002, reported that of some 6,000 languages spoken world-wide, about one-half were endangered. In October 2003 the UNESCO General Conference adopted a Convention for the Safeguarding of Intangible Cultural Heritage, which provided for the establishment of an intergovernmental committee and for participating states to formulate national inventories of intangible heritage.

UNESCO encourages the translation and publication of literary works, publishes albums of art, and produces records, audiovisual programmes and travelling art exhibitions. It supports the development of book publishing and distribution, including the free flow of books and educational material across borders, and the training of editors and managers in publishing. UNESCO is active in preparing and encouraging the enforcement of international legislation on copyright.

In December 1992 UNESCO established the World Commission on Culture and Development, to strengthen links between culture and development and to prepare a report on the issue. The first World Conference on Culture and Development was held in June 1999, in Havana, Cuba. Within the context of the UN's World Decade for Cultural Development (1988–97) UNESCO launched the Silk Roads Project, as a multi-disciplinary study of the interactions among cultures and civilizations along the routes linking Asia and Europe, and established an International Fund for the Promotion of Culture, awarding two annual prizes for music and the promotion of arts. In April 1999 UNESCO celebrated the completion of a major international project, the *General History of Africa*.

COMMUNICATION AND INFORMATION

In 2001 UNESCO introduced a major programme, 'Information for All', as the principal policy-guiding framework for the Communication and Information sector. The organization works towards establishing an open, non-exclusive knowledge society based on information-sharing and incorporating the socio-cultural and ethical dimensions of sustainable development. It promotes the free flow of, and universal access to, information, knowledge, data and best practices, through the development of communications infrastructures, the elimination of impediments to freedom of expression, and the promotion of the right to information; through encouraging international co-operation in maintaining libraries and archives; and through efforts to harness informatics for development purposes and strengthen member states' capacities in this field. Activities include assistance with the development of legislation and training programmes in countries where independent and pluralistic media are emerging; assistance in the monitoring of media independence, pluralism and diversity; promotion of exchange programmes and study tours; and improving access and opportunities for women in the media. UNESCO recognizes that the so-called global 'digital divide', in addition to other developmental differences between countries, generates exclusion and marginalization, and that increased participation in the democratic process can be attained through strengthening national communication and information capacities. UNESCO promotes the upholding of human rights in the use of cyberspace. The organization participated in the first phase of the World Summit on the Information Society, held in Geneva, Switzerland, in December 2003; the second phase was scheduled to take place in Tunis, Tunisia, in November 2005. The work programme on Communication and Information comprises the following components: Promoting equitable access to information and knowledge, especially in the public domain, and Promoting freedom of expression and strengthening communication capacities. UNES-CO's Memory of the World project aims to preserve in digital form, and thereby to promote wide access to, the world's documentary heritage.

In regions affected by conflict UNESCO supports efforts to establish and maintain an independent media service. This strategy is largely implemented through an International Programme for the Development of Communication (IPDC). In Cambodia, Haiti and Mozambique UNESCO participated in the restructuring of the media in the context of national reconciliation and in Bosnia and Herzegovina it assisted in the development of independent media. In December 1998 the Israeli-Palestinian Media Forum was established, to foster professional co-operation between Israeli and Palestinian journalists. IPDC provides support to communication and media development projects in the developing world, including the establishment of news agencies and newspapers and training editorial and technical staff. Since its establishment in 1982 IPDC, has financed some 1,000 projects in more than 130 countries.

In March 1997 the first International Congress on Ethical, Legal and Societal Aspects of Digital Information ('INFOethics') was held in Monte Carlo, Monaco. At the second INFOethics Congress, held in October 1998, experts discussed issues concerning privacy, confidentiality and security in the electronic transfer of information. In November 2000 a third INFOethics conference was held, on the theme of the 'Right to universal access to information in the 21st century'. UNESCO maintains an Observatory on the Information Society, which provides up-to-date information on the development of new information and communications technologies, analyses major trends, and aims to raise awareness of related ethical, legal and societal issues. A UNESCO Institute for Information Technologies in Education was established in Moscow, Russia in 1998. In 2001 the UNESCO Institute for Statistics was established in Montréal, Canada.

Finance

UNESCO's activities are funded through a regular budget provided by contributions from member states and extrabudgetary funds from other sources, particularly UNDP, the World Bank, regional banks and other bilateral Funds-in-Trust arrangements. UNESCO co-operates with many other UN agencies and international non-governmental organizations.

UNESCO's Regular Programme budget for the two years 2004–05 was US $610m. Extrabudgetary funds for 2004–05 were estimated at $347m.

Publications

(mostly in English, French and Spanish editions; Arabic, Chinese and Russian versions are also available in many cases)

Atlas of the World's Languages in Danger of Disappearing.
Copyright Bulletin (quarterly).
Encyclopedia of Life Support Systems (internet-based).
International Review of Education (quarterly).
International Social Science Journal (quarterly).
Museum International (quarterly).
Nature and Resources (quarterly).
Prospects (quarterly review on education).
UNESCO Courier (monthly, in 27 languages).
UNESCO Sources (monthly).
UNESCO Statistical Yearbook.
World Communication Report.
World Educational Report (every 2 years).
World Heritage Review (quarterly).
World Information Report.
World Science Report (every 2 years).

Books, databases, video and radio documentaries, statistics, scientific maps and atlases.

INTERGOVERNMENTAL COMMITTEE FOR PHYSICAL EDUCATION AND SPORT

Address: 7 place de Fontenoy, 75352 Paris, France.

Established by UNESCO in 1978 to serve as a permanent intergovernmental body in the field of physical education and sport.

The Committee is composed of 30 representatives of member states of UNESCO, elected by the General Conference.

Among its many activities aimed at further development of physical education and sport throughout the world, the Committee is responsible for supervising the planning and implementation of UNESCO's programme of activities in physical education and sport, promoting international co-operation in this area and facilitating the adoption and implementation of an International Charter of physical education and sport.

INTERNATIONAL BUREAU OF EDUCATION (IBE)

Address: POB 199, 1211 Geneva 20, Switzerland.

Telephone: (22) 9177800; **fax:** (22) 9177801; **e-mail:** doc.centre@ibe.unesco.org; **internet:** www.ibe.unesco.org.

Founded in 1925, the IBE became an intergovernmental organization in 1929 and was incorporated into UNESCO in 1969. The Bureau's fundamental mission is to deal with matters concerning educational content, methods, and teaching/learning strategies. In addition, the IBE, as an observatory of educational trends and innovations, has assumed responsibilities in the field of educational information. It publishes a quarterly review of education and a newsletter, in addition to various monographs and reference works. The Council of the IBE is composed of representatives of 28 member states of UNESCO, designated by the General Conference. The International Conference on Education is held periodically.

Director: Cecilia Braslavsky (Argentina).

INTERNATIONAL CENTRE FOR TECHNICAL AND VOCATIONAL EDUCATION AND TRAINING

Address: Gorrestr. 15, 53113 Bonn, Germany.

Telephone: (228) 243370; **fax:** (228) 2433777; **e-mail:** info@unevoc.unesco.org; **internet:** www.unevoc.unesco.org.

The Institute, inaugurated in April 2002, promotes high-quality lifelong technical and vocational education in UNESCO's member states, with a particular focus on young people, girls and women, and the disadvantaged.

Director: Rupert Maclean.

INTERNATIONAL INSTITUTE FOR EDUCATIONAL PLANNING (IIEP)

Address: 7–9 rue Eugène Delacroix, 75116 Paris, France.

Telephone: 1-45-03-77-00; **fax:** 1-40-72-83-66; **e-mail:** information@iiep.unesco.org; **internet:** www.unesco.org/iiep.

The Institute was established by UNESCO in 1963 to serve as a world centre for advanced training and research in educational planning. Its purpose is to help all member states of UNESCO in their social and economic development efforts, by enlarging the fund of knowledge about educational planning and the supply of competent experts in this field.

Legally and administratively a part of UNESCO, the Institute is autonomous, and its policies and programme are controlled by its own Governing Board, under special statutes voted by the General Conference of UNESCO.

A satellite office of the IIEP was opened in Buenos Aires, Argentina, in June 1998.

Director: Gudmund Hernes (Norway).

UNESCO INSTITUTE FOR EDUCATION

Address: Feldbrunnenstr. 58, 20148 Hamburg, Germany.

Telephone: (40) 448-0410; **e-mail:** uie@unesco.org; **internet:** www.unesco.org/education/uie/institute/about.shtml.

UNESCO established the Institute in 1951 as a research, training, information, documentation and publishing centre, with a particular focus on adult basic and further education and adult literacy.

Director: Adama Ouane (Mali).

UNESCO INSTITUTE FOR INFORMATION TECHNOLOGIES IN EDUCATION

Address: 8 Kedrova St, 117292 Moscow, Russia.

Telephone: (95) 1292990; **fax:** (95) 1291225; **e-mail:** info@iite.ru; **internet:** www.iite.ru/iite.

The Institute aims to formulate policies regarding the development of, and to support and monitor the use of, information and communication technologies in education. The Institute also conducts research and organizes training programmes.

Director: Dr Vladimir Kinelev.

UNESCO INSTITUTE FOR STATISTICS

Address: CP 6128, Succursale Centre-Ville, Montréal, QC, H3C 3J7, Canada.

Telephone: (514) 343-6880; **fax:** (514) 343-6882; **e-mail:** uis@unesco.org; **internet:** www.uis.unesco.org.

The Institute for Statistics, established in 2001, collects and analyzes national statistics on education, science, technology, culture and communications.

Director: DENISE LIEVESLEY.

UNESCO INSTITUTE FOR WATER EDUCATION

Address: Westvest 7, 2611 AX Delft, The Netherlands.

Telephone: (15) 2151–715; **fax:** (15) 2122–921; **internet:** www.ihe.nl.

The activities of the Institute for Water Education, established in 2003, include advisory and policy-making functions; setting international standards for postgraduate education programmes and professional training in the water sector; education, training and research; and co-ordination of a global network of water sector organizations.

Director: Prof. Dr RICHARD A. MEGANCK.

United Nations Industrial Development Organization— UNIDO

Address: Vienna International Centre, POB 300, 1400 Vienna, Austria.

Telephone: (1) 260260; **fax:** (1) 2692669; **e-mail:** unido@unido.org; **internet:** www.unido.org.

UNIDO began operations in 1967, as an autonomous organization within the UN Secretariat, and became a specialized agency of the UN in 1985. UNIDO's objective is to promote sustainable industrial development in developing nations and states with economies in transition. It aims to assist such countries to integrate fully into the global economic system by mobilizing knowledge, skills, information and technology to promote productive employment, competitive economies and sound environment.

MEMBERS

UNIDO has 171 members.

Organization

(March 2005)

GENERAL CONFERENCE

The General Conference, which consists of representatives of all member states, meets once every two years. It is the chief policy-making organ of the Organization, and reviews UNIDO's policy concepts, strategies on industrial development and budget. The 10th General Conference was held in Vienna, Austria, in December 2003.

INDUSTRIAL DEVELOPMENT BOARD

The Board consists of 53 members elected by the General Conference for a four-year period. It reviews the implementation of the approved work programme, the regular and operational budgets and other General Conference decisions, and, every four years, recommends a candidate for the post of Director-General to the General Conference for appointment.

PROGRAMME AND BUDGET COMMITTEE

The Committee, consisting of 27 members elected by the General Conference for a two-year term, assists the Industrial Development Board in preparing work programmes and budgets.

SECRETARIAT

The Secretariat comprises the office of the Director-General and three divisions, each headed by a Managing Director: Programme Development and Technical Co-operation; Programme Co-ordination and Field Operations; and Administration. In January 2004 UNIDO employed 558 staff members at its headquarters.

Director-General: CARLOS ALFREDO MAGARIÑOS (Argentina).

FIELD REPRESENTATION

In January 2005 UNIDO had 21 country offices, nine regional offices and five focal points. There were more than 90 permanent field staff.

Activities

In its efforts to promote the advancement and integration of industry, UNIDO fulfils two core functions. Firstly, as a global forum, it generates and disseminates knowledge relating to indus-trial matters and provides a platform for policy- and decision-makers to enhance co-operation, establish dialogue and develop partnerships to address effectively challenges to sustainable industrialization. Secondly, as a technical co-operation agency, UNIDO designs and implements programmes to support national industrial development efforts. It also offers specialized support for programme development. The two core functions are complementary and mutually supportive: policy-makers benefit from experience gained in technical co-operation projects, while, by helping to define priorities, the Organization's analytical work identifies where technical co-operation will have greatest impact.

UNIDO's services are designed to be easily integrated into country-specific packages, and local ownership ensures a custom-made approach. The comprehensive services provided by UNIDO cover:

(i) Industrial governance and statistics;

(ii) Promotion of investment and technology;

(iii) Industrial competitiveness and trade;

(iv) Private-sector development;

(v) Agro-industries;

(vi) Sustainable energy and climate change;

(vii) The Montreal Protocol;

(viii) Environment management.

In December 1997 the seventh session of the General Conference endorsed a Business Plan on the Future Role and Functions of UNIDO, which regrouped the Organization's activities into two main areas—Strengthening of industrial capacities, and Cleaner and sustainable industrial development. According to the Plan, activities were to be concentrated in support of the development and mainstreaming of small and medium-sized enterprises (SMEs, identified as the principal means for achieving equitable and sustainable industrial development), in support of agro-based industries and their integration into national industrial structures, and in least-developed countries (LDCs), in particular in Africa, with emphasis on service provision at regional and sub-regional level. In December 1999, at its eighth session, the General Conference approved funding arrangements for a new strategy of developing integrated industrial service packages designed specifically for individual countries. (By 2003 some US \$146.3m. had been committed towards integrated industrial services packages—with 40% of the total allocated to African countries, 40% to central and eastern Europe, Asia and Latin America, and 20% to Arab countries—and 51 packages were in place. The first regional integrated programme was initiated in 2001, covering six West African countries—see below.)

In 2003 UNIDO's investment promotion and institutional capacity-building activities delivered US \$94.6m. in technical co-operation to developing countries and economies in transition. There are seven priority areas: industrial policy formulation and implementation; statistics and information networks; metrology, standardization, certification and accreditation; continuous improvement and quality management; investment and technology promotion; policy framework for SMEs; policy for women's entrepreneurship and entrepreneurship development. New project approvals in 2003 totalled some US \$84.4m. UNIDO has extended its networking with the private sector while assisting developing countries and economies in transition with capacity-building for sustained industrial growth. Promotion of business partnerships, for example, has been strengthened through the Organization's world-wide network of investment and technology promotion offices, investment promotion units, and subcontracting and partnership exchanges, as well as through the Asia-Africa Investment and Technology Promotion

Centre. UNIDO has pursued efforts to overcome the so-called 'digital divide' between and within countries. The Organization has helped to develop electronic and mobile business for SMEs in developing countries and economies in transition. It has also launched an internet-based electronic platform, UNIDO Exchange (accessible at www.unido.org/exchange), for sharing intelligence and fostering business partnerships. UNIDO's Technology Foresight initiative, launched in 1999, involves the systematic visualization of long-term developments in the areas of science, technology, industry, economy and society, with the aim of identifying technologies capable of providing future economic and social benefits. The initiative is being implemented in Latin America and the Caribbean and in Central and Eastern Europe and the CIS.

Through strategic alliances with international certification and standards organizations UNIDO is assisting enterprises in developing countries to overcome technical barriers while improving product quality and access to international markets. UNIDO's industrial business development services—such as business incubators, rural entrepreneurship development and SME cluster development—for SME support institutions are aimed at enabling SMEs to play a key role in economic growth.

UNIDO provides advice to governmental agencies and industrial institutions to improve the management of human resources. The Organization also undertakes training projects to develop human resources in specific industries, and aims to encourage the full participation of women in economic progress through gender awareness programmes and practical training to improve women's access to employment and business opportunities.

UNIDO participated in the Third United Nations Conference on the Least-Developed Countries (UN-LDCs III), held in Brussels, Belgium, in May 2001. The Organization launched a package of 'deliverables' (special initiatives) in support of the Programme of Action adopted by the Conference, which emphasized the importance of productive capacity in the international development agenda. These related to energy, market access (the enablement of LDCs to participate in international trade), and SME networking and cluster development (with a particular focus on agro-processing and metal-working). A new post of UNIDO Co-ordinator for LDCs was created in 2001.

In 2002 UNIDO participated in the International Conference on Financing and Development, held in Monterrey, Mexico, in March, and the World Summit on Sustainable Development (WSSD), held in Johannesburg, South Africa, in August–September. At the Monterrey conference UNIDO launched an initiative designed to facilitate access to international markets for developing countries and countries with transitional economies by assisting them in overcoming barriers to trade. A similar initiative, seeking to promote rural energy for productive use, especially in the poorest countries, was launched at the WSSD.

As a result of the reforms introduced in the 1990s, UNIDO shifted its programming modality from a project-based framework to one with a national scope. Emphasis was given to industrialization in Africa, owing to the prevalence there of LDCs and the necessity to reduce regional inequalities in view of increasing globalization. The national integrated industrial service packages (see above) emphasize capacity-building for the enhancement of industrial competitiveness and private-sector development, which is regarded as a major priority for the transformation of African economies. The basic philosophy has been to identify, jointly with key stakeholders in major industrial sub-sectors, the basic tools required to determine their national industrial development needs and priorities. This process has facilitated the definition and establishment of comprehensive national medium-term and long-term industrial development agendas. By 2003 national programmes, to which some US $51.4m. had been committed, had been developed for 24 African countries. In 2001 a West African regional integrated programme was launched, with a special focus on agro-industries in Benin, Burkina Faso, Guinea, Niger, Senegal and Togo. In 1996 UNIDO formally inaugurated the Alliance for Africa's Industrialization, which constituted the industrial sector element of the UN System-wide Special Initiative on Africa. This aimed to promote development of the continent's natural resources, strengthen labour resources and build government capacities in order to exploit new global markets, in particular in the agro-industrial sector. The Organization supported the Conference on Industrial Partnership and Investment in Africa, held in October 1999 in Dakar, Senegal, which aimed to provide a forum for developing industrial partnerships and promote industrial development. UNIDO was to be responsible for the technical implementation of a regional programme on quality management and standardization, covering the member countries of the Union économique et monétaire ouest-africaine (UEMOA), to be undertaken in collaboration with the European Union, that was approved in 2000. In addition, a technical support programme to improve the level of fish exports has been approved.

UNIDO is increasingly involved in general environmental projects. As one of the implementing agencies of the Multilateral Fund for the Implementation of the Montreal Protocol, UNIDO assists developing countries in efforts gradually to reduce the use of ozone-depleting substances. It is also involved in implementing the Kyoto Protocol of the Framework Convention on Climate Change (relating to greenhouse gas emissions) in old factories world-wide. By late 2004 UNIDO had helped to develop 10 national ozone units responsible for designing, monitoring and implementing programmes to phase-out ozone-depleting substances. In 1994 UNIDO and UNEP launched the National Cleaner Production Centres Programme to promote the use and development of environmentally sustainable technologies and to build national capacities in cleaner production. By early 2005 30 Centres had been established world-wide (including one, in Cuba, which was a national network).

UNIDO also supports collaborative efforts between countries with complementary experience or resources in specific sectors. The investment and technology promotion network publicizes investment opportunities, provides information to investors and promotes business contacts between industrialized and developing countries and economies in transition. UNIDO is increasingly working to achieve investment promotion and transfer of technology and knowledge among developing countries. The Organization has developed several databases, including the Biosafety Information Network Advisory Service (BINAS), the Business Environment Strategic Toolkit (BEST), Industrial Development Abstracts (IDA, providing information on technical co-operation), and the International Referral System on Sources of Information (IRS).

UNIDO has helped to establish and operate the following International Technology Centres: the International Centre for Science and High Technology (based in Trieste, Italy); the International Centre for Advancement of Manufacturing Technology (Bangalore, India); the UNIDO Regional Centre for Small Hydro Power (Trivandum, India); the Centre for the Application of Solar Energy (Perth, Australia); the International Centre of Medicine Biotechnology (Obolensk, Russia); and the International Materials Assessment and Application Centre (in Rio de Janeiro, Brazil). Four others—the International Centre for Materials Technology Promotion, the Shenzhen International Technology Promotion Centre, the Shanghai International Technology Promotion Centre (all in the People's Republic of China) and the International Centre for Materials Evaluation Technology (Republic of Korea)—were under development in early 2005.

Finance

The regular budget for the two years 2004–05 amounted to €144.3m., financed by assessed contributions payable by member states. There was an operational budget of some €21.5m. for the same period, financed from the reimbursement of support costs pertaining to technical co-operation and other services for the same period. The Organization's technical co-operation expenditure was budgeted at some €190m. Technical co-operation activities are financed mainly by voluntary contributions from member countries and donor institutions, and by UNDP, the Multilateral Fund for the Implementation of the Montreal Protocol on Substances that Deplete the Ozone Layer, the Global Environment Facility, and the Common Fund for Commodities. Voluntary contributions for the 2004–05 biennium were projected at €189.8m. The Industrial Development Fund is used by UNIDO to finance development projects that fall outside the usual systems of multilateral funding.

Publications

African Industry 2000: The Challenge of Going Global.

Annual Report.

Development of Clusters and Networks of SMEs.

Gearing up for a New Development Agenda.

Industry for Growth into the New Millennium.

International Yearbook of Industrial Statistics (annually).

Manual for the Evaluation of Industrial Projects.

Manual for Small Industrial Businesses.

Reforming the UN System—UNIDO's Need-Driven Model.

UNIDOScope (monthly, electronic newsletter).

Using Statistics for Process Control and Improvement: An Introduction to Basic Concepts and Techniques.

World Industrial Development Report.

World Information Directory of Industrial Technology and Investment Support Services.

Several other manuals, guide-lines, numerous working papers and reports.

Universal Postal Union—UPU

Address: Case Postale 13, 3000 Bern 15, Switzerland.
Telephone: (31) 3503111; **fax:** (31) 3503110; **e-mail:** info@upu.int; **internet:** www.upu.int.

The General Postal Union was founded by the Treaty of Berne (1874), beginning operations in July 1875. Three years later its name was changed to the Universal Postal Union. In 1948 the UPU became a specialized agency of the UN. The UPU promotes the sustainable development of high-quality, universal, efficient and accessible postal services.

MEMBERS

The UPU has 190 members.

Organization

(March 2005)

CONGRESS

The supreme body of the Union is the Universal Postal Congress, which meets, in principle, every five years. Congress focuses on general principles and broad policy issues. It is responsible for the Constitution (the basic act of the Union), the General Regulations (which contain provisions relating to the application of the Constitution and the operation of the Union), changes in the provision of the Universal Postal Convention, approval of the strategic plan and budget parameters, formulation of overall policy on technical co-operation, and for elections and appointments. Amendments to the Constitution are recorded in Additional Protocols, of which there are currently six. The 22nd Congress was held in Beijing, People's Republic of China, in August–September 1999, the 23rd Congress in Bucharest, Romania, in September–October 2004 and the 24th Congress was scheduled to be held in Nairobi, Kenya, in 2008. The 23rd Congress adopted the Bucharest World Postal Strategy as a four-year framework for the Union's activities in 2005–08 (see below).

COUNCIL OF ADMINISTRATION

The Council, created by the Seoul Congress, 1994, to replace the former Executive Council, meets annually at Bern. It is composed of a Chairman and representatives of 41 member countries of the Union elected by the Universal Postal Congress on the basis of an equitable geographical distribution. It is responsible for supervising the affairs of the Union between Congresses. The Council also considers policies that may affect other sectors, such as standardization and quality of service, provides a forum for considering the implications of governmental policies with respect to competition, deregulation, and trade-in-service issues for international postal services, and considers intergovernmental aspects of technical co-operation. The Council approves the Union's budget, supervises the activities of the International Bureau and takes decisions regarding UPU contacts with other international agencies and bodies. It is also responsible for promoting and co-ordinating all aspects of technical assistance among member countries.

POSTAL OPERATIONS COUNCIL (POC)

As the technical organ of the UPU, the Council, which holds annual sessions and comprises 40 elected member countries, is responsible for the operational, economic and commercial aspects of international postal services. The POC has the authority to amend and enact the Detailed Regulations of the Universal Postal Convention, on the basis of decisions made at Congress. It promotes the studies undertaken by some postal services and the introduction of new postal products. It also prepares and issues recommendations for member countries concerning uniform standards of practice. On the recommendation of the 1999 Beijing Congress the POC established a Standards Board with responsibility for approving standards relating to telematics, postal technology and Electronic Data Interchange (EDI). The POC aims to assist national postal services to modernize postal products, including letter and parcel post, financial services and expedited mail services.

CONSULTATIVE COMMITTEE

The Consultative Committee was established in September 2004 by the 23rd Congress, meeting in Bucharest, Romania. Membership of the Committee was to be open to private companies and other non-government organizations with an involvement or concern in international postal services. All members were to be extended full observer status in all organs of the Union. The Committee was to twice a year, in Bern, to coincide with meetings of the Council of Administration and the Postal Operations Council. The Committee replaced an Advisory Group which had been constituted in 2000 upon recommendation of a high-level group, established at the Beijing Congress to consider the future development of the organization.

INTERNATIONAL BUREAU

The day-to-day administrative work of the UPU is executed through the International Bureau, which provides secretariat and support facilities for the UPU's bodies. It serves as an instrument of liaison, information and consultation for the postal administration of the member countries and promotes technical co-operation among Union members. It also acts as a clearing house for the settlement of accounts between postal administrations for inter-administration charges related to the exchange of postal items and international reply coupons. The Bureau supports the technical assistance programmes of the UPU and serves as an intermediary between the UPU, the UN, its agencies and other international organizations, customer organizations and private delivery services. Increasingly the Bureau has assumed a greater role in certain areas of postal administration, for example, the application of telematics, postal technology and EDI through its Postal Technology Centre, the development of postal markets, and the monitoring of quality of postal services world-wide.

Director-General of the International Bureau: EDOUARD DAYAN (France).

Activities

The essential principles of the Union are the following:

(i) to develop social, cultural and commercial communication between people through the efficient operation of the postal services;

(ii) to guarantee freedom of transit and free circulation of postal items;

(iii) to ensure the organization, development and modernization of the postal services;

(iv) to promote and participate in postal technical assistance between member countries;

(v) to ensure the interoperability of postal networks by implementing a suitable policy of standardization;

(vi) to meet the changing needs of customers; and

(vii) to improve the quality of service.

In addition to the Constitution and the General Regulations, the Universal Postal Convention is also a compulsory Act of the UPU (binding on all member countries), in view of its importance in the postal field and historical value. The Convention and its Detailed Regulations contain the common rules applicable to the international postal service and provisions concerning letter- and parcel-post. The Detailed Regulations are agreements concluded by the national postal administrations elected by Congress to the POC. The POC is empowered to revise and enact these, taking into account decisions made at Congress.

The Postal Payment Services Agreement and its Regulations, adopted by the 1999 Beijing Congress to replace the former Money Orders, Giro and Cash-on-Delivery Agreements, is an optional arrangement. Not all member countries have acceded to this Agreement.

In recent years the UPU has reviewed its activities and has focused on the following factors underlying the modern postal environment: the growing role played by technology, the expanding reach of the effects of globalization, and the need to make the customer the focus of new competitive strategies. The 1999 Beijing Congress authorized the establishment of a high-level group to make recommendations on the future development of the UPU, which proposed the reorganization of the Union around three circles of member interest: (i) governments and state regulatory bodies; (ii) postal operators; and (iii) external stakeholders in postal systems, to be represented on a new Consultative Committee. In October 2002 the UPU organized a strategy conference entitled 'Future Post', at which delegates representing governments and postal services addressed challenges confronting the postal industry. The 23rd Congress, held in September–October 2004 adopted the Bucharest World Postal Strategy, detailing a number of objectives to be pursued by governments, postal administrations and restricted unions, and the UPU permanent bodies, over the period 2005–08. The strategy incorporated the following objectives: to ensure the provision of a good quality, affordable universal post service; to improve the quality and level of efficiency of the international postal network; to facilitate the development of markets to respond to customer needs; to undertake reform of the postal sector in order to ensure the sustainable development of postal services; and to strengthen and broaden co-operation with all stakeholders of the postal sector. The Bucharest Congress also adopted a new package of proposals for so-called terminal dues; a new quality of service standard and targets for international mail services; a resolution relating to security, the combating of terrorism and prevention of money-laundering through use of the mail network; and a proposal to amend the UPU Convention to recognize legally the Electronic Postmark as an optional postal service.

The 1999 Congress approved the establishment of a Quality Service Fund, which was to be financed by industrialized member countries (by a 7.5% increase in dues) in order to support service improvement projects in developing member states. It was anticipated to be a temporary arrangement, to be dissolved at the end of 2008. New projects approved by the Fund in September 2004 included improvement of the delivery time in Paraguay, a conveyor belt system in South Africa, extension of a tracking system for international mail in Nepal, and the refitting of airmail facility in Bermuda. Other efforts to generate resources available for postal development and reform are undertaken by the Postal Development Action Group, established in 1991.

On 1 October 2003 a new UPU clearing system became operational to enable postal operators to exchange bills electronically. During 2004 the UPU sponsored an application to the Internet Corporation for Assigned Names and Numbers to obtain a top-level internet domain, .post, for use, *inter alia*, by national and other postal operators, postal-related organizations, regional associations, UPU-regulated services, and trademarks and brand names.

Finance

All of the UPU's regular budget expenses are financed by member countries, based on a contribution class system. During the period 2001–04 the annual budget was not to exceed 37m. Swiss francs.

Publications

Letter Post Compendium.

Postal Statistics.

Union Postale (quarterly, in French, German, English, Arabic, Chinese, Spanish and Russian).

UPU Technical Standards.

Other guides and industry reports.

World Health Organization—WHO

Address: Ave Appia 20, 1211 Geneva 27, Switzerland.
Telephone: (22) 7912111; **fax:** (22) 7913111; **e-mail:** info@who.int; **internet:** www.who.int.

WHO, established in 1948, is the lead agency within the UN system concerned with the protection and improvement of public health.

MEMBERS

WHO has 192 members and two associate members.

Organization

(March 2005)

WORLD HEALTH ASSEMBLY

The Assembly meets in Geneva, once a year. It is responsible for policy making and the biennial programme and budget; appoints the Director-General; admits new members; and reviews budget contributions.

EXECUTIVE BOARD

The Board is composed of 32 health experts designated by, but not representing, their governments; they serve for three years, and the World Health Assembly elects 10–12 member states each year to the Board. It meets at least twice a year to review the Director-General's programme, which it forwards to the Assembly with any recommendations that seem necessary. It advises on questions referred to it by the Assembly and is responsible for putting into effect the decisions and policies of the Assembly. It is also empowered to take emergency measures in case of epidemics or disasters.

Chairman: D. Á. GUNNARSON (Iceland).

SECRETARIAT

Director-General: Dr JONG-WOOK LEE (Republic of Korea).

Assistant Directors-General: DENIS AITKEN (United Kingdom) (Director of the Office of the Director-General), LIU PEILONG (People's Republic of China) (Adviser to the Director-General), ANARFI ASAMOA-BAAH (Ghana) (Communicable Diseases), KAZEM BEHBEHANI (Kuwait) (External Relations and Governing Bodies), JACK C. CHOW (USA) (HIV/AIDS, TB and Malaria), TIMOTHY G. EVANS (Canada) (Evidence and Information for Policy), CATHERINE LE GALÈS-CAMUS (France) (Non-Communicable Diseases and Mental Health), KERSTIN LEITNER (Germany) (Sustainable Development & Healthy Environments), VLADIMIR LEPAKHIN (Russia) (Health Technology and Pharmaceuticals), ANDERS NORDSTRÖM (Sweden) (General Management), JOY PHU-MAPHI (Botswana) (Family & Community Health).

REGIONAL OFFICES

Each of WHO's six geographical regions has its own organization, consisting of a regional committee representing relevant member states and associate members, and a regional office staffed by experts in various fields of health.

Africa: Cité du Djoue BP 06, Brazzaville, Republic of the Congo; tel. 83-09-00; fax 83-95-01; e-mail regafro@whoafr.org; internet www.afro.who.int/; Dir Dr EBRAHIM MALICK SAMBA (The Gambia).

Americas: Pan-American Health Organization, 525 23rd St, NW, Washington, DC 20037, USA; tel. (202) 974-3000; fax (202) 974-3663; e-mail director@paho.org; internet www.paho.org; Dir Dr MIRTA ROSES PERIAGO (Argentina).

Eastern Mediterranean: POB 7608, Abdul Razzak al Sanhouri St, Cairo (Nasr City) 11371, Egypt; tel. (2) 6702535; fax (2) 6702492; e-mail postmaster@emro.who.int; internet www.emro.who.int; Dir Dr HUSSEIN ABDUL RAZZAQ GEZAIRY.

Europe: 8 Scherfigsvej, 2100 Copenhagen Ø, Denmark; tel. (1) 39-17-17-17; fax (1) 39-17-18-18; e-mail postmaster@euro.who.int; internet www.euro.who.int; Dir Dr MARC DANZON (France).

South-East Asia: World Health House, Indraprastha Estate, Mahatma Gandhi Rd, New Delhi 110002, India; tel. (11) 23370804; fax (11) 23379507; e-mail pandeyh@whosea.org; internet w3.whosea.org; Dir Dr SAMLEE PLIANBANGCHANG.

Western Pacific: POB 2932, Manila 1000, Philippines; tel. (2) 5288001; fax (2) 5211036; e-mail postmaster@wpro.who.int; internet www.wpro.who.int; Dir Dr SHIGERU OMI (Japan).

Activities

WHO's objective is stated in its constitution as 'the attainment by all peoples of the highest possible level of health'. 'Health' is defined as 'a state of complete physical, mental and social well-being and not merely the absence of disease and infirmity'. In November 2001 WHO issued the International Classification of Functioning, Disability and Health (ICF) to act as an international standard and guide-lines for determining health and disability.

WHO acts as the central authority directing international health work, and establishes relations with professional groups and government health authorities on that basis.

It provides, on request from member states, technical and policy assistance in support of programmes to promote health, prevent and control health problems, control or eradicate disease, train health workers best suited to local needs and strengthen national health systems. Aid is provided in emergencies and natural disasters.

A global programme of collaborative research and exchange of scientific information is carried out in co-operation with about 1,200 national institutions. Particular stress is laid on the widespread communicable diseases of the tropics, and the countries directly concerned are assisted in developing their research capabilities.

It keeps diseases and other health problems under constant surveillance, promotes the exchange of prompt and accurate information and of notification of outbreaks of diseases, and administers the International Health Regulations. It sets standards for the quality control of drugs, vaccines and other substances affecting health. It formulates health regulations for international travel.

It collects and disseminates health data and carries out statistical analyses and comparative studies in such diseases as cancer, heart disease and mental illness.

It receives reports on drugs observed to have shown adverse reactions in any country, and transmits the information to other member states.

It promotes improved environmental conditions, including housing, sanitation and working conditions. All available information on effects on human health of the pollutants in the environment is critically reviewed and published.

Co-operation among scientists and professional groups is encouraged. The organization negotiates and sustains national and global partnerships. It may propose international conventions and agreements, and develops and promotes international norms and standards. The organization promotes the development and testing of new technologies, tools and guide-lines. It assists in developing an informed public opinion on matters of health.

HEALTH FOR ALL

WHO's first global strategy for pursuing 'Health for all' was adopted in May 1981 by the 34th World Health Assembly. The objective of 'Health for all' was identified as the attainment by all citizens of the world of a level of health that would permit them to lead a socially and economically productive life, requiring fair distribution of available resources, universal access to essential health care, and the promotion of preventive health care. In May 1998 the 51st World Health Assembly renewed the initiative, adopting a global strategy in support of 'Health for all in the 21st century', to be effected through regional and national health policies. The new approach was to build on the primary health care approach of the initial strategy, but was to strengthen the emphasis on quality of life, equity in health and access to health services. The following have been identified as minimum requirements of 'Health for All':

Safe water in the home or within 15 minutes' walking distance, and adequate sanitary facilities in the home or immediate vicinity;

Immunization against diphtheria, pertussis (whooping cough), tetanus, poliomyelitis, measles and tuberculosis;

Local health care, including availability of essential drugs, within one hour's travel;

Trained personnel to attend childbirth, and to care for pregnant mothers and children up to at least one year old.

WHO's technical programmes are divided into the following groups, or 'clusters': Communicable Diseases; Non-communicable Diseases and Mental Health; Family and Community Health; Sustainable Development and Healthy Environments; Health Technology and Pharmaceuticals; and Evidence and Information for Policy. In 2004–05 the following areas of work were designated as organization-wide priorities: HIV/AIDS; TB; malaria; cancer, cardiovascular diseases and diabetes; tobacco; mental health; making pregnancy safer and children's health; health and environment; food safety; health systems, including essential medicines; and blood safety. In 2000 WHO adopted a new corporate strategy, entailing a stronger focus on performance and programme delivery through standardized plans of action, and increased consistency and efficiency throughout the organization.

The Tenth General Programme of Work, for the period 2002–05, defined a policy framework for pursuing the principal objectives of building healthy populations and combating ill health. The Programme took into account: increasing understanding of the social, economic, political and cultural factors involved in achieving better health and the role played by better health in poverty reduction; the increasing complexity of health systems; the importance of safeguarding health as a component of humanitarian action; and the need for greater co-ordination among development organizations. It incorporated four interrelated strategic directions: lessening excess mortality, morbidity and disability, especially in poor and marginalized populations; promoting healthy lifestyles and reducing risk factors to human health arising from environmental, economic, social and behavioural causes; developing equitable and financially fair health systems; and establishing an enabling policy and an institutional environment for the health sector and promoting an effective health dimension to social, economic, environmental and development policy.

COMMUNICABLE DISEASES

WHO identifies infectious and parasitic communicable diseases as a major obstacle to social and economic progress, particularly in

developing countries, where, in addition to disabilities and loss of productivity and household earnings, they cause nearly one-half of all deaths. Emerging and re-emerging diseases; those likely to cause epidemics; increasing incidence of zoonoses (diseases passed from animals to humans either directly or by insects), attributable to environmental changes; outbreaks of unknown etiology; and the undermining of some drug therapies by the spread of antimicrobial resistance are main areas of concern. In recent years WHO has noted the global spread of communicable diseases through international travel, voluntary human migration and involuntary population displacement.

WHO's Communicable Diseases group works to reduce the impact of infectious diseases world-wide through surveillance and response; prevention, control and eradication strategies; and research and product development. The group seeks to identify new technologies and tools, and to foster national development through strengthening health services and the better use of existing tools. It aims to strengthen global monitoring of important communicable disease problems. The group advocates a functional approach to disease control. It aims to create consensus and consolidate partnerships around targeted diseases and collaborates with other groups at all stages to provide an integrated response. In April 2000 WHO and several partner institutions in epidemic surveillance established a Global Outbreak Alert and Response Network. Through the Network WHO aims to maintain constant vigilance regarding outbreaks of disease and to link world-wide expertise to provide an immediate response capability. From March 2003 WHO, through the Network, was co-ordinating the international investigation into the global spread of Severe Acute Respiratory Syndrome (SARS), a previously unknown atypical pneumonia. From the end of that year WHO was monitoring the spread through several Asian countries of the virus A/H5N1 (a rapidly mutating strain of zoonotic highly pathogenic avian influenza). In February 2005 WHO issued guide-lines for the global surveillance of the spread of A/H5N1 infection in human and animal populations. WHO has urged all countries to develop influenza pandemic preparedness plans.

One of WHO's major achievements was the eradication of smallpox. Following a massive international campaign of vaccination and surveillance (begun in 1958 and intensified in 1967), the last case was detected in 1977 and the eradication of the disease was declared in 1980. In May 1996 the World Health Assembly resolved that, pending a final endorsement, all remaining stocks of the smallpox virus were to be destroyed on 30 June 1999, although 500,000 doses of smallpox vaccine were to remain, along with a supply of the smallpox vaccine seed virus, in order to ensure that a further supply of the vaccine could be made available if required. In May 1999, however, the Assembly authorized a temporary retention of stocks of the virus until 2002. In late 2001, in response to fears that illegally-held virus stocks could be used in acts of biological terrorism (see below), WHO reassembled a team of technical experts on smallpox. In January 2002 the Executive Board determined that stocks of the virus should continue to be retained, to enable research into more effective treatments and vaccines.

In 1988 the World Health Assembly declared its commitment to the eradication of poliomyelitis by the end of 2000 and launched the Global Polio Eradication Initiative. In August 1996 WHO, UNICEF and Rotary International, together with other national and international partners, initiated a campaign to 'Kick Polio out of Africa', with the aim of immunizing more than 100m. children in 46 countries against the disease over a three-year period. In 2000 WHO adopted a strategic plan for the eradication of polio covering the period 2001–05, which envisaged the effective use of National Immunization Days (NIDs) to secure global interruption of polio transmission by the end of 2002, with a view to achieving certification of the global eradication of polio by the end of 2005. (In conflict zones so-called 'days of tranquility' have been negotiated to facilitate the implementation of NIDs. Vitamin A has also been administered during NIDS in order to combat nutritional deficiencies in children and thereby boost their immunity.) Meanwhile, routine immunization services were to be strengthened. A post-certification immunization policy for polio was to be formulated. In January 2004 the ministers of health of six countries (Afghanistan, Egypt, India, Niger, Nigeria and Pakistan) that had been designated as still 'polio-endemic' at the end of 2003, and global partners, meeting under the auspices of WHO and UNICEF, adopted the Geneva Declaration on the Eradication of Poliomyelitis, in which they made a commitment to accelerate the drive towards eradication of the disease, by improving the scope of vaccination programmes. Significant progress in eradication of the virus was reported in Asia during that year. In sub-Saharan Africa, however, an outbreak originating in northern Nigeria had spread, by mid-2004, to 12 previously polio-free countries. These included Côte d'Ivoire and Sudan, where ongoing civil unrest and population displacements were impeding control efforts. By that time 257 new cases had been reported in the northern Nigerian outbreak, which had been caused by a temporary cessation of vaccination activities in response to local opposition to the vaccination programme. During September and October the governments of affected West and Central African countries organized a number of synchronized immunization days, which resulted in the vaccination of more than 80m. children. A renewed co-ordinated mass vaccination drive across West and Central Africa was launched in late February 2005; this was expected to reach 100,000 children in 22 countries, with further vaccination rounds scheduled for April and May. At December 2004 the number of confirmed polio cases world-wide stood at 1,252, of which 786 were in Nigeria and 135 were in India. (In 1988 35,000 cases had been confirmed in 125 countries, with the actual number of cases estimated at around 350,000.) WHO has declared the following regions 'polio-free': the Americas (1994); Western Pacific (2000); and Europe (2002).

The Onchocerciasis Control Programme in West Africa (OCP) was initiated in 1974 to eliminate onchocerciasis, which can cause blindness, as a major public health problem and an impediment to socio-economic development in 11 countries of the region. In January 1996 a new initiative, the African Programme for Onchocerciasis Control (APOC), covering 19 countries outside West Africa, became operational, with funding co-ordinated by the World Bank and with WHO as the executing agency. In December 1994 WHO announced that the OCP was to be terminated by the end of 2002, by which time it was estimated that 40m. people would have been protected from the disease and 600,000 people prevented from blindness. In May 1999 WHO reported that the OCP, based in Ouagadougou, Burkina Faso, was to be transformed into a Multi-disease Surveillance Centre.

The Onchocerciasis Elimination Programme in the Americas (OEPA), launched in 1992, co-ordinates work to control the disease in six endemic countries of Latin America. In January 1998 a new 20-year programme to eliminate lymphatic filariasis was initiated, with substantial funding and support from two major pharmaceutical companies, and in collaboration with the World Bank, the Arab Fund for Economic and Social Development and the governments of Japan, the United Kingdom and the USA. South American trypanosomiasis ('Chagas disease') is endemic in Central and South America, causing the deaths of some 45,000 people each year and infecting a further 16m.–18m. A regional intergovernmental commission is implementing a programme to eliminate Chagas from the Southern Cone region of Latin America; it is hoped that this goal will be achieved by 2010. The countries of the Andean region of Latin America initiated a plan for the elimination of transmission of Chagas disease in February 1997, and a similar plan was launched by Central American governments in October.

WHO is committed to the elimination of leprosy (the reduction of the prevalence of leprosy to less than one case per 10,000 population). The use of a highly effective combination of three drugs (known as multi-drug therapy—MDT) resulted in a reduction in the number of leprosy cases world-wide from 10m.–12m. in 1988 to 458,000 in 2004. The number of countries having more than one case of leprosy per 10,000 had declined to 10 by 2003, compared with 122 in 1985. The Global Alliance for the Elimination of Leprosy, launched in November 1999 by WHO, in collaboration with governments of affected countries and several private partners, including a major pharmaceutical company, aimed to bring about the eradication of the disease by the end of 2005, through the continued use of MDT treatment. In March 2005 WHO transferred responsibility for its global leprosy programme from the Organization's Geneva headquarters to the South-East Asia Regional Office, based in New Delhi, India. Responsibility for supplying MDT remained with WHO headquarters. At that time leprosy control activities were being intensified in the most endemic countries: Angola, Brazil, India, Madagascar, Mozambique, Nepal and Tanzania. (India had more than one-half of all active leprosy cases, while Brazil was the second most endemic country.) In 1998 WHO launched the Global Buruli Ulcer Initiative, which aimed to co-ordinate control of and research into Buruli ulcer, another mycobacterial disease. In July of that year the Director-General of WHO and representatives of more than 20 countries, meeting in Yamoussoukro, Côte d'Ivoire, signed a declaration on the control of Buruli ulcer. In May 2004 the World Health Assembly adopted a resolution urging improved research into, and detection and treatment of, Buruli ulcer.

The Special Programme for Research and Training in Tropical Diseases, established in 1975 and sponsored jointly by WHO, UNDP and the World Bank, as well as by contributions from donor countries, involves a world-wide network of some 5,000 scientists working on the development and application of vaccines, new drugs, diagnostic kits and preventive measures, and an applied field research on practical community issues affecting the target diseases.

The objective of providing immunization for all children by 1990 was adopted by the World Health Assembly in 1977. Six diseases (measles, whooping cough, tetanus, poliomyelitis, tuberculosis and diphtheria) became the target of the Expanded Programme on Immunization (EPI), in which WHO, UNICEF and many other organizations collaborated. As a result of massive international and national efforts, the global immunization coverage increased from 20% in the early 1980s to the targeted rate of 80% by the end of 1990. This coverage signified that more than 100m. children in the developing world under the age of one had been successfully vaccinated

against the targeted diseases, the lives of about 3m. children had been saved every year, and 500,000 annual cases of paralysis as a result of polio had been prevented. In 1992 the Assembly resolved to reach a new target of 90% immunization coverage with the six EPI vaccines; to introduce hepatitis B as a seventh vaccine (with the aim of an 80% reduction in the incidence of the disease in children by 2001); and to introduce the yellow fever vaccine in areas where it occurs endemically.

In June 2000 WHO released a report entitled 'Overcoming Antimicrobial Resistance', in which it warned that the misuse of antibiotics could render some common infectious illnesses unresponsive to treatment. At that time WHO issued guide-lines which aimed to mitigate the risks associated with the use of antimicrobials in livestock reared for human consumption.

HIV/AIDS, TB AND MALARIA

Combating HIV/AIDS, tuberculosis (TB) and malaria are organization-wide priorities and, as such, are supported not only by their own areas of work but also by activities undertaken in other areas. In July 2000 a meeting of the Group of Seven industrialized nations and Russia (G-8), convened in Genoa, Italy, announced the formation of a new Global Fund to Fight AIDS, TB and Malaria (as previously proposed by the UN Secretary-General and recommended by the World Health Assembly). By early 2005 the Fund, a partnership between governments, UN bodies (including WHO) and other agencies, and private-sector interests, had committed around US $3,000m. in grants to prevention and treatment programmes in 128 countries.

The HIV/AIDS epidemic represents a major threat to human well-being and socio-economic progress. Some 95% of those known to be infected with HIV/AIDS live in developing countries, and AIDS-related illnesses are the leading cause of death in sub-Saharan Africa. At December 2004 an estimated 39.4m. people world-wide were living with HIV/AIDS (including some 2.2m. children under 15 years); 4.9m. people were newly infected during that year. WHO's Global Programme on AIDS, initiated in 1987, was concluded in December 1995. A Joint UN Programme on HIV/AIDS (UNAIDS) became operational on 1 January 1996, sponsored by WHO and other UN agencies. The UNAIDS secretariat is based at WHO headquarters. WHO established an Office of HIV/AIDS and Sexually-Transmitted Diseases in order to ensure the continuity of its global response to the problem, which included support for national control and education plans, improving the safety of blood supplies and improving the care and support of AIDS patients. In addition, the Office was to liaise with UNAIDS and to make available WHO's research and technical expertise. HIV/AIDS are an organization-wide priority. Sufferers of HIV/AIDS in developing countries have often failed to receive advanced antiretroviral (ARV) treatments that are widely available in industrialized countries, owing to their high cost. In May 2000 the World Health Assembly adopted a resolution urging WHO member states to improve access to the prevention and treatment of HIV-related illnesses and to increase the availability and affordability of drugs. A WHO-UNAIDS HIV Vaccine Initiative was launched in that year. In June 2001 governments participating in a special session of the UN General Assembly on HIV/AIDS adopted a Declaration of Commitment on HIV/AIDS. WHO, with UNAIDS, UNICEF, UNFPA, the World Bank, and major pharmaceutical companies, participates in the 'Accelerating Access' initiative, which aims to expand access to care, support and ARVs for people with HIV/AIDS. In March 2002, under its 'Access to Quality HIV/AIDS Drugs and Diagnostics' programme, WHO published a comprehensive list of HIV-related medicines deemed to meet standards recommended by the Organization. In April WHO issued the first treatment guide-lines for HIV/AIDS cases in poor communities, and endorsed the inclusion of HIV/AIDS drugs in its *Model List of Essential Medicines* (see below) in order to encourage their wider availability. The secretariat of the International HIV Treatment Access Coalition, founded in December of that year by governments, non-governmental organizations, donors and others to facilitate access to ARVs for people in low- and middle-income countries, is based at WHO headquarters. WHO, jointly with UNAIDS and the Global Fund to Fight AIDS, TB and Malaria, supports the so-called '3-by-5' target of providing 3m. people in developing countries with ARVs by the end of 2005. WHO supports governments in developing effective health-sector responses to the HIV/AIDS epidemic through enhancing the planning and managerial capabilities, implementation capacity, and resources of health systems. In February 2003 WHO and FAO jointly published a manual on nutritional care for people living with HIV/AIDS.

By the late 1990s many countries had failed significantly to reduce inequalities in healthcare, to improve the health of poor and disadvantaged people or to improve the sustainability of health systems, owing to weak national health systems and the insufficient use of evidence-based, cost-effective treatment methods. In addition, there was a lack of systems to monitor improvements in health services and to determine overall changes in health. WHO, therefore, aims to address these problems and works to ensure that treatment concerning children, adolescents and women, and reproductive health, HIV/AIDS and other sexually transmitted infections, is effectively provided. WHO assists countries to expand and improve the functioning of their health infrastructure in order to ensure wider access to care, hospital services and health education. It works with countries to ensure continuity and quality of care at all levels, by well-trained health personnel.

Joint UN Programme on HIV/AIDS (UNAIDS): 20 ave Appia, 1211 Geneva 27, Switzerland; tel. (22) 7913666; fax (22) 7914187; e-mail unaids@unaids.org; internet www.unaids.org; established in 1996 to lead, strengthen and support an expanded response to the global HIV/AIDS pandemic; activities focus on prevention, care and support, reducing vulnerability to infection, and alleviating the socioeconomic and human effects of HIV/AIDS; launched the Global Coalition on Women and AIDS in Feb. 2004; co-sponsors: WHO, UNICEF, UNDP, UNFPA, UNODC, ILO, UNESCO, the World Bank, WFP, UNHCR; Exec. Dir PETER PIOT (Belgium).

In 1995 WHO established a Global Tuberculosis Programme to address the challenges of the TB epidemic, which had been declared a global emergency by the Organization in 1993. According to WHO estimates, one-third of the world's population carries the TB bacillus, generating around 9m. active cases and killing around 2m. people each year. The largest concentration of TB cases is in south-east Asia. WHO provides technical support to all member countries, with special attention given to those with high TB prevalence, to establish effective national tuberculosis control programmes. WHO's strategy for TB control includes the use of DOTS (direct observation treatment, short-course), standardized treatment guide-lines, and result accountability through routine evaluation of treatment outcomes. Simultaneously, WHO is encouraging research with the aim of further disseminating DOTS, adapting DOTS for wider use, developing new tools for prevention, diagnosis and treatment, and containing new threats such as the HIV/TB co-epidemic. 'Stop TB', launched by WHO in 1999, in partnership with the World Bank, the US Government and a coalition of non-governmental organizations, aims to promote the use of DOTS to ensure a one-half reduction in global TB cases by 2010 (compared with levels at 2000). However, inadequate control of DOTS in some areas, leading to partial and inconsistent treatments, has resulted in the development of drug-resistant and, often, incurable strains of the disease. The incidence of so-called multidrug-resistant TB (MDR-TB) strains, that are unresponsive to at least two of the four most commonly used anti-TB drugs, has risen in recent years; in 2004 WHO estimated that, annually, 300,000 new MDR-TB cases were arising world-wide, of which some 79% were 'super strains', resistant to at least three of the main anti-TB drugs. WHO has developed DOTS-Plus, a strategy for controlling the spread of MDR-TB in areas of high prevalence. TB is the principal cause of death for people infected with the HIV virus and an estimated one-third of people living with HIV/AIDS globally are co-infected with TB. In March 2001 the Global TB Drug Facility was launched under the 'Stop TB' initiative; this aims to increase access to high-quality anti-TB drugs for sufferers in developing countries. The 'Stop TB' partnership has co-ordinated the development of the Global Plan to Stop TB, which represents a 'roadmap' for TB control, envisaging the expansion of access to DOTS; the advancement of MDR-TB prevention measures; the development of anti-TB drugs entailing a shorter treatment period; and the implementation of new strategies for treating people with HIV and TB. The first phase of the Global Plan covered the period 2000–05, while the second stage was to cover 2006–15.

In October 1998 WHO, jointly with UNICEF, the World Bank and UNDP, formally launched the Roll Back Malaria (RBM) programme, which aimed to halve the prevalence of malaria by 2010. The disease acutely affects at least 350m.–500m. people, and kills an estimated 1m. people, every year. Some 90% of all malaria cases occur in sub-Saharan Africa. It is estimated that the disease directly causes 18% of all child deaths in that region. The global RBM Partnership, linking governments, development agencies, and other parties, aims to mobilize resources and support for controlling malaria. An RBM Partnership Global Strategic Plan for the period 2005–15 was expected to be adopted in November 2005. In January 2004 WHO's RBM department recommended a number of guide-lines for malaria control, focusing on the need for prompt, effective antimalarial treatment, and the issue of drug resistance; vector control, including the use of insecticide-treated bednets; malaria in pregnancy; malaria epidemics; and monitoring and evaluation activities. WHO, with several private- and public-sector partners, supports the development of more effective anti-malaria drugs and vaccines through the 'Medicines for Malaria' venture.

NON-COMMUNICABLE DISEASES AND MENTAL HEALTH

The Non-communicable Diseases and Mental Health group comprises departments for the surveillance, prevention and management of uninfectious diseases, such as those arising from an unhealthy diet, and departments for health promotion, disability, injury prevention and rehabilitation, mental health and substance abuse. Surveillance, prevention and management of non-communicable diseases, tobacco, and mental health are organization-wide priorities.

Tobacco use, unhealthy diet and physical inactivity are regarded as common, preventable risk factors for the four most prominent non-communicable diseases: cardiovascular diseases, cancer, chronic respiratory disease and diabetes. WHO aims to monitor the global epidemiological situation of non-communicable diseases, to co-ordinate multinational research activities concerned with prevention and care, and to analyse determining factors such as gender and poverty. In 1998 the organization adopted a resolution on measures to be taken to combat non-communicable diseases; their prevalence was anticipated to increase, particularly in developing countries, owing to rising life expectancy and changes in lifestyles. For example, between 1995 and 2025 the number of adults affected by diabetes world-wide was projected to increase from 135m. to 300m. In 2001 chronic diseases reportedly accounted for about 59% of the estimated 56.5m. total deaths globally and for 46% of the global burden of disease. In February 1999 WHO initiated a new programme, 'Vision 2020: the Right to Sight', which aimed to eliminate avoidable blindness (estimated to be as much as 80% of all cases) by 2020. Blindness was otherwise predicted to increase by as much as twofold, owing to the increased longevity of the global population. In May 2004 the World Health Assembly endorsed a Global Strategy on Diet, Physical Activity and Health; it was estimated at that time that more than 1,000m. adults world-wide were overweight, and that, of these, some 300,000 were clinically obese. WHO has studied obesity-related issues in co-operation with the International Association for the Study of Obesity (IASO). The International Task Force on Obesity, affiliated to the IASO, aims to encourage the development of new policies for managing obesity. WHO and FAO jointly commissioned an expert report on the relationship of diet, nutrition and physical activity to chronic diseases, which was published in March 2003.

WHO's programmes for diabetes mellitus, chronic rheumatic diseases and asthma assist with the development of national initiatives, based upon goals and targets for the improvement of early detection, care and reduction of long-term complications. WHO's cardiovascular diseases programme aims to prevent and control the major cardiovascular diseases, which are responsible for more than 14m. deaths each year. It is estimated that one-third of these deaths could have been prevented with existing scientific knowledge. The programme on cancer control is concerned with the prevention of cancer, improving its detection and cure, and ensuring care of all cancer patients in need. In May 2004 the World Health Assembly adopted a resolution on cancer prevention and control, recognizing an increase in global cancer cases, particularly in developing countries, and stressing that many cases and related deaths could be prevented. The resolution included a number of recommendations for the improvement of national cancer control programmes. WHO is a co-sponsor of the Global Day Against Pain, which was held for the first time in 2004 and was to take place thereafter annually on 11 October. The Global Day highlights the need for improved pain management and palliative care for sufferers of diseases such as cancer and AIDS, with a particular focus on patients living in low-income countries with minimal access to opioid analgesics, and urges recognition of access to pain relief as a basic human right.

The WHO Human Genetics Programme manages genetic approaches for the prevention and control of common hereditary diseases and of those with a genetic predisposition representing a major health importance. The Programme also concentrates on the further development of genetic approaches suitable for incorporation into health care systems, as well as developing a network of international collaborating programmes.

WHO works to assess the impact of injuries, violence and sensory impairments on health, and formulates guide-lines and protocols for the prevention and management of mental problems. The health promotion division promotes decentralized and community-based health programmes and is concerned with developing new approaches to population ageing and encouraging healthy life-styles and self-care. It also seeks to relieve the negative impact of social changes such as urbanization, migration and changes in family structure upon health. WHO advocates a multi-sectoral approach—involving public health, legal and educational systems—to the prevention of injuries, which represent 16% of the global burden of disease. It aims to support governments in developing suitable strategies to prevent and mitigate the consequences of violence, unintentional injury and disability. Several health promotion projects have been undertaken, in collaboration between WHO regional and country offices and other relevant organizations, including: the Global School Health Initiative, to bridge the sectors of health and education and to promote the health of school-age children; the Global Strategy for Occupational Health, to promote the health of the working population and the control of occupational health risks; Community-based Rehabilitation, aimed at providing a more enabling environment for people with disabilities; and a communication strategy to provide training and support for health communications personnel and initiatives. In 2000 WHO, UNESCO, the World Bank and UNICEF adopted the joint Focusing Resources for Effective School Health (FRESH Start) approach to promoting life skills among adolescents.

In July 1997 the fourth International Conference on Health Promotion (ICHP) was held in Jakarta, Indonesia, where a declaration on 'Health Promotion into the 21st Century' was agreed. The fifth ICHP was convened in June 2000, in Mexico City, Mexico.

Mental health problems, which include unipolar and bipolar affective disorders, psychosis, epilepsy, dementia, Parkinson's disease, multiple sclerosis, drug and alcohol dependency, and neuro-psychiatric disorders such as post-traumatic stress disorder, obsessive compulsive disorder and panic disorder, have been identified by WHO as significant global health problems. Although, overall, physical health has improved, mental, behavioural and social health problems are increasing, owing to extended life expectancy and improved child mortality rates, and factors such as war and poverty. WHO aims to address mental problems by increasing awareness of mental health issues and promoting improved mental health services and primary care.

The Substance Abuse department is concerned with problems of alcohol, drugs and other substance abuse. Within its Programme on Substance Abuse (PSA), which was established in 1990 in response to the global increase in substance abuse, WHO provides technical support to assist countries in formulating policies with regard to the prevention and reduction of the health and social effects of psychoactive substance abuse. PSA's sphere of activity includes epidemiological surveillance and risk assessment, advocacy and the dissemination of information, strengthening national and regional prevention and health promotion techniques and strategies, the development of cost-effective treatment and rehabilitation approaches, and also encompasses regulatory activities as required under the international drugs-control treaties in force.

The Tobacco or Health Programme aims to reduce the use of tobacco, by educating tobacco-users and preventing young people from adopting the habit. In 1996 WHO published its first report on the tobacco situation world-wide. According to WHO, about one-third of the world's population aged over 15 years smoke tobacco, which causes approximately 3.5m. deaths each year (through lung cancer, heart disease, chronic bronchitis and other effects). In 1998 the 'Tobacco Free Initiative', a major global anti-smoking campaign, was established. In May 1999 the World Health Assembly endorsed the formulation of a Framework Convention on Tobacco Control (FCTC) to help to combat the increase in tobacco use (although a number of tobacco growers expressed concerns about the effect of the convention on their livelihoods). The FCTC entered into force in February 2005. The greatest increase in tobacco use is forecast to occur in developing countries.

FAMILY AND COMMUNITY HEALTH

WHO's Family and Community Health group addresses the following areas of work: child and adolescent health, research and programme development in reproductive health, making pregnancy safer and men and women's health. Making pregnancy safer is an organization-wide priority. The group's aim is to improve access to sustainable health care for all by strengthening health systems and fostering individual, family and community development. Activities include newborn care; child health, including promoting and protecting the health and development of the child through such approaches as promotion of breast-feeding and use of the mother-baby package, as well as care of the sick child, including diarrhoeal and acute respiratory disease control, and support to women and children in difficult circumstances; the promotion of safe motherhood and maternal health; adolescent health, including the promotion and development of young people and the prevention of specific health problems; women, health and development, including addressing issues of gender, sexual violence, and harmful traditional practices; and human reproduction, including research related to contraceptive technologies and effective methods. In addition, WHO aims to provide technical leadership and co-ordination on reproductive health and to support countries in their efforts to ensure that people: experience healthy sexual development and maturation; have the capacity for healthy, equitable and responsible relationships; can achieve their reproductive intentions safely and healthily; avoid illnesses, diseases and injury related to sexuality and reproduction; and receive appropriate counselling, care and rehabilitation for diseases and conditions related to sexuality and reproduction.

In September 1997 WHO, in collaboration with UNICEF, formally launched a programme advocating the Integrated Management of Childhood Illness (IMCI), following successful regional trials in more than 20 developing countries during 1996–97. IMCI recognizes that pneumonia, diarrhoea, measles, malaria and malnutrition cause some 70% of the approximately 11m. childhood deaths each year, and recommends screening sick children for all five conditions, to obtain a more accurate diagnosis than may be achieved from the results of a single assessment. WHO's Division of Diarrhoeal and Acute Respiratory Disease Control encourages national programmes aimed at reducing childhood deaths as a result of diarrhoea, particularly through the use of oral rehydration therapy and preventive measures. The Division is also seeking to reduce deaths from pneumonia in infants through the use of a simple case-management strategy involving the recognition of danger signs and treatment with an appropriate antibiotic.

In March 1996 WHO's Centre for Health Development opened at Kobe, Japan. The Centre researches health developments and other determinants to strengthen policy decision-making within the health sector.

SUSTAINABLE DEVELOPMENT AND HEALTHY ENVIRONMENTS

The Sustainable Development and Healthy Environments group focuses on the following areas of work: health in sustainable development; nutrition; health and environment; food safety; and emergency preparedness and response. Food safety is an organization-wide priority.

WHO promotes recognition of good health status as one of the most important assets of the poor. The Sustainable Development and Healthy Environment group seeks to monitor the advantages and disadvantages for health, nutrition, environment and development arising from the process of globalization (i.e. increased global flows of capital, goods and services, people, and knowledge); to integrate the issue of health into poverty reduction programmes; and to promote human rights and equality. Adequate and safe food and nutrition is a priority programme area. WHO collaborates with FAO, the World Food Programme, UNICEF and other UN agencies in pursuing its objectives relating to nutrition and food safety. An estimated 780m. people world-wide cannot meet basic needs for energy and protein, more than 2,000m. people lack essential vitamins and minerals, and 170m. children are estimated to be malnourished. In December 1992 WHO and FAO hosted an international conference on nutrition, at which a World Declaration and Plan of Action on Nutrition was adopted to make the fight against malnutrition a development priority. Following the conference, WHO promoted the elaboration and implementation of national plans of action on nutrition. WHO aims to support the enhancement of member states' capabilities in dealing with their nutrition situations, and addressing scientific issues related to preventing, managing and monitoring protein-energy malnutrition; micronutrient malnutrition, including iodine deficiency disorders, vitamin A deficiency, and nutritional anaemia; and diet-related conditions and non-communicable diseases such as obesity (increasingly affecting children, adolescents and adults, mainly in industrialized countries), cancer and heart disease. In 1990 the World Health Assembly resolved to eliminate iodine deficiency (believed to cause mental retardation); a strategy of universal salt iodization was launched in 1993. In collaboration with other international agencies, WHO is implementing a comprehensive strategy for promoting appropriate infant, young child and maternal nutrition, and for dealing effectively with nutritional emergencies in large populations. Areas of emphasis include promoting healthcare practices that enhance successful breast-feeding; appropriate complementary feeding; refining the use and interpretation of body measurements for assessing nutritional status; relevant information, education and training; and action to give effect to the International Code of Marketing of Breast-milk Substitutes. The food safety programme aims to protect human health against risks associated with biological and chemical contaminants and additives in food. With FAO, WHO establishes food standards (through the work of the Codex Alimentarius Commission and its subsidiary committees) and evaluates food additives, pesticide residues and other contaminants and their implications for health. The programme provides expert advice on such issues as food-borne pathogens (e.g. listeria), production methods (e.g. aquaculture) and food biotechnology (e.g. genetic modification). In July 2001 the Codex Alimentarius Commission adopted the first global principles for assessing the safety of genetically-modified (GM) foods. In March 2002 an intergovernmental task force established by the Commission finalized 'principles for the risk analysis of foods derived from biotechnology', which were to provide a framework for assessing the safety of GM foods and plants. In the following month WHO and FAO announced a joint review of their food standards operations. In February 2003 the FAO/WHO Project and Fund for Enhanced Participation in Codex was launched to support the participation of poorer countries in the Commission's activities.

WHO's programme area on environment and health undertakes a wide range of initiatives to tackle the increasing threats to health and well-being from a changing environment, especially in relation to air pollution, water quality, sanitation, protection against radiation, management of hazardous waste, chemical safety and housing hygiene. Some 1,100m. people world-wide have no access to clean drinking water, while a further 2,400m. people are denied suitable sanitation systems. WHO helped launch the Water Supply and Sanitation Council in 1990 and regularly updates its *Guidelines for Drinking Water Quality*. In rural areas, the emphasis continues to be on the provision and maintenance of safe and sufficient water supplies and adequate sanitation, the health aspects of rural housing, vector control in water resource management, and the safe use of agrochemicals. In urban areas, assistance is provided to identify local environmental health priorities and to improve municipal governments' ability to deal with environmental conditions and health problems in an integrated manner; promotion of the 'Healthy City' approach is a major component of the Programme. Other Programme activities include environmental health information development and management, human resources development, environmental health planning methods, research and work on problems relating to global environment change, such as UV-radiation. A report considering the implications of climate change on human health, prepared jointly by WHO, WMO and UNEP, was published in July 1996. The WHO Global Strategy for Health and Environment, developed in response to the WHO Commission on Health and Environment which reported to the UN Conference on Environment and Development in June 1992, provides the framework for programme activities. In December 2001 WHO published a report on the relationship between macroeconomics and health.

Through its International EMF Project WHO is compiling a comprehensive assessment of the potential adverse effects on human health deriving from exposure to electromagnetic fields (EMF). In June 2004 WHO organized a workshop on childhood sensitivity to EMF.

WHO's work in the promotion of chemical safety is undertaken in collaboration with ILO and UNEP through the International Programme on Chemical Safety (IPCS), the Central Unit for which is located in WHO. The Programme provides internationally-evaluated scientific information on chemicals, promotes the use of such information in national programmes, assists member states in establishment of their own chemical safety measures and programmes, and helps them strengthen their capabilities in chemical emergency preparedness and response and in chemical risk reduction. In 1995 an Inter-organization Programme for the Social Management of Chemicals was established by UNEP, ILO, FAO, WHO, UNIDO and OECD, in order to strengthen international co-operation in the field of chemical safety. In 1998 WHO led an international assessment of the health risk from bendocine disruptors (chemicals which disrupt hormonal activities).

In January 2001 WHO sent a team of experts to Kosovo and Metohija (Federal Republic of Yugoslavia—FRY, now Serbia and Montenegro) to assess the potential impact on the health of the local population of exposure to depleted uranium, which had been used by NATO in ammunition during its aerial offensive against the FRY in 1999.

Since the major terrorist attacks perpetrated against targets in the USA in September 2001, WHO has focused renewed attention on the potential malevolent use of bacteria (such as bacillus anthracis, which causes anthrax), viruses (for example, the variola virus, causing smallpox) or toxins, or of chemical agents, in acts of biological or chemical terrorism. In September 2001 WHO issued draft guide-lines entitled 'Health Aspects of Biological and Chemical Weapons'.

Within the UN system, WHO's Department of Emergency and Humanitarian Action co-ordinates the international response to emergencies and natural disasters in the health field, in close co-operation with other agencies and within the framework set out by the UN's Office for the Co-ordination of Humanitarian Affairs. In this context, WHO provides expert advice on epidemiological surveillance, control of communicable diseases, public health information and health emergency training. Its emergency preparedness activities include co-ordination, policy-making and planning, awareness-building, technical advice, training, publication of standards and guide-lines, and research. Its emergency relief activities include organizational support, the provision of emergency drugs and supplies and conducting technical emergency assessment missions. The Division's objective is to strengthen the national capacity of member states to reduce the adverse health consequences of disasters. In responding to emergency situations, WHO always tries to develop projects and activities that will assist the national authorities concerned in rebuilding or strengthening their own capacity to handle the impact of such situations. Under the UN's Consolidated Appeals Process (CAP) for 2005, launched in November 2004, WHO appealed for US $51.5m. to fund emergency activities in 14 countries and regions.

In January 2005, following a massive earthquake in the Indian Ocean in December 2004, which caused a series of tidal waves, or tsunamis, that devastated coastal regions in 12 countries in South and South-East Asia and East Africa, WHO requested emergency funding of US $67.1m. to support an initial six-month relief operation. Priorities included the establishment of a local disease surveillance and early warning system; co-ordination of humanitarian

health assistance at international and national level; guidance on critical public health matters (such as disease outbreak response, water quality and sanitation, and mental health and pre-existing disease management); ensuring equitable access to essential health care; and ensuring the prompt provision of medical supplies.

HEALTH TECHNOLOGY AND PHARMACEUTICALS

WHO's Health Technology and Pharmaceuticals group, made up of the departments of essential drugs and other medicines, vaccines and other biologicals, and blood safety and clinical technology, covers the following areas of work: essential medicines—access, quality and rational use; immunization and vaccine development; and world-wide co-operation on blood safety and clinical technology. Blood safety and clinical technology are an organization-wide priority.

The Department of Essential Drugs and Other Medicines promotes public health through the development of national drugs policies and global guide-lines and through collaboration with member countries to promote access to essential drugs, the rational use of medicines and compliance with international drug-control requirements. The department comprises four teams: Policy Access and Rational Use; the Drug Action Programme; Quality, Safety and the Regulation of Medicines; and Traditional Medicine.

The Department of Vaccines and Other Biologicals undertakes activities related to quality assurance and safety of biologicals; vaccine development; vaccine assessment and monitoring; access to technologies; and the development of policies and strategies aimed at maximizing the use of vaccines.

The Policy Access and Rational Use team and the Drug Action Programme assist in the development and implementation by member states of pharmaceutical policies, in ensuring a supply of essential drugs of good quality at low cost, and in the rational use of drugs. Other activities include global and national operational research in the pharmaceutical sector, and the development of technical tools for problem solving, management and evaluation. The Policy Access and Rational Use team also has a strong advocacy and information role, promulgated through a periodical, the *Essential Drugs Monitor,* an extensive range of technical publications, and an information dissemination programme targeting developing countries.

The Quality, Safety and Regulation of Medicines team supports national drug-regulatory authorities and drug-procurement agencies and facilitates international pharmaceutical trade through the exchange of technical information and the harmonization of internationally respected norms and standards. In particular, it publishes the *International Pharmacopoeia,* the *Consultative List of International Nonproprietary Names for Pharmaceutical Substances,* and annual and biennial reports of Expert Committees responsible for determining relevant international standards for the manufacture and specification of pharmaceutical and biological products in international commerce. It provides information on the safety and efficacy of drugs, with particular regard to counterfeit and substandard projects, to health agencies and providers of health care, and it maintains the pharmaceuticals section of the UN *Consolidated List of Products whose Consumption and/or Sale have been Banned, Withdrawn, Severely Restricted or Not Approved by Governments.* The *WHO Model List of Essential Medicines* is updated about every two years and is complemented by corresponding model prescribing information; the 13th *Model List* was published in 2003 and identified 316 essential drugs, including 12 ARVs and 60 further essential medicines for HIV/AIDS. In September 2002 WHO issued the first *WHO Model Formulary,* which gives detailed information on the safe and effective use of all essential drugs.

The Traditional Medicine team encourages and supports member states in the integration of traditional medicine into national health-care systems and in the appropriate use of traditional medicine, in particular through the provision of technical guide-lines, standards and methodologies. In May 2002 WHO adopted a strategy on the regulation of traditional medicine and complementary or alternative medicines (TM/CAM)

In January 1999 the Executive Board adopted a resolution on WHO's Revised Drug Strategy which placed emphasis on the inequalities of access to pharmaceuticals, and also covered specific aspects of drugs policy, quality assurance, drug promotion, drug donation, independent drug information and rational drug use. Plans of action involving co-operation with member states and other international organizations were to be developed to monitor and analyse the pharmaceutical and public health implications of international agreements, including trade agreements. In April 2001 experts from WHO and the World Trade Organization participated in a workshop to address ways of lowering the cost of medicines in less developed countries. In the following month the World Health Assembly adopted a resolution urging member states to promote equitable access to essential drugs, noting that this was denied to about one-third of the world's population. WHO participates with other partners in the 'Accelerating Access' initiative, which aims to expand access to antiretroviral drugs for people with HIV/AIDS (see above).

WHO reports that 2m. children die each year of diseases for which common vaccines exist. In September 1991 the Children's Vaccine Initiative (CVI) was launched, jointly sponsored by the Rockefeller Foundation, UNDP, UNICEF, the World Bank and WHO, to facilitate the development and provision of children's vaccines. The CVI has as its ultimate goal the development of a single oral immunization shortly after birth that will protect against all major childhood diseases. An International Vaccine Institute was established in Seoul, Republic of Korea, as part of the CVI, to provide scientific and technical services for the production of vaccines for developing countries. In September 1996 WHO, jointly with UNICEF, published a comprehensive survey, entitled *State of the World's Vaccines and Immunization.* In 1999 WHO, UNICEF, the World Bank and a number of public- and private-sector partners formed the Global Alliance for Vaccines and Immunization (GAVI), which aimed to expand the provision of existing vaccines and to accelerate the development and introduction of new vaccines and technologies, with the ultimate goal of protecting children of all nations and from all socio-economic backgrounds against vaccine-preventable diseases.

WHO supports states in ensuring access to safe blood, blood products, transfusions, injections, and healthcare technologies.

EVIDENCE AND INFORMATION FOR HEALTH POLICY

The Evidence and Information for Health Policy group addresses the following areas of work: evidence for health policy; health information management and dissemination; and research policy and promotion and organization of health systems. Through the generation and dissemination of evidence the Evidence and Information for Health Policy group aims to assist policy-makers assess health needs, choose intervention strategies, design policy and monitor performance, and thereby improve the performance of national health systems. The group also supports international and national dialogue on health policy.

WHO co-ordinates the Health InterNetwork Access to Research Initiative (HINARI), which was launched in July 2001 to enable relevant authorities in developing countries to access more than 2,000 biomedical journals through the internet at no or greatly reduced cost, in order to improve the world-wide circulation of scientific information; some 28 medical publishers participate in the initiative.

HEALTH DAYS

World Health Day is observed on 7 April every year, and is used to promote awareness of a particular health topic ('Make every mother and child count', in 2005). World Leprosy Day is held every year on 30 January, World TB Day on 24 March, World No Tobacco Day on 31 May, World Heart Day on 24 September, World Mental Health Day on 10 October, World Diabetes Day, in association with the International Diabetes Federation, on 14 November, World AIDS Day on 1 December, and World Asthma Day on 11 December.

ASSOCIATED AGENCY

International Agency for Research on Cancer: 150 Cours Albert Thomas, 69372 Lyon Cédex 08, France; tel. 4-72-73-84-85; fax 4-72-73-85-75; e-mail com@iarc.fr; internet www.iarc.fr; established in 1965 as a self-governing body within the framework of WHO, the

Agency organizes international research on cancer. It has its own laboratories and runs a programme of research on the environmental factors causing cancer. Members: Australia, Belgium, Canada, Denmark, Finland, France, Germany, Italy, Japan, Netherlands, Norway, Spain, Sweden, Switzerland, United Kingdom, USA; Dir Dr P. Boyle (United Kingdom).

Finance

WHO's regular budget is provided by assessment of member states and associate members. An additional fund for specific projects is provided by voluntary contributions from members and other sources, including UNDP and UNFPA.

A regular budget of US $901.5m. was proposed for the two years 2004–05.

WHO budget appropriations by region, 2004–05

Region	Amount ('000 US dollars)	% of total budget
Africa	198,149	22.8
Americas	75,399	8.7
South-East Asia	96,230	11.1
Europe	56,295	6.5
Eastern Mediterranean	84,689	9.8
Western Pacific	74,116	8.5
Global	282,597	32.6
Total	901,475	100.0

Publications

Bulletin of the World Health Organization (monthly).

Eastern Mediterranean Health Journal (annually).

International Classification of Functioning, Disability and Health— ICF.

Model List of Essential Medicines (biennially).

Pan-American Journal of Public Health (annually).

3 By 5 Progress Report.

Toxicological Evaluation of Certain Veterinary Drug Residues in Food (annually).

Weekly Epidemiological Record (in English and French, paper and electronic versions available).

WHO Drug Information (quarterly).

WHO Global Atlas of Traditional, Complementary and Alternative Medicine.

WHO Model Formulary.

World Health Report (annually, in English, French and Spanish).

World Malaria Report (with UNICEF).

Zoonoses and Communicable Diseases Common to Man and Animals.

Technical report series; catalogues of specific scientific, technical and medical fields available.

World Intellectual Property Organization—WIPO

Address: 34 chemin des Colombettes, BP 18, 1211 Geneva 20, Switzerland.

Telephone: (22) 3389111; **fax:** (22) 7335428; **e-mail:** wipo.mail@wipo.int; **internet:** www.wipo.int.

WIPO was established by a Convention signed in Stockholm in 1967, which came into force in 1970. It became a specialized agency of the UN in December 1974.

MEMBERS

WIPO has 182 members.

Organization

(March 2005)

GENERAL ASSEMBLY

The General Assembly is one of the three WIPO governing bodies, and is composed of all states that are party to the WIPO Convention and that are also members of any of the WIPO-administered Unions (see below). In March 2005 the Assembly comprised 172 members. The Assembly meets in ordinary session once a year to agree on programmes and budgets. It elects the Director-General, who is the executive head of WIPO.

CONFERENCE

All member states are represented in the Conference, which meets in ordinary session once every two years.

CO-ORDINATION COMMITTEE

Countries belonging to the Committee are elected from among the member states of WIPO, the Paris and Berne Unions, and, *ex officio*, Switzerland. At March 2005 there were 80 members of the Committee, including three *ad hoc* members and Switzerland. It meets in ordinary session once a year.

INTERNATIONAL BUREAU

The International Bureau, as WIPO's secretariat, prepares the meetings of the various bodies of WIPO and the Unions, mainly through the provision of reports and working documents. It organizes the meetings, and sees that the decisions are communicated to all concerned, and, as far as possible, that they are carried out.

The International Bureau implements projects and initiates new ones to promote international co-operation in the field of intellectual property. It acts as an information service and publishes reviews. It is also the depositary of most of the treaties administered by WIPO.

Director-General: Dr KAMIL IDRIS (Sudan).

More than 170 non-governmental organizations have observer status at WIPO. There are two advisory bodies: the Policy Advisory Commission (comprising eminent politicians, diplomats, lawyers and public officials) and the Industry Advisory Commission (comprising senior business representatives).

Activities

WIPO works to ensure that the rights of creators and owners of intellectual property are protected throughout the world, with a view to facilitating the advancement of science, technology and the arts and promoting international trade. Intellectual property comprises two principal branches: industrial property (patents and other rights in technological inventions, rights in trademarks, industrial designs, appellations of origin, etc.) and copyright and neighbouring rights (in literary, musical, artistic, photographic and audiovisual works).

WIPO administers and encourages member states to sign and enforce international treaties relating to the protection of intellectual property, of which the most fundamental are the Paris Convention for the Protection of Industrial Property (1883), the Berne Convention for the Protection of Literary and Artistic Works (1886), and the Patent Co-operation Treaty (PCT). WIPO's main areas of activity are progressive development of international intellectual property law, global protection systems and services, and co-operation for development. The Organization seeks to simplify and harmonize national intellectual property legislation and procedures (for example through implementation of the Trademark Law Treaty, 1994, and development of the Patent Law Treaty, 2000, scheduled to enter into force in April 2005), provide services for international applications for industrial property rights, exchange information on intellectual property, provide training and legal and technical assistance to developing countries, facilitate the resolution of private intellectual property disputes, and develop the use of information technology for storing, accessing and using valuable intellectual property information.

The rapid advancement of digital communications networks has posed challenges regarding the protection and enforcement of intellectual property rights. WIPO has undertaken a range of initiatives to address the implications for copyright and industrial property law, and for electronic commerce transcending national jurisdictions. WIPO's Electronic Commerce Section co-ordinates programmes and activities relating to the intellectual property aspects of electronic commerce. In September 1999 WIPO organized the first International Conference on Electronic Commerce and Intellectual Property; a 'Digital Agenda' was launched by the Organization at the Conference. The second International Conference on Electronic Commerce and Intellectual Property was held in September 2001. A planned WIPO Summit on Intellectual Property and the Knowledge Economy, scheduled to be held in Beijing, People's Republic of China, in April 2003, was postponed.

In view of the advances in technology and economic globalization in recent years WIPO has focused increasingly on the relationship between intellectual property and issues such as traditional knowledge, biological diversity, environmental protection and human rights. In 1998–99 WIPO prepared the first ever report on the intellectual property concerns of holders of traditional knowledge. In April 2000 the organization convened its first Meeting on Intellec-

tual Property and Genetic Resources. A WIPO Intergovernmental Committee on Intellectual Property and Genetic Resources, Traditional Knowledge and Folklore was established in September. In January 2002 an international forum organized by WIPO adopted the Muscat Declaration on Intellectual Property and Traditional Knowledge, recognizing the contribution of traditional knowledge to international co-operation.

In September 2001 member states approved the WIPO Patent Agenda, a process of global consultations aimed at creating a blueprint for the development of the international patent system.

PROGRESSIVE DEVELOPMENT OF INTERNATIONAL PROPERTY LAW

One of WIPO's major activities is the progressive development and application of international norms and standards. The Organization prepares new treaties and undertakes the revision of the existing treaties that it administers. WIPO administers international classifications established by treaties and relating to inventions, marks and industrial designs: periodically it reviews these to ensure their improvement in terms of coverage and precision. WIPO also carries out studies on issues in the field of intellectual property that could be the subject of model laws or guide-lines for implementation at national or international levels. The organization is increasingly active in harmonizing and simplifying procedures in order to make the registration of intellectual property more easily accessible. WIPO aims to keep pace with rapid developments in the intellectual property domain. Standing committees have been formed by member states to examine questions of substantive law or harmonization in the organization's main fields of activity and to ensure that the interests of member states are addressed promptly.

CO-OPERATION FOR DEVELOPMENT

WIPO aims to modernize national intellectual property systems. It offers assistance to increase the capabilities of developing countries to benefit from the international intellectual property framework, with a view to promoting the optimal use of human and other resources and thereby contributing to national prosperity. WIPO supports governments with intellectual property-related institution-building, human resources development, and preparation and implementation of legislation. The WIPO Worldwide Academy, created in 1998, undertakes training, teaching and research on intellectual property matters, focusing particularly on developing countries. The Academy maintains a Distance Learning Centre using on-line facilities, digital multimedia technology and video conferencing. WIPO's Information and Documentation Centre holds extensive reference materials. Under its Digital Agenda WIPO aims to assist the integration of developing countries into the internet environment, particularly through the use of WIPOnet, a global digital network of intellectual property information capable of transmitting confidential data that was launched in January 2001. The organization is also implementing the Intellectual Property Digital Libraries database project and maintains the WIPO Collection of Laws for Electronic Access (CLEA) multi-lingual database.

WIPO advises countries on obligations under the World Trade Organization's agreement on Trade-Related Aspects of Intellectual Property Rights (TRIPS). The two organizations are undertaking a joint technical co-operation initiative to assist least-developed countries to harmonize their national legislative and administrative structures in compliance with the TRIPS accord by 1 January 2006.

WIPO presented a programme of action to the Third UN Conference on the Least-Developed Countries (UN-LDCs III, held in Brussels, Belgium in May 2001), which was aimed at strengthening LDC's intellectual property systems. In May 2002 WIPO convened a Sino-African Intellectual Property Forum.

A new programme focusing on the intellectual property concerns of small and medium-sized enterprises was approved by the WIPO General Assembly in September 2000. An International Forum on Intellectual Property and SMEs, organized jointly by WIPO and the Italian Government in Milan, Italy in February 2001, adopted the Milan Plan of Action for helping SMEs to benefit fully from the intellectual property system.

GLOBAL PROTECTION SYSTEMS AND SERVICES

WIPO administers a small number of treaties, covering inventions (patents), trademarks and industrial designs, under which one international registration or filing has effect in any of the relevant signatory states. The services provided by WIPO under such treaties simplify the registration process and reduce the cost of making individual applications or filings in each country in which protection for a given intellectual property right is sought. The most widely used of these treaties is the PCT, under which a single international patent application is valid in all signatory countries selected by the applicant. The PCT system has expanded rapidly in recent years. The PCT-SAFE (Secure Applications Filed Electronically) system became operational in February 2004, safeguarding the electronic filing of patent applications. Through its Information Management for the PCT (IMPACT) project WIPO aims to automate fully the operations of the PCT. The corresponding treaties concerning the international registration of trademarks and industrial designs are, respectively, the Madrid Agreement (and its Protocol), and the Hague Agreement. WIPO's Advisory Committee on Enforcement of Industrial Property Rights assesses best practices and procedures for the effective enforcement of intellectual property rights.

WIPO maintains the following international registration services:

International registration of trademarks: operating since 1893; during 2002 there were 22,236 registrations and renewals of trademarks; publ. *WIPO Gazette of International Marks* (every two weeks).

International deposit of industrial designs: operating since 1928; during 2002 4,300 applications were made for deposits, renewals and prolongations of 20,705 industrial designs; publ. *International Designs Bulletin* (monthly).

International applications for patents: operating since 1978; during 2004 120,100 record copies of international applications for patents under the PCT were received; publ. *PCT Gazette* (weekly).

WIPO also maintains the WIPO Arbitration and Mediation Centre, which became operational on 1 October 1994, to facilitate the settlement of intellectual property disputes between private parties. The Centre also organizes arbitrator and mediator workshops and assists in the development of WIPO model contract clauses and industry-specific resolution schemes. The Centre operates a Domain Name Dispute Resolution Service, which plays a leading role in reviewing cases of conflict between trademarks and internet domain names, in accordance with the Uniform Domain Name Dispute Resolution Policy that was, on WIPO's recommendation, adopted by the Internet Corporation for Assigned Names and Numbers—ICANN (see p. 398) in October 1999. In 2003 1,100 new cases concerning disputes over generic top-level domains were filed with the Centre. WIPO's first Internet Domain Name Process, a series of international consultations, undertaken in 1999, issued several recommendations for controlling the abuse of trademarks on the internet. A second Internet Domain Name Process, completed in 2001, addressed the improper registration of other identifiers ('cybersquatting'), including standard non-proprietary names for pharmaceutical substances, names and acronyms of intergovernmental organizations, geographical indications and terms, and trade names. WIPO maintains an online database of cybersquatting cases (accessible at arbiter.wipo.int/domains/search).

PARIS AND BERNE CONVENTIONS

International Union for the Protection of Industrial Property (Paris Convention): the treaty was signed in Paris in 1883, and last revised in 1967; there were 167 members of the Union's Assembly at March 2005 and two parties to the Convention that were not Assembly members. Member states must accord to nationals and residents of other member states the same advantages under their laws relating to the protection of inventions, trademarks and other subjects of industrial property as they accord to their own nationals.

International Union for the Protection of Literary and Artistic Works (Berne Union): the treaty was signed in Bern in 1886 and last revised in 1971; there were 156 members of the Union's Assembly at March 2005 and three parties to the Convention that were not Assembly members. Members of the Union's Assembly must accord the same protection to the copyright of nationals of other member states as to their own. The treaty also prescribes minimum standards of protection, for example, that copyright protection generally continues throughout the author's life and for 50 years after. It includes special provision for the developing countries.

OTHER AGREEMENTS
(Status at March 2005, unless otherwise indicated)

International Protection of Industrial Property:

Madrid Agreement of 14 April 1891, for the Repression of False or Deceptive Indications of Source on Goods; 34 states party to the Agreement.

Madrid Agreement of 14 April 1891, Concerning the International Registration of Marks; 76 states party to the Agreement.

The Hague Agreement of 6 November 1925, Concerning the International Deposit of Industrial Designs; 41 states party to the Agreement.

Nice Agreement of 15 June 1957, Concerning the International Classification of Goods and Services for the Purposes of the Registration of Marks; 74 states party to the Agreement.

Lisbon Agreement of 31 October 1958, for the Protection of Appellations of Origin and their International Registration; 23 states party to the Agreement.

Locarno Agreement of 8 October 1968, Establishing an International Classification for Industrial Designs; 45 states party to the Agreement.

Patent Co-operation Treaty of 19 June 1970 (PCT); 126 states party to the Treaty.

Strasbourg Agreement of 24 March 1971, Concerning the International Patent Classification (IPC); 55 states party to the Agreement.

Vienna Agreement of 12 June 1973, Establishing an International Classification of the Figurative Elements of Marks; 20 states party to the Agreement.

Budapest Treaty of 28 April 1977, on the International Recognition of the Deposit of Micro-organisms for the Purposes of Patent Procedure; 60 states party to the Treaty.

Nairobi Treaty of 26 September 1981, on the Protection of the Olympic Symbol; 43 states party to the Treaty.

Trademark Law Treaty of 27 October 1994; 33 states party to the Treaty.

Protocol Relating to the Madrid Agreement Concerning the International Registration of Marks, signed on 28 June 1989; 66 contracting states.

Geneva Act of the Hague Agreement Concerning the International Registration of Industrial Designs, 1999; entered into force 23 December 2003, at which time there were 11 states party to the Agreement.

Patent Law Treaty, 2000; entry into force: 28 April 2005, 10 states party.

Copyright and Special International Protection of the Rights of Performers, Producers of Phonograms and Broadcasting Organizations ('Neighbouring Rights'):

Rome Convention, 26 October 1961, for the Protection of Performers, Producers of Phonograms and Broadcasting Organizations; 79 states party to the Convention.

Geneva Convention, 29 October 1971, for the Protection of Producers of Phonograms against Unauthorized Duplication of their Phonograms; 73 states party to the Convention.

Brussels Convention, 21 May 1974, Relating to the Distribution of Programme-carrying Signals Transmitted by Satellite; 26 states party to the Convention.

Treaty on the International Registration of Audiovisual Works (Film Register Treaty), 1989; 13 states party to the Treaty.

Performances and Phonograms Treaty, 1996; 49 states party to the Treaty.

Copyright Treaty, 1996; 51 states party to the Treaty.

Finance

The approved budget for the two years 2004–05 amounted to 638.8m. Swiss francs. Some 86% of WIPO's revenue derives from the international registration systems maintained by the Organization; the remainder derives mainly from contributions by member states.

Publications

Annual Report.

Les appellations d'origine (annually, in French).

Essential Elements of Intellectual Property (CD-Rom).

Industrial Property and Copyright (monthly in English and French; bimonthly in Spanish).

Intellectual Property for Small and Medium-sized Enterprises (CD-Rom).

Industrial Property Statistics (CD-Rom).

Intellectual Property in Asia and the Pacific (quarterly in English).

Intellectual Property Profile of the Least-Developed Countries.

International Designs Bulletin (monthly in English and French, also on CD-Rom).

PCT Gazette (weekly in English and French).

PCT Newsletter (monthly in English).

WIPO Academy Review.

WIPO Gazette of International Marks (every two weeks, in English and French, also on CD-Rom).

WIPO Magazine (monthly in English, French and Spanish).

A collection of industrial property and copyright laws and treaties; a selection of publications related to intellectual property.

World Meteorological Organization—WMO

Address: 7 bis, ave de la Paix, CP 2300, 1211 Geneva 2, Switzerland.

Telephone: (22) 7308111; **fax:** (22) 7308181; **e-mail:** ipa@wmo.int; **internet:** www.wmo.int.

The WMO was established in 1950 and was recognized as a Specialized Agency of the UN in 1951, operating in the fields of meteorology, climatology, operational hydrology and related fields, as well as their applications.

MEMBERS

WMO has 187 members.

Organization

(March 2005)

WORLD METEOROLOGICAL CONGRESS

The supreme body of the Organization, the Congress, is convened every four years and represents all members; it adopts regulations, and determines policy, programme and budget. Fourteenth Congress: May 2003.

EXECUTIVE COUNCIL

The Council has 37 members and meets at least once a year to prepare studies and recommendations for the Congress; it supervises the implementation of Congress resolutions and regulations, informs members on technical matters and offers advice.

SECRETARIAT

The Secretariat acts as an administrative, documentary and information centre; undertakes special technical studies; produces publications; organizes meetings of WMO constituent bodies; acts as a link between the meteorological and hydrometeorological services of the world, and provides information for the general public.

Secretary-General: MICHEL JARRAUD (France).

REGIONAL ASSOCIATIONS

Members are grouped in six Regional Associations (Africa, Asia, Europe, North and Central America, South America and South-West Pacific), whose task is to co-ordinate meteorological activity within their regions and to examine questions referred to them by the Executive Council. Sessions are held at least once every four years.

TECHNICAL COMMISSIONS

The Technical Commissions are composed of experts nominated by the members of the Organization. Sessions are held at least once every four years. The Commissions cover the following areas: Basic Systems; Climatology; Instruments and Methods of Observation; Atmospheric Sciences; Aeronautical Meteorology; Agricultural Meteorology; Hydrology; Oceanography and Marine Meteorology.

Activities

WORLD WEATHER WATCH PROGRAMME

Combining facilities and services provided by the members, the Programme's primary purpose is to make available meteorological and related geophysical and environmental information enabling them to maintain efficient meteorological services. Facilities in regions outside any national territory (outer space, ocean areas and Antarctica) are maintained by members on a voluntary basis.

Antarctic Activities: co-ordinates WMO activities related to the Antarctic, in particular the surface and upper-air observing programme, plan the regular exchange of observational data and products needed for operational and research purposes, study problems related to instruments and methods of observation peculiar to the Antarctic, and develop appropriate regional coding practices. Contacts are maintained with scientific bodies dealing with Antarctic research and with other international organizations on aspects of Antarctic meteorology.

Data Management: monitors the integration of the different components of the World Weather Watch (WWW) Programme, with the intention of increasing the efficiency of, in particular, the Global Observing System, the Global Data Processing System and the Global Telecommunication System. The Data Management component of the WWW Programme develops data handling procedures and

standards for enhanced forms of data representation, in order to aid member countries in processing large volumes of meteorological data.

Emergency Response Activities: assists national meteorological services to respond effectively to man-made environmental emergencies, particularly nuclear accidents, through the development, co-ordination and implementation of WMO/IAEA established procedures and response mechanisms for the provision and exchange of observational data and specialized transport model products.

Global Data Processing and Forecasting System: consists of World Meteorological Centres (WMCs) in Melbourne (Australia), Moscow (Russia) and Washington, DC (USA); 40 Regional/Specialized Meteorological Centres (RSMCs); and 187 National Meteorological Centres. The WMCs and RSMCs provide analyses, forecasts and warnings for exchange on the Global Telecommunications System. Some centres concentrate on the monitoring and forecasting of environmental quality and special weather phenomena, such as tropical cyclones, monsoons, droughts, etc., which have a major impact on human safety and national economies. These analyses and forecasts are designed to assist the members in making local and specialized forecasts.

Global Observing System: makes simultaneous observations at more than 10,000 land stations. Meteorological information is also received from 3,000 aircraft, 7,000 ships, 600 drifting buoys, and nine polar orbiting and six geostationary meteorological satellites. About 160 members operate some 1,300 ground stations equipped to receive picture transmissions from geostationary and polar-orbiting satellites.

Global Telecommunication System: provides telecommunication services for the rapid collection and exchange of meteorological information and related data; consists of: the Main Telecommunication Network (MTN), six Regional Meteorological Telecommunication networks, and the national telecommunication networks. The system operates through 183 National Meteorological Centres, 29 Regional Telecommunications Hubs and the three WMCs.

Instruments and Methods of Observation Programme: promotes the world-wide standardization of meteorological and geophysical instruments and methods of observation and measurement to meet agreed accuracy requirements. It provides related guidance material and training assistance in the use and maintenance of the instruments.

System Support Activity: provides guidance and support to members in the planning, establishment and operation of the WWW. It includes training, technical co-operation support, system and methodology support, operational WWW evaluations, advanced technology support, an operations information service, and the WWW referral catalogue.

Tropical Cyclone Programme: established in response to UN General Assembly Resolution 2733 (XXV), aims to develop national and regionally co-ordinated systems to ensure that the loss of life and damage caused by tropical cyclones and associated floods, landslides and storm surges are reduced to a minimum. The Programme supports the transfer of technology, and includes five regional tropical cyclone bodies covering more than 60 countries, to improve warning systems and for collaboration with other international organizations in activities related to disaster mitigation.

WORLD CLIMATE PROGRAMME

Adopted by the Eighth World Meteorological Congress (1979), the World Climate Programme (WCP) comprises the following components: World Climate Data and Monitoring Programme (WCDMP), World Climate Applications and Climate Information Services (CLIPS) Programme (WCASP), World Climate Impact Assessment and Response Strategies Programme (WCIRP), World Climate Research Programme (WCRP). The WCP is supported by the Global Climate Observing System (GCOS), which provides comprehensive observation of the global climate system, involving a multi-disciplinary range of atmospheric, oceanic, hydrologic, cryospheric and biotic properties and processes. In 1997–98 the GCOS was particularly active in monitoring the impact of the El Niño weather phenomenon on the climate system. The objectives of the WCP are: to use existing climate information to improve economic and social planning; to improve the understanding of climate processes through research, so as to determine the predictability of climate and the extent of man's influence on it; and to detect and warn governments of impending climate variations or changes, either natural or man-made, which may significantly affect critical human activities.

Co-ordination of the overall Programme is the responsibility of the WMO, together with direct management of the WCDMP and WCASP. The UN Environment Programme (UNEP) has accepted responsibility for the WCIRP, while the WCRP is jointly administered by WMO, the International Council for Science (ICSU) and UNESCO's Intergovernmental Oceanographic Commission. Other organizations involved in the Programme include FAO, WHO, and the Consultative Group on International Agricultural Research (CGIAR). In addition, the WCP supports the WMO/UNEP Intergovernmental Panel on Climate Change and the implementation of international agreements, such as the UN Framework Convention on Climate Change (see below); and co-ordinates climate activities within WMO.

World Climate Applications and Climate Information and Services Programme (WCASP): promotes applications of climate knowledge in the areas of food production, water, energy (especially solar and wind energy), urban planning and building, human health, transport, tourism and recreation.

World Climate Data and Monitoring Programme (WCDMP): aims to make available reliable climate data for detecting and monitoring climate change for both practical applications and research purposes. The major projects are: the Climate Change Detection Project (CCDP); development of climate databases; computer systems for climate data management (CLICOM); the World Data and Information Referral Service (INFOCLIMA); the Climate Monitoring System; and the Data Rescue (DARE) project.

World Climate Impact Assessment and Response Strategies Programme (WCIRP): aims to make reliable estimates of the socio-economic impact of climate changes, and to assist in forming national policies accordingly. It concentrates on: study of the impact of climate variations on national food systems; assessment of the impact of man's activities on the climate, especially through increasing the amount of carbon dioxide and other radiatively active gases in the atmosphere; and developing the methodology of climate impact assessments.

World Climate Research Programme (WCRP): organized jointly with the Intergovernmental Oceanographic Commission of UNESCO and the ICSU, to determine to what extent climate can be predicted, and the extent of man's influence on climate. Its three specific objectives are: establishing the physical basis for weather predictions over time ranges of one to two months; understanding and predicting the variability of the global climate over periods of several years; and studying the long-term variations and the response of climate to natural or man-made influence over periods of several decades. Studies include: changes in the atmosphere caused by emissions of carbon dioxide, aerosols and other gases; the effect of cloudiness on the radiation balance; the effect of ground water storage and vegetation on evaporation; the Arctic and Antarctic climate process; and the effects of oceanic circulation changes on the global atmosphere. The 10-year Tropical Ocean and Global Atmosphere Project, which ended in 1994, developed forecasting techniques used to monitor the climate phenomenon, El Niño, in 1997–98.

Global Climate Observing System (GCOS): aims to ensure that data on climate are obtained and made available for: climate system monitoring and climate change detection and attribution; assessing impacts of, and vulnerability to, climate variability and change, e.g. extreme events, terrestrial ecosystems, etc., and analysing options for adaptation; research to improve understanding, modelling and prediction of the climate system; and application to sustainable economic development. The strategy of the GCOS has been to work with its international and regional partners and to engage countries both directly and through international fora such as WMO, other GCOS sponsors and the UN Framework Convention on Climate Change.

ATMOSPHERIC RESEARCH AND ENVIRONMENT PROGRAMME

This major Programme aims to help members to implement research projects; to disseminate relevant scientific information; to draw the attention of members to outstanding research problems of major importance, such as atmospheric composition and environment changes; and to encourage and help members to incorporate the results of research into operational forecasting or other appropriate techniques, particularly when such changes of procedure require international co-ordination and agreement.

Global Atmosphere Watch (GAW): a world-wide system that integrates most monitoring and research activities involving the long-term measurement of atmospheric composition, and is intended to serve as an early warning system to detect further changes in atmospheric concentrations of 'greenhouse' gases, changes in the ozone layer and as associated ultraviolet radiation, and in long-range transport of pollutants, including acidity and toxicity of rain, as well as the atmospheric burden of aerosols. The instruments of these globally standardized observations and related research are a set of 22 global stations in remote areas and, in order to address regional effects, some 200 regional stations measuring specific atmospheric chemistry parameters, such as ozone and acid deposition. GAW is the main contributor of data on chemical composition

and surface ultraviolet radiation to the GCOS. Through GAW, WMO has collaborated with the UN Economic Commission for Europe (ECE) and has been responsible for the meteorological part of the Monitoring and Evaluation of the Long-range Transmission of Air Pollutants in Europe. In this respect, WMO has arranged for the establishment of two Meteorological Synthesizing Centres (Oslo, Norway, and Moscow, Russia) which provide daily analysis of the transport of pollution over Europe. GAW also gives attention to atmospheric chemistry studies, prepares scientific assessments and encourages integrated environmental monitoring. Quality Assurance/Science Activity Centres have been established to ensure an overall level of quality in GAW. Atmospheric composition information is maintained by and available through a series of six GAW World Data Centres. GAW operates the GAW Urban Environment Meteorological Research Programme (GURME), which assists National Meteorological and Hydrological Services (NMHSs) in dealing with regional and urban pollution monitoring and forecasting, through the provision of guide-lines and information on the requisite measuring and modelling infrastructures, and by bringing together NMHSs, regional and city administrations and health authorities. GURME is being developed in co-operation with the World Health Organization.

Physics of Clouds and Weather Modification Research Programme: encourages scientific research on cloud physics and chemistry, with special emphasis on interaction between clouds and atmospheric chemistry, as well as weather modification such as precipitation enhancement ('rain-making') and hail suppression. It provides information on world-wide weather modification projects, and guidance in the design and evaluation of experiments. It also studies the chemistry of clouds and their role in the transport, transformation and dispersion of pollution.

Tropical Meteorology Research Programme: aims to promote and co-ordinate members' research efforts into such important problems as monsoons, tropical cyclones, meteorological aspects of droughts in the arid zones of the tropics, rain-producing tropical weather systems, and the interaction between tropical and mid-latitude weather systems. This should lead to a better understanding of tropical systems and forecasting, and thus be of economic benefit to tropical countries.

World Weather Research Programme (WWRP): promotes the development and application of improved weather forecasting techniques. The Programme is primarily concerned with forecasting weather events that have the potential to cause considerable socio-economic dislocation. Advances in forecasting capability are pursued through a combination of improved scientific understanding (gained through field experiments and research), forecast technique development, the demonstration of new forecasting capabilities, and the transfer of these advances to all NMHSs in conjunction with related training through various Research Developments Projects (RDPs) and Forecast Demonstration Projects (FDPs). In particular, THORPEX: a Global Atmospheric Research Programme, is being developed and implemented as part of the WWRP to accelerate improvements in the accuracy of 1–14-day weather forecasts in order to achieve social and economic benefits. The Programme builds upon ongoing advances within the basic research and operational forecasting communities. It aims to make progress by enhancing international collaboration between these communities and with users of forecast products.

APPLICATIONS OF METEOROLOGY PROGRAMME

Public Weather Services Programme: assists members in providing reliable and effective weather and related services for the benefit of the public. The main objectives of the Programme are: to strengthen members' capabilities to meet the needs of the community through the provision of comprehensive weather and related services, with particular emphasis on public safety and welfare; and to foster a better understanding by the public of the capabilities of national meteorological services and how best to use their services.

Agricultural Meteorology Programme: the study of weather and climate as they affect agriculture and forestry, the selection of crops and their protection from disease and deterioration in storage, soil conservation, phenology and physiology of crops and productivity and health of farm animals; the Commission for Agricultural Meteorology supervises the applications projects and also advises the Secretary-General in his efforts to co-ordinate activities in support of food production. There are also special activities in agrometeorology to monitor and combat drought and desertification, to apply climate and real-time weather information in agricultural planning and operations, and to help improve the efficiency of the use of human labour, land, water and energy in agriculture; close co-operation is maintained with FAO, centres of CGIAR and UNEP.

Aeronautical Meteorology Programme: provides operational meteorological information required for safe, regular and efficient air navigation, as well as meteorological assistance to non-real-time activities of the aviation industry. The objective is to ensure the world-wide provision of cost-effective and responsive aviation operations. The Programme is implemented at global, regional and national levels, the Commission for Aeronautical Meteorology (CAeM) playing a major role, taking into account relevant meteorological developments in science and technology, studying aeronautical requirements for meteorological services, promoting international standardization of methods, procedures and techniques, and considering requirements for basic and climatological data as well as aeronautical requirements for meteorological observations and specialized instruments and enhanced understanding and awareness of the impact of aviation on the environment. Activities under this Programme are carried out, where relevant, with the International Civil Aviation Organization (ICAO) and in collaboration with users of services provided to aviation.

Marine Meteorology and Oceanography Programme: undertakes operational monitoring of the oceans and the maritime atmosphere; collection, exchange, archival recording and management of marine data; processing of marine data, and the provision of marine meteorological and oceanographic services in support of the safety of life and property at sea and of the efficient and economic operation of all sea-based activities. The joint WMO/Intergovernmental Oceanographic Commission (IOC) Technical Commission for Oceanography and Marine Meteorology (JCOMM) has broad responsibilities in the overall management of the Programme. Many programme elements are undertaken jointly with the IOC, within the context of JCOMM, and also of the Global Ocean Observing System (GOOS). Close co-operation also occurs with the International Maritime Organization (IMO), as well as with other bodies both within and outside the UN system.

HYDROLOGY AND WATER RESOURCES PROGRAMME

The overall objective of this major Programme is to apply hydrology to meet the needs of sustainable development and use of water and related resources; for the mitigation of water-related disasters; and to ensure effective environment management at national and international levels. The Programme consists of the following mutually supporting component programmes:

Programme on Basic Systems in Hydrology (BSH): provides the basis and framework for the majority of the scientific and technical aspects of WMO activities in hydrology and water resources. The BSH covers the collection, transmission and storage of data, the transfer of operationally proven technology through the Hydrological Operational Multipurpose System (HOMS), and the development of the World Hydrological Cycle Observing System (WHYCOS), with the aim of improving countries' capacity to supply reliable water-related data, and manage and exchange accurate and timely water resources information.

Programme on Forecasting and Applications in Hydrology (FAH): covers aspects of the Hydrology and Water Resources Programme relating to hydrological modelling and forecasting, and to the application of hydrology in studies of global change. The FAH organizes activities in support of water resources development and management, and hazard mitigation, and promotes interdisciplinary co-operation to enhance flood forecasting at the national, regional and global level. The Programme is linked to the World Climate and Tropical Cyclone programmes.

Programme on Sustainable Development of Water Resources (SDW): encourages the full participation of hydrological services in national planning and in the implementation of actions consequent to the relevant recommendations of the United Nations Conference on Environment and Development (UNCED, held in Rio de Janeiro, Brazil, in 1992), and the World Summit on Sustainable Development (WSSD, held in Johannesburg, South Africa, in 2002).

Programme on Capacity Building in Hydrology and Water Resources (CBH): provides a framework under which National Hydrological Services (NHSs) are supported in their institutional development, through education and training activities, development of guidance material, assistance in the preparation of water legislation, reorganization of services and changes in administrative and legal frameworks.

Programme on Water-related Issues (WRI): maintains WMO's important role in international activities relating to water resource assessment and hydrological forecasting. A major aspect of this component programme is the Organization's collaboration with other UN agencies.

Other WMO programmes contain hydrological elements, which are closely co-ordinated with the Hydrology and Water Resources Programme. These include the Tropical Cyclone Programme, the World Climate Programme, and the Global Energy and Water Budget Experiment of the World Climate Research Programme.

EDUCATION AND TRAINING PROGRAMME

The overall objective of this Programme is to assist members in developing adequately trained staff to meet their responsibilities for providing meteorological and hydrological information services.

Activities include surveys of the training requirements of member states, the development of appropriate training programmes, the monitoring and improvement of the network of 23 Regional Meteorological Training Centres, the organization of training courses, seminars and conferences and the preparation of training materials. The Programme also arranges individual training programmes and the provision of fellowships. The Panel of Experts on Education and Training was established by the Executive Council to serve as an advisory body on all aspects of technical and scientific education and of training in meteorology and operational hydrology.

TECHNICAL CO-OPERATION PROGRAMME

The objective of the WMO Technical Co-operation Programme is to assist developing countries in improving their meteorological and hydrological services so that they can serve the needs of their people more effectively. This is achieved through improving, *inter alia,* their early warning systems for severe weather; their agricultural-meteorological services, to facilitate more reliable and fruitful food production; and the assessment of climatological factors for economic planning. At a regional level the Programme concentrates on disaster prevention and mitigation. In 2003 the cost of assistance to developing countries, administered or arranged by the Technical Co-operation Programme, was US $23.6m.

Programme for the Least Developed Countries: has as its long-term objective enhancement of the capacities of the NMHSs of LDCs so that they can contribute efficiently and in a timely manner to socio-economic development efforts. Priority areas are poverty alleviation and natural disaster preparedness and mitigation. Specific projects will be developed for individual countries and at a subregional level for countries in Africa, Asia and the Pacific.

Voluntary Co-operation Programme (VCP): WMO assists members in implementing the World Weather Watch Programme to develop an integrated observing and forecasting system. Member governments contribute equipment, services and fellowships for training, in addition to cash donations. During 2003 133 projects in 64 countries received support under the VCP. Contributions to the VCP totalled US $7.7m. in 2003.

WMO also carries out assistance projects under Trust Fund arrangements, financed by national authorities, either for activities in their own country or in a beneficiary country and managed by UNDP, the World Bank, regional development banks, the European Union and others. Such arrangements provided US $12.8m. of assistance in 2003. WMO provides assistance to UNDP in the development of national meteorological and hydrological services, in the application of meteorological and hydrological data to national economic development, and in the training of personnel. Assistance in the form of expert missions, fellowships and equipment was provided to 18 countries in 2003 at a cost of $2.2m., financed by UNDP. Financial support from WMO's regular budget for fellowships, group training, technical conferences and study tours amounted to $900,000 in 2003.

REGIONAL PROGRAMME

WMO's Regional Programme cuts across the other major WMO programmes of relevance to the regions and addresses meteorological, hydrological and other geophysical issues which are unique to and of common concern to a region or group of regions. It provides a framework for the formulation of most of the global WMO Programmes and serves as a mechanism for their implementation at the national, subregional and regional levels. The Programme provides support to the WMO regional associations and contributes to the development of NMHSs through capacity-building and other priority activities identified by members or relevant economic groups and organizations within the respective regions.

NATURAL DISASTER PREVENTION AND MITIGATION PROGRAMME

The purpose of this cross-cutting Programme is to ensure the integration of relevant activities being carried out by the various WMO programmes in the area of disaster prevention and mitigation, and to provide for the effective co-ordination of pertinent WMO activities with the related activities of international, regional and national organizations, including civil defence organizations. The Programme should also provide scientific and technical support to WMO actions made in response to disaster situations, and its activities should emphasize pre-disaster preparedness and be based on activities within a number of WMO programmes, including the Public Weather Services and other components of the Applications of Meteorology Programme. The Programme will serve as a vehicle for enabling the delivery of increasingly accurate and reliable warnings of severe events, especially through co-ordinating WMO actions aimed at improving mechanisms and communications for the delivery, use and evaluation of warnings, provision of prompt advice and assistance to members; and at enhancing effective international co-operation and collaboration.

SPACE PROGRAMME

The 14th WMO Congress initiated this new, cross-cutting programme to increase the effectiveness of, and contributions from, satellite systems for WMO programmes. Congress recognized the critical importance of data, products and services provided by the expanded space-based component of the GOS. In recent years the use by WMO members of satellite data, products and services has grown tremendously, to the benefit of almost all WMO programmes and WMO-supported programmes. The 53rd session of the Executive Council adopted a landmark decision to expand the space-based component of the GOS to include appropriate research and development ('R&D') and environmental satellite missions. The Congress agreed that the Commission for Basic Systems should continue to play a leading role, in full consultation with the other technical commissions for the Space Programme. Anticipated benefits from the Programme include an increasing contribution to the development of the GOS, as well as to that of other WMO-supported programmes and associated observing systems, through the provision of continuously improved data, products and services, from both operational and R&D satellites. The Programme also aims to facilitate and promote the wider availability and meaningful utilization world-wide of such improved data.

CO-OPERATION WITH OTHER BODIES

As a Specialized Agency of the UN, WMO actively participates in the UN system. In addition, WMO has concluded a number of formal agreements and working arrangements with international organizations both within and outside the UN system, at the intergovernmental and non-governmental level. As a result, WMO participates in major international conferences convened under the auspices of the UN or other organizations.

Intergovernmental Panel on Climate Change (IPCC): established in 1988 by WMO and UNEP; comprises some 3,000 scientists as well as other experts and representatives of all UN member governments. Approximately every five years the IPCC assesses all available scientific, technical and socio-economic information on anthropogenic climate change. The IPCC provides, on request, scientific, technical and socio-economic advice to the parties to the Conference of the Parties to the UN Framework Convention on Climate Change (UNFCCC) and to its subsidiary bodies, and compiles reports on specialized topics, such as *Aviation and the Global Atmosphere* and *Regional Impacts of Climate Change.* The IPCC informs and guides, but does not prescribe, policy. In December 1995 the IPCC presented evidence to 120 governments, demonstrating 'a discernible human influence on global climate'. In 2001 the Panel issued its *Third Assessment Report,* in which it confirmed this finding and presented new and strengthened evidence attributing most global climate warming over the past 50 years to human activities. IPCC's fourth report was scheduled to be issued in 2007.

Secretariat of the UN Framework Convention on Climate Change: Haus Carstanjen, Martin-Luther-King-Strasse 8, 53175 Bonn, Germany; tel. (228) 815-1000; fax (228) 815-1999; e-mail secretariat@unfccc.int; internet unfccc.int; WMO and UNEP worked together to formulate the Convention, in response to the first report of the IPCC, issued in August 1990, which predicted an increase in the concentration of 'greenhouse' gases (i.e. carbon dioxide and other gases that have a warming effect on the atmosphere) owing to human activity. The UNFCCC was signed in May 1992 and formally adopted at the UN Conference on Environment and Development, held in June. It entered into force in March 1994. It committed countries to submitting reports on measures being taken to reduce the emission of greenhouse gases and recommended stabilizing these emissions at 1990 levels by 2000; however, this was not legally-binding. In July 1996, at the second session of the Conference of the Parties (COP) of the Convention, representatives of developed countries declared their willingness to commit to legally-binding objectives for emission limitations in a specified timetable. Multilateral negotiations ensued to formulate a mandatory treaty on greenhouse gas emissions. At the third COP, held in Kyoto, Japan, in December 1997, 38 industrial nations endorsed mandatory reduc-

tions of combined emissions of the six major gases by an average of 5.2% during the five-year period 2008–12, to pre-1990 levels. The so-called Kyoto Protocol was to enter into force on being ratified by at least 55 countries party to the UNFCCC, including industrialized countries with combined emissions of carbon dioxide in 1990 accounting for at least 55% of the total global greenhouse gas emissions by developed nations. Many of the Protocol's operational details, however, remained to be determined. The fourth COP, convened in Buenos Aires, Argentina, in November 1998, adopted a plan of action to promote implementation of the UNFCCC and to finalize the operational details of the Kyoto Protocol. These included the Clean Development Mechanism, by which industrialized countries may obtain credits towards achieving their reduction targets by assisting developing countries to implement emission-reducing measures, and a system of trading emission quotas. The fifth COP, held in Bonn, Germany, in October–November 1999, and the first session of the sixth COP, convened in The Hague, Netherlands, in November 2000, failed to reach agreement on the implementation of the Buenos Aires plan of action, owing to a lack of consensus on several technical matters, including the formulation of an effective mechanism for ascertaining compliance under the Kyoto Protocol, and adequately defining a provision of the Protocol under which industrialized countries may obtain credits towards achieving their reduction targets in respect of the absorption of emissions resulting from activities in the so-called land-use, land-use change and forestry (LULUCF) sector. Further, informal, talks were held in Ottawa, Canada, in early December. Agreement on implementing the Buenos Aires action plan was finally achieved at the second session of the sixth COP, held in Bonn in July 2001. The seventh COP, convened in Marrakech, Morocco, in October–November, formally adopted the decisions reached in July, and elected 15 members to the Executive Board of the Clean Development Mechanism. The eighth COP, convened in New Dehli, India, in October–November 2002, issued the Dehli Declaration, urging states parties that had not done so already to ratify the Kyoto Protocol, and urging the integration of climate change objectives in key areas into national sustainable development strategies. In March the USA (the most prolific national producer of harmful gas emissions) announced that it would not ratify the Kyoto Protocol. A major advance achieved at the ninth COP was agreement on the modalities and scope for carbon-absorbing forest-management projects in the Clean Development Mechanism. The Kyoto Protocol eventually entered into force on 16 February 2005, 90 days after its ratification by Russia. By that time the Protocol had received 141 ratifications, including ratifications by industrialized nations with combined responsibility for 61.6% of greenhouse gas emissions by developed nations in 1990 (although excluding participation by Australia and the USA).

INTERNATIONAL DAY

World Meteorological Day is observed every year on 23 March. The theme in 2005 was 'Weather, Climate, Water and Sustainable Development'.

Finance

WMO is financed by contributions from members on a proportional scale of assessment. For the fourteenth financial period, the four years 2004–07, a programme and budget of 253.8m. was approved, of which 249.8m. Swiss francs were to be funded from assessed contributions and 4.0m. Swiss francs would be made available from any cash surplus arising from the previous financial period. Outside this budget, WMO implements a number of projects as executing agency for UNDP or else under trust-fund arrangements.

Publications

Annual Report.
Statements on the Status of the Global Climate.
WMO Bulletin (quarterly in English, French, Russian and Spanish).
Reports, technical regulations, manuals and notes and training publications.

World Tourism Organization

Address: Capitán Haya 42, 28020 Madrid, Spain.
Telephone: (91) 5678100; **fax:** (91) 5713733; **e-mail:** omt@world-tourism.org; **internet:** www.world-tourism.org.

The World Tourism Organization (WTO) was formally established in 1975 following transformation of the International Union of Official Travel Organisations into an intergovernmental body, in accordance with a resolution of the UN General Assembly approved in 1969. The Organization became a specialized agency of the UN in December 2003. It aims to promote and develop sustainable tourism, in particular in support of socio-economic growth in developing countries.

MEMBERS

145 member states, seven associate members, 305 affiliate members.

Organization

(March 2005)

GENERAL ASSEMBLY

The General Assembly meets once every two years to approve the budget and programme of work of the Organization and to consider issues of concern for the tourism sector. It consists of representatives of all full and associate members; affiliate members and representatives of other international organizations participate as observers.

EXECUTIVE COUNCIL

The Council, comprising 29 members elected by the General Assembly, is the Organization's governing body responsible for supervising the activities of the Organization. It meets twice a year. The following specialized committees are subsidiary organs of the Council and advise on management and programme content: Programme; Budget and Finance; Statistics and Macroeconomic Analysis of Tourism; Market Intelligence and Promotion; Sustainable Development of Tourism; and Quality Support. There is also a Subcommittee for the Review of Applications for Affiliate Membership.

REGIONAL COMMISSIONS

There are six regional commissions, comprising all members and associate members from that region, which meet at least once a year to determine the Organization's priorities and future activities in the region. The commissions cover Africa, the Americas, East Asia and the Pacific, Europe, the Middle East, and South Asia.

SECRETARIAT

The Secretariat is responsible for implementing WTO's work programme. A regional support office for Asia and the Pacific is based in Osaka, Japan. Six regional representatives, based at the Secretariat, support national tourism authorities, act as a liaison between those authorities and international sources of finance, and represent the WTO at national and regional events.
Secretary-General: Francesco Frangialli (France).

AFFILIATE MEMBERS

The World Tourism Organization is unique as an intergovernmental body in extending membership to operational representatives of the industry and other related sectors, for example transport companies, educational institutions, insurance companies, publishing groups. A WTO Education Council aims to supports WTO's education and human resource development activities. It undertakes research projects, grants awards for innovation and the application of knowledge in tourism, and co-ordinates a tourism labour market observatory project. The WTO Business Council groups together the affiliate members from the private sector and aims to promote and facilitate partnerships between the industry and governments. A third group of the affiliate membership is the WTO Task Force on Destination Management, which acts as an informal advisory body of WTO with particular concern for issues relevant to tourist destinations, for example local tourism marketing, economic measurements and management of congestion.
CEO of WTO Affiliate Members: Antonio de la Morena (Spain).

Activities

The World Tourism Organization (WTO) promotes the development of responsible, sustainable and universally accessible tourism within the broad context of contributing to economic development, international prosperity and peace and respect for human rights. As a specialized agency of the UN (a status which was achieved in 2003) WTO aims to emphasize the role of tourism as a means of supporting socio-economic development and achieve the so-called Millennium Development Goals. Through its network of more than 300 affiliated members WTO extends its activities and objectives to the private sector, tourism authorities and educational institutions.

In January 2005 the Executive Council convened its first ever emergency session in response to the devastation of many coastal areas in the Indian Ocean caused by an earthquake and tsunami which struck 12 countries at the end of 2004. The Council, meeting in Phuket, Thailand, along with other regional organizations, private sector representatives and tourism experts, adopted an action plan to support the recovery of the tourism sector in many of the affected areas, help to restore tourist confidence in the region and rehabilitate tourism infrastructure, in particular in Thailand, the Maldives, Indonesia and Sri Lanka.

CO-OPERATION FOR DEVELOPMENT

In 1976 WTO became an executing agency of the United Nations Development Programme (UNDP) and has subsequently been concerned with the contribution of tourism to the sustainable development objectives of member states. Activities to transfer technical skills and knowledge to developing countries are fundamental tasks for the Organization. It aims to assist member countries to develop tourism plans and strategies and helps to secure and manage specific development projects, for example the formulation of tourism legislation in Syria, hotel classification in Bolivia and statistics development in Botswana.

In September 2002 at the World Summit on Sustainable Development, held in Johannesburg, South Africa, WTO, in collaboration with the UN Conference on Trade and Development (UNCTAD), launched the Sustainable Tourism-Eliminating Poverty (ST-EP) initiative. It aimed to encourage social, economic and ecologically sustainable tourism with the aim of alleviating poverty in the world's poorest countries. In September 2004 WTO signed an agreement with the Republic of Korea providing for the establishment of a ST-EP Foundation in the capital, Seoul.

In 1994 WTO, in co-operation with the UN Educational, Scientific and Cultural Organization (UNESCO) initiated a project to promote tourism, in support of economic development, along the traditional Silk Road trading routes linking Asia and Europe. A fourth international meeting of participants in the project was convened in Bukhara, Uzbekistan, in October 2002. In October 2004 a Silk Road Tourism Office was opened in Samarkand, Uzbekistan. In 1995 WTO and UNESCO launched the Slave Route project to stimulate tourism and raise cultural awareness in several West African countries.

QUALITY

WTO aims to ensure that quality standards and safety and security aspects are incorporated into all tourism products and services. It is also concerned with the social impact of tourism and the regulatory trading framework. Under its programme on quality and trade there was also a greater focus on the economics of tourism.

In 1991 WTO's General Assembly approved a series of Recommended Measures for Tourism Safety which member states were encouraged to apply. WTO has established a Safety and Security in Tourism Network to consider aspects of the recommended measures and to facilitate collaboration between institutions and experts concerned with safety and security issues. The Network publishes national factsheets on safety and security in countries and tourist destinations, compiled by a designated national tourism administration focal point, for use by tourism professionals and the general public. WTO works to ensure safety and security measures are incorporated into products and services. Other essential quality standards promoted by the Organization are hygiene and food safety, accessibility, product and pricing transparency and authenticity. WTO is also concerned with ensuring that tourist activities are in keeping with the surrounding environment.

A Task Force for the Protection of Children from Sexual Exploitation in Tourism was established in 1997 as a forum for governments, industry associations and other organizations to work together with the aim of identifying, preventing and eradicating the sexual exploitation of children. A series of regional consultations was held in 2003. In 1999 the General Assembly adopted a Global Code of Ethics for Tourism. The Code was endorsed by a special resolution of the UN General Assembly in 2001. The Code aims to protect resources upon which tourism depends and to ensure that the economic benefits of tourism are distributed equitably. A World Committee on Tourism Ethics, established in 2003 to support the implementation of the Code, held its first meeting in Rome, Italy, in February 2004.

WTO participates as an observer at the World Trade Organization on issues relating to trade in tourism services, with particular concern to negotiations under the General Agreement on Trade in Services (GATS) for a separate annex on tourism. WTO hosts a voluntary working group on liberalization.

SUSTAINABLE TOURISM DEVELOPMENT

WTO aims to encourage and facilitate the application of sustainable practices within the tourism industry. It publishes guides on sustainable development for use by local authorities as well as compilations for good practices. WTO has also published several manuals for tourism planning at regional, national and local level and has organized seminars on planning issues in developing countries. WTO actively promotes voluntary initiatives for sustainability including labelling schemes, certification systems and awards. In 2003–04 WTO organized a series of regional conferences to consider further sustainability certification of tourism activities at the regional and local level.

In 1999 WTO was mandated, together with the UN Environment Programme, to assume responsibility for the International Year of Ecotourism which was held in 2002, as well as all preparatory and follow-up activities. A World Ecotourism Summit, which was convened in Québec, Canada in May, was attended by delegates from 132 countries. It resulted in the Québec Declaration containing guide-lines for sustainable ecotourism development and management. WTO publishes a series of compilations of good practices for small and medium-sized businesses involved with ecotourism. WTO sponsored the first International Conference on Climate Change and Tourism, which was held in Djerba, Tunisia, in April 2003. A final declaration of the conference urged that WTO take the lead in focusing international attention on the issue and called upon all parties to continue research efforts, to encourage sustainability in tourism, to generate awareness and to implement defined actions.

STATISTICS AND ECONOMIC MANAGEMENT

WTO has established international standards for tourism measurement and reporting. It also compiles comprehensive tourism statistics and forecasts. A Tourism Satellite Account (TSA) was developed to analyse the economic impact of tourism. It was endorsed by the UN Statistical Commission in 2000 and is recognized as a framework for providing internationally comparable data. The TSA is also considered by WTO to be a strategic project within the broader objective of developing a system of tourism statistics.

In early 2003 WTO initiated a study on sustainable tourism indicators with the aim of compiling a comprehensive resource and guidebook for planners and managers within the industry.

MARKET INTELLIGENCE AND PROMOTION

WTO assists governments and tourist professionals to analyse and forecast tourism trends and to assess the relative performance of each country's tourist industry. The Organization also assist member states with tourism promotion through marketing tools and the formulation of tourism development strategies. A Market Intelligence and Promotion Committee was formally established in October 2002. Following the terrorism attacks against targets in the USA in September 2001 a Tourism Recovery Committee was established to monitor events affecting tourism, help to restore confidence in the industry and strengthen WTO activities concerned with safety and security.

In order to generate awareness of tourism among the international community WTO sponsors a World Tourism Day, held each year on 27 September. In 2004 the official events were hosted by Malaysia, on the theme of 'Sport and tourism: two living forces for mutual understanding, culture and the development of societies'.

DOCUMENTATION

WTO aims to act as a clearing house of information for the tourist industry. A WTO Documentation Centre collates extensive information on tourism activities and promotes access to and exchange of information among members states and affiliated partners. The Centres offers access to tourism legislation and other regulatory procedures through its LEXTOUR database on the internet. The Centre also administers a tourism information database (INFO-DOCTOUR).

Institute

WTO Themis Foundation: Avinguda Dr Vilanova 9, Edif. Thaïs 4c, Andorra la Vella, Andorra; tel. 802600; fax 829955; e-mail wto .themis@andorra.ad; internet www.themis.ad; aims to promote quality and efficiency in tourism education and training. Works closely with the human resource development programme of WTO and promotes WTO's specialized training products and services, in particular the TedQual certification and the practicum programme for tourism officials; Dir-Gen. JAVIER GALLEGO.

Publications

Compendium of Tourism Statistics.

Tourism Market Trends (annually).

Yearbook of Tourism Statistics.

WTO World Tourism Barometer (3 a year).

WTOBC Interactive (monthly).

WTO News (quarterly).

Other research or statistical reports, studies, guide-lines and fact-sheets.

AFRICAN DEVELOPMENT BANK—ADB

Address: Headquarters: rue Joseph Anoma, 01 BP 1387, Abidjan 01, Côte d'Ivoire.

Telephone: 20-20-44-44; **fax:** 20-20-49-59; **e-mail:** afdb@afdb.org; **internet:** www.afdb.org.

Address: Temporary relocation agency: angle des trois rues, ave du Ghana, rue Pierre de Coubertin et rue Hedi Nouira, BP 323, 1002 Tunis Belvedere, Tunisia.

Telephone: (71) 333-511; **fax:** (71) 251-933.

Established in 1964, the Bank began operations in July 1966, with the aim of financing economic and social development in African countries. The Bank's headquarters are based in Abidjan, Côte d'Ivoire. From February 2003, however, in view of ongoing insecurity in Côte d'Ivoire, the Bank's operations were relocated on a temporary basis to Tunis, Tunisia (see above).

AFRICAN MEMBERS

Algeria	Equatorial Guinea	Namibia
Angola	Eritrea	Niger
Benin	Ethiopia	Nigeria
Botswana	Gabon	Rwanda
Burkina Faso	The Gambia	São Tomé and
Burundi	Ghana	Príncipe
Cameroon	Guinea	Senegal
Cape Verde	Guinea-Bissau	Seychelles
Central African	Kenya	Sierra Leone
Republic	Lesotho	Somalia
Chad	Liberia	South Africa
Comoros	Libya	Sudan
Congo,	Madagascar	Swaziland
Democratic	Malawi	Tanzania
Republic	Mali	Togo
Congo, Republic	Mauritania	Tunisia
Côte d'Ivoire	Mauritius	Uganda
Djibouti	Morocco	Zambia
Egypt	Mozambique	Zimbabwe

There are also 24 non-African members.

Organization

(April 2005)

BOARD OF GOVERNORS

The highest policy-making body of the Bank. Each member country nominates one Governor, usually its Minister of Finance and Economic Affairs, and an alternate Governor or the Governor of its Central Bank. The Board meets once a year. It elects the Board of Directors and the President.

BOARD OF DIRECTORS

The Board consists of 18 members (of whom six are non-African), elected by the Board of Governors for a term of three years, renewable once; it is responsible for the general operations of the Bank. The Board meets on a weekly basis.

OFFICERS

The President is responsible for the organization and the day-to-day operations of the Bank under guidance of the Board of Directors. The President is elected for a five-year term and serves as the Chairman of the Board of Directors. In 2000 the Bank initiated a process of organizational restructuring as part of a new Bank Vision, approved by the Board of Governors in the previous year. The objectives of the reorganization were to give greater priority to client needs, strategically oriented planning, and human resources management. A new structure was introduced on 1 January 2002. Accordingly, the number of Vice-Presidents was increased from three to five, responsible for Planning, Policy and Research; Corporate Management; Operations, Central and West Regions; Operations, North, East and South Regions; and Finance.

Executive President and Chairman of Board of Directors: OMAR KABBAJ (Morocco).

Secretary-General: CHEIKH IBRAHIMA FALL (Senegal).

FINANCIAL STRUCTURE

The ADB Group of development financing institutions comprises the African Development Fund (ADF) and the Nigeria Trust Fund (NTF), which provide concessionary loans, and the African Develop-

ment Bank itself. The group uses a unit of account (UA), which, at December 2002, was valued at US $1.3595.

The capital stock of the Bank was at first exclusively open for subscription by African countries, with each member's subscription consisting of an equal number of paid-up and callable shares. In 1978, however, the Governors agreed to open the capital stock of the Bank to subscription by non-regional states on the basis of nine principles aimed at maintaining the African character of the institution. The decision was finally ratified in May 1982, and the participation of non-regional countries became effective on 30 December. It was agreed that African members should still hold two-thirds of the share capital, that all loan operations should be restricted to African members, and that the Bank's President should always be an African national. In May 1998 the Board of Governors approved an increase in capital of 35%, and resolved that the non-African members' share of the capital be increased from 33.3% to 40%. In 2003 the ADB's authorized capital was US $32,498m. At the end of 2003 subscribed capital was $32,043m. (of which the paid-up portion was $3,241m.).

Activities

At the end of 2003 total loan and grant approvals by the ADB Group since the beginning of its operations amounted to US $47,556.5m. Of that amount agriculture received the largest proportion of assistance (18.5%), while transport received 16.0%, multi-sector activities 14.6%, and finance 13.4%. In 2003 the group approved 145 loans and grants amounting to $2,624.7m., compared with $2,772m. for 118 loans and grants in the previous year.

A new credit policy, adopted in May 1995, effectively disqualified 39 low-income regional members, deemed to be non-creditworthy, from receiving non-concessional ADB financing, in an attempt to reduce the accumulation of arrears. The ADB Group estimated that its capital requirements for the period 1997–2001 would amount to US $46,500m. to allow for greater flexibility in its lending. In September 1997 the Bank established a Supplementary Financing Mechanism, to provide countries eligible for ADF funds with quick-disbursing resources to meet interest payments on outstanding Bank debt. The Bank allocated UA 222m. for the mechanism, which became operational in March 1998.

The ADB contributed funds for the establishment, in 1986, of the Africa Project Development Facility, which assists the private sector in Africa by providing advisory services and finance for entrepreneurs: it is managed by the International Finance Corporation (IFC). In 1989 the ADB, in co-ordination with IFC and UNDP, created the African Management Services Company (AMSCo) which provides management support and training to private companies in Africa. The Bank is one of three multilateral donors, with the World Bank and UNDP, supporting the African Capacity Building Foundation, which was established in 1991 to strengthen and develop institutional and human capacity in support of sustainable development activities.

The Bank also provides technical assistance to regional member countries in the form of experts' services, pre-investment feasibility studies, and staff training; much of this assistance is financed through bilateral aid funds contributed by non-African member states. The Bank's African Development Institute provides training for officials of regional member countries in order to enhance the management of Bank-financed projects and, more broadly, to strengthen national capacities for promoting sustainable development. In 1990 the ADB established the African Business Round Table (ABR), which is composed of the chief executives of Africa's leading corporations. The ABR aims to strengthen Africa's private sector, promote intra-African trade and investment, and attract foreign investment to Africa. The ABR is chaired by the ADB's Executive President. At its fourth annual meeting, held in Arusha, Tanzania, in March 1994, the ABR resolved to establish an African Investment Bank, in co-operation with the ADB, which was to provide financial services to African companies. In November 1999 a Joint Africa Institute, which had been established by the Bank, the World Bank and the IMF, was formally inaugurated in Abidjan, Côte d'Ivoire. The Institute aimed to enhance training opportunities in economic policy and management and to strengthen capacity-building in the region.

In 1990 a Memorandum of Understanding (MOU) for the Reinforcement of Co-operation between the Organization of African Unity, now African Union, the UN Economic Commission for Africa and the ADB was signed by the three organizations. A joint secretariat supports co-operation activities between the organizations. In 1999 a Co-operation Agreement was formally concluded between the

Bank and the Common Market for Eastern and Southern Africa (COMESA). In March 2000 the Bank signed an MOU on its strategic partnership with the World Bank. Other MOUs were signed during that year with the United Nations Industrial Development Organization, the World Food Programme, and the Arab Maghreb Union. Since 1996 the Bank has collaborated closely with international partners, in particular the World Bank, in efforts to address the problems of heavily indebted poor countries—HIPCs (see IBRD). Following the introduction of an enhanced framework for the initiative, extending the number of eligible African countries from 25 to 31, the Bank has been actively involved in the preparation of Poverty Reduction Strategy Papers, that provide national frameworks for poverty reduction programmes. At December 2003 the Bank had approved US $2,385.7m. under the enhanced HIPC initiative. In 2002 the Bank's Board of Directors approved a Strategic Plan for 2003–07 incorporating four fundamental principles for Bank activities: country ownership; greater selectivity; participatory approaches; and enhanced co-operation with development partners.

AFRICAN DEVELOPMENT BANK (ADB)

The Bank makes loans at a variable rate of interest, which is adjusted twice a year, plus a commitment fee of 0.75%. Loan approvals amounted to US $1,108.3m. for 28 loans in 2003. Since October 1997 new fixed and floating rate loans have also been made available.

AFRICAN DEVELOPMENT FUND (ADF)

The Fund commenced operations in 1974. It grants interest-free loans to low-income African countries for projects with repayment over 50 years (including a 10-year grace period) and with a service charge of 0.75% per annum. Grants for project feasibility studies are made to the poorest countries.

Negotiations for a seventh replenishment of the Fund's resources commenced in May 1993. However, in May 1994, donor countries withheld any new funds owing to dissatisfaction with the Bank's governance. In May 1996, following the implementation of various institutional reforms to strengthen the Bank's financial management and decision-making capabilities and to reduce its administrative costs, an agreement was concluded on the seventh replenishment of the ADF. Donor countries pledged some US $2,690m. for the period 1996–98. An additional allocation of $420m. was endorsed at a special donors' meeting held in Osaka, Japan, in June. The ADF aimed to offer concessional assistance to 42 African countries over the period 1996–98. The seventh replenishment provided for the establishment of an ADF Microfinance Initiative (AMINA), initially for a two-year period, to support small-scale capacity-building projects. In January 1999 negotiations on the eighth replenishment of the Fund were concluded with an agreement to provide additional resources amounting to $3,437m. The replenishment was approved by the Board of Governors in May, and came into effect in December. In September 2002 donor countries pledged resources of around $3,500m. for the ninth replenishment of the Fund, covering the period 2002–04.

In 2003 112 ADF loans and grants were approved amounting to US $1,482.9m.

NIGERIA TRUST FUND (NTF)

The Agreement establishing the Nigeria Trust Fund was signed in February 1976 by the Bank and the Government of Nigeria. The Fund is administered by the Bank and its loans are granted for up to 25 years, including grace periods of up to five years, and carry 0.75% commission charges and 4% interest charges. The loans are intended to provide financing for projects in co-operation with other lending institutions. The Fund also aims to promote the private sector and trade between African countries by providing information on African and international financial institutions able to finance African trade.

During 1999 negotiations on a revised Agreement and replenishment of the Fund's resources were undertaken. Five loans were approved during 2003 amounting to US $33.5m.

SUMMARY OF BANK GROUP ACTIVITIES

(US $ million)

	2002	2003	Cumulative total*
ADB loans			
Number	31	28	934
Amount approved . . .	1,452.05	1,108.30	27,917.68
Disbursements . . .	679.45	969.45	18,356.17
ADF loans and grants			
Number	84	112	1,769
Amount approved . . .	1,306.14	1,482.93	19,250.96
Disbursements . . .	740.97	546.94	10,847.79

— continued	2002	2003	Cumulative total*
NTF loans			
Number	3	5	70
Amount approved . . .	13.79	33.45	387.83
Disbursements	4.56	3.63	247.73
Group total			
Number	118	145	2,740
Amount approved . . .	2,771.99	2,624.69	47,556.45
Disbursements	1,424.97	1,519.83	29,451.68

* Since the initial operations of the three institutions (1967 for ADB, 1974 for ADF and 1976 for NTF).

Source: *Annual Report 2003*.

ASSOCIATED INSTITUTIONS

The ADB actively participated in the establishment of five associated institutions:

African Reinsurance Corporation—Africa-Re: Africa Re House, Plot 1679, Karimu Kotun St, Victoria Island, PMB 12765, Lagos, Nigeria; tel. (1) 2626660; fax (1) 2668802; e-mail info@africa-re.com; internet www.africa-re.com; f. 1977; started operations in 1978; its purpose is to foster the development of the insurance and reinsurance industry in Africa and to promote the growth of national and regional underwriting capacities; auth. cap. US $100m., of which the ADB holds 10%; there are 12 directors, one appointed by the Bank; mems: 41 countries, the ADB, and some 110 insurance and reinsurance cos; Man. Dir Bakary Kamara; publ. *The African Reinsurer* (annually).

African Export-Import Bank—Afreximbank: POB 404 Gezira, Cairo 11568; World Trade Centre Bldg, 1191 Corniche el-Nil, Cairo 11221, Egypt; tel. (2) 5780282; fax (2) 5780277; e-mail mail@afreximbank.com; internet www.afreximbank.com; f. 1993; aims to increase the volume of African exports and to expand intra-African trade by financing exporters and importers directly and indirectly through trade finance institutions, such as commercial banks; in Nov. 2001, under the auspices of Afreximbank, a Memorandum of General Principles was signed by African bankers for the establishment of an African Bankers Forum; auth. cap. US $750m.; paid-up cap. $146.6m. (Dec. 2003); Pres. Jean-Louis Ekra; publ. *Annual Report*.

Association of African Development Finance Institutions—AADFI: Immeuble AIAFD, blvd Latrille, rue J61, Cocody Deux Plateaux, Abidjan 04, Côte d'Ivoire; tel. 22-52-33-89; fax 22-52-25-84; e-mail adfi@aviso.ci; f. 1975; aims to promote co-operation among financial institutions in the region in matters relating to economic and social development, research, project design, financing and the exchange of information; mems: 92 in 43 African and non-African countries; Pres. Gershom Mumba; Sec.-Gen. J. A. Amihere (acting); publs *Annual Report*, *AADFI Information Bulletin* (quarterly), *Finance and Development in Africa* (2 a year).

Shelter-Afrique (Société pour l'habitat et le logement territorial en Afrique): Longonot Rd, POB 41479, Nairobi, Kenya; tel. (20) 2722305; fax (20) 2722024; e-mail info@shelterafrique.org; internet www.shelterafrique.org; f. 1982 to finance housing in mem. countries; auth. share cap. is US $300m., held by 41 African countries, the ADB, Africa-Re and CDC Group plc (formerly the Commonwealth Development Corpn); Man. Dir P. M'Baye.

Société Internationale Financière pour les Investissements et le Développement en Afrique—SIFIDA: 22 rue François-Perréard, CP 310, 1225 Chêne-Bourg/Geneva, Switzerland; tel. (22) 8692000; fax (22) 8692001; e-mail headoffice@sifida.com; internet www.sifida.com; f. 1970 by 120 financial and industrial institutions, including the ADB and the IFC following a restructuring in 1996, the main shareholders are BNP/Paribas and its six banking affiliates in West and Central Africa. SIFIDA is active in the fields of trade and equity participation finance in Africa and also provides financial advisory services, notably in the context of project finance, privatizations and debt conversion; auth. cap. US $75m., subscribed cap. $12.5m; Chair. Pierre Mariani; Man. Dir Philippe Séchaud; publ. *African Banking Directory* (annually).

Publications

Annual Report.
ADB Business Bulletin (10 a year).
ADB Statistical Pocketbook.
ADB Today (every 2 months).
African Development Report (annually).
African Development Review.

African Economic Outlook (annually, with OECD).

Annual Procurement Report.

Basic Information (annually).

Economic Research Papers.

Quarterly Operational Summary.

Summaries of operations in each member country and various background documents.

AFRICAN UNION—AU

Address: POB 3243, Addis Ababa, Ethiopia.

Telephone: (1) 51-7700; **fax:** (1) 51-7844; **e-mail:** general@africa-union.org; **internet:** www.africa-union.org.

In May 2001 the Constitutive Act of the African Union entered into force. In July 2002 the African Union (AU) became fully operational, replacing the Organization of African Unity (OAU), which had been founded in 1963. The AU aims to support unity, solidarity and peace among African states; to promote and defend African common positions on issues of shared interest; to encourage human rights, democratic principles and good governance; to advance the development of member states by encouraging research and by working to eradicate preventable diseases; and to promote sustainable development and political and socio-economic integration, including co-ordinating and harmonizing policy between the continent's various 'regional economic communities' (see below).

MEMBERS*

Algeria	Eritrea	Nigeria
Angola	Ethiopia	Rwanda
Benin	Gabon	São Tomé and
Botswana	The Gambia	Príncipe
Burkina Faso	Ghana	Senegal
Burundi	Guinea	Seychelles
Cameroon	Guinea-Bissau	Sierra Leone
Cape Verde	Kenya	Somalia
Central African	Lesotho	South Africa
Republic	Liberia	Sudan
Chad	Libya	Swaziland
Comoros	Madagascar	Tanazania
Congo, Democratic	Malawi	Togo
Republic	Mali	Tunisia
Congo, Republic	Mauritania	Uganda
Côte d'Ivoire	Mauritius	Zambia
Djibouti	Mozambique	Zimbabwe
Egypt	Namibia	
Equatorial Guinea	Niger	

* The Sahrawi Arab Democratic Republic (SADR–Western Sahara) was admitted to the OAU in February 1982, following recognition by more than one-half of the member states, but its membership was disputed by Morocco and other states which claimed that a two-thirds' majority was needed to admit a state whose existence was in question. Morocco withdrew from the OAU with effect from November 1985, and has not applied to join the AU. The SADR ratified the Constitutive Act in December 2000 and is a full member of the AU.

Note: The Constitutive Act stipulates that member states in which Governments accede to power by unconstitutional means are liable to suspension from participating in the Union's activities and to the imposition of sanctions by the Union.

Organization

(April 2005)

ASSEMBLY

The Assembly, comprising member countries' heads of state and government, is the supreme organ of the Union and meets at least once a year (with alternate sessions held in Addis Ababa, Ethiopia) to determine and monitor the Union's priorities and common policies and to adopt its annual work programme. Resolutions are passed by a two-thirds' majority, procedural matters by a simple majority. Extraordinary sessions may be convened at the request of a member state and on approval by a two-thirds' majority. A chairperson is elected at each meeting from among the members, to hold office for one year. The Assembly ensures compliance by member states with decisions of the Union, adopts the biennial budget, will appoint judges of the planned Court of Human and Peoples' Rights, and hears and settles disputes between member states. The first regular Assembly meeting was held in Durban, South Africa, in July 2002.

A first extraordinary summit meeting of the Assembly was convened in Addis Ababa in February 2003. In July delegates convened in Maputo, Mozambique for the second regular Assembly. The third regular Assembly meeting was held in July 2004 in Addis Ababa, and the fourth took place in Abuja, Nigeria, in January 2005.

Chairperson: (2004/05) OLUSEGUN OBASANJO (Pres. of Nigeria).

EXECUTIVE COUNCIL

Consists of ministers of foreign affairs and others and meets at least twice a year (in February and July), with provision for extraordinary sessions. The Council's Chairperson is the minister of foreign affairs (or another competent authority) of the country that has provided the Chairperson of the Assembly. Prepares meetings of, and is responsible to, the Assembly. Determines the issues to be submitted to the Assembly for decision, co-ordinates and harmonizes the policies, activities and initiatives of the Union in areas of common interest to member states, monitors the implementation of policies and decisions of the Assembly.

PERMANENT REPRESENTATIVES COMMITTEE

The Committee, which comprises Ambassadors accredited to the AU and meets at least once a month, is responsible to, advises and prepares meetings of the Executive Council, including its agenda and draft decisions.

COMMISSION

The Commission is the permanent secretariat of the organization. It comprises a Chairperson (elected for a four-year term of office by the Assembly), Deputy Chairperson and eight Commissioners (responsible for: peace and security; political affairs; infrastructure and energy; social affairs; human resources, science and technology; trade and industry; rural economy and agriculture; and economic affairs) who are elected on the basis of equal geographical distribution. Members of the Commission serve a term of four years and may stand for re-election for one further term of office. Further support staff assist the smooth functioning of the Commission. The Commission represents the Union under the guidance of and as mandated by the Assembly and the Executive Council, and reports to the Executive Council. It deals with administrative issues, implements the decisions of the Union, and acts as the custodian of the Constitutive Act and Protocols, and other agreements. Its work covers the following domains: control of pandemics; disaster management; international crime and terrorism; environmental management; negotiations relating to external trade; negotiations relating to external debt; population, migration, refugees and displaced persons; food security; socio-economic integration; and all other areas where a common position has been established by Union member states. It has responsibility for the co-ordination of AU activities and meetings.

Chairperson: ALPHA OUMAR KONARÉ (Mali).

SPECIALIZED TECHNICAL COMMITTEES

There are specialized committees for monetary and financial affairs; rural economy and agricultural matters; trade, customs and immigration matters; industry, science and technology, energy, natural resources and environment; transport, communications and tourism; health, labour and social affairs; and education, culture and human resources. These have responsibility for implementing the Union's programmes and projects.

PAN-AFRICAN PARLIAMENT

The Pan-African Parliament, inaugurated in March 2004, comprises five deputies (including at least one woman) from each AU member state, presided over by an elected President assisted by four Vice-Presidents. The President and Vice-Presidents must equitably represent the central, northern, eastern, southern and western African states. The Parliament convenes at least twice a year; an extraordinary session may be called by a two-thirds majority of the members. The Parliament currently has only advisory and consultative powers. Its eventual evolution into an institution with full legislative authority is planned. In July 2004 it was announced that

South Africa would host the permanent seat of the Parliament. The Parliament's second session was convened in September at temporary headquarters in Midrand.

President: GERTRUDE MONGELA (Tanzania).

ECONOMIC, SOCIAL AND CULTURAL COUNCIL

The Economic, Social and Cultural Council (ECOSOCC), inaugurated in March 2005, is to have an advisory function and to comprise representatives of civic, professional and cultural bodies at national, regional and diaspora levels. It's main organs are to be: an elected General Assembly; Standing Committee; Credential Committee; and Sectoral Cluster Communities. It is envisaged that the Council will strengthen the partnership between member governments and African civil society. Following ECOSOCC's inauguration a consultation process was launched for the eventual organization of elections to the planned General Assembly. Prior to the activation of the Assembly an interim elected Standing Committee was to hold office for a two-year period. The Sectoral Cluster Communities were to be established to formulate opinions and influence AU decision-making in the following 10 areas: peace and security; political affairs; infrastructure and energy; social affairs and health; human resources, science and technology; trade and industry; rural economy and agriculture; economic affairs; women and gender; and cross-cutting programmes.

Note: In early 2005 the planned Court of Human and Peoples' Rights, which was to pass judgment on alleged human rights abuses, remained to be established. In addition three financial instititions were to be created to manage the financing of programmes and projects: an African Central Bank, an African Monetary Fund, and an African Investment Bank.

Activities

There were various attempts at establishing an inter-African organization from the 1950s. In November 1958 Ghana and Guinea (later joined by Mali) drafted a Charter that was to form the basis of a Union of African States. In January 1961 a conference was held at Casablanca, attended by the heads of state of Ghana, Guinea, Mali, Morocco, and representatives of Libya and of the provisional government of the Algerian Republic (GPRA). Tunisia, Nigeria, Liberia and Togo declined the invitation to attend. An African Charter was adopted and it was decided to set up an African Military Command and an African Common Market. Between October 1960 and March 1961 three conferences were held by French-speaking African countries, at Abidjan, Brazzaville and Yaoundé, Cameroon. None of the 12 countries that attended these meetings had been present at the Casablanca Conference. These conferences led eventually to the signing in September 1961, at Tananarive, of a charter establishing the Union africaine et malgache, later the Organisation commune africaine et mauricienne (OCAM). In May 1961 a conference was held at Monrovia, Liberia, attended by the heads of state or representatives of 19 countries: Cameroon, Central African Republic, Chad, Congo Republic (ex-French), Côte d'Ivoire, Dahomey, Ethiopia, Gabon, Liberia, Madagascar, Mauritania, Niger, Nigeria, Senegal, Sierra Leone, Somalia, Togo, Tunisia and Upper Volta. Meeting again (with the exception of Tunisia and with the addition of the ex-Belgian Congo Republic) in January 1962 at Lagos, Nigeria, they established a permanent secretariat and a standing committee of finance ministers, and accepted a draft charter for an Organization of Inter-African and Malagasy States.

It was the Conference of Addis Ababa, convened in 1963, which finally brought together African states despite the regional, political and linguistic differences that divided them. The foreign ministers of 32 African states attended the Preparatory Meeting held in mid-May: Algeria, Burundi, Cameroon, Central African Republic, Chad, Congo (Brazzaville—now Republic of the Congo), Congo (Léopoldville—now Democratic Republic of the Congo), Côte d'Ivoire, Dahomey (now Benin), Ethiopia, Gabon, Ghana, Guinea, Liberia, Libya, Madagascar, Mali, Mauritania, Morocco, Niger, Nigeria, Rwanda, Senegal, Sierra Leone, Somalia, Sudan, Tanganyika (now Tanzania), Togo, Tunisia, Uganda, the United Arab Republic (Egypt) and Upper Volta (now Burkina Faso). The topics discussed by the meeting were: (i) creation of an Organization of African States; (ii) co-operation among African states in the following fields: economic and social; education, culture and science; collective defence; (iii) decolonization; (iv) apartheid and racial discrimination; (v) effects of economic grouping on the economic development of Africa; (vi) disarmament; (vii) creation of a Permanent Conciliation Commission; and (viii) Africa and the United Nations. The Heads of State Conference that opened on 23 May 1963 drew up the Charter of the Organization of African Unity, which was then signed by the heads of 30 states on 25 May. The Charter was essentially functional and reflected a compromise between the concept of a loose associa-

tion of states favoured by the Monrovia Group and the federal idea supported by the Casablanca Group, and in particular by Ghana.

In May 1994 the Abuja Treaty Establishing the African Economic Community (AEC, signed in June 1991) entered into force. The formation of the Community was expected to be a gradual process, to be completed by 2028. An extraordinary summit meeting, convened in September 1999, in Sirte, Libya, at the request of the Libyan leader Col al-Qaddafi, determined to establish an African Union, based on the principles and objectives of the OAU and AEC, but furthering African co-operation, development and integration. Heads of state declared their commitment to accelerating the establishment of regional institutions, including a pan-African parliament, court of human and peoples' rights and central bank, as well as the implementation of economic and monetary union, as provided for by the Abuja Treaty Establishing the AEC. In July 2000 at the annual OAU summit meeting, held at Lomé, Togo, 27 heads of state and government signed the draft Constitutive Act of the African Union, which was to enter into force one month after ratification by two-thirds of member states' legislatures; this was achieved on 26 May 2001. The Union was inaugurated, replacing the OAU, on 9 July 2002, at a summit meeting of heads of state and government held in Durban, South Africa, following a transitional period of one year after the endorsement of the Act in July 2001. During the transitional year, pending the transfer of all assets and liabilities to the Union, the OAU Charter remained in effect. A review of all OAU treaties was implemented, with those deemed relevant retained by the AU. The four key organs of the AU were launched in July 2002. Morocco is the only African country that is not a member of the AU. The AU aims to strengthen and advance the process of African political and socio-economic integration initiated by the OAU. The Union operates on the basis of both the Constitutive Act and the Abuja Treaty. It is envisaged that the process of implementing the Abuja Treaty will be accelerated.

The AU has the following areas of interest: peace and security; political affairs; infrastructure and energy; social affairs; human resources, science and technology; trade and industry; rural economy and agriculture; and economic affairs. In July 2001 the OAU adopted a New African Initiative, which was subsequently renamed the New Partnership for Africa's Development—NEPAD (see below). NEPAD, which was officially launched in October, represents a long-term strategy for socio-economic recovery in Africa and aims to promote the strengthening of democracy and economic management in the region. The heads of state of Algeria, Egypt, Nigeria, Senegal and South Africa played leading roles in its preparation and management. In June 2002 NEPAD heads of state and government adopted a Declaration on Democracy, Political, Economic and Corporate Governance and announced the development of an African Peer Review Mechanism (APRM—whose secretariat was to be hosted by the UN Economic Commission for Africa). Meeting during that month the Group of Seven industrialized nations and Russia (the G-8) welcomed the formation of NEPAD and adopted an Africa Action Plan in support of the initiative. NEPAD is ultimately answerable to the AU Assembly. The inaugural summit of the Assembly, held in Durban, South Africa, in July 2002, issued a Declaration on the Implementation of NEPAD, which urged all member states to adopt the Declaration on Democracy, Political, Economic and Corporate Governance and to participate in the peer-review process. Ghana, Kenya, Mauritius and Rwanda were selected as the first countries to be examined under the APRM. By February 2005 19 other nations had agreed to participate in the review process. In 2005 NEPAD was continuing to focus on: promoting the improvement of transport and energy infrastructures; the elimination of the so-called 'digital divide' through the establishment of a Digital Solidarity Fund; the production of generic drugs in Africa to combat AIDS, malaria and other endemic diseases; the development of large areas of agricultural production, particularly in the Horn of Africa, the Sahel, Southern Africa and Madagascar; the advancement of industrialisation projects; and the establishment of new centres of excellence in the fields of research, training and education. The summit meeting of the Assembly convened in Maputo, Mozambique, in July 2003, determined that NEPAD should be integrated into AU structures and processes.

In March 2005 the UN Secretary-General issued a report on the functioning of the United Nations which included a clause urging donor nations to focus particularly on the need for a 10-year plan for capacity-building within the AU.

PEACE AND SECURITY

The Protocol to the Constitutive Act of the African Union Relating to the Establishment of the Peace and Security Council, adopted by the inaugural AU summit of heads of state and government in July 2002, entered into force in December 2003, superseding the 1993 Cairo Declaration on the OAU Mechanism for Conflict Prevention, Management and Resolution. The Protocol provides for the inauguration of an AU collective security and early warning mechanism, comprising a 15-country Peace and Security Council, operational at the levels of heads of state and government, ministers of foreign affairs, and permanent representatives, to be supported by a five-member advisory Panel of the Wise, a Continental Early Warning System, an African Standby Force and a Peace Fund (superseding the OAU Peace Fund, which was established in June 1993 and had received contributions of US $42m. by March 2002). In March 2004 the Executive Council elected 15 member states to serve on the inaugural Peace and Security Council. Gabon, Ethiopia, Algeria, South Africa and Nigeria (representing, respectively, the central, eastern, northern, southern and western regions of the continent) were to serve terms of three years on the Council. Ten other countries (Cameroon, Republic of the Congo, Kenya, Sudan, Libya, Lesotho, Mozambique, Ghana, Senegal and Togo) were elected for two-year periods of service. The activities of the Peace and Security Council were to include the promotion of peace, security and stability; early warning and preventive diplomacy; peace-making mediation; peace support operations and intervention; peace-building activities and post-conflict reconstruction; and humanitarian action and disaster management. The Council was to implement the common defence policy of the Union, and to ensure the implementation of the 1999 OAU Convention on the Prevention and Combating of Terrorism (which provided for the exchange of information to help counter terrorism and for signatory states to refrain from granting asylum to terrorists). Member states were to set aside standby troop contingents for the planned African Standby Force, which was to be mandated to undertake observation, monitoring and other peace-support missions; to deploy in member states as required to prevent the resurgence or escalation of violence; to intervene in member states as required to restore stability; to conduct post-conflict disarmament and demobilization and other peace-building activities; and to provide emergency humanitarian assistance. The Council was to harmonize and co-ordinate the activities of other regional security mechanisms. An extraordinary AU summit meeting, convened in Sirte, Libya, in February 2004, adopted a declaration approving the establishment of the multinational African Standby Force, which was to be deployed at five regional bases, with some 15,000 troops mainly from Egypt, Kenya, Nigeria and South Africa, by 2005, and expanded to a full continent-wide force by 2010. A Policy Framework Document on the establishment of the African Standby Force and the Military Staff Committee, adopted in May 2003 by the third meeting of the African chiefs of defence staff, was approved by the third regular summit of AU heads of state, held in July 2004.

The extraordinary OAU summit meeting convened in Sirte, Libya in September 1999 determined to hold a regular ministerial Conference on Security, Stability, Development and Co-operation in Africa (CSSDCA): the first CSSDCA took place in Abuja, Nigeria, in May 2000. The CSSDCA process provides a forum for the development of policies aimed at advancing the common values of the AU and AEC in the areas of peace, security and co-operation. In December 2000 OAU heads of state and government adopted the Bamako Declaration, concerning arresting the circulation of small arms on the continent.

In June 2003 a meeting of the G-8 and NEPAD adopted a Joint Africa/G-8 Plan to enhance African capabilities to undertake Peace Support Operations. Within the framework of the Plan, a consultation between the AU, the NEPAD Secretariat, the G-8, the African regional economic communities, as well as the European Union (EU) and UN and other partners, was convened in Addis Ababa in April 2005. In September 2002 and October 2004 the AU organized high-level intergovernmental meetings on preventing and combating terrorism in Africa. An AU Special Representative on Protection of Civilians in Armed Conflict Situations in Africa was appointed in September 2004.

In recent years the OAU was involved in peace-making and peace-building activities in several African countries and regions. Military observer missions were deployed in Rwanda (1991–93), Burundi (1993–96), the Comoros (1998–2002), the Democratic Republic of the Congo (from 1999) and Eritrea and Ethiopia (from 2000). In February 2002 the OAU mediated talks between President Didier Ratsiraka of Madagascar and the official opposition leader Marc Ravalomanana, who established a rival Madagascan government during that month, having also claimed victory at the presidential election held in that country in December 2001. In March 2002 the OAU held talks with each of the disputing sides in the Madagascan political crisis, facilitating the conclusion in mid-April of the so-called Dakar Agreement, providing for the formation of an interim government of national unity, pending the staging of a new presidential election. However, in the following month Ravalomanana was declared President by a Madagascan constitutional court. In view of significant opposition to this decision, the OAU determined not to recognize the Ravalomanana administration and, in June, suspended Madagascar from its meetings. In July the newly inaugurated AU upheld this decision, suspending the country from AU meetings pending the staging of free and fair elections leading to the establishment of a legitimate and democratic government. In July 2003, however, following new parliamentary elections, held in

December 2002 (resulting in a majority of seats for supporters of Ravalomanana), Madagascar's suspension was formally revoked. An extraordinary summit meeting of the Assembly, held in February 2003, urged support for a peace accord concluded in January by parties to the conflict that had erupted in Côte d'Ivoire in September 2002. In March 2003 the AU unequivocally condemned the military *coup d'état* that had taken place in Central African Republic, and subsequently banned that country's leaders from participating at the July Assembly meeting convened in Maputo. In April the AU authorized the establishment of a 3,500-member African Mission in Burundi (AMIB) to oversee the implementation of cease-fire accords in that country, support the disarmament and demobilization of former combatants, and ensure favourable conditions for the deployment of a future UN peace-keeping presence. In June 2004 AMIB was terminated and its troops 'rehatted' as participants in the newly-authorized UN Operation in Burundi—ONUB. In May 2003 the AU, UNDP and UN Office for Project Services agreed a US $6.4m. project entitled 'Support for the Implementation of the Peace and Security Agenda of the African Union'.

The July 2003 Maputo Assembly determined to establish a post-conflict reconstruction ministerial committee on the Sudan. The first meeting of the committee, convened in March 2004, resolved to dispatch an AU team of experts to southern Sudan to compile a preliminary assessment of that region's post-conflict requirements; this was undertaken in late June. In early April, meeting in N'Djamena, Chad, the Sudan Government and other Sudanese parties signed, under AU auspices, a Humanitarian Cease-fire Agreement providing for the establishment of an AU-led Cease-fire Commission and for the deployment of an AU military observer mission (the AU Mission in the Sudan—AMIS) to the western Sudanese region of Darfur, where widespread violent unrest (including reportedly systematic attacks on the indigenous civilian population by pro-government militias), resulting in a grave humanitarian crisis, had prevailed since early 2003. Following the adoption in late May 2004 of an accord on the modalities for the implementation of the Humanitarian Cease-fire Agreement (also providing for the future deployment of a an armed protection force as an additional component of AMIS, as requested by a recent meeting of the Peace and Security Council), the Cease-fire Commission was inaugurated at the end of that month and, at the beginning of June, the Commission's headquarters were opened in El-Fasher, Sudan; some 60 AMIS military observers were dispatched to the headquarters during that month. In early July the AU Assembly agree to increase the strength of AMIS to 80. The cost of the Mission was estimated at US $26m., of which some $12m. was provided by the EU, see below. From mid-2004 the AU mediated negotiations between the parties to the conflict in Darfur on the achievement of a comprehensive peace agreement; the fourth round of talks was held in December. AMIS's military component, agreed in May, initially comprising 310 troops from Nigeria and Rwanda and mandated to monitor the cease-fire and protect the Mission, began to be deployed in mid-August. In October the Peace and Security Council decided to expand AMIS into a full peace-keeping operation, eventually to comprise 3,300 troops, police and civilian support staff. The mission's mandate was enhanced to include promoting increased compliance by all parties with the cease-fire agreement and helping with the process of confidence-building; responsibility for monitoring compliance with any subsequent agreements; assisting IDP and refugee returns; and contributing to the improvement of the security situation throughout Darfur. By March 2005 some 1,900 troops had been deployed to AMIS. Most of the funding required for AMIS, estimated at $220m. for 2005, was to be provided by international donors, including the EU ($100m.) and the USA ($45m.).

Meeting in January 2005 the Peace and Security Council accepted in principle the future deployment of an AU Peace Support Mission in Somalia, with a mandate to support that member country's transitional federal institutions; meanwhile, an IGAD peace support mission (approved by IGAD in January 2005 and endorsed by that month's AU summit) was to be stationed in Somalia. The AU strongly condemned the unconstitutional transfer of power effected in Togo in early February, describing it as a *coup d'état*, and suspended that country's participation in activities of the Union pending the restoration of constitutional rule; this was achieved at the end of that month.

The EU assists the AU financially in the areas of peace and security (including €25m. funding granted in December 2003 towards AMIB and support to AMIS, see above); institutional development; governance; and regional economic integration and trade. In June 2004 the European Commission activated for the first time its newly-established Africa Peace Facility, which provided €12m. in support of the AU's humanitarian and peace monitoring efforts in Darfur.

INFRASTRUCTURE, ENERGY AND THE ENVIRONMENT

Meeting in Lomé, Togo, in July 2001, OAU heads of state and government authorized the establishment of an African Energy

Commission—AFREC, which was to increase co-operation in energy matters between Africa and other regions. The convention establishing AFREC had been ratified by seven states at April 2005.

In 1964 the OAU adopted a Declaration on the Denuclearization of Africa, and in April 1996 it adopted the African Nuclear Weapons Free Zone Treaty (also known as the 'Pelindaba Treaty'), which identifies Africa as a nuclear weapon-free zone and promotes co-operation in the peaceful uses of nuclear energy.

In 1968 OAU member states adopted the African Convention on the Conservation of Nature and Natural Resources. The Bamako Convention on the Ban of the Import into Africa and the Control of Transboundary Movement and Management of Hazardous Wastes within Africa was adopted by OAU member states in 1991 and entered into force in April 1998.

POLITICAL AND SOCIAL AFFAIRS

The African Charter on Human and People's Rights, which was adopted by the OAU in 1981 and entered into force in October 1986, provided for the establishment of an 11-member African Commission on Human and People's Rights, based in Banjul, The Gambia. A Protocol to the Charter, establishing an African Court of People's and Human Rights, was adopted by the OAU Assembly of Heads of State in June 1998 and entered into force in January 2004. A further Protocol, relating to the Rights of Women, was adopted by the July 2003 Maputo Assembly. The African Charter on the Rights and Welfare of the Child was opened for signature in July 1990 and entered into force in November 1999. A Protocol to the Abuja Treaty Establishing the AEC relating to the Pan-African Parliament, adopted by the OAU in March 2001, entered into force in December 2003. The Parliament was inaugurated in March 2004 and was, initially, to exercise advisory and consultative powers only, although its eventual evolution into an institution with full legislative powers is envisaged. In March 2005 the advisory Economic, Social and Cultural Council was inaugurated.

The July 2002 inaugural summit meeting of AU heads of state and government adopted a Declaration Governing Democratic Elections in Africa, providing guide-lines for the conduct of national elections in member states and outlining the AU's electoral observation and monitoring role. In March an OAU observer team found the Zimbabwean presidential election, held in controversial circumstances during that month, to have been conducted freely and fairly. In April 2003 the AU Commission and the South African Independent Electoral Commission jointly convened an African Conference on Elections, Democracy and Governance, in Pretoria, South Africa. In recent years several large population displacements have occurred in Africa, mainly as a result of violent conflict. In 1969 OAU member states adopted the Convention Governing the Specific Aspects of Refugee Problems in Africa, which entered into force in June 1974 and had been ratified by 45 states at April 2005. The Convention promotes close co-operation with UNHCR. The AU maintains a Special Refugee Contingency Fund to provide relief assistance and to support repatriation activities, education projects, etc., for displaced people in Africa. The AU aims to address pressing health issues affecting member states, including the eradication of endemic parasitic and infectious diseases and improving access to medicines. An African Summit on HIV/AIDS, Tuberculosis and other related Infectious Diseases was convened, under OAU auspices, in March 2001. An AU Scientific, Technical and Research Commission is based in Lagos, Nigeria, and a Centre for Linguistic and Historical Studies by Oral Tradition is based in Niamey, Niger.

TRADE, INDUSTRY AND ECONOMIC CO-OPERATION

In October 1999 a conference on Industrial Partnerships and Investment in Africa was held in Dakar, Senegal, jointly organized by the OAU with UNIDO, the ECA, the African Development Bank and the Alliance for Africa's Industrialization. In June 1997 the first meeting between ministers of the OAU and the EU was convened in New York, USA. In April 2000 the first EU–Africa summit of heads of state and government was held in Cairo, Egypt, under the auspices of the EU and OAU. The summit adopted the Cairo Plan of Action, which addressed areas including economic integration, trade and investment, private-sector development in Africa, human rights and good governance, peace and security, and development issues such as education, health and food security. A second EU–Africa summit meeting, scheduled to be held in April 2003, in Lisbon, Portugal, was postponed, owing to disagreements concerning the participation of President Mugabe of Zimbabwe, against whom the EU had imposed sanctions. More than 200 business representatives participated in an AU Business Summit, convened in July 2002, in Durban, South Africa, alongside the inaugural AU summit of heads of state and government.

The AU aims to reduce obstacles to intra-African trade and to reverse the continuing disproportionate level of trade conducted by many African countries with their former colonial powers.

In June 1991 the OAU Assembly of Heads of State signed the Abuja Treaty Establishing the African Economic Community (AEC).

The Treaty was to enter into force after ratification by two-thirds of member states. The Community was to be established by 2028, following a gradual six-phase process involving the co-ordination, harmonization and progressive integration of the activities of all existing and future sub-regional economic unions. (There are 14 so-called 'regional economic communities'—RECs in Africa, including the following major RECs that are regarded as the five pillars, or building blocks, of the AEC: the Common Market for Eastern and Southern Africa—COMESA, the Communauté économique des états de l'Afrique centrale—CEEAC, the Economic Community of West African States—ECOWAS, the Southern African Development Community—SADC, and the Union of the Arab Maghreb. The subsidiary RECs are: the Communauté économique et monétaire de l'Afrique centrale—CEMAC, the Community of Sahel-Saharan States—CEN-SAD, the East African Community—EAC, the Economic Community of the Great Lakes Countries, the Intergovernmental Authority on Development—IGAD, the Indian Ocean Commission—IOC, the Mano River Union, the Southern African Customs Union, and the Union économique et monétaire ouest-africaine—UEMOA.) The Abuja Treaty entered into force on 12 May 1994, having been ratified by the requisite number of OAU member states. The inaugural meeting of the AEC took place in June 1997.

RURAL ECONOMY AND AGRICULTURE

In July 2003 the second Assembly of heads of state and government adopted a Declaration on Agriculture and Food Security in Africa, focusing on the need to revitalize the agricultural sector and to combat hunger on the continent by developing food reserves based on African production. The leaders determined to deploy policies and budgetary resources to remove current constraints on agricultural production, trade and rural development; and to implement the Comprehensive Africa Agriculture Programme (CAADP), which had been developed by NEPAD and FAO in 2002–03. The CAADP focused on increasing investment in the areas of water management, rural infrastructure, programmes to increase productivity, and capacity development for market access; and also on means of addressing emergencies, and the advancement of research and technology. The heads of state and government agreed that, by 2008/09, at least 10% of national budgets should be allocated to agriculture and rural development.

Finance

The AU inherited more than US $50m. in debts owed by member states to the OAU. The programme budget for 2005 totalled $158m., of which $75m. was allocated to peace and security. Some $63m. of the 2005 budget was to be financed by contributions from member states, with the remainder to be derived from international donor support.

Specialized Agencies

African Accounting Council: POB 11223, Kinshasa, Democratic Republic of the Congo; tel. (12) 33567; f. 1979; provides assistance to institutions in member countries on standardization of accounting; promotes education, further training and research in accountancy and related areas of study; publ. *Information and Liaison Bulletin* (every two months).

African Civil Aviation Commission (AFCAC): 15 blvd de la République, BP 2356, Dakar, Senegal; tel. 893-93-73; fax 823-26-61; e-mail secretariat@afcac-cafac.org; internet www.afcac-cafac.org; f. 1969 to encourage co-operation in all civil aviation activities; 43 mem states; promotes co-ordination and better utilization and development of African air transport systems and the standardization of aircraft, flight equipment and training programmes for pilots and mechanics; organizes working groups and seminars, and compiles statistics; Pres. MAMDOUH HESHMAT (Egypt); Sec. CHARLES M. DIOP.

Pan-African Institution of Education for Development (PIED): 29 ave de la Justice, BP 1764, Kinshasa I, Democratic Republic of the Congo; tel. (12) 34527; e-mail baseeduc@hotmail.com; f. 1973, became specialized agency in 1986, present name adopted 2001; undertakes educational research and training, focuses on co-operation and problem-solving, acts as an observatory for education; publs *Bulletin d'Information* (quarterly), *Revue africaine des sciences de l'éducation* (2 a year), *Répertoire africain des institutions de recherche* (annually).

Pan-African News Agency (PANAPRESS): BP 4056, ave Bourjuiba, Dakar, Senegal; tel. 824-13-95; fax 824-13-90; e-mail quoiset@sonatel.senet.net; internet www.panapress.com; f. 1979 as PanAfrican News Agency, restructured under current name in 1997; regional headquarters in Khartoum, Sudan; Lusaka, Zambia; Kinshasa, Democratic Republic of the Congo; Lagos, Nigeria; Tripoli,

Libya; began operations in May 1983, restructured in late 1990s; receives information from national news agencies and circulates news in English, French and Arabic; Dir-Gen. BABACAR FALL; publs *Press Review In-Focus*.

Pan-African Postal Union (PAPU): POB 6026, Arusha, Tanzania; tel. (27) 2508604; fax (27) 2508606; e-mail sg@papu.co.tz; internet www.upap-papu.org; f. 1980 to extend members' co-operation in the improvement of postal services; 43 mem countries; Sec.-Gen. JILANI BEN HADDADA; publ. *PAPU News*.

Pan-African Railways Union: BP 687, Kinshasa, Democratic Republic of the Congo; tel. (12) 23861; f. 1972 to standardize, expand, co-ordinate and improve members' railway services; the ultimate aim is to link all systems; main organs: Gen. Assembly, Exec. Bd, Gen. Secr., five tech. cttees; mems in 30 African countries.

Pan-African Telecommunications Union: POB 7248, Kinshasa, Democratic Republic of the Congo; f. 1977; co-ordinates devt of telecommunications networks and services in Africa.

Supreme Council for Sports in Africa: BP 1363, Yaoundé, Cameroon; tel. and fax 23-95-80; f. 1965; Sec.-Gen. Dr AWOTURE

ELEYAE (Nigeria); publs *SCSA News* (6 a year), *African Sports Movement Directory* (annually).

ASSOCIATED PARTNERSHIP

New Partnership for Africa's Development (NEPAD): POB 1234, Midrand, Halfway House, 1685 South Africa (secretariat); tel. (11) 313-3716; fax (11) 313-3684; e-mail africam@nepad.org; internet www.nepad.org; f. 2001 as a long-term strategy to promote socio-economic development in Africa; adopted Declaration on Democracy, Political, Economic and Corporate Governance and the African Peer Review Mechanism in June 2002; heads of state implementation cttee comprises representatives of 20 countries (four from each of the AU's five regions: northern, eastern, southern, western and central); steering cttee, comprising Algeria, Egypt, Nigeria, Senegal and South Africa, meets once a month; the UN allocated US \$9,344m. in support of NEPAD under its 2004–05 budget; the July 2003 AU Maputo summit decided that NEPAD should be integrated into AU structures and processes; Implementation Cttee Chair. Gen. (retd) OLUSEGUN OBASANJO (Pres. of Nigeria); Steering Cttee Chair. Prof. WISEMAN NKUHLU (South Africa).

ANDEAN COMMUNITY OF NATIONS
(COMUNIDAD ANDINA DE NACIONES—CAN)

Address: Paseo de la República 3895, San Isidro, Lima 27; Apdo 18-1177, Lima 18, Peru.

Telephone: (1) 4111400; **fax:** (1) 2213329; **e-mail:** contacto@comunidadandina.org; **internet:** www.comunidadandina.org.

The organization was established in 1969 as the Acuerdo de Cartagena (the Cartagena Agreement), also referred to as the Grupo Andino (Andean Group) or the Pacto Andino (Andean Pact). In March 1996 member countries signed a Reform Protocol of the Cartagena Agreement, in accordance with which the Andean Group was superseded in August 1997 by the Andean Community of Nations (CAN, generally referred to as the Andean Community). The Andean Community was to promote greater economic, commercial and political integration under a new Andean Integration System (Sistema Andino de Integración), comprising the organization's bodies and institutions. The Community covers an area of 4,710,000 sq km, with some 115m. inhabitants.

MEMBERS

Bolivia Colombia Ecuador Peru Venezuela

Note: Chile, which withdrew from the Andean Group in 1976, was granted observer status with the Andean Community in December 2004. Panama also has observer status with the Community.

Organization
(April 2005)

ANDEAN PRESIDENTIAL COUNCIL

The presidential summits, which had been held annually since 1989, were formalized under the 1996 Reform Protocol of the Cartagena Agreement as the Andean Presidential Council. The Council is the highest-level body of the Andean Integration System, and provides the political leadership of the Community.

COMMISSION

The Commission consists of a plenipotentiary representative from each member country, with each country holding the presidency in turn. The Commission is the main policy-making organ of the Andean Community, and is responsible for co-ordinating Andean trade policy.

COUNCIL OF FOREIGN MINISTERS

The Council of Foreign Ministers meets annually or whenever it is considered necessary, to formulate common external policy and to co-ordinate the process of integration.

GENERAL SECRETARIAT

The General Secretariat (formerly the Junta) is the body charged with implementation of all guide-lines and decisions issued by the bodies listed above. It submits proposals to the Commission for facilitating the fulfilment of the Community's objectives. Members are appointed for a three-year term. They supervise technical offi-

cials assigned to the following Departments: External Relations, Agricultural Development, Press Office, Economic Policy, Physical Integration, Programme of Assistance to Bolivia, Industrial Development, Programme Planning, Legal Affairs, Technology. Under the reforms agreed in March 1996 the Secretary-General is elected by the Council of Foreign Ministers for a five-year term, and has enhanced powers to adjudicate in disputes arising between member states. In August 1997 the General Secretariat assumed the functions of the Board of the Cartagena Agreement.

Secretary-General: ALLAN WAGNER TIZÓN (Peru).

PARLIAMENT

Parlamento Andino: Avda 13, No. 70–61, Santafé de Bogotá, Colombia; tel. (1) 249-3400; fax (1) 348-2805; e-mail pandino@cable.net.co; internet www.parlamentoandino.org; f. 1979; comprises five members from each country, and meets in each capital city in turn; makes recommendations on regional policy; in April 1997 a new protocol was adopted which provided for the election of members by direct and universal voting; in November 1998 Venezuela put the new voting mechanism into practice; the remaining Community countries were expected to complete the process by 2007; Pres. VICTOR ENRIQUE URQUIDI HODGKINSON.

COURT OF JUSTICE

Tribunal de Justicia de la Comunidad Andina: Calle Roca 450 y Seis de Diciembre, Quito, Ecuador; tel. (2) 529998; fax (2) 565007; e-mail tjca@tribunalandino.org.ec; internet www.tribunalandino.org.ec; f. 1979, began operating in 1984; a protocol approved in May 1996 (which came into force in August 1999) modified the Court's functions; its main responsibilities are to resolve disputes among member countries and interpret community legislation; comprises five judges, one from each member country, appointed for a renewable period of six years; the Presidency is assumed annually by each judge in turn.

Activities

In May 1979, at Cartagena, Colombia, the Presidents of the five member countries signed the 'Mandate of Cartagena', which envisaged greater economic and political co-operation, including the establishment of more sub-regional development programmes (especially in industry). In May 1989 the Group undertook to revitalize the process of Andean integration, by withdrawing measures that obstructed the programme of trade liberalization, and by complying with tariff reductions that had already been agreed upon. In May 1991, in Caracas, Venezuela, a summit meeting of the Andean Group agreed the framework for the establishment of a free-trade area on 1 January 1992 (achieved in February 1993) and for an eventual Andean common market (see below, under Trade).

In March 1996 heads of state, meeting in Trujillo, Peru, agreed to a substantial restructuring of the Andean Group. The heads of state signed the Reform Protocol of the Cartagena Agreement, providing for the establishment of the Andean Community of Nations, which was to have more ambitious economic and political objectives than the Group. Consequently, in August 1997 the Andean Community was inaugurated, and the Group's Junta was replaced by a new General Secretariat, headed by a Secretary-General with enhanced executive and decision-making powers. The initiation of these reforms was designed to accelerate harmonization in economic matters, particularly the achievement of a common external tariff. In September 1996 the Group agreed to negotiate a free-trade agreement with the Mercado Común del Sur—Mercosur. (Disunity among the Andean nations had been evident in June, when Bolivia had agreed to enter into free-trade negotiations with Mercosur on a unilateral basis, thus becoming an associate member of that grouping.) In April 1997 the Peruvian Government announced its intention to withdraw from the Cartagena Agreement, owing to disagreements about the terms of Peru's full integration into the Community's trading system. Later in that month the heads of state of the four other members attended a summit meeting, in Sucre, Bolivia, and reiterated their commitment to strengthening regional integration. A high-level group of representatives was established to pursue negotiations with Peru regarding its future relationship with the Community (agreement was reached in June—see below). In April 2001 Venezuela announced that it intended to apply for membership of Mercosur (while retaining its membership of the Community).

At the 13th presidential summit, held in Valencia, Venezuela, in June 2001, heads of state adopted an Andean Co-operation Plan for the Control of Illegal Drugs and Related Offences, which was to promote a united approach to combating these problems. An executive committee was to be established under the accord to oversee implementation of an action plan. It was also agreed that an Andean passport system should enter into effect no later than December 2005. In January 2002 a special Andean presidential summit, held in Santa Cruz, Bolivia, reiterated the objective of creating a common market and renewing efforts to strengthen sub-regional integration, including the adoption of a common agricultural policy and the standardization of macroeconomic policies.

In June 2002 ministers of defence and of foreign affairs of the Andean Community approved an Andean Charter for Peace and Security, establishing principles and commitments for the formulation of a policy on sub-regional security, the establishment of a zone of peace, joint action in efforts to counter terrorism, and the limitation of external defence spending. Other provisions of the Charter included commitments to eradicate illegal trafficking in firearms, ammunition and explosives, to expand and reinforce confidence-building measures, and to establish verification mechanisms to strengthen dialogue and efforts in those areas. In January 2003 the Community concluded a co-operation agreement with Interpol providing for collaboration in combating national and transnational crime, and in June the presidential summit, adopted an Andean Plan for the Prevention, Combating and Eradication of Small, Light Weapons. The heads of state, convened in Quirama, Colombia, also endorsed a new strategic direction for the Andean integration process based on the following core themes: developing the Andean common market, common foreign policy and social agenda, the physical integration of South America, and sustainable development. In July 2004 the 15th presidential summit, held in Quito, Ecuador, formulated priority objectives for a New Strategic Scheme.

TRADE

A council for customs affairs met for the first time in January 1982, aiming to harmonize national legislation within the group. In December 1984 the member states launched a common currency, the Andean peso, aiming to reduce dependence on the US dollar and to increase regional trade. The new currency was to be supported by special contributions to the Fondo Andino de Reservas (now the Fondo Latinoamericano de Reservas) amounting to US $80m., and was to be 'pegged' to the US dollar, taking the form of financial drafts rather than notes and coins.

The 'Caracas Declaration' of May 1991 provided for the establishment of an Andean free-trade area, which entered into effect (excluding Peru—see below) in February 1993. Heads of state also agreed in May 1991 to create a common external tariff (CET), to standardize member countries' trade barriers in their dealings with the rest of the world, and envisaged the eventual creation of an Andean common market. In December heads of state defined four main levels of external tariffs (between 5% and 20%). In August 1992 the Group approved a request by Peru for the suspension of its rights and obligations under the Pact, thereby enabling the other members to proceed with hitherto stalled negotiations on the CET. Peru was readmitted as a full member of the Group in 1994, but participated only as an observer in the ongoing negotiations.

In November 1994 ministers of trade and integration, meeting in Quito, Ecuador, concluded a final agreement on a four-tier structure of external tariffs (although Bolivia was to retain a two-level system). The CET agreement, which came into effect in February 1995, covered 90% of the region's imports which were to be subject to the following tariff bands: 5% for raw materials; 10%–15% for semi-manufactured goods; and 20% for finished products. In order to reach an agreement, special treatment and exemptions were granted, while Peru, initially, was to remain a 'non-active' member of the accord: Bolivia was to maintain external tariffs of 5% and 10%, Ecuador was permitted to apply the lowest rate of 5% to 990 items and was granted an initial exemption from tariffs on 400 items, while Colombia and Venezuela were granted 230 items to be subject to special treatment for four years. In June 1997 an agreement was concluded to ensure Peru's continued membership of the Community, which provided for that country's integration into the free-trade area. The Peruvian Government determined to eliminate customs duties on some 2,500 products with immediate effect, and it was agreed that the process be completed by 2005. However, negotiations were to continue with regard to the replacement of Peru's single tariff on products from outside the region with the Community's scale of external duties.

In May 1999 the 11th presidential summit agreed to establish the Andean Common Market by 2005; the Community adopted a policy on border integration and development to prepare the border regions of member countries for the envisaged free circulation of people, goods, capital and services, while consolidating sub-regional security. In June 2001 the Community agreed to recognize national identification documents issued by member states as sufficient for tourist travel in the sub-region. Community heads of state, meeting in January 2002 at a special Andean presidential summit, agreed to consolidate and improve the free-trade zone by mid-2002 and apply a new CET (with four levels, i.e. 0%, 5%, 10% and 20%). To facilitate this process a common agricultural policy was to be adopted and macro-economic policies were to be harmonized. In June 2002 ministers of foreign affairs approved a schedule of activities relating to the new CET. In October member governments determined the new tariff levels applicable to 62% of products and agreed the criteria for negotiating levels for the remaining 38%. The CET was to become effective on 1 January 2004. This date was subsequently postponed until 1 March, and then until 10 May. In early May ministers of foreign trade agreed to postpone the effective date of the CET until 10 May 2005.

EXTERNAL RELATIONS

In September 1995 heads of state of member countries identified the formulation of common positions on foreign relations as an important part of the process of relaunching the integration initiative. A Protocol Amending the Cartagena Agreement was signed in June 1997 to confirm the formulation of a common foreign policy. During 1998 the General Secretariat held consultations with government experts, academics, representatives of the private sector and other interested parties to help formulate a document on guide-lines for a common foreign policy. The guide-lines, establishing the principles, objectives and mechanisms of a common foreign policy, were approved by the Council of Foreign Ministers in 1999. In July 2004 Andean ministers of foreign affairs approved new guide-lines for an Andean common policy on external security, which aimed to prevent and counter new security threats more effectively through co-operation and co-ordination. The ministers, meeting in Quito, Ecuador, also adopted a Declaration on the Establishment of an Andean Peace Area, free from nuclear, chemical or biological weapons.

The Group has sought to strengthen relations with the European Union, and a co-operation agreement was signed between the two blocs in April 1993. A Euro-Andean Forum is held periodically to promote mutual co-operation, trade and investment. In February 1998 the Community signed a co-operation and technical assistance agreement with the EU in order to combat drugs trafficking. At the first summit meeting of Latin American, Caribbean and EU leaders held in Rio de Janeiro, Brazil, in June 1999, Community–EU discussions were held on strengthening economic, trade and political co-operation and on the possibility of eventually concluding an Association Agreement. In May 2002 the European Union adopted a Regional Strategy for the Andean Community covering the period 2002–06. The second Latin America, Caribbean and EU summit meeting, held in May 2002 in Madrid, Spain, welcomed a new initiative to negotiate an accord on political dialogue and co-operation, envisaging that this would strengthen the basis for subsequent bilateral negotiations. Consequently, the Political Dialogue and Co-operation Agreement was negotiated during May–October 2003, and signed in December. In May 2004 a meeting of the two sides during the third Latin American, Caribbean and EU summit, held in Guadalajara, Mexico, confirmed that an EU-CAN Association Agreement was a common strategic objective. It was agreed that a Joint Committee would meet in late 2004 to define a timetable of activities and objectives which would lead to the start of substantive negotiations on the Association Agreement.

In March 2000 the Andean Community concluded an agreement to establish a political consultation and co-operation mechanism with the People's Republic of China. At the first ministerial meeting within this framework, which took place in October 2002, it was agreed that consultations would be held thereafter on a biennial basis. A high-level meeting between senior officials from Community member states and Japan was organized in December; further consultations were to be convened, aimed at cultivating closer relations.

In April 1998, at the 10th Andean presidential summit, an agreement was signed with Panama establishing a framework for negotiations providing for the conclusion of a free-trade accord by the end of 1998 and for Panama's eventual associate membership of the Community. Also in April 1998 the Community signed a framework agreement with Mercosur on the establishment of a free-trade accord. Although negotiations between the Community and Mercosur were subsequently delayed, bilateral agreements between the countries of the two groupings were extended. A preferential tariff agreement was concluded between Brazil and the Community in July 1999; the accord entered into effect, for a period of two years, in August. In August 2000 a preferential tariff agreement concluded with Argentina entered into force. The Community commenced negotiations on drafting a preferential tariff agreement with (jointly) El Salvador, Guatemala and Honduras in March of that year. In September leaders of the Community and Mercosur, meeting at a summit of Latin American heads of state, determined to relaunch negotiations, with a view to establishing a free-trade area. In July 2001 ministers of foreign affairs of the two groupings approved the establishment of a formal mechanism for political dialogue and co-ordination in order to facilitate negotiations and to enhance economic and social integration. In December 2003 Mercosur and the Andean Community signed an Economic Complementary Agreement providing for free-trade provisions, according to which tariffs on 80% of trade between the two groupings is to be phased out by 2014 and tariffs to be removed from the remaining 20% of, initially protected, products by 2019. The entry into force of the accord, scheduled for 1 July 2004, was postponed owing to delays in drafting the tariff reduction schedule. Members of the Latin American Integration Association remaining outside Mercosur and the Andean Community—Cuba, Chile and Mexico—were to be permitted to apply to join the envisaged larger free-trade zone. In December leaders from 12 Latin American countries (excluding Argentina, Ecuador, Paraguay and Uruguay) attending a pan-South American summit, convened in Cuzco, Peru, approved in principle the creation of a new South American Community of Nations. It was envisaged that negotiations on the formation of the new Community, which was to entail the merger of the Andean Community, Mercosur and the Rio Group, would be completed within 15 years. In that month the Andean Community agreed to grant observer status to Chile.

In March 1998 ministers of trade from 34 countries, meeting in San José, Costa Rica, concluded an agreement on the structure of negotiations for the establishment of a Free Trade Area of the Americas (FTAA). The process was formally initiated by heads of state, meeting in Santiago, Chile, in the following month. The Community negotiated as a bloc to obtain chairmanship of three of the nine negotiating groups: on market access (Colombia), on competition policy (Peru), and on intellectual property (Venezuela). The Community insisted that the final declaration issued by the meeting include recognition that the varying levels of development of the participating countries should be taken into consideration throughout the negotiating process. In April 2001, convened in Québec, Canada, leaders of the participating countries determined to conclude negotiations on the FTAA by January 2005. At a special summit of the Americas, held in January 2004 in Monterrey, Mexico, however, the leaders did not specify a completion date for the negotiations, although they adopted a declaration committing themselves to its eventual establishment. Negotiations were stalled during 2004.

In August 1999 the Secretary-General of the Community visited Guyana in order to promote bilateral trading opportunities and to strengthen relations with the Caribbean Community. The Community held a meeting on trade relations with the Caribbean Community during 2000.

INDUSTRY

Negotiations began in 1970 for the formulation of joint industrial programmes, particularly in the petrochemicals, metal-working and motor vehicle sectors, but disagreements over the allocation of different plants, and the choice of foreign manufacturers for co-operation, prevented progress and by 1984 the more ambitious schemes had been abandoned. Instead, emphasis was to be placed on assisting small and medium-sized industries, particularly in the agro-industrial and electronics sectors, in co-operation with national industrial organizations.

An Andean Agricultural Development Programme was formulated in 1976 within which 22 resolutions aimed at integrating the Andean agricultural sector were approved. In 1984 the Andean Food Security System was created to develop the agrarian sector, replace

imports progressively with local produce, and improve rural living conditions. In April 1998 the Presidential Council instructed the Commission, together with ministers of agriculture, to formulate an Andean Common Agricultural Policy, including measures to harmonize trade policy instruments and legislation on animal and plant health. The 12th Andean presidential summit, held in June 2000, authorized the adoption of the concluded Policy and the enforcement of a plan of action for its implementation. In January 2002, at the special Andean presidential summit, it was agreed that all countries in the bloc would adopt price stabilization mechanisms for agricultural products.

In May 1987 member countries signed the Quito Protocol, modifying the Cartagena Agreement, to amend the strict rules that had formerly been imposed on foreign investors in the region. The Protocol entered into force in May 1988. Accordingly, each government was to decide which sectors were to be closed to foreign participation, and the period within which foreign investors must transfer a majority shareholding to local investors was extended to 30 years (37 years in Bolivia and Ecuador). In March 1991 the Protocol was amended, with the aim of further liberalizing foreign investment and stimulating an inflow of foreign capital and technology. External and regional investors were to be permitted to repatriate their profits (in accordance with the laws of the country concerned) and there was no stipulation that a majority shareholding must eventually be transferred to local investors. A further directive, adopted in March, covered the formation of 'Empresas Multinacionales Andinas' (multinational enterprises) in order to ensure that at least two member countries have a shareholding of 15% or more of the capital, including the country where the enterprise was to be based. These enterprises were entitled to participate in sectors otherwise reserved for national enterprises, subject to the same conditions as national enterprises in terms of taxation and export regulations, and to gain access to the markets of all member countries.

In November 1988 member states established a bank, the Banco Intermunicipal Andino, which was to finance public works.

In May 1995 the Group initiated a programme to promote the use of cheap and efficient energy sources and greater co-operation in the energy sector. The programme planned to develop a regional electricity grid. During 2003 efforts were undertaken to establish an Andean Energy Alliance, with the aim of fostering the development of integrated electricity and gas markets.

In September 1999 Colombia, Ecuador and Venezuela signed an accord to facilitate the production and sale of vehicles within the region. The agreement became effective in January 2000, with a duration of 10 years.

TRANSPORT AND COMMUNICATIONS

The Andean Community has pursued efforts to improve infrastructure throughout the region. In 1983 the Commission formulated a plan to assist land-locked Bolivia, particularly through improving roads connecting it with neighbouring countries and the Pacific Ocean. An 'open skies' agreement, giving airlines of member states equal rights to airspace and airport facilities within the grouping, was signed in May 1991. In June 1998 the Commission approved the establishment of an Andean Commission of Land Transportation Authorities, which was to oversee the operation and development of land transportation services. Similarly, an Andean Committee of Water Transportation Authorities has been established to ensure compliance with Community regulations regarding ocean transportation activities. The Community aims to facilitate the movement of goods throughout the region by the use of different modes of transport ('multimodal transport') and to guarantee operational standards. It also intends to harmonize Community transport regulations and standards with those of Mercosur countries.

In August 1996 a regulatory framework was approved for the development of a commercial Andean satellite system. In December 1997 the General Secretariat approved regulations for granting authorization for the use of the system; the Commission subsequently granted the first Community authorization to an Andean multinational enterprise (Andesat), comprising 48 companies from all five member states. In 1994 the Community initiated efforts to establish digital technology infrastructure throughout the Community: the resulting Andean Digital Corridor comprises ground, underwater and satellite routes providing a series of cross-border interconnections between the member countries. The Andean Internet System, which aims to provide internet protocol-based services throughout the Community, was operational in Colombia, Ecuador and Venezuela in 2000, and was due to be extended to all five member countries. In May 1999 the Andean Committee of Telecommunications Authorities agreed to remove all restrictions to free trade in telecommunications services (excluding sound broadcasting and television) by 1 January 2002. The Committee also determined to formulate provisions on interconnection and the safeguarding of free competition and principles of transparency within the sector.

Asociación de Empresas de Telecomunicaciones de la Comunidad Andina (ASETA): Calle La Pradera 510 y San Salvador, Casilla 17-1106042, Quito, Ecuador; tel. (2) 2563-812; fax (2) 2562-499; e-mail info@aseta.org; internet www.aseta.org; f. 1974; co-ordinates improvements in national telecommunications services, in order to contribute to the further integration of the countries of the Andean Community; Sec.-Gen. MARCELO LÓPEZ ARJONA.

SOCIAL INTEGRATION

Several formal agreements and institutions have been established within the framework of the grouping to enhance social development and welfare (see below). The Community aims to incorporate these bodies into the process of enhanced integration and to promote greater involvement of representatives of civil society. In May 1999 the 11th Andean presidential summit adopted a 'multidimensional social agenda' focusing on job creation and on improvements in the fields of education, health and housing throughout the Community. In June 2000 the 12th presidential summit instructed the Andean institutions to prepare individual programmes aimed at consolidating implementation of the Community's integration programme and advancing the development of the social agenda. At a special presidential summit in January 2002, corresponding ministers were directed to meet during the first half of the year to develop a Community strategy to complement national efforts in this area. In June 2003 ministers of foreign affairs and foreign trade at the 14th presidential summit adopted 16 legal provisions aimed at giving maximum priority to the social dimension of integration within the Community, including a measure providing for mobility of workers between member countries (see above). In July 2004 Community heads of state declared support for a new Andean Council of Social Development Ministers and a draft Comprehensive Social Development Plan. Other bodies established in 2003/04 included Councils of Ministers of Education and of Ministers responsible for Cultural Policies, and a Consultative Council of Municipal Authorities

INSTITUTIONS

Consejo Consultivo Empresarial Andino (Andean Business Advisory Council): Paseo de la República 3895, Lima, Peru; tel. (1) 4111400; fax (1) 2213329; e-mail rsuarez@comunidadandina.org; first meeting held in November 1998; an advisory institution within the framework of the Sistema Andino de Integración; comprises elected representatives of business organizations; advises Community ministers and officials on integration activities affecting the business sector; Pres. ROBERTO PEÑA DURINI (Ecuador).

Consejo Consultivo Laboral Andino (Andean Labour Advisory Council): Unitary General Workers' Union, Calle 35, No. 7–25, 9°, Cartegena, Colombia; tel. (5) 323-7550; fax (5) 664-1460; e-mail presidencia@ccla.org.pe; internet www.ccla.org.pe; an advisory institution within the framework of the Sistema Andino de Integración; comprises elected representatives of labour organizations; advises Community ministers and officers on related labour issues; Chair. JOSÉ CHÁVEZ CHÁVEZ (Ecuador).

Convenio Andrés Bello (Andrés Bello Agreement): Paralela Autopista Norte, Avda 13 85–60, Santafé de Bogotá, Colombia; tel. (1) 618-1701; fax (1) 610-0139; e-mail ecobello@col1.telecom.com.co; internet www.cab.int.co; f. 1970, modified in 1990; aims to promote integration in the educational, technical and cultural sectors; a new Interinstitutional Co-operation Agreement was signed with the Secretariat of the CAN in August 2003; mems: Bolivia, Chile, Colombia, Cuba, Ecuador, Panama, Paraguay, Peru, Spain, Venezuela.

Convenio Hipólito Unanue (Hipólito Unanue Agreement): Edif. Cartagena, Paseo de la República 3832, 3°, San Isidro, Lima, Peru;

tel. (1) 2210074; fax (1) 4409285; e-mail postmaster@conhu.org.pe; internet www.conhu.org.pe; f. 1971 on the occasion of the first meeting of Andean ministers of health; became part of the institutional structure of the Community in 1998; aims to enhance the development of health services, and to promote regional co-ordination in areas such as environmental health, disaster preparedness and the prevention and control of drug abuse.

Convenio Simón Rodríguez (Simón Rodríguez Agreement): Paseo de la República 3895, esq. Aramburú, San Isidro, Lima 27, Peru; tel. (1) 4111400; fax (1) 2213329; promotes a convergence of social and labour conditions throughout the Community, for example, working hours and conditions, employment and social security policies, and to promote the participation of workers and employers in the subregional integration process.

Corporación Andina de Fomento (CAF) (Andean Development Corporation): Torre CAF, Avda Luis Roche, Altamira, Apdo 5086, Caracas, Venezuela; tel. (2) 2092111; fax (2) 2092394; e-mail infocaf@caf.com; internet www.caf.com; f. 1968, began operations in 1970; aims to encourage the integration of the Andean countries by specialization and an equitable distribution of investments; conducts research to identify investment opportunities, and prepares the resulting investment projects; gives technical and financial assistance; and attracts internal and external credit; auth. cap. US $5,000m.; subscribed or underwritten by the governments of member countries, or by public, semi-public and private-sector institutions authorized by those governments; the Board of Directors comprises representatives of each country at ministerial level; mems: the Andean Community, Argentina, Brazil, Chile, Jamaica, Mexico, Panama, Paraguay, Spain, Trinidad and Tobago, and 22 private banks in the Andean region; Exec. Pres. ENRIQUE GARCÍA RODRÍGUEZ (Bolivia).

Fondo Latinoamericano de Reservas (FLAR) (Latin American Reserve Fund): Avda 82, 12–18, 7°, Santafé de Bogotá, Colombia; tel. (1) 634-4360; fax (1) 634-4384; e-mail flar@flar.net; internet www.flar.net; f. 1978 as the Fondo Andino de Reservas to support the balance of payments of member countries, provide credit, guarantee loans, and contribute to the harmonization of monetary and financial policies; adopted present name in 1991, in order to allow the admission of other Latin American countries; in 1992 the Fund began extending credit lines to commercial for export financing; it is administered by an Assembly of the ministers of finance and economy of the member countries, and a Board of Directors comprising the Presidents of the central banks of the member states; subscribed cap. US $2,109.4m. (31 March 2003); Exec. Pres. JULIO VELARDE; Gen. Sec. ANA MARÍA CARRASQUILLA.

Universidad Andina Simón Bolívar (Simón Bolívar Andean University): Calle Real Audiencia 73, Casilla 608-33, Sucre, Bolivia; tel. (64) 60265; fax (64) 60833; e-mail uasb@uasb.edu.bo; internet www.uasb.edu.bo; f. 1985; institution for postgraduate study and research; promotes co-operation between other universities in the Andean region; branches in Quito (Ecuador), La Paz (Bolivia), Caracas (Venezuela) and Cali (Colombia); Pres. Dr JULIO GARRET AILLÓN.

Publications

Andean Apparel for the Third Millennium.

Trade and Investment Guide.

Reports, working papers.

ARAB FUND FOR ECONOMIC AND SOCIAL DEVELOPMENT—AFESD

Address: POB 21923, Safat, 13080 Kuwait.

Telephone: 4844500; **fax:** 4815760; **e-mail:** hq@arabfund.org; **internet:** www.arabfund.org.

Established in 1968 by the Economic Council of the Arab League, the Fund began its operations in 1974. It participates in the financing of economic and social development projects in the Arab states.

MEMBERSHIP

Twenty-one members (see table of subscriptions below)

Organization

(April 2005)

BOARD OF GOVERNORS

The Board of Governors consists of a Governor and an Alternate Governor appointed by each member of the Fund. The Board of Governors is considered as the General Assembly of the Fund, and has all powers.

BOARD OF DIRECTORS

The Board of Directors is composed of eight Directors elected by the Board of Governors from among Arab citizens of recognized experience and competence. They are elected for a renewable term of two years.

The Board of Directors is charged with all the activities of the Fund and exercises the powers delegated to it by the Board of Governors.

Director-General and Chairman of the Board of Directors: ABDLATIF YOUSUF AL-HAMAD.

FINANCIAL STRUCTURE

In 1982 the authorized capital was increased from 400m. Kuwaiti dinars (KD) to KD 800m., divided into 80,000 shares having a value of KD 10,000 each. At the end of 2003 paid-up capital was KD 663.04m.

SUBSCRIPTIONS*
(KD million, December 2003)

Algeria	64.78	Oman	17.28
Bahrain	2.16	Palestine	1.10
Djibouti	0.02	Qatar	6.75
Egypt	40.50	Saudi Arabia	159.07
Iraq	31.76	Somalia	0.21
Jordan	17.30	Sudan	11.06
Kuwait	169.70	Syria	24.00
Lebanon	2.00	Tunisia	6.16
Libya	59.85	United Arab Emirates	28.00
Mauritania	0.82	Yemen	4.52
Morocco	16.00	**Total**	663.04

* 100 Kuwaiti dinars = US $339.33 (December 2003).

Activities

Pursuant to the Agreement Establishing the Fund (as amended in 1997 by the Board of Governors), the purpose of the Fund is to contribute to the financing of economic and social development projects in the Arab states and countries by:

1. Financing economic development projects of an investment character by means of loans granted on concessionary terms to governments and public enterprises and corporations, giving preference to projects which are vital to the Arab entity, as well as to joint Arab projects;

2. Financing private sector projects in member states by providing all forms of loans and guarantees to corporations and enterprises (possessing juridical personality), participating in their equity capital, and providing other forms of financing and the requisite financial, technical and advisory services, in accordance with such regulations and subject to such conditions as may be prescribed by the Board of Directors;

3. Forming or participating in the equity capital of corporations possessing juridical personality, for the implementation and financing of private sector projects in member states, including the provision and financing of technical, advisory and financial services;

4. Establishing and administering special funds with aims compatible with those of the Fund and with resources provided by the Fund or other sources;

5. Encouraging, directly or indirectly, the investment of public and private capital in a manner conducive to the development and growth of the Arab economy;

6. Providing expertise and technical assistance in the various fields of economic development.

LOANS BY MEMBER, 2003

Member	Project	Amount (KD million)
Djibouti	Boulaos power generating station (phase III)	3.0
Egypt	Nubaria power generating station (phase I)	30.0
	Nubaria power generating station (phase II)	30.0
	Educational buildings	30.0
Jordan	Education development (school buildings)	10.0
Lebanon	Lebanese University project (phase II)	6.0
Libya	Conversion of Zawya power station to a combined cycle	28.0
Morocco	Rural electrification	20.0
	Tetuan-Fenideq motorway	14.0
	Settat-Marakesh motorway (phase I)	30.0
Oman	Improvement of Nazwa-Thamreet road (phase II)	6.0
	Khasb port development	4.5
Syria	Conversion of Zeizoun power station to a combined cycle	22.0
Tunisia	Modernization of transmission network	30.0
Yemen	Upgrading electric grid	30.0
	Dhamar-Housainieh road	15.0

LOANS BY SECTOR, 2003

Sector	Amount (KD million)	%
Energy and electricity	193.0	62.6
Transport and telecommunications	69.5	22.5
Social services	46.0	14.9
Total	308.5	100.0

The Fund co-operates with other Arab organizations such as the Arab Monetary Fund, the League of Arab States and OAPEC in preparing regional studies and conferences, for example in the areas of human resource development, demographic research and private sector financing of infrastructure projects. It also acts as the secretariat of the Co-ordination Group of Arab National and Regional Development Financing Institutions. These organizations also work together to produce a *Joint Arab Economic Report*, which considers economic and social developments in the Arab states.

During 2003 the Fund approved 16 new loans, totalling KD 308.5m., for projects in 10 member countries. At the end of that year total lending since 1974 amounted to KD 4,460.7m., which helped to finance more than 375 projects in 17 Arab countries. In 2003 some 63% of financing was for projects in the energy and electricity sector, while 23% was for transport and telecommunications projects. During the period 1974–2003 31% of project financing was for energy and electricity, 20% for transport and telecommunications and for agriculture and rural development, 10% for water and sewerage, 9% for social services and 8% for industry and mining.

The total number of technical assistance grants provided by the end of 2003 was 735, with a value of KD 100.2m. During 2003 the Fund extended 27 new grants, totalling KD 7.0m. Some 47% of the grant financing was allocated to implement emergency programmes in southern Sudan and rehabilitation of infrastructure and services affected by flooding of the al-Qash River in Kassala province. A further 31% of grants was directed to institutional support and training, while 14% was for the preparation of general studies and research.

In December 1997 AFESD initiated an Arab Fund Fellowships Programme, which aimed to provide grants to Arab academics to conduct university teaching or advanced research.

ARAB MONETARY FUND

Address: Arab Monetary Fund Bldg, Corniche Rd, POB 2818, Abu Dhabi, United Arab Emirates.
Telephone: (2) 6171400; **fax:** (2) 6326454; **e-mail:** centralmail@amfad.org.ae; **internet:** www.amf.org.ae.

The Agreement establishing the Arab Monetary Fund was approved by the Economic Council of Arab States in Rabat, Morocco, in April 1976 and entered into force on 2 February 1977.

MEMBERS

Algeria	Morocco
Bahrain	Oman
Comoros	Palestine
Djibouti	Qatar
Egypt	Saudi Arabia
Iraq*	Somalia*
Jordan	Sudan*
Kuwait	Syria
Lebanon	Tunisia
Libya	United Arab Emirates
Mauritania	Yemen

* From July 1993 loans to Iraq, Somalia and Sudan were suspended as a result of non-repayment of debts to the Fund. Sudan was readmitted in April 2000, following a settlement of its arrears; a memorandum of understanding, to incorporate new loan repayments was concluded in September 2001. At 31 December 2003 the arrears to the Fund by Iraq and Somalia totalled AAD 150.2m.

Organization

(April 2005)

BOARD OF GOVERNORS

The Board of Governors is the highest authority of the Arab Monetary Fund. It formulates policies on Arab economic integration and liberalization of trade among member states. With certain exceptions, it may delegate to the Board of Executive Directors some of its powers. The Board of Governors is composed of a governor and a deputy governor appointed by each member state for a term of five years. It meets at least once a year; meetings may also be convened at the request of half the members, or of members holding half of the total voting power.

BOARD OF EXECUTIVE DIRECTORS

The Board of Executive Directors exercises all powers vested in it by the Board of Governors and may delegate to the Director-General such powers as it deems fit. It is composed of the Director-General and eight non-resident directors elected by the Board of Governors. Each director holds office for three years and may be re-elected.

DIRECTOR-GENERAL

The Director-General of the Fund is appointed by the Board of Governors for a renewable five-year term, and serves as Chairman of the Board of Executive Directors.

The Director-General supervises a Committee on Loans and a Committee on Investments to make recommendations on loan and investment policies to the Board of Executive Directors, and is required to submit an Annual Report to the Board of Governors.

Director-General and Chairman of the Board of Executive Directors: Dr JASSIM ABDULLAH AL-MANNAI.

FINANCE

The Arab Accounting Dinar (AAD) is a unit of account equivalent to three IMF Special Drawing Rights. (The average value of the SDR in 2003 was $1.39883.)

Each member paid, in convertible currencies, 5% of the value of its shares at the time of its ratification of the Agreement and another 20% when the Agreement entered into force. In addition, each member paid 2% of the value of its shares in its national currency regardless of whether it is convertible. The second 25% of the capital was to be subscribed by the end of September 1979, bringing the total paid-up capital in convertible currencies to AAD 131.5m. An increase in requests for loans led to a resolution by the Board of Governors in April 1981, giving members the option of paying the balance of their subscribed capital. This payment became obligatory in July 1981, when total approved loans exceeded 50% of the already paid-up capital in convertible currencies. In April 1983 the authorized capital of the Fund was increased from AAD 288m. to AAD

600m. The new capital stock comprised 12,000 shares, each having the value of AAD 50,000. At the end of 2003 total paid-up capital was AAD 324.3m.

CAPITAL SUBSCRIPTIONS
(million Arab Accounting Dinars, 31 December 2003)

Member	Paid-up capital
Algeria	42.40
Bahrain	5.00
Comoros	0.25
Djibouti	0.25
Egypt	32.00
Iraq	42.40
Jordan	5.40
Kuwait	32.00
Lebanon	5.00
Libya	13.44
Mauritania	5.00
Morocco	15.00
Oman	5.00
Palestine	2.16
Qatar	10.00
Saudi Arabia	48.40
Somalia	4.00
Sudan	10.00
Syria	7.20
Tunisia	7.00
United Arab Emirates	19.20
Yemen	15.40
Total*	**324.34**

* Excluding Palestine's share (AAD 2.16m.), which was deferred by a Board of Governors' resolution in 1978.

Activities

The creation of the Arab Monetary Fund was seen as a step towards the goal of Arab economic integration. It assists member states in balance of payments difficulties, and also has a broad range of aims.

The Articles of Agreement define the Fund's aims as follows:

(*a*) to correct disequilibria in the balance of payments of member states;

(*b*) to promote the stability of exchange rates among Arab currencies, to render them mutually convertible, and to eliminate restrictions on current payments between member states;

(*c*) to establish policies and modes of monetary co-operation to accelerate Arab economic integration and economic development in the member states;

(*d*) to tender advice on the investment of member states' financial resources in foreign markets, whenever called upon to do so;

(*e*) to promote the development of Arab financial markets;

(*f*) to promote the use of the Arab dinar as a unit of account and to pave the way for the creation of a unified Arab currency;

(*g*) to co-ordinate the positions of member states in dealing with international monetary and economic problems; and

(*h*) to provide a mechanism for the settlement of current payments between member states in order to promote trade among them.

The Arab Monetary Fund functions both as a fund and a bank. It is empowered:

(*a*) to provide short- and medium-term loans to finance balance of payments deficits of member states;

(*b*) to issue guarantees to member states to strengthen their borrowing capabilities;

(*c*) to act as intermediary in the issuance of loans in Arab and international markets for the account of member states and under their guarantees;

(*d*) to co-ordinate the monetary policies of member states;

(*e*) to manage any funds placed under its charge by member states;

(*f*) to hold periodic consultations with member states on their economic conditions; and

(*g*) to provide technical assistance to banking and monetary institutions in member states.

Loans are intended to finance an overall balance of payments deficit and a member may draw up to 75% of its paid-up subscription, in convertible currencies, for this purpose unconditionally (automatic loans). A member may, however, obtain loans in excess of this limit, subject to agreement with the Fund on a programme aimed at reducing its balance of payments deficit (ordinary and extended loans, equivalent to 175% and 250% of its quota respectively). From 1981 a country receiving no extended loans was entitled to a loan under the Inter-Arab Trade Facility (discontinued in 1989) of up to 100% of its quota. In addition, a member has the right to borrow up to 50% of its paid-up capital in order to cope with an unexpected deficit in its balance of payments resulting from a decrease in its exports of goods and services or a large increase in its imports of agricultural products following a poor harvest (compensatory loans).

Automatic and compensatory loans are repayable within three years, while ordinary and extended loans are repayable within five and seven years respectively. Loans are granted at concessionary and uniform rates of interest which increase with the length of the period of the loan. In 1988 the Fund's executive directors agreed to modify their policy on lending, placing an emphasis on the correction of economic imbalances in recipient countries. In 1996 the Fund established the Structural Adjustment Facility, initially providing up to 75% of a member's paid-up subscription and later increased to 175%. This may include a technical assistance component comprising a grant of up to 2% of the total loan.

Over the period 1978–2003 the Fund extended 127 loans amounting to AAD 998,453m. During 2003 the Fund approved three loans, amounting to AAD 66,593m., while loan disbursements amounted to AAD 33,266m.

The Fund's technical assistance activities are extended through either the provision of experts to the country concerned or in the form of specialized training of officials of member countries. In view of the increased importance of this type of assistance, the Fund established, in 1988, the Economic Policy Institute (EPI) which offers regular training courses and specialized seminars for middle-level and senior staff, respectively, of financial and monetary institutions of the Arab countries. During 2003 the EPI organized nine training courses, covering areas such as banking supervision, price statistics and anti-money laundering, two seminars and a workshop on debt management. In April 1999 the Fund signed a memorandum of understanding with the International Monetary Fund to establish a joint regional training programme.

AMF collaborates with AFESD, the Arab League and OAPEC in writing and publishing a *Joint Arab Economic Report*. The Fund also co-operates with AFESD, with the technical assistance of the International Monetary Fund and the World Bank, in organizing an annual seminar. The 15th joint seminar was held in Kuwait, in October 2003, on the theme of 'Arab Women and Economic Development'.

LOANS APPROVED, 1978–2003

Type of loan	Number of loans	Amount (AAD '000)
Automatic	57	293,925
Ordinary	11	104,567
Compensatory	14	99,085
Extended	21	278,944
Structural Adjustment Facility	13	157,202

Type of loan— *continued*	Number of loans	Amount (AAD '000)
Inter-Arab Trade Facility (cancelled in 1989)	11	64,730
Total	127	998,453

LOANS APPROVED, 2003

Borrower	Type of loan	Amount (AAD thousand)
Djibouti	Extended	367.5
Egypt	Extended	55,125.0
Morocco	Structural Adjustment Facility	11,100.0
Total		66,592.5

TRADE PROMOTION

Arab Trade Financing Program (ATFP): POB 26799, Arab Monetary Fund Bldg, 7th Floor, Corniche Rd, Abu Dhabi, United Arab Emirates; tel. (2) 6316999; fax (2) 6316793; e-mail atfphq@atfp.org.ae; internet www.atfp.org.ae; f. 1989 to develop and promote trade between Arab countries and to enhance the competitive ability of Arab exporters; operates by extending lines of credit to Arab exporters and importers through national agencies (some 152 agencies designated by the monetary authorities of 19 Arab countries in Dec. 2004); the Arab Monetary Fund provided 50% of ATFP's authorized capital of US $500m.; participation was also invited from private and official Arab financial institutions and joint Arab/foreign institutions; ATFP administers the Inter-Arab Trade Information Network (IATIN), and organizes Buyers-Sellers meetings to promote Arab goods; Chair. and Chief Exec. Dr JASSIM ABDULLAH AL-MANNAI; publs *Annual Report* (Arabic and English), *IATIN Quarterly Bulletin* (Arabic).

Publications

Annual Report.

AMDB Bulletin (quarterly).

Arab Countries: Economic Indicators (annually).

Balance of Payments and External Public Debt of the Arab Countries (annually).

Foreign Trade of the Arab Countries (annually).

Joint Arab Economic Report (annually).

Money and Credit in the Arab Countries.

National Accounts of the Arab Countries (annually).

Reports on commodity structure (by value and quantity) of member countries' imports from and exports to other Arab countries; other studies on economic, social, management and fiscal issues.

ASIA-PACIFIC ECONOMIC CO-OPERATION—APEC

Address: 35 Heng Mui Keng Terrace, Singapore 119616.
Telephone: 67756012; **fax:** 67756013; **e-mail:** info@apec.org; **internet:** www.apec.org.

Asia-Pacific Economic Co-operation (APEC) was initiated in November 1989, in Canberra, Australia, as an informal consultative forum. Its aim is to promote multilateral economic co-operation on issues of trade and investment.

MEMBERS

Australia	Japan	Philippines
Brunei	Korea, Republic	Russia
Canada	Malaysia	Singapore
Chile	Mexico	Taiwan*
China, People's	New Zealand	Thailand
Republic	Papua New Guinea	USA
Hong Kong	Peru	Viet Nam
Indonesia		

*Admitted as Chinese Taipei.
Note: APEC has three official observers: the Association of South East Asian Nations Secretariat; the Pacific Economic Co-operation Council; and the Pacific Islands Forum Secretariat (formerly the South Pacific Forum Secretariat). Observers may participate in APEC meetings and have full access to all related documents and information.

Organization

(April 2005)

ECONOMIC LEADERS' MEETINGS

The first meeting of APEC heads of government was convened in November 1993, in Seattle, Washington, USA. Subsequently, each annual meeting of APEC ministers of foreign affairs and of economic affairs has been followed by an informal gathering of the leaders of the APEC economies, at which the policy objectives of the grouping are discussed and defined. The 12th Economic Leaders' Meeting was held in November 2004, in Santiago, Chile. The 13th Economic Leaders' Meeting was scheduled to be convened in November 2005, in Busan, Republic of Korea.

MINISTERIAL MEETINGS

APEC ministers of foreign affairs and ministers of economic affairs meet annually. These meetings are hosted by the APEC Chair, which rotates each year, although it was agreed, in 1989, that alternate Ministerial Meetings were to be convened in an ASEAN member country. A Senior Officials' Meeting (SOM) convenes regularly between Ministerial Meetings to co-ordinate and administer the budgets and work programmes of APEC's committees and working groups. Other meetings of ministers are held on a regular basis to enhance co-operation in specific areas.

SECRETARIAT

In 1992 the Ministerial Meeting, held in Bangkok, Thailand, agreed to establish a permanent secretariat to support APEC activities, and approved an annual budget of US $2m. The Secretariat became operational in February 1993. The Executive Director is appointed from the member economy chairing the group and serves a one-year term. A Deputy Executive Director is appointed by the member economy designated to chair APEC in the following year.

Executive Director: CHOI SEOK YOUNG (Republic of Korea).

Deputy Executive Director: TRAN TRONG TOAN (Viet Nam).

COMMITTEES AND GROUPS

Budget and Management Committee (BMC): f. 1993 as Budget and Administrative Committee, present name adopted 1998; advises APEC senior officials on budgetary, administrative and managerial issues. The Committee reviews the operational budgets of APEC committees and groups, evaluates their effectiveness and conducts assessments of group projects.

Committee on Trade and Investment (CTI): f. 1993 on the basis of a Declaration signed by ministers meeting in Seattle, Washington, USA, in order to facilitate the expansion of trade and the development of a liberalized environment for investment among member countries; undertakes initiatives to improve the flow of goods, services and technology in the region. An Investment Experts' Group was established in 1994, initially to develop non-binding investment principles. In May 1997 an APEC Tariff Database was inaugurated, with sponsorship from the private sector. A new Market Access Group was established in 1998 to administer CTI activities concerned with non-tariff measures. In 2001 the CTI finalized a set of non-binding Principles on Trade Facilitation. The development of the nine principles was intended to help eliminate procedural and administrative impediments to trade and to increase trading opportunities. A Trade Facilitation Action Plan was approved in 2002. In 2003 a Transparency By 2005 strategy was adopted to incorporate transparency standards.

Economic Committee (EC): f. 1994 following an agreement, in November, to transform the existing *ad hoc* group on economic trends and issues into a formal committee; aims to enhance APEC's capacity to analyse economic trends and to research and report on issues affecting economic and technical co-operation in the region. In addition, the Committee is considering the environmental and development implications of expanding population and economic growth.

SOM Committee on Economic and Technical Co-operation (ESC): f. 1998 to assist the SOM with the co-ordination of APEC's economic and technical co-operation programme (ECOTECH); monitors and evaluates project implementation and also identifies initiatives designed to strengthen economic and technical co-operation in infrastructure. The ESC co-ordinated the development of APEC's Human-Capacity Building Strategy in 2001.

In addition, the following Working Groups promote and co-ordinate practical co-operation between member countries in different activities: Agricultural technical co-operation; Energy; Fisheries; Human resources development; Industrial science and technology; Marine resource conservation; Small and medium enterprises (SMEs); Telecommunications and Information; Tourism; Trade promotion; and Transportation. (See below for more detailed information.)

ADVISORY COUNCIL

APEC Business Advisory Council (ABAC): Philamlife Tower, 43rd Floor, 8767 Paseo de Roxas, Makati City 1226, Philippines; tel. (2) 8454564; fax (2) 8454832; e-mail abacsec@pfgc.ph; internet www.abaconline.org; an agreement to establish ABAC, comprising up to three senior representatives of the private sector from each APEC member economy, was concluded at the Ministerial Meeting held in November 1995. ABAC was mandated to advise member states on the implementation of APEC's Action Agenda and on other business matters, and to provide business-related information to APEC fora. ABAC meets three or four times each year and holds a dialogue with APEC economic leaders prior to their annual informal meeting. ABAC's first meeting, convened in June 1996 in Manila, the Philippines, resolved to accelerate the liberalization of regional trade; in 2005 ABAC determined to support the World Trade Organization's Doha Development Agenda, in preparation for a ministerial meeting to be held in November (see below); Exec. Dir RENE MUGA.

Activities

APEC was initiated in 1989 as a forum for informal discussion between the then six ASEAN members and their six dialogue partners in the Pacific, and, in particular, to promote trade liberalization in the Uruguay Round of negotiations, which were being conducted under the General Agreement on Tariffs and Trade (GATT). The Seoul Declaration, adopted by ministers meeting in the Republic of Korea in November 1991, defined the objectives of APEC.

ASEAN countries were initially reluctant to support any more formal structure of the forum, or to admit new members, owing to concerns that it would undermine ASEAN's standing as a regional grouping and be dominated by powerful non-ASEAN economies. In August 1991 it was agreed to extend membership to the People's Republic of China, Hong Kong and Taiwan (subject to conditions imposed by the People's Republic of China, including that a Taiwanese official of no higher than vice-ministerial level should attend the annual meeting of ministers of foreign affairs). Mexico and Papua New Guinea acceded to the organization in November 1993, and Chile joined in November 1994. The summit meeting held in November 1997 agreed that Peru, Russia and Viet Nam should be admitted to APEC at the 1998 meeting, but imposed a 10-year moratorium on further expansion of the grouping.

In September 1992 APEC ministers agreed to establish a permanent secretariat. In addition, the meeting created an 11-member non-governmental Eminent Persons Group (EPG), which was to assess trade patterns within the region and propose measures to promote co-operation. At the Ministerial Meeting in Seattle, Washington, USA, in November 1993, members agreed on a framework for expanding trade and investment among member countries, and to establish a permanent committee (the CTI, see above) to pursue these objectives.

In August 1994 the EPG proposed the following timetable for the liberalization of all trade across the Asia-Pacific region: negotiations for the elimination of trade barriers were to commence in 2000 and be completed within 10 years in developed countries, 15 years in newly-industrialized economies and by 2020 in developing countries. Trade concessions could then be extended on a reciprocal basis to non-members in order to encourage world-wide trade liberalization, rather than isolate APEC as a unique trading bloc. In November 1994 the meeting of APEC heads of government adopted the Bogor Declaration of Common Resolve, which endorsed the EPG's timetable for free and open trade and investment in the region by the year 2020. Other issues incorporated into the Declaration included the implementation of GATT commitments in full and strengthening the multilateral trading system through the forthcoming establishment of the World Trade Organization (WTO), intensifying development co-operation in the Asia-Pacific region and expanding and accelerating trade and investment programmes.

During 1995 meetings of APEC officials and other efforts to substantiate the trade liberalization agreement revealed certain differences among members regarding the timetable and means of implementing the measures, which were to be agreed upon at the 1995 Economic Leaders' Meeting. The principal concern, expressed notably by the USA, focused on whether tariff reductions were to be achieved by individual trade liberalization plans or based on some reciprocal or common approach. In August the EPG issued a report, to be considered at the November Leaders' Meeting, which advocated acceleration of tariff reductions and other trade liberalization measures agreed under GATT; the establishment of a dispute mediation service to reduce and settle regional trade conflicts; and a review of new trade groupings within the APEC region. Further proposals for the implementation of the Bogor Declaration objectives were presented, in September, by the Pacific Business Forum, comprising APEC business representatives. The recommendations included harmonization of product quality, the establishment of one-stop investment agencies in each APEC country, training and technology transfers and the implementation of visa-free business travel by 1999. In November 1995 the Ministerial Meeting decided to dismantle the EPG, and to establish an APEC Business Advisory Council (ABAC), consisting of private-sector representatives.

In November 1995 APEC heads of government, meeting in Osaka, Japan, adopted an Action Agenda as a framework to achieve the commitments of the Bogor Declaration. Part One of the Agenda identified action areas for the liberalization of trade and investment and the facilitation of business, for example, customs procedures, rules of origin and non-tariff barriers. It incorporated agreements that the process was to be comprehensive, consistent with WTO commitments, comparable among all APEC economies and non-discriminatory. Each member economy was to ensure the transparency of its laws, regulations and procedures affecting the flow of goods, services and capital among APEC economies and to refrain from implementing any trade protection measures. A second part of the Agenda was to provide a framework for further economic and technical co-operation between APEC members in areas such as energy, transport, infrastructure, SMEs and agricultural technology. In order to resolve a disagreement concerning the inclusion of agricultural products in the trade liberalization process, a provision for flexibility was incorporated into the Agenda, taking into account diverse circumstances and different levels of development in APEC member economies. Liberalization measures were to be implemented from January 1997 (i.e. three years earlier than previously agreed) and were to be subject to annual reviews. A Trade and Investment Liberalization and Facilitation Special Account was established to finance projects in support of the implementation of the Osaka Action Agenda. In May 1996 APEC senior officials met in Cebu, the Philippines, to review Individual Action Plans—IAPs, annual reports submitted by each member state on progress in the implementation of trade liberalization measures—and to achieve some coherent approach to tariff liberalization prior to the Leaders' Meeting in November.

In November 1996 the Economic Leaders' Meeting, held in Subic Bay, the Philippines, approved the Manila Action Plan for APEC (MAPA), which had been formulated at the preceding Ministerial Meeting, held in Manila. MAPA incorporated the IAPs and other collective measures aimed at achieving the trade liberalization and co-operation objectives of the Bogor Declaration, as well as the joint activities specified in the second part of the Osaka Agenda. Heads of government also endorsed a US proposal to eliminate tariffs and other barriers to trade in information technology products by 2000 and determined to support efforts to conclude an agreement to this effect at the forthcoming WTO conference; however, they insisted on the provision of an element of flexibility in achieving trade liberalization in this sector.

The 1997 Economic Leaders' Meeting, held in Vancouver, Canada, in November, was dominated by concern at the financial instability that had affected several Asian economies during 1997. The final declaration of the summit meeting endorsed a framework of measures that had been agreed by APEC deputy ministers of finance and central bank governors at an emergency meeting convened in the previous week in Manila, the Philippines (the so-called Manila Framework for Enhanced Asian Regional Co-operation to Promote Financial Stability). The meeting, attended by representatives of the IMF, the World Bank and the Asian Development Bank, committed all member economies receiving IMF assistance to undertake specified economic and financial reforms, and supported the establishment of a separate Asian funding facility to supplement international financial assistance (although this was later rejected by the IMF). APEC ministers of finance and governors of central banks were urged to accelerate efforts for the development of the region's financial and capital markets and to liberalize capital flows in the region. Measures were to include strengthening financial market supervision and clearing and settlement infrastructure, the reform of pension systems, and promoting co-operation among export credit agencies and financing institutions. The principal item on the Vancouver summit agenda was an initiative to enhance trade liberalization, which, the grouping insisted, should not be undermined by the financial instability in Asia. The following 15 economic sectors were identified for 'early voluntary sectoral liberalization' ('EVSL'): environmental goods and services; fish and fish products; forest products; medical equipment and instruments; toys; energy; chemicals; gems and jewellery; telecommunications; oilseeds and oilseed products; food; natural and synthetic rubber; fertilizers; automobiles; and civil aircraft. The implementation of EVSL was to encompass market opening, trade facilitation, and economic and technical co-operation activities. The heads of government subsequently requested the authorities in each member state to formulate details of tariff reductions in these sectors by mid-1998, with a view to implementing the measures in 1999. (In June 1998, however, ministers of trade, meeting in Malaysia, failed to conclude an agreement on early tariff reductions, in part owing to Japan's reluctance to liberalize trade in fish and forest products.) In Vancouver APEC Economic Leaders also declared their support for an agreement to liberalize financial services (which was successfully negotiated under the auspices of the WTO in December 1997) and for the objective of reducing the emission of 'greenhouse gases', which was under consideration at a global conference, held in Kyoto, Japan, in December (resulting in the adoption of the Kyoto Protocol to the UN Framework Convention on Climate Change).

In May 1998 APEC finance ministers met in Canada to consider the ongoing financial and economic crisis in Asia and to review progress in implementing efforts to alleviate the difficulties experienced by several member economies. The ministers agreed to pursue activities in the following three priority areas: capital market development, capital account liberalization and strengthening financial systems (including corporate governance). The region's economic difficulties remained the principal topic of discussion at the Economic Leaders' Meeting held in Kuala Lumpur, Malaysia, in November. A final declaration reiterated their commitment to co-operation in pursuit of sustainable economic recovery and growth, in particular through the restructuring of financial and corporate sectors, promoting and facilitating private-sector capital flows, and efforts to strengthen the global financial system. The meeting endorsed a proposal of ABAC to establish a partnership for equitable growth, with the aim of enhancing business involvement in APEC's programme of economic and technical co-operation. Other initiatives approved included an Agenda of APEC Science and Technology Industry Co-operation into the 21st Century (for which the People's Republic of China announced it was to establish a special fund), and an Action Programme on Skills and Development in APEC. Japan's persisting opposition to a reduction of tariffs in the fish and forestry sectors again prevented the conclusion of tariff negotiations under the EVSL scheme, and it was therefore agreed that responsibility for managing the tariff reduction element of the initiative should be transferred to the WTO. The meeting was divided by political differences regarding human rights, and in particular, the treatment by the Malaysian authorities of the imprisoned former Deputy Prime Minister, Anwar Ibrahim. A declaration of support for the democratic reform movement in Malaysia by the US representative dominated discussions at the start of the summit meeting and provoked a formal complaint from the Malaysian Government.

In September 1999 political dialogue regarding the civil conflict in East Timor (now Timor-Leste) dominated the start of the annual meetings of the grouping, held in Auckland, New Zealand, although the issue remained separate from the official agenda. Ministers of foreign affairs, convened in emergency session, declared their support for the establishment of a multinational force, under UN auspices, to restore peace in the territory and determined to provide humanitarian and technical assistance to facilitate the process of reconstruction and rehabilitation. The Economic Leaders' Meeting considered measures to sustain the economic recovery in Asia and endorsed the APEC Principles to Enhance Competition and Regulatory Reform (for example, transparency, accountability, non-discrimination) as a framework to strengthen APEC markets and to enable further integration and implementation of the IAPs. The meeting endorsed a report prepared during the year by an *ad hoc* task force concerning an ABAC proposal for the development of an APEC food system. Also under discussion was the forthcoming round of multilateral trade negotiations, to be initiated by the WTO. The heads of government proposed the objective of completing a single package of trade agreements within three years and endorsed the abolition of export subsidies for agricultural products. The meeting determined to support the efforts of the People's Republic of China, Russia, Taiwan and Viet Nam to accede to WTO membership.

The Economic Leaders' Meeting for 2000, held in Brunei in November, urged that an agenda for the now-stalled round of multilateral trade negotiations should be formulated without further delay. The meeting endorsed a plan of action to promote the utilization of advances in information and communications technologies in member economies, for the benefit of all citizens. It adopted the aim of tripling the number of people in the region with access to the internet by 2005, and determined to co-operate with business and education sector interests to attract investment and expertise in the pursuit of this goal. A proposal that the Democratic People's Republic of Korea be permitted to participate in APEC working groups was approved at the meeting.

The 2001 Economic Leaders' Meeting, held in October, in Shanghai, People's Republic of China, condemned the terrorist attacks against targets in the USA of the previous month and resolved to take action to combat the threat of international terrorism. The heads of government declared terrorism to be a direct challenge to APEC's vision of free, open and prosperous economies, and concluded that the threat made the continuing move to free trade, with its aim of bolstering economies, increasing prosperity and encouraging integration, even more of a priority. The meeting emphasized the importance of sharing the benefits of globalization. The leaders also expressed their determination to address the effects on APEC countries of the prevailing global economic downturn, advocating timely policy actions in the coming year to rebuild confidence and boost growth. Human capacity-building was a central theme. The meeting adopted the Shanghai Accord, which identified development goals for APEC during its next decade and clarified measures for achieving the Bogor goals within the agreed timetable. The meeting also outlined the e-APEC Strategy developed by the e-APEC Task Force established after the Brunei Economic Leaders' meeting. Considering issues of entrepreneurship, structural and regulatory reform, competition, intellectual property rights and information security, the strategy aimed to facilitate technological development in the region. Finally, the meeting adopted a strategy document relating to infectious diseases in the Asia Pacific region, which aimed to promote a co-ordinated response to combating HIV/AIDS and other infectious diseases.

In September 2002 a meeting of APEC ministers of finance was held in Los Cabos, Mexico. Ministers discussed the importance of efforts to combat money-laundering and the financing of terrorism. The meeting also focused on ways to strengthen global and regional economic growth, to advance fiscal and financial reforms and to improve the allocation of domestic savings for economic development. The theme of the 2002 Economic Leaders' Meeting, held in the following month in Los Cabos, Mexico, was 'Expanding the Benefits of Co-operation for Economic Growth and Development—Implementing the Vision'. The meeting issued a statement on the implementation of APEC standards of transparency in trade and investment liberalization and facilitation. Leaders also issued a statement on fighting terrorism and promoting growth. In February 2003 a Counter Terrorism Task Force was established to co-ordinate implementation of the leaders' statement. In the same month the first conference to promote the Secure Trade in the APEC Region (STAR) initiative was convened in Bangkok, Thailand, and attended by representatives of all APEC member economies as well as senior officers of private sector companies and relevant international organizations. A second STAR conference was held in March 2004, in Chile.

In September 2003 APEC finance ministers, meeting in Phuket, Thailand, emphasized the importance of the following in achieving their goal of sustainable growth in the APEC region: good governance within the private and public sectors; stable and efficient financial markets; greater economic integration and openness among member economies; and heightened vigilance towards money-laundering for the financing of terrorism. The 2003 Economic Leaders' Meeting, convened in mid-October, in Bangkok, Thailand, considered means of advancing the WTO's stalled Doha round of trade negotiations, emphasizing the central importance of its development dimension, and noted progress made hitherto in facilitating intra-APEC trade. The meeting also addressed regional security issues, reiterating the Community's commitment to ensuring the resilience of APEC economies against the threat of terrorism. The Leaders adopted the Bangkok Declaration on Partnership for the

Future which identified the following areas as priority concerns for the group: the promotion of trade and investment liberalization; enhancing human security; and helping people and societies to benefit from globalization. The Bangkok meeting also issued a statement on health security, which expressed APEC's determination to strengthen infrastructure for the detection and prevention of infectious diseases, as well as the surveillance of other threats to public health, and to ensure a co-ordinated response to public health emergencies, with particular concern to the outbreak, earlier in the year, of Severe Acute Respiratory Syndrome (SARS). Health security activities were to be implemented by a newly-established *ad hoc* Health Task Force, which subsequently convened for the first time in Taiwan (Chinese Taipei), in April 2004. At that time the Task Force was also considering ways of contributing to the global and regional response to outbreaks of so-called 'avian flu'.

The 12th Economic Leaders' Meeting was held in Santiago, Chile, in November 2004, on the theme 'One Community, Our Future'. The meeting reaffirmed the grouping's commitment to the Doha Development Agenda, and endorsed the package of agreements concluded by the WTO in July. The meeting approved a Santiago Initiative for Expanded Trade in APEC, to promote further trade and investment liberalization in the region and advance trade facilitation measures. Other areas discussed were human security, HIV/AIDS and other emerging infectious diseases, and energy security. Efforts to promote good governance included a Santiago Commitment to Fight Corruption and Ensure Transparency and a Leaders' Agenda to Implement Structural Reform.

WORKING GROUPS

APEC's structure of working groups aims to promote practical and technical co-operation in specific areas, and to help implement individual and collective action plans in response to the directives of the Economic Leaders and meetings of relevant ministers. APEC recognizes sustainable development as a key issue cross-cutting all forum activities. In 1997 APEC leaders declared their commitment to the integration of women into the mainstream of APEC activities. A Gender Focal Point Network (GFPN) was established in May 2003 as a mechanism for the implementation of the Framework for the Integration of Women in APEC.

Agricultural Technical Co-operation: Formally established as an APEC Expert's Group in 1996, and incorporated into the system of working groups in 2000. The group aims to enhance the role of agriculture in the economic growth of the region and to promote co-operation in the following areas: conservation and utilization of plant and animal genetic resources; research, development and extension of agricultural biotechnology; processing, marketing, distribution and consumption of agricultural products; plant and animal quarantine and pest management; development of an agricultural finance system; sustainable agriculture; and agricultural technology transfer and training. The group has primary responsibility for undertaking recommendations connected with the implementation of the proposed APEC food system. The group has conducted projects on human resource development in post-harvest technology and on capacity-building, safety assessment and communication in biotechnology. A high level policy dialogue on agricultural biotechnology was initiated in 2002.

Energy: Responsible for the development of the energy component of the 1995 Action Agenda. APEC ministers responsible for energy convened for the first time in 1996 to discuss major energy challenges confronting the region and to provide guidance for the working group. The group's main objectives were determined as: the enhancement of regional energy security and improvement of the fuel supply market for the power sector; the development and implementation of programmes of work promoting the adoption of environmentally sound energy technologies and promoting private-sector investment in regional power infrastructure; the development of energy efficiency guide-lines; and the standardization of testing facilities and results. In March 1999 the group resolved to establish a business network to improve relations and communications with the private sector. The first meeting of the network took place in April. In October 1998 APEC energy ministers, meeting in Okinawa, Japan, emphasized the role of the energy sector in stimulating economic activity and stressed the need to develop infrastructure, improve energy efficiency and accelerate the development of natural gas reserves. In May 2000 ministers meeting in San Diego, California, USA, launched the APEC 21st Century Renewable Energy Initiative, which aims to encourage co-operation in and advance the utilization of renewable energy technologies, envisaging the establishment of a Private Sector Renewable Energy Forum. In July 2002 APEC energy ministers, convened in Mexico City, proposed several initiatives, including the cross-border interconnection of natural gas pipelines and improvements in energy security. Meeting in Portland, Oregon, USA, in June 2003 ministers agreed on a framework to implement APEC's Energy Security Initiative. The first meeting of ministers responsible for mining was convened in Santiago, Chile, in June 2004.

Fisheries: Aims to maximize the economic benefits and sustainability of fisheries resources for all APEC members. Recent concerns include food safety, the quality of fish products and resource management. In 1996 the group initiated a four-year study on trade and investment liberalization in the sector, in the areas of tariffs, non-tariff barriers and investment measures and subsidies. In 1997 the group organized two technical workshops on seafood inspection systems, and conducted a workshop addressing destructive fishing techniques. The first APEC Aquaculture Forum, which considered the sustainable development of aquaculture in the region and the development of new markets for APEC fish products, was held in Taipei, Taiwan, in June 1998. In May 1999 new guide-lines were adopted to encourage the participation of the private sector in the activities of the working group. The group's first business forum was convened in July 2000. In April 2002 the first ocean-related ministerial meeting, held in Seoul, Republic of Korea, adopted the Seoul Oceans Declaration, detailing recommendations on marine environmental protection and integrated coastal management.

Human Resources Development: Established in 1990, comprising three networks: the Capacity Building Network, with a focus on human capacity-building, including management and technical skills development and corporate governance; the Education Network, promoting effective learning systems and supporting the role of education in advancing individual, social and economic development; and the Labour and Social Protection Network, concerned with promoting social integration through the strengthening of labour markets, the development of labour market information and policy, and improvements in working conditions and social safety net frameworks. The working group undertakes activities through these networks to implement ministerial and leaders' directives, as well as the 'Medium Term Strategic Priorities', which were formulated in January 1997. A voluntary network of APEC study centres links higher education and research institutions in member economies. In January 1998 the working group established a Task Force on the Human Resource and Social Impacts of the Financial Crisis. Private-sector participation in the working group has been strengthened by the establishment of a network of APEC senior executives responsible for human resources management. Recent initiatives have included a cyber-education co-operation project, a workshop on advanced risk management, training on the prevention and resolution of employment and labour disputes, and an educators' exchange programme on the use of information technology in education.

Industrial Science and Technology: Aims to contribute to sustainable development in the region, improve the availability of information, enhance human resources development in the sector, improve the business climate, promote policy dialogue and review and facilitate networks and partnerships. Accordingly, the group has helped to establish an APEC Virtual Centre for Environmental Technology Exchange in Japan; a Science and Technology Industrial Parks Network; an International Molecular Biology Network for the APEC Region; an APEC Centre for Technology Foresight, based in Thailand; and the APEC Science and Technology Web, an online database. During 1997 and 1998 the group formulated an APEC Action Framework on Emerging Infectious Diseases and developed an Emerging Infections Network (EINet), based at the University of Washington, Seattle, USA.

Marine Resource Conservation: Promotes initiatives within APEC to protect the marine environment and its resources. In 1996 a five-year project was initiated for the management of red tide and harmful algal blooms in the APEC region. An APEC Action Plan for Sustainability of the Marine Environment was adopted by ministers responsible for the environment, meeting in June 1997. The Plan aimed to promote regional co-operation, an integrated approach to coastal management, the prevention, reduction and control of marine pollution, and sustainable development. Efforts were also being undertaken to establish an Ocean Research Network of centres of excellence in the Pacific. Strategies to encourage private-sector participation in promoting the sustainable management of marine resources were endorsed by the group in June 2000. Four main themes were identified for the Action Plan in the 21st century: balancing coastal development and resource protection; ensuring sustainable fisheries and aquaculture; understanding and observing the oceans and seas; and promoting economic and technical co-operation in oceans management. The Seoul Oceans Declaration, endorsed in April 2002 (see above), established the direction of the group's future activities. A new strategic framework for the group was adopted in May 2004, at a meeting held in Puerto Varas, Chile.

Small and Medium Enterprises: The group was established in 1995, as the Ad Hoc Policy Level Group on Small and Medium Enterprises, with a temporary mandate to oversee all APEC activities relating to SMEs. It supported the establishment of an APEC Centre for Technical Exchange and Training for Small and Medium Enterprises, which was inaugurated at Los Baños, near Manila, the Philippines, in September 1996. A five-year action plan for SMEs was endorsed in 1998. The group was redesignated as a working

group, with permanent status, in 2000. In 2000 and 2001 the group considered issues relating to globalization, innovation, human resource development, information technology and e-commerce, financing, and the forming of strategic alliances with other SMEs and larger firms. In August 2002 the group's action plan was revised to include an evaluation framework to assist APEC and member economies in identifying and analysing policy issues. In the same month a sub-group specialising in micro-enterprises was established. The first APEC Incubator Forum was held in July-August 2003, in Taiwan (Chinese Taipei), to promote new businesses and support their early development. During 2003 the Group undertook efforts to develop a special e-APEC Strategy for SMEs.

Telecommunications and Information: Incorporates four steering groups concerned with different aspects of the development and liberalization of the sector—Liberalization; Business facilitation; Development co-operation; and Human resource development. Activities are guided by directives of ministers responsible for telecommunications, who first met in 1995, in the Republic of Korea, and adopted a Seoul Declaration on Asia Pacific Information Infrastructure (APII). The second ministerial meeting, held in Gold Coast, Australia, in September 1996, adopted more detailed proposals for liberalization of the sector in member economies. In June 1998 ministers, meeting in Singapore, agreed to remove technical barriers to trade in telecommunications equipment (although Chile and New Zealand declined to sign up to the arrangement). At their fourth meeting, convened in May 2000 in Cancún, Mexico, telecommunications ministers approved a programme of action that included measures to bridge the 'digital divide' between developed and developing member economies, and adopted the APEC Principles on International Charging Arrangements for Internet Services and the APEC Principles of Interconnection. The fifth ministerial meeting, held in May 2002, issued a Statement on the Security of Information and Communications Infrastructures; a compendium of IT security standards has been disseminated in support of the Statement. A report entitled Stocktake of Progress Towards the Key Elements of a Fully Liberalized Telecommunications Sector in the APEC Region was completed in 2004.

Tourism: Established in 1991, with the aim of promoting the long-term sustainability of the tourism industry, in both environmental and social terms. The group administers a Tourism Information Network and an APEC International Centre for Sustainable Tourism, which in mid-2003 comprised 11 member countries. In 1998 the group initiated a project to assess the impact of the Asian financial crisis on regional tourism and to identify strategies to counter any negative effects. The first meeting of APEC ministers of tourism, held in the Republic of Korea in July 2000, adopted the Seoul Declaration on the APEC Tourism Charter. The group's work plan is based on four policy goals inherent in the Seoul Declaration, namely, the removal of impediments to tourism business and investment; increased mobility of visitors and increased demand for tourism goods and services; sustainable management of tourism; and enhanced recognition of tourism as a vehicle for economic and social development. At a meeting of the working group in April 2001, APEC and the Pacific Asia Travel Association (PATA) adopted a Code for Sustainable Tourism. The Code is designed for adoption and implementation by a variety of tourism companies and government agencies. It urges members to conserve the natural environment, ecosystems and biodiversity; respect local traditions and cultures; conserve energy; reduce pollution and waste; and ensure that regular environmental audits are carried out. In November 2001 the working group considered the impact on tourism of the September terrorist attacks on the USA. The group advocated work to improve the quality and timeliness of tourism data, to enable accurate assessment of the situation. In 2004 the group published its report on Best Practices in Safety and Security to Safeguard Tourism against Terrorism.

Trade Promotion: Aims to promote trade, as a key aspect of regional economic co-operation, through activities to enhance trade financing, skills and training, information and networking (for example, through the establishment of APECNet, providing information to the business community via the internet, accessible at www.apecnet.org.sg), and co-operation with the private sector and public agencies, including trade promotion organizations. Organizes an APEC International Trade Fair.

Transportation: Undertakes initiatives to enhance the efficiency and safety of the regional transportation system, in order to facilitate the development of trade. The working group focuses on three main areas: improving the competitiveness of the transportation industry; promoting a safe and environmentally-sound regional transportation system; and human resources development, including training, research and education. The group has published surveys, directories and manuals on all types of transportation systems, and has compiled an inventory on regional co-operation on oil spills preparedness and response arrangements. A Road Transportation Harmonization Project aims to provide the basis for common standards in the automotive industry in the Asia-Pacific region. The group has established an internet database on ports and the internet-based Virtual Centre for Transportation Research, Development and Education. It plans to develop a regional action plan on the implementation of Global Navigation Satellite Systems, in consultation with the relevant international bodies. In 2003 the group was involved in discussions on means of enhancing security throughout international and domestic supply chains in the region while facilitating cross-border movement of legitimate commerce. The group was also responsible for overseeing various projects in respect of counter-terrorism. A Special Task Force was established to assist member economies to implement a new International Ship and Port Facility Security Code, sponsored by the International Maritime Organization, which entered into force on 1 July 2004. In April 2004 an Aviation Safety Experts' Group met for the first time since 2000.

Publications

ABAC Report to APEC Leaders (annually).

APEC Business Travel Handbook.

APEC Economic Outlook (annually).

APEC Economies Beyond the Asian Crisis.

APEC Energy Handbook (annually).

APEC Energy Statistics (annually).

Foreign Direct Investment and APEC Economic Integration (irregular).

Guide to the Investment Regimes of the APEC Member Economies.

Key APEC Documents (annually).

Towards Knowledge-based Economies in APEC.

Trade and Investment Liberalization in APEC.

Working group reports, regional directories, other irregular surveys.

ASIAN DEVELOPMENT BANK—ADB

Address: 6 ADB Ave, Mandaluyong City, 0401 Metro Manila, Philippines; POB 789, 0980 Manila, Philippines.

Telephone: (2) 6324444; **fax:** (2) 6362444; **e-mail:** information@adb .org; **internet:** www.adb.org.

The ADB commenced operations in December 1966. The Bank's principal functions are to provide loans and equity investments for the economic and social advancement of its developing member countries, to give technical assistance for the preparation and implementation of development projects and programmes and advisory services, to promote investment of public and private capital for development purposes, and to respond to requests from developing member countries for assistance in the co-ordination of their development policies and plans.

MEMBERS

There are 45 member countries and territories within the ESCAP region and 18 others (see list of subscriptions below).

Organization

(April 2005)

BOARD OF GOVERNORS

All powers of the Bank are vested in the Board, which may delegate its powers to the Board of Directors except in such matters as admission of new members, changes in the Bank's authorized capital stock, election of Directors and President, and amendment of the Charter. One Governor and one Alternate Governor are appointed by each member country. The Board meets at least once a year. The 37th Bank Annual Meeting was convened in Juju Island, Republic of Korea, in May 2004, and the 39th meeting was scheduled to be held in Istanbul, Turkey, in May 2005.

BOARD OF DIRECTORS

The Board of Directors is responsible for general direction of operations and exercises all powers delegated by the Board of Governors, which elects it. Of the 12 Directors, eight represent constituency groups of member countries within the ESCAP region (with about 65% of the voting power) and four represent the rest of the member countries. Each Director serves for two years and may be re-elected.

Three specialized committees (the Audit Committee, the Budget Review Committee and the Inspection Committee), each comprising six members, assist the Board of Directors in exercising its authority with regard to supervising the Bank's financial statements, approving the administrative budget, and reviewing and approving policy documents and assistance operations.

The President of the Bank, though not a Director, is Chairman of the Board.

Chairman of Board of Directors and President: Haruhiko Kuroda (Japan).

Vice-Presidents: Joseph B. Eichenberger (USA), Khempheng Pholsena (Laos), Liquin Jin (People's Republic of China), Geert van der Linden (Netherlands).

ADMINISTRATION

The Bank had 2,311 staff at 31 December 2003.

On 1 January 2002 the Bank implemented a new organizational structure. The reorganization aimed to strengthen the Bank's country and sub-regional focus, as well as its capacity for poverty reduction and implementing its long-term strategic framework. Five regional departments cover East and Central Asia, the Mekong, the Pacific, South Asia, and South East Asia. Other departments and offices include Private Sector Operations, Central Operations Services, Regional and Sustainable Development, Strategy and Policy, Cofinancing Operations, and Economics and Research, as well as other administrative units.

There are Bank Resident Missions in Afghanistan, Azerbaijan, Bangladesh, Cambodia, the People's Republic of China, India, Indonesia, Kazakhstan, Kyrgyzstan, Laos, Mongolia, Nepal, Pakistan, Papua New Guinea, Sri Lanka, Tajikistan, Uzbekistan and Viet Nam, all of which report to the head of the regional department. In addition, the Bank has established a country office in the Philippines, Extended Missions in Gujarat, India and in Thailand, a Special Office in Timor-Leste, a Liaison Office in Turkmenistan, and a South Pacific Regional Mission, based in Vanuatu. Representative Offices are located in Tokyo, Japan, Frankfurt am Main, Germany (for Europe), and Washington, DC, USA (for North America).

Secretary: Jeremy Hovland.

General Counsel: Arthur M. Mitchell.

INSTITUTE

ADB Institute—ADBI: Kasumigaseki Bldg, 8th Floor, 2–5 Kasumigaseki 3-chome, Chiyoda-ku, Tokyo 100-6008, Japan; tel. (3) 3593-5500; fax (3) 3593-5571; e-mail info@adbi.org; internet www .adbi.org; f. 1997 as a subsidiary body of the ADB to research and analyse long-term development issues and to disseminate development practices through training and other capacity-building activities; Dean Dr Peter McCawley (Australia).

FINANCIAL STRUCTURE

The Bank's ordinary capital resources (which are used for loans to the more advanced developing member countries) are held and used entirely separately from its Special Funds resources (see below). A fourth General Capital Increase (GCI IV), amounting to US $26,318m. (or some 100%), was authorized in May 1994. At the final deadline for subscription to GCI IV, on 30 September 1996, 55 member countries had subscribed shares amounting to $24,675.4m.

At 31 December 2003 the position of subscriptions to the capital stock was as follows: authorized US $51,996.6m.; 'callable' subscribed $48,339.5m.

The Bank also borrows funds from the world capital markets. Total borrowings during 2003 amounted to US $4,141m. (compared with $6,145m. in 2002). At 31 December 2003 total outstanding borrowings amounted to $26,359m.

In July 1986 the Bank abolished the system of fixed lending rates, under which ordinary operations loans had carried interest rates fixed at the time of loan commitment for the entire life of the loan. Under the new system the lending rate is adjusted every six months, to take into account changing conditions in international financial markets.

SPECIAL FUNDS

The Asian Development Fund (ADF) was established in 1974 in order to provide a systematic mechanism for mobilizing and administering resources for the Bank to lend on concessionary terms to the least-developed member countries. In 1998 the Bank revised the terms of ADF. Since 1 January 1999 all new project loans are repayable within 32 years, including an eight-year grace period, while quick-disbursing programme loans have a 24-year maturity, also including an eight-year grace period. The previous annual service charge was redesignated as an interest charge, including a portion to cover administrative expenses. The new interest charges on all loans are 1%–1.5% per annum. During 2003 47 ADF loans were approved, amounting to US $1,379m.

Successive replenishments of the Fund's resources amounted to US $809m. for the period 1976–78, $2,150m. for 1979–82, $3,214m. for 1983–86, $3,600m. for 1987–90, $4,200m. for 1992–95, $6,300m. for 1997–2000, and $5,650m. for 2001–04. In May 2004 28 donor countries pledged $3,200m. towards the ADF's eighth replenishment (ADF IX), which totalled $7,000m. to provide resources for the period 2005–08

The Bank provides technical assistance grants from its Technical Assistance Special Fund (TASF). By the end of 2003, the Fund's total resources amounted to US $1,005.5m., of which $901.4m. had been utilized or committed. The Japan Special Fund (JSF) was established in 1988 to provide finance for technical assistance by means of grants, in both the public and private sectors. The JSF aims to help developing member countries restructure their economies, enhance the opportunities for attracting new investment, and recycle funds. The Japanese Government had committed a total of 99,200m. yen (equivalent to some $852.7m.) to the JSF by the end of 2003. During 2003 the Bank approved 66 technical assistance projects for the JSF, amounting to $36.9m. An Asian Currency Crisis Support Facility (ACCSF) was operational for the three-year period March 1999–March 2002, as an independent component of the JSF to provide additional technical assistance, interest payment assistance and guarantees to countries most affected by financial instability, i.e. Indonesia, Republic of Korea, Malaysia, Philippines and Thailand. At the end of 2002 the Japanese Government, as the sole financier of the fund, had contributed 27,500m. yen (some $241.0m.) to the ACCSF. The Japanese Government funds the Japan Scholarship Program, under which 1,621 scholarships had been awarded to recipients from 34 member countries between 1988 and 2003, and the ADB Institute Special Fund, which was established to finance the ADB Institute's initial operations. By 31 December 2003 cumulative commitments to the Special Fund amounted to 10,100m. yen (or $83.1m.). In May 2000 the Japan Fund for Poverty Reduction was established, with an initial contribution of 10,000m. yen (approximately $92.6m.) from the Japanese Government, to support ADB-financed poverty reduction and social development activities. By the end of 2003 cumulative commitments to the Fund totalled $302.4m. and 38 projects, amounting to $116m., had been approved for implementation. A Japan Fund for Information and Communication Technology (ICT) was established in July 2001, for a three-year period, to promote the advancement and use of ICT in developing member countries. The Fund was established with an initial contribution of 1,273m. yen (or $10.7m.) from the Japanese Government.

The majority of grant funds in support of the Bank's technical assistance activities are provided by bilateral donors under channel financing arrangements (CFAs), the first of which was negotiated in 1980. CFAs may also be processed as a thematic financing tool, for example concerned with renewable energy, water or poverty reduction, enabling more than one donor to contribute. In 2002 a new multi-donor thematic CFA with a focus on poverty reduction was introduced. In 2003 two new co-operative funds were established under CFA terms, relating to gender and development and to poverty and the environment.

Activities

Loans by the ADB are usually aimed at specific projects. In responding to requests from member governments for loans, the Bank's staff assesses the financial and economic viability of projects and the way in which they fit into the economic framework and priorities of development of the country concerned. In 1987 the Bank adopted a policy of lending in support of programmes of sectoral adjustment, not limited to specific projects; such loans were not to exceed 15% of total Bank public sector lending. In 1999 the Board of Directors increased the ceiling on programme lending to 20% of the annual total. In 1985 the Bank decided to expand its assistance to the private sector, hitherto comprising loans to development finance institutions, under government guarantee, for lending to small and medium-sized enterprises; a programme was formulated for direct financial assistance, in the form of equity and loans without government guarantee, to private enterprises. In 1992 a Social Dimensions

Unit was established as part of the central administrative structure of the Bank, which contributed to the Bank's increasing awareness of the importance of social aspects of development as essential components of sustainable economic growth. During the early 1990s the Bank also aimed to expand its role as project financier by providing assistance for policy formulation and review and promoting regional co-operation, while placing greater emphasis on individual country requirements. In accordance with its medium-term strategy for 1995–98 the Bank resolved to promote sound development management, by integrating into its operations and projects the promotion of governance issues, such as capacity-building, legal frameworks, and openness of information. During that period the Bank also introduced a commitment to assess development projects for their impact on the local population and to avoid all involuntary resettlement where possible and established a formal procedure for grievances, under which the Board may authorize an inspection of a project, by an independent panel of experts, at the request of the affected community or group. In 1998 the Bank approved a new anticorruption strategy.

The currency instability and ensuing financial crises affecting many Asian economies in the second half of 1997 and in 1998 prompted the Bank to reflect on its role in the region. The Bank resolved to strengthen its activities as a broad-based development institution, rather than solely as a project financier, through lending policies, dialogue, co-financing and technical assistance. A Task Force on Financial Sector Reform was established to review the causes and effects of the regional financial crisis. The Task Force identified the Bank's initial priorities as being to accelerate banking and capital market reforms in member countries, to promote market efficiency in the financial, trade and industrial sectors, to promote good governance and sound corporate management, and to alleviate the social impact of structural adjustments. In mid-1999 the Bank approved a technical assistance grant to establish an internet-based Asian Recovery Information Centre, within a new Regional Monitoring Unit, which aimed to facilitate access to information regarding the economic and social impact of the Asian financial crisis, analyses of economic needs of countries, reform programmes and monitoring of the economic recovery process. In November the Board of Directors approved a new overall strategy objective of poverty reduction, which was to be the principal consideration for all future Bank lending, project financing and technical assistance. The strategy incorporated key aims of supporting sustainable, grass-roots based economic growth, social development and good governance. The Board also approved a health sector policy, to concentrate resources on basic primary healthcare, and initiated reviews of the Bank's private sector strategy and the efficiency of resident missions. During 2000 the Bank began to refocus its country strategies, projects and lending targets to complement the poverty reduction strategy. In addition, it initiated a process of wide-ranging discussions to formulate a long-term strategic framework for the next 15 years, based on the target of reducing by 50% the incidence of extreme poverty by 2015, one of the so-called Millennium Development Goals identified by the UN General Assembly. The framework, establishing the operational priorities and principles for reducing poverty, was approved in March 2001. At the same time a medium-term strategy, for the period 2001–05, was approved, which aimed to enhance the development impact of the Bank's assistance and to define the operational priorities within the context of the strategic agenda.

On 1 June 2004 the Bank approved a new policy to provide rehabilitation and reconstruction assistance following disasters or other emergencies. The policy also aimed to assist developing member countries with prevention, preparation and mitigation of the impact of future disasters. At the end of December the Bank announced assistance amounting to US $325m. to finance immediate reconstruction and rehabilitation efforts in Indonesia, the Maldives and Sri Lanka, which had been severely damaged by a series of large waves, or tsunamis, that had spread throughout the Indian Ocean as a result of a massive earthquake that had occurred close to the west coast of Sumatra, Indonesia. Of the total amount $150m. was to be drawn as new lending commitments from the Asian Development Fund. Teams of Bank experts undertook to identify priority operations and initiated efforts, in co-operation with governments and other partner organizations, to prepare for more comprehensive reconstruction activities. In January 2005, at a Special ASEAN Leaders' Meeting, held in Jakarta, Indonesia, the Bank pledged assistance amounting to $500m.; later in that month the Bank announced its intention to establish a $600m. Multi-donor Asian Tsunami Trust Fund to accelerate the provision of reconstruction and technical assistance to countries most affected by the disaster. In March the Bank hosted a high-level co-ordination meeting on rehabilitation and reconstruction assistance to tsunami-affected countries.

In 2003 the Bank approved 85 loans for 66 projects amounting to US $6,104.8m. (compared with $5,658m. for 70 projects in 2002). Loans from ordinary capital resources in 2003 totalled $4,725.7m., while loans from the ADF amounted to $1,379.2m. Private-sector operations approved amounted to $562.7m., including loans of $187.0m., equity investments of $35.7m. and guarantees of $240.0m. The largest proportion of assistance, amounting to some 42% of total lending, was allocated to transport and communications projects. The largest borrowers were India (25% of total lending), the People's Republic of China (24%), and Pakistan (14%). Disbursements of loans during 2003 amounted to $3,816.2m., bringing cumulative disbursements to $70,186.3m.

In 2003 grants approved for technical assistance (e.g. project preparation, consultant services and training) amounted to US $176.5m. for 315 projects, with $86.7m. deriving from the TASF, $36.9m. from the JSF, and $52.9m. from other bilateral and multi-lateral sources. The Bank's Operations Evaluation Office prepares reports on completed projects, in order to assess achievements and problems. In April 2000 the Bank announced that, from 2001, some new loans would be denominated in local currencies, in order to ease the repayment burden on recipient economies.

The Bank co-operates with other international organizations active in the region, particularly the World Bank group, the IMF, UNDP and APEC, and participates in meetings of aid donors for developing member countries. In May 2001 the Bank and UNDP signed a memorandum of understanding (MOU) on strategic part-nership, in order to strengthen co-operation in the reduction of poverty, for example the preparation of common country assess-ments and a common database on poverty and other social indica-tors. Also in 2001 the Bank signed an MOU with the World Bank on administrative arrangements for co-operation, providing a frame-work for closer co-operation and more efficient use of resources. In early 2002 the Bank worked with the World Bank and UNDP to assess the preliminary needs of the interim administration in Afghanistan, in preparation for an International Conference on Reconstruction Assistance to Afghanistan, held in late January, in Tokyo. The Bank pledged to work with its member governments to provide highly concessional grants and loans of some US $500m. over two-and-a-half years, with a particular focus on road recon-struction, basic education, and agricultural irrigation rehabilitation. A new policy concerning co-operation with non-governmental organ-izations (NGOs) was approved by the Bank in 1998.

Finance

Internal administrative expenses totalled US $252.6m. in 2003. The budget for 2004 amounted to $279.5m.

Publications

ADB Business Opportunities (monthly).

ADB Institute Newsletter.

ADB Review (6 a year).

Annual Report.

Asian Development Outlook (annually).

Asian Development Review (2 a year).

Basic Statistics (annually).

Key Indicators of Developing Asian and Pacific Countries (annually).

Law and Policy Reform Bulletin (annually).

Loan Disbursement Handbook.

Studies and technical assistance reports, information brochures, guide-lines, sample bidding documents, staff papers.

Statistics

SUBSCRIPTIONS AND VOTING POWER
(31 December 2003)

Country	Subscribed capital (% of total)	Voting power (% of total)
Regional:		
Afghanistan	0.034	0.345
Australia	5.851	4.998
Azerbaijan	0.450	0.677
Bangladesh	1.032	1.143
Bhutan	0.006	0.322
Cambodia	0.050	0.357
China, People's Republic	6.516	5.530
Cook Islands	0.003	0.320
Fiji	0.069	0.372

Country— *continued*	Subscribed capital (% of total)	Voting power (% of total)
Hong Kong	0.551	0.758
India	6.402	5.439
Indonesia	5.507	4.723
Japan	15.781	12.942
Kazakhstan	0.816	0.970
Kiribati	0.004	0.321
Korea, Republic	5.094	4.393
Kyrgyzstan	0.302	0.559
Laos	0.014	0.329
Malaysia	2.754	2.520
The Maldives	0.004	0.321
Marshall Islands	0.003	0.320
Micronesia, Federated States	0.004	0.321
Mongolia	0.015	0.330
Myanmar	0.551	0.758
Nauru	0.004	0.321
Nepal	0.149	0.436
New Zealand	1.558	1.560
Pakistan	2.203	2.080
Palau	0.003	0.320
Papua New Guinea	0.095	0.393
Philippines	2.409	2.245
Samoa	0.003	0.320
Singapore	0.344	0.593
Solomon Islands	0.007	0.323
Sri Lanka	0.586	0.787
Taiwan	1.101	1.199
Tajikistan	0.290	0.549
Thailand	1.377	1.419
Timor-Leste	0.010	0.325
Tonga	0.004	0.321
Turkmenistan	0.256	0.522
Tuvalu	0.001	0.319
Uzbekistan	0.681	0.862
Vanuatu	0.007	0.323
Viet Nam	0.345	0.594
Sub-total	63.241	64.878
Non-regional:		
Austria	0.344	0.593
Belgium	0.344	0.593
Canada	5.289	4.549
Denmark	0.344	0.593
Finland	0.344	0.593
France	2.354	2.200
Germany	4.374	3.871
Italy	1.828	1.780
Luxembourg	0.344	0.593
Netherlands	1.037	1.147
Norway	0.344	0.593
Portugal	0.344	0.593
Spain	0.344	0.593
Sweden	0.344	0.593
Switzerland	0.590	0.790
Turkey	0.344	0.593
United Kingdom	2.065	1.970
USA	15.781	12.942
Sub-total	36.759	35.122
Total	100.000	100.000

LENDING ACTIVITIES BY SECTOR

	Loan Approvals (US $ million)		
	2003		1968–2003
Sector	Amount	%	%
Agriculture and natural resources	391.90	6.42	17.06
Energy	756.70	12.40	20.33
Finance	483.00	7.91	14.17
Industry and non-fuel minerals	0.00	—	3.16
Social infrastructure	1,130.51	18.52	16.24
Transport and communications	2,577.70	42.22	21.88
Multi-sector and others	765.00	12.54	7.17
Total	6,104.81	100.00	100.00

LENDING ACTIVITIES BY COUNTRY
(US $ million)

	Loans approved in 2003		
Country	Ordinary Capital	ADF	Total
Afghanistan	—	150.00	150.00
Azerbaijan	—	22.00	22.00
Bangladesh	286.00	246.00	532.00
Bhutan	—	9.40	9.40
Cambodia	—	98.26	98.26
China, People's Republic	1,488.00	—	1,488.00
Fiji	47.00	—	47.00
India	1,532.00	—	1,532.00
Indonesia	187.40	74.20	261.60
Kazakhstan	34.60	—	34.60
Kyrgyzstan	—	15.50	15.50
Laos	—	46.00	46.00
The Maldives	—	6.00	6.00

	Loans approved in 2003		
Country— *continued*	Ordinary Capital	ADF	Total
Mongolia	—	29.50	29.50
Nepal	—	94.00	94.00
Pakistan	692.70	178.00	870.70
Philippines	183.76	—	183.76
Samoa	—	8.00	8.00
Sri Lanka	90.00	185.29	275.29
Tajikistan	—	38.00	38.00
Thailand	40.00	—	40.00
Uzbekistan	99.20	—	99.20
Viet Nam	—	179.00	179.00
Regional	45.00	—	45.00
Total	**4,725.66**	**1,379.15**	**6,104.81**

Source: *ADB Annual Report 2003.*

ASSOCIATION OF SOUTH EAST ASIAN NATIONS— ASEAN

Address: 70A Jalan Sisingamangaraja, POB 2072, Jakarta 12110, Indonesia.
Telephone: (21) 7262991; **fax:** (21) 7398234; **e-mail:** public@aseansec.org; **internet:** www.aseansec.org.

ASEAN was established in August 1967 in Bangkok, Thailand, to accelerate economic progress and to increase the stability of the South-East Asian region.

MEMBERS

Brunei	Malaysia	Singapore
Cambodia	Myanmar	Thailand
Indonesia	Philippines	Viet Nam
Laos		

Organization

(April 2005)

SUMMIT MEETING

The highest authority of ASEAN, bringing together the heads of government of member countries. The first meeting was held in Bali, Indonesia, in February 1976. The 30th anniversary of the founding of ASEAN was commemorated at an informal gathering of heads of government in Kuala Lumpur, Malaysia, in December 1997. The ninth summit meeting was held in Bali, Indonesia, in October 2003, and the 10th meeting was held in Vientiane, Laos, in November 2004.

MINISTERIAL MEETINGS

The ASEAN Ministerial Meeting (AMM), comprising ministers of foreign affairs of member states, meets annually, in each member country in turn, to formulate policy guide-lines and to co-ordinate ASEAN activities. These meetings are followed by 'post-ministerial conferences' (PMCs), where ASEAN ministers of foreign affairs meet with their counterparts from countries that are 'dialogue partners' as well as with ministers from other countries. Ministers of economic affairs also meet once a year, to direct ASEAN economic co-operation. Joint Ministerial Meetings, consisting of ministers of foreign affairs and of economic affairs are convened prior to a summit meeting, and may be held at the request of either group of ministers. Other ministers meet regularly to promote co-operation in different sectors.

STANDING COMMITTEE

The Standing Committee normally meets every two months. It consists of the minister of foreign affairs of the host country and ambassadors of the other members accredited to the host country.

SECRETARIATS

A permanent secretariat was established in Jakarta, Indonesia, in 1976 to form a central co-ordinating body. The Secretariat comprises four bureaux relating to: Programme Co-ordination and External Relations; Trade, Industry and Services; Investment, Finance and Surveillance; and Economic and Functional Co-operation. The Secretary-General holds office for a five-year term, and is assisted by two Deputy Secretaries-General. In each member country day-to-day work is co-ordinated by an ASEAN National Secretariat.

Secretary-General: ONG KENG YONG (Singapore).

Deputy Secretaries-General: Dr WILFRIDO V. VILLACORTA (Philippines), Pengiran MASHOR Pengiran AHMAD (Brunei).

COMMITTEES AND SENIOR OFFICIALS' MEETINGS

Ministerial meetings are serviced by 29 committees of senior officials, supported by 122 technical working groups. There is a network of subsidiary technical bodies comprising sub-committees, expert groups, *ad hoc* working groups and working parties.

To support the conduct of relations with other countries and international organizations, ASEAN committees (composed of heads of diplomatic missions) have been established in 15 foreign capitals: those of Australia, Belgium, Canada, the People's Republic of China, France, Germany, India, Japan, the Republic of Korea, New Zealand, Pakistan, Russia, Switzerland, the United Kingdom and the USA. There is also an ASEAN committee in New York (USA).

Activities

ASEAN was established in 1967 with the signing of the ASEAN Declaration, otherwise known as the Bangkok Declaration, by the ministers of foreign affairs of Indonesia, Malaysia, the Philippines, Singapore and Thailand. In February 1976 the first ASEAN summit meeting adopted the Treaty of Amity and Co-operation and the Declaration of ASEAN Concord. Brunei joined the organization in January 1984, shortly after attaining independence. Viet Nam was admitted as the seventh member of ASEAN in July 1995. Laos and Myanmar joined in July 1997 and Cambodia was formally admitted in April 1999, fulfilling the organization's ambition to incorporate all 10 countries in the sub-region. In October 2003 ASEAN leaders adopted a declaration known as 'Bali Concord II', which committed signatory states to the creation of an ASEAN Economic Community, an ASEAN Security Community and an ASEAN Sociocultural Community. In early January 2005 a Special ASEAN Leaders' Meeting was convened in Jakarta, Indonesia, to consider the needs of countries affected by an earthquake and devastating tsunamis that had occurred in the Indian Ocean on 26 December 2004. The meeting, which was also attended the Secretary-General of the United Nations, the President of the World Bank and other senior envoys of donor countries and international organizations, adopted a Declaration on Action to Strengthen Emergency Relief, Rehabilitation,

Reconstruction and Prevention on the Aftermath of Earthquake and Tsunami Disaster.

TRADE AND ECONOMIC CO-OPERATION

A Basic Agreement on the Establishment of ASEAN Preferential Trade Arrangements was concluded in 1977. In December 1987, by which time the system covered only about 5% of trade between member states, the meeting of ASEAN heads of government resolved to reduce exclusions of any 'sensitive' products from preferential import tariffs to a maximum of 10% of the number of items traded and to a maximum of 50% of the value of trade, over the next five years (seven years for Indonesia and the Philippines).

In January 1992 heads of government, meeting in Singapore, signed an agreement to create an ASEAN Free Trade Area (AFTA) by 2008. In accordance with the agreement, a common effective preferential tariff (CEPT) scheme came into effect in January 1993. The CEPT covered all manufactured products, including capital goods, and processed agricultural products (which together accounted for two-thirds of intra-ASEAN trade), but was to exclude unprocessed agricultural products. Tariffs were to be reduced to a maximum of 20% within a period of five to eight years and to 0%–5% during the subsequent seven to 10 years. Fifteen categories were designated for accelerated tariff reduction. Member states were, however, still to be permitted exclusion for certain 'sensitive' products. In October 1993 ASEAN trade ministers agreed to modify the CEPT, with only Malaysia and Singapore having adhered to the original tariff reduction schedule. The new AFTA programme, under which all member countries except Brunei were scheduled to begin tariff reductions from 1 January 1994, substantially enlarged the number of products to be included in the tariff-reduction process (i.e. on the so-called 'inclusion list') and reduced the list of products eligible for protection. In September 1994 ASEAN ministers of economic affairs agreed to accelerate the implementation of AFTA, advancing the deadline for its entry into operation from 2008 to 1 January 2003. Tariffs were to be reduced to 0%–5% within seven to 10 years, or within five to eight years for products designated for accelerated tariff cuts. In July 1995 Viet Nam was admitted as a member of ASEAN and was granted until 2006 to implement the AFTA trade agreements. In December 1995 heads of government, at a meeting convened in Bangkok, Thailand, agreed to extend liberalization to certain service industries, including banking, telecommunications and tourism. In July 1997 Laos and Myanmar became members of ASEAN and were granted a 10-year period, from 1 January 1998, to comply with the AFTA schedule.

In December 1998, meeting in Hanoi, Viet Nam, heads of government approved a Statement on Bold Measures, detailing ASEAN's strategies to deal with the economic crisis that had prevailed in the region since late 1997. These included incentives to attract investors, for example a three-year exemption on corporate taxation, accelerated implementation of the ASEAN Investment Area (AIA, see below), and advancing the AFTA deadline, for the original six members, to 2002, with some 85% of products to be covered by the arrangements by 2000, and 90% by 2001. It was envisaged that the original six members and the new members would achieve the elimination of all tariffs by 2015 and 2018, respectively. The Hanoi Plan of Action, which was also adopted at the meeting as a framework for the development of the organization over the period 1999–2004, incorporated a series of measures aimed at strengthening macroeconomic and financial co-operation and enhancing economic integration. In April 1999 Cambodia, on being admitted as a full member of ASEAN, signed an agreement to implement the tariff reduction programme over a 10-year period, commencing 1 January 2000. Cambodia also signed a declaration endorsing the commitments of the 1998 Statement on Bold Measures. In May 2000 Malaysia was granted a special exemption to postpone implementing tariff reductions on motor vehicles for two years from 1 January 2003. In November 2000 a protocol was approved permitting further temporary exclusion of products from the CEPT scheme for countries experiencing economic difficulties. On 1 January 2002 AFTA was formally realized among the original six signatories (Brunei, Indonesia, Malaysia, the Philippines, Singapore and Thailand), which had achieved the objective of reducing to less than 5% trade restrictions on 96.24% of products on the inclusion list. Some 98.36% of tariff lines for the core six AFTA members were on the inclusion list at that time. Tariffs on trade in products on the inclusion list for these countries averaged less than 2.9% in 2002.

To complement AFTA in facilitating intra-ASEAN trade, member countries are committed to the removal of non-tariff barriers (such as quotas), the harmonization of standards and conformance measures, and the simplification and harmonization of customs procedures. In June 1996 the Working Group on Customs Procedures completed a draft legal framework for regional co-operation, designed to simplify and harmonize customs procedures, legislation and product classification. The agreement was signed in March 1997 at the inaugural meeting of ASEAN finance ministers. (Laos and Myanmar signed the customs agreement in July and Cambodia

assented to it in April 1999.) In 2001 ASEAN finalized its system of harmonized tariff nomenclature, implementation of which commenced in the following year.

At the seventh summit meeting, held in Brunei, in November 2001 heads of government discussed moving beyond the group's existing free-trade and investment commitments by deepening market liberalization. Specifically, it was proposed that negotiations on the liberalization of intra-ASEAN trade in services be accelerated. The third round of negotiations on liberalizing trade in services began at the end of 2001. Members also agreed to start negotiations on mutual recognition arrangements for professional services. The summit meeting stated that tariff preferences would be extended to ASEAN's newer members from January 2002, under the ASEAN Integration System of Preferences (AISP), thus allowing Cambodia, Laos, Myanmar and Viet Nam tariff-free access to the more developed ASEAN markets earlier than the previously agreed target date of 2010.

In November 2000 heads of government endorsed an Initiative for ASEAN Integration (IAI), which aimed to reduce economic disparities within the region through effective co-operation, in particular, in training and other educational opportunities. In July 2002 the AMM endorsed an IAI Work Plan, which focused on the following priority areas: human resources development; infrastructure; information and communications technology (ICT); and regional economic integration. The Plan was to be implemented over the six-year period 2002–08. An IAI Development Co-operation Forum was held in August.

At the eighth summit meeting, held in November 2002, in Phnom-Penh, Cambodia, ASEAN heads of state considered the Phnom-Penh Agenda, comprising the following four elements: collaboration with an ongoing initiative to promote economic co-operation in the Greater Mekong subregion, with a view to accelerating the pace of ASEAN integration; promoting ASEAN as a single tourist destination; solidarity for peace and security, especially in combating terrorism; and progress in sustainable natural resources management, including the ratification of the Kyoto Protocol to the UN Framework Convention on Climate Change.

In 1991 ASEAN ministers discussed a proposal of the Malaysian Government for the formation of an economic grouping, to be composed of ASEAN members, the People's Republic of China, Hong Kong, Japan, the Republic of Korea and Taiwan. In July 1993 ASEAN ministers of foreign affairs agreed a compromise, whereby the grouping was to be a caucus within APEC, although it was to be co-ordinated by ASEAN's meeting of economy ministers. In July 1994 ministers of foreign affairs of nine prospective members of the group held their first informal collective meeting; however, no progress was made towards forming the proposed East Asia Economic Caucus. There was renewed speculation on the formation of an East Asian grouping following the onset of the Asian financial crisis of the late 1990s. At an informal meeting of leaders of ASEAN countries, China, Japan and the Republic of Korea, held in November 1999, all parties (designating themselves 'ASEAN + 3') issued a Joint Statement on East Asian Co-operation, in which they agreed to strengthen regional unity, and addressed the long-term possibility of establishing an East Asian common market and currency. Meeting in May 2000, in Chiang Mai, Thailand, ASEAN + 3 ministers of economic affairs proposed the establishment of an enhanced currency-swap mechanism, enabling countries to draw on liquidity support to defend their economies during balance-of-payments difficulties or speculative currency attacks and to prevent future financial crises. In July ASEAN + 3 ministers of foreign affairs convened an inaugural formal summit in Bangkok, Thailand, and in October ASEAN + 3 economic affairs ministers agreed to hold their hitherto twice-yearly informal meetings on an institutionalized basis. In November an informal meeting of ASEAN + 3 leaders approved further co-operation in various sectors and initiated a feasibility study into a proposal to establish a regional free trade area. In May 2001 ASEAN + 3 ministers of economic affairs endorsed a series of projects for co-operation in ICT, environment, small and medium-sized enterprises, Mekong Basin development, and harmonization of standards. In the same month the so-called Chiang Mai Initiative on currency-swap arrangements was formally approved by ASEAN + 3 finance ministers. A meeting of the ASEAN + 3 leaders was held alongside the seventh ASEAN summit in November 2001. In October ASEAN + 3 agriculture and forestry ministers met for the first time, and discussed issues of poverty alleviation, food security, agricultural research and human resource development. The first meeting of ASEAN + 3 tourism ministers was held in January 2002. In July ASEAN + 3 ministers of foreign affairs declared their support for other regional initiatives, namely an Asia Co-operation Dialogue, which was initiated by the Thai Government in June, and an Initiative for Development in East Asia (IDEA), which had been announced by the Japanese Government in January. An IDEA ministerial meeting was convened in Tokyo, in August. ASEAN + 3 ministers of labour convened in May 2003. In August a meeting of ASEAN + 3 finance ministers agreed to establish a Finance Co-operation Fund, to be administered by the ASEAN

Secretariat; the Fund was to support ongoing economic reviews relating to projects such as the Chiang Mai Initiative. In September the sixth consultation between ASEAN + 3 ministers of economic affairs was held, at which several new projects were endorsed, including two on e-commerce. During 2004 an ASEAN + 3 Unit was established in the ASEAN Secretariat. The first meeting of ASEAN + 3 energy ministers was held in June. In November the ASEAN summit meeting agreed to convene an East Asia Summit in 2005.

The Bali Concord II, adopted in October 2003 (see above), affirmed commitment to existing ASEAN economic co-operation frameworks, including the Hanoi Plan of Action (and any subsequently agreed regional plans of action) and the IAI, and outlined plans for the creation, by 2020, of an integrated ASEAN Economic Community (AEC), entailing: the harmonization of customs procedures and technical regulations by the end of 2004; the removal of non-tariff trade barriers and the establishment of a network of free-trade zones by 2005; and the progressive withdrawal of capital controls and strengthening of intellectual property rights. An ASEAN legal unit was to be established to strengthen and enhance existing dispute settlement systems. The free movement of professional and skilled workers would be facilitated by standardizing professional requirements and simplifying visa procedures, with the adoption of a single ASEAN visa requirement envisaged by 2005. In 2004 ASEAN economic and trade ministers worked closely, in co-operation with the private sector, to produce a 'road map' for the integration of 11 sectors identified as priority areas in the AEC plan of action . In July the ASEAN Ministerial Meeting reviewed progress in preparing the Vientiane Action Programme (VAP), the proposed successor to the Hanoi Plan of Action. In November the 10th meeting of ASEAN heads of state, held in Vientiane, Laos, endorsed the VAP with commitments to deepen regional integration and narrow the development gap within the grouping. An ASEAN Development Fund was to be established to support the implementation of the VAP and other action programmes. The leaders adopted two plans of action (concerning security and socio-cultural affairs) to further the implementation of the Bali Concord II regarding the establishment of a three-pillared ASEAN Community. An ASEAN Framework Agreement for Integration of the Priority Sectors was also signed. Import duties were to be eliminated by 2007 for the original members (including Brunei) and by 2012 for newer member states on the following 11 sectors, accounting for more than 50% of intra-ASEAN trade in 2003: agro-based products, air travel, automotive, electronics, fisheries, healthcare, information and communications technology, rubber-based products, textiles and apparels, tourism and wood-based products.

INDUSTRY

The ASEAN-Chambers of Commerce and Industry (CCI) aims to enhance ASEAN economic and industrial co-operation and the participation in these activities of the private sector. In March 1996 a permanent ASEAN-CCI secretariat became operational at the ASEAN Secretariat. The first AIA Council-Business Sector Forum was convened in September 2001, with the aim of developing alliances between the public and private sectors. The seventh ASEAN summit in November resolved to encourage the private sector to convene a regular ASEAN Business Summit. It was also agreed to establish an ASEAN Business Advisory Council, which held its inaugural meeting in April 2003.

The ASEAN Industrial Co-operation (AICO) scheme, initiated in 1996, encourages companies in the ASEAN region to undertake joint manufacturing activities. Products derived from an AICO arrangement benefit immediately from a preferential tariff rate of 0%–5%. The AICO scheme superseded the ASEAN industrial joint venture scheme, established in 1983. The attractiveness of the scheme is expected slowly to diminish as ASEAN moves towards the full implementation of the CEPT scheme. ASEAN has initiated studies of new methods of industrial co-operation within the grouping, with the aim of achieving further integration. In April 2004 ASEAN economic ministers signed a Protocol to Amend the Basic Agreement on the AICO Scheme, which aimed to maintain it relevance and further efforts towards setting the tariff rate at 0%.

The ASEAN Consultative Committee on Standards and Quality (ACCSQ) aims to promote the understanding and implementation of quality concepts, considered to be important in strengthening the economic development of a member state and in helping to eliminate trade barriers. ACCSQ comprises three working groups: standards and information; conformance and assessment; and testing and calibration. By 2004 all member states had harmonized standards for 20 priority products and 81 safety standards. A Standards and Quality Bulletin is published regularly to disseminate information and promote transparency on standards, technical regulations and conformity assessment procedures. In September 1994 an *ad hoc* Working Group on Intellectual Property Co-operation was established, with a mandate to formulate a framework agreement on intellectual property co-operation and to strengthen ASEAN activities in intellectual property protection. An ASEAN Intellectual

Property Right Action Plan 2004–10 aimed, *inter alia,* to accelerate IP asset creation and to develop and harmonize regional mechanisms for IPR registration, protection and enforcement.

In 1988 the ASEAN Fund was established, with capital of US \$150m., to provide finance for portfolio investments in ASEAN countries, in particular for small and medium-sized enterprises (SMEs). The Hanoi Plan of Action, which was adopted by ASEAN heads of state in December 1998, incorporated a series of initiatives to enhance the development of SMEs, including training and technical assistance, co-operation activities and greater access to information. In September 2004 ASEAN economic ministers approved an ASEAN Policy Blueprint for SME Development 2004–14, first proposed by a working group in 2001, which comprised strategic work programmes and policy measures for the development of SMEs in the region.

FINANCE, BANKING AND INVESTMENT

In 1987 heads of government agreed to accelerate regional financial co-operation, to support intra-ASEAN trade and investment. They adopted measures to increase the role of ASEAN currencies in regional trade, to assist negotiations on the avoidance of double taxation, and to improve the efficiency of tax and customs administrators. An ASEAN Reinsurance Corporation was established in 1988, with initial authorized capital of US \$10m. In December 1995 the summit meeting proposed the establishment of an ASEAN Investment Area (AIA). Other measures to attract greater financial resource flows in the region, including an ASEAN Plan of Action for the Promotion of Foreign Direct Investment and Intra-ASEAN Investment, were implemented during 1996.

In February 1997 ASEAN central bank governors agreed to strengthen efforts to combat currency speculation through the established network of foreign-exchange repurchase agreements. However, from mid-1997 several Asian currencies were undermined by speculative activities. Subsequent unsuccessful attempts to support the foreign-exchange rates contributed to a collapse in the value of financial markets in some countries and to a reversal of the region's economic growth, at least in the short term, while governments undertook macroeconomic structural reforms. In early December ASEAN ministers of finance, meeting in Malaysia, agreed to liberalize markets for financial services and to strengthen surveillance of member country economies, to help prevent further deterioration of the regional economy. The ministers also endorsed a proposal for the establishment of an Asian funding facility to provide emergency assistance in support of international credit and structural reform programmes. At the informal summit meeting held later in December, ASEAN leaders issued a joint statement in which they expressed the need for mutual support to counter the region's financial crisis and urged greater international assistance to help overcome the situation and address the underlying problems. The heads of government also resolved to accelerate the implementation of the AIA.

In July 1998 the ASEAN Ministerial Meeting endorsed the decisions of finance ministers, taken in February, to promote greater use of regional currencies for trade payments and to establish an economic surveillance mechanism. In October ministers of economic affairs, meeting in Manila, the Philippines, signed a framework agreement on the AIA, which was expected to provide for equal treatment of domestic and other ASEAN direct investment proposals within the grouping by 2010, and of all foreign investors by 2020. The meeting also confirmed that the proposed ASEAN Surveillance Process (ASP), to monitor the economic stability and financial systems of member states, would be implemented with immediate effect, and would require the voluntary submission of economic information by all members to a monitoring committee, to be based in Jakarta, Indonesia. The ASP and the framework agreement on the AIA were incorporated into the Hanoi Plan of Action, adopted by heads of state in December 1998. The December summit meeting also resolved to accelerate reforms, particularly in the banking and financial sectors, in order to strengthen the region's economies, and to promote the liberalization of the financial services sector.

In March 1999 ASEAN ministers of trade and industry, meeting in Phuket, Thailand, as the AIA Council, agreed to open their manufacturing, agriculture, fisheries, forestry and mining industries to foreign investment. Investment restrictions affecting those industries were to be eliminated by 2003 in most cases, although Laos and Viet Nam were granted until 2010. In addition, ministers adopted a number of measures to encourage investment in the region, including access to three-year corporate income-tax exemptions, and tax allowances of 30% for investors. The AIA agreement formally entered into force in June 1999, having been ratified by all member countries. Under the agreement, member countries submitted individual action plans for 2000–04, noting specific action to be taken in the areas of investment promotion, facilitation and liberalization. In September 2001 ministers agreed to accelerate the full realization of the AIA for non-ASEAN investors in manufacturing, agriculture, forestry, fishing and mining sectors. The date for full implementation was advanced to 2010 for the original six ASEAN members and to 2015 for the newer members.

In November 2001 ASEAN heads of state considered the difficulties facing member countries as a result of the global economic and political uncertainties following the terrorist attacks on the USA in September. The summit meeting noted the recent decline in foreign direct investment and the erosion of the region's competitiveness. Short-term priorities were stated to be the stimulation of economies to lessen the impact of reduced external demand, and the adoption of appropriate fiscal and monetary policies, together with a renewed commitment to structural reform.

In April 2002 ASEAN economy ministers signed an agreement to facilitate intra-regional trade in electrical and electronic equipment by providing for the mutual recognition of standards (for example, testing and certification). The agreement was also intended to lower the costs of trade in those goods, thereby helping to maintain competitiveness.

SECURITY

In 1971 ASEAN members endorsed a declaration envisaging the establishment of a Zone of Peace, Freedom and Neutrality (ZOPFAN) in the South-East Asian region. This objective was incorporated in the Declaration of ASEAN Concord, which was adopted at the first summit meeting of the organization, held in Bali, Indonesia, in February 1976. (The Declaration also issued guide-lines for co-operation in economic development and the promotion of social justice and welfare.) Also in February 1976 a Treaty of Amity and Co-operation was signed by heads of state, establishing principles of mutual respect for the independence and sovereignty of all nations, non-interference in the internal affairs of one another and settlement of disputes by peaceful means. The Treaty was amended in December 1987 by a protocol providing for the accession of Papua New Guinea and other non-member countries in the region; it was reinforced by a second protocol, signed in July 1998. In July 2004 Indonesia, Japan, the Republic of Korea, Pakistan and Russia acceded to the Treaty.

In December 1995 ASEAN heads of government, meeting in Bangkok, Thailand, signed a treaty establishing a South-East Asia Nuclear-Weapon Free Zone (SEANWFZ). The treaty was also signed by Cambodia, Myanmar and Laos. It was extended to cover the offshore economic exclusion zones of each country. On ratification by all parties, the Treaty was to prohibit the manufacture or storage of nuclear weapons within the region. Individual signatories were to decide whether to allow port visits or transportation of nuclear weapons by foreign powers through territorial waters. The Treaty entered into force on 27 March 1997. ASEAN senior officials were mandated to oversee implementation of the Treaty, pending the establishment of a permanent monitoring committee. In July 1999 the People's Republic of China and India agreed to observe the terms of the SEANWFZ.

In January 1992 ASEAN leaders agreed that there should be greater co-operation on security matters within the grouping, and that ASEAN's post-ministerial conferences (PMCs) should be used as a forum for discussion of questions relating to security with dialogue partners and other countries. In July 1992 the ASEAN Ministerial Meeting issued a statement calling for a peaceful resolution of the dispute concerning the strategically significant Spratly Islands in the South China Sea, which are claimed, wholly or partly, by the People's Republic of China, Viet Nam, Taiwan, Brunei, Malaysia and the Philippines. (In February China had introduced legislation that defined the Spratly Islands as belonging to its territorial waters.) Viet Nam's accession to ASEAN in July 1995, bringing all the Spratly Islands claimants except China and Taiwan into the grouping, was expected to strengthen ASEAN's position of negotiating a multilateral settlement on the islands. In 1999 ASEAN established a special committee to formulate a code of conduct for the South China Sea to be observed by all claimants to the Spratly Islands. A draft code of conduct was approved in November 1999. In November 2002 ASEAN and China's foreign ministers adopted a Declaration on the Conduct of Parties in the South China Sea, agreeing to promote a peaceful environment and durable solutions for the area, to resolve territorial disputes by peaceful means, to refrain from undertaking activities that would aggravate existing tensions (such as settling unpopulated islands and reefs), and to initiate a regular dialogue of defence officials.

In July 1997 ASEAN ministers of foreign affairs reiterated their commitment to the principle of non-interference in the internal affairs of other countries. However, the group's efforts in Cambodia (see below) marked a significant shift in diplomatic policy towards one of 'constructive intervention', which had been proposed by Malaysia's Deputy Prime Minister in recognition of the increasing interdependence of the region. At the Ministerial Meeting in July 1998 Thailand's Minister of Foreign Affairs, supported by his Philippine counterpart, proposed that the grouping formally adopt a policy of 'flexible engagement'. The proposal, based partly on concerns that the continued restrictions imposed by the Myanma

authorities on dissident political activists was damaging ASEAN relations with its dialogue partners, was to provide for the discussion of the affairs of other member states when they have an impact on neighbouring countries. While rejecting the proposal, other ASEAN ministers agreed to pursue a more limited version, referred to as 'enhanced interaction', and to maintain open dialogue within the grouping. In September 1999 the unrest prompted by the popular referendum on the future of East Timor (now Timor-Leste) and the resulting humanitarian crisis highlighted the unwillingness of some ASEAN member states to intervene in other member countries and undermined the political unity of the grouping. A compromise agreement, enabling countries to act on an individual basis rather than as representatives of ASEAN, was formulated prior to an emergency meeting of ministers of foreign affairs, held during the APEC meetings in Auckland, New Zealand. Malaysia, the Philippines, Singapore and Thailand declared their support for the establishment of a multinational force to restore peace in East Timor and committed troops to participate in the Australian-led operation. At their informal summit in November 1999 heads of state approved the establishment of an ASEAN Troika, which was to be constituted as an *ad hoc* body comprising the foreign ministers of the Association's current, previous and future chairmanship with a view to providing a rapid response mechanism in the event of a regional crisis.

On 12 September 2001 ASEAN issued a ministerial statement on international terrorism, condemning the attacks of the previous day in the USA and urging greater international co-operation to counter terrorism. The seventh summit meeting in November issued a Declaration on a Joint Action to Combat Terrorism. This condemned the September attacks, stated that terrorism was a direct challenge to ASEAN's aims, and affirmed the grouping's commitment to strong measures to counter terrorism. The summit encouraged member countries to sign (or ratify) the International Convention for the Suppression of Financing of Terrorism, to strengthen national mechanisms against terrorism, and to work to deepen co-operation, particularly in the area of intelligence exchange; international conventions to combat terrorism would be studied to see if they could be integrated into the ASEAN structure, while the possibility of developing a regional anti-terrorism convention was discussed. The summit noted the need to strengthen security co-operation to restore investor confidence. In its Declaration and other notes, the summit explicitly rejected any attempt to link terrorism with religion or race, and expressed concern for the suffering of innocent Afghanis during the US military action against the Taliban authorities in Afghanistan. The summit's final Declaration was worded so as to avoid any mention of the US action, to which Muslim ASEAN states such as Malaysia and Indonesia were strongly opposed. In November 2002 the eighth summit meeting adopted a Declaration on Terrorism, reiterating and strengthening the measures announced in the previous year. In January 2003 ASEAN police chiefs proposed the establishment of a network of national anti-terrorism task forces, to work in close co-operation with one another.

In June 1999 the first ministerial meeting to consider issues relating to transnational crime was convened. Regular meetings of senior officials and ministers were subsequently held. The third ministerial meeting, in October 2001, considered initiatives to combat transnational crime, which was defined as including terrorism, trafficking in drugs, arms and people, money-laundering, cyber-crime, piracy and economic crime. In May 2002 ministers responsible for transnational crime issues convened a Special Ministerial Meeting on Terrorism, held in Kuala Lumpur, Malaysia. The meeting approved a work programme to implement a plan of action to combat transnational crime, including information exchange, the development of legal arrangements for extradition, prosecution and seizure, the enhancement of co-operation in law enforcement, and the development of regional security training programmes. In a separate initiative Indonesia, Malaysia and the Philippines signed an agreement on information exchange and the establishment of communication procedures. Cambodia acceded to the agreement in July. In November 2004 ASEAN leaders adopted an ASEAN Declaration against Trafficking in Persons, Particularly Women and Children, which aimed to strengthen co-operation to prevent and combat trafficking, through, *inter alia*, the establishment of a new regional focal network, information-sharing procedures and standardized immigration controls.

ASEAN Regional Forum (ARF): In July 1993 the meeting of ASEAN ministers of foreign affairs sanctioned the establishment of a forum to discuss and promote co-operation on security issues within the region, and, in particular, to ensure the involvement of the People's Republic of China in regional dialogue. The ARF was informally initiated during that year's PMC, comprising the ASEAN countries, its dialogue partners (at that time Australia, Canada, the EC, Japan, the Republic of Korea, New Zealand and the USA), and the People's Republic of China, Laos, Papua New Guinea, Russia and Viet Nam. The first formal meeting of the ARF was conducted in July 1994, following the Ministerial Meeting held in Bangkok,

Thailand, and it was agreed that the ARF would be convened on an annual basis. The 1995 meeting, held in Brunei, in August, attempted to define a framework for the future of the Forum. It was perceived as evolving through three stages: the promotion of confidence-building (including disaster relief and peace-keeping activities); the development of preventive diplomacy; and the elaboration of approaches to conflict. The 19 ministers of foreign affairs attending the meeting (Cambodia participated for the first time) recognized that the ARF was still in the initial stage of implementing confidence-building measures. The ministers, having conceded to a request by China not to discuss explicitly the Spratly Islands, expressed concern at overlapping sovereignty claims in the region. In a further statement, the ministers urged an 'immediate end' to the testing of nuclear weapons, then being undertaken by the French Government in the South Pacific region. The third ARF, convened in July 1996, which was attended for the first time by India and Myanmar, agreed a set of criteria and guiding principles for the future expansion of the grouping. In particular, it was decided that the ARF would only admit as participants countries that had a direct influence on the peace and security of the East Asia and Pacific region. The ARF held in July 1997 reviewed progress made in developing the first two 'tracks' of the ARF process, through the structure of inter-sessional working groups and meetings. The Forum's consideration of security issues in the region was dominated by concern at the political situation in Cambodia; support was expressed for ASEAN mediation to restore stability within that country. Myanmar and Laos attended the ARF for the first time. Mongolia was admitted into the ARF at its meeting in July 1998. India rejected a proposal that Pakistan attend the meeting to discuss issues relating to both countries' testing of nuclear weapons. The meeting ultimately condemned the testing of nuclear weapons in the region, but declined to criticize specifically India and Pakistan. In July 1999 the ARF warned the Democratic People's Republic of Korea (DPRK) not to conduct any further testing of missiles over the Pacific. At the seventh meeting of the ARF, convened in Bangkok, Thailand, in July 2000, the DPRK was admitted to the Forum. The meeting considered the positive effects and challenges of globalization, including the possibilities for greater economic interdependence and for a growth in transnational crime. The eighth ARF meeting in July 2001 in Hanoi, Viet Nam, pursued these themes, and also discussed the widening development gap between nations. The meeting agreed to enhance the role of the ARF Chairman, enabling him to issue statements on behalf of ARF participants and to organize events during the year. In March and April 2002 ARF workshops were held on financial measures against terrorism and on the prevention of terrorism, respectively. The ninth ARF meeting, held in Bandar Seri Begawan, Brunei, in July, assessed regional and international security developments, and issued a statement of individual and collective intent to prevent any financing of terrorism. The statement included commitments by participants to freeze the assets of suspected individuals or groups, to implement international financial standards and to enhance co-operation and the exchange of information. In October the Chairman, on behalf of all ARF participants, condemned the terrorist bomb attacks committed against tourist targets in Bali, Indonesia. Pakistan joined the ARF process as its 24th participant in July 2004.

Since 2000 the ARF has published the *Annual Security Outlook*, to which participating countries submit assessments of the security prospects in the region.

EXTERNAL RELATIONS

ASEAN's external relations have been pursued through a dialogue system, initially with the objective of promoting co-operation in economic areas with key trading partners. The system has been expanded in recent years to encompass regional security concerns and co-operation in other areas, such as the environment. The ARF (see above) emerged from the dialogue system, and more recently the formalized discussions of ASEAN with Japan, China and the Republic of Korea (ASEAN + 3) has evolved as a separate process with its own strategic agenda.

European Union: In March 1980 a co-operation agreement was signed between ASEAN and the European Community (EC, as the EU was known prior to its restructuring on 1 November 1993), which provided for the strengthening of existing trade links and increased co-operation in the scientific and agricultural spheres. A Joint Co-operation Committee met in November (and annually thereafter). An ASEAN-EC Business Council was launched in December 1983, and three European Business Information Councils have since been established, in Malaysia, the Philippines and Thailand, to promote private-sector co-operation. The first meeting of ministers of economic affairs from ASEAN and EC member countries took place in October 1985. In December 1990 the Community adopted new guidelines on development co-operation, with an increase in assistance to Asia, and a change in the type of aid given to ASEAN members, emphasizing training, science and technology and venture capital,

rather than assistance for rural development. In October 1992 the EC and ASEAN agreed to promote further trade between the regions, as well as bilateral investment, and made a joint declaration in support of human rights. An EU-ASEAN Junior Managers Exchange Programme was initiated in November 1996, as part of efforts to promote co-operation and understanding between the industrial and business sectors in both regions. An ASEAN-EU Business Network was established in Brussels in 2001, to develop political and commercial contacts between the two sides.

In May 1995 ASEAN and EU senior officials endorsed an initiative to strengthen relations between the two economic regions within the framework of an Asia-Europe Meeting of heads of government (ASEM). The first ASEM was convened in Bangkok, Thailand, in March 1996, at which leaders approved a new Asia-Europe Partnership for Greater Growth. The second ASEM summit meeting, held in April 1998, focused heavily on economic concerns. In February 1997 ministers of foreign affairs of countries participating in ASEM met in Singapore. Despite ongoing differences regarding human rights issues, in particular concerning ASEAN's granting of full membership status to Myanmar and the situation in East Timor (which precluded the conclusion of a new co-operation agreement), the Ministerial Meeting issued a final joint declaration, committing both sides to strengthening co-operation and dialogue on economic, international and bilateral trade, security and social issues. A protocol to the 1980 co-operation agreement was signed, enabling the participation of Viet Nam in the dialogue process. In November 1997 a session of the Joint Co-operation Committee was postponed and later cancelled, owing to a dispute concerning objections by the EU to the participation of Myanmar. A compromise agreement, allowing Myanma officials to attend meetings as 'silent' observers, was concluded in November 1998. However, a meeting of the Joint Co-operation Committee, scheduled to take place in January 1999, was again cancelled, owing to controversy over perceived discrimination by the EU against Myanmar's status. The meeting was finally convened in Bangkok, Thailand, in late May. The third ASEM summit meeting was convened in Seoul, Korea in October 2000. In December an ASEAN-EU Ministerial Meeting was held in Vientiane, Laos. Both sides agreed to pursue dialogue and co-operation and issued a joint declaration that accorded support for the efforts of the UN Secretary-General's special envoy towards restoring political dialogue in Myanmar. Myanmar agreed to permit an EU delegation to visit the country, and opposition leaders, in early 2001. In September 2001 the Joint Co-operation Committee met for the first time since 1999 and resolved to strengthen policy dialogue, in particular in areas fostering regional integration. Four new EU delegations were to be established—in Cambodia, Laos, Myanmar and Singapore. At the 14th ASEAN-EU Ministerial Meeting, held in Brussels, Belgium, in January 2003, delegates adopted an ASEAN-EU Joint Declaration on Co-operation to Combat Terrorism. An ASEM seminar on combating terrorism was held in Beijing, People's Republic of China, in October. In February the EU awarded ASEAN €4.5m. under the ASEAN-EU Programme on Regional Integration Support (APRIS) to enhance progress towards establishing AFTA. In April the EU proposed the creation of a regional framework, the Trans-Regional EU-ASEAN Trade Initiative (TREATI), to address mutual trade facilitation, investment and regulatory issues. It was suggested that the framework might eventually result in a preferential trade agreement. In January 2004 a joint statement was issued announcing a 'road map' for implementing the TREATI and an EU-ASEAN work plan for that year. The fifth ASEM meeting of heads of state and government was held in Hanoi, Viet Nam, in October, attended for the first time by the 10 new members of the EU and by Cambodia, Laos, and Myanmar.

People's Republic of China: Efforts to develop consultative relations between ASEAN and China were initiated in 1993. Joint Committees on economic and trade co-operation and on scientific and technological co-operation were subsequently established. The first formal consultations between senior officials of the two sides were held in April 1995. In July 1996, in spite of ASEAN's continued concern at China's territorial claims to the Spratly Islands in the South China Sea, China was admitted to the PMC as a full dialogue partner. In February 1997 a Joint Co-operation Committee was established to co-ordinate the China-ASEAN dialogue and all aspects of relations between the two sides. Relations were further strengthened by the decision to form a joint business council to promote bilateral trade and investment. China participated in the informal summit meeting held in December, at the end of which both sides issued a joint statement affirming their commitment to resolving regional disputes through peaceful means. A second meeting of the Joint Co-operation Committee was held in March 1999. China was a participant in the first official ASEAN + 3 meeting of foreign ministers, which was convened in July 2000. An ASEAN-China Experts Group was established in November, to consider future economic co-operation sond free-trade opportunities. The Group held its first meeting in April 2001 and proposed a framework agreement on economic co-operation and the establishment of an ASEAN-China free-trade area within 10 years (with differential treatment and flexibility for newer ASEAN members). Both proposals were endorsed at the seventh ASEAN summit meeting in November 2001. China also agreed to grant preferential tariff treatment for some goods from Cambodia, Laos and Myanmar. In November 2002 an agreement on economic co-operation was concluded by the ASEAN member states and China. The Framework Agreement on Comprehensive Economic Co-operation between ASEAN and China entered into force in July 2003,and envisaged the establishment of an ASEAN-China Free Trade Area (ACFTA) by 2010. The Agreement provided for strengthened co-operation in key areas including agriculture, information and telecommunications, and human resources development. It was also agreed to implement the consensus of the Special ASEAN-China Leaders' Meeting on SARS, held the previous April, and set up an ASEAN + 1 special fund for health co-operation. In October China acceded to the Treaty on Amity and Co-operation and signed a joint declaration with ASEAN on Strategic Partnership for Peace and Prosperity on strengthening co-operation in politics, economy, social affairs, security and regional and international issues. It was also agreed to continue consultations on China's accession to the SEANWFZ and to expedite the implementation of the Joint Statement on Co-operation in the Field of Non-Traditional Security Issues and the Declaration on the Conduct of Parties in the South China Sea.

Japan: The ASEAN-Japan Forum was established in 1977 to discuss matters of mutual concern in trade, investment, technology transfer and development assistance. The first meeting between the two sides at ministerial level was held in October 1992. At this meeting, and subsequently, ASEAN requested Japan to increase its investment in member countries and to make Japanese markets more accessible to ASEAN products, in order to reduce the trade deficit with Japan. Since 1993 ASEAN-Japanese development and cultural co-operation has expanded under schemes including the Inter-ASEAN Technical Exchange Programme, the Japan-ASEAN Co-operation Promotion Programme and the ASEAN-Japan Friendship Programme. In December 1997 Japan, attending the informal summit meeting in Malaysia, agreed to improve market access for ASEAN products and to provide training opportunities for more than 20,000 young people in order to help develop local economies. In December 1998 ASEAN heads of government welcomed a Japanese initiative, announced in October, to allocate US $30,000m. to promote economic recovery in the region. In mid-2000 a new Japan-ASEAN General Exchange Fund (JAGEF) was established to promote and facilitate the transfer of technology, investment and personnel. In November 1999 Japan, along with the People's Republic of China and the Republic of Korea, attending an informal summit meeting of ASEAN, agreed to strengthen economic and political co-operation with the ASEAN countries, to enhance political and security dialogue, and to implement joint infrastructure and social projects. Japan participated in the first official ASEAN + 3 meeting of foreign ministers, which was convened in July 2000. An ASEAN-Japan Experts Group, similar to that for China, was to be established to consider how economic relations between the two sides can be strengthened. In recent years Japan has provided ICT support to ASEAN countries, and has offered assistance in environmental and health matters and for educational training and human resource development (particularly in engineering). In October 2003 ASEAN and Japan signed a Framework for Comprehensive Partnership. In mid-December Japan concluded a joint action plan with ASEAN with provisions on reinforcing economic integration within ASEAN and enhancing competitiveness, and on addressing terrorism, piracy and other transnational issues. A joint declaration was also issued on starting discussions in 2005 on the possibility of establishing an ASEAN-Japan FTA by 2012. In November 2004 the ASEAN-Japan summit meeting agreed to commence negotiations on a Comprehensive Economic Partnership agreement in April 2005.

Australia and New Zealand: In 1999 ASEAN and Australia undertook to establish the ASEAN-Australia Development Co-operation Programme (AADCP), to replace an economic co-operation programme which had begun in 1974. In August 2002 the two sides signed a formal memorandum of understanding on the AADCP. It was to comprise three core elements, with assistance amounting to $A45m.: a Program Stream, to address medium-term issues of economic integration and competitiveness; a Regional Partnerships Scheme for smaller collaborative activities; and the establishment of a Regional Economic Policy Support Facility within the ASEAN Secretariat. All components were to be fully operational by 2003. Co-operation relations with New Zealand are based on the Inter-Institutional Linkages Programme and the Trade and Investment Promotion Programme, which mainly provide assistance in forestry development, dairy technology, veterinary management and legal aid training. An ASEAN-New Zealand Joint Management Committee was established in November 1993, to oversee the implementation of co-operation projects. New Zealand's English Language Training for Officials Programme is among the most important of these projects. In September 2001 ASEAN ministers of

economic affairs signed a Framework for Closer Economic Partnership (CEP) with their counterparts from Australia and New Zealand (the Closer Economic Relations—CER—countries), and agreed to establish a Business Council to involve the business communities of all countries in the CEP. The CEP was perceived as a first step towards the creation of a free-trade area between ASEAN and CER countries. The establishment of such an area would strengthen the grouping's bargaining position regionally and multilaterally, and bring benefits such as increased foreign direct investment and the possible relocation of industry.

Other countries: The USA gives assistance for the development of small and medium-sized businesses and other projects, and supports a Center for Technology Exchange. In 1990 ASEAN and the USA established an ASEAN-US Joint Working Group, whose purpose is to review ASEAN's economic relations with the USA and to identify measures by which economic links could be strengthened. In recent years, dialogue has increasingly focused on political and security issues. In August 2002 ASEAN ministers of foreign affairs met with their US counterpart, and signed a Joint Declaration for Co-operation to Combat International Terrorism. At the same time, the USA announced the ASEAN Co-operation Plan, which was to include activities in the fields of ICT, agricultural biotechnology, health, disaster response and training for the ASEAN Secretariat. ASEAN-Canadian co-operation projects include fisheries technology, the telecommunications industry, use of solar energy, and a forest seed centre. A Working Group on the Revitalization of ASEAN-Canada relations met in February 1999. At a meeting in Bangkok, Thailand, in July 2000, the two sides agreed to explore less formal avenues for project implementation.

In July 1991 the Republic of Korea was accepted as a 'dialogue partner' in ASEAN, and in December a joint ASEAN-Korea Chamber of Commerce was established. In 1995 co-operation projects on human resources development, science and technology, agricultural development and trade and investment policies were implemented. The Republic of Korea participated in ASEAN's informal summit meetings in December 1997 and November 1999 (see above), and took part in the first official ASEAN + 3 meeting of foreign ministers, convened in July 2000. The Republic's assistance in the field of ICT has become particularly valuable in recent years. In March 2001, in a sign of developing co-operation, ASEAN and the Republic of Korea exchanged views on political and security issues in the region for the first time. The ASEAN-Korea Work Programme for 2001–03 covered, among other areas, the environment, transport, science and technology and cultural sectors. In November 2004 an ASEAN-Korea summit meeting agreed to initiate negotiations in early 2005 on the establishment of a free-trade area between the two sides, with the aim of eliminating tariffs on 80% of products by 2009.

In July 1993 both India and Pakistan were accepted as sectoral partners, providing for their participation in ASEAN meetings in sectors such as trade, transport and communications and tourism. An ASEAN-India Business Council was established, and met for the first time, in New Delhi, in February 1995. In December 1995 the ASEAN summit meeting agreed to enhance India's status to that of a full dialogue partner; India was formally admitted to the PMC in July 1996. At a meeting of the ASEAN-India Working Group in March 2001 the two sides agreed to pursue co-operation in new areas, such as health and pharmaceuticals, social security and rural development. The fourth meeting of the ASEAN-India Joint Co-operation Committee in January 2002 agreed to strengthen co-operation in these areas and others, including technology. The first ASEAN-India consultation between ministers of economic affairs, which took place in September, resulted in the adoption as a long-term objective, of the ASEAN-India Regional Trade and Investment Area. The first ASEAN-India summit at the level of heads of state was held in Phnom Penh, Cambodia, in November. An ASEAN-Pakistan Joint Business Council met for the first time in February 2000. In early 2001 both sides agreed to co-operate in projects relating to new and renewable energy resources, ICT, agricultural research and transport and communications. In October 2003 India acceded to the Treaty of Amity and Co-operation and signed a joint Framework Agreement on Comprehensive Economic Co-operation, which was to enter into effect in July 2004. The objectives of the Agreement included: strengthening and enhancing economic, trade and investment co-operation; liberalizing and promoting trade in goods and services; and facilitating economic integration within ASEAN. Various initiatives were discussed in the fields of agriculture, biotechnology, and human resources development; and both sides adopted the Joint Declaration for Co-operation to Combat International Terrorism. It was also agreed that negotiations would begin on establishing an ASEAN-India Regional Trade and Investment Area (RTIA), including a free-trade area, by 2016.

In March 2000 the first ASEAN-Russia business forum opened in Kuala Lumpur, Malaysia. In 2003 an economic co-operation agreement between Russia and ASEAN was under consideration. In 2004 Russia acceded to the Treaty of Amity and Co-operation in Southeast

Asia. The first ASEAN-Russia summit meeting was scheduled to be held in 2005.

Indo-China: In July 1992 Viet Nam and Laos signed ASEAN's Treaty of Amity and Co-operation and subsequently participated in ASEAN meetings and committees as observers. Viet Nam was admitted as a full member of ASEAN in July 1995. In that month Myanmar signed the Treaty of Amity and Co-operation. In July 1996 ASEAN granted Myanmar observer status and admitted it to the ARF, despite the expression of strong reservations by (among others) the Governments of Australia, Canada and the USA owing to the human rights situation in Myanmar. In November ASEAN heads of government, attending an informal summit meeting in Jakarta, Indonesia, agreed to admit Myanmar as a full member of the grouping at the same time as Cambodia and Laos. While Cambodia's membership was postponed, Laos and Myanmar were admitted to ASEAN in July 1997.

Cambodia was accorded observer status in July 1995. In May 1997 ASEAN ministers of foreign affairs confirmed that Cambodia, together with Laos and Myanmar, was to be admitted to the grouping in July of that year. In mid-July, however, Cambodia's membership was postponed owing to the deposition of Prince Ranariddh, and the resulting civil unrest. Later in that month Cambodia's *de facto* leader, Second Prime Minister Hun Sen, agreed to ASEAN's pursuit of a mediation role in restoring stability in the country and in preparing for democratic elections. In early August the ministers of foreign affairs of Indonesia, the Philippines and Thailand, representing ASEAN, met Hun Sen to confirm these objectives. A team of ASEAN observers joined an international monitoring mission to supervise the election held in Cambodia in July 1998. International approval of the conduct of the election, and consequently of Hun Sen's victory, prompted ASEAN to agree to reconsider Cambodia's admission into the Association. In December, following the establishment of a coalition administration in Cambodia, the country was welcomed, by the Vietnamese Government, as the 10th member of ASEAN, despite an earlier meeting of ministers of foreign affairs failing to reach a consensus decision. Its formal admission took place on 30 April 1999.

In June 1996 ministers of ASEAN countries, and of the People's Republic of China, Cambodia, Laos and Myanmar adopted a framework for ASEAN-Mekong Basin Development Co-operation. The initiative aimed to strengthen the region's cohesiveness, with greater co-operation on issues such as drugs-trafficking, labour migration and terrorism, and to facilitate the process of future expansion of ASEAN. Groups of experts and senior officials were to be convened to consider funding issues and proposals to link the two regions, including a gas pipeline network, rail links and the establishment of a common time zone. In December 1996 the working group on rail links appointed a team of consultants to conduct a feasibility study of the proposals. The completed study was presented at the second ministerial conference on ASEAN-Mekong Basin Development Co-operation, convened in Hanoi, Viet Nam, in July 2000. At the November 2001 summit China pledged US $5m. to assist with navigation along the upper stretches of the Mekong River, while other means by which China could increase its investment in the Mekong Basin area were considered. At the meeting the Republic of Korea was invited to become a core member of the grouping. Other growth regions sponsored by ASEAN include the Brunei, Indonesia, Malaysia, Philippines, East ASEAN Growth Area (BIMP-EAGA), the Indonesia, Malaysia, Singapore Growth Triangle (IMS-GT), and the West-East Corridor within the Mekong Basin Development initiative.

AGRICULTURE, FISHERIES AND FORESTRY

In October 1983 a ministerial agreement on fisheries co-operation was concluded, providing for the joint management of fish resources, the sharing of technology, and co-operation in marketing. In July 1994 a Conference on Fisheries Management and Development Strategies in the ASEAN region resolved to enhance fish production through the introduction of new technologies, aquaculture development, improvements of product quality and greater involvement by the private sector.

Co-operation in forestry is focused on joint projects, funded by ASEAN's dialogue partners, which include a Forest Tree Seed Centre, an Institute of Forest Management and the ASEAN Timber Technology Centre. In April 1995 representatives of the ASEAN Secretariat and private-sector groups met to co-ordinate the implementation of a scheme to promote the export of ASEAN agricultural and forestry products. In recent years ASEAN has urged member countries to take action to prevent illegal logging in order to prevent the further degradation of forest resources.

ASEAN holds an emergency rice reserve, amounting to 87,000 metric tons, as part of its efforts to ensure food security in the region. There is an established ASEAN programme of training and study exchanges for farm workers, agricultural experts and members of agricultural co-operatives. During 1998 ASEAN was particularly concerned with the impact of the region's economic crisis on the

agricultural sector, and the possible effects of climatic change. In September ministers of agriculture and forestry, meeting in Hanoi, Viet Nam, endorsed a Strategic Plan of Action on ASEAN Co-operation in Food, Agriculture and Forestry for 1999–2004. The Plan focused on programmes and activities aimed at enhancing food security, the international competitiveness of ASEAN food, agriculture and forestry products, promoting the sustainable use and conservation of natural resources, encouraging greater involvement by the private sector in the food and agricultural industry, and strengthening joint approaches on international and regional issues. An ASEAN Task Force has been formed to harmonize regulations on agricultural products derived from biotechnology. In December 1998 heads of state determined to establish an ASEAN Food Security Information Service to enhance the capacity of member states to forecast and manage food supplies. In 1999 agriculture ministers endorsed guide-lines on assessing risk from genetically modified organisms (GMOs) in agriculture, to ensure a common approach. In 2001 work was undertaken to increase public and professional awareness of GMO issues, through workshops and studies. In October 2004 ministers of agriculture and forestry, meeting in Yangon, Myanmar, endorsed a Strategic Plan of Action on ASEAN Co-operation in Food, Agriculture and Forestry 2005–10. The ministers also approved certain regional food standards, endorsed the establishment of an ASEAN Animal Health Trust Fund, and resolved to establish a Task Force to co-ordinate regional co-operation for the control and eradication of highly pathogenic avian influenza ('avian flu').

MINERALS AND ENERGY

The ASEAN Centre for Energy (ACE), based in Jakarta, Indonesia, provides an energy information network, promotes the establishment of interconnecting energy structures among ASEAN member countries, supports the development of renewable energy resources and encourages co-operation in energy efficiency and conservation. An ASEAN energy business forum is held annually and attended by representatives of the energy industry in the private and public sectors. Efforts to establish an ASEAN electricity grid were initiated in 1990. An ASEAN Interconnection Masterplan Study Working Group was established in April 2000 to formulate a study on the power grid. In November 1999 a Trans-ASEAN Gas Pipeline Task Force was established. In July 2002 ASEAN ministers of energy signed a Memorandum of Understanding to implement the pipeline project, involving seven interconnections. The meeting also approved initial plans for the implementation of the regional power grid initiative. ASEAN has forged partnerships with the EU and Japan in the field of energy, under the ASEAN Plan of Action for Energy Co-operation, running from 1999–2004. In June 2004 ASEAN ministers of energy adopted the Plan of Action for Energy Co-operation 2004–09.

A Framework of Co-operation in Minerals was adopted by an ASEAN working group of experts in August 1993. The group has also developed a programme of action for ASEAN co-operation in the development and utilization of industrial minerals, to promote the exploration and development of mineral resources, the transfer of mining technology and expertise, and the participation of the private sector in industrial mineral production. The programme of action is implemented by an ASEAN Regional Development Centre for Mineral Resources, which also conducts workshops and training programmes relating to the sector.

TRANSPORT AND COMMUNICATIONS

ASEAN aims to promote greater co-operation in the transport and communications sector, and in particular, to develop multi-modal transport; to harmonize road transport laws and regulations; to improve air space management; to develop ASEAN legislation for the carriage of dangerous goods and waste by land and sea; and to achieve interoperability and interconnectivity in telecommunications. The summit meeting of December 1998 agreed to work to develop a trans-ASEAN transportation network by 2000, comprising principal routes for the movement of goods and people. In September 1999 ASEAN ministers of transport and communications resolved to establish working groups to strengthen co-operation within the sector and adopted a programme of action for development of the sector in 1999–2004. By September 2001, under the action programme, a harmonized road route numbering system had been completed, a road safety implementation work plan agreed, and two pilot courses, on port management and traffic engineering and safety, had been adopted. A Framework Agreement on Facilitation of Goods in Transit entered into force in October 2000. In September 2002 ASEAN transport ministers signed Protocol 9 on Dangerous Goods, one of the implementing protocols under the framework agreement, which provided for the simplification of procedures for the transportation of dangerous goods within region using internationally accepted rules and guide-lines.

ASEAN is seeking to develop a Competitive Air Services Policy, possibly as a first step towards the creation of an ASEAN Open Skies

Policy. In September 2000 a meeting of transport ministers agreed to embark on a study to formulate maritime shipping policy, to cover, *inter alia*, issues of transshipment, the competitiveness of ports, liberalization, and the integration of maritime shipping into the overall transport system. In October 2001 ministers approved the third package of commitments for the air and transport sectors under the ASEAN framework agreement on services (according to which member countries were to liberalize the selling and marketing of air and maritime transport services). A protocol to implement the forth package of commitments was signed by ministers in November 2004. In September 2002 ASEAN senior transport officials signed the Memorandum of Understanding on Air Freight Services, which represented the first stage in full liberalization of air freight services in the region.

In October 1999 an e-ASEAN initiative was launched, aiming to promote and co-ordinate e-commerce and internet utilization. In November 2000 the informal meeting of ASEAN heads of government approved an e-ASEAN Framework Agreement to further the aims of the initiative. The Agreement incorporated commitments to develop and strengthen ASEAN's information infrastructure, in order to provide for universal and affordable access to communications services. Tariff reduction on ICT products was to be accelerated, with the aim of eliminating all tariffs in the sector by 2010. In July 2001 ministers of foreign affairs discussed measures for the economic liberalization of ICT products and for developing ICT capabilities in poorer member countries. In the same month the first meeting of ASEAN ministers responsible for telecommunications was held, in Kuala Lumpur, Malaysia, during which a Ministerial Understanding on ASEAN co-operation in telecommunications and ICT was signed. In September ASEAN ministers of economic affairs approved a list of ICT products eligible for the elimination of duties under the e-ASEAN Framework Agreement. This was to take place in three annual tranches, commencing in 2003 for the six original members of ASEAN and in 2008 for the newer member countries. During 2001 ASEAN continued to develop a reference framework for e-commerce legislation; it aimed to have e-commerce legislation in place in all member states by 2003. The second ASEAN telecommunications ministerial meeting was held in Manila, the Philippines, in August 2002. The meeting issued a declaration incorporating commitments to exploit ASEAN's competitive position in the field of ICT and to fulfil the obligations of the e-ASEAN Framework Agreement. The ministers also resolved to enhance co-operation with China, Japan and Korea with regard to ICT.

SCIENCE AND TECHNOLOGY

ASEAN's Committee on Science and Technology (COST) supports co-operation in food science and technology, meteorology and geophysics, microelectronics and ICT, biotechnology, non-conventional energy research, materials science and technology, space technology applications, science and technology infrastructure and resources development, and marine science. There is an ASEAN Science Fund, used to finance policy studies in science and technology and to support information exchange and dissemination.

The Hanoi Plan of Action, adopted in December 1998, envisaged a series of measures aimed at promoting development in the fields of science and technology, including the establishment of networks of science and technology centres of excellence and academic institutions, the creation of a technology scan mechanism, the promotion of public- and private-sector co-operation in scientific and technological (particularly ICT) activities, and an increase in research on strategic technologies. In September 2001 the ASEAN Ministerial Meeting on Science and Technology, convened for its first meeting since 1998, approved a new framework for implementation of ASEAN's Plan of Action on Science and Technology during the period 2001–04. The Plan aimed to help less developed member countries become competitive in the sector and integrate into regional co-operation activities. In September 2003 ASEAN and the People's Republic of China inaugurated a Network of East Asian Think-tanks to promote scientific and technological exchange.

ENVIRONMENT

A ministerial meeting on the environment in April 1994 approved long-term objectives on environmental quality and standards for the ASEAN region, aiming to enhance joint action in addressing environmental concerns. At the same time, ministers adopted standards for air quality and river water to be achieved by all ASEAN member countries by 2010. In June 1995 ministers agreed to co-operate to counter the problems of transboundary pollution.

In December 1997 ASEAN heads of state endorsed a Regional Haze Action Plan to address the environmental problems resulting from forest fires, which had afflicted several countries in the region throughout that year. A Haze Technical Task Force undertook to implement the plan in 1998, with assistance from the UN Environment Programme. In March ministers of the environment requested international financial assistance to help mitigate the dangers of forest fires in Indonesia, which had suffered an estimated US

$1,000m. in damage in 1997. Sub-regional fire-fighting arrangement working groups for Sumatra and Borneo were established in April 1998 and in May the Task Force organized a regional workshop to strengthen ASEAN capacity to prevent and alleviate the haze caused by the extensive fires. A pilot project of aerial surveillance of the areas in the region most at risk of forest fires was initiated in July. In December heads of government resolved to establish an ASEAN Regional Research and Training Centre for Land and Forest Fire Management. In March 2002 members of the workings groups on sub-regional fire-fighting arrangements for Sumatra and Borneo agreed to intensify early warning efforts and surveillance activities in order to reduce the risks of forest fires. In June ASEAN ministers of the environment signed an Agreement on Transboundary Haze Pollution, which was intended to provide a legal basis for the Regional Haze Action Plan. The Agreement, which entered into force in November 2003, required member countries to co-operate in the prevention and mitigation of haze pollution, for example, by responding to requests for information by other states and facilitating the transit of personnel and equipment in case of disaster. The Agreement also provided for the establishment of an ASEAN Co-ordination Centre for Transboundary Haze Pollution Control. An ASEAN Specialized Meteorological Centre (ASMC) based in Singapore, plays a primary role in long-range climatological forecasting, early detection and monitoring of fires and haze.

In April 2000 ministers adopted a Strategic Plan of Action on the Environment for 1999–2004. Activities under the Plan focused on issues of coastal and marine erosion, nature conservation and biodiversity, the implementation of multilateral environmental agreements, and forest fires and haze. Other ASEAN environmental objectives include the implementation of a water conservation programme and the formation and adoption of an ASEAN protocol on access to genetic resources. An ASEAN Regional Centre for Biodiversity Conservation (ARCBC) was established in February 1999. It held several workshops in 2000 and 2001, on issues including genetically modified organisms, access to genetic resources and data sharing. In May 2001 environment ministers launched the ASEAN Environment Education Action Plan (AEEAP), with the aim of making citizens 'environmentally literate', and willing and able to participate in sustainable regional development. In November 2003 ASEAN + 3 ministers of environment agreed to prioritize environmental activities in ten key areas: environmentally sustainable cities; global environmental issues; land and forest fires and transboundary haze pollution; coastal and marine environment; sustainable forest management; freshwater resources; public awareness and environmental education; promotion of green technologies and cleaner production; sustainable development monitoring and reporting.

SOCIAL DEVELOPMENT

ASEAN concerns in social development include youth development, the role of women, health and nutrition, education, labour affairs and disaster management. In December 1993 ASEAN ministers responsible for social affairs adopted a Plan of Action for Children, which provided a framework for regional co-operation for the survival, protection and development of children in member countries. ASEAN supports efforts to combat drug abuse and illegal drugs-trafficking. It aims to promote education and drug-awareness campaigns throughout the region, and administers a project to strengthen the training of personnel involved in combating drug abuse. In October 1994 a meeting of ASEAN Senior Officials on Drug Matters approved a three-year plan of action on drug abuse, providing a framework for co-operation in four priority areas: preventive drug education; treatment and rehabilitation; law enforcement; and research. In July 1998 ASEAN ministers of foreign affairs signed a Joint Declaration for a Drug-Free ASEAN, which envisaged greater co-operation among member states, in particular in information exchange, educational resources and legal procedures, in order to eliminate the illicit production, processing and trafficking of narcotic substances by 2020. (This deadline was subsequently advanced to 2015.)

The seventh ASEAN summit meeting, held in November 2001, declared work on combating HIV and AIDS to be a priority. The second phase of a work programme to combat AIDS and provide help for sufferers was endorsed at the meeting. Heads of government expressed their readiness to commit the necessary resources for prevention and care, and to attempt to obtain access to cheaper drugs. More than 1.5m. people in South-East Asia were known to be infected with HIV. An ASEAN task force on AIDS has been operational since March 1993. An ASEAN Co-operation Forum on HIV/AIDS was held in February 2003, in Bangkok, Thailand. In April a Special ASEAN Leaders' Meeting on Severe Acute Respiratory Syndrome (SARS) endorsed the recommendations of ministers of health, who convened in special session a few days previously, and agreed to establish an *ad hoc* ministerial-level Joint Task Force to follow-up and monitor implementation of those decisions. Co-operation measures approved included public information and education campaigns, health and immigration control procedures, and the establishment of an early-warning system on emerging infectious diseases.

In December 1998 ASEAN leaders approved a series of measures aimed at mitigating the social impact of the financial and economic crises that had affected many countries in the region. Plans of Action were formulated on issues of rural development and poverty eradication, while Social Safety Nets, which aimed to protect the most vulnerable members of society, were approved. The summit meeting emphasized the need to promote job generation as a key element of strategies for economic recovery and growth. The fourth meeting of ministers of social welfare in August 2001 noted the need for a holistic approach to social problems, integrating social and economic development. The summit meeting in November considered the widening development gap between ASEAN members and concluded that bridging this gap was a priority. The meeting approved an Initiative for ASEAN Integration Work Plan, which identified infrastructure development, human resource development, access to ICT and the promotion of regional economic integration as priority areas of activity, in particular to assist the newer signatory states, i.e. Cambodia, Laos, Myanmar and Viet Nam.

In January 1992 the ASEAN summit meeting resolved to establish an ASEAN University Network (AUN) to hasten the development of a regional identity. A draft AUN Charter and Agreement were adopted in 1995. The Network aims to strengthen co-operation within the grouping, develop academic and professional human resources and transmit information and knowledge. The 17 universities linked in the network carry out collaborative studies and research programmes. At the seventh ASEAN summit in November 2001 heads of government agreed to establish the first ASEAN University, in Malaysia.

TOURISM

National tourist organizations from ASEAN countries meet regularly to assist in co-ordinating the region's tourist industry, and a Tourism Forum is held annually to promote the sector. The first formal meeting of ASEAN ministers of tourism was held in January 1998, in Cebu, the Philippines. The meeting adopted a Plan of Action on ASEAN Co-operation in Tourism, which aimed to promote intra-ASEAN travel, greater investment in the sector, joint marketing of the region as a single tourist destination and environmentally sustainable tourism. In January 1999 the second meeting of ASEAN ministers of tourism agreed to appoint country co-ordinators to implement various initiatives, including the designation of 2002 as 'Visit ASEAN Millennium Year'; research to promote the region as a tourist destination in the 21st century, and to develop a cruise-ship industry; and the establishment of a network of ASEAN Tourism Training Centres to develop new skills and technologies in the tourist industry. The third meeting of tourism ministers, held in Bangkok, Thailand, in January 2000, agreed to reformulate the Visit ASEAN Millennium Year initiative as a long-term Visit ASEAN programme. This was formally launched in January 2001 at the fourth ministerial meeting. The first phase of the programme promoted brand awareness through an intense marketing effort; the second phase, initiated at the fifth meeting of tourism ministers, held in Yogyakarta, Indonesia, in January 2002, was to direct campaigns towards end-consumers. Ministers urged member states to abolish all fiscal and non-fiscal travel barriers, to encourage tourism, including intra-ASEAN travel. In November 2002 the eighth summit of heads of state adopted a framework agreement on ASEAN co-operation in tourism, aimed at facilitating domestic and intra-regional travel. ASEAN national tourism organizations signed an implementation plan for the agreement in May 2003, when they also announced a Declaration on Tourism Safety and Security. In December 2003 an online heritage network was established with a view to boosting tourism by promoting the region's cultural diversity. In February 2004 ASEAN tourism ministers adopted an Action Plan for the Implementation of the ASEAN Tourism Agreement, which aimed to promote integration of the region's tourist industry. The third phase of the Visit ASEAN initiative commenced in early 2004 and aimed to promote intra-ASEAN travel.

CULTURE AND INFORMATION

Regular workshops and festivals are held in visual and performing arts, youth music, radio, television and films, and print and interpersonal media. In addition, ASEAN administers a News Exchange and provides support for the training of editors, journalists and information officers. In 2000 ASEAN adopted new cultural strategies, with the aims of raising awareness of the grouping's objectives and achievements, both regionally and internationally. The strategies included: producing ASEAN cultural and historical educational materials; promoting cultural exchanges (especially for young people); and achieving greater exposure of ASEAN cultural activities and issues in the mass media. ASEAN ministers responsible for culture and arts met for the first time in October 2003.

In July 1997 ASEAN ministers of foreign affairs endorsed the establishment of an ASEAN Foundation to promote awareness of the organization and greater participation in its activities; this was inaugurated in July 1998 and is based at the ASEAN secretariat building (www.aseanfoundation.org).

Publications

Annual Report.

Annual Security Report.

ASEAN Investment Report (annually).

ASEAN State of the Environment Report (1st report: 1997; 2nd report: 2000).

Business ASEAN (quarterly).

Public Information Series, Briefing Papers, Documents Series, educational materials

BANK FOR INTERNATIONAL SETTLEMENTS—BIS

Address: Centralbahnplatz 2, 4002 Basel, Switzerland.
Telephone: (61) 2808080; **fax:** (61) 2809100; **e-mail:** email@bis.org; **internet:** www.bis.org.

The Bank for International Settlements was founded pursuant to the Hague Agreements of 1930 to promote co-operation among national central banks and to provide additional facilities for international financial operations.

Organization

(April 2005)

GENERAL MEETING

The General Meeting is held annually in June and is attended by representatives of the central banks of countries in which shares have been subscribed. At early 2005 the central banks of the following authorities were entitled to attend and vote at General Meetings of the BIS: Algeria, Argentina, Australia, Austria, Belgium, Bosnia and Herzegovina, Brazil, Bulgaria, Canada, the People's Republic of China, Croatia, the Czech Republic, Denmark, Estonia, Finland, France, Germany, Greece, Hong Kong, Hungary, Iceland, India, Indonesia, Ireland, Israel, Italy, Japan, the Republic of Korea, Latvia, Lithuania, the former Yugoslav republic of Macedonia, Malaysia, Mexico, the Netherlands, New Zealand, Norway, the Philippines, Poland, Portugal, Romania, Russia, Saudi Arabia, Singapore, Slovakia, Slovenia, South Africa, Spain, Sweden, Switzerland, Thailand, Turkey, the United Kingdom and the USA. Since the redefinition in February 2003 of the Federal Republic of Yugoslavia (FRY) as Serbia and Montenegro, with two central banks, the status of the FRY's issue of capital at the BIS remains under review. The European Central Bank became a shareholder in December 1999.

BOARD OF DIRECTORS

The Board of Directors is responsible for the conduct of the Bank's operations at the highest level, and comprises the Governors in office of the central banks of Belgium, Canada, France, Germany, Italy, Japan, the Netherlands, Sweden, Switzerland, the United Kingdom and the USA, and also appointed directors from six of these countries. The statutes also provide for the election to the Board of not more than nine Governors of other member central banks: those of Canada, Japan, the Netherlands, Sweden and Switzerland are elected members of the Board.

Chairman of the Board and President of the Bank: Nout Wellink (Netherlands).

MANAGEMENT

The Bank has a staff of about 550 employees, from 49 countries. In July 1998 the BIS inaugurated its first overseas administrative unit, the Representative Office for Asia and the Pacific, which is based in Hong Kong. A Regional Treasury dealing room became operational at the Hong Kong office in October 2000, with the aim of improving access for Asian central banks to BIS financial services during their trading hours. In November 2002 a Representative Office for the Americas was inaugurated in Mexico City, Mexico.

General Manager: MALCOLM D. KNIGHT (Canada).

Activities

The BIS is an international financial institution whose role is to promote international monetary and financial co-operation, and to fulfil the function of a 'central banks' bank'. Although it has the legal form of a company limited by shares, it is an international organization governed by international law, and enjoys special privileges and immunities in keeping with its role (a Headquarters Agreement was concluded with Switzerland in 1987). The participating central banks were originally given the option of subscribing the shares themselves or arranging for their subscription in their own countries. In January 2001, however, an extraordinary general meeting amended the Bank's statutes to restrict ownership to central banks. Accordingly, all shares then held by private shareholders (representing 14% of the total share capital) were repurchased at a compensation rate of 16,000 Swiss francs per share.

FINANCE

Until the end of the 2002/03 financial year the Bank's unit of account was the gold franc. An extraordinary general meeting in March 2003 amended the Bank's statutes to redenominate the Bank's share capital in Special Drawing Rights (SDRs), the unit of account of the International Monetary Fund, with effect from 1 April 2003, in order to enhance the efficiency and transparency of the Bank's operations. The meeting decided that the nominal value of shares would be rounded down from SDR 5,696 at 31 March 2003 to SDR 5,000, entailing a reduction of 12.2% in the total share capital. The excess of SDR 92.1m. was transferred to the Bank's reserve funds. The average value of the SDR in 2003 was US $1.39883. The authorized capital of the Bank at 31 March 2004 was 1,500m. gold francs (SDR 3,000), divided into 600,000 shares of equal value.

Statement of Account
(In SDR millions; 31 March 2004)

Assets		%
Gold and gold deposits	9,073.8	5.4
Cash on hand and on sight a/c		
with banks	18.9	0.0
Treasury bills	30,240.7	18.0
Time deposits and advances . .	68,162.4	40.6
Securities	55,318.3	32.9
Miscellaneous	3,528.1	2.1
Total	167,934.8	100.0

Liabilities		%
Deposits (gold)	7,293.5	4.3
Deposits (currencies)	133,152.5	79.3
Accounts payable	12,169.4	7.2
Other liabilities	5,709.4	3.4
Shareholders' equity	9,610.0	5.7
Total	167,934.8	100.0

BANKING OPERATIONS

The BIS assists central banks in managing and investing their monetary reserves: in 2004 some 140 international financial institutions and central banks from all over the world had deposits with the BIS, representing around 6% of world foreign exchange reserves.

The BIS uses the funds deposited with it partly for lending to central banks. Its credit transactions may take the form of swaps against gold; covered credits secured by means of a pledge of gold or marketable short-term securities; credits against gold or currency deposits of the same amount and for the same duration held with the BIS; unsecured credits in the form of advances or deposits; or standby credits, which in individual instances are backed by guarantees given by member central banks.

The BIS also engages in traditional types of investment: funds not required for lending to central banks are placed in the market as deposits with commercial banks and purchases of short-term nego-tiable paper, including Treasury bills. Such operations constitute a major part of the Bank's business. Increasingly the Bank has developed its own investment services for central banks, including short-term products and longer-term financial instruments.

Central banks' monetary reserves often need to be available at short notice, and need to be placed with the BIS at short term, for fixed periods and with clearly defined repayment terms. The BIS has to match its assets to the maturity structure and nature of its commitments, and must therefore conduct its business with special regard to maintaining a high degree of liquidity.

The Bank's operations must be in conformity with the monetary policy of the central banks of the countries concerned. It is not permitted to make advances to governments or to open current accounts in their name. Real estate transactions are also excluded.

INTERNATIONAL MONETARY CO-OPERATION

Governors of central banks meet for regular discussions at the BIS to co-ordinate international monetary policy and ensure orderly conditions on the international financial markets. There is close co-operation with the IMF and the World Bank. The BIS participates in meetings of the so-called Group of 10 (G-10) industrialized nations (see IMF, see p. 111), which has been a major forum for discussion of international monetary issues since its establishment in 1962. Governors of central banks of the G-10 countries convene for regular Basel Monthly Meetings. In 1971 a Standing Committee of the G-10 central banks was established at the BIS to consider aspects of the development of Euro-currency markets. In February 1999 the G-10 renamed the body the Committee on the Global Financial System, and approved a revised mandate to undertake systematic short-term monitoring of global financial system conditions; longer-term analysis of the functioning of financial markets; and the articulation of policy recommendations aimed at improving market functioning and promoting stability. A Markets Committee (formerly known as the Committee on Gold and Foreign Exchange, established in 1962) comprises senior officials responsible for market operations in the G-10 central banks. It meets regularly to consider developments in foreign exchange and related financial markets, possible future trends and short-run implications of events on market functioning. In 1990 a Committee on Payment and Settlement Systems was established to monitor and analyse developments in domestic payment, settlement and clearing systems, and cross-border and multi-currency systems. It meets three times a year.

In 1974 the Governors of central banks of the G-10 set up the Basel Committee on Banking Supervision (whose secretariat is provided by the BIS) to co-ordinate banking supervision at the international level. The Committee pools information on banking supervisory regulations and surveillance systems, including the supervision of banks' foreign currency business, identifies possible danger areas and proposes measures to safeguard the banks' solvency and liquidity. An International Conference of Banking Supervisors is held every two years. In 1997 the Committee published new guidelines, entitled Core Principles for Effective Banking Supervision, that were intended to provide a comprehensive set of standards to ensure sound banking. In 1998 the Committee was concerned with the development and implementation of the Core Principles, particularly given the ongoing financial and economic crisis affecting several Asian countries and instability of other major economies. In January 2001 the Committee issued preliminary proposals on capital adequacy rules. In June 2004 the Committee approved a revised framework of the International Convergence of Capital Measurement and Capital Standards (also known as Basel II) which aimed to promote improvements in risk management and strengthen the stability of the financial system. A Financial Stability Institute was established in 1998, jointly by the BIS and Basel Committee, to enhance the capacity of central banks and supervisory bodies to implement aspects of the Core Principles, through the provision of training programmes and other policy workshops.

The BIS hosts the secretariat of the Financial Stability Forum, which was established following a meeting in February 1999 of ministers of finance and governors of the central banks of the Group of Seven (G-7) industrialized nations. The Forum aims to strengthen co-operation among the world's largest economies and economic bodies to improve the monitoring of international finance, to reduce the tendency for financial shocks to spread from one economy to another, and thus to prevent a recurrence of economic crises such as those that occurred in 1997 and 1998. The first meeting of the Forum, comprising representatives of G-7 ministries of finance and central banks, and of international financial institutions and regulatory bodies, took place at the headquarters of the IMF in Washington, DC, USA, in April 1999. Three working groups were established to study aspects of highly leveraged, or unregulated, institutions, offshore financial centres, and short-term capital flows. In November the Forum constituted additional groups to review deposit insurance schemes and to consider measures to promote implementation of international standards. Since 2001 the Forum has convened regular regional meetings with non-member financial authorities in Latin America, Asia and the Pacific, and Central and Eastern Europe.

Since January 1998 the BIS has hosted the secretariat of the International Association of Insurance Supervisors, which aims to promote co-operation within the insurance industry with regard to effective supervision and the development of domestic insurance markets. It also hosts the secretariat of the International Association of Deposit Insurers, founded in May 2002.

RESEARCH

The Bank's Monetary and Economic Department conducts research, particularly into monetary and financial questions; collects and publishes data on securities markets and international banking developments; and organizes a data bank for central banks. Examples of recent research and policy analysis include inflation targeting procedures, structural changes in foreign exchange markets, financial risks and the business cycle, international capital flows, and transmission mechanism of monetary policy. The BIS Annual Report provides an independent analysis of monetary and economic developments. Statistics on international banking and on external indebtedness are also published regularly.

AGENCY AND TRUSTEE FUNCTIONS

Throughout its history the BIS has undertaken various duties as Trustee Fiscal Agent or Depository with regard to international loan agreements. From October 1986 the BIS performed the functions of Agent for the private European Currency Unit (ECU) clearing and settlement system, in accordance with the provisions of successive agreements concluded between the then ECU Banking Association (now Euro Banking Association—EBA), based in Paris, and the BIS. This arrangement was terminated following the introduction of the

euro on 1 January 1999, when the ECU clearing system was replaced by a new euro clearing system of the EBA. At that time 62 banks had been granted the status of clearing bank by the EBA.

In April 1994 the BIS assumed new functions in connection with the rescheduling of Brazil's external debt, which had been agreed by the Brazilian Government in November 1993. In accordance with two collateral pledge agreements, the BIS acts in the capacity of Collateral Agent to hold and invest collateral for the benefit of the holders of certain US dollar-denominated bonds, maturing in 15 or 30 years, which have been issued by Brazil under the rescheduling arrangements. The Bank acts in a similar capacity for Peru, in accordance with external debt agreements concluded in November 1996 and a collateral agreement signed with the BIS in March 1997, and for Côte d'Ivoire, under a restructuring agreement signed in May 1997 and collateral agreement signed in March 1998.

Publications

Annual Report (in English, French, German and Italian).
The BIS Consolidated International Banking Statistics (every 6 months).
BIS Papers (series).
Central Bank Survey of Foreign Exchange and Derivatives Market Activity (3 a year).
Joint BIS-IMF-OECD-World Bank Statistics on External Debt (quarterly).
Quarterly Review: International Banking and Financial Market Developments (English, French, German and Italian).
Regular OTC Derivatives Market Statistics (every 6 months).

CARIBBEAN COMMUNITY AND COMMON MARKET— CARICOM

Address: POB 10827, Avenue of the Republic, Georgetown, Guyana.
Telephone: (2) 226-9280; **fax:** (2) 226-7816; **e-mail:** carisec3@caricom.org; **internet:** www.caricom.org.

CARICOM was formed in 1973 by the Treaty of Chaguaramas, signed in Trinidad, as a movement towards unity in the Caribbean; it replaced the Caribbean Free Trade Association (CARIFTA), founded in 1965. A revision of the Treaty of Chaguaramas (by means of nine separate Protocols), in order to institute greater regional integration and to establish a CARICOM single market and economy (CSME), was instigated in the 1990s and completed in July 2001.

MEMBERS

Antigua and Barbuda	Jamaica
Bahamas*	Montserrat
Barbados	Saint Christopher and Nevis
Belize	Saint Lucia
Dominica	Saint Vincent and the Grenadines
Grenada	Suriname
Guyana	Trinidad and Tobago
Haiti	

* The Bahamas is a member of the Community but not the Common Market.

ASSOCIATE MEMBERS

Anguilla	Cayman Islands
Bermuda	Turks and Caicos Islands
British Virgin Islands	

Note: Aruba, Colombia, the Dominican Republic, Mexico, the Netherlands Antilles, Puerto Rico and Venezuela have observer status with the Community.

Organization

(April 2005)

HEADS OF GOVERNMENT CONFERENCE AND BUREAU

The Conference is the final authority of the Community and determines policy. It is responsible for the conclusion of treaties on behalf

of the Community and for entering into relationships between the Community and international organizations and states. Decisions of the Conference are generally taken unanimously. Heads of government meet annually, although inter-sessional meetings may be convened.

At a special meeting of the Conference, held in Trinidad and Tobago in October 1992, participants decided to establish a Heads of Government Bureau, with the capacity to initiate proposals, to update consensus and to secure the implementation of CARICOM decisions. The Bureau became operational in December, comprising the Chairman of the Conference, as Chairman, as well as the incoming and outgoing Chairmen of the Conference, and the Secretary-General of the Conference, in the capacity of Chief Executive Officer.

COMMUNITY COUNCIL OF MINISTERS

In October 1992 CARICOM heads of government agreed that a Caribbean Community Council of Ministers should be established to replace the existing Common Market Council of Ministers as the second highest organ of the Community. Protocol I amending the Treaty of Chaguaramas, to restructure the organs and institutions of the Community, was formally adopted at a meeting of CARICOM heads of government in February 1997 and was signed by all member states in July. The inaugural meeting of the Community Council of Ministers was held in Nassau, the Bahamas, in February 1998. The Council consists of ministers responsible for community affairs, as well as other government ministers designated by member states, and is responsible for the development of the Community's strategic planning and co-ordination in the areas of economic integration, functional co-operation and external relations.

COURT OF JUSTICE

Caribbean Court of Justice (CCJ): Unit Trust Building, 5th Floor, Independence Sq., Port-of-Spain, Trinidad and Tobago; tel. 623-2225; e-mail info@caribbeancourtofjustice.org; internet www.caribbeancourtofjustice.org; inaugurated in April 2005; an agreement establishing the Court was formally signed by 10 member countries in February 2001; in January 2004 a revised agreement on the establishment of the CCJ, which incorporated provision for a Trust Fund, entered into force; serves as a tribunal to enforce rights and to consider disputes relating to the CARICOM Single Market and Economy; intended to replace the Judicial Committee of the Privy Council as the Court of Final Appeal (effective for Barbados and Guyana at April 2005); Pres. MICHAEL DE LA BASTIDE.

MINISTERIAL COUNCILS

The principal organs of the Community are assisted in their functions by the following bodies, established under Protocol I amending the Treaty of Chaguaramas: the Council for Trade and Economic Development (COTED); the Council for Foreign and Community Relations (COFCOR); the Council for Human and Social Development (COHSOD); and the Council for Finance and Planning (COFAP). The Councils are responsible for formulating policies, promoting their implementation and supervising co-operation in the relevant areas.

SECRETARIAT

The Secretariat is the main administrative body of the Caribbean Community. The functions of the Secretariat are: to service meetings of the Community and of its Committees; to take appropriate follow-up action on decisions made at such meetings; to carry out studies on questions of economic and functional co-operation relating to the region as a whole; to provide services to member states at their request in respect of matters relating to the achievement of the objectives of the Community.

Secretary-General: EDWIN W. CARRINGTON (Trinidad and Tobago).

Deputy Secretary-General: LOLITA APPLEWHAITE (Barbados).

Activities

REGIONAL INTEGRATION

In 1989 CARICOM heads of government established the 15-member West Indian Commission to study regional political and economic integration. The Commission's final report, submitted in July 1992, recommended that CARICOM should remain a community of sovereign states (rather than a federation), but should strengthen the integration process and expand to include the wider Caribbean region. It recommended the formation of an Association of Caribbean States (ACS), to include all the countries within and surrounding the Caribbean Basin. In November 1997 the Secretaries-General of CARICOM and the ACS signed a Co-operation Agreement to formalize the reciprocal procedures through which the organizations work to enhance and facilitate regional integration. The Heads of Government Conference that was held in October 1992 established an Inter-Governmental Task Force, which was to undertake preparations for a reorientation of CARICOM. In February 1993 it presented a draft Charter of Civil Society for the Community, which set out principles in the areas of democracy, government, parliament, freedom of the press and human rights. The Charter was signed by Community heads of government in February 1997. Suriname was admitted to the organization in July 1995. In July 1997 the Heads of Government Conference agreed to admit Haiti as a member, although the terms and conditions of its accession to the organization had yet to be negotiated. These were finalized in July 1999. In July 2001 the CARICOM Secretary-General formally inaugurated a CARICOM Office in Haiti, which aimed to provide technical assistance in preparation of Haiti's accession to the Community. In January 2002 a CARICOM special mission visited Haiti, following an escalation of the political violence which had started in the previous month. Ministers of foreign affairs emphasized the need for international aid for Haiti when they met their US counterpart in February. Haiti was admitted as the 15th member of CARICOM at the Heads of Government Conference, held in July.

In August 1998 CARICOM and the Dominican Republic signed a free-trade accord, covering trade in goods and services, technical barriers to trade, government procurement, and sanitary and phytosanitary measures and standards. A protocol to the agreement was signed in April 2000, following the resolution of differences concerning exempted items. The accord was ratified by the Dominican Republic in February 2001 and entered partially into force on 1 December (except in Guyana, Suriname and the Bahamas).

In July 1999 CARICOM heads of government endorsed proposals to establish a Caribbean Court of Justice (CCJ), which, it was provisionally agreed, would be located in Port of Spain, Trinidad and Tobago. The Court was intended to replace the Judicial Committee of the Privy Council as the Court of Final Appeal for those countries recognizing its jurisdiction, and was also to adjudicate on trade disputes and on the interpretation of the CARICOM Treaty. It was finally inaugurated in April 2005 (see above).

In November 2001 the CARICOM Secretary-General formally inaugurated a Caribbean Regional Technical Assistance Centre (CARTAC), in Barbados. The Centre was intended to provide technical advice and training to officials from member countries and the

Dominican Republic in support of the region's development, with particular focus on fiscal management, financial sector supervision and regulation, and the compilation of statistics. The IMF was to manage the Centre's operations, while UNDP was to provide administrative and logistical support.

In July 2002 a conference was held, in Liliendaal, Guyana, attended by representatives of civil society and the CARICOM heads of government. The meeting issued a statement of principles on 'Forward Together', recognizing the role of civil society in meeting the challenges to the region. It was agreed to hold regular meetings and to establish a task force to develop a regional strategic framework for pursuing the main recommendations of the conference.

CO-ORDINATION OF FOREIGN POLICY

The co-ordination of foreign policies of member states is listed as one of the main objectives of the Community in its founding treaty. Activities include: strengthening of member states' position in international organizations; joint diplomatic action on issues of particular interest to the Caribbean; joint co-operation arrangements with third countries and organizations; and the negotiation of free-trade agreements with third countries and other regional groupings. This last area of activity has assumed increasing importance since the agreement in 1994 by almost all the governments of countries in the Americas to establish a 'Free Trade Area of the Americas' (FTAA). In April 1997 CARICOM inaugurated a Regional Negotiating Machinery body to co-ordinate and strengthen the region's presence at external economic negotiations. The main focus of activities has been the establishment of the FTAA, ACP relations with the European Union (EU), and multilateral trade negotiations under the WTO.

In July 1991 Venezuela applied for membership of CARICOM, and offered a non-reciprocal free-trade agreement for CARICOM exports to Venezuela, over an initial five-year period. In October 1993 the newly-established Group of Three (Colombia, Mexico and Venezuela) signed joint agreements with CARICOM and Suriname on combating drugs-trafficking and environmental protection. In June 1994 CARICOM and Colombia concluded an agreement on trade, economic and technical co-operation, which, *inter alia*, gives special treatment to the least-developed CARICOM countries. CARICOM has observer status in the Latin American Rio Group.

In 1992 Cuba applied for observer status within CARICOM, and in July 1993 a joint commission was inaugurated to establish closer ties between CARICOM and Cuba and to provide a mechanism for regular dialogue. In July 1997 the heads of government agreed to pursue consideration of a free-trade accord between the Community and Cuba. A Trade and Economic Agreement was signed by the two sides in July 2000, and a CARICOM office was established in Cuba, in February 2001. In July 2004 a meeting between with two sides was held in Havana, Cuba, at ministerial level. A CARICOM-Cuba meeting of heads of state and government was scheduled to be convened in December 2005. In February 1992 ministers of foreign affairs from CARICOM and Central American states met to discuss future co-operation, in view of the imminent conclusion of the North American Free Trade Agreement—NAFTA between the USA, Canada and Mexico. It was agreed that a consultative forum would be established to discuss the possible formation of a Caribbean and Central American free-trade zone. In October 1993 CARICOM declared its support for NAFTA, but requested a 'grace period', during which the region's exports would have parity with Mexican products, and in March 1994 requested that it should be considered for early entry into NAFTA. In July 1996 the heads of government expressed strong concern over the complaint lodged with the World Trade Organization (WTO) by the USA, Ecuador, Guatemala and Honduras regarding the European Union's import regime on bananas, which gives preferential access to bananas from the ACP countries (see the European Union). CARICOM requested the US Government to withdraw its complaint and to negotiate a settlement. Nevertheless, WTO panel hearings on the complaint were initiated in September. Banana producers from the ACP countries were granted third-party status, at the insistence of the Eastern Caribbean ambassador to the EU, Edwin Laurent. In December a special meeting of the Heads of Government Conference was convened, in Barbados, in order to formulate a common position on relations with the USA, in particular with respect to measures to combat illegal drugs-trafficking, following reports that the US Government was planning to impose punitive measures against certain regional authorities, owing to their perceived failure to implement effective controls on illicit drugs.

In May 1997 CARICOM heads of government met the then US President, Bill Clinton, to discuss issues of mutual concern. A partnership for prosperity and security was established at the meeting, and arrangements were instituted for annual consultations between the ministers of foreign affairs of CARICOM countries and the US Secretary of State. However, the Community failed to secure a commitment by the USA to grant the region's exports 'NAFTA-parity' status, or to guarantee concessions to the region's banana industry, following a temporary ruling of the WTO, issued in March, upholding the US trade complaint. The WTO ruling was confirmed in May and endorsed by the WTO dispute settlement body in September. The USA's opposition to a new EU banana policy (which was to terminate the import licensing system, extending import quotas to 'dollar' producers, while maintaining a limited duty-free quota for Caribbean producers) was strongly criticized by CARICOM leaders, meeting in July 1998. In March 1999 the Inter-Sessional meeting of the Conference of Heads of Government issued a statement condemning the imposition by the USA of sanctions against a number of EU imports, in protest at the revised EU banana regime, and the consequences of this action on Caribbean economies, and agreed to review its co-operation with the USA under the partnership for prosperity and security.

During 1998 CARICOM was particularly concerned by the movement within Nevis to secede from its federation with Saint Christopher. In July heads of government agreed to dispatch a mediation team to the country (postponed until September). The Heads of Government Conference held in March 1999 welcomed the establishment of a Constitutional Task Force by the local authorities to prepare a draft constitution, on the basis of recommendations of a previous constitutional commission and the outcome of a series of public meetings. In July 1998 heads of government expressed concern at the hostility between the Government and opposition groupings in Guyana. The two sides signed an agreement, under CARICOM auspices, and in September a CARICOM mediation mission visited Guyana to promote further dialogue. CARICOM has declared its support for Guyana in its territorial disputes with Venezuela and Suriname. In June 2000 CARICOM initiated negotiations following Suriname's removal of petroleum drilling equipment from Guyanan territorial waters. In March 2000 heads of government issued a statement supporting the territorial integrity and security of Belize in that country's ongoing border dispute with Guatemala. CARICOM subsequently urged both countries to implement the provisions of an agreement signed in November. In December 2001 a CARICOM mission observed a general election in Trinidad and Tobago. Following an inconclusive outcome to the election, a delegation from CARICOM visited that country in late January 2002.

In July 2000 the Heads of Government meeting issued a statement strongly opposing the OECD Harmful Tax Initiative, under which punitive measures had been threatened against 35 countries, including CARICOM member states, if they failed to tighten taxation legislation. The meeting also condemned a separate list, issued by the OECD's Financial Task Force on Money Laundering—FATF, which identified 15 countries, including five Caribbean states, of failing to counter effectively international money-laundering. The statement reaffirmed CARICOM's commitment to fighting financial crimes and support for any necessary reform of supervisory practices or legislation, but insisted that national taxation jurisdictions, and specifically competitive regimes designed to attract offshore business, was not a matter for OECD concern. CARICOM remained actively involved in efforts to counter the scheme, and in April 2001 presented its case to the US President. In September the FATF issued a revised list of 19 'unco-operative jurisdictions', including Dominica, Grenada, St Christopher and Nevis and St Vincent and the Grenadines. In early 2002 most Caribbean states concluded a provisional agreement with the OECD to work to improve the transparency and supervision of offshore sectors.

In February 2002 the first meeting of heads of state and of government of CARICOM and the Central American Integration System convened in Belize City. The meeting aimed to strengthen co-operation between the groupings, in particular in international negotiations, efforts to counter transnational organized crime, and support for the regions' economies. In March 2004 CARICOM signed a free-trade agreement with Costa Rica.

In January 2004 CARICOM heads of government resolved to address the escalating political crisis in Haiti. Following a visit by a high-level delegation to that country early in the month discussions were held with representatives of opposition political parties and civil society groups. A few days later the Prime Minister of the Bahamas met with Haiti's President Aristide. At the end of January several CARICOM leaders met with Aristide and members of his government and announced a Prior Action Plan, incorporating opposition demands for political reform. The Plan, however, was rejected by opposition parties since it permitted President Aristide to complete his term-in-office. CARICOM, together with the OAS, continued to pursue diplomatic efforts to secure a peaceful solution to the crisis. On 29 February Aristide resigned and left the country and a provisional president was appointed. In July CARICOM heads of government resolved to send a five-member ministerial team to Haiti to discuss developments in that country with the new interim administration, and to discuss the conditions of participation by that authority in the councils of the Community.

ECONOMIC CO-OPERATION

The Caribbean Community's main field of activity is economic integration, by means of a Caribbean Common Market which replaced the former Caribbean Free Trade Association. The Secretariat and the Caribbean Development Bank undertake research on the best means of facing economic difficulties, and meetings of the Chief Executives of commercial banks and of central bank officials are also held with the aim of strengthening regional co-operation.

In July 1984 heads of government agreed to establish a common external tariff (CET) on certain products, in order to protect domestic industries, although implementation of the CET was considerably delayed (see below). They also urged the necessity of structural adjustment in the economies of the region, including measures to expand production and reduce imports. In 1989 the Conference of Heads of Government agreed to implement, by July 1993, a series of measures to encourage the creation of a single Caribbean market. These included the establishment of a CARICOM Industrial Programming Scheme; the inauguration of the CARICOM Enterprise Regime; abolition of passport requirements for CARICOM nationals travelling within the region; full implementation of the rules of origin and the revised scheme for the harmonization of fiscal incentives; free movement of skilled workers; removal of all remaining regional barriers to trade; establishment of a regional system of air and sea transport; and the introduction of a scheme for regional capital movement. A CARICOM Export Development Council, established in November 1989, undertook a three-year export development project to stimulate trade within CARICOM and to promote exports outside the region.

In August 1990 CARICOM heads of government mandated the governors of CARICOM members' central banks to begin a study of the means to achieve a monetary union within CARICOM; they also institutionalized meetings of CARICOM ministers of finance and senior finance officials, to take place twice a year.

The initial deadline of 1 January 1991 for the establishment of a CET was not achieved, and in July a new deadline of 1 October was set for those members which had not complied—Antigua and Barbuda, Belize, Montserrat, Saint Christopher and Nevis and Saint Lucia, whose governments feared that the tariff would cause an increase in the rate of inflation and damage domestic industries. This deadline was later (again unsuccessfully) extended to February 1992. The tariff, which imposed a maximum level of duty of 45% on imports, was also criticized by the World Bank, the IMF and the US Government as being likely to reduce the region's competitiveness. At a special meeting, held in October 1992, CARICOM heads of government agreed to reduce the maximum level of tariffs to between 30% and 35%, to be in effect by 30 June 1993 (the level was to be further lowered, to 25%–30% by 1995). The Bahamas, however, was not party to these trading arrangements (since it is a member of the Community but not of the Common Market), and Belize was granted an extension for the implementation of the new tariff levels. At the Heads of Government Conference, held in July 1995 in Guyana, Suriname was admitted as a full member of CARICOM and acceded to the treaty establishing the Common Market. It was granted until 1 January 1996 for implementation of the tariff reductions.

The 1995 Heads of Government Conference approved additional measures to promote the single market. The free movement of skilled workers (mainly graduates from recognized regional institutions) was to be permitted from 1 January 1996. At the same time an agreement on the mutual protection and provision of social security benefits was to enter into force. In July 1996 the heads of government decided that CARICOM ministers of finance, central bank governors and planning agencies should meet more frequently to address single market issues and agreed to extend the provisions of free movement to sports people, musicians and others working in the arts and media.

In July 1997 the heads of government, meeting in Montego Bay, Jamaica, agreed to accelerate economic integration, with the aim of completing a single market by 1999. At the meeting 11 member states signed Protocol II amending the Treaty of Chaguaramas, which constituted a central element of a CARICOM Single Market and Economy (CSME), providing for the right to establish enterprises, the provision of services and the free movement of capital and labour throughout participating countries. A regional collaborative network was established to promote the CSME. In July 1998, at the meeting of heads of government, held in Saint Lucia, an agreement was signed with the Insurance Company of the West Indies to accelerate the establishment of a Caribbean Investment Fund, which was to mobilize foreign currency from extra-regional capital markets for investment in new or existing enterprises in the region. Some 60% of all funds generated were to be used by CARICOM countries and the remainder by non-CARICOM members of the ACS.

In November 2000 a special consultation on the single market and economy was held in Barbados, involving CARICOM and government officials, academics, and representatives of the private sector, labour organizations, the media, and other regional groupings. In February 2001 heads of government agreed to establish a new high-level sub-committee to accelerate the establishment of the CSME and to promote its objectives. The sub-committee was to be supported by a Technical Advisory Council, comprising representatives of the public and private sectors. By June all member states had signed and declared the provisional application of Protocol II, which had received two ratifications. By March 2005 11 countries had completed the fourth phase of the CET.

In October 2001 CARICOM heads of government, meeting in a special emergency meeting, considered the impact on the region's economy of the terrorist attacks perpetrated against targets in the USA in the previous month. The meeting resolved to enhance aviation security, to implement promotion and marketing campaigns in support of the tourist industry, and to approach international institutions to assist with emergency financing. The economic situation, which had been further adversely affected by the reduced access to the EU banana market, the economic downturn in the USA, and the effects on the investment climate of the OECD Harmful Taxation Initiative, was considered at the Heads of Government Conference, held in Guyana, in July 2002. Heads of government agreed to meeting in August in special session to elaborate a programme to revive the economy, on the basis of the work of a newly-appointed technical team. A technical committee was also established in July to develop proposals for a regional stabilization programme, and a Stabilization Fund, with initial capital of US $60m. An inter-sessional Heads of Government Conference that was held in March 2004, however, agreed that there was insufficient support for the Fund to be established at that time.

CRIME AND SECURITY

In December 1996 CARICOM heads of government determined to strengthen comprehensive co-operation and technical assistance to combat illegal drugs-trafficking. The Conference decided to establish a Caribbean Security Task Force to help formulate a single regional agreement on maritime interdiction, incorporating agreements already concluded by individual members. A Regional Drugs Control Programme at the CARICOM Secretariat aims to co-ordinate regional initiatives with the overall objective of reducing the demand and supply of illegal substances. In July 2001 the Prime Minister of Antigua and Barbuda, Lester Bird, proposed the establishment of a rapid response unit to deal with drugs-related and other serious crimes. Heads of government agreed, instead, to establish a task force to be responsible for producing recommendations for a forthcoming meeting of national security advisers. In October, heads of government convened an emergency meeting in Nassau, the Bahamas, to consider the impact of the terrorist attacks against the USA which had occurred in September. The meeting determined to convene immediately the so-called Task Force on Crime and Security in order to implement new policy directives. It was agreed to enhance co-ordination and collaboration of security services throughout the region, in particular in intelligence gathering, analysis and sharing in relation to crime, illicit drugs and terrorism, and to strengthen security at airports, seaports and borders. In July 2002 heads of government agreed on a series of initiatives recommended by the Task Force to counter the escalation in crime and violence. These included strengthening border controls, preparing national anti-crime master plans, establishing broad-based National Commissions on law and order and strengthening the exchange of information and intelligence.

INDUSTRY AND ENERGY

A protocol relating to the CARICOM Industrial Programming Scheme (CIPS), approved in 1988, is the Community's instrument for promoting the co-operative development of industry in the region. Protocol III amending the Treaty of Chaguaramas, with respect to industrial policy, was opened for signature in July 1998. At June 2001 it had been signed by 13 member states, provisionally applied by 12, and ratified by one.

The Secretariat has established a national standards bureau in each member country to harmonize technical standards, and supervises the metrication of weights and measures. In 1999 members agreed to establish a new CARICOM Regional Organization of Standards and Quality (CROSQ) to develop common regional standards and resolve disputes. CROSQ, located in Barbados, became operational in 2002.

The CARICOM Alternative Energy Systems Project provides training, assesses energy needs and conducts energy audits. Efforts in regional energy development are directed at the collection and analysis of data for national energy policy documents.

TRANSPORT, COMMUNICATIONS AND TOURISM

A Caribbean Confederation of Shippers' Councils represents the interests of regional exporters and importers. In July 1990 the Caribbean Telecommunications Union was established to oversee developments in regional telecommunications.

In 1988 a Consultative Committee on Caribbean Regional Information Systems (CCCRIS) was established to evaluate and monitor the functioning of existing information systems and to seek to co-ordinate and advise on the establishment of new systems.

A Summit of Heads of Government on Tourism, Trade and Transportation was held in Trinidad and Tobago, in August 1995, to which all members of the ACS and regional tourism organizations were invited. In 1997 CARICOM heads of government considered a number of proposals relating to air transportation, tourism, human resource development and capital investment, which had been identified by Community ministers of tourism as critical issues in the sustainable development of the tourist industry. The heads of government requested ministers to meet regularly to develop tourism policies, and in particular to undertake an in-depth study of human resource development issues in early 1998. A new fund to help train young people from the region in aspects of the tourist industry was inaugurated in July 1997, in memory of the former Prime Minister of Jamaica, Michael Manley. A regional summit on tourism, in recognition of the importance of the industry to the economic development of the region, was held in the Bahamas, in December 2001.

A Multilateral Agreement Concerning the Operations of Air Services within the Caribbean Community entered into force in November 1998, providing a formal framework for the regulation of the air transport industry and enabling CARICOM-owned and -controlled airlines to operate freely within the region. In July 1999 heads of government signed Protocol VI amending the Treaty of Chaguaramas providing for a common transportation policy, with harmonized standards and practices, which was to be an integral component of the development of a single market and economy. In November 2001 representatives of national civil aviation authorities signed a memorandum of understanding, providing for the establishment of a regional body, the Regional Aviation Oversight Safety System.

AGRICULTURE AND FISHERIES

In July 1996 the CARICOM summit meeting agreed to undertake wide-ranging measures in order to modernize the agricultural sector and to increase the international competitiveness of Caribbean agricultural produce. The CARICOM Secretariat was to support national programmes with assistance in policy formulation, human resource development and the promotion of research and technology development in the areas of productivity, marketing, agri-business and water resources management. During 1997 CARICOM Governments continued to lobby against a complaint lodged at the WTO with regard to the EU's banana import regime (offering favourable conditions to ACP producers—see above) and to generate awareness of the economic and social importance of the banana industry to the region. Protocol V amending the Treaty of Chaguaramas, which was concerned with agricultural policy, was opened for signature by heads of government in July 1998. At June 2001 it had been signed and provisionally applied by 13 member states, and ratified by one (Guyana). In July 2002 heads of government approved an initiative to develop a CARIFORUM Special Programme for Food Security.

In February 2003 the CARICOM Secretariat was mandated to draft a proposal for a common fisheries policy.

HEALTH AND EDUCATION

In 1986 CARICOM and the Pan-American Health Organization launched 'Caribbean Co-operation in Health' with projects to be undertaken in six main areas: environmental protection, including the control of disease-bearing pests; development of human resources; chronic non-communicable diseases and accidents; strengthening health systems; food and nutrition; maternal and child health care; and population activities. In 2001 CARICOM co-ordinated a new regional partnership to reduce the spread and impact of HIV and AIDS in member countries. All countries were to prepare national strategic plans to facilitate access to funding to combat the problem. A meeting of the so-called Pan-Caribbean Partnership against HIV/AIDS (PANCAP) was convened in November. In February 2002 PANCAP initiated regional negotiations with pharmaceutical companies to secure reductions in the cost of anti-retroviral drugs. A Caribbean Environmental Health Institute (see below) aims to promote collaboration among member states in all areas of environmental management and human health. In July 2001 heads of government, meeting in the Bahamas, issued the Nassau Declaration on Health, advocating greater regional strategic co-ordination and planning in the health sector, institutional reform, and increased resources.

CARICOM educational programmes have included the improvement of reading in schools through assistance for teacher-training; and ensuring the availability of low-cost educational material throughout the region. In July 1997 CARICOM heads of government adopted the recommendations of a ministerial committee, which identified priority measures for implementation in the education sector. These included the objective of achieving universal, quality secondary education and the enrolment of 15% of post-secondary students in tertiary education by 2005, as well as improved training in foreign languages and science and technology. From the late 1990s youth activities have been increasingly emphasized by the Community. These have included new programmes for disadvantaged youths, a mechanism for youth exchange and the convening of a Caribbean Youth Parliament.

EMERGENCY ASSISTANCE

A Caribbean Disaster Emergency Response Agency (CDERA) was established in 1991 to co-ordinate immediate disaster relief, primarily in the event of hurricanes. In May 2004 the Community determined to contribute to relief and rehabilitation efforts following the devastation caused by flooding and mudslides in the Dominican Republic and Haiti, which had killed more than 1,000 people. In January 2005, meeting on the sidelines of the fifth Summit of the Alliance of Small Island States, in Port Louis, Mauritius, the Secretaries-General of CARICOM, the Commonwealth, the Pacific Islands Forum and the Indian Ocean Commission determined to take collective action to strengthen the disaster preparedness and response capabilities of their member countries in the Caribbean, Pacific and Indian Ocean areas.

INSTITUTIONS

The following are among the institutions formally established within the framework of CARICOM.

Assembly of Caribbean Community Parliamentarians: c/o CARICOM Secretariat; an intergovernmental agreement on the establishment of a regional parliament entered into force in August 1994; inaugural meeting held in Barbados, in May 1996. Comprises up to four representatives of the parliaments of each member country, and up to two of each associate member. It aims to provide a forum for wider community involvement in the process of integration and for enhanced deliberation on CARICOM affairs; authorized to issue recommendations for the Conference of Heads of Government and to adopt resolutions on any matter arising under the Treaty of Chaguaramas.

Caribbean Agricultural Research and Development Institute (CARDI): UWI Campus, St Augustine, Trinidad and Tobago; tel. 645-1205; fax 645-1208; e-mail info@cardi.org; internet www.cardi.org; f. 1975; aims to contribute to the competitiveness and sustainability of Caribbean agriculture by generating and transferring new and appropriate technologies and by developing effective partnerships with regional and international entities; Exec. Dir FRANK B. LAUCKNER; publs *CARDI Weekly*, *CARDI Review*, technical bulletin series.

Caribbean Centre for Development Administration (CARICAD): 1st Floor, Weymouth Corporate Centre, Roebuck St, St Michael, Barbados; tel. 427-8535; fax 436-1709; e-mail caricad@caribsurf.com; internet www.caricad.org; f. 1980; aims to assist governments in the reform of the public sector and to strengthen their managerial capacities for public administration; promotes the involvement of the private sector, non-governmental organizations and other bodies in all decision-making processes; Exec. Dir Dr P. I. GOMES.

Caribbean Disaster Emergency Response Agency (CDERA): Bldg 1, Manor Lodge, Lodge Hill, St Michael, Barbados; tel. 425-0386; fax 425-8854; e-mail cdera@caribsurf.com; internet www

.cdera.org; f. 1991 for activities, see Emergency Assistance above; Regional Co-ordinator JEREMY COLLYMORE.

Caribbean Environmental Health Institute (CEHI): POB 1111, The Morne, Castries, St Lucia; tel. 4522501; fax 4532721; e-mail cehi@candw.lc; internet www.cehi.org.lc; f. 1980 (began operations in 1982); provides technical and advisory services to member states in formulating environmental health policy legislation and in all areas of environmental management (for example, solid waste management, water supplies, beach and air pollution, and pesticides control); promotes, collates and disseminates relevant research; conducts courses, seminars and workshops throughout the region; Exec. Dir VINCENT SWEENEY.

Caribbean Food and Nutrition Institute (CFNI): UWI Campus, POB 140, St Augustine, Trinidad and Tobago; tel. 663-1544; e-mail cfni@cablenett.net; internet www.cfni.paho.org; f. 1967 to serve the governments and people of the region and to act as a catalyst among persons and organizations concerned with food and nutrition through research and field investigations, training in nutrition, dissemination of information, advisory services and production of educational material; mems: all English-speaking Caribbean territories, including the mainland countries of Belize and Guyana; Dir Dr FITZROY HENRY; publs *Cajanus* (quarterly), *Nyam News* (monthly), *Nutrient-Cost Tables* (quarterly), educational material.

Caribbean Meteorological Organization (CMO): POB 461, Port of Spain, Trinidad and Tobago; tel. 624-4481; fax 623-3634; e-mail hqcmo@tstt.net.tt; f. 1951 to co-ordinate regional activities in meteorology, operational hydrology and allied sciences; became an associate institution of CARICOM in 1973; comprises a headquarters unit, a Council of Government Ministers, the Caribbean Meteorological Foundation and the Caribbean Meteorological Institute, located in Barbados; mems: govts of 16 countries and territories represented by the National Meteorological and Hydro-meteorological Services; Co-ordinating Dir TYRONE W. SUTHERLAND.

ASSOCIATE INSTITUTIONS

Caribbean Development Bank: POB 408, Wildey, St Michael, Barbados; tel. 431-1600; fax 426-7269; e-mail info@caribank.org; internet www.caribank.org; f. 1969 to stimulate regional economic growth through support for agriculture, industry, transport and other infrastructure, tourism, housing and education; subscribed cap. US $705.0m. (April 2004); in 1999 net approvals totalled $146.6m. for 16 projects; at the end of 1999 cumulative grant and loan disbursements totalled $1,275.0m.; the Special Development Fund was replenished in 1996; mems: CARICOM states, and Canada, the People's Republic of China, Colombia, Germany, Italy, Mexico, United Kingdom, Venezuela; Pres. Dr. COMPTON BOURNE.

Caribbean Law Institute: University of the West Indies, Cave Hill Campus, POB 64, Bridgetown, Barbados; tel. 417-4560; fax 417-4138; f. 1988 to harmonize and modernize commercial laws in the region; Exec. Dir Dr WINSTON C. ANDERSON.

Other Associate Institutions of CARICOM, in accordance with its constitution, are the University of Guyana, the University of the West Indies and the Secretariat of the Organisation of Eastern Caribbean States.

Publications

CARICOM Perspective (annually).
CARICOM View (6 a year).

CENTRAL AMERICAN INTEGRATION SYSTEM
(SISTEMA DE LA INTEGRACIÓN CENTROAMERICANA—SICA)

Address: Blv. Orden de Malta 470, Urb. Santa Elena, Antiguo Cuscatlán, San Salvador, El Salvador.

Telephone: 248-8800; **fax:** 248-8899; **e-mail:** info@sgsica.org; **internet:** www.sgsica.org.

Founded in December 1991, when the heads of state of six Central American countries signed the Protocol of Tegucigalpa to the agreement establishing the Organization of Central American States (f. 1951), creating a new framework for regional integration. A General Secretariat of the Sistema de la Integración Centroamericana (SICA) was inaugurated in February 1993 to co-ordinate the process of political, economic, social cultural and environmental integration

and to promote democracy and respect for human rights throughout the region.

MEMBERS

Belize	Guatemala	Nicaragua
Costa Rica	Honduras	Panama
El Salvador		

OBSERVERS

Dominican Republic	Taiwan

Organization

(April 2005)

SUMMIT MEETINGS

The meetings of heads of state of member countries serve as the supreme decision-making organ of SICA.

COUNCIL OF MINISTERS

Ministers of Foreign Affairs of member states meet regularly to provide policy direction for the process of integration.

CONSULTATIVE COMMITTEE

The Committee comprises representatives of business organizations, trade unions, academic institutions and other federations concerned with the process of integration in the region. It is an integral element of the integration system and assists the Secretary-General in determining the policies of the organization.

President: RICARDO SOL.

GENERAL SECRETARIAT

The General Secretariat of SICA was established in February 1993 to co-ordinate the process of enhanced regional integration. It comprises the following divisions: inter-institutional relations; research and co-operation; legal and political affairs; economic affairs; and communications and information.

In September 1997 Central American Common Market (CACM) heads of state, meeting in the Nicaraguan capital, signed the Managua Declaration in support of further regional integration and the establishment of a political union. A commission was to be established to consider all aspects of the policy and to formulate a timetable for the integration process. In February 1998 SICA heads of state resolved to establish a Unified General Secretariat to integrate the institutional aspects of SICA (see below) in a single office, to be located in San Salvador. The process was ongoing in 2005.

Secretary-General: ANÍBAL ENRIQUE QUIÑÓNEZ ABARCA.

SPECIALIZED TECHNICAL SECRETARIATS

Secretaría Ejecutiva de la Comisión Centroamericana de Ambiente y Desarrollo (SE-CCAD): Blv. Orden de Malta 470, Santa Elena, Antiguo Cuscatlán, San Salvador, El Salvador; tel. 289-6131; fax 289-6126; e-mail mcastro@sgsica.org; internet www.ccad.ws; f. 1989 to enhance collaboration in the promotion of sustainable development and environmental protection; Exec. Sec. MARCO GONZÁLEZ PASTORA.

Secretaría General de la Coordinación Educativa y Cultural Centroamericana (SG-CECC): 175m norte de la esquina oeste del ICE, Sabana Norte, San José, Costa Rica; tel. 232-3783; fax 231-2366; e-mail sgcecc@sol.racsa.co.cr; f. 1982; promotes development of regional programmes in the fields of education and culture; Sec.-Gen. MARVIN HERRERA ARAYA.

Secretaría de Integración Económica Centroamericana (SIECA): 4A Avda 10–25, Zona 14, Apdo 1237, 01901 Guatemala City, Guatemala; tel. (2) 368-2151; fax (2) 368-1071; e-mail info@sieca.org.gt; internet www.sieca.org.gt; f. 1960 to assist the process of economic integration and the creation of a Central American Common Market (CACM—established by the organization of Central American States under the General Treaty of Central American Economic Integration, signed in December 1960 and ratified by Costa Rica, Guatemala, El Salvador, Honduras and Nicaragua in September 1963); supervises the correct implementation of the legal instruments of economic integration, carries out relevant studies at the request of the CACM, and arranges meetings; comprises departments covering the working of the CACM: negotiations and external trade policy; external co-operation; systems and statistics; finance and administration; also includes a unit for co-operation with the private sector and finance institutions, and a legal consultative committee; Sec.-Gen. RÓGER HAROLDO RODAS MELGAR; publs *Anuario Estadístico Centroamericano de Comercio Exterior*, *Carta Informativa* (monthly), *Cuadernos de la SIECA* (2 a year), *Estadísticas Macroeconómicas de Centroamérica* (annually), *Series Estadísticas Seleccionadas de Centroamérica* (annually), *Boletín Informativo* (fortnightly).

Secretaría de la Integración Social Centroamericana (SISCA): Blv. Orden de Malta 470, Santa Elena, Antiguo Cuscatlán, San Salvador, El Salvador; tel. 289-6131; fax 289-6124; e-mail hmorgado@sgsica.org.sv; f. 1995; Dir-Gen. Dr HUGO MORGADO.

OTHER SPECIALIZED SECRETARIATS

Secretaría de Integración Turística Centroamericana (SITCA): Blv. Orden de Malta 470, Santa Elena, Antiguo Cuscatlán, San Salvador, El Salvador; tel. 248-8837; fax 248-8897; e-mail csilva@sgsica.org; f. 1965 to develop regional tourism activities; Dir. MERCEDES DE MENA.

Secretaría del Consejo Agropecuario Centroamericano (SCAC): Sacretarion Isidro de Coronado, Apdo Postal 55-2200, San José, Costa Rica; tel. 216-0303; fax 216-0285; e-mail rguillen@iica.ac.cr; internet www.coreca.org; f. 1991 to determine and co-ordinate regional policies and programmes relating to agriculture and agro-industry; Sec-Gen. RÓGER GUILLÉN BUSTOS.

Secretaría Ejecutiva del Consejo Monetario Centroamericano (SECMCA) (Central American Monetary Council): Ofiplaza del Este, Edif. C, 75m. oeste de la Rotonda la Bandera, San Pedro Montes de Oca, Apdo Postal 5438-1000, San José, Costa Rica; tel. 280-9522; fax 280-2511; e-mail secma@secma.org; internet www.secma.org; f. 1964 by the presidents of Central American central banks, to co-ordinate monetary policies; Exec. Sec. MIGUEL CHORRO; publs *Boletín Estadístico* (annually), *Informe Económico* (annually).

Comisión Centroamericana de Transporte Marítimo (COCATRAM): Frente al Costado Oeste del Hotel Mansión Teodolinda, Barrio Bolonia, Apdo Postal 2423, Managua, Nicaragua; tel. (2) 222-3482; fax (2) 222-2759; e-mail cocatram@ibw.com.ni; internet www.cocatram.org.ni; f. 1981; Exec. Dir ALFONSO BREUILLET GALINDO; publ. *Boletín Informativo*.

PARLIAMENT

Address: 12A Avda 33-04, Zona 5, Guatemala City, Guatemala 01005.

Telephone: (2) 339-0466; **fax:** (2) 334-6670; **e-mail:** guatemala@parlacen.org.gt; **internet:** www.parlacen.org.gt.

Officially inaugurated in 1991. Comprises representatives of El Salvador, Guatemala, Honduras, Nicaragua and Panama. In 2004 Honduras announced its intention temporarily to withdraw from the Parliament.

President: FABIO GADEA MANTILLA.

COURT OF JUSTICE

Address: Apdo Postal 907 Managua, Nicaragua.

Telephone: 266-6273; **fax:** 266-8486; **e-mail:** cortecen@tmx.com.ni; **internet:** www.ccj.org.ni.

Officially inaugurated in 1994. Tribunal authorized to consider disputes relating to treaties agreed within the regional integration system. In February 1998 Central American heads of state agreed to limit the number of magistrates in the Court to one per country.

President: ADOLFO LEÓN GÓMEZ.

Secretary-General: ORLANDO GUERRERO MAYORGA.

AD HOC INTERGOVERNMENTAL SECRETARIATS

Comisión de Ciencia y Tecnología de Centroamérica y Panamá (CTCAP) (Committee for Science and Technology of Central America and Panama): Antigua base de Clayton, Edif. 213, Panama; tel. 317-0014; fax 317-0026; e-mail espinoza@ns.hondunet.net; internet www.senacyt.gob.pa/ctcap; f. 1976.

Consejo Centroamericano de Instituciones de Seguridad Social (COCISS) (Central American Council of Social Security Institutions): Apdo 10105, San José, Costa Rica; tel. 257-0122; fax 233-1850; e-mail cociss@ccss.sa.cr; internet www.ccss.sa.cr/cociss/idcociss.htm; f. 1992.

Consejo del Istmo Centroamericano de Deportes y Recreación (CODICADER) (Committee of the Central American Isthmus for Sport and Recreation): Palacio Nacional de los Deportes, Edif. Administrativo, 3°, San Salvador, El Salvador; tel. 231-9993; fax 231-9990; e-mail jorgehernandez@indes.gob.sv; f. 1992.

Unidad Técnica del Consejo Centroamericano de Vivienda y Asentamientos Humanos (CCVAH) (Central American Council on Housing and Human Settlements): Avda la Paz 244, Tegucigalpa, Honduras; tel. 236-5804; fax 236-6560; f. 1992.

Secretaría Ejecutiva del Consejo de Electrificación de América Central (CEAC) (Central American Electrification Council): 9A Calle Pte 950, Edif. CEL, Centro de Gobierno, San Salvador, El Salvador; tel. 211-6175; fax 211-6239; e-mail jmontesi@cel.gob.sv; internet www.ceac-ca.org.sv; f. 1985.

Organización Centroamericana de Entidades Fiscalizadores Superiores: e-mail cdcr@es.com.sv; internet www.sgsica.org.ir/ocefs.htm.

OTHER REGIONAL INSTITUTIONS

Finance

Banco Centroamericano de Integración Económica (BCIE) (Central American Bank for Economic Integration): Blv. Suyapa,

Contigua a Banco de Honduras, Apdo 772, Tegucigalpa, Honduras; tel. 228-2243; fax 228-2185; e-mail jarevalo@bcie.org; internet www .bcie.hn; f. 1961 to promote the economic integration and balanced economic development of member countries; finances public and private development projects, particularly those related to industrialization and infrastructure; loan approvals in 2002/03 totalled US $728.5m.; auth. cap. $2,000m; regional mems: Costa Rica, Dominican Republic, El Salvador, Guatemala, Honduras, Nicaragua; non-regional mems: Argentina, the People's Republic of China, Colombia, Mexico; Pres. HARRY BRAUTIGAM; publs *Annual Report*, *Revista de la Integración y el Desarrollo de Centroamérica*.

Public Administration

Centro de Coordinación para la Prevención de Desastres Naturales en América Central (CEPREDENAC): Antigua base de Howard, Ave Rencher, Edif. 707, Panamá, Panama; tel. 316-0065; fax 316-0074; e-mail secretaria@cepredenac.org; internet www .cepredenac.org; f. 1988, integrated into SICA in 1995; aims to strengthen the capacity of the region to reduce its vulnerability to natural disasters; Exec. Sec. GERONIMO GIUSTO-ROBELO.

Instituto Centroamericano de Administración Pública (ICAP) (Central American Institute of Public Administration): Apdo Postal 10025-1000 San José, Costa Rica; tel. 234-1011; fax 225-2049; e-mail icapcr@racsa.co.cr; internet www.icap.ac.cr; f. 1954 by the five Central American Republics and the United Nations, with later participation by Panama; the Institute aims to train the region's public servants, provide technical assistance and carry out research leading to reforms in public administration; Dir Dr HUGO ZELAYA CÁLIX.

Secretaría Ejecutiva de la Comisión Regional de Recursos Hidráulicos (SE-CRRH): Apdo Postal 21–2300, Curridabat, San José, Costa Rica; tel. 231-5791; fax 296-0047; e-mail crrhcr@sol .racsa.co.cr; internet aguayclima.com; f. 1966; mems: Belize, Costa Rica, El Salvador, Guatemala, Honduras, Nicaragua, Panama; Exec. Sec. MAX CAMPOS ORTIZ.

Agriculture and Fisheries

Organismo Internacional Regional de Sanidad Agropecuaria (OIRSA ()) (International Regional Organization of Plant Protection and Animal Health): Avda Las Camelias 14, Col. San Francisco, Apdo 61, San Salvador, El Salvador; tel. 223-9545; fax 279-0189; e-mail orgoirsa@gbm.net; internet ns1.oirsa.org.sv; f. 1953 for the prevention of the introduction of animal and plant pests and diseases unknown in the region; research, control and eradication programmes of the principal pests present in agriculture; technical assistance and advice to the ministries of agriculture and livestock of member countries; education and qualification of personnel; mems: Belize, Costa Rica, Dominican Republic, El Salvador, Guatemala, Honduras, Mexico, Nicaragua, Panama; Exec. Dir Dr CELIO HUMBERTO BARRETO ORTEGA.

Unidad Coordinadora de la Organización del Sector Pesquero y Acuícola del Istmo Centroamericano: Blv. Orden de Malta 470, Santa Elena, Antiguo Cuscatlán, San Salvador, El Salvador; tel. 248-8800; fax 248-8899; e-mail mgonzalez@sgsica.org; f. 1995, incorporated into SICA in 1999; Regional Co-ordinator MARIO GONZÁLEZ RECINOS.

Education and Health

Comité Coordinador Regional de Instituciones de Agua Potable y Saneamiento de Centroamérica, Panamá y República Dominicana (CAPRE): Avda Bo. 1A, El Obelisco Comayagüela, Tegucigalpa, Honduras; tel. 237-8552; fax 237-2575; e-mail capregtz@sol.racsa.co.cr; f. 1979; Dir LILIANA ARCE UMAÑA.

Consejo Superior Universitario Centroamericano (CSUCA) (Central American University Council): Avda Las Américas 1–03, Zona 14, International Club Los Arcos, Guatemala City, Guatemala; tel. (2) 367-1833; fax (2) 367-4517; e-mail sp@csuca.edu.gt; internet www.csuca.edu.gt; f. 1948 to guarantee academic, administrative and economic autonomy for universities and to encourage regional integration of higher education; maintains libraries and documentation centres; Council of 32 mems; mems: 16 universities, in Belize, Costa Rica (four), El Salvador, Guatemala, Honduras (two), Nicaragua (four) and Panama (three); Sec.-Gen. EFRAIN MEDINA GUERRA; publs *Estudios Sociales Centroamericanos* (quarterly), *Cuadernos de Investigación* (monthly), *Carta Informativa de la Secretaría General* (monthly).

Instituto de Nutrición de Centroamérica y Panamá (Institute of Nutrition of Central America and Panama—INCAP): Calzada Roosevelt, Zona 11, Apdo Postal 1188, Guatemala City, Guatemala; tel. (2) 472-3762 ; fax (2) 473-6529; e-mail hdelgado@incap.ops-oms .org; internet www.incap.org.gt; f. 1949 to promote the development of nutritional sciences and their application and to strengthen the technical capacity of member countries to reach food and nutrition security; provides training and technical assistance for nutrition education and planning; conducts applied research; disseminates information; maintains library (including about 600 periodicals); administered by the Pan American Health Organization (PAHO) and the World Health Organization; mems: CACM mems and Belize and Panama; Dir Dr HERNÁN L. DELGADO; publ. *Annual Report*.

Transport and Communications

Comisión Técnica de Telecomunicaciones—COMTELCA (Technical Commission for Telecommunications): Col. Palmira, Edif. Alfa, 608 Avda Brasil, Apdo 1793, Tegucigalpa, Honduras; tel. 220-6666; fax 220-1197; e-mail sec@comtelca.hn; internet www.comtelca .hn; f. 1966 to co-ordinate and improve the regional telecommunications network; Dir-Gen. HÉCTOR LEONEL RODRÍGUEZ MILLA.

Corporación Centroamericana de Servicios de Navegación Aérea—COCESNA (Central American Air Navigation Service Corporation): Apdo 660, Aeropuerto de Toncontín, Tegucigalpa, Honduras; tel. 234-3360; fax 234-2550; e-mail sec-interna@cocesna.org; internet www.cocesna.org; f. 1960; offers radar air traffic control services, aeronautical telecommunications services, flight inspections and radio assistance services for air navigation; administers the Central American Aeronautical School; Exec. Pres. EDUARDO JOSÉ MARÍN.

Activities

In June 1990 the presidents of the Central American Common Market (CACM) countries (Costa Rica, El Salvador, Guatemala, Honduras and Nicaragua) signed a declaration welcoming peace initiatives in El Salvador, Guatemala and Nicaragua, and appealing for a revitalization of CACM, as a means of promoting lasting peace in the region. In December the presidents committed themselves to the creation of an effective common market, proposing the opening of negotiations on a comprehensive regional customs and tariffs policy by March 1991, and the introduction of a regional 'anti-dumping' code by December 1991. They requested the support of multilateral lending institutions through investment in regional development, and the cancellation or rescheduling of member countries' debts. In December 1991 the heads of state of the five CACM countries and Panama signed the Protocol of Tegucigalpa, and in February 1993 the General Secretariat of SICA was inaugurated to co-ordinate the integration process in the region.

In February 1993 the European Community (EC, now European Union—EU) signed a new framework co-operation agreement with the CACM member states extending the programme of economic assistance and political dialogue initiated in 1984; a further co-operation agreement with the EU (EC, now European Union—EU) was signed in early 1996. A political dialogue and co-operation agreement was concluded in December 2003.

In October 1993 the presidents of the CACM countries and Panama signed a protocol to the 1960 General Treaty, committing themselves to full economic integration in the region (with a common external tariff of 20% for finished products and 5% for raw materials and capital goods) and creating conditions for increased free trade. The countries agreed to accelerate the removal of internal non-tariff barriers, but no deadline was set. Full implementation of the protocol was to be 'voluntary and gradual', owing to objections on the part of Costa Rica and Panama. In May 1994, however, Costa Rica committed itself to full participation in the protocol. In March 1995 a meeting of the Central American Monetary Council discussed and endorsed a reduction in the tariff levels from 20% to 15% and from 5% to 1%. However, efforts to adopt this as a common policy were hindered by the implementation of these tariff levels by El Salvador on a unilateral basis, from 1 April, and the subsequent modifications by Guatemala and Costa Rica of their external tariffs. In March 2002 Central American leaders adopted the San Salvador Plan of Action for Central American Economic Integration, establishing several objectives as the basis for the creation, by 1 January 2004, of a regional customs union, with a single tariff.

In December 1994 the SICA member states and the USA signed the Central American-United States of America Joint Declaration (CONCAUSA), covering co-operation in the following areas: conservation of biodiversity, sound management of energy, environmental legislation, and sustainable economic development. In June 2001 the SICA states and the USA signed a renewed and expanded CONCAUSA, now also covering co-operation in addressing climate change, and in disaster preparedness. In May 1997 the heads of state of CACM member countries, together with the Prime Minister of Belize, conferred with the then US President, Bill Clinton, in San José, Costa Rica. The leaders resolved to establish a Trade and Investment Council to promote trade relations; however, Clinton failed to endorse a request from CACM members that their products receive preferential access to US markets, on similar terms to those from Mexico agreed under the NAFTA accord. During the 1990s the Central American Governments pursued negotiations to conclude free-trade agreements with Mexico, Panama and the members of the Caribbean Community and Common Market (CARICOM). Nicaragua signed a bilateral accord with Mexico in December (Costa Rica already having done so in 1994). El Salvador, Guatemala and Honduras jointly concluded a free-trade arrangement with Mexico in May 2000. In November 1997, at a special summit meeting of CACM heads of state, an agreement was reached with the President of the Dominican Republic to initiate a gradual process of incorporating that country into the process of Central American integration, with the aim of promoting sustainable development throughout the region. The first sectors for increased co-operation between the two sides were to be tourism, health, investment promotion and air transport. A free-trade accord with the Dominican Republic was concluded in April 1998, and formally signed in November.

In November 1998 Central American heads of state held an emergency summit meeting to consider the devastation in the region caused by 'Hurricane Mitch'. The Presidents urged international creditors to write off the region's estimated debts of US $16,000m. to assist in the economic recovery of the countries worst-affected. They also reiterated requests for preferential treatment for the region's exports within the NAFTA framework. In October 1999 the heads of state adopted a strategic framework for the period 2000–04 to strengthen the capacity for the physical, social, economic and environmental infrastructure of Central American countries to withstand the impact of natural disasters. In particular, programmes for the integrated management and conservation of water resources, and for the prevention of forest fires were to be implemented.

In June 2001 the heads of state and representatives of Belize, Costa, Rica, El Salvador, Guatemala, Honduras, Mexico, Nicaragua and Panama agreed to activate the Puebla-Panama Plan (PPP) to promote sustainable social and economic development in the region and to reinforce integration efforts among Central America and the southern states of Mexico (referred to as Mesoamerica). The heads of state identified the principal areas for PPP initiatives, including tourism, road integration, telecommunications, energy interconnection, and the prevention and mitigation of disasters. In June 2002 the heads of state of seven countries, and the Vice-President of Panama, convened in Mérida, Mexico during an investment fair to promote the Plan and reiterated their support for the regional initiatives. The meeting was also held within the framework of the Tuxtla dialogue mechanism, so-called after an agreement signed in 1991 between Mexico and Central American countries, to discuss co-ordination between the parties, in particular in social matters, health, education and the environment.

In April 2001 Costa Rica concluded a free-trade accord with Canada; the other four CACM countries commenced negotiations with Canada in November with the aim of reaching a similar agreement. In February 2002 heads of state of SICA countries convened an extraordinary summit meeting in Managua, Nicaragua, at which they resolved to implement measures to further the political and economic integration of the region. The leaders determined to pursue initial proposals for a free-trade pact with the USA

during the visit to the region of US President George W. Bush in the following month, and, more generally, to strengthen trading relations with the EU. They also pledged to resolve all regional conflicts by peaceful means. Earlier in February the first meeting of heads of state or government of SICA and CARICOM countries took place in Belize, with the aim of strengthening political and economic relations between the two groupings. The meeting agreed to work towards concluding common negotiating positions, for example in respect of the FTAA and World Trade Organization.

In May 2002 ministers of foreign affairs of Central America and the EU agreed upon a new agenda for a formalized dialogue and on priority areas of action, including environmental protection, democracy and governance, and poverty reduction. The meeting determined to work towards the eventual conclusion of an Association Agreement. It was agreed that meetings between the two sides, at ministerial level, were to be held each year. In December 2003 a new EU-Central America Political Dialogue and Co-operation Agreement was signed to replace an existing (1993) framework accord. The EU has allocated €74.5m. to finance co-operation programmes under its Regional Strategy for Central America covering the period 2002–06; these were to focus on strengthening the role of civil society in the process of regional integration, reducing vulnerability to natural disasters, and environmental improvement.

The summit meeting of CACM heads of state, convened in December 2002, in San José, Costa Rica, adopted the 'Declaration of San José', supporting the planned establishment of the Central American customs union (see above), and endorsing the initiation of negotiations with the USA on the creation of a new Central American Free-Trade Area (CAFTA). The establishment of a new Central American Tourism Agency was also announced at the summit.

Negotiations on CAFTA between the CACM countries and the USA were initiated in January 2003. An agreement was concluded between the USA and El Salvador, Guatemala, Honduras and Nicaragua in December, and with Costa Rica in January 2004. Under the resulting US-Central America Free-Trade Agreement some 80% of US exports of consumer and industrial goods and more than 50% of US agricultural exports to CAFTA countries were to become duty-free immediately upon its entry into force, with remaining tariffs to be eliminated over a 10-year period for consumer and industrial goods and over a 15-year period for agricultural exports. Almost all CAFTA exports of consumer and industrial products to the USA were to be duty-free on the Agreement's entry into force. The Agreement was signed by the US Trade Representative and CACM ministers of trade and economy, convened in Washington, DC, in May 2004. It required ratification by all national legislatures before entering into effect. Negotiations on a US-Dominican Republic free-trade agreement, to integrate the Dominican Republic into CAFTA, were concluded in March.

A meeting of SICA heads of state, held in December 2004, was concerned with economic and regional security issues. In March 2005 SICA ministers responsible for security, defence and the interior resolved to establish a special regional force to combat crime, drugs and arms trafficking and terrorism.

COMMON MARKET FOR EASTERN AND SOUTHERN AFRICA—COMESA

Address: COMESA Centre, Ben Bella Rd, POB 30051, 101101 Lusaka, Zambia.
Telephone: (1) 229726; **fax:** (1) 225107; **e-mail:** comesa@comesa .int; **internet:** www.comesa.int.

The COMESA treaty was signed by member states of the Preferential Trade Area for Eastern and Southern Africa (PTA) in November 1993. COMESA formally succeeded the PTA in December 1994. COMESA aims to promote regional economic and social development.

MEMBERS

Angola	Malawi
Burundi	Mauritius
Comoros	Rwanda
Congo, Democratic Republic	Seychelles
Djibouti	Sudan
Egypt	Swaziland
Eritrea	Uganda
Ethiopia	Zambia
Kenya	Zimbabwe
Madagascar	

Organization

(April 2005)

AUTHORITY

The Authority of the Common Market is the supreme policy organ of COMESA, comprising heads of state or of government of member countries. The inaugural meeting of the Authority took place in Lilongwe, Malawi, in December 1994. The ninth summit meeting was convened in Kampala, Uganda, in June 2004, and the 10th summit was scheduled to be held in Kigali, Rwanda, in May 2005.

COUNCIL OF MINISTERS

Each member government appoints a minister to participate in the Council. The Council monitors COMESA activities, including supervision of the Secretariat, recommends policy direction and development, and reports to the Authority.

A Committee of Governors of Central Banks advises the Authority and the Council of Ministers on monetary and financial matters.

COURT OF JUSTICE

The inaugural session of the COMESA Court of Justice was held in March 2001. The sub-regional Court is vested with the authority to settle disputes between member states and to adjudicate on matters concerning the interpretation of the COMESA treaty. The Court is composed of seven judges, who serve terms of five years' duration.

President: AKILANO MOLADE AKIWUMI (Kenya).

SECRETARIAT

COMESA's Secretariat comprises the following divisions: Trade, customs and monetary harmonization; Investment promotion and private sector development; Infrastructure development; and Information and networking. The COMESA/SADC task force operates from the secretariats of both organizations.

Secretary-General: J. E. O. (ERASTUS) MWENCHA (Kenya).

Activities

COMESA aims to promote economic and social progress in member states. Since its establishment in 1994 COMESA has pursued efforts to strengthen the process of regional economic integration that was initiated under the PTA, in order to help member states achieve sustainable economic growth. In May 1999 COMESA established a Free-Trade Area (FTA) Committee to facilitate and co-ordinate preparations for the establishment of the common market envisaged under the COMESA treaty. An extraordinary summit of COMESA heads of state or government, held in October 2000, established the FTA, with nine initial members: Djibouti, Egypt, Kenya, Madagascar, Malawi, Mauritius, Sudan, Zambia and Zimbabwe. The final deadline for all states to join was initially 30 April 2002. This was, however, subsequently extended to the end of 2005. Burundi and Rwanda became members of the FTA in February 2004. Trading practices within the FTA have been fully liberalized, including the elimination of non-tariff barriers, thereby enabling the free internal movement of goods, services and capital. It was envisaged that a regional customs union would be established in May 2005 (by the 10th summit meeting of the Authority), with a common external tariff set at 0%, 5%, 15% and 30% for, respectively, capital goods, raw materials, intermediate goods and final goods. In the early 2000s a COMESA Fund was under development, in order to assist member states address structural imbalances in their economies. COMESA also plans to form an economic community (entailing monetary union and the free movement of people between member states) by 2014. COMESA aims to formulate a common investment procedure to promote domestic, cross-border and direct foreign investment by ensuring the free movement of capital, services and labour. Heads of regional investment agencies, meeting in August 2000, developed a plan of action for the creation of a common investment agency to facilitate the establishment of a COMESA common investment area (CCIA), in accordance with recommendations by the Authority. A draft framework document on the CCIA was submitted for review by member states in December 2004, and the first of a planned four rounds of negotiations on this was held in March 2005. The development of a protocol to the COMESA treaty on the Free Movement of Persons, Labour, Services, the Right of Establishment and Residence is under way. In October 2001 COMESA concluded a Trade and Investment Framework Agreement with the USA.

A clearing house (based in Harare, Zimbabwe) dealing with credit arrangements and balance of payments issues became operational under the PTA in 1984 in order to facilitate intra-regional trade. The role of the clearing house was diminished by the liberalization of foreign exchange markets in the majority of member countries, and it ceased operating in 1996. In the early 2000s preparations were under way to create a regional payments and settlement system (REPSS). An Automated System of Customs Data (ASYCUDA) has been established to facilitate customs administration in all COMESA member states. Through support for capacity-building activities and the establishment of other specialized institutions (see below) COMESA aims to reinforce its objectives of regional integration. In August 2001 COMESA inaugurated the African Trade Insurance Agency (ATI), based in Nairobi, Kenya. The ATI manages COMESA's Regional Trade Facilation Project, promoting trade and investment activities throughout the region. The electronic African Commerce Exchange (ACE) was launched by the Authority in 2000.

Co-operation programmes have been implemented by COMESA in the agricultural, transport and communications, industrial, and energy sectors. A regional food security programme aims to ensure continuous adequate food supplies. In 1997 COMESA Heads of State advocated that the food sector be supported by the implementation of an irrigation action plan for the region. The organization also supports the establishment of common agricultural standards and phytosanitary regulations throughout the region in order to stimulate trade in food crops. In March 2005 more than 100 standards on quality assurance, covering mainly agricultural products, were adopted. Meeting for the first time in November 2002, COMESA ministers of agriculture determined to formulate a regional policy on genetically-modified organisms. At their second meeting, held in October 2004, ministers of agriculture agreed to prioritize agriculture in their development efforts and (in accordance with a Declaration of the African Union) to allocate at least 10% of national budgets to agriculture and rural development by 2008/09. Other organization-wide initiatives include a road customs declaration document, a scheme for third party motor vehicle insurance, a system of regional travellers cheques, and a regional customs bond guarantee scheme. A Trade Information Network co-ordinates information on the production and marketing of goods manufactured and traded in the region. COMESA is implementing the new COMESA Information Network, which aims to develop the utilization by member states of advanced information and communication technologies. A COMESA Telecommunications Company (COMTEL) was registered in May 2000. In January 2003 the Association of Regulators of Information and Communication for Eastern and Southern Africa was launched, under the auspices of COMESA. The first COMESA trade fair was held in Nairobi, Kenya, in May 1999. The first COMESA economic forum was held in Cairo, Egypt, in February 2000. The inaugural COMESA business summit was convened in June 2004 in Kampala, Uganda, concurrently with the ninth annual meeting of the Authority.

In May 1999 the COMESA Authority resolved to establish a Committee on Peace and Security comprising ministers of foreign affairs from member states. It was envisaged that the Committee would convene at least once a year to address matters concerning regional stability. (Instability in certain member states was regarded as a potential threat to the successful implementation of the FTA.) The Committee met for the first time in 2000. It was announced in September 2002 that the COMESA Treaty was to be amended to provide for the establishment of a formal conflict prevention and resolution structure to be governed by member countries' heads of state.

Since COMESA's establishment there have been concerns on the part of member states, as well as other regional non-member countries, in particular South Africa, of adverse rivalry between COMESA and the Southern African Development Community (SADC) and of a duplication of roles. In 1997 Lesotho and Mozambique terminated their membership of COMESA owing to concerns that their continued participation in the organization was incompatible with their SADC membership. Tanzania withdrew from COMESA in September 2000, reportedly also in view of its dual commitment to that organization and to SADC. The summit meeting of COMESA heads of state or government held in May of that year expressed support for an ongoing programme of co-operation by the secretariats of COMESA and SADC aimed at reducing the duplication of roles between the two organizations, and urged further mutual collaboration. A co-ordinating COMESA/SADC task force was established in 2001. COMESA has co-operated with other sub-regional organizations to finalize a common position on co-operation between African ACP countries and the EU under the Cotonou Agreement (concluded in June 2000, see chapter on the European Union). In June 2003 Namibia announced its withdrawal from COMESA.

COMESA INSTITUTIONS

African Trade Insurance Agency (ATI): based in Nairobi, Kenya; f. 2001; Man. Dir BERNARD DE HALDERANG.

COMESA Bankers Association: Private Bag 271, Kapeni House, 1st Floor, Blantyre, Malawi; tel. (1) 674236; fax (1) 674236; e-mail info@comesabankers.org; internet www.comesabankers.org; aims to strengthen co-operation between banks in the region; organizes training activities; conducts studies to harmonize banking laws and operations; initiated a project to combat bank fraud and money laundering in 2000; mems: commercial banking orgs in Burundi, Egypt, Eritrea, Ethiopia, Malawi, Rwanda, Swaziland, Sudan, Uganda; Exec. Sec. ERIC C. CHIKANDA (acting).

COMESA Leather and Leather Products Institute (LLPI): POB 5538, Addis Ababa, Ethiopia; tel. (1) 510361; fax (1) 512799; e-mail comesa.llpi@telecom.net.et; f. 1990 as the PTA Leather Institute; mems: Govts of 16 COMESA mem. states; Dir Dr GEREMEW DEBELE.

COMESA Metallurgical Industries Association (COMESAMIA): Kampala, Uganda; f. 1999; aims to advance capabilities in the production, processing and marketing of metals and allied engineering products, and to develop co-operation and networking in the sector.

Compagnie de réassurance de la Zone d'échanges préférentiels (ZEP-RE) (PTA Reinsurance Co): Anniversary Towers, University Way, POB 42769, Nairobi, Kenya; tel. (20) 212792; fax (20) 224102; e-mail mail@zep-re.com; internet www.zep-re.com; f.

1992 (began operations on 1 January 1993); provides local reinsurance services and training to personnel in the insurance industry; auth. cap. CMD 27.3m; Man. Dir S. M. LUBASI.

Eastern and Southern African Trade and Development Bank: NSSF Bldg, 23rd Floor, Bishop's Rd, POB 48596, Nairobi, Kenya; tel. (20) 712260; fax (20) 711510; e-mail official@ptabank.co.ke; internet www.ptabank.co.ke; f. 1983 as PTA Development Bank; aims to mobilize resources and finance COMESA activities to foster regional integration; promotes investment and co-financing within the region; in Jan. 2003 the US dollar replaced the UAPTA (PTA unit of account) as the Bank's reporting currency; shareholders 16 COMESA mem. states and the African Development Bank; cumulative project approvals (comprising 110 project loans and seven equity investments) totalled UAPTA 182.5m. at 31 Dec. 2002; cap. p.u. UAPTA 73.5m. (Dec. 2002); Pres. Dr MICHAEL GONDWE; Chair. Bd of Dirs MARGARET CHEMENGICH.

Federation of National Associations of Women in Business (FEMCOM): c/o COMESA Secretariat; f. 1993 to provide links between female business executives throughout the region and to promote greater awareness of relevant issues at policy level.

Finance

COMESA is financed by member states. The organization's activities have been undermined by delays by some countries in paying membership dues.

Publications

Annual Report of the Council of Ministers.

Asycuda Newsletter.

COMESA Journal.

COMESA Trade Directory (annually).

COMESA Trade Information Newsletter (monthly).

Demand/supply surveys, catalogues and reports.

THE COMMONWEALTH

Address: Commonwealth Secretariat, Marlborough House, Pall Mall, London, SW1Y 5HX, United Kingdom.

Telephone: (20) 7747-6500; **fax:** (20) 7930-0827; **e-mail:** info@commonwealth.int; **internet:** www.thecommonwealth.org.

The Commonwealth is a voluntary association of 53 independent states, comprising about one-quarter of the world's population. It includes the United Kingdom and most of its former dependencies, and former dependencies of Australia and New Zealand (themselves Commonwealth countries).

The evolution of the Commonwealth began with the introduction of self-government in Canada in the 1840s; Australia, New Zealand and South Africa became independent before the First World War. At the Imperial Conference of 1926 the United Kingdom and the Dominions, as they were then called, were described as 'autonomous communities within the British Empire, equal in status', and this change was enacted into law by the Statute of Westminster, in 1931.

The modern Commonwealth began with the entry of India and Pakistan in 1947, and of Sri Lanka (then Ceylon) in 1948. In 1949, when India decided to become a republic, the Commonwealth Heads of Government agreed to replace allegiance to the British Crown with recognition of the British monarch as Head of the Commonwealth, as a condition of membership. This was a precedent for a number of other members (see Heads of State and Heads of Government, below).

MEMBERS*

Antigua and Barbuda	Jamaica	Saint Vincent and the Grenadines
Australia	Kenya	Samoa
Bahamas	Kiribati	Seychelles
Bangladesh	Lesotho	Sierra Leone
Barbados	Malawi	Singapore
Belize	Malaysia	Solomon Islands
Botswana	The Maldives	South Africa
Brunei	Malta	Sri Lanka
Cameroon	Mauritius	Swaziland
Canada	Mozambique	Tanzania
Cyprus	Namibia	Tonga
Dominica	Nauru	Trinidad and Tobago
Fiji	New Zealand	Tuvalu
The Gambia	Nigeria	Uganda
Ghana	Pakistan	United Kingdom
Grenada	Papua New Guinea	Vanuatu
Guyana	Saint Christopher and Nevis	Zambia
India	Saint Lucia	

*Ireland, South Africa and Pakistan withdrew from the Commonwealth in 1949, 1961 and 1972 respectively. In October 1987 Fiji's membership was declared to have lapsed (following the proclamation of a republic there). It was readmitted in October 1997, but was suspended from participation in meetings of the Commonwealth in June 2000. Fiji was formally readmitted to Commonwealth meetings in December 2001 following the staging of free and fair legislative elections in August–September. Pakistan rejoined the Commonwealth in October 1989; however, it was suspended from participation in meetings in October 1999. South Africa rejoined in June 1994. Nigeria's membership was suspended in November 1995; it formally resumed membership in May 1999, when a new civilian government was inaugurated. Tuvalu, previously a special member of the Commonwealth with the right to participate in all activities except full Meetings of Heads of Government, became a full member in September 2000.

Note: In March 2002 Zimbabwe was suspended from participation in meetings of the Commonwealth. Zimbabwe announced its withdrawal from the Commonwealth in December 2003.

Dependencies and Associated States

Australia:	British Antarctic Territory
Ashmore and Cartier Islands	British Indian Ocean
Australian Antarctic	Territory
Territory	British Virgin Islands
Christmas Island	Cayman Islands
Cocos (Keeling) Islands	Channel Islands
Coral Sea Islands Territory	Falkland Islands
Heard Island and the	Gibraltar
McDonald Islands	Isle of Man
Norfolk Island	Montserrat
New Zealand:	Pitcairn Islands
Cook Islands	St Helena
Niue	Ascension
Ross Dependency	Tristan da Cunha
Tokelau	South Georgia and the South
United Kingdom:	Sandwich Islands
Anguilla	Turks and Caicos Islands
Bermuda	

HEADS OF STATE AND HEADS OF GOVERNMENT

At April 2005 21 member countries were monarchies and 32 were republics. All Commonwealth countries accept Queen Elizabeth II as the symbol of the free association of the independent member nations and as such the Head of the Commonwealth. Of the 32 republics, the offices of Head of State and Head of Government were combined in 21: Botswana, Cameroon, Cyprus, The Gambia, Ghana, Guyana, Kenya, Kiribati, Malawi, The Maldives, Mozambique, Namibia, Nauru, Nigeria, Seychelles, Sierra Leone, South Africa, Sri Lanka, Tanzania, Uganda and Zambia. The two offices were separated in the remaining 11: Bangladesh, Dominica, Fiji, India, Malta, Mauritius, Pakistan, Samoa, Singapore, Trinidad and Tobago and Vanuatu.

Of the monarchies, the Queen is Head of State of the United Kingdom and of 15 others, in each of which she is represented by a Governor-General: Antigua and Barbuda, Australia, the Bahamas, Barbados, Belize, Canada, Grenada, Jamaica, New Zealand, Papua New Guinea, Saint Christopher and Nevis, Saint Lucia, Saint Vincent and the Grenadines, Solomon Islands and Tuvalu. Brunei, Lesotho, Malaysia, Swaziland and Tonga are also monarchies, where the traditional monarch is Head of State.

The Governors-General are appointed by the Queen on the advice of the Prime Ministers of the country concerned. They are wholly independent of the Government of the United Kingdom.

HIGH COMMISSIONERS

Governments of member countries are represented in other Commonwealth countries by High Commissioners, who have a status equivalent to that of Ambassadors.

Organization

(April 2005)

The Commonwealth is not a federation: there is no central government nor are there any rigid contractual obligations such as bind members of the United Nations.

The Commonwealth has no written constitution but its members subscribe to the ideals of the Declaration of Commonwealth Principles unanimously approved by a meeting of heads of government in Singapore in 1971. Members also approved the 1977 statement on apartheid in sport (the Gleneagles Agreement); the 1979 Lusaka Declaration on Racism and Racial Prejudice; the 1981 Melbourne Declaration on relations between developed and developing countries; the 1983 New Delhi Statement on Economic Action; the 1983 Goa Declaration on International Security; the 1985 Nassau Declaration on World Order; the Commonwealth Accord on Southern Africa (1985); the 1987 Vancouver Declaration on World Trade; the Okanagan Statement and Programme of Action on Southern Africa (1987); the Langkawi Declaration on the Environment (1989); the Kuala Lumpur Statement on Southern Africa (1989); the Harare Commonwealth Declaration (1991); the Ottawa Declaration on Women and Structural Adjustment (1991); the Limassol Statement on the Uruguay Round of multilateral trade negotiations (1993); the Millbrook Commonwealth Action Programme on the Harare Declaration (1995); the Edinburgh Commonwealth Economic Declaration (1997); the Fancourt Commonwealth Declaration on Globalization and People-centred Development (1999); the Coolum Declaration on the Commonwealth in the 21st Century: Continuity and Renewal (2002); and the Aso Rock Commonwealth Declaration and Statement on Multilateral Trade (2003).

MEETINGS OF HEADS OF GOVERNMENT

Commonwealth Heads of Government Meetings (CHOGMs) are private and informal and operate not by voting but by consensus. The emphasis is on consultation and exchange of views for co-operation. A communiqué is issued at the end of every meeting. Meetings are normally held every two years in different capitals in the Commonwealth. The last meeting was held in Abuja, Nigeria, in December 2003. The next meeting was scheduled to be held in Malta in 2005.

OTHER CONSULTATIONS

Meetings at ministerial and official level are also held regularly. Since 1959 finance ministers have met in a Commonwealth country in the week prior to the annual meetings of the IMF and the World Bank. Meetings on education, legal, women's and youth affairs are held at ministerial level every three years. Ministers of health hold annual meetings, with major meetings every three years, and ministers of agriculture meet every two years. Ministers of finance, trade, labour and employment, industry, science, and the environment also hold periodic meetings. The first meeting of Commonwealth ministers of tourism was convened in March 2004.

Senior officials—cabinet secretaries, permanent secretaries to heads of government and others—meet regularly in the year between meetings of heads of government to provide continuity and to exchange views on various developments.

COMMONWEALTH SECRETARIAT

The Secretariat, established by Commonwealth heads of government in 1965, operates as an international organization at the service of all Commonwealth countries. It organizes consultations between governments and runs programmes of co-operation. Meetings of heads of government, ministers and senior officials decide these programmes and provide overall direction. A Board of Governors, on which all eligible member governments are represented, meets annually to review the Secretariat's work and approve its budget. The Board is supported by an Executive Committee which convenes four times a year to monitor implementation of the Secretariat's work programme. The Secretariat is headed by a secretary-general, elected by heads of government.

In 2002 the Secretariat was restructured, with a view to strengthening the effectiveness of the organization to meet the priorities determined by the meeting of Heads of Government held in Coolum, Australia, in March 2002. Under the reorganization the number of deputy secretaries-general was reduced from three to two. Certain work divisions were amalgamated, while new units or sections, concerned with youth affairs, human rights and good offices, were created to strengthen further activities in those fields. Accordingly, the new divisional structure was as follows: Legal and constitutional affairs; Political affairs; Corporate services; Communications and public affairs; Strategic planning and evaluation; Economic affairs; Governance and institutional development; Social transformation programmes; and Special advisory services. In addition there were units responsible for human rights, youth affairs, and project management and referrals, and an Office of the Secretary-General.

The main programme areas of the Secretariat's strategic plan for 2004–06 were: Good offices for peace; Democracy and consensus building; Rule of law; Human rights; International trade; Investment; Finance and debt; Public sector development; Environmentally sustainable development; Small states; Education; Health; Young people; Gender equality and equity; Capacity-building and institutional development; and Secretariat governance, management and communications.

Secretary-General: Rt Hon. Donald (Don) C. McKinnon (New Zealand).

Deputy Secretaries-General: Florence Mugasha (Uganda), Winston A. Cox (Barbados).

Activities

INTERNATIONAL AFFAIRS

In October 1991 heads of government, meeting in Harare, Zimbabwe, issued the Harare Commonwealth Declaration, in which they reaffirmed their commitment to the Commonwealth Principles declared in 1971, and stressed the need to promote sustainable development and the alleviation of poverty. The Declaration placed emphasis on the promotion of democracy and respect for human rights and resolved to strengthen the Commonwealth's capacity to assist countries in entrenching democratic practices. In November 1995 Commonwealth heads of government, convened in New Zealand, formulated and adopted the Millbrook Commonwealth Action Programme on the Harare Declaration, to promote adherence by member countries to the fundamental principles of democracy and human rights (as proclaimed in the 1991 Declaration). The Programme incorporated a framework of measures to be pursued in support of democratic processes and institutions, and actions to be taken in response to violations of the Harare Declaration principles, in particular the unlawful removal of a democratically-elected government. A Commonwealth Ministerial Action Group on the Harare Declaration (CMAG) was to be established to implement this process and to assist the member country involved to comply with the Harare principles. On the basis of this Programme, the leaders suspended Nigeria from the Commonwealth with immediate effect, following the execution by that country's military Government of nine environmental and human rights protesters and a series of other violations of human rights. The meeting determined to expel Nigeria from the Commonwealth if no 'demonstrable progress' had been made towards the establishment of a democratic authority by the time of the next summit meeting. In addition, the Programme formulated measures to promote sustainable development in member countries, which was considered to be an important element in sustaining democracy, and to facilitate consensus-building within the international community.

In December 1995 CMAG convened for its inaugural meeting in London. The Group, comprising the ministers of foreign affairs of Canada, Ghana, Jamaica, Malaysia, New Zealand, South Africa, the United Kingdom and Zimbabwe (with membership to be reconstituted periodically), commenced by considering efforts to restore democratic government in the three Commonwealth countries then under military regimes, i.e. The Gambia, Nigeria and Sierra Leone. At the second meeting of the Group, in April 1996, ministers commended the conduct of presidential and parliamentary elections in Sierra Leone and the announcement by The Gambia's military leaders to proceed with a transition to civilian rule. In June a three-member CMAG delegation visited The Gambia to reaffirm Commonwealth support of the transition process in that country and to identify possible areas of further Commonwealth assistance. In August the Gambian authorities issued a decree removing the ban on political activities and parties, although shortly afterwards they prohibited certain parties and candidates involved in political life prior to the military take-over from contesting the elections. CMAG recommended that in such circumstances no Commonwealth observers should be sent to either the presidential or parliamentary elections, which were held in September 1996 and January 1997 respectively. Following the restoration of a civilian Government in early 1997, CMAG requested the Commonwealth Secretary-General to extend technical assistance to The Gambia in order to consolidate the democratic transition process. In April 1996 it was noted that the human rights situation in Nigeria had continued to deteriorate. CMAG, having pursued unsuccessful efforts to initiate dialogue with the Nigerian authorities, outlined a series of punitive and restrictive measures (including visa restrictions on members of the administration, a cessation of sporting contacts and an embargo on the export of armaments) that it would recommend for collective Commonwealth action in order to exert further pressure for reform in Nigeria. Following a meeting of a high-level delegation of the Nigerian Government and CMAG in June, the Group agreed to postpone the implementation of the sanctions, pending progress on the dialogue. (Canada, however, determined, unilaterally, to impose the measures with immediate effect; the United Kingdom did so in accordance with a decision of the European Union to implement limited sanctions against Nigeria.) A proposed CMAG mission to Nigeria was postponed in August, owing to restrictions imposed by the military authorities on access to political detainees and other civilian activists in that country. In September the Group agreed to proceed with the visit and to delay further a decision on the implementation of sanction measures. CMAG, without the participation of the representative of the Canadian Government, undertook its ministerial mission in November. In July 1997 the Group reiterated the Commonwealth Secretary-General's condemnation of a military coup in Sierra Leone in May, and decided that the country's participation in meetings of the Commonwealth should be suspended pending the restoration of a democratic government.

In October 1997 Commonwealth heads of government, meeting in Edinburgh, United Kingdom, endorsed CMAG's recommendation that the imposition of sanctions against Nigeria be held in abeyance pending the scheduled completion of a transition programme towards democracy by October 1998. It was also agreed that CMAG be formally constituted as a permanent organ to investigate abuses of human rights throughout the Commonwealth. Jamaica and South Africa were to be replaced as members of CMAG by Barbados and Botswana, respectively.

In March 1998 CMAG commended the efforts of the Economic Community of West African States (ECOWAS) in restoring the democratically-elected Government of President Ahmed Tejan Kabbah in Sierra Leone, and agreed to remove all restrictions on Sierra Leone's participation in Commonwealth activities. Later in that month, a representative mission of CMAG visited Sierra Leone to express its support for Kabbah's administration and to consider the country's needs in its process of reconstruction. At the CMAG meeting held in October members agreed that Sierra Leone should no longer be considered under the Group's mandate; however, they urged the Secretary-General to continue to assist that country in the process of national reconciliation and to facilitate negotiations with opposition forces to ensure a lasting cease-fire. A Special Envoy of the Secretary-General was appointed to co-operate with the UN, ECOWAS and the OAU (now African Union—AU) in monitoring the implementation of the Sierra Leone peace process, and the Commonwealth has supported the rebuilding of the Sierra Leone police force. In September 2001 CMAG recommended that Sierra Leone be removed from its remit, but that the Secretary-General should continue to monitor developments there.

In April 1998 the Nigerian military leader, Gen. Sani Abacha, confirmed his intention to conduct a presidential election in August, but indicated that, following an agreement with other political organizations, he was to be the sole candidate. In June, however, Abacha died suddenly. His successor, Gen. Abdulsalam Abubakar, immediately released several prominent political prisoners, and in early July agreed to meet with the Secretaries-General of the UN and the Commonwealth to discuss the release of the imprisoned opposition leader, Chief Moshood Abiola. Abubakar also confirmed his intention to abide by the programme for transition to civilian rule by October. In mid-July, however, shortly before he was to have been liberated, Abiola died. The Commonwealth Secretary-General subsequently endorsed a new transition programme, which provided for the election of a civilian leader in May 1999. In October 1998 CMAG, convened for its 10th formal meeting, acknowledged Abubakar's efforts towards restoring a democratic government and recommended that member states begin to remove sanctions against Nigeria and that it resume participation in certain Commonwealth activities. The Commonwealth Secretary-General subsequently announced a programme of technical assistance to support Nigeria in the planning and conduct of democratic elections. Staff teams from the Commonwealth Secretariat observed local government, and state and governorship elections, held in December and in January 1999, respectively. A Commonwealth Observer Group was also dispatched to Nigeria to monitor preparations and conduct of legislative and presidential elections, held in February. While the Group reported several irregularities in the conduct of the polling, it confirmed that, in general, the conditions had existed for free and fair elections and that the elections were a legitimate basis for the transition of power to a democratic, civilian government. In April CMAG voted to readmit Nigeria to full membership on 29 May, upon the installation of the new civilian administration.

In 1999 the Commonwealth Secretary-General appointed a Special Envoy to broker an agreement in order to end a civil dispute in Honiara, Solomon Islands. An accord was signed in late June, and it was envisaged that the Commonwealth would monitor its implementation. In October a Commonwealth Multinational Police Peace

Monitoring Group was stationed in Solomon Islands; this was renamed the Commonwealth Multinational Police Assistance Group in February 2000. Following further internal unrest, however, the Group was disbanded. In June CMAG determined to send a new mission to Solomon Islands in order to facilitate negotiations between the opposing parties, to convey the Commonwealth's concern and to offer assistance. The Commonwealth welcomed the peace accord concluded in Solomon Islands in October, and extended its support to the International Peace Monitoring Team which was established to oversee implementation of the peace accords. CMAG welcomed the conduct of parliamentary elections held in Solomon Islands in December 2001. CMAG removed Solomon Islands from its agenda in December 2003 but was to continue to receive reports from the Secretary General on future developments.

In June 1999 an agreement was concluded between opposing political groups in Zanzibar, having been facilitated by the good offices of the Secretary-General; however, this was only partially implemented. In mid-October a special meeting of CMAG was convened to consider the overthrow of the democratically-elected Government in Pakistan in a military coup. The meeting condemned the action as a violation of Commonwealth principles and urged the new authorities to declare a timetable for the return to democratic rule. CMAG also resolved to send a four-member delegation, comprising the ministers of foreign affairs of Barbados, Canada, Ghana and Malaysia, to discuss this future course of action with the military regime. Pakistan was suspended from participation in meetings of the Commonwealth with immediate effect. The suspension, pending the restoration of a democratic government, was endorsed by heads of government, meeting in November, who requested that CMAG keep the situation in Pakistan under review. At the meeting, held in Durban, South Africa, CMAG was reconstituted to comprise the ministers of foreign affairs of Australia, Bangladesh, Barbados, Botswana, Canada, Malaysia, Nigeria and the United Kingdom. It was agreed that no country would serve for more than two consecutive two-year terms. CMAG was requested to remain actively involved in the post-conflict development and rehabilitation of Sierra Leone and the process of consolidating peace. In addition, it was urged to monitor persistent violations of the Harare Declaration principles in all countries. Heads of government also agreed to establish a new ministerial group on Guyana and to reconvene a ministerial committee on Belize, in order to facilitate dialogue in ongoing territorial disputes with neighbouring countries. The meeting established a 10-member Commonwealth High Level Review Group to evaluate the role and activities of the Commonwealth. In 2000 the Group initiated a programme of consultations to proceed with its mandate and established a working group of experts to consider the Commonwealth's role in supporting information technology capabilities in member countries.

In June 2000, following the overthrow in May of the Fijian Government by a group of armed civilians, and the subsequent illegal detention of members of the elected administration, CMAG suspended Fiji's participation in meetings of the Commonwealth pending the restoration of democratic rule. In September, upon the request of CMAG, the Secretary-General appointed a Special Envoy to support efforts towards political dialogue and a return to democratic rule in Fiji. The Special Envoy undertook his first visit in December. In December 2001, following the staging of democratic legislative elections in August–September, Fiji was readmitted to Commonwealth meetings on the recommendation of CMAG. Fiji was removed from CMAG's agenda in May 2004, although the Group determined to continue to note developments there, as judgments were still pending in the Fiji Supreme Court on unresolved matters concerning the democratic process.

In March 2001 CMAG resolved to send a ministerial mission to Zimbabwe, in order to relay to the government the Commonwealth's concerns at the ongoing violence and abuses of human rights in that country, as well as to discuss the conduct of parliamentary elections and extend technical assistance. The mission was rejected by the Zimbabwe Government, which queried the basis for CMAG's intervention in the affairs of an elected administration. In September, under the auspices of a group of Commonwealth foreign ministers partly derived from CMAG, the Zimbabwe Government signed the Abuja Agreement, which provided for the cessation of illegal occupations of white-owned farms and the resumption of the rule of law, in return for financial assistance to support the ongoing process of land reform in that country. In January 2002 CMAG expressed strong concern at the continuing violence and political intimidation in Zimbabwe. The summit of Commonwealth heads of government convened in early March (see below) also expressed concern at the situation in Zimbabwe, and, having decided on the principle that CMAG should be permitted to engage with any member Government deemed to be in breach of the organization's core values, mandated a Commonwealth Chairperson's Committee on Zimbabwe to determine appropriate action should an impending presidential election (scheduled to be held during that month) be found not to have been conducted freely and fairly. Following the publication by a Commonwealth observer team of an unfavourable report on the conduct of the election, the Committee decided to suspend Zimbabwe from meetings of the Commonwealth for one year. In March 2003 the Committee concluded that the suspension should remain in force pending consideration by the next summit of heads of government.

In March 2002, meeting in Coolum, near Brisbane, Australia, Commonwealth heads of government adopted the Coolum Declaration on the Commonwealth in the 21st Century: Continuity and Renewal, which reiterated commitment to the organization's principles and values. Leaders at the meeting condemned all forms of terrorism; welcomed the Millennium Development Goals declared by the UN; called on the Secretary-General to constitute a high-level expert group on implementing the objectives of the Fancourt Declaration; pledged continued support for small states; and urged renewed efforts to combat the spread of HIV/AIDS. The meeting adopted a report on the future of the Commonwealth drafted by the High Level Review Group. The document recommended strengthening the Commonwealth's role in conflict prevention and resolution and support of democratic practices; enhancing the good offices role of the Secretary-General; better promoting member states' economic and development needs; strengthening the organization's role in facilitating member states' access to international assistance; and promoting increased access to modern information and communications technologies. The meeting expanded CMAG's mandate to enable the Group to consider action against serious violations of the Commonwealth's core values perpetrated by elected administrations (such as that in Zimbabwe, see above) as well as by military regimes. At the summit CMAG was reconstituted to comprise the ministers of foreign affairs of Australia, the Bahamas, Bangladesh, Botswana, India, Malta, Nigeria and Samoa.

A Commonwealth team of observers dispatched to monitor legislative and provincial elections that were held in Pakistan, in October 2002, found them to have been well-organized and conducted in a largely transparent manner. The team made several recommendations on institutional and procedural issues. CMAG subsequently expressed concern over the promulgation of new legislation in Pakistan following the imposition earlier in the year of a number of extra-constitutional measures. CMAG determined that Pakistan should continue to be suspended from meetings of the Commonwealth, pending a review of the role and functioning of its democratic institutions. Pakistan's progress in establishing democratic institutions was welcomed by a meeting of CMAG in May 2003. In November 2002 a Commonwealth Expert Group on Papua New Guinea, established in the previous month to review the electoral process in that country (in view of unsatisfactory legislative elections that were conducted there in July), made several recommendations aimed at enhancing the future management of the electoral process.

In December 2003 the meeting of Heads of Government, held in Abuja, Nigeria, resolved to maintain the suspension of Pakistan and Zimbabwe from participation in Commonwealth meetings. President Mugabe of Zimbabwe responded by announcing his country's immediate withdrawal from the Commonwealth and alleging a pro-Western bias within the grouping. Support for Zimbabwe's position was declared by a number of members, including South Africa, Mozambique, Namibia and Zambia. A Commonwealth committee, consisting of six heads of government, was established to monitor the situation in Zimbabwe and only when the committee believed sufficient progress had been made towards consolidating democracy and promoting development within Zimbabwe would the Commonwealth be consulted on readmitting the country. At the meeting CMAG was reconstituted to comprise the ministers of foreign affairs of the Bahamas, Canada, India, Lesotho, Malta, Samoa, Sri Lanka and Tanzania.

In concluding the 2003 meeting heads of government issued the Aso Rock Commonwealth Declaration, which emphasized their commitment to strengthening development and democracy, and incorporated clear objectives in support of these goals. Priority areas identified included efforts to eradicate poverty and attain the Millennium Development Goals, strengthening democratic institutions, empowering women, promoting the involvement of civil society, combating corruption and recovering assets (for which a working group was to be established), facilitating finance for development, efforts to address the spread of HIV/AIDS and other diseases, combating the illicit trafficking in human beings, and promoting education. The leaders also adopted a separate statement on multilateral trade, in particular in support of the stalled Doha round of World Trade Organization negotiations.

In response to the earthquake and tsunami that devastated coastal areas of several Indian Ocean countries (including Bangladesh, India, Malaysia, the Maldives and Sri Lanka) in late December 2004, the Commonwealth Secretary-General appealed for assistance from Commonwealth Governments for the mobilization of emergency humanitarian relief. In early January 2005 the Secretariat dispatched a Disaster Relief Co-ordinator to the Maldives to assess the needs of that country and to co-ordinate ongoing relief and rehabilitation activities, and later in that month the Secretariat sent emergency medical doctors from other member states to the Mal-

dives. In mid-January, meeting during the fifth Summit of the Alliance of Small Island States, in Port Louis, Mauritius, the Secretaries-General of the Commonwealth, CARICOM, Pacific Islands Forum and Indian Ocean Commission determined to take collective action to strengthen the disaster preparedness and response capacities of their member countries in the Caribbean, Pacific and Indian Ocean areas.

Meeting in February 2005, CMAG expressed serious concern that President Musharraf of Pakistan had failed to relinquish the role of chief of army staff; at meetings held in May and September 2004 CMAG had urged the separation of the military and civilian offices held by the President, deeming this arrangement to be undemocratic. The Group recommended that the Secretary-General should maintain high-level contacts with Pakistan.

Political Affairs Division: assists consultation among member governments on international and Commonwealth matters of common interest. In association with host governments, it organizes the meetings of heads of government and senior officials. The Division services committees and special groups set up by heads of government dealing with political matters. The Secretariat has observer status at the United Nations, and the Division manages a joint office in New York to enable small states, which would otherwise be unable to afford facilities there, to maintain a presence at the United Nations. The Division monitors political developments in the Commonwealth and international progress in such matters as disarmament and the Law of the Sea. It also undertakes research on matters of common interest to member governments, and reports back to them. The Division is involved in diplomatic training and consular co-operation.

In 1990 Commonwealth heads of government mandated the Division to support the promotion of democracy by monitoring the preparations for and conduct of parliamentary, presidential or other elections in member countries at the request of national governments. During 2004 Commonwealth observer groups attended legislative elections in Antigua and Barbuda (in March); legislative elections in Sri Lanka (April); legislative and presidential elections in Malawi (May); local government elections in Sierra Leone (also May); a presidential election in Cameroon (October); legislative elections in Saint Christopher and Nevis (also October); and legislative and presidential elections in Mozambique (December). In January 2005 an observer group was dispatched to observe legislative elections in the Maldives.

Under the reorganization of the Secretariat in 2002 a Good Offices Section was established within the Division to strengthen and support the activities of the Secretary-General in addressing political conflict in member states and in assisting countries to adhere to the principles of the Harare Declaration. The Secretary-General's good offices may be directed to preventing or resolving conflict and assisting other international efforts to promote political stability.

Human Rights Unit: undertakes activities in support of the Commonwealth's commitment to the promotion and protection of fundamental human rights. It develops programmes, publishes human rights materials, co-operates with other organizations working in the field of human rights, in particular within the UN system, advises the Secretary-General, and organizes seminars and meetings of experts. The Unit aims to integrate human rights standards within all divisions of the Secretariat.

LAW

Legal and Constitutional Affairs Division: promotes and facilitates co-operation and the exchange of information among member governments on legal matters and assists in combating financial and organized crime, in particular transborder criminal activities. It administers, jointly with the Commonwealth of Learning, a distance training programme for legislative draftsmen and assists governments to reform national laws to meet the obligations of international conventions. The Division organizes the triennial meeting of ministers, Attorneys General and senior ministry officials concerned with the legal systems in Commonwealth countries. It has also initiated four Commonwealth schemes for co-operation on extradition, the protection of material cultural heritage, mutual assistance in criminal matters and the transfer of convicted offenders within the Commonwealth. It liaises with the Commonwealth Magistrates' and Judges' Association, the Commonwealth Legal Education Association, the Commonwealth Lawyers' Association (with which it helps to prepare the triennial Commonwealth Law Conference for the practising profession), the Commonwealth Association of Legislative Counsel, and with other international non-governmental organizations. The Division provides in-house legal advice for the Secretariat. The *Commonwealth Law Bulletin*, published twice a year, reports on legal developments in and beyond the Commonwealth. The Division promotes the exchange of information regarding national and international efforts to combat serious commercial crime through a quarterly publication, *Commonwealth Legal Assistance News*, and the *Crimewatch* bulletin.

The Heads of Government meeting, held in Coolum, Australia, in March 2002 endorsed a Plan of Action for combating international terrorism. A Commonwealth Committee on Terrorism, convened at ministerial level, was subsequently established to oversee its implementation.

A new expert group on good governance and the elimination of corruption in economic management convened for its first meeting in May 1998. In November 1999 Commonwealth heads of government endorsed a Framework for Principles for Promoting Good Governance and Combating Corruption, which had been drafted by the group. The conference of heads of government that met in Coolum in March 2002, endorsed a Commonwealth Local Government Good Practice Scheme, to be managed by the Commonwealth Local Government Forum (established in 1995).

ECONOMIC CO-OPERATION

In October 1997 Commonwealth heads of government, meeting in Edinburgh, the United Kingdom, signed an Economic Declaration that focused on issues relating to global trade, investment and development and committed all member countries to free-market economic principles. The Declaration also incorporated a provision for the establishment of a Trade and Investment Access Facility within the Secretariat in order to assist developing member states in the process of international trade liberalization and promote intra-Commonwealth trade.

In May 1998 the Commonwealth Secretary-General appealed to the Group of Eight industrialized nations to accelerate and expand the initiative to ease the debt burden of the most heavily indebted poor countries (HIPCs—see World Bank and IMF). In October Commonwealth finance ministers, convened in Ottawa, Canada, reiterated their appeal to international financial institutions to accelerate the HIPC initiative. The meeting also issued a Commonwealth Statement on the global economic crisis and endorsed several proposals to help to counter the difficulties experienced by several countries. These measures included a mechanism to enable countries to suspend payments on all short-term financial obligations at a time of emergency without defaulting, assistance to governments to attract private capital and to manage capital market volatility, and the development of international codes of conduct regarding financial and monetary policies and corporate governance. In March 1999 the Commonwealth Secretariat hosted a joint IMF-World Bank conference to review the HIPC scheme and initiate a process of reform. In November Commonwealth heads of government, meeting in South Africa, declared their support for measures undertaken by the World Bank and IMF to enhance the HIPC initiative. At the end of an informal retreat the leaders adopted the Fancourt Commonwealth Declaration on Globalization and People-Centred Development, which emphasized the need for a more equitable spread of wealth generated by the process of globalization, and expressed a renewed commitment to the elimination of all forms of discrimination, the promotion of people-centred development and capacity-building, and efforts to ensure developing countries benefit from future multilateral trade liberalization measures. In June 2002 the Commonwealth Secretary-General urged more generous funding of the HIPC initiative. Meetings of ministers of finance from Commonwealth African member countries participating in the HIPC initiative are convened periodically (most recently in March 2005). The Secretariat aims to assist HIPCs and other small economies through its Debt Recording and Management System, which was first used in 1985 and updated in 2002.

In February 1998 the Commonwealth Secretariat hosted the first Inter-Governmental Organizations Meeting to promote co-operation between small island states and the formulation of a unified policy approach to international fora. A second meeting was convened in March 2001, where discussions focused on the forthcoming WTO ministerial meeting and OECD's harmful tax competition initiative. In September 2000 Commonwealth finance ministers, meeting in Malta, reviewed the OECD initiative and agreed that the measures, affecting many member countries with offshore financial centres, should not be imposed on governments. The ministers mandated the involvement of the Commonwealth Secretariat in efforts to resolve the dispute; a joint working group was subsequently established by the Secretariat with the OECD. In April 2002 a meeting on international co-operation in the financial services sector, attended by representatives of international and regional organizations, donors and senior officials from Commonwealth countries, was held under Commonwealth auspices in Saint Lucia.

The first meeting of governors of central banks from Commonwealth countries was held in June 2001 in London.

The Commonwealth Secretariat was to contribute funding of €4m. towards the €20m. 'Hub and Spokes' project, launched in October 2004 by the European Commission as a capacity-building initiative in the areas of trade policy formulation, mainstreaming trade in poverty reduction strategies, and participation in international trade negotiations for the African, Caribbean and Pacific (ACP)

group of countries. The Secretariat was to manage the project in 55 of the 78 ACP member states.

Economic Affairs Division: organizes and services the annual meetings of Commonwealth ministers of finance and the ministerial group on small states and assists in servicing the biennial meetings of heads of government and periodic meetings of environment ministers. It engages in research and analysis on economic issues of interest to member governments and organizes seminars and conferences of government officials and experts. The Division undertook a major programme of technical assistance to enable developing Commonwealth countries to participate in the Uruguay Round of multilateral trade negotiations and has assisted the African, Caribbean and Pacific (ACP) group of countries in their trade negotiations with the European Union. It continues to help developing countries to strengthen their links with international capital markets and foreign investors. The Division also services groups of experts on economic affairs that have been commissioned by governments to report on, among other things, protectionism; obstacles to the North-South negotiating process; reform of the international financial and trading system; the debt crisis; management of technological change; the impact of change on the development process; environmental issues; women and structural adjustment; and youth unemployment. A separate section within the Division addresses the specific needs of small states and provides technical assistance. The work of the section covers a range of issues including trade, vulnerability, environment, politics and economics. A Secretariat Task Force services a Commonwealth Ministerial Group of Small States which was established in 1993 to provide strategic direction in addressing the concerns of small states and to mobilise support for action and assistance within the international community. The Economic Affairs Division also co-ordinates the Secretariat's environmental work and manages the Iwokrama International Centre for Rainforest Conservation and Development.

The Division played a catalytic role in the establishment of a Commonwealth Equity Fund, initiated in September 1990, to allow developing member countries to improve their access to private institutional investment, and promoted a Caribbean Investment Fund. The Division supported the establishment of a Commonwealth Private Investment Initiative (CPII) to mobilize capital, on a regional basis, for investment in newly-privatized companies and in small and medium-sized businesses in the private sector. The first regional fund under the CPII was launched in July 1996. The Commonwealth Africa Investment Fund (Comafin), was to be managed by the United Kingdom's official development institution, the Commonwealth Development Corporation, to assist businesses in 19 countries in sub-Saharan Africa, with initial resources of US $63.5m. In August 1997 a fund for the Pacific Islands was launched, with an initial capital of $15.0m. A $200m. South Asia Regional Fund was established at the Heads of Government Meeting in October. In October 1998 a fund for the Caribbean states was inaugurated, at a meeting of Commonwealth finance ministers. The 2001 summit of Commonwealth heads of government authorized the establishment of a new fund for Africa (Comafin II): this was inaugurated in March 2002, and attracted initial capital in excess of $200m.

SOCIAL WELFARE

Social Transformation Programmes Division: consists of three sections concerned with education, gender and health.

The **Education Section** arranges specialist seminars, workshops and co-operative projects, and commissions studies in areas identified by ministers of education, whose three-yearly meetings it also services. Its present areas of emphasis include improving the quality of and access to basic education; strengthening the culture of science, technology and mathematics education in formal and non-formal areas of education; improving the quality of management in institutions of higher learning and basic education; improving the performance of teachers; strengthening examination assessment systems; and promoting the movement of students between Commonwealth countries. The Section also promotes multi-sectoral strategies to be incorporated in the development of human resources. Emphasis is placed on ensuring a gender balance, the appropriate use of technology, promoting good governance, addressing the problems of scale particular to smaller member countries, and encouraging collaboration between governments, the private sector and other non-governmental organizations.

The **Gender Affairs Section** is responsible for the implementation of the Commonwealth Plan of Action for Gender Equality, covering the period 2005–15, which succeeded the Commonwealth Plan of Action on Gender and Development (adopted in 1995 and updated in 2000). The Plan of Action support efforts towards the achievement of the Millennium Development Goals, adopted by 189 governments attending a summit meeting of the UN General Assembly in September 2000, and the objectives of gender equality adopted by the 1995 Beijing Declaration and Platform for Action and the follow–up Beijing + 5 review conference held in 2000. Gender equality, poverty eradication, promotion of human rights, and strengthening democracy are recognized as intrinsically inter-related, and the Plan has a particular focus on the advancement of gender mainstreaming in the following areas: democracy, peace and conflict; human rights and law; poverty eradication and economic empowerment; and HIV/AIDS. In February–March 2005 Commonwealth ministers responsible for gender affairs attended the Beijing + 10 review conference.

The **Health Section** organizes ministerial, technical and expert group meetings and workshops, to promote co-operation on health matters, and the exchange of health information and expertise. The Section commissions relevant studies and provides professional and technical advice to member countries and to the Secretariat. It also supports the work of regional health organizations and promotes health for all people in Commonwealth countries.

Youth Affairs: A Youth Affairs Unit, reporting directly to a Deputy Secretary-General, was established within the Secretariat in 2002.

The Unit administers the **Commonwealth Youth Programme (CYP)** , which was initiated in 1973 to promote the involvement of young people in the economic and social development of their countries. The CYP, funded through separate voluntary contributions from governments, was awarded a budget of £2.5m. for 2005/06. The Programme's activities are centred on four key programmes: Youth enterprise and development; Youth networks and governance; Youth participation; and Youth work, education and training. Regional centres are located in Zambia (for Africa), India (for Asia), Guyana (for the Caribbean), and Australia (for the South Pacific). The Programme administers a Youth Study Fellowship scheme, a Youth Project Fund, a Youth Exchange Programme (in the Caribbean), and a Youth Service Awards Scheme. It also holds conferences and seminars, carries out research and disseminates information. The Commonwealth Youth Credit Initiative, launched in 1995, provides funds, training and advice to young entrepreneurs. A Plan of Action on Youth Empowerment to the Year 2005 was approved by a Commonwealth ministerial meeting held in Kuala Lumpur, Malaysia, in May 1998.

In March 2002 Commonwealth heads of government approved the Youth for the Future initiative to encourage and use the skills of young people throughout the Commonwealth. It was to comprise four main components: Youth enterprise development; Youth volunteers; Youth mentors; and Youth leadership awards.

TECHNICAL ASSISTANCE

Commonwealth Fund for Technical Co-operation (CFTC): f. 1971 to facilitate the exchange of skills between member countries and to promote economic and social development; it is administered by the Commonwealth Secretariat and financed by voluntary subscriptions from member governments. The CFTC responds to requests from member governments for technical assistance, such as the provision of experts for short- or medium-term projects, advice on economic or legal matters, in particular in the areas of natural resources management and public-sector reform, and training programmes. The CFTC also administers the Langkawi awards for the study of environmental issues, which is funded by the Canadian Government; the CFTC budget for 2005/06 amounted to £24.1m.

CFTC activities are mainly implemented by the following divisions:

Governance and Institutional Development Division: strengthens good governance in member countries, through advice, training and other expertise in order to build capacity in national public institutions. The Division administers the Commonwealth Service Abroad Programme (CSAP), which is funded by the CFTC. The Programme extends short-term technical assistance through highly qualified volunteers. The main objectives of the scheme are to provide expertise, training and exposure to new technologies and practices, to promote technology transfers and sharing of experiences and knowledge, and to support community workshops and other grassroots activities.

Special Advisory Services Division: advises on economic and legal issues, such as debt and financial management, natural resource development, multilateral trade issues, export marketing, trade facilitation, competitiveness and the development of enterprises.

Finance

The Secretariat's budget for 2005/06 was £12.4m. Member governments meet the cost of the Secretariat through subscriptions on a scale related to income and population.

Publications

Commonwealth Currents (quarterly).
International Development Policies (quarterly).

Report of the Commonwealth Secretary-General (every 2 years).
Numerous reports, studies and papers (catalogue available).

Commonwealth Organizations

(In the United Kingdom, unless otherwise stated)

PRINCIPAL BODIES

Commonwealth Business Council: 18 Pall Mall, London, SW1Y 5LU; tel. (20) 7024-8200; fax (20) 7930-3944; e-mail info@cbcglobelink.org; internet www.cbcglobelink.org; f. 1997 by the Commonwealth Heads of Government Meeting to promote co-operation between governments and the private sector in support of trade, investment and development; the Council aims to identify and promote investment opportunities, in particular in Commonwealth developing countries, to support countries and local businesses to work within the context of globalization, to promote capacity-building and the exchange of skills and knowledge (in particular through its Information Communication Technologies for Development programme), and to encourage co-operation among Commonwealth members; promotes good governance; supports the process of multilateral trade negotiations and other liberalization of trade and services; represents the private sector at government level; Dir-Gen. and CEO Dr MOHAN KAUL.

Commonwealth Foundation: Marlborough House, Pall Mall, London, SW1Y 5HY; tel. (20) 7930-3783; fax (20) 7839-8157; e-mail geninfo@commonwealth.int; internet www.commonwealthfoundation.com; f. 1966; intergovernmental body promoting people-to-people interaction, and collaboration within the non-governmental sector of the Commonwealth; supports non-governmental organizations, professional associations and Commonwealth arts and culture; awards an annual Commonwealth Writers' Prize; funds are provided by Commonwealth govts; Chair. Prof. GUIDO DE MARCO (Mozambique); Dir COLIN BALL (United Kingdom); publ. *Commonwealth People* (quarterly).

Commonwealth of Learning (COL): 1055 West Hastings St, Suite 1200, Vancouver, BC V6E 2E9, Canada; tel. (604) 775-8200; fax (604) 775-8210; e-mail info@col.org; internet www.col.org; f. 1987 by Commonwealth Heads of Government to promote the devt and sharing of distance education and open learning resources, including materials, expertise and technologies, throughout the Commonwealth and in other countries; implements and assists with national and regional educational programmes; acts as consultant to international agencies and national governments; conducts seminars and studies on specific educational needs; COL is financed by Commonwealth governments on a voluntary basis; in 1999 heads of government endorsed an annual core budget for COL of US $9m; Pres. and CEO Sir JOHN DANIEL (Canada/UK); publs *Connections*, *EdTech News*.

The following represents a selection of other Commonwealth organizations:

AGRICULTURE AND FORESTRY

Commonwealth Forestry Association: 2 Webbs Barn Cottage, Witney Rd, Kingston Bagpuize, Abingdon, Oxon, OX13 5AN; tel. (1865) 820935; fax (870) 0116645; e-mail alan.pottinger@cfa-international.org; internet www.cfa-international.org; f. 1921; produces, collects and circulates information relating to world forestry and promotes good management, use and conservation of forests and forest lands throughout the world; mems: 1,000; Chair. Prof. J. BURLEY; publs *International Forestry Review* (quarterly), *Commonwealth Forestry News* (quarterly), *Commonwealth Forestry Handbook* (irregular).

Standing Committee on Commonwealth Forestry: Forestry Commission, 231 Corstorphine Rd, Edinburgh, EH12 7AT; tel. (131) 314-6137; fax (131) 316-4344; e-mail libby.jones@forestry.gsi.gov.uk; f. 1923 to provide continuity between Confs, and to provide a forum for discussion on any forestry matters of common interest to mem. govts which may be brought to the Cttee's notice by any mem. country or organization; 54 mems; 2005 Conference: Sri Lanka; Sec. LIBBY JONES; publ. *Newsletter* (quarterly).

COMMONWEALTH STUDIES

Institute of Commonwealth Studies: 28 Russell Sq., London, WC1B 5DS; tel. (20) 7862-8844; fax (20) 7862-8820; e-mail ics@sas.ac.uk; internet www.sas.ac.uk/commonwealthstudies; f. 1949 to promote advanced study of the Commonwealth; provides a library and meeting place for postgraduate students and academic staff engaged in research in this field; offers postgraduate teaching; Dir Prof. TIMOTHY SHAW; publs *Annual Report, Collected Seminar Papers, Newsletter, Theses in Progress in Commonwealth Studies*.

COMMUNICATIONS

Commonwealth Telecommunications Organization: Clareville House, 26–27 Oxendon St, London, SW1Y 4EL; tel. (20) 7930-5511; fax (20) 7930-4248; e-mail info@cto.int; internet www.cto.int; f. 1967 as an international development partnership between Commonwealth and non-Commonwealth governments, business and civil society organizations; aims to help to bridge the digital divide and to achieve social and economic development by delivering to developing countries knowledge-sharing programmes in the use of information and communication technologies (ICT) in the specific areas of telecommunications, IT, broadcasting and the internet; CEO Dr EKWOW SPIO-GARBRAH; publs *CTO Update* (quarterly), *Annual Report, Research Reports*.

EDUCATION AND CULTURE

Association of Commonwealth Universities (ACU): John Foster House, 36 Gordon Sq., London, WC1H 0PF; tel. (20) 7380-6700; fax (20) 7387-2655; e-mail info@acu.ac.uk; internet www.acu.ac.uk; f. 1913; promotes international co-operation and understanding; provides assistance with staff and student mobility and development programmes; researches and disseminates information about universities and relevant policy issues; organizes major meetings of Commonwealth universities and their representatives; acts as a liaison office and information centre; administers scholarship and fellowship schemes; operates a policy research unit; mems: 500 universities in 36 Commonwealth countries or regions; Sec.-Gen. Dr JOHN ROWETT; publs include *Yearly Review* (annually), *Commonwealth Universities Yearbook* (annually), *ACU Bulletin* (quarterly), *Report of the Council of the ACU* (annually), *Who's Who of Executive Heads: Vice-Chancellors, Presidents, Principals and Rectors, International Awards*, student information papers (study abroad series).

Commonwealth Association for Education in Journalism and Communication (CAEJC): c/o Faculty of Law, University of Western Ontario, London, ON N6A 3K7, Canada; tel. (519) 661-3348; fax (519) 661-3790; e-mail caejc@julian.uwo.ca; f. 1985; aims to foster high standards of journalism and communication education and research in Commonwealth countries and to promote co-operation among institutions and professions; c. 700 mems in 32 Commonwealth countries; Pres. Prof. SYED ARABI IDID (Malaysia); Sec. Prof. ROBERT MARTIN (Canada); publ. *CAEJAC Journal* (annually).

Commonwealth Association of Science, Technology and Mathematics Educators (CASTME): 7 Lion Yard, Tremadoc Rd, London, SW4 7NQ; tel. (20) 7819-3932; fax (20) 7720-5403; e-mail ann.powell@lect.org.uk; internet www.castme.org; f. 1974; special emphasis is given to the social significance of education in these subjects; organizes an Awards Scheme to promote effective teaching and learning in these subjects, and biennial regional seminars; Hon. Sec. Dr LYN HAINES; publ. *CASTME Journal* (quarterly).

Commonwealth Council for Educational Administration and Management: International Educational Leadership and Management Centre, Lincoln School of Management, Lincoln University Campus, Brayford Pool, Lincoln LNG 7TS; tel. (1522) 886071; fax (1522) 886023; f. 1970; aims to foster quality in professional development and links among educational administrators; holds nat. and regional confs, as well as visits and seminars; mems: 24 affiliated groups representing 3,000 persons; Pres. Prof. ANGELA THODAY; publ. *International Studies in Educational Administration* (2 a year).

Commonwealth Institute: 230 Kensington High St, London, W8 6NQ; tel. (20) 7603-4535; fax (20) 7603-4525; e-mail info@commonwealth.org.uk; internet www.commonwealth.org.uk; f. 1893 as the Imperial Institute; restructured as an independent pan-Commonwealth agency Jan. 2000; governed by a Bd of Trustees elected by the Bd of Governors; Commonwealth High Commissioners to the United Kingdom act as *ex-officio* Governors; the Inst. houses a Commonwealth Resource and Literature Library and a Conference and Events Centre; supplies educational resource materials and training throughout the United Kingdom; provides internet services to the Commonwealth; operates as an arts and conference centre, running a Commonwealth-based cultural programme; a five-year strategic plan, entitled 'Commonwealth 21', was inaugurated in 1998; in 2004 the Institute, in collaboration with Cambridge University, established a Centre of Commonwealth Education; Chair. JUDITH HANRATTY; Chief Exec. DAVID FRENCH; publ. *Annual Review*.

League for the Exchange of Commonwealth Teachers: 7 Lion Yard, Tremadoc Rd, London, SW4 7NQ; tel. (20) 7498-1101; fax (20) 7720-5403; e-mail info@lect.org.uk; internet www.lect.org.uk; f. 1901; promotes educational exchanges between teachers in Aus-

tralia, the Bahamas, Barbados, Bermuda, Canada, Guyana, India, Jamaica, Kenya, Malawi, New Zealand, Pakistan, South Africa and Trinidad and Tobago; Dir ANNA TOMLINSON; publs *Annual Report, Exchange Teacher* (annually).

HEALTH

Commonwealth Medical Trust (COMMAT): BMA House, Tavistock Sq., London, WC1H 9JP; tel. (20) 7272-8492; fax (20) 7272-8569; e-mail office@commat.org; internet www.commat.org; f. 1962 (as the Commonwealth Medical Association) for the exchange of information; provision of tech. co-operation and advice; formulation and maintenance of a code of ethics; promotes the Right to Health; liaison with WHO and other UN agencies on health issues; meetings of its Council are held every three years; mems: medical asscns in Commonwealth countries; Dir MARIANNE HASLEGRAVE.

Commonwealth Pharmaceutical Association: 1 Lambeth High St, London, SE1 7JN; tel. (20) 7572-2364; fax (20) 7572-2508; e-mail admin@commonwealthpharmacy.org; internet www.commonwealthpharmacy.org; f. 1970 to promote the interests of pharmaceutical sciences and the profession of pharmacy in the Commonwealth to maintain high professional standards, encourage links between members and the creation of nat. asscns; and to facilitate the dissemination of information; holds confs (every four years) and regional meetings; mems: pharmaceutical asscns from over 40 Commonwealth countries; Pres. GRACE ALLEN YOUNG; publ. *Quarterly Newsletter*.

Commonwealth Society for the Deaf: 34 Buckingham Palace Rd, London, SW1W 0RE; tel. (20) 7233-5700; fax (20) 7233-5800; e-mail sound.seekers@btinternet.com; internet www.sound-seekers.org.uk; undertakes initiatives to establish audiology services in developing Commonwealth countries, including mobile clinics to provide outreach services; aims to educate local communities in aural hygiene and the prevention of ear infection and deafness; provides audiological equipment and organizes the training of audiological maintenance technicians; conducts research into the causes and prevention of deafness; Chief Exec. GARY WILLIAMS; publ. *Annual Report*.

Sight Savers International: Grosvenor Hall, Bolnore Rd, Haywards Heath,West Sussex, RH16 4BX; tel. (1444) 446600; fax (1444) 446688; e-mail generalinformation@sightsavers.org.uk; internet www.sightsavers.org; f. 1950 to prevent blindness and restore sight in developing countries, and to provide education and community-based training for incurably blind people; operates in collaboration with local partners, with high priority given to training local staff; Chair. Sir JOHN COLES; Dir RICHARD PORTER; publ. *Sight Savers News*.

INFORMATION AND THE MEDIA

Commonwealth Broadcasting Association: 17 Fleet St, London, EC4Y 1AA; tel. (20) 7583-5550; fax (20) 7583-5549; e-mail cba@cba.org.uk; internet www.cba.org.uk; f. 1945; gen. confs are held every two years (2004: Fiji); mems: 97 in 57 countries; Pres. GEORGE VALARINO; Sec.-Gen. ELIZABETH SMITH; publs *Commonwealth Broadcaster* (quarterly), *Commonwealth Broadcaster Directory* (annually).

Commonwealth Institute: see under Education and Culture.

Commonwealth Journalists Association: internet www.commonwealthjournalists.org; f. 1978 to promote co-operation between journalists in Commonwealth countries, organize training facilities and confs, and foster understanding among Commonwealth peoples; Pres. RAY EKPU; Exec. Dir LAWRIE BREEN; publ. *Newsletter* (3 a year).

Commonwealth Press Union (Association of Commonwealth Newspapers, News Agencies and Periodicals): 17 Fleet St, London, EC4Y 1AA; tel. (20) 7583-7733; fax (20) 7583-6868; e-mail lindsay@cpu.org.uk; internet www.cpu.org.uk; f. 1950; promotes the welfare of the Commonwealth press; provides training for journalists and organizes biennial confs; mems: c. 700 newspapers, news agencies, periodicals in 42 Commonwealth countries; Exec. Dir LINDSAY ROSS; publ. *Annual Report*.

LAW

Commonwealth Lawyers' Association: c/o Institute of Commonwealth Studies, 28 Russell Sq., London, WC1B 5DS; tel. (20) 7862-8824; fax (20) 7862-8816; e-mail cla@sas.ac.uk; internet www.commonwealthlawyers.com; f. 1983 (fmrly the Commonwealth Legal Bureau); seeks to maintain and promote the rule of law throughout the Commonwealth, by ensuring that the people of the Commonwealth are served by an independent and efficient legal profession; upholds professional standards and promotes the availability of legal services; assists in organizing the triennial Commonwealth law confs; Exec. Sec. CLAIRE MARTIN; publs *The Commonwealth Lawyer, Clarion*.

Commonwealth Legal Advisory Service: c/o British Institute of International and Comparative Law, Charles Clore House, 17 Russell Sq., London, WC1B 5DR; tel. (20) 7636-5802; fax (20) 7323-2016; e-mail bicl@dial.pipex.com; f. 1962; financed by the British Institute and by contributions from Commonwealth govts; provides research facilities for Commonwealth govts and law reform commissions; Chair. Rt Hon. Lord BROWNE-WILKINSON; publ. _New Memoranda_ series.

Commonwealth Legal Education Association: c/o Legal and Constitutional Affairs Division, Commonwealth Secretariat, Marlborough House, Pall Mall, London, SW1Y 5HX; tel. (20) 7747-6415; fax (20) 7747-6406; e-mail clea@commonwealth.int; internet www.clea.org.uk; f. 1971 to promote contacts and exchanges and to provide information regarding legal education; Gen. Sec. JOHN HATCHARD; publs _Commonwealth Legal Education Association Newsletter_ (3 a year), _Directory of Commonwealth Law Schools_ (every 2 years).

Commonwealth Magistrates' and Judges' Association: Uganda House, 58/59 Trafalgar Sq., London, WC2N 5DX; tel. (20) 7976-1007; fax (20) 7976-2395; e-mail info@cmja.org; internet www.cmja.org; f. 1970 to advance the administration of the law by promoting the independence of the judiciary, to further education in law and crime prevention and to disseminate information; confs and study tours; corporate membership for asscns of the judiciary or courts of limited jurisdiction; assoc. membership for individuals; Pres. Hon. Chief Justice RICHARD BANDA; Exec. Vice-Pres. MICHAEL A. LAMBERT; publs _Commonwealth Judicial Journal_ (2 a year), _CMJA News_.

PARLIAMENTARY AFFAIRS

Commonwealth Parliamentary Association: Westminster House, Suite 700, 7 Millbank, London, SW1P 3JA; tel. (20) 7799-1460; fax (20) 7222-6073; e-mail hq.sec@cpahq.org; internet www.cpahq.org; f. 1911 to promote understanding and co-operation between Commonwealth parliamentarians; organization: Exec. Cttee of 35 MPs responsible to annual Gen. Assembly; 170 brs in national, state, provincial and territorial parliaments and legislatures throughout the Commonwealth; holds annual Commonwealth Parliamentary Confs and seminars; also regional confs and seminars; Sec.-Gen. Hon. DENIS MARSHALL; publ. _The Parliamentarian_ (quarterly).

PROFESSIONAL AND INDUSTRIAL RELATIONS

Commonwealth Association of Architects: 66 Portland Pl., London, W1N 4AD; tel. (20) 7490-3024; fax (20) 7253-2592; e-mail info@comarchitect.org; internet comarchitect.org; f. 1964; an asscn of 38 socs of architects in various Commonwealth countries; objectives: to facilitate the reciprocal recognition of professional qualifications; to provide a clearing house for information on architectural practice; and to encourage collaboration. Plenary confs every three years; regional confs are also held; Exec. Dir TONY GODWIN; publs _Handbook, Objectives and Procedures: CAA Schools Visiting Boards, Architectural Education in the Commonwealth_ (annotated bibliography of research), _CAA Newsnet_ (2 a year), a survey and list of schools of architecture.

Commonwealth Association for Public Administration and Management (CAPAM): 1075 Bay St, Suite 402, Toronto, ON M5S 2B1, Canada; tel. (416) 920-3337; fax (416) 920-6574; e-mail capam@capam.ca; internet www.capam.comnet.mt/; f. 1994; aims to promote sound management of the public sector in Commonwealth countries and to assist those countries undergoing political or financial reforms; an international awards programme to reward innovation within the public sector was introduced in 1997, and is awarded every 2 years; more than 1,200 individual mems and 80 institutional memberships in some 80 countries; Pres. Hon. JOCELYNE BOURGON (Canada); Exec. Dir GILLIAN MASON (Canada).

SCIENCE AND TECHNOLOGY

Commonwealth Engineers' Council: c/o Institution of Civil Engineers, One Great George St, London, SW1P 3AA; tel. (20) 7222-7722; fax (20) 7223-1806; e-mail international@ice.org.uk; internet www.ice.org.uk/cec; f. 1946; the Council meets every two years to provide an opportunity for engineering institutions of Commonwealth countries to exchange views on collaboration; Pres. Prof. TONY RIDLEY; Sec.-Gen. TOM FOULKES.

Commonwealth Geological Surveys Forum: c/o Commonwealth Science Council, CSC Earth Sciences Programme, Marlborough House, Pall Mall, London, SW1Y 5HX; tel. (20) 7839-3411; fax (20) 7839-6174; e-mail comsci@gn.apc.org; f. 1948 to promote collaboration in geological, geochemical, geophysical and remote sensing techniques and the exchange of information; Geological Programme Officer Dr SIYAN MALOMO.

SPORT

Commonwealth Games Federation: 4th Floor, 26 Upper Brooke Street, London, W1K 7QE; tel. (20) 7491-8801; fax (20) 7409-7803; e-mail info@thecgf.com; internet www.thecgf.com; the Games were first held in 1930 and are now held every four years; participation is limited to competitors representing the mem. countries of the Commonwealth; 2006 games: Melbourne, Australia, in March; mems: 72 affiliated bodies; Pres. HRH The Earl of WESSEX; CEO MICHAEL HOOPER.

YOUTH

Commonwealth Youth Exchange Council: 7 Lion Yard, Tremadoc Rd, London, SW4 7NQ; tel. (20) 7498-6151; fax (20) 7622-4365; e-mail mail@cyec.org.uk; internet www.cyec.org.uk; f. 1970; promotes contact between groups of young people of the United Kingdom and other Commonwealth countries by means of educational exchange visits, provides information for organizers and allocates grants; provides host governments with technical assistance for delivery of the Commonwealth Youth Forum, held every two years (2005: Malta); 222 mem. orgs; Chief Exec. V. S. G. CRAGGS; publs _Contact_ (handbook), _Exchange_ (newsletter), _Final Communiqués_ (of the Commonwealth Youth Forums), _Safety and Welfare_ (guide-lines for Commonwealth Youth Exchange groups).

Duke of Edinburgh's Award International Association: Award House, 7-11 St Matthew St, London, SW1P 2JT; tel. (20) 7222-4242; fax (20) 7222-4141; e-mail sect@intaward.org; internet www.intaward.org; f. 1956; offers a programme of leisure activities for young people, comprising Service, Expeditions, Physical Recreation, and Skills; operates in more than 60 countries (not confined to the Commonwealth); International Sec.-Gen. DAVID MANSON; publs _Award World_ (2 a year), _Annual Report_, handbooks and guides.

MISCELLANEOUS

Commonwealth Countries League: 96 High Street, Hampton Wick, Kingston-upon-Thames KT1 4DQ; tel. (20) 8943-3001; fax (20) 8458-0763; e-mail info@ccl-int.org.uk; internet www.ccl-int.org.uk; f. 1925 to secure equal opportunities and status between men and women in the Commonwealth, to act as a link between Commonwealth women's orgs, and to promote and finance secondary education of disadvantaged girls of high ability in their own countries, through the CCL Educational Fund; holds meetings with speakers and an annual conf., organizes the annual Commonwealth Fair for fund-raising; individual mems and affiliated socs in the Commonwealth; Exec. Chair. LEOLYNN JONES; publs _CCL Newsletter_ (3 a year), _Annual Report_.

Commonwealth War Graves Commission: 2 Marlow Rd, Maidenhead, Berks, SL6 7DX; tel. (1628) 634221; fax (1628) 771208; internet www.cwgc.org; casualty and cemetery enquiries e-mail casualty.enq@cwgc.org; f. 1917 (as Imperial War Graves Commission); responsible for the commemoration in perpetuity of the 1.7m. members of the Commonwealth Forces who died during the wars of 1914–18 and 1939–45; provides for the marking and maintenance of war graves and memorials at some 23,000 locations in 150 countries; mems: Australia, Canada, India, New Zealand, South Africa, United Kingdom; Pres. HRH The Duke of KENT; Dir-Gen. RICHARD KELLAWAY.

Joint Commonwealth Societies' Council: c/o Royal Commonwealth Society, 18 Northumberland Ave, London, WC2N 5BJ; tel. (20) 7930-6733; fax (20) 7930-9705; e-mail jcsc@rcsint.org; internet www.commonwealthday.com; f. 1947; provides a forum for the exchange of information regarding activities of mem. orgs which promote understanding among countries of the Commonwealth; co-ordinates the distribution of the Commonwealth Day message by Queen Elizabeth, organizes the observance of the Commonwealth Day and produces educational materials relating to the occasion; mems: 13 unofficial Commonwealth orgs and four official bodies; Chair. Sir PETER MARSHALL; Sec. Sir DAVID THORNE.

Royal Commonwealth Ex-Services League: 48 Pall Mall, London, SW1Y 5JG; tel. (20) 7973-7263; fax (20) 7973-7308; internet www.commonwealthveterans.org.uk; links the ex-service orgs in the Commonwealth, assists ex-servicemen of the Crown who are resident abroad; holds triennial confs; 57 mem. orgs in 48 countries; Grand Pres. HRH The Duke of EDINBURGH; publ. _Annual Report_.

Royal Commonwealth Society: 18 Northumberland Ave, London, WC2N 5BJ; tel. (20) 7930-6733; fax (20) 7930-9705; e-mail info@rcsint.org; internet www.rcsint.org; f. 1868 to promote international understanding of the Commonwealth and its people; organizes meetings and seminars on topical issues, and cultural and social events; library housed by Cambridge University Library; more than 10,000 mems; Chair. Baroness PRASHAR; Dir STUART MOLE; publs _Annual Report, Newsletter_ (3 a year), conference reports.

Royal Over-Seas League: Over-Seas House, Park Place, St James's St, London, SW1A 1LR; tel. (20) 7408-0214; fax (20) 7499-6738; e-mail info@rosl.org.uk; internet www.rosl.org.uk; f. 1910 to promote friendship and understanding in the Commonwealth; club-houses in London and Edinburgh; membership is open to all British subjects and Commonwealth citizens; Chair. Sir COLIN IMRAY; Dir-Gen. ROBERT F. NEWELL; publ. *Overseas* (quarterly).

Victoria League for Commonwealth Friendship: 55 Leinster Sq., London, W2 4PU; tel. (20) 7243-2633; fax (20) 7229-2994; e-mail victorialeaguehq@btconnect.com; internet www.victorialeague.co.uk; f. 1901; aims to further personal friendship among Commonwealth peoples and to provide hospitality for visitors; maintains Student House, providing accommodation for students from Commonwealth countries; has brs elsewhere in the UK and abroad; Chair. JOHN KELLY; Gen. Sec. JOHN M. W. ALLAN; publ. *Annual Report*.

THE COMMONWEALTH OF INDEPENDENT STATES— CIS

Address: 220000 Minsk, Kirava 17, Belarus.
Telephone: (172) 22-35-17; **fax:** (172) 27-23-39; **e-mail:** postmaster@www.cis.minsk.by; **internet:** www.cis.minsk.by.

The Commonwealth of Independent States is a voluntary association of 12 (originally 11) states, established at the time of the collapse of the USSR in December 1991.

MEMBERS

Armenia	Moldova
Azerbaijan	Russia
Belarus	Tajikistan
Georgia	Turkmenistan
Kazakhstan	Ukraine
Kyrgyzstan	Uzbekistan

Note: Azerbaijan signed the Alma-Ata Declaration (see below), but in October 1992 the Azerbaijan legislature voted against ratification of the foundation documents by which the Commonwealth of Independent States had been established in December 1991. Azerbaijan formally became a member of the CIS in September 1993, after the legislature voted in favour of membership. Georgia was admitted to the CIS in December 1993.

Organization

(April 2005)

COUNCIL OF HEADS OF STATE

This is the supreme body of the CIS, on which all the member states of the Commonwealth are represented at the level of head of state, for discussion of issues relating to the co-ordination of Commonwealth activities and the development of the Minsk Agreement. Decisions of the Council are taken by common consent, with each state having equal voting rights. The Council meets at least once a year. An extraordinary meeting may be convened on the initiative of the majority of Commonwealth heads of state. From January 2003 the chairmanship of the Council was to be rotated among member states; in September 2004, however, the Russian President was reappointed as chairman of the Council.

COUNCIL OF HEADS OF GOVERNMENT

This Council convenes for meetings at least once every three months; an extraordinary sitting may be convened on the initiative of a majority of Commonwealth heads of government. The two Councils may discuss and take necessary decisions on important domestic and external issues, and may hold joint sittings.

Working and auxiliary bodies, composed of authorized representatives of the participating states, may be set up on a permanent or interim basis on the decision of the Council of Heads of State and the Council of Heads of Government.

CIS EXECUTIVE COMMITTEE

The Executive Committee was established by the Council of Heads of State in April 1999 to supersede the existing Secretariat, the Inter-state Economic Committee and other working bodies and committees, in order to improve the efficient functioning of the organization. The Executive Committee co-operates closely with other CIS bodies including the councils of foreign ministers and defence ministers; the Economic Council; Council of Border Troops Commanders; the Collective Security Council; the Secretariat of the

Council of the Inter-parliamentary Assembly; and the Inter-state Committee for Statistics.

Executive Secretary and Chairman of the Executive Committee: VLADIMIR RUSHAYLO.

Activities

On 8 December 1991 the heads of state of Belarus, Russia and Ukraine signed the Minsk Agreement, providing for the establishment of a Commonwealth of Independent States. Formal recognition of the dissolution of the USSR was incorporated in a second treaty (the Alma-Ata Declaration), signed by 11 heads of state in the then Kazakh capital, Alma-Ata (Almaty), later in that month.

In March 1992 a meeting of the CIS Council of Heads of Government decided to establish a commission to examine the resolution that 'all CIS member states are the legal successors of the rights and obligations of the former Soviet Union'. Documents relating to the legal succession of the Soviet Union were signed at a meeting of Heads of State in July. In April an agreement establishing an Inter-parliamentary Assembly (IPA), signed by Armenia, Belarus, Kazakhstan, Kyrgyzstan, Russia, Tajikistan and Uzbekistan, was published. The first Assembly was held in Bishkek, Kyrgyzstan, in September, attended by delegates from all these countries, with the exception of Uzbekistan.

A CIS Charter was formulated at the meeting of the heads of state in Minsk, Belarus, in January 1993. The Charter, providing for a defence alliance, an inter-state court and an economic co-ordination committee, was to serve as a framework for closer co-operation and was signed by all of the members except Moldova, Turkmenistan and Ukraine.

In May 1994 the CIS and UNCTAD signed a co-operation accord. A similar agreement was concluded with the UN Economic Commission for Europe in June 1996. Working contacts have also been established with ILO, UNHCR, WHO and the European Union. In June 1998 the IPA approved a decision to sign the European Social Charter (see Council of Europe); a declaration of co-operation between the Assembly and the OSCE Parliamentary Assembly was also signed.

In November 1995, at the Council of Heads of Government meeting, Russia expressed concern at the level of non-payment of debts by CIS members, which, it said, was hindering further integration. At the meeting of the Council in April 1996 a long-term plan for the integrated development of the CIS, incorporating measures for further socio-economic, military and political co-operation, was approved.

In March 1997 the then Russian President, Boris Yeltsin, admitted that the CIS institutional structure had failed to ameliorate the severe economic situation of certain member states. Nevertheless, support for the CIS as an institution was reaffirmed by the participants during the meeting. At the heads of state meeting held in Chişinău, Moldova, in October, Russia was reportedly criticized by the other country delegations for failing to implement CIS agreements, for hindering development of the organization and for failing to resolve regional conflicts. Russia, for its part, urged all member states to participate more actively in defining, adopting and implementing CIS policies. Meeting in April 1998 heads of state emphasized the necessity of improving the activities of the CIS and of reforming its bureaucratic structure. Reform of the CIS was also the main item on the agenda of the eleventh IPA, held in June. It was agreed that an essentially new institution needed to be created, taking into account the relations between the states in a new way. In the same month the first plenary meeting of a special forum, convened to address issues of restructuring the CIS, was held. Working groups were to be established to co-ordinate proposals and draft documents. However, in October reform proposals drawn up by 'experienced specialists' and presented by the Executive Secretary were unanimously rejected as inadequate by the 12 member states. In March 1999 Boris Yeltsin, acting as Chairman of the Council of Heads of State, dismissed the then Executive Secretary, Boris Berezovskii, owing to alleged misconduct and neglect of duties. The decision was endorsed by the Council of Heads of Government meeting in April. The Council also adopted guide-lines for restructuring the CIS and for the future development of the organization. Economic co-operation was to be a priority area of activity, and in particular, the establishment of a free-trade zone. Vladimir Putin, then acting President of the Russian Federation, was elected as the new Chairman of the Council of Heads of State at a CIS summit held in Moscow in January 2000. Meeting in June, a summit of the Councils of Heads of State and Government issued a declaration concerning the maintenance of strategic stability, approved a plan and schedule for pursuing economic integration, and adopted a short-term programme for combating international terrorism (perceived to be a significant threat in central Asia). The Council of Heads of Government also approved a programme of action to guide the organization's activities until 2005. An informal CIS 10-year 'jubilee' summit, convened in November 2001, adopted a statement identifying the collective pursuit of stable socio-economic development and integration on a global level as the organization's principal objective. A summit of heads of state convened in January 2003 agreed that the position of Chairman of the Council of Heads of State (hitherto held by consecutive Russian presidents) should be rotated henceforth among member states. Leonid Kuchma, the President of Ukraine, was elected as the new Chairman. (In September 2004, however, Russia's President Putin was reappointed as the Chairman of the Council, owing to a perceived deterioration in the international security situation and a declared need for experienced leadership.) A summit meeting convened in September 2003, in Yalta, Ukraine, focused on measures to combat crime and terrorism, and endorsed an economic plan for 2003–10. In late November, following a popular uprising against the Georgian regime, an emergency meeting of CIS foreign ministers was convened in Kiev, Ukraine. The meeting issued a statement reaffirming Georgia's territorial integrity and calling for the restoration of the constitutional and democratic process; a CIS envoy was dispatched to the capital, Tbilisi, to mediate in a handover of power from the deposed President, Eduard Shevardnadze. In early January 2004 a team of some 70 CIS observers were present at elections to choose a new Georgian President.

In September 2004 the CIS Council of Heads of State, meeting in Astana, Kazakhstan, was dominated by consideration of measures to combat terrorism and extremist violence, following a month in which Russia, including North Ossetia, had experienced several atrocities committed against civilian targets. As part of a wider consideration of a reorganization of the CIS, the Council resolved to establish a Security Council, comprising the ministers responsible for foreign affairs and for defence, and heads of security and border control. The meeting was attended by all heads of state, except those of Turkmenistan and Moldova.

Member states of the CIS have formed alliances of various kinds among themselves, thereby potentially undermining the unity of the Commonwealth. In March 1996 Belarus, Kazakhstan, Kyrgyzstan and the Russian Federation signed the Quadripartite Treaty for greater integration. This envisaged the establishment of a 'New Union', based, initially on a common market and customs union, and was to be open to all CIS members and the Baltic states. Consequently these countries (with Tajikistan) became founding members of the Eurasian Economic Community, inaugurated in October 2001. In April 1996 Belarus and Russia signed the Treaty on the Formation of a Community of Sovereign Republics (CSR), which provided for extensive economic, political and military co-operation. In April 1997 the two countries signed a further Treaty of Union and, in addition, initialled the Charter of the Union, which detailed the procedures and institutions designed to develop a common infrastructure, a single currency and a joint defence policy within the CSR, with the eventual aim of 'voluntary unification of the member states'. The Charter was signed in May and ratified by the respective legislatures the following month. The Union's Parliamentary Assembly, comprising 36 members from the legislature of each country, convened in official session for the first time shortly afterwards. Azerbaijan, Georgia, Moldova and Ukraine co-operated increasingly during the late 1990s as the so-called GUAM Group, which envisaged implementing joint economic and transportation initiatives and establishing a sub-regional free-trade zone. In October 1997 the GUAM countries agreed collectively to establish a Eurasian Trans-Caucasus transportation corridor. Uzbekistan joined in April 1999, creating GUAAM. The group agreed in September 2000 to convene regular annual summits of member countries' heads of state and to organize meetings of ministers of foreign affairs at least twice a year. Russia, Armenia, Azerbaijan and Georgia convene regular meetings as the 'Caucasian Group of Four'. The formation of a new regional security organization, the Central

Asian Co-operation Organization, was announced in February 2002 by Kazakhstan, Kyrgyzstan, Tajikistan and Uzbekistan; and in April 2003 Armenia, Belarus, Kazakhstan, Kyrgyzstan, Tajikistan and Russia established the Collective Security Treaty Organization (see below).

The CIS regularly sends observer teams to monitor legislative and presidential elections in member states, most recently to Belarus, in October 2004, to observe elections to the National Assembly and a referendum to extend the president's term-in-office; to Ukraine, in November and December, to monitor the restaged presidential election; to Kyrgyzstan and Tajikistan, in February 2005, to monitor legislative elections; and to Moldova, in March, again to monitor legislative elections.

A number of multilateral meetings of senior representatives of CIS member states held during early 2005, including a meeting of foreign ministers convened in mid-March and a meeting of prime ministers in early April, discussed recommendations for restructuring the organs of the CIS, with a view to increasing the overall efficiency of the organization. The recommendations (which included the establishment of the CIS Security Council) were to be considered at the next summit of the Council of Heads of State, scheduled to be held in Kazan, Russia, in August.

ECONOMIC AFFAIRS

At a meeting of the Council of Heads of Government in March 1992 agreement was reached on repayment of the foreign debt of the former USSR. Agreements were also signed on pensions, joint tax policy and the servicing of internal debt. In May an accord on repayment of inter-state debt and the issue of balance-of-payments statements was adopted by the heads of government, meeting in Tashkent, Uzbekistan. In July it was decided to establish an economic court in Minsk.

The CIS Charter, formulated in January 1993 and signed by seven of the 10 member countries, provided for the establishment of an economic co-ordination committee. In February, at a meeting of the heads of foreign economic departments, a foreign economic council was formed. In May all member states, with the exception of Turkmenistan, adopted a declaration of support for increased economic union and, in September, agreement was reached by all states except Ukraine and Turkmenistan on a framework for economic union, including the gradual removal of tariffs and creation of a currency union. Turkmenistan was subsequently admitted as a full member of the economic union in December 1993 and Ukraine as an associate member in April 1994.

At the Council of Heads of Government meeting in September 1994 all member states, except Turkmenistan, agreed to establish an Inter-state Economic Committee to implement economic treaties adopted within the context of an economic union. The establishment of a payments union to improve the settlement of accounts was also agreed. In April 1998 CIS heads of state resolved to incorporate the functions of the Inter-state Economic Committee, along with those of other working bodies and sectional committees, into a new CIS Executive Committee.

In October 1997 seven heads of government signed a document on implementing the 'concept for the integrated economic development of the CIS'. The development of economic co-operation between the member states was a priority task of the special forum on reform held in June 1998. In the same month an economic forum, held in St Petersburg, Russia, acknowledged the severe economic conditions prevailing in certain CIS states.

Guide-lines adopted by the Council of Heads of State in April 1999 concerning the future development of the CIS identified economic co-operation and the establishment of a free-trade zone (see Trade) as priority areas for action. The plan of action for the development of the CIS until 2005, adopted by the Council of Heads of Government in June 2000, outlined medium-term economic co-operation measures, including the formulation of intergovernmental accords to provide the legal basis for the free movement of services, capital, people, etc.; the development of private business and markets; and joint participation in the implementation of major economic projects. At the summit meeting held in September 2003 CIS foreign ministers approved a draft plan aimed at improving and enhancing economic co-operation until 2010.

TRADE

Agreement was reached on the free movement of goods between republics at a meeting of the Council of Heads of State in February 1992, and in April 1994 an agreement on the creation of a CIS free-trade zone (envisaged as the first stage of economic union) was concluded. In July a council of the heads of customs committees, meeting in Moscow, approved a draft framework for customs legislation in CIS countries, to facilitate the establishment of a free-trade zone. The framework was approved by all the participants, with the exception of Turkmenistan. In April 1999 CIS heads of state signed a protocol to the 1994 free-trade area accord, which aimed to accelerate co-operation. In June 2000 the Council of Heads of State adopted a plan and schedule for the implementation of priority measures related to the creation of the free-trade zone, and at the September 2003 summit meeting Russia, Belarus, Kazakhstan and Ukraine signed the Union of Four agreement establishing the framework for a Single Economic Space (SES) that was open to accession by all CIS members. The agreement envisaged the creation of a free-trade zone and the gradual harmonization of tariffs, customs and transport legislation. While participation at each stage would remain optional, decisions would be obligatory and certain areas of sovereignty would eventually be ceded to a council of heads of state and a commission.

At the first session of the Inter-state Economic Committee in November 1994 draft legislation regarding a customs union was approved. In March 1998 Russia, Belarus, Kazakhstan and Kyrgyzstan signed an agreement establishing a customs union, which was to be implemented in two stages: firstly, the removal of trade restrictions and the unification of trade and customs regulations; followed by the integration of economic, monetary and trade policies (see above). The development of a customs union and the strengthening of intra-CIS trade were objectives endorsed by all participants, with the exception of Georgia, at the Council of Heads of Government meeting held in March 1997. In February 1999 Tajikistan signed the 1998 agreement to become the fifth member of the customs union. In October 1999 the heads of state of the five member states of the customs union reiterated their political determination to implement the customs union and approved a programme to harmonize national legislation to create a single economic space. In May 2000 the heads of state announced their intention to raise the status of the customs union to that of an inter-state economic organization, and, in October, the leaders signed a treaty establishing the Eurasian Economic Community. Under the new structure member states aimed to formulate a unified foreign economic policy, and collectively to pursue the creation of the planned single economic space. In the following month the five member governments signed an agreement enabling visa-free travel within the new Community. (Earlier in 2000 Russia had withdrawn from a CIS-wide visa-free travel arrangement agreed in 1992.) In December 2000 member states of the Community adopted several documents aimed at facilitating economic co-operation. The Eurasian Economic Community, governed by an inter-state council based in Astana, Kazakhstan, was formally inaugurated in October 2001. In October 2003 the Community was granted observer status at the UN.

The CIS maintains a 'loose co-ordination' on issues related to applications by member states to join the WTO.

BANKING AND FINANCE

In February 1992 CIS heads of state agreed to retain the rouble as the common currency for trade between the republics. However, in July 1993, in an attempt to control inflation, notes printed before 1993 were withdrawn from circulation and no new ones were issued until January 1994. Despite various agreements to recreate the 'rouble zone', including a protocol agreement signed in September 1993 by six states, it effectively remained confined to Tajikistan, which joined in January 1994, and Belarus, which joined in April. Both those countries proceeded to introduce national currencies in May 1995. In January 1993, at the signing of the CIS Charter, all 10 member countries endorsed the establishment of an inter-state bank to facilitate payments between the republics and to co-ordinate monetary-credit policy. Russia was to hold 50% of shares in the bank, but decisions were to be made only with a two-thirds majority approval. In December 2000, in accordance with the CSR and Treaty of Union (see above), the Presidents of Belarus and Russia signed an agreement providing for the adoption by Belarus of the Russian currency from 1 January 2005, and for the introduction of a new joint Union currency by 1 January 2008; the adoption by Belarus of the Russian currency was, however, subsequently postponed until 1 January 2006.

In October 2004 Russia and Kazakhstan announced a proposal to establish a CIS Development Bank, with a capital of €1m.

DEFENCE

An Agreement on Armed Forces and Border Troops was concluded on 30 December 1991, at the same time as the Agreement on Strategic Forces. This confirmed the right of member states to set up their own armed forces and appointed Commanders-in-Chief of the Armed Forces and of the Border Troops, who were to elaborate joint security procedures. In February 1992 an agreement was signed stipulating that the commander of the strategic forces was subordinate to the Council of Heads of States. Eight states agreed on a unified command for general-purpose (i.e. non-strategic) armed forces for a transitional period of two years. Azerbaijan, Moldova and Ukraine resolved to establish independent armed forces.

In January 1992 Commissions on the Black Sea Fleet (control of which was disputed by Russia and Ukraine) and the Caspian Flotilla (the former Soviet naval forces on the Caspian Sea) were established. The defence and stability of CIS external borders and the

status of strategic and nuclear forces were among topics discussed at the meeting of heads of state and of government, in Bishkek, in October. The formation of a defence alliance was provided for in the CIS Charter formulated in January 1993 and signed by seven of the 10 member countries; a proposal by Russia to assume control of all nuclear weapons in the former USSR was rejected at the same time.

In June 1993 CIS defence ministers agreed to abolish CIS joint military command and to abandon efforts to maintain a unified defence structure. The existing CIS command was to be replaced, on a provisional basis, by a 'joint staff for co-ordinating military co-operation between the states of the Commonwealth'. It was widely reported that Russia had encouraged the decision to abolish the joint command, owing to concerns at the projected cost of a CIS joint military structure and support within Russia's military leadership of bilateral military agreements with the country's neighbours. In December the Council of Defence Ministers agreed to establish a secretariat to co-ordinate military co-operation as a replacement to the joint military command. In November 1995 the Council of Defence Ministers authorized the establishment of a Joint Air Defence System, to be co-ordinated largely by Russia. A CIS combat duty system was to be created in 1999–2005. Russia and Belarus were also developing a joint air-defence unit in the context of the CSR (see above).

In September 1996 the first meeting of the inter-state commission for military economic co-operation was held; a draft agreement on the export of military projects and services to third countries was approved. The basic principles of a programme for greater military and technical co-operation were approved by the Council of Defence Ministers in March 1997. In April 1998 the Council proposed drawing up a draft programme for military and technical co-operation between member countries and also discussed procedures advising on the use and maintenance of armaments and military hardware. The programme was approved by CIS heads of state in October 2002. Draft proposals relating to information security for the military were approved by the Council in December. It was remarked that the inadequate funding of the Council was impeding co-operation. In May 2001 a draft plan for military co-operation until 2005 was agreed.

In August 1996 the Council of Defence Ministers condemned what it described as the political, economic and military threat implied in any expansion of NATO. The statement was not signed by Ukraine. The eighth plenary session of the IPA, held in November, urged NATO countries to abandon plans for the organization's expansion. Strategic co-operation between NATO and CIS member states increased from the mid-1990s, particularly with Russia and Ukraine. In the late 1990s the USA established bilateral military assistance programmes for Azerbaijan, Georgia, and Uzbekistan. Uzbekistan and other central Asian CIS states played a support role in the US-led action initiated in late 2001 against the then Taliban-held areas of Afghanistan (see below).

REGIONAL SECURITY

At a meeting of heads of government in March 1992 agreements on settling inter-state conflicts were signed by all participating states (except Turkmenistan). At the same meeting an agreement on the status of border troops was signed by five states. In May a five-year Collective Security Agreement was signed. In July further documents were signed on collective security and it was agreed to establish joint peacemaking forces to intervene in CIS disputes. In April 1999 Armenia, Belarus, Kazakhstan, Kyrgyzstan, Russia and Tajikistan signed a protocol to extend the Collective Security Agreement for a further five-year period. The signatories to the Collective Security Agreement planned to adopt an agreement on military technical cooperation in mid-2005.

In September 1993 the Council of Heads of State agreed to establish a Bureau of Organized Crime, to be based in Moscow. A meeting of the Council of Border Troop Commanders in January 1994 prepared a report on the issue of illegal migration and drug trade across the external borders of the CIS; Moldova, Georgia and Tajikistan did not attend. A programme to counter organized crime within the CIS was approved by heads of government, meeting in Moscow, in April 1996. In March 2001 CIS interior ministers agreed to strengthen co-operation in combating transnational organized crime, in view of reportedly mounting levels of illicit drugs-trafficking in the region.

The fourth plenary session of the IPA in March 1994 established a commission for the resolution of the conflicts in the secessionist regions of Nagornyi Karabakh (Azerbaijan) and Abkhazia (Georgia) and endorsed the use of CIS peace-keeping forces. In the following month Russia agreed to send peace-keeping forces to Georgia, and the dispatch of peace-keeping forces was approved by the Council of Defence Ministers in October. The subsequent session of the IPA in October adopted a resolution to send groups of military observers to Abkhazia and to Moldova. The inter-parliamentary commission on the conflict between Abkhazia and Georgia proposed initiating direct negotiations with the two sides in order to reach a peaceful settlement.

In December 1994 the Council of Defence Ministers enlarged the mandate of the commander of the CIS collective peace-keeping forces in Tajikistan: when necessary CIS military contingents were permitted to engage in combat operations without the prior consent of individual governments. At the Heads of State meeting in Moscow in January 1996 Georgia's proposal to impose sanctions against Abkhazia was approved, in an attempt to achieve a resolution of the conflict. Provisions on arrangements relating to collective peace-keeping operations were approved at the meeting; the training of military and civilian personnel for these operations was to commence in October. In March 1997 the Council of Defence Ministers agreed to extend the peace-keeping mandates for CIS forces in Tajiskistan and Abkhazia (following much disagreement, the peace-keepers' mandate in Abkhazia was further renewed in October). At a meeting of the Council in January 1998 a request from Georgia that the CIS carry out its decisions to settle the conflict with Abkhazia was added to the agenda. The Council discussed the promotion of military co-operation and the improvement of peace-making activities, and declared that there was progress in the formation of the collective security system, although the situation in the North Caucasus remained tense. In April President Yeltsin requested that the Armenian and Azerbaijani presidents sign a document to end the conflict in Nagornyi Karabakh; the two subsequently issued a statement expressing their support for a political settlement of the conflict. A document proposing a settlement of the conflict in Abkhazia was also drawn up, but the resolutions adopted were not accepted by Abkhazia. Against the wishes of the Abkhazian authorities, the mandate for the CIS troops in the region was extended to cover the whole of the Gali district. The mandate expired in July 1998, but the forces remained in the region while its renewal was debated. In April 1999 the Council of Heads of State agreed to a retrospective extension of the operation's mandate; the mandate subsequently continued to be renewed at six-monthly intervals until March 2003 when it was extended indefinitely. At the end of 2003 the force comprised some 3,000 Russian troops. The mandate of the CIS peace-keeping operation in Tajikistan was terminated in June 2000. In February 2001 it was reported that regulations had been drafted for the institution of a CIS Special Envoy for the Settlement of Conflicts.

In February 1995 a non-binding memorandum on maintaining peace and stability was adopted by heads of state, meeting in Almaty. Signatories were to refrain from applying military, political, economic or other pressure on another member country, to seek the peaceful resolution of border or territorial disputes and not to support or assist separatist movements active in other member countries. In April 1998 the Council of Defence Ministers approved a draft document proposing that coalition forces be provided with technical equipment to enhance collective security.

In June 1998, at a session of the Council of Border Troop Commanders, some 33 documents were signed relating to border co-operation. A framework protocol on the formation and expedient use of a border troops reserve in critical situations was discussed and signed by several participants. A register of work in scientific and engineering research carried out in CIS countries in the interests of border troops was also adopted. A programme aimed at enhancing co-operation between border troops was adopted by heads of state in October 2002. In February 2004 an expert group drafted regulations for the establishment of a common system to register foreign nationals and stateless persons.

In June 1998 CIS interior ministers, meeting in Tashkent, Uzbekistan, adopted a number of co-operation agreements, including a framework for the exchange of information between CIS law-enforcement agencies; it was also decided to maintain contact with Interpol.

An emergency meeting of heads of state in October 1996 discussed the ongoing conflict in nearby Afghanistan and the consequent threat to regional security. The participants requested the UN Security Council to adopt measures to resolve the situation. The IPA subsequently reiterated the call for a cessation of hostilities in that country. In May 2000 the six signatory states to the Collective Security Agreement pledged to strengthen military co-operation in view of the perceived threat to their security from the Taliban regime in Afghanistan. In October the parties to the Collective Security Agreement signed an agreement on the Status of Forces and Means of Collective Security Systems, establishing a joint rapid deployment function. The so-called CIS Collective Rapid Reaction Force was to be assembled to combat insurgencies, with particular reference to trans-border terrorism from Afghanistan, and also to deter trans-border illegal drugs trafficking (see above). In June 2001

a CIS anti-terrorism centre was established in Moscow. The centre was to co-ordinate counter-terrorism activities and to compile a database of international terrorist organizations operating in member states. In October, in response to the major terrorist attacks perpetrated in September against targets in the USA—allegedly co-ordinated by militant fundamentalist Islamist leader Osama bin Laden—the parties to the Collective Security Treaty adopted a new anti-terrorism plan. In November the head of the co-ordinating Collective Security Council identified combating international terrorism as the main focus of the Collective Security Agreement at that time. In December 2002 the committee of the Collective Security Treaty member countries adopted a protocol on the exchange of expertise and information on terrorist organizations and their activities. In April 2003 the members determined to establish the Collective Security Treaty Organization (CSTO); ratification of its founding documents was completed by September, when it applied for UN observer status. In early November CSTO co-ordinated an operation targeting drugs-traffickers involving some 30,000 law enforcement officers. The signatory countries to the Collective Security Agreement participate in regular so-called 'CIS Southern Shield' joint military exercises. A CSTO joint anti-terrorism exercise, involving some 2,000 troops, was held in Kazakhstan and Kyrgyzstan in August 2004. In October 2002 a central Asian subdivision of the CIS anti-terrorism centre was established in Bishkek, Kyrgyzstan. The CIS summit in September 2003 approved draft decisions to control the sale of portable anti-aircraft missiles and to set up a joint co-ordination structure to address illegal immigration.

In September 2004 CIS ministers of the interior, convened in Kiev, Ukraine, agreed to draft joint programmes to combat crime and drugs-trafficking in the period 2005–07. In October CIS directors of security agencies and intelligence services, meeting in Minsk, Belarus, discussed regional counter-terrorism measures, including efforts to exchange information and restrict sources of terrorist finance. The meeting adopted a new CIS programme on combating international terrorism and manifestations of extremism, to cover the period 2005–07.

LEGISLATIVE CO-OPERATION

An agreement on legislative co-operation was signed at an Inter-Parliamentary Conference in January 1992; joint commissions were established to co-ordinate action on economy, law, pensions, housing, energy and ecology. The CIS Charter, formulated in January 1993, provided for the establishment of an inter-state court. In October 1994 a Convention on the rights of minorities was adopted at the meeting of the Heads of State. In May 1995, at the sixth plenary session of the IPA, several acts to improve co-ordination of legislation were approved, relating to migration of labour, consumer rights, and the rights of prisoners of war.

The creation of a Council of Ministers of Internal Affairs was approved at the Heads of State meeting in January 1996; the Council was to promote co-operation between the law-enforcement bodies of member states. The IPA has approved a number of model laws, relating to areas including banking and financial services; charity; defence; the economy; education; ecology; the regulation of refugee problems; and social issues, including obligatory social insurance against production accidents and occupational diseases. In November 2003 IPA approved 12 model laws relating to the economy, defence, social policy and ecology; and in early 2004 it was preparing a model law on combating terrorism.

OTHER ACTIVITIES

The CIS has held a number of discussions relating to the environment. In July 1992 agreements were concluded to establish an Inter-state Ecological Council. It was also agreed in that month to establish *Mir*, an inter-state television and radio company. In October 2002 a decision was made by CIS heads of government to enhance mutual understanding and co-operation between members countries through *Mir* radio and television broadcasts. In February 1995 the IPA established a Council of Heads of News Agencies, in order to promote the concept of a single information area.

A Petroleum and Gas Council was created at a Heads of Government meeting in March 1993, to guarantee energy supplies and to invest in the Siberian petroleum industry. The Council was to have a secretariat based in Tyumen, Siberia. In October 2002 the Council of Heads of Government signed a co-operation agreement on energy effectiveness and power supply. In the field of civil aviation, the inter-state economic committee agreed in February 1997 to establish an Aviation Alliance to promote co-operation between the countries' civil aviation industries.

CO-OPERATION COUNCIL FOR THE ARAB STATES OF THE GULF

Address: POB 7153, Riyadh 11462, Saudi Arabia.
Telephone: (1) 482-7777; **fax:** (1) 482-9089; **internet:** www.gcc-sg .org.
More generally known as the Gulf Co-operation Council (GCC), the organization was established on 25 May 1981 by six Arab states.

MEMBERS

Bahrain	Oman	Saudi Arabia
Kuwait	Qatar	United Arab Emirates

Organization

(April 2005)

SUPREME COUNCIL

The Supreme Council is the highest authority of the GCC. It comprises the heads of member states and meets annually in ordinary session, and in emergency session if demanded by two or more members. The Council also convenes an annual consultative meeting. The Presidency of the Council is undertaken by each state in turn, in alphabetical order. The Supreme Council draws up the overall policy of the organization; it discusses recommendations and laws presented to it by the Ministerial Council and the Secretariat General in preparation for endorsement. The GCC's charter provided for the creation of a commission for the settlement of disputes between member states, to be attached to and appointed by the Supreme Council. The Supreme Council convenes the commission for the settlement of disputes on an *ad hoc* basis to address altercations between member states as they arise.

MINISTERIAL COUNCIL

The Ministerial Council consists of the foreign ministers of member states (or other ministers acting on their behalf), meeting every three months, and in emergency session if demanded by two or more members. It prepares for the meetings of the Supreme Council, and draws up policies, recommendations, studies and projects aimed at developing co-operation and co-ordination among member states in various spheres. GCC ministerial committees have been established in a number of areas of co-operation; sectoral ministerial meetings are held periodically.

CONSULTATIVE COMMISSION

The Consultative Commission, comprising 30 members (five from each member state) nominated for a three-year period, acts as an advisory body, considering matters referred to it by the Supreme Council.

SECRETARIAT GENERAL

The Secretariat assists member states in implementing recommendations by the Supreme and Ministerial Councils, and prepares reports and studies, budgets and accounts. The Secretary-General is appointed by the Supreme Council for a three-year term renewable once. The position is rotated among member states in order to ensure equal representation. Assistant Secretary-Generals are appointed by the Ministerial Council upon the recommendation of the Secretary-General. The Secretariat comprises the following divisions and departments: political affairs; economic affairs; military affairs; human and environmental affairs; legal affairs; the Office of the Secretary-General, Finance and Administrative Affairs; a patent bureau; an administrative development unit; an internal auditing unit; an information centre; and a telecommunications bureau (based in Bahrain). All member states contribute in equal proportions towards the budget of the Secretariat.

Secretary-General: ABDUL RAHMAN BIN HAMAD AL-ATTIYA (Qatar).

Assistant Secretary-General for Political Affairs: Dr HAMAD ALI AS-SULAYTI (Bahrain).

Assistant Secretary-General for Economic Affairs: MOHAMED BIN OBAID AL-MAZROUI.

Assistant Secretary-General for Military Affairs: Maj.-Gen. ALI IBN SALEM AL-MUAMARI (Oman).

Note: In December 2001 the Supreme Council admitted Yemen (which applied to join the organization as a full member in 1996) as a member of the GCC's Arab Bureau of Education for the Gulf States), as a participant in meetings of GCC ministers of health and of labour and social affairs, and, alongside the GCC member states, as a participant in the biennial Gulf Cup football tournament. The Council also authorized the establishment of a Supreme Defence Council. This was to be composed of defence ministers meeting on an annual basis to consider security matters and supervise the implementation of the organization's joint defence pact.

Activities

The GCC was established following a series of meetings of foreign ministers of the states concerned, culminating in an agreement on the basic details of its charter on 10 March 1981. The Charter was signed by the six heads of state on 25 May. It describes the organization as providing 'the means for realizing co-ordination, integration and co-operation' in all economic, social and cultural affairs.

ECONOMIC CO-OPERATION

In November 1981 GCC ministers drew up a 'unified economic agreement' covering freedom of movement of people and capital, the abolition of customs duties, technical co-operation, harmonization of banking regulations and financial and monetary co-ordination. At the same time GCC heads of state approved the formation of a Gulf Investment Corporation, to be based in Kuwait (see below). In March 1983 customs duties on domestic products of the Gulf states were abolished, and new regulations allowing free movement of workers and vehicles between member states were also introduced. A common minimum customs levy (of between 4% and 20%) on foreign imports was imposed in 1986. In February 1987 the governors of the member states' central banks agreed in principle to co-ordinate their rates of exchange, and this was approved by the Supreme Council in November. It was subsequently agreed to link the Gulf currencies to a 'basket' of other currencies. In April 1993 the Gulf central bank governors decided to allow Kuwait's currency to become part of the GCC monetary system that was established following Iraq's invasion of Kuwait in order to defend the Gulf currencies. In May 1992 GCC trade ministers announced the objective of establishing a GCC common market. Meeting in September GCC ministers reached agreement on the application of a unified system of tariffs by March 1993. A meeting of the Supreme Council, held in December 1992, however, decided to mandate GCC officials to formulate a plan for the introduction of common external tariffs, to be presented to the Council in December 1993. Only the tax on tobacco products was to be standardized from March 1993, at a rate of 50% (later increased to 70%). In April 1994 ministers of finance agreed to pursue a gradual approach to the unification of tariffs. A technical committee, which had been constituted to consider aspects of establishing a customs union, met for the first time in June 1998. In November 1999 the Supreme Council concluded an agreement to establish the customs union by 1 March 2005. However, in December 2001 the Supreme Council, meeting in Muscat, Oman, adopted a new agreement on regional economic union ('Economic Agreement Between the Arab GCC States'), which superseded the 1981 'unified economic agreement'. The new accord brought forward the deadline for the establishment of the proposed customs union to 1 January 2003 and provided for a standard tariff level of 5% for foreign imports (with the exception of 53 essential commodities previously exempted by the Supreme Council). The agreement also provided for the introduction, by 1 January 2010, of a GCC single currency, linked to the US dollar. The necessary economic performance measures for monetary union were to be established by the end of 2005. The Supreme Council also authorized the creation of a new independent authority for overseeing the unification of specifications and standards throughout member states. The GCC customs union was launched, as planned, on 1 January 2003. In July the GCC entered into negotiations with Yemen on harmonizing economic legislation.

In April 1993 GCC central bank governors agreed to establish a joint banking supervisory committee, in order to devise rules for GCC banks to operate in other member states. In December 1997 GCC heads of state authorized guide-lines to this effect. These were to apply only to banks established at least 10 years previously with a share capital of more than US $100m.

A GCC Economic Forum has been convened annually since 2002.

TRADE AND INDUSTRY

In 1982 a ministerial committee was formed to co-ordinate trade policies and development in the region. Technical subcommittees were established to oversee a strategic food reserve for the member states, and joint trade exhibitions (which were generally held every year until responsibility was transferred to the private sector in 1996). In 1986 the Supreme Council approved a measure whereby citizens of GCC member states were enabled to undertake certain retail trade activities in any other member state, with effect from 1 March 1987. In September 2000 GCC ministers of commerce agreed to establish a technical committee to promote the development of electronic commerce and trade among member states.

In 1976 the GCC member states formed the Gulf Organization for Industrial Consulting, based in Doha, Qatar, which promotes regional industrial development. In 1985 the Supreme Council endorsed a common industrial strategy for the Gulf states. It approved regulations stipulating that priority should be given to imports of GCC industrial products, and permitting GCC investors to obtain loans from GCC industrial development banks. In November 1986 resolutions were adopted on the protection of industrial products, and on the co-ordination of industrial projects, in order to avoid duplication. In 1989 the Ministerial Council approved the Unified GCC Foreign Capital Investment Regulations, which aimed to attract foreign investment and to co-ordinate investments amongst GCC countries. Further guide-lines to promote foreign investment in the region were formulated during 1997. In December 1999 the Supreme Council amended the conditions determining rules of origin on industrial products in order to promote direct investment and intra-Community trade. In December 1992 the Supreme Council endorsed Patent Regulations for GCC member states to facilitate regional scientific and technological research. A GCC Patent Office for the protection of intellectual property in the region, was established in 1998.

In December 1998 the Supreme Council approved a long-term strategy for regional development, covering the period 2000–25, which had been formulated by GCC ministers of planning. The strategy aimed to achieve integrated, sustainable development in all member states and the co-ordination of national development plans. The Supreme Council also approved a framework Gulf population strategy formulated by the ministers of planning. In December 2000 the Supreme Council agreed gradually to limit, by means of the imposition of quotas and deterrent taxation measures, the numbers of foreign workers admitted to member states, in order to redress the current demographic imbalance resulting from the large foreign population resident in the region (believed to comprise more than one-third of the overall population). Unified procedures and measures for facilitating the intra-regional movement of people and commercial traffic were adopted by the Supreme Council in December 2001, as well as unified standards in the areas of education and health care. In August 2003 the GCC adopted new measures permitting nationals of its member states to work in, and to seek loans from financial institutions in, any other member state.

AGRICULTURE

A unified agricultural policy for GCC countries was endorsed by the Supreme Council in November 1985. Co-operation in the agricultural sector extends to consideration of the water resources in the region. Between 1983 and 1990 ministers also approved proposals for harmonizing legislation relating to water conservation, veterinary vaccines, insecticides, fertilizers, fisheries and seeds. A permanent committee on fisheries aims to co-ordinate national fisheries policies, to establish designated fishing periods and to undertake surveys of the fishing potential in the Arabian (Persian) Gulf. In February 2001 GCC ministers responsible for water and electricity determined to formulate a common water policy for the region, which experiences annual shortfalls of water. Unified agricultural quarantine laws were adopted by the Supreme Council in December 2001.

TRANSPORT, COMMUNICATIONS AND INFORMATION

During 1985 feasibility studies were undertaken on new rail and road links between member states, and on the establishment of a joint coastal transport company. A scheme to build a 1,700-km railway to link all the member states and Iraq (and thereby the European railway network) was postponed, owing to its high estimated cost. In November 1993 ministers agreed to request assistance from the International Telecommunication Union on the establishment of a joint telecommunications network, which had been approved by ministers in 1986. The region's telecommunications systems were to be integrated through underwater fibre-optic cables and a satellite-based mobile telephone network. In the mid-1990s GCC ministers of information began convening on a regular basis with a view to formulating a joint external information policy. In November 1997 GCC interior ministers approved a simplified passport system to facilitate travel between member countries.

ENERGY

In 1982 a ministerial committee was established to co-ordinate hydrocarbons policies and prices. Ministers adopted a petroleum security plan to safeguard individual members against a halt in their production, to form a stockpile of petroleum products, and to organize a boycott of any non-member country when appropriate. In December 1987 the Supreme Council adopted a plan whereby a member state whose petroleum production was disrupted could 'borrow' petroleum from other members, in order to fulfil its export obligations. GCC petroleum ministers hold occasional co-ordination meetings to discuss the agenda and policies of OPEC, to which all six member states belong.

During the early 1990s proposals were formulated to integrate the electricity networks of the six member countries. In the first stage of the plan the networks of Saudi Arabia, Bahrain, Kuwait and Qatar would be integrated; those of the United Arab Emirates (UAE) and Oman would be interconnected and finally linked to the others in the second stage. In December 1997 GCC heads of state declared that work should commence on the first stage of the plan, under the management of an independent authority. The estimated cost of the project was more than US $6,000m. However, it was agreed not to invite private developers to participate in construction of the grid, but that the first phase of the project be financed by member states (to contribute 35% of the estimated $2,000m. required), and by loans from commercial banking and international monetary institutions. The Gulf Council Interconnection Authority was established in 1999, with its headquarters in Dammam, Saudi Arabia.

CULTURAL CO-OPERATION

The GCC Folklore Centre, based in Doha, Qatar, was established in 1983 to collect, document and classify the regional cultural heritage, publish research, sponsor and protect regional folklore, provide a database on Gulf folklore, and to promote traditional culture through education.

REGIONAL SECURITY

Although no mention of defence or security was made in the original charter, the summit meeting which ratified the charter also issued a statement rejecting any foreign military presence in the region. The Supreme Council meeting in November 1981 agreed to include defence co-operation in the activities of the organization: as a result, defence ministers met in January 1982 to discuss a common security policy, including a joint air defence system and standardization of weapons. In November 1984 member states agreed to form the Peninsula Shield Force for rapid deployment against external aggression, comprising units from the armed forces of each country under a central command to be based in north-eastern Saudi Arabia.

In October 1987 (following an Iranian missile attack on Kuwait, which supported Iraq in its war against Iran) GCC ministers of foreign affairs issued a statement declaring that aggression against one member state was regarded as aggression against them all. In December the Supreme Council approved a joint pact on regional co-operation in matters of security. In August 1990 the Ministerial Council condemned Iraq's invasion of Kuwait as a violation of sovereignty, and demanded the withdrawal of all Iraqi troops from Kuwait. The Peninsula Shield Force was not sufficiently developed to be deployed in defence of Kuwait. During the crisis and the ensuing war between Iraq and a multinational force which took place in January and February 1991, the GCC developed closer links with Egypt and Syria, which, together with Saudi Arabia, played the most active role among the Arab countries in the anti-Iraqi alliance. In March the six GCC nations, Egypt and Syria formulated the 'Declaration of Damascus', which announced plans to establish a regional peace-keeping force. The Declaration also urged the abolition of all weapons of mass destruction in the area, and recommended the resolution of the Palestinian question by an international conference. In June Egypt and Syria, whose troops were to have formed the largest proportion of the proposed peace-keeping force, announced their withdrawal from the project, reportedly as a result of disagreements with the GCC concerning the composition of the force and the remuneration involved. A meeting of ministers of foreign affairs of the eight countries took place in July, but agreed only to provide mutual military assistance when necessary. In September 1992 the signatories of the Damascus Declaration adopted a joint statement on regional questions, including the Middle East peace process and the dispute between the UAE and Iran (see below), but rejected an Egyptian proposal to establish a series of rapid deployment forces which could be called upon to defend the interests of any of the eight countries. A meeting of GCC ministers of defence in November agreed to maintain the Peninsula Shield Force. In November 1993 GCC ministers of defence approved a proposal for the significant expansion of the Force and for the incorporation of air and naval units. Ministers also agreed to strengthen the defence of the region by developing joint surveillance and early warning systems. A GCC military committee was established, and convened for the first time in April 1994, to discuss the implementation of the proposals. However, the expansion of the Peninsula Shield Force was not implemented. Joint military training exercises were conducted by troops from five GCC states (excluding Qatar) in northern Kuwait in March 1996. In December 1997 the Supreme Council approved plans for linking the region's military telecommunications networks and establishing a common early warning system. In December 2000 GCC leaders adopted a joint defence pact aimed at enhancing the grouping's defence capability. The pact formally committed member states to defending any other member state from external attack, envisaging the expansion of the Peninsula Shield Force from 5,000 to 22,000 troops and the creation of a new rapid deployment function within the Force. In March 2001 the GCC member states inaugurated the first phase of the long-envisaged joint air defence system. In December GCC heads of state authorized the establishment of a supreme defence council, comprising member states' ministers of defence, to address security-related matters and supervise the implementation of the joint defence pact. The council was to convene on an annual basis. Meeting in emergency session in early February 2003 GCC ministers of defence and foreign affairs agreed to deploy the Peninsula Field Force in Kuwait, in view of the then impending US military action against neighbouring Iraq. The full deployment of 3,000 Peninsula Shield troops to Kuwait was completed in early March; the force was withdrawn two months later. At a consultative meeting held in May, following the perpetration of terrorist attacks in Riyadh, Saudi Arabia, the Supreme Council considered the possible development of a regional missile defence system, to be based on its pre-existing early warning and communications network.

In 1992 Iran extended its authority over the island of Abu Musa, which it had administered under a joint arrangement with the UAE since 1971. In September 1992 the GCC Ministerial Council condemned Iran's continued occupation of the island and efforts to consolidate its presence, and reiterated support of UAE sovereignty over Abu Musa, as well as the largely uninhabited Greater and Lesser Tunb islands (also claimed by Iran). All three islands are situated the approach to the Strait of Hormuz, through which petroleum exports are transported. In December 1994 the GCC supported the UAE's request that the dispute be referred to the International Court of Justice (ICJ).

In September 1992 a rift within the GCC was caused by an incident on the disputed border between Saudi Arabia and Qatar. Qatar's threat to boycott a meeting of the Supreme Council in December was allayed at the last minute as a result of mediation efforts by the Egyptian President. At the meeting, which was held in UAE, Qatar and Saudi Arabia agreed to establish a joint technical committee to demarcate the disputed border. In November 1994 a security agreement, to counter regional crime and terrorism, was concluded by GCC states. The pact, however, was not signed by Kuwait, which claimed that a clause concerning the extradition of offenders was in contravention of its constitution; Qatar did not attend the meeting, held in Riyadh, owing to its ongoing dispute with Saudi Arabia. During 1995 the deterioration of relations between Qatar and other GCC states threatened to undermine the Council's solidarity. In December Qatar publicly displayed its dissatisfaction at the appointment, without a consensus agreement, of Saudi Arabia's nominee as the new Secretary-General by failing to attend the final session of the Supreme Council, held in Muscat, Oman. However, at a meeting of ministers of foreign affairs in March 1996, Qatar endorsed the new Secretary-General, following an agreement on future appointment procedures, and reasserted its commitment to the organization. In June Saudi Arabia and Qatar agreed to reactivate the joint technical committee in order to finalize the demarcation of their mutual border: border maps drafted by the committee were approved by both sides in December 1999. In December 1996 Qatar hosted the annual GCC summit meeting; however, Bahrain refused to attend, owing to Qatar's 'unfriendly attitude' and a long-standing dispute between the two countries (referred by Qatar to the ICJ in 1991) concerning the sovereignty of the Hawar islands, and of other islands, maritime and border areas. The issue dominated the meeting, which agreed to establish a four-member committee to resolve the conflicting sovereignty claims. In January 1997 the ministers of foreign affairs of Kuwait, Oman, Saudi Arabia and the UAE, meeting in Riyadh, formulated a seven-point memorandum of understanding to ease tensions between Bahrain and Qatar. The two countries refused to sign the agreement; however, in March both sides announced their intention to establish diplomatic relations at ambassadorial level. In March 2001 the ICJ ruled on the dispute between Bahrain and Qatar concerning the sovereignty of the Hawar Islands and other territorial boundaries, awarding Bahrain sovereignty of the Hawar islands, while supporting Qatar's sovereignty over other disputed territories. The GCC welcomed the judgment, which was accepted by the Governments of both countries.

In May 1997 the Ministerial Council, meeting in Riyadh, expressed concern at Turkey's cross-border military operation in northern Iraq and urged a withdrawal of Turkish troops from Iraqi territory. In December the Supreme Council reaffirmed the need to ensure the sovereignty and territorial integrity of Iraq. At the same time, however, the Council expressed concern at the escalation of tensions in the region, owing to Iraq's failure to co-operate with the UN Special Commission (UNSCOM). The Council also noted the opportunity to strengthen relations with Iran, in view of political developments in that country. In February 1998 the US Defense Secretary visited each of the GCC countries in order to generate regional support for any punitive military action against Iraq, given that country's obstruction of UN weapons inspectors. Kuwait was the only country to declare its support for the use of force (and to permit the use of its bases in military operations against Iraq), while other member states urged a diplomatic solution to the crisis. Qatar pursued a diplomatic initiative to negotiate directly with the Iraqi authorities, and during February, the Qatari Minister of Foreign Affairs became the most senior GCC government official to visit Iraq since 1990. The GCC supported an agreement concluded between the UN Secretary-General and the Iraqi authorities at the end of February 1998, and urged Iraq to co-operate with UNSCOM in order to secure an end to the problem and a removal of the international embargo against the country. This position was subsequently reiterated by the Supreme Council. (In December 1999 UNSCOM was replaced by a new arms inspection body, the UN Monitoring, Verification and Inspection Commission—UNMOVIC.) In December 2000 Kuwait and Saudi Arabia rejected a proposal by the Qatari Government, supported by the UAE, that the GCC should soften its policy on Iraq and demand the immediate removal of the international embargo against that country. During that month the Supreme Council determined to establish a committee with the function of touring Arab states to explain the GCC's Iraq policy. In September 2002 the US Secretary of State met representatives of the GCC to discuss ongoing US pressure on the UN Security Council to draft a new resolution insisting that Iraq comply with previous UN demands, setting a time frame for such compliance and authorizing the use of force against Iraq in response to non-compliance. In March 2003, in response to the initiation of US-led military action against Iraq for perceived non-compliance with the resulting Security Council resolution (1441, adopted in November 2002), the GCC Secretary-General urged the resumption of negotiations in place of military conflict. He also expressed regret that the Saddam Hussein regime had failed to co-operate sufficiently with the UN, in disregard of the GCC's recommendations. The GCC summit meeting held in Kuwait, in December 2003, issued a statement accepting the USA's policies towards Iraq at that time, emphasizing the importance of UN participation there, condemning ongoing operations by terrorist forces, and denoting the latter as anti-Islamic. In December 2004 the summit meeting, convened in Manama, Bahrain, urged participation by Iraqi citizens in the January 2005 elections to the Iraq Transitional National Assembly.

The GCC has condemned repeated military exercises conducted by Iran in the waters around the disputed islands of Abu Musa and Greater and Lesser Tunb as a threat to regional security and a violation of the UAE's sovereignty. Nevertheless, member countries have pursued efforts to strengthen relations with Iran. In May 1999 President Khatami undertook a state visit to Qatar, Saudi Arabia and Syria, prompting concern on the part of the UAE that its support within the GCC and the solidarity of the grouping were being undermined. In June a meeting of GCC ministers of foreign affairs was adjourned, owing to reported disagreements between Saudi Arabia and the UAE. Diplomatic efforts secured commitments, issued by both countries later in that month, to co-operate fully within the GCC. In early July the Ministerial Council reasserted GCC support of the UAE's sovereignty claim over the three disputed islands and determined to establish a committee, comprising the ministers of foreign affairs of Oman, Qatar and Saudi Arabia and the GCC Secretary-General, to resolve the dispute. In December the Supreme Council extended the mandate of the committee to establish a mechanism for direct negotiations between UAE and Iran. Iran, however, refused to co-operate with the committee; consequently, the committee's mandate was terminated in January 2001. In March the Ministerial Council demanded that Iran cease the construction of buildings for settlement on the disputed islands, and reiterated its support for the UAE's sovereignty claim. In December 2004 GCC leaders issued a declaration in support of the UAE's sovereignty claim; this was rejected by Iran.

EXTERNAL RELATIONS

In June 1988 an agreement was signed by GCC and European Community (EC) ministers on economic co-operation; this took effect from January 1990. Under the accord a joint ministerial council (meeting on an annual basis) was established, and working groups were subsequently created to promote co-operation in several specific areas, including business, energy, the environment and industry. In October 1990 GCC and EC ministers of foreign affairs commenced negotiations on formulating a free-trade agreement. In October 1995 a conference was held in Muscat, Oman, which aimed to strengthen economic co-operation between European Union (EU, as the restructured EC was now known) and GCC member states, and to promote investment in both regions. GCC heads of state, meeting in December 1997, condemned statements issued by the European Parliament, as well as by other organizations, regarding human rights issues in member states and insisted they amounted to interference in GCC judicial systems. In January 2003 the GCC established a customs union (see above), which was a precondition of the proposed GCC-EU free-trade agreement. It was envisaged that the GCC-EU agreement would be adopted by the end of 2005.

In September 1994 GCC ministers of foreign affairs decided to end the secondary and tertiary embargo on trade with Israel. In February 1995 a ministerial meeting of signatories of the Damascus Declaration adopted a common stand, criticizing Israel for its refusal to renew the nuclear non-proliferation treaty. In December 1996 the foreign ministers of the Damascus Declaration states, convened in Cairo, requested the USA to exert financial pressure on Israel to halt the construction of settlements on occupied Arab territory. In December 2001 GCC heads of state issued a statement holding Israeli government policy responsible for the escalating crisis in the Palestinian territories. The consultative meeting of heads of state held in May 2002 declared its support for a Saudi-proposed initiative aimed at achieving a peaceful resolution of the crisis.

In June 1997 ministers of foreign affairs of the Damascus Declaration states agreed to pursue efforts to establish a free-trade zone throughout the region, which they envisaged as the nucleus of a future Arab common market. Meanwhile, the Greater Arab Free-Trade Area, an initiative of the League of Arab States, entered into effect on 1 January 2005.

The GCC-USA Economic Dialogue, which commenced in 1985, convenes periodically as a government forum to promote co-operation between the GCC economies and the USA. Since the late 1990s private-sector interests have been increasingly represented at sessions of the Dialogue. It was announced in March 2001 that a business forum was to be established under the auspices of the Dialogue, to act as a permanent means of facilitating trade and investment between the GCC countries and the USA. Crown Prince Abdullah of Saudi Arabia withdrew as leader of the Saudi Arabian delegation to the December 2004 GCC summit in protest at the conclusion, in September, of a bilateral free-trade agreement between Bahrain and the USA and also at ongoing negotiations of proposed similar agreements between the USA and Kuwait, Oman, Qatar and the UAE, all of which were perceived by his government to be in contravention of certain existing agreements.

The GCC Secretary-General denounced the major terrorist attacks that were perpetrated in September 2001 against targets in the USA. Meeting in an emergency session in mid-September, in Riyadh, Saudi Arabia, GCC foreign ministers agreed to support the aims of the developing international coalition against terrorism. Meanwhile, however, member states urged parallel international resolve to halt action by the Israeli security forces against Palestinians. In December the Supreme Council declared the organization's full co-operation with the anti-terrorism coalition.

INVESTMENT CORPORATION

Gulf Investment Corporation (GIC): POB 3402, Safat 13035, Kuwait; tel. 2225000; fax 2448894; e-mail gic@gic.com.kw; internet www.gulfinvestmentcorp.com; f. 1983 by the six member states of the GCC, each contributing 16.6% of the total capital; total assets US $6,695 (Dec. 2003); investment chiefly in the Gulf region, financing industrial projects (including pharmaceuticals, chemicals, steel wire, aircraft engineering, aluminium, dairy produce and chicken-breeding); provides merchant banking and financial advisory services, and in 1992 was appointed to advise the Kuwaiti Government on a programme of privatization; CEO Hisham Abdul-razzak Al-Razzuqi; publ. *The GIC Gazetteer* (annually).

Gulf International Bank: POB 1017, Al-Dowali Bldg, 3 Palace Ave, Manama 317, Bahrain; tel. 534000; fax 522633; e-mail info@gib.com.bh; internet www.gibonline.com; f. 1976 by the six GCC states and Iraq; became a wholly-owned subsidiary of the GIC (without Iraqi shareholdings) in 1991; in April 1999 a merger with Saudi Investment Bank was concluded; cap. US $1,000m., total liabilities $15,913m., total assets $17,302m. (Dec. 2003); Chair. Ebrahim bin Khalifa al-Khalifa; CEO Dr Khaled M. al-Fayez.

Publications

GCC News (monthly).

At-Ta'awun (periodical).

COUNCIL OF ARAB ECONOMIC UNITY

Address: 1113 Corniche en-Nil, 4th Floor, POB 1 Mohammed Fareed, 11518 Cairo, Egypt.

Telephone: (2) 5755321; **fax:** (2) 5754090; **e-mail:** caeu@idsc.net.eg; **internet:** www.caeu.org.eg.

Established in 1957 by the Economic Council of the League of Arab States. The first meeting of the Council of Arab Economic Unity was held in 1964.

MEMBERS

Egypt	Palestine
Iraq	Somalia
Jordan	Sudan
Libya	Syria
Mauritania	Yemen

Organization

(April 2005)

COUNCIL

The Council consists of representatives of member states, usually ministers of economy, finance and trade. It meets twice a year; meetings are chaired by the representative of each country for one year.

GENERAL SECRETARIAT

Entrusted with the implementation of the Council's decisions and with proposing work plans, including efforts to encourage participation by member states in the Arab Economic Unity Agreement. The Secretariat also compiles statistics, conducts research and publishes studies on Arab economic problems and on the effects of major world economic trends.

General Secretary: Dr Ahmed Goweili (Egypt).

COMMITTEES

There are seven standing committees: preparatory, follow-up and Arab Common Market development; Permanent Delegates; budget; economic planning; fiscal and monetary matters; customs and trade planning and co-ordination; statistics. There are also seven *ad hoc* committees, including meetings of experts on tariffs, trade promotion and trade legislation.

Activities

The Council undertakes to co-ordinate measures leading to a customs union subject to a unified administration; conduct market and commodity studies; assist with the unification of statistical terminology and methods of data collection; conduct studies for the formation of new joint Arab companies and federations; and to formulate specific programmes for agricultural and industrial co-ordination and for improving road and railway networks.

ARAB COMMON MARKET

Based on a resolution passed by the Council in August 1964; its implementation was to be supervised by the Council. Customs duties and other taxes on trade between the member countries were to be eliminated in stages prior to the adoption of a full customs union, and ultimately all restrictions on trade between the member countries, including quotas, and restrictions on residence, employment and transport, were to be abolished. In practice little progress was achieved in the development of an Arab common market during 1964–2000. However, the Council's efforts towards liberalizing intra-Arab trade were intensified in 2001. A meeting of Council ministers of economy and trade convened in Baghdad, Iraq, in June, issued the 'Baghdad Declaration' on establishing an, initially, quadripartite free-trade area comprising Egypt, Iraq, Libya and Syria; future participation by other member states was urged by the Council's General Secretary. The initiative was envisaged as a cornerstone of the Greater Arab Free Trade Area—GAFTA, which was being implemented by the Arab League. The meeting also approved an executive programme for developing the common market, determined to establish a compensation fund to support the integration of the least developed Arab states into the regional economy, and agreed to provide technical assistance for Arab states aiming to join the WTO. It was reported in late 2001 that Palestine had also applied to join the sub-regional free-trade area, and that consideration of its application would delay the zone's entry into force. In May Egypt, Jordan, Morocco and Tunisia (all participants in the Euro-Mediterranean Partnership—see European Union), meeting in Agadir, Morocco, had issued the 'Agadir Declaration' in which they determined to establish by 2010 the Mediterranean Arab Free Trade Area (MAFTA) as a cornerstone of a planned larger Arab-Mediterranean free trade area. The so-called Agadir Agreement on MAFTA was signed in February 2004. Other Arab states that had concluded Association Agreements with the EU and were signatories of GAFTA were invited to join MAFTA. In the early 2000s the Council was considering a draft 20-year general framework for joint Arab economic action in the areas of investment, infrastructure, human resources development, technology, trade and joint ventures (see below). In December 2002 the Secretary-General of the Council announced the finalization of an Arab investment plan detailing some 4,000 investment opportunities; the Council launched a related internet site, www.arabinvestmap.com, in June 2004. Tariff-free trade between the 17 participants in GAFTA entered into force on 1 January 2005. In early 2005 the Council planned to launch an Arab electronic commerce market; it was envisaged that small and medium-sized enterprises in the region would benefit from this facility.

JOINT VENTURES

A number of multilateral organizations in industry and agriculture have been formed on the principle that faster development and economies of scale may be achieved by combining the efforts of member states. In industries that are new to the member countries Arab Joint Companies are formed, while existing industries are co-ordinated by the setting up of Arab Specialized Unions. The unions are for closer co-operation on problems of production and marketing, and to help companies deal as a group in international markets. The companies are intended to be self-supporting on a purely commercial basis; they may issue shares to citizens of the participating countries. The joint ventures are:

Arab Joint Companies:

Arab Company for Drug Industries and Medical Appliances—ACDIMA: POB 925161, Amman 11190, Jordan; tel. (6) 5821618; fax (6) 5821649; e-mail acdima@go.com.jo; internet www.acdima.com; f. 1976.

Arab Company for Electronic Commerce: f. 2001.

Arab Company for Industrial Investment: POB 3385, Alwiyah, Baghdad, Iraq; tel. (1) 718-9215; fax (1) 718-0710; e-mail aiic@warkaa.net; f. 1978; sponsors and establishes metal and engineering enterprises in the Arab region.

Arab Company for Livestock Development: POB 5305, Damascus, Syria; tel. 666037.

Arab Mining Company: POB 20198, Amman, Jordan; tel. (6) 5663148; fax (6) 5684114; e-mail armico@go.com.jo; f. 1974.

Specialized Arab Unions and Federations:

Arab Co-operative Federation: POB 57640, Baghdad, Iraq; tel. (1) 888-8121; f. 1985.

Arab Federation for Paper, Printing and Packaging Industries: POB 5456, Baghdad, Iraq; tel. (1) 887-2384; fax (1) 886-9639; f. 1977; 250 mems.

Arab Federation of Chemical Fertilizers Producers: Cairo, Egypt; f. 1976.

Arab Federation of Engineering Industries: POB 509, Baghdad, Iraq; tel. (1) 776-1101; f. 1975.

Arab Federation of Leather Industries: POB 2188, Damascus, Syria; f. 1978; activities currently suspended.

Arab Federation of Shipping: POB 1161, Baghdad, Iraq; tel. (1) 717-4540; fax (1) 717-7243; f. 1979; 22 mems.

Arab Federation of Textile Industries: POB 620, Damascus, Syria; f. 1976; activities currently suspended.

Arab Federation of Travel Agents: POB 7090, Amman, Jordan.

Arab Seaports Federation: Alexandria, Egypt; f. 1977.

Arab Steel Union: Algiers, Algeria; f. 1972.

Arab Sugar Federation: POB 195, Khartoum, Sudan; f. 1977; activities currently suspended.

Arab Union for Cement and Building Materials: POB 9015, Damascus, Syria; tel. (11) 6118598; fax (11) 6111318; e-mail aucbm@scs-net.org; internet www.aucbm.org; f. 1977; 22 mem. countries, 103 mem. cos.; *Cement and Building Materials Review* (quarterly).

Arab Union for Information Technology.

Arab Union of Fish Producers: POB 15064, Baghdad, Iraq; tel. (1) 551-1261; f. 1976.

Arab Union of Food Industries: POB 13025, Baghdad, Iraq; f. 1976.

Arab Union of Hotels and Tourism: Beirut, Lebanon; f. 1994.

Arab Union of Land Transport: POB 926324, Amman 11190, Jordan; tel. (6) 5663153; fax (6) 5664232; e-mail ault@go.com.jo; internet www.auolt.net; f. 1978.

Arab Union of the Manufacturers of Pharmaceuticals and Medical Appliances: POB 81150, Amman 11181, Jordan; tel. (6) 4654306; fax (6) 4648141; f. 1986.

Arab Union of the Manufacturers of Tyres and Rubber Products: Alexandria, Egypt; f. 1993.

Arab Union of Railways: POB 6599, Aleppo, Syria; tel. (21)2667270; fax (21) 2686000; f. 1979.

General Arab Insurance Federation: 8 Kaser El Nil St, POB 611, 11511 Cairo, Egypt; tel. (2) 5743177; fax (2) 5762310; e-mail info@gaif.org; internet www.gaif.org; f. 1964.

General Union of Arab Agricultural Workers and Co-operatives: Tripoli, Libya; f. 1993.

Union of Arab Contractors: Cairo, Egypt; f. 1995.

Union of Arab Investors: Cairo, Egypt; f. 1995.

Publications

Annual Bulletin for Arab Countries' Foreign Trade Statistics.
Annual Bulletin for Official Exchange Rates of Arab Currencies.
Arab Economic Unity Bulletin (2 a year).
Demographic Yearbook for Arab Countries.
Economic Report of the General Secretary (2 a year).
Guide to Studies prepared by Secretariat.
Progress Report (2 a year).
Statistical Yearbook for Arab Countries.
Yearbook for Intra-Arab Trade Statistics.
Yearbook of National Accounts for Arab Countries.

COUNCIL OF BALTIC SEA STATES—CBSS

Address: Strömsborg, POB 2010, 103 11 Stockhölm, Sweden.
Telephone: (8) 440-19-20; **fax:** (8) 440-19-44; **e-mail:** cbss@cbss.st;
internet: www.cbss.st.

The Council of Baltic Sea States (CBSS) was established in 1992 to develop co-operation between member states.

MEMBERS

Denmark	Iceland	Poland
Estonia	Latvia	Russia
Finland	Lithuania	Sweden
Germany	Norway	

The European Commission also has full membership status.

Organization

(April 2005)

PRESIDENCY

The presidency is occupied by member states for one year, on a rotating basis. Summit meetings of heads of government are convened every two years. The fifth summit meeting was convened in Laulasmaa, Estonia, in June 2004, and the sixth was scheduled to be held in Iceland in 2006.

COUNCIL

The Council comprises the ministers of foreign affairs of each member state and a representative of the European Commission. The Council meets annually and aims to serve as a forum for guidance, direction of work and overall co-ordination among participating states. The minister of foreign affairs of the presiding country acts as Chairman of the Council and is responsible for co-ordinating the Council's activities between ministerial sessions, with assistance from the Committee of Senior Officials. (Other ministers also convene periodically, on an *ad hoc* basis by their own decision.)

COMMITTEE OF SENIOR OFFICIALS—CSO

The Committee consists of senior officials of the ministries of foreign affairs of the member states and of the European Commission. It serves as a discussion forum for matters relating to the work of the Council and undertakes inter-sessional activities. The Chairman of the Committee, from the same country serving as President of the CBSS, meets regularly with the previous and future Chairmen. The so-called Troika aims to maintain information co-operation, promote better exchange of information, and ensure more effective decision-making.

SECRETARIAT

In October 1998 the presidency inaugurated a permanent secretariat in Stockholm. The tasks of the secretariat include the preparation of summit meetings, annual sessions of ministers of foreign affairs, and other meetings of high-level officials and experts, the provision of technical support to the presidency regarding the implementation of plans, maintaining contacts with other sub-regional organizations, and strengthening awareness of the Council and its activities. The Secretariat includes an Energy Unit (established in April 2000), Baltic 21 Unit (January 2001) and a Children's Unit (June 2002).

Director: Hannu Halinen (Finland).

Activities

The CBSS was established in March 1992 as a forum to enhance and strengthen co-operation between countries in the Baltic Sea region. At a meeting of the Council in Kalmar, Sweden, in July 1996, ministers adopted an Action Programme as a guide-line for CBSS activities. The main programme areas covered stable and participatory political development; economic integration and prosperity; and protection of the environment. The third summit meeting of CBSS heads of government, held at Kolding, Denmark, in April 2000, recommended a restructuring of the organization to consolidate regional intergovernmental, multilateral co-operation in all sectors. In June the ninth meeting of the CBSS Council approved the summit's recommendations. The 10th ministerial session, held in Hamburg, Germany, in June 2001, adopted a set of guide-lines regarding the strengthening of the CBSS.

The ministerial session held in May 1994 determined to appoint an independent Commissioner on Democratic Development, concerned with democratic institutions and human rights, to serve a three-year term of office, from October of that year. The Commissioner's mandate was subsequently extended twice for three years, in July 1997 and June 2000, and was terminated in mid-December 2003.

At the first Baltic Sea States summit, held in Visby, Sweden, in May 1996, heads of government agreed to establish a Task Force on Organized Crime to counter drugs-trafficking, strengthen judicial co-operation, increase the dissemination of information, impose regional crime-prevention measures, improve border controls and provide training. In January 1998 the second summit meeting, convened in Riga, Latvia, agreed to extend the mandate of the Task Force until the end of 2000 and to enhance co-operation in the areas of civic security and border control. In April 2000 the third Baltic Sea States summit prolonged the Task Force's mandate further, until the end of 2004, and in June 2004 the fifth summit extended it until end-2008. The 2000 summit also authorized the establishment of a Task Force on Communicable Disease Control, which was mandated to formulate a joint plan aimed at improving disease control throughout the region, and also to strengthen regional co-operation in combating the threat to public health posed by a significant increase in communicable diseases, in particular HIV/AIDS. The Task Force presented its final report to the CBSS summit meeting held in June 2004. It was recognized that some of the structures of the Task Force could be pursued through a Northern Dimension Partnership in Public Health and Social Well-Being, which was established in late 2003.

The Council has founded a number of working groups, comprising experts in specific fields, which aim to report on and recommend action on issues of concern to the Council. In early 2005 there were five groups working under the auspices of the CSO: the Working Group on Assistance to Democratic Institutions; the Working Group on Economic Co-operation; the Working Group on Nuclear Radiation Safety; the Working Group on Youth Affairs; and the Working Group for Co-operation on Children at Risk. There was also an *ad hoc* Working Group on Transportation Issues.

A Baltic Business Advisory Council was established in 1996 with the aim of facilitating the privatization process in the member states in transition and promoting small and medium-sized enterprises.

In January 2001 the CBSS Council agreed to establish a unit in the CBSS secretariat to implement Baltic 21, the regional variant (adopted by the CBSS in 1998) of 'Agenda 21', the programme of action agreed by the UN Conference on Environment and Development, held in Rio de Janeiro, Brazil, in June 1992. Baltic 21 comprised a programme of 30 projects throughout the region, which aim to promote sustainable development in the agriculture, forestry and fisheries, energy, industry, tourism, transport, and spatial planning sectors. The Baltic Sea Region Energy Co-operation (BASREC) has its own secretariat function and council of senior energy officials, administered by the CBSS secretariat. BASREC also has *ad hoc* groups on electricity markets, gas markets, energy efficiency and climate change.

The CBSS contributed to the implementation of the European Union's Northern Dimension Action Plan (NDAP) for 2000–03 through the formulation, in collaboration with other regional groupings, of a 'List of Priorities and Projects'; and it also contributed to the implementation of the second phase of NDAP, covering 2004–06. In 2000 CBSS heads of government approved a Northern e-Dimension Action Plan (NeDAP) to co-ordinate efforts to strengthen information technologies through the region.

Finance

The Secretariat is financed by contributions of the governments of the Council's 11 member states. Ongoing activities and co-operation projects are funded through voluntary contributions from member states on the basis of special contribution schemes.

Publication

Newsletter (monthly).

THE COUNCIL OF EUROPE

Address: 67075 Strasbourg Cédex, France.
Telephone: 3-88-41-20-33; **fax:** 3-88-41-27-45; **e-mail:** infopoint@coe.int; **internet:** www.coe.int.

The Council was founded in May 1949 to achieve a greater unity between its members, to facilitate their social progress and to uphold the principles of parliamentary democracy, respect for human rights and the rule of law. Membership has risen from the original 10 to 46.

MEMBERS*

Albania	Lithuania
Andorra	Luxembourg
Armenia	Macedonia, former Yugoslav
Austria	republic
Azerbaijan	Malta
Belgium	Moldova
Bulgaria	Monaco
Bosnia and Herzegovina	Netherlands
Croatia	Norway
Cyprus	Poland
Czech Republic	Portugal
Denmark	Romania
Estonia	Russia
Finland	San Marino
France	Serbia and Montenegro
Georgia	Slovakia
Germany	Slovenia
Greece	Spain
Hungary	Sweden
Iceland	Switzerland
Ireland	Turkey
Italy	Ukraine
Latvia	United Kingdom
Liechtenstein	

*The Holy See, Canada, Japan, Mexico and the USA have observer status with the organization. The parliaments of Canada, Israel and Mexico have observer status with the Parliamentary Assembly.

Organization

(April 2005)

COMMITTEE OF MINISTERS

The Committee consists of the ministers of foreign affairs of all member states (or their deputies); it decides with binding effect all matters of internal organization, makes recommendations to governments and draws up conventions and agreements; it also discusses matters of political concern, such as European co-operation, compliance with member states' commitments, in particular concerning the protection of human rights, and considers possible co-ordination with other institutions, such as the European Union (EU) and the Organization for Security and Co-operation in Europe (OSCE). The Committee meets weekly at deputy level and once a year (usually in May) at ministerial level. Six two-day meetings are convened every year to supervise the execution of judgments of the European Court of Human Rights (see below).

CONFERENCES OF SPECIALIZED MINISTERS

There are 19 Conferences of specialized ministers, meeting regularly for intergovernmental co-operation in various fields.

PARLIAMENTARY ASSEMBLY

President: RENÉ VAN DER LINDEN (Netherlands).
Chairman of the Socialist Group: LLUÍS MARIA DE PUIG (Spain).
Chairman of the Group of the European People's Party: LUC VAN DEN BRANDE (Belgium).
Chairman of the Liberal, Democratic and Reformers' Group: MÁTYÁS EÖRSI (Hungary).
Chairman of the European Democratic Group: MIKHAIL MARGELOV (Russia).
Chairman of the Unified European Left Group: MATS EINARSSON (Sweden).

Members are elected or appointed by their national parliaments from among the members thereof; political parties in each delegation follow the proportion of their strength in the national parliament.

Members do not represent their governments, speaking on their own behalf. At March 2005 the Assembly had 315 members (and 315 substitutes): 18 each for France, Germany, Italy, Russia and the United Kingdom; 12 each for Poland, Spain, Turkey and Ukraine; 10 for Romania; seven each for Belgium, the Czech Republic, Greece, Hungary, the Netherlands, Portugal and Serbia and Montenegro; six each for Austria, Azerbaijan, Bulgaria, Sweden and Switzerland; five each for Bosnia and Herzegovina, Croatia, Denmark, Finland, Georgia, Moldova, Norway and Slovakia; four each for Albania, Armenia, Ireland and Lithuania; three each for Cyprus, Estonia, Iceland, Latvia, Luxembourg, the former Yugoslav republic of Macedonia, Malta and Slovenia; and two each for Andorra, Liechtenstein, Monaco and San Marino. The parliaments of Israel, Canada and Mexico have permanent observer status. (Belarus's special 'guest status' was suspended in January 1997.)

The Assembly meets in ordinary session once a year. The session is divided into four parts, generally held in the last full week of January, April, June and September. The Assembly submits Recommendations to the Committee of Ministers, passes Resolutions, and discusses reports on any matters of common European interest. It is also a consultative body to the Committee of Ministers, and elects the Secretary-General, the Deputy Secretary-General, the Secretary-General of the Assembly, the Council's Commissioner for Human Rights, and the members of the European Court of Human Rights.

Standing Committee: represents the Assembly when it is not in session, and may adopt Recommendations to the Committee of Ministers and Resolutions on behalf of the Assembly. Consists of the President, Vice-Presidents, Chairmen of the Political Groups, Chairmen of the Ordinary Committees and Chairmen of national delegations. Meetings are usually held three times a year.

Ordinary Committees: political; legal and human rights; economic and development; social, health and family affairs; culture, science and education; environment, agriculture, and local and regional authorities; migration, refugees and population; rules of procedure and immunities; equal opportunities; honouring of obligations and commitments by member states of the Council of Europe.

SECRETARIAT

The Secretariat incorporates the Secretariats and Registry of the principal institutions of the Council. There are Directorates of Communication and Research, Strategic Planning, Protocol and Internal Audit, and the following Directorates General: Political Affairs; Legal Affairs; Human Rights; Social Cohesion; Education, Culture and Heritage, Youth and Sport; and Administration and Logistics.

Secretary-General: TERRY DAVIS (United Kingdom).
Deputy Secretary-General: MAUD DE BOER-BUQUICCHIO (Netherlands).
Secretary-General of the Parliamentary Assembly: BRUNO HALLER (France).

EUROPEAN COURT OF HUMAN RIGHTS

The Court was established in 1959 under the European Convention on Human Rights (see below). It has compulsory jurisdiction and is competent to consider complaints lodged by states party to the European Convention and by individuals, groups of individuals or non-governmental organizations claiming to be victims of breaches of the Convention's guarantees. The Court comprises one judge for each contracting state. The Court sits in three-member Committees, empowered to declare applications inadmissible in the event of unanimity and where no further examination is necessary, seven-member Chambers, and a 17-member Grand Chamber. Chamber judgments become final three months after delivery, during which period parties may request a rehearing before the Grand Chamber, subject to acceptance by a panel of five judges. Grand Chamber judgments are final. The Court's final judgments are binding on respondent states and their execution is supervised at regular intervals by the Committee of Ministers. Execution of judgments includes payment of pecuniary just satisfaction awarded by the Court, adoption of specific individual measures to erase the consequences of the violations found (such as striking out of impugned convictions from criminal records, reopening of judicial proceedings, etc.), and general measures to prevent new similar violations (e.g. constitutional and legislative reforms, changes of domestic case-law and administrative practice, etc.) At its meeting in February 2005 the Committee of Ministers supervised the payment of just satisfaction in 507 cases, the adoption, in 30 cases, of individual measures and 64 cases or groups of cases requiring the adoption of new general measures. In addition, the Committee started examining 124 new judgements of the Court. When the Committee of Ministers considers that the measures taken comply with the respondent state's obligation to give effect to the judgment, a final resolution is adopted that terminates the supervision of the case.

President: Luzius Wildhaber (Switzerland).

Registrar: Paul Mahoney (United Kingdom).

CONGRESS OF LOCAL AND REGIONAL AUTHORITIES OF THE COUNCIL OF EUROPE (CLRAE)

The Congress was established in 1994, incorporating the former Standing Conference of Local and Regional Authorities, in order to protect and promote the political, administrative and financial autonomy of local and regional European authorities by encouraging central governments to develop effective local democracy. The Congress comprises two chambers—a Chamber of Local Authorities and a Chamber of Regions—with a total membership of 315 elected representatives (and 315 elected substitutes). Annual sessions are mainly concerned with local government matters, regional planning, protection of the environment, town and country planning, and social and cultural affairs. A Standing Committee, drawn from all national delegations, meets between plenary sessions of the Congress. Four Statutory Committees (Institutional; Sustainable Development; Social Cohesion; Culture and Education) meet twice a year in order to prepare texts for adoption by the Congress.

The Congress advises the Council's Committee of Ministers and the Parliamentary Assembly on all aspects of local and regional policy and co-operates with other national and international organizations representing local government. The Congress monitors implementation of the European Charter of Local Self-Government, which was opened for signature in 1985 and provides common standards for effective local democracy. Other legislative guide-lines for the activities of local authorities and the promotion of democracy at local level include the 1980 European Outline Convention on Transfrontier Co-operation, and its Additional Protocol which was opened for signature in 1995, a Convention on the Participation of Foreigners in Public Life at Local Level (1992), and the European Charter for Regional or Minority Languages (1992). In addition, the European Urban Charter (1992) defines citizens' rights in European towns and cities, for example in the areas of transport, urban architecture, pollution and security; the European Landscape Convention (2000) details an obligation for public authorities to adopt policies and measures at local, regional, national and international level for the protection, management and planning of landscapes; and the Charter on the Participation of Young People in Municipal and Regional Life (1992), revised in 2003, sets out guide-lines for encouraging the active involvement of young people in the promotion of social change in their municipality or region.

President: Giovanni di Stasi (Italy).

Activities

In an effort to harmonize national laws, to put the citizens of member countries on an equal footing and to pool certain resources and facilities, the Council of Europe has concluded a number of conventions and agreements covering particular aspects of European co-operation. Since 1989 the Council has undertaken to increase co-operation with all countries of the former Eastern bloc and to facilitate their accession to the organization. In October 1997 heads of state or government of member countries convened for only the second time (the first meeting took place in Vienna, in October 1993—see below) with the aim of formulating a new social model to consolidate democracy throughout Europe. The meeting endorsed a Final Declaration and an Action Plan, which established priority areas for future Council activities, including fostering social cohesion; protecting civilian security; promoting human rights; enhancing joint measures to counter cross-border illegal trafficking; and strengthening democracy through education and other cultural activities. In addition, the meeting generated renewed political commitment to the Programme of Action against Corruption, which has become a key element of Council activities. In July 2004 members states decided to convene a third meeting of heads of state, to be held in May 2005 in Warsaw, Poland, in order to identify the political priorities and framework for the Council's activities in the future.

A Multidisciplinary Group on International Action against Terrorism, established in 2001, has updated the 1977 European Convention on the Suppression of Terrorism. In 2002 the Council's Committee of Ministers adopted a set of 'Guide-lines on Human Rights and the Fight against Terrorism'.

HUMAN RIGHTS

The protection of human rights is one of the Council of Europe's basic goals, to be achieved in four main areas: the effective supervision and protection of fundamental rights and freedoms; identification of new threats to human rights and human dignity; development of public awareness of the importance of human rights; and promotion of human rights education and professional training. The most significant treaties in this area include: the European Convention for the Protection of Human Rights and Fundamental Freedoms (European Convention on Human Rights) (which was adopted in 1950 and entered into force in 1953); the European Social Charter; the European Convention for the Prevention of Torture and Inhuman or Degrading Treatment or Punishment; and the Framework Convention for the Protection of National Minorities.

The Steering Committee for Human Rights is responsible for inter-governmental co-operation in the field of human rights and fundamental freedoms; it works to strengthen the effectiveness of systems for protecting human rights and to identify potential threats and challenges to human rights. The Committee has been responsible for the elaboration of several conventions and other legal instruments including the following protocols to the European Convention on Human Rights: Protocol No. 11, which entered into force in November 1998, resulting in the replacement of the then existing institutions—the European Commission of Human Rights and the European Court of Human Rights—by a single Court, working on a full-time basis; Protocol No. 12, adopted in June 2000, enforcing a general prohibition of discrimination; and No. 13, adopted in May 2002, guaranteeing the abolition of the death penalty in all circumstances (including in time of war).

The Committee was responsible for the preparation of the European Ministerial Conference on Human Rights, held in Rome in November 2000, to commemorate the 50th anniversary of the adoption of the European Convention on Human Rights. The Conference highlighted, in particular, 'the need to reinforce the effective protection of human rights in domestic legal systems as well as at the European level'. Protocol No. 14, adopted in May 2004, aimed to enhance the effectiveness of the European Court of Human Rights by improving implementation of the Convention at national level and the processing of applications, and accelerating the execution of the Court's decisions.

The second summit meeting of the Council's heads of state and government, held in Strasbourg, France, in October 1997, welcomed a proposal to institute a Council of Europe Commissioner for Human Rights to promote respect for human rights in member states; this office was established by a resolution of the Council's Committee of Ministers in May 1999.

Commissioner for Human Rights: Alvaro Gil-Robles (Spain).

European Committee for the Prevention of Torture and Inhuman or Degrading Treatment or Punishment (CPT)

The Committee was established under the 1987 Convention for the Prevention of Torture as an integral part of the Council of Europe's system for the protection of human rights. The Committee, comprising independent experts, aims to examine the treatment of persons deprived of their liberty with a view to strengthening, if necessary, the protection of such persons from torture and from inhuman or degrading treatment or punishment. It conducts periodic visits to police stations, prisons, detention centres, and all other sites where persons are deprived of their liberty by a public authority, in all states parties to the Convention, and may also undertake *ad hoc* visits when the Committee considers them necessary. After each visit the Committee drafts a report of its findings and any further advice or recommendations, based on dialogue and co-operation. By March 2005 the Committee had published 140 reports. In 2005 the Committee's programme of periodic visits was to include Albania, Belgium, Germany, Greece, Hungary, Norway, Russia, San Marino, Slovakia and Ukraine.

President: Silvia Casale (United Kingdom).

European Social Charter

The European Social Charter, in force since 1965, is the counterpart of the European Convention on Human Rights, in the field of protection of economic and social rights. A revised Charter, which amended existing guarantees and incorporated new rights, was opened for signature in May 1996, and entered into force on 1 July 1999. By March 2005 35 member states had ratified the Charter and 19 had ratified the revised Charter. Rights guaranteed by the Charter concern all individuals in their daily lives in matters of housing, health, education, employment, social protection, movement of persons and non-discrimination. The European Committee of Social Rights considers reports submitted to it annually by member states. It also considers collective complaints submitted in the framework of an Additional Protocol (1995), providing for a system which entered into force in July 1998, permitting trade unions, employers' organizations and NGOs to lodge complaints on alleged violations of the Charter. The Committee, composed of 15 members, decides on the conformity of national situations with the Charter. When a country does not bring a situation into conformity, the Committee of Ministers may, on the basis of decisions prepared by a Governmental Committee (composed of representatives of each Contracting Party), issue recommendations to the state concerned, inviting it to change its legislation or practice in accordance with the Charter's requirements.

President of the European Committee of Social Rights: JEAN-MICHEL BELORGEY (France).

FRAMEWORK CONVENTION FOR THE PROTECTION OF NATIONAL MINORITIES

In 1993 the first summit meeting of Council of Europe heads of state and government, held in Vienna, mandated the Committee of Ministers to draft 'a framework convention specifying the principle that States commit themselves to respect in order to assure the protection of national minorities'. A special committee was established to draft the so-called Framework Convention for the Protection of National Minorities, which was then adopted by the Committee in November 1994. The Convention was opened for signature in February 1995, entering into force in February 1998. Contracting parties (35 States at January 2005) are required to submit reports on the implementation of the treaty at regular intervals to an Advisory Committee composed of 18 independent experts. The Advisory Committee adopts an opinion on the implementation of the Framework Convention by the contracting party, on the basis of which the Committee of Ministers adopts a resolution. At January 2005 34 opinions and recommendations in respect of 29 countries had been adopted.

Executive Secretary: ANTTI KORKEAKIVI.

RACISM AND INTOLERANCE

In October 1993 heads of state and of government, meeting in Vienna, resolved to reinforce a policy to combat all forms of intolerance, in response to the increasing incidence of racial hostility and intolerance towards minorities in European societies. A European Commission against Racism and Intolerance (ECRI) was established by the summit meeting to analyse and assess the effectiveness of legal, policy and other measures taken by member states to combat these problems. It became operational in March 1994. The European conference against racism, held in October 2000, requested that ECRI should be reinforced and, in June 2002, the Committee of Ministers of the Council of Europe adopted a new Statute for ECRI that consolidated its role as an independent human rights monitoring body focusing on issues related to racism and radial discrimination. Members of ECRI are appointed on the basis of their recognized expertise in the field; they are independent and impartial in fulfilling their mandate. ECRI undertakes activities in three programme areas: country-by-country approach; work on general themes; and relations with civil society. In the first area of activity, ECRI analyses the situation regarding racism and intolerance in each of the member states, in order to advise governments on measures to combat these problems. In December 1998 ECRI completed a first round of reports for all Council members. A second series of reports was prepared during 1999–2002 and a third monitoring cycle was initiated in 2004. ECRI's work on general themes includes the preparation of policy recommendations and guide-lines on issues of importance to combating racism and intolerance. ECRI also collects and disseminates examples of good practices relating to these issues. Under the third programme area ECRI aims to disseminate information and raise awareness of the problems of racism and intolerance among the general public.

EQUALITY BETWEEN WOMEN AND MEN

The Steering Committee for Equality between Women and Men (CDEG—an intergovernmental committee of experts) is responsible for encouraging action at both national and Council of Europe level to promote equality of rights and opportunities between the two sexes. Assisted by various specialist groups and committees, the CDEG is mandated to establish analyses, studies and evaluations, to examine national policies and experiences, to devise concerted policy strategies and measures for implementing equality and, as necessary, to prepare appropriate legal and other instruments. It is also responsible for preparing the European Ministerial Conferences on Equality between Women and Men. The main areas of CDEG activities are the comprehensive inclusion of the rights of women (for example, combating violence against women and trafficking in human beings) within the context of human rights; the issue of equality and democracy, including the promotion of the participation of women in political and public life; projects aimed at studying the specific equality problems related to cultural diversity, migration and minorities; positive action in the field of equality between men and women and the mainstreaming of equality into all policies and programmes at all levels of society. In October 1998 the Committee of Ministers adopted a Recommendation to member states on gender mainstreaming; in May 2000 it approved a Recommendation on action against trafficking in human beings for the purpose of sexual exploitation; and in April 2002 it adopted a Recommendation on the protection of women from violence.

MEDIA AND COMMUNICATIONS

Article 10 of the European Convention on Human Rights (freedom of expression and information) forms the basis for the Council of Europe's mass media activities. Implementation of the Council of Europe's work programme concerning the media is undertaken by the Steering Committee on the Mass Media (CDMM), which comprises senior government officials and representatives of professional organizations, meeting in plenary session twice a year. The CDMM is mandated to devise concerted European policy measures and appropriate legal instruments. Its underlying aims are to further freedom of expression and information in a pluralistic democracy, and to promote the free flow of information and ideas. The CDMM is assisted by various specialist groups and committees. Policy and legal instruments have been developed on subjects including: exclusivity rights; media concentrations and transparency of media ownership; protection of journalists in situations of conflict and tension; independence of public-service broadcasting, protection of rights holders; legal protection of encrypted television services; media and elections; protection of journalists' sources of information; the independence and functions of broadcasting regulatory authorities; and coverage of legal proceedings by the media. These policy and legal instruments (mainly in the form on non-binding recommendations addressed to member governments) are complemented by the publication of studies, analyses and seminar proceedings on topics of media law and policy. The CDMM has also prepared a number of international binding legal instruments, including the European Convention on Transfrontier Television (adopted in 1989 and ratified by 30 countries by March 2005), the European Convention on the legal protection of services based on or consisting of conditional access (ratified by five countries at March 2005), and the European Convention relating to questions on copyright law and neighbouring rights in the context of transfrontier broadcasting by satellite (ratified by two countries at March 2005). In March 2005 the Council's Committee of Ministers adopted a declaration on freedom of expression and information in the media in the context of the fight against terrorism.

SOCIAL COHESION

In June 1998 the Committee of Ministers established the European Committee for Social Cohesion (CDCS). The CDCS has the following responsibilities: to co-ordinate, guide and stimulate co-operation between member States with a view to promoting social cohesion in Europe, to develop and promote integrated, multidisciplinary responses to social issues, and to promote the social standards embodied in the European Social Charter and other Council of Europe instruments, including the European Code of Social Security. In November 2002 the CDCS published the *Report on Access to Social Rights in Europe*, concerning access to employment, housing and social protection. The Committee supervises an extensive programme of work on children, families and elderly. In March 2004 the Committee of Ministers approved a revised version of the Council's strategy for social cohesion (adopted in July 2000).

The European Code of Social Security and its Protocol entered into force in 1968; by March 2005 the Code and Protocol had been ratified by Belgium, Germany, Luxembourg, the Netherlands, Norway, Portugal and Sweden, while the Code alone had, additionally, been ratified by Cyprus, the Czech Republic, Denmark, France, Greece, Ireland, Italy, Slovenia, Spain, Switzerland, Turkey and the United Kingdom. These instruments set minimum standards for medical care and the following benefits: sickness, old-age, unemployment, employment injury, family, maternity, invalidity and survivor's benefit. A revision of these instruments, aiming to provide higher standards and greater flexibility, was completed for signature in 1990 and had been signed by 14 states at March 2005.

The European Convention on Social Security, in force since 1977, now applies in Austria, Belgium, Italy, Luxembourg, the Netherlands, Portugal, Spain and Turkey; most of the provisions apply automatically, while others are subject to the conclusion of additional multilateral or bilateral agreements. The Convention is concerned with establishing the following four fundamental principles of international law on social security: equality of treatment, unity of applicable legislation, conservation of rights accrued or in course of acquisition, and payment of benefits abroad. In 1994 a Protocol to the Convention, providing for the enlargement of the personal scope of the Convention, was opened for signature. By March 2005 it had been signed by Austria, the Czech Republic, Greece and Luxembourg, and had been ratified by Portugal.

HEALTH

Through a series of expert committees, the Council aims to ensure constant co-operation in Europe in a variety of health-related fields, with particular emphasis on patients' rights, for example: equity in access to health care, quality assurance, health services for institutionalized populations (prisoners, elderly in homes), discrimination resulting from health status and education for health. These efforts are supplemented by the training of health personnel.

Improvement of blood transfusion safety and availability of blood and blood derivatives has been ensured through European Agreements and guide-lines. Advances in this field and in organ transplantation are continuously assessed by expert committees.

Eighteen states co-operate in a Partial Agreement to protect the consumer from potential health risks connected with commonplace or domestic activities. The committees of experts of the Public Health Committee provide the scientific base for national and international regulations regarding products which have a direct or indirect impact on the human food chain, pesticides, pharmaceuticals and cosmetics.

The 1992 Recommendation on A Coherent Policy for People with Disabilities contains the policy principles for the rehabilitation and integration of people with disabilities. This model programme recommends that governments of all member states develop comprehensive and co-ordinated national disability policies taking account of prevention, diagnosis, treatment education, vocational guidance and training, employment, social integration, social protection, information and research. It has set benchmarks, both nationally and internationally. The 1995 Charter on the Vocational Assessment of People with Disabilities states that a person's vocational abilities and not disabilities should be assessed and related to specific job requirements. The 2001 Resolution on Universal Design aims to improve accessibility, recommending the inclusion of Universal Design principles in the training for vocations working on the built environment. The 2001 Resolution on New Technologies recommends formulating national strategies to ensure that people with disabilities benefit from new technologies. Current activities include: air travel, community living, disability prevention, and women with disabilities. Tailor-made programmes for Central and Eastern European countries take account of their specific requirements. The Council of Europe designated 2003 as the European Year of People with Disabilities.

In the co-operation group to combat drug abuse and illicit drugs trafficking (Pompidou Group), 34 states work together, through meetings of ministers, officials and experts, to counteract drug abuse. The Group follows a multidisciplinary approach embracing, in particular, legislation, law enforcement, prevention, treatment, rehabilitation and data collection.

The Convention on the Elaboration of a European Pharmacopoeia (establishing legally binding standards for medicinal substances, auxiliary substances, pharmaceutical preparations, vaccines for human and veterinary use and other articles) entered into force in eight signatory states in May 1974: in October 2004 35 states and the European Union were parties to the Convention. WHO and 16 European and non-European states participate as observers in the sessions of the European Pharmacopoeia Commission. In 1994 a procedure on certification of suitability to the European Pharmacopoeia monographs for manufacturers of substances for pharmaceutical use was established. A network of official control laboratories for human and veterinary medicines was established in 1995, open to all signatory countries to the Convention and observers at the Pharmacopoeia Commission. The fourth edition of the European Pharmacopoeia, in force since 1 January 2002, is updated three times a year in its electronic version, and includes some 1,800 harmonized European standards, or 'monographs', 300 general methods of analysis and 2,002 reagents. The fifth edition entered into force in January 2005.

In April 1997 the first international convention on biomedicine was opened for signature at a meeting of health ministers of member states, in Oviedo, Spain. The so-called Convention for the Protection of Human Rights and the Dignity of Human Beings with Respect to the Applications of Biology and Medicine incorporated provisions on scientific research, the principle of informed patient consent, organ and tissue transplants and the prohibition of financial gain and disposal of a part of the human body. It entered into force on 1 November 1999 (see below), and by March 2005 had been ratified by 19 states.

POPULATION AND MIGRATION

The European Convention on the Legal Status of Migrant Workers, in force since 1983, has been ratified by France, Italy, the Netherlands, Norway, Portugal, Spain, Sweden and Turkey. The Convention is based on the principle of equality of treatment for migrant workers and the nationals of the host country as to housing, working conditions, and social security. The Convention also upholds the principle of the right to family reunion. An international consultative committee, representing the parties to the Convention, monitors the application of the Convention.

In 1996 the European Committee on Migration concluded work on a project entitled 'The Integration of Immigrants: Towards Equal Opportunities' and the results were presented at the sixth conference of European ministers responsible for migration affairs, held in

Warsaw, Poland. At the conference a new project, entitled 'Tensions and Tolerance: Building better integrated communities across Europe' was initiated; it was concluded in 1999. The Committee was responsible for activities concerning Roma/Gypsies in Europe, in co-ordination with other relevant Council of Europe bodies. The Committee is also jointly responsible, with the *ad hoc* Committee of Experts on the legal aspects of territorial asylum, refugees and stateless persons, for the examination of migration issues arising at the pan-European level. In December 2004 a European Roma and Travellers' Forum, established in partnership with the Council of Europe, was inaugurated.

The European Population Committee, an intergovernmental committee of scientists and government officials responsible for population matters, monitors and analyses population trends throughout Europe and informs governments, research centres and the public of demographic developments and their impact on policy decisions. It compiles an annual statistical review of demographic developments (covering 46 European states) and publishes the results of studies on population issues.

COUNCIL OF EUROPE DEVELOPMENT BANK

The Council of Europe Development Bank was established in April 1956 by the Committee of Ministers, initially as the Resettlement Fund, and later as the Council of Europe Social Development Fund, and then renamed again in November 1999. It is a multilateral development bank with a social mandate, promoting social development by granting loans for projects with a social purpose. Projects aimed at solving social problems related to the presence of refugees, displaced persons or forced migrants are a priority. In addition, the Bank finances projects in other fields that contribute directly to strengthening social cohesion in Europe: job creation and preservation in small and medium-sized enterprises; social housing; improving urban living conditions; health and education infrastructure, protection of the environment, and rural modernization; protection and rehabilitation of the historic heritage. At September 2003 the Bank had a subscribed capital of €3,240m. In 2004 the Bank approved 33 new projects with a value of €1,751m. Its lending activities have been increasingly targeted at central and eastern European countries.

LEGAL AFFAIRS

The European Committee on Legal Co-operation develops co-operation between member states in the field of law, with the objective of harmonizing and modernizing public and private law, including administrative law and the law relating to the judiciary. The Committee is responsible for expert groups which consider issues relating to administrative law, efficiency of justice, family law, nationality, information technology and data protection.

Numerous conventions and Recommendations have been adopted, and followed up by appropriate committees or groups of experts, on matters which include: efficiency of justice, nationality, legal aid, rights of children, data protection, information technology, children born out of wedlock, animal protection, adoption, information on foreign law, and the legal status of non-governmental organizations. In addition, a new draft Convention on contact concerning children was adopted in May 2002. By March 2005 it had received 14 signatures and been ratified by two states (requiring three to enter into force).

In December 1999 the Convention for the Protection of Human Rights and the Dignity of Human Beings with Respect to the Applications of Biology and Medicine: Convention on Human Rights and Biomedicine entered into force, as the first internationally-binding legal text to protect people against the misuse of biological and medical advances. It aims to preserve human dignity and identity, rights and freedoms, through a series of principles and rules. Additional protocols develop the Convention's general provisions by means of specialized texts. A Protocol prohibiting the medical cloning of human beings was approved by Council heads of state and government in October 1997 and entered into force on 1 March 2001. A Protocol on the transplantation of human organs and tissue was opened for signature in January 2002, and a Protocol concerning biomedical research opened for signature in January 2005. Work on draft protocols relating to protection of the human embryo and foetus, and genetics is ongoing. A Recommendation on xenotransplantation was adopted by the Committee of Ministers in 2003.

In 2001 an Additional Protocol to the Convention for the protection of individuals with regard to automatic processing of personal data was adopted. The Protocol, which opened for signature in November, concerned supervisory authorities and transborder data flows. It entered into force in July 2004 and by March 2005 had been ratified by eight states.

In 2001 the European Committee for Social Cohesion (CDCS) approved three new conventions on contact concerning children, legal aid, and 'Information Society Services'. In 2002 the CDCS approved a Recommendation on mediation on civil matters and a resolution establishing the European Commission for the Efficiency of Justice (CEPEJ). The aims of the CEPEJ are: to improve the efficiency and functioning of the justice system of member states, with a view to ensuring that everyone within their jurisdiction can enforce their legal rights effectively, increasing citizen confidence in the system; and enabling better implementation of the international legal instruments of the Council of Europe concerning efficiency and fairness of justice.

The Consultative Council of European Judges has prepared a framework global action plan for judges in Europe. In addition, it has contributed to the implementation of this programme by the adoption of opinions on standards concerning the independence of the judiciary and the irremovability of judges, and on the funding and management of courts.

A Committee of Legal Advisers on Public and International Law (CAHDI), comprising the legal advisers of ministers of foreign affairs of member states and of several observer states, is authorized by the Committee of Ministers to examine questions of public international law, and to exchange and, if appropriate, to co-ordinate the views of member states. The CAHDI functions as a European observatory of reservations to international treaties. Recent activities of the CAHDI include the preparation of a Recommendation on reactions to inadmissible reservations to international treaties, the publication of a report on state practice with regard to state succession and recognition, and another on expression of consent of states to be bound by a treaty. In 2003 the CAHDI concerned itself, *inter alia*, with the implementation of the pilot project of the Council of Europe on state practice regarding State immunities.

An *ad hoc* Committee of Experts on the Legal Aspects of Territorial Asylum, Refugees and Stateless Persons (CAHAR) proposes solutions to practical and legal problems relating to its area of expertise and works towards harmonizing rules and practices to be followed in Europe in matters of asylum and refugees. It reviews national and international developments and formulates appropriate legal instruments (mainly Recommendations) for discussion and adoption by the Committee of Ministers. Over the years the Committee has drafted a number of pan-European standards, and in 2002 it prepared a draft recommendation relating to the detention of asylum seekers. The CAHAR has also adopted a series of opinions for the Committee of Ministers on issues relating to refugees and displaced persons in member states. It works closely with other international bodies, in particular UNHCR and the Council's Parliamentary Assembly.

With regard to crime, expert committees and groups operating under the authority of the European Committee on Crime Problems have prepared conventions on such matters as extradition, mutual assistance, recognition and enforcement of foreign judgments, transfer of proceedings, suppression of terrorism, transfer of prisoners, compensation payable to victims of violent crime, money-laundering, confiscation of proceeds from crime and corruption. A Convention on Cybercrime, adopted in 2001, entered into force in July 2004 and by March 2005 had received nine ratifications. In 2002 member states concluded an additional Protocol to the Convention relating to the criminalization of acts of a racist and xenophobic nature committed through computer systems.

The Group of States Against Corruption (GRECO) became operational in 1999 and became a permanent body of the Council in 2002. In March 2005 it had 39 members (including the USA). A monitoring mechanism, based on mutual evaluation and peer pressure, GRECO assesses members' compliance with Council instruments for combating corruption. Its first round evaluations were completed by the end of 2002. A second round evaluations commenced in 2003, reviewing Proceeds of Corruption, Public Administration and Corruption, and Legal Persons and Corruption. It was then to cover member states' compliance with, *inter alia*, requirements of the Criminal Law Convention on Corruption, which entered into force in July 2002 (and by March 2005 had been ratified by 30 states). The evaluation procedure of GRECO is confidential but it has become practice to make reports public after their adoption.

The select committee of Experts on the Evaluation of Anti-Money laundering Measures (MONEYVAL) became operational in 1998. It is responsible for mutual evaluation of the anti-money laundering measures in place in 25 Council of Europe states that are not members of the Financial Action Task Force (FATF). The MONEYVAL mechanism is based on FATF practices and procedures. States are evaluated against the relevant international standards in the legal, financial and law enforcement sectors. In the legal sector this includes evaluation of states' obligations under the Council of Europe Convention on Laundering, Search Seizure and Confiscation of the Proceeds from Crime. After the terrorist attacks against targets in the USA on 11 September 2001, the Committee of Ministers adopted revised terms of reference, which specifically include the evaluation of measures to combat the financing of terrorism. MONEYVAL completed its first round of onsite visits in 2000 and subsequently adopted all first round reports. Its second round, focusing even more closely on the effectiveness of national systems, began in 2001 and was completed in 2003. A third round commenced

in early 2005. The evaluations of MONEYVAL are confidential, but summaries of adopted reports are made public.

A Criminological Scientific Council, composed of specialists in law, psychology, sociology and related sciences, advises the Committee and organizes criminological research conferences and colloquia. A Council for Penological Co-operation organizes regular high-level conferences of directors of prison administration and is responsible for collating statistical information on detention and community sanctions in Europe. The Council prepared the European Prison Rules in 1987 and the European Rules on Community Sanctions (alternatives to imprisonment) in 1992. A council for police matters was established in 2002.

In May 1990 the Committee of Ministers adopted a Partial Agreement to establish the European Commission for Democracy through Law, to be based in Venice, Italy. The so-called Venice Commission was enlarged in February 2002 and in late 2004 comprised all Council of Europe member states and Kyrgyzstan. The Commission is composed of independent legal and political experts, mainly senior academics, supreme or constitutional court judges, members of national parliaments, and senior public officers. Its main activity is constitutional assistance and it may supply opinions upon request, made through the Committee of Ministers, by the Parliamentary Assembly, the Secretary-General or any member states of the Commission. Other states and international organizations may request opinions with the consent of the Committee of Ministers. The Commission is active throughout the constitutional domain, and has worked on issues including legislation on constitutional courts and national minorities, electoral law and other legislation with implications for national democratic institutions. The creation of the Council for Democratic Elections institutionalized co-operation in the area of elections between the Venice Commission, the Parliamentary Assembly of the Council of Europe, and the Congress of Regional and Local Authorities of the Council of Europe. The Commission disseminates its work through the UniDem (University for Democracy) programme of seminars, the CODICES database, and the *Bulletin of Constitutional Case-Law*.

The promotion of local and regional democracy and of transfrontier co-operation constitutes a major aim of the Council's intergovernmental programme of activities. The Steering Committee on Local and Regional Democracy (CDLR) serves as a forum for representatives of member states to exchange information and pursue co-operation in order to promote the decentralization of powers, in accordance with the European Charter on Local Self-Government. The CDLR's principal objective is to improve the legal, institutional and financial framework of local democracy and to encourage citizen participation in local and regional communities. In December 2001 the Committee of Ministers adopted a Recommendation on citizens' participation in public life at local level, drafted on the basis of the work conducted by the CDLR. The CDLR publishes comparative studies and national reports, and aims to identify guide-lines for the effective implementation of the principles of subsidiarity and solidarity. Its work also constitutes a basis for the provision of aid to central and eastern European countries in the field of local democracy. The CDLR is responsible for the preparation and follow-up of Conferences of Ministers responsible for local and regional government.

Intergovernmental co-operation with the CDLR is supplemented by specific activities aimed at providing legislative advice, supporting reform and enhancing management capabilities and democratic participation in European member and non-member countries. These activities are specifically focused on the democratic stability of central and eastern European countries. The programmes for democratic stability in the field of local democracy draw inspiration from the European Charter of Local Self-Government, operating at three levels of government: at intergovernmental level, providing assistance in implementing reforms to reinforce local or regional government, in compliance with the Charter; at local or regional level, co-operating with local and regional authorities to build local government capacity; and at community level, co-operating directly with individual authorities to promote pilot initiatives. Working methods include: awareness-raising conferences; legislative opinion involving written opinions, expert round-tables and working groups; and seminars, workshops and training at home and abroad.

The policy of the Council of Europe on transfrontier co-operation between territorial communities or authorities is implemented through two committees. The Committee of Experts on Transfrontier Co-operation, working under the supervision of the CDLR, aims to monitor the implementation of the European Outline Convention on Transfrontier Co-operation between Territorial Communities or Authorities; to make proposals for the elimination of obstacles, in particular of a legal nature, to transfrontier and interterritorial co-operation; and to compile 'best practice' examples of transfrontier co-operation in various fields of activity. In 2002 the Committee of Ministers adopted a draft recommendation on the mutual aid and assistance between central and local authorities in the event of disasters affecting frontier areas. A Committee of

Advisers for the development of transfrontier co-operation in central and eastern Europe is composed of six members appointed or elected by the Secretary-General, the Committee of Ministers and the Congress of Local and Regional Authorities of Europe. Its task is to guide the promotion of transfrontier co-operation in central and eastern European countries, with a view to fostering good neighbourly relations between the frontier populations, especially in particularly sensitive regions. Its programme comprises: conferences and colloquies designed to raise awareness on the Outline Convention; meetings in border regions between representatives of local communities with a view to strengthening mutual trust; and legal assistance to, and restricted meetings with, national and local representatives responsible for preparing the legal texts for ratification and/or implementation of the Outline Convention. The priority areas outlined by the Committee of Advisers include South-East Europe, northern Europe around the Baltic Sea, the external frontiers of an enlarged European Union, and the Caucasus.

EDUCATION, CULTURE AND HERITAGE

The European Cultural Convention covers education, culture, heritage, sport and youth. Programmes on education, higher education, culture and cultural heritage are managed by four steering committees.

The education programme consists of projects on education for democratic citizenship and human rights, history teaching, the European dimension of education and interreligious dialogue, instruments and policies for plurilingualism, equitable education policies responding to new social, economic and technological realities, and bilateral co-operation for education renewal. Other activities include the partial agreement for the European Centre for Modern Languages located in Graz, Austria, the In Service Educational Staff Training Programme, the Network for School Links and Exchanges, and the European Schools Day competition, organized in co-operation with the European Union. The Council of Europe's main focus in the field of higher education is on the Bologna Process aiming to establish a European Higher Education Area by 2010.

In December 2000 the Committee of Ministers adopted a Declaration on Cultural Diversity, formulated in consultation with other organizations (including the European Union and UNESCO), which created a framework for developing a European approach to valuing cultural diversity. A European Charter for Regional or Minority languages entered into force in 1998, with the aim of protecting regional or minority languages, which are considered to be a threatened aspect of Europe's cultural heritage. It was intended to promote the use in private and public life of languages traditionally used within a state's territory. The Charter provides for a monitoring system enabling states, the Council of Europe and individuals to observe and follow up its implementation.

The Council of Europe's activities related to cultural policy focus on the following priority areas: standard-setting; cultural policy reviews; conflict prevention; comparative studies on cultural diversity, and partnership programmes; archives; the MOSAIC and STAGE projects (co-operation with South-East Europe and the South Caucasus, respectively); and the Action Plan for Russia.

The European Convention for the Protection of Audiovisual Heritage and its Protocol were opened for signature in November 2001. By March 2005 both documents had been ratified by Lithuania and Monaco (requiring five ratifications to enter into force). The Eurimages support fund, in which 32 member states participate, helps to finance co-production of films. The Convention for the Protection of the Architectural Heritage and the Protection of the Archaeological Heritage provide a legal framework for European co-operation in these areas. The European Heritage Network is being developed to facilitate the work of professionals and state institutions and the dissemination of good practices in more than 30 countries of the states party to the European Cultural Convention.

YOUTH

In 1972 the Council of Europe established the European Youth Centre (EYC) in Strasbourg. A second residential centre was created in Budapest in 1995. The centres, run with and by international non-governmental youth organizations representing a wide range of interests, provide about 50 residential courses a year (study sessions, training courses, symposia). A notable feature of the EYC is its decision-making structure, by which decisions on its programme and general policy matters are taken by a Programming Committee composed of an equal number of youth organizations and government representatives. In May 2005 a European Youth Summit was to be convened, in Warsaw, Poland, to coincide with the summit of heads of state and of government.

The European Youth Foundation (EYF) aims to provide financial assistance to European activities of non-governmental youth organizations and began operations in 1973. Since that time more than 280,000 young people have benefited directly from EYF-supported activities. The European Steering Committee for Intergovernmental Co-operation in the Youth Field conducts research in youth-related matters and prepares for ministerial conferences.

SPORT

The Committee for the Development of Sport, founded in November 1977, oversees sports co-operation and development on a pan-European basis, bringing together all the 48 states party to the European Cultural Convention. Its activities focus on the implementation of the European Sport Charter and Code of Sports Ethics (adopted in 1992 and revised in 2002), the role of sport in society, the provision of assistance in sports reform to new member states in central and eastern Europe, and the practice of both recreational and high level sport. A Charter on Sport for Disabled Persons was adopted in 1986. The Committee also prepares the Conferences of European Ministers responsible for Sport (usually held every four years) and has been responsible for drafting two important conventions to combat negative influences on sport. The European Convention on Spectator Violence and Misbehaviour at Sport Events (1985) provides governments with practical measures to ensure crowd security and safety, particularly at football matches. The Anti-Doping Convention (1989) has been ratified by 46 European countries (as at March 2005), and is also open to non-European states. In October 2004 the ministerial conference, convened in Budapest, Hungary, adopted principles of good governance in sport, and a resolution on European sports co-operation in 2004–08.

ENVIRONMENT AND SUSTAINABLE DEVELOPMENT

In 1995 a pan-European biological and landscape diversity strategy, formulated by the Committee of Ministers, was endorsed at a ministerial conference of the UN Economic Commission for Europe, which was held in Sofia, Bulgaria. The strategy was to be implemented jointly by the Council of Europe and UNEP, in close co-operation with the European Community. In particular, it provided for implementation of the Convention on Biological Diversity.

The Convention on the Conservation of European Wildlife and Natural Habitats (Bern Convention), which was signed in 1979 and entered into force in June 1982, gives total protection to 693 species of plants, 89 mammals, 294 birds, 43 reptiles, 21 amphibians, 115 freshwater fishes, 113 invertebrates and their habitats. The Convention established a network of protected areas known as the 'Emerald Network'. The Council's NATUROPA Centre provides information and documentation on the environment, through periodicals and campaigns. The Council awards the European Diploma for protection of sites of European significance, supervises a network of biogenetic reserves, and co-ordinates conservation action for threatened animals and plants. A European Convention on Landscape, to provide for the management and protection of the natural and cultural landscape in Europe, was adopted by the Committee of Ministers in 2000 and entered into force in July 2004.

Regional disparities constitute a major obstacle to the process of European integration. Conferences of ministers responsible for regional planning (CEMAT) are held to discuss these issues. In 2000 they adopted guiding principles for sustainable development of the European continent and, in 2001, a resolution detailing a 10-point programme for greater cohesion among the Regions of Europe. In September the 13th CEMAT, convened in Ljubljana, Slovenia, agreed on strategies to promote the sustainable spatial development of the continent, including greater public participation in decision-making, an initiative to revitalise the countryside and efforts to prevent flooding. The 14th meeting was to be held in Portugal, in 2006.

EXTERNAL RELATIONS

Agreements providing for co-operation and exchange of documents and observers have been concluded with the United Nations and its agencies, and with most of the European inter-governmental organizations and the Organization of American States. Relations with non-member states, other organizations and non-governmental organizations are co-ordinated by the Directorate General of Political Affairs. In 2001 the Council and European Commission signed a joint declaration on co-operation and partnership, which provided for the organization and funding of joint programmes.

Israel, Canada and Mexico are represented in the Parliamentary Assembly by observer delegations, and certain European and other non-member countries participate in or send observers to certain meetings of technical committees and specialized conferences at intergovernmental level. Full observer status with the Council was granted to the USA in 1995, to Canada and Japan in 1996 and to Mexico in 1999. The Holy See has had a similar status since 1970.

The European Centre for Global Interdependence and Solidarity (the 'North–South Centre') was established in Lisbon, Portugal, in 1990, in order to provide a framework for European co-operation in this area and to promote pluralist democracy and respect for human rights. The Centre is co-managed by parliamentarians, governments, non-governmental organizations and local and regional authorities. Its activities are divided into three programmes: public information and media relations; education and training for global interdependence; and dialogue for global partnership. The Centre organizes workshops, seminars and training courses on global interdependence and convenes international colloquies on human rights.

During the early 1990s the Council of Europe established a structure of programmes to assist the process of democratic reform in central and eastern European countries that had formerly been under communist rule. In October 1997 the meeting of heads of state or of government of Council members agreed to extend the programmes as the means by which all states are assisted to meet their undertakings as members of the Council. These specific co-operation programmes were mainly concerned with the development of the rule of law; the protection and promotion of human rights; and strengthening local democracy. A scheme of Democratic Leadership Programmes has also been established for the training of political leaders. Within the framework of the co-operation programme 22 information and documentation centres/offices have been established in 17 countries of central and eastern Europe. A secretariat representation to co-ordinate the Council's contribution to the UN operation in Kosovo was established in Priština (the capital of Kosovo and Metohija), in mid-1999.

Finance

The budget is financed by contributions from members on a proportional scale of assessment (using population and gross domestic product as common indicators). The 2004 budget totalled €180.5m.

Publications

Activities Report (in English and French).

The Bulletin (newsletter of the CLRAE, 3 a year).

Bulletin On Constitutional Case-Law (3–4 times a year, in English and French).

The Council of Europe: 800 million Europeans (introductory booklet).

The Europeans (electronic bulletin of the Parliamentary Assembly).

The Fight Against Terrorism, Council of Europe Standards (in English and French).

Human Rights and the Environment (in English, French and Italian).

Human Rights Information Bulletin (monthly, in English and French).

Naturopa (3 a year, in 15 languages).

Penological Information Bulletin (annually, in English and French).

The Pompidou Group Newsletter (3 a year).

Recent Demographic Developments in Europe (annually, in English and French).

Yearbook of Film, Television and Multimedia in Europe (in English and French).

ECONOMIC COMMUNITY OF WEST AFRICAN STATES—ECOWAS

Address: ECOWAS Executive Secretariat, 60 Yakubu Gowon Crescent, Asokoro, Abuja, Nigeria.

Telephone: (9) 3147647; **fax:** (9) 3147646; **e-mail:** info@ecowasmail.net; **internet:** www.ecowas.int.

The Treaty of Lagos, establishing ECOWAS, was signed in May 1975 by 15 states, with the object of promoting trade, co-operation and self-reliance in West Africa. Outstanding protocols bringing certain key features of the Treaty into effect were ratified in November 1976. Cape Verde joined in 1977. A revised ECOWAS treaty, designed to accelerate economic integration and to increase political co-operation, was signed in July 1993.

MEMBERS

Benin	Ghana	Niger
Burkina Faso	Guinea	Nigeria
Cape Verde	Guinea-Bissau	Senegal
Côte d'Ivoire	Liberia	Sierra Leone
The Gambia	Mali	Togo*

* Togo's membership of ECOWAS was suspended briefly in February 2005, following the unconstitutional appointment in that country of a new head of state.

Organization

(April 2005)

AUTHORITY OF HEADS OF STATE AND GOVERNMENT

The Authority is the supreme decision-making organ of the Community, with responsibility for its general development and realization of its objectives. The Chairman is elected annually by the Authority from among the member states. The Authority meets at least once a year in ordinary session.

COUNCIL OF MINISTERS

The Council consists of two representatives from each member country; the chairmanship is held by a minister from the same member state as the Chairman of the Authority. The Council meets at least twice a year, and is responsible for the running of the Community.

EXECUTIVE SECRETARIAT

The Executive Secretary is elected for a four-year term, which may be renewed once only.

Executive Secretary: MOHAMED IBN CHAMBAS (Ghana).

SPECIALIZED TECHNICAL COMMISSIONS

There are eight commissions, comprising representatives of each member state, which prepare Community projects and programmes in the following areas:

(i) Food and Agriculture;

(ii) Industry, Science and Technology, and Energy;

(iii) Environment and Natural Resources;

(iv) Transport, Communications, and Tourism;

(v) Trade, Customs, Taxation, Statistics, and Money and Payments;

(vi) Political, Judicial and Legal Affairs, Regional Security, and Immigration;

(vii) Human Resources, Information, and Social and Cultural Affairs; and

(viii) Administration and Finance.

ECOWAS PARLIAMENT

The inaugural session of the 120-member ECOWAS Parliament, based in Abuja, Nigeria, was held in November 2000. Members of the Parliament are elected for five-year terms. Each ECOWAS member state is allocated a minimum of five seats; the distribution of the remaining 45 seats is proportionate to the relative sizes of member states' populations. There is a co-ordinating administrative bureau, comprising a speaker, elected for a five-year term of office, and other elected officials. There are 13 technical committees covering the Parliament's areas of activity, including defence and security, economics and finance, energy, environment and natural resources, foreign affairs, human rights, laws and regulations, rural development, transport and communications, and women's and children's affairs.

Speaker: Prof. ALI NOUHOUM DIALLO (Mali).

ECOWAS COURT OF JUSTICE

The Court of Justice, established in January 2001, is based in Abuja, Nigeria, and comprises seven judges who serve a five-year renewable term of office.

Chief Justice: HASSINE DONLI (Nigeria).

ECOWAS BANK FOR INVESTMENT AND DEVELOPMENT

BP 2704, 128 blvd du 13 Janvier, Lomé, Togo; tel. 216864; fax 218684.

At a summit of ECOWAS heads of state and government in December 1999 it was announced that the former ECOWAS Fund for Co-operation, Compensation and Development was to be converted into the ECOWAS Bank for Investment and Development, with two divisions, a Regional Investment Bank and a Regional Development Fund. This was achieved in 2001.

President: Dr GEORGE SIPA-ADJAH YANKEY (Ghana).

Activities

ECOWAS aims to promote co-operation and development in economic, social and cultural activity, particularly in the fields for which specialized technical commissions (see above) are appointed, to raise the standard of living of the people of the member countries, increase and maintain economic stability, improve relations among member countries and contribute to the progress and development of Africa. ECOWAS is committed to abolishing all obstacles to the free movement of people, services and capital, and to promoting: harmonization of agricultural policies; common projects in marketing, research and the agriculturally-based industries; joint development of economic and industrial policies and elimination of disparities in levels of development; and common monetary policies. The ECOWAS treaty provides for compensation for states whose import duties are reduced through trade liberalization and contains a clause permitting safeguard measures in favour of any country affected by economic disturbances through the application of the treaty.

Initial slow progress in achieving many of ECOWAS' aims was attributed to the reluctance of some governments to implement policies at the national level, their failure to provide the agreed financial resources, and the absence of national links with the Secretariat; to the high cost of compensating loss of customs revenue; and to the existence of numerous other intergovernmental organizations in the region (in particular the Union économique et monétaire ouest-africaine—UEMOA (see p. 267), which replaced the francophone Communauté économique de l'Afrique de l'ouest in 1994). In respect of the latter obstacle to progress, however, ECOWAS and UEMOA resolved in February 2000 to create a single monetary zone (see below). In October ECOWAS and the European Union (EU) held their first joint high-level meeting, at which the EU pledged financial support for ECOWAS' economic integration programme, and, in April 2001 it was announced that the IMF had agreed to provide technical assistance for the programme.

A revised treaty for the Community was drawn up by an ECOWAS Committee of Eminent Persons in 1991–92, and was signed at the ECOWAS summit conference that took place in Cotonou, Benin, in July 1993. The treaty, which was to extend economic and political co-operation among member states, designated the achievement of a common market and a single currency as economic objectives, while in the political sphere it envisaged the establishment of an ECOWAS parliament, an economic and social council, and an ECOWAS court of justice to enforce Community decisions. The treaty also formally assigned the Community with the responsibility of preventing and settling regional conflicts. At a summit meeting held in Abuja, Nigeria, in August 1994, ECOWAS heads of state and government signed a protocol agreement for the establishment of a regional parliament. The meeting also adopted a Convention on Extradition of non-political offenders. The new ECOWAS treaty entered into effect in August 1995, having received the required number of ratifications. A draft protocol providing for the creation of a mechanism for the prevention, management and settlement of conflicts, and for the maintenance of peace in the region, was approved by ECOWAS heads of state and government in December 1999. The protocol establishing the ECOWAS Parliament came into effect in March 2000. The inaugural session of the Parliament was held in Abuja, Nigeria, in November, and in January 2001 the seven judges of the ECOWAS Court of Justice were sworn in. In December Mauritania withdrew from ECOWAS.

In February 2005 ECOWAS briefly suspended Togo's membership of the Community and imposed an arms embargo on that country and a travel ban on its leaders, owing to the unconstitutional installation of a new President; the sanctions against Togo were reversed when the illegal appointment was withdrawn at the end of the month.

In May 2002 the ECOWAS Authority met in Yamoussoukro, Côte d'Ivoire, to develop a regional plan of action for the implementation of the New Partnership for Africa's Development (NEPAD).

TRADE AND MONETARY UNION

Under the founding ECOWAS treaty elimination of tariffs and other obstructions to trade among member states, and the establishment

of a common external tariff, were planned over a transitional period of 15 years, from 1975. At the 1978 Conference of Heads of State and Government it was decided that from May 1979 no member state might increase its customs tariff on goods from another member. This was regarded as the first step towards the abolition of customs duties within the Community. During the first two years import duties on intra-community trade were to be maintained, and then eliminated in phases over the next eight years. Quotas and other restrictions of equivalent effect were to be abolished in the first 10 years. It was envisaged that in the remaining five years all differences between external customs tariffs would be abolished.

In 1980 ECOWAS heads of state and government decided to establish a free-trade area for unprocessed agricultural products and handicrafts from May 1981. Tariffs on industrial products made by specified community enterprises were also to be abolished from that date, but implementation was delayed by difficulties in defining the enterprises. From 1 January 1990 tariffs were eliminated on 25 listed items manufactured in ECOWAS member states. Over the ensuing decade, tariffs on other industrial products were to be eliminated as follows: the 'most-developed' countries of ECOWAS (Côte d'Ivoire, Ghana, Nigeria and Senegal) were to abolish tariffs on 'priority' products within four years and on 'non-priority' products within six years; the second group (Benin, Guinea, Liberia, Sierra Leone and Togo) were to abolish tariffs on 'priority' products within six years, and on 'non-priority' products within eight years; and the 'least-developed' members (Burkina Faso, Cape Verde, The Gambia, Guinea-Bissau, Mali and Niger) were to abolish tariffs on 'priority' products within eight years and on 'non-priority' products within 10 years. By December 2000 only Benin had removed tariffs on all industrial products.

In 1990 ECOWAS heads of state and government agreed to adopt measures that would create a single monetary zone and remove barriers to trade in goods that originated in the Community. ECOWAS regards monetary union as necessary to encourage investment in the region, since it would greatly facilitate capital transactions with foreign countries. In September 1992 it was announced that, as part of efforts to enhance monetary co-operation and financial harmonization in the region, the West African Clearing House was to be restructured as the West African Monetary Agency—WAMA. As a specialized agency of ECOWAS, WAMA was to be responsible for administering an ECOWAS exchange rate system (EERS) and for establishing the single monetary zone. A credit guarantee scheme and travellers' cheque system were to be established in association with the EERS. The agreement founding WAMA was signed by the Governors of the central banks of ECOWAS member states, meeting in Banjul, The Gambia, in March 1996. In July the Authority agreed to impose a common value-added tax (VAT) on consumer goods, in order to rationalize indirect taxation and to stimulate greater intra-Community trade. In August 1997 ECOWAS heads of state and government appointed an *ad hoc* monitoring committee to promote and oversee the implementation of trade liberalization measures and the establishment of a single monetary zone. The meeting also authorized the introduction of the regional travellers' cheque scheme. In October 1998 the travellers' cheque scheme was formally inaugurated at a meeting of ECOWAS heads of state. The cheques were to be issued by WAMA in denominations of a West African Unit of Account and convertible into each local currency at the rate of one Special Drawing Right (SDR—see IMF). The cheques entered into circulation on 1 July 1999. In March 1998 senior customs officials of ECOWAS countries agreed to harmonize customs policies and administrations, in order to facilitate intra-Community trade, and to pursue the objective of establishing a common external tariff by 2000. However, this deadline was not met. In December 1999 the ECOWAS Authority determined to pursue a 'Fast Track Approach' to economic integration, involving a two-track implementation of related measures. In April 2000 seven, predominantly anglophone, ECOWAS member states—Cape Verde, The Gambia, Ghana, Guinea, Liberia, Nigeria and Sierra Leone—issued the 'Accra Declaration', in which they agreed to establish by 1 January 2003 a second West African monetary union (the West African Monetary Zone—WAMZ) to co-exist initially alongside UEMOA, which unites eight, mainly francophone, ECOWAS member states. As preconditions for adopting a single currency and common monetary and exchange rate policy, the member states of the second West African monetary union were to attain a number of convergence criteria, including: a satisfactory level of price stability; sustainable budget deficits; a reduction in inflation; and the maintenance of an adequate level of foreign exchange reserves. The two complementary monetary unions were expected to harmonize their economic programmes, with a view to effecting an eventual merger, as outlined in an action plan adopted by ECOWAS and UEMOA in February 2000. The ECOWAS Authority summit held in December in Bamako, Mali, adopted an Agreement Establishing the WAMZ, approved the establishment of a West African Monetary Institute to prepare for the formation of a West African Central Bank, and determined that the harmonization of member countries' tariff structures should be accelerated to facilitate the implementation of the planned customs union. In December 2001 the Authority determined that the currency of the WAMZ (and eventually the ECOWAS-wide currency) would be known as the 'eco' and authorized the establishment during 2002 of an exchange rate mechanism. (This was achieved in April.) In November 2002 the heads of state and government of the planned WAMZ determined to postpone its inauguration and the launch of the eco until 1 July 2005, owing to slower than anticipated progress in achieving the convergence criteria required for monetary union. The establishment of the proposed West African Central Bank was to be effected during 2003–05. The heads of state and government also agreed that a forum of ministers of finance from the planned second monetary union should be convened on a regular basis to ensure the effective implementation of fiscal policies. In May 2004 ECOWAS and UEMOA signed a co-operation agreement that provided for the establishment of a Joint Technical Secretariat to enhance the co-ordination of their programmes.

The summit of the Authority held in January 2005 decided to postpone the launch of the 'eco' that had been planned for July. In early April ECOWAS member states agreed to establish a customs union over the period May 2005–end-2007, entailing a four-band common external tariff regime, as follows: a 0% tariff would be applied to social goods (for example, educational and medical equipment); 5% would be levied on raw materials and most agricultural inputs; 10% on intermediate goods and rice; and 20% on finished consumer products.

In December 1992 ECOWAS ministers agreed on the institutionalization of an ECOWAS trade fair, in order to promote trade liberalization and intra-Community trade. The first trade fair was held in Dakar, Senegal, in May–June 1995; the second was staged in Accra, Ghana, in March 1999; and a third fair was held in Lomé, Togo, in March 2003.

TRAVEL, TRANSPORT AND COMMUNICATIONS

In 1979 ECOWAS heads of state signed a Protocol relating to free circulation of the region's citizens and to rights of residence and establishment of commercial enterprises. The first provision (the right of entry without a visa) came into force in 1980. An optional ECOWAS travel certificate, valid for travel within the Community in place of a national passport, was established in July 1985. The second provision of the 1979 Protocol, allowing unlimited rights of residence, was signed in 1986 (although Nigeria indicated that unskilled workers and certain categories of professionals would not be allowed to stay for an indefinite period) and came into force in 1989. The third provision, concerning the right to establish a commercial enterprise in another member state was signed in 1990. In July 1992 the ECOWAS Authority formulated a Minimum Agenda for Action for the implementation of Community agreements regarding the free movement of goods and people, for example the removal of non-tariff barriers, the simplification of customs and transit procedures and a reduction in the number of control posts on international roads. However, implementation of the Minimum Agenda was slow. In April 1997 Gambian and Senegalese finance and trade officials concluded an agreement on measures to facilitate the export of goods via Senegal to neighbouring countries, in accordance with ECOWAS protocols relating to inter-state road transit arrangements. An Inter-state Road Transit Authority has been established. A Brown Card scheme provides recognized third-party liability insurance throughout the region. In October 2001 an ECOWAS passport was reported to be ready for issuance; the ECOWAS travel certificate was to remain in operation, while national passports were to be gradually eliminated over a period of five years.

In February 1996 ECOWAS and several private-sector partners established ECOAir Ltd, based in Abuja, Nigeria, which was to develop a regional airline. The airline became operative in April 2002. A regional shipping company, ECOMARINE, commenced operations in February 2003.

In August 1996 the initial phase of a programme to improve regional telecommunications was reported to have been completed. Some US $35m. had been granted for project financing in eight ECOWAS countries. A second phase of the programme (INTELCOM II), which aimed to modernize and expand the region's telecommunications services, was initiated by ECOWAS heads of state in August 1997. A West African Telecommunications Regulators' Association was established, under the auspices of ECOWAS, in September 2000. A harmonization programme to create a common, liberalized telecommunications market was expected to be completed by 2008.

A programme for the development of an integrated regional road network was adopted in 1980. Under the programme, two major trans-regional roads were to be completed: the Trans-Coastal Highway, linking Lagos, Nigeria, with Nouackchott, Mauritania (4,767 km); and the Trans-Sahelian Highway, linking Dakar, Senegal, with N'Djamena, Chad (4,633 km). By the end of 2000 about 83% of the trans-coastal route was reportedly complete, and about

87% of the trans-Sahelian route. In 2003 the African Development Bank agreed to finance a study on interconnection of the region's railways.

ECONOMIC AND INDUSTRIAL DEVELOPMENT

In November 1984 ECOWAS heads of state and government approved the establishment of a private regional investment bank, to be known as Ecobank Transnational Inc. The bank, which was based in Lomé, Togo, opened in March 1988. ECOWAS has a 10% share in the bank.

The West African Industrial Forum, sponsored by ECOWAS, is held every two years to promote regional industrial investment. Community ministers of industry are implementing an action plan on the formulation of a West African Industrial Master Plan identifying strategies for stimulating regional economic development and attracting external investment.

In September 1995 Nigeria, Ghana, Togo and Benin resolved to develop a gas pipeline to connect Nigerian gas supplies to the other countries. In August 1999 the participating countries, together with two petroleum companies operating in Nigeria, signed an agreement on the financing and construction of the 600-km West African Gas Pipeline, which was to extend from the Nigerian capital Lagos to Takoradi, Togo. The first shipment of gas through the pipeline was expected to be made in June 2005. The implementation of a planned energy exchange scheme, known as the West African Power Pool Project (WAPP), is envisaged as a means of efficiently utilizing the region's hydro-electricity and thermal power capabilities by transferring power from surplus producers to countries unable to meet their energy requirements. In May 2003 the Community decided to initiate the first phase of WAPP, which was to be implemented in Benin, Côte d'Ivoire, Ghana, Niger, Nigeria and Togo at an estimated cost of US $335m. In January 2005 the Authority endorsed a revised masterplan for the implementation of WAPP, which was scheduled to be completed by 2020. ECOWAS is developing an initiative aimed at promoting the use of renewable energy resources.

REGIONAL SECURITY

In 1990 a Standing Mediation Committee was formed to mediate disputes between member states. Member states reaffirmed their commitment to refrain from aggression against one another at a summit conference in 1991. The revised ECOWAS treaty, signed in July 1993, incorporates a separate provision for regional security, requiring member states to work towards the maintenance of peace, stability and security.

In December 1997 an extraordinary meeting of ECOWAS heads of state and government was convened in Lomé, Togo, to consider the future stability and security of the region. It was agreed that a permanent mechanism be established for conflict prevention and the maintenance of peace. ECOWAS leaders also reaffirmed their commitment to pursuing dialogue to prevent conflicts, co-operating in the early deployment of peace-keeping forces and implementing measures to counter trans-border crime and the illegal trafficking of armaments and drugs. At the meeting ECOWAS leaders acknowledged ECOMOG's role in restoring constitutional order in Liberia and expressed their appreciation of the force's current efforts in Sierra Leone (see below). In March 1998 ECOWAS ministers of foreign affairs, meeting in Yamoussoukro, Côte d'Ivoire, resolved that ECOMOG should become the region's permanent peace-keeping force, and upheld the decision of heads of state regarding the establishment of a new body, which should be used to observe, analyse and monitor the security situation in the West African region. Ministers agreed to undertake a redefinition of the command structure within the organization in order to strengthen decision-making and the legal status of the ECOMOG force.

In July 1998 ECOWAS ministers of defence and of security adopted a draft mechanism for conflict management, peace-keeping and security, which provided for ECOWAS intervention in the internal affairs of member states, where a conflict or military uprising threatened the region's security. In October the ECOWAS Authority determined to implement a renewable three-year ban on the import, export or manufacture of small armaments in order to enhance the security of the sub-region. (The ban was renewed for a further three years in July 2001.) The Authority also issued a declaration on the control and prevention of drug abuse, agreeing to allocate US $150,000 to establish an Eco-Drug Fund to finance regional activities in countering substance abuse.

The summit meeting of ECOWAS heads of state and government held in December 1999 in Lomé, Togo, approved a draft protocol to the organization's treaty, providing for the establishment of a Permanent Mechanism for the Prevention, Management and Settlement of Conflicts and the Maintenance of Peace in the Region, as envisaged at their conference in December 1997, and for the creation in connection with the Mechanism of a Mediation and Security Council, to comprise representatives of 10 member states, elected for two-year terms. The Mediation and Security Council was to be supported by an advisory Council of Elders, comprising 32 eminent statesmen from the region; this was inaugurated in July 2001. ECOMOG was to be transformed from an *ad hoc* cease-fire monitoring group into a permanent standby force available for immediate deployment to avert emerging conflicts in the region.

In 2002 ECOWAS, with assistance from the USA, was developing an early warning system for monitoring threats to regional security. In June 2004 the Community approved the establishment of a standby unit of 6,500 troops, including a core rapid reaction component—the ECOWAS Task Force—comprising 1,500 soldiers (deployable within 30 days), a reserve of 1,500 troops, and 3,500 additional troops that could, as necessary, augment the numbers of the Task Force to brigade level (deployable with up to 90 days notice).

Peace-keeping Operations

In August 1990 an ECOWAS Cease-fire Monitoring Group (ECOMOG—initially comprising about 4,000 troops from The Gambia, Ghana, Guinea, Nigeria and Sierra Leone) was dispatched to Liberia in an attempt to enforce a cease-fire between conflicting factions there, to restore public order, and to establish an interim government, until elections could be held. In November a temporary cease-fire was agreed by the protagonists in Liberia, and an interim president was installed by ECOMOG. Following the signature of a new cease-fire agreement a national conference, organized by ECOWAS in March 1991, established a temporary government, pending elections to be held in early 1992. In June 1991 ECOWAS established a committee (initially comprising representatives of five member states, later expanded to nine) to co-ordinate the peace negotiations. In September, at a meeting in Yamoussoukro, Côte d'Ivoire, held under the aegis of the ECOWAS committee, two of the rival factions in Liberia agreed to encamp their troops in designated areas and to disarm under ECOMOG supervision. During the period preceding the proposed elections, ECOMOG was to occupy Liberian air and sea ports, and create a 'buffer zone' along the country's border with Sierra Leone. By September 1992, however, ECOMOG had been unable either to effect the disarmament of two of the principal military factions, the National Patriotic Front of Liberia (NPFL) and the United Liberation Movement of Liberia for Democracy (ULIMO), or to occupy positions in substantial areas of the country, as a result of resistance on the part of the NPFL. The proposed elections were consequently postponed indefinitely.

In October 1992 ECOMOG began offensive action against NPFL positions, with a campaign of aerial bombardment. In November ECOWAS imposed a land, sea and air blockade on the NPFL's territory, in response to the Front's refusal to comply with the Yamoussoukro accord of October 1991. In April 1993 ECOMOG announced that the disarmament of ULIMO had been completed, amid widespread accusations that ECOMOG had supported ULIMO against the NPFL, and was no longer a neutral force. An ECOWAS-brokered cease-fire agreement was signed in Cotonou, Benin, in July, and took effect on 1 August. In September a UN observer mission (UNOMIL) was established in Liberia to work alongside ECOMOG in monitoring the process of disarming troops, as well as to verify the impartiality of ECOMOG.

In September 1994 leaders of Liberia's main military factions, having negotiated with representatives of ECOWAS, the Organization of African Unity (OAU, now the African Union—AU) and the UN, signed an amendment to the Cotonou accord in Akosombo, Ghana. This provided for a new five-member Council of State, in the context of a cease-fire, as a replacement to the expired interim executive authority, and established a new timetable for democratic elections. In early 1995 negotiations to secure a peace settlement, conducted under ECOWAS auspices, collapsed, owing to disagreement on the composition of the new Council of State. In May, in an attempt to ease the political deadlock, ECOWAS heads of state and of government met leaders of the six main warring factions. Under continuing pressure from the international community, the leaders of the Liberian factions signed a new peace accord, in Abuja, Nigeria, in August. This political development led to renewed efforts on the part of ECOWAS countries to strengthen ECOMOG, and by October Burkina Faso, Nigeria, Ghana and Guinea had pledged troop contributions to increase the force strength from 7,268 to 12,000. In accordance with the peace agreement, ECOMOG forces, with UNOMIL, were to be deployed throughout Liberia and along its borders to prevent the flow of arms into the country and to monitor the disarmament of the warring parties. In December an attack on ECOMOG troops, by a dissident ULIMO faction (ULIMO–J), disrupted the deployment of the multinational forces and the disarmament process, which was scheduled to commence in mid-January 1996. At least 16 members of the peace-keeping force were killed in the fighting that ensued. Clashes between ECOMOG and the ULIMO–J forces continued in the west of the country in late December 1995 and early January 1996, during which time 130 Nigerian members of ECOMOG were held hostage. In April, following a series of violations of the cease-fire, serious hostilities erupted in the Liberian capital, Monrovia, between government forces and dissident troops. An initial agreement to end the fighting, negotiated under ECOWAS auspices, was unsuccessful; however, it

secured the release of several civilians and soldiers who had been taken hostage during the civil disruption. Later in April a further cease-fire agreement was concluded, under the aegis of the US Government, the UN and ECOWAS. In May ministers of foreign affairs of the countries constituting the ECOWAS Committee of Nine advocated that all armed factions be withdrawn from Monrovia and that ECOMOG troops be deployed throughout the capital in order to re-establish the city's 'safe-haven' status. According to the Committee's demands, all property, armaments and equipment seized unlawfully from civilians, ECOMOG and other international organizations during the fighting were to be returned, while efforts to disarm the warring factions and to pursue the restoration of democracy in the country were to be resumed. At the end of May the deployment of ECOMOG troops was initiated. In August a new cease-fire accord was signed by the leaders of the principal factions in Liberia, which envisaged the completion of the disarmament process by the end of January 1997, with elections to be held in May. The disarmament process began in November 1996, and by the end of January 1997 ECOMOG confirmed that 23,000 of the targeted 30,000–35,000 soldiers had been disarmed. The deadline for disarmament was extended by seven days, during which time a further 1,500 soldiers were reported to have been disarmed. However, vigilante attacks by remaining armed faction fighters persisted. The Committee of Nine announced in February that presidential and legislative elections would be held in May, later revising the election schedule to mid-July. ECOMOG was to withdraw from Liberia six months after the election date, until which time it had proposed to offer security for the incoming government and to provide training for a new unified Liberian army. The Committee also agreed, in consultation with the Council of State, to replace the existing Electoral Commission with a new Commission comprising seven members, to reflect all aspects of Liberian society. The Chairman would be selected from among the seven, in consultation with ECOWAS, which along with the UN and the OAU, would act as a 'technical adviser' to the Commission. ECOMOG deployed additional troops, who were joined by other international observers in ensuring that the elections were conducted in the necessary conditions of security. In August, following the inauguration of Charles Taylor (formerly leader of the NPFL) as Liberia's democratically-elected President, ECOWAS heads of state agreed that the ECOMOG force in Liberia was to be reconstituted and would henceforth assist in the process of national reconstruction, including the restructuring of the armed and security forces, and the maintenance of security; it was further envisaged that ECOMOG's mandate (officially due to expire in February 1998) would be extended in agreement with the Liberian Government. A Status of Forces Agreement, which defined ECOMOG's post-conflict responsibilities (i.e. capacity-building and maintenance of security) and imposed conditions on the peace-keeping forces remaining in the country, was signed by the Liberian Government and ECOWAS in June 1998. Relations with the Taylor administration, however, deteriorated, owing to accusations that ECOMOG was providing assistance to opposition groupings. The tense political situation, therefore, and the need for greater resources in Sierra Leone, resulted in ECOMOG transferring its headquarters from Monrovia to Freetown in Sierra Leone. The transfer was reported to have been completed by October, with just two ECOMOG battalions remaining in Liberia. The ECOMOG mission in Liberia was effectively terminated in October 1999 when the final declared stocks of rebel armaments were destroyed. In April 2001 the ECOWAS Authority determined to send a Mediation and Security Council mission to Liberia to monitor compliance with a resolution of the UN Security Council imposing sanctions on the Liberian regime. An ECOWAS military team was sent to Liberia in June 2002 to assess continuing unrest in the country. ECOWAS welcomed a Liberian Leadership Forum that was staged in the following month, in Ouagadougou, Burkina Faso, to address means of achieving peace and reconciliation. In September President Taylor lifted the state of emergency in Liberia. In mid-2003, however, rebel groups began to seize territory in south-eastern areas and to launch a siege on Monrovia. In June a cease-fire brokered by ECOWAS was signed, which provided for a transitional government excluding Taylor. One week later, following the President's announcement that he would stay in power until the expiry of his term of office in January 2004, fighting in the capital resumed, resulting in hundreds of civilian casualties. In July 2003 ECOWAS agreed to send a 3,000-strong force to Liberia; later that month, after considerable international pressure, US President George W. Bush agreed to deploy three US warships to the region to support the Community's troops. In early August troops of the ECOWAS Mission in Liberia (ECOMIL) began to arrive in Monrovia, prompting President Taylor to stand down and to leave the country for exile in Nigeria. At the beginning of October authority was transferred from ECOMIL to a newly-inaugurated UN Mission in Liberia (UNMIL), mandated to support the implementation of the cease-fire accord agreed in June and a Comprehensive Peace Agreement concluded by the parties to the conflict in August. ECOMIL's 3,600 troops were reassigned to UNMIL. ECOWAS was to co-operate with UNMIL and other partners to assist the National Transitional Government (inaugurated in mid-October) with the training of a national police force and the restructuring of the military. It was envisaged that national elections would be staged by 2005.

In May 1997 the democratically-elected Sierra Leonean leader, President Ahmed Tejan Kabbah, was overthrown by a military coup involving officers of the national army and RUF rebels. Nigerian forces based in Sierra Leone as part of a bilateral defence pact attempted to restore constitutional order. Their numbers were strengthened by the arrival of more than 700 Nigerian soldiers and two naval vessels which had been serving under the ECOMOG mandate in neighbouring Liberia. At the end of June ECOWAS ministers of foreign affairs, convened in Conakry, Guinea, agreed to pursue the objective of restoring a democratic government in Sierra Leone through dialogue and the imposition of economic sanctions. In July a five-member ECOWAS committee, comprising the foreign ministers of Côte d'Ivoire, Ghana, Guinea, Liberia and Nigeria, together with representatives of the OAU, negotiated an agreement with the so-called Armed Forces Revolutionary Council (AFRC) in Sierra Leone to establish an immediate cease-fire and to pursue efforts towards the restoration of constitutional order. In August ECOWAS heads of state reaffirmed the Community's condemnation of the removal of President Kabbah and officially endorsed a series of punitive measures against the AFRC authorities in order to accelerate the restoration of democratic government. The meeting mandated ECOMOG to maintain and monitor the cease-fire and to prevent all goods, excepting essential humanitarian supplies, from entering that country. It was also agreed that the committee on Sierra Leone include Liberia and be convened at the level of heads of state. In October the UN Security Council imposed an embargo on the sale or supply of armaments to Sierra Leone and authorized ECOWAS to ensure implementation of these measures. ECOMOG conducted a number of attacks against commercial and military targets, with the aim of upholding the international sanctions, and clashes occurred between ECOMOG troops and AFRC/RUF soldiers, in particular around the area of Freetown's Lungi international airport which had been seized by ECOMOG. Despite the escalation in hostilities, the ECOWAS Committee of Five pursued negotiations with the military authorities, and at the end of October both sides signed a peace agreement, in Conakry, Guinea, providing for an immediate end to all fighting and the reinstatement of Kabbah's Government by April 1998; all combatants were to be disarmed and demobilized under the supervision of a disarmament committee comprising representatives of ECOMOG, the military authorities and local forces loyal to President Kabbah. In November 1997, however, the peace process was undermined by reports that ECOMOG forces had violated the cease-fire agreement following a series of air raids on Freetown, which ECOMOG claimed to have been in retaliation for attacks by AFRC/RUF-operated anti-aircraft equipment, and a demand by the AFRC authorities that the Nigerian contingent of ECOMOG leave the country. In mid-February 1998, following a series of offensive attacks against forces loyal to the military authorities, ECOMOG assumed control of Freetown and arrested several members of the AFRC/RUC regime. Some 50 AFRC officials were arrested by troops serving under ECOMOG on arrival at James Spriggs Payne Airport in Liberia, prompting protests from the Liberian Government at the Nigerian military intervention. An 11-member supervisory task force, which included the ECOMOG Commander, was established in Sierra Leone to maintain order, pending Kabbah's return from exile. ECOMOG troops subsequently also monitored the removal of the embargo against the use of the airport and port facilities in Freetown. Kabbah returned to Sierra Leone in March and installed a new administration. It was agreed that ECOMOG forces were to remain in the country in order to ensure the full restoration of peace and security, to assist in the restructuring of the armed forces and to help to resolve the problems of the substantial numbers of refugees and internally displaced persons. In early May ECOWAS Chiefs of Staff, meeting in Accra, Ghana, urged member states to provide more troops and logistical support to strengthen the ECOMOG force in Sierra Leone (at that time numbering some 10,000 troops), which was still involved in ongoing clashes with remaining rebel soldiers in eastern regions of the country. The UN established an Observer Mission in Sierra Leone (UNOMSIL) in July, which was to monitor the cease-fire, mainly in areas secured by ECOMOG troops. In October ECOMOG transferred its headquarters to Freetown, in order, partly, to reinforce its presence in the country. In January 1999 rebel soldiers attacked the capital and engaged in heavy fighting with ECOMOG forces, amid reports that the Liberian Government was supporting the rebels. Nigeria dispatched several thousand additional troops to counter the rebel advance and to secure the border with Liberia. In February, however, once ECOMOG had regained control of Freetown, the Nigerian Government expressed its desire to withdraw all its troops from the peace-keeping force by May, owing to financial restraints. Efforts to negotiate a peace settlement were initiated, with the Chairman of ECOWAS at that time, President Gnassingbé Eyadéma of Togo,

actively involved in mediation between the opposing groups, despite persisting reports of fighting between ECOMOG and rebel soldiers in areas east of the capital. A cease-fire agreement was concluded in May, and a political settlement was signed, by Kabbah and the RUF leader, in Lomé, Togo, in July. ECOMOG's mandate in Sierra Leone was adapted to support the consolidation of peace in that country and national reconstruction. In October UNOMSIL was replaced by the UN Mission in Sierra Leone (UNAMSIL), which was to assist with the implementation of the Lomé accord and to assume many of the functions then being performed by ECOMOG, including the provision of security at Lungi international airport and at other key installations, buildings and government institutions in the Freetown area. In consequence the ECOMOG contingent was withdrawn in April 2000. However, following a resurgence of RUF violence in April and May, when as many as 500 members of UNAMSIL (which had not been deployed to full strength) were captured by the rebels, ECOWAS heads of government agreed to reinforce the UN peace-keeping operation with some 3,000 regional troops. A UN Security Council mission to Sierra Leone in September recommended the establishment of a mechanism to co-ordinate the formulation and implementation by the UN, ECOWAS, the Sierra Leone Government and other parties of a unified strategy to resolve the insecurity in Sierra Leone. A new cease-fire accord was agreed by the Sierra Leone Government and the RUF in November, in Abuja, Nigeria, and in January 2002 the process (monitored by UNAMSIL) of disarming, demobilizing and reintegrating former combatants was completed. An ECOWAS observer team was dispatched to monitor legislative and presidential elections that were held in Sierra Leone in May. In April 2001 representatives of the Mediation and Security Council were dispatched to Liberia to monitor, jointly with a UN delegation, the Liberian Government's compliance with a UN Security Council Resolution aimed at ending support for and eradicating RUF activity in that country, and at terminating illicit trading there in Sierra Leonean diamonds.

At the end of September 2002 an extraordinary summit meeting of ECOWAS heads of state and government was convened in Accra, Ghana, to address the violent unrest that had erupted in Côte d'Ivoire during that month, commencing with an attempted *coup d'état* by disloyal elements of the country's armed forces. The summit meeting condemned the attempt to overthrow democratic rule and constitutional order and established a high-level contact group, comprising the heads of state of Ghana, Guinea-Bissau, Mali, Niger, Nigeria and Togo, to prevail upon the rebels to end hostilities, and to negotiate a general framework for the resolution of the crisis. The contact group helped to mediate a cease-fire in the following month; this was to be monitored by an ECOWAS military mission in Côte d'Ivoire (ECOMICI), which was also to be responsible for ensuring safe passage for deliveries of humanitarian assistance. In March 2003, following the conclusion in January by the parties to the conflict of a peace agreement, signed at Marcoussis, France, ECOWAS chiefs of staff endorsed the expansion of ECOMICI from 1,264 to a maximum of 3,411 men, to monitor the implementation of the peace agreement in co-operation with the UN Mission in Côte d'Ivoire (MINUCI), and French forces. In early April 2004 authority was transferred from ECOMICI and MINUCI to the newly-inaugurated UN Operation in Côte d'Ivoire (UNOCI). In mid-June ECOWAS heads of state and government convened at a summit to address means of reviving the implementation of the stalled Marcoussis peace accord. A high-level meeting of ECOWAS heads of state and government, other African leaders, the Chairperson of the AU, and the parties to the Côte d'Ivoire conflict, held in Accra in late July, affirmed that a monitoring mechanism, comprising representatives of ECOWAS, the AU, Côte d'Ivoire and the United Nations, should produce regular reports on progress towards peace in Côte d'Ivoire.

In May 2000 the ECOWAS Authority authorized the initiation of an inquiry into the link between illicit trading in diamonds and ongoing rebel activity in the region, with a particular focus on Liberia and Sierra Leone.

ENVIRONMENTAL PROTECTION

ECOWAS promotes implementation of the UN Convention on Desertification Control and supports programmes initiated at national and sub-regional level within the framework of the treaty. Together with the Permanent Inter-State Committee on Drought Control in the Sahel—CILSS, ECOWAS has been designated as a project leader for implementing the Convention in West Africa. Other environmental initiatives include a regional meteorological project to enhance meteorological activities and applications, and in particular to contribute to food security and natural resource management in the sub-region. ECOWAS pilot schemes have formed the basis of integrated control projects for the control of floating weeds in five water basins in West Africa, which had hindered the development of the local fishery sectors. A rural water supply programme aims to ensure adequate water for rural dwellers in order to improve their living standards. The first phase of the project focused on schemes to develop village and pastoral water points in Burkina Faso, Guinea, Mali, Niger and Senegal, with funds from various multilateral donors.

AGRICULTURE AND FISHING

In November 1995 an agro-industrial forum, jointly organized by ECOWAS and the EU, was held in Dakar, Senegal. The forum aimed to facilitate co-operation between companies in the two regions, to develop the agro-industrial sector in West Africa and to promote business opportunities.

In February 2001 ECOWAS ministers of agriculture adopted an action plan for the formulation of a common agricultural policy, as envisaged under the ECOWAS treaty. A draft of the common agricultural policy was endorsed by the January 2005 Authority summit. The Community enforces a transhumance certification scheme for facilitating the monitoring of animal movement and animal health surveillance and protection in the sub-region.

SOCIAL PROGRAMME

Four organizations have been established within ECOWAS by the Executive Secretariat: the Organization of Trade Unions of West Africa, which held its first meeting in 1984; the West African Youth Association; the West African Universities' Association; and the West Africa Women's Association (whose statutes were approved by a meeting of ministers of social affairs in May 1987). Regional sports competitions are held annually. The West African Health Organization (WAHO) was established in 2000 by merger of the West African Health Community and the Organization for Co-ordination and Co-operation in the Struggle against Endemic Diseases. In December 2001 the ECOWAS summit of heads of state and government adopted a plan of action aimed at combating trafficking in human beings and authorized the establishment of an ECOWAS Criminal Intelligence Bureau.

INFORMATION AND MEDIA

In March 1990 ECOWAS ministers of information formulated a policy on the dissemination of information about ECOWAS throughout the region and the appraisal of attitudes of its population towards the Community. The ministers established a new information commission. In November 1991 a conference on press communication and African integration, organized by ECOWAS, recommended the creation of an ECOWAS press card, judicial safeguards to protect journalists, training programmes for journalists and the establishment of a regional documentation centre and data bank. In November 1994 the commission of social and cultural affairs, meeting in Lagos, Nigeria, endorsed a series of measures to promote west African integration. These included special radio, television and newspaper features, sporting events and other competitions or rallies. In December 2000 the Council of Ministers approved a new policy on the dissemination of information about the Community's activities.

SPECIALIZED AGENCIES

West African Monetary Agency: 11–13 ECOWAS St, PMB 218, Freetown, Sierra Leone; tel. 224485; fax 223943; e-mail wama@sierratel.sl; f. 1975 as West African Clearing House; administers transactions between its 10 member central banks in order to promote sub-regional trade and monetary co-operation; administers ECOWAS travellers' cheques scheme. Mems: Banque Centrale des Etats de l'Afrique de l'Ouest (serving Benin, Burkina Faso, Côte d'Ivoire, Guinea-Bissau, Mali, Niger, Senegal, Togo) and the central banks of Cape Verde, The Gambia, Ghana, Guinea, Liberia, Mauritania, Nigeria and Sierra Leone; Dir-Gen. ANTOINE M. F. NDIAYE (Senegal); publ. *Annual Report*.

West African Monetary Institute: Premier Towers, 8th/9th Floors, Cantonments 75, Accra, Ghana; tel. (21) 676-901; fax (21) 676-903; e-mail info@wami-imao.org; internet www.ecowas.int/wami-imao/; f. by the ECOWAS Authority summit in December 2000 to prepare for the establishment of a West African Central Bank; Dir-Gen. Dr MICHAEL OLUFEMI OJO.

West African Health Organization—WAHO: BP 153 Bobo-Dioulasso 01, Burkina Faso; tel. (226) 975772; fax (226) 975772; e-mail wahooas@fasonet.bf; f. 2000 by merger of the West African Health Community (f. 1978) and the Organization for Co-ordination and Co-operation in the Struggle against Endemic Diseases (f. 1960); aims to harmonize member states' health policies and to promote research, training, the sharing of resources and diffusion of information; Dir-Gen. Dr KABBA T. JOINER; publ. *Bulletin Bibliographique* (quarterly).

Finance

ECOWAS is financed by contributions from member states, although there is a poor record of punctual payment of dues, which has hampered the work of the Secretariat. Under the revised treaty, ECOWAS was to receive revenue from a community tax, based on the total value of imports from member countries. In July 1996 the summit meeting approved a protocol on a community levy, providing for the imposition of a 0.5% tax on the value of imports from a third country. In August 1997 the Authority of Heads of State and Government determined that the community levy should replace budgetary contributions as the organization's principal source of finance. The protocol came into force in January 2000, having been ratified by nine member states, with the substantive regime entering into effect on 1 January 2003.

Publications

Annual Report.
Contact.
ECOWAS National Accounts.
ECOWAS News.
West African Bulletin.

ECONOMIC CO-OPERATION ORGANIZATION—ECO

Address: 1 Golbou Alley, Kamranieh St, POB 14155-6176, Tehran, Iran.

Telephone: (21) 2831733; **fax:** (21) 2831732; **e-mail:** registry@ecosecretariat.org; **internet:** www.ecosecretariat.org.

The Economic Co-operation Organization (ECO) was established in 1985 as the successor to the Regional Co-operation for Development, founded in 1964.

MEMBERS

Afghanistan	Kyrgyzstan	Turkey
Azerbaijan	Pakistan	Turkmenistan
Iran	Tajikistan	Uzbekistan
Kazakhstan		

The 'Turkish Republic of Northern Cyprus' has been granted special guest status.

Organization

(April 2005)

SUMMIT MEETING

The first summit meeting of heads of state and of government of member countries was held in Tehran in February 1992. Summit meetings are generally held at least once every two years. The eighth summit meeting was convened in Dushanbe, Tajikistan, in September 2004.

COUNCIL OF MINISTERS

The Council of Ministers, comprising ministers of foreign affairs of member states, is the principal policy- and decision-making body of ECO. It meets at least once a year.

REGIONAL PLANNING COUNCIL
The Council, comprising senior planning officials or other representatives of member states, meets at least once a year. It is responsible for reviewing programmes of activity and evaluating results achieved, and for proposing future plans of action to the Council of Ministers.

COUNCIL OF PERMANENT REPRESENTATIVES
Permanent representatives or Ambassadors of member countries accredited to Iran meet regularly to formulate policy for consideration by the Council of Ministers and to promote implementation of decisions reached at ministerial or summit level.

SECRETARIAT
The Secretariat is headed by a Secretary-General, who is supported by two Deputy Secretaries-General. The following Directorates administer and co-ordinate the main areas of ECO activities: Trade and investment; Transport and communications; Energy, minerals and environment; Industry and agriculture (to be renamed Human development); Project research; Economic research and statistics; and Co-ordination and international relations.

Secretary-General: ASKHAT ORAZBAY.

Activities

The Regional Co-operation for Development (RCD) was established in 1964 as a tripartite arrangement between Iran, Pakistan and Turkey, which aimed to promote economic co-operation between member states. ECO replaced the RCD in 1985, and seven additional members were admitted to the Organization in November 1992. The main areas of co-operation are transport (including the building of road and rail links, of particular importance as seven member states are landlocked), telecommunications and post, trade and investment, energy (including the interconnection of power grids in the region), minerals, environmental issues, industry, and agriculture. ECO priorities and objectives for each sector are defined in the Quetta Plan of Action and the İstanbul Declaration; an Almaty Outline Plan, which was adopted in 1993, is specifically concerned with the development of regional transport and communication infrastructure. The period 1998–2007 has been designated as the ECO Decade of Transport and Communications.

In 1990 an ECO College of Insurance was inaugurated. A joint Chamber of Commerce and Industry was established in 1993. The third ECO summit meeting, held in Islamabad, Pakistan, in March 1995, concluded formal agreements on the establishment of several other regional institutes and agencies: an ECO Trade and Development Bank, in İstanbul, Turkey (with main branches in Tehran, Iran, and Islamabad, Pakistan), a joint shipping company, airline, and an ECO Cultural Institute, all to be based in Iran, an ECO Reinsurance Company and an ECO Science Foundation, with headquarters in Pakistan. In addition, heads of state and of government endorsed the creation of an ECO eminent persons group and signed the following two agreements in order to enhance and facilitate trade throughout the region: the Transit Trade Agreement (which entered into force in December 1997) and the Agreement on the Simplification of Visa Procedures for Businessmen of ECO Countries (which came into effect in March 1998). The sixth ECO summit meeting, held in June 2000 in Tehran, urged the completion of the necessary formalities for the creation of the planned ECO Trade and Development Bank and ECO Reinsurance Company. The ECO Cultural Institute was inaugurated in that year. The Shipping Company is now also operational. In May 2001 the Council of Ministers agreed to terminate the ECO airline project, owing to its unsustainable cost, and to replace it with a framework agreement on co-operation in the field of air transport.

In September 1996, at an extraordinary meeting of the ECO Council of Ministers, held in İzmir, Turkey, member countries signed a revised Treaty of İzmir, the Organization's fundamental charter. An extraordinary summit meeting, held in Ashgabat, Turkmenistan, in May 1997, adopted the Ashgabat Declaration, emphasizing the importance of the development of the transport and communications infrastructure and the network of transnational petroleum and gas pipelines through bilateral and regional arrangements in the ECO area. In May 1998, at the fifth summit meeting, held in Almaty, Kazakhstan, ECO heads of state and of government

signed a Transit Transport Framework Agreement and a memorandum of understanding to help combat the cross-border trafficking of illegal goods. The meeting also agreed to establish an ECO Educational Institute in Ankara, Turkey. In June 2000 the sixth ECO summit encouraged member states to participate in the development of information and communication technologies through the establishment of a database of regional educational and training institutions specializing in that field. ECO heads of state and government also reconfirmed their commitment to the Ashgabat Declaration. In December 2001 ECO organized its first workshop on energy conservation and efficiency in Ankara. The seventh ECO summit, held in İstanbul, Turkey, in October 2002, adopted the İstanbul Declaration, which outlined a strengthened and more proactive economic orientation for the Organization.

Convening in conference for the first time in March 2000, ECO ministers of trade signed a Framework Agreement on ECO Trade Co-operation (ECOFAT), which established a basis for the expansion of intra-regional trade. The Framework Agreement envisaged the eventual adoption of an accord providing for the gradual elimination of regional tariff and non-tariff barriers between member states. The so-called ECO Trade Agreement (ECOTA) was endorsed at the eighth summit meeting, held in Dushanbe, Tajikistan, in September 2004. Heads of state and government urged member states to ratify ECOTA at the earliest opportunity, in order to achieve their vision of an ECO free-trade area by 2015. The meeting also requested members to ratify and implement the Transit Transport Framework Agreement (see above), to support economic co-operation throughout the region.

In November 2000 the first meeting of ECO ministers responsible for energy and petroleum, convened in Islamabad, Pakistan, adopted a plan of action for regional co-operation on energy and petroleum matters over the period 2001–05. The first meeting of ECO ministers of agriculture, convened in July 2002, in Islamabad, adopted a declaration on co-operation in the agricultural sector, which specified that member states would contribute to agricultural rehabilitation in Afghanistan and considered instigating a mechanism for the regional exchange of agricultural and cattle products. The second meeting of ministers of agriculture, held in December 2004, in Antalya, Turkey, approved the Antalya Declaration on ECO Co-operation in Agriculture and adopted an ECO Plan of Action on Drought Management and Mitigation. In December 2002 the first meeting of ECO ministers of the environment, held in Tehran, adopted an action plan for co-operation in environmental issues covering the period 2003–07; the second environment ministers meeting was held in October 2004, in Istanbul. The first meeting of ECO ministers of industry took place in Tehran, in January 2004.

ECO staged its third trade fair in Bandar Anzali, Iran, in July 1998. The fourth fair, scheduled to be held in Karachi, Pakistan, in May 2002, was postponed. It was rescheduled to be held in Kabul, Afghanistan, in May–June 2005. The Organization maintains ECO TradeNet, an internet-based repository of regional trade information. ECO has co-operation agreements with several UN agencies and other international organizations in development-related activities. An ECO-UNODC Project on Drug Control and Co-ordination Unit commenced operations in Tehran in July 1999. ECO has been granted observer status at the UN, OIC and WTO.

In November 2001 the UN Secretary-General requested ECO to take an active role in efforts to restore stability in Afghanistan and to co-operate closely with his special representative in that country. In June 2002 the ECO Secretary-General participated in a tripartite ministerial conference on co-operation for development in Afghanistan that was convened under the auspices of the UN Development Programme and attended by representatives from Afghanistan, Iran and Pakistan. The ECO summit meeting in October authorized the establishment of a fund to provide financial assistance for reconstruction activities in Afghanistan.

Finance
Member states contribute to a centralized administrative budget.

Publications
ECO Annual Economic Report.
ECO Bulletin (quarterly).

EUROPEAN BANK FOR RECONSTRUCTION AND DEVELOPMENT—EBRD

Address: One Exchange Square, 175 Bishopsgate, London, EC2A 2JN, United Kingdom.

Telephone: (20) 7338-6000; **fax:** (20) 7338-6100; **e-mail:** generalenquiries@ebrd.com; **internet:** www.ebrd.com.

The EBRD was founded in May 1990 and inaugurated in April 1991. Its object is to contribute to the progress and the economic reconstruction of the countries of central and eastern Europe which undertake to respect and put into practice the principles of multi-party democracy, pluralism, the rule of law, respect for human rights and a market economy.

MEMBERS

Countries of Operations:

Albania	Lithuania
Armenia	Macedonia, former Yugoslav
Azerbaijan	republic
Belarus	Moldova
Bosnia and Herzegovina	Poland
Bulgaria	Romania
Croatia	Russia
Czech Republic	Serbia and Montenegro
Estonia	Slovakia
Georgia	Slovenia
Hungary	Tajikistan
Kazakhstan	Turkmenistan
Kyrgyzstan	Ukraine
Latvia	Uzbekistan

Other EU members*:

Austria	Italy
Belgium	Luxembourg
Denmark	Netherlands
Finland	Portugal
France	Spain
Germany	Sweden
Greece	United Kingdom
Ireland	

EFTA members:

Iceland	Norway
Liechtenstein	Switzerland

Other countries:

Australia	Malta
Canada	Mexico
Cyprus	Mongolia†
Egypt	Morocco
Israel	New Zealand
Japan	Turkey
Republic of Korea	USA

* The European Community and the European Investment Bank are also shareholder members in their own right.

† Receives assistance through a technical co-operation fund.

Organization

(April 2005)

BOARD OF GOVERNORS

The Board of Governors, to which each member appoints a Governor and an alternate, is the highest authority of the EBRD.

BOARD OF DIRECTORS

The Board is responsible for the organization and operations of the EBRD. The Governors elect 23 directors for a three-year term and a President for a term of four years. Vice-Presidents are appointed by the Board on the recommendation of the President.

ADMINISTRATION

The EBRD's operations are conducted by its Banking Department, headed by the First Vice-President. The other departments are: Finance; Risk Management; Human Resources and Administration; Internal Audit; and Offices of the President, the Secretary-General, the General Counsel, the Chief Economist and the Chief Compliance Officer. A structure of country teams, industry teams and operations support units oversee the implementation of projects. The EBRD has 32 local offices in all 27 of its countries of operations. At December 2003 there were 906 regular staff at the Bank's headquarters.

President: JEAN LEMIERRE (France).

First Vice-President: NOREEN DOYLE (USA) (until Aug. 2005).

Activities

In April 1996 EBRD shareholders, meeting in Sofia, Bulgaria, agreed to increase the Bank's capital from ECU 10,000m. to ECU 20,000m., to enable the Bank to continue, and to enhance, its lending programme (the ECU was replaced by the euro, with an equivalent value, from 1 January 1999). It was agreed that 22.5% of the new resources, was to be paid-up, with the remainder as 'callable' shares. Contributions were to be paid over a 13-year period from April 1998. At 31 December 2003 paid-up capital amounted to €5,197m.

The Bank aims to assist the transition of the economies of central Europe, southern and eastern Europe and the Caucasus, and central Asia and Russia towards a market economy system, and to encourage private enterprise. The Agreement establishing the EBRD specifies that 60% of its lending should be for the private sector, and that its operations do not displace commercial sources of finance. The Bank helps the beneficiaries to undertake structural and sectoral reforms, including the dismantling of monopolies, decentralization, and privatization of state enterprises, to enable these countries to become fully integrated in the international economy. To this end, the Bank promotes the establishment and improvement of activities of a productive, competitive and private nature, particularly small and medium-sized enterprises (SMEs), and works to strengthen financial institutions. It mobilizes national and foreign capital, together with experienced management teams, and helps to develop an appropriate legal framework to support a market-orientated economy. The Bank provides extensive financial services, including loans, equity and guarantees, and aims to develop new forms of financing and investment in accordance with the requirements of the transition process. The EBRD's founding Agreement specifies that all operations are to be undertaken in the context of promoting environmentally sound and sustainable development. It undertakes environmental audits and impact assessments in areas of particular concern, which enable the Bank to incorporate environmental action plans into any project approved for funding. An Environment Advisory Council assists with the development of policy and strategy in this area.

In the year ending 31 December 2003 the EBRD approved 119 operations, involving funds of €3,722m., compared with €3,899m. for 102 operations in the previous year. During 2003 one-third of all project financing committed was allocated to the financial sector. By the end of 2003 the Bank had approved more than 1,000 projects, for which financing of €22,669m. had been approved. In addition, the Bank had mobilized resources amounting to an estimated €45,822m.

The economic crisis in Russia, in August 1998, undermined the viability of many proposed projects and adversely affected the Bank's large portfolio of Russian investments. In March 1999, partly in response to the region's economic difficulties, the Board of Directors approved a new medium-term strategy for 2000–03, which focused on advancing the process of transition. Key aspects of the strategy were to develop a sound financial sector and investment climate in its countries of operations; to provide leadership for the development of SMEs; to promote infrastructure development; and to ensure a balanced and focused project portfolio. Since 2002 EBRD, together with the World Bank, IMF and Asian Development Bank, has sponsored the CIS-7 initiative which aimed to generate awareness of the difficulties of transition for seven low-income countries of the Commonwealth of Independent States (Armenia, Azerbaijan, Georgia, Kyrgyzstan, Moldova, Tajikistan, Uzbekistan), strengthen international and regional co-operation, and promote reforms to achieve economic growth. A review of the initiative was published in April 2004.

During 1999 the Bank participated in international efforts to secure economic and political stability in the Balkans, following the conflict in Kosovo. Subsequently the Bank has promoted the objectives of the Stability Pact for South-Eastern Europe by expanding its commitments in the region and by taking a lead role among international financial institutions in promoting private sector development. In July 2000 a US/EBRD SME Financing Facility was established for South East Europe and other early transition countries. In April 1999 the Bank and the European Commission launched a new

EU/EBRD SME Finance Facility, to provide equity and loan financing for SMEs in countries seeking accession to the EU. The Facility was also to extend technical assistance in areas including financial regulation, competition policy and telecommunications. At the end of 2003 the Bank had committed some €645m. to signed projects under the Facility. During 2003 an EU/EBRD Municipal Finance Facility became operational, with funds of €120m., to assist small municipalities to undertake infrastructure projects to meet EU standards. Following the accession of eight Central European and Baltic countries to the EU in May 2004 the Bank envisaged continuing to provide support in restructuring, encouraging private sector investment and the expansion of local businesses. A Trade Facilitation Programme extends bank guarantees in order to promote trading capabilities in the region. By the end of 2003 79 issuing banks in the region, together with 450 confirming banks in countries world-wide, were participating in the Programme. In October 2001 the Bank developed an Action Plan for Central Asia in order to accelerate development and economic stability in the countries neighbouring Afghanistan, as part of a wider objective of securing peace in the region. From 2002 the EBRD was involved in negotiations concerning the construction of a Baku-Tbilisi-Ceyhan (BTC) oil pipeline.

A high priority is given to attracting external finance for Bank-sponsored projects, in particular in countries at advanced stages of transition, from government agencies, international financial institutions, commercial banks and export credit agencies. The EBRD's Technical Co-operation Funds Programme (TCFP) aims to facilitate access to the Bank's capital resources for countries of operations by providing support for project preparation, project implementation and institutional development. In 2003 technical co-operation funding from donor countries and institutions amounted to €73m. Resources for technical co-operation originate from regular TCFP contributions, specific agreements and contributions to Special Funds. The Baltic Investment Programme, which is administered by Nordic countries, consists of two special funds to co-finance investment and technical assistance projects in the private sectors of Baltic states. The Funds are open to contributions from all EBRD member states. The Russia Small Business Fund (RSBF) was established in 1994 to support local SMEs through similar investment and technical co-operation activities over a period of 10 years. Other financing mechanisms that the EBRD uses to address the needs of the region include Regional Venture Funds, which invest equity in privatized companies, in particular in Russia, and provide relevant management assistance, and the Central European Agency Lines, which disburse lines of credit to small-scale projects through local intermediaries. A TurnAround Management Programme (TAM) provides practical assistance to senior managers of industrial enterprises to facilitate the expansion of businesses in a market economy. A Business Advisory Services programme complements TAM by undertaking projects to improve competitiveness, strategic planning, marketing and financial management in SMEs. In 2001 the EBRD collaborated with other donor institutions and partners to initiate a Northern Dimension Environmental Partnership (NDEP) to strengthen and co-ordinate environmental projects in northern Europe; the Partnership, which became operational in November 2002, includes a 'nuclear window' to address the nuclear legacy of the Russian Northern Fleet. The Bank manages the NDEP Support Fund.

The Bank administers a number of other funds specifically to support the promotion of nuclear safety. By the end of 2003 donor countries and the European Union had pledged more than €1,600m. to funds including the Nuclear Safety Account (NSA), a multilateral programme of action established in 1993, the Chernobyl Shelter Fund (CSF), established in 1997, and international decommissioning support funds (IDSFs) for Bulgaria, Lithuania and the Slovak Republic.

In 1997 the G-7, together with the European Community and Ukraine, endorsed the creation of the CSF-financed Chornobyl Unit 4 Shelter Implementation Plan (SIP) to assist Ukraine in stabilizing the protective sarcophagus covering the damaged Chornobyl (Chernobyl) reactor. The plan also provides for the construction of a new confinement structure safely to enclose the building, to be completed by 2007. In 1995 the G-7 requested that the Bank fund the com-

pletion of two new nuclear reactors in Ukraine, to provide alternative energy sources to the Chornobyl power-station. A study questioning the financial viability of the proposed reactors threatened funding in early 1997; a second survey, however, carried out by the EBRD, pronounced the plan viable, although environmental groups continued to dispute the proposals.

The funds have enabled the closure of nuclear plants for safety reasons in countries where this would otherwise have been prohibitively costly. In December 2000 Chornobyl unit 3 was closed, and in 2002 two units were closed in Bulgaria. The closure of a further two units in Bulgaria and units in Lithuania and the Slovak Republic are expected in the next few years. The NSA was also financing the construction of two major pre-decommissioning facilities in Ukraine, and a review of a safety report for a Russian reactor.

Publications

Annual Report.
EBRD Report to the Donor and Co-financing Community (annually).
Environments in Transition (2 a year).
Law in Transition (2 a year).
Transition Report (annually).

EBRD Statistics

PROJECT FINANCING COMMITTED BY COUNTRY

	2003		Cumulative to 31 Dec. 2003	
	Number	Amount (€ million)	Number	Amount (€ million)
Albania	2	47	15	170
Armenia	0	5	6	90
Azerbaijan . . .	3	25	16	280
Belarus	1	19	7	158
Bosnia and Herzegovina . .	2	36	19	259
Bulgaria	8	240	46	848
Croatia	5	125	51	1,232
Czech Republic . .	4	82	41	916
Estonia	1	26	42	451
Georgia	3	17	20	185
Hungary	6	379	66	1,526
Kazakhstan . . .	6	264	32	872
Kyrgyzstan . . .	2	2	14	123
Latvia	1	45	24	332
Lithuania . . .	1	16	27	393
Macedonia, former Yugoslav republic	3	102	20	307
Moldova	1	15	20	162
Poland	10	315	129	2,843
Romania	14	385	75	2,361
Russia	27	1,100	171	5,174
Serbia and Montenegro . .	9	149	24	509
Slovakia	1	138	38	1,012
Slovenia	1	44	26	506
Tajikistan . . .	0	3	6	29
Turkmenistan . .	0	1	5	125
Ukraine	6	116	58	1,279
Uzbekistan . . .	1	34	18	612
Total	119	3,722	1,019	22,669

Note: Operations may be counted as fractional numbers if multiple sub-loans are grouped under one framework agreement.

Source: EBRD, *Annual Report 2003.*

EUROPEAN FREE TRADE ASSOCIATION—EFTA

Address: (secretariat headquarters): 9–11 rue de Varembé, 1211 Geneva 20, Switzerland.
Telephone: (22) 3322626; **fax:** (22) 3322677; **e-mail:** mail.gva@efta .int; **internet:** www.efta.int.

Established in 1960, EFTA aimed to bring about free trade in industrial goods and to contribute to the liberalization and expansion of world trade. EFTA now serves as the structure through which three of its members participate in the European Economic Area (EEA), together with the member states of the European Union. In June 2002 a revised EFTA Convention entered into force, replacing the original Convention that had been in effect since 1960.

MEMBERS

Iceland	Norway
Liechtenstein	Switzerland

Three founder members subsequently left EFTA and joined the European Community (EC): Denmark (1973), the United Kingdom (1973) and Portugal (1986). Finland, formerly an associate member of EFTA, became a full member on 1 January 1986. Liechtenstein joined EFTA as a full member in September 1991, having hitherto had associate status through its customs union with Switzerland. Austria, Sweden (both founder members) and Finland left the Association on 31 December 1994 to become members of the European Union (as the EC had been restyled).

Organization

(April 2005)

EFTA COUNCIL

The Council is EFTA's governing body. The Chair is held for six months by each country in turn. The Council's decisions are binding on member states and must be unanimous. The Council is assisted by a substructure of committees and expert groups.

EFTA STANDING COMMITTEES

Board of Auditors.
Budget Committee.
Committee of Members of Parliament of the EFTA Countries.
Committee of Origin and Customs Experts.
Committee on Technical Barriers to Trade.
Committee on Third Country Relations.
Committee of Trade Experts.
Consultative Committee.
Economic Committee.
Steering Committee of the Portuguese Fund.

MATTERS RELATED TO THE EEA

The treaty establishing the EEA, which entered into force in 1994, provided for an institutional structure to enhance its operations. An EEA Council, comprising ministers of all signatory countries, provides policy direction, while a Joint Committee, comprising representatives of the EFTA states in the EEA, the European Commission and EU member states, is responsible for the day-to-day management of EEA matters. A Standing Committee serves as the forum of consultation within EFTA, consisting of representatives from Iceland, Liechtenstein and Norway and observers from Switzerland. It is assisted by five Subcommittees (for free movement of goods; free movement of capital and services; free movement of persons; flanking and horizontal policies; and legal and institutional matters) and a number of Working Groups. An independent EFTA Surveillance Authority and an EFTA Court have also been established to provide judicial control.

SECRETARIAT

The secretariat headquarters, in Geneva, Switzerland, provides support to the EFTA Council and on third country relations, as well as servicing the operation of certain conventions and schemes. About one-third of secretariat staff are deployed at headquarters. The secretariat division, based in Brussels, Belgium, and employing most of the remaining staff, assists member states on EEA matters. The Office of the Statistical Adviser is based in Luxembourg, and a Customs Officer is based in Paris, France. (Brussels

division): 74 rue de Trèves, 1040 Brussels, Belgium; tel. (2) 286-17-11; fax (2) 286-17-50; e-mail mail.bxl@efta.int
Secretary-General: WILLIAM ROSSIER (Switzerland).

Activities

The creation of a single market including all the countries in Western Europe was the ultimate objective of EFTA when it was created in 1960. Member states were, however, not ready or able to accept the far-reaching political and economic implications of joining the EC, which was established in 1958. EFTA's first target, the creation of free trade in industrial goods between its members, was achieved by the end of 1966. By 1991 tariffs or import duties had been removed on all imports except agricultural products. The revised EFTA Convention that was adopted by member states in Vaduz, Liechtenstein, in June 2001, and entered into force in June 2002, provided for strengthened economic integration between the four countries.

EEA

In 1972 EFTA member states signed bilateral agreements with the EC, which established free trade in most industrial goods between them from 1 July 1977. The last restrictions on free industrial trade were abolished from 1 January 1984. In April of that year ministers from all EFTA and EC member countries agreed on general guidelines for developing the EFTA-EC relationship. Their Declaration (known as the Luxembourg Declaration) recommended intensified efforts to improve the free circulation of industrial products between their countries, and closer co-operation beyond the framework of the free-trade agreements, in fields such as education, the environment, social policy, and research and development. In March 1989 the EFTA heads of government issued a declaration reaffirming their commitment to establish a European Economic Area (EEA), consisting of all the member states of EFTA and the EC. Formal negotiations on the establishment of the EEA commenced in June 1990, and the Agreement was signed in Oporto, Portugal, in May 1992. In December a Swiss referendum voted to oppose ratification of the EEA treaty. The ministers of trade of the remaining 18 member countries, however, signed an adjustment protocol in March 1993, allowing the EEA to be established without Switzerland. The EEA entered into force on 1 January 1994. Liechtenstein joined the EEA on 1 May 1995, having amended its customs union agreement and secured the support of the majority of its population in a national referendum. The EEA Agreement provided for the removal of all restrictions on the movement of goods, persons, services and capital within the area, effectively extending the internal market of the EU to the three EFTA countries within the EEA. In addition, the Agreement provided for co-operation in areas such as the environment, social policy, education and training, tourism, culture, consumer protection and small and medium-sized enterprises. To maintain homogeneity within the EEA, the Agreement is amended on a continuous basis to ensure that relevant EU legislation is extended to the EFTA EEA grouping. Bilateral agreements on strengthening Switzerland–EU trade entered into force in June 2002. The revised EFTA Convention that entered into force in that month extended to Iceland, Liechtenstein and Norway the main provisions of these bilateral trade agreements. In November 2003 the EEA member states, the EU Commission and the EU's ten candidate countries signed an agreement on the enlargement of the EEA following the accession of the candidate countries to the EU (which took place as planned on 1 May 2004 with the entry into force of the EU Accession Treaty, adopted in April 2003). The legal text of the EEA Enlargement Instrument, including EEA-relevant technical adaptations and transitional arrangements, was prepared on the basis of the EU Accession Treaty.

THIRD COUNTRY RELATIONS

In recent years EFTA developed an extensive network of contractual relations in central and eastern Europe and in the Mediterranean region. EFTA is currently in the process of extending the geographical scope of its third country relations, and has engaged in negotiations with other countries, and regional and sub-regional groupings, from beyond Europe and the Mediterranean. In a declaration adopted in Geneva in December 1999, to commemorate the 40th anniversary of EFTA's foundation, ministers reaffirmed their commitment to the further development of the Association's network of free-trade agreements, and indicated the potential for broadening the scope of the agreements to include fields such as services and investment, these being of growing importance in the increasingly interdependent global economy. The network was extended across the Atlantic by the declaration on trade and investment co-operation concluded with Mercosur in 2000 and the free-trade agreements concluded with Mexico in 2001 and with Chile in 2003 (see below); the latter agreements have been the most comprehensive developed to date, covering areas including services and investment and public procurement.

EFTA has concluded free-trade agreements with: Turkey (in December 1991); with Israel (September 1992); with Romania (December 1992); with Bulgaria (March 1993); with Morocco (which was granted a 12-year transitional period to phase out customs duties) (June 1997); with the Palestinian National Authority (November 1998); with the former Yugoslav Republic of Macedonia (June 2000); with Croatia and Jordan (June 2001); with Mexico (July 2001); with Singapore (June 2002); with Chile (June 2003); and with Lebanon and Tunisia (June and December 2004, respectively). In addition, declarations on co-operation (with a view to securing a free-trade agreement) are in force with: Albania (signed in December 1992); with Egypt (December 1995); with Ukraine and the Co-operation Council for the Arab States of the Gulf (June 2000); with Serbia and Montenegro (then the Federal Republic of Yugoslavia) and Mercosur (the latter a declaration on trade and investment co-operation) (December 2000); and with Algeria (December 2002). EFTA is pursuing negotiations on free-trade agreements with Canada, the Republic of Korea and the Southern African Customs Union. An exploratory meeting on initiating negotiations with Thailand was scheduled for May 2005.

Although Portugal withdrew from EFTA in 1985, EFTA decided to maintain an industrial development fund (established in 1976) for that country, for the 25-year period originally foreseen. Free-trade agreements concluded with Czechoslovakia (in March 1992) (with protocols on succession with the Czech Republic and Slovakia in April 1993), Poland (December 1992), Hungary (March 1993), Slovenia (July 1995), and with Estonia, Latvia and Lithuania (in December 1995) were dissolved upon the accession of these countries to the European Union on 1 May 2004.

Finance

Net budget for 2005: 22.3m. Swiss francs.

Publications

EEA Supplement to the Official Journal of the European Union (weekly).
EFTA Annual Report.
EFTA Bulletin.
EFTA Traders' ABC (CD-Rom).
Factsheets, legal documents.

EUROPEAN SPACE AGENCY—ESA

Address: 8–10 rue Mario Nikis, 75738 Paris Cédex 15, France.

Telephone: 1-53-69-76-54; **fax:** 1-53-69-75-60; **e-mail:** contactesa@esa.int; **internet:** www.esa.int.

ESA was established in 1975 to provide for, and to promote, European co-operation in space research and technology, and their applications, for exclusively peaceful purposes. It replaced the European Space Research Organisation (ESRO) and the European Launcher Development Organisation (both founded in 1962)

MEMBERS*

Austria	Italy
Belgium	Netherlands
Denmark	Norway
Finland	Portugal
France	Spain
Germany	Sweden
Greece	Switzerland
Ireland	United Kingdom

* Canada has signed an agreement for close co-operation with ESA, including representation on the ESA Council. In March 2004 the Council approved the accession of Greece and Luxembourg to the ESA Convention; Greece ratified the Convention and became a full member of the Agency in March 2005, and Luxembourg was expected to become a full member by 1 December 2005.

Organization

(April 2005)

Director-General: JEAN-JACQUES DORDAIN (France).

COUNCIL

The Council is composed of representatives of all member states. It is responsible for formulating policy and meets at ministerial or delegate level.

PROGRAMME BOARDS AND COMMITTEES

The Council is assisted in its work by five specialized Programme Boards, which oversee the management of the following ESA activities: Communication Satellite Programmes; Satellite Navigation; Earth Observation; Human Spaceflight, Research and Applications; and Launchers. The other principal bodies of the ESA administrative structure are the Committees for Administration and Finance, Industrial Policy, Science Programme, International Relations, and Security.

ESA CENTRES

European Space Research and Technology Centre (ESTEC): Noordwijk, Netherlands. ESA's principal technical establishment, at which the majority of project teams are based, together with the space science department and the technological research and support engineers; provides the appropriate testing and laboratory facilities.

European Space Operations Centre (ESOC): Darmstadt, Germany. Responsible for all satellite operations and the corresponding ground facilities and communications networks.

European Space Research Institute (ESRIN): Frascati, Italy. Responsible for the corporate exploitation of Earth observation data from space.

European Astronaut Centre (EAC): Köln, Germany. As a subsidiary of the Directorate of Human Spaceflight, manages all European astronaut activities and trains European and international partner astronauts on the European elements of the International Space Station. The Centre employs 16 European astronauts.

ESA also helps to maintain the Space Centre at Kourou, French Guyana, which is used for the Ariane launchers.

ESA had some 1,907 permanent staff in February 2005.

Activities

ESA's tasks are to define and put into effect a long-term European space policy of scientific research and technological development and to encourage all members to co-ordinate their national programmes with those of ESA to ensure that Europe maintains a competitive position in the field of space technology. ESA's basic activities cover studies on future projects, technological research, shared technical investments, information systems and training programmes. These, and the science programme, are mandatory activities to which all members must contribute; other programmes are optional and members may determine their own level of participation. In November 2000 the ESA Council and the Council of the European Union adopted parallel resolutions endorsing a European strategy for space. The strategy, which had been jointly prepared in 1999 and was entitled *Europe and Space: A New Chapter*, aimed to strengthen the foundation for European space activities; advance scientific knowledge; and to use the technical capabilities developed in connection with space activities to secure wider economic and social benefits. ESA collaborated with the European Commission in the preparation of a Green Paper on EU Space Policy, which assessed Europe's strengths and weaknesses in the sector. The Green Paper, which addressed such issues as the EU's independent access to space, international co-operation and environmental and security issues, was released in January 2003 as the basis for a period of consultation, involving national and international organizations, the EU space industry, the scientific community and citizens. Meanwhile, in March 2001, ESA and the European Commission had established a Joint Task Force to implement the European strategy for space. In November 2003 negotiations on a framework agreement for structured co-operation between ESA and the European Community were concluded. The framework agreement aimed to facilitate the coherent and progressive development of an overall European space policy; and to establish a common basis and appropriate practical arrangements for efficient and mutually beneficial co-operation between ESA and the EU. Immediately prior to the conclusion of the framework agreement the European Commission had adopted a White Paper on space policy that had been drafted with ESA's support. The White Paper incorporated an action plan for implementing an enlarged European space policy, and included proposals for joint ESA-EU space programmes that took as their basis the framework agreement.

ESA is committed to pursuing international co-operation to achieve its objective of developing the peaceful applications of space technology. ESA works closely with both the US National Aeronautics and Space Administration (NASA) and the Russian Aviation and Space Agency (Rosaviakosmos). In 2003 ESA and the Russian Government signed an Agreement on Co-operation and Partnership in the Exploration and Use of Outer Space for Peaceful Purposes (to be implemented by Rosaviakosmos), succeeding a similar agreement concluded with the USSR in 1990. In recent years ESA has developed a co-operative relationship with Japan, in particular in data relay satellites and the exchange of materials for the International Space Station. ESA has also concluded co-operation agreements with the Czech Republic, Greece, Hungary, Poland and Romania, providing for technical training and joint projects in the fields of space science, Earth observation and telecommunications. In 2003 ESA and Hungary concluded a 'European Co-operating State Agreement', a legal instrument designed to replace existing co-operation agreements between ESA and European states seeking closer relations with the Agency. ESA assists other transitional and developing countries to expand their space activities. It works closely with other international organizations, in particular the European Union and EUMETSAT. ESA has observer status with the UN Committee on the Peaceful Uses of Outer Space and co-operates closely with the UN's Office of Outer Space Affairs, in particular through the organization of a training and fellowship programme.

SCIENCE

The first European scientific space programmes were undertaken under the aegis of ESRO, which launched seven satellites during 1968–72. The Science Programme is a mandatory activity of the Agency and forms the basis of co-operation between member states. The first astronomical satellite (COS–B) was launched by ESA in August 1975. By March 2002 ESA had launched 17 scientific satellites and probes, among the most successful being the Giotto probe, launched in 1985 to study the composition of Halley's comet and reactivated in 1990 to observe the Grigg-Skjellerup comet in July 1992, and Hipparcos, which, between 1989 and 1993, determined the precise astronomic positions and distances of more than 1m. stars. In November 1995 ESA launched the Infrared Space Observatory, which has successfully conducted pre-planned scientific studies providing data on galaxy and star formation and on interstellar matter. ESA is collaborating with NASA in the Ulysses space project (a solar polar mission), the Solar and Helispheric Observatory (SOHO), launched in 1995 to study the internal structure of the sun, and the Hubble Space Telescope. In October 1997 the Huygens space probe was launched under the framework of a joint NASA–ESA project (the Cassini/Huygens mission) to study the planet Saturn and its largest moon, Titan, where it landed in mid-January 2005. In December 1999 the X-Ray Multimirror Mission (XMM–Newton) was launched from Kourou, French Guyana. It was envisaged that XMM–Newton, the most powerful x-ray telescope ever placed in orbit, would investigate the origin of galaxies, the formation of black holes, etc. Four cluster satellites, launched from Baikonur, Russia, in July-August 2000, were, in association with SOHO, to explore the interaction between the Earth's magnetic field and electrically-charged particles transported on the solar wind. In October 2002 INTEGRAL (International Gamma-Ray Astrophysical Laboratory) was successfully launched by a Russian Proton vehicle, to study the most violent events perceptible in the Universe.

ESA's space missions are an integral part of its long-term science programme, Horizon 2000, which was initiated in 1984. In 1994 a new set of missions was defined, to enable the inclusion of projects using new technologies and participation in future international space activities, which formed the Horizon 2000 Plus extension covering the period 2005–16. Together they were called Horizons 2000.

In May 2002 the Science Programme Committee initiated a new programme, COSMIC VISION, covering the period 2002–12. Under the programme three main projects—Astrophysics, Solar System Science, and Fundamental Physics—were to be developed in pro-

duction groups, missions within each to be built synergistically, where possible using common technologies and engineering teams:

Astrophysics: Production Group 2: Herschel, exploring the infrared and microwave Universe; Planck, studying the cosmic microwave background; Eddington, searching for extra-solar planets and studying the stellar seismology. (These missions were to be launched during 2007–08.) Group 3: GAIA, the ultimate galaxy mapper (to be launched no later than 2012).

Solar System Science: Group 1: Rosetta, launched in March 2004, to 'rendez-vous' and land on a comet); Mars Express, a Mars orbiter carrying the Beagle2 lander (launched in 2003); Venus Express, a Venus orbiter (2005). Group 2: SMART-1, which was to demonstrate solar propulsion technology while on course to the Moon (2003); BepiColombo, a mission to Mercury; Solar Orbiter to take a closer look at the Sun. (These missions were to be launched in 2011–12.)

Fundamental Physics: SMART 2, a technology demonstration mission (to be launched in 2006); a joint mission with NASA, searching for gravitational waves (2011).

In addition, the Agency is committed to co-operation with NASA on JWST (James Webb Space Telescope), the successor of the Hubble Space telescope, scheduled to be launched in 2010. The Herschel Space Observatory, designed to investigate the formation of stars and galaxies, was scheduled to be launched in 2007.

EARTH OBSERVATION

ESA has contributed to the understanding and monitoring of the Earth's environment through its satellite projects. Since 1977 ESA has launched seven Meteosat spacecraft into geosynchronous orbit, which have provided continuous meteorological data, mainly for the purposes of weather forecasting. The Meteosat systems are financed and owned by EUMETSAT, but were operated by ESA until December 1995. ESA and EUMETSAT have collaborated on the development of a successor to the Meteosat weather satellites (Meteosat Second Generation—MSG) to provide enhanced geostationary data coverage. The first satellite, MSG-1, was launched in August 2002. ESA and EUMETSAT have also begun development of the METOP/EPS (EUMETSAT Polar System) programme, to provide observations from polar orbit. The first METOP satellite was scheduled for launch in 2005.

In 1991 ESA launched the ERS-1 satellite, which carried sophisticated instruments to measure the Earth's surface and its atmosphere. A second ERS satellite was launched in April 1995 with the specific purpose of measuring the stratospheric and tropospheric ozone. ENVISAT, the largest and most advanced European-built observation satellite, was launched in February 2002 from Kourou, French Guyana. ENVISAT aims to provide a detailed assessment of the impact of human activities on the Earth's atmosphere, and land and coastal processes, and to monitor exceptional natural events, such as volcanic eruptions.

In June 1998 the ESA Council approved the initiation of activities related to the Living Planet Programme, designed to increase understanding of environmental issues. In May 1999 the Council committed funds for a research mission, Cryosat, to be undertaken, in order to study the impact of global warming on polar ice caps. Cryosat was due to be launched in 2005. Future missions also include the Gravity Field and Steady-State Ocean Circulation Explorer (GOCE), scheduled to be launched in 2006; the GOCE mission was to use a unique measurement technique to recover geodetic precision data on the Earth's gravity field.

As part of the Treaty Enforcement Services using Earth Observation (TESEO) initiative, agreed in 2001, ESA satellites provide data for a wide range of environmental activities including monitoring wetlands, ensuring compliance with Kyoto Protocol emission targets and combating desertification. Similarly, ESA has agreements with UNESCO to protect wildlife and sites of historic interest, in support of the Convention Concerning the Protection of the World Cultural and Natural Heritage.

TELECOMMUNICATIONS

ESA commenced the development of communications satellites in 1968. These have since become the largest markets for space use and have transformed global communications, with more than 100 satellites circling the Earth for the purposes of telecommunications. The main series of operational satellites developed by ESA are the European Communications Satellites (ECS), based on the original orbital test satellite and used by EUTELSAT, and the Maritime Communications Satellites (MARECS), which have been leased for operations to INMARSAT.

In 1989 ESA launched an experimental civilian telecommunications satellite, Olympus, to develop and demonstrate new broadcasting services. Its mission terminated in 1993, however, after it ran out of fuel. An Advanced Relay and Technology Mission Satellite (ARTEMIS) has been developed by ESA to test and operate new telecommunications techniques, and in particular to enable the relay of information directly between satellites. ARTEMIS was launched in July 2001. In 1998 ESA, together with the EU and

EUROCONTROL continued to implement a satellite-based navigation system to be used for civilian aircraft and maritime services, similar to the two existing systems operational for military use. ESA was also working with the EU and representatives of the private sector to enhance the region's role in the development of electronic media infrastructure to meet the expanding global demand. In May 1999 the Council approved funding for a satellite multimedia programme, Artes 3, which aimed to support the development of satellite systems and services for delivering information through high-speed internet access.

NAVIGATION

ESA, in co-operation with the European Commission and Eurocontrol, is implementing the EGNOS System. EGNOS is the European contribution to the Global Navigation Satellite System phase 1 (GNSS-1) and will provide an improved navigation and positioning service for all users of the (American) GPS and (Russian) GLONASS systems. EGNOS was to become fully operational in 2005, and was to serve as a major regional component of a seamless, world-wide augmentation system for navigation, aimed at meeting the demanding requirements for aircraft navigation, and comprising (in addition to EGNOS in Europe): WAAS in the USA, MSAS in Japan and GAGAN in India. ESA and the European Commission are also collaborating to design and develop a European satellite and navigation system, *Galileo*. The project will consist of about 30 satellites, a global network of tracking stations, and central control facilities in Europe. The satellites are due to be launched during 2005–08, with an initial *Galileo* service to be available from 2006. The GNSS aims to use the *Galileo*, GPS and GLONASS systems to provide an integrated satellite navigation service of unprecedented accuracy and global coverage under civilian control.

LAUNCHERS

The European requirement for independent access to space first manifested itself in the early 1970s against the background of strategic and commercial interests in telecommunications and Earth observation. As a consequence, and based on knowledge gained through national programmes, ESA began development of a space launcher. The resulting Ariane rocket was first launched in December 1979. The project, which incorporated four different launchers; Ariane-1 to Ariane-4, subsequently became an essential element of ESA's programme activities and, furthermore, developed a successful commercial role in placing satellites into orbit. The last flight of Ariane-4 took place in February 2003. From 1985 ESA worked to develop the more powerful Ariane-5 launcher, which has been in commercial operation since 1999, launched from the ESA facility at the Guyana Space Centre. In December 2000 the ESA Council approved the Vega Small Launcher Development and the P80 Advanced Solid Propulsion Stage programmes. The first Vega launch is due to take place in mid-2006. A Future Launcher Preparatory Programme is being defined.

HUMAN SPACEFLIGHT

Europe has gained access to human space technology and operations through Spacelab, which ESA developed as the European contribution to the US Space Shuttle Programme, and through the two joint Euromir missions on the Russian space station, Mir. Spacelab has flown into space 25 times and, with the Euromir projects, has enabled ESA to conduct, using its own astronauts, research into life and physical sciences under microgravity conditions. Since the mid-1980s ESA has supported space research in the life and physical sciences through its microgravity programmes. A considerable scientific output has been achieved in key areas such as crystal growth, solidification physics, fluid sciences, thermophysical properties, molecular and cell biology, developmental biology, exobiology and human physiology. The latest microgravity programme, approved in November 2001, is the ESA Programme in Life and Physical Sciences and Applications (ELIPS). ESA is a partner in the International Space Station (ISS), which was initiated by the US Government in 1984, and subsequently developed as a joint project between five partners-Canada, Europe, Japan, Russia and the USA. ESA's main contributions to the ISS are the Columbus Laboratory (due to be launched in 2006); and the Automated Transfer Vehicle—ATV (due to be launched by Ariane-5 in 2006), which is to provide logistical support to the Space Station. The Columbus laboratory will accommodate European multi-user research facilities: Biolab; Fluid Science Laboratory, European Physiology Modules, Material Science Laboratory (all being developed within the Microgravity Facilities for the Columbus Programme); and European Drawer Rack and European Stowage Rack (both within the ISS Utilization Programme). Once in orbit, Columbus will accommodate 10 active racks. In the framework of the ISS agreements with the USA, ESA is allocated 51% usage of Columbus, the other five racks being allocated to NASA. In addition to the experiment accommodation capabilities on Columbus, the European Zero-G Airbus, operated under ESA contract by Novespace, provides European researchers short-duration access to microgravity conditions for a wide variety of experiments, ranging from precursor experiments for the ISS to student experiments. Droptowers and sounding rockets provide additional short-duration opportunities. The ESA Directorate of Human Spaceflight also provides European researchers with flight opportunities on unmanned Russian Foton and Bion capsules.

Finance

All member states contribute to ESA's mandatory programme activities, on a scale based on their national income, and are free to decide on their level of commitment in optional programmes. The 2004 budget amounted to about €3,175m., of which 21.7% was allocated to mandatory programme activities (including 11.7% for space science); 78.3% to optional programmes (21.2% of the total budget was for human spaceflight and microgravity; 19.0% for launchers; 13.2% for earth observation; 11.0% for navigation; 7.6% for telecommunications; and 2.2% for technology); and 4.1% to third party programmes. ESA's budget for 2005 is €2,977m.

Publications

ESA Annual Report.
ESA Bulletin (quarterly).
EDUnews.
Earth Observation Quarterly.
On Station.
Reaching for the Skies (quarterly).
PFF—Preparing for the Future.
CONNECT.
Spacelink (newsletter).
Eurocomp (newsletter).
ECSL News.

Monographs and conference proceedings.

EUROPEAN UNION—EU

The European Coal and Steel Community (ECSC) was created by a treaty signed in Paris on 18 April 1951 (effective from 25 July 1952) to pool the coal and steel production of the six original members. It was seen as a first step towards a united Europe. The European Economic Community (EEC) and European Atomic Energy Community (Euratom) were established by separate treaties signed in Rome on 25 March 1957 (effective from 1 January 1958), the former to create a common market and to approximate economic policies, the latter to promote growth in nuclear industries. The common institutions of the three Communities were established by a treaty signed in Brussels on 8 April 1965 (effective from 1 July 1967).

The EEC was formally changed to the European Community (EC) under the Treaty on European Union (effective from 1 November 1993), although in practice the term EC had been used for several years to describe the three Communities together. The new Treaty established a European Union (EU), which introduced citizenship thereof and aimed to increase intergovernmental co-operation in economic and monetary affairs; to establish a common foreign and security policy; and to introduce co-operation in justice and home affairs. The EU was placed under the supervision of the European Council (comprising Heads of State or of Government of member countries), while the EC continued to exist, having competence in matters relating to the Treaty of Rome and its amendments.

The Treaty of Paris establishing the ECSC expired on 23 July 2002. A series of events and ceremonies were held to mark the occasion, including a symposium on the history and future of the EU. Upon expiry of the Treaty, which resulted in the termination of the ECSC legal regime and procedures and the dissolution of the ECSC Consultative Committee, the ECSC's assets and liabilities were transferred to the overall EU budget, while rights and obligations arising from international agreements drawn up between the ECSC and third countries were devolved to the EC.

Meetings of the principal organs take place in Brussels, Luxembourg and Strasbourg.

Presidency of the Council of the European Union: Luxembourg (January–June 2005); United Kingdom (July–December 2005).

Secretary-General of the Council of the European Union and High Representative for Common Foreign and Security Policy: JAVIER SOLANA MADARIAGA (Spain).

President of the European Commission: JOSÉ MANUEL DURÃO BARROSO (Portugal).

President of the European Parliament: JOSEP BORRELL FONTELLES (Spain).

MEMBERS

Austria	Greece	Netherlands*
Belgium*	Hungary	Poland
Cyprus	Ireland	Portugal
Czech Republic	Italy*	Slovakia
Denmark	Latvia	Slovenia
Estonia	Lithuania	Spain
Finland	Luxembourg*	Sweden
France*	Malta	United Kingdom
Germany*		

*Original members.

ENLARGEMENT

The six original members (Belgium, France, Germany, Italy, Luxembourg and the Netherlands) were joined in the European Communities (later the European Union—EU) on 1 January 1973 by Denmark, Ireland and the United Kingdom, and on 1 January 1981 by Greece. In a referendum held in February 1982, the inhabitants of Greenland voted to end their membership of the Community, entered into when under full Danish rule. Greenland's withdrawal took effect from 1 February 1985. Portugal and Spain became members on 1 January 1986. Following the reunification of Germany in October 1990, the former German Democratic Republic immediately became part of the Community, although a transitional period was allowed before certain Community legislation took effect there. Austria, Finland and Sweden became members on 1 January 1995.

At the Copenhagen summit on 13 December 2002, an historic agreement was reached when the European Council agreed that 10 candidate countries, comprising eight in central and eastern Europe (the Czech Republic, Estonia, Hungary, Latvia, Lithuania, Poland, Slovakia and Slovenia) and Malta and Cyprus should join the EU on 1 May 2004. The leaders of the 10 new member states signed the accession treaty in Athens on 16 April 2003. The Treaty of Athens had to be ratified by all 25 states prior to accession on 1 May 2004. The 15 current member states opted to ratify the Treaty in parliament whereas the future member states, except Cyprus (the Cypriot Parliament unanimously approved accession to the EU on 14 July 2003) adopted the Treaty by referendum. A referendum took place in Malta on 8 March, Slovenia on 23 March, Hungary on 12 April, Lithuania on 10 and 11 May, Slovakia on 16 and 17 May, Poland on 7 and 8 June, the Czech Republic on 15 and 16 June, Estonia on 14 September and Latvia on 20 September; each poll recorded a majority in favour of accession. Under the terms of the Treaty, only the Greek Cypriot sector of Cyprus was to be admitted to the EU in the absence of a settlement on the divided status of the island, although the EU made clear its preference for the accession of a united Cyprus. Negotiations in pursuit of a settlement regarding the reunification of Cyprus continued in early 2004. In April, however, in a referendum held only a few days before Cyprus was scheduled to join the EU, some 76% of Greek Cypriot voters rejected a reunification settlement proposed by the UN. At the same time, some 65% of Turkish Cypriot voters endorsed the settlement. Both communities would have had to approve the proposed reunification in order for Cyprus to commence its membership of the EU undivided. The results of the referendums meant that only the Greek sector of the island assumed EU membership from 1 May.

Romania submitted its formal application for EU membership on 22 June 1995 while Bulgaria applied for membership on 14 December 1995. Following the Helsinki European Council's decision in December 1999, accession negotiations started with Romania and Bulgaria in February 2000. The Commission concluded in November 2003 that Bulgaria had a functioning market economy and would be able to perform within the EU in the near future provided it continued to implement its reform programme. In October 2004 a report by the European Commission described Romania as a functioning market economy for the first time, although it confirmed that endemic corruption, ethnic minority rights and human trafficking remained, *inter alia*, areas of concern in both countries. In the same strategy document the Commission proposed a new clause in accession treaties under which membership negotiations could be suspended if candidate countries failed to fulfil the economic and political criteria established in Copenhagen in December 2002, according to which a prospective member must: be a stable democracy, respecting human rights, the rule of law, and the protection of minorities; have a functioning market economy; and adopt the common rules, standards and policies that make up the body of EU law. Bulgaria and Romania provisionally completed formal negotiations in June and December respectively and this was confirmed at the Brussels European Council of 17 December 2004. The Commission formally approved the accession applications of Romania and Bulgaria on 22 February 2005. Bulgaria and Romania signed a joint accession treaty on 25 April 2005, which would enter into force on 1 January 2007. However, under the new clause, accession could be delayed by one year should either country fail to implement all the commitments undertaken during entry negotiations (notably with regard to the independence of their judiciaries and with tackling corruption).

The third candidate country, Turkey, which had signed an association agreement with the EC in 1963 (although this was suspended between 1980 and 1986 following a military coup), applied for membership of the EU on 14 April 1987. As a populous Muslim nation with a poor record on human rights and low average income levels, Turkey encountered objections to its prospective membership of the EU, which opponents claimed would disturb the balance of power within the EU and place an intolerable strain on the organization's finances. The Helsinki European Council of 1999, however, granted Turkey applicant status and encouraged it to undertake the requisite political and economic reforms for eventual membership. By accelerating the pace of reforms, Turkey had made significant progress towards achieving compliance with the Copenhagen criteria by 2004, including far-reaching reforms of the Constitution and the penal code. Turkish ambitions for EU membership were adversely affected in April 2004 by the failure of the UN plan for the reunification of Cyprus, which was rejected in a referendum by the Greek Cypriots in the south of the island. Cyprus has been divided since 1974 when Turkey invaded the northern third of the country in response to a Greek-sponsored coup aiming to unite the island with Greece. Turkey refuses to recognize the Greek-Cypriot Government and is the only country to recognize the Government of the northern section of the country, known as the 'Turkish Republic of Northern Cyprus', where it has 30,000 troops deployed. The requirement for the successful resolution of all territorial disputes with members of the EU meant that failure to reach a settlement in Cyprus remained a significant impediment to Turkey's accession to the EU, although the Turkish authorities had expressed strong support for the peace plan. In December 2004, however, the EU agreed to begin accession talks with Turkey on 3 October 2005, although it specified a number of conditions, including the right to impose 'permanent safeguard' clauses in any accession accord. The safeguard clauses had regard to the freedom of movement of Turkish citizens within the EU (seeking to allay fears about large numbers of low-paid Turkish workers entering other EU member states) and restrictions on the level of subsidy available to Turkey for its infrastructure development or agriculture. The EU warned that negotiations could last between 10 and 15 years and that eventual membership was not guaranteed. Turkey was also obliged to give a written commitment to sign a protocol to update its association agreement with the EU by the start of accession negotiations in October, to cover the 10 new members that had joined the organization in May 2004, including Cyprus. The Turkish Government had previously refused to grant effective recognition to the Greek Cypriot Government and still insisted that the extension of the association agreement did not constitute formal recognition.

Croatia submitted its application for membership of the European Union on 21 February 2003. Croatia is preparing for membership on the basis of an association agreement signed on 29 October 2001 and the interim agreement, which entered into force in March 2002. In April 2004 the European Commission declared that Croatia had fulfilled the political and economic criteria needed to begin EU membership negotiations. Also in that month Croatia was deemed to be co-operating fully with the International Criminal Tribunal for the former Yugoslavia (ICTY). Croatia's progress towards accession had been hindered by its previous reluctance to co-operate with the ICTY. However, since the election of Ivo Sanader to the premiership of Croatia in November 2003, considerable progress had been made in the transfer of suspects to the war crimes tribunal in The Hague. In early 2005 the only outstanding issue between Croatia and the ICTY was the arrest and transfer to The Hague of the retired Gen. Ante Gotovina, who went into hiding in 2001 when the ICTY charged him with war crimes against ethnic Serbs during a military operation in Croatia's war of independence from the former Yugoslavia in 1995. Although further progress was required in the areas of minority rights, refugee returns, judiciary reform, regional co-operation and anti-corruption measures, the Commission recommended that negotiations for accession to the European Union should be opened with Croatia. Accession talks were scheduled to start in April 2005 but were advanced to 17 March, pending continuing full co-operation with the ICTY. However on 16 March the EU suspended membership negotiations with Croatia, on the grounds that it had not co-operated fully with the ICTY, owing to its failure to arrest Gotovina. Croatia's objective, which was to join the EU in 2007 with Bulgaria and Romania, seemed increasingly unlikely to be achieved.

The former Yugoslav republic of Macedonia made a formal application to join the EU on 22 March 2004.

THE TREATY ESTABLISHING A CONSTITUTION FOR EUROPE

In February 2002 a Convention on the Future of Europe was opened in Brussels, chaired by the former French President, Valéry Giscard d'Estaing. The Convention, which had been agreed upon at the Laeken summit in December 2001, when the European Council adopted the Declaration on the Future of the European Union, included in its remit 60 or more topics aimed at reforming EU institutions to ensure the smooth functioning of the Union after enlargement. The full text of the draft constitutional treaty was submitted to the Council of the European Union on 18 July 2003. The draft was discussed at the Intergovernmental Conference (IGC), which was composed of the representatives of the member states and the accession countries, from October to December.

At an EU summit in Brussels on 12–13 December 2003 under the chairmanship of the Italian Prime Minister, Silvio Berlusconi, the Heads of State and of Government failed to reach agreement on the final text of the constitution. Although agreement was reached in many policy areas, the summit collapsed over the issue of voting rights. Poland, supported by Spain, resisted the loss of voting rights promised at the Nice summit three years previously. Under the complex voting arrangements agreed under the Treaty of Nice (which, failing agreement on a new constitution, were not due to lapse until 2009), Poland and Spain were both awarded 27 votes on the Council of the European Union (almost as many as the 29 accorded to Germany, France, Italy and the United Kingdom). The German Government, which controls a population almost twice the size of that of Poland and makes the largest contribution to the EU budget, was particularly concerned to redress this imbalance. The draft constitution proposed a more transparent system whereby a simple majority of countries would carry a vote if they represented at least 60% of the EU's population (thus benefiting countries with larger populations). The failure to reach agreement on the constitution provoked fears that France, Germany and Belgium could lead a more integrationist group within the EU, creating a 'two-speed Europe'. The IGC continued to discuss the draft constitution under the Irish Presidency of the Council of the European Union during the first half of 2004. At a summit meeting held in Brussels on 18 June the Heads of State and of Government of the 25 EU member states finally approved the draft constitutional treaty, following a compromise proposal by the incumbent President of the Council of the European Union, the Irish Prime Minister, Bertie Ahern. The constitutional treaty provided for a permanent president for the Council of the European Union (replacing the current system of a six-month rotating presidency), an EU minister of foreign affairs, a new system of voting weights for member states in the Council of the European Union (proposals must have the support of at least 55% of the members of the Council, comprising at least 15 of them, representing at least 65% of the total population, in order to be passed), the expansion of majority voting in certain policy areas and the retention of national vetoes for foreign policy, defence and taxation. It required unanimous ratification by the member states over the next two years either by national legislatures or by popular referendums. The compromise reached over voting rights meant that smaller member states—particularly the new Eastern European members—could not be simply overruled by a small but powerful group of senior members, such as France, Germany and the United Kingdom. Opposition to the constitution was expected to be most intense in the United Kingdom and the new Eastern European member states where anti-European parties had performed well in the elections to the European Parliament on 10–13 June. The constitution was formally signed in Rome on 29 October by the Heads of State or of Government of the 25 member states and the three candidate countries (Bulgaria, Romania and Turkey), although it remained subject to ratification by each individual member nation, either by a vote in the national legislature or by a popular referendum, by the end of October 2006. On 12 January 2005 the European Parliament endorsed the constitution by 500 votes to 137 (there were 40 abstentions). By the end of 2004 two countries had already ratified the constitutional treaty, both by parliamentary vote—Lithuania in November and Hungary in December. Slovenia became the third country to ratify the treaty, also by parliamentary vote, on 1 February 2005. Spain was the first member state to hold a popular referendum on the issue of accepting or rejecting the draft document. At the poll, which took place on 20 February 2005, 76.7% voted in favour of the treaty and 17.2%

against; the turnout was low at 42.3%. Both Italy and Greece ratified the constitution, by parliamentary votes, in April. Referendums on the constitutional treaty were scheduled for 29 May in France, 1 June in the Netherlands and 27 September in Denmark.

Principal Elements of the Treaty Establishing a Constitution for Europe

If ratified, the Treaty establishing a Constitution for Europe would constitute a single foundation for the EU, replacing the EU and EC Treaties and all the treaties amending and supplanting them. The constitutional treaty clarifies the role of the institutions of the EU. It provides for the creation of an EU minister of foreign affairs (who would be appointed by the European Council by qualified majority with the agreement of the President of the Commission) to represent the EU internationally, combining the roles of EU commissioner responsible for external relations and EU High Representative for the Common Foreign and Security Policy (although foreign policy would still be subject to a national veto). The minister of foreign affairs would be mandated by the Council but also be a member of the Commission and would chair the External Relations Council. The treaty also envisages the creation of a new permanent president of the European Council, elected by the European Council for a period of two and one-half years, renewable once, to replace the current system of a six-month rotating presidency. The Council of the European Union, however, contrary to the Convention's proposal, would retain the system of a six-month rotating presidency for the different Council formations, except for the External Relations Council (which would be chaired by the new EU minister of foreign affairs), although it would comprise a 'team presidency' of three countries. The system of qualified majority voting in the Council of the European Union would be extended and redefined, ending the system of national vetoes in 20 new areas. A qualified majority would be defined as at least 55% of the members of the Council, composed of at least 15 of them and representing member states comprising 65% of the EU's population (although a blocking minority would have to include at least four member states). The constitutional treaty also includes a provision that the European Council could agree, by unanimity and subject to prior unanimous approval by national legislatures, to introduce qualified majority voting in an area currently requiring unanimity (thus obviating the need for treaty change). The European Parliament's legislative powers are consolidated in the constitutional treaty, which grants the Parliament the right of co-decision with the Council of the European Union in policy areas requiring qualified majority voting, giving it a more prominent role in framing legislation. The maximum number of seats in the European Parliament was raised to 750, with member states accorded a minimum of six and a maximum of 96 seats on a proportional basis (the precise number of seats allocated to each country would be decided prior to the elections to the European Parliament in 2009). The European Commission was to retain its current composition of one commissioner for each member state until 2014; thereafter the Commission would comprise a number of commissioners corresponding to two-thirds of the member states, according to a system of equal rotation. The constitution attempts to improve democracy and transparency within the Union, introducing the right for EU citizens to petition the Commission to introduce new legislation and enshrining the principles of subsidiarity (that the EU should only act when an objective can be better achieved at the supranational level, implying that national powers are the norm) and proportionality (that the action should be proportional to the desired objective)—national parliaments were to be given the opportunity to examine EU legislation to ensure that it was within the EU's remit and to return legislation to the Commission for reconsideration if one-third of member states found that a proposed law breached these principles. The constitutional treaty provides a legal basis for the EU defence force, with a mutual defence clause, and (although not written into the constitution itself) a separate operational planning capability, and includes the stipulation that the EU has the power to sign treaties and sit on international bodies as a legal body in its own right. The document also provides for the establishment of a European public prosecutor's office to combat EU fraud and cross-border crime, the right to dual citizenship (i.e. of the EU as well as of a member state) and includes arrangements for the formal withdrawal of a member state from the EU.

Diplomatic Representation

PERMANENT REPRESENTATIVES OF MEMBER STATES

Austria: Gregor Woschnagg, 30 ave de Cortenbergh, 1040 Brussels; tel. (2) 234-51-00; fax (2) 235-63-00; e-mail presse.bruessel-ov@bmaa .gv.at; internet www.bmaa.gv.at.

Belgium: JAN DE BOCK, Rond-point Schuman 6, 1040 Brussels; tel. (2) 233-21-11; fax (2) 231-10-75; e-mail belrep@belgoeurop.diplobel.fgov.be.

Cyprus: NICHOLAS EMILIOU, 2 square Ambiorix, 1000 Brussels; tel. (2) 735-35-10; fax (2) 735-45-52; e-mail cyprus.embassy@skynet.be.

Czech Republic: JAN KOHOUT, 15 rue Caroly, 1050 Brussels; tel. and fax (2) 213-01-85; e-mail eu.brussels@embassy.mzv.cz; internet www.mfa.cz/missionEU.

Denmark: CLAUS GRUBE, 73 rue d'Arlon, 1040 Brussels; tel. (2) 233-08-11; fax (2) 230-93-84; e-mail brurep@um.dk.

Estonia: VÄINO REINART, 11–13 rue Guimard, 1040 Brussels; tel. (2) 227-39-10; fax (2) 227-39-25; e-mail mission@estemb.be; internet www.estemb.be.

Finland: EIKKA KOSONEN, 100 rue de Trèves, 1040 Brussels; tel. (2) 287-84-11; fax (2) 287-84-00; e-mail press.eue@formin.fi; internet www.uunet.be/finland.

France: PIERRE SELLAL, 14 place de Louvain, 1000 Brussels; tel. (2) 229-82-11; fax (2) 229-82-82; e-mail firstname.lastname@diplomatie.fr; internet www.rpfrance.org.

Germany: Dr WILHELM SCHÖNFELDER, 19–21 rue Jacques de Lalaing, 1040 Brussels; tel. (2) 238-18-11; fax (2) 238-19-78; e-mail eurogerma.eu@bruessel.auswaertiges-amt.de; internet www.eu-vertretung.de.

Greece: VASSILIS KASKARELIS, 25 rue Montoyer, 1000 Brussels; tel. (2) 551-56-11; fax (2) 551-56-51; e-mail mea.bruxelles@rp-grece.be.

Hungary: TIBOR KISS, 92–98 rue de Trèves, 1040 Brussels; tel. (2) 234-12-00; fax (2) 372-07-84; e-mail sec@hunrep.be; internet www.hunrep.be.

Ireland: ANNE ANDERSON, 89–93 rue Froissart, 1040 Brussels; tel. (2) 230-85-80; fax (2) 230-32-03; e-mail reppermirl@online.be.

Italy: ROCCO ANTONIO CANGELOSI, 9–11 rue du Marteau, 1000 Brussels; tel. (2) 220-04-11; fax (2) 219-34-49; e-mail rpue@rpue.it; internet www.italiaue.it.

Latvia: EDUARDS STIPRAIS, 39–41 rue d'Arlon, Boîte 6, 1000 Brussels; tel. (2) 282-03-60; fax (2) 282-03-69; e-mail missioneu@mfa.gov.lv.

Lithuania: Dr OSKARAS JUSYS, 41–43 rue Belliard, 1040 Brussels; tel. (2) 771-01-40; fax (2) 771-45-97; e-mail office@lt-mission-eu.be; internet www.lt-mission-eu.be.

Luxembourg: MARTINE SCHOMMER, 75 ave de Cortenbergh, 1000 Brussels; tel. (2) 737-56-00; fax (2) 737-56-10; e-mail secretariat@rpue.etat.lu.

Malta: RICHARD CACHIA CARUANA, 65–67 rue Belliard, 1040 Brussels; tel. (2) 343-01-95; fax (2) 343-01-06.

Netherlands: THOM DE BRUIJN, 48 ave Herrmann Debroux, 1160 Brussels; tel. (2) 679-15-11; fax (2) 679-17-75.

Poland: MAREK GRELA, 282–284 ave de Tervuren, 1150 Brussels; tel. (2) 777-72-00; fax (2) 777-72-97; e-mail mail@pol-mission-eu.be; internet www.pol-mission-eu.be.

Portugal: ÁLVARO MENDONÇA E MOURA, 12/22 ave de Cortenbergh, 1040 Brussels; tel. (2) 286-42-11; fax (2) 231-00-26; e-mail reper@reper-portugal.be; internet www.reper-portugal.be.

Slovakia: MIROSLAV ADAMIS, 79 ave de Cortenbergh, 1000 Brussels; tel. (2) 743-68-11; fax (2) 743-68-88; e-mail slovakmission@pmsreu.be; internet www.eubrussels.mfa.sk.

Slovenia: Dr CIRIL STOKELJ, 30 ave Marnix, 1000 Brussels; tel. (2) 512-44-66; fax (2) 512-09-97; e-mail mission.bruxelles@gov.si.

Spain: CARLOS BASTARRECHE SAGÜES, 52 blvd du Régent, 1000 Brussels; tel. (2) 509-86-11; fax (2) 511-19-40.

Sweden: SVEN-OLOF PETERSSON, 30 square de Meeûs, 1000 Brussels; tel. (2) 289-56-11; fax (2) 289-56-00; e-mail representationen.bryssel@foreign.ministry.se; internet www.utrikes.regeringen.se/eu/startsidan.htm.

United Kingdom: Sir JOHN GRANT, 10 ave d'Auderghem, 1040 Brussels; tel. (2) 287-82-11; fax (2) 287-83-98; e-mail firstname.lastname@fco.gov.uk; internet www.ukrep.be.

PERMANENT MISSIONS TO THE EUROPEAN UNION
(March 2005)

Afghanistan: 281 rue François Gay, 1150 Brussels; tel. (2) 761-31-66; fax (2) 761-31-67; e-mail ambassade.afghanistan@brutele.be; internet www.ambafghane.web.com; Ambassador HOMAYOUN TANDAR.

Albania: 30 rue Tenbosch, 1000 Brussels; tel. (2) 640-35-44; fax (2) 640-31-77; e-mail albanian.ec2@skynet.be; Ambassador ARTUR KUKO.

Algeria: 209 ave Molière, 1050 Brussels; tel. (2) 343-50-78; fax (2) 343-51-68; e-mail info@algerian-embassy.be; internet www.algerian-embassy.be.htm; Ambassador HALIM BENATTALLAH.

Andorra: 10 rue de la Montagne, 1000 Brussels; tel. (2) 502-12-11; fax (2) 513-07-41; e-mail ambassade@andorra.be; internet www.andorra.be; Ambassador MERITXELL MATEU I PI.

Angola: 182 rue Franz Merjay, 1050 Brussels; tel. (2) 346-18-72; fax (2) 344-08-94; e-mail angola.embassy.brussels@skynet.be; Chargé d'affaires a.i. MARIA EUGÉNIA FEIJO DE ALMEIDA FERREIRA DOS SANTOS.

Antigua and Barbuda: 42 rue de Livourne, 1000 Brussels; tel. (2) 534-36-11; fax (2) 539-40-09; e-mail ecs.embassies@skynet.be; internet www.caribisles.org; Ambassador (vacant).

Argentina: 225 ave Louise (7e étage), Boîte 2, 1050 Brussels; tel. (2) 648-93-71; fax (2) 648-08-04; e-mail info@eceur.org; internet www.eceur.org; Ambassador JORGE REMES LENICOV.

Armenia: 157 rue Franz Merjay, 1050 Brussels; tel. and fax (2) 348-44-00; e-mail armembel@tiscali.be; internet www.armenian-embassy.be; Ambassador VIGUEN TCHITETCHIAN.

Australia: Guimard Centre, 6–8 rue Guimard, 1040 Brussels; tel. (2) 286-05-00; fax (2) 230-68-02; e-mail austemb.brussels@dfat.gov.au; internet www.austemb.be; Ambassador PETER GREY.

Azerbaijan: 78 ave Général Lartigue, 1200 Brussels; tel. (2) 735-98-80; fax (2) 735-92-70; e-mail az.missioneu@chello.be; Ambassador ARIF MAMEDOV.

Bahamas: 10 Chesterfield St, London, W1J 5JI, United Kingdom; tel. (20) 7408-4488; fax (20) 7499-9937; e-mail info@bahamashclondon.net; Ambassador BASIL G. O'BRIEN.

Bahrain: 3 bis place des Etats-Unis, 75016 Paris, France; tel. 1-47-23-48-68; Ambassador SHAIKHA HAYA BINT RASHID AL-KHALIFA.

Bangladesh: 29–31 rue Jacques Jordaens, 1000 Brussels; tel. (2) 640-55-00; fax (2) 646-59-98; e-mail bdootbrussels@skynet.be; Ambassador SYED MAUDUD ALI.

Barbados: 100 ave F. D. Roosevelt, 1050 Brussels; tel. (2) 732-17-37; fax (2) 732-32-66; e-mail brussels@foreign.gov.bb; internet www.foreign.barbadosgov.org; Ambassador ERROL L. HUMPHREY.

Belarus: 192 ave Molière, 1050 Brussels; tel. (2) 340-02-70; fax (2) 340-02-87; e-mail embbel@skynet.be; Ambassador (vacant).

Belize: 136 blvd Brand Whitlock, 1200 Brussels; tel. (2) 732-62-04; fax (2) 732-62-46; e-mail embel.bru@pophost.eunet.be; internet www.belize.gov.bz; Ambassador YVONNE HYDE.

Benin: 5 ave de l'Observatoire, 1180 Brussels; tel. (2) 375-06-74; fax (2) 375-83-26; e-mail ambabenin_benelux@yahoo.fr; Ambassador EULOGE HINVI.

Bhutan: 17–19 chemin du Champ d'Anier, 1209 Geneva, Switzerland; tel. (22) 799-08-90; fax (22) 799-08-99; e-mail mission.bhutan@ties.itu.int; Ambassador BAP KESANG.

Bolivia: 176 ave Louise, Boîte 6, 1050 Brussels; tel. (2) 627-00-10; fax (2) 647-47-82; e-mail embajada.bolivia@embolbrus.be; Ambassador FERNANDO LAREDO AGUAYO.

Bosnia and Herzegovina: 34 rue Tenbosch, 1000 Brussels; tel. (2) 644-20-08; fax (2) 644-16-98; e-mail bh-mission-07@skynet.com; Ambassador ZDENKO MARTINOVIĆ.

Botswana: 169 ave de Tervuren, 1150 Brussels; tel. (2) 735-20-70; fax (2) 735-63-18; e-mail embasofbotswana@yahoo.co.uk; internet www.gov.bw; Ambassador SASARA CHASALA GEORGE.

Brazil: 30 ave F. D. Roosevelt, 1050 Brussels; tel. (2) 640-20-40; fax (2) 648-80-40; e-mail missao@braseuropa.be; Ambassador JOSÉ ALFREDO GRAÇA LIMA.

Brunei: 238 ave F. D. Roosevelt, 1050 Brussels; tel. (2) 675-08-78; fax (2) 672-93-58; e-mail kedutaan-brunei.brussels@skynet.be; Chargé d'affaires a.i. AMALINA MURAD.

Bulgaria: 108 rue d'Arlon, 1040 Brussels; tel. (2) 374-84-68; fax (2) 374-91-88; e-mail info@missionbg.be; internet www.missionbg.be; Ambassador STANISLAV DASKALOV.

Burkina Faso: 16 place Guy d'Arezzo, 1180 Brussels; tel. (2) 345-99-12; fax (2) 345-06-12; e-mail ambassade.burkina@skynet.be; Ambassador KADRÉ DÉSIRÉ OUEDRAOGO.

Burundi: 46 square Marie-Louise, 1040 Brussels; tel. (2) 230-45-35; fax (2) 230-78-83; e-mail ambassade.burundi@skynet.be; internet www.burundi.gov.bi; Ambassador FERDINAND NYABENDA.

Cambodia: 4 rue Adolphe Yvon, 75116 Paris, France; tel. 1-45-03-47-20; fax 1-45-03-47-40; e-mail ambcambodgeparis@mangoosta.fr; Ambassador (vacant).

Cameroon: 131–133 ave Brugmann, 1190 Brussels; tel. (2) 345-18-70; fax (2) 344-57-35; Ambassador ISABELLE BASSONG.

Canada: 2 ave de Tervuren, 1040 Brussels; tel. (2) 741-06-60; fax (2) 741-06-29; e-mail breec@dfait-maeci.gc.ca; internet www

.dfait-maeci.gc.ca/eu-mission/index.htm; Ambassador Jeremy Kinsman.

Cape Verde: 29 ave Jeanne, 1050 Brussels; tel. (2) 643-62-70; fax (2) 646-33-85; e-mail emb.caboverde@skynet.be; Ambassador Fernando Wahnon Ferreira.

Central African Republic: 416 blvd Lambermont, 1030 Brussels; tel. (2) 242-28-80; fax (2) 215-13-11; e-mail ambassade .centreafrique@skynet.be; Ambassador Armand-Guy Zounguere-Sokambi.

Chad: 52 blvd Lambermont, 1030 Brussels; tel. (2) 215-19-75; fax (2) 216-35-26; e-mail ambassade.tchad@skynet.be; Ambassador Abderahim Yacoub N'Diaye.

Chile: 106 rue des Aduatiques, 1040 Brussels; tel. (2) 743-36-60; fax (2) 736-49-94; e-mail embachile@embachile.be; internet www .misionchile-ue.org; Ambassador Alberto van Klaveren.

China, People's Republic: 443–445 ave de Tervuren, 1150 Brussels; tel. (2) 771-33-09; fax (2) 772-37-45; Ambassador Chengyuan Guan.

Colombia: 96A ave F. D. Roosevelt, 1050 Brussels; tel. (2) 649-56-79; fax (2) 646-54-91; e-mail colombia@emcolbru.org; internet www .emcolbru.org; Ambassador Nicolas Echavarria Resa.

Comoros: 128 ave Paul Hymans, 1200 Brussels; tel. and fax (2) 779-58-38; e-mail ambacom.bxl@skynet.be; Ambassador Sultan Chouzour.

Congo, Democratic Republic: 30 rue Marie de Bourgogne, 1000 Brussels; tel. (2) 503-04-52; fax (2) 503-04-54; Ambassador Jean-Pierre Mavungu-di-Ngoma.

Congo, Republic: 16–18 ave F. D. Roosevelt, 1050 Brussels; tel. (2) 648-38-56; fax (2) 648-42-13; Ambassador Jacques Obia.

Cook Islands: 10 rue Berckmans, 1060 Brussels, Belgium; tel. (2) 543-10-00; fax (2) 543-10-01; e-mail cookislands@prmltd.com; Ambassador Todd McClay.

Costa Rica: 489 ave Louise (4e étage), 1050 Brussels; tel. (2) 640-55-41; fax (2) 648-31-92; e-mail embcrbel@coditel.net; Ambassador Maria Salvadora Ortiz.

Côte d'Ivoire: 234 ave F. D. Roosevelt, 1050 Brussels; tel. (2) 672-23-57; fax (2) 672-04-91; e-mail mailbox@ambacibnl.be; Ambassador Marie Gosset.

Croatia: 50 ave des Arts, Boîte 14, 1000 Brussels; tel. (2) 500-09-30; fax (2) 646-56-64; e-mail cromiss.eu@mvp.hr; Ambassador Mirjana Mladineo.

Cuba: 77 rue Robert Jones, 1180 Brussels; tel. (2) 343-00-20; fax (2) 344-96-91; e-mail mision@embacuba.be; Ambassador Rodrigo Malmierca Diaz.

Djibouti: 204 ave F. D. Roosevelt, 1050 Brussels; tel. (2) 347-69-67; fax (2) 347-69-63; e-mail amb_djib@yahoo.fr; Ambassador Mohamed Moussa Chehem.

Dominica: 42 rue de Livourne, 1000 Brussels; tel. (2) 534-26-11; fax (2) 539-40-09; e-mail ecs.embassies@skynet.be; internet www .caribisles.org; Ambassador George Randolph Earle Bullen.

Dominican Republic: 12 ave Bel Air, 1180 Brussels; tel. (2) 346-49-35; fax (2) 346-51-52; e-mail embajada@dominicana.be; Ambassador Clara Quiñones de Longo.

Ecuador: 363 ave Louise, BP 1, 1050 Brussels; tel. (2) 644-30-50; fax (2) 644-28-13; e-mail amb.equateur@skynet.be; Ambassador Méntor Villagomez Merino.

Egypt: 19 ave de l'Uruguay, 1000 Brussels; tel. (2) 663-58-00; fax (2) 675-58-88; e-mail embassy.egypt@skynet.be; Ambassador Soliman Awaad.

El Salvador: 171 ave de Tervuren, 1150 Brussels; tel. (2) 733-04-85; fax (2) 735-02-11; e-mail amb.elsalvador@brutele.be; Ambassador Héctor Gonzalez Urrutia.

Equatorial Guinea: 17 ave Jupiter, 1190 Brussels; tel. (2) 346-25-09; fax (2) 346-33-09; e-mail guineaecuatorial.brux@skynet.be; Ambassador Vitorino N. K. A. Obiang.

Eritrea: 15–17 ave de Wolvendael, 1180 Brussels; tel. (2) 374-44-34; fax (2) 372-07-30; e-mail eri_emba_brus@hotmail.com; Ambassador Andebrhan Woldegiorgis.

Ethiopia: 231 ave de Tervuren, Brussels; tel. (2) 771-32-94; fax (2) 771-49-14; e-mail etebru@brutele.be; Ambassador Berhane Gebre Christos.

Fiji: 92–94 square Plasky, 1030 Brussels; tel. (2) 736-90-50; fax (2) 736-14-58; e-mail info@fijiembassy.be; internet www.fijiembassy.be; Ambassador Isikeli Uluinairai Mataitoga.

Gabon: 112 ave Winston Churchill, 1180 Brussels; tel. (2) 340-62-10; fax (2) 346-46-69; e-mail bs.175335@skynet.be; Ambassador René Makongo.

The Gambia: 126 ave F. D. Roosevelt, 1050 Brussels; tel. (2) 640-10-49; fax (2) 646-32-77; e-mail gambianmission@hotmail.com; Ambassador Yusuoha Alieu Kah.

Georgia: 58 ave Orban, 1150 Brussels; tel. (2) 761-11-90; fax (2) 761-11-99; e-mail mdgadc@skynet.be; Ambassador Konstantin Zaldastanishvili.

Ghana: 7 blvd Général Wahis, 1030 Brussels; tel. (2) 705-82-20; fax (2) 705-66-53; e-mail ghanaemb@chello.be; internet www.ghanabru .net; Ambassador Kobina Wudu.

Grenada: 123 rue de Laeken, 1000 Brussels; tel. (2) 223-73-03; fax (2) 223-73-07; internet www.caribisles.org; Chargé d'affaires Joan Marie Coutain.

Guatemala: 185 ave Winston Churchill, 1180 Brussels; tel. (2) 345-90-58; fax (2) 344-64-99; e-mail obguab@infoboard.be; Ambassador Edmond Mullet Lesieur.

Guinea: 75 ave Roger Vandendriessche, 1150 Brussels; tel. (2) 771-01-26; fax (2) 762-60-36; Ambassador Kazaliou Balde.

Guinea-Bissau: 70 ave F. D. Roosevelt, 1050 Brussels; tel. (2) 647-08-90; fax (2) 640-43-12; Chargé d'affaires a.i. Serafim Ianga.

Guyana: 12 ave du Brésil, 1000 Brussels; tel. (2) 675-62-16; fax (2) 675-55-98; e-mail embassy.guyana@skynet.be; Ambassador Dr Kenneth F. S. King.

Haiti: 139 chaussée de Charleroi, 1060 Brussels; tel. (2) 649-73-81; fax (2) 640-60-80; e-mail amb.haiti@brutele.be; Ambassador Yolette Azor-Charles.

Holy See: 289 ave Brugmann, 1180 Brussels; tel. (2) 340-77-00; fax (2) 340-77-04; e-mail nonciature.ue.chancellerie@pro.tiscali.be; Apostolic Nuncio Mgr Faustino Sainz Muñoz.

Honduras: 3 ave des Gaulois (5e étage), 1040 Brussels; tel. (2) 734-00-00; fax (2) 735-26-26; e-mail ambassade.honduras@chello.be; Ambassador Teodolinda Benegas Morazan.

Iceland: 11 rond point Schuman, 1040 Brussels; tel. (2) 238-50-00; fax (2) 230-69-38; e-mail icemb.brussel@utn.stjr.is; internet www .iceland.org/be; Ambassador Kjartan Jóhannsson.

India: 217 chaussée de Vleurgat, 1050 Brussels; tel. (2) 640-91-40; fax (2) 648-96-38; e-mail admin@indembassy.be; internet www .indembassy.be; Ambassador Pradeep Kumar Singh.

Indonesia: 38 blvd de la Woluwe, 1200 Brussels; tel. (2) 779-09-15; fax (2) 772-82-10; e-mail primebxl@skynet.be; Ambassador Abdurachman Mattalitti.

Iran: 415 ave de Tervuren, 1150 Brussels; tel. (2) 762-37-45; fax (2) 762-39-15; e-mail eiri.bxl@skynet.be; Ambassador Abolghasem Delfi.

Iraq: 23 ave des Aubépines, 1180 Brussels; tel. (2) 374-59-92; fax (2) 374-76-15; e-mail ambassade.irak@skynet.be; Ambassador (vacant).

Israel: 40 ave de l'Observatoire, 1180 Brussels; tel. (2) 373-55-24; fax (2) 373-56-77; e-mail info-eu@brussels.mfa.gov.il; internet www .israeli-mission.org; Ambassador Oded Eran.

Jamaica: 2 ave Palmerston, 1000 Brussels; tel. (2) 230-11-70; fax (2) 230-37-09; e-mail emb.jam.brussels@skynet.be; Ambassador Evadne Coye.

Japan: 5–6 square de Meeûs, 1000 Brussels; tel. (2) 500-77-11; fax (2) 513-32-41; e-mail inf@jmission-eu.be; internet www.jmission-eu .be; Ambassador Kazuo Asakai.

Jordan: 104 ave F. D. Roosevelt, 1050 Brussels; tel. (2) 640-77-55; fax (2) 640-27-96; e-mail jordan.embassy@skynet.be; Chargé d'affaires a.i. Malek E. Twal.

Kazakhstan: 30 ave Van Bever, 1180 Brussels; tel. (2) 374-95-62; fax (2) 374-50-91; e-mail kazakstan.embassy@swing.be; internet www.kazakstanembassy.be; Ambassador Konstantin V. Zhigalov.

Kenya: 208 ave Winston Churchill, 1180 Brussels; tel. (2) 340-10-40; fax (2) 340-10-50; e-mail kenbrussels@hotmail.com; Ambassador Peter O. Ole Nkuraiyia.

Korea, Democratic People's Republic: Glinkastr. 5/7, 1017 Berlin, Germany; tel. (30) 2293189; fax (30) 2293191.

Korea, Republic: 173–175 chaussée de la Hulpe, 1170 Brussels; tel. (2) 675-57-77; fax (2) 675-52-21; e-mail eukorea@skynet.be; Ambassador Haeng-Kyeom Oh.

Kuwait: 43 ave F. D. Roosevelt, 1050 Brussels; tel. (2) 647-79-50; fax (2) 646-12-98; e-mail embassy.kwt@skynet.be; Ambassador Abdulazeez A. ash-Sharikh.

Kyrgyzstan: 47 rue de l'Abbaye, 1050 Brussels; tel. (2) 640-18-68; fax (2) 640-01-31; Ambassador Chingiz Torekulovitch Aitmatov.

Laos: 19–21 ave de la Brabançonne, 1000 Brussels; tel. (2) 740-09-50; fax (2) 734-16-66; e-mail secretaire@yucom.be; Ambassador Thongphachanh Sonnasinh.

Lebanon: 2 rue Guillaume Stocq, 1050 Brussels; tel. (2) 645-77-65; fax (2) 645-77-69; e-mail ambassade.liban@brutele.be; Ambassador FAWZI FAWAZ.

Lesotho: 44 blvd Général Wahis, 1030 Brussels; tel. (2) 705-39-76; fax (2) 705-67-79; e-mail lesothobrussels@hotmail.com; Ambassador MOLIEHI MATHATO ADEL MATLANYANE.

Liberia: 50 ave du Château, 1081 Brussels; tel. (2) 411-01-12; fax (2) 411-09-12; e-mail liberia.embassy@pro.tiscali.be; Chargéd'affaires a.i. YOUNGOR S. TELEWODA.

Libya: 28 ave Victoria, 1000 Brussels; tel. (2) 649-37-37; fax (2) 640-90-76; Ambassador HAMED AHMED EL HOUDERI.

Liechtenstein: 1 place du Congrès, 1000 Brussels; tel. (2) 229-39-00; fax (2) 219-35-45; e-mail ambassade.liechtenstein@bbru.llv.li; Ambassador Prince NIKOLAUS DE LIECHTENSTEIN.

Macedonia, former Yugoslav republic: 209A ave Louise, 1050 Brussels; tel. (2) 732-91-08; fax (2) 732-91-11; e-mail mk.mission@skynet.be; Ambassador SAŠKO STEFKOV.

Madagascar: 276 ave de Tervuren, 1150 Brussels; tel. (2) 770-17-26; fax (2) 772-37-31; e-mail info@ambassademadagascar.be; internet www.ambassademadagascar.be; Ambassador JEAN OMER BERIZIKY.

Malawi: 15 rue de la Loi, 1040 Brussels; tel. (2) 231-09-80; fax (2) 231-10-66; e-mail malawi.embassy@pi.be; Ambassador JERRY ALEXANDER ALIKOPAGA JANA.

Malaysia: 414A ave de Tervuren, 1150 Brussels; tel. (2) 776-03-40; fax (2) 762-50-49; e-mail mwbrusel@euronet.be; Ambassador Dato' DEVA MOHD RIDZAM BIN ABDULLAH.

Maldives: East 47th St, Apt 15B, New York, NY 10017, USA; tel. (212) 688-0776.

Mali: 487 ave Molière, 1050 Brussels; tel. (2) 345-74-32; fax (2) 344-57-00; e-mail ambamali@skynet.be; Ambassador IBRAHIM B. BA.

Marshall Islands: 800 2nd Ave, 18th Floor, New York, NY 10017, USA; tel. (212) 983-30-40; fax (212) 983-32-02; e-mail rmiun@aol.com.

Mauritania: 6 ave de la Colombie, 1000 Brussels; tel. (2) 672-18-02; fax (2) 672-20-51; e-mail amb.bxl.mauritanie@skynet.be; internet www.mauritania.com; Ambassador ALIOU IBRA BA.

Mauritius: 68 rue des Bollandistes, 1040 Brussels; tel. (2) 733-99-88; fax (2) 734-40-21; e-mail ambmaur@skynet.be; Ambassador SUTIWAN GUNESSEE.

Mexico: 94 ave F. D. Roosevelt, 1050 Brussels; tel. (2) 629-07-11; fax (2) 644-08-19; e-mail embamexbelgica-ue.skynet.be; Ambassador PORFIRIO A. MUÑOZ-LEDO Y LAZO DE LA VEGA.

Moldova: 54 rue Tenbosch, 1050 Brussels; tel. (2) 732-96-59; fax (2) 732-96-60; e-mail moldovamission@brutele.be; Ambassador MIHAI POPOV.

Monaco: 17 place Guy d'Arezzo, 1180 Brussels; tel. (2) 347-49-87; fax (2) 343-49-20; Ambassador JEAN PASTORELLI.

Mongolia: 18 ave Besme, 1190 Brussels; tel. (2) 344-69-74; fax (2) 344-32-15; e-mail brussels.mn.embassy@chello.be; internet users .skynet.be/mongolia; Ambassador ONON SODOV.

Morocco: 275 ave Louise, 1050 Brussels; tel. (2) 626-34-10; fax (2) 626-34-34; e-mail mission.maroc@skynet.be; Ambassador FATH'ALLAH SIJILMASSI.

Mozambique: 97 blvd Saint-Michel, 1040 Brussels; tel. (2) 736-25-64; fax (2) 735-62-07; e-mail embamoc.bru@skynet.be; Ambassador MARIA MANUELA DOS SANTOS LUCAS.

Myanmar: 60 rue de Courcelles, 75008 Paris, France; tel. 1-42-25-56-95; fax 1-42-56-49-41; e-mail me-paris@wanadoo.fr; internet www.myanmarembassyparis.com; Ambassador U WUNNA MAUNG LWIN.

Namibia: 454 ave de Tervuren, 1150 Brussels; tel. (2) 771-14-10; fax (2) 771-96-89; e-mail nam.emb@brutele.be; Ambassador PETER HITJITEVI KATJAVIVI.

Nepal: 68 ave Winston Churchill, 1180 Brussels; tel. (2) 346-26-58; fax (2) 344-13-61; e-mail rne.bru@skynet.be; Ambassador NARAYAN SHUMSHERE THAPA.

New Zealand: 1 square de Meeûs, 1000 Brussels; tel. (2) 512-10-40; fax (2) 513-48-56; e-mail kiwmb.brussels@skynet.be; internet www.nzembassy.com/belgium; Ambassador WADE ARMSTRONG.

Nicaragua: 55 ave de Wolvendael, 1180 Brussels; tel. (2) 375-65-00; fax (2) 375-71-88; e-mail sky77706@skynet.be; Chargé d'affaires a.i. RICARDO PAÚL LIRA.

Niger: 78 ave F. D. Roosevelt, 1050 Brussels; tel. (2) 648-61-40; fax (2) 648-27-84; e-mail ambnigerbxl@advalvas.be; Ambassador ABDOU AGBARRY.

Nigeria: 288 ave de Tervuren, 1150 Brussels; tel. (2) 762-52-00; fax (2) 762-37-63; e-mail nigeriaembassy@belgacom.net; internet www.nigeriabru.net; Chargé d'affaires a.i. V. A. OKOEDION.

Niue: 10 rue Berckmans, 1060 Brussels, Belgium; tel. (2) 543-10-00; fax (2) 543-10-01; e-mail cookislands@prmltd.com; Ambassador TODD MCCLAY.

Norway: 17 rue Archimède, 1000 Brussels; tel. (2) 234-11-11; fax (2) 234-11-50; e-mail eu.brussels@mfa.no; internet www.eu-norway.org; Ambassador BJORN T. GRYDELAND.

Oman: 27 Koninginnegracht, 2514 AB The Hague, Netherlands; tel. (70) 361-58-00; fax (70) 360-53-64; e-mail embassyoman@wanadoo.nl; Ambassador KHADIJA H. S. AL-LAWATI.

Pakistan: 57 ave Delleur, 1170 Brussels; tel. (2) 673-80-07; fax (2) 675-83-94; e-mail parepbrussels@skynet.be; Ambassador TARIQ FATEMI.

Panama: 390–392 ave Louise, 1050 Brussels; tel. (2) 649-07-29; fax (2) 648-92-16; e-mail embajada.panama@skynet.be; Ambassador ROLANDO GUEVARA ALVARADO.

Papua New Guinea: 430 ave de Tervuren, 1150 Brussels; tel. (2) 779-06-09; fax (2) 772-70-88; e-mail kundu.brussels@skynet.be; Chargé d'affaires a.i. KAPI MARO.

Paraguay: 475 ave Louise (12e étage), 1050 Brussels; tel. (2) 649-90-55; fax (2) 647-42-48; e-mail embapar@skynet.be; Ambassador EMILIO GIMENEZ FRANCO.

Peru: 179 ave de Tervuren, 1150 Brussels; tel. (2) 733-33-19; fax (2) 733-48-19; e-mail comunicaciones@embassy-of-peru.be; Ambassador JOSÉ URRUTIA.

Philippines: 297 ave Molière, 1050 Brussels; tel. (2) 340-33-77; fax (2) 345-64-25; e-mail brusselspe@brutele.be; internet www.philembassy.be; Ambassador CLEMENCIO F. MONTESA.

Qatar: 57 quai d'Orsay, 75007 Paris, France; tel. 1-45-51-90-71; fax 1-45-51-77-07; Chargé d'affaires a.i. KHAMIS B. AS-SAHOTI.

Romania: 12 rue Montoyer, 1000 Brussels; tel. (2) 270-00-60; fax (2) 270-00-61; e-mail bru@roumisue.org; internet www.ue.mae.ro; Ambassador LAZAR COMANESCU.

Russia: 31–33 blvd du Régent, 1000 Brussels; tel. (2) 502-18-55; fax (2) 513-76-49; e-mail misrusce@coditel.net; Ambassador Dr VASILIY LIKHACHEV.

Rwanda: 1 ave des Fleurs, 1150 Brussels; tel. (2) 763-07-21; fax (2) 763-07-53; e-mail ambarwanda.@skynet.be; internet www.ambarwanda.be; Ambassador EMMANUEL KAYITANA IMANZI.

Saint Christopher and Nevis: 42 rue de Livourne, 1000 Brussels; tel. (2) 534-26-11; fax (2) 539-40-09; e-mail ecs.embassies@skynet.be; internet www.caribisles.org; Ambassador GEORGE R. E. BULLEN.

Saint Lucia: 42 rue de Livourne, 1000 Brussels; tel. (2) 534-26-11; fax (2) 539-40-09; e-mail ecs.embassies@skynet.be; internet www.caribisles.org; Ambassador GEORGE R. E. BULLEN.

Saint Vincent and the Grenadines: 42 rue de Livourne, 1000 Brussels; tel. (2) 534-26-11; fax (2) 539-40-09; e-mail ecs.embassies@skynet.be; internet www.caribisles.org; Ambassador GEORGE R. E. BULLEN.

Samoa: 20 ave de l'Orée, Boîte 4, 1000 Brussels; tel. (2) 660-84-54; fax (2) 675-03-36; e-mail samoaembassy@skynet.be; Ambassador TAU'ILI'ILI UILI MEREDITH.

San Marino: 62 ave F. D. Roosevelt, 1050 Brussels; tel. (2) 644-22-24; fax (2) 644-20-57; e-mail ambrsm.bxl@coditel.net; Ambassador SAVINA ZAFFERANI.

São Tomé and Príncipe: 175 ave de Tervuren, 1150 Brussels; tel. and fax (2) 734-88-15; e-mail ambassade.sao.tome@skynet.be; Chargé d'affaires a.i. ANTÓNIO DE LIMA VIEGAS.

Saudi Arabia: 45 ave F. D. Roosevelt, 1050 Brussels; tel. (2) 649-20-44; fax (2) 647-24-92; Ambassador NASSER A. H. AL-ASSAF.

Senegal: 196 ave F. D. Roosevelt, 1050 Brussels; tel. (2) 673-00-97; fax (2) 675-04-60; e-mail senegal.ambassade@coditel.net; Ambassador SALIOU CISSE.

Serbia and Montenegro: 19 ave Emile de Mot, 1000 Brussels; tel. (2) 649-82-42; fax (2) 649-08-78; e-mail mission.rfy@skynet.be; Ambassador PAVLE JEVREMOVIĆ.

Seychelles: 51 ave Mozart, 75016 Paris, France; tel. 1-42-30-57-47; fax 1-42-30-57-40; e-mail ambsey@aol.com; Ambassador CALLIXTE FRANÇOIS-XAVIER D'OFFAY.

Sierra Leone: 410 ave de Tervuren, 1150 Brussels; tel. (2) 771-00-53; fax (2) 771-82-30; e-mail sierraleoneembassy@brutele.be; Ambassador FODE MACLEAN DABOR.

Singapore: 198 ave F. D. Roosevelt, 1050 Brussels; tel. (2) 660-29-79; fax (2) 660-86-85; e-mail amb.eu@singembbru.be; Ambassador WALTER WOON.

Solomon Islands: 17 ave Edouard Lacomblé, 1040 Brussels; tel. (2) 732-70-85; fax (2) 732-68-85; e-mail siembassy@compuserve.com; internet www.commerce.gov.sb; Ambassador Robert Sisilo.

South Africa: 26 rue de la Loi, Boîtes 7–8, 1040 Brussels; tel. (2) 285-44-00; fax (2) 285-44-02; e-mail embassy@southafrica.be; internet www.ambassade.net/southafrica/index.html; Ambassador Jerry M. Matjila.

Sri Lanka: 27 rue Jules Lejeune, 1050 Brussels; tel. (2) 344-53-94; fax (2) 344-67-37; e-mail sri.lanka@tiscali.be; Ambassador Chrysantha R. Jayasinghe.

Sudan: 124 ave F. D. Roosevelt, 1050 Brussels; tel. (2) 647-51-59; fax (2) 648-34-99; e-mail sudanbxl@yahoo.com; Ambassador Dr Ali Yousef Ahmed.

Suriname: 379 ave Louise, 1050 Brussels; tel. (2) 640-11-72; fax (2) 646-39-62; e-mail sur.amb.bru@online.be; Ambassador Gerard Otmar Hiwat.

Swaziland: 188 ave Winston Churchill, 1180 Brussels; tel. (2) 347-47-71; fax (2) 347-46-23; Ambassador Dr Thembayena Annastasia Dlamini.

Switzerland: 1 place du Luxembourg, 1050 Brussels; tel. (2) 286-13-11; fax (2) 230-45-09; e-mail vertretung@brm.rep.admin.ch; internet www.eda.admin.ch/brussels_miss/f/home.html; Ambassador Bernhard Marfurt.

Syria: 3 ave F. D. Roosevelt, 1050 Brussels; tel. (2) 648-01-35; fax (2) 646-40-18; Ambassador Toufic Salloum.

Tajikistan: 363–365 ave Louise, BP 14, 1050 Brussels; tel. (2) 640-69-33; fax (2) 649-01-95; e-mail tajemb-belgium@skynet.be; Ambassador Sharif Rakhimov.

Tanzania: 363 ave Louise (7e étage), 1050 Brussels; tel. (2) 640-65-00; fax (2) 646-80-26; e-mail tanzania@skynet.be; Ambassador Ali Abeid Aman Karume.

Thailand: 2 square du Val de la Cambre, 1050 Brussels; tel. (2) 640-68-10; fax (2) 648-30-66; e-mail thaibxl@pophost.eunet.be; internet www.waw.be/rte-be; Ambassador (vacant).

Timor-Leste: 12 ave Cortenbergh, 1000 Brussels; tel. (2) 280-00-96; fax (2) 280-02-77; Ambassador José Antonio Amorim Dias.

Togo: 264 ave de Tervuren, 1150 Brussels; tel. (2) 770-17-91; fax (2) 771-50-75; Ambassador Kati Ohara Korga.

Tonga: 36 Molyneux St, London, W1H 5BQ, United Kingdom; tel. (20) 7724-5828; fax (20) 7723-9074; e-mail fetu@btinternet.com; Ambassador Col Fetu'utolu Tupou.

Trinidad and Tobago: 14 ave de la Faisanderie, 1150 Brussels; tel. (2) 762-94-00; fax (2) 772-27-83; e-mail info@embtrinbago.be; Ambassador Learie Rousseau.

Tunisia: 278 ave de Tervuren, 1150 Brussels; tel. (2) 771-73-95; fax (2) 771-94-33; e-mail amb.detunisie@brutele.be; Ambassador Mehrez Ben Rhouma.

Turkey: 4 rue Montoyer, 1000 Brussels; tel. (2) 513-28-36; fax (2) 511-04-50; e-mail info@turkdeleg.org; Ambassador Oguz Demiralp.

Turkmenistan: 106 ave F. D. Roosevelt, 1050 Brussels; tel. (2) 648-18-74; fax (2) 648-19-06; Ambassador Niyazklych Nurklychev.

Uganda: 317 ave de Tervuren, 1150 Brussels; tel. (2) 762-58-25; fax (2) 763-04-38; e-mail ugembrus@brutele.be; Chargé d'affaires Lewis D. Balinda.

Ukraine: 99–101 ave Louis Lepoutre, 1180 Brussels; tel. (2) 340-98-60; fax (2) 340-98-79; e-mail pm_eu@mfa.gov.ua; internet www.ukraine-eu.mfa.gov.ua; Ambassador Roman Shpek.

United Arab Emirates: 73 ave F. D. Roosevelt, 1050 Brussels; tel. (2) 640-60-00; fax (2) 646-24-73; e-mail uae_embassy@skynet.be; Ambassador Abdel Hadi Abdel Wahid al-Khaja.

USA: 13 rue Zinner, 1000 Brussels; tel. (2) 508-22-22; fax (2) 512-57-20; e-mail useu-pa@state.gov; internet www.useu.be; Ambassador Rockwell A. Schnabel.

Uruguay: 22 ave F. D. Roosevelt, 1050 Brussels; tel. (2) 640-11-69; fax (2) 648-29-09; e-mail uruemb@skynet.be; Ambassador Elbio Oscar Rosselli Frieri.

Uzbekistan: 99 ave F. D. Roosevelt, 1050 Brussels; tel. (2) 672-88-44; fax (2) 672-39-46; e-mail eumission@uzbekistan.be; internet www.eu.uzbekembassy.com; Ambassador Alisher Shaykhov.

Venezuela: 10 ave F. D. Roosevelt, 1050 Brussels; tel. (2) 639-03-40; fax (2) 647-88-20; e-mail embajada@venezuela-eu.org; internet www.venezuela-eu.org; Ambassador Luisa Romero-Bermúdez.

Viet Nam: 1 blvd Général Jacques, 1050 Brussels; tel. (2) 379-27-37; fax (2) 374-93-76; e-mail vnem.brussels@skynet.be; internet vietnamfestival.com; Ambassador Phan Thuy Thanh.

Yemen: 114 ave F. D. Roosevelt, 1050 Brussels; tel. (2) 646-52-90; fax (2) 646-29-11; e-mail gazem@skynet.be; Ambassador Dr Jaffer Mohamed Jaffer.

Zambia: 469 ave Molière, 1060 Brussels; tel. (2) 343-56-49; fax (2) 347-43-33; e-mail zambiansbrussels@skynet.be; Ambassador Irene Mumba Kamanga.

Zimbabwe: 11 square Joséphine Charlotte, 1200 Brussels; tel. (2) 762-58-08; fax (2) 762-96-05; e-mail zimbrussels@skynet.be; Ambassador Gift Punungwe.

Union Institutions

EUROPEAN COMMISSION

Address: 200 rue de la Loi, 1049 Brussels, Belgium.

Telephone: (2) 299-11-11; **fax:** (2) 295-01-38; **e-mail:** forename.surname@cec.eu.int; **internet:** www.europa.eu.int/index-en.htm.

Please note: in an e-mail address when the forename and/or the surname are composed of more than one word, the different words are linked by a hyphen. If help is needed, you may send a message to address-information@cec.eu.int requesting the correct e-mail address of the correspondent.

Members of the Commission
(March 2005)

President: José Manuel Durão Barroso (Portugal).

Vice President, responsible for Institutional Relations and Communication Strategy: Margot Wallström (Sweden).

Vice President, responsible for Enterprise and Industry: Günter Verheugen (Germany).

Vice President, responsible for Transport: Jacques Barrot (France).

Vice President, responsible for Administrative Affairs, Audit and Anti-fraud: Siim Kallas (Estonia).

Vice President, responsible for Justice, Freedom and Security: Franco Frattini (Italy).

Commissioner, responsible for Information Society and Media: Viviane Reding (Luxembourg).

Commissioner, responsible for the Environment: Stavros Dimas (Greece).

Commissioner, responsible for Economic and Monetary Affairs: Joaquín Almunia (Spain).

Commissioner, responsible for Regional Policy: Danuta Hübner (Poland).

Commissioner, responsible for Fisheries and Maritime Affairs: Joe Borg (Malta).

Commissioner, responsible for Financial Programming and the Budget: Dalia Grybauskaitė (Lithuania).

Commissioner, responsible for Science and Research: Janez Potočnik (Slovenia).

Commissioner, responsible for Education, Training, Culture and Multilingualism: Ján Figel (Slovakia).

Commissioner, responsible for Health and Consumer Protection: Markos Kyprianou (Cyprus).

Commissioner, responsible for Enlargement: Olli Rehn (Finland).

Commissioner, responsible for Development and Humanitarian Aid: Louis Michel (Belgium).

Commissioner, responsible for Energy: Andris Piebalgs (Latvia).

Commissioner, responsible for Competition: Neelie Kroes-Smit (Netherlands).

Commissioner, responsible for Agriculture and Rural Development: Mariann Fischer Boel (Denmark).

Commissioner, responsible for External Relations and European Neighbourhood Policy: Benita Ferrero-Waldner (Austria).

Commissioner, responsible for the Internal Market and Services: Charlie McCreevy (Ireland).

Commissioner, responsible for Employment, Social Affairs and Equal Opportunities: Vladimír Špidla (Czech Republic).

Commissioner, responsible for Trade: Peter Mandelson (United Kingdom).

Commissioner, responsible for Taxation and Customs Union: László Kovács (Hungary).

European Union

The European Commission, like the European Parliament and Council of the European Union, was established in the 1950s under the EU's founding Treaties. The functions of the Commission are fourfold: to propose legislation to the European Parliament and the Council of the European Union; to implement EU policies and programmes adopted by the European Parliament and to manage and implement the budget; to enforce European law, in conjunction with the Court of Justice, in all the member states; and to represent the EU in international affairs and to negotiate agreements between the EU and other organizations or countries.

A new Commission is appointed for a five-year term, within six months of the elections to the European Parliament. The Governments of the member states agree on an individual to designate as the new Commission President. The President-designate then selects the other members of the Commission, following discussions with the member state Governments. In the performance of their duties, the members of the Commission are forbidden to seek or accept instructions from any government or other body, or to engage in any other paid or unpaid professional activity. The nominated President and other members of the Commission must be approved as a body by the European Parliament before they can take office. Once approved, the Commission may nominate a number of its members as Vice President. Any member of the Commission, if he or she no longer fulfils the conditions required for the performance of his or her duties, or commits a serious offence, may be declared removed from office by the Court of Justice. The Court may furthermore, on the petition of the Council of the European Union or of the Commission itself, provisionally suspend any member of the Commission from his or her duties. The European Parliament has the authority to dismiss the entire Commission by adopting a motion of censure. The number of members of the Commission may be amended by a unanimous vote of the Council of the European Union.

The members of the Commission, also known as the College, meet once a week and a collective decision is made on policy following a presentation by the relevant Commissioner. The Commission's staff is organized into 36 departments, known as Directorates-General and services. The Directorates-General are each responsible for a particular policy area and they devise and draft the Commission's legislative proposals, which become official when adopted by the Commission at the weekly meeting.

In January 1999 Commissioners accused of mismanagement and corruption retained their positions following a vote of censure by Parliament. However, Parliament proceeded to appoint a five-member Committee of Independent Experts to investigate allegations of fraud, mismanagement and nepotism within the Commission. In early March two new codes of conduct for Commissioners were announced. On 15 March the Committee published a report that criticized the Commission's failure to control the administration and to take responsibility for the budget and other measures implemented by each department. The report also identified individual Commissioners as guilty of nepotism and mismanagement and proposed the establishment of a new independent unit to investigate fraud. As a consequence of the report the Commission agreed, collectively, to resign, although Commissioners were to retain their positions, and exercise limited duties, until their successors were appointed. In late March EU Heads of State and of Government nominated Romano Prodi, the former Italian Prime Minister, as the next President of the Commission. His appointment, and the team of Commissioners that he had appointed in the interim, were duly ratified by Parliament in September. However, Parliament made ratification subject to conditions, forming the foundation of a future inter-institutional agreement between itself and the Commission: while it did not lose any of its powers, the Commission undertook to be more open in its future dealings with the Parliament. The Commission's term of office was to expire on 31 October 2004.

On 1 May 2004, following the accession of 10 new member states, the 20 existing members of the Commission were joined by 10 new members (one from each new member state). For the first six months of their term of office, although considered full members, they were to work alongside existing Commissioners and were not allocated their own departments. From 1 November 2004, when a new Commission was to begin its mandate, there were to be 25 members of the Commission, one from each member state (prior to 1 May 2004 large countries were allowed two Commissioners while the smaller countries had one). In late October, however, the incoming President of the European Commission, José Manuel Durão Barroso, was forced to withdraw his proposed team of commissioners and to reconsider the composition of his Commission to avoid an unprecedented defeat in the scheduled parliamentary investiture vote in the European Parliament on 27 October. The reconstituted Commission (two members were replaced and one was allocated a new portfolio) was approved by the European Parliament and finally took office on 22 November 2004.

In January 2004 the Commission launched legal proceedings against the Economic and Financial Council of Ministers (ECOFIN—which comprises the national ministers responsible for

finance), one of the formats of the Council of the European Union. The Commission was seeking a ruling from the European Court of Justice on the legality of ECOFIN's decision to suspend disciplinary procedures against France and Germany, both of which were intending to exceed the budget deficit limit of 3% of gross domestic product (GDP), imposed under the Stability and Growth Pact, for the third consecutive year. In July the European Court of Justice ruled that ECOFIN's intervention was not compatible with EU legislation but that ministers retained ultimate control over the implementation of the pact.

DIRECTORATES-GENERAL AND SERVICES

General Services

European Anti-Fraud Office: 30 rue Joseph II, 1000 Brussels; tel. (2) 296-54-25; fax (2) 296-08-53; e-mail olaf-courrier@cec.eu.int; internet www.europa.eu.int/olaf; Dir-Gen. FRANZ-HERMANN BRÜNER.

Eurostat (Statistical Office of the European Communities): Bâtiment Jean Monnet, rue Alcide de Gasperi, 2920 Luxembourg; tel. 43-01-33-048; fax 43-01-35-349; e-mail eurostat-mediasupport@cec.eu.int; internet www.europa.eu.int/comm/eurostat; Dir-Gen. GÜNTHER HANREICH.

Directorate-General Press and Communication Service: 45 ave d'Auderghem, 1049 Brussels; tel. (2) 299-11-11; fax (2) 295-01-43; e-mail forename.surname@cec.eu.int; internet www.europa.eu.int/comm/dgs/press_communication/index_en.htm; Dir-Gen. JORGE DE OLIVEIRA E SOUSA.

Office for Official Publications of the European Communities (Office des Publications Officielles des Communautés—OPOCE): 2 rue Mercier, 2985 Luxembourg; tel. 29-291; fax 29-29-44-619; e-mail info-info-opoce@cec.eu.int; internet www.publications.eu.int; Dir-Gen. THOMAS L. CRANFIELD.

Secretariat-General of the Commission: 45 ave d'Auderghem, 1049 Brussels; tel. (2) 299-11-11; fax (2) 296-05-54; e-mail sg-info@cec.eu.int; internet www.europa.eu.int/comm/dgs/secretariat_general/index_en.htm; Sec.-Gen. DAVID O'SULLIVAN.

Policies

Agriculture Directorate-General: 130 rue de la Loi, 1040 Brussels; tel. (2) 295-32-40; fax (2) 295-01-30; e-mail agri-library@cec.eu.int; internet www.europa.eu.int/comm/dgs/agriculture/index_en.htm; Dir-Gen. JOSÉ MANUEL SILVA RODRÍGUEZ.

Competition Directorate-General: 70 rue Joseph II, Brussels; tel. (2) 299-11-11; fax (2) 296-59-93; e-mail infocomp@cec.eu.int; internet www.europa.eu.int/comm/competition/index_en.htm; Dir-Gen. PHILIP LOWE.

Directorate-General for Economic and Financial Affairs: 1 ave de Beaulieu, 1160 Brussels; tel. (2) 299-11-11; fax (2) 296-94-28; e-mail ecfin-info@cec.eu.int; internet www.europa.eu.int/comm/dgs/economic_financial_affairs/index_en.htm; Dir-Gen. KLAUS REGLING.

Directorate-General for Education and Culture: 2 rue Van Maerlant, 1040 Brussels; tel. (2) 299-11-11; fax (2) 295-60-85; e-mail eac-info@cec.eu.int; internet www.europa.eu.int/comm/dgs/education_culture/index_en.htm; Dir-Gen. NIKOLAUS VAN DER PAS.

Directorate-General for Employment, Social Affairs and Equal Opportunities: 27 and 37 rue Joseph II, 1000 Brussels; tel. (2) 299-11-11; fax (2) 295-65-07; e-mail empl-info@cec.eu.int; internet www.europa.eu.int/comm/dgs/employment_social/index.en.htm; Dir-Gen. ODILE QUINTIN.

Enterprise and Industry Directorate-General: 15 rue de la Science, 1040 Brussels; tel. (2) 299-11-11; fax (2) 295-97-92; e-mail info-enterprises@cec.eu.int; internet www.europa.eu.int/comm/dgs/enterprise/index_en.htm; Dir-Gen. HORST REICHENBACH.

Directorate-General for the Environment: 5 ave de Beaulieu, 1160 Brussels; tel. (2) 299-11-11; fax (2) 299-11-05; e-mail envinfo@cec.eu.int; internet www.europa.eu.int/comm/dgs/environment/index_en.htm; Dir-Gen. CATHERINE DAY.

Fisheries and Maritime Affairs Directorate-General: 99 rue de Joseph II, 1000 Brussels; tel. (2) 299-11-11; fax (2) 295-25-69; e-mail fisheries-info@cec.eu.int; internet www.europa.eu.int/comm/dgs/fisheries/index_en.htm; Dir-Gen. JÖRGEN HOLMQUIST.

Health and Consumer Protection Directorate-General: 232 rue Belliard, 1040 Brussels; tel. (2) 299-11-11; fax (2) 296-62-98; e-mail sanco-mailbox@cec.eu.int; internet www.europa.eu.int/comm/dgs/health_consumer/index_en.htm; Dir-Gen. ROBERT MADELIN.

Information Society and Media Directorate-General: 24 ave Beaulieu, 1060 Brussels; tel. (2) 296-88-00; fax (2) 299-41-70; e-mail infso-desk@cec.eu.int; internet www.europa.eu.int/comm/dgs/information_society/index_en.htm; Dir-Gen. FABIO COLASANTI.

Internal Market and Services Directorate-General: 107 ave de Cortenbergh, 1000 Brussels; tel. (2) 299-11-11; fax (2) 295-65-00; e-mail markt-info@cec.eu.int; internet www.europa.eu.int/comm/dgs/internal_market/index_en.htm; Dir-Gen. ALEXANDER SCHAUB.

Joint Research Centre (JRC): 8 square de Meeûs, 1000 Brussels; tel. (2) 299-11-11; fax (2) 295-05-46; e-mail forename.surname@cec.eu.int; internet www.jrc.cec.eu.int; Acting Dir-Gen. ROLAND SCHENKEL.

Directorate-General for Justice, Freedom and Security: 46 rue du Luxembourg, 1050 Brussels; tel. (2) 299-11-11; fax (2) 296-74-81; e-mail forename.surname@cec.eu.int; internet www.europa.eu.int/comm/dgs/justice_home/index_en.htm; Dir-Gen. JONATHAN FAULL.

Regional Policy Directorate-General: 23 rue Père de Deken, 1040 Brussels; tel. (2) 299-11-11; fax (2) 295-01-49; e-mail dgregio@inforegio.cec.eu.int; internet www.europa.eu.int/comm/dgs/regional_policy/index_en.htm; Dir-Gen. GRAHAM MEADOWS.

Research Directorate-General: 8 square de Meeûs, 1000 Brussels; tel. (2) 299-11-11; fax (2) 295-01-45; e-mail research@cec.eu.int; internet www.europa.eu.int/comm/dgs/research/index_en.htm; Dir-Gen. ACHILLEAS MITSOS.

Directorate-General for Taxation and the Customs Union: 59 rue Montoyer, 1000 Brussels; tel. (2) 299-11-11; fax (2) 295-07-56; e-mail librarian-information@cec.eu.int; internet www.europa.eu.int/comm/dgs/taxation_customs/index_en.htm; Dir-Gen. ROBERT VERRUE.

Directorate-General for Transport and Energy: 28 rue de Mot, 1040 Brussels; tel. (2) 299-11-11; fax (2) 295-01-50; e-mail tren-info@cec.eu.int; internet www.europa.eu.int/comm/dgs; Dir-Gen. FRANÇOIS LAMOUREUX.

External Relations

Directorate-General for Development (DG DEV): 12 rue de Genève, 1140 Brussels; tel. (2) 299-11-11; fax (2) 299-10-25; e-mail development@cec.eu.int; internet www.europa.eu.int/comm/dgs/development/index_en.htm; Dir-Gen. STEFANO MANSERVISI.

Directorate-General for Enlargement: 170 rue de la Loi, 1040 Brussels; tel. (2) 299-11-11; fax (2) 296-84-90; e-mail elarg-info@cec.eu.int; internet www.europa.eu.int/comm/dgs/enlargement/index_en.htm; Acting Dir-Gen. FABRIZIO BARBASO.

EuropeAid Co-operation Office: 41 rue de la Loi, 1040 Brussels; tel. (2) 299-32-71; fax (2) 296-94-89; e-mail forename.surname@cec.eu.int; internet www.europa.eu.int/comm/europeaid/general; Dir-Gen. KOOS RICHELLE.

External Relations Directorate-General: 170 rue de la Loi, 1040 Brussels; tel. (2) 299-11-11; fax (2) 299-65-29; e-mail relex-feedback@cec.eu.int; internet www.europa.eu.int/comm/dgs/external_relations/index_en.htm; Dir-Gen. ENEKO LANDÁBURU ILLARRAMENDI.

Humanitarian Aid Office (ECHO): 1 rue de Genève, 1140 Brussels; tel. (2) 299-11-11; fax (2) 295-45-78; e-mail echo-info@cec.eu.int; internet www.europa.eu.int/comm/dgs/humanitarian_aid/index_en.htm; Dir ANTÓNIO CAVACO.

Directorate-General for Trade (DG Trade): 170 rue de la Loi, 1140 Brussels; tel. (2) 299-11-11; fax (2) 299-10-29; e-mail trade-unit3@cec.eu.int; internet www.europa.eu.int/comm/dgs/trade/index_en.htm; Dir-Gen. MOGENS PETER CARL.

Internal Services

Budget Directorate-General: 19 ave d'Auderghem, 1040 Brussels; tel. (2) 299-11-11; fax (2) 295-95-85; e-mail budget@cec.eu.int; internet www.europa.eu.int/comm/dgs/budget/index_en.htm; Dir-Gen. LUIS ROMERO REQUENA.

Group of Policy Advisers: 45 ave d'Auderghem, 1040 Brussels; tel. (2) 299-11-11; fax (2) 295-23-05; e-mail forename.surname@cec.eu.int; internet www.europa.eu.int/comm/dgs/policy_advisers/index_en.htm; Dir CARLOS TAVARES.

Directorate General for Informatics: e-mail DIGIT-EUROPA@cec.eu.int; Dir-Gen. FRANCISCO GARCÍA MORÁN.

Office for Infrastructure and Logistics: e-mail oib-info@cec.eu.int; Dir P. VERLEYSEN.

Internal Audit Service: 200 rue de la Loi, 1049 Brussels; tel. (2) 299-11-11; fax (2) 295-41-40; e-mail ias-europa@cec.eu.int; internet www.europa.eu.int/comm/dgs/internal_audit/index_en.htm; Dir-Gen. WALTER DEFFAA.

Directorate-General for Interpretation: 24 rue de Mot, 1049 Brussels; tel. (2) 299-11-11; fax (2) 295-95-84; e-mail euroscic@cec.eu.int; internet www.europa.eu.int/comm/dgs/interpretation/index_en.htm; Head of Service MARCO BENEDETTI.

Legal Service: 85 ave des Nerviens, 1049 Brussels; tel. (2) 299-11-11; fax (2) 296-30-86; e-mail forename.surname@cec.eu.int; internet www.europa.eu.int/comm/dgs/legal_service/index_en.htm; Dir-Gen. MICHEL PETITE.

Personnel and Administration Directorate-General: 11 rue de la Science, 1000 Brussels; tel. (2) 299-11-11; fax (2) 299-62-76; e-mail forename.surname@cec.eu.int; internet www.europa.eu.int/comm/dgs/personnel_administration/index_en.htm; Dir-Gen. CLAUDE CHÈNE.

Directorate-General for Translation (DGT): 1 ave de Cortenbergh, 1049 Brussels; tel. (2) 299-11-11; fax (2) 295-65-03; e-mail sdt-webmaster@cec.eu.int; internet www.europa.eu.int/comm/dgs/translation/index_en.htm; Dir-Gen. KARL-JOHAN LÖNNROTH.

EUROPEAN COUNCIL

The European Council is the name used to describe summit meetings of the Heads of State or of Government of the EU member states, their foreign ministers, and senior officials of the European Commission. The Council meets at least twice a year, in the member state that currently exercises the Presidency of the Council of the European Union, or in Brussels.

Until 1975 summit meetings were held less frequently, on an *ad hoc* basis, usually to adopt major policy decisions regarding the future development of the Community. In answer to the evident need for more frequent consultation at the highest level, it was decided at the summit meeting in Paris, in December 1974, to hold the meetings on a regular basis, under the rubric of the European Council. There was no provision made for the existence of the European Council in the Treaty of Rome, but its position was acknowledged and regularized in the Single European Act (1987). Its role was further strengthened in the Treaty on European Union, which entered into force on 1 November 1993. As a result of the Treaty, the European Council became directly responsible for common policies within the fields of Common Foreign and Security Policy and Justice and Home Affairs.

When policy decisions are taken by the European Council that conform to the constitutional requirements of the founding treaties, they have the force of EC legislation. More generally, however, European Council agreements are framed as general principles or a broad consensus on future action, which are subsequently transferred to the European Commission and the Council of the European Union for further investigation, discussion and possible adoption.

COUNCIL OF THE EUROPEAN UNION

Address: Justus Lipsius Bldg, 175 rue de la Loi, 1048 Brussels, Belgium.

Telephone: (2) 285-65-41; **fax:** (2) 285-87-74; **e-mail:** public.relations@consilium.eu.int; **internet:** ue.eu.int.

The Council of the European Union (until November 1993 known formally as the Council of Ministers of the European Communities and still frequently referred to as the Council of Ministers) is the only institution that directly represents the member states. It is the Community's principal decision-making body, acting, as a rule, only on proposals made by the Commission, and has six key responsibilities: to pass EC legislation (in many fields it legislates jointly with the European Parliament); to co-ordinate the broad economic policies of the member states; to conclude international agreements between the EU and one or more states or international organizations; to approve the EU budget (in conjunction with the European Parliament); to develop the EU's Common Foreign and Security Policy (CFSP), on the basis of guide-lines drawn up by the European Council; and to co-ordinate co-operation between the national courts and police forces in criminal matters. The Council is composed of representatives of the member states, each Government delegating to it one of its members, according to the subject to be discussed (the Council has nine different configurations). These meetings are generally referred to as the Agriculture and Fisheries Council, the Transport, Telecommunications and Energy Council, etc. The General Affairs and External Relations Council, the Economic and Financial Affairs Council (ECOFIN) and the Agriculture and Fisheries Council each normally meet once a month. The Presidency is exercised for a term of six months by each member of the Council in rotation (January–June 2005: Luxembourg; July–December 2005: the United Kingdom; January–June 2006: Austria; July–December 2006 Finland). The foreign minister of the state currently holding the Presidency (which coincides with that of the European Council) becomes President of the Council and is responsible during those six months for organizing the business of the Council, in conjunction with the General Secretariat. Meetings of the Council are convened and :chaired by the President, acting on his or her own initiative or at the request of a member or of the Commission.

The Treaty of Rome prescribed three types of voting (depending on the issue under discussion): simple majority, qualified majority and unanimity. Prior to May 2004 the votes of its members were weighted as follows: France, Germany, Italy and the United Kingdom 10 votes each; Spain eight votes; Belgium, Greece, the Netherlands and Portugal five votes each; Austria and Sweden four votes each; Denmark, Finland and Ireland three votes each; and Luxembourg two votes. Out of a total number of votes of 87, 62 were required for a qualified majority decision, making 26 votes sufficient for a blocking minority. During negotiations regarding the impending enlargement of the EU, an agreement was reached, in March 1994, on new rules regulating voting procedures in the expanded Council, in response to concerns on the part of Spain and the United Kingdom that their individual influence would be diminished. Under the 'Ioannina compromise' (named after the Greek town where the agreement was concluded), 23–25 opposing votes ensured the continued debate of legislation for a 'reasonable period' until a consensus decision was reached. Amendments to the Treaty of Rome (the Single European Act), effective from July 1987, restricted the right of 'veto', and were expected to accelerate the development of a genuine common market: they allowed proposals relating to the dismantling of barriers to the free movement of goods, persons, services and capital to be approved by a majority vote in the Council, rather than by a unanimous vote. Unanimity would still be required, however, for certain areas, including harmonization of indirect taxes, legislation on health and safety, veterinary controls, and environmental protection; individual states would also retain control over immigration rules, prevention of terrorism and drugs-trafficking. The Treaty of Amsterdam, which came into force on 1 May 1999, extended the use of qualified majority voting (QMV) to a number of areas previously subject to unanimous decision. Under the terms of the Treaty of Nice, which came into force on 1 February 2003, a further range of areas (mostly minor in nature and relating to appointments to various EU institutions) that had previously been subject to national vetoes became subject to QMV. With the expansion of the EU to 25 members in 2004 and the decreased likelihood of Council decisions being unanimous, the use of QMV in an even broader range of decisions was expected to minimize so-called 'policy drag'.

The Single European Act introduced a 'co-operation procedure' whereby a proposal adopted by a qualified majority in the Council must be submitted to the European Parliament for approval: if the Parliament rejects the Council's common position, unanimity shall be required for the Council to act on a second reading, and if the Parliament suggests amendments, the Commission must re-examine the proposal and forward it to the Council again. A 'co-decision procedure' was introduced in 1993 by the Treaty on European Union. The procedure allows a proposal to be submitted for a third reading by a so-called 'Conciliation Committee', composed equally of Council representatives and members of the European Parliament. The Treaty of Amsterdam simplified the co-decision procedure, and extended it to matters previously resolved under the co-operation procedure, although the latter remained in place for matters concerning economic and monetary union.

Under the Treaty of Amsterdam, the Secretary-General of the Council also took the role of 'High Representative', responsible for the co-ordination of the common foreign and security policy. The Secretary-General is supported by a policy planning and early warning unit. In June 1999 Javier Solana Madariaga, at that time Secretary-General of NATO, was designated as the first Secretary-General of the Council.

The Treaty of Nice, which came into force in February 2003, addresses institutional issues that remained outstanding under the Treaty of Amsterdam and that had to be settled before the enlargement of the EU in 2004, and various other issues not directly connected with enlargement. The main focus of the Treaty is the establishment of principles governing the new distribution of seats in the European Parliament, the new composition of the Commission and a new definition of QMV within the Council of the European Union. From 1 May 2004 (when the 10 accession states joined the EU) until 31 October 2004 there were transitional arrangements for changing the weighting of votes in the Council. In accordance with the provisions incorporated in the Treaty of Nice, from 1 November 2004 the new weighting system would be as follows: France, Germany, Italy and the United Kingdom 29 votes each; Poland and Spain 27 votes each; the Netherlands 13 votes; Belgium, the Czech Republic, Greece, Hungary and Portugal 12 votes each; Austria and Sweden 10 votes each; Denmark, Finland, Ireland, Lithuania and Slovakia seven votes each; Cyprus, Estonia, Latvia, Luxembourg and Slovenia four votes each; and Malta three votes. From this date a qualified majority was to be reached if a majority of member states (in some cases a two-thirds' majority) approve and if a minimum of 232 votes out of a total of 321 is cast in favour (which is 72.3% of the total—approximately the same share as under the previous system). In addition, a member state may request confirmation that the votes in favour represent at least 62% of the total population of the EU. Should this not be the case, the decision would not be adopted by the Council. The number of weighted votes required for the adoption of a decision (referred to as the 'qualified majority threshold') was to be reassessed on the accession of any additional new member state. However, it was widely held that the voting system according to the Treaty of Nice was overly complicated and that it gave undue power to certain less populous countries, notably Spain and Poland (which both held 27 votes each, compared with Germany, which, with a population of at least twice the size of those in Spain and Poland, controlled 29 votes—only two votes more). Accordingly, the draft treaty establishing a constitution for the EU, which was published by the Convention on the Future of Europe in mid-2003, proposed a simpler system of voting for the Council—a vote could be passed when it had the support of 50% of the member states representing at least 60% of the EU's population. Not surprisingly, Spain and Poland rejected these proposals (which would entail a considerable diminution of their voting strength), and the European Council summit meeting that was held in Brussels in December to discuss the draft constitution collapsed as a result of the *impasse* over voting rights. Following intense negotiations, a compromise was achieved under the auspices of the incumbent President of the Council of the European Union, the Irish Prime Minister, Bertie Ahern, and the European Council finally approved text of the constitution at a summit meeting in Brussels on 18 June 2004. Part of the compromise package was a proposed new system of voting weights for member states in the Council of the European Union (measures would require the support of at least 55% of the EU member states, comprising 15 of them, representing at least 65% of the total population, in order to be passed). The compromise reached over voting rights meant that smaller member states—particularly the new Eastern European members—could not be simply overruled by a small but powerful group of more long-standing members, such as France, Germany and the United Kingdom.

PERMANENT REPRESENTATIVES

Preparation and co-ordination of the Council's work (with the exception of agricultural issues, which are handled by the Special Committee on Agriculture) is entrusted to a Committee of Permanent Representatives (COREPER), which meets in Brussels on a weekly basis and which consists of the permanent representatives of the member countries to the Union (who have senior ambassadorial status). A staff of national civil servants assists each ambassador.

GENERAL SECRETARIAT

Secretary-General and High Representative for Common Foreign and Security Policy: JAVIER SOLANA MADARIAGA.

Deputy Secretary-General: PIERRE DE BOISSIEU.

Secretary-General's Private Office: Dir, High Representative and Head of Cabinet ALBERTO NAVARRO GONZÁLEZ.

Directorate for General Political Questions: Dir MAX J. KELLER-NOËLLET.

Legal Service: Dir-Gen./Legal Adviser JEAN-CLAUDE PIRIS.

Directorates-General:

A (Personnel and Administration): Dir-Gen. VITTORIO GIFFO.

B (Agriculture and Fisheries): Dir-Gen. ÁNGEL BOIXAREU CARRERA.

C (Internal Market; Customs Union; Industrial Policy; Telecommunications; Information Society; Research; Energy; Transport): Dir-Gen. KLAUS GRETSCHMANN.

E (External Economic Relations; Common Foreign and Security Policy) (*): Dir-Gen. ROBERT COOPER.

F (Press, Communications and Protocol): Dir-Gen./Head of Protocol HANS BRUNMAYR.

G (Economic and Social Affairs): Dir-Gen. SIXTEN KORKMAN.

H (Justice and Home Affairs): Dir-Gen. CHARLES ELSEN.

I (Protection of the Environment and of Consumers; Civil Protection; Health; Food Legislation; Drug Addiction; AIDS; Education and Youth; Culture; Audio-visual Media): Dir-Gen. KERSTIN NIBLAEUS.

* Directorate-General D no longer exists.

EUROPEAN PARLIAMENT

Address: Centre Européen, Plateau du Kirchberg, BP 1601, 2929 Luxembourg.

Telephone: 4300-1; **fax:** 4300-29494; **internet:** www.europarl.eu.int.

PRESIDENT AND MEMBERS
(March 2005)

President: JOSEP BORRELL FONTELLES (Spain).

Members: According to the Treaty of Nice, which came into force in February 2003, following the accession of the 10 new member states in May 2004 the next Parliament (elected in June 2004) was composed of 732 members and the distribution of seats among the 25 members was as follows: Germany 99 members; France, Italy and the United Kingdom 78 members each; Spain and Poland 54; the Netherlands 27; Belgium, Greece, Portugal, the Czech Republic and Hungary 24 each; Sweden 19; Austria 18; Denmark, Finland and Slovakia 14 each; Ireland and Lithuania 13; Latvia nine; Slovenia seven; Luxembourg, Cyprus and Estonia six each; and Malta five. Members are elected for a five-year term by direct universal suffrage by the citizens of the member states. Members sit in the Chamber in transnational political, not national, groups.

The European Parliament has three main roles: sharing with the Council of the European Union the power to legislate; holding authority over the annual Union budget (again, jointly with the Council), including the power to adopt or reject it in its entirety; and exercising a measure of democratic control over the executive organs of the European Communities, the Commission and the Council. Notably, it has the power to dismiss the European Commission as a whole by a vote of censure (requiring a two-thirds' majority of the votes cast, which must also be a majority of the total parliamentary membership)—the Parliament does not exercise the authority, however, to dismiss individual Commissioners. Increases in parliamentary powers have been brought about through amendments to the Treaty of Rome. The Single European Act, which entered into force on 1 July 1987, introduced, in certain circumstances where the Council normally adopts legislation through majority voting, a co-operation procedure involving a second parliamentary reading, enabling the Parliament to amend legislation. Community agreements with third countries require parliamentary approval. The Treaty on European Union, which came into force in November 1993, introduced the co-decision procedure, permitting a third parliamentary reading (see Council of the European Union, above). The Treaty also gives the Parliament potentially the right to veto legislation, and allows it to approve or reject the nomination of Commissioners (including the President of the Commission). The Parliament appoints the European Ombudsman from among its members, who investigates reports of maladministration in Community institutions. The Treaty of Amsterdam, which entered into force in May 1999, expanded and simplified the Parliament's legislative role. The co-decision procedure between the Parliament and the Council was extended into a wider range of policy areas. The Treaty also stipulated that the President of the Commission must be formally approved by the Parliament. In addition, international agreements, treaty decisions and the accession of new member states all require the assent of the Parliament. The Treaty of Nice, which came into force in February 2003, further extended the use of co-decision and introduced a new distribution of seats in the Parliament, which took effect at the elections on 10–13 June 2004, following the accession of the new member states on 1 May 2004 (see above). According to the draft constitution, which was approved by the European Council in June 2004 and by the European Parliament itself in January 2005, the European Parliament was granted the right of co-decision with the Council of the European Union in policy areas requiring qualified majority voting, thus giving it a more prominent role in framing legislation.

Political Groupings

	Distribution of seats (25 April 2005)
Group of the European People's Party (Christian Democrats) and European Democrats (PPE-ED)	268
Socialist Group in the European Parliament (PSE)	202
Group of the Alliance of Liberals and Democrats for Europe (ALDE)	88
Group of the Greens/European Free Alliance (Verts/ALE)	42
Confederal Group of the European United Left/Nordic Green Left (GUE/NGL)	41
Independence/Democracy Group (IND/DEM) . .	36
Union for Europe of the Nations Group (UEN) .	27
Non-affiliated (NI)	28
Total	**732**

The Parliament has an annual session, divided into about 12 one-week meetings, which are (or, at least, should be) attended by all the members and which are normally held in Strasbourg, France. The session opens with the March meeting. Committee meetings, political group meetings and additional plenary sittings of the Parliament are held in Brussels, while the parliamentary administrative offices are based in Luxembourg.

The budgetary powers of the Parliament (which, together with the Council of the European Union, forms the Budgetary Authority of the Communities) were increased to their present status by a treaty of 22 July 1975. Under this treaty, it can amend non-agricultural

spending and reject the draft budget, acting by a majority of its members and two-thirds of the votes cast. The Parliament debates the draft budget in two successive readings, and it does not come into force until it has been signed by the President of the Parliament. The Parliament's Committee on Budgetary Control (COCOBU) monitors how the budget is expended, and each year the Parliament decides whether to approve the Commission's handling of the budget for the previous financial year (a process technically known as 'granting a discharge').

The Parliament is run by a Bureau comprising the President, 14 Vice-Presidents elected from its members by secret ballot to serve for two-and-a-half years, and the five members of the College of Quaestors. The Conference of Presidents is the political governing body of the Parliament, with responsibility for formulating the agenda for plenary sessions and the timetable for the work of parliamentary bodies, and for establishing the terms of reference and the size of committees and delegations. It comprises the President of the Parliament and the Chairmen of the political groupings.

The majority of the Parliament's work is conducted by 20 Standing Parliamentary Committees (increased from 17 Committees in July 2004), which correspond to different policy areas and various European Commission agencies: Foreign Affairs, Human Rights, Security and Defence; Budgets; Budgetary Control; Civil Liberties, Justice and Home Affairs; Economic and Monetary Affairs; the Internal Market and Consumer Protection; Industry, Research and Energy; Employment and Social Affairs; the Environment, Public Health and Food Safety; Agriculture; Fisheries; Regional Development; Transport and Tourism; Culture and Education; Legal Affairs; Constitutional Affairs; Women's Rights and Gender Equality; Development; International Trade; and Petitions.

The first direct elections to the European Parliament took place in June 1979, and Parliament met for the first time in July. The second elections were held in June 1984 (with separate elections held in Portugal and Spain in 1987, following the accession of these two countries to the Community), the third in June 1989, and the fourth in June 1994. Direct elections to the European Parliament were held in Sweden in September 1995, and in Austria and Finland in October 1996. The fifth European Parliament was elected in June 1999. Elections to the sixth European Parliament were held on 10–13 June 2004, following the accession of the 10 new member states in May. The turnout at these elections reached a record low of only 45.3% of the electorate; among the 10 new member states public apathy towards the elections was particularly notable, with turnout averaging a mere 26.4%.

EUROPEAN OMBUDSMAN

Address: ave du Président Robert Schuman 1, BP 403, 67001 Strasbourg Cédex, France.

Telephone: 3-88-17-23-13; **fax:** 3-88-17-90-62; **e-mail:** euro-ombudsman@europarl.eu.int; **internet:** www .euro-ombudsman.eu.int.

The position was created by the Treaty on European Union (the Maastricht Treaty), and the first Ombudsman took office in July 1995. The Ombudsman is appointed by the European Parliament (from among its own members) for a renewable five-year term. He is authorized to receive complaints (from EU citizens, businesses and institutions, and from anyone residing or having their legal domicile in an EU member state) regarding maladministration in Community institutions and bodies (except in the Court of Justice and Court of First Instance), to make recommendations, and to refer any matters to the Parliament. The Ombudsman submits an annual report on his activities to the European Parliament.

European Ombudsman: Prof. NIKIFOROS DIAMANDOUROS (Greece).

COURT OF JUSTICE OF THE EUROPEAN COMMUNITIES

Address: Cour de justice des Communautés européennes, L-2925 Luxembourg.

Telephone: 4303-1; **fax:** 4303-2600; **e-mail:** info@curia.eu.int; **internet:** www.curia.eu.int/en/index.htm.

As the European Union's judicial institution the Court of Justice acts as a safeguard of EU legislation (technically known as Community law) and has jurisdiction over cases concerning member states, EU institutions, undertakings or individuals. The Court ensures uniform interpretation and application of Community law throughout the EU. The 25 Judges and the eight Advocates-General are each appointed for a term of six years, after which they may be reappointed for one or two further periods of three years. The role of the Advocates-General is—publicly and impartially—to deliver reasoned opinions on the cases brought before the Court. There is normally one Judge per member state, whose name is put forward by the Government of that member state. These proposed appointments are then subject to a vote in the Council of the European

Union. Following the enlargement of the EU to 25 member states in May 2004 there was still one Judge per member state, but, for the sake of efficiency, when the Court held a plenary session only 13 Judges—sitting as a 'Grand Chamber'—would have to attend. The President of the Court, who has overall charge of the Court's work and presides at hearings and deliberations, is elected by the Judges from among their number for a renewable term of three years. The majority of cases are dealt with by one of the five chambers, each of which consists of a President of Chamber and three or six Judges. The Court may sit in plenary session in cases of particular importance or when a member state or Community institution that is a party to the proceedings so requests. Judgments are reached by a majority vote and are signed by all Judges involved in the case, irrespective of how they voted. The Court has jurisdiction to award damages. It may review the legality of acts (other than recommendations or opinions) of the Council, the Commission or the European Central Bank, of acts adopted jointly by the European Parliament and the Council, and of Acts adopted by the Parliament and intended to produce legal effects *vis-à-vis* third parties. It is also competent to give judgment on actions by a member state, the Council or the Commission on grounds of lack of competence, of infringement of an essential procedural requirement, of infringement of a Treaty or of any legal rule relating to its application, or of misuse of power. The Court of Justice may hear appeals, on a point of law only, from the Court of First Instance.

The Court is also empowered to hear certain other cases concerning the contractual and non-contractual liability of the Communities and disputes between member states in connection with the objects of the Treaties. It also gives preliminary rulings at the request of national courts on the interpretation of the Treaties, of Union legislation, and of the Brussels Convention on Jurisdiction and the Enforcement of Judgments in Civil and Commercial Matters.

COMPOSITION OF THE COURT
(in order of precedence, from 14 October 2004)

President of the Court of Justice: VASSILIOS SKOURIS (Greece).

Judge: PETER JANN (Austria—President of the First Chamber).

Judge: CHRISTIAAN TIMMERMANS (Netherlands—President of the Second Chamber).

Judge: ALLAN ROSAS (Finland—President of the Third Chamber).

First Advocate-General: LEENDERT A. GEELHOED (Netherlands).

Judge: ROSARIO SILVA DE LAPUERTA (Spain—President of the Fifth Chamber).

Judge: KOEN LENAERTS (Belgium—President of the Fourth Chamber).

Judge: ANTHONY BORG BARTHET (Malta—President of the Sixth Chamber).

Advocate-General: FRANCIS JACOBS (United Kingdom).

Judge: CLAUS GULMANN (Denmark).

Judge: ANTONIO MARIO LA PERGOLA (Italy).

Judge: JEAN-PIERRE PUISSOCHET (France).

Advocate-General: PHILIPPE LÉGER (France).

Advocate-General: DAMASO RUIZ-JARABO COLOMER (Spain).

Judge: ROMAIN SCHINTGEN (Luxembourg).

Judge: NINON COLNERIC (Germany).

Judge: STIG VON BAHR (Sweden).

Advocate-General: ANTONIO TIZZANO (Italy).

Judge: JOSÉ NARCISO DA CUNHA RODRIGUES (Portugal).

Advocate-General: CHRISTINE STIX-HACKL (Austria).

Advocate-General: JULIANNE KOKOTT (Germany).

Advocate-General: LUÍS MIGUEL POIARES PESSOA MADURA (Portugal).

Judge: Sir KONRAD HERMANN THEODOR SCHIEMANN (United Kingdom).

Judge: JERZY MAKARCZYK (Poland).

Judge: PRANAS KŪRIS (Lithuania).

Judge: ENDRE JUHÁSZ (Hungary).

Judge: GEORGE ARESTIS (Cyprus).

Judge: MARKO ILEŠIČ (Slovenia).

Judge: JIŘÍ MALENOVSKÝ (Czech Republic).

Judge: JÁN KLUČKA (Slovakia).

Judge: UNO LÕHMUS (Estonia).

Judge: EGILS LEVITS (Latvia).

Judge: AINDRIAS Ó CAOIMH (Ireland).

Registrar: ROGER GRASS (France).

COURT OF FIRST INSTANCE OF THE EUROPEAN COMMUNITIES

Address: Cour de justice des Communautés européennes, L-2925 Luxembourg .

Telephone: 4303-1; **fax:** 4303-2100; **internet:** www.curia.eu.int.

In order to help the Court of Justice deal with the thousands of cases brought before it and to offer citizens better legal protection, the Court of First Instance was established by the European Council by a decision of October 1988, and began operations in 1989. Since 1994, irrespective of the subject matter concerned, the Court (which, although independent, is attached to the Court of Justice) has dealt with all actions brought by individuals (both natural and legal) and undertakings against measures of the EU institutions that are addressed to them or that are of direct and individual concern to them. As with the Court of Justice, the composition of the Court of First Instance is based on 25 Judges (one from each member state, appointed for a renewable term of six years), one President (elected from among the 25 Judges for a renewable period of three years) and five chambers.

COMPOSITION OF THE COURT OF FIRST INSTANCE
(in order of precedence, from 10 September 2004–30 September 2005)

President of the Court of First Instance: BO VESTERDORF (Denmark).

President of Chamber: MARC JAEGER (Luxembourg).

President of Chamber: JÖRG PIRRUNG (Germany).

President of Chamber: MIHALIS VILARAS (Greece).

President of Chamber: HUBERT LEGAL (France).

President of Chamber: JOHN D. COOKE (Ireland).

Judge: RAFAEL GARCÍA-VALDECASAS Y FERNÁNDEZ (Spain).

Judge: VIRPI TIILI (Finland).

Judge: PERNILLA LINDH (Sweden).

Judge: JOSEF AZIZI (Austria).

Judge: PAOLO MENGOZZI (Italy).

Judge: ARJEN MEIJ (Netherlands).

Judge: NICHOLAS J. FORWOOD (United Kingdom).

Judge: MARIA EUGÉNIA MARTINS DE NAZARÉ RIBEIRO (Portugal).

Judge: FRANKLIN DEHOUSSE (France).

Judge: ENA CREMONA (Malta).

Judge: OTTÓ CZÚCZ (Hungary).

Judge: IRENA WISZNIEWSKA-BIALECKA (Poland).

Judge: IRENA PELIKÁNOVÁ (Czech Republic).

Judge: DANIEL ŠVÁBY (Slovakia).

Judge: VILENAS VADAPALAS (Lithuania).

Judge: KÜLLIKE JÜRIMÄE (Estonia).

Judge: INGRIDA LABUCKA (Latvia).

Judge: SAVVAS S. PAPASAVVAS (Cyprus).

Judge: VERICA TRSTENJAK (Slovenia).

Registrar: HANS JUNG (Germany).

EUROPEAN COURT OF AUDITORS

Address: 12 rue Alcide de Gasperi, 1615 Luxembourg.

Telephone: 4398-45410; **fax:** 4398-46430; **e-mail:** firstname .surname@eca.eu.int; **internet:** www.eca.eu.int.

The European Court of Auditors (ECA) was created by the Treaty of Brussels, which was signed on 22 July 1975, and commenced its duties in late 1977. It was given the status of an institution on a par with the Commission, the Council, the Court of Justice and the Parliament by the Treaty on European Union. It is the institution responsible for the external audit of the resources managed by the European Communities and the European Union. It consists of 25 members (one from each member state) who are appointed for renewable six-year terms (under a qualified majority voting system) by the Council of the European Union, after consultation with the European Parliament (in practice, however, the Council simply endorses the candidates put forward by the member states). The members elect the President of the Court from among their number for a renewable term of three years.

The Court is organized and acts as a collegiate body. It adopts its decisions by a majority of its members. Each member, however, has a direct responsibility for the audit of certain sectors of Union activities.

The Court examines the accounts of all expenditure and revenue of the European Communities and of any body created by them in so far as the relevant constituent instrument does not preclude such examination. It examines whether all revenue has been received and all expenditure incurred in a lawful and regular manner and whether the financial management has been sound. The audit is based on records, and if necessary is performed directly in the institutions of the Communities, in the member states and in other countries. In the member states the audit is carried out in co-operation with the national audit bodies. The Court of Auditors draws up an annual report after the close of each financial year. The Court provides the Parliament and the Council with a statement of assurance as to the reliability of the accounts, and the legality and regularity of the underlying transactions. It may also, at any time, submit observations on specific questions (usually in the form of special reports) and deliver opinions at the request of one of the institutions of the Communities. It assists the European Parliament and the Council in exercising their powers of control over the implementation of the budget, in particular in the framework of the annual discharge procedure, and gives its prior opinion on the financial regulations, on the methods and procedure whereby the budgetary revenue is made available to the Commission, and on the formulation of rules concerning the responsibility of authorizing officers and accounting officers and concerning appropriate arrangements for inspection.

President: JUAN MANUEL FABRA VALLÉS (Spain).

Members: GIORGIO CLEMENTE (Italy), HUBERT WEBER (Austria), AUNUS SALMI (Finland), FRANÇOIS COLLING (Luxembourg), MAARTEN B. ENGWIRDA (Netherlands), JEAN-FRANÇOIS BERNICOT (France), ROBERT REYNDERS (Belgium), MÁIRE GEOGHEGAN-QUINN (Ireland), VÍTOR MANUEL SILVA CALDEIRA (Portugal), LARS TOBISSON (Sweden), HEDDA VON WEDEL (Germany), DAVID BOSTOCK (United Kingdom), MORTEN LOUIS LEVYSOHN (Denmark), IOANNIS SARMAS (Greece), JÚLIUS MOLNÁR (Slovakia), VOJKO ANTON ANTONČIČ (Slovenia), GEJZA HALÁSZ (Hungary), JOSEF BONNICI (Malta), JACEK UCZKIEWICZ (Poland), IRENA PETRUŠKEVIČIENE (Lithuania), IGORS LUDBORŽS (Latvia), JAN KINŠT (Czech Republic), KERSTI KALJULAID (Estonia).

Secretary-General: MICHEL HERVÉ (France).

Audit Group I—Agricultural Policies: JEAN-FRANÇOIS BERNICOT, HEDDA VON WEDEL, DAVID BOSTOCK.

Audit Group II—Structural and Internal Policies: GIORGIO CLEMENTE, LARS TOBISSON, FRANÇOIS COLLING.

Audit Group III—External Actions: HUBERT WEBER, MAARTEN B. ENGWIRDA, ROBERT REYNDERS.

Audit Group IV—Own Resources, Banking Activities, Administrative Expenditure, Community Institutions and Bodies: AUNUS SALMI, MORTEN LOUIS LEVYSOHN, IOANNIS SARMAS.

CEAD Group—Co-ordination, Evaluation, Assurance, Development: VÍTOR MANUEL SILVA CALDEIRA, JUAN MANUEL FABRA VALLÉS, DAVID BOSTOCK, LARS TOBISSON, MAARTEN B. ENGWIRDA, MORTEN LOUIS LEVYSOHN.

EUROPEAN CENTRAL BANK

Address: Kaiserstr. 29, D-60311 Frankfurt am Main, Germany; .

Address: Postfach 160319, D-60066 Frankfurt am Main, Germany.

Telephone: (69) 13440; **fax:** (69) 13446000; **e-mail:** info@ecb.int; **internet:** www.ecb.int.

The European Central Bank (ECB) was formally established on 1 June 1998, replacing the European Monetary Institute, which had been operational since January 1994. The Bank has the authority to issue the single currency, the euro, which replaced the European Currency Unit (ECU) on 1 January 1999, at the beginning of Stage III of Economic and Monetary Union (EMU), in accordance with the provisions of the Treaty on European Union (the Maastricht Treaty). One of the ECB's main tasks is to maintain price stability in the euro area (i.e. in those member states that have adopted the euro as their national currency)—this is achieved primarily by controlling the money supply and by monitoring price trends. The Bank's leadership is provided by a six-member Executive Board, appointed by common agreement of the presidents or prime ministers of the euro area countries (Austria, Belgium, Finland, France, Germany, Greece, Ireland, Italy, Luxembourg, the Netherlands, Portugal and Spain) for a non-renewable term of eight years (it should be noted that the Statute of the European System of Central Banks—ESCB—provides for a system of staggered appointments to the first Executive Board for members other than the President in order to ensure continuity). The Executive Board is responsible for the preparation of meetings of the Governing Council, the implementation of monetary policy in accordance with the guide-lines and decisions laid down by the Governing Council and for the current business of the ECB. The ECB and the national central banks of all EU member states together comprise the ESCB. The Governing Council, which is the ECB's highest decision-making body and which consists of the six members of the Executive Board and the governors of the central banks of countries participating in EMU, meets twice a month. The prime mission of the Governing Council is to define the monetary policy of the euro area, and, in particular, to fix the interest rates at which the commercial banks can obtain money from the ECB. The General Council is the ECB's third decision-making body; it comprises the ECB's President, the Vice-President and the governors of the central banks of all EU member states.

President: JEAN-CLAUDE TRICHET (France).

Vice-President: LUCAS D. PAPADEMOS (Greece).

Executive Board: JOSÉ MANUEL GONZÁLEZ-PÁRAMO (Spain), GERTRUDE TUMPEL-GUGERELL (Austria), OTMAR ISSING (Germany), TOMMASO PADOA-SCHIOPPA (Italy).

EUROPEAN INVESTMENT BANK

Address: 100 blvd Konrad Adenauer, 2950 Luxembourg.

Telephone: 4379-1; **fax:** 4377-04; **e-mail:** info@eib.org; **internet:** www.eib.org.

The European Investment Bank (EIB) is the EU's international financing institution, and was created in 1958 by the six founder member states of the European Economic Community. The shareholders are the member states of the EU, which have all subscribed to the bank's capital. The bulk of the EIB's resources comes from borrowings, principally public bond issues or private placements on capital markets inside and outside the Union.

The EIB's principal task, defined by the Treaty of Rome, is to work on a non-profit basis, making or guaranteeing loans for investment projects which contribute to the balanced and steady development of EU member states. Throughout the Bank's history, priority has been given to financing investment projects which further regional development within the Community. The EIB also finances projects that improve communications, protect and improve the environment, promote urban development, strengthen the competitive position of industry and encourage industrial integration within the Union, support the activities of small and medium-sized enterprises (SMEs), and help ensure the security of energy supplies. Following a recommendation of the Lisbon European Council in March 2000 for greater support for SMEs, the Board of Governors set up the EIB Group, consisting of the EIB and the European Investment Fund. The EIB also provides finance for developing countries in Africa, the Caribbean and the Pacific, under the terms of the Cotonou Agreement (see p. 262), the successor agreement to the Lomé Convention; for countries in the Mediterranean region, under a new Euro-Mediterranean investment facility established in 2002; and for accession countries in central and eastern Europe.

In 2003 total financing contracts signed by the EIB, both inside and outside the European Union, amounted to €46,600m., of which €37,000m. was directed towards investments within the EU and €5,700m. to the accession states.

The Board of Governors of the EIB, which usually meets only once a year, lays down general directives on credit policy, approves the annual report and accounts and decides on capital increases. The Board of Directors meets once a month, and has sole power to take decisions in respect of loans, guarantees and borrowings. The Bank's President presides over meetings of the Board of Directors. The day-to-day management of operations is the responsibility of the Management Committee, which is the EIB's collegiate executive body and recommends decisions to the Board of Directors. The Audit Committee, which reports to the Board of Governors regarding the management of operations and the maintenance of the Bank's accounts, is an independent body comprising three members who are appointed by the Board of Governors for a renewable three-year term.

Board of Governors: The Board of Governors comprises one minister (usually the minister with responsibility for finance or economic affairs) from each member state.

Chair: PEDRO SOLBES MIRA (Spain).

Board of Directors: The Board of Directors consists of 26 directors, appointed for a renewable five-year term, with one director appointed by each member state and one by the European Commission. There are 16 alternates, also appointed for a renewable five-year term, meaning that some of these positions will be shared by groupings of countries. Since 1 May 2004, decisions have been taken by a majority consisting of at least one-third of members entitled to vote and representing at least 50% of the subscribed capital.

Management Committee

The President and seven Vice-Presidents, nominated for a renewable six-year term by the Board of Directors and approved by the Board of Governors. The President presides over the meetings of the Management Committee but does not vote.

President: PHILIPPE MAYSTADT (Belgium).

Vice-Presidents: Wolfgang Roth (Germany), Peter Sedgwick (United Kingdom), Isabel Martín Castellá (Spain), Gerlando Genuardi (Italy), Philippe de Fontaine Vive Curtaz (France), Torsten Gersfelt (Denmark), Sauli Niinistö (Finland), Ivan Pilip (Czech Republic).

Audit Committee

The Audit Committee is composed of three members and three observers, appointed by the Governors for a term of office of three years

Chair: Marc Colas (Luxembourg).

FINANCE CONTRACTS SIGNED

Recipient	2003 Amount (€ million)	%	1998–2003 Amount (€ million)	%
Austria	900	2.6	4,031	2.2
Belgium	540	1.6	2,112	1.1
Denmark	907	2.7	4,988	2.7
Finland	780	2.3	3,257	1.8
France	4,095	12.0	19,506	10.5
Germany	6,433	18.8	30,449	16.4
Greece	1,190	3.5	7,061	3.8
Ireland	538	1.6	1,937	1.0
Italy	5,925	17.3	26,988	14.5
Luxembourg . . .	184	0.5	572	0.3
Netherlands . . .	522	1.5	2,391	1.3
Portugal	1,645	4.8	8,662	4.7
Spain	6,291	18.4	24,479	13.2
Sweden	890	2.6	3,708	2.0
United Kingdom . .	3,239	9.5	15,424	8.3
Other*	99	0.3	991	0.5
EU total	34,187	80.8	156,556	84.2
Central and eastern European candidate and accession countries	4,354	10.3	15,479	8.3
Cyprus and Malta . .	235	0.6	730	0.4
Candidate countries total	4,589	10.8	16,209	8.7
Pre-accession facility .	3,867	9.1	12,378	6.7
Mediterranean countries (except Cyprus and Malta)†	2,088	4.9	7,092	3.8
ACP-Overseas countries and territories and South Africa	723	1.7	2,790	1.5
Asia and Latin America	348	0.8	1,907	1.0
Balkans	372	0.9	1,330	0.7
Russia	25	0.1	25	0.0
Partner countries total	3,556	8.4	13,144	7.1
Total	42,332	100.0	185,909	100.0

* Projects with a European dimension located outside the member states.
† Including Turkey.

EUROPEAN ECONOMIC AND SOCIAL COMMITTEE

Address: 99 rue Belliard, 1040 Brussels.

Telephone: (2) 546-90-11; **fax:** (2) 513-48-93; **e-mail:** info@esc.eu.int; **internet:** www.esc.eu.int.

The Committee was set up by the 1957 Rome Treaties. It is advisory and is consulted by the Council of the European Union or by the European Commission, particularly with regard to agriculture, free movement of workers, harmonization of laws and transport, as well as legislation adopted under the Euratom Treaty. In certain cases consultation of the Committee by the Commission or the Council is mandatory. In addition, the Committee has the power to deliver opinions on its own initiative.

The Committee has a tripartite structure with members belonging to one of three groupings: the Employers' Group, the Employees' Group and the Various Interests Group, which includes representatives of social, occupational, economic and cultural organizations. The Committee is appointed for a renewable term of four years by the unanimous vote of the Council of the European Union. The 317 members are nominated by national governments, but are appointed in their personal capacity and are not bound by any mandatory instructions. Germany, France, Italy and the United Kingdom have

24 members each, Spain and Poland have 21, Belgium, Greece, the Netherlands, Portugal, Austria, Sweden, Czech Republic and Hungary 12, Denmark, Ireland, Finland, Lithuania and Slovakia 9, Estonia, Latvia and Slovenia 7, Luxembourg and Cyprus 6 and Malta 5. The Committee is served by a permanent and independent General Secretariat, headed by the Secretary-General.

President: Ann-Marie Sigmund (Austria).

Vice-Presidents: Roger Briesch (Germany) (Employees), Dimitrios Dimitriadis (Greece) (Employers).

Secretary-General: Patrick Venturini (France).

COMMITTEE OF THE REGIONS

Address: 101 rue Belliard, 1040 Brussels.

Telephone: (2) 282-22-11; **fax:** (2) 282-23-25; **e-mail:** info@cor.eu.int; **internet:** www.cor.eu.int.

The Treaty on European Union provided for a committee to be established, with advisory status, comprising representatives of regional and local bodies throughout the EU. The first meeting of the Committee was held in March 1994. It may be consulted on EU proposals concerning economic and social cohesion, trans-European networks, public health, education and culture, and may issue an opinion on any issue with regional implications. The Committee meets in plenary session five times a year.

The number of members of the Committee is equal to that of the European Economic and Social Committee. Members are appointed for a renewable term of four years by the Council, acting unanimously on the proposals from the respective member states. The Committee elects its principal officers from among its members for a two-year term.

President: Peter Straub (Germany).

First Vice-President: Albert Bore (United Kingdom).

OTHER BODIES

EUROPEAN INVESTMENT FUND—EIF

Address: 43 ave J. F. Kennedy, 2968 Luxembourg.

Telephone: 4266-881; **fax:** 4266-88200; **e-mail:** info@eif.org; **internet:** www.eif.org.

The European Investment Fund was founded in 1994 as a specialized financial institution to support the growth of small and medium-sized enterprises (SMEs). Its operations are focused on the provision of venture capital, through investment in funds that support SMEs, and on guarantee activities to facilitate access to finance for SMEs. In all its activities the Fund aims to maintain a commercial approach to investment, and to apply risk-sharing principles. Since 1998 the Fund has managed the European Technology Faculty (ETF)—Start-Up, and the SME Guarantee Facility.

Chief Executive: Francis Carpenter (United Kingdom).

ADVISORY COMMITTEES

There are advisory committees dealing with all aspects of EU policy. Consultation with some committees is compulsory in the procedure for drafting EC legislation.

In addition to the consultative bodies listed above there are several hundred special interest groups representing every type of interest within the Union. All these hold unofficial talks with the Commission.

AGENCIES

Community Plant Variety Office (CPVO)

POB 62141, 49021 Angers Cedex 2; 3 blvd du Maréchal Foch, 49100 Angers, France; tel. 2-41-25-64-00; fax 2-41-25-64-10; e-mail cpvo@cpvo.eu.int; internet www.cpvo.eu.int.

Began operations in April 1995, with responsibility for granting intellectual property rights for plant varieties. Supervised by an Administrative Council, and managed by a President, appointed by the Council of the European Union. A Board of Appeal has been established to consider appeals against certain technical decisions taken by the Office.

President: Barteld P. Kiewiet.

European Agency for Reconstruction (EAR)

Egnatia 4, 546 26 Thessaloniki, Greece; POB 10177, 541 10 Thessaloniki, Greece; tel. (2310) 505100; fax (2310) 505172; e-mail info@ear.eu.int; internet www.ear.eu.int.

Established in February 2000 (upon a Council regulation of November 1999) to assume the responsibilities of the European Commission's Task Force for the Reconstruction of Kosovo (which had become operational in July 1999 following the end of hostilities in the southern Serbian province of Kosovo and Metohija). The Agency is responsible for the management of the main assistance programmes in Serbia and Montenegro (UN-administered Kosovo and Metohija, the Republic of Serbia and the Republic of Montenegro) and the former Yugoslav republic of Macedonia (FYRM). The Agency has operational centres in Belgrade (Serbia), Priština (Kosovo), Podgorica (Montenegro) and Skopje (FYRM).

Director: Richard Zink (Germany).

European Agency for Safety and Health at Work (EU-OSHA)

Gran Vía 33, 48009 Bilbao, Spain; tel. (94) 479-43-60; fax (94) 479-43-83; e-mail information@osha.eu.int; internet agency.osha.eu.int.

Began operations in 1996. Aims to encourage improvements in the working environment, and to make available all necessary technical, scientific and economic information for use in the field of health and safety at work. An Administrative Board comprising representatives from each member state's government, employers' and workers' organizations, and three representatives from the European Commission, adopts the Agency's work programme and other strategic decisions of the Agency, and appoints the Director. The Agency supports a network of Focal Points in the member states of the EU, in the member states of the European Free Trade Association (EFTA, see p. 214) and in the candidate states of the EU.

Director: Hans-Horst Konkolewsky (Denmark).

European Aviation Safety Agency (EASA)

Postfach 101253, 50452 Köln, Germany; tel. (221) 89990 0000; fax (221) 89990 9501; e-mail info@easa.eu.int; internet www.easa.eu .int.

Established by regulation of the European Parliament in July 2002; the mission of the agency is to establish and maintain a high, uniform level of civil aviation safety and environmental protection in Europe. The Agency commenced operating fully in September 2003, and its permanent seat, in Köln, Germany, was officially opened in December 2004.

Executive Director: Patrick Goudou (France).

European Centre for the Development of Vocational Training (Cedefop)

POB 22427, 551 02 Thessaloniki, Greece; Evropis 123, 570 01 Thessaloniki, Greece; tel. (31) 490111; fax (31) 490102; e-mail info@cedefop.eu.int; internet www.cedefop.eu.int.

Established in 1975, Cedefop assists policy-makers and other officials in member states and partner organizations in issues relating to vocational training policies, and assists the European Commission in the development of these policies. Manages a European Training Village internet site.

Director: Johan van Rens (Netherlands).

European Environment Agency (EEA)

6 Kongens Nytorv, 1050 Copenhagen K, Denmark; tel. 33-36-71-00; fax 33-36-71-99; e-mail eea@eea.eu.int; internet www.eea.eu.int.

Became operational in 1994, having been approved in 1990, to gather and supply information to assist the drafting and implementation of EU policy on environmental protection and improvement. Iceland, Liechtenstein, Norway, Bulgaria, Romania and Turkey are also members of the Agency. In 2005 the Agency's budget amounted to around €32m. The Agency publishes frequent reports on the state of the environment and on environmental trends.

Executive Director: Prof. Jacqueline McGlade (United Kingdom).

Chairman of the Management Board: Lars-Erik Liljelund (Sweden).

Chairman of the Scientific Committee: Prof. Bedrich Moldan (Czech Republic).

European Food Safety Authority (EFSA)

10 rue de Genève, 1140 Brussels, Belgium; Largo N. Palli 5/A, 43100 Parma, Italy; tel. (2) 337-21-11; fax (2) 726-68-13; e-mail info@efsa .eu.int; internet www.efsa.eu.int.

Established by a regulation of the European Parliament in February 2002; the primary responsibility of the Authority is to provide independent scientific advice on all matters with a direct or indirect impact on food safety. The Authority will carry out assessments of risks to the food chain and scientific assessment on any matter that may have a direct or indirect effect on the safety of the food supply, including matters relating to animal health, animal welfare and plant health. The Authority will also give scientific advice on genetically modified organisms (GMOs), and on nutrition in relation to Community legislation. The permanent seat of the Authority will be

Parma, Italy. By January 2005 the Executive Director and 22 other staff were located in Parma and the rest of the staff were due to relocate from Brussels by late 2005.

Executive Director: Geoffrey Podger (United Kingdom).

Chairman of Management Board: Stuart Slorach (Sweden).

European Foundation for the Improvement of Living and Working Conditions (Eurofound)

Wyattville Rd, Loughlinstown, Dublin 18, Ireland; tel. (1) 204-3100; fax (1) 282-6456; e-mail postmaster@eurofound.eu.int; internet www.eurofound.eu.int.

Established in 1975 to develop strategies for the improvement of industrial relations, living conditions and working conditions. The Foundation publishes a bi-monthly newsletter.

Director: Willy Buschak (acting).

Chairman of the Administrative Board: Dr Jan Willem Van den Braak (Employers' Group).

European Maritime Safety Agency (EMSA)

12 rue de Genève, 1049 Brussels, Belgium; tel. (2) 298-58-12; fax (2) 299-80-59; e-mail tren-emsa-info@cec.eu.int; internet www.emsa.eu .int.

Established by a regulation of the European Parliament in June 2002; the primary responsibility of the Agency is to provide technical and scientific advice to the Commission in the field of maritime safety and prevention of pollution by ships. The Agency held its inaugural meeting in December 2002, and in December 2003 it was decided that the permanent seat of the Agency would be Lisbon, Portugal.

Executive Director: Willem de Ruiter (Netherlands).

Chairman of the Board: Brian Wadsworth (United Kingdom).

European Medicines Agency (EMEA)

7 Westferry Circus, Canary Wharf, London, E14 4HB, United Kingdom; tel. (20) 7418-8400; fax (20) 7418-8416; e-mail mail@emea .eu.int; internet www.emea.eu.int.

Established in 1993 for the authorization and supervision of medicinal products for human and veterinary use.

Executive Director: Thomas Lönngren (Sweden).

Chairman of the Management Board: Hannes Wahlroos (Finland).

Chairman of the Committee for Medicinal Products for Human Use (CHMP): Dr Daniel Brasseur (Belgium).

Chairman of the Committee for Medicinal Products for Veterinary Use (CVMP): Dr Gérard Moulin (France).

Chairman of the Committee for Orphan Medicinal Products (COMP): Prof. Josep Torrent-Farnell (Spain).

Chairman of the Committee for Herbal Medicinal Products (HMPC): Dr Konstantin Keller (Germany).

European Monitoring Centre for Drugs and Drug Addiction (EMCDDA)

Rua da Cruz de Sta. Apolónia 23–25, 1149-045 Lisbon, Portugal; tel. (1) 21811-30-00; fax (1) 21811-17-11; e-mail info@emcdda.eu.int; internet www.emcdda.eu.int.

Founded in 1993, and became fully operational at the end of 1995, with the aim of providing member states with objective, reliable and comparable information on drugs and drug addiction in order to assist in combating the problem. The Centre co-operates with other European and international organizations and non-Community countries. The Centre publishes an *Annual Report on the State of the Drugs Problem in the European Union and Norway*. A newsletter, *Drugnet Europe*, is published quarterly.

Executive Director: Jaume Bardolet (acting).

Chairman of the Management Board: Armand Wagner (Luxembourg).

Chairman of the Scientific Committee: Salme Ahlström (Finland).

European Monitoring Centre on Racism and Xenophobia (EUMC)

Rahlgasse 3, 1060 Vienna, Austria; tel. (1) 580300; fax (1) 5803093; e-mail information@eumc.eu.int; internet www.eumc.eu.int.

Established by a decision of the European Council in June 1997, and began operations in July 1998. The EUMC aims to provide objective, reliable and comparable information and data on racism, xenophobia, islamophobia and anti-semitism at the European level and to promote best practices to combat these problems. Central to the work of the EUMC is the creation of the European Information Network on Racism and Xenophobia (RAXEN), which is designed to collect data and information at national as well as European level.

Director: Dr Beate Winkler (Germany).

Chairman of Executive Board: Anastasia Crickley (Ireland).

European Network and Information Security Agency (ENISA)

33 ave de Beaulieu, Brussels, Belgium; fax (2) 299-43-74; e-mail enisa-info@cec.eu.int; internet www.enisa.eu.int.

Established by a regulation of the European Parliament in March 2004; the primary responsibilities of the Agency are to promote closer European co-ordination on information security and to provide assistance in the application of EU measures in this field. The Agency was expected to commence operations during 2005. ENISA's seat will be in Heraklion (Greece).

Executive Director: Andrea Pirotti (Italy).

Chairman of the Management Board: Kristiina Pietikainen (Finland).

European Railway Agency (ERA)

Brussels.

Established by a regulation of the European Parliament in April 2004; the primary responsibility of the Agency is to reinforce the safety and interoperability of railways in the EU. The Agency (the permanent seat of which was to be situated in Lille/Valenciennes, France) held its inaugural meeting in July 2004.

Executive Director: Marcel Verslype (Belgium).

Chairman of the Administrative Board: Reino Lampinen (Finland).

European Training Foundation (ETF)

Villa Gualino, Viale Settimio Severo 65, 10133 Turin, Italy; tel. (011) 630-22-22; fax (011) 630-22-00; e-mail info@etf.eu.int; internet www.etf.eu.int.

This Foundation, which was established in 1995, provides policy advice to the European Commission and to the EU's partner countries (which numbered 29 at the beginning of 2005), to support vocational education and training reform. The partner countries where ETF initiates and supports reform are the beneficiaries of four EU support programmes: countries taking part in the enlargement process (Bulgaria, Romania, Croatia and Turkey—PHARE and MEDA Programmes), south-eastern Europe (Albania, Bosnia-Herzegovina, Kosovo, Macedonia (FYR), Serbia and Montenegro—Community Assistance for Reconstruction, Development and Stabilization—CARDS Programme), Eastern Europe and Central Asia (Armenia, Azerbaijan, Belarus, Georgia, Kazakhstan, Kyrgyzstan, Moldova, the Russian Federation, Tajikistan, Ukraine and Uzbekistan—Technical Assistance to the Commonwealth of Independent States—TACIS Programme) and non-EU Mediterranean countries and territories (Algeria, Egypt, Israel, Jordan, Lebanon, Morocco, Syria, Tunisia, West Bank and Gaza Strip—MEDA Programme). The ETF also gives technical assistance to the European Commission for the implementation of the Trans-European Mobility Scheme for University Studies (TEMPUS), which focuses on the reform of higher education systems in partner countries.

Director: Dr Muriel Dunbar (United Kingdom).

Chairman of the Governing Board: Nikolaus van der Pas (Germany).

Office for Harmonisation in the Internal Market (Trade Marks and Designs) (OHIM)

Apartado de Correos 77, 03080 Alicante, Spain; Avda de Europa 4, 03008 Alicante, Spain; tel. (96) 513-91-00; fax (96) 513-91-73; e-mail information@oami.eu.int; internet www.oami.eu.int.

Established in 1993 to promote and control trade marks and designs throughout the European Union.

President: Wubbo de Boer (Netherlands).

Chairman of the Administrative Board: Martti Enäjärvi (Finland).

Chairman of the Budget Committee: Peter Lawrence (United Kingdom).

Translation Centre for the Bodies of the European Union (CdT)

Bâtiment Nouvel Hémicycle, 1 rue de Fort Thüngen, 1499 Luxembourg; tel. 4217-11-1; fax 4217-11-220; e-mail cdt@cdt.eu.int; internet www.cdt.eu.int.

Established in 1994 to meet the translation needs of other decentralized Community agencies.

Director: Marie-Anne Fernandez (acting).

A European Agency for the Management of Operational Co-operation at the External Borders of the European Union was established by a regulation of the European Parliament in October 2004, the primary responsibility of which would be the creation of an integrated border management system, which would ensure a high and uniform level of control and surveillance. The Agency was scheduled to commence operations on 1 May 2005.

Activities of the Community

AGRICULTURE

Co-operation in the Community has traditionally been at its most highly organized in the area of agriculture. The Common Agricultural Policy (CAP), which took effect from 1962, was originally devised to ensure food self-sufficiency for Europe following the food shortages of the post-war period and to ensure a fair standard of living for the agricultural community. Its objectives are described in the Treaty of Rome. The markets for agricultural products have been progressively organized following three basic principles: unity of the market (products must be able to circulate freely within the Community and markets must be organized according to common rules); Community preference (products must be protected from low-cost imports and from fluctuations on the world market); common financial responsibility: the European Agricultural Guidance and Guarantee Fund (EAGGF) finances, through its Guarantee Section, all public expenditure intervention, storage costs, marketing subsidies and export rebates.

Agricultural prices are, in theory, fixed each year at a common level for the Community as a whole, taking into account the rate of inflation and the need to discourage surplus production of certain commodities. Export subsidies are paid to enable farmers to sell produce at the lower world market prices without loss. When market prices of certain cereals, sugar, some fruits and vegetables, dairy produce and meat fall below a designated level the Community intervenes, and buys a certain quantity which is then stored until prices recover.

Agriculture is by far the largest item on the Community budget, accounting for 47% of annual expenditure in 2001 (although this represented a significant reduction from 68% in 1988), mainly for supporting prices through the EAGGF Guarantee Section (appropriations for which amounted to €44,505m., or 45% of total commitment appropriations, in 2002). A system of stabilizers was introduced in February 1988, imposing an upper limit on the production of certain products. Any over-production would result in a decrease in the guaranteed intervention price for the following year.

Serious reform of the CAP began in 1992, following strong criticism of the EC's agricultural and export subsidies during the 'Uruguay Round' of negotiations on the General Agreement on Tariffs and Trade (GATT, see World Trade Organization—WTO, see p. 357) in 1990. In May 1992 ministers adopted a number of reforms, which aimed to transfer the Community's agricultural support from upholding prices to maintaining farmers' incomes, thereby removing the incentive to over-produce. Intervention prices were reduced and farmers were compensated by receiving additional grants, which, in the case of crops, took the form of a subsidy per hectare of land planted. To qualify for these subsidies, arable farmers (except for those with the smallest farms) were obliged to remove 15% of their land from cultivation (the 'set-aside' scheme). Incentives were given for alternative uses of the withdrawn land (e.g. forestry).

In May 1992 the US Government threatened to impose a large increase in import tariffs on European products, in retaliation against subsidies paid by the EC to oilseed producers, which, the US Government claimed, led to unfair competition for US exports of soya beans. In November, however, agreement was reached between the USA and the European Commission: the USA agreed that limits should be imposed on the area of EC land on which cultivation of oilseeds was permitted. The USA also agreed to accept a reduction in the volume and value of the EC's subsidized exports of farm produce, over a six-year period. These agreements formed the basis of the GATT agricultural accord, which was concluded as part of the Uruguay Round trade agreement in December 1993.

In March 1999 at the Berlin European Council the EU Heads of Government concluded an agreement on a programme, Agenda 2000, which aimed to reinforce Community policies and to restructure the financial framework of the EU with a view to enlargement. In terms of agriculture it was decided to continue the process of agricultural reform begun in 1992 with particular emphasis on environmental concerns, safeguarding a fair income for farmers, streamlining legislation and decentralizing its application. A further element of reform was the increased emphasis on rural development, which was described as the 'second pillar' of the CAP in Agenda 2000. The objective was to restore and increase the competitiveness of rural areas, through supporting employment, diversification and population growth. In addition, producers were to be rewarded for the preservation of rural heritage. Specifically, the policy would provide funds for the modernization of agricultural holdings, for establishing young farmers, for training and for early retirement. Forestry was recognized as an integral part of rural development (previous treaties of the EU had made no provision for a comprehensive common forestry policy). During 1999 and 2000 member states developed rural development programmes for 2000–06. In late 2000 rural development programmes for a number of applicant countries were also adopted. These were drawn up under the EU's Special Accession Programme for Agriculture and Rural Development (SAPARD), which aimed to help candidate countries manage structural adjustment in their agricultural sectors.

The accession of 10 new states to the EU in May 2004 was expected to have major implications for the CAP, in that the enlargement would double the EU's arable land area and its farming population. In October 2002 it was agreed that the enlargement process would be part-funded by a deal to cap farm subsidies at 2006 levels until 2013, with a 1% annual correction for inflation, and that the new members would be offered direct farm payments at 25% of the level paid to existing member states, rising in stages to 100% over 10 years.

In his mid-term review of the Agenda 2000 CAP reforms, which was published in July 2002, the Commissioner responsible for Agriculture, Rural Development and Fisheries, Franz Fischler, proposed directing more funds towards the rural development policy and severing the link between direct payments to farmers and production (a policy styled 'decoupling'). The latter proposals were partly aimed at preparing for the next meeting of the Doha Development Round of the WTO negotiations, which began in November 2001, where the EU was under pressure to reduce policies that distorted world trade; production-linked subsidies promoted over-production and thus high levels of export subsidies and the dumping of surplus foodstuffs in the markets of developing countries, harming both their export capacity and their domestic market. The reforms suggested by the Commission were, however, vigorously opposed by the main beneficiaries of the current system, notably France. Fischler was obliged to submit a revised plan which restored the link between subsidies and production for certain products whilst still adhering to the principle of decoupling.

The compromise deal for CAP reform was agreed on 26 June 2003 by 14 votes to one (Portugal opposed the agreement in protest at the milk quota allocated to the Azores) and the agreement was finally ratified by the Council of the European Union and the accession states on 29 September. Production-linked subsidies were to be replaced by a Single Farm Payment, which was to be calculated from the subsidies received in the years 2000–02 rather than tied to current production levels and was also to be linked to environmental, food safety and animal welfare standards. This decoupling was to begin in 2005, but France won a concession for countries, including itself, Ireland and Spain, to choose to delay its introduction until 2007. The United Kingdom, the Netherlands and Sweden were all permitted to opt for more radical reform, and the United Kingdom announced its intention to end all production-linked subsidies in 2004. Obligatory decoupling was only partial for beef, cereal and mutton, with production still accounting for up to 25% of payments for cereals and up to 40% for beef. Overall, however, 90% of payments would no longer be linked to production. The Commission was forced to abandon proposed reductions in the intervention price for cereals, following a threat by France to veto the whole agreement. The intervention price for butter was to be cut by 25% over four years and that for skimmed milk powder by 15% over three years. However, reforms to the dairy sector were to be delayed until 2008. The Commission had wanted to impose an upper limit of €300,000 on payments to individual farmers but this was blocked by the United Kingdom. The agreement finally contained instead a commitment to reduce all payments above €5,000 a year by 3% in 2005, 4% in 2006 and 5% in 2007. Increased resources were to be directed towards rural development projects, protecting the environment and improvements to food quality; organic farmers and those offering high-quality produce with special guarantees were to receive grants of up to €3,000 a year for five years. Under the principle of 'modulation', an increasing percentage of direct farm subsidies was to be retained by individual member states to finance rural development measures. Funds were to be collected at a rate of 3% in 2005, 4% in 2006 and 5% in 2007, a level at which they would remain for subsequent years (although the United Kingdom was likely to apply a previously planned modulation rate of 4.5% in 2005 and 2006); the equivalent of at least 80% of the funds gathered in each member state (90% in Germany) should be spent in that country. The issue of sugar (the heavily-subsidized production of which was dominated by France and Germany) proved so divisive that it was removed from discussion and no action was taken regarding olive oil, tobacco and cotton. Since these crops were all of great significance to the developing world and since the overall level of subsidy had not been reduced, the reforms were viewed by many aid agencies and developing countries as inadequate.

In April 2004 the EU Council of Ministers of Agriculture reached agreement for CAP reform of the olive oil, cotton, hops and tobacco sectors. The principle of decoupling aid from production was to be extended to these commodities. A significant share of the current production-linked payments were to be transferred to the single farm payment (which was provided independently of production), although production-linked subsidies were permitted of up to 60% for tobacco, 40% for olive oil, 35% for cotton and 25% for hops. Moreover full decoupling in the tobacco sector was to be introduced progressively over the four years to 2010 and rural development aid was to finance conversion to other crops in tobacco-producing areas. The remaining production aid for olive oil was to be directed at maintaining olive groves with environmental or social value. The reforms were criticized by some non-governmental organizations (NGOs) on the grounds that the partial decoupling of cotton was insufficient to act as an incentive to farmers to convert to other crops and would thus fail to alleviate the problems of cotton-exporting developing countries.

The European Commission finally published proposals to reform the sugar industry in July 2004. Currently the EU sugar sector is characterized by large subsidies, high internal prices and imports by African, Caribbean and Pacific (ACP) countries on favourable terms under quotas. The EU produces large surpluses of sugar, which are disposed of on the world market to the detriment of more competitive producers, notably developing countries. The proposed reforms included: the gradual reduction of the internal EU market price (which was currently three times the international price for the commodity) by about one-third; direct aid payments to sugar producers as compensation; the reduction of quotas (which currently exceeded domestic consumption by about 25%); and the transferability of quotas between member states. The Commission also proposed to review the price and quota levels of the proposed reform, which were originally to take effect in 2005/06, after a three-year period. The proposals were criticized by NGOs as they would not help create a sustainable international sugar market and by ACP countries, which claimed the measures would have a severe adverse affect on ACP economies. A new draft of the proposals was due in June 2005 and the objective was to reach political agreement within the EU on the reforms by December. In October 2004 the WTO ruled that EU sugar subsidies breach world trade rules, upholding complaints by Brazil, Australia and Thailand. The EU announced it would continue with its planned reforms and lodged an appeal against the ruling in January 2005.

On 1 January 2005 10 EU countries began implementation of the CAP reforms agreed in June 2003: Austria, Belgium, Denmark, Germany, Ireland, Italy, Luxembourg, Portugal, Sweden and the United Kingdom. Initially the reform applied only to the main agricultural sectors, including cereals, meat and dairy products (and hops), while tobacco, olive oil and cotton were to be added in 2006. France, Finland, Greece, the Netherlands and Spain were to begin application of the Single Farm Payment in January 2006. Malta and Slovenia were to implement the reforms in 2007 and the other eight new EU members were obliged to participate by 2009.

In 2004 the Commission proposed the adoption of new basic regulation on the financing of the CAP (as part of the EU rural development policy 2007–13) and recommended setting up two new funds, reflecting the two pillars of the CAP: a European Agricultural Guarantee Fund (EAGF) and a single instrument for financing and programming rural development policy, the European Agricultural Fund for Rural Development (EAFRD). Under the EAFRD the member states, regions and action groups were to have greater influence in the design of rural development programmes to meet local needs.

At the Doha Round of the WTO in Cancún, Mexico, in September 2003 the USA and the EU submitted a joint proposal on agriculture that offered far fewer reductions in protectionism than developing countries were seeking. The EU also demanded new rules for foreign investment as well as the right to retain the exclusive use of names of quality products such as parma ham, feta cheese and champagne. The negotiations collapsed without agreement. In May 2004 the EU agreed to phase out its farm export refunds on condition that its trading partners removed their export subsidy programmes, and requested the opening of tariff negotiations on banana imports. A meeting in Mombasa, Kenya, in March 2005 identified ways to accelerate agreement in the Doha Round and progress was expected during 2005 prior to a meeting in Hong Kong in December.

Food safety has become an issue of increasing significance in the EU, especially since the first case of bovine spongiform encephalopathy (BSE), a transmissible disease that causes the brain tissue to degenerate, was diagnosed in cattle in the United Kingdom in 1986. The use of meat and bone meal (MBM) in animal feed was identified as possibly responsible for the emergence of the disease, and was banned for use in cattle feed in the United Kingdom in 1988. MBM was banned throughout the EU from 1994 for ruminants and in December 2000 for all animals. The possible link between BSE and new variant Creutzfeldt-Jakob disease (v-CJD), a degenerative brain disease that affects humans, led to a collapse in consumer confidence in the European beef market in early 1996. By January 2005 148 people had died of v-CJD in the United Kingdom, the location of the vast majority of cases, (France had recorded nine deaths and Ireland two and Italy one), although the number of deaths per year declined to 9 in 2004 from a peak of 28 in 2000. In

March 1996 the Commission accepted that member countries could unilaterally stop imports of British beef on health grounds, pending a decision by a committee of scientific and veterinary experts from all member states. At the end of the month the Commission agreed a full ban on exports from the United Kingdom of live cattle, beef and beef products.

In July 1997 agriculture ministers voted to introduce a complete ban on the use for any purpose of 'specified risk materials' (SRMs—i.e. those parts and organs most likely to carry the BSE prion disease agent) from cattle, sheep and goats. The introduction of the ban was postponed until January 1999, as a result of opposition from a number of EU member states, particularly Germany, as well as the USA. The scope of legislation on undesirable substances in animal feed was extended in May 2002, to cover additives, with the aim of enhancing the safety of animal feed.

In October 1998 Portugal was banned from exporting beef and live cattle, following a twofold increase in reported cases of BSE in the country. In July 1999 the United Kingdom was deemed to have met all of the conditions pertaining to the lifting of the ban on its beef exports; the European Commission announced that exports would be permitted to resume from 1 August in the framework of the Date-based Exportation System, under which animals were tracked by an official monitoring system. The French Government finally lifted its ban on imports of British beef in October 2002, following a ruling by the European Court of Justice in December 2001 ordering it to revoke its unilateral ban.

In May 2001 new legislation was adopted by the European Parliament and the Agriculture Council that consolidated much of the existing legislation on BSE and other transmissible spongiform encephalopathies (TSEs) in bovine, ovine and caprine animals. The new TSE Regulation, which replaced previous emergency legislation and clarified the rules for the prevention, control and eradication of TSEs, came into force on 1 July 2001. It comprised two main elements: the passive surveillance of animals manifesting clinical symptoms compatible with BSE, which was introduced from 1998 at EU level, and active monitoring based on the use of rapid *post mortem* tests, which was introduced from January 2001. The *post mortem* screening was obligatory for all cattle subject to emergency slaughtering, all bovine animals aged over 30 months slaughtered in normal conditions and intended for human consumption, all bovine animals found dead or slaughtered during transport but not for human consumption, and all sheep and goats slaughtered aged at over 18 months. In 2003 about 10m. bovine animals were tested in this way. All the new member states that joined the EU in May 2004 were fully committed to comply with EU legislation on combating BSE, and prior to accession were already removing the SRMs from the food chain and testing healthy cattle aged over 30 months.

By early 2005 Sweden was the only country in the EU that was free of BSE. In 2002 a total of 1,889 cases of BSE were recorded in the whole of the EU. This was reduced to 922 cases in the first 11 months of 2003. In most member states the recorded incidence of the disease was declining; in the United Kingdom, which still had the most registered cases, the number of animals infected declined from 912 in 2002 to 426 in 2003 and 309 in 2004. However, in Spain and Portugal recorded incidences of the disease increased from 118 in 2002 to 145 in 2003 and from 63 in 2002 to 89 in 2003, respectively. This increase presented an obstacle to the lifting of the EU ban on Portuguese beef, as the tendency for cases to decline exhibited since 1999 had been reversed. Although the United Kingdom had many more individual cases, Portugal had the highest incidence rate of the disease in 2003, with 157 BSE cases per million head of cattle compared with 154 in the United Kingdom. The Portuguese authorities claimed that the increase in recorded cases was a direct result of improvements in the diagnostic testing of dead animals and the slaughter of animals born prior to the introduction of the ban on suspect animal feed. EU member states, with the exception of France, agreed to lift the ban on Portuguese beef exports in September 2004. In December 2003 the EU Commission announced that the testing of sheep and goats for BSE-like diseases was to be reduced following the failure of widespread testing to reveal any evidence of infection. However, in January 2005 a goat slaughtered in France in 2002 tested positive for BSE, the first animal other than a cow to have the disease. The EC planned to test an additional 200,000 goats in the 25 EU member states in the following six months.

Following an outbreak of foot-and-mouth disease on farms in the United Kingdom in February 2001, the EU imposed a temporary ban on imports of British livestock products. Three days after the first cases were reported, all movement of susceptible livestock in the United Kingdom was stopped. The culling of sheep imported from the United Kingdom by other member states began in February. An EU-wide ban on assembly points and markets for all potentially affected species was imposed (with exceptions for direct transport to slaughter-houses and other farms) and measures were adopted requiring the disinfection of vehicles travelling from the United Kingdom to other member states. Cases of foot-and-mouth disease were also noted in the Netherlands, France and Ireland. These three

countries were declared free of the disease in September. During the outbreak, the USA and other third countries imposed import restrictions on fresh meat and livestock from the EU. In January 2002 the United Kingdom regained 'clear' status, without recourse to vaccination. In September 2003 the Council of Agriculture Ministers adopted new legislation on measures to control foot-and-mouth disease in the EU in the light of the outbreak in the United Kingdom. The new regulations included the use of emergency vaccination as a preventative option in the event of any future outbreak and the introduction of measures to ensure a high level of preparedness against a potential outbreak, including contingency planning and vaccine banks. Member states had to comply with the provisions by the end of June 2004.

In October 2003 the European Commission announced that it was strengthening a ban on beef from cattle treated with artificial growth hormones, which was originally imposed in 1988, on the grounds that it was dangerous to human health. The USA and Canada, the principal exporters of hormone-treated beef, filed a suit against the ban in 1996 within the WTO, which ruled in 1998 that the ban was illegal as the scientific studies demonstrating the harmfulness of the hormones were inadequate. The EU refused to repeal the ban by the May 1999 deadline set by the WTO, which then granted the USA and Canada leave to impose retaliatory sanctions of US $116.8m. and C $11m. respectively for each year that the ban was in place. The EU subsequently conducted further scientific studies on the alleged harmful effects of the six types of hormones, confirming that one was a proven carcinogen while the others posed an undetermined risk to consumers. The EU claimed in October 2003 that the new scientific studies together with fresh EU legislation meant that the ban now complied with WTO regulations and called for the USA and Canada to lift the punitive trade sanctions on European goods. In early 2005 the EU requested a WTO panel to review the trade sanctions.

The EU's Food and Veterinary Office was established in April 1997 to ensure that the laws on food safety, animal health and welfare and plant health are applied in all member states. The office carries out audits and checks on food safety in member states and in third countries exporting agricultural produce to the EU. Legislation establishing the European Food Safety Authority (EFSA) was signed in January 2002; the new body was to provide independent scientific advice and support on matters with a direct or indirect impact on food safety. It will have no regulatory or judicial power, but will co-operate closely with similar bodies in the member states. The first meeting of the EFSA management board took place in September 2002, while its Advisory Forum was convened for the first time in March 2003.

The EU has also adopted a number of protective measures to prevent the introduction of organisms harmful to plants and plant products. Regulations governing the deliberate release of genetically-modified organisms (GMOs) into the environment have been in force since October 1991, with an approval process based on a case-by-case analysis of the risks to human health and the environment. A total of 18 GMOs were authorized for use in the EU under this directive. An updated directive took effect in October 2002 which introduced principles for risk assessment, long-term monitoring requirements and full labelling and traceability obligations for food and feed containing more than 0.9% GM ingredients. Labelling was not to be limited to foods containing genetically modified DNA or proteins but would also be extended to foods and food ingredients produced from GMOs but containing no detectable GM material, thus providing the consumer with the ability to choose whether or not to consume food derived from GMOs. A new regulation adopted by the Commission in January 2004, which specified a system precisely to identify and trace each GMO product used in the production of all food and animal feeds, completed the EU's regulatory framework on the authorization, labelling and traceability of GMOs. In May 2003 the USA filed a case at the WTO, with the support of Argentina and Canada, demanding that Europe repeal a *de facto* moratorium on new GM food product approvals, which had been in place since 1998, owing to widespread public concern about the technology. The EU claimed that the new rules on the release of GMOs would be sufficiently stringent to allow the issue of marketing permits for new GM products, with EFSA producing risk assessments and participating in the authorization process. Some of the 10 new member states, notably Poland, have been cultivating GM crops for several years. Although by early 2004 all of the accession states had adopted EU regulations on GM products, many had inadequate testing facilities and fears were raised by environmental groups that they would be unable to implement labelling procedures effectively. However, the moratorium was lifted in May 2004 and in September the Commission approved for use across the EU a GM variety of maize that had been endorsed by the Governments of Spain and France in 1998.

In 2004 the Commission, with support from the Council, presented a European action plan for organic food and farming, comprising 21 measures, aimed at promoting the development of organic farming in the EU. This was a response to the strong demand from consumers and the rapid growth in the number of organic producers evident in the Community. The Council also adopted a regulation improving legal protection for organic farming methods and established a programme on the conservation, collection and utilization of genetic resources in agriculture.

In June 1995 the Agriculture Council agreed to new rules on the welfare of livestock during transport. The agreement, which came into effect in 1996, limited transport of livestock to a maximum of eight hours in any 24-hour period, and stipulated higher standards for their accommodation and care while in transit. In January 1996 the Commission proposed a ban on veal crates, which came into effect from January 1998. In April 2001 the Commission adopted new rules for long-distance animal transport, setting out the required standards of ventilation, temperature and humidity control. In June 1999 EU agriculture ministers agreed to end battery egg production within the EU by 2012; in December 2000 a regulation was adopted requiring EU producers to indicate the rearing method on eggs and egg-packaging. A new directive laying out minimum standards for the protection of pigs, including provisions banning the use of individual stalls for pregnant sows and gilts, increasing their living space and allowing them to have permanent access to materials for rooting, was applicable from January 2003 to holdings newly built or rebuilt and from January 2013 to all holdings. Following 13 years of negotiations, in November 2002 agreement was finally reached between the European Parliament and the member states to ban the sale of virtually all animal-tested cosmetic products in the EU from 2009 and to halt all animal testing for cosmetics, ending a system under which about 38,000 animals were used and killed every year. The French Government, however, filed a suit in the European Court of Justice demanding that the ban be quashed on legal and technical grounds.

FISHERIES

The Common Fisheries Policy (CFP) came into effect in January 1983 after seven years of negotiations, particularly concerning the problem of access to fishing-grounds. In 1973 a 10-year agreement had been reached, whereby member states could have exclusive access to waters up to six nautical miles (11.1 km) or, in some cases, 12 miles from their shores; 'historic rights' were reserved in certain cases for foreign fishermen who had traditionally fished within a country's waters. In 1977 the Community set up a 200-mile (370-km) fishing zone around its coastline (excluding the Mediterranean) within which all members would have access to fishing. The 1983 agreement confirmed the 200-mile zone and allowed exclusive national zones of six miles with access between six and 12 miles from the shore for other countries according to specified historic rights. Rules furthering conservation (e.g. standards for fishing tackle) were imposed under the policy, with checks by a Community fisheries inspectorate. Total allowable catches (TACs) were fixed annually by species and were divided into national quotas (prior to 2003 these targets were set under the renewable Multiannual Guidance Programme—MAGP). A body of inspectors answerable to the Commission monitored compliance with the quotas and TACs and with technical measures in Community and some international waters.

In 1990 it was reported that stocks of certain species of fish in EC waters had seriously diminished. Consequently a reduction in quotas was agreed, together with the imposition of a compulsory eight-day period in each month during which fishermen in certain areas (chiefly the North Sea) would stay in port, with exemptions for fishermen using nets with larger meshes that would allow immature fish to escape. In 1992 the compulsory non-fishing period was increased to 135 days between February and December (with similar exemptions).

In December 1992 EC ministers agreed to extend the CFP for a further 10-year period. Two years later ministers concluded a final agreement on the revised CFP, allowing Spain and Portugal to be integrated into the policy by 1 January 1996. A compromise accord was reached regarding access to waters around Ireland and off south-west Great Britain (referred to as the 'Irish box'), by means of which up to 40 Spanish vessels were granted access to 80,000 sq miles of the 90,000 sq mile area. However, the accord was strongly opposed by Irish and British fishermen. In April 1995 seven Spanish vessels were seized by the Irish navy, allegedly for fishing illegally in the Irish Sea. In October fisheries ministers agreed a regime to control fishing in the 'Irish box', introducing stricter controls and instituting new surveillance measures.

The organization of fish marketing involves common rules on size, weight, quality and packing and a system of guide prices established annually by the Council of the European Union. Fish are withdrawn from the market if prices fall too far below the guide price, and compensation may then be paid to the fishermen. Export subsidies are paid to enable the export of fish onto the lower-priced world market and import levies are imposed to prevent competition from low-priced imports. A new import regime took effect from May 1993. This enables regional fishermen's associations to increase prices to a maximum of 10% over the Community's reference price, although this applies to both EU and imported fish.

Initially, structural assistance actions for fisheries were financed by the European Agricultural Guidance and Guarantee Fund (EAGGF). Following the reform of the structural funds in 1993, a separate fund, the Financial Instrument for Fisheries Guidance (FIFG), was set up. The instrument's principal responsibilities include the decommissioning of vessels and the creation, with foreign investors, of joint ventures designed to reduce the fishing effort in EU waters. The fund also supports the building and modernizing of vessels, developments in the aquaculture sector and the creation of protected coastal areas. In addition, it finances contributions to redundancy payments.

The proposals put forward in May 1996 by the European Commission for the fourth MAGP, covering 1997–2002, envisaged catch reductions of up to 40% for species most at risk, and set targets and detailed rules for restructuring fishing fleets in the EU. However, the draft MAGP IV failed to gain approval at the meeting of fisheries ministers held in November 1996. The British Government, in October, insisted that it would not accept additional limits on catches without action to stop 'quota-hopping', in which UK-registered boats were bought by operators in other EU countries (mainly Spain and the Netherlands), which were thus able to gain part of the British fishing quotas. (In mid-1998 the British Government received approval from the Commission to introduce new licensing conditions from 1 January 1999 that would compel the owners of boats involved in 'quota-hopping' to establish economic links with the United Kingdom.) In April 1997, following a number of concessions by the Commission, ministers approved MAGP IV. The programme fixed catch reductions at 30% for species most at risk and at 20% for other over-fished species.

In June 1998 the Council of the European Union overcame long-standing objections from a number of member states and adopted a ban on the use of drift nets in the Atlantic Ocean and the Mediterranean Sea, in an attempt to prevent the unnecessary deaths of marine life such as dolphins and sharks. The ban, which was introduced in January 2002, partially implemented a 1992 UN resolution demanding a complete cessation of drift-net fishing. A series of compensatory measures aimed to rectify any short-term detrimental impact on EU fishing fleets. In July 2003 the Commission proposed the implementation of a total ban on the use of drift nets in the Baltic Sea within four years, and the use of acoustic warning devices on fishing nets throughout most EU waters to prevent dolphins and porpoises from becoming fatally entangled in the nets. These proposals were welcomed by animal welfare organizations, and, in an attempt to head off protests from the fishing industry at the costs involved in fitting the warning devices, the Commission indicated that some of the initial expenditure could be met from EU funds.

With concern over stocks continuing to mount, an emergency 11-week ban on deep-sea cod fishing over 40,000 sq miles of the North Sea was introduced in February 2001. In March similar emergency measures for the west of Scotland entered into effect, while emergency measures for the northern hake catch were adopted in June. Measures for the Irish Sea had been instituted in 2000. In December 2001 the Fisheries Council fixed TACs for 2002, incorporating further substantial reductions, with the aim of achieving 'biologically acceptable' levels of stocks. In June 2002 the Commission presented its long-term recovery plans for cod and hake. Under the plans, the Commission proposed establishing a procedure for setting TACs so as to achieve a significant increase in mature fish stocks, with limits on the fishing effort fixed in accordance with the TACs. The plans also provided for the temporary closure of areas where endangered species had congregated, and allowed for more generous EU aid for the decommissioning of vessels (aid for the modernization of vessels, which tends to increase the fishing catch, was to be reduced). The Commission proposed catch limits for deep-water fish stocks (including blue ling, red seabream and black scabbardfish) for the first time in December.

Radical reform of the CFP, aimed at ensuring the sustainable development of the industry, was announced during 2002; the Commission proposed a new multi-annual framework for the efficient conservation of resources and the management of fisheries, incorporating environmental concerns; under the new framework—which was to replace the MAGP system—a long-term approach to attaining/maintaining fish stocks was to be adopted which was designed to give greater responsibility to member states to achieve a better balance between the fishing capacity of their fleets and the available resources (the erstwhile short-term approach, which had focused mainly on annual objectives, had prevented fishermen from planning ahead and, more seriously, had failed to conserve fish stocks). Under the terms of the new framework, quotas for catches of cod, whiting and haddock were substantially reduced, fishermen were to be guaranteed only nine days a month at sea (with a degree of leeway to extend this to 15 days in some circumstances) and public funding for the renewal or modernization of fishing boats was to be abolished after 2004 (although the provision of aid to improve security and working conditions on board was to be maintained). In addition, it was announced that measures were to be taken to develop co-operation among the various fisheries authorities concerned and to strengthen the uniformity of control and sanctions (imposed against rule-breakers) throughout the EU. The powers of the Commission inspectors were to be extended to ensure the equity and effectiveness of the enforcement of EU regulations. Regional advisory councils were also to be established to enable scientists, fishermen and other interested parties to work together to identify modes of achieving sustainable fisheries in the region concerned. In an attempt to compensate for the ongoing decline of the EU fishing fleet, a number of socio-economic measures were introduced, including the provision of aid from member states to fishermen and vessel owners who have temporarily to halt their fishing activities and the granting of aid to fishermen to help them retrain to convert to professional activities outside the fisheries sector, while permitting them to continue fishing on a part-time basis. The new measures were instigated on 1 January 2003. They replaced the basic rules governing the CFP since 1993 and substantially amended the regulation on structural assistance in the fisheries sector through the FIFG. A new regulation setting up an emergency fund to encourage the decommissioning of vessels (known as the 'Scrapping Fund') was also adopted.

In December 2003 the EU fisheries ministers and the European Commission reached an agreement on quotas for 2004 that aimed to strike a balance between conserving stocks and protecting the industry. Quotas for cod and hake catches in the North Sea were frozen at the levels set for 2003, while the North Sea fishing fleet was permitted to catch 30% more prawns and 53% more haddock, compared with the previous year, owing to flourishing stocks of these species. The Commission stopped short of following scientific advice that fishing for cod and some other species should be suspended entirely in the North and Irish Seas; many scientists claimed that, unless a complete ban were imposed, cod stocks could disappear completely, as had happened off the east coast of Canada in the early 1990s following many years of over-fishing. According to scientific calculations, in the early 2000s cod stocks in the North Sea had fallen to a mere one-tenth of their level at 1970. In addition to the setting of annual quotas, longer-term recovery programmes for cod and hake were also agreed, in an effort to establish sustainable conservation measures which would (ideally) avoid the necessity of continuing with the existing annual bartering system. In a further attempt to ease stocks, restrictions on the number of days fishermen were permitted to spend at sea were maintained for 2004 and the area covered by these restrictions was extended, and the Commission proposed the imposition of stricter controls to clamp down on illegal fishing, which the existing system was poorly equipped to prevent.

In November 2004 the North Sea Regional Advisory Council (RAC) was established in Edinburgh, Scotland; six other RACs were to be created in the near future as part of the 2002 reform of the CFP (see above). In December, following opposition from the United Kingdom and other EU member states with a North Sea coastline, the European Commission abandoned proposals to close depleted cod grounds in parts of the North Sea, the Irish Sea, the west of Scotland, the Baltic Sea and the English Channel. Later that month the Fisheries Council reached agreement on national fishing quotas for 2005. Overall, TACs were to be reduced by approximately 10% (a smaller reduction than originally envisaged) and the number of fishing days per month was to be cut by one day for white fish vessels in the North Sea and by two days for white fish vessels in the west of Scotland. In addition, new catch limitations were agreed for a number of deep-sea stocks not previously covered by TACs, more stringent monitoring restrictions were to be imposed to ensure that fishermen did not exceed quotas, and the Commission presented a communication aiming to simplify the implementation of the CFP. As in previous years, various environmentalist groups expressed their disappointment at the outcome of the negotiations and claimed that the adopted measures would fail to prevent the irreversible destruction of cod stocks in EU waters.

Bilateral fisheries agreements have been signed with other countries (Norway, Sweden, Canada and the USA) allowing limited reciprocal fishing rights and other advantages ('reciprocity agreements'), and with some African and Indian Ocean countries that receive technical and financial assistance in strengthening their fishing industries in return for allowing EU boats to fish in their waters ('development co-operation agreements'). Following the withdrawal of Greenland from the Community in February 1985, Community vessels retained fishing rights in Greenland waters, in exchange for financial compensation. In recent years, however, owing to growing competition for scarce fish resources, it has become increasingly difficult for the EU to conclude bilateral fisheries agreements giving its fleets access to surplus fish stocks in the waters of third countries.

The enlargement of the EU in May 2004 was expected to have a limited impact on the CFP, owing to the fact that, of the 10 accession states, only four had sizeable fishing industries (namely Poland,

Estonia, Latvia and Lithuania); moreover, the combined total annual catch of these four states in the early 2000s was equivalent to less than 7% of the EU total. Prior to their joining the EU in 2004 the accession states were obliged to establish the necessary administrative capacity for applying the obligations arising from the CFP, including the modernization and renewal of old fishing vessels, the joint conservation of resources, the training of fisheries inspectors, the implementation and monitoring of common marketing standards, the introduction of EU health and hygiene standards, the management of structural policy in fisheries and aquaculture, and the compilation of a register of fishing vessels.

RESEARCH AND TECHNOLOGY

In the amendments to the Treaty of Rome, effective from July 1987, a section on research and technology was included for the first time, defining the extent of Community co-operation in this area. Most of the funds allocated to research and technology are granted to companies or institutions that apply to participate in EU research programmes. In March 1996 task forces established by the Commission presented a report identifying priority topics for European research: the car of tomorrow; educational software and multimedia; new generation aircraft; vaccines and viral diseases; trains and railway systems of the future; intermodal transport; maritime systems; and the environment, with a particular focus on water resources.

In January 2000 the Commission launched an initiative to establish a European Research Area (ERA). The aim was to promote the more effective use of scientific resources within a single area, in order to enhance the EU's competitiveness and create jobs. ERA was to provide venture capital and tax breaks for research and high-technology start-up companies. The creation of ERA was to be supported through the Sixth Framework Programme for research and technological development (FP6), which was launched in 2002. Covering the period 2002–06, the programme, which had a budget of €17,500m. (€16,270m. allocated to the European Community and €1,230m. to the European Atomic Energy Community), aimed to integrate research capacities in Europe (for example by establishing networks of excellence and jointly-implemented national programmes), and to concentrate on priority areas such as genomics, sustainable development, aeronautics and space, information technology and food safety. During 2003–04 plans were discussed regarding the proposed establishment of a European Research Council, which, as an independent funding body for science, would play a vital role in the ERA. Many observers claimed that, unless such a body were set up, hundreds of European scientists would relocate to the USA and parts of Asia, where research funding was substantially greater than in Europe. The FP6 funding system was widely criticized as being overly bureaucratic, biased towards large, complex collaborations and subject to political pressures.

The European Strategic Programme for Research and Development in Information Technology (ESPRIT) was inaugurated in 1984 and concentrated on five key areas: advanced micro-electronics; software technology; advanced information processing; office automation; and computer integrated manufacturing. One-half of the programme was financed by the EU and one-half by the participating research institutes, universities and industrial companies. In 1998 ESPRIT was integrated into the EU's Information Society Technologies (IST) initiative under the fifth framework programme (FP5, 1998–2002). The IST initiative is designed to accelerate the emergence of an information society in Europe by promoting the development of high-quality, affordable services.

In July 1997 the European Parliament approved the Life Patent Directive, a proposal aiming to harmonize European rules on gene patenting in order to promote research into genetic diseases, despite objections over the ethical implications. In December 2000 the EU agreed to establish a parliamentary committee to examine new developments in human genetics. In late 2001 the Commission set up a website to encourage debate on embryonic stem cell research (which could help in the treatment of diseases such as diabetes and Parkinson's), aiming to create a dialogue between experts and the public. The EU is also participating actively in the international human genome project, which seeks to characterize the genomes of humans and other organisms, through mapping and sequencing of their DNA. Despite bitter condemnation from a number of campaign groups, in November 2003 the European Parliament voted to allow EU funds to be spent on controversial stem cell research; the following month, however, at a meeting of the Council of the European Union, Germany, Austria and Italy reiterated their strong opposition to EU funding of embryo research; the proposal was blocked and the moratorium on central funding was extended indefinitely. Despite opposition on religious and ethical grounds, Europe is leading the way in stem cell research, which is regarded by many as one of the most promising and potentially profitable areas of biotechnology.

The EU is making efforts to integrate space science into its research activities, and is increasingly collaborating with the European Space Agency (ESA). In September 2000 the EU and the ESA adopted a joint European strategy for space, and in the following year the two bodies established a joint task force. In November 2001 the European Commission and the ESA agreed to launch a Global Monitoring for Environment and Security (GMES) initiative—based on a combination of *in situ* (land, sea and air) and space-based monitoring—which was expected to be fully operational by 2008. In March 2002 the EU approved the development of the 'Galileo' civil satellite navigation and positioning system, which was to be based on a network of 30 orbiting satellites and which was to be compatible and interoperable with the global positioning system (GPS) currently operated by the US military and with the Russian Glonass system. Start-up costs for Galileo, which was to be financed jointly by the ESA and the EU, were projected at €3,600m.; the system was expected to require €220m. a year for maintenance from the date of its launch (which was set at 2008). Galileo Industries was to be located in Germany, which was also to take charge of the space sector, while a second base was to be located in Rome, with Italy in charge of systems engineering. In October 2003, despite objections from the USA, it was announced that the People's Republic of China and India both intended to invest considerable sums of money in the Galileo project. In December 2004 the Council of the EU approved the deployment phase of Galileo, covering the construction and launch of satellites and the building of ground receiving stations. This phase of the project was to be undertaken by Galileo Industries and was estimated to cost around €2,100m. Galileo, which was expected to lead to the creation of about 150,000 jobs, was projected to improve greatly the accuracy and reliability of navigation and timing signals received across the planet. The system was to have many practical applications: e.g. traffic management, direct information for the emergency services, and the prevention of natural disasters such as floods and fires. Four satellites were expected to be launched in 2008, with the whole constellation of 30 projected to be in orbit by the end of the decade.

In January 2005, following four years of negotiations, the ESA and Russia signed an agreement to allow closer co-operation over the use of facilities and exchange of information. Russia was accorded special status in the ESA and was to be permitted to use the Agency's space port in Kourou, French Guiana, for rocket launches. The first launch of a Russian Soyuz craft from Kourou was tentatively scheduled for December 2006.

In February 2000 the European Parliament called for action to be taken to combat the under-representation of women in science. The Commission is working towards a target of 40% participation by women at all levels in the implementation and management of research programmes.

The Joint Research Centre (JRC) was established under the European Atomic Energy Community. Directed by the European Commission, but relying for much of its funding on individual contracts, the JRC is, in fact, a collection of seven institutes, based at five different sites around Europe—Ispra (Italy), Geel (Belgium), Karlsruhe (Germany), Seville (Spain) and Petten (Netherlands). The Directorate-General and the Institutional and Scientific Relations Directorate are based in Brussels—the former co-ordinates the research undertaken at the seven institutes, while the latter serves as a link between the institutes and European policy-makers. While nuclear research and development remain major concerns of the institutes, their research efforts have diversified substantially over the years. In 2000 the JRC restructured its work around four areas: safety of food and chemicals; the environment (including climate change, sustainability and biodiversity); the dependability of information systems and services; and nuclear safety and safeguards. In particular, it prioritized work on genetically-modified organisms. Nuclear work accounted for about 27% of total JRC activities in 2000, with the share accounted for by non-nuclear work increasing. The JRC also provides technical assistance to applicant countries. The JRC's budget for the FP6 period was €1,050m. (€760m. for non-nuclear activities and €290m. for nuclear activities).

The EU also co-operates with non-member countries (particularly EFTA states) in bilateral research projects. The Commission and 35 (mainly European) countries—including the members of the EU as individuals—participate, as full members, in the EUREKA programme of research and development in market-orientated industrial technology, which was launched in 1985; in addition to the full members, a number of countries have some sort of associate status. EUREKA (the acronym of the European Research Co-ordination Agency), which is more a sponsor of projects than a programme, focuses on robotics, engineering, IT and environmental science, allows resources to be pooled and promotes collaboration. Most of EUREKA's funding is provided by private sources. The Community research and development information service (CORDIS) disseminates findings in the field of advanced technology, with nine databases, while the 'Value' programme funds the publication and dissemination of technical reports from specific research projects. In 1994 a European Technology Assessment Network (ETAN) was developed to improve the dissemination of technological research findings; under the FP5 this was replaced by the Strategic Analysis

of Specific Political Issues (STRATA) programme, which aims to promote dialogue between researchers and policy-makers on general science, technology and innovation policy issues of European relevance. The programme supports the establishment of networks and expert groups to improve the development of science and technology policies at all levels and to aid interaction with other policy fields.

ENERGY

The treaty establishing the European Atomic Energy Community ('Euratom') came into force on 1 January 1958. This was designed to encourage the growth of the nuclear energy industry in the Community by conducting research, providing access to information, supplying nuclear fuels, building reactors and establishing common laws and procedures. A common market for nuclear materials was introduced in 1959 and there is a common insurance scheme against nuclear risks. In 1977 the Commission began granting loans on behalf of Euratom to finance investment in nuclear power stations and the enrichment of fissile materials. An agreement with the International Atomic Energy Authority entered into force in 1977, to facilitate co-operation in research on nuclear safeguards and controls. The EU's Joint Research Centre (JRC, see Research and Technology) conducts research on nuclear safety and the management of radioactive waste.

The Joint European Torus (JET) is an experimental thermonuclear machine designed to pioneer new processes of nuclear fusion, using the 'Tokamak' system of magnetic confinement to heat gases to very high temperatures and bring about the fusion of tritium and deuterium nuclei. Fusion powers stars and is viewed as a 'cleaner' approach to energy production than nuclear fission and fossil fuels. Switzerland and Romania are also members of the JET project (formally inaugurated in 1984), which is based at Culham in the United Kingdom and which is funded by the European Commission. The project is a collaboration between all European fusion organizations, and involves technology and physics research from the global scientific and engineering community. In 1991 JET became the first fusion facility in the world to achieve significant production of controlled fusion power. The European Fusion Development Agreement (EFDA), which entered into force in January 1999 (and was subsequently extended until 2004), and a new JET implementing agreement, which came into force in January 2000, provide the framework for the collective use of the JET facilities. In 1988 work began with representatives of Japan, the former USSR and the USA on the joint design of an International Thermonuclear Experimental Reactor (Iter), based on JET but with twice its capacity. The aim of Iter was to demonstrate the scientific and technical capacities of fusion energy for peaceful, commercial purposes. By early 2005 Iter had become very much an international project, with participant teams from the People's Republic of China, the EU (represented by Euratom), Japan, the Republic of Korea, Russia and the USA. All of the participants were under the auspices of the International Atomic Energy Association. Design work on Iter was being carried out at two joint work sites, at Naka in Japan and at Garching in Germany. Two candidate sites for the construction of the vast trial reactor were under consideration in early 2005—Cadarache in France and Rokkasho-Mura in Japan—but the six participant teams were evenly split over which of the two to choose. Once activated, the reactor would be the first fusion device to produce thermal energy at the level of conventional electricity-producing power stations, and would pave the way for commercial power production.

Legislation on the completion of the 'internal energy market', adopted in 1990, aimed to encourage the sale of electricity and gas across national borders in the Community by opening national networks to foreign supplies, obliging suppliers to publish their prices and co-ordinating investment in energy. Energy ministers reached agreement in June 1996 on rules for the progressive liberalization of the electricity market. In December 1997 the Council agreed rules to allow the gas market to be opened up in three stages, over a 10-year period.

In 2001 the Commission amended the timetable for liberalizing the electricity and gas markets: by 2003 all non-domestic consumers were to have the freedom to choose their electricity supplier; by 2004 non-domestic consumers were to have the freedom to choose their gas supplier; and by 2005 all consumers, domestic and non-domestic, would be able to choose both suppliers. The Commission further proposed that the management of transmission and distribution grids should be legally separated from production and sales activities (except for small-scale distribution companies). It was suggested that network access tariffs should be published and approved by national regulators before entering into force, and that a regulator should be established for each member state. To create a genuine single market, the Commission proposed adopting rules on tariff-setting across borders, developing a European infrastructure plan for electricity and gas, and negotiating reciprocal agreements on the opening of electricity markets with the EU's neighbours. In June 2002 the European Council confirmed amended target dates for the complete two-stage liberalization of the markets: opening up by July 2004 for non-domestic users and by July 2007 for domestic users. The European Regulators Group for electricity and gas was established in November 2003 to act as an advisory group of independent national regulatory authorities to assist the European Commission in consolidating the internal market for electricity and gas.

The Commission has consistently urged the formation of an effective overall energy policy. The five-year programmes, SAVE and SAVE II, introduced respectively in 1991 and 1995, aimed to establish energy efficiency (e.g. reduction in the energy consumption of vehicles and the use of renewable energy) as a criterion for all EU projects. In February 2002 SAVE was integrated into the 'Energy, Environment and Sustainable Development—EESD' thematic programme initiated under the Fifth Framework Programme (FP5) for 1998–2002. In 2002 the Commission proposed a new multi-annual programme (as part of the Sixth Framework Programme—FP6) for action in the field of energy for the period 2002–06. The programme aimed to focus on security of energy supply, rational and effective use of energy, and promotion of renewable energy. In November 2002 a budget of €190m. was agreed for the energy programme incorporated in FP6.

Renewable energy sources (RES), such as wind, solar, biomass and small-scale hydropower, provided less than 6% of the total energy produced in the EU in 1996. In May 1998, following the publication of a report by the Commission in late 1997, the Council committed the EU to increasing the use of RES to 12% by 2010. In May 2000 the EU set out a fourfold strategy on the promotion of electricity from RES in the internal energy market, based on the 1997 report. In December 2000 an action plan on energy efficiency was adopted, setting out measures to integrate energy efficiency into other EU policies and programmes. In June 2003 the EU adopted a new programme entitled Intelligent Energy for Europe (EIE), the aim of which was to strengthen the security of supply and to promote energy efficiency and RES. The EIE, which was basically a support programme for non-technological actions, was to run from 2003 until 2006, and was to receive funding totalling €200m. (rising to around €250m. on the enlargement of the EU in May 2004). A new campaign, the Campaign for Sustainable Energy (2004–07), was launched in mid-2004 to succeed the Campaign for Take-Off (1999–2003). The Renewable Energy Partnership scheme was used in both campaigns to involve public and private partners in supporting RES and energy efficiency.

Energy ministers from the EU member states and 12 Mediterranean countries agreed at a meeting held in June 1996 in Trieste, Italy, to develop a Euro-Mediterranean gas and electricity network. The first Euro-Med Energy Forum was held in May 1997, and an action plan (covering the years 1998–2002) to develop an integrated network was adopted in May 1998. In May 2003 the energy ministers of the Euro-Med partnership (including the ministers from the 10 accession states) adopted a declaration launching the Second Regional Energy Plan (2003–06). The Energy Forum's objectives, which promoted massive projects for the creation of North-South and South-South transmission infrastructures, were criticized by environmentalist groups in respect of both environmental and financial concerns.

In 1997 the Community agreed to help a number of newly independent eastern European countries to overcome energy problems by means of the Interstate Oil and Gas Transport to Europe programme (INOGATE). The overall aim of this programme was to improve the security of Europe's energy supply by promoting the regional integration of the oil and gas pipeline systems both within eastern Europe itself and towards the export markets of Europe and the West in general, while acting as a catalyst for attracting private investors and international financial institutions to these pipeline projects. INOGATE originally formed part of the TACIS (Technical Assistance to the Commonwealth of Independent States) programme (see External Relations). Under the Umbrella Agreement of INOGATE, which officially came into force as an international treaty in February 2001, however, the programme is now open to all interested countries (regardless of their individual status as an oil- and gas-producing country or as a transit country). By early 2004 the Agreement had been signed by 21 states of Central Asia, the Caucasus, Eastern Europe and the EU. One of the stated objectives of INOGATE in the mid-2000s was to encourage other key countries, such as Iran and other Mediterranean countries (in addition to Greece and Turkey, which were already signatories) to sign the Umbrella Agreement.

At the sixth EU-Russia summit, held in Paris in October 2000, the two sides agreed to institute an energy dialogue on a regular basis with a view to establishing a strategic EU-Russia energy partnership.

In addition, the EU promotes trans-European networks (TENs, see also Transport Policy), with the aim of developing European energy, telecommunications and transport through the interconnection and opening-up of national networks. Over the years progress on the development of EU energy networks has proved slow, partly owing to difficulties in co-operation and co-ordination between member states regarding cross-border issues. In 2003 a revision of the guide-lines for TEN-Energy (TEN-E) was undertaken to take into account the priorities of the enlarged EU, in particular the competitive operation of the internal energy market and the improvement of the energy supply for the 25 member states. An important target, therefore, was to integrate fully the new member states in these guide-lines and lists of projects. The revised guide-lines were as follows: to enhance the security of energy supplies in Europe; to strengthen the internal energy market of the enlarged EU; to support the modernization of energy systems in partner countries; to increase the share of renewable energies, in particular in electricity generation; and to facilitate the realization of major new energy infastructure projects. It was estimated that the funding required for the creation of the TEN-E infrastructure considered necessary over the following decade would total €40,000m. (€26,000m. for investments within the EU and €14,000m. for investments outside the EU).

In November 1999 the Commission indicated the need to strengthen the EU's 'Northern Dimension' energy policy (covering Scandinavia, the Baltic states and northwest Russia) through the reinforcement of international co-operation, the opening-up of markets, the promotion of competition and the improvement of nuclear safety. In a communication in September 2000 the Commission set out the broad lines of a new EU strategy on nuclear safety in central and eastern Europe and the former Soviet states. The strategy entailed supporting those countries in their efforts to improve operating safety, strengthening their regulatory frameworks, and closing reactors that could not be upgraded to an acceptable standard. The enlargement of the EU had implications for nuclear safety, since five of the 10 new member states that joined the Union in May 2004 had nuclear reactors, mostly of the old Soviet design.

In November 2000 the Commission adopted a Green Paper on the security of energy supply, which was aimed at launching a broad debate on the role of each energy source, with regard to the security of supply, sustainable development, questions of enlargement, and action needed to combat climate change. Security of supply is of vital importance as the EU currently meets around 50% of its energy requirements through imports (this figure was expected to increase substantially over the next decade or so). Following the outbreak of hostilities in Iraq in March 2003, the Commission expressed particular concern about the risk of oil price fluctuations, stock management, use of national fiscal measures and security of the energy infrastructure.

ENTERPRISE AND INDUSTRY

Industrial co-operation was the earliest activity of the Community. The treaty establishing the European Coal and Steel Community (ECSC) came into force in July 1952, and by the end of 1954 nearly all barriers to trade in coal, coke, steel, pig-iron and scrap iron had been removed. The ECSC treaty expired in July 2002, and the provisions of the ECSC treaty were incorporated in the EEC treaty, on the grounds that it was no longer appropriate to treat the coal and steel sectors separately.

In the late 1970s and 1980s measures were adopted radically to restructure the steel industry in response to a dramatic reduction in world demand for steel. These included production capacity quotas, a reduction in state subsidies and financial compensation for job losses (in the mid-1970s the European steel industry employed around 774,000 workers). During the 1990s, however, new technologies and modern production processes were introduced, and the European steel sector showed signs of substantial recovery. Privatization and cross-border mergers also improved the industry's competitive performance and by the early 2000s Europe was very much a world leader in high-quality steel production and a competitive global exporter. In the early 2000s the European steel industry had a total annual production of around 160m. metric tons, it generated about €90,000m.–€100,000m. per year, and it directly employed more than 250,000 EU citizens (with several times this number employed in the steel-processing, usage and recycling industries).In 1996 the Commission adopted a new code on steel aid, for the period 1997–2002. The new code stipulated the conditions under which member states could grant aid to steel companies, namely for research and development, environmental protection, and for full or partial closures of capacity. In March 2004 the European Commission and major stakeholders in the European steel industry launched the European Steel Technology Platform. This high-level group included research institutes in the steel industry, key stakeholders, trade unions, national regulators, universities, etc. The long-term aim of the Platform was to help the sector meet the challenges of the global marketplace, changing supply and demand patterns, environmental objectives (e.g. a reduction in harmful emissions), and the streamlining of EU and national legislation and regulation in this field. In addition, with the May 2004 enlargement of the EU, the need for extensive restructuring of the steel industries was pressing. The steel industry played a relatively larger role in the

10 new member states, compared with the existing 15 members (in 2002 steel production in the accession states amounted to 26.1m. tons). In 2002 the Commission adopted a report on state aid to the coal industry, and in particular the results of restructuring, rationalization and modernization in the member states that still produce coal.

The European textile and clothing industry has been seriously affected by overseas competition over an extended period. From 1974 the Community participated in the Multi-fibre Arrangement (MFA, see WTO, see p. 357), to limit imports from low-cost suppliers overseas. However, as a result of the Uruguay Round of GATT (General Agreement on Tariffs and Trade) trade negotiations, the MFA was progressively eliminated during 1994–2004. An action plan for the European textile and clothing industry was drawn up in 1997. This was designed to improve competitiveness, facilitate structural adjustment in the industry and improve conditions of employment and training. A report published by the Commission in 2000 established future priorities for the sector, focusing on preparations for the enlargement of the EU and systems for co-operation in the 'new economy'. Particular importance was attached to ensuring a smooth transition to the quota-free world environment (from 1 January 2005), to enable third countries currently exporting to the EU to maintain their competitive position, and to secure for EU textile and clothing industries in third countries market access conditions similar to those offered by the EU. In 2002 the EU was the world's largest exporter of textile products, with a 15% share, and the world's second largest (after the People's Republic of China) exporter of textiles and clothing, with an 11% share. In the same year the EU accounted for around 20% of total global textile and clothing imports (valued at about €71,000m.), second after the USA, which accounted for around 24%.

Production in EU member states' shipyards has fallen drastically since the 1970s, mainly as a result of competition from shipbuilders in the Far East. In the first half of the 1980s a Council directive allowed for subsidies to help reorganize the shipbuilding industry and to increase efficiency, but subsequently rigorous curbs on state aid to the industry were introduced. In July 1994 the EU signed an accord with Japan, the USA, the Republic of Korea and the Nordic countries to end subsidies to the shipbuilding industry from 1996, subject to ratification by member states. However, subsidies available in several EU countries in 1996 were higher than the official ceiling, and state aid was also given for industrial restructuring (for example, for modernization of east German shipyards) and for rescuing state-owned yards in difficulties (as in Spain). State aid was eventually phased out in early 2001. In April 2002 the Commission adopted its fifth report on the state of world shipbuilding. It confirmed previous observations that, in the absence of an international agreement, the market was facing a serious crisis, owing to the extremely low prices offered by South Korean shipyards. In May 2002 the EU agreed to launch WTO procedures against South Korea, and to establish a 'temporary defensive mechanism' (TDM) of state subsidies to protect European shipbuilding against unfair South Korean practices. In 2003 a report entitled 'LeaderSHIP 2015' was presented by the Commission and a high-level group of shipping experts, which included 30 recommendations for the future development of the EU shipbuilding and ship repair sector. The report indicated that the strength of the European shipbuilding industry lay in the construction of sophisticated vessels, and consequently suggested that aid should be diverted from production aid to development aid. It also stated that the shipyards of Europe should promote safer and more 'environmentally friendly' ships.

Harmonization of national company law to form a common legal structure within the Community has led to the adoption of directives on disclosure of information, company capital, internal mergers, the accounts of companies and of financial institutions, the division of companies, the qualification of auditors, single-member private limited companies, mergers, take-over bids and the formation of joint ventures. In March 2004 the European Commission proposed stringent new rules for auditors in an attempt to prevent accounting scandals; the proposed directive stated that all companies listed on the stock market would be obliged to have independent audit committees which would recommend an auditor for shareholder approval. In September the Commission launched a broad strategy to prevent financial and corporate malpractice. The strategy recommended timely and effective implementation of the Financial Services Action Plan and the Action Plan for Company Law and Corporate Governance, and its key elements were enhanced transparency, improved traceability and better co-ordinated enforcement. In October a 15-member European Corporate Governance Forum was established to monitor corporate governance practices throughout the EU with a view to bringing them closer together.

The European Patent Convention was signed in 1973 and entered into force in 1977. In June 1997 the Commission published proposals to simplify the European patent system through the introduction of a unitary Community patent, which would remove the need to file patent applications with individual member states. The Commission hoped to have the patent in place by the end of 2001, but disagreements between member states resulted in this deadline being missed and in early 2005 the patent had still not been introduced (the main obstacle was the issue of the translation of the claims in the patent). Once established, the Community patent was to be issued by the European Patent Office (EPO), based in Munich.

An Office for Harmonization in the Internal Market (OHIM), based in Alicante, Spain, was established in December 1993, and is responsible for the registration of Community trade marks and for ensuring that these receive uniform protection throughout the EU. Numerous directives have been adopted on the technical harmonization and standardization of products (e.g. on safety devices in motor vehicles, labelling of foodstuffs and of dangerous substances, and classification of medicines).

The liberalization of Community public procurement has played an important role in the establishment of the internal market. A directive on public supplies contracts (effective from January 1989, or from March 1992 in Greece, Portugal and Spain) stipulated that major purchases of supplies by public authorities should be offered for tender throughout the Community. Public contracts for construction or civil engineering works in excess of ECU 5m. were to be offered for tender throughout the EC from July 1990 (March 1992 for Greece, Portugal and Spain). From January 1993 the liberalization of procurement was extended to include public utilities in the previously excluded sectors of energy, transport, drinking-water and telecommunications. In 1996 the Commission launched the Système d'information pour les marchés publics (SIMAP) programme, which gives information on rules, procedures and opportunities in the public procurement market, and aims to encourage the optimum use of information technology in public procurement. During 2002 the European Parliament adopted a regulation aimed at simplifying the rules on procurement of contract notices, by introducing a single system for classifying public procurement, to be used by all public authorities. The European Public Procurement Network was established in January 2003. The objective of this network, which comprises all of the EU member states, EU candidate countries, EEA members, Switzerland and other European countries, was to strengthen the application of public procurement rules through a mutual exchange of experience. In December 2003 reforms to the EU's public procurement legislation were introduced in an attempt to make the often complex rules more transparent, efficient and comprehensible.

In 1990 the European Council adopted two directives with the aim of removing the tax obstacles faced by companies operating across borders: the Merger Directive was designed to reduce tax measures that could hamper business reorganization and the Parent-Subsidiary Directive abolished double taxation of profit distributed between parent companies in one member state and their subsidiaries in others. In October 2001 the Commission presented a strategy for company taxation in the EU, suggesting the introduction of a single consolidated tax base, to eliminate the large variations in effective company tax rates across the EU. The Commission noted that a new approach was needed, in view of increasing globalization and economic integration in the internal market as well as developments such as economic and monetary union (EMU, see Economic Co-operation). In that month the European Council also adopted two legislative instruments enabling companies to form a European Company (known as a Societas Europaea—SE). A vital element of the internal market, the legislation gave companies operating in more than one member state the option of establishing themselves as single companies, thereby able to function throughout the EU under one set of rules and through a unified management system; companies might be merged to establish an SE. The legislation was aimed at making cross-border enterprise management more flexible and less bureaucratic, and at helping to improve competitiveness. In 2003 the Commission launched public consultations on two initiatives aimed at establishing a common tax base: one concerned the possibilty of using the International Accounting Standards as a starting point to develop an EU-wide consolidated tax base for companies, and the other involved a 'Home State Taxation' pilot project for small and medium-sized enterprises (SMEs). At a meeting of the EU's finance ministers held in the Netherlands in September 2004 there were wide divergences of opinion expressed over the proposals to co-ordinate tax policy throughout the Union; the United Kingdom and Ireland were among those member states which rejected any centralized interference in domestic taxation.

The Business Co-operation Centre, established in 1973, supplies information to businesses and introduces firms from 70 different countries wishing to co-operate or form links. The Business Co-operation Network (BC-Net) links enterprises, both public and private, which wish to form alliances with others (e.g. licensing agreements), on a confidential basis. The Business Environment Simplification Task Force (BEST) was established in 1997 to consider ways of improving legislation and of removing hindrances to the development of businesses, especially SMEs. BEST presented its final report in 1998; the subsequent action plan, designed to improve the overall environment for business, was endorsed in April 1999.

In September 1995 a Commission report outlined proposals to improve the business environment for SMEs in particular, by improving fiscal policies and access to finance, and introducing measures aimed at reducing delays in payments and lowering the costs of international transactions. In March 1996 the Commission agreed new guide-lines for state aid to SMEs. Aid for the acquisition of patent rights, licences, expertise, etc., was to be allowed at the same level as that for tangible investment. In July 1997 the I-TEC scheme was inaugurated to encourage SMEs to invest in new technology. A Charter for Small Enterprises, approved in June 2000, aimed to support SMEs in areas such as education and training, the development of regulations, and taxation and financial matters, and to increase representation of the interests of small businesses at national and EU level. In October 2001 SMEs comprised 98% of all EU enterprises and employed almost 75m. people. The EU has repeatedly stated that it views small businesses as a vital source of economic growth and employment creation. In January 2005 the Commission launched a €36m. programme to provide finance to SMEs through local banks and other credit institutions, with particular emphasis on the EU's new member states.

The European Investment Bank (see p. 229) provides finance for small businesses by means of 'global loans' to financial intermediaries. A mechanism providing small businesses with subsidized loans was approved by ministers in April 1992. In 2001, noting that SMEs were gradually switching from loan finance to other instruments, including equity, the EU began an initiative to develop European venture capital markets.

A network of 39 Euro Info Centres (EICs), aimed particularly at small businesses, began work in 1987. A total of 314 EICs and 14 Euro Info Correspondence Centres were in operation by early 2005. The EU's other information services for business include the Community Research and Development Information Service (Cordis, see Research and Technology) and the internet-based Dialogue with Business, which brings together advice and data from various sources.

Meeting in Lisbon, in March 2000, the European Council set the EU the new strategic goal of transforming itself into the most competitive and dynamic economy in the world over the following decade. In January 2000 the EU's Directorates-General for Industry and SMEs and for Innovation were transformed into one Directorate-General for Enterprise Policy (subsequently restyled the Enterprise and Industry Directorate General). The Commission subsequently adopted a multiannual programme on enterprise and entrepreneurship covering the period 2001–05, aimed particularly at SMEs. It was noted that business start-ups should be made easier and the cost of doing business in Europe lowered. Stronger measures were proposed for the protection of intellectual property rights (IPRs), and the harmonization of legislation on IPRs was advocated (differences between national laws in this respect could constitute protectionist barriers to the EU's principle of free movement of goods and services). The programme's overall objective was to create a dynamic, sustainable, innovation-based environment for EU businesses and to develop a climate of confidence among investors. In January 2003 the Commission presented a draft directive on the enforcement of IPRs, which aimed to make it dramatically easier to enforce copyrights, patents and trademarks in the EU and to punish those who tampered with technical mechanisms designed to prevent copying or counterfeiting. The proposals were welcomed by the music, film and fashion industries, but were strongly opposed by sections of the telecommunications and information technology industries, which viewed the draft directive as a threat to competition and freedom. In March 2004 the European Parliament voted in favour of the draft directive (with a number of amendments). In November the Commission announced plans to commence monitoring certain countries (particularly the People's Republic of China, Ukraine and Russia) to check that they were making genuine efforts to put a stop to the production of counterfeit goods. The Commission estimated that between 1998 and 2002 the number of counterfeit goods intercepted at the EU's external borders had increased by more than 800%.

In order to analyse the EU's performance, the Commission has established innovation and enterprise policy scoreboards; these involve a set of performance indicators that serve as a benchmark for evaluating progress, looking at indicators such as home internet access, high technology patents, public research and development, ICT expenditure as a proportion of GDP, employment in high-technology manufacturing, etc. The European Innovation Scoreboard (EIS) for 2003 noted that the EU's general innovation performance continued to lag behind that of the USA; particularly large disparities between the USA and the EU were noted in tertiary education and in levels of patenting. The EIS for 2004 confirmed that the innovation gap between the EU and the USA had not been reduced; the USA led Europe in nine of the 11 comparable indicators. Sweden and Finland maintained their leadership positions within the EU, while the new member states were catching up with the other members (although from relatively low levels). The innovation performance of the EU was found to have been relatively constant since 1996, whereas that of the USA and of Japan had further improved, thus widening the innovation gap. The main challenges that the EU needed to address in order to catch up with the USA were the weaknesses in patenting, the lower qualifications of the work-force and the lower levels of expenditure on research and development. The 2004 EIS examined for the first time the differences between various sectors in terms of innovation; the most innovative sector was found to be electrical and optical equipment, while the least innovative sector was textiles and textile products. A network of Innovation Relay Centres (IRCs) has been established to facilitate the transfer of technologies throughout Europe; by 2004 a total of 71 IRCs had been set up.

Through its joint European venture programme, the EU backs the establishment of joint ventures between enterprises from at least two member states. The European Business Angels Network (EBAN) provides a means of introduction between SMEs and investors and encourages the exchange of expertise. The Commission also promotes inter-industry co-operation between enterprises in the EU and in third countries through the Euro-Med Industrial Co-operation working party, the TransAtlantic Business Dialogue (TABD), the EU-Japan Centre for Industrial Co-operation, and the Mercosur-EU Business Forum (MEBF).

COMPETITION

The Treaty of Rome establishing the European Economic Community provided for the creation of a common market based on the free movement of goods, persons, services and capital. The EU's competition policy aims to guarantee the unity of this internal market, by providing access to a range of high-quality goods and services, at competitive prices. It seeks to prevent anti-competitive practices by companies or national authorities, and to outlaw monopolization, protective agreements and abuses of dominant positions. Overall, it aims to create a climate favourable to innovation, while protecting the interests of consumers.

The Commission has wide investigative powers in the area of competition policy. It may act on its own initiative, or after a complaint from a member state, firm or individual, or after being notified of agreements or planned state aid. Before taking a decision, the Commission organizes hearings; its decisions can be challenged before the Court of First Instance and the Court of Justice, or in national courts.

State aid—which ranges from discrimination in favour of public enterprises to the granting of aid to private-sector companies—is contrary to the principles of competition policy. The EU does not attempt to ban state aid completely, but encourages a reduction in its overall level and works to ensure that all aid granted is compatible with the principles of the common market. The procedural rules on state aid were consolidated and clarified in a regulation in 1999. There are several exemptions, notably regarding the provision of aid to small and medium-sized enterprises (SMEs) and for training. The EU has drawn up 'regional aid maps' designed to concentrate aid in those regions with the most severe development problems.

The Treaty of Rome prohibits agreements and concerted practices between firms resulting in the prevention, restriction or distortion of competition within the common market. This ban applies both to horizontal agreements (between firms at the same stage of the production process) and vertical agreements (between firms at different stages). The type of agreements and practices that are prohibited include: price-fixing; imposing conditions on sale; seeking to isolate market segments; imposing production or delivery quotas; agreements on investments; establishing joint sales offices; market-sharing agreements; creating exclusive collective markets; agreements leading to discrimination against other trading parties; collective boycotting; and voluntary restraints on competitive behaviour. Certain types of co-operation considered to be positive, such as agreements promoting technical and economic progress, may be exempt.

In addition, mergers that would significantly impede competition in the common market are banned. The Commission examines prospective mergers in order to decide whether they are compatible with competition principles. In July 2001 the EU blocked a merger between two US companies for the first time, on the grounds that EU companies would be adversely affected. In December 2001 the Commission launched a review of its handling of mergers and acquisitions, focusing on the speed of decisions and on bringing European competition standards in line with those in the USA and elsewhere.

The Commission is attempting to abolish monopolies in the networks supplying basic services to member states. In June 2002 the Council adopted a directive on the opening up of postal services. Liberalization is also being pursued in the gas and electricity, telecommunications and transport sectors. In July 2002 the Commission approved a plan to open the car industry to greater competition, by applying new Europe-wide rules for car sales, giving car dealers the freedom to operate anywhere in the EU. The reforms, which were strongly opposed by car manufacturers and by the

French and German Governments, were due to come into effect in 2005. In January 2005 the Commission launched a new initiative, in collaboration with the European Automobile Manufacturers' Association, to boost the competitiveness of the car industry in the EU. A high-level group, entitled a 'Competitive Automotive Regulatory System for the 21st Century—CARS 21', was to be established in March to look at the challenges of increasing labour productivity, lowering labour costs and promoting technological innovation.

In 2003 the Commission worked to establish detailed provisions of a modernized framework for anti-trust and merger control in advance of the enlargement of the EU in May 2004. In May 2004 major changes to EU competition law and policy (including substantive and procedural reform of the European Community Merger Regulation) entered into force. As part of the reforms, national competition authorities, acting as a network, and national courts were expected to become much more involved in the enforcement of competition rules, and companies were to be required to conduct more self-assessment of their commercial activities. In March 2004 the US Department of Justice criticized the EU's anti-trust action against the US computer software company Microsoft. The EU imposed a fine of €497m. and instructed the company to disclose key elements of its programming (within 120 days) to facilitate the development of competitive products. Microsoft appealed against the decision in the Court of First Instance in Luxembourg in June and the EU penalties were temporarily suspended pending the final outcome of the appeal. In December the court rejected Microsoft's appeal; the US company was widely expected, however, to contest the ruling in the long term at a higher level of the EU judiciary. In October 2004 the USA threatened to launch a dispute at the WTO in protest at alleged massive state subsidies to the civil aircraft manufacturers Airbus. However, the EU threatened retaliatory action regarding state subsidies to the US aircraft manufacturer Boeing. The EU and the USA agreed in January 2005 to attempt to settle the dispute through bilateral talks and refrain from further hostile action at the WTO. In January 2005 the Commission officially launched an investigation into whether the Italian airline Alitalia was receiving illegal state aid.

The international affairs unit of the Directorate-General for Competition co-operates with foreign competition authorities (particularly in the USA) and promotes competition instruments in applicant countries, where it also provides technical assistance. The unit works within the framework of international organizations such as the WTO, the Organisation for Economic Co-operation and Development (OECD) and the United Nations Conference on Trade and Development (UNCTAD).

TELECOMMUNICATIONS, INFORMATION TECHNOLOGY AND BROADCASTING

In 1990 proposals were adopted by the European Council on the co-ordinated introduction of a European public paging system and of cellular digital land-based mobile communications. In 1991 the Council adopted a directive requiring member states to liberalize their rules on the supply of telecommunications terminal equipment, thus ending the monopolies of national telecommunications authorities. In the same year the Council adopted a plan for the gradual introduction of a competitive market in satellite communications; a directive relating to the liberalization of satellite telecommunications equipment and services came into force in late 1994, but allowed for deferment until 1 January 1996. In October 1995 the Commission adopted a directive liberalizing the use of cable telecommunications, requiring member states to permit a wide range of services, in addition to television broadcasts, on such networks. The EU market for mobile telephone networks was opened to full competition as a result of a directive adopted by the Commission in January 1996, according to which member states were to abolish all exclusive and special rights in this area, and establish open and fair licensing procedures for digital services. The telecommunications market was to be fully deregulated by 1998, although extensions to the deregulation schedule were agreed for a number of member states. In October 1997 the Commission announced plans to commence legal proceedings against those member states that had not yet adopted the legislation necessary to permit the liberalization of the telecommunications market. Spain agreed to bring forward the full deregulation of its telecommunications market from January 2003 to 1998, which meant that all the major EU telecommunications markets were, in principle, open to competition from 1998.

In July 1998 the Commission identified 14 cases of unfair pricing after commencing an investigation into the charges imposed by telecommunications companies for interconnection between fixed and mobile telephone networks. In December the Commission suspended some of its investigations, after a number of companies introduced price reductions. In February 2000 the Commission requested that national competition authorities, telecommunications regulators, mobile network operators and service providers give information on conditions and price structures for national and international mobile services.

In July 2000 a comprehensive reform of the regulatory framework for telecommunications—the so-called 'telecoms package'—was launched. The reform aimed to update EU regulations to take account of changes in the telecommunications, media and information technology (IT) sectors. Noting the continuing convergence of these sectors, the Commission aimed to develop a single regulatory framework for all transmission networks and associated services, in order to exploit the full potential for growth, competition and job creation. The Commission recommended, as a priority, introducing a regulation on unbundled access to the local loop (the final connection of telephone wires into the home). The lack of competition in this part of the network was considered a significant obstacle to the widespread provision of low-cost internet access. The regulation obliged incumbent operators to permit shared and full access to the local loop by the end of 2000. In December 2001 the European Parliament voted to adopt a compromise telecoms package. This gave the Commission powers to oversee national regulatory regimes and, in some cases, to overrule national regulatory authorities. It was designed to reduce the dominant market position of monopolies and to open the market to competition. The package included a framework directive and three specific directives (covering issues of authorization, access and interconnection, universal service and users' rights) and measures to ensure harmonized conditions in radio spectrum policy. By the end of 2003 the EU regulatory framework for electronic communications had been completely implemented; during 2004, however, the Commission took a number of member states to court for their failure fully to transpose the new rules of competition in their national laws. A report published by the Commission in December 2004 stated that broadband and mobile telephone services in the newly enlarged EU were benefiting from intensifying competition and strong growth.

The EU is undertaking efforts to make the internet more user-friendly, with targeted online services, technical support and IT training for those at risk of 'digital exclusion'. At the European Council meeting held in January 2000, referred to as the 'dot.com summit', the Commission agreed to put all remaining e-commerce legislation in place by the end of the year. In December 2000 the Commission's programme on European digital content was adopted. Recognizing that a large proportion of the material on the internet originated in the USA, this sought to develop the regional potential in this area. The 'eu' domain name was formally adopted by the European Parliament in April 2002, giving a European identity for providers of services and information. During 2002 the European Council approved a new eEurope 2005 action plan, following on from the earlier eEurope 2002 plan. The new plan aimed to create a dynamic electronic business environment (eBusiness) favourable to private investment and job creation, to modernize—in electronic terms—public services (notably government—eGovernment, hospitals—eHealth and schools—eLearning) and to give everyone the opportunity to participate in the global information society. Particular emphasis was to be placed on the widespread availability and use of broadband networks (at competitive prices) by 2005. In early 2005 a new initiative, entitled i2010, was announced, which was to replace the eEurope 2005 plan when it expired at the end of the year. The three main focuses of the new plan were the promotion of a borderless European 'information space' with the aim of establishing an internal market for electronic communications and digital services; the stimulation of innovation through investment in research and the encouragement of industrial application; and the continuance of the policy of making the EU information society as inclusive and accessible as possible.

The EU maintains several information society programmes. The Community's overall Information Society Technologies (IST) programme (see Research and Technology) is designed to accelerate the emergence of an information society and promotes the development of high-quality, efficient, affordable services. The Interchange of Data between Administrations (IDA) initiative supported the rapid electronic exchange of information between EU administrations—in January 2005 the IDA was renamed the Interoperable Delivery of pan-European eGovernment Services to Public Administrations, Businesses and Citizens (IDAbc) programme. An action plan promoting safer use of the internet, extended in March 2002 until December 2004, aimed to combat illegal and harmful content on global networks. In December 2004 the EU approved a new programme, called Safer Internet plus (2005–08), to promote safer use of the internet and new online technologies and to combat illegal and harmful content (particularly child pornography and violent and racist material).

In 1992 a White Paper proposed the establishment of trans-European networks (TENs) in telecommunications, energy and transport, in order to improve infrastructure and assist in the development of the common market. Following the liberalization of the telecommunications market in 1998, efforts in this area were concentrated on support (through the eTEN programme) for the development of broadband networks and multimedia applications.

The eTen programme focuses strongly on public services, particularly in areas where Europe has a competitive advantage, and its objectives are based on the EU's stated aim of 'an information society for all'.

In October 2003 new digital privacy legislation aimed at stemming the tide of unwanted commercial e-mails (known collectively as 'spam') came into force across the EU. The new rules required companies to gain consent before sending e-mails and introduced a ban on the use of 'spam' throughout the EU. The Commission claimed that 'spam' cost European business almost US$3,000m. in lost productivity in 2002 and that unwanted e-mails accounted for more than one-half of all e-mail traffic. It was widely recognized, however, that concerted international action was required, since most of the 'spam' entering Europe originated from abroad (particularly from the USA). In November 2003 a European Network and Information Security Agency (ENISA) was established in Brussels (on a temporary basis) by a regulation of the European Parliament. The main aims of the Agency, which became fully operational in October 2004 and which was to establish its headquarters in Heraklion, Greece, in the near future, were to promote closer European co-ordination on information security and to provide assistance in the application of EU measures in this field.

In 1991 a controversial directive ('Television without Frontiers') came into force, establishing minimum standards for television programmes to be broadcast freely throughout the Community: limits were placed on the amount of time devoted to advertisements, a majority of programmes broadcast were to be from the Community, where practicable, and governments were allowed to forbid the transmission of programmes considered morally harmful. The 'Media' programme was introduced in the same year to provide financial support to the television and film industry. 'Media III' (2001–05), which aimed to strengthen further the competitiveness of the European audiovisual industry through pre- and post-production support, incorporated two major initiatives—Media Plus, which, while taking account of the new regulatory environment, aimed to encourage the development, distribution and marketing of European audiovisual material; and Media Training, which basically involved the implementation of a training programme for professionals working in the audiovisual industry.

During 2002 the scope of the Media programme was extended to include nine candidate countries, and in 2004 the programme was extended until the end of 2006. In November 2002 the Commission adopted a communication on the promotion and distribution of television programmes, and proposed a revision of the 'Television without Frontiers' directive in the light of technological developments in the field of television broadcasting. In July 2003 the Commission reiterated proposals (originally presented at the Lisbon summit in March 2000) to help film and audiovisual production companies to have access to external funding from banks and other financial institutions by covering some of the costs of the guarantees demanded by these institutions and/or part of the cost of a loan ('discount contract loan') for financing the production of their works.

TRANSPORT

The establishment of a common transport policy is stipulated in the Treaty of Rome, with the aim of gradually standardizing the national regulations that hinder the free movement of traffic within the Community, such as the varying safety and licensing rules, diverse restrictions on the size of lorries, and frontier-crossing formalities. A White Paper in 1992 set out a common transport policy for the EU. The paper proposed the establishment of trans-European networks (TENs) to improve transport, telecommunications and energy infrastructure throughout the Community, as well as the integration of transport systems and measures to protect the environment and improve safety. Significant progress has been made on the trans-European transport network (TEN-T), through harmonization and liberalization; however, it must be noted that work has not advanced as rapidly as expected (partly owing to deficiencies in funding resources and partly owing to the complexities arising from the 2004 enlargement). The overall aim of the EU's TEN-T policy, which included so-called intelligent transport systems and services, was to unite the various national networks into a single European network, by eliminating bottlenecks and adding missing links. The 2000–06 budget for the 14 TEN-T projects totalled €4,600m., funded in part by the European Regional Development Fund, the European Investment Bank and the European Investment Fund. In addition, efforts are being made to increase the private-sector involvement in financing TEN-T, through the development of public-private partnerships (PPPs). The majority of the financial backing, however, is provided by individual member states.

In recent years the EU has focused on integrating environmental issues and questions of sustainable development into transport policy. In September 2001 the Commission adopted a White Paper on Transport Policy for 2010. This set out a framework designed to accommodate the forecast strong growth in demand for transport on a sustainable basis. The new policy aimed to shift the balance between modes of transport by 2010, by revitalizing railways, promoting maritime and inland waterway transport systems, and by linking up different kinds of transport. The paper proposed an action plan and a strategy designed gradually to break the link between economic and transport growth, with the aim of reducing pressure on the environment and relieving congestion.

In 1986 transport ministers agreed on a system of Community-wide permits for commercial vehicles, to facilitate the crossing of frontiers, and in 1993 they agreed on measures concerning road haulage. A common tax system for trucks using EC roads led to the full liberalization of road 'cabotage' (whereby road hauliers may provide services in the domestic market of another member state) by July 1998. In May 1998 transport ministers approved legislation compelling member governments to clear serious obstructions, such as truck blockades, that hinder the free movement of goods. The White Paper on Transport Policy adopted in September 2001 proposed the harmonization of petrol taxes across the EU.

In 1991 directives were adopted by the Council on the compulsory use of safety belts in vehicles weighing less than 3.5 metric tons. Further regulations applying to minibuses and coaches were introduced in mid-1996. In June 2000 the Commission issued a communication setting out measures to improve the safety and efficiency of road transport and to ensure fair competition. These included road traffic monitoring, the regulation of employed drivers' working time, and regularity of employment conditions. In November 2002 the European Parliament adopted a directive on speed limitation devices for certain categories of motor vehicles, including haulage vehicles and passenger vehicles carrying more than eight passengers.

In the late 1980s ministers of transport approved measures to contribute to the liberalization of air transport within the Community. In 1990 ministers agreed to make further reductions in guaranteed quotas for a country's airlines on routes to another country, and to liberalize air cargo services. In 1992 they approved an 'open skies' arrangement that would allow any EC airline to operate domestic flights within another member state (with effect from 1 April 1997). In June 1996 the ministers of transport approved a limited mandate for the Commission to negotiate an 'open skies' agreement with the USA, under which a common EU-US aviation area would be created. However, the USA wished to negotiate on the basis of a full mandate. In October 1998 ministers failed to award a full mandate to the Commission. In November 2002 the European Court of Justice ruled that bilateral 'open-skies' treaties between countries were illegal if they discriminated against airlines from other member states; the ruling was in response to a case brought by the Commission against eight member states that had concluded such agreements with the USA.

In July 1994, despite EU recommendations for tighter controls on subsidies awarded to airlines, as part of efforts to increase competitiveness within the industry, the Commission approved substantial subsidies that had been granted by the French and Greek governments to their respective national airlines. Subsequently, the Commission specified that state assistance could be granted to airlines 'in exceptional, unforeseen circumstances, outside the control of the company'. Following the terrorist attacks perpetrated against targets in the USA in September 2001, and the consequent difficulties suffered by the air transport sector, the EU ruled that a degree of aid or compensation was permissible, but stressed that this must not lead to distortion of competition.

In early 1999 a dispute arose between the EU and the USA over the introduction of new EU legislation to curb aircraft noise. Initially, the EU proposed to prevent aircraft fitted with 'hush kits' from flying in the EU after 1 April 2002 unless they were already operating there before 1 April 1999 (aircraft fitted with hush kits create more noise than newer aircraft, use more fuel and cause more pollution). The legislation was subsequently amended to avert the threat of a temporary boycott of some European flights by the US authorities, and a new directive on the use of a 'balanced approach' to noise management around airports was adopted in March 2002.

In July 2002 the European Parliament adopted a regulation creating a European Aviation Safety Agency (EASA). The EASA (which officially opened its permanent seat in Köln, Germany, in December 2004) was to cover all aircraft registered in member states, unless agreed otherwise. The Commission has also formulated ground rules for enquiries into civil air incidents and has issued proposals for assessing the safety of aircraft registered outside the EU. In October 2001 the Commission proposed establishing common rules in the field of civil aviation safety, to strengthen public confidence in air transport following the terrorist attacks on the USA. Issues addressed included securing cockpits, improving air-ground communications and using video cameras in aircraft. Member states also agreed to incorporate into Community law co-operation arrangements on security measures. These measures covered control of access to sensitive areas of airports and aircraft, control of passengers and hand luggage, control and monitoring of hold luggage, and training of ground staff. In January 2004 the EU reached an agreement on the creation of 'blacklists' of unsafe airlines, through which the Union will be able to name and ban airlines causing concern.

In December 1999 the Commission presented a communication on streamlining air-traffic control to create a Single European Sky, of which the overall aim was to restructure the EU's airspace on the basis of traffic, rather than national frontiers. In December 2002 EU transport ministers agreed on a package of measures under which the separate European air traffic control providers would be regulated as a single entity, and EU airspace over 28,500 feet (approximately 8,690 m) would be under unified control.

In 1986 progress was made towards the establishment of a common maritime transport policy, with the adoption of regulations on unfair pricing practices, safeguard of access to cargoes, application of competition rules and the eventual elimination of unilateral cargo reservation and discriminatory cargo-sharing arrangements. In December 1990 the Council approved, in principle, the freedom for shipping companies to provide maritime transport anywhere within the Community. Cabotage by sea began to be phased in from January 1993 and was virtually complete by January 1999. Cabotage was also introduced in the inland waterways transport sector in 1993. By January 2000 the inland waterways market had been liberalized, although obstacles to the functioning of the single market subsequently persisted, including differing technical regulations among member states.

In March 2000 the Commission adopted a communication on the safety of the seaborne oil trade. It proposed the introduction of a first package of short-term measures to strengthen controls, including the right to refuse access to substandard ships, more stringent inspections and a generalization of the ban on single-hull oil tankers. In May the Commission adopted a proposal to harmonize procedures between bulk carriers and terminals, in order to reduce the risk of accidents caused by incorrect loading and unloading. In the same month the Commission signed a memorandum of understanding with several countries on the establishment of the Equasis database, intended to provide information on the safety and quality of ships. In December the Commission set out a second package of safety measures, broad agreement was reached on the first package, and the EU agreed to accelerate the phasing in of double-hull tankers (single-hull tankers were to be completely phased out by 2010). In June 2002 the European Parliament established by regulation the European Maritime Safety Agency (the permanent seat of which was to be established in Lisbon, Portugal); its tasks were to include preparing legislation in the field of maritime safety, co-ordination of investigations following accidents at sea, assisting member states in implementing maritime safety measures, and providing assistance to candidate countries.

In April 1998 the Commission published a report on railway policy, with the aim of achieving greater harmonization, the regulation of state subsidies and the progressive liberalization of the rail-freight market. In October 1999 EU transport ministers concluded an agreement that was regarded as a precursor to the full liberalization and revitalization of the rail-freight market. Rail transport's share of the total freight market had declined substantially since the 1970s, but it was widely recognized that, in terms of environmental protection and safety, transport of freight by rail was greatly preferable to road haulage. The agreement provided for the extension of access to a planned core Trans-European Rail Freight Network (TERFN, covering some 50,000 km), with a charging system designed to ensure optimum competitiveness. During 2000–04 the EU adopted three 'railway packages' which dealt with the progressive deregulation of the rail-freight market. However, a number of EU member states vehemently opposed granting full access to their national railway networks, and, consequently, the liberalization process (including cabotage) and full implementation of the TERFN was not expected to be completed before 2008. Other measures incorporated in the packages included developing a common approach to rail safety; bolstering principles of interoperability; and setting up a European Railway Agency (ERA). The ERA was established by a regulation of the European Parliament in April 2004 and held its inaugural meeting in July. The main aim of the Agency, the permanent seat of which was to be in Lille/Valenciennes, France, was to reinforce the safety and interoperability of railways in the EU. The EU aims also to carry out a progressive liberalization of passenger rail services.

The Marco Polo programme (2003–06), which succeeded the earlier PACT (pilot action for combined transport) scheme, aimed to reduce road congestion and to improve the environmental performance of the freight transport system within the Community and to enhance intermodality, thereby contributing to an efficient and sustainable transport system. To achieve this objective, the programme supported actions in the freight transport, logistics and other relevant markets. These actions were aimed at maintaining the distribution of freight between various modes of transport at 1998 levels by helping to shift the expected aggregate increase in road freight traffic to short sea shipping, rail and inland waterways or to a combination of modes of transport in which road journeys were as short as possible. The programme, which had a budget of

€100m., was also supported by non-EU countries such as Norway, Iceland and Liechtenstein. In July 2004 the Commission proposed the establishment of a significantly expanded Marco Polo II programme, which would run from 2007–13. The budget for Marco Polo II was projected at €740m. and the scope of the programme was to be extended to countries bordering the EU.

A draft directive tabled by the Commission in April 2003 aimed to establish an electronic toll collection system across the EU that would apply to roads, tunnels, bridges, ferries and urban congestion-charging schemes. Transfer to the new system, which would be based on satellite positioning and mobile telephones, would be progressive, beginning in 2007 at the earliest.

JUSTICE AND HOME AFFAIRS

Under the Treaty on European Union, EU member states undertook to co-operate in the areas of justice and home affairs, particularly in relation to the free movement of people between member states. Issues of common interest were defined as asylum policy; border controls; immigration; drug addiction; fraud; judicial co-operation in civil and criminal matters; customs co-operation; and police co-operation for the purposes of combating terrorism, drugs-trafficking and other serious forms of international crime. In view of the sensitivity of many of the issues involved in this sphere, the EU affords great weight to the positions and opinions of individual states. There tends to be a greater degree of flexibility than in other areas, and requirements are frequently less stringent.

A European Police Office (Europol), facilitating the exchange of information between police forces, operates from The Hague, Netherlands. A special Europol unit dealing with the trafficking of illicit drugs and nuclear and radioactive materials began work in 1994. Europol's mandate has been extended to cover illegal immigrants, stolen vehicles, paedophilia and terrorist activities, and money-laundering.

The EU convention on extradition, signed by ministers of justice in September 1996 prior to ratification by national governments, simplified and accelerated procedures in this area, reduced the number of cases where extradition could be refused, and made it easier to extradite members of criminal organizations. In November 1997 the Commission proposed an extension to European law to allow civil and commercial judgments made in the courts of member states to be enforced throughout the whole of the EU. A regulation on the mutual recognition and enforcement of such judgments came into force in March 2001 across the EU, with the exception of Denmark. In 2000 a convention on mutual assistance in criminal matters (such as criminal hearings by video and telephone conference and cross-border investigations) was adopted.

The Grotius-Civil programme of incentives and exchanges for legal practitioners was established in 1996. It was designed to aid judicial co-operation between member states by improving reciprocal knowledge of legal and judicial systems. The successor programme, Grotius II, focused on general and criminal law. In February 2002 the EU established a 'Eurojust' unit, composed of prosecutors, magistrates and police-officers from member states, to help co-ordinate prosecutions and support investigations into incidences of serious organized crime. A European Police College (CEPOL) has also been created to train senior members of Community police departments, as well as officers from the central and eastern European states. CEPOL initially consisted of a network of existing national training institutes; in December 2003, however, the European Council decided that a permanent CEPOL institution would be established at Bramshill in the United Kingdom.

In March 2000 an action programme entitled 'The prevention and control of organized crime: a European strategy' was adopted. A European crime prevention network was formally established in May 2001. There are also agreements within the EU on co-operation between financial intelligence units and between police forces for the purposes of combating child pornography. In addition, the EU has a common strategy designed to help Russia combat organized crime. The EU ran the FALCONE programme—a series of incentives, training opportunities and exchanges for those responsible for the fight against organized crime in individual member states. The STOP (sexual treatment of persons) programme operated a similar system for those responsible for combating trade in humans and the sexual exploitation of children. Several programmes, including Grotius II, STOP and FALCONE, were merged into a single framework programme, called AGIS, in January 2003. AGIS (2003–07) covers police and judicial co-operation in criminal matters. In September 2001 member states harmonized their definitions of human trafficking and set common minimum jail sentences. The European Monitoring Centre for Drugs and Drug Addiction (EMCDDA) is based in Lisbon, Portugal. In 2000 Norway became the first non-EU state to be admitted to EMCDDA. The EU is working with other third countries to tackle issues of drugs demand and supply.

The EU's draft Charter of Fundamental Rights, which was signed in December 2000 and which was incorporated into the draft treaty on establishing a constitution for Europe in 2003, outlines the rights and freedoms recognized by the EU. It includes civil, political, economic and social rights, with each based on a previous charter, convention, treaty or jurisprudence. The charter may be used to challenge decisions taken by the Community institutions and by member states when implementing EU law.

The Justice and Home Affairs Council held an emergency meeting in September 2001 following the terrorist attacks on the USA. It determined a number of measures to be taken to improve security in the Community. First, the Council sought to reach a common definition of acts of terrorism, and to establish higher penalties for such acts. The new definition included cyber and environmental attacks. The Council decided that, for the perpetrators of terrorist attacks, as well as those involved in other serious crimes (including trafficking in arms, people and drugs and money-laundering), the process of extradition would ultimately be replaced by a procedure for handover based on a European arrest warrant. In the mean time, member states were urged to take the necessary steps to allow the existing conventions on extradition to enter into force. The member states reached agreement on the arrest warrant in December; under the agreement, covering 32 serious offences, EU countries may no longer refuse to extradite their own nationals. The warrant entered into force in eight of the then 15 EU member states on 1 January 2004 (the seven other member states having failed to meet the implementation deadline of 31 December 2003). The Council also determined to accelerate the implementation of the convention on mutual assistance in criminal matters and to establish a joint investigation team. Member states were encouraged to ratify the convention on combating the financing of terrorism and to exercise greater rigour in the issuing of travel documents. The heads of the security and intelligence services of member states met in October 2001, in the first EU-wide meeting of this kind, to discuss the co-ordinated action to be taken to curb terrorism. They were to meet in regular sessions thereafter. A team of counter-terrorist specialists, established within Europol, was to produce an assessment of terrorist threats to EU states, indicating the likely nature and location of any such attacks. Rapid links were forged with US counterparts—in December Europol signed a co-operation agreement on the exchange of strategic information (excluding personal data) with the USA; in December 2002 the agreement was extended also to include the exchange of personal data. The heads of the EU's anti-terrorist units also held a meeting following the September 2001 attacks, to discuss issues such as joint training exercises, equipment sharing, the joint procurement of equipment and possible joint operations. Prior to these emergency meetings, intelligence and security information had been shared bilaterally and on a small scale, impeding Europol's effectiveness. The terrorist bombings in Madrid, Spain, in March 2004 injected a greater sense of urgency into EU counter-terrorism efforts, and gave added impetus to EU initiatives aimed at improving travel document security and impeding the cross-border movements of terrorists. Following the attacks the EU created the new position of Counter-terrorist Co-ordinator, whose main task it would be to tackle ongoing challenges facing the EU as it sought to translate its various counter-terrorist initiatives into effective law enforcement tools. Key among the Co-ordinator's responsibilities would be enhancing intelligence-sharing among EU members and promoting the implementation of already-agreed EU anti-terrorism measures, some of which had been impeded by the legislative processes of individual member states.

Measures related to the abolition of customs formalities at intra-community frontiers were completed by mid-1991, and entered into force in January 1993. However, disagreements remained among member governments concerning the free movement of persons: discussions continued in 1992 on the abuse of open frontiers by organized crime, particularly for drugs-trafficking; on extradition procedures; and on rules of asylum and immigration. In June 1990 Belgium, France, Germany, Luxembourg and the Netherlands, meeting in Schengen, Luxembourg, signed a convention to implement an earlier agreement (concluded in 1985 at the same location), abolishing frontier controls on the free movement of persons from 1993. Delay in the establishment of the Schengen Information System (SIS), providing a computer network on suspect persons or cargo for use by the police forces of signatory states, resulted in the postponement of the implementation of the new agreement. Seven countries (Belgium, France, Germany, Luxembourg, the Netherlands, Portugal and Spain) agreed to implement the agreement with effect from March 1995. Frontier controls at airports on those travelling between the seven countries were dismantled during a three-month transition period, which ended on 1 July 1995. However, after that date the French Government announced that it would retain land-border controls for a further six months, claiming that drugs-trafficking and illegal immigration had increased as a result of the agreement. In March 1996 France decided to lift its border controls with Spain and Germany while maintaining controls on borders with the Benelux countries, mainly owing to fears concerning the transportation of illicit drugs from the Netherlands via Belgium and Luxembourg. Italy joined the 'Schengen Group' in October 1997, and Austria in December. Border controls for both

countries were removed in 1998. Denmark, Finland and Sweden (and non-EU members Norway and Iceland) were admitted as observers of the accord from 1 May 1996, and all five countries joined the 'Schengen Group' in March 2001. Meanwhile, in March 1999 signatories of the Schengen accords on visa-free border crossings began to waive visa requirements with Estonia, Latvia and Lithuania. The Treaty of Amsterdam, which came into effect on 1 May 1999, incorporated the so-called Schengen 'acquis' (comprising the 1985 agreement, 1990 convention and additional accession protocols and executive decisions), in order to integrate it into the framework of the EU. The Treaty permitted the United Kingdom and Ireland to maintain permanent jurisdiction over their borders and rules of asylum and immigration. Countries acceding to the EU after 2000 were automatically to adhere to the Schengen arrangements. In February 2002 the Council approved Ireland's participation in some of the provisions of the Schengen *acquis*.

Following the enlargement of the EU in May 2004 border controls between the 15 existing members and the 10 new members were to stay in force until 2007. Although the 10 new states technically belonged to the Schengen agreement, the Commission decided that the SIS computer network was not large enough to incorporate data from 10 more countries. Work on a new computerized information system began in 2002 but was not expected to be completed until 2006 at the earliest. The EU allocated €960m. in aid to the former communist countries acceding to the EU in 2004 to secure their eastern borders to prevent illegal immigrants trying to gain access to the more prosperous members of the EU. The members of the Schengen agreement were to reassess the border situation in 2007.

The need to develop a common EU policy on immigration became increasingly important in the late 1990s, with the number of immigrants forecast to rise considerably in the near future. In November 2000 the Commission adopted a communication outlining a common asylum procedure and providing for a uniform status, valid throughout the EU, for persons granted asylum. In March 2001 a common list of countries whose citizens required visas to enter the EU was finally adopted. The EU has also developed the so-called 'Eurodac' database for co-ordinating information on the movements of asylum-seekers; Eurodac allows for the comparison of fingerprints of refugees. In September 2001 the Commission launched a directive establishing a common European definition of a refugee, aimed at curtailing so-called 'asylum shopping' (in which a person moves from one state to another until reaching one prepared to give protection). The EU was also seeking to develop common repatriation procedures for unsuccessful claimants. (Under current arrangements refugees may simply be repatriated to the EU state from which they arrived.) The European Commission adopted a new action programme, entitled ARGO, which was to cover the period 2002–06 and which was to advocate EU administrative co-operation in the fields of asylum, visas, immigration and external borders. In February 2002 the European Council adopted a comprehensive plan to combat illegal immigration. Priority areas included visa policy, readmission and repatriation policies, the monitoring of borders, the role of Europol and penalties. In June 2002 a summit of the European Council in Seville, Spain, discussed the issues of asylum and immigration. The meeting's priority was to continue the progress towards a common asylum policy, by establishing minimum standards and procedures for member states. In March 2004 the last two draft directives aimed at harmonizing asylum policy across the EU were being finalized in advance of the accession of 10 new member states in May. A European Agency for the Management of Operational Co-operation at the External Borders of the European Union was established by a regulation of the European Parliament in October, the primary responsibility of which would be the creation of an integrated border management system, which would ensure a high and uniform level of control and surveillance. The Agency was scheduled to commence operations on 1 May 2005. In November 2004 the EU agreed an ambitious five-year programme, known as the Hague programme, which was aimed at making the EU an area of common 'freedom, justice and security'. The programme incorporated many new policies, including a common European asylum system, a common repatriation policy for illegal immigrants, an EU diplomatic corps, common issuing of visas, harmonization of divorce and family laws to help to settle cross-border disputes, mutual recognition of court judgments, complete sharing of police information, and a European criminal record.

All 15 of the existing members of the EU, except the United Kingdom and Ireland, planned to impose at least a two-year period of restrictions on immigrants from the eight former communist countries (the Czech Republic, Estonia, Hungary, Latvia, Lithuania, Poland, Slovenia and Slovakia) from their accession to the EU in May 2004, to prevent their labour markets being inundated with inexpensive labour. Germany indicated that it was likely to extend the employment restrictions for the full seven years allowed under the accession treaties of the new members. Even the United Kingdom and Ireland planned to impose restrictions on the welfare benefits non-residents could claim. Workers from the new member states Malta and Cyprus were to be allowed into existing EU countries without any restrictions.

A high-level working group on asylum and migration was set up in December 1998. It implements action plans in the main source countries for immigration to western Europe (Afghanistan and the surrounding region; Iraq; Morocco; Somalia; Sri Lanka; and Albania and Kosovo). The European Refugee Fund was established in September 2000. It aims to support the efforts of member states to receive refugees and, with a reserve of €10m., allows emergency measures to be taken in the event of a sudden, mass influx.

EDUCATION, TRAINING AND CULTURE

The Treaty of Rome, although not covering education directly, gave the Community the role of establishing general principles for implementing a common vocational training policy. The Treaty on European Union urged greater co-operation on education policy, including encouraging exchanges and mobility for students and teachers, distance learning and the development of European studies. In July 2000 the EU's Economic and Social Committee adopted a report on education in Europe. The Committee considered the development of a more integrated education strategy for Europe and advocated the study of new approaches to schooling, including differing structures and wider objectives, more diverse fields of learning and greater use of modern technologies.

The postgraduate European University Institute (EUI) was founded in Florence, Italy, in 1972, with departments of history, economics, law, and political and social sciences, together with a European Policy Unit and a European Culture Research Centre. The EUI is also the depository for the historical archives of the EC institutions. In 2003 there were some 330 research students enrolled at the Institute. In 1998 the establishment of 25 Jean Monnet European Centres of Excellence was approved; by 2003 the number of these Centres had risen to 82. The Jean Monnet project for 'European Integration in University Studies' also finances the establishment of Jean Monnet chairs at universities world-wide; there were 601 such chairs by 2002. The Jean Monnet project targets disciplines in which Community developments are an increasingly important part of the subject studied—e.g. Community law, European economic and political integration, and the history of the European construction process.

In 1980 an educational information network, 'Eurydice', began operations, with a central unit in Brussels and national units providing data on the widely varying systems of education within member states. In 1987 the Council adopted a European Action Scheme for the Mobility of University Students ('Erasmus'). The scheme was expanded to include EFTA member states from 1992. The 'Lingua' programme promoted the learning and teaching of foreign languages in the Community. From 1 January 1995 the Erasmus and Lingua schemes were incorporated into a new Community programme, 'Socrates'. This programme prioritizes the learning of EU languages; the promotion of mobility in education (for example, through educational exchanges); innovation in educational practices (particularly focusing on information and communications technologies); and lifelong learning.

The Trans-European Mobility Programme for University Studies (TEMPUS) was launched in 1990 to foster co-operation between institutions of higher education and their counterparts in central and eastern Europe, as part of the wider aid programme to those countries. Under the second phase of the scheme (TEMPUS II, covering 1994–98), the former Soviet republics were eligible to participate. Under TEMPUS III (2000–06), the programme widened its remit to incorporate certain non-academic institutions, as well as extending geographical coverage to include Mediterranean non-member countries. The European Training Foundation (ETF), which was established in Turin, Italy, in 1995, supports TEMPUS projects as part of its general assistance for the development of vocational training and retraining in EU partner countries. The Foundation deals with those countries eligible to participate in the EU's PHARE, CARDS, TACIS and MEDA programmes (see External Relations). Prior to the enlargement of the EU in May 2004, however, the activities of the ETF were gradually wound down in the various accession states in central and eastern Europe that were preparing to become full members of the Union. The ETF was expected to sustain its involvement in human resources development in Romania and Bulgaria, and to increase its activities in Turkey.

In 1975 a European Centre for the Development of Vocational Training (Centre Européen pour le Développement de la Formation Professionnelle—CEDEFOP) was established in Berlin, Germany. The centre relocated to Thessaloniki, Greece, in 1995. Much of CEDEFOP's recent work has focused upon the employment problems faced by women, especially those who wish to return to work after a long absence. In January 2000 a programme for the promotion of European pathways for work-linked training, including apprenticeship, came into force. (According to the Commission, European pathways for training refer to any period of vocational

training completed by a person undergoing work-linked training as part of their training in another member state, complying with a number of quality criteria.) The programme involved the introduction of the new EU 'EUROPASS Training' document, which attests to periods of training completed in another member state. The EUROPASS programme, which was officially launched in February 2005 and which brought into a single framework several existing tools for the transparency of diplomas, certificates and competences, was aimed at promoting both occupational mobility, between countries as well as across sectors, and mobility for learning purposes.

In April 2000 the EU's 'Youth' community action programme for 2000–06 was adopted, with a budget of €520m. This incorporated all the previous youth programmes and related activities, including Youth for Europe, which covered the period 1995–99, and the European Voluntary Service (EVS) programmes. The overall objective of the new programme was to help young people (aged between 15 and 25 years) to contribute to the building of Europe and to foster a spirit of initiative. From the outset Youth included applicant countries; it also runs a Euro-Med partnership programme.

In May 2000 the Commission adopted an initiative entitled 'eLearning: designing tomorrow's education' as part of its overall 'eEurope' action plan (see Telecommunications, Information Technology and Broadcasting). One of the main objectives of the eEurope programme was to encourage the use of the internet in schools and universities.

The Commission organizes the annual so-called 'Netd@ys' Europe (launched in 1997), aimed at exchanging and disseminating experience in the use of new media, especially the internet, as a teaching, learning and cultural resource. People of all ages and backgrounds can participate in Netd@ys, but the target group is primarily those in the 15–25 age range. Non-member countries are involved in the initiative, which is held over the course of one week. In 2003 the EU accession states were invited to appoint representatives to become Netd@ys National Correspondents, and the participation of representatives of European Mediterranean countries was also encouraged.

The EU's Culture 2000 framework programme (2000–06) replaced the Raphael, Kaleidoscope and Ariane programmes. The programme (which in 2003 included the participation of all 10 accession states as well as Romania and Bulgaria), focused on the following themes: legislation of benefit to cultural projects; the cultural aspects of existing support policies; and the incorporation of culture into the field of external relations. Its main aim was to promote a 'common cultural area' inclusive of cultural diversity and common cultural heritage; this objective provoked a certain amount of opposition on the grounds that it could lead to transnational cultural conformity and that it could damage national and regional cultural diversity. As part of the so-called Cardiff process of integration of environmental and sustainable development issues, however, (see Environment Policy), the Commission is bound to make efforts to preserve cultural heritage in the formulation of other policies.

The European City of Culture initiative was launched in 1985 (it was renamed the European Capital of Culture initiative in 1999). Member states designate cities, which receive a subsidy from the Commission. In the mid-2000s the following cities were selected as capitals of culture: Genoa (Italy) and Lille (France) for 2004, Cork (Ireland) for 2005, Patras (Greece) for 2006, Luxembourg and Sibiu (Romania) for 2007, and Liverpool (United Kingdom) and Stavanger (Norway) for 2008.

SOCIAL AFFAIRS AND EMPLOYMENT

The Single European Act, which entered into force in 1987, added to the original Treaty of Rome articles that emphasized the need for 'economic and social cohesion' in the Community, i.e. the reduction of disparities between the various regions. This was to be achieved principally through the existing 'structural funds' (see p. 264)—the European Regional Development Fund, the European Social Fund, and the Guidance Section of the European Agricultural Guidance and Guarantee Fund (EAGGF). In 1988 the Council declared that Community operations through the structural funds, the European Investment Bank (EIB) and other financial instruments should have five priority objectives: (i) promoting the development and structural adjustment of the less-developed regions (where gross domestic product per head is less than 75% of the Community average); (ii) converting the regions, frontier regions or parts of regions seriously affected by industrial decline; (iii) combating long-term unemployment among people above the age of 25; (iv) providing employment for young people (aged under 25); and (v) with a view to the reform of the common agricultural policy (CAP), speeding up the adjustment of agricultural structures and promoting the development of rural areas.

In 1989 the Commission proposed a Charter of Fundamental Social Rights of Workers (later known as the Social Charter), covering freedom of movement, fair remuneration, improvement of working conditions, the right to social security, freedom of association and collective wage agreements, the development of participation by workers in management, and sexual equality. The Charter was approved (with some modifications) by the heads of government of all Community member states, except the United Kingdom, in December. On the insistence of the United Kingdom, the chapter on social affairs of the Treaty on European Union, negotiated in December 1991, was omitted from the Treaty to form a separate protocol (the so-called Social Chapter, complete with an opt-out arrangement for the United Kingdom).

In September 1994 ministers adopted the first directive to be approved under the Social Charter, concerning the establishment of mandatory works councils in multinational companies. After lengthy negotiations, it was agreed that the legislation was to apply to companies employing more than 1,000 people, of whom 150 worked in at least two EU member states. The United Kingdom was excluded from the directive; however, British companies operating in other European countries were to participate in the scheme (although without counting UK-based employees towards the applicability thresholds). The directive came into force in September 1996. In April 1996 the Commission proposed that part-time, fixed-term and temporary employees should receive comparable treatment to permanent, full-time employees. A directive ensuring equal treatment for part-time employees was adopted by the Council in December 1997. A directive on parental leave, the second directive to be adopted under the Social Charter, provided for a statutory minimum of three months' unpaid leave to allow parents to care for young children, and was adopted in June 1996.

In May 1997 the new Labour Government of the United Kingdom approved the Social Charter, which was to be incorporated into the Treaty of Amsterdam. The Treaty, which entered into force in May 1999, consequently removed the opt-out clause and incorporated the Social Chapter in the revised Treaty of Rome. In December 1999 the Council adopted amendments extending the two directives adopted under the Charter to include the United Kingdom.

The Treaty of Amsterdam authorized the European Council to take action against all types of discrimination. Several directives and programmes on gender equality and equal opportunities have been approved and the Commission has initiated legal proceedings against a number of member states before the European Court of Justice for infringements. In June 2000 the Council adopted a directive implementing the principle of equal treatment regardless of racial or ethnic origin in employment, education, social security, healthcare and access to goods and services. This was followed in November by a directive establishing a framework for equal treatment regardless of religion or belief, disability, age or sexual orientation. The European Monitoring Centre on Racism and Xenophobia, which was established in Vienna, Austria, in 1997, maintains an information network (the European Information Network on Racism and Xenophobia—RAXEN) and database. In February 2004 the Commission held a joint seminar with the European Jewish Congress in Brussels to discuss the concerns of the Jewish community that anti-Semitism was increasing in Europe; Jewish leaders accused the EU authorities of inaction and indifference in the face of a rise in anti-Semitic incidents (some violent) in Europe.

Numerous directives on health and safety in the workplace have been adopted by the Community. The Major Accident Hazards Bureau (MAHB), which was established in 1996 and is based at the Joint Research Centre at Ispra in Italy, helps to prevent and to mitigate industrial accidents in the EU. To this end, MAHB maintains a Major Accident Reporting System database and a Community Documentation Centre on Industrial Risk. There is also a European Agency for Health and Safety at Work, which was established in 1995 in Bilbao, Spain. The Agency has a health and safety information network composed of 'focal points' in each member state, in the four EFTA states and in the three candidate countries.

In June 1993 the Working Time Directive (WTD) was approved, restricting the working week to 48 hours, except where overtime arrangements are agreed with trade unions. The WTD also prescribed minimum rest periods and a minimum of four weeks' paid holiday a year. However, certain categories of employee were exempt from the maximum 48-hour week rule, including those in the transport sector, those employed in offshore oil extraction, fishermen and junior hospital doctors. In April 2000 agreement was reached on extending some or all of the rights of the WTD to cover most excluded workers; this extension was to be phased in under transitional arrangements. A Road Transport Directive, which applies to mobile workers who participate in road transport activities covered by EU drivers' hours rules, was adopted in March 2002. In January 2004 the Commission launched a review of the WTD following an increase in the use of the opt-out clause by a number of member states.

The European Foundation for the Improvement of Living and Working Conditions, which was established in Dublin, Ireland, in 1975, undertakes four-year research and development programmes in the field of employment, sustainable development, equal opportunities, social cohesion, health and well-being, and participation. By the end of 2003 the focus of the Foundation's key monitoring tools had been extended to include fully the 10 accession states and the

three candidate states. Prior to the EU's enlargement in May 2004, the Foundation made available wide-ranging new data and analysis on living and working conditions in the existing member states and in the accession and candidate states. A much-anticipated Quality of Life in Europe survey, which was conducted during 2003 in 28 countries, was published in 2004. The survey, which was the first of its kind, focused on employment, economic resources, family life, community life, health and education.

The European Confidence Pact for Employment was launched by the Commission in 1996 as a comprehensive strategy to combat unemployment, involving a common approach by public authorities, employers and employees. An employment body, European Employment Services (EURES), launched in 1994, operates as a network of more than 500 specialist advisers across Europe, who (with the co-operation of national public employment services, trade unions, employers' organizations, local authorities, etc., and with access to a detailed database) provide the three basic EURES services of information, guidance and placement to both job-seekers and employers interested in the European job market. EURES has a particularly effective role to play in cross-border regions where there are significant degrees of cross-border commuting amongst employees. EURES, which covers the countries of the European Economic Area (as well as Switzerland), also provides a public database that lists 50,000–100,000 employment vacancies daily, and a CV search database, through which job-seekers can make their CVs available to a wide range of employers.

An employment summit held in Luxembourg in November 1997 committed member governments to providing training or work placements for unemployed young people within six months, and for the long-term unemployed within 12 months. Member states also agreed to reduce taxation on labour-intensive service industries from 1 July 1998 and to produce national action plans for employment. Under the European employment strategy, initiated in 1997 and incorporated in the Treaty of Amsterdam, an Employment Committee was established to oversee the co-ordination of the employment strategies of the member states and an employment package was to be presented (as a joint effort by the Council of the European Union and the Commission) each year. The package contains reports on member states' performances, individual recommendations and policy guide-lines for the future. The overall EU employment rate averaged 64.2% in 2002 (55.5% for women), while the employment rate for the 10 accession states in that year stood at 56.1% (50.3% for women). The employment rates across Europe differ greatly between men and women.

A European Social Protection Committee was established in June 2000. In addition, the EU runs MISSOC—the Mutual Information System on Social Protection in the EU member states and the European Economic Area. In the early 2000s the system was extended to include MISSCEEC—the Mutual Information System on Social Protection in the Central and Eastern European Countries in order to take into account the 10 accession states. In February 2005 the European Commission launched its new Social Agenda (2005–10) for modernizing the EU's social model. The new Agenda focused on providing jobs and equal opportunities for all and ensuring that the benefits of the EU's growth and employment-creation schemes reached all levels of society. By modernizing labour markets and social protection systems, it was hoped that the Agenda would help people to seize the opportunities created by international competition, technological advances and changing population patterns, while protecting the most vulnerable in society. The Agenda had three key priorities: employment, the fight against poverty and the promotion of equal opportunities.

The Charter of Fundamental Rights (CFR) was proclaimed at the Nice Summit of the European Council in December 2000. The text of the CFR consists of seven chapters covering dignity, freedoms, equality, solidarity, citizens' rights, justice and general provisions. No new rights were actually created as part of the CFR; rather, it presents in a single document the existing rights and freedoms enjoyed by EU citizens through the European Convention on Human Rights, the Charter of Fundamental Social Rights of Workers and various other EU treaties. Despite the fact that it contained nothing new, the member states were not willing to make the CFR a legally-binding document. However, the CFR was incorporated into the draft treaty establishing a constitution for Europe, which was finally approved by the European Council in mid-2004.

The EU Disability Strategy has three main focuses: co-operation between the Commission and the member states; the full participation of people with disabilities; and the mainstreaming of disability in policy formulation (particularly with regard to employment). EU activities relating to disability include dialogue with the European Disability Forum, and the Technology Initiative for Disabled and Elderly people (TIDE), which aims to develop technologies to improve the living conditions of these groups. Awareness-raising includes the 'European Day of People with Disabilities', which takes place in December each year.

CONSUMER PROTECTION AND HEALTH

Consumer protection is one of the stated priorities of EU policy, and has been implemented via a series of action programmes covering areas such as safety of products and services (e.g. food additives, safety of toys and childcare articles, packaging and labelling of goods), protecting consumers' economic and legal interests, and promoting consumer representation. A number of measures have been taken to strengthen consumer power, by promoting consumer associations and drawing up a requirement for fair commercial practices.

In February 1997 the Commission extended the function of its directorate-general on consumer policy to incorporate consumer health protection. This decision (which followed widespread consumer concerns regarding the bovine spongiform encephalopathy (BSE) crisis—see Agriculture), was designed to ensure that sufficient importance was given to food safety. In November a Scientific Steering Committee was established to provide advice on consumer health issues. Eight sectoral steering committees were formed at the same time, covering a range of public health and consumer protection issues. Five of the committees were devoted to food safety, one to cosmetic and non-food products, one to medicinal products and medical devices, and one to issues of toxicity and the environment. In March 2004 the Commission adopted a decision to establish three new scientific steering committees in the fields of consumer products, health and environmental risks, and emerging and newly identified health risks. The new committees were to replace the existing committees for consumer products and non-food products intended for consumers, for toxicity, ecotoxicity and the environment, and for medicinal products and medical devices. In July 1998 an Institute for Health and Consumer Protection (IHCP), attached to the Commission's Joint Research Centre, was established to improve research in this field.

In January 2000 the Commission adopted a White Paper on food safety, proposing a comprehensive, integrated approach covering foodstuffs from 'farm to table'. The paper envisaged a programme of measures, including legislation on the responsibilities of food and feedstuff manufacturers, the welfare of animals during transport and the traceability of products. Stringent rules and appropriate checks at all stages of the production chain were to be introduced and the importance of clear labelling, presentation and advertising was emphasized. The paper proposed that certain substances recognized scientifically as being sources of allergies should be included in lists of ingredients on labels. From October 1999 food products labelled as 'GM-free' in the EU were permitted to contain up to 1% of GM material. In July 2001 the Commission developed its rules on the labelling and tracing of GM organisms (GMOs, see Agriculture). In 2002 the European Food Safety Authority was formally established (see Agriculture), with a wide brief to cover all stages of food production and supply right through to consumers; the Authority became fully operational in 2003. In July the Commission proposed the implementation of stringent regulations requiring that all health claims on food, drinks or food supplements be substantiated by independent experts. During 2004 a framework was developed for the creation of international guidelines on the measurement of chemical and biological elements in food and other products. The system would facilitate the detection of GMOs and the measurement of sulphur content in motor fuels. In December 2004 the Commission proposed extending until 1 July 2007 the transitional measures to combat BSE.

In May 2002 the Commission presented its new strategy for consumer policy for 2002–06. Specific measures agreed included a proposal for a harmonization of rules for consumer credit, as well as a resolution on labelling of video and computer games, aimed at ensuring their suitability for young people. The same year saw an extension of the monitoring of certain foodstuffs, to include labelling of irradiated foods, authorization of two new sweeteners, and labelling and marketing of food supplements. In October 2004 the European Parliament and the Council adopted a regulation establishing a network of public authorities responsible for enforcing legislation to protect the interests of consumers in the event of cross-border disputes. Legislation increasing the compensation rights of air travellers took effect in February 2005. New rights to compensation and assistance in the event of cancellations or long delays were introduced, compensation was increased for passengers unable to board a flight owing to overbooking by the airline and cover was extended to passengers travelling on charter or domestic flights.

In February 2005 the European Parliament approved a new law to harmonize the framework across the EU for banning unfair commercial practices. The new legislation, which was proposed by the Commission in 2003, clarified consumers' rights, banned pressure selling and misleading marketing and facilitated cross-border trade; it was to be implemented throughout the EU by 2007. In February 2003 the Commission adopted an action plan for a more coherent and standardized European contract law. A communication outlining the next stage of the plan was adopted in October 2004.

In September 2002 the European Parliament adopted a programme of Community action in the field of public health for the period 2003–08, with a budget of €312m. The three basic objectives of the programme were: to improve health-related information; to encourage swift and co-ordinated responses to threats to health; and to promote health and prevent diseases.

Various epidemiological surveillance systems are in operation, covering major communicable diseases. An early warning and response system to help member states deal with outbreaks of diseases was in place by the end of 2000. Partly in response to the outbreak of severe acute respiratory syndrome (SARS) in the Far East in 2003 and the outbreak of avian influenza in the Netherlands in early 2003 and in Viet Nam in early 2004, in April 2004 the European Parliament and the Council adopted a regulation establishing a European Centre for Disease Prevention and Control, which would enable the EU to pool its disease control expertise more effectively and would allow multinational investigation teams to be drawn up quickly and efficiently. The initial focus of the Centre would be on communicable diseases and outbreaks of diseases of unknown origin. The new independent European agency would also assist the work on monitoring and preparedness planning against bioterrorist attacks being pursued by the EU's Health Security Task Force (which was established in May 2002). The Centre, which was to be based in Sweden, was due to become operational in May 2005. In March 2004 the Commission presented a plan for coping with an influenza pandemic. The EU implements a number of individual action plans, including one to combat cancer. Under the Treaty on European Union, the EU assumed responsibility for the problem of drug addiction; a European Monitoring Centre for Drugs and Drug Addiction (EMCDDA, see Justice and Home Affairs) was established in Lisbon, Portugal, in 1995.

A new €72m. anti-smoking campaign was launched in March 2005, aimed at children and young adults. The campaign, which followed a previous three-year €18m. programme that ended in December 2004, was to last four years and was to include a series of television and cinema advertisements across the EU. The commissioner responsible for health urged member states to ban smoking in public places.

An Advocate-General of the European Court of Justice announced in April 2005 that the Food Supplements Directive, which was approved in 2002 and was designed to strengthen controls on the sale of natural remedies, vitamin supplements and mineral plant extracts, infringed EU guide-lines. Under the legislation, which had been due to come into effect in August 2005, only vitamins and minerals on an approved list could be used in supplements and restrictions were to be placed on the upper limits of vitamin doses. A final ruling on the directive was expected in July.

The enlargement of the EU in May 2004 to incorporate 10 new member states was expected to cause a number of problems for the EU with regard to public health policy given that, in general, the health status indicators of the majority of the accession states compared poorly with the EU average. Some of the new member states, which (with only one or two exceptions) had few resources to spend on health, faced serious problems with communicable diseases (particularly HIV/AIDS), and the health systems of most were in need of improvement. An EU report in 2004 stated that some new EU members, notably Lithuania, Latvia and Estonia, had experienced a significant increase in the level of HIV infections in the 2000s. The report also confirmed that the number of newly reported cases in western Europe had doubled in the previous decade.

ENVIRONMENT

Environmental action by the EU was initiated in 1972. Five successive action programmes were complemented by a variety of legislation, including regulations on air and water pollution (e.g. 'acid rain', pollution by fertilizers and pesticides, and emissions from vehicles), directives on the transport of hazardous waste across national boundaries, measures on waste treatment, noise abatement and the protection of natural resources, and legislation to guarantee freedom of access to information on the environment held by public authorities. The Maastricht Treaty on European Union, which entered into force in November 1993, gave environmental action policy status, and the Treaty of Amsterdam identified sustainable development as one of the Community's overall aims.

The Community's fifth environmental action programme (1993–2000), entitled 'Towards Sustainability', aimed to address the root causes of environmental degradation, by raising public awareness and working to change the behaviour of authorities, enterprises and the general public. The programme focused on anticipating, as well as addressing, environmental problems. A 1998 communication on the so-called 'Cardiff Process' of integrating environmental considerations into all EU policies confirmed this programme's broad approach. The Commission recognized that full integration was a long-term aim. For the short term, it identified two priority objectives: the fulfilment of the environmental measures contained in the Agenda 2000 action programme (relating for example to the reform of the Common Agricultural Policy and to EU enlargement), and the implementation of the Kyoto Protocol (see below). The programme listed several initiatives that were to be pursued, including better resource management by industry, the curbing of consumer demand for products that generate pollution, the development of more 'environmentally friendly' agriculture and a more effective management of mass tourism.

The EU's sixth environmental action programme (2001–10), entitled 'Environment 2010: Our Future, Our Choice', was adopted by the European Parliament in July 2002, and emphasized the continuing importance of the integration of environmental considerations into other EU policies, focusing on four priority areas: climate change, nature and biodiversity, environment, health and quality of life, and the management of natural resources and waste. The programme also identified explicitly the measures required to implement successfully the EU's sustainable development strategy. In addition, it encouraged an extended dialogue with the administrations of all the applicant states (10 of which joined the EU in May 2004), and sought to encourage greater public participation in environmental debates.

The Community's programme of research and technological development on the environment, carried out on a shared-cost basis by various scientific institutions, covers the economic and social aspects of environmental issues and the EU's participation in global change programmes. The programme is open to all European countries. A separate programme covers research in marine science and technology. In 1990 the EC established the European Environment Agency (EEA, see p. 231) to monitor environmental issues and provide advice. The agency, which is located in Copenhagen and which became operational in November 1994, also provides targeted information to policy-makers and the public and disseminates comparable environmental data. The agency is open to non-EU countries and it was the first EU body to have members from the accession states. In February 2004 the Commission and the EEA launched the European Pollutant Emission Register, the first Europe-wide register of industrial emissions into air and water. The European Parliament approved legislation in April 2004 that made firms causing pollution liable for the costs of repairing the damage caused to natural habitats, water resources and wildlife. EU Governments were obliged to introduce the law at national level within three years.

In 1992 the LIFE programme was established as a financial instrument to promote the development and implementation of environmental policy. LIFE funds priority activities in EU member states and provides technical assistance to countries in central and eastern Europe and the Mediterranean. The LIFE programme is subdivided into LIFE-Environment (addressing the further development of environmental policy); LIFE-Nature (managing conservation of wild flora and fauna and natural habitats); and LIFE-Third Countries (contributing to the development of environmental policy and action programmes in third countries). Following the 2004 enlargement of the EU, the poor state of the environment in some central and eastern European countries has become a pressing issue.

In 1985 the Community (and a number of individual member states) ratified the Vienna Convention for the Protection of the Ozone Layer, and in 1987 the Community signed a protocol to the treaty, controlling the production of chlorofluorocarbons (CFCs). In 1990 ministers of the environment undertook to ban the production of CFCs by mid-1997 (the introduction of the ban was later brought forward to 1996), and in 1998 the Commission proposed committing EU countries to the progressive elimination of remaining ozone-depleting substances, by introducing a ban on the sale and use of CFCs and imposing production limits on hydrochlorofluorocarbons (HCFCs), which were originally introduced to replace CFCs. In 1990 ministers agreed to stabilize emissions of carbon dioxide, believed to be responsible for 'global warming', at 1990 levels by 2000 (2005 for the United Kingdom). In December 1997, at the third conference of parties to the UN Framework Convention on Climate Change (UNFCCC), agreement was reached on the Kyoto Protocol, under which emissions of six greenhouse gases were to be reduced by 8% between 2008 and 2012, in comparison with 1990 levels. In June 1998 ministers of the environment agreed upon individual emission targets for each EU member state. The Kyoto Protocol was formally approved by the European Council in April 2002.

In March 2000 the Commission noted that emissions were actually rising in relation to 1990 levels. In that month the Commission adopted a Green Paper on the trading of greenhouse gas emissions within the EU in order to fulfil its commitments under the Kyoto Protocol. The EU Greenhouse Gas Emissions Trading Scheme, which was launched in January 2005, obliges companies that exceed their allocation of carbon dioxide emissions to buy extra allowances from more efficient companies or incur considerable fines. However, experts criticized certain EU Governments, notably Italy and Austria, for allowing industry to increase emissions through generous permit limits. The European Climate Change Programme (ECCP) was adopted in 2000. This outlined the strategy

needed to meet commitments under the Kyoto Protocol and aimed to incorporate climate-change concerns into various EU policies. In January 2000 the EU's Theseo 2000-Solve experiment was launched; this was the largest experiment ever undertaken to study the ozone layer above northern Europe.

In June 1996 the Commission agreed a strategy, drawn up in collaboration with the European petroleum and car industries and known as the Auto-Oil Programme, for reducing harmful emissions from road vehicles by between 60% and 70% by 2010 in an effort to reduce air pollution. The programme committed member states to the progressive elimination of leaded petrol by 2000 (with limited exemptions until 2005). From 2000 petrol-powered road vehicles were to be fitted with 'on-board diagnostic' (OBD) systems to monitor emissions. Diesel vehicles were to be installed with OBD systems by 2005. Under Auto-Oil II the directive was revised in 2003, establishing specifications to come into force on 1 January 2005, with new limits on sulphur content of both petrol and diesel. Moreover, even lower limits would come into force for all fuel marketed from December 2009, although there would be limited availability from 2005. In July 1998 the Commission announced plans to decrease pollution from nuclear power stations by reducing emissions of sulphur dioxides, nitrogen oxides and dust by one-half. The European Commission was developing a thematic strategy on air pollution under the auspices of Clean Air for Europe (CAFE), a programme of technical analysis and policy development, which was launched in March 2001. An air-quality policy covering all emissions sources was expected to be published in mid-2005.

In December 2004 EEA projections stated that in total the EU was likely to reduce its greenhouse gas emissions by more than its 8% commitment under the Kyoto Protocol, although some member states, notably Denmark, Italy, Portugal, Spain and Ireland, were likely to exceed their targets by a wide margin.

As part of the sixth environmental action programme (2001–10), the EU is aiming for a significant reduction in the amount of rubbish generated, through new waste prevention initiatives, better use of resources, and a shift to more sustainable consumption patterns. Its goal is to reduce the quantity of waste going to 'final disposal' by 20%, compared with 2000, by 2010, and by 50% by 2050 (with special emphasis on reducing hazardous waste).

In September 2000 the EU adopted a directive on end-of-life vehicles (ELVs), containing measures for the collection, treatment, recovery and disposal of such waste. The ruling forced manufacturers to pay for the disposal of new cars from July 2002 and of old cars from January 2007. The directive set recycling and recovery targets, restricted the use of heavy metals in new cars from 2003, and specified that ELVs might only be dismantled by authorized agencies. In June 2000 the Commission adopted two proposals on the management of waste from electronic and electrical equipment to complement its measures on landfill and incineration of waste. EU directives on waste electrical and electronic equipment and the restriction of the use of certain hazardous substances in electronic and electrical equipment came into force in February 2003. The directives were based on the premise of producer responsibility and aimed to persuade producers to improve product design in order to facilitate recycling and disposal. Increased recycling of electrical and electronic equipment would limit the total quantity of waste going to final disposal. Under the legislation consumers would be able to return equipment free of charge. In order to prevent the generation of hazardous waste, the second directive required the substitution of various heavy metals (lead, mercury, cadmium, and hexavalent chromium) and brominated flame retardants in new electrical and electronic equipment marketed from 1 July 2006.

A regulation revising EU laws on trade in wild animals and plants was adopted by ministers of the environment in December 1996. This aimed to tighten controls and improve the enforcement of restrictions on trade in endangered species. A series of directives adopted in 2002 formulated new EU policy on the conservation of wild birds, fishing and protection for certain species of whales. Every three years the Commission publishes an official report on the conservation of wild birds; a report, in March 2002, identified a decline of almost 25% in wild bird species in Europe, despite efforts made over the last 20 years. A report published by Birdlife International in November 2004 claimed that 226 bird species (43% of the total in Europe) were threatened by intensive agriculture and changes in climate. The EU has pledged to attempt to halt the decline of wildlife in Europe by 2010.

As part of the EU's efforts to promote awareness of environmental issues and to encourage companies to do likewise, the voluntary Eco-Management and Audit Scheme (EMAS) was launched in April 1995. Under the scheme, participating industrial companies undergo an independent audit of their environmental performance. In addition, the EU awards 'eco-labels' for products that limit harmful effects on the environment (including foodstuffs, beverages and pharmaceutical products, among others). The criteria to be met are set by the EU Eco-Labelling Board (EUEB).

In October 2003 the Commission presented a new environmental policy—the Registration, Evaluation and Authorisation of Chemicals system (REACH)—which was originally intended to collate crucial safety information on tens of thousands of potentially dangerous chemicals used in consumer goods industries. However, following intensive lobbying by the chemical industry sector, the scope of REACH was reduced (for example, the number of chemicals to be tested was cut to 6,000 and the number of chemicals that would require licences was also substantially curtailed). Legislative work concerning REACH continued throughout 2004 and the European Parliament began discussing the proposed legislation in January 2005.

SECURITY AND DEFENCE

Under the Single European Act, which came into force on 1 July 1987 (amending the Treaty of Rome), it was formally stipulated for the first time that member states should inform and consult each other on foreign policy matters (as was already, in practice, often the case). In June 1992 the Petersberg Declaration of Western European Union (WEU, see p. 352) defined the role of WEU as the defence component of the EU and outlined the 'Petersberg tasks' relating to crisis management, including humanitarian, peace-keeping and peace-making operations, which could be carried out under WEU authority (now EU authority). In 1992 France and Germany established a joint force called Eurocorps, based in Strasbourg, France, which was later joined by Belgium, Spain and Luxembourg. An agreement was signed in January 1993 that specified that Eurocorps troops could serve under NATO command, thus relieving concern, particularly from the United Kingdom and the USA, that the Eurocorps would undermine NATO's role in Europe. In May 1993 member states of the Eurocorps agreed to make the Eurocorps available to WEU. WEU also ratified in May 1995 the decision by Spain, France, Italy and Portugal to establish land and sea forces, European Operational Rapid Force (EUROFOR) and the European Maritime Force (EUROMARFOR) respectively, which were also to undertake the Petersberg tasks under the auspices of WEU. Several other multinational forces also belonged to Forces Answerable to the WEU (FAWEU). At the EU summit in Köln, Germany, in June 1999 EU member states accepted a proposal for the Eurocorps to be placed at the disposal of the EU for crisis response operations. At the end of that year Eurocorps member states agreed to transform the Eurocorps into a rapid reaction corps headquarters available both to the EU and NATO. In 2002 NATO certified the Eurocorps as a NATO high readiness force, which required the headquarters to be open to all NATO members as well as those from the EU; thus representatives from Austria, Canada, Finland, Greece, Italy, the Netherlands, Poland, Turkey and the United Kingdom are integrated into the headquarters.

The Maastricht Treaty on European Union, which came into force on 1 November 1993, provided for joint action by member governments in matters of common foreign and security policy (CFSP), and envisaged the eventual formation of a European security and defence policy (ESDP), with the possibility of a common defence force, although existing commitments to NATO were to be honoured. The Treaty raised WEU to the rank of an 'integral part of the development of the Union', while preserving its institutional autonomy, and gave it the task of elaborating and implementing decisions and actions with defence implications.

The Treaty of Amsterdam, which entered into force in May 1999, aimed to strengthen the concept of a CFSP within the Union and incorporated a process of common strategies to co-ordinate external relations with a third party. Under the Amsterdam Treaty, WEU was to provide the EU with access to operational capability for undertaking the so-called 'Petersberg tasks'. In late March 1999 representatives of the Commission and NATO held a joint meeting, for the first time, to discuss the conflict in the southern Serbian province of Kosovo and Metohija. In April a meeting of NATO Heads of State and of Government determined that NATO's equipment, personnel and infrastructure would be available to any future EU military operation. In June the European Council, meeting in Köln, Germany, determined to strengthen the ESDP, stating that the EU needed a capacity for autonomous action, without prejudice to actions by NATO and acknowledging the supreme prerogatives of the UN Security Council. The European Council initiated a process of assuming direct responsibility for the Petersberg tasks, which were placed at the core of the ESDP process. In December 1999, following consultation with NATO, the European Council, meeting in Helsinki, adopted the European Defence Initiative, comprising the following goals: by 2003 the EU should be able to deploy within 60 days and for a period of up to one year a rapid reaction force, comprising up to 60,000 national troops from member states, capable of implementing the full range of Petersberg tasks. At the Helsinki meeting the establishment of three permanent military institutions was proposed: a Political and Security Committee (PSC), a Military Body and a Military Staff. In February 2000 the EU set up an interim PSC and an interim Military Body. The PSC, which was fully established by 2001, monitors the international situation, helps define policies and assess their implementation,

encourages dialogue and, under the auspices of the Council, takes responsibility for the political direction of capability development. In the event of a crisis situation, it oversees the strategic direction of any military response, proposes political objectives and supervises their enactment. The Military Body gives military advice to the PSC, and comprises the chiefs of defence of member states, represented by military delegates. It serves as a forum for military consultation and co-operation and deals with risk assessment, the development of crisis management and military relations with non-EU European NATO members, accession countries, and NATO itself. Meanwhile, the Military Staff, comprising experts seconded by the member states, provides the EU with an early-warning capability, takes responsibility for strategic planning for the Petersberg tasks and implements the Military Body's policies. Permanent arrangements have been agreed for EU-NATO consultation and co-operation in this area. The process of transferring the crisis-management responsibilities of WEU to the EU was finalized by July 2001.

In December 2001 the EU announced that the rapid reaction force was, theoretically, ready, although only as yet capable of undertaking small-scale crisis management tasks. Further negotiations on the organization and funding of the force took place in 2002, but were hampered by disputes between Greece and Turkey on the role of the new body; a deal was finally agreed at the Copenhagen summit in December about sharing planning resources with NATO, in theory clearing the way for the beginning of EU military operations. In January 2003 EU forces were deployed for the first time in an international peace-keeping role, when 500 police officers were dispatched to Bosnia and Herzegovina to take over policing duties from the existing UN force. In March the European Parliament voted to approve the EU's first military mission, setting the stage for 450 lightly-armed EU troops to take over from NATO peace-keepers in the former Yugoslav republic of Macedonia in the following month. The EU announced in June its first military operation outside the continent of Europe, agreeing to send 1,400 peace-keepers to attempt to curb the ethnic violence in the Democratic Republic of the Congo. In July 2004 ministers responsible for foreign affairs agreed that EU-led military forces would take over from NATO in Bosnia and Herzegovina by the end of 2004. The EU duly assumed control of operations in November; 7,000 troops were deployed under EU command with a mission to ensure stability in the country.

At a meeting in Brussels in November 2004 EU ministers responsible for defence agreed to create up to 13 battle groups for deployment to crisis areas by 2007. Battle groups were to comprise between 1,000 and 1,500 troops and were to be capable of being deployed within 10 days of a unanimous decision from EU member states and the creation of a battle plan and would be equipped to stay in an area for up to four months. Each group was to be commanded by a 'lead nation' and associated with a force headquarters. France, Italy, Spain and the United Kingdom were to set up their own battle groups, which were likely to be ready before 2007. Ireland was not to participate in the battle groups for constitutional reasons. The creation of the battle groups was partly to compensate for the inadequacies of the rapid reaction force of 60,000 troops, which while theoretically declared ready for action in May 2003, in practice was adversely affected by shortfalls in equipment, owing to a lack of investment in procurement and research and a failure to co-ordinate purchases among member states.

According to the draft constitutional treaty of the EU, which was approved by the European Council in June 2004, the EU defence force would be given a legal basis; a mutual defence clause was included, and (although not written into the constitution itself) a separate operational planning capability. Although in April 2003 France, Germany, Belgium and Luxembourg had originally proposed a separate headquarters to plan joint military operations by EU nations, a compromise was reached in December under which a small cell of planning staff would be created, situated in NATO's military headquarters in Belgium, which would only be used if NATO declined involvement and national European headquarters needed support.

In June 2004 the European Council approved the creation of a European Defence Agency. A Council Joint Action on the establishment of the Agency was adopted in July. The new European Defence Agency was to be responsible for improving the EU's defence capabilities in relation to crisis management and for promoting co-operation on research and procurement, strengthening the European defence industrial and technological base and developing a competitive European defence equipment market.

In June 2000 the EU established a civilian crisis management committee. In the same month the European Council defined four priority areas for civilian crisis management: developing the role of the police; strengthening the rule of law; strengthening civilian administrations; and improving civil protection. As part of the general rapid reaction force (see above), the EU aimed to be able to deploy up to 5,000 police-officers for international missions by 2003. In February 2001 the Council adopted a regulation creating a rapid reaction mechanism (RRM) to improve the EU's civilian capacity to respond to crises. The mechanism bypasses cumbersome decision-making processes, to enable civilian experts in fields such as mine clearance, customs, police training, election-monitoring, institution-building, media support, rehabilitation and mediation to be mobilized speedily.

In September 2004 five European ministers responsible for defence signed an agreement in Noordwijk, the Netherlands, to establish a 3,000-member police force, which could be deployed internationally for post-conflict peace-keeping duties and maintaining public order. The European Gendarmerie Force, which was to be based in Vicenza, north-eastern Italy, would initially comprise members from France, Italy, Spain, Portugal and the Netherlands and it was hoped that it could be active by the end of 2005.

In October 2002 an extraordinary session of the Brussels European Council adopted a European action plan to combat terrorism, which aimed to contribute to a global anti-terrorism strategy. Its priority objectives included deepening political dialogue with third countries, strengthening arrangements for shared intelligence and using military or civilian capabilities to protect civilian populations in the event of terrorist attack. In December EU ministers of justice agreed to allow the exchange of information on crime and terrorist suspects between European and US agencies. In the wake of the bomb attacks carried out by suspected Islamist extremists in Madrid, Spain, in March 2004, the leaders of the EU agreed to implement a series of counter-terrorism measures, including monitoring data from mobile telephone calls and the internet; introducing a single EU-wide arrest warrant; harmonizing penalties for terrorist crimes; freezing assets held by outlawed groups; and appointing a senior counter-terrorism co-ordinator to help efforts to pool intelligence across Europe. The draft EU constitutional treaty includes a solidarity clause, under which member states would act jointly in the event of a terrorist attack, natural disaster or a man-made catastrophe. In May 2004, despite challenges to the legality of the move by the European Parliament on the grounds that it infringed civil liberties, the EU agreed to pass airline passenger data to US security agencies to enhance its capacity to fight terrorism.

Under the European code of conduct on arms exports, the EU publishes an annual report on defence exports based on confidential information provided by each member state. EU member states must withhold export licences to countries where it is deemed that arms sales might lead to political repression or external aggression. The Community funds projects aimed at the collection and destruction of weapons in countries emerging from conflict. The EU is strongly committed to nuclear non-proliferation. Under its programme of co-operation with Russia, the Union works to dismantle or destroy nuclear, chemical and biological weapons and weapons of mass destruction.

FINANCIAL SERVICES AND CAPITAL MOVEMENTS

Freedom of capital movement and the creation of a uniform financial area were regarded as vital for the completion of the EU's internal market by 1992. In 1987, as part of the liberalization of the flow of capital, a Council directive came into force whereby member states were obliged to remove restrictions on three categories of transactions: long-term credits related to commercial transactions; acquisition of securities; and the admission of securities to capital markets. In June 1988 the Council of Ministers approved a directive whereby all restrictions on capital movements (financial loans and credits, current and deposit account operations, transactions in securities and other instruments normally dealt in on the money market) were to be removed by 1 July 1990. A number of countries were permitted to exercise certain restrictions until the end of 1992, and further extensions were then granted to Portugal and Greece. With the entry into force of the Maastricht Treaty in November 1993, the principle of full freedom of capital movements was incorporated into the structure of the EU.

The EU worked to develop a single market in financial services throughout the 1990s. In October 1998 the Commission drew up a framework for action in the financial services sector. This communication was followed by a Financial Services Action Plan (FSAP) in May 1999, with three strategic objectives: to establish a single market in wholesale financial services; to make retail markets open and secure; and to strengthen the rules on prudential supervision in order to keep pace with new sources of financial risk. The prudential supervision of financial conglomerates (entities offering a range of financial services in areas such as banking, insurance and securities), which are developing rapidly, has been identified as an area of particular importance. During 2002 a directive was drawn up on the supplementary supervision of such businesses, in recognition of the increasing consolidation in the financial sector and the emergence of cross-sector financial groups. Individual targets specified in the 1999 FSAP included removing the outstanding barriers to raising capital within the EU; creating a coherent legal framework for supplementary pension funds; and providing greater legal certainty in cross-border securities trading.

The legislative timetable for the adoption of the FSAP measures set a deadline of 2005. During 2003 several important steps were taken regarding the FSAP, and by mid-2004 93% of the FSAP measures had been completed on schedule. In November 2003 the Commission adopted a package of seven measures aiming to establish a new organizational architecture in all financial services sectors. The Commission stressed that this initiative was required urgently if the FSAP was to be implemented and enforced effectively.

In July 2001 progress towards the creation of a single financial market was impeded by the European Parliament's rejection of a proposed takeover directive that had been under negotiation for 12 years. The directive had aimed to ensure that shareholders were treated in the same way throughout the EU after takeover bids, and had sought to create a single Community framework governing takeovers. The proposed directive was eventually approved by the European Parliament (with a number of strategic amendments) in mid-December 2003, but was subject to final approval by the Council of the EU.

A directive on Community banking, adopted in 1977, laid down common prudential criteria for the establishment and operation of banks in member states. A second banking directive, adopted in 1989, aimed to create a single community licence for banking, thereby permitting a bank established in one member country to open branches in any other. The directive entered into force on 1 January 1993. Related measures were subsequently adopted, with the aim of ensuring the capital adequacy of credit institutions and the prevention of 'money-laundering' by criminals. In September 1993 ministers approved a directive on a bank deposit scheme to protect account-holders. These directives were consolidated into one overall banking directive in March 2000. Non-bank institutions may be granted a 'European passport' once they have complied with the principles laid down in the EU's first banking directive on the mutual recognition of licences, prudential supervision and supervision by the home member state. Non-bank institutions must also comply with the directive on money-laundering.

In September 2000 a directive was issued governing the actions of non-bank institutions with regard to the issuance of 'electronic money' (money stored on an electronic device, for example, a chip card or in a computer memory). The directive authorized non-bank institutions to issue electronic money on a non-professional basis, with the aim of promoting a 'level playing field' with other credit institutions. Other regulations oblige the institutions to redeem electronic money at par value in coins and bank notes, or by transfer without charge.

In May 2001 a directive on the reorganization and winding up of failed credit institutions with branches in more than one member state was agreed; it entered into force in May 2004.

In July 1994 the third insurance co-ordination directives, relating to life assurance and non-life insurance, came into effect, creating a framework for an integrated Community insurance market. The Directive on the Reorganisation and Winding-Up of Insurance Undertakings was adopted by the EU in February 2001 and came into force in April 2003. The main aim of the directive was to provide greater consumer protection and it formed part of a wider drive to achieve a consistent approach to insolvency proceedings across the EU. A new directive on life assurance was adopted in November 2002, superseding all previous directives in this field. The EU's insurance committee works to improve co-operation with national supervisory authorities.

In May 1993 ministers adopted a directive on investment services, which (with effect from 1 January 1996) allowed credit institutions to offer investment services in any member state, on the basis of a licence held in one state. The 1999 FSAP aimed to achieve the further convergence of national approaches to investment, in order to increase the effectiveness of the 1993 directive.

In late 1999 the Commission put forward proposals to remove tax barriers and investment restrictions affecting cross-border pension schemes. At present, variations among member states in the tax liability of contributions to supplementary pension schemes obstruct the transfer of pension rights from one state to another, contradicting the Treaty of Rome's principles of free movement. In October 2000 a specific legal framework for institutions for occupational retirement provision (IORPs) was proposed. This seeks to abolish barriers to investment by pension funds and would permit the cross-border management of IORP pension schemes, with mutual recognition of the supervisory methods in force. In September 2003 the occupational pensions directive (IORP directive), which was designed to allow workers of multinational companies to have access to cross-border employer pension schemes, became EU law.

In November 1997 the Commission adopted proposals to co-ordinate tax policy among member states. The measures aimed to simplify the transfer of royalty and interest payments between member states and to prevent the withholding of taxes. In February 1999 Parliament endorsed a proposal by the Commission to harmonize taxation further, through the co-ordination of savings taxes. In November 2000 finance ministers agreed on a proposed savings tax directive, the details of which were endorsed in July 2001. This directive set out rules on the exchange of information on savings accounts of individuals resident in one EU country and receiving interest in another. However, in December 2001 Austria, Luxembourg and Belgium abandoned the agreement, insisting that they would only comply if other 'tax havens' in Europe, such as Monaco, Liechtenstein and Switzerland, were compelled to amend their banking secrecy laws.

Two other proposed directives were issued in November 2000, the first relating to interest and royalties and the second concerning the code of conduct for business taxation. Together with the tax savings directive, these were known as the 'EU tax package'. The EU finance ministers finally reached agreement on the terms of the package in June 2003. The package consisted of a political code of conduct to eliminate harmful business tax regimes; a legislative measure to ensure an effective minimum level of taxation of savings income; and a legislative measure to eliminate source taxes on cross-border payments of interest and royalties between associated companies. The Council of the EU reached agreement on the controversial savings tax directive (after 15 years of negotiation) in June 2004; the directive was due to be enforced from 1 July 2005. The aim of the directive was to prevent EU citizens from avoiding taxes on savings by keeping their money in foreign bank accounts. Under the directive, each member state would ultimately be expected to provide information to other member states on interest paid from that member state to individual savers resident in those other member states. For a transitional period, Belgium, Luxembourg and Austria were to be allowed to apply a withholding tax instead, at a rate of 15% for the first three years (2005–07), 20% for the subsequent three years (2008–10) and 35% from 1 July 2011 onwards. Negotiations had been concluded with Switzerland, Liechtenstein, Monaco, Andorra and San Marino to ensure the adoption of equivalent measures in those countries to allow effective taxation of savings income paid to EU residents.

The May 2000 convention on mutual assistance in criminal matters (see Justice and Home Affairs) committed member states to co-operation in combating economic and financial crime. In May 2001 the Council adopted a framework decision on preventing fraud and counterfeiting in non-cash means of payment, recognizing this as a criminal offence. An EU conference in Paris, France, in February 2002 (which was also attended by representatives of seven candidate countries and Russia) agreed to tackle money-laundering by setting minimum secrecy levels and compelling internet service providers to identify operators of suspect financial deals. Following the terrorist attacks on the USA in September 2001, the EU attempted to accelerate the adoption of the convention combating the financing of terrorism, and began work on a new directive on 'freezing' assets or evidence related to terrorist crimes. In early 2005 the Council of the EU approved a proposal for the compulsory declaration at EU borders of large amounts (i.e. more than €10,000) of cash (including banknotes and cheques); the proposal applied only to the external borders of the Union. The aim of this measure was to prevent the entry into the EU of untraceable money, which could then be used to fund criminal or terrorist activities. A proposed third money-laundering directive (which was extended to cover terrorist financing as well as money-laundering) was also under discussion in early 2005.

In February 2001 the Commission launched a complaints network for out-of-court settlements in the financial sector (FIN-NET), to help consumers find amicable solutions in cases where the supplier is in another member state. In September the EU agreed harmonized rules on the cross-border distance-selling of financial services.

ECONOMIC CO-OPERATION

A review of the economic situation is presented annually by the Commission, analysing recent developments and short- and medium-term prospects. Economic policy guide-lines for the following year are adopted annually by the Council.

The following objectives for the end of 1973 were agreed by the Council in 1971, as the first of three stages towards European economic and monetary union: the narrowing of exchange-rate margins to 2.25%; creation of a medium-term pool of reserves; co-ordination of short- and medium-term economic and budgetary policies; a joint position on international monetary issues; harmonization of taxes; creation of the European Monetary Co-operation Fund (EMCF); and creation of the European Regional Development Fund.

The narrowing of exchange margins (the 'snake') came into effect in 1972; however, Denmark, France, Ireland, Italy and the United Kingdom later floated their currencies, with only Denmark permanently returning to the arrangement. Sweden and Norway also linked their currencies to the 'snake', but Sweden withdrew from the arrangement in August 1977, and Norway withdrew in December 1978.

The European Monetary System (EMS) came into force in March 1979, with the aim of creating closer monetary co-operation, leading to a zone of monetary stability in Europe, principally through an exchange-rate mechanism (ERM), supervised by the ministries of finance and the central banks of member states. Not all Community members participated in the ERM: Greece did not join, Spain joined only in June 1989, the United Kingdom in October 1990 and Portugal in April 1992. To prevent wide fluctuations in the value of members' currencies against each other, the ERM fixed for each currency a central rate in European Currency Units (ECUs, see below), based on a 'basket' of national currencies; a reference rate in relation to other currencies was fixed for each currency, with established fluctuation margins. Central banks of the participating states intervened by buying or selling currencies when the agreed margin was likely to be exceeded. Each member placed 20% of its gold reserves and dollar reserves, respectively, into the EMCF, and received a supply of ECUs to regulate central bank interventions. Short- and medium-term credit facilities were given to support the balance of payments of member countries. The EMS was initially put under strain by the wide fluctuations in the exchange rates of non-Community currencies and by the differences in economic development among members, which led to nine realignments of currencies in 1979–83. Subsequently, greater stability was achieved, with only two realignments of currencies between 1984 and 1988. In 1992–93, however, there was great pressure on currency markets, necessitating further realignments; in September 1992 Italian and British membership of the ERM was suspended. In late July 1993, as a result of intensive currency speculation on European financial markets (forcing the weaker currencies to the very edge of their permitted margins), the ERM almost collapsed. In response to the crisis, EC finance ministers decided to widen the fluctuation margins allowed for each currency, except in the cases of Germany and the Netherlands, which agreed to maintain their currencies within the original limits. The new margins were regarded as allowing for so much fluctuation in exchange rates as to represent a virtual suspension of the ERM, although some countries, notably France and Belgium, expressed their determination to adhere as far as possible to the original 'bands' in order to fulfil the conditions for eventual monetary union. In practice, during 1994, most currencies remained within the former narrower bands. Austria became a member of the EMS in January 1995, and its currency was subject to ERM conditions. While Sweden decided to remain outside the EMS, Finland joined in October 1996. In November of that year the Italian lira was readmitted to the ERM.

In September 1988 a committee (chaired by Jacques Delors, then President of the European Commission, and comprising the governors of member countries' central banks, representatives of the European Commission and outside experts) was established to discuss European monetary union. The resulting 'Delors plan' was presented to heads of government in June 1989, who agreed to begin the first stage of the process of monetary union—the drafting of a treaty on the subject—in 1990. The Intergovernmental Conference on Economic and Monetary Union was initiated in December 1990, and continued to work (in parallel with the Intergovernmental Conference on Political Union) throughout 1991. The Intergovernmental Conference was responsible for the drafting of the economic and monetary provisions of the Treaty on European Union, which was agreed by the European Council in December 1991 and which came into force on 1 November 1993. The principal feature of the Treaty's provisions on Economic and Monetary Union (EMU) was the gradual introduction of a single currency, to be administered by a single central bank. During the remainder of Stage I, member states were to adopt programmes for the 'convergence' of their economies and ensure the complete liberalization of capital movements. Stage II began on 1 January 1994, and included the establishment of a European Monetary Institute (EMI), replacing the EMCF and comprising governors of central banks and a president appointed by heads of government. Heads of government were to decide, not later than 31 December 1996, whether a majority of member states fulfilled the necessary conditions for the adoption of a single currency: if so, they were to establish a date for the beginning of Stage III. If no date had been set by the end of 1997, Stage III was to begin on 1 January 1999, and was to be confined to those members that did fulfil the necessary conditions. After the establishment of a starting date for Stage III, the European Central Bank (ECB) and a European System of Central Banks were to be set up to replace the EMI. During Stage III, exchange rates were to be irrevocably fixed, and a single currency introduced. Member states that had not fulfilled the necessary conditions for the adoption of a single currency would be exempt from participating. The United Kingdom was to be allowed to make a later, separate decision on whether to proceed to Stage III, while Denmark reserved the right to submit its participation in Stage III to a referendum. The near-collapse of the ERM in July 1993 cast serious doubts on the agreed timetable for monetary union, although in October the EC heads of government reaffirmed their commitment to the objective.

In December 1995 the European Council confirmed that Stage III of EMU was to begin on 1 January 1999. The economic conditions for member states wishing to enter Stage III (including an annual budget deficit of no more than 3% of annual gross domestic product—GDP—and total public debt of no more than 60% of annual GDP) were also confirmed. The meeting decided that the proposed single currency would be officially known as the 'euro'. Participants in EMU were to be selected in early 1998, on the basis of economic performance during 1997. In October 1996 the Commission issued a draft regulation on a proposed Stability and Growth Pact (SGP), intended to ensure that member countries maintained strict budgetary discipline during Stage III of monetary union. Another draft regulation formed the legal framework for the euro, confirming that it would be the single currency of participating countries from 1 January 1999. During a transitional period of up to three years, national currencies would remain in circulation, having equivalent legal status to the euro. The communication outlined the main features of a new ERM, which would act as a 'waiting room' for countries preparing to join the single currency. Member countries remaining outside the monetary system, whether or not by choice, would still be part of the single market.

Although all of the then 15 members of the EU endorsed the principle of monetary union, with France and Germany the most ardent supporters, certain countries were known to have political doubts about joining. In October 1997 both the United Kingdom and Sweden confirmed that they would not participate in EMU from 1999. Denmark was also to remain outside the single currency.

Technical preparations for the euro were confirmed during a meeting of the European Council in Dublin in December 1996. The heads of government endorsed the new ERM and the legal framework for the euro and agreed to the proposed SGP. In March 1998 the Commission and the European Investment Bank (EIB) published reports on the progress made by member states towards the fulfilment of convergence criteria. The Commission concluded that Greece alone failed to satisfy the necessary conditions. However, the EIB warned that Italy and Belgium, with public-debt ratios of over 100% of GDP, had made insufficient progress towards the reduction of debt levels. In March Greece was admitted to the ERM, causing a 14% devaluation of its national currency. In early May 1998 heads of state and of government confirmed that Greece failed to fulfil the conditions required for the adoption of a single currency from 1999, and that 11 countries would take part in Stage III of EMU. The meeting agreed that existing ERM central rates were to be used to determine the final rates of exchange between national currencies and the euro, which would be adopted on 1 January 1999. The ECB, which was established on 1 June 1998 and ceremonially launched on 30 June, was to be accountable to a European Forum, comprising members of the European Parliament (MEPs) and chairmen of the finance committees of the national parliaments of EU member countries.

In September 1998 Sweden and the United Kingdom came under pressure to join the successor to the ERM, ERMII, launched on 1 January 1999, as a precondition of future participation in EMU. In October 1998 ministers discussed Greece's convergence programme for 1998–2001; this sought to allow Greece to join the single currency from 1 January 2001. On 31 December 1998 the ECOFIN Council adopted the conversion rates for the national currencies of the countries participating in the single currency. The euro was formally launched on 1 January 1999. Both Greece and Denmark joined ERMII. In September 2000 some 53% of Danish voters participating in a national referendum rejected the adoption of the euro. On 1 January 2001 Greece became the twelfth EU member state to adopt the euro, in the first enlargement of the euro area since its inception. In September 2003 the majority of Swedish voters—some 56%—participating in a national referendum chose to reject Sweden's adoption of the euro.

The SGP, which was designed to sustain confidence in the euro, is seen as the cornerstone of monetary union. Under its original terms member states were obliged to keep budget deficits within 3% of GDP, or face fines, and to bring their budgets close to balance by 2004. However, during 2002 the Pact was heavily criticized for being inflexible, when a number of countries (including Portugal and Germany) could not meet its requirements. In September 2002 the 2004 deadline for reaching a balanced budget was extended by two years (benefiting France, Germany, Italy and Portugal), although the 3% limit for budgetary deficit remained, while some concessionary provision was introduced to allow countries with low levels of long-term debt, such as the United Kingdom and Ireland, to increase investment spending by running larger short-term budget deficits.

In November 2003 France and Germany, which were both likely to breach the budget deficit limit of 3% for a third consecutive year, persuaded the EU ministers responsible for finance to suspend the disciplinary procedure (triggered by their failure to meet the 3% limit in 2002) under which they could have faced punitive fines. The two countries had argued that further fiscal austerity could have precipitated a recession in their economies. Under compromise agreements Germany and France were to reduce their budget deficits by 0.6% and 0.77% of GDP respectively in 2004 and by 0.5% and 0.6% respectively in 2005. However, even these reductions would not be required if growth in the French and German economies were

unexpectedly low. The refusal of France and Germany to restrict their expenditure provoked anger among some smaller EU countries that had implemented strict austerity programmes in order to comply with the Pact. In January 2004 the European Commission launched a legal action against the Council of Finance Ministers in the European Court of Justice. The Court ruled in July that the Council had acted illegally in temporarily suspending the budget rules.However, prior to this ruling, in June, the economic affairs commissioner had announced a review of the SGP in order to clarify the rules of the pact, citing the need for combining fiscal discipline with considerations of growth and aiming to focus more on debt, sustainability and the specific state of a country's finances. Critics of the SGP, notably Germany, complained that the pact was too inflexible and prevented countries from increasing public investment to stimulate the economy in an economic downturn. However, discussions by member states on the reform of the SGP in January and March 2005 were inconclusive.

All 10 countries that joined the EU on 1 May 2004 (Cyprus, the Czech Republic, Estonia, Hungary, Latvia, Lithuania, Malta, Poland, Slovakia and Slovenia) were obliged to participate in EMU; however, adoption of the euro was dependent on the fulfilment of the same Maastricht convergence criteria as the initial entrants, which comprised conditions regarding inflation, debt, budget deficit, long-term interest rates and exchange-rate stability. The exchange-rate criteria included the requirement to spend at least two years in ERMII. Although the currency was permitted to fluctuate 15% either side of a central rate or, by common agreement, within a narrower band, the ECB specified that the limit of 2.25% would be applied when judging whether countries had achieved sufficient stability to join the euro area. Although many of the new member countries were keen to adopt the euro as soon as possible, the ECB warned of the risks associated with early membership of ERMII, sharing widespread concerns that the required fiscal austerity and loss of flexibility over exchange-rate policy would stifle economic growth in the accession countries. Moreover, economies would also become vulnerable to speculative attacks once they entered ERMII. Owing to differences in the economies of the new member states, progress towards membership in EMU was likely to vary significantly. In June 2004 Estonia, Lithuania and Slovenia joined ERM II. They were thus expected to be assessed in mid-2006 ready for admission to EMU in January 2007. Latvia, Malta, Cyprus and Slovakia were expected to meet the convergence criteria in 2008–09, while Poland, Hungary and the Czech Republic were unlikely to be ready to adopt the euro before 2010. The entry into EMU of the new member states was not expected to have an impact on the ECB's monetary policy as the new member states only accounted for about 5% of the GDP of the enlarged EU.

In May 2004 Portugal was deemed to have complied with the recommendations made following the Council's announcement that it had an excessive budgetary deficit in 2002. In June and July the Council noted excessive budgetary deficits in the Czech Republic, Greece, Cyprus, Hungary, Malta, the Netherlands, Poland and Slovenia and recommended measures to remedy the position. In September 2004 revised figures released by Greece revealed previous gross under-reporting of the country's national budgetary deficit and debt figures. It was subsequently established that Greece had not complied with membership rules for the single currency in 2000, the year in which it qualified to join. Greece received a formal warning from the Commission in December for publishing inaccurate data concerning its public finances for 1997–2003. The Netherlands was found in October 2004 to have taken effective action to redress the situation and the measures adopted by the Czech Republic, Cyprus, Malta, Poland and Slovenia were similarly approved in December. However, Hungary's response was deemed to have been inadequate. At a meeting in January 2005 the ministers responsible for finance from the member states abandoned disciplinary action against France and Germany after concluding that both countries would meet the target budgetary deficit of 3% in 2005.

In November 2004 the former Dutch Prime Minister, Wim Kok, published a report on the progress of the EU states toward the objectives established at a meeting in Lisbon, Portugal, in 2000, known as the Lisbon Agenda. The Lisbon Agenda called on EU Governments to implement economic and social changes, including tax reductions, health-care and pension-system reform and the introduction of more flexible employment systems, in order to perform better than the US economy by 2010. Kok's report concluded that the agenda had been too broad and that many targets would be missed, and recommended a future focus on only 14 key indicators with an emphasis on job creation and economic growth.

The Euro

With the creation of the European Monetary System (EMS) in 1999, a new monetary unit, the European Currency Unit (ECU), was adopted. Its value and composition were identical to those of the European Unit of Account (EUA) already used in the administrative fields of the Community. The ECU was a composite monetary unit, in which the relative value of each currency was determined by the gross national product and the volume of trade of each country.

The ECU, which was assigned the function of the unit of account used by the European Monetary Co-operation Fund (EMCF), was also used as the denominator for the Exchange Rate Mechanism (ERM); as the denominator for operations in both the intervention and the credit mechanisms; and as a means of settlement between monetary authorities of the European Community. From April 1979 the ECU was also used as the unit of account for the purposes of the Common Agricultural Policy (CAP). From 1981 it replaced the EUA in the general budget of the Community; the activities of the European Development Fund (EDF) under the Lomé Convention; the balance sheets and loan operations of the European Investment Bank (EIB); and the activities of the European Coal and Steel Community (ECSC). In June 1985 measures were adopted by the governors of the Community's central banks, aiming to strengthen the EMS by expanding the use of the ECU, for example, by allowing international monetary institutions and the central banks of non-member countries to become 'other holders' of ECUs.

In June 1989 it was announced that, with effect from 20 September, the Portuguese and Spanish currencies were to be included in the composition of the ECU. From that date the amounts of the national currencies included in the composition of the ECU were 'weighted' as follows (in percentages): Belgian franc 7.6; Danish krone 2.5; French franc 19.0; Deutsche Mark 30.1; Greek drachma 0.8; Irish pound 1.1; Italian lira 10.2; Luxembourg franc 0.3; Netherlands guilder 9.4; Portuguese escudo 0.8; Spanish peseta 5.3; and the United Kingdom pound sterling 13.0. The composition of the ECU 'basket' of currencies was 'frozen' with the entry into force of the Treaty on European Union on 1 November 1993. This was not affected by the accession to the EU of Austria, Finland and Sweden; consequently those countries' currencies were not represented in the ECU 'basket'.

As part of Stage III of the process of Economic and Monetary Union (EMU), the ECU was replaced by a single currency, the euro (€), on 1 January 1999, at a conversion rate of 1:1.

In April 1998 ministers agreed that banks should make no charge for the conversion of accounts or payments of national currency into euros, during a transitional period. In July agreement was reached with trade and consumer groups to establish a voluntary scheme allowing retailers to display prices in euros and to accept payments made in euros without imposing any additional charges.

A payments settlement system, known as Target (Trans-European Automated Real-time Gross Settlement Express Transfer), was introduced for countries participating in EMU on 4 January 1999. By 2002 Target had become one of the world's largest payment systems, and was considered to be making a considerable contribution to the integration of the euro money market and the smooth implementation of the single monetary policy.

On 1 January 2002 the euro entered into circulation in the 12 participating countries. By the end of February the former national currencies of all of the participating countries had been withdrawn. The introduction of the new currency took place without major problems, and even ahead of the official phasing-out of national currencies the changeover was functioning smoothly; by the beginning of February the euro was used in over 95% of cash transactions.

The euro's value in national currencies is calculated and published daily. By mid-1999 the value of the euro had declined by some 12% against the US dollar compared with its value on introduction. Its decline was attributed to the relatively high degree of economic growth taking place in the USA compared with rates in the euro zone. Signs of economic recovery, especially in Germany, led to the strengthening of the euro against the US dollar in the second half of 1999. However, this renewal of confidence was not sustained and the euro dropped below parity level with the dollar in December. The ECB raised interest rates four times during the six months to May 2000, in an attempt to combat the failure in confidence. In September 2000 the monetary authorities of the USA and Japan, concerned about the impact of the weakness of the euro on the world economy, intervened jointly with the ECB in exchange markets. In November 2000 the currency reached its lowest recorded level. The euro rallied briefly in early 2001, but by June its value was declining once again. The ECB lowered interest rates four times during 2001 (including in September, as part of a joint effort by central banks to counteract the economic effects of the terrorist attacks on the USA). By November the currency had lost about one-fifth of its value against the US dollar since its launch in 1999.

Immediately following the introduction of the euro in the 12 participating countries in January 2002, its value rose significantly; during 2002 it continued to appreciate against other currencies, reaching parity with the US dollar in June, a stage which marked its highest level since February 2000. The euro continued to appreciate sharply against the dollar, by 20% in 2003, largely as a result of the large US current-account deficit and its financing requirements. In early 2004 the euro weakened slightly against the dollar, owing partly to the disparity between growth rates in the USA and the euro zone, declining to €1=US $1.18 in late April, its lowest rate since

November 2003, although it recovered swiftly to €1=US $1.19 before the end of the month.

The euro appreciated sharply against the dollar in 2004, reaching its highest ever rate of €1=US $1.37 in December. However, the ECB resisted pressure to lower interest rates; the last change in interest rates was in early June 2003 when the ECB reduced its key refinancing rate to 2.0%. By February 2005 the exchange rate had stabilized at about €1=US $1.30. Although the high value of the euro had an adverse effect on exports it had a favourable impact on imports, keeping imported inflation low and partially protecting the euro area from the negative effects of high petroleum prices.

External Relations

CENTRAL AND EASTERN EUROPE

During the late 1980s the extensive political changes and reforms in eastern European countries led to a strengthening of links with the EC. Agreements on trade and economic co-operation were concluded with Hungary (1988), Poland (1989), the USSR (1989), Czechoslovakia (1988—on trade only—and 1990), Bulgaria (1990), the German Democratic Republic (GDR—1990) and Romania (1990). In July 1989 the EC was entrusted with the co-ordination of aid from member states of the Organisation for Economic Co-operation and Development—OECD (see p. 307) to Hungary and Poland ('Operation PHARE'—Poland/Hungary Aid for Restructuring of Economies): this programme was subsequently extended to include Albania, Bulgaria, the Czech Republic, Slovakia, Romania and the Baltic states (Estonia, Latvia and Lithuania). Community heads of government agreed in December 1989 to establish a European Bank for Reconstruction and Development—EBRD (see p. 212), with participation by member states of the OECD and the Council for Mutual Economic Assistance, to promote investment in eastern Europe; the EBRD began operations in April 1991. In June 1995 the European Council agreed to provide total funding under the PHARE programme of ECU 6,693m. to central and eastern European countries for the period 1995–99.

'Europe Agreements' between the EC and Czechoslovakia, Hungary and Poland were signed in December 1991, with the aim of establishing a free-trade area within 10 years and developing political co-operation. In April 1994 Hungary and Poland submitted formal applications for EU membership. The Czech Republic applied formally in January 1996. In June 1991 the EC established diplomatic relations with Albania, and in May 1992 an agreement on trade and co-operation was signed. Europe Agreements were initialled with Romania in October, and with Bulgaria in March 1993. In June 1995 Romania formally applied for EU membership, followed by Bulgaria in December. In June 1993 the European Council approved measures to accelerate the opening of EC markets to goods from central and eastern European countries, with customs duties on many industrial items to be removed by the end of 1994. In September 1993 a co-operation agreement with Slovenia came into force; a Europe Agreement was signed in 1996, and Slovenia then formally applied for EU membership. An interim agreement, implementing the measures approved in June 1993, entered into force on 1 January 1997, providing for the gradual establishment of a free-trade area during a transitional period of six years. In December 2000 a preferential trade regime between Slovenia and the EU entered into effect.

Trade and co-operation agreements with the three Baltic states were signed in May 1992. In July 1994 free-trade agreements with these countries were finalized by the EU, coming into effect on 1 January 1995. The EU concluded Europe Agreements with the Baltic states in June 1995. In October 1995 Latvia submitted a formal application for EU membership. Formal applications by Estonia and Lithuania were submitted in December.

In 1991 the EC established the Technical Assistance to the Commonwealth of Independent States (TACIS) programme, to promote the development of successful market economies and foster democracy in the countries of the former USSR through the provision of expertise and training. (TACIS initially extended assistance to the Baltic states. In 1992, however, these became eligible for assistance under PHARE and withdrew from TACIS.) The TACIS/EBRD Bangkok Facility provides EU financing to assist in the preparation for, and implementation of, EBRD investment in the CIS region. In 1994 Mongolia also became eligible for TACIS assistance. The TACIS programme's budget for 2000–06 was €3,138m.

In 1992 EU heads of government decided to replace the agreement on trade and economic co-operation that had been concluded with the USSR in 1989 with new Partnership and Co-operation Agreements (PCAs), providing a framework for closer political, cultural and economic relations between the EU and the former republics of the USSR. The PCAs are preceded by preliminary Interim Agreements. An Interim Agreement with Russia on trade concessions came into effect in February 1996, giving EU exporters improved access to the Russian market for specific products, and at the same time abolishing quantitative restrictions on some Russian exports to the EU. In December 1997 a PCA with Russia entered into force. The first meeting of the Co-operation Council for the EU-Russia PCA took place in January 1998, and, in July, an EU-Russia Space Dialogue was established. In June 1999 the EU adopted a Common Strategy on Russia. This aimed to promote the consolidation of democracy and rule of law in the country; the integration of Russia into the common European economic and social space; and regional stability and security. At the sixth EU-Russia summit in October 2000 the two sides agreed to initiate a regular energy dialogue, with the aim of establishing an EU-Russia Energy Partnership. During 2002 two EU-Russia summits were held, at which each party reconfirmed its commitment to democratic principles and human rights, and its determination to continue the fight against international terrorism, drugs-trafficking and illegal immigration. Discussion also centred on the issue of Kaliningrad, a Russian enclave between Poland and Lithuania, and its future status following the accession of these two countries. In the face of opposition from Russia, the EU insisted that residents of Kaliningrad would need a visa to cross EU territory; the matter was eventually resolved by a compromise agreement on a special multiple re-entry transit pass for residents of the enclave. The enlargement of the EU in May 2004 was likely to have a detrimental effect on the Russian economy as some of its neighbouring countries (significant markets for Russian goods) would be obliged to introduce EU quotas and tariffs; Russia requested compensation for these potential trade losses. At a summit in St. Petersburg in May 2003 the EU and Russia agreed to improve their co-operation by creating four 'common spaces' in the framework of the Partnership and Cooperation Agreement. The four areas related to the economy (in particular energy and the environment), freedom and justice, external security and research and education. However, relations between the EU and Russian remained strained by Russia's hostility to EU enlargement. In February 2004 the EU released a policy paper criticizing Russian human rights abuses in Chechnya, the Government's failure to promote democracy and the country's refusal to sign the Kyoto Protocol on climate change. In May 2004, at a bilateral summit in Moscow, the EU agreed to support Russia's membership of the World Trade Organization (WTO), following Russia's extension in April of its co-operation agreement with the EU to the 10 new member states of the EU. In June, however, Russia halted imports of meat from nearly one-half of EU countries, owing to a disagreement about veterinary certificates. A meeting between the Russian President, Vladimir Putin, with EU leaders in The Hague, Netherlands, was held in November. The meeting, at which discussions took place concerning cross-border policing, the liberalization of visa arrangements, Russian access to Kaliningrad and the situation in Chechnya, was affected by differences over a controversial presidential election in Ukraine. However, in early 2005 bilateral relations improved significantly.

In February 1994 the EU Council of Ministers agreed to pursue closer economic and political relations with Ukraine, following an agreement by that country to renounce control of nuclear weapons on its territory. A PCA was signed by the two sides in June. In December EU ministers of finance approved a loan totalling ECU 85m., conditional on Ukraine's implementation of a strategy to close the Chernobyl (Chornobyl) nuclear power plant. An Interim Trade Agreement with Ukraine came into force in February 1996; this was replaced by a PCA in March 1998. In December 1999 the EU adopted a Common Strategy on Ukraine, aimed at developing a strategic partnership on the basis of the PCA. The Chernobyl plant closed in December 2000. The EU has provided funding to cover the interim period prior to the completion of two new reactors (supported by the EBRD and the European Atomic Energy Community—Euratom) to replace the plant's generating capacity. The EU has also been involved in social regeneration projects in the Chernobyl area. The EU refused to grant Ukraine market economy status, following an EU-Ukraine summit in The Hague in July 2004. Relations with Ukraine improved following EU mediation in the crisis in Ukraine over the fraudulent presidential elections in 2004. The EU welcomed the inauguration as President of the pro-Western opposition leader, Viktor Yushchenko, in January 2005 who emphasized that future co-operation would be dependent on genuine democratic reform in Ukraine. The EU announced its intention to proceed with the Action Plan for Ukraine which would offer Ukraine, in principle, complete access to the EU's single market.

An Interim Agreement with Belarus was signed in March 1996. However, in February 1997 the EU suspended negotiations for the conclusion of the Interim Agreement and for a PCA in view of serious reverses to the development of democracy in that country. EU technical assistance programmes were suspended, with the exception of aid programmes and those considered directly beneficial to the democratic process. In 1999 the EU announced that the punitive measures would be withdrawn gradually upon the attainment of certain benchmarks. In 2000 the EU criticized the Belarus Government for failing to accept its recommendations on the conduct of

legislative elections held in October. By July 1999 PCAs had entered into force with all the CIS states except for Belarus, Tajikistan and Turkmenistan. In November 2002 the EU member states imposed a travel ban on President Alyaksandr Lukashenka of Belarus, as a protest against his authoritarian rule and the declining human rights situation in the country; the ban was lifted in April 2003. Unlike Russia and Ukraine, Belarus was reluctant to negotiate with the EU about border concerns, as the new EU member states were forced to introduce a visa regime. In September 2004 the European Parliament condemned Lukashenka's attempt to gain a third term of office by calling a referendum to change the country's constitution, which currently permitted a maximum of two terms. The EU subsequently imposed a travel ban on officials responsible for the allegedly fraudulent legislative elections and referendum held in Belarus in October that gave Lukashenka the right to an unlimited period in office. In January 2005 the EU condemned the imprisonment of a former opposition presidential candidate on allegedly politically motivated charges.

A co-operation agreement was signed with Yugoslavia in 1980 (but not ratified until April 1983), allowing tariff-free imports and Community loans. New financial protocols were signed in 1987 and 1991. However, EC aid was suspended in July 1991, following the declarations of independence by the Yugoslav republics of Croatia and Slovenia, and the subsequent outbreak of civil conflict. Efforts were made in the ensuing months by EC ministers of foreign affairs to negotiate a peaceful settlement between the Croatian and Serbian factions, and a team of EC observers was maintained in Yugoslavia from July onwards, to monitor successive cease-fire agreements. In October the EC proposed a plan for an association of independent states, to replace the Yugoslav federation: this was accepted by all the Yugoslav republics except Serbia, which demanded a redefining of boundaries to accommodate within Serbia all predominantly Serbian areas. In November the application of the Community's co-operation agreements with Yugoslavia was suspended (with exemptions for the republics which co-operated in the peace negotiations). In January 1992 the Community granted diplomatic recognition to the former Yugoslav republics of Croatia and Slovenia, and in April it recognized Bosnia and Herzegovina, while withholding recognition from Macedonia (owing to pressure from the Greek Government, which feared that the existence of an independent Macedonia would imply a claim on the Greek province of the same name). In May EC ambassadors were withdrawn from Belgrade, in protest at Serbia's support for aggression by Bosnian Serbs against other ethnic groups in Bosnia and Herzegovina, and in the same month the Community imposed a trade embargo on Serbia and Montenegro.

New proposals for a settlement of the Bosnian conflict, submitted by EC and UN mediators in 1993, were accepted by the Bosnian Croats and by the Bosnian Government in March, but rejected by the Bosnian Serbs. In June the European Council pledged more rigorous enforcement of sanctions against Serbia. In July, at UN/EC talks in Geneva, all three parties to the Bosnian war agreed on a plan to divide Bosnia and Herzegovina into three separate republics; however, the Bosnian Government rejected the proposals for the share of territory to be allotted to the Muslim community.

In April 1994, following a request from EU ministers of foreign affairs, a Contact Group, consisting of France, Germany, the United Kingdom, the USA and Russia, was initiated to undertake peace negotiations. The following month ministers of foreign affairs of the USA, Russia and the EU (represented by five member states) jointly endorsed a proposal to divide Bosnia and Herzegovina in proportions of 49% to the Bosnian Serbs and 51% to the newly-established Federation of Muslims and Croats. The proposal was rejected by the Bosnian Serb assembly in July and had to be abandoned after the Muslim-Croat Federation withdrew its support subsequent to the Bosnian Serb vote. In July the EU formally assumed political control of Mostar, in southern Bosnia and Herzegovina, in order to restore the city's administrative infrastructure and secure peace.

Despite some criticism of US policy towards the former Yugoslavia, in September 1995 the EU supported US-led negotiations in Geneva to devise a plan to end the conflict in Bosnia and Herzegovina. The plan closely resembled the previous proposals of the Contact Group: two self-governing entities were to be created within Bosnia and Herzegovina, with 51% of territory being allocated to the Muslim-Croat Federation, and 49% to Bosnian Serbs. The proposals were finally agreed after negotiations in Dayton, USA, in November 1995, and an accord was signed in Paris in December. During 1991–2000 Bosnia and Herzegovina received a total of €1,032m. in assistance from the EU. In 2000 the EU published a 'road map' for Bosnia and Herzegovina, outlining measures that must be undertaken by the Government prior to the initiation of a feasibility study on the formulation of a Stabilization and Association Agreement (SAA). In September 2002 the Commission reported that Bosnia and Herzegovina had essentially adhered to the terms of the road map. In January 2003 a new European Union Police Mission (EUPM) took over from the UN peace-keeping force in Bosnia and Herzegovina, with a budget of €38m. for 2003. This was the first operation under the common European security and defence policy.

Negotiations towards a trade and co-operation agreement with Croatia began in June 1995, but talks were suspended in early August, following Croatia's military offensive in the Krajina region, which was strongly criticized by the EU. A Consultative Task Force was established in Croatia in February 2000. An SAA with Croatia entered into force in October 2001. In 2004 the EU determined to establish a new mission in Bosnia and Herzegovina following the planned termination at the end of that year of the mandate (approved in December 1996) of the NATO-led Stabilization Force (SFOR).

In January 1996 the EU announced its intention to recognize Yugoslavia (Serbia and Montenegro), despite the opposition of the USA. During 1996–99 the EU allocated ECU 1,000m. for the repatriation of refugees, restructuring the economy and technical assistance, in addition to ECU 1,000m. in humanitarian aid provided since the beginning of the conflict in the former Yugoslavia.

In December 1993 six member states of the EU formally recognized the former Yugoslav republic of Macedonia (FYRM) as an independent state, but in February 1994 Greece imposed a commercial embargo against the FYRM, on the grounds that the use of the name and symbols (e.g. on the state flag) of 'Macedonia' was a threat to Greek national security. In March, however, ministers of foreign affairs of the EU decided that the embargo was in contravention of EU law, and in April the Commission commenced legal proceedings in the European Court of Justice against Greece. In September 1995 Greece and the FYRM began a process of normalizing relations, after the FYRM agreed to change the design of its state flag. In October Greece ended its economic blockade of the FYRM. A trade and co-operation agreement with the FYRM entered into force in January 1998. In April 2001 an SAA was signed with the FYRM. At the same time, an interim agreement was adopted, allowing for trade-related matters of the SAA to enter into effect in June, without the need for formal ratification by the national parliaments of the EU member states. (The SAA provided for the EU to open its markets to 95% of exports from the FYRM.) However, the Macedonian Government was informed that it would be required to deliver concessions to the ethnic Albanian minority population prior to entering into the agreement. In 2002 the remit of the European Agency for Reconstruction, which had been originally established to implement aid programmes in Kosovo, was extended to include the FYRM.

In March 1997 the EU sent two advisory delegations to Albania to help to restore order after violent unrest and political instability erupted in that country. A request by the Albanian Government for the deployment of EU peace-keeping troops was refused, but it was announced in early April that the EU was to provide humanitarian aid of some ECU 2m., to be used for emergency relief. In September 2002 the European Parliament voted in support of opening negotiations for an SAA with Albania, following satisfactory progress in that country, with regard to presidential elections and electoral reform. In January 2004 negotiations for an SAA were officially opened with Albania.

In 1998 the escalation of violence in Kosovo and Metohija (Federal Republic of Yugoslavia), between Serbs and the ethnic Albanian majority, prompted the imposition of sanctions by EU ministers of foreign affairs. In March ministers agreed to impose an arms embargo, to halt export credit guarantees to Yugoslavia and to restrict visas for Serbian officials. A ban on new investment in the region was imposed in June. In the same month military observers from the EU, Russia and the USA were deployed to Kosovo. During October the Yugoslav Government allowed a team of international experts to investigate atrocities in the region, under an EU mandate. Several EU countries participated in the NATO military offensive against Yugoslavia, which was initiated in March 1999 owing to the continued repression of ethnic Albanians in Kosovo by Serbian forces. Ministers approved a new series of punitive measures in April, including an embargo on the sale or supply of petroleum to the Yugoslav authorities and an extension of a travel ban on Serbian official and business executives. Humanitarian assistance was extended to provide relief for the substantial numbers of refugees who fled Kosovo amid the escalating violence, in particular to assist the Governments of Albania and the FYRM.

In September 1999 EU foreign ministers agreed to ease sanctions in force against Kosovo and Montenegro. In October the EU began to implement an 'Energy for Democracy' initiative, with the objective of supplying some €5m.-worth of heating oil to Serbian towns controlled by groups in opposition to the then Yugoslav President Slobodan Milošević. In February 2000 the EU suspended its ban on the Yugoslav national airline. However, the restrictions on visas for Serbian officials were reinforced. Kosovo received a total of €474.7m. under EU programmes in 2000 and the EU remained the largest financial contributor to the province in 2001.

In May 2000 the EU agreed an emergency aid package to support Montenegro against destabilization by Serbia. Following the election of a new administration in the former Republic of Yugoslavia (FRY) in late 2000 the EU immediately withdrew all remaining sanctions, with the exception of those directed against Milošević and his associates, and pledged financial support of €200m. The FRY was welcomed as a full participant in the stabilization and association process (see below). It was announced that a Consultative Task Force would be set up when conditions permitted. The EU insisted that the FRY must co-operate fully with the International Criminal Tribunal for the Former Yugoslavia (ICTY). Following the arrest of Milošević by the FRY authorities in April 2001, the first part of the EU's aid package for that year (amounting to €240m.) was released. During 2002 EU humanitarian aid to Serbia totalled €37.5m., to assist the large numbers of refugees and displaced persons.

At a Balkan summit convened in Zagreb, Croatia, in November 2000, the EU pledged €4,650m. for reconstruction aid to the region over the period 2000–06. The allocation of aid in 2002 for the Balkans was half that of 2001, owing to the return to relative normality in the region and the decline in humanitarian needs.

In June 1999 the EU, in conjunction with the Group of Seven industrialized nations and Russia (the G-8), regional governments and other organizations concerned with the stability of the region, launched the Stability Pact for South-Eastern Europe, which was placed under the auspices of the Organization for Security and Co-operation in Europe (OSCE). For its part, the EU proposed to offer customized SAAs (see above) to Albania, Bosnia, Croatia, the FYRM and, eventually, the FRY, provided that they fulfilled certain conditions. The FRY (renamed Serbia and Montenegro in February 2003) was excluded from the Pact until October 2000, following the staging there of democratic presidential elections. Since the establishment of the Pact, the heads of state and government of the South-East European countries have met regularly in the framework of the South East Europe Co-operation Process (SEECP). The FYRM Government signed an SAA with the EU in April 2001. A formal application for membership of the EU was submitted on 22 March 2004. Negotiations on the signature of an initial SAA with Albania, which officially commenced at the end of January 2003, were effectively suspended later in the year. In November EU officials declared that the Albanian Government had made inadequate progress in the implementation of the reforms, and urged immediate remedial measures. On 28 January 2004 the Bosnian Government issued a decree, providing for the reunification of Mostar (divided between Croat- and Bosnian-controlled municipalities since 1993) into a single administration, thereby fulfilling one of the major preconditions for signature of an SAA with the EU. In February 2003 Croatia submitted a formal application for membership of the EU.

On 31 March 2003 a NATO contingent in the FYRM was replaced by an EU-led mission, entitled Operation Concordia, comprising 350 military personnel; 13 EU member states and 14 non-EU nations participated in the force. It was replaced in December 2003 by a 200-member EU police mission, Operation Proxima, which, in addition to maintaining security and combating organized crime in the country, was to advise the Macedonian police forces. Proxima was extended for a further year in December 2004.

An EU-Western Balkans summit was held in June 2004, to continue the progress made at the Thessaloniki European Council of June 2003. A joint declaration was adopted confirming EU support for the future of the Balkan countries in the EU under the SAA process and the Thessaloniki agenda was published, which provided a framework for progress towards European integration for the Balkans. It was announced that in future meetings would take place between ministers responsible for foreign affairs, justice and home affairs as well as Heads of State. The first of these meetings took place in November and December.

OTHER EUROPEAN COUNTRIES

The members of the European Free Trade Association (EFTA) concluded bilateral free-trade agreements with the EEC and the ECSC during the 1970s. On 1 January 1984 the last tariff barriers were eliminated, thus establishing full free trade for industrial products between the Community and EFTA members. Some EFTA members subsequently applied for membership of the EC: Austria in 1989, Sweden in 1991, and Finland, Switzerland and Norway in 1992. Formal negotiations on the creation of a 'European Economic Area' (EEA), a single market for goods, services, capital and labour among EC and EFTA members, began in June 1990, and were concluded in October 1991. The agreement was signed in May 1992 (after a delay caused by a ruling of the Court of Justice of the EC that a proposed joint EC-EFTA court, for adjudication in disputes, was incompatible with the Treaty of Rome; EFTA members then agreed to concede jurisdiction to the Court of Justice on cases of competition involving both EC and EFTA members, and to establish a special joint committee for other disputes). In a referendum in December Swiss voters rejected ratification of the agreement, and the remaining 18 countries signed an adjustment protocol in March 1993, allowing the EEA to be established without Switzerland (which was to have observer status). The EEA entered into force on 1 January 1994. Despite the rejection of the EEA by the Swiss electorate, the Swiss Government declared its intention to continue to pursue its application for membership of the EU. Formal negotiations on the accession to the EU of Austria, Finland and Sweden began on 1 February, and those on Norway's membership started on 1 April. Negotiations were concluded with Austria, Finland and Sweden on 1 March 1994, and with Norway on 16 March, having been delayed by issues concerning the fisheries sector. Heads of government of the four countries signed treaties of accession to the EU in June, which were to come into effect from 1995, subject to approval by a national referendum in each country. Accession to the EU was endorsed by the electorates of Austria, Finland and Sweden in June, October and November 1994 respectively. Norway's accession, however, was rejected in a national referendum (by 52.4% of voters) conducted at the end of November. The success of the campaign opposing Norway's entry to the EU was attributed to several factors: in particular, fears were expressed by farmers that the influx of cheaper agricultural goods from the EU would lead to bankruptcies and unemployment in the agricultural sector, and by workers in the fishing industry that stocks of fish would be severely depleted if EU boats were granted increased access to Norwegian waters. There was also widespread concern that national sovereignty would be compromised by the transfer to the EU of certain executive responsibilities. Since the 1994 referendum Norway's relations with the EU have been based on full participation in the EEA as well as involvement (at non-signatory level) in the EU's Schengen Agreement. Austria, Finland and Sweden became members of the EU on 1 January 1995. Liechtenstein, which became a full member of EFTA in September 1991, joined the EEA on 1 May 1995. Negotiations conducted with Switzerland since 1992 on the formulation of a new bilateral economic arrangement proceeded slowly. The main obstacles to an agreement concerned Switzerland's work permit quotas for EU citizens, and the weight limit on trucks passing through its territory. In February 1994, in defiance of a government campaign, 52% of Swiss voters in a referendum approved a proposal to ban transit freight by road through Switzerland within 10 years (requiring its transportation by rail), in order to protect the Swiss Alps. In April 1996 the Swiss Government approved the Neue Eisenbahn-Alpen-Transversale (NEAT) project to construct two new Alpine tunnels in order to expedite international freight transport by rail; it was announced that this was to be financed mainly by levying a weight and distance toll on heavy goods vehicles crossing Swiss territory. Agreement was reached in December 1996 to phase out Swiss work permit quotas for citizens of EU member states within six years of an economic treaty being signed between the EU and Switzerland. In early December 1998 political agreement was reached with Switzerland to abolish the weight limit and instead impose road-haulage charges on trucks weighing 40 metric tons or more. Later in that month an interim EU-Swiss trade agreement was concluded. By February 2000 the Swiss Government had negotiated seven bilateral free-trade agreements with the EU. The accords included the gradual elimination of immigration controls between Switzerland and the EU over a 12-year period in order to allay popular anxiety regarding the possibility of EU workers depriving the Swiss of employment. While the Swiss Government had taken care to ensure that Swiss sovereignty was not affected by the trade agreements, popular resentment at the EU's imposition of sanctions against Austria during 1999 in protest at the presence of the far-right in the Austrian Government prompted Swiss opponents of the EU to submit a petition to the Swiss Government, thereby forcing a referendum on the trade agreements. At the referendum, which was held in May 2000, 67.2% of those who voted approved the agreements. Following the submission of a petition by pro-EU lobbyists, a referendum was held in March 2001 on whether to begin 'fast-track' accession negotiations with the EU; the ballot attracted an unusually high participation rate and the motion was rejected by an unexpectedly large majority, 77% of the vote. The Swiss Government, however, announced that the vote did not represent a rejection of the EU, but rather reflected the desire to move towards membership at a slower pace, and that its plans for eventual membership of the EU remained unchanged. In December 2002 talks aimed at combating fraud and tax evasion took place between EU and Swiss officials; the EU was keen to gain further concessions from Switzerland regarding improved access to information for EU tax authorities. The first EU-Switzerland summit meeting took place in Brussels in May 2004, following which nine new sectoral agreements (covering areas such as savings tax, fraud, the Schengen Agreement and the environment) were signed by the two parties.

Despite the fact that Iceland joined EFTA in 1970 and ratified the EEA in 1993 (although the extension of the single market legislation excluded agriculture and fisheries management, as in Norway and Liechtenstein), it did not thereafter apply for EU membership. Although opposition to Iceland's joining the EU persisted at government level in the first half of the 2000s, relations between the EU and Iceland had generally developed smoothly since 1993—notably Iceland negotiated participation in the Schengen Agreement

(although, as a signatory, it was not involved in decision-making within the agreement).

A trade agreement with Andorra entered into force on 1 January 1991, establishing a customs union for industrial products, and allowing duty-free access to the EC for certain Andorran agricultural products. In January 1998 negotiations on a co-operation agreement with Andorra (covering a wide range of issues) were finalized. Negotiations on a co-operation and customs union agreement between the EC and San Marino were concluded in December 1991; the agreement, however, did not enter into force until May 2002. In January 1999 San Marino adopted the euro, which became the sole currency in circulation at the start of 2002.

THE MIDDLE EAST AND THE MEDITERRANEAN

A scheme to negotiate a series of parallel trade and co-operation agreements encompassing almost all of the non-member states on the coast of the Mediterranean was formulated by the EC in 1972. Association agreements, intended to lead to customs union or the eventual full accession of the country concerned, had been signed with Greece (which eventually became a member of the Community in 1981) in 1962, Turkey in 1964 and Malta in 1971; a fourth agreement was signed with Cyprus in 1972. These established free access to the Community market for most industrial products and tariff reductions for most agricultural products. Annexed were financial protocols under which the Community was to provide concessional finance. During the 1970s a series of agreements covering trade and economic co-operation were concluded with the Arab Mediterranean countries and Israel, all establishing free access to EC markets for most industrial products. Access for agricultural products was facilitated, although some tariffs remained. In 1982 the Commission formulated an integrated plan for the development of its own Mediterranean regions and recommended the adoption of a new policy towards the non-Community countries of the Mediterranean. This was to include greater efforts towards diversifying agriculture, in order to avoid surpluses of items such as citrus fruits, olive oil and wine (which the Mediterranean countries all wished to export to the Community) and to reduce these countries' dependence on imported food. From 1 January 1993 the majority of agricultural exports from Mediterranean non-Community countries were granted exemption from customs duties.

In June 1995 the European Council endorsed a proposal by the Commission to reform and strengthen the Mediterranean policy of the EU. The initiative envisaged the eventual establishment of a Euro-Mediterranean Economic Area (EMEA), to be preceded by a gradual liberalization of trade within the region through bilateral and regional free-trade arrangements, and the adoption of financial and technical measures to support the implementation of structural reforms in Mediterranean partner countries. In November 1995 a conference of foreign affairs ministers of the EU member states, 11 Mediterranean non-member countries (excluding Libya) and the Palestinian authorities was convened in Barcelona, Spain. The conference endorsed the agreement on the EMEA and resolved to establish a permanent Euro-Mediterranean ministerial dialogue. It issued the 'Barcelona Declaration', endorsing commitments to uphold democratic principles and to pursue greater co-operation in the control of international crime, drugs-trafficking and illegal migration. The Declaration set the objective of establishing a Euro-Mediterranean free-trade area by 2010. The process of co-operation and dialogue under this agreement became known as the Euro-Mediterranean Partnership (or 'Barcelona Process'). In September 1998 the Commission proposed measures to extend the single market to the Mediterranean countries and sought to formulate common rules on customs and taxation, free movement of goods, public procurement, intellectual property, financial services, data protection and accounting.

In April 1997 the second Euro-Mediterranean Conference of ministers of foreign affairs was held, in Malta, to review implementation of the partnership strategy. Euro-Mediterranean foreign ministers convened for a third conference in April 1999, in Stuttgart, Germany. The Stuttgart conference agreed that Libya could eventually become a partner in the process, following the removal of UN sanctions on that country (which took place in September 2003) and acceptance of the full terms of the Barcelona Declaration. Libya subsequently attended some meetings as an observer. A fourth conference, convened in November 2000, in Marseilles, France, focused on the adoption of a new common strategy for the Mediterranean, aimed at strengthening the Barcelona Process. With economic, financial, social and cultural components, the new approach involved increased political dialogue with partnership countries as well as further efforts to improve security, democracy and human rights. The fifth Euro-Mediterranean Conference, in Valencia, Spain, in April 2002, reaffirmed the principles of the Barcelona Declaration and adopted an action plan covering different fields of the partnership, and in particular accelerating progress towards the creation of the Euro-Mediterranean free-trade area. The sixth Euro-Mediterranean Conference, held in December 2003, in

Naples, Italy, was the last such meeting before the enlargement of the EU in May 2004, and, as such, stressed the political importance of the partnership and emphasized the potential for closer integration between Europe and Mediterranean countries (as offered by the EU's 'Wider Europe' policy, which covered areas such as transport, energy and telecommunications). At the conference agreement was reached on the establishment of a Euro-Mediterranean Parliamentary Assembly, to allow partners to meet on a more formal basis; a reinforced lending facility by the European Investment Bank (EIB, see p. 229) was agreed, in order to stimulate growth in the private sector; and, finally, it was agreed that a Euro-Mediterranean Foundation for the Dialogue of Cultures would be set up, which would aim to increase dialogue and promote exchanges, co-operation and mobility between people at all levels (with particular focus on young people). The seventh Euro-Mediterranean Conference was due to be held in Luxembourg in late May 2005.

The EU's primary financial instrument for the implementation of the Euro-Mediterranean Partnership has been the MEDA programme, providing support for the reform of economic and social structures within partnership countries. The legal basis of the MEDA programme was the MEDA Regulation, adopted in July 1996. In 1999 the MEDA Regulation was reviewed and revised. The amended programme was named MEDA II. Covering the period 2000–06, MEDA II was granted a budget of €5,350m.

The first Euro-Mediterranean Energy Forum was convened in May 1997 and a second Energy Forum was held in May 1998; a number of other sectoral conferences have been organized (covering the following areas: transport, culture, health, the environment, water, the information society and industrial co-operation). The inaugural meeting of a Euro-Mediterranean Parliamentary Forum was convened in Brussels in October 1998. The second meeting of the Forum took place in Brussels in February 2001. (The meeting was, thereafter, to be held annually.) The first Euro-Mediterranean ministerial conference on trade was convened in May 2001, in Brussels; ministers agreed to hold regular meetings within this framework, and the second such meeting took place in Toledo, Spain, in March 2002.

Turkey, which had signed an association agreement with the EC in 1963 (although this was suspended between 1980 and 1986 following a military coup), applied for membership of the EU in April 1987 (see Enlargement).

Co-operation agreements concluded in the 1970s with the Maghreb countries (Algeria, Morocco and Tunisia), the Mashreq countries (Egypt, Jordan, Lebanon and Syria) and Israel covered free access to the Community market for industrial products, customs preferences for certain agricultural products, and financial aid in the form of grants and loans from the EIB. A co-operation agreement negotiated with the Republic of Yemen was non-preferential. In June 1992 the EC approved a proposal to conclude new bilateral agreements with the Maghreb countries, incorporating the following components: political dialogue; financial, economic, technical and cultural co-operation; and the eventual establishment of a free-trade area. A Euro-Mediterranean Association Agreement with Tunisia was signed in July 1995 and entered into force in March 1998. A similar agreement with Morocco entered into force in March 2000. (In July 1987 Morocco applied to join the Community, but its application was rejected on the grounds that it is not a European country.) The EU's relations with Algeria have been affected by political and civil instability in that country and by concerns regarding the Government's respect for human rights and democratic principles. In March 1997 negotiations were initiated between the European Commission and representatives of the Algerian Government on a Euro-Mediterranean Association Agreement that would incorporate political commitments relating to democracy and human rights; this was signed in December 2001. An Association Agreement with Jordan was signed in November 1997 and entered into force in May 2002. A Euro-Mediterranean Association Agreement with Egypt (which has been a major beneficiary of EU financial co-operation since the 1970s) was signed in June 2001 and was fully ratified in June 2004. In May 2001 Egypt, together with Jordan, Tunisia and Morocco, issued the Agadir Declaration, providing for the establishment of a free-trade area, as a cornerstone of the planned Euro-Mediterranean free-trade area. An interim Association Agreement with Lebanon was signed in June 2002, and it was expected to be fully ratified by mid-2005. While Association Agreements with all other Mediterranean partner countries had been signed by 2003, negotiations with Syria were still in process in early 2005.

In January 1989 the EC and Israel eliminated the last tariff barriers to full free trade for industrial products. A Euro-Mediterranean Association Agreement with Israel was signed in 1995, providing further trade concessions and establishing an institutional political dialogue between the two parties. The agreement entered into force in June 2000. Following the signing of the September 1993 Israeli-Palestine Liberation Organization (PLO) peace agreement, the EC committed substantial funds in humanitarian assistance for the Palestinians. A Euro-Mediterranean Interim Association Agreement on Trade and Co-operation was signed with the PLO in February 1997 and entered into force in July. The agreement confirmed existing trade concessions offered to the Palestinians since 1986 and provided for free trade to be introduced during an initial five-year period. In April 1998 the EU and the Palestinian (National) Authority (PA) signed a security co-operation agreement, which provided for regular meetings to promote joint efforts on security issues, in particular in combating terrorism. In April 1999 the European Parliament demanded an investigation into the handling of Commission funds to Palestinian-controlled areas of the West Bank and Gaza. At that time the EU was reported to be the largest donor to the PA. The escalation of violence between Israel and the Palestinians from September 2000 resulted in a significant deterioration in EU-Israel relations. During 2002 the EU criticized Israel for its policy of restricting the movements of Yasser Arafat, the Palestinian President, and in May of that year Israel alleged that EU funding to the PA was being diverted for terrorist activities, although the EU insisted that its aid was closely monitored by the IMF. The EU formed part of the Quartet (alongside the UN, the USA and Russia), which was established in July 2002 to monitor and aid the implementation of Palestinian civil reforms, and to guide the international donor community in its support of the Palestinian reform agenda. In September 2002 the Quartet put forward a three-stage peace plan (the so-called 'Roadmap', which was published in April 2003), including provision for free elections for the Palestinian people, the creation of a Palestinian state and negotiations between Israel and Palestine, aiming at a final settlement by 2005. In February 2005 the European Commission announced that during that year it intended to allocate funds of around €250m. to supporting further steps towards the creation of a viable Palestinian state. The Commission stressed that it considered the following to be the priority areas for Palestinian reform: a well-functioning judiciary, a democratic and independent election process, and public financial transparency.

Following successful negotiations during 1997, a new, expanded co-operation agreement with Yemen, incorporating a political element (i.e. commitments to democratic principles and respect for human rights), and providing for 'most favoured nation' treatment, entered into force in July 1998. In 2003 bilateral relations between the EU and Yemen were strengthened through the decision to launch a political dialogue. The establishment of the political dialogue was announced at the Joint Co-operation Committee in October 2003. A first meeting took place in July 2004 and focused on democracy, human rights, democratization and co-operation in the fight against terrorism.

Talks were held with Iran in April 1992 on the establishment of a co-operation accord. In December the Council of Ministers recommended that a 'critical dialogue' be undertaken with Iran, owing to the country's significance to regional security. In April 1997 the 'critical dialogue' was suspended and ambassadors were recalled from Iran, following a German court ruling that found the Iranian authorities responsible for ordering the murder of four Kurdish dissidents in Berlin in 1992. Later that month ministers of foreign affairs resolved to restore diplomatic relations with Iran, in order to protect the strong trading partnership. In November 2000 an EU-Iran Working Group on Trade and Investment met for the first time to discuss the possibility of increasing and diversifying trade and investment. By November 2003 four such meetings had taken place. During 2002 attempts were made to improve relations with Iran, as negotiations began in preparation for a Trade and Co-operation Agreement. An eventual trade deal was to be linked to progress in political issues, including human rights, weapons proliferation and counter-terrorism. In mid-2003 the EU (in line with US policy) warned Iran to accept stringent new nuclear inspections, and threatened the country with economic repercussions (including the abandonment of the proposed trade agreement) unless it restored international trust in its nuclear programme. In January 2005 the EU resumed trade talks with Iran after the Iranian authorities agreed to suspend uranium enrichment.

A co-operation agreement between the EC and the countries of the Gulf Co-operation Council (GCC), which entered into force in January 1990, provided for co-operation in industry, energy, technology and other fields. Negotiations on a full free-trade pact began in October 1990, but it was expected that any agreement would involve transition periods of some 12 years for the reduction of European tariffs on 'sensitive products' (i.e. petrochemicals). In November 1999 the GCC Supreme Council agreed to establish a customs union (a precondition of the proposed EU-GCC free-trade agreement) by March 2005. In December 2001 the GCC countries decided to advance the introduction of the customs union by two years; the union was consequently established in January 2003. Free-trade negotiations between the EU and the GCC countries continued throughout 2002–05.

Contacts with the Arab world in general take place within the framework of the 'Euro-Arab Dialogue', established in 1973 to provide a forum for discussion of economic issues through working groups on specific topics. Following a decision in 1989 to reactivate the Dialogue, meetings were suspended in 1990 as a result of Iraq's invasion of Kuwait. In April 1992 senior EC and Arab officials agreed to resume the process.

The increased tension in the Middle East in the run-up to the US-led military action in Iraq in March 2003 placed considerable strain on relations between member states of the EU, and exposed the lack of a common EU policy on Iraq. A summit of EU foreign ministers in Denmark in August 2002 emphasized the EU's support for the UN weapons inspectors in Iraq, and in January 2003 the EU warned the USA that only the UN Security Council could determine whether military action was justified. In the same month (which saw the beginning of the six-month Greek presidency of the EU) an EU diplomatic mission led by the Greek foreign minister visited seven Arab states in an effort to avert war. Divisions remained between member states, with the United Kingdom, Spain, Italy, Portugal and Denmark supporting the US policy, while France and Germany led the other members in opposing the impending conflict, or, at the least, in insisting on a second UN resolution. In February 2003 the European Council held an extraordinary meeting to discuss the crisis in Iraq, and issued a statement reconfirming its commitment to the UN. In April, however, the EU leaders reluctantly accepted a dominant role for the USA and the United Kingdom in post-war Iraq, and Denmark, Spain and the Netherlands announced plans to send peace-keeping troops to Iraq. At the Madrid Donors' Conference for Iraq in October the EU and its accession states pledged more than €1,250m. (mainly in grants) for Iraq's reconstruction. Of this total, €200m. was pledged for 2003–04 (in addition to the €100m. in humanitarian assistance that the EU had already set aside for Iraq in 2003). In March 2004 the Commission adopted a programme setting three priorities for reconstruction assistance to Iraq in that year: restoring the delivery of key public services; boosting employment and reducing poverty; and strengthening governance, civil society and human rights. The EU welcomed the handover of power by the Coalition Provisional Authority to the Iraqi Interim Government in June 2004 and supported the holding of legislative elections in Iraq in January 2005. The EU planned to provide further substantial amounts of aid towards Iraq's reconstruction and recovery during 2005.

LATIN AMERICA

A non-preferential trade agreement was signed with Uruguay in 1974, and economic and commercial co-operation agreements with Mexico in 1975 and Brazil in 1980. A five-year co-operation agreement with the members of the Central American Common Market and with Panama entered into force in 1987, as did a similar agreement with the member countries (see below) of the Andean Group (now the Andean Community, see p. 148). Co-operation agreements were signed with Argentina and Chile in 1990, and in that year tariff preferences were approved for Bolivia, Colombia, Ecuador and Peru, in support of those countries' efforts to combat drugs-trafficking. In May 1992 an interinstitutional co-operation agreement was signed with the Southern Common Market (Mercosur); in the following month the EC and the member states of the Andean Group (Bolivia, Colombia, Ecuador, Peru and Venezuela) initialled a new co-operation agreement, which was to broaden the scope of economic and development co-operation and enhance trade relations, and a new co-operation agreement was signed with Brazil. In July 1993 the EC introduced a tariff regime to limit the import of bananas from Latin America, in order to protect the banana-producing countries of the ACP group, then linked to the EC by the Lomé Convention.

During 1996–2000 the EU forged closer links with Latin America, by means of strengthened political ties, an increase in economic integration and free trade, and co-operation in other areas. In April 1997 the EU extended further trade benefits to the countries of the Andean Community. In July the EU and Mexico concluded an Economic Partnership, Political Co-operation and Co-operation Agreement and an interim agreement on trade. The accords were signed in December. The main part of the interim agreement entered into effect in July 2000 and the co-operation agreement entered into force in October. In November 1999 the EU and Mexico concluded a free-trade agreement which, on implementation, was to lead to the removal of all tariffs on bilateral trade in industrial products by 2007.

In June 1996 the EU and Chile signed a framework agreement on political and economic co-operation, which provided for a process of bilateral trade liberalization, as well as co-operation in other industrial and financial areas. An EU-Chile Joint Council was established. In November 1999 the EU and Chile commenced practical negotiations on developing closer political and economic co-operation, within the framework of a proposed association agreement. In November 2002 the EU and Chile signed an association and free-trade agreement in Brussels; it provided for the liberalization of trade within seven years for industrial products and 10 years for agricultural products. The first meeting of the Association Council

set up by the agreement took place in Athens, Greece, in March 2003.

In late December 1994 the EU and Mercosur signed a joint declaration that aimed to promote trade liberalization and greater political co-operation. In September 1995, at a meeting in Montevideo, Uruguay, a framework agreement on the establishment of a free-trade regime between the two organizations was initialled. The agreement was formally signed in December. In July 1998 the Commission voted to commence negotiations towards an inter-regional association agreement with Mercosur and Chile, which would strengthen existing co-operation agreements. Negotiations were initiated in April 2000. The association agreement was expected to be finalized before the end of 2004, but by April 2005 it had still not been concluded.

The first ministerial conference between the EC and the then 11 Latin American states of the Rio Group took place in April 1991; thereafter high-level joint ministerial meetings have been held on a regular basis. The first summit meeting of all EU and Latin American heads of state or government was held in Rio de Janeiro, Brazil, in June 1999, when a strategic partnership was launched. A second EU-Latin America/Caribbean (EU-LAC) summit took place in Madrid, Spain, in May 2002, and covered co-operation in political, economic, social and cultural fields. A political dialogue and co-operation agreement with the Andean Community and its member states was signed in December 2003. At the third EU-LAC summit meeting held in Guadalajara, Mexico, in May 2004 it was agreed by the two parties that an association agreement, which included a free-trade area, was a common objective.

During 2002 the Argentine economy was severely affected by recession, and the EU responded by temporarily increasing import quotas for Argentine meat in response to a request from the Argentine Government. In November 2002 the EU signed a memorandum of agreement on co-operation with Brazil for the period 2001–06.

In 2004 Cuba remained the only Latin American country that did not have a formal economic co-operation agreement with the EU. In June 1995 a Commission communication advocated greater economic co-operation with Cuba. This policy was strongly supported by a resolution of the European Parliament in January 1996, but was criticized by the US Government, which continued to maintain an economic embargo against Cuba. Later that year the EU agreed to make the extent of economic co-operation with Cuba (which was a one-party state) contingent on progress towards democracy. In 2000 Cuba withdrew its application to join the successor to the Lomé Convention, the Cotonou Agreement, following criticism by some European governments of its human rights record. However, improvements in bilateral relations between Cuba and the EU led to the opening of an EU legation office in Havana in March 2003 and support for Cuba's renewed application to join the Cotonou Agreement. However, human rights abuses perpetrated by the Cuban regime in April (the imprisonment of a large number of dissidents) led to the downgrading of diplomatic relations with Cuba by the EU, the instigation of an EU policy of inviting dissidents to embassy receptions in Havana (the so-called 'cocktail wars') and the indefinite postponement of Cuba's application to join the Cotonou Agreement. In May Cuba withdrew its application for membership and in July the Cuban President announced that the Government would not accept aid from the EU and would terminate all political contact with the organization. In December 2004 the EU proposed a compromise—namely not to invite any Cubans, whether government ministers or dissidents, to future embassy receptions, but reiterated its demand that Cuba unconditionally release all political prisoners who remained in detention (several dissidents had already been released). In response to this amelioration in relations, Cuba announced in early January 2005 that it was restoring diplomatic ties with all EU states. In February the EU temporarily suspended the diplomatic sanctions imposed on Cuba in mid-2003 and announced its intention to resume a constructive dialogue with the Cuban authorities.

In 2003 the EU pledged €637m. to finance co-operation with Latin America, including €249m. for financial and technical co-operation and €13m. for rehabilitation and construction measures in developing countries.

ASIA AND AUSTRALASIA

Relations between the EU and the Association of South-East Asian Nations (ASEAN) are based on the Co-operation Agreement of 1980. Under this agreement, joint committee meetings are held approximately every 18 months. There are also regular ministerial meetings and post-ministerial conferences. In addition, the EU is a member of the ASEAN Regional Forum (ARF), a security grouping designed to promote peace and stability, established in 1994. In December of that year the European Council endorsed a new strategy for Asia, which recognized the region's increasing economic and political importance and pledged to strengthen bilateral and regional dialogue. The strategy aimed to enhance the development of trade and investment, promote peace and security, and assist the

INTERNATIONAL ORGANIZATIONS

European Union

less-developed countries in Asia. In May 1995 ASEAN and EU senior officials endorsed an initiative to convene an Asia-Europe Meeting of heads of government (ASEM). The first Asia-Europe meeting (ASEM) was held in March 1996 in Bangkok, Thailand. It was agreed to launch an Asia-Europe Partnership for Greater Growth, in order to expand trade, investment and technology transfer. An Asia-Business Forum was to be formed, as well as an Asia-Europe Foundation in Singapore to promote educational and cultural exchanges. The second ASEM summit, convened in the United Kingdom in April 1998, was dominated by economic and financial concerns, and both sides' declared intention to prevent a return to protectionist trading policies. The meeting established an ASEM Trust Fund, under the auspices of the World Bank, to alleviate the social impact of the financial crisis. Other initiatives adopted by ASEM were an Asia-Europe Co-operation Framework to co-ordinate political, economic and financial co-operation, a Trade Facilitation Action Plan, and an Investment Promotion Action Plan, which incorporated a new Investment Experts Group. The meeting resolved to promote efforts to strengthen relations in all areas, and to establish a series of working bodies to promote specific areas of co-operation. ASEM heads of government convened for the third time in Seoul, Republic of Korea, in October 2000. ASEM III welcomed the ongoing *rapprochement* between the two Korean nations, declared a commitment to the promotion of human rights, and endorsed several initiatives related to globalization and information technology. The meeting established a new Asia-Europe Co-operation Framework (AECF), identifying ASEM's principles and priorities for the next 10 years. ASEM IV took place in Copenhagen, Denmark, in September 2002. Statements were subsequently adopted on co-operation in the fight against international terrorism, and on the situation in the Korean peninsula. Economic issues were also discussed, and in particular the need to continue the WTO 'Doha' negotiating round. At the same time the first EU-Korea summit was held; discussion centred on the reduction in customs barriers and aid to shipbuilding. ASEM V took place in Hanoi, Viet Nam, in October 2004; at the meeting international developments and global challenges were reviewed, and regional developments in Europe and Asia, including the recent EU enlargement and the human rights situation in Myanmar, were addressed.

In September 2001 the EU adopted a new Communication on relations with Asia for the coming decade. Representing an updating of the 1994 strategy, this focused on strengthened partnership, particularly in the areas of politics, security, trade and investment. It aimed to reduce poverty and to promote democracy, good governance and the rule of law throughout the region. Partnerships and alliances on global issues were to be forged. A fundamental aim was to strengthen the EU's presence in Asia, promoting mutual awareness and knowledge on both sides.

Bilateral non-preferential co-operation agreements were signed with Bangladesh, India, Pakistan and Sri Lanka between 1973 and 1976. A further agreement with India, extended to include co-operation in trade, industry, energy, science and finance, came into force in December 1981. A third agreement, which entered into effect in August 1994, included commitments to develop co-operation between the two sides and improve market access, as well as for the observance of human rights and democratic principles. The first EU-India summit meeting was held in Lisbon, Portugal, in June 2000. In November 2003 the EU called on India to reciprocate the EU's open market stance towards India by lowering its import tariffs on European products. In November 2004 the EU and India signed a 'strategic partnership' agreement, which was expected significantly to boost their relationship; the agreement—described as a reflection of 'India's growing stature and influence'—meant that India became a special EU partner alongside the USA, Canada, the Pepole's Republic of China and Russia. A new and extended agreement with Pakistan on commercial and economic co-operation entered into force in May 1986; in May 1992 an agreement was signed on measures to stimulate private investment in Pakistan. A new accord with Sri Lanka, designed to promote co-operation in areas such as trade, investment and protection of the environment, entered into force in April 1995. A similar agreement with Nepal entered into force in June 1996. In July of that year EU Governments authorized the European Commission to conclude similar agreements with Bangladesh and Pakistan. A draft co-operation agreement was initialled with Pakistan in April 1998. However, following the October 1999 military coup in Pakistan, the agreement was suspended. Political dialogue with Pakistan recommenced on an *ad hoc* basis in November 2000, and the co-operation agreement was signed in Islamabad in November 2001; a joint statement was issued on the occasion in which Pakistan reiterated its firm commitment to return to democratic government. The new co-operation accord with Bangladesh (which replaced the 1976 commercial co-operation agreement) was signed in May 2000 and came into force in March 2001.

A trade agreement was signed with the People's Republic of China (PRC) in 1978, and renewed in May 1985. In June 1989, following the violent repression of the Chinese pro-democracy movement by the PRC Government, the EC imposed economic sanctions and an

embargo on arms sales on that country. In October 1990 it was decided that relations with the PRC should be 'progressively normalized'. The EU has supported the PRC's increased involvement in the international community and, in particular, supported its application for membership of the WTO. The first EU-PRC meeting of heads of government was convened in April 1998. In November the President of the Commission made an official visit to the PRC and urged that country to remove trade restrictions imposed on European products. In the same month the EU and Hong Kong signed a co-operation agreement to combat drugs-trafficking and copyright piracy. A bilateral trade agreement between the EU and the PRC was concluded in May 2000, removing a major barrier to the PRC's accession to the WTO; this was approved in November 2001. A third EU-PRC summit meeting was held in Beijing in October 2000. At the fourth summit, convened in September 2001, the two sides agreed to strengthen and widen political dialogue and to continue discussions on human rights issues. In March 2002 the European Commission approved a strategy document setting out a framework for co-operation between the EU and the PRC over the period 2002–06, and in September the fifth EU-PRC summit discussed trade relations and future co-operation on illegal immigrants and tourism. At the sixth EU-PRC summit, held in Beijing in October 2003, two agreements were signed establishing a new dialogue on industrial policy and confirming the PRC's participation in the 'Galileo' project (the EU's system of radiosatellite navigation); in addition, a memorandum of understanding was initialled, paving the way for Chinese tourist groups to travel to the EU more easily. At the seventh EU-PRC summit, which took place in The Hague, Netherlands, in December 2004, the two sides further strengthened their maturing strategic partnership. The EU raised the topics of human rights and the fight against illegal migration, and discussions also focused on economic issues, including the Doha Development Round, textiles and other trade concerns. In addition a number of international issues, including the Democratic People's Republic of Korea (DPRK) and Myanmar, featured in the talks. A joint declaration was signed on non-proliferation and arms control and agreements were also concluded on customs co-operation, and science and technology. Meanwhile, in March 2004 there were reports that the EU was considering lifting the arms embargo against the PRC. This proposal was strongly supported by France; a number of other member states (as well as the USA) were opposed to it on the grounds of the PRC's continuing poor human rights record. In April 2005 the EU shifted its position somewhat when senior officials stated that the PRC would have to make a significant gesture with regard to human rights in order that the arms embargo be lifted.

A framework agreement on trade and co-operation between the EU and the Republic of Korea was signed in 1996 and entered into force in April 2001. In October 1997 the EU and the Republic of Korea signed an agreement regarding a reciprocal opening of markets for telecommunications equipment, following a protracted dispute, which had led the EU to lodge a complaint with the WTO. In September 1997, however, the Commission submitted a further complaint to the WTO, accusing the Republic of Korea of tax discrimination against European spirits exporters. In the same month the EU joined the Korean Peninsula Energy Development Organization, an initiative founded in 1995 to increase nuclear safety and reduce the risk of nuclear proliferation from the energy programme of the DPRK. In September 1999, for the first time ever, ministerial-level discussions took place between the EU and the DPRK at the UN General Assembly. In May 2001 the EU announced that it was to establish diplomatic relations with the DPRK to facilitate the Union's efforts in support of reconciliation in the Korean Peninsula and, in particular, in support of economic reform and the easing of the acute food and health problems in the DPRK. In October 2002 the EU expressed its deep concern that the DPRK had admitted conducting a clandestine nuclear weapons programme, in serious breach of the country's international non-proliferation commitments. The following month the EU stated that failure to resolve the nuclear issue would jeopardize the future development of EU-DPRK relations.

In June 1992 the EC signed trade and co-operation agreements with Mongolia and Macao, with respect for democracy and human rights forming the basis of envisaged co-operation. The eighth EU-Mongolia joint committee met in Brussels in March 2005. A co-operation accord was formally signed with Viet Nam in July 1995, under which the EU agreed to increase quotas for Vietnamese textile products, to support the country's efforts to join the WTO and to provide aid for environmental and public management projects. The agreement entered into force in June 1996. A permanent EU mission to Viet Nam was established in February 1996. In October the EU imposed strict limits on entry visas for Myanmar officials, because of Myanmar's refusal to allow the Commission to send a mission to investigate allegations of forced labour. In March 1997 EU ministers of foreign affairs agreed to revoke Myanmar's special trade privileges under the Generalized System of Preferences (GSP). In November a meeting of EU and ASEAN officials was postponed, owing to Myanmar's insistence (then as a full member of the ASEAN

www.europaworld.com

259

grouping) that it should attend with full observer status. After several further delays, the meeting was finally convened, with Myanmar as a 'silent' observer, in late May 1999. The EU has successively extended its ban on arms exports to Myanmar and its prohibition on the issuing of visas, and in October 2002 the European Council confirmed its so-called 'Common Position' that progress on human rights and democratization in Myanmar was insufficient. In April 2003 a new Common Position was adopted by the EU, which consolidated and extended the scope of existing sanctions against Myanmar and strengthened the arms embargo; EU sanctions were further extended in April 2004 in view of the military regime's failure to make any significant progress in normalizing the administration of the country and addressing any of the EU's concerns as regards human rights. Non-preferential co-operation agreements were signed with Laos and Cambodia in April 1997. The agreement with Laos (which emphasized development assistance and economic co-operation) entered into force on 1 December; the agreement with Cambodia was postponed owing to adverse political developments in that country. The EU concluded a textile agreement with Laos, which provisionally entered into force in December 1998; as a result of the agreement exports of textiles to the EU from Laos increased significantly. In 1998 the EU provided financial assistance to support preparations for a general election in Cambodia, and dispatched observers to monitor the election, which was held in July. The EU co-operation agreement with Cambodia entered into force in November 1999. EU-Cambodia relations were further enhanced with the opening of an EU delegation in Phnom-Penh in early 2002. In September 1999 the EU briefly imposed an arms embargo against Indonesia, which was at that time refusing to permit the deployment of an international peace-keeping force in East Timor (now Timor-Leste). The main objective of the 2002–06 EU Country Strategy Paper for aid co-operation with Indonesia was to encourage the consolidation of democracy and good governance through EU support to Indonesia's sustainable economic, social and environmental development. In April 2005 the EU extended preferential trade conditions to Indonesia, which meant that the country would benefit from lower customs duty in certain sectors.

Textiles exports by Asian countries have caused concern in the EU, owing to the depressed state of its textiles industry. In 1982 bilateral negotiations were held under the Multi-fibre Arrangement (MFA, see WTO) with Asian producers, notably Hong Kong, the Republic of Korea and Macao. Agreements were eventually reached involving reductions in clothing quotas and 'anti-surge' clauses to prevent flooding of European markets. In 1986 new bilateral negotiations were held and agreements were reached with the principal Asian textile exporters, for the period 1987–91 (later extended to December 1993, when the 'Uruguay Round' of GATT negotiations was finally concluded): in most cases a slight increase in quotas was permitted. Under the conclusions of the Uruguay Round, the MFA was to be progressively eliminated over a 10-year period. In January 1995 bilateral textiles agreements, signed by the EU with India, Pakistan and the PRC, specified certain trade liberalization measures to be undertaken, including an increase of the PRC's silk export quota and a removal of trade barriers on small-business and hand-loom textile products from India, while including commitments from the Asian countries for greater efforts to combat textile and design fraud. In March 1998 the Commission signed an agreement with Nepal on trade in textile products in order to secure an orderly and equitable development of trade in these products. In March 2001 the EU and Sri Lanka signed an agreement to open their mutual textiles markets. The agreement lifted all textiles quotas with Sri Lanka in exchange for tariff reductions by Sri Lanka and the binding of all its tariffs for the textiles and clothing sector at the WTO.

Numerous discussions have been held since 1981 on the Community's increasing trade deficit with Japan, and on the failure of the Japanese market to accept more European exports. In July 1991 the heads of government of Japan and of the EC signed a joint declaration on closer co-operation in both economic and political matters. In the same month an agreement was reached on limiting exports of Japanese cars to the EC until the end of 1999. The agreement did not include vehicles produced in Europe by Japanese companies. The European office of the EU-Japan Industrial Co-operation Centre was opened in Brussels in June 1996; the Centre, which was established in 1987 as a joint venture between the Japanese Government and the European Commission, sought to boost industrial co-operation between the EU and Japan. In October 1996 the WTO upheld a long-standing complaint brought by the EU that Japanese taxes on alcoholic spirits discriminated against certain European products. In January 1998 an EU-Japan summit meeting was held, followed by a meeting at ministerial level in October. Subsequent summits (the 13th was held in Tokyo, Japan, in June 2004) have aimed to strengthen dialogue.

The EU pledged assistance for the reconstruction of Afghanistan following the removal of the Taliban regime in late 2001, and in 2002 announced development aid of €1,000m. for the period 2002–06, in addition to humanitarian aid. In March 2003 the European Commission hosted, along with the World Bank, the Afghanistan High Level Strategic Forum. The Government of Afghanistan convened the meeting to discuss with its key partners, donors and multilateral organizations the progress and future vision for state-building in Afghanistan, as well as the long-term funding requirements for reconstruction. In 2004 the EU provided substantial support for the election process in Afghanistan and dispatched a Democracy and Election Support Mission in August to assess key aspects of the presidential election, which was held in October, and to make recommendations for the holding of legislative elections in the first half of 2005.

In 2000 the EU contributed €19m. to a Trust Fund established by the World Bank to finance reconstruction activities in East Timor. In December the EU hosted the third multilateral conference of donors to the territory. During 2002 the EU provided €650,000 in development aid for East Timor. The EU's long-term assistance strategy for Timor-Leste was focused on two sectors: basic health services provision and rural development.

Regular consultations are held with Australia at ministerial level. In January 1996 the Commission proposed a framework agreement to formalize the EU's trade and political relationship with that country. However, in September negotiations were suspended, following the Australian Government's objections to the human rights clause contained in all EU international agreements. In June 1997 a joint declaration was signed, committing both sides to greater political, cultural and economic co-operation. Despite intensive negotiations between the EU and the New Zealand Government in 1996, no conclusion was reached regarding import duties. In March 1997 New Zealand took the case to the WTO, which later ruled against the EU. A joint declaration detailing areas of co-operation and establishing a consultative framework to facilitate the development of these was signed in May 1999. Mutual recognition agreements were also signed with Australia and New Zealand in 1999, with the aim of facilitating bilateral trade in industrial products.

THE USA AND CANADA

A framework agreement for commercial and economic co-operation between the Community and Canada was signed in Ottawa in 1976. It was superseded in 1990 by a Declaration on EC-Canada Relations. In 1995 relations with Canada were strained as a result of a dispute regarding fishing rights in the north-west Atlantic Ocean. An agreement on a new division of quotas between EU and Canadian fishermen was concluded in April. In February 1996 the Commission proposed closer ties with Canada, and an action plan including early warning to avoid trade disputes, elimination of trade barriers, and promotion of business contacts. An action plan and joint political declaration were signed in December. Two EU-Canada summits took place in 2002; numerous issues were discussed, including improved co-operation to combat terrorism, heightened co-operation in research, science and technology, the strengthening of trade relations, and collaboration on environmental issues.

At the Ottawa summit in December 2002 the Canadian Government and the EU decided to initiate a review of bilateral relations and to develop a Trade and Investment Enhancement Agreement (TIEA). Negotiations on the TIEA, which would aim to reduce the impediments to trade and investment flows, were initiated at the Ottawa summit meeting held in March 2004 and were expected to last for three years. An important aspect of the proposed accord was to promote the mutual recognition of professional qualifications and quality standards, in order to facilitate investment. Also at the summit Canada and the EU adopted a Partnership Agenda to promote political and economic co-operation. In March an outbreak of avian influenza in Canada prompted a temporary EU ban on imports of eggs and poultry from Canada.

A number of specific agreements have been concluded between the Community and the USA: a co-operation agreement on the peaceful use of atomic energy entered into force in 1959, and agreements on environmental matters and on fisheries came into force in 1974 and 1984 respectively. Additional agreements provide for co-operation in other fields of scientific research and development, while bilateral contacts take place in many areas not covered by a formal agreement.

The USA has frequently criticized the Common Agricultural Policy, which it sees as creating unfair competition for US exports by its system of export refunds and preferential agreements. In 1998 the WTO upheld a US complaint about the EU ban on imports of hormone-treated beef, which had led to a retaliatory US ban on meat imports from the EU. Following the EU's refusal to repeal the ban by the deadline of May 1999, the WTO authorized the imposition by the USA and Canada of retaliatory sanctions of US $116.8m. and C $11m. respectively for each year that the ban was in place. The USA rejected claims by the EU in October 2003 that new scientific studies and EU legislation meant that the ban now complied with WTO regulations and the sanctions should be lifted. In June 2003 at a US-EU summit in Washington, DC, it was acknowledged that agriculture remained a major obstacle to agreement in the Doha round of the WTO. In May the USA had further strained relations by announcing that it was filing a WTO complaint to end the EU's *de facto* moratorium on genetically modified food, which began in 1998 and was based on European safety concerns, on the grounds that it was an unfair trade barrier. Another issue of contention between the USA and the EU was the EU's banana import regime (see EU-ACP Partnership, see p. 263).

A 'Transatlantic Declaration' on EC-US relations was agreed in November 1990: the two parties agreed to consult each other on important matters of common interest, and to increase formal contacts. A new Trans-Atlantic Agenda for EU-US relations was signed by the US President and the Presidents of the European Commission and European Council at a meeting in Madrid, Spain, in December 1995. In October 1996 EU ministers of foreign affairs agreed to pursue in the WTO a complaint regarding the effects on European businesses of the USA's trade embargo against Cuba, formulated in the Helms-Burton Act. In April 1997 the EU and the USA approved a temporary resolution of the Helms-Burton dispute, whereby the US Administration was to limit the application of sanctions in return for a formal suspension of the WTO case. In mid-1996 the US Congress had adopted legislation imposing an additional trade embargo (threatening sanctions against any foreign company investing more than US $40m. in energy projects in a number of prescribed states, including Iran and Libya), the presence of which further complicated the EU-US debate in September 1997, when a French petroleum company, Total, provoked US anger, owing to its proposed investment in an Iranian natural gas project. In May 1998 an EU-USA summit meeting reached agreement on a 'Trans-Atlantic Economic Partnership' (TEP), to remove technical trade barriers, eliminate industrial tariffs, establish a free-trade area in services, and further liberalize measures relating to government procurement, intellectual property and investment. The agricultural and audiovisual sectors were to be excluded from the agreement. Initial objections from France were overcome when the EU and the USA reached a resolution to the dispute on sanctions legislation. The USA agreed to exempt European companies from the trade embargo on Iran and Libya, and to seek congressional approval for an indefinite waiver for the Helms-Burton Act, thereby removing the threat of sanctions from Total. The EU had allowed the WTO case to lapse in April, but it warned that a new WTO panel would be established if the USA took action against European companies trading with Cuba. In return, the EU agreed to increase co-operation in combating terrorism and the proliferation of weapons of mass destruction and to discourage investment in expropriated property. Following approval by the Council in November, it was agreed that implementation of the TEP would begin in advance of an EU-USA summit meeting in December.

In July 1997 the EU became involved in intensive negotiations with the US aircraft company Boeing over fears that its planned merger with McDonnell Douglas would harm European interests. In late July the EU approved the merger, after Boeing accepted concessions including an agreement to dispense with exclusivity clauses for 20-year supply contracts and to maintain McDonnell Douglas as a separate company for a period of 10 years. In June the EU and the USA agreed to introduce a mutual recognition agreement, which was to enable goods (including medicines, pharmaceutical products, telecommunications equipment and electrical apparatus) undergoing tests in Europe to be marketed in the USA or Canada without the need for further testing. In August 2004 a fresh trade dispute erupted between the USA and the EU over the subsidies that the two sides paid to their respective aircraft industries. The USA claimed that the financial support European governments provided to aircraft manufacturer Airbus was in breach of world trade rules, while the EU stated that the same was true of the US Administration's subsidies for Boeing. The USA made a formal complaint to the WTO over the EU's support for Airbus in October; the EU immediately responded in kind by filing a complaint regarding the US financial assistance to Boeing.

In July 2002 the Commission submitted a complaint to the WTO regarding tax exemptions granted to US companies exporting goods via subsidiaries established in tax-free countries (foreign sales corporations). The WTO found in favour of the Commission and authorized the EU to levy punitive tariffs of up to US $4,000m. in compensation for the US tax exemptions, which benefited large companies, including Boeing and Microsoft, and which the WTO ruled were discriminatory and should be abolished. In February 2003 the EU released a final list of about 50,000 goods that would be subjected to tariffs of 100% but postponed implementation of the sanctions, pending the progress of a bill to amend the tax law in the US Congress. In March 2004, however, the legislation remained in place and the EU began the phased imposition of duties (initially at 5% but increasing by 1% every month) on a range of US exports, including jewellery, toys, honey, refrigerators, paper, nuclear reactors and roller skates. This represented the first time that the EU had taken retaliatory action against the USA in a trade dispute. Consideration was also being given to imposing further trade sanctions against the USA for its failure to revoke a clause in its anti-dumping legislation, known as the Byrd Amendment. The Byrd Amendment, which was

promulgated in October 2000, made provision for funds accruing from the payment of anti-dumping and anti-subsidy duties to be paid to the US companies that filed the complaint. The WTO ruled the Amendment illegal in 2002, but the USA failed to repeal the legislation by the deadline of December 2003. In March 2005 the EU proposed sanctions on a range of US goods as punishment for the failure of the USA to repeal the Amendment; paper, farm goods, textiles and machinery were to face an extra 15% duty from 1 May. In September 2004 the USA filed a complaint with the WTO against the EU, charging that the lack of uniform customs rules and procedures among the 25 member states was a barrier to US exports.

In December 2003 the US President, George W. Bush, announced his decision to repeal US tariffs of up to 30% on imports of steel, which had been imposed in March 2002. The decision followed a ruling by the WTO in January that the imposition of tariffs by the USA was illegal. The EU had threatened the imposition of retaliatory tariffs worth US $2,200m. if the USA did not comply with the WTO ruling by cancelling the duties before the permitted deadline of January 2004.

In political matters, some member states also criticized the USA's objections to the establishment of the International Criminal Court (which eventually came into effect in The Hague in 2003), while the EU also criticized the USA for its strategy on Iraq in early 2003 (see The Middle East and the Mediterranean), adopting the line that only the UN Security Council could determine whether military action was justified. The EU-US annual summit held in June, however, emphasized the need for transatlantic co-operation following the overthrow by a US-led coalition force of Saddam Hussain's regime in Iraq, stressing the need to unite against global terrorism and the proliferation of weapons of mass destruction. In February 2005 President George W. Bush made a 'good will' tour of Europe in an attempt to improve the strained relations between the USA and Europe; although there were claims on both sides of a new spirit of co-operation, many issues of contention remained (including Iraq, EU plans to lift its arms embargo on China and Bush's continued refusal to sign the Kyoto Protocol on climate change). A few days prior to the US President's visit, the EU foreign ministers had, as a conciliatory gesture, agreed in principle to help train 700–800 Iraqi judges, police-officers and prison wardens.

GENERALIZED PREFERENCES

In July 1971 the Community introduced a generalized system of preferences (GSP) for tariffs in favour of developing countries, ensuring duty-free entry to the EC of all otherwise dutiable manufactured and semi-manufactured industrial products, including textiles—but subject in certain circumstances to preferential limits. Preferences, usually in the form of a tariff reduction, are also offered on some agricultural products. In 1980 the Council agreed to the extension of the scheme for a second decade (1981–90): at the same time it adopted an operational framework for industrial products, which gives individual preferential limits based on the degree of competitiveness of the developing country concerned. From the end of 1990 an interim scheme was in operation, pending the introduction of a revised scheme based on the outcome of the 'Uruguay Round' of GATT negotiations on international trade (which were finally concluded in December 1993). Since 1977 the Community has progressively liberalized GSP access for the least-developed countries by according them duty-free entry on all products and by exempting them from virtually all preferential limits. In 1992–93 the GSP was extended to Albania, the Baltic states, the CIS and Georgia; in September 1994 it was extended to South Africa.

In December 1994 the European Council adopted a revised GSP to operate during 1995–98. It provided additional trade benefits to encourage the introduction by governments of environmentally sound policies and of internationally-recognized labour standards. Conversely, a country's preferential entitlement could be withdrawn, for example, if it permitted forced labour. Under the new scheme preferential tariffs amounted to 85% of the common customs duty for very sensitive products (for example, most textile products), and 70% or 35% for products classified as sensitive (for example, chemicals, electrical goods). The common customs duty was suspended for non-sensitive products (for example, paper, books, cosmetics). In accordance with the EU's foreign policy objective of focusing on the development of the world's poorest countries, duties were eliminated in their entirety (with the exception of arms and ammunition) for 49 least-developed countries. Duties were also suspended for a further five Latin American countries, conditional on the implementation of campaigns against the production and trade of illegal drugs.

A new GSP for 1999–2001 largely extended the existing scheme unchanged. The next GSP regulation, for 2002–04, was revised to expand product coverage and improve preferential margins. In May 2003 new regulations were adopted enabling certain countries to be exempted from the abolition of tariff preferences on export of their products to the EU if that sector was judged to be in crisis. In February 2005, in response to the tsunami disaster that struck south-east Asia in December 2004, the European Commission proposed to accelerate (by three months) the entry into force of the new EU preferential trade regime for developing countries. The new GSP consequently came into effect on 1 April. The focus of the new regime was on developing countries most in need, such as the Maldives, Sri Lanka, Thailand and Indonesia, and it provided for further tariff concessions, in particular in the clothing and fishery sectors.

AID TO DEVELOPING AND NON-EU COUNTRIES

The main channels for Community aid to developing countries are the Cotonou Agreement and the Mediterranean Financial Protocols, but technical and financial aid, and assistance for refugees, training, trade promotion and co-operation in industry, energy, science and technology is also provided to about 30 countries in Asia and Latin America. The EC International Investment Partners facility, established in 1988, promotes private-sector investment in Asian, Latin American and Mediterranean countries, especially in the form of joint ventures. The European Community Humanitarian Office (ECHO) was established in 1991 with a mandate to co-ordinate emergency humanitarian assistance and food aid provided by the Community and became fully operational in early 1993. ECHO, which is based in Brussels, finances operations conducted by non-governmental organizations and international agencies, with which it works in partnership. ECHO aims to meet the immediate needs of victims of mostly man-made disasters world-wide, in such areas as assisting displaced persons, health, sanitary and mine-clearing programmes. During 2004 the main recipient areas for humanitarian aid were the Horn of Africa, the Great Lakes Region of Africa, Western and Southern Africa and certain parts of Asia (notably Iraq and Afghanistan). ECHO also planned to pay particular attention to the deteriorating situation in the Middle East, notably in the Palestinian territories. In 2004 through ECHO the EU provided humanitarian aid worth a total of €570.4m. In early 2005 the EU released €100m. from its budgetary reserve to provide immediate, short-term emergency aid to those countries in south-east Asia that had been affected by the devastating tsunami in December 2004 (namely Indonesia, Sri Lanka, the Maldives, Thailand and India). In April 1999 ECHO signed a framework partnership agreement with the International Federation of Red Cross and Red Crescent Societies to promote effective co-operation in the provision of humanitarian assistance.

EU-ACP PARTNERSHIP

From 1976 to February 2000 the principal means of co-operation between the Community and developing countries were the Lomé Conventions, concluded by the EU and African, Caribbean and Pacific (ACP) countries. The First Lomé Convention (Lomé I), which was concluded at Lomé, Togo, in February 1975 and came into force on 1 April 1976, replaced the Yaoundé Conventions and the Arusha Agreement. Lomé I was designed to provide a new framework of co-operation, taking into account the varying needs of developing ACP countries. The Second Lomé Convention entered into force on 1 January 1981. The Third Lomé Convention came into force on 1 March 1985 (trade provisions) and 1 May 1986 (aid). The Fourth Lomé Convention, which had a 10-year commitment period, was signed in December 1989: its trade provisions entered into force on 1 March 1990, and the remainder entered into force in September 1991. In June 2000, meeting in Cotonou, Benin, EU and ACP heads of state and government concluded a new 20-year partnership accord with the 77 ACP states. The so-called Cotonou Agreement entered into force on 1 April 2003 (although many of its provisions had been applicable for a transitional period since August 2000), following ratification by the then 15 EU member states and more than the requisite two-thirds of the ACP countries.

ACP-EU Institutions

Council of Ministers: one minister from each signatory state; one co-chairman from each of the two groups; meets annually.

Committee of Ambassadors: one ambassador from each signatory state; chairmanship alternates between the two groups; meets at least every six months.

Joint Assembly: EU and ACP are equally represented; attended by parliamentary delegates from each of the ACP countries and an equal number of members of the European Parliament; one co-chairman from each of the two groups; meets twice a year.

Secretariat of the ACP-EC Council of Ministers: 175 rue de la Loi, 1048 Brussels; tel. (2) 285-61-11; fax (2) 285-74-58.

Centre for the Development of Enterprise (CDE): 52 ave Herrmann Debroux, 1160 Brussels, Belgium; tel. (2) 679-18-11; fax (2) 679-26-03; e-mail info@cde.be; internet www.cde.be; f. 1977 to encourage and support the creation, expansion and restructuring of industrial companies (mainly in the fields of manufacturing and

agro-industry) in the ACP states by promoting co-operation between ACP and European companies, in the form of financial, technical or commercial partnership, management contracts, licensing or franchise agreements, sub-contracts, etc.; manages the Pro€Invest programme; Dir FERNANDO MATOS ROSA.

Technical Centre for Agricultural and Rural Co-operation: Postbus 380, 6700 AJ Wageningen, Netherlands; tel. (317) 467100; fax (317) 460067; e-mail cta@cta.int; internet www.agricta.org; f. 1983 to provide ACP states with better access to information, research, training and innovations in agricultural development and extension; Dir CARL B. GREENIDGE.

ACP Institutions

ACP Council of Ministers.

ACP Committee of Ambassadors.

ACP Secretariat: ACP House, 451 ave Georges Henri, Brussels, Belgium; tel. (2) 743-06-00; fax (2) 735-55-73; e-mail info@acpsec.org; internet www.acpsec.org; Sec.-Gen. Sir JOHN KAPUTIN (Papua New Guinea).

The ACP States

Angola	Mali
Antigua and Barbuda	Marshall Islands
Bahamas	Mauritania
Barbados	Mauritius
Belize	Federated States of
Benin	Micronesia
Botswana	Mozambique
Burkina Faso	Namibia
Burundi	Nauru
Cameroon	Niger
Cape Verde	Nigeria
Central African Republic	Niue
Chad	Palau
Comoros	Papua New Guinea
Congo, Democratic Republic	Rwanda
Congo, Republic	Saint Christopher and Nevis
Cook Islands	Saint Lucia
Côte d'Ivoire	Saint Vincent and the
Cuba	Grenadines
Djibouti	Samoa
Dominica	São Tomé and Príncipe
Dominican Republic	Senegal
Equatorial Guinea	Seychelles
Eritrea	Sierra Leone
Ethiopia	Solomon Islands
Fiji	Somalia
Gabon	South Africa
The Gambia	Sudan
Ghana	Suriname
Grenada	Swaziland
Guinea	Tanzania
Guinea-Bissau	Timor-Leste
Guyana	Togo
Haiti	Tonga
Jamaica	Trinidad and Tobago
Kenya	Tuvalu
Kiribati	Uganda
Lesotho	Vanuatu
Liberia	Zambia
Madagascar	Zimbabwe
Malawi	

Under Lomé I, the Community committed ECU 3,052.4m. for aid and investment in developing countries, through the European Development Fund (EDF) and the European Investment Bank (EIB). Provision was made for over 99% of ACP (mainly agricultural) exports to enter the EC market duty free, while certain products that compete directly with Community agriculture, such as sugar, were given preferential treatment but not free access. The Stabex (Stabilization of Export Earnings) scheme was designed to help developing countries to withstand fluctuations in the price of their agricultural products, by paying compensation for reduced export earnings.

The Second Lomé Convention (1981–85) envisaged Community expenditure of ECU 5,530m.: it extended some of the provisions of Lomé I, and introduced new fields of co-operation, including a scheme (Sysmin) to safeguard exports of mineral products.

Lomé III made commitments of ECU 8,500m., including loans of ECU 1,100m. from the EIB. Innovations included an emphasis on agriculture and fisheries, and measures to combat desertification; assistance for rehabilitating existing industries or sectoral improvements; improvements in the efficiency of the Stabex system (now covering a list of 48 agricultural products) and of Sysmin; simplification of the rules of origin of products; the promotion of private investment; co-operation in transport and communications; cultural and social co-operation; restructuring of emergency aid, and more efficient procedures for technical and financial assistance.

The Fourth Lomé Convention covered the period 1990–99 (but was subsequently extended to February 2000). The budget for financial and technical co-operation for 1990–95 amounted to ECU 12,000m., of which ECU 10,800m. was from the EDF (including ECU 1,500m. for Stabex and ECU 480m. for Sysmin) and ECU 1,200m. from the EIB. The budget for the second five years was ECU 14,625m., of which ECU 12,967m. was from the EDF, and ECU 1,658m. from the EIB. Under Lomé IV, the obligation of most of the ACP states to contribute to the replenishment of Stabex resources, including the repayment of transfers made under the first three Conventions, was removed. In addition, special loans made to ACP member countries were to be cancelled, except in the case of profit-orientated businesses. Other innovations included the provision of assistance for structural adjustment programmes (amounting to ECU 1,150m.); increased support for the private sector, environmental protection, and control of growth in population; and measures to avoid increasing the recipient countries' indebtedness (e.g. by providing Stabex and Sysmin assistance in the form of grants, rather than loans).

In September 1993 the Community announced plans to revise and strengthen its relations with the ACP countries under the Lomé Convention. In May 1994 representatives of EU member states and ACP countries initiated the mid-term review of Lomé IV. The Community reiterated its intention to maintain the Convention as an aid instrument but emphasized that stricter conditions relating to the awarding of aid would be imposed, based on standards of human rights, human resource development and environmental protection. In March 1997 the Commission proposed granting debt relief assistance of ECU 25m. each year for the period 1997–2000 to the 11 heavily-indebted poor countries (as identified by the World Bank and the IMF) forming part of the ACP group. Funding was to be used to support international efforts to reduce debt and encourage the economic prospects of such countries. In May 2001 the EU announced that it would cancel all outstanding debts arising from its trade accords with former colonies of member states.

The Cotonou Agreement was to cover a 20-year period from 2000 and was subject to revision every five years. A financial protocol was attached to the Agreement which indicated the funds available to the ACP through the EDF. The first financial protocol, covering the initial five-year period from March 2000, provided a total budget of €13,500m., of which €1,300m. was allocated to regional co-operation and €2,200m. was for the new investment facility for the development of the private sector. In addition, uncommitted balances from previous EDFs amounted to a further €2,500m. The new Agreement envisaged a more participatory approach with more effective political co-operation to encourage good governance and democracy, increased flexibility in the provision of aid to reward performance and a new framework for economic and trade co-operation. Its objectives were to alleviate poverty, contribute to sustainable development and integrate the ACP economies into the global economy.

Under the provisions of the new accord, the EU was to negotiate free-trade arrangements (replacing the previous non-reciprocal trade preferences) with the most developed ACP countries during 2000–08; these would be structured around a system of regional free-trade zones, and would be designed to ensure full compatibility with WTO provisions. Once in force, the agreements would be subject to revision every five years. An assessment to be conducted in 2004 would identify those mid-ranking ACP nations also capable of entering into such free-trade deals. Meanwhile, the least-developed ACP nations were to benefit from an EU initiative to allow free access for most of their products by 2005. The preferential agreements currently in force would be retained initially (phase I), in view of a waiver granted by the WTO; thereafter ACP-EU trade was to be gradually liberalized over a period of 12–15 years (phase II). It was envisaged that Stabex and Sysmin would be eliminated gradually. In February 2001 the EU agreed to phase out trade barriers on imports of everything but military weapons from the world's 48 least-developed countries, 39 of which were in the ACP group. Duties on sugar, rice, bananas and some other products were to remain until 2009.

In 2001 the Commission created the EuropeAid Co-operation Office to begin a programme of devolving responsibility for the administration of the EDF to Delegations, ensuring that operational decisions were taken in the country to improve efficiency. The fourth plenary session of the joint ACP-EU Joint Parliamentary Assembly was held in Cape Town, South Africa, in March 2002, at which the ninth EDF was discussed. The plan was to be organized along sub-regional lines, with countries grouped into west Africa, central Africa, the Caribbean, the Pacific region, eastern and southern Africa (partly via the Southern Africa Development Community, SADC). One major programme set up on behalf of the ACP countries and financed by the EDF was the new Pro€Invest programme, which was launched in 2002, with funding of €110m. over a seven-year period. In October 2003 the EU proposed to 'budgetize' the EDF, that is to incorporate it into the EU budget (previously the EDF had always been a fund outside the EU budget, based on direct voluntary contributions from the EU member states).

The first general stage of negotiations for the Economic Partnership Agreements (EPA), involving discussions with all ACP countries regarding common procedures, began in September 2002. The regional phase of EPA negotiations to establish a new framework for trade and investment commenced in October 2003, including discussions with the central African region in Brazzaville (the Republic of the Congo) and talks with the west African region in Cotonou. In May 2003 Timor-Leste became the 79th member of the ACP and the ACP-EC Council of Ministers approved its accession to the ACP-EC Partnership Agreement; Cuba, which had been admitted to the ACP in December 2000, was granted observer status. Cuba withdrew its application to join the Cotonou Agreement in July 2003.

On 1 July 1993 the EC introduced a regime to allow the preferential import into the Community of bananas from former French and British colonies in the Caribbean. This was designed to protect the banana industries of ACP countries from the availability of cheaper bananas, produced by countries in Latin America. The new regime guaranteed 30% of the European market to ACP producers, and established an annual quota of 2m. metric tons for bananas imported from Latin America, which would incur a uniform duty of 20%, while imports above this level were to be subject to a tariff of ECU 850 per ton. In February 1994 a dispute panel of GATT upheld a complaint, brought by five Latin American countries, that the EU banana import regime was in contravention of free-trade principles. An agreement was reached in March, under which the EU increased the annual quota for Latin American banana imports. However, in 1995 the USA, supported by Guatemala, Honduras and Mexico (and subsequently by Ecuador), filed a complaint with the WTO against the EU's banana regime. In May 1997 the WTO concluded that the EU banana import regime violated 19 free-trade regulations. The EU appealed against the ruling in July, but in September the WTO's dispute settlement body endorsed the original verdict. However, the allocation of preferential tariffs to ACP producers, covered by a waiver since late 1994, was upheld. In October 1997 the EU agreed to amend its banana import regime to comply with the WTO ruling. An arbitration report, published in January 1998, compelled the EU to implement changes by 1 January 1999. In June 1998 EU ministers of agriculture approved a reform of the import regime, providing for two separate quota systems, granting Latin American producers greater access to the European market, with a quota of 2.53m. tons (at a tariff of ECU 75 per ton), while ACP countries would have a quota of 857,000 tons (tariff-free). The quota systems, which were to apply from 1 January 1999, were approved by the Commission in October. However, in November the USA proposed the imposition of duties of 100% on a number of European imports, in protest at the reform, which it continued to regard as discriminatory and incompatible with WTO provisions. In March 1999, the USA imposed provisional measures against a diverse range of EU products, prompting the EU to issue a complaint with the WTO. In April an arbitration panel of the WTO confirmed that the EU had failed to conform its banana regime with WTO rules and formally authorized the USA to impose trade sanctions, valued at US $191.4m. An accord, involving the adoption by the EU of a new system of licences and quotas to cover the period 2001–06 and the introduction of a new tariff-only system from 2006, was eventually reached by the EU and USA in April 2001, subject to approval by EU member states; the USA consequently agreed to suspend its punitive trade sanctions. In 2003 the ACP Council expressed concerns about the continuing decline in prices for ACP bananas on the European market, which threatened banana production in the Windward Islands and Belize. The ACP Council requested further funds to ensure that the increase in quotas pursuant to EU enlargement in May 2004 did not further jeopardize the future of ACP banana producers.

In June 1995 negotiations opened with a view to concluding a wide-ranging trade and co-operation agreement with South Africa, including the eventual creation of a free-trade area (FTA). The accord was approved by heads of state and of government in March 1999, after agreement was reached to eliminate progressively, over a 12-year period, the use of the terms 'port' and 'sherry' to describe South African fortified wines. The accord provided for the removal of duties from about 99% of South Africa's industrial exports and some 75% of its agricultural products within 10 years, while South Africa was to liberalize its market for some 86% of EU industrial goods (with protection for the motor vehicle and textiles industries), within a 12-year period. The accord also introduced increased development assistance for South Africa after 1999. The long-delayed agreement was finally signed in January 2002, allowing South African wines freer access to the European market. Under the terms of the agreement South Africa was allowed to export 42m. litres of wine a year duty-free to the EU, in exchange for abandoning the use of names such as 'sherry', 'port', 'ouzo' or 'grappa'. In March 1997 the Commission approved a Special Protocol for South Africa's accession to the Lomé Convention, and in April South Africa attained partial membership. Full membership was withheld, as South Africa was not regarded as, in all respects, a developing country, and was therefore not entitled to aid provisions.

Prior to its ratification, parts of the Cotonou Agreement were able to be put into practice owing to measures giving effect to some of its provisions in advance. Article 96 of the Agreement, which provides for suspension of the Agreement in specific countries in the event of violation of one of its essential elements (respect for human rights, democratic principles and the rule of law) was invoked against Haiti in 2001 and was extended annually to December 2004. In January 2002 action was taken against Zimbabwe, when financing of most projects was suspended. In contrast, co-operation was resumed with Côte d'Ivoire and the Comoros in February, but Fiji and Liberia still remained subject to Article 96. During 2002 the European Council condemned the worsening human rights situation in Zimbabwe, describing the elections held there in 2002 as deeply flawed, and imposed a range of targeted sanctions including a travel ban and freezing of assets of certain members of the leadership, an arms embargo, and the suspension of development aid. In February 2003 it was announced that the second Europe-Africa summit, scheduled to take place in Lisbon, Portugal, in April, had been postponed indefinitely when EU leaders decided that they could not find a way to exclude the Zimbabwean leader, Robert Mugabe. At the same time the EU sanctions against Zimbabwe were renewed for a further year. The number of senior administration officials subject to a travel ban was increased from 79 to 95 in February 2004 as EU sanctions against Zimbabwe were extended for a further year. The EU claimed that the elections held in Zimbabwe in February 2005 were fraudulent and non-democratic, and consequently extended its sanctions for a further year. In December 2003 restrictive measures imposed on Fiji in 2000 were lifted as a result of the normalization of the democratic process in that country. The comprehensive Liberian peace agreement signed in Accra, Ghana, led to the lifting in 2003 of certain restrictions imposed on Liberia in 2002 in order to liberate funds to finance peace-keeping operations and promote the restoration of democracy.

Finance

THE COMMUNITY BUDGET

The general budget of the European Union covers all EEC and Euratom expenditure. The Commission is responsible for implementing the budget. Under the Council decision of 24 June 1988 all revenue (except that expressly designated for supplementary research and technological development programmes) is used without distinction to finance all expenditure, and all budget expenditure must be covered in full by the revenue entered in the budget. Any amendment of this decision requires the unanimous approval of the Council and must be ratified by the member states. The Treaty of Rome requires member states to release funds to cover the appropriations entered in the budget.

Each Community institution draws up estimates of its expenditure, and sends them to the Commission before 1 July of the year preceding the financial year (1 January–31 December) in question. The Commission consolidates these estimates in a preliminary draft budget, which it sends to the Council by 1 September. Expenditure is divided into two categories: that necessarily resulting from the Treaties (compulsory expenditure) and other (non-compulsory) expenditure. The draft budget must be approved by a qualified majority in the Council, and presented to Parliament by 5 October. Parliament may propose modifications to compulsory expenditure, and may (within the limits of the 'maximum rate of increase', dependent on growth of member states' gross national income—GNI—and budgets) amend non-compulsory expenditure. The budget must normally be declared finally adopted 75 days after the draft is presented to Parliament. If the budget has not been adopted by the beginning of the financial year, monthly expenditure may amount to one-twelfth of the appropriations adopted for the previous year's budget. The Commission may (even late in the year during which the budget is being executed) revise estimates of revenue and expenditure, by presenting supplementary and/or amending budgets.

Expenditure under the general budget is financed by 'own resources', comprising agricultural duties (on imports of agricultural produce from non-member states), customs duties, application of value-added tax (VAT) on goods and services, and (since 1988) a levy based on the GNI of member states. Member states are obliged to collect 'own resources' on the Community's behalf. From May 1985 arrangements were introduced for the correction of budgetary imbalances, as a result of which the United Kingdom received compensation in the form of reductions in VAT payments. In 1988 it was decided by the Community's heads of government to set a maximum amount for 'own resources' that might be called up in any one year.

The general budget contains the expenditures of the six main Community institutions—the Commission, the Council, Parliament,

the Court of Justice, the Court of Auditors, and the Economic and Social Committee and the Committee of the Regions—of which Commission expenditure (covering administrative costs and expenditure on operations) forms the largest proportion. The Common Agricultural Policy accounts for about 50% of total expenditure, principally in agricultural guarantees. In 1988 it was decided (as part of a system of budgetary discipline agreed by the Council) that the rate of increase in spending on agricultural guarantees between 1988 and a given year was not to exceed 74% of the growth rate of Community GNI during the same period. In December 1992 it was agreed to increase the upper limit on Community expenditure from 1.2% of the EC's combined GNI to 1.27% in 1999. In December 1994, taking into account the enlargement of the EU to 15 countries (from 1 January 1995), it was agreed to set a level of maximum expenditure at ECU 75,500m. in 1995, increasing to ECU 87,000m. in 1999, at constant 1992 prices. 'Agenda 2000', concerning financial arrangements for the period 2000–06, proposed maintaining the upper limit on Community expenditure at 1.27% of GNI from 2000. Agenda 2000 proposed that maximum annual expenditure would increase to €104,600m., at 1999 prices, by 2006. In early 2004 the Commission disclosed plans to boost EU expenditure following the enlargement of the EU by 10 new members in May of that year. At least six existing member states, however, including the EU's biggest financial contributors, wanted the budget capped at a lower level than its current rate (which was 1.24% of GNI in 2004). A clear division was increasingly apparent between net donors, who feared that expansion would cost them billions of euros, and net receivers, who were eager to maintain their levels of aid. The Commission wanted to set the level of expenditure at 1.22% of the EU's GNI from 2007, while the United Kingdom, France, Germany, the Netherlands, Austria and Sweden wanted to lower the limit to 1.0% of GNI. The Commission proposed to increase total expenditure to €125,000m. in 2007 and to €143,000m. in 2013.

The budget for 2005 was adopted by the European Parliament on 8 March 2005. Adopted on an EU-25 basis, it totalled €116,544.1m. for commitments (an increase of 6.3% compared with 2004) and €106,300.0m. for payments (an increase of 4.4% compared with 2004). The 2005 payments budget represented 0.99% of the 25 member states' GNI, the authorized ceiling still being 1.24%. Of the total commitment appropriations in the budget for 2005, €6.4m. were for administration, €49.1m. were for agriculture, €32.4m. for structural operations, €7.9m. for internal policies, €5.5m. for external action, €3.3m. for pre-accession strategy, €1.3m. for compensation and €0.4m. for reserves.

STRUCTURAL FUNDS

The Community's 'structural funds' comprise the Guidance Section of the European Agricultural Guidance and Guarantee Fund, the European Regional Development Fund, the European Social Fund and the Cohesion Fund. There is also a financial instrument for fisheries guidance (the Financial Instrument for Fisheries Guidance—FIFG—which was established in 1993). In accordance with the Single European Act (1987), reforms of the Community's structural funds were adopted by the Council with effect from 1 January 1989, with the aim of more accurate identification of priority targets, and greater selectivity to enable action to be concentrated in the least-favoured regions (see Social Policy). 'Agenda 2000', which was approved by the Council in March 1999, provided for the reform of the structural funds to make available some €213,000m. for 2000–06, at 1999 prices. During 2002 the European Council established a new European Union Solidarity Fund, designed as a disaster relief fund in response to the flooding that affected Germany, Austria and several candidate countries during the summer of that year. A budget of €1,000m. per year was agreed for the Fund in November 2002.

Cohesion Fund

The Treaty on European Union and its protocol on economic and social cohesion provided for the establishment of a 'Cohesion Fund', which began operating on 1 April 1993, with a budget of ECU 1,500m. for the first year. This was to subsidize projects in the fields of the environment and trans-European energy and communications networks in member states with a per caput GNP of less than 90% of the Community average (in practice, this was to mean Greece, Ireland, Portugal and Spain). Commitments under the Fund in the budget appropriations for 2004 amounted to €5,621m. The Fund's total budget for the period 2000–06 was €18,000m.

European Agricultural Guidance and Guarantee Fund (EAGGF)—Guidance Section

Created in 1962, the European Agricultural Guidance and Guarantee Fund is administered by the Commission. The Guidance section covers expenditure on Community aid for projects to improve farming conditions in the member states. It includes aid for poor rural areas and the structural adjustment of rural areas, particularly in the context of the reform of the Common Agricultural Policy (CAP). This aid is usually granted in the form of financial contributions to programmes also supported by the member governments themselves. Commitments to the EAGGF in 2004 amounted to €3,311.5m.

European Regional Development Fund—ERDF

Payments began in 1975. The Fund is intended to compensate for the unequal rate of development in different regions of the Community, by encouraging investment and improving infrastructure in 'problem regions'. In 2004 commitments to the Fund totalled €19,059.9m.

European Social Fund

The Fund (established in 1960) provides resources with the aim of combating long-term unemployment and facilitating the integration into the labour market of young people and the socially disadvantaged. It also supports schemes to help workers to adapt to industrial changes. Commitments to the Fund in 2004 amounted to €9,895.4m.

Financial Instrument for Fisheries Guidance—FIFG

The FIFG was set up in 1993, following the reform of the structural funds (previous to this, structural assistance actions for fisheries were financed by the EAGGF). The FIFG aims to contribute to achieving a sustainable balance between fishery resources and their exploitation. It also seeks to strengthen the competitiveness of the sector and the development of areas dependent upon it. Commitments to the FIFG totalled €622.9m. in 2004.

BUDGET EXPENDITURE APPROPRIATIONS FOR THE ACTIVITIES OF THE EUROPEAN COMMISSION
(€ million)

	2002	2003
Section III 'Commission' (part B)		
EAGGF Guarantee Section	44,480.2	44,762.5
Structural operations, other agricultural and regional operations, transport and fisheries	32,287.1	33,330.5
Training, youth, culture, audiovisual media, information and other social operations	888.2	879.6
Energy, Euratom nuclear safeguards and environment	189.3	250.8
Consumer protection, internal market, industry and trans-European networks	1,124.2	1,165.7
Research and technological development	3,751.7	3,650.0
External actions	7,387.0	7,687.6
Common foreign and security policy .	35.0	50.0
Guarantees, reserves and compensation	335.2	366.2
Subtotal	90,477.9	92,142.9
Section III 'Commission' (part A) . .	3,424.8	3,489.5
Other institutions	1,753.7	1,870.6
Total expenditure	95,656.4	97,502.9

Note: The funds allocated to the other Community institutions were to be supplemented by the institutions' own resources.

REVENUE
(€ million)

Source of revenue	2003	2004
Agricultural duties	1,313.4	819.4
Sugar and isoglucose levies	401.6	793.6
Customs duties	10,580.4	10,750.0
VAT own resources	13,679.3	15,313.5
GNI-based own resources	69,061.6	77,583.0
Balance and adjustments to balances of VAT own resources from previous years	232.8	n.a.
Balance and adjustments to balances of GNI own resources from previous years	−232.2	n.a.
Surplus available from previous year .	5,693.0	n.a.
Other revenue	2,623.6	1,040.5
Total	103,353.5	106,300.0

Source: European Commission, *General Report* (2004).

MEMBER STATES' PAYMENTS

Country	Contribution for 2003 (€ million)	% of total
Austria	2,177.8	2.3
Belgium	3,667.0	3.8
Denmark	2,016.9	2.1
Finland	1,448.6	1.5
France	16,576.5	17.3
Germany	22,010.2	23.0
Greece	1,639.4	1.7
Ireland	1,252.5	1.3
Italy	13,606.5	14.2
Luxembourg	231.7	0.2
Netherlands	5,741.9	6.0
Portugal	1,427.9	1.5
Spain	7,800.2	8.2
Sweden	2,550.9	2.7
United Kingdom	13,517.6	14.1
Total	95,665.6	100.0

Publications*

Bulletin of the European Union (10 a year).

The Courier (every 2 months, on ACP-EU affairs).

European Economy (every 6 months, with supplements).

European Voice (weekly).

General Report on the Activities of the European Union (annually).

Official Journal of the European Communities.

Publications of the European Communities (quarterly).

EUR-Lex Website (treaties, legislation and judgments, internet europa.eu.int/eur-lex/en/index.html).

Information sheets, background reports and statistical documents.

* Most publications are available in all of the official languages of the Union. They are obtainable from the Office for Official Publications of the European Communities, 2 rue Mercier, 2985 Luxembourg; tel. 29291; fax 495719; email europ@opoce.cec.be; internet europ.eu.int.

THE FRANC ZONE

Address: Direction des Relations Internationales et Européennes (Service de la Zone Franc), Banque de France, 39 rue Croix-des-Petits-Champs, 75049, Paris Cédex 01, France.

Telephone: 1-42-92-31-46; **fax:** 1-42-92-39-88; **e-mail:** comozof@banque-france.fr; **internet:** www.banque-france.fr/fr/eurosys/zonefr/.

MEMBERS*

Benin	French Overseas
Burkina Faso	Territories
Cameroon	Gabon
Central African Republic	Guinea-Bissau
Chad	Mali
Comoros	Niger
Republic of the Congo	Senegal
Côte d'Ivoire	Togo
Equatorial Guinea	

* Prior to 1 January 2002, when the transition to a single European currency (euro) was finalized (see below), the Franc Zone also included Metropolitan France, the French Overseas Departments (French Guiana, Guadeloupe, Martinique and Réunion), the French Overseas Collectivité Départementale (Mayotte) and the French Overseas Collectivité Territoriale (St Pierre and Miquelon). The French Overseas Territory (French Polynesia) and the French Overseas Countries (New Caledonia and the Wallis and Futuna Islands) have continued to use the franc CFP (franc des Comptoirs français du Pacifique, 'French Pacific franc').

Apart from Guinea and Mauritania (see below), all of the countries that formerly comprised French West and Equatorial Africa are members of the Franc Zone. The former West and Equatorial African territories are still grouped within the two currency areas that existed before independence, each group having its own variant on the CFA, issued by a central bank: the franc de la Communauté Financière d'Afrique ('franc CFA de l'Ouest'), issued by the Banque centrale des états de l'Afrique de l'ouest—BCEAO, and the franc Coopération financière en Afrique centrale ('franc CFA central'), issued by the Banque des états de l'Afrique centrale—BEAC.

The following states withdrew from the Franc Zone during the period 1958–73: Guinea, Tunisia, Morocco, Algeria, Mauritania and Madagascar. Equatorial Guinea, formerly a Spanish territory, joined the Franc Zone in January 1985, and Guinea-Bissau, a former Portuguese territory, joined in May 1997.

The Comoros, formerly a French Overseas Territory, did not join the Franc Zone following its unilateral declaration of independence in 1975. However, the franc CFA was used as the currency of the new state and the Institut d'émission des Comores continued to function as a Franc Zone organization. In 1976 the Comoros formally assumed membership. In July 1981 the Banque centrale des Comores replaced the Institut d'émission des Comores, establishing its own currency, the Comoros franc.

The Franc Zone operates on the basis of agreements concluded between France and each group of member countries, and the Comoros. The currencies in the Franc Zone were formerly linked with the French franc at a fixed rate of exchange. However, following the introduction of the euro (European single currency) in January 1999, within the framework of European economic and monetary union, in which France was a participant, the Franc Zone currencies were effectively linked at fixed parity to the euro (i.e. parity was based on the fixed conversion rate for the French franc and the euro). From 1 January 2002, when European economic and monetary union was finalized and the French franc withdrawn from circulation, the franc CFA, Comoros franc and franc CFP became officially pegged to the euro, at a fixed rate of exchange. (In accordance with Protocol 13 on France, appended to the 1993 Maastricht Treaty on European Union, France was permitted to continue issuing currencies in its Overseas Territories—i.e. the franc CFP—following the completion of European economic and monetary union.) All the convertability arrangements previously concluded between France and the Franc Zone remained in force. Therefore Franc Zone currencies are freely convertible into euros, at the fixed exchange rate, guaranteed by the French Treasury. Each group of member countries, and the Comoros, has its own central issuing bank, with overdraft facilities provided by the French Treasury. (The issuing authority for the French Overseas Territories is the Institut d'émission d'outre-mer, based in Paris.) Monetary reserves are held mainly in the form of euros. The BCEAO and the BEAC are authorized to hold up to 35% of their foreign exchange holdings in currencies other than the euro. Franc Zone ministers of finance normally meet twice a year to review economic and monetary co-operation. The meeting

is normally attended by the French Minister of Co-operation and Francophony.

During the late 1980s and early 1990s the economies of the African Franc Zone countries were adversely affected by increasing foreign debt and by a decline in the prices paid for their principal export commodities. The French Government, however, refused to devalue the franc CFA, as recommended by the IMF. In 1990 the Franc Zone governments agreed to develop economic union, with integrated public finances and common commercial legislation. In April 1992, at a meeting of Franc Zone ministers, a treaty on the insurance industry was adopted, providing for the establishment of a regulatory body for the industry, the Conférence Intrafricaine des Marchés d'Assurances (CIMA), and for the creation of a council of Franc Zone ministers responsible for the insurance industry, with its secretariat in Libreville, Gabon. (A code of conduct for members of CIMA entered into force in February 1995.) At the meeting held in April 1992 ministers also agreed that a further council of ministers was to be created with the task of monitoring the social security systems in Franc Zone countries. A programme drawn up by Franc Zone finance ministers concerning the harmonization of commercial legislation in member states through the establishment of l'Organisation pour l'Harmonisation du Droit des Affaires en Afrique (OHADA) was approved by the Franco-African summit in October. A treaty to align corporate and investment regulations was signed by 11 member countries in October 1993.

In August 1993, in view of financial turmoil related to the continuing weakness of the French franc and the abandonment of the European exchange rate mechanism, the BCEAO and the BEAC determined to suspend repurchasing of francs CFA outside the Franc Zone. Effectively this signified the temporary withdrawal of guaranteed convertibility of the franc CFA with the French franc. Devaluations of the franc CFA and the Comoros franc (by 50% and 33.3%, respectively) were implemented in January 1994. Following the devaluation the CFA countries embarked on programmes of economic adjustment, including restrictive fiscal and wage policies and other monetary, structural and social measures, designed to stimulate growth and to ensure eligibility for development assistance from international financial institutions. France established a special development fund of FFr 300m. to alleviate the immediate social consequences of the devaluation, and announced substantial debt cancellations. In April the French Government announced assistance amounting to FFr 10,000m. over three years to Franc Zone countries undertaking structural adjustment programmes. The IMF, which had strongly advocated a devaluation of the franc CFA, and the World Bank approved immediate soft-credit loans, technical assistance and cancellations or rescheduling of debts. In June 1994 heads of state (or representatives) of African Franc Zone countries convened in Libreville, Gabon, to review the effects of the currency realignment. The final communiqué of the meeting urged further international support for the countries' economic development efforts. In April 1995 Franc Zone finance ministers, meeting in Paris, recognized the positive impact of the devaluation on agricultural export sectors, in particular in west African countries. In January 1996 Afristat, a research and training institution based in Bamako, Mali, commenced activities, having been established in accordance with a decision by the Franc Zone member countries and the French Government made in September 1993. Afristat aims to support national statistical organizations in participating states in order to strengthen their economic management capabilities. The IMF and the World Bank have continued to support economic development efforts in the Franc Zone. France provides debt relief to Franc Zone member states eligible under the World Bank's HIPC. In April 2001 the African Franc Zone member states determined jointly to develop anti-money laundering legislation.

In February 2000 UEMOA and ECOWAS adopted an action plan for the creation of a single West African Monetary Zone and consequent replacement of the franc Communauté financière africaine by a single West African currency (see below).

CURRENCIES OF THE FRANC ZONE

1 franc CFA = €0.00152. CFA stands for Communauté financière africaine in the West African area and for Coopération financière en Afrique centrale in the Central African area. Used in the monetary areas of West and Central Africa respectively.

1 Comoros franc = €0.00201. Used in the Comoros, where it replaced the franc CFA in 1981.

1 franc CFP = €0.00839. CFP stands for Comptoirs français du Pacifique. Used in New Caledonia, French Polynesia and the Wallis and Futuna Islands.

WEST AFRICA

Union économique et monétaire ouest-africaine (UEMOA):
BP 543, Ouagadougou, Burkina Faso; tel. 31-88-73; fax 31-88-72;
e-mail commission@uemoa.bf; internet www.uemoa.int; f. 1994; promotes regional monetary and economic convergence, and envisages
the eventual creation of a sub-regional common market. A preferential tariff scheme, eliminating duties on most local products and
reducing by 30% import duties on many Union-produced industrial
goods, became operational on 1 July 1996; in addition, from 1 July,
a community solidarity tax of 0.5% was imposed on all goods from
third countries sold within the Union, in order to strengthen
UEMOA's capacity to promote economic integration. (This was
increased to 1% in December 1999.) In June 1997 UEMOA heads of
state and government agreed to reduce import duties on industrial
products originating in the Union by a further 30%. An inter-
parliamentary committee, recognized as the predecessor of a
UEMOA legislature, was inaugurated in Mali in March 1998. In
September Côte d'Ivoire's stock exchange was transformed into the
Bourse regionale des valeurs mobilières, a regional stock exchange
serving the Union, in order to further economic integration. On 1
January 2000 internal tariffs were eliminated on all local products
(including industrial goods) and a joint external tariff system,
reportedly in five bands of between 0% and 20%, was imposed on
goods deriving from outside the new customs union. Guinea-Bissau
was excluded from the arrangement owing to its unstable political
situation. The UEMOA member countries also belong to ECOWAS
and, in accordance with an action plan adopted by the two organizations in February 2000, aim to harmonize UEMOA's economic
programme with that of a planned second West African monetary
union (the West African Monetary Zone—WAMZ), to be established
by the remaining—mainly anglophone—ECOWAS member states.
(In January 2005 the previous deadline for the establishment of
WAMZ, 1 July 2005, was postponed indefinitely.) A merger of the
two complementary monetary unions, and the replacement of the
franc Communauté financière africaine by a new single West
African currency, is eventually envisaged. On 29 January 2003
member states adopted a treaty on the establishment of a UEMOA
parliament. Mems: Benin, Burkina Faso, Côte d'Ivoire, Guinea-
Bissau, Mali, Niger, Senegal and Togo; Pres. SOUMAILA CISSE (Mali).

Union monétaire ouest-africaine (UMOA) (West African
Monetary Union): established by Treaty of November 1973,
entered into force 1974; in 1990 the UMOA Banking Commission
was established, which is responsible for supervising the activities
of banks and financial institutions in the region, with the
authority to prohibit the operation of a banking institution.
UMOA constitutes an integral part of UEMOA.

Banque centrale des états de l'Afrique de l'ouest (BCEAO):
ave Abdoulaye Fadiga, BP 3108, Dakar, Senegal; tel. 839-05-00; fax
823-93-35; e-mail akangni@bceao.int; internet www.bceao.int; f.
1962; central bank of issue for the mems of UEMOA; cap. and res
850,504m. francs CFA (Dec. 2001); mems: Benin, Burkina Faso,
Côte d'Ivoire, Guinea-Bissau, Mali, Niger, Senegal and Togo; Gov.
CHARLES KONAN BANNY (Côte d'Ivoire); Sec.-Gen. AMADOU SADICKH
DIOP; publs *Annual Report, Notes d'Information et Statistiques*
(monthly), *Annuaire des banques, Bilan des banques et établissements financiers* (annually).

Banque ouest-africaine de développement (BOAD): 68 ave de
la Libération, BP 1172, Lomé, Togo; tel. 221-42-44; fax 221-52-67;
e-mail boadsiege@boad.org; internet www.boad.org; f. 1973 to promote the balanced development of mem. states and the economic
integration of West Africa; cap. and res 90,406m. francs CFA (Dec.
2001); a Guarantee Fund for Private Investment in West Africa,
established jtly by BOAD and the European Investment Bank in
Dec. 1994, aims to guarantee medium- and long-term credits to
private sector businesses in the region; mems: Benin, Burkina Faso,
Côte d'Ivoire, Guinea-Bissau, Mali, Niger, Senegal, Togo; Pres. Dr
YAYI BONI (Benin); Vice-Pres. ISSA COULIBALY; publs *Rapport Annuel,
BOAD en Bref* (quarterly).

Bourse Régionale des Valeurs Mobilières (BVRM): 18 ave
Joseph Anoma, BP 3802, Abidjan 01, Côte d'Ivoire; tel. 20-32-66-85;
fax 20-32-66-84; e-mail brvm@brvm.org; internet www.brvm.org; f.
1998; Pres. COULIBALY TIEMKOKO YADE; Man. JEAN-PAUL GILLET.

CENTRAL AFRICA

**Communauté économique et monétaire de l'Afrique centrale
(CEMAC):** BP 969, Bangui, Central African Republic; tel. and fax
61-21-35; e-mail sgudeac@intnet.cf; f. 1998; formally inaugurated as
the successor to the Union douanière et économique de l'Afrique
centrale (UDEAC, f. 1966) at a meeting of heads of state held in

Malabo, Equatorial Guinea, in June 1999; aims to promote the
process of sub-regional integration within the framework of an
economic union and a monetary union; CEMAC was also to comprise
a parliament and sub-regional tribunal; UDEAC established a
common external tariff for imports from other countries and administered a common code for investment policy and a Solidarity Fund
to counteract regional disparities of wealth and economic development; mems: Cameroon, Central African Republic, Chad, Republic
of the Congo, Equatorial Guinea, Gabon; Sec.-Gen. JEAN NKUETE.

At a summit meeting in December 1981, UDEAC leaders agreed in
principle to form an economic community of Central African states
(Communauté économique des états de l'Afrique centrale—CEEAC),
to include UDEAC members and Burundi, Rwanda, São Tomé and
Príncipe and Zaire (now Democratic Republic of the Congo). CEEAC
began operations in 1985.

**Banque de développement des états de l'Afrique centrale
(BDEAC):** place du Gouvernement, BP 1177, Brazzaville, Republic
of the Congo; tel. 81-18-85; fax 81-18-80; f. 1975; cap. and res
29,528m. francs CFA (Dec. 2001); shareholders: Cameroon, Central
African Republic, Chad, Republic of the Congo, Gabon, Equatorial
Guinea, ADB, BEAC, France, Germany and Kuwait; Pres. ANICET
GEORGES DOLOGUÉLÉ.

Banque des états de l'Afrique centrale (BEAC): 736 ave Mgr
François Xavier Vogt, BP 1917, Yaoundé, Cameroon; tel. 223-40-30;
fax 223-33-29; e-mail beac@beac.int; internet www.beac.int; f. 1973
as the central bank of issue of Cameroon, the Central African
Republic, Chad, Republic of the Congo, Equatorial Guinea and
Gabon; a monetary market, incorporating all national financial
institutions of the BEAC countries, came into effect on 1 July 1994;
cap. and res 221,114m. francs CFA (Dec. 2001); Gov. JEAN-FÉLIX
MAMALEPOT; publs *Rapport annuel, Etudes et statistiques* (monthly).

CENTRAL ISSUING BANKS

Banque centrale des Comores: place de France, BP 405, Moroni,
Comoros; tel. (73) 1002; fax (73) 0349; e-mail bcc@snpt.km; f. 1981;
cap. 1,100m. Comoros francs (Dec. 1999); Gov. SALIM AHMED
ABDALLAH.

Banque centrale des états de l'Afrique de l'ouest: see above.

Banque des états de l'Afrique centrale: see above.

Institut d'émission d'outre-mer (IEOM): 5 rue Roland Barthes,
75598 Paris Cédex 12, France; tel. 1-53-44-41-41; fax 1-43-47-51-34;
e-mail contact@ieom.fr; internet www.ieom.fr; f. 1966; issuing
authority for the French Overseas Territories; Pres. JEAN-PAUL
REDOUIN; Dir-Gen. JEAN-MICHEL SEVERINO; Dir THIERRY CORNAILLE.

FRENCH ECONOMIC AID

France's connection with the African Franc Zone countries involves
not only monetary arrangements, but also includes comprehensive
French assistance in the forms of budget support, foreign aid,
technical assistance and subsidies on commodity exports.

Official French financial aid and technical assistance to developing countries is administered by the following agencies:

Agence française de développement (AFD): 5 rue Roland
Barthes, 75598 Paris Cédex 12, France; tel. 1-53-44-31-31; fax 1-44-
87-99-39; e-mail com@afd.fr; internet www.afd.fr/; f. 1941; fmrly the
Caisse française de développement—CFD; French development
bank which lends money to member states and former member
states of the Franc Zone and several other states, and executes the
financial operations of the FSP (see below). Following the devaluation of the franc CFA in January 1994, the French Government
cancelled some FFr 25,000m. in debt arrears owed by member states
to the CFD. The CFD established a Special Fund for Development
and the Exceptional Facility for Short-term Financing to help alleviate the immediate difficulties resulting from the devaluation. In
early 1994 the CFD made available funds totalling 2,420m. francs
CFA to assist the establishment of CEMAC (see above). Serves as
the secretariat for the Fonds français pour l'environnement mondial
(f. 1994). Since 2000 the AFD has been implementing France's
support of the World Bank's HIPC initiative; a total of €11.7m. was
lent to Franc Zone countries in 2004; Dir-Gen. JEAN-MICHEL SEVERINO.

Fonds de Solidarité Prioritaire (FSP): 20 rue Monsieur, 75007
Paris, France; tel. 1-53-69-37-29; fax 1-53-69-37-55; f. 2000, taking
over from the Fonds d'aide et de coopération (f. 1959) the administration of subsidies from the French Government to 54 countries of
the Zone de Solidarité prioritaire; FSP is administered by the
Ministry of Co-operation and Francophony, which allocates budgetary funds to it.

INTER-AMERICAN DEVELOPMENT BANK—IDB

Address: 1300 New York Ave, NW, Washington, DC 20577, USA.
Telephone: (202) 623-1000; **fax:** (202) 623-3096; **e-mail:** pic@iadb
.org; **internet:** www.iadb.org.

The Bank was founded in 1959 to promote the individual and collective development of Latin American and Caribbean countries through the financing of economic and social development projects and the provision of technical assistance. From 1976 membership extended to include countries outside the region.

MEMBERS

Argentina	El Salvador	Norway
Austria	Finland	Panama
Bahamas	France	Paraguay
Barbados	Germany	Peru
Belgium	Guatemala	Portugal
Belize	Guyana	Slovenia
Bolivia	Haiti	Spain
Brazil	Honduras	Suriname
Canada	Israel	Sweden
Chile	Italy	Switzerland
Colombia	Jamaica	Trinidad and
Costa Rica	Japan	Tobago
Croatia	Republic of	United Kingdom
Denmark	Korea	USA
Dominican	Mexico	Uruguay
Republic	Netherlands	Venezuela
Ecuador	Nicaragua	

Organization

(April 2005)

BOARD OF GOVERNORS

All the powers of the Bank are vested in a Board of Governors, consisting of one Governor and one alternate appointed by each member country (usually ministers of finance or presidents of central banks). The Board meets annually, with special meetings when necessary. The 45th annual meeting of the Board of Governors took place in Lima, Peru, in March 2004, and the 46th meeting was scheduled to be convened in Okinawa, Japan, in April 2005.

BOARD OF EXECUTIVE DIRECTORS

The Board of Executive Directors is responsible for the operations of the Bank. It establishes the Bank's policies, approves loan and technical co-operation proposals that are submitted by the President of the Bank, and authorizes the Bank's borrowings on capital markets.

There are 14 executive directors and 14 alternates. Each Director is elected by a group of two or more countries, except the Directors representing Canada and the USA. The USA holds 30% of votes on the Board, in respect of its contribution to the Bank's capital. The Board has five permanent committees, relating to: Policy and evaluation; Organization, human resources and board matters; Budget, financial policies and audit; Programming; and a Steering Committee.

ADMINISTRATION

The Bank comprises three Regional Operations Departments, as well as the following principal departments: Finance; Legal; Research; Integration and Regional Operations; Private Sector; External Relations; Sustainable Development; Information Technology and General Services; Strategic Planning and Budget; and Human Resources. There are also Offices of the Auditor-General, the Vice-President for Planning and Administration, and of Evaluation and Oversight. In October 2003 an Office of Institutional Integrity was established. In March 2004 the Board of Governors approved the establishment of a new Office of Development Effectiveness. The Bank has country offices in each of its borrowing member states, and special offices in Paris, France and in Tokyo, Japan. At the end of 2003 there were 1,891 Bank staff (excluding the Board of Executive Directors and the Evaluation Office), of whom 540 were based in country offices. The administrative budget for 2003 amounted to US $387m.

President: Enrique V. Iglesias (Uruguay).

Executive Vice-President: Dennis E. Flannery (USA).

Activities

Loans are made to governments, and to public and private entities, for specific economic and social development projects and for sectoral reforms. These loans are repayable in the currencies lent and their terms range from 12 to 40 years. Total lending authorized by the Bank by the end of 2003 amounted to US $128,857m. During 2003 the Bank approved loans totalling $6,810m., compared with $4,549m. in 2002. Disbursements on authorized loans amounted to $8,902m. in 2003, compared with $5,837m. in the previous year.

The subscribed ordinary capital stock, including inter-regional capital, which was merged into it in 1987, totalled US $100,951.4m. at the end of 2003, of which $4,340.2m. was paid-in and $96,611.2m. was callable. The callable capital constitutes, in effect, a guarantee of the securities which the Bank issues in the capital markets in order to increase its resources available for lending. In July 1995 the eighth general increase of the Bank's authorized capital was ratified by member countries: the Bank's resources were to be increased by $41,000m. to $102,000m.

In 2003 the Bank borrowed the equivalent of US $9,309m. on the international capital markets, bringing total borrowings outstanding to more than $50,821m. at the end of the year. During 2003 net earnings amounted to $2,433m. in ordinary capital resources and $114m. from the Fund for Special Operations (see below), and at the end of that year the Bank's total reserves were $12,659m.

The Fund for Special Operations enables the Bank to make concessional loans for economic and social projects where circumstances call for special treatment, such as lower interest rates and longer repayment terms than those applied to loans from the ordinary resources. The Board of Governors approved US $200m. in new contributions to the Fund in 1990, and in 1995 authorized $1,000m. in extra resources for the Fund. During 2003 the Fund made 23 loans totalling $578m., bringing the cumulative total of Fund lending to $16,652m. for 1,122 loans. Assistance may be provided to countries adversely affected by economic crises or natural disasters through an Emergency Lending Program. In September 2004 the Bank announced emergency relief to assist five Caribbean countries affected by Hurricane Ivan, including $200,000 for construction materials and medical supplies in Grenada, and $200,000 to assist the rehabilitation of housing in Jamaica. A Disaster Prevention Sector Facility assists countries to reduce their vulnerability to natural disasters and provides grants for identification, mitigation and preparedness projects.

In January 1993 a Multilateral Investment Fund was established, as an autonomous fund administered by the Bank, to promote private sector development in the region. The 21 Bank members who signed the initial draft agreement in 1992 to establish the Fund pledged to contribute US $1,200m. The Fund's activities are undertaken through three separate facilities concerned with technical co-operation, human resources development and small enterprise development. In 2000 a specialist working group, established to consider MIF operations, recommended that it target its resources on the following core areas of activity: small business development; microenterprise; market functioning; and financial and capital markets. In June 2002 the Fund approved $1.2m. to assist the financial intelligence units in eight South American countries in their efforts to counter money laundering. During 2003 the Fund approved some $70m. for 70 projects. The Bank's Social Entrepreneurship Program makes available credit to individuals or groups without access to commercial or development loans. Some $10m. is awarded under the programme to fund projects in 26 countries.

In 1998 the Bank agreed to participate in a joint initiative by the International Monetary Fund and the World Bank to assist heavily indebted poor countries (HIPCs) to maintain a sustainable level of debt. Four member countries were eligible for assistance under the initiative (Bolivia, Guyana, Honduras and Nicaragua). Also in 1998, following projections of reduced resources for the Fund for Special Operations, borrowing member countries agreed to convert about US $2,400m. in local currencies held by the Bank, in order to maintain a convertible concessional Fund for poorer countries, and to help to reduce the debt-servicing payments under the HIPC initiative. In mid-2000 a committee of the Board of Governors endorsed a financial framework for the Bank's participation in an enhanced HIPC initiative, which aimed to broaden the eligibility criteria and accelerate the process of debt reduction. The Bank's total contribution to the initiative was estimated to be $1,100m. By December 2001 the Bank had approved interim debt relief for all four eligible member countries under the enhanced HIPC initiative, and had assisted the preparation of national Poverty Reduction Strategy Papers, a condition of reaching the 'completion point' of the process.

The Bank supports a range of consultative groups, in order to strengthen donor co-operation with countries in the Latin America and Caribbean region. In December 1998 the Bank established an emergency Consultative Group for the Reconstruction and Transformation of Central America to co-ordinate assistance to countries that had suffered extensive damage as a result of Hurricane Mitch. The Bank hosted the first meeting of the group in the same month, which was attended by government officials, representatives of donor agencies and non-governmental organizations and academics. A total of US $6,200m. was pledged in the form of emergency aid, longer-term financing and debt relief. A second meeting of the group was held in May 1999, in Stockholm, Sweden, at which the assistance package was increased to some $9,000m., of which the Bank and World Bank committed $5,300m. In March 2001 the group convened, in Madrid, Spain, to promote integration and foreign investment in Central America. The meeting, organized by the Bank, was also used to generate $1,300m. in commitments from international donors to assist emergency relief and reconstruction efforts in El Salvador following an earthquake earlier in the year. In October the Bank organized a consultative group meeting in support of a Social Welfare and Alternative Preventive Development Programme for Ecuador, to which donor countries committed $266m. Other consultative groups co-ordinated by the Bank include ones to support the peace process in Colombia, and in Guatemala. In November the Bank hosted the first meeting of a Network for the Prevention and Mitigation of Natural Disasters in Latin America and the Caribbean, which was part of a regional policy dialogue, sponsored by the Bank to promote broad debate on strategic issues. In July 2004 the Bank co-hosted an international donor conference, together with the World Bank, the European Union and the United Nations, to consider the immediate and medium-term needs for Haiti following a period of political unrest. Some $1,080m. was pledged at the conference, of which the Bank's contribution was $260m.

An increasing number of donor countries have placed funds under the Bank's administration for assistance to Latin America, outside the framework of the Ordinary Resources and the Bank's Special Operations. These trust funds, totalling 52 in 2003, include the Social Progress Trust Fund (set up by the USA in 1961); the Venezuelan Trust Fund (set up in 1975); the Japan Special Fund (1988); and other funds administered on behalf of Austria, Belgium, Canada, Denmark, Finland, France, Israel, Italy, Japan, the Netherlands, Norway, Portugal, Spain, Sweden, Switzerland, the United Kingdom and the EU. A Program for the Development of Technical Co-operation was established in 1991, which is financed by European countries and the EU. Total cumulative lending from all these trust funds was $1,769m. for loans approved by the end of 2003. During 2003 cofinancing by bilateral and multilateral sources amounted to $1,318.8m., which helped to finance 11 projects.

The Bank provides technical co-operation to help member countries to identify and prepare new projects, to improve loan execution, to strengthen the institutional capacity of public and private agencies, to address extreme conditions of poverty and to promote small- and micro-enterprise development. The Bank has established a special co-operation programme to facilitate the transfer of experience and technology among regional programmes. In 2003 the Bank approved 327 technical co-operation operations, totalling US $63.6m., mainly financed by income from the Fund for Special Operations and donor trust funds. The Bank supports the efforts of the countries of the region to achieve economic integration and has provided extensive technical support for the formulation of integration strategies in the Andean, Central American and Southern Cone regions. The Bank is also supporting the initiative to establish a Free Trade Area of the Americas (FTAA) and has provided technical assistance, developed programming strategies and produced a number of studies on relevant integration and trade issues. During the period 1998–2000 the Bank contributed an estimated $15,000m. to projects in support of the goals of the summit meetings of the Americas, for example, strengthening democratic systems, alleviating poverty, and promoting economic integration. From March 2003 the Bank supported the transfer of the Administrative Secretariat of the FTAA from Panama City, Panama to Puebla, Mexico. In 2001 the Bank took a lead role in a Central American regional initiative, the Puebla-Panama Plan, which aimed to consolidate integration and support for social and economic development.

ASSOCIATED BODY

Inter-American Investment Corporation—IIC: 1300 New York Ave, NW, Washington, DC 20057, USA; tel. (202) 623-3900; fax (202) 623-2360; e-mail iicmail@iadb.org; internet www.iadb.org/iic; f. 1986 as a legally autonomous affiliate of the Inter-American Development Bank, to promote the economic development of the region; commenced operations in 1989; initial capital stock was US $200m., of which 55% was contributed by developing member nations, 25.3% by the USA, and the remainder by non-regional members; in total, the IIC has 42 shareholders (26 Latin American and Caribbean coun-

tries, 13 European countries, Israel, Japan and the USA); in 2001 the Board of Governors of the IADB agreed to increase the IIC's capital to $500m.; places emphasis on investment in small and medium-sized enterprises without access to other suitable sources of equity or long-term loans; in 2003 the IIC approved 26 projects in 15 countries amounting to $193.7m.; Gen. Man. JACQUES ROGOZINSKI; publ. *Annual Report* (in English, French, Portuguese and Spanish).

INSTITUTIONS

Instituto para la Integración de América Latina y el Caribe (Institute for the Integration of Latin America and the Caribbean): Esmeralda 130, 17°, 1035 Buenos Aires, Argentina; tel. (11) 4320-1850; fax (11) 4320-1865; e-mail int/inl@iadb.org; internet www.iadb.org/intal; f. 1965 under the auspices of the Inter-American Development Bank; forms part of the Bank's Integration and Regional Programmes Department; undertakes research on all aspects of regional integration and co-operation and issues related to international trade, hemispheric integration and relations with other regions and countries of the world; activities come under four main headings: regional and national technical co-operation projects on integration; policy fora; integration fora; and journals and information; maintains an extensive Documentation Center and various statistical databases; Dir JUAN JOSÉ TACCONE; publs *Integración y Comercio/Integration and Trade* (2 a year), *Intal Monthly Newsletter, Informe Andino/Andean Report, CARICOM Report, Informe Centroamericano/Central American Report, Informe Mercosur/Mercosur Report* (2 a year).

Inter-American Institute for Social Development—INDES: 1350 New York Ave, NW, Washington, DC, 20057, USA; fax (202) 623–2008; e-mail indes@iadb.org; internet www.iadb.org/indes; commenced operations in 1995; aims to support the training of senior officials from public sector institutions and organizations involved with social policies and social services; organizes specialized sub-regional courses and seminars and national training programmes; produces teaching materials and also serves as a forum for the exchange of ideas on social reform; during 2003 more than 1,000 people participated in regional and national training courses; Dir NOHRA REY DE MARULANDA.

Publications

Annual Report (in English, French, Portuguese and Spanish).

Annual Report on Oversight and Evaluation.

Annual Report on the Environment and Natural Resources (in English and Spanish).

Equidad (2 a year).

Ethics and Development (weekly).

IDBamérica (monthly, English and Spanish).

IDB Projects (10 a year, in English).

IFM (Infrastructure and Financial Markets) Review (quarterly).

Latin American Economic Policies (quarterly).

Micro Enterprise Américas (annually).

Proceedings of the Annual Meeting of the Boards of Governors of the IDB and IIC (in English, French, Portuguese and Spanish).

Social Development Newsletter (2 a year).

Brochure series, occasional papers, working papers, reports.

Statistics

DISTRIBUTION OF LOANS
(US $ million)

Sector	2003	%	1961–2003	%
Competitiveness				
Energy	221.4	3.3	18,272.4	14.2
Transportation and communication	235.0	3.5	14,270.2	11.1
Agriculture and fisheries .	94.4	1.4	14,105.6	10.6
Industry, mining and tourism	126.5	1.9	12,410.5	9.6
Multisector credit and preinvestment	70.0	1.0	2,610.8	2.0
Science and technology . .	5.4	0.1	1,705.5	1.3
Trade financing	50.0	0.7	1,604.8	1.2
Support for private sector .	506.4	7.4	1,549.9	1.2
Capital market development	10.0	0.1	15.2	0.0
Social Sector Reform				
Social investment . .	3,540.5	52.0	14,565.6	11.3
Water and sanitation . .	157.0	2.3	9,277.3	7.2

Sector— *continued*	2003	%	1961–2003	%
Urban development . . .	311.9	4.6	7,583.1	5.9
Education	284.4	4.2	5,510.6	4.3
Health	406.4	6.0	2,685.4	2.1
Environment	19.0	0.3	1,945.9	1.5
Microenterprise . . .	0.0	0.0	428.2	0.3
Reform and Modernization of the State				
Public sector planning and reform	78.7	1.1	10,063.3	7.8

Sector— *continued*	2003	%	1961–2003	%
Financial sector reform . .	506.6	7.4	5,688.3	4.4
Fiscal reform	98.9	1.5	3,718.0	2.9
Decentralization policies .	67.8	1.0	426.4	0.3
Modernization and administration of justice .	0.0	0.0	311.7	0.2
Modernization of legislatures	7.0	0.1	71.0	0.1
Strengthening of civil society	0.0	0.0	24.7	0.0
Trade policy development .	12.9	0.2	12.9	0.0
Total	6,810.0	100.0	128,857.3	100.0

YEARLY AND CUMULATIVE LOANS AND GUARANTEES, 1961–2003
(US $ million; after cancellations and exchange adjustments)

	Total Amount		Ordinary Capital*		Fund for Special Operations		Funds in Administration	
Country	2003	1961–2003	2003	1961–2003	2003	1961–2003	2003	1961–2003
Argentina	1,986.0	19,634.3	1,986.0	18,940.3	—	644.9	—	49.1
Bahamas	—	357.1	—	355.1	—	—	—	2.0
Barbados	—	419.2	—	360.4	—	39.8	—	19.0
Belize	—	92.2	—	92.2	—	—	—	—
Bolivia	223.8	3,472.1	—	1,223.2	223.8	2,176.3	—	72.6
Brazil	339.3	26,134.1	339.3	24,444.2	—	1,558.1	—	131.8
Chile	143.1	5,295.3	143.1	5,047.8	—	204.3	—	43.2
Colombia	1,814.0	10,978.5	1,814.0	10,152.1	—	763.6	—	62.8
Costa Rica	6.4	2,312.8	6.4	1,815.5	—	355.0	—	142.3
Dominican Republic . . .	30.8	2,616.0	30.8	1,798.6	—	730.6	—	86.8
Ecuador	232.9	4,172.2	232.9	3,130.2	—	952.9	—	89.1
El Salvador	100.0	3,004.8	100.0	2,082.5	—	773.2	—	149.1
Guatemala	112.5	2,684.4	112.5	1,962.5	—	647.5	—	74.4
Guyana	4.9	848.3	—	117.5	4.9	723.9	—	6.9
Haiti	201.9	971.4	—	—	201.9	965.1	—	6.3
Honduras	84.1	2,476.0	—	566.3	84.1	1,837.9	—	71.8
Jamaica	30.0	1,786.0	30.0	1,420.1	—	167.0	—	198.9
Mexico	510.0	17,220.6	510.0	16,604.8	—	559.0	—	56.8
Nicaragua	63.1	2,122.0	—	277.3	63.1	1,772.4	—	72.3
Panama	53.3	2,098.0	53.3	1,762.8	—	288.3	—	46.9
Paraguay	66.0	1,911.1	66.0	1,300.7	—	597.8	—	12.6
Peru	524.6	6,602.6	524.6	5,950.1	—	431.4	—	221.1
Suriname	12.5	90.2	12.5	88.2	—	2.0	—	—
Trinidad and Tobago . . .	10.0	1,056.0	10.0	1,000.2	—	30.6	—	25.2
Uruguay	260.0	3,676.1	260.0	3,530.2	—	104.1	—	41.8
Venezuela	0.8	3,993.2	0.8	3,818.9	—	101.4	—	72.9
Regional	—	2,832.7	—	2,594.4	—	224.8	—	13.5
Total	6,810.0	128,857.3	6,232.2	110,436.0	577.8	16,651.9	—	1,769.4

* Includes private sector loans, net of participations.

Source: *Annual Report, 2003.*

INTERGOVERNMENTAL AUTHORITY ON DEVELOPMENT—IGAD

Address: BP 2653, Djibouti.

Telephone: 354050; **fax:** 356994; **e-mail:** igad@intnet.dj; **internet:** www.igad.org.

The Intergovernmental Authority on Development (IGAD), established in 1996 to supersede the Intergovernmental Authority on Drought and Development (IGADD, founded in 1986), aims to co-ordinate the sustainable socio-economic development of member countries, to combat the effects of drought and desertification, and to promote regional food security.

MEMBERS

Djibouti	Kenya	Sudan
Eritrea	Somalia	Uganda
Ethiopia		

Organization
(April 2005)

ASSEMBLY

The Assembly, consisting of heads of state and of government of member states, is the supreme policy-making organ of the Authority. It holds a summit meeting at least once a year. The chairmanship of the Assembly rotates among the member countries on an annual basis.

Chairman: Lt-Gen. Yoweri Kaguta Museveni (Uganda).

COUNCIL OF MINISTERS

The Council of Ministers is composed of the minister of foreign affairs and one other minister from each member state. It meets at least twice a year and approves the work programme and the annual budget of the Secretariat.

COMMITTEE OF AMBASSADORS

The Committee of Ambassadors comprises the ambassadors or plenipotentiaries of member states to Djibouti. It convenes as regularly as required to advise and assist the Executive Secretary concerning the interpretation of policies and guide-lines and the realization of the annual work programme.

SECRETARIAT

The Secretariat, the executive body of IGAD, is headed by the Executive Secretary, who is appointed by the Assembly for a term of four years, renewable once. In addition to the Office of the Executive Secretary, the Secretariat comprises the following three divisions: Agriculture and Environment; Economic Co-operation; and Political and Humanitarian Affairs, each headed by a director.

Executive Secretary: Dr ATTALLA HAMAD BASHIR (Sudan).

Activities

IGADD was established in 1986 by Djibouti, Ethiopia, Kenya, Somalia, Sudan and Uganda, to combat the effects of aridity and desertification arising from the severe drought and famine that has periodically affected the Horn of Africa. Eritrea became a member of IGADD in September 1993, following its proclamation as an independent state. In April 1995, at an extraordinary summit meeting held in Addis Ababa, Ethiopia, heads of state and of government resolved to reorganize and expand the Authority. In March 1996 IGAD was endorsed to supersede IGADD, at a second extraordinary summit meeting of heads of state and of government, held in Nairobi, Kenya. The meeting led to the adoption of an agreement for a new organizational structure and the approval of an extended mandate to co-ordinate and harmonize policy in the areas of economic co-operation and political and humanitarian affairs, in addition to its existing responsibilities for food security and environmental protection.

IGAD aims to achieve regional co-operation and economic integration. To facilitate this IGAD assists the governments of member states to maximize resources and co-ordinates efforts to initiate and implement regional development programmes and projects. In this context, IGAD promotes the harmonization of policies relating to agriculture and natural resources, communications, customs, trade and transport; the implementation of pro-grammes in the fields of social sciences, research, science and technology; and effective participation in the global economy. Meetings between IGAD foreign affairs ministers and the IGAD Joint Partners' Forum, comprising the grouping's donors, are convened periodically to discuss issues such as food security and humanitarian affairs. In October 2001 delegates from IGAD and representatives of government and civil society in member states initiated a process to establish an IGAD-Civil Society Forum; the founding assembly of the Forum was convened in Nairobi, Kenya in July 2003.

FOOD SECURITY AND ENVIRONMENTAL PROTECTION

IGAD seeks to achieve regional food security, the sustainable development of natural resources and environmental protection, and to encourage and assist member states in their efforts to combat the consequences of drought and other natural and man-made disasters. The region suffers from recurrent droughts, which severely impede crop and livestock production. Natural and man-made disasters increase the strain on resources, resulting in annual food deficits. About 80% of the IGAD sub-region is classified as arid or semi-arid, and some 40% of the region is unproductive, owing to severe environmental degradation. Activities to improve food security and preserve natural resources have included: the introduction of remote-sensing services; the development of a Marketing Information System and of a Regional Integrated Information System (RIIS); the establishment of training and credit schemes for fishermen; research into the sustainable production of drought-resistant, high-yielding crop varieties; transboundary livestock disease control and vaccine production; the control of environmental pollution; the promotion of alternative sources of energy in the home; the management of integrated water resources; the promotion of community-based land husbandry; training programmes in grain marketing; and the implementation of the International Convention to Combat Desertification.

ECONOMIC CO-OPERATION

The Economic Co-operation division concentrates on the development of a co-ordinated infrastructure for the region, in particular in the areas of transport and communications, to promote foreign, cross-border and domestic trade and investment opportunities. IGAD seeks to harmonize national transport and trade policy and

thereby facilitate the free movement of people, goods and services. The improvements to infrastructure also aim to facilitate more timely interventions to conflicts, disasters and emergencies in the sub-region. Projects under way in the early 2000s included: the construction of missing segments of the Trans-African Highway and the Pan African Telecommunications Network; the removal of barriers to trade and communications; improvements to ports and inland container terminals; and the modernization of railway and telecommunications services. In November 2000 the IGAD Assembly determined to establish an integrated rail network connecting all member countries. In addition, the heads of state and government considered the possibility of drafting legislation to facilitate the expansion of intra-IGAD trade. The development of economic co-operation has been impeded by persisting conflicts in the sub-region (see below). An IGAD Business Forum is to be established in Asmara, Eritrea.

POLITICAL AND HUMANITARIAN AFFAIRS

The field of political and humanitarian affairs focuses on conflict prevention, management and resolution through dialogue. The division's primary aim is to restore peace and stability to member countries affected by conflict, in order that resources may be diverted for development purposes. Efforts have been pursued to strengthen capacity for conflict prevention and to relieve humanitarian crises. The ninth IGAD summit meeting, held in Khartoum in January 2002, adopted a protocol to IGAD's founding agreement establishing a conflict early warning and response mechanism (CEWARN). CEWARN, which was to be based in Addis Ababa, Ethiopia, was to collect and analyse information for the preparation of periodic early warning reports concerning the potential outbreak of violent conflicts in the region. The inaugural meeting of CEWARN was held in June.

In September 1995 negotiations between the Sudanese Government and opposition leaders were initiated, under the auspices of IGAD, with the aim of resolving the conflict in southern Sudan; these were subsequently reconvened periodically. In March 2001 IGAD's mediation committee on southern Sudan, chaired by President Daniel arap Moi of Kenya, publicized a seven-point plan for a peaceful settlement of the conflict. In early June, at a regional summit on the situation in Sudan convened by IGAD, it was agreed that a permanent negotiating forum comprising representatives of the parties to the conflict would be established at the Authority's secretariat. In mid-July 2002 the Sudanese Government and the main rebel grouping in that country signed, under IGAD auspices, in Machakos, Kenya, a protocol providing for a six-year period of autonomy for southern Sudan to be followed by a referendum on self-determination, and establishing that northern Sudan would be governed in accordance with *Shari'a* law and southern Sudan by a secular judicial system. Peace negotiations subsequently continued under IGAD auspices. A cease-fire agreement was concluded by the parties to the conflict in October, to which an addendum was adopted in February 2003, recommending the deployment of an IGAD verification and monitoring team to oversee compliance with the agreement. In September of that year the parties to the conflict signed an accord on interim security arrangements. During 2003–04 IGAD mediated several further security accords, paving the way for the conclusion, in January 2005, of a final, comprehensive peace agreement.

In May–August 2000 a conference aimed at securing peace in Somalia was convened in Arta, Djibouti, under the auspices of IGAD. The conference appointed a transitional Somali legislature, which then elected a transitional national president. The eighth summit of IGAD heads of state and government, held in Khartoum, Sudan, in November, welcomed the conclusion in September of an agreement on reconciliation between the new Somali transitional administration and a prominent opposition alliance, and determined that those member countries that neighboured Somalia (the 'frontline states' of Djibouti, Ethiopia and Kenya) should co-operate in assisting the process of reconstruction and reconciliation in that country. The summit appointed a special envoy to implement IGAD's directives concerning the Somali situation. In January 2002 the ninth IGAD summit meeting determined that a new conference for promoting reconciliation in Somalia (where insecurity continued to prevail) should be convened, under IGAD's auspices. The leaders also issued a statement condemning international terrorism and urged Somalia, in particular, to make a firm commitment to eradicating terrorism. The second Somalia reconciliation conference, initiated in October, in Eldoret, Kenya, under IGAD auspices, issued, towards the end of that month, a Declaration on Cessation of Hostilities, Structures and Principles of the Somalia National Reconciliation Process, as a basis for the pursuit of a peace settlement. In February 2003 the conference was relocated to Nairobi. In July delegates at the ongoing Nairobi conference reached a provisional agreement on the formation of a Somali interim government; however, this was rejected by the president of the transitional government. Progress at the conference stalled further in early October, owing to disagreement between participating groups concerning the adoption of a federal system for the country; later in that month Djibouti withdrew its support from the negotiations, owing to a perceived lack of neutrality on the part of the IGAD technical committee. The Nairobi conference resumed in January 2004 and, later in that month, determined to establish a new parliament; this was inaugurated in August. In January 2005 IGAD heads of state and government authorized the deployment of a Peace Support Mission in Somalia to assist the transitional federal authorities there, pending the subsequent deployment of an African Union (AU) peace force; this arrangement was endorsed in the same month by the AU. Initially Sudan and Uganda would deploy troops to the mission, while other IGAD member states would provide logistics, equipment and emergency assistance, as well as training to the Somali army and police.

Following the violent escalation of a border dispute between Eritrea and Ethiopia in mid-1998 IGAD supported efforts by the Organization of African Unity (now AU) to mediate a cease-fire between the two sides. This was achieved in mid-2000.

Publications

Annual Report.

IGAD News (2 a year).

Proceedings of the Summit of Heads of State and Government; Reports of the Council of Ministers' Meetings.

INTERNATIONAL CHAMBER OF COMMERCE—ICC

Address: 38 cours Albert 1er, 75008 Paris, France.

Telephone: 1-49-53-28-28; **fax:** 1-49-53-28-59; **e-mail:** webmaster@ iccwbo.org; **internet:** www.iccwbo.org.

The ICC (now also referred to as the World Business Organization) was founded in 1919 to promote free trade and private enterprise, provide practical services and represent business interests at governmental and intergovernmental levels.

MEMBERS

ICC membership comprises corporations, national professional and sectoral associations, business and employer federations, chambers of commerce, and individuals involved in international business from more than 130 countries. National Committees or Groups have been formed in some 70 countries and territories to co-ordinate ICC objectives and functions at the national level.

Organization

(April 2005)

COUNCIL

The Council is the governing body of the organization. It meets twice a year and is composed of members nominated by the National Committees. Ten direct members, from countries where no National Committee exists, may also be invited to participate. The Council elects the Chairman and Vice-Chairman for terms of two years.

Chairman: YONG SUNG PARK (Republic of Korea).

EXECUTIVE BOARD

The Executive Board consists of 15–30 members appointed by the Council on the recommendation of the Chairman and nine *ex-officio*members. Members serve for a three-year term, one-third of the members retiring at the end of each year. It ensures close direction of ICC activities and meets at least three times each year.

INTERNATIONAL SECRETARIAT

The ICC secretariat is based at International Headquarters in Paris, with additional offices maintained in Geneva and New York principally for liaison with the United Nations and its agencies. The Secretary-General is appointed by the Council on the recommendation of the Executive Board.

Secretary-General: MARIA LIVANOS CATTAUI (Switzerland).

NATIONAL COMMITTEES AND GROUPS

Each affiliate is composed of leading business organizations and individual companies. It has its own secretariat, monitors issues of concern to its national constituents, and draws public and government attention to ICC policies.

CONGRESS

The ICC's supreme assembly, to which all member companies and organizations are invited to send senior representatives. Congresses are held regularly, in a different place on each occasion, with up to 2,000 participants. The 35th Congress was held in Marrakesh, Morocco, in June 2004, on the theme of 'Standing up for Global Economy'.

CONFERENCES

ICC Conferences was created in 1996 to disseminate ICC expertise in the fields of international arbitration, trade, banking and commercial practice, by means of a world-wide programme of conferences and seminars.

Activities

The various Commissions of the ICC (listed below) are composed of at least 500 practising business executives and experts from all sectors of economic life, nominated by National Committees. ICC recommendations must be adopted by a Commission following consultation with National Committees, and then approved by the Council or Executive Board, before they can be regarded as official ICC policies. Meetings of Commissions are generally held twice a year. Working Parties are frequently constituted by Commissions to undertake specific projects and report back to their parent body. Officers of Commissions, and specialized Working Parties, often meet in the intervals between Commission sessions. The Commissions produce a wide array of specific codes and guide-lines of direct use to the world business community; formulate statements and initiatives for presentation to governments and international bodies; and comment constructively and in detail on proposed actions by intergovernmental organizations and governments that are likely to affect business. In January 1997 the ICC opened its first regional office, in the Hong Kong Special Administrative Region.

ICC works closely with other international organizations. ICC members, the heads of UN economic organizations and the OECD convene for annual discussions on the world economy. The Commission on International Trade and Investment Policy campaigns against protectionism in world trade and in support of the World Trade Organization (WTO). The ICC also works closely with the European Union, commenting on EU directives and making recommendations on, for example, tax harmonization and laws relating to competition.

ICC plays a part in combating international crime connected with commerce through its Commercial Crime Services, based in London, United Kingdom, and Kuala Lumpur, Malaysia. These comprise: the Commercial Crime Bureau; the International Maritime Bureau, which combats maritime fraud, including insurance fraud and the theft of cargoes; and the Counterfeiting Intelligence Bureau, established in 1985 to investigate counterfeiting in trade-marked goods, copyrights and industrial designs.

The ICC provides a framework for international commercial disputes, mainly through the ICC International Court of Arbitration, which was established in 1923. The Court received 561 requests for arbitration in 2004. Other ICC services for dispute resolution include its Rules of Arbitration, its Alternative Dispute Resolution, and the International Centre for Expertise, which administers ICC Rules of Expertise and Rules for Documentary Credit and Dispute Resolution Expertise (DOCDEX).

The ICC has developed rules and guide-lines relating to electronic transactions, including guide-lines for ethical advertising on the internet and for data protection. In September 1999 it presented model clauses for company contracts involving the electronic transfer of personal information. The Geneva Business Dialogue was held in Switzerland in September. The primary subjects discussed were the importance of globalization in business and the need to avoid protectionist reactions to recent economic upheaval. The ICC has also devised a system of standard trade definitions most commonly used in international sales contracts. A fully revised and updated version of these, Incoterms 2000, entered into effect on 1 January 2000.

Policy and Technical Commissions:
Commission on Air Cargo
Commission on Air Transport
Commission on Arbitration
Commission on Banking Technique and Practice
Commission on Business in Society
Commission on Competition
Commission on Customs and Trade Regulations
Commission on Energy
Commission on Environment
Commission on Extortion and Bribery
Commission on Financial Services and Insurance
Commission on Intellectual and Industrial Property
Commission on International Commercial Practice
Commission on Maritime Transport
Commission on Marketing, Advertising and Distribution
Commission on Surface Transport
Commission on Taxation
Commission on Telecommunications and Information Technologies
Commission on Trade and Investment Policy

Special Groups:
Corporate Economist Advisory Group
Electronic Commerce Project
Standing Committee on Extortion and Bribery

Bodies for the Settlement of Disputes:
International Centre for Technical Expertise
International Court of Arbitration
International Maritime Arbitration Organization

Other Bodies:
ICC Centre for Maritime Co-operation

ICC Commercial Crime Bureau
ICC Corporate Security Services
ICC Counterfeiting Intelligence Bureau
ICC Cybercrime Unit
ICC Institute of International Business Law and Practice
ICC International Maritime Bureau
ICC-WTO Economic Consultative Committee
Institute of World Business Law
World Chambers Federation

Finance

The International Chamber of Commerce is a private organization financed partly by contributions from National Committees and other members, according to the economic importance of the country which each represents, and partly by revenue from fees for various services and from sales of publications.

Publications

Annual Report.
Business World (electronic magazine).
Documentary Credits Insight (quarterly).
Handbook.
ICC Contact (newsletter).
ICC International Court of Arbitration Bulletin.
IGO Report.
Numerous publications on general and technical business and trade-related subjects.

INTERNATIONAL CONFEDERATION OF FREE TRADE UNIONS—ICFTU

Address: 5 blvd du Roi Albert II, bte 1, 1210 Brussels, Belgium.
Telephone: (2) 224-0211; **fax:** (2) 201-5815; **e-mail:** internetpo@icftu.org; **internet:** www.icftu.org.

ICFTU was founded in 1949 by trade union federations which had withdrawn from the World Federation of Trade Unions (see p. 356). It aims to promote the interests of working people and to secure recognition of workers' organizations as free bargaining agents; to reduce the gap between rich and poor; and to defend fundamental human and trade union rights. It campaigns for the adoption by the World Trade Organization of a social clause, with legally-binding minimum labour standards, and regularly provides economic analysis and proposals at international meetings. In March 2001 ICTFU launched a two-year campaign to promote the eradication of child labour. In March 2002 it presented a report on the social dimensions of globalization, at the first meeting of the ILO World Commission on Globalization. See also the World Confederation of Labour).

MEMBERS

233 organizations in 154 countries with 148m. members (December 2004).

Organization

(April 2005)

WORLD CONGRESS

The Congress, the highest authority of ICFTU, normally meets every four years. The 18th Congress was held in Miyakazi, Japan, in December 2004.

Delegations from national federations vary in size according to membership. The Congress examines past activities, maps out future plans, elects the Executive Board and the General Secretary, considers the functioning of the regional machinery, examines financial reports and social, economic and political situations. It works through plenary sessions and through technical committees which report to the plenary sessions.

EXECUTIVE BOARD

The Board meets not less than once a year, for about three days, usually at Brussels, or at the Congress venue; it comprises 53 members elected by Congress and nominated by areas of the world. The General Secretary is an *ex-officio* member. After each Congress the Board elects a President and at least seven Vice-Presidents.

The Board considers administrative questions; hears reports from field representatives, missions, regional organizations and affiliates, and makes resultant decisions; and discusses finances, applications for affiliation, and problems affecting world labour. It elects a steering committee of 19 to deal with urgent matters between Board meetings.

President: Sharan Burrow (Australia).

PERMANENT COMMITTEES

Steering Committee: Administers the General Fund, comprising affiliation fees, and the International Solidarity Fund, constituting additional voluntary contributions.

Economic and Social Committee.

Human and Trade Union Rights Committee.

ICFTU/ITS Working Party on Trade Union Education.

*ICFTU/ITS Occupational Health, Safety, and the Environment Working Party.

*ICFTU/ITS Working Party on Multinational Companies.

Peace, Security and Disarmament Committee.

Youth Committee.

Women's Committee.
* A joint body of the ICFTU and International Trade Secretariats.

SECRETARIAT

Departments at headquarters include: Economic and Social Policy; Trade Union Rights; Projects, Co-ordination and Education (comprising units for Projects and Trade Union Education); Equality (including Youth); Finance and Administration; Press and Publications. There are also the Co-ordination Unit for Central and Eastern Europe, the Electronic Data Processing Unit, Personnel,

Co-ordination and Regional Liaison Desks for the Americas, Africa and Asia.

General Secretary: GUY RYDER (United Kingdom).

BRANCH OFFICES

ICFTU Amman Office: POB 925875, Amman 11190, Jordan; tel. (6) 5603181; fax (6) 5603185; e-mail icftuamm@go.com.jo; Co-ordinator NEZAM QAHOUSH.

ICFTU Geneva Office: 46 ave Blanc, 1202 Geneva, Switzerland; tel. (22) 7384202; fax (22) 7381082; e-mail icftu.ge@geneva.icftu.org; Dir ANNA BIONDI.

ICFTU Moscow Office: 2142, Leninsky Prospekt 42, 117119 Moscow, Russia; tel. (95) 938-7356; fax (95) 938-7304; e-mail icftumos@cq.ru; Rep. VADIM BORISOV.

ICFTU South East European Office: 71000 Sarajevo, Koturova 8, Bosnia and Herzegovina; tel. (33) 238976; fax (33) 238984; e-mail icftubux@bih.net.ba; Rep. JASMIN RADZEPOVIC.

ICFTU United Nations Office: 211 East 43rd St, Suite 710, New York, NY 10017, USA; tel. (212) 370-0180; fax (212) 370-0188; e-mail icftuny@igc.org; Perm. Rep. GEMMA ADABA.

There are also Permanent Representatives accredited to FAO (Rome), IMO (London), UNIDO and IAEA (Vienna), and to UNEP and UN-Habitat (Nairobi).

REGIONAL ORGANIZATIONS

ICFTU African Regional Organization (AFRO): POB 67273, Kenya Re Towers, 4th Floor, Upper Hill, Off Ragati Rd, POB 67273, Nairobi, Kenya; tel. (20) 244336; fax (20) 215072; e-mail info@ictfuafro.org; internet www.icftu-afro.org; f. 1957; mems: 5m. workers in 36 African countries; Gen. Sec. ANDREW KAILEMBO (Tanzania).

ICFTU Asian and Pacific Regional Organization (APRO): 73 Bras Basah Rd, NTUC Trade Union House, Singapore 189556; tel. (65) 6222-6294; fax (65) 6221-7380; e-mail gs@icftu-apro.org; internet www.icftu-apro.org; f. 1951; mems: 33m. in 38 orgs in 29 countries; Gen. Sec. NORIYUKI SUZUKI.

Inter-American Regional Organization of Workers (ORIT): Avda Andrés Eloy Blanco, Edif. José Vargas, 15 Los Caobos, Caracas, Venezuela; tel. (2) 578-3538; fax (2) 578-1702; e-mail sedeorit@cioslorit.org; internet www.cioslorit.org; f. 1951; mems: national unions in 28 countries and territories; Gen. Sec. VÍCTOR BÁEZ (Paraguay).

There are Field Representatives in various parts of Africa. In addition, a number of Project Planners for development co-operation travel in different countries.

Finance

Affiliated federations pay a standard fee of €175.15 (2005), or its equivalent in other currencies, per 1,000 members per annum, which covers the establishment and routine activities of the ICFTU headquarters in Brussels, and partly subsidizes the regional organizations.

An International Solidarity Fund was set up in 1956 to assist unions in developing countries, and workers and trade unionists victimized by repressive political measures. It provides legal assistance and supports educational activities. In cases of major natural disasters affecting workers token relief aid is granted.

Publications

Survey of Trade Union Rights (annually).

Trade Union World (official journal, monthly).

These periodicals are issued in English, French and Spanish. In addition the Congress report is issued in English. Numerous other publications on labour, social protection and trade union training have been published in various languages.

Associated International Trade Secretariats

Education International (EI): 5 blvd du Roi Albert II (8ème étage), 1210 Brussels, Belgium; tel. (2) 224-06-80; fax (2) 224-06-06; e-mail headoffice@ei-ie.org; internet www.ei-ie.org; f. 1993 by merger of the World Confederation of Organizations of the Teaching Profession (f. 1952) and the International Federation of Free Teach-

ers' Unions (f. 1951); mems: 319 national orgs of teachers' trade unions representing more than 26m. members in 162 countries and territories; holds Congress every three years (July 2004: Porto Alegre, Brazil); Pres. MARY HATWOOD FUTRELL (USA); Sec.-Gen. FRED VAN LEEUWEN (Netherlands); publs *Worlds of Education Education International* (quarterly) (both in English, French and Spanish).

International Federation of Building and Woodworkers (IFBWW): 54 route des Acacias, 1227 Carouge, Switzerland; tel. (22) 8273777; fax (22) 8273770; e-mail info@ifbww.org; internet www.ifbww.org; f. 1934; mems: 287 national unions with a membership of more than 10m. workers in 124 countries; organization: Congress, Executive Committee; Pres. ROEL DE VRIES (Netherlands); Sec.-Gen. ANITA NORMARK (Sweden); publ. *IFBWW News* (2 a month).

International Federation of Chemical, Energy, Mine and General Workers' Unions (ICEM): 109 ave Emile de Béco, B-1050 Brussels, Belgium; tel. (2) 626-20-20; fax (2) 648-43-16; e-mail info@icem.org; internet www.icem.org; f. 1995 by merger of the International Federation of Chemical, Energy and General Workers' Unions (f. 1907) and the Miners' International Federation (f. 1890); mems: 403 trade unions covering approximately 20m. workers in 115 countries; main sectors cover energy industries; chemicals; pharmaceuticals and biotechnology; mining and extraction; pulp and paper; rubber; ceramics; glass; building materials; and environmental services; Pres. JOHN MAITLAND; Gen. Sec. FRED HIGGS; publs *ICEM Info* (quarterly), *ICEM Focus on Health, Safety and Environment* (2 a year), *ICEM Update* Irregular.

International Federation of Journalists (IFJ): International Press Centre, 155 rue de la Loi, 1040 Brussels, Belgium; tel. (2) 235-22-00; fax (2) 235-22-19; e-mail ifj@ifj.org; internet www.ifj.org; f. 1952 to link national unions of professional journalists dedicated to the freedom of the press, to defend the rights of journalists, and to raise professional standards; it conducts surveys, assists in trade union training programmes, organizes seminars and provides information; it arranges fact-finding missions in countries where press freedom is under pressure, and issues protests against the persecution and detention of journalists and the censorship of the mass media; holds Congress every three years: (May 2004: Athens, Greece); mems: 147 unions in 106 countries, comprising 450,000 individuals; Pres. CHRISTOPHER WARREN (Australia); Gen. Sec. AIDAN WHITE (UK); publ. *IFJ Direct Line* every two months.

International Metalworkers' Federation (IMF): 54 bis, route des Acacias, CP 1516, 1227 Geneva, Switzerland; tel. (22) 3085050; fax (22) 3085055; e-mail info@imfmetal.org; internet www.imfmetal.org; f. 1893; Mems: national orgs covering 24.8m. workers in 207 unions in 101 countries; holds Congress every four years; has six regional offices; seven industrial departments; World Company Councils for unions in multinational corporations; Pres. JÜRGEN PETERS (Germany); Gen. Sec. MARCELLO MALENTACCHI; publs *IMF News Briefs* (weekly), *Metal World* (quarterly).

International Textile, Garment and Leather Workers' Federation (ITGLWF): rue Joseph Stevens 8 (boîte 4), 1000 Brussels, Belgium; tel. (2) 512-26-06; fax (2) 511-09-04; e-mail office@itglwf.org; internet www.itglwf.org; f. 1970; mems: 217 unions covering 10m. workers in 110 countries; holds Congress every four years: (October 2004: Istanbul, Turkey); Pres. MANFRED SCHALLMEYER (Germany); Gen. Sec. NEIL KEARNEY (Ireland); publ. *ITGLWF Newsletter* (quarterly).

International Transport Workers' Federation (ITF): 49–60 Borough Rd, London, SE1 1DR, United Kingdom; tel. (20) 7403-2733; fax (20) 7357-7871; e-mail mail@itf.org.uk; internet www.itfglobal.org; f. 1896; mems: national trade unions covering 5m. workers in 604 unions in 137 countries; holds Congress every four years; has eight Industrial Sections; Pres. UMRAOMAL PUROHIT (India); Gen. Sec. DAVID COCKROFT (UK); publ. *Transport International* (quarterly).

International Union of Food, Agricultural, Hotel, Restaurant, Catering, Tobacco and Allied Workers' Associations (IUF): 8 rampe du Pont-Rouge, 1213 Petit-Lancy, Switzerland; tel. (22) 7932233; fax (22) 7932238; e-mail iuf@iuf.org; internet www.iuf.org; f. 1920; mems: 336 affiliated organizations covering about 12m. workers in 120 countries; holds Congress every five years; Pres. GARY NEBEKER (USA); Gen. Sec. TOMOJI MISATO; publs bi-monthly bulletins.

Public Services International (PSI): 45 ave Voltaire, BP9, 01211 Ferney-Voltaire Cédex, France; tel. 4-50-40-64-64; fax 4-50-40-73-20; e-mail psi@world-psi.org; internet www.world-psi.org; f. 1907; mems: 620 unions and professional associations covering 20m. workers in 149 countries; holds Congress every five years (Sept. 2002: Ottawa, Canada); Pres. YLVA THÖRN (Sweden); Gen. Sec. HANS ENGELBERTS (Netherlands); publ. *Focus* (quarterly).

Union Network International (UNI): ave Reverdil 8–10, 1260 Nyon, Switzerland; tel. (22) 3652100; fax (22) 3652121; e-mail contact@union-network.org; internet www.union-network.org; f. 2000 by merger of Communications International (CI), the International Federation of Commercial, Clerical, Professional and Technical Employees (FIET), the International Graphical Federation (IGF), and Media and Entertainment International (MEI); mems: 900 unions in more than 140 countries, representing 15.5m. people; activities cover the following 12 sectors: commerce; electricity; finance; graphical; hair and beauty; professional and information technology staff; media, entertainment and the arts; postal; property

services; social insurance and private health care; telecommunications; and tourism; first World Congress convened in Berlin, Germany, in September 2001; second World Congress scheduled to be held in Chicago, USA, in August 2005, where UNI was to be relaunched as UNI Global Union; Pres. JOE HANSEN (USA); Gen. Sec. PHILIP J. JENNINGS (United Kingdom); publs *UNIinfo* (quarterly), *UNInet News* (monthly).

INTERNATIONAL CRIMINAL COURT

Address: Maanweg 174, 2516 AB The Hague, Netherlands.
Telephone: (70) 515-8515; **fax:** (70) 515-8555; **e-mail:** pio@icc-cpi.int; **internet:** www.icc-cpi.int.

The International Criminal Court (ICC) was established by the Rome Statute of the International Criminal Court, adopted by 120 states participating in a United Nations Diplomatic Conference in July 1998. The Rome Statute (and therefore the temporal jurisdiction of the ICC) entered into force on 1 July 2002, 60 days after ratification by the requisite 60th signatory state in April. The ICC is a permanent, independent body, in relationship with the United Nations, that aims to promote the rule of law and punish the most serious international crimes. The Rome Statute reaffirms the principles of the UN Charter and states that the relationship between the Court and the United Nations system is to be determined by a framework relationship agreement to be concluded by the states parties to the Rome Statute and the UN General Assembly. Under the draft agreement, approved by the Assembly of States Parties to the Rome Statute in September 2002, there was to be mutual exchange of information and documentation to the fullest extent and co-operation and consultation on practical matters, and the Court might, if deemed appropriate, submit reports on its activities to the UN Secretary-General and propose to the Secretary-General items for consideration by the United Nations. The so-called negotiated relationship agreement was concluded and entered into force in October 2004, upon signature by the Court's President and the Secretary-General of the United Nations.

The Court comprises the Presidency (consisting of a President and first and second Vice-Presidents), Chambers (including a Pre-Trial Division, Trial Division and Appeals Division) with 18 permanent judges, Office of the Prosecutor (comprising the Chief Prosecutor and up to two Deputy Prosecutors), and Registry. The judges must each have a different nationality and equitably represent the major legal systems of the world, a fair geographical distribution, and a fair proportion of men and women. They are elected by the Assembly of States Parties to the Rome Statute from two lists, the first comprising candidates with established competence in criminal law and procedures and the second comprising candidates with established competence in relevant areas of international law, to terms of office of three, six or nine years. The President and Vice-Presidents are elected by an absolute majority of the judges for renewable three-year terms of office. The Chief Prosecutor is elected by an absolute majority of states parties to the Rome Statute to an unrenewable nine-year term of office. The first judges were elected to the Court in February 2003, the first Presidency in March, and the first Chief Prosecutor in April. By March 2005 138 states had signed and 98 states had ratified the Rome Statute.

The Court has established a Victims Trust Fund to finance compensation, restitution or rehabilitation for victims of crimes (individ-

uals or groups of individuals). The Fund is administered by the Registry and supervised by an independent board of directors.

By the end of March 2005 three states party to the Rome Statute had referred cases to the Court: Uganda (in January 2004, relating to the long-term unrest in the north of that country); the Democratic Republic of the Congo (in April 2004, relating to alleged war crimes); and the Central African Republic (in January 2005, relating to war crimes and crimes against humanity allegedly committed during the period October 2002–March 2003). Also, in March 2005, the UN Security Council referred to the Court the situation prevailing in Darfur, Sudan, since 1 July 2002. By the end of March 2005 the Chief Prosecutor had agreed to open investigations into two of the referred cases: the situation in the DRC (agreed in June 2004) and the situation in Uganda (agreed in July 2004).

THE JUDGES
(April 2005)

	Term
President: PHILIPPE KIRSCH (Canada)	6 years
First Vice-President: AKUA KUENYEHIA (Ghana) . .	3 years
Second Vice President: ELIZABETH ODIO BENITO (Costa Rica)	9 years
RENÉ BLATTMANN (Bolivia)	6 years
MAUREEN HARDING CLARK (Ireland)	9 years
FATOUMATA DEMBELE DIARRA (Mali)	9 years
Sir ADRIAN FULFORD (United Kingdom)	9 years
KARL HUDSON-PHILLIPS (Trinidad and Tobago) . . .	9 years
CLAUDE JORDA (France)	6 years
HANS-PETER KAUL (Germany)	3 years
ERKKI KOURULA (Finland)	3 years
GHEORGHIOS PIKIS (Cyprus)	6 years
NAVANETHEM PILLAY (South Africa)	6 years
MAURO POLITI (Italy)	6 years
TUILOMA NERONI SLADE (Samoa)	3 years
SANG-HYUN SONG (Republic of Korea)	3 years
SYLVIA DE FIGUEIREDO STEINER (Brazil)	9 years
ANITA UŠACKA (Latvia)	6 years

Chief Prosecutor: LUIS MORENO OCAMPO (Argentina).

Registrar: BRUNO CATHALA (France).

Finance

The proposed budget for the International Criminal Court for 2005 amounted to €66.8m.

INTERNATIONAL OLYMPIC COMMITTEE

Address: Château de Vidy, 1007 Lausanne, Switzerland.
Telephone: (21) 6216111; **fax:** (21) 6216216; **internet:** www
.olympic.org.
The International Olympic Committee was founded in 1894 to
ensure the regular celebration of the Olympic Games.

Organization

(April 2005)

INTERNATIONAL OLYMPIC COMMITTEE

The International Olympic Committee (IOC) is a non-governmental
international organization comprising 128 members, who are
representatives of the IOC in their countries and not their countries'
delegates to the IOC. In addition there are 25 Honorary members
and five Honor members. The members meet in session at least once
a year. In accordance with reforms adopted in December 1999, the
Committee was to comprise a maximum of 115 members (130 until
31 December 2003), including 15 active Olympic athletes, 15
National Olympic Committee presidents, 15 International Sports
Federation presidents, and 70 other individuals. A nominations
committee has been established under the reform programme to
select qualified candidates to stand for election to the IOC.

The IOC is the final authority on all questions concerning the
Olympic Games and the Olympic movement. There are 199 recognized National Olympic Committees, which are the sole authorities responsible for the representation of their respective countries
at the Olympic Games. The IOC may give recognition to International Federations which undertake to adhere to the Olympic
Charter, and which govern sports that comply with the IOC's
criteria.

An International Council for Arbitration for Sport (ICAS) has been
established. ICAS administers the Court of Arbitration for Sport
which hears cases brought by competitors.

EXECUTIVE BOARD

The session of the IOC delegates to the Executive Board the
authority to manage the IOC's affairs. The President of the Board is
elected for an eight-year term, and is eligible for re-election once for
an additional term of four years. The Vice-Presidents are elected for
four-year terms, and may be re-elected after a minimum interval of
four years. Members of the Board are elected to hold office for four
years. The Executive Board generally meets four to five times per
year.

President: Dr JACQUES ROGGE (Belgium).

Vice-Presidents: THOMAS BACH (Germany), VITALY SMIRNOV
(Russia), JAMES L. EASTON (USA), GUNILLA LINDBERG (Sweden).

Members of the Board: SERGEI BUBKA (Ukraine), TONI KHOURY
(Lebanon), LAMBIS W. NIKOLAOU (Greece), DENIS OSWALD (Switzer-
land), MARIO VÁZQUEZ RAÑA (Mexico), OTTAVIO CINQUANTA (Italy), GER-
HARD HEIBERG (Norway), ALPHA IBRAHIM DIALLO (Guinea), ZAIQING YU
(People's Republic of China), RICHARD L. CARRIÓN (Puerto Rico).

IOC COMMISSIONS

Athletes' Commission: f. 1981; comprising active and retired
athletes, represents their interests; may issue recommendations to
the Executive Board.

Commission for Culture and Olympic Education: f. 2000 by
merger of the Culture Commission (f. 1968) and the IOC Commission for the International Olympic Academy and Olympic Education
(f. 1961).

Co-ordination Commission for the Olympic Games: f. after the
election of a host city to oversee and assist the organizing committee
in the planning and management of the games.

Ethics Commission: f. 1999 to develop and monitor rules and
principles to guide the selection of hosts for the Olympic Games, and
the organization and execution of the Games.

Medical Commission: f. 1967; concerned with the protection of the
health of athletes, respect for medical and sport ethics, and equality
for all competing athletes.

Olympic Collectors' Commission: f. 1993; aims to increase
awareness of Olympic philately, numismatics, and other memora-
bilia.

Olympic Games Study Commission: f. 2002; makes recommendations on means of controlling the cost, complexity and size of the
Summer and Winter Games.

Olympic Programme Commission: reviews, and analyses the
Olympic programme of sports, disciplines and events; develops
recommendations on the principles and structure of the programme.

Olympic Solidarity Commission: f. 1961; assists National
Olympic Committees (NOCs); responsible for managing and administering the share of television rights allocated to NOCs.

Sport and Environment Commission: f. 1995 to promote environmental protection and sustainable development.

Sport for All Commission: f. 1983 to encourage and support the
principles of Sport for All.

Women and Sport Commission: f. 2004 (by transformation of a
working group, f. 1995 to advise the Executive Board on policies to
promote women in sport).

ADMINISTRATION

The administration of the IOC is under the authority of the Director-
General, who is appointed by the Executive Board, on the proposal
of the President, and is assisted by Directors responsible for the
following administrative sectors: international co-operation;
Olympic Games co-ordination; finance, marketing and legal affairs;
technology; control and co-ordination of operations; communications; and medical.

Director-General: URS LACOTTE.

Activities

The fundamental principles of the Olympic movement are:

Olympism is a philosophy of life, exalting and combining, in a
balanced whole, the qualities of body, will and mind. Blending sport
with culture, education and respect for the environment, Olympism
seeks to create a way of life based on the joy found in effort, the
educational value of good example and respect for universal fundamental ethical principles.

Under the supreme authority of the IOC, the Olympic movement
encompasses organizations, athletes and other persons who agree to
be guided by the Olympic Charter. The criterion for belonging to the
Olympic movement is recognition by the IOC.

The goal of the Olympic movement is to contribute to building a
peaceful and better world by educating youth through sport practised without discrimination of any kind and in the Olympic spirit,
which requires mutual understanding with a spirit of friendship,
solidarity and fair-play.

The activity of the Olympic movement is permanent and universal.
It reaches its peak with the bringing together of the athletes of the
world at the great sport festival, the Olympic Games.

The Olympic Charter is the codification of the fundamental principles, rules and bye-laws adopted by the IOC. It governs the
organization and operation of the Olympic movement and stipulates
the conditions for the celebration of the Olympic Games.

In March 1998, at a meeting organized with other international
sports governing bodies, it was agreed to form a working group to
defend the principle of self-regulation in international sports organizations, against possible interference by the EU. At a meeting in
August methods of containing the increase in drugs abuse in sport
were discussed. In January 1999, following publication of the results
of an investigation into allegations of corruption and bribery, six
members of the Committee were recommended for expulsion while
investigations into the conduct of other officials were to be pursued.
In March an extraordinary session of the IOC was convened, at
which the six Committee members were expelled for violating rules
relating to Salt Lake City's bid to host the Olympic Winter Games in
2002 (four other members had already resigned, while Executive
Board member Un Yong Kim had received disciplinary action). The
President of the IOC retained his position after receiving a vote of
confidence. The session approved far-reaching reforms, including
the introduction of an interim procedure to select the host city for the
Winter Games in 2006, by means of which an election college was to
choose two finalists from the six cities submitting bids. Visits by IOC
members to any of the bid cities were prohibited. In addition, the
meeting approved the establishment of an independent Ethics Commission to oversee cities' bids to host the Olympic Games (see above)
and an IOC 2000 Commission to review the bidding process after
2006 and the internal structure of the organization. A declaration on

drugs and sport was also adopted by the meeting. In November 1999, an independent World Anti-Doping Agency (WADA, see below) was established by the IOC, and an Anti-Doping Code entered into effect on 1 January 2000. In December 1999 the IOC adopted 50 reforms proposed by the IOC 2000 Commission during the Extraordinary 110th Session. The changes aimed to create a more open, responsive and accountable organization, and included the elimination of member visits to bid cities, the application of terms of office, limiting the expansion of the Summer Games, and the election of 15 active athletes to the IOC membership. In 2000, prior to the Sydney 'Summer' Olympic Games, held in September of that year, WADA conducted about 2,200 out-of-competition drugs tests, involving competitors from more than 80 nations and supplementing significantly the IOC's ongoing out-of-competition drugs testing programme. The Agency established a 15-member team of independent observers to oversee doping control operations at the Sydney Games. Participants attending the World Conference on Doping in Sport, held in Copenhagen, Denmark, in March 2003, adopted the Copenhagen Declaration on Doping in Sport and promoted the World Anti-Doping Code, formulated by WADA, as the basis for combating doping in sport.

In July 2000 the International Olympic Committee established a subsidiary International Olympic Truce Foundation, and an International Olympic Truce Centre, based in Athens, Greece, with the aim of promoting a culture of peace through the pursuit of sport and the Olympic ideals. A new president of the IOC's Executive Board was elected at the 112th Session, held in Moscow, Russia, in July 2001. In early 2002 the Olympic Games Study Commission was established to address means of reducing the cost and complexity of the Games. The Commission presented a full report of its findings, incorporating several recommendations for the future organization of the Games, to the 115th Session of the IOC, held in Prague, Czech Republic, in July 2003. The Commission was subsequently dissolved. In November 2002 the Olympic Programme Commission made a full review of the sports programme for the first time since 1936. It decided to cap the number of sports at 28, the number of events at 300, and the number of participating athletes at 10,500.

ASSOCIATED AGENCY

World Anti-Doping Agency—WADA: f. 1999 to promote and coordinate efforts to achieve drug-free sport; has five committees: Ethics and Education; Finance and Administration; Health, Medical and Research; Legal; Standards and Harmonization; Chair. RICHARD W. POUND; Dir Gen. HARRI SYVÄSALMI.

THE GAMES OF THE OLYMPIAD

The Olympic Summer Games take place during the first year of the Olympiad (period of four years) which they are to celebrate. They are the exclusive property of the IOC, which entrusts their organization to a host city seven years in advance.

1896	Athens	1960	Rome
1900	Paris	1964	Tokyo
1904	St Louis	1968	Mexico City
1908	London	1972	Munich
1912	Stockholm	1976	Montreal
1920	Antwerp	1980	Moscow
1924	Paris	1984	Los Angeles
1928	Amsterdam	1988	Seoul
1932	Los Angeles	1992	Barcelona
1936	Berlin	1996	Atlanta
1948	London	2000	Sydney
1952	Helsinki	2004	Athens
1956	Melbourne	2008	Beijing

The programme of the Games must include at least 15 of the total number of Olympic sports (sports governed by recognized International Federations and admitted to the Olympic programme by decision of the IOC at least seven years before the Games). The Olympic summer sports are: aquatics (including swimming, diving and water polo), archery, athletics, badminton, baseball, basketball, boxing, canoeing, cycling, equestrian sports, fencing, football, gymnastics, handball, field hockey, judo, modern pentathlon, rowing, sailing, shooting, softball, table tennis, tae kwondo, tennis, triathlon, volleyball, weight-lifting, wrestling.

OLYMPIC WINTER GAMES

The Olympic Winter Games comprise competitions in sports practised on snow and ice. From 1994 onwards, they were to be held in the second calendar year following that in which the Games of the Olympiad take place.

1924	Chamonix	1976	Innsbruck
1928	St Moritz	1980	Lake Placid
1932	Lake Placid	1984	Sarajevo
1936	Garmisch-Partenkirchen	1988	Calgary
1948	St Moritz	1992	Albertville
1952	Oslo	1994	Lillehammer
1956	Cortina d'Ampezzo	1998	Nagano
1960	Squaw Valley	2002	Salt Lake City
1964	Innsbruck	2006	Turin
1968	Grenoble	2010	Vancouver
1972	Sapporo		

The Winter Games may include biathlon, bobsleigh, curling, ice hockey, luge, skating and skiing.

Finance

The International Olympic Committee derives marketing revenue from the sale of broadcast rights, the Olympic Partners sponsorship Programme, local sponsorship, ticketing, and licensing. Some 8% of this is retained for the Committee's operational budget, with the remainder allocated to Olympic organizing committees, National Olympic Committees and teams, and international sports federations.

Publication

Olympic Review (3 a year).

INTERNATIONAL ORGANIZATION FOR MIGRATION— IOM

Address: 17 route des Morillons, CP 71, 1211 Geneva 19, Switzerland.

Telephone: (22) 7179111; **fax:** (22) 7986150; **e-mail:** info@iom.int; **internet:** www.iom.int.

The Intergovernmental Committee for Migration (ICM) was founded in 1951 as a non-political and humanitarian organization with a predominantly operational mandate, including the handling of orderly and planned migration to meet specific needs of emigration and immigration countries; and the processing and movement of refugees, displaced persons and other individuals in need of international migration services to countries offering them resettlement opportunities. In 1989 ICM's name was changed to the International Organization for Migration (IOM). IOM was admitted as an observer to the UN General Assembly in October 1992.

MEMBERS

Albania	France	Nigeria
Algeria	The Gambia	Norway
Angola	Georgia	Pakistan
Argentina	Germany	Panama
Armenia	Greece	Paraguay
Australia	Guatemala	Peru
Austria	Guinea	Philippines
Azerbaijan	Guinea-Bissau	Poland
Bangladesh	Haiti	Portugal
Belgium	Honduras	Romania
Belize	Hungary	Rwanda
Benin	Iran	Senegal
Bolivia	Ireland	Serbia and
Bulgaria	Israel	Montenegro
Burkina Faso	Italy	Sierra Leone
Cambodia	Japan	Slovakia
Canada	Jordan	Slovenia
Cape Verde	Kazakhstan	South Africa
Chile	Kenya	Sri Lanka
Colombia	Korea, Republic	Sudan
Congo, Democratic	Kyrgyzstan	Sweden
Republic	Latvia	Switzerland
Congo, Republic	Liberia	Tajikistan
Costa Rica	Lithuania	Tanzania
Côte d'Ivoire	Luxembourg	Thailand
Croatia	Madagascar	Tunisia
Cyprus	Mali	Uganda
Czech Republic	Malta	Ukraine
Denmark	Mauritania	United Kingdom
Dominican	Mexico	USA
Republic	Moldova	Uruguay
Ecuador	Morocco	Venezuela
Egypt	Netherlands	Yemen
El Salvador	New Zealand	Zambia
Finland	Nicaragua	Zimbabwe

Observers: Afghanistan, Belarus, Bhutan, Bosnia and Herzegovina, Brazil, Burundi, People's Republic of China, Cuba, Estonia, Ethiopia, Ghana, Holy See, India, Indonesia, Jamaica, Libya, former Yugoslav republic of Macedonia, Mozambique, Namibia, Nepal, Papua New Guinea, Russia, San Marino, São Tomé and Príncipe, Somalia, Spain, Turkey, Turkmenistan and Viet Nam. In addition, some 68 international, governmental and non-governmental organizations hold observer status with IOM.

Organization

(April 2005)

IOM is governed by a Council which is composed of representatives of all member governments, and has the responsibility for making final decisions on policy, programmes and financing. An Executive Committee of nine member governments elected by the Council prepares the work of the Council and makes recommendations on the basis of reports from the Sub-Committee on Budget and Finance and the Sub-Committee on the Co-ordination of Transport.

Director General: BRUNSON MCKINLEY (USA).

Deputy Director General: NDIORO NDIAYE (Senegal).

Activities

IOM aims to provide assistance to member governments in meeting the operational challenges of migration, to advance understanding of migration issues, to encourage social and economic development through migration and to work towards effective respect of the human dignity and well-being of migrants. It provides a full range of migration assistance to, and sometimes *de facto* protection of, migrants, refugees, displaced persons and other individuals in need of international migration services. This includes recruitment, selection, processing, medical examinations, and language and cultural orientation courses, placement, activities to facilitate reception and integration and other advisory services. IOM co-ordinates its refugee activities with the UN High Commissioner for Refugees (UNHCR) and with governmental and non-governmental partners. In May 1997 IOM and UNHCR signed a memorandum of understanding which aimed to facilitate co-operation between the two organizations. Since it commenced operations in February 1952 IOM is estimated to have provided assistance to more than 11m. migrants.

IOM was designated as one of the implementing organizations of the settlement agreement concluded between survivors of the Nazi holocaust and Swiss banks. IOM established the Holocaust Victim Assets Programme (HVAP) to process claims made by certain target groups. A German Forced Labour Compensation Programme (GFLCP) was founded to process applications for claims of forced labour and personal injury and for property loss. The deadline for filing claims under both programmes was 31 December 2001. By May 2004 45,000 claims had been received under the HVAP; IOM had recommended payment of US $13.9m. to 9,196 of those claims. IOM aimed to conclude the Programme by the end of 2005. By July 2004 claims received under the GFLCP included 330,600 for slave and forced labour, 41,830 for personal injury and 34,000 for property loss. Under the terms of the settlement agreement, with regard to 'looted assets', IOM was mandated to distribute $20.5m. to humanitarian programmes, specifically to assist elderly Roma and Sinti, Jehovah's Witnesses, disabled and homosexual victims and targets of Nazi persecution.

In January 2005, following a massive earthquake in the Indian Ocean in December 2004, which caused a series of tidal waves, or tsunamis, that devastated coastal regions in 12 countries in South and South-East Asia and East Africa, IOM initiated a US $57m. six-month emergency relief operation to provide temporary shelter; IDP management; assistance with family reunification; and provision of medical supplies, safe water, food and non-food items to about 500,000 people in Aceh, Indonesia (close to the epicentre of the earthquake). IOM's field office in Banda Aceh, Aceh, was to serve as a logistics centre for other agencies conducting humanitarian operations there. A further operation, requiring funding of $16.3m., was to provide relief assistance to about 300,000 Sri Lankans affected by the natural disaster. In addition to pre-existing counter-trafficking programmes in countries in the region, IOM was to undertake a rapid response mass information project to raise awareness of human trafficking among vulnerable IDPs (with a particular focus on women and children) in Indonesia, Sri Lanka and Thailand.

IOM operates within the framework of the main service areas outlined below. It also administers special programmes. In June 2001 IOM established a Migration Policy and Research Programme to strengthen the capacity of governments to manage migration effectively, and to contribute to a better understanding of migration issues.

MOVEMENTS

IOM's constitution mandates the organization to provide for the organized transfer of migrants, refugee displaced persons, and others to countries offering to receive them. Accordingly, IOM provides assistance to persons fleeing conflict situations, to refugees being resettled in third countries or repatriated, to stranded individuals, to internally and externally displaced persons, to other persons compelled to leave their homelands, to individuals seeking to reunite with other members of their families and to migrants involved in regular migration, including qualified migrants travelling under the Facilitated Passage Programme. IOM provides these individuals with secure, reliable, cost-effective services, including counselling, document processing, medical examination, transportation, language training, and cultural orientation and integration assistance. IOM offers discounted transport services and assistance during departure, transit and arrival.

IOM movements are undertaken by the Movement Management Department, which is also responsible for statistical recording of IOM activities and for the development of effective procedures and operational guide-lines. In a humanitarian emergency situation, the department assumes the focal point of IOM operations until field missions are prepared to co-ordinate activities. From April–June 1999 IOM co-operated with UNHCR and the OSCE to facilitate the evacuation of refugees from Kosovo and Metohija (Federal Republic of Yugoslavia, now Serbia and Montenegro), following an escalation of violence against the local Albanian population by Serbian forces and the initiation of a NATO military offensive. The joint Humanitarian Evacuation Programme included land transportation to move substantial numbers of refugees away from overcrowded camps in the border region of the former Yugoslav republic of Macedonia (FYRM), and the provision of charter flights to evacuate those refugees most at need to third countries. IOM was also involved in implementing a programme to register the refugees in Albania, the FYRM and Montenegro, and to reissue identification documents where necessary.

ASSISTED RETURNS SERVICE

IOM assists migrants to return home, on a voluntary basis. These people may include unsuccessful asylum seekers, stranded students, labour migrants, qualified nationals and refugees referred by UNHCR. IOM provides return services directly to the migrant, as well as in co-operation with other organizations to assist wider groups of people. As with its movements service, IOM provides assistance at each stage of the process, i.e. pre-departure, transportation, and post-arrival. It aims to act in a mediating role between the countries and governments of origin, transit and destination and often extends assistance through a period of rehabilitation, to longer-term reconstruction and development efforts.

Since its establishment IOM has been involved in the voluntary repatriation of refugees, displaced persons, and other vulnerable groups. Between 1996 and 1998 more than 160,000 Bosnians were assisted to return voluntarily under IOM auspices. In June 1999, following the end of the conflict in Kosovo and Metohija, IOM co-ordinated the return movement of refugees and worked with the UN mission and UNHCR to assist returnees to move to their final destination in Kosovo. From July 1999–December 2000 IOM assisted some 170,000 Kosovars to return to the province.

In the period October 1999–December 2000 IOM assisted 115,000 East Timorese, who had fled violence between Indonesian forces and separatist groups in September 1999, to return to the territory (now independent Timor-Leste) from camps in West Timor, and participated in reconstruction activities. A joint IOM/UNHCR programme to facilitate the return of Afghan refuees from Iran commenced in April 2000. From late 2001 the IOM was actively involved in assisting Afghans who had left their homes during renewed fighting between Taliban and oposition forces and the US bombing raids against Taliban and other military targets in Afghanistan. IOM was the co-ordinating agency for the largest camp, located in Maslakh, which had an estimated population of 120,000. A registration process was conducted in February 2002. IOM aimed to provide transport assistance, in co-operation with UNHCR, to 400,000 Afghan refugees from Iran by the end of 2002; however, transport assistance activities were suspended indefinitely in May, owing to insufficient funding. In 2001 IOM assisted with the repatriation of Sierra Leonean refugees from Guinea, following an escalation of violence in the south of that country which had rendered refugee camps vulnerable to attack and largely inaccessible to humanitarian aid agencies. In April 2003, following the US-led military action initiated in March against the Saddam Hussain regime in Iraq, IOM launched the Iraq Transition Initiative, aimed at addressing the priority community requirements of post-conflict Iraq. The programme was to facilitate the reintegration of internally displaced people, refugees and former combatants, to stabilize populations, and to establish links between local communities and regional and national authorities. During that month IOM announced that it would launch a programme to repatriate some 21,500 third-country nationals (mainly from Burkina Faso, Guinea and Mali) who had been displaced by the ongoing violent unrest in Côte d'Ivoire and had become stranded in that country, Liberia and Mali.

IOM aims to contribute towards alleviating economic and social problems through the recruitment and selection of high-level workers and professionals to fill positions in priority sectors of the economy in developing countries for which qualified persons are not available locally, taking into account national development priorities as well as the needs and concerns of receiving communities. IOM screens possible returnees, identifies employment opportunities and provides reintegration assistance. Selection Migration programmes help qualified professionals to migrate to countries in need of specific expertise when the country cannot find the required skills from within or through the return of nationals. Integrated Experts programmes provide temporary expatriate expertise to states for up to six years: these experts transfer their skills to their

working partners and contribute directly to productive output. Programmes of Intraregional Co-operation in the field of qualified human resources encourage collective self-reliance among developing countries by fostering the exchange of governmental experts and the transfer of professionals and technicians within a given region. IOM maintains recruitment offices throughout the world. In November 1996 IOM established a Return of Qualified Nationals (RQN) programme to facilitate the employment of refugees returning to Bosnia and Herzegovina. By December 1999, when the programme was terminated, more than 750 professionals had been placed in jobs in that country. In 2001 IOM initiated a Programme for the Return of Judiciary and Prosecutors to Minority Areas in Bosnia and Herzegovina.

An RQN programme has been established for Timor-Leste, and a programme to encourage the Return and Reintegration of Qualified Afghan Nationals is under way. In addition, IOM operates a Return of Qualified African Nationals scheme. IOM and the EU jointly fund a scheme to support Rwandan students abroad and encourage their return to Rwanda.

In recent years IOM has increasingly assisted in the return home and reintegration of demobilized soldiers, police officials, and their dependents.

COUNTER TRAFFICKING

IOM aims to counter the growing problem of smuggling and trafficking in migrants, which has resulted in several million people being exploited by criminal agents and employers. IOM aims to provide shelter and assistance for victims of trafficking; to provide legal and medical assistance to migrants uncovered in transit or in the receiving country; and to offer voluntary return and reintegration assistance. IOM organizes mass information campaigns in countries of origin, in order to highlight the risks of smuggling and trafficking, and aims to raise general awareness of the problem. In October 2001 IOM initiated a campaign for the prevention of trafficking in women in the Baltic states. IOM also provides training to increase the capacity of governments and other organizations to counter irregular migration. Since 1996 IOM has worked in Cambodia and Thailand to help victims of trafficking to return home. A transit centre has been established on the border between the two countries, where assessments are carried out, advice is given, and the process of tracing families is undertaken.

TECHNICAL CO-OPERATION ON MIGRATION

Through its technical co-operation programmes IOM offers advisory services on migration to governments, intergovernmental agencies and non-governmental organizations. They aim to assist in the formation and implementation of effective and coherent migration policy, legislation and administration. IOM technical co-operation also focuses on capacity building projects such as training courses for government migration officials, and analysis of and suggestions for solving emerging migration problems. Throughout these activities IOM aims to maintain an emphasis on the rights and well-being of migrants, and in particular to ensure that the specific needs of migrant women are incorporated into programmes and policies.

MASS INFORMATION

IOM furthers the understanding of migration through mass information campaigns, in particular to provide migrants with enough knowledge to make informed decisions. In recent years information campaigns have addressed migrant rights, trafficking in women and children, migration and health, promoting the image of migrants, and amnesty programmes. Information campaigns may also inform refugees and displaced persons on the nature and extent of humanitarian aid during an emergency. Information programmes may be implemented to address a specific need, or as part of a wider strategy for migration management. Through its research IOM has developed mechanisms to gather information on potential migrants' attitudes and motivations, as well as on situations which could lead to irregular migration flows. Trends in international migration point to information as an essential resource for individuals making life-changing decisions about migrating; for governments setting migration policies; for international, regional or non-governmental organizations designing migration programmes; and for researchers, the media and individuals analyzing and reporting on migration.

MIGRATION HEALTH

IOM's migration health services aim to ensure that migrants are fit to travel, do not pose a danger to those travelling with them, and that they receive medical attention and care when necessary. IOM also undertakes research and other technical support and policy development activities in the field of health care. Medical screening of prospective migrants is routinely conducted, along with immunizations and specific counselling, e.g. for HIV/AIDS. IOM administers programmes for disabled refugees and undertakes medical evacuation of people affected by conflict. Under its programmes for health assistance and advice, IOM conducts health education programmes, training for health professionals in post-conflict regions, and assessments of availability and access to health care for migrant populations. IOM provides assistance for post-emergency returning populations, through the rehabilitation of health infrastructures, provision of medical supplies, mental health programmes, and training of personnel. In September 1999 IOM established a one-year Psychosocial and Trauma Response in Kosovo project, to enhance the local capacity to respond to problems arising from the conflict and mass displacement. Following the end of the project, during which 37 people graduated as counsellors, IOM developed a new programme to establish community psychosocial centres, to train a further 40 counsellors and to enhance access to psychosocial support for ethnic minorities.

IOM collaborates with government health authorities and relevant intergovernmental and non-governmental organizations. In September 1999 IOM and UNAIDS signed a co-operation framework to promote awareness on HIV/AIDS issues relating to displaced populations, and to ensure the needs of migrants are incorporated into national and regional AIDS strategies. In October IOM and WHO signed an agreement to strengthen collaborative efforts to improve the health care of migrants. IOM maintains a database of its tuberculosis diagnostic and treatment programmes, which facilitates the management of the disease. An information system on immigration medical screening data was being developed to help to analyse disease trends among migrants.

International Centre for Migration and Health

11 route du Nant-d'Avril, 1214 Geneva, Vernier, Switzerland; tel. (22) 7831080; fax (22) 7831087; e-mail admin@icmh.ch; internet www.icmh.ch.

Established in March 1995, by IOM and the University of Geneva, with the support of WHO, to respond to the growing needs for information, documentation, research, training and policy development in migration health; designated a WHO collaborating centre, in August 1996, for health-related issues among people displaced by disasters.

Executive Director: Dr Manuel Carballo.

Finance

IOM's provisional operational budget for 2005 was about US $800m.

Publications

International Migration (quarterly).

IOM News (quarterly, in English, French and Spanish).

Migration and Health (quarterly).

Report by the Director General (in English, French and Spanish).

Trafficking in Migrants (quarterly).

World Migration Report (annually).

Research reports, *IOM Info Sheets* surveys and studies.

INTERNATIONAL RED CROSS AND RED CRESCENT MOVEMENT

The International Red Cross and Red Crescent Movement is a worldwide independent humanitarian organization, comprising three components: the International Committee of the Red Cross (ICRC), founded in 1863; the International Federation of Red Cross and Red Crescent Societies (the Federation), founded in 1919; and National Red Cross and Red Crescent Societies in 181 countries.

Organization

INTERNATIONAL CONFERENCE

The supreme deliberative body of the Movement, the Conference comprises delegations from the ICRC, the Federation and the National Societies, and of representatives of States Parties to the Geneva Conventions (see below). The Conference's function is to determine the general policy of the Movement and to ensure unity in the work of the various bodies. It usually meets every four to five years, and is hosted by the National Society of the country in which it is held. The 28th International Conference was held in Geneva, Switzerland, in December 2003.

STANDING COMMISSION

The Commission meets at least twice a year in ordinary session. It promotes harmony in the work of the Movement, and examines matters which concern the Movement as a whole. It is formed of two representatives of the ICRC, two of the Federation, and five members of National Societies elected by the Conference.

COUNCIL OF DELEGATES

The Council comprises delegations from the National Societies, from the ICRC and from the Federation. The Council is the body where the representatives of all the components of the Movement meet to discuss matters that concern the Movement as a whole.

In November 1997 the Council adopted an Agreement on the organization of the activities of the Movement's components. The Agreement aimed to promote increased co-operation and partnership between the Movement's bodies, clearly defining the distribution of tasks between agencies. In particular, the Agreement aimed to ensure continuity between international operations carried out in a crisis situation and those developed in its aftermath.

Fundamental Principles of the Movement

Humanity: The International Red Cross and Red Crescent Movement, born of a desire to bring assistance without discrimination to the wounded on the battlefield, endeavours, in its international and national capacity, to prevent and alleviate human suffering wherever it may be found. Its purpose is to protect life and health and to ensure respect for the human being. It promotes mutual understanding, friendship, co-operation and lasting peace amongst all peoples.

Impartiality: It makes no discrimination as to nationality, race, religious beliefs, class or political opinions. It endeavours to relieve the suffering of individuals, being guided solely by their needs, and to give priority to the most urgent cases of distress.

Neutrality: In order to continue to enjoy the confidence of all, the Movement may not take sides in hostilities or engage in controversies of a political, racial, religious or ideological nature.

Independence: The Movement is independent. The National Societies, while auxiliaries in the humanitarian services of their governments and subject to national laws, must retain their autonomy so that they may always be able to act in accordance with the principles of the Movement.

Voluntary Service: It is a voluntary relief movement not prompted by desire for gain.

Unity: There can be only one Red Cross or Red Crescent Society in any one country. It must be open to all. It must carry on its humanitarian work throughout the territory.

Universality: The International Red Cross and Red Crescent Movement, in which all National Societies have equal status and share equal responsibilities and duties in helping each other, is worldwide.

In 1997 all constituent parts of the Movement (National Societies, the ICRC and the International Federation of Red Cross and Red Crescent Societies) adopted the Seville Agreement on co-operation in the undertaking of international relief activities. The Agreement excludes activities that are entrusted to individual components by the statutes of the Movement or the Geneva Conventions.

International Committee of the Red Cross—ICRC

Address: 19 ave de la Paix, 1202 Geneva, Switzerland.
Telephone: (22) 7346001; **fax:** (22) 7332057; **e-mail:** press.gva@icrc
.org; **internet:** www.icrc.org.

Founded in 1863, the ICRC is at the origin of the Red Cross and Red
Crescent Movement, and co-ordinates all international humanitarian activities conducted by the Movement in situations of conflict.
New statutes of the ICRC, incorporating a revised institutional
structure, were adopted in June 1998 and came into effect in July.

Organization

(April 2005)

INTERNATIONAL COMMITTEE

The ICRC is an independent institution of a private character
composed exclusively of Swiss nationals. Members are co-opted, and
their total number may not exceed 25. The international character of
the ICRC is based on its mission and not on its composition.

President: JAKOB KELLENBERGER.

Vice-Presidents: JACQUES FORSTER, ANNE PETITPIERRE.

ASSEMBLY

Under the new decision-making structures, approved in 1998, the
Assembly was defined as the supreme governing body of the ICRC.
It formulates policy, defines the Committee's general objectives and
strategies, oversees its activities, and approves its budget and
accounts. The Assembly is composed of the members of the ICRC,
and is collegial in character. The President and Vice-Presidents of
the ICRC hold the same offices in the Assembly.

ASSEMBLY COUNCIL

The Council (formerly the Executive Board) is a subsidiary body of
the Assembly, to which the latter delegates certain of its responsibilities. It prepares the Assembly's activities and takes decisions on
matters within its competence. The Council is composed of five
members elected by the Assembly and is chaired by the President of
the ICRC.

Members: JAKOB KELLENBERGER, JACQUES FORSTER, JEAN ABT, JEAN DE
COURTEN, JACQUES MOREILLON.

DIRECTORATE

The Directorate is the executive body of the ICRC, overseeing the
efficient running of the organization and responsible for the application of the general objectives and institutional strategies decided by
the Assembly. Members are appointed by the Assembly to serve a
four-year term.

Director-General: ANGELO GNAEDINGER.

Members: PIERRE KRAEHENBUEL (Director of Operations), JACQUES
STROUN (Director of Human Resources), DORIS PFISTER (Director of
Resources and Operational Support), YVES DACCORD (Director of
Communication), FRANÇOIS BUGNION (Director for International Law
and Co-operation within the Movement).

Activities

The International Committee of the Red Cross was founded in 1863
in Geneva, by Henry Dunant and four of his friends. The original
purpose of the Committee was to promote the foundation, in every
country, of a voluntary relief society to assist wounded soldiers on
the battlefield (the origin of the National Societies of the Red Cross
or Red Crescent), as well as the adoption of a treaty protecting
wounded soldiers and all those who come to their rescue. The
mission of the ICRC was progressively extended through the Geneva
Conventions (see below). The present activities of the ICRC consist
in giving legal protection and material assistance to military and
civilian victims of wars (international wars, internal strife and
disturbances) and in promoting and monitoring the application of
international humanitarian law. The ICRC takes into account the
legal standards and the specific cultural, ethical and religious features of the environment in which it operates. It aims to influence
the conduct of all actual and potential perpetrators of violence by
seeking direct dialogue with combatants. In 1990 the ICRC was
granted observer status at the United Nations General Assembly.
The ICRC overall programme of activities covers the following areas:

The protection of vulnerable individuals and groups under international humanitarian law, including activities related to

ensuring respect for detainees (monitoring prison conditions),
respect for civilians, reuniting relatives separated in conflict situations and restoring family links, and tracing missing persons.

The implementation of assistance activities, aimed at restoring a
sufficient standard of living to victims of armed conflict, including
the provision of medical aid and emergency food supplies, initiatives to improve water supply, basic infrastructure and access
to health care, and physical rehabilitation assistance (for example
to assist civilians injured by land-mines).

Preventive action, including the development and implementation
of international humanitarian law and dissemination of humanitarian principles, with a view to protecting non-combatants from
violence.

The use of humanitarian diplomacy to raise awareness of humanitarian issues among states and within international organizations.

Building private sector relations.

Co-operation with National Societies.

In January 1996 an ICRC Advisory Service became operational; this
was intended to assist national authorities in their implementation
of humanitarian law and to provide a basis for consultation, analysis
and harmonization of legislative texts. A Documentation Centre has
also been established for exchanging information on national measures and activities aimed at promoting humanitarian law in countries. The Centre is open to all states and National Societies, as well
as to interested institutions and the general public.

In 1996 the ICRC launched the 'Avenir' project to define the
organization's future role, in recognition of significant changes in
the world situation and the consequent need for changes in humanitarian action. Four main priorities were identified: improving the
status of international humanitarian action and knowledge of and
respect for humanitarian law; carrying out humanitarian action in
closer proximity to victims, with long-term plans and identified
priorities; strengthening dialogue with all parties (including
launching joint appeals with other organizations if necessary, and
the establishment of a combined communication and information
dissemination unit); and increasing the ICRC's efficiency. In April
1998 the Assembly endorsed a plan of action, based on these priorities. The 28th International Conference of the Red Cross and Red
Crescent, held in December 2003, adopted an Agenda for Humanitarian Action.

The ICRC consistently reviews the 1980 UN Convention on prohibitions or restrictions on the use of certain conventional weapons
which may be deemed to be excessively injurious or to have indiscriminate effects and its protocols. In September 1997 the ICRC
participated in an international conference, held in Oslo, Norway, at
which a Convention was adopted, prohibiting 'the use, stockpiling,
production and transfer of anti-personnel mines' and ensuring their
destruction. The treaty was opened for signature in December and
entered into force on 1 March 1999. In April 1998 the Swiss Government established a Geneva International Centre for Humanitarian
Demining, in co-operation with the United Nations and the ICRC, to
co-ordinate the destruction of landmines world-wide.

In 1995 the ICRC adopted a 'Plan of Action concerning Children in
Armed Conflicts', to promote the principle of non-recruitment and
non-participation in armed conflict of children under the age of 18
years. A co-ordinating group was established, with representatives
of the individual National Societies and the International Federation of Red Cross and Red Crescent Societies. The ICRC participated in drafting the Optional Protocol to the Convention on the
Rights of the Child, which was adopted by the UN General Assembly
in May 2000 and entered into force in February 2002, raising from 15
to 18 years the minimum age for recruitment in armed conflict.

In February 2003 the ICRC launched 'The Missing', a major
initiative that aimed to raise awareness of the issue of persons
unaccounted for owing to armed conflict or internal violence.

The ICRC's presence in the field is organized under the following
three categories: responsive action, aimed at addressing the immediate effects of crises; remedial action, with an emphasis on rehabilitation; and environment-building activities, aimed at creating
political, institutional, humanitarian and economic situations that
are suitable for generating respect for human rights. ICRC operational delegations focus on responsive action and remedial action,
while environment-building is undertaken by ICRC regional delegations. The regional delegations undertake humanitarian diplomacy efforts (e.g. networking, promoting international humanitarian law and distributing information), logistical support to operational delegations, and their own operations; they also have an early
warning function, alerting the ICRC to developing conflict situations. The ICRC targets its activities at the following groups:
'victims', comprising civilians affected by violent crises, people

deprived of their freedom, and the wounded and sick; and institutions and individuals with influence, i.e. national and local authorities, security forces, representatives of civil society, and Red Cross or Red Crescent National Societies. Children, women and girls, internally displaced people and missing persons are of particular concern to the ICRC. The ICRC's 'FamilyLinks' internet pages (accessible at www.icrc.org/home.nsf/home/webfamilylinks) aim to reunite family members separated by conflict or disaster situations.

During 2003 ICRC representatives visited some 469,648 prisoners held in about 80 countries. A total of 1.3m. messages were collected from or distributed to family members separated by conflict, and more than 4,142 persons reported as missing were traced. Regular substantial assistance was provided to 67 hospitals and 305 other health-care facilities world-wide. During the year the ICRC participated in orthopaedic projects in 26 countries, including the manufacturing and fitting of artificial limbs. In early 2005 the ICRC was actively concerned with around 80 conflicts and was undertaking major operations in (in order of budgetary priority): Sudan, Iraq, Israel and the Palestinian territories, Afghanistan, Liberia, the Caucasus, the Democratic Republic of the Congo, Ethiopia, Colombia, and Somalia. In 2005 operations in Africa were allocated the highest proportion of the total field budget (some 47.6%), followed by Europe and the Americas (17.1%) and Asia and the Pacific (16.5%).

In January 2005, following a massive earthquake in the Indian Ocean in December 2004, which caused a series of tidal waves, or tsunamis, that devastated coastal regions in 12 countries in South and South-East Asia and East Africa, the ICRC focused its relief efforts in northern and north-eastern Sri Lanka and Aceh, Indonesia (close to the epicentre of the earthquake). In other areas of Sri Lanka and Indonesia, and in other affected countries, the International Federation of Red Cross and Red Crescent Societies was co-ordinating the Movement's response. The ICRC established new 'FamilyLinks' internet pages (see above) to reunite family members separated by the natural disaster in India, Indonesia, Sri Lanka and Thailand.

THE GENEVA CONVENTIONS

In 1864, one year after its foundation, the ICRC submitted to the states called to a Diplomatic Conference in Geneva a draft international treaty for 'the Amelioration of the Condition of the Wounded in Armies in the Field'. This treaty was adopted and signed by 12 states, which thereby bound themselves to respect as neutral wounded soldiers and those assisting them. This was the first Geneva Convention.

With the development of technology and weapons, the introduction of new means of waging war, and the manifestation of certain phenomena (the great number of prisoners of war during World War I; the enormous number of displaced persons and refugees during World War II; the internationalization of internal conflicts in recent years), the necessity was felt of having other international treaties to protect new categories of war victims. The ICRC, for more than 134 years, has been the leader of a movement to improve and complement international humanitarian law.

There are now four Geneva Conventions, adopted on 12 August 1949: I—to protect wounded and sick in armed forces on land, as well as medical personnel; II—to protect the same categories of people at sea, as well as the shipwrecked; III—concerning the treatment of prisoners of war; IV—for the protection of civilians in time of war; and there are two Additional Protocols of 8 June 1977, for the protection of victims in international armed conflicts (Protocol I) and in non-international armed conflicts (Protocol II).

By January 2005 192 states were parties to the Geneva Conventions; 162 were parties to Protocol I and 158 to Protocol II.

In April 2000 a joint working group on the emblems of the National Red Cross and Red Crescent Societies recommended the formulation of a Third Additional Protocol to the Geneva Conventions, designating a new official emblem so that National Societies could be recognized in countries that did not wish to be represented by either current symbol or did not wish to choose between the two.

Finance

The ICRC's work is financed by a voluntary annual grant from governments parties to the Geneva Conventions, voluntary contributions from National Red Cross and Red Crescent Societies and by gifts and legacies from private donors. The ICRC's total budget for 2005 amounted to some 971.8m. Swiss francs, of which 819.7m. Swiss francs were allocated to field operations.

Publications

Annual Report (editions in English, French and Spanish).

The Geneva Conventions (texts and commentaries).

ICRC News (weekly, English, French, German and Spanish editions).

International Review of the Red Cross (quarterly in English and French; annually in Arabic, Russian and Spanish).

The Additional Protocols (texts and commentaries).

FORUM series.

Various publications on subjects of Red Cross interest (medical studies, international humanitarian law, etc.), some in electronic form.

International Federation of Red Cross and Red Crescent Societies

Address: 17 chemin des Crêts, Petit-Saconnex, CP 372, 1211 Geneva 19, Switzerland.

Telephone: (22) 7304222; **fax:** (22) 7330395; **e-mail:** secretariat@ifrc.org; **internet:** www.ifrc.org.

The Federation was founded in 1919 (as the League of Red Cross Societies). It works on the basis of the Principles of the Red Cross and Red Crescent Movement to inspire, facilitate and promote all forms of humanitarian activities by the National Societies, with a view to the prevention and alleviation of human suffering, and thereby contribute to the maintenance and promotion of peace in the world. The Federation acts as the official representative of its member societies in the field. The Federation maintains close relations with many inter-governmental organizations, the United Nations and its Specialized Agencies, and with non-governmental organizations. It has permanent observer status with the United Nations.

MEMBERS

National Red Cross and Red Crescent Societies in 181 countries in April 2005, with a total of 97m. members and volunteers.

Organization

(April 2005)

GENERAL ASSEMBLY

The General Assembly is the highest authority of the Federation and meets every two years in commission sessions (for development, disaster relief, health and community services, and youth) and plenary sessions. It is composed of representatives from all National Societies that are members of the Federation.

GOVERNING BOARD

The Board (formerly the Executive Council) meets every six months and is composed of the President of the Federation, nine Vice-Presidents, representatives of 16 National Societies elected by the Assembly, and the Chairman of the Finance Commission. Its functions include the implementation of decisions of the General Assembly; it also has powers to act between meetings of the Assembly.

President:: Juan Manuel Suárez del Toro Rivero (Spain).

COMMISSIONS

Development Commission.
Disaster Relief Commission.
Finance Commission.
Health and Community Services Commission.
Youth Commision.

The Commissions meet, in principle, twice a year, just before the Governing Board. Members are elected by the Assembly under a system that ensures each Society a seat on one Commission.

SECRETARIAT

The Secretariat assumes the statutory responsibilities of the Federation in the field of relief to victims of natural disasters, refugees and civilian populations who may be displaced or exposed to abnormal hardship. In addition, the Secretariat promotes and co-ordinates assistance to National Societies in developing their basic structure and their services to the community. From 2000 the Secretariat underwent a process of restructuring. In 2003 there were some 230 staff at the Secretariat, employed in the following divisions: co-operation and development, disaster management and co-ordination, external relations, support services, monitoring and evaluation, and governance and planning.

Secretary-General: MARKKU NISKALA (Finland).

Activities

In October 1999 the Assembly adopted Strategy 2010, outlining the Federation's objectives and strategies for the next 10 years, in order to address new demands placed on it, for example by the proliferation of other humanitarian groups, restricted finance, and pressure from donors for efficiency, transparency and results. The Strategy involved a significant restructuring of the organization.

DISASTER RESPONSE

The Federation supports the establishment of emergency response units, which aim to act effectively and independently to meet the needs of victims of natural or man-made disasters. The units cover basic health care provision, referral hospitals, water sanitation, logistics, telecommunications and information units. The Federation advises National Societies in relief health. In the event of a disaster the following areas are covered: communicable disease alleviation and vaccination; psychological support and stress management; health education; the provision of medicines; and the organization of mobile clinics and nursing care. The Societies also distribute food and clothing to those in need and assist in the provision of shelter and adequate sanitation facilities and in the management of refugee camps.

DEVELOPMENT

The Federation undertakes capacity-building activities with the National Societies to train and develop staff and volunteers and to improve management structures and processes, in particular in the area of disaster-preparedness. Blood donor programmes are often undertaken by National Societies, sometimes in conjunction with WHO. The Federation supports the promotion of these programmes and the implementation of quality standards. Other activities in the health sector aim to strengthen existing health services and promote community-based health care and first aid; the prevention of HIV/AIDS and substance abuse; and health education and family planning initiatives. The Federation also promotes the establishment and development of education and service programmes for children and for other more vulnerable members of society, including the elderly and disabled. Education projects support the promotion of humanitarian values.

Finance

The permanent Secretariat of the Federation is financed by the contributions of member Societies on a pro-rata basis. Each relief action is financed by separate, voluntary contributions, and development programme projects are also financed on a voluntary basis.

Publications

Annual Report.
Handbook of the International Red Cross and Red Crescent Movement (with the ICRC).
Red Cross, Red Crescent (quarterly, English, French and Spanish).
Weekly News.
World Disasters Report (annually).
Newsletters on several topics; various guides and manuals for Red Cross and Red Crescent activities.

INTERNATIONAL SEABED AUTHORITY

Address: 14–20 Port Royal St, Kingston, Jamaica.
Telephone: 922-9105; **fax:** 922-0195; **e-mail:** webmaster@isa.org.jm; **internet:** www.isa.org.jm.

The Authority is an autonomous international organization established in accordance with the 1982 United Nations Convention on the Law of the Sea and 1994 Agreement Relating to the Implementation of Part XI of the Convention. The Authority was founded in November 1994 and became fully operational in June 1996.

Organization

(April 2005)

ASSEMBLY

The Assembly is the supreme organ of the Authority, consisting of representatives of all member states. It formulates policies, approves the budget and elects Council members. The first session of the Assembly was initiated in November 1994 and was continued at a meeting in February–March 1995. The session was concluded in August 1995, having failed to reach agreement on the composition of the Council (see below) and to elect a Secretary-General of the Authority. In March 1996 the Assembly concluded the first part of its second session, having constituted the 36-member Council and elected, by consensus, the first Secretary-General of the Authority. The 10th session of the Assembly was held in May–June 2004.

COUNCIL

The Council, elected by the Assembly, acts as the executive organ of the Authority. It consists of 36 members, comprising the four states that are the largest importers or consumers of seabed minerals, the four largest investors in seabed minerals, the four major exporters of seabed minerals, six developing countries representing special interests, and 18 members covering all the geographical regions.

LEGAL AND TECHNICAL COMMISSION

The Legal and Technical Commission, comprising 24 experts, assists the Council by making recommendations concerning sea-bed activities, assessing the environmental implications of activities in the area and proposing measures to protect the marine environment.

FINCANCE COMMITTEE

The Committee, comprising 15 experts, was established to make recommendations to the Assembly and the Council on all financial and budgetary issues.

SECRETARIAT

The Secretariat provides administrative services to all the bodies of the Authority and implements the relevant work programmes. It comprises the Office of the Secretary-General, Offices of Resources and Environmental Monitoring, Legal Affairs, and Administration and Management. Under the terms of the 1994 Agreement Relating to the Implementation of Part XI of the Convention, the Secretariat is performing the functions of the Enterprise, the organ through which the Authority carries out deep sea-bed mining operations (directly or through joint ventures). It is envisaged that the Enterprise will eventually operate independently of the Secretariat.

Secretary-General: SATYA N. NANDAN (Fiji).

Activities

The Authority, functioning as an autonomous international organization in relationship with the UN, implements the Convention on the Law of the Sea (which was adopted in April 1982 and entered into force in November 1994). All states party to the Convention (148 at April 2005) are members. The Convention covers the uses of ocean space: navigation and overflight, resource exploration and exploitation, conservation and pollution, and fishing and shipping; as well as governing conduct on the oceans; defining maritime zones; establishing rules for delineating sea boundaries; assigning legal rights, duties and responsibilities to states; and providing machinery for the settlement of disputes. Its main provisions are as follows:

Coastal states are allowed sovereignty over their territorial waters of up to 12 nautical miles in breadth; foreign vessels are to be allowed 'innocent passage' through these waters;

Ships and aircraft of all states are allowed 'transit passage' through straits used for international navigation;

Archipelagic states (composed of islands) have sovereignty over a sea area enclosed by straight lines drawn between the outermost points of the islands;

Coastal states and inhabited islands are entitled to proclaim a 200-mile exclusive economic zone with respect to natural resources and jurisdiction over certain activities (such as protection and preservation of the environment), and rights over the adjacent continental shelf, up to 350 miles from the shore under specified circumstances;

All states have freedom of navigation, overflight, scientific research and fishing on the high seas, but must co-operate in measures to conserve living resources;

A 'parallel system' is to be established for exploiting the international seabed, where all activities are to be supervised by the International Seabed Authority;

States are bound to control pollution and co-operate in forming preventive rules, and incur penalties for failing to combat pollution;

Marine scientific research in the zones under national jurisdiction is subject to the prior consent of the coastal state, but consent may be denied only under specific circumstances;

States must submit disputes on the application and interpretation of the Convention to a compulsory procedure entailing decisions binding on all parties.

The Convention provides for the establishment of an International Tribunal for the Law of the Sea (see below).

In July 1994 the UN General Assembly adopted the Agreement Relating to the Implementation of Part XI of the Convention. The original Part XI, concerning the exploitation of the international ocean bed, and particularly the minerals to be found there (chiefly manganese, cobalt, copper and nickel), envisaged as the 'common heritage of mankind', had not been supported by the USA and other industrialized nations on the grounds that countries possessing adequate technology for deep-sea mining would be insufficiently represented in the Authority; that the operations of private mining consortia would be unacceptably limited by the stipulations that their technology should be shared with the Authority's 'Enterprise' and that production should be limited in order to protect land-based mineral producers. Under the 1994 Agreement there was to be no mandatory transfer of technology, the Enterprise was to operate according to commercial principles and there were to be no production limits, although a compensation fund was to assist land-based producers adversely affected by seabed mining. Several industrial nations then ratified the Convention and Agreement (which entered into force in July 1996), although the USA had not yet

ratified either by early 2004. An agreement on the implementation of the provisions of the Convention relating to the conservation and management of straddling and highly migratory fish stocks was opened for signature in December 1995 and entered into force in December 2001.

In July 2000 the Authority adopted the Regulations for Prospecting and Exploration for Polymetallic Nodules in the Area. In 2001 and 2002, pursuant to the Regulations, exploration contracts were signed with six out of seven registered pioneer investors who had submitted plans of work for deep seabed exploration. During 1998–2002 the Authority organized five workshops on (i) development of guide-lines for the assessment of the possible environmental impacts arising from exploration for polymetallic nodules; (ii) proposed technologies for deep seabed mining of polymetallic nodules; (iii) the available knowledge on mineral resources other than polymetallic nodules in the deep seabed; (iv) a standardized system of data interpretation; and (v) international co-operation and collaboration in marine scientific research on the deep oceans. A sixth workshop was held in May 2003 on the establishment of a geologic model for the assessment of polymetallic nodule resources in the Clarion-Clipperton Fracture Zone (CCFZ) of the equatorial north Pacific Ocean. The Authority is developing a database on polymetallic nodules (POLYDAT), and has also made significant progress towards the establishment of a central data repository for all marine minerals in the seabed.

Finance

The Authority's budget is the responsibility of the Finance Committee. The budget for the Authority for the biennium 2005–06 was US $10.8m. The administrative expenses of the Authority are met by assessed contributions of its members.

Publications

Handbook (annually).

The Law of the Sea: Compendium of Basic Documents.

Selected decisions of sessions of the Authority, consultations, documents, rules of procedure, etc.

Associated Institutions

The following were also established under the terms of the Convention:

Commission on the Limits of the Continental Shelf: Division for Ocean Affairs and the Law of the Sea, Room DC2-0450, United Nations, New York, NY 10017, USA; tel. (212) 963-3966; fax (212) 963-5847; e-mail doalos@un.org; internet www.un.org/Depts/los/clcs_new/clcs_home.htm; 21 members, serving a five-year term (the first election of members took place in March 1997 and the second was held in April 2002); responsible for making recommendations regarding the establishment of the outer limits of the continental shelf of a coastal state, where the limit extends beyond 200 nautical miles (370 km).

International Tribunal for the Law of the Sea: Am internationalen Seegerichtshof 1, 22609 Hamburg, Germany; tel. (40) 356070; fax (40) 35607245; e-mail itlos@itlos.org; internet www.itlos.org; inaugurated in Oct. 1996; 21 judges; responsible for interpreting the Convention and ruling on disputes brought by states party to the Convention on matters within its jurisdiction; Registrar Philippe Gautier (Belgium).

INTER-PARLIAMENTARY UNION—IPU

Address: 5 chemin du Pommier, CP 330, 1218 Le Grand Saconnex/Geneva, Switzerland.
Telephone: (22) 9194150; **fax:** (22) 9194160; **e-mail:** postbox@mail.ipu.org; **internet:** www.ipu.org.

Founded in 1889, the IPU aims to promote peace, co-operation and representative democracy by providing a forum for multilateral political debate between representatives of national parliaments.

MEMBERS

National parliaments of 141 sovereign states; seven international parliamentary associations (associate members).

Organization

(April 2005)

ASSEMBLY

The Assembly (formerly known as the Inter-Parliamentary Conference and renamed in April 2003) is the main statutory body of the IPU, comprising eight to 10 representatives from each member parliament. It meets twice a year to discuss current issues in world affairs and to make political recommendations. Other specialized meetings of parliamentarians may also be held, on a global or regional basis. The Assembly is assisted by the following three plenary Standing Committees: on Peace and International Security; Sustainable Development, Finance and Trade; and Democracy and Human Rights.

GOVERNING COUNCIL

The Governing Council (formerly the Inter-Parliamentary Council, renamed in April 2003) comprises two representatives of each member parliament, usually from different political groups. It is responsible for approving membership and the annual programme and budget of the IPU, and for electing the Secretary-General. The Council may consider substantive issues and adopt resolutions and policy statements, in particular on the basis of recommendations from its subsidiary bodies.

President: SERGIO PÁEZ VERDUGO (Chile).

MEETING OF WOMEN PARLIAMENTARIANS

The Meeting is a mechanism for co-ordination between women parliamentarians. Since 1975 the Meeting has been convened twice a year, on the occasion of IPU statutory meetings, to discuss subjects of common interest, to formulate strategies to develop the IPU's women's programme, to strengthen their influence within the organization and to ensure that women are elected to key positions. The Meeting is assisted by a Co-ordinating Committee.

SUBSIDIARY BODIES

In addition to the thematic Standing Committees of the IPU Assembly, various other committees and groups undertake and co-ordinate IPU activities in specific areas. All these bodies are subsidiary to the IPU Council:

Committee on the Human Rights of Parliamentarians;

Committee on Middle East Questions;

Group of Facilitators for Cyprus;

Ad Hoc Committee to Promote Respect for International Humanitarian Law;

CSCM Co-ordinating Committee (concerned with security and co-operation in the Mediterranean);

Co-ordinating Committee of the Meeting of Women MPs;

Gender Partnership Group;

Management Board of the Staff Pension Fund.

EXECUTIVE COMMITTEE

The Committee, comprising 17 members and presided over by the President of the Council, oversees the administration of the IPU and advises the Council on membership, policy and programme, and any other matters referred to it.

SECRETARIAT

Secretary-General: ANDERS B. JOHNSSON (Sweden).

Activities

PROMOTION OF REPRESENTATIVE DEMOCRACY

This is one of the IPU's core areas of activity, and covers a wide range of concerns, such as democracy, gender issues, human rights and ethnic diversity, parliamentary action to combat corruption, and links between democracy and economic growth. In September 1997 the Council adopted a Universal Declaration on Democracy. The IPU subsequently published a study entitled *Democracy: Its Principles and Achievements*.

The IPU administers a Programme for the Study and Promotion of Representative Institutions, which aims to improve knowledge of the functioning of national parliaments by gathering and disseminating information on their constitutional powers and responsibilities, structure, and membership, and on the electoral systems used. The IPU also organizes international seminars and gatherings for parliamentarians, officials, academics and other experts to study the functioning of parliamentary institutions. A Technical Co-operation Programme aims to mobilize international support in order to improve the capabilities, infrastructure and technical facilities of national parliaments and enhance their effectiveness. Under the Programme, the IPU may provide expert advice on the structure of legislative bodies, staff training, and parliamentary working procedures, and provide technical equipment and other resources. The IPU provided technical assistance for the drafting of Timor-Leste's Constitution, which was adopted by the then East Timor Constituent Assembly in March 2002. The IPU aims to establish a Parliamentary Resource Centre at its headquarters.

IPU teams of observers have overseen elections in Namibia, in 1989, in Cambodia (1993), and in El Salvador (1994). Their duties included observing the process of voter registration, the election campaign and voting, and verifying the results. In 1993 the Council resolved that the IPU be present at all national elections organized, supervised or verified by the United Nations. The IPU has reported on the rights and responsibilities of election observers and issued guide-lines on the holding of free and fair elections. These include a *Declaration on Criteria for Free and Fair Elections*, together with a study on the subject, and Codes of Conduct for Elections. In January 2005 IPU observers world-wide monitored the expatriate vote in the elections for the Transitional National Assembly in Iraq.

The IPU maintains a special database (PARLINE) on parliaments of the world, giving access to information on the structure and functioning of all existing parliaments, and on national elections. It conducts regular world studies on matters regarding the structure and functioning of parliaments. It also maintains a separate database (PARLIT) comprising literature from around the world on constitutional, electoral and parliamentary matters.

In August–September 2000 the IPU organized the first international conference of presiding officers of national parliaments. The second speakers' conference was scheduled to take place in late 2005.

INTERNATIONAL PEACE AND SECURITY

The IPU aims to promote conflict resolution and international security through political discussion. Certain areas of conflict are monitored by the Union on an ongoing basis (for example, Cyprus and the Middle East), while others are considered as they arise. In the 1990s the IPU was particularly concerned with the situation in the former Yugoslavia, and condemned incidents of violations of humanitarian law and supported efforts to improve the lives of those affected by the conflict. A meeting in July 2003 of Israeli and Palestinian parliamentarians agreed to establish an Israeli-Palestinian parliamentary working group on co-operation. In April 2003 the 108th Inter-Parliamentary Conference adopted a resolution urging an end to the unilateral military action against Iraq launched in March by a US-led coalition. The resolution also emphasized the importance of international law and urged full co-operation with the United Nations. In October 2004 the Assembly discussed an emergency item on the need for parliamentary action to restore peace and security in Iraq. An extensive programme of activities is undertaken by the IPU with regard to the Mediterranean region. In June 1992 the first Conference on Security and Co-operation in the Mediterranean (CSCM) took place; the objectives outlined at the Conference have been integrated as a structured process of the IPU. A second CSCM was held in Valletta, Malta, in November 1995, and a third was convened at Marseilles, France, in March–April 2000. Intermediary thematic meetings are held between plenary conferences, while consultations among parties to the CSCM process take place every six months. In February 2005 participants attending the fourth CSCM, held in Nafplion, Greece, agreed to terminate the process and establish in its place a Parliamentary Assembly of the

Mediterranean. The inaugural session of the Assembly was provisionally scheduled to be convened in Jordan, in late 2005.

The IPU has worked constantly to promote international and regional efforts towards disarmament, as part of the process of enhancing peace and security. Issues that have been discussed by the Assembly include nuclear non-proliferation, a ban on testing of nuclear weapons, and a global register of arms transfers.

SUSTAINABLE DEVELOPMENT

The Standing Committee for Sustainable Development, Finance and Trade guides the IPU's work in this area, with a broad approach of linking economic growth with social, democratic, human welfare and environmental considerations. Issues of world economic and social development on which the IPU has approved recommendations include employment in a globalizing world, the globalization of economy and liberalization of trade, Third World debt and its impact on the integration of those countries affected into the process of globalization, international mass migration and other demographic problems, and the right to food. The IPU co-operates with programmes and agencies of the UN, in particular in the preparation of major socio-economic conferences, including the World Summit for Social Development, which was held in Copenhagen, Denmark, in March 1995, the Fourth World Conference on Women, held in Beijing, People's Republic of China, in September 1995, and the World Food Summit, held in Rome, Italy, in November 1996. In September 1996 a tripartite meeting of parliamentary, governmental and inter-governmental representatives, convened at the UN headquarters in New York, considered legislative measures to pursue the objectives of the World Summit for Social Development; a follow-up meeting was held in March 1999. In November–December 1998 the IPU, in co-operation with FAO, organized an Inter-Parliamentary Conference concerned with 'Attaining the World Food Summit's Objectives through a Sustainable Development Strategy'. The IPU assisted with preparations for the World Food Summit: Five Years Later, held in Rome, Italy, in June 2002. In February 2003 the IPU and the European Parliament jointly organized a parliamentary conference on the WTO, which addressed issues including access to markets, the development dimension of the multilateral trading system, agriculture and subsidies. The conference aimed to add a parliamentary dimension to multilateral co-operation on trade matters and thereby to enhance the transparency of the WTO's activities and to strengthen democracy at international level.

Activities to protect the environment are undertaken within the framework of sustainable development. In 1984 the first Inter-Parliamentary Conference on the Environment, convened in Nairobi, Kenya, advocated the inclusion of environmental considerations into the development process. The IPU was actively involved in the preparation of the UN Conference on Environment and Development (UNCED), which was held in Rio de Janeiro, Brazil, in June 1992. Subsequently the IPU's environment programme has focused on implementing the recommendations of UNCED, and identifying measures to be taken at parliamentary level to facilitate that process. The IPU also monitors the actual measures taken by national parliaments to pursue the objective of sustainable development, as well as emerging environmental problems. In 1997 the IPU published the *World Directory of Parliamentary Bodies for Environment*. In April 2005 the Assembly held an emergency debate on the role of parliaments in the prevention of natural disasters and the protection of vulnerable groups.

HUMAN RIGHTS AND HUMANITARIAN LAW

The IPU aims to incorporate human rights concerns, including employment, the rights of minorities, and gender issues, in all areas of activity. The Assembly and specialized meetings of parliamentarians frequently consider and make relevant recommendations on human rights issues. A five-member Committee on the Human Rights of Parliamentarians is responsible for the consideration of complaints relating to alleged violations of the human rights of members of parliament, for example state harassment, arbitrary arrest and detention, unfair trail and violation of parliamentary immunity, based on a procedure adopted by the IPU in 1976. The Committee conducts hearings and site missions to investigate a complaint and communicates with the authorities of the country concerned. If no settlement is reached at that stage, the Committee may then publish a report for the Governing Council and submit recommendations on specific measures to be adopted. In early 2004 the Committee was addressing 48 cases of allegations of human rights violations against 190 current or former members of parliament in 28 countries.

The IPU works closely with the International Committee of the Red Cross to uphold respect for international humanitarian law. It supports the implementation of the Geneva Conventions and their Additional Protocols, and the adoption of appropriate national legislation. In 1995 the Council adopted a special resolution to establish a reporting mechanism at the parliamentary level to ensure respect for international humanitarian law. Consequently IPU initiated a world survey on legislative action regarding the application of international humanitarian law, as well as efforts to ban anti-personnel land-mines. In April and September 1998 the Council adopted special resolutions on parliamentary action to secure the entry into force and implementation of the Convention on the Prohibition of the Use, Stockpiling, Production and Transfer of Anti-personnel Mines and on their Destruction, which was signed by representatives of some 120 countries meeting in Ottawa, Canada, in December 1997. Further resolutions to that effect were adopted by the Inter-Parliamentary Conference in October 1999 and in April 2001.

In 1998 the IPU published a *World Directory of Parliamentary Human Rights Bodies*

WOMEN IN POLITICS

The IPU aims to promote the participation of women in the political and parliamentary decision-making processes, and, more generally, in all aspects of society. It organizes debates and events on these issues and compiles a statistical database on women in politics, compiled by regular world surveys. The IPU also actively addresses wider issues of concern to women, such as literacy and education, women in armed conflicts, women's contribution to development, and women in the electoral process. The eradication of violence against women was the subject of a special resolution adopted by the Conference in 1991. The Meeting of Women MPs has monitored efforts by national authorities to implement the recommendations outlined in the resolution. In 1996 the IPU promoted the Framework for Model Legislation on Domestic Violence, formulated by the UN Special Rapporteur on the issue, which aimed to assist national parliaments in preparing legislation to safeguard women. At the Fourth World Conference on Women, held in Beijing, in September 1995, the IPU organized several events to bring together parliamentarians and other leading experts, diplomats and officials to promote the rights of women and of children. In February 1997 the IPU organized a Specialized Inter-Parliamentary Conference, in New Delhi, India, entitled 'Towards partnership between men and women in politics'. Following the Conference the IPU decided to establish a Gender Partnership Group, comprising two men and two women, within the Executive Committee, to ensure that IPU activities and decisions serve the interests and needs of all members of the population. The Group was authorized to report to the IPU Council.

The IPU aims to promote the importance of women's role in economic and social development and their participation in politics as a democratic necessity, and recognizes the crucial role of the media in presenting the image of women. Within the context of the 1997 New Delhi Conference, the IPU organized a second Round Table on the Image of Women Politicians in the Media (the first having been convened in November 1989). The debate urged fair and equal representation of women politicians by the media and for governments to revise their communications policies to advance the image of female parliamentarians.

EDUCATION, SCIENCE AND CULTURE

Activities in these sectors are often subject to consideration by statutory meetings of the Assembly. Assembly resolutions have focused on the implementation of educational and cultural policies designed to foster greater respect for demographic values, adopted in April 1993; on bioethics and its implications world-wide for human rights protection, adopted in April 1995; and on the importance of education and culture as prerequisites for securing sustainable development (with particular emphasis on the education of women and the application of new information technologies), necessitating their high priority status in national budgets, adopted in April 2001. Specialized meetings organized by the IPU have included the Asia and Pacific Inter-Parliamentary Conference on 'Science and technology for regional sustainable development', held in Tokyo, Japan, in June 1994, and the Inter-Parliamentary Conference on 'Education, science, culture and communication on the threshold of the 21st century', organized jointly with UNESCO, and held in Paris, France, in June 1996. In October 2003 the IPU and UNESCO launched a network of national focal points linking the IPU's member parliaments and UNESCO, with the aim of circulating information and improving co-operation in the area of education, science, culture and communications.

Finance

The IPU is financed by its members from public funds. The 2004 annual budget totalled 9.9m. Swiss francs. In addition external financial support, primarily from UNDP, is received for some special activities.

Publications

Activities of the Inter-Parliamentary Union (annually).

IPU Information Brochure (annually).

World Directory of Parliaments (annually).

The World of Parliaments (quarterly).

Other handbooks, reports and surveys, documents, proceedings of the Assembly.

ISLAMIC DEVELOPMENT BANK

Address: POB 5925, Jeddah 21432, Saudi Arabia.

Telephone: (2) 6361400; **fax:** (2) 6366871; **e-mail:** idbarchives@isdb.org.sa; **internet:** www.isdb.org.

The Bank was established following a conference of Ministers of Finance of member countries of the Organization of the Islamic Conference (OIC), held in Jeddah in December 1973. Its aim is to encourage the economic development and social progress of member countries and of Muslim communities in non-member countries, in accordance with the principles of the Islamic *Shari'a* (sacred law). The Bank formally opened in October 1975. The Bank and its associated entities—the Islamic Research and Training Institute, the Islamic Corporation for the Development of the Private Sector, and the Islamic Corporation for the Insurance of Investment and Export Credit—constitute the Islamic Development Bank Group.

MEMBERS

There are 55 members.

Organization

(April 2005)

BOARD OF GOVERNORS

Each member country is represented by a governor, usually its Minister of Finance, and an alternate. The Board of Governors is the supreme authority of the Bank, and meets annually. The 29th meeting was held in Tehran, Iran, in September 2004, and the 30th meeting was scheduled to be convened in Kuala Lumpur, Malaysia, in June 2005.

BOARD OF EXECUTIVE DIRECTORS

The Board consists of 14 members, seven of whom are appointed by the seven largest subscribers to the capital stock of the Bank; the remaining seven are elected by Governors representing the other subscribers. Members of the Board of Executive Directors are elected for three-year terms. The Board is responsible for the direction of the general operations of the Bank.

ADMINISTRATION

In addition to the President of the Bank, there are three Vice-Presidents, responsible for Operations, Trade and Policy, and Corporate Resources and Services.

President of the Bank and Chairman of the Board of Executive Directors: Dr AHMED MOHAMED ALI.

Vice-President Operations: Dr AMADOU BOUBACAR CISSE.

Vice-President Trade and Policy: Dr SYED JAAFAR AZNAN.

Vice-President Corporate Resources and Services: MUZAFAR AL HAJ MUZAFAR.

REGIONAL OFFICES

Kazakhstan: 65/69 Naurizbay St, 480091 Almaty; tel. (3272) 62-35-55; fax (3272) 62-34-11; e-mail idb-roa@nursat.kz; Dir NIK ZEINAL ABIDIN.

Malaysia: Banguan Bank Industri & Teknologi, 13th Floor, 1016 Jalan Sultan Ismail, POB 13671, 50818 Kuala Lumpur; tel. (3) 2946627; fax (3) 2946626; e-mail idbkul@po.jaring.my; Dir AHMAD SALEH HARIRI.

Morocco: 177 Ave John Kennedy, Souissi 10105, POB 5003, Rabat; tel. (7) 757191; fax (7) 775726; Dir HANI SALIM SUNBUL.

FINANCIAL STRUCTURE

The Bank's unit of account is the Islamic Dinar (ID), which is equivalent to the value of one Special Drawing Right of the IMF (SDR 1 = US \$1.52188 at 18 January 2005). In 2001 the Bank's Board of Governors approved an increase in the authorized capital from ID 6,000m. to ID 15,000m. Subscribed capital was increased from ID 4,100m. to ID 8,100m. At 20 February 2004 total subscriptions amounted to ID 7,960.71m.

SUBSCRIPTIONS

(million Islamic Dinars, as at 20 February 2004)

Afghanistan	5.00	Malaysia	. .	157.89
Albania	2.50	Maldives	. .	2.50
Algeria	124.67	Mali	. .	9.76
Azerbaijan	9.76	Mauritania	. .	9.76
Bahrain	13.89	Morocco	. .	49.24
Bangladesh	97.82	Mozambique	. .	4.96
Benin	9.76	Niger	. .	24.63
Brunei	24.63	Oman	. .	27.35
Burkina Faso	24.63	Pakistan	. .	246.59
Cameroon	24.63	Palestine	. .	9.85
Chad	9.76	Qatar	. .	97.70
Comoros	2.50	Saudi Arabia	. .	1,987.87
Côte d'Ivoire	2.50	Senegal	. .	24.65
Djibouti	2.50	Sierra Leone	. .	4.96
Egypt	686.84	Somalia	. .	2.50
Gabon	29.32	Sudan	. .	39.07
The Gambia	4.96	Suriname	. .	4.96
Guinea	24.63	Syria	. .	9.92
Guinea-Bissau	4.96	Tajikistan	. .	4.96
Indonesia	185.47	Togo	. .	4.96
Iran	694.51	Tunisia	. .	19.55
Iraq	13.05	Turkey	. .	626.05
Jordan	39.47	Turkmenistan	. .	2.50
Kazakhstan	4.96	Uganda	. .	24.63
Kuwait	985.88	United Arab		
Kyrgyzstan	4.96	Emirates	. .	561.67
Lebanon	9.76	Uzbekistan	. .	2.50
Libya	793.79	Yemen	. .	49.62

Activities

The Bank adheres to the Islamic principle forbidding usury, and does not grant loans or credits for interest. Instead, its methods of project financing are: provision of interest-free loans (with a service fee), mainly for infrastructural projects which are expected to have a marked impact on long-term socio-economic development; provision of technical assistance (e.g. for feasibility studies); equity participation in industrial and agricultural projects; leasing operations, involving the leasing of equipment such as ships, and instalment sale financing; and profit-sharing operations. Funds not immediately needed for projects are used for foreign trade financing. Under the Import Trade Financing Operations (ITFO) scheme, funds are used for importing commodities for development purposes (i.e. raw materials and intermediate industrial goods, rather than consumer goods), with priority given to the import of goods from other member countries (see table). The Export Financing Scheme (EFS), established as the Longer-term Trade Financing Scheme (LTTFS) in 1987/88, aims to provide financing for the export of non-traditional and capital goods. A special programme under the EFS became operational in AH 1419, on the basis of a memorandum of understanding signed between the Bank and the Arab Bank for Economic Development in Africa (BADEA), to finance Arab exports to non-Arab League members of the OAU (now African Union).

The Bank's Special Assistance Programme was initiated in AH 1400 to support the economic and social development of Muslim communities in non-member countries, in particular in the education and health sectors. It also aimed to provide emergency aid in times of natural disasters, and to assist Muslim refugees throughout the world. Operations undertaken by the Bank are financed by the Waqf Fund (formerly the Special Assistance Account). Other assistance activities include scholarship programmes, technical co-operation projects and the sacrificial meat utilization project. In early 2004 some US \$201m. was approved for reconstruction projects following the devastating earthquake that occurred in Bam, eastern

Iran, in December. In January 2005 the Bank allocated $500m. to assist the survivors of the Indian Ocean earthquake and *tsunami* which struck coastal areas in 11 countries in late December 2004. The Bank announced that it was to dispatch missions to provide emergency relief to Indonesia, the Maldives and Sri Lanka, and planned to send further teams to assess the requirements for reconstruction. The Bank increasingly has worked to assist post-conflict member countries in rehabilitation and reconstruction. It is a member of the management committee of the Afghanistan Reconstruction Trust Fund, which was established in 2001, and in AH 1424 the Bank approved an operation to assist Afghan refugees. In December 2003 the Bank approved a Programme for Reconstruction of Iraq, with funding of ID 365.5m. ($500m.) to be implemented over a five-year period. In October 2002 the Bank's Board of Governors, meeting in Burkina Faso, adopted the Ouagadougou Declaration on the co-operation between the Bank group and Africa, which identified priority areas for Bank activities, for example education and the private sector. The Bank pledged $2,000m. to finance implementation of the Declaration over the five years 2004–08.

By 20 February 2004 the Bank had approved a total of ID 9,648.39m. for project financing and technical assistance since operations began in 1976, ID 16,038.96m. for foreign trade financing, and ID 450.78m. for special assistance operations, excluding amounts for cancelled operations. During the Islamic year 1424 (4 March 2003 to 20 February 2004) the Bank approved a net total of ID 2,799.93m., for 344 operations.

The Bank approved 53 loans in the year ending 20 February 2004, amounting to ID 236.53m. These loans supported projects concerned with the education and health sectors, infrastructural improvements, and agricultural developments. During the year ending 20 February 2004 the Bank's disbursements totalled ID 1,350.84m., bringing the total cumulative disbursements since the Bank began operations to ID 18,142.45m.

During the Islamic Year 1424 the Bank approved ID 162.42m. for 13 projects co-financed with other institutions, amounting to 25% of the total cost of the projects.

OPERATIONS APPROVED, ISLAMIC YEAR 1424
(4 March 2003–20 February 2004)

Type of operation	Number of operations	Total amount (million Islamic Dinars)
Ordinary operations	122	931.37
Project financing . . .	98	923.27
Technical assistance . .	24	8.10
Other project financing . .	41	411.21
Trade financing operations* .	133	1,440.65
Waqf Fund operations . . .	45	16.70
Total †	344	2,799.93

* Including ITFO, the EFS, the Islamic Bank's Portfolio, the UIF, and the Awqaf Properties Investment Fund.
† Excluding cancelled operations.

PROJECT FINANCING AND TECHNICAL ASSISTANCE BY SECTOR, ISLAMIC YEAR 1424
(4 March 2003–20 February 2004)

Sector	Number of operations	Amount (million Islamic Dinars)	%
Agriculture and agro-industry	23	133.74	16.19
Industry and mining . .	1	2.78	0.34
Transport and communications . .	17	176.49	21.36
Public utilities	22	281.99	34.13
Social sectors . . .	38	216.02	26.15
Financial services/Other* .	16	15.21	1.84
Total †	117	826.22	100.00

* Mainly approved amounts for Islamic banks.
† Excluding cancelled operations and projects financed from the International Islamic Sukuk bond issue.

During AH 1424 the Bank approved 24 technical assistance operations in the form of grants and loans, amounting to ID 8.10m., of which ID 4.81m. (59%) was for least developed member countries.

Import trade financing approved during the Islamic year 1424 amounted to ID 1,162.25m. for 88 operations in 17 member countries. By the end of that year cumulative import trade financing amounted to ID 16,807.5m., of which 41% was for imports of crude petroleum, 25% for intermediate industrial goods and 6% for refined petroleum products. By the end of AH 1424 26 member countries were participating in the EFS. At that time total export financing approved under the scheme amounted to ID 917.13m. for operations

in 19 countries. The Bank also finances other trade financing operations, including the Islamic Corporation for the Development of the Private Sector (see below), the Awqaf Properties Investment Fund and the Treasury Department. In addition, a Trade Co-operation and Promotion Programme supports efforts to enhance trade among OIC member countries.

In AH 1407 (1986–87) the Bank established an Islamic Bank's Portfolio for Investment and Development (IBP) in order to promote the development and diversification of Islamic financial markets and to mobilize the liquidity available to banks and financial institutions. During AH 1424 the IBP approved 13 operations amounting to US $161.25m. The Bank's Unit Investment Fund (UIF) became operational in 1990, with the aim of mobilizing additional resources and providing a profitable channel for investments conforming to *Shari'a*. The initial issue of the UIF was $100m., which has subsequently been increased to $325m. The Fund finances mainly private-sector industrial projects in middle-income countries and also finances short-term trade operations. In October 1998 the Bank announced the establishment of a new fund to invest in infrastructure projects in member states. The Bank committed $250m. to the fund, which was to comprise $1,000m. equity capital and a $500m. Islamic financing facility. In November 2001 the Bank signed an agreement with Malaysia, Bahrain, Indonesia and Sudan for the establishment of an Islamic financial market. In April 2002 the Bank, jointly with governors of central banks and the Accounting and Auditing Organization for Islamic Financial Institutions, concluded an agreement, under the auspices of the IMF, for the establishment of an Islamic Financial Services Board. The Board, which was to be located in Kuala Lumpur, Malaysia, was intended to elaborate and harmonize standards for best practices in the regulation and supervision of the Islamic financial services industry.

During AH 1424 the Bank approved 45 Waqf Fund operations, amounting to ID 16.69m. Of the total financing, 31 operations provided assistance for Muslim organizations and communities in 20 non-member countries.

In AH 1404 (1983–84) the Bank established a scholarship programme for Muslim communities in non-member countries to provide opportunities for students to pursue further education or other professional training. The programme also assists nine member countries on an exceptional basis. By the end of the Islamic year 1424 the programme had benefited some 6,827 students, at a cost of ID 38.10m., from 56 countries. The Merit Scholarship Programme, initiated in AH 1412 (1991–92), aims to develop scientific, technological and research capacities in member countries through advanced studies and/or research. A total of 244 scholarships had been awarded, at a cost of US $10.1m., by the end of AH 1424. In AH 1419 (1998–99) a Scholarship Programme in Science and Technology for IDB Least Developed Member Countries became operational for students in 20 eligible countries. By the end of AH 1424 120 students had been selected under the programme to study in other Bank member countries.

The Bank's Programme for Technical Co-operation aims to mobilize technical capabilities among member countries and to promote the exchange of expertise, experience and skills through expert missions, training, seminars and workshops. During AH 1424 92 projects were approved under the programme. In December 1999 the Board of Executive Directors approved two technical assistance grants to support a programme for the eradication of illiteracy in the Islamic world, and one for self-sufficiency in human vaccine production. By the end of AH 1424 11 operations amounting to ID 2.5m. had been approved under the illiteracy programme, while six projects, amounting to ID 1.5 m., had been approved under the vaccine programme. The Bank also undertakes the distribution of meat sacrificed by Muslim pilgrims. The Bank was the principal source of funding of the International Center for Biosaline Agriculture, which was established in Dubai, UAE, in September 1999.

BANK GROUP ENTITIES

Islamic Corporation for the Development of the Private Sector: POB 54069, Jeddah 21514, Saudi Arabia; tel. (2) 6441644; fax (2) 6444427; e-mail icd@isdb.org; internet www.icd-idb.org; f. 1999 to identify opportunities in the private sector, provide financial products and services compatible with Islamic law, mobilize additional resources for the private sector in member countries, and encourage the development of Islamic financing and capital markets; auth. cap. ID 675.2m. (of which the Bank's share is 50%, member countries 30% and public financial institutions of member countries 20%), subscribed cap. ID 337.6m. (July 2004); mems: 42 countries, the Bank, and five public financial institutions (a further seven countries have signed the Articles of Agreement and are in the process of ratification); CEO and Gen. Man. Dr ALI A. SULAIMAN.

Islamic Corporation for the Insurance of Investment and Export Credit (ICIEC): POB 15722, Jeddah 21454, Saudi Arabia; tel. (2) 6445666; fax (2) 6379504; e-mail idb.iciec@isdb.org.sa; internet www.iciec.com; f. 1994; aims to promote trade and the flow of investments among member countries of the OIC through the provision of export credit and investment insurance services; auth. cap. ID 100m., subscribed cap. ID 97.0m. (July 2004); mems: 34 member states and the Islamic Development Bank (which contributes 50% of its capital); Man. Dr ABDEL RAHMAN A. TAHA.

Islamic Research and Training Institute: POB 9201, Jeddah 21413, Saudi Arabia; tel. (2) 6361400; fax (2) 6378927; e-mail maljarhi@isdb.org.sa; internet www.irti.org; f. 1982 to undertake research enabling economic, financial and banking activities to conform to Islamic law, and to provide training for staff involved in

development activities in the Bank's member countries; the Institute also organizes seminars and workshops, and holds training courses aimed at furthering the expertise of government and financial officials in Islamic developing countries; Deputy Dir BASHIR ALI KHALLAT; publs *Annual Report*, *Islamic Economic Studies* (2 a year), various research studies, monographs, reports.

Publication

Annual Report.

LATIN AMERICAN INTEGRATION ASSOCIATION—LAIA
(ASOCIACIÓN LATINOAMERICANA DE INTEGRACIÓN—ALADI)

Address: Cebollatí 1461, Casilla 577, 11200 Montevideo, Uruguay.
Telephone: (2) 410-1121; **fax:** (2) 419-0649; **e-mail:** sgaladi@aladi .org; **internet:** www.aladi.org.

The Latin American Integration Association was established in August 1980 to replace the Latin American Free Trade Association, founded in February 1960.

MEMBERS

Argentina	Colombia	Paraguay
Bolivia	Cuba	Peru
Brazil	Ecuador	Uruguay
Chile	Mexico	Venezuela

Observers: People's Republic of China, Costa Rica, Dominican Republic, El Salvador, Guatemala, Honduras, Italy, Japan, Republic of Korea, Nicaragua, Panama, Portugal, Romania, Russia, Spain and Switzerland; also the UN Economic Commission for Latin America and the Caribbean (ECLAC), the UN Development Programme (UNDP), the European Union, the Inter-American Development Bank, the Organization of American States, the Andean Development Corporation, the Inter-American Institute for Co-operation on Agriculture, the Latin American Economic System, and the Pan American Health Organization.

Organization

(April 2005)

COUNCIL OF MINISTERS

The Council of Ministers of Foreign Affairs is responsible for the adoption of the Association's policies. It meets when convened by the Committee of Representatives.

EVALUATION AND CONVERGENCE CONFERENCE

The Conference, comprising plenipotentiaries of the member governments, assesses the Association's progress and encourages negotiations between members. It meets when convened by the Committee of Representatives.

COMMITTEE OF REPRESENTATIVES

The Committee, the permanent political body of the Association, comprises a permanent and a deputy representative from each member country. Permanent observers have been accredited by 15 countries and eight international organizations (see above). The Committee is the main forum for the negotiation of ALADI's initiatives and is responsible for the correct implementation of the Treaty and its supplementary regulations. There are the following auxiliary bodies:

Advisory Commission for Financial and Monetary Affairs.

Advisory Commission on Customs Valuation.

Advisory Council for Enterprises.

Advisory Council for Export Financing.

Advisory Council for Customs Matters.

Budget Commission.

Commission for Technical Support and Co-operation.

Council for Financial and Monetary Affairs: comprises the Presidents of member states' central banks, who examine all aspects of financial, monetary and exchange co-operation.

Council of National Customs Directors.

Council on Transport for Trade Facilitation.

Labour Advisory Council.

Nomenclature Advisory Commission.

Sectoral Councils.

Tourism Council.

GENERAL SECRETARIAT

The General Secretariat is the technical body of the Association; it submits proposals for action, carries out research and evaluates activities. The Secretary-General is elected for a three-year term, which is renewable. There are two Assistant Secretaries-General.

Secretary-General: Dr DIDIER OPERTTI BADÁN (Uruguay).

Activities

The Latin American Free Trade Association (LAFTA) was an intergovernmental organization, created by the Treaty of Montevideo in February 1960 with the object of increasing trade between the Contracting Parties and of promoting regional integration, thus contributing to the economic and social development of the member countries. The Treaty provided for the gradual establishment of a free-trade area, which would form the basis for a Latin American Common Market. Reduction of tariff and other trade barriers was to be carried out gradually until 1980.

By 1980, however, only 14% of annual trade among members could be attributed to LAFTA agreements, and it was the richest states which were receiving most benefit. In June it was decided that LAFTA should be replaced by a less ambitious and more flexible organization, the Latin American Integration Association (Asociación Latinoamericana de Integración—ALADI), established by the 1980 Montevideo Treaty, which came into force in March 1981, and was fully ratified in March 1982. The Treaty envisaged an area of economic preferences, comprising a regional tariff preference for goods originating in member states (in effect from 1 July 1984) and regional and partial scope agreements (on economic complementation, trade promotion, trade in agricultural goods, scientific and technical co-operation, the environment, tourism, and other matters), taking into account the different stages of development of the members, and with no definite timetable for the establishment of a full common market.

The members of ALADI are divided into three categories: most developed (Argentina, Brazil and Mexico); intermediate (Chile, Colombia, Peru, Uruguay and Venezuela); and least developed (Bolivia, Cuba—which joined the Association in August 1999, Ecuador and Paraguay), enjoying a special preferential system. By 2003 intra-ALADI exports were estimated to total US $42,880m., an increase of 11% compared with the previous year, representing some 17% of the total value of the region's trade.

Certain LAFTA institutions were retained and adapted by ALADI, e.g. the Reciprocal Payments and Credits Agreement (1965, modified in 1982) and the Multilateral Credit Agreement to Alleviate Temporary Shortages of Liquidity, known as the Santo Domingo Agreement (1969, extended in 1981 to include mechanisms for counteracting global balance-of-payments difficulties and for assisting in times of natural disaster).

By August 1998 98 agreements had entered into force. Seven were 'regional agreements' (in which all member countries participate). These agreements included a regional tariff preference agreement, whereby members allow imports from other member states to enter with tariffs 20% lower than those imposed on imports from other countries, and a Market Opening Lists agreement in favour of the three least developed member states, which provides for the total elimination of duties and other restrictions on imports of certain products. The remaining 91 agreements were 'partial scope agreements' (in which two or more member states participate), including: renegotiation agreements (pertaining to tariff cuts under LAFTA); trade agreements covering particular industrial sectors; the agreements establishing (Mercosur) and the Group of Three (G3); and agreements covering agriculture, gas supply, tourism, environmental protection, books, transport, sanitation and trade facilitation. A new system of tariff nomenclature, based on the 'harmonized system', was adopted from 1 January 1990 as a basis for common trade negotiations and statistics. General regimes on safeguards and rules of origin entered into force in 1987.

The Secretariat convenes meetings of entrepreneurs in various private industrial sectors, to encourage regional trade and co-operation. In early 2001 ALADI conducted a survey on small and medium-sized enterprises in order to advise the Secretary-General in formulating a programme to assist those businesses and enhance their competitiveness.

A feature of ALADI is its 'outward' projection, allowing for multilateral links or agreements with Latin American non-member countries or integration organizations, and with other developing countries or economic groups outside the continent. In February 1994 the Council of Ministers of Foreign Affairs urged that ALADI should become the co-ordinating body for the various bilateral, multilateral and regional accords (with the Andean Community, Mercosur and G3, etc.), with the aim of eventually forming a region-wide common market. The General Secretariat initiated studies in preparation for a programme to undertake this co-ordinating work. At the same meeting in February there was a serious disagreement regarding the proposed adoption of a protocol to the Montevideo Treaty to enable Mexico to participate in the North American Free Trade Agreement (NAFTA), while remaining a member of ALADI. Brazil, in particular, opposed such a solution. However, in June the first Interpretative Protocol to the Montevideo Treaty was signed by the Ministers of Foreign Affairs: the Protocol allows member states to establish preferential trade agreements with developed nations, with a temporary waiver of the most-favoured nation clause (article 44 of the Treaty), subject to the negotiation of unilateral compensation.

Mercosur (which comprises Argentina, Brazil, Paraguay and Uruguay, with Chile and Bolivia as associate members) aims to conclude free-trade agreements with the other members of ALADI. In March 2001 ALADI signed a co-operation agreement with the Andean Community to facilitate the exchange of information and consolidate regional and subregional integration. In December 2003 Mercosur and the Andean Community signed an Economic Complementary Agreement, and in April 2004 concluded a free-trade agreement, to come into effect on 1 July 2004 (although later postponed). Those ALADI member states remaining outside Mercosur and the Andean Community—Cuba, Chile and Mexico—would be permitted to apply to join the envisaged larger free-trade zone.

Publications

Empresarios en la Integración (monthly, in Spanish).
Noticias ALADI (monthly, in Spanish).
Estadísticas y Comercio (quarterly, in Spanish).
Reports, studies, brochures, texts of agreements.

LEAGUE OF ARAB STATES

Address: POB 11642, Arab League Bldg, Tahrir Square, Cairo, Egypt.

Telephone: (2) 575-0511; **fax:** (2) 574-0331; **internet:** www.arableagueonline.org/arableague/index.jsp.

The League of Arab States (more generally known as the Arab League) is a voluntary association of sovereign Arab states, designed to strengthen the close ties linking them and to co-ordinate their policies and activities and direct them towards the common good of all the Arab countries. It was founded in March 1945.

MEMBERS

Algeria	Lebanon	Somalia
Bahrain	Libya*	Sudan
Comoros	Mauritania	Syria
Djibouti	Morocco	Tunisia
Egypt	Oman	United Arab
Iraq	Palestine†	Emirates
Jordan	Qatar	Yemen
Kuwait	Saudi Arabia	

* In October 2002 Libya announced that it was to withdraw from the League.

† Palestine is considered an independent state, and therefore a full member of the League.

Organization

(April 2005)

COUNCIL

The supreme organ of the Arab League, the Council consists of representatives of the member states, each of which has one vote, and a representative for Palestine. The Council meets ordinarily every March, normally at the League headquarters, at the level of heads of state ('kings, heads of state and emirs'), and in March and September at the level of foreign ministers. The summit-level meeting reviews all issues related to Arab national security strategies, co-ordinates supreme policies of the Arab states towards regional and international issues, reviews recommendations and reports submitted to it by meetings at foreign minister level, appoints the Secretary-General of the League, and is mandated to amend the League's Charter. Decisions of the summit-level Council are passed on a consensus basis. Foreign ministers' meetings assess the implementation of summit resolutions, prepare relevant reports, and make arrangements for subsequent summits. Committees comprising a smaller group of foreign ministers may be appointed to follow up closely summit resolutions. Extraordinary summit-level meetings may be held at the request of one member state or the Secretary-General, if approved by a two-thirds majority of member states. Extraordinary sessions of ministers of foreign affairs may, be held at the request of two member states or of the Secretary-General. The presidency of ordinary meetings is rotated in accordance with the alphabetical order of the League's member states. Unanimous decisions of the Council are binding upon all member states of the League; majority decisions are binding only on those states which have accepted them.

The Council is supported by technical and specialized committees advising on financial and administrative affairs, information affairs and legal affairs. In addition, specialized ministerial councils have been established to formulate common policies for the regulation and the advancement of co-operation in the following sectors: communications; electricity; environment; health; housing and construction; information; interior; justice; social affairs; tourism; transportation; and youth and sports.

GENERAL SECRETARIAT

The administrative and financial offices of the League. The Secretariat carries out the decisions of the Council, and provides financial and administrative services for the personnel of the League. General departments comprise: the Bureau of the Secretary-General, Arab Affairs, Economic Affairs, Information Affairs, Legal Affairs, Palestine Affairs, Political International Affairs, Military Affairs, Social Affairs, Administrative and Financial Affairs, and Internal Audit. In addition, there is a Documentation and Information Centre, an Arab League Centre in Tunis, an Arab Fund for Technical Assistance in African States, a Higher Arab Institute for Translation in Algiers, a Music Academy in Baghdad, and a Special Bureau for Boycotting Israel, based in Damascus, Syria (see below). The following bodies have also been established: an administrative court, an investment arbitration board and a higher auditing board.

The Secretary-General is appointed at summit meetings of the Council by a two-thirds' majority of the member states, for a five-year, renewable term. He appoints the Assistant Secretaries-General and principal officials, with the approval of the Council. He has the rank of ambassador, and the Assistant Secretaries-General have the rank of ministers plenipotentiary.

Secretary-General: Amr Muhammad Moussa (Egypt).

DEFENCE AND ECONOMIC CO-OPERATION

Groups established under the Treaty of Joint Defence and Economic Co-operation, concluded in 1950 to complement the Charter of the League.

Arab Unified Military Command: f. 1964 to co-ordinate military policies for the liberation of Palestine.

Economic and Social Council: compares and co-ordinates the economic policies of the member states; supervises the activities of the Arab League's specialized agencies. The Council is composed of ministers of economic affairs or their deputies; decisions are taken by majority vote. The first meeting was held in 1953. In February 1997 the Economic and Social Council adopted the Executive Programme of the League's (1981) Agreement to Facilitate and Develop Trade Among Arab Countries, with a view to establishing a Greater Arab Free Trade Area (see below).

Joint Defence Council: supervises implementation of those aspects of the treaty concerned with common defence. Composed of foreign and defence ministers; decisions by a two-thirds majority vote of members are binding on all.

Permanent Military Commission: established 1950; composed of representatives of army general staffs; main purpose: to draw up plans of joint defence for submission to the Joint Defence Council.

ARAB DETERRENT FORCE

Created in June 1976 by the Arab League Council to supervise successive attempts to cease hostilities in Lebanon, and afterwards to maintain the peace. The mandate of the Force has been successively renewed. The Arab League summit conference in October 1976 agreed that costs were to be paid in the following percentage contributions: Saudi Arabia and Kuwait 20% each, the United Arab Emirates 15%, Qatar 10% and other Arab states 35%.

OTHER INSTITUTIONS OF THE LEAGUE

Other bodies established by resolutions adopted by the Council of the League:

Administrative Tribunal of the Arab League: f. 1964; began operations 1966.

Arab Fund for Technical Assistance to African Countries: f. 1975 to provide technical assistance for development projects by providing African and Arab experts, grants for scholarships and training, and finance for technical studies.

Higher Auditing Board: comprises representatives of seven member states, elected every three years; undertakes financial and administrative auditing duties.

Investment Arbitration Board: examines disputes between member states relating to capital investments.

Special Bureau for Boycotting Israel: POB 437, Damascus, Syria; f. 1951 to prevent trade between Arab countries and Israel, and to enforce a boycott by Arab countries of companies outside the region that conduct trade with Israel.

SPECIALIZED AGENCIES

All member states of the Arab League are also members of the Specialized Agencies, which constitute an integral part of the Arab League. (See also entries on Arab Fund for Economic and Social Development, the Arab Monetary Fund, Council of Arab Economic Unity and the Organization of Arab Petroleum Exporting Countries.)

Arab Academy for Science, Technology and Maritime Transport—AASTMT: POB 1029, Alexandria, Egypt; tel. (3) 5622388; fax (3) 5622525; internet www.aast.edu; f. 1975 as Arab Maritime Transport Academy; provides specialized training in marine transport, engineering, technology and management; Dir-Gen. Dr GAMAL ED-DIN MOUKHTAR; publs *Maritime Research Bulletin* (monthly), *Journal of the Arab Academy for Science Technology and Maritime Transport* (2 a year).

Arab Administrative Development Organization—ARADO: 2 El Hegaz St, POB 2692 Al-Horreia, Heliopolis, Cairo, Egypt; tel. (2) 2587744; fax (2) 2580077; e-mail arado@arado.org; internet www .arado.org.eg; f. 1961 (as Arab Organization of Administrative Sciences), became operational in 1969; administration development, training, consultancy, research and studies, information, documentation; promotes Arab and international co-operation in administrative sciences; includes Arab Network of Administrative Information; 20 Arab state members; library of 26,000 volumes, 400 periodicals; Dir-Gen. Dr MUHAMMAD IBRAHIM AT-TWEGRI; publs *Arab Journal of Administration* (biannual), *Management Newsletter* (quarterly), research series, training manuals.

Arab Atomic Energy Agency—AAEA: POB 402, al-Manzah 1004, 1004 Tunis, Tunisia; tel. (71) 800099; fax (71) 781820; e-mail aaea@ aaea.org.tn; f. 1988 to co-ordinate research into the peaceful uses of atomic energy; Dir-Gen. Prof. Dr MAHMOUD NASREDDINE (Lebanon);

publs *The Atom and Development* (quarterly), other publs in the field of nuclear sciences and their applications in industry, biology, medicine, agriculture, food irradiation and seawater desalination.

Arab Bank for Economic Development in Africa (Banque arabe pour le développement économique en Afrique—BADEA): Sayed Abd ar-Rahman el-Mahdi St, POB 2640, Khartoum 11111, Sudan; tel. (11) 773646; fax (11) 770600; e-mail badea@badea.org; internet www.badea.org; f. 1973 by Arab League; provides loans and grants to African countries to finance development projects; paid-up cap. US $1,500m. (Dec. 2003); in 2003 the Bank approved loans and grants totalling $140m.; by the end of 2003 total loans and grants approved since funding activities began in 1975 amounted to $2,485m.; subscribing countries: all countries of Arab League, except the Comoros, Djibouti, Somalia and Yemen; recipient countries: all countries of the African Union, except those belonging to the Arab League; Chair. AHMAD ABDALLAH AL-AKEIL (Saudi Arabia); Dir-Gen. MEDHAT SAMI LOTFY (Egypt); publs *Annual Report Co-operation for Development* (quarterly), Studies on Afro-Arab co-operation, periodic brochures.

Arab Centre for the Study of Arid Zones and Dry Lands—ACSAD: POB 2440, Damascus, Syria; tel. (11) 5743039; fax (11) 5743063; e-mail acsad@net.sy; internet www.acsad.org; f. 1968 to conduct regional research and development programmes related to water and soil resources, plant and animal production, agrometeorology, and socio-economic studies of arid zones; the Centre holds conferences and training courses and encourages the exchange of information by Arab scientists; Dir-Gen. Prof. Dr FAROUK FARES.

Arab Industrial Development and Mining Organization: rue France, Zanagat Al Khatawat, POB 8019, Rabat, Morocco; tel. (7) 772600; fax (7) 772188; e-mail aidmo@arifonet.org.ma; internet www.arifonet.org.ma; f. 1990 by merger of Arab Industrial Development Organization, Arab Organization for Mineral Resources and Arab Organization for Standardization and Metrology; comprises a 13-member Executive Council, a High Consultative Committee of Standardization, a High Committee of Mineral Resources and a Co-ordination Committee for Arab Industrial Research Centres; a Ministerial Council, of ministers of member states responsible for industry, meets every two years; Dir-Gen. TALA'AT BEN DAFER; publs *Arab Industrial Development* (monthly and quarterly newsletters).

Arab Labour Organization: POB 814, Cairo, Egypt; tel. (2) 3362721; fax (2) 3484902; internet www.arab-labor.org; f. 1965 for co-operation between member states in labour problems; unification of labour legislation and general conditions of work wherever possible; research; technical assistance; social insurance; training, etc.; the organization has a tripartite structure: governments, employers and workers; Dir-Gen. IBRAHIM GUDIR; publs *ALO Bulletin* (monthly), *Arab Labour Review* (quarterly), *Legislative Bulletin* (annually), series of research reports and studies concerned with economic and social development issues in the Arab world.

Arab League Educational, Cultural and Scientific Organization—ALECSO: POB 1120, Tunis, Tunisia; tel. (71) 784-466; fax (71) 784-965; e-mail alecso@email.ati.tn; internet www.alecso.org .tn; f. 1970 to promote and co-ordinate educational, cultural and scientific activities in the Arab region; 21 mem. states; Regional units: Arab Centre for Arabization, Translation, Authorship, and Publication—Damascus, Syria; Institute of Arab Manuscripts—Cairo, Egypt; Institute of Arab Research and Studies—Cairo, Egypt; Khartoum International Institute for Arabic Language—Khartoum, Sudan; and the Arabization Co-ordination Bureau—Rabat, Morocco; Dir-Gen. Dr MONGI BOUSNINA; publs *Arab Journal of Culture* (2 a year), *Arab Journal of Education* (2 a year), *Arab Journal of Science and Information* (2 a year), *Arab Bulletin of Publications* (annually), *ALECSO Newsletter* (monthly).

Arab Organization for Agricultural Development—AOAD: St no. 7, Al-Amarat, POB 474, Khartoum, Sudan; tel. (11) 472176; fax (11) 471402; e-mail aoad@sudanmail.net; internet www.aoad.org; f. 1970; began operations in 1972 to contribute to co-operation in agricultural activities, and in the development of natural and human resources for agriculture; compiles data, conducts studies, training and food security programmes; includes Information and Documentation Centre, Arab Centre for Studies and Projects, and Arab Institute of Forestry and Biodiversity; Dir-Gen. Dr SALEM AL-LOZI; publs *Agricultural Statistics Yearbook Annual Report on Agricultural Development the State of Arab Food Security* (annually), *Agriculture and Development in the Arab World* (quarterly), *Accession Bulletin* (every 2 months), *AOAD Newsletter* (monthly), *Arab Agricultural Research Journal, Arab Journal for Irrigation Water Management* (2 a year).

Arab Satellite Communications Organization—ARABSAT: POB 1038, Diplomatic Quarter, Riyadh 11431, Saudi Arabia; tel. (1) 4820000; fax (1) 4887999; e-mail market@arabsat.com; internet www.arabsat.com; f. 1976; regional satellite telecommunications organization providing television, telephone and data exchange services to members and private users; operates five satellites, which cover all Arab and Western European countries; Dir-Gen. KHALID AHMED BALKHEYOUR.

Arab States Broadcasting Union—ASBU: POB 250, 1080 Tunis Cedex; 6 rue des Entrepreneurs, zone industrielle Charguia 2, Ariana Aéroport, Tunisia; tel. (71) 703854; fax (71) 704705; e-mail asbu@asbu.intl.tn; internet www.asbu.org.tn; f. 1969 to promote Arab fraternity, co-ordinate and study broadcasting subjects, to exchange expertise and technical co-operation in broadcasting; conducts training and audience research; 29 active mems, five participating mems, three assoc. mems; Exec. Chair. Dr FAYEZ AS- SAYEGH (Syria); publ. *Arab Broadcasters* (quarterly).

Inter-Arab Investment Guarantee Corporation: POB 23568, Safat 13096, Kuwait; tel. 4844500; fax 4815741; internet www.iaigc .org; f. 1975; insures Arab investors for non-commercial risks, and export credits for commercial and non-commercial risks; undertakes research and other activities to promote inter-Arab trade and investment; cap. p.u. US \$82.5m., res \$158m. (Dec. 2002); mems: 22 Arab governments; Dir-Gen. MAMOUN IBRAHIM HASSAN; publs *News Bulletin* (monthly), *Arab Investment Climate Report* (annually).

ARAB LEAGUE OFFICES AND INFORMATION CENTRES ABROAD

Established by the Arab League to co-ordinate work at all levels among Arab embassies abroad.

Austria: Kärntner Ring 17, 1010 Vienna; e-mail arab.league .vienna@aon.at.

Belgium: 28 ave de l'Uruguay, 1000 Brussels; e-mail ligue.etats .arabes@skynet.be.

China, People's Republic: 1-14-2 Lian Ma He, Tayuan Diplomatic Building, Beijing 100600; e-mail lasj@a-1.net.cn.

Ethiopia: POB 5768, Addis Ababa; e-mail arague.et@telecom.net .et.

France: 36 rue Fortuny, 75017 Paris; e-mail leap@pelnet.com.

Germany: Markgrafenstr. 25, 10117 Berlin.

India: F-63 Poorvo MargVasant Vihar, New Delhi; e-mail las@ mantraonline.com.

Italy: Piazzale delle Belle Arti 6, 00196 Rome; e-mail legaarab@ shareware.it.

Russia: 123242 Moscow, ul. Konyushkovskaya 28; e-mail ligarab@ granit.ru.

Spain: Paseo de la Castellana 180, 60°, 28046 Madrid; e-mail liga .arabe@terra.es.

Switzerland: 9 rue du Valais, 1202 Geneva; e-mail saad.alfarargi@ ties.itu.int.

United Kingdom: 52 Green St, London, W1Y 3RH.

USA: 1100 17th St, NW, Suite 602, Washington, DC 20036; 747 Third Ave, 35th Floor, New York, NY 10017 (UN Office); e-mail arableague@aol.com.

Activities

The League of Arab States was founded in 1945 with the signing of the Pact of the Arab League. A Cultural Treaty was signed in the following year. In 1952 agreements were concluded on extradition, writs, letters of request and the nationality of Arabs outside their country of origin, and in the following year a Convention was adopted on the privileges and immunities of the League. In 1954 a Nationality Agreement was concluded. At an emergency summit meeting held in 1985 two commissions were established to mediate in disagreements between Arab states (between Jordan and Syria, Iraq and Syria, Iraq and Libya, and Libya and the Palestine Liberation Organization (PLO). The League's headquarters, which had been transferred from Cairo, Egypt, to Tunis, Tunisia, in 1979, were relocated to Cairo in 1990. In 1993 the Council of the League admitted the Comoros as the League's 22nd member. At a meeting of the Council held in September 2000 foreign ministers of member states adopted an Appendix to the League's Charter that provided for the Council to meet ordinarily every March at the level of a summit conference of heads of state ('kings, heads of state and emirs'). The Council was to continue to meet at foreign ministerial level every March and September. In 2001 Amr Moussa, hitherto Egypt's minister of foreign affairs, was appointed as the League's new Secretary-General. In October 2002 Libya announced plans to withdraw from the League, although these were subsequently suspended. In April 2003 Libya reiterated its decision to terminate its membership, citing the organization's failure to take 'a firm and strong position' over the war in Iraq. (Libya's move, however, did not yet represent an official demand one year after which, under the terms of the League's Charter, its withdrawal would become effec-

tive.) In July the Egyptian Government unveiled a series of measures aimed at strengthening the League. The proposed reforms included the adoption of majority voting and the establishment of a body to resolve conflicts in the region (previously agreed at the 1996 summit and sanctioned by member states' foreign ministers in 2000). The plan, which was supported by Saudi Arabia and Jordan, was to be presented to the next summit conference. The 2004 summit meeting of Arab League heads of state, scheduled to be held in Tunis in late March, was postponed by the Tunisian Government two days in advance following disagreements among member states over a number of issues on the summit's agenda, including democratic reforms in Arab states and reforms to the League. The meeting, which was eventually held in May in Tunis, approved a *Pledge of Accord and Solidarity* that committed them to fully implementing decisions of the League. The Arab leaders also stated their commitment to conducting political, economic and social reforms, respect for human rights, and strengthening the role of women, despite continuing opposition from several member states. The 2005 heads of state summit meeting, convened in Algiers, Algeria, in mid-March, commemorated the 60th anniversary of the League's foundation.

SECURITY

In 1950 Arab League member states concluded a Joint Defence and Economic Co-operation Treaty. In 1995 the Council discussed plans for a regional court of justice and for an Arab Code of Honour to prevent the use of force in disputes between Arab states. In April 1998 Arab League ministers of the interior and justice adopted the Arab Convention for the Suppression of Terrorism, which incorporated security and judicial measures, such as extradition arrangements and the exchange of evidence. The agreement was to enter into effect 30 days after being ratified by at least seven member countries. (This was achieved in May 2000.) In August 1998 the League denounced terrorist bomb attacks against the US embassies in Kenya and Tanzania. Nevertheless, it condemned US retaliatory military action, a few days later, against suspected terrorist targets in Afghanistan and Sudan, and endorsed a request by the Sudanese Government that the Security Council investigate the incident. An emergency meeting of the League's Council, convened in mid-September 2001 in response to recent major terrorist attacks on the USA, allegedly perpetrated by militant Islamist fundamentalists, condemned the atrocities, while urging respect for the rights of Arab and Muslim US citizens. The Secretary-General subsequently emphasized the need for co-ordinated global anti-terrorist action to have clearly defined goals and to be based on sufficient consultations and secure evidence. He also deplored anti-Islamic prejudice, stated that US-led action against any Arab state would not be supported and that Israeli participation in an international anti-terrorism alliance would be unacceptable. A meeting of League foreign ministers in Doha, Qatar, in early October condemned international terrorism but did not express support for retaliatory military action by the USA and its allies. In December a further emergency meeting of League foreign affairs ministers was held to discuss the deepening Middle East crisis. In January 2002 the League appointed a commissioner responsible for promoting dialogue between civilizations. The commissioner was mandated to encourage understanding in Western countries of Arab and Muslim civilization and viewpoints, with the aim of redressing perceived negative stereotypes (especially in view of the Islamist fundamentalist connection to the September 2001 terrorist atrocities). In early April 2003 the Secretary-General expressed his regret that the Arab states had failed to prevent the ongoing war in Iraq, and urged the development of a new regional security order. In November the UN Secretary-General, Kofi Annan, appointed the Secretary-General of the League to serve as the Arab region's representative on the UN High-Level Panel on Threats, Challenges and Change.

TRADE AND ECONOMIC CO-OPERATION

In 1953 Arab League member states formed an Economic and Social Council. In 1956 an agreement was concluded on the adoption of a Common Tariff Nomenclature. In 1962 an Arab Economic Unity Agreement was concluded. The first meeting of the Council of Arab Economic Unity took place in June 1964. An Arab Common Market Agreement was endorsed by the Council in August. In February 1997 the Economic and Social Council adopted the Executive Programme of the (1981) Agreement to Facilitate and Develop Trade Among Arab Countries, with a view to creating a Greater Arab Free Trade Area (GAFTA), which aimed to facilitate and develop trade among participating countries through the reduction and eventual elimination of customs duties over a 10-year period (at a rate of 10% per year), with effect from January 1998. In February 2002 the Economic and Social Council agreed to bring forward the inauguration of GAFTA to 1 January 2005. Consequently customs duties, which, according to schedule, had been reduced by 50% from January 1998–January 2002, were further reduced by 10% by January 2003, 20% by January 2004, and a final 20% by January 2005, when

GAFTA entered into force as planned with 17 participating countries (accounting for about 94% of the total volume of intra-Arab trade). The Council agreed to supervise the implementation of the free-trade agenda and formally to review its progress twice a year.

WATER RESOURCES

In April 1993 the Council approved the creation of a committee to consider the political and security aspects of water supply in Arab countries. In March 1996, following protests by Syria and Iraq that extensive construction work in southern Turkey was restricting water supply in the region, the Council determined that the waters of the Euphrates and Tigris rivers be shared equitably between the three countries. In April an emergency meeting of the Council issued a further endorsement of Syria's position in the dispute with Turkey.

ARAB–ISRAELI AFFAIRS

In 1964 the second summit conference of Arab heads of state welcomed the establishment of the PLO. The fifth summit conference, held in 1969, issued a call for the mobilization of all Arab nations against Israel. In 1977, by the so-called Tripoli Declaration, Algeria, Iraq, Libya and the People's Democratic Republic of Yemen decided to boycott meetings of the Arab League held in Egypt in response to a visit by President Sadat of Egypt to Israel. In 1979 a meeting of the League's Council resolved to withdraw Arab ambassadors from Egypt; to recommend severance of political and diplomatic relations with Egypt; to suspend Egypt's membership of the League on the date of the signing of its formal peace treaty with Israel (26 March); to transfer the headquarters of the League to Tunis; to condemn US policy regarding its role in concluding the Camp David agreements (in September 1978) and the peace treaty; to halt all bank loans, deposits, guarantees or facilities, as well as all financial or technical contributions and aid to Egypt; to prohibit trade exchanges with the Egyptian state and with private establishments dealing with Israel.

In November 1981 the 12th summit conference of the Arab League, held in Fez, Morocco, was suspended owing to disagreement over a Saudi Arabian proposal, known as the Fahd Plan, which included not only the Arab demands on behalf of the Palestinians, as approved by the UN General Assembly, but also an implied *de facto* recognition of Israel. In September 1982 the 12th summit conference was reconvened. It adopted a peace plan, which demanded Israel's withdrawal from territories occupied in 1967, and removal or Israeli settlements in these areas; freedom of worship for all religions in the sacred places; the right of the Palestinian people to self-determination, under the leadership of the PLO; temporary supervision for the West Bank and the Gaza Strip; the creation of an independent Palestinian state, with Jerusalem as its capital; and a guarantee of peace for the states of the region by the UN Security Council.

In 1983 a summit meeting of the League due to be held in November was postponed owing to members' differences of opinion concerning Syria's opposition to the Yasser Arafat chairmanship of the PLO, and Syrian support for Iran in the war against Iraq. In July 1986 King Hassan of Morocco announced that he was resigning as chairman of the next League summit conference, after criticism by several Arab leaders of his meeting with the Israeli Prime Minister earlier that month. A ministerial meeting held in October condemned any attempt at direct negotiation with Israel. In November 1987 an extraordinary summit conference stated, *inter alia*, that the resumption of diplomatic relations with Egypt was a matter to be decided by individual states. In June 1988 a summit conference agreed to provide finance for the PLO to continue the Palestinian uprising in Israeli-occupied territories. It reiterated a demand for a peaceful settlement in the Middle East (thereby implicitly rejecting recent proposals by the US Government for a conference that would exclude the PLO). At a summit conference held in May 1989 Egypt was readmitted to the League. The conference expressed support for the then chairman of the PLO, Yasser Arafat, in his recent peace proposals made before the UN General Assembly, and reiterated the League's support for proposals that an international conference should be convened to discuss the rights of Palestinians: in so doing, it accepted UN Security Council Resolutions 242 and 338 on a peaceful settlement in the Middle East and thus gave tacit recognition to the State of Israel. The meeting also supported Arafat in rejecting Israeli proposals for elections in the Israeli-occupied territories of the West Bank and the Gaza Strip.

In September 1991, in spite of deep divisions between Arab League member states, it was agreed that a committee should be formed to co-ordinate Arab positions in preparation for the US-sponsored peace talks between Arab countries and Israel. (In the event an *ad hoc* meeting, attended by Egypt, Jordan, Syria, the PLO, Saudi Arabia—representing the Gulf Co-operation Council (GCC)—and Morocco—representing the Union of the Arab Maghreb—was held in October, prior to the start of the talks.) In April 1993 the League pledged its commitment to the Middle East peace talks, but warned that Israel's continued refusal to repatriate the Palestinians based in Lebanon remained a major obstacle to the process. Fol-

lowing the signing of the Israeli-PLO peace accord in September the Council convened in emergency session, at which it approved the agreement, despite opposition from some members, notably Syria. In November it was announced that the League's boycott of commercial activity with Israel was to be maintained. In 1994 the League condemned a decision of the GCC, announced in late September, to end the secondary and tertiary trade embargo against Israel, by which member states refuse to trade with international companies that have investments in Israel. A statement issued by the League insisted that the embargo could be removed only on the decision of the Council. Earlier in September the Council had endorsed a recommendation that the UN conduct a census of Palestinian refugees, in the absence of any such action taken by the League.

In March 1995 Arab ministers of foreign affairs approved a resolution urging Israel to renew the Nuclear Non-Proliferation Treaty (NPT). The resolution stipulated that failure by Israel to do so would cause Arab states to seek to protect legitimate Arab interests by alternative means. In May an extraordinary session of the Council condemned a decision by Israel to confiscate Arab-owned land in East Jerusalem for resettlement. The Israeli Government announced the suspension of its expropriation plans. In April 1996 an emergency meeting of the Council was convened at the request of Palestine, in order to attract international attention to the problem of radiation from an Israeli nuclear reactor. The Council requested an immediate technical inspection of the site by the UN, and further demanded that Israel be obliged to sign the NPT to ensure the eradication of its nuclear weaponry.

In June 1996 an extraordinary summit conference of Arab League heads of state was convened, the first since 1990, in order to formulate a united Arab response to the election, in May, of a new government in Israel and to the prospects for peace in the Middle East. At the conference, which was attended by heads of state of 13 countries and senior representatives of seven others (Iraq was excluded from the meeting in order to ensure the attendance of the Gulf member states), Israel was urged to honour its undertaking to withdraw from the Occupied Territories, including Jerusalem, and to respect the establishment of an independent Palestinian state, in order to ensure the success of the peace process. A final communiqué of the meeting warned that Israeli co-operation was essential to prevent Arab states from reconsidering their participation in the peace process and the re-emergence of regional tensions. In September the League met in emergency session following an escalation of civil unrest in Jerusalem and the Occupied Territories. The League urged the UN Security Council to prevent further alleged Israeli aggression against the Palestinians. In November the League criticized Israel's settlement policy, and at the beginning of December convened in emergency session to consider measures to end any expansion of the Jewish population in the West Bank and Gaza. In March 1997 the Council met in emergency session in response to the Israeli Government's decision to proceed with construction of a new settlement at Har Homa (Jabal Abu-Ghunaim) in East Jerusalem. The Council pledged its commitment to seeking a reversal of the decision and urged the international community to support this aim. At the end of March ministers of foreign affairs of Arab League states agreed to end all efforts to secure normal diplomatic relations with Israel (although binding agreements already in force with Egypt, Jordan and Palestine were exempt) and to close diplomatic offices and missions while construction work continued in East Jerusalem. In addition, ministers recommended reactivating the economic boycott against Israel until comprehensive peace was achieved in the region and suspending Arab participation in the multilateral talks that were initiated in 1991 to further the peace process. In September 1997 ministers of foreign affairs of member states voted to pursue the decision, adopted in March, not to strengthen relations with Israel. Several countries urged a formal boycott of the forthcoming Middle East and North Africa conference, in protest at the lack of progress in the peace process (for which the League blamed Israel, which was due to participate in the conference). However, the meeting upheld a request by the Qatari Government, the host of the conference, that each member should decide individually whether to attend. In the event, only seven Arab League member countries participated in the conference, which was held in Doha in mid-November, while the Secretary-General of the League decided not to attend as the organization's official representative.

A meeting of the Council in March 1998, attended by ministers of foreign affairs of 16 of the League's member states, rejected Israel's proposal to withdraw from southern Lebanon, which was conditional on the deployment by the Lebanese Government of extra troops to secure Israeli territory from attack, and, additionally, urged international support to secure Israel's withdrawal from the Golan Heights. Among items concluded by the Council at its meeting in September were condemnation of Turkey's military co-operation with Israel and a request that the UN dispatch a fact-finding mission to examine conditions in the Israeli-occupied territories and alleged violations of Palestinian property rights.

In March 1999 a meeting of the League's Council expressed support for a UN resolution convening an international conference to facilitate the implementation of agreements applying to Israel and the Occupied Territories, condemned Israel's refusal to withdraw from the Occupied Territories without a majority vote in favour from its legislature, as well as its refusal to resume the peace negotiations with Lebanon and Syria that had ended in 1996, and advocated the publication of evidence of Israeli violence against Palestinians. The Council considered other issues, including the need to prevent further Israeli expansion in Jerusalem and the problem of Palestinian refugees, and reiterated demands for international support to secure Israel's withdrawal from the Golan Heights. In June the League condemned an Israeli aerial attack on Beirut and southern Lebanon. In September 1999 the Council considered, among other things, the Middle East peace process, US military aid to Israel, and a dispute with the Walt Disney corporation regarding a forthcoming exhibition which appeared to depict Jerusalem as the capital of Israel. Later in September an extraordinary meeting of League senior media and information officials was convened to discuss the latter issue. Negotiations with representatives of Disney were pursued and the implied threat of an Arab boycott of the corporation was averted following assurances that the exhibition would be apolitical. In October the Secretary-General of the League condemned the Mauritanian authorities for concluding an agreement with Israel to establish diplomatic relations. In November the League demanded that Israel compensate Palestinians for alleged losses incurred by their enforced use of the Israeli currency. In late December, prior to a short-lived resumption of Israeli-Syrian peace negotiations, the League reaffirmed its full support for Syria's position.

In February 2000 the League strongly condemned an Israeli aerial attack on southern Lebanon; the League's Council changed the venue of its next meeting, in March, from the League's Cairo headquarters to Beirut as a gesture of solidarity with Lebanon. The League welcomed the withdrawal of Israeli forces from southern Lebanon in May, although it subsequently condemned continuing territorial violations by the Israeli military. At a meeting of the Council in early September resolutions were passed urging international bodies to avoid participating in conferences in Jerusalem, reiterating a threatened boycott of a US chain of restaurants which was accused of operating a franchise in an Israeli settlement in the West Bank, and opposing an Israeli initiative for a Jewish emblem to be included as a symbol of the International Red Cross and Red Crescent Movement. At an emergency summit meeting convened in late October in response to mounting insecurity in Jerusalem and the Occupied Territories, 15 Arab heads of state, senior officials from six countries and Yasser Arafat, the then Palestinian National Authority (PA) leader, strongly rebuked Israel, which was accused of inciting the ongoing violent disturbances by stalling the progress of the peace process. The summit determined to 'freeze' co-operation with Israel, requested the formation of an international committee to conduct an impartial assessment of the situation, urged the UN Security Council to establish a mechanism to bring alleged Israeli 'war criminals' to trial, and requested the UN to approve the creation of an international force to protect Palestinians residing in the Occupied Territories. The summit also endorsed the establishment of an 'Al-Aqsa Fund', with a value of US $800m., which was to finance initiatives aimed at promoting the Arab and Islamic identity of Jerusalem, and a smaller 'Jerusalem Intifada Fund' to support the families of Palestinians killed in the unrest. A follow-up committee was subsequently established to implement the resolutions adopted by the emergency summit.

In early January 2001 a meeting of Arab League foreign ministers reviewed a proposed framework agreement, presented by outgoing US President Clinton, which aimed to resolve the continuing extreme tension between the Israeli and Palestinian authorities. The meeting agreed that the issues dominating the stalled Middle East peace process should not be redefined, strongly objecting to a proposal that, in exchange for Palestinian assumption of control over Muslim holy sites in Jerusalem, Palestinians exiled at the time of the foundation of the Israeli state in 1948 should forgo their claimed right to return to their former homes. In late March 2001 the League's first ordinary annual summit-level Council was convened, in Amman, Jordan. The summit issued the Amman Declaration, which emphasized the promotion of Arab unity, and demanded the reversal of Israel's 1967 occupation of Arab territories. Heads of state attending the summit meeting requested that the League consider means of reactivating the now relaxed Arab economic boycott of Israel. In May a meeting of League ministers of foreign affairs determined that all political contacts with Israel should be suspended in protest at aerial attacks by Israel on Palestinian targets in the West Bank. In July representatives of 13 member countries met in Damascus, Syria, under the auspices of the Special Bureau for Boycotting Israel. The meeting declared unanimous support for reactivated trade measures against Israeli companies and foreign businesses dealing with Israel. In August an emergency meeting of ministers of foreign affairs of the member states was

convened at the request of the Palestinian authorities to address the recent escalation of hostilities and Israel's seizure of institutions in East Jerusalem. The meeting, which was attended by the League's Secretary-General and the leader of the PA at that time, Yasser Arafat, aimed to formulate a unified Arab response to the situation. The meeting followed an emergency gathering of information ministers of member countries, at which it was agreed to provide political and media support to the Palestinian position.

In early March 2002 a meeting of League foreign ministers agreed to support an initiative proposed by Crown Prince Abdullah of Saudi Arabia aimed at brokering a peaceful settlement in the, by then, critical Palestinian-Israeli crisis. The Saudi-backed plan—entailing the restoration of 'normal' Arab relations with Israel and acceptance of its right to exist in peace and security, in exchange for a full Israeli withdrawal from the Occupied Territories, the establishment of an independent Palestinian state with East Jerusalem at its capital, and the return of refugees—was unanimously endorsed, as the first-ever pan-Arab Palestinian-Israeli peace initiative, by the summit-level Council held in Beirut in late March. The plan urged compliance with UN Security Council Resolution 194 concerning the return of Palestinian refugees to Israel, or appropriate compensation for their property; however, precise details of eligibility criteria for the proposed return, a contentious issue owing the potentially huge numbers of refugees and descendants of refugees involved, were not elaborated. Conditions imposed by Israel on Yasser Arafat's freedom of movement deterred him from attending the summit. At the end of March the League's Secretary-General condemned the Israeli military's siege of Arafat's presidential compound in Ramallah (initiated in retaliation against a succession of Palestinian bomb attacks on Israeli civilians). In April an extraordinary Council meeting, held at the request of Palestine to consider the 'unprecedented deterioration' of the situation in the Palestinian territories, accused certain states (notably the USA) of implementing a pro-Israeli bias that enabled Israel to act outside the scope of international law and to ignore relevant UN resolutions, and accused Israel of undermining international co-operation in combating terrorism by attempting to equate its actions towards the Palestinian people with recent anti-terrorism activities conducted by the USA. A meeting organized by the Special Bureau for Boycotting Israel at the end of April in Damascus, Syria, was attended by representatives of League member states, except for Egypt, Jordan and Mauritania (which have relations with Israel). The meeting agreed to expand boycott measures and assessed the status of 17 companies believed to have interests in Israel. Israel's termination of its siege of Arafat's Ramallah compound in early May was welcomed by the Secretary-General. A meeting of Arab information ministers in mid-June launched a US $22.5m. campaign to combat Israel's Palestine policy through the international media. Following an aerial raid by the Israeli military on targets in Gaza in late July, the League urged a halt to the export of weaponry, particularly F-16 military aircraft, to Israel. A Council meeting held in early September agreed to intensify Arab efforts to expose Israeli atrocities against the Palestinians and urged the international community to provide protection and reparations for Palestinians. The Council authorized the establishment of a committee to address the welfare of imprisoned Palestinians and urged the USA and the United Kingdom to reconsider their policies on exporting weaponry to Israel, while issuing a resolution concerning the danger posed by Israel's possession of weapons of mass destruction. In early October the Secretary-General expressed concern at new US legislation aimed at securing the relocation of the USA's embassy in Israel from Tel-Aviv to Jerusalem, stating that this represented a symbolic acceptance of Jerusalem as the Israeli capital, in contravention of relevant UN resolutions.

In November 2003 the League welcomed the adoption by the UN Security Council of a resolution endorsing the adoption in April by the so-called 'Quartet', comprising envoys from the UN, European Union, Russia and the USA, of a 'performance-based roadmap to a permanent two-state solution to the Israeli-Palestinian conflict'. In January 2004 the International Court of Justice (ICJ) authorized the participation of the League in proceedings relating to request for an advisory opinion on the *Legal Consequences of the Construction of a Wall in the Occupied Palestinian Territory*, referred to the ICJ by the UN General Assembly in late 2003; the League welcomed the ICJ's conclusions on the case, published in July 2004. The 2004 summit meeting of Arab League heads of state, held in Tunis in May, condemned contraventions of international law by the Israeli Government, in particular continuing settlement activities and the use of unjudicial killings and other violence, and focused on the humanitarian situation of Palestinians recently displaced by large-scale house demolitions in Rafah, Gaza. In January 2005 the League welcomed the election of Mahmud Abbas as the new Executive President of the PA, following the death in November 2004 of Yasser Arafat.

CONFLICT IN THE PERSIAN (ARABIAN) GULF

In March 1984 an emergency meeting established an Arab League committee to encourage international efforts to bring about a negotiated settlement of the Iran–Iraq War. In May ministers of foreign affairs adopted a resolution urging Iran to stop attacking non-belligerent ships and installations in the Gulf region; similar attacks by Iraq were not mentioned. An extraordinary summit conference was held in November 1987, mainly to discuss the war between Iran and Iraq. Contrary to expectations, the participants unanimously agreed on a statement expressing support for Iraq in its defence of its legitimate rights, and criticizing Iran for its procrastination in accepting the UN Security Council Resolution 598 of July, which had recommended a cease-fire and negotiations on a settlement of the conflict. In March 2001 the League's Council accused Iran of theatening regional security by conducting military manoeuvres on the three disputed islands in the Persian (Arabian) Gulf that were also claimed by the United Arab Emirates (UAE). In September 1992 the League's Council issued a condemnation of Iran's alleged occupation of three islands in the Persian (Arabian) Gulf that were claimed by the UAE, and decided to refer the issue to the UN.

In May 1990 a summit conference, held in Baghdad, Iraq (which was boycotted by Syria and Lebanon), criticized recent efforts by Western governments to prevent the development of advanced weapons technology in Iraq. In August an emergency summit conference was held to discuss the invasion and annexation of Kuwait by Iraq. Twelve members (Bahrain, Djibouti, Egypt, Kuwait, Lebanon, Morocco, Oman, Qatar, Saudi Arabia, Somalia, Syria and the UAE) approved a resolution condemning Iraq's action, and demanding the withdrawal of Iraqi forces from Kuwait and the reinstatement of the Government. The 12 states expressed support for the Saudi Arabian Government's invitation to the USA to send forces to defend Saudi Arabia; they also agreed to impose economic sanctions on Iraq, and to provide troops for an Arab defensive force in Saudi Arabia. The remaining member states, however, condemned the presence of foreign troops in Saudi Arabia, and their ministers of foreign affairs refused to attend a meeting, held at the end of August, to discuss possible solutions to the crisis. In November King Hassan of Morocco urged the convening of an Arab summit conference, in an attempt to find an 'Arab solution' to Iraq's annexation of Kuwait. However, the divisions in the Arab world over the issue meant that conditions for such a meeting could not be agreed.

In September 1996 the League condemned US missile attacks against Iraq as an infringement of that country's sovereignty. In addition, it expressed concern at the impact on Iraqi territorial integrity of Turkish intervention in the north of Iraq. In June 1997 the League condemned Turkey's military incursion into northern Iraq and demanded a withdrawal of Turkish troops from Iraqi territory. In November 1997 the League expressed concern at the tensions arising from Iraq's decision not to co-operate fully with UN weapons inspectors, and held several meetings with representatives of the Iraqi administration in an effort to secure a peaceful conclusion to the impasse.

In early 1998 the Secretary-General of the League condemned the use or threat of force against Iraq and continued to undertake diplomatic efforts to secure Iraq's compliance with UN Security Council resolutions. The League endorsed the agreement concluded between the UN Secretary-General and the Iraqi authorities in late February, and reaffirmed its commitment to facilitating the eventual removal of the international embargo against Iraq. In November, following an escalation of tensions between the Iraqi authorities and UN weapons inspectors, the Secretary-General reiterated the League's opposition to the use of force against Iraq, but urged Iraq to maintain a flexible approach in its relations with the UN. The League condemned the subsequent bombing of strategic targets in Iraq, conducted by US and British military aircraft from mid-December, and offered immediate medical assistance to victims of the attacks.

An emergency meeting of ministers of foreign affairs, held in late January 1999 to formulate a unified Arab response to the aerial attacks on targets in Iraq and attended by representatives of 18 member states, expressed concern at the military response to the stand-off between Iraq and the UN, and agreed to establish a seven-member *ad hoc* committee to consider the removal of punitive measures against Iraq within the framework of UN resolutions. However, the Iraqi delegation withdrew from the meeting in protest at the final statement, which included a request that Iraq recognize Kuwait's territorial integrity.

During March 2000 the Secretary-General of the League expressed regret over Iraq's failure to join the *ad hoc* committee established in early 1999 and also over Iraq's refusal to co-operate with the recently established UN Monitoring, Verification and Inspection Commission (UNMOVIC).

In late March 2001 the League's first ordinary annual summit-level Council was convened in Amman, Jordan, where, among other things, it demanded the removal of the UN sanctions against Iraq. At the summit-level Council, held in Beirut in late March 2002, a *rapprochement* occurred between Iraq and Kuwait when the Iraqi envoy representing Saddam Hussain declared Iraq's respect for Kuwait's sovereignty and security. In early August 2002 the Secretary-General expressed strong concern at US threats to attack Iraq in view of its failure to implement UN resolutions, stating that such action would seriously undermine regional stability. A Council meeting held in early September reiterated its complete opposition to the threat of aggression against any Arab country, including Iraq, and demanded the withdrawal of the sanctions against that country. In mid-September, following an ultimatum by the USA that military action against Iraq would ensue were the UN to fail within a short time limit to ensure the elimination of any Iraqi-held weapons of mass destruction, the League urged Iraq to negotiate the return of UN weapons inspectors with a view to avoiding confrontation. Soon afterwards, following tripartite consultations between the Secretary-General of the League, the UN Secretary-General and the Iraqi foreign minister concerning the implementation of UN resolutions and eventual withdrawal of UN sanctions, Iraq agreed to admit UNMOVIC personnel. An emergency meeting of the Council, convened in early November 2002, reviewed the recent adoption by the UN Security Council of Resolution 1441, establishing a strict time frame for Iraqi compliance with UN demands and authorizing the use of force against Iraq in response to non-compliance. The Council urged Iraq to co-operate with UNMOVIC and IAEA inspection teams, requested the inclusion of Arab weapons inspectors on the teams, and urged that the resolution should not be used as a pretext to launch a war against Iraq, emphasizing the importance of a peaceful resolution of the situation.

A summit-level meeting of the Council, held in Sharm esh-Sheikh, Egypt, at the beginning of March 2003, issued a final communiqué rejecting threatened aggression against Iraq, reiterating that the Saddam Hussain regime should co-operate with UN weapons inspectors, urging that the inspectors be given enough time to complete their work, and declaring that the League would form a committee of diplomats to explain its position to concerned international parties. In late March, following the initiation of US-led military action against the Saddam Hussain regime, the League participated in a joint meeting of Arab organizations convened to consider means of assisting the Iraqi people.

LIBYA AND THE INTERNATIONAL COMMUNITY

In December 1991 the League expressed solidarity with Libya, which was under international pressure to extradite two government agents who were suspected of involvement in the explosion which destroyed a US passenger aircraft over Lockerbie, United Kingdom, in December 1988. In March 1992 the League appointed a committee to seek to resolve the disputes between Libya and the USA, the United Kingdom and France over the Lockerbie bomb and the explosion which destroyed a French passenger aircraft over Niger in September 1989. The League condemned the UN's decision, at the end of March, to impose sanctions against Libya, and appealed for a negotiated solution. In September 1997 Arab League ministers of foreign affairs advocated a gradual removal of international sanctions against Libya, and agreed that member countries should permit international flights to leave Libya for specific humanitarian and religious purposes and when used for the purpose of transporting foreign nationals. In August 1998 the USA and United Kingdom accepted a proposal of the Libyan Government, supported by the Arab League, that the suspects in the Lockerbie case be tried in The Hague, the Netherlands, under Scottish law. In March 1999 the League's Council determined that member states would suspend sanctions imposed against Libya, once arrangements for the trial of the suspects in the Lockerbie case had been finalized. (The suspects were transferred to a detention centre in the Netherlands in early April, whereupon the UN Security Council suspended its sanctions against Libya.) At the end of January 2001, following the completion of the trial in The Hague of the two Libyans accused of complicity in the Lockerbie case (one of whom was found guilty and one of whom was acquitted), the Secretary-General of the League urged the UN Security Council fully to terminate the sanctions against Libya that had been suspended in 1999. Meeting in mid-March, the League's Council pledged that member states would not consider themselves bound by the (inactive) UN sanctions. In early September 2002 the Council deplored the USA's continuing active imposition of sanctions against Libya and endorsed Libya's right to claim compensation in respect of these.

LEBANON

In January 1989 an Arab League group, comprising six ministers of foreign affairs, began discussions with the two rival Lebanese governments on the possibility of a political settlement in Lebanon. In May a new mediation committee was established, with a six-month mandate to negotiate a cease-fire in Lebanon, and to reconvene the Lebanese legislature with the aim of holding a presidential election and restoring constitutional government in Lebanon. In September the principal factions in Lebanon agreed to observe a cease-fire, and the surviving members of the Lebanese legislature (originally elected in 1972) met at Ta'if, in Saudi Arabia, in October, and approved the League's proposed 'charter of national reconciliation'.

CONFLICT IN SUB-SAHARAN AFRICA

In November 1997 the League criticized the decision of the US Government to impose economic sanctions against Sudan. In March 2001 the Council reiterated the League's opposition to the economic sanctions maintained by the USA against Sudan. In early September 2002 the Council established a committee to encourage peace efforts in Sudan.

In 1992 the League attempted to mediate between the warring factions in Somalia. In early June 2002 the League appointed a special representative to Somalia to assist with the ongoing reconciliation efforts in that country.

In May 1999 the League expressed its concern at the political situation in the Comoros, following the removal of the government and the establishment of a new military regime in that country at the end of April. In March 2001 the Council welcomed the political *rapprochement* achieved in the Comoros in February.

In May 2004 representatives of the League participated in an African Union fact-finding mission to assess the ongoing human-itarian crisis in Darfur, Sudan. In August an emergency meeting of League foreign ministers convened to address the situation in Darfur declared support for the Sudanese Government's measures to disarm Arab militias and punish human rights violations there. In November the League was asked to join a panel appointed to monitor the cease-fire agreement that had been adopted in April by the parties to the Darfur conflict.

Finance

In September 2002 the Council approved a budget of US $35m. for the Secretariat in 2003.

Publications

Arab Perspectives—Sh'oun Arabiyya (monthly).

Journal of Arab Affairs (monthly).

Bulletins of treaties and agreements concluded among the member states, essays, regular publications circulated by regional offices.

NORDIC COUNCIL

Address: Store Strandstræde 18, 1021 Copenhagen K, Denmark.

Telephone: 3396-0400; **fax:** 3311-1870; **e-mail:** nordisk-rad@norden.org; **internet:** www.norden.org.

The Nordic Council was founded in 1952 for co-operation between the Nordic parliaments and governments. The four original members were Denmark, Iceland, Norway and Sweden; Finland joined in 1955, and the Faroe Islands and Åland Islands were granted representation in 1970 within the Danish and Finnish delegations respectively. Greenland had separate representation within the Danish delegation from 1984. Co-operation was first regulated by a Statute, and subsequently by the Helsinki Treaty of 1962. The Nordic region has a population of about 24m.

MEMBERS

Denmark (with the autonomous territories of the Faroe Islands and Greenland)	Finland (with the autonomous territory of the Åland Islands)	Iceland Norway Sweden

Organization

(April 2005)

COUNCIL

The Nordic Council is not a supranational parliament, but a forum for co-operation between the parliaments and governments of the Nordic countries. The Nordic Council of Ministers co-ordinates the activities of the governments of the Nordic countries when decisions are to be implemented.

The Council comprises 87 members, elected annually by and from the parliaments of the respective countries (Denmark 16 members; Faroes 2; Greenland 2; Finland 18; Åland 2; Iceland 7; Norway 20; Sweden 20). The various parties are proportionately represented in accordance with their representation in the national parliaments. Sessions of the Council consider proposals submitted by Council members, by the Council of Ministers or national governments. The sessions also follow up the outcome of past decisions and the work of the various Nordic institutions. The Plenary Assembly, which convenes once a year, is the highest body of the Nordic Council. Government representatives participate in the Assembly, but do not have the right to vote.

The Council has initiated and overseen extensive efforts to strengthen Nordic co-operation at the political, economic and social level. In 1995 the following were adopted as the priority focus areas ('pillars') of Nordic co-operation: intra-Nordic co-operation, with the emphasis on cultural, education and research co-operation; co-operation with the EU and the European Economic Area, focusing on promoting Nordic values and interests in a broader European context; and co-operation with the Adjacent Areas, i.e. the Baltic States, north-west Russia and the Arctic Area/Barents Sea, where Nordic governments are committed to furthering democracy, security and sustainable development. In September 2000 a Nordic Advisory Panel, appointed in 1999, recommended that the three-pillar basis of Nordic co-operation should be replaced by a theme-based, 'circular' structure. Meeting in Copenhagen, Denmark, in November 2000, the Council endorsed new guide-lines for policy and administrative reforms, in order to develop a better correspondence between the work of the Council and national parliaments. The reform process was also intended to facilitate co-operation with the Nordic Council of Ministers and the implementation of recommendations. Co-operation with non-member states remained a priority focus of the Council's activities.

STANDING COMMITTEES

Council members are assigned to the following Standing Committees: the Culture and Education and Training Committee, Citizens and Consumer Rights Committee, Environment and Natural Resource Committee, Welfare Committee, and the Business and Industry Committee.

PRESIDIUM

The day-to-day work of the Nordic Council is directed by a Presidium, consisting of 13 members of national legislatures. The Presidium is the Council's highest decision-making body between sessions. The Presidium secretariat is headed by a Council Director. Each delegation to the Nordic Council has a secretariat at its national legislature.

Director: FRIDA NOKKEN (Norway).

Publications

Note: the titles listed below are joint publications of the Nordic Council and Nordic Council of Ministers.

Norden this Week (electronic newsletter in the languages of the region and English).

Norden the Top of Europe (monthly newsletter in English, German and French).

Politik i Norden (magazine in the languages of the region).

Yearbook of Nordic Statistics (in English, Finnish and Swedish).

Books and pamphlets on Nordic co-operation; summaries of Council sessions.

NORDIC COUNCIL OF MINISTERS

Address: Store Strandstræde 18, 1255 Copenhagen K, Denmark.
Telephone: 3396-0200; **fax:** 3393-8955; **e-mail:** nmr@norden.org; **internet:** www.norden.org.

The Governments of Denmark, Finland, Iceland, Norway and Sweden co-operate through the Nordic Council of Ministers. This co-operation is regulated by the Treaty of Co-operation between Denmark, Finland, Iceland, Norway and Sweden of 1962 (amended in 1971, 1974, 1983, 1985, 1993 and 1995) and the Treaty between Denmark, Finland, Iceland, Norway and Sweden concerning cultural co-operation of 1971 (amended in 1983 and 1985). Although the Prime Ministers do not meet formally within the Nordic Council of Ministers, they have decided to take a leading role in overall Nordic co-operation. The Ministers of Defence and Foreign Affairs do not meet within the Council of Ministers. These ministers, however, meet on an informal basis.

MEMBERS

Denmark Finland Iceland Norway Sweden

Greenland, the Faroe Islands and the Åland Islands also participate as autonomous regions.

Organization

(April 2005)

COUNCIL OF MINISTERS

The Nordic Council of Ministers holds formal and informal meetings and is attended by ministers with responsibility for the subject under discussion. Each member state also appoints a minister in its own cabinet as Minister for Nordic Co-operation.

Decisions of the Council of Ministers must be unanimous, except for procedural questions, which may be decided by a simple majority of those voting. Abstention constitutes no obstacle to a decision. Decisions are binding on the individual countries, provided that no parliamentary approval is necessary under the constitution of any of the countries. If such approval is necessary, the Council of Ministers must be so informed before its decision.

Meetings are concerned with: agreements and treaties, guidelines for national legislation, recommendations from the Nordic Council, financing joint studies, setting up Nordic institutions.

The Council of Ministers reports each year to the Nordic Council on progress in all co-operation between member states, as well as on future plans.

SECRETARIAT

The Office of the Secretary-General is responsible for co-ordination and legal matters (including co-ordination of work related to the European integration process and to the development of eastern Europe).

The work of the Secretariat is divided into the following departments:

Cultural and educational co-operation, research, advanced education, computer technology

Budget and administration

Environmental protection, finance and monetary policy, fisheries, industry and energy, regional policy, agriculture and forestry

Information

Labour market issues, social policy and health care, occupational environment, consumer affairs, equal opportunities

Secretary-General: PER UNCKEL (Sweden).

COMMITTEES

Nordic Co-operation Committee: for final preparation of material for the meetings of Ministers of Nordic Co-operation.

Senior Executives' Committees: prepare the meetings of the Council of Ministers and conduct research at its request. There are a number of sub-committees. The Committees cover the subjects listed under the Secretariat (above).

Activities

The Nordic Council of Ministers has designated the following as priority areas of activity: technological development; welfare; the internal market in the Nordic countries; the environment and sustainable development; and co-operation with neighbouring countries

and regions, and adopted the following strategic objectives for the period 2003–05: active support for the implementation of the European Union's Action Plan for the Northern Dimension (see below); increased co-operation with Northwest Russia and Kaliningrad; the identification of new projects in the Arctic; restructuring co-operation with the Baltic states; and improved co-operation and division of activities among actors in the Adjacent Areas. A long-term cross-sectoral Strategy for a Sustainable Nordic Region and the Adjacent Areas covering the period 2001–20 was adopted in 2001. The strategy established targets for regional sustainable development, focusing on climate change, biodiversity, genetics, cultural environment, the oceans, chemicals and food safety.

ECONOMIC AND FINANCIAL CO-OPERATION

Nordic economic and financial co-operation aims to promote regional economic, ecological and socially sustainable growth, without inflation, with high employment, and supporting the Nordic social welfare model. It also aims to continue preparing the way for economic integration within the Nordic area and with Europe, and to promote issues of common Nordic concern internationally. Co-operation is undertaken in the following areas: freer markets for goods and services; measures on training and employment; elimination of trade barriers; liberalization of capital movements; research and development; export promotion; taxes and other levies; and regional policy. The Environment and Economics Group commissions environmental and economic analyses of areas of joint Nordic interest, e.g. ecological taxes and duties, cost-effective solutions to international environmental problems, and financing; and disseminates internationally analyses of and other information on Nordic environmental/economic issues.

Nordic Development Fund: f. 1989; supports activities by national administrations for overseas development with resources amounting to €330m.

Nordic Environmental Finance Corporation—NEFCO: f. 1990 to finance environmental projects in Central and Eastern Europe; cap. €80m.

Nordic Industrial Fund: f. 1973 to provide grants, subsidies and loans for industrial research and development projects of interest to more than one member country.

Nordic Investment Bank—NIB: f. under an agreement of December 1975 to provide finance and guarantees for the implementation of investment projects and exports; total assets €16,700m. (Dec. 2003); the main sectors of the Bank's activities are energy, metal and wood-processing industries (including petroleum extraction) and manufacturing; in 1982 a separate scheme for financing investments in developing countries was established; in 1997 an Environmental Loan Facility was established to facilitate environmental investments in the Nordic Adjacent Areas.

Nordic Project Fund—NoPEF: f. 1982 to strengthen the international competitiveness of Nordic exporting companies, and to promote industrial co-operation in international projects (e.g. in environmental protection); grants loans to Nordic companies for feasibility expenses relating to projects.

NORDTEST: f. 1973 as an inter-Nordic agency for technical testing and standardization of methods and of laboratory accreditation.

RELATIONS WITH THE EU, EASTERN EUROPE AND THE ARCTIC

In 1991 the theme 'Norden in Europe' was identified as an area of high priority for the coming years by the Council. Nordic co-operation was to be used to co-ordinate member countries' participation in the western European integration process, based on EC and EC/EFTA co-operation. Since 1995, when Finland and Sweden acceded to the European Union (joining Denmark, already a member of that organization), Europe and the EU have been an integrated part of the work of Nordic co-operation. Under the Finnish presidency of the EU in the second half of 1999 the 'Northern Dimension', a strategy covering the Nordic region and Adjacent Areas, was adopted by the EU. The Nordic Council of Ministers actively supports the EU's Northern Dimension Action Plan (NDAP). The first phase of NDAP covered the period 2000–03, while the second phase covers 2004–06.

Since 1991 the Nordic Council of Ministers has developed its co-operation relating to the Baltic countries and north-west Russia, in order to contribute to peace, security and stability in Europe. Co-operation measures aim to promote democracy, the establishment of market economies, respect for civil rights and the responsible use of resources in these areas. The Nordic Council of Ministers has co-operated with the Arctic Council since that body's establishment in

1996. The Nordic 'Working Programme of the Adjacent Areas' comprises the following major components: Nordic Information Offices in Tallinn, Riga, Vilnius and St Petersburg, which co-ordinate Nordic projects and activities, promote regional contact at all levels and provide information about the Nordic countries in general and Nordic co-operation specifically; the Nordic Grants Scheme for the Baltic States and Northwest Russia, which supports networks linking universities and research institutions, and also awards grants to facilitate network-building in the NGO sector; a grants scheme for public servants and an exchange programme for parliamentarians; and the Nordic Council of Ministers Project Activities. In 1998 the Council of Ministers adopted a Framework Action Plan for Children and Young Adults in the Adjacent Areas. In 2000 the Council of Ministers implemented a review of the strategic goals for co-operation with the Adjacent Areas in view of the administrative, democratic and economic reforms implemented by the Baltic States and their planned accession to the EU; progress achieved towards strengthening regional and EU co-operation with Russia; and an increase in Nordic and international bilateral co-operation measures in the Adjacent Areas. In March of that year the Nordic Investment Bank and the Nordic Environmental Finance Corporation signed a framework agreement with the EU and other partners on providing funding to assist the planned accession to the EU of the Baltic states and other central and east European countries. In June 2003 the Nordic Council of Ministers organized a conference, in Tartu, Estonia, on regional cross-border co-operation following the enlargement of the EU in May 2004. The conference was attended by about 120 delegates from the Nordic and Baltic states and Russia.

A new strategy for activities in the Adjacent Areas and a separate Arctic Programme of Co-operation were approved by the Council of Ministers in 2001. It was agreed that co-operation should focus primarily on the following themes: the Nordic welfare model (including healthcare and gender equality); sustainable utilization of resources (including environmental and energy issues); children and youth issues; culture mediation; and consumer policy and food safety. It was envisaged that cross-border co-operation along the boundaries with Russia and Belarus would assume a growing significance. The programme for co-operation with the Arctic (introduced in 2003) was to take into account subsequent developments since the formation of the Arctic Council.

The budget for co-operation with the Adjacent Areas and the Arctic totalled 86m. Danish kroner in 2003, jointly funded by NEFCO, NOPEF, NIB and bilateral financing.

COMMUNICATIONS AND TRANSPORT

The main areas of co-operation have been concerned with international transport, the environment, infrastructure, road research, transport for the disabled and road safety.

EMPLOYMENT

In 1954 an agreement entered into force on a free labour market between Denmark, Finland, Norway and Sweden. Iceland became a party to the agreement in 1982 and the Faroe Islands in 1992. In 1982 an agreement on worker training and job-oriented rehabilitation came into effect. There is a joint centre for labour market training at Övertorneå in Sweden. A convention on the working environment was signed in 1989. The Nordic Institute for Advanced Training in Occupational Health is based in Helsinki, Finland.

GENDER EQUALITY

A Nordic co-operation programme on equality between women and men began in 1974. The main areas of co-operation have been the integration of equality aspects into all activities covered by the organization (i.e. 'mainstreaming'), working conditions, education, social welfare and family policy, housing and social planning, and women's participation in politics. In June 2000 the Council of Ministers determined that each ministerial group should take responsibility for gender equality in its own sphere of activities. In 2001–05 the main areas of concern were: incorporating the equality dimension into national budgetary policy; men and equality; and the prevention of violence against women.

ENVIRONMENT

A Nordic Environmental Action Plan constituted the overall guidelines for Nordic co-operation in this field in the early 2000s. The long-term cross-sectoral Strategy for a Sustainable Nordic Region and the Adjacent Areas covering the period 2001–20, adopted in 2001, had a strong focus on climate change, biodiversity, and the oceans. Under the Strategy environmental considerations were applied across a wide spectrum of issues, such as globalization, communications technology, natural resources, consumption patterns, renewable resources, air and sea pollutants and poverty reduction. In 2002 the Nordic Council of Ministers launched a Nordic Millennium Ecosystem Assessment. The Nordic countries promote a high level of ambition as the basis for the environmental work conducted in the EU and at an international level.

ENERGY AND INDUSTRY

Co-operation in the energy sector focuses on energy-saving, energy and the environment, climate policy, the energy market, and the introduction of new and renewable sources of energy. A Nordic Co-operation Programme on Business Policy for 2002–05 represented the first joint Nordic initiative concerning the trade and industry sector.

CONSUMER AFFAIRS

The main areas of co-operation are in safety legislation, consumer education and information and consumers' economic and legal interests. The Nordic Council of Ministers promotes changes in consumption habits and production that are conducive to sustainable development.

AGRICULTURE, FORESTRY, FISHERIES AND FOOD

Efforts to develop co-operation in both the fisheries and agriculture and forestry sectors have been undertaken with the aim of integrating environmental aspects into the relevant policies and strategies. The Nordic Council of Ministers promotes sustainable development in agricultural production within the framework of the Strategy for a Sustainable Nordic Region and the Adjacent Areas for 2001–20. Priorities included ensuring food security through ecologically and economically sustainable production methods and an emphasis on quality, with reference to related areas such as food safety, biological diversity and genetic resources. Nordic co-operation on forestry issues includes joint participation in international processes concerned with forestry management. Co-operation on fisheries aims to promote the sustainable development of the fishing industry as an important economic asset and to ensure a balanced approach to the exploitation of regional marine resources.

LAW

The five countries have similar legal systems and tend towards uniformity in legislation and interpretation of law. Much of the preparatory committee work within the national administrations on new legislation involves consultation with the neighbour countries.

Citizens of one Nordic country working in another are in many respects given the status of nationals. In all the Nordic countries they already have the right to vote in local elections in the country of residence. The changing of citizenship from one Nordic country to another has been simplified, and legislation on marriage and on children's rights amended to achieve the greatest possible parity.

There are special extradition facilities between the countries and further stages towards co-operation between the police and the courts have been adopted. In October 1996 justice ministers of the Nordic countries agreed to strengthen police co-operation in order to counter an increase in violent crime perpetrated by gangs. Emphasis is also placed on strengthening co-operation to combat the sexual abuse of children.

There is a permanent Council for Criminology and a Nordic Institute for Maritime Law in Oslo.

REGIONAL POLICY

The Council of Ministers has aimed to develop cross-border co-operation between the Nordic countries and co-operation with the EU and the Baltic countries, and to give greater priority to exchanging knowledge and information.

SOCIAL WELFARE AND HEALTH

Existing conventions and other co-operation directives ensure that Nordic citizens have the same rights, benefits and obligations in each Nordic country, with regard to sickness, parenthood, occupational injury, unemployment, disablement and old-age pension. Uniform provisions exist concerning basic pension and supplementary pension benefits when moving from one Nordic country to another. In 1993 Nordic representatives signed an agreement providing for a common Nordic labour market for health professionals. Numerous joint initiatives have been undertaken in the social welfare and health sectors within the framework of the co-operating institutions. A programme on Nordic co-operation on illicit drugs for 2001–05 aimed to include the Adjacent Areas in the Council of Ministers' activities in this field.

Institutions:
Nordic Committee on Disability
Nordic Committee on Social Security Statistics
Nordic Council for Alcohol and Drug Research, Helsinki, Finland
Nordic Council on Medicines, Uppsala, Sweden
Nordic Education Programme for Social Service Development, Gothenburg, Sweden
Nordic Medico-statistical Committee, Copenhagen, Denmark
Nordic School of Public Health, Gothenburg, Sweden
Nordic Staff Training Centre for Deaf-blind Services, Dronninglund, Denmark
Scandinavian Institute of Dental Materials, Haslum, Norway

EDUCATIONAL AND SCIENTIFIC CO-OPERATION

Education: Nordic co-operation in the educational field includes the objective content and means of education, the structure of the educational system and pedagogical development work. Strategic, long-term investment in human resources, particularly education and research, form part of the basis of the Nordic welfare model. Nordic co-operation on information and communication technology aims to promote universal access to information, with a view to strengthening democracy, Nordic culture, electronic commerce and business networking.

The Nordic Council of Ministers finances the following co-operating bodies, permanent institutions and joint programmes:

Nordic-Baltic Scholarship Scheme;

Nordic Folk Academy;

Nordic Institute in Finland;

Nordic Language and Literature Courses;

NORDPLUS (Nordic Programme for Mobility of University Students and Teachers);

Nordic programmes for mobility of pupils, students, and teachers at primary and secondary school level (NORDPLUS-Junior and others);

Nordic School Data Network (ODIN);

Nordic Summer University;

Programme of Action for Nordic Language Co-operation;

Steering Committee for Nordic Co-operation on General and Adult Education;

Steering Committee for Nordic Co-operation in Higher Education;

Steering Committee for Nordic Educational Co-operation (primary and secondary school).

Research: Nordic co-operation in research comprises information on research activities and research findings, joint research projects, joint research institutions, the methods and means in research policy, the organizational structure of research and co-ordination of the national research programmes. Much of the research co-operation activities at the more permanent joint research institutions consists of establishing science contacts in the Nordic areas by means of grants, visiting lecturers, courses and symposia.

The research institutions and research bodies listed below receive continuous financial support via the Nordic cultural budget. In many cases, these joint Nordic institutions ensure a high international standard that would otherwise have been difficult to maintain at a purely national level.

Nordic Academy for Advanced Study;

Nordic Committee for Bioethics;

Nordic Council for Scientific Information and Research Libraries;

Nordic Institute of Asian Studies;

Nordic Institute of Maritime Law;

Nordic Institute for Theoretical Physics;

Nordic Programme for Arctic Research;

Nordic Sámi Institute;

Nordic Science Policy Council;

Nordic Vulcanological Institute;

Research Programme on the Nordic Countries and Europe.

Cultural activities: Cultural co-operation is based on the Nordic Agreement on Cultural Affairs Co-operation, adopted in 1971, and aims to promote the linguistic and cultural heritage of the Nordic nations. Co-operation includes artistic and other cultural exchange between the Nordic countries; activities relating to libraries, museums, radio, television, film and digitalized culture; promotion of activities within organizations with general cultural aims, including youth and sports organizations; the improvement of conditions for the creative and performing arts; and encouragement for artists and cultural workers. Exhibitions and performances of Nordic culture are organized abroad. A Nordic Multimedia Fund is planned. In 2000 Nordic ministers responsible for Sámi affairs and the leaders of Sámi parliaments (the Sámi being the indigenous population of the northern areas of Norway, Sweden, Finland and north-western Russia) established a permanent co-operation, with the aim of strengthening Sámi languages, culture, business and community life. The Sámi co-operation was to be informally linked to the Nordic Council of Ministers. In October 2001 the ministers for Sámi affairs agreed to appoint a committee of experts to draft a Nordic Sámi Convention.

Joint projects include:

Fund for Mobility of Young Nordic Artists—SLEIPNIR;

Nordic Amateur Theatre Council;

Nordic Art Centre;

Nordic Co-operation in Athletics;

Nordic Council Literature Prize;

Nordic Council Music Prize;

Nordic Documentation Centre for Mass Communication Research;

Nordic Film and Television Fund;

Nordic House in the Faroe Islands;

Nordic House in Reykjavík;

Nordic Institute in Åland;

Nordic Institute of Contemporary Art;

Nordic Institute in Greenland;

Nordic Literature and Libraries Committee;

Nordic Music Committee;

Nordic Theatre and Dance Committee;

Nordic Visual Art Committee;

Steering Committee on Culture and Mass Media;

Steering Committee on Nordic Cultural Projects Abroad;

Valhalla (a network for children's and youth culture).

NORDIC CULTURAL FUND

The Nordic Cultural Fund was established through a separate agreement between the governments of the Nordic countries in 1966, and began operating in 1967, with the aim of supporting the needs of cultural life in the Nordic countries. A Board of 11 members administers and distributes the resources of the Fund and supervises its activities. Five of the members are appointed by the Nordic Council and five by the Nordic Council of Ministers (of culture and education), for a period of two years. The autonomous territories (the Åland islands, the Faroe Islands and Greenland) are represented by one member on the Board, appointed alternately by the Nordic Council and the Nordic Council of Ministers. The Fund is located within and administered by the Secretariat of the Nordic Council of Ministers. It considers applications for assistance for research, education and general cultural activities; grants may also be awarded for the dissemination of information concerning Nordic culture within and outside the region.

Finance

Joint expenses are divided according to an agreed scale in proportion to the relative national product of the member countries. The 2005 budget of the Nordic Council of Ministers amounted to 826m. Danish kroner. Various forms of co-operation are also financed directly from the national budgets.

NORTH AMERICAN FREE TRADE AGREEMENT—NAFTA

Address: Canadian section: Royal Bank Centre, 90 Sparks St, Suite 705, Ottawa, ON K1P 5B4.
Telephone: (613) 992-9388; **fax:** (613) 992-9392; **e-mail:** canada@nafta-sec-alena.org; **internet:** www.nafta-sec-alena.org/canada.
Address: Mexican section: Blvd Adolfo López Mateos 3025, 2°, Col Héroes de Padierna, 10700 México, DF.
Telephone: (5) 629-9630; **fax:** (5) 629-9637; **e-mail:** mexico@nafta-sec-alena.org.
Address: US section: 14th St and Constitution Ave, NW, Room 2061, Washington, DC 20230.

Telephone: (202) 482-5438; **fax:** (202) 482-0148; **e-mail:** usa@nafta-sec-alena.org; **internet:** www.nafta-sec-alena.org.

The North American Free Trade Agreement (NAFTA) grew out of the free-trade agreement between the USA and Canada that was signed in January 1988 and came into effect on 1 January 1989. Negotiations on the terms of NAFTA, which includes Mexico in the free-trade area, were concluded in October 1992 and the Agreement was signed in December. The accord was ratified in November 1993 and entered into force on 1 January 1994. The NAFTA Secretariat is composed of national sections in each member country.

MEMBERS

Canada	Mexico	USA

MAIN PROVISIONS OF THE AGREEMENT

Under NAFTA almost all restrictions on trade and investment between Canada, Mexico and the USA were to be gradually removed over a 15-year period. Most tariffs were eliminated immediately on agricultural trade between the USA and Mexico, with tariffs on 6% of agricultural products (including corn, sugar, and some fruits and vegetables) to be abolished over the 15 years. Tariffs on automobiles and textiles were to be phased out over 10 years in all three countries. Mexico was to open its financial sector to US and Canadian investment, with all restrictions to be removed by 2007. Barriers to investment were removed in most sectors, with exemptions for petroleum in Mexico, culture in Canada and airlines and radio communications in the USA. Mexico was to liberalize government procurement, removing preferential treatment for domestic companies over a 10-year period. In transport, heavy goods vehicles were to have complete freedom of movement between the three countries by 2000. An interim measure, whereby transport companies could apply for special licences to travel further within the borders of each country than the existing limit of 20 miles (32 km), was postponed in December 1995, shortly before it was scheduled to come into effect. The postponement was due to concerns, on the part of the US Government, relating to the implementation of adequate safety standards by Mexican truck-drivers. The 2000 deadline for the free circulation of heavy goods vehicles was not met, owing to the persistence of these concerns. In February 2001 a five-member NAFTA panel of experts appointed to adjudicate on the dispute ruled that the USA was violating the Agreement. In December the US Senate approved legislation entitling Mexican long-haul trucks to operate anywhere in the USA following compliance with rigorous safety checks to be enforced by US inspectors. In April 1998 the fifth meeting of the three-member ministerial Free Trade Commission (see below), held in Paris, France, agreed to remove tariffs on some 600 goods, including certain chemicals, pharmaceuticals, steel and wire products, textiles, toys, and watches, from 1 August. As a result of the agreement, a number of tariffs were eliminated as much as 10 years earlier than had been originally planned.

In April 2003 the Mexican Government announced that, in order to protect the livelihoods of local producers, it was planning to renegotiate provisions of the Agreement that would permit, with effect from January 2008, the tariff-free importation of maize and beans from Canada and the USA.

In the case of a sudden influx of goods from one country to another that adversely affects a domestic industry, the Agreement makes provision for the imposition of short-term 'snap-back' tariffs.

Disputes are to be settled in the first instance by intergovernmental consultation. If a dispute is not resolved within 30 to 40 days, a government may call a meeting of the Free Trade Commission. In October 1994 the Commission established an Advisory Committee on Private Commercial Disputes to recommend procedures for the resolution of such disputes. If the Commission is unable to settle the issue a panel of experts in the relevant field is appointed to adjudicate. In June 1996 Canada and Mexico announced their decision to refer the newly-enacted US 'Helms-Burton' legislation on trade with Cuba to the Commission. They claimed that the legislation, which provides for punitive measures against foreign companies that engage in trade with Cuba, imposed undue restrictions on Canadian and Mexican companies and was, therefore, in contravention of NAFTA. However, at the beginning of 1997 certain controversial provisions of the Helms-Burton legislation were suspended for a period of six months by the US administration. In April these were again suspended, as part of a compromise agreement with the European Union. The relevant provisions continued to be suspended at six-monthly intervals, and remained suspended in 2005. An Advisory Committee on Private Commercial Disputes Regarding Agricultural Goods was formed in 1998.

In December 1994 NAFTA members issued a formal invitation to Chile to seek membership of the Agreement. Formal discussions on Chile's entry began in June 1995, but were stalled in December when the US Congress failed to approve 'fast-track' negotiating authority for the US Government, which was to have allowed the latter to negotiate a trade agreement with Chile, without risk of incurring a line-by-line veto from the US Congress. In February 1996 Chile began high-level negotiations with Canada on a wide-ranging bilateral free-trade agreement. Chile, which already had extensive bilateral trade agreements with Mexico, was regarded as advancing its position with regard to NAFTA membership by means of the proposed accord with Canada. The bilateral agreement, which provided for the extensive elimination of customs duties by 2002, was signed in November 1996 and ratified by Chile in July 1997. However, in November 1997 the US Government was obliged to request the removal of the 'fast-track' proposal from the legislative agenda, owing to insufficient support within Congress.

In April 1998 heads of state of 34 countries, meeting in Santiago, Chile, agreed formally to initiate the negotiating process to establish a Free Trade Area of the Americas (FTAA). The US Government had originally proposed creating the FTAA through the gradual extension of NAFTA trading privileges on a bilateral basis. However, the framework agreed upon by ministers of trade of the 34 countries, meeting in March, provided for countries to negotiate and accept FTAA provisions on an individual basis and as part of a sub-regional economic bloc. It was envisaged that the FTAA would exist alongside the sub-regional associations, including NAFTA. In April 2001, meeting in Québec, QC, Canada, leaders of the participating countries agreed to conclude the negotiations on the FTAA by January 2005 and implement it by the end of that year. At a special summit of the Americas, held in January 2004 in Monterrey, Mexico, however, the leaders did not specify a completion date for the negotiations, although they adopted a declaration committing themselves to its eventual establishment.

ADDITIONAL AGREEMENTS

During 1993, as a result of domestic pressure, the new US Government negotiated two 'side agreements' with its NAFTA partners, which were to provide safeguards for workers' rights and the environment. A Commission for Labour Co-operation was established under the North American Agreement on Labour Co-operation (NAALC) to monitor implementation of labour accords and to foster co-operation in that area. The North American Commission for Environmental Co-operation (NACEC) was initiated to combat pollution, to ensure that economic development was not environmentally damaging and to monitor compliance with national and NAFTA environmental regulations. Panels of experts, with representatives from each country, were established to adjudicate in cases of alleged infringement of workers' rights or environmental damage. The panels were given the power to impose fines and trade sanctions, but only with regard to the USA and Mexico; Canada, which was opposed to such measures, was to enforce compliance with NAFTA by means of its own legal system. In 1995 the North American Fund for Environmental Co-operation (NAFEC) was established. NAFEC, which is financed by the NACEC, supports community environmental projects.

In February 1996 the NACEC consented for the first time to investigate a complaint brought by environmentalists regarding non-compliance with domestic legislation on the environment. Mexican environmentalists claimed that a company that was planning to build a pier for tourist ships (a project that was to involve damage to a coral reef) had not been required to supply adequate environmental impact studies. The NACEC was limited to presenting its findings in such a case, as it could only make a ruling in the case of complaints brought by one NAFTA government against another. The NACEC allocates the bulk of its resources to research undertaken to support compliance with legislation and agreements on the environment. However, in October 1997 the council of NAFTA ministers of the environment, meeting in Montréal, Canada, approved a new structure for the NACEC's activities. The NACEC's main objective was to be the provision of advice concerning the environmental impact of trade issues. It was also agreed that the Commission was further to promote trade in environmentally-sound products and to encourage private-sector investment in environmental trade issues.

With regard to the NAALC, National Administration Offices have been established in each of the three NAFTA countries in order to monitor labour issues and to address complaints about non-compliance with domestic labour legislation. However, punitive measures in the form of trade sanctions or fines (up to US $20m.) may only be imposed in the specific instances of contravention of national legislation regarding child labour, a minimum wage or health and safety standards. A Commission for Labour Co-operation has been established (see below) and incorporates a council of ministers of labour of the three countries.

In August 1993 the USA and Mexico agreed to establish a Border Environmental Co-operation Commission (BECC) to assist with the co-ordination of projects for the improvement of infrastructure and to monitor the environmental impact of the Agreement on the US–Mexican border area, where industrial activity was expected to intensify. The Commission is located in Ciudad Juárez, Mexico. By April 2005 the BECC had certified 105 projects, at a cost of US $2180.6m. In October 1993 the USA and Mexico concluded an agreement to establish the North American Development Bank (NADB or NADBank), which was mandated to finance environmental and infrastructure projects along the US–Mexican border.

Commission for Labour Co-operation: 1211 Connecticut Ave, NW Suite 200, Washington, DC 20036, USA; tel. (202) 464-1100; fax (202) 464-9487; e-mail info@naalc.org; internet www.naalc.org; f. 1994; Exec. Dir MARK S. KNOUSE (USA); publ. *Annual Report*.

North American Commission for Environmental Co-oper-ation (NACEC): 393 rue St Jacques Ouest, Bureau 200, Montréal, QC H2Y 1N9, Canada; tel. (514) 350-4300; fax (514) 350-4314; e-mail info@ccemtl.org; internet www.cec.org; f. 1994; Exec. Dir WILLIAM V. KENNEDY; publs *Annual Report*, *Taking Stock* (annually), industry reports, policy studies.

North American Development Bank (NADB/NADBank): 203 St Mary's, Suite 300, San Antonio, TX 78205, USA; tel. (210) 231-8000; fax (210) 231-6232; internet www.nadbank.org; at 31 March 2004 the NADB had authorized capital of US $3,000m., subscribed equally by Mexico and the USA, of which $349m. was paid-up; Man. Dir RAUL RODRIGUEZ (Mexico); publs *Annual Report*, *NADBank News*.

NORTH ATLANTIC TREATY ORGANIZATION—NATO

Address: blvd Léopold III, 1110 Brussels, Belgium.

Telephone: (2) 707-41-11; **fax:** (2) 707-45-79; **e-mail:** natodoc@hq.nato.int; **internet:** www.nato.int.

The Atlantic Alliance was established on the basis of the 1949 North Atlantic Treaty as a defensive political and military alliance of a group of European states (then numbering 10) and the USA and Canada. The Alliance aims to provide common security for its members through co-operation and consultation in political, military and economic fields, as well as scientific, environmental, and other non-military aspects. The objectives of the Alliance are implemented by NATO. Following the collapse of the communist governments in Central and Eastern Europe, from 1989 onwards, and the dissolution of the Warsaw Pact (which had hitherto been regarded as the Alliance's principal adversary) in 1991, NATO has undertaken a fundamental transformation of its structures and policies to meet the new security challenges in Europe.

MEMBERS*

Belgium	Hungary	Portugal
Bulgaria	Iceland	Romania
Canada	Italy	Slovakia
Czech Republic	Latvia	Slovenia
Denmark	Lithuania	Spain
Estonia	Luxembourg	Turkey
France	Netherlands	United Kingdom
Germany	Norway	USA
Greece	Poland	

* Greece and Turkey acceded to the Treaty in 1952, and the Federal Republic of Germany in 1955. France withdrew from the integrated military structure of NATO in 1966, although remaining a member of the Atlantic Alliance; in 1996 France resumed participation in some, but not all, of the military organs of NATO. Spain acceded to the Treaty in 1982, but remained outside the Alliance's integrated military structure until 1999. The Czech Republic, Hungary and Poland were formally admitted as members of NATO in March 1999. In March 2003 protocols of accession, amending the North Atlantic Treaty, were adopted by the 19 NATO member states with a view to admitting Bulgaria, Estonia, Latvia, Lithuania, Romania, Slovakia and Slovenia to the Alliance. In March 2004, the protocols of accession having been ratified by all of the member states, those seven countries were formally invited to join NATO and, on 29 March, they acceded to the Treaty.

Organization

(April 2005)

NORTH ATLANTIC COUNCIL

The Council, the highest authority of the Alliance, is composed of representatives of the 26 member states. It meets at the level of Permanent Representatives, ministers of foreign affairs, or heads of state and government, and, at all levels, has effective political and decision-making authority. Ministerial meetings are held at least twice a year. Occasional meetings of defence ministers are also held. At the level of Permanent Representatives the Council meets at least once a week.

The Secretary-General of NATO is Chairman of the Council, and each year a minister of foreign affairs of a member state is nominated honorary President, following the English alphabetical order of countries.

Decisions are taken by common consent and not by majority vote. The Council is a forum for wide consultation between member governments on major issues, including political, military, economic and other subjects, and is supported by the Senior or regular Political Committee, the Military Committee and other subordinate bodies.

PERMANENT REPRESENTATIVES

Belgium: DOMINIQUE STRUYE DE SWIELANDE.
Bulgaria: LUBOMIR IVANOV.
Canada: JEAN-PIERRE JUNEAU.
Czech Republic: KAREL KOVANDA.
Denmark: PER POULSEN-HANSEN.
Estonia: HARRI TIIDO.
France: BENOÎT D'ABOVILLE.
Germany: Dr RÜDIGER REYELS.
Greece: YANNIS-ALEXIS ZEPOS.
Hungary: JÁNOS HERMAN.
Iceland: GUNNAR GUNNARSSON.
Italy: MAURIZIO MORENO.
Latvia: AIVIS RONIS.
Lithuania: GINTE B. DAMUŠIS.
Luxembourg: JOSEPH WEYLAND.
Netherlands: MICHIEL PATIJN.
Norway: KAI EIDE.
Poland: JERZY NOWAK.
Portugal: JOSÉ PACHECO LUIS GOMES.
Romania: BOGDAN MAZURU.
Slovakia: IGOR SLOBODNIK.
Slovenia: Matjaž ŠINKOVEC.
Spain: PABLO BENAVIDES ORGAZ.
Turkey: ÜMIT PAMIR.
United Kingdom: Sir PETER RICKETTS.
USA: R. NICHOLAS BURNS.

Note: NATO partner countries are represented by heads of diplomatic missions or liaison officers located at NATO headquarters.

DEFENCE PLANNING COMMITTEE

Most defence matters are dealt with in the Defence Planning Committee, composed of representatives of all member countries except France. The Committee provides guidance to NATO's military authorities and, within the field of its responsibilities, has the same functions and authority as the Council. Like the Council, it meets regularly at ambassadorial level and assembles twice a year in ministerial sessions, when member countries are represented by their ministers of defence.

NUCLEAR PLANNING GROUP

Defence ministers of countries participating in the Defence Planning Committee meet regularly in the Nuclear Planning Group (NPG) to discuss specific policy issues relating to nuclear forces, such as safety, deployment issues, nuclear arms control and proliferation. The NPG is supported by a Staff Group, composed of representatives of all members participating in the NPG, which meets at least once a week. The NPG High Level Group, chaired by the USA and comprising national policy-makers and experts, exists as a senior advisory body to the NPG in respect of nuclear policy and planning issues.

OTHER COMMITTEES

There are also committees for political affairs, economics, military medical services, armaments, defence review, science, infrastructure, logistics, communications, civil emergency planning, information and cultural relations, and civil and military budgets. In addition, other committees consider specialized subjects such as NATO pipelines, air traffic management, etc. Since 1992 most of these committees consult on a regular basis with representatives from central and eastern European countries.

INTERNATIONAL SECRETARIAT

The Secretary-General is Chairman of the North Atlantic Council, the Defence Planning Committee and the Nuclear Planning Group. He is the head of the International Secretariat, with staff drawn from the member countries. He proposes items for NATO consultation and is generally responsible for promoting consultation and co-operation in accordance with the provisions of the North Atlantic Treaty. He is empowered to offer his help informally in cases of disputes between member countries, to facilitate procedures for settlement.

Secretary-General: JAKOB GIJSBERT (JAAP) DE HOOP SCHEFFER (Netherlands).

Deputy Secretary-General: ALESSANDRO MINUTO RIZZO (Italy).

There is an Assistant Secretary-General for each of the operational divisions listed below.

PRINCIPAL DIVISIONS

Division of Defence Investment: responsible for enhancing NATO's defence capacity (including armaments planning, air defence and security investment) by developing and investing in the Alliance's assets and capabilities; Asst Sec. Gen. MARSHALL S. BILLINGSLEA (USA).

Division of Defence Policy and Planning: responsible for defence planning, nuclear policy and defence against weapons of mass destruction; Asst Sec. Gen. JOHN COLSTON (United Kingdom).

Division of Political Affairs and Security Policy: is concerned with regional, economic and security affairs and relations with other international organizations and partner countries; Asst Sec. Gen. GÜNTHER ALTENBURG (Germany).

Division of Public Diplomacy: responsible for dissemination of information on NATO's activities and policies through the media, the official website and print publications as well as seminars and conferences; Asst Sec. Gen. JEAN FOURNET (France).

Executive Management Division: ensures the efficient running of the International Secretariat and provides support to elements such as conference services, information management and human and financial resources; Asst Sec. Gen. JUAN MARTINEZ ESPARZA (Spain).

Operations Division: responsible for the Alliance's crisis management and peace-keeping activities and civil emergency planning and exercises; Asst Sec. Gen. ADAM KOBIERACKI (Poland).

Military Organization

MILITARY COMMITTEE

Composed of the allied Chiefs-of-Staff, or their representatives, of all member countries: the highest military body in NATO under the authority of the Council. Meets at least twice a year at Chiefs-of-Staff level and remains in permanent session with Permanent Military Representatives. It is responsible for making recommendations to the Council and Defence Planning Committee and Nuclear Planning Group on military matters and for supplying guidance on military questions to Supreme Allied Commanders and subordinate military authorities. The Committee is supported by an International Military Staff.

In December 1995 France agreed to rejoin the Military Committee, which it had formally left in 1966.

Chairman: Gen. HARALD KUJAT (Germany).

COMMANDS

Allied Command Operations: Casteau, Belgium—Supreme Headquarters Allied Powers Europe—SHAPE; Supreme Allied Commander Europe—SACEUR Gen. JAMES L. JONES (USA).

Allied Command Transformation: Norfolk, Virginia, USA; Supreme Allied Commander Transformation—SACT Adm. EDMUND P. GIAMBASTIANI, JR (USA).

Activities

The common security policy of the members of the North Atlantic Alliance is to safeguard peace through the maintenance of political solidarity and adequate defence at the lowest level of military forces needed to deter all possible forms of aggression. Each year, member countries take part in a Defence Review, designed to assess their contribution to the common defence in relation to their respective capabilities and constraints. Allied defence policy is reviewed periodically by ministers of defence.

Since the 1980s the Alliance has been actively involved in co-ordinating policies with regard to arms control and disarmament issues designed to bring about negotiated reductions in conventional forces, intermediate and short-range nuclear forces and strategic nuclear forces. A Verification Co-ordinating Committee was established in 1990. In April 1999 the summit meeting determined to improve co-ordination on issues relating to weapons of mass destruction through the establishment of a separate centre at NATO headquarters.

Political consultations within the Alliance take place on a permanent basis, under the auspices of the North Atlantic Council (NAC), on all matters affecting the common security interests of the member countries, as well as events outside the North Atlantic Treaty area.

Co-operation in scientific and technological fields as well as co-operation on environmental challenges takes place in the NATO Science Committee and in its Committee on the Challenges of Modern Society. Both these bodies operate an expanding international programme of science fellowships, advance study institutes and research grants. NATO has also pursued co-operation in relation to civil emergency planning. These activities represent NATO's 'Third Dimension'.

At a summit meeting of the Conference on Security and Co-operation in Europe—CSCE, now renamed the Organization for Security and Co-operation in Europe—OSCE, in November 1990 the member countries of NATO and the Warsaw Pact signed an agreement limiting Conventional Armed Forces in Europe (CFE), whereby conventional arms would be reduced to within a common upper limit in each zone. The two groups also issued a Joint Declaration, stating that they were no longer adversaries and that none of their weapons would ever be used 'except in self-defence'. Following the dissolution of the USSR the eight former Soviet republics with territory in the area of application of the CFE Treaty committed themselves to honouring its obligations in June 1992. In March 1992, under the auspices of the CSCE, the ministers of foreign affairs of the NATO and of the former Warsaw Pact countries (with Russia, Belarus, Ukraine and Georgia taking the place of the USSR) signed the 'Open Skies' treaty. Under this treaty, aerial reconnaissance missions by one country over another were to be permitted, subject to regulation. At the summit meeting of the OSCE in December 1996 the signatories of the CFE Treaty agreed to begin negotiations on a revised treaty governing conventional weapons in Europe. In July 1997 the CFE signatories concluded an agreement on Certain Basic Elements for Treaty Adaptation, which provided for substantial reductions in the maximum levels of conventional military equipment at national and territorial level, replacing the previous bloc-to-bloc structure of the Treaty.

An extensive review of NATO's structures was initiated in June 1990, in response to the fundamental changes taking place in Central and Eastern Europe. In November 1991 NATO heads of government, convened in Rome, recommended a radical restructuring of the organization in order to meet the demands of the new security environment, which was to involve further reductions in military forces in Europe, active involvement in international peace-keeping operations, increased co-operation with other international institutions and close co-operation with its former adversaries, the USSR and the countries of Eastern Europe. The basis for NATO's new force structure was incorporated into a new Strategic Concept, which was adopted in the Rome Declaration issuing from the summit meeting. The concept provided for the maintenance of a collective defence capability, with a reduced dependence on nuclear weapons. Substantial reductions in the size and levels of readiness of NATO forces were undertaken, in order to reflect the Alliance's strictly defensive nature, and forces were reorganized within a streamlined integrated command structure. Forces were categorized into immediate and rapid reaction forces (including the ACE Rapid Reaction Corps—ARRC, which was inaugurated in October 1992), main defence forces and augmentation forces, which may be used to reinforce any NATO region or maritime areas for deterrence, crisis management or defence. In December the NAC, meeting at ministerial level, endorsed a new military structure, which envisaged a reduction in the number of NATO command headquarters from 65 to 20. During 1998 work was undertaken on the formulation of a new Strategic Concept, reflecting the changing security environment and defining NATO's future role and objectives, which recognized a broader sphere of influence of NATO in the 21st century and confirmed NATO to be the principal generator of security in the Euro-Atlantic area. It emphasized NATO's role in crisis management and a renewed commitment to partnership and dialogue. The document was approved at a special summit meeting, convened in Washington, DC, USA, in April 1999, to commemorate the 50th anniversary of the Alliance. A separate initiative was approved to assist member states to adapt their defence capabilities to meet changing security requirements, for example improving the means of troop deployment and equipping and protecting forces. The Washington meeting, which had been envisaged as a celebration of NATO's achievements since its foundation, was, however, dominated by consideration of the situation in the southern Serbian province of Kosovo and Metohija and the conduct of its military offensive against the Federal Republic of Yugoslavia, initiated in late March (see below).

In January 1994 NATO heads of state and government welcomed the entry into force of the Maastricht Treaty, establishing the European Union (EU, superseding the EC). The Treaty included an agreement on the development of a common foreign and security policy, which was intended to be a mechanism to strengthen the European pillar of the Alliance. NATO subsequently co-operated with Western European Union (WEU) in support of the development of a European Security and Defence Identity. In June 1996 NATO ministers of foreign affairs reached agreement on the implementation of the 'Combined Joint Task Force (CJTF) concept', which had been adopted in January 1994. Measures were to be taken to establish the 'nuclei' of these task forces at certain NATO headquarters, which would provide the basis for missions that could be activated at short notice for specific purposes such as crisis management and peace-keeping. It was also agreed to make CJTFs available for operations undertaken by WEU. In conjunction with this, WEU was to be permitted to make use of Alliance hardware and capabilities (in practice, mostly belonging to the USA) subject to the endorsement of the NAC. The summit meeting, held in April 1999, confirmed NATO's willingness to establish a direct NATO-EU relationship. In February 2000 the first joint NATO-WEU crisis management exercise was conducted. However, in accordance with decisions taken by the EU in late 1999 and 2000 to implement a common security and defence policy, it was agreed that routine NATO-WEU consultation mechanisms were to be suspended. The first formal meeting of the Military Committees of the EU and NATO took place in June 2001 to exchange information relating to the development of EU-NATO security co-operation. In order to support an integrated security structure in Europe, NATO also co-operates with the OSCE and has provided assistance for the development of the latter's conflict prevention and crisis management activities.

In January 2001 NATO established an *ad hoc* working committee in response to concerns expressed by several member governments regarding the health implications of the use of depleted uranium munitions during the Alliance's military intervention in the Balkans. The committee was to co-ordinate the compilation of information regarding the use of depleted uranium and to co-operate with the Yugoslav authorities in the rehabilitation of the local environment. An extraordinary meeting of chiefs of military medical services, including surgeons-general and medical experts, was also convened to consider the issue.

On 12 September 2001 the NAC agreed to invoke, for the first time, Article 5 of the North Atlantic Treaty, providing for collective self-defence, in response to terrorist attacks against targets in the USA that took place on the previous day. The measure was formally implemented in early October after the US authorities presented evidence substantiating claims that the attacks had been directed from abroad. The NAC endorsed eight specific US requests for logistical and military support in its efforts to counter terrorism, including enhanced sharing of intelligence and full access to airfields and ports in member states. It also agreed to dispatch five surveillance aircraft to help to patrol US airspace and directed the standing naval force to the Eastern Mediterranean. Accordingly, Operation Active Endeavour, conducting the surveillance and monitoring of maritime trade in the region, was subsequently launched. In December NATO ministers of defence initiated a review of military capabilities and defences with a view to strengthening its ability to counter international terrorism. In March 2004 the NAC determined to extend Operation Active Endeavour to the whole of the Mediterranean and to seek the support of this extension, through their active participation in the Operation, by participants in the Euro-Atlantic Partnership Council and the Partnership for Peace programme.

In February–early May 2003 NATO deployed surveillance aircraft and missile defences in Turkey, and provided assistance with civil emergency planning, to defend that country from possible repercussions of the US-led military action against neighbouring Iraq that was initiated in March.

On 7 April 2003 an agreement was signed by six member states—the Czech Republic, Denmark, Germany, the Netherlands, Norway and Poland—formally establishing the Civil-Military Co-operation Group North. The group, which was conceived in 2000, was to be based at Budel, Netherlands, and was intended to provide NATO commanders with a co-ordinated approach to civil-military co-operation during crises and in post-conflict areas. In mid-June NATO defence ministers agreed an historic reform of the Alliance's command which was to reflect its new missions and enable the transition to smaller, more flexible forces. The number of commands was to be reduced from 20 to 11 and their responsibilites redefined. The restructuring included a Response Force, which was inaugurated in October 2003. In August NATO undertook its first mission outside of

the Euro-Atlantic area when it assumed command of the UN-mandated International Security Assistance Force (ISAF) in Kabul, Afghanistan. NATO ministers of defence agreed in December to progressively extend ISAF's mission in Afghanistan beyond Kabul. In November the EU and NATO conducted a joint crisis management exercise for the first time. The June 2004 summit meeting, held in Istanbul, Turkey, determined to expand the ISAF. The meeting also agreed to offer assistance to the newly-inaugurated Iraqi Interim Government with the training of its security forces. The meeting endorsed a new NATO Policy on Combating Trafficking in Human Beings, with the aim of supporting the efforts of countries and international organizations to counter the problem. In July a NATO Training Implementation Mission was initiated to undertake the training commitments in Iraq. In December the NAC authorized an expansion of the Mission, of up to 300 personnel, and the establishment of an Iraq Training, Education and Doctrine Centre. The expanded operation was to be called the NATO Training Mission–Iraq.

In March 2005 the NAC approved a charter formally to establish an organization to manage an Active Layered Theatre Ballistic Missile Defence programme, which aimed to establish a new collective defence capability. The specifications of the new system were approved by NATO ministers of defence in June 2004.

PARTNERSHIPS

In May 1997 a Euro-Atlantic Partnership Council (EAPC) was inaugurated as a successor to the North Atlantic Co-operation Council (NACC), that had been established in December 1991 to provide a forum for consultation on political and security matters with the countries of central and eastern Europe, including the former Soviet republics. An EAPC Council was to meet monthly at ambassadorial level and twice a year at ministerial level. It was to be supported in its work by a steering committee and a political committee. The EAPC was to pursue the NACC Work Plan for Dialogue, Partnership and Co-operation and incorporate it into a new Work Plan, which was to include an expanded political dimension of consultation and co-operation among participating states. The Partnership for Peace (PfP) programme, which was established in January 1994 within the framework of the NACC, was to remain an integral element of the new co-operative mechanism. The PfP incorporated practical military and defence-related co-operation activities that had originally been part of the NACC Work Plan. Participation in the PfP requires an initial signature of a framework agreement, establishing the common principles and objectives of the partnership, the submission of a presentation document, indicating the political and military aspects of the partnership and the nature of future co-operation activities, and thirdly, the development of individual partnership programmes establishing country-specific objectives. In June 1994 Russia, which had previously opposed the strategy as being the basis for future enlargement of NATO, signed the PfP framework document, which included a declaration envisaging an 'enhanced dialogue' between the two sides. Despite its continuing opposition to any enlargement of NATO, in May 1995 Russia agreed to sign a PfP Individual Partnership Programme, as well as a framework document for NATO-Russian dialogue and co-operation beyond the PfP. During 1994 a Partnership Co-ordination Cell (PCC), incorporating representatives of all partnership countries, became operational in Mons, Belgium. The PCC, under the authority of the NAC, aims to co-ordinate joint military activities and planning in order to implement PfP programmes. The first joint military exercises with countries of the former Warsaw Pact were conducted in September. NATO began formulating a PfP Status of Forces Agreement (SOFA) to define the legal status of Allies' and partners' forces when they are present on each other's territory; the PfP SOFA was opened for signature in June 1995. The new EAPC was to provide a framework for the development of an enhanced PfP programme, which NATO envisaged would become an essential element of the overall European security structure. Accordingly, the military activities of the PfP were to be expanded to include all Alliance missions and incorporate all NATO committees into the PfP process, thus providing for greater co-operation in crisis management, civil emergency planning and training activities. In addition, all PfP member countries were to participate in the CJTF concept through a structure of Partners Staff Elements, working at all levels of the Alliance military structure. Defence ministers of NATO and the 27 partner countries were to meet regularly to provide the political guidance for the enhanced Planning and Review Process of the PfP. In December 1997 NATO ministers of foreign affairs approved the establishment of a Euro-Atlantic Disaster Response Co-ordination Centre (EDRCC), and a non-permanent Euro-Atlantic Disaster Response Unit. The EDRCC was inaugurated in June 1998 and immediately commenced operations to provide relief to ethnic Albanian refugees fleeing the conflict in the Serbian province of Kosovo. In November the NAC approved the establishment of a network of PfP training centres, the first of which was inaugurated in Ankara, Turkey. The centres were a key element of a Training and

Education Programme, which was endorsed at the summit meeting in April 1999. During 2000 *ad hoc* working groups were convened to consider EAPC involvement in global humanitarian action against mines, the challenge of small arms and light weapons, and prospects for regional co-operation in South-Eastern Europe and in the Caucasus. The EAPC Action Plan for 2002–04 aimed to promote new approaches to co-operation in combating international terrorism. The Istanbul summit meeting in June 2004 agreed to strengthen co-operation with partner countries in the Caucasus and Central Asia. A Special Representative of the Secretary-General to the two regions was appointed in September.

The enlargement of NATO, through the admission of new members from the former USSR and Central and Eastern European countries, was considered to be a progressive means of contributing to the enhanced stability and security of the Euro-Atlantic area. In December 1996 NATO ministers of foreign affairs announced that invitations to join the Alliance would be issued to some former eastern bloc countries during 1997. The NATO Secretary-General and member governments subsequently began intensive diplomatic efforts to secure Russia's tolerance of these developments. It was agreed that no nuclear weapons or large numbers of troops would be deployed on the territory of any new member country in the former Eastern bloc. In May 1997 NATO and Russia signed the Founding Act on Mutual Relations, Co-operation and Security, which provided for enhanced Russian participation in all NATO decision-making activities, equal status in peace-keeping operations and representation at the Alliance headquarters at ambassadorial level, as part of a recognized shared political commitment to maintaining stability and security throughout the Euro-Atlantic region. A NATO-Russian Permanent Joint Council (PJC) was established under the Founding Act, and met for the first time in July; the Council provided each side the opportunity for consultation and participation in the other's security decisions, but without a right of veto. In March 1999 Russia condemned NATO's military action against the Federal Republic of Yugoslavia and announced the suspension of all relations within the framework of the Founding Act, as well as negotiations on the establishment of a NATO mission in Moscow. The PJC convened once more in May 2000, and subsequent meetings were held in June and December. In February 2001 the NATO Secretary-General agreed with the then acting Russian President a joint statement of commitment to pursuing dialogue and co-operation. A NATO information office was opened in Moscow in that month. The PJC condemned terrorist attacks perpetrated against the USA in September and pledged to strengthen Russia-NATO co-operation with a view to combating international terrorism. In December an agreement was concluded by NATO ministers of foreign affairs and their Russian counterpart to establish an eventual successor body to the PJC. The new NATO-Russia Council, in which NATO member states and Russia were to have equal status in decision-making, was inaugurated in May 2002. The Council aimed to strengthen co-operation in issues including counter-terrorism, crisis management, nuclear non-proliferation, and arms control. The third NATO-Russia conference on the role of the military in combating terrorism was convened in April 2004. In September the Council issued a joint statement condemning atrocities committed against civilians in North Ossetia and other parts of the Russian Federation.

In May 1997 NATO ministers of foreign affairs, meeting in Sintra, Portugal, concluded an agreement with Ukraine providing for enhanced co-operation between the two sides; the so-called Charter on a Distinctive Relationship was signed at the NATO summit meeting held in Madrid, Spain, in July. In May 1998 NATO agreed to appoint a permanent liaison officer in Ukraine to enhance co-operation between the two sides and assist Ukraine to formulate a programme of joint military exercises. The first NATO-Ukraine meeting at the level of heads of state took place in April 1999. A NATO-Ukraine Commission met for the first time in March 2000.

The Madrid summit meeting in July 1997 endorsed the establishment of a Mediterranean Co-operation Group to enhance NATO relations with Egypt, Israel, Jordan, Mauritania, Morocco and Tunisia. The Group was to provide a forum for regular political dialogue between the two groupings and to promote co-operation in training, scientific research and information exchange. In April 1999 NATO heads of state endorsed measures to strengthen the so-called Mediterranean Dialogue. Algeria joined the Mediterranean Dialogue in February 2000. The June 2004 summit meeting determined to enhance the Mediterranean Dialogue and launched a new 'Istanbul Co-operation Initiative' aimed at promoting broader co-operation with the Middle East.

In July 1997 heads of state and government formally invited the Czech Republic, Hungary and Poland to begin accession negotiations, with the aim of extending membership to those countries in April 1999. During 1997 concern was expressed on the part of some member governments with regard to the cost of expanding the Alliance; however, in November the initial cost of incorporating the Czech Republic, Hungary and Poland into NATO was officially estimated at US $1,300m. over a 10-year period, which was widely deemed to be an acceptable figure. Accession Protocols for the admission of those countries were signed in December and required ratification by all member states. The three countries formally became members of NATO in March 1999. In April the NATO summit meeting, held in Washington, DC, USA, initiated a new Membership Action Plan to extend practical support to aspirant member countries and to formalize a process of reviewing applications. In March 2003 protocols of accession, amending the North Atlantic Treaty, were adopted by the then 19 NATO member states with a view to admitting Bulgaria, Estonia, Latvia, Lithuania, Romania, Slovakia and Slovenia to the Alliance. In March 2004, the protocols of accession having been ratified by all of the member states, those seven countries were formally invited to join NATO and, on 29 March, they acceded to the Treaty. Albania, Croatia and the former Yugoslav republic of Macedonia were participating in the Membership Action Plan in April 2004.

PEACE-KEEPING ACTIVITIES

During the 1990s NATO increasingly developed its role as a mechanism for peace-keeping and crisis management. In June 1992 NATO ministers of foreign affairs, meeting in Oslo, Norway, announced the Alliance's readiness to support peace-keeping operations under the aegis of the CSCE on a case-by-case basis: NATO would make both military resources and expertise available to such operations. In July NATO, in co-operation with WEU, undertook a maritime operation in the Adriatic Sea to monitor compliance with the UN Security Council's resolutions imposing sanctions against the Yugoslav republics of Serbia and Montenegro. In October NATO was requested to provide, staff and finance the military headquarters of the United Nations peace-keeping force in Bosnia and Herzegovina, the UN Protection Force in Yugoslavia (UNPROFOR). In December NATO ministers of foreign affairs expressed the Alliance's readiness to support peace-keeping operations under the authority of the UN Security Council. From April 1993 NATO fighter and reconnaissance aircraft began patrolling airspace over Bosnia and Herzegovina in order to enforce the UN prohibition of military aerial activity over the country. In addition, from July NATO aircraft provided protective cover for UNPROFOR troops operating in the 'safe areas' established by the UN Security Council. In February 1994 NATO conducted the first of several aerial strikes against artillery positions that were violating heavy-weapons exclusion zones imposed around 'safe areas' and threatening the civilian populations. Throughout the conflict the Alliance also provided transport, communications and logistics to support UN humanitarian assistance in the region.

The peace accord for the former Yugoslavia, which was initialled in Dayton, USA, in November 1995, and signed in Paris in December, provided for the establishment of a NATO-led Implementation Force (IFOR) to ensure compliance with the treaty, in accordance with a strictly defined timetable and under the authority of a UN Security Council mandate. In early December a joint meeting of allied foreign and defence ministers endorsed the military structure for the peace mission, entitled Operation Joint Endeavour, which was to involve approximately 60,000 troops from 31 NATO and non-NATO countries. The mission was to be under the overall authority of the Supreme Allied Commander Europe (ACE), with the Commander of the ACE Rapid Reaction Corps providing command on the ground. IFOR, which constituted NATO's largest military operation ever, formally assumed responsibility for peace-keeping in Bosnia and Herzegovina from the UN on 20 December.

By mid-1996 the military aspects of the Dayton peace agreement had largely been implemented under IFOR supervision, including the withdrawal of former warring parties to behind agreed lines of separation and the release of prisoners of war. Substantial progress was achieved in the demobilization of soldiers and militia and in the cantonment of heavy weaponry. However, in August and September the Bosnian Serbs obstructed IFOR weapons inspections and the force was obliged to threaten the Serbs with strong military retaliation to secure access to the arms sites. During 1996 IFOR personnel undertook many activities relating to the civilian reconstruction of Bosnia and Herzegovina, including the repair of roads, railways and bridges; reconstruction of schools and hospitals; delivery of emergency food and water supplies; and emergency medical transportation. IFOR also co-operated with, and provided logistical support for, the Office of the High Representative of the International Community in Bosnia and Herzegovina, which was charged with overseeing implementation of the civilian aspects of the Bosnian peace accord. IFOR assisted the OSCE in preparing for and overseeing the all-Bosnia legislative elections that were held in September, and provided security for displaced Bosnians who crossed the inter-entity boundary in order to vote in their towns of origin. In December NATO ministers of foreign affairs approved a follow-on operation, with an 18-month mandate, to be known as the Stabilization Force (SFOR). SFOR was to be about one-half the size of IFOR, but was to retain 'the same unity of command and robust rules of engagement' as the previous force. SFOR became operational on 20 December. Its principal objective was to maintain a safe environment at a military level to ensure that the civil aspects of the Dayton peace accord could be fully implemented, including the completion of the de-mining process, the repatriation of refugees and preparations for municipal elections. In July 1997 NATO heads of government expressed their support for a more determined implementation of SFOR's mandate permitting the arrest of people sought by the International Criminal Tribunal for the Former Yugoslavia—ICTY if they were discovered within the normal course of duties. A few days later troops serving under SFOR seized two former Serb officials who had been indicted on charges of genocide. SFOR has subsequently undertaken this objective as part of its operational activities. From mid-1997 SFOR assisted efforts to maintain the security and territorial integrity of the Republika Srpska in the face of violent opposition from nationalist supporters of the former President, Radovan Karadžić, based in Pale. In August NATO authorized SFOR to use force to prevent the use of the local media to incite violence, following attacks on multinational forces by Serb nationalists during attempts to regain control of police buildings. In November SFOR provided the general security framework, as well as logistical and communications assistance, in support of the OSCE's supervision of legislative elections that were conducted in the Republika Srpska. In December NATO ministers of defence confirmed that SFOR would be maintained at its current strength of some 31,000 troops, subject to the periodic six-monthly reviews. In February 1998 NATO resolved to establish within SFOR a specialized unit to respond to civil unrest and uphold public security. At the same time the NAC initiated a series of security co-operation activities to promote the development of democratic practices and defence mechanisms in Bosnia and Herzegovina. In October 1999 the NAC formally agreed to implement a reduction in SFOR's strength to some 20,000 troops, as well as a revision of its command structure, in response to the improved security situation in Bosnia and Herzegovina. In 2001 some 35 countries contributed troops to SFOR. Its main activities continued to be in support of the peace process, assisting the collection and disposal of illegal weapons, distributing humanitarian aid, and rebuilding the country's infrastructure. In May 2002, in view of the improved security environment in Bosnia and Herzegovina, NATO determined to reduce SFOR to 12,000 troops by the end of the year. The reduction was reported to have been implemented by January 2003. In December of that year NATO defence ministers undertook to reduce NATO's presence in Bosnia and Herzegovina to some 7,000 troops by mid-2004. The June 2004 summit meeting determined to terminate SFOR's mandate at the end of 2004, and endorsed an EU initiative to establish a new mission in Bosnia and Herzegovina.

In March 1998 an emergency session of the NAC was convened at the request of the Albanian Government, which was concerned at the deteriorating security of its border region with the Serbian province of Kosovo and Metohija, following intensified action by the Kosovo Liberation Army (KLA) and retaliatory attacks by Serbian security forces. In mid-June NATO defence ministers authorized the formulation of plans for airstrikes against Serbian targets. A few days later some 80 aircraft dispatched from 15 NATO bases flew close to Albania's border with Kosovo, in an attempt to demonstrate the Alliance's determination to prevent further reprisals against the ethnic Albanian population. In September NATO defence ministers urged a diplomatic solution to the conflict, but insisted that, with an estimated 50,000 refugees living without shelter in the mountainous region bordering Albania, their main objective was to avert a humanitarian disaster. In late September the UN Security Council issued a resolution (1199) demanding an immediate cease-fire in Kosovo, the withdrawal of the majority of Serbian military and police forces, co-operation by all sides with humanitarian agencies, and the initiation of political negotiations on some form of autonomy for the province. Plans for NATO airstrikes were finalized in early October. However, the Russian Government remained strongly opposed to the use of force and there was concern among some member states over whether there was sufficient legal basis for NATO action without further UN authorization. Nevertheless, in mid-October, following Security Council condemnation of the humanitarian situation in Kosovo, the NAC agreed on limited airstrikes against Serbian targets, with a 96-hour delay on the 'activation order'. At the same time the US envoy to the region, Richard Holbrooke, concluded an agreement with President Milošević to implement the conditions of UN Resolution 1199. A 2,000-member international observer force, under the auspices of the OSCE, was to be established to monitor compliance with the agreement, supported by a NATO Co-ordination Unit, based in the former Yugoslav republic of Macedonia (FYRM), to assist with aerial surveillance. In mid-November NATO ambassadors approved the establishment of a 1,200–1,800 strong multinational force, under French command, to assist in any necessary evacuation of OSCE monitors. A NATO Kosovo Verification Command Centre was established in Kumanovo, north-east FYRM, in late November; however, President Milošević warned that the dispatch of foreign troops into Kosovo would be treated as an act of aggression.

In January 1999 NATO ambassadors convened in an emergency session following the discovery of the bodies of 45 ethnic Albanians in the Kosovan village of Racak. The meeting demanded that Serbia co-operate with an inquiry into the incident by the Prosecutor of the ICTY, guarantee the security and safety of all international personnel, withdraw security forces (which had continued to undertake offensives within Kosovo), and uphold the cease-fire. Intensive diplomatic efforts, co-ordinated by the six-country 'Contact Group' on the former Yugoslavia, succeeded in bringing both sides in the dispute to talks on the future of Kosovo. During the first stage of negotiations, held in Rambouillet, France, a provisional framework for a political settlement was formulated, based on a form of autonomy for Kosovo (to be reviewed after a three-year period), and incorporating a mandate for a NATO force of some 28,000 troops to monitor its implementation. The talks were suspended in late February with neither side having agreed to the accord. On the resumption of negotiations in mid-March representatives of the KLA confirmed that they would sign the peace settlement. President Milošević, however, continued to oppose the establishment of a NATO force in Kosovo and, despite further diplomatic efforts by Holbrooke, declined to endorse the agreement in accordance with a deadline imposed by the Contact Group. Amid reports of renewed Serbian violence against Albanian civilians in Kosovo, the NAC subsequently reconfirmed its support for NATO military intervention.

On 24 March 1999 an aerial offensive against the Federal Republic of Yugoslavia (now Serbia and Montenegro) was initiated by NATO, with the declared aim of reducing that country's capacity to commit attacks on the Albanian population. The first phase of the allied operation was directed against defence facilities, followed, a few days later, by the second phase which permitted direct attacks on artillery positions, command centres and other military targets in a declared exclusion zone south of the 44th parallel. The escalation of the conflict prompted thousands of Albanians to flee Kosovo, while others were reportedly forced from their homes by Serbian security personnel, creating massive refugee populations in neighbouring countries. In early April NATO ambassadors agreed to dispatch some 8,000 troops, as an ACE Mobile Force Land operation (entitled 'Operation Allied Harbour'), to provide humanitarian assistance to the estimated 300,000 refugees in Albania at that time and to provide transportation to relieve overcrowded camps, in particular in border areas. Refugees in the FYRM were to be assisted by the existing NATO contingent (numbering some 12,000 troops by early April), which was permitted by the authorities in that country to construct new camps for some 100,000 displaced Kosovans. An additional 1,000 troops were transferred from the FYRM to Albania in mid-May in order to construct a camp to provide for a further 65,000 refugees. In mid-April NATO ministers of foreign affairs, meeting in special session, expressed extreme concern at the refugee situation throughout the region. The ministers also clarified the conditions necessary to halt the offensive, which included Serbia's agreement to an international military presence in Kosovo, provision for the safe return of all refugees and an undertaking to work on the basis of the Rambouillet accord. Russia continued to pursue diplomatic efforts to secure a peaceful settlement to the conflict; however, Milošević's reported agreement to allow an unarmed international force in Kosovo, conditional on the immediate end to the NATO campaign, was dismissed by NATO governments. From early April there was increasing evidence of civilian casualties resulting from NATO's aerial bombing of transport, power and media infrastructure and suspected military targets. In mid-April NATO initiated an inquiry following the bombing of a convoy of lorries which resulted in the deaths of some 69 refugees. In the following month NATO was obliged to apologize to the authorities of the People's Republic of China after the accidental bombing of its embassy in Belgrade. At the same time there was widespread concern among governments at increasing evidence of systematic killings and ethnic violence being committed by Serbian forces within Kosovo, and at the estimated 100,000 Albanian men unaccounted for among the massive displaced population. NATO's 50th anniversary summit meeting, held in Washington, DC, USA, in late April, was dominated by consideration of the conflict and of the future stability of the region. A joint statement declared the determination of all Alliance members to increase economic and military pressure on President Milošević to withdraw forces from Kosovo. In particular, the meeting agreed to prevent shipments of petroleum reaching Serbia through Montenegro, to complement the embargo imposed by the EU and a new focus of the bombing campaign which aimed to destroy the fuel supply within Serbia. However, there was concern on the part of several NATO governments with regard to the legal and political aspects of implementing the embargo. The meeting failed to adopt a unified position on the use of ground forces, which many expert commentators insisted, throughout the campaign, were necessary to secure NATO's objectives. In May ministers of foreign affairs of the Group of Seven industrialized nations and Russia (the G-8) agreed on general principles for a political solution, which was to form the basis of a UN Security Council resolution. Later in that month NATO estimated that a future Kosovo Peace Implementation Force (KFOR), installed to guarantee a settlement, would require at least 48,000 troops. Following further intensive diplomatic efforts to secure a cease-fire in Kosovo, on 9 June a Military Technical Agreement was signed between NATO and the Federal Republic of Yugoslavia, incorporating a timetable for the withdrawal of all Serbian security personnel. On the following day the UN Security Council adopted Resolution 1244, which authorized an international security presence in Kosovo, under NATO, and an international civilian presence, the UN Interim Administration Mission in Kosovo (UNMIK). The NAC subsequently suspended the airstrike campaign, which, by that time, had involved some 38,000 sorties. KFOR was organized into six brigades, under the leadership of France, Germany, Italy, USA and the United Kingdom (with responsibility for two brigades). An initial force of 20,000 troops entered Kosovo on 12 June. A few days later an agreement was concluded with Russia, whose troops had also entered Kosovo and taken control of Pristina airport, which provided for the joint responsibility of the airstrip with a NATO contingent and for the participation of some 3,600 Russian troops in KFOR, reporting to the country command in each sector. On 20 June the withdrawal of Yugoslav troops from Kosovo was completed, providing for the formal ending of NATO's air campaign. The KLA undertook to demilitarize and transform the force, as required under Resolution 1244, which was reported to have been achieved in September. KFOR's immediate responsibility was to provide a secure environment to facilitate the safe return of refugees, and, pending the full deployment of UNMIK, to assist the reconstruction of infrastructure and civil and political institutions. In addition, NATO troops were to assist personnel of the international tribunal to investigate sites of alleged violations of human rights and mass graves. From August an escalation of ethnic violence and deterioration of law and order in some parts of the province was an outstanding concern. In January 2000 NATO agreed that the Eurocorps defence force (see under WEU) would assume command of KFOR headquarters in April. At that time KFOR's main concerns were to protect the minority populations, maintain security and reintegrate members of the KLA into civilian life. KFOR was also to continue to work closely with UNMIK in the provision of humanitarian aid, the rehabilitation of infrastructure and the development of civil administration. In February an emergency meeting of the NAC was convened to review the situation in the divided town of Titova Mitrovica, northern Kosovo, where violent clashes had occurred between the ethnic populations and five people had died during attempts by KFOR to impose order. The NAC expressed its determination to reinforce KFOR's troop levels. In September KFOR undertook to protect ethnic Serbians who were eligible to vote in a general election in the Federal Republic of Yugoslavia, and in the following month KFOR worked with OSCE and UN personnel to maintain a secure environment and provide logistical assistance for the holding of municipal elections in Kosovo. During the year KFOR attempted to prevent the movement and stockpiling of illegal armaments in the region. In November there was a marked deterioration in the security situation in Kosovo, and KFOR attempted to halt several outbreaks of cross-border violence. In February 2001 NATO conducted negotiations with the Yugoslav Government regarding new security arrangements to prevent further attacks on the local population in southern Serbia and to counter illegal arms-trafficking. A Weapons Destruction Programme was successfully conducted by KFOR between April 2000–December 2001; a second programme was initiated in March 2002, while an Ammunition Destruction Programme commenced in January. In May the NAC approved a modification of KFOR's mission that was designed to facilitate the introduction of a more regional approach to operations and, among other things, permit a reduction in KFOR's strength from 38,000 troops to some 33,200 by the end of the year. In July 2003, in view of progress made in the security situation, the withdrawal of the Russian contingent from KFOR was effected. In March 2004, in response to renewed inter-ethnic violence in Kosovo, NATO deployed additional troops from previously designated operational and strategic reserve forces in order to support operations undertaken by KFOR (whose strength totalled some 18,500 troops at this time) to protect Kosovar Serbs and other ethnic minorities in addition to ethnic Albanians.

In March 2001 Albanian separatists in the FYRM escalated their campaign in the north of that country. KFOR troops attempted to prevent Kosovo Albanians from supporting the rebels, fighting as the National Liberation Army (NLA), in order to avert further violence and instability. NATO dispatched military and political missions to meet with the Macedonian authorities, and agreed that Serbian troops were to be permitted to enter the ground safety zone in the Presevo valley (bordering on Kosovo and the FYRM) to strengthen security and prevent it becoming a safe haven for the rebel fighters. The Secretary-General also requested an additional 1,400 troops from member countries to reinforce border security. In mid-March the NLA seized strategic positions around Tetovo, in north-west FYRM. After several days of conflict Macedonian troops initiated an offensive against the rebel strongholds, prompting thousands of Albanians to flee into Kosovo. Nevertheless, hostilities intensified again from late April, resulting in further population displacements. In June NATO troops supervised the withdrawal of

some 300 armed Albanian rebels who had been besieged in a town neighbouring Skopje, the Macedonian capital. A cease-fire agreement, mediated by NATO, was concluded by the Macedonian authorities and Albanian militants in early July, as a prelude to negotiations on a political settlement. Meanwhile, NATO, at the request of the Macedonian Government, was drafting contingency plans to deploy troops in the FYRM with a mandate to supervise the voluntary disarmament of the Albanian militants and to collect and destroy their weapons, on condition that both sides showed commitment to maintaining the cease-fire and pursuing peace talks. In mid-July, however, ethnic Albanian insurgents in the Tetovo area were reportedly violating the cease-fire accord. An agreement regarding disarmament and conditions for ethnic minorities, as well as for the immediate withdrawal of troops, was concluded in August. Some 3,800 NATO troops were deployed at the end of that month, under so-called Operation Essential Harvest. At the end of the operation's 30-day mandate almost 4,300 guns had been surrendered, together with 400,000 mines, grenades and ammunition rounds. The NLA formally disbanded, in accordance with the peace agreement. The NAC approved a successor mission, Task Force Fox, comprising 700 troops, initially with a three-month mandate (subsequently extended), to protect the civilian observers of the accord (to be deployed by the EU and OSCE). In June 2002 a team from NATO headquarters met with the Macedonian authorities to discuss measures to enhance the country's co-operation with the Alliance. In November, as the expiry of the extended mandate of Task Force Fox approached, NATO agreed, at the request of the FYRM authorities, to deploy a new peace-keeping mission, 'Operation Allied Harmony', from December in order to afford continued protection to the civilian observers of the cease-fire accord and to assist the Macedonian authorities to assume responsibility for security. In March 2003 NATO's peace-keeping mission in the FYRM was replaced by an EU-led operation.

In April 2003 NATO determined to enhance its support to the International Security Assistance Force in Afghanistan, mandated by the United Nations Security Council in December 2001 to assist the Afghan Interim Authority in maintaining security; NATO assumed responsibility for command, co-ordination and planning of the operation in early August 2003. In December NATO ministers of defence determined progressively to expand the mission in Afghanistan beyond the capital, Kabul. The transfer of command of the Kunduz Provincial Reconstruction Team to NATO in January 2004 represented the first step of that expansion. In December the North Atlantic Council authorized further deployment of Provincial Reconstruction Teams to the west of the country.

Nato Agencies

Civilian production and logistics organizations responsible to the NAC:

Central Europe Pipeline Management Agency (CEPMA): BP 552, 78005 Versailles, France; tel. 1-39-24-49-00; fax 1-39-55-65-39; f. 1957; responsible for the 24-hour operation of the Central Europe Pipeline System and its storage and distribution facilities.

NATO Air Command and Control System Management Agency (NACMA): Bldg Z, blvd Léopold III, 1110 Brussels, Belgium; tel. (2) 707-41-11; fax (2) 707-87-77; internet www.nacma.nato .int; conducts planning, system engineering, implementation and configuration management for NATO's ACCS programme.

NATO Airborne Early Warning and Control Programme Management Organisation (NAPMO): Akerstraat 7, 6445 CL Brunssum, Netherlands; fax (45) 5254373; f. 1978; responsible for the management and implementation of the NATO Airborne Early Warning and Control Programme.

NATO Consultation, Command and Control Agency (NC3A): 1110 Brussels, Belgium; tel. (2) 707-43-58; fax (2) 707-57-09; internet www.nc3a.nato.int; works within the framework of the NATO C3 Organization (f. 1996 by restructuring of the NATO Communications and Information Systems Organization and the Tri-Service Group on Communications and Electronics, incorporating the former Allied Data Systems Interoperability Agency, the Allied Naval Communications Agency and the Allied Tactical Communications Agency); provides scientific advice and assistance to NATO military and political authorities; helps to develop, procure and implement cost-effective system capabilities to support political consultations and military command and control functions; also maintains offices in The Hague.

NATO CIS Operating and Support Agency (NACOSA): maintains NATO's communications and information system (CIS); supervised by the NC3 Board.

NATO Communications and Information Systems (NCISS) School: 04010 Borgo Piave, Latina, Italy; tel. (0773) 6771; fax

(0773) 662467; f. 1959; provides advanced training to civilian and military personnel in the operation and maintenance of NATO's communications and information systems; conducts orientation courses for partner countries.

NATO EF 2000 and Tornado Development, Production and Logistics Management Agency (NETMA): Insel Kammerstrasse 12–14, Postfach 1302, 82008 Unterhaching, Germany; tel. (89) 666800; fax (89) 66680555; replaced the NATO Multirole Combat Aircraft (MRCA) Development and Production Management Agency (f. 1969) and the NATO European Fighter (EF) Aircraft Development, Production and Logistics Management Agency (f. 1987); responsible for the joint development and production of the European Fighter Aircraft and the MRCA (Tornado).

NATO HAWK Management Office: 26 rue Galliéni, 92500 Rueil-Malmaison, France; tel. 1-47-08-75-00; fax 1-47-52-10-99; e-mail bgohnhmo@csi.com; f. 1959 to supervise the multinational production and upgrading programmes of the HAWK surface-to-air missile system in Europe; Gen. Man. A. BOCCHI.

NATO Helicopter Design and Development Production and Logistics Management Agency (NAHEMA): Le Quatuor, Bâtiment A, 42 route de Galice, 13082 Aix-en-Provence Cédex 2, France; tel. 4-42-95-92-00; fax 4-42-64-30-50.

NATO Maintenance and Supply Agency (NAMSA): 8302 Capellen, Luxembourg; tel. 30-631; fax 30-87-21; internet www.namsa.nato.int; f. 1958; supplies spare parts and logistical support for a number of jointly-used weapon systems, missiles and electronic systems; all member nations except Iceland participate.

Responsible to the Military Committee:

NATO Defense College (NDC): Via Giorgia Pelosi 1, 00143 Rome-Cecchiguola, Italy; tel. (06) 505259; fax (06) 50525799; internet www.ndc.nato.int; f. 1951 to train officials for posts in NATO organizations or in national ministries; organizes international research seminars; Commandant Lt-Gen. MARC VANKEIRSBILCK (Belgium).

NATO Frequency Management Sub-Committee (FMSC): 1100 Brussels, Belgium; tel. (2) 707-55-28; replaced the Allied Radio Frequency Agency (f. 1951); the FMSC is the frequency authority of the Alliance and establishes and co-ordinates all policy concerned with the military use of the radio frequency spectrum.

NATO Standardisation Agency (NSA): 1110 Brussels, Belgium; tel. (2) 707-55-76; fax (2) 707-57-18; e-mail nsa@hq.nato.int; lead agent for the development, co-ordination and assessment of operational standardization, in order to enhance interoperability; initiates, co-ordinates, supports and administers standardization activities conducted under the authority of the NATO Committee for Standardisation.

Research and Technology Organisation (RTO): BP 25, 7 rue Ancelle, 92201 Neuilly-sur-Seine Cédex, France; tel. 1-55-61-22-00; fax 1-55-61-22-99; e-mail mailbox@rta.nato.int; internet www.rta.nato.int; f. 1998 by merger of the Advisory Group for Aerospace Research and Development and the Defence Research Group; brings together scientists and engineers from member countries for exchange of information and research co-operation (formally established 1998); provides scientific and technical advice for the Military Committee, for other NATO bodies and for member nations; comprises a Research and Technology Board and a Research and Technology Agency, responsible for implementing RTO's work programme.

Responsible to Supreme Allied Commander Europe (SACEUR):

NATO (SHAPE) School: Am Rainenbichl 54, 82487 Oberammergau, Germany; tel. (88) 22922353; fax (88) 221035; e-mail postmaster@natoschool-shape.de; internet www.natoschool-shape.de; f. 1975; acts as a centre for training military and civilian personnel of NATO countries, and, since 1991, for officials from partner countries, in support of NATO policies, operations and objectives.

Responsible to Supreme Allied Commander Transformation:

NATO Undersea Research Centre: Viale San Bartolomeo 400, 19138 La Spezia, Italy; tel. (0187) 5271; fax (0187) 524600; e-mail library@saclantc.nato.int; internet www.saclantc.nato.int; f. 1959; conducts maritime research in support of NATO's operational and transformational requirements, in particular through its science programme.

Finance

As NATO is an international, not a supra-national, organization, its member countries themselves decide the amount to be devoted to their defence effort and the form which the latter will assume. Thus, the aim of NATO's defence planning is to develop realistic military plans for the defence of the Alliance at reasonable cost. Under the annual defence planning process, political, military and economic factors are considered in relation to strategy, force requirements and available resources. The procedure for the co-ordination of military plans and defence expenditures rests on the detailed and comparative analysis of the capabilities of member countries. All installations for the use of international forces are financed under a common-funded infrastructure programme. In accordance with the terms of the Partnership for Peace strategy, partner countries undertake to make available the necessary personnel, assets, facilities and capabilities to participate in the programme. The countries also share the financial cost of military exercises in which they participate. The administrative (or 'civil') budget, which includes the NATO Science Programme, amounted to €124.7m. in 2002. The total military budget approved for 2001 amounted to €746m. (including the operating costs of NATO command structures in the former Yugoslavia, but excluding the costs of assignment of military personnel, met by the contributing countries).

Publications

NATO publications (in English and French, with some editions in other languages) include:

NATO Basic Texts.
NATO Handbook.
NATO in the 21st Century.
NATO Ministerial Communiqués.
NATO Review (quarterly in 17 languages).
NATO Update (weekly, electronic version only).
Economic and scientific publications

ORGANISATION FOR ECONOMIC CO-OPERATION AND DEVELOPMENT—OECD

Address: 2 rue André-Pascal, 75775 Paris Cédex 16, France.

Telephone: 1-45-24-82-00; **fax:** 1-45-24-85-00; **e-mail:** webmaster@oecd.org; **internet:** www.oecd.org.

OECD was founded in 1961, replacing the Organisation for European Economic Co-operation (OEEC) which had been established in 1948 in connection with the Marshall Plan. It constitutes a forum for governments to discuss, develop and attempt to co-ordinate their economic and social policies. The Organisation aims to promote policies designed to achieve the highest level of sustainable economic growth, employment and increase in the standard of living, while maintaining financial stability and democratic government, and to contribute to economic expansion in member and non-member states and to the expansion of world trade.

MEMBERS

Australia	Hungary	Norway
Austria	Iceland	Poland
Belgium	Ireland	Portugal
Canada	Italy	Slovakia
Czech Republic	Japan	Spain
Denmark	Republic of Korea	Sweden
Finland	Luxembourg	Switzerland
France	Mexico	Turkey
Germany	Netherlands	United Kingdom
Greece	New Zealand	USA

The European Commission also takes part in OECD's work.

Organization
(April 2005)

COUNCIL

The governing body of OECD is the Council, at which each member country is represented. The Council meets from time to time (usually once a year) at the level of government ministers, with the chairmanship rotated among member states. It also meets regularly at official level, when it comprises the Secretary-General and the Permanent Representatives of member states to OECD. It is responsible for all questions of general policy and may establish subsidiary bodies as required, to achieve the aims of the Organisation. Decisions and recommendations of the Council are adopted by mutual agreement of all its members.

Heads of Permanent Delegations
(with ambassadorial rank)

Australia: Véronique Ingram.

Austria: Ulrich Stacher.

Belgium: Patrick van Haute.

Canada: Jocelyne Bourgon.

Czech Republic: Jiří Maceška.

Denmark: Peter Brückner.

Finland: Jorma Julin.

France: Dominique Perreau.

Germany: Hans-Stefan Kruse.

Greece: Anthony Courakis.

Hungary: Károly Lotz.

Iceland: Tómas Ingi Olrich.

Ireland: John Rowan.

Italy: Francesco Olivieri.

Japan: Shinichi Kitajima.

Republic of Korea: Dr O-Kyu Kwon.

Luxembourg: Hubert Wurth.

Mexico: Carlos Elizondo Mayer-Serra.

Netherlands: Joan Boer.

New Zealand: Adrian H. Macey.

Norway: Tanya H. Storm.

Poland: Jan Bielawski.

Portugal: Basílio Horta.

Slovakia: Dušan Bella.

Spain: Fernando Ballestero Díaz.

Sweden: Gun-Britt Andersson.

Switzerland: Wilhelm B. Jaggi.

Turkey: Sencar Özsoy.

United Kingdom: David Lyscom.

USA: Constance Albanese Morella.

Participant with Special Status

European Commission: Michel Vanden Abeele (Belgium).

EXECUTIVE COMMITTEE

The Executive Committee prepares the work of the Council. It is also called upon to carry out specific tasks where necessary. In addition to its regular meetings, the Committee meets occasionally in special sessions attended by senior government officials.

SECRETARIAT

The Council, the committees and other bodies in OECD are assisted by an independent international secretariat headed by the Secretary-General. An Executive Director is responsible for the management of administrative support services.

Secretary-General: Donald J. Johnston (Canada) (until May 2006).

Deputy Secretaries-General: Richard E. Hecklinger (USA), Herwig Schlögl (Germany), Kiyotaka Akasaka (Japan), Berglind Asgeirsdóttir (Iceland).

AUTONOMOUS AND SEMI-AUTONOMOUS BODIES

Centre for Educational Research and Innovation (CERI): f. 1968; includes all member countries; Head Tom Schuller.

Development Centre.
European Conference of Ministers of Transport.
Financial Action Task Force on Money Laundering.
Sahel and West Africa Club.
International Energy Agency.
Nuclear Energy Agency.

Activities

The greater part of the work of OECD, which covers all aspects of economic and social policy, is prepared and carried out in about 200 specialized bodies (committees, working parties, etc.); all members are normally represented on these bodies, except on those of a restricted nature.

ECONOMIC POLICY

Through its work on economic policy, OECD aims to promote stable macroeconomic environments in member and non-member countries and to identify priority concerns. *Economic Outlook*, analysing the major trends in short-term economic prospects and key policy issues, is published twice a year. The main organ for the consideration and direction of economic policy is the Economic Policy Committee, which comprises governments' chief economic advisers and central bankers, and meets two or three times a year. It has several working parties and groups, including Working Party No. 1 on Macro-Economic and Structural Policy Analysis, Working Party No. 3 on Policies for the Promotion of Better International Payments Equilibrium, and the Working Party on Short-Term Economic Prospects.

The Economic and Development Review Committee, comprising all member countries, is responsible for surveys of the economic situation and macroeconomic and structural policies of each member country. A report, including specific policy recommendations, is issued every 12 to 18 months on each country, after an examination carried out by the Committee. This process of peer review has been extended to other branches of the Organisation's work (agriculture, environment, manpower and social affairs, scientific policy and development aid efforts).

STATISTICS

Statistical data and related methodological information are collected from member governments and, where possible, consolidated, or converted into an internationally comparable form. The Statistics Directorate maintains and makes available data required for macro-economic forecasting, i.e. national accounts, the labour force, foreign trade, prices, output, and monetary, financial, industrial and other short-term statistics. Work is also undertaken to develop new statistics and new statistical standards and systems in areas of emerging policy interest (such as sustainable development). In addition, the Directorate passes on to non-member countries member states' experience in compiling statistics. In the early 2000s OECD undertook a strategy to improve and reform its statistical activities. A new Statistical Information System, incorporating new technical infrastructure, was developed which aimed to improve the efficiency of data collection, processing, storage etc, to improve the quality of OECD statistics, and to enhance accessibility to the data. In April 2004 a new Experts Group on Statistical and Metadata Exchange began work to foster dialogue with external partners on strategic issues relating to the development and practical implementation of new technologies and procedures for statistical data exchange.

DEVELOPMENT CO-OPERATION

The Development Assistance Committee (DAC) is the principal body through which the Organisation deals with issues relating to co-operation with developing countries and is one of the key forums in which the major bilateral donors work together to increase their effectiveness in support of sustainable development. The DAC is supported by the Development Co-operation Directorate, which monitors aid programmes and resource flows, compiles statistics and seeks to establish codes of practice in aid. There are also working parties on statistics, on aid evaluation, on gender equality and on development co-operation and environment; and networks on poverty reduction, on good governance and capacity development, and on conflict, peace and development co-operation. Other development work is undertaken by the Development Centre, a research body that promotes a better understanding of the economic and social problems of developing countries, the Sahel and West Africa Club, which aims to support links between the public and private sectors of OECD and African countries, and the Centre for the Co-operation with Non-Members

Guided by the Development Partnerships Strategy formulated in 1996, the DAC's mission is to foster co-ordinated, integrated, effective and adequately financed international efforts in support of sustainable economic and social development. Recognizing that developing countries themselves are ultimately responsible for their own development, the DAC concentrates on how international co-operation can contribute to the population's ability to overcome poverty and participate fully in society. Principal activities include: adopting authoritative policy guide-lines; conducting periodic critical reviews of members' programmes of development co-operation; providing a forum for dialogue, exchange of experience and the building of international consensus on policy and management issues; and publishing statistics and reports on aid and other resource flows to developing countries and countries in transition. A working set of indicators of development progress has been established by the DAC, in collaboration with experts from UN agencies (including the World Bank) and from developing countries.

The DAC holds an annual high-level meeting of ministers responsible for international aid, and heads of aid agencies from member governments, with senior officials from the World Bank, IMF and UNDP. In February–March 2005 OECD/DAC co-sponsored a High-Level Forum on Aid Effectiveness, held in Paris, France. The key issues arising from the Forum were considered at the DAC high level meeting, convened in mid-March. In addition, the meeting reviewed OECD's contribution to achieving the UN Millennium Development Goals, issues relating to development, peace and security, and a report commissioned by heads of state participating in the New Partnership for Africa's Development (NEPAD), the *Mutual Review of Development Effectiveness in the NEPAD context*.

PUBLIC GOVERNANCE AND TERRITORIAL DEVELOPMENT

The Public Governance and Territorial Development Directorate is concerned with identifying changing needs in society and in markets, and with helping countries to adapt their governmental systems and territorial policies. One of the Directorate's primary functions is to provide a forum for exchanging ideas on how to meet the challenges countries face in the area of governance. It is concerned with improving public sector governance through comparative data and analysis, the setting and promotion of standards, and the facilitation of transparency and peer review, as well as to encourage the participation of civil society in public governance. In 2005 the Directorate was particularly concerned with the implementation by member countries of so-called e-government and knowledge management techniques in the public sector. The Public Management Committee (PUMA) serves as a forum for senior officials responsible for the central management systems of government, providing information, analysis and recommendations on public management and governing capacity. A Working Party of Senior Budget Officials is the principal international forum for issues concerning international budgeting. In November 2004 the Global Forum on Governance considered methods of preventing and detecting corruption in public procurement. In 1992 a joint initiative of OECD and the European Union (EU), operating within OECD, was established to support good governance in the countries of Central and Eastern Europe that were to accede to, or were candidates for either accession to or association with, the European Union (EU). The so-called Support for Improvement in Governance and Management (SIGMA) programme assists in the reform and modernization of public institutions in those countries and assesses their progress in those areas.

The Territorial Development Policy Committee assists central governments with the design and implementation of more effective, area-based strategies, encourages the emergence of locally driven initiatives for economic development, and promotes better integration of local and national approaches. Generally, the Committee's work programme emphasizes the need for innovative policy initiatives and exchange of knowledge in a wide range of policies, such as entrepreneurship and technology diffusion and issues of social exclusion and urban deprivation. National and regional territorial reviews are undertaken to analyse economic and social trends and highlight governance issues.

INTERNATIONAL TRADE

The analytical work of OECD's Trade Directorate, which is generally performed under the auspices of the OECD Trade Committee, supports the continued liberalization and efficient operation of the multilateral trading system, with the aim of contributing to the expansion of world trade on a non-discriminatory basis. Its activities include examination of issues concerning trade relations among member countries as well as relations with non-member countries, and consideration and discussion of trade measures taken by a member country which adversely affect another's interests. Through its working parties, the Committee analyses trade issues relating to, for example, the environment and agriculture. It holds regular consultations with civil society organizations.

A Working Party on Export Credits and Credit Guarantees serves as a forum for the discussion and co-ordination of export credit policies. OECD maintains an Export Credit Arrangement, which

provides a framework for the use of officially supported export credits, stipulating the most generous financial terms and conditions available. Governments participating in the Arrangement meet regularly. In November 2004 they agreed to implement a two-year pilot programme to enhance transparency and effectiveness of untied overseas development aid credits.

The Trade Committee considers the challenges that are presented to the existing international trading system by financial or economic instability, the process of globalization of production and markets and the ensuing deeper integration of national economies. OECD provided support to the multilateral trade negotiations conducted under the General Agreement on Tariffs and Trade (GATT), assisting member countries to analyse the effects of the trade accords and promoting its global benefits. Following the entry into force of the World Trade Organization (WTO) agreements in 1995, OECD continued to study and assess aspects of the international trade agenda. In November 1999 OECD published a report on the impact of further trade liberalization on developing countries, in preparation for the next round of multilateral trade negotiations (which were launched by WTO in November 2001). In 2000 all OECD governments adopted a set of revised guide-lines for multinational enterprises. OECD sought to ensure, in the approach to the WTO ministerial meeting held in Cancún, Mexico, in 2003 that development issues occupied the mainstream of all aspects of its trade and investment work. OECD is addressing various agricultural trade issues related to WTO negotiations. A report published in 2002, *Agricultural Policies in OECD Countries: A Positive Reform Agenda*, examined the costs and benefits of agricultural trade reform. *GATS: the Case for Open Services Markets*, meanwhile, also published in 2002, sought to show the benefits of market openness in services trade and investment. OECD is committed to the Doha Development Agenda, the framework for the multilateral trade negotiations currently under way in WTO. OECD and WTO have established a joint database that provides information about trade-related technical assistance and capacity-building in respect of trade policy and regulation; trade development; and infrastructure.

FINANCIAL AND ENTERPRISE AFFAIRS

Promoting the efficient functioning of markets and enterprises and strengthening the multilateral framework for trade and investment is the responsibility of the main OECD committees and working groups supported by the Directorate for Financial and Enterprise Affairs. The Directorate analyses emerging trends, provides policy guide-lines and recommendations, gives examples of best practice and maintains benchmarks to measure progress.

The Committee on Capital Movements and Invisible Transactions monitors the implementation of the Codes of Liberalization of Invisible Transactions and of Current Invisible Operations as legally binding norms for all member countries. The Committee on International Investment and Multinational Enterprises monitors the OECD Guide-lines for Multinational Enterprises, a corporate Code of Conduct recommended by OECD member governments, business and labour units. A Declaration on International Investment and Multinational Enterprises, while non-binding, contains commitments on the conduct and treatment of foreign-owned enterprises established in member countries. A comprehensive review of the Declaration was completed in 2000. Negotiations on a Multilateral Agreement on Investment (MAI), initiated by OECD ministers in 1995 to provide a legal framework for international investment, broke down in October 1998, although 'informal consultation' on the issue was subsequently continued.

The Committee on Competition Law and Policy promotes the harmonization of national competition policies, co-operation in competition law enforcement, common merger reporting rules and procompetitive regulatory reform, the development of competition laws and institutions, and efforts to change policies that restrain competition. The Committee on Financial Markets exercises surveillance over recent developments, reform measures and structural and regulatory conditions in financial markets. It aims to promote international trade in financial services, to encourage the integration of non-member countries into the global financial system, and to improve financial statistics. The Insurance Committee monitors structural changes and reform measures in insurance markets, for example the liberalization of insurance markets, financial insolvency, co-operation on insurance and reinsurance policy, the monitoring and analysis of regulatory and structural developments, and private pensions and health insurance. A working party on private pensions meets twice a year. In 2002 OECD member governments approved guide-lines for the administration of private pension funds, the first initiative they had taken to set international standards for the governance and supervision of collective pension funds. Specialized work on public debt is undertaken by the Working Party on Government Debt Management. An OECD Global Forum on Public Debt Management and Emerging Government Securities Markets is convened each year.

In May 1997 the OECD Council endorsed plans to introduce a global ban on the corporate bribery of public officials; the OECD Convention on Bribery of Foreign Public Officials in International Business Transactions entered into force in February 1999. By January 2005 the Convention had been ratified by 36 countries, of which 35 had undergone a 'phase I' review of legislation conformity with anti-bribery standards. In May 1999 ministers endorsed a set of OECD Principles for Corporate Governance, covering ownership and control of corporate entities, the rights of shareholders, the role of stakeholders, transparency, disclosure and the responsibilities of boards. In 2000 these became one of the 12 core standards of global financial stability, and they are used as a benchmark by other international financial institutions. In 2002 OECD mandated a Steering Group on Corporate Governance to review and update the Principles. The revised set of Principles was published in 2004. OECD collaborates with the World Bank and other organizations to promote good governance world-wide, for example through regional round tables and the Global Corporate Governance Forum. OECD provides the secretariat for the Financial Action Task Force on Money Laundering (FATF), which develops and promotes policies to combat money-laundering.

TAXATION

OECD promotes internationally-accepted standards and practices of taxation, and provides a forum for the exchange of information and experience of tax policy and administration. The Committee on Fiscal Affairs is concerned with promoting the removal of tax barriers, monitoring the implementation and impact of major tax reforms, developing a neutral tax framework for electronic commerce, and studying the tax implications of the globalization of national economies. A Centre for Policy and Administration supports the work of the Committee. Other activities include the publication of comparable statistics on taxation and guide-lines on transfer pricing, and the study of tax evasion and tax and electronic commerce. OECD is a sponsor, with the IMF and World Bank, of an International Tax Dialogue, the first global forum of which was convened in March 2005 on the topic of value-added taxation. OECD also convenes a Global Forum on Taxation. In June 2004 the Forum, held in Berlin, Germany, agreed proposals to achieve higher standards of transparency and information exchange in taxation issues.

Since 1998 OECD has promoted co-ordinated action for the elimination of so-called 'harmful' tax practices, designed to reduce the incidence of international money-laundering, and the level of potential tax revenue lost by OECD members. In mid-2000 it launched an initiative to abolish 'harmful tax systems', identifying a number of offshore jurisdictions as 'tax havens' lacking financial transparency, and inviting these to co-operate with the Organisation by amending national financial legislation. Several of the countries and territories named agreed to follow a timetable for reform, with the aim of eliminating such practices by the end of 2005. Others, however, were reluctant to participate. (The USA also strongly opposed the initiative.) In April 2002 OECD announced that co-ordinated defensive measures would be implemented against non-complying jurisdictions ('un-co-operative tax havens') from early 2003. The Organisation has also highlighted examples of preferential tax regimes in member countries. In February 2004 the Committee on Fiscal Affairs published a Progress Report on the elimination of harmful tax practices.

FOOD, AGRICULTURE AND FISHERIES

OECD's Directorate of Food, Agriculture and Fisheries undertakes analysis of relevant issues and advises governments, in particular in relation to policy reform and trade liberalization. OECD provides analytical support to agricultural trade liberalization under review by the WTO. It is also a focal point for global efforts in the certification and standardisation of products, packaging and control schemes. A Committee for Agriculture reviews major developments in agricultural policies, deals with the adaptation of agriculture to changing economic conditions, elaborates forecasts of production and market prospects for the major commodities, manages a programme to develop product standards in agriculture, identifies best practices for limiting the impact of agricultural production on the environment, promotes the use of sustainable practices in the sector and considers questions of agricultural development in emerging and transition economies. A separate Fisheries Committee carries out similar tasks in its sector, and, in particular, analyses the consequences of policy measures with a view to promoting responsible and sustainable fisheries. The Directorate administers a Biological Resources in Agriculture programme, which sponsors research fellowships as well as workshops and conferences, to enhance international co-operation in priority areas of agro-food research.

ENVIRONMENT

The OECD Environment Directorate works in support of the Environment Policy Committee (EPOC) on environmental issues.

EPOC assesses performance; encourages co-operation on environmental policy; promotes the integration of environmental and economic policies; works to develop principles, guide-lines and strategies for effective environmental management; provides a forum for member states to address common problems and share data and experience; and promotes the sharing of information with non-member states. The Directorate conducts peer reviews of environmental conditions and progress. A first cycle of 32 Environmental Performance Reviews of member and selected non-member countries was completed in 2000, and a second cycle commenced in 2001. The Directorate aims to improve understanding of past and future trends through the collection and dissemination of environmental data.

OECD programmes and working parties on the environment consider a range of issues, including the harmonization of biotechnology regulation, the environmental impact of production and consumption, natural resource management, trade and investment and the environment, and chemical safety. In some cases working parties collaborate with other Directorates (for example, the Working Parties on Trade and Environment and on Agriculture and Environment). An Experts Group on Climate Change, based in the Environment Directorate, undertakes studies related to international agreements on climate change. In 1995 the BioTrack Online programme was developed to disseminate information relating to the regulatory oversight of biotechnology, with particular emphasis on environmental and food safety.

In May 2001 OECD ministers of the environment, convened in Paris, France, adopted the OECD Environmental Strategy for the 21st Century, containing recommendations for future work. The Strategy, which was to be implemented by 2010, focused on fostering sustainable development, and strengthening co-operation with non-member countries and partnerships with the private sector and civil society. Fundamental objectives included the efficient use of renewable and non-renewable resources; the avoidance of irreversible damage; the maintenance of ecosystems; and separating environmental pressures from economic growth. The Strategy identified several issues requiring urgent action, such as the generation of municipal waste, increased car and air travel, greenhouse gas emissions, groundwater pollution, and the exploitation of marine fisheries. The meeting endorsed guide-lines for the provision of environmentally sustainable transport, as well as the use of a set of key environmental indicators. A review of the key indicators was presented to a meeting of environment ministers, convened in April 2004.

The Environment Directorate also provides the secretariat for the Task Force for the Implementation of the Environmental Action Programme in Central and Eastern Europe, which encourages countries in Eastern Europe and the CIS to take environmental issues into consideration in the process of economic restructuring.

SCIENCE, TECHNOLOGY AND INDUSTRY

The Directorate for Science, Technology and Industry aims to assist member countries in formulating, adapting and implementing policies that optimize the contribution of science, technology, industrial development and structural change to economic growth, employment and social development. It provides indicators and analysis on emerging trends in these fields, identifies and promotes best practices, and offers a forum for dialogue.

Areas considered by the Committee for Scientific and Technological Policy include the management of public research, technology and innovation, and intellectual property rights. A Working Party on Biotechnology was established in 1993 to pursue study of biotechnology and its applications, including issues such as scientific and technological infrastructure, and the relation of biotechnology to sustainable industrial development. Statistical work on biotechnology is undertaken by a Working Party of National Experts on Science and Technology Indicators. In 1992 a megascience forum was established to bring together senior science policy officials to identify and pursue opportunities for international co-operation in scientific research. It was succeeded, in 1999, by the Global Science Forum, which meets twice a year. In 2000 multilateral negotiations on establishing a Global Biodiversity Information Facility (GBIF) were concluded. The GBIF began operations in 2001 to connect global biodiversity databases in order to make available a wide range of online data.

The Committee for Information, Computer and Communications Policy monitors developments in telecommunications and information technology and their impact on competitiveness and productivity, with a new emphasis on technological and regulatory convergence. It also promotes the development of new rules (e.g. guide-lines on information security) and analyses trade and liberalization issues. The Committee maintains a database of communications indicators and telecommunications tariffs. In December 1999 the OECD Council adopted a set of Guide-lines for Consumer Protection in the Context of Electronic Commerce. A Working Party on Information Security and Privacy promotes a co-ordinated approach to efforts to enhance trust in the use of electronic commerce. In August 2004 an OECD Task Force was established to co-ordinate efforts to counter unsolicited e-mail ('spam'). OECD supports the Digital Opportunities Task Force (Dot.force) which was established in June 2000 by the Group of Seven industrialized nations and Russia (the G-8) to recommend action with a view to eliminating the so-called 'digital divide' between developed and less developed countries and between different population sectors within nations. OECD's Global Conference on Telecommunications Policy for the Digital Environment, held in January 2002, emphasized the importance of competition in the sector and the need for regulatory reform.

The Committee on Industry and the Business Environment focuses on industrial production; business performance; innovation and competitiveness in industrial and services sectors; and policies for private-sector development in member and selected non-member economies. In recent years the Committee has addressed issues connected with globalization, regulatory reform, small and medium-sized enterprises (SMEs), and the role of industry in sustainable development. Business and industry policy fora explore a variety of issues with the private sector and develop recommendations. Issues addressed recently include environmental strategies for industry and new technologies. A working party on SMEs conducts an ongoing review of the contribution of SMEs to growth and employment and carries out a comparative assessment of best practice policies. OECD, in conjunction with the Italian Government, organized its first ministerial conference on SMEs in Bologna, Italy, in 2000. Monitoring implementation of the SME policies agreed at the conference is undertaken under the so-called Bologna Process. A second ministerial conference was held in Istanbul, Turkey, in 2004. In July 2004 a Centre for Entrepreneurship, SMEs and Local Development was established to foster entrepreneurial initiatives and to address the needs of new and existing business.

The Transport Division of the Directorate for Science, Technology and Industry considers aviation, maritime, shipbuilding, road and intermodal transport issues. Maritime Transport and Steel Committees aim to promote multilateral solutions to sectoral friction and instability based on the definition and monitoring of rules. The Working Party on Shipbuilding seeks to establish normal competitive conditions in that sector, especially through dialogue with non-OECD countries. The Tourism Committee promotes sustained growth in the tourism sector and encourages the integration of tourism issues into other policy areas. On 1 January 2004 a new Transport Research Centre was established by merger of OECD's road transport and intermodal linkages research programme and the economic research activities of the European Conference of Ministers of Transport.

EMPLOYMENT, LABOUR AND SOCIAL AFFAIRS

The Employment, Labour and Social Affairs Committee is concerned with the development of the labour market and selective employment policies to ensure the utilization of human capital at the highest possible level and to improve the quality and flexibility of working life, as well as the effectiveness of social policies; it plays a central role in addressing OECD's concern to reduce high and persistent unemployment through the creation of high-quality jobs. The Committee's work covers such issues as the role of women in the economy, industrial relations, measurements of unemployment, and the development of an extensive social database. The Committee also carries out single-country and thematic reviews of labour-market policies and social assistance systems. It has assigned a high priority to work on the policy implications of an ageing population and on indicators of human capital investment.

OECD undertakes analysis of health-care and health expenditure issues, and reviews the organization and performance of health systems. In 2001 a three-year OECD Health Project was launched with the aim of evaluating and analysing the performance of health-care systems in member countries and the factors affecting their performance. In May 2004 OECD ministers responsible for health convened for the first time to consider the completed Project. Upon their recommendation, in January 2005 a new Group on Health was established to direct a further programme of work, to be supported by a new Health Division within the Directorate of Employment, Labour and Social Affairs. Social policy areas of concern include benefits and wages, family-friendly policies, and the social effects of population ageing.

A Non-Member Economies and International Migration Division works on social policy issues in emerging economies and economies in transition, especially relating to education and labour market reforms and to the economic and social aspects of migration. The Directorate undertakes regular analysis of trends in international migration, including consideration of its economic and social impact, the integration of immigrants, and international co-operation in the control of migrant flows.

EDUCATION

In 2002 a new Directorate for Education was created in order to raise the profile of OECD's work, which is conducted in the context of its view of education as a lifelong activity. The Directorate comprises Divisions on Education and Training, Indicators and Analysis, Education Management, and Infrastructure. It also incorporates a Programme for Co-operation with non-member Economies and the Centre for Educational Research and Innovation (CERI), which promotes the development of research activities in education, together with experiments of an advanced nature, designed to test innovations in educational systems and to stimulate research and development. Other programmes undertaken by the Directorate include the Programme of International Student Assessments, the Programme on Institutional Management in Higher Education, and the Programme on Education Building. In 2004 OECD, in collaboration with UNESCO, began drafting Guide-lines on Quality Provision in Cross-border Higher Education.

CO-OPERATION WITH NON-MEMBER ECONOMIES

The Centre for Co-operation with Non-Members (CCNM) was established in January 1998, by merger of the Centre for Co-operation with Economies in Transition (founded in 1990) and the Liaison and Co-ordination Unit. It serves as the focal point for the development of policy dialogue with non-member economies, managing multi-country, thematic, regional and country programmes. These include a Baltic Regional Programme, a Common Programme for Transition Economies of Europe and Central Asia, Programmes for Russia and for Brazil, an Emerging Asian Economies Programme and the OECD Programme of Dialogue and Co-operation with China. The Centre also manages OECD's various Global Forums, which discuss a wide range of specific issues that defy resolution in a single country or region, for example international investment, sustainable development, biotechnology, and trade. The Centre co-ordinates and maintains OECD's relations with other international organizations.

Non-member economies are invited by the CCNM, on a selective basis, to participate in or observe the work of certain OECD committees and working parties. The Centre also provides a limited range of training activities in support of policy implementation and institution building. In 1994 the OECD Centre for Private Sector Development, based in Istanbul, Turkey, commenced operations as a joint project between the OECD and the Turkish Government to provide policy advice and training to administrators from transitional economies in Eastern Europe, Central Asia and Transcaucasus. Subsequently, the Centre has evolved into a regional forum for policy dialogue and co-operation with regard to issues of interest to transitional economies. The CCNM is also a sponsor of the Joint Vienna Institute, which offers a variety of administrative, economic and financial management courses to participants from transition economies.

Finance

In 2004 OECD's total budget amounted to €307m.

Publications

Activities of OECD (Secretary-General's Annual Report).

Agricultural Outlook (annually).

Development Co-operation Report (annually).

Energy Balances (quarterly).

Energy Prices and Taxes (quarterly).

Financial Market Trends (3 a year).

Financial Statistics (Part 1 (domestic markets): monthly; Part 2 (international markets): monthly; Part 3 (OECD member countries): 25 a year).

Foreign Trade Statistics (monthly).

Higher Education Management and Policy (3 a year).

Indicators of Industry and Services Activity (quarterly).

International Trade by Commodities Statistics (5 a year).

Joint BIS-IMF-OECD-World Bank Statistics on External Debt (quarterly).

Main Developments in Trade (annually).

Main Economic Indicators (monthly).

Monthly Statistics of International Trade.

National Accounts Quarterly.

OECD Economic Outlook (2 a year).
OECD Economic Studies (2 a year).
OECD Economic Surveys (every 12 to 18 months for each country).
OECD Employment Outlook (annually).
OECD Factbook (annually).
OECD Journal of Competition Law and Policy (quarterly).
OECD Observer (every 2 months).

Oil, Gas, Coal and Electricity Statistics (quarterly).
PEB Exchange (newsletter of the Programme on Educational Building, 3 a year).
Short-term Economic Indicators: Transition Economies (quarterly).
Trends in International Migration (annually).
Numerous specialized reports, working papers, books and statistics on economic and social subjects (about 130 titles a year, both in English and French) are also published.

International Energy Agency—IEA

Address: 9 rue de la Fédération, 75739 Paris Cédex 15, France.
Telephone: 1-40-57-65-00; **fax:** 1-40-57-65-59; **e-mail:** info@iea.org; **internet:** www.iea.org.

The Agency was established by the OECD Council in 1974 to develop co-operation on energy questions among participating countries.

MEMBERS

Australia	Greece	Norway
Austria	Hungary	Portugal
Belgium	Ireland	Spain
Canada	Italy	Sweden
Czech Republic	Japan	Switzerland
Denmark	Republic of Korea	Turkey
Finland	Luxembourg	United Kingdom
France	Netherlands	USA
Germany	New Zealand	

The European Commission is also represented.

Organization

(April 2005)

GOVERNING BOARD

Composed of ministers or senior officials of the member governments. Meetings are held every two years at ministerial level and five times a year at senior official level. Decisions may be taken by a weighted majority on a number of specified subjects, particularly concerning emergency measures and the emergency reserve commitment; a simple weighted majority is required for procedural decisions and decisions implementing specific obligations in the agreement. Unanimity is required only if new obligations, not already specified in the agreement, are to be undertaken.

SECRETARIAT

The Secretariat comprises the following offices: Energy Technology and Research and Development; Co-operation with Non-member Countries; Oil Markets and Emergency Preparedness; and Long-term Co-operation and Policy Analysis. There are also the following Standing Groups and Committes: Standing Group on Long-Term Co-operation; Standing Group on the Oil Market; Standing Group on Emergency Questions; Committee on Energy Research and Technology (with working parties); Committee on Non-Member Countries; Coal Industry Advisory Board; and Industry Advisory Board.

Executive Director: CLAUDE MANDIL (France).

Activities

The Agreement on an International Energy Programme was signed in November 1974 and formally entered into force in January 1976. The Programme commits the participating countries of the International Energy Agency to share petroleum in emergencies, to strengthen their long-term co-operation in order to reduce dependence on petroleum imports, to increase the availability of information on the petroleum market, to co-operate in the development and co-ordination of energy policies, and to develop relations with the petroleum-producing and other petroleum-consuming countries. The IEA issues energy statistics and publications and provides information and analysis on the energy sector. It sponsors conferences, symposia and workshops to enhance international co-operation among member and non-member states.

An emergency petroleum-sharing plan has been established, and the IEA ensures that the necessary technical information and faci-

lities are in place so that it can be readily used in the event of a reduction in petroleum supplies. The IEA undertakes emergency response reviews and workshops, and publishes an Emergency Management Manual to facilitate a co-ordinated response to a severe disruption in petroleum supplies. A separate division monitors and reports on short-term developments in the petroleum market. It also considers other related issues, including international crude petroleum pricing, petroleum trade and stock developments and investments by major petroleum-producing countries.

The IEA Long-Term Co-operation Programme is designed to strengthen the security of energy supplies and promote stability in world energy markets. It provides for co-operative efforts to conserve energy, to accelerate the development of alternative energy sources by means of both specific and general measures, to strengthen research and development of new energy technologies and to remove legislative and administrative obstacles to increased energy supplies. Regular reviews of member countries' efforts in the fields of energy conservation and accelerated development of alternative energy sources assess the effectiveness of national programmes in relation to the objectives of the Agency.

The IEA also reviews the energy situation in non-member countries, in particular the petroleum-producing countries of the Middle East and Central and Eastern European countries. In the latter states the IEA has provided technical assistance for the development of national energy legislation, regulatory reform and energy efficiency projects.

The IEA aims to contribute to the energy security of member countries through energy technology and research and development projects, in particular those concerned with energy efficiency, conservation and protection of the environment. The IEA promotes international collaboration in this field and the participation of energy industries to facilitate the application of new technologies, through effective transfer of knowledge, technology innovation and training. Member states adopt Implementing Agreements, which provide mechanisms for collaboration and information exchange in specific areas, for example, electric vehicle technologies, electric demand-side management and photovoltaic power systems. Non-member states are encouraged to participate in these Agreements. The Agency sponsors conferences, symposia and workshops to further enhance international co-operation among member and non-member countries.

In recent years the IEA has increased its focus on issues related to the environment and sustainable development. It supports analysis of actions to mitigate climate change, studies of the implications of the Kyoto Protocol to the UN Framework Convention on Climate Change, and analysis of policies designed to reduce greenhouse gas emissions, including emissions trading. Since 2001 IEA has organized, with the International Emissions Trading Association and the Electric Power Research Institute, an annual workshop of greenhouse gas emissions trading. The Agency also analyses the regulation and reform of energy markets, especially for electricity and gas. The IEA Regulatory Forum held in February 2002 considered the implications for security of supply and public service of competition in energy markets.

Publications

Coal Information (annually).
Electricity Information (annually).
Natural Gas Information (annually).
Oil Information (annually).
Oil Market Report (monthly).
World Energy Outlook (annually).
Reports, studies, statistics, country reviews.

OECD Nuclear Energy Agency—NEA

Address: Le Seine Saint-Germain, 12 blvd des Îles, 92130 Issy-les-Moulineaux, France.

Telephone: 1-45-24-10-10; **fax:** 1-45-24-11-10; **e-mail:** nea@nea.fr; **internet:** www.nea.fr.

The NEA was established in 1958 to further the peaceful uses of nuclear energy. Originally a European agency, it has since admitted OECD members outside Europe.

MEMBERS

All members of OECD (except New Zealand and Poland).

Organization

(April 2005)

STEERING COMMITTEE FOR NUCLEAR ENERGY

Meets twice a year. Comprises senior representatives of member governments, presided over by a chairman.

SECRETARIAT

Director-General: Luis Enrique Echávarri (Spain).
Deputy Director-General: Dr Gail Marcus (USA).

MAIN COMMITTEES

Committee on Nuclear Regulatory Activities.
Committee on Radiation Protection and Public Health.
Committee on the Safety of Nuclear Installations.
Committee for Technical and Economic Studies on Nuclear Development and the Fuel Cycle (Nuclear Development Committee).
Nuclear Law Committee.
Nuclear Science Committee.
Radioactive Waste Management Committee.

NEA DATA BANK

The Data Bank was established in 1978, as a successor to the Computer Programme Library and the Neutron Data Compilation Centre. The Data Bank develops and supplies data and computer programmes for nuclear technology applications to users in laboratories, industry, universities and other areas of interest. Under the supervision of the Nuclear Science Committee, the Data Bank collates integral experimental data, and functions as part of a network of data centres to provide direct data services. It was responsible for co-ordinating the development of the Joint Evaluation Fission and Fusion (JEFF) data reference library, and works with the Radioactive Waste Management Division of the NEA on the Thermonuclear Database project (see below).

Activities

The mission of the Agency is to assist its member countries in maintaining and further developing—through international co-operation—the scientific, technological and legal bases required for the safe, environmentally-friendly and economical use of nuclear energy for peaceful purposes. The Agency maintains a continual survey with the co-operation of other organizations, notably the International Atomic Energy Agency (IAEA), of world uranium resources, production and demand, and of economic and technical aspects of the nuclear fuel cycle.

A major part of the Agency's work is devoted to the safety and regulation of nuclear power, including co-operative studies and projects related to the prevention of nuclear accidents and the long-term safety of radioactive waste disposal systems. It is also concerned with the harmonization of nuclear legislation and the dissemination of information on nuclear law issues. A Nuclear Development Committee provides members with statistics and analysis on nuclear resources, economics, technology and prospects. There are Joint NEA/IAEA Groups concerned with uranium, and isotope supply and demand, and Expert Groups on international collaboration to achieve nuclear support excellence, the impact of advanced fuel cycle options on waste management policies, innovation in nuclear energy technology, nuclear energy products, society and nuclear energy, and partitioning and transmutation. The NEA also co-operates with non-member countries of Central and Eastern Europe and the CIS in areas such as nuclear safety, radiation protection and nuclear law.

JOINT PROJECTS

Nuclear Safety

OECD Fire Project: covers the period 2002–05; aims to encourage multilateral co-operation in the collection and analysis of data relating to fire events; eight initial participants.

OECD Halden Reactor Project: Halden, Norway; experimental boiling heavy water reactor, which became an OECD project in 1958; from 1964, under successive agreements with participating countries, the reactor has been used for long-term testing of water reactor fuels and for research into automatic computer-based control of nuclear power stations; the main focus is on nuclear fuel safety and man-machine interface; some 100 nuclear energy research institutions and authorities in 20 countries support the project.

OECD International Common Cause Failure Data Exchange (ICDE Project): initiated in 1994 and formally operated by the NEA since April 1998; encourages multilateral co-operation in the collection and analysis of data on common cause failure (CCF) events occurring at nuclear power plants, with the aim of enabling greater understanding and prevention of such events; 11 participating countries.

OECD-IRSN Cabri Water Loop Project: revised eight-year programme initiated in 2000; conducted at the Institute for Protection and Nuclear Safety (IPSN), based in France; investigates the capacity of high burn-up fuel to withstand sharp power peaks that may occur in power reactors owing to rapid reactivity insertion in the reactor core (i.e. reactivity-initiated accidents); 12 participating countries.

OECD MASCA-2 Project: three-year project running July 2003–June 2006; extension of a project which conducted tests in order to resolve remaining uncertainties related to the heat load that the reactor vessel can support during an accident involving core melt; aimed to enhance the application of MACSA results; 15 participating countries.

OECD Melt Coolability and Concrete Interaction (MCCI Project): initiated 2002; conducted at the Argonne National Laboratory, USA; aims to provide experimental data on severe accident molten core coolability and interaction with containment concrete, contributing to improved accident management; 13 participating countries.

OECD Piping Failure Data Exchange Project (OPDE): covers the period 2002–05; aims to collect and analyse piping failure event data with the aim of generating qualitative insights into the root causes of such events; 12 participating countries.

OECD PSB VVER Project: covers the period Feb. 2003–Dec. 2006; conducted at a large-scale, thermal-hydraulics facility located at the Electrogorsk Research and Engineering Centre in Russia; is intended to provide the experimental data needed to allow full validation of the computer codes used in the thermal-hydraulic analysis of Russian-designed VVER-1000 reactors; six participating countries.

OECD SETH Project: covers the period 2001–05; conducted at the Paul Scherrer Institute PANDA facility, based in Switzerland, and the Siemens Primär Kreislauf, Germany; researches important thermal-hydraulic phenomena in support of accident management; 15 participating countries.

OECD PKL Project: three-year project initiated in Jan. 2004; to investigate pressurised water reactor safety issues, in particular boron dilution accidents and loss of residual heat removal in mid-loop operation; 13 participating countries.

OECD Studsvik Project: five-year project initiated in July 2004; aims to study dominant failure mechanisms for light water reactor fuel cladding under pellet-clad mechanism interaction loading; 10 participating countries.

Radioactive Waste Management

International Co-operative Programme on Decommissioning: initiated in 1985; promotes exchange of technical information and experience for ensuring that safe, economic and optimum environmental options for decommissioning are used; 14 participating countries.

Sorption Project: phase II commenced in 2000; comprises benchmark exercises co-ordinated by the NEA; aims to evaluate various approaches used to model sorption phenomena in the context of performance assessments of geologic disposal concepts for the disposal of radioactive waste in deep geological formations; 10 participating countries and 16 participating organizations.

Thermonuclear Database (TDB Project): aims to develop a quality-assured, comprehensive thermodynamic database of selected chemical elements for use in the safety assessment of radioactive waste repositories; data are selected by review teams; phase II commenced in 1998 and is ongoing; phase III commenced in Feb. 2003 focusing on new reviews of inorganic species and compounds of other elements; 12 participating countries and 17 participating organizations.

Radiation Protection

Information System on Occupational Exposure (ISOE): initiated in 1992 and co-sponsored by the IAEA; maintains largest database world-wide on occupational exposure to ionizing radiation at nuclear power plants; participants: 461 reactors (some of which are either defunct or actively decommissioning) in 29 countries.

Nuclear Development

International Advisory Group for the Jules Horowitz Reactor Project: initiated in 2003; aims to support the establish-

ment of the Jules Horowitz reactor as an international research and development infrastructure project for the testing of nuclear fuels and materials, and to monitor progress in the design, development, construction and operation phases; 11 participating countries.

Finance

The Agency's annual budget amounts to some €9.2m., while funding of €2.6m. is made available for the Data Bank. These sums may be supplemented by members' voluntary contributions.

Publications

Annual Report.
NEA News (2 a year).
Nuclear Energy Data (annually).
Nuclear Law Bulletin (2 a year).
Publications on a range of issues relating to nuclear energy, reports and proceedings.

ORGANIZATION FOR SECURITY AND CO-OPERATION IN EUROPE—OSCE

Address: 1010 Vienna, Kärntner Ring 5–7, Austria.
Telephone: (1) 514-36-180; **fax:** (1) 514-36-105; **e-mail:** info@osce .org; **internet:** www.osce.org.

The OSCE was established in 1972 as the Conference on Security and Co-operation in Europe (CSCE), providing a multilateral forum for dialogue and negotiation. It produced the Helsinki Final Act of 1975 on East–West relations (see below). The areas of competence of the CSCE were expanded by the Charter of Paris for a New Europe (1990), which transformed the CSCE from an *ad hoc* forum into an organization with permanent institutions, and the Helsinki Document 1992 (see 'Activities'). In December 1994 the summit conference adopted the new name of OSCE, in order to reflect the Organization's changing political role and strengthened secretariat.

PARTICIPATING STATES

Albania	Greece	Romania
Andorra	Hungary	Russia
Armenia	Iceland	San Marino
Austria	Ireland	Serbia and
Azerbaijan	Italy	Montenegro
Belarus	Kazakhstan	Slovakia
Belgium	Kyrgyzstan	Slovenia
Bosnia and	Latvia	Spain
Herzegovina	Liechtenstein	Sweden
Bulgaria	Lithuania	Switzerland
Canada	Luxembourg	Tajikistan
Croatia	Macedonia, former	Turkey
Cyprus	Yugoslav republic	Turkmenistan
Czech Republic	Malta	Ukraine
Denmark	Moldova	United Kingdom
Estonia	Monaco	USA
Finland	Netherlands	Uzbekistan
France	Norway	Vatican City (Holy
Georgia	Poland	See)
Germany	Portugal	

Organization

(April 2005)

SUMMIT CONFERENCES

Heads of state or government of OSCE participating states convene periodically (normally every two to three years) to set priorities and political orientation of the Organization. The most recent conference was held in İstanbul, Turkey, in November 1999.

MINISTERIAL COUNCIL

The Ministerial Council (formerly the Council of Foreign Ministers) comprises ministers of foreign affairs of member states. It is the central decision-making and governing body of the OSCE and meets every year in which no summit conference is held.

SENIOR COUNCIL

The Senior Council (formerly the Council of Senior Officials—CSO) is responsible for the supervision, management and co-ordination of OSCE activities. Member states are represented by senior political officers, who convene at least twice a year in Prague, Czech Republic, and once a year as the Economic Forum.

PERMANENT COUNCIL

The Council, which is based in Vienna, is responsible for day-to-day operational tasks. Members of the Council, comprising the permanent representatives of member states to the OSCE, convene weekly. The Council is the regular body for political consultation and decision-making, and may be convened for emergency purposes.

FORUM FOR SECURITY CO-OPERATION (FSC)

The FSC, comprising representatives of delegations of member states, meets weekly in Vienna to negotiate and consult on measures aimed at strengthening security and stability throughout Europe. Its main objectives are negotiations on arms control, disarmament, and confidence- and security-building; regular consultations and intensive co-operation on matters related to security; and the further reduction of the risks of conflict. The FSC is also responsible for the implementation of confidence- and security-building measures (CSBMs); the preparation of seminars on military doctrine; the holding of annual implementation assessment meetings; and the provision of a forum for the discussion and clarification of information exchanged under agreed CSBMs.

CHAIRMAN-IN-OFFICE (CIO)

The CIO is vested with overall responsibility for executive action. The position is held by a minister of foreign affairs of a member state for a one-year term. The CIO may be assisted by a troika, consisting of the preceding, current and succeeding chairpersons; *ad hoc* steering groups; or personal representatives, who are appointed by the CIO with a clear and precise mandate to assist the CIO in dealing with a crisis or conflict.

Chairman-in-Office: DIMITRIJ RUPEL (Slovenia) (2005).

SECRETARIAT

The Secretariat comprises two principal departments: the Conflict Prevention Centre (including an Operations Centre), which focuses on the support of the CIO in the implementation of OSCE policies, in particular the monitoring of field activities and co-operation with other international bodies; and the Department of Management and Finance, responsible for technical and administrative support activities. The OSCE maintains an office in Prague, Czech Republic, which assists with documentation and information activities, and a centre in Tashkent, Uzbekistan.

The position of Secretary-General was established in December 1992 and the first appointment to the position was made in June 1993. The Secretary-General is appointed by the Ministerial Council for a three-year term of office. The Secretary-General is the representative of the CIO and is responsible for the management of OSCE structures and operations.

Secretary-General: JÁN KUBIŠ (Slovakia).

Co-ordinator of OSCE Economic and Environmental Activities: MARCIN SWIECICKI (Poland).

HIGH COMMISSIONER ON NATIONAL MINORITIES

POB 20062, 2500 EB The Hague, Netherlands; tel. (70) 3125500; fax (70) 3635910; e-mail hcnm@hcnm.org; internet www.osce.org/hcnm.

The establishment of the office of High Commissioner on National Minorities was proposed in the 1992 Helsinki Document, and endorsed by the Council of Foreign Ministers in Stockholm, Sweden, in December 1992. The role of the High Commissioner is to identify ethnic tensions that might endanger peace, stability or relations between OSCE participating states, and to promote their early resolution. The High Commissioner may issue an 'early warning' for the attention of the Senior Council of an area of tension likely to degenerate into conflict. The High Commissioner is appointed by the Ministerial Council, on the recommendation of the Senior Council, for a three-year term.

High Commissioner: ROLF EKÉUS (Sweden).

OFFICE FOR DEMOCRATIC INSTITUTIONS AND HUMAN RIGHTS (ODIHR)

Aleje Ujazdowskie 19, 00-557 Warsaw, Poland; tel. (22) 520-06-00; fax (22) 520-06-05; e-mail office@odihr.pl; internet www.osce.org/odihr.

Established in July 1999, the ODIHR has responsibility for promoting human rights, democracy and the rule of law. The Office provides a framework for the exchange of information on and the promotion of democracy-building, respect for human rights and elections within OSCE states. In addition, it co-ordinates the monitoring of elections and provides expertise and training on constitutional and legal matters.

Director: CHRISTIAN STROHAL (Austria).

OFFICE OF THE REPRESENTATIVE ON FREEDOM OF THE MEDIA

Kärntner Ring 5–7, 1010 Vienna, Austria; tel. (1) 512-21-450; fax (1) 512-21-459; e-mail pm-fom@osce.org; internet www.osce.org/fom.

The office was founded in 1998 to strengthen the implementation of OSCE commitments regarding free, independent and pluralistic media.

Representative: MIKLOS HARASZTI (Hungary).

PARLIAMENTARY ASSEMBLY

Rädhusstraede 1, 1466 Copenhagen K, Denmark; tel. 33-37-80-40; fax 33-37-80-30; e-mail osce@oscepa.dk; internet www.osce.org/pa.

The OSCE Parliamentary Assembly, which is composed of 317 parliamentarians from 55 participating countries, was inaugurated in July 1992, and meets annually. The Assembly comprises a Standing Committee, a Bureau and three General Committees and is supported by a Secretariat in Copenhagen, Denmark.

President: ALCEE L. HASTINGS (USA).

Secretary-General: R. SPENCER OLIVER (USA).

OSCE Related Bodies

COURT OF CONCILIATION AND ARBITRATION

266 route de Lausanne, 1292 Chambésy, Geneva, Switzerland; tel. (22) 7580025; fax (22) 7582510; e-mail cca.osce@bluewin.ch.

The establishment of the Court of Conciliation and Arbitration was agreed in 1992 and effected in 1994. OSCE states that have ratified the OSCE Convention on Conciliation and Arbitration may submit a dispute to the Court for settlement by the Arbitral Tribunal or the Conciliation Commission.

President: ROBERT BADINTER.

JOINT CONSULTATIVE GROUP (JCG)

The states that are party to the Treaty on Conventional Armed Forces in Europe (CFE), which was concluded within the CSCE framework in 1990, established the Joint Consultative Group (JCG). The JCG, which meets in Vienna, addresses questions relating to compliance with the Treaty; enhancement of the effectiveness of the Treaty; technical aspects of the Treaty's implementation; and disputes arising out of its implementation. There are currently 30 states participating in the JCG.

OPEN SKIES CONSULTATIVE COMMISSION

The Commission represents all states parties to the 1992 Treaty on Open Skies, and promotes its implementation. Its regular meetings are serviced by the OSCE secretariat.

Activities

In July 1990 heads of government of the member countries of the North Atlantic Treaty Organization (NATO) proposed to increase the role of the CSCE 'to provide a forum for wider political dialogue in a more united Europe'. The Charter of Paris for a New Europe, which undertook to strengthen pluralist democracy and observance of human rights, and to settle disputes between participating states by peaceful means, was signed in November. At the summit meeting the Treaty on Conventional Armed Forces in Europe (CFE), which had been negotiated within the framework of the CSCE, was signed by the member states of NATO and of the Warsaw Pact. The Treaty limits non-nuclear air and ground armaments in the signatory countries. In April 1991 parliamentarians from the CSCE countries agreed on the creation of a pan-European parliamentary assembly. Its first session was held in Budapest, Hungary, in July 1992.

The Council of Foreign Ministers met for the first time in Berlin, Germany, in June 1991. The meeting adopted a mechanism for consultation and co-operation in the case of emergency situations, to be implemented by the Council of Senior Officials (CSO, which was subsequently renamed the Senior Council). A separate mechanism regarding the prevention of the outbreak of conflict was also adopted, whereby a country can demand an explanation of 'unusual military activity' in a neighbouring country. These mechanisms were utilized in July in relation to the armed conflict in Yugoslavia between the Republic of Croatia and the Yugoslav Government. In mid-August a meeting of the CSO resolved to reinforce considerably the CSCE's mission in Yugoslavia and in September the CSO agreed to impose an embargo on the export of armaments to Yugoslavia. In October the CSO resolved to establish an observer mission to monitor the observance of human rights in Yugoslavia.

In January 1992 the Council of Foreign Ministers agreed that the Conference's rule of decision-making by consensus was to be altered to allow the CSO to take appropriate action against a participating state 'in cases of clear and gross violation of CSCE commitments'. This development was precipitated by the conflict in Yugoslavia, where the Yugoslav Government was held responsible by the majority of CSCE states for the continuation of hostilities. It was also agreed at the meeting that the CSCE should undertake factfinding and conciliation missions to areas of tension, with the first such mission to be sent to Nagornyi Karabakh, the largely Armenian-populated enclave in Azerbaijan.

In March 1992 CSCE participating states reached agreement on a number of confidence-building measures, including commitments to exchange technical data on new weapons systems; to report activation of military units; and to prohibit military activity involving very large numbers of troops or tanks. Later in that month at a meeting of the Council of Foreign Ministers, which opened the Helsinki Follow-up Conference, the members of NATO and the former members of the Warsaw Pact (with Russia, Belarus, Ukraine and Georgia taking the place of the USSR) signed the Open Skies Treaty. Under the treaty, aerial reconnaissance missions by one country over another were permitted, subject to regulation. An Open Skies Consultative Commission was subsequently established (see above).

The summit meeting of heads of state and government that took place in Helsinki, Finland, in July 1992 adopted the Helsinki Document 1992, in which participating states defined the terms of future CSCE peace-keeping activities. Conforming broadly to UN practice, peace-keeping operations would be undertaken only with the full consent of the parties involved in any conflict and only if an effective cease-fire were in place. The CSCE may request the use of the military resources of NATO, the CIS, the EU, Western European Union (WEU) or other international bodies. The Helsinki Document declared the CSCE a 'regional arrangement' in the sense of Chapter VIII of the UN's Charter, which states that such a regional grouping should attempt to resolve a conflict in the region before referring it to the Security Council. In 1993 the First Implementation Meeting on Human Dimension Issues (the CSCE term used with regard to issues concerning human rights and welfare) took place. The Meeting, for which the ODIHR serves as a secretariat, provides a now annual forum for the exchange of news regarding OSCE commitments in the fields of human rights and democracy.

In December 1993 a Permanent Committee (now renamed the Permanent Council) was established in Vienna, providing for greater political consultation and dialogue through its weekly meetings. In December 1994 the summit conference redesignated the CSCE as the Organization for Security and Co-operation in Europe (OSCE) and endorsed the role of the Organization as the primary instrument for early warning, conflict prevention and crisis management in the region. The conference adopted a 'Code of Conduct on Politico-Military Aspects of Security', which set out principles to guide the role of the armed forces in democratic societies. The summit conference that was held in Lisbon, Portugal, in December 1996 agreed to adapt the CFE Treaty, in order to further arms-reduction negotiations on a national and territorial basis. The conference also adopted the 'Lisbon Declaration on a Common and

Comprehensive Security Model for Europe for the 21st Century', committing all parties to pursuing measures to ensure regional security. A Security Model Committee was established and began to meet regularly during 1997 to consider aspects of the Declaration, including the identification of risks and challenges to future European security; enhancing means of joint co-operative action within the OSCE framework in the event of non-compliance with OSCE commitments by participating states; considering other new arrangements within the OSCE framework that could reinforce security and stability in Europe; and defining a basis of co-operation between the OSCE and other relevant organizations to co-ordinate security enforcement. In November 1997 the Office of the Representative on Freedom of the Media was established in Vienna, to support the OSCE's activities in this field. In the same month a new position of Co-ordinator of OSCE Economic and Environmental Activities was created.

In November 1999 OSCE heads of state and of government, convened in İstanbul, Turkey, signed a new Charter for European Security, which aimed to formalize existing norms regarding the observance of human rights and to strengthen co-operation with other organizations and institutions concerned with international security. The Charter focused on measures to improve the operational capabilities of the OSCE in early warning, conflict prevention, crisis management and post-conflict rehabilitation. Accordingly, Rapid Expert Assistance and Co-operation (REACT) teams were to be established to enable the Organization to respond rapidly to requests from participating states for assistance in crisis situations. The REACT programme became operational in April 2001. The 1999 summit meeting also adopted a Platform for Co-operative Security as a framework for co-operation with other organizations and institutions concerned with maintaining security in the OSCE area. At the İstanbul meeting a revised CFE Treaty was signed, providing for a stricter system of limitations and increased transparency, which was to be open to other OSCE states not currently signatories. The US and EU governments determined to delay ratification of the Agreement of the Adaptation of the Treaty until Russian troop levels in the Caucasus had been reduced.

In April 2000 the OSCE High Commissioner on National Minorities issued a report reviewing the problems confronting Roma and Sinti populations in OSCE member states. In April 2001 the ODIHR launched a programme of assistance for the Roma communities of south-eastern Europe. The OSCE and UN Office for Drug Control and Crime Prevention (ODCCP, renamed the UN Office on Drugs and Crime in October 2002) jointly organized a conference in October 2000, supported by the Governments of Kazakhstan, Kyrgyzstan, Tajikistan, Turkmenistan and Uzbekistan and attended by representatives of 67 states and 44 international organizations, which aimed to promote co-operation, democratization, security and stability in Central Asia and to address the threat of drugs-trafficking, organized crime and terrorism in the sub-region. In November an OSCE Document on Small Arms and Light Weapons was adopted, aimed at curtailing the spread of armaments in member states. A workshop on implementation of the Document was held in February 2002. In mid-November 2000 the Office of the Representative on Freedom of the Media organized a conference, staged in Dushanbe, Tajikistan, of journalists from Kazakhstan, Kyrgyzstan, Tajikistan and Uzbekistan. In February 2001 the ODIHR established an Anti-Trafficking Project Fund to help to finance its efforts to combat trafficking in human beings. In July the OSCE Parliamentary Assembly adopted a resolution concerned with strengthening transparency and accountability within the Organization.

In September 2001 the Secretary-General condemned terrorist attacks perpetrated against targets in the USA, allegedly by militant Islamist fundamentalists. In early October OSCE member states unanimously adopted a statement in support of the developing US-led global coalition against international terrorism. Meanwhile, the Organization determined to establish a working group on terrorism to draft an action plan on counter-terrorism measures. In December the Ministerial Council, meeting in Romania, approved the 'Bucharest Action Plan' outlining the Organization's contribution to countering terrorism. A Personal Representative for Terrorism was appointed by the CIO in January 2002 to co-ordinate the implementation of the initiatives. Later in December 2001 the OSCE sponsored, with the ODCCP, an International Conference on Security and Stability in Central Asia, held in Bishek, Kyrgyzstan. The meeting, which was attended by representatives of more than 60 countries and organizations, was concerned with strengthening efforts to counter terrorism and providing effective support to the Central Asian states. In October 2002 the ODIHR and the Government of Azerbaijan organized an international conference on religious freedom and combating terrorism. At a Ministerial Council meeting held in Porto, Portugal, in December the OSCE issued a Charter on Preventing Terrorism, which condemned terrorism 'in all its forms and manifestations' and called upon member states to work together to counter, investigate and prosecute terrorist acts. The charter also acknowledged the links between terrorism, organized crime and trafficking in human beings. At the same time, a political declaration entitled 'Responding to Change' was adopted, in which member states pledged their commitment to mutual co-operation in combating threats to security. At the OSCE's first Annual Security Review Conference, held in Vienna, in July 2003, a range of practical options for addressing the new threats and challenges to security were set out. These included the introduction of common security features on travel documentation, stricter controls on manual portable air defence systems, and the improvement of border security and policing methods. Security issues were also the subject of the Rotterdam Declaration, adopted by some 300 members of the Parliamentary Assembly in July, which stated that it was imperative for the OSCE to maintain a strong field presence and for field missions to be provided with sufficient funding and highly trained staff. It also recommended that the OSCE assume a role in unarmed peace-keeping operations.

During July 2003 the first OSCE conference on the effects of globalization was convened in Vienna, attended by some 200 representatives from international organizations. Participants called for the advancement of good governance in the public and private sectors, the development of democratic institutions, and the creation of conditions that would enable populations to benefit from the global economy. At a meeting of the Ministerial Council, convened in Maastricht, Netherlands, in December, member states endorsed a document that aimed to address risks to regional security and stability arising from stockpiles of conventional ammunition through, *inter alia*, detailing practical steps for their destruction. In December 2004 the ministerial council, held in Sofia, Bulgaria, condemned terrorist attacks that had been committed during the year, including in Madrid, Spain, in March, and in Beslan, Russia, in September. The meeting issued a statement expressing determination to pursue all measures to prevent and combat international terrorism.

In July 2003 the Permanent Council adopted a new Action Plan to Combat Trafficking in Human Beings. The Plan was endorsed by the Ministerial Council, held in Maastricht, Netherlands, in December. The Council approved the appointment of a Special Representative on Combating Trafficking in Human Beings, mandated to raise awareness of the issues and to ensure member governments comply with international procedures and conventions, and the establishment of a special unit within the secretariat. In July 2004 the Special Representative, Helga Konrad, organized an international conference to consider issues relating to human trafficking, including human rights, labour, migration, organized crime, and minors. Participants agreed to establish an Alliance against Trafficking in Persons, which aimed to consolidate co-operation among international and non-governmental organizations.

OSCE MISSIONS AND FIELD ACTIVITIES

In 2005 there were long-term OSCE missions in Bosnia and Herzegovina, Croatia, Georgia, Kosovo, the former Yugoslav republic of Macedonia, Moldova, Serbia and Montenegro and Tajikistan. The OSCE was also undertaking field activities in Albania, Armenia, Azerbaijan, Belarus, Kazakhstan, Kyrgyzstan, Turkmenistan Ukraine and Uzbekistan. The OSCE has institutionalized structures to assist in the implementation of certain bilateral agreements. At early 2005 there were OSCE representatives to the Russian-Latvian Joint Commission on Military Pensioners and to the Estonian Government Commission on Military Pensioners.

In August 1995 the CIO appointed a Personal Representative concerned with the conflict between Armenia and Azerbaijan in the Nagornyi Karabakh region. The OSCE provided a framework for discussions between the two countries through its 11-nation Minsk Group, which from early 1997 was co-chaired by France, Russia and the USA. In October 1997 Armenia and Azerbaijan reached agreement on OSCE proposals for a political settlement; however, the concessions granted by the Armenian President, Levon Ter-Petrossian, which included the withdrawal of troops from certain strategic areas of Nagornyi Karabakh, precipitated his resignation in February 1998. The proposals were rejected by his successor, Robert Kocharian. Nevertheless, meetings of the Minsk Group continued in 1998 and both countries expressed their willingness to recommence negotiations. The then CIO, Bronisław Geremek, met with the leaders of both countries in November and persuaded them to exchange prisoners of war. In July 1999 the OSCE Permanent Council approved the establishment of an Office in Yerevan (Armenia), which began operations in February 2000. The Office works independently of the Minsk Group, to promote OSCE principles within the country in order to support political and economic stability. It aims to contribute to the development of democratic institutions and to the strengthening of civil society. An Office in Baku (Azerbaijan) opened in July 2000 with a mandate to undertake activities in democratization, human rights, economy and the environment, and media. In November 2001 the Office in Yerevan presented a report on trafficking in human beings in Armenia, which had been compiled as a joint effort by the OSCE, IOM and UNICEF.

In March 2002 the CIO visited the region to discuss prospects for peace, and the OSCE's role in the process. In that year a programme on military and security issues was initiated in Armenia which was to enhance the OSCE's role in police-related activities in conflict prevention, crisis management and post-conflict rehabilitation. In July 2003 the Armenian police service signed a Memorandum of Understanding with the OSCE, launching a major police assistance programme with the particular aim of creating a constructive partnership between the police and the general population. The first phase of the programme, the renovation of a police training centre, was initiated in March 2005. In February the OSCE and Azerbaijani authorities agreed to increase co-operation in judicial and legal reform, after consideration of a report on trial monitoring compiled by the Office in Baku and ODIHR in 2003 and 2004.

In December 1999 the Permanent Council, at the request of the Government of Georgia expanded the mandate of the existing OSCE Mission to Georgia to include monitoring that country's border with the Chechen Republic of Ichkeriya (Chechnya). The first permanent observation post opened in February 2000 and the monitoring team was fully deployed by July. In December 2001 the Permanent Council approved an expansion in the border monitoring mission to cover the border between Georgia and Ingushetia. A further expansion, to include monitoring Georgia's border with Dagestan, was effected from January 2003. The OSCE Mission to Georgia was established in 1992 to work towards a political settlement between disputing factions within the country. Since 1994 the Mission has contributed to efforts to define the political status of South Ossetia and has supported UN peace-keeping and human rights activities in Abkhazia. A special envoy of the OSCE Chairman visited Georgia in July 2004 following a deterioration in the security situation. In November the Mission assisted the Georgian Government to develop an Action Plan to combat trafficking in human beings. In the same month the Mission helped to organize a national workshop on combating money laundering and suppressing the financing of terrorism.

In late 1996 the OSCE declared the constitutional referendum held in Belarus in November to be illegal and urged that country's Government to ensure political freedoms and respect for human rights. In September 1997 the Permanent Council determined to establish an OSCE Advisory and Monitoring Group to assist with the process of democratization; the Group commenced operations in February 1998. It was subsequently active in strengthening civil society, organizing training seminars and workshops in electoral practices, monitoring the human rights situation, including the registration of political parties and the development of an independent media, and in mediating between the President and opposition parties. In October 1998 the OSCE Parliamentary Assembly formed an *ad hoc* Committee on Belarus, to act as a working group to support and intensify the Organization's work in the country. The OSCE/ODIHR declared legislative elections staged in Belarus in October 2000 not to have been conducted freely and fairly, and pronounced that presidential elections held in September 2001 had not met the standards required by the Organization. In December 2002 the decision was taken to terminate the Group and to establish in its place an OSCE Office in Minsk; the Office was opened in January 2003. In May the OSCE Representative on Freedom of the Media requested urgent clarification on a decision by the Belarus Government to ban publication of two independent newspapers. In September the ODIHR entered into dialogue with the Belarus authorities on reforming electoral legislation. In the same month the Minsk Office expressed its concern at the recent closure of non-governmental organizations in Belarus for alleged violations of the law. In October 2004 some 270 observers from 38 countries participated in an joint mission of the ODIHR and the OSCE Parliamentary Assembly to monitor parliamentary elections in Belarus. The mission concluded that several fundamental democratic principles had not been adhered to during the electoral process.

An OSCE Mission to Moldova was established in February 1993, in order to assist conflicting parties in that country to pursue negotiations on a political settlement, as well as to observe the military situation in the region and to provide advice on issues of human and minority rights, democratization and the repatriation of refugees. In December 1999 the Permanent Council, with the approval of the Russian Government, authorized an expansion of the Mission's mandate to ensure the full removal and destruction of Russian ammunition and armaments and to co-ordinate financial and technical assistance for the withdrawal of foreign troops and the destruction of weapons. In June 2001 the Mission established a tripartite working group, with representatives of the Russian Ministry of Defence and the local authorities in Transdniestrian to assist and support the process of disposal of munitions. Destruction of heavy weapons began in mid-2002, under the supervision of the Mission. In May 2003 a seminar on federalism, organized by the OSCE Parliamentary Assembly, was held further to promote negotiations between Moldova and the Transdniestrian region on the development of a new Moldovan constitution, based on the principles of federalism. A second parliamentary conference on federalism was

convened in September. In late September 2004 the OSCE Mission financed a workshop as part of a two-year project concerned with 'strengthening protection and assistance to victims of trafficking, adults and minors'. In March 2005 observers from the ODIHR and OSCE Parliamentary Assembly participated in an international mission to monitor parliamentary elections in Moldova.

In 1999 an OSCE Project Co-ordinator in Ukraine was established, following the successful conclusion of the OSCE Mission to Ukraine (which had been established in November 1994). The Project Co-ordinator is responsible for pursuing co-operation between Ukraine and the OSCE and providing technical assistance in areas including legal reform, freedom of the media, trafficking in human beings, and the work of the human rights Ombudsman. In April 2002 an ODIHR Election Observation Mission monitored parliamentary elections in Ukraine. In July 2003 the Project Co-ordinator and the Ukrainian defence ministry launched a joint programme to assist former military personnel with adaptation to civilian life. In September 2004 an ODIHR mission was deployed to observe forthcoming presidential elections. More than 300 short-term observers monitored the first and second round polls, which were held in October and November respectively. In December the country's Supreme Court ruled that, owing to electoral irregularities, the second round voting should be re-run at the end of that month. The OSCE/ODIHR mission remained in the country to observer the process, and produced preliminary recommendations on the conduct of the re-run. In late January 2005 the CIO attended the inauguration of the newly-elected President, Viktor Yuschchenko.

In March 1997 the OSCE dispatched a fact-finding mission to Albania to help restore political and civil stability, which had been undermined by the collapse of national pyramid saving schemes at the start of the year. An agreement was negotiated between Albania's President Sali Berisha and opposition parties to hold elections in mid-1997 and to establish a government of national reconciliation. In March the Permanent Council agreed to establish an OSCE Presence in Albania, and confirmed that the organization should provide the framework for co-ordinating other international efforts in the country. OSCE efforts focused on reaching a political consensus on new legislation for the conduct of the forthcoming elections to establish a government of national reconciliation. Voting took place in June–July, with 500 OSCE observers providing technical electoral assistance and helping to monitor the voting. In December the Permanent Council confirmed that the Presence should provide the framework for co-ordinating other international efforts in the country. In March 1998 the OSCE Presence was mandated to monitor the country's borders with the Kosovan region of southern Serbia and to prevent any spillover effects from the escalating crisis. (This role was reduced following the political settlement for Kosovo and Metohija concluded in mid-1999.) In June 1998 the OSCE observed local elections in Albania. It became the Co-Chair, with the EU, of the Friends of Albania group, which then brought together countries and international bodies concerned with the situation in Albania for the first time in September. In October the Permanent Council determined to enhance the Presence's role in border-monitoring activities. With other organizations, the OSCE was involved in the preparation of the country's draft constitution, finalized in October, and an ODIHR Election Observation Mission was established to observe the referendum on the constitution held in November. The OSCE Presence in Albania has subsequently provided advice and support to the Albanian Government regarding democratization, the rule of law, the media, human rights, election preparation and monitoring, and the development of civil society. It supports an Economics and Environment Unit and an Elections Unit, which, since the parliamentary elections of 2001, has facilitated the process of electoral reform. The Presence also monitors the Government's weapons collection programme. An ODIHR election observation mission was deployed in early 2005 to monitor local elections in March.

The OSCE Mission to Bosnia and Herzegovina was established in December 1995 to achieve the objectives of the peace accords for the former Yugoslavia, in particular to oversee the process of democratization. The OSCE's efforts to organize and oversee the Bosnian national elections, which were held in September 1996, was the largest-ever electoral operation undertaken by the organization, with some 1,200 electoral observers deployed. The OSCE subsequently monitored Bosnian municipal elections, held in September 1997, and the elections to the National Assembly of the Serb Republic and to the Bosnian Serb presidency in November. In 1998 the mission was charged with organizing the second post-war general elections in Bosnia and Herzegovina. The mission assisted with the registration of voters and, in September, was responsible for the supervision of the elections at polling stations within and outside the country. The final results of the election to the Bosnian Serb presidency were delayed, owing to the unexpected victory of an extreme nationalist, which, it was feared, could jeopardize the peace process. The OSCE immediately emphasized the necessity of maintaining the process. It also insisted on the need to transfer responsibility for the electoral process to the national authorities for future elections. In March 1999 the OSCE initiated an educational campaign relating to new election laws. However, a permanent electoral legal framework had not been approved by the time of legislative elections held in November 2000; the OSCE was therefore active in both preparing and monitoring these. The Mission's responsibility for elections in the country ended in November 2001 when a new permanent Election Commission was inaugurated. However, it was to continue to provide support for the Commission's secretariat. Other key areas of Mission activity are the promotion of democratic values, monitoring and promoting respect for human rights, strengthening the legal system, assisting with the creation of a modernized, non-discriminatory education system and establishing democratic control over the armed forces. An Agreement on Regional Arms Control was signed in 1995, providing for confidence- and security-building measures and a reduction in excess armaments. The Mission has established consultative commissions to promote dialogue among military personnel from different entities within the country. An audit of the entities' defence budgets was conducted in 2001. In late 2002 an OSCE-sponsored audit of several public enterprises and government ministries in Bosnia and Herzegovina was initiated. The results of the audits of three utility companies and of the Ministry of Social Policy, Displaced Persons and Refugees were published in March 2003. In January–August 2004 the Mission undertook monitoring of the criminal justice system. A report, concerned with the implementation of new procedural codes, was presented in December. In September the agreement on confidence and security-building measures, mandated under the Dayton peace accords, was suspended in acknowledgement of the country's extensive political reforms. In December the Mission transferred its co-chairmanship of the country's Defence Reform Commission (DRC) to the new NATO headquarters in Sarajevo, although representatives of the Mission continued to be involved in work of the DRC. The Mission's work in the first half of 2005 was, increasingly, to be focused on ensuring peoples' rights to social welfare, healthcare and adequate housing.

The OSCE Mission to Croatia was established in April 1996 to provide assistance and expertise in the field of human and minority rights, and to assist in the implementation of legislation and the development of democratic institutions. The Mission's mandate was extended in June 1997 in order to enhance its capacity to protect human rights, in particular the rights of minorities, to monitor the return and treatment of refugees and displaced persons, and to make specific recommendations to the Croatian authorities. In March 1998, following the integration of the disputed region into Croatia, the OSCE criticized the conditions imposed by the Croatian Government for the return of Serb refugees, stating that the right to return to one's own country was inalienable and must not depend on the fulfilment of conditions. The Mission conducts extensive field monitoring to facilitate the return of refugees and displaced persons. In October 1998 the Mission assumed the responsibilities of the United Nations Police Support Group (UNPSG). The OSCE Police Monitoring Group, comprising a maximum of 120 unarmed OSCE civilian police monitors, was deployed in the region, representing the Organization's first police-monitoring role. The Group was terminated in October 2000, although the OSCE has continued to advise on and monitor police activities in Croatia. The OSCE was also to be responsible for monitoring the border regions, with particular concern for customs activities. The OSCE/ODIHR monitored legislative and presidential elections held in Croatia in January 2000. Local government elections were held in May 2001. The OSCE welcomed the adoption of the Constitutional Law on National Minorities adopted in December 2002 and urged ethnic minorities to participate in elections for minority self-government that took place in May 2003, in respect of which the OSCE funded a public information campaign. The OSCE likewise urged the Government to facilitate the participation of expatriate refugee voters in legislative elections held in November. In June the Mission initiated an 18-month public awareness campaign to promote reconciliation and the sustainable return of refugees.

In mid-1998 the OSCE was involved in the mediation effort to resolve the conflict between the Serbian authorities and ethnic Albanian separatists in the formerly autonomous province of Kosovo and Metohija. In October, following months of diplomatic effort and the threat of NATO air strikes, Yugoslav President Slobodan Milošević agreed to comply with UN Security Council Resolution 1199, which required an immediate cease-fire, Serbian troop withdrawals, the commencement of meaningful peace negotiations, and unrestricted access for humanitarian aid. Under a peace plan proposed by the US special envoy, Richard Holbrooke, President Milošević agreed to the formation of a 2,000-member OSCE Kosovo Verification Mission (KVM) to monitor compliance, in addition to surveillance flights by unarmed NATO aircraft. The KVM was to patrol the region to ensure the withdrawal of Serbian military and police units, and to oversee the safe return of refugees and the non-harassment of ethnic Albanian inhabitants. It was also to monitor border control activities and accompany police units in Kosovo, when

necessary, to assist them to perform their normal policing roles. The Mission's mandate was formally established on 25 October 1998 for a period of one year. Upon achievement of a political settlement defining the area's self-government, and its subsequent implementation, the KVM was to be responsible for supervising elections in Kosovo, assisting in the establishment of democratic institutions and developing a Kosovo police force. The long-term mission was accepted in return for the eventual removal of Yugoslavia's suspension from the OSCE. However, sporadic fighting continued in the province, and the monitoring force began unofficially to assume a peace-keeping role. In January 1999 the KVM successfully negotiated for the release of eight Yugoslav soldiers held hostage by the separatist forces. Later in that month following the KVM's denunciation of the killing of some 45 ethnic Albanians by Serbian security forces in the village of Racak, President Milošević ordered the head of the mission, William Walker, to leave the region. The order was later revoked. Meanwhile, OSCE monitors were forced to withdraw from Racak under fire from Serbian troops. An emergency meeting of the OSCE in Vienna agreed to maintain the mission. However, on 19 March, following the failure of negotiations to resolve the crisis, the CIO decided to evacuate the 1,380 unarmed monitors, owing to the deteriorating security situation in Kosovo. NATO commenced an aerial offensive against Yugoslavia in late March. In early April the CIO condemned the mass expulsion of ethnic Albanians from Kosovo and other violations of human rights committed by Serbian forces. Later in the same month the CIO, at a meeting of a ministerial troika attended by the Secretary-General, announced that the OSCE was willing to assist in the implementation of a political settlement in Kosovo. The OSCE was also concerned with measures to prevent the crisis affecting the other Balkan states. Within the framework of a political settlement for Kosovo, which was formally concluded in June, the OSCE (whose Mission in Kosovo, mandated to comprise 1,400 personnel, was established on 1 July) was responsible for democracy- and institution-building under the auspices of the UN Interim Administration Mission for Kosovo (UNMIK). OSCE monitors were deployed to assess the human rights situation throughout the region, and in August a new OSCE-administered police training school was inaugurated. (By October 2004 6,925 police-officers had trained under the OSCE police education programme.) In December 1999 the OSCE published a report on the situation in Kosovo, which confirmed that Serbian forces had conducted systematic abuses of human rights but also raised suspicion against the Kosovo Liberation Army (KLA) for organizing retribution attacks against Serbian civilians later in the year. In February 2000 the OSCE Mission established an Institute for Civil Administration to train public officials in principles of democratic governance. A Kosovo Law Centre was established in June to provide technical assistance to the legal community, with a view to promoting democratic principles and human rights. In the following month the Department for Democratic Governance and Civil Society was established by UNMIK, and was to be administered by the OSCE Mission. In August an Ombudsperson, nominated by the OSCE, was appointed to a new Office of the Ombudsperson, which became operational in November: the role of the Ombudsperson was to investigate and mediate claims of human rights violations arising within Kosovo. The OSCE was responsible for registering about 1m. voters prior to municipal elections that were held in Kosovo in October. During 2001 the Mission assisted the registration process for voting in a general election, and supervised the polling which took place in November. In early 2002 the Mission initiated training sessions for members of the new Kosovo Assembly. At that time the Mission was restructured, consolidating the number of field offices from 21 to nine. Among the priorities of the Mission's programme for 2004 were work on the sustainability of institutions created; developing the capacity of Kosovars to administer their own institutions and ensure that they adhere to democratic standards; and the promotion of reconciliation and tolerance and of the right to return. In June 2004 the Mission initiated an Out-of-Kosovo voting scheme to update the voter registration for upcoming Assembly elections. In early 2005 the Mission commended the signing of a new Press Code and determined to facilitate the establishment of a Press Council.

In November 2000 the Federal Republic of Yugoslavia (FRY, now Serbia and Montenegro) was admitted into the OSCE. In March 2001 an OSCE Mission to the FRY was inaugurated. (In February 2003, following the State Union of Serbia and Montenegro, the OSCE Mission to the FRY was renamed the OSCE Mission to Serbia and Montenegro.) This was to assist in the areas of democracy and protection of human rights and in the restructuring and training of law enforcement agencies and the judiciary, to provide advice to government authorities with regard to reform of the media, and, in close co-operation with the United Nations High Commissioner for Refugees, to facilitate the return of refugees to and from neighbouring countries as well as within the FRY. In March 2002 members of the Mission were facilitating the census process in southern Serbia. In June 2003 the Mission announced the launch of a border-policing project in an effort to reduce human trafficking and organized crime in Serbia and Montenegro. ODIHR deployed election observation missions for presidential and parliamentary elections held in Serbia and Montenegro in late 2003. An ODIHR team observed a presidential election in the Serb Republic, conducted in June 2004. In September the Mission financed monitoring of municipal elections by a local non-governmental organization.

The OSCE Spillover Monitor Mission to Skopje was established in September 1992 to help to prevent the conflict in the former Yugoslavia from destabilizing the former Yugoslav republic of Macedonia (FYRM). Its initial mandate was to monitor the border region, as well as monitoring human rights and promoting the development of democratic institutions, including an independent media. The Mission is also concerned with mediating between inter-ethnic groups in the country, and has provided support for implementation of a framework political agreement signed in August 2001 through the deployment of international confidence-building monitors and police advisers. In December OSCE monitors accompanied multi-ethnic police officers to areas of early conflict, as part of the August agreement. In March 2002 OSCE signed its first memorandum of understanding with the European Commission, in respect of policing operations in FYRM. The Mission supports a Police Academy and ongoing police training programmes. In September 2002 the OSCE participated with monitoring of parliamentary elections in FYRM. In mid-2003 the Mission initiated a trial observation programme, in order to build confidence in the country's legal system. Preliminary findings were published in 2004. ODIHR led international election observation missions to monitor a popular referendum, held in November in relation to legislation to establish municipal boundaries, and to observe local elections, held in March 2005.

In March 2000 the OSCE adopted a Regional Strategy for South-Eastern Europe, aimed at enhancing co-operation amongst its presences in the region. The OSCE was actively involved in co-ordinating the Stability Pact for South-Eastern Europe, which was initiated, in June 1999, as a collaborative plan of action by the EU, Group of Seven industrialized nations and Russia (the G-8), regional governments and other organizations concerned with the stability of the region. (This can be accessed at www.stabilitypact.org.) A meeting of participants in the Pact was convened to coincide with the OSCE summit meeting, held in November. In October 2001 the OSCE organized a Stability Pact regional conference, held in Bucharest, Romania. A memorandum of understanding between the OSCE Mission to the FRY and the Stability Pact was signed in December.

The OSCE Mission to Tajikistan was established in December 1993, and began operations in February 1994. The Mission worked with the UN Mission of Observers to Tajikistan (UNMOT) to promote a peace process in that country, and was a guarantor of the peace agreement concluded in June 1997. The Mission remained actively concerned with promoting respect for human rights, assisting the development of the local media, locating missing persons, and the fair distribution of humanitarian aid. Following multi-party parliamentary elections, held in February 2000, the Mission's focus was to be on post-conflict rehabilitation. In October 2002 the Permanent Council, taking into account the progress made in Tajikistan since the end of the civil conflict, decided to adapt the OSCE's mandate in the country and to replace the mission with a Centre in Dushanbe, with effect from the beginning of November. On 1 January 2004 the Centre initiated a two-year Mine Action Programme. In February 2005 an ODIHR mission observed the first round of parliamentary elections in Tajikistan, and reported a failure to meet certain OSCE commitments and other international standards.

In December 2000 the Permanent Council renamed the OSCE Liaison Office in Central Asia the OSCE Centre in Tashkent. The Centre aims to promote OSCE principles within Uzbekistan; it also functions as an information exchange between OSCE bodies and participating Central Asian states and as a means of liaising with OSCE presences in the region. In July 1998 the Permanent Council determined to establish OSCE Centres in Bishkek (Kyrgyzstan), Almaty (Kazakhstan), and Ashgabad (Turkmenistan), all of which opened in January 1999. In general the Centres were to encourage each country's integration into the OSCE, and implementation of its principles, and to focus on the economic, environmental, human and political aspects of security. In January 2000, for the first time, the OSCE refused to dispatch official observers to monitor presidential elections in a member state, owing to concerns about the legitimacy of elections held in Kazakhstan. Subsequently the Centre in Almaty, with the ODIHR and the OSCE Parliamentary Assembly, initiated a round table on elections project to improve electoral legislation, thus strengthening the political system. The project concluded in January 2002, when participants presented a list of recommendations to the national parliament. In September 2004 an OSCE mission observed parliamentary elections held in Kazakhstan. In a joint statement with a parliamentary delegation of the Council of Europe, the mission declared concern at procedural standards in relation to election legislation in that country. In mid-October the OSCE Centres in Bishkek and Almaty organized a roundtable concerned with the electoral processes in Kazakhstan and Kyrgyzstan attended by some 20 participants from state institutions and civil society organizations. A joint ODIHR and OSCE Parliamentary Assembly mission observed parliamentary elections held in Kyrgyzstan in February and March 2005. The mission reported many procedural and democratic shortcomings in the election process. Following an escalation of civil and political tensions after the polls, the Centre in Bishkek offered to provide a forum for dialogue between the authorities and opposition groups. In 2004 all five Central Asian OSCE Centres launched a Central Asian Youth Network to promote collaboration among the region's students and study of OSCE's fundamental principles. An OSCE Academy in Bishkek was inaugurated in December 2002 as a regional centre for training, research and dialogue, in particular in security-related issues.

Japan, the Republic of Korea, Thailand and Afghanistan have the status of 'partners for co-operation' with the OSCE, while Algeria, Egypt, Israel, Jordan, Morocco and Tunisia are 'Mediterranean partners for co-operation'. Regular consultations are held with these countries in order to discuss security issues of common concern.

Finance

All activities of the institutions, negotiations, *ad hoc* meetings and missions are financed by contributions from member states. The budget for 2004 amounted to €180.3m., of which 78% was allocated to OSCE field operations. Some 72% of the total field expenditure was for south-eastern Europe, 18% for the Caucasus, 7% for central Asia, and 3% for eastern Europe.

Publications

Annual Report of the Secretary-General.
The Caucasus: In Defence of the Future.
Decision Manual (annually).
OSCE Handbook (annually).
OSCE Newsletter (monthly).
Factsheets on OSCE missions, institutions and other structures appear regularly.

ORGANIZATION OF AMERICAN STATES—OAS

(ORGANIZACIÓN DE LOS ESTADOS AMERICANOS—OEA)

Address: 17th St and Constitution Ave, NW, Washington, DC 20006, USA.

Telephone: (202) 458-3000; **fax:** (202) 458-6319; **e-mail:** pi@oas .org; **internet:** www.oas.org.

The ninth International Conference of American States (held in Bogotá, Colombia, in 1948) established the Organization of American States by adopting the Charter (succeeding the International Union of American Republics, founded in 1890). The Charter was subsequently amended by the Protocol of Buenos Aires (creating the annual General Assembly), signed in 1967, enacted in 1970, and by the Protocol of Cartagena de Indias, which was signed in 1985 and enacted in 1988. The purpose of the Organization is to strengthen the peace and security of the continent; to promote and consolidate representative democracy, with due respect for the principle of non-intervention; to prevent possible causes of difficulties and to ensure the peaceful settlement of disputes that may arise among the member states; to provide for common action in the event of aggression; to seek the solution of political, juridical and economic problems that may arise among them; to promote, by co-operative action, their economic, social and cultural development; to achieve an effective limitation of conventional weapons; and to devote the largest amount of resources to the economic and social development of the member states.

MEMBERS

Antigua and Barbuda	Guyana
Argentina	Haiti
Bahamas	Honduras
Barbados	Jamaica
Belize	Mexico
Bolivia	Nicaragua
Brazil	Panama
Canada	Paraguay
Chile	Peru
Colombia	Saint Christopher and Nevis
Costa Rica	Saint Lucia
Cuba*	Saint Vincent and the Grenadines
Dominica	Suriname
Dominican Republic	Trinidad and Tobago
Ecuador	USA
El Salvador	Uruguay
Grenada	Venezuela
Guatemala	

*The Cuban Government was suspended from OAS activities in 1962.

Permanent Observers: Algeria, Angola, Armenia, Austria, Azerbaijan, Belgium, Bosnia and Herzegovina, Bulgaria, People's Republic of China, Croatia, Cyprus, Czech Republic, Denmark, Egypt, Equatorial Guinea, Estonia, Finland, France, Georgia, Germany, Ghana, Greece, Holy See, Hungary, India, Ireland, Israel, Italy, Japan, Kazakhstan, Republic of Korea, Latvia, Lebanon, Luxembourg, Morocco, Netherlands, Nigeria, Norway, Pakistan, Philippines, Poland, Portugal, Qatar, Romania, Russia, Saudi Arabia, Serbia and Montenegro, Slovakia, Slovenia, Spain, Sri Lanka, Sweden, Switzerland, Thailand, Tunisia, Turkey, Ukraine, United Kingdom, Yemen and the European Union.

Organization

(May 2005)

GENERAL ASSEMBLY

The Assembly meets annually and may also hold special sessions when convoked by the Permanent Council. As the supreme organ of the OAS, it decides general action and policy. The 34th regular session of the General Assembly was convened in Quito, Ecuador, in June 2004.

MEETINGS OF CONSULTATION OF MINISTERS OF FOREIGN AFFAIRS

Meetings are convened, at the request of any member state, to consider problems of an urgent nature and of common interest to member states, or to serve as an organ of consultation in cases of armed attack or other threats to international peace and security. The Permanent Council determines whether a meeting should be convened and acts as a provisional organ of consultation until ministers are able to assemble.

PERMANENT COUNCIL

The Council meets regularly throughout the year at OAS headquarters. It is composed of one representative of each member state with the rank of ambassador; each government may accredit alternate representatives and advisers and when necessary appoint an interim representative. The office of Chairman is held in turn by each of the representatives, following alphabetical order according to the names of the countries in Spanish. The Vice-Chairman is determined in the same way, following reverse alphabetical order. Their terms of office are three months.

The Council acts as an organ of consultation and oversees the maintenance of friendly relations between members. It supervises the work of the OAS and promotes co-operation with a variety of other international bodies including the United Nations. It comprises a General Committee and Committees on Juridical and Political Affairs, Hemispheric Security, Inter-American Summits Management and Civil Society Participation in OAS Activities, and Administrative and Budgetary Affairs. There are also *ad hoc* working groups. The official languages are English, French, Portuguese and Spanish.

INTER-AMERICAN COUNCIL FOR INTEGRAL DEVELOPMENT (CIDI)

The Council was established in 1996, replacing the Inter-American Economic and Social Council and the Inter-American Council for Education, Science and Culture. Its aim is to promote co-operation among the countries of the region, in order to accelerate economic and social development. CIDI's work focuses on eight areas: social development and education; cultural development; the generation of productive employment; economic diversification, integration and trade liberalization; strengthening democratic institutions; the exchange of scientific and technological information; the development of tourism; and sustainable environmental development. An Executive Secretary for Integral Development provides CIDI with technical and secretarial services.

Executive Secretary: BRIAN J. R. STEPHENSON.

Inter-American Agency for Co-operation and Development: f. November 1999 as a subsidiary body of CIDI to accelerate the development of Latin America and the Caribbean through technical co-operation and training programmes. In particular, the Agency aimed to formulate strategies for mobilizing external funds for OAS co-operation initiatives; establish criteria for the promotion and exchange of co-operation activities; prepare co-operation accords and evaluate project requests and results; and review mechanisms for promoting scholarships and professional exchange programmes. The Agency has developed an Educational Portal of the Americas providing comprehensive electronic access to information regarding distance learning; a Virtual Classroom was launched in May 2003. A Trust for the Americas works within the Agency to enable the private sector to participate OAS development programmes. The Executive Secretary for Integral Development serves as the Agency's Director-General.

GENERAL SECRETARIAT

The Secretariat, the central and permanent organ of the Organization, performs the duties entrusted to it by the General Assembly, Meetings of Consultation of Ministers of Foreign Affairs and the Councils.

Secretary-General: JOSÉ MIGUEL INSULZA (Chile).

Assistant Secretary-General: LUIGI R. EINAUDI (USA).

INTER-AMERICAN COMMITTEES AND COMMISSIONS

Inter-American Juridical Committee (IAJC) (Comissão Jurídica Interamericana/Comité Jurídico Interamericano): Av. Marechal Floriano 196, 3° andar, Palácio Itamaraty, Centro, 20080-002, Rio de Janeiro, RJ , Brazil; tel. (21) 2206-9903; fax (21) 2203-2090; e-mail cjioea.trp@terra.com.br; composed of 11 jurists, nationals of different member states, elected for a period of four years, with the possibility of re-election. The Committee's purposes are: to serve as an advisory body to the Organization on juridical matters; to promote the progressive development and codification of international law; and to study juridical problems relating to the integration of the developing countries in the hemisphere, and, in so far as may appear desirable, the possibility of attaining uniformity in legislation; Chair. MAURICIO HERDOCIA SACASA.

Inter-American Commission on Human Rights (Comisión Interamericana de Derechos Humanos): 1889 F St, NW, Washington, DC 20006, USA; tel. (202) 458-6002; fax (202) 458-3992; e-mail cidhoea@oas.org; internet www.cidh.oas.org; f. 1960; comprises seven members; promotes the observance and protection of human rights in the member states of the OAS; examines and reports on the human rights situation in member countries; considers individual petitions relating to alleged human rights violations by member states; in Feb. 2005 established a Special Rapporteurship on the Rights of People of Afro-Descendants, and against Racial Discrimination; Pres. CLARE K. ROBERTS; Exec. Sec. SANTIAGO CANTON.

Inter-American Court of Human Rights (IACHR) (Corte Interamericana de Derechos Humanos): Apdo Postal 6906-1000, San José, Costa Rica; tel. 234-0581; fax 234-0584; e-mail corteidh@corteidh.or.cr; internet www.corteidh.or.cr; f. 1978, as an autonomous judicial institution whose purpose is to apply and interpret the American Convention on Human Rights (which entered into force in 1978: at late 2004 the Convention had been ratified by 25 OAS member states, of which 21 had accepted the competence of the Court); comprises seven jurists from OAS member states; Pres. SERGIO GARCÍA-RAMIREZ; Sec. PABLO SAAVEDRA-ALESSANDRI (Chile); publ. *Annual Report.*

Inter-American Drug Abuse Control Commission (Comisión Interamericana para el Control del Abuso de Drogas—CICAD): 1889 F St, NW, Washington, DC 20006, USA; tel. (202) 458-3178; fax (202) 458-3658; e-mail oidcicad@oas.org; internet www.cicad.oas.org; f. 1986 by the OAS to promote and facilitate multilateral co-operation in the control and prevention of the trafficking, production and use of illegal drugs, and related crimes; mems: 34 countries; Exec. Sec. JAMES F. MACK; publs *Statistical Survey* (annually), *Directory of Governmental Institutions Charges with the Fight Against the Illicit Production, Trafficking, Use and Abuse of Narcotic Drugs and Psychotropic Substances Evaluation of Progress in Drug Control Progress Report in Drug Control—Implementation in Recommendations* (twice a year).

Inter-American Telecommunication Commission (Comisión Interamericana de Telecomunicaciones—CITEL): 1889 F St, NW, Washington, DC 20006, USA; tel. (202) 458-3004; fax (202) 458-6854; e-mail citel@oas.org; internet www.citel.oas.org; f. 1993 to promote the development of telecommunications in the region; mems: 35 countries; Exec. Sec. CLOVIS JOSÉ BAPTISTA NETO.

Inter-American Committee on Ports (Comisión Interamericana de Puertos—CIP): 1889 F St, NW, Washington, DC 20006, USA; tel. (202) 458-3871; fax (202) 458-3517; e-mail cgallegos@oas.org; f. 1998 to further OAS activities in the sector (previously undertaken by Inter-American Port Conferences); aims to develop and co-ordinate member state policies in port administration and management; the first meeting of the Committee took place in October 1999; three technical advisory groups were established to advise on port operations, port security, and navigation control and environmental protection; an Executive Board meets annually; Sec. CARLOS GALLEGOS.

Activities

In December 1994 the first Summit of the Americas was convened in Miami, USA. The meeting endorsed the concept of a Free Trade Area of the Americas (FTAA), and also approved a Plan of Action to strengthen democracy, eradicate poverty and promote sustainable development throughout the region. The OAS subsequently embarked on an extensive process of reform and modernization to strengthen its capacity to undertake a lead role in implementing the Plan. The Organization realigned its priorities in order to respond to the mandates emerging from the Summit and developed a new institutional framework for technical assistance and co-operation, although many activities continued to be undertaken by the specialized or associated organizations of the OAS (see below). In 1998, following the second Summit of the Americas, held in April, in Santiago, Chile, the OAS established an Office of Summit Follow-Up, in order to strengthen its servicing of the meetings, and to co-ordinate tasks assigned to the Organization. The third Summit, convened in Québec, QC, Canada, in April 2001, reaffirmed the central role of the OAS in implementing decisions of the summit meetings and instructed the Organization to pursue the process of reform in order to enhance its operational capabilities, in particular in the areas of human rights, combating trade in illegal drugs, and enforcement of democratic values. The Summit declaration stated that commitment to democracy was a requirement for a country's participation in the summit process. The meeting also determined that the OAS was to be the technical secretariat for the process, assuming many of the responsibilities previously taken by the host country. Further to its mandate the OAS established a Summits of the Americas Secretariat, which assists countries in planning and follow-up and provides technical, logistical and administrative support for the Summit Implementation Review Group and the summit process. A Special Summit of the Americas was held in January 2004, in Monterrey, Mexico, to reaffirm commitment to the process and to advance the implementation of measures, in particular to combat poverty to promote social development and equitable economic growth and to strengthen democratic governance. The fourth Summit was scheduled to be convened in Argentina, in November 2005.

TRADE AND ECONOMIC INTEGRATION

A trade unit was established in 1995 in order to strengthen the Organization's involvement in trade issues and the process of economic integration, which became a priority area following the first Summit of the Americas. The unit was to provide technical assistance in support of the establishment of the FTAA, and to co-ordinate activities between regional and sub-regional integration organizations. Subsequently the unit has provided technical support to the nine FTAA negotiating groups: market access; investment; services; government procurement; dispute settlement; agriculture; intellectual property rights; subsidies, anti-dumping and counter-vailing duties; and competition policy. In April 2001 the third Summit of the Americas requested the OAS to initiate an analysis of corporate social responsibility. At the Summit it was agreed that negotiations to establish the FTAA should be concluded by January 2005. At a special summit of the Americas, held in January 2004 in Monterrey, Mexico, however, the leaders failed to specify a completion date for the negotiations, although they adopted a declaration committing themselves to its eventual establishment. Negotiations on the FTAA stalled during 2004. The trade unit supports a Hemispheric Co-operation Programme, which was established by ministers of trade of the Americas, meeting in November 2002, to assist smaller economies to gain greater access to resources and technical assistance.

The unit operates in consultation with a Special Committee on Trade, which was established in 1993, comprising high-level officials representing each member state. The Committee studies trade issues, provides technical analyses of the economic situation in member countries and the region, and prepares reports for ministerial meetings of the FTAA. The OAS also administers an Inter-American Foreign Trade Information System which facilitates the exchange of information.

DEMOCRACY AND CIVIL SOCIETY

Two principal organs of the OAS, the Inter-American Commission on Human Rights and the Inter-American Court of Human Rights, work to secure respect for human rights in all member countries. The OAS aims to encourage more member governments to accept jurisdiction of the Court. The OAS also collaborates with member states in the strengthening of representative institutions within government and as part of a democratic civil society. The third Summit of the Americas, convened in April 2001, mandated the OAS to formulate an Inter-American Democratic Charter. The Charter was adopted in September at a special session of the Assembly. Central to the Charter's five chapters was democracy and its relationship to human rights, integral development and combating poverty. It aimed to establish procedures to strengthen and promote democracy and to respond to violations of or threats to democracy in member countries.

Through its Unit for the Promotion of Democracy, established in 1990, the OAS provides electoral technical assistance to member states and undertakes missions to observe the conduct of elections. By mid-2004 the OAS had conducted more than 70 electoral missions in 20 member countries. In 2004 missions included observing presidential elections in El Salvador in March, and in Panama and Dominican Republic in May. The OAS also supports societies in post-conflict situations and recently-installed governments to promote democratic practices. In November 2003 the OAS sponsored the third Inter-American Forum on Political Parties, held in Cartagena, Colombia, during which leaders of political parties considered means of enhancing campaign transparency, implementing structural party reforms and strengthening links to grass-roots membership.

In June 1991 the OAS General Assembly approved a resolution on representative democracy, which authorized the Secretary-General to summon a session of the Permanent Council in cases where a democratically-elected government had been overthrown or democratic procedures abandoned in member states. The Council could then convene an *ad hoc* meeting of ministers of foreign affairs to consider the situation. The procedure was invoked following political developments in Haiti, in September 1991, and Peru, in April 1992. Ministers determined to impose trade and diplomatic sanctions against Haiti and sent missions to both countries. The resolution was incorporated into the Protocol of Washington, amending the OAS charter, which was adopted in December 1992 and entered into force in September 1997. A high-level OAS mission was dispatched to Peru in June 2000 to assist with the process of 'strengthening its institutional democratic system', following allegations that the Peruvian authorities had manipulated the re-election of that country's President in May. The mission subsequently co-ordinated negotiations between the Peruvian Government and opposition organizations.

In August 2000 the OAS Secretary-General undertook the first of several high-level missions to negotiate with the authorities in Haiti in order to resolve the political crisis resulting from a disputed general election in May. (An OAS electoral monitoring team was withdrawn from Haiti in July prior to the second round of voting owing to concern at procedural irregularities.) In January 2001, following a meeting with the Haitian Prime Minister, the Assistant Secretary-General recommended that the OAS renew its efforts to establish a dialogue between the government, opposition parties and representatives of civil society in that country. In May the OAS and CARICOM undertook a joint mission to Haiti in order to assess prospects for a democratic resolution to the political uncertainties, and in June the OAS General Assembly issued a resolution urging all parties in Haiti to respect democratic order. At the end of that month the OAS Secretary-General led a visit of the joint mission to Haiti, during which further progress was achieved on the establishment of a new electoral council. Following political and social unrest in Haiti in December 2001, the OAS and CARICOM pledged to conduct an independent investigation into the violence, and in March 2002 an agreement to establish a Special OAS Mission for Strengthening Democracy in Haiti was signed in the capital, Port-au-Prince. The independent commission of inquiry reported to the OAS at the beginning of July, and listed a set of recommendations relating to law reform, security and other confidence-building measures to help to secure democracy in Haiti. In September, in acknowledgement of the perceived efforts of the Government to resolve the political *impasse* (including a commitment by the President to staging legislative and municipal elections by the end of 2003), the OAS issued a resolution releasing aid to Haiti that had been blocked since the controversial May 2000 elections. Release of the funds, however, was contingent upon certain political and social reforms (such as reform of the police force and the disarming of partisans), and by mid-2003 it appeared that few of the conditions set by the OAS had been met. In January 2004 the OAS Special Mission condemned the escalation of political violence in Haiti and in February took a lead in drafting a plan of action to implement a CARICOM-brokered action plan to resolve the crisis. In late February the Permanent Council met in special session, and urged the United Nations to take necessary and appropriate action to address the deteriorating situation in Haiti. On 29 February President Aristide resigned and left the country; amidst ongoing civil unrest, a provisional president was sworn in. The OAS Mission continued to attempt to maintain law and order, in co-operation with a UN-authorized Multinational Interim Force, and facilitated political discussions on the establishment of a transitional government. From March the Special Mission participated in the process to develop an Interim Co-operation Framework, identifying the urgent and medium-term needs of Haiti, which was presented to a meeting of international donors held in July. In June the OAS General Assembly adopted a resolution instructing the Permanent Council to undertake all necessary diplomatic initiatives to foster the restoration of democracy in Haiti, and called upon the Special Mission to work with the new UN Stabilization Mission in Haiti in preparing, organizing and monitoring future elections. In early 2005 OAS technical experts were to start co-ordinating the process of voter registration for elections scheduled for later in that year.

In April 2002 a special session of the General Assembly was convened to discuss the ongoing political instability in Venezuela. The Assembly applied its authority granted under the Inter-American Democratic Charter to condemn the alteration of the constitutional order in Venezuela which forced the temporary eviction of President Hugo Chávez from office. In January 2003 the OAS announced the establishment of a Group of Friends, composed of representatives from Brazil, Chile, Mexico, Spain, Portugal and the USA, to support its efforts to resolve the ongoing crisis in Venezuela. In March the OAS Secretary-General was invited by Venezuelan opposition groupings to mediate negotiations with the Government. The talks culminated in May with the signing of an OAS-brokered agreement which, it was hoped, would lead to mid-term referendums on elected officials, including the presidency. The OAS, with the Carter Center, has subsequently undertaken to oversee and verify the collection of signatures.

In April 2005 a special session of the Permanent Council expressed concern at recent political developments in Ecuador and determined to send a high-level mission to work with officials and political and civil organizations in that country in order to strengthen democratic processes.

An OAS Assistance Programme for Demining in Central America was established in 1992, based in Managua, Nicaragua, to contribute to the social and economic rehabilitation of the region. The programme was to provide training, oversee clearance of anti-personnel devices, undertake risk education, and assist victims of mines, including assistance with medical treatment and retraining activities. The mine clearance operation in Costa Rica was concluded in December 2002 and in Honduras by the end of 2004. In 2002 OAS began to support demining operations in Ecuador and Peru, and in 2003 opened an office in Bogotá, Colombia, to help support mine action programmes, in particular victim rehabilitation and the development of a mine action database. Since mid-2002 the programme, together with the Inter-American Defense Board (see below), had assisted the destruction of an estimated 1m. landmines from military stock-piles in Argentina, Colombia, Chile, Ecuador, Honduras, Nicaragua, Peru and Suriname (which, in April 2005, became the third member state to conclude its demining programme). In November 1997 an Inter-American Convention against the Illicit Manufacture of and Trafficking in Firearms, Ammunition, Explosives, and Other related materials was adopted; it entered into force in July 1998. By June 2004 the Convention had been ratified by 23 countries. An Inter-American Convention on Transparency in Conventional Weapons was adopted in 1999.

The OAS formulated an Inter-American Programme of Co-operation to Combat Corruption in order to address the problem at national level and, in 1996, adopted a Convention against Corruption. The first conference of the parties to the Convention was held in Buenos Aires, Argentina, in May 2001. In June the General Assembly approved the proposed establishment of a verification mechanism, including a policy-making annual conference and an intergovernmental committee of experts. At June 2004 the Convention had been ratified by 33 member states. A working group on transparency aims to promote accountability throughout the public sector and supports national institutions responsible for combating corruption. In 1997 the OAS organized a meeting of experts to consider measures for the prevention of crime. The meeting adopted a work programme which included commitments to undertake police training in criminology and crime investigation, to exchange legal and practical knowledge, and to measure crime and violence in member countries.

REGIONAL SECURITY

In 1991 the General Assembly established a working group to consider issues relating to the promotion of co-operation in regional security. A Special Commission on Hemispheric Security was subsequently established, while two regional conferences have been held on security and confidence-building measures. Voluntary practices agreed by member states include the holding of border meetings to co-ordinate activities, co-operation in natural disaster management, and the exchange of information on military exercises and expenditure. From 1995 meetings of ministers of defence have been convened regularly, which provide a forum for discussion of security matters. The OAS aims to address the specific security concerns of small-island states, in particular those in the Caribbean, by adopting a multidimensional approach to counter their vulnerability, for example through efforts to strengthen democracy, to combat organized crime, to mitigate the effects of natural disasters and other environmental hazards, and to address the problem of HIV/AIDS.

In June 2000 the OAS General Assembly, convened in Windsor, Canada, established a Fund for Peace in support of the peaceful settlement of territorial disputes. In the early 2000s the Fund was supported efforts to resolve disputes between Belize and Guatemala and between Honduras and Nicaragua. In June 2001 an agreement was concluded to enable an OAS Civilian Verification Mission to visit Honduras and Nicaragua in order to monitor compliance with previously agreed confidence-building measures. The Mission was to be financed by the Fund for Peace.

The OAS is actively involved in efforts to combat the abuse and trafficking of illegal drugs, and in 1996 members approved a Hemispheric Anti-drug Strategy, reiterating their commitment to addressing the problem. In 1998 the Inter-American Drug Abuse Control Commission (CICAD) established a Multilateral Evaluation Mechanism (MEM) to measure aspects of the drug problem and to co-ordinate an evaluation process under which national plans of action to combat drugs trafficking were to be formulated. The first hemispheric drugs report was published by MEM in January 2001 and in February 34 national reports produced under MEM were issued together with a series of recommendations for action. In January 2002 MEM published a progress report on the implementation of the recommendations, in which it stated that the countries of the Americas had made a 'significant effort' to adopt the recommendations, although in some instances they had encountered difficulties owing to a lack of technical or financial resources. It was reported that advances had been made in developing national anti-drugs plans, measuring land under illicit cultivation, and adopting procedures against money-laundering. Since 1996 an OAS group of experts has undertaken efforts to assist countries in reducing the demand for illegal substances. Activities include the implementation of prevention programmes for street children; the development of communication strategies; and education and community projects relating to the prevention of drug dependence.

The first Specialized Inter-American Conference on Terrorism was held in Lima, Peru, in April 1996. A Declaration and Plan of Action were adopted, according to which member states agreed to co-operate and implement measures to combat terrorism and organized crime. A second conference was held in Mar del Plata, Argentina, in 1998, which culminated in the adoption of the Commitment of Mar del Plata. Member states recommended the establishment of an Inter-American Committee against Terrorism (CICTE) to implement decisions relating to judicial, police and intelligence co-operation. The Committee held its first session in Miami, USA, in October 1999; a second meeting was convened in January 2002. Two special sessions of the CICTE were held in October and November 2001, following the terrorist attacks on targets in the USA in September. A CICTE On-Line Anti-terrorism Database came into operation during 2002. In June 2002, at the OAS General Assembly, held in Bridgetown, Barbados, 30 heads of state and of government signed an Inter-American Convention against Terrorism. The Assembly also adopted a Declaration of Bridgetown on the multidimensional approach to hemispheric security. The Convention entered into force in July 2003, following its ratification by the required six member states. By February 2005 the Convention had been signed by all member states and ratified by 12 states. A Special Conference on Security was convened in October 2003 to review the security structure throughout the Americas.

SOCIAL DEVELOPMENT AND EDUCATION

In June 1996 the OAS established a specialized unit for social development and education to assist governments and social institutions of member states to formulate public policies and implement initiatives relating to employment and labour issues, education development, social integration and poverty elimination. It was also to provide technical and operational support for the implementation of inter-American programmes in those sectors, and to promote the exchange of information among experts and professionals working in those fields. In June 1997 the OAS approved an Inter-American

Programme to Combat Poverty. The unit serves as the technical secretariat for annual meetings on social development that were to be convened within the framework of the Programme. The unit also administers the Social Networks of Latin America and the Caribbean project, and its co-ordinating committee, which promotes sub-regional co-operation to combat poverty and discrimination. From 1999 the unit implemented a project funded by the Inter-American Development Bank to place interns and trainees within the Social Network institutions and to promote exchanges between the institutions.

The first meeting of ministers of education of the Americas was held in Brasília, Brazil, in July 1998, based on the mandate of the second Summit of the Americas. The meeting approved an Inter-American Education Programme, formulated by the unit for social development and education, which incorporated the following six priority initiatives: education for priority social sectors; strengthening educational management and institutional development; education for work and youth development; education for citizenship and sustainability in multicultural societies; training in the use of new technologies in teaching the official languages of the OAS; and training of teachers and education administrators. Other programmes in the education sector are undertaken with international agencies and non-governmental organizations (NGOs). In April 2004 OAS convened a special meeting on the promotion of a democratic culture through education, which was attended by ministers of education and other officials, education experts and representatives of NGOs. The meeting agreed upon guide-lines for the development of an Inter-American Values Programme, which was to carry out goals identified by OAS ministers of education and principles expressed in the Inter-American Democratic Charter.

The OAS supports member states to formulate and implement programmes to promote productive employment and vocational training, to develop small businesses and other employment generation initiatives, and to regulate labour migration. In 1998 the OAS initiated the Labour Market Information System project, which aimed to provide reliable and up-to-date indicators of the labour situation in member countries, to determine the impact of economic policy on the labour situation, and to promote the exchange of information among relevant national and regional institutions. Labour issues were addressed by the second Summit of the Americas, and, following an Inter-American Conference of Labour Ministers, held in Viña del Mar, Chile, in October 1998, two working groups were established to consider the globalization of the economy and its social and labour dimension and the modernization of the state and labour administration. In June 2002 the Pan-American Health Organization (PAHO) and Inter-American Institute for Co-operation on Agriculture (IICA) signed an agreement to increase co-operation in matters relating to health and agriculture, in order to combat poverty in rural communities.

SUSTAINABLE DEVELOPMENT AND THE ENVIRONMENT
In 1996 a summit meeting on social development adopted a plan of action, based on the objectives of the UN Conference on the Environment and Development, which was held in Rio de Janeiro, Brazil, in June 1992. The OAS was to participate in an inter-agency group to monitor implementation of the action plan. The OAS has subsequently established new financing mechanisms and networks of experts relating to aspects of sustainable development. Technical co-operation activities include multinational basin management; a strategic plan for the Amazon; natural disaster management; and the sustainable development of border areas in Central America and South America. In December 1999 the Inter-American Council for Integral Development approved a policy framework and recommendations for action of a new Inter-American Strategy for Public Participation in Decision-making for Sustainable Development.

The following initiatives have also been undertaken by the OAS Unit for Sustainable Development and Environment: a Caribbean Disaster Mitigation Project, to help those countries to counter and manage the effects of natural disasters; a Post-Georges Disaster Mitigation initiative specifically to assist countries affected by Hurricane Georges; a Natural Hazards Project to provide a general programme of support to assess member states' vulnerability, to provide technical assistance and training to mitigate the effects of a disaster, and to assist in the planning and formulation of development and preparedness policies; the Renewable Energy in the Americas initiative to promote co-operation and strengthen renewable energy and energy efficiency; an Inter-American Water Resources Network, which aims to promote collaboration, training and the exchange of information within the sector; and a Water Level Observation Network for Central America to provide support for coastal resources management, navigation and disaster mitigation in the countries affected by Hurricane Mitch. In mid-2003 the OAS was also facilitating two further projects: the Caribbean Hazard Mitigation Capacity Building Programme to assist countries in the region in formulating policies to reduce their vulnerability to natural disaster; and, in St Lucia, the Hurricane-Resistant Home Improve-

ment Programme, aimed at creating safer housing for low-income earners.

SCIENCE AND TECHNOLOGY
The OAS supports and develops activities to contribute to the advancement of science and technology throughout the Americas, and to promote its contribution to social and sustainable development. In particular, it promotes collaboration, dissemination of information and improved communication between experts and institutions working in the sector. Specialized bodies and projects have been established to promote activities in different fields, for example metrology; co-operation between institutions of accreditation, certification and inspection; the development of instruments of measurements and analysis of science and technology; chemistry; the development of technical standardization and related activities; and collaboration between experts and institutions involved in biotechnology and food technology. The OAS also maintains an information system to facilitate access to databases on science and technology throughout the region.

TOURISM AND CULTURE
A specialized unit for tourism was established in 1996 in order to strengthen and co-ordinate activities for the sustainable development of the tourism industry in the Americas. The unit supports regional and sub-regional conferences and workshops, as well as the Inter-American Travel Congress, which was convened for the first time in 1993 to serve as a forum to formulate region-wide tourism policies. The unit also undertakes research and analysis of the industry.

In 1998 the OAS approved an Inter-American Programme of Culture to support efforts being undertaken by member states and to promote co-operation in areas such as cultural diversity; protection of cultural heritage; training and dissemination of information; and the promotion of cultural tourism. The OAS also assists with the preparation of national and multilateral cultural projects, and co-operates with the private sector to protect and promote cultural assets and events in the region.

COMMUNICATIONS
In June 1993 the OAS General Assembly approved the establishment of an Inter-American Telecommunication Commission. The body has technical autonomy, within the statute and mandate agreed by the Assembly. It aims to facilitate and promote the development of communications in all member countries, in collaboration with the private sector and other organizations, and serves as the principal advisory body of the OAS on matters related to telecommunications.

Finance
The OAS budget for 2005, approved by the General Assembly in mid-2004, amounted to US $84.4m., of which $76.3m. was to come from the regular fund, and $8.2m. from the Special Fund for Integral Development (FEMCIDI).

Publications
(in English and Spanish)

Américas (6 a year).
Annual Report.
Catalog of Publications (annually).
Newsletter (online, 6 a year).
Numerous cultural, legal and scientific reports and studies.

Specialized Organizations and Associated Agencies

Inter-American Children's Institute (Instituto Americano del Niño—IIN): Avda 8 de Octubre 2904, POB 16212, Montevideo 11600, Uruguay; tel. (2) 487-2150; fax (2) 487-3242; e-mail iin@redfacil.com.uy; internet www.iin.oea.org; f. 1927; promotes the regional implementation of the Convention on the Rights of the Child, assists in the development of child-oriented public policies; promotes co-operation between states; and aims to develop awareness of problems affecting children and young people in the region. The Institute organizes workshops, seminars, courses, training programmes and conferences on issues relating to children, including, for example, the rights of children, children with disabilities, and the child welfare system. It also provides advisory services, statistical data and other relevant information to authorities and experts throughout the region; Dir-Gen. ALEJANDRO BONASSO; publ. *IINfancia* (2 a year).

Inter-American Commission of Women (Comisión Interamericana de Mujeres—CIM): 1889 F St, NW, Suite 350 Washington, DC 20006, USA; tel. (202) 458-6084; fax (202) 458-6094; e-mail spcim@oas.org; f. 1928 for the extension of civil, political, economic, social and cultural rights for women; in 1991 a Seed Fund was established to provide financing for grass-roots projects consistent with the Commission's objectives; Pres. NILCÉA FREIRE (Brazil); Exec. Sec. CARMEN LOMELLIN (USA).

Inter-American Committee Against Terrorism (Comité Interamericano Contra el Terrorismo—CICTE): 17th St and Constitution Ave, NW, Washington, DC 20006, USA; tel. (202) 458-3000; fax (202) 458-3857; internet www.cicte.oas.org; f. 1999 to enhance the exchange of information via national authorities (including the establishment of an Inter-American database on terrorism issues), formulate proposals to assist member states in drafting counter-terrorism legislation in all states, compile bilateral, sub-regional, regional and multilateral treaties and agreements signed by member states and promote universal adherence to international counter-terrorism conventions, strengthen border co-operation and travel documentation security measures, and develop activities for training and crisis management; Exec. Sec. STEVEN MONBLATT (USA).

Inter-American Defense Board (Junta Interamericana de Defensa—JID): 2600 16th St, NW, Washington, DC 20441, USA; tel. (202) 939-7490; internet www.jid.org; works in liaison with member governments to plan and train for the common security interests of the western hemisphere; operates the Inter-American Defense College; Chair. Maj.-Gen. KEITH M. HUBER (USA).

Inter-American Indigenous Institute (Instituto Indigenista Interamericano—III): Avda de las Fuentes 106, Col. Jardines del Pedregal, Delegación Álvaro Obregón, 01900 México, DF, Mexico; tel. (55) 5595-8410; fax (55) 5595-4324; e-mail ininin@data.net.mx; internet www.indigenista.org; f. 1940; conducts research on the situation of the indigenous peoples of America; assists the exchange of information; promotes indigenous policies in member states aimed at the elimination of poverty and development within Indian communities, and to secure their position as ethnic groups within a democratic society; Hon. Dir Dr GUILLERMO ESPINOSA VELASCO (Mexico); publs *América Indígena* (quarterly), *Anuario Indigenista*.

Inter-American Institute for Co-operation on Agriculture (IICA) (Instituto Interamericano de Cooperación para la Agricultura): Apdo Postal 55–2200 San Isidro de Coronado, San José, Costa Rica; tel. 216-0222; fax 216-0233; e-mail iicahq@iica.ac.cr; internet www.iica.int; f. 1942 (as the Inter-American Institute of Agricultural Sciences, present name adopted 1980); supports the efforts of member states to improve agricultural development and rural well-being; encourages co-operation between regional organizations, and provides a forum for the exchange of experience; Dir-Gen. Dr CHELSTON W. D. BRATHWAITE (Barbados).

Pan American Development Foundation (PADF) (Fundación Panamericana para el Desarrollo): 1889 F St, NW, Washington, DC 20006, USA; tel. (202) 458-3969; fax (202) 458-6316; e-mail padf-dc@padf.org; internet www.padf.org; f. 1962 to promote and facilitate economic and social development in Latin America and the Caribbean by means of innovative partnerships and integrated involvement of the public and private sectors; provides low-interest credit for small-scale entrepreneurs, vocational training, improved health care, agricultural development and reafforestation, and strengthening local non-governmental organizations; provides emergency disaster relief and reconstruction assistance; Pres. RUTH ESPEY-ROMERO; Exec. Dir YOLANDA MELLON SUÁREZ.

Pan American Health Organization (PAHO) (Organización Panamericana de la Salud): 525 23rd St, NW, Washington, DC 20037, USA; tel. (202) 974-3000; fax (202) 974-3663; e-mail webmaster@paho.org; internet www.paho.org; f. 1902; co-ordinates regional efforts to improve health; maintains close relations with national health organizations and serves as the Regional Office for the Americas of the World Health Organization; Dir Dr MIRTA ROSES PERIAGO (Argentina).

Pan-American Institute of Geography and History—PAIGH (Instituto Panamericano de Geografía e Historia–IPGH): Ex-Arzobispado 29, 11860 México, DF, Mexico; tel. (55) 5277-5888; fax (55) 5271-6172; e-mail secretariageneral@ipgh.org.mx; internet www.ipgh.org.mx; f. 1928; co-ordinates and promotes the study of cartography, geophysics, geography and history; provides technical assistance, conducts training at research centres, distributes publications, and organizes technical meetings; Sec.-Gen. SANTIAGO BORRERO MUTIS; Publs *Revista Cartográfica* (2 a year), *Revista Geográfica* (2 a year), *Revista Historia de América* (2 a year), *Revista Geofísica* (2 a year), *Revista de Arqueología Americana* (annually), *Folklore Americano* (annually), *Boletín de Antropología Americana* (annually).

ORGANIZATION OF ARAB PETROLEUM EXPORTING COUNTRIES—OAPEC

Address: POB 20501, Safat 13066, Kuwait.
Telephone: 4844500; **fax:** 4815747; **e-mail:** oapec@qualitynet.net; **internet:** www.oapecorg.org.

OAPEC was established in 1968 to safeguard the interests of members and to determine ways and means for their co-operation in various forms of economic activity in the petroleum industry. OAPEC member states contributed 27.4% of total world petroleum production in 2003 and 12.6% of total global natural gas output in 2002. At the end of 2003 OAPEC member states accounted for an estimated 58.3% of total global oil reserves and 29.7% of total global reserves of natural gas.

MEMBERS

Algeria	Kuwait	Saudi Arabia
Bahrain	Libya	Syria
Egypt	Qatar	United Arab Emirates
Iraq		

Organization

(April 2005)

MINISTERIAL COUNCIL

The Council consists normally of the ministers of petroleum of the member states, and forms the supreme authority of the Organization, responsible for drawing up its general policy, directing its activities and laying down its governing rules. It meets twice yearly, and may hold extraordinary sessions. Chairmanship is on an annual rotation basis.

EXECUTIVE BUREAU

Assists the Council to direct the management of the Organization, approves staff regulations, reviews the budget, and refers it to the Council, considers matters relating to the Organization's agreements and activities and draws up the agenda for the Council. The Bureau comprises one senior official from each member state. Chairmanship is by rotation on an annual basis, following the same order as the Ministerial Council chairmanship. The Bureau convenes at least three times a year.

GENERAL SECRETARIAT

Secretary-General: ABDUL AZIZ A. AL-TURKI (Saudi Arabia).

Besides the Office of the Secretary-General, there are four departments: Finance and Administrative Affairs, Information and Library, Technical Affairs, and Economics. The last two form the Arab Centre for Energy Studies (which was established in 1983). At the end of 2003 there were 21 professional staff members and 30 general personnel at the General Secretariat.

JUDICIAL TRIBUNAL

The Tribunal comprises seven judges from Arab countries. Its task is to settle differences in interpretation and application of the OAPEC Agreement, arising between members and also between OAPEC and its affiliates; disputes among member countries on petroleum activities falling within OAPEC's jurisdiction and not under the sovereignty of member countries; and disputes that the Ministerial Council decides to submit to the Tribunal.

President: FARIS ABDUL RAHMAN AL-WAGAYAN.
Registrar: Dr RIAD RASHAD AL-DAOUDI.

Activities

OAPEC co-ordinates different aspects of the Arab petroleum industry through the joint undertakings described below. It co-operates with the League of Arab States and other Arab organizations, and attempts to link petroleum research institutes in the Arab states. It organizes or participates in conferences and seminars, many of which are held jointly with non-Arab organizations in order to enhance Arab and international co-operation. OAPEC collaborates with AFESD, the Arab Monetary Fund and the League of Arab States in compiling the annual *Joint Arab Economic Report*, which is issued by the Arab Monetary Fund.

OAPEC provides training in technical matters and in documentation and information. The General Secretariat also conducts technical and feasibility studies and carries out market reviews. It provides information through a library, 'databank' and the publications listed below.

In association with AFESD, OAPEC organizes the Arab Energy Conference every four years. The conference is attended by OAPEC ministers of petroleum and energy, senior officials from other Arab states, and representatives of invited institutions and organizations concerned with energy issues. The seventh Conference, with the theme of 'Energy and Arab Co-operation', was convened in May 2002, in Cairo, Egypt. The eighth Arab Energy Conference, focusing on the same theme, was scheduled to be held in Amman, Jordan, in May 2006. OAPEC, with other Arab organizations, participates in the Higher Co-ordination Committee for Higher Arab Action.

In December 2003 a delegation of the then Iraq Interim Cabinet briefed government representatives from other OAPEC member states on the planned reactivation of the Baghdad-based Arab Well Logging Company and Arab Petroleum Training Institute (see below), which had both suspended operations in 1990.

Finance

The combined General Secretariat and Judicial Tribunal budget for 2004 amounted to 1,643,930 Kuwaiti dinars (KD).

Publications

Annual Statistical Report.

Energy Resources Monitor (quarterly, Arabic).

OAPEC Monthly Bulletin (Arabic and English editions).

Oil and Arab Co-operation (quarterly, Arabic).

Secretary-General's Annual Report (Arabic and English editions).

Papers, studies, conference proceedings.

OAPEC-Sponsored Ventures

Arab Maritime Petroleum Transport Company—AMPTC: POB 22525, Safat 13086, Kuwait; tel. 4844500; fax 4842996; e-mail amptc.kuwait@amptc.net; internet www.amptc.net; f. 1973 to undertake transport of crude petroleum, gas, refined products and petro-chemicals, and thus to increase Arab participation in the tanker transport industry; auth. cap. US $200m.; Gen. Man. SULAYMAN AL-BASSAM.

Arab Petroleum Investments Corporation—APICORP: POB 9599, Dammam 31423, Saudi Arabia; tel. (3) 847-0444; fax (3) 847-0022; e-mail apicorp@apicorp-arabia.com; internet www .apicorp-arabia.com; f. 1975 to finance investments in petroleum and petrochemicals projects and related industries in the Arab world and in developing countries, with priority being given to Arab joint ventures; projects financed include gas liquefaction plants, petrochemicals, tankers, oil refineries, pipelines, exploration, detergents, fertilizers and process control instrumentation; auth. cap. US $1,200m.; subs. cap. $460m.; shareholders: Kuwait, Saudi Arabia and United Arab Emirates (17% each), Libya (15%), Iraq and Qatar (10% each), Algeria (5%), Bahrain, Egypt and Syria (3% each); Chair. ABDULLAH A. AZ-ZAID (Saudi Arabia); Gen. Man. and CEO RASHEED AL-MARAJ.

Arab Detergent Chemicals Company—ARADET: POB 27864, el-Monsour, Baghdad, Iraq; tel. (1) 541-9893; f. 1981; produces and markets linear alkyl benzene; construction of a sodium multiphosphate plant is under way; APICORP holds 32% of shares in the co; auth. cap. 72m. Iraqi dinars; subs. cap. 60m. Iraqi dinars.

Arab Petroleum Services Company—APSCO: POB 12925, Tripoli, Libya; tel. (21) 45861; fax (21) 3331930; f. 1977 to provide petroleum services through the establishment of companies specializing in various activities, and to train specialized personnel; auth. cap. 100m. Libyan dinars; subs. cap. 15m. Libyan dinars; Chair. AYAD HUSSEIN AD-DALI; Gen. Man. ISMAIL AL-KORAITLI.

Arab Drilling and Workover Company: POB 680, Suani Rd, km 3.5, Tripoli, Libya; tel. (21) 800064; fax (21) 805945; f. 1980; 40% owned by APSCO; auth. cap. 12m. Libyan dinars; Gen. Man. MUHAMMAD AHMAD ATTIGA.

Arab Geophysical Exploration Services Company— AGESCO: POB 84224, Airport Rd, Tripoli, Libya; tel. (21) 4804863; fax (21) 4803199; f. 1985; 40%-owned by APSCO; auth. cap. 12m. Libyan dinars; subs. cap. 4m. Libyan dinars; Gen. Man. AYAD HUSSEIN AD-DALI.

Arab Well Logging Company (AWLCO): POB 6225, Baghdad, Iraq; tel. (1) 541-8259; f. 1983 to provide well-logging services and data interpretation; wholly-owned subsidiary of APSCO; operations suspended in 1990; auth. cap. 7m. Iraqi dinars.

Arab Petroleum Training Institute—APTI: POB 6037, Al-Tajeyat, Baghdad, Iraq; tel. (1) 523-4100; fax (1) 521-0526; f. 1978 to provide instruction in many technical and managerial aspects of the oil industry; operations suspended in 1990.

Arab Shipbuilding and Repair Yard Company—ASRY: POB 50110, Hidd, Bahrain; tel. 671111; fax 670236; e-mail asryco@ batelco.com.bh; internet www.asry.net; f. 1974 to undertake repairs and servicing of vessels; operates a 500,000 dwt dry dock in Bahrain; two floating docks operational since 1992; has recently diversified it activities, e.g. into building specialized service boats and upgrading oil rigs; cap. (auth. and subs.) US $170m.; Chair. EID ABDULLA YOUSIF (Bahrain); Chief Exec. MOHAMED M. ALKHATEEB.

ORGANIZATION OF THE BLACK SEA ECONOMIC CO-OPERATION—BSEC

Address: İstinye Cad. Müşir Fuad Paşa Yalısı, Eski Tersane 80860 İstinye-İstanbul, Turkey.

Telephone: (212) 229-63-30; **fax:** (212) 229-63-36; **e-mail:** bsec@tnn .net; **internet:** www.bsec.gov.tr.

The Black Sea Economic Co-operation (BSEC) was established in 1992 to strengthen regional co-operation, particularly in the field of economic development. In June 1998, at a summit meeting held in Yalta, Ukraine, participating countries signed the BSEC Charter, thereby officially elevating BSEC to regional organization status. The Charter entered into force on 1 May 1999, at which time BSEC formally became the Organization of the Black Sea Economic Co-operation, retaining the same acronym.

MEMBERS

Albania	Georgia	Russia
Armenia	Greece	Serbia and Montenegro
Azerbaijan	Moldova	Turkey
Bulgaria	Romania	Ukraine

Note: Observer status has been granted to Egypt, France, Germany, Israel, Italy, Poland, Slovakia and Tunisia. The BSEC Business Council, International Black Sea Club, and the Energy Charter Conference also have observer status. Iran, the former Yugoslav republic of Macedonia and Uzbekistan have applied for full membership.

Organization

(April 2005)

PRESIDENTIAL SUMMIT

The Presidential Summit, comprising heads of state or government of member states, represents the highest authority of the body.

COUNCIL

The Council of Ministers of Foreign Affairs is BSEC's principal decision-making organ. Ministers meet twice a year to review progress and to define new objectives. Chairmanship of the Council rotates among members; the Chairman-in-Office co-ordinates the activities undertaken by BSEC. The Council is supported by a Committee of Senior Officials.

PARLIAMENTARY ASSEMBLY

Address: 1 Hareket Kösku, Dolmabahçe Sarayi, Besiktas, 80680 İstanbul, Turkey.

Telephone: (212) 227-6070; **fax:** (212) 227-6080; **e-mail:** pabsec@pabsec.org; **internet:** www.pabsec.org.

The Parliamentary Assembly, consisting of the representatives of the national parliaments of member states, was created in February 1993 to provide a legal basis for the implementation of decisions within the BSEC framework. It comprises three committees concerning economic, commercial, technological and environmental affairs; legal and political affairs; and cultural, educational and social affairs. The presidency rotates every six months.

Secretary-General: ALEXEY KUDRIAVTSEV.

PERMANENT INTERNATIONAL SECRETARIAT

The Secretariat's tasks are, primarily, of an administrative and technical nature, and include the maintenance of archives, and the preparation and distribution of documentation. Much of the organization's activities are undertaken by 15 working groups, each headed by an Executive Manager, and by various *ad hoc* groups and meetings of experts.

Secretary-General: TEDO JAPARIDZE (Georgia).

Activities

In June 1992, at a summit meeting held in İstanbul, heads of state and of government signed the summit declaration on BSEC, and adopted the Bosphorus statement, which established a regional structure for economic co-operation. The grouping attained regional organization status in May 1999 (see above). The Organization's main areas of co-operation include transport; communications; trade and economic development; banking and finance; energy; tourism; agriculture and agro-industry; health care and pharmaceuticals; environmental protection; science and technology; the exchange of statistical data and economic information; collaboration between customs authorities; and combating organized crime, drugs-trafficking, trade in illegal weapons and radioactive materials, and terrorism. In order to promote regional co-operation, the organization also aims to strengthen the business environment by providing support for small and medium-sized enterprises; facilitating closer contacts between businesses in member countries; progressively eliminating obstacles to the expansion of trade; creating appropriate conditions for investment and industrial co-operation, in particular through the avoidance of double taxation and the promotion and protection of investments; encouraging the dissemination of information concerning international tenders organized by member states; and promoting economic co-operation in free-trade zones.

In recent years BSEC has undergone a process of reform aimed at developing a more project-based orientation. In April 2001 the

Council adopted the so-called BSEC Economic Agenda for the Future Towards a More Consolidated, Effective and Viable BSEC Partnership, which provided a roadmap for charting the implementation of the Organization's goals. In 2002 a project development fund was established and a regional programme of governance and institutional renewal was launched. Under the new orientation the roles of BSEC's Committee of Senior Officials and network of country-co-ordinators were to be enhanced.

BSEC aims to foster relations with other international and regional organizations, and has been granted observer status at the UN General Assembly. In 1999 BSEC agreed upon a Platform of Co-operation for future structured relations with the European Union. The main areas in which BSEC determined to develop co-operation with the EU were transport, energy and telecommunications infrastructure; trade and the promotion of foreign direct investment; sustainable development and environmental protection, including nuclear safety; science and technology; and combating terrorism and organized crime. BSEC supports the Stability Pact for South-Eastern Europe, initiated in June 1999 as a collaborative plan of action by the EU, the Group of Seven industrialized nations and Russia (the G-8), regional governments and other organizations concerned with the stability of the region. The Declaration issued by BSEC's decennial anniversary summit, held in Istanbul in June 2002, urged that collaboration with the EU should be enhanced. In April 2005 representatives of BSEC and the EU met in Brussels, Belgium, to address possibilities for such co-operation, focusing in particular on the EU's policy in the Black Sea region and on the development of regional transport and energy networks (see Alexandroupolis Declaration, below).

A BSEC Business Council was established in İstanbul in December 1992 by the business communities of member states. It has observer status at the BSEC, and aims to identify private and public investment projects, maintain business contacts and develop programmes in various sectors. A Black Sea Trade and Development Bank has been established, in Thessaloníki, Greece, as the organization's main funding institution, to finance and implement joint regional projects. It began operations on 1 July 1999. The European Bank for Reconstruction and Development (EBRD) was entrusted as the depository for all capital payments made prior to its establishment. A BSEC Co-ordination Centre, located in Ankara, Turkey, aims to promote the exchange of statistical and economic information. An International Center for Black Sea Studies (ICBSS) was established in Athens, Greece, in March 1998, in order to undertake research concerning the BSEC, in the fields of economics, industry and technology. In March 2001 the transport ministers of BSEC member states adopted a Transport Action Plan, which envisaged reducing the disparities in regional transport systems and integrating the BSEC regional transport infrastructure with wider international networks and projects. In March 2005 ministers of BSEC member states responsible for energy adopted the Alexandroupolis Declaration, approving a common framework for future collaboration on the creation of a regional energy market, and urging the liberalization of electricity and natural gas markets in accordance with EU directives as a basis for this.

BSEC has supported implementation of the Bucharest Convention on the Protection of the Black Sea Against Pollution, adopted by Bulgaria, Georgia, Romania, Russia, Turkey and Ukraine in April 1992. In October 1996 those countries adopted the Strategic Action Plan for the Rehabilitation and Protection of the Black Sea (BSSAP), to be implemented by the Commission of the Bucharest Convention.

Finance

BSEC is financed by annual contributions from member states on the following scale: Greece, Russia, Turkey and Ukraine each contribute 15% of the budget; Bulgaria, Romania and Serbia and Montenegro contribute 7.5%; the remaining members each contribute 3.5%.

ORGANIZATION OF THE ISLAMIC CONFERENCE—OIC

Address: Kilo 6, Mecca Rd, POB 178, Jeddah 21411, Saudi Arabia.
Telephone: (2) 690-0001; **fax:** (2) 275-1953; **e-mail:** oiccabinet@arab.net.sa; **internet:** www.oic-oci.org.

The Organization was formally established in May 1971, when its Secretariat became operational, following a summit meeting of Muslim heads of state at Rabat, Morocco, in September 1969, and the Islamic Foreign Ministers' Conference in Jeddah in March 1970, and in Karachi, Pakistan, in December 1970.

MEMBERS

Afghanistan	Indonesia	Qatar
Albania	Iran	Saudi Arabia
Algeria	Iraq	Senegal
Azerbaijan	Jordan	Sierra Leone
Bahrain	Kazakhstan	Somalia
Bangladesh	Kuwait	Sudan
Benin	Kyrgyzstan	Suriname
Brunei	Lebanon	Syria
Burkina Faso	Libya	Tajikistan
Cameroon	Malaysia	Togo
Chad	The Maldives	Tunisia
Comoros	Mali	Turkey
Côte d'Ivoire	Mauritania	Turkmenistan
Djibouti	Morocco	Uganda
Egypt	Mozambique	United Arab
Gabon	Niger	Emirates
The Gambia	Nigeria	Uzbekistan
Guinea	Oman	Yemen
Guinea-Bissau	Pakistan	
Guyana	Palestine	

Note: Observer status has been granted to Bosnia and Herzegovina, the Central African Republic, Thailand, the Muslim community of the 'Turkish Republic of Northern Cyprus', the Moro National Liberation Front (MNLF) of the southern Philippines, the United Nations, the African Union, the Non-Aligned Movement, the League of Arab States, the Economic Co-operation Organization, the Union of the Arab Maghreb and the Co-operation Council for the Arab States of the Gulf.

Organization

(April 2005)

SUMMIT CONFERENCES

The supreme body of the Organization is the Conference of Heads of State, which met in 1969 at Rabat, Morocco, in 1974 at Lahore, Pakistan, and in January 1981 at Mecca, Saudi Arabia, when it was decided that ordinary summit conferences would normally be held every three years in future. An extraordinary summit conference was convened in Doha, Qatar, in March 2003, to consider the situation in Iraq. The 10th Conference was held in Putrajaya, Malaysia, in October 2003. A further extraordinary summit was scheduled to take place in late 2005, with the 11th ordinary Conference to be hosted by Senegal in 2007.

CONFERENCE OF MINISTERS OF FOREIGN AFFAIRS

Conferences take place annually, to consider the means for implementing the general policy of the Organization, although they may also be convened for extraordinary sessions.

SECRETARIAT

The executive organ of the Organization, headed by a Secretary-General (who is elected by the Conference of Ministers of Foreign Affairs for a four-year term, renewable only once) and four Assistant Secretaries-General (similarly appointed).

Secretary-General: Prof. Dr EKMELEDDIN IHSANOGLU (Turkey).

At the summit conference in January 1981 it was decided that an International Islamic Court of Justice should be established to adjudicate in disputes between Muslim countries. Experts met in January 1983 to draw up a constitution for the court; however, by 2005 it was not yet in operation.

STANDING COMMITTEES

Al-Quds Committee: f. 1975 to implement the resolutions of the Islamic Conference on the status of Jerusalem (Al-Quds); it meets at the level of foreign ministers; maintains the Al-Quds Fund; Chair. King MUHAMMAD VI OF MOROCCO.

Standing Committee for Economic and Commercial Co-operation—COMCEC: f. 1981; Chair. AHMET NECDET SEZER (Pres. of Turkey).

Standing Committee for Information and Cultural Affairs—COMIAC: f. 1981; Chair. ABDOULAYE WADE (Pres. of Senegal).

Standing Committee for Scientific and Technological Co-operation—COMSTECH: f. 1981; Chair. Gen. PERVEZ MUSHARRAF (Pres. of Pakistan).

Other committees comprise the Islamic Peace Committee, the Permanent Finance Committee, the Committee of Islamic Solidarity with the Peoples of the Sahel, the Eight-Member Committee on the Situation of Muslims in the Philippines, the Six-Member Committee on Palestine, the Committee on United Nations reform, and the *ad hoc* Committee on Afghanistan. In addition, there is an Islamic Commission for Economic, Cultural and Social Affairs, and there are OIC contact groups on Bosnia and Herzegovina, Kosovo, Jammu and Kashmir, Sierra Leone, and Somalia. A Commission of Eminent Persons was inaugurated in January 2005.

Activities

The Organization's aims, as proclaimed in the Charter that was adopted in 1972, are:

(i) To promote Islamic solidarity among member states;

(ii) To consolidate co-operation among member states in the economic, social, cultural, scientific and other vital fields, and to arrange consultations among member states belonging to international organizations;

(iii) To endeavour to eliminate racial segregation and discrimination and to eradicate colonialism in all its forms;

(iv) To take necessary measures to support international peace and security founded on justice;

(v) To co-ordinate all efforts for the safeguard of the Holy Places and support of the struggle of the people of Palestine, and help them to regain their rights and liberate their land;

(vi) To strengthen the struggle of all Muslim people with a view to safeguarding their dignity, independence and national rights; and

(vii) To create a suitable atmosphere for the promotion of co-operation and understanding among member states and other countries.

The first summit conference of Islamic leaders (representing 24 states) took place in 1969 following the burning of the Al Aqsa Mosque in Jerusalem. At this conference it was decided that Islamic governments should 'consult together with a view to promoting close co-operation and mutual assistance in the economic, scientific, cultural and spiritual fields, inspired by the immortal teachings of Islam'. Thereafter the foreign ministers of the countries concerned met annually, and adopted the Charter of the Organization of the Islamic Conference in 1972.

At the second Islamic summit conference (Lahore, Pakistan, 1974), the Islamic Solidarity Fund was established, together with a committee of representatives which later evolved into the Islamic Commission for Economic, Cultural and Social Affairs. Subsequently, numerous other subsidiary bodies have been set up (see below).

ECONOMIC CO-OPERATION

A general agreement for economic, technical and commercial co-operation came into force in 1981, providing for the establishment of joint investment projects and trade co-ordination. This was followed by an agreement on promotion, protection and guarantee of investments among member states. A plan of action to strengthen economic co-operation was adopted at the third Islamic summit conference in 1981, aiming to promote collective self-reliance and the development of joint ventures in all sectors. In 1994 the 1981 plan of action was revised; the reformulated plan placed greater emphasis on private-sector participation in its implementation. Although several meetings of experts were subsequently held to discuss some of the 10 priority focus areas of the plan, little progress was achieved in implementing it during the 1990s and early 2000s. In October 2003 a meeting of COMCEC endorsed measures aimed at accelerating the implementation of the plan of action.

The fifth summit conference, held in 1987, approved proposals for joint development of modern technology, and for improving scientific and technical skills in the less developed Islamic countries. The first international Islamic trade fair was held in Jeddah, Saudi Arabia, in March 2001.

In 1991 22 OIC member states signed a Framework Agreement on a Trade Preferential System among the OIC Member States; this entered into force in 2003, following the requisite ratification by more than 10 member states, and was envisaged as representing the first step towards the eventual establishment of an Islamic common market. By April 2005 14 countries had ratified the Framework Agreement and four rounds of trade negotiations, concerning finalizing tariff-reduction modalities and an implementation schedule for the Agreement, had been convened.

CULTURAL CO-OPERATION

The Organization supports education in Muslim communities throughout the world, and was instrumental in the establishment of Islamic universities in Niger and Uganda. It organizes seminars on various aspects of Islam, and encourages dialogue with the other monotheistic religions. Support is given to publications on Islam both in Muslim and Western countries. The OIC organizes meetings at ministerial level to consider aspects of information policy and new technologies.

HUMANITARIAN ASSISTANCE

Assistance is given to Muslim communities affected by wars and natural disasters, in co-operation with UN organizations, particularly UNHCR. The countries of the Sahel region (Burkina Faso, Cape Verde, Chad, The Gambia, Guinea, Guinea-Bissau, Mali, Mauritania, Niger and Senegal) receive particular attention as victims of drought. OIC member states have provided humanitarian assistance to the Muslim population affected by the conflict in Chechnya. In October 2001 the OIC established an Afghan People Assistance Fund. The OIC also administers a Trust Fund for the urgent return of refugees and the displaced to Bosnia and Herzegovina and a Fund for the Reconstruction of Sierra Leone. A resolution on the status of refugees in the Muslim world that was adopted by the 10th OIC summit meeting, held in October 2003, urged all member states to accede to the 1951 UN Convention on the Status of Refugees. In June 2004 the OIC dispatched a mission to assess the situation in Darfur, Sudan. The OIC organized urgent emergency assistance for survivors of the December 2004 Indian Ocean tsunami, and planned to support reconstruction projects in affected countries. In January 2005 the OIC launched an emergency appeal to fund its tsunami-related operations.

POLITICAL CO-OPERATION

Since its inception the OIC has called for vacation of Arab territories by Israel, recognition of the rights of Palestinians and of the Palestine Liberation Organization (PLO) as their sole legitimate representative, and the restoration of Jerusalem to Arab rule. The 1981 summit conference called for a *jihad* (holy war—though not necessarily in a military sense) 'for the liberation of Jerusalem and the occupied territories'; this was to include an Islamic economic boycott of Israel. In 1982 Islamic ministers of foreign affairs decided to establish Islamic offices for boycotting Israel and for military co-operation with the PLO. The 1984 summit conference agreed to reinstate Egypt (suspended following the peace treaty signed with Israel in 1979) as a member of the OIC, although the resolution was opposed by seven states.

In August 1990 a majority of ministers of foreign affairs condemned Iraq's recent invasion of Kuwait, and demanded the withdrawal of Iraqi forces. In August 1991 the Conference of Ministers of Foreign Affairs obstructed Iraq's attempt to propose a resolution demanding the repeal of economic sanctions against the country. The sixth summit conference, held in Senegal in December, reflected the divisions in the Arab world that resulted from Iraq's invasion of Kuwait and the ensuing war. Twelve heads of state did not attend, reportedly to register protest at the presence of Jordan and the PLO at the conference, both of which had given support to Iraq. Disagreement also arose between the PLO and the majority of other OIC members when a proposal was adopted to cease the OIC's support for the PLO's *jihad* in the Arab territories occupied by Israel, in an attempt to further the Middle East peace negotiations.

In August 1992 the UN General Assembly approved a non-binding resolution, introduced by the OIC, that requested the UN Security Council to take increased action, including the use of force, in order to defend the non-Serbian population of Bosnia and Herzegovina (some 43% of Bosnians being Muslims) from Serbian aggression, and to restore its 'territorial integrity'. The OIC Conference of Ministers of Foreign Affairs, which was held in December, demanded anew that the UN Security Council take all necessary measures against Serbia and Montenegro, including military intervention, in order to protect the Bosnian Muslims.

A report by an OIC fact-finding mission, which in February 1993 visited Azad Kashmir while investigating allegations of repression of the largely Muslim population of the Indian state of Jammu and Kashmir by the Indian armed forces, was presented to the 1993 Conference. The meeting urged member states to take the necessary measures to persuade India to cease the 'massive human rights violations' in Jammu and Kashmir and to allow the Indian Kashmiris to 'exercise their inalienable right to self-determination'. In September 1994 ministers of foreign affairs, meeting in Islamabad, Pakistan, agreed to establish a contact group on Jammu and Kashmir, which was to provide a mechanism for promoting international awareness of the situation in that region and for seeking a peaceful solution to the dispute. In December OIC heads of state approved a resolution condemning reported human rights abuses by Indian security forces in Kashmir.

In July 1994 the OIC Secretary-General visited Afghanistan and proposed the establishment of a preparatory mechanism to promote national reconciliation in that country. In mid-1995 Saudi Arabia, acting as a representative of the OIC, pursued a peace initiative for Afghanistan and issued an invitation for leaders of the different factions to hold negotiations in Jeddah.

A special ministerial meeting on Bosnia and Herzegovina was held in July 1993, at which seven OIC countries committed themselves to making available up to 17,000 troops to serve in the UN Protection Force in the former Yugoslavia (UNPROFOR). The meeting also decided to dispatch immediately a ministerial mission to persuade influential governments to support the OIC's demands for the removal of the arms embargo on Bosnian Muslims and the convening of a restructured international conference to bring about a political solution to the conflict. In December 1994 OIC heads of state, convened in Morocco, proclaimed that the UN arms embargo on Bosnia and Herzegovina could not be applied to the Muslim authorities of that Republic. The Conference also resolved to review economic relations between OIC member states and any country that supported Serbian activities. An aid fund was established, to which member states were requested to contribute between US $500,000 and $5m., in order to provide further humanitarian and economic assistance to Bosnian Muslims. In relation to wider concerns the conference adopted a Code of Conduct for Combating International Terrorism, in an attempt to control Muslim extremist groups. The code commits states to ensuring that militant groups do not use their territory for planning or executing terrorist activity against other states, in addition to states refraining from direct support or participation in acts of terrorism. In a further resolution the OIC supported the decision by Iraq to recognize Kuwait, but advocated that Iraq comply with all UN Security Council decisions.

In July 1995 the OIC contact group on Bosnia and Herzegovina (at that time comprising Egypt, Iran, Malaysia, Morocco, Pakistan, Saudi Arabia, Senegal and Turkey), meeting in Geneva, declared the UN arms embargo against Bosnia and Herzegovina to be 'invalid'. Several Governments subsequently announced their willingness officially to supply weapons and other military assistance to the Bosnian Muslim forces. In September a meeting of all OIC ministers of defence and foreign affairs endorsed the establishment of an 'assistance mobilization group' which was to supply military, economic, legal and other assistance to Bosnia and Herzegovina. In a joint declaration the ministers also demanded the return of all territory seized by Bosnian Serb forces, the continued NATO bombing of Serb military targets, and that the city of Sarajevo be preserved under a Muslim-led Bosnian Government. In November the OIC Secretary-General endorsed the peace accord for the former Yugoslavia, which was concluded, in Dayton, USA, by leaders of all the conflicting factions, and reaffirmed the commitment of Islamic states to participate in efforts to implement the accord. In the following month the OIC Conference of Ministers of Foreign Affairs, convened in Conakry, Guinea, requested the full support of the international community to reconstruct Bosnia and Herzegovina through humanitarian aid as well as economic and technical co-operation. Ministers declared that Palestine and the establishment of fully-autonomous Palestinian control of Jerusalem were issues of central importance for the Muslim world. The Conference urged the removal of all aspects of occupation and the cessation of the construction of Israeli settlements in the occupied territories. In addition, the final statement of the meeting condemned Armenian aggression against Azerbaijan, registered concern at the persisting civil conflict in Afghanistan, demanded the elimination of all weapons of mass destruction and pledged support for Libya (affected by the US trade embargo). Ministers determined that an intergovernmental group of experts should be established in 1996 to address the situation of minority Muslim communities residing in non-OIC states.

In December 1996 OIC ministers of foreign affairs, meeting in Jakarta, Indonesia, urged the international community to apply pressure on Israel in order to ensure its implementation of the terms of the Middle East peace process. The ministers reaffirmed the importance of ensuring that the provisions of the Dayton Peace Agreement for the former Yugoslavia were fully implemented, called for a peaceful settlement of the Kashmir issue, demanded that Iraq fulfil its obligations for the establishment of security, peace and stability in the region and proposed that an international conference on peace and national reconciliation in Somalia be convened. In March 1997, at an extraordinary summit held in Pakistan, OIC heads of state and of government reiterated the organization's objective of increasing international pressure on Israel to ensure the full implementation of the terms of the Middle East peace process. An 'Islamabad Declaration' was also adopted, which pledged to increase co-operation between members of the OIC. In June the OIC condemned the decision by the US House of Representatives to recognize Jerusalem as the Israeli capital. The Secretary-General of the OIC issued a statement rejecting the US decision as counter to the role of the USA as sponsor of the Middle East peace plan.

In early 1998 the OIC appealed for an end to the threat of US-led military action against Iraq arising from a dispute regarding access granted to international weapons inspectors. The crisis was averted by an agreement concluded between the Iraqi authorities and the UN Secretary-General in February. In March OIC ministers of foreign affairs, meeting in Doha, Qatar, requested an end to the international sanctions against Iraq. Additionally, the ministers urged all states to end the process of restoring normal trading and diplomatic relations with Israel pending that country's withdrawal from the occupied territories and acceptance of an independent Palestinian state. In April the OIC, jointly with the UN, sponsored new peace negotiations between the main disputing factions in Afghanistan, which were conducted in Islamabad, Pakistan. In early May, however, the talks collapsed and were postponed indefinitely. In September the Secretaries-General of the OIC and UN agreed to establish a joint mission to counter the deteriorating security situation along the Afghan–Iranian border, following the large-scale deployment of Taliban troops in the region and consequent military manoeuvres by the Iranian authorities. They also reiterated the need to proceed with negotiations to conclude a peaceful settlement in Afghanistan. In December the OIC appealed for a diplomatic solution to the tensions arising from Iraq's withdrawal of co-operation with UN weapons inspectors, and criticized subsequent military air-strikes, led by the USA, as having been conducted without renewed UN authority. An OIC Convention on Combating International Terrorism was adopted in 1998. An OIC committee of experts responsible for formulating a plan of action for safeguarding the rights of Muslim communities and minorities met for the first time in 1998.

In early April 1999 ministers of foreign affairs of the countries comprising OIC's contact group met to consider the crisis in Kosovo. The meeting condemned Serbian atrocities being committed against the local Albanian population and urged the provision of international assistance for the thousands of people displaced by the conflict. The group resolved to establish a committee to co-ordinate relief aid provided by member states. The ministers also expressed their willingness to help to formulate a peaceful settlement and to participate in any subsequent implementation force. In June an OIC Parliamentary Union was inaugurated; its founding conference was convened in Tehran, Iran.

In early March 2000 the OIC mediated contacts between the parties to the conflict in Afghanistan, with a view to reviving peace negotiations. Talks, held under OIC auspices, ensued in May. In November OIC heads of state attended the ninth summit conference, held in Doha, Qatar. In view of the significant deterioration in relations between Israel and the Palestinian (National) Authority (PA) during late 2000, the summit issued a Declaration pledging solidarity with the Palestinian cause and accusing the Israeli authorities of implementing large-scale systematic violations of human rights against Palestinians. The summit also issued the Doha Declaration, which reaffirmed commitment to the OIC Charter and undertook to modernize the organization's organs and mechanisms. Both the elected Government of Afghanistan and the Taliban sent delegations to the Doha conference. The summit determined that Afghanistan's official participation in the OIC, suspended in 1996, should not yet be reinstated. In early 2001 a high-level delegation from the OIC visited Afghanistan in an attempt to prevent further destruction of ancient statues by Taliban supporters.

In May 2001 the OIC convened an emergency meeting, following an escalation of Israeli–Palestinian violence. The meeting resolved to halt all diplomatic and political contacts with the Israeli government, while restrictions remained in force against Palestinian-controlled territories. In June the OIC condemned attacks and ongoing discrimination against the Muslim Community in Myanmar. In the same month the OIC Secretary-General undertook a tour of six African countries—Burkina Faso, The Gambia, Guinea, Mali, Niger and Senegal—to promote co-operation and to consider further OIC support for those states. In August the Secretary-General condemned Israel's seizure of several Palestinian institutions in East Jerusalem and aerial attacks against Palestinian settlements. The OIC initiated high-level diplomatic efforts to convene a meeting of the UN Security Council in order to discuss the situation.

In September 2001 the OIC Secretary-General strongly condemned major terrorist attacks perpetrated against targets in the USA. Soon afterwards the US authorities rejected a proposal by the Taliban regime that an OIC observer mission be deployed to monitor the activities of the Saudi Arabian-born exiled militant Islamist

fundamentalist leader Osama bin Laden, who was accused by the US Government of having co-ordinated the attacks from alleged terrorist bases in the Taliban-administered area of Afghanistan. An extraordinary meeting of OIC ministers of foreign affairs, convened in early October, in Doha, Qatar, to consider the implications of the terrorist atrocities, condemned the attacks and declared its support for combating all manifestations of terrorism within the framework of a proposed collective initiative co-ordinated under the auspices of the UN. The meeting, which did not pronounce directly on the recently-initiated US-led military retaliation against targets in Afghanistan, urged that no Arab or Muslim state should be targeted under the pretext of eliminating terrorism. It determined to establish a fund to assist Afghan civilians. In February 2002 the Secretary-General expressed concern at statements of the US administration describing Iran and Iraq (as well as the Democratic People's Republic of Korea) as belonging to an 'axis of evil' involved in international terrorism and the development of weapons of mass destruction. In early April OIC foreign ministers convened an extraordinary session on terrorism, in Kuala Lumpur, Malaysia. The meeting issued the 'Kuala Lumpur Declaration', which reiterated member states' collective resolve to combat terrorism, recalling the organization's 1994 code of conduct and 1998 convention to this effect; condemned attempts to associate terrorist activities with Islamists or any other particular creed, civilization or nationality, and rejected attempts to associate Islamic states or the Palestinian struggle with terrorism; rejected the implementation of international action against any Muslim state on the pretext of combating terrorism; urged the organization of a global conference on international terrorism; and urged an examination of the root causes of international terrorism. In addition, the meeting strongly condemned Israel's ongoing military intervention in areas controlled by the PA. The meeting adopted a plan of action on addressing the issues raised in the declaration. Its implementation was to be co-ordinated by a 13-member committee on international terrorism. Member states were encouraged to sign and ratify the Convention on Combating International Terrorism in order to accelerate its implementation. In June ministers of foreign affairs, meeting in Khartoum, Sudan, issued a declaration reiterating the OIC call for an international conference to be convened, under UN auspices, in order clearly to define terrorism and to agree on the international procedures and mechanisms for combating terrorism through the UN. The conference also repeated demands for the international community to exert pressure on Israel to withdraw from all Palestinian-controlled territories and for the establishment of an independent Palestinian state. It endorsed the peace plan for the region that had been adopted by the summit meeting of the League of Arab States in March.

In June 2002 the OIC Secretary-General expressed his concern at the escalation of tensions between Pakistan and India regarding Kashmir. He urged both sides to withdraw their troops and to refrain from the use of force. In the following month the OIC pledged its support for Morocco in a territorial dispute with Spain over the small island of Perejil, but called for a negotiated settlement to resolve the issue.

An extraordinary summit conference of Islamic leaders convened in Doha, Qatar, in early March 2003 to consider the ongoing Iraq crisis welcomed the Saddam Hussain regime's acceptance of UN Security Council Resolution 1441 and consequent co-operation with UN weapons inspectors, and emphatically rejected any military strike against Iraq or threat to the security of any other Islamic state. The conference also urged progress towards the elimination of all weapons of mass destruction in the Middle East, including those held by Israel. In May the 30th session of the Conference of Ministers of Foreign Affairs, entitled 'Unity and Dignity', issued the Tehran Declaration, in which it resolved to combat terrorism and to contribute to preserving peace and security in Islamic countries. The Declaration also pledged its full support for the Palestinian cause and rejected the labelling as 'terrorist' of those Muslim states deemed to be resisting foreign aggression and occupation. The 10th OIC summit meeting, held in October in Putrajaya, Malaysia, issued the Putrajaya Declaration, in which Islamic leaders resolved to enhance Islamic states' role and influence in international affairs. The leaders adopted a plan of action that entailed: reviewing and strengthening OIC positions on international issues; enhancing dialogue among Muslim thinkers and policy-makers through relevant OIC insitutions; promoting constructive dialogue with other cultures and civilizations; completing an ongoing review of the structure and efficacy of the OIC Secretariat; establishing a working group to address means of enhancing the role of Islamic education; promoting among member states the development of science and technology, discussion of ecological issues, and the role of information communication technology in development; improving mechanisms to assist member states in post-conflict situations; and advancing trade and investment through data-sharing and encouraging access to markets for products from poorer member states.

In mid-May 2004 the OIC Secretary-General urged combat forces in Iraq to respect the inviolability of that country's holy places.

Shortly afterwards he condemned the ongoing destruction of Palestinian homes by Israeli forces, and consequent population displacement, particularly in Rafah, Gaza. He urged international organizations to condemn Israel's actions and appealed to the UN Security Council to intervene promptly in the situation and to compel Israel to respect international law. In June the Secretary-General welcomed progress achieved by a round of expert-level talks on nuclear confidence-building measures conducted during that month by India and Pakistan. An observer mission dispatched by the OIC to monitor presidential elections held in the Palestinian territories in early January 2005, at the request of the PA, was rejected by Israel. Later in that month the inaugural meeting of an OIC Commission of Eminent Persons was convened in Putrajaya, Malaysia. The Commission was mandated to finalize recommendations in the following areas: the preparation of a strategy and plan of action enabling the Islamic community to meet the challenges of the 21st century; the preparation of a comprehensive plan for promoting enlightened moderation, both within Islamic societies and universally; and the preparation of proposals for the future reform and restructuring of the OIC system.

Finance

The OIC's activities are financed by mandatory contributions from member states. The budget for 2002/03 totalled US $11.4m.

Subsidiary Organs

Islamic Centre for the Development of Trade: Complexe Commercial des Habous, ave des FAR, BP 13545, Casablanca, Morocco; tel. (2) 314974; fax (2) 310110; e-mail icdt@icdt.org; internet www.icdt.org; f. 1983 to encourage regular commercial contacts, harmonize policies and promote investments among OIC mems; Dir-Gen. ALLAL RACHDI; publs *Tijaris: International and Inter-Islamic Trade Magazine* (bi-monthly), *Inter-Islamic Trade Report* (annually).

Islamic Jurisprudence (Fiqh) Academy: POB 13917, Jeddah, Saudi Arabia; tel. (2) 667-1664; fax (2) 667-0873; internet www.fiqhacademy.org.sa; f. 1982; Sec.-Gen. SHEIKH MOHAMED HABIB IBN AL-KHODHA.

Islamic Solidarity Fund: c/o OIC Secretariat, POB 178, Jeddah 21411, Saudi Arabia; tel. (2) 680-0800; fax (2) 687-3568; f. 1974 to meet the needs of Islamic communities by providing emergency aid and the finance to build mosques, Islamic centres, hospitals, schools and universities; Chair. Sheikh NASIR ABDULLAH BIN HAMDAN; Exec. Dir ABDULLAH HERSI.

Islamic University in Uganda: POB 2555, Mbale, Uganda; Kampala Liaison Office: POB 7689, Kampala; tel. (45) 33502; fax (45) 34452; e-mail iuiu@info.com.co.ug; tel. (41) 236874; fax (41) 254576; f. 1988 to meet the educational needs of Muslim populations in English-speaking African countries; mainly financed by OIC; Principal Officer Prof. MAHDI ADAMU.

Islamic University of Niger: BP 11507, Niamey, Niger; tel. 723903; fax 733796; f. 1984; provides courses of study in *Shari'a* (Islamic law) and Arabic language and literature; also offers courses in pedagogy and teacher training; receives grants from Islamic Solidarity Fund and contributions from OIC member states; Rector Prof. ABDELALI OUDHRIRI.

Islamic University of Technology—IUT: Board Bazar, Gazipur 1704, Dhaka, Bangladesh; tel. (2) 980-0960; fax (2) 980-0970; e-mail vc@iut-dhaka.edu; internet www.iutoic-dhaka.edu; f. 1981 as the Islamic Centre for Technical and Vocational Training and Resources, named changed to Islamic Institute of Technology in 1994, current name adopted in June 2001; aims to develop human resources in OIC mem. states, with special reference to engineering, technology, tech. and vocational education and research; 135 staff and 646 students; library of 26,500 vols; Vice-Chancellor Prof. Dr M. FAZLI ILAHI; publs *News Bulletin* (annually), *Journal of Engineering and Technology* (2 a year), annual calendar and announcement for admission, reports, human resources development series.

Research Centre for Islamic History, Art and Culture—IRCICA: POB 24, Beşiktaş 80692, İstanbul, Turkey; tel. (212) 2591742; fax (212) 2584365; e-mail ircica@superonline.com; internet www.ircica.org; f. 1980; library of 60,000 vols; Dir-Gen. Prof. Dr EKMELEDDİN IHSANOĞLU; publs *Newsletter* (3 a year), monographical studies.

Statistical, Economic and Social Research and Training Centre for the Islamic Countries: Attar Sok 4, GOP 06700, Ankara, Turkey; tel. (312) 4686172; fax (312) 4673458; e-mail oicankara@sesrtcic.org; internet www.sesrtcic.org; f. 1978; Dir-Gen. ERDİNÇ ERDÜN; publs *Journal of Economic Co-operation among Islamic Countries* (quarterly), *InfoReport* (quarterly), *Statistical Yearbook* (annually).

Specialized Institutions

International Islamic News Agency—IINA: King Khalid Palace, Madinah Rd, POB 5054, Jeddah 21422, Saudi Arabia; tel. (2) 665-8561; fax (2) 665-9358; e-mail iina@cyberia.net.sa; internet www.islamicnews.org; f. 1972; distributes news and reports daily on events in the Islamic world, in Arabic, English and French; Dir-Gen. ABDULWAHAB KASHIF.

Islamic Educational, Scientific and Cultural Organization—ISESCO: BP 755, Rabat 10104, Morocco; tel. (7) 772433; fax (7) 772058; e-mail cid@isesco.org.ma; internet www.isesco.org.ma; f. 1982; Dir-Gen. Dr ABDULAZIZ BIN OTHMAN AT-TWAIJRI; publs *ISESCO Newsletter* (quarterly), *Islam Today* (2 a year), *ISESCO Triennial*.

Islamic States Broadcasting Organization—ISBO: POB 6351, Jeddah 21442, Saudi Arabia; tel. (2) 672-1121; fax (2) 672-2600; e-mail isbo@isbo.org; internet www.isbo.org; f. 1975; Sec.-Gen. HUSSEIN AL-ASKARY.

Affiliated Institutions

International Association of Islamic Banks—IAIB: King Abdulaziz St, Queen's Bldg, 23rd Floor, Al-Balad Dist, POB 9707, Jeddah 21423, Saudi Arabia; tel. (2) 651-6900; fax (2) 651-6552; f. 1977 to link financial institutions operating on Islamic banking principles; activities include training and research; mems: 192 banks and other financial institutions in 34 countries; Sec.-Gen. SAMIR A. SHAIKH.

Islamic Chamber of Commerce and Industry: POB 3831, Clifton, Karachi 75600, Pakistan; tel. (21) 5874756; fax (21) 5870765; e-mail icci@icci-oic.org; internet icci-oic.org; f. 1979 to promote trade and industry among member states; comprises nat. chambers or feds of chambers of commerce and industry; Sec.-Gen. AQEEL AHMAD AL-JASSEM.

Islamic Committee for the International Crescent: POB 17434, Benghazi, Libya; tel. (61) 95823; fax (61) 95829; f. 1979 to attempt to alleviate the suffering caused by natural disasters and war; Sec.-Gen. Dr AHMAD ABDALLAH CHERIF.

Islamic Solidarity Sports Federation: POB 5844, Riyadh 11442, Saudi Arabia; tel. and fax (1) 482-2145; f. 1981; Sec.-Gen. Dr MOHAMMAD SALEH GAZDAR.

Organization of Islamic Capitals and Cities—OICC: POB 13621, Jeddah 21414, Saudi Arabia; tel. (2) 698-1953; fax (2) 698-1053; e-mail secrtriat@oicc.org; internet www.oicc.org; f. 1980 to promote and develop co-operation among OICC mems, to preserve their character and heritage, to implement planning guide-lines for the growth of Islamic cities and to upgrade standards of public services and utilities in those cities; Sec.-Gen. OMAR ABDULLAH KADI.

Organization of the Islamic Shipowners' Association: POB 14900, Jeddah 21434, Saudi Arabia; tel. (2) 663-7882; fax (2) 660-4920; e-mail oisa@sbm.net.sa; f. 1981 to promote co-operation among maritime cos in Islamic countries; In 1998 mems approved the establishment of a new commercial venture, the Bakkah Shipping Company, to enhance sea transport in the region; Sec.-Gen. Dr ABDULLATIF A. SULTAN.

World Federation of Arab-Islamic Schools: POB 3446, Jeddah, Saudi Arabia; tel. (2) 670-0019; fax (2) 671-0823; f. 1976; supports Arab-Islamic schools world-wide and encourages co-operation between the institutions; promotes the dissemination of the Arabic language and Islamic culture; supports the training of personnel.

ORGANIZATION OF THE PETROLEUM EXPORTING COUNTRIES—OPEC

Address: Obere Donaustrasse 93, 1020 Vienna, Austria.
Telephone: (1) 211-12-279; **fax:** (1) 214-98-27; **e-mail:** prid@opec.org; **internet:** www.opec.org.

OPEC was established in 1960 to link countries whose main source of export earnings is petroleum; it aims to unify and co-ordinate members' petroleum policies and to safeguard their interests generally. In 1976 OPEC member states established the OPEC Fund for International Development.

OPEC's share of world petroleum production was 40.7% in 2003 (compared with 44.7% in 1980 and 54.7% in 1974). OPEC members were estimated to possess 80.5% of the world's known reserves of crude petroleum in 2003; about three-quarters of these were in the Middle East. In that year OPEC members possessed about 51.7% of known reserves of natural gas, and in 2002 OPEC members accounted for 22.1% of total global output of natural gas.

MEMBERS

Algeria	Kuwait	Saudi Arabia
Indonesia	Libya	United Arab Emirates
Iran	Nigeria	Venezuela
Iraq	Qatar	

Organization

(April 2005)

CONFERENCE

The Conference is the supreme authority of the Organization, responsible for the formulation of its general policy. It consists of representatives of member countries, who examine reports and recommendations submitted by the Board of Governors. It approves the appointment of Governors from each country and elects the Chairman of the Board of Governors. It works on the unanimity principle, and meets at least twice a year. In September 2000 the Conference agreed that regular meetings of heads of state or government should be convened every five years.

BOARD OF GOVERNORS

The Board directs the management of the Organization; it implements resolutions of the Conference and draws up an annual budget. It consists of one governor for each member country, and meets at least twice a year.

MINISTERIAL MONITORING COMMITTEE

The Committee (f. 1982) is responsible for monitoring price evolution and ensuring the stability of the world petroleum market. As such, it is charged with the preparation of long-term strategies, including the allocation of quotas to be presented to the Conference. The Committee consists of all national representatives, and is normally convened four times a year. A Ministerial Monitoring Sub-committee, reporting to the Committee on production and supply figures, was established in 1993.

ECONOMIC COMMISSION

A specialized body operating within the framework of the Secretariat, with a view to assisting the Organization in promoting stability in international prices for petroleum at equitable levels; consists of a Board, national representatives and a commission staff; meets at least twice a year.

SECRETARIAT

Secretary-General: AHMAD FAHAD AL-AHMAD AL-SABAH (Kuwait) (acting).

Research Division: comprises three departments:

Data Services Department: Maintains and expands information services to support the research activities of the Secretariat and those of member countries; collects, collates and analyses statistical information and provides essential data for forecasts and estimates necessary for OPEC medium- and long-term strategies.

Energy Studies Department: Energy Section monitors, forecasts and analyses developments in the energy and petrochemical industries and their implications for OPEC, and prepares forecasts of demands for OPEC petroleum and gas. Petroleum Section assists the Board of the Economic Commission in determining the relative values of OPEC crude petroleum and gases and in developing alternative methodologies for this purpose.

Petroleum Market Analysis Department: Monitors and analyses short-term oil market indicators and world economic developments, factors affecting the supply and demand balance, policy developments affecting prices and petroleum demand, crude oil and product market performance, stocks, spot price movements and refinery utilization.

Division Director: Dr ADNAN SHIHAB-ELDIN (Kuwait).

Administration and Human Resources Department: Responsible for all organization methods, provision of administrative services for all meetings, personnel matters, budgets, accounting and internal control; reviews general administrative policies and industrial relations practised throughout the oil industry; Head S. J. SENUSSI.

Public Relations and Information Department: Concerned with communicating OPEC objectives, decisions and actions; produces and distributes a number of publications, films, slides and tapes; and disseminates news of general interest regarding the Organization and member countries on energy and other related issues. Operates a daily on-line news service, the OPEC News Agency (OPECNA). An OPEC Library contains an extensive collection of energy-related publications; Head Dr O. F. IBRAHIM.

Legal Office: Provides legal advice, supervises the Secretariat's legal commitments, evaluates legal issues of concern to the Organization and member countries, and recommends appropriate action; Senior Legal Counsel Dr IBIBIA LUCKY WORIKA.

Office of the Secretary-General: Provides the Secretary-General with executive assistance in maintaining contacts with governments, organizations and delegations, in matters of protocol and in the preparation for and co-ordination of meetings; Head KARIN CHACIN.

Record of Events

1960　The first OPEC Conference was held in Baghdad in September, attended by representatives from Iran, Iraq, Kuwait, Saudi Arabia and Venezuela.

1961　Second Conference, Caracas, January. Qatar was admitted to membership; a Board of Governors was formed and statutes agreed.

1962　Fourth Conference, Geneva, April and June. Protests were addressed to petroleum companies against price cuts introduced in August 1960. Indonesia and Libya were admitted to membership.

1965　In July the Conference reached agreement on a two-year joint production programme, implemented from 1965 to 1967, to limit annual growth in output to secure adequate prices.

1967　Abu Dhabi was admitted to membership.

1969　Algeria was admitted to membership.

1970　Twenty-first Conference, Caracas, December. Tax on income of petroleum companies was raised to 55%.

1971　A five-year agreement was concluded in February between the six producing countries in the Gulf and 23 international petroleum companies (Tehran Agreement). Nigeria was admitted to membership.

1972　In January petroleum companies agreed to adjust petroleum revenues of the largest producers after changes in currency exchange rates (Geneva Agreement).

1973　OPEC and petroleum companies concluded an agreement whereby posted prices of crude petroleum were raised by 11.9% and a mechanism was installed to make monthly adjustments to prices in future (Second Geneva Agreement). Negotiations with petroleum companies on revision of the Tehran Agreement collapsed in October, and the Gulf states unilaterally declared 70% increases in posted prices, from US $3.01 to $5.11 per barrel. In December the Conference resolved to increase the posted price by nearly 130%, to $11.65 per barrel, from 1 January 1974. Ecuador was admitted to full membership and Gabon became an associate member.

1974　As a result of Saudi opposition to the December price increase, prices were held at current levels for first quarter (and subsequently for the remainder of 1974). Abu Dhabi's membership was transferred to the United Arab Emirates (UAE). A meeting in June increased royalties charged to petroleum companies from 12.5% to 14.5% in all member states except Saudi Arabia. A meeting in September increased governmental take by about 3.5% through further increases in royalties on equity crude to 16.67% and in taxes to 65.65%, except in Saudi Arabia.

1975 OPEC's first summit meeting of heads of state or government was held in Algiers in March. Gabon was admitted to full membership. A ministerial meeting in September agreed to raise prices by 10% for the period until June 1976.

1976 The OPEC Fund for International Development was created in May. In December 11 member states endorsed a rise in basic prices of 10% as of 1 January 1977, and a further 5% rise as of 1 July 1977. However, Saudi Arabia and the UAE decided to raise their prices by 5% only.

1977 Following an earlier waiver by nine members of the 5% second stage of the price increase, Saudi Arabia and the UAE announced in July that they would both raise their prices by 5%. As a result, a single level of prices throughout the organization was restored. Because of continued disagreements between the 'moderates', led by Saudi Arabia and Iran, and the 'radicals', led by Algeria, Libya and Iraq, the Conference, held in December, was unable to settle on an increase in prices.

1978 The June Conference agreed that price levels should remain stable until the end of the year. In December it was decided to raise prices in four instalments, in order to compensate for the effects of the depreciation of the US dollar. These would bring a rise of 14.5% over nine months, but an average increase of 10% for 1979.

1979 At an extraordinary meeting in March members decided to raise prices by 9%. In June the Conference agreed minimum and maximum prices that seemed likely to add between 15% and 20% to import bills of consumer countries. The December Conference agreed in principle to convert the OPEC Fund into a development agency with its own legal personality.

1980 In June the Conference decided to set the price for a marker crude at US $32 per barrel, and that the value differentials which could be added above this ceiling (on account of quality and geographical location) should not exceed $5 per barrel. The planned OPEC summit meeting in Baghdad in November was postponed indefinitely because of the Iran–Iraq war, but the scheduled ministerial meeting went ahead in Bali in December, with both Iranians and Iraqis present. A ceiling price of $41 per barrel was fixed for premium crudes.

1981 In May attempts to achieve price reunification were made, but Saudi Arabia refused to increase its US $32 per barrel price unless the higher prices charged by other countries were lowered. Most of the other OPEC countries agreed to cut production by 10% so as to reduce the surplus. An emergency meeting in Geneva in August again failed to unify prices, although Saudi Arabia agreed to reduce production by 1m. barrels per day (b/d). In October OPEC countries agreed to increase the Saudi marker price to $34 per barrel, with a ceiling price of $38 per barrel.

1982 In March an emergency meeting of petroleum ministers was held in Vienna and agreed (for the first time in OPEC's history) to defend the Organization's price structure by imposing an overall production ceiling of 18m. b/d. In December the Conference agreed to limit OPEC production to 18.5m. b/d in 1983 but postponed the allocation of national quotas pending consultations among the respective governments.

1983 In January an emergency meeting of petroleum ministers, fearing a collapse in world petroleum prices, decided to reduce the production ceiling to 17.5m. b/d, but failed to agree on individual production quotas or on adjustments to the differentials in prices charged for the high-quality crude petroleum produced by Algeria, Libya and Nigeria compared with that produced by the Gulf States. In February Nigeria cut its prices to US $30 per barrel, following a collapse in its production. To avoid a 'price war' OPEC set the official price of marker crude at $29 per barrel, and agreed to maintain existing price differentials at the level agreed on in March 1982, with the temporary exception that the differentials for Nigerian crudes should be $1 more than the price of the marker crude. It also agreed to maintain the production ceiling of 17.5m. b/d and allocated quotas for each member country except Saudi Arabia, which was to act as a 'swing producer' to supply the balancing quantities to meet market requirements.

1984 In October the production ceiling was lowered to 16m. b/d. In December price differentials for light (more expensive) and heavy (cheaper) crudes were slightly altered in an attempt to counteract price-cutting by non-OPEC producers, particularly Norway and the United Kingdom.

1985 In January members (except Algeria, Iran and Libya) effectively abandoned the marker price system. During the year production in excess of quotas by OPEC members, unofficial discounts and barter deals by members, and price cuts by non-members (such as Mexico, which had hitherto kept its prices in line with those of OPEC) contributed to a weakening of the market.

1986 During the first half of the year petroleum prices dropped to below US $10 per barrel. In April ministers agreed to set OPEC production at 16.7m. b/d for the third quarter of 1986 and at 17.3m. b/d for the fourth quarter. Algeria, Iran and Libya dissented. Discussions were also held with non-member countries (Angola, Egypt, Malaysia, Mexico and Oman), which agreed to co-operate in limiting production, although the United Kingdom declined. In August all members, with the exception of Iraq (which demanded to be allowed the same quota as Iran and, when this was denied it, refused to be a party to the agreement), agreed upon a return to production quotas, with the aim of cutting production to 14.8m. b/d (about 16.8m. b/d including Iraq's production) for the ensuing two months. This measure resulted in an increase in prices to about $15 per barrel, and was extended until the end of the year. In December members (with the exception of Iraq) agreed to return to a fixed pricing system at a level of $18 per barrel as the OPEC reference price, with effect from 1 February 1987. OPEC's total production for the first half of 1987 was not to exceed 15.8m. b/d.

1987 In June, with prices having stabilized, the Conference decided that production during the third and fourth quarters of the year should be limited to 16.6m. b/d (including Iraq's production). However, total production continued to exceed the agreed levels. In December ministers decided to extend the existing agreement for the first half of 1988, although Iraq, once more, refused to participate.

1988 By March prices had fallen below US $15 per barrel. In April non-OPEC producers offered to reduce the volume of their petroleum exports by 5% if OPEC members would do the same. Saudi Arabia, however, refused to accept further reductions in production, insisting that existing quotas should first be more strictly enforced. In June the previous production limit (15.06m. b/d, excluding Iraq's production) was again renewed for six months, in the hope that increasing demand would be sufficient to raise prices. By October, however, petroleum prices were below $12 per barrel. In November a new agreement was reached, limiting total production (including that of Iraq) to 18.5m. b/d, with effect from 1 January 1989. Identical quotas were agreed for Iran and Iraq.

1989 In June (when prices had returned to about US $18 per barrel) ministers agreed to increase the production limit to 19.5m. b/d for the second half of 1989. However, Kuwait and the UAE indicated that they would not feel bound to observe this limit. In September the production limit was again increased, to 20.5m. b/d, and in November the limit for the first half of 1990 was increased to 22m. b/d.

1990 In May members resolved to adhere more strictly to the agreed production quotas, in response to a sharp decline in prices. By late June, however, it was reported that total production had decreased by only 400,000 b/d, and prices remained at about US $14 per barrel. In July Iraq threatened to take military action against Kuwait unless it reduced its petroleum production. In the same month OPEC members agreed to limit output to 22.5m. b/d. In August Iraq invaded Kuwait, and petroleum exports by the two countries were halted by an international embargo. Petroleum prices immediately increased to exceed $25 per barrel. Later in the month an informal consultative meeting of OPEC ministers placed the July agreement in abeyance, and permitted a temporary increase in production of petroleum, of between 3m. and 3.5m. b/d (mostly by Saudi Arabia, the UAE and Venezuela). In September and October prices fluctuated in response to political developments in the Gulf region, reaching a point in excess of $40 per barrel in early October, but falling to about $25 per barrel by the end of the month. In December a meeting of OPEC members voted to maintain the high levels of production and to reinstate the quotas that had been agreed in July, once the Gulf crisis was over. During the period August 1990–February 1991 Saudi Arabia increased its petroleum output from 5.4m. to 8.5m. b/d. Seven of the other OPEC states also produced in excess of their agreed quotas.

1991 In March, in an attempt to reach the target of a minimum reference price of US $21 per barrel, ministers agreed to reduce production from 23m. b/d to 22.3m. b/d, although Saudi Arabia refused to return to its pre-August 1990 quota. In June ministers decided to maintain the ceiling of 22.3m. b/d into the third quarter of the year, since Iraq and Kuwait were still unable to export their petroleum. In September it was agreed that OPEC members' production for the last quarter of 1991 should be raised to 23.65m. b/d, and in November the OPEC Conference decided to maintain the increased production ceiling during the first quarter of 1992. From early November, however, the price of petroleum declined sharply, owing to lower than anticipated demand.

1992 The Ministerial Monitoring Committee, meeting in February, decided to impose a production ceiling of 22.98m. b/d with immediate effect. In May ministers agreed to maintain the production restriction during the third quarter of 1992. Kuwait, which was resuming production in the wake of the extensive damage inflicted on its oil-wells by Iraq during the Gulf War, was granted a special dispensation to produce without a fixed quota. During the first half of 1992 member states' petroleum output consistently exceeded agreed levels, with Saudi Arabia and Iran the principal over-producers. In June, at the UN Conference on Environment and Development, OPEC's Secretary-General expressed its member countries' strong objections to the tax on fossil fuels (designed to reduce pollution) proposed by the EC. In September agreement was reached on a production ceiling of 24.2m. b/d for the final quarter of 1992, in an attempt to raise the price of crude petroleum to the OPEC target of US $21 per barrel. At the Conference, held in November, Ecuador formally resigned from OPEC, the first country ever to do so, citing as reasons the high membership fee and OPEC's refusal to increase Ecuador's quota. The meeting agreed to restrict production to 24.58m. b/d for the first quarter of 1993 (24.46m. b/d, excluding Ecuador).

1993 In February a quota was set for Kuwait for the first time since the onset of the Gulf crisis. Kuwait agreed to produce 1.6m. b/d (400,000 less than current output) from 1 March, on the understanding that this would be substantially increased in the third quarter of the year. The quota for overall production from 1 March was set at 23.58m. b/d. A Ministerial Monitoring Sub-committee was established to supervise compliance with quotas. In June OPEC ministers decided to 'roll over' the overall quota of 23.58m. b/d into the third quarter of the year. However, Kuwait rejected its new allocation of 1.76m. b/d, demanding a quota of at least 2m. In July discussions between Iraq and the UN on the possible supervised sale of Iraqi petroleum depressed petroleum prices to below US $16 per barrel. The Monitoring Sub-committee urged member states to adhere to their production quotas (which were exceeded by a total of 1m. b/d in July). At the end of September an extraordinary meeting of the Conference agreed on a raised production ceiling of 24.52m. b/d, to be effective for six months from 1 October. Kuwait accepted a quota of 2m. b/d, which brought the country back into the production ceiling mechanism. Iran agreed on an allocation of 3.6m. b/d, while Saudi Arabia consented to freeze production at current levels, in order to support petroleum prices which remained persistently low. In November the Conference rejected any further reduction in production. Prices subsequently fell below $14.

1994 In March OPEC ministers opted to maintain the output quotas agreed in September 1993 until the end of the year, and urged non-OPEC producers to freeze their production levels. (Iraq failed to endorse the agreement, recognizing only the production agreement adopted in July 1990.) At the meeting Saudi Arabia resisted a proposal from Iran and Nigeria, both severely affected by declines in petroleum revenue, to reduce its production by 1m. b/d in order to boost prices. In November ministers endorsed a proposal by Saudi Arabia to maintain the existing production quota (of 24.52m. b/d) until the end of 1995.

1995 In January it was reported that Gabon was reconsidering its membership of OPEC, owing to difficulties in meeting its budget contribution. In June the ministerial Conference expressed concern at OPEC's falling share of the world petroleum market. The Conference criticized the high level of North Sea production, by Norway and the United Kingdom, and urged collective production restraint in order to stimulate prices. In November the Conference agreed to extend the existing production quota (24.52m. b/d) for a further six months, in order to stabilize prices. During the year, however, output remained in excess of the production quotas, at some 25.58m. b/d.

1996 The possibility of a UN-Iraqi agreement permitting limited petroleum sales dominated OPEC concerns in the first half of the year and contributed to price fluctuations in the world markets. By early 1996 output by OPEC countries was estimated to be substantially in excess of quota levels; however, the price per barrel remained relatively buoyant (the average basket price reaching US $21 in March), owing largely to unseasonal cold weather in the northern hemisphere. In May a memorandum of understanding was signed between Iraq and the UN to allow the export of petroleum, up to a value of $2,000m. over a six-month period, in order to fund humanitarian relief efforts within that country. In June the Conference agreed to increase the overall output ceiling by 800,000 b/d, i.e. the anticipated level of exports from Iraq in the first six months of the agreement. Gabon's withdrawal from the Organization was confirmed at the meeting. As a result of these developments, the new production ceiling was set at 25.03m. b/d. Independent market observers expressed concern that, without any formal agreement to reduce overall production and given the actual widespread violation of the quota system, the renewed export of Iraqi petroleum would substantially depress petroleum prices. In September the Monitoring Sub-committee acknowledged that members were exceeding their production quotas, but declined to impose any punitive measures (owing to the steady increase in petroleum prices). In November the Conference agreed to maintain the existing production quota for a further six months. Also in that month, Iraq accepted certain disputed technical terms of the UN agreement, enabling the export of petroleum to commence in December.

1997 During the first half of the year petroleum prices declined, reaching a low of US $16.7 per barrel in early April, owing to the Iraqi exports, depressed world demand and persistent over-production. In June the Conference agreed to extend the existing production ceiling, of 25.03m. b/d, for a further six-month period. Member states resolved to adhere to their individual quotas in order to reduce the cumulative excess production of an estimated 2m. b/d; however, Venezuela, which (some sources claimed) was producing almost 800,000 b/d over its quota of 2.4m. b/d, declined to co-operate. An escalation in political tensions in the Gulf region in October, in particular Iraq's reluctance to co-operate with UN inspectors, prompted an increase in the price of crude petroleum to some $21.2 per barrel. In November the OPEC Conference, meeting in Jakarta, approved a proposal by Saudi Arabia, to increase the overall production ceiling by some 10%, with effect from 1 January 1998, in order to meet the perceived stable world demand and to reflect more accurately current output levels. At the same time the Iranian Government announced its intention to increase its production capacity and maintain its share of the quota by permitting foreign companies to conduct petroleum exploration in its territory.

1998 A decline in petroleum prices at the start of the year caused widespread concern, and speculation that this had resulted from the decision to increase production to 27.5m. b/d, coinciding with the prospect of a decline in demand from Asian economies that had been undermined by extreme financial difficulties and of a new Iraqi agreement with the UN with provision for increased petroleum exports. A meeting of the Monitoring Sub-committee, in late January, urged members to implement production restraint and resolved to send a monitoring team to member states to encourage compliance with the agreed quotas. (Venezuela remained OPEC's principal over-producer.) In February the UN Security Council approved a new agreement permitting Iraq to export petroleum valued at up to US $5,256m. every 180 days, although the Iraqi Government insisted that its production and export capacity was limited to $4,000m. In March Saudi Arabia, Venezuela and Mexico announced a joint agreement to reduce domestic production by 300,000 b/d, 200,000 b/d and 100,000 b/d respectively, with effect from 1 April, and agreed to co-operate in persuading other petroleum producing countries to commit to similar reductions. At the end of March an emergency ministerial meeting ratified the reduction proposals (the so-called 'Riyadh Pact'), which amounted to 1.245m. b/d pledged by OPEC members and 270,000 b/d by non-member states. Nevertheless, prices remained low, with over-production, together with lack of market confidence in member states' willingness to comply with the restricted quotas, an outstanding concern. In June Saudi Arabia, Venezuela and Mexico reached agreement on further reductions in output of some 450,000 b/d. Later in that month the Conference, having reviewed the market situation, agreed to implement a new reduction in total output of some 1.36m b/d, with effect from 1 July, reducing the total production target for OPEC members to 24.387m. b/d. Iran, which had been criticized for not adhering to the reductions agreed in March, confirmed that it would reduce output by 305,000 b/d. In early August petroleum prices fell below $12 per barrel. In September Iraq's petroleum production reached an estimated 2.4m. b/d, contributing to concerns of over-supply in the world market. In early November OPEC members attending a conference of the parties to the UN Framework Convention on Climate Change, held in Buenos Aires, Argentina, warned that they would claim compensation for any lost revenue resulting from initiatives to limit the emission of 'greenhouse gases' and reduce the consumption of petroleum. Later in November OPEC ministers, meeting in Vienna, resolved to maintain the existing production levels, but improve compliance. Subsequently, despite an escalation of tensions between the UN and Iraqi authorities, prices remained consistently around the level of $11 per barrel.

1999   In March ministers from Algeria, Iran, Mexico, Saudi Arabia and Venezuela, meeting in The Hague, Netherlands, agreed further to reduce petroleum production, owing to the continued weakness of the global market. Subsequently, petroleum prices rose by nearly 40%, after reaching the lowest price of US $9.9 per barrel in mid-February. Later in March OPEC confirmed a new reduction in output of 2.104m. b/d from 1 April, including commitments from non-OPEC members Mexico, Norway, Oman and Russia to decrease production by a total of 388,000 b/d. The agreement envisaged a total production target for OPEC member countries of 22.976m. b/d. By June total production by OPEC member states (excluding Iraq) had declined to a reported 23.25m. b/d (compared with 27.72m. in March). The evidence of almost 90% compliance with the new production quotas contributed to market confidence that stockpiles of petroleum would be reduced, and resulted in sustained price increases. In September OPEC ministers confirmed that the existing quotas would be maintained for a further six-month period. At the end of September the reference price for petroleum rose above $24, its highest level since January 1997. Prices remained buoyant during the rest of the year; however, there was increasing speculation at whether the situation was sustainable. At the end of November Iraq temporarily suspended its petroleum exports, totalling some 2.2m. b/d, pending agreement on a new phase of the 'oil-for-food' arrangement and concern at the lack of progress on the removal of international sanctions.

2000   In March petroleum prices attained their highest level since the 1990 Gulf crisis, with the the reference price briefly exceeding US $34. At the end of that month OPEC ministers, meeting in Vienna, agreed to raise output by 1.45m. b/d, in order to ease supply shortages and thereby contain the surge in prices, with a view to restoring these to a more moderate level. They also introduced an informal price band mechanism that was to signal the need for adjustments in production should prices deviate for more than 20 days from an average bracket of $22–$28 per barrel. A further increase in production, of 500,000 b/d, was approved by member states in June, to take effect from July (contingent on the reference price continuing to exceed $28 for 20 consecutive days). Prices remained high, reaching $34.6 in early September and leading to intense international pressure on OPEC to resolve the situation. OPEC ministers immediately announced that an increase in production of 800,000 b/d would take effect from 1 October and indicated that, were the reference price still to exceed $28 at the end of that month, an additional increase in output would be implemented. The production agreement was supported by five non-OPEC member countries: Angola, Mexico, Norway, Oman and Russia. In late September both the Group of Seven industrialized nations (G-7) and the IMF issued warnings about the potential economic and social consequences of sustained high petroleum prices. Meanwhile the US administration agreed to release part of its strategic petroleum reserve. Towards the end of the month OPEC heads of state or government, convened at their first summit since 1975, issued the so-called 'Caracas Declaration' in which they resolved to promote market stability by developing 'remunerative, stable and competitive' pricing policies in conjunction with implementing a production policy that would secure OPEC member states an equitable share of world supply; by strengthening co-operation between the organization and other oil-exporting nations; and by developing communication between petroleum producers and consumers. The declaration also affirmed the organization's commitment to environmentally sound practice and to promoting sustainable global economic growth, social development and the eradication of poverty; supported research in technical and scientific fields; expressed concern that government taxation policies significantly inflate the end cost of petroleum;

and agreed to convene future heads of state summits at regular five-yearly intervals. By the end of September petroleum prices had declined to just above $30 per barrel; this was attributed in part to an announcement by the Saudi Arabian Government that it would consider unilaterally raising output if prices were to remain at a high level. However, the decline in prices was short-lived, as the political crisis in the Middle East prompted a further series of increases: by 12 October the London Brent crude price exceeded $35 per barrel. From 31 October an additional increase in production, of 500,000 b/d was implemented, as planned for in early September. Meeting in mid-November the Conference appointed Dr Alí Rodríguez Araque as the new OPEC Secretary-General, with effect from January 2001. Addressing the Conference, Rodríguez identified the following contributory factors to the high level of petroleum prices other than the relationship between production and price levels: a decline in recent years in the refining capacity of the USA (the world's largest market), the high national taxes on consumption (particularly within the European Union), and price distortions deriving from speculation on futures markets. Attending the sixth conference of parties to the UN Framework Convention on Climate Change later in November OPEC reiterated its concern over the lost revenue that limits on 'greenhouse gas' emissions and reduced petroleum consumption would represent for member states, estimating this at $63,000m. per year.

2001   In mid-January, with a view to stabilizing petroleum prices that by now had fallen back to around US $25 per barrel, the Conference agreed to implement a reduction in production of 1.5m. b/d, to take effect on 1 February. A further reduction, of 1m. b/d, effective from 1 April, was approved by the Conference in mid-March, limiting overall production to 24.2m. b/d. In early June an extraordinary meeting of the Conference determined to maintain the production level, given that prices had stabilized within the agreed price range of $22–$28 per barrel, in spite of market reports forecasting reduced demand. A further extraordinary meeting was convened in early July, following Iraq's decision temporarily to suspend its petroleum exports under the UN programme, which again resolved to make no adjustment to the output ceiling. Later in that month, however, OPEC responded to a gradual decline in petroleum prices, which reached $22.78 in mid-July, by announcing a ministerial agreement to reduce production by 1m. b/d, with effect from 1 September. Meeting in late September the Conference addressed the repercussions of recent major terrorist attacks on targets in the USA, which had caused significant market uncertainty. OPEC's spot basket reference price had fallen back to around $20 per barrel. The Conference declared its commitment to stabilizing the market and determined to leave production levels unchanged (at 23.2m. b/d) in order to ensure sufficient supplies. It agreed to establish an expert working group, comprising representatives of OPEC and non-OPEC producer countries, to evaluate future market developments and advance dialogue and co-operation. At a further meeting in December the Conference decided, in view of the prevailing global economic uncertainty and a decline in the average basket price level to $17–$18 in November and December, to prevent a further deterioration in petroleum prices by reducing output by a further 1.5m. b/d for six months from 1 January 2002, contingent upon the non-OPEC producers concurrently implementing a reduction in production amounting to 500,000 b/d. The Conference resolved to continue to develop contacts with the non-OPEC producer states. By the end of December 2001 the non-OPEC producers had committed themselves to a reduction in output totalling 462,500 b/d, which was considered by OPEC an adequate basis for lowering its own production ceiling to 21.70m. b/d from the start of 2002, as planned. The OPEC reference basket price averaged $23.1 in 2001.

2002   Meeting in March the OPEC Conference welcomed a gradual improvement in the reference price (the spot basket price had averaged nearly US $19 in February), attributing this to a high level of compliance by member countries with their agreed production quotas and to ongoing support from non-OPEC producers. The latter were urged to maintain their voluntarily-imposed reductions in output. Six non-OPEC producers—Angola, Egypt, Mexico, Oman, Russia and Syria—attended the meeting as observers. Concern was expressed over the potentially destabilizing effects of the ongoing Middle East crisis. Prices rose significantly in early April following the imposition by Iraq of a one-month suspension of its oil exports in protest at the ongoing Israeli military intervention in areas controlled by the Palestinian (National) Authority. The ensuing reduction in global supply was compounded by constraints on Venezuelan production caused by a strike in the oil sector. It was reported at this time that the Iranian Government advocated the implementation of a general embargo by the Arab states on oil exports to Western countries perceived to be supporting Israeli actions. During April–early August the reference price stabilized at around $25. Meeting in June the Conference determined to maintain the existing production quota (21.7m. b/d) and appointed a new Secretary-General, Dr Alvaro Silva Calderón, hitherto Venezuela's Minister of Energy and Mines. In September the Conference agreed to maintain existing production levels until the end of 2002. In view of the threat to prices posed by persistent overproduction by some member states, the Conference, convened in December, determined to effect an increase in production quotas to 23m. b/d from 1 January 2003 while simultaneously reducing market supply; strict compliance by member states with the new quotas was urged. The OPEC reference basket price averaged $24.4 in 2002.

2003 Petroleum prices rose above OPEC's target range of US $22–$28 from mid-December 2002, exceeding $30 by early January 2003, owing to the reduction in actual output agreed in December 2002, compounded by the continuing industrial action in Venezuela (which was reducing overall levels of supply by about 2m. b/d), and the ongoing threat of US military action against Iraq (and consequent medium-term threat to Iraq's production of about 2.2m. b/d under the UN 'oil-for-food' arrangement). Meeting early in January the Conference agreed to raise the production ceiling to 24.5m. b/d from 1 February with the aim of stabilizing the market. Prices subsequently continued to rise, with the spot basket reference price reaching $32 in February, but fell back to within the desired $22–$28 price range in March, mainly owing to a recovery in Venezuelan production by that time. Meeting in early March the Conference welcomed the resolution of Venezuela's previous supply difficulties, and decided to maintain the production ceiling at the level approved in January. The meeting resolved that, to ensure continuing stable supply, member states would make up from their available excess capacities the shortfall in production that would result in the event of war against Iraq. Later in that month, following the initiation of US-led military action against Iraq and the consequent temporary interruption in that country's production, the Secretary-General reiterated the cartel's resolve to implement this decision. In April, however, the rapid overthrow of Saddam Hussain's regime raised fears of a surplus that might drive down prices, and at the end of the month, at an extraordinary session, the Conference set the production ceiling at 25.4m. b/d, effective from the beginning of June. Although this represented a 900,000 b/d increase on the previous limit it necessitated a 2m. b/d reduction in actual production at this time. Despite OPEC's move, prices continued to fall. Meeting again in extraordinary session in mid-June members agreed to maintain output at its current level; a further meeting at the end of July produced the same result. In late September, in view of the gradual revival of Iraqi petroleum exports, the Conference determined to reinstate the production ceiling of 24.5m. b/d with effect from 1 November. The UN 'oil-for-food' arrangement was terminated in November. An extraordinary meeting of the Conference convened in December agreed to maintain current production levels. The Conference failed to reach a consensus on the appointment of a new General-Secretary and it was agreed that Indonesia would temporarily assume responsibility for the position, with effect from 1 January 2004. The OPEC reference basket price averaged $28.1 in 2003.

2004 An extraordinary meeting of the Conference held in February, in Algiers, Algeria, determined to lower the production ceiling to 23.5m. b/d, with effect from 1 April; the reduction was implemented, accordingly, having been reaffirmed at the March gathering of the Conference. In early June an extraordinary meeting of the Conference was convened in Beirut, Lebanon, in response to a sharp escalation in petroleum prices, intense market speculation and international concern regarding the security of petroleum supplies. The Conference agreed to increase the production ceiling to 25.5m. b/d (excluding Iraq) with effect from 1 July, and to 26m. b/d from 1 August. A second extraordinary meeting, scheduled to be held in late July, was cancelled following a market review that reaffirmed the Conference's decisions. In August OPEC reported that production had exceeded 29m. b/d in July (27.5m. b/d excluding Iraq) in order to meet market demands and to attempt to stabilize prices. However, the markets remained volatile owing to continuing geopolitical tensions, speculation on the futures markets and growth in demand, in particular in the People's Republic of China and the USA, and the reference basket price rose above US $40 per barrel. In September the Conference determined to increase the production ceiling to 27m. b/d (excluding Iraq), with effect from 1 November. Meeting in December, the Conference decided to maintain the existing production ceiling, owing to a stabilization in prices at that time. However, member countries pledged to reduce overproduction over quota levels by 1m. b/d, with effect from 1 January 2005. The OPEC reference basket price averaged $36.0 in 2004.

2005 In late January the Conference agreed to maintain current production levels and urged all member states to comply strictly with these. It also temporarily suspended the US $22–$28 price band mechanism, acknowledging this to be unrealistic in the prevailing climate. The reference basket price rose steeply from the start of February, attributable to particularly cold weather in the Northern Hemisphere and recent disruptions to supply, as well as continuing expectations of strong demand, speculation on the futures markets, and ongoing geopolitical tensions. Meeting in Isfahan, Iran, in mid-March, the Conference expressed concern at the 'unsustainable' price increases and determined to raise the production ceiling to 27.5m. b/d, with immediate effect, while authorizing the President to implement a further increase of 500,000 b/d, until the next meeting of the Conference (scheduled for June), should there be no decrease in the reference basket price. The Conference stressed ongoing initiatives to stabilize the market, including the accelerated implementation in some member countries of capacity expansion plans aimed at improving national refinery capabilities and thereby enhancing OPEC's ability to cope with possible future disruptions in supply. At 4 April the reference basket price stood at a record $52.9.

Finance

The budget for 2005, approved in January, amounted to €19.8m.

Publications

Annual Report.
Annual Statistical Bulletin.
Monthly Oil Market Report.
OPEC Bulletin (monthly).
OPEC Review (quarterly).
Reports, information papers, press releases.

OPEC FUND FOR INTERNATIONAL DEVELOPMENT

Address: POB 995, 1011 Vienna, Austria.

Telephone: (1) 515-64-0; **fax:** (1) 513-92-38; **e-mail:** info@opecfund.org; **internet:** www.opecfund.org.

The Fund was established by OPEC member countries in 1976.

MEMBERS

Member countries of OPEC.

Organization

(April 2005)

ADMINISTRATION

The Fund is administered by a Ministerial Council and a Governing Board. Each member country is represented on the Council by its minister of finance. The Board consists of one representative and one alternate for each member country.

Chairman, Ministerial Council: Dr MOHAMED KHALFAN BIN KHIRBASH (UAE).

Chairman, Governing Board: Dr SALEH A. AL-OMAIR (Saudi Arabia).

Director-General of the Fund: SULEIMAN JASIR AL-HERBISH (Saudi Arabia).

FINANCIAL STRUCTURE

The resources of the Fund, whose unit of account is the US dollar, consist of contributions by OPEC member countries, and income received from operations or otherwise accruing to the Fund.

The initial endowment of the Fund amounted to US $800m. Its resources have been replenished three times, and have been further increased by the profits accruing to seven OPEC member countries through the sales of gold held by the International Monetary Fund. The pledged contributions to the OPEC Fund amounted to $3,435m. at the end of 2003, and paid-in contributions totalled some $2,920m.

Activities

The OPEC Fund for International Development is a multilateral agency for financial co-operation and assistance. Its objective is to reinforce financial co-operation between OPEC member countries and other developing countries through the provision of financial support to the latter on appropriate terms, to assist them in their economic and social development. The Fund was conceived as a collective financial facility which would consolidate the assistance extended by its member countries; its resources are additional to those already made available through other bilateral and multilateral aid agencies of OPEC members. It is empowered to:

(i) Provide concessional loans for balance-of-payments support;

(ii) Provide concessional loans for the implementation of development projects and programmes;

(iii) Make contributions and/or provide loans to eligible international agencies; and

(iv) Finance technical assistance and research through grants.

The eligible beneficiaries of the Fund's assistance are the governments of developing countries other than OPEC member countries, and international development agencies whose beneficiaries are developing countries. The Fund gives priority to the countries with the lowest income.

The Fund may undertake technical, economic and financial appraisal of a project submitted to it, or entrust such an appraisal to an appropriate international development agency, the executing national agency of a member country, or any other qualified agency. Most projects financed by the Fund have been co-financed by other development finance agencies. In each such case, one of the co-financing agencies may be appointed to administer the Fund's loan in association with its own. This practice has enabled the Fund to extend its lending activities to more than 100 countries over a short period of time and in a simple way, with the aim of avoiding duplication and complications. As its experience grew, the Fund increasingly resorted to parallel, rather than joint financing, taking up separate project components to be financed according to its rules and policies. In addition, it started to finance some projects completely on its own. These trends necessitated the issuance in 1982 of guide-lines for the procurement of goods and services under the Fund's loans, allowing for a margin of preference for goods and services of local origin or originating in other developing countries: the general principle of competitive bidding is, however, followed by the Fund. The loans are not tied to procurement from Fund member countries or from any other countries. The margin of preference for goods and services obtainable in developing countries is allowed on the request of the borrower and within defined limits. Fund assistance in the form of programme loans has a broader coverage than project lending. Programme loans are used to stimulate an economic sector or sub-sector, and assist recipient countries in obtaining inputs, equipment and spare parts. Besides extending loans for project and programme financing and balance of payments support, the Fund also undertakes other operations, including grants in support of technical assistance and other activities (mainly research), and financial contributions to other international institutions. In 1998 the Fund began to extend lines of credit to support private-sector activities in beneficiary countries. The so-called Private-Sector Facility aims to encourage the growth of private enterprises, in particular small and medium-sized enterprises, and to support the development of local capital markets.

OPEC FUND COMMITMENTS AND DISBURSEMENTS IN 2003
(US $ million)

	Commitments	Disbursements
Public-sector lending operations:	236.24	175.74
Project financing	216.74	132.64
Programme financing	9.50	—
HIPC initiative financing*	10.00	43.10
Private-sector lending operations	47.95	56.61
Grant Programme:	31.64	26.15
Technical assistance	3.58	1.94
Research and other activities	1.01	0.58
Emergency aid	1.25	1.43
HIV/AIDS Special Account	0.30	2.90
Special Grant Account for Palestine	5.50	2.00
Food Aid Special Grant Account	20.00	16.91
Common Fund for Commodities	—	0.39
Total	315.83	258.50

* Heavily Indebted Poor Countries initiative, jointly implemented by the International Monetary Fund and World Bank.

PROJECT LOANS APPROVED IN 2003
(US $ million)

	Loans approved
Sector:	
Transportation	90.00
Agriculture and agro-industry	22.00
Education	23.32
Energy	13.20
Water supply and sewerage	4.00
Multisectoral	51.42
Total	216.74
Region:	
Africa	110.64
Asia	86.10
Latin America and the Caribbean	20.00

Source: *OPEC Annual Report 2003.*

By the end of December 2003 the Fund had approved 981 public sector loans since operations began in 1976, totalling US $5,382.4m., of which $4,169.3m. (or 77%) was for project financing, $724.2m. (14%) was for balance-of-payments support, $314.8m. (6%) was for programme financing and $164.0m. (3%) was allocated as financing for the Heavily Indebted Poor Countries (HIPC) initiative (see World Bank). Private sector financing totalled $238.1m. for 47 operations at that time. The Fund's 15th lending programme, approved for a three-year period, became effective on 1 January 2002.

Direct loans are supplemented by grants to support technical assistance, food aid and research. By the end of December 2003 658 grants, amounting to US $303.6m., had been committed, including $83.6m. to the Common Fund for Commodities (established by the UN Conference on Trade and Development—UNCTAD), $47.2m. in support of emergency relief operations, $104.2m. in technical assistance often in co-operation with UN agencies or other development organizations, and a special contribution of $20m. to the International Fund for Agricultural Development (IFAD). In addition, the OPEC Fund had committed $971.8m. to other international institutions by the end of 2003, comprising OPEC members' contributions to the resources of IFAD, and irrevocable transfers in the name of its members to the IMF Trust Fund. By the end of 2003 66.5% of total commitments had been disbursed.

During the year ending 31 December 2003 the Fund's total commitments amounted to US $315.8m. (compared with $272.4m. in 2002). These commitments included 26 public sector project loans, amounting to $216.7m., one loan of $9.5m. to fund a commodity imports programme and another of $10m. to finance debt-relief under the HIPC initiative. The largest proportion of project loans (41.5%) was to support improvements in the transportation sector in 11 countries and included road upgrades and improvements in Azerbaijan, Burkina Faso, Cambodia, Ethiopia, Lebanon, Malawi and Sierra Leone; developing road connections to remote rural areas in Botswana and Tajikistan; re-commissioning a railway line in Ghana; and rehabilitating marine transport infrastructure in Papua New Guinea. Six multisectoral loans (23.7% of the total) were approved for the development of rural infrastructure and capacity-building activities in Guatemala, Madagascar and Viet Nam; expansion of the scope of a rural development project in Guinea; technical assistance to co-operatives and producers' groups and the establishment of training schemes in Turkey; and social development initiatives in Yemen. Three loans (10.8%) were allocated to education projects in Namibia, Tunisia and Seychelles. The remainder of lending distribution was for agriculture and agro-industry (10.2%), energy (6.1%), health (5.9%), and water supply and sewerage (1.8%). Private sector operations in 2003 amounted to $47.95m., of which 40% was allocated to telecommunications projects, 31.3% to regional and development banks, 16.2% to transportation, 6.3% to commercial banks, and 6.3% to microfinance. In 2003, following the completion of a five-year review of the Fund's Private Sector Facility, the Ministerial Council pledged significant additional funding in support of the increasing demand from developing countries for risk capital and long-term financing.

During 2003 the Fund approved US $31.64m. for 57 grants, of which $3.58m. (11%) was for technical assistance activities, $5.5m. (9%) was for the Special Grant Account for Palestine, $1.2m. (4%) to provide emergency assistance to Algeria and Iran (following earthquakes in those countries), $1.01m. (3%) for research, and $300,000

(1%) was allocated to the HIV/AIDS Special Account. Both the Special Grant Account for Palestine and the HIV/AIDS Special Account became operational in 2002. In 2003 the former funded psychological, medical, educational, training, vocational, rehabilitation and other activities in Palestine and the latter supported the newly-established UN Commission for HIV/AIDS and Governance in Africa (see Economic Commission for Africa). The Food Aid Special Grant Account was established in 2003 to combat famine in Africa.

Publications

Annual Report (in Arabic, English, French and Spanish).
OPEC Fund Newsletter (3 a year).
Occasional papers and documents.

PACIFIC COMMUNITY

Address: BP D5, 98848 Nouméa Cédex, New Caledonia.
Telephone: 26-20-00; **fax:** 26-38-18; **e-mail:** spc@spc.int; **internet:** www.spc.org.nc.

In February 1947 the Governments of Australia, France, the Netherlands, New Zealand, the United Kingdom, and the USA signed the Canberra Agreement establishing the South Pacific Commission, which came into effect in July 1948. (The Netherlands withdrew from the Commission in 1962, when it ceased to administer the former colony of Dutch New Guinea, now Papua, formerly known as Irian Jaya, part of Indonesia.) In October 1997 the 37th South Pacific Conference, convened in Canberra, Australia, agreed to rename the organization the Pacific Community, with effect from 6 February 1998. The Secretariat of the Pacific Community (SPC) services the Community, and provides research, technical advice, training and assistance in economic, social and cultural development to 22 countries and territories of the Pacific region. It serves a population of about 6.8m., scattered over some 30m. sq km, more than 98% of which is sea.

MEMBERS

American Samoa	Niue
Australia	Northern Mariana Islands
Cook Islands	Palau
Fiji	Papua New Guinea
France	Pitcairn Islands
French Polynesia	Samoa
Guam	Solomon Islands
Kiribati	Tokelau
Marshall Islands	Tonga
Federated States of	Tuvalu
Micronesia	United Kingdom
Nauru	USA
New Caledonia	Vanuatu
New Zealand	Wallis and Futuna Islands

Organization

(April 2005)

CONFERENCE OF THE PACIFIC COMMUNITY

The Conference is the governing body of the Community (replacing the former South Pacific Conference) and is composed of representatives of all member countries and territories. The main responsibilities of the Conference, which meets annually, are to appoint the Director-General, to determine major national or regional policy issues in the areas of competence of the organization and to note changes to the Financial and Staff Regulations approved by the Committee of Representatives of Governments and Administrations (CRGA).

COMMITTEE OF REPRESENTATIVES OF GOVERNMENTS AND ADMINISTRATIONS (CRGA)

This Committee comprises representatives of all member states and territories, having equal voting rights. It meets annually to consider the work programme evaluation conducted by the Secretariat and to discuss any changes proposed by the Secretariat in the context of regional priorities; to consider and approve any policy issues for the

organization presented by the Secretariat or by member countries and territories; to consider applicants and make recommendations for the post of Director-General; to approve the administrative and work programme budgets; to approve amendments to the Financial and Staff Regulations; and to conduct annual performance evaluations of the Director-General.

SECRETARIAT

The Secretariat of the Pacific Community—SPC—is headed by a Director-General, a Senior Deputy Director-General and a Deputy Director-General, based in Suva, Fiji. Three administrative Divisions cover Land Resources, Marine Resources and Social Resources. The Secretariat also provides information services, including library facilities, publications, translation and computer services. The organization has about 250 staff members.

Director-General: Lourdes Pangelinan (Guam).

Senior Deputy Director-General: Dr Jimmie Rodgers (Solomon Islands).

Deputy Director-General: Yves Corbel (France).

Regional Office: Private Mail Bag, Suva, Fiji; tel. 3370733; fax 3370021; e-mail spcsuva@spc.org.fj.

Activities

The SPC provides, on request of its member countries, technical assistance, advisory services, information and clearing-house services aimed at developing the technical, professional, scientific, research, planning and management capabilities of the regional population. The SPC also conducts regional conferences and technical meetings, as well as training courses, workshops and seminars at the regional or country level. It provides small grants-in-aid and awards to meet specific requests and needs of members. In November 1996 the Conference agreed to establish a specific Small Islands States fund to provide technical services, training and other relevant activities. The organization's three programme divisions are: land resources, marine resources and social resources. The Pacific Community oversees the maritime programme and telecommunications policy activities of the Pacific Islands Forum Secretariat.

In 1998 the SPC adopted a Corporate Plan for 1999–2003, the main objectives of which included developing national capabilities in 'value-adding' technology; enhancing the integration of cross-sectoral issues (such as economics, gender, culture and community education) into national planning and policy-making processes; and developing a co-ordinated human resources programme as a focal point for providing information, advice and support to the regional population. The 1999 Conference, held in Tahiti in December, adopted the 'Déclaration de Tahiti Nui', a mandate that detailed the operational policies and mechanisms of the Pacific Community, taking into account operational changes not covered by the founding Canberra Agreement. The Déclaration was regarded as a 'living document' that would be periodically revised to record subsequent modifications of operational policy. The SPC has signed memoranda of understanding with WHO, the Forum Fisheries Agency, the South Pacific Regional Environment Programme (SPREP), and several other partners. The organization participates in meetings of the Council of Regional Organizations in the Pacific (CROP, see under

Pacific Islands Forum Secretariat). Representatives of the SPC, SPREP and the South Pacific Applied Geoscience Commission hold periodic 'troika' meetings to develop regional technical co-operation and harmonization of work programmes.

LAND RESOURCES

The land resources division comprises two major programmes: agriculture (incorporating advice and specific activities in crop improvement and plant protection; animal health and production services; and agricultural resource economics and information); and forestry (providing training, technical assistance and information in forestry management and agroforestry). Objectives of the agriculture programme, based in Suva, Fiji, include the promotion of land and agricultural management practices that are both economically and environmentally sustainable; strengthening national capabilities to reduce losses owing to crop pests (insects, pathogens and weeds) and animal diseases already present, and to prevent the introduction of new pests and diseases; and facilitating trade through improved quarantine procedures. A Regional Animal Health Service was established in 1991. A Pacific Regional Agricultural Programme (PRAP), funded by the European Union (EU), was introduced by eight member states in 1990. The SPC assumed responsibility for administering PRAP in 1998. Funding through PRAP and the Australian Government enabled the establishment of the Regional Germplasm Centre in March 1999, which was to address the issue of conservation of plant genetic resources in the region. In 2003 an EU-funded Development of Sustainable Agriculture in the Pacific (DSAP) project was initiated to assist 10 member countries to implement sustainable agriculture measures and to improve food production and security. A further six Pacific countries joined the programme in 2004. The Regional Forestry Programme, based at the Pacific Islands Forum Secretariat, was formally established in January 2000. The programme's strategic plan for 2001–04 stated the following as among its key objectives: strengthening the capacity of member states to formulate and implement sound forestry polices and practices; promoting the application and adoption of multiple land-use systems; promoting awareness and participation on the part of local communities in the management, use and protection of forests; and providing a focal point for advocacy, collaboration, information dissemination and resource mobilization. The programme also incorporates the Forests and Trees Project, funded by the Australian Government, and the Pacific–German Regional Forestry Project.

In September 2004 the SPC hosted the first joint conference of Pacific Ministers of Agriculture and of Forestry to reflect activities to integrate the two activities under a single management of the Land Resources Division. The meeting considered a new strategic plan for the division for 2005–08, which focused on the following themes: Food security and health; Sustainable agriculture and forestry; and Biosecurity and trade facilitation. The meeting was followed by the first combined regional meeting of the Heads of Agriculture and Forestry Services.

MARINE RESOURCES

The SPC aims to support and co-ordinate the sustainable development and management of inshore fisheries resources in the region, to undertake scientific research in order to provide member governments with relevant information for the sustainable development and management of tuna and billfish resources in and adjacent to the South Pacific region, and to provide data and analytical services to national fisheries departments. The main components of the Community's fisheries activities are the Coastal Fisheries Programme (CFP), the Oceanic Fisheries Programme (OFP), and the Regional Maritime Programme (RMP). The CFP is divided into the following sections: community fisheries (research and assessment of and development support for people occupied in subsistence and artisanal fisheries); fisheries training; sustainable fisheries development; reef fisheries assessment and management; fisheries information; and post-harvest development (offering advice and training in order to improve handling practices, storage, seafood product development, quality control and marketing). The OFP consists of the following three sections: statistics and monitoring; tuna ecology and biology; and stock assessment and modelling. The statistics and monitoring section maintains a database of industrial tuna fisheries in the region. The OFP contributed research and statistical information for the formulation of the Convention for the Conservation and Management of Highly Migratory Fish Stocks in the Western and Central Pacific, which aimed to establish a regime for the sustainable management of tuna reserves. The Convention was opened for signature in Honolulu in September 2000, and entered into force in June 2004. In March 2002 the SPC and European Commission launched a Pacific Regional Oceanic and Coastal Fisheries Project (PROCFISH). The oceanic component of the project aimed to assist the OFP with advancing knowledge of tuna fisheries ecosystems,

while the coastal element was to produce the first comparative regional baseline assessment of reef fisheries. The RMP advises member governments in the fields of policy, law and training. In early 2002 the RMP launched the model Pacific Islands Maritime Legislation and Regulations as a framework for the development of national maritime legislation. The SPC administers the Pacific Island Aquaculture Network, a forum for promoting regional aquaculture development.

The SPC hosts the Pacific Office of the WorldFish Center (the International Centre for Living Aquatic Resources Management—ICLARM); the SPC and the WorldFish Center have jointly implemented a number of projects.

SOCIAL RESOURCES

The Social Resources Division comprises the Public Health Programme and the Socio-economic Programme (including sub-programmes and sections on statistics; population and demography; rural energy development; youth issues; culture; women's and gender equality; community education training; and media training).

The Public Health Programme aims to implement health promotion programmes; to assist regional authorities to strengthen health information systems and to promote the use of new technology for health information development and disease control (for example, through the Public Health Surveillance and Disease Control Programme); to promote efficient health services management; and to help all Pacific Islanders to attain a level of health and quality of life that will enable them to contribute to the development of their communities. The Public Health Services also work in the areas of non-communicable diseases and nutrition (with particular focus on the high levels of diabetes and heart disease in parts of the region); environmental health, through the improvement of water and sanitation facilities; and reducing the incidence of HIV/AIDS and other sexually-transmitted infections (STIs), tuberculosis, and vector-borne diseases such as malaria and dengue fever. The SPC operates a project (mainly funded by Australia and New Zealand), to prevent AIDS and STIs among young people through peer education and awareness. In August 2004 a new grants scheme was launched to fund the development and implementation of national HIV/AIDS and STI strategic plans. A Lifestyle Health Section aims to assist member countries to improve and sustain health, in particular in nutrition.

The Statistics Programme assists governments and administrations in the region to provide effective and efficient national statistical services through the provision of training activities, a statistical information service and other advisory services. A Regional Meeting of Heads of Statistics facilitates the integration and co-ordination of statistical services throughout the region, while the Pacific Regional Information System (PRISM), initiated by the National Statistics Office of the Pacific Islands and developed with British funding, provides statistical information about member countries and territories. Activities of a new Pacific Regional Poverty Programme are to be integrated into PRISM.

The Population and Demography Programme provides technical support in population, demographic and development issues to member governments, other SPC programmes, and organizations active in the region. The Programme aims to assist governments effectively to analyse data and utilize it into the formulation of national development policies and programmes. The Programme organizes national workshops in population and development planning, provides short-term professional attachments, undertakes demographic research and analysis, and disseminates information.

The Pacific Youth Bureau (PYB) co-ordinates the implementation of the Pacific Youth Strategy 2005, which aims to develop opportunities for young people to play an active role in society. The PYB provides non-formal education and support for youth, community workers and young adults in community development subjects and provides grants to help young people find employment. It also advises and assists the Pacific Youth Council in promoting a regional youth identity. The Pacific Women's Bureau (PWB) aims to promote the social, economic and cultural advancement of women in the region by assisting governments and regional organizations to include women in the development planning process. The PWB also provides technical and advisory services, advocacy and management support training to groups concerned with women in development and gender and development, and supports the production and exchange of information regarding women.

The Cultural Affairs Programme aims to preserve and promote the cultural heritage of the Pacific Islands. The Programme assists with the training of librarians, archivists and researchers and promotes instruction in local languages, history and art at schools in member states and territories. The SPC acts as the secretariat of the Council of Pacific Arts, which organizes the Festival of Pacific Arts on a four-yearly basis. The ninth Festival was held in July 2004, in Palau.

The SPC regional office in Suva, Fiji, administers a Community Education Training Centre (CETC), which conducts a seven-month training course for up to 40 women community workers annually, with the objective of training women in methods of community development so that they can help others to achieve better living conditions for island families and communities. The Regional Media Centre provides training, technical assistance and production materials in all areas of the media for member countries and territories, community work programmes, donor projects and regional non-governmental organizations. The Centre comprises a radio broadcast unit, a graphic design and publication unit and a TV and video unit.

In 2000 the SPC's Information Technology and Communication Unit launched ComET, a satellite communications project aimed at linking more closely the organization's headquarters in New Caledonia and regional office in Fiji. The Information and Communications Programme is developing the use of modern communication technology as an invaluable resource for problem-solving, regional networking, and uniting the Community's scattered, often physically isolated, island member states. In conjunction with the Secretariat of the Pacific Islands Forum the SPC convened the first regional meeting of Information and Communication Technology workers, researchers and policy-makers in August 2001. The meeting addressed strategies for the advancement of new information technologies in member countries.

Finance

The organization's core budget, funded by assessed contributions from member states, finances executive and administrative expenditures, the Information and Communications Programme, and several professional and support positions that contribute to the work of the three programme divisions (i.e. Land Resources, Marine Resources and Social Resources). The non-core budget, funded mainly by aid donors and in part by Community member states, mostly on a contractual basis, finances the SPC's technical services. Administrative expenditure for 2004 amounted to CFP 3,211m.

Publications

Annual Report.
Fisheries Newsletter (quarterly).
Pacific Aids Alert Bulletin (quarterly).
Pacific Island Nutrition (quarterly).
Regional Tuna Bulletin (quarterly).
Report of the Conference of the Pacific Community.
Women's Newsletter (quarterly).

Technical publications, statistical bulletins, advisory leaflets and reports.

PACIFIC ISLANDS FORUM

Address: c/o Pacific Islands Forum Secretariat, Private Mail Bag, Suva, Fiji.
Telephone: 3312600; **fax:** 3305573; **e-mail:** info@forumsec.org.fj; **internet:** www.forumsec.org.fj.

MEMBERS

Australia	Niue
Cook Islands	Palau
Fiji	Papua New Guinea
Kiribati	Samoa
Marshall Islands	Solomon Islands
Federated States of	Tonga
Micronesia	Tuvalu
Nauru	Vanuatu
New Zealand	

Note: New Caledonia was admitted as an observer at the Forum in 1999. Timor-Leste was granted 'special observer' status in 2002 and French Polynesia was admitted as an observer in August 2004.

The Pacific Islands Forum (which changed its name from South Pacific Forum in October 2000) was founded as the gathering of Heads of Government of the independent and self-governing states of the South Pacific. Its first meeting was held on 5 August 1971, in Wellington, New Zealand. It provides an opportunity for informal discussions to be held on a wide range of common issues and problems and meets annually or when issues require urgent attention. The Forum has no written constitution or international agreement governing its activities nor any formal rules relating to its purpose, membership or conduct of meeting. Decisions are always reached by consensus, it never having been found necessary or desirable to vote formally on issues. In October 1994 the Forum was granted observer status by the General Assembly of the United Nations.

Since 1989 each Forum has been followed by 'dialogues' with representatives of other countries with a long-term interest in and commitment to the region. In October 1995 the Forum Governments suspended France's 'dialogue' status, following that country's resumption of the testing of nuclear weapons in French Polynesia. France was reinstated as a 'dialogue partner' in September 1996. In 2004 'dialogue partners' comprised Canada, the People's Republic of China, France, India, Indonesia, Japan, the Republic of Korea, Malaysia, Philippines, the United Kingdom, the USA, and the European Union. Thailand was to participate in the dialogue meetings from 2005.

The South Pacific Nuclear-Free Zone Treaty (Treaty of Rarotonga), prohibiting the acquisition, stationing or testing of nuclear weapons in the region, came into effect in December 1986, following ratification by eight states. The USSR signed the protocols to the treaty (whereby states possessing nuclear weapons agree not to use or threaten to use nuclear explosive devices against any non-nuclear party to the Treaty) in December 1987 and ratified them in April 1988; the People's Republic of China did likewise in December 1987 and October 1988 respectively. In July 1993 the Forum petitioned the USA, the United Kingdom and France, asking them to reconsider their past refusal to sign the Treaty in the light of the end of the 'Cold War'. In July 1995, following the decision of the French Government to resume testing of nuclear weapons in French Polynesia, members of the Forum resolved to increase diplomatic pressure on the three Governments to sign the Treaty. In October the United Kingdom, the USA and France announced their intention to accede to the Treaty, by mid-1996. Following France's decision, announced in January 1996, to end the programme four months earlier than scheduled, representatives of the Governments of the three countries signed the Treaty in March.

In 1990 five of the Forum's smallest island member states formed an economic sub-group to address their specific concerns, in particular economic disadvantages resulting from a poor resource base, absence of a skilled work-force and lack of involvement in world markets. In September 1997 the 28th Forum, convened in Rarotonga, the Cook Islands, endorsed the inclusion of the Marshall Islands as the sixth member of the Smaller Island States (SIS) sub-group. Representatives of the grouping, which also includes Kiribati, the Cook Islands, Nauru, Niue and Tuvalu, meet regularly. In February 1998 senior Forum officials, for the first time, met with representatives of the Caribbean Community and the Indian Ocean Commission, as well as other major international organizations, to discuss means to enhance consideration and promotion of the interests of small island states. Small island member states have been particularly concerned about the phenomenon of global warming and its potentially damaging effects on the region (see below).

At the 24th Forum, held in Yaren, Nauru, in August 1993 it was agreed that effective links needed to be established with the broader Asia-Pacific region, with participation in Asia-Pacific Economic Cooperation (APEC), where the Forum has observer status, to be utilized to the full. The Forum urged an increase in intra-regional trade and asked for improved opportunities for Pacific island countries exporting to Australia and New Zealand. New Caledonia's right to self-determination was supported. Environmental protection measures and the rapid growth in population in the region, which was posing a threat to economic and social development, were also discussed by the Forum delegates.

The 25th Forum was convened in Brisbane, Australia, in August 1994 under the theme of 'Managing Our Resources'. In response to the loss of natural resources as well as of income-earning potential resulting from unlawful logging of timber by foreign companies, Forum members agreed to impose stricter controls on the exploitation of forestry resources and to begin negotiations to standardize monitoring of the region's resources. The Forum also agreed to strengthen its promotion of sustainable exploitation of fishing stocks, reviewed preparations of a convention to control the movement and management of radioactive waste within the South Pacific and discussed the rationalization of national airlines, on a regional or sub-regional basis, to reduce operational losses.

The 26th Forum, held in Madang, Papua New Guinea, in September 1995, was dominated by extreme hostility on the part of Forum Governments to the resumption of testing of nuclear weapons by France in the South Pacific region. The decision to recommence testing, announced by the French Government in June, had been instantly criticized by Forum Governments. The 26th Forum reiterated their demand that France stop any further testing, and also condemned the People's Republic of China for conducting nuclear tests in the region. The meeting endorsed a draft Code of Conduct on the management and monitoring of indigenous forest resources in selected South Pacific countries, which had been initiated at the 25th Forum; however, while the six countries concerned committed themselves to implementing the Code through national legislation, its signing was deferred, owing to an initial unwillingness on the part of Papua New Guinea and Solomon Islands. The Forum did adopt a treaty to ban the import into the region of all radioactive and other hazardous wastes, and to control the transboundary movement and management of these wastes (the so-called Waigani Convention). The Forum agreed to reactivate the ministerial committee on New Caledonia, comprising Fiji, Nauru and Solomon Islands, which was to monitor political developments in that territory prior to its referendum on independence, scheduled to be held in 1998. In addition, the Forum resolved to implement and pursue means of promoting economic co-operation and long-term development in the region. In December 1995 Forum finance ministers, meeting in Port Moresby, Papua New Guinea, discussed the issues involved in the concept of 'Securing Development Beyond 2000' and initiated an assessment project to further trade liberalization efforts in the region.

The 27th Forum, held in Majuro, the Marshall Islands, in September 1996, supported the efforts of the French Government to improve relations with countries in the South Pacific and agreed to readmit France to the post-Forum dialogue. The Forum meeting recognized the importance of responding to the liberalization of the global trading system by reviewing the region's economic tariff policies, and of assisting members in attracting investment for the development of the private sector. The Forum advocated that a meeting of economy ministers of member countries be held each year. The Forum was also concerned with environmental issues: in particular, it urged the ratification and implementation of the Waigani Convention by all member states, the promotion of regional efforts to conserve marine resources and to protect the coastal environment, and the formulation of an international, legally-binding agreement to reduce emissions by industrialized countries of so-called 'greenhouse gases'. Such gases contribute to the warming of the earth's atmosphere (the 'greenhouse effect') and to related increases in global sea-levels, and have therefore been regarded as a threat to low-lying islands in the region. The Forum requested the ministerial committee on New Caledonia (established by the 1990 Forum to monitor, in co-operation with the French authorities, political developments in the territory) to pursue contacts with all parties there and to continue to monitor preparations for the 1998 referendum.

In July 1997 the inaugural meeting of Forum economy ministers was convened in Cairns, Australia. It formulated an Action Plan to encourage the flow of foreign investment into the region by committing members to economic reforms, good governance and the implementation of multilateral trade and tariff policies. The meeting also commissioned a formal study of the establishment of a free-trade agreement between Forum island states. The 28th Forum, held in Rarotonga, the Cook Islands, in September, considered the economic challenges confronting the region. However, it was marked by a failure to conclude a common policy position on mandatory targets for reductions in 'greenhouse gas' emissions, owing to an ongoing dispute between Australia and other Forum Governments.

The 29th Forum, held in Pohnpei, Federated States of Micronesia, in August 1998, considered the need to pursue economic reforms and to stimulate the private sector and foreign investment in order to ensure economic growth. Leaders reiterated their support for efforts to implement the economic Action Plan and to develop a framework for a free-trade agreement, and endorsed specific recommendations of the second Forum Economic Ministers Meeting, which was held in Fiji, in July, including the promotion of competitive telecommunications markets, the development of information infrastructures and support for a new economic vulnerability index at the UN to help determine least developed country status. The Forum was also concerned with environmental issues, notably the shipment of radioactive wastes, the impact of a multinational venture to launch satellites from the Pacific, the need for ongoing radiological monitoring of the Mururoa and Fangataufa atolls, and the development of a South Pacific Whale Sanctuary. The Forum adopted a Statement on Climate Change, which urged all countries to ratify and implement the gas emission reductions agreed upon by UN member states in December 1997 (the so-called Kyoto Protocol of the UN Framework Convention on Climate Change), and emphasized the

Forum's commitment to further measures for verifying and enforcing emission limitation.

In October 1999 the 30th Forum, held in Koror, Palau, endorsed in principle the establishment of a regional free-trade area (FTA), which had been approved at a special ministerial meeting held in June. The FTA was to be implemented from 2002 over a period of eight years for developing member countries and 10 years for smaller island states and least developed countries. The Forum requested officials from member countries to negotiate the details of a draft agreement on the FTA (the so-called Pacific Island Countries Trade Agreement—PICTA), including possible extensions of the arrangements to Australia and New Zealand. The heads of government adopted a Forum Vision for the Pacific Information Economy, which recognized the importance of information technology infrastructure for the region's economic and social development and the possibilities for enhanced co-operation in investment, job creation, education, training and cultural exchange. Forum Governments also expressed concern at the shipment of radioactive waste through the Pacific and determined to pursue negotiations with France, Japan and the United Kingdom regarding liability and compensation arrangements; confirmed their continued support for the multinational force and UN operations in East Timor (now Timor-Leste); and urged more countries to adopt and implement the Kyoto Protocol to limit the emission of 'greenhouse gases'. In addition, the Forum agreed to rename the grouping (hitherto known as the South Pacific Forum) the Pacific Islands Forum, to reflect the expansion of its membership since its establishment; the new designation took effect at the 31st Forum, which was convened in Tarawa, Kiribati, at the end of October 2000.

At the 31st Forum the heads of government discussed the escalation in regional insecurity that had occurred since the previous Forum. Concern was expressed over the unrest that prevailed during mid-2000 in Fiji and Solomon Islands, and also over ongoing political violence in the Indonesian province of Irian Jaya (now Papua). The Forum adopted the Biketawa Declaration, which outlined a mechanism for responding to any future such crises in the region while urging members to undertake efforts to address the fundamental causes of instability. The detrimental economic impact of the disturbances in Fiji and Solomon Islands was noted. The Forum endorsed a proposal to establish a Regional Financial Information Sharing Facility and national financial intelligence units, and welcomed the conclusion in June by the European Union and ACP states (which include several Forum members) of the Cotonou Agreement. The Forum also reiterated support for the prompt implementation of the Kyoto Protocol.

In August 2001, convened at the 32nd Forum, in Nauru, nine regional leaders adopted PICTA, providing for the establishment of the FTA (as envisaged at the 30th Forum). A related Pacific Agreement on Closer Economic Relations (PACER), envisaging the phased establishment of a regional single market including the signatories to PICTA and Australia and New Zealand, was also adopted. The Forum expressed concern at the refusal of the USA (responsible for about one-quarter of world-wide 'greenhouse gas' emissions) to ratify the Kyoto Protocol. In response to an ongoing initiative by the Organisation of Economic Co-operation and Development (OECD) to eliminate the operation of 'harmful tax systems', the Forum reaffirmed the sovereign right of nations to establish individual tax regimes and urged the development of a new co-operative framework to address issues relating to financial transparency. (OECD had identified the Cook Islands, the Marshall Islands, Nauru and Niue as so-called 'tax havens' lacking financial transparency and had demanded that they impose stricter legislation to address the incidence of international money-laundering on their territories.) Forum leaders also reiterated protests against the shipment of radioactive materials through the region.

The 33rd Forum, held in Suva, Fiji, in August 2002, adopted the Nasonini Declaration on Regional Security, which recognized the need for immediate and sustained regional action to combat international terrorism and transnational crime, in view of the perceived increased threat to global and regional security following the major terrorist attacks perpetrated against targets in the USA in September 2001. Regional leaders also approved a Pacific Island Regional Ocean Policy, which aimed to ensure the future sustainable use of the ocean and its resources by Pacific Island communities and external partners. In addition the Forum urged OECD to adopt a more flexible approach in the implementation of its ongoing harmful tax initiative; welcomed the third assessment report on climate change issued in 2001 by the WMO/UNEP Intergovernmental Panel on Climate Change and reiterated demands for a world-wide reduction in greenhouse gas emissions; invited member island states to declare their coastal waters as whale sanctuaries; and urged the development of a Pacific Regional Plan of Action against HIV/AIDS.

Regional leaders convened at the 34th Forum, held in August 2003, in Auckland, New Zealand, commended the swift response by member countries and territories in deploying a Regional Assistance Mission in Solomon Islands, which had been approved by Forum ministers of foreign affairs at a meeting held in Sydney, Australia, in

June, in accordance with the Biketawa Declaration. The Forum also welcomed the entry into force of the PICTA and PACER trade agreements and agreed, in principle, that the USA and France should become parties to both agreements. Regional leaders adopted a set of Forum Principles of Good Leadership, establishing key requirements for good governance, including respect for law and the system of government, and respect for cultural values, customs and traditions, and for freedom of religion. The leaders determined that a review of the activities of the Forum and its Secretariat should be undertaken, and established an Eminent Persons Group to initiate that process.

In April 2004 a Special Leaders' Retreat was convened in Auckland, New Zealand, in order to consider the future activities and direction of the Forum. The meeting concluded that the following four areas were key priorities for the grouping: economic growth; sustainable development; security; and good governance. The heads of government mandated the development of a Pacific Plan to strengthen co-operation throughout Forum countries and to achieve their objectives, which included the sustainable management of resources, the observation of democratic values and good governance, economic sustainability, peaceful relations with neighbours, and improved communications throughout the region. They also recognized the specific needs of Small Island States. The 35th Forum was held in August, in Apia, Samoa. Leaders commended the work

already being undertaken on the Pacific Plan by a newly-established Task Force, and anticipated a substantial document to be presented to the 36th Forum. Leaders adopted new Principles on Regional Transport Services, based on the results of a study requested by the 34th Forum, 'to improve the efficiency, effectiveness and sustainability of air and shipping services'. The 35th Forum also reiterated the importance of fisheries to the region's economy and population, and resolved to pursue an increase in sustainable returns through greater participation of resource-owning countries in the fishing industry. Furthermore, Forum leaders approved an HIV/AIDS Regional Strategy and requested its implementation with immediate effect, resolved to support a request from the Government of Nauru for economic and technical assistance in accordance with the Biketawa Declaration (2000), and determined to review the region's response to national disasters and other emergencies, with particular concern given to the recovery efforts of Niue following a devastating cyclone which struck the territory in January. In this respect, in January 2005, meeting on the fringes of the fifth Summit of the Alliance of Small Island States, in Port Louis, Mauritius, the Secretaries-General of the Pacific Islands Forum Secretariat, the Commonwealth, CARICOM, and the Indian Ocean Commission determined to take collective action to strengthen the disaster preparedness and response capacities of their member countries in the Pacific, Caribbean and Indian Ocean areas.

Pacific Islands Forum Secretariat

Address: Private Mail Bag, Suva, Fiji.
Telephone: 3312600; **fax:** 3301102; **e-mail:** info@forumsec.org.fj; **internet:** www.forumsec.org.fj.

The South Pacific Bureau for Economic Co-operation (SPEC) was established by an agreement signed on 17 April 1973, at the third meeting of the South Pacific Forum (now Pacific Islands Forum) in Apia, Western Samoa (now Samoa). SPEC was renamed the South Pacific Forum Secretariat in 1988; this, in turn, was redesignated as the Pacific Islands Forum Secretariat in October 2000.

Organization

(April 2005)

FORUM OFFICIALS COMMITTEE

The Forum Officials Committee is the Secretariat's executive board. It comprises representatives and senior officials from all member countries. It meets twice a year, immediately before the meetings of the Pacific Islands Forum and at the end of the year, to discuss in detail the Secretariat's work programme and annual budget.

SECRETARIAT

The Secretariat undertakes the day-to-day activities of the Forum. It is headed by a Secretary-General, with a staff of some 70 people drawn from the member countries. The Secretariat comprises the following four Divisions: Corporate Services; Development and Economic Policy; Trade and Investment; and Political, International and Legal Affairs.

Secretary-General: GREGORY (GREG) URWIN (Australia).

Deputy Secretary-General: IOSEFA MAIAVA (Samoa).

Activities

The Secretariat's aim is to enhance the economic and social well-being of the people of the South Pacific, in support of the efforts of national governments.

The Secretariat's trade and investment services extend advice and technical assistance to member countries in policy, development, export marketing, and information dissemination. Trade policy activities are mainly concerned with improving private sector policies, for example investment promotion, assisting integration into the world economy (including the provision of information and technical assistance to member states on WTO-related matters and supporting Pacific Island ACP states with preparations for negotiations on trade partnership with the EU under the Cotonou Agreement), and the development of businesses. The Secretariat aims to assist both island governments and private sector companies to enhance their capacity in the development and exploitation of export markets, product identification and product development. A regional

trade and investment database is being developed. The Trade and Investment Division of the Secretariat co-ordinates the activities of the regional trade offices located in Australia, New Zealand and Japan (see below). A representative trade office in Beijing, People's Republic of China, opened in January 2002. A Forum office was opened in Geneva, Switzerland, in 2004 to represent member countries at the WTO.

In 1981 the South Pacific Regional Trade and Economic Co-operation Agreement (SPARTECA) came into force. SPARTECA aimed to redress the trade deficit of the Pacific Island countries with Australia and New Zealand. It is a non-reciprocal trade agreement under which Australia and New Zealand offer duty-free and unrestricted access or concessional access for specified products originating from the developing island member countries of the Forum. In 1985 Australia agreed to further liberalization of trade by abolishing (from the beginning of 1987) duties and quotas on all Pacific products except steel, cars, sugar, footwear and garments. In August 1994 New Zealand expanded its import criteria under the agreement by reducing the rule of origin requirement for garment products from 50% to 45% of local content. In response to requests from Fiji, Australia agreed to widen its interpretation of the agreement by accepting as being of local content manufactured products that consist of goods and components of 50% Australian content. A new Fiji/Australia Trade and Economic Relations Agreement (AFTERA) was concluded in March 1999 to complement SPARTECA and compensate for certain trade benefits that were in the process of being withdrawn.

Two major regional trade accords signed by Forum heads of state in August 2001 entered into force in April 2003 and October 2002, respectively: the Pacific Island Countries Trade Agreement (PICTA), providing for the establishment of a Pacific Island free-trade area (FTA); and the related Pacific Agreement on Closer Economic Relations (PACER), incorporating trade and economic co-operation measures and envisaging an eventual single regional market comprising the PICTA FTA and Australia and New Zealand. It was envisaged that negotiations on free-trade agreements between Pacific Island states and Australia and New Zealand, with a view to establishing the larger regional single market envisaged by PACER, would commence within eight years of PICTA's entry into force. SPARTECA (see above) would remain operative pending the establishment of the larger single market, into which it would be subsumed. Under the provisions of PACER, Australia and New Zealand were to provide technical and financial assistance to PICTA signatory states in pursuing the objectives of PACER. In September 2004 Forum trade officials adopted a Regional Trade Facilitation Programme, within the framework of PACER, which included measures concerned with customs procedures, quarantine, standards and other activities to harmonize and facilitate trade between Pacific Island states and Australia and New Zealand, as well as with other international trading partners.

In April 2001 the Secretariat convened a meeting of seven member island states—the Cook Islands, the Marshall Islands, Nauru, Niue, Samoa, Tonga and Vanuatu—as well as representatives from Australia and New Zealand, to address the regional implications of the

OECD's Harmful Tax Competition Initiative. The meeting requested the OECD to engage in conciliatory negotiations with the listed Pacific Island states. The August Forum reiterated this stance, proclaiming the sovereign right of nations to establish individual tax regimes, and supporting the development of a new co-operative framework to address financial transparency concerns. In December the Secretariat hosted a workshop for officials from nine member states concerned with combating financial crime. The workshop was attended and sponsored by several partner organizations and bodies, including the IMF. In 2004 the Secretariat undertook work to prepare a Pacific Plan that had been mandated a the Special Leaders' Retreat held in April.

The Political, International and Legal Affairs Division of the Secretariat organizes and services the meetings of the Forum, disseminates its views, administers the Forum's observer office at the United Nations, and aims to strengthen relations with other regional and international organizations, in particular APEC and ASEAN. The Division's other main concern is to promote regional co-operation in law enforcement and legal affairs, and it provides technical support for the drafting of legal documents and for law enforcement capacity-building. In 1997 the Secretariat undertook an assessment to survey the need for specialist training in dealing with money laundering in member countries. In recent years the Forum Secretariat has been concerned with assessing the legislative reforms and other commitments needed to ensure implementation of the 1992 Honiara Declaration on Law Enforcement Co-operation. The Division assists member countries to ratify and implement the 1988 UN Convention against Illicit Trafficking in Narcotic Drugs and Psychotropic Substances. In December 1998 the Secretariat initiated a five-year programme to strengthen regional law enforcement capabilities, in particular to counter cross-border crimes such as money-laundering and drugs-trafficking. All member states, apart from Australia and New Zealand, were to participate in the initiative. In December 2001 the first ever Forum Election Observer Group was dispatched to monitor legislative elections held in Solomon Islands. In July 2004 a joint mission, with officials from the Commonwealth Secretariat, observed elections to the National Assembly in Vanuatu. A similar joint observer mission was to monitor elections in Nauru, in October. At the end of 2001 a conference of Forum immigration ministers expressed concern at rising levels of human-trafficking and illegal immigration in the region, and recommended that member states become parties to the 2000 UN Convention Against Transnational Organized Crime. In February 2003 the Forum hosted a seminar of Pacific Island lawmakers under a regional initiative to draft legislation on combating money laundering and the financing of terrorism. A Pacific Transnational Crime Co-ordination Centre was established in Suva, Fiji, in 2004, to enhance and gather law enforcement intelligence generated by national transnational crime units. Under the proposed Pacific Plan, to be formulated in 2004–05, the Forum Secretariat requested the establishment of a Pacific Islands Regional Security Technical Co-operation Unit to support legislative efforts in, *inter alia*, transnational organized crime, counter-terrorism and financial intelligence.

The Secretariat helps to co-ordinate environmental policy. With support from the Australian Government, it administers a network of stations to monitor sea-levels and climate change throughout the Pacific region. In recent years the Secretariat has played an active role in supporting regional participation at meetings of the Conference of the Parties to the UN Framework Convention on Climate Change.

The Development and Economic Policy Division of the Secretariat aims to co-ordinate and promote co-operation in development activities and programmes throughout the region. The Division administers a Short Term Advisory Service, which provides consultancy services to help member countries meet economic development priorities, and a Fellowship Scheme to provide practical training in a range of technical and income-generating activities. A Small Island Development Fund aims to assist the economic development of this sub-group of member countries (i.e. the Cook Islands, Kiribati, the Marshall Islands, Nauru, Niue and Tuvalu) through project financing. A separate fellowship has also been established to provide training to the Kanak population of New Caledonia, to assist in their social, economic and political development. The Division aims to assist regional organizations to identify development priorities and to provide advice to national governments on economic analysis, planning and structural reforms. The Secretariat chairs the Council of Regional Organizations in the Pacific (CROP), an *ad hoc* committee comprising the heads of eight regional organizations, which aims to discuss and co-ordinate the policies and work programmes of the various agencies in order to avoid duplication of or omissions in their services to member countries.

The Secretariat services the Pacific Group Council of ACP states receiving assistance from the EU, and in 1993 a joint unit was established within the Secretariat headquarters to assist Pacific ACP countries and regional organizations in submitting projects to the EU for funding. In October 2002 the Secretariat signed, on behalf of the Pacific Island ACP states, a framework agreement providing for EU-Pacific co-operation over a period of five years, and making a €29m. contribution in support of trade and economic integration (in particular the implementation of PICTA), the development of human resources (with particular emphasis on basic education), and the fisheries sector.

The Forum established the Pacific Forum Line and the Association of South Pacific Airlines (see below), as part of its efforts to promote co-operation in regional transport. On 1 January 1997 the work of the Forum Maritime Programme, which included assistance for regional maritime training and for the development of regional maritime administrations and legislation, was transferred to the regional office of the South Pacific Commission (renamed the Pacific Community from February 1998) at Suva. At the same time responsibility for the Secretariat's civil aviation activities was transferred to individual countries, to be managed at a bilateral level. Telecommunications policy activities were also transferred to the then South Pacific Commission at the start of 1997. In May 1998 ministers responsible for aviation in member states approved a new regional civil aviation policy, which envisaged liberalization of air services, common safety and security standards and provisions for shared revenue. During 2003–04 the Forum Secretariat worked with member countries to ensure their compliance with a new International Shipping and Port Facility Code. In accordance with the Principles on Regional Transport Services, which were adopted by Forum Leaders in August 2004, the Secretariat was to support efforts to enhance air and shipping services, as well as develop a regional digital strategy.

Finance

The Governments of Australia and New Zealand each contribute some one-third of the annual budget and the remaining amount is shared by the other member Governments. Extra-budgetary funding is contributed mainly by Australia, New Zealand, Japan, the EU and France. The Forum's 2004 budget amounted to FJ $15.4m.

Publications

Annual Report.

Forum News (quarterly).

Forum Trends.

Forum Secretariat Directory of Aid Agencies.

South Pacific Trade Directory.

SPARTECA (guide for Pacific island exporters).

Reports of meetings; profiles of Forum member countries.

Associated and Affiliated Organizations

Association of South Pacific Airlines—ASPA: POB 9817, Nadi Airport, Nadi, Fiji; tel. 6723526; fax 6720196; f. 1979 at a meeting of airlines in the South Pacific, convened to promote co-operation among the member airlines for the development of regular, safe and economical commercial aviation within, to and from the South Pacific; mems: 16 regional airlines, two associates; Chair. SEMISI TAUMOEPEAU; Sec.-Gen. GEORGE E. FAKTAUFON.

Forum Fisheries Agency—FFA: POB 629, Honiara, Solomon Islands; tel. (677) 21124; fax (677) 23995; e-mail info@ffa.int; internet www.ffa.int; f. 1979 to promote co-operation in fisheries among coastal states in the region; collects and disseminates information and advice on the living marine resources of the region, including the management, exploitation and development of these resources; provides assistance in the areas of law (treaty negotiations, drafting legislation, and co-ordinating surveillance and enforcement), fisheries development, research, economics, computers, and information management; the FFA was closely involved in the legal process relating to the establishment of a Western and Central Pacific Fisheries Commission, which was inaugurated in 2004; a Vessel Monitoring System, to provide automated data collection and analysis of fishing vessel activities throughout the region, was inaugurated by the FFA in 1998; on behalf of its 16 member countries, the FFA administers a multilateral fisheries treaty, under which vessels from the USA operate in the region, in exchange for an annual payment; Dir VICTORIO UHERBELAU; publs *FFA News Digest* (every two months), *FFA Reports*, *MCS Newsletter* (quarterly), *Tuna Market Newsletter* (monthly).

Pacific Forum Line: POB 796, Auckland, New Zealand; tel. (9) 356-2333; fax (9) 356-2330; e-mail info@pflnz.co.nz; internet www

.pflnz.co.nz; f. 1977 as a joint venture by South Pacific countries, to provide shipping services to meet the special requirements of the region; operates three container vessels; conducts shipping agency services in Australia, Fiji, New Zealand and Samoa, and stevedoring in Samoa; Chair. A. Vocea; CEO W. J. MacLennan.

Pacific Islands Centre—PIC: Sotobori Sky Bldg, 5th Floor, 2-11 Ichigayahonmura-cho, Shinjuku-ku, Tokyo 162-0845, Japan; tel. (3) 3268-8419; fax (3) 3268-6311; e-mail info@pic.or.jp; internet www.pic.or.jp; f. 1996 to promote and to facilitate trade, investment and tourism among Forum members and Japan; Dir Akira Ouchi.

Pacific Islands Trade and Investment Commission (Australia Office): Level 11, 171 Clarence St, Sydney, NSW 20010, Australia; tel. (2) 9290-2133; fax (2) 9299-2151; e-mail info@pitic.org.au; internet www.sptc.gov.au; f. 1979; assists Pacific Island Governments and business communities to identify market opportunities in Australia and promotes investment in the Pacific Island countries; Senior Trade Commr Aivu Tauvasa (Papua New Guinea).

Pacific Islands Trade and Investment Commission (New Zealand Office): Flight Centre, 48 Emily Pl., Auckland, New Zealand; tel. (9) 3020465; fax (9) 3776642; e-mail info@pitic.org.nz; internet www.pitic.org.nz; Senior Trade Commr Christopher Roy Cocker.

SOUTH ASIAN ASSOCIATION FOR REGIONAL CO-OPERATION—SAARC

Address: POB 4222, Tridevi Marg, Kathmandu, Nepal.
Telephone: (1) 4221785; **fax:** (1) 4227033; **e-mail:** saarc@saarc-sec.org; **internet:** www.saarc-sec.org.

The South Asian Association for Regional Co-operation (SAARC) was formally established in 1985 in order to strengthen and accelerate regional co-operation, particularly in economic development.

MEMBERS

Bangladesh	Nepal
Bhutan	Pakistan
India	Sri Lanka
Maldives	

Organization

(April 2005)

SUMMIT MEETING

Heads of state and of government of member states represent the body's highest authority, and a summit meeting is normally held annually. The 12th SAARC summit meeting was convened in Islamabad, Pakistan, in January 2004. The 13th summit meeting was to be held in Dhaka, Bangladesh, in mid-2005.

COUNCIL OF MINISTERS

The Council of Ministers comprises the ministers of foreign affairs of member countries, who meet twice a year. The Council may also meet in extraordinary session at the request of member states. The responsibilities of the Council include formulation of policies, assessing progress and confirming new areas of co-operation.

STANDING COMMITTEE

The Committee consists of the secretaries of foreign affairs of member states. It has overall responsibility for the monitoring and co-ordination of programmes and financing, and determines priorities, mobilizes resources and identifies areas of co-operation. It usually meets twice a year, and submits its reports to the Council of Ministers. The Committee is supported by an *ad hoc* Programming Committee made up of senior officials, who meet to examine the budget of the Secretariat, confirm the Calendar of Activities and resolve matters assigned to it by the Standing Committee.

TECHNICAL COMMITTEES

SAARC's Integrated Programme of Action is implemented by seven Technical Committees covering: Agriculture and rural development; Energy; Environment, meteorology and forestry; Human resource development; Science and technology; Social development; and Transport and communications. Each committee is headed by a representative of a member state and meets annually.

SECRETARIAT

The Secretariat was established in 1987 to co-ordinate and oversee SAARC activities. It comprises the Secretary-General and a Director from each member country. The Secretary-General is appointed by the Council of Ministers, after being nominated by a member state, and serves a three-year term of office. The Director is nominated by member states and appointed by the Secretary-General for a term of

three years, although this may be increased in special circumstances.
Secretary-General: Chenkyab Dorji (Bhutan).

Activities

The first summit meeting of SAARC heads of state and government, held in Dhaka, Bangladesh, in December 1985, resulted in the signing of the Charter of the South Asian Association for Regional Co-operation (SAARC). In August 1993 ministers of foreign affairs of seven countries, meeting in New Delhi, India, adopted a Declaration on South Asian Regional Co-operation and launched an Integrated Programme of Action (IPA), which identified the main areas for regional co-operation. The ninth summit meeting, held in May 1997, authorized the establishment of a Group of Eminent Persons to review the functioning of the IPA. On the basis of the group's recommendations a reconstituted IPA, to be administered by a more efficient arrangement of Technical Committees, was initiated in June 2000.

SAARC is committed to improving quality of life in the region by accelerating economic growth, social progress and cultural development; promoting self-reliance; encouraging mutual assistance; increasing co-operation with other developing countries; and co-operating with other regional and international organizations. The SAARC Charter stipulates that decisions should be made unanimously, and that 'bilateral and contentious issues' should not be discussed. Regular meetings, at all levels, are held to further co-operation in areas covered by the Technical Committees (see above). A priority objective is the eradication of poverty in the region, and in 1993 SAARC endorsed an Agenda of Action to help achieve this. A framework for exchanging information on poverty eradication has also, since, been established. The 11th SAARC summit meeting, held in Kathmandu, Nepal, in January 2002, adopted a convention on regional arrangements for the promotion of child welfare in South Asia. The 11th summit also determined to reinvigorate regional poverty reduction activities in the context of the UN General Assembly's Millennium Development Goal of halving extreme poverty by 2015, and of other internationally-agreed commitments. The summit also urged the development of a regional strategy for preventing and combating HIV/AIDS and other communicable diseases; the SAARC Tuberculosis Centre (see below) was to play a co-ordinating role in this area. In April 2003 SAARC ministers of health convened an emergency meeting to consider the regional implications of the spread of Severe Acute Respiratory Syndrome (SARS), a previously unknown atypical pneumonia. In November of that year SAARC ministers of health determined to establish a regional surveillance and rapid reaction system for managing health crises and natural disasters. An emergency meeting of health and agriculture and livestock ministers was convened in New Delhi, India, in January 2004 to address the spread of Avian Influenza. Heads of state participating in the 12th summit meeting, held in Islamabad, Pakistan, in that month, adopted a SAARC Social Charter that had been drafted by with assistance from representatives of civil society, academia, non-governmental organizations and government, under the auspices of an inter-governmental expert group, and incorporated objectives in areas including poverty eradication, promotion of health and nutrition, food security, water supply and sanitation, children's development and rights, participation by women, and human resources development.

A Committee on Economic Co-operation (CEC), comprising senior trade officials of member states, was established in July 1991 to monitor progress concerning trade and economic co-operation issues. In the same year the summit meeting approved the creation of an inter-governmental group to establish a framework for the promotion of specific trade liberalization measures. A SAARC Chamber of Commerce (SCCI) became operational in 1992, with headquarters in Karachi, Pakistan. (The SCCI headquarters were subsequently transferred to Islamabad, Pakistan.) In April 1993 ministers signed a SAARC Preferential Trading Arrangement (SAPTA), which came into effect in December 1995. The 10th summit meeting proposed a series of measures to accelerate progress in the next round of SAPTA trade negotiations, including a reduction in the domestic content requirements of SAPTA's rules of origin, greater tariff concessions on products being actively traded and the removal of certain discriminatory and non-tariff barriers. In December 1995 the Council resolved that the ultimate objective for member states should be the establishment of a South Asian Free Trade Area (SAFTA), superseding SAPTA. An Agreement on SAFTA was signed in January 2004, at the 12th summit. It was scheduled to enter into force on 1 January 2006 providing for the phased elimination of tariffs: these were to be reduced to 30% in least developed member countries and to 20% in the others over a two-year period following the Agreement's entry into force, and subsequently to 0–5% over a period of five years. The Agreement established a mechanism for administering SAFTA and for settling disputes at ministerial level.

In January 1996 the first SAARC Trade Fair was held, in New Delhi, India, to promote intra-SAARC commerce. At the same time SAARC ministers of commerce convened for their first meeting to discuss regional economic co-operation. SAARC Trade Fairs have since been held in Colombo, Sri Lanka, in 1998; Islamabad, Pakistan, in September 2001; Kathmandu, Nepal, in October 2002; and in Dhaka, Bangladesh, in December 2003. The sixth trade fair was scheduled to be held in New Delhi, India, in 2005. A group on customs co-operation was established in 1996 to harmonize trading rules and regulations within the grouping, to simplify trade procedures and to upgrade facilities. In 1999 a regional action plan to harmonize national standards, quality control and measurements came into effect. In August 2001 SAARC commerce ministers met, in New Delhi, to discuss a co-ordinated approach to the World Trade Organization negotiations.

An Agricultural Information Centre was founded in 1988, in Dhaka, Bangladesh, to serve as a central institution for the dissemination of knowledge and information in the agricultural sector. It maintains a network of centres in each member state, which provide for the efficient exchange of technical information and for strengthening agricultural research. An agreement establishing a Food Security Reserve to meet emergency food requirements was signed in November 1987, and entered into force in August 1988. The Board of the Reserve meets annually to assess the food security of the region. At December 2002 the Reserve contained some 241,580 metric tons of grain. Other regional institutions include the SAARC Tuberculosis Centre in Thimi, Nepal, which opened in July 1992 with the aim of preventing and reducing the prevalence of the disease in the region through the co-ordination of tuberculosis control programmes, research and training; a SAARC Documentation Centre, established in New Delhi in May 1994; and a SAARC Meteorological Research Centre which opened in Dhaka in January 1995. A Human Resources Development Centre was established in Islamabad, Pakistan in 1999. In January 2004 the summit meeting endorsed the establishment of a Cultural Centre, to be based in Sri Lanka, a Coastal Zone Management Centre, in the Maldives, and an Information Centre in Nepal. In July the Council of Ministers approved the establishment of additional regional centres for forestry, to be based in Bhutan, and for energy, to be located in Pakistan. Regional funds include a SAARC-Japan Special Fund established in September 1993. One-half of the fund's resources, provided by the Japanese Government, was to be used to finance projects identified by Japan, including workshops and cultural events, and one-half was to be used to finance projects identified by SAARC member states. The eighth SAARC summit meeting, held in New Delhi in May 1996, established a South Asian Development Fund, comprising a Fund for Regional Projects, a Regional Fund and a fund for social development and infrastructure building.

A SAARC Youth Volunteers Programme (SYVOP) enables young people to work in other member countries in the agriculture and forestry sectors. The Programme is part of a series of initiatives designed to promote intra-regional exchanges and contact. A Youth Awards Scheme to reward outstanding achievements by young people was inaugurated in 1996. Founded in 1987, the SAARC Audio-visual Exchange Programme (SAVE) broadcasts radio and television programmes on social and cultural affairs to all member countries, twice a month, in order to disseminate information about SAARC and its members. From 2001 SAVE was to organize an annual SAARC Teleflim festival. The SAARC Consortium of Open and Distance Learning was established in 2000. A Visa Exemption Scheme, exempting 21 specified categories of person from visa requirements, with the aim of promoting closer regional contact, became operational in March 1992. A SAARC citizens forum promotes interaction among the people of South Asia. In addition, SAARC operates a fellowships, scholarships and chairs scheme and a scheme for the promotion of organized tourism. The 12th SAARC summit meeting designated 2005 as South Asia Tourism Year. The 13th summit, due to be held in Dhaka, Bangladesh, in mid-2005, was to consider the regional impact of the devastating earthquake and tsunami that struck the Indian Ocean in December 2004.

At the third SAARC summit, held in Kathmandu in November 1987, member states signed a regional convention on measures to counteract terrorism. The convention, which entered into force in August 1988, commits signatory countries to the extradition or prosecution of alleged terrorists and to the implementation of preventative measures to combat terrorism. Monitoring desks for terrorist and drugs offences have been established to process information relating to those activities. The first SAARC conference on co-operation in police affairs, attended by the heads of the police forces of member states, was held in Colombo in July 1996. The conference discussed the issues of terrorism, organized crime, the extradition of criminals, drugs-trafficking and drug abuse. A convention on narcotic drugs and psychotropic substances was signed during the fifth SAARC summit meeting, held in Malé in 1990. The convention entered into force in September 1993, following its ratification by member states. It is implemented by a co-ordination group of drug law enforcement agencies. At the 11th SAARC summit member states adopted a convention on the prevention of trafficking of women and children for prostitution. The 12th summit adopted an Additional Protocol on Suppression of Terrorism with a view to preventing the financing of terrorist activities.

SAARC co-operates with other regional and international organizations. In February 1993 SAARC signed a memorandum of understanding with UNCTAD, whereby both parties agreed to exchange information on trade control measures regionally and in 50 developed and developing countries, respectively, in order to increase transparency and thereby facilitate trade. In February 1994 SAARC signed a framework co-operation agreement with ESCAP to enhance co-operation on development issues through a framework of joint studies, workshops and information exchange. A memorandum of understanding with the European Commission was signed in July 1996. SAARC has also signed co-operation agreements with UNICEF (in 1993), the Asia Pacific Telecommunity (1994), UNDP (1995), UN Drug Progamme (1995), the International Telecommunication Union (1997), the Canadian International Development Agency (1997), WHO (2000), and UNIFEM (2001). An informal dialogue at ministerial level has been conducted with ASEAN and the European Union since 1998. SAARC and WIPO hold regular consultations concerning regional co-operation on intellectual property rights, and regular consultations are convened with the WTO. In July 2004 a memorandum of understanding was signed with the South Asia Co-operative Environment Programme (SACEP).

Finance

The national budgets of member countries provide the resources to finance SAARC activities. The Secretariat's annual budget is shared among member states according to a specified formula.

Publications

SAARC News (3/4 a year).
Other official documents, regional studies, reports.

Regional Apex Bodies

Association of Persons of the Legal Communities of the SAARC Countries (SAARCLAW): Pioneer House, Shahayog Marg, Anamnagar, Kathmandu, Nepal; tel. (1) 221340; fax (1) 226770; e-mail saarclaw@wlink.com.np; internet www.saarclaw.org; f. 1991; recognized as a SAARC regional apex body in July 1994; aims to enhance exchanges and co-operation amongst the legal communities of the sub-region and to promote the development of law; Pres. Laxman Aryal (Nepal); Sec.-Gen. Bharat Raj Upreti (Nepal).

SAARC Chamber of Commerce and Industry (SCCI): House 5, St 59, F-8/4, Islamabad, Pakistan; tel. (51) 2281395; fax (51) 2281390; e-mail saarc@isb.comsats.net.pk; internet www.saarcnet .org; f. 1992; promotes economic and trade co-operation throughout the sub-region and greater interaction between the business communities of member countries; organizes SAARC Economic Co-operation Conferences and Trade Fairs; Pres. Padma Jyoti (Nepal); Sec.-Gen. Abul Hasan.

South Asian Federation of Accountants (SAFA): f. 1984; recognized as a SAARC regional apex body in Jan. 2002; aims to develop regional co-ordination for the accountancy profession.

Other recognized regional bodies include the South Asian Association for Regional Co-operation of Architects, the Association of Management Development Institutions, the SAARC Federation of University Women, the SAARC Association of Town Planners, the SAARC Cardiac Society, the Association of SAARC Speakers and Parliamentarians, the Federation of State Insurance Organizations of SAARC Countries, the Federation of State Insurance Organizations of SAARC Countries, the SAARC Diploma Engineers Forum, the Radiological Society of SAARC Countries, the SAARC Teachers' Federation, the SAARC Surgical Care Society and the Foundation of SAARC Writers and Literature.

SOUTHERN AFRICAN DEVELOPMENT COMMUNITY— SADC

Address: SADC House, Government Enclave, Private Bag 0095, Gaborone, Botswana.

Telephone: 3951863; **fax:** 3972848; **e-mail:** registry@sadc.int; **internet:** www.sadc.int.

The first Southern African Development Co-ordination Conference (SADCC) was held at Arusha, Tanzania, in July 1979, to harmonize development plans and to reduce the region's economic dependence on South Africa. In August 1992 the 10 member countries of the SADCC signed a treaty establishing the Southern African Development Community (SADC), which replaced SADCC. The treaty places binding obligations on member countries, with the aim of promoting economic integration towards a fully developed common market. A tribunal was to be established to arbitrate in the case of disputes between member states arising from the treaty. By September 1993 all of the member states had ratified the treaty; it came into effect in early October. A protocol on the establishment of the long-envisaged SADC tribunal was adopted in 2000. The Protocol on Politics, Defence and Security Co-operation, regulating the structure, operations and functions of the Organ on Politics, Defence and Security, established in June 1996 (see under Regional Security), entered into force in March 2004. A troika system, comprising the current, incoming and outgoing SADC chairmanship, operates at the level of the Summit, Council of Ministers and Standing Committee of Officials, and co-ordinates the Organ on Politics, Defence and Security. Other member states may be co-opted into the troika as required. A system of SADC national committees, comprising representatives of government, civil society and the private sector, oversees the implementation of regional programmes at country level and helps to formulate new regional strategies. In recent years SADC institutions have been undergoing a process of intensive restructuring.

MEMBERS*

Angola	Malawi	Swaziland
Botswana	Mauritius	Tanzania
Congo, Democratic	Mozambique	Zambia
Republic	Namibia	Zimbabwe
Lesotho	South Africa	

*Seychelles withdrew from SADC in July 2004. In the following month Madagascar applied for membership of the Community; it was expected to be admitted at the summit meeting of heads of state and government scheduled to be held in August 2005.

Organization

(April 2005)

SUMMIT MEETING

The meeting is held at least once a year and is attended by heads of state and government or their representatives. It is the supreme policy-making organ of SADC and is responsible for the appointment of the Executive Secretary. A report on the restructuring of SADC, adopted by an extraordinary summit held in Windhoek, Namibia, in March 2001, recommended that biannual summit meetings should be convened. A summit meeting of heads of state and government was scheduled to be held in Gaborone, Botswana, in August 2005.

COUNCIL OF MINISTERS

Representatives of SADC member countries at ministerial level meet at least once a year.

INTEGRATED COMMITTEE OF MINISTERS

The Integrated Committee of Ministers (ICM), comprising at least two ministers from each member state and responsible to the Council of Ministers, oversees the four priority areas of integration (trade, industry, finance and investment; infrastructure and services; food, agriculture and natural resources; and social and human development and special programmes) and monitors the Directorates that administer these; facilitates the co-ordination and harmonization of cross-sectoral activities; and provides policy guidance to the Secretariat. The ICM also supervises the implementation of the Regional Indicative Strategic Development Plan (see below).

STANDING COMMITTEE OF OFFICIALS

The Committee, comprising senior officials, usually from the ministry responsible for economic planning or finance, acts as the technical advisory body to the Council. It meets at least once a year. Members of the Committee also act as a national contact point for matters relating to SADC.

SECRETARIAT

Executive Secretary: Dr Pakereesamy ('Prega') Ramsamy (Mauritius).

The extraordinary summit held in March 2001 determined that the mandate and resources of the Secretariat should be strengthened. A Department of Strategic Planning, Gender and Development and Policy Harmonization was established, comprising permanently-staffed Directorates covering the four priority areas of integration (see above).

Activities

In July 1979 the first Southern African Development Co-ordination Conference was attended by delegations from Angola, Botswana, Mozambique, Tanzania and Zambia, with representatives from donor governments and international agencies. In April 1980 a regional economic summit conference was held in Lusaka, Zambia, and the Lusaka Declaration, a statement of strategy entitled 'Southern Africa: Towards Economic Liberation', was approved. The members aimed to reduce their dependence on South Africa for rail and air links and port facilities, imports of raw materials and manufactured goods, and the supply of electric power. In 1985, however, an SADCC report noted that since 1980 the region had become still more dependent on South Africa for its trade outlets, and the 1986 summit meeting, although it recommended the adoption of economic sanctions against South Africa, failed to establish a timetable for doing so.

In January 1992 a meeting of the SADCC Council of Ministers approved proposals to transform the organization (by then expanded to include Lesotho, Malawi, Namibia and Swaziland) into a fully integrated economic community, and in August the treaty establishing SADC (see above) was signed. An SADC Programme of Action—SPA was to combine the strategies and objectives of the organization's sectoral programmes. South Africa became a member of SADC in August 1994, thus strengthening the objective of regional co-operation and economic integration. Mauritius became a member in August 1995. In September 1997 SADC heads of state agreed to admit the Democratic Republic of the Congo (DRC) and Seychelles as members of the Community; Seychelles withdrew in July 2004.

A possible merger between SADC and the Preferential Trade Area for Eastern and Southern African States (PTA), which consisted of all the members of SADC apart from Botswana and had similar aims of enhancing economic co-operation, was rejected by SADC's Executive Secretary in January 1993. He denied that the two organizations were duplicating each other's work, as had been suggested. However, concerns of regional rivalry with the PTA's successor, the Common Market for Eastern and Southern Africa (COMESA), persisted. In August 1996 an SADC–COMESA ministerial meeting advocated the continued separate functioning of the two organizations. A programme of co-operation between the secretariats of

SADC and COMESA, aimed at reducing all duplication of roles between the two organizations, is under way. A co-ordinating SADC/COMESA task force was established in 2001.

In September 1994 the first meeting of ministers of foreign affairs of SADC and the European Union (EU) was held in Berlin, Germany. The two sides agreed to establish working groups to promote closer trade, political, regional and economic co-operation. In particular, a declaration issued from the meeting specified joint objectives, including a reduction of exports of weapons to southern Africa and of the arms trade within the region, promotion of investment in the region's manufacturing sector and support for democracy at all levels. A consultative meeting between representatives of SADC and the EU was held in February 1995, in Lilongwe, Malawi, at which both groupings resolved to strengthen security in the southern African region. A second SADC–EU ministerial meeting, held in Namibia in October 1996, endorsed a Regional Indicative Programme to enhance co-operation between the two organizations over the next five years. The third ministerial meeting took place in Vienna, Austria, in November 1998. In September 1999 SADC signed a co-operation agreement with the US Government, which incorporated measures to promote US investment in the region, and commitments to support HIV/AIDS assessment and prevention programmes and to assist member states to develop environmental protection capabilities. The fourth SADC–EU ministerial meeting, convened in Gaborone, Botswana, in November 2000, adopted a joint declaration on the control of small arms and light weapons in the SADC region. The meeting also emphasized that the termination of illicit trading in diamonds would be a major contributory factor in resolving the ongoing conflicts in Angola and the DRC (see below). The fifth SADC–EU ministerial meeting was held in Maputo, Mozambique, in November 2002.

In July 1996 the SADC Parliamentary Forum was inaugurated, with the aim of promoting democracy, human rights and good governance throughout the region. Membership of the Forum, which is headquartered in Windhoek, Namibia, is open to national parliaments of all SADC countries, and offers fair representation for women. Representatives serve for a period of five years. The Forum receives funds from member parliaments, governments and charitable and international organizations. In September 1997 SADC heads of state endorsed the establishment of the Forum as an autonomous institution. The Forum frequently deploys missions to monitor parliamentary and presidential elections in the region. A regional women's parliamentary caucus was inaugurated in April 2002.

The August 2004 summit meeting of heads of state and government, held in Grand Baie, Mauritius, adopted a new Protocol on Principles and Guide-lines Governing Democratic Elections, which advocated: full participation by citizens in the political process; freedom of association; political tolerance; elections at regular intervals; equal access to the state media for all political parties; equal opportunity to exercise the right to vote and be voted for; independence of the judiciary; impartiality of the electoral institutions; the right to voter education; the respect of election results proclaimed to be free and fair by a competent national electoral authority; and the right to challenge election results as provided for in the law.

The extraordinary summit meeting convened in March 2001 adopted a report detailing recommendations on the restructuring of SADC's institutions, with a view to facilitating the effective application of the objectives of the organization's treaty and of the SPA. During 2001–03 the Community's former system comprising 21 sectors was, accordingly, reorganized under four new directorates: trade, industry, finance and investment; infrastructure and services; food, agriculture and natural resources; and social and human development and special programmes. The directorates are administered from the secretariat in Gaborone, in order to ensure greater efficiency (the previous sectoral system had been decentralized). The report adopted in March 2001 outlined a Common Agenda for the organization, which covered the promotion of poverty reduction measures and of sustainable and equitable socio-economic development, promotion of democratic political values and systems, and the consolidation of peace and security. The extraordinary summit meeting also authorized the establishment of an integrated committee of ministers mandated to formulate a five-year Regional Indicative Strategic Development Plan (RISDP), intended as the key policy framework for managing the SADC Common Agenda. A draft of the RISDP, adopted by the SADC Council of Ministers in March 2003, was approved by the summit meeting convened in Dar es Salaam, Tanzania, in August.

In August 2001 SADC established a task force, comprising representatives of five member countries, to address the ongoing political crisis in Zimbabwe. The Community sent two separate observer teams to monitor the controversial presidential election held in Zimbabwe in March 2002; the SADC Council of Ministers team found the election to have been conducted freely and fairly, while the Parliamentary Forum group was reluctant to endorse the poll. Having evaluated both reports, the Community approved the election. An SADC Council of Ministers group was convened to observe

the parliamentary elections held in Zimbabwe in March 2005; however, the Zimbabwean Government refused to invite a delegation from the SADC Parliamentary Forum. The Zimbabwean Government claimed to have enacted electoral legislation in accordance with the provisions of the August 2004 SADC Protocol on Principles and Guide-lines Governing Democratic Elections (see above).

In 2005 SADC, with the other African regional economic communities, was considering a draft protocol on the relations between the regional economic communities and the African Union (AU). A high-level meeting concerned with integrating the objectives of the New Partnership for Africa's Development (NEPAD) into SADC's regional programme activities was convened in August 2004.

REGIONAL SECURITY

In November 1994 SADC ministers of defence, meeting in Arusha, Tanzania, approved the establishment of a regional rapid-deployment peace-keeping force, which could be used to contain regional conflicts or civil unrest in member states. In April 1997 a training programme was organized in Zimbabwe, which aimed to inform troops from nine SADC countries of UN peace-keeping doctrines, procedures and strategies. A peace-keeping exercise involving 4,000 troops was held in South Africa, in April 1999. A further SADC peace-keeping exercise was conducted in February 2002 in Tanzania, jointly with Tanzanian and Ugandan forces. An SADC Mine Action Committee has been established to monitor and co-ordinate the process of removing anti-personnel land devices from countries in the region.

In June 1996 SADC heads of state and government, meeting in Gaborone, Botswana, inaugurated an Organ on Politics, Defence and Security, which was expected to enhance co-ordination of national policies and activities in these areas. The objectives of the body were, *inter alia*, to safeguard the people and development of the region against instability arising from civil disorder, inter-state conflict and external aggression; to undertake conflict prevention, management and resolution activities, by mediating in inter-state and intra-state disputes and conflicts, pre-empting conflicts through an early-warning system and using diplomacy and peace-keeping to achieve sustainable peace; to promote the development of a common foreign policy, in areas of mutual interest, and the evolution of common political institutions; to develop close co-operation between the police and security services of the region; and to encourage the observance of universal human rights, as provided for in the charters of the UN and OAU (now AU). There were, however, disagreements within SADC regarding its future status, either as an integrated part of the Community (favoured by South Africa) or as a more autonomous body (supported by Zimbabwe).

In August 1998 the Zimbabwean Government convened a meeting of the heads of state of seven SADC member states to discuss the escalation of civil conflict in the DRC and the threat to regional security, with Rwanda and Uganda reportedly having sent troops to assist anti-government forces. Later in that month ministers of defence and defence officials of several SADC countries declared their support for an initiative of the Zimbabwean Government to send military assistance to the forces loyal to President Kabila in the DRC. South Africa, which did not attend the meeting, rejected any military intervention under SADC auspices and insisted that the organization would pursue a diplomatic initiative. Zimbabwe, Angola and Namibia proceeded to send troops and logistical support to counter rebel Congolese forces. The Presidents of those countries failed to attend an emergency meeting of heads of state, convened by President Mandela of South Africa, which called for an immediate cease-fire and presented a 10-point-peace plan. A further emergency meeting, held in early September and attended by all SADC leaders, agreed to pursue negotiations for a peaceful settlement of the conflict. Some unity within the grouping was restored by Mandela's endorsement of the objective of supporting Kabila as the legitimate leader in the DRC. Furthermore, at the annual SADC summit meeting, held in Mauritius, it was agreed that discussion of the report on the security Organ, scheduled to have been presented to the conference, would be deferred to a specially convened summit meeting (although no date was agreed). Talks attended by Angola, the DRC, Namibia, Rwanda, Uganda, Zambia and Zimbabwe, conducted in mid-September, in Victoria Falls, agreed in principle on a cease-fire in the DRC but failed to conclude a detailed peace accord. Fighting continued to escalate, and in October Zimbabwe, Angola and Namibia resolved to send reinforcements to counter the advancing rebel forces. Meanwhile, in September representatives of SADC attempted to mediate between government and opposition parties in Lesotho amidst a deteriorating security situation in that country. At the end of the month, following an attempt by the Lesotho military to seize power, South Africa, together with Botswana, sent troops into Lesotho to restore civil order. The operation, which was declared to have been conducted under SADC auspices, prompted widespread criticism owing to the troops' involvement in heavy fighting with opposition forces. A committee was established by SADC to secure a cease-fire in Lesotho. Also at the end of

September SADC chiefs of staff agreed that the Community would assist the Angolan Government to eliminate the UNITA movement, owing to its adverse impact on the region's security. In October an SADC ministerial team, comprising representatives of South Africa, Botswana, Mozambique and Zimbabwe, negotiated an accord between the opposing sides in Lesotho providing for the conduct of democratic elections. The withdrawal of foreign troops from Lesotho was initiated at the end of April 1999, and was reported to have been completed by mid-May.

During the first half of 1999 Zambia's President Chiluba pursued efforts, under SADC auspices, to negotiate a political solution to the conflict in the DRC. Troops from the region, in particular from Angola and Zimbabwe, remained actively involved in the struggle to uphold Kabila's administration. SADC ministers of defence and of foreign affairs convened in Lusaka, in June, in order to secure a cease-fire agreement. An accord was finally signed in July between Kabila, leaders of the rebel forces and foreign allies of both sides. All foreign troops were to be withdrawn within nine months according to a schedule to be drawn up by the UN, OAU and a Joint Military Commission. However, the disengagement and redeployment of troops from front-line positions did not commence until February 2001. SADC welcomed peace accords signed by the DRC Government with Ugandan-backed rebels and with the Rwandan Government, respectively in July and August 2002. In August 2001 SADC heads of state resolved to support the continuing imposition of sanctions by the UN Security Council against the UNITA rebels in Angola; it was agreed to promote the international certification system for illicit trade in rough diamonds (believed to finance UNITA's activities), to install mobile radar systems that would detect illegal cross-border flights in the region, and to establish a body to compile information and to devise a strategy for terminating the supply of petroleum products to UNITA. SADC welcomed the cease-fire that was signed by the Angolan Government and UNITA in April 2002; all UN sanctions against UNITA were withdrawn by December.

In June 2004 SADC recommended that a fact-finding mission should be sent to the DRC to investigate continuing armed military activities, particularly in eastern areas.

In August 2000 proposals were announced (strongly supported by South Africa, see above) to develop the Organ for Politics, Defence and Security as a substructure of SADC, with subdivisions for defence and international diplomacy, to be chaired by a member country's head of state, working within a troika system; these were approved at the extraordinary summit held in March 2001. A Protocol on Politics, Defence and Security Co-operation, regulating the structure, operations and functions of the Organ, was adopted and opened for signature in August and entered into force in March 2004. The protocol was to be implemented by an Inter-state Politics and Diplomacy Committee.

The March 2001 extraordinary SADC summit adopted a Declaration on Small Arms, promoting the curtailment of the proliferation of and illicit trafficking in light weapons in the region. A Protocol on the Control of Firearms, Ammunition and Other Related Materials was adopted in August of that year. In July SADC ministers of defence approved a draft regional defence pact, providing for a mechanism to prevent conflict involving member countries and for member countries to unite against outside aggression. In January 2002 an extraordinary summit of SADC heads of state, held in Blantyre, Malawi, adopted a Declaration against Terrorism.

TRADE, INDUSTRY AND INVESTMENT

Under the treaty establishing SADC, efforts were to be undertaken to achieve regional economic integration. The Directorate of Trade, Industry, Finance and Investment aims to facilitate such integration, and poverty eradication, through the creation of an enabling investment and trade environment in SADC countries. Objectives include the establishment of a single regional market; the progressive removal of barriers to the movement of goods, services and people; and the promotion of cross-border investment. SADC supports programmes for industrial research and development and standardization and quality assurance, and aims to mobilize industrial investment resources and to co-ordinate economic policies and the development of the financial sector. In August 1996, at a summit meeting held in Lesotho, SADC member states signed the Protocol on Trade, providing for the establishment of a regional free-trade area, through the gradual elimination of tariff barriers (with an eight-year implementation schedule envisaged at that time). (Angola and the DRC are not signatories to the Protocol.) In October 1999 representatives of the private sector in SADC member states established the Association of SADC Chambers of Commerce, based in Mauritius. The Protocol on Trade entered into force in January 2000, and an Amendment Protocol on Trade came into force in August, incorporating renegotiated technical details on the gradual elimination of tariffs, rules of origin, customs co-operation, special industry arrangements and dispute settlement procedures. The implementation phase of the Protocol on Trade commenced in September. In accordance with a revised schedule, all intra-SADC trade

tariffs were to be removed by 2012, with about 85% to be withdrawn by 2008. Annual meetings are convened to review the work of expert teams in the areas of standards, quality, assurance, accreditation and metrology.

The mining sector contributes about 10% of the SADC region's annual GDP. The principal objective of SADC's programme of action on mining is to stimulate increased local and foreign investment in the sector, through the assimilation and dissemination of data, prospecting activities, and participation in promotional fora. In December 1994 SADC held a mining forum, jointly with the EU, in Lusaka, Zambia, with the aim of demonstrating to potential investors and promoters the possibilities of mining exploration in the region. A second mining investment forum was held in Lusaka in December 1998. A further SADC-EU mining investment forum ('Mines 2000') was held in Lusaka, Zambia, in October 2000. Subsequently a Mines 2000 follow-up programme has been implemented. Other objectives of the mining sector are the improvement of industry training, increasing the contribution of small-scale mining, reducing the illicit trade in gemstones and gold, increasing co-operation in mineral exploration and processing, and minimizing the adverse impact of mining operations on the environment. In February 2000 a Protocol on Mining entered into force, providing for the harmonization of policies and programmes relating to the development and exploitation of mineral resources in the region. SADC supports the Kimberley Process Certification Scheme aimed at preventing illicit trade in illegally mined rough diamonds. (The illicit trade in so-called 'conflict diamonds' and other minerals is believed to have motivated and financed many incidences of rebel activity in the continent, for example in Angola and the DRC.)

In July 1998 a Banking Association was officially constituted by representatives of SADC member states. The Association was to establish international banking standards and regional payments systems, organize training and harmonize banking legislation in the region. In April 1999 governors of SADC central banks determined to strengthen and harmonize banking procedures and technology in order to facilitate the financial integration of the region. Efforts to harmonize stock exchanges in the region were also initiated in 1999.

INFRASTRUCTURE AND SERVICES

The Directorate of Infrastructure and Services focuses on transport, communications and meteorology, energy, tourism and water. At SADC's inception transport was seen as the most important area to be developed, on the grounds that, as the Lusaka Declaration noted, without the establishment of an adequate regional transport and communications system, other areas of co-operation become impractical. Priority was to be given to the improvement of road and railway services into Mozambique, so that the landlocked countries of the region could transport their goods through Mozambican ports instead of South African ones. The Southern African Transport and Communications Commission (SATCC) was established, in Maputo, Mozambique, in order to undertake SADC's activities in this sector. During 1995 the SATCC undertook a study of regional transport and communications to provide a comprehensive framework and strategy for future courses of action. A task force was also established to identify measures to simplify procedures at border crossings throughout southern Africa. In 1996 the SATCC Road Network Management and Financing Task Force was established. An SADC Transport Investment Forum was convened in Windhoek, Namibia, in April 2001. In March the Association of Southern African National Road Agencies (ASANRA) was established to foster the development of an integrated regional transportation system. Eleven railways in the region form the Interconnected Regional Rail Network (IRRN), comprising nearly 34,000 km of route track.

SADC development projects have aimed to address missing links and over-stretched sections of the regional network, as well as to improve efficiency, operational co-ordination and human resource development, such as management training projects. Other objectives have been to ensure the compatibility of technical systems within the region and to promote the harmonization of regulations relating to intra-regional traffic and trade. In 1997 Namibia announced plans, supported by SADC, to establish a rail link with Angola in order to form a trade route similar to that created in Mozambique, on the western side of southern Africa. In March 1998 the final stage of the trans-Kalahari highway, linking ports on the east and west coasts of southern Africa, was officially opened. In July 1999 a 317-km rail link between Bulawayo, Zimbabwe, and the border town of Beitbridge, administered by SADC as its first build-operate-transfer project, was opened. SADC promotes greater co-operation in the civil aviation sector, in order to improve efficiency and to reverse a steady decline in the region's airline industries. Within the telecommunications sector efforts have been made to increase the capacity of direct exchange lines and international subscriber dialling (ISD) services. In January 1997 the Southern African Telecommunications Regional Authority (SATRA), a regulatory authority, was established.

SADC policy guide-lines on 'making information and communications technology a priority in turning SADC into an information-based economy' were adopted in November 2001. Policy guide-lines and model regulations on tariffs for telecommunications services have also been adopted. An SADC Expedited Mail Service operates in the postal services sector. The SATCC's Technical Unit oversees the region's meteorological services and issues a regular *Drought-Watch for Southern Africa* bulletin, a monthly *Drought Overview* bulletin and forewarnings of impending natural disasters. SADC is developing a regional strategy aimed at improving the early warning capabilities of national meteorological services.

Areas of activity in the energy sector include: joint petroleum exploration, training programmes for the petroleum sector and studies for strategic fuel storage facilities; promotion of the use of coal; development of hydroelectric power and the co-ordination of SADC generation and transmission capacities; new and renewable sources of energy, including pilot projects in solar energy; assessment of the environmental and socio-economic impact of wood-fuel scarcity and relevant education programmes; and energy conservation. In July 1995 SADC energy ministers approved the establishment of the Southern African Power Pool, whereby all member states were to be linked into a single electricity grid. (Several grids are already integrated and others are being rehabilitated.) At the same time, ministers endorsed a protocol to promote greater co-operation in energy development within SADC, providing for the establishment of an Energy Commission, responsible for 'demand-side' management, pricing, ensuring private-sector involvement and competition, training and research, collecting information, etc.; the protocol entered into force in September 1998. SADC implements a Petroleum Exploration Programme. In September 1997 heads of state endorsed an Energy Action Plan to proceed with the implementation of co-operative policies and strategies in four key areas of energy: trade, information exchange, training and organizational capacity-building, and investment and financing. A technical unit of the Energy Commission was to be responsible for implementation of the Action Plan. Two major regional energy supply projects were under development in the mid-2000s: utilities from Angola, Botswana, the DRC, Namibia and South Africa were participating in the Western Power Corridor project, approved in October 2002, and a feasibility study was initiated in 2003 for a planned Zambia–Tanzania Inter-connector Project.

The tourism sector operates within the context of national and regional socio-economic development objectives. It comprises four components: tourism product development; tourism marketing and research; tourism services; and human resources development and training. SADC has promoted tourism for the region at trade fairs in Europe, and has initiated a project to provide a range of promotional material and a regional tourism directory. In 1993 the Council approved the implementation of a project to design a standard grading classification system for tourist accommodation in the region, which had been completed with the assistance of the World Tourism Organization. In September 1997 the legal charter for the establishment of a new Regional Tourism Organization for Southern Africa (RETOSA), to be administered jointly by SADC officials and private-sector operators, was signed by ministers of tourism. RETOSA assists member states to formulate tourism promotion policies and strategies. During 1999 a feasibility study on the development of the Upper Zambezi basin as a site for eco-tourism was initiated. Consultations are under way on the development of a common visa (UNIVISA) system to promote tourism in the region.

SADC aims to promote equitable distribution and effective management of water resources. A Protocol on Shared Watercourse Systems entered into force in April 1998, and a Revised Protocol on Shared Watercourses came into force in September 2003. A regional strategic action plan for integrated water resources development and management in the SADC region was launched in 1999.

FOOD, AGRICULTURE AND NATURAL RESOURCES

The Directorate of Food, Agriculture and Natural Resources aims to develop, co-ordinate and harmonize policies and programmes on agriculture and natural resources with a focus on sustainability. The Directorate covers the following sectors: agricultural research and training; inland fisheries; forestry; wildlife; marine fisheries and resources; food security; livestock production and animal disease control; and environment and land management. According to SADC figures, agriculture contributes one-third of the region's GNP, accounts for about one-quarter of total earnings of foreign exchange and employs some 80% of the labour force. The principal objectives in this field are regional food security, agricultural development and natural resource development.

The Southern African Centre for Co-operation in Agricultural Research (SACCAR), was established in Gaborone, Botswana, in 1985. It aims to strengthen national agricultural research systems, in order to improve management, increase productivity, promote the development and transfer of technology to assist local farmers, and improve training. Examples of activity include: a sorghum and

millet improvement programme; a land and water management research programme; a root crop research network; agroforestry research, implemented in Malawi, Tanzania, Zambia and Zimbabwe; and a grain legume improvement programme, comprising separate research units for groundnuts, beans and cowpeas. SADC's Plant Genetic Resources Centre, based near Lusaka, Zambia, aims to collect, conserve and utilize indigenous and exotic plant genetic resources and to develop appropriate management practices. In 2003 an SADC fact-finding mission on genetically-modified organisms (GMOs) visited Belgium and the USA and made a number of recommendations for consideration by a newly-established advisory committee on biosafety and biotechnology based at the SADC Secretariat; the recommendations were endorsed by senior officials of ministries of agriculture in June. SADC member states were to develop national legislation on GMOs by the end of 2004.

SADC aims to promote inland and marine fisheries as an important, sustainable source of animal protein. Marine fisheries are also considered to be a potential source of income of foreign exchange. In May 1993 the first formal meeting of SADC ministers of marine fisheries convened in Namibia, and it was agreed to hold annual meetings. Meeting in May 2002 marine fisheries ministers expressed concern about alleged ongoing illegal, unregulated and unreported (IUU) fisheries activities in regional waters. The development of fresh water fisheries is focused on aquaculture projects, and their integration into rural community activities. The SADC Fisheries Protocol entered into force in September 2003. Environment and land management activities have an emphasis on sustainability as an essential quality of development. SADC aims to protect and improve the health, environment and livelihoods of people living in the southern African region; to preserve the natural heritage and biodiversity of the region; and to support regional economic development on a sustainable basis. There is also a focus on capacity-building, training, regional co-operation and the exchange of information in all areas related to the environment and land management. SADC operates an Environmental Exchange Network and implements a Land Degradation and Desertification Control Programme. Projects on the conservation and sustainable development of forestry and wildlife are under implementation. An SADC Protocol on Forestry was signed in October 2002, and in November 2003 the Protocol on Wildlife Conservation and Law Enforcement entered into force.

Under the food security programme, the Regional Early Warning Unit aims to anticipate and prevent food shortages through the provision of information relating to the food security situation in member states. As a result of the drought crisis experience, SADC member states have agreed to inform the food security sector of their food and non-food requirements on a regular basis, in order to assess the needs of the region as a whole. A regional food reserve project was also to be developed. In June 2002 SADC predicted a regional cereals deficit of 5.3m. metric tons for 2002/03, owing to both severe drought and flooding, and estimated that 12.8m. people throughout the region would require food assistance, mainly in Lesotho, Malawi, Mozambique, Swaziland, Zambia and Zimbabwe. The SADC Regional Disaster Response Task Force recommended a number of strategies for managing the situation. SADC aims to establish a Regional Strategic Food Reserve Facility, aimed at better prevention of/preparation for potential future emergencies. A programme on irrigation development and water management aims to reduce regional dependency on rain-fed agricultural production, while a programme on the promotion of agricultural trade and food safety aims to increase intra-regional and inter-regional trade with a view to improving agriculture growth and rural incomes. An SADC extraordinary summit on agriculture and food security, held in May 2004 in Dar es Salaam, Tanzania, considered strategies for accelerating development in the agricultural sector and thereby securing food security and reducing poverty in the region. A regional cereals deficit of 1.5m. tons was forecast for 2004/05.

The sector for livestock production and animal disease control has aimed to improve breeding methods in the region through the Management of Farm Animal Genetic Research Programme. It also seeks to control diseases such as contagious bovine pleuropneumonia, foot-and-mouth disease and African swine fever through diagnosis, monitoring and vaccination programmes. An *Animal Health Mortality Bulletin* is published, as is a monthly *Animal Disease Situation Bulletin*, which alerts member states to outbreaks of disease in the region. An emergency audit of foot and mouth cases undertaken in Botswana, Mozambique, South Africa and Zimbabwe during April–May 2003 indicated emergency vaccine requirements amounting to 10m. doses to control the spread of the disease in Zimbabwe. SADC aims to finalize a regional foot-and-mouth disease policy by 2006.

SOCIAL AND HUMAN DEVELOPMENT AND SPECIAL PROGRAMMES

SADC helps to supply the region's requirements in skilled manpower by providing training in the following categories: high-level managerial personnel; agricultural managers; high- and medium-level technicians; artisans; and instructors. The Technical Committee on Accreditation and Certification aims to harmonize and strengthen the education and training systems in SADC through initiatives such as the standardization of curricula and examinations. Human resources development activities focus on determining active labour market information systems and institutions in the region, improving education policy analysis and formulation, and addressing issues of teaching and learning materials in the region. SADC administers an Intra-regional Skills Development Programme. SADC has initiated a programme of distance education to enable greater access to education, and operates a scholarship and training awards programme. In September 1997 heads of state, meeting in Blantyre, Malawi, endorsed the establishment of a Gender Department within the Secretariat to promote the advancement and education of women. A Declaration on Gender and Development was adopted. At the same time representatives of all member countries (except Angola) signed a Protocol on Education and Training, which was to provide a legal framework for co-operation in this sector; this entered into force in July 2000. In 2001 a gender audit study of aspects of the SADC SPA was finalized. An SADC regional human development report for 2000 was published in 2001 by UNDP and the Southern African Regional Institute for Policy Studies. An SADC Protocol on Combating Illicit Drugs entered into force in March 1999. In October 2000 an SADC Epidemiological Network on Drug Use was established to enable the systematic collection of narcotics-related data. SADC operates a regional drugs control programme, funded by the EU.

In August 1999 an SADC Protocol on Health was adopted. SADC has adopted a strategic framework (currently covering the period 2004–07) and programme of action for tackling HIV/AIDS, which are endemic in the region. In December 1999 a multisectoral sub-committee on HIV/AIDS was established. In August 2000 SADC adopted a set of guide-lines to underpin any future negotiations with major pharmaceutical companies on improving access to and reducing the cost of drugs to combat HIV/AIDS. In July 2003 an SADC special summit on HIV/AIDS, convened in Maseru, Lesotho, and attended by representatives of the World Bank, UNAIDS and WHO, issued the Maseru Declaration on HIV/AIDS, identifying priority areas for action, including prevention, access to testing and treatment, and social mobilization. The implementation of the stategic framework and Maseru Declaration were to be co-ordinated through an SADC Business Plan on HIV/AIDS, which was under development in 2004. The Plan was to focus on harmonizing regional guide-lines on mother-to-child transmission and anti-retroviral therapy; and to address issues related to access to affordable essential drugs, including bulk procurement and regional production. An SADC Protocol on Sexually Transmitted Infections Treatment was expected to be adopted by the end of 2007 and a regional policy on Orphans and Vulnerable Children was to be introduced by the end of 2006. SADC is implementing a Southern African Tuberculosis Control Initiative (SATCI); the SATCI TB/HIV Co-ordinator took office in February 2001. In May 2000 an SADC Malaria Task Force was established.

SADC seeks to promote employment and harmonize legislation concerning labour and social protection. Activities include: the implementation of International Labour Standards, the improvement of health and safety standards in the workplace, combating child labour and the establishment of a statistical database for employment and labour issues.

Following the ratification of the treaty establishing the Community, regional socio-cultural development was to be emphasized as part of the process of greater integration. The SADC Press Trust was established, in Harare, Zimbabwe, to disseminate information about SADC and to articulate the concerns and priorities of the region. Public education initiatives have commenced to encourage the involvement of people in the process of regional integration and development, as well as to promote democratic and human rights' values. In 1994 the SADC Festival on Arts and Culture project was initiated. Interdisciplinary and monodisciplinary festivals are alternated on a two-yearly basis. The following monodisciplinary festivals are planned: theatre (in 2008) and visual arts (2012). An SADC Cultural Fund was established in 1996. A draft SADC protocol on piracy and protection of copyright and neighbouring rights has been prepared.

Finance

SADC's administrative budget for 2005/06, approved by the Council in February 2005, amounted to US $37.5m., to be financed mainly by contributions from member states.

Publications

Quarterly Food Security Bulletin.

SACCAR Newsletter (quarterly).

SADC Annual Report.

SADC Energy Bulletin.

SADC Today (six a year).

SATCC Bulletin (quarterly).

SKILLS.

SPLASH.

SOUTHERN COMMON MARKET— MERCOSUR/MERCOSUL

(MERCADO COMÚN DEL SUR/MERCADO COMUM DO SUL)

Address: Edif. Mercosur, Luis Piera 1992, 1°, 11200 Montevideo, Uruguay.

Telephone: (2) 412-9024; **fax:** (2) 418-0557; **e-mail:** sam@mercosur .org.uy; **internet:** www.mercosur.org.uy.

Mercosur (known as Mercosul in Portuguese) was established in March 1991 by the heads of state of Argentina, Brazil, Paraguay and Uruguay with the signature of the Treaty of Asunción. The primary objective of the Treaty is to achieve the economic integration of member states by means of a free flow of goods and services between member states, the establishment of a common external tariff, the adoption of common commercial policy, and the co-ordination of macroeconomic and sectoral policies. The Ouro Preto Protocol, which was signed in December 1994, conferred on Mercosur the status of an international legal entity with the authority to sign agreements with third countries, group of countries and international organizations.

MEMBERS

Argentina	Brazil	Paraguay	Uruguay

Bolivia, Chile, Colombia, Ecuador, Peru and Venezuela are associate members.

Organization

(April 2005)

COMMON MARKET COUNCIL

The Common Market Council (Consejo del Mercado Común) is the highest organ of Mercosur and is responsible for leading the integration process and for taking decisions in order to achieve the objectives of the Asunción Treaty.

COMMON MARKET GROUP

The Common Market Group (Grupo Mercado Común) is the executive body of Mercosur and is responsible for implementing concrete measures to further the integration process.

TRADE COMMISSION

The Trade Commission (Comisión de Comercio del Mercosur) has competence for the area of joint commercial policy and, in particular, is responsible for monitoring the operation of the common external tariff (see below). The Brasília Protocol may be referred to for the resolution of trade disputes between member states.

JOINT PARLIAMENTARY COMMISSION

The Joint Parliamentary Commission (Comisión Parlamentaria Conjunta) is made up of parliamentarians from the member states and is charged with accelerating internal national procedures to implement Mercosur decisions, including the harmonization of country legislation.

CONSULTATIVE ECONOMIC AND SOCIAL FORUM

The Consultative Economic and Social Forum (Foro Consultivo Económico-Social) comprises representatives from the business community and trade unions in the member countries and has a consultative role in relation to Mercosur.

ADMINISTRATIVE SECRETARIAT

Director: REGINALDO BRAGA ARCURI (Brazil).

Activities

Mercosur's free-trade zone entered into effect on 1 January 1995, with tariffs removed from 85% of intra-regional trade. A regime of gradual removal of duties on a list of special products was agreed, with Argentina and Brazil given four years to complete this process while Paraguay and Uruguay were allowed five years. Regimes governing intra-zonal trade in the automobile and sugar sectors remained to be negotiated. Mercosur's customs union also came into force at the start of 1995, comprising a common external tariff of 0%–20%. A list of exceptions from the common external tariff was also agreed; these products were to lose their special status and be subject to the general tariff system concerning foreign goods by 2006. The value of intra-Mercosur trade was estimated to have tripled during the period 1991–95 and was reported to have amounted to US $20,400m. in 1998. However, intra-subregional trade was reported to have declined to $15,200m. in 1999, stabilizing at about 15,000m. in 2000. The financial crisis that escalated in Argentina during late 2001 had a detrimental effect on intra-Mercosur trade.

In December 1995 Mercosur presidents affirmed the consolidation of free trade as Mercosur's 'permanent and most urgent goal'. To this end they agreed to prepare norms of application for Mercosur's customs code, accelerate paper procedures and increase the connections between national computerized systems. It was also agreed to increase co-operation in the areas of agriculture, industry, mining, energy, communications, transport and tourism, and finance. At this meeting Argentina and Brazil reached an accord aimed at overcoming their dispute regarding the trade in automobiles between the two countries. They agreed that cars should have a minimum of 60% domestic components and that Argentina should be allowed to complete its balance of exports of cars to Brazil, which had earlier imposed a unilateral quota on the import of Argentine cars. In June 1995 Mercosur ministers responsible for the environment agreed to harmonize environmental legislation and to form a permanent sub-group of Mercosur

In May 1996 Mercosur parliamentarians met with the aim of harmonizing legislation on patents in member countries. In December Mercosur heads of state, meeting in Fortaleza, Brazil, approved agreements on harmonizing competition practices (by 2001), integrating educational opportunities for post-graduates and human resources training, standardizing trading safeguards applied against third-country products (by 2001) and providing for intra-regional cultural exchanges. An Accord on Subregional Air Services was signed at the meeting (including by the heads of state of Bolivia and Chile) to liberalize civil transport throughout the region. In addition, the heads of state endorsed texts on consumer rights that were to be incorporated into a Mercosur Consumers' Defence Code, and agreed to consider the establishment of a bank to finance the integration and development of the region.

In June 1996 the Joint Parliamentary Commission agreed that Mercosur should endorse a 'Democratic Guarantee Clause', whereby a country would be prevented from participation in Mercosur unless democratic, accountable institutions were in place. The clause was adopted by Mercosur heads of state at the summit meeting held in San Luis de Mendoza, Argentina, later in the month. The presidents approved the entry into Mercosur of Bolivia and Chile as associate members. An Economic Complementation Accord with Bolivia, which includes Bolivia in Mercosur's free-trade zone, but not in the customs union, was signed in December 1995 and was to come into force on 1 January 1997. In December 1996 the Accord was extended until 30 April 1997, when a free-trade zone between Bolivia and Mercosur was to become operational. Measures of the free-trade agreement, which was signed in October 1996, were to be implemented over a transitional period commencing on 28 February 1997 (revised from 1 January). Chile's Economic Complementation Accord with Mercosur entered into effect on 1 October 1996, with duties on most products to be removed over a 10-year period (Chile's most sensitive products were given 18 years for complete tariff

elimination). Chile was also to remain outside the customs union, but was to be involved in other integration projects, in particular infrastructure projects designed to give Mercosur countries access to both the Atlantic and Pacific Oceans (Chile's Pacific coast was regarded as Mercosur's potential link to the economies of the Far East).

In June 1997 the first meeting of tax administrators and customs officials of Mercosur member countries was held, with the aim of enhancing information exchange and promoting joint customs inspections. During 1997 Mercosur's efforts towards regional economic integration were threatened by Brazil's adverse external trade balance and its Government's measures to counter the deficit, which included the imposition of import duties on certain products. In November the Brazilian Government announced that it was to increase its import tariff by 3%, in a further effort to improve its external balance. The measure was endorsed by Argentina as a means of maintaining regional fiscal stability. The new external tariff, which was to remain in effect until 31 December 2000, was formally adopted by Mercosur heads of state at a meeting held in Montevideo, Uruguay, in December 1997. At the summit meeting a separate Protocol was signed providing for the liberalization of trade in services and government purchases over a 10-year period. In order to strengthen economic integration throughout the region, Mercosur leaders agreed that Chile, while still not a full member of the organization, be integrated into the Mercosur political structure, with equal voting rights. In December 1998 Mercosur heads of state agreed on the establishment of an arbitration mechanism for disputes between members, and on measures to standardize human, animal and plant health and safety regulations throughout the grouping. In March 1998 the ministers of the interior of Mercosur countries, together with representatives of the Governments of Chile and Bolivia, agreed to implement a joint security arrangement for the border region linking Argentina, Paraguay and Brazil. In particular, the initiative aimed to counter drugs-trafficking, money-laundering and other illegal activities in the area.

Tensions within Mercosur were compounded in January 1999 owing to economic instability in Brazil and its Government's decision effectively to devalue the national currency, the real. In March the grouping's efforts at integration were further undermined by political instability in Paraguay. As a consequence of the devaluation of its currency, Brazil's important automotive industry became increasingly competitive, to the detriment of that of Argentina. In April Argentina imposed tariffs on imports of Brazilian steel and, in July, the Argentine authorities approved a decree permitting restrictions on all imports from neighbouring countries, in order to protect local industries, prompting Brazil to suspend negotiations to resolve the trading differences between the two countries. Argentina withdrew the decree a few days later, but reiterated its demand for some form of temporary safeguards on certain products as compensation for their perceived loss of competitiveness resulting from the devalued real. An extraordinary meeting of the Common Market Council was convened, at Brazil's request, in August, in order to discuss the dispute, as well as measures to mitigate the effects of economic recession throughout the sub-region. However, little progress was made and the bilateral trade dispute continued to undermine Mercosur. Argentina imposed new restrictions on textiles and footwear, while, in September, Brazil withdrew all automatic import licences for Argentine products, which were consequently to be subject to the same quality control, sanitary measures and accounting checks applied to imports from non-Mercosur countries. The volume of intra-Mercosur trade shrank during 1999 as a consequence of the continuing dispute. In January 2000, however, the Argentine and Brazilian Governments agreed to refrain from adopting potentially divisive unilateral measures and resolved to accelerate negotiations on the resolution of ongoing differences. In March Mercosur determined to promote and monitor private accords to cover the various areas of contention, and also established a timetable for executing a convergence of regional macroeconomic policies. In June Argentina and Brazil signed a bilateral automobile agreement. The motor vehicle agreement, incorporating new tariffs and a nationalization index, was endorsed by all Mercosur leaders at a meeting convened in Florianopolis, Brazil, in December. The significant outcome of that meeting was the approval of criteria, formulated by Mercosur finance ministers and central bank governors, determining monetary and fiscal targets to achieve economic convergence. Annual inflation rates were to be no higher than 5% in 2002–05, and reduced to 4% in 2006 and 3% from 2007 (with an exception for Paraguay). Public debt was to be reduced to 40% of GDP by 2010, and fiscal deficits were to be reduced to no more than 3% of GDP by 2002. The targets aimed to promote economic stability throughout the region, as well as to reduce competitive disparities affecting the unity of the grouping. The Florianopolis summit meeting also recommended the formulation of social indicators to facilitate achieving targets in the reduction of poverty and the elimination of child labour. However, political debate surrounding the meeting was dominated by the Chilean Government's announcement that it had initiated bilateral free-trade discussions with the

USA, which was considered, in particular by the Brazilian authorities, to undermine Mercosur's unified position at multilateral free-trade negotiations. Procedures to incorporate Chile as a full member of Mercosur were suspended. (Chile and the USA concluded negotiations on a bilateral free-trade agreement in December 2002.)

In early 2001 Argentina imposed several emergency measures to strengthen its domestic economy, in contradiction of Mercosur's external tariffs. In March Brazil was reported to have accepted the measures, which included an elimination of tariffs on capital goods and an increase in import duties on consumer goods, as an exceptional temporary trade regime; this position was reversed by mid-2001 following Argentina's decision to exempt certain countries from import tariffs. In February 2002, at a third extraordinary meeting of the Common Market Council, held in Buenos Aires, Argentina, Mercosur heads of state expressed their support for Argentina's application to receive international financial assistance, in the wake of that country's economic crisis. Although there were fears that the crisis might curb trade and stall economic growth across the region, Argentina's adoption of a floating currency made the prospect of currency harmonization between Mercosur member countries appear more viable. During the meeting it was also agreed that a permanent panel to consider trade disputes would be established in Asunción, Paraguay, comprising one legal representative from each of Mercosur's four member countries, plus one 'consensus' member. The summit meeting held in July in Buenos Aires, Argentina, adopted an agreement providing for reduced tariffs and increased quotas in the grouping's automotive sector, with a view to establishing a fully liberalized automotive market by 2006. In December 2002 Mercosur ministers of justice signed an agreement permitting citizens of Mercosur member and associate member states to reside in any other Mercosur state, initially for a two-year period. At a summit convened in Asunción in June 2003 heads of state of the four member countries agreed to strengthen integration of the bloc and to harmonize all import tariffs by 2006, thus creating the basis for a single market. They also agreed to establish a directly-elected Mercosur legislature by 2006. The July 2004 summit of Mercosur heads of state announced that an Asunción-based five-member tribunal responsible for ruling on appeals in cases of disputes between member countries was to become operational in the following month. Peru and Venezuela became Mercosur's third and fourth associate members, respectively, in December 2003 and July 2004. Colombia and Ecuador were granted associate membership in December 2004. In July of that year Mexico was invited to attend all meetings of the organization with a view to future accession to associate membership. Bilateral negotiations on a free-trade agreement between Mexico and Mercosur had been initiated in 2001.

EXTERNAL RELATIONS

In December 1995 Mercosur and the EU signed a framework agreement for commercial and economic co-operation, which provided for co-operation in the economic, trade, industrial, scientific, institutional and cultural fields and the promotion of wider political dialogue on issues of mutual interest. In June 1997 Mercosur heads of state, convened in Asunción, reaffirmed the group's intention to pursue trade negotiations with the EU, Mexico and the Andean Community, as well as to negotiate as a single economic bloc in discussions with regard to the establishment of a Free Trade Area of the Americas (FTAA). Chile and Bolivia were to be incorporated into these negotiations. During 1997 negotiations to establish a free-trade accord with the Andean Community were hindered by differences regarding schedules for tariff elimination and Mercosur's insistence on a local content of 60% to qualify for rules of origin preferences. However, in April 1998 the two groupings signed an accord that committed them to the establishment of a free-trade area by January 2000. Negotiations in early 1999 failed to conclude an agreement on preferential tariffs between the two blocs, and the existing arrangements were extended on a bilateral basis. In March the Andean Community agreed to initiate free-trade negotiations with Brazil; a preferential tariff agreement was concluded in July. In

August 2000 a similar agreement between the Community and Argentina entered into force. In September leaders of Mercosur and the Andean Community, meeting at a summit of Latin American heads of state, determined to relaunch negotiations. The establishment of a mechanism to support political dialogue and co-ordination between the two groupings, which aimed to enhance the integration process, was approved at the first joint meeting of ministers of foreign affairs in July 2001. In April 2004 Mercosur and the Andean Community signed a free-trade accord, providing for tarrifs on 80% of trade between the two groupings to be phased out by 2014 and for tariffs to be removed from the remaining 20% of, initially protected, products by 2019. The entry into force of the accord, scheduled for 1 July 2004, was postponed owing to delays in drafting the tariff reduction schedule. Negotiations between Mercosur and the EU on the conclusion of an Association Agreement commenced in 1999 and were ongoing in 2005. In March 2003 Argentina and Brazil, with the backing of other Mercosur member states, formed the Southern Agricultural Council (CAS), which was to represent the interests of the grouping as a whole in negotiations with third countries. In December 2004 leaders from 12 Latin American countries (excluding Argentina, Ecuador, Paraguay and Uruguay) attending a pan-South American summit, convened in Cuzco, Peru, approved in principle the creation of a new South American Community of Nations. It was envisaged that negotiations on the formation of the new Community, which was to entail the merger of Mercosur, the Andean Community and the Rio Group, would be completed within 15 years.

In March 1998 ministers of trade of 34 countries agreed a detailed framework for negotiations on the establishment of the FTAA. Mercosur secured support for its request that a separate negotiating group be established to consider issues relating to agriculture, as one of nine key sectors to be discussed. The FTAA negotiating process was formally initiated by heads of state of the 34 countries meeting in Santiago, Chile, in April 1998. In June Mercosur and Canada signed a Trade and Investment Co-operation Arrangement, which aimed to remove obstacles to trade and to increase economic co-operation between the two signatories. In July the European Commission proposed obtaining a mandate to commence negotiations with Mercosur and Chile towards a free-trade agreement, which, it was envisaged, would provide for the elimination of tariffs over a period of 10 years. However, Mercosur requested that the EU abolish agricultural subsidies as part of any accord. Negotiations between Mercosur, Chile and the EU were initiated in April 2000. Specific discussion of tariff reductions and market access commenced at the fifth round of negotiations, held in July 2001, at which the EU proposed a gradual elimination of tariffs on industrial imports over a 10-year period and an extension of access quotas for agricultural products. The summit meeting held in December 2000 was attended by the President of South Africa, and it was agreed that Mercosur would initiate free-trade negotiations with that country. (These commenced in October 2001.) In June 2001 Mercosur leaders agreed to pursue efforts to conclude a bilateral trade agreement with the USA, an objective previously opposed by the Brazilian authorities, while reaffirming their commitment to the FTAA process. Leaders attending a special summit of the Americas, convened in January 2004 in Monterrey, Mexico, did not specify a completion date for the ongoing negotiations on the FTAA, although they adopted a declaration committing themselves to its eventual establishment.

Finance

The annual budget for the secretariat is contributed by the four full member states.

Publication

Boletín Oficial del Mercosur (quarterly).

WESTERN EUROPEAN UNION—WEU

Address: 15 rue de l'Association, 1000 Brussels, Belgium.

Telephone: (2) 500-44-50; **fax:** (2) 500-44-70; **e-mail:** ueo
.secretarygeneral@skynet.be; **internet:** www.weu.int.

Based on the Brussels Treaty of 1948, the Western European Union
(WEU) was set up in 1955 as an intergovernmental organization for
European co-operation in the field of security and defence. In the
1990s WEU was developed as the defence component of the European Union—EU, and as the means of strengthening the European
pillar of the Atlantic Alliance under NATO. However, in June 1999
the European Council resolved to formulate a common European
security and defence policy, incorporating the main crisis management responsibilities of WEU. Consequently, WEU relinquished
these functions to the EU by July 2001. WEU's residual functions
include commitments relating to collective defence, institutional
dialogue within the Assembly of Western European Union, support
to related armaments co-operation bodies, and other administrative
tasks.

MEMBERS*

Belgium	Luxembourg
France	Netherlands
Germany	Portugal
Greece	Spain
Italy	United Kingdom

* WEU has invited the other members of the EU to join the organ-
ization and has invited other European members of NATO to
become Associate Members to enable them to participate fully in
WEU activities. In November 1992 Denmark and Ireland took up
observer status and on 1 January 1995 Austria, Finland and
Sweden became Observers following their accession to the EU.
Associate Member status was granted to Iceland, Norway and
Turkey in November 1992. Associate Partner status was granted to
Bulgaria, the Czech Republic, Estonia, Hungary, Latvia, Lith-
uania, Poland, Romania and Slovakia in May 1994 and to Slovenia
in June 1996. The Czech Republic, Hungary and Poland became
Associate Partners in March 1999.

Organization

(April 2005)

COUNCIL

The Council is WEU's main body and is organized so as to be able to
function on a permanent basis and may be convened as necessary at
any time at the request of a member state. The Permanent Council,
chaired by the WEU Secretary-General, is the central body responsible for day-to-day management of the organization and for
assigning tasks to and co-ordinating the activities of the various
working groups. It is composed of permanent representatives, supported by military delegates, and meets as often as required. The
presidency of the Council is rotated between member states on a six-
monthly basis. Since July 2001 two Council working groups have
been operational: the Budget and Organization Committee and an
ad hoc group concerned with other administrative matters.

SECRETARIAT-GENERAL

Secretary-General: Dr JAVIER SOLANA MADARIAGA (Spain).

WEU's Secretariat also headquarters the secretariats of the
Western European Armaments Group (WEAG), a forum for armaments co-operation, and the Western European Armaments Organization (WEAO), which operates as a research cell.

ASSEMBLY

43 ave du Président Wilson, 75775 Paris Cédex 16, France; tel. 1-53-
67-22-00; fax 1-53-67-22-01; e-mail info@assembly.weu.int; internet
www.assembly-weu.org.

The Assembly of Western European Union is composed of the
representatives of the Brussels Treaty powers to the Parliamentary
Assembly of the Council of Europe. It meets at least twice a year,
usually in Paris. The Assembly may proceed on any matter
regarding the application of the Brussels Treaty and on any matter
submitted to the Assembly for an opinion by the Council. Resolutions
may be adopted in cases where this form is considered appropriate.
When so directed by the Assembly, the President transmits such
resolutions to international organizations, governments and
national parliaments. An annual report is presented to the Assembly
by the Council. In March 2000 an extraordinary meeting of the

Assembly determined to initiate a process of transforming the body
into the European Security and Defence Assembly (ESDA).

President: STEF GORIS (Belgium).

PERMANENT COMMITTEES OF THE ASSEMBLY

There are permanent committees on: Political Defence Questions;
Technological and Aerospace Questions; Budgetary Affairs and
Administration; Rules of Procedure and Privileges; and Parlia-
mentary and Public Relations.

Activities

The Brussels Treaty was signed in 1948 by Belgium, France, Luxembourg, the Netherlands and the United Kingdom. It foresaw the
potential for international co-operation in Western Europe and
provided for collective defence and collaboration in economic, social
and cultural activities. Within this framework, NATO and the
Council of Europe (see chapters) were formed in 1949.

On the collapse in 1954 of plans for a European Defence Community, a nine-power conference was convened in London to try to
reach a new agreement. This conference's decisions were embodied
in a series of formal agreements drawn up by a ministerial conference held in Paris in October. The agreements entailed: arrangements for the Brussels Treaty to be strengthened and modified to
include the Federal Republic of Germany and Italy, the ending of the
occupation regime in the Federal Republic of Germany, and the
invitation to the latter to join NATO. These agreements were ratified on 6 May 1955, on which date the seven-power Western European Union came into being. WEU was reactivated in October 1984
by restructuring its organization and by holding more frequent
ministerial meetings, in order to harmonize members' views on
defence questions, arms control and disarmament, developments in
East-West relations, Europe's contribution to the Atlantic alliance,
and European armaments co-operation.

In April 1990 ministers of foreign affairs and defence discussed
the implications of recent political changes in central and eastern
Europe, and mandated WEU to develop contacts with democratically elected governments there. In June 1992 an extraordinary
meeting of WEU's Ministerial Council with the ministers of defence
and foreign affairs of Hungary, Czechoslovakia, Poland, Romania,
Bulgaria, Estonia, Latvia and Lithuania agreed on measures to
enhance co-operation. The ministers were to meet annually, while a
forum of consultation was to be established between the WEU
Council and the ambassadors of the countries concerned, which was
to meet at least twice a year. The focus of consultations was to be the
security structure and political stability of Europe; the future development of the CSCE (now the OSCE); and arms control and disarmament, in particular the implementation of the Treaty on Conventional Armed Forces in Europe (the CFE Treaty) and the 'Open
Skies' Treaty (see NATO for both). In May 1994 the Council of
Ministers, meeting in Luxembourg, issued the Kirchberg Declaration, according the nine countries concerned (including the Czech
Republic and Slovakia, which were the legal successors to Czechoslovakia) the status of Associate Partners of WEU, thereby suspending
the forum of consultation.

The EC Treaty on European Union, which was agreed at Maastricht, in the Netherlands, in December 1991, and entered into force
on 1 November 1993, referred to WEU as an 'integral part of the
development of European Union' and requested WEU 'to elaborate
and implement decisions and actions of the Union which have
defence implications'. The Treaty also committed EU member countries to the 'eventual framing of a common defence policy which
might in time lead to a common defence'. A separate declaration,
adopted by WEU member states in Maastricht, defined WEU's role
as being the defence component of the European Union but also as
the instrument for strengthening the European pillar of the Atlantic
Alliance, thus maintaining a role for NATO in Europe's defence and
retaining WEU's identity as distinct from that of the EU. In January
1993 WEU's Council and Secretariat-General moved to Brussels
(from Paris and London, respectively), in order to promote closer co-
operation with both the EU and NATO, which have their headquarters there.

In June 1992 WEU ministers of defence and foreign affairs convened in Petersberg, Germany, to consider the implementation of
the Maastricht decisions. In the resulting 'Petersberg Declaration'
member states declared that they were prepared to make available
military units from the whole spectrum of their conventional armed
forces for military tasks conducted under the authority of WEU. In
addition to contributing to the common defence in accordance with

Article V of the modified Brussels Treaty, three categories of missions were identified for the possible employment of military units under the aegis of WEU: humanitarian and rescue tasks; peace-keeping tasks; and crisis management, including peace-making. (Missions of this kind are often described as 'Petersberg tasks'.) The Petersberg Declaration stated that WEU was prepared to support peace-keeping activities of the CSCE and UN Security Council on a case-by-case basis. A WEU planning cell was established in Brussels in October, which was to be responsible for preparing contingency plans for the employment of forces under WEU auspices for humanitarian operations, peace-keeping and crisis-management activities. It was expected that the same military units identified by member states for deployment under NATO would be used for military operations under WEU: this arrangement was referred to as 'double-hatting'. In May 1995 WEU ministers, convened in Lisbon, Portugal, agreed to strengthen WEU's operational capabilities through new structures and mechanisms, including the establishment of a politico-military group to advise on crises and crisis management, a Situation Centre able to monitor WEU operations and support decisions taken by the Council, and an Intelligence Section within the planning cell. WEU rules of engagement, with a view to implementing the missions identified in the Petersberg Declaration, were to be formulated.

In January 1994 NATO heads of state gave their full support to the development of a European Security and Defence Identity (ESDI) and to the strengthening of WEU. They declared their readiness to make collective assets of the Alliance available for WEU operations, and endorsed the concept of Combined Joint Task Forces (CJTFs), which was to provide separable, but not separate, military capabilities that could be employed by either organization. In May 1996 NATO and WEU signed a security agreement, which provided for the protection and shared use of classified information. In June NATO ministers, meeting in Berlin, Germany, agreed on a framework of measures to enable the implementation of the CJTF concept and the development of an ESDI within the Alliance. WEU was to be permitted to request the use of a CJTF headquarters for an operation under its command and to use Alliance planning capabilities and military infrastructure. In May 1998 the Council of both organizations approved a set of consultation arrangements as a guide to co-operation in a crisis situation. A framework document on principles and guide-lines for detailed practicalities of cases where NATO assets and/or capabilities were loaned to WEU was subsequently prepared.

In November 1994 a WEU ministerial meeting in Noordwijk, the Netherlands, adopted a set of preliminary conclusions on the formulation of a common European defence policy. The role and place of WEU in further European institutional arrangements were addressed by the EU's Intergovernmental Conference, which commenced in March 1996. The process was concluded in June 1997 with agreement having been reached on the Treaty of Amsterdam. The Treaty, which was signed in October and entered into force on 1 May 1999, confirmed WEU as providing the EU with access to operational capability for undertaking the Petersberg tasks, which were incorporated into the revised Treaty. It advocated enhanced EU-WEU co-operation and referred to the possible integration of WEU into the EU, should the European Council so decide (the United Kingdom being the main opponent). Following the entry into force of the Treaty of Amsterdam WEU and the EU approved a set of arrangements for enhanced co-operation. In June the EU determined to strengthen its common security and defence policy, and initiated a process of assuming direct responsibility for the Petersberg tasks. Javier Solana was appointed as the EU's first High Representative for foreign and security policy, and subsequently named as the new WEU Secretary-General, providing for the highest level of co-operation between the two organizations. In November WEU ministers adopted a series of recommendations, based on the results of an audit of assets, to enable European countries to respond rapidly to conduct crisis management operations, to enhance collective capabilities in strategic intelligence and planning, and to strengthen military air, sea and transport equipment and capabilities for use in humanitarian and peace-keeping operations. By July 2001 the transfer of WEU's crisis management functions to the EU had been finalized, leaving commitments relating to collective defence as WEU's key focus area. The EU assumed responsibility for two former subsidiary bodies of WEU (a Satellite Centre and the Paris-based Institute for Strategic Studies) in January 2002. The remaining functions of the restructured WEU related to the provision of military and other aid and assistance should a member state become the object of an armed attack in Europe, as provided for under the Brussels Treaty; institutional dialogue within the Assembly, support to the Western European Armaments Group and the Western European Armaments Organization, and other administrative tasks.

In the early 1990s WEU's operational capabilities were substantially developed. From mid-July 1992 warships and aircraft of WEU members undertook a monitoring operation in the Adriatic Sea, in co-ordination with NATO, to ensure compliance with the UN Security Council's resolutions imposing a trade and armaments embargo on Serbia and Montenegro. In mid-November the UN Security Council gave the NATO/WEU operation the power to search vessels suspected of attempting to flout the embargo. In June 1993 the Councils of WEU and NATO agreed to establish a unified command for the operation, which was to implement a Security Council resolution to strengthen the embargo against Serbia and Montenegro. Under the agreement, the Councils were to exert joint political control, and military instructions were to be co-ordinated within a joint *ad hoc* headquarters. In April WEU ministers offered civil assistance to Bulgaria, Hungary and Romania in enforcing the UN embargo on the Danube, and a monitoring mission began operations in June. In June 1996 the NATO/WEU naval monitoring mission in the Adriatic Sea was suspended, following the decision of the UN Security Council to remove the embargo on the delivery of armaments to the former Yugoslavia. WEU provided assistance for the administration of Mostar, Bosnia and Herzegovina, for which the EU assumed responsibility in July 1994.

In May 1997 WEU dispatched a Multinational Advisory Police Element (MAPE) to Albania to provide training and advice on restructuring the police force in that country. By the end of 1999 a new State Police Law, formulated with MAPE's support, had been ratified by the Albanian legislature, while some 3,000 police officers had been trained at centres in Tirana and Dürres and through field programmes. In February the WEU Council approved plans for an enhanced MAPE, with greater geographical coverage and operational mobility, with an initial mandate until April 2000. MAPE was being conducted by WEU at the request of the EU, enabling a large part of the costs to be met from the EU budget. In response to the escalation of conflict in the Serbian province of Kosovo and Metohija in 1999, MAPE assisted the Albanian authorities to establish an Emergency Crisis Group to help to administer and to assist the massive refugee population which entered Albania in March and April. MAPE terminated its operational activities in Albania on 31 May 2001.

In April 1999 WEU and Croatia signed an agreement to establish a WEU De-mining Assistance Mission (WEUDAM) in that country, upon a request by the Council of the EU. WEUDAM, which commenced activities in May, provided advice, technical expertise and training to the Croatian Mine Action Centre. WEUDAM was terminated on 31 November 2001.

In May 1992 France and Germany announced their intention to establish a joint defence force, the 'Eurocorps', which was to be based in Strasbourg, France, and which was intended to provide a basis for a European army under the aegis of WEU. This development caused concern among some NATO member countries, particularly the USA and United Kingdom, which feared that it represented a fresh attempt (notably on the part of France, which is outside NATO's military structure) to undermine the Alliance's role in Europe. In November, however, France and Germany stated that troops from the joint force could serve under NATO military command. This principle was recognized in an agreement signed in January 1993, which established links between the proposed joint force and NATO's military structure. In June Belgium opted to participate in the Eurocorps. In December Spain agreed to provide troops for the force. Luxembourg agreed to participate in May 1994. Eurocorps formally became operational on 30 November 1995. In June 1999 EU ministers decided that Eurocorps was to be transformed into a rapid reaction force, under EU authority. In May 1995 France, Italy, Spain and Portugal announced the establishment of two new forces, which were to be at the disposal of WEU as well as NATO and the UN: EUROFOR, consisting of up to 14,000 ground troops, to be based in Florence, Italy; and EUROMARFOR, a maritime force serving the Mediterranean. A number of other multinational forces are also designated as forces answerable to WEU (FAWEU) or that were to be available to WEU: the Multinational Division (Central), comprising Belgium, Germany, the Netherlands and the United Kingdom; the Headquarters of the First German-Netherlands Corps; the United Kingdom-Netherlands Amphibious Force; the Spanish-Italian Amphibious Force; and the European Air Group (EAG), comprising Belgium, France, Germany, Italy, Netherlands, Spain and the United Kingdom.

Publications

Account of the Session (WEU Assembly, 2 a year).

Annual Report of the Council.

Assembly of Western European Union: Texts adopted and Brief Account of the Session (2 a year).

Assembly documents and reports.

WORLD CONFEDERATION OF LABOUR—WCL

Address: 33 rue de Trèves, 1040 Brussels, Belgium.
Telephone: (2) 285-47-00; **fax:** (2) 230-87-22; **e-mail:** info@cmt-wcl
.org; **internet:** www.cmt-wcl.org.
Founded in 1920 as the International Federation of Christian Trade
Unions (IFCTU); reconstituted under present title in 1968. (See also
the International Confederation of Free Trade Unions and the World
Federation of Trade Unions.)

MEMBERS

Affiliated national federations and trade union internationals; about
30m. members in 116 countries.

Organization

(April 2005)

CONGRESS

The supreme and legislative authority, which convenes every four
years (October 2001: Bucharest, Romania). Congress consists of
delegates from national confederations and trade internationals.
Delegates have votes according to the size of their organization.
Congress receives official reports, elects the Executive Board, considers the future programme and any proposals.

CONFEDERAL BOARD

The Board meets annually, and consists of 47 members (including 23
representatives of national confederations and eight representatives
of trade internationals) elected by Congress from among its members for four-year terms. It issues executive directions and instructions to the Secretariat.

SECRETARIAT-GENERAL

Secretary-General: WILLY THYS (Belgium).

Deputy Secretaries-General: EDUARDO ESTÉVEZ (Argentina), JAAP
WIENEN (Netherlands).

REGIONAL AND OTHER OFFICES

Africa: Democratic Organization of African Workers' Trade Unions
(ODSTA), BP 4401, Route International d'Atakpamé, Lomé, Togo;
tel. 250710; fax 256113; e-mail odsta@café.tg; Pres. BENYDIN TOOL-
SYRAJ.

Asia: Brotherhood of Asian Trade Unionists (BATU), POB 163,
Manila, Philippines; tel. (2) 500709; fax (2) 5218335; e-mail
necielucero@eastern.com.ph; Pres. J. TAN.

Latin America: Latin-American Confederation of Workers (CLAT),
Apdo 6681, Caracas 1010, Venezuela; tel. (32) 720794; fax (32)
720463; e-mail clat@telcel.net.ve; internet www.clat.org; Sec.-Gen.
EDUARDO GARCÍA.

North America: c/o National Alliance of Postal and Federal
Employees, 1628 11th St, NW, Washington, DC 20001, USA; tel.
(202) 939-6325; fax (202) 939-6389; e-mail jmcgee@napfe.org; Pres.
JAMES MCGEE.

Eastern Europe Liaison Office: Bucharest, Splaiul Indepen-
dentei, nr 202, cam. 324, Sector 6, Romania; tel. and fax (1) 3101586;
e-mail cmtest@cartelalfa.ro.

Geneva Liaison Office: CP 122, 1 rue de Varembé, 1211 Geneva
20, Switzerland; tel. (22) 7482080; fax (22) 7482088; e-mail herve
.sea@cmt-wcl.org; e-mail ramon.vivanco@cmt-wcl.org.

INTERNATIONAL INSTITUTES OF TRADE UNION
STUDIES

Africa: Fondation panafricaine pour le développement économique,
social et culturel (Fopadesc), Lomé, Togo.

Asia: BATU Social Institute, Manila, Philippines.

Latin America:
Instituto Andino de Estudios Sociales, Lima, Peru
Instituto Centro-Americano de Estudios Sociales (ICAES), San José,
  Costa Rica
Instituto del Cono Sur (INCASUR), Buenos Aires, Argentina
Instituto de Formación del Caribe, Willemstad, Curaçao, Nether-
  lands Antilles
Universidad de Trabajadores de América Latina (UTAL).

Finance

Income is derived from affiliation dues, contributions, donations and
capital interest.

Publications

Tele-flash (every 2 weeks).
Labor magazine (3 a year).
Reports of Congresses; Study Documents.

International Trade Union Federations

Federation of Professional Sportsmen: rue des Chartreux 70,
1040 Brussels, Belgium; tel. (2) 500-28-32; fax (2) 500-28-39; e-mail
sporta@acv-csv.be; Sec. DIRK DE VOS.

**International Federation of Textile and Clothing Workers—
IFTC:** 33 rue de Trèves, 1040 Brussels, Belgium; tel. (9) 285-47-36;
fax (9) 230-87-22; e-mail piet.nelissen@cmt-wcl.org; f. 1901; mems:
unions covering 800,000 workers in 39 countries; Organization:
Congress (every three years), Board, Exec. Committee; Pres. DIRK
UYTTENHOVE (Belgium); Gen. Sec. JAAP JONGEJAN (Netherlands).

**International Federation of Trade Unions of Employees in
Public Service—INFEDOP:** 33 rue de Trèves, 1040 Brussels,
Belgium; tel. (2) 230-38-65; fax (2) 231-14-72; e-mail info@
infedop-eurofedop.com; f. 1922; mems: national federations of
workers in public service, covering 4m. workers; Organization:
World Congress (at least every five years), World Confederal Board
(meets every year), 10 Trade Groups, Secretariat; Pres. FRITZ NEU-
GEBAUER (Austria); publ. _Servus_ (monthly).

> **European Federation of Employees in Public Services—
> EUROFEDOP:** 33 rue de Trèves, 1040 Brussels, Belgium; tel. (2)
> 230-38-65; fax (2) 231-14-72; e-mail info@infedop-eurofedop.com;
> internet www.eurofedop.org; Chair. FRITZ NEUGEBAUER (Austria);
> Sec.-Gen. BERT VAN CAELENBERG (Belgium).

**International Federation of Trade Unions of Transport
Workers—FIOST:** 33 rue de Trèves, 1040 Brussels, Belgium; tel.
(2) 285-47-35; fax (2) 230-87-22; e-mail olga.nicolae@cmt-wcl.org;
internet www.cmt-wcl.org; f. 1921; mems: national federations in 28
countries covering 600,000 workers; Organization: Congress (every
four years), Committee (meets twice a year), Executive Board; Pres.
MICHEL BOVY (Belgium); Exec. Sec. OLGA NICOLAE (Belgium).

World Confederation of Teachers—WCT: 33 rue de Trèves, 1040
Brussels, Belgium; tel. (2) 285-47-29; fax (2) 230-87-22; e-mail ;
internet www.wctcsme.org; f. 1963; mems: national federations of
unions concerned with teaching; Organization: Congress (every four
years), Council (at least once a year), Steering Committee; Pres.
CLAUDIO CORRIES; Sec.-Gen. GASTON DE LA HAYE.

**World Federation of Agriculture, Food, Hotel and Allied
Workers—WFAFW:** 33 rue de Trèves, 1040 Brussels, Belgium; tel.
(2) 285-47-35; fax (2) 230-87-22; e-mail olga.nicolae@cmt-wcl.org;
internet www.cmt-wcl.org; f. 1982; merger of former World Federation of Agricultural Workers and World Federation of Workers in
the Food, Drink, Tobacco and Hotel Industries; mems: national
federations covering 2,800,000 workers in 38 countries; Organization: Congress (every five years), World Board, Daily Management Board; Pres. CARLOS ANCIZAR RICO (Colombia); Exec. Sec. OLGA
NICOLAE (Belgium); Gen. Sec. TIMOTHÉE T. BOKO (Benin).

**World Federation of Building and Woodworkers Unions—
WFBW:** 33 rue de Trèves, 1040 Brussels, Belgium; tel. (2) 285-47-33;
fax (2) 230-87-22; e-mail piet.nelissen@cmt-wcl.org;; internet
www.wflw-fmcb.org; f. 1936; mems: national federations
covering 2,438,000 workers in several countries; Organization: Congress, Bureau, Permanent Secretariat; Pres. JACKY JACKERS; Sec.-
Gen. BERT VAN DER SPEK (Netherlands); publ. _Bulletin_.

World Federation of Clerical Workers—WFCW: 33 rue de
Trèves, 1040 Brussels, Belgium; tel. (2) 285-47-35; fax (2) 230-87-22;
e-mail olga.nicolae@cmt-wcl.org; internet www.cmt-wcl.org; f. 1921;
mems: national federations of unions and professional associations
covering 700,000 workers in 57 countries; Organization: Congress
(every four years), Council, Executive Board, Secretariat; Pres.
ERNST GFRERER (Austria); Sec. OLGA NICOLAE.

World Federation of Industry Workers—WFIW: 33 rue de Trèves, 1040 Brussels, Belgium; e-mail isabelle.voss@cmt-wcl.org; f. 1985; mems: regional and national federations covering about 600,000 workers in 45 countries; Organization: Congress (every five years), World Board (every year), Executive Committee, six World Trade Councils; Pres. BART BRUGGEMAN; Gen. Sec. ITALO RODOMONTI.

WORLD COUNCIL OF CHURCHES—WCC

Address: 150 route de Ferney, POB 2100, 1211 Geneva 2, Switzerland.

Telephone: (22) 7916111; **fax:** (22) 7910361; **e-mail:** infowcc@wcc-coe.org; **internet:** www.wcc-coe.org.

The Council was founded in 1948 to promote co-operation between Christian Churches and to prepare for a clearer manifestation of the unity of the Church.

MEMBERS

There are 347 member Churches in more than 120 countries. Chief denominations: Anglican, Baptist, Congregational, Lutheran, Methodist, Moravian, Old Catholic, Orthodox, Presbyterian, Reformed and Society of Friends. The Roman Catholic Church is not a member but sends official observers to meetings.

Organization

(April 2005)

ASSEMBLY

The governing body of the World Council, consisting of delegates of the member Churches, it meets every seven or eight years to frame policy and consider some main themes. It elects the Presidents of the Council, who serve as members of the Central Committee. The eighth Assembly was held at Harare, Zimbabwe, in December 1998. The ninth Assembly was to be held in Porto Alegre, Brazil, in 2006.

Presidium: Dr AGNES ABOUM (Kenya), Rev. KATHRYN K. BANNISTER (USA), Bishop JABEZ L. BRYCE (Fiji), His Eminence CHRYSOSTOMOS OF EPHESUS (Greece), Dr MOON-KYU KANG (Republic of Korea), Bishop FEDERICO J. PAGURA (Argentina), Bishop EBERHARDT RENZ (Germany), His Holiness IGNATIUS ZAKKA I (Syria).

CENTRAL COMMITTEE

Appointed by the Assembly to carry out its policies and decisions, the Committee consists of 158 members chosen from Assembly delegates. It meets every 12 to 18 months.

The Central Committee comprises the Programme Committee and the Finance Committee. Within the Programme Committee there are advisory groups on issues relating to communication, women, justice, peace and creation, youth, ecumenical relations, and inter-religious relations. There are also five commissions and boards.

Moderator: His Holiness ARAM I (CATHOLICOS OF CILICIA) (Armenian Apostolic Church, Lebanon).

Vice-Moderators: Justice SOPHIA O. A. ADINYIRA (Ghana), Dr MARION S. BEST (Canada).

EXECUTIVE COMMITTEE

Consists of the Presidents, the Officers and 20 members chosen by the Central Committee from its membership to prepare its agenda, expedite its decisions and supervise the work of the Council between meetings of the Central Committee. Meets every six months.

GENERAL SECRETARIAT

The General Secretariat implements the policies laid down by the WCC and co-ordinates the Council's work through seven divisions: Church and Ecumenical Relations; Interreligious Relations and Dialogue; Human Resources and Technical Services; Finance; Budgeting and Planning; Public Information; and Publications and Research (including the Ecumenical Library). The General Secretariat is also responsible for an Ecumenical Institute, at Bossey, Switzerland, which provides training in ecumenical leadership.

General Secretary: Rev. Dr SAMUEL KOBIA (Kenya).

Activities

The WCC's activities are organized under five 'historic' themes: faith and order; mission and ecumenical formation; justice, peace and creation; international affairs, peace and human security; and Dia-

konia (Christian service) and Solidarity. Special programmes include the Decade to Overcome Violence (2001–10), the Ecumenical Accompaniment Programme in Palestine and Israel (EAPPI), the Ecumenical Focus on Africa, and the Ecumenical HIV/AIDS Initiative in Africa (EHAIA).

FAITH AND ORDER

The World Council's Faith and Order programme promotes unity among different Christian confessions. The Council organizes meetings of theologians to address means of resolving potentially divisive so-called 'boundary' issues that define and differentiate the various member communities. In 2004 the following boundary questions were under consideration: ecclesiology; baptism; hermeneutics; theological anthropology; ethnic identity, national identity and the search for unity; theological reflection on peace; worship; and ministries of women in the Church.

MISSION AND ECUMENICAL FORMATION

During 2003–05 the WCC was undertaking preparations for the World Mission Conference, scheduled to be held in Athens, Greece, in 2005, on the theme of healing and reconciliation. The Council also works with churches and associated organizations (such as schools, colleges and seminaries) and networks to promote ecumenical learning.

JUSTICE, PEACE AND CREATION

The Justice, Peace and Creation programme promotes the values and practices underpinning a culture of peace, and promotes a culture of solidarity between young people, women, indigenous and oppressed populations.

INTERNATIONAL AFFAIRS, PEACE AND SECURITY

The International Affairs, Peace and Human Security programme addresses and provides information on public issues, such as international political trends (e.g. global security), and on international crises and critical processes, such as the Israeli–Palestinian conflict and the situation in Iraq. Through the programme the Council offers an ecumenical forum and guidance on human rights and religious freedom, disarmament and arms control, peace and conflict resolution, global governance, and truth and reconciliation. The Council maintains consultative relations with the United Nations.

DIAKONIA AND SOLIDARITY

The programme on *Diakonia* and Solidarity is founded on principles and values approved at ecumenical consultations held in Larnaca, Cyprus, in 1986 and at El Escorial, Spain in 1987. The programme aims to to promote just relationships (based on shared power and resources) between member churches and to encourage member churches and related bodies to support the marginalized and excluded.

Finance

The main contributors to the WCC's budget are the churches and their agencies, with funds for certain projects contributed by other organizations. The 2003 budget amounted to 46.8m. Swiss francs.

Publications

Catalogue of periodicals, books and audio-visuals.
Current Dialogue (2 a year).
Ecumenical News International (weekly).
Ecumenical Review (quarterly).
International Review of Mission (quarterly).
Ministerial Formation (quarterly).
Overcoming Violence (quarterly).
WCC News (quarterly).
WCC Yearbook.

WORLD FEDERATION OF TRADE UNIONS—WFTU

Address: POB 80, 14200 Prague 4, Czech Republic.
Telephone: (2) 4446-2085; **fax:** (2) 4446-1378; **e-mail:** wftu@login
.cz; **internet:** www.wftu.cz.

The Federation was founded in 1945, on a world-wide basis. A number of members withdrew from the Federation in 1949 to establish the International Confederation of Free Trade Unions (see p. 273). (See also the World Confederation of Labour (see p. 354).)

MEMBERS

Affiliated or associated national federations (including the six Trade Unions Internationals) in 126 countries representing some 135m. individuals.

Organization

(April 2005)

WORLD TRADE UNION CONGRESS

The Congress meets every five years. It reviews WFTU's work, endorses reports from the executives, and elects the General Council. The size of the delegations is based on the total membership of national federations. The Congress is also open to participation by non-affiliated organizations. The 14th Congress was held in New Delhi, India, in March 2000. The 15th Congress was scheduled to be convened in Havana, Cuba, in November 2005, marking the 60th anniversary of the founding of the organization.

GENERAL COUNCIL

The General Council meets three times between Congresses, and comprises members and deputies elected by Congress from nominees of national federations. Every affiliated or associated organization and Trade Unions International has one member and one deputy member.

The Council receives reports from the Presidential Council, approves the plan and budget and elects officers.

PRESIDENTIAL COUNCIL

The Presidential Council meets twice a year and conducts most of the executive work of WFTU. It comprises a President, elected each year from among its members, the General Secretary and 18 Vice-Presidents.

SECRETARIAT

The Secretariat consists of the General Secretary, and six Deputy General Secretaries. It is appointed by the General Council and is responsible for general co-ordination, regional activities, national trade union liaison, press and information, administration and finance.

WFTU has regional offices in New Delhi, India (for the Asia-Pacific region), Havana, Cuba (covering the Americas), Dakar, Senegal (for Africa), Damascus, Syria (for the Middle East) and in Moscow, Russia (covering the CIS countries).

General Secretary: ALEKSANDR ZHARIKOV (Russia).

Finance

Income is derived from affiliation dues, which are based on the number of members in each trade union federation.

Publication

Flashes from the Trade Unions (fortnightly, in English, French and Spanish; monthly in Arabic and Russian).

Trade Unions Internationals

The following autonomous Trade Unions Internationals (TUIs) are associated with WFTU:

Trade Unions International of Agriculture, Food, Commerce, Textile and Allied Workers: f. 1997 by merger of the TUI of Agricultural, Forestry and Plantation Workers (f. 1949), the TUI of Food, Tobacco, Hotel and Allied Industries Workers (f. 1949), the TUI of Workers in Commerce (f. 1959) and the TUI of Textile, Clothing, Leather and Fur Workers (f. 1949); Pres. FREDDY HUCK (France); Gen. Sec. DMITRII DOZORIN (Russia).

Trade Unions International of Public and Allied Employees: 4 Windsor Pl., New Delhi 110 001, India; tel. (11) 331-1829; fax (11) 331-1849; e-mail aisgeff@ca12.vsnl.net.in; internet www .tradeunionindia.org; f. 1949; mems: 34m. in 152 unions in 54 countries; Branch Commissions: State, Municipal, Postal and Telecommunications, Health, Banks and Insurance; Pres. CHRISTOS ALEKKOU CHRISTOU (Cyprus); Gen. Sec. SUKOMAL SEN (India); publ. *Information Bulletin* (in three languages).

Trade Unions International of Transport Workers: Tengerszem U. 21/B , 1142 Budapest, Hungary; tel. and fax (1) 2851593; f. 1949; holds International Trade Conference (every 4 years) and General Council (annually); mems: 95 unions from 37 countries; Pres. NASR ZARIF MOUHREZ (Syria); Gen. Sec. JÓZSEF TÓTH (Hungary); publ. *TUI Reporter* (every 2 months, in English and Spanish).

Trade Unions International of Workers of the Building, Wood and Building Materials Industries (Union Internationale des Syndicats des Travailleurs du Bâtiment, du Bois et des Matériaux de Construction—UITBB): Box 281, 00101 Helsinki, Finland; tel. (9) 693-1130; fax (9) 693-1020; e-mail rguitbb@kaapeli.fi; internet www .uitbb.org; f. 1949; mems: unions in 50 countries, grouping 2m. workers; Sec.-Gen. JOSÉ DINIS (Portugal); publ. *Bulletin*.

Trade Unions International of Workers in the Energy, Metal, Chemical, Oil and Related Industries: c/o 3a Calle Maestro Antonio Caso 45, Col. Tabacalera, 06470 Mexico City, Mexico; tel. and fax (55) 5546-3200; e-mail uis@uis-tui.org; internet www.uis-tui .org; f. 1998 by merger of the TUI of Chemical, Oil and Allied Workers (f. 1950), the TUI of Energy Workers (f. 1949) and the TUI of Workers in the Metal Industry (f. 1949); Gen. Sec. ROSENDO FLORES FLORES (Mexico); publ. *Bulletin*.

World Federation of Teachers' Unions: 6/6 Kalicharan Ghosh Rd, Kolkata 700 050, India; tel. (33) 2528-4786; fax (33) 2557-1293; f. 1946; mems: 132 national unions of teachers and educational and scientific workers in 78 countries, representing over 24m. individuals; Pres. LESTURUGE ARIYAWANSA (Sri Lanka); Gen. Sec. MRINMOY BHATTACHARYYA (India); publ. *Teachers of the World* (quarterly, in English).

WORLD TRADE ORGANIZATION—WTO

Address: Centre William Rappard, rue de Lausanne 154, 1211 Geneva, Switzerland.

Telephone: (22) 7395111; **fax:** (22) 7314206; **e-mail:** enquiries@wto .org; **internet:** www.wto.org.

The WTO is the legal and institutional foundation of the multilateral trading system. It was established on 1 January 1995, as the successor to the General Agreement on Tariffs and Trade (GATT).

MEMBERS*

Albania	The Gambia	New Zealand
Angola	Georgia	Nicaragua
Antigua and	Germany	Niger
Barbuda	Ghana	Nigeria
Argentina	Greece	Norway
Armenia	Grenada	Oman
Australia	Guatemala	Pakistan
Austria	Guinea	Panama
Bahrain	Guinea-Bissau	Papua New Guinea
Bangladesh	Guyana	Paraguay
Barbados	Haiti	Peru
Belgium	Honduras	Philippines
Belize	Hong Kong	Poland
Benin	Hungary	Portugal
Bolivia	Iceland	Qatar
Botswana	India	Romania
Brazil	Indonesia	Rwanda
Brunei	Ireland	Saint Christopher
Bulgaria	Israel	and Nevis
Burkina Faso	Italy	Saint Lucia
Burundi	Jamaica	Saint Vincent and the
Cambodia	Japan	Grenadines
Cameroon	Jordan	Senegal
Canada	Kenya	Sierra Leone
Central African	Korea, Republic	Singapore
Republic	Kuwait	Slovakia
Chad	Kyrgyzstan	Slovenia
Chile	Latvia	Solomon Islands
China, People's	Lesotho	South Africa
Republic	Liechtenstein	Spain
China, Republic†	Lithuania	Sri Lanka
Colombia	Luxembourg	Suriname
Congo, Democratic	Macau	Swaziland
Republic	Macedonia, former	Sweden
Congo, Republic	Yugoslav republic	Switzerland
Costa Rica	Madagascar	Tanzania
Côte d'Ivoire	Malawi	Thailand
Croatia	Malaysia	Togo
Cuba	The Maldives	Trinidad and
Cyprus	Mali	Tobago
Czech Republic	Malta	Tunisia
Denmark	Mauritania	Turkey
Djibouti	Mauritius	Uganda
Dominica	Mexico	United Arab
Dominican Republic	Moldova	Emirates
Ecuador	Mongolia	United Kingdom
Egypt	Morocco	USA
El Salvador	Mozambique	Uruguay
Estonia	Myanmar	Vanuatu
Fiji	Namibia	Venezuela
Finland	Nepal	Zambia
France	Netherlands	Zimbabwe
Gabon		

* The European Community also has membership status.
† Admitted as the Separate Customs Territory of Taiwan, Penghu, Kinmen and Matsu (referred to as Chinese Taipei).

Note: At April 2005 a further 27 governments had requested to join the WTO, and their applications were under consideration by accession working parties. An accession request had also been received from Syria in 2001; however, a working party for this had not yet been established.

Organization

(April 2005)

MINISTERIAL CONFERENCE

The Ministerial Conference is the highest authority of the WTO. It is composed of representatives of all WTO members at ministerial level, and may take decisions on all matters under any of the multilateral trade agreements. The Conference is required to meet at least every two years. The fourth Conference was held in Doha, Qatar, in November 2001; the fifth Conference was convened in Cancún, Mexico, in September 2003. The sixth Conference was scheduled to take place in December 2005, in Hong Kong.

GENERAL COUNCIL

The General Council, which is also composed of representatives of all WTO members, is required to report to the Ministerial Conference and conducts much of the day-to-day work of the WTO. The Council convenes as the Dispute Settlement Body, to oversee the trade dispute settlement procedures, and as the Trade Policy Review Body, to conduct regular reviews of the trade policies of WTO members. The Council delegates responsibility to three other major Councils: for trade-related aspects of intellectual property rights, for trade in goods and for trade in services.

TRADE NEGOTIATIONS COMMITTEE

The Committee was established in November 2001 by the Declaration of the fourth Ministerial Conference, held in Doha, Qatar, to supervise the agreed agenda of trade negotiations. It was to operate under the authority of the General Council and was mandated to establish negotiating mechanisms and subsidiary bodies for each subject under consideration. A structure of negotiating groups and a declaration of principles and practices for the negotiations were formulated by the Committee in February 2002

SECRETARIAT

The WTO Secretariat comprises some 550 staff. Its responsibilities include the servicing of WTO delegate bodies, with respect to negotiations and the implementation of agreements, undertaking accession negotiations for new members and providing technical support and expertise to developing countries. In July 1999 member states reached a compromise agreement on the appointment of a new Director-General, having postponed the decision several times after failing to achieve the required consensus. Two candidates were appointed to serve consecutive three-year terms-in-office. In December 2001 the Director-General announced that the Secretariat was to be reorganized, in order to provide greater support to developing countries.

In June 2001 a WTO Training Institute was established, at the Secretariat, to extend the provision of training activities previously undertaken. Courses were to be held on trade policy, WTO dispute settlement rules and procedures, and other specialized topics; other programmes included training-of-trainers programmes and distance-learning services.

Director-General: SUPACHAI PANITCHPAKDI (Thailand).

Deputy Directors-General: RODERICK ABBOT (United Kingdom), KIPKORIR ALY AZAD RANA (Kenya), FRANCISCO THOMPSON-FLÔRES (Brazil), RUFUS YERXA (USA).

Activities

The Final Act of the Uruguay Round of GATT multilateral trade negotiations, which were concluded in December 1993, provided for extensive trade liberalization measures and for the establishment of a permanent structure to oversee international trading procedures. The Final Act was signed in April 1994, in Marrakesh, Morocco. At the same time a separate accord, the Marrakesh Declaration, was signed by the majority of GATT contracting states, endorsing the establishment of the WTO. The essential functions of the WTO are: to administer and facilitate the implementation of the results of the Uruguay Round; to provide a forum for multilateral trade negotiations; to administer the trade dispute settlement procedures; to review national trade policies; and to co-operate with other international institutions, in particular the IMF and World Bank, in order to achieve greater coherence in global economic policy-making.

The WTO Agreement contains some 29 individual legal texts and more than 25 additional Ministerial declarations, decisions and understandings, which cover obligations and commitments for member states. All these instruments are based on a few fundamental principles, which form the basis of the WTO Agreement. An integral part of the Agreement is 'GATT 1994', an amended and updated version of the original GATT Agreement of 1947, which was formally concluded at the end of 1995. Under the 'most-favoured nation' (MFN) clause, members are bound to grant to each other's products treatment no less favourable than that accorded to the products of any third parties. A number of exceptions apply, principally for customs unions and free-trade areas and for measures in favour of and among developing countries. The principle of 'national treatment' requires goods, having entered a market, to be treated no less favourably than the equivalent domestically-produced goods. Secure and predictable market access, to encourage trade, investment and job creation, may be determined by 'binding' tariffs, or customs duties. This process means that a tariff level for a particular product becomes a commitment by a member state, and cannot be increased without compensation negotiations with its main trading partners. Other WTO agreements also contribute to predictable trading conditions by demanding commitments from member countries and greater transparency of domestic laws and national trade policies. By permitting tariffs, whilst adhering to the guide-lines of being non-discriminatory, the WTO aims to promote open, fair and undistorted competition.

The WTO aims to encourage development and economic reform among the increasing number of developing countries and countries with economies in transition participating in the international trading system. These countries, particularly the least-developed states, have been granted transition periods and greater flexibility to implement certain WTO provisions. Industrial member countries are encouraged to assist developing nations by their trading conditions and by not expecting reciprocity in trade concession negotiations. In addition, the WTO operates a limited number of technical assistance programmes, mostly relating to training and the provision of information technology.

Finally, the WTO Agreement recognizes the need to protect the environment and to promote sustainable development. A new Committee on Trade and Environment was established to identify the relationship between trade policies, environmental measures and sustainable development and to recommend any appropriate modifications of the multilateral trading provisions.

At the 1996 Conference representatives of some 28 countries signed a draft Information Technology Agreement (ITA), which aimed to eliminate tariffs on the significant global trade in IT products by 2000. By late February 1997 some 39 countries, representing the required 90% share of the world's IT trade, had consented to implement the ITA. It was signed in March, and was to cover the following main product categories: computers; telecommunications products; semiconductors or manufacturing equipment; software; and scientific instruments. Tariff reductions in these sectors were to be undertaken in four stages, commencing in July, and subsequently on 1 January each year, providing for the elimination of all tariffs by the start of 2000. (In April 2005 there were 63 participants in the ITA.) In February 1999 the WTO announced plans to investigate methods of removing non-tariff barriers to trade in IT products, such as those resulting from non-standardization of technical regulations. A one-year work programme on non-tariff measures was approved by the Committee of Participants on the Expansion of Trade in IT Products in November 2000.

At the end of the Uruguay Round a 'built-in' programme of work for the WTO was developed. In addition, the Ministerial Conferences in December 1996 and May 1998 addressed a range of issues. The final declaration issued from the Ministerial Conference in December 1996 incorporated a text on the contentious issue of core labour standards, although it was emphasized that the relationship between trade and labour standards was not part of the WTO agenda. The text recognized the International Labour Organization's competence in establishing and dealing with core labour standards and endorsed future WTO/ILO co-operation. The declaration also included a plan of action on measures in favour of the world's least-developed countries, to assist these countries in enhancing their trading opportunities. The second Conference, convened in May 1998, decided against imposing customs duties on international electronic transactions, and agreed to establish a comprehensive work programme to address the issues of electronic commerce. The Conference also supported the creation of a framework of international rules to protect intellectual property rights and provide security and privacy in transactions. Developing countries were assured that their needs in this area would be taken into account. Members agreed to begin preparations for the launch of comprehensive talks on global trade liberalization. In addition, following repeated mass public demonstrations against free trade, it was agreed to try to increase the transparency of the WTO and improve public understanding of the benefits of open global markets.

Formal negotiations on the agenda of a new multilateral trade 'round', which was initially scheduled to be launched at the third Ministerial Conference, to be held in Seattle, USA, in late November–December 1999, commenced in September 1998. While it was confirmed that further liberalization of agriculture and services was to be considered, no consensus was reached (in particular between the Cairns Group of countries and the USA, and the European Union (EU), supported by Japan) on the terms of reference or procedures for these negotiations prior to the start of the Conference. In addition, developing countries criticized renewed efforts, mainly by the USA, to link trade and labour standards and to incorporate environmental considerations into the discussions.

Efforts by the EU to broaden the talks to include investment and competition policy were also resisted by the USA. The conduct of the Ministerial Conference was severely disrupted by public demonstrations by a diverse range of interest groups concerned with the impact of WTO accords on the environment, workers' rights and developing countries. The differences between member states with regard to a formal agenda failed to be resolved during extensive negotiations, and the Conference was suspended. At a meeting of the General Council, convened later in December, member countries reached an informal understanding that any agreements concluding on 31 December would be extended. Meanwhile, the Director-General attempted to maintain a momentum for proceeding with a new round of trade negotiations. In February 2000 the General Council agreed to resume talks with regard to agriculture and services, and to consider difficulties in implementing the Uruguay Accord, which was a main concern of developing member states. The Council also urged industrialized nations to pursue an earlier initiative to grant duty-free access to the exports of least developed countries. In May the Council resolved to initiate a series of Special Sessions to consider implementation of existing trade agreements, and approved more flexible provisions for implementation of TRIPS (see below), as part of ongoing efforts to address the needs of developing member states and strengthen their confidence in the multilateral trading system.

During 2001 negotiations were undertaken to reach agreement on further trade liberalization. A draft accord was approved by the General Council in October. The fourth Ministerial Conference, held in Doha, Qatar, in November, adopted a final declaration providing a mandate for a three-year agenda for negotiations on a range of subjects, commencing 1 January 2002. Most of the negotiations were scheduled to be concluded, on 1 January 2005, as a single undertaking, i.e. requiring universal agreement on all matters under consideration. (This deadline was subsequently advanced to end-2006.) A new Trade Negotiations Committee was established to supervise the process, referred to as the Doha Development Round. Several aspects of existing agreements were to be negotiated, while new issues included WTO rules, such as subsidies, regional trade agreements and anti-dumping measures, and market access. The Declaration incorporated a commitment to negotiate issues relating to trade and the environment, including fisheries subsidies, environmental labelling requirements, and the relationship between trade obligations of multilateral environment agreements and WTO rules. The Conference approved a separate decision on implementation-related issues, to address the concerns of developing countries in meeting their WTO commitments. Several implementation issues were agreed at the meeting, while others were incorporated into the Development Agenda. Specific reference was made in the Declaration to providing greater technical co-operation and capacity-building assistance to WTO developing country members. A Doha Development Agenda Global Trust Fund was established in late 2001, with a core budget of CHF 15m., to help finance technical support for trade liberalization in less developed member states. On assuming office in September 2002 the new WTO Director-General, Supachai Panitchpakdi, announced that the ongoing trade negotiations should be brought to a swift conclusion, and that this goal would be supported by the strengthening of the following four pillars of the Organization: beneficial use of the legal framework binding together the multilateral system; technical and capacity-building assistance to least-developed and developing countries; greater coherence in international economic policy-making; and the WTO's functioning as an institution.

The fifth Ministerial Conference, however, convened in Cancún, Mexico, in September 2003 to advance the Doha Development Round, failed to achieve consensus on a number of issues, in particular investment and competition policy. Senior officials from member states convened in December to discuss the future of the Doha Round, but no major breakthrough was achieved. Members did, however, indicate their willingness to recommence work in negotiating groups, which had been suspended after the Cancún conference. The General Council, meanwhile, was to continue working to explore the possibilities of agreements on a multilateral approach on trade facilitation and transparency in government procurement. At the Cancún meeting membership applications from Nepal and Cambodia were approved; they acceded to the WTO in April and October 2004, respectively.

AGRICULTURE

The Final Act of the Uruguay Round extended previous GATT arrangements for trade in agricultural products through new rules and commitments to ensure more predictable and fair competition in the sector. All quantitive measures limiting market access for agricultural products were to be replaced by tariffs (i.e. a process of 'tariffication'), enabling more equal protection and access opportunities. All tariffs on agricultural items were to be reduced by 36% by developed countries, over a period of six years, and by 24% by developing countries (excluding least-developed member states) over 10 years. A special treatment clause applied to 'sensitive' products (mainly rice) in four countries, for which limited import restrictions could be maintained. Efforts to reduce domestic support measures for agricultural products were to be based on calculations of total aggregate measurements of support (Total AMS) by each member state. A 20% reduction in Total AMS was required by developed countries over six years, and 13% over 10 years by developing countries. No reduction was required of least-developed countries. Developed member countries were required to reduce the value and quantity of direct export subsidies by 36% and 21% respectively (on 1986–90 levels) over six years. For developing countries these reductions were to be two-thirds those of developed nations, over 10 years. A specific concern of least-developed and net-food importing developing countries, which had previously relied on subsidized food products, was to be addressed through other food aid mechanisms and assistance for agricultural development. The situation was to be monitored by WTO's Committee on Agriculture. Negotiations on the further liberalization of agricultural markets were part of the WTO 'built-in' programme for 2000 or earlier, but remained a major area of contention. In March 2000 negotiations on market access in the agricultural sector commenced, under an interim chairman owing to a disagreement among participating states. By November 2001 121 countries had submitted proposals for the next stage of negotiations. The Doha Declaration, approved in that month, established a timetable for further negotiations on agriculture, which were initially scheduled to be concluded as part of the single undertaking on 1 January 2005. (The deadline was subsequently advanced to end-2006.) A compromise agreement was reached with the EU to commit to a reduction in export subsidies, with a view to phasing them out (without a firm deadline for their elimination). Member states agreed to aim for further reductions in market access restrictions and domestic support mechanisms, and to incorporate non-trade concerns, including environmental protection, food security and rural development, into the negotiations.

The Agreement on the Application of Sanitary and Phytosanitary Measures aims to regulate world-wide standards of food safety and animal and plant health in order to encourage the mutual recognition of standards and conformity, so as to facilitate trade in these products. The Agreement includes provisions on control inspection and approval procedures. In September 1997, in the first case to be brought under the Agreement, a dispute panel of the WTO ruled that the EU's ban on imports of hormone-treated beef and beef products from the USA and Canada was in breach of international trading rules. In January 1998 the Appellate Body upheld the panel's ruling, but expressed its support for restrictions to ensure food standards if there was adequate scientific evidence of risks to human health. The EU maintained the ban, against resistance from the USA, while it carried out scientific risk assessments.

TEXTILES AND CLOTHING

From 1974 the Multi-fibre Arrangement (MFA) provided the basis of international trade concerning textiles and clothing, enabling the major importers to establish quotas and protect their domestic industries, through bilateral agreements, against more competitive low-cost goods from developing countries. MFA restrictions that were in place on 31 December 1994 were carried over into the new agreement and were to be phased out through integration into GATT 1994, under which they would be subject to the same rules applying to other industrial products. This was to be achieved in four stages: products accounting for 16% of the total volume of textiles and clothing imports (at 1990 levels) were to be integrated from 1 January 1995; a further 17% on 1 January 1998; and not less than a further 18% on 1 January 2002, with all remaining products to be integrated by 1 January 2005. (This deadline was subsequently advanced to end-2006.)

TRADE IN SERVICES

The General Agreement on Trade in Services (GATS), which was negotiated during the GATT Uruguay Round, is the first set of multilaterally-agreed and legally-enforceable rules and disciplines ever negotiated to cover international trade in services. The GATS comprises a framework of general rules and disciplines, annexes addressing special conditions relating to individual sectors and national schedules of market access commitments. A Council for Trade in Services oversees the operation of the agreement.

The GATS framework consists of 29 articles, including the following set of basic obligations: total coverage of all internationally-traded services; national treatment, i.e. according services and service suppliers of other members no less favourable treatment than that accorded to domestic services and suppliers; MFN treatment (see above), with any specific exemptions to be recorded prior to the implementation of the GATS, with a limit of 10 years duration; transparency, requiring publication of all relevant national laws and legislations; bilateral agreements on recognition of standards and qualifications to be open to other members who wish to negotiate accession; no restrictions on international payments and transfers;

progressive liberalization to be pursued; and market access and national treatment commitments to be bound and recorded in national schedules. These schedules, which include exemptions to the MFN principles, contain the negotiated and guaranteed conditions under which trade in services is conducted and are an integral part of the GATS.

Annexes to the GATS cover the movement of natural persons, permitting governments to negotiate specific commitments regarding the temporary stay of people for the purpose of providing a service; the right of governments to take measures in order to ensure the integrity and stability of the financial system; the role of telecommunications as a distinct sector of economic activity and as a means of supplying other economic activities; and air transport services, excluding certain activities relating to traffic rights.

At the end of the Uruguay Round governments agreed to continue negotiations in the following areas: basic telecommunications, maritime transport, movement of natural persons and financial services. The Protocol to the GATS relating to movement of natural persons was concluded in July 1995. In May 1996 the USA withdrew from negotiations to conclude an agreement on maritime transport services. At the end of June the participating countries agreed to suspend the discussions and to recommence negotiations in 2000.

In July 1995 some 29 members signed an interim agreement to grant greater access to the banking, insurance, investment and securities sectors from August 1996. Negotiations to strengthen the agreement and to extend it to new signatories (including the USA, which had declined to sign the agreement, claiming lack of reciprocity by some Asian countries) commenced in April 1997. A final agreement was successfully concluded in mid-December: 102 countries endorsed the elimination of restrictions on access to the financial services sectors from 1 March 1999, and agreed to subject those services to legally-binding rules and disciplines. In late January 1999 some 35 signatory states had yet to ratify the financial services agreement, and its entry into force was postponed. Negotiations on trade in basic telecommunications began in May 1994 and were scheduled to conclude in April 1996. Before the final deadline, however, the negotiations were suspended, owing to US concerns, which included greater access to satellite telecommunications markets in Asia and greater control over foreign companies operating from the domestic markets. An agreement was finally concluded by the new deadline of 15 February 1997. Accordingly the largest telecommunications markets, i.e. the USA, the EU and Japan, were to eliminate all remaining restrictions on domestic and foreign competition in the industry by 1 January 1998 (although delays were granted to Spain, until December 1998, Ireland, until 2000, and Greece and Portugal, until 2003). The majority of the 69 signatories to the accord also agreed on common rules to ensure that fair competition could be enforced by the WTO disputes settlement mechanism, and pledged their commitment to establishing a regulatory system for the telecommunications sector and guaranteeing transparency in government licensing. The agreement entered into force on 5 February 1998, having been rescheduled, owing to the delay on the part of some signatory countries (then totalling 72 states) in ratifying the accord and incorporating the principles of industry regulation into national legislation. The negotiations to liberalize trade in services were formally reopened in 2000, while new guide-lines and procedures for the negotiations were approved in March 2001. The negotiations were incorporated into the Doha Agenda and were to be concluded as part of a single undertaking, initially by 1 January 2005, although the deadline was subsequently advanced to end-2006.

INTELLECTUAL PROPERTY RIGHTS

The WTO Agreement on Trade-Related Aspects of Intellectual Property Rights (TRIPS) recognizes that widely varying standards in the protection and enforcement of intellectual property rights and the lack of multilateral disciplines dealing with international trade in counterfeit goods have been a growing source of tension in international economic relations. The TRIPS agreement aims to ensure that nationals of member states receive equally favourable treatment with regard to the protection of intellectual property and that adequate standards of intellectual property protection exist in all WTO member countries. These standards are largely based on the obligations of the Paris and Berne Conventions of WIPO, however, and the agreement aims to expand and enhance these where necessary, for example: computer programmes, to be protected as literary works for copyright purposes; definition of trade marks eligible for protection; stricter rules of geographical indications of consumer products; a 10-year protection period for industrial designs; a 20-year patent protection available for all inventions; tighter protection of layout design of integrated circuits; and protection for trade secrets and 'know-how' with a commercial value.

Under the agreement member governments are obliged to provide procedures and remedies to ensure the effective enforcement of intellectual property rights. Civil and administrative procedures outlined in the TRIPS include provisions on evidence, injunctions, judicial authority to order the disposal of infringing goods, and criminal procedures and penalties, in particular for trademark counterfeiting and copyright piracy. A one-year period was envisaged for developed countries to bring their legislation and practices into conformity with the agreement. Developing countries were to do so in five years (or 10 years if an area of technology did not already have patent protection) and least-developed countries in 11 years. A Council for Trade-Related Property Rights monitors the compliance of governments with the agreement and its operation. During 2000 the implementation of TRIPS was one the key areas of contention among WTO members. In November WTO initiated a review of TRIPS, although this was expected to consider alteration of the regime rather than of its implementation. At that time some 70 developing countries were failing to apply TRIPS rules. In November 2001 the WTO Ministerial Conference sought to resolve the ongoing dispute regarding the implementation of TRIPS in respect of pharmaceutical patents in developing countries. A separate declaration aimed to clarify a flexible interpretation of TRIPS in order for governments to meet urgent public health priorities. The deadline for some of the poorest countries to apply provisions on pharmaceutical patents was extended to 1 January 2016. The TRIPS Council was mandated to undertake further consideration of problems concerning compulsory licensing. The Doha Declaration also committed the Council to concluding, by the next Ministerial Conference, negotiations on a multilateral registration system for geographical indications for wines and spirits.

LEGAL FRAMEWORK

In addition to the binding agreements mentioned above, WTO aims to provide a comprehensive legal framework for the international trading system. Under GATT 1994 'anti-dumping' measures were permitted against imports of a product with an export price below its normal value, if these imports were likely to cause damage to a domestic industry. The WTO agreement provides for greater clarity and more-detailed rules determining the application of these measures and determines settlement procedures in disputes relating to anti-dumping actions taken by WTO members. In general, anti-dumping measures were to be limited to five years. WTO's Agreement on Subsidies and Countervailing Measures is intended to expand on existing GATT agreements. It classifies subsidies into three categories: prohibited, which may be determined by the Dispute Settlement Body and must be immediately withdrawn; actionable, which must be withdrawn or altered if the subsidy is found to cause adverse effects on the interests of other members; and non-actionable, for example subsidies involving assistance to industrial research, assistance to disadvantaged regions or adaptation of facilities to meet new environmental requirements. The Agreement also contains provisions on the use of duties to offset the effect of a subsidy (so-called countervailing measures) and establishes procedures for the initiation and conduct of investigations into this action. Countervailing measures must generally be terminated within five years of their imposition. Least-developed countries, and developing countries with gross national product per capita of less than US $1,000, are exempt from disciplines on prohibited export subsidies; however, these were to be eliminated by 2003 in all other developing countries and by 2002 in countries with economies in transition.

WTO members may take safeguard actions to protect a specific domestic industry from a damaging increase of imported products. However, the WTO agreement aims to clarify criteria for imposing safeguards, their duration (normally to be no longer than four years, which may be extended to eight years) and consultations on trade compensation for the exporting countries. At 1 December 1995 50 member states had notified the Committee on Safeguards of the WTO Secretariat of their existing domestic safeguard legislations, as required under the agreement. Any measures to protect domestic industries through voluntary export restraints or other market-sharing devices were to be phased out by the end of 1998, or a year later for one specific safeguard measure, subject to mutual agreement of the members directly concerned. Safeguard measures are not applicable to products from developing countries as long as their share of imports of the product concerned does not exceed 3%.

Further legal arrangements act to ensure the following: that technical regulations and standards (including testing and certification procedures) do not create unnecessary obstacles to trade; that import licensing procedures are transparent and predictable; that the valuation of goods for customs purposes are fair and uniform; that GATT principles and obligations apply to import preshipment inspection activities; the fair and transparent administration of rules of origin; and that no investment measures which may restrict or distort trade may be applied. A Working Group on Notification Obligations and Procedures aims to ensure that members fulfil their notification requirements, which facilitate the transparency and surveillance of the trading rules.

PLURILATERAL AGREEMENT

The majority of GATT agreements became multilateral obligations when the WTO became operational in 1995; however, four agreements, which had a selective group of signatories, remained in effect. These so-called plurilateral agreements, the Agreement on Trade in Civil Aircraft, the Agreement on Government Procurement, the International Dairy Agreement and the International Bovine Meat Agreement, aimed to increase international co-operation and fair and open trade and competition in these areas. The bovine meat and dairy agreements were terminated in 1997. The remaining two plurilateral agreements establish their own management bodies, which are required to report to the General Council.

TRADE POLICY REVIEW MECHANISM

The mechanism, which was established provisionally in 1989, was given a permanent role in the WTO. Through regular monitoring and surveillance of national trade policies the mechanism aims to increase the transparency and understanding of trade policies and practices and to enable assessment of the effects of policies on the world trading system. In addition, it records efforts made by governments to bring domestic trade legislation into conformity with WTO provisions and to implement WTO commitments. Reviews are conducted in the Trade Policy Review Body on the basis of a policy statement of the government under review and an independent report prepared by the WTO Secretariat. Under the mechanism the world's four largest traders, the EU, the USA, Japan and Canada, were to be reviewed every two years. Special groups were established to examine new regional free-trade arrangements and the trade policies of acceding countries. In February 1996 a single Committee on Regional Trade Agreements was established, superseding these separate working parties. The Committee aimed to ensure that these groupings contributed to the process of global trade liberalization and to study the implications of these arrangements on the multilateral system. At the Ministerial Conference held in December 1996 it was agreed to establish a new working group to conduct a study of transparency in government procurement practices.

SETTLEMENT OF DISPUTES

A separate annex to the WTO agreement determines a unified set of rules and procedures to govern the settlement of all WTO disputes, substantially reinforcing the GATT procedures. WTO members are committed not to undertake unilateral action against perceived violations of the trade rules, but to seek recourse in the dispute settlement mechanism and abide by its findings.

The first stage of the process requires bilateral consultations between the members concerned in an attempt to conclude a mutually-acceptable solution to the issue. These may be undertaken through the good offices and mediation efforts of the Director-General. Only after a consultation period of 60 days may the complainant ask the General Council, convened as the Dispute Settlement Body (DSB), to establish an independent panel to examine the case, which then does so within the terms of reference of the agreement cited. Each party to the dispute submits its arguments and then presents its case before the panel. Third parties which notify their interest in the dispute may also present views at the first substantive meeting of the panel. At this stage an expert review group may be appointed to provide specific scientific or technical advice. The panel submits sections and then a full interim report of its findings to the parties, who may then request a further review involving additional meetings. A final report should be submitted to the parties by the panel within six months of its establishment, or within three months in cases of urgency, including those related to perishable goods. Final reports are normally adopted by the DSB within 60 days of issuance. In the case of a measure being found to be inconsistent with the relevant WTO agreement, the panel recommends ways in which the member may bring the measure into conformity with the agreement. However, under the WTO mechanism either party has the right to appeal against the decision and must notify the DSB of its intentions before adoption of the final report. Appeal proceedings, which are limited to issues of law and the legal interpretation covered by the panel report, are undertaken by three members of the Appellate Body within a maximum period of 90 days. The report of the Appellate Body must be unconditionally accepted by the parties to the dispute (unless there is a consensus within the DSB against its adoption). If the recommendations of the panel or appeal report are not implemented immediately, or within a 'reasonable period' as determined by the DSB, the parties are obliged to negotiate mutually-acceptable compensation pending full implementation. Failure to agree compensation may result in the DSB authorizing the complainant to suspend concessions or obligations against the other party. In any case the DSB monitors the implementation of adopted recommendations or rulings, while any outstanding cases remain on its agenda until the issue is resolved. By April 2005 329 trade complaints had been notified to the WTO since 1995, on more than 180 different issues.

In late 1997 the DSB initiated a review of the WTO's understanding on dispute settlement, as required by the Marrakesh Agreement. The Doha Declaration, which was adopted in November 2001, mandated further negotiations to be conducted on the review and on additional proposals to amend the dispute procedure as a separate undertaking from the rest of the work programme. Negotiations were to be concluded by May 2003. In July of that year, however, the General Council acknowledged that the special session on dispute procedure required more time to conclude its work.

CO-OPERATION WITH OTHER ORGANIZATIONS

WTO is mandated to pursue co-operation with the IMF and the World Bank, as well as with other multilateral organizations, in order to achieve greater coherence in global economic policy-making. In November 1994 the preparatory committee of the WTO resolved not to incorporate the new organization into the UN structure as a specialized agency. Instead, co-operation arrangements with the IMF and World Bank were to be developed. In addition, efforts were pursued to enhance co-operation with UNCTAD in research, trade and technical issues. The Directors-General of the two organizations agreed to meet at least twice a year in order to develop the working relationship. In particular, co-operation was to be undertaken in WTO's special programme of activities for Africa, which aimed to help African countries expand and diversify their trade and benefit from the global trading system. Since 1997 WTO has co-operated with the IMF, ITC, UNCTAD, UNDP and World Bank in an Integrated Framework for trade-related technical assistance to least developed countries.

International Trade Centre (UNCTAD/WTO): Palais des Nations, 1211 Geneva 10, Switzerland; tel. (22) 7300111; fax (22) 7334439; e-mail itcreg@intracen.org; internet www.intracen.org; f. 1964 by GATT; jointly operated with the UN (through UNCTAD) since 1968; ITC works with developing countries in product and market development, the development of trade support services, trade information, human resource development, international purchasing and supply management, and needs assessment and programme design for trade promotion; publs *International Trade Forum* (quarterly), market studies, handbooks, etc.

Executive Director: J. DENIS BÉLISLE.

Finance

The WTO's 2005 budget amounted to 164m. Swiss francs, financed mainly by contributions from members in proportion to their share of total trading conducted by WTO members.

Publications

Annual Report (2 volumes).
International Trade Statistics (annually).
World Trade Report (annually).
World Trade Review (3 a year).
WTO Focus (monthly).

OTHER INTERNATIONAL ORGANIZATIONS

OTHER INTERNATIONAL ORGANIZATIONS

Agriculture, Food, Forestry and Fisheries

(For organizations concerned with agricultural commodities, see Commodities)

African Timber Organization (ATO): BP 1077, Libreville, Gabon; tel. 732928; fax 734030; e-mail oab-gabon@internetgabon .com; f. 1976 to enable members to study and co-ordinate ways of ensuring the optimum utilization and conservation of their forests; mems: 13 African countries; Sec.-Gen. (vacant); publs *ATO Information Bulletin* (quarterly), *International Magazine of African Timber* (2 a year).

Asian Vegetable Research and Development Center (AVRDC): POB 42, Shanhua, Tainan 741, Taiwan; tel. (6) 5837801; fax (6) 5830009; e-mail avrdcbox@netra.avrdc.org.tw; internet www .avrdc.org.tw; f. 1971; aims to enhance the nutritional well-being and raise the incomes of the poor in rural and urban areas of developing countries, through improved varieties and methods of vegetable production, marketing and distribution; runs an experimental farm, laboratories, gene-bank, greenhouses, quarantine house, insectarium, library and weather station; provides training for research and production specialists in tropical vegetables; exchanges and disseminates vegetable germplasm through regional centres in the developing world; serves as a clearing-house for vegetable research information; and undertakes scientific publishing; mems: Australia, France, Germany, Japan, Republic of Korea, Philippines, Taiwan, Thailand, USA; Dir-Gen. Dr THOMAS A. LUMPKIN; publs *Annual Report*, *Technical Bulletin*, *Proceedings*, *Centerpoint* (quarterly).

CAB International (CABI): Wallingford, Oxon, OX10 8DE, United Kingdom; tel. (1491) 832111; fax (1491) 833508; e-mail cabi@cabi .org; internet www.cabi.org; f. 1929 as the Imperial Agricultural Bureaux (later Commonwealth Agricultural Bureaux), current name adopted in 1985; aims to improve human welfare world-wide through the generation, dissemination and application of scientific knowledge in support of sustainable development; places particular emphasis on sustainable agriculture, forestry, human health and the management of natural resources, with priority given to the needs of developing countries; compiles and publishes extensive information (in a variety of print and electronic forms) on aspects of agriculture, forestry, veterinary medicine, the environment and natural resources, Third World rural development and others; maintains regional centres in the People's Republic of China, India, Kenya, Malaysia, Pakistan, Switzerland, Trinidad and Tobago, and the United Kingdom; mems: 40 countries; Dir-Gen. Dr DENIS BLIGHT.

CABI Bioscience: Bakeham Lane, Egham, Surrey, TW20 9TY, United Kingdom; tel. (1491) 829080; fax (1491) 829100; e-mail bioscience.egham@cabi.org; internet www.cabi-bioscience.org; f. 1998 by integration of the following four CABI scientific institutions: International Institute of Biological Control; International Institute of Entomology; International Institute of Parasitology; International Mycological Institute; undertakes research, consultancy, training, capacity-building and institutional development measures in sustainable pest management, biosystematics and molecular biology, ecological applications and environmental and industrial microbiology; maintains centres in Kenya, Malaysia, Pakistan, Switzerland, Trinidad and Tobago, and the United Kingdom; Dir DAVID DENT.

Collaborative International Pesticides Analytical Council Ltd (CIPAC): c/o Dr M. D. Müller, Swiss Federal Res. Station, 8820 Waedenswil, Switzerland; tel. (1) 7836412; fax (1) 7836439; e-mail markus.mueller@faw.admin.ca; internet www.cipac.org; f. 1957 to organize international collaborative work on methods of analysis for pesticides used in crop protection; mems: in 46 countries; Chair. Dr MARKUS D. MÜLLER (Switzerland); Sec. Dr LÁZLÓ BURA (Hungary).

Desert Locust Control Organization for Eastern Africa (DLCOEA): POB 30023, Nairobi, Kenya; tel. (20) 602305; fax (20) 601575; e-mail dlco@wananchi.com; f. 1962 to promote effective control of desert locust in the region and to conduct research into the locust's environment and behaviour; also assists member states in the monitoring, forecasting and extermination of other migratory pests; mems: Djibouti, Eritrea, Ethiopia, Kenya, Somalia, Sudan, Tanzania, Uganda; Dir PETER O. ODIYO; Co-ordinator J. M. GATIMU;

publs *Desert Locust Situation Reports* (monthly), *Annual Report*, technical reports.

European and Mediterranean Plant Protection Organization (EPPO): 1 rue Le Nôtre, 75016 Paris, France; tel. 1-45-20-77-94; fax 1-42-24-89-43; e-mail hq@eppo.fr; internet www.eppo.org; f. 1951, present name adopted in 1955; aims to promote international co-operation between government plant protection services to prevent the introduction and spread of pests and diseases of plants and plant products; mems: governments of 46 countries and territories; Chair. OLIVER FÉLIX; Dir-Gen. Dr IAN M. SMITH; publs *EPPO Bulletin*, *Data Sheets on Quarantine Organisms*, *Guidelines for the Efficacy Evaluation of Pesticides*, *Crop Growth Stage Keys*, *Summary of the Phytosanitary Regulations of EPPO Member Countries*, *Reporting Service*.

European Association for Animal Production (EAAP) (Fédération européenne de zootechnie): Via Nomentana 134A, 00162 Rome, Italy; tel. (06) 86329141; fax (06) 86329263; e-mail eaap@eaap.org; internet www.eaap.org; f. 1949 to help improve the conditions of animal production and meet consumer demand; holds annual meetings; mems: asscns in 37 countries; Pres. A. AUMAITRE (France); publ. *Livestock Production Science* (16 a year).

European Association for Research on Plant Breeding (EUCARPIA): c/o Instituto Valenciano de Investigaciones Agrarias, Apdo Oficial, E-46113 Moncada, Valencia, Spain; tel. (9364) 24049; fax (9634) 24106; e-mail eucarpia.secretariat@ivia.es; internet www .eucarpia.org; f. 1956 to promote scientific and technical co-operation in the plant breeding field; mems: 1,100 individuals, 65 corporate mems; Pres. Prof. JAIME PROHENS-TOMÁS (Spain); Sec. Dr MARIA LUISA BADENES (Spain); publ. *EUCARPIA Bulletin*.

European Confederation of Agriculture (CEA): 23 rue de la Science, bte 23, 1040 Brussels, Belgium; tel. (2) 230-43-80; fax (2) 230-46-77; e-mail cea@pophost.eunet.be; f. 1889 as International Confederation, re-formed in 1948 as European Confederation; represents the interests of European agriculture in the international field; provides social security for independent farmers and foresters in the member countries; mems: 300 mems. in 30 countries; Pres. BEN GILL (UK); Gen. Sec. CHRISTOPHE HÉMARD (France); publs *CEA Dialog*, *Annual Report*.

European Grassland Federation: c/o Dr Willy Kessler, Swiss Federal Research Station for Agroecology and Agriculture, Reckenholzstr. 191, Postfach 8046 Zürich, Switzerland; tel. (1) 3777376; fax (1) 3770201; e-mail fedsecretary@europeangrassland.org; internet www.europeangrassland.org; f. 1963 to facilitate and maintain liaison between European grassland organizations and to promote the interchange of scientific and practical knowledge and experience; holds General Meeting every two years and symposia at other times; mems: 30 full and seven corresponding mem. countries in Europe; Pres. Dr JUAN PIÑEIRO; Sec. Dr WILLY KESSLER; publ. *Proceedings (Grassland Science in Europe)*.

European Livestock and Meat Trading Union (UECBV): 81A rue de la Loi, 1040 Brussels, Belgium; tel. (2) 230-46-03; fax (2) 230-94-00; e-mail uecbv@pophost.eunet.be; internet uecbv.eunet.be; f. 1952 to study problems of the European livestock and meat trade and inform members of all relevant legislation; acts as an international arbitration commission; conducts research on agricultural markets, quality of livestock, and veterinary regulations; mems: national organizations in 23 countries, and the European Association of Livestock Markets; Pres. LAURENT SPANGHERO; Sec.-Gen. JEAN-LUC MERIAUX.

Inter-American Association of Agricultural Librarians, Documentalists and Information Specialists (Asociación Interamericana de Bibliotecarios, Documentalistas y Especialistas en Información Agrícolas—AIBDA): c/o IICA-CIDIA, Apdo 55-2200 Coronado, Costa Rica; tel. 216-0290; fax 216-0291; e-mail aibda@iica .ac.cr; internet www.iica.int/servicios/aibda; f. 1953 to promote professional improvement through technical publications and meetings, and to promote improvement of library services in agricultural sciences; mems: c. 400 in 29 countries and territories; Pres. GERARDO SÁNCHEZ AMBRIZ (Mexico); Exec. Sec. AURA MATA (Costa Rica); publs *Boletín Informativo* (3 a year), *Boletín Especial* (irregular), *Revista AIBDA* (2 a year), *AIBDA Actualidades* (4 or 5 a year).

Inter-American Tropical Tuna Commission (IATTC): 8604 La Jolla Shores Drive, La Jolla, CA 92037-1508, USA; tel. (858) 546-7100; fax (858) 546-7133; e-mail rallen@iattc.org; internet www.iattc

.org; f. 1950; administers two programmes, the Tuna-Billfish Programme and the Tuna-Dolphin Programme. The principal responsibilities of the Tuna-Billfish Programme are: to study the biology of the tunas and related species of the eastern Pacific Ocean to estimate the effects of fishing and natural factors on their abundance; to recommend appropriate conservation measures in order to maintain stocks at levels which will afford maximum sustainable catches; and to collect information on compliance with Commission resolutions. The principal functions of the Tuna-Dolphin Programme are: to monitor the abundance of dolphins and their mortality incidental to purse-seine fishing in the eastern Pacific Ocean; to study the causes of mortality of dolphins during fishing operations and promote the use of fishing techniques and equipment that minimize these mortalities; to study the effects of different fishing methods on the various fish and other animals of the pelagic ecosystem; and to provide a secretariat for the International Dolphin Conservation Programme; mems: Costa Rica, Ecuador, El Salvador, France, Guatemala, Japan, Mexico, Nicaragua, Panama, Peru, Spain, USA, Vanuatu, Venezuela; Dir ROBIN ALLEN; publs *Bulletin* (irregular), *Annual Report, Fishery Status Report, Stock Assessment Report* (annually), *Special Report* (irregular).

International Association for Cereal Science and Technology (ICC): Marxergasse 2, Postfach 47, 1033 Vienna, Austria; tel. (1) 707-72-02; fax (1) 707-72-04; e-mail gen.sec@icc.or.at; internet www .icc.or.at; f. 1955 (as the International Association for Cereal Chemistry; name changed 1986); aims to promote international co-operation in the field of cereal science and technology through the dissemination of information and the development of standard methods of testing and analysing products; mems: 49 mem. and six observer mem. states; Pres. JAN WILLEM VAN DER KAMP (Netherlands); Sec.-Gen. Dr HELMUT GLATTES (Austria).

International Association for Vegetation Science (IAVS): Alterra, Green World Research, POB 47, 6700 AA Wageningen, Netherlands; tel. (317) 477914; fax (317) 424988; e-mail j.h.j .schaminee@alterra.wag-ur.nl; internet www.iavs.org; f. 1938; mems: 1,500 in 70 countries; Chair. Prof. Dr E. O. BOX; Gen Sec. Dr J. H. J. SCHAMINÉE (Netherlands); publs *Phytocoenologia, Journal of Vegetation Science, Applied Vegetation Science.*

International Association of Agricultural Economists (IAAE): c/o Farm Foundation, 1211 West 22nd St, Suite 216, Oak Brook, IL 60523-2197, USA; tel. (630) 571-9393; fax (630) 571-9580; e-mail iaae@farmfoundation.org; internet www.iaae-agecon.org; f. 1929 to foster development of agricultural economic sciences; aims to further the application of research into agricultural processes; works to improve economic and social conditions for agricultural and rural life; mems: in 83 countries; Pres. PRABHU PINGALI (Italy); Sec. and Treas. WALTER J. ARMBRUSTER (USA); publs *Agricultural Economics* (8 a year), *IAAE Newsletter* (2 a year).

International Association of Agricultural Information Specialists: c/o Margot Bellamy, 14 Queen St, Dorchester-on-Thames, Wallingford, Oxon OX10 7HR, United Kingdom; tel. (1865) 340054; e-mail margot.bellamy@fritillary.demon.co.uk; internet www.iaald .org; f. 1955 to promote agricultural library science and documentation and the professional interests of agricultural librarians and documentalists; affiliated to INFITA; mems: 400 in 84 countries; Pres. a.i. PAMELA ANDRÉ (USA); Sec.-Treas. MARGOT BELLAMY (UK); publs *Quarterly Bulletin, World Directory of Agricultural Information Resource Centres.*

International Association of Horticultural Producers (IAHP): Louis Pasteurlaan 6, POB 280,2700 AG Zoetermeen, Netherlands; tel. (79) 3470707; fax (79) 3470405; e-mail aiph@tuinbouw .nl; internet www.aiph.org; f. 1948; represents the common interests of commercial horticultural producers in the international field; authorizes international horticultural exhibitions; mems: national asscns in 25 countries; Pres. DOEKE FABER (Netherlands); Gen. Sec. PETER RUHNKE (Denmark); publ. *Yearbook of International Horticultural Statistics.*

International Bee Research Association (IBRA): 18 North Rd, Cardiff, CF10 3DT, United Kingdom; tel. (29) 2037-2409; fax (29) 2066-5522; e-mail info@ibra.org.uk; internet www.ibra.org.uk; f. 1949 to further bee research and provide an information service for bee scientists and bee-keepers world-wide; mems: 1,200 in 130 countries; Dir RICHARD JONES; Asst Dir Dr PAMELA MUNN; publs *Bee World* (quarterly), *Apicultural Abstracts* (quarterly), *Journal of Apicultural Research* (quarterly), *Buzz Extra* (quarterly).

International Centre for Tropical Agriculture (Centro Internacional de Agricultura Tropical—CIAT): Apdo Aéreo 6713, Cali, Colombia; tel. (2) 445-0000; fax (2) 445-0073; e-mail ciat@cgiar.org; internet www.ciat.cgiar.org; f. 1967 to contribute to the alleviation of hunger and poverty in tropical developing countries by using new techniques in agriculture research and training; focuses on production problems in field beans, cassava, rice and tropical pastures in the tropics; Dir-Gen. Dr JOACHIM VOSS; publs *Annual Report,*

Growing Affinities (2 a year), *Pasturas Tropicales* (3 a year), catalogue of publications.

International Commission for the Conservation of Atlantic Tunas (ICCAT): Calle Corazón de Maria 8, 28020 Madrid, Spain; tel. (91) 4165600; fax (91) 4152612; e-mail info@iccat.es; internet www.iccat.es; f. 1969 under the provisions of the International Convention for the Conservation of Atlantic Tunas (1966) to maintain the populations of tuna and tuna-like species in the Atlantic Ocean and adjacent seas at levels that permit the maximum sustainable catch; collects statistics; conducts studies; mems: 40 contracting parties; Chair. M. MIYAHARA (Japan); Exec. Sec. DRISS MESKI (Morocco); publs *ICCAT Biennial Report, ICCAT Collective Vol. of Scientific Papers, Statistical Bulletin* (annually), *Data Record* (annually).

International Commission of Sugar Technology (Commission Internationale Technique de Sucrerie—CITS): Marktbreiter Str. 74, 97199 Ochsenfurt, Germany; tel. (9331) 91450; fax (9331) 91462; f. 1949 to discuss investigations and promote scientific and technical research work; Pres. LÉON SUÉ (Belgium); Hon. Sec.-Gen. ROBERT PIECK.

International Committee for Animal Recording (ICAR): Villa del Ragno, Via Nomentana 134, 00161 Rome, Italy; tel. (06) 86329141; fax (06) 86329263; e-mail icar@eap.org; internet www .icar.org; f. 1951 to extend and improve the work of recording and to standardize methods; mems: in 58 countries; Pres. MARK JEFFRIES (New Zealand).

International Crops Research Institute for the Semi-Arid Tropics (ICRISAT): Patancheru 502 324, Andhra Pradesh, India; tel. (40) 23296161; fax (40) 23241239; e-mail icrisat@cgiar.org; internet www.icrisat.org; f. 1972 to promote the genetic improvement of crops and for research on the management of resources in the world's semi-arid tropics, with the aim of reducing poverty and protecting the environment; research covers all physical and socioeconomic aspects of improving farming systems on unirrigated land; Dir Dr WILLIAM D. DAR (Philippines); publs *ICRISAT Report* (annually), *SAT News* (2 a year), *International Chickpea and Pigeonpea Newsletter, International Arachis Newsletter, International Sorghum and Millet Newsletter* (annually), information and research bulletins.

International Dairy Federation (IDF): Diamant Bldg, 80 blvd Auguste Reyers, 1030 Brussels, Belgium; tel. (2) 733-98-88; fax (2) 733-04-13; e-mail info@fil-idf.org; internet www.fil-idf.org; f. 1903 to link all dairy asscns, in order to encourage the solution of scientific, technical and economic problems affecting the dairy industry; mems: national cttees in 41 countries; Dir-Gen. EDWARD HOPKIN (UK); publs *Bulletin of IDF, IDF Standards.*

International Federation of Agricultural Producers (IFAP): 60 rue St-Lazare, 75009 Paris, France; tel. 1-45-26-05-53; fax 1-48-74-72-12; e-mail ifap@ifap.org; internet www.ifap.org; f. 1946 to represent, in the international field, the interests of agricultural producers; encourages the exchange of information and ideas; works to develop understanding of world problems and their effects upon agricultural producers; encourages sustainable patterns of agricultural development; holds conference every two years; mems: national farmers' organizations and agricultural co-operatives of 71 countries; Pres. JACK WILKINSON (Canada); Sec.-Gen. DAVID KING; publs *The World Farmer* (monthly), *Proceedings of General Conferences.*

International Federation of Beekeepers' Associations (APIMONDIA): Corso Vittorio Emanuele II 101, 00186 Rome, Italy; tel. and fax (06) 6852286; e-mail apimondia@mclink.it; internet www .apimondia.org; f. 1949; collects and brings up to date documentation on international beekeeping; carries out studies into the particular problems of beekeeping; organizes international congresses, seminars, symposia and meetings; co-operates with other international organizations interested in beekeeping, in particular, with the FAO; mems: 65 asscns from 56 countries; Pres. ASGER SØGAARD JØRGENSEN (Denmark); Sec.-Gen. RICCARDO JANNONI-SEBASTIANINI (Italy); publs *Apiacta* (quarterly, in English, French, German and Spanish), *Dictionary of Beekeeping Terms,* AGROVOC (thesaurus of agricultural terms), studies.

International Hop Growers' Convention: c/o Inštitut za hmeljarstvo in pivovarstvo, POB 51, 3310 Žalec, Slovenia; tel. (63) 712-16-18; fax (63) 712-16-20; e-mail martin.pavlovic@uni-lj.si; internet www.hmelj-giz.si/ihgc; f. 1950; acts as a centre for the collection of data and reports on hop production, beer exports and imports and sales, estimates the world crop and promotes scientific research; mems: national asscns in 19 countries, two hop trading companies; Pres. BERNARD INGWILLER (France); Gen. Sec. Dr MARTIN PAVLOVIĆ.

International Institute for Beet Research (IIRB): ave de Tervuren 195, 1150 Brussels, Belgium; tel. (2) 737-70-90; fax (2) 737-70-99; e-mail mail@iirb.org; internet www.iirb.org; f. 1932 to promote research and the exchange of information; organizes meetings

Agriculture, Food, Forestry and Fisheries

and study groups; mems: 600 in 33 countries; Pres. HANS-JÖRG GEBHARD (German); Sec.-Gen. RALPH BECKERS (Belgium).

International Institute of Tropical Agriculture (IITA): Oyo Rd, PMB 5320, Ibadan, Oyo State, Nigeria; tel. (2) 2412626; fax (2) 2412221; e-mail iita@cgiar.org; internet www.iita.org; f. 1967; principal financing arranged by the Consultative Group on International Agricultural Research—CGIAR, co-sponsored by the FAO, the IBRD and the UNDP; research programmes comprise crop management, improvement of crops and plant protection and health; conducts a training programme for researchers in tropical agriculture; maintains a library of 75,000 vols and data base; administers six agro-ecological research stations; Dir-Gen. Dr PETER HARTMAN (USA); publs *Annual Report, IITA Research* (quarterly), technical bulletins, research reports.

International Livestock Research Institute (ILRI): POB 30709, Nairobi, Kenya; tel. (20) 632311; fax (20) 631499; e-mail ilri-kenya@cgiar.org; internet www.cgiar.org/ilri; f. 1995 to supersede the International Laboratory for Research on Animal Diseases and the International Livestock Centre for Africa; conducts laboratory and field research on animal health and other livestock issues; carries out training programmes for scientists and technicians; maintains a specialized science library; Dir Dr CARLOS SERÉ; publs *Annual Report, Livestock Research for Development* (newsletter, 2 a year).

International Maize and Wheat Improvement Centre (CIMMYT): Apdo Postal 6-641, 06600 México, DF, Mexico; tel. (55) 5804-2004; fax (55) 5804-7558; e-mail cimmyt@cgiar.org; internet www.cimmyt.org; conducts world-wide research programme for sustainable maize and wheat cropping systems to help the poor in developing countries; Dir-Gen. Dr MASA IWANAGA.

International Organization for Biological Control of Noxious Animals and Plants: IOBC Permanent Secretariat, AGROPOLIS, ave Agropolis, 34394 Montpellier Cédex 5, France; e-mail iobc@agropolis.fr; internet www.oilb.agropolis.fr; f. 1955 to promote and co-ordinate research on the more effective biological control of harmful organisms; re-organized in 1971 as a central council with world-wide affiliations and six largely autonomous regional sections; Pres. Dr L.E. EHLER (USA); Sec.-Gen. Dr A. GASSMANN (Switzerland); publs *BioControl, Newsletter*.

International Organization of Citrus Virologists (IOCV): c/o C. N. Roistacher, Dept of Plant Pathology, Univ. of California, Riverside, CA 92521-0122, USA; tel. (909) 684-0934; fax (909) 684-4324; e-mail chester.r@worldnet.att.net; f. 1957 to promote research on citrus virus diseases at international level by standardizing diagnostic techniques and exchanging information; mems: 250; Chair. PEDRO MORENO; Sec. CHESTER N. ROISTACHER.

International Red Locust Control Organization for Central and Southern Africa (IRLCO-CSA): POB 240252, Ndola, Zambia; tel. (2) 612057; fax (2) 614285; e-mail locust@zamnet.zm; f. 1971 to control locusts in eastern, central and southern Africa; also assists in the control of African army-worm and quelea-quelea; mems: seven countries; Dir Dr AFETE DIVELIAS GADABU; publs *Annual Report, Quarterly Report, Monthly Report*, scientific reports.

International Rice Research Institute (IRRI): Los Baños, Laguna, DAPO Box 7777, Metro Manila, Philippines; tel. (2) 8450563; fax (2) 8911292; e-mail irri@cgiar.org; internet www.irri.org; f. 1960; conducts research on rice, with the aim of developing technologies of environmental, social and economic benefit; works to enhance national rice research systems and offers training; operates Riceworld, a museum and learning centre about rice; maintains a library of technical rice literature; organizes international conferences and workshops; Dir-Gen. Dr RONALD P. CANTRELL; publs *Rice Literature Update, Hotline, Facts about IRRI, News about Rice and People, International Rice Research Notes*.

International Seed Testing Association (ISTA): Zürichstrasse 50, Postfach 308, 8303 Bassersdorf, Switzerland; tel. (1) 8386000; fax (1) 8386001; e-mail ista.office@ista.ch; internet www.seedtest.org; f. 1924 to promote uniformity and accurate methods of seed testing and evaluation in order to facilitate efficiency in production, processing, distribution and utilization of seeds; organizes meetings, workshops, symposia, training courses and triennial congresses; mems: 72 countries; Sec.-Gen. Dr M. MUSCHICK; Pres. PIETER OOSTERVELD (Netherlands); publs *Seed Science and Technology* (3 a year), *Seed Testing International (ISTA News Bulletin)* (2 a year), *International Rules for Seed Testing* (annually).

International Sericultural Commission (ISC): 25 quai Jean-Jacques Rousseau, 69350 La Mulatière, France; tel. 4-78-50-41-98; fax 4-78-86-09-57; e-mail info@inserco.org; internet www.inserco.org; f. 1948 to encourage the development of silk production; mems: governments of Brazil, Egypt, France, Greece, India, Indonesia, Iran, Japan, Lebanon, Madagascar, Romania, Thailand, Tunisia, Turkey; Sec.-Gen. Dr GÉRARD CHAVANCY (France); publ. *Sericologia* (quarterly).

International Service for National Agricultural Research (ISNAR): Laan van Nieuw Oost Indie 133, 2593 BM The Hague; POB 93375, 2509 AJ The Hague, Netherlands ; tel. (70) 349-61-00; fax (70) 381-96-77; e-mail isnar@cgiar.org; internet www.isnar.cgiar.org; f. 1980 by the Consultative Group on International Agricultural Research—CGIAR to strengthen national agricultural research systems in developing countries; promotes appropriate research policies, the creation of sustainable research institutions and improved research management; provides advisory, training and research services and information; Chair. MOÏSE MENSAH; Dir-Gen. STEIN W. BIE.

International Society for Horticultural Science (ISHS): Decroylaan 42 (01.21), POB 500, 3001 Leuven 1, Belgium; tel. (16) 22-94-27; fax (16) 22-94-50; e-mail info@ishs.org; internet www.ishs.org; f. 1959 to promote co-operation in horticultural science research; mems: 54 mem. countries, 300 organizations, 6,000 individuals; Pres. Dr NORMAN E. LOONEY (Canada); Exec. Dir Ir JOZEF VAN ASSCHE (Belgium); publs *Chronica Horticulturae* (quarterly), *Acta Horticulturae, Horticultural Research International*.

International Union of Forest Research Organizations (IUFRO): 1140 Vienna-Hadersdorf, Austria; tel. (1) 877-01-51-0; fax (1) 877-01-51-50; e-mail office@iufro.org; internet www.iufro.org; f. 1892; mems: 700 organizations in 115 countries, involving more than 15,000 scientists; Pres. Prof. RISTO SEPPÄLÄ (Finland); Exec. Sec. PETER MAYER (Austria); publs *Annual Report, IUFRO News* (10 a year, electronic format only), *IUFRO World Series, IUFRO Occasional Paper Series, IUFRO Research Series*.

International Union for the Protection of New Varieties of Plant (Union internationale pour la protection des obtentions végétales—UPOV): c/o 34 chemin des Colombettes, 1211 Geneva 20, Switzerland; tel. (22) 3389111; fax (22) 7330336; e-mail upov.mail@upov.int; internet www.upov.int; f. 1961 by the International Convention for the Protection of New Varieties of Plants (entered into force 1968, revised in 1972, 1978 and 1991); aims to encourage the development of new plant varieties and provide an effective system of protection. Admin. support provided by WIPO; mems: 58 states; Pres. ENRIQUETA MOLINA MACÍAS; Sec.-Gen. Dr KAMIL IDRIS.

International Union of Soil Sciences: c/o Department of Soil Science, University of Reading, POB 233, Reading RG6 6DW, United Kingdom; tel. (118) 378-6559; fax (118) 378-6666; e-mail iuss@rdg.ac.uk; internet www.iuss.org; f. 1924; mems: national academies or national soil science societies from 143 countries; Pres. Prof. DONALD SPARKS (UK); Sec.-Gen. Prof. STEPHEN NORTCLIFF (UK); publ. *Bulletin* (2 a year).

International Whaling Commission (IWC): The Red House, 135 Station Rd, Impington, Cambridge, CB4 9NP, United Kingdom; tel. (1223) 233971; fax (1223) 232876; e-mail secretariat@iwcoffice.com; internet www.iwcoffice.org; f. 1946 under the International Convention for the Regulation of Whaling, for the conservation of world whale stocks; reviews the regulations covering whaling operations; encourages research; collects, analyses and disseminates statistical and other information on whaling. A ban on commercial whaling was passed by the Commission in July 1982, to take effect three years subsequently (in some cases, a phased reduction of commercial operations was not completed until 1988). A revised whale-management procedure was adopted in 1992, to be implemented after the development of a complete whale management scheme; mems: governments of 49 countries; Chair. Prof. BO FERNHOLM (Sweden); Sec. Dr NICOLA GRANDY; publ. *Annual Report*.

North Pacific Anadromous Fish Commission: 889 W. Pender St, Suite 502, Vancouver, BC V6C 3B2, Canada; tel. (604) 775-5550; fax (604) 775-5577; e-mail secretariat@npafc.org; f. 1993; mems: Canada, Japan, Republic of Korea, Russia, USA; Exec. Dir VLADIMIR FEDORENKO; publs *Annual Report, Newsletter* (2 a year), *Statistical Yearbook, Scientific Bulletin, Technical Report*.

Northwest Atlantic Fisheries Organization (NAFO): 2 Morris Drive, POB 638, Dartmouth, NS B2Y 3Y9, Canada; tel. (902) 468-5590; fax (902) 468-5538; e-mail info@nafo.int; internet www.nafo.int; f. 1979 (formerly International Commission for the Northwest Atlantic Fisheries); aims at optimum use, management and conservation of resources; promotes research and compiles statistics; Pres. D. BEVAN (Canada); Exec. Sec. Dr J. FISHER; publs *Annual Report* (electronic format only), *Statistical Bulletin, Journal of Northwest Atlantic Fishery Science* (in electronic and print formats), *Scientific Council Reports, Scientific Council Studies, Sampling Yearbook, Meeting Proceedings*.

Western and Central Pacific Fisheries Commission: c/o Ministerial Task Force on IUU Fishing, OECD, 2 rue André Pascal, Paris Cédex 16, France; e-mail contact@wcpfc.org; internet www.wcpfc.org; f. 2004 under the Convention for the Conservation and Management of Highly Migratory Fish Stocks in the Western and Central Pacific, which entered into force in June of that year, six months after the deposit of the 13th ratification; inaugural session convened in December, in Pohnpei, Federated States of Micronesia; Head of Interim Secretariat MICHAEL LODGE.

World Association for Animal Production (WAAP): Villa del Ragno, Via Nomentana 134, 00162 Rome, Italy; tel. (06) 86329141; fax (06) 86329263; e-mail waap@waap.it; internet www.waap.it; f. 1965; holds world conference on animal production every five years; encourages, sponsors and participates in regional meetings, seminars and symposia; mems: 17 mem. organizations; Pres. AKKE J. VAN DER ZIJPP (Netherlands); Sec.-Gen. JEAN GEORGES BOYAZOGLU (Greece); publ. *WAAP Newsletter*.

World Association of Veterinary Food-Hygienists (WAVFH): Federal Institute for Health Protection of Consumers and Veterinary Medicine (BgVV), Diedersdorfer Weg 1, 12277 Berlin, Germany; tel. (30) 8412-2101; fax (30) 8412-2951; e-mail p.teufel@bgvv.de; f. 1955 to promote hygienic food control and discuss research; mems: national asscns in 40 countries; Pres. Prof. PAUL TEUFEL; Sec. Treas. Dr L. ELLERBROEK.

World Association of Veterinary Microbiologists, Immunologists and Specialists in Infectious Diseases: Ecole Nationale Vétérinaire d'Alfort, 7 ave du Général de Gaulle, 94704 Maisons-Alfort Cédex, France; tel. 1-43-96-70-21; fax 1-43-96-70-22; f. 1967 to facilitate international contacts in the fields of microbiology, immunology and animal infectious diseases; Pres. Prof. C. PILET (France); publs *Comparative Immunology, Microbiology and Infectious Diseases*.

WorldFish Center (International Centre for Living Aquatic Resources Management—ICLARM): Jalan Batu Maung, Batu Maung, 11960 Bayan Lepas, Penang, Malaysia; POB 500, 10670 Penang; tel. (4) 626-1606; fax (4) 626-5530; e-mail worldfishcenter@cgiar.org; internet www.worldfishcenter.org; f. 1973; became a mem. of the Consultative Group on International Agricultural Research—CGIAR in 1992; aims to contribute to food security and poverty eradication in developing countries through the sustainable development and use of living aquatic resources; carries out research and promotes partnerships; Dir-Gen. MERYL J. WILLIAMS; publ. *NAGA* (quarterly newsletter).

World Ploughing Organization (WPO): Søkildevej 17, 5270 Odense N, Denmark; tel. 65-97-80-06; fax 65-97-80-35; internet www.worldploughing.org; f. 1952 to promote the World Ploughing Contest in a different country each year, to improve techniques and promote better understanding of soil cultivation practices through research and practical demonstrations; arranges tillage clinics world-wide; mems: affiliates in 29 countries; Gen. Sec. CARL ALLESØ; publ. *WPO Handbook* (annually).

World's Poultry Science Association (WPSA): c/o Dr P. C. M. Simons, POB 31, 7360 AA Beekbergen, Netherlands; tel. (55) 506-3250; fax (55) 506-4858; e-mail piet.simons@wur.nl; internet www.wpsa.com; f. 1912 to exchange knowledge in the industry, to encourage research and teaching, to publish information relating to production and marketing problems, to promote World Poultry Congresses and co-operate with governments; mems: individuals in more than 100 countries, branches in 70 countries; Pres. Prof. Dr RÜVEYDE AKBAY (Turkey); Sec. Dr PIET C. M. SIMONS (Netherlands); publ. *The World Poultry Science Journal* (quarterly).

World Veterinary Association: Rosenlunds Allé 8, 2720 Vanlose, Denmark; tel. 38-71-01-56; fax 38-71-03-22; e-mail wva@ddd.dk; internet www.worldvet.org; f. 1959 as a continuation of the International Veterinary Congresses; organizes quadrennial congress; mems: organizations in 76 countries, 19 organizations of veterinary specialists as associate members; Pres. Dr HERBERT SCHNEIDER; Exec. Sec. Dr LARS HOLSAAE.

Arts and Culture

Europa Nostra—Pan-European Federation for Heritage: Lange Voorhout 35, 2514 EC The Hague, Netherlands; tel. (70) 302-4050; fax (70) 361-7865; e-mail office@europanostra.org; internet www.europanostra.org; f. 1963; groups organizations and individuals concerned with the protection and enhancement of the European architectural and natural heritage and of the European environment; has consultative status with the Council of Europe; mems: 220 mem. organizations, around 170 supporting bodies, more than 1,200 individual mems; Pres. HRH The Prince Consort of Denmark; Exec. Pres. OTTO VON DER GABLENTZ (Germany); Sec.-Gen. SNESKA QUAEDVLIEG-MIHAILOVIĆ.

European Association of Conservatoires, Music Academies and Music High Schools: POB 805, 3500 AV Utrecht, Netherlands; tel. (30) 236-12-42; fax (30) 236-12-90; e-mail aecinfo@aecinfo.org; internet www.aecinfo.org; f. 1953; aims to establish and foster contacts and exchanges between and represent the interests of members; initiates and supports international collaboration through research projects, congresses and seminars; mems: 190 full mems, 28 associate mems; Pres. JOHANNES JOHANSSON; Gen. Sec. GEORGE

CAIRD; publs *The European Cultural Heritage Review* (annually), *Europa Nostra Scientific Bulletin,* conference proceedings.

European Society of Culture: Guidecca 54P (Calle Michelangelo, Villa Hériot), 30133 Venice, Italy; tel. (041) 5230210; fax (041) 5231033; e-mail info@societaeuropeacultura.it; internet www.societaeuropeacultura.it; f. 1950 to unite artists, poets, scientists, philosophers and others through mutual interests and friendship in order to safeguard and improve the conditions required for creative activity; maintains a library of 10,000 volumes; mems: national and local centres, and 2,000 individuals, in 60 countries; Pres. Prof. VINCENZO CAPPELLETTI (Italy); Gen. Sec. Dott. MICHELLE CAMPAGNOLO-BOUVIER.

Inter-American Music Council (Consejo Interamericano de Música—CIDEM): 2511 P St NW, Washington, DC 20007, USA; f. 1956 to promote the exchange of works, performances and information in all fields of music, to study problems relative to music education, to encourage activity in the field of musicology, to promote folklore research and music creation, and to establish distribution centres for music material of the composers of the Americas; mems: national music societies of 33 American countries; Sec.-Gen. EFRAÍN PAESKY.

International Association of Art (IAA): Maison de l'UNESCO, 1 rue Miollis, 75732 Paris Cédex 15, France; tel. 1-45-68-26-55; fax 1-45-67-22-87; f. 1954; mems: 104 national committees; Pres. UNA WALKER; Sec.-Gen. J. C. DE SALINS; publ. *IAA Newsletter* (quarterly).

International Association of Art Critics: 32 rue Yves Toudic, 75010 Paris, France; tel. 1-47-70-17-42; fax 1-47-70-17-81; e-mail office.paris@aica-int.org; internet www.aica-int.org; f. 1949 to increase co-operation in plastic arts, promote international cultural exchanges and protect the interests of mems; mems: 4,062 in 77 countries; Pres. HENRY MEYRIC HUGHES (UK); Sec.-Gen. RAMON TIO BELLIDO (France); publs *Annuaire, Newsletter* (quarterly).

International Association of Bibliophiles: Réserve des livres rares, Quai François Mauriac, 75706 Cédex 13, France; fax 1-53-79-54-60; f. 1963 to create contacts between bibliophiles and encourage book-collecting in different countries; organizes and encourages congresses, meetings, exhibitions and the award of scholarships; mems: 450; Pres. Conde DE ORGAZ (Spain); Sec.-Gen. JEAN-MARC CHATELAIN (France); publs *Le Bulletin du Bibliophile* (2 a year), yearbooks.

International Association of Literary Critics: 38 rue du Faubourg St-Jacques, 75014 Paris, France; tel. 1-53-10-12-13; fax 1-53-10-12-12; internet www.aicl.org; f. 1969; national centres in 34 countries; organizes congresses; Pres. ROBERT ANDRÉ; publ. *Revue* (2 a year).

International Association of Museums of Arms and Military History (IAMAM): c/o Senior Curator, Koninklijk Nederlands Leger en Wapenmuseum, Delft, Netherlands; tel. (4) 221-94-16; fax (4) 221-94-01; e-mail claude.gaier@museedarmes.be; internet www.klm-mra.be/ICOMAM/index.htm; f. 1957; links museums and other scientific institutions with public collections of arms and armour and military equipment, uniforms, etc.; holds triennial conferences and occasional specialist symposia; mems: 260 institutions in 60 countries; name change to International Cttee of Museums of Arms and Military History pending in 2004; Pres. GUY M. WILSON (UK); Sec.-Gen. JAN PIET PUYPE (Netherlands); publ.*The Mohonk Courier*.

International Board on Books for Young People (IBBY): Nonnenweg 12, Postfach, 4003 Basel, Switzerland; tel. (61) 272-2917; fax (61) 272-2757; e-mail ibby@eye.ch; internet www.ibby.org; f. 1953 to support and link bodies in all countries connected with children's book work; encourages the distribution of good children's books; promotes scientific investigation into problems of juvenile books; presents the Hans Christian Andersen Award every two years to a living author and a living illustrator whose work is an outstanding contribution to juvenile literature; presents the IBBY-Asahi Reading Promotion Award (every two years) to an organization that has made a significant contribution towards the encouragement of reading; sponsors International Children's Book Day (2 April); mems: national sections and individuals in more than 60 countries; Pres. PETER SCHNECK (Austria); Exec. Dir KIMETE BASHA; publs *Bookbird* (quarterly, in English), *Congress Papers, IBBY Honour List* (every 2 years), special bibliographies.

International Centre for the Study of the Preservation and Restoration of Cultural Property (ICCROM): Via di San Michele 13, 00153 Rome, Italy; tel. (06) 585531; fax (06) 58553349; e-mail iccrom@iccrom.org; internet www.iccrom.org; f. 1959; assembles documents on the preservation and restoration of cultural property; stimulates research and proffers advice; organizes missions of experts; undertakes training of specialists; mems: 113 countries; Dir-Gen. Dr NICHOLAS STANLEY-PRICE (UK); publ. *Newsletter* (annually, in Arabic, English, French and Spanish).

International Centre of Films for Children and Young People (Centre international du film pour l'enfance et la jeunesse—CIFEJ):

3774 rue Saint-Denis, Bureau 200, Montréal, QC H2W 2M1, Canada; tel. (514) 284-9388; fax (514) 284-0168; e-mail info@cifej .com; internet www.cifej.com; f. 1955; serves as a clearing house for information about: entertainment films (cinema and television) for children and young people, the influence of films on the young, and the regulations in force for the protection and education of young people; promotes production and distribution of suitable films and their appreciation; awards the CIFEJ prize at selected film festivals; mems: 163 mems in 53 countries; Exec. Dir Jo-Anne Blouin; publ. *CIFEJ Info* (monthly).

International Committee for the Diffusion of Arts and Literature through the Cinema (Comité international pour la diffusion des arts et des lettres par le cinéma—CIDALC): 24 blvd Poissonnière, 75009 Paris, France; tel. 1-42-46-13-60; f. 1930 to promote the creation and release of educational, cultural and documentary films and other films of educational value, in order to contribute to closer understanding between peoples; awards medals and prizes for films of exceptional merit; mems: national committees in 19 countries; Pres. Jean-Pierre Foucault (France); Sec.-Gen. Mario Verdone (Italy); publs *Annuaire CIDALC*, *Cinéma éducatif et culturel*.

International Comparative Literature Association (ICLA) (Association Internationale de Littérature Comparée): c/o Paola Mildonian, Letterature Comparate, Dipartim. di Studi Anglo-Americani e Ibero-Americani, Università Ca' Foscari-Venezia, Ca' Garzoni, S. Marco 3417, 30124 Venice, Italy; tel. (041) 2578427; fax (041) 2578476; e-mail iclaweb@byu.edu; internet www.byu.edu/icla; f. 1954 to work for the development of the comparative study of literature in modern languages; mems: societies and individuals in 78 countries; Pres. Koji Kawamoto; publs *ICLA Bulletin* (annually), *Literary Research* (2 a year).

International Confederation of Societies of Authors and Composers—World Congress of Authors and Composers: 20–26 blvd du Parc, 92200 Neuilly-sur-Seine, France; tel. 1-55-62-08-50; fax 1-55-62-08-60; e-mail cisac@cisac.org; internet www.cisac.org; f. 1926 to protect the rights of authors and composers; organizes biennial congress; mems: 204 mem. societies from 105 countries; Sec.-Gen. Eric Baptiste.

International Council of Graphic Design Associations (ICOGRADA): POB 5, Forest 2, 1190 Brussels, Belgium; tel. (2) 344-58-43; fax (2) 344-71-38; e-mail secretariat@icograda.org; internet www .icograda.org; f. 1963; aims to raise standards of graphic design; promotes the exchange of information; organizes exhibitions and congresses; maintains library, slide collection and archive; mems: 68 asscns in 43 countries; Pres. Robert L. Peters (Canada); Sec.-Gen. Tiffany Turkington (South Africa); publs *Newsletter* (quarterly), *Regulations and Guidelines governing International Design Competitions*, *Model Code of Professional Conduct*, other professional documents.

International Council of Museums (ICOM): Maison de l'UNESCO, 1 rue Miollis, 75732 Paris Cédex 15, France; tel. 1-47-34-05-00; fax 1-43-06-78-62; e-mail secretariat@icom.museum; internet www.icom.museum; f. 1946 to further international co-operation among museums and to advance museum interests; maintains with UNESCO the organization's documentation centre; mems: 20,000 individuals and institutions in 140 countries; Pres. Alissandra Cummins (Barbados); Sec.-Gen. John S. Zvereff (USA); publ. *ICOM News—Nouvelles de l'ICOM—Noticias del ICOM* (quarterly).

International Council on Monuments and Sites (ICOMOS): 49–51 rue de la Fédération, 75015 Paris, France; tel. 1-45-67-67-70; fax 1-45-66-06-22; e-mail secretariat@icomos.org; internet www .icomos.org; f. 1965 to promote the study and preservation of monuments and sites and to arouse and cultivate the interest of public authorities and people of every country in their cultural heritage; disseminates the results of research into the technical, social and administrative problems connected with the conservation of the architectural heritage; holds triennial General Assembly and Symposium; mems: c. 7,000, 21 international committees, 105 national committees; Pres. Dr Michael Petzet (Germany); Sec.-Gen. Dinu Bumbaru (Canada); publs *ICOMOS Newsletter* (quarterly), *Scientific Journal* (quarterly).

International Federation for Theatre Research (IFTR) (Fédération Internationale pour la Recherche Théâtrale): c/o Dean of Arts & Humanities, Lancaster University, Lancaster, LA1 4YN, United Kingdom; e-mail d.whitton@lancaster.ac.uk; internet www .firt-iftr.org; f. 1955 by 21 countries at the International Conference on Theatre History, London; Pres. Prof. Janelle Reinelt (USA); Joint Secs-Gen. Prof. David Whitton (UK), Prof. Frédéric Maurin (Canada); publs *Theatre Research International* (in association with Cambridge University Press, 3 a year).

International Federation of Film Archives (Fédération Internationale des Archives du Film—FIAF): rue Defacqz 1, B-1000 Brussels, Belgium; tel. (2) 538-30-65; fax (2) 534-47-74; e-mail info@ fiafnet.org; internet www.fiafnet.org; f. 1938 to encourage the creation of audio-visual archives for the collection and conservation of the moving image heritage of every country; facilitates co-operation and exchanges between film archives; promotes public interest in the art of the cinema; aids and conducts research; compiles new documentation; holds annual congress; mems: in 65 countries; Pres. Eva Orbanz (Germany); Sec.-Gen. Meg Labrom (Australia); publs *Journal of Film Preservation* (2 a year), *FIAF International Film Archive Database* (2 a year).

International Federation of Film Producers' Associations (Fédération Internationale des associations de Producteurs de Films—FIAPF): 9 rue de l'Echelle, 75002 Paris, France; tel. 1-44-77-97-50; fax 1-42-56-16-52; e-mail infos@fiapf.org; internet fiapf.org; f. 1933 to represent film production internationally, to defend its general interests and promote its development; studies all cultural, legal, economic, technical and social problems related to film production; mems: national asscns in 23 countries; Pres. Aurelio de Laurentiis (Italy); Dir-Gen. André Chaubeau (France).

International Institute for Children's Literature and Reading Research (Internationales Institut für Jugendliteratur und Leseforschung): 1040 Vienna, Mayerhofgasse 6, Austria; tel. (1) 50503-59; fax (1) 50503-5917; e-mail office@jugendliteratur.net; internet www.jugendliteratur.net; f. 1965 as an international documentation, research and advisory centre of juvenile literature and reading; maintains specialized library; arranges conferences and exhibitions; compiles recommendation lists; mems: individual and group members in 28 countries; Pres. Dr Hilde Hawlicek; Dir Karin Haller; publ. *1000 & 1 Buch* (quarterly).

International Institute for Conservation of Historic and Artistic Works: 6 Buckingham St, London, WC2N 6BA, United Kingdom; tel. (20) 7839-5975; fax (20) 7976-1564; e-mail iicon@ compuserve.com; internet www.iiconservation.org; f. 1950; mems: 3,350 individual, 450 institutional mems; Pres. Andrew Oddy; Exec. Sec. Graham Voce; publs *Studies in Conservation* (quarterly), *Reviews in Conservation* (annually).

International Liaison Centre for Cinema and Television Schools (Centre international de liaison des écoles de cinéma et de television—CILECT): 8 rue Thérésienne, 1000 Brussels, Belgium; tel. (2) 511-98-39; fax (2) 511-98-39; e-mail hverh.cilect@skynet.be; internet www.cilect.org; f. 1955 to link higher teaching and research institutes and improve education of makers of films and television programmes; organizes conferences and student film festivals; runs a training programme for developing countries; mems: 107 institutions in 52 countries; Pres. Caterina D'Amico (Italy); Exec. Sec. Henry Verhasselt (Belgium); publ. *Newsletter*.

International Music Council (IMC): Maison de l'UNESCO, 1 rue Miollis, 75732 Paris Cédex 15, France; tel. 1-45-68-48-50; fax 1-43-06-87-98; e-mail imc@unesco.org; internet www.unesco.org/imc; f. 1949 to promote musical diversity and cultural rights for all; mems: 34 international non-governmental organizations, national committees in 74 countries; Pres. Kifah Fakhouri (Jordan); Sec.-Gen. Damien M. Pwono (Germany).

Members of IMC include:

European Festivals Association: Kastel Borluut, Kleine Gentstraat 46, 9051 Ghent, Belgium; tel. (9) 243-94-94; e-mail ghent@ euro-festival.net; internet www.euro-festival.net; f. 1952 to maintain high artistic standards and the representative character of art festivals; holds annual General Assembly; a Eurofest Research and Training Centre is based in Coppet, Switzerland; mems: 92 regular international performing arts festivals in 30 European countries, Israel, Japan, Lebanon and Mexico; Pres. Gavin Henderson; publ. *Festivals* (annually).

International Association of Music Libraries, Archives and Documentation Centres (IAML): c/o Music Room, National Library of New Zealand, POB 1467, Wellington, New Zealand; tel. (4) 474-3039; fax (4) 474-3035; e-mail roger.flury@natlib.govt.nz; internet www.iaml.info; f. 1951; mems: 2,003 institutions and individuals in 58 countries; Pres. Massimo Gentili-Tedeschi (Italy); Sec.-Gen. Roger Flury (New Zealand); publ. *Fontes artis musicae* (quarterly).

International Council for Traditional Music (ICTM): Dept of Ethnomusicology, UCLA, 2539 Schoenberg, Box 957178, Los Angeles, California, CA 90095-7178, USA; tel. (310) 794-1858; fax (310) 206-4738; e-mail ictm@arts.ucla.edu; internet www .ethnomusic.ucla.edu/ictm; f. 1947 (as International Folk Music Council) to further the study, practice, documentation, preservation and dissemination of traditional music of all countries; holds conference every two years; mems: 1,650; Pres. Dr Krister Malm (Sweden); Sec.-Gen. Prof. Anthony Seeger (USA); publs *Yearbook for Traditional Music*, *ICTM Bulletin* (2 a year), *Directory of Traditional Music* (every 2 years).

International Federation of Musicians: 21 bis rue Victor Massé, 75009 Paris, France; tel. 1-45-26-31-23; fax 1-45-26-31-57; e-mail office@fim-musicians.com; internet www.fim-musicians

.com/; f. 1948 to promote and protect the interests of musicians in affiliated unions; mems: 69 unions totalling 250,000 individuals in 57 countries; Pres. John F. Smith (UK); Gen. Sec. Benoît Machuel (France).

International Music and Media Centre (Internationales Musik + Medienzentrum): 1230 Vienna, Speisinger Str. 121–127, Austria; tel. (1) 889 03-15; fax (1) 889 03-1577; e-mail office@imz .at; internet www.imz.at; f. 1961 for the study and dissemination of music through technical media (film, television, radio, gramophone); organizes congresses, seminars and screenings on music in audio-visual media; holds courses and competitions designed to strengthen the relationship between performing artists and audio-visual media; mems: 110 ordinary mems and 30 associate mems in 33 countries, including 50 broadcasting organizations; Pres. Henk van der Meulen (Netherlands); Sec.-Gen. Franz A. Patay (Austria).

International Society for Contemporary Music (ISCM): c/o Gaudeamus, Swammerdamstraat 38, 1091 RV Amsterdam, Netherlands; tel. (20) 6947349; fax (20) 6947258; e-mail info@iscm.nl; internet www.iscm.nl; f. 1922 to promote the development of contemporary music; organizes annual World Music Day; mems: organizations in 48 countries; Pres. Richard Tsang; Sec.-Gen. Henk Heuvelmans.

Jeunesses Musicales International (JMI): Palais des Beaux-Arts, 10 rue Royale, 1000 Brussels, Belgium; tel. (2) 513-97-74; fax (2) 514-47-55; e-mail mail@jmi.net; internet www.jmi.net; f. 1945 to enable young people to develop, through music, and to stimulate contacts between member countries; mems: organizations in 40 countries; Sec.-Gen. Dag Franzén; publ. *JMI News* (6 a year).

World Federation of International Music Competitions (WFIMC): 104 rue de Carouge, 1205 Geneva, Switzerland; tel. (22) 3213620; fax (22) 7811418; e-mail fmcim@iprolink.ch; internet www.wfimc.org; f. 1957 to co-ordinate the arrangements for affiliated competitions and to exchange experience; holds General Assembly annually; mems: 118; Pres. Marianne Granvig; Sec.-Gen. Renate Ronnefeld.

International PEN (World Association of Writers): 9–10 Charterhouse Bldgs, Goswell Rd, London, EC1M 7AT, United Kingdom; tel. (20) 7253-4308; fax (20) 7253-5711; e-mail intpen@dircon.co.uk; internet www.internationalpen.org; f. 1921 to promote co-operation between writers; mems: c. 14,000, 138 centres world-wide. International; Pres. Jiří Gruša; International Sec. Joanne Leedom-Ackerman; publ. *PEN International* (2 a year, in English, French and Spanish, with the assistance of UNESCO).

International Theatre Institute (ITI): Maison de l'UNESCO, 1 rue Miollis, 75732 Paris Cédex 15, France; tel. 1-45-68-48-80; fax 1-45-66-50-40; e-mail iti@unesco.org; internet iti-worldwide.org; f. 1948 to facilitate cultural exchanges and international understanding in the domain of the theatre; holds conferences; mems: 87 member nations, each with an ITI national centre; Pres. Manfred Beilharz (Germany); Sec.-Gen. a.i. André-Louis Perinetti (France); publs *ITI News* (3 times a year in English and French), *World Theatre Directory* (every 2 years), *The World of Theatre* (every 2 years).

Organization of World Heritage Cities: 15 rue Saint-Nicolas, Québec, QC G1K 1MB, Canada; tel. (418) 692-0000; fax (418) 692-5558; e-mail secretariat@ovpm.org; internet www.ovpm.org; f. 1993 to assist cities inscribed on the UNESCO World Heritage List to implement the Convention concerning the Protection of the World Cultural and Natural Heritage (1972); promotes co-operation between city authorities, in particular in the management and sustainable development of historic sites; holds a General Assembly, comprising the mayors of member cities, at least every two years; mems: 208 cities world-wide; Sec.-Gen. Denis Ricard.

Pan-African Writers' Association (PAWA): PAWA House, Roman Ridge, POB C456, Cantonments, Accra, Ghana; tel. (21) 773-062; fax (21) 773-042; e-mail pawa@ghana.com; f. 1989 to link African creative writers, defend the rights of authors and promote awareness of literature; Sec.-Gen. Atukwei Okai (Ghana).

Royal Asiatic Society of Great Britain and Ireland: 60 Queen's Gardens, London, W2 3AF, United Kingdom; tel. (20) 7724-4742; fax (20) 7706-4008; e-mail info@royalasiaticsociety.org; internet www .royalasiaticsociety.org; f. 1823 for the study of history and cultures of the East; mems: c. 700, branch societies in Asia; Pres. Prof. F. C. R. Robinson; Sec. Alison Ohta; publ. *Journal* (3 a year).

Society of African Culture (Société Africaine de Culture): 25 bis rue des Ecoles, 75005 Paris, France; tel. 1-43-54-15-88; fax 1-43-25-96-67; f. 1956 to create unity and friendship among scholars in Africa, for the encouragement of their own cultures; mems: national asscns and individuals in 44 countries and territories; Pres. Aimé Césaire; Gen. Sec. Christiane Yandé Diop; publ. *La Revue Présence Africaine* (2 a year).

United World Federation of United Cities: 41 rue de la République, 93200 Saint Denis, France; tel. 1-55-84-23-50; fax 1-55-84-23-51; e-mail contact@fmcu-uto.org; internet www.fmcu-uto.org; f. 1957, as the United Towns Organization, by Le Monde Bilingue (f. 1951); aims to set up permanent links between towns throughout the world, leading to social, cultural, economic and other exchanges favouring world peace, understanding and development; involved in sustainable development and environmental activities at municipal level; mem. of the Habitat II follow-up group; mems: 4,000 local and regional authorities throughout the world; World Pres. Mercedes Bresso; Sec.-Gen. Paolo Morello; publs *Cités Unies* (quarterly, in French, English and Spanish), *Newsletter* (3 a year in English, French, Italian and Spanish).

World Crafts Council International: Anthrakitou 5 and Tsechouli Street, Kastro Ioanninon, 452 21 Ioannina, Greece; tel. (30) 26510-72315; fax (30) 26510-36695; e-mail wis@epcon.gr; internet www.wccwis.gr; f. 1964; aims to strengthen the status of crafts as a vital part of cultural life, to link crafts people around the world, and to foster wider recognition of their work; mems: national organizations in more than 87 countries; Pres. Elena Averoff (Greece); publs *Annual Report*, *Newsletter* (2 a year), *WCC News* (in English and French).

Commodities

African Groundnut Council (AGC): Trade Fair Complex, Badagry Expressway Km 15, POB 3025, Lagos, Nigeria; tel. (1) 4715257; fax (1) 887811; e-mail afrgroundnut_council@yahoo.com; f. 1964 to advise producing countries on marketing policies; mems: Gambia, Mali, Niger, Nigeria, Senegal, Sudan; Chair. Choguel Maïga; Exec. Sec. Elhadj Mour Mamadou Samb (Senegal); publ. *Groundnut Review*.

African Oil Palm Development Association (AFOPDA): 15 BP 341, Abidjan 15, Côte d'Ivoire; tel. 25-15-18; fax 21-97-06; f. 1985; seeks to increase production of, and investment in, palm oil; mems: Benin, Cameroon, Democratic Republic of the Congo, Côte d'Ivoire, Ghana, Guinea, Nigeria, Togo; Exec. Sec. Baudelaire Hounsinou Sourou.

African Petroleum Producers' Association (APPA): POB 1097, Brazzaville, Republic of the Congo; tel. 83-64-38; fax 83-67-99; f. 1987 by African petroleum-producing countries to reinforce co-operation among regional producers and to stabilize prices; council of ministers responsible for the hydrocarbons sector meets twice a year; holds annual Congress and Exhibition: Algiers, Algeria (Feb. 2004); mems: Algeria, Angola, Benin, Cameroon, Democratic Republic of the Congo, Republic of the Congo, Côte d'Ivoire, Egypt, Equatorial Guinea, Gabon, Libya, Nigeria; Exec. Sec. Maxime Obiang-Nze; publ. *APPA Bulletin* (2 a year).

Asian and Pacific Coconut Community (APCC): 3rd Floor, Lina Bldg, Jalan H. R. Rasuna Said Kav. B7, Kuningan, Jakarta 10002, Indonesia; POB 1343, Jakarta 10013; tel. (21) 5221712; fax (21) 5221714; e-mail apcc@indo.net.id; internet www.apccsec.sg; f. 1969 to promote and co-ordinate all activities of the coconut industry, to achieve higher production and better processing, marketing and research; organizes annual Coconut Technical Meeting (COCOTECH); mems: Fiji, India, Indonesia, Kiribati, Malaysia, Marshall Islands, Federated States of Micronesia, Papua New Guinea, Philippines, Samoa, Solomon Islands, Sri Lanka, Thailand, Vanuatu, Viet Nam; assoc. mem.: Palau; Chair. Ioteba Redfern; Exec. Dir Dr P. Rathinam; publs *Cocomunity* (fortnightly), *CORD* (2 a year), *Statistical Yearbook*, *Cocoinfo International* (2 a year).

Association of Natural Rubber Producing Countries (ANRPC): Bangunan Getah Asli, 148 Jalan Ampang, 7th Floor, 50450 Kuala Lumpur, Malaysia; tel. (3) 2611900; fax (3) 2613014; e-mail anrpc@capo.jaring.my; f. 1970 to co-ordinate the production and marketing of natural rubber, to promote technical co-operation amongst members and to bring about fair and stable prices for natural rubber; holds seminars, meetings and training courses on technical and statistical subjects; a joint regional marketing system has been agreed in principle; mems: India, Indonesia, Malaysia, Papua New Guinea, Singapore, Sri Lanka, Thailand, Viet Nam; Sec.-Gen. G. W. S. K. de Silva; publs *ANRPC Statistical Bulletin* (quarterly), *ANRPC Newsletter*.

Cocoa Producers' Alliance (CPA): Old National Assembly, Tafawa Balewa Sq., POB 1718, Lagos, Nigeria; tel. (1) 2635574; fax (1) 2635684; e-mail copal@alphalinkserve.com; internet www .copal-cpa.org; f. 1962 to exchange technical and scientific information, to discuss problems of mutual concern to producers, to ensure adequate supplies at remunerative prices and to promote consumption; mems: Brazil, Cameroon, Côte d'Ivoire, Dominican Republic, Gabon, Ghana, Malaysia, Nigeria, São Tomé and Príncipe, Togo; Sec.-Gen. Hope Sona Ebai.

Common Fund for Commodities: Postbus 74656, 1070 BR, Amsterdam, Netherlands; tel. (20) 575-4949; fax (20) 676-0231; e-mail managing.director@common-fund.org; internet www .common-fund.org; f. 1989 as the result of an UNCTAD negotiation conference; finances commodity development measures including research, marketing, productivity improvements and vertical diversification, with the aim of increasing the long-term competitiveness of particular commodities; paid-in capital US $165m; mems: 106 countries and the AU, EC and COMESA; Man. Dir (also Chief Exec. and Chair.) ROLF BOEHNKE.

European Aluminium Association (EEA): 12 ave de Broqueville, 1150 Brussels, Belgium; tel. (2) 775-63-63; fax (2) 779-05-31; e-mail eaa@eaa.be; internet www.eaa.net; f. 1981 to encourage studies, research and technical co-operation, to make representations to international bodies and to assist national asscns in dealing with national authorities; mems: individual producers of primary aluminium, 17 national groups for wrought producers, the Organization of European Aluminium Smelters, representing producers of recycled aluminium, and the European Aluminium Foil Association, representing foil rollers and converters; Chair. D. BRAUN; Sec.-Gen. P. DE SCHRYNMAKERS; publs *Annual Report, EAA Quarterly Report.*

European Association for the Trade in Jute and Related Products: Adriaan Goekooplaan 5, POB 29822, 2502 LV, The Hague, Netherlands; tel. (70) 338-4659; fax (70) 351-2777; e-mail info@eurojute.com; internet www.eurojute.com; f. 1970 to maintain contacts between national asscns, permit the exchange of information and represent the interests of the trade; carries out scientific research; mems: enterprises in eight European countries; Sec.-Gen. H. J. J. KRUIPER.

European Committee of Sugar Manufacturers: 182 ave de Tervueren, 1150 Brussels, Belgium; tel. (2) 762-07-60; fax (2) 771-00-26; e-mail cefs@cefs.org; internet www.cefs.org; f. 1954 to collect statistics and information, conduct research and promote co-operation between national organizations; mems: national asscns in 15 European countries; Pres. JOHANN MARIHART; Dir-Gen. J. L. BARJOL.

Group of Latin American and Caribbean Sugar Exporting Countries (Grupo de Países Latinoamericanos y del Caribe Exportadores de Azúcar—GEPLACEA): Paseo de la Reforma 1030, Lomas de Chapultepec, 11000 México DF, Mexico; tel. (55) 5520-9711; fax (55) 5520-5089; e-mail geplacea@dns.telecom.ipn.mx; internet www .geplacea.ipn.mx; f. 1974 to serve as a forum for consultation on the production and sale of sugar to contribute to the adoption of agreed positions at international meetings on sugar; to provide training and the transfer of technology; to exchange scientific and technical knowledge on agriculture and the sugar industry; to co-ordinate the various branches of sugar processing; and to co-ordinate policies of action, in order to achieve fair and remunerative prices; mems: 23 Latin American and Caribbean countries (accounting for about 45% of world sugar exports and 66% of world cane sugar production); Exec. Sec. LUIS EDUARDO ZEDILLO PONCE DE LEÓN.

Inter-African Coffee Organization (IACO) (Organisation internationale du café—OIAC): BP V210, Abidjan, Côte d'Ivoire; tel. 20-21-61-31; fax 20-21-62-12; e-mail oiac-iaco@aviso.ci; f. 1960 to adopt a common policy on the marketing and consumption of coffee; aims to foster greater collaboration in research technology transfer through the African Coffee Research Network (ACRN); seeks to improve the quality of coffee exports, and implement poverty reduction programmes focusing on value added product (VAP) and the manufacturing of green coffee; mems: 25 coffee-producing countries in Africa; Chair. AMADOU SOUMAHORO (Côte d'Ivoire); Sec.-Gen. JOSEFA LEONEL CORREIA SACKO (Angola).

International Cadmium Association: 12110 Sunset Hills Rd, Suite 110, Reston, VA 22090, USA; tel. (703) 709-1400; fax (703) 709-1402; f. 1976; covers all aspects of the production and use of cadmium and its compounds; includes almost all producers and users of cadmium; Chair. DAVID SINCLAIR (USA).

International Cocoa Organization (ICCO): 22 Berners St, London, W1P 3DB, United Kingdom; tel. (20) 7637-3211; fax (20) 7631-0114; e-mail exec.dir@icco.org; internet www.icco.org; f. 1973 under the first International Cocoa Agreement, 1972; the ICCO supervises the implementation of the agreements, and provides member governments with up-to-date information on the world cocoa economy; the sixth International Cocoa Agreement (2001) entered into force in October 2003; mems: 12 exporting countries and 18 importing countries; and the European Union; Council Chair. 2004–05 S. P. ESSOMBA ABANDA (Cameroon); Acting Exec. Dir Dr J. VINGERHOETS (Netherlands); publs *Quarterly Bulletin of Cocoa Statistics, Annual Report, World Cocoa Directory, Cocoa Newsletter,* studies on the world cocoa economy.

International Coffee Organization (ICO): 22 Berners St, London, W1T 4DD, United Kingdom; tel. (20) 7580-8591; fax (20) 7580-6129; e-mail info@ico.org; internet www.ico.org; f. 1963 under the International Coffee Agreement, 1962, which was renegotiated in 1968, 1976, 1983, 1994 (extended in 1999) and 2001; aims to improve international co-operation and provide a forum for intergovernmental consultations on coffee matters; to facilitate international trade in coffee by the collection, analysis and dissemination of statistics; to act as a centre for the collection, exchange and publication of coffee information; to promote studies in the field of coffee; and to encourage an increase in coffee consumption; mems: 40 exporting and 15 importing countries; Chair. of Council JACQUES THINSY (Belgium); Exec. Dir NÉSTOR OSORIO (Colombia).

International Confederation of European Sugar Beet Growers (Confédération internationale des betteraviers européens—CIBE): 29 rue du Général Foy, 75008 Paris, France; tel. 1-44-69-39-00; fax 1-42-93-28-93; f. 1925 to act as a centre for the co-ordination and dissemination of information about beet sugar production and the industry to represent the interests of sugar beet growers at an international level; mems: asscns in Austria, Belgium, Czech Republic, Denmark, Finland, France, Germany, Greece, Hungary, Ireland, Italy, Lithuania, Netherlands, Poland, Portugal, Romania, Slovakia, Spain, Sweden, Switzerland, United Kingdom; Pres. OTTO VON ARNOLD (Sweden); Sec.-Gen. H. CHAVANES (France).

International Cotton Advisory Committee (ICAC): 1629 K St, NW, Suite 702, Washington, DC 20006-1636, USA; tel. (202) 463-6660; fax (202) 463-6950; e-mail secretariat@icac.org; internet www .icac.org; f. 1939 to observe developments in world cotton; to collect and disseminate statistics; to suggest measures for the furtherance of international collaboration in maintaining and developing a sound world cotton economy; and to provide a forum for international discussions on cotton prices; mems: 41 countries; Exec. Dir Dr TERRY TOWNSEND (USA); publs *Cotton This Week!* (internet/e-mail only), *Cotton This Month, Cotton: Review of the World Situation*(every 2 months), *Cotton: World Statistics* (annually), *The ICAC Recorder,World Textile Demand* (annually), other surveys, studies, trade analyses and technical publications.

International Grains Council (IGC): 1 Canada Sq., Canary Wharf, London, E14 5AE, United Kingdom; tel. (20) 7513-1122; fax (20) 7513-0630; e-mail igc@igc.org.uk; internet www.igc.org.uk; f. 1949 as International Wheat Council, present name adopted in 1995; responsible for the administration of the International Grains Agreement, 1995, comprising the Grain Trade Convention (GTC) and the Food Aid Convention (FAC, under which donors pledge specified minimum annual amounts of food aid for developing countries in the form of grain and/or other eligible products); aims to further international co-operation in all aspects of trade in grains, to promote international trade in grains, and to achieve a free flow of this trade, particularly in developing member countries; seeks to contribute to the stability of the international grain market; acts as a forum for consultations between members; provides comprehensive information on the international grain market; mems: 25 countries and the EU; Exec. Dir G. DENIS; publs *World Grain Statistics* (annually), *Wheat and Coarse Grain Shipments* (annually), *Report for the Fiscal Year* (annually), *Grain Market Report* (monthly), *IGC Grain Market Indicators* (weekly).

International Jute Study Group (IJSG): 145 Monipuriparu, Near Farmgate, Tejgaon, Dhaka 1215, Bangladesh; tel. (2) 9125581; fax (2) 9125248; e-mail ijoinf@bdmail.net; f. 2002 as successor to International Jute Organization (f. 1984 in accordance with an agreement made by 48 producing and consuming countries in 1982, under the auspices of UNCTAD); aims to improve the jute economy and the quality of jute and jute products through research and development projects and market promotion; Sec.-Gen T. NANADA-KUMAR.

International Lead and Zinc Study Group (ILZSG): 1 Mill St, London, SE1 2DF, United Kingdom; tel. (20) 7740-2750; fax (20) 7740-2983; e-mail root@ilzsg.org; internet www.ilzsg.org; f. 1959 for intergovernmental consultation on world trade in lead and zinc; conducts studies and provides information on trends in supply and demand; mems: 28 countries; Chair. A. IGNATOW (Canada); Sec.-Gen. DON SMALE; publ. *Lead and Zinc Statistics* (monthly).

International Molybdenum Association (IMOA): 2 Baron's Gate, 33 Rothschild Rd, London, W4 5HT, United Kingdom; tel. (20) 8742-2274; fax (20) 8742-7345; e-mail info@imoa.info; internet www .imoa.info; f. 1989; collates statistics; promotes the use of molybdenum; monitors health and environmental issues in the molybdenum industry; mems: 49; Pres. J. GRAELL; Sec.-Gen. MICHAEL MABY.

International Olive Oil Council: Príncipe de Vergara 154, 28002 Madrid, Spain; tel. (91) 5903638; fax (91) 5631263; e-mail iooc@ internationaloliveoil.org; internet www.internationaloliveoil.org; f. 1959 to administer the International Agreement on Olive Oil and Table Olives, which aims to promote international co-operation in connection with problems of the world economy for olive products; works to prevent unfair competition, to encourage the production and consumption of, and international trade in, olive products, and to reduce the disadvantages caused by fluctuations of supplies on the market; mems: of the 1986 Agreement (Fourth Agreement, amended and extended in 1993; last prolonged in 2003): nine mainly producing countries, four mainly importing country, and the European Community; Exec. Dir HABIB ESSID; publs *Information Sheet of the IOOC* (fortnightly, in French and Spanish), *OLIVAE* (5 a year, in English, French, Italian and Spanish).

International Pepper Community (IPC): 4th Floor, Lina Bldg, Jalan H. R. Rasuna Said, Kav. B7, Kuningan, Jakarta 12920, Indonesia; tel. (21) 5224902; fax (21) 5224905; e-mail ipc@indo.net .id; internet www.ipcnet.org; f. 1972 for promoting, co-ordinating and harmonizing all activities relating to the pepper economy; mems: Brazil, India, Indonesia, Malaysia, Federated States of Micronesia, Papua New Guinea, Sri Lanka, Thailand; Exec. Dir Dr K. P. G. MENON; publs *Pepper Statistical Yearbook, International Pepper News Bulletin* (quarterly), *Directory of Pepper Exporters, Directory of Pepper Importers, Weekly Prices Bulletin, Pepper Market Review*.

International Platinum Association: Kroegerstr. 5, Frankfurt-am-Main, 60313, Germany; tel. (69) 287941; fax (69) 283601; e-mail info@platinuminfo.net; internet www.platinuminfo.net; links principal producers and fabricators of platinum; Pres. DEREK G. ENGEL-BRECHT; Man. Dir MARCUS NURDIN.

International Rubber Study Group: Heron House, 109–115 Wembley Hill Rd, Wembley, HA9 8DA, United Kingdom; tel. (20) 8900-5400; fax (20) 8903-2848; e-mail irsg@rubberstudy.com; internet www.rubberstudy.com; f. 1944 to provide a forum for the discussion of problems affecting synthetic and natural rubber and to provide statistical and other general information on rubber; mems: 17 governments; Sec.-Gen. Dr A. F. S. BUDIMAN (Indonesia); publs *Rubber Statistical Bulletin* (every 2 months), *Rubber Industry Report* (every 2 months), *Proceedings of International Rubber Forums* (annually), *World Rubber Statistics Handbook, Key Rubber Indicators, Rubber Statistics Yearbook* (annually), *Rubber Economics Yearbook* (annually), *Outlook for Elastomers* (annually).

International Silk Association: 34 rue de la Charité, 69002 Lyon, France; tel. 4-78-42-10-79; fax 4-78-37-56-72; e-mail isa-silk .ais-sole@wanadoo.fr; f. 1949 to promote closer collaboration between all branches of the silk industry and trade, develop the consumption of silk, and foster scientific research; collects and disseminates information and statistics relating to the trade and industry; organizes biennial congresses; mems: employers' and technical organizations in 40 countries; Gen. Sec. X. LAVERGNE; publs *ISA Newsletter* (monthly), congress reports, standards, trade rules, etc.

International Spice Group: c/o International Trade Centre (UNCTAD/WTO), 54–56 rue de Montbrillant, 1202 Geneva, Switzerland; tel. (22) 7300101; fax (22) 7300254; e-mail itcreg@intracen.org; f. 1983 to provide a forum for producers and consumers of spices; works to increase the consumption of spices; mems: 33 producer countries, 15 importing countries; Chair. HERNAL HAMILTON (Jamaica).

International Sugar Organization: 1 Canada Sq., Canary Wharf, London, E14 5AA, United Kingdom; tel. (20) 7513-1144; fax (20) 7513-1146; e-mail exdir@isosugar.org; internet www.isosugar.org; administers the International Sugar Agreement (1992), with the objectives of stimulating co-operation, facilitating trade and encouraging demand; aims to improve conditions in the sugar market through debate, analysis and studies; serves as a forum for discussion; holds annual seminars and workshops; sponsors projects from developing countries; mems: 71 countries producing some 83% of total world sugar; Exec. Dir Dr PETER BARON; publs *Sugar Year Book, Monthly Statistical Bulletin, Market Report and Press Summary, Quarterly Market Outlook*, seminar proceedings.

International Tea Committee Ltd (ITC): Sir John Lyon House, 5 High Timber St, London, EC4V 3NH, United Kingdom; tel. (20) 7248-4672; fax (20) 7329-6955; e-mail info@intteacomm.co.uk; internet www.inttea.com; f. 1933 to administer the International Tea Agreement; now serves as a statistical and information centre; in 1979 membership was extended to include consuming countries; producer mems: national tea boards or asscns in seven countries; consumer mems: United Kingdom Tea Asscn, Tea Asscn of the USA Inc., Irish Tea Traders' Asscn, Netherland Coffee Roasters and Tea Packers' Asscn, and the Tea Council of Canada; assoc. mems: Netherlands and UK ministries of agriculture, Japan and national tea boards/asscns in six producing countries; Chair. M. J. BUNSTON; Chief Exec. MANUJA PEIRIS; publs *Annual Bulletin of Statistics, Monthly Statistical Summary*.

International Tea Promotion Association (ITPA): c/o Tea Board of Kenya, POB 20064, 00200 Nairobi, Kenya; tel. (20) 572421; fax (20) 562120; e-mail teaboardk@kenyaweb.com; internet www .teaboard.or.ke; f. 1979; mems: eight countries; Chair. GEORGE M. KIMANI; publ. *International Tea Journal* (2 a year).

International Tobacco Growers' Association (ITGA): Apdo 5, 6001-081 Castelo Branco, Portugal; tel. (272) 325901; fax (272) 325906; e-mail itga@mail.telepac.pt; internet www.tobaccoleaf.org; f. 1984 to provide a forum for the exchange of views and information

of interest to tobacco producers; mems: 22 countries producing over 80% of the world's internationally traded tobacco; Pres. ALBERT KAMULAGA (Malawi); Exec. Dir ANTONIO ABRUNHOSA (Portugal); publs *Tobacco Courier* (quarterly), *Tobacco Briefing*.

International Tropical Timber Organization (ITTO): International Organizations Center, 5th Floor, Pacifico-Yokohama, 1-1-1, Minato-Mirai, Nishi-ku, Yokohama 220-0012, Japan; tel. (45) 223-1110; fax (45) 223-1111; e-mail itto@itto.or.jp; internet www.itto.or .jp; f. 1985 under the International Tropical Timber Agreement (1983); a new treaty, ITTA 1994, came into force in 1997; provides a forum for consultation and co-operation between countries that produce and consume tropical timber, and is dedicated to the sustainable development and conservation of tropical forests; facilitates progress towards 'Objective 2000', which aims to move as rapidly as possible towards achieving exports of tropical timber and timber products from sustainably managed resources; encourages, through policy and project work, forest management, conservation and restoration, the further processing of tropical timber in producing countries, and the gathering and analysis of market intelligence and economic information; mems: 33 producing and 26 consuming countries and the EU; Exec. Dir Dr MANOEL SOBRAL FILHO; publs *Annual Review and Assessment of the World Timber Situation, Tropical Timber Market Information Service* (every 2 weeks), *Tropical Forest Update* (quarterly).

International Tungsten Industry Association (ITIA): 2 Baron's Gate, 33 Rothschild Rd, London, W4 5HT, United Kingdom; tel. (20) 8742-2274; fax (20) 8742-7345; e-mail info@itia.info; internet www .itia.info; f. 1988 (fmrly Primary Tungsten Asscn, f. 1975); promotes use of tungsten; collates statistics; prepares market reports; monitors health and environmental issues in the tungsten industry; mems: 51; Pres. R. FILLNOW; Sec.-Gen. MICHAEL MABY.

International Vine and Wine Organisation (Organisation Internationale de la Vigne et du Vin—OIV): 18 rue d'Aguesseau, 75008 Paris, France; tel. 1-44-94-80-80; fax 1-42-66-90-63; e-mail oiv@oiv .int; internet www.oiv.int; f. 1924 to study all the scientific, technical, economic and human problems concerning the vine and its products to spread knowledge and facilitate contacts between researchers; mems: 18 countries; Dir-Gen. FEDERICO CASTELLUCCI (Italy); publs *Bulletin de l'OIV* (every 2 months), *Lettre de l'OIV* (monthly), *Lexique de la Vigne et du Vin, Recueil des méthodes internationales d'analyse des vins, Code international des Pratiques oenologiques, Codex oenologique international*, numerous scientific publications.

International Zinc Association: 168 ave de Tervueren, Box 4, 1150 Brussels, Belgium; tel. (2) 776-00-70; fax (2) 776-00-89; e-mail email@iza.com; internet www.iza.com; f. 1990 to represent the world zinc industry; provide a forum for senior executives to address global issues requiring industry-wide action; consider new applications for zinc and zinc products; foster understanding of zinc's role in the environment; build a sustainable development policy; mems: 28 zinc-producing countries; Exec. Dir EDOUARD GERVAIS; publ. *Zinc Protects* (quarterly).

Lead Development Association International: 42 Weymouth St, London, W1G 6NP, United Kingdom; tel. (20) 7499-8422; fax (20) 7493-1555; e-mail enq@ldaint.org; internet www.ldaint.org; f. 1956; provides authoritative information on the use of lead and its compounds; Financed by lead producers and users in the United Kingdom, Europe and elsewhere; Dir Dr D. N. WILSON (UK).

Regional Association of Oil and Natural Gas Companies in Latin America and the Caribbean (Asociación Regional de Empresas de Petróleo y Gas Natural en Latinoamérica y el Caribe—ARPEL): Javier de Viana 2345, Casilla de correo 1006, 11200 Montevideo, Uruguay; tel. (2) 4106993; fax (2) 4109207; e-mail bsettembri@arpel.org.uy; internet www.arpel.org; f. 1965 as the Mutual Assistance of the Latin American Oil Companies; aims to initiate and implement activities for the development of the oil and natural gas industry in Latin America and the Caribbean; promotes the expansion of business opportunities and the improvement of the competitive advantages of its members; promotes guide-lines in support of competition in the sector; and supports the efficient and sustainable exploitation of hydrocarbon resources and the supply of products and services. Works in co-operation with international organizations, governments, regulatory agencies, technical institutions, universities and non-governmental organizations; mems: state enterprises, representing more than 90% of regional operations, in Argentina, Bolivia, Brazil, Canada, Chile, Colombia, Costa Rica, Cuba, Ecuador, Jamaica, Mexico, Nicaragua, Paraguay, Peru, Suriname, Trinidad and Tobago, Uruguay, Venezuela; Exec. Sec. JOSÉ FÉLIX GARCÍA GARCÍA; publ. *Boletín Técnico*.

Sugar Association of the Caribbean (Inc.): c/o Caroni (1975) Ltd, Brechin Castle, Conva, Trinidad and Tobago; tel. 636-2449; fax 636-2847; f. 1942; mems: national sugar cos of Barbados, Belize, Guyana, Jamaica and Trinidad and Tobago, and Sugar Asscn of St Kitts–Nevis–Anguilla; Chair. RODERICK KARL JAMES; Sec. AZIZ

MOHAMMED; publs *SAC Handbook, SAC Annual Report, Proceedings of Meetings of WI Sugar Technologists.*

Union of Banana-Exporting Countries (Unión de Paises Exportadores de Banano—UPEB): Apdo 4273, Bank of America, 7°, Panamá 5, Panama; tel. 263-6266; fax 264-8355; e-mail iicapan@pan.gbm.net; f. 1974 as an intergovernmental agency to assist in the cultivation and marketing of bananas and to secure prices; collects statistics; mems: Colombia, Costa Rica, Guatemala, Honduras, Nicaragua, Panama, Venezuela; Exec. Dir a.i. ROLANDO GABRIELLI; publs *Informe UPEB, Fax UPEB, Anuario de Estadísticas,* bibliographies.

West Africa Rice Development Association (WARDA): 01 BP 2551 Bouaké 01, Côte d'Ivoire; tel. 22-52-62-00; fax 22-41-18-07; e-mail warda@cgiar.org; internet www.cgiar.org/warda; f. 1971 as a mem. of the network of agricultural research centres supported by the Consultative Group on International Agricultural Research (CGIAR); aims to contribute to food security and poverty eradication in poor rural and urban populations, particularly in West and Central Africa, through research, partnerships, capacity strengthening and policy support on rice-based systems; promotes sustainable agricultural development based on environmentally-sound management of natural resources; maintains research stations in Côte d'Ivoire, Nigeria and Senegal; provides training and consulting services; mems: 17 west African countries; Dir-Gen. Dr KANAYO F. NWANZE (Nigeria); publs *Program Report* (annually), *Participatory Varietal Selection* (annually), *Rice Interspecific Hybridization Project Research Highlights* (annually), *Biennial WARDA / National Experts Committee Meeting Reports, Inland Valley Newsletter, ROCARIZ Newsletter,* training series, proceedings, leaflets.

West Indian Sea Island Cotton Association (Inc.): c/o Barbados Agricultural Development Corporation, Fairy Valley, Christ Church, Barbados; mems: organizations in Antigua-Barbuda, Barbados, Jamaica, Montserrat and St Christopher and Nevis; Pres. LEROY ROACH; Sec. MICHAEL I. EDGHILL.

World Association of Beet and Cane Growers (WABCG): c/o IFAP, 60 rue St Lazare, 75009 Paris, France; tel. 1-45-26-05-53; fax 1-48-74-72-12; e-mail wabcg@ifap.org; internet www.ifap.org/wabcg; f. 1983 (formal adoption of Constitution, 1984); groups national organizations of independent sugar beet and cane growers; aims to boost the economic, technical and social development of the beet- and cane-growing sector; works to strengthen professional representation in international and national fora; serves as a forum for discussion and exchange of information; mems: 21 beet-growing organizations, 14 cane-growing organizations, from 30 countries; Pres. ROGER STEWART (South Africa); Sec. HUGUES BEYLER; publs *World Sugar Farmer News* (quarterly), *World Sugar Farmer Fax Sheet, WABCG InfoFlash,* study reports.

World Federation of Diamond Bourses: 62 Pelikaanstraat, 2018 Antwerp, Belgium; tel. (3) 234-91-21; fax (3) 226-40-73; e-mail info@worldfed.com; internet www.worldfed.com; f. 1947 to protect the interests of affiliated bourses and their individual members and to settle disputes by arbitration; mems: 24 bourses in 15 countries; Pres. SHMUEL. SCHNITZER (Israel); Sec.-Gen. MICHAEL H. VAUGHAN (Belgium).

World Gold Council: 55 Old Broad St, London, EC2M 1RX, United Kingdom; tel. (20) 7826-4700; fax (20) 7826-4799; e-mail info@gold.org; internet www.gold.org; f. 1987 as world-wide international asscn of gold producers, to promote the demand for gold; Chair. PIERRE LASSONDE; Chief Exec. JAMES E. BURTON.

World Sugar Research Organisation (WSRO): Science and Technology Centre, University of Reading, Earley Gate, Whiteknights Rd, Reading, RG6 6BZ, United Kingdom; tel. (118) 935-7000; fax (118) 935-7301; e-mail wsro@wsro.org; internet www.wsro.org; an alliance of sugar producers, processors, marketers and users; monitors and communicates research on role of sugar and other carbohydrates in nutrition and health; organizes conferences and symposia; operates a database of information; serves as a forum for exchange of views; mems: 73 orgs in 30 countries; Dir-Gen. Dr RIAZ KHAN; publs *WSRO Research Bulletin* (on-line, monthly), *WSRO Newsletter,* papers and conference proceedings.

Development and Economic Co-operation

African Capacity Building Foundation (ACBF): Intermarket Life Towers, 7th and 15th Floors, cnr Jason Moyo Ave/Sam Nujoma St, POB 1562, Harare, Zimbabwe; tel. (4) 790398; fax (4) 702915; e-mail root@acbf-pact.org; internet www.acbf-pact.org; f. 1991 by the World Bank, UNDP, the African Development Bank, African and non-African governments; assists African countries to strengthen and build local capacity in economic policy analysis and development management. Implementing agency for the Partnership for Capacity Building in Africa (PACT, established in 1999); Exec. Sec. Dr SOUMANA SAKO.

African Training and Research Centre in Administration for Development (Centre africain de formation et de recherche administratives pour le développement—CAFRAD): blvd Pavillon International, BP 310, Tangier, 90001 Morocco; tel. (3) 9322707; fax (3) 9325785; e-mail cafrad@cafrad.org; internet www.cafrad.org; f. 1964 by agreement between Morocco and UNESCO; undertakes research into administrative problems in Africa and documents results; provides a consultation service for governments and organizations; holds workshops to train senior civil servants; prepares the Biennial Pan-African Conference of Ministers of the Civil Service; mems: 37 African countries; Chair. MOHAMED BOUSSAID; Dir-Gen. a.i. Dr SIMON MAMOSI LELO; publs *African Administrative Studies* (2 a year), *Research Studies, Newsletter* (internet), *Collection: Etudes et Documents, Répertoires des Consultants et des institutions de formation en Afrique.*

Afro-Asian Rural Development Organization (AARDO): No. 2, State Guest Houses Complex, Chanakyapuri, New Delhi 110 021, India; tel. (11) 24100475; fax (11) 24672045; e-mail aardohq@nde.vsnl.net.in; internet www.aardo.org; f. 1962 to act as a catalyst for the co-operative restructuring of rural life in Africa and Asia and to explore opportunities for the co-ordination of efforts to promote rural welfare and to eradicate hunger, thirst, disease, illiteracy and poverty; carries out collaborative research on development issues; organizes training; encourages the exchange of information; holds international conferences and seminars; awards 100 individual training fellowships at nine institutes in Egypt, India, Japan, the Republic of Korea, Malaysia and Taiwan; mems: 13 African countries, 14 Asian countries, one African associate; Sec.-Gen. ABDALLA YAHIA ADAM (Sudan); publs *Afro-Asian Journal of Rural Development* (2 a year), *Annual Report, AARDO Newsletter* (2 a year).

Agence Intergouvernementale de la Francophonie: 13 quai André Citroën, 75015 Paris, France; tel. 1-44-37-33-00; fax 1-45-79-14-98; e-mail com@francophonie.org; internet agence.francophonie.org; f. 1970 as l'Agence de coopération culturelle et technique; promotes co-operation among French-speaking countries in the areas of education, culture, peace and democracy, and technology; implements decisions of the Sommet francophone; technical and financial assistance has been given to projects in every member country, many to aid rural people; mems: 50 states; Gen. Administrator ROGER DEHAYBE (Belgium); publ. *Journal de l'Agence de la Francophonie* (quarterly).

Arab Authority for Agricultural Investment and Development (AAAID): POB 2102, Khartoum, Sudan; tel. (11) 780777; fax (11) 772600; e-mail info@aaaid.org; internet www.aaaid.org; f. 1976 to accelerate agricultural development in the Arab world and to ensure food security; acts principally by equity participation in agricultural projects in Iraq, Sudan and Tunisia; signed a co-operation agreement with IFAD in Nov. 2000; mems: 16 countries; Pres. and Chair. ABDUL KAREEM MOHAMMAD AL-AMRI; publs *Journal of Agricultural Investment* (English and Arabic), *Extension and Investment Bulletins, Annual Report* (Arabic and English), *AAAID Newsletter* (quarterly).

Arab Gulf Programme for the United Nations Development Organizations (AGFUND): POB 18371, Riyadh 11415, Saudi Arabia; tel. (1) 4418888; fax (1) 4412962; e-mail info@agfund.org; internet www.agfund.org; f. 1981 to provide grants for projects in mother and child care carried out by United Nations organizations, Arab non-governmental organizations and other international bodies, and to co-ordinate assistance by the nations of the Gulf; financing comes mainly from member states, all of which are members of OPEC; mems: Bahrain, Kuwait, Oman, Qatar, Saudi Arabia, UAE; Pres. HRH Prince TALAL BIN ABDAL-AZIZ.

Arctic Council: c/o Ministry of Foreign Affairs, Smolenskaya–Sennaya pl. 32/34, Moscow, Russia; tel. (095) 244-1239; fax (095) 244-2559; e-mail e-mail: ac-chair@mid.ru; internet www.arctic-council.org; f. 1996 to promote co-ordination of activities in the Arctic region, in particular in the areas of education, development and environmental protection; mems: Canada, Denmark, Finland, Iceland, Norway, Russia, Sweden, USA; chairmanship of the Council rotates on a two-yearly basis (Nov. 2004–Nov. 2006: Russia).

Association of Caribbean States (ACS): 5–7 Sweet Briar Rd, St Clair, POB 660, Port of Spain, Trinidad and Tobago; tel. 622-9575; fax 622-1653; e-mail communications@acs-aec.org; internet www.acs-aec.org; f. 1994 by the Governments of the 13 CARICOM countries and Colombia, Costa Rica, Cuba, Dominican Republic, El Salvador, Guatemala, Haiti, Honduras, Mexico, Nicaragua, Suriname and Venezuela; aims to promote economic integration, sustainable development and co-operation in the region; to co-ordinate participation in multilateral forums; to undertake concerted action to protect the environment, particularly the Caribbean Sea; and to co-operate in the areas of science and technology, health, trade, transport, tourism, education and culture. Policy is determined by a

Ministerial Council and implemented by a Secretariat based in Port of Spain. In December 2001 a third Summit of Heads of State and Government was convened in Venezuela; a Plan of Action focusing on issues of sustainable tourism, trade, transport and natural disasters was agreed; mems: 25 signatory states, three associate members, 18 observer countries; Sec.-Gen. Dr RUBÉN ARTURO SILIÉ VALDEZ.

Association of Development Financing Institutions in Asia and the Pacific (ADFIAP): Skyland Plaza, 2nd Floor, Sen. Gil J. Puyat Ave, Makati City, Metro Manila, 1200 Philippines; tel. (2) 8161672; fax (2) 8176498; e-mail inquire@adfiap.org; internet www.adfiap.org; f. 1976 to promote the interests and economic development of the respective countries of its member institutions, through development financing; mems: 65 institutions in 30 countries; Chair. ISOA KALOUMAIRA (Fiji); Sec.-Gen. ORLANDO P. PEÑA (Philippines); publs *Asian Banking Digest*, *Journal of Development Finance* (2 a year), *ADFIAP Newsletter*, *ADFIAP Accompli*, *DevTrade Finance*.

Benelux Economic Union: 39 rue de la Régence, 1000 Brussels, Belgium; tel. (2) 519-38-11; fax (2) 513-42-06; e-mail info@benelux.be; internet www.benelux.be; f. 1960 to bring about the economic union of Belgium, Luxembourg and the Netherlands; aims to introduce common policies in the field of cross-border co-operation and harmonize standards and intellectual property legislation; structure comprises: Committee of Ministers; Council; Court of Justice; Consultative Inter-Parliamentary Council; the Economic and Social Advisory Council; and the General Secretariat; Sec.-Gen. Dr B. M. J. HENNEKAM (Netherlands); publs *Benelux Newsletter*, *Bulletin Benelux*.

Caribbean-Britain Business Council: Westminster Palace Gdns, Suite 18, 1–7 Artillery Row, London, SW1P 1RR, United Kingdom; tel. (20) 7799-1521; e-mail admin@caribbean-council.org; f. 2001; promotes trade and investment development between the United Kingdom, the Caribbean and the European Union; Chair. JEFFRIES BRIGINSHAW; Exec. Dir S. MONTEATH; publ. *Caribbean Briefing* (weekly).

Caritas Internationalis (International Confederation of Catholic Organizations for charitable and social action): Palazzo San Calisto, 00120 Città del Vaticano; tel. (06) 6987-9799; fax (06) 6988-7237; e-mail caritas.internationalis@caritas.va; internet www.caritas.org; f. 1950 to study problems arising from poverty, their causes and possible solutions; national mem. organizations undertake assistance and development activities. The Confederation co-ordinates emergency relief and development projects, and represents mems at international level; mems: 154 national orgs; Pres. Mgr YOUHANNA-FOUAD EL-HAGE (Bishop of Imperatriz, Brazil); Sec.-Gen. DUNCAN MACLAREN; publs *Caritas Matters* (quarterly), *Emergency Calling* (2 a year).

Central European Free Trade Association: internet www.cefta.org; f. 1992, entered into force 1993; free-trade agreement covering a number of sectors; mems: Bulgaria, Czech Republic, Hungary, Poland, Romania, Slovakia, Slovenia.

Colombo Plan: Bank of Ceylon Merchant Tower, 28 St Michael's Rd, Colombo 03, Sri Lanka; tel. (1) 564448; fax (1) 564531; e-mail cplan@slt.lk; internet www.colombo-plan.org; f. 1950 by seven Commonwealth countries, to encourage economic and social development in Asia and the Pacific; the Plan comprises the Programme for Public Administration, to provide training for officials in the context of a market-orientated economy; the Programme for Private Sector Development, which organizes training programmes to stimulate the economic benefits of development of the private sector; a Drug Advisory Programme, to encourage regional co-operation in efforts to control drug-related problems, in particular through human resources development; a programme to establish a South-South Technical Co-operation Data Bank, to collate, analyse and publish information in order to facilitate South-South co-operation; and a Staff College for Technician Education (see below). All programmes are voluntarily funded; developing countries are encouraged to become donors and to participate in economic and technical co-operation activities among developing mems; mems: 24 countries; Sec.-Gen. U. SARAT CHANDRAN (India); publs *Annual Report*, *Colombo Plan Focus* (quarterly), Consultative Committee proceedings (every 2 years).

Colombo Plan Staff College for Technician Education: POB 7500, Domestic Airport Post Office, NAIA, Pasay City 1300, Philippines; tel. (2) 631-0991; fax (2) 631-0996; e-mail cpsc@skyinet.net; internet www.cpsc.org.ph; f. 1973 with the support of member Governments of the Colombo Plan; aims to enhance the development of technician education systems in developing mem. countries; Dir MAN-GON PARK; publ. *CPSC Quarterly*.

Communauté économique des états de l'Afrique centrale (CEEAC) (Economic Community of Central African States): BP 2112, Libreville, Gabon; tel. 73-35-48; internet www.ceeac.org; f. 1983, operational 1 January 1985; aims to promote co-operation between member states by abolishing trade restrictions, establishing a common external customs tariff, linking commercial banks,

and setting up a development fund, over a period of 12 years; works to combat drug abuse and to promote regional security; mems: 10 African countries; Sec.-Gen. LOUIS-SYLVAIN GOMA.

Community of Sahel-Saharan States (Communauté des états Sahelo–Sahariens—CEN-SAD): POB 4041, Aljazaer Sq., Tripoli, Libya; tel. and fax (21) 361-4832; fax (21) 333-2116; e-mail info@cen-sad.org; internet www.cen-sad.org; f. 1998; fmrly known as COMESSA; aims to strengthen co-operation between signatory states in order to promote their economic, social and cultural integration and to facilitate conflict resolution and poverty alleviation; partnership agreements concluded with many orgs, including the AU, the UN and ECOWAS; mems: Benin, Burkina Faso, Central African Republic, Chad, Côte d'Ivoire, Djibouti, Egypt, Eritrea, The Gambia, Ghana, Guinea-Bissau, Liberia, Libya, Mali, Morocco, Niger, Nigeria, Senegal, Somalia, Sudan, Togo, Tunisia; Sec.-Gen. Dr MOHAMMED AL-MADANI AL-AZHARI (Libya).

Conseil de l'Entente (Entente Council): 01 BP 3734, angle ave Verdier/rue de Tessières, Abidjan 01, Côte d'Ivoire; tel. 20-33-28-35; fax 20-33-11-49; e-mail fegece@conseil-entente.org; f. 1959 to promote economic development in the region; the Council's Mutual Aid and Loan Guarantee Fund (Fonds d' entraide et de garantie des emprunts) finances development projects, including agricultural projects, support for small and medium-sized enterprises, vocational training centres, research into new sources of energy and building of hotels to encourage tourism. A Convention of Assistance and Co-operation was signed in Feb. 1996. Holds annual summit; mems: Benin, Burkina Faso, Côte d'Ivoire, Niger, Togo; Sec.-Gen. OUSMANE TAMIMOU; publ. *Rapport d'activité* (annually).

> **Communauté économique du bétail et de la viande (CEBV) du Conseil de l'Entente** (Livestock and Meat Economic Community of the Entente Council): 01 BP 638 Ouagadougou, Burkina Faso; tel. 21-30-62-67; fax 21-30-62-68; e-mail cebv@cenatrin.bf; internet www.cenatrin.bf/cebv; f. 1970 to promote the production, processing and marketing of livestock and meat; negotiates between members and with third countries on technical and financial co-operation and co-ordinated legislation; attempts to co-ordinate measures to combat drought and cattle diseases; mems: states belonging to the Conseil de l'Entente; Exec. Sec. Dr ELIE LADIKPO (Togo).

Council of American Development Foundations (Consejo de Fundaciones Americanas de Desarrollo—SOLIDARIOS): Calle 6 No. 10 Paraíso, Apdo Postal 620, Santo Domingo, Dominican Republic; tel. 549-5111; fax 544-0550; e-mail solidarios@codetel.net.do; f. 1972; exchanges information and experience, arranges technical assistance, raises funds to organize training programmes and scholarships; administers development fund to finance programmes carried out by members through a loan guarantee programme; provides consultancy services. Mem. foundations provide technical and financial assistance to low-income groups for rural, housing and micro-enterprise development projects; mems: 18 institutional mems in 14 Latin American and Caribbean countries; Pres. MERCEDES P. DE CANALDA; Sec.-Gen. ISABEL C. ARANGO; publs *Solidarios* (quarterly), *Annual Report*.

Developing Eight (D-8): Muşir Fuad Paşa Yalisi, Eski Tersane, Emirgan, Cad. 90, 80860 İstanbul, Turkey; tel. (212) 2775513; fax (212) 2775519; e-mail edoffice@d8net.org; internet www.mfa.gov.tr/d-8; inaugurated at a meeting of heads of state in June 1997; aims to foster economic co-operation between member states and to strengthen the role of developing countries in the global economy; project areas include trade and industry, agriculture, human resources, telecommunications, rural development, finance (including banking and privatization), energy, environment, and health; fourth Summit meeting, convened in Tehran, Iran, in Feb. 2004, addressed the need for improved implementation by mem. states of specific projects and the facilitation of intra-D-8 trade; mems: Bangladesh, Egypt, Indonesia, Iran, Malaysia, Nigeria, Pakistan, Turkey; Exec. Dir AYHAN KAMEL.

Earth Council: POB 319-6100, San José, Costa Rica; tel. 205-1600; fax 249-3500; e-mail eci@ecouncil.ac.cr; internet www.ecouncil.ac.cr; f. 1992, following the UN Conference on Environment and Development; aims to promote and support sustainable development; supported the establishment of National Councils for Sustainable Development (NCSDs) and administers a programme to promote co-operation and dialogue and to facilitate capacity-building and training, with NCSDs; works, with other partner organizations, to generate support for an Earth Charter. The Earth Council Institute, comprising 18 members, functions as an advisory board to the Council; Chair. MAURICE STRONG (Canada); Pres. and CEO of Earth Council Institute FRANS VAN HAREN (Netherlands).

East African Community (EAC): AICC Bldg, Kilimanjaro Wing, 5th Floor, POB 1096, Arusha, Tanzania; tel. (27) 2504253; fax (27) 2504255; e-mail eac@eachq.org; internet www.eac.int; f. Jan. 2001, following the adoption of a treaty on political and economic integration (signed in November 1999) by the heads of state of Kenya,

Tanzania and Uganda, replacing the Permanent Tripartite Commission for East African Co-operation (f. 1993) and reviving the former East African Community (f. 1967; dissolved 1977); initial areas for co-operation were to be trade and industry, security, immigration, transport and communications, and promotion of investment; further objectives were the elimination of trade barriers and ensuring the free movement of people and capital within the grouping; a customs union came into effect on 1 Jan. 2005; it was envisaged that Rwanda would become a full member of the EAC in 2005; Sec.-Gen. NUWE AMANYA-MUSHEGA.

Economic Community of the Great Lakes Countries (Communauté économique des pays des Grands Lacs—CEPGL): POB 58, Gisenyi, Rwanda; tel. 61309; fax 61319; f. 1976 main organs: annual Conference of Heads of State, Council of Ministers of Foreign Affairs, Permanent Executive Secretariat, Consultative Commission, Security Commission, three Specialized Technical Commissions; there are four specialized agencies: a development bank, the Banque de Développement des Etats des Grands Lacs (BDEGL) at Goma, Democratic Republic of the Congo; an energy centre at Bujumbura, Burundi; the Institute of Agronomic and Zootechnical Research, Gitega, Burundi; and a regional electricity company (SINELAC) at Bukavu, Democratic Republic of the Congo; mems: Burundi, the Democratic Republic of the Congo, Rwanda; publs *Grands Lacs* (quarterly review), *Journal* (annually).

Food Aid Committee: c/o International Grains Council, 1 Canada Sq., Canary Wharf, London, E14 5AE, United Kingdom; tel. (20) 7513-1122; fax (20) 7513-0630; e-mail igc-fac@igc.org.uk; internet www.igc.org.uk; f. 1967; responsible for administration of the Food Aid Convention—FAC (1999), a constituent element of the International Grains Agreement (1995); aims to make appropriate levels of food aid available on a consistent basis to maximize the impact and effectiveness of such assistance; provides a framework for co-operation, co-ordination and information-sharing among members on matters related to food aid. The 23 donor members pledge to supply a minimum of 5m. metric tons of food annually to developing countries and territories, mostly as gifts: in practice aid has usually exceeded 8m. tons annually. Secretariat support is provided by the International Grains Council; Exec. Dir G. DENIS; publ. *Report on shipments* (annually).

Gambia River Basin Development Organization (Organisation de mise en valeur du fleuve Gambie—OMVG): BP 2353, 13 passage Leblanc, Dakar, Senegal; tel. 822-31-59; fax 822-59-26; e-mail omvg@sentoo.sn; f. 1978 by Senegal and The Gambia; Guinea joined in 1981 and Guinea-Bissau in 1983. A masterplan for the integrated development of the Kayanga/Geba and Koliba/Corubal river basins has been developed, encompassing a projected natural resources management project; work on a hydraulic development plan for the Gambia river commenced in late 1996 and was completed in mid-1998; a pre-feasibility study on connecting the national electric grids of the four member states has been completed, and a feasibility study for the construction of the proposed Sambangalou hydro-electric dam, providing for energy transmission to all member states, commenced in Feb. 2002; maintains documentation centre; Exec. Sec. MAMADOU NASSIROU DIALLO.

Group of Three (G3): c/o Secretaría de Relaciones Exteriores, 1 Tlatelolco, Del. Cuauhtémoc 06995 México, DF; e-mail gtres@sre.gob .mx; internet g3.sre.gob.mx; f. 1990 by Colombia, Mexico and Venezuela to remove restrictions on trade between the three countries; the trade agreement covers market access, rules of origin, intellectual property, trade in services, and government purchases, and entered into force in early 1994. Tariffs on trade between member states were to be removed on a phased basis. Co-operation was also envisaged in employment creation, the energy sector and the fight against cholera. The secretariat function rotates between the three countries on a two-yearly basis.

Indian Ocean Commission (IOC) (Commission de l'Océan Indien—COI): Q4, Ave Sir Guy Forget, BP 7, Quatre Bornes, Mauritius; tel. 425-9564; fax 425-2709; e-mail coi7@intnet.mu; internet www.coi-info.org; f. 1982 to promote regional co-operation, particularly in economic development; projects include tuna-fishing development, protection and management of environmental resources and strengthening of meteorological services; tariff reduction is also envisaged; organizes an annual regional trade fair; mems: Comoros, France (representing the French Overseas Department of Réunion), Madagascar, Mauritius, Seychelles; Sec.-Gen. WILFRID BERTILE; publ. *La Lettre de l'Océan Indien*.

Indian Ocean Rim Association for Regional Co-operation (IOR–ARC): Sorèze House, Wilson Ave, Vacoas, Mauritius; tel. 698-3979; fax 698-5390; e-mail iorarchq@intnet.mu; internet www.iornet .org; the first intergovernmental meeting of countries in the region to promote an Indian Ocean Rim initiative was convened in March 1995; charter to establish the Asscn was signed at a ministerial meeting in March 1997; aims to promote the sustained growth and balanced devt of the region and of its mem. states and to create

common ground for regional economic co-operation, *inter alia* through trade, investment, infrastructure, tourism, and science and technology; fifth meeting of Council of Ministers held in Colombo, Sri Lanka, Aug. 2004; mems: Australia, Bangladesh, India, Indonesia, Iran, Kenya, Madagascar, Malaysia, Mauritius, Mozambique, Oman, Singapore, South Africa, Sri Lanka, Tanzania, Thailand, United Arab Emirates and Yemen. Dialogue Partner countries: People's Republic of China, Egypt, France, Japan, United Kingdom. Observer: Indian Ocean Tourism Orgn; Chair. LAKSHMAN KADIRGAMAR (Sri Lanka); Exec. Dir TUAN ZAROOK AMJADEEN (Sri Lanka).

Inter-American Planning Society (Sociedad Interamericana de Planificación—SIAP): c/o Revista Interamericana de Planificación, Casilla 01-05-1978, Cuenca, Ecuador; tel. (7) 823-860; fax (7) 823-949; e-mail siap1@siap.org.ec; f. 1956 to promote development of comprehensive planning; mems: institutions and individuals in 46 countries; Pres. Prof. PATRICIA A. WILSON (USA); Exec. Sec. LUIS E. CAMACHO (Colombia); publs *Correo Informativo* (quarterly), *Inter-American Journal of Planning* (quarterly).

International Co-operation for Development and Solidarity (Co-opération internationale pour le développement et la solidarité—CIDSE): 16 rue Stévin, 1000 Brussels, Belgium; tel. (2) 230-77-22; fax (2) 230-70-82; e-mail postmaster@cidse.org; internet www .cidse.org; f. 1967 to link Catholic development organizations and assist in the co-ordination of projects; co-ordinates advocacy and lobbying; provides information; mems 15 Catholic agencies in 14 countries and territories; Pres. JEAN-MARIE FARDEAU; Sec.-Gen. CHRISTIANE OVERKAMP.

Inuit Circumpolar Conference: 170 Laurier Ave West, Suite 504, Ottawa, ON K1P 5V5, Canada; tel. (613) 563-2642; fax (613) 565-3089; e-mail icc@magma.ca; internet www.inuit.org; f. 1977 to protect the indigenous culture, environment and rights of the Inuit people (Eskimoes), and to encourage co-operation among the Inuit; conferences held every four years; mems: Inuit communities in Canada, Greenland, Alaska and Russia; Pres. AQQALUK LYNGE; Exec. Dir HJALMAR DAHL; publ. *Silarjualiriniq*.

Lake Chad Basin Commission (LCBC): BP 727, N'Djamena, Chad; tel. 52-41-45; fax 52-41-37; e-mail lcbc@intnet.td; f. 1964 to encourage co-operation in developing the Lake Chad region and to promote the settlement of regional disputes; work programmes emphasize the regulation of the utilization of water and other natural resources in the basin; the co-ordination of natural resources development projects and research; holds annual summit of heads of state; mems: Cameroon, Central African Republic, Chad, Niger, Nigeria; Exec. Sec. MUHAMMAD SANI ADAMU; publ. *Bibliographie générale de la cblt* (2 a year).

Latin American Association of Development Financing Institutions (Asociación Latinoamericana de Instituciones Financieras para el Desarrollo—ALIDE): Apdo Postal 3988, Paseo de la República 3211, Lima 100, Peru; tel. (1) 442-2400; fax (1) 442-8105; e-mail sg@alide.org.pe; internet www.alide.org.pe; f. 1968 to promote co-operation among regional development financing bodies; programmes: technical assistance; training; studies and research; technical meetings; information; projects and investment promotion; mems: 62 active, 8 assoc. and 8 collaborating (banks and financing institutions and development organizations in 22 Latin American countries, Slovenia and Spain); Sec.-Gen. ROMMEL ACEVEDO; publs *ALIDE Bulletin* (6 a year), *ALIDENOTICIAS Newsletter* (monthly), *Annual Report, Latin American Directory of Development Financing Institutions*.

Latin American Economic System (Sistema Económico Latinoamericano—SELA): Torre Europa, 4°, Urb. Campo Alegre, Avda Francisco de Miranda, Caracas 1061, Venezuela; Apdo 17035, Caracas 1010-A, Venezuela; tel. (212) 955-7111; fax (212) 951-5292; e-mail difusion@sela.org; internet www.sela.org; f. 1975 in accordance with the Panama Convention; aims to foster co-operation and integration among the countries of Latin America and the Caribbean, and to provide a permanent system of consultation and co-ordination in economic and social matters; conducts studies and other analysis and research; extends technical assistance to sub-regional and regional co-ordination bodies; provides library, information service and data bases on regional co-operation. The Latin American Council, the principal decision-making body of the System, meets annually at ministerial level and high-level regional consultation and co-ordination meetings are held; there is also a Permanent Secretariat; mems: 28 countries; Perm. Sec. ROBERTO GUARNIERI (Venezuela); publs *Capítulos del SELA* (3 a year), *Bulletin on Latin America and Caribbean Integration* (monthly), *SELA Antenna in the United States* (quarterly).

Liptako-Gourma Integrated Development Authority (LGA): POB 619, ave M. Thevenond, Ouagadougou, Burkina Faso; tel. (3) 30-61-48; f. 1972; scope of activities includes water infrastructure, telecommunications and construction of roads and railways; in 1986 undertook study on development of water resources in the basin of

Development and Economic Co-operation

the Niger river (for hydroelectricity and irrigation); mems: Burkina Faso, Mali, Niger; Dir-Gen. GISANGA DEMBÉLE (Mali).

Mano River Union: Private Mail Bag 133, Delco House, Lightfoot Boston St, Freetown, Sierra Leone; tel. (22) 226883; f. 1973 to establish a customs and economic union between member states to accelerate development via integration; a common external tariff was instituted in 1977. Intra-union free trade was officially introduced in May 1981, as the first stage in progress towards a customs union. A non-aggression treaty was signed by heads of state in 1986. The Union was inactive for three years until mid-1994, owing to regional conflict and disagreements regarding funding. In January 1995 a Mano River Centre for Peace and Development was established, which was to be temporarily based in London. The Centre aims to provide a permanent mechanism for conflict prevention and resolution, and monitoring of human rights violations, and to promote sustainable peace and development. A new security structure was approved in 2000. In Aug. 2001 ministers of foreign affairs, security, internal affairs, and justice, meeting as the Joint Security Committee, resolved to deploy joint border security and confidence-building units, and to work to reestablish the free movement of people and goods; mems: Guinea, Liberia, Sierra Leone; Dir Dr ABDOULAYE DIALLO.

Mekong River Commission (MRC): 364 M. V. Preah Monivong, Sangkat Phsar Doerm Thkouv, Khan Chamkar Mon, POB 1112, Phnom Penh, Cambodia; tel. (23) 720979; fax (23) 720972; e-mail mrcs@mrcmekong.org; internet www.mrcmekong.org; f. 1995 as successor to the Committee for Co-ordination of Investigations of the Lower Mekong Basin (f. 1957); aims to promote and co-ordinate the sustainable development and use of the resources of the Mekong River Basin for navigational and non-navigational purposes, in order to assist the social and economic development of member states and preserve the ecological balance of the basin. Provides scientific information and policy advice; supports the implementation of strategic programmes and activities; organizes an annual donor consultative group meeting; maintains regular dialogue with Myanmar and the People's Republic of China; mems: Cambodia, Laos, Thailand, Viet Nam; Chief Exec. JOERN KRISTENSEN; publ. *Mekong News* (quarterly).

Niger Basin Authority (Autorité du bassin du Niger): BP 729, Niamey, Niger; tel. 723102; fax 735310; e-mail abasec@intnet.ne; internet www.abn-nba.org; f. 1964 (as River Niger Commission; name changed 1980) to harmonize national programmes concerned with the River Niger Basin and to execute an integrated development plan; compiles statistics; regulates navigation; runs projects on hydrological forecasting, environmental control; infrastructure and agro-pastoral development; mems: Benin, Burkina Faso, Cameroon, Chad, Côte d'Ivoire, Guinea, Mali, Niger, Nigeria; Exec. Sec. MOHAMMED BELLO TUGA (Nigeria); publ. *Bulletin*.

Nile Basin Initiative: POB 192, Entebbe, Uganda; tel. (41) 321329; fax (41) 320971; e-mail nbisec@nilesec.org; internet www.nilebasin .org; f. 1999; aims to achieve sustainable socio-economic development through the equitable use and benefits of the Nile Basin water resources and to create an enabling environment for the implementation of programmes with a shared vision. Highest authority is the Nile Basin Council of Ministers (Nile-COM); other activities undertaken by a Nile Basin Technical Advisory Committee (Nile-TAC); mems: Burundi, Democratic Republic of the Congo, Egypt, Eritrea, Ethiopia, Kenya, Rwanda, Sudan, Tanzania, Uganda; Exec. Dir Meraji O. Y. MSUYA (Tanzania).

Organization for the Development of the Senegal River (Organisation pour la mise en valeur du fleuve Sénégal—OMVS): c/o Haut-Commissariat, 46 rue Carnot, BP 3152, Dakar, Senegal; tel. 823-45-30; fax 823-47-62; e-mail omvssphc@sentoo.sn; internet www .omvs-hc.org; f. 1972 to promote the use of the Senegal river for hydroelectricity, irrigation and navigation; the Djama dam in Senegal provides a barrage to prevent salt water from moving upstream, and the Manantali dam in Mali is intended to provide a reservoir for irrigation of about 375,000 ha of land and for production of hydroelectricity and provision of year-round navigation for ocean-going vessels. In 1997 two companies were formed to manage the dams: Société de gestion de l'énergie de Manantali (SOGEM) and Société de gestion et d'exploitation du barrage de Djama (SOGED). Work began in 1997 on a hydro-electric power station on the Senegal River; mems: Mali, Mauritania, Senegal; Guinea has observer status; Pres. ABOUBACARY COULIBALY (Mali).

Organization for the Management and Development of the Kagera River Basin (Organisation pour l'aménagement et le développement du bassin de la rivière Kagera—OBK): BP 297, Kigali, Rwanda; tel. (7) 84665; fax (7) 82172; f. 1978; envisages joint development and management of resources, including the construction of an 80-MW hydroelectric dam at Rusumo Falls, on the Rwanda-Tanzania border, a 2,000-km railway network between the four member countries, road construction (914 km), and a tele-communications network between member states; mems: Burundi, Rwanda, Tanzania, Uganda; Exec. Sec. JEAN-BOSCO BALINDA.

Pacific Basin Economic Council (PBEC): 900 Fort St, Suite 1080, Honolulu, HI 96813, USA; tel. (808) 521-9044; fax (808) 521-8530; e-mail info@pbec.org; internet www.pbec.org; f. 1967; an asscn of business representatives aiming to promote business opportunities in the region, in order to enhance overall economic development; advises governments and serves as a liaison between business leaders and government officials; encourages business relationships and co-operation among members; holds business symposia; mems: 20 economies (Australia, Canada, Chile, People's Republic of China, Colombia, Ecuador, Hong Kong, Indonesia, Japan, Republic of Korea, Malaysia, Mexico, New Zealand, Peru, Philippines, Russia, Singapore, Taiwan, Thailand, USA); Chair. SUCK-RAI CHO; Pres. DALTON TANONAKA; publs *Pacific Journal* (quarterly), *Executive Summary* (annual conference report).

Pacific Economic Co-operation Council (PECC): 4 Nassim Rd, Singapore 258372; tel. 67379823; fax 67379826; e-mail pecc@pecc .org; internet www.pecc.org; f. 1980; an independent, policy-orientated organization of senior research, government and business representatives from 25 economies in the Asia-Pacific region; aims to foster economic development in the region by providing a forum for discussion and co-operation in a wide range of economic areas; holds a General Meeting every 2 years; mems: Australia, Brunei, Canada, Chile, the People's Republic of China, Colombia, Ecuador, Hong Kong, Indonesia, Japan, the Republic of Korea, Malaysia, Mexico, Mongolia (assoc. mem.), New Zealand, Peru, Philippines, Russia, Singapore, Taiwan, Thailand, USA, Viet Nam and the Pacific Islands Forum; French Pacific Territories (assoc. mem.); Dir-Gen. EDUARDO PEDROSA (acting); publs *Issues PECC* (quarterly), *Pacific Economic Outlook* (annually), *Pacific Food Outlook* (annually).

Pan-African Institute for Development (PAID): BP 4056, Douala, Cameroon; tel. and fax 342-80-30; e-mail ipd.sg@camnet.cm; internet www.paid-wa.org; f. 1964; gives training to people from African countries involved with development at grassroots, intermediate and senior levels (48 countries in 1998); emphasis is given to: development management and financing; agriculture and rural development; issues of gender and development; promotion of small and medium-sized enterprises; training policies and systems; environment, health and community development; research, support and consultancy services; and specialized training. There are four regional institutes: Central Africa (Douala), Sahel (Ouagadougou, Burkina Faso), West Africa (Buéa, Cameroon), Eastern and Southern Africa (Kabwe, Zambia) and a European office in Geneva; Pres. of the Governing Council Dr MBUKI V. MWAMUFIYA; publs *Newsletter* (2 a year), *Annual Progress Report*, *PAID Report* (quarterly).

Permanent Inter-State Committee on Drought Control in the Sahel (Comité permanent inter états de lutte contre la sécheresse au Sahel—CILSS): POB 7049, Ouagadougou 03, Burkina Faso; tel. 37-41-25; fax 37-41-32; e-mail cilss@fasonet.bf; internet www .cilssnet.org; f. 1973; works in co-operation with UNDP Drylands Development Centre; aims to combat the effects of chronic drought in the Sahel region, by improving irrigation and food production, halting deforestation and creating food reserves; initiated a series of projects to improve food security and to counter poverty, entitled Sahel 21; the heads of state of all members had signed a convention for the establishment of a Fondation pour le Développement Durable du Sahel; maintains Institut du Sahel at Bamako (Mali) and centre at Niamey (Niger); mems: Burkina Faso, Cape Verde, Chad, The Gambia, Guinea-Bissau, Mali, Mauritania, Niger, Senegal; Pres. AMADOU TOUMANI TOURÉ (Mali); Exec. Sec. MOUSSA S. MBENGA (The Gambia); publ. *Reflets Sahéliens* (quarterly).

Population Council: 1 Dag Hammarskjöld Plaza, New York, NY 10017, USA; tel. (212) 339-0500; fax (212) 755-6052; e-mail pubinfo@ popcouncil.org; internet www.popcouncil.org; f. 1952; aims to improve reproductive health and achieve a balance between people and resources; analyses demographic trends; conducts biomedical research to develop new contraceptives; works with private and public agencies to improve the quality and scope of family planning and reproductive health services; helps governments to design and implement population policies; communicates results of research. Four regional offices, in India, Mexico, Egypt and Ghana, and 15 country offices. Additional office in Washington, DC, USA, carries out world-wide operational research and activities for reproductive health and the prevention of HIV and AIDS; Pres. LINDA G. MARTIN; publs *Studies in Family Planning* (quarterly), *Population and Development Review* (quarterly), *Population Briefs* (quarterly).

Society for International Development: Via Panisperna 207, 00184 Rome, Italy; tel. (06) 4872172; fax (06) 4872170; e-mail info@ sidint.org; internet www.sidint.org; f. 1957; a global network of individuals and institutions wishing to promote participative, pluralistic and sustainable development; builds partnerships with civil society groups and other sectors; fosters local initiatives and new forms of social experimentation; mems: over 3,000 in 125 countries, 60 local chapters; Pres. ENRIQUE IGLESIAS; Sec.-Gen. ROBERTO SAVIO; publs *Development* (quarterly), *Bridges* (newsletter, every 2 months).

South Centre: Chemin du Champ-d'Anier 17–19, BP 228, 1211 Geneva 19, Switzerland; tel. (22) 7918050; fax (22) 7988531; e-mail south@southcentre.org; internet www.southcentre.org; f. 1990 as a follow-up mechanism of the South Commission (f. 1987); in 1995 established as an intergovernmental body to promote South–South solidarity and co-operation by generating ideas and action-oriented proposals on major policy issues; Chair. BOUTROS BOUTROS-GHALI (Egypt); publs *South Bulletin* (every 2 weeks), *South Letter* (occasional).

Union of the Arab Maghreb (Union du Maghreb arabe—UMA): 14 rue Zalagh, Agdal, Rabat, Morocco; tel. (37) 671-274; fax (37) 671-253; e-mail sg.uma@maghrebarabe.org; internet www .maghrebarabe.org; f. 1989; aims to encourage joint ventures and to create a single market; structure comprises a council of heads of state (meeting annually), a council of ministers of foreign affairs, a follow-up committee, a consultative council of 30 delegates from each country, a UMA judicial court, and four specialized ministerial commissions. Chairmanship rotates annually between heads of state. A Maghreb Investment and Foreign Trade Bank, funding joint agricultural and industrial projects, has been established and a customs union created. In May 1999 the follow-up committee convened to formulate a programme to reactivate the Union; mems: Algeria, Libya, Mauritania, Morocco, Tunisia; Sec.-Gen. HABIB BOU-LARES (Tunisia).

Vienna Institute for Development and Co-operation (Wiener Institut für Entwicklungsfragen und Zusammenarbeit): Möllwald-platz 5/3, 1040 Vienna, Austria; tel. (1) 713-35-94; fax (1) 713-35-94-73; e-mail office@vidc.org; internet www.vidc.org; f. 1987 (fmrly Vienna Institute for Development, f. 1964); manages development policy research on sectoral, regional and cross-cutting issues (for example, gender issues); arranges cultural exchanges between Austria and countries from Africa, Asia and Latin America; deals with conception and organization of anti-racist and integrative measures in sport, in particular football; Pres. BARBARA PRAMMER; Dir ERICH ANDLIK; publs *Report Series*, *Echo*.

Economics and Finance

African Centre for Monetary Studies (ACMS): 15 blvd Franklin Roosevelt, BP 4128, Dakar, Senegal; tel. 821-93-80; fax 822-73-43; e-mail caem@syfed.refer.sn; began operations 1978; aims to promote better understanding of banking and monetary matters; studies monetary problems of African countries and the effect on them of international monetary developments; seeks to enable African countries to co-ordinate strategies in international monetary affairs; established as an organ of the Association of African Central Banks (AACB) following a decision by the OAU Heads of State and Government; mems: all mems of the AACB; Chair. Dr PAUL A. OGWUMA (Nigeria); Dir MAMADOU SIDIBE.

African Insurance Organization (AIO): SNAC Building, 3rd Floor Flatters St, BP 5860, Douala, Cameroon; tel. 342-47-58; fax 343-20-08; e-mail aio@sprynet.com; internet www.africaninsurance .org; f. 1972 to promote the expansion of the insurance and reinsurance industry in Africa, and to increase regional co-operation; holds annual conference, periodic seminars and workshops, and arranges meetings for reinsurers, brokers, consultant and regulators in Africa; has established African insurance 'pools' for aviation, petroleum and fire risks, and created asscns of African insurance educators, supervisory authorities and insurance brokers and consultants; Pres. TEWODROS TILAHUN (Ethiopia); Sec.-Gen. YOSEPH ASEFFA (Cameroon); publ. *African Insurance Annual Review*.

Asian Clearing Union (ACU): 207/1 Pasdaran Ave, POB 15875/7177, Tehran, Iran; tel. (21) 2842076; fax (21) 2847677; e-mail acusecret@cbi.ir; internet www.asianclearingunion.org; f. 1974 to provide clearing arrangements, whereby members settle payments for intra-regional transactions among the participating central banks, on a multilateral basis, in order to economize on the use of foreign exchange and promote the use of domestic currencies in trade transactions among developing countries; part of ESCAP's Asian trade expansion programme; the Central Bank of Iran is the Union's agent; in September 1995 the ACU unit of account was changed from SDR to US dollars, with effect from 1 January 1996; mems: central banks of Bangladesh, Bhutan, India, Iran, Myanmar, Nepal, Pakistan, Sri Lanka; Sec.-Gen. BAHEREH MIRZAEI-TEHRANI; publs *Annual Report*, *Newsletter* (monthly).

Asian Reinsurance Corporation: 17th Floor, Tower B, Chamnan Phenjati Business Center, 65 Rama 9 Rd, Huaykwang, Bangkok 10320, Thailand; tel. (2) 245-2169; fax (2) 248-1377; e-mail asianre@ asianrecorp.com; internet www.asianrecorp.com; f. 1979 by ESCAP

with UNCTAD, to operate as a professional reinsurer, giving priority in retrocessions to national insurance and reinsurance markets of member countries, and as a development organization providing technical assistance to countries in the Asia-Pacific region; cap. (auth.) US \$15m., (p.u.) \$8m.; mems: Afghanistan, Bangladesh, Bhutan, People's Republic of China, India, Iran, Republic of Korea, Philippines, Sri Lanka, Thailand; Gen. Man. A. S. MALABANAN.

Association of African Central Banks (AACB): 15 blvd Franklin Roosevelt, BP 4128, Dakar, Senegal; tel. 821-93-80; fax 822-73-43; f. 1968 to promote contacts in the monetary and financial sphere, in order to increase co-operation and trade among member states; aims to strengthen monetary and financial stability on the African continent; mems: 36 African central banks representing 47 states; Chair. Dr PAUL A. OGWUMA (Nigeria).

Association of African Tax Administrators (AATA): POB 13255, Yaoundé, Cameroon; tel. 22-41-57; fax 23-18-55; f. 1980 to promote co-operation in the field of taxation policy, legislation and administration among African countries; mems: 20 states; Exec. Sec. OWONA PASCAL-BAYLON.

Association of Asian Confederations of Credit Unions (AACCU): 36/2 Moo 3, Soi Malee Suanson Ramkanheang Rd, Bangkapi, Bangkok 10240, Thailand; tel. (2) 374-3170; fax (2) 374-5321; e-mail accu@aaccu.com; internet www.aaccu.net; links and promotes credit unions in Asia, provides research facilities and training programmes; mems: in 20 Asian countries; Pres. CHARLES YIP WAI KWONG (Hong Kong); CEO RANJITH HETTIARACHICHI (Thailand); publs *ACCU News* (every 2 months), *Annual Report and Directory*.

Association of European Institutes of Economic Research (AIECE) (Association d'instituts européens de conjoncture économique): 3 place Montesquieu, 1348 Louvain-la-Neuve, Belgium; tel. (10) 47-34-26; fax (10) 47-39-45; e-mail olbrechts@aiece.org; internet www.aiece.org; f. 1957; provides a means of contact between member institutes; organizes two meetings annually, at which discussions are held on the economic situation and on a special theoretical subject; mems: 40 institutes in 20 European countries; Admin. Sec. PAUL OLBRECHTS.

Central Asian Bank for Co-operation and Development (CABCD): 115A Abay, Almaty, Kazakhstan; tel. (2) 422737; fax (2) 428627; f. 1994 to support trade and development in the sub-region; mems: Kazakhstan, Kyrgyzstan, Tajikistan, Uzbekistan.

Centre for Latin American Monetary Studies (Centro de Estudios Monetarios Latinoamericanos—CEMLA): Durango 54, Col. Roma, Del. Cuauhtémoc, 06700 México, DF, Mexico; tel. (55) 5533-0300; fax (55) 5525-4432; e-mail estudios@cemla.org; internet www .cemla.org; f. 1952; organizes technical training programmes on monetary policy, development finance, etc; runs applied research programmes on monetary and central banking policies and procedures; holds regional meetings of banking officials; mems: 31 associated members (Central Banks of Latin America and the Caribbean), 28 co-operating members (supervisory institutions of the region and non-Latin American Central Banks); Dir-Gen. KENNETH GILMORE COATES SPRY; publs *Bulletin* (every 2 months), *Monetaria* (quarterly), *Money Affairs* (2 a year).

Comité Européen des Assurances (CEA): 3 bis rue de la Chaussée d'Antin, F-75009 Paris, France; tel. 1-44-83-11-83; fax 1-47-70-03-75; internet www.cea.assur.org; f. 1953 to represent the interests of European insurers, to encourage co-operation between members, to allow the exchange of information and to conduct studies; mems: national insurance asscns of 32 countries; Pres. GÉRARD DE LA MARTINIÈRE (France); Dir-Gen. DANIEL G. SCHANTÉ (France); publs *CEA Executive Update* (monthly newsletter), *European Insurance in Figures* (annually), *The European Life Insurance Market* (annually).

East African Development Bank: 4 Nile Ave, POB 7128, Kampala, Uganda; tel. (41) 230021; fax (41) 259763; e-mail admin@eadb .com; internet www.transafrica.org/eadb; f. 1967 by the former East African Community to promote development within Kenya, Tanzania and Uganda, which each hold 25.78% of the equity capital; the remaining equity is held by the African Development Bank and other institutional investors; total assets SDR 145m. (31 Dec. 2002); Chair. MWAGHAZI MWACHOFI; Dir-Gen. F. R. TIBEITA.

Eastern Caribbean Central Bank (ECCB): POB 89, Basseterre, St Christopher and Nevis; tel. 465-2537; fax 465-9562; e-mail eccbinfo@caribsurf.com; internet www.eccb-centralbank.org; f. 1983 by OECS governments; maintains regional currency (Eastern Caribbean dollar) and advises on the economic development of member states; mems: Anguilla, Antigua and Barbuda, Dominica, Grenada, Montserrat, Saint Christopher and Nevis, Saint Lucia, Saint Vincent and the Grenadines; Gov. Sir K. DWIGHT VENNER.

Econometric Society: Dept of Economics, Northwestern University, Evanston, IL 60208, USA; tel. (847) 491-3615; internet www .econometricsociety.org; f. 1930 to promote studies aiming at a unification of the theoretical-quantitative and the empirical-quantitative approaches to economic problems; mems: c. 7,000; Exec. Dir and Sec. JULIE P. GORDON; publ. *Econometrica* (6 a year).

Eurasian Economic Community (EurAsEC): Interparliamentary Assembly, 193015 St Petersburg, ul. Shpalernaya 47, Tavricheslkii dvorets; tel. (812) 326-69-32; fax (812) 326-69-72; e-mail kanz@iacis.ru; internet www.ipaeurasec.org; f. 2000; formerly a Customs Union agreed between Belarus, Kazakhstan, Kyrgyzstan, Russia and Tajikistan in 1999; aims to create a common economic space with a single currency; a free trade zone was established at the end of 2002; mems co-operate on issues including customs tariff harmonization, migration, border security and negotiating admission to the WTO; Armenia, Moldova and Ukraine have observer status; Sec.-Gen. GRIGORII RAPOTA.

European Federation of Finance House Associations (Eurofinas): 267 ave de Tervueren, 1150 Brussels, Belgium; tel. (2) 778-05-60; fax (2) 778-05-79; internet www.eurofinas.org; f. 1959 to study the development of instalment credit financing in Europe, to collate and publish instalment credit statistics, and to promote research into instalment credit practice; mems: finance houses and professional asscns in 16 European countries; Chair. GREGORIO D'OTTAVIANO CHIARAMONTI (Italy); Sec.-Gen. MARC BAERT; publs *Eurofinas Newsletter* (monthly), *Annual Report, Study Reports.*

European Federation of Financial Analysts Societies (EFFAS): Palais de la Bourse, Place de la Bourse, 75002 Paris, France; tel. 1-03-58-33-48; fax 1-03-58-33-35; e-mail claudia .stinnes@effas.com; internet www.effas.com; f. 1962 to co-ordinate the activities of European asscns of financial analysts; aims to raise the standard of financial analysis and improve the quality of information given to investors; encourages unification of national rules and draws up rules of profession; holds biennial congress; mems: 14,000 in 18 European countries; Pres. FRITZ H. RAU.

European Financial Management and Marketing Association (EFMA): 16 rue d'Aguesseau, 75008 Paris, France; tel. 1-47-42-52-72; fax 1-47-42-56-76; e-mail info@efma.com; internet www.efma .com; f. 1971 to link financial institutions by organizing seminars, conferences and training sessions and an annual Congress and World Convention, and by providing information services; mems: over 200 European financial institutions; Chair. ALFREDO SÁENZ ABAD (Spain); publ. *Newsletter.*

European Private Equity and Venture Capital Association (EVCA): 4 Minervastraat, 1930 Zaventem, Belgium; tel. (2) 715-00-20; fax (2) 725-07-04; e-mail evca@evca.com; internet www.evca .com; f. 1983 to link private equity and venture capital companies within Europe; provides information services; supports networking; organizes lobbies and campaigns; works to promote the asset class in Europe and world-wide; holds three conferences each year as well as seminars, organizes EVCA Institute training courses; mems: over 950; Chair. MAX BURGER; Sec.-Gen. JAVIER ECHARRI; publs *Yearbook*, research and special papers, legal documents, industry guide-lines.

Financial Action Task Force on Money Laundering (FATF) (Groupe d'action financière sur le blanchiment de capitaux—GAFI): 2 rue André-Pascal, 75775 Paris Cédex 16, France; tel. 1-45-24-82-00; fax 1-45-24-85-00; e-mail contact@fatf.gafi.org; internet www1 .oecd.org/fatf; f. 1989, on the recommendation of the Group of Seven industrialized nations (G-7), to develop and promote policies to combat money laundering and the financing of terrorism; formulated a set of recommendations for member countries to implement; established regional task forces in the Caribbean, Asia-Pacific, Europe, Africa and South America; mems: 31 countries, the European Commission, and the Co-operation Council for the Arab States of the Gulf; Pres. CLAES NORGREN (Sweden); Exec. Sec. PATRICK MOULETTE; publ. *Annual Report.*

Fonds Africain de Garantie et de Co-opération Economique (FAGACE) (African Guarantee and Economic Co-operation Fund): 01 BP 2045 RP, Cotonou, Benin; tel. 30-03-76; fax 30-02-84; e-mail fagace@intnet.bj; internet www.fagace.org; commenced operations in 1981; guarantees loans for development projects, provides loans and grants for specific operations and supports national and regional enterprises; mems: nine African countries; Dir-Gen. LIBASSE SAMB.

International Accounting Standards Board (IASB): 30 Cannon St, London, EC4M 6XH, United Kingdom; tel. (20) 7246-6410; fax (20) 7246-6411; e-mail iasb@iasb.org.uk; internet www.iasb.org.uk; f. 1973 as International Accounting Standards Committee, reorganized and present name adopted 2001; aims to develop, in the public interest, a single set of high-quality, uniform, clear and enforceable global accounting standards requiring the submission of high-quality, transparent and comparable information in financial statements and other financial reporting, in order to assist participants in world-wide capital markets and other end-users to make informed decisions on economic matters; aims also to promote the use and rigorous application of these global accounting standards, and to bring about the convergence of these with national accounting standards; Chair. and CEO Sir DAVID TWEEDIE; publs *IASB Insight*

(quarterly), *Bound Volume of International Accounting Standards* (annually), *Interpretations of International Accounting Standards.*

International Association for Research in Income and Wealth: Dept of Economics, New York University, 269 Mercer St, Room 700, New York, NY 10003, USA; tel. (212) 924-4386; fax (212) 366-5067; e-mail iariw@nyu.edu; internet www.econ.nyu.edu/iariw; f. 1947 to further research in the general field of national income and wealth and related topics by the organization of biennial conferences and other means; mems: approx. 375; Chair. TIM SMEEDING; Exec. Sec. JANE FORMAN (USA); publ. *Review of Income and Wealth* (quarterly).

International Bureau of Fiscal Documentation (IBFD): H. J. E. Wenckebachweg 210, POB 20237, 1096 AS Amsterdam, Netherlands; tel. (20) 55-40-100; fax (20) 62-28-658; e-mail info@ibfd.org; internet www.ibfd.org; f. 1938 to supply information on fiscal law and its application; maintains library on international taxation; Pres. Prof. G. MAISTO; Chair. Prof. HUBERT M. A. L. HAMAEKERS; publs *Bulletin for International Fiscal Documentation, Asia Pacific Tax Bulletin, Derivatives and Financial Instruments, European Taxation, International VAT Monitor, International Transfer Pricing Journal, Supplementary Service to European Taxation* (all monthly), *Tax News Service* (weekly); studies, data bases, regional tax guides.

International Centre for Local Credit: Koninginnegracht 2, 2514 AA The Hague, Netherlands; tel. (70) 3750850; fax (70) 3454743; e-mail centre@bng.nl; f. 1958 to promote local authority credit by gathering, exchanging and distributing information and advice on member institutions and on local authority credit and related subjects; studies important subjects in the field of local authority credit; mems: 22 financial institutions in 16 countries; Sec.-Gen. P. P. VAN BESOUW (Netherlands); publs *Bulletin, Newsletter* (quarterly).

International Economic Association: 23 rue Campagne Première, 75014 Paris, France; tel. 1-43-27-91-44; fax 1-42-79-92-16; e-mail iea@iea-world.org; internet www.iea-world.com; f. 1949 to promote international collaboration for the advancement of economic knowledge and develop personal contacts between economists, and to encourage the provision of means for the dissemination of economic knowledge; mems: asscns in 59 countries; Pres. Prof. JANOS KORNAI (Hungary); Sec.-Gen. Prof. JEAN-PAUL FITOUSSI (France).

International Federation of Accountants: 545 5th Ave, 14th Floor, New York, NY 10017, USA; tel. (212) 286-9344; fax (212) 286-9570; internet www.ifac.org; f. 1977 to develop a co-ordinated world-wide accounting profession with harmonized standards; mems: 159 accountancy bodies in 118 countries; Pres. RENÉ RICOL; Chief Exec. IAN BALL; publ. *International Standards on Auditing.*

International Fiscal Association (IFA): World Trade Center, POB 30215, 3001 DE Rotterdam, Netherlands; tel. (10) 4052990; fax (10) 4055031; e-mail n.gensecr@ifa.nl; internet www.ifa.nl; f. 1938 to study international and comparative public finance and fiscal law, especially taxation; holds annual congresses; mems in 96 countries and branches in 50 countries; Pres. JEROME B. LIBIN (USA); Sec.-Gen. M. J. ELLIS (Netherlands); publs *Cahiers de Droit Fiscal International, Yearbook of the International Fiscal Association, IFA Congress Seminar Series.*

International Institute of Public Finance: University of the Saar, PO Box 151150, 66041 Saarbrücken, Germany; fax (681) 302-4369; e-mail schneider@iipf.net; internet www.iipf.org; f. 1937; a private scientific organization aiming to establish contacts between people of every nationality, whose main or supplementary activity consists in the study of public finance; holds one meeting a year devoted to a certain scientific subject; Pres. MICHAEL KEEN (UK); Exec. Sec. BIRGIT SCHNEIDER.

International Organization of Securities Commissions (IOSCO): Calle Oquendo 12, 28006 Madrid, Spain; tel. (91) 417-5549; fax (91) 555-9368; e-mail mail@oicv.iosco.org; internet www .iosco.org; f. 1983 to facilitate co-operation between securities and futures regulatory bodies at the international level; mems: 168 agencies; Chair. FERNANDO TEIXEIRA DOS SANTOS; Sec.-Gen. PHILIPPE RICHARD; publ. *IOSCO News* (3 a year).

International Securities Market Association (ISMA): Rigistr. 60, POB, 8033 Zürich, Switzerland; tel. (1) 3634222; fax (1) 3637772; e-mail info@isma.org; internet www.isma.org; f. 1969 for discussion of questions relating to the international securities market, to issue rules governing their functions, and to maintain a close liaison between the primary and secondary markets in international securities; mems: 568 banks and major financial institutions in 48 countries; Chair. RIJNHARD W. F. VAN TETS (Netherlands); Chief Exec. and Sec.-Gen. JOHN L. LANGTON; publs *International Bond Manual*, daily Eurobond listing, electronic price information, weekly Eurobond guide, ISMA formulae for yield, members' register, ISMA quarterly comment, reports, etc.

International Union for Housing Finance: 3 Savile Row, London, W1S 3PB, United Kingdom; tel. (20) 7494-2995; fax (20) 7734-6826; e-mail iuhf@housingfinance.org; internet www .housingfinance.org; f. 1914 to foster world-wide interest in savings and home-ownership and co-operation among members; encourages comparative study of methods and practice in housing finance; promotes development of appropriate legislation on housing finance; mems: 350 in 51 countries, 8 regional affiliates; Sec.-Gen. ADRIAN COLES; publs *Housing Finance International* (quarterly), *Directory*, *International Housing Finance Factbook* (every 2 years), *IUHF Newsletter* (3 a year).

Latin American Banking Federation (Federación Latino-americana de Bancos—FELABAN): Santafé de Bogotá, DC, Colombia Cra 11A No. 93-67 Of. 202 A.A 091959; tel. (1) 621-8617; fax (1) 621-7659; internet www.latinbanking.com; f. 1965 to co-ordinate efforts towards wide and accelerated economic development in Latin American countries; mems: 19 Latin American national banking asscns; Pres. of Board IGNACIO SALVATIERRA (Venezuela); Sec.-Gen. MARICIELO GLEN DE TOBÓN (Colombia).

World Council of Credit Unions (WOCCU): POB 2982, 5710 Mineral Point Rd, Madison, WI 53705, USA; tel. (608) 231-7130; fax (608) 238-8020; e-mail mail@woccu.org; internet www.woccu.org; f. 1970 to link credit unions and similar co-operative financial institutions and assist them in expanding and improving their services; provides technical and financial assistance to credit union asscns in developing countries; mems: 35,000 credit unions in 86 countries; CEO ARTHUR ARNOLD; publs *WOCCU Annual Report*, *Credit Union World* (3 a year), *Spotlights On Development*; technical monographs and brochures.

World Federation of Exchanges (International Federation of Stock Exchanges): 22 boulevard de Courcelles, 75017 Paris, France; tel. 1-44-01-05-45; fax 1-47-54-94-22; e-mail secretariat@ world-exchanges.org; internet www.world-exchanges.org; f. 1961; formerly Fédération Internationale des Bourses de Valeurs—FIBV; central reference point for the securities industry; offers member exchanges guidance in business strategies, and improvement and harmonization of management practices; works with public financial authorities to promote increased use of regulated securities and derivatives exchanges; mems: 59, and 23 corresponding exchanges; Pres. RICHARD A. GRASSO; Sec-Gen. THOMAS KRANTZ.

World Savings Banks Institute: 11 rue Marie Thérèse, 1000 Brussels, Belgium; tel. (2) 211-11-11; fax (2) 211-11-99; internet www.savings-banks.org; f. 1924 as International Savings Banks Institute, present name and structure adopted in 1994; promotes co-operation among members and the development of savings banks world-wide; mems: 104 banks and asscns in 89 countries; Pres. Dr HOLGEN BERNDT (Germany); publs *Annual Report*, *International Savings Banks Directory*, *Perspectives* (4–5 a year).

Education

Agence Universitaire de la Francophonie (AUF): BP 400, succ. Côte-des-Neiges, Montréal, QC H3S 2S7, Canada; tel. (514) 343-6630; fax (514) 343-5783; e-mail recteur@auf.org; internet www.auf .org; f. 1961; aims to develop a francophone university community, through building partnerships with students, teachers, institutions and governments; mems: 535 institutions; Pres. JEAN DU BOIS DE GAUDUSSON (Canada); Dir-Gen. and Rector MICHÈLE GENDREAU-MASSA-LOUX (France); publ. *Le Français à l'Université* (quarterly).

Asian and South Pacific Bureau of Adult Education (ASPBAE): c/o MAAPL, Eucharistic Congress Bldg No. 3, 9th Floor, 5 Convent St, Colaba, Mumbai 400 039, India; tel. (22) 22021391; fax (22) 22832217; e-mail aspbae@vsnl.com; internet www.aspbae.org; f. 1964 to assist non-formal education and adult literacy; organizes training courses and seminars; provides material and advice relating to adult education; mems in 36 countries and territories; Sec.-Gen. MARIA-LOURDES ALMAZAN-KHAN; publ. *ASPBAE News* (3 a year) .

Asian Confederation of Teachers: c/o FIT, 55 Abhinav Apt, Mahturas Rd Extn, Kandivli, Mumbai 400 067, India; tel. (22) 8085437; fax (22) 6240578; e-mail vsir@hotmail.com; f. 1990; mems in 10 countries and territories; Pres. MUHAMMAD MUSTAPHA; Sec.-Gen. VINAYAK SIRDESAI.

Association for Childhood Education International: 17904 Georgia Ave, Suite 215, Olney, MD 20832, USA; tel. (301) 570-2111; fax (301) 570-2212; e-mail aceihq@aol.com; internet www.acei.org; f. 1892 to work for the education of children (from infancy through early adolescence) by promoting desirable conditions in schools, raising the standard of teaching, co-operating with all groups concerned with children, informing the public of the needs of children; mems: 12,000; Pres. JACQUELINE BLACKWELL; Exec. Dir GERALD C. ODLAND; publs *Childhood Education* (6 a year), *Professional Focus*

Newsletters, *Journal of Research in Childhood Education* (quarterly), books on current educational subjects.

Association Montessori Internationale: Koninginneweg 161, 1075 CN Amsterdam, Netherlands; tel. (20) 6798932; fax (20) 6767341; e-mail info@montessori-ami.org; internet www .montessori-ami.org; f. 1929 to propagate the ideals and educational methods of Dr Maria Montessori on child development, without racial, religious or political prejudice; organizes training courses for teachers in 15 countries; Pres. RENILDE MONTESSORI; publ. *Communications* (quarterly).

Association of African Universities (AAU) (Association des universités africaines): POB 5744, Accra North, Ghana; tel. (21) 774495; fax (21) 774821; e-mail info@aau.org; internet www.aau.org; f. 1967 to promote exchanges, contact and co-operation among African university institutions and to collect and disseminate information on research and higher education in Africa; mems: 132 university institutions; Sec.-Gen. Prof. FRANÇOIS RAJAOSON (Madagascar); publs *AAU Newsletter* (3 a year), *Directory of African Universities* (every 2 years).

Association of Arab Universities: POB 401, Jubeyha, Amman, Jordan; tel. (6) 5345131; fax (6) 5332994; e-mail secgen@aaru.edu.jo; internet www.aaru.edu.jo; f. 1964; a scientific conference is held every 3 years; council meetings held annually; mems: 161 universities; Sec.-Gen. Dr MARWAN RASIM KAMAL; publ. *AARU Bulletin* (annually and quarterly, in Arabic).

Association of Caribbean University and Research Institutional Libraries (ACURIL): Apdo postal 23317, San Juan 00931-3317, Puerto Rico; tel. 790-8054; fax 764-2311; e-mail acuril@rrpac .upr.clu.edu; internet acuril.rrp.upr.edu; f. 1968 to foster contact and collaboration between mem. universities and institutes; holds conferences, meetings and seminars; circulates information through newsletters and bulletins; facilitates co-operation and the pooling of resources in research; encourages exchange of staff and students; mems: 250; Pres. LUISA VIGO-CEPEDA (Puerto Rico); Exec.-Sec. ONEIDA R. ORTIZ (Puerto Rico); publ. *Newsletter* (2 a year).

Association of South-East Asian Institutions of Higher Learning (ASAIHL): Secretariat, Ratasastra Bldg 2, Chulalongkorn University, Henri Dunant Rd, Bangkok 10330, Thailand; tel. (2) 251-6966; fax (2) 253-7909; e-mail oninnat@chula.ac.th; internet www.seameo.org/asaihl; f. 1956 to promote the economic, cultural and social welfare of the people of South-East Asia by means of educational co-operation and research programmes; and to cultivate a sense of regional identity and interdependence; collects and disseminates information, organizes discussions; mems: 160 university institutions in 14 countries; Pres. Prof. Tan Sri Dr SYED JALALUDIN SYED SALIM; Sec.-Gen. Dr NINNAT OLANVORAVUTH; publs *Newsletter*, *Handbook* (every 3 years).

Caribbean Examinations Council: The Garrison, St Michael 20, Barbados; tel. 436-6261; fax 429-5421; e-mail ezo@cxc.org; internet www.cxc.org; f. 1972; develops syllabuses and conducts examinations; mems: govts of 16 English-speaking countries and territories.

Catholic International Education Office: 60 rue des Eburons, 1000 Brussels, Belgium; tel. (2) 230-72-52; fax (2) 230-97-45; e-mail oiec@pophost.eunet.be; internet www3.planalfa.es/oiec; f. 1952 for the study of the problems of Catholic education throughout the world; co-ordinates the activities of members; represents Catholic education at international bodies; mems: 102 countries, 18 assoc. mems, 13 collaborating mems, 6 corresponding mems; Pres. Mgr CESARE NOSIGLIA; Sec.-Gen. ANDRÉS DELGADO HERNÁNDEZ; publs *OIEC Bulletin* (every 3 months, in English, French and Spanish), *OIEC Tracts on Education*.

Comparative Education Society in Europe (CESE): Institut für Augemeine Pädagogik, Humboldt-Universität zu Berlin, Unter den Linden 6, 10099 Berlin, Germany; tel. (30) 20934094; fax (30) 20931006; e-mail juergen.schriewer@educat.hu-berlin.de; internet www.ceseurope.org; f. 1961 to promote teaching and research in comparative and international education; organizes conferences and promotes literature; mems: in 49 countries; Pres. Prof. DONATELLA PALOMBA (Italy); Sec. and Treas. Prof. MIGUEL A. PEREYRA (Spain); publ. *Newsletter* (quarterly).

Council of Legal Education (CLE): c/o Registrar, POB 323, Tunapuna, Trinidad and Tobago; tel. 662-5860; fax 662-0927; f. 1971; responsible for the training of members of the legal profession; mems: govts of 12 countries and territories.

European Association for the Education of Adults: rue Liedts 27, 1030 Brussels, Belgium; tel. (2) 513-5205; fax (2) 513-5734; e-mail eaea-main@eaea.org; internet www.eaea.org; f. 1953; aims to create a 'learning society' by encouraging demand for learning, particularly from women and excluded sectors of society; seeks to improve response of providers of learning opportunities and authorities and agencies; mems: 100 organizations in 34 countries; Pres. JÁNOS TÓTH; Gen. Sec. ELLINOR HAASE; publs *EAEA Monograph Series*, newsletter.

European Cultural Foundation: Jan van Goyenkade 5, 1075 HN Amsterdam, Netherlands; tel. (20) 6760222; fax (20) 6752231; e-mail eurocult@eurocult.org; internet www.eurocult.org; f. 1954 as a non-governmental organization, supported by private sources, to promote activities of mutual interest to European countries on aspects of culture; maintains national committees in 23 countries and a transnational network of institutes and centres: European Institute of Education and Social Policy, Paris; Institute for European Environmental Policy, London, Madrid and Berlin; Association for Innovative Co-operation in Europe (AICE), Brussels; EURYDICE Central Unit (the Education Information Network of the European Community), Brussels; European Institute for the Media, Düsseldorf; European Foundation Centre, Brussels; Fund for Central and East European Book Projects, Amsterdam; Institute for Human Sciences, Vienna; East West Parliamentary Practice Project, Amsterdam; and Centre Européen de la Culture, Geneva; a grants programme, for European co-operation projects is also conducted; Pres. Princess MARGRIET OF THE NETHERLANDS; Sec.-Gen. GOTTFRIED WAGNER; publs *Annual Report*, *Newsletter* (3 a year).

European Federation for Catholic Adult Education (Federation Européene pour l'Éducation Catholique des Adultes—FEECA): ave de Tervueren 221, 1150, Brussels, Belgium; tel. (2) 738-07-90; fax (2) 738-07-95; e-mail feeca@brutele.be; f. 1963 to strengthen international contact between mems and to assist with international research and practical projects in adult education; holds conference every two years; Pres. ERICA SCHUSTER (Austria); Sec. GEORG DÜCHS.

European Foundation for Management Development (EFMD): 88 rue Gachard, 1050 Brussels, Belgium; tel. (2) 629-08-10; fax (2) 629-08-11; e-mail info@efmd.be; internet www.efmd.be; f. 1971 through merger of European Association of Management Training Centres and International University Contact for Management Education; aims to help improve the quality of management development, disseminate information within the economic, social and cultural context of Europe and promote international co-operation; mems: over 390 institutions in 41 countries world-wide (26 in Europe); Pres. GERARD VAN SCHAIK; Dir-Gen. ERIC CORNUEL; publs *Forum* (3 a year), *The Bulletin* (3 a year), *Guide to European Business Schools and Management Centres* (annually).

European Union of Arabic and Islamic Scholars (Union Européenne des Arabisants et Islamisants—UEAI): c/o Prof. S. Naef, Univ. de Genève, Faculté des Lettres, 3 rue de Candolle, 1211 Geneva 4, Switzerland; tel. (22) 3797138; fax (22) 3797281; e-mail silvia.naef@lettres.unige.ch; f. 1964 to organize congresses of Arabic and Islamic Studies; holds congresses every two years; mems: 300 in 28 countries; Pres. Prof. JUAN SOUTO (Spain); Sec. Prof. SILVIA NAEF (Switzerland).

European University Association (EUA): 13 rue d'Egmont, 1000 Brussels, Belgium; tel. (2) 230-55-44; fax (2) 230-57-51; e-mail info@eua.be; internet www.eua.be; f. 2001 by merger of the Association of European Universities and the Confederation of EU Rectors' Conferences; represents European universities and national rectors' conferences; promotes the development of a coherent system of European higher education and research through projects and membership services; provides support and guidance to mems. mems: 732 in 45 countries; Pres. ERIC FROMENT; Sec.-Gen. LESLEY WILSON; publs *Thema*, *Directory*, *Annual Report*.

Graduate Institute of International Studies (Institut universitaire de hautes études internationales—HEI): POB 36, 132 rue de Lausanne, 1211 Geneva 21, Switzerland; tel. (22) 9085700; fax (22) 9085710; e-mail info@hei.unige.ch; internet heiwww.unige.ch; f. 1927 to establish a centre for advanced studies in international relations of the present day; maintains a library of 147,000 vols; Pres. Prof. JEAN-MICHEL JACQUET; Sec.-Gen. SIMON WERMELINGER.

Inter-American Centre for Research and Documentation on Vocational Training (Centro Interamericano de Investigación y Documentación sobre Formación Profesional—CINTER-FOR): Avda Uruguay 1238, Casilla de correo 1761, Montevideo, Uruguay; tel. (2) 9020557; fax (2) 9021305; e-mail dirmvd@cinterfor.org.uy; internet www.ilo.org/public/english/region/ampro/cinterfor; f. 1964 by the International Labour Organization for mutual help among the Latin American and Caribbean countries in planning vocational training; services are provided in documentation, research, exchange of experience; holds seminars and courses; Dir PEDRO DANIEL WEINBERG; publs *Bulletin* (3 a year), *Documentation* (2 a year), *Herramientas para la transformación*, *Trazos de la formación*, studies, monographs and technical office papers.

Inter-American Confederation for Catholic Education (Confederación Interamericana de Educación Católica—CIEC): Calle 78 No 12–16 (of. 101), Apdo Aéreo 90036, Santafé de Bogotá 8 DE, Colombia; tel. (1) 255-3676; fax (1) 255-0513; e-mail ciec@cable.net.co; internet www.ciec.to; f. 1945 to defend and extend the principles and rules of Catholic education, freedom of education, and human rights; organizes congress every three years; Pres. RAMÓN E. RIVAS

TOMASI (Venezuela); Sec.-Gen. MARIA CONSTANZA ARANGO; publ. *Educación Hoy*.

International Association for Educational and Vocational Guidance (IAEVG): c/o Linda Taylor, Essex Careers and Business Partnership, Westergaard House, The Matchyns, London Rd, Rivenhall, Essex, CM8 3HA, United Kingdom; tel. (1376) 391303; fax (1376) 391498; e-mail linda.taylor@careersbp.co.uk; internet www.iaevg.org; f. 1951 to contribute to the development of vocational guidance and promote contact between persons associated with it; mems: 40,000 from 60 countries; Pres. Dr BERNHARD JENSCHKE (Germany); Sec.-Gen. LINDA TAYLOR (UK); publs *Bulletin* (2 a year), *Newsletter* (3 a year).

International Association for the Development of Documentation, Libraries and Archives in Africa: Villa 2547 Dieuppeul II, BP 375, Dakar, Senegal; tel. 824-09-54; f. 1957 to organize and develop documentation and archives in all African countries; mems: national asscns, institutions and individuals in 48 countries; Sec.-Gen. ZACHEUS SUNDAY ALI (Nigeria).

International Association of Educators for World Peace: POB 3282, Mastin Lake Station, Huntsville, AL 35810-0282, USA; tel. (256) 534-5501; fax (256) 536-1018; e-mail mercieca@hiwaay.net; internet www.earthportals.com/portal_messenger/executivelistiaewp1.html; f. 1969 to develop education designed to contribute to the promotion of peaceful relations at personal, community and international levels; aims to communicate and clarify controversial views in order to achieve maximum understanding; helps put into practice the Universal Declaration of Human Rights; mems: 35,000 in 102 countries; Pres. Dr CHARLES MERCIECA (USA); Sec.-Gen. Dr SURYA NATH PRASAD (India); publs *Peace Progress* (annually), *IAEWP Newsletter* (6 a year), *Peace Education* (2 a year), *UN News* (monthly).

International Association of Papyrologists (Association Internationale de Papyrologues): Fondation Egyptologique Reine Elisabeth, Parc du Cinquantenaire 10, 1000 Brussels, Belgium; tel. (2) 741-73-64; e-mail amartin@ulb.ac.be; internet www.ulb.ac.be/assoc/aip; f. 1947; links all those interested in Graeco-Roman Egypt, especially Greek texts; mem. of the International Federation of the Societies of Classical Studies; mems: about 400; Pres. Prof. DOROTHY J. THOMPSON (UK); Sec. Prof. ALAIN MARTIN (Belgium).

International Association of Physical Education in Higher Education (Association Internationale des Écoles Supérieures d'Éducation Physique—AIESEP): Faculdade de Motricidade Humana, Universidade Técnica de Lisboa, 1495-688 Cruz Quebrada, Lisbon, Portugal; tel. (21) 419-66-08; fax (21) 415-12-48; e-mail fcosta@fmh.utl.pt; f. 1962; organizes congresses, exchanges, and research in physical education; mems: institutions in 51 countries; Sec.-Gen. Dr FRANCISCO CARREIRO DA COSTA.

International Association of Universities (IAU)/ International Universities Bureau (IUB): 1 rue Miollis, 75732 Paris cédex 15, France; tel. 1-45-68-48-00; fax 1-47-34-76-05; e-mail iau@unesco.org; internet www.unesco.org/iau; f. 1950 to allow co-operation at the international level among universities and other institutions of higher education; provides clearing-house services and operates the joint IAU/UNESCO Information Centre on Higher Education; conducts meetings and research on issues concerning higher education; mems: about 607 universities and institutions of higher education in some 118 countries, 25 international and national university organizations; Pres. HANS VAN GINKEL; Sec.-Gen. EVA EGRON-POLAK; publs *Higher Education Policy* (quarterly), *IAU Newsletter* (every 2 months), *International Handbook of Universities* (every 2 years), *Issues in Higher Education* (monographs), *World Higher Education Database* (CD-ROM, annually), *World List of Universities and other Institutions of Higher Education* (every 2 years).

International Association of University Professors and Lecturers (IAUPL) (Association Internationale des Professeurs et Maîtres de Conférence Universitaires): 87 rue de Rome, 75017 Paris, France; tel. 1-44-90-01-01; fax 1-44-90-08-87; e-mail autonomesup@aol.com; f. 1945 for the development of academic fraternity amongst university teachers and research workers; the protection of independence and freedom of teaching and research; the furtherance of the interests of all university teachers; and the consideration of academic problems; mems: federations in 13 countries.

International Baccalaureate Organization (IBO): Route des Morillons 15, Grand-Saconnex 1218, Geneva, Switzerland; tel. (22) 7917740; fax (22) 7910277; e-mail ibhq@ibo.org; internet www.ibo.org; f. 1967 to plan curricula and an international university entrance examination, the International Baccalaureate, recognized by major universities world-wide; offers the Primary Years Programme for children aged between 3 and 12, the Middle Years Programme for students in the 11–16 age range, and the Diploma Programme for 17–18 year olds; mems: 1,425 participating schools in 115 countries; Pres. of Council GREG CRAFTER (Australia); Dir-Gen. Prof. GEORGE WALKER.

International Catholic Federation for Physical and Sports Education (Fédération Internationale Catholique d'Education Physique et Sportive—FICEP): 22 rue Oberkampf, 75011 Paris, France; tel. 1-43-38-50-57; fax 1-43-14-06-65; f. 1911 to group Catholic asscns for physical education and sport of different countries and to develop the principles and precepts of Christian morality by fostering meetings, study and international co-operation; mems: 14 affiliated national federations representing about 3.5m. members; Pres. DICK WIJTE (Netherlands); Sec.-Gen. CLÉMENT SCHERTZINGER (France).

International Council for Adult Education (ICAE): 720 Bathurst St, Suite 500, Toronto, ON M5S 2R4, Canada; tel. (416) 588-1211; fax (416) 588-5725; e-mail icae@icae.ca; internet www.web.net/icae; f. 1973 as a partnership of adult learners, teachers and organizations; General Assembly meets every four years; mems: seven regional organizations and 85 national asscns in more than 80 countries; Pres. PAUL BÉLANGER; publs *Convergence, ICAE News.*

International Council for Open and Distance Education (ICDE): Lilleakerveien 23, 0283 Oslo, Norway; tel. 22-06-26-30; fax 22-06-26-31; e-mail icde@icde.no; internet www.icde.org; f. 1938 (name changed 1982); furthers distance (correspondence) education by promoting research, encouraging regional links, providing information and organizing conferences; mems: institutions, corporations and individuals in 120 countries; Pres. JIM TAYLOR (Australia); Sec.-Gen. REIDAR ROLL (Norway); publ. *Open Praxis* (2 a year).

International Federation for Parent Education (IFPE) (Fédération internationale pour l'éducation des parents–FIEP): 1 ave Léon Journault, 92311 Sèvres Cédex, France; tel. 1-45-07-21-64; fax 1-46-26-69-27; e-mail fiep@sympatico.ca; f. 1964 to gather in congresses and colloquia experts from different scientific fields and those responsible for family education in their own countries and to encourage the establishment of family education where it does not exist; mems: 120; Pres. MONEEF GUITOUNI (Canada); publ. *Lettre de la FIEP* (2 a year).

International Federation of Catholic Universities (Fédération internationale d'universités catholiques—FIUC): 21 rue d'Assas, 75270 Paris Cédex 06, France; tel. 1-44-39-52-26; fax 1-44-39-52-28; e-mail sgfiuc@bureau.fiuc.org; internet www.fiuc.org/; f. 1948; aims to ensure a strong bond of mutual assistance among all Catholic universities in the search for truth; to help to solve problems of growth and development, and to co-operate with other international organizations; mems: 196 in 52 countries; Pres. Rev. JAN PETERS (Netherlands); Sec.-Gen. GUY-RÉAL THIVIERGE (Canada); publ. *Monthly Newsletter.*

International Federation of Library Associations and Institutions (IFLA): POB 95312, 2509 CH The Hague, Netherlands; tel. (70) 3140884; fax (70) 3834827; e-mail ifla@ifla.org; internet www.ifla.org; f. 1927 to promote international co-operation in librarianship and bibliography; mems: 1,700 members in 150 countries; Pres. Elect (2005–07) ALEX BYRNE; Sec.-Gen. PETER LOR; publs *IFLA Annual Report, IFLA Directory, IFLA Journal, International Cataloguing and Bibliographic Control* (quarterly), *IFLA Professional Reports.*

International Federation of Organizations for School Correspondence and Exchange: Via Torino 256, 10015 Ivrea, Italy; tel. (0125) 234433; e-mail fioces@ipfs.org; internet ipfs.org/fioces.htm; f. 1929; aims to contribute to the knowledge of foreign languages and civilizations and to bring together young people of all nations by furthering international scholastic correspondence; mems: 78 national bureaux of scholastic correspondence and exchange in 21 countries; Pres. ALBERT V. RUTTER (Malta); Gen. Sec. LIVIO TONSO (Italy).

International Federation of Physical Education (Fédération internationale d'éducation physique—FIEP): c/o Prof. Robert Decker, 7–9 rue du X Octobre, 7243 Bereldange, Luxembourg; tel. and fax 33-94-81; e-mail robert.decker@education.lu; f. 1923; studies physical education on scientific, pedagogic and aesthetic bases, with the aim of stimulating health, harmonious development or preservation, healthy recreation, and the best adaptation of the individual to the general needs of social life; organizes international congresses and courses; awards research prize; mems: from 112 countries; Vice-Pres. (Europe) Prof. ROBERT DECKER; publ. *FIEP Bulletin* (trilingual edition in English, French, and Spanish, 3 a year).

International Federation of Teachers of Modern Languages (Fédération des Professeurs de Langues Vivantes): POB 216, Belgrave 3160, Australia; tel. (6139) 754-4714 ; fax (6139) 416-9899; e-mail djc@netspace.net.au; internet www.fiplv.org; f. 1931; holds meetings on every aspect of foreign-language teaching; has consultative status with UNESCO; mems: 28 national and regional language asscns and nine international unilingual asscns (teachers of English, Esperanto, French, German, Hungarian, Portuguese, Russian, and Spanish); Pres. DENIS CUNNINGHAM; Sec.-Gen. EYNAR LEUPOLD; publ. *FIPLV World News* (quarterly, in English, French, German and Spanish).

International Federation of University Women (IFUW): 8 rue de l'Ancien Port, 1201 Geneva, Switzerland; tel. (22) 7312380; fax (22) 7380440; e-mail ifuw@ifuw.org; internet www.ifuw.org; f. 1919 to promote understanding and friendship among university women of the world to encourage international co-operation; to further the development of education; to represent university women in international organizations; to encourage the full application of members' skills to the problems which arise at all levels of public life; Affiliates: 77 national asscns with over 160,000 mems; Pres. Prof. REIKO AOKI (Japan); publs *IFUW News* (6 a year), triennial report.

International Federation of Workers' Education Associations: c/o POB 8703, Youngstorget, 0028 Oslo 1, Norway; tel. (161) 445-9272; fax (161) 445-3625; e-mail dave.spooner@ifwea.org; internet www.ifwea.org; f. 1947 to promote co-operation between non-governmental bodies concerned with workers' education; organizes clearing-house services; promotes exchange of information; holds international seminars, conferences and summer schools; Pres. JOÃO PROENCA (Portugal); Gen. Sec. DAVE SPOONER (UK); publ. *Worker's Education* (quarterly).

International Institute for Adult Education Methods: POB 19395/6194, 5th Floor, Golfam St, 19156 Tehran, Iran; tel. (21) 2220313; f. 1968 by UNESCO and the Government of Iran, to collect, analyse and distribute information on activities concerning methods of literacy training and adult education; sponsors seminars; maintains documentation service and library on literacy and adult education; Dir Dr MOHAMMAD REZA HAMIDIZADE; publs *Selection of Adult Education Issues* (monthly), *Adult Education and Development* (quarterly), *New Library Holdings* (quarterly).

International Institute of Philosophy (IIP) (Institut international de philosophie): 8 rue Jean-Calvin, 75005 Paris, France; tel. 1-43-36-39-11; e-mail inst.intern.philo@wanadoo.fr; f. 1937 to clarify fundamental issues of contemporary philosophy and to promote mutual understanding among thinkers of different backgrounds and traditions; mems: 103 in 38 countries; Pres. A. FAGOT-LARGEAULT (France); Sec.-Gen. P. AUBENQUE (France); publs *Bibliography of Philosophy* (quarterly), *Proceedings* of annual meetings, *Chroniques, Philosophy and World Community* (series), *Philosophical Problems Today, Controverses philosophiques.*

International Reading Association: 800 Barksdale Rd, POB 8139, Newark, DE 19714-8139, USA; tel. (302) 731-1600; fax (302) 731-1057; internet www.reading.org; f. 1956 to improve the quality of reading instruction at all levels, to promote the habit of lifelong reading, and to develop every reader's proficiency; mems: 90,000 in 99 countries; Pres. JERRY L. JOHNS; publs *The Reading Teacher* (8 a year), *Journal of Adolescent and Adult Literacy* (8 a year), *Reading Research Quarterly, Lectura y Vida* (quarterly in Spanish), *Reading Today* (6 a year).

International Schools Association (ISA): 10333 Diego Drive South, Boca Raton, FL 33428, USA; tel. (561) 883-3854; fax (561) 483-2004; e-mail info@isaschools.org; internet www.isaschools.org; f. 1951 to co-ordinate work in international schools and promote their development; supports the maintenance of high standards and equal opportunities in international schools; carries out curriculum research; convenes annual conferences on problems of curriculum and educational reform; organizes occasional teachers' training workshops and specialist seminars; mems: 72 schools throughout the world; Pres. CLIVE CARTHEW; Exec. Dir BERT TIMMERMANS; publs *Education Bulletin* (2 a year), *ISA Magazine* (annually), *Conference Report* (annually), curriculum studies (occasional).

International Society for Business Education: POB 20457, Carson City, NV 89721, USA; tel. (775) 882-1445; fax (775) 882-1449; e-mail kantin@charter.net; internet www.siec-isbe.org; f. 1901; encourages international exchange of information; organizes international courses and congresses on business education; mems: 2,200 national organizations and individuals in 23 countries; Pres. Dr HANS WEBER (Switzerland); Gen. Sec. G. LEE KANTIN (USA); publ. *International Review for Business Education.*

International Society for Education through Art (INSEA): c/o Peter Hermans, Citogroep, POB 1109, 6801 BC Arnhem, Netherlands; fax (26) 3521202; e-mail insea@citogroep.nl; internet insea.unb.ca; f. 1951 to unite art teachers throughout the world, to exchange information and to co-ordinate research into art education; organizes international congresses and exhibitions of children's art; Pres. DOUG BOUGHTON (USA); Sec.-Gen. DEBORAH SMITH-SHANK; publ. *INSEA News* (3 a year).

International Society for Music Education (ISME): POB 909, Nedlands, WA 6909, Australia; tel. (8) 9386-2654; fax (8) 9386-2658; e-mail isme@isme.org ; internet www.isme.org; f. 1953 to organize international conferences, seminars and publications on matters pertaining to music education; acts as advisory body to UNESCO in matters of music education; mems: national committees and individuals in more than 70 countries; Pres. GARY McPHERSON (USA); Sec.-Gen. JUDY THÖNELL (Australia); publs *ISME Newsletter, International Journal of Music Education.*

International Society for the Study of Medieval Philosophy: Collège Mercier, place du Cardinal Mercier 14, 1348 Louvain-la-Neuve, Belgium; tel. (10) 47-48-07; fax (10) 47-82-85; e-mail siepm@isp.vcp.ac.be; internet www.isp.ucl.ac.be/isp/siepm/siepm.html; f. 1958 to promote the study of medieval thought and the collaboration between individuals and institutions in this field; organizes international congresses; mems: 576; Pres. Prof. DAVID LUSCOMBE (UK); Sec. Prof. JACQUELINE HAMESSE (Belgium); publ. *Bulletin de Philosophie Médiévale* (annually).

International Youth Library (Internationale Jugendbibliothek): Schloss Blutenburg, 81247 Munich, Germany; tel. (89) 8912110; fax (89) 8117553; e-mail bib@ijb.de; internet www.ijb.de; f. 1949, since 1953 an associated project of UNESCO; promotes the international exchange of children's literature; provides study opportunities for specialists in childrens' books; maintains a library of 540,000 volumes in about 130 languages; Dir Dr BARBARA SCHARIOTH; publs *The White Ravens*, *IJB Report*, catalogues.

League of European Research Libraries (Ligue des bibliothèques européennes de recherche—LIBER): c/o Secretariat, Susan Vejlsgaard, Det Kongelige Bibliotek, POB 2149, 1016 Copenhagen K, Denmark; tel. 33-93-62-22; fax 33-91-95-96; e-mail sv@kb.dk; internet www.kb.dk/liber; f. 1971 to encourage collaboration between the general research libraries of Europe, and national and university libraries in particular; gives assistance in finding practical ways of improving the quality of the services provided; mems: 329 libraries and individuals in 33 countries; Dir-Gen. ERLAND KOLDING NIELSEN; Sec. PETER K. FOX (UK); publ. *LIBER Quarterly*.

Organization of Ibero-American States for Education, Science and Culture (Organización de Estados Iberoamericanos para la Educación, la Ciencia y la Cultura—OEI): Centro de Recursos Documentales e Informáticos, Calle Bravo Murillo 38, 28015 Madrid, Spain; tel. (91) 594-43-82; fax (91) 594-32-86; e-mail oeimad@oei.es; internet www.oei.es; f. 1949 (as the Ibero-American Bureau of Education); promotes peace and solidarity between member countries, through education, science, technology and culture; provides information, encourages exchanges and organizes training courses; the General Assembly (at ministerial level) meets every four years; mems: govts of 20 countries; Sec.-Gen. FRANCISCO JOSÉ PIÑÓN; publ. *Revista Iberoamericana de Educación* (quarterly).

Organization of the Catholic Universities of Latin America (Organización de Universidades Católicas de América Latina—ODUCAL): c/o Dr J. A. Tobías, Universidad del Salvador, Viamonte 1856, CP 1056, Buenos Aires, Argentina; tel. (11) 4813-1408; fax (11) 4812-4625; e-mail udes-rect@salvador.edu.ar; f. 1953 to assist the social, economic and cultural development of Latin America through the promotion of Catholic higher education in the continent; mems: 43 Catholic universities in 15 Latin American countries; Pres. Dr JUAN ALEJANDRO TOBÍAS (Argentina); publs *Anuario*, *Sapientia*, *Universitas*.

Pan-African Association for Literacy and Adult Education: c/o ANAFA, BP 10358, Dakar, Senegal; tel. 825-48-50; fax 824-43-30; e-mail anafa@metissacana.sn; f. 2000 to succeed African Assen for Literacy and Adult Education (f. 1984); Co-ordinator Dr LAMINE KANE.

Southeast Asian Ministers of Education Organization (SEAMEO): M. L. Pin Malakul Bldg, 920 Sukhumvit Rd, Bangkok 10110, Thailand; tel. (2) 391-0144; fax (2) 381-2587; e-mail secretariat@seameo.org; internet www.seameo.org; f. 1965 to promote co-operation among the Southeast Asian nations through projects in education, science and culture; SEAMEO has 15 regional centres including: BIOTROP for tropical biology, in Bogor, Indonesia; INNOTECH for educational innovation and technology; an Open-Learning Centre in Indonesia; RECSAM for education in science and mathematics, in Penang, Malaysia; RELC for languages, in Singapore; RIHED for higher education development in Bangkok, Thailand; SEARCA for graduate study and research in agriculture, in Los Baños, Philippines; SPAFA for archaeology and fine arts in Bangkok, Thailand; TROPMED for tropical medicine and public health with regional centres in Indonesia, Malaysia, Philippines and Thailand and a central office in Bangkok; VOCTECH for vocational and technical education; the SEAMEO Training Centre in Ho Chi Minh City, Viet Nam; and the SEAMEO Centre for History and Tradition (CHAT) in Yangon, Myanmar; mems: Brunei, Cambodia, Indonesia, Laos, Malaysia, Philippines, Singapore, Thailand, Viet Nam; assoc. mems: Australia, Canada, France, Germany, Netherlands, New Zealand; Pres. Prof. NGUYEN MINH HIEN; Dir Dr EDILBERTO DE JESUS (Philippines); publs *Annual Report*, *Journal of Southeast Asian Education*.

Union of Latin American Universities (Unión de Universidades de América Latina—UDUAL): Edificio UDUAL, Apdo postal 70-232, Ciudad Universitaria, Del. Coyoacán, 04510 México, DF, Mexico; tel. (55) 5622-0991; fax (55) 5616-1414; e-mail udual@servidor.unam.mx; internet www.unam.mx udual; f. 1949 to organize exchanges between professors, students, research fellows and graduates and generally encourage good relations between the Latin American universities; arranges conferences; conducts statistical research; maintains centre for university documentation; mems: 165 universities; Pres. Dr SALOMÓN LERNER FEBRES (Peru); Sec.-Gen. Dr JUAN JOSÉ SÁNCHEZ SOSA (Mexico); publs *Universidades* (2 a year), *Gaceta UDUAL* (quarterly), *Censo* (every 2 years).

Universal Esperanto Association (Universala Esperanto-Asocio): Nieuwe Binnenweg 176, 3015 BJ Rotterdam, Netherlands; tel. (10) 4361044; fax (10) 4361751; e-mail uea@inter.nl.net; internet www.uea.org; f. 1908 to assist the spread of the international language, Esperanto, and to facilitate the practical use of the language; mems: 62 affiliated national asscns and 19,750 individuals in 120 countries; Pres. RENATO CORSETTI (Italy); Gen. Sec. IVO OSIBOV (Croatia); publs *Esperanto* (monthly), *Kontakto* (every 2 months), *Jarlibro* (yearbook), *Esperanto Documents*.

World Association for Educational Research (WAER) (Association mondiale des sciences de l'éducation—AMSE): c/o Denise Lauzon, Faculty of Education, Sherbrooke Univ., 2500 blvd de l'Université Sherbrooke, QC J1K 2R1, Canada; e-mail denise .lauzon@usherbrooke.ca; f. 1953, present title adopted 1977; aims to encourage research in educational sciences by organizing congresses, issuing publications and supporting the exchange of information; mems: societies and individual members in 50 countries; Pres. Prof. Dr YVES LENOIR; Gen. Sec. and Treas. CÉLINE GARANT.

World Education Fellowship: 54 Fox Lane, London N13 4AL, United Kingdom; f. 1921 to promote education for international understanding, and the exchange and practice of ideas, together with research into progressive educational theories and methods; mems: sections and groups in 20 countries; Pres. Prof. SHINJO OKUDA (Japan); Chair. CHRISTINE WYKES (UK); Gen. Sec. GUADALUPE G. DE TURNER (UK); publ. *The New Era in Education* (3 a year).

World Union of Catholic Teachers (Union mondiale des enseignants catholiques—UMEC): Piazza San Calisto 16, 00120 Città del Vaticano; tel. (06) 69887286; f. 1951; encourages the grouping of Catholic teachers for the greater effectiveness of Catholic schools, distributes documentation on Catholic doctrine with regard to education, and facilitates personal contacts through congresses, and seminars, etc; nationally and internationally; mems: 32 organizations in 29 countries; Pres. ARNOLD BACKX (Netherlands); Sec.-Gen. MICHAEL EMM (UK); publ. *Nouvelles de l'UMEC*.

World University Service (WUS): International Co-ordination Office, c/o WUSC, 1404 Scott St, Ottawa, ON K1Y 2N2, Canada; tel. (613) 798-7477; fax (613) 798-0990; internet www.wusc.ca; f. 1920; links students, faculty and administrators in post-secondary institutions concerned with economic and social development, and seeks to protect their academic freedom and autonomy; seeks to extend technical, personal and financial resources of post-secondary institutions to under-developed areas and communities; provides scholarships at university level for refugees, displaced people, and returnees, and supports informal education projects for women; governed by an assembly of national committees; Chair. LEONARD W. CONOLLY (Canada); publs *WUS News*, *WUS and Human Rights* (quarterly).

Environmental Conservation

BirdLife International: Wellbrook Ct, Girton Rd, Cambridge, CB3 0NA, United Kingdom; tel. (1223) 277318; fax (1223) 277200; e-mail birdlife@birdlife.org.uk; internet www.birdlife.net; f. 1922 as the International Council for Bird Preservation; a global partnership of organizations that determines status of bird species throughout the world and compiles data on all endangered species; identifies conservation problems and priorities; initiates and co-ordinates conservation projects and international conventions; mems: partners in 60 countries, representatives in 31 countries; Chair. GERARD A. BERTRAND; Dir Dr MICHAEL RANDS (UK); publs *Bird Red Data Book*, *World Birdwatch* (quarterly), *Bird Conservation Series*, study reports.

Friends of the Earth International: Prins Hendrikkade 48, POB 19199, 1000 GD Amsterdam, Netherlands; tel. (20) 6221369; fax (20) 6392181; e-mail foei@foei.org; internet www.foei.org; f. 1971 to promote the conservation, restoration and rational use of the environment and natural resources through public education and campaigning; mems: 68 national groups; publ. *Link* (quarterly).

Greencross International: 160A route de Florissant, 1231 Conches/Geneva, Switzerland; tel. (22) 7891662; fax (22) 7891695; e-mail gcinternational@gci.ch; internet www.greencrossinternational.net; f. 1993; aims to promote Earth Charter, to mitigate the environmental legacy of conflicts, to deter conflict in water-stressed regions, to combat desertification, to promote new energy consumption patterns, and to promote international conferences on and awareness of environmental issues; Pres. and CEO ALEXANDER LIKHOTAL (Russia).

Greenpeace International: Keizersgracht 176, 1016 DW Amsterdam, Netherlands; tel. (20) 5236222; fax (20) 5236200; e-mail supporter.services@ams.greenpeace.org; internet www.greenpeace .org; f. 1971 to campaign for the protection of the environment; aims to bear witness to environmental destruction, and to demonstrate solutions for positive change; mems: offices in 41 countries; Chair. Anne Summers (Australia); Exec. Dir Gerd Leipold (Germany).

Independent World Commission on the Oceans (IWCO): c/o Palácio de Belém, 1300 Lisbon, Portugal; tel. (1) 3637141; fax (1) 3636603; e-mail secretariat@world-oceans.org; internet www .world-oceans.org; f. 1995 to study ways of protecting maritime resources and coastal areas; Chair. Mário Soares.

International Commission for the Protection of the Rhine: Postfach 200253 56002 Koblenz; Hohenzollernstrasse 18, 56068 Koblenz, Germany; tel. (261) 12495; fax (261) 36572; e-mail sekretariat@iksr.de; internet www.iksr.org; f. 1950; prepares and commissions research on the nature of the pollution of the Rhine; proposes protection, ecological rehabilitation and flood prevention measures; mems: 23 delegates from France, Germany, Luxembourg, Netherlands, Switzerland and the EU; Pres. Prof. M. Krafft; Sec. J. H. Oterdoom; publ. *Annual Report*.

International Emissions Trading Association: 20 Eglinton Ave West, Suite 1305, POB 2017, Toronto, Canada, ON M4R 1K8; tel. (416) 487-8591; fax (416) 481-2625; e-mail marcu@ieta.org; internet www.ieta.org; f. 1999; aims to establish a functional international framework for trading greenhouse gas emissions, in accordance with the objectives of the UN Framework Convention on Climate Change; serves as a specialized information centre on emissions trading and the greenhouse gas market; mems: 45 international companies from all sectors of the industry; Exec. Dir Andrei Marcu.

IUCN—The World Conservation Union: 28 rue Mauverney, 1196 Gland, Switzerland; tel. (22) 9990000; fax (22) 9990002; e-mail mail@hq.iucn.org; internet www.iucn.org; f. 1948, as the International Union for Conservation of Nature and Natural Resources; supports partnerships and practical field activities to promote the conservation of natural resources, to secure the conservation of biological diversity as an essential foundation for the future; to ensure wise use of the earth's natural resources in an equitable and sustainable way; and to guide the development of human communities towards ways of life in enduring harmony with other components of the biosphere, developing programmes to protect and sustain the most important and threatened species and eco-systems and assisting governments to devise and carry out national conservation strategies; maintains a conservation library and documentation centre and units for monitoring traffic in wildlife; mems: more than 1,000 states, government agencies, non-governmental organizations and affiliates in some 140 countries; Pres. Yolanda Kakabadse Navarro (Ecuador); Dir-Gen. Achim Steiner; publs *World Conservation Strategy, Caring for the Earth, Red List of Threatened Plants, Red List of Threatened Species, United Nations List of National Parks and Protected Areas, World Conservation* (quarterly), *IUCN Today*.

South Asia Co-operative Environment Programme (SACEP): 10 Anderson Rd, Colombo 5, Sri Lanka; tel. (1) 589787; fax (1) 589369; e-mail sacep@eureka.lk; f. 1982; aims to promote and support the protection and management of the environment in the subregion; Governing Council meets regularly; specific projects managed by individual mem. states, e.g. conservation of coral, mangroves, deltas and coastal areas (Bangladesh), training in wildlife management (India); mems: Afghanistan, Bangladesh, Bhutan, India, The Maldives, Nepal, Pakistan, Sri Lanka; Dir-Gen. Mahboob Elahi; publ. *SACEP Newsletter*.

South Pacific Regional Environment Programme (SPREP): POB 240, Apia, Samoa; tel. 21929; fax 20231; e-mail sprep@sprep .org.ws; internet www.sprep.org.ws; f. 1978 by the South Pacific Commission (where it was based; now Pacific Community), the South Pacific (now Pacific Islands) Forum, ESCAP and UNEP; formally established as an independent institution in June 1993; aims to promote regional co-operation in environmental matters, to assist members to protect and improve their shared environment, and to help members work towards sustainable development; mems: 22 Pacific islands, Australia, France, New Zealand, USA; Dir Asterio Takesy (Federated States of Micronesia); publs *SPREP Newsletter* (quarterly), *CASOLink* (quarterly), *La lettre de l'environnement* (quarterly), *South Pacific Sea Level and Climate Change Newsletter* (quarterly).

Wetlands International: POB 471, 6700 AL Wageningen, Netherlands; tel. (317) 478854; fax (317) 478850; e-mail post@wetlands.org; internet www.wetlands.org; f. 1995 by merger of several regional wetlands organizations; aims to sustain and restore wetlands, their resources and biodiversity through research, information exchange and conservation activities; promotes implementation of the 1971 Ramsar Convention on Wetlands; Chair. Stew Morrison; CEO Jane Madgwick; publs *Wetlands* (2 a year), other studies, technical publications, manuals, proceedings of meetings.

World Society for the Protection of Animals (WSPA): 89 Albert Embankment, London, SE1 7TP, United Kingdom; tel. (20) 7587-5000; fax (20) 7793-0208; e-mail wspa@wspa.org.uk; internet www .wspa.org.uk; f. 1981, incorporating the World Federation for the Protection of Animals (f. 1950) and the International Society for the Protection of Animals (f. 1959); promotes animal welfare and conservation by humane education, practical field projects, international lobbying and legislative work; mems: 489 member societies in 123 countries; Pres. Hugh Wirth; Dir-Gen. Maj.-Gen. Peter Davis.

WWF International: ave du Mont-Blanc, 1196 Gland, Switzerland; tel. (22) 3649111; fax (22) 3645358; e-mail info@wwfint.org; internet www.panda.org; f. 1961 (as World Wildlife Fund), name changed to World Wildlife Fund for Nature 1986, current nomenclature adopted 2001; aims to stop the degradation of the natural environment, conserve bio-diversity, ensure the sustainable use of renewable resources, and promote the reduction of both pollution and wasteful consumption; addresses six priority issues: forests, fresh water programmes, endangered seas, species, climate change, and toxins; has identified, and focuses its activities in, 200 'ecoregions' (the 'Global 200'), believed to contain the best part of the world's remaining biological diversity; actively supports and operates conservation programmes in 90 countries; mems: 28 national organizations, four associates, c. 5m. individual mems world-wide; Pres. Chief Emeka Anyaoku (Nigeria); Dir-Gen. Claude Martin; publs *Annual Report, Living Planet Report*.

Government and Politics

African Association for Public Administration and Management (AAPAM): Britak Centre, Ragati and Mara Rds, POB 48677, 00100 GPO, Nairobi, Kenya; tel. (20) 2730555; fax (20) 2731153; e-mail aapam@africaonline.co.ke; internet www.aapam.org; f. 1971 to promote good practices, excellence and professionalism in public administration through training, seminars, research, publications; convenes regular conferences to share learning experiences among members, and an annual Roundtable Conference; funded by membership contributions, government and donor grants; mems: 500 individual, 50 corporate; Pres. John Mitala (Uganda); Sec.-Gen. Dr Yolama Rufunda Barongo (Uganda); publs *Newsletter* (quarterly), *Annual Seminar Report, Newsletter* (quarterly), *African Journal of Public Administration and Management* (2 a year), studies.

Afro-Asian Peoples' Solidarity Organization (AAPSO): 89 Abdel Aziz Al-Saoud St, POB 11559-61 Manial El-Roda, Cairo, Egypt; tel. (2) 3636081; fax (2) 3637361; e-mail aapso@tedata.net.eg; f. 1958; acts among and for the peoples of Africa and Asia in their struggle for genuine independence, sovereignty, socio-economic development, peace and disarmament; mems: national committees and affiliated organizations in 66 countries and territories, assoc. mems in 15 European countries; Sec.-Gen. Nouri Abdel Razzak Hussein (Iraq); publs *Solidarity Bulletin* (monthly), *Socio-Economic Development* (3 a year).

Agency for the Prohibition of Nuclear Weapons in Latin America and the Caribbean (Organismo para la Proscripción de las Armas Nucleares en la América Latina y el Caribe—OPANAL): Schiller 326, 5°, Col. Chapultepec Morales, 11570 México, DF, Mexico; tel. (55) 5255-2914; fax (55) 5255-3748; internet www .opanal.org; f. 1969 to ensure compliance with the Treaty for the Prohibition of Nuclear Weapons in Latin America (Treaty of Tlatelolco), 1967 to ensure the absence of all nuclear weapons in the application zone of the Treaty; to contribute to the movement against proliferation of nuclear weapons; to promote general and complete disarmament; to prohibit all testing, use, manufacture, acquisition, storage, installation and any form of possession, by any means, of nuclear weapons; the organs of the Agency comprise the General Conference, meeting every two years, the Council, meeting every two months, and the secretariat; a General Conference is held every two years; mems: 33 states that have fully ratified the Treaty; the Treaty has two additional Protocols: the first signed and ratified by France, the Netherlands, the United Kingdom and the USA, the second signed and ratified by China, the USA, France, the United Kingdom and Russia; Sec.-Gen. Edmundo Vargas Carreño (Chile).

Alliance of Small Island States (AOSIS): c/o 211 East 43rd St, 15th Floor, New York, NY 10017, USA; tel. (212) 949-0190; fax (212) 697-3829; e-mail mauritius@un.int; internet www.sidsne.org/aosis; f. 1990 as an *ad hoc* intergovernmental grouping to focus on the special problems of small islands and low-lying coastal developing states; mems: 43 island nations; Chair. Jagdish Koonjul (Mauritius); publ. *Small Islands, Big Issues*.

ANZUS: c/o Dept of Foreign Affairs and Trade, Locked Bag 40, Queen Victoria Terrace, Canberra, ACT 2600, Australia; tel. (2) 6261-9111; fax (2) 6273-3577; internet www.dfat.gov.au; the ANZUS Security Treaty was signed in 1951 by Australia, New Zealand and the USA, and ratified in 1952 to co-ordinate partners' efforts for collective defence for the preservation of peace and security in the

Pacific area, through the exchange of technical information and strategic intelligence, and a programme of exercises, exchanges and visits. In 1984 New Zealand refused to allow visits by US naval vessels that were either nuclear-propelled or potentially nuclear-armed, and this led to the cancellation of joint ANZUS military exercises: in 1986 the USA formally announced the suspension of its security commitment to New Zealand under ANZUS. Instead of the annual ANZUS Council meetings, bilateral talks were subsequently held every year between Australia and the USA. ANZUS continued to govern security relations between Australia and the USA, and between Australia and New Zealand; security relations between New Zealand and the USA were the only aspect of the treaty to be suspended. Senior-level contacts between New Zealand and the USA resumed in 1994. The Australian Govt invoked the Anzus Security Treaty for the first time following the international terrorist attacks against targets in the USA that were perpetrated in September 2001.

Association of Secretaries General of Parliaments: c/o Table Office, House of Commons, London, SW1, United Kingdom; tel. (20) 7219-8195; e-mail phillipsris@parliament.uk; internet www.asgp.info; f. 1938; studies the law, practice and working methods of different Parliaments; proposes measures for improving those methods and for securing co-operation between the services of different Parliaments; operates as a consultative body to the Inter-Parliamentary Union, and assists the Union on subjects within the scope of the Association; mems: c. 200 representing 145 countries; five assoc. institutions; Pres. IAN HARRIS (Australia); Jt Secs FRÉDÉRIC SLAMA (France), ROGER PHILLIPS (UK); publ. *Constitutional and Parliamentary Information* (2 a year).

Atlantic Treaty Association: Ryvangs Allé 1, 2100 Copenhagen Ø, Denmark; tel. 39-27-19-44; fax 39-27-56-26; e-mail troels@atlant.dk; internet www.atasec.org; f. 1954 to inform public opinion on the North Atlantic Alliance and to promote the solidarity of the peoples of the North Atlantic; holds annual assemblies, seminars, study conferences for teachers and young politicians; mems: national asscns in 19 member countries of NATO; 19 assoc. mems from central and eastern Europe, two observer mems; Pres. ROBERT E. HUNTER (USA); Sec.-Gen. TROELS FRØLING (Denmark).

Baltic Council: f. 1993 by the Baltic Assembly, comprising 60 parliamentarians from Estonia, Latvia and Lithuania; the Council of Ministers of the three Baltic countries co-ordinates policy in the areas of foreign policy, justice, the environment, education and science.

Celtic League: 11 Cleiy Rhennee, Kirk Michael, Isle of Man, IM6 1HT, United Kingdom; tel. (1624) 877918; e-mail b.moffatt@advsys.co.im; internet www.manxman.co.im/cleague; f. 1961 to foster co-operation between the six Celtic nations (Ireland, Scotland, Man, Wales, Cornwall and Brittany), especially those actively working for political autonomy by non-violent means; campaigns politically on issues affecting the Celtic countries; monitors military activity in the Celtic countries; co-operates with national cultural organizations to promote the languages and culture of the Celts; mems: approx. 1,400 individuals in the Celtic communities and elsewhere; Chair. CATHAL Ó LUAIN; Gen. Sec. BERNARD MOFFAT; publ. *Carn* (quarterly).

Central European Initiative (CEI): CEI Executive Secretariat, Via Genova 9, 34121 Trieste, Italy; tel. (040) 7786777; fax (040) 360640; e-mail cei-es@cei-es.org; internet www.ceinet.org; f. 1989 as 'Quadrilateral' co-operation between Austria, Italy, Hungary and Yugoslavia, became 'Pentagonal' in 1990 with the admission of Czechoslovakia, and 'Hexagonal' with the admission of Poland in 1991, present name adopted in 1992, when Bosnia and Herzegovina, Croatia and Slovenia were admitted; the Czech Republic and Slovakia became separate mems in January 1993, and Macedonia also joined in that year; Albania, Belarus, Bulgaria, Romania and Ukraine joined the CEI in 1995 and Moldova in 1996; the Federal Republic of Yugoslavia (now Serbia and Montenegro) was admitted in 2000; encourages regional political and economic co-operation; Dir-Gen. Dr HARALD KREID; publ. *Newsletter* (monthly).

Christian Democrat and Peoples' Parties International: 67 rue d'Arlon, 1040 Brussels, Belgium; tel. (2) 285-41-60; fax (2) 285-41-66; e-mail idc@idc-cdi.org; internet www.idc-cdi.org; f. 1961 to serve as a platform for the co-operation of political parties of Christian Social inspiration; mems: parties in 64 countries (of which 47 in Europe); Pres. JOSÉ MARÍA AZNAR (Spain); Exec. Sec. ANTONIO LÓPEZ ISTURIZ; publs *DC-Info* (quarterly), *Human Rights* (5 a year), *Documents* (quarterly).

Comunidade dos Países de Língua Portuguesa (CPLP) (Community of Portuguese-Speaking Countries): rua S. Caetano 32, 1200-829 Lisbon, Portugal; tel. (21) 392-8560; fax (21) 392-8588; e-mail comunicacao@cplp.org; internet www.cplp.org; f. 1996; aims to produce close political, economic, diplomatic and cultural links between Portuguese-speaking countries and to strengthen the influence of the Lusophone commonwealth within the international community; mems: Angola, Brazil, Cape Verde, Guinea-Bissau, Mozambique, Portugal, São Tomé e Príncipe, Timor-Leste; Exec. Sec. LUIS FONSECA (Cape Verde).

Eastern Regional Organization for Public Administration (EROPA): One Burgundy Plaza, Suite 12M, 307 Katipunan Ave, Loyola Heights, Quezon City 1105, Metro Manila, Philippines; tel. (2) 4338175; fax (2) 4349223; e-mail eropa@eropa.org.ph; internet www.eropa.org.ph; f. 1960 to promote regional co-operation in improving knowledge, systems and practices of governmental administration, to help accelerate economic and social development; organizes regional conferences, seminars, special studies, surveys and training programmes. There are three regional centres: Training Centre (New Delhi), Local Government Centre (Tokyo), Development Management Centre (Seoul); mems: 12 countries, 112 organizations/groups, 489 individuals; Chair. O. P. AGARWAL; Sec.-Gen. PATRICIA A. STO TOMAS (Philippines); publs *EROPA Bulletin* (quarterly), *Asian Review of Public Administration* (2 a year).

European Movement: 25 Square de Meeus, 1000 Brussels, Belgium; tel. (2) 508-30-88; fax (2) 508-30-89; e-mail secretariat@europeanmovement.org; internet www.europeanmovement.org; f. 1947 by a liaison committee of representatives from European organizations, to study the political, economic and technical problems of a European Union and suggest how they could be solved and to inform and lead public opinion in the promotion of integration; Conferences have led to the creation of the Council of Europe, College of Europe, etc; mems: national councils and committees in 41 European countries, and several international social and economic organizations, 21 assoc. mems; Pres. JOSÉ MARIA GIL-ROBLES (Spain); Sec.-Gen. HENRIK H. KRÖNER.

European Union of Women (EUW): 2 Pittakou St, 105 58 Athens, Greece; tel. (1) 3314847; fax (1) 3314817; e-mail fpetralia@parliament.gr; f. 1955 to increase the influence of women in the political and civic life of their country and of Europe; mems: national organizations in 21 countries; Chair. FANNY PALLI PETRALIA; Sec.-Gen. VASSO KOLLIA.

La Francophonie: 28 rue de Bourgogne, 75007 Paris, France; tel. 1-44-11-12-50; fax 1-44-11-12-76; e-mail oif@francophonie.org; internet www.francophonie.org; political grouping of French-speaking countries; conference of heads of state convened every two years to promote co-operation throughout the French-speaking world (2004: Ouagadougou, Burkina Faso); mems: govts of 51 countries; five countries with observer status; Sec.-Gen. ABDOU DIOUF (Senegal).

Gulf of Guinea Commission (Commission du Golfe de Guinée—CGG): f. 2001 to promote co-operation among mem; countries and the peaceful and sustainable development of natural resources in the sub-region; mems: Angola, Cameroon, the Repub. of the Congo, Equatorial Guinea, Gabon, Nigeria, Sao Tomé and Príncipe.

Hansard Society: 9 Kingsway, London, WC2B 6FX, United Kingdom; tel. (20) 7955-7459; fax (20) 7955-7492; e-mail hansard@hansard.lse.ac.uk; internet www.hansardsociety.org.uk; f. 1944 as Hansard Society for Parliamentary Government; aims to promote political education and research and the informed discussion of all aspects of modern parliamentary government; Dir CLARE ETTINGHAUSEN; publ. *Parliamentary Affairs* (quarterly).

International Alliance of Women: c/o Lenaustr. 5/2/12, 4053 Haid bei Ansfelden, Austria; tel. (7229) 876-34; e-mail mab@liwest.at; internet www.womenalliance.com; f. 1904 to obtain equality for women in all fields and to encourage women to assume decision-making responsibilities at all levels of society; lobbies at international organizations; mems: 60 national affiliates; Pres. ROSY WEISS; Sec. ALISON BROWN; publ. *International Women's News* (3 a year).

International Association for Community Development (IACD): 179 rue du Débarcadère, 6001 Marcinelle, Belgium; tel. (71) 44-72-78; fax (71) 47-11-04; internet www.iacdglobal.org; organizes annual international colloquium for community-based organizations; Sec.-Gen. PIERRE ROZEN; publ. *IACD Newsletter* (2 a year).

International Commission for the History of Representative and Parliamentary Institutions (CHRPI): c/o Dr David Dean, Dept of History, Carleton Univ., 400 Peterson Hall, 1125 Colonel By Drive, Ottawa, ON KIS 511, Canada; tel. (613) 520-2828; fax (613) 520-2819; internet www.univie.ac.at/ichrpi; f. 1936; promotes research into the origin and development of representative and parliamentary institutions world-wide; encourages wide and comparative study of such institutions, both current and historical; facilitates the exchange of information; mems: 300 individuals in 31 countries; Pres. WILHELM BRAUNEDER (Austria); Sec.-Gen. Dr DAVID DEAN (Canada); publs *Parliaments, Estates and Representation* (annually), studies.

International Democrat Union: 100 Pall Mall, London, SW1P 5HP, United Kingdom; tel. (20) 7222-0847; fax (20) 7664-8711; e-mail rnormington@idu.org; internet www.idu.org; f. 1983 as a group of centre and centre-right political parties; facilitates the exchange of information and views; promotes networking; organizes campaigning seminars for politicians and party workers; holds Party Leaders' meetings every three or four years, also executive meetings and a Young Leaders' Forum; mems: political parties in some 60 countries, 46 assoc. mems in regions; Exec. Sec. RICHARD NORMINGTON.

International Federation of Resistance Movements (FIR): c/o R. Maria, 5 rue Rollin, 75005 Paris, France; tel. 1-43-26-84-29; f. 1951; supports the medical and social welfare of former victims of fascism; works for peace, disarmament and human rights, and against fascism and neo-fascism; mems: 82 national organizations in 29 countries; Pres. ALIX LHOTE (France); Sec.-Gen. OSKAR WIES-FLECKER (Austria); publs *Feuille d'information* (in French and German), *Cahier d'informations médicales, sociales et juridiques* (in French and German).

International Institute for Democracy and Electoral Assistance (IDEA): Strömsborg, S-103 34 Stockholm, Sweden; tel. (8) 698-3700; fax (8) 20-2422; e-mail info@idea.int; internet www.idea .int; f. 1995; aims to promote sustainable democracy in new and established democracies; provides world-wide electoral assistance and focuses on broader democratic issues in Africa, the Caucasus and Latin America; 21 mem. states; Sec.-Gen. KAREN FOGG (UK).

International Institute for Peace: Möllwaldplatz 5, 1040 Vienna, Austria; tel. (1) 504-43-76; fax (1) 505-32-36; e-mail director@iip.at; internet www.iip.at; f. 1957; non-governmental organization with consultative status at ECOSOC and UNESCO; studies conflict prevention; new structures in international law; security issues in Europe and world-wide; mems: individuals and corporate bodies invited by the executive board; Pres. ERWIN LANC (Austria); Dir PETER STANIA (Austria); publ. *Peace and Security* (quarterly, in English).

International Institute for Strategic Studies (IISS): Arundel House, 13–15 Arundel St, London, WC2R 3DX, United Kingdom; tel. (20) 7379-7676; fax (20) 7836-3108; e-mail iiss@iiss.org; internet www.iiss.org; f. 1958; concerned with the study of the role of force in international relations, including problems of international strategy, the ethnic, political and social sources of conflict, disarmament and arms control, peace-keeping and intervention, defence economics, etc.; independent of any government; mems: c. 3,000; Dir Dr JOHN M. W. CHIPMAN; publs *Survival* (quarterly), *The Military Balance* (annually), *Strategic Survey* (annually), *Adelphi Papers* (10 a year), *Strategic Comments* (10 a year).

International Lesbian and Gay Association (ILGA): 37 Villa-laan, 1060 Belgium; tel. and fax (2) 502-24-71; e-mail ilga@ilga.org; internet www.ilga.org; f. 1978; works to abolish legal, social and economic discrimination against homosexual and bisexual women and men, and transexuals, throughout the world; co-ordinates political action at an international level; co-operates with other supportive movements; 2005 world conference: Geneva. Switzerland; mems: 350 national and regional asscns in 80 countries; Co-Secs-Gen. KURSAD KAHRAMANOGLU, ROSANNA FLAMER-CALDERA; publs *ILGA Bulletin* (quarterly), *GBLT Human Rights Annual Report*.

International Peace Bureau (IPB): 41 rue de Zürich, 1201 Geneva, Switzerland; tel. (22) 7316429; fax (22) 7389419; e-mail mailbox@ipb.org; internet www.ipb.org; f. 1892; promotes international co-operation for general and complete disarmament and the non-violent solution of international conflicts; co-ordinates and represents peace movements at the UN; conducts projects on the abolition of nuclear weapons and the role of non-governmental organizations in conflict prevention and resolution; mems: 220 peace organizations in 53 countries; Pres. CORA WEISS; Sec.-Gen. COLIN ARCHER; publs *IPB News* (quarterly), *IPB Geneva News*.

International Political Science Association (IPSA) (Association Internationale de Science Politique—AISP): c/o Concordia Univ., 331 ave Docteur Penfield, Montréal, QC H3G 1C5, Canada; tel. (514) 848-8717; fax (514) 848-4095; e-mail info@ipsa.com; internet www.ipsa.ca; f. 1949; aims to promote the development of political science; organizes World Congress (July 2006: Fukuoka, Japan, "Is Democracy Working?"); mems: 41 national asscns, 100 institutions, 1,350 individual mems; Pres. MAX KAASE (Germany); Sec.-Gen. GUY LACHAPELLE (Canada); publs *Participation* (3 a year), *International Political Science Abstracts* (6 a year), *International Political Science Review* (quarterly).

International Union of Local Authorities (IULA): POB 90646, 2509 LP, The Hague, Netherlands; tel. (70) 3066066; fax (70) 3500496; e-mail iula@iula.org; internet www.iula.org; f. 1913 to promote local government, improve local administration and encourage popular participation in public affairs; activities include organization of a biennial international congress; operation of specific 'task forces' (Association Capacity-Building, Women in Local Government, Information Technology); development of intermunicipal relations to provide a link between local authorities of countries; maintenance of a permanent office for the collection and distribution of information on municipal affairs; mems: in over 110 countries, seven regional sections; Pres. ALAN LLOYD; Sec.-Gen. JEREMY SMITH; publs various, on a range of local government issues.

International Union of Young Christian Democrats (IUYCD): 16 rue de la Victoire, 1060 Brussels, Belgium; tel. (2) 537-77-51; fax (2) 534-50-28; f. 1962; mems: national organizations in 59 countries and territories; Sec.-Gen. MARCOS VILLASMIL (Venezuela); publs *IUYCD Newsletter* (fortnightly), *Debate* (quarterly).

Jewish Agency for Israel (JAFI): POB 92, 48 King George St, Jerusalem, Israel; tel. (2) 6202297; fax (2) 6202412; e-mail elibir@jazo.org.il; internet www.jafi.org.il; f. 1929; reconstituted 1971 as an instrument through which world Jewry can work to develop a national home; constituents are: World Zionist Organization, United Israel Appeal, Inc. (USA), and Keren Hayesod; Chair. Exec. SALLAI MERIDOR; Chair. Bd. ALEX GRASS; Dir-Gen. Maj.-Gen. (retd) GIORA ROMM.

Latin American Parliament (Parlamento Latinoamericano): Avda Auro Soares de Moura Andrade 564, São Paulo, Brazil; tel. (11) 3824-6325; fax (11) 3824-0621; internet www.parlatino.org.br; f. 1965; permanent democratic institution, representative of all existing political trends within the national legislative bodies of Latin America; aims to promote the movement towards economic, political and cultural integration of the Latin American republics, and to uphold human rights, peace and security; Sec.-Gen. RAFAEL CORREA FLORES; publs *Acuerdos, Resoluciones de las Asambleas Ordinarias* (annually), *Parlamento Latinoamericano–Actividades de los Órganos, Revista Patria Grande* (annually), statements and agreements.

Liberal International: 1 Whitehall Place, London, SW1A 2HD, United Kingdom; tel. (20) 7839-5905; fax (20) 7925-2685; e-mail all@liberal-international.org; internet www.liberal-international.org; f. 1947; world union of 90 liberal parties in 65 countries; co-ordinates foreign policy work of member parties, and promotes freedom, tolerance, democracy, international understanding, protection of human rights and market-based economics; has consultative status at ECOSOC of United Nations and the Council of Europe; Pres. ANNEMIE NEYTS-UYTTEBROECK; Sec.-Gen. FEDERICA SABBATI; publ. *Liberal Aerogramme* (quarterly).

Nato Parliamentary Assembly: 3 place du Petit Sablon, 1000 Brussels, Belgium; tel. (2) 513-28-65; fax (2) 514-18-47; e-mail secretariat@nato-pa.int; internet www.nato-pa.int; f. 1955 as the NATO Parliamentarians' Conference; name changed 1966 to North Atlantic Assembly; renamed as above 1999; the inter-parliamentary assembly of the North Atlantic Alliance; holds two plenary sessions a year and meetings of committees (Political, Defence and Security, Economics and Security, Civil Dimension of Security, Science and Technology) to facilitate parliamentary awareness and understanding of key Alliance security issues, to provide the Alliance governments with a collective parliamentary voice, to contribute to a greater degree of transparency of NATO policies, and to strengthen the transatlantic dialogue; Pres. PIERRE LELLOUCHE (France); Sec.-Gen. SIMON LUNN (UK).

Non-aligned Movement (NAM): c/o Permanent Representative of Malaysia to the UN, 313 East 43rd St, New York, NY 10016, USA (no permanent secretariat); tel. (212) 986-6310; fax (212) 490-8576; e-mail malaysia@un.int; internet www.namkl.org.my; f. 1961 by a meeting of 25 Heads of State, with the aim of linking countries that had refused to adhere to the main East/West military and political blocs; co-ordination bureau established in 1973; works for the establishment of a new international economic order, and especially for better terms for countries producing raw materials; maintains special funds for agricultural development, improvement of food production and the financing of buffer stocks; South Commission promotes co-operation between developing countries; seeks changes in the United Nations to give developing countries greater decision-making power; holds summit conference every three years; 13th conference (February 2003): Kuala Lumpur, Malaysia; mems: 116 countries.

Open Door International (for the Economic Emancipation of the Woman Worker): 16 rue Américaine, 1060 Brussels, Belgium; tel. (2) 537-67-61; f. 1929 to obtain equal rights and opportunities for women in the whole field of work; mems: in 10 countries; Hon. Sec. ADÈLE HAUWEL (Belgium).

Organisation of Eastern Caribbean States (OECS): POB 179, The Morne, Castries, Saint Lucia; tel. 452-2537; fax 453-1628; e-mail oesec@oecs.org; internet www.oecs.org; f. 1981 by the seven states which formerly belonged to the West Indies Associated States (f. 1966); aims to promote the harmonized development of trade and industry in member states; single market created on 1 January 1988; principal institutions are: the Authority of Heads of Government (the supreme policy-making body), the Foreign Affairs Committee, the Defence and Security Committee, and the Economic Affairs Committee; there is also an Export Development and Agricultural Diversification Unit—EDADU (based in Dominica); mems: Antigua and Barbuda, Dominica, Grenada, Montserrat, Saint Christopher and Nevis, Saint Lucia, Saint Vincent and the Grenadines;

assoc. mems: Anguilla, British Virgin Islands; Dir-Gen. Dr LEN ISHMAEL.

Organization for the Prohibition of Chemical Weapons (OPCW): Johan de Wittlaan 32, 2517JR The Hague, Netherlands; tel. (70) 4163300; fax (70) 3063535; e-mail media@opcw.org; internet www.opcw.org; f. 1997 to oversee implementation of the Chemical Weapons Convention, which aims to ban the development, production, stockpiling, transfer and use of chemical weapons; the Convention was negotiated under the auspices of the UN Conference on Disarmament and entered into force in April 1997, at which time the OPCW was inaugurated; governed by an Executive Council, comprising representatives of 41 States Parties, elected on a regional basis; undertakes mandatory inspections of member states party to the Convention (167 at November 2004); 2004 budget: €73.1m; Dir-Gen. ROGELIO PFIRTER.

Organization of Solidarity of the Peoples of Africa, Asia and Latin America (OSPAAAL) (Organización de Solidaridad de los Pueblos de África, Asia y América Latina): Apdo 4224, Calle C No 670 esq. 29, Vedado, Havana 10400, Cuba; tel. (7) 830-5136; fax (7) 833-3985; e-mail ospaal1966@enet.cu; internet www.tricontinental.cubaweb.cu; f. 1966 at the first Conference of Solidarity of the Peoples of Africa, Asia and Latin America, to unite, co-ordinate and encourage national liberation movements in the three continents, to oppose foreign intervention in the affairs of sovereign states, colonial and neo-colonial practices, and to fight against racialism and all forms of racial discrimination; favours the establishment of a new international economic order; mems: 56 organizations in 46 countries; Sec.-Gen. HUMBERTO HERNÁNDEZ; publ. *Tricontinental* (quarterly).

Organization of the Co-operatives of America (Organización de las Cooperativas de América—OCA): Apdo Aéreo 241263, Carrera 11, No. 86-32 Of. 101, Santafé de Bogotá, DC, Colombia; tel. (1) 610-3296; fax (1) 610-1912; f. 1963 for improving socio-economic, cultural and moral conditions through the use of the co-operative system; works in every country of the continent; regional offices sponsor plans of activities based on the most pressing needs and special conditions of individual countries; mems: organizations in 23 countries and territories; Pres. Dr ARMANDO TOVAR PARADA; Exec. Sec. Dr CARLOS JULIO PINEDA; publs *OCA News* (monthly), *América Cooperativa* (3 a year).

Parliamentary Association for Euro-Arab Co-operation (PAEAC): 10 ave de la Renaissance, 1040 Brussels, Belgium; tel. (2) 231-13-00; fax (2) 231-06-46; e-mail paeac@medea.be; internet www.medea.be; f. 1974 as an asscn of 650 parliamentarians of all parties from the national parliaments of the Council of Europe countries and from the European Parliament, to promote friendship and co-operation between Europe and the Arab world; Executive Committee holds annual joint meetings with Arab Inter-Parliamentary Union; represented in Council of Europe, Western European Union and European Parliament; works for the progress of the Euro-Arab Dialogue and a settlement in the Middle East that takes into account the national rights of the Palestinian people; Jt Chair. MICHAEL LANIGAN (Ireland), ROY PERRY (UK); Sec.-Gen. POL MARCK (Belgium); publs *Information Bulletin* (quarterly), *Euro-Arab and Mediterranean Political Fact Sheets* (2 a year), conference notes.

Party of European Socialists (PES): 60 rue Wiertz, 1047 Brussels, Belgium; tel. (2) 284-29-76; fax (2) 230-17-66; e-mail pes@pes.org; internet www.pes.org; f. 1992 to replace the Confederation of the Socialist Parties of the EC (f. 1974); affiliated to Socialist International; mems: 28 member parties, 7 associate parties and 6 observer parties; Chair. ROBIN COOK (UK); Sec.-Gen. ANTONY BEUMER; publs various, including statutes, manifestos and Congress documents.

Rio Group: f. 1987 at a meeting in Acapulco, Mexico, of eight Latin American government leaders, who agreed to establish a 'permanent mechanism for joint political action'; additional countries subsequently joined the Group (see below); holds annual summit meetings at presidential level. At the ninth presidential summit (Quito, Ecuador, September 1995) a 'Declaration of Quito' was adopted, which set out joint political objectives, including the strengthening of democracy; combating corruption, drugs-production and -trafficking and 'money-laundering'; and the creation of a Latin American and Caribbean free trade area by 2005 (supporting the efforts of the various regional groupings). Opposes US legislation (the 'Helms-Burton' Act), which provides for sanctions against foreign companies that trade with Cuba; a pan-South American summit convened in December 2004, in Cuzco, Peru, approved in principle the creation within 15 years of a new South American Community of Nations, entailing the eventual merger of the Rio Group, the Andean Community and Mercosur; also concerned with promoting sustainable development in the region, the elimination of poverty, and economic and financial stability. The Rio Group holds annual ministerial conferences with the European Union (11th meeting held in Greece in March 2003; third summit of heads of state and govt held in

Guadalajara, Mexico in May 2004); mems: Argentina, Bolivia, Brazil, Chile, Colombia, Costa Rica, Dominican Republic, Ecuador, El Salvador, Guatemala, Guyana, Honduras, Mexico, Nicaragua, Panama, Paraguay, Peru, Uruguay, Venezuela.

Shanghai Co-operation Organization—SCO: f. 2001, replacing the Shanghai Five (f. 1996 to address border disputes); comprises People's Republic of China, Kazakhstan, Kyrgyzstan, Russia, Tajikistan and Uzbekistan; aims to achieve security through mutual co-operation: promotes economic co-operation and measures to eliminate terrorism and drugs-trafficking; agreement on combating terrorism signed June 2001; a Convention on the Fight against Terrorism, Separatism and Extremism signed June 2002; a SCO anti-terrorism centre was to be established in Bishkek, Kyrgyzstan; holds annual summit meeting (June 2004: Tashkent, Uzbekistan).

Socialist International: Maritime House, Clapham, London, SW4 0JW, United Kingdom; tel. (20) 7627-4449; fax (20) 7720-4448; e-mail secretariat@socialistinternational.org; internet www.socialistinternational.org; f. 1864; re-established in 1951; the world's oldest and largest asscn of political parties, grouping democratic socialist, labour and social democratic parties from every continent; provides a forum for political action, policy discussion and the exchange of ideas; works with many international organizations and trades unions (particularly members of ICFTU; holds Congress every three years. The Council meets twice a year, and regular conferences and meetings of party leaders are also held; committees and councils on a variety of subjects and in different regions meet frequently; mems: 89 full member, 25 consultative and 15 observer parties in 110 countries; There are three fraternal organizations and nine associated organizations, including: the Party of European Socialists (PES), the Group of the PES at the European Parliament and the International Federation of the Socialist and Democratic Press; Pres. ANTÓNIO GUTERRES (Portugal); Gen. Sec. LUIS AYALA (Chile); publ. *Socialist Affairs* (quarterly).

International Falcon Movement—Socialist Educational International: 3 rue Quinaux, 1030 Brussels, Belgium; tel. (2) 215-79-27; fax (2) 245-00-83; e-mail contact@ifm.sei.org; internet www.ifm.sei.org; f. 1924 to help children and adolescents develop international understanding and a sense of social responsibility and to prepare them for democratic life; co-operates with several institutions concerned with children, youth and education; mems: about 1m., 62 co-operating organizations in all countries; Pres. ÖSTEN LÖUGREN (Sweden); Sec.-Gen. UWE OSTENDORFF (Germany); publs *IFM-SEI Bulletin* (quarterly), *IFM-SEI World News*, *EFN Newsletter* (6 a year), *Asian Regional Bulletin*, *Latin American Regional Bulletin*.

International Union of Socialist Youth (IUSY): Amtshausgasse 4, 1050 Vienna, Austria; tel. (1) 523-12-67; fax (1) 523-12-679; e-mail iusy@iusy.org; internet www.iusy.org; f. 1907 as Socialist Youth International (present name adopted 1946), to educate young people in the principles of free and democratic socialism and further the co-operation of democratic socialist youth organizations; conducts international meetings, symposia, etc; mems: 143 youth and student organizations in 100 countries; Pres. FIKILE MBALULA; Gen. Sec. ENZO AMENDOLA (Italy); publs *IUSY Newsletter*, *FWG News*, *IUSY—You see us in Action*.

Socialist International Women: Maritime House, Old Town, Clapham, London, SW4 0JW, United Kingdom; tel. (20) 7627-4449; fax (20) 7720-4448; e-mail socintwomen@gn.apc.org; internet socintwomen.org; f. 1907 to promote the understanding among women of the aims of democratic socialism to facilitate the exchange of experience and views; to promote programmes opposing discrimination in society; and to work for human rights in general and for development and peace; mems: 152 organizations; Pres. PIA LOCATELLI; Gen. Sec. MARLÈNE HAAS; publ. *Women and Politics* (quarterly).

Stockholm International Peace Research Institute—SIPRI: Signalistgatan 9, 169 70 Solna, Sweden; tel. (8) 655-97-00; fax (8) 655-97-33; e-mail sipri@sipri.org; internet www.sipri.org; f. 1966; carries out studies on international security and arms control issues, including on conflict and crisis management, peace-keeping and regional security, and chemical and biological warfare; mems: about 50 staff mems, half of whom are researchers; Dir ALYSON J. K. BAILES (UK); Chair. ROLF EKÉUS (Sweden); publs *SIPRI Yearbook: Armaments, Disarmament and International Security*, monographs and research reports.

Transparency International: Otto-Suhr-Allee 97–99, 10585 Berlin, Germany; tel. (30) 3438200; fax (30) 34703912; e-mail ti@transparency.org; internet www.transparency.org; f. 1993; aims to promote governmental adoption of anti-corruption practices and accountability at all levels of the public sector; works to ensure that international business transactions are conducted with integrity and without resort to corrupt practices; formulates an annual Corruption Perceptions Index, and a Bribe Payers Index, and an annual

Global Corruption Report; holds International Anti-Corruption Conference every two years; Chair. Dr PETER EIGEN.

Trilateral Commission: 1156 15th St, NW, Washington, DC 20005, USA; tel. (202) 467-5410; fax (202) 467-5415; e-mail admin@ trilateral.org; internet www.trilateral.org; also offices in Paris and Tokyo; f. 1973 by private citizens of western Europe, Japan and North America, to encourage closer co-operation among these regions on matters of common concern; through analysis of major issues the Commission seeks to improve public understanding of problems, to develop and support proposals for handling them jointly, and to nurture the habit of working together in the 'trilateral' area. The Commission issues 'task force' reports on such subjects as monetary affairs, political co-operation, trade issues, the energy crisis and reform of international institutions; mems: about 335 individuals eminent in academic life, industry, finance, labour, etc.; those currently engaged as senior government officials are excluded; Chair. THOMAS S. FOLEY, YOTARO KOBYASHI, PETER SUTHERLAND; Dirs MICHAEL J. O'NEIL, TADASHI YAMAMOTO, PAUL REVAY; publs *Task Force Reports, Triangle Papers*.

Unrepresented Nations' and Peoples' Organization (UNPO): POB 85878, 2508 CN The Hague, Netherlands; tel. (70) 364-6504; fax (70) 364-6608; e-mail unpo@unpo.org; internet www.unpo.org; f. 1991 to provide an international forum for indigenous and other unrepresented peoples and minorities; provides training in human rights, law, diplomacy and public relations to UNPO members; provides conflict resolution services; mems: 61 organisations representing occupied nations, indigenous peoples and minorities; Gen. Sec. MARINO BUSDACHIN; publs *UNPO News, UNPO Yearbook*.

War Resisters' International: 5 Caledonian Rd, London, N1 9DX, United Kingdom; tel. (20) 7278-4040; fax (20) 7278-0444; e-mail office@wri-irg.org; internet www.wri-irg.org; f. 1921; encourages refusal to participate in or support wars or military service, collaborates with movements that work for peace and non-violent social change; mems: approx. 150,000; Chair. JOANNE SHEEHAN; Co-ordinator ANDREAS SPECK; publ. *Peace News* (quarterly).

Women's International Democratic Federation (WIDF) (Fédération Démocratique Internationale des Femmes—FDIF): c/o 'Femmes solidaires', 25 rue du Charolais, 75012 Paris, France; tel. 1-40-01-90-90; fax 1-40-01-90-81; e-mail fdif@fdif.eu.org; internet www.fdif.eu.org; f. 1945 to unite women regardless of nationality, race, religion or political opinion to enable them to work together to win and defend their rights as citizens, mothers and workers; to protect children; and to ensure peace and progress, democracy and national independence; structure: Congress, Secretariat and Executive Committee; mems: 629 organizations in 104 countries; Pres. SYLVIE JAN (France); publs *Women of the Whole World* (6 a year), *Newsletter*.

World Council of Indigenous Peoples: 100 Argyle Ave, 2nd Floor, Ottawa, ON K2P 1B6, Canada; tel. (613) 230-9030; fax (613) 230-9340; e-mail wcip@net.web; f. 1975 to promote the rights of indigenous peoples and to support their cultural, social and economic development; comprises representatives of indigenous organizations from five regions: North, South and Central America, Pacific-Asia and Scandinavia; holds General Assembly every three years; Pres. CONRADO JORGE VALIENTE QUILPILDOR; publ. *WCIP Newsletter* (4–6 a year).

World Disarmament Campaign: 45–47 Blythe St, London, E2 6LN, United Kingdom; tel. (20) 7729-2523; f. 1980 to encourage governments to take positive and decisive action to end the arms race, acting on the four main commitments called for in the Final Document of the UN's First Special Session on Disarmament; aims to mobilize people of every country in a demand for multilateral disarmament, to encourage consideration of alternatives to the nuclear deterrent for ensuring world security, and to campaign for a strengthened role for the UN in these matters; Chair. Dr FRANK BARNABY, Dr TONY HART; publ. *World Disarm!* (6 a year).

World Federalist Movement: 708 Third Ave, 24th Floor, New York, NY 10017, USA; tel. (212) 599-1320; fax (212) 599-1332; e-mail info@wfm.org; internet www.wfm.org; f. 1947 to achieve a just world order through a strengthened United Nations to acquire for the UN the authority to make and enforce laws for the peaceful settlement of disputes, and to raise revenue under limited taxing powers; to establish better international co-operation in the areas of environment, development and disarmament; and to promote federalism throughout the world; mems: 27 member organizations and 17 assoc. organizations; Pres. LOIS WILSON (acting); Exec. Dir WILLIAM R. PACE; publs *World Federalist News* (quarterly), *International Criminal Court Monitor* (quarterly).

World Federation of United Nations Associations (WFUNA) (Fédération Mondiale des Associations Pour les Nations Unies—FMANU): 1 United Nations Plaza, DC1-1177, New York, NY 10017, USA; tel. (212) 963-5610; fax (212) 963-0447; e-mail wfunany@ wfuna.org; internet www.wfuna.org; f. 1946 to encourage popular interest and participation in United Nations programmes, discus-

sion of the role and future of the UN, and education for international understanding; Plenary Assembly meets every two years; WFUNA has founded International Youth and Student Movement for the United Nations; mems: national asscns in more than 100 countries; Pres. Lady RHYL JANSEN (New Zealand); Sec.-Gen. JAMES SITRICK; publ. *WFUNA News*.

World Peace Council: Othonos 10, Athens, Greece; tel. (210) 331-6326; fax (210) 322-4302; e-mail info@wpc-in.org; internet www .wpc-in.org; f. 1950 at the Second World Peace Congress, Warsaw; principles: the prevention of nuclear war; the peaceful co-existence of the various socio-economic systems in the world; settlement of differences between nations by negotiation and agreement; complete disarmament; elimination of colonialism and racial discrimination; and respect for the right of peoples to sovereignty and independence; mems: representatives of national organizations, groups and individuals from 140 countries, and of 30 international organizations; Executive Committee of 40 mems elected by world assembly held every three years; Exec. Sec. ATHANASSIOS PAFILIS; publ. *Peace Courier* (monthly).

Youth of the European People's Party (YEPP): 67 rue d'Arlon, 1040 Brussels, Belgium; tel. (2) 285-41-65; fax (2) 285-41-65; e-mail yepp@evppe.be; internet www.yepp.org; f. 1997 to unite national youth organizations of member parties of European Young Christian Democrats and Democrat Youth Community of Europe; aims to develop contacts between youth movements and advance general political debate among young people; mems: 50 organizations in some 35 European countries; Pres. DANIEL BAUTISTA (Spain); Sec.-Gen. RIIKA KERVINEN (Finland).

Industrial and Professional Relations

Arab Federation of Petroleum, Mining and Chemicals Workers: POB 5339, Tripoli, Libya; tel. (21) 444-7597; fax (21) 444-9139; f. 1961 to establish industrial relations policies and procedures for the guidance of affiliated unions; promotes establishment of trade unions in the relevant industries in countries where they do not exist; publs *Arab Petroleum* (monthly), specialized publications and statistics.

European Association for Personnel Management (EAPM): c/o CIPD, CIPD House, Camp Rd, Wimbledon, London, SW19 4OX; tel. (20) 8263-3273; fax (20) 8263-3806; e-mail f.wilson@ipd.co.uk; internet www.eapm.org; f. 1962 to disseminate knowledge and information concerning the personnel function of management, to establish and maintain professional standards, to define the specific nature of personnel management within industry, commerce and the public services, and to assist in the development of national asscns; mems: 26 national asscns; Pres. CHRISTOPH SCHAUB (Switzerland); Sec.-Gen. GEOFFREY ARMSTRONG (UK).

European Civil Service Federation (ECSF) (Fédération de la Fonction Publique Européenne—FFPE): 200 rue de la Loi, L 102 6/14,1049 Brussels, Belgium; e-mail secretariat.politique@ffpe.org; internet www.ffpe.org; f. 1962 to foster the idea of a European civil service of staff of international organizations operating in western Europe or pursuing regional objectives; upholds the interests of civil service members; mems: local cttees in 12 European countries and individuals in 66 countries; Sec.-Gen. L. RIJNOUDT; publ. *Eurechos*.

European Construction Industry Federation (Fédération de l'Industrie Européenne de la Construction—FIEC): 66 ave Louise, 1050 Brussels, Belgium; tel. (2) 514-55-35; fax (2) 511-02-76; e-mail info@fiec.org; internet www.fiec.org; f. 1905 as International European Construction Federation, present name adopted 1999; mems: 32 national employers' organizations in 25 countries; Pres. WILHELM KÜCHLER (Germany); Dir-Gen. ULRICH PAETZOLD; publs *FIEC News* (2 a year), *Annual Report, Construction Activity in Europe*.

European Federation of Conference Towns: 39 rue le Corrège, 1000 Brussels, Belgium; tel. (2) 732-69-54; fax (2) 735-48-40; e-mail secretariat@efct.com; internet www.efct.com; lays down standards for conference towns; provides advice and assistance to its members and other organizations holding conferences in Europe; undertakes publicity and propaganda for promotional purposes; helps conference towns to set up national centres; Pres. HENRI CÉRAN (France); Exec. Dir ALINE LEGRAND.

European Federation of Lobbying and Public Affairs (Fédération européenne du lobbying et public afairs—FELPA): rue du Trône 61, 1050 Brussels, Belgium; tel. (2) 511-74-30; fax (2) 511-12-84; aims to enhance the development and reputation of the industry; encourages professionals active in the industry to sign a code of conduct outlining the ethics and responsibilities of people involved in lobbying or public relations work with the institutions of the EU; Pres. Y. DE LESPINAY.

European Industrial Research Management Association (EIRMA): 46 rue Lauriston, 75116 Paris, France; tel. 1-53-23-83-10; fax 1-47-20-05-30; e-mail info@eirma.asso.fr; internet www.eirma .asso.fr; f. 1966 under auspices of the OECD; a permanent body in which European science and technology firms meet to consider approaches to industrial innovation, support research and development, and take joint action to improve performance in their various fields; mems: 160 in 21 countries; Pres. HANS DE WIT; Gen. Sec. ANDREW DEARING; publs *Annual Report, Conference Reports, Working Group Reports, Workshop Reports.*

European Trade Union Confederation (ETUC) (Confédération européenne des syndicats): 5 blvd du Roi Albert II, 1210 Brussels, Belgium; tel. (2) 224-04-11; fax (2) 224-04-54; e-mail etuc@etuc.org; internet www.etuc.org; f. 1973; comprises 77 national trade union confederations and 11 European industrial federations in 35 European countries, representing 60m. workers; holds congress every four years; Pres. FRITZ VERZETNITSCH (Austria); Gen. Sec. EMILIO GABAGLIO (Italy).

Federation of International Civil Servants' Associations (FICSA): Palais des Nations, 1211 Geneva 10, Switzerland; tel. (22) 9173150; fax (22) 9170660; e-mail ficsa@ficsa.org; internet www .ficsa.org; f. 1952 to co-ordinate policies and activities of member asscns and unions, to represent staff interests before inter-agency and legislative organs of the UN and to promote the development of an international civil service; mems: 26 asscns and unions consisting of staff of UN organizations, 2 associate mems from non-UN organizations, 25 consultative asscns and 17 inter-organizational federations with observer status; Pres. ALI K. BASARAN; Gen. Sec. JANICE ALBERT; publs *Annual Report, FICSA Newsletter, FICSA Update, FICSA circulars.*

International Association of Conference Interpreters: 10 ave de Sécheron, 1202 Geneva, Switzerland; tel. (22) 9081540; fax (22) 7324151; e-mail info@aiic.net; internet www.aiic.net; f. 1953 to represent professional conference interpreters, ensure the highest possible standards and protect the legitimate interests of mems; establishes criteria designed to improve the standards of training; recognizes schools meeting the required standards; has consultative status with the UN and several of its agencies; mems: 2,300 in 53 countries; Pres. JENNIFER MACKINTOSH (Switzerland); Exec. Sec. JOSYANE CRISTINA; publs *Code of Professional Conduct, Yearbook* (listing interpreters), etc.

International Association of Conference Translators: 15 route des Morillons, 1218 Le Grand-Saconnex, Geneva, Switzerland; tel. (22) 7910666; fax (22) 7885644; e-mail secretariat@aitc.ch; internet www.aitc.ch; f. 1962; represents revisers, translators, précis writers and editors working for international conferences and organizations; aims to protect the interests of those in the profession and help maintain high standards; establishes links with international organizations and conference organizers; mems: c. 450 in 33 countries; Pres. LUIS TURIANSKY; Exec. Sec. MARIE EL-ACHKAR; publs *Directory, Bulletin.*

International Association of Crafts and Small and Medium-Sized Enterprises (IACME): c/o Centre patronal, CP 1215, 1001 Lausanne, Switzerland; tel. (21) 7963326; fax (21) 7963390; e-mail iacme@centrepatronal.ch; f. 1947 to defend undertakings and the freedom of enterprise within private economy, to develop training, to encourage the creation of national organizations of independent enterprises and promote international collaboration, to represent the common interests of members and to institute exchange of ideas and information; mems: organizations in 26 countries; Chair. FRANCO MUSCARA; Gen. Sec. JACQUES DESGRAZ.

International Association of Mutual Insurance Companies (AISAM) (Association internationale des sociétés d'assurance mutuelle): 29 Square de Meeûs, 1000, Brussels, Belgium; tel. (2) 503-38-78; fax (2) 503-30-55; e-mail aisam@aisam.org; internet www .aisam.org; f. 1963 for the establishment of good relations between members and the protection of the general interests of private insurance based on the principle of mutuality; mems: over 200 in 25 countries; Pres. FILOMENO MIRA (Spain); Sec.-Gen. GÉRARD OUTTERS; publs *Mutuality* (2 a year), *AISAM Directory, Newsletter.*

International Federation of Actors (Fédération internationale des acteurs—FIA): Guild House, Upper St Martin's Lane, London, WC2H 9EG, United Kingdom; tel. (20) 7379-0900; fax (20) 7379-8260; e-mail info@fia-actors.com; internet www.fia-actors.com; f. 1952; Exec. Cttee meets annually, Congress convened every four years; mems: 100 performers' unions in 75 countries; Pres. TOMAS BOLME (Sweden); Gen. Sec. DOMINICK LUQUER.

International Federation of Air Line Pilots' Associations (IFALPA): Interpilot House, Gogmore Lane, Chertsey, Surrey, KT16 9AP, United Kingdom; tel. (1932) 571711; fax (1932) 570920; e-mail admin@ifalpa.org; internet www.ifalpa.org; f. 1948 to represent pilots at the ICAO and other industry fora and organizations, especially in technical and safety matters; establishes standards for air safety world-wide; seeks to ensure fair conditions of employment

for pilots; mems: 95 asscns, over 100,000 pilots; Pres. Capt. TED MURPHY; publs *Interpilot* (2 a year), safety bulletins and news-sheets.

International Federation of Biomedical Laboratory Science (IFBLS): Office POB 2830, Hamilton, Ontario, ON L8N 3N8, Canada; tel. (905) 528-8642; fax (905) 528-4968; e-mail office@ifbls .org; internet www.ifbls.org; f. 1954 to allow discussion of matters of common professional interest; fmrly the International Association of Medical Laboratory Technologists (f. 1954); aims to promote globally the highest standards in the delivery of care, of professional training, and ethical and professional practices; develops and promotes active professional partnerships in health care at the international level; promotes and encourages participation of members in international activities; holds international congress every second year; mems: 180,000 in 40 countries; Pres. (2005) RUTH PIERCE (Canada); publ. *Biomedical Laboratory Science International* (quarterly).

International Federation of Business and Professional Women: POB 568, Horsham RH13 9ZP, United Kingdom; tel. (1403) 739343; fax (1403) 734432; e-mail members@bpw-international.org .uk; internet www.bpwi.org; f. 1930 to promote interests of business and professional women and secure combined action by such women; mems: national federations, associate clubs and individual associates, totalling more than 100,000 mems in over 100 countries; Pres. ANTOINETTE RUEGG (Switzerland); Exec. Sec. ANN R. TODD-LAMBIE (New Zealand); publ. *BPW News International* (every 2 months).

International Federation of Insolvency Professionals (INSOL): 2–3 Philpot Lane, London, EC3M 8AQ, United Kingdom; tel. (20) 7929-6679; fax (20) 7929-6678; e-mail pennyr@insol.ision.co .uk; internet www.insol.org; f. 1982; comprises national asscns of accountants and lawyers specializing in corporate turnaround and insolvency; holds annual conference; mems: 36 asscns, with more than 7,700 individual members; Pres. JOHN LEES (Hong Kong); Exec. Dir CLAIRE BROUGHTON; publs *INSOL World* (quarterly newsletter), *International Insolvency Review* (2 a year).

International Graphical Federation (Fédération graphique internationale): 17 rue des Fripiers, Galerie du Centre, bloc 2, 1000 Brussels, Belgium; tel. (2) 223-02-20; fax (2) 223-18-14; e-mail igf-fgi@enter.org; f. 1925; mems: national federations in 15 countries, covering 100,000 workers; Pres. L. VAN HAUDT (Belgium); Sec.-Gen. R. E. VAN KESTEREN (Netherlands).

International Industrial Relations Association (IIRA): c/o International Labour Office, 1211 Geneva 22, Switzerland; tel. (22) 7996841; fax (22) 7998541; e-mail iira@ilo.org; internet www.ilo.org/ iira; f. 1966 to encourage development of national asscns of specialists, facilitate the spread of information, organize conferences, and promote internationally planned research, through study groups and regional meetings; a World Congress is held every three years; mems: 39 asscns, 47 institutions and 1,100 individuals; Pres. Prof. MANFRED WEISS; Sec. Prof. TAYO FASHOYIN; publs *IIRA Bulletin* (3 a year), *IIRA Membership Directory, IIRA Congress proceedings.*

International Organisation of Employers (IOE): 26 chemin de Joinville, BP 68, 1216 Cointrin/Geneva, Switzerland; tel. (22) 9290000; fax (22) 9290001; internet www.ioe-emp.org; f. 1920; aims to establish and maintain contacts between mems and to represent their interests at the international level; works to promote free enterprise; and to assist the development of employers' organizations; General Council meets annually; there is a Management Board and a General Secretariat; mems: 136 federations in 132 countries; Chair. FRANÇOIS PERIGOT (France); Sec.-Gen. ANTONIO PEÑALOSA (Spain); publ. *IOE.net.*

International Organization of Experts (ORDINEX): 19 blvd Sébastopol, 75001 Paris, France; tel. 1-40-28-06-06; fax 1-40-28-03-13; e-mail contact@ordinex.org; internet www.ordinex.org; f. 1961 to establish co-operation between experts on an international level; mems: 600; Pres. FRANZ SCHREINER (Austria); Sec.-Gen. PIERRE ROYER (France); publ. *General Yearbook.*

International Public Relations Association (IPRA): 1 Dunley Hill Court, Ranmore Common, Dorking, Surrey RH5 6SX, United Kingdom; tel. (1483) 280130; fax (1483) 280131; e-mail secretariat@ ipra.org; internet www.ipra.org; f. 1955 to provide for an exchange of ideas, technical knowledge and professional experience among those engaged in international public relations, and to foster the highest standards of professional competence; mems: 1,000 in 95 countries; CEO JAMES HOLT; publs *Frontline* (quarterly), *Directory of Members* (annually).

International Society of City and Regional Planners (ISo-CaRP): POB 983, 2501 CZ, The Hague, Netherlands; tel. (70) 3462654; fax (70) 3617909; e-mail isocarp@isocarp.org; internet www.isocarp.org; f. 1965 to promote better planning practice through the exchange of knowledge; holds annual international congress (2005: Bilbao, Spain); mems: 480 in 70 countries; Exec. Dir

JUDY VAN HEMERT; publs *News Bulletin* (quarterly), seminar and congress reports.

International Union of Architects (Union internationale des architectes—UIA): 51 rue Raynouard, 75016 Paris, France; tel. 1-45-24-36-88; fax 1-45-24-02-78; e-mail uia@uia-architectes.org; internet www.uia-architectes.org; f. 1948; holds triennial congress; mems: 106 countries; Pres. JAIME LERNER (Brazil); Sec.-Gen JEAN-CLAUDE RIGUET (France); publ. *Lettre d'informations* (monthly).

Latin American Federation of Agricultural Workers (Federación Latinoamericana de Trabajadores Agrícolas, Pecuarios y Afines—FELTRA): Antiguo Local Conadi, B° La Granja, Comayaguela, Tegucigalpa, Honduras; tel. 2252526; fax 2252525; internet www.acmoti.org; f. 1999 by reorganization of FELTACA (f.1961) to represent the interests of workers in agricultural and related industries in Latin America; mems: national unions in 28 countries and territories; Sec.-Gen. MARCIAL REYES CABALLERO; publ. *Boletín Luchemos* (quarterly).

Nordic Industry Workers' Federation (Nordiska Industriarbetarefederationen—NIF): Olof Palmes gata 11, 5th Floor, Box 1114, 111 81 Stockholm, Sweden; tel. (8) 7868500; fax (8) 105968; e-mail kent.karrlander.nif@industrifacket.se; f. 1901; promotes collaboration between affiliates representing workers in the chemicals, energy, garment, manufacturing, mining, paper and textile sectors in Denmark, Finland, Iceland, Norway and Sweden; supports sister unions economically and in other ways in labour market conflicts; mems: 400,000 in 17 unions; Pres. LEIF OHLSSON; Sec. KENT KÄRRLANDER.

Organisation of African Trade Union Unity (OATUU): POB M386, Accra, Ghana; tel. (21) 508855; fax (21) 508851; e-mail oatuu@lghmail.com; internet www.ecouncil.ac.cr/ngoexch/oatuu2.htm; f. 1973 as a single continental trade union org., independent of international trade union organizations; has affiliates from all African trade unions. Congress, the supreme policy-making body, is composed of four delegates per country from affiliated national trade union centres, and meets at least every four years; the General Council, composed of one representative from each affiliated trade union, meets annually to implement Congress decisions and to approve the annual budget; mems: trade union movements in 53 independent African countries; Sec.-Gen. Gen. HASSAN A. SUNMONU (Nigeria); publ. *The African Worker*.

Pan-African Employers' Confederation (PEC): c/o Mauritius Employers' Federation, Cerné House, 13 La Chaussée, Port Louis, Mauritius; tel. 212-1599; fax 212-6725; e-mail mef@intnet.mu; f. 1986 to link African employers' organizations and represent them at the AU, UN and ILO; representation in 39 countries on the continent; Sec.-Gen. AZAD JEETUN (Mauritius).

World Movement of Christian Workers (WMCW): 124 blvd du Jubilé, 1080 Brussels, Belgium; tel. (2) 421-58-40; fax (2) 421-58-49; e-mail mmtc@skynet.be; internet www.mmtc-wmcw-wbca.be; f. 1961 to unite national movements that advance the spiritual and collective well-being of workers; holds General Assembly every four years; mems: 47 affiliated movements in 39 countries; Sec.-Gen. NORBERT KLEIN; publ. *Infor-WMCW*.

World Federation of Scientific Workers (WFSW) (Fédération mondiale des travailleurs scientifiques—FMTS): Case 404, 263 rue de Paris, 93516 Montreuil, Cédex, France; tel. 1-48-18-81-75; fax 1-48-18-80-03; e-mail fmts@wanadoo.fr; internet assoc.wanadoo.fr/fmts.wfsw; f. 1946 to improve the position of science and scientists, to assist in promoting international scientific co-operation and to promote the use of science for beneficial ends; studies and publicizes problems of general, nuclear, biological and chemical disarmament; surveys the position and activities of scientists; mems: organizations in 37 countries, totalling over 500,000 mems; Pres. ANDRÉ JAEGLÉ; Sec.-Gen. CHARLES DEMONS (UK); publ. *Scientific World* (quarterly, in English, Esperanto, German and Russian).

World Union of Professions (Union mondiale des professions libérales): 38 rue Boissière, 75116 Paris, France; tel. 1-44-05-90-15; fax 1-44-05-90-17; e-mail info@umpl.com; internet www.umpl.com; f. 1987 to represent and link members of the liberal professions; mems: 27 national inter-professional organizations, two regional groups and 12 international federations; Pres. Dr CHRISTIAN RONDEAU.

Law

African Bar Association: 29/31 Obafemi Awolowo Way, Ikeja, Lagos, Nigeria (temporary address); tel. (1) 4936907; fax (1) 7752202; f. 1972; aims to uphold the rule of law, maintain the independence of the judiciary, and improve legal services; Pres. PETER ALA ADJETY (Ghana); Sec.-Gen. FEMI FELANA (Nigeria).

African Society of International and Comparative Law (ASICL): 402 Holloway Rd, London, N7 6PZ, United Kingdom; tel.

(20) 7609-3800; fax (20) 7609-5400; e-mail asicl@compuserve.com; f. 1986; promotes public education on law and civil liberties; aims to provide a legal aid and advice system in each African country, and to facilitate the exchange of information on civil liberties in Africa; Pres. MOHAMED BEDJAOUI; Sec. EMILE YAKPO (Ghana); publs *Newsletter* (every 2 months), *African Journal of International and Comparative Law* (quarterly).

Asian-African Legal Consultative Organization (AALCO): E-66, Vasant Marg, Vasant Vihar, New Delhi 110057, India; tel. (11) 26152251; fax (11) 26152041; e-mail mail@aalco.org; internet www.aalco.org; f. 1956 to consider legal problems referred to it by member countries and to serve as a forum for Afro-Asian co-operation in international law, including international trade law, and economic relations; provides background material for conferences, prepares standard/model contract forms suited to the needs of the region; promotes arbitration as a means of settling international commercial disputes; trains officers of member states; has permanent UN observer status; mems: 46 countries; Pres. CHOI YOUNG-JIN (Republic of Korea); Sec.-Gen. Dr WAFIK ZAHER KAMIL (Egypt).

Centre for International Environmental Law (CIEL): 1367 Connecticut Ave, NW, Suite 300, Washington, DC 20036, USA; tel. (202) 785-8700; fax (202) 785-8701; e-mail info@ciel.org; internet www.ciel.org; f. 1989; aims to solve environmental problems and promote sustainable societies through use of law; works to strengthen international and comparative environmental law and policy and to incorporate fundamental ecological principles into international law; provides a range of environmental legal services; educates and trains environmental lawyers; Exec. Dir DANIEL B. MAGRAW.

Comité maritime international (CMI): Mechelsesteensweg 196, 2018 Antwerp, Belgium; tel. (3) 227-35-26; fax (3) 227-35-28; e-mail admin@cmi-imc.org; internet www.comitemaritime.org; f. 1897 to contribute to the unification of maritime law and to encourage the creation of national asscns; work includes drafting of conventions on collisions at sea, salvage and assistance at sea, limitation of shipowners' liability, maritime mortgages, etc.; mems: national asscns in more than 50 countries; Pres. JEAN-SERGE ROHART (France) (2004); Sec. Gen. a.i. NIGEL FRAWLEY (Canada); publs *CMI Newsletter, Year Book*.

Council of the Bars and Law Societies of Europe (CCBE): 1–5 ave de la Joyeuse Entrée, 1040 Brussels, Belgium; tel. (2) 234-65-10; fax (2) 234-65-11; e-mail ccbe@ccbe.org; internet www.ccbe.org; f. 1960; the officially recognized representative organization for the legal profession in the European Union and European Economic Area; liaises between the bars and law societies of member states and represents them before the European institutions; also maintains contact with other international organizations of lawyers; principal objective is to study all questions affecting the legal profession in member states and to harmonize professional practice; mems: 28 delegations (representing more than 700,000 European lawyers), and observer delegations from seven countries; Pres. BERNARD VATIER; Sec.-Gen. JONATHAN GOLDSMITH.

Hague Conference on Private International Law: Scheveningseweg 6, 2517 KT, The Hague, Netherlands; tel. (70) 3633303; fax (70) 3604867; e-mail secretariat@hcch.net; internet www.hcch.net; f. 1893 to work for the unification of the rules of private international law; Permanent Bureau f. 1955; mems: 40 European and 24 other countries; Sec.-Gen. J. H. A. VAN LOON; publs *Proceedings of Diplomatic Sessions* (every 4 years), *Collection of Conventions, The Judges' Newsletter on International Child Protection*.

Institute of International Law (Institut de droit international): IUHEI, 132 rue de Lausanne, CP 36, 1211 Geneva 21, Switzerland; tel. (22) 9085720; fax (22) 9085710; e-mail gerardi@hei.unige.ch; internet www.idi-iil.org; f. 1873 to promote the development of international law through the formulation of general principles, in accordance with civilized ethical standards; provides assistance for the gradual and progressive codification of international law; mems: limited to 132 members and associates world-wide; Sec.-Gen. JOE VERHOEVEN (Belgium); publ. *Annuaire de l'Institut de Droit international*.

Inter-African Union of Lawyers (IAUL) (Union interafricaine des avocats): BP14409, Libreville, Gabon ; tel. 76-41-44; fax 74-54-01; f. 1980; holds congress every three years; Pres. ABDELAZIZ BENZAKOUR (Morocco); Sec.-Gen. FRANÇOIS XAVIER AGONDJO-OKAWE (Gabon); publ. *L'avocat africain* (2 a year).

Inter-American Bar Association (IABA): 1211 Connecticut Ave, NW, Suite 202, Washington, DC 20036, USA; tel. (202) 466-5944; fax (202) 466-5946; e-mail iaba@iaba.org; internet www.iaba.org; f. 1940 to promote the rule of law and to establish and maintain relations between asscns and organizations of lawyers in the Americas; mems: 90 asscns and 3,500 individuals in 27 countries; Sec.-Gen. HARRY A. INMAN (USA); publs *Newsletter* (quarterly), *Conference Proceedings*.

Intergovernmental Committee of the Universal Copyright Convention: Division of Arts and Cultural Enterprise, UNESCO, 7 place de Fontenoy, 75700 Paris, France; tel. 1-45-68-47-05; fax 1-45-68-55-89; e-mail rsy@unesco.org; established to study the application and operation of the Universal Copyright Convention and to make preparations for periodic revisions of this Convention; studies other problems concerning the international protection of copyright, in co-operation with various international organizations; mems: 18 states; publ. *Copyright Bulletin* (quarterly: digital format in English, French and Spanish; print format in Chinese and Russian).

International Association for the Protection of Industrial Property (AIPPI): Tödistrasse 16, 8027 Zürich 27, Switzerland; tel. (1) 2805880; fax (1) 2805885; e-mail mail@aippi.org; internet www.aippi.org; f. 1897 to encourage the development of legislation on the international protection of industrial property and the development and extension of international conventions, and to make comparative studies of existing legislation with a view to its improvement and unification; holds triennial congress; mems: 8,200 (national and regional groups and individual mems) in 108 countries; Pres. Dr GERD F. KUNZE (Australia); Sec.-Gen. VINCENZO M. PEDRAZZINI (Switzerland); publs *Yearbook*, reports.

International Association of Democratic Lawyers: 21 rue Brialmont, 1210 Brussels, Belgium; tel. and fax (2) 223-33-10; e-mail jsharma@del3.vsnl.net.in; internet www.iadllaw.org; f. 1946 to facilitate contacts and exchange between lawyers, encourage study of legal science and international law and support the democratic principles favourable to the maintenance of peace and co-operation between nations; promotes the preservation of the environment; conducts research on labour law, private international law, agrarian law, etc.; has consultative status with UN; mems: in 96 countries; Pres. JITENDRA SHARMA (India); Sec.-Gen. BEINUSZ SZMUKLER (Argentina); publ. *International Review of Contemporary Law* (2 a year, in French, English and Spanish).

International Association of Youth and Family Judges and Magistrates (IAYFJM): 175 Andersonstown Rd, Belfast, BT11 9EA, Northern Ireland; tel. (28) 9061-5164; fax (28) 9061-8374; e-mail w.mccarney@btconnect.com; internet www .judgesandmagistrates.org; f. 1928 to support the protection of youth and family, and criminal behaviour and juvenile maladjustment; members exercise functions as juvenile and family court judges or within professional services linked to youth and family justice and welfare; organizes study groups, meetings and an international congress every four years (Nov.–Dec. 2005: Amsterdam); mems: 23 national asscns and mems in more than 80 countries; Pres. WILLIE MCCARNEY (United Kingdom).

International Association of Law Libraries (IALL): POB 5709, Washington, DC 20016-1309, USA; e-mail morriso6@is.dal.ca; internet www.iall.org; f. 1959 to encourage and facilitate the work of librarians and others concerned with the bibliographic processing and administration of legal materials; mems: 600 from more than 50 countries (personal and institutional); Pres. HOLGER KNUDSEN (Germany); Sec. ANN MORRISON (Canada); publ. *International Journal of Legal Information* (3 a year).

International Association of Legal Sciences (IALS) (Association internationale des sciences juridiques): c/o CISS, 1 rue Miollis, 75015 Paris, France; tel. 1-45-68-25-59; fax 1-45-66-76-03; f. 1950 to promote the mutual knowledge and understanding of nations and the increase of learning by encouraging throughout the world the study of foreign legal systems and the use of the comparative method in legal science; governed by a president and an executive committee of 11 members known as the International Committee of Comparative Law; sponsored by UNESCO; mems: national committees in 47 countries; Pres. Prof. WLADIMIR TOUMANOV (Russia); Sec.-Gen. M. LEKER (Israel).

International Association of Penal Law: 41 rue Bonado, 640000 Pau, France; tel. 5-59-98-08-24; fax 5-59-27-24-56; e-mail aidp-pau@ infonie.fr; internet www.penal.org; f. 1924 to promote collaboration between those from different countries working in penal law, studying criminology, or promoting the theoretical and practical development of international penal law; mems: 1,800; Pres. Prof. M. C. BASSIOUNI; Sec.-Gen. Dr H. EPP; publs *Revue Internationale de Droit Pénal* (2 a year), *Nouvelles Etudes Penales*.

International Bar Association (IBA): 271 Regent St, London W1B 2AQ, United Kingdom; tel. (20) 7629-1206; fax (20) 7409-0456; e-mail iba@int-bar.org; internet www.ibanet.org; f. 1947; a non-political federation of national bar asscns and law societies; aims to discuss problems of professional organization and status; to advance the science of jurisprudence; to promote uniformity and definition in appropriate fields of law; to promote administration of justice under law among peoples of the world; to promote in their legal aspects the principles and aims of the United Nations; mems: 154 member organizations in 164 countries, 17,500 individual members in 173 countries; Pres. EMILIO CÁRDENAS (Argentina); Sec. Gen. FERNANDO POMBO (Spain); publs *International Business Lawyer* (11 a year),

International Bar News (3 a year), *International Legal Practitioner* (quarterly), *Journal of Energy and Natural Resources Law* (quarterly).

International Commission of Jurists (ICJ): POB 216, 81A ave de Châtelaine, 1219 Châtelaine/Geneva, Switzerland; tel. (22) 9793800; fax (22) 9793801; e-mail info@icj.org; internet www.icj.org; f. 1952 to promote the implementation of international law and principles that advance human rights; provides legal expertise to ensure that developments in international law adhere to human rights principles and that international standards are implemented at the national level; maintains Centre for the Independence of Judges and Lawyers (f. 1978); mems: 81 sections and affiliates; Pres. Chief Justice ARTHUR CHASKALSON (Canada); Sec.-Gen. NICHOLAS HOWEN; publs: special reports.

International Commission on Civil Status: 3 place Arnold, 67000 Strasbourg, France; e-mail ciec-sg@ciec1.org; internet www .ciec1.org; f. 1950 for the establishment and presentation of legislative documentation relating to the rights of individuals; carries out research on means of simplifying the judicial and technical administration with respect to civil status; mems: governments of Austria, Belgium, Croatia, France, Germany, Greece, Hungary, Italy, Luxembourg, Netherlands, Poland, Portugal, Spain, Switzerland, Turkey, United Kingdom; Pres. MIGUEL TEIXEIRA DE SOUSA (Portugal); Sec.-Gen. P. LAGARDE (France); publs *Guide Pratique international de l'état civil* (available on-line), various studies on civil status.

International Copyright Society (Internationale Gesellschaft für Urheberrecht e. V.—INTERGU): Rosenheimer Strasse 11, 81667 Munich, Germany; tel. (89) 48003-00; fax (89) 48003-969; f. 1954 to enquire scientifically into the natural rights of the author and to put the knowledge obtained to practical application worldwide, in particular in the field of legislation; mems: 187 individuals and corresponding organizations in 37 countries; CEO Prof. REINHOLD KREILE; publs *Schriftenreihe* (61 vols), *Yearbook*.

International Council for Commercial Arbitration (ICCA): c/o Ulf Franke, POB 16050, 103 21 Stockholm, Sweden; tel. (8) 555-100-00; fax (8) 5663-16-50; e-mail info@arbitration-icca.org; internet www.arbitration-icca.org; promotes international arbitration and other forms of dispute resolution; convenes Congresses and Conferences for discussion and the presentation of papers; mems: 33 mems, 12 advisory mems; Pres. FALI S. NARIMAN (India); Sec.-Gen. ULF FRANKE (Sweden); publs *Yearbook on Commercial Arbitration*, *International Handbook on Commercial Arbitration*, *ICCA Congress Series*.

International Council of Environmental Law: Adenauerallee 214, 53113 Bonn, Germany; tel. (228) 2692-240; fax (228) 2692-250; e-mail 100651.317@compuserve.com; internet www.law.pace.edu/ env/icelsite/icelhome.html; f. 1969 to exchange information and expertise on legal, administrative and policy aspects of environmental questions; Exec. Governors Dr WOLFGANG E. BURHENNE (Germany), Dr ABDULBAR AL-GAIN (Saudi Arabia); publs *Directory*, *References*, *Environmental Policy and Law*, *International Environmental Law—Multilateral Treaties*, etc.

International Criminal Police Organization (INTERPOL): 200 quai Charles de Gaulle, 69006 Lyon, France; tel. 4-72-44-70-00; fax 4-72-44-71-63; e-mail cp@interpol.int; internet www.interpol.int; f. 1923, reconstituted 1946; aims to promote and ensure mutual assistance between police forces in different countries; co-ordinates activities of police authorities of member states in international affairs; works to establish and develop institutions with the aim of preventing transnational crimes; centralizes records and information on international criminals; operates a telecommunications network of 179 stations; holds General Assembly annually; mems: official bodies of 179 countries; Sec.-Gen. RONALD K. NOBLE (USA); publs *International Criminal Police Review*, *International Crime Statistics*, *Stolen Works of Art* (CD Rom), *Interpol Guide to Vehicle Registration Documents* (annually).

International Customs Tariffs Bureau: 38 rue de l'Association, 1000 Brussels, Belgium; tel. (2) 501-87-74; fax (2) 218-30-25; e-mail info@bitd.org; internet www.bitd.org; f. 1890; serves as the executive instrument of the International Union for the Publication of Customs Tariffs; translates and publishes all customs tariffs in five languages—English, French, German, Italian, Spanish; mems: 71; Pres. MARC VAN CRAEN (Belgium); Dir EMILE GOFFIN; publs *International Customs Journal*, *Annual Report*.

International Development Law Organization (IDLO): Via di San Sebastianello 16, 00187 Rome, Italy; tel. (06) 6979261; fax (06) 6781946; e-mail idlo@idlo.int; internet www.idlo.int; f. 1983; designs and conducts courses and seminars for lawyers, legal advisors and judges from developing countries, central and eastern Europe and the former USSR; also provides in-country training workshops; training programme addresses legal skills, international commercial law, economic law reform, governance and the role of the judiciary; Chair. JAMES HURLOCK; Dir-Gen. WILLIAM T. LORIS.

International Federation for European Law (Fédération Internationale pour le Droit Européen—FIDE): 113 ave Louise, 1050 Brussels, Belgium; tel. (2) 534-71-63; fax (2) 534-28-58; e-mail pia .conseil@euronet.be; internet www.fidelaw.org; f. 1961 to advance studies on European law among members of the European Community by co-ordinating activities of member societies; organizes conferences every two years; mems: 12 national asscns; Pres. ZACHARIAS SÜNDSTRÖM; Sec.-Gen. Prof. PETER-CHRISTIAN MÜLLER-GRAFF.

International Federation of Senior Police Officers (Federation Internationale des Fonctionnaires Superieures de Police—FIFSP): FIFSP, Ministère de l'Intérieur, 127 rue Faubourg Saint Honoré, 75008 Paris, France; tel. 1-49-27-40-67; fax 1-45-62-48-52; f. 1950 to unite policemen of different nationalities, adopting the general principle that prevention should prevail over repression, and that the citizen should be convinced of the protective role of the police; established International Centre of Crime and Accident Prevention, 1976 and International Association against Counterfeiting, 1994; mems: 34 national organizations; Pres. JUAN GARCÍA LLOVERA; Sec.-Gen. JEAN-PIERRE HAVRIN (France); publ. *International Police Information* (quarterly, in English, French and German).

International Institute for the Unification of Private Law (UNIDROIT): Via Panisperna 28, 00184 Rome, Italy; tel. (06) 696211; fax (06) 69941394; e-mail info@unidroit.org; internet www .unidroit.org; f. 1926 to undertake studies of comparative law, to prepare for the establishment of uniform legislation, to prepare drafts of international agreements on private law and to organize conferences and publish works on such subjects; holds international congresses on private law and meetings of organizations concerned with the unification of law; maintains a library of 215,000 vols; mems: govts of 58 countries; Pres. Prof. BERARDINO LIBONATI (Italy); Sec.-Gen. Prof. HERBERT KRONKE (Germany); publs *Uniform Law Review* (quarterly), *Digest of Legal Activities of International Organizations*, etc.

International Institute of Space Law (IISL): c/o IAF, 3–5 rue Mario Nikis, 75015 Paris, France; tel. 1-45-67-42-60; fax 1-42-73-21-20; e-mail iaf@wanadoo.fr; internet www.iafastro.com; f. 1959 at the XI Congress of the International Astronautical Federation; organizes annual Space Law colloquium; studies juridical and sociological aspects of astronautics; makes awards; Pres. NANDASIRI JASENTULIYANAARBOSA (USA); publs *Proceedings of Annual Colloquium on Space Law*, *Survey of Teaching of Space Law in the World*.

International Juridical Institute (IJI): Permanent Office for the Supply of International Legal Information, Spui 186, 2511 BW, The Hague, Netherlands; tel. (70) 3460974; fax (70) 3625235; e-mail iji@ worldonline.nl; internet www.iji.nl; f. 1918 to supply information on any non-secret matter of international interest, respecting international, municipal and foreign law and the application thereof; Pres. A. V. M. STRUYCKEN; Dir A. L. G. A. STILLE.

International Law Association (ILA): Charles Clore House, 17 Russell Sq., London, WC1B 5DR, United Kingdom; tel. (20) 7323-2978; fax (20) 7323-3580; e-mail secretariat@ila-hq.org; internet www.ila-hq.org; f. 1873 for the study and advancement of international law, both public and private and the promotion of international understanding and goodwill; mems: 4,000 in 51 regional branches; 25 international cttees; Pres. Hon. Justice. S. P. BHARUCHA (Taiwan); Chair. Exec. Council Lord SLYNN OF HADLEY (UK); Sec.-Gen. DAVID J. C. WYLD (UK).

International Nuclear Law Association (INLA): 29 sq. de Meeûs, 1000 Brussels, Belgium; tel. (2) 547-58-41; fax (2) 503-04-40; e-mail info@aidn-inla.be; internet www.aidn-inla.be; f. 1972 to promote international studies of legal problems related to the peaceful use of nuclear energy; holds conference every two years; mems: 500 in 30 countries; Sec.-Gen. V. VERBRAEKEN; publs *Congress reports*, *Une Histoire de 25 ans*.

International Penal and Penitentiary Foundation (IPPF) (Fondation internationale pénale et pénitentiaire—FIPP): c/o Dr K. Hobe, Bundesministerium der Justiz, 10104 Berlin, Germany; tel. (30) 20259226; fax (30) 20259525; f. 1951 to encourage studies in the field of prevention of crime and treatment of delinquents; mems in 23 countries (membership limited to three people from each country) and corresponding mems; Pres. JORGE DE FIGUEIREDO DIAS (Portugal); Sec.-Gen. KONRAD HOBE (Germany).

International Police Association (IPA): 1 Fox Rd, West Bridgford, Nottingham, NG2 6AJ, United Kingdom; tel. (115) 945-5985; fax (115) 982-2578; e-mail isg@ipa-iac.org; internet www.ipa-iac.org; f. 1950 to permit the exchange of professional information, create ties of friendship between all sections of the police service and organize group travel and studies; mems: 350,000 in more than 59 countries; International Pres. MICHAEL ODYSSEOS; International Sec.-Gen. A. F. CARTER.

International Society for Labour and Social Security Law (ISLSSL): CP 500, CH-1211 Geneva 22, Switzerland; tel. (22) 7996961; fax (22) 7998749; e-mail bronstein@ilo.org; internet www .asociacion.org.ar/ISLLSS; f. 1958 to encourage collaboration between labour law and social security specialists; holds World Congress every three years, as well as irregular regional congresses (Europe, Africa, Asia and Americas); mems: 66 national asscns of labour law officers; Pres. CLYDE SUMMERS (USA); Sec.-Gen. ARTURO BRONSTEIN.

International Union of Latin Notaries (Union Internationale du Notariat Latin—UINL): Alsina 2280, 2°, 1090 Buenos Aires, Argentina; tel. (11) 4952-8848; fax (11) 4952-7094; internet www.iunl.org; f. 1948 to study and standardize notarial legislation and promote the progress, stability and advancement of the Latin notarial system; mems: organizations and individuals in 70 countries; Sec. BERNARDO PÉREZ FERNÁNDEZ DEL CASTILLO (Mexico); publs *Revista Internacional del Notariado* (quarterly), *Notarius International*.

Law Association for Asia and the Pacific (LAWASIA): LAWASIA Secretariat, GPO Box 980, Brisbane, Qld 4001, Australia; tel. (7) 3222-5888; fax (7) 3222-5850; e-mail lawasia@lawasia.asn .au; internet www.lawasia.asn.au; f. 1966; provides an international, professional network for lawyers to update, reform and develop law within the region; comprises six Sections and 21 Standing Committees in Business Law and General Practice areas, which organize speciality conferences; also holds a biennial conference (2005: Gold Coast, Australia; 2007: Hong Kong); mems: national orgs in 23 countries; 2,500 mems in 55 countries; publs *Directory* (annually), *Journal*(annually), *LAWASIA Update* (3 times a year: April, Aug., Dec.).

Permanent Court of Arbitration: Peace Palace, Carnegieplein 2, 2517 KJ, The Hague, Netherlands; tel. (70) 3024165; fax (70) 3024167; e-mail bureau@pca-cpa.org; internet www.pca-cpa.org; f. by the Convention for the Pacific Settlement of International Disputes (1899, 1907); provides for the resolution of disputes involving combinations of states, private parties and intergovernmental organizations, under its own rules of procedure, by means of arbitration, conciliation and fact-finding; operates a secretariat, the International Bureau, which provides registry services and legal support to ad hoc tribunals and commissions; draws up lists of adjudicators with specific expertise; and maintains documentation on mass claims settlement processes; mems: governments of 101 countries; Sec.-Gen. TJACO VAN HOUT (Netherlands); publs *Kluwer Law International Database* (ed), *Journal of International Arbitration* (ed), *World Trade and Arbitration Materials* (ed), *Peace Palace Papers* (ed), *International Law Seminars* (annually).

Society of Comparative Legislation: 28 rue Saint-Guillaume, 75007 Paris, France; tel. 1-44-39-86-23; fax 1-44-39-86-28; e-mail slc@legiscompare.com; internet www.legiscompare.com; f. 1869 to study and compare laws of different countries, and to investigate practical means of improving the various branches of legislation; mems: 600 in 48 countries; Pres. JEAN-LOUIS DEWOST (France); Sec.-Gen. DAVID CAPITANT (France); publ. *Revue Internationale de Droit Comparé* (quarterly).

Union Internationale des Avocats (International Association of Lawyers): 25 rue du Jour, 75001 Paris, France; tel. 1-44-88-55-66; fax 1-44-88-55-77; e-mail uiacentre@wanadoo.fr; internet www .uianet.org; f. 1927 to promote the independence and freedom of lawyers, and defend their ethical and material interests on an international level; aims to contribute to the development of international order based on law; mems: 250 asscns and 3,000 lawyers in over 120 countries; Pres. PAUL NEMO; Exec. Dir MARIE-PIERRE RICHARD.

Union of Arab Jurists (UAJ): POB 6026, Al-Mansour, Baghdad, Iraq; tel. (1) 537-2371; fax (1) 537-2369; f. 1975 to facilitate contacts between Arab lawyers, to safeguard the Arab legislative and judicial heritage, to encourage the study of Islamic jurisprudence; and to defend human rights; mems: national jurists asscns in 15 countries; Sec.-Gen. SHIBIB LAZIM AL-MALIKI; publ. *Al-Hukuki al-Arabi* (Arab Jurist).

Union of International Associations (UIA): 40 rue Washington, 1050 Brussels, Belgium; tel. (2) 640-41-09; fax (2) 643-61-99; e-mail uia@uia.be; internet www.uia.org; f. 1907, present title adopted 1910; aims to facilitate the evolution of the activities of the worldwide network of non-profit organizations, especially non-governmental and voluntary asscns; collects and disseminates information on such organizations; promotes research on the legal, administrative and other problems common to these asscns; mems: 200 in 54 countries; Sec.-Gen. ANDRÉ ONKELINX (Belgium); publs *Transnational Associations* (quarterly), *International Congress Calendar* (quarterly), *Yearbook of International Organizations*, *International Organization Participation* (annually), *Global Action Network* (annually), *Encyclopedia of World Problems and Human Potential*, *Documents for the Study of International Non-Governmental Relations*, *International Congress Science* series, *International Association Statutes* series, *Who's Who in International Organizations*.

World Jurist Association (WJA): 1000 Connecticut Ave, NW, Suite 202, Washington, DC 20036, USA; tel. (202) 466-5428; fax

(202) 452-8540; e-mail wja@worldjurist.org; internet www .worldjurist.org; f. 1963; promotes the continued development of international law and the legal maintenance of world order; holds biennial world conferences, World Law Day and demonstration trials; organizes research programmes; mems: lawyers, jurists and legal scholars in 155 countries; Pres. Hans Thümmel (Germany); Exec. Vice-Pres. Margaretha M. Henneberry (USA); publs *The World Jurist* (6 a year), Research Reports, *Law and Judicial Systems of Nations*, 4th revised edn (directory), *World Legal Directory*, *Law/Technology* (quarterly), *World Law Review* Vols I–V (World Conference Proceedings), *The Chief Justices and Judges of the Supreme Courts of Nations* (directory), work papers, newsletters and journals.

World Association of Judges (WJA): 1000 Connecticut Ave, NW, Suite 202, Washington, DC 20036, USA; tel. (202) 466-5428; fax (202) 452-8540; e-mail wja@worldjurist.org; f. 1966 to advance the administration of judicial justice through co-operation and communication among ranking jurists of all countries; Pres. Prince Bola Ajibola (Nigeria).

World Association of Law Professors (WALP): 1000 Connecticut Ave, NW, Suite 202, Washington, DC 20036, USA; tel. (202) 466-5428; fax (202) 452-8540; e-mail wja@worldjurist.org; internet www.worldjurist.org; f. 1975 to improve scholarship and education in matters related to international law; Pres. Salvador B. Lao (Philippines).

World Association of Lawyers (WAL): 1000 Connecticut Ave, NW, Suite 202, Washington, DC 20036, USA; tel. (202) 466-5428; fax (202) 452-8540; e-mail wja@worldjurist.org; internet www .worldjurist.org; f. 1975 to develop international law and improve lawyers' effectiveness in this field; Pres. Alexander Belohlavek (Czech Republic).

Medicine and Health

Aerospace Medical Association (AsMA): 320 S. Henry St, Alexandria, VA 22314-3579, USA; tel. (703) 739-2240; fax (703) 739-9652; e-mail rrayman@asma.org; internet www.asma.org; f. 1929 as Aero Medical Association; aims to advance the science and art of aviation and space medicine; establishes and maintains co-operation between medical and allied sciences concerned with aerospace medicine; works to promote, protect, and maintain safety in aviation and astronautics; mems: individual, constituent and corporate in 75 countries; Pres. Dr Claude Thibeault (Canada); Exec. Dir Russell B. Rayman (USA); publ. *Aviation Space and Environmental Medicine* (monthly).

Asia Pacific Academy of Ophthalmology (APAO): c/o Prof. Arthur S. M. Lim, Eye Clinic Singapura, 6A Napier Rd, 02-38 Gleneagles Annexe Block, Gleneagles Hospital, Singapore 258500; tel. 64666666; fax 67333360; f. 1956; holds Congress every two years; Pres. Ian Constable (Australia); Sec.-Gen. Prof. Arthur S. M. Lim (Singapore).

Asia Pacific Dental Federation (APDF): c/o Dr J. Annan, 16 The Terrace, Wellington, New Zealand; tel. 4472-5516; fax 4472-5448; e-mail jannan@apdf.info; internet www.apdf.info; f. 1955 to establish closer relationships among dental asscns in Asian and Pacific countries and to encourage research on dental health in the region; holds congress every year; mems: 27 national dental asscns; Pres. Dr Jeffrey Y. S. Tsang; Sec.-Gen. Dr Jeff Annan.

Association for Paediatric Education in Europe (APEE) (Association pour l'Enseignement de la Pédatrie en Europe—AEPE): c/o Dr Claude Billeaud, Dept Néonatal Médicine, Maternité-CHU Pellegrin, 33076 Bordeaux Cédex, France; tel. 5-56-79-55-39; fax 5-56-79-61-56; e-mail claude.billeaud@neonata.u-bordeaux2.fr; internet www.atinternet.com/apee; f. 1970 to promote research and practice in educational methodology in paediatrics; mems: 120 in 20 European countries; Pres. Dr Juan Brines (Spain); Sec.-Gen. Dr Claude Billeaud (France).

Association of National European and Mediterranean Societies of Gastroenterology (ASNEMGE): c/o Andrea Bauer, Vereinsmanagement Lassingleithnerplatz 2/3, 1020 Vienna, Austria; tel. (1) 533-35-42; fax (1) 535-10-45; e-mail info@asnemge.org; internet www.asnemge.org; f. 1947 to facilitate the exchange of ideas between gastroenterologists and to disseminate knowledge; organizes International Congress of Gastroenterology every four years; mems: in 37 countries, national societies and sections of national medical societies; Pres. Prof. Peter Ferenci (Austria); Sec. Prof. Jørgen Rask-Madsen (Denmark).

Balkan Medical Union (Uniunii Medicale Balcanice—UMB): POB 149, 1 rue G. Clémenceau, 70148 Bucharest, Romania; tel. (1) 3137857; fax (1) 3121570; f. 1932; studies medical problems, particularly ailments specific to the Balkan region; promotes a regional programme of public health; facilitates the exchange of information between doctors in the region; organizes research programmes and congresses; mems: doctors and specialists from Albania, Bulgaria, Cyprus, Greece, Moldova, Romania, Turkey and the countries of the former Yugoslavia; Pres. Prof. H. Ciobanu (Moldova); publs *Archives de l'union médicale Balkanique* (quarterly), *Bulletin de l'union médicale Balkanique* (6 a year), *Annuaire*.

Council for International Organizations of Medical Sciences (CIOMS): c/o WHO, ave Appia, 1211 Geneva 27, Switzerland; tel. (22) 7913467; fax (22) 7913111; e-mail cioms@who.int; internet www .cioms.ch; f. 1949 to serve the scientific interests of the international biomedical community; aims to facilitate and promote activities in biomedical sciences; runs long-term programmes on bioethics, health policy, ethics and values, drug development and use, and the international nomenclature of diseases; maintains collaborative relations with the UN; holds a general assembly every three years; mems: 67 organizations; Pres. Prof. Michel B. Vallotton; Sec.-Gen. Prof. J. E. Idánpáán-Heikkilä; publs *Reports on Drug Development and Use*, *Proceedings of CIOMS Conferences*, *International Nomenclature of Diseases*, *International Ethical Guide-lines for Biomedical Research Involving Human Subjects*.

Cystic Fibrosis Worldwide: POB 677, 5600 AR Eindhoven, Netherlands; tel. (40) 259-2760; fax (40) 259-2701; e-mail info@cfww.org; internet www.cfww.org; f. 2003 by merger of the International Association of Cystic Fibrosis Adults and International Cystic Fibrosis (Muscoviscidosis) Association (f. 1964); promotes the development of lay organizations and the advancement of knowledge among medical, scientific and health professionals in underdeveloped areas; convenes annual conference, 2004: Birmingham, UK; Pres. Herman Weggen (Netherlands); Sec. Gina Steekamer (Netherlands); publs *Annual Report*, *CFW Newsletter* (quarterly), *Joseph Levy Lecture*, Physiotherapy booklet.

European Association for Cancer Research (EACR): c/o P. Saunders, The School of Pharmacy, Univ. of Nottingham, University Park, Nottingham, NG7 2RD, United Kingdom; tel. (115) 9515114; fax (115) 9515115; e-mail paul.saunders@nottingham.ac.uk; internet www.eacr.org; f. 1968 to facilitate contact between cancer research workers and to organize scientific meetings in Europe; mems: over 5,000 in more than 40 European and other countries; Pres. W. J. Gullick; Sec. R. Marais (UK).

European Association for the Study of Diabetes (EASD): Rheindorfer Weg 3 40591 Düsseldorf, Germany Germany; tel. (211) 75-84-69; fax (211) 75-84-69; e-mail secretariat@easd.org; internet www.easd.org; f. 1965 to support research in the field of diabetes, to promote the rapid diffusion of acquired knowledge and its application; holds annual scientific meetings within Europe; mems: 6,000 in 101 European and other countries; Pres. Prof. P. A. Halban (Switzerland); Exec. Dir Dr Viktor Jörgens (Germany); publ. *Diabetologia* (13 a year).

European Association of Radiology: c/o EAR Office, Neutorgasse 9/2A, Vienna, Austria; e-mail office@ear-online.org; internet www.ear-online.org; f. 1962 to develop and co-ordinate the efforts of radiologists in Europe by promoting radiology in both biology and medicine, studying its problems, developing professional training and establishing contact between radiologists and professional, scientific and industrial organizations; mems: national asscns in 40 countries; Pres. Prof. N. Gourtsoyiannis; Sec.-Gen. Prof. G. Frila; publs *EAR Newsletter*, *European Radiology* (monthly).

European Association of Social Medicine: Corso Bramante 83, 10126 Turin, Italy; f. 1953 to provide co-operation between national asscns of preventive medicine and public health; mems: asscns in 14 countries; Pres. Dr Jean-Paul Fournier (France); Sec.-Gen. Prof. Dr Enrico Belli (Italy).

European Brain and Behaviour Society (EBSS): c/o Dr M. Ammassari-Teule, CNR Institute of Neuroscience, IRCCS S. Lucia Foundation, Via del Fosso di Riorano, 64–65, 00143 Rome, Italy; tel. (06) 501-703082; fax (06) 501-703082; e-mail ebbs-science@hsantalucia.it; internet www.ebbs-science.org; f. 1969; holds one conference a year and organizes workshops; Pres. Prof. John Aggleton (UK); Sec.-Gen. Dr Martine Ammassari-Teule (Italy); publ. *Newsletter* (annually).

European Federation of Internal Medicine (EFIM): c/o Dr Christopher Davidson, Royal Sussex County Hospital, Eastern Rd, Brighton, BN2 5BE, United Kingdom; tel. (1273) 696955; fax (1273) 684554; e-mail chris.davidson@bsuh.nhs.uk; internet www.efim.org; f. 1969 as European Asscn of Internal Medicine (present name adopted 1996); aims to bring together European specialists, and establish communication between them, to promote internal medicine; organizes congresses and meetings; provides information; mems: 29 European societies of internal medicine; Pres. Prof. Daniel Sereni; Sec. Dr Christopher Davidson; publ. *European Journal of Internal Medicine* (8 a year).

European Health Management Association (EHMA): Vergemount Hall, Clonskeagh, Dublin 6, Ireland; tel. (1) 2839299; fax (1) 2838653; e-mail pcberman@ehma.org; internet www.ehma.org; f.

1966; aims to improve health care in Europe by raising standards of managerial performance in the health sector; fosters co-operation between health service organizations and institutions in the field of health-care management education and training; mems: 225 in 30 countries; Pres. Dr ROBERT F. KONING; Dir PHILIP C. BERMAN; publs *Newsletter, Eurobriefing* (quarterly).

European League against Rheumatism (EULAR): Witikonerstr. 15, 8032 Zürich, Switzerland; tel. (1) 3839690; fax (1) 3839810; e-mail secretariat@eular.org; internet www.eular.org; f. 1947 to co-ordinate research and treatment of rheumatic complaints; holds an annual Congress; mems: in 41 countries; Exec. Sec. F. WYSS; publ. *Annals of the Rheumatic Diseases.*

European Organization for Caries Research (ORCA): c/o Lutz Stösser, Dept of Preventive Dentistry, Dental School of Erfurt, Univ. of Jena, Nordhauser Str. 78, 99089 Erfurt, Germany; tel. (361) 7411205; e-mail stoesser@zmkh.ef.uni-jena.de; internet www .orca-caries-research.org; f. 1953 to promote and undertake research on dental health, encourage international contacts, and make the public aware of the importance of care of the teeth; mems: research workers in 23 countries; Pres. Prof. BIRGIT ANGMAR-MANSSON (Sweden); Sec.-Gen. Prof. L. STÖSSER (Germany); publ. *Caries Research.*

European Orthodontic Society (EOS): Flat 20, 49 Hallam St, London, W1W 6JN, United Kingdom; tel. (20) 7935-2795; fax (20) 7323-0410; e-mail eoslondon@compuserve.com; internet www .eoseurope.org; f. 1907 (name changed in 1935), to advance the science of orthodontics and its relations with the collateral arts and sciences; mems: 2,725 in 85 countries; Sec. Prof. L. DERMAUT; publ. *European Journal of Orthodontics* (6 a year).

European Union of Medical Specialists (Union Européenne des Médecins Spécialistes—UEMS): 20 ave de la Couronne, Brussels 1050, Belgium; tel. (2) 649-51-64; fax (2) 640-37-30; e-mail uems@ skynet.be; internet www.uems.be; f. 1958 to harmonize and improve the quality of medical specialist practices in the EU and safeguard the interests of medical specialists; seeks formulation of common training policy; mems: two representatives each from Austria, Belgium, Denmark, Finland, France, Germany, Greece, Iceland, Ireland, Italy, Luxembourg, Netherlands, Norway, Portugal, Spain, Sweden, Switzerland, United Kingdom; Pres. Dr H. HALILA (Finland); Sec.-Gen. Dr B. MAILLET (Belgium).

Eurotransplant International Foundation: POB 2304, 2301 CH Leiden, Netherlands; tel. (71) 5795795; fax (71) 5790057; internet www.eurotransplant.nl; f. 1967; co-ordinates the exchange of organs for transplants in Austria, Belgium, Germany, Luxembourg, Netherlands and Slovenia; keeps register of c. 15,000 patients with all necessary information for matching with suitable donors in the shortest possible time; organizes transport of the organ and transplantation; collaborates with similar organizations in western and eastern Europe; Dirs Dr B. COHEN, Dr G. G. PERSIJN.

FDI World Dental Federation: L'Avant Centre, 13 chemin du Levant, 01210 Ferney Voltaire, France; tel. and fax 4-50-40-55-55; e-mail info@fdiworldental.org; internet www.fdiworldental.org; f. 1900; mems: 152 national dental asscns and 31 affiliates; Pres. Dr H. R. YOON (Republic of Korea); Exec. Dir Dr J. T. BARNARD (South Africa); publ. *International Dental Journal* (every 2 months).

Federation of French-Language Obstetricians and Gynaecologists (Fédération des gynécologues et obstetriciens de langue française—FGOLF): Clinique Baudelocque, 123 blvd de Port-Royal, 75674 Paris Cédex 14, France; tel. 1-42-34-11-43; fax 1-42-34-12-31; f. 1920 for the scientific study of phenomena having reference to obstetrics, gynaecology and reproduction in general; mems: 1,500 in 50 countries; Pres. Prof. H. RUF (France); Gen. Sec. Prof. J. R. ZORN (France); publ. *Journal de Gynécologie Obstétrique et Biologie de la Reproduction* (8 a year).

Federation of the European Dental Industry (Fédération de l'Industrie Dentaire en Europe—FIDE): Kirchweg 2, 50858 Cologne, Germany; tel. (221) 50068712; fax (221) 50068721; e-mail shelton@ fide-online.org; internet www.fide-online.org; f. 1957 to promote the interests of dental industry manufacturers; mems: national asscns in 12 European countries; Pres. and Chair. Dr ALESSANDRO GAMBERINI (Italy); Sec. HARALD RUSSEGGER (Germany).

General Association of Municipal Health and Technical Experts: 83 ave Foch, BP 3916, 75761 Paris Cédex 16, France; tel. 1-53-70-13-53; fax 1-53-70-13-40; e-mail aghtm@aghtm.org; internet www.aghtm.org; f. 1905 to study all questions related to urban and rural health; mems: in 35 countries; Dir-Gen. ALAIN LASALMONIE (France); publ. *TSM-Techniques, Sciences, Méthodes* (monthly).

ICDDR, B: Centre for Health and Population Research: GPO Box 128, Dhaka 1000, Bangladesh; tel. (2) 8811751; fax (2) 8823116; e-mail info@icddrb.org; internet www.icddrb.org; f. 1960 as Pakistan-SEATO Cholera Research Laboratory, international health research institute (International Centre for Diarrhoeal Disease Research, Bangladesh—ICDDR, B since 1978; undertakes research,

training and information dissemination on diarrhoeal diseases, child health, nutrition, emerging infectious diseases, environmental health, sexually transmitted diseases, HIV/AIDS, poverty and health, vaccine evaluation and case management, with particular reference to developing countries; supported by 50 governments and international orgs; Exec. Dir Prof. DAVID A. SACK; publs *Annual Report, Journal of Health, Population and Nutrition* (quarterly), *Glimpse* (quarterly), *Shasthya Sanglap* (3 a year), *Health and Science Bulletin* (quarterly), *SUZY* (newsletter, 2 a year), scientific reports, working papers, monographs, special publications.

Inter-American Association of Sanitary and Environmental Engineering (Asociación Interamericana de Ingeniería Sanitaria y Ambiental—AIDIS): Rua Nicolau Gagliardi 354, 05429-010 São Paulo, SP, Brazil; tel. (11) 3812-4080; fax (11) 3814-2441; e-mail aidis@aidis.org.br; internet www.aidis.org.br; f. 1948 to assist in the development of water supply and sanitation; mems: 32 countries; Pres. HORST OTTERSTETTER (Brazil); Exec. Dir LUIZ AUGUSTO DE LIMA PONTES (Brazil); publs *Revista Ingeniería Sanitaria* (quarterly), *Desafío* (quarterly).

International Academy of Aviation and Space Medicine (IAASM): c/o Dr G. Takahashi, 40 Wallford Way, Nepean, ON K2E 6B6, Canada; tel. (613) 228-9345; fax (613) 228-0422; e-mail g .takahashi@sympatico.ca; internet www.iaasm.org; f. 1955 to facilitate international co-operation in research and teaching in the fields of aviation and space medicine; mems: in 46 countries; Pres. Dr ERIC DONALDSON (Australia); Sec.-Gen. Dr GEORGE TAKAHASHI (Canada).

International Academy of Cytology: Burgunderstr. 1, 79104 Freiburg, Germany; tel. (761) 292-3801; fax (761) 292-3802; e-mail centraloffice@cytology-iac.org; internet www.cytology-iac.org; f. 1957 to facilitate the international exchange of information on specialized problems of clinical cytology, to stimulate research and to standardize terminology; mems: 2,400; Pres. (2004–07) MATÍAS JIMÉNEZ AYALA; Sec. VOLKER SCHNEIDER; publs *Acta Cytologica, Analytical and Quantitative Cytology and Histology* (both every 2 months).

International Agency for the Prevention of Blindness (IAPB): L. V. Prasad Eye Institute, L. V. Prasad Marg, Banjara Hills, Hyderabad 500 034, India; tel. (40) 2354-5389; fax (40) 2354-8271; e-mail iapb@lvpeye.stph.net; internet www.iapb.org; f. 1975; promotes advocacy and information sharing on the prevention of blindness; aims to encourage the formation of national prevention of blindness committees and programmes; has an official relationship with WHO; Pres. Dr HANNAH B. FAAL (The Gambia); Sec.-Gen. Dr GULLAPALLI N. RAO (India); publ. *IAPB News.*

International Anatomical Congress: c/o Prof. Dr Wolfgang Kühnel, Institut für Anatomie, Medizinische Universität zu Lübeck, Ratzeburger Allee 160, 23538 Lübeck, Germany; tel. (451) 500-4030; fax (451) 500-4034; e-mail buchuel@anet.mu-luebeck.de; internet www.anet.mu-luebeck.de/anetpes.html; f. 1903; runs international congresses for anatomists to discuss research, teaching methods and terminology in the fields of gross and microscopical anatomy, histology, cytology, etc; Pres. J. ESPERENCA-PINE (Portugal); Sec.-Gen. Prof. Dr WOLFGANG KÜHNEL (Germany); publ. *Annals of Anatomy.*

International Association for Child and Adolescent Psychiatry and Allied Professions (IACAPAP): c/o Dr I. M. Goodyer, Univ. of Cambridge, Douglas House, 18B Trumpington Rd, Cambridge CB2 2AH, United Kingdom; tel. (1223) 336098; fax (1223) 746122; e-mail ig104@cus.cam.ac.uk; internet www.iacapap.org; f. 1937 to promote scientific research in the field of child psychiatry by collaboration with allied professions; mems: national asscns and individuals in 42 countries; Pres. Prof. HELMUT REMSCHMIDT; Sec.-Gen. Dr IAN M. GOODYER; publs *The Child in the Family* (Yearbook of the IACAPP), *Newsletter.*

International Association for Dental Research (IADR): 1619 Duke St, Alexandria, VA 22314, USA; tel. (703) 548-0066; fax (703) 548-1883; e-mail research@iadr.com; internet www.dentalresearch .org; f. 1920 to encourage research in dentistry and related fields; holds annual meetings, triennial conferences and divisional meetings; Pres. Dr JOHN CLARKSON; Exec. Dir Dr ROBERT COLLINS.

International Association for the Study of Obesity (IASO): 231 North Gower St, London, NW1 2NS, United Kingdom; e-mail inquiries@iaso.org; internet www.iaso.org; f. 1986; supports research into the prevention and management of obesity throughout the world and disseminates inormation regarding disease and accompanying health and social issues; incorporates the International Obesity Task Force; international congress every four years (2002: Sao Paulo, Brazil); Exec. Dir KATE BAILLIE.

International Association of Agricultural Medicine and Rural Health (IAAMRH): ul.Marszalkowska 82, 00517 Warsaw, Poland; tel. and fax (22) 623-6551; e-mail kris@krus.gov.pl; internet www.iaamrh.org; f. 1961 to study the problems of medicine in agriculture in all countries and to prevent the diseases caused by the conditions of work in agriculture; mems: 405; Pres. Dr ASHOK PATIL (India); Gen. Sec. Dr ANDRZEJ WOJTYLA (Poland).

International Association of Applied Psychology (IAAP): c/o Prof. José M. Prieto, Universidad Complutense, Facultad de Psicología, Despacho 2222, Somosaguas, 28223 Madrid, Spain; fax (91) 351-0091; e-mail iaap@psi.ucm.es; internet www.iaapsy.org; f. 1920, present title adopted in 1955; aims to establish contacts between those carrying out scientific work on applied psychology, to promote research and to encourage the adoption of measures contributing to this work; organizes International Congress of Applied Psychology every four years (2006: Athens, Greece) and co-sponsors International Congress of Psychology every two years (2004: Beijing, People's Republic of China); mems: 2,200 in 94 countries; Pres. Prof. MICHAEL FRESE (Germany); Sec.-Gen. Prof. JOSÉ. M. PRIETO (Spain); publ. *Applied Psychology: An International Review* (quarterly).

International Association of Asthmology (INTERASMA): c/o Prof. Hugo Neffen, Irigoyen Freyre 2670, 3000 Santa Fé, Argentina; tel. (42) 453-7638; fax (42) 456-9773; e-mail interasm@neffen.satlink .net; internet www.asmanet.com; f. 1954 to advance medical knowledge of bronchial asthma and allied disorders; mems: 1,100 in 54 countries; Pres. Prof. GAETANO MELILLO (Italy); Sec./Treas. Prof. H. NEFFEN; publs *Interasma News, Journal of Investigative Allergology and Clinical Immunology* (every 2 months), *Allergy and Clinical Immunology International* (every 2 months).

International Association of Bioethics: POB 137, University of the Philippines, Diliman, Quezon City 1101, Philippines; tel. (2) 426-9593; fax (2) 926-1008; internet www.bioethics-international.org; f. 1992; aims to facilitate contact and to promote exchange of information among people working in the bioethics field; aims to promote the development of research and training in bioethics; organizes international conferences (7th World Congress of Bioethics: Nov. 2004, Sydney, Australia); Sec. Prof. LEONARDO DE CASTRO (Philippines); publs *Bioethics Journal, IAB News* (2 a year).

International Association of Gerontology (IAG): IAG Secretariat, Gerontology Research Centre, Simon Fraser Univ. at Harbour Centre 2800, 515 West Hastings St, Vancouver, BC V3C 5K3, Canada; tel. (604) 268-7972; fax (604) 291-5066; e-mail iag@sfu.ca; internet www.sfu.ca/iag; f. 1950 to promote research and training in all fields of gerontology and to protect the interests of gerontologic societies and institutions; holds World Congress every four years; mems: 63 national societies in 60 countries; Pres. Prof. GLORIA M. GUTMAN (Canada); Sec.-Gen. JOHN E. GRAY (Canada); publ. *IAG Newsletter* (2 a year).

International Association of Group Psychotherapy: IAGP Postfach, 8126 Zumikon, Switzerland; tel. (71) 6885650; fax (71) 6885651; e-mail office@iagp.com; internet www.iagp.com; f. 1954; holds congresses every three years; mems: in 35 countries; Pres. CHRISTER SANDAHL (Sweden); Sec. HOWARD D. KIBEL (USA); publs *The Forum, Globeletter* (2 a year).

International Association of Hydatidology: Florida 460, 3°, 1005 Buenos Aires, Argentina; tel. (11) 4322-2030; fax (11) 4325-8231; f. 1941; mems: 1,200 in 41 countries; Pres. Dr RAÚL MARTÍN MENDY; Sec.-Gen. Dr JORGE ALFREDO IRIARTE (Argentina); publs *Archivos Internacionales de la Hidatidosis* (every 2 years), *Boletín de Hidatidosis* (quarterly).

International Association of Logopedics and Phoniatrics (IALP): Tilweg 1, 9971 Ulrum, Netherlands; e-mail h.k.schutte@ med.rug.nl; internet www.ialp.info; f. 1924 to promote standards of training and research in human communication disorders, to establish information centres and communicate with kindred organizations; mems: 125,000 in 60 societies from 54 countries; Pres. Prof. HARM SCHUTTE (Netherlands); Sec. and Pres. Elect DOLORES E. BATTLE (USA); publ. *Folia Phoniatrica et Logopedica* (6 a year).

International Association of Medicine and Biology of the Environment (IAMBE): c/o 115 rue de la Pompe, 75116 Paris, France; tel. 1-45-53-45-04; fax 1-45-53-41-75; e-mail aimbe.world@ free.fr; f. 1971 with assistance from the UN Environment Programme; aims to contribute to the solution of problems caused by human influence on the environment; structure includes 13 technical commissions; mems: individuals and orgs in 79 countries; Hon. Pres. Prof. R. DUBOS; Pres. Dr R. ABBOU.

International Association of Oral and Maxillofacial Surgeons (IAOMS): 17 W 220, 22nd St, Suite 420, Oakbrook Terrace, IL 60181-4480, USA; fax (630) 833-1382; e-mail info@iaoms.org; internet www.iaoms.org; f. 1963 to advance the science and art of oral and maxillofacial surgery; organizes biennial international conference; mems: over 3,000; Pres. Dr JOSÉ LUIS FERRERIA (Argentina); Exec. Dir Dr JOHN F. HELFRICK (USA); publs *International Journal of Oral and Maxillofacial Surgery* (2 a year), *Newsletter*.

International Brain Research Organization (IBRO): 51 blvd de Montmorency, 75016 Paris, France; tel. 1-46-47-92-92; fax 1-45-20-60-06; e-mail ibro@wanadoo.fr; internet www.ibro.org; f. 1958 to further all aspects of brain research; mems: 45 corporate, 16 aca-

demic and 51,000 individual; Pres. Prof. T. N. WIESEL (USA); Sec.-Gen. Prof. A. J. AGUAYO (Canada); publs *IBRO News, Neuroscience* (bi-monthly).

International Bronchoesophagological Society: Mayo Clinic, 13400 E. Shea Blvd, Scottsdale, AZ 85259, USA; e-mail helmers .richard@mayo.edu; f. 1951 to promote the progress of bronchoesophagology and to provide a forum for discussion among bronchoesophagologists with various medical and surgical specialities; holds Congress every two years; mems: 500 in 37 countries; Exec. Sec. Dr RICHARD A. HELMERS.

International Bureau for Epilepsy (IBE): POB 21, 2100 AA Heemstede, Netherlands; tel. (23) 5588411; fax (23) 5588419; e-mail ibe@sein.nl; internet www.ibe-epilepsy.org; f. 1961; collects and disseminates information about social and medical care for people with epilepsy; organizes international and regional meetings; advises and answers questions on social aspects of epilepsy; mems: 699 national epilepsy orgs; Sec.-Gen. ESPER CAVALHEIRO; publ. *International Epilepsy News* (quarterly).

International Catholic Committee of Nurses and Medico-Social Assistants (Comite International Catholique des Infirmières et Assistantes Médico-Sociales—CICIAMS): 43 Square Vergote, 1040 Brussels, Belgium; tel. (2) 732-10-50; fax (2) 734-84-60; e-mail an.verlinde@adamco.be; f. 1933 to group professional Catholic nursing asscns to represent Christian thought in the general professional field at international level; to co-operate in the general development of the profession and to promote social welfare; mems: 49 full, 20 corresponding mems; Pres. RICHARD LAI; Gen. Sec. AN VERLINDE; publ. *Nouvelles/News/Nachrichten* (3 a year).

International Cell Research Organization (ICRO) (Organisation Internationale de Recherche sur la Cellule): c/o UNESCO, SC/BES/LSC, 1 rue Miollis, 75015 Paris, France; fax 1-45-68-58-16; e-mail icro@unesco.org; internet www.unesco.org/icro; f. 1962 to create, encourage and promote co-operation between scientists of different disciplines throughout the world for the advancement of fundamental knowledge of the cell, normal and abnormal; organizes international laboratory courses on modern topics of cell and molecular biology and biotechnology for young research scientists; mems: 400; Pres. Prof. JORGE E. ALLENDE (Chile); Exec. Sec. Prof. GEORGES N. COHEN (France).

International Chiropractors' Association: 1110 North Glebe Rd, Suite 1000, Arlington, VA 22201, USA; tel. (703) 528-5000; fax (703) 528-5023; e-mail chiro@chiropractic.org; internet www .chiropractic.org; f. 1926 to promote advancement of the art and science of chiropractors; mems: 7,000 individuals, and affiliated asscns; Pres. Dr D. D. HUMBER; Exec. Dir RONALD M. HENDRICKSON; publs *International Review of Chiropractic* (every 2 months), *ICA Today* (every 2 months).

International College of Surgeons (ICS): 1516 N. Lake Shore Drive, Chicago, IL 60610, USA; tel. (312) 642-3555; fax (312) 787-1624; e-mail info@icsglobal.org; internet www.icsglobal.org; f. 1935, as a world-wide federation of surgeons and surgical specialists for the advancement of the art and science of surgery; aims to create a common bond among the surgeons of all nations and promote the highest standards of surgery, without regard to nationality, creed, or colour; sends teams of surgeons to developing countries to teach local surgeons; provides research and scholarship grants, organizes surgical congresses around the world; manages the International Museum of Surgical Science in Chicago; mems: c. 8,000 in 112 countries; Pres. RAY A. DIETER (USA); Exec. Dir MAX C. DOWNHAM (USA); publ. *International Surgery* (quarterly).

International Commission on Occupational Health (ICOH): c/o National Institute for Occupational Safety and Prevention, Via Fontana Candida 1, 1-00040 Monteporzio Catone (Rome), Italy; internet www.icoh.org.sg; f. 1906, present name adopted 1985; aims to study and prevent pathological conditions arising from industrial work; arranges congresses on occupational medicine and the protection of workers' health; provides information for public authorities and learned societies; mems: 1,944 in 89 countries; Pres. Prof. BENGT KNAVE (Sweden); Sec.-Gen. Dr SERGIO IAVICOLI (Italy); publ. *Newsletter* (electronic version).

International Commission on Radiological Protection (ICRP): 17116 Stockholm, Sweden; tel. (8) 729-72-75; fax (8) 729-72-98; e-mail jack.valentin@ssi.se; internet www.icrp.org; f. 1928 to provide technical guidance and promote international co-operation in the field of radiation protection; committees on Radiation Effects, Doses from Radiation Exposure, Protection in Medicine, and the Application of Recommendations; mems: c. 70; Chair. Prof. R. H. CLARKE (UK); Scientific Sec. Dr J. VALENTIN (Sweden); publ. *Annals of the ICRP*.

International Committee of Military Medicine (ICMM) (Comité international de médecine militaire—CIMM): Hôpital Militaire Reine Astrid, rue Bruyn, 1120 Brussels, Belgium; tel. (2) 264-43-48; fax (2) 264-43-67; e-mail info@cimm-icmm.org; internet www

.cimm-icmm.org; f. 1921 as Permanent Committee of the International Congresses of Military Medicine and Pharmacy; name changed 1990; aims to increase co-operation and promote activities in the field of military medicine; considers issues relating to mass medicine, dentistry, military pharmacy, veterinary sciences and the administration and organization of medical care missions, among others; mems: official delegates from 100 countries; Chair. Lt-Gen. IGOR BYKOV (Russia); Sec.-Gen. Col Dr J. SANABRIA (Belgium); publ. *Revue Internationale des Services de Santé des Forces Armées* (quarterly).

International Council for Laboratory Animal Science (ICLAS): Canadian Council on Animal Care, 1510–130 Albert St, Ottawa, ON K1P 5G4, Canada; tel. (450) 467-4221; fax (450) 467-6308; e-mail gdemers@ccac.ca; internet www.iclas.org; f. 1956; promotes the ethical care and use of laboratory animals in research, with the aim of advancing human and animal health; establishes standards and provides support resources; encourages international collaboration to develop knowledge; Pres. Dr GILLES DEMERS (Canada); Sec.-Gen. Dr PATRI VERGARA (Spain).

International Council for Physical Activity and Fitness Research (ICPAFR): Prof. F. G. Viviani, Faculty of Psychology, Univ. of Padua, via Venezia 8, 35131 Padua, Italy; tel. (049) 880-4668; fax (048) 827-6600; e-mail franco.viviani@unipd.it; internet www.unipid.it/esterni/wwwmedic/servizi.htm; f. 1964 to construct international standardized physical fitness tests, to encourage research based upon the standardized tests and to enhance participation in physical activity; mems: some 35 countries; Pres. Prof. FRANCO G. VIVIANI (Italy); Sec./Treas. A. MACMANUS; publs *International Guide to Fitness and Health*, proceedings of seminars and symposia, other fitness and health publs.

International Council of Nurses (ICN): 3 place Jean-Marteau, 1201 Geneva, Switzerland; tel. (22) 9080100; fax (22) 9080101; e-mail icn@icn.ch; internet www.icn.ch; f. 1899 to allow national asscns of nurses to work together to develop the contribution of nursing to the promotion of health; holds quadrennial Congresses; mems: 124 national nurses' asscns; Pres. CHRISTINE HANCOCK (UK); Exec. Dir JUDITH OULTON; publ. *The International Nursing Review* (quarterly).

International Diabetes Federation (IDF): 19 ave Emile de Mot, 1000 Brussels, Belgium; tel. (2) 538-55-11; fax (2) 538-51-14; e-mail luc.hendrickx@idf.org; internet www.idf.org; f. 1949 to help in the collection and dissemination of information on diabetes and to improve the welfare of people suffering from diabetes; mems: 175 asscns in 138 countries; Exec. Dir LUC HENDRICKX; publs *Diabetes Voice*, *Bulletin of the IDF* (quarterly).

International Epidemiological Association (IEA): Epidemiology Dept, High Institute of Public Health, Alexandria University, 38 Ismailah St, Apt 201, Mostafa Kamal, Alexandria, Egypt; tel. and fax (3) 5467576; e-mail IEAsecretariat@link.net; internet www.IEAweb.org; f. 1954; mems: 2,237; promotes epidemiology and organizes international scientific meetings and region-specific meetings; Pres. Dr JORN OLSEN (USA); Sec. Prof. AHMED MANDIL (Egypt); publ. *International Journal of Epidemiology* (6 a year).

International Federation for Medical and Biological Engineering (IFMBE): 10000 Zagreb, Unska 3, Faculty of Electrical Engineering and Computing, Univ. of Zagreb, Croatia; tel. (1) 6129938; fax (1) 6129652; e-mail office@ifmbe.org; internet www.ifmbe.org; f. 1959; mems: 50 societies; Pres. Prof. JOACHIM NAGEL; Sec.-Gen. RATKO MAGJAREVIC (Croatia).

International Federation for Medical Psychotherapy—IFMP: c/o Prof. E. Heim, Tannackstr. 3, 3653 Oberhofen, Switzerland; tel. and fax (33) 2431141; e-mail senf-blum@t-online.de; f. 1946 to further research and teaching of psychotherapy; organizes international congresses; mems: c. 6,000 psychotherapists from around 40 countries, 36 societies; Pres. Dr EDGAR HEIM (Switzerland); Sec.-Gen. Prof. Dr WOLFGANG SENE (Germany).

International Federation of Clinical Chemistry and Laboratory Medicine (IFCC): via Carlo Farini 81, 20159 Milan, Italy; tel. (02) 6680-9912; fax (02) 6078-1846; e-mail ifcc@ifcc.org; internet www.ifcc.org; f. 1952; mems: 78 national societies (about 33,000 individuals) and 33 corporate mems; Pres. Prof. MATHIAS M. MÜLLER (Austria); Sec. Dr RENZE BAIS (Australia); publs *Journal* (electronic version), *Annual Report*.

International Federation of Clinical Neurophysiology: c/o Concorde Administration Ltd, 42 Canham Rd, London, W3 7SR, United Kingdom; tel. (20) 8743-3106; fax (20) 8743-1010; e-mail ifcn@ifcn.info; internet www.elsevier.nl/homepage/sah/ifcn; f. 1949 to attain the highest level of knowledge in the field of electroencephalography and clinical neurophysiology in all the countries of the world; mems: 48 organizations; Pres. Prof. FRANÇOIS MAUGUIÈRE (France); Sec. Prof. G. F. A. HARDING (UK); publs *Clinical Neurophysiology* (monthly), *Evoked Potentials* (every 2 months), *EMG and Motor Control* (every 2 months).

International Federation of Fertility Societies (IFFS): c/o CSI, 337 rue de la Combe Caude, 34090 Montpellier, France; tel. 4-67-63-53-40; fax 4-67-41-94-27; e-mail algcsi@mnet.fr; f. 1951 to study problems of fertility and sterility; Pres. ROBERT F. HARRISON; Sec.-Gen. Prof. BERNARD HEDON; publ. *Newsletter* (2 a year).

International Federation of Gynecology and Obstetrics (FIGO): FIGO House, Suite 3, Waterloo Court, 10 Theed St, London, SE1 8ST, United Kingdom; tel. (20) 7928-1166; fax (20) 7928-7099; e-mail figo@figo.org; internet www.figo.org; f. 1954; aims to improve standards in gynaecology and obstetrics, promote better health care for women, facilitate the exchange of information, and perfect methods of teaching; mems: national societies in 102 countries; Pres. Dr ARNALDO ACOSTA (Paraguay); Sec.-Gen. Prof. SABARATNAM ARULKUMARAN (UK); publ. *International Journal of Obstetrics and Gynecology*.

International Federation of Ophthalmological Societies: c/o Dr Bruce E. Spivey, 945 Green St, San Francisco, CA 94133, USA; tel. (415) 409-8410; fax (415) 409-8403; e-mail icoph@icoph.org; internet www.icoph.org; f. 1933; works to support and develop ophthalmology, especially in developing countries; carries out education and assessment programmes; promotes clinical standards; holds World Ophthalmology Congress every two years; Pres. Prof. G. O. H. NAUMANN (Germany); Sec. Dr BRUCE E. SPIVEY.

International Federation of Oto-Rhino-Laryngological Societies (IFOS): Oosterveldlaan 24, 2610 Wilrijk-Antwerp, Belgium; tel. and fax (3) 443-36-11; e-mail ifos@uia.ua.ac.be; internet www.ifosworld.org; f. 1965 to initiate and support programmes to protect hearing and prevent hearing impairment; holds Congresses every four years; Pres. NASSER KOTBY (Egypt); Sec.-Gen. JAN J. GROTE (Netherlands); publ. *IFOS Newsletter* (quarterly).

International Federation of Surgical Colleges: c/o Prof. S. W. A. Gunn, La Panetiere, 1279 Bogis-Bossey, Switzerland; tel. (22) 7762161; fax (22) 7766417; e-mail swagunn@bluewin.ch; internet www.ifsc-net.org; f. 1958 to encourage high standards in surgical training; accepts volunteers to serve as surgical teachers in developing countries and co-operates with WHO in these countries; provides journals and text books for needy medical schools; conducts international symposia; offers grants; mems: colleges or asscns in 77 countries, 420 individual associates; Pres. Prof. ALBRECHT ENCKE (Germany); Hon. Sec. Prof. S. WILLIAM. A. GUNN (Switzerland); publ. *IFSC News*.

International Hospital Federation (IHF) (Fédération Internationale des Hôpitaux—FIH): 13 chemin du Levant, 01210 Ferney Voltaire, France; tel. 4 -50-42-60-00; fax 4-50-42-60-01; e-mail info@ihf-fih.org; internet www.hospitalmanagement.net; f. 1947 for information exchange and education in hospital and health service matters; represents institutional health care in discussions with WHO; conducts conferences and courses on management and policy issues; mems in five categories: national hospital and health service organizations; professional asscns, regional organizations and individual hospitals; individual mems; professional and industrial mems; honorary mems; Dir-Gen. Prof. PER-GUNNAR SVENSSON; publs *World Hospitals and Health Services* (quarterly), *Hospitals International* (quarterly), *Hospital Management International (Yearbook1)*, *New World Health (Yearbook 2)*.

International League against Epilepsy (ILAE): 204 ave Marcel Thiry, 1200 Brussels, Belgium; tel. (2) 774-95-47; fax (2) 774-96-90; e-mail dsartiaux@ilae-epilepsy.org; internet www.ilae-epilepsy.org; f. 1909 to link national professional asscns and to encourage research, including classification and the development of anti-epileptic drugs; collaborates with the International Bureau for Epilepsy and with WHO; mems: 93 chapters; Pres. PETER WOLF; Sec.-Gen. NATALIO FEJERMAN.

International League of Associations for Rheumatology (ILAR): c/o Prof. of Rheumatology and Rehabilitation, Univ. of Cairo, 19 Ismail Mohammed St, Jeddah Tower, Zamalek, Egypt; tel. (615) 343-9324; fax (615) 343-6478; internet www.ilar.org; f. 1927 to promote international co-operation for the study and control of rheumatic diseases to encourage the foundation of national leagues against rheumatism; to organize regular international congresses and to act as a connecting link between national leagues and international organizations; mems: 13,000; Pres. Prof. TAHSIN HADIDI (Chile); Sec.-Gen. Prof. SAMIR EL-BADAWY (USA); publs *Annals of the Rheumatic Diseases* (in the UK), *Revue du Rhumatisme* (in France), *Reumatismo* (in Italy), *Arthritis and Rheumatism* (in the USA), etc.

International Leprosy Association (ILA): c/o Univ. of Oxford, International Leprosy Association Global Project on the History of Leprosy, Wellcome Unit for The History of Medicine, 45–47 Banbury Rd, Oxford, OX2 6PE, United Kingdom; tel. (1865) 284627; fax (1865) 274605 ; f. 1931 to promote international co-operation in work on leprosy; holds congress every five years (2002: Brazil); Pres. Dr S. K. NOORDEEN; publ. *International Journal of Leprosy and Other Mycobacterial Diseases* (quarterly).

International Narcotics Control Board (INCB): 1400 Vienna, POB 500, Austria; tel. (1) 260-60-42-77; fax (1) 260-60-58-67; e-mail secretariat@incb.org; internet www.incb.org; f. 1961 by the Single Convention on Narcotic Drugs, to supervise implementation of drug control treaties by governments; mems: 13 individuals; Pres. PHILIP EMAFO (Nigeria); Sec. HERBERT SCHAEPE (Germany); publ. *Annual Report* (with three technical supplements).

International Opticians' Association: Godmersham Park Mansion, Godmersham, Canterbury, Kent, CT4 7DT, United Kingdom; tel. (1227) 733901; fax (1227) 733900; e-mail general@abdo.org.uk; internet www.abdo.org.uk; f. 1951 to promote the science of opthalmic dispensing, and to maintain and advance standards and effect co-operation in optical dispensing; Pres. JAMES RUSSELL; Gen. Sec. Sir ANTHONY GARRETT; publs *ABDO Frame Rule*, *Dispensing Optics* (monthly).

International Organization for Medical Physics (IOMP): c/o Prof. Gary D. Fullerton, UTHSCSA, Dept of Radiology, MSC 7800, 7703 Floyd Curl Drive, San Antonio, TX 78229-3900, USA; tel. (210) 567-5551; fax (210) 567-5549; e-mail iomp@uthscsa.edu; internet www.iomp.org; f. 1963 to organize international co-operation in medical physics, to promote communication between the various branches of medical physics and allied subjects, to contribute to the advancement of medical physics in all its aspects and to advise on the formation of national organizations; mems: national organizations of medical physics in over 70 countries; Pres. Prof. OSKAR CHOMICKI (Poland); Sec.-Gen. Prof. GARY FULLERTON; publ. *Medical Physics World*.

International Pediatric Association (IPA): c/o Hôpital Necker-Enfants Malades, 149 rue de Sèvres, 75743 Paris Cédex 15, France; tel. 1- 42-19-26-45; fax 1-42-19-26-44; internet www.ipa-france.net; f. 1912; holds triennial congresses and regional and national workshops; mems: 135 national paediatric societies in 131 countries, 9 regional affiliate societies, 9 paediatric specialty societies; Pres. Dr. JANE SCHALLER (USA); Exec. Dir JACQUES SCMITZ (France); publ. *International Child Health* (quarterly).

International Pharmaceutical Federation (Fédération Internationale Pharmaceutique—FIP): POB 84200, 2508 AE, The Hague, Netherlands; tel. (70) 302-1970; fax (70) 302-1999; e-mail secretariat@fip.org; internet www.fip.org; f. 1912; aims to represent and serve pharmacy and pharmaceutical sciences world-wide and to improve access to medecines; holds World Congress of Pharmacy and Pharmaceutical Sciences annually; mems: 86 national pharmaceutical organizations in 62 countries, 55 associate, supportive and collective mems, 4,000 individuals; Dir A. J. M (TON) HOEK (Netherlands); publ. *International Pharmacy Journal* (2 a year).

International Psycho-Analytical Association (IPA): Broomhills, Woodside Lane, London, N12 8UD, United Kingdom; tel. (20) 8446-8324; fax (20) 8445-4729; e-mail ipa@ipa.org.uk; internet www.ipa.org.uk; f. 1908; holds meetings to define and promulgate the theory and teaching of psychoanalysis; acts as a forum for scientific discussions; controls and regulates training; contributes to the interdisciplinary area common to the behavioural sciences; mems: 11,000 in 34 countries; Pres. Prof. DANIEL WIDLÖCHER; Sec.-Gen. ALAIN GIBEAULT; publs *Bulletin*, *Newsletter*.

International Rhinologic Society: c/o Prof. Clement, ENT-Dept, AZ-VUB, Laarbeeklaan 101, 1090 Brussels, Belgium; tel. (2) 477-68-89; fax (2) 477-68-80; e-mail knoctp@az.vub.ac.be; f. 1965; holds congress every four years; Pres. IN-YONG PARK (Republic of Korea); Sec. Prof. P. A. R. CLEMENT (Belgium); publ. *Rhinology*.

International Society for Cardiovascular Surgery (ISCVS): 900 Cummings Center, Beverly, MA 01915, USA; tel. (978) 927-8330; fax (978) 524-8890; e-mail iscvs@prri.com; internet iscvs.vascularweb.org; f. 1950 to stimulate research on the diagnosis and therapy of cardiovascular diseases and to exchange ideas on an international basis; Pres. JAMES MAY (USA); Sec.-Gen. Dr LAZAR J. GREENFIELD (USA); publ. *Cardiovascular Surgery*.

International Society for Oneiric Mental Imagery Techniques: c/o Odile Dorkel, 56 rue Sedaine, 75011 Paris, France; tel. 1-47-00-16-63; e-mail odile.orkel@wanadoo.fr; links a group of research workers, technicians and psychotherapists using oneirism techniques under waking conditions, with the belief that a healing action cannot be dissociated from the restoration of creativity; mems: in 17 countries; Pres. ODILE DORKEL (France); Sec.-Gen. JEAN-FRANÇOIS CESARO (France).

International Society for the Psychopathology of Expression and Art Therapy (SIPE): c/o Dr G. Roux, 27 rue du mal Joffre, 64000 Pau, France; tel. and fax 5-59-27-69-74; e-mail sipearther@aol.com; internet online-art-therapy.com; f. 1959 to bring together specialists interested in the problems of expression and artistic activities in connection with psychiatric, sociological and psychological research; mems: 625; Pres. Dr G. ROUX (France); Sec.-Gen. J. L. SUDRES (France); publ. *Newsletter* (quarterly).

International Society of Audiology: University Hospital Rotterdam, Audiological Centre, Molewaterplein 40, 3015 GD Rotterdam, Netherlands; tel. (10) 4634586; fax (10) 4634240; e-mail info@isa-audiology.org; internet www.isa-audiology.org; f. 1952 to facilitate the knowledge, protection and rehabilitation of human hearing and to represent the interests of audiology professionals and of the hearing-impaired; organizes biannual Congress and workshops and seminars; mems: 400 individuals; Pres. Dr BILL NOBLE; Gen. Sec. Dr J. VERSCHUURE; publ. *International Journal of Audiology* (every 2 months).

International Society of Blood Transfusion (ISBT): c/o Eurocongress Conference Management, Jan van Goyenkade 11, 1075 HP Amsterdam, Netherlands; tel. (20) 6794311; fax (20) 6737306; e-mail isbt@eurocongres.org; internet www.isbt-web.org; f. 1937; mems: c. 1,000 in 100 countries; Pres. H. E. HEIER; Sec.-Gen. Dr P. T. W. STRENGERS; publ. *Transfusion Today* (quarterly).

International Society of Dermatopathology (ISVD): c/o Mill House Veterinary Surgery, Kings Lynn, Norfolk, United Kingdom; tel. (1553) 771457; e-mail vets@vetcutis.freeserve.co.uk; internet www.vetcutis.freeserve.co.uk/vetcutis.freeserve.co.uk; f. 1958; groups professionals interested in the microscopic interpretation of skin diseases; aims to advance veterinary and comparative dermatopathology; encourages the development of technologies for the diagnosis of skin diseases in animals; promotes professional training; Pres. Dr THELMA LEE GROSS (USA); Sec. Dr DAVID H. SHEARER (UK).

International Society of Developmental Biologists: c/o Dr Paul T. van der Saag, Hubrecht Laboratorium/Netherlands Institute for Developmental Biology, Uppsalalaan 8, 3584 CT, Utrecht, Netherlands; tel. (30) 2510211; e-mail directie@niob.knaw.nl; internet www.elsevier.com/inca/homepage/sah/isdb; f. 1911 as International Institute of Embryology; aims to promote the study of developmental biology and to encourage international co-operation among investigators in the field; mems: 850 in 33 countries; Pres. Prof. EDWARD M. DE ROBERTIS (USA); International Sec. Prof. BEN SCHERES (Netherlands); publ. *Mechanisms of Development*.

International Society of Internal Medicine: Dept. of Medicine, SRO Hospital, 4901 Langenthal, Switzerland; tel. (62) 9163102; fax (62) 9164155; e-mail r.streuli@sro.ch; internet www.acponline.org/isim; f. 1948 to encourage research and education in internal medicine; mems: 58 national societies, 1,500 individuals in 65 countries; 2004 congress: Granada, Spain ; 2008 congress: Buenos Aires, Argentina; Pres. Prof. THOMAS KJELLSTRÖM (Sweden); Sec. Prof. ROLF A. STREULI (Switzerland).

International Society of Lymphology: Room 4406, University of Arizona, 1501 North Campbell Ave, POB 245063, Tucson, AZ 85724-5063, USA; tel. (520) 626-6118; fax (520) 626-0822; e-mail lymph@u.arizona.edu; internet www.u.arizona.edu/~witte/ISL.htm; f. 1966 to further progress in lymphology through personal contacts and the exchange of ideas; mems: 375 in 42 countries; Pres. M. OHKUMA (Japan); Sec.-Gen. M. H. WITTE (USA); publ. *Lymphology* (quarterly).

International Society of Neuropathology: c/o Prof. Hannu Kalimo, Dept of Pathology, Turku University Hospital, 20520 Turku, Finland; tel. (2) 2611685; fax (2) 3337456; e-mail hkalimo@mailhost.utu.fi; internet brainpath.medsch.ucla.edu/isn/isnhome.htm; Pres. Prof. SAMUEL K. LUDWIN (Canada); Sec.-Gen. Prof. HANNU KALIMO (Finland).

International Society of Orthopaedic Surgery and Traumatology (Société Internationale de Chirurgie Orthopédique et de Traumatologie): 40 rue Washington, bte 9, 1050 Brussels, Belgium; tel. (2) 648-68-23; fax (2) 649-86-01; e-mail hq@sicot.org; internet www.sicot.org; f. 1929; convenes an annual conference and world congresses every three years; mems: 102 countries, 3,000 individuals; Pres. Prof. JOHN C. Y. LEONG; Sec.-Gen. MAURICE HINSENKAMP; publ. *Newsletter* (every 2 months).

International Society of Physical and Rehabilitation Medicine (ISPRM): ISPRM Central Office, Werner van Cleemputte, Medicongress, 28–34 Waalpoel, 9960 Assenede, Belgium; tel. (9) 344-39-59; fax (9) 344-40-10; e-mail isprm@medicongress.com; internet www.isprm.org; f. 1999 by merger of International Federation of Physical Medicine and Rehabilitation (f. 1952) and International Rehabilitation Medicine Association (f. 1968); mems: in 68 countries; second international congress: Prague, Czech Republic (May 2003); Pres. Dr HAIM RING (Israel); Sec. Dr NAOICHI CHINO (Japan).

International Society of Radiology (ISR): 7910 Woodmont Ave, Suite 400, Bethesda, Maryland 20814-3095, USA; tel. (301) 657-2652; fax (301) 907-8768; e-mail isr@isradiology.org; internet www.isradiology.org; f. 1953 to promote radiology world-wide; International Commissions on Radiation Units and Measurements (ICRUM), on Radiation Protection (ICRP), and on Radiological Education (ICRE); organizes biannual International Congress of Radiology; collaborates with WHO; mems: more than 50 national radiological societies; Pres. F. ARREDONDO; Sec.-Gen. CLAUDE MANELFE; Exec. Dir OTHA W. LINTON; publ. *Newsletter*.

International Society of Surgery (ISS): Netzibodenstr. 34, POB 1527, 4133 Pratteln, Switzerland; tel. (61) 8159666; fax (61) 8114775; e-mail surgery@iss-sic.ch; internet www.iss-sic.ch; f. 1902 to promote understanding between surgical disciplines; groups surgeons to address issues of interest to all surgical specialists; supports general surgery as a training base for abdominal surgery, surgery with integuments and endocrine surgery; organizes congresses, 40th World Congress of Surgery: Durban, South Africa (August 2005); mems: 4,000; Admin. Dir. VICTOR BERTSCHI; Sec.-Gen. Prof. FELIX HARDER; publ. *World Journal of Surgery* (monthly).

International Spinal Cord Society (ISCoS): National Spinal Injuries Centre, Stoke Mandeville Hospital, Aylesbury, Bucks, HP21 8AL, United Kingdom; tel. (1296) 315866; fax (1296) 315870; e-mail admin@iscos.org.uk; internet www.iscos.org.uk; f. 2001; formerly the International Medical Society of Paraplegia (f.1961); studies all problems relating to traumatic and non-traumatic lesions of the spinal cord, including causes, prevention, research and rehabilitation; promotes the exchange of information; assists in efforts to guide and co-ordinate research; Pres. Prof. T. IKATA; Hon. Sec. W. EL-MASRY; publ. *Spinal Cord*.

International Union against Cancer (Union internationale contre le cancer—UICC): 3 rue du Conseil Général, 1205 Geneva, Switzerland; tel. (22) 8091811; fax (22) 8091810; e-mail info@uicc .org; internet www.uicc.org; f. 1933 to promote the campaign against cancer on an international level; organizes International Cancer Congress every four years; administers the American Cancer Society UICC International Fellowships for Beginning Investigators (ACSBI), the Astrazeneca and Novartis UICC Transnational Cancer Research Fellowships (TCRF), the UICC International Cancer Technology Transfer Fellowships (ICRETT), the Yamagiwa-Yoshida Memorial UICC International Cancer Study Grants (YY), the Trish Greene UICC International Oncology Nursing Fellowships (IONF), the UICC Asia-Pacific Cancer Society Training Grants (APCASOT), and the Latin America UICC COPES Training and Education Fellowship (LACTEF); conducts worldwide programmes of campaign organization; public and professional education; and patient support, detection and diagnosis; and programmes on epidemiology and prevention; tobacco and cancer; the treatment of cancer; and tumour biology; mems: voluntary national organizations, cancer research and treatment organizations, institutes and governmental agencies in more than 80 countries; Pres. Dr JOHN SEFFRIN (USA); Exec. Dir ISABEL MORTARA (Switzerland); publs *UICC International Directory of Cancer Institutes and Organizations* (electronic version), *International Journal of Cancer* (36 a year), *UICC News* (quarterly), *International Calendar of Meetings on Cancer* (2 a year).

International Union against Tuberculosis and Lung Disease (IUATLD): 68 blvd St Michel, 75006 Paris, France; tel. 1-44-32-03-60; fax 1-43-29-90-87; e-mail union@iuatld.org; internet www.iuatld .org; f. 1920 to co-ordinate the efforts of anti-tuberculosis and respiratory disease asscns, to mobilize public interest, to assist control programmes and research around the world, to collaborate with governments and WHO and to promote conferences; mems: asscns in 165 countries, 3,000 individual mems; Pres. Prof. ANNE FANNING; Exec. Dir Dr NILS BILLO; publs *The International Journal of Tuberculosis and Lung Disease* (in English, with summaries in French and Spanish; incl. conference proceedings), *Newsletter*.

International Union for Health Promotion and Education (IUHPE): Immeuble le Berry, 2 rue Auguste Comte, 92170 Vanves, France; tel. 1-46-45-00-59; fax 1-46-45-00-45; e-mail mclamarre@ iuhpe.org; internet www.iuhpe.org; f. 1951; provides an international network for the exchange of practical information on developments in health promotion and education; promotes research; encourages professional training for health workers, teachers, social workers and others; holds a World Conference on Health Promotion and Health Education every three years; organizes regional conferences and seminars; mems: in more than 90 countries; Pres. Prof. MAURICE MITTELMARK (Norway); Exec. Dir MARIE-CLAUDE LAMARRE (France); publs. *Health Promotion International*, *Promotion and Education* (quarterly, in English, French and Spanish).

International Union of Therapeutics: c/o Prof. A. Pradalier, Hôpital Louis Mourier, 178 rue des Renouillers, 92701 Colombes, France; tel. 1-47-60-67-05; e-mail secretariat.medecine4@emr .ap-hop-paris.fr; f. 1934; international congress held every other year; mems: 500 from 22 countries; Pres. Prof. A. PRADALIER.

Latin American Association of National Academies of Medicine: Carrera 7, Santafé de Bogotá, Colombia; tel. and fax (1) 249-3122; e-mail alanam_colombia@hotmail.com; f. 1967; mems: 11 national Academies; Exec. Sec. Dr ZOÍLO CUÉLLAR-MONTOYA (Colombia).

Medical Women's International Association (MWIA): Wilhelm-Brand-Str.3, 44141 Dortmund, Germany; tel. (231) 94-32-771; fax (231) 94-32-773; e-mail secretariat@mwia.net; internet www

.mwia.net; f. 1919 to facilitate contacts between women in medicine and to encourage co-operation in matters connected with international health problems; mems: national asscns in 47 countries, and individuals; Pres. Dr SHELLEY ROSS (Canada); Sec.-Gen. Dr WALTRAUD DIEKHAUS (Germany); publ. *MWIA UPDATE* (3 a year).

Middle East Neurosurgical Society: c/o Dr Gamal Azab, 20 Amine Fikri St, Ramleh Station, Alexandria, Egypt; f. 1958 to promote clinical advances and scientific research among its members and to spread knowledge of neurosurgery and related fields among all members of the medical profession in the Middle East; mems: 684 in nine countries; Pres. Dr GAMAL AZAB; Hon. Sec. IZAT SHERIF.

Multiple Sclerosis International Federation (MSIF): 3rd Floor, Skyline House, 200 Union St, London, SE1 0LX, United Kingdom; tel. (20) 7620-1911; fax (20) 7620-1922; e-mail info@msif.org; internet www.msif.org; f. 1967; promotes shared scientific research into multiple sclerosis and related neurological diseases; stimulates the active exchange of information; provides support for new and existing multiple sclerosis societies; Pres. PETER W. SCHMIDT; Chief Exec. CHRISTINE PURDY; publs *MSIF Annual Review* (annually), *MS: The Guide to Treatment and Management* (every 2 years), *MS in Focus* (2 a year), *MSIF Directory* (annually), *How To* series (annually).

Organisation panafricaine de lutte contre le SIDA (OPALS): 15/21 rue de L'École de Médecine, 75006 Paris, France; tel. 1-43-26-72-28; fax 1-43-29-70-93; e-mail opals@croix-rouge.fr; f. 1988; disseminates information relating to the treatment and prevention of AIDS; provides training of medical personnel; promotes co-operation between African medical centres and specialized centres in the USA and Europe; Pres. Prof. MARC GENTILINI; publ. *OPALS Liaison*.

Organization for Co-ordination in the Struggle against Endemic Diseases in Central Africa (Organisation de coordination pour la lutte contre les endémies en Afrique Centrale—OCEAC): BP 288, Yaoundé, Cameroon; tel. 23-22-32; fax 23-00-61; e-mail oceac@camnet.cm; internet www.cm.refer.org/site_oceac; f. 1965 to standardize methods of controlling endemic diseases, to co-ordinate national action, and to negotiate programmes of assistance and training on a regional scale; mems: Cameroon, Central African Republic, Chad, Republic of the Congo, Equatorial Guinea, Gabon; Sec.-Gen. Dr AUGUSTE BILONGO-MANÉNÉ; publ. *Bulletin de Liaison et de Documentation* (quarterly).

Pan-American Association of Ophthalmology (PAAO): 1301 South Bowen Rd, Suite 365, Arlington, TX 76013, USA; tel. (817) 275-7553; fax (817) 275-3961; e-mail info@paao.org; internet www .paao.org; f. 1939 to promote friendship within the profession and the dissemination of scientific information; holds biennial Congress (2005: Chile); mems: national ophthalmological societies and other bodies in 39 countries; Pres. Dr BRONWYN BATEMAN; Exec. Dir Dr CRISTIÁN LUCO (Chile); publ. *Vision Panamerica* (quarterly).

Pan-Pacific Surgical Association: POB 61479 Honolulu, HI 96839, Hawaii, USA; tel. (808) 941-1010 ; fax (808) 536-4141; e-mail ppsa.info@panpacificsurgical.org; internet www.panpacificsurgical .org; f. 1929 to bring together surgeons to exchange scientific knowledge relating to surgery and medicine, and to promote the improvement and standardization of hospitals and their services and facilities; congresses are held every two years; mems: 2,716 regular, associate and senior mems from 44 countries; Pres. JOHN WONG; Chair. THOMAS KOSASA.

Rehabilitation International: 25 East 21st St, New York, NY 10010, USA; tel. (212) 420-1500; fax (212) 505-0871; e-mail ri@ riglobal.org; internet www.riglobal.org; f. 1922 to improve the lives of disabled people through the exchange of information and research on equipment and methods of assistance; organizes international conferences and co-operates with UN agencies and other international organizations; mems: organizations in 81 countries; Pres. MICHAEL FOY; Sec.-Gen. TOMAS LAGERWALL; publs *International Rehabilitation Review* (annually), *Rehabilitación* (2 or 3 a year).

Society of French-speaking Neuro-Surgeons (Société de neurochirurgie de langue française—SNLF): c/o Prof. C. Raftopoulos, ave Hippocrate 10, 1200, Brussels, Belgium; tel. (2) 764-10-88; fax (2) 764-89-61; e-mail Raftopoulos@chir.ucl.ac.be; internet www.snclf .com; f. 1949; holds annual convention and congress; mems: 700; Pres. Prof. JEAN CHAZAL (France); Sec. Prof. CHRISTIAN RAFTOPOULOS (Belgium); publ. *Neurochirurgie* (6 a year).

Transplantation Society (Société de Transplantation): Central Business Office, 205 Viger Ave West, Suite 201, Montreal, QC H2Z 1G2, Canada; tel. (514) 874-1998; fax (514) 874-1580; e-mail info@ transplantation-soc.org; internet www.transplantation-soc.org; f. 1966; over 3,000 members in 65 countries; Pres. Dr DAVID E. R. SUTHERLAND; Exec. Sec. PHILIP DOMBROSKI.

World Allergy Organization (IAACI): 611 East Wells St, Milwaukee, WI 53202, USA; tel. (414) 276-1791; fax (414) 276-3349; e-mail info@worldallergy.org; internet www.worldallergy.org; f.

1945, as International Association of Allergology and Clinical Immunology, to further work in the educational, research and practical medical aspects of allergic and immunological diseases; 2003 Congress: Vancouver, Canada; mems: 56 national societies and three regional orgs; Pres. Prof. CARLOS E. BAENA-CAGNANI (Argentina); Sec.-Gen. Prof. G. WALTER CANONICA (Italy); publ. *Allergy and Clinical Immunology International* (6 a year).

World Association for Disaster and Emergency Medicine (WADEM): c/o Marvin L. Birnbaum, 600 N. Highland Ave, Mail Code 6733, Madison, WI 53792–6733, USA; e-mail mlb@medicine.wisc.edu; internet wadem.medicine.wisc.edu; f. 1976 to improve the world-wide delivery of emergency and humanitarian care in mass casualty and disaster situations, through training, symposia, and publications; mems: 600 in 62 countries; Pres. KNUT OLE SUNDNES (Norway); Sec. DEMETRIOS PYRROS (Greece); publ. *Prehospital and Disaster Medicine.*

World Association of Societies of Pathology and Laboratory Medecine (WASPaLM): c/o Japan Clinical Pathology Foundation for International Exchange, Sakura-Sugamo Bldg 7F, Sugamo 2-11-1, Toshima-ku, Tokyo 170, Japan; tel. (3) 3918-8161; fax (3) 3949-6168; internet www.waspalm.org; f. 1947 to link national societies and co-ordinate their scientific and technical means of action; promotes the development of anatomic and clinical pathology, especially by convening conferences, congresses and meetings, and through the interchange of publications and personnel; mems: 54 national asscns; Pres. Dr MIKIO MORI (Japan); Sec. KENNETH D. McCLATCHEY (USA); publ. *Newsletter* (quarterly).

World Confederation for Physical Therapy (WCPT): 46–48 Grosvenor Gdns, London, SW1W 0EB, United Kingdom; tel. (20) 7881-9234; fax (20) 7881-9239; e-mail info@wcpt.org; internet www.wcpt.org; f. 1951; represents physical therapy internationally; encourages high standards of physical therapy education and practice; promotes exchange of information among members, and the development of a scientific professional base through research; aims to contribute to the development of informed public opinion regarding physical therapy; holds seminars and workshops and quadrennial General Assembly; mems: 93 national physical therapy orgs; Pres. SANDRA MERCER MOORE; Sec.-Gen. B. J. MYERS; publ. *Newsletter* (2 a year).

World Council of Optometry (WCO): 8360 Old York West, 4th Floor, Elkins Park, PA 19027, USA; e-mail wco@pco.edu; internet www.worldoptometry.org; f. 1927 to co-ordinate efforts to provide a good standard of ophthalmic optical (optometric) care throughout the world; enables exchange of ideas between different countries; focuses on optometric education; gives advice on standards of qualification; considers optometry legislation throughout the world; mems: 70 optometric organizations in 50 countries and four regional groups; Pres. Dr SCOTT D. BRISBIN (Canada); Exec. Dir Dr ANTONY DI STEFANO (USA); publ. *Interoptics* (quarterly).

World Federation for Medical Education (WFME) (Fédération mondiale pour l'enseignement de la médecine): Univ. of Copenhagen Faculty of Health Sciences, Blegdamsvej 3, 2200 Copenhagen N, Denmark; tel. (353) 27103; fax (35) 27070; e-mail wfme@wfme.org; internet www.wfme.org; f. 1972; aims to promote and integrate medical education world-wide; links regional and international asscns; has official relations with WHO, UNICEF, UNESCO, UNDP and the World Bank; Pres. Dr HANS KARLE; Exec. Dir ULRIK MEYER.

World Federation for Mental Health (WFMH): POB 16810, Alexandria, VA 22302-0810, USA; tel. (703) 838-7543; fax (703) 519-7648; e-mail info@wfmh.com; internet www.wfmh.org; f. 1948 to promote the highest standards of mental health; works with agencies of the United Nations in promoting mental health; assists other voluntary asscns in improving mental health services; mems: 250 national and international asscns in 115 countries; Pres. and Chief Exec. PRESTON J. GARRISON; publs *Newsletter* (quarterly), *Annual Report.*

World Federation of Associations of Paediatric Surgeons (WOFAPS): c/o Prof. J. Boix-Ochoa, Clinica Infantil 'Vall d'Hebron', Departamento de Cirugía Pediátrica, Valle de Hebron 119–129, Barcelona 08035, Spain; f. 1974; mems: 80 asscns; Pres. Prof. J. L. GROSFELD; Sec. Prof. J. BOIX-OCHOA.

World Federation of Associations of Poison Centres and Clinical Toxicology Centres: c/o Prof. Louis Roche, CIRC, 150 cours Albert-Thomas, 69372 Lyon, Cédex 2, France; tel. 4-78-74-16-74; f. 1975 as World Federation of Associations of Clinical Toxicology Centres and Poison Control Centres; mems: 37; Pres. Dr HANS PERSSON (Sweden); Sec.-Gen. Prof. LOUIS ROCHE; publ. *Bulletin of the World Federation* (quarterly).

World Federation of Hydrotherapy and Climatotherapy: Cattedra di Terapia Med. E Medic. Termal, Università degli Studi, via Cicognara 7, 20129 Milan, Italy; tel. (02) 50318456; fax (02) 50318461; e-mail umberto.solimene@unimi.it; internet www.femteconline.com; f. 1947 as International Federation of Ther-

malism and Climatism; recognized by WHO in 1986; present name adopted 1999; mems: in 36 countries; Pres. M. NIKOLAI A. STOROJENKO; Gen. Sec. Prof. UMBERTO SOLIMENE.

World Federation of Neurology (WFN): 12 Chandos St, London, W1G 9DR, United Kingdom; tel. (20) 7323-4011; fax (20) 7323-4012; e-mail wfnlondon@aol.com; internet www.wfneurology.org; f. 1955 as International Neurological Congress, present title adopted 1957; aims to assemble members of various congresses associated with neurology and promote co-operation among neurological researchers. Organizes Congress every four years; mems: 23,000 in 89 countries; Pres. JUN KIMURA (Japan); Sec.-Treas. Dr RICHARD GODWIN-AUSTEN (UK); publs *Journal of the Neurological Sciences, World Neurology* (quarterly).

World Federation of Neurosurgical Societies (WFNS): c/o Prof. Edward R. Laws, Dept. of Neurological Surgery, Univ. of Virginia, Box 212, Health Science Center, Charlottesville, VA 22908, USA; tel. (804) 924-2650; fax (804) 924-5894; internet www.wfns.org; f. 1957 to assist in the development of neurosurgery and to help the formation of asscns; facilitates the exchange of information and encourages research; mems: 57 societies in 56 countries; Pres. Prof. ARMANDO BASSO; Sec. Prof. EDWARD R. LAWS, Jr.

World Federation of Occupational Therapists (WFOT): POB 30, Forrestfield, 6058 Western Australia, Australia; tel. (8) 9453-9746 ; e-mail wfot@multiline.com.au; internet wfot.org.au; f. 1952 to further the rehabilitation of the physically and mentally disabled by promoting the development of occupational therapy in all countries; facilitates the exchange of information and publications; promotes research in occupational therapy; holds international congresses every four years; mems: national professional asscns in 50 countries, with total membership of c. 100,000; Pres. KIT SINCLAIR (Hong Kong); Hon. Sec. MARILYN PATTISON (Australia); publ. *Bulletin* (2 a year).

World Federation of Public Health Associations: c/o Stacey Succop, Program Co-ordinator, APHA, 800 I St, NW, Washington, DC 20001-3710, USA; tel. (202) 777-2506; fax (202) 777-2534; e-mail stacey.succop@apha.org; internet www.wfpha.org; f. 1967; brings together researchers, teachers, health service providers and workers in a multidisciplinary environment of professional exchange, studies and action; endeavours to influence policies and to set priorities to prevent disease and promote health; holds a triennial Congress: Brighton, United Kingdom (2004); mems: 67 national public health asscns; Sec.-Gen. ALLEN JONES (USA); publs *WFPHA Report* (in English), and occasional technical papers.

World Federation of Societies of Anaesthesiologists (WFSA): 21 Portland Place, London, W1B 1PY, United Kingdom; tel. (20) 7631-8880; fax (20) 7631-8882; e-mail wfsahq@anaesthesiologists.org; internet www.anaesthesiologists.org; f. 1955; aims to make available the highest standards of anaesthesia to all peoples of the world; mems: 116 national societies; Pres. Prof. A. E. E. MEURSING (Netherlands); Sec. Prof. JOHN MOYERS (USA); publs *World Anaesthesia Newsletter* (2 a year), *Annual Report.*

World Heart Federation: 5 ave du Mail, 1205 Geneva 12, Switzerland; tel. (22) 8070320; fax (22) 8070339; e-mail admin@worldheart.org; internet www.worldheart.org; f. 1978 as International Society and Federation of Cardiology, through merger of the International Society of Cardiology and the International Cardiology Federation, name changed as above 1998; aims to promote the study, prevention and relief of cardiovascular diseases through scientific and public education programmes and the exchange of materials; organizes world congresses every four years; mems: national cardiac societies and heart foundations in 84 countries; Pres. Dr PHILIP POOLE-WILSON (UK); Sec. Dr AYRTON BRANDÃO (Hungary); publs *CVD Prevention, Heartbeat* (quarterly).

World Medical Association (WMA): 13 chemin du Levant, POB 63, 01210 Ferney-Voltaire, France; tel. 4-50-40-75-75; fax 4-50-40-59-37; e-mail wma@wma.net; internet www.wma.net; f. 1947 to achieve the highest international standards in all aspects of medical education and practice, to promote closer ties among doctors and national medical asscns by personal contact and all other means, to study problems confronting the medical profession, and to present its views to appropriate bodies; holds an annual General Assembly; mems: 83 national medical asscns; Pres. Dr Y. D. COBLE (USA); Sec.-Gen. Dr O. KLOIBER (Germany); publ. *The World Medical Journal* (quarterly).

World Organization of Gastroenterology (Organisation mondiale de gastro-entérologie—OMGE): c/o Bridget Fischer, Medconnect GmbH, Brünnsteinstr. 10, 81541 München, Germany; tel. (89) 41419240; fax (89) 41419245; e-mail omge@omge.org; internet www.omge.org; f. 1958 to promote clinical and academic gastroenterological practice throughout the world, and to ensure high ethical standards; mems: in 80 countries; Pres. Prof. GUIDO N. J. TYTGAT; Sec.-Gen. Dr HENRY COHEN.

World Psychiatric Association (WPA): Elmhurst Hospital/Mt Sinai School of Medicine, 79 Broadway, Room D-10-20, Elmhurst,

NY 11373, USA; tel. (718) 334-5094; fax (718) 334-5096; e-mail wpasecretariat@wpanet.org; internet www.wpanet.org; f. 1961 for the exchange of information on problems of mental illness and to strengthen relations between psychiatrists in all countries; organizes World Psychiatric Congresses and regional and inter-regional scientific meetings; mems: 150,000 psychiatrists in 100 countries; Pres. AHMED OKASHA (Egypt); Sec.-Gen. JOHN COX (UK).

World Self-Medication Industry (WSMI): Centre International de Bureaux, 13 chemin du Levant, 01210 Ferney-Voltaire, France; tel. 4-50-28-47-28; fax 4-50-28-40-24; e-mail dwebber@wsmi.org; internet www.wsmi.org; Dir-Gen. Dr DAVID E. WEBBER.

Posts and Telecommunications

African Telecommunications Union: Posta Sacco Plaza, 11th Floor, Uhuru Highway, POB 35282 Nairobi, Kenya; tel. (20) 216678; fax (20) 219445; e-mail sg@atu-uat.org; internet www.atu-uat.org; f. 1999 as successor to Pan-African Telecommunications Union (f. 1977); promotes the rapid development of information communications in Africa, with the aim of making Africa an equal participant in the global information society; works towards universal service and access and full inter-country connectivity; promotes development and adoption of appropriate policies and regulatory frameworks; promotes financing of development; encourages co-operation between members and the exchange of information; advocates the harmonization of telecommunications policies; mems: in 46 countries; Sec.-Gen. AKOSSI AKOSSI.

Arab Permanent Postal Commission: c/o Arab League Bldg, Tahrir Sq., Cairo, Egypt; tel. (2) 5750511; fax (2) 5775626; f. 1952; aims to establish stricter postal relations between the Arab countries than those laid down by the Universal Postal Union, and to pursue the development and modernization of postal services in member countries; publs *APU Bulletin* (monthly), *APU Review* (quarterly), *APU News* (annually).

Arab Telecommunications Union: POB 2397, Baghdad, Iraq; tel. (1) 555-0642; f. 1953 to co-ordinate and develop telecommunications between member countries to exchange technical aid and encourage research; promotes establishment of new cable telecommunications networks in the region; Sec.-Gen. ABDUL JAFFAR HASSAN KHALAF IBRAHIM AL-ANI; publs *Arab Telecommunications Union Journal* (2 a year), *Economic and Technical Studies.*

Asia-Pacific Telecommunity: No. 12/49, Soi 5, Chaengwattana Rd, Thungsonghong, Bangkok 10210, Thailand; tel. (2) 573-0044; fax (2) 573-7479; e-mail aptmail@aptsec.org; internet www.aptsec.org; f. 1979 to cover all matters relating to telecommunications in the region; mems: Afghanistan, Australia, Bangladesh, Brunei, the People's Republic of China, India, Indonesia, Iran, Japan, the Republic of Korea, Laos, Malaysia, Maldives, Myanmar, Nauru, Nepal, Pakistan, the Philippines, Singapore, Sri Lanka, Thailand, Viet Nam; assoc. mems: Cook Islands, Hong Kong; two affiliated mems each in Indonesia, Japan and Thailand, three in the Republic of Korea, four in Hong Kong, one in Maldives and six in the Philippines; Exec. Dir AMARENDRA NARAYAN.

Asian-Pacific Postal Union: Post Office Bldg, 1000 Manila, Philippines; tel. (2) 470760; fax (2) 407448; f. 1962 to extend, facilitate and improve the postal relations between the member countries and to promote co-operation in the field of postal services; mems: 23 countries; Dir JORGE SARMIENTO; publs *Annual Report, Exchange Program of Postal Officials, APPU Newsletter.*

European Conference of Postal and Telecommunications Administrations: Ministry of Transport and Communications, Odos Xenofontos 13, 10191 Athens, Greece; tel. (1) 9236494; fax (1) 9237133; internet www.cept.org; f. 1959 to strengthen relations between member administrations and to harmonize and improve their technical services; set up Eurodata Foundation, for research and publishing; mems: 26 countries; Sec. Z. PROTOPSALTI; publ. *Bulletin.*

European Telecommunications Satellite Organization (EUTELSAT): 70 rue Balard, 75502, Paris Cédex 15, France; tel. 1-53-98-47-47; fax 1-53-98-37-00; internet www.eutelsat.com; f. 1977 to operate satellites for fixed and mobile communications in Europe; EUTELSAT's in-orbit resource comprises 18 satellites; commercialises capacity in three satellites operated by other companies; mems: public and private telecommunications operations in 47 countries; Chair. and CEO GIULIANO BERRETTA.

INMARSAT (International Mobile Satellite Organization): 99 City Rd, London, EC1Y 1AX, United Kingdom; tel. (20) 7728-1000; fax (20) 7728-1044; internet www.inmarsat.org; f. 1979, as International Maritime Satellite Organization, to provide (from February 1982) global communications for shipping via satellites on a commercial basis; satellites in geo-stationary orbit over the Atlantic, Indian and Pacific Oceans provide telephone, telex, facsimile, telegram, low to high speed data services and distress and safety communications for ships of all nations and structures such as oil rigs; in 1985 the operating agreement was amended to include aeronautical communications, and in 1988 amendments were approved which allow provision of global land-mobile communications; in April 1999 INMARSAT was transferred to the private sector and became a limited company; an intergovernmental secretariat was to be maintained to monitor INMARSAT's public service obligations; mems: 86 countries; Chair. and CEO ANDY SUKAWATY.

International Telecommunications Satellite Organization (INTELSAT): 3400 International Drive, NW, Washington, DC 20008-3098, USA; tel. (202) 944-6800; fax (202) 944-7860; internet www.intelsat.com; f. 1964 to establish a global commercial satellite communications system; Assembly of Parties attended by representatives of member governments, meets every two years to consider policy and long-term aims and matters of interest to members as sovereign states; meeting of Signatories to the Operating Agreement held annually; 24 INTELSAT satellites in geosynchronous orbit provide a global communications service; provides most of the world's overseas traffic; in 1998 INTELSAT agreed to establish a private enterprise, incorporated in the Netherlands, to administer six satellite services; mems: 143 governments; Dir-Gen. and Chief Exec. CONNY L. KULLMAN (Sweden).

Internet Corporation for Assigned Names and Numbers (ICANN): 4676 Admiralty Way, Suite 330, Marina del Rey, CA 90292-6601, USA; tel. (310) 823-9358; fax (310) 823-8649; e-mail icann@icann.org; internet www.icann.org; f. 1998; non-profit, private-sector body; aims to co-ordinate the technical management and policy development of the internet; comprises three Supporting Organizations to assist, review and develop recommendations on internet policy and structure relating to addresses, domain names, and protocol; Pres. and CEO PAUL TWOMEY (Australia).

Pacific Telecommunications Council (PTC): 2454 S. Beretania St, 302 Honolulu, HI 96826, USA; tel. (808) 941-3789; fax (808) 944-4874; e-mail info@ptc.org; internet www.ptc.org; f. 1980 to promote the development, understanding and beneficial use of telecommunications and information systems/services throughout the Pacific region; provides forum for users and providers of communications services; sponsors annual conference and seminars; mems: 650 (corporate, government, academic and individual); Pres. BRUCE DRAKE (Canada).

Postal Union of the Americas, Spain and Portugal (Unión Postal de las Américas, España y Portugal): Cebollatí 1468/70, 1°, Casilla de Correos 20.042, Montevideo, Uruguay; tel. (2) 4100070; fax (2) 4105046; e-mail secretaría@upaep.com.uy; internet www.upaep.com.uy; f. 1911 to extend, facilitate and study the postal relationships of member countries; mems: 27 countries; Sec.-Gen. MARIO FELMER KLENNER (Chile).

Press, Radio and Television

Asia-Pacific Broadcasting Union (ABU): POB 1164, 59700 Kuala Lumpur, Malaysia; tel. (3) 22823592; fax (3) 22825292; e-mail info@abu.org.my; internet www.abu.org.my; f. 1964 to foster and co-ordinate the development of broadcasting in the Asia-Pacific area, to develop means of establishing closer collaboration and co-operation among broadcasting orgs, and to serve the professional needs of broadcasters in Asia and the Pacific; holds annual General Assembly; mems: 102 in 50 countries and territories; Pres. KATSUJI EBISAWA (Japan); Sec.-Gen. DAVID ASTLEY (Australia); publs *ABU News* (every 2 months), *ABU Technical Review* (every 2 months).

Association for the Promotion of the International Circulation of the Press (DISTRIPRESS): Beethovenstrasse 20, 8002 Zürich, Switzerland; tel. (1) 2024121; fax (1) 2021025; e-mail info@distripress.ch; internet www.distripress.ch; f. 1955 to assist in the promotion of the freedom of the press throughout the world, supporting and aiding UNESCO in promoting the free flow of ideas; organizes meetings of publishers and distributors of newspapers, periodicals and paperback books, to promote the exchange of information and experience among members; mems: 470 in 97 countries; Pres. JOËL FILLON (France); Man. Dir Dr PETER EMÖD (Switzerland); publs *Distripress Gazette, Who's Who.*

Association of European Journalists (AEJ): Balistraat 46, Den Haag, 2585 Netherlands; tel. (70) 3635857; fax (70) 3107217; e-mail helmut@helmuthetzel.com; internet www.aej.org; f. 1963 to participate actively in the development of a European consciousness to promote deeper knowledge of European problems and secure appreciation by the general public of the work of European institutions; to facilitate members' access to sources of European information; and to defend freedom of the press; mems: 2,100 individuals and national asscns in 25 countries; Pres. HELMUT HETZEL (Netherlands); Sec.-Gen. JURAJ ALNER (Slovakia); publ. *Newsletter.*

Association of Private European Cable Operators: 1 blvd Anspach, boîte 25, 1000 Brussels, Belgium; tel. (2) 223-25-91; fax (2)

223-06-96; internet www.apecops.org; f. 1995 to promote the interests of independent cable operators and to ensure exchange of information on cable and telecommunications; carries out research on relevant technical and legal questions; mems: 27 organizations in 19 countries; Pres. M. DE SUTTER.

Broadcasting Organization of Non-aligned Countries (BONAC): c/o Cyprus Broadcasting Corpn, POB 4824, 1397 Nicosia, Cyprus; tel. (2) 422231; fax (2) 314050; e-mail rik@cybc.com.cy; f. 1977 to ensure an equitable, objective and comprehensive flow of information through broadcasting; Secretariat moves to the broadcasting organization of host country; mems: in 102 countries.

European Alliance of News Agencies: Norrbackagatan 23, 11341 Stockholm; tel. (8) 301-324; e-mail erik-n@telia.com; internet www.pressalliance.com; f. 1957 as European Alliance of Press Agencies (name changed 2002); aims to promote co-operation among members and to study and protect their common interests; annual assembly; mems: in 30 countries; Pres. PAUL TESSELAAR; Sec.-Gen. ERIK NYLÉN.

European Broadcasting Union (EBU): CP 45, Ancienne-Route 17A, 1218 Grand-Saconnex, Geneva, Switzerland; tel. (22) 7172111; fax (22) 7474000; e-mail ebu@ebu.ch; internet www.ebu.ch; f. 1950 in succession to the International Broadcasting Union; a professional asscn of broadcasting organizations, supporting the interests of members and assisting the development of broadcasting in all its forms; activities include the Eurovision news and programme exchanges and the Euroradio music exchanges; mems: 72 active (European) in 52 countries, and 50 associate in 30 countries; Pres. ARNE WESSBERG (Finland); Sec.-Gen. JEAN RÉVEILLON (France); publs *EBU Technical Review* (annually), *Dossiers* (2 a year).

IFRA: Washingtonplatz 1, 64287 Darmstadt, Germany; tel. (6151) 7336; fax (6151) 733800; e-mail info@ifra.com; internet www.ifra .com; f. 1961 as Inca-Fiej Research Asscn to develop methods and techniques for the newspaper industry to evaluate standard specifications for raw materials for use in newspaper production; and to investigate economy and quality improvements for newspaper printing and publishing; mems: more than 1,300 newspapers, 400 suppliers; Pres. WILLEM O. KOK; Man. Dir REINER MITTELBACH; publ. *Newspaper Techniques* (monthly, in English, French and German).

Inter-American Press Association (IAPA) (Sociedad Interamericana de Prensa): Jules Dubois Bldg, 1801 SW 3rd Ave, Miami, FL 33129, USA; tel. (305) 634-2465; fax (305) 635-2272; e-mail info@ sipiapa.org; internet www.sipiapa.org; f. 1942 to guard the freedom of the press in the Americas to promote and maintain the dignity, rights and responsibilities of the profession of journalism; to foster a wider knowledge and greater interchange among the peoples of the Americas; mems: 1,400; Exec. Dir JULIO E. MUÑOZ; publ. *IAPA News* (monthly).

International Association of Broadcasting (Asociación Internacional de Radiodifusión—AIR): Edif. Torre Uruguay, Cnel Brandzen 1961, Of. 402, 11200 Montevideo, Uruguay; tel. (2) 4088129; fax (2) 4088121; e-mail airiab@distrinet.com.uy; internet www.airiab.com; f. 1946 to preserve free and private broadcasting to promote co-operation between the corporations and public authorities; to defend freedom of expression; mems: national asscns of broadcasters; Pres. Dr LUIS H. TARSITANO; Dir-Gen. Dr HÉCTOR OSCAR AMENGUAL; publ. *La Gaceta de AIR* (every 2 months).

International Association of Sound and Audiovisual Archives: c/o Eva Fønss-Jørgensen, Statsbiblioteket, 8000 Aarhus C, Denmark; tel. 89-46-2051; fax 89-46-2220; e-mail efj@ statsbiblioteket.dk; internet www.iasa-web.org; f. 1969; supports the professional exchange of sound and audiovisual documents, and fosters international co-operation between audiovisual archives in all fields, in particular in the areas of acquisition, documentation, access, exploitation copyright, and preservation; holds annual conference; mems: 410 individuals and institutions in 48 countries; Sec.-Gen. EVA FØNSS-JØRGENSEN; publs *IASA Journal* (2 a year), *IASA Information Bulletin* (quarterly).

International Catholic Union of the Press (Union catholique internationale de la presse—UCIP): 37–39 rue de Vermont, Case Postale 197, 1211 Geneva 20, Switzerland; tel. (22) 7340017; fax (22) 7340053; e-mail helo@ucip.ch; internet www.ucip.ch; f. 1927 to link all Catholics who influence public opinion through the press, to inspire a high standard of professional conscience and to represent the interest of the Catholic press at international organizations; mems: Federation of Catholic Press Agencies, Federation of Catholic Journalists, Federation of Catholic Dailies, Federation of Catholic Periodicals, Federation of Teachers in the Science and Technics of Information, Federation of Church Press Associations, Federation of Book Publishers, eight regional asscns; Pres. RERESA EE-CHOOI; Sec.-Gen. JOSEPH CHITTILAPPILLY (India); publ. *UCIP-Information*.

International Council for Film, Television and Audiovisual Communication (Conseil international du cinema de la television et de la communication audiovisuelle): 1 rue Miollis, 75732 Paris

Cédex 15, France; tel. 1-45-68-48-55; fax 1-45-67-28-40; e-mail cict@ unesco.org; internet www.unesco.org/iftc; f. 1958 to support collaboration between UNESCO and professionals engaged in cinema, television and audiovisual communications; mems: 36 international film and television organizations; Pres. HISANORI ISOMURA; Sec.-Gen. GUILIO C. GIORDANO; publ. *Letter of Information* (monthly).

International Council of French-speaking Radio and Television Organizations (Conseil international des radios-télévisions d'expression française): 52 blvd Auguste-Reyers, 1044 Brussels, Belgium; tel. (2) 732-45-85; fax (2) 732-62-40; e-mail cirtef@rtlf.be; internet www.cirtef.org; f. 1978 to establish links between French-speaking radio and television organizations; mems: 46 organizations; Pres. TORIDEN CHELLAPERMAL (Mauritius); Sec.-Gen. GUILA THIAM (Senegal).

International Federation of Film Critics (Fédération Internationale de la Presse Cinématographique—FIPRESCI): Schleissheimerstr. 83, 80797 Munich, Germany; tel. (89) 182303; fax (89) 184766; e-mail info@fipresci.org; internet www.fipresci.org; f. 1930 to develop the cinematographic press and promote cinema as an art; organizes international meetings and juries in film festivals; mems: national organizations or corresponding members in 68 countries; Pres. MICHEL CIMENT (France); Sec.-Gen. KLAUS EDER (Germany).

International Federation of Press Cutting Agencies: Streulistr. 19, POB 8030 Zürich, Switzerland; tel. (1) 3888200; fax (1) 3888201; e-mail fibep@bluewin.ch; f. 1953 to improve the standing of the profession, prevent infringements, illegal practices and unfair competition; and to develop business and friendly relations among press cuttings agencies throughout the world; mems: 81 agencies; Pres. CARLOS BEGAS (Israel); Gen. Sec. THOMAS HENNE (Switzerland).

International Federation of the Periodical Press (FIPP): Queen's House, 55/56 Lincoln's Inn Fields, London, WC2A 3LJ, United Kingdom; tel. (20) 7404-4169; fax (20) 7404-4170; e-mail info@fipp.com; internet www.fipp.com; f. 1925; works through national asscns to promote optimum conditions for the development of periodical publishing; fosters formal and informal alliances between magazine publishers; mems: 42 national asscns, 104 publishing cos and 31 assoc. mems; Pres. and CEO DONALD KUMMERFELD; publ. *Magazine World* (6 a year).

International Federation of the Socialist and Democratic Press: CP 737, 1-2021 Milan, Italy; tel. (02) 8050105; f. 1953 to promote co-operation between editors and publishers of socialist newspapers; affiliated to the Socialist International; mems: about 100; Sec. UMBERTO GIOVINE.

International Institute of Communications: Regent House, 24/25 Nutford Place, London, W1H 5YN, United Kingdom; tel. (20) 7323-9622; fax (20) 7323-9623; e-mail enquiries@iicom.org; internet www.iicom.org; f. 1969 (as the International Broadcast Institute) to link all working in the field of communications, including policy makers, broadcasters, industrialists and engineers; holds local, regional and international meetings; undertakes research; mems: over 1,000 corporate, institutional and individual; Pres. BERNARD COURTOIS (Canada); Dir-Gen. BRIAN QUINN; publs *Intermedia* (quarterly).

International Maritime Radio Association: South Bank House, Black Prince Rd, London, SE1 7SJ, United Kingdom; tel. (20) 7587-1245; fax (20) 7587-1436; e-mail secgen@cirm.org; internet www .cirm.org; f. 1928 to study and develop means of improving marine radio communications and radio aids to marine navigation; mems: over 80 organizations and companies from the major maritime nations involved in marine electronics in the areas of radio communications and navigation; Pres. BRUNO MUSELLA (Italy); Sec.-Gen. and Chair. of Technical Cttee MICHAEL RAMBAUT.

International Press Institute (IPI): Spiegelgasse 2/29, 1010 Vienna, Austria; tel. (1) 5129011; fax (1) 5129014; e-mail ipi@ freemedia.at; internet www.freemedia.at; f. 1951 as a non-governmental organization of editors, publishers and news broadcasters supporting the principles of a free and responsible press; aims to defend press freedom; conducts training programmes and research; maintains a library; holds regional meetings and an annual World Congress; mems: about 2,000 from 110 countries; Pres. WILFRED KIBORO (Kenya); Dir JOHANN FRITZ (Austria); publs *IPI Global Journalist* (quarterly), *World Press Freedom Review* (annually).

International Press Telecommunications Council (IPTC): Royal Albert House, Sheet St, Windsor, Berks, SL4 1BE, United Kingdom; tel. (1753) 705051; fax (1753) 831541; e-mail m_director_iptc@iptc.org; internet www.iptc.org; f. 1965 to safeguard and promote the interests of the Press on all matters relating to telecommunications; keeps its members informed of current and future telecommunications developments; acts as the news information formal standards body; meets three times a year and maintains four committees and 10 working parties; mems: 44 press asscns, newspapers, news agencies and industry vendors; Chair. JOHN IOBST;

Man. Dir MICHAEL STEIDL; publs *IPTC Spectrum* (annually), *IPTC Mirror* (monthly).

Latin-American Catholic Press Union: Apdo Postal 17-21-178, Quito, Ecuador; tel. (2) 548-046; fax (2) 501-658; f. 1959 to co-ordinate, promote and improve the Catholic press in Latin America; mems: national asscns and local groups in most Latin American countries; Pres. ISMAR DE OLIVEIRA SOARES (Brazil); Sec. CARLOS EDUARDO CORTÉS (Colombia).

Organization of Asia-Pacific News Agencies (OANA): c/o Xinhua News Agency, 57 Xuanwumen Xidajie, Beijing 100803, People's Republic of China; tel. (10) 3074762; fax (10) 3072707; internet www.oananews.com; f. 1961 to promote co-operation in professional matters and mutual exchange of news, features, etc. among the news agencies of Asia and the Pacific via the Asia-Pacific News Network (ANN); mems: Anadolu Ajansi (Turkey), Antara (Indonesia), APP (Pakistan), Bakhtar (Afghanistan), BERNAMA (Malaysia), BSS (Bangladesh), ENA (Bangladesh), Hindustan Samachar (India), IRNA (Iran), ITAR-TASS (Russia), Kaz-TAG (Kazakhstan), KABAR (Kyrgyzstan), KCNA (Korea, Democratic People's Republic), KPL (Laos), Kyodo (Japan), Lankapuvath (Sri Lanka), Montsame (Mongolia), PNA (Philippines), PPI (Pakistan), PTI (India), RSS (Nepal), Samachar Bharati (India), TNA (Thailand), UNB (Bangladesh), UNI (India), Viet Nam News Agency, Xinhua (People's Republic of China), Yonhap (Republic of Korea); Pres. GUO CHAOREN; Sec.-Gen. MIKHAIL GUSMANN.

Press Foundation of Asia: POB 1843, S & L Bldg, 3rd Floor, 1500 Roxas Blvd, Manila, Philippines; tel. (2) 5233223; fax (2) 5224365; e-mail pfa@pressasia.org; internet www.pressasia.org; f. 1967; an independent, non-profit-making organization governed by its newspaper members; acts as a professional forum for about 200 newspapers in Asia; aims to reduce cost of newspapers to potential readers, to improve editorial and management techniques through research and training programmes and to encourage the growth of the Asian press; operates *Depthnews* feature service; mems: 200 newspapers; Exec. Chair. MAZLAN NORDIN (Malaysia); Chief Exec. MOCHTAR LUBIS (Indonesia); publs *Pressasia* (quarterly), *Asian Women* (quarterly).

Reporters sans Frontières: 5 rue Geoffroy Marie, 75009 Paris, France; tel. 1-44-83-84-84; fax 1-45-23-11-51; e-mail rsf@rsf.org; internet www.rsf.org; f. 1985 to defend press freedom throughout the world; generates awareness of violations of press freedoms and supports journalists under threat or imprisoned as a result of their work; mems in 77 countries; Dir ROBERT MÉNARD; publs *Annual Report*, *La Lettre de Reporters sans Frontières* (6 a year).

Union of National Radio and Television Organizations of Africa (URTNA): 101 rue Carnot, BP 3237, Dakar, Senegal; tel. 821-16-25; fax 822-51-13; e-mail urtnadkr@telecomplus.sn; f. 1962; co-ordinates radio and television services, including monitoring and frequency allocation, the exchange of information and coverage of national and international events among African countries; maintains programme exchange centre (Nairobi, Kenya), technical centre (Bamako, Mali), a centre for rural radio studies (Ouagadougou, Burkina Faso) and a centre for the exchange of television news (Algiers, Algeria); mems: 48 organizations and six associate members; Sec.-Gen. ABDELHAMID BOUKSANI; publ. *URTNA Review* (2 a year, in English and French).

World Association for Christian Communication (WACC): 357 Kennington Lane, London, SE11 5QY, United Kingdom; tel. (20) 7582-9139; fax (20) 7735-0340; e-mail wacc@wacc.org.uk; internet www.wacc.org.uk; f. 1975 to promote human dignity, justice and peace through freedom of expression and the democratization of communication; offers professional guidance on communication policies; interprets developments in and the consequences of global communication methods; works towards the empowerment of women; assists the training of Christian communicators; mems: more than 800 corporate and personal mems in 115 countries, organized in eight regional asscns; Pres. ALBERT VAN DEN HEUVEL; Gen.-Sec. R. L. NAYLOR; publs *Action*, newsletter (10 a year), *Media Development* (quarterly), *Communication Resource*, *Media and Gender Monitor* (both occasional).

World Association of Newspapers (WAN): 7 rue Geoffroy Saint Hilaire, 75005 Paris, France; tel. 1-47-42-85-00; fax 1-47-42-49-48; e-mail tbalding@wan.asso.fr; internet www.wan-press.org; f. 1948 to defend the freedom of the press, to safeguard the ethical and economic interests of newspapers and to study all questions of interest to newspapers at international level; mems: 71 national newspaper asscns, individual newspaper executives in 100 countries, 13 news agencies and nine regional and world-wide press groups; Pres. SEOK HYUN HONG (Republic of Korea); Dir-Gen. TIMOTHY BALDING; publ. *Newsletter*.

Religion

Agudath Israel World Organisation: Hacherut Sq., POB 326, Jerusalem 91002, Israel; tel. (2) 5384357; fax (2) 5383634; f. 1912 to help solve the problems facing Jewish people all over the world in the spirit of the Jewish tradition; holds World Congress (every five years) and an annual Central Council; mems: over 500,000 in 25 countries; Chair. J. M. ABRAMOWITZ (Jerusalem); Secs Rabbi MOSHE GEWIRTZ, Rabbi CHAIM WEINSTOCK; publs *Hamodia* (Jerusalem daily newspaper, in Hebrew; weekly in English), *Jewish Tribune* (London, weekly), *Jewish Observer* (New York, monthly), *Dos Yiddishe Vort* (New York, monthly), *Coalition* (New York), *Perspectives* (Toronto, monthly), *La Voz Judia* (Buenos Aires, monthly), *Jüdische Stimme* (Zürich, monthly).

All Africa Conference of Churches (AACC): POB 14205, 00800 Westlands, Nairobi, Kenya; tel. (20) 4441483; fax (20) 4443241; e-mail secretariat@aacc-ceta.org; f. 1963; an organ of co-operation and continuing fellowship among Protestant, Orthodox and independent churches and Christian Councils in Africa; 2003 Assembly: Yaoundé, Cameroon; mems: 169 churches and affiliated Christian councils in 39 African countries; Pres. The Right Rev. Dr NYANSAKO-NI-NKU (Cameroon); Gen. Sec. Rev. Dr MVUME DANDALA (South Africa); publs *ACIS/APS Bulletin*, *Tam Tam*.

Alliance Israélite Universelle (AIU): 45 rue La Bruyère, 75425 Paris Cédex 09, France; tel. 1-53-32-88-55; fax 1-48-74-51-33; e-mail info@aiu.org; internet www.aiu.org; f. 1860 to work for the emancipation and moral progress of the Jews; maintains 40 schools in eight countries; library of 120,000 vols; mems: 8,000 in 16 countries; Pres. ADY STEG; Dir JEAN-JACQUES WAHL (France); publs *Les Cahiers de l'Alliance Israélite Universelle* (3 a year, in French), *Les Cahiers du Judaïsme*, *The Alliance Review* (in English).

Bahá'í International Community: Bahá'í World Centre, POB 155, 31 001 Haifa, Israel; tel. (4) 8358394; fax (4) 8313312; e-mail opi@bwc.org; internet www.bahai.org; f. 1844 in Persia to promote the unity of mankind and world peace through the teachings of the Bahá'í religion, including the equality of men and women and the elimination of all forms of prejudice; maintains schools for children and adults world-wide, operates educational and cultural radio stations in the USA, Asia and Latin America; has 32 publishing trusts throughout the world; governing body: Universal House of Justice (nine mems elected by 182 National Spiritual Assemblies); mems: in 111,000 local communities (in 190 countries and 45 dependent territories or overseas departments); Sec.-Gen. ALBERT LINCOLN (USA); publs *Bahá'í World* (annually), *One Country* (quarterly, in 6 languages).

Baptist World Alliance: 405 North Washington St, Falls Church, VA 22046, USA; tel. (703) 790-8980; fax (703) 893-5160; e-mail bwa@bwanet.org; internet www.bwanet.org; f. 1905; aims to unite Baptists, lead in evangelism, respond to people in need and defend human rights; mems: 191 Baptist unions and conventions comprising 42m. people in 200 countries and territories; Pres. BILLY JANG HURAN KIM (Republic of Korea); Gen. Sec. Dr DENTON LOTZ; publ. *The Baptist World* (quarterly).

Caribbean Conference of Churches: 8 Gallus St, Woodbrook, POB 876, Port of Spain, Trinidad and Tobago; tel. 623-0588; fax 624-9002; e-mail ccchq@tstt.net.tt; internet www.cariblife.com/pub/ccc; f. 1973; holds Assembly every five years; the recognized Regional Ecumenical Organization of the Caribbean and a major development agency in the region; initiatives include human development programmes (designated as Priority Regional Initiatives), sustainable socio-economic development programmes, an advocacy and communications programme and the international relations programme; maintains the Caribbean Ecumenical Institute; mems: 34 churches; Gen. Sec. GERARD GRANADO; publ. *Ecuscope Caribbean*.

Christian Conference of Asia (CCA): 96, 2nd District, Pak Tin Village, Mei Tin Rd, Shatin, NT, Hong Kong; tel. 26911068; fax 26924378; e-mail cca@cca.org.hkt; internet www.cca.org.hk; f. 1957 (present name adopted 1973) to promote co-operation and joint study in matters of common concern among the Churches of the region and to encourage interaction with other regional Conferences and the World Council of Churches; mems: more than 100 churches and councils of churches from 18 Asian countries; Gen. Sec. Dr AHN JAE WOONG; publ. *CCA News* (quarterly).

Christian Peace Conference: Prokopova 4, 130 00 Prague 3, Czech Republic; tel. (2) 22781800; fax (2) 22781801; e-mail christianpeace@volny.cz; internet www.volny.cz/christianpeace; f. 1958 as an international movement of theologians, clergy and lay-people, aiming to bring Christendom to recognize its share of guilt in both world wars and to dedicate itself to the service of friendship, reconciliation and peaceful co-operation of nations, to concentrate on united action for peace and justice, and to co-ordinate peace groups in individual churches and facilitate their effective participation in the peaceful development of society; works through five continental asscns, regional groups and member churches in many countries; Moderator Dr Sergio Arce Martínez; Co-ordinator Rev. Brian G. Cooper; publs *CPC Information* (8 a year in English and German), occasional *Study Volume*.

Conference of European Churches (CEC): POB 2100, 150 route de Ferney, 1211 Geneva 2, Switzerland; tel. (22) 7916111; fax (22) 7916227; e-mail cec@cec-kek.org; internet www.cec-kek.org; f. 1959 as a regional ecumenical organization for Europe and a meeting-place for European churches, including members and non-members of the World Council of Churches; holds assemblies every six years; mems: 125 Protestant, Anglican, Orthodox and Old Catholic churches in all European countries; Gen. Sec. Rev. Dr Keith Clements; publs *Monitor* (quarterly), CEC communiqués, reports.

Conference of International Catholic Organizations: 37–39 rue de Vermont, 1202 Geneva, Switzerland; tel. (22) 7338392; internet www.oic-ico.org; f. 1927 to encourage collaboration and agreement between the different Catholic international organizations in their common interests, and to contribute to international understanding; organizes international assemblies and meetings to study specific problems; permanent commissions deal with human rights, the new international economic order, social problems, the family health, education, etc.; mems: some 40 Catholic international organizations; Pres. Ernest Koenig.

Consultative Council of Jewish Organizations (CCJO): 420 Lexington Ave, New York, NY 10170, USA; tel. (212) 808-5437; f. 1946 to co-operate and consult with the UN and other international bodies directly concerned with human rights and to defend the cultural, political and religious rights of Jews throughout the world; Sec.-Gen. Warren Green (USA).

European Baptist Federation (EBF): Postfach 610340, 22423 Hamburg, Germany; tel. (40) 5509723; fax (40) 5509725; e-mail office@ebf.org; internet www.ebf.org; f. 1949 to promote fellowship and co-operation among Baptists in Europe to further the aims and objects of the Baptist World Alliance; to stimulate and co-ordinate evangelism in Europe; to provide for consultation and planning of missionary work in Europe and elsewhere in the world; mems: 49 Baptist Unions in European countries and the Middle East; Pres. David Coffey; Sec.-Treas. Rev. Karl-Heinz Walter (Germany).

European Evangelical Alliance: Wilhelmshoeher Allee 258, 34131 Kassel, Germany; tel. (561) 3149711; fax (561) 9387520; e-mail 100341.550@compuserve.com; internet www.hfe.org; f. 1953 to promote understanding and co-operation among evangelical Christians in Europe and to stimulate evangelism; mems: 25 national alliances from 24 countries, 6 pan-European asscns; Pres. Derek Copley (UK); Sec. Gordon Showell-Rogers.

Federation of Jewish Communities of the CIS: 5A 2nd Vysheslavtzev Pereulok, Moscow, Russia; tel. (095) 737-8275; fax (095) 681-6316; e-mail info@fjc.ru; internet www.fjc.ru; f. 1998 to restore Jewish society, culture and religion throughout the countries of the fmr Soviet Union through the provision of professional assistance, educational support and funding to member communities; Pres. Lev Leviev.

Friends World Committee for Consultation: 4 Byng Pl., London, WC1E 7LE, United Kingdom; tel. (20) 7388-0497; fax (20) 7383-4644; e-mail world@fwcc.quaker.org; internet www.quaker.org/fwcc/; f. 1937 to encourage and strengthen the spiritual life within the Religious Society of Friends (Quakers) to help Friends to a better understanding of their vocation in the world; and to promote consultation among Friends of all countries; representation at the United Nations as a non-governmental organization with general consultative status; mems: appointed representatives and individuals from 70 countries; Gen. Sec. Elizabeth Duke; publs *Friends World News* (2 a year), *Calendar of Yearly Meetings* (annually), *Quakers around the World* (handbook).

Initiatives of Change International: POB 3, 1211 Geneva 20, Switzerland; tel. (22) 7335668; fax (22) 7330267; e-mail iofc.int-gva@caux.ch; internet www.iofc.org; f. 1921; an international network specializing in conflict resolution that is open to people of all cultures, nationalities, religions and beliefs, and works towards change, both locally and globally, commencing at the personal level; has special consultative status with ECOSOC and participatory status with the Council of Europe; supports and publicizes the grassroots work of the National Societies of Initiatives of Change; works in 60 countries; Pres. of Swiss foundation Cornelio Sommaruga; publs *Changer International* (French, 6 a year), *For a Change* (English, 6 a year), *Caux Information* (German, monthly).

International Association for Religious Freedom (IARF): 2 Market St, Oxford OX1 3EF, United Kingdom; tel. (1865) 202-744; fax (1865) 202-746; e-mail hq@iarf.net; internet iarf-religiousfreedom.net; f. 1900 as a world community of religions, subscribing to the principle of openness and upholding the United Nation's Universal Declaration on freedom of religion or belief; conducts religious freedom programmes, focusing on inter-religious

harmony; holds regional conferences and triennial congress; mems: 100 groups in 27 countries; Pres. Ellen Campbell (Canada); Gen. Sec. Andrew C. Clark (UK); publ. *IARF World* (2 a year).

International Association of Buddhist Studies (IABS): c/o Prof. T. J. F. Tillemans, Section des langues et civilisations orientales, Université de Lausanne, 1015 Lausanne, Switzerland; tel. (761) 2033158; fax (761) 2033152; e-mail iabs.treasurer@orient.unil.ch; f. 1976; supports studies of Buddhist religion, philosophy and literature; holds international conference every three or four years; Gen. Sec. Tom J. F. Tillemans; publ. *Journal* (2 a year).

International Council of Christians and Jews (ICCJ): Martin Buber House, Werléstrasse 2, 64646 Heppenheim, Germany; tel. (6252) 93120; fax (6252) 68331; e-mail iccj_buberhouse@t-online.de; internet www.iccj.org; f. 1947 to promote mutual respect and co-operation; holds annual international colloquium, seminars, meetings for young people and for women; maintains a forum for Jewish–Christian–Muslim relations; mems: 36 national councils in 32 countries; Pres. Rev. Prof. John T. Pawilowski; Sec.-Gen. Rev. Friedhelm Pieper; publs *ICCJ History*, *ICCJ Brochure*, conference documents.

International Council of Jewish Women: POB 12130, Local 4, Montevideo, Uruguay; tel. and fax (2) 6285874; e-mail icjw@montevideo.org.uy; internet www.icjw.org; f. 1912 to promote friendly relations and understanding among Jewish women throughout the world; campaigns for human and women's rights, exchanges information on community welfare activities, promotes volunteer leadership, sponsors field work in social welfare, co-sponsors the International Jewish Women's Human Rights Watch and fosters Jewish education; mems: affiliates totalling over 1.5m. members in 46 countries; Pres. Sara Winkowski; publs *Newsletter*, *Links around the World* (2 a year, English and Spanish), *International Jewish Women's Human Rights Watch* (2 a year).

International Fellowship of Reconciliation (IFOR): Spoorstraat 38, 1815 BK Alkmaar, Netherlands; tel. (72) 512-30-14; fax (72) 515-11-02; e-mail office@ifor.org; internet www.ifor.org; f. 1919; international, spiritually-based movement committed to active non-violence as a way of life and as a means of building a culture of peace and non-violence; maintains branches, affiliates and groups in more than 50 countries; Int. Pres. John Sisson (Switzerland); publs *IFOR in Action* (quarterly), *Patterns in Reconciliation*, *Cross the Lines* (3 a year, in Arabic, English, French, Russian and Spanish), occasional paper series.

International Humanist and Ethical Union (IHEU): 47 Theobald's Rd, London, WC1X 8SP, United Kingdom; tel. (20) 7831-4817; fax (20) 7404-8641; internet www.iheu.org; f. 1952 to bring into asscn all those interested in promoting ethical and scientific humanism and human rights; mems: national organizations and individuals in 37 countries; Exec. Dir Babu R. R. Gogineni; publ. *International Humanist News* (quarterly).

International Organization for the Study of the Old Testament: c/o Prof. Gordon, St Catharine's College, Cambridge CB2 1RL, United Kingdom; tel. (1223) 335118; fax (1223) 335110; f. 1950; holds triennial congresses; Pres. Prof. A. van der Kooij (Netherlands); Sec. Prof. R. P. Gordon (UK); publ. *Vetus Testamentum* (quarterly).

Latin American Council of Churches (Consejo Latinoamericano de Iglesias—CLAI): Casilla 17-08-8522, Calle Inglaterra N.32–113 y Mariana de Jesús, Quito, Ecuador; tel. and fax (2) 2553996; fax (2) 2529933; e-mail israel@clai.org.ec; internet www.clai.org.ec; f. 1982; mems: 147 churches in 19 countries; Gen. Sec. Rev. Israel Batista.

Latin American Episcopal Council (Consejo Episcopal Latinoamericano—CELAM): Apartado Aéreo 51086, Santafé de Bogotá, Colombia; tel. (1) 612-1620; fax (1) 612-1929; e-mail celam@celam.org; internet www.celam.org; f. 1955 to co-ordinate Church activities in and with the Latin American and the Caribbean Catholic Bishops' Conferences; mems: 22 Episcopal Conferences of Central and South America and the Caribbean; Pres. Cardinal Francisco Javier Errázuriz O.; publ. *Boletín* (a a year).

Lutheran World Federation: 150 route de Ferney, POB 2100, 1211 Geneva 2, Switzerland; tel. (22) 7916111; fax (22) 7916111; e-mail info@lutheranworld.org; internet www.lutheranworld.org; f. 1947; groups 128 Lutheran Churches in 70 countries; provides inter-church aid and relief work in various areas of the globe; gives service to refugees, including resettlement; carries out theological research, conferences and exchanges; grants scholarship aid in various fields of church life; conducts inter-confessional dialogue with Roman Catholic, Seventh-day Adventist, Anglican and Orthodox churches; Pres. Rt Rev. Dr Christian Krause (Germany); Gen. Sec. Rev. Dr Ishmael Noko (Zimbabwe); publs *Lutheran World Information* (English and German, daily e-mail news service and monthly print edition), *LWF Today* and *LWF Documentation* (both irregular).

Middle East Council of Churches: Makhoul St, Deep Bldg, POB 5376, Beirut, Lebanon; tel. and fax (1) 344894; internet www.mecchurches.org; f. 1974; mems: 28 churches; Pres Pope Shenoudah,

III; Rev. Dr Selim Sahyouni; Archbishop Kyrillos Bustros; Gen. Sec. Rev. Dr Riad Jarjour; publs *MECC News Report* (monthly), *Al Montada News Bulletin* (quarterly, in Arabic), *Courrier oecuménique du Moyen-Orient* (quarterly), *MECC Perspectives* (3 a year).

Muslim World League (MWL) (Rabitat al-Alam al-Islami): POB 537, Makkah, Saudi Arabia; tel. (2) 5600919; fax (2) 5601319; e-mail info@muslimworldleague.org; internet www.muslimworldleague .org; f. 1962; aims to advance Islamic unity and solidarity, and to promote world peace and respect for human rights; provides financial assistance for education, medical care and relief work; has 30 offices throughout the world; Sec.-Gen. Dr Abdullah bin Abdulmoshin al-Turki; publs *Al-Aalam al Islami* (weekly, Arabic), *Dawat al-Haq* (monthly).

Opus Dei (Prelature of the Holy Cross and Opus Dei): Viale Bruno Buozzi 73, 00197 Rome, Italy; tel. (06) 808961; e-mail newyork@ opusdei.org; internet www.opusdei.org; f. 1928 by St Josemaría Escrivá de Balaguer to spread, at every level of society, an increased awareness of the universal call to sanctity and apostolate in the exercise of one's work; mems: 84,541 Catholic laypeople and 1,875 priests; Prelate Most Rev. Javier Echevarría; publ. *Romana (Bulletin of the Prelature)* (2 a year).

Pacific Conference of Churches: POB 208, 4 Thurston St, Suva, Fiji; tel. 3311277; fax 3303205; e-mail pacific@is.com.fj; f. 1961; organizes assembly every five years, as well as regular workshops, meetings and training seminars throughout the region; mems: 36 churches and councils; Moderator Pastor Reuben Magekon; Gen. Sec. Rev. Valamotu Palu.

Pax Romana International Catholic Movement for Intellectual and Cultural Affairs (ICMICA); and International Movement of Catholic Students (IMCS): 15 rue du Grand-Bureau, POB 315, 1211 Geneva 24, Switzerland; tel. (22) 8230707; fax (22) 8230708; e-mail miicmica@paxromana.int.ch; internet www .pax-romana.org; f. 1921 (IMCS), 1947 (ICMICA), to encourage in members an awareness of their responsibilities as people and Christians in the student and intellectual milieux to promote contacts between students and graduates throughout the world and co-ordinate the contribution of Catholic intellectual circles to international life; mems: 80 student and 60 intellectual organizations in 80 countries; ICMICA—Pres. Mary J. Mwingira (Tanzania); Gen. Sec. Anselmo Lee Seong-Hoon (Republic of Korea); IMCS—Gen. Secs Walter Prysthon (Brazil), Roland Ranaivoarison (Madagascar); publ. *Convergence* (3 a year).

Salvation Army: International HQ, 101 Queen Victoria St, London, EC4P 4EP, United Kingdom; tel. (20) 7332-0101; fax (20) 7236-4981; e-mail websa@salvationarmy.org; internet www.salvationarmy.org; f. 1865 to spread the Christian gospel and relieve poverty; emphasis is placed on the need for personal discipleship, and to make its evangelism effective it adopts a quasi-military form of organization. Social, medical and educational work is also performed in the 109 countries where the Army operates; Pres. Gen. John Larsson; Chief of Staff Commissioner Israel L. Gaither; publ. *The War Cry* (weekly).

Theosophical Society: Adyar, Chennai 600 020, India; tel. (44) 24915552; fax (44) 24902706; e-mail theossoc@satyam.net.in; internet www.ts-adyar.org; f. 1875; aims at universal brotherhood, without distinction of race, creed, sex, caste or colour; study of comparative religion, philosophy and science; investigation of unexplained laws of nature and powers latent in man; mems: 32,000 in 70 countries; Pres. Radha S. Burnier; Int. Sec. Mary Anderson; publs *The Theosophist* (monthly), *Adyar News Letter* (quarterly), *Brahmavidya* (annually).

United Bible Societies: 7th Floor, Reading Bridge House, Reading, RG1 8PJ, United Kingdom; tel. (118) 950-0200; fax (118) 950-0857; e-mail jphillips@ubs-wsc.org; internet www.biblesociety .org; f. 1946; co-ordinates the translation, production and distribution of the Bible by Bible Societies world-wide; works with national Bible Societies to develop religious programmes; mems: 136 Bible Societies in more than 200 countries; Pres. Dr Samuel Escobar (Peru/USA); Gen. Sec. Neil Crosbie (UK); publs *Bulletin (1 or 2 a year), The Bible Translator* (quarterly), *Publishing World* (3 a year), *Prayer Booklet* (annually), *Special Report* (3 or 4 a year), *World Report* (monthly).

Watch Tower Bible and Tract Society: 25 Columbia Heights, Brooklyn, NY 11201–2483, USA; tel. (718) 560-5000; internet www .watchtower.org; f. 1881; 110 branches; serves as legal agency for Jehovah's Witnesses.

World Alliance of Reformed Churches (Presbyterian and Congregational): Box 2100, 150 route de Ferney, 1211 Geneva 2, Switzerland; tel. (22) 7916240; fax (22) 7916505; e-mail sn@warc.ch; internet www.warc.ch; f. 1970 by merger of WARC (Presbyterian) (f.1875) with International Congregational Council (f. 1891) to promote fellowship among Reformed, Presbyterian and Congregational churches; mems: 214 churches in 106 countries; Pres. Prof. Choan-

Seng Song; Gen. Sec. Rev. Dr Setri Nyomi (Ghana); publs *Reformed World* (quarterly), *Up-Date*.

World Christian Life Community: Borgo S. Spirito 8, Casella Postale 6139, 00195 Rome, Italy; tel. (06) 6868079; fax (06) 6813-2497; e-mail mcvx.wclc@agora.it; f. 1953 as World Federation of the Sodalities of our Lady (first group f.1563) as a lay organization based on the teachings of Ignatius Loyola, to integrate Christian faith and daily living; mems: groups in 55 countries representing about 100,000 individuals; Pres. José María Riera; Exec. Sec. Gilles Michaud; publ. *Progressio* (in English, French and Spanish).

World Conference of Religions for Peace: 777 United Nations Plaza, New York, NY 10017, USA; tel. (212) 687-2163; fax (212) 983-0566; e-mail info@wcrp.org; internet www.wcrp.org; f. 1970 to co-ordinate education and action of various world religions for world peace and justice; mems: more than 50 inter-religious councils in Africa, Asia, Europe and Latin America; Sec.-Gen. Dr William Vendley; publ. *Religion for Peace*.

World Congress of Faiths: 125 Salusbury Rd, London, NW6 6RG, United Kingdom; tel. (20) 89593129; fax (20) 76043052; e-mail admin@worldfaiths.org; internet www.worldfaiths.org; f. 1936 to promote a spirit of fellowship among mankind through an understanding of one another's religions, to bring together people of all nationalities, backgrounds and creeds in mutual respect and tolerance, to encourage the study and understanding of issues arising out of multi-faith societies, and to promote welfare and peace; sponsors lectures, conferences, retreats, etc.; works with other interfaith organizations; mems: about 400; Pres. Rev. Marcus Braybrooke; Chair. Rabbi Jacqueline Tabick; publ. *Interreligious Insight* (quarterly), *One Family*.

World Evangelical Alliance: 141 Middle Rd 05-05, GSM Bldg, Singapore 188976, Singapore; tel. 3397900; fax 3383756; e-mail 100012.345@compuserve.com; internet www.worldevangelical.org; f. 1951 as World Evangelical Fellowship, on reorganization of World Evangelical Alliance (f. 1846), reverted to original name Jan. 2002; an int. grouping of national and regional bodies of evangelical Christians; encourages the organization of national fellowships and assists national mems in planning their activities; mems: national evangelical asscns in 110 countries; International Dir Augustin B. Vencer, Jr; publs *Evangelical World* (monthly), *Evangelical Review of Theology* (quarterly).

World Fellowship of Buddhists: 616 Benjasiri Pk, Soi Medhinivet off Soi Sukhumvit 24, Bangkok 10110, Thailand; tel. (2) 661-1284; fax (2) 661-0555; e-mail wfb-hq@asianet.co.th; internet www .wfb-hq.org; f. 1950 to promote strict observance and practice of the teachings of the Buddha; holds General Conference every 2 years; 146 regional centres in 37 countries; Pres. Phan Wannamethee; Hon. Sec.-Gen. Phallop Thaiarry; publs *WFB Journal* (6 a year), *WFB Review* (quarterly), *WFB Newsletter* (monthly), documents, booklets.

World Hindu Federation: c/o Dr Jogendra Jha, Pashupati Kshetra, Kathmandu, Nepal; tel. (1) 470182; fax (1) 470131; e-mail hem@karki.com.np; f. 1981 to promote and preserve Hindu philosophy and culture and to protect the rights of Hindus, particularly the right to worship; executive board meets annually; mems: in 45 countries and territories; Sec.-Gen. Dr Jogendra Jha (Nepal); publ. *Vishwa Hindu* (monthly).

World Jewish Congress: 501 Madison Ave, New York, NY 10022, USA; tel. (212) 755-5770; fax (212) 755-5883; internet www.wcj.org .il; f. 1936 as a voluntary asscn of representative Jewish communities and organizations throughout the world; aims to foster the unity of the Jewish people and ensure the continuity and development of their heritage; mems: Jewish communities in 84 countries; Pres. Edgar M. Bronfman; Chair. Israel Singer; publs *Gesher* (Hebrew quarterly, Israel), *Boletín Informativo OJI* (fortnightly, Buenos Aires),*World Jewry* (monthly, New York).

World Methodist Council: International Headquarters, POB 518, Lake Junaluska, NC 28745, USA; tel. (704) 456-9432; fax (704) 456-9433; e-mail georgefreeman@mindspring.com; internet www .worldmethodistcouncil.org; f. 1881 to deepen the fellowship of the Methodist peoples, encourage evangelism, foster Methodist participation in the ecumenical movement and promote the unity of Methodist witness and service; mems: 76 churches in 132 countries, comprising 38m. individuals; Gen. Sec. George H. Freeman (USA); publ. *World Parish* (quarterly).

World Sephardi Federation: 13 rue Marignac, 1206 Geneva, Switzerland; tel. (22) 3473313; fax (22) 3472839; f. 1951 to strengthen the unity of Jewry and Judaism among Sephardi and Oriental Jews, to defend and foster religious and cultural activities of all Sephardi and Oriental Jewish communities and preserve their spiritual heritage, to provide moral and material assistance where necessary and to co-operate with other similar organizations; mems: 50 communities and organizations in 33 countries; Pres. Nessim D. Gaon; Sec.-Gen. Shimon Dery.

World Student Christian Federation (WSCF): 5 route des Morillons, Grand-Saconnex, 1218 Geneva, Switzerland; tel. (22) 7988953; fax (22) 7982370; e-mail wscf@wscf.ch; internet www.wscf.org; f. 1895 to proclaim Jesus Christ as Lord and Saviour in the academic community, and to present students with the claims of the Christian faith over their whole life; holds General Assembly every four years; mems: 67 national Student Christian Movements, and 34 national correspondents; Chair. Rev. EJIKE OKORD (Nigeria); Secs-Gen. BEATE FAGERLI (Norway), LAWRENCE BREW (Ghana).

World Union for Progressive Judaism: 633 Third Ave, New York, NY 10017, USA; tel. (212) 249-0100; fax (212) 650-4099; internet wupj.org; f. 1926; promotes and co-ordinates efforts of Reform, Liberal, Progressive and Reconstructionist congregations throughout the world; supports new congregations; assigns and employs rabbis; sponsors seminaries and schools; organizes international conferences; maintains a youth section; mems: organizations and individuals in 30 countries; Pres. AUSTIN BEUTEL; Exec. Dir Rabbi RICHARD G. HIRSCH (Israel); publs *News Updates*, *International Conference Reports*, *European Judaism* (bi-annual).

World Union of Catholic Women's Organisations: 18 rue Notre-Dame-des-Champs, 75006 Paris, France; tel. 1-45-44-27-65; fax 1-42-84-04-80; e-mail wucwoparis@wanadoo.fr; internet www.wucwo.org; f. 1910 to promote and co-ordinate the contribution of Catholic women in international life, in social, civic, cultural and religious matters; mems: 20m.; Pres. MARÍA EUGENIA DÍAZ DE PFENNICH (Mexico); Sec.-Gen. GILLIAN BADCOCK (UK); publ. *Women's Voice* (quarterly, in four languages).

Science

Association for the Taxonomic Study of the Flora of Tropical Africa: National Botanic Garden of Belgium, Domein van Bouchout, 1860 Meise, Belgium; tel. (2) 260-09-28; fax (2) 260-08-45; e-mail rammeloo@br.fgov.be; f. 1950 to facilitate co-operation and liaison between botanists engaged in the study of the flora of tropical Africa south of the Sahara including Madagascar; maintains a library; mems: c. 800 botanists in 63 countries; Sec.-Gen. Prof. J. RAMMELOO; publs *AETFAT Bulletin* (annually), *Proceedings*.

Association of Geoscientists for International Development (AGID): Institute of Geoscience, University of São Paulo, Rua do Lago 562, São Paulo, 05508-900 Brazil; tel. (11) 818-4206; fax (11) 210-4958; e-mail kmellito@usp.br; internet agid.igc.usp.br; f. 1974 to encourage communication and the exchange of knowledge between those interested in the application of the geosciences to international development; contributes to the funding of geoscience development projects; provides postgraduate scholarships; mems: 2,000 individual and institutional mems in over 120 countries; Pres. Dr S. D. LIMAYE (India); Sec. Dr A. J. REEDMAN (UK); publs *Geoscience and Developments* (2 or 3 a year), reports on geoscience and development issues.

Council for the International Congresses of Entomology: c/o FAO, POB 3700 MCPO, 1277 Makati, Philippines; tel. (2) 8134229; fax (2) 8127725; e-mail joliver@gasou.edu; f. 1910 to act as a link between quadrennial congresses and to arrange the venue for each congress; the committee is also the entomology section of the International Union of Biological Sciences; Chair. Dr M. J. WHITTAM (Australia); Sec. Dr J. OLIVER (USA).

European Association of Geoscientists and Engineers (EAGE): c/o EAGE Holdings, 3990 DB Houten, Netherlands; tel. (30) 6354055; fax (30) 6343524; e-mail eage@eage.nl; internet www.eage.nl; f. 1997 by merger of European Asscn of Exploration Geophysicists and Engineers (f. 1951) and the European Asscn of Petroleum Geoscientists and Engineers (f. 1988); these two organizations have become, respectively, the Geophysical and the Petroleum Divisions of the EAGE; aims to promote the applications of geoscience and related subjects and to foster co-operation between those working or studying in the fields; organizes conferences, workshops, education programmes and exhibitions; seeks global co-operation with organizations with similar objectives; mems: approx. 5,400 in 95 countries; Exec. Dir A. VAN GERWEN; publs *Geophysical Prospecting* (6 a year), *First Break* (monthly), *Petroleum Geoscience* (quarterly).

European Atomic Forum (FORATOM): 57 rue de la Loi, 1040 Brussels, Belgium; tel. (2) 502-45-95; fax (2) 502-39-02; e-mail foratom@foratom.org; internet www.foratom.org; f. 1960; promotes the peaceful use of nuclear energy; provides information on nuclear energy issues to the EU, the media and the public; represents the nuclear industry within the EU institutions; holds periodical conferences; mems: atomic forums in 16 countries; Pres. ÉDUARDO GONZALEZ GOMEZ; Dir Gen. Dr PETER HAUG.

European Molecular Biology Organization (EMBO): Meyerhofstr. 1, Postfach 1022.40, 69012 Heidelberg, Germany; tel. (6221) 8891-0; fax (6221) 8891-200; e-mail embo@embo.org; internet www .embo.org; f. 1962 to promote collaboration in the field of molecular biology and to establish fellowships for training and research; has established the European Molecular Biology Laboratory where a majority of the disciplines comprising the subject are represented; mems: 1,200; Exec. Dir Prof. FRANK GANNON; publs *Annual Report*, *EMBO Journal* (24 a year), *EMBO Reports* (monthly).

European Organization for Nuclear Research (CERN): European Laboratory for Particle Physics, 1211 Geneva 23, Switzerland; tel. (22) 7676111; fax (22) 7676555; internet www.cern.ch; f. 1954 to provide for collaboration among European states in nuclear research of a pure scientific and fundamental character, for peaceful purposes only; Council comprises two representatives of each member state; major experimental facilities: Proton Synchrotron (of 25–28 GeV), and Super Proton Synchrotron (of 450 GeV). Budget (1998) 875m. Swiss francs; mems: 20 European countries; observers: Israel, Japan, Russia, Turkey, USA, European Commission, UNESCO; Dir-Gen. LUCIANO MAIANI (Italy); publs *CERN Courier* (monthly), *Annual Report*, *Scientific Reports*.

European-Mediterranean Seismological Centre: c/o LDG, BP 12, 91680 Bruyères-le-Châtel, France; tel. 1-69-26-78-14; fax 1-69-26-70-00; e-mail csem@emsc-csem.org; internet www.emsc-csem.org; f. 1976 for rapid determination of seismic hypocentres in the region; maintains data base; mems: institutions in 37 countries; Pres. C. BROWITT; Sec.-Gen. R. BOSSU; publ. *Newsletter* (2 a year).

Federation of Arab Scientific Research Councils: POB 13027, Al Karkh/Karadat Mariam, Baghdad, Iraq; tel. (1) 888-1709; fax (1) 886-6346; f. 1976 to encourage co-operation in scientific research, promote the establishment of new institutions and plan joint regional research projects; mems: national science bodies in 15 countries; Sec.-Gen. Dr TAHA AL-NUEIMI; publs *Journal of Computer Research*, *Journal of Environmental and Sustained Development*, *Journal of Biotechnology*.

Federation of Asian Scientific Academies and Societies (FASAS): c/o Malaysian Scientific Association (MSA), Room 1, 2nd Floor, Bangunan Sultan, Salahuddin Abdul Aziz Shah, 16 Jalan Utara, POB 48, 46700 Petaling Jaya, Malaysia; tel. (3) 7954-1644; fax (3) 7957-8930; e-mail malsci@tm.net.my; f. 1984 to stimulate regional co-operation and promote national and regional self-reliance in science and technology, by organizing meetings, training and research programmes and encouraging the exchange of scientists and of scientific information; mems: national scientific academies and societies from Afghanistan, Australia, Bangladesh, People's Republic of China, India, Republic of Korea, Malaysia, Nepal, New Zealand, Pakistan, Philippines, Singapore, Sri Lanka, Thailand; Pres. Prof. TING-KUEH SOON (Philippines); Sec. Prof. INDIRA NATH (India).

Federation of European Biochemical Societies: c/o Institute of Cancer Biology and Danish Centre for Human Genome Research, Danish Cancer Society, Strandboulevarden 49, 2100 Copenhagen Ø, Denmark; tel. 3525-7364; fax 3525-7376; e-mail secretariat@febs.org; internet www.febs.org; f. 1964 to promote the science of biochemistry through meetings of European biochemists, advanced courses and the provision of fellowships; mems: 40,000 in 34 societies; Chair. Prof. C. RODRIGUES-POUSADA; Sec.-Gen. Prof. JULIO E. CELIS; publs *The FEBS Journal*, *FEBS News*, *FEBS Letters*, *FEBS Newsletter*.

Foundation for International Scientific Co-ordination (Fondation 'Pour la science', Centre international de synthèse): Revue de Synthèse, Centre International de Synthèse, CNRS UMS 2267 ACTA, 4 rue Lhomond, 75005, Paris, France; tel. 1-55-42-83-11; fax 1-55-42-83-19; e-mail revuedesynthese@ens.fr; internet www.ehess .fr/acta/synthese; f. 1925; Dirs MICHEL BLAY, ERIC BRIAN; publs *Revue de Synthèse*, *Revue d'Histoire des Sciences*, *Semaines de Synthèse*, *L'Evolution de l'Humanité*.

Intergovernmental Oceanographic Commission: UNESCO, 1 rue Miollis, 75732 Paris Cédex 15, France; tel. 1-45-68-39-83; fax 1-45-68-58-10; internet ioc.unesco.org/iocweb; f. 1960 to promote scientific investigation of the nature and resources of the oceans through the concerted action of its members; mems: 127 govts; Chair. SU JILAN (China); Exec. Sec. Dr PATRICIO BERNAL; publs *IOC Technical Series* (irregular), IOC *Manuals and Guides* (irregular), *IOC Workshop Reports* (irregular) and *IOC Training Course Reports* (irregular), annual reports.

International Academy of Astronautics (IAA): 6 rue Galilee, POB 1268–16, 75766 Paris Cédex 16, France; tel. 1-47-23-82-15; fax 1-47-23-82-16; internet www.iaanet.org; f. 1960; fosters the development of astronautics for peaceful purposes, holds scientific meetings and makes scientific studies, reports, awards and book awards; maintains 19 scientific cttees and a multilingual terminology data base (20 languages); mems: 681, and 382 corresponding mems, in basic sciences, engineering sciences, life sciences and social sciences, from 57 countries; Sec.-Gen. Dr JEAN-MICHEL CONTANT; publ. *Acta Astronautica* (monthly).

International Association for Biologicals (IABS): 8 chemin de la Gravière, 1227 Acacias, Geneva, Switzerland; tel. (22) 3011036; fax (22) 3011037; e-mail iabs@iabs.org; internet www.iabs.org; f. 1955 to connect producers and controllers of immunological products (sera, vaccines, etc.), for the study and development of methods of standardization; supports international organizations in their efforts to solve problems of standardization; mems: c. 500; Pres. J. PETRICCIANI (USA); Sec. D. GAUDRY (France); publs *Newsletter* (quarterly), *Biologicals* (quarterly).

International Association for Earthquake Engineering: Kenchiku Kaikan, 3rd Floor, 5-26-20, Shiba, Minato-ku, Tokyo 108, Japan; tel. (3) 3453-1281; fax (3) 3453-0428; e-mail secretary@iaee .or.jp; internet www.iaee.or.jp; f. 1963 to promote international co-operation among scientists and engineers in the field of earthquake engineering through exchange of knowledge, ideas and results of research and practical experience; mems: national cttees in 49 countries; Pres. Prof. LUIS ESTEVA (Mexico); Sec.-Gen. HIROKAZU IEMURA.

International Association for Ecology (INTECOL): Lunigiana Museum of Natural History, 54011 Aulla, Italy; tel. (0187) 400252; fax (0187) 420727; e-mail afarina@tamnet.it; internet www.intecol .org; f. 1967 to provide opportunities for communication between ecologists world-wide to co-operate with organizations and individuals having related aims and interests; to encourage studies in the different fields of ecology; affiliated to the International Union of Biological Sciences; mems: 35 national and international ecological societies, and 1,000 individuals; Pres. J. A. LEE (UK); Sec.-Gen. A. FARINA (Italy).

International Association for Mathematical Geology (IAMG): c/o T. A. Jones, POB 2189, Houston, TX 77252-2189, USA; tel. (713) 431-6546; fax (713) 431-6336; internet www.iamg.org; f. 1968 for the preparation and elaboration of mathematical models of geological processes; the introduction of mathematical methods in geological sciences and technology; assistance in the development of mathematical investigation in geological sciences; the organization of international collaboration in mathematical geology through various forums and publications; educational programmes for mathematical geology; affiliated to the International Union of Geological Sciences; mems: c. 600; Pres. Dr R. A. OLEA (USA); Sec.-Gen. Dr T. A. JONES (USA); publs *Mathematical Geology* (8 a year), *Computers and Geosciences* (10 a year), *Natural Resources Research* (quarterly), *Newsletter* (2 a year).

International Association for Mathematics and Computers in Simulation: c/o Free University of Brussels, Automatic Control, CP 165, 50 ave F. D. Roosevelt, 1050 Brussels, Belgium; tel. (2) 650-20-97; fax (2) 650-35-64; internet www.first.gmd.de/imacs97/imacs; f. 1955 to further the study of mathematical tools and computer software and hardware, analogue, digital or hybrid computers for simulation of soft or hard systems; mems: 1,100 and 27 assoc. mems; Pres. R. VICHNEVETSKY (USA); Sec. Prof. RAYMOND HANUS; publs *Mathematics and Computers in Simulation* (6 a year), *Applied Numerical Mathematics* (6 a year), *Journal of Computational Acoustics*.

International Association for the Physical Sciences of the Ocean (IAPSO): POB 820440, Vicksburg, MS 39182-0440, USA; tel. (601) 636-1363; fax (601) 629-9640; e-mail camfield@vicksburg .com; internet www.olympus.net/IAPSO; f. 1919 to promote the study of scientific problems relating to the oceans and interactions occurring at its boundaries, chiefly in so far as such study may be carried out by the aid of mathematics, physics and chemistry; to initiate, facilitate and co-ordinate research; and to provide for discussion, comparison and publication; affiliated to the International Union of Geodesy and Geophysics; mems: 81 member states; Pres. PAOLA RIZZOLI; Sec.-Gen. Dr FRED E. CAMFIELD (USA); publ. *Publications Scientifiques* (irregular).

International Association for Plant Physiology (IAPP): c/o Dr D. Graham, Div. of Food Science and Technology, CSIRO, POB 52, North Ryde, NSW, Australia 2113; tel. (2) 9490-8333; fax (2) 9490-3107; e-mail douglasgraham@dfst.csiro.au; f. 1955 to promote the development of plant physiology at the international level through congresses, symposia and workshops, by maintaining communication with national societies and by encouraging interaction between plant physiologists in developing and developed countries; affiliated to the International Union of Biological Sciences; Pres. Prof. S. MIYACHI; Sec.-Treas. Dr D. GRAHAM.

International Association for Plant Taxonomy (IAPT): Institute of Botany, University of Vienna, Rennweg 14, 1030 Vienna, Austria; tel. (1) 4277-54098; fax (1) 4277-54099; e-mail office@ iapt-taxon.org; internet www.botanik.univie.ac.at/iapt; f. 1950 to promote the development of plant taxonomy and encourage contacts between people and institutes interested in this work; maintains the International Bureau for Plant Taxonomy and Nomenclature; affiliated to the International Union of Biological Sciences; mems: institutes and individuals in 85 countries; Man. Sec. Dr ALESSANDRA

RICCIUTI LAMONEA; publs *Taxon* (quarterly), *Regnum vegetabile* (irregular).

International Association of Botanic Gardens (IABG): c/o Prof. J. E. Hernández-Bermejo, Córdoba Botanic Garden, Avda de Linneo, s/n, 14004 Córdoba, Spain; tel. (957) 200077; fax (957) 295333; e-mail jardinbotcord@telefonica.net; f. 1954 to promote co-operation between scientific collections of living plants, including the exchange of information and specimens to promote the study of the taxonomy of cultivated plants; and to encourage the conservation of rare plants and their habitats; affiliated to the International Union of Biological Sciences; Pres. Prof. H. E. SHANAN (People's Republic of China); Sec. Prof. J. ESTEBAN HERNÁNDEZ-BERMEJO (Spain).

International Association of Geodesy: Dept of Geophysics, Juliane Maries Vej 30, 2100 Copenhagen Oe, Denmark; tel. (45) 3532-0582; fax (45) 3536-5357; e-mail cct@gfy.ku.dk; internet www .gfy.ku.dk/niag; f. 1922 to promote the study of all scientific problems of geodesy and encourage geodetic research to promote and co-ordinate international co-operation in this field; to publish results; affiliated to the International Union of Geodesy and Geophysics; mems: national committees in 73 countries; Pres. F. SANSÓ (Italy); Sec.-Gen. C. C. TSCHERNING (Denmark); publs *Journal of Geodesy*, *Travaux de l'AIG*.

International Association of Geomagnetism and Aeronomy (IAGA): c/o Prof. Bengt Hultqvist, Swedish Institute of Space Physics, POB 812, 98128, Kiruna, Sweden; tel. (980) 84340; e-mail hultqv@irf.se; f. 1919 for the study of questions relating to geomagnetism and aeronomy and the encouragement of research; holds General and Scientific Assemblies every two years; affiliated to the International Union of Geodesy and Geophysics; mems: countries that adhere to the IUGG; Pres. H. C. BARTON (Australia); Sec.-Gen. Prof. BENGT HULTQVIST (Sweden); publs *IAGA Bulletin* (including annual *Geomagnetic Data*), *IAGA News* (annually).

International Association of Hydrological Sciences: Dept of Geography, Wilfrid Laurier Univ., Waterloo, ON N2L 3C5, Canada; tel. (519) 884-1970; fax (519) 846-0968; e-mail 44iahs@mach1.wlu .ca; internet www.wlu.ca/wwwiahs; f. 1922 to promote co-operation in the study of hydrology and water resources; Pres. Dr J. C. RODDA (UK); Sec.-Gen. Dr GORDON J. YOUNG (Canada); publs *Journal* (every 2 months), *Newsletter* (3 a year).

International Association of Meteorology and Atmospheric Sciences (IAMAS): Dept of Physics, Univ. of Toronto, Toronto, ON M5S 1A7, Canada; internet iamas.org; f. 1919; maintains permanent commissions on atmospheric ozone, radiation, atmospheric chemistry and global pollution, dynamic meteorology, polar meteorology, clouds and precipitation, climate, atmospheric electricity, planetary atmospheres and their evolution, and meteorology of the upper atmosphere; holds general assemblies every four years, special assemblies between general assemblies; affiliated to the International Union of Geodesy and Geophysics; Pres. Prof. R. DUCE (USA); Sec.-Gen. Prof. R. LIST (Canada).

International Association of Sedimentologists: c/o Prof. José-Pedro Calvo, Departamento de Petrologia y Geoquimica, Facultad CC Geológicas, Universidad Complutense, 28040 Madrid, Spain; tel. (913) 944905; fax (915) 442535; e-mail jpcalvo@geo.ucm.es; internet www.iasnet.org; f. 1952; affiliated to the International Union of Geological Sciences; mems: 2,200; Pres. Prof. J. A. McKENZIE (Switzerland); Gen. Sec. Prof. JOSÉ-PEDRO CALVO (Spain); publ. *Sedimentology* (every 2 months).

International Association of Theoretical and Applied Limnology (Societas Internationalis Limnologiae): Dept of Environmental Sciences and Engineering, University of North Carolina, Chapel Hill, NC 2755–7431, USA; tel. (919) 843-4916; fax (919) 843-4072; e-mail rwetzel@unc.edu; internet www.limnology.org; f. 1922 for the study of physical, chemical and biological phenomena of lakes and rivers; affiliated to the International Union of Biological Sciences; mems: c. 3,200; Pres. G. E. LIKENS (USA); Gen. Sec. and Treas. ROBERT G. WETZEL (USA).

International Association of Volcanology and Chemistry of the Earth's Interior (IAVCEI): Geophysical Institute, University of Alaska Fairbanks, POB 757320, Fairbanks, AK 99775, USA; tel. (907) 474-7131; fax (907) 474-5618; f. 1919 to examine scientifically all aspects of volcanology; affiliated to the International Union of Geodesy and Geophysics; Pres. O. NAVON (Israel); Sec.-Gen. S. R. McNUTT (USA); publs *Bulletin of Volcanology*, *Catalogue of the Active Volcanoes of the World*, *Proceedings in Volcanology*.

International Association of Wood Anatomists: USDA Forest Service, Forest Products, Laboratory, 1 Gifford Pinchot Drive, Madison WI 53726-2398, USA; tel. (608) 231-9200; fax (608) 231-9508; f. 1931 for the purpose of study, documentation and exchange of information on the structure of wood; holds annual conference; mems: 650 in 68 countries; Exec. Sec. REGIS B. MILLER; publ. *IAWA Journal*.

International Astronautical Federation (IAF): 3–5 rue Mario-Nikis, 75015 Paris, France; tel. 1-45-67-42-60; fax 1-42-73-21-20; e-mail iaf@wanadoo.fr; internet www.iafastro.com; f. 1950 to foster the development of astronautics for peaceful purposes at national and international levels; the IAF has created the International Academy of Astronautics (IAA) and the International Institute of Space Law (IISL); mems: 165 national astronautical societies in 44 countries; Pres. MARCIO BARBOSA (Brazil); Deputy Exec. Dir. ANNIE MOULIN.

International Astronomical Union (IAU): 98 bis blvd d'Arago, 75014 Paris, France; tel. 1-43-25-83-58; fax 1-43-25-26-16; e-mail iau@iap.fr; internet www.iau.org; f. 1919 to facilitate co-operation between the astronomers of various countries and to further the study of astronomy in all its branches; organizes colloquia every two months; mems: organizations in 65 countries, and 9,000 individual mems; Pres. FRANCO PACINI (Italy); Gen. Sec. HANS RICKMAN (Sweden); publs *IAU Information Bulletin* (2 a year), *Symposia Series* (6 a year), *Highlights* (every 3 years).

International Biometric Society: c/o Prof. E. Baráth, Chair. of Statistics, 2103 Gödöllö, Hungary; tel. (28) 410-694; fax (28) 430-336; internet www.tibs.org; f. 1947 for the advancement of quantitative biological science through the development of quantitative theories and the application, development and dissemination of effective mathematical and statistical techniques; the Society has 16 regional organizations and 17 national groups, is affiliated with the International Statistical Institute and WHO, and constitutes the Section of Biometry of the International Union of Biological Sciences; mems: over 6,000 in more than 70 countries; Pres. Prof. SUE WILSON (Australia); Sec. Prof. E. BARÁTH (Hungary); publs *Biometrics* (quarterly), *Biometric Bulletin* (quarterly), *Journal of Agricultural, Biological and Environmental Statistics* (quarterly).

International Botanical Congress: c/o Dr Peter Hoch, Missouri Botanical Garden, PO Box 299, St Louis, MO 63166-0299, USA; tel. (314) 577-5175; fax (314) 577-9589; e-mail ibc16@mobot.org; f. 1864 to inform botanists of recent progress in the plant sciences; the Nomenclature Section of the Congress attempts to provide a uniform terminology and methodology for the naming of plants; other Divisions deal with developmental, metabolic, structural, systematic and evolutionary, ecological botany; genetics and plant breeding; 2005 Congress: Vienna, Austria; affiliated to the International Union of Biological Sciences; Sec. Dr PETER HOCH.

International Bureau of Weights and Measures (Bureau international des poids et mesures—BIPM): Pavillon de Breteuil, 92312 Sèvres Cédex, France; tel. 1-45-07-70-70; fax 1-45-34-20-21; e-mail info@bipm.org; internet www.bipm.org; f. 1875 works to ensure the international unification of measurements and their traceability to the International System of Unification; carries out research and calibration; organizes international comparisons of national measurement standards; mems: 51 member states and 10 associates; Pres. J. KOVALEVSKY (France); Sec. R. KAARLS (Netherlands); publs *Le Système International d'Unités* (in English and French), *Metrologia* (6 a year), scientific articles, reports and monographs, committee reports.

International Cartographic Association: 136 bis rue de Grenelle, 75700 Paris 07 SP, France; tel. 1-43-98-82-95; fax 1-43-98-84-00; internet www.icaci.org; f. 1959 for the advancement, instigation and co-ordination of cartographic research involving co-operation between different nations; particularly concerned with furtherance of training in cartography, study of source material, compilation, graphic design, drawing, scribing and reproduction techniques of maps; organizes international conferences, symposia, meetings, exhibitions; mems: 80 countries; Pres. MICHAEL WOOD; publ. *ICA Newsletter* (2 a year).

International Centre of Insect Physiology and Ecology: POB 30772, Nairobi, Kenya; tel. (20) 861680; fax (20) 803360; e-mail icipe@africaonline.co.ke; internet www.icipe.org; f. 1970; specializes in research and development of environmentally sustainable and affordable methods of managing tropical arthropod plant pests and disease vectors, and in the conservation and utilization of biodiversity of insects of commercial and ecological importance; organizes training programmes; Dir-Gen. Dr HANS RUDOLPH HERREN; publs *Insect Science and its Application* (quarterly), *Annual Report*, training manuals, technical bulletins, newsletter.

International Commission for Optics (ICO): Departamento de Optica, Facultad de Ciencias Fisicas, Universidad Complutense de Madrid, Ciudad Universitaria s/n, 28040 Madrid, Spain; tel. (91) 394-4684; fax (91) 394-4683; e-mail icosec@fis.ucm.es; internet www.ico-optics.org; f. 1948 to contribute to the progress of theoretical and instrumental optics, to assist in research and to promote international agreement on specifications; holds Gen. Assembly every three years; mems: committees in 48 territories, and five international societies; Pres. Prof. R. DÄNDLIKER; Sec.-Gen. Prof. M. L. CALVO (Spain); publ. *ICO Newsletter*.

International Commission for Plant-Bee Relationships: c/o Prof. I. Williams, Plant and Invertebrate Ecology Division, Rothamsted Research, Harpenden, Herts, AL5 2JQ, United Kingdom; e-mail ingrid.williams@bbsrc.ac.uk; f. 1950 to promote research and its application in the field of bee botany, and collect and spread information to organize meetings, etc., and collaborate with scientific organizations; affiliated to the International Union of Biological Sciences; mems: 240 in 41 countries; Pres. Prof. INGRID WILLIAMS; Sec. Dr J. L. OSBORNE.

International Commission for the Scientific Exploration of the Mediterranean Sea (Commission internationale pour l'exploration scientifique de la mer Méditerranée—CIESM): 16 blvd de Suisse, 98000 Monaco; tel. 93-30-38-79; fax 92-16-11-95; e-mail fbriand@ciesm.org; internet www.ciesm.org; f. 1919 for scientific exploration of the Mediterranean Sea; organizes multilateral research investigations; includes 6 scientific committees; mems: 23 member countries, 2,500 scientists; Pres. SAS Prince ALBERT OF MONACO; Sec.-Gen. Prof. F. DOUMENGE; Dir-Gen. Prof. F. BRIAND; publs Congress reports, science and workshop series.

International Commission on Physics Education: c/o Prof. J. Barojas, POB 55534, 09340 México DF, Mexico; tel. (5) 686-35-19; internet www.physics.umd.edu/ripe/icpe; f. 1960 to encourage and develop international collaboration in the improvement and extension of the methods and scope of physics education at all levels; collaborates with UNESCO and organizes international conferences; mems: appointed triennially by the International Union of Pure and Applied Physics; Sec. Prof. J. BAROJAS.

International Commission on Radiation Units and Measurements (ICRU): 7910 Woodmont Ave, Suite 400, Bethesda, MD 20814, USA; tel. (301) 657-2652; fax (301) 907-8768; e-mail icru@icru.org; internet www.icru.org; f. 1925 to develop internationally acceptable recommendations regarding: (1) quantities and units of radiation and radioactivity, (2) procedures suitable for the measurement and application of these quantities in clinical radiology and radiobiology, (3) physical data needed in the application of these procedures; makes recommendations on quantities and units for radiation protection (see International Radiation Protection Association); mems: from about 18 countries; Chair. A. WAMBERSIE; Sec. S. SELTZER; publs reports.

International Commission on Zoological Nomenclature: c/o The Natural History Museum, Cromwell Rd, London, SW7 5BD, United Kingdom; tel. (20) 7942-5653; e-mail iczn@nhm.ac.uk; internet www.iczn.org; f. 1895; has judicial powers to determine all matters relating to the interpretation of the International Code of Zoological Nomenclature and also plenary powers to suspend the operation of the Code where the strict application of the Code would lead to confusion and instability of nomenclature; also responsible for maintaining and developing the Official Lists and Official Indexes of Names in Zoology; affiliated to the International Union of Biological Sciences; Pres. Dr N. L. EVENHUIS (USA); Exec. Sec. Dr A. POLASZEK (UK); publs *Bulletin of Zoological Nomenclature* (quarterly), *International Code of Zoological Nomenclature*, *Official Lists and Indexes of Names and Works in Zoology*, *Towards Stability in the Names of Animals*.

International Council for Science (ICSU): 51 blvd de Montmorency, 75016 Paris, France; tel. 1-45-25-03-29; fax 1-42-88-94-31; e-mail secretariat@icsu.org; internet www.icsu.org; f. 1919 as International Research Council; present name adopted 1931; new statutes adopted 1996; to co-ordinate international co-operation in theoretical and applied sciences and to promote national scientific research through the intermediary of affiliated national organizations; General Assembly of representatives of national and scientific members meets every three years to formulate policy. The following committees have been established: Cttee on Science for Food Security, Scientific Cttee on Antarctic Research, Scientific Cttee on Oceanic Research, Cttee on Space Research, Scientific Cttee on Water Research, Scientific Cttee on Solar-Terrestrial Physics, Cttee on Science and Technology in Developing Countries, Cttee on Data for Science and Technology, Programme on Capacity Building in Science, Scientific Cttee on Problems of the Environment, Steering Cttee on Genetics and Biotechnology and Scientific Cttee on International Geosphere-Biosphere Programme. The following services and Inter-Union Committees and Commissions have been established: Federation of Astronomical and Geophysical Data Analysis Services, Inter-Union Commission on Frequency Allocations for Radio Astronomy and Space Science, Inter-Union Commission on Radio Meteorology, Inter-Union Commission on Spectroscopy, Inter-Union Commission on Lithosphere; national mems: academies or research councils in 98 countries; Scientific mems and assocs: 26 international unions and 28 scientific associates; Pres. W. ARBER; Sec.-Gen. H. A. MOONEY; publs *ICSU Yearbook*, *Science International* (quarterly), *Annual Report*.

International Council for Scientific and Technical Information: 51 blvd de Montmorency, 75016 Paris, France; tel. 1-45-25-65-

92; fax 1-42-15-12-62; e-mail icsti@icsti.org; internet www.icsti.org; f. 1984 as the successor to the International Council of Scientific Unions Abstracting Board (f. 1952); aims to increase accessibility to scientific and technical information; fosters communication and interaction among all participants in the information transfer chain; mems: 50 organizations; Pres. GÉRARD GIROUD (Netherlands); Gen. Sec. ELLIOT SIEGEL (USA).

International Council for the Exploration of the Sea (ICES): Palægade 2–4, 1261 Copenhagen K, Denmark; tel. 33-15-42-25; fax 33-93-42-15; e-mail ices.info@ices.dk; internet www.ices.dk; f. 1902 to encourage and facilitate research on the utilization and conservation of living resources and the environment in the North Atlantic Ocean and its adjacent seas; publishes and disseminate results of research; advises member countries and regulatory commissions; mems: 19 mem. countries and five countries or bodies with observer status; Gen. Sec. D. DE G. GRIFFITH; publs *ICES Journal of Marine Science, ICES Marine Science Symposia, ICES Fisheries Statistics, ICES Cooperative Research Reports, ICES Oceanographic Data Lists and Inventories, ICES Techniques in Marine Environmental Sciences, ICES Identification Leaflets for Plankton, ICES Identification Leaflets for Diseases and Parasites of Fish and Shellfish, ICES/CIEM Information.*

International Council of Psychologists: Dept of Psychology, Southwest Texas State University, San Marcos, TX 78666, USA; tel. (512) 245-7605; fax (512) 245-3153; internet www.geocities.com/icpsych; f. 1941 to advance psychology and the application of its scientific findings throughout the world; holds annual conventions; mems: 1,200 qualified psychologists; Sec.-Gen. Dr JOHN M. DAVIS; publs *International Psychologist* (quarterly), *World Psychology* (quarterly).

International Council of the Aeronautical Sciences (ICAS): c/o FOI, SE-17290 Stockholm, Sweden; tel. 5550-4229; e-mail secr.exec@icas.org; internet www.icas.org; f. 1957 to encourage free interchange of information on aeronautical science and technology; holds biennial Congresses; mems: national asscns in more than 30 countries; Pres. BILLY FREDRIKSSON (Sweden); Exec. Sec. ANDERS GUSTAFSSON (Sweden).

International Earth Rotation Service: Central Bureau, Paris Observatory, 61 ave de l'Observatoire, 75014 Paris, France; tel. 1-40-51-22-26; fax 1-40-51-22-91; e-mail iers@obspm.fr; internet hpiers.obspm.fr; f. 1988 (fmrly International Polar Motion Service and Bureau International de l'Heure); maintained by the International Astronomical Union and the International Union of Geodesy and Geophysics; defines and maintains the international terrestrial and celestial reference systems; determines earth orientation parameters (terrestrial and celestial co-ordinates of the pole and universal time) connecting these systems; monitors global geophysical fluids; organizes collection, analysis and dissemination of data; Pres. Directing Bd Prof. C. REIGBER.

International Federation for Cell Biology: c/o Dr Ivan Cameron, Dept of Cellular and Structural Biology, Univ. of Texas Health Science Center, 7703 Floyd Curl Drive, San Antonio, Texas 78229, USA; internet lonestar.texas.net/icameron/ifcb.htm; f. 1972 to foster international co-operation, and organize conferences; Pres. Dr JUDIE WALTON; Sec.-Gen. Dr IVAN CAMERON; publs *Cell Biology International* (monthly), reports.

International Federation of Operational Research Societies (IFORS): c/o Loretta Peregrina, Richard Ivey School of Business, University of Western Ontario, London, ON N6A 3K7, Canada; tel. (519) 661-4220; fax (519) 661-3485; e-mail ifors@ivey.uwo.ca; internet www.ifors.org; f. 1959 for development of operational research as a unified science and its advancement in all nations of the world; mems: c. 30,000 individuals, 44 national societies, four kindred societies; Pres. Prof. PAOLO TOTH (Italy); Sec. LORETTA PEREGRINA; publs *International Abstracts in Operational Research, IFORS Bulletin, International Transactions in Operational Research.*

International Federation of Science Editors: School for Scientific Communication, Abruzzo Science Park, Via Antica Arischia 1, 67100 L'Aquila, Italy; tel. (0862) 3475308; fax (0862) 3475213; e-mail miriam.balaban@aquila.infn.it; f. 1978; links editors in different branches of science with the aim of improving scientific writing, editing, ethics and communication internationally; Pres. MIRIAM BALABAN (Italy).

International Federation of Societies for Microscopy (IFSM): Dept of Chemical Engineering and Materials Science, University of Minnesota, 151 Amundson Hall, 421 Washington Ave, SE, Minneapolis, MN 554455, USA; tel. (612) 625-8805; fax (612) 626-7246; e-mail carter@cems.umn.edu; internet www.ifsm.umn.edu; f. 1955 to contribute to the advancement of all aspects of electron microscopy; promotes and co-ordinates research; sponsors meetings and conferences; holds International Congress every four years; mems: representative organizations of 40 countries; Pres. Prof. DAVID J. H. COCKAYNE (UK); Gen.-Sec. C. BARRY CARTER (USA).

International Food Information Service (IFIS): UK Office (IFIS Publishing), Lane End House, Shinfield Rd, Shinfield, Reading, RG2 9BB, United Kingdom; tel. (118) 988-3895; fax (118) 988-5065; e-mail ifis@ifis.org; internet www.ifis.org; f. 1968; board of governors comprises two members each from CAB-International (UK), Bundesministerium für Landwirtschaft, Ernährung und Forsten (represented by Deutsche Landwirtschafts-Gesellschaft e.V.) (Germany), the Institute of Food Technologists (USA), and the Centrum voor Landbouwpublikaties en Landbouwdocumentaties (Netherlands); collects and disseminates information on all disciplines relevant to food science, food technology and human nutrition; Man. Dir Prof. J. D. SELMAN; publ. *Food Science and Technology Abstracts* (monthly, also available via the internet and on CD-Rom).

International Foundation of the High-Altitude Research Stations Jungfraujoch and Gornergrat: Sidlerstrasse 5, 3012 Berne, Switzerland; tel. (31) 6314052; fax (31) 6314405; e-mail louise.wilson@phim.unibe.ch; internet www.ifjungo.ch; f. 1931; international research centre which enables scientists from many scientific fields to carry out experiments at high altitudes. Six countries contribute to support the station: Austria, Belgium, Germany, Italy, Switzerland, United Kingdom; Pres. Prof. E. FLÜCKIGER.

International Geographical Union (IGU): Dept of Geography, University of Bonn, 53115 Bonn, Meckenheimer Allee 166, Germany; tel. (228) 739287; fax (228) 739272; e-mail secretariat@igu.bn.eunet.be; internet www.helsinki.fi/science/igu; f. 1922 to encourage the study of problems relating to geography, to promote and co-ordinate research requiring international co-operation, and to organize international congresses and commissions; mems: 83 countries, 11 associates; Pres. Prof. BRUNO MESSERLI (Switzerland); Sec.-Gen. Prof. ECKART EHLERS (Germany); publ. *IGU Bulletin* (2 a year).

International Glaciological Society: Lensfield Rd, Cambridge, CB2 1ER, United Kingdom; tel. (1223) 355974; fax (1223) 354931; e-mail igsoc@igsoc.org; internet www.igsoc.org; f. 1936 to stimulate interest in and encourage research into the scientific and technical problems of snow and ice in all countries; mems: 850 in 30 countries; Pres. Dr ELIZABETH MORRIS; Sec.-Gen. MAGNÚS MÁRMAGNÚSSON; publs *Journal of Glaciology* (quarterly), *Ice* (News Bulletin, 3 a year), *Annals of Glaciology.*

International Hydrographic Organization (IHO): 4 quai Antoine 1er, BP 445, Monte-Carlo, 98011 Monaco; tel. 93-10-81-00; fax 93-10-81-40; e-mail info@ihb.mc; internet www.iho.shom.fr; f. 1921 to link the hydrographic offices of member governments and co-ordinate their work, with a view to rendering navigation easier and safer; seeks to obtain, as far as possible, uniformity in charts and hydrographic documents; fosters the development of electronic chart navigation; encourages adoption of the best methods of conducting hydrographic surveys; encourages surveying in those parts of the world where accurate charts are lacking; provides IHO Data Centre for Digital Bathymetry; and organizes quinquennial conference; mems: 75 states; Directing Committee: Pres. Vice Adm. A. MARATOS (Greece); Dirs Rear-Adm. K. BARBOR (USA), Capt. H. GORZIGLIA (Chile); publs *International Hydrographic Bulletin, IHO Yearbook,* other documents (available on the IHO website).

International Institute of Refrigeration: 177 blvd Malesherbes, 75017 Paris, France; tel. 1-42-27-32-35; fax 1-47-63-17-98; e-mail iifiir@iifiir.org; internet www.iifiir.org; f. 1908 to further the science of refrigeration and its applications on a world-wide scale; to investigate, discuss and recommend any aspects leading to improvements in the field of refrigeration; maintains FRIDOC database (available via internet); mems: 61 national, 1,500 associates; Dir DIDIER COULOMB (France); publs *Bulletin* (every 2 months), *International Journal of Refrigeration* (8 a year), *Newsletter* (quarterly), books, proceedings, recommendations.

International Mathematical Union (IMU): c/o Institute for Advanced Study (IAS), Einstein Drive, Princeton, NJ 08540, USA; e-mail imu@ias.edu; internet elib.zib.de/imu; f. 1952 to support and assist the International Congress of Mathematicians and other international scientific meetings or conferences and to encourage and support other international mathematical activities considered likely to contribute to the development of mathematical science—pure, applied or educational; mems: 63 countries; Pres. Prof. JACOB PALIS; Sec.-Gen. Prof. PHILLIP GRIFFITHS.

International Mineralogical Association: Institute of Mineralogy, University of Marburg, 3550 Marburg, Germany; tel. 285617; fax 285831; internet www.dst.unipi.it/ima; f. 1958 to further international co-operation in the science of mineralogy; affiliated to the International Union of Geological Sciences; mems: national societies in 31 countries; Sec. Prof. S. S. HAFNER.

International Organization of Legal Metrology: 11 rue Turgot, 75009 Paris, France; tel. 1-48-78-12-82; fax 1-42-82-17-27; internet www.oiml.org; f. 1955 to serve as documentation and information centre on the verification, checking, construction and use of measuring instruments, to determine characteristics and standards to which measuring instruments must conform for their use to be recommended internationally, and to determine the general principles of legal metrology; mems: governments of 50 countries; Dir B. ATHANÉ (France); publ. *Bulletin* (quarterly).

International Palaeontological Association: c/o Prof. R. F. Maddocks, Room 336, Science and Research Bldg 1, Dept of Geosciences, Univ. of Houston, Houston, TX 77204-5503, USA., Paleontologisk Museum, Box 1172 Blindern, 0318 Oslo, Norway; tel. (713) 743-3429; fax (713) 748-7906; e-mail rmaddocks@uh.edu; internet ipa.geo.ukans.edu; f. 1933; affiliated to the International Union of Geological Sciences and the International Union of Biological Sciences; Pres. Dr J. TALENT (Australia); Sec.-Gen. Prof. ROSALIE F. MADDOCKS (Norway); publs *Lethaia* (quarterly), *Directory of Paleontologists of the World, Directory of Fossil Collectors of the World.*

International Peat Society: Vapaudenkatu 12, 40100 Jyväskylä, Finland; tel. (14) 3385440; fax (14) 3385410; e-mail ips@peatsociety.fi; internet www.peatsociety.fi; f. 1968 to encourage co-operation in the study and use of mires, peatlands, peat and related material, through international meetings, research groups and the exchange of information; mems: 21 Nat. Cttees, research institutes and other organizations, and individuals from 37 countries; Pres. MARKKU MÄKELÄ (Finland); Sec.-Gen. JAAKO SILPOLA (Finland); publs *Peat News* (monthly electronic newsletter), *International Peat Journal* (annually), *Peatlands International* (2 a year).

International Phonetic Association (IPA): Dept of Linguistics, University of Victoria, POB 3045, Victoria, BC V8W 3P4, Canada; e-mail esling@uvic.ca; internet www.arts.gla.ac.uk/ipa/ipa.html; f. 1886 to promote the scientific study of phonetics and its applications; organizes International Congress of Phonetic Sciences every four years (2003: Barcelona, Spain); mems: 1,000; Pres. K. KOHLER (Germany); Sec. Prof. JOHN ESLING; publ. *Journal* (2 a year).

International Phycological Society: c/o Harbor Branch Oceanographic Institution, 5600 Old Dixie Highway, Fort Pierce, FL 34946, USA; fax (561) 468-0757; e-mail hanisak@hboi.edu; internet seaweed.ucg.ie/phycologia/ips.html; f. 1961 to promote the study of algae, the distribution of information, and international co-operation in this field; mems: about 1,000; Pres. C. J. BIRD; Sec. M. D. HANISAK; publ. *Phycologia* (every 2 months).

International Primatological Society: c/o Dr D. Fragaszy, Dept of Psychology, Univ. of Georgia, Athens, GA 30602, USA; tel. (706) 542-3036; fax (706) 542-3275; e-mail doree@arches.uga.edu; internet www.primate.wisc.edu/pin/ips.html; f. 1964 to promote primatological science in all fields; mems: about 1,500; Pres. Dr D. FRAGASZY; Sec.-Gen. Dr J. A. R. A. M. VAN HOOFF; publs *Bulletin, International Journal of Primatology, Codes of Practice.*

International Radiation Protection Association (IRPA): POB 662, 5600 AR Eindhoven, Netherlands; tel. (40) 247-33-55; fax (40) 243-50-20; e-mail irpa.exof@sbd.tue.nl; internet www.irpa.net; f. 1966 to link individuals and societies throughout the world concerned with protection against ionizing radiations and allied effects, and to represent doctors, health physicists, radiological protection officers and others engaged in radiological protection, radiation safety, nuclear safety, legal, medical and veterinary aspects and in radiation research and other allied activities; mems: 16,000 in 42 societies; Pres. Prof. K. DUFTSCMID (Austria); Sec.-Gen. C. J. HUYSKENS (Netherlands); publ. *IRPA Bulletin.*

International Society for General Semantics: POB 728, Concord, CA 94522, USA; tel. (925) 798-0311; e-mail isgs@generalsemantics.org; internet www.generalsemantics.org; f. 1943 to advance knowledge of and inquiry into non-Aristotelian systems and general semantics; mems: 2,000 individuals in 40 countries; Pres. CHARLES RUSSELL, Jr (USA); Exec. Dir PAUL D. JOHNSTON (USA).

International Society for Human and Animal Mycology (ISHAM): Mycology Unit, Women's and Children's Hospital, N. Adelaide 5006, Australia; tel. (8) 8204-7365; fax (8) 8204-7589; e-mail dellis@mad.adelaide.edu.au; internet www.leeds.ac.uk/isham; f. 1954 to pursue the study of fungi pathogenic for man and animals; holds congresses (2003 Congress: San Antonio, USA); mems: 1,100 in 70 countries; Pres. Prof. M. R. McGINNIS; Gen. Sec. Dr D. H. ELLIS; publ. *Medical Mycology* (6 a year).

International Society for Rock Mechanics: c/o Laboratório Nacional de Engenharia Civil, 101 Av. do Brasil, 1700-066 Lisboa, Portugal; tel. (21) 8443419; fax (21) 8443021; e-mail isrm@lnec.pt; internet www.isrm.net; f. 1962 to encourage and co-ordinate international co-operation in the science of rock mechanics; assists individuals and local organizations in forming national bodies; maintains liaison with organizations representing related sciences, including geology, geophysics, soil mechanics, mining engineering, petroleum engineering and civil engineering; organizes international meetings; encourages the publication of research; mems: c. 6,000; Pres. NIELEN VAN DER MERWE; Sec.-Gen. Dr LUÍS LAMAS; publ. *News Journal* (3 a year).

International Society for Stereology: c/o CMM—Ecole des Mines de Paris, 77305 Fontainebleau, France; tel. 1-64-69-47-06; fax 1-64-69-47-07; e-mail iss@cmm.ensmp.fr; internet www.stereologysociety.org; f. 1962; an interdisciplinary society gathering scientists from metallurgy, geology, mineralogy and biology to exchange ideas on three-dimensional interpretation of two-dimensional samples (sections, projections) of their material by means of stereological principles; mems: 300; Pres. Prof. DOMINIQUE JEULIN; Treas./Sec. Dr ETIENNE DECENCIÈRE.

International Society for Tropical Ecology: c/o Botany Dept, Banaras Hindu University, Varanasi, 221 005 India; tel. (542) 368399; fax (542) 368174; e-mail tropecol@banaras.ernet.in; f. 1956 to promote and develop the science of ecology in the tropics in the service of humanity to publish a journal to aid ecologists in the tropics in communication of their findings; and to hold symposia from time to time to summarize the state of knowledge in particular or general fields of tropical ecology; mems: 500; Sec. Prof. J. S. SINGH (India); Editor Prof. K. P. SINGH; publ. *Tropical Ecology* (2 a year).

International Society of Biometeorology (IBS): c/o Dr M. Shibata, Dept of Biometeorology, Yamanashi Institute of Environmental Sciences, Fuji-Yoshida, Yamanashi 403-0005, Japan; tel. 555-72-6184; fax 555-72-6205; e-mail mshibata@yies.pref.yamanashi.jp; internet www.biometeorology.org; f. 1956 to unite all biometeorologists working in the fields of agricultural, botanical, cosmic, entomological, forest, human, medical, veterinarian, zoological and other branches of biometeorology; mems: 250 individuals, nationals of 46 countries; Pres. Dr IAN BURTON (Canada); Sec. Dr MASAKI SHIBATA (Japan); publs *Biometeorology* (Proceedings of the Congress of ISB), *International Journal of Biometeorology* (quarterly), *Biometeorology Bulletin.*

International Society of Criminology (Société internationale de criminologie): 4 rue Ferrus, 75014 Paris, France; tel. 1-45-88-00-23; fax 1-45-88-96-40; e-mail crim.sic@wanadoo.fr; f. 1934 to promote the development of the sciences in their application to the criminal phenomenon; mems: in 63 countries; Sec.-Gen. GEORGES PICCA; publ. *Annales internationales de Criminologie.*

International Union for Physical and Engineering Sciences in Medicine (IUPESM): c/o Prof. G. Fullerton, UTHSCSA, Dept of Radiology, MSC 7800, 7703 Floyd Curl Drive, San Antonio, TX 78229-3900, USA; tel. (210) 567-5551; fax (210) 567-5549; e-mail fullerton@uthscsa.edu; internet www.iupesm.org; f. 1980 by its two constituent orgs (International Federation for Medical and Biological Engineering, and International Organization for Medical Physics); promotes international co-operation in health care science and technology and represents the professional interests of members; organizes seminars, workshops, scientific conferences; holds World Congress every three years (2003: Sydney, Australia); Sec.-Gen. Prof. GARY FULLERTON (USA); publs *IUPESM Newsletter* (2 a year), Congress proceedings.

International Union for Pure and Applied Biophysics (IUPAB): School of Biochemistry and Molecular Biology, University of Leeds, Leeds, LS2 9JT, United Kingdom; tel. (113) 2333023; fax (113) 2333167; e-mail a.c.t.north@leeds.ac.uk; internet www.iupab.org; f. 1961 to organize international co-operation in biophysics and promote communication between biophysics and allied subjects, to encourage national co-operation between biophysical societies, and to contribute to the advancement of biophysical knowledge; mems: 50 adhering bodies; Pres. I. PECHT (Israel); Sec.-Gen. Prof. A. C. T. NORTH (UK); publ. *Quarterly Reviews of Biophysics.*

International Union for Quaternary Research (INQUA): Dept of Soil and Water Sciences, Agricultural University of Norway, POB 3028, 1432, Aas, Norway; e-mail sylvi.haldorsen@ijvf.nlh.no; internet inqua.nlh.no; f. 1928 to co-ordinate research on the Quaternary geological era throughout the world; holds congress every four years (2003: Reno, USA); mems: in 38 countries and states; Sec.-Gen. Prof. SYLVI HALDORSEN (Norway); publs *Quarternary International, Quarternary Perspectives.*

International Union of Biochemistry and Molecular Biology (IUBMB): Institute for Biophysical Chemistry and Biochemistry, Technical University Berlin, Franklinstr. 29, 10587 Berlin, Germany; tel. (30) 31424205; fax (30) 31424783; e-mail kleinkauf@chem.tu-berlin.de; internet www.iubmb.unibe.ch; f. 1955 to sponsor the International Congresses of Biochemistry, to co-ordinate research and discussion, to organize co-operation between the societies of biochemistry and molecular biology, to promote high standards of biochemistry and molecular biology throughout the world and to contribute to the advancement of biochemistry and molecular biology in all its international aspects; mems: 65 bodies; Pres. W. WHELAN (USA); Gen. Sec. Prof. Dr H. KLEINKAUF (Germany).

International Union of Biological Sciences (IUBS): 51 blvd de Montmorency, 75016 Paris, France; tel. 1-45-25-00-09; fax 1-45-25-20-29; e-mail secretariat@iubs.org; internet www.iubs.org; f. 1919; serves as an international forum for the promotion of biology; runs scientific programmes on subjects including biosystematics, bionomenclature, reproductive biology, biological diversity, integrative biology, biological education and aquaculture; carries out international collaborative research programmes; convenes General Assembly every 3 years; mems: 44 national bodies, 80 scientific bodies; Exec. Dir Dr T. YOUNES; publs *Biology International* (quarterly), *IUBS Monographs, IUBS Methodology, Manual Series*.

International Union of Crystallography: c/o M. H. Dacombe, 2 Abbey Sq., Chester, CH1 2HU, United Kingdom; tel. (1244) 345431; fax (1244) 344843; internet www.iucr.org; f. 1947 to facilitate the international standardization of methods, units, nomenclature and symbols used in crystallography; and to form a focus for the relations of crystallography to other sciences; mems: in 40 countries; Pres. Prof. W. L. DUAX (USA); Gen. Sec. S. LARSEN (Denmark); Exec. Sec. M. H. DACOMBE; publs *IUCR Newsletter, Acta Crystallographica, Journal of Applied Crystallography, Journal of Synchroton Radiation, International Tables for Crystallography, World Directory of Crystallographers, IUCr/OUP Crystallographic Symposia, IUCr/OUP Monographs on Crystallography, IUCr/OUP Texts on Crystallography*.

International Union of Food Science and Technology: POB 61021, 511 Maplegrove Rd, Oakville, ON L6J 6X0, Canada; tel. (905) 815-1926; fax (905) 815-1574; e-mail iufost@ca.inter.net; internet home.inforamp.net/-iufost; f. 1970; sponsors international symposia and congresses; mems: 60 national groups; Pres. ALAN MORTIMER (Australia); Sec.-Gen. JUDITH MEECH (Canada); publ. *IUFOST Newsline* (3 a year).

International Union of Geodesy and Geophysics (IUGC): Cires Campus Box 216, University of Colorado, Boulder, CO 80309, USA; tel. (303) 497-5147; fax (303) 497-3645; e-mail jjoselyn@cires.colorado.edu; internet www.iugg.org; f. 1919; federation of seven asscns representing Geodesy, Seismology and Physics of the Earth's Interior, Physical Sciences of the Ocean, Volcanology and Chemistry of the Earth's Interior, Hydrological Sciences, Meteorology and Atmospheric Physics, Geomagnetism and Aeronomy, which meet in committees and at the General Assemblies of the Union; organizes scientific meetings and sponsors various permanent services to collect, analyse and publish geophysical data; mems: in 66 countries; Pres. Prof. MASARU KONO (Japan); Sec.-Gen. Dr JOANN JOSELYN (USA); publs *IUGG Yearbook, Journal of Geodesy* (quarterly), *IASPEI Newsletter* (iregular), *Bulletin Volcanologique* (2 a year), *Hydrological Sciences Journal* (quarterly), *Bulletin de l'Association Internationale d'Hydrologie Scientifique* (quarterly), *IAMAP News Bulletin* (irregular).

International Union of Geological Sciences (IUGS): c/o Norges Geologiske Underskelse, N-7491 Trondheim, Norway; tel. 73-90-40-40; fax 73-50-22-30; e-mail iugs.secretariat.ngu.no; internet www.iugs.org/; f. 1961 to encourage the study of geoscientific problems, facilitate international and inter-disciplinary co-operation in geology and related sciences, and support the quadrennial International Geological Congress; organizes international meetings and cosponsors joint programmes, including the International Geological Correlation Programme (with UNESCO); mems: in 114 countries; Pres. Prof. ED DE MULDER (Netherlands); Sec.-Gen. Prof. A. BORIANI (Italy).

International Union of Immunological Societies (IUIS): Executive Manager, IUIS Central Office, c/o Vienna Academy of Postgraduate Medical Education and Research, Alser Strasse 4, 1090 Vienna, Austria; tel. (1) 405-13-83-13; fax (1) 405-13-83-23; e-mail iuis-central-office@medacad.org; internet www.iuisonline.org; f. 1969; holds triennial international congress; mems: national societies in 57 countries and territories; Pres. ROLF ZINKERNAGEL; Sec.-Gen. Dr MOHAMED R. DAHA; Exec. Man. SYLVIA TRITTINGER.

International Union of Microbiological Societies (IUMS): c/o Prof. John S. Mackenzie, Dept of Microbiology, University of Queensland, Brisbane QLD 4072, Australia; tel. (7) 3365-4648; fax (7) 3365-6265; e-mail john.mackenzie@uq.edu.au; internet www.iums.org; f. 1930; mems: 106 national microbiological societies; Pres. Prof. JULIAN DAVIES (Canada); Sec.-Gen. Prof. JOHN S. MACKENZIE; publs *International Journal of Systematic Bacteriology* (quarterly), *International Journal of Food Microbiology* (every 2 months), *Advances in Microbial Ecology* (annually), *Archives of Virology*.

International Union of Nutritional Sciences (IUNS): c/o Dr Galal, UCLA School of Public Health, 10833 Le Conte Ave, POB 951772, Los Angeles, CA 90095-1772, USA; tel. (310) 2069639; fax (310) 7941805; e-mail ogalal@ucla.edu; internet www.iuns.org; f. 1946 to promote international co-operation in the scientific study of nutrition and its applications, to encourage research and exchange of scientific information by holding international congresses and issuing publications; mems: 69 organizations; Pres. Dr MARK WHALQVIST; Sec.-Gen. Dr OSMAN GALAL; publs *Annual Report, IUNS Directory, Newsletter*.

International Union of Pharmacology: c/o Prof. Sue Piper Duckles, Dept of Pharmacology, College of Medicine, University of California, Irvine, CA 92697, USA; tel. (949) 824-4265; fax (924) 824-4855; e-mail spduckle@uci.edu; internet www.iuphar.org; f. 1963 to promote co-ordination of research, discussion and publication in the field of pharmacology, including clinical pharmacology, drug metabolism and toxicology; co-operates with WHO in all matters concerning drugs and drug research; holds international congresses; mems: 54 national and three regional societies; Pres. PAUL M. VANHOUTTE (France); Sec.-Gen. Prof. SUE PIPER DUCKLES; publ. *PI (Pharmacology International)*.

International Union of Photobiology: c/o Dr Tom Dubbelman, POB 9503, 2300 RA Leiden, Netherlands; tel. (71) 5276053; fax (71) 5276125; e-mail t.m.a.r.dubbelman@mcb.medfac.leidenuniv.nl; internet www.pol.us.net/iupb; f. 1928 (frmly International Photobiology Asscn); stimulation of scientific research concerning the physics, chemistry and climatology of non-ionizing radiations (ultraviolet, visible and infra-red) in relation to their biological efffects and their applications in biology and medicine; 18 national committees represented; affiliated to the International Union of Biological Sciences. International Congresses held every four years; Pres. Prof. PILL SOON SONG; Sec.-Gen. Dr TOM DUBBELMAN.

International Union of Physiological Sciences (IUPS): IUPS Secretariat, LGN, Bâtiment CERVI, Hôpital de la Pitié-Salpêtrière, 83 blvd de l'Hôpital, 75013 Paris, France; tel. 1-42-17-75-37; fax 1-42-17-75-75; e-mail suorsoni@infobiogen.fr; internet www.iups.org; f. 1955; mems: 50 national, six asscn, four regional, two affiliated and 14 special mems; Pres. Prof. ALAN W. COWLEY, Jr (USA); Sec. Prof. OLE PETERSEN (UK).

International Union of Psychological Science: c/o Prof. P. L.-J. Ritchie, Ecole de psychologie, Université d'Ottawa, 145 Jean-Jacques-Lussier, CP 450, Succ. A, Ottawa, ON KIN 6N5, Canada; tel. (613) 562-5289; fax (613) 562-5169; e-mail pritchie@uottawa.ca; internet www.iupsys.org; f. 1951 to contribute to the development of intellectual exchange and scientific relations between psychologists of different countries; mems: 68 national and 12 affiliate orgs; Pres. Prof. M. DENIS (France); Sec.-Gen. Prof. P. L.-J. RITCHIE (Canada); publs *International Journal of Psychology* (quarterly), *The IUPsyS Directory* (irregular), *Psychology CD Rom Resource File* (annually).

International Union of Pure and Applied Chemistry (IUPAC): Bldg 19, 104 T. W. Alexander Dr., Research Triangle Park, POB 13757, NC 27709-3757, USA; tel. (919) 485-8700; fax (919) 485-8706; e-mail secretariat@iupac.org; internet www.iupac.org; f. 1919 to organize permanent co-operation between chemical asscns in the member countries, to study topics of international importance requiring standardization or codification, to co-operate with other international organizations in the field of chemistry and to contribute to the advancement of all aspects of chemistry; holds a biennial General Assembly; mems: in 43 countries; Pres. Prof. P. S. STEYN (South Africa); Sec.-Gen. Dr E. D. BECKER (USA); publs *Chemistry International* (2 a month), *Pure and Applied Chemistry* (monthly).

International Union of Pure and Applied Physics (IUPAP): c/o ESRF, BP 220, 38043 Grenoble Cédex, France; tel. 4-76-88-20-30; fax 4-76-88-24-18; e-mail petroff@esrf.fr; internet www.iupap.org; f. 1922 to promote and encourage international co-operation in physics and facilitate the world-wide development of science; mems: in 46 countries; Pres. Y. PETROFF; Sec.-Gen. Dr RENÉ TURLAY (France).

International Union of Radio Science: c/o INTEC, Ghent University, Sint-Pietersnieuwstraat 41, 9000 Ghent, Belgium; tel. (9) 264-33-20; fax (9) 264-42-88; e-mail ursi@intec.rug.ac.be; internet www.ursi.org; f. 1919 to stimulate and co-ordinate, on an international basis, studies, research, applications, scientific exchange and communication in the field of radio science; aims to encourage the adoption of common methods of measurement and the standardization of measuring instruments used in scientific work; represents radio science at national and international levels; there are 48 national committees; Pres. Prof. K. SCHLEGEL (Germany); Sec.-Gen. Prof. P. LAGASSE (Belgium); publs *The Radio Science Bulletin* (quarterly), *Proceedings of General Assemblies* (every 3 years), *Handbook on Radiopropagation related to Satellite Communications in Tropical and Subtropical Countries, Review of Radio Science* (every 3 years).

International Union of the History and Philosophy of Science: Division of the History of Science (DHS): Centre d'Histoire des Sciences et des Techniques, 5 quai Banning, 4000 Liège, Belgium; tel. (4) 366-94-79; fax (4) 366-94-47; e-mail chst@ulg.ac.be; Division of the History of Logic, Methodology and Philosophy of Science (DLMPS): 161 rue Ada, 34392 Montpellier, France; f. 1956 to promote research into the history and philosophy of science; DHS has 44 national committees and DLMPS has 35 committees; DHS Council: Pres. Prof. B. V. SUBBARAYAPPA (India); Sec. Prof. R. HALLEUX (Belgium); DLMPS Council: Pres. Prof. M. RABIN (Israel); Sec.-Gen. Prof. D. WESTERSTAHL (Sweden).

International Union of Theoretical and Applied Mechanics: c/o Prof. Dick H. van Campen, Dept of Mechanical Engineering, Eindhoven University of Technology, POB 513, 5600 Eindhoven, Netherlands; tel. (40) 2472768; fax (40) 2461418; e-mail sg@iutam.net; internet www.iutam.net; f. 1947 to form links between those engaged in scientific work (theoretical or experimental) in mechanics or related sciences; organizes international congresses of theoretical and applied mechanics, through a standing Congress Committee, and other international meetings; engages in other activities designed to promote the development of mechanics as a science; mems: from 49 countries; Pres. Prof. H. K. MOFFATT (UK); Sec.-Gen. Prof. D. H. VAN CAMPEN (Netherlands); publs *Annual Report, Newsletter.*

International Union of Toxicology: c/o Dept of Environmental and Occupational Health, Graduate School of Public Health, University of Pittsburgh, Pittsburgh, PA 15261, USA; tel. (412) 383-9473; fax (412) 624-3040; e-mail mhk@pitt.edu; internet www.iutox .org; f. 1980 to foster international co-operation among toxicologists and promote world-wide acquisition, dissemination and utilization of knowledge in the field; sponsors International Congresses and other education programmes; mems: 43 national societies; Sec.-Gen. MERYL H. KAROL; publs *IUTOX Newsletter*, Congress proceedings.

International Water Association (IWA): Alliance House, 12 Caxton St, London SW1H OQS, United Kingdom; tel. (20) 7654-5500; fax (20) 7654-5555; e-mail water@iwahq.org.uk; internet www .iwahq.org.uk; f. 1999 by merger of the International Water Services Association and the International Association on Water Quality; aims to encourage international communication, co-operative effort, and exchange of information on water quality management, through conferences, electronic media and publication of research reports; mems: c. 9,000 in 130 countries; Pres. Prof. N. TAMBO (Japan); Exec. Dir ANTHONY MILBURN (UK); publs *Water Research* (monthly), *Water Science and Technology* (24 a year), *Water 21* (6 a year), *Yearbook*, *Scientific and Technical Reports*.

Pacific Science Association: 1525 Bernice St, POB 17801, Honolulu, HI 96817; tel. (808) 848-4139; fax (808) 847-8252; e-mail psa@ bishop.bishop.hawaii.org; internet www.pacificscience.org; f. 1920 to promote co-operation in the study of scientific problems relating to the Pacific region, more particularly those affecting the prosperity and well-being of Pacific peoples; sponsors Pacific Science Congresses and Inter-Congresses; mems: institutional representatives from 35 areas, scientific societies, individual scientists. Tenth Inter-Congress: Guam, 2001; 20th Congress: Bangkok, Thailand, 2003; Pres. Dr R. GERARD WARD (Japan); Exec. Sec. Dr LUCIUS G. ELDREDGE; publ. *Information Bulletin* (2 a year).

Pan-African Union of Science and Technology: POB 2339, Brazzaville, Republic of the Congo; tel. 832265; fax 832185; f. 1987 to promote the use of science and technology in furthering the development of Africa; organizes triennial congress; Pres. Prof. EDWARD AYENSU; Sec.-Gen. Prof. LÉVY MAKANY.

Pugwash Conferences on Science and World Affairs: Ground Floor Flat, 63A Great Russell St, London, WC1B 3BJ, United Kingdom; tel. (20) 7405-6661; fax (20) 7831-5651; e-mail pugwash@ mac.com; internet www.pugwash.org; f. 1957 to organize international conferences of scientists to discuss problems arising from the development of science, particularly the dangers to mankind from weapons of mass destruction; mems: national Pugwash groups in 38 countries; Pres. Prof. M. S. SWAMINATHAN; Sec.-Gen. Prof. PAOLO COTTA-RAMUSINO; publs *Pugwash Newsletter* (2 a year), occasional papers, monographs.

Scientific, Technical and Research Commission (STRC): Nigerian Ports Authority Bldg, PMB 2359, Marina, Lagos, Nigeria; tel. (1) 2633430; fax (1) 2636093; e-mail oaustrcl@hyperia.com; f. 1965 to succeed the Commission for Technical Co-operation in Africa (f. 1954); implements priority programmes of the African Union relating to science and technology for development; supervises the Inter-African Bureau for Animal Resources (Nairobi, Kenya), the Inter-African Bureau for Soils (Lagos, Nigeria) and the Inter-African Phytosanitary Commission (Yaoundé, Cameroon) and several joint research projects; provides training in agricultural man., and conducts pest control programmes; services various inter-African committees of experts, including the Scientific Council for Africa; publishes and distributes specialized scientific books and documents of original value to Africa; organizes training courses, seminars, symposia, workshops and technical meetings; Exec. Dir KOLAWOLE O. ADENIJI.

Unitas Malacologica (Malacological Union): c/o Dr P. B. Mordan, The Natural History Museum, Science Depts, Zoology: Mollusca, Cromwell Rd, London, SW7 5BD, United Kingdom; tel. (20) 7938-9359; fax (20) 7938-8754; e-mail p.mordan@nhm.ac.uk; f. 1962 to further the study of molluscs; affiliated to the International Union of Biological Sciences; holds triennial congress; mems: 400 in over 30 countries; Pres. Dr F. WELLS (Australia); Sec. Dr PETER B. MORDAN (UK); publ. *UM Newsletter* (2 a year).

World Organisation of Systems and Cybernetics (WOSC) (Organisation Mondiale pour la Systémique et la Cybernétique): c/o Dr Alex M. Andrew, 95 Finch Rd, Earley, Reading, Berskshire RG6 7JX, United Kingdom; tel. and fax (118) 926-9328; internet www .cybsoc.org/wosc; f. 1969 to act as clearing-house for all societies

concerned with cybernetics and systems, to aim for the recognition of cybernetics as fundamental science, to organize and sponsor international exhibitions of automation and computer equipment, congresses and symposia, and to promote and co-ordinate research in systems and cybernetics; sponsors an honorary fellowship and awards a Norbert Wiener memorial gold medal; mems: national and international societies in 30 countries; Pres. Prof. R. VALLÉE (France); Dir-Gen. Dr ALEX M. ANDREW; publs *Kybernetes, the International Journal of Cybernetics and Systems.*

Social Sciences

African Social and Environmental Studies Programme: Box 4477, Nairobi, Kenya; tel. (20) 747960; fax (20) 740817; f. 1968; develops and disseminates educational material on social and environmental studies in eastern and southern Africa; mems: 18 African countries; Chair. Prof. WILLIAM SENTEZA-KAJUBI; Exec. Dir Prof. PETER MUYANDA MUTEBI; publs *African Social and Environmental Studies Forum* (2 a year), teaching guides.

Arab Towns Organization (ATO): POB 68160, Kaifan 71962, Kuwait; tel. 4849705; fax 4849322; e-mail ato@ato.net; internet www.ato.net; f. 1967; aims to promote co-operation and the exchange of expertise with regard to urban administration; works to improve the standard of municipal services and utilities in Arab towns and to preserve the character and heritage of Arab towns. Administers an Institute for Urban Development (AUDI), based in Riyadh, Saudi Arabia, which provides training and research for municipal officers; the Arab Towns Development Fund, to help member towns implement projects; and the ATO Award, to encourage the preservation of Arab architecture; mems: 413 towns; Dir-Gen. MOHAMMED ABDUL HAMID AL-SAQR; Sec.-Gen. ABD AL-AZIZ Y. AL-ADASANI; publ. *Al-Madinah Al-Arabiyah* (every 2 months).

Association for the Study of the World Refugee Problem (AWR): Piazzale di Porta Pia 121, 00198 Rome, Italy; tel. (06) 44250159; f. 1951 to promote and co-ordinate scholarly research on refugee problems; mems: 475 in 19 countries; Pres. FRANCO FOSCHI (Italy); Sec.-Gen. ALDO CLEMENTE (Italy); publs *AWR Bulletin* (quarterly, in English, French, Italian and German), treatises on refugee problems (17 vols).

Council for the Development of Social Science Research in Africa (CODESRIA): BP 3304, Dakar, Senegal; tel. 825-98-22; fax 824-12-89; e-mail codesria@sentoo.sn; internet www.codesria.org; f. 1973; promotes research, organizes conferences, working groups and information services; mems: research institutes and university faculties and researchers in African countries; Exec. Sec. ADEBAYO OLUKOSHI; publs *Africa Development* (quarterly), *CODESRIA Bulletin* (quarterly), *Index of African Social Science Periodical Articles* (annually), *African Journal of International Affairs* (2 a year), *African Sociological Review* (2 a year), *Afrika Zameni* (annually), *Identity, Culture and Politics* (2 a year), *Afro Arab Selections for Social Sciences* (annually), directories of research.

Council for Research in Values and Philosophy (CRVP): c/o Prof. G. F. McLean, School of Philosophy, Catholic University of America, Washington, DC 20064, USA; tel. and fax (202) 319-6089; e-mail cua-rvp@cua.edu; internet www.crvp.org; organizes conferences and an annual 10-week seminar; mems: 70 teams from 60 countries; Pres. Prof. KENNETH L. SCHMITZ (Canada); Sec.-Gen. Prof. GEORGE F. MCLEAN (USA); publs *Cultural Heritage and Contemporary Change* series.

Eastern Regional Organisation for Planning and Housing: POB 10867, 50726 Kuala Lumpur, Malaysia; tel. (3) 718-7068; fax (3) 718-3931; f. 1958 to promote and co-ordinate the study and practice of housing and regional town and country planning; maintains offices in Japan, India and Indonesia; mems: 57 organizations and 213 individuals in 28 countries; Sec.-Gen. JOHN KOH SENG SIEW; publs *EAROPH News and Notes* (monthly), *Town and Country Planning* (bibliography).

English-Speaking Union of the Commonwealth: Dartmouth House, 37 Charles St, Berkeley Sq., London, W1J 5ED, United Kingdom; tel. (20) 7529-1550; fax (20) 7495-6108; e-mail esu@esu .org; internet www.esu.org; f. 1918 to promote international understanding between Britain, the Commonwealth, the United States and Europe, in conjunction with the ESU of the USA; mems: 70,000 (incl. USA); Chair. Lord ALAN WATSON; Dir-Gen. VALERIE MITCHELL; publ. *Concord.*

European Association for Population Studies (EAPS): POB 11676, 2502 AR The Hague, Netherlands; tel. (70) 3565200; fax (70) 3647187; e-mail contact@eaps.nl; internet www.eaps.nl; f. 1983 to foster research and provide information on European population problems; organizes conferences, seminars and workshops; mems: demographers from 40 countries; Exec. Sec. GYS BEETS; publ. *European Journal of Population/Revue Européenne de Démographie* (quarterly).

European Society for Rural Sociology: c/o M. Lehtola, Swedish School of Social Science, POB 16, University of Helsinki, Finland; tel. (9) 19128483; fax (9) 19128485; e-mail minna.lehtola@sockom .helsinki.fi; internet esrs.hu/execom03.htm; f. 1957 to further research in, and co-ordination of, rural sociology and provide a centre for documentation of information; mems: 300 individuals, institutions and asscns in 29 European countries and nine countries outside Europe; Pres. Dr IMRE KOVÁCH (Hungary); Sec. MINNA LEHTOLA (Finland); publ. *Sociologia Ruralis* (quarterly).

Experiment in International Living: POB 595, Main St, Putney, VT 05346, USA; tel. (802) 387-4210; fax (802) 387-5783; e-mail federation@experiment.org; internet www.experiment.org; f. 1932 as an international federation of non-profit educational and cultural exchange institutions; works to create mutual understanding and respect among people of different nations, as a means of furthering peace; mems: organizations in 24 countries; Dir ILENE TODD.

International African Institute (IAI): School of Oriental and African Studies, Thornhaugh St, Russell Sq., London, WC1H 0XG, United Kingdom; tel. (20) 7898-4420; fax (20) 7898-4419; e-mail iai@ soas.ac.uk; internet www.oneworld.org/iai; f. 1926 to promote the study of African peoples, their languages, cultures and social life in their traditional and modern settings; organizes an international seminar programme bringing together scholars from Africa and elsewhere; links scholars in order to facilitate research projects, especially in the social sciences; mems: 1,500 in 97 countries; Chair. Prof. V. Y. MUDIMBE; Dir Prof. PAUL SPENCER; publs *Africa* (quarterly), *Africa Bibliography* (annually).

International Association for Media and Communication Research: c/o Ole Prehn, Aalborg University, Kroghstr. 3, 9220 Aalborg East, Denmark; tel. 96-35-90-38; fax 98-15-68-69; e-mail prehn@hum.aau.dk; internet www.iamcr.net; f. 1957 (fmrly International Asscn for Mass Communication Research) to stimulate interest in mass communication research and the dissemination of information about research and research needs, to improve communication practice, policy and research and training for journalism, and to provide a forum for researchers and others involved in mass communication to meet and exchange information; mems: over 2,300 in c.70 countries; Pres. FRANK MORGAN; Sec.-Gen. OLE PREHN; publ. *Newsletter*.

International Association for the History of Religions (IAHR): c/o Prof. Armin W. Geertz, Institut for Religionsvidenskab, Aarhus Universitet, Taasingegade 3, 8000 Aarhus C, Denmark; tel. 89-42-23-06; fax 86-13-04-90; e-mail geertz@teologi.au.dk; internet www.iahr.dk; f. 1950 to promote international collaboration of scholars, to organize congresses and to stimulate research; mems: 33 countries; Pres. PETER ANTES; Sec.-Gen. Prof. ARMIN W. GEERTZ.

International Association of Applied Linguistics (Association internationale de linguistique appliquée—AILA): c/o Susan M. Gass, Dept of Linguistics and German, Slavic, Asian and African Languages, Michigan State Univ., A-714 Wells Hall, East Langing, MI 48824; tel. (517) 353-0800; fax (517) 432-1149; e-mail gass@cal.msu .edu; internet www.aila.ac; f. 1964; organizes seminars on applied linguistics, and a World Congress every three years; mems: asscns in 38 countries; Pres. SUSAN M. GASS (USA); Sec.-Gen. Prof. KARLFRIED KNAPP (Germany); publs *AILA Review* (annually), *AILA News* (2 a year).

International Association of Metropolitan City Libraries (INTAMEL): c/o Frans Meijer, Bibliotheek Rotterdam, Hoogstraat 110, 3011 PV Rotterdam, Netherlands; tel. (10) 281-6140; fax (10) 281-6221; e-mail f.meijer@bibliotheek.rotterdam.nl; f. 1967; serves as a platform for libraries in cities of over 400,000 inhabitants or serving a wide and diverse geographical area; promotes the exchange of ideas and information on a range of topics including library networks, automation, press relations and research; mems: 98 libraries in 28 countries; Pres. FRANS MEIJER (Netherlands); publs *INTAMEL Metro* (2 a year), conference reports.

International Committee for Social Sciences Information and Documentation: c/o Dr A. F. Marks, Herengracht 410 (Swidoc), 1017BX Amsterdam, Netherlands; tel. (20) 6225061; fax (20) 6238374; internet www.unesco.org/most/icssd.htm; f. 1950 to collect and disseminate information on documentation services in social sciences, to help improve documentation, to advise societies on problems of documentation and to draw up rules likely to improve the presentation of documents; mems: from international asscns specializing in social sciences or in documentation, and from other specialized fields; Sec.-Gen. ARNAUD F. MARKS (Netherlands); publs *International Bibliography of the Social Sciences* (annually), *Newsletter* (2 a year).

International Committee for the History of Art: 13 rue de Seine, 75006 Paris, France; e-mail philippe.senechal@inha.fr; internet www.esteticas.unam.mx/ciha; f. 1930 by the 12th International Congress on the History of Art, for collaboration in the scientific study of the history of art; holds international congress every four years, and at least two colloquia between congresses;

mems: National Committees in 34 countries; Pres. Prof. STEPHEN BANN (UK); Sec. PHILIPPE SENECHAL (France); publ. *Bibliographie d'Histoire de l'Art—Bibliography of the History of Art* (quarterly).

International Committee of Historical Sciences: Département d'histoire, UQAM, CP 8888, Succursale Centre-ville, Montréal, QC H3C 3P8, Canada; e-mail cish@uqam.ca; internet www.cish.org; f. 1926 to work for the advancement of historical sciences by means of international co-ordination; holds international congress every five years, 2005: Sydney, Australia; mems: 54 national committees, 28 affiliated international organizations and 12 internal commissions; Pres. JÜRGEN KOCKA (Germany); Sec.-Gen. JEAN-CLAUDE ROBERT (Canada); publ. *Bulletin d'Information du CISH*.

International Congress of African Studies: c/o International African Institute, School of Oriental and African Studies, Thornhaugh St, London, WC1H 0XG, United Kingdom; tel. (20) 7898-4420; fax (20) 7898-4419; e-mail iai@soas.ac.uk; f. 1962.

International Council for Philosophy and Humanistic Studies (ICPHS): Maison de l'UNESCO, 1 rue Miollis, 75732 Paris Cédex 15, France; tel. 1-45-68-26-85; fax 1-40-65-94-80; e-mail cipsh@unesco.org; internet www.unesco.org/cipsh; f. 1949 under the auspices of UNESCO to encourage respect for cultural autonomy by the comparative study of civilization and to contribute towards international understanding through a better knowledge of humanity; works to develop international co-operation in philosophy, humanistic and kindred studies; encourages the setting up of international organizations; promotes the dissemination of information in these fields; sponsors works of learning, etc.; mems: some 13 organizations representing 145 countries; Pres. MADELEINE H. CAVINESS; Sec.-Gen. MAURICE AYMARD; publs *Bulletin of Information* (biennially), *Diogenes* (quarterly).

International Council on Archives (ICA): 60 rue des Francs-Bourgeois, 75003 Paris, France; tel. 1-40-27-63-06; fax 1-42-72-20-65; e-mail ica@ica.org; internet www.ica.org; f. 1948 to develop relationships between archivists in different countries; aims to protect and enhance archives, to ensure preservation of archival heritage; facilitates training of archivists and conservators; promotes implementation of a professional code of conduct; encourages ease of access to archives; has 11 regional branches; mems: 1,680 in 180 countries; Pres. ELISA DE SANTOS (Spain); Sec.-Gen. JOAN VAN ALBADA; publs *Comma* (quarterly), *Flash Newsletter* (3 a year).

International Ergonomics Association (IEA): BP 2025, 3500 HA Utrecht, Netherlands; tel. (30) 35-44-55; fax (30) 35-76-39; internet www.iea.cc; f. 1957 to bring together organizations and persons interested in the scientific study of human work and its environment to establish international contacts among those specializing in this field, to co-operate with employers' asscns and trade unions in order to encourage the practical application of ergonomic sciences in industries, and to promote scientific research in this field; mems: 17 federated societies; Pres. ILKKA KUORINKA (Finland); Sec.-Gen. Prof. D. P. ROOKMAAKER; publ. *Ergonomics* (monthly).

International Federation for Housing and Planning (IFHP): Wassenaarseweg 43, 2596 CG The Hague, Netherlands; tel. (70) 3244557; fax (70) 3282085; e-mail info@ifhp.org; internet www.ifhp .org; f. 1913 to study and promote the improvement of housing and the theory and practice of town planning; holds world congress and international conference every 2 years; mems: 200 organizations and 300 individuals in 65 countries; Pres. IRENE WIESE-VON OFEN (Germany); Sec.-Gen. E. E. VAN HYLCKAMA VLIEG (Netherlands); publ. *Newsletter* (quarterly).

International Federation for Modern Languages and Literatures: c/o D. A. Wells, Dept of German, Birkbeck College, Malet St, London, WC1E 7HX, United Kingdom; tel. (20) 7631-6103; fax (20) 7383-3729; e-mail d.wells@bbk.ac.uk; f. 1928 to establish permanent contact between historians of literature, to develop or perfect facilities for their work and to promote the study of modern languages and literature; holds Congress every three years; mems: 19 asscns, with individual mems in 98 countries; Sec.-Gen. D. A. WELLS (UK).

International Federation of Institutes for Socio-religious Research: 1 pl. Montesquieu, bte 13, 1348 Louvain-la-neuve, Belgium; e-mail gendebien@anso.ucl.ac.be; f. 1958; federates centres engaged in scientific research in order to analyse and discover the social and religious phenomena at work in contemporary society; mems: institutes in 26 countries; Pres. Canon Fr HOUTART (Belgium); Sec. F. GENDEBIEN; publ. *Social Compass (International Review of Sociology of Religion)* (quarterly, in English and French).

International Federation of Philosophical Societies: c/o I. Kuçuradi, Ahmet Rasim Sok. 8/4, Çankaya, 06550 Ankara, Turkey; tel. (312) 4407408; fax (312) 4410297; e-mail ioanna@fisp.org.tr; internet www.fisp.org.tr; f. 1948 under the auspices of UNESCO, to encourage international co-operation in the field of philosophy; holds World Congress of Philosophy every five years; mems: 110 societies from 50 countries; 27 international societies; Pres. IOANNA KUÇURADI (Turkey); Sec.-Gen. PETER KEMP (Denmark); publs *Newsletter*, *Inter-*

national Bibliography of Philosophy, Chroniques de Philosophie, Contemporary Philosophy, Philosophical Problems Today, Philosophy and Cultural Development, Ideas Underlying World Problems,The Idea of Values.

International Federation of Social Science Organizations (IFSSO): Institute of Law, nardoni 18, 110 000 Prague 1, Czech Republic; tel. (2) 24913858; fax (2) 24913858; f. 1979 to assist research and teaching in the social sciences, and to facilitate co-operation and enlist mutual assistance in the planning and evaluation of programmes of major importance to members; mems: 31 national councils or academies in 29 countries; Pres. Prof. CARMEN-CITA T. AGUILAR; Sec.-Gen. Prof. J. BLAHOZ; publs *IFSSO Newsletter* (2 a year), *International Directory of Social Science Organizations.*

International Federation of Societies of Classical Studies: c/o Prof. P. Schubert, 7 rue des Beaux-Arts, 2000 Neuchatel, Switzerland; tel. (22) 3797035; fax (22) 3797932; e-mail paul.schubert@ lettres.unige.ch; internet www.fiecnet.org; f. 1948 under the auspices of UNESCO; mems: 79 societies in 44 countries; Pres. HEINRICH VON STADEN (USA); Sec.-Gen. Prof. PAUL SCHUBERT (Switzerland); publs *L'Année Philologique, Thesaurus linguae Latinae.*

International Federation of Vexillological Associations: Box 580, Winchester, MA 01890, USA; tel. (781) 729-9410; fax (781) 721-4817; e-mail vexor@atthi.com; internet www.crwflags.com/fotw/flags/vex-fiav.html; f. 1967 to promote through its member organizations the scientific study of the history and symbolism of flags; sanctions international standards for scientific flag study; holds International Congresses every two years; mems: 42 institutions and asscns in 27 countries; Pres. Prof. MICHEL LUPANT (Belgium); Liaison Officer WHITNEY SMITH; publs *Recueil* (every 2 years), *The Flag Bulletin* (every 2 months), *Info FIAV* (every 4 months).

International Institute for Ligurian Studies: Via Romana 39, 18012 Bordighera, Italy; tel. (0184) 263601; fax (0184) 266421; e-mail istituto@üsl.it; internet www.üsl.it; f. 1947 to conduct research on ancient monuments and regional traditions in the northwest arc of the Mediterranean (France and Italy); maintains library of 80,000 vols; mems: in France, Italy, Spain, Switzerland; Dir Prof. CARLO VARALDO (Italy).

International Institute of Administrative Sciences (IIAS): 1 rue Defacqz, 1000 Brussels, Belgium; tel. (2) 538-91-65; fax (2) 537-97-02; e-mail iias@iiasiisa.be; internet www.iiasiisa.be; f. 1930 for the comparative examination of administrative experience; carries out research and programmes designed to improve administrative law and practices; maintains library of 15,000 vols; has consultative status with UN, UNESCO and ILO; organizes international congresses; mems: 46 mem. states, 55 national sections, nine international governmental organizations, 51 corporate mems, 13 individual members; Pres. IGNACIO PICHARDO PAGAZA (Mexico); Dir-Gen. GIANCARLO VILELLA (Italy); publs *International Review of Administrative Sciences* (quarterly), *Newsletter* (3 a year).

International Institute of Sociology (IIS): c/o Dr K. Cook, Dept of Sociology, Stanford University, Stanford CA 94305, USA; f. 1893 to enable sociologists to meet and to study sociological questions; mems: c. 300 in 47 countries; Pres. PAOLO AMMASSARI (Italy); Sec.-Gen. Dr KAREN COOK; publ. *The Annals of the IIS.*

International Musicological Society (IMS): CP 1561, 4001 Basel, Switzerland; fax (1) 9231027; e-mail imsba@swissonline.ch; internet www.ims-online.ch; f. 1927; holds international congresses every five years; Pres. DAVID FALLOWS; Sec.-Gen. Dr DOROTHEA BAUMANN (Switzerland); publ. *Acta Musicologica* (2 a year).

International Numismatic Commission: Cabinet des Médailles de la Bibliothèque nationale de France, 58 rue de Richelieu, 75084 Paris Cédex 02, France; tel. 1-53-79-83-63; fax 1-53-79-89-47; e-mail michel.amandry@bnf.fr; internet www.inc-cin.org; f. 1936; facilitates co-operation between scholars studying coins and medals; mems: numismatic orgs in 38 countries; Pres. MICHEL AMANDRY; Sec. C. ARNOLD-BIUCCHI.

International Peace Academy (IPA): 777 United Nations Plaza, New York, NY 10017, USA; tel. (212) 687-4300; fax (212) 983-8246; e-mail ipa@ipacademy.org; internet www.ipacademy.org; f. 1970 to promote the prevention and settlement of armed conflicts between and within states through policy research and development; educates government officials in the procedures needed for conflict resolution, peace-keeping, mediation and negotiation, through international training seminars and publications; off-the-record meetings are also conducted to gain complete understanding of a specific conflict; Chair. RITA E. HAUSER; Pres. DAVID M. MALONE; publ. *Annual Report.*

International Peace Research Association (IPRA): c/o K. Kodama, Mie University, Dept of Humanities, Kamihama, Tsu 514, Japan; tel. and fax (592) 319156; e-mail kkodama@human.mie-u.ac .jp; internet www.human.mie-u.ac.jp/~peace/; f. 1964 to encourage interdisciplinary research on the conditions of peace and the causes of war; mems: 150 corporate, five regional branches, 1,000 individ-

uals, in 93 countries; Sec.-Gen. KATSUYA KODAMA (Japan); publ. *IPRA Newsletter* (quarterly).

International Social Science Council (ISSC): Maison de l'UNESCO, 1 rue Miollis, 75732 Paris Cédex 15, France; tel. 1-45-68-48-60; fax 1-45-66-76-03; e-mail issc@unesco.org; internet www .unesco.org/ngo/issc; f. 1952; aims to promote the advancement of the social sciences throughout the world and their application to the major problems of the world; encourages co-operation at an international level between specialists in the social sciences. ISSC has a Senior Board; and programmes on International Human Dimensions of Global Environmental Change (IHDP), Gender, Globalization and Democratization, and Comparative Research on Poverty (CROP); mems: International Association of Legal Sciences, International Economic Association, International Federation of Social Science Organizations, International Geographical Union, International Institute of Administrative Sciences, International Law Association, International Peace Research Association, International Political Science Association, International Sociological Association, International Union for the Scientific Study of Population, International Union of Anthropological and Ethnological Sciences, International Union of Psychological Science, World Association for Public Opinion Research, World Federation for Mental Health; 22 national organizations; 18 associate member organizations; Pres. Prof. LOURDES ARIZPE (Mexico); Sec.-Gen. Dr ALI KAZANCIGIL (Turkey).

International Society of Social Defence and Humane Criminal Policy (ISSD): c/o Centro nazionale di prevenzione e difesa sociale, Piazza Castello 3, 20121 Milan, Italy; tel. (02) 86460714; fax (02) 72008431; e-mail cnpds.ispac@iol.it; f. 1945 to combat crime, to protect society and to prevent citizens from being tempted to commit criminal actions; mems: in 43 countries; Pres. SIMONE ROZÈS (France); Sec.-Gen. EDMONDO BRUTI LIBERATI (Italy); publ. *Cahiers de défense sociale* (annually).

International Sociological Association: c/o Faculty of Political Sciences and Sociology, Universidad Complutense, 28223 Madrid, Spain; tel. (91) 3527650; fax (91) 3524945; e-mail isa@sis.ucm.es; internet www.ucm.es/info/isa; f. 1949 to promote sociological knowledge, facilitate contacts between sociologists, encourage the dissemination and exchange of information and facilities and stimulate research; has 53 research committees on various aspects of sociology; holds World Congresses every four years (15th Congress: Brisbane, Australia, 2002); Pres. A. MARTINELLI (Italy); Exec. Sec. IZABELA BARLINSKA; publs *Current Sociology* (3 a year), *International Sociology* (quarterly), *Sage Studies in International Sociology* (based on World Congress).

International Statistical Institute (ISI): POB 950, Prinses Beatrixlaan 428, 2270 AZ Voorburg, Netherlands; tel. (70) 3375737; fax (70) 3860025; e-mail isi@cbs.nl; internet www.cbs.nl/isi; f. 1885; devoted to the development and improvement of statistical methods and their application throughout the world; administers a statistical education centre in Calcutta, in co-operation with the Indian Statistical Institute; executes international research programmes; mems: 2,000 ordinary mems, nine hon. mems, 166 *ex-officio* mems, 69 corporate mems, 45 affiliated organizations, 32 national statistical societies; Pres. NIELS KEIDING (Denmark); Dir Permanent Office DANIEL BERZE; publs *Bulletin of the International Statistical Institute* (proceedings of biennial sessions), *International Statistical Review* (3 a year), *Short Book Reviews* (3 a year), *Statistical Theory and Method Abstracts–Z* (available on CD-Rom and online), *ISI Newsletter* (3 a year), *Membership Directory* (available online).

International Studies Association (ISA): Social Science 324, Univ. of Arizona, Tucson, AZ 85721, USA; tel. (520) 621-7715; fax (520) 621-5780; e-mail isa@u.arizona.edu; internet www.isanet.org; f. 1959; links those whose professional concerns extend beyond their own national boundaries (government officials, representatives of business and industry, and scholars); mems: 3,500 in 60 countries; Pres. MICHAEL BRECHER; Exec. Dir THOMAS J. VOLGY; publs *International Studies Quarterly, International Studies Perspectives, International Studies Review, ISA Newsletter.*

International Union for Oriental and Asian Studies: Közraktar u. 12A 11/2, 1093 Budapest, Hungary; f. 1951 by the 22nd International Congress of Orientalists under the auspices of UNESCO, to promote contacts between orientalists throughout the world, and to organize congresses, research and publications; mems: in 24 countries; Sec.-Gen. Prof. GEORG HAZAI; publs *Philologiae Turcicae Fundamenta, Materialien zum Sumerischen Lexikon, Sanskrit Dictionary, Corpus Inscriptionum Iranicarum, Linguistic Atlas of Iran, Matériels des parlers iraniens, Turcology Annual, Bibliographie égyptologique.*

International Union for the Scientific Study of Population (IUSSP): 34 rue des Augustins, 4000 Liège, Belgium; tel. (4) 222-40-80; fax (4) 222-38-47; e-mail iussp@iussp.org; internet www.iussp .org; f. 1928 to advance the progress of quantitative and qualitative demography as a science; mems: 1,917 in 121 countries; Pres. JOSÉ

Social Welfare and Human Rights

ALBERTO M. DE CARVALHO; publs *IUSSP Bulletin* and books on population.

International Union of Academies (IUA) (Union académique internationale—UAI): Palais des Académies, 1 rue Ducale, 1000 Brussels, Belgium; tel. (2) 550-22-00; fax (2) 550-22-05; e-mail info@uai-iua.org; internet www.uai-iua.org; f. 1919 to promote international co-operation through collective research in philology, archaeology, art history, history and social sciences; mems: academic institutions in 56 countries; Pres. S. SHAKED (Israel); Secs L HOUZIAUX, J.-L. DE PAEPE.

International Union of Anthropological and Ethnological Sciences (IUAES): c/o Dr P. J. M. Nas, Faculty of Social Sciences, Univ. of Leiden, Wassenaarseweg 52, POB 9555, 2300 RB Leiden, Netherlands; tel. (71) 5273992; fax (71) 5273619; e-mail nas@rulfsw.leidenuniv.nl; internet lucy.ukc.ac.uk/IUAES; f. 1948 under the auspices of UNESCO, to enhance exchange and communication between scientists and institutions in the fields of anthropology and ethnology; aims to promote harmony between nature and culture; organizes 22 international research commissions; mems: institutions and individuals in 100 countries; Pres. Prof. ERIC SUNDERLAND (UK); Sec.-Gen. Dr P. J. M. NAS (Netherlands); publ. *IUAES Newsletter* (3 a year).

International Union of Prehistoric and Protohistoric Sciences: c/o Prof. J. Bourgeois, Dept of Archaeology and Ancient History of Europe, University of Ghent, Blandijnberg 2, 9000 Ghent, Belgium; tel. (9) 264-41-06; fax (9) 264-41-73; e-mail jean.bourgeois@rug.ac.be; internet www.geocities.com/athens/ithaca/7152; f. 1931 to promote congresses and scientific work in the fields of pre- and proto-history; mems: 120 countries; Pres. Prof. P. BONENFANT (Belgium); Sec.-Gen. Prof. J. BOURGEOIS (Belgium).

Mensa International: 15 The Ivories, 6–8 Northampton St, London, N1 2HY, United Kingdom; tel. (20) 7226-6891; fax (20) 7226-7059; internet www.mensa.org/mensa-international; f. 1946 to identify and foster intelligence for the benefit of humanity; mems: individuals who score in a recognized intelligence test higher than 98% of people in general may become mems; there are 100,000 mems world-wide; Exec. Dir E. J. VINCENT (UK); publ. *Mensa International Journal* (monthly).

Permanent International Committee of Linguists: Instituut voor Nederlandse Lexicologie, Matthias de Vrieshof 2, 2311 BZ Leiden, Netherlands; tel. (71) 5141648; fax (71) 5272115; e-mail secretariaat@inl.nl; internet www.ciplnet.com; f. 1928; aims to further linguistic research, to co-ordinate activities undertaken for the advancement of linguistics, and to make the results of linguistic research known internationally; holds Congress every five years; mems: 34 countries and two international linguistic organizations; Pres. F. KIEFER (Hungary); Sec.-Gen. P. G. J. VAN STERKENBURG (Netherlands); publ. *Linguistic Bibliography* (annually).

Third World Forum: 39 Dokki St, POB 43, Orman Giza, Cairo, Egypt; tel. (2) 7488092; fax (2) 7480668; e-mail 20sabry2@gega.net; internet www.egypt2020.org; f. 1973 to link social scientists and others from the developing countries, to discuss alternative development policies and encourage research; currently undertaking Egypt 2020 research project; maintains regional offices in Egypt, Mexico, Senegal and Sri Lanka; mems: individuals in more than 50 countries; Chair. ISMAIL-SABRI ABDALLA.

World Association for Public Opinion Research: c/o University of Nebraska-Lincoln, UNL Gallup Research Center, 200 N 11th St, Lincoln, NE 68588-0241, USA; tel. (402) 458-2030; fax (402) 458-2038; e-mail wapor@unl.edu; internet www.wapor.org; f. 1947 to establish and promote contacts between persons in the field of survey research on opinions, attitudes and behaviour of people in the various countries of the world; works to further the use of objective, scientific survey research in national and international affairs; mems: 450 from 72 countries; Man. Dir RENAE REIS; publs *WAPOR Newsletter* (quarterly), *International Journal of Public Opinion* (quarterly).

World Society for Ekistics: c/o Athens Center of Ekistics, 24 Strat. Syndesmou St, 106 73 Athens, Greece; tel. (1) 3623216; fax (1) 3629337; e-mail ekistics@otenet.gr; internet www.ekistics.org; f. 1965; aims to promote knowledge and ideas concerning human settlements through research, publications and conferences; encourages the development and expansion of education in ekistics; aims to recognize the benefits and necessity of an inter-disciplinary approach to the needs of human settlements; mems: 170 individuals; Pres. Dr SUZANNE KELLER; Sec.-Gen. and Treas. P. PSOMOPOULOS.

Social Welfare and Human Rights

African Commission on Human and People's Rights: Kairaba Ave, POB 673, Banjul, The Gambia; e-mail idoc@achpr.org; internet www.achpr.org; tel. 392962; fax 390764; f. 1987; mandated to monitor compliance with the African Charter on Human and People's Rights (ratified in 1986); investigates claims of human rights abuses perpetrated by govts that have ratified the Charter (claims may be brought by other African govts, the victims themselves, or by a third party); meets twice a year for 15 days in March and Oct.; mems: 11; Sec. GERMAIN BARICAKO (Burundi).

Aid to Displaced Persons and its European Villages: 35 rue du Marché, 4500 Huy, Belgium; tel. (85) 21-34-81; fax (85) 23-01-47; e-mail aidepersdepl.huy@proximedia.be; internet www.proximedia.com/aideperso.html; f. 1957 to carry on and develop work begun by the Belgian asscn Aid to Displaced Persons; aims to provide material and moral aid for refugees; European Villages established at Aachen, Bregenz, Augsburg, Berchem-Ste-Agathe, Spiesen, Euskirchen, Wuppertal as centres for refugees; Pres. LUC DENYS (Belgium).

Amnesty International: 1 Easton St, London, WC1X ODW, United Kingdom; tel. (20) 7413-5500; fax (20) 7956-1157; e-mail amnestyis@amnesty.org; internet www.amnesty.org; f. 1961; an independent world-wide movement that campaigns impartially for the release of all prisoners of conscience, for fair and prompt trials for all political prisoners, for the abolition of torture and the death penalty and for an end to extrajudicial executions and 'disappearances'; also opposes abuses by opposition groups (hostage-taking, torture and arbitrary killings); financed by donations; mems: more than 1.5m. represented by 7,800 local, youth, student and other specialist groups, in more than 140 countries and territories; nationally organized sections in 58 countries and pre-section co-ordinating structures in another 22 countries; Sec.-Gen. IRENE KHAN (Bangladesh); publs *International Newsletter* (monthly), *Annual Report*, other country reports.

Anti-Slavery International: Thomas Clarkson House, The Stableyard, Broomgrove Rd, London, SW9 9TL, United Kingdom; tel. (20) 7501-8920; fax (20) 7738-4110; e-mail antislavery@antislavery.org; internet www.antislavery.org; f. 1839; aims to eliminate all forms of slavery by exposing manifestations of it around the world and campaigning against it; supports initiatives by local organizations to release people from slavery, and develops rehabilitation programmes aimed at preventing people from re-entering slavery; pressures governments to implement international laws prohibiting slavery and to develop and enforce similar national legislation; mems: more than 5,000 world-wide; Chair. DEE SULLIVAN; Dir MARY CUNNEEN; publs *Annual Review* (quarterly), *Reporter* (quarterly), special reports and research documentation.

Associated Country Women of the World (ACWW): Mary Sumner House, 24 Tufton St, London, SW1P 3RB, United Kingdom; tel. (20) 7799-3875; fax (20) 7340-9950; e-mail info@acww.org.uk; internet www.acww.org.uk; f. 1933; aims to aid the economic and social development of countrywomen and home-makers of all nations, to promote international goodwill and understanding, and to work to alleviate poverty, and promote good health and education; Pres. URSULA GOM; publ. *The Countrywoman* (quarterly).

Association Internationale de la Mutualité (AIM) (International Association of Mutual Health Funds): 50 rue d'Arlon, 1000 Brussels, Belgium; tel. (2) 234-57-00; fax (2) 234-57-08; e-mail aim.secretariat@aim-mutual.org; internet www.aim-mutual.org; f. 1950 as a grouping of autonomous health insurance and social protection bodies; aims to promote and reinforce access to health care by developing the sound management of mutualities; serves as a forum for exchange of information and debate; mems: 43 national federations in 31 countries; Pres. RON HENDRIKS (Netherlands); Dir WILLY PALM (Belgium); publs *AIMS* (newsletter), reports on health issues.

Aviation sans Frontières (ASF): Brussels National Airport, Brucargo 706, POB 7339, 1931 Brucargo, Belgium; tel. (2) 753-24-70; fax (2) 753-24-71; e-mail office@asfbelgium.org; internet www.asfbelgium.org; f. 1983 to make available the resources of the aviation industry to humanitarian organizations, for carrying supplies and equipment at minimum cost, both on long-distance flights and locally; Pres. PHILIPPE DEHENNIN; Gen. Man. XAVIER FLAMENT.

Co-ordinating Committee for International Voluntary Service (CCIVS): Maison de l'UNESCO, 1 rue Miollis, 75732 Paris Cédex 15, France; tel. 1-45-68-49-36; fax 1-42-73-05-21; e-mail ccivs@unesco.org; internet www.unesco.org/ccivs; f. 1948 to co-ordinate youth voluntary service organizations world-wide; Organizes seminars and conferences; publishes relevant literature; undertakes planning and execution of projects in collaboration with UNESCO, the UN, the EU etc; generates funds for member organizations' projects; Affiliated mems: 140 orgs in more than 90 countries; Pres. G. ORSINI; Dir S. COSTANZO-SOW; publs *News from CCIVS* (3 a year), *The Volunteer's Handbook*, other guides, handbooks and directories.

Co-ordinator of the Indigenous Organizations of the Amazon Basin (COICA): e-mail com@coica.org; internet www.coica.org; f. 1984; aims to co-ordinate the activities of national organizations concerned with the indigenous people and environment of the Amazon basin, and promotes respect for human rights and the self-determination of the indigenous populations; nine member orgs; Co-

Social Welfare and Human Rights

ordinator-General Sebastião Manchineri; publ. *Nuestra Amazonia* (quarterly, in English, Spanish, French and Portuguese).

EIRENE (International Christian Service for Peace): 56503 Neuwied, Postfach 1322, Germany; tel. (2631) 83790; fax (2631) 31160; e-mail eirene-int@eirene.org; internet www.eirene.org; f. 1957; carries out professional training, apprenticeship programmes, agricultural work and work to support co-operatives in Africa and Latin America; runs volunteer programmes in co-operation with peace groups in Europe and the USA; Gen. Sec. Eckehard Fricke.

European Federation of Older Persons (EURAG): Wielandgasse 9, 1 Stock, 8010 Graz, Austria; tel. (316) 81-46-08; fax (316) 81-46-08; e-mail office@eurag-europe.org; internet www.eurag-europe .org; f. 1962 as the European Federation for the Welfare of the Elderly (present name adopted 2002); serves as a forum for the exchange of experience and practical co-operation among member organizations; represents the interests of members before international organizations; promotes understanding and co-operation in matters of social welfare; draws attention to the problems of old age; mems: organizations in 33 countries; Pres. Edmée Mangers-Anen (Luxembourg); Sec.-Gen. Dr Ulla Herfort-Wörndle (Austria); publs (in English, French, German and Italian) *EURAG Newsletter* (quarterly), *EURAG Information* (monthly).

Federation of Asia-Pacific Women's Associations (FAWA): Centro Escolar University, 9 Mendiola St, San Miguel, Manila, Philippines; tel. (2) 741-04-46; e-mail zmaustria@ceu.edu.ph; f. 1959 to provide closer relations, and bring about joint efforts among Asians, particularly women, through mutual appreciation of cultural, moral and socio-economic values; mems: 415,000; Pres. Susy Chia-Isai (Singapore); Sec. Woo Choon Mei (Singapore); publ. *FAWA News Bulletin* (quarterly).

Inclusion Europe: Galeries de la Toison d'Or, 29 ch. d'Ixelles, Ste 393/32, 1050 Brussels, Belgium; tel. (2) 502-28-15; fax (2) 502-80-10; e-mail secretariat@inclusion-europe.org; internet www .inclusion-europe.org; f. 1988 to advance the human rights and defend the interests of people with learning or intellectual disabilities, and their families, in Europe; mems: 40 societies in 28 European countries; Pres. Françoise Jan; Dir Geert Freyhoff; publs *INCLUDE* (in English and French), *Information Letter* (weekly online, in English and French), *Human Rights Observer* (in English and French), *Enlargement Update* (on-line every 2 weeks, in English and French), other papers and publs.

Inter-American Conference on Social Security (Conferencia Interamericano de Seguridad Social—CISS): Calle San Ramon s/n esq. Avda San Jerónimo, UCol. San Jerónimo Lídice, Del. Magdalena Contreras, CP 10100 México, DF, Mexico; tel. (55) 5595-0011; fax (55) 5683-8524; e-mail ciss@ciss.org.mx; internet www.ciss.org .mx; f. 1942 to contribute to the development of social security in the countries of the Americas and to co-operate with social security institutions; CISS bodies are: the General Assembly, the Permanent Inter-American Committee on Social Security, the Secretariat General, six American Commissions of Social Security and the Inter-American Center for Social Security Studies; mems: 66 social security institutions in 36 countries; Pres. Santiago Levy Algazi (Mexico); Sec.-Gen. Dr Gabriel Martínez González (Mexico); publs *Social Security Journal/Seguridad Social* (every 2 months), *The Americas Social Security Report* (annually), *Social Security Bulleting* (monthly, online), monographs, study series.

International Abolitionist Federation: 11 rue des Savoies, 1205 Geneva, Switzerland; tel. (22) 7813060; fax (22) 7813133; e-mail iaf@ iaf-online.org; f. 1875; aims to abolish traffic in persons, the exploitation of the prostitution of others, state regulation of prostitution, degradation, humiliation and marginalizing of women and children, all forms of discrimination based on gender, and all contemporary forms of slavery and slavery-like practices; holds international congress every three years and organizes regional conferences to raise awareness of the cultural, religious and traditional practices that affect adversely the lives of women and children; Affiliated organizations in 17 countries, corresponding mems in 40 countries; Sec.-Gen. Hélène Sackstein; publ. *IAF Information* (1-2 a year).

International Association for Education to a Life without Drugs (Internationaler Verband für Erziehung zu suchtmittelfreiem Leben—IVES): c/o Uljas Syväniemi, Haiharankatu 15 G 64, 33710 Tampere, Finland; e-mail uljas.syvaniemi@koti.tpo.ti; f. 1954 (as the International Association for Temperance Education) to promote international co-operation in education on the dangers of alcohol and drugs; collects and distributes information on drugs; maintains regular contact with national and international organizations active in these fields; holds conferences; mems: 77,000 in 10 countries; Pres. Uljas Syväniemi; Sec. Dag Magne Johannessen.

International Association for Suicide Prevention: c/o Ms M. Campos, IASP Central Administrative Office, 1725 West Harrison St, Suite 955, Chicago, IL 60612, USA; tel. (312) 942-7208; fax (312) 942-2177; internet www.iasp1960.org; f. 1960; serves as a common platform for interchange of acquired experience, literature and

information about suicide; disseminates information; arranges special training; encourages and carries out research; organizes the Biennial International Congress for Suicide Prevention; mems: 340 individuals and societies, in 55 countries of all continents; Pres. Dr Diego de Leo; publ. *Crisis* (quarterly).

International Association of Children's International Summer Villages (CISV International Ltd): Mea House, Ellison Pl., Newcastle upon Tyne, NE1 8XS, United Kingdom; tel. (191) 232-4998; fax (191) 261-4710; e-mail international@cisv.org; internet www.cisv.org; f. 1950 to promote peace, education and cross-cultural friendship; conducts International Camps for children and young people mainly between the ages of 11 and 19; mems: c. 49,000; International Pres. Cathy Knoop; Sec.-Gen. Gabrielle Mandell; publs *CISV News, Annual Review, Local Work Magazine, Interspectives* (all annually).

International Association of Schools of Social Work: School of Social Sciences, University of Southampton, Highfield, Southampton SO17 1BJ, United Kingdom; tel. (2380) 593054; fax (2380) 594800; e-mail ld@socsci.soton.ac.uk; internet www.iassw.soton.ac .uk; f. 1928 to provide international leadership and encourage high standards in social work education; mems: 1,600 schools of social work in 70 countries, and 25 national asscns of schools; Pres. Lena Dominelli (UK); Sec. Bertha Mary Rodriguez Villa; publs *Newsletters* (in English, French and Spanish), *Directory of Schools of Social Work, Journal of International Social Work*, reports and case studies.

International Association of Social Educators (AIEJI): 22 rue Halévy, 59000 Lille, France; tel. 3-20-93-70-16; fax 3-20-09-18-39; internet www.aieji.net; f. 1951 (as International Asscn of Workers for Troubled Children and Youth); provides a centre of information about child welfare; encourages co-operation between members; 2005 Congress: Montevideo, Uruguay; mems: national and regional public or private asscns from 22 countries and individual members in many other countries; Pres. Arlin E. Ness (USA); Gen. Sec. Lars Steinov (Denmark).

International Catholic Migration Commission: CP 96, 37–39 rue de Vermont, POB 96, 1211 Geneva 20, Switzerland; tel. (22) 9191020; fax (22) 9191048; e-mail secretariat.ch@icmc.net; internet www.icmc.net; f. 1951; offers migration aid programmes; grants interest-free travel loans; assists refugees on a world-wide basis, helping with social and technical problems; mems: in 85 countries; Pres. Prof. Stefano Zamagni (Italy); Sec.-Gen. Johan Ketelers (Belgium); publ. *Annual Report*.

International Christian Federation for the Prevention of Alcoholism and Drug Addiction: 20a Ancienne Route, Apt. No 42, 1218 Grand-Saconnex, Geneva, Switzerland; tel. (22) 7888158; fax (22) 7888136; e-mail jonathan@iprolink.ch; f. 1960, reconstituted 1980 to promote world-wide education and remedial work through the churches and to co-ordinate Christian concern about alcohol and drug abuse, in co-operation with the World Council of Churches and WHO; Chair. Karin Israelsson (Sweden); Gen. Sec. Jonathan N. Gnanadason.

International Civil Defence Organization (ICDO) (Organisation internationale de protection civile—OIPC): POB 172, 10–12 chemin de Surville, 1213 Petit-Lancy 2, Geneva, Switzerland; tel. (22) 8796969; fax (22) 8796979; e-mail icdo@icdo.org; internet www .icdo.org; f. 1931, present statutes in force 1972; aims to contribute to the development of structures ensuring the protection of populations and the safeguarding of property and the environment in the face of natural and man-made disasters; promotes co-operation between civil defence organizations in member countries; Sec.-Gen. Nawaf B. S. al Sleibi (Jordan); publ. *International Civil Defence Journal* (quarterly, in Arabic, English, French, Russian and Spanish).

International Commission for the Prevention of Alcoholism and Drug Dependency: 12501 Old Columbia Pike, Silver Spring, MD 20904-6600, USA; tel. (301) 680-6719; fax (301) 680-6707; e-mail the_icpa@hotmail.com; internet www.adventist.org/icpa; f. 1952 to encourage scientific research on intoxication by alcohol, its physiological, mental and moral effects on the individual, and its effect on the community; 50th anniversary conference (eleventh World Congress): Bethesda, USA, 2002; mems: individuals in 120 countries; Exec. Dir Dr Peter N. Landless; publ. *ICPA Reporter*.

International Council of Voluntary Agencies (ICVA): 48 Chemin du Grand-Montfleury, 1290 Versoix, Switzerland; tel. (22) 9509600; fax (22) 9509609; e-mail secretariat@icva.ch; internet www .icva.ch; f. 1962 as a global network of human rights and humanitarian and development NGOs; focuses on information exchange and advocacy, primarily in the areas of humanitarian affairs and refugee issues; mems: 78 non-governmental organizations; Chair. Anders Ladekarl; Co-ordinator Ed Schenkenberg van Mierop; publ. *Talk Back* (newsletter; available on website).

International Council of Women (ICW) (Conseil international des femmes—CIF): 13 rue Caumartin, 75009 Paris, France; tel. 1-47-42-19-40; fax 1-42-66-26-23; e-mail icw-cif@wanadoo.fr; internet www.icw-cif.org; f. 1888 to bring together in international affiliation Nat. Councils of Women from all continents, for consultation and joint action; promotes equal rights for men and women and the integration of women in development and decision-making; has five standing committees; mems: 63 national councils; Pres. ANAMAH TAN; Sec.-Gen. MARIE-CHRISTINE LAFARGUE; publ. *Newsletter*.

International Council on Alcohol and Addictions (ICAA): CP 189, 1001 Lausanne, Switzerland; tel. (21) 3209865; fax (21) 3209817; e-mail secretariat@icaa.ch; internet www.icaa.de; f. 1907; provides an international forum for all those concerned with the prevention of harm resulting from the use of alcohol and other drugs; offers advice and guidance in development of policies and pro-grammes; organizes training courses, congresses, symposia and seminars in different countries; mems: affiliated organizations in 74 countries, as well as individual members; Pres. Dr IBRAHIM AL-AWAJI (Saudi Arabia); Exec. Dir Dr JÖRG SPIELDENNER (Germany); publs *ICAA News, Alcoholism* (2 a year).

International Council on Jewish Social and Welfare Services (INTERCO): World Jewish Relief, The Forum, 74–80 Camden St, London, NW1 OEG, United Kingdom; tel. (20) 7691-1771; fax (20) 7691-1780; e-mail info@wjr.org.uk; internet www.tolife.info; f. 1961; functions include the exchange of views and information among member agencies concerning the problems of Jewish social and welfare services; represents views to governments and international organizations. mems: organizations in France, Switzerland, United Kingdom and the USA; Exec. Sec. VIVIENNE LEWIS.

International Council on Social Welfare (ICSW): 380 St Antoine St West, Suite 3200, Montreal H2Y 3X7, Canada; tel. (514) 287-3280; fax (514) 287-9702; e-mail icsw@icsw.org; internet www.icsw.org; f. 1928 to provide an international forum for the discussion of social work and related issues and to promote interest in social welfare; holds international conference every two years; provides documentation and information services; mems: 45 national com-mittees, 12 international organizations, 33 other organizations; Pres. JULIAN DISNEY (Australia); Exec. Dir STEPHEN KING (UK); publ. *Social Development Review* (quarterly).

International Dachau Committee: 2 rue Chauchat, 75009 Paris, France; tel. 1-45-23-39-99; fax 1-48-00-06-73; f. 1958 to perpetuate the memory of the political prisoners of Dachau to manifest the friendship and solidarity of former prisoners whatever their beliefs or nationality; to maintain the ideals of their resistance, liberty, tolerance and respect for persons and nations; and to maintain the former concentration camp at Dachau as a museum and interna-tional memorial; mems: national asscns in 20 countries; Pres. Gen. ANDRÉ DELPECH; Sec.-Gen. JEAN SAMUEL; publ. *Bulletin Officiel du Comité International de Dachau* (2 a year).

International Federation of the Blue Cross: CP 6813, 3001 Bern, Switzerland; tel. (31) 3005860; fax (31) 3005869; e-mail ifbc.bern@bluewin.ch; internet www.eurocare.org/bluecross; f. 1877 to aid the victims of intemperance and drug addicts, and to take part in the general movement against alcoholism; Pres. Pastor RAYMOND BASSIN (Switzerland); Gen. Sec. HANS RÜTTIMAN.

International Federation of Educative Communities (FICE): Piazza S.S. Annunziale 12, 50122 Florence, Italy; tel. (055) 2469162; fax (055) 2347041; e-mail fice@lycosmail.com; f. 1948 under the auspices of UNESCO to co-ordinate the work of national asscns, and to promote the international exchange of knowledge and experience in the field of childcare; mems: national asscns from 21 European countries, India, Israel, Canada, Morocco, the USA and South Africa; Pres. ROBERT SOISSON (Luxembourg); Gen. Sec. GIANLUCA BARBANOTTI (Italy); publ. *Bulletin* (2 a year).

International Federation of Human Rights Leagues (FIDH): 17 passage de la Main d'Or, 75011 Paris, France; tel. 1-43-55-25-18; fax 1-43-55-18-80; e-mail fidh@fidh.org; internet www.fidh.imaginet.fr; f. 1922; promotes the implementation of the Universal Declara-tion of Human Rights and other instruments of human rights protection; aims to raise awareness and alert public opinion to issues of human rights violations; undertakes investigation and observa-tion missions; carries out training; uses its consultative and observer status to lobby international authorities; mems: 105 national leagues in over 86 countries; Pres. SIDIKI KABA; publs *Lettre* (2 a month), mission reports.

International Federation of Persons with Physical Disability (FIMITIC): Plittersdorfer Str. 103, 53173 Bonn, Germany; tel. (228) 9359-191; fax (228) 9359-192; e-mail fimitic@t-online.de; internet www.fimitic.org; f. 1953; an international, humanitarian, non-profit, politically and religiously neutral non-governmental umbrella feder-ation of persons with physical disability under the guidance of the disabled themselves; focuses activities on ensuring the equalization of opportunities and full participation of persons with physical disabilities in society and fights against any kind of discrimination

against persons with disabilities; mems: national groups from 28 European countries; Pres. MARIJA-LIDIJA STIGLIC (Germany); publs *Bulletin, Nouvelles*.

International Federation of Social Workers (IFSW): POB 6875, Schwarztorstrasse 20, 3001 Bern, Switzerland; tel. (31) 3826015; fax (31) 3811222; e-mail global@ifsw.org; internet www.ifsw.org; f. 1928 as International Permanent Secretariat of Social Workers; present name adopted 1956; aims to promote social work as a profession through international co-operation on standards, training, ethics and working conditions; organizes international conferences; represents the profession at the UN and other interna-tional bodies; supports national asscns of social workers; mems: national asscns in 80 countries; Pres. IMELDA DODDS (Australia); Sec.-Gen. TOM JOHANNESEN (Switzerland); publs *IFSW update* (available on-line), policy statements and manifestos.

International League against Racism and Antisemitism: CP 1754, 1211 Geneva 1, Switzerland; tel. (22) 7310633; fax (22) 7370634; e-mail licra@mnet.ch; internet www.licra.ch; f. 1927; mems in 17 countries; Pres. PIERRE AIDENBAUM (France).

International League for Human Rights: 228 E 45th St. 5th Floor, New York, NY 10017, USA; tel. (212) 661-0480; fax (212) 661-0416; e-mail info@ilhr.org; internet www.ilhr.org; f. 1942 to imple-ment political, civil, social, economic and cultural rights contained in the Universal Declaration of Human Rights adopted by the United Nations and to support and protect defenders of human rights world-wide; mems: individuals, national affiliates and correspondents throughout the world; Exec. Dir LOUISE KANTROW; publs various human rights reports.

International Planned Parenthood Federation (IPPF): Regent's College, Inner Circle, Regent's Park, London, NW1 4NS, United Kingdom; tel. (20) 7487-7900; fax (20) 7487-7950; e-mail info@ippf.org; internet www.ippf.org; f. 1952; aims to promote and support sexual and reproductive health rights and choices world-wide, with a particular focus on the needs of young people; works to bring relevant issues to the attention of the media, parliamentar-ians, academics, governmental and non-governmental organiza-tions, and the general public; mobilizes financial resources to fund programmes and information materials; offers technical assistance and training; collaborates with other international organizations. The International Medical Panel of the IPPF formulates guide-lines and statements on current medical and scientific advice and best practices; mems: independent family planning asscns in over 150 countries; Pres. NINA PURI; Dir-Gen. Dr STEVEN SINDING.

International Prisoners Aid Association: c/o Dr Ali, Depart-ment of Sociology, University of Louisville, Louisville, KY 40292, USA; tel. (502) 588-6836; fax (502) 852-7042; f. 1950; works to improve prisoners' aid services, with the aim of promoting the rehabilitation of the individual and increasing the protection of society; mems: national federations in 29 countries; Pres. Dr WOLF-GANG DOLEISCH (Austria); Exec. Dir Dr BADR-EL-DIN ALI; publ. *News-letter* (3 a year).

International Scout and Guide Fellowship (ISGF): 38 ave de la Porte de Hal, 1060 Brussels, Belgium; tel. and fax (2) 511-46-95; e-mail isgf-aisg@euronet.be; internet www.isgf.org; f. 1953 to help adult scouts and guides to keep alive the spirit of the Scout and Guide Promise and Laws in their own lives and to bring that spirit into the communities in which they live and work; promotes liaison and co-operation between national organizations for adult scouts and guides; encourages the founding of an organization in any country where no such organization exists; mems: 90,000 in 57 mem. states; Chair. of Cttee RICCARDO DELLA ROCCA; Sec.-Gen. FAOUZIA KCHOUK; publ. *World Gazette Mondiale* (quarterly).

International Social Security Association (ISSA): CP 1, 1211 Geneva 22, Switzerland; tel. (22) 7996617; fax (22) 7998509; e-mail issa@ilo.org; internet www.issa.int; f. 1927 to promote the develop-ment of social security throughout the world, mainly through the improvement of techniques and administration, in order to advance social and economic conditions on the basis of social equality; mems: 367 institutions in 151 countries; Pres. CORAZON DE LA PAZ (Philip-pines); Sec.-Gen. DALMER D. HOSKINS (USA); publs *International Social Security Review* (quarterly, in English, French, German, Spanish), *Trends in Social Security* (quarterly, in English, French, German, Spanish), *Social Security Documentation* (African, Asian-Pacific and European series), *Social Security Worldwide* (CD Rom and internet), *Compendia of Conference Reports* (in English, French, German, Spanish), various news bulletins.

International Social Service (SSI) (Service social inter-national—SSI): 32 quai du Seujet, 1201 Geneva, Switzerland; tel. (22) 9067700; fax (22) 9067701; e-mail info@iss-ssi.org; internet www.iss-ssi.org; f. 1921 to aid families and individuals whose prob-lems require services beyond the boundaries of the country in which they live, and where the solution of these problems depends upon co-ordinated action on the part of social workers in two or more countries; studies from an international standpoint the conditions and consequences of emigration in their effect on individual, family, and social life; operates on a non-sectarian and non-political basis; mems: branches in 14 countries, four affiliated offices, and correspondents in some 100 other countries; Pres. Prof. Dr RAINER FRANK (Germany); Sec.-Gen. VINCENT FABER; publs *ISS Reports, Newsletter* (available on-line).

International Union of Family Organisations: 28 place Saint-Georges, 75009 Paris, France; tel. 1-48-78-07-59; fax 1-42-82-95-24; f. 1947 to bring together all organizations throughout the world working for family welfare; maintains commissions and working groups on issues including standards of living, housing, marriage guidance, rural families, etc.; there are six regional organizations: the Pan-African Family Organisation (Rabat, Morocco), the North America organization (Montréal, Canada), the Arab Family Organisation (Tunis, Tunisia), the Asian Union of Family Organisations (New Delhi, India), the European regional organization (Berne, Switzerland) and the Latin American Secretariat (Curitiba, Brazil); mems: national asscns, groups and governmental departments in over 55 countries; Pres. MARIA TERESA DA COSTA MACEDO (Portugal).

International Union of Tenants: Box 7514, 10392 Stockholm, Sweden; tel. (8) 791-02-00; fax (8) 20-43-44; e-mail info@iut.nu; internet www.iut.nu; f. 1955 to collaborate in safeguarding the interests of tenants; participates in activities of UN-Habitat; has working groups for EC matters, eastern Europe, developing countries and for future development; holds annual council meeting and triennial congress; mems: national tenant orgs in 29 European countries, Australia, Benin, Canada, India, Kenya, New Zealand, Nigeria, Tanzania Togo, Uganda, and USA; Chair. ELISABET LÖNNGREN; Sec.-Gen. MAGNUS HAMMAR; publ. *The Global Tenant* (quarterly).

Inter-University European Institute on Social Welfare (IEISW): 179 rue du Débarcadère, 6001 Marcinelle, Belgium; tel. (71) 44-72-67; fax (71) 47-27-44; e-mail ieiasmayence@hotmail.com; f. 1970 to promote, carry out and publicize scientific research on social welfare and community work; Pres. JOSEPH GILLAIN; Gen. Dir SERGE MAYENCE; publ. *COMM*.

Lions Clubs International: 300 West 22nd St, Oak Brook, IL 60523-8842, USA; tel. (630) 571-5466; fax (630) 571-8890; e-mail lions@lionsclubs.org; internet www.lionsclubs.org; f. 1917 to foster understanding among people of the world to promote principles of good government and citizenship and an interest in civic, cultural, social and moral welfare and to encourage service-minded people to serve their community without financial reward; mems: 1.4m. in over 44,500 clubs in 185 countries and geographic areas; Exec. Admin. WIN HAMILTON; publ. *The Lion* (10 a year, in 20 languages).

Médecins sans frontières (MSF): 39 rue de la Tourelle, 1040 Brussels, Belgium; tel. (2) 280-18-81; fax (2) 280-01-73; internet www.msf.org; f. 1971; independent medical humanitarian org. composed of physicians and other members of the medical profession; aims to provide medical assistance to victims of war and natural disasters; operates longer-term programmes of nutrition, immunization, sanitation, public health, and rehabilitation of hospitals and dispensaries; awarded the Nobel peace prize in Oct. 1999; mems: national sections in 18 countries in Europe, Asia and North America; Pres. Dr ROWAN GILLIES; Sec.-Gen. MARINE BUISONNIERE; publ. *Activity Report* (annually).

Pan-Pacific and South East Asia Women's Association (PPSEAWA): POB 119, Nuku'alofa, Tonga; tel. 24003; fax 41404; e-mail nanasi@kalianet.to; internet www.ppseawa.org; f. 1928 to foster better understanding and friendship among women in the region, and to promote co-operation for the study and improvement of social conditions; holds international conference every three years; mems: 19 national member organizations; Pres. HRH Princess NANASIPAU'U TUKU'AHO; publ. *PPSEAWA Bulletin* (2 a year).

Rotary International: 1560 Sherman Ave, Evanston, IL 60201, USA; tel. (847) 866-3000; fax (847) 328-8554; e-mail wenerm@rotaryintl.org; internet www.rotary.org; f. 1905 to carry out activities for the service of humanity, to promote high ethical standards in business and professions and to further international understanding, goodwill and peace; mems: some 1.2m. in 30,462 Rotary Clubs in 162 countries; Pres. RICHARD D. KING; Gen. Sec. EDWIN H. FUTA (USA); publs *The Rotarian* (monthly, English), *Rotary World* (5 a year, in 9 languages), *News Basket* (weekly).

Service Civil International (SCI): St-Jacobsmarkt 82, 2000 Antwerp, Belgium; tel. (3) 226-57-27; fax (3) 232-03-44; e-mail info@sciint.org; internet www.sciint.org; f. 1920 to promote peace and understanding through voluntary service projects; mems: 14,000 in 36 countries; Pres. I. DANCKAERTS; publ. *Action* (quarterly).

Society of Saint Vincent de Paul: 5 rue du Pré-aux-Clercs, 75007 Paris, France; tel. 1-53-45-87-53; fax 1-42-61-72-56; e-mail cgi .information@ozanet.org; internet www.ozanet.org; f. 1833 to conduct charitable activities such as childcare, youth work, work with immigrants, adult literacy programmes, residential care for the sick,

handicapped and elderly, social counselling and work with prisoners and the unemployed, through personal contact; mems: over 600,000 in 130 countries; Pres. JOSÉ RAMÓN DÍAZ TORREMOCHA; Sec.-Gen. YVES VERRÉ; publ. *Vincenpaul* (quarterly, in English, French, Portuguese and Spanish).

SOLIDAR: 22 rue de Commerce, 1000 Brussels, Belgium; tel. (2) 500-10-20; fax (2) 500-10-30; e-mail solidar@skynet.be; internet www.solidar.org; f. 1951 (fmrly International Workers' Aid); an asscn of independent development and social welfare agencies based in Europe, linked to the labour and democratic socialist movements; aims to contribute to the creation of radical models of economic and social development, and to advance practical solutions that enable people to have increased control over their future; mems: agencies in 90 countries; Sec.-Gen. GIAMPIERO ALHADEFF.

Soroptimist International: 87 Glisson Rd, Cambridge, CB1 2HG, United Kingdom; tel. (1223) 311833; fax (1223) 467951; e-mail hq@soroptimistinternational.org; internet www .soroptimistinternational.org/; f. 1921 to strive for the advancement of the status of women, high ethical standards, human rights for all, equality and development of peace through international goodwill, understanding and friendship; convention held every 4 years (2007: Glasgow, United Kingdom); mems: 95,000 in 3,000 clubs in 122 countries and territories; International Pres. LYNN DUNNING; Exec. Officer ROSIE COUTTS; publ. *International Soroptimist* (quarterly).

World Blind Union: c/o CBC ONCE, 18 La Coruña, 28020 Madrid, Spain; tel. (91) 5713675; fax (91) 5715777; e-mail umc@once.es; internet www.once.es/wbu; f. 1984 (amalgamating the World Council for the Welfare of the Blind and the International Federation of the Blind) to work for the prevention of blindness and the welfare of blind and visually-impaired people; encourages development of braille, talking book programmes and other media for the blind; organizes rehabilitation, training and employment; works on the prevention and cure of blindness in co-operation with the International Agency for the Prevention of Blindness; co-ordinates aid to the blind in developing countries; maintains the Louis Braille birthplace as an international museum; mems: in 146 countries; Pres. EUCLID HERIE (Canada); Sec.-Gen. PEDRO ZURITA (Spain); publ. *World Blind* (2 a year, in English, English Braille and on cassette, in Spanish and Spanish Braille and on cassette, and in French).

World Federation of the Deaf (WFD): POB 65, 00401 Helsinki, Finland; e-mail generalsecretary@wfdeaf.org; internet www.wfdeaf .org; f. 1951 to serve the interests of deaf people and their national organizations and represent these in international fora; works towards the goal of full participation by deaf people in society; encourages deaf people to set up and run their own organizations; priority is given to the promotion of the recognition and use of national sign languages, the education of deaf people and deaf people in the developing world; mems: 127 member countries; Pres. MARKKU JOKINEN; Gen. Sec. CAROL-LEE AQUILINE; publ. *WFD News* (2–3 a year).

World ORT: ORT House, 126 Albert St, London, NW1 7NE, United Kingdom; tel. (20) 7446-8500; fax (20) 7446-8650; e-mail wo@ort.org; internet www.ort.org; f. 1880 for the development of industrial, agricultural and artisanal skills among Jews; now, one of the world's largest educational and training organizations active in 60 countries; conducts vocational training programmes for adolescents and adults, including instructors' and teachers' education and apprenticeship training, including technical assistance programmes in co-operation with interested governments; mems: committees in more than 40 countries; Dir-Gen. ROBERT SINGER; publs *Annual Report, World ORT Times*.

World Veterans Federation: 17 rue Nicolo, 75116 Paris, France; tel. 1-40-72-61-00; fax 1-40-72-80-58; e-mail fmacwvf@noos.fr; internet www.wvf-fmac.org; f. 1950 to maintain international peace and security by the application of the San Francisco Charter and work to help implement the Universal Declaration of Human Rights and related international conventions; aims to defend the spiritual and material interests of war veterans and war victims; promotes practical international co-operation in disarmament, legislation concerning war veterans and war victims, and development of international humanitarian law, etc; in 1986 established International Socio-Medical Information Centre (United Kingdom) for psychomedical problems resulting from stress. Regional committees for Africa, Asia and the Pacific, and Europe and Standing Committee on Women; mems: national organizations in 84 countries, representing about 27m. war veterans and war victims; Pres. ABDUL HAMID IBRAHIM; Sec.-Gen. MAREK HAGMAJER (Poland); publs special studies (disarmament, human rights, rehabilitation).

Zonta International: 557 W. Randolph St, Chicago, IL 60661-2206, USA; tel. (312) 930-5848; fax (312) 930-0951; e-mail zontaint@zonta.org; internet www.zonta.org; f. 1919; links executives in business and the professions, with the aim of advancing the status of women world-wide; carries out local and international projects; supports women's education and leadership; makes fellowship awards in various fields; mems: 35,000 in 69 countries and areas; Pres. Margit Webjorn; Exec. Dir Janet Halstead; publ. *The Zontian* (quarterly).

Sport and Recreations

Arab Sports Confederation: POB 62997, Riyadh 11595, Saudi Arabia; tel. (1) 482-4927; fax (1) 482-1944; f. 1976 to encourage regional co-operation in sport; mems: 21 Arab national Olympic Committees, 53 Arab sports federations; Sec.-Gen. Othman M. Al-Saad; publ. *Annual Report*.

Fédération Aéronautique Internationale (FAI) (World Air Sports Federation): 24 ave Mon Repos, 1005 Lausanne, Switzerland; e-mail sec@fai.org; internet www.fai.org; f. 1905 to promote all aeronautical sports; organizes world championships; develops rules through Air Sports Commissions; endorses world aeronautical and astronautical records; mems: in 100 countries and territories; Pres. Wolfgang Weinreich; Sec.-Gen. Max Bishop; publ. *Air Sports International*.

General Association of International Sports Federations (GAISF) (Association générale de fédérations internationales de sports): 4 blvd du Jardin Exotique, Monte Carlo, Monaco; tel. 97-97-65-10; fax 93-25-28-73; e-mail info@agfisonline.com; internet www.agfisonline.com; f. 1967 to act as a forum for the exchange of ideas and discussion of common problems in sport; collects and circulates information; and provides secretarial, translation, documentation and consultancy services for members; mems: 99 international sports organizations; Pres. Dr Un Yong Kim (Republic of Korea); Sec.-Gen. Don Porter (USA); publs *AGFIS / GAISF Magazine* (quarterly, in English and French), *GAISF Calendar*, *Sport and Education* and *Sport and Media*.

International Amateur Athletic Federation (IAAF): 17 rue Princesse Florestine, BP 359, 98007 Monte Carlo Cédex, Monaco; tel. 93-10-88-88; fax 93-15-95-15; e-mail headquarters@iaaf.org; f. 1912 to ensure co-operation and fairness and to combat discrimination in athletics; compiles athletic competition rules and organizes championships at all levels; frames regulations for the establishment of World, Olympic and other athletic records; settles disputes between members; conducts a programme of development consisting of coaching, judging courses, etc.; and affiliates national governing bodies; mems: national asscns in 211 countries and territories; Gen. Sec. István Gyulai (Hungary); publs *IAAF Handbook* (every 2 years), *IAAF Review* (quarterly), *IAAF Directory* (annually), *New Studies in Athletics* (quarterly).

International Amateur Boxing Association (AIBA): POB 76343, Atlanta, GA 30358, USA; tel. (770) 455-8350; fax (770) 454-6467; e-mail lbaker27@mindspring.com; internet www.aiba.net; f. 1946 as the world body controlling amateur boxing for the Olympic Games, continental, regional and inter-nation championships and tournaments in every part of the world; mems: 191 national asscns; Pres. Prof. A. Chowdhry (Pakistan); Sec.-Gen. Loring K. Baker (USA); publ. *World Amateur Boxing Magazine* (quarterly).

International Amateur Radio Union: POB 310905, Newington, CT 06131-0905, USA; tel. (860) 594-0200; fax (860) 594-0259; internet www.iaru.org; f. 1925 to link national amateur radio societies and represent the interests of two-way amateur radio communication; mems: 150 national amateur radio societies; Pres. Larry E. Price; Sec. David Sumner.

International Archery Federation (Fédération internationale de tir à l'arc—FITA): 135 ave de Cour, 1007 Lausanne, Switzerland; tel. (21) 6143050; fax (21) 6143055; e-mail info@archery.org; internet www.archery.org; f. 1931 to promote international archery; organizes world championships and Olympic tournaments; holds Biennial Congress (2003: New York, USA); mems: national amateur asscns in 135 countries; Pres. James L. Easton (USA); Sec.-Gen. Giuseppe Cinnirella (Italy); publs *Information FITA* (monthly), *The Target* (2 a year).

International Automobile Federation (Fédération Internationale de l'Automobile—FIA): Administration office: 2 chemin de Blandonnet, CP 296, 1215 Geneva, Switzerland; tel. (22) 5444400; fax (22) 5444450; internet www.fia.com; f. 1904; manages world motor sport and organizes international championships; mems: 163 national automobile clubs and asscns in 118 countries; Pres. Max Mosley; Sec.-Gen. (Sport) Pierre de Coninck; Sec.-Gen. (Mobility) Peter Doggwiler.

International Badminton Federation (IBF): Manor Park Place, Rutherford Way, Cheltenham, Gloucestershire, GL51 9TU, United Kingdom; tel. (1242) 234904; fax (1242) 221030; e-mail info@intbadfed.org; internet www.intbadfed.org; f. 1934 to oversee the sport of badminton world-wide; mems: affiliated national organizations in 156 countries and territories; Pres. Korn Thapparansi; Chief Operating Officer Andrew Ryan; publs *World Badminton* (available on internet), *Statute Book* (annually).

International Basketball Federation (Fédération Internationale de Basketball): 8 chemin Blandonnet. 1214 Vernier/Geneva, Switzerland; e-mail info@fiba.com; internet www.fiba.com; f. 1932 as International Amateur Basketball Federation (present name adopted 1989); aims to promote, supervise and direct international basketball; organizes quadrennial congress; mems: affiliated national federations in 212 countries; Sec.-Gen. Patrick Baumann (Switzerland); publs *FIBA Assist* (monthly), *FIBA Media Guide*.

International Canoe Federation: Calle de la Antracita 7, 4th Floor, 28045 Madrid, Spain; tel. (91) 506-1150; fax (91) 506-1155; e-mail message@canoeicf.com; internet www.canoeicf.com; f. 1924; administers canoeing at the Olympic Games; promotes canoe/kayak activity in general; mems: 114 national federations; Pres. Ulrich Feldhoff; Sec.-Gen. José Perurena Lopez.

International Council for Health, Physical Education, Recreation, Sport and Dance (ICHPERSD): 1900 Association Drive, Reston, VA 20191, USA; tel. (800) 213-7193; internet www.ichpersd.org; f. 1958 to encourage the development of programmes in health, physical education, recreation, sport and dance throughout the world, by linking teaching professionals in these fields.

International Cricket Council: Lord's Cricket Ground, London, NW8 8QN, United Kingdom; tel. (20) 7266-1818; fax (20) 7266-1777; internet www.cricket.org; f. 1909 as the governing body for international cricket; holds an annual conference; mems: Australia, England, India, New Zealand, Pakistan, South Africa, Sri Lanka, West Indies, Zimbabwe, and 23 associate and 13 affiliate mems; Chief Exec. D. L. Richards.

International Cycling Union (UCI): 1860 Aigle, Switzerland; tel. (24) 4685811; fax (24) 4685812; e-mail admin@uci.ch; internet www.uci.ch; f. 1900 to develop, regulate and control all forms of cycling as a sport; mems: 160 federations; Pres. Hein Verbruggen (Netherlands); publs *International Calendar* (annually), *Velo World* (6 a year).

International Equestrian Federation: CP 157, ave Mon-Repos 24, 1000 Lausanne 5, Switzerland; tel. (21) 3104747; fax (21) 3104760; e-mail info@horsesport.org; internet www.horsesport.org; f. 1921; international governing body of equestrian sport recognized by the International Olympic Committee; establishes rules and regulations for conduct of international equestrian events, including on the health and welfare of horses; mems: 127 member countries; Sec.-Gen. Dr Bo Helander.

International Federation of Associated Wrestling Styles: 17 ave Juste-Olivier, 1006 Lausanne, Switzerland; tel. (21) 3128426; fax (21) 3236073; e-mail filalausanne@bluewin.ch; internet www.fila_wrestling.org; f. 1912 to encourage the development of amateur wrestling and promote the sport in countries where it is not yet practised and to further friendly relations between all members; mems: 142 federations; Pres. Milan Ercegan; Sec.-Gen. Michel Dusson; publs *News Bulletin*, *Wrestling Revue*.

International Federation of Association Football (Fédération internationale de football association—FIFA): FIFA House, Hitzigweg 11, POB 85, 8030 Zürich, Switzerland; tel. (1) 3849595; fax (1) 3849696; e-mail media@fifa.org; internet www.fifa.com; f. 1904 to promote the game of association football and foster friendly relations among players and national asscns; to control football and uphold the laws of the game as laid down by the International Football Association Board to prevent discrimination of any kind between players; and to provide arbitration in disputes between national asscns; organizes World Cup competition every four years; mems: 204 national asscns, six continental confederations; Pres. Joseph S. Blatter (Switzerland); Gen. Sec. Urs Linsi; publs *FIFA News* (monthly), *FIFA Magazine* (every 2 months) (both in English, French, German and Spanish), *FIFA Directory* (annually), *Laws of the Game* (annually), *Competitions' Regulations* and *Technical Reports* (before and after FIFA competitions).

International Federation of Park and Recreation Administration (IFPRA): Globe House, Crispin Close, Caversham, Reading, Berks, RG4 7JS, United Kingdom; tel. and fax (118) 946-1680; e-mail ifpraworld@aol.com; internet www.ifpra.org; f. 1957 to provide a world centre for members of government departments, local authorities, and all organizations concerned with recreational and environmental services to discuss relevant matters; mems: 550 in over 50 countries; Gen. Sec. Alan Smith (UK); publ. *IFPRA World*.

International Fencing Federation (Fédération internationale d'escrime—FIE): ave Mon-Repos 24, CP 128, 1000 Lausanne 5, Switzerland; tel. (21) 3203115; fax (21) 3203116; e-mail contact@fie.ch; internet www.fie.ch; f. 1913; promotes development and co-operation between amateur fencers; determines rules for international events; organizes World Championships; mems: 109 national federations; Pres. René Roch.

International Gymnastic Federation: rue des Oeuches 10, CP 359, 2740 Moutier 1, Switzerland; tel. (32) 4946410; fax (32) 4946419; e-mail gymnastics@fig.worldsport.org; f. 1881 to promote the exchange of official documents and publications on gymnastics; mems: in 122 countries and territories; Pres. BRUNO GRANDI; Gen. Sec. NORBERT BUECHE (Switzerland); publs *FIG Bulletin* (quarterly), *World of Gymnastics Magazine* (quarterly).

International Hockey Federation: 1 ave des Arts, Boîte 5, 1210 Brussels, Belgium; tel. (2) 219-45-37; fax (2) 219-27-61; e-mail info@ fihockey.org; internet www.fihockey.org; f. 1924 to fix the rules of outdoor and indoor hockey for all affiliated national asscns to control the game of hockey and indoor hockey and to control the organization of international tournaments, such as the Olympic Games and the World Cup; mems: 120 national asscns; Pres. JUAN ANGEL CALZADO; Sec.-Gen. ELS VAN BREDA-VRIESMAN; publ. *World Hockey* (quarterly).

International Judo Federation: BP 333, El Menzah 1004, Tunis, Tunisia; tel. (71) 750-105; fax (71) 743-424; e-mail sgfij@gnet.tn; internet www.ijf.org; f. 1951 to promote cordial and friendly relations between members to protect the interests of judo throughout the world; to organize World Championships and the judo events of the Olympic Games; to develop and spread the techniques and spirit of judo throughout the world; and to establish international judo regulations; Pres. YONG SUNG PARK (Republic of Korea); Gen. Sec. Dr HEDI DHOUIB (Tunisia).

International Paralympic Committee (IPC): Adenauerallee 212–214, 53113 Bonn, Germany; tel. (228) 2097200; fax (228) 2097209; e-mail info@paralympic.org; internet www.paralympic .org; f. 1989 as the international governing body of sports for athletes with a disability; supervises and co-ordinates the Paralympic summer and winter games (held every four years) and other multi-disability competitions, including the World and Regional Championships; mems: 157 national paralympic committees and four disability-specific international sports federations; Pres. PHIL CRAVEN (UK); Chief Operating Officer a.i. XAVIER GONZALEZ (Spain); publ. *The Paralympian* (3 a year).

International Philatelic Federation: Jupiterstrasse 49, 9032 Zürich, Switzerland; tel. (1) 4223839; fax (1) 4223843; e-mail heiri@ f-i-p.ch; internet www.f-i-p.ch/; f. 1926 to promote philately internationally; Pres. KOH SEOW CHUAN; Sec.-Gen. MARIE-LOUISE HEIRI.

International Rowing Federation (Fédération internationale des sociétés d'aviron—FISA): 135 ave de Cour, CP 18, 1000 Lausanne 3, Switzerland; tel. (21) 6178373; fax (21) 6178375; e-mail info@fisa.org; internet www.worldrowing.com; f. 1892 to establish contacts between rowers in all countries and to draw up racing rules; serves as the world controlling body of the sport of rowing; mems: 118 national federations; Pres. DENIS OSWALD; Sec.-Gen. and Exec. Dir MATTHEW SMITH; publs *FISA Guide* (annually), *FISA World Rowing Magazine* (quarterly), *FISA Bulletins* (annually).

International Sailing Federation (ISAF): Ariadne House, Town Quay, Southampton, Hants, SO14 2AQ, United Kingdom; tel. (2380) 635111; fax (2380) 635789; e-mail secretariat@isaf.co.uk; internet www.sailing.org; f. 1907; serves as the controlling authority of sailing in all its forms throughout the world; establishes and amends international yacht racing rules; organizes the Olympic Sailing Regatta and other championships; mems: 117 national yachting federations; Pres. PAUL HENDERSON; Sec.-Gen. ARVE SUNDHEIM; publ. *Making Waves.*

International Shooting Sport Federation (ISSF): 80336 Munich, Bavariaring 21, Germany; tel. (89) 5443550; fax (89) 54435544; e-mail munich@issf-shooting.org; internet www .issf-shooting.org; f. 1907 to promote and guide the development of amateur shooting sports; organizes World Championships and controls the organization of continental and regional championships; supervises the shooting events of the Olympic and Continental Games under the auspices of the International Olympic Committee; mems: 151 federations in 146 countries; Pres. OLEGARIO VÁZQUEZ-RAÑA (Mexico); Sec.-Gen. HORST G. SCHREIBER (Germany); publs *ISSF News*, *International Shooting Sport* (6 a year).

International Skating Union (ISU): chemin de Primerose 2, 1007 Lausanne, Switzerland; tel. (21) 6126666; fax (21) 6126677; e-mail info@isu.ch; internet www.isu.org; f. 1892; holds regular conferences; mems: 73 national federations in 57 countries; Pres. OTTAVIO CINQUANTA; Gen.-Sec. FREDI SCHMID; publs Judges' manuals, referees' handbooks, general and special regulations.

International Ski Federation (Fédération internationale de ski—FIS): 3653 Oberhofen am Thunersee, Switzerland; tel. (33) 2446161; fax (33) 2446171; internet www.fis-ski.com; f. 1924 to further the sport of skiing to prevent discrimination in skiing matters on racial, religious or political grounds; to organize World Ski Championships and regional championships and, as supreme international skiing authority, to establish the international competition calendar and rules for all ski competitions approved by the FIS, and to arbitrate in any disputes; mems: 104 national ski asscns; Pres. GIAN-FRANCO KASPER (Switzerland); Sec.-Gen. SARAH LEWIS (UK); publ. *FIS Bulletin* (2 a year).

International Swimming Federation (Fédération internationale de natation—FINA): POB 4, ave de l'Avant, 1005 Lausanne, Switzerland; tel. (21) 3126602; fax (21) 3126610; internet www.fina.org; f. 1908 to promote amateur swimming and swimming sports internationally; administers rules for swimming sports, competitions and for establishing records; organizes world championships and FINA events; runs a development programme to increase the popularity and quality of aquatic sports; mems: 180 federations; Pres. MUSTAPHA LARFAOUI (Algeria); Exec. Dir CORNEL MARCULESCU; publs *Handbook* (every 4 years), *FINA News* (monthly), *World of Swimming* (quarterly).

International Table Tennis Federation: ave Mon-Repos 30, 1005 Lausanne, Switzerland; tel. (21) 3407090; fax (21) 3407099; e-mail ittf@ittf.com; internet www.ittf.com; f. 1926; Pres. ADHAM SHARARA; Exec. Dir JORDI SERRA; publs *Table Tennis Illustrated*, *Table Tennis News* (both bimonthly), *Table Tennis Legends*, *Table Tennis Fascination*, *Table Tennis: The Early Years.*

International Tennis Federation: Bank Lane, Roehampton, London, SW15 5XZ, United Kingdom; tel. (20) 8878-6464; fax (20) 8878-7799; e-mail communications@itftennis.com; internet www .itftennis.com; f. 1913 to govern the game of tennis throughout the world, promote its teaching and preserve its independence of outside authority; produces the Rules of Tennis; promotes the Davis Cup Competition for men, the Fed. Cup for women, the Olympic Games Tennis Event, wheelchair tennis, 16 cups for veterans, the ITF Sunshine Cup and the ITF Continental Connelly Cup for players of 18 years old and under, the World Youth Cup for players of 16 years old and under, and the World Junior Tennis Tournament for players of 14 years old and under; organizes tournaments; mems: 141 full and 57 associate; Pres. FRANCESCO RICCI BITTI; publs *World of Tennis* (annually), *Davis Cup Yearbook*, *ITF World* (quarterly), *ITF This Week* (weekly).

International Volleyball Federation (Fédération internationale de volleyball—FIVB): ave de la Gare 12, 1001 Lausanne, Switzerland; tel. (21) 3453535; fax (21) 3453545; e-mail info@mail.fivb.ch; internet www.fivb.ch; f. 1947 to encourage, organize and supervise the playing of volleyball, beach volleyball, and park volley; organizes biennial congress; mems: 218 national federations; Pres. Dr RUBÉN ACOSTA HERNÁNDEZ; Gen. Man. JEAN-PIERRE SEPPEY; publs *VolleyWorld* (every 2 months), *X-Press* (monthly).

International Weightlifting Federation (IWF): PF 614, 1374 Budapest, Hungary; tel. (1) 3530530; fax (1) 3530199; e-mail iwf@iwf .net; internet www.iwf.net; f. 1905 to control international weightlifting; draws up technical rules; trains referees; supervises World Championships, Olympic Games, regional games and international contests of all kinds; registers world records; mems: 167 national organizations; Pres. Dr THOMÁS AJAN (Hungary); Gen. Sec. YANNIS SGOUROS (Greece); publs *IWF Constitution and Rules* (every 4 years), *World Weightlifting* (quarterly).

International World Games Association: Ekeby House, Luiksestraat 23, 2587 The Hague, Netherlands; tel. (70) 3512774; fax (70) 3509911; e-mail iwga@hetnet.nl; internet www.worldgames-iwga .org; f. 1980; organizes World Games every four years (2001: Akita, Japan), comprising 26 sports that are not included in the Olympic Games; Sec.-Gen. J. A. P. KOREN.

Union of European Football Associations (UEFA): route de Genève 46, 1260 Nyon 2, Switzerland; tel. (22) 9944444; fax (22) 9944488; internet www.uefa.com; f. 1954; works on behalf of Europe's national football asscns to promote football; aims to foster unity and solidarity between national asscns; mems: 52 national asscns; Pres. LENNART JOHANSSON; CEO LARS-CHRISTER OLSSON; publ. *Magazine* (available online).

World Boxing Organization: c/o 100 West Randolph St, 9th Floor, Chicago, IL 60601, USA; tel. (312) 814-3145; fax (312) 814-2719; internet www.wbo-int.com; f. 1962; regulates professional boxing.

World Bridge Federation: 56 route de Vandoeuvres, 1253 Geneva, Switzerland; tel. (22) 7501541; fax (22) 7501620; internet www.bridge.gr; f. 1958 to promote the game of contract bridge throughout the world; federates national bridge asscns in all countries; conducts world championships competitions; establishes standard bridge laws; mems: 89 countries; Pres. ERNESTO D'ORSI (Brazil); publ. *World Bridge News* (quarterly).

World Chess Federation (Fédération internationale des echecs—FIDE): 9 Syggrou Ave, Athens 11743, Greece; tel. (210) 9212047; fax (210) 9212859; e-mail office@fide.com; internet www.fide.com; f. 1924; controls chess competitions of world importance and awards international chess titles; mems: national orgs in more than 160 countries; Pres. KIRSAN ILYUMZHINOV; publ. *International Rating List* (2 a year).

World Squash Federation Ltd: 6 Havelock Rd, Hastings, East Sussex, TN34 1BP, United Kingdom; tel. (1424) 429245; fax (1424) 429250; e-mail wsf@worldsquash.org; internet www.worldsquash .org; f. 1966 to maintain quality and reputation of squash and increase its popularity; monitors rules and makes recommendations for change; trains, accredits and assesses international and world referees; sets standards for all technical aspects of squash; co-ordinates coaching training and awards; runs World Championships; mems: 125 national orgs; Exec. Dir CHRISTIAN LEIGHTON.

World Underwater Federation: Viale Tiziano 74, 00196 Rome, Italy; tel. (06) 32110594; fax (06) 32110595; e-mail cmas@cmas.org; internet www.cmas2000.org; f. 1959 to develop underwater activities to form bodies to instruct in the techniques of underwater diving; to perfect existing equipment, encourage inventions and experiment with newly marketed products; and to organize international competitions; mems: organizations in 100 countries; Pres. ACHILLE FERRERO (Italy); Sec. PIERRE DERNIER (Belgium); publs *International Year Book of CMAS, Scientific Diving: A Code of Practice,* manuals.

Technology

African Organization of Cartography and Remote Sensing: 5 Route de Bedjarah, BP 102, Hussein Dey, Algiers, Algeria; tel. (2) 77-79-34; fax (2) 77-79-34; e-mail oact@wissal.dz; f. 1988 by amalgamation of African Association of Cartography and African Council for Remote Sensing; aims to encourage the development of cartography and of remote sensing by satellites; organizes conferences and other meetings, promotes establishment of training institutions; maintains four regional training centres (in Burkina Faso, Kenya, Nigeria and Tunisia); mems: national cartographic institutions of 24 African countries; Sec.-Gen. UNIS MUFTAH.

African Regional Centre for Technology: Imm. Fahd, 17th Floor, blvd Djilly Mbaye, BP 2435, Dakar, Senegal; tel. 823-77-12; fax 823-77-13; e-mail arct@sonatel.senet.net; f. 1977 to encourage the development of indigenous technology and to improve the terms of access to imported technology; assists the establishment of national centres; mems: govts of 31 countries; Exec. Dir Dr OUSMANE KANE; publs *African Technodevelopment, Alert Africa.*

AIIM International: 1100 Wayne Ave, Suite 1100, Silver Spring, Maryland 20910, USA; tel. (301) 587–8202; fax (301) 587–2711; e-mail aiim@aiim.org; internet www.aiim.org; f. 1999 by merger of the Association for Information and Image Management (f. 1943) and the International Information Management Congress (f. 1962); serves as the international body of the document technologies industry.

Bureau International de la Recupération et du Recyclage (Bureau of International Recycling): 24 ave Franklin Roosevelt, 1050 Brussels, Belgium; tel. (2) 627-57-70; fax (2) 627-57-73; e-mail bir@bir.org; internet www.bir.org; f. 1948 as the world federation of the reclamation and recycling industries; promotes international trade in scrap iron and steel, non-ferrous metals, paper, textiles, plastics and glass; mems: asscns and individuals in 53 countries; Dir-Gen. FRANCIS VEYS.

Ecma International: 114 rue de Rhône, 1204 Geneva, Switzerland; tel. (22) 8496000; fax (22) 8496001; e-mail helpdesk@ecma-international.org; internet www.ecma-international.org; f. 1961 to develop standards and technical reports, in co-operation with the appropriate national, European and international organizations, in order to facilitate and standardize the use of information processing and telecommunications systems; promulgates various standards applicable to the functional design and use of these systems; mems: 21 ordinary and 12 associate mems; Sec.-Gen. JAN VAN DEN BELD; publs *Ecma Standards, Ecma Memento, Ecma Technical Reports.*

EUREKA: 107 rue Neerveld, bte 5, 1200 Brussels, Belgium; tel. (2) 777-09-50; fax (2) 770-74-95; e-mail eureka.secretariat@es.eureka.be; internet www.eureka.be; f. 1985; aims to promote industrial collaboration between member countries on non-military research and development activities; enables joint development of technology; supports innovation and systematic use of standardization in new technology sectors; mems: 34 in 33 countries; Sec.-Gen. Dr HEIKKI KOTILAINEN; publs *Annual Report, Eureka Bulletin.*

European Convention for Constructional Steelwork (ECCS): 32-36 ave des Ombrages, bte 20, 1200 Brussels, Belgium; tel. (2) 762-04-29; fax (2) 762-09-35; e-mail eccs@steelconstruct.com; internet www.steelconstruct.com; f. 1955 for the consideration of problems involved in metallic construction; mems: in 25 countries; Sec.-Gen. G. GENDEBEN; publs Information sheets and documents, symposia reports, model codes.

European Federation of Chemical Engineering: c/o Institution of Chemical Engineers, Davis Bldg, 165–189 Railway Terrace, Rugby, Warwickshire, CV21 3HQ, United Kingdom; tel. (1788) 578214; fax (1788) 560833; internet www.icheme.org; f. 1953 to encourage co-operation between non-profit-making scientific and technical societies, for the advancement of chemical engineering and its application in the processing industries; mems: 65 societies in 25

European countries, 15 corresponding societies in other countries; Chief Exec. Dr T. J. EVANS.

European Federation of Corrosion: 1 Carlton House Terrace, London, SW1Y 5DB, United Kingdom; tel. (20) 7451-7336; fax (20) 8392-2289; e-mail paul.mcintyre@iom3.org; internet www.materials.org; f. 1955 to encourage co-operation in research on corrosion and methods of combating this; mems: societies in 24 countries; Pres. D. HARROP (UK); Hon. Secs J. P. BERGE (France), G. KREYSA (Germany), B. A. RICKINSON (UK); Scientific Sec. P. McINTYRE (UK).

European Federation of National Engineering Associations (Fédération européenne d'associations nationales d'ingénieurs— FEANI): 18 ave R. Vandendriessche, 1150 Brussels, Belgium; tel. (2) 639-03-90; fax (2) 639-03-99; e-mail rita.heissner@feani.org; internet www.feani.org; f. 1951 to affirm the professional identity of the engineers of Europe and to strive for the unity of the engineering profession in Europe; mems: 26 mem. countries; Pres. K. ALEXOPOULOS (Greece); Sec.-Gen. PHILIPPE WAUTERS (Belgium); publs *FEANI News, INDEX.*

European Metal Union: Einsteinbaan 1, POB 2600, 3430 GA Nieuwegein, Netherlands; tel. (30) 605-33-44; fax (30) 605-31-15; e-mail info@metaalunie.nl; f. 1954 as International Union of Metal; liaises between national craft organizations and small and medium-sized enterprises in the metal industry; represents members' interests at a European level; provides for the exchange of information and ideas; mems: national federations from Austria, Germany, Hungary, Luxembourg, Netherlands and Switzerland; Pres. PIET TOLSMA (Netherlands); Sec. HARM-JAN KEIJER (Netherlands).

European Organisation for the Exploitation of Meteorological Satellites (EUMETSAT): 64295 Darmstadt, Am Kavalleriesand 31, Germany; tel. (6151) 807345; fax (6151) 807555; e-mail press@eumetsat.de; internet www.eumetsat.de; f. 1986; establishes, maintains and exploits European systems of operational meteorological satellites; projects include a second generation Meteosat programme for gathering weather data; mems: 18 European countries and seven co-operating states; Dir-Gen. Dr LARS PRAHM; publs *Annual Report, IMAGE Newsletter,* brochures, conference and workshop proceedings.

European Organization for Civil Aviation Equipment (EURO-CAE): 17 rue Hamelin, 75783 Paris Cédex 16, France; tel. 1-45-05-71-88; fax 1-45-05-72-30; e-mail eurocae@eurocae.com; internet www.eurocae.org; f. 1963; studies and advises on problems related to the equipment used in aeronautics; assists international bodies in the establishment of international standards; mems: 92 manufacturers, and regulatory and research bodies; Pres. TERRENCE KNIBB; Sec.-Gen. FRANCIS GRIMAL; publs Reports, documents and specifications on civil aviation equipment.

Eurospace: 15-17 ave de Ségur, 75005 Paris, France; tel. 1-44-42-00-70; fax 1-44-42-00-79; e-mail letterbox@eurospace.org; internet www.eurospace.org; f. 1961 as an asscn of European aerospace industrial companies responsible for promotion of European Space activity; carries out studies on the legal, economic, technical and financial aspects of space activity; acts as an industrial adviser to the European Space Agency, in particular with regard to future space programmes and industrial policy matters; mems: 60 in 13 European countries; Pres. PASCALE SOURISSE (France); Sec.-Gen. ALAIN GAUBERT.

International Association for Bridge and Structural Engineering (IABSE): ETH—Hönggerberg, 8093 Zürich, Switzerland; tel. (1) 6332647; fax (1) 6331241; e-mail secretariat@iabse.org; internet www.iabse.org; f. 1929 to exchange knowledge and advance the practice of structural engineering world-wide; mems: 4,100 government departments, local authorities, universities, institutes, firms and individuals in over 100 countries; Pres. MANABU ITO (Japan); Exec. Dir A. GOLAY; publs *Structural Engineering International* (quarterly), *Structural Engineering Documents, Congress Report, IABSE Report.*

International Association for Cybernetics (Association internationale de cybernétique): Palais des Expositions, ave Sergent Vrithoff 2, 5000 Namur, Belgium; tel. (81) 71-71-71; fax (81) 71-71-00; e-mail cyb@info.fundp.ac.be; internet pespmc1.vub.ac.be/iac.html; f. 1957 to ensure liaison between research workers engaged in various sectors of cybernetics; promotes the development of the science and its applications; disseminates information; mems: firms and individuals in 42 countries; Chair. J. RAMAEKERS; Gen. Sec. CARINE AIGRET; publ. *Cybernetica* (quarterly).

International Association of Hydraulic Engineering and Research (IAHR): Paseo Bajo Virgen del Puerto 3, 28005 Madrid, Spain; tel. (91) 3357908; fax (91) 3357935; e-mail iahr@iahr.org; internet www.iahr.org; f. 1935; promotes advancement and exchange of knowledge on hydraulic engineering; holds biennial congresses and symposia; mems: 1,850 individual, 300 corporate; Sec.-Gen. C. MATEOS (Spain); publs *Journal of River Basin Management, IAHR Newsletter, Journal of Hydraulic Research, Proceedings* of Biennial Conferences, *Fluvial Processes Monograph*, *Fluvial Processes Solutions Manual*, *Hydraulicians in Europe 1800–2000*.

International Association of Lighthouse Authorities: 20 ter rue Schnapper, 78100 St Germain en Laye, France; tel. 1-34-51-70-01; fax 1-34-51-82-05; e-mail aismiala@easynet.fr; internet www.iala-aism.org; f. 1957; holds technical conference every four years; working groups study special problems and formulate technical recommendations, guide-lines and manuals; mems in 80 countries; Sec.-Gen. Torsten Kruuse; publ. *Bulletin* (quarterly).

International Association of Technological University Libraries (IATUL): c/o Dr Judith Palmer, Radcliffe Science Library, Oxford University, Parks Rd, Oxford OX1 3QP, United Kingdom; tel. (1865) 272820; fax (1865) 272832; e-mail judith.palmer@bodley.ox.ac.uk; internet www.iatul.org; f. 1955 to promote co-operation between member libraries and stimulate research on library problems; mems: 202 university libraries in 41 countries; Pres. Dr Michael Breaks (UK); Sec. Dr Judith Palmer (UK); publs *IATUL Proceedings*, *IATUL Newsletter* (electronic version only).

International Bridge, Tunnel and Turnpike Association: 1146 19th St, NW, Suite 800, Washington, DC 20036-3725, USA; tel. (202) 659-4620; fax (202) 659-0500; e-mail ibtta@ibtta.org; internet www.ibtta.org; f. 1932 to serve as a forum for sharing knowledge, with the aim of promoting toll-financed transportation services; mems: 240 mems in 22 countries; Exec. Dir. Patrick D. Jones; publ. *Tollways* (monthly).

International Cargo Handling Co-ordination Association (ICHCA): Suite 2, 85 Western Rd, Romford, Essex RM1 3LS, United Kingdom; tel. (1708) 734787; fax (1708) 734877; e-mail info@ichca.org.uk; internet www.ichca.org.uk; f. 1952 to foster economy and efficiency in the movement of goods from origin to destination; mems: 2,000 in 90 countries; Pres. Ken Hoggat; Chief Exec. Gerry Askham; publs *Cargo Tomorrow: Cargo Handling News* (bimonthly), *World of Cargo Handling* (annually), *Who's Who in Cargo Handling* (annually), technical publs and reviews.

International Colour Association: c/o Frank Rochow, LMT Lichtmesstechnik GmbH Berlin, Helmholtzstr. 9, 10587 Berlin, Germany; tel. (30) 3934028; fax (30) 3918001; f. 1967 to encourage research in colour in all its aspects, disseminate the knowledge gained from this research and promote its application to the solution of problems in the fields of science, art and industry; holds international congresses and symposia; mems: organizations in 28 countries; Pres. Paula Alessi (USA); Sec. and Treas. Frank Rochow (Germany).

International Commission of Agricultural Engineering (CIGR): Institut für Landtechnik, Universität Bonn, Nussallee 5, 53 115 Bonn, Germany; tel. (228) 732389; fax (228) 739644; e-mail cigr@uni-bonn.de; internet www.cigr.org; f. 1930; aims to stimulate development of science and technology in agricultural engineering; encourages education, training and mobility of professionals; facilitates exchange of research; represents profession at international level; mems: asscns from 92 countries; Pres. Prof. A. Munack (Germany); Sec.-Gen. P. Schulze Lammers (Germany); publs *Bulletin de la CIGR*, *Newsletter* (quarterly), technical reports.

International Commission on Glass: Stazione Sperimentale del Vetro, Via Briati 10, 30141 Murano, Venice, Italy; tel. (041) 739422; fax (041) 739420; e-mail spevetro@ve-nettuno.it; internet www.nettuno.it/fiera/spevetro; f. 1933 to co-ordinate research in glass and allied products, exchange information and organize conferences; mems: 30 organizations; Pres. D. Pye; Sec.-Gen. F. Nicoletti.

International Commission on Illumination (CIE): Kegelgasse 27, 1030 Vienna, Austria; tel. (1) 714-31-87-0; fax (1) 713-08-38-18; e-mail ciecb@ping.at; internet www.cie.co.at; f. 1900 as International Commission on Photometry, present name adopted 1913; aims to provide an international forum for all matters relating to the science and art of light and lighting; serves as a forum for the exchange of information; develops and publishes international standards and provides guidance in their application; mems: 40 national committees and four individuals; Gen. Sec. C. Hermann; publs standards, technical reports.

International Commission on Irrigation and Drainage (ICID) (Commission Internationale des Irrigations et du Drainage): 48 Nyaya Marg, Chanakyapuri, New Delhi 110 021, India; tel. (11) 26115679; fax (11) 26115962; e-mail icid@icid.org; internet www.icid.org; f. 1950; holds triennial congresses; mems: 140 national committees; Pres. Keizrul bin Abdullah (Malaysia); Sec.-Gen. Er. M. Gopalakrishnan (India); publs *Journal* (quarterly), *World Irrigation*, *Multilingual Technical Dictionary*, *Historical Dams*, *Indus Basin*, *Danube Valley*, *Application of Geosynthetics in Irrigation and Drainage Projects*, technical books.

International Commission on Large Dams: 151 blvd Haussmann, 75008 Paris, France; tel. 1-40-42-68-24; fax 1-40-42-60-71; e-mail secretaire.general@icold-cigb.org; internet www.icold-cigb.org/; f. 1928; holds triennial congresses (2003 congress: Montréal,

Canada); mems: in 82 countries; Pres. B. Viotti (Brazil); Sec.-Gen. and Treas. A. Bergeret; publs *Technical Bulletin* (3 or 4 a year), *World Register of Dams*, *World Register of Mine and Industrial Wastes*, *Technical Dictionary on Dams*, studies.

International Committee on Aeronautical Fatigue (ICAF): c/o Prof. O. Buxbaum, Fraunhofer-Institut für Betriebsfestigkeit LBF, 64289 Darmstadt, Bartningstrasse 47, Germany; tel. (6151) 7051; fax (6151) 705214; internet www.icaf2003.com; f. 1951 for collaboration between aeronautical bodies and laboratories on questions of fatigue of aeronautical structures; organizes periodical conferences; mems: national centres in 13 countries; Sec. Prof. O. Buxbaum (Germany).

International Council on Large High-Voltage Electric Systems (Conseil international des grands réseaux électriques—CIGRE): 21 rue d'Artois, 75008 Paris, France; tel. 1-53-89-12-90; fax 1-53-89-12-99; e-mail secretary-general@cigre.org; internet www.cigre.org; f. 1921 to facilitate and promote the exchange of technical knowledge and information in the general field of electrical generation and transmission at high voltages; holds general sessions (every 2 years) and symposia; mems: 5,000 in 80 countries; Pres. D. Croft (Australia); Sec.-Gen. J. Kowal (France); publ. *Electra* (every 2 months).

International Council for Research and Innovation in Building and Construction: Postbox 1837, 3000 BV Rotterdam, Netherlands; tel. (10) 4110240; fax (10) 4334372; e-mail secretariat@cibworld.nl; internet www.cibworld.nl; f. 1953 to encourage and facilitate co-operation in building research, studies and documentation in all aspects; mems: governmental and industrial organizations and qualified individuals in 70 countries; Pres. Dr S. A. Barakat (Canada); Sec.-Gen. W. J. P. Bakens; publs *Information Bulletin* (bi-monthly), conference proceedings and technical, best practice and other reports.

International Electrotechnical Commission (IEC): 3 rue de Varembé, POB 131, 1211 Geneva 20, Switzerland; tel. (22) 9190211; fax (22) 9190300; e-mail info@iec.ch; internet www.iec.ch; f. 1906 as the authority for world standards for electrical and electronic engineering: its standards are used as the basis for regional and national standards, and are used in the preparation of specifications for international trade; mems: national committees representing all branches of electrical and electronic activities in some 60 countries; Gen.-Sec. A. Amit; publs *International Standards and Reports*, *IEC Bulletin*, *Annual Report*, *Catalogue of Publications*.

International Special Committee on Radio Interference: British Electrotechnical Committee, British Standards Institution, 389 Chiswick High Rd, London, W4 4AL, United Kingdom; tel. (20) 8996-9000; fax (20) 8996-7400; e-mail chris_beckley@electricity.org.uk; f. 1934; special committee of the IEC, promoting international agreement on the protection of radio reception from interference by equipment other than authorized transmitters; recommends limits of such interference and specifies equipment and methods of measurement; mems: national committees of IEC and seven other international organizations; Sec. Christopher Beckley.

International Federation for Information and Documentation: POB 90402, 2509 LK The Hague, Netherlands; tel. (70) 3140671; fax (70) 3140667; e-mail fid@fid.nl; internet www.fid.nl; f. 1895; aims to promote, and improve, through international co-operation, research in and development of information science, information management and documentation; maintains regional commissions for Latin America, North America and the Caribbean, Asia and Oceania, Western, Eastern and Southern Africa, North Africa and the Near East, and for Europe; mems: 62 national, five international, 330 institutional and individual mems; Pres. K. Brunnstein; Exec. Dir J. Stephen Parker; publs *FID Review* (every 2 months), *FID Directory* (every 2 years).

International Federation for Information Processing (IFIP): Hofstrasse 3, 2361 Laxenburg, Austria; tel. (2236) 73616; fax (2236) 736169; e-mail ifip@ifip.or.at; internet www.ifip.or.at; f. 1960 to promote information science and technology; encourages research, development and application of information processing in science and human activities; furthers the dissemination and exchange of information on information processing; mems: 45 organizations, 3 corresponding mems, 1 assoc. mem. and 11 affiliate mems; Pres. P. Bollerslev (Denmark); Exec. Dir Plamen Nedkov.

International Federation for the Promotion of Machine and Mechanism Science: Laboratory of Robotics and Mechantronics, Univ. of Cassino, via di Biasio 43, 03043 Cassino, Italy; tel. (776) 299-3663; fax (776) 299-3989; e-mail ceccarelli@unicas.it; internet www.iftomm.org; f. 1969 to study mechanisms, robots, man-machine systems, etc.; Pres. K. Waldron; Sec.-Gen. M. Ceccarelli; publ. *Mechanism and Machine Theory*, *Journal of Applied Mechanics*, *Journal of Gearing and Transmissions*, *Electronic Journal on Computational Kinematics*.

International Federation of Airworthiness (IFA): 14 Railway Approach, East Grinstead, West Sussex RH19 1BP, United Kingdom; tel. (1342) 301788; fax (1342) 317808; e-mail sec@ifairworthy.org; internet www.ifairworthy.org; f. 1964 to provide a forum for the exchange of international experience in maintenance, design and operations; holds annual conference; awards international aviation scholarship annually; mems: 120, comprising 50 airlines, 17 airworthiness authorities, 23 aerospace manufacturing companies, 17 service and repair organizations, three consultancies, six professional societies, two aviation insurance companies, one aircraft leasing company, and the Flight Safety Foundation (USA); Pres. JOHN K LAUBER (USA); Exec. Dir J. W. SAULL (UK); publ. *IFA News* (quarterly).

International Federation of Automatic Control (IFAC): 2361 Laxenburg, Schlossplatz 12, Austria; tel. (2236) 71447; fax (2236) 72859; e-mail secr@ifac.co.at; internet www.ifac-control.org; f. 1957 to serve those concerned with the theory and application of automatic control and systems engineering; mems: 50 national asscns; Pres. Prof. VLADIMIR KUCERA (Czech Republic); Sec. G. HENCSEY; publs *Annual Reviews in ControlAutomatica and Control Engineering Practice* (bi-monthly), *Journal of Process Control, Newsletter, Engineering Applications of Artificial Intelligence* .

International Federation of Automotive Engineering Societies (FISITA): 1 Birdcage Walk, London SW1H 9JJ, United Kingdom; tel. (20) 7973-1275; fax (20) 7973-1285; e-mail info@fisita.com; internet www.fisita.com; f. 1947 to promote the technical and sustainable development of all forms of automotive transportation; maintains electronic job centre for automotive engineers (www.fisitajobs.com); holds congresses every two years; mems: national orgs in 34 countries; Chief Exec. IAN DICKIE; publ. *AutoTechnology*.

International Federation of Consulting Engineers (Fédération internationale des ingénieurs-conseils—FIDIC): POB 311, 1215 Geneva 15, Switzerland; tel. (22) 7994900; fax (22) 7994901; e-mail fidic@fidic.org; internet www.fidic.org; f. 1913 to encourage international co-operation and the establishment of standards for consulting engineers; mems: national asscns in 66 countries, comprising some 500,000 design professionals; Pres. EIGIL STEEN PEDERSEN; publs *FIDIC Report, Annual Survey, Annual Review*.

International Federation of Hospital Engineering: 2 Abingdon House, Cumberland Business Centre, Northumberland Rd, Portsmouth, PO5 1DS, United Kingdom; tel. (2392) 823186; fax (2392) 815927; e-mail ifhc@iheem.org.uk; internet www.ifhc.info; f. 1970 to promote internationally standards of hospital engineering and to provide for the exchange of knowledge and experience in the areas of hospital and healthcare facility design, construction, engineering, commissioning, maintenance and estate management; mems: 50, in more than 30 countries; Pres. GUNNAR BÆKKEN (Norway); Gen. Sec. BERNARD SHAPIRO (South Africa); publ. *Hospital Engineering* (quarterly).

International Gas Union: c/o Dong A/S, POB 550, Agern Alle 24–26, 2970 Hoersholm, Denmark; tel. 45-17-12-00; fax 45-17-19-00; e-mail secr.igu@dong.dkl; internet www.igu.org; f. 1931; represents the gas industry world-wide; mems: 66 Charter mems, 14 Associate mems; Pres. GEORGE H. VORBERG (Netherlands); Sec.-Gen. PETER K. STORM (Denmark).

International Institute of Seismology and Earthquake Engineering (IISEE): Building Research Institute, 1 Tatehara, Tsukuba City, Ibaraki Pref., Japan; tel. (298) 79-0677; fax (298) 64-6777; e-mail iisee@kenken.go.jp; internet iisee.kenken.go.jp; f. 1962 to work on seismology and earthquake engineering for the purpose of reducing earthquake damage in the world; trains seismologists and earthquake engineers from the earthquake-prone countries; undertakes surveys, research, guidance and analysis of information on earthquakes and related matters; mems: 75 countries; Dir T. FUKUTA; publs *Year Book, Bulletin* (annually), *Individual Studies* (annually).

International Institute of Welding: 90 rue des Vanesses, ZI Paris Nord II, 93420 Villepinte, France; tel. 1-49-90-36-08; fax 1-49-90-36-80; e-mail iiw@wanadoo.fr; internet www.iiw-iis.org; f. 1948; mems: 53 societies in 45 countries; Pres. B. PEKKARI (Sweden); Chief Exec. D. BEAUFILS (France); publ. *Welding in the World* (7 a year).

International Institution for Production Engineering Research: 9 rue Mayran, 75009 Paris, France; tel. 1-45-26-21-80; fax 1-45-26-92-15; e-mail cirp@cirp.net; internet www.cirp.net; f. 1951 to promote by scientific research the study of the mechanical processing of all solid materials; mems: 510 in 40 countries; Pres. F. JOVANE (Italy); Sec.-Gen. M. VERON (France); publ. *Annals* (2 a year).

International Iron and Steel Institute (IISI): 120 rue Col Bourg, 1140 Brussels, Belgium; tel. (2) 702-89-00; fax (2) 702-88-99; e-mail steel@iisi.be; internet www.worldsteel.org; f. 1967 to promote the welfare and interests of the world's steel industries; undertakes research into all aspects of steel industries; serves as a forum for exchange of knowledge and discussion of problems relating to steel industries; collects, disseminates and maintains statistics and information; serves as a liaison body between international and national steel organizations; mems: in over 50 countries; Sec.-Gen. IAN CHRISTMAS; publs *Worldsteel Newsletter*, policy statements and reports.

International Measurement Confederation (IMEKO): POB 457, 1371 Budapest 5, Hungary; tel. and fax (1) 353-1562; e-mail imeko.ime@mtesz.hu; internet www.imeko.org; f. 1958 as a federation of member organizations concerned with the advancement of measurement technology; aims to promote exchange of scientific and technical information in field of measurement and instrumentation and to enhance co-operation between scientists and engineers; holds World Congress every 3 years (2006: Rio de Janeiro); mems: 35 orgs; Pres. Prof. L. VAN BIESEN (Belgium); Sec.-Gen. Dr TAMÁS KEMÉNY (Hungary); publs *Acta IMEKO* (proceedings of World Congresses), *IMEKO TC Events Series, Measurement* (quarterly), *IMEKO Bulletin* (2 a year).

International Navigation Association: Graaf de Ferraris, 11e étage, bte 3, 156 blvd Roi Albert II, 1000 Brussels, Belgium; tel. (2) 553-71-60; fax (2) 553-71-55; e-mail info@pianc-aipcn.org; internet www.pianc-aipcn.org; f. 1885; fmrly Permanent International Assoc. of Navigation Congresses (PIANC); fosters progress in the construction, maintenance and operation of inland and maritime waterways, of inland and maritime ports and of coastal areas; holds Congresses every four years; mems: 40 governments, 2,780 others; Pres. Ir R. DE PAEPE; Sec.-Gen. C. VAN BEGIN; publs *Bulletin* (quarterly), *Illustrated Technical Dictionary* (in 6 languages), technical reports, Congress papers.

International Organization for Standardization: POB 56, 1 rue de Varembé, 1211 Geneva 20, Switzerland; tel. (22) 7490111; fax (22) 7333430; e-mail central@iso.org; internet www.iso.org; f. 1947 to reach international agreement on industrial and commercial standards; mems: national standards bodies of c. 150 countries; Pres. MASAMI TANAKA (Japan); Sec.-Gen. ALAN BRYDEN; publs *ISO International Standards, ISO Memento* (annually), *ISO Management Systems* (6 a year), *ISO Focus* (11 a year), *ISO Catalogue* (annually, updated regularly online), *ISO Annual Report*.

International Research Group on Wood Protection: Drottning Kristinas väg 33A, Stockholm, Sweden; tel. (8) 10-14-53; fax (8) 10-80-81; e-mail irg@sp.se; internet www.irg-wp.com; f. 1965 as Wood Preservation Group by OECD; independent since 1969; consists of five sections; holds plenary annual meeting; mems: 327 in 52 countries; Pres. Dr JEFFREY MORRELL (USA); Sec.-Gen. JÖRAN JERMER (Sweden); publs technical documents.

International Rubber Research and Development Board (IRRDB): POB 10150, 50908 Kuala Lumpur, Malaysia; fax (3) 21620414; e-mail draziz@pop.jaring.my; internet www.irrdb.org; f. 1937; mems: 15 research institutes; Sec. Datuk Dr A. AZIZ.

International Society for Photogrammetry and Remote Sensing (ISPRS): c/o Orhan Altan, Istanbul Technical Univ., Division of Photogrammetry, 34469 Ayazaga-Istanbul, Turkey; tel. (212) 285-3810; fax (212) 285-6587; e-mail oaltan@itu.edu.tr; internet www.isprs.org/; f. 1910; holds congress every four years, and technical symposia; mems: 103 countries; Pres. IAN DOWMAN (UK); Sec.-Gen. ORHAN ALTAN (Turkey); publs *Journal of Photogrammetry and Remote Sensing* (6 a year), *ISPRS Highlights* (quarterly), *International Archives of Photogrammetry and Remote Sensing* (every 2 years).

International Society for Soil Mechanics and Geotechnical Engineering: City University, Northampton Sq., London, EC1V 0HB, United Kingdom; tel. (20) 7040-8154; fax (20) 7040-8832; e-mail secretariat@issmge.org; internet www.issmge.org; f. 1936 to promote international co-operation among scientists and engineers in the field of geotechnics and its engineering applications; maintains 30 technical committees; holds quadrennial international conference, regional conferences and specialist conferences; mems: 17,000 individuals, 74 national societies, 23 corporate members; Pres. Prof. W. F. VAN IMPE; Sec.-Gen. Prof. R. N. TAYLOR; publs *ISSMGE News* (quarterly), *Lexicon of Soil Mechanics Terms* (in eight languages).

International Solar Energy Society: Wiesentalstrasse 50, 79115 Freiburg, Germany; tel. (761) 459060; fax (761) 4590699; e-mail hq@ises.org; internet www.ises.org; f. 1954; addresses all aspects of renewable energy, including characteristics, effects and methods of use; undertakes projects in several countries on various aspects of renewable energy technology and implementation; organizes major international, regional and national congresses; mems: c. 30,000 in some 100 countries; Pres. Dr YOGI GOSWAMI (Norway); Exec. Dir RIAN VAN STADEN (South Africa); publs *Solar Energy Journal* (monthly), *Refocus* (6 a year).

International Solid Waste Association (ISWA): Overgaden Oven Vandet 48E, 1415 Copenhagen K, Denmark; tel. 32-96-15-88;

fax 32-96-15-84; e-mail iswa@iswa.dk; internet www.iswa.org; f. 1970 to promote the exchange of information and experience in solid waste management, in order to protect human health and the environment; promotes research and development activities; provides advice; organizes conferences; Pres. CHRISTOPH SCHARFF (Austria); Man. Dir SUZANNE ARUP VELTZÉ (Denmark); publs *Waste Management World*, *Waste Management and Research* (6 a year).

International Union for Electricity Applications: 5 rue Chante-Coq, 92808 Puteaux Cédex, France; tel. 1-41-26-56-48; fax 1-41-26-56-49; e-mail uie@uie.org; internet www.uie.org; f. 1953, present title adopted 1994; aims to study all questions relative to electricity applications, except commercial questions; links national groups and organizes international congresses on electricity applications; mems: national committees, corporate associated and individual members in 18 countries; Pres. RONNIE BELMANS (Belgium); Gen. Sec. Prof. MICHEL MACHIELS; publ. UIE proceedings.

International Union for Vacuum Science, Technique and Applications (IUVSTA): c/o Dr R. J. Reid, 84 Oldfield Drive, Vicars Cross, Chester CH3 5LW, United Kingdom; tel. (1244) 342-675; e-mail iuvsta.secretary.general@ronreid.me.uk; internet www.iuvsta.org; f. 1958; collaborates with the International Standards Organization in defining and adopting technical standards; holds triennial International Vacuum Congress, European Vacuum Conference, triennial International Conference on Thin Films, and International Conference on Solid Surfaces; administers the Welch Foundation scholarship for postgraduate research in vacuum science and technology; mems: organizations in 30 countries; Pres. Prof. UGO VALBUSA (Italy); Sec.-Gen. Dr R. J. REID (UK); publ. *News Bulletin* (2 a year).

International Union of Air Pollution Prevention and Environmental Protection Associations: 44 Grand Parade, Brighton, BN2 2QA, United Kingdom; tel. (1273) 878772; fax (1273) 606626; e-mail iuappa@nsca.org.uk; internet www.iuappa.fsnet.co.uk; f. 1963; organizes triennial World Clean Air Congress and regional conferences for developing countries (several a year); undertakes policy development and research programmes on international environmental issues; Pres. Prof. M. LURIA (Israel); Dir-Gen. R. MILLS; publs *IUAPPA Newsletter* (quarterly), *Clean Air around the World*.

International Union of Technical Associations and Organizations (Union internationale des associations et organismes techniques—UATI): UNESCO House, 1 rue Miollis, 75015 Paris Cédex 15, France; tel. 1-45-68-27-70; fax 1-43-06-29-27; e-mail uati@unesco.org; internet www.unesco.org/uati; f. 1951 (fmrly Union of International Technical Associations) under the auspices of UNESCO; aims to promote and co-ordinate activities of member organizations and represent their interests; facilitates relations with international organizations, notably UN agencies; receives proposals and makes recommendations on the establishment of new international technical assocns; mems: 25 organizations; Chair. PHILIPPE AUSSOURD (France); publ. *Convergence* (3 a year).

International Union of Testing and Research Laboratories for Materials and Structures: École Normale Supérieure, 61 ave du Président Wilson, 94235 Cachan Cédex, France; tel. 1-47-40-23-97; fax 1-47-40-01-13; e-mail sg@rilem.ens-cachan.fr; internet www.iabse.ethz.ch/lc/rilem.html; f. 1947 for the exchange of information and the promotion of co-operation on experimental research concerning structures and materials; studies research methods with a view to improvement and standardization; mems: laboratories and individuals in 73 countries; Pres. Dr JACQUES BRESSON (France); Sec.-Gen. M. BRUSIN (France); publ. *Materials and Structures—Testing and Research* (10 a year).

International Water Resources Association (IWRA): University of New Mexico, 1915 Roma NE, Albuquerque, NM 87131-1436, USA; tel. (505) 277-9400; fax (505) 277-9405; e-mail iwra@unm.edu; internet www.iwra.siu.edu; f. 1972 to promote collaboration in and support for international water resources programmes; holds conferences; conducts training in water resources management; Pres. GLENN E. STOUT (USA); Sec.-Gen. VICTOR DE KOSINSKY (Belgium); publ. *Water International* (quarterly).

Latin-American Energy Organization (Organización Latinoamericana de Energía—OLADE): Avda Mariscal Antonio José de Sucre, No N58–63 y Fernándes Salvador, Edif. OLADE, Sector San Carlos, POB 17-11-6413 CCI, Quito, Ecuador; tel. (2) 598-122; fax (2) 531-691; e-mail oladel@olade.org.ec; internet www.olade.org.ec; f. 1973 to act as an instrument of co-operation in using and conserving the energy resources of the region; mems: 26 Latin-American and Caribbean countries; Exec. Sec. Dr DIEGO PÉREZ PALLARES; publ. *Energy Magazine*.

Latin-American Iron and Steel Institute: Benjamín 2944, 5°, Las Condes, Santiago, Chile; tel. (2) 233-0545; fax (2) 233-0768; e-mail ilafa@entelchile.net; internet www.ilafa.org; f. 1959 to help achieve the harmonious development of iron and steel production, manufacture and marketing in Latin America; conducts economic surveys on the steel sector; organizes technical conventions and meetings; disseminates industrial processes suited to regional conditions; prepares and maintains statistics on production, end uses, prices, etc., of raw materials and steel products within this area; mems: 18 hon. mems; 63 mems; 68 assoc. mems; Chair. JULIO CÉSAR VILLARREAL; Sec.-Gen. ENRIQUE ALVAREZ; publs *Acero Latinoamericano* (every 2 months), *Statistical Year Book*, *Directory of Latin American Iron and Steel Companies* (every 2 years).

Regional Centre for Mapping of Resources for Development: POB 632, 00618 Ruaraka, Nairobi, Kenya; tel. (20) 860654; fax (20) 802767; e-mail rcmrd@rcmrd.org; internet www.rcmrd.org; f. 1975; present name adopted 1997; provides services for the professional techniques of map-making and the application of satellite and remote sensing data in resource analysis and development planning; undertakes research and provides advisory services to African governments; mems: 14 signatory and 10 non-signatory governments; Dir-Gen. Dr WILBER K. OTTICHILO.

Regional Centre for Training in Aerospace Surveys (RECTAS) (Centre Regional de formation aux techniques des leves aerospatiaux): PMB 5545, Ile-Ife, Nigeria; tel. (36) 230050; fax (36) 230481; e-mail rectas@oauife.edu.ng; internet www.rectas.org; f. 1972; provides training, research and advisory services in aerospace surveys and geoinformatics; administered by the ECA; mems: eight governments; Exec. Dir Dr OLAJIDE KUFONIYI.

Regional Council of Co-ordination of Central and East European Engineering Organizations: c/o MTESZ, 1055 Budapest, Kossuth Lajos tér 6–8, Hungary; tel. (361) 353-4795; fax (361) 353-0317; e-mail mtesz@mtesz.hu; f. 1992; Hon. Pres. JÁNOS TÓTH.

Union of the Electricity Industry (EURELECTRIC): Blvd de l'Impératrice 66, Box 2, 1000 Brussels, Belgium; tel. (2) 515-10-00; fax (2) 510-10-10; e-mail eurelectric@eurelectric.org; internet www.eurelectric.org; f. 1999 by merger of International Union of Producers and Distributors of Electrical Energy (UNIPEDE, f. 1925) and European Grouping of the Electricity Industry (EEIG, f. 1989); aims to study all questions relating to the production, transmission and distribution of electrical energy, and to promote the image of and defend the interests of the electricity supply industry; Pres. HANS HAIDER; Sec.-Gen. PAUL BULTEEL; publ. *Watt's New* (newsletter).

World Association of Industrial and Technological Research Organizations (WAITRO): c/o SIRIM Berhad, 1 Persiaran Dato' Menteri, Section 2, POB 7035, 40911 Shah Alam, Malaysia; tel. 5544-6635; fax 5544-6735; e-mail info@waitro.sirim.my; internet www.waitro.org; f. 1970 by the UN Industrial Development Organization to organize co-operation in industrial and technological research; provides financial assistance for training and joint activities; arranges international seminars; facilitates the exchange of information; mems: 200 research institutes in 80 countries; Pres. BJORN LUNDBERG (Sweden); Contact MOSES MENGU; publs *WAITRO News* (quarterly), *WAITRO News* (quarterly).

World Association of Nuclear Operators (WANO-CC): Cavendish Court, 11–15 Wigmore St, London, W1U 1PF, United Kingdom; tel. (20) 7478-4200; fax (20) 7495-4502; internet www.wano.org.uk; f. 1989 by operators of nuclear power plants; aims to improve the safety and reliability of nuclear power plants through the exchange of information; operates four regional centres (in France, Japan, Russia and the USA) and a co-ordinating centre in the UK; mems: in 34 countries; Man. Dir SIG BERG.

World Bureau of Metal Statistics: 27A High St, Ware, Herts, SG12 9BA, United Kingdom; tel. (1920) 461274; fax (1920) 464258; e-mail wbms@world-bureau.co.uk; internet www.world-bureau.com; f. 1949; produces statistics of production, consumption, stocks, prices and international trade in copper, lead, zinc, tin, nickel, aluminium and several other minor metals; Man. Dir S. M. EALES; publs *World Metal Statistics* (monthly), *World Tin Statistics* (monthly), *World Nickel Statistics* (monthly), *World Metal Statistics Yearbook*, *World Metal Statistics Quarterly Summary*, *World Stainless Steel Statistics* (annually), *World Wrought Copper Statistics* (annually).

World Energy Council: 5th Floor, Regency House, 1–4 Warwick St, London, W1B 5LT, United Kingdom; tel. (20) 7734-5996; fax (20) 7734-5926; e-mail info@worldenergy.org; internet www.worldenergy.org; f. 1924 to link all branches of energy and resources technology and maintain liaison between world experts; holds congresses every three years; mems: 99 committees; Chair. ANTONIO DEL ROSARIO (Philippines); Sec.-Gen. GERALD DOUCET (Canada); publs *Annual Report*, energy supply and demand projections, resources surveys, technical assessments, reports.

World Federation of Engineering Organizations (WFEO): Maison de l'UNESCO, 1 rue Miollis, 75015 Paris, France; tel. 1-45-68-48-47; fax 1-43-06-29-27; e-mail peb.fmoi@unesco.org; internet www.unesco.org/wfeo; f. 1968 to advance engineering as a profession; fosters co-operation between engineering organizations throughout the world; undertakes special projects in co-operation with other international bodies; mems: 80 national mems, nine international mems; Pres. JOSÉ MEDEM SANJUAN (Spain); Exec. Dir

PIERRE EDOUARD DE BOIGNE (France); publ. *WFEO Newsletter* (2 a year).

World Foundrymen Organization (WFO): National Metalforming Centre, 47 Birmingham Rd, West Bromwich, B70 6PY, United Kingdom; tel. (121) 601-6979; fax (121) 601-6981; e-mail secretary@thewfo.com; internet www.thewfo.com; Pres. MIKE CLIFFORD; Gen. Sec. Eng. A. TURNER.

World Petroleum Congresses: 4th Floor, Suite 1, 1 Duchess St, London, W1N 3DE, United Kingdom; tel. (20) 7637-4958; e-mail pierce@world-petroleum.org; internet www.world-petroleum.org; f. 1933 to serve as a forum for petroleum science, technology, economics and management; undertakes related information and liaison activities; 2002 Congress: Rio de Janeiro, Brazil; mems: Permanent Council includes 59 mem. countries; Pres. Dr E. ROREN (Norway); Dir-Gen. Dr PIERCE W. F. RIEMER (UK).

World Road Association (PIARC): La Grande Arche, Paroi Nord, Niveau 8, 92055 La Défense Cédex, France; tel. 1-47-96-81-21; fax 1-49-00-02-02; e-mail piarc@wanadoo.fr; internet www.piarc.org; f. 1909 as the Permanent International Association of Road Congresses; aims to promote the construction, improvement, maintenance, use and economic development of roads; organizes technical committee and study sessions; mems: governments, public bodies, organizations and private individuals in 100 countries; Pres. O. MICHAUD (Switzerland); Sec.-Gen. J. F. CORTÉ (France); publs *Bulletin*, *Technical Dictionary*, *Lexicon*, technical reports.

Tourism

Alliance Internationale de Tourisme: 2 Chemin de Blandonnet, CP 111, 1215 Geneva 15, Switzerland; tel. (22) 5444501; fax (22) 5444550; e-mail webmaster@aitfia.ch; internet www.aitgva.ch; f. 1898, present title adopted 1919; represents motoring organizations and touring clubs around the world; aims to study all questions relating to international touring and to suggest reforms; mems: 140 asscns with 100m. members in 102 countries; Pres. W. KRAUS (Austria); Dir-Gen. P. DOGGWILER (Switzerland); publ. *AIT News*.

Caribbean Tourism Organization: One Financial Pl., Collymore Rock, St Michael, Barbados; tel. 427-5242; fax 429-3065; e-mail ctobar@caribsurf.com; internet www.onecaribbean.org; f. 1989, by merger of the Caribbean Tourism Association (f. 1951) and the Caribbean Tourism Research and Development Centre (f. 1974); aims to encourage tourism in the Caribbean region; organizes annual Caribbean Tourism Conference, Sustainable Tourism Development Conference and Tourism Investment Conference; conducts training and other workshops on request; maintains offices in New York, Canada and London; mems: 33 Caribbean governments, 400 allied mems; Sec.-Gen. JEAN HOLDER; publs *Caribbean Tourism Statistical News* (quarterly), *Caribbean Tourism Statistical Report* (annually).

European Travel Commission: 19A ave Marnix, 1000 Brussels, Belgium; tel. (2) 548-90-00; fax (2) 514-18-43; e-mail info@etc-corporate.org; internet www.etc-corporate.org; f. 1948 to promote tourism in and to Europe, to foster co-operation and the exchange of information, and to organize research; mems: national tourist organizations in 31 European countries; Exec. Dir ROB FRANKLIN (United Kingdom).

International Association of Scientific Experts in Tourism: Dufourstr. 40A, 9000 St Gallen, Switzerland; tel. (71) 2242530; fax (71) 2242536; e-mail aiest@unisg.ch; internet www.aiest.org; f. 1949 to encourage scientific activity in tourism, to support tourist institutions of a scientific nature and to organize conventions; mems: 400 from 40 countries; Pres. Prof. Dr PETER KELLER (Switzerland); Gen. Sec. Prof. Dr THOMAS BIEGER (Switzerland); publ. *The Tourism Review* (quarterly).

International Congress and Convention Association (ICCA): Entrada 121, 1096 EB Amsterdam, Netherlands; tel. (20) 398-19-19; fax (20) 699-07-81; e-mail icca@icca.nl; internet www.iccaworld.com; f. 1963 to establish world-wide co-operation between all involved in organizing congresses, conventions and exhibitions; mems: over 680 from 80 countries; CEO MARTIN SIRK; publ. *ICCA Intelligence* (quarterly).

International Hotel and Restaurant Association: 48 blvd de Sébastopol, 75003, Paris, France; tel. 1-44-88-92-20; fax 1-44-88-92-30; e-mail ohrner@ih-ra.com; internet www.ih-ra.com; f. 1946 to act as the authority on matters affecting the international hotel and restaurant industry, to promote its interests and to contribute to its growth, profitability and quality; membership extended to restaurants in 1996; mems: 120 national hospitality asscns, 100 national and international hotel and restaurant chains; Dir and CEO DAVID I. MCMILLAN; publs *Hotels* (monthly), *Yearbook and Directory* (annually).

Latin-American Confederation of Tourist Organizations (Confederación de Organizaciones Turísticas de la América Latino—COTAL): Viamonte 640, 8°, 1053 Buenos Aires, Argentina; tel. (11) 4322-4003; fax (11) 4393-5696; e-mail cotal@cscom.com.ar; internet www.cotal.org.ar; f. 1957 to link Latin American national asscns of travel agents and their members with other tourist bodies around the world; mems: in 21 countries; Pres. ENZO U. FURNARI; publ. *Revista COTAL* (every 2 months).

Pacific Asia Travel Association (PATA): Unit B1, 28th Floor, Siam Tower, 989 Rama 1 Rd, Pratumwan, Bangkok 10330, Thailand; tel. (2) 658-2000; fax (2) 658-2010; e-mail patabkk@pata.org; internet www.pata.org; f. 1951; aims to enhance the growth, value and quality of Pacific Asia travel and tourism for the benefit of PATA members; holds annual conference and travel fair; divisional offices in Germany, Australia (Sydney), USA; mems: more than 1,200 governments, carriers, tour operators, travel agents and hotels; publs *PATA Compass* (every 2 months), *Statistical Report* (quarterly), *Forecasts Book*, research reports, directories, newsletters.

South Pacific Tourism Organization: POB 13119, Suva, Fiji; tel. 3304177; fax 3301995; e-mail info@spto.org; internet www.tcsp.com; fmrly the Tourism Council of the South Pacific; aims to foster regional co-operation in the development, marketing and promotion of tourism in the island nations of the South Pacific; receives EU funding and undertakes sustainable activities; mems: 13 countries in the South Pacific; Chief Exec. LISIATE AKOLO; publ. *Weekly Newsletter*.

United Federation of Travel Agents' Associations (UFTAA): 1 ave des Castelans, Stade Louis II-Entrée H, 98000 Monaco; tel. 92-05-28-29; fax 92-05-29-87; e-mail uftaa@uftaa.org; internet www.uftaa.org; f. 1966 to unite travel agents' asscns; represents the interests of travel agents at the international level; helps in international legal differences; issues literature on travel; mems: regional and national asscns of travel agencies in 112 countries; Sec.-Gen. BIRGER BÄCKMAN.

World Association of Travel Agencies (WATA): 11 chaussée Riant-Coteau, 1196 Gland, Switzerland; tel. (22) 9951545; fax (22) 9951546; e-mail wata@wata.net; internet www.wata.net; f. 1949 to foster the development of tourism, to help the rational organization of tourism in all countries, to collect and disseminate information and to participate in commercial and financial operations to foster the development of tourism; mems: more than 100 individual travel agencies in some 50 countries; Sec.-Gen. MARCO AGUSTONI (Switzerland); publ. *WATA Gazette* (quarterly).

World Travel and Tourism Council (WTTC): 1–2 Queen Victoria Terrace, Sovereign Court, London, E1W 3HA, United Kingdom; tel. (20) 7481-8007; fax (20) 7488-1008; e-mail enquiries@wttc.org; internet www.wttc.org; f. 1989; promotes the development of the travel/tourism industry; analyses impact of tourism on employment levels and local economies and promotes greater expenditure on tourism infrastructure; administers a 'Green Globe' certification programme to enhance environmental management throughout the industry; mems: 57 global mems, five hon. mems; Pres. JEAN-CLAUDE BAUMGARTEN; publs *WTTC Backgrounder*, *Travel and Tourism Review*, *Viewpoint* (quarterly), *Blueprint for New Tourism*, regional and country reports.

Trade and Industry

African Regional Organization for Standardization: POB 57363, Nairobi, Kenya; tel. (20) 224561; fax (20) 218792; e-mail arso@bidii.com; internet www.arso-oran.org; f. 1977 to promote standardization, quality control, certification and metrology in the African region, to formulate regional standards, and to co-ordinate participation in international standardization activities; mems: 24 states; Sec.-Gen. Dr ADEBAYO O. OYEJOLA; publs *ARSO Bulletin* (2 a year), *ARSO Catalogue of Regional Standards* (annually), *ARSO Annual Report*.

Arab Iron and Steel Union (AISU): BP 4, Chéraga, Algiers, Algeria; tel. (21) 37-15-80; fax (21) 37-19-75; e-mail relex@solbarab.com; internet www.solbarab.com; f. 1972 to develop commercial and technical aspects of Arab steel production by helping member asscns commercialize their production in Arab markets, guaranteeing them high quality materials and intermediary products, informing them of recent developments in the industry and organizing training sessions; also arranges two annual symposia; mems: 80 companies in 15 Arab countries; Gen. Sec. MUHAMMAD LAID LACHGAR; publs *Arab Steel Review* (monthly), *Information Bulletin*, *News Steel World* (2 a month), *Directory* (annually).

Asian Productivity Organization: Hirakawacho Daiichi Seimei Bldg 2F, 1-2-10 Hirakawa-cho, Chiyoda-ku, Tokyo 102–0093, Japan; tel. (3) 5226-3920; fax (3) 3226-3950; e-mail apo@apo-tokyo.org; internet www.apo-tokyo.org; f. 1961 as non-political, non-profit making, non-discriminatory regional intergovernmental organization with the aim of contributing to the socio-economic development of Asia and the Pacific through productivity promotion; activities cover industry, agriculture and service sectors, with the primary focus on human resources development; five key areas are incorporated into its activities: knowledge management, green productivity, strengthening small and medium enterprises, integrated community development and development of national productivity organizations; serves its members as a think tank, catalyst, regional adviser, institution builder and clearing house; mems: 20 countries; Sec.-Gen. SHIGEO TAKENAKA; publs *APO News* (monthly), *Annual Report*, *APO Asia-Pacific Productivity Data and Analysis* (annually), other books and monographs.

Association of African Trade Promotion Organizations (AATPO): Pavillion International, BP 23, Tangier, Morocco; tel. (9) 324465; fax (9) 943779; e-mail aoapc@mtds.com; f. 1975 under the auspices of the OAU (now AU) and the ECA to foster regular contact between African states in trade matters and to assist in the harmonization of their commercial policies, in order to promote intra-African trade; conducts research and training; organizes meetings and trade information missions; mems: 26 states; Sec.-Gen. Prof. ADEYINKA W. ORIMALADE; publs *FLASH: African Trade* (monthly), *Directory of African Consultants and Experts in Trade Promotion*, *Directory of Trade Information Contacts in Africa*, *Directory of Trade Information Sources in Africa*, *Directory of State Trading Organizations*, *Directory of Importers and Exporters of Food Products in Africa*, *Basic Information on Africa*, studies.

Association of European Chambers of Commerce and Industry (EUROCHAMBRES): 5 rue d'Archimède, 1000 Brussels, Belgium; tel. (2) 282-08-50; fax (2) 230-00-38; e-mail eurochambres@eurochambres.be; internet www.eurochambres.be; f. 1958 to promote the exchange of experience and information among its members and to bring their joint opinions to the attention of the institutions of the European Union; conducts studies and seminars; coordinates EU projects; mems: 15 full and 18 affiliated mems; Pres. JÖRG MITTELSTEN SCHEID (Germany); Sec.-Gen. ARNALDO ABRUZZINI (Italy).

CAEF—The European Foundry Association: Sohnstrasse 70, D-40237 Düsseldorf, Germany; tel. (211) 687-1215; fax (211) 687-1205; e-mail info@caef-eurofoundry.org; internet www.caef-eurofoundry.org; f. 1953 to safeguard the common interests of European foundry industries and to collect and exchange information; mems: asscns in 18 countries; Sec.-Gen. Dr KLAUS URBAT; publ. *The European Foundry Industry* (annually).

Cairns Group: (no permanent secretariat); internet www.cairnsgroup.org; f. 1986 by major agricultural exporting countries; aims to bring about reforms in international agricultural trade, including reductions in export subsidies, in barriers to access and in internal support measures; represents members' interests in WTO negotiations; mems: Argentina, Australia, Bolivia, Brazil, Canada, Chile, Colombia, Costa Rica, Fiji, Guatemala, Indonesia, Malaysia, New Zealand, Paraguay, Philippines, South Africa, Thailand, Uruguay; Chair. MARK VAILE (Australia).

Caribbean Association of Industry and Commerce (CAIC): POB 442, Trinidad Hilton and Conference Centre, Rooms 1238–1241, Lady Young Rd, St Ann's, Trinidad and Tobago; tel. (868) 623-4830; fax (868) 623-6116; e-mail sifill@wow.net; internet www.caic.wow.net; f. 1955; aims to encourage economic development through the private sector; undertakes research and training and gives assistance to small enterprises; encourages export promotion; mems: chambers of commerce and enterprises in 20 countries and territories; Exec. Dir SEAN IFILL; publ. *Caribbean Investor* (quarterly).

Committee for European Construction Equipment (CECE): c/o Diamant Bldg, blvd Reyers 80, 1030 Brussels, Belgium; tel. (2) 706-82-25; fax (2) 706-82-10; e-mail info@cece-eu.org; internet www.cece-eu.org; f. 1959 to further contact between manufacturers, to improve market conditions and productivity and to conduct research into techniques; mems: representatives from 10 European countries; Sec.-Gen. RALF WEZEL.

Confederation of Asia-Pacific Chambers of Commerce and Industry (CACCI): 13th Floor, 3 Sungshou Rd, Taipei 110, Taiwan; tel. (2) 27255663; fax (2) 27255665; e-mail cacci@ttn.net; internet www.cacci.org.tw; f. 1966; holds biennial conferences to examine regional co-operation; liaises with governments to promote laws conducive to regional co-operation; serves as a centre for compiling and disseminating trade and business information; encourages contacts between businesses; conducts training and research; mems: national chambers of commerce and industry the region, also affiliate and special mems; Dir-Gen. Dr WEBSTER KIANG; publs *CACCI Profile* (monthly), *CACCI Journal of Commerce and Industry*.

Confederation of International Soft Drinks Associations (CISDA): 79 blvd St Michel, 1040 Brussels, Belgium; tel. (2) 743-40-50; fax (2) 732-51-02; e-mail mail@unesda-cisda.org; internet www.unesda-cisda.org; f. 1951 to promote co-operation among the national asscns of soft drinks manufacturers on all industrial and commercial matters, to stimulate the sales and consumption of soft drinks, to deal with matters of interest to all member asscns and to represent the common interests of member asscns; holds a congress every year; Gen. Sec. ALAIN BEAUMONT.

Consumers International: 24 Highbury Cres., London, N5 1RX, United Kingdom; tel. (20) 7226-6663; fax (20) 7354-0607; e-mail consint@consint.org; internet www.consumersinternational.org; f. 1960 as International Organization of Consumers' Unions—IOCU; links consumer groups world-wide through information networks and international seminars; supports new consumer groups and represents consumers' interests at the international level; maintains four regional offices; mems: 250 asscns in 115 countries; Dir-Gen. JULIAN EDWARDS; publs *The African Consumer/Le Consommateur African* (3 a year, English and French), *Asia Pacific Consumer* (online, quarterly), *Consumer 21* (online, quarterly, in English, French and Russian), *Consumidores y Desarollo* (quarterly).

CropLife International: ave Louise 143, 1050 Brussels, Belgium; tel. (2) 542-04-10; fax (2) 542-04-19; e-mail croplife@croplife.org; internet www.croplife.org; f. 1960 as European Group of National Asscns of Pesticide Manufacturers, international body since 1967, present name adopted in 2001, evolving from Global Crop Protection Federation; represents the plant science industry, with the aim of promoting sustainable agricultural methods; aims to harmonize national and international regulations concerning crop protection products and agricultural biotechnology; promotes observation of the FAO Code of Conduct on the Distribution and Use of Pesticides; holds an annual General Assembly; mems: 6 regional bodies and national asscns in 85 countries; Dir-Gen. CHRISTIAN VERSCHUEREN.

Energy Charter Secretariat: blvd de la Woluwe 56, 1200 Brussels, Belgium; tel. (2) 775-98-00; fax (2) 775-98-01; e-mail info@encharter.org; internet www.encharter.org; f. 1995 under the provisions of the Energy Charter Treaty (1994); aims to promote trade and investment in the energy industries; mems: 51 signatory states; Sec.-Gen. Dr RIA KEMPER (Germany); publs *Promoting Energy Efficiency*, *Trade in Energy*, *The Energy Charter Treaty—A Reader's Guide*, reports.

ESOMAR—World Association of Opinion and Marketing Research Professionals: Vondelstraat 172, 1054 GV Amsterdam, Netherlands; tel. (20) 664-21-41; fax (20) 664-29-22; e-mail email@esomar.org; internet www.esomar.org; f. 1948 (as European Society for Opinion and Marketing Research); aims to further professional interests and encourage high technical standards in the industry; mems: over 4,000 in 100 countries; Pres. FREDERIK NAUCKHOFF (Switzerland); publs *Research World* (monthly), *ESOMAR Directory* (annually).

European Association of Communications Agencies (EACA): 152 blvd Brand Whitlock, 1200 Brussels, Belgium; tel. (2) 740-07-10; fax (2) 740-07-17; e-mail dominic.lyle@eaca.be; internet www.eaca.be; f. 1959 (as European Association of Advertising Agencies) to maintain and raise the standards of service of all European advertising, media and sales promotions agencies; aims to strive towards uniformity in fields where this would be of benefit; and to serve the interests of all agency members in Europe; mems: 18 national advertising agency asscns and 23 multinational agency groups; Pres. JAMES BEST (United Kingdom); Dir-Gen. DOMINIC LYLE.

European Association of Electrical Contractors (AIE): 1 J. Chantraineplantsoen, 3070 Kortenberg, Belgium; tel. (2) 253-43-22; fax (2) 253-67-63; e-mail info@aie-elec.org; internet www.aie-elec.org; mems: national asscns in 20 countries and territories; Gen. Sec. EVELYNE SCHELLEHEUS; publ. *AIE Brochure* (every 2 years).

European Association of Manufacturers of Radiators—EURORAD: Konradstr. 9, 8023 Zürich, Switzerland; tel. (1) 2719090; fax (1) 2719292; f. 1966 to represent the national asscns of manufacturers of radiators made of steel and cast iron, intended to be attached to central heating plants and which convey heat by natural convection and radiation without the need for casing; mems: in 15 countries; Pres. Dr H. GASSER (Belgium); Gen. Sec. K. EGLI (Switzerland).

European Association of National Productivity Centres (EANPC): 60 rue de la Concorde, 1050 Brussels, Belgium; tel. (2) 511-71-00; fax (2) 511-02-97; e-mail eanpc@skynet.be; internet www.eanpc.org; f. 1966 to enable members to pool knowledge about their policies and activities; mems: 19 European centres; Pres. PETER REHNSTRÖM; Sec.-Gen. A. C. HUBERT; publs *EPI* (quarterly), *Annual Report*.

European Brewery Convention: POB 510, 2380 BB Zoeterwoude, Netherlands; tel. (71) 545-60-47; fax (71) 541-00-13; e-mail secretariat@ebc-nl.com; internet www.ebc-nl.com; f. 1947, present name adopted 1948; aims to promote scientific co-ordination in malting and brewing; mems: national asscns in 23 European countries; Pres. J. VESELÝ (Czech Republic); Sec.-Gen. M. VAN WIJNGAARDEN

(Netherlands); publs *Analytica, Thesaurus, Dictionary of Brewing*, monographs, conference proceedings, manuals of good practice.

European Chemical Industry Council: ave van Nieuwenhuyse 4, 1160 Brussels, Belgium; tel. (2) 676-72-11; fax (2) 676-73-00; e-mail mail@cefic.be; internet www.cefic.org; f. 1972; represents and defends the interests of the chemical industry in legal and trade policy, internal market, environmental and technical matters; liaises with intergovernmental organizations; provides secretariat for some 100 product sector groups; mems: 16 national federations; Dir-Gen. Dr HUGO LEVER; Sec.-Gen. JEAN-MARIE DEVOS.

European Committee for Standardization (Comité européen de normalisation—CEN): 36 rue de Stassart, 1050 Brussels, Belgium; tel. (2) 550-08-11; fax (2) 550-08-19; e-mail infodesk@cenorm.be; internet www.cenorm.be; f. 1961 to promote European standardization; works to eliminate obstacles caused by technical requirements, in order to facilitate the exchange of goods and services; mems: 22 national standards bodies, 7 associated and 11 affiliated bodies in central and eastern Europe and 4 partnership standardization bodies; Sec.-Gen. GEORG HONGLER; publs *Catalogue of European Standards, Work Programme* (both 2 a year), *CEN Networking* (newsletter, every 2 months), *Bulletin* (quarterly), *Directories and related standards* (in English, French and German), *Directions European Standardization in a Global Context, The Benefits of Standards.*

European Committee of Associations of Manufacturers of Agricultural Machinery: 19 rue Jacques Bingen, 75017 Paris, France; tel. 1-42-12-85-90; fax 1-40-54-95-60; e-mail cema@sygma .org; f. 1959 to study economic and technical problems in field of agricultural machinery manufacture, to protect members' interests and to disseminate information; mems: 13 mem. countries; Pres. G. WEIJERS (Netherlands); Sec.-Gen. J. DEHOLLAIN (France).

European Committee of Textile Machinery Manufacturers (CEMATEX): POB 190, 2700 AD Zoetermeer, Netherlands; tel. (79) 531-100; fax (79) 531-365; f. 1952; promotes general interests of the industry; mems: organizations in eight European countries; Pres. Dr F. PAETZOLD (Germany); Gen. Sec. R. BICKER CAARTEN.

European Confederation of Iron and Steel Industries (EURO-FER): 211 rue du Noyer, 1000 Brussels, Belgium; tel. (2) 738-79-20; fax (2) 736-30-01; e-mail mail@eurofer.be; internet www .eurofer.org; f. 1976 as a confederation of national federations and companies in the European steel industry; aims to foster co-operation between the member federations and companies and to represent their common interests to the EU and other international organizations; mems: in 13 European countries, assoc. mems from central and eastern European countries; Dir-Gen. D. VON HÜLSEN.

European Confederation of Woodworking Industries: 5/4 allée Hof-ter-Vleest, 1070 Brussels, Belgium; tel. (2) 556-25-85; fax (2) 556-25-95; e-mail info@cei-bois.org; internet www.cei-bois.org; f. 1952 to liaise between national organizations, undertake research and defend the interests of the industry; mems: national federations in 24 European countries, eight branch federations; Pres. BO BORG-STRÖM (Finland); Sec.-Gen. FILIP DE JAEGER; publ. *Brochure.*

European Council of Paint, Printing Ink and Artists' Colours Industry: ave E. van Nieuwenhuyse 4, 1160 Brussels, Belgium; tel. (2) 676-74-80; fax (2) 676-74-90; e-mail secretariat@cepe.org; internet www.cepe.org; f. 1951 to study questions relating to the paint and printing ink industries, to take or recommend measures for the development of these industries or to support their interests, and to exchange information; mems: national asscns in 17 European countries and 13 company members; Pres. N. PETERSEN; Gen. Sec. J. SCHODER; publs *Annual Review*, guidance documents.

European Federation of Associations of Insulation Enterprises: Kurfürstenstr. 129, 10785 Berlin, Germany; tel. (30) 212-86163; fax (30) 212-86160; e-mail bfa.wksb@bauindustrie.de; f. 1970; groups organizations in Europe representing insulation firms; aims to facilitate contacts between member asscns; studies problems of interest to the profession; works to safeguard the interests of the profession and represent it in international fora; mems: professional organizations in 16 European countries; Sec.-Gen. M. SCHMOLDT.

European Federation of Insurance Intermediaries (BIPAR): 40 ave Albert-Elisabeth, 1200 Brussels, Belgium; tel. (2) 735-60-48; fax (2) 732-14-18; e-mail bipar@skynet.be; internet www.biparweb .org; f. 1937; represents, promotes and defends the interests of national asscns of professional insurance agents and brokers at the European and international level; works to co-ordinate members' activities; mems: 41 asscns from 25 countries, representing approx. 250,000 brokers and agents; Pres. CLAUDIO RUZZI; Dir HARALD KRAUSS; publ. *BIPAR Intern* (quarterly).

European Federation of Marketing Research Organisations (EFAMRO): Studio 38, Wimbledon Business Centre, Riverside Road, London, SW17 0BA, United Kingdom; tel. (20) 8879-0709; fax (20) 8947-2637; internet www.efamro.org; f. 1965 (frmly known as FEMRA) to facilitate contacts between researchers; maintains spe-

cialist divisions on European chemical marketing research, European technological forecasting, paper and related industries, industrial materials, automotives, textiles, methodology, and information technology; mems: 500; Pres. DAVID A. CLARK (Belgium).

European Federation of Management Consultants' Associations: 3–5 ave des Arts, 1210 Brussels, Belgium; tel. (2) 250-06-50; fax (2) 250-06-51; e-mail feaco@feaco.org; internet www.feaco.org; f. 1960 to bring management consultants together and promote a high standard of professional competence, by encouraging discussions of, and research into, problems of common professional interest; mems: 24 asscns; Pres. and Chair. RÉMI REDLEY; Exec. Man. ELSE GROEN; publs *Newsletter* (3 a year), *Annual Survey of the European Management Consultancy Market.*

European Federation of Materials Handling and Storage Equipment: Diamant Bldg, 80 blvd A. Reyers, 1030 Brussels, Belgium; tel. (2) 706-82-30; fax (2) 706-82-50; e-mail guy .vandoorslaer@orgalime.org; internet www.fem-eur.com; f. 1953 to facilitate contact between members of the profession, conduct research, standardize methods of calculation and construction and promote standardized safety regulations; mems: organizations in 12 European countries; Pres. STIG GUSTAVSON; Sec.-Gen. GUY VAN DOOR-SLAER.

European Federation of the Plywood Industry (FEIC): Allée Hof-ter-Vleest, bte 4, 1070 Brussels, Belgium; tel. (2) 556-25-84; fax (2) 556-25-95; e-mail info@europards.org; internet www .europlywood.org; f. 1957 to organize co-operation between members of the industry at the international level; mems: asscns in 15 European countries; Pres. N. RENI; Sec.-Gen. K. WYNENDAELE.

European Federation of Tile and Brick Manufacturers: c/o Cérame-Unie, 18–24 rue des Colonies, BP 17, 1000 Brussels, Belgium; tel. (2) 511-30-12; fax (2) 511-51-74; e-mail sec@cerameunie .net; internet www.cerameunie.net; f. 1952 to co-ordinate research between members of the industry, improve technical knowledge and encourage professional training; mems: asscns in 23 European and east European countries; Chair. (2005/06) CHRISTIAN SCHENCK.

European Furniture Manufacturers Federation (Union européenne de l'ameublement—UEA): 35 chaussé de Haecht, 1210 Brussels; tel. (2) 218-18-89; fax (2) 219-27-01; e-mail secretariat@ uea.be; internet www.ueanet.com; f. 1950 to determine and support the general interests of the European furniture industry and facilitate contacts between members of the industry; mems: organizations in 19 European countries; Pres. J. ENGELS; Sec.-Gen. B. DE TURCK; publs *UEA Newsletter* (bi-monthly), *Focus on Issues, Strategy Survey.*

European General Galvanizers Association—EGGA: Maybrook House, Godstone Rd, Caterham, Surrey, CR3 6RE, United Kingdom; tel. (1883) 331277; fax (1883) 331287; e-mail mail@egga .com; internet www.egga.com; f. 1955 to promote co-operation between members of the industry, especially in improving processes and finding new uses for galvanized products; mems: asscns in 18 European countries; Pres. J. VERSTAPPEN (Netherlands).

European Glass Container Manufacturers' Committee: Northumberland Rd, Sheffield, S10 2UA, United Kingdom; tel. (114) 268-6201; fax (114) 268-1073; e-mail l.roe@britglass.co.uk; internet www.britglass.co.uk; f. 1951 to facilitate contacts between members of the industry and inform them of relevant legislation; mems: representatives from 15 European countries; Sec. Dr W. G. A. COOK.

European Organization for Quality (EOQ): 3 rue de Luxembourg, 1000 Brussels, Belgium; tel. (2) 501-07-35; fax (2) 501-07-36; e-mail bjouslin@compuserve.com; internet www.eoq.org; f. 1956 to encourage the use and application of quality management, with the aim of improving quality, lowering costs and increasing productivity; organizes the exchange of information and documentation; mems: organizations in 31 European countries; Sec.-Gen. BERTRAND JOUSLIN DE NORAY; publs *European Quality* (6 a year), *Annual Report.*

European Packaging Federation: c/o Institut Français de l'Emballage et du Conditionnement IFEC, 33 rue Louis Blanc, 93582 St-Ouen Cédex, France; tel. 1-40-11-22-12; fax 1-40-11-01-06; e-mail info@ifecpromotion.tm.fr; internet www.ifecpromotion.tm.fr/epf .htm; f. 1953 to encourage the exchange of information between national packaging institutes and to promote technical and economic progress; mems: organizations in 12 European countries; Pres. J. P. POTHET (France); Sec.-Gen. A. FREIDINGER-LEGAY (France).

European Panel Federation: allée Hof-ter-Vleest 5, 1070 Brussels, Belgium; tel. (2) 556-25-89; fax (2) 556-25-94; e-mail info@ europanels.org; internet www.europanels.org; f. 1958 as European Federation of Associations of Particle Board Manufacturers; present name adopted 1999; works to develop and encourage international co-operation in the particle board and MDF industry; Pres. L. DÖRY; Sec.-Gen. K. WIJNENDALE (Belgium); publ. *Annual Report.*

European Patent Office (EPO): 80298 Munich, Germany; tel. (89) 2399-0; fax (89) 2399-4560; internet www.european-patent-office

.org; f. 1977 as the executive branch of the European Patent Organisation, established under the Munich convention of 1973; conducts searches and examination of patent applications; grants patents; mems: 30 European countries; Pres. Prof. ALAIN POMPIDOU (France); Chair. Admin. Council ROLAND GROSSENBACHER; publs *Annual Report, Official Journal* (monthly), *European Patent Bulletin, European Patent Applications, Granted Patents*.

European Union of the Natural Gas Industry (EUROGAS): 4 ave Palmerston, 1000 Brussels, Belgium; tel. (2) 237-11-11; fax (2) 230-62-91; e-mail eurogas@eurogas.org; internet www.eurogas.org/; mems: orgs, federations and companies in 19 European countries; Pres. P. GADONNEIX (France); Gen. Sec. JEAN-MARIE DEVOS (Belgium).

Fairtrade Labelling Organizations International: Kaiser-Fried-rich-str. 13, 53113 Bonn, Germany; tel. (228) 949230; fax (228) 2421713; e-mail info@fairtrade.net; internet www.fairtrade.net; world-wide fairtrade standards and certification organization; works with other orgs in the fairtrade movement to contribute to sustainable development and to support the rights of producers and workers; Man.-Dir LUUK ZONNEVELD.

Federación de Cámaras de Comercio del Istmo Centroamericano (Federation of Central American Chambers of Commerce): 10A Calle 3-80, Zona 1, 01001 Guatemala City, Guatemala; internet www.fecamco.com; f. 1961; plans and co-ordinates industrial and commercial exchanges and exhibitions; Pres. EMILIO BRUCE JIMÉNEZ (Costa Rica); Sec. JORGE E. BRIZ ABULARACH (Guatemala).

General Union of Chambers of Commerce, Industry and Agriculture for Arab Countries: POB 11-2837, Beirut, Lebanon; tel. (1) 814269; fax (1) 862841; e-mail admin@gucciaac.org.lb; internet www.gucciaac.org.lb; f. 1951 to enhance Arab economic development, integration and security through the co-ordination of industrial, agricultural and trade policies and legislation; mems: chambers of commerce, industry and agriculture in 22 Arab countries; Sec. Gen. Dr ELIAS GHANTOUS; publs *Arab Economic Report, Al-Omran Al-Arabi* (every 2 months), economic papers, proceedings.

Gulf Organization for Industrial Consulting (GOIC): POB 5114, Doha, Qatar; tel. 4858888; fax 4831465; e-mail goic@goic.org .qa; internet www.goic.org.qa; f. 1976 by the Gulf Arab states to encourage industrial co-operation among Gulf Arab states, to pool industrial expertise and to encourage joint development of projects; undertakes feasibility studies, market diagnosis, assistance in policy-making, legal consultancies, project promotion, promotion of small and medium industrial investment profiles and technical training; maintains industrial data bank; mems: mem. states of the Co-operation Council for the Arab States of the Gulf; Sec.-Gen. MOHAMED BIN ALI BIN ABDULLAH AL-MUSALLAM; publs *GOIC Monthly Bulletin* (in Arabic), *Al Ta'awon al Sina'e* (quarterly, in Arabic and English).

Instituto Centroamericano de Administración de Empresas (INCAE) (Central American Institute for Business Administration): Apdo 960, 4050 Alajuela, Costa Rica; tel. 443-0506; fax 433-9101; e-mail artaviar@mail.incae.ac.cr; internet www.incae.ac.cr; f. 1964; provides a postgraduate programme in business administration; runs executive training programmes; carries out management research and consulting; maintains a second campus in Nicaragua; libraries of 85,000 vols; Rector Dr ROBERTO ARTAVIA; publs *Alumni Journal* (in Spanish), *Bulletin* (quarterly), books and case studies.

Inter-American Commercial Arbitration Commission: OAS Administration Bldg, Rm 211, 19th and Constitution Ave, NW, Washington, DC 20006, USA; tel. (202) 458-3249; fax (202) 458-3293; f. 1934 to establish an inter-American system of arbitration for the settlement of commercial disputes by means of tribunals; mems: national committees, commercial firms and individuals in 22 countries; Dir-Gen. Dr ADRIANA POLANIA.

International Advertising Association Inc: 521 Fifth Ave, Suite 1807, New York, NY 10175, USA; tel. (212) 557-1133; fax (212) 983-0455; e-mail iaa@iaaglobal.org; internet www.iaaglobal.org; f. 1938 as a global partnership of advertisers, agencies, the media and other marketing communications professionals; aims to protect freedom of commercial speech and consumer choice; holds World Congress every 2 years (2006: Dubai, UAE); mems: more than 3,000 in 81 countries; World Pres. MICHAEL LEE; CEO FRANK J. CUTITTA (USA); publs *IAA Membership Directory, Annual Report*.

International Association of Buying and Marketing Groups: Vorgebirgsstr. 43, 53119 Bonn, Germany; tel. (228) 9858420; fax (228) 9858410; e-mail g.olesch@zgv-online.de; f. 1951 to research, document and compile statistics; holds annual conference; mems: 300 buying groups in 13 countries; Sec.-Gen. Dr GÜNTER OLESCH.

International Association of Department Stores: 4 rue de Rome, 75008 Paris, France; tel. 1-42-94-02-02; fax 1-42-94-02-04; e-mail iads@iads.org; internet www.iads.org; f. 1928 to conduct research and exchange information and statistics on management, organization and technical problems; maintains a documentation centre; mems: large-scale retail enterprises in 18 countries; Pres.

JORGE ZONT (Spain); Gen. Sec. M. DE GROOT VAN EMBDEN (Netherlands); publ. *Retail News Letter* (monthly).

International Association of Scholarly Publishers: c/o Michael Huter, Berggasse 5, 1090 Vienna, Austria; tel. (1) 3105356; fax (1) 3197050; e-mail huter@wuv.co.at; internet www.iasp.at; f. 1970 for the exchange of information and experience on scholarly and academic publishing by universities and others; assists in the transfer of publishing skills to developing countries; mems: over 140 in 38 countries; Pres. MICHAEL HUTER (Austria); publs *IASP Newsletter* (every 2 months), *International Directory of Scholarly Publishers*.

International Association of the Soap, Detergent and Maintenance Products Industry (AISE) (Association internationale de la savonnerie, de la détergence et des produits d'entretien): 49 sq. Marie-Louise, 1000 Brussels, Belgium; tel. (2) 230-83-71; fax (2) 230-82-88; e-mail aise.main@aise-net.org; internet www.aise-net.org; f. 1967 to promote the manufacture and use of a wide range of cleaning products, polishes, bleaches, disinfectants and insecticides, to develop the exchange of statistical information and to study technical, scientific, economic and social problems of interest to its members; mems: 35 national asscns in 30 countries; Dir M. G. LABBERTON; publs *Annual Review*, technical documents and reports.

International Booksellers Federation (IBF): rue du Grand Hospice 34a, 1000 Belgium; tel. (2) 223-49-40; fax (2) 223-49-41; e-mail eurobooks@skynet.be; internet www.ibf-world.org; f. 1956 to promote the book trade and the exchange of information, and to protect the interests of booksellers when dealing with other international organizations; special committees deal with questions of postage, resale price maintenance, book market research, advertising, customs and tariffs, the problems of young booksellers, etc; mems: 200 in 22 countries; Pres. YVONNE STEINBERGER; Sec.-Gen. CHRISTIANE VUIDAR; publs *IBF-bulletin* (2 a year), *Booksellers International*.

International Bureau for the Standardization of Man-Made Fibres (BISFA): 4 ave van Nieuwenhuyse, 1160 Brussels, Belgium; tel. (2) 676-74-55; fax (2) 676-74-54; e-mail van@cirfs.org; internet www.bisfa.org; f. 1928 to examine and establish rules for the standardization, classification and naming of various categories of man-made fibres; mems: 49; Sec.-Gen. J. SPIJKERS.

International Butchers' Confederation: bte 10, 4 rue Jacques de Lalaing, 1040 Brussels, Belgium; tel. (2) 230-38-76; fax (2) 230-34-51; e-mail info@cibc.be; f. 1907; aims to defend the interests of small and medium-sized enterprises in the meat trading and catering industry; Pres. EUGEN NAGEL; Sec.-Gen. MARTIN FUCHS.

International Confederation for Printing and Allied Industries (INTERGRAF): 7 pl. E. Flagey, 1050 Brussels, Belgium; tel. (2) 230-86-46; fax (2) 231-14-64; internet www.intergraf.org; f. 1983 to defend the common interests of the printing and allied interests in mem. countries; mems: federations in 20 countries; Pres. LARS FREDRIKSON; Sec.-Gen. BEATRICE KLOSE.

International Confederation of Art Dealers: 33 rue Ernest-Allard, 1000 Brussels, Belgium; tel. (2) 511-67-77; e-mail secretary@ cinoa.org; internet www.cinoa.org; f. 1936 to co-ordinate the work of asscns of dealers in works of art and paintings and to contribute to artistic and economic expansion; mems: asscns in 24 countries; Pres. HENRY NEVILLE; Sec.-Gen. DORIS AMMANN.

International Co-operative Alliance (ICA): 15 route des Morillons, 1218 Grand-Saconnex, Geneva, Switzerland; tel. (22) 9298888; fax (22) 7984122; e-mail ica@coop.org; internet www.coop .org; f. 1895 for the pursuit of co-operative aims; a General Assembly and four Regional Assemblies meet every two years, on an alternating basis; a 20-member ICA Board controls the affairs of the organization between meetings of the General Assembly; specialized bodies have been established to promote co-operative activities in the following fields: agriculture, banking, fisheries, consumer affairs, energy, tourism, communications, co-operative research, health, human resources, wholesale distribution, housing, insurance, women's participation and industrial, artisanal and service producers' co-operatives; mems: 242 affiliated national orgs, with a total membership of more than 760m. individuals in 100 countries, and four int. orgs; Pres. IVANO BARBERINI (Italy); Dir-Gen. BRUCE THORDARSON (Canada); publs *Review of International Co-operation* (quarterly), *ICA News* (every 2 months), *Co-op Dialogue* (2 a year).

International Council of Societies of Industrial Design (ICSID): POB 100820, 45008 Essen, Germany; tel. (201) 3010420; fax (201) 3010440; e-mail office@icsid.org; internet www.icsid.org; f. 1957 to encourage the development of high standards in the practice of industrial design; works to improve and expand the contribution of industrial design throughout the world; mems: 150 in 53 countries; Pres. LUIGI FERRARA (Italy); Sec.-Gen. DILI DE SILVA; publs *ICSID News, World Directory of Design Schools*.

International Council of Tanners: Leather Trade House, Kings Park Rd, Moulton Park, Northampton, NN3 6JD, United Kingdom; tel. (1604) 679917; fax (1604) 679998; e-mail sec@tannerscouncilct .org; internet www.tannerscouncilct.org; f. 1926 to study all questions relating to the leather industry and maintain contact with national asscns; mems: national tanners' organizations in 33 countries; Pres. TONY MOSSOP (South Africa); Sec. PAUL PEARSON (UK).

International Council on Mining and Metals (ICMM): 19 Stratford Place, London W1C 1BQ, United Kingdom; tel. (20) 7290-4920; e-mail info@icmm.com; internet www.icmm.com; f. 1991 (as the International Council on Metals and the Environment, present name adopted 2002); aims to promote sustainable development practices and policies in the mining, use, recycling and disposal of minerals and metals; mems: 15 cos, 27 asscns; Chair. DAVID KERR (Canada); Sec.-Gen. PAUL MITCHELL (UK); publ. *ICMM Newsletter* (quarterly).

International Exhibitions Bureau: 34 ave d'Iéna, 75116 Paris, France; tel. 1-45-00-38-63; fax 1-45-00-96-15; e-mail bie@bie-paris.org; internet www.bie-paris.org; f. 1931, revised by Protocol 1972, for the authorization and registration of international exhibitions falling under the 1928 Convention; mems: 91 states; Pres. JIANMIN WU; Sec.-Gen. VICENTE GONZALES LOSCERTALES.

International Federation for Alternative Trade: 30 Murdock Rd, Bicester, Oxon, OX6 7RF, United Kingdom; tel. (1869) 249819; fax (1869) 246381; e-mail info@ifat.org.uk; internet www.catgen.com/ifat; f. 1989; coalition of trading and producer organizations; supports the market development of fairtrade products and conducts monitoring and advocacy; mems: 70 alternative trade organizations from 30 countries; Exec. Dir CAROL WILLS.

International Federation of Associations of Textile Chemists and Colourists (IFATCC): Postfach 403, 4153 Reinach 1, Switzerland; e-mail markus.krayer@cibasc.com; f. 1930 for liaison on professional matters between members and the furtherance of scientific and technical collaboration in the development of the textile finishing industry and the colouring of materials; mems: in 22 countries; Pres. Dr W. STREIT (Germany); Sec. MARKUS KRAYER (Switzerland).

International Federation of Grocers' Associations (IFGA): Vakcentrum, Woerden, Netherlands; tel. (348) 419771; fax (348) 421801; f. 1927; initiates special studies and works to further the interests of members, with special regard to conditions resulting from European integration and developments in consuming and distribution; mems: 30 asscns representing 125,000 sales outlets.

International Federation of Pharmaceutical Manufacturers Associations (IFPMA): 30 rue de St Jean, POB 758, 1211 Geneva 13, Switzerland; tel. (22) 3383200; fax (22) 3383299; e-mail admin@ifpma.org; internet www.ifpma.org; f. 1968 for the exchange of information and international co-operation in all questions of interest to the pharmaceutical industry, particularly in the field of health legislation, science and research; develops ethical principles and practices; co-operates with national and international organizations; mems: the national pharmaceutical asscn of 60 countries and one regional asscn (representing Latin America); Pres. Prof. ROLF KREBS (Germany); Dir-Gen. Dr HARVEY E. BALE, Jr (USA); publs *IPFMA Code of Pharmaceutical Marketing Practices*, action papers, occasional publications.

International Federation of the Phonographic Industry (IFPI): 54 Regent St, London, W1R 5PJ, United Kingdom; tel. (20) 7878-7900; fax (20) 7878-7950; e-mail info@ifpi.org; internet www.ifpi.org; f. 1933; represents the interests of record producers by campaigning for the introduction, improvement and enforcement of copyright and related rights legislation; co-ordinates the recording industry's anti-piracy activities; mems: 1,476 in 73 countries; Chair. and Chief Exec. JASON BERMAN.

International Fertilizer Industry Association: 28 rue Marbeuf, 75008 Paris, France; tel. 1-53-93-05-00; fax 1-53-93-05-45; e-mail ifa@fertilizer.org; internet www.fertilizer.org; Pres. C. E. CHILDERS; Sec.-Gen. L. M. MAENE.

International Fragrance Association (IFRA): 49 sq. Marie Louise, 1000 Brussels, Belgium; tel. (2) 2389904; fax (2) 2300265; e-mail secretariat@ifraorg.org; internet www.ifraorg.org; f. 1973 to develop and advance the fragrance industry, to collect and study scientific data on fragrance materials and to make recommendations on their safe use; mems: national asscns in 17 countries; Pres. R. CARRAHER; Dir-Gen. J.-P. HOURI; publs *Code of Practice, Information Letters*.

International Fur Trade Federation: POB 495, Weybridge, KT13 8WD, United Kingdom; internet www.iftf.com; f. 1949 to promote and organize joint action by fur trade organizations in order to develop and protect the trade in fur skins and the processing of skins; mems: 33 organizations in 27 countries; Exec. Dir J. BAILEY.

International Meat Secretariat (Office international de la viande): 6 rue de la Victoire, 75009 Paris, France; tel. 1-45-26-68-97; fax 1-45-26-68-98; e-mail info@meat-ims.org; internet www.meat-ims.org; Pres. PATRICK MOORE; Sec.-Gen. LAURENCE WRIXON.

International Organization of Motor Manufacturers (Organisation internationale des constructeurs d'automobiles—OICA): 4 rue de Berri, 75008 Paris; tel. 1-43-59-00-13; fax 1-45-63-84-41; e-mail oica@oica.net; internet www.oica.net; f. 1919 to co-ordinate and further the interests of the automobile industry, to promote the study of economic and other matters affecting automobile construction, and to control automobile manufacturers' participation in international exhibitions in Europe; mems: manufacturers' asscns of 16 European countries, China, Japan, the Republic of Korea and the USA; 40 assoc. mems; Gen. Sec. Y. VAN DER SRAATEN; publ. *Yearbook of the World's Motor Industry*.

International Organization of the Flavour Industry (IOFI): 5 Chemin de la Parfumerie, 1214 Vernier, Switzerland; tel. (22) 4318250; fax (22) 4318806; e-mail secretariat@iofi.org; internet www.iofi.org; f. 1969 to support and promote the flavour industry; active in the fields of safety evaluation and regulation of flavouring substances; mems: national asscns in 21 countries; Exec. Dir R. HONCY; publs *Documentation Bulletin, Information Letters, Code of Practice*.

International Publishers' Association: 3 ave de Miremont, 1206 Geneva, Switzerland; tel. (22) 3463018; fax (22) 3475717; e-mail secretariat@ipa-uie.org; internet www.ipa-uie.org; f. 1896 to defend the freedom of publishers, promote their interests and foster international co-operation; promotes the international trade in books; carries out work on international copyright; mems: 79 professional book publishers' organizations in 66 countries; Pres. PERE VICENS; Sec.-Gen. BENOÎT MÜLLER.

International Rayon and Synthetic Fibres Committee (Comité international de la rayonne et des fibres synthétiques—CIRFS): 4 ave van Nieuwenhuyse, 1160 Brussels, Belgium; tel. (2) 676-74-55; fax (2) 676-74-54; e-mail info@cirfs.org; internet www.cirfs.org; f. 1950 to improve the quality and promote the use of man-made fibres and products made from fibres; mems: individual producers in 24 countries; Pres. OMER SABANCI; Dir-Gen. C. PURVIS (UK); publs *Statistical Booklet* (annually), market reports, technical test methods.

International Shopfitting Organisation: Gladbachstr. 80, 8044 Zürich, Switzerland; tel. (1) 2678100; fax (1) 2678150; e-mail petra.isenberg@vssm.ch; internet www.shopfitting.org; f. 1959 to promote the interchange of ideas between individuals and firms concerned with shopfitting; mems: companies in 13 countries; Pres. J. BREITENMOSER; Sec. PETRA ISENBERG.

International Textile Manufacturers Federation (ITMF): Am Schanzengraben 29, Postfach, 8039 Zürich, Switzerland; tel. (1) 2017080; fax (1) 2017134; e-mail secretariat@itmf.org; internet www.itmf.org; f. 1904, present title adopted 1978; aims to protect and promote the interests of its members, disseminate information, and encourage co-operation; mems: national textile trade asscns in c. 50 countries; Pres. HERBERT SCHMID (Brazil); Dir-Gen. Dr HERWIG STROLZ (Austria); publs *State of Trade Report* (quarterly), *Country Statements, Annual Conference Report, Directory*, various statistics, sectoral reports and guidelines.

International Union of Marine Insurance (IUMI): Gotthardstr. 3, POB 6304, Zug, Switzerland; tel. (41) 7293966; fax (41) 7293967; e-mail mail@iumi.com; internet www.iumi.com; f. 1873 to collect and distribute information on marine insurance on a world-wide basis; mems: 54 asscns; Pres. GEORG MEHL (Germany); Gen. Sec. STEFAN PELLER.

International Wool Textile Organisation (IWTO) (Fédération lanière internationale—FLI): 4 rue de l'Industrie, 1000 Brussels, Belgium; tel. (2) 505-40-10 ; fax (2) 503-47-85; e-mail info@iwto.org; internet www.iwto.org; f. 1929 to link wool textile organizations in member-countries and represent their interests; holds annual Wool Forum (2005: Biella, Italy); mems: in 23 countries; Pres. JUAN CASANOVAS (Spain); Gen. Man. HENRIK KUFFNER (Germany); publs *Wool Statistics* (annually), *Global Wool Supplies and Wool Textile Manufacturing Activity* (annually), *Blue Book, Red Book*.

International Wrought Copper Council: 6 Bathurst St, Sussex Sq., London, W2 2SD, United Kingdom; tel. (20) 7724-7465; fax (20) 7724-0308; e-mail iwcc@coppercouncil.org; internet www.coppercouncil.org; f. 1953 to link and represent copper fabricating industries and represent the views of copper consumers to raw material producers; organizes specialist activities on technical work and the development of copper; mems: 17 national groups in Europe, Australia, Japan and Malaysia, 13 corporate mems; Chair. A. BAGRI; Sec.-Gen. SIMON PAYTON; publs *Annual Report*, surveys.

Liaison Group of the European Mechanical, Electrical, Electronic and Metalworking Industries (Orgalime): Diamant Bldg, 80 blvd Reyers, 1030 Brussels, Belgium; tel. (2) 511-34-84; fax (2) 512-99-70; e-mail secretariat@orgalime.be; internet www.orgalime.org; f. 1954 to provide a permanent liaison between the mechanical, electrical and electronic engineering, and metalworking industries of member countries; mems: 25 trade asscns in 16 European countries; Pres. Prof. Dr EDWARD GEORG KRUBASIK (Germany) (designate); Sec.-Gen. ADRIAN HARRIS.

UFI (Global Association of the Exhibition Industry): 35 bis, rue Jouffroy d'Abbans, 75017 Paris, France; tel. 1-42-67-99-12; fax 1-42-27-19-29; e-mail info@ufi.org; internet www.ufi.org; f. 1925 as Union des Foires Internationales; works to increase co-operation between international trade fairs/exhibitions, safeguard their interests and extend their operations; imposes quality criteria and defines standards; approves 680 events; mems: 295, including 39 asscns, in 72 countries; Pres. RUUD VAN INGEN (Netherlands); Man. Dir VINCENT GÉRARD (Belgium).

Union of Industrial and Employers' Confederations of Europe (UNICE): 168 ave de Cortenbergh, 1000 Brussels, Belgium; tel. (2) 237-65-11; fax (2) 231-14-45; e-mail main@unice.be; internet www.unice.org; f. 1958; aims to ensure that European Union policy-making takes account of the views of European business; committees and working groups develop joint positions in fields of interest to business and submit these to the Community institutions concerned; the Council of Presidents (of member federations) lays down general policy; the Executive Committee (of Directors-General of member federations) is the managing body; and the Committee of Permanent Delegates, consisting of federation representatives in Brussels, ensures permanent liaison with mems; mems: 29 industrial and employers' federations from the EU member states, and nine federations from non-EU countries, three observer federations; Pres. JÜRGEN STRUBE; publ. *UNICE@News* (monthly, by e-mail).

World Customs Organization (WCO): 30 rue du Marché, 1210 Brussels, Belgium; tel. (2) 209-92-11; fax (2) 209-92-92; e-mail info@wcoomd.org; internet www.wcoomd.org; f. 1952 as Customs Co-operation Council; aims to enhance the effectiveness and efficiency of customs administrations in the areas of compliance with trade regulations, the protection of society and revenue collection; mems: governments of 165 countries; Chair. Dr PRAVIN GORDHAN (South Africa); Sec.-Gen. MICHEL DANET (France); publ. *WCO News* (quarterly).

World Federation of Advertisers: 120 ave Louise, 1050 Brussels; tel. (2) 502-57-40; fax (2) 502-56-66; e-mail info@wfanet.org; internet www.wfanet.org; f. 1953; promotes and studies advertising and its related problems; holds World Congress (2003: Brussels, Belgium); mems: asscns in 46 countries and 35 international companies; Pres. PAUL CAROTHERS; Man. Dir STEPHAN HOERKE; publ. *EU Brief* (weekly).

World Packaging Organisation: c/o STFI-Packforsk, POB 5604, SE-114 86 Stockholm, Sweden; e-mail carl.olsmats@stfi.se; internet www.worldpacking.org; f. 1968 to provide a forum for the exchange of knowledge of packaging technology and, in general, to create conditions for the conservation, preservation and distribution of world food production; holds annual congress and competition; mems: Asian, North American, Latin American, European and African packaging federations; Pres. ALEXIS STASSINOUPOLOS (Greece); Gen. Sec. CARL OLSMATS (Sweden).

World Trade Centers Association: 60 East 42nd St, Suite 1901, New York, NY 10165, USA; tel. (212) 432-2626; fax (212) 488-0064; internet www.wtca.org; f. 1968 to promote trade through the establishment of world trade centres, including education facilities, information services and exhibition facilities; operates an electronic trading and communication system (WTC On-Line); mems: trade centres, chambers of commerce and other organizations in 95 countries; Pres. GUY F. TOZZOLI; Chair. BRYAN MONTGOMERY; publ. *WTCA News* (monthly).

Transport

African Airlines Association: POB 20116, Nairobi, Kenya; tel. (20) 604925; fax (20) 601173; e-mail afraa@africaonline.co.ke; internet www.afraa.org; f. 1968 to give African air companies expert advice in technical, financial, juridical and market matters to improve air transport in Africa through inter-carrier co-operation; and to develop manpower resources; mems: 34 national carriers; publs *Newsletter*, reports.

Airports Council International (ACI): POB 16, 1215 Geneva 15-Airport, Switzerland; tel. (22) 7178585; fax (22) 7178888; e-mail aci@aci.aero.org; internet www.airports.org; f. 1991, following merger of Airport Operators Council International and International Civil Airports Association; aims to represent and develop co-operation among airports of the world; mems: 554 mems operating more than 1,400 airports in 170 countries and territories; Chair. A. GHANEM AL-HAJRI; Dir-Gen. ROBERT J. AARONSON; publs *World Report* (6 a year), *Airport World Magazine*, *Policy Handbook*, reports.

Arab Air Carriers' Organization (AACO): PO Box 13-5468, Beirut, Lebanon; tel. (1) 861297; fax (1) 863168; e-mail info@aaco.org; internet www.aaco.org; f. 1965 to promote co-operation in the activities of Arab airline companies; mems: 22 Arab air carriers;

Pres. ABDEL RAHMAN AL-BUSAEDI (Qatar); Sec.-Gen. ABDUL WAHAB TEFFAHA; publs bulletins, reports and research documents.

Association of Asia Pacific Airlines: 9th Floor, Kompleks Antarabangsa, Jalan Sultan Ismail, 50250 Kuala Lumpur, Malaysia; tel. (3) 2145-5600; fax (3) 2145-2500; e-mail info@aapa.org.my; internet www.aapairlines.org; f. 1966 as Orient Airlines Asscn; present name adopted in 1997; represents the interests of Asia Pacific airlines; encourages the exchange of information and increased co-operation between airlines; seeks to develop safe, efficient, profitable and environmentally friendly air transport; mems: 17 scheduled international airlines; Dir-Gen. RICHARD T. STIRLAND; publs *Annual Report*, *Annual Statistical Report*, *Monthly International Statistics*, *Orient Aviation* (10 a year).

Association of European Airlines: 350 ave Louise, bte 4, 1050 Brussels, Belgium; tel. (2) 639-89-89; fax (2) 639-89-90; e-mail aea.secretariat@aca.be; internet www.aea.be; f. 1954 to carry out research on political, commercial, economic and technical aspects of air transport; maintains statistical data bank; mems: 29 airlines; Chair. LEO M. VAN WIJK (Netherlands); Sec.-Gen. KARL-HEINZ NEUMEISTER (Germany).

Baltic and International Maritime Council (BIMCO): Bagsvaerdvej 161, 2880 Bagsvaerd, Denmark; tel. 44-36-68-00; fax 44-36-68-68; e-mail mailbox@bimco.dk; internet www.bimco.dk; f. 1905 to unite shipowners and other persons and organizations connected with the shipping industry; mems: in 122 countries, representing over 65% of world merchant tonnage; Pres. MICHAEL EVERARD (UK); Sec.-Gen. TRULS W. L'ORANGE; publs *BIMCO Review* (annually), *BIMCO Bulletin* (6 a year), *Vessel* (CD-ROM), manuals.

Central Commission for the Navigation of the Rhine: Palais du Rhin, Place de la République, 67000 Strasbourg, France; tel. 3-88-52-20-10; fax 3-88-32-10-72; e-mail ccmr@ccr-zkr.org; internet www.ccnr-zkr.org; f. 1815 to ensure free movement of traffic and standard river facilities for ships of all nations; draws up navigational rules; standardizes customs regulations; arbitrates in disputes involving river traffic; approves plans for river maintenance work; there is an administrative centre for social security for boatmen; mems: Belgium, France, Germany, Netherlands, Switzerland; Sec.-Gen. JEAN-MARIE WOEHRLING (France); publs guides, rules and directives (in French and German).

Danube Commission: Benczúr utca 25, 1068 Budapest, Hungary; tel. (1) 352-1835; fax (1) 352-1839; e-mail secretariat@danubecom-intern.org; internet www.danubecom-intern.org; f. 1948; supervises implementation of the Belgrade Convention on the Regime of Navigation on the Danube; approves projects for river maintenance; supervises a uniform system of traffic regulations on the whole navigable portion of the Danube and on river inspection; mems: Austria, Bulgaria, Croatia, Germany, Hungary, Moldova, Romania, Russia, Serbia and Montenegro, Slovakia, Ukraine; Pres. Dr S. NICK; Dir-Gen. Capt. D. NEDIALKOV; publs *Basic Regulations for Navigation on the Danube*, *Hydrological Yearbook*, *Statistical Yearbook*, proceedings of sessions.

European Civil Aviation Conference (ECAC): 3 bis Villa Emile-Bergerat, 92522 Neuilly-sur-Seine Cédex, France; tel. 1-46-41-85-44; fax 1-46-24-18-18; e-mail secretariat@ecac-ceac.org; internet www.ecac-ceac.org; f. 1955; aims to promote the continued development of a safe, efficient and sustainable European air transport system; mems: 41 European states; Pres. LASZLO KISS; Exec. Sec. RAYMOND BENJAMIN.

European Conference of Ministers of Transport (ECMT): 2 rue André Pascal, 75775 Paris Cédex 16, France; tel. 1-45-24-82-00; fax 1-45-24-97-42; e-mail marian.ashworth@oecd.org; internet www.oecd.org/cem; f. 1953 to achieve the maximum use and most rational development of European transport; aims to create a safe, sustainable, efficient, integrated transport system; provides a forum for analysis and discussion; holds round tables, seminars and symposia; shares Secretariat staff with OECD; mems: 43 member countries, six associate mems, one observer country; Sec.-Gen. JACK SHORT; publs *Annual Report*, *ECMT News* (2 a year), *Trends in the Transport Sector*, various statistical publications and surveys.

European Organisation for the Safety of Air Navigation (EUROCONTROL): 96 rue de la Fusée, 1130 Brussels, Belgium; tel. (2) 729-90-11; fax (2) 729-90-44; internet www.eurocontrol.int; f. 1960; aims to develop a coherent and co-ordinated air traffic control system in Europe. A revised Convention was signed in June 1997, incorporating the following institutional structure: a General Assembly (known as the Commission in the transitional period), a Council (known as the Provisional Council) and an Agency under the supervision of the Director General; there are directorates, covering human resources and finance matters and a general secretariat. A special organizational structure covers the management of the European Air Traffic Management Programme. EUROCONTROL also operates the Experimental Centre (at Brétigny-sur-Orge, France), the Institute of Air Navigation Services (in Luxembourg), the Central Route Charges Office, the Central Flow Management Unit (both in Brussels) and the Upper Area Control Centre (in Maastricht, Netherlands); mems: 31 European countries; Dir-Gen. VÍCTOR M. AGUADO (Spain).

Forum Train Europe (FTE): Direction générale des chemins de fer fédéraux suisses, Hochschulstrasse 6, 3030 Bern, Switzerland; internet www.fte-rail.com; f. 1923 as the European Passenger Train Time-Table Conference to arrange international passenger connections by rail and water; since 1997 concerned also with rail freight; mems: rail and steamship companies and administrations. Administered by the Directorate of the Swiss Federal Railways; Pres. P. A. URECH.

Institute of Air Transport: 103 rue la Boétie, 75008 Paris, France; tel. 1-43-59-38-68; fax 1-43-59-47-37; e-mail contac@ita-paris.com; internet www.ita-paris.com; f. 1945 as an international centre of research on economic, technical and policy aspects of air transport, and on the economy and sociology of transport and tourism; acts as economic and technical consultant in research requested by members on specific subjects; maintains a data bank, a library and a consultation and advice service; organizes training courses on air transport economics; mems: organizations involved in air transport, production and equipment, universities, banks, nsurance companies, private individuals and government agencies in 79 countries; Dir-Gen. JACQUES PAVAUX; publs (in French and English), *ITA Press* (2 a month), *ITA Studies and Reports* (quarterly), *Aviation Industry Barometer* (quarterly).

Intergovernmental Organization for International Carriage by Rail: Gryphenhübeliweg 30, 3006 Bern, Switzerland; tel. (31) 3591010; fax (31) 3591011; e-mail info@otif.org; internet www.otif.org; f. 1893 as Central Office for International Carriage by Rail, present name adopted 1985; aims to establish and develop a uniform system of law governing the international carriage of passengers and goods by rail in member states; mems: 42 states; Dir-Gen. STEFAN SCHIMMING; publ. *Bulletin des Transports Internationaux ferroviaires* (quarterly, in English, French and German).

International Air Transport Association (IATA): 33 route de l'Aéroport, CP 416, 1215 Geneva 15, Switzerland; tel. (22) 7992525; fax (22) 7983553; e-mail information@iata.org; internet www.iata.org; f. 1945 to represent and serve the airline industry; Aims to promote safe, reliable and secure air services; to assist the industry to attain adequate levels of profitability while developing cost-effective operational standards; to promote the importance of the industry in global social and economic development; and to identify common concerns and represent the industry in addressing these at regional and international level; maintains regional offices in Amman, Brussels, Dakar, London, Nairobi, Santiago, Singapore and Washington, DC; mems: 258 airline cos; Dir-Gen. and CEO GIOVANNI BISIGNANI; publ. *Airlines International* (every 2 months).

IVR: Vasteland 12E, 3011 BL Rotterdam (POB 23210, 3001 KE Rotterdam), Netherlands; tel. (10) 4116070; fax (10) 4129091; e-mail info@ivr.nl; internet www.ivr.nl; f. 1947 for the classification of Rhine ships, the organization and publication of a Rhine ships register, the unification of general average rules, and the harmonization of European inland navigation law; mems: shipowners and asscns, insurers and asscns, shipbuilding engineers, average adjusters and others interested in Rhine traffic; Gen. Sec. T. K. HACK-STEINER.

International Association of Ports and Harbors (IAPH): Kono Bldg, 1-23-9 Nishi-Shimbashi, Minato-ku, Tokyo 105, Japan; tel. (3) 3591-4261; fax (3) 3580-0364; e-mail iaph@msn.com; internet www.iaph.or.jp; f. 1955 to increase the efficiency of ports and harbours through the dissemination of information on port organization, management, administration, operation, development and promotion; encourages the growth of water-borne commerce; holds conference every two years; mems: 350 in 85 states; Pres. DOMINIC J. TADDEO (Canada); Sec.-Gen. SATOSHI INOUE (Japan); publs *Ports and Harbors* (10 a year), *Membership Directory* (annually).

International Association of Public Transport: 17 ave Herrmann-Debroux, 1160 Brussels, Belgium; tel. (2) 673-61-00; fax (2) 660-10-72; e-mail administration@uitp.com; internet www.uitp.com; f. 1885 to study all problems connected with the urban and regional public passenger transport industry; mems: 2,000 in 80 countries; Pres. WOLFGANG MEIER (Germany); Sec.-Gen. HANS RAT; publs *Public Transport International* (every 2 months), *EUExpress*, *Mobility News* (monthly, electronic), statistics reports.

International Chamber of Shipping: Carthusian Court, 12 Carthusian St, London, EC1M 6EZ, United Kingdom; tel. (20) 7417-8844; fax (20) 7417-8877; e-mail ics@marisec.org; internet www.marisec.org; f. 1921 to co-ordinate the views of the international shipping industry on matters of common interest, in the policy-making, technical and legal fields of shipping operations; mems: national asscns representing free-enterprise shipowners and operators in 39 countries; Sec.-Gen. J. C. S. HORROCKS.

International Container Bureau: 167 rue de Courcelles, 75017 Paris, France; tel. 1-47-66-03-90; fax 1-47-66-08-91; e-mail bis@bic-code.org; internet www.bic-code.org; f. 1933 to group representatives of all means of transport and activities concerning containers, to promote combined door-to-door transport by the successive use of several means of transport, to examine and bring into effect administrative, technical and customs advances, and to centralize data on behalf of mems; mems: 1,200; Sec.-Gen. JEAN REY; publs *Containers Bulletin*, *Containers Bic-Code* (annually).

International Federation of Freight Forwarders' Associations (FIATA): Schaffhauserstr. 104, 8152 Glattbrugg, Switzerland; tel. (43) 2116550; fax (43) 2116565; e-mail info@fiata.com; internet www.fiata.com; f. 1926 to protect and represent its members at international level; mems: 94 organizations and more than 4,500 associate members in 150 countries; Pres. ISLA BALUCH (UAE); Dir MARCO A. SANGALETTI; publ. *FIATA Review* (every 2 months).

International Rail Transport Committee (Comité international des transports ferroviaires—CIT): Weltpoststr. 20, 3015 Bern 15, Switzerland; tel. (31) 350-0190; fax (31) 350-0199; e-mail info@cit-rail.org; internet www.cit-rail.org; f. 1902 for the development of international law relating to railway transport, on the basis of the Convention concerning International Carriage by Rail (COTIF) and its Appendices (CIV, CIM), and for the adoption of standard rules on other questions relating to international transport law; mems: 102 transport undertakings in 37 countries; Pres. KOUNKA KIRKOVA; Sec. M. LEIMGRUBER (Switzerland).

International Railway Congress Association: Section 10, 85 rue de France, 1060 Brussels, Belgium; tel. (2) 520-78-31; fax (2) 525-40-84; e-mail secretariat@aiccf.org; internet www.aiccf.org; f. 1885 to facilitate the progress and development of railways; mems: governments, railway administrations, national and international organizations; Pres. E. SCHOUPPE; Sec.-Gen. A. MARTENS; publ. *Rail International* (monthly).

International Road Federation (IRF): Washington office: 1010 Massachusetts Ave, NW, Suite 410, Washington, DC 20037, USA; Geneva Office: 2 chemin de Blandonnet 1214, Vernier, Geneva, Switzerland; tel. (22) 3715544; fax (22) 3715565; e-mail info@irfnet.org; internet www.irfnet.org; tel. (22) 3060260; fax (22) 3060270; f. 1948 to encourage the development and improvement of highways and highway transportation; organizes IRF world and regional meetings; mems: 70 national road asscns and 500 individual firms and industrial asscns; Dir-Gen. (Washington) C. PATRICK SANKEY; Dir-Gen. (Geneva) M. W. WESTERHUIS; publs *World Road Statistics* (annually), *World Highways* (8 a year).

International Road Safety Association (La prevention routière internationale—PRI): Estrada da Luz, 90-1°, 1600-160 Lisbon, Portugal; tel. (21) 7222230; fax (21) 7222232; e-mail info@lapri.org; internet www.lapri.org; f. 1959 for exchange of ideas and material on road safety; organizes international action and congresses; assists non-member countries; mems: 74 national organizations; Pres. JOSÉ MIGUEL TRIGOSO (Portugal); Sec.-Gen. MARTINE PETERS; publ. *Newsletter* (6 a year).

International Road Transport Union (IRU): Centre International, 3 rue de Varembé, BP 44, 1211 Geneva 20, Switzerland; tel. (22) 9182700; fax (22) 9182741; e-mail iru@iru.org; internet www.iru.org; f. 1948 to study all problems of road transport, to promote unification and simplification of regulations relating to road transport, and to develop the use of road transport for passengers and goods; represents and promotes the industry at an international level; mems: 178 national asscns in 67 countries; Sec.-Gen. MARTIN MARMY; publs studies, congress and conference reports, regulations and statistics.

International Shipping Federation: Carthusian Court, 12 Carthusian St, London, EC1M 6EZ, United Kingdom; tel. (20) 7417-8844; fax (20) 7417-8877; e-mail isf@marisec.org; internet www.marisec.org; f. 1909 to consider all personnel questions affecting the interests of shipowners; responsible for Shipowners' Group at conferences of the International Labour Organisation; represents shipowners at International Maritime Organization; mems: national shipowners' organizations in 34 countries; Pres. R. WESTFAL-LARSON (Norway); Sec.-Gen. J. C. S. HORROCKS; publs conference papers, guidelines and training records.

International Union for Inland Navigation: 7 quai du Général Koenig, 67085 Strasbourg Cédex, France; tel. 3-88-36-28-44; fax 3-88-37-04-82; f. 1952 to promote the interests of inland waterways carriers; mems: national waterways organizations of Austria, Belgium, France, Germany, Italy, Luxembourg, Netherlands, Switzerland; Pres. P. GRULOIS (Belgium); Sec. M. RUSCHER; publs annual and occasional reports.

International Union of Railways (Union internationale des chemins de fer—UIC): 16 rue Jean-Rey, 75015 Paris, France; tel. 1-44-49-20-20; fax 1-44-49-20-29; e-mail communication@uic.asso.fr; internet www.uic.asso.fr; f. 1922 for the harmonization of railway operations and the development of international rail transport; aims to ensure international interoperability of the rail system; compiles information on economic, management and technical aspects of railways; co-ordinates research and collaborates with industry and the EU; organizes international conferences; mems: 172 railways in 87 countries; Pres. BENEDIKT WEIBEL; Chief Exec. PHILIPPE ROUME-GUÈRE; publs *International Railway Statistics* (annually), *Activities Reports*, *UIC Panorama* (newsletter).

Northern Shipowners' Defence Club (Nordisk Skibsrederforening): Kristinelundv. 22, POB 33, Elisenberg, 0207 Oslo, Norway; tel. 22-13-56-00; fax 22-43-00-35; e-mail post@nordisk.no; internet www.nordisk.org; f. 1889 to assist members in disputes over charter parties, contracts and sale and purchase, taking the necessary legal steps on behalf of members and bearing the cost of such claims; mems: mainly Finnish, Swedish and Norwegian and some non-Scandinavian shipowners, representing about 1,800 ships and drilling rigs with gross tonnage of about 50m.; Man. Dir GEORG SCHEEL; Chair. MORTEN WERRING; publ. *A Law Report of Scandinavian Maritime Cases* (annually).

Organisation for the Collaboration of Railways: Hozà 63–67, 00681 Warsaw, Poland; tel. (22) 6573600; fax (22) 6573654; e-mail osjd@osjd.org.pl; internet www.osjd.org; f. 1956; aims to improve standards and co-operation in railway traffic between countries of Europe and Asia; promotes co-operation on issues relating to traffic policy and economic and environmental aspects of railway traffic; ensures enforcement of a number of rail agreements; aims to elaborate and standardize general principles for international transport law. Conference of Ministers of mem. countries meets annually; Conference of Gen. Dirs of Railways meets at least once a year; mems: ministries of transport of 27 countries world-wide; Chair. TADEUSZ SZOZDA; publ. *OSShD Journal* (every 2 months, in Chinese, German and Russian).

Pan American Railway Congress Association (Asociación del Congreso Panamericano de Ferrocarriles): Av. 9 de Julio 1925, 13°, 1332 Buenos Aires, Argentina; tel. (11) 4381-4625; fax (11) 4814-1823; e-mail acpf@nat.com.ar; f. 1907, present title adopted 1941; aims to promote the development and progress of railways in the American continent; holds Congresses every three years; mems: government representatives, railway enterprises and individuals in 21 countries; Pres. JUAN CARLOS DE MARCHI (Argentina); Gen. Sec. LUIS V. DONZELLI (Argentina); publ. *Boletín ACPF* (5 a year).

Union of European Railway Industries (UNIFE): 221 ave Louise, 1050 Brussels, Belgium; tel. (2) 626-12-60; fax (2) 626-12-61; e-mail mail@unife.org; internet www.unife.org; f. 1975 to represent companies concerned in the manufacture of railway equipment in Europe to European and international organizations; mems: 140 companies in 14 countries; Chair. PHILIPPE MELLIER; Dir-Gen. DREWIN NIEUWENHUIS.

World Airlines Clubs Association (WACA): c/o IATA, 800 Pl. Victoria, POB 113, Montréal, Québec, QC H4Z 1M1, Canada; tel. (514) 874-0202; fax (514) 874-1753; e-mail info@waca.org; internet www.waca.org; f. 1966; holds a General Assembly annually, regional meetings, international events and sports tournaments; mems: clubs in 38 countries; Man. AUBREY WINTERBOTHAM; publs *WACA Contact*, *WACA World News*, annual report.

Youth and Students

AIESEC International: Teilingerstraat 126–128, 3032 Rotterdam, Netherlands; tel. (10) 4434383; fax (10) 2651386; e-mail info@ai.aiesec.org; internet www.aiesec.org; f. 1948 as International Association of Students in Economics and Management; works to develop leadership skills and socio-economic and international understanding among young people, through exchange programmes and related educational activities; mems: 50,000 students in more than 650 higher education institutions in 88 countries and territories; Pres. SAHIL KAUL; Vice-Pres. ANDREW SCHURGOTT; publ. *Annual Report*.

Asia Students Association: 353 Shanghai St, 14/F, Kowloon, Hong Kong; tel. 23880515; fax 27825535; e-mail asasec@netvigator.com; f. 1969; aims to promote students' solidarity in struggling for democracy, self-determination, peace, justice and liberation; conducts campaigns, training of activists, and workshops on human rights and other issues of importance; there are Student Commissions for Peace, Education and Human Rights; mems: 40 national or regional student unions in 25 countries and territories; Secretariat LINA CABAERO (Philippines), STEVEN GAN (Malaysia), CHOW WING-HANG (Hong Kong); publs *Movement News* (monthly), *ASA News* (quarterly).

Council on International Educational Exchange (CIEE): 7 Custom House St, 3rd Floor, Portland, ME 04101, USA; tel. (207) 553-7600; fax (207) 553-7699; e-mail info@ciee.org; internet www.ciee.org; f. 1947; issues International Student Identity Card enti-

tling holders to discounts and basic insurance; arranges overseas work and study programmes for students; co-ordinates summer work programme in the USA for foreign students; administers programmes for teachers and other professionals and sponsors conferences on educational exchange; operates a voluntary service programme; mems: 307 colleges, universities and international educational organizations; Chair. CHARLES PING; publs include *Work, Study, Travel Abroad: The Whole World Handbook*, *Update*, *Volunteer!*, *High-School Student's Guide to Study, Travel and Adventure Abroad*.

European Law Students' Association (ELSA): 1 rue Defacqz, 1050 Brussels, Belgium; tel. (2) 534-56-79; fax (2) 534-65-86; internet www.elsa-online.org; f. 1981 to foster mutual understanding and promote social responsibility of law students and young laywers; publs *ELSA Law Review*, *Legal Studies in Europe*.

European Students' Forum (Association des Etats Généraux des Etudiants de l'Europe—AEGEE): 15 rue Nestor de Tière, 1030 Brussels, Belgium; tel. (2) 245-23-00; fax (2) 245-62-60; e-mail headoffice@aegee.org; internet www.aegee.org; promotes cross-border communication, co-operation and integration between students; fosters inter-cultural exchange; holds specialized conferences; mems: 17,000 students in 260 university cities in 42 countries; Sec.-Gen. WEIBKE HAHN.

European Youth Forum: 120 rue Joseph II, 1000 Brussels, Belgium; tel. (2) 230-64-90; fax (2) 230-21-23; e-mail youthforum@youthforum.org; internet www.youthforum.org; f. 1996; promotes development of a coherent and integrated youth policy; promotes the rights of young people, as well as understanding and respect for human rights; consults with international organizations and governments on issues relevant to young people; Pres. GIACOMO FILIBECK (Italy); Sec.-Gen. JOHANNA TZANIKAKI (Greece).

International Association for the Exchange of Students for Technical Experience (IAESTE): e-mail webmaster@iaeste.org; internet www.iaeste.org; f. 1948; mems: 63 national committees; publs *Activity Report*, *Annual Report*.

International Association of Dental Students (IADS): c/o FDI World Dental Federation, 13 chemin du Levant l'Avent Centre, 01210 Ferney-Voltaire, France; tel. 4-50-40-50-50; fax 4-50-40-55-55; e-mail gsecretary@iads-web.org; internet www.iads-web.org; f. 1951 to represent dental students and their opinions internationally, to promote dental student exchanges and international congresses; mems: 60,000 students in 45 countries, 15,000 corresponding mems; Pres. TASKIN TUNA (Germany); Sec. Dr AHMED HAWAS (Egypt); publ. *IADS Newsletter* (3 a year).

International Federation of Medical Students' Associations (IFMSA): Institute of Social Medicine, Academisch Medisch Centrum, Meibergdreef 15, 1105 Amsterdam, Netherlands; tel. (20) 5665366; fax (20) 6972316; e-mail f.w.hilhorst@amc.uva.nl; internet www.ifmsa.org; f. 1951 to promote international co-operation in professional treatment and the achievement of humanitarian ideals; provides forum for medical students; maintains standing committees on professional exchange, electives exchange, medical education, public health, refugees and AIDS; organizes annual General Assembly; mems: 57 asscns; Sec.-Gen. MIA HILHORST; publ. *IFMSA Newsletter* (quarterly).

International Pharmaceutical Students' Federation (IPSF): POB 84200, 2508 AE The Hague, Netherlands; tel. (70) 3021992; fax (70) 3021999; e-mail ipsf@fip.nl; internet www.pharmweb.net/ipsf.html; f. 1949 to study and promote the interests of pharmaceutical students and to encourage international co-operation; mems: 31 full mems from national organizations and 23 mems in assoc. from national or local organizations; Pres. GONÇALO SOUSA PINTO; Sec.-Gen. HELENA WESTERMARK; publ. *IPSF News Bulletin* (3 a year).

International Union of Students: POB 58, 17th November St, 110 01 Prague 01, Czech Republic; tel. (2) 312812; fax (2) 316100; internet www.stud.uni-hannover/delgruppen/ius; f. 1946 to defend the rights and interests of students and strive for peace, disarmament, the eradication of illiteracy and of all forms of discrimination; operates research centre, sports and cultural centre and student travel bureau; activities include conferences, meetings, solidarity campaigns, relief projects; awards 30–40 scholarships annually; mems: 140 organizations from 115 countries; Pres. JOSEF SKALA; Vice-Pres. MARTA HUBIČKOVÁ; Gen. Sec. GIORGOS MICHAELIDES (Cyprus); publs *World Student News* (quarterly), *IUS Newsletter*, *Student Life* (quarterly), *DE—Democratization of Education* (quarterly).

International Young Christian Workers: 4 ave G. Rodenbach, 1030 Brussels, Belgium; tel. (2) 242-18-11; fax (2) 242-48-00; e-mail postmaster@jociycw.net; internet www.jociycw.net; f. 1925, on the inspiration of the Priest-Cardinal Joseph Cardijn; aims to educate young workers to take on present and future responsibilities in their commitment to the working class, and to gain personal fulfilment through their actions; Pres. JOSÉE DESROSIERS (Canada); Sec.-Gen.

ANNA CIROCCO (Australia); publs *International INFO* (3 a year), *IYCW Bulletin* (quarterly).

International Youth Hostel Federation: Gate House, 2nd Floor, Fretherne Rd, Welwyn Garden City, Herts., AL8 6RD, United Kingdom; tel. (1707) 324170; fax (1707) 323980; e-mail iyhf@iyhf .org; internet www.HIhostels.com; f. 1932; facilitates international travel by members of the various youth hostel asscns; advises and helps in the formation of youth hostel asscns in countries where no such organizations exist; records over 35m. overnight stays annually in around 4,000 youth hostels; mems: 60 national asscns with over 3.2m. national members and 1m. international guest members; 12 associated national orgns; Pres. Dr HARISH SAXENA (India); Sec.-Gen. ULRICH BUNJES (Germany); publs *Annual Report, Guidebook on World Hostels* (annually), *Manual, News Bulletin.*

Junior Chamber International (JCI), Inc.: 16120 Chesterfield Parkway West, Suite 250, Chesterfield, MO 63017, USA; tel. (636) 449-3100; fax (636) 449-3107; e-mail ekodama@jci.cc; internet www .jci.cc; f. 1944 to encourage and advance international understanding and goodwill; aims to solve civic problems by arousing civic consciousness; Junior Chamber organizations throughout the world provide opportunities for leadership training and for the discussion of social, economic and cultural questions; mems: 200,000 in more than 100 countries; Pres. FERNANDO SÁNCHEZ-ARIAS (Venezuela); Sec.-Gen. (interim) EDSON KODAMA (Brazil); publ. *JCI News* (quarterly, in English and more than six other languages).

Latin American and Caribbean Confederation of Young Men's Christian Associations (Confederación Latinoamericana y del Caribe de Asociaciones Cristianas de Jóvenes): Culpina 272, 1406 Buenos Aires, Argentina; tel. (11) 4373-4156; fax (11) 4374-4408; e-mail clacj@wamani.apc.org; f. 1914; aims to encourage the moral, spiritual, intellectual, social and physical development of young men; to strengthen the work of national Asscns and to sponsor the establishment of new Asscns; mems: affiliated YMCAs in 25 countries (comprising 350,000 individuals); Pres. GERARDO VITUREIRA (Uruguay); Gen. Sec. MARCO ANTONIO HOCHSCHEIT (Brazil); publs *Diecisiete/21* (bulletin), *Carta Abierta, Brief*, technical articles and other studies.

Pan-African Youth Movement (Mouvement pan-africain de la jeunesse): 19 rue Debbih Chérif, BP 72, Didouch Mourad, 16000 Algiers, Algeria; tel. and fax (2) 71-64-71; f. 1962; aims to encourage the participation of African youth in socio-economic and political development and democratization; organizes conferences and seminars, youth exchanges and youth festivals; mems: youth groups in 52 African countries and liberation movements; publ. *MPJ News* (quarterly).

WFUNA Youth: c/o Palais des Nations, 16 ave Jean-Tremblay, 1211 Geneva 10, Switzerland; tel. (22) 7985850; fax (22) 7334838; internet www.wfuna-youth.org; f. 1948 by the World Federation of United Nations Associations (WFUNA) as the International Youth and Student Movement for the United Nations (ISMUN), independent since 1949; an international non-governmental organization of students and young people dedicated especially to supporting the principles embodied in the United Nations Charter and Universal Declaration of Human Rights; encourages constructive action in building economic, social and cultural equality and in working for national independence, social justice and human rights on a world-wide scale; maintains regional offices in Austria, France, Ghana, Panama and the USA; mems: asscns in 53 countries world-wide; Head Co-ordinator TIM JARMAN.

World Alliance of Young Men's Christian Associations: 12 clos. Belmont, 1208 Geneva, Switzerland; tel. (22) 8495100; fax (22) 8495110; e-mail office@ymca.int; internet www.ymca.int; f. 1855 to unite the National Alliances of Young Men's Christian Associations throughout the world; mems: national alliances and related asscns in 128 countries; Pres. CAESAR MOLEBATSI (South Africa); Sec.-Gen. SHAHA BARTHOLOMEW; publ. *YMCA World* (quarterly).

World Assembly of Youth: International Youth Centre, Jalan Tenteram, Bandar Tun Razak, 56000 Kuala Lumpur, Malaysia; tel. (3) 9732722; fax (3) 9736011; internet www.jaring.my/way; f. 1949 as co-ordinating body for youth councils and organizations; organizes conferences, training courses and practical development projects; Pres. Datuk ALI RUSTAM; Sec.-Gen. HEIKKI PAKARINEN; publs *WAY Information* (every 2 months), *Youth Roundup* (monthly), *WAY Forum* (quarterly).

World Association of Girl Guides and Girl Scouts (WAGGGS): World Bureau, Olave Centre, 12c Lyndhurst Rd, London, NW3 5PQ, United Kingdom; tel. (20) 7794-1181; fax (20) 7431-3764; e-mail wagggs@wagggsworld.org; internet www.wagggsworld.org; f. 1928 to enable girls and young women to develop their full potential as responsible citizens, and to support friendship and mutual understanding among girls and young women world-wide; World Conference meets every three years; mems: about 10m. individuals in 140 organizations; Chair. World Board GINNY RADFORD; Dir World Bureau LESLEY BULMAN; publs *Triennial Report, Annual Report, Trefoil Round the World* (every 3 years), *Our World News* (quarterly).

World Council of Service Clubs: POB 148, Wallaroo, South Australia 5556, Australia; e-mail kelly@kadina.mtx.net.au; internet www.woco.org; f. 1946 to provide a means for the exchange of information and news, with the aim of furthering international understanding and co-operation; aims to create in young people a sense of civic responsibility; works to facilitate the extension of service clubs; mems: over 3,000 clubs in 83 countries; Sec.-Gen. SHANE KELLY.

World Federation of Democratic Youth (WFDY): POB 147, 1389 Budapest, Hungary; tel. (1) 3502202; fax (1) 3501204; e-mail wfdy@mail.matav.hu; internet www.wfdy.org; f. 1945 to strive for peace, disarmament and joint action by democratic and progressive youth movements and for the creation of a new and more just international economic order; promotes national independence, democracy, social progress and youth rights; supports the liberation struggles in Asia, Africa and Latin America; mems: 152 members in 102 countries; Pres. IRAKLIS TSAVDARIDIS (Greece); publ. *WFDY News* (every 3 months, in English, French and Spanish).

World Organization of the Scout Movement: Case Postale 241, 1211 Geneva 4, Switzerland; tel. (22) 7051010; fax (22) 7051020; e-mail worldbureau@world.scout.org; internet www.scout.org; f. 1922 to promote unity and understanding of scouting throughout the world to develop good citizenship among young people by forming their characters for service, co-operation and leadership; and to provide aid and advice to members and potential member asscns. The World Scout Bureau (Geneva) has regional offices in Chile, Egypt, Kenya and the Philippines (the European Region has its offices in Brussels and Geneva); mems: over 25m. in 215 countries and territories; Sec.-Gen. Dr JACQUES MOREILLON (Switzerland); publ. *Worldinfo Triennial Report.*

World Union of Jewish Students (WUJS): POB 7114, 58 King George St, Jerusalem 91070, Israel; tel. (2) 6251682; fax (2) 6251688; e-mail office@wujs.org.il; internet www.wujs.org.il; f. 1924 (by Albert Einstein); organization for national student bodies concerned with educational and political matters, where possible in co-operation with non-Jewish student organizations, UNESCO, etc.; divided into six regions; organizes Congress every two years; mems: 52 national unions representing over 1.5m. students; Chair. PELEG RESHEF; publs *The Student Activist Yearbook, Heritage and History, Forum, WUJS Report.*

World Young Women's Christian Association (World YWCA): 16 Ancienne Route, 1218 Grand-Saconnex, Geneva, Switzerland; tel. (22) 9296040; fax (22) 9296044; e-mail worldoffice@worldywca.org; internet www.worldywca.org; f. 1894; global movement which aims to empower women and girls to change their lives and communities; works to achieve social and economic justice through grassroots development and global advocacy; addresses critical issues affecting women, such as HIV/AIDS and violence; promotes the sharing of human and financial resources among member asscns; mems: in 122 countries; Pres. MÓNICA ZETZSCHE; Gen. Sec. MUSIMBI KANYORO; publs *Annual Report, Common Concern, Week of Prayer* (booklet), other reports.

Youth for Development and Co-operation (YDC): Rijswijkstrasse 141, 1062 HN Amsterdam, Netherlands; tel. (20) 6142510; fax (20) 6175545; e-mail ydc@geo2.geonet.de; aims to strengthen youth structures promoting co-operation between young people in the industrialized and developing worlds, in order to achieve development that is environmentally sustainable and socially just; holds seminars, conferences and campaigns on issues related to youth and development; mems: 51 organizations; Sec.-Gen. B. AUER; publ. *FLASH Newsletter* (irregular).

PART TWO
Afghanistan–Jordan

AFGHANISTAN

Introductory Survey

Location, Climate, Language, Religion, Flag, Capital

The Islamic State of Afghanistan is a land-locked country in south-western Asia. It is bordered by Turkmenistan, Uzbekistan and Tajikistan to the north, Iran to the west, the People's Republic of China to the north-east and Pakistan to the east and south. The climate varies sharply between the highlands and lowlands; the temperature in the south-west in summer reaches 49°C (120°F), but in the winter, in the Hindu Kush mountains of the north-east, it falls to –26°C (–15°F). Of the many languages spoken in Afghanistan, the principal two are Pashto (Pakhto) and Dari (a dialect of Farsi or Iranian). The majority of Afghans are Muslims of the Sunni sect; there are also minority groups of Shi'a Muslims, Hindus, Sikhs and Jews. The state flag (proportions 1 by 2) has three equal vertical stripes from hoist to fly of black, red and green, bearing in the centre in white and red the state arms and an inscription reading 'There is no God but Allah, and Muhammad is his Prophet, and Allah is Great', in Arabic. The Islamic date 1298 appears under the inscription. The flag was first introduced in 1928, modified in 1964, and banned following the coup in 1978. The only difference featured in the current flag, introduced in June 2002, following the collapse of the Taliban, is the inscription bearing the word 'Afghanistan'. The capital is Kabul.

Recent History

The last King of Afghanistan, Mohammad Zahir Shah, reigned from 1933 to 1973. His country was neutral during both World Wars and became a staunch advocate of non-alignment. In 1953 the King's cousin, Lt-Gen. Sardar Mohammad Daoud Khan, was appointed Prime Minister and, securing aid from the USSR, initiated a series of economic plans for the modernization of the country. In 1963 Gen. Daoud resigned and Dr Mohammad Yusuf became the first Prime Minister not of royal birth. Dr Yusuf introduced a new democratic Constitution in the following year, which combined Western ideas with Islamic religious and political beliefs; the King, however, did not permit political parties to operate. Afghanistan made little progress under the succeeding Prime Ministers.

In July 1973, while King Zahir was in Italy, the monarchy was overthrown by a coup, in which the main figure was the former Prime Minister, Gen. Daoud. The 1964 Constitution was abolished and Afghanistan was declared a republic. Daoud renounced his royal titles and took office as Head of State, Prime Minister and Minister of Foreign Affairs and Defence.

A Loya Jirga (Grand National Council), appointed from among tribal elders by provincial governors, was convened in January 1977 and adopted a new Constitution, providing for presidential government and a one-party state. Daoud was elected to continue as President for six years and the Loya Jirga was then dissolved. In March President Daoud formed a new civilian Government, nominally ending military rule. However, during 1977 there was growing discontent with Daoud, especially within the armed forces, and in April 1978 a coup, known (from the month) as the 'Saur Revolution', ousted the President, who was killed with several members of his family. Nur Mohammad Taraki, the imprisoned leader of the formerly banned People's Democratic Party of Afghanistan (PDPA), was released and installed as President of the Revolutionary Council and Prime Minister. The country was renamed the Democratic Republic of Afghanistan, the year-old Constitution was abolished and no political parties other than the communist PDPA were allowed to function. Afghanistan's already close relations with the USSR were further strengthened. However, opposition to the new regime led to armed insurrection, particularly by fiercely traditionalist Islamist rebel tribesmen (known, collectively, as the *mujahidin*), in almost all provinces, and the flight of thousands of refugees to Pakistan and Iran. In spite of purges of the army and civil service, Taraki's position became increasingly insecure, and in September 1979 he was ousted by Hafizullah Amin, an erstwhile Deputy Prime Minister and Minister of Foreign Affairs. Amin's imposition of rigorous communist policies proved unsuccessful and unpopular. In December he was killed in a coup, which was supported by the entry into

Afghanistan of about 80,000 combat troops from the USSR. This incursion by Soviet armed forces into a traditionally non-aligned neighbouring country aroused world-wide condemnation. Babrak Karmal, a former Deputy Prime Minister under Taraki, was installed as the new Head of State, having been flown into Kabul by a Soviet aircraft from virtual exile in Eastern Europe.

Riots, strikes and inter-factional strife and purges continued into 1980 and 1981. Sultan Ali Keshtmand, hitherto a Deputy Prime Minister, replaced Karmal as Prime Minister in June 1981. In the same month the regime launched the National Fatherland Front (NFF), incorporating the PDPA and other organizations, with the aim of promoting national unity. Despite a series of government reorganizations carried out in the early 1980s, the PDPA regime continued to fail to win widespread popular support. Consequently, the Government attempted to broaden the base of its support: in April 1985 it summoned a Loya Jirga, which ratified a new Constitution for Afghanistan, and during the second half of 1985 and the first half of 1986 elections were held for new local government organs (it was claimed that 60% of those elected were non-party members) and several non-party members were appointed to high-ranking government posts (including the chairmanship of the NFF).

In May 1986 Dr Najibullah (the former head of the state security service, KHAD) succeeded Karmal as General Secretary of the PDPA. Karmal retained the lesser post of President of the Revolutionary Council. In the same month Najibullah announced the formation of a collective leadership comprising himself, Karmal and Prime Minister Keshtmand. In November, however, Karmal was relieved of all party and government posts. Haji Muhammad Chamkani, formerly First Vice-President (and a non-PDPA member), became Acting President of the Revolutionary Council, pending the introduction of a new constitution and the establishment of a permanent legislature.

In December 1986 an extraordinary plenum of the PDPA Central Committee approved a policy of national reconciliation, involving negotiations with opposition groups, and the proposed formation of a coalition government of national unity. In early January 1987 a Supreme Extraordinary Commission for National Reconciliation, led by Abd ar-Rahim Hatif (the Chairman of the National Committee of the NFF), was formed to conduct the negotiations. The NFF was renamed the National Front (NF), and became a separate organization from the PDPA. The new policy of reconciliation won some support from former opponents, but the seven-party *mujahidin* alliance (Ittehad-i-Islami Afghan Mujahidin, Islamic Union of Afghan Mujahidin—IUAM), which was based in Peshawar, Pakistan, refused to observe the cease-fire or to participate in negotiations, while continuing to demand a complete and unconditional Soviet withdrawal from Afghanistan.

In July 1987, as part of the process of national reconciliation, several important developments occurred: a law permitting the formation of other political parties (according to certain provisions) was introduced; Najibullah announced that the PDPA would be prepared to share power with representatives of opposition groups in the event of the formation of a coalition government of national unity; and the draft of a new Constitution was approved by the Presidium of the Revolutionary Council. The main innovations incorporated in the draft Constitution were: the formation of a multi-party political system, under the auspices of the NF; the formation of a bicameral legislature, called the Meli Shura (National Assembly), composed of a Sena (Senate) and a Wolasi Jirga (House of Representatives); the granting of a permanent constitutional status to the PDPA; the bestowal of unlimited power on the President, who was to hold office for seven years; and the reversion of the name of the country from the Democratic Republic to the Republic of Afghanistan. A Loya Jirga ratified the new Constitution in November.

Meanwhile, a considerable proportion of the successful candidates in local elections held throughout the country in August 1987 were reported to be non-PDPA members. On 30 September Najibullah was unanimously elected as President of the Revolutionary Council, and Haji Muhammad Chamkani resumed his former post as First Vice-President. In order to strengthen his position, Najibullah ousted all the remaining supporters of former President Karmal from the Central Committee and Politburo of the PDPA in October. In the following month a Loya Jirga unanimously elected Najibullah as President of the State.

In April 1988 elections were held to both houses of the new National Assembly, which replaced the Revolutionary Council. Although the elections were boycotted by the *mujahidin*, the Government left vacant 50 of the 234 seats in the House of Representatives, and a small number of seats in the Senate, in the hope that the guerrillas would abandon their armed struggle and present their own representatives to participate in the new administration. The PDPA itself won only 46 seats in the House of Representatives, but was guaranteed support from the NF, which secured 45, and from the various newly recognized left-wing parties, which won a total of 24 seats. In May Dr Muhammad Hasan Sharq (a non-PDPA member and a Deputy Prime Minister since June 1987) replaced Keshtmand as Prime Minister, and in June a new Council of Ministers was appointed.

On 18 February 1989, following the completion of the withdrawal of Soviet troops from Afghanistan (see below), Najibullah implemented a government reorganization, involving the replacement of non-communist ministers with loyal PDPA members. On the same day, Prime Minister Sharq (who had been one of the main promoters of the policy of national reconciliation) resigned from his post and was replaced by Keshtmand. Following the declaration of a state of emergency by Najibullah (citing allegations of repeated violations of the Geneva accords by Pakistan and the USA—see below) on 19 February, a PDPA-dominated 20-member Supreme Council for the Defence of the Homeland was established. The Council, which was headed by President Najibullah and was composed of ministers, members of the PDPA Politburo and high-ranking military figures, assumed full responsibility for the country's economic, political and military policies (although the Council of Ministers continued to function).

In early March 1990 the Minister of Defence, Lt-Gen. Shah-nawaz Tanay, with the alleged support of the air force and some divisions of the army, led an unsuccessful coup attempt against Najibullah's Government. Najibullah subsequently enacted thorough purges of PDPA and army leaders and decided to revert rapidly to some form of constitutional civilian government. On 20 May the state of emergency was lifted; the Supreme Council for the Defence of the Homeland was disbanded; and a new Council of Ministers, under the premiership of Fazle Haq Khalikyar, was appointed. At the end of the month a Loya Jirga was convened in Kabul, which ratified constitutional amendments, greatly reducing Afghanistan's socialist orientation; ending the PDPA's and the NF's monopoly over executive power and paving the way for fully democratic elections; introducing greater political and press freedom; encouraging the development of the private sector and further foreign investment; lessening the role of the State and affording greater prominence to Islam. The extensive powers of the presidency were, however, retained. In addition, in late June the PDPA changed its name to the Homeland Party (HP—Hizb-i Watan), and dissolved the Politburo and the Central Committee, replacing them with an Executive Board and a Central Council, respectively. The party adopted a new programme, of which the hallmark was hostility to ideology. Najibullah was unanimously elected as Chairman of the HP. An important factor in Najibullah's decision to continue with, and to extend, the process of national reconciliation was the fact that the USSR's own internal problems meant that the Soviet administration was unwilling to sustain, for much longer, the supplies of weapons, goods and credits that were helping to support the Kabul regime.

Fighting between the *mujahidin* and Afghan army units had begun in the eastern provinces after the 1978 coup and was aggravated by the implementation of unpopular social and economic reforms by the new administrations. The Afghan army relied heavily upon Soviet military aid in the form of weapons, equipment and expertise, but morale and resources were severely affected by defections to the rebels' ranks: numbers fell from around 80,000 men in 1978 to about 40,000 in 1985. During 1984–89 the guerrilla groups, which had been poorly armed at first, received ever-increasing support (both military and financial) from abroad, notably from the USA (which began to supply them with sophisticated anti-aircraft weapons in 1986), the United Kingdom and the People's Republic of China. Despite the Government's decision to seal the border with Pakistan, announced in September 1985, and the strong presence of Soviet forces there, foreign weapons continued to reach the guerrillas

via Pakistan. Many of the guerrillas established bases in the North-West Frontier Province of Pakistan (notably in the provincial capital, Peshawar). From 1985 the fighting intensified, especially in areas close to the border between Afghanistan and Pakistan. There were many violations of the border, involving shelling, bombing and incursions into neighbouring airspace. The general pattern of the war, however, remained the same: the regime held the main towns and a few strategic bases, and relied on bombing of both military and civilian targets, and occasional attacks in force, together with conciliatory measures such as the provision of funds for local development, while the rebel forces dominated rural areas and were able to cause serious disruption.

The civil war brought famine to parts of Afghanistan, and there was a mass movement of population from the countryside to Kabul, and of refugees to Pakistan and Iran. In mid-1988 the office of the UN High Commissioner for Refugees (UNHCR) estimated the number of Afghan refugees in Pakistan at 3.15m., and the number in Iran at 2.35m. Supply convoys were often prevented from reaching the cities, owing to the repeated severing of major road links by the guerrillas. Kabul, in particular, began to suffer from severe shortages of food and fuel, which were only partially alleviated by airlifts of emergency aid supplies.

From 1980 extensive international negotiations took place to try to achieve the complete withdrawal of Soviet forces from Afghanistan. Between June 1982 and September 1987 seven rounds of indirect talks took place between the Afghan and Pakistani Ministers of Foreign Affairs in Geneva, Switzerland, under the auspices of the UN. In October 1986 the USSR made a token withdrawal of six regiments (6,000–8,000 men) from Afghanistan. As a result of the discussions in Geneva, an agreement was finally signed on 14 April 1988. The Geneva accords consisted of five documents: detailed undertakings by Afghanistan and Pakistan, relating to non-intervention and non-interference in each other's affairs; international guarantees of Afghan neutrality (with the USA and the USSR as the principal guarantors); arrangements for the voluntary and safe return of Afghan refugees; a document linking the preceding documents with a timetable for a Soviet withdrawal; and the establishment of a UN monitoring force, which was to oversee both the Soviet troop departures and the return of the refugees. The withdrawal of Soviet troops (numbering 100,000, according to Soviet figures, or 115,000, according to Western sources) commenced on 15 May.

Neither the *mujahidin* nor Iran played any role in the formulation of the Geneva accords, and, in spite of protests by Pakistan, no agreement was incorporated regarding the composition of an interim coalition government in Afghanistan, or the 'symmetrical' cessation of Soviet aid to Najibullah's regime and US aid to the *mujahidin*. Therefore, despite the withdrawal of the Soviet troops, the supply of weapons to both sides was not halted, and the fighting continued. Pakistan repeatedly denied accusations that it had violated the accords by continuing to harbour Afghan guerrillas and to act as a conduit for the supply of weapons. At the end of November 1988 Soviet officials held direct talks with representatives of the *mujahidin* in Peshawar, Pakistan, the first such meeting since the start of the 10-year conflict. High-level discussions were held in early December in Saudi Arabia between Prof. Burhanuddin Rabbani, the Chairman of the IUAM, and the Soviet ambassador to Afghanistan. These discussions collapsed, however, when the *mujahidin* leaders reiterated their demand that no members of Najibullah's regime should be incorporated in any future Afghan government, while the Soviet officials continued to insist on a government role for the PDPA. In spite of the unabated violence, the USSR, adhering to the condition specified in the Geneva accords, had withdrawn all of its troops from Afghanistan by mid-February 1989.

In mid-1988 the *mujahidin* had intensified their military activities, attacking small provincial centres and launching missiles against major cities. By the end of 1990 the *mujahidin* had failed to achieve any significant military successes and their control was confined to rural areas (including several small provincial capitals). The guerrillas also failed to make any important advances on the political front. Talks between the IUAM and the Iranian-based Hizb-i Wahadat-i Islami (Islamic Unity Party), an alliance of eight Shi'a Afghan resistance groups, repeatedly failed to reach any agreement as to the composition of a broadly-based interim government. Consequently, in February 1989 the IUAM convened its own *shura* (council) in Rawalpindi, Pakistan, at which an interim government-in-exile (known as the Afghan Interim Government, AIG) was elected. The AIG, however, was officially recognized by only four countries. It also failed to gain any substantial support or recognition from the guerrilla commanders, who were beginning to establish their own unofficial alliances inside the country. In March, however, the AIG received a form of diplomatic recognition, when it was granted membership of the Organization of the Islamic Conference (OIC). In addition, in June the US Government appointed a special envoy to the *mujahidin*, with the rank of personal ambassador. In mid-1989 the unity of the *mujahidin* forces was seriously weakened by an increase in internecine violence among the various guerrilla groups, while the AIG was riven by disputes between the moderates and the fundamentalists. The USA, Saudi Arabia and Pakistan began to reduce financial aid and military supplies to the IUAM in Peshawar, and to undertake the difficult task of delivering weapons and money directly to guerrilla commanders and tribal leaders inside Afghanistan.

Following extensive negotiations with the regional powers involved in the crisis, the UN Secretary-General made a declaration in May 1991, setting out five principles for a settlement, the main points of which were: recognition of the national sovereignty of Afghanistan; the right of the Afghan people to choose their own government and political system; the establishment of an independent and authorized mechanism to oversee free and fair elections to a broadly-based government; a UN-monitored cease-fire; and the donation of sufficient financial aid to facilitate the return of the refugees and internal reconstruction. The declaration received the approval of the Afghan and Pakistani Governments, but was rejected by the AIG.

Reflecting its disenchantment with the guerrilla cause, the US Government substantially reduced its aid to the *mujahidin* in 1991. New military campaigns had been launched by the *mujahidin* in the second half of 1990 in an attempt to impress their international supporters, disrupt the return of refugees and obstruct contacts between the Government and moderate guerrillas. At the end of March 1991, following more than two weeks of heavy fighting, the south-eastern city of Khost was captured by the *mujahidin*, representing the most severe reversal sustained by the Government since the Soviet withdrawal. The *mujahidin* also carried out attacks on Gardez, Jalalabad, Ghazni, Qandahar and Herat in 1991.

An unexpected breakthrough towards resolving the Afghan crisis occurred in mid-September 1991, when the USA and the USSR announced that they would stop supplying arms to the warring factions, and would encourage other countries (namely Pakistan, Saudi Arabia and Iran) to do likewise. Although both the Afghan Government and the *mujahidin* welcomed this pledge, neither side showed any sign of implementing the proposed cease-fire, and, indeed, the fighting intensified around Kabul. In February 1992, however, the peace process was given a major boost when Pakistan made it clear that, rather than continuing actively to encourage the *mujahidin*, through arms supplies and training, it was urging all the guerrilla factions to support the five-point UN peace plan (see above). In doing so, Pakistan was effectively abandoning its insistence on the installation of a fundamentalist government in Kabul. There were growing fears, none the less, that the peace process might be placed in jeopardy by an increase in ethnic divisions within both the government forces and a number of *mujahidin* groups, between the majority Pashtuns and minority groups such as the Tajiks and Uzbeks. As a result of a mutiny staged by Uzbek militia forces in the Afghan army, under the command of Gen. Abdul Rashid Dostam, the northern town of Mazar-i-Sharif was captured by the *mujahidin* in March.

On 16 April 1992 events took an unexpected turn when Najibullah was forced to resign by his own ruling party, following the capture of the strategically important Bagram air base and the nearby town of Charikar, only about 50 km north of Kabul, by the Jamiat-i Islami guerrilla group under the command of the Tajik general, Ahmad Shah Masoud. Najibullah went into hiding in the capital, under UN protection, while one of the Vice-Presidents, Abd ar-Rahim Hatif, assumed the post of acting President. Within a few days of Najibullah's downfall, every major town in Afghanistan was under the control of different coalitions of *mujahidin* groups co-operating with disaffected army commanders. Masoud was given orders by the guerrilla leaders in Peshawar to secure Kabul. On 25 April the forces of both Masoud and of Gulbuddin Hekmatyar, the leader of a rival guerrilla group, the Pashtun-dominated Hizb-i Islami

(Islamic Party), whose men were massed to the south of the capital, entered Kabul. The army surrendered its key positions, and immediately the city was riven by *mujahidin* faction-fighting. The military council that had, a few days earlier, replaced the Government relinquished power to the *mujahidin*. Having discarded the UN's proposal to form a neutral body, the guerrilla leaders in Peshawar agreed to establish a 51-member interim Islamic Jihad Council, composed of military and religious leaders, which was to assume power in Kabul. The leader of the small, moderate Jebha-i-Nejat-i-Melli (National Liberation Front), Prof. Sibghatullah Mojaddedi, was to chair the Islamic Jihad Council for two months, after which period a 10-member Leadership Council, comprising *mujahidin* chiefs and presided over by the head of the Jamiat-i Islami, Prof. Burhanuddin Rabbani, would be set up for a period of four months. Within the six months a special council was to meet to designate an interim administration which was to hold power for up to a year pending elections.

Mojaddedi arrived in Kabul on 28 April 1992 as the President of the new interim administration. The Islamic Jihad Council was not, however, supported by Hekmatyar, whose radical stance differed substantially from Mojaddedi's more tolerant outlook. At the end of the month Hekmatyar's forces lost control of their last stronghold in the centre of Kabul. Within a few weeks the Government of the newly proclaimed Islamic State of Afghanistan had won almost universal diplomatic recognition, and by early May about one-half of the Islamic Jihad Council had arrived in the capital. An acting Council of Ministers was formed, in which Masoud was given the post of Minister of Defence and the premiership was set aside for Ustad Abdol Sabur Farid, a Tajik commander from the Hizb-i Islami (Hekmatyar declined to accept the post). As part of the process of 'Islamization', the death penalty was introduced, alcohol and narcotics were banned and the wearing of strict Islamic dress by all women was enforced. Despite Mojaddedi's repeated pleas to Hekmatyar and his followers to lay down their arms, Hekmatyar, who was particularly angered by the presence of Gen. Dostam's Uzbek forces in the capital, continued to bombard Kabul with artillery and indiscriminate rocket launches from various strongholds around the city, killing and wounding scores of citizens.

On 28 June 1992 Mojaddedi surrendered power to the Leadership Council, which immediately offered Burhanuddin Rabbani the presidency of the country and the concomitant responsibility for the interim Council of Ministers for four months, as set forth in the Peshawar Agreement (see above). In early July Farid assumed the premiership, which had been held open for him since late April. On assuming the presidency Rabbani announced the adoption of a new Islamic flag, the establishment of an economic council, which was to address the country's severe economic problems, and the appointment of a commission to draw up a new constitution. A Deputy President was appointed in late July. In early August the withdrawal of the members of the Hizb-i Islami faction led by Maulvi Muhammad Yunus Khalis from the Leadership Council revealed serious rifts within the Government. A further problem was the continuing inter-*mujahidin* violence in Kabul. Within days the violence had escalated into a full-scale ground offensive, launched by Hekmatyar's forces against the capital. The airport was closed, hundreds of people were killed or wounded, and tens of thousands of civilians fled Kabul. In response, President Rabbani expelled Hekmatyar from the Leadership Council and dismissed Prime Minister Farid. Hekmatyar demanded the expulsion of the 75,000 Uzbek militia from Kabul as a precondition to peace talks, alleging that Gen. Dostam was still closely allied to former members of the communist regime. At the end of the month a cease-fire agreement was reached between Rabbani and Hekmatyar and, after a few days of relative peacefulness, the airport was reopened. Sporadic fighting involving various *mujahidin* and militia groups (notably Gen. Dostam's Uzbek forces) continued, however, in Kabul itself and in the provinces throughout the remainder of the year. At the end of October the Leadership Council agreed to extend Rabbani's tenure of the presidency by two months. On 30 December a special advisory council, known as the Resolution and Settlement Council (Shura-e Ahl-e Hal wa Aqd), which was composed of 1,335 tribal leaders, was convened in Kabul. The Council elected Rabbani, who was the sole candidate, as President of the country for a period of a further two years. In early January 1993 200 members of the advisory council were selected to constitute the future membership of the country's legislature.

The establishment of the advisory council and the re-election of President Rabbani provoked yet further heavy fighting in Kabul and other provinces in early 1993. Owing to the worsening violence, all Western diplomats had left the capital by the end of January. In early March, however, President Rabbani, Hekmatyar, Mojaddedi and leaders of other major *mujahidin* factions held negotiations in Islamabad, Pakistan, at the end of which a peace accord was signed. Under the terms of the accord, an interim Government was to be established, which would hold power for 18 months; President Rabbani was to remain as Head of State, and Hekmatyar (or his nominee) was to assume the premiership of the acting Council of Ministers; a cease-fire was to be imposed with immediate effect; legislative elections were to be held within six months; a 16-member defence commission was to be formed, which would be responsible for the establishment of a national army; and all weaponry was to be seized from the warring factions in an attempt to restore peace and order. The peace accord was officially approved and signed by the Governments of Pakistan, Saudi Arabia and Iran.

Confronted with the difficult task of satisfying the demands of all the *mujahidin* groups, Hekmatyar was not able to present a new Council of Ministers until late May 1993 (it was sworn in the following month). Each *mujahidin* faction was allocated two ministerial posts, with further positions left vacant for other representatives (representatives from Gen. Dostam's group of predominantly Uzbek militiamen—known collectively as the National Islamic Movement (NIM) (Jonbesh-i Melli-i Islami)—were offered two posts in July). One of Hekmatyar's most noteworthy decisions in the formation of the new Council of Ministers was to remove one of his most powerful rivals, Ahmad Shah Masoud, from the crucial post of Minister of Defence. The new Prime Minister promised to hold a general election by October. The temporary headquarters of the Government were situated in Charasiab, Hekmatyar's military base, about 25 km south of Kabul.

Despite the signing of the Islamabad peace accord in March 1993, the violence between the various *mujahidin* groups did not cease, and hundreds of people continued to be killed and wounded. The interim Government was beset by internal dissension and proved rather ineffectual. Hekmatyar refused to co-operate with Rabbani, and frequently demanded the President's resignation. In September, however, it was reported that a new draft Constitution (known as the Basic Law) had been drawn up and approved by a special commission, in preparation for the holding of a general election. The fighting intensified in late December, when Gen. Dostam transferred his allegiance to his hitherto arch-enemy, Hekmatyar, and the supporters of the two combined to confront the forces of Rabbani and Masoud. The violence spread throughout the provinces, resulting in large numbers of military and civilian casualties and the internal displacement of thousands of people. Various unsuccessful attempts were made in 1994 by neighbouring countries and by international organizations, such as the UN and the OIC, to achieve a negotiated settlement between the main warring factions. In late June the Supreme Court ruled that Rabbani could retain the presidency for a further six months, but failed to grant a similar extension to Hekmatyar's premiership. Although President Rabbani's extended term in office expired at the end of December, he did not resign.

In the latter half of 1994, a new, hitherto unknown, militant grouping emerged in Afghanistan, known as the Taliban (the plural form of 'Talib', meaning 'seeker of religious knowledge'). The movement, which at the outset comprised an estimated 25,000 fighters (the majority of whom were reported to be young Pashtun graduates of fundamentalist Islamist schools established by Afghan refugees in Pakistan), advocated the adoption of extremist practices, including the complete seclusion of women from society. Although initially claiming that they had no interest in actually assuming power in Afghanistan, the Taliban, who were led by Mullah Mohammad Omar, won a major victory in October, when they captured the city of Qandahar from the forces of Hekmatyar, which had hitherto dominated the southern provinces of the country. In February 1995 the Taliban routed Hekmatyar's men from their headquarters in Charasiab, and within a month they controlled 10 provinces, mostly in southern and south-eastern Afghanistan. However, the Taliban retreated from their advance on Kabul when Rabbani's troops launched a massive counter-offensive. By mid-1995, with both the Taliban and Hekmatyar's men held in check, President Rabbani and his supporters were enjoying an unprecedented level of authority and confidence in Kabul and its

environs. This was reflected in Rabbani's reneging on his earlier promise of standing down from the presidency in late March and in the growing number of countries that were considering reopening their embassies in the Afghan capital (the Indian embassy reopened in May). In mid-1995 talks were held between Rabbani and the Taliban, but relations between the two sides remained extremely strained. In early September the Taliban achieved a notable gain when they captured the key north-western city of Herat and the surrounding province from government forces. The resurgence of the Taliban apparently provoked an attack on the Pakistani embassy in Kabul by hundreds of pro-Government demonstrators protesting against Pakistan's alleged support for the student militia; the embassy was destroyed by fire, one employee was killed and a number wounded (including the ambassador himself). In response, the Afghan ambassador to Pakistan and six other Afghan diplomats were expelled from Islamabad. In October the Taliban launched a massive ground and air assault on Kabul, but by early January 1996 had failed to breach the capital's defences. The constant bombardment of the besieged city, however, resulted in hundreds of civilian deaths, and the road blockades around the capital caused serious shortages of vital supplies.

Despite the holding of exploratory negotiations between the Rabbani Government and major opposition parties in the first quarter of 1996, the fighting in and around Kabul intensified. The President's attempts at conciliation finally proved successful, however, in late May when, in a critical development (known as the Mahipar Agreement), he persuaded Hekmatyar to rejoin the Government. Hekmatyar's forces arrived in the capital during May to defend the city against the Taliban. In late June Hekmatyar resumed the post of Prime Minister and President Rabbani appointed a new Council of Ministers in early July, which was to hold power for a period of six–12 months pending the staging of a general election. In addition, under the terms of the Mahipar Agreement, a Constitution to cover the interim period was drawn up and published.

The political situation was radically altered in late September 1996 when, as a culmination of two weeks of sweeping military advances (including the capture of the crucial eastern city of Jalalabad), the Taliban seized control of Kabul following fierce clashes with government troops, who fled northwards together with the deposed Government. One of the Taliban movement's first actions in the captured capital was the summary execution of former President Najibullah and his brother. On assuming power, the Taliban declared Afghanistan a 'complete' Islamic state and appointed an interim Council of Ministers, led by Mullah Mohammad Rabbani, to administer the country (of which it now controlled about two-thirds). Pakistan, which was widely suspected of actively aiding the Islamist militia, was the first country officially to recognize the new regime. (By mid-November, however, few other countries or international organizations had followed suit—neither the UN, India, Russia nor Iran had given official recognition to the Taliban administration.) The Taliban imposed a strict and intimidatory Islamic code—women were not permitted to enter employment or be formally educated beyond the age of eight years; television, non-religious music, gambling and alcohol were all banned; amputations and public stonings were enforced as forms of punishment; compulsory attendance at mosques by all men was introduced; and women were ordered into purdah.

Taliban hopes that the opposition would remain divided were thwarted following the formation in October 1996 of a powerful military and logistical alliance by Gen. Dostam, the former Minister of Defence, Masoud, and the leader of the Shi'a Hizb-i Wahadat-i Islami, Gen. Abdol Karim Khalili. Gen. Dostam, who controlled six northern provinces, apparently decided to establish this unlikely alliance after cease-fire talks between himself and the Taliban broke down. By late October the anti-Taliban forces, whose leaders were now collectively known as the Supreme Council for the Defence of Afghanistan (the headquarters of which were situated in Gen. Dostam's stronghold of Mazar-i-Sharif), had launched a concerted offensive against Kabul in the hope of ousting the Islamist militia. Despite repeated calls for a cease-fire from various foreign governments and the UN and despite complaints by the human rights organization Amnesty International regarding civilian casualties and abuses of human rights, the fighting between the Taliban and the allied opposition continued into January 1997. In mid-January, following the rapid collapse of UN-sponsored talks in Islamabad, the Taliban launched an unexpected offensive, advancing north and capturing Bagram air base and the provincial capital of Charikar. By late January the Taliban had made significant military gains and had pushed the front line to about 100 km north of Kabul. There was a dramatic development in mid-May when, following the defection of the Uzbek Gen. Abdul Malik and his men to the Taliban, the latter were able to capture the strategically important northern town of Mazar-i-Sharif with relatively little bloodshed. Gen. Dostam was reported to have fled to Turkey, and his position as leader of the NIM was assumed by Gen. Malik. The Taliban now controlled about 80% of the country, including all of the major towns and cities. Their position was also strengthened by Pakistan's decision to be the first country to accord formal recognition to the Taliban Government (closely followed by Saudi Arabia and the United Arab Emirates—UAE). Taliban control of Mazar-i-Sharif, however, was extremely brief, and within only three days of entering the town the movement was in full retreat. It appeared that Gen. Malik's tenuous alliance with the Taliban had collapsed almost immediately and his troops, together with Shi'a militia, forced the newcomers out after ferocious fighting. The Taliban were soundly routed, and by early June their forces had retreated almost 200 km south of Mazar-i-Sharif.

The regional aspect of the Afghan conflict was highlighted at the beginning of June 1997 by the Taliban decision to close down the Iranian embassy in Kabul; the Iranian Government was widely suspected of actively aiding the anti-Taliban northern alliance. The alliance was reported to have been expanded and strengthened in early June by the inclusion of the forces of Hekmatyar and of the Mahaz-i-Melli-i-Islami (National Islamic Front), led by Pir Sayed Ahmad Gailani. This new coalition, which superseded the Supreme Council for the Defence of Afghanistan, was known as the United National Islamic Front for the Salvation of Afghanistan, commonly known as the United Front and the Northern Alliance. The United Front was the military wing of the exiled Government, the 'Islamic State of Afghanistan'. Despite the arrival of thousands of reinforcements from training camps in Pakistan (many of whom, however, were inexperienced teenagers), the Taliban suffered a series of military defeats in northern Afghanistan, and by late July the United Front forces were within firing range of Kabul, having recaptured Charikar and the air base at Bagram. In the same month the UN Security Council demanded a cease-fire and an end to all foreign intervention in Afghanistan. In mid-1997 it was widely believed that the Taliban were supported by Pakistan and Saudi Arabia; on the opposing side, to various degrees, were ranged Iran, India, the Central Asian states (which feared the encroachment of Taliban fundamentalism) and Russia.

In mid-August 1997 it was reported that the United Front had appointed a new Government, based in Mazar-i-Sharif, with Rabbani continuing as President, Abdorrahim Ghafurzai as Prime Minister, Masoud as Minister of Defence and Gen. Malik as Minister of Foreign Affairs. The former Prime Minister in the anti-Taliban administration, Gulbuddin Hekmatyar, refused to recognize the new Government. Within a few days of its appointment, however, seven members of the new Government, including Prime Minister Ghafurzai, were killed in an aeroplane crash. In late August the anti-Taliban opposition alliance appointed Abdolghaffur Rawanfarhadi as the new Prime Minister.

In September 1997 Gen. Dostam was reported to have returned to Mazar-i-Sharif from Turkey, and in the following month the member parties of the United Front re-elected him as commander of the forces of the alliance and appointed him as Vice-President of the anti-Taliban administration. However, there were reports of a bitter rivalry between Gen. Dostam and Gen. Malik and skirmishes between their respective forces. Dostam's battle for supremacy with his rival led him to make overtures to the Taliban, including offers of exchanges of prisoners-of-war. Gen. Dostam also accused Gen. Malik of having massacred about 3,000 Taliban prisoners earlier in the year. By late November Gen. Dostam had resumed the leadership of the NIM, ousting Gen. Malik. In late October the Taliban unilaterally decided to change the country's name to the Islamic Emirate of Afghanistan and altered the state flag, moves that were condemned by the opposition alliance and all of Afghanistan's neighbours except Pakistan. In late 1997 the World Food Programme (WFP) launched an emergency operation to help people facing starvation in the impoverished central region of Hazarajat (held by the Shi'a Hizb-i Wahadat-i Islami), which had been blockaded by the Taliban since August. In January 1998, however, the UN was forced to suspend its airlifts of emergency supplies when Taliban aircraft bombed the area.

Meanwhile, in mid-December 1997 the UN Security Council issued a communiqué expressing its concern at the alleged massacres of civilians and prisoners-of-war being perpetrated by various factions in Afghanistan. In May 1998 a UN exploratory mission visited the sites of alleged atrocities to assess the feasibility of a full-scale war-crimes investigation being carried out.

In late March 1998 the UN ceased operating aid programmes in the southern province of Qandahar (where the political headquarters of the Taliban were located) following attacks on staff and constant harassment by the Taliban. In the same month there were reports of factional fighting between rival members of the United Front in and around Mazar-i-Sharif, highlighting the fragile nature of the anti-Taliban alliance. In late April, following the launch of a major diplomatic initiative by the USA, the Taliban and the United Front held talks, sponsored by the UN and the OIC, in Islamabad, the first formal peace negotiations between the two opposing sides for more than a year. In early May, however, the talks broke down, and fighting resumed to the north of Kabul. One of the main reasons cited for the failure of the negotiations was the refusal of the Taliban to lift the blockade on Hazarajat, where thousands of people were reported to be at risk of imminent starvation.

Relations between the Taliban Government and the UN deteriorated in June 1998, as a result of the former's decision to close more than 100 private schools and numerous small, home-based vocational courses in Kabul, many of which were educating girls. The living conditions of the 1.2m. inhabitants of the capital were expected to worsen considerably as a result of the expulsion in July of almost all international aid agencies by the Taliban.

On 1 August 1998 the Taliban captured the northern city of Shiberghan, Gen. Dostam's new headquarters, after a number of his Uzbek commanders allegedly accepted bribes from the Taliban and switched allegiance. Gen. Dostam was reported to have fled to the Uzbek border and thence to Turkey. Following the recapture of Mazar-i-Sharif by the Taliban (who allegedly now included considerable numbers of extremist volunteers from various other Islamic countries, including Pakistan, Saudi Arabia, Algeria and Egypt) in early August, 10 Iranian diplomats and one Iranian journalist who were based in the city were reported to have been captured and killed by Taliban militia. The Taliban, however, initially denied any knowledge of the whereabouts of the Iranian nationals. In early September Afghanistan and Iran appeared to be on the verge of open warfare, as 70,000 Iranian troops were deployed on the mutual border, and it emerged that nine of the missing Iranian nationals had, in fact, been murdered by members of the Taliban as they stormed Mazar-i-Sharif. (It was later reported that 2,000–6,000 Shi'a Hazara civilians had been systematically massacred by the guerrillas after recapturing the city.) Both Iran and Afghanistan massed more troops on the border; by mid-September 500,000 Iranian troops had reportedly been placed on full military alert. In mid-October, in an attempt to defuse the tension, the Taliban agreed to free all Iranian prisoners being held in Afghanistan and to punish those responsible for the killing of the nine Iranian diplomats (or military advisers, according to the Taliban). By the end of the year the situation appeared much calmer, with the Taliban having expressed regret for the deaths of the Iranian nationals and Iran having scaled down its border forces and having announced that it had no intention of invading Afghanistan.

Meanwhile, on 20 August 1998 the USA launched simultaneous air-strikes against alleged terrorist bases in eastern Afghanistan and Sudan, reportedly operated by the Saudi-born militant leader of the al-Qa'ida (Base) organization, Osama bin Laden (who was supported by the Taliban), in retaliation for the bombing of two US embassies in East Africa earlier that month. Many aid agencies withdrew their remaining expatriate staff from Afghanistan, fearing terrorist acts of vengeance. In September the Taliban suffered a considerable set-back when Saudi Arabia (one of only three countries officially to recognize the regime) withdrew its funding and political support and recalled its envoy from Kabul. The decision by the Saudi Government substantially to downgrade its relations with the Taliban appeared to have been prompted by its opposition to the reported brutality of the guerrilla authorities and to their sheltering of bin Laden. In the following month the Taliban stated that, although they were not willing to extradite the Saudi dissident, in the event of a lawsuit being filed against him, they would be prepared to place him on trial in Afghanistan. The

Taliban also insisted that bin Laden (who had reportedly been resident in Afghanistan for at least two years) was under close supervision, with his activities and media access suitably restricted. In late November evidence submitted by the US Government to the Afghan Supreme Court was deemed by the latter as inadequate grounds for bin Laden's arrest.

In mid-September 1998 the Taliban captured the capital of Bamian province, a Shi'a stronghold; this victory meant that any substantial anti-Taliban opposition was effectively restricted to Masoud's stronghold in north-eastern Afghanistan. Taliban advances in the north alarmed Russia and the Central Asian states, which feared the unsettling potential of a militant Islamist army along their southern borders. In December the UN Security Council threatened the Taliban with the imposition of sanctions and called on the regime to commence negotiations with the opposition. Pakistan, on the other hand, demonstrated its diplomatic isolation with regard to the Afghan situation, by defending the Taliban and urging the other members of the UN to recognize their Government.

In January 1999 it was reported that the United Front had established a multi-ethnic Supreme Military Council, under the command of Masoud, the aim of which was to give fresh impetus to the anti-Taliban movement and to co-ordinate manoeuvres against Taliban forces in northern Afghanistan. Despite a certain degree of optimism being raised by the holding of UN-monitored direct peace talks between representatives of the Taliban and the United Front in February, March and July, ultimately very little was achieved as a result of the negotiations. In March, however, the first UN personnel returned to Afghanistan since their evacuation in August 1998 (following the murder of three UN employees); this represented the beginning of a phased return of UN international staff to Afghanistan.

In July 1999, following reports that bin Laden was being sheltered in eastern Afghanistan, the USA imposed financial and economic sanctions on the Taliban regime in a further attempt to persuade it to hand over the militant leader (who the US authorities suspected of planning more atrocities) to stand trial in the USA. In response, the Taliban claimed that the sanctions would have very little impact and again refused to extradite bin Laden.

The Taliban continued to campaign for international recognition, to no avail. At the 1999 session of the UN General Assembly (held in September–November) the UN again rejected the Taliban request to represent Afghanistan; the seat remained under the control of President Rabbani, the leader of the 'Islamic State of Afghanistan'. In October 1999 the UN Secretary-General's Special Envoy to Afghanistan, Lakhdar Brahimi, announced his withdrawal from his mission, owing to the lack of progress (and particularly to the alleged negative attitude of the Taliban). In February 2000 Francesc Vendrell was appointed Head of the UN Special Mission to Afghanistan and Personal Representative of the UN Secretary-General, with the rank of Assistant Secretary-General. Relations between the UN and Afghanistan, however, remained tense, culminating in the UN's temporary withdrawal of its expatriate staff from Qandahar at the end of March, following an assault on UN offices by the Taliban.

In mid-November 1999 the UN Security Council imposed an embargo on all Taliban-controlled overseas assets and a ban on the international flights of the national airline, Ariana Afghan Airlines, as a result of the Afghan regime's continuing refusal to relinquish the suspected terrorist leader, bin Laden, to stand trial in the USA or in a third (possibly Islamic) country. Following the imposition of the sanctions, there were reports of large-scale demonstrations throughout Afghanistan, and international aid organizations once again came under attack. The impact of the sanctions was expected to be alleviated, however, by the reopening of key trade routes along the Afghan–Iranian border in late November. The Taliban Government expressed hopes that the trade with Iran would compensate for the significant decrease in imports of wheat and flour from Pakistan caused by the recent imposition of stricter border controls by the new military regime in Pakistan. Although the price of basic foodstuffs in Kabul and other towns duly declined dramatically as a result of renewed trade with Iran, the general economic circumstances in Kabul worsened. In February 2000 the UN relaxed the sanctions to permit the Taliban to operate flights to Mecca, in Saudi Arabia. In October an agreement was signed to allow weekly flights from Sharjah, in the UAE, to Qandahar, in southern Afghanistan.

During 2000 the Taliban and United Front suffered internal discord, with defections of senior officials occurring on both sides. In March a partial reorganization of the Taliban Interim Council of Ministers was announced. Heavy fighting, concentrated in the north of Kabul, resumed in early March. In the same month the military commander Ismail Khan escaped from prison in Qandahar and fled to Iran. The OIC hosted peace negotiations between representatives of the Taliban and the United Front in March and May, during which the two parties decided to exchange prisoners-of-war. No agreement, however, was reached on a cease-fire. In early June there was renewed fighting in northern and central Afghanistan, and by the end of July the Taliban had acquired more territory in the north of the country. As the fighting intensified throughout August, the Taliban became more confident of victory in the north, reopening training camps that had been previously closed down owing to international pressure.

At the beginning of September 2000 the Taliban captured Taloqan, the capital of Takhar province in the north of Afghanistan and the headquarters of the United Front. This victory represented a serious military and political set-back for Masoud and the United Front. In December the Taliban and the United Front entered negotiations conducted by Francesc Vendrell. Meanwhile, the conflict exacerbated the effects of severe drought and famine, which the country had endured from early 2000.

Despite renewed attempts by the Taliban from September 2000 to end their diplomatic isolation, the UN continued to refute the Taliban claim to the Afghan seat at the UN. In December the UN Security Council passed a resolution, which stated that unless the Taliban surrendered bin Laden and closed down militant training camps by 19 January 2001, the international community would impose an arms embargo on the Taliban, tighten an existing embargo on flights and the 'freeze' on Taliban assets abroad, restrict the sale of chemicals used to produce heroin from poppies and close Ariana Afghan Airlines offices abroad. The weapons embargo would not affect the anti-Taliban forces. The Taliban refused to concede to the demands and, immediately after the UN's decision, shut down the UN special mission to Afghanistan and cancelled planned peace negotiations. By early January 2001 24 of the original 64 UN foreign workers had returned to Kabul. The sanctions were imposed in mid-January. Consequently, Francesc Vendrell's attempts to persuade the Taliban and their opposition to participate in open-ended negotiations collapsed.

In February 2001 the Taliban ordered the destruction of all statues in Afghanistan depicting living creatures, including the world's tallest standing Buddhas in Bamian. Despite intense international opposition, destruction of Afghanistan's pre-Islamic cultural heritage was carried out in March. However, Hindu and Sikh statues, acknowledged as fundamental to the respective religious practices, were preserved. The order contravened a 1999 decree, which ordered the preservation of all ancient relics, thereby prompting speculation that members of bin Laden's al-Qa'ida had taken control of the Taliban, by ousting the more moderate leaders.

In mid-April 2001 the Chairman of the Taliban Interim Council of Ministers, and Gen. Commander of the Armed Forces of the Taliban, Mullah Mohammad Rabbani, died, owing to illness. He was later replaced as Gen. Commander by his brother, Mullah Ahmed. In May all UN political staff left Afghanistan in accordance with a Taliban order, a consequence of fresh sanctions imposed on the Taliban in January. At the end of the month the Taliban issued a decree commanding all non-Muslim minorities to display distinctive yellow badges or cloths as marks of identification. Sikhs were distinguished by their turbans and were thus not required to identify themselves. This pronouncement provoked international outrage; the Taliban defended their decision, claiming that they intended to prevent the unnecessary detention of non-Muslims for not conducting Muslim practices. At the end of June, however, the Taliban yielded to international pressure and withdrew their controversial decree. The militant policies of the Taliban caused increasing difficulties for humanitarian agencies. In June WFP threatened to close down its 130 bakeries in Kabul unless the Taliban withdrew their restriction on the employment of Afghan women to conduct an essential survey of food requirements in the capital. However, WFP was faced with a dilemma: although the employment of women was forbidden, male employees were not allowed direct contact with females. A compromise was reached to allow the bakeries to continue operating. In July the

Taliban issued another set of controversial edicts: the use of the internet was outlawed; women were banned from visiting picnic areas; and items such as tape recorders, telephone sets, musical instruments and lipstick were proscribed as non-Islamic.

In early August 2001 eight foreign and 16 Afghan aid workers of a German-based Christian non-governmental organization were arrested by the Taliban on charges of Christian proselytization. A trial under the rules of *Shari'a* (Islamic religious law) of the foreign aid workers began in early September. Shortly afterwards the Taliban offer to release the detained humanitarian workers in return for the release of Sheikh Omar Abdul Rahman, an Egyptian militant Islamist sentenced to life imprisonment in the USA, was rejected. Meanwhile, the Taliban closed down two other Christian aid organizations and ordered the foreign staff to leave the country.

At the end of June 2001 the US ambassador to Pakistan issued a statement in which he warned the Taliban that they would be held accountable if bin Laden carried out an attack against US interests. In response, the Taliban Minister of Foreign Affairs stated that the regime was not responsible for safeguarding US security outside Afghanistan. In late July the UN Security Council adopted a resolution which reinforced the sanctions imposed in January. Some 15 UN officials were to be posted in and around Afghanistan to monitor the success of the existing arms embargo. The resolution was censured for focusing solely on the Taliban and for failing to curb the United Front's arms supply.

Meanwhile, following the coup in Pakistan in October 1999, there were indications that relations between the Taliban and the new Pakistani administration, headed by Gen. Pervez Musharraf, might not prove as amicable as they had been since 1996. In his first major address to the Pakistani nation shortly after assuming power, Gen. Musharraf pledged to work for a 'truly representative government' in Afghanistan, and in the following month the State Bank of Pakistan complied with the UN sanctions in ordering a 'freeze' on all Taliban financial assets in Pakistan. In late January 2000, however, a delegation of the Islamic Emirate of Afghanistan, led by the Chairman of the Taliban Interim Council of Ministers, accepted a formal invitation to enter negotiations with Pakistani officials. Pakistan continued to offer economic aid and support to the Taliban and condemned the UN sanctions against Afghanistan. Although Gen. Musharraf strongly denied giving military assistance to the Taliban, allegations relating to the involvement of Pakistan's special forces in the Taliban campaign grew, following the latter's successful offensive in August–September 2000.

On 9 September 2001 Masoud was seriously injured in an attack by suicide bombers; some six days later he died. His deputy, Gen. Muhammed Fahim, was appointed acting military leader of the United Front. Evidence that emerged from deserted al-Qa'ida camps following the fall of the Taliban in Kabul in mid-November indicated that the Arab suicide bombers were linked to bin Laden.

The situation in Afghanistan drastically changed as a result of the terrorist attacks on New York and Washington, DC, USA, on 11 September 2001. Although bin Laden denied his involvement in the attacks, some two days after the events the US Secretary of State, Colin Powell, publicly identified bin Laden and his al-Qa'ida organization as principally responsible. The Taliban initially claimed that neither bin Laden nor Afghanistan had the means to carry out the attacks, warning that they would retaliate if the USA attacked Afghanistan. On 16 September the UN imposed diplomatic sanctions and an arms embargo on the Taliban. Meanwhile, the USA began to form an anti-terrorism coalition, with the assistance of the United Kingdom.

Pakistan, a supporter of the Taliban, under considerable pressure reversed its policy and agreed to co-operate with the US-led coalition. On 17 September 2001 a Pakistani delegation issued Taliban leaders with an ultimatum to surrender bin Laden or face retaliation from the USA. A few days later a *shura* of Afghan clerics under the leadership of Mullah Mohammad Omar issued an edict for bin Laden to leave Afghanistan voluntarily. The *shura* also demanded that the UN and OIC held independent investigations, and threatened to instigate a *jihad* (holy war) if the USA attacked Afghanistan. US officials, calling for unconditional surrender, considered the edict insufficient. At the same time, US President George W. Bush warned that the Taliban would also be targeted if they refused to extradite bin Laden and the rest of al-Qa'ida. It remained highly improbable that the Taliban would surrender bin Laden. Al-Qa'ida had

become increasingly involved in Taliban affairs: in late August bin Laden reportedly was appointed Commander-in-Chief of the Taliban forces.

In the mean time, the USA deployed aircraft around Afghanistan, in preparation for attack. The Taliban responded to the developments with preparations for *jihad*. On 26 September 2001 thousands of protesters set fire to the abandoned US embassy in Kabul. The next day Taliban officials announced that an edict had been delivered to bin Laden ordering him to leave the country. The US Government dismissed the edict and restated demands for the Taliban to surrender bin Laden to the US authorities. The USA also rejected an offer by Mullah Mohammad Omar to enter negotiations regarding the extradition of bin Laden.

The United Front had suffered a serious set-back when Masoud was shot days before the terrorist attacks. However, speculation that it would receive military assistance from the anti-terrorism coalition as a result of the likely military intervention in Afghanistan encouraged the anti-Taliban coalition, which reported military successes against the Taliban in late September 2001. In early October there were reports that the USA was militarily assisting anti-Taliban groups within Afghanistan.

The Taliban reportedly repeated their request to enter negotiations with the US-led coalition in early October 2001, an offer rejected by the US President. Meanwhile, the Taliban continued forcibly to conscript men to bolster their army, which in early October numbered 40,000 fighters. There were reports that al-Qa'ida provided the Taliban with several thousand fighters. In the mean time, the trial of the foreign aid workers continued. On 6 October an offer by a Taliban official to release the detainees in exchange for the withdrawal of the US-led military threats was dismissed. In mid-November the aid workers were rescued by anti-Taliban fighters and flown by helicopter to Pakistan.

On 12 September 2001 the UN and other aid organizations began to remove their foreign staff from Afghanistan, owing to fears that the USA would launch retaliatory attacks against al-Qa'ida and the Taliban. Less than two weeks later the Taliban seized the UN Kabul office and shut down the Afghan communications network. The number of displaced people increased considerably; although accurate estimates of new refugees were not known, some reports estimated that 1.5m. Afghans had abandoned their homes in the latter half of September. Pakistan restricted entry to those at the border considered to be most in need of assistance. Thousands of refugees managed to enter Pakistan illegally, nevertheless. At the end of September communications were restored with Afghan humanitarian workers. WFP resumed emergency food deliveries to Kabul and Herat and northern Afghanistan on a trial basis; local aid workers were expected to distribute the aid. At the same time the Red Cross transported medical supplies to Kabul. In early October the US President announced a humanitarian aid programme for Afghans in order to undermine the Taliban and to show Muslim countries that the USA was planning war against terrorism and not Islam. However, the proposal to link humanitarian aid with a pending military operation concerned humanitarian organizations.

On the evening of 7 October 2001 US-led forces began the aerial bombardment of suspected al-Qa'ida camps and strategic Taliban positions in Afghanistan. In addition to military strikes, aircraft released food and medicine parcels to Afghan civilians near the southern border with Pakistan; leaflets were also dropped offering protection and a reward in return for information on the whereabouts of al-Qa'ida leaders. Mullah Mohammad Omar responded by appealing to all Muslims to help defend Afghanistan, and as a result several thousand pupils of *madrassas* (mosque schools) in Pakistan and some Arab countries arrived in Afghanistan during October. A pre-recorded videotape of bin Laden's response to the military strikes was broadcast by the Qatar-based satellite television company Al-Jazeera. In the recording bin Laden declared war on the 'infidels' and warned the USA that attacks against it would continue until it withdrew from the Middle East. Although he did not claim responsibility for the attacks, bin Laden's comments were widely seen to be an implicit admission of his organization's involvement. Bin Laden also encouraged Muslims in countries that had offered assistance to the anti-terrorism coalition to rebel against their Governments, thus provoking the sentiment that the US-led military strikes were against Afghanistan and Islam, as opposed to terrorism.

The US-led military operation, named 'Operation Enduring Freedom', achieved rapid results. After 10 days President George W. Bush announced that the Taliban regime's air defences had been destroyed. The nature of the attack changed when US and British ground forces, with Russian assistance, began an assault on Afghanistan on 20 October 2001. Some three days later it was announced that all of the identified al-Qa'ida training camps had been destroyed by air-strikes. The US-led military operation, however, also incurred failures, which resulted in civilian deaths. Evidence of civilian casualties adversely affected support for the US-led military operation. Saudi Arabia, which had hitherto remained silent about the military strikes, voiced its discontent in mid-October. In addition, tension rose in Pakistan; thousands of pro-Taliban fighters attempted to cross the border into Afghanistan. The USA's strategy also concerned members of the United Front; the bombing had not transformed the military balance in Afghanistan and by the end of October the United Front forces were still outnumbered. Nevertheless, rival commanders in the United Front launched a joint assault against the Taliban to recapture Mazar-i-Sharif and Taloqan. US servicemen were also killed in the conflict.

Initially, the US-led coalition avoided targeting Kabul in order to prevent the fractious United Front from capturing the capital. There were fears that while no alternative transitional government existed, the defeat of the Taliban in Kabul and other major cities would leave a power vacuum, resulting in anarchy. Some members of the United Front also voiced their concerns over occupying Kabul without a mandate; however, others regarded this strategy as a US-Pakistani plot to prevent the anti-Taliban opposition from advancing on Kabul and began to plan an early assault. In the mean time, the USA, the United Kingdom, other UN Security Council members and countries neighbouring Afghanistan began discussions for a broad-based transitional government for Afghanistan. At a meeting of United Front leaders in mid-October 2001 it was decided that the alliance would postpone an attack on Kabul for at least one month. At the same time, a delegation headed by the moderate religious leader, Pir Sayed Ahmad Gailani, held negotiations with the former King, Zahir Shah, in Rome, Italy, during which Gailani agreed to create a council, to be led by the former King. However, a meeting of more than 1,000 exiled Afghan commanders and tribal elders, chaired by Gailani, in Pakistan in late October revealed deep divisions between rival opposition groups. Some warned against the inclusion of the United Front, which was mainly composed of Tajiks, Uzbeks and Hazaras, in a transitional government that was to represent a majority Pashtun population. Senior representatives of the United Front and the former King were absent from the assembly. The outcome of the meeting caused grave concern for Western Governments and the UN; many believed that Pakistan had sanctioned the conference in an attempt to encourage a resolute stand against support given by the West to the United Front. Plans to establish an alternative transitional council were hampered further by the capture and assassination of the Pashtun leader Abdul Haq by the Taliban. Haq entered Afghanistan on 21 October to attempt to mobilize Pashtuns to rebel against the Taliban; he was killed five days later.

The UN Secretary-General appointed a special representative for Afghanistan, Lakhdar Brahimi, to assist the formation of a transitional government. His first task was to negotiate an agreement between Afghanistan's neighbours regarding the council's composition. The USA had already requested the UN to supply a peace-keeping force that could secure Kabul; the UN refused, stating that it could not become involved while the war continued. Meanwhile, the humanitarian situation worsened. On 10 October 2001 the UN resumed food aid. At the same time, the number of Afghan refugees attempting to leave the country increased dramatically; in early November UNHCR estimated that 135,000 refugees had entered Pakistan since the suicide attacks on the USA.

In early November 2001 attacks against the Taliban in northern Afghanistan escalated. On 9 November the United Front captured Mazar-i-Sharif and continued to seize almost all of northern Afghanistan at an astonishing pace. The USA, United Kingdom and Pakistan advised the United Front not to enter Kabul until a leadership council was formed; however, on the night of 12 November the Taliban fled the capital and the next day, facing very little resistance, the United Front took over Kabul. Although the United Front immediately requested assistance from the US-led coalition to create a transitional govern-

ment, it was impossible to do so while the majority Pashtun ethnic group remained under-represented. The USA and Pakistan hitherto had failed to attract defectors from the Pashtun Taliban leadership to join the council; in addition, US-led forces had given little support to anti-Taliban Pashtun leaders attempting to capture southern Afghanistan. Commanders of the United Front were soon in disagreement over the running of provinces in northern Afghanistan. Anti-Taliban forces from all ethnic backgrounds quickly advanced on southern Afghanistan and by the end of November had captured the Taliban stronghold of Kunduz. Unlike the factions belonging to the United Front, these groups were not united under a political alliance.

On 27 November 2001 the UN hosted a conference of 28 Afghan leaders representing the United Front, the Rome Group led by Zahir Shah, the pro-Iranian Cyprus Process and the Pakistan-backed Peshawar process (composed of Pashtun exiles and headed by Gailani), as well as other leading figures, in Bonn, Germany. On 5 December the leaders signed the Agreement on Provisional Arrangements in Afghanistan Pending the Re-establishment of Permanent Government Institutions, also known as the Bonn Agreement, stipulating the establishment of a 30-member multi-ethnic Interim Authority to preside for six months from 22 December. A Pashtun tribal chief, Hamid Karzai, was named Chairman of the Interim Authority, which was to comprise 11 Pashtuns, eight Tajiks, five Hazaras, three Uzbeks and three members of smaller tribal and religious groups. The United Front received the most seats; three of the leading members, Younis Qanooni, Gen. Muhammed Fahim and Dr Abdullah Abdullah, were allocated the interior, defence and foreign affairs portfolios, respectively. Two female doctors were also granted posts in the executive council. Some leaders who were excluded from the government were dissatisfied with the outcome, including the former President Burhanuddin.

The Taliban regime's sole official contact with the outside world ended in late November 2001, when Pakistan severed all diplomatic links with the Taliban and closed their last remaining embassy. On 7 December the remaining members of the Taliban finally surrendered Qandahar and disappeared, marking the end of the Taliban regime. In the mean time, US ground forces were strengthened in an effort to find bin Laden and his supporters. Following unconfirmed reports that bin Laden and Mullah Mohammad Omar were hiding in the Tora Bora caves with the rest of the Islamist forces, the US-led coalition and United Front intensified the air and ground assault on the cave complex. However, after much of the region had been destroyed, there was no sign of the two leaders and their close associates. Some unconfirmed reports suggested that bin Laden had fled to Pakistan. Meanwhile, the USA and its allies continued to search for remaining Taliban and al-Qa'ida forces in Afghanistan. On 9 December WFP began a massive aid distribution programme in Kabul. The reopening of the Friendship Bridge between Afghanistan and Uzbekistan on the same day was a momentous occasion and provided humanitarian agencies with a much-needed route by which to transport supplies. However, the poor weather conditions hampered the international relief campaign and most rural areas remained inaccessible, owing to safety concerns. Meanwhile, following the defeat of the Taliban regime, tens of thousands of refugees began to return to Afghanistan.

On 22 December 2001 the Interim Authority was inaugurated; Karzai was sworn in as Chairman. The country returned to the Constitution of 1964, which combined *Shari'a* with Western concepts of justice. One of Karzai's first decisions was to appoint Gen. Dostam, who initially boycotted the Government in protest at his exclusion, as Vice-Chairman and Deputy Minister of Defence. At the end of December the UN Security Council authorized, as envisaged in the Bonn Agreement, the deployment of an International Security Assistance Force (ISAF) to help maintain security in Kabul over the next six months. Some 19 countries were authorized to form a 5,000-strong security force, led by the United Kingdom.

In January 2002 the international community agreed to donate US $4,500m. over two-and-a-half years towards the reconstruction of Afghanistan. Also in that month a 21-member Special Independent Commission for the Convening of the Emergency Loya Jirga (commonly known as the Loya Jirga Commission) was established to devise the selection process and conduct of the Emergency Loya Jirga. Deployment of the ISAF began in mid-January and remained confined to Kabul, despite Karzai's requests for the number of ISAF troops to be increased and the international force's mandate to be expanded to include security operations for the entire country. In May a UN Security Council Resolution approved the extension of the ISAF for six months beyond June. In June Turkey took over command of the security force. The ISAF participated in joint patrols with Afghan police and assisted in creating and training a new Afghan National Army (ANA). It was intended that the ANA would eventually be a force of some 60,000, supported by a border guard of 12,000 and an air force of 8,000. Meanwhile, however, regional military commanders continued to reorganize their own armies, preventing scarce resources from being sent to the ANA and making the task of creating a multi-ethnic national army even more difficult. In early 2002 reports were already emerging of fighting among ethnic groups. In mid-February the Minister of Civil Aviation and Tourism, Abdul Rahman, was assassinated by a rival faction within the Interim Authority. The murder of Rahman, a staunch supporter of Zahir Shah, was evidently an attempt to deter the former monarch from returning to Afghanistan. In early April the Interim Authority claimed to have prevented an attempt allegedly organized by Hekmatyar to assassinate Karzai. Government officials accused Hekmatyar of seeking to depose the Interim Authority and assume control. Despite security concerns, former King Zahir Shah returned to Afghanistan as a 'private citizen' on 18 April.

In mid-January 2002 Afghanistan's main route connecting Kabul with the north, the Salang Pass, was reopened for the first time in 10 years, following a clearance operation by Russian and French teams. At the same time UN sanctions imposed on Ariana Afghan Airlines were lifted. The Interim Authority issued a decree banning poppy cultivation and the processing, trafficking and abuse of opiates. In February, however, reports were emerging that the large-scale planting of poppies had already taken place during the collapse of law and order in late 2001. In early April 2002 the Interim Administration introduced a radical programme to eradicate the crop. In accordance with the scheme, farmers would receive compensation for destroying their opium crops; those who refused would have their land seized by the Government and risk prosecution. However, the offer of compensation did not compare well with the lucrative sale of opium, and farmers carried out violent demonstrations throughout the country against the initiative. Despite attempts by the Government and the UN to curb the drugs trade, the annual survey conducted by the UN Office on Drugs and Crime, published in October, reported that, owing to the planting of poppies in late 2001, Afghanistan had resumed its place as the world's biggest producer of opium.

The number of refugees returning in 2002 surpassed all expectations. In early April UNHCR reported that more than 50,000 Afghan refugees were returning from Pakistan every week. In the same month UNHCR and the Iranian Government embarked on a joint voluntary repatriation programme to facilitate the return of more than 400,000 Afghans from Iran. By early December that target had almost been reached. At the end of 2002 UNHCR announced that more than 1.5m. refugees had returned from Pakistan. An estimated 2.5m. refugees remained outside Afghanistan, including 1.1m. in Iran and 1.2m. in Pakistan. In September, however, concerns were raised that Afghanistan was incapable of meeting the nutritional requirements of its population. Officials estimated that only 20%–30% of the country's land was cultivated in 2002, largely owing to the fourth successive year of drought. The crisis was exacerbated by the lack of sufficient humanitarian assistance from the international donor community. The rapid return of refugees placed an even greater strain on the humanitarian programme. Some 80% of the funds provided by the international agencies had been allocated to humanitarian aid, thus leaving only 20% available for the country's reconstruction programme. In mid-September Japan, Saudi Arabia and the USA announced a joint aid programme worth US $180m. for the repair and improvement of roads throughout Afghanistan.

Internecine fighting escalated as tribal commanders attempted to consolidate territorial and political influence in preparation for the Loya Jirga. The human rights organization Human Rights Watch issued a report in March 2002 detailing a rise in incidents of violence, killing, rape and ethnic persecution in northern Afghanistan, particularly aimed at Pashtun villagers. Many of the commanders held responsible for the violence were supposed supporters of the Interim Authority. The USA and UN attempted to mediate between rival commanders as violent clashes between ethnic factions continued. In February the UN brokered an agreement between the leaders of the three feuding factions in northern and north-western Afghani-

stan, Gen. Dostam, Gen. Atta Mohammed and Mohammed Mohaqqeq, according to which a 600-strong security force was to be established in the region representing all three factions. However, factional fighting continued in the region and throughout Afghanistan.

In the mean time, the US-led coalition continued its search for the leaders of al-Qa'ida and the Taliban. In early February 2002 the former Taliban Minister of Foreign Affairs, Mawlawi Wakil Ahmad Motawakkil, surrendered himself to US forces in Qandahar. The search was often thwarted by the activities of regional Afghan (non-Taliban) military commanders. In early January, for example, the Interim Authority confirmed that seven senior Taliban members, who had surrendered to a local Afghan commander, had been released without the approval of the Interim Administration or the US-led coalition forces. 'Operation Anaconda', conducted by US-led forces against alleged Taliban and al-Qa'ida forces in the Shah-i Kot valley of Paktia province in March, was planned as a three-day assault, but developed into a 17-day conflict resulting in the deaths of coalition soldiers. Many al-Qa'ida and Taliban members fled to Khost province. US forces depended heavily on information provided by military commanders regarding the whereabouts of militant Islamists. This tactic was often to the USA's detriment, as complex tribal allegiances and enmities regularly dictated the type of information given by tribal commanders. Indeed, it was largely believed that bin Laden had been allowed to escape from Tora Bora in December 2001 (see above) by Afghans who claimed to be US allies. The USA's policy of hiring and arming local soldiers, in the hope of capturing Islamist militants, at times compounded the unstable political situation. In March 2002 the funds provided by the US forces in return for the assistance of Afghan soldiers were reportedly used by various military commanders in their attempt to secure control of Khost province. In April the mission to find the remnants of al-Qa'ida and the Taliban became more dangerous and volatile. US-led and Afghan forces encountered considerable security threats. In mid-April British troops launched their first major military assault, joining US and Afghan soldiers in Paktia. US-led forces conducted several smaller operations in eastern Afghanistan in May–June, with the support of Afghan ground troops, with some success. The USA's military strategy came under severe criticism after a wedding party in Uruzgan province was bombed by mistake in early July. It appeared that US forces, not for the first time, had mistaken the traditional celebratory firing of weapons at an Afghan wedding for Taliban activity.

The election of 1,051 delegates to attend the Emergency Loya Jirga by district representatives took place in May–June 2002 under the monitoring of the UN and Loya Jirga Commission. International aid agencies, universities and other organizations chosen by the Commission appointed an additional 600 members to ensure that the assembly was balanced in terms of gender, geography, ethnicity and political beliefs. The Emergency Loya Jirga, due to commence on 10 June, was delayed by about 36 hours, largely owing to tension over the former King Zahir Shah's candidature for the presidency. Zahir Shah eventually withdrew his candidature, reportedly after pressure by the USA, and announced his support for Karzai. The former President, Burhanuddin Rabbani, also renounced his candidature and declared his support for Karzai. The Emergency Loya Jirga convened the following day, on 11 June, and was attended by an estimated 1,650 delegates. Karzai won the presidential election, with 1,295 of the approximately 1,575 votes cast. Masooda Jalal, a doctor and the first woman ever to participate in an Afghan presidential election, came second with 171 votes; Mahfouz Nedai secured 109 votes. Some 83 voters abstained. The UN declared the elections flawed, with incidents of malpractice and intimidation of candidates, but fair. The Loya Jirga was also expected to choose the structure of the Transitional Authority and its principal staff; however, the decision-making took place largely outside the assembly tent. Debate in the assembly was reportedly obstructed by poor chairmanship and the lack of a clear agenda. Nevertheless, on 19 June the Loya Jirga approved the Transitional Authority cabinet, retaining most of the incumbent members of the Interim Authority. However, it failed to establish a Meli Shura (National Assembly). Instead, it was decided that a National Assembly Commission would be convened at a future date to discuss this issue. Karzai announced the creation of a number of other commissions to address the issues of defence, human rights, internal security reform and a new constitution.

In early July 2002 the Vice-President and Minister of Reconstruction, Haji Abdul Qadir, was assassinated, raising new
concerns over the Transitional Authority's stability. Many
observers held the remnants of the Taliban or al-Qa'ida responsible for the attack. Later that month US authorities declared
that they would provide armed guards for Karzai, in response to
fears for the President's safety. An ISAF report published in
mid-August on the assassination of Qadir stated that Afghan
officials were inadequately protected and that it was unlikely
that the assassins would be found, since the Afghan security
agencies were ill-equipped to investigate the incident. In early
September Karzai escaped an assassination attempt in Qandahar; hours later a bomb explosion in Kabul killed 30 people
and injured at least 160 others. Afghan officials and Western
diplomats believed that Hekmatyar had joined forces with remnants of the Taliban and al-Qa'ida in south and east Afghanistan and had perpetrated the attacks in an attempt to depose
the Transitional Authority. Hekmatyar had allegedly also held
negotiations with other discontented regional leaders in an
effort to form a wider alliance against the Afghan Government
and US military presence in Afghanistan. Following the bomb
attack some 800 additional ISAF troops were deployed across
Kabul to carry out random searches of vehicles and to construct
security checkpoints; police officers arrested more than 100
people in connection with the attack.

Reported incidents of factional fighting increased significantly in late June and July 2002. In some parts of Afghanistan
the fighting hindered humanitarian relief efforts. In mid-July
Karzai announced the establishment of a UN-supported
security commission, which would begin the disarming of rebel
troops and precipitate the creation of a national army. Despite
commanding little control outside Kabul, Karzai warned military commanders that their powers would be removed unless
they denounced factional fighting and joined the Government.
In early November the President dismissed more than 20 senior
regional officials—including Gen. Abdul Hamid, the military
commander of Mazar-i-Sharif—in an attempt to consolidate the
Transitional Authority's jurisdiction outside Kabul.

In the mean time, rival military commanders Gen. Dostam
and Gen. Atta Mohammed eventually negotiated a cease-fire in
October 2002 and agreed to support the security commission;
however, violence was reportedly renewed in mid-November.
The disarmament programme resumed after Gen. Dostam and
Gen. Atta Mohammed agreed to co-operate; by mid-January
2003 thousands of weapons had been collected, but regional
commanders remained as powerful as before. Meanwhile,
fighting continued in Khost and Paktia provinces. At a conference focusing on Afghanistan's reconstruction in Germany in
early December 2002, Karzai officially announced the plan to
build a 70,000-strong multi-ethnic army. In January 2003
Karzai established four committees to accelerate the disarmament process and to recruit a national army. In October a three-
year programme of disarmament, demobilization and reintegration established by the Transitional Administration and the
USA, was launched. Shortly before, a law proscribing the participation of military commanders and armed factions in political life was approved by the authorities. In December Gen.
Dostam and Gen. Mohammed surrendered army tanks and
weapons to the ANA under a deal brokered by the Minister of
Interior Affairs and British forces. Meanwhile, Karzai continued
attempts to extend his control outside Kabul. In May 12 Afghan
provincial governors signed an agreement to transfer customs
revenues to the Transitional Administration after Karzai
threatened to resign if the governors refused to accede to this
demand.

In early September 2002 the Transitional Authority
announced a currency reform programme designed to end the
problem of hyperinflation and to stop regional commanders from
printing their own banknotes to fund military operations.
During a two-month period, commencing 7 October, old afghani
notes were exchanged for new afghani notes at a rate of 1,000 old
afghanis to one new afghani. In late November Afghan authorities prevented an attempt to assassinate Marshal (formerly
Gen.) Fahim. At the same time, the UN Security Council
approved the extension of the mandate of the ISAF for one year
beyond 20 December; Germany and the Netherlands agreed to
assume joint command of the force from Turkey.

In early March 2003 a number of new political parties were
established and united under a single 'umbrella' movement: the
National Front for Democracy in Afghanistan. The parties were
not officially recognized by the Government, however, as the

formation of political parties remained illegal. In August supporters of former King Zahir Shah launched Jonbesh-i Wahadat-
i Melli (the Afghan National Unity Movement); Sultan Mahmoud Ghazi was elected Chairman of the new political party.
Later that month the activities of a new political organization,
Hizb-i Muttahid-i Melli (United National Party), established by
supporters of the former communist PDPA, were proscribed by
the Supreme Court after being deemed 'anti-Islamic'. On 9
September the Government approved legislation allowing the
creation of political parties. Meanwhile, in mid-August Gul
Agha Sherzai was removed from his post as Governor of Qandahar and appointed as Minister of Housing and Town Planning, as part of a major reshuffle of provincial governors and
military officials. In early September Gen. Besmellah Khan was
appointed Chief of Staff of the Army, replacing Gen. Asif
Dilawar. Some two months later Wahidullah Sabaoon was
appointed as presidential adviser and Minister of Tribal Affairs.
In August, meanwhile, the North Atlantic Treaty Organization
(NATO) assumed formal control of the ISAF. In mid-October the
UN Security Council passed a resolution authorizing the expansion of the mandate of the ISAF.

In the mean time, in April 2003 the Afghan Constitutional
Drafting Commission, which had been meeting since November
2002, completed its draft of a new constitution. A 35-member
Constitutional Commission was established to review the draft
by October 2003, at which point it would submit the proposed
charter to a constitutional loya jirga for discussion and ratification. The Commission did not reveal its official draft of a
proposed constitution until early November, however, and the
convening of the council was postponed until mid-December.
The charter, envisaging a strong presidential system of government and a bicameral legislature, provoked a wide range of
reactions. There were concerns that the draft failed to protect
adequately the rights of women and religious freedoms. On 14
December the Constitutional Loya Jirga convened. Some 502
delegates representing all 32 provinces of Afghanistan, as well
as the country's ethnic groups, minorities and refugees, were
divided into 10 committees to debate the draft constitution.
Some three weeks of intense negotiations, marred by ethnic
divisions and arguments, followed. There were fears that an
agreement would not be reached when more than 40% of the
delegates boycotted the voting process on 1 January 2004;
however, following closed-door negotiations led by Brahimi and
the US ambassador to Afghanistan, a compromise was secured
two days later. On 4 January Afghanistan's Constitution was
approved by consensus rather than actual vote, after the
Chairman of the Loya Jirga called for endorsement of the
document by asking the delegates to rise and stand. In certain
respects the new charter differed little from the draft released in
November: it still provided for a strongly presidential political
system following presidential elections scheduled for June,
despite a campaign by former *mujahidin* parties for a parliamentary state. The new Constitution, however, added a second
vice-presidential post and gave the National Assembly veto
powers over major presidential appointments and policies. The
document made no specific reference to the role of *Shari'a*. The
status of languages was one of the main issues that delayed the
agreement; eventually, Pashto and Dari were identified as the
national languages, with provision made for a third national
language in areas where the language of the ethnic group
forming the majority population differed. The charter also contained new human rights provisions and articulated the equal
rights of men and women before the law. One of the most
significant achievements was the ensuring of greater political
representation for women: it was agreed that approximately
25% of seats in the Wolasi Jirga (House of the Representatives)
would be reserved for women; the President would appoint
additional women to the Meshrano Jirga (House of Elders).
After the ratification of the Constitution, however, Human
Rights Watch expressed concern that military commanders,
factional leaders and ministers had been involved in political
intimidation and vote-buying before and during the assembly.
This proved that local factions continued to dominate Afghanistan's political processes and raised doubts about whether the
country could hold free and fair presidential elections in June
and parliamentary elections by the end of the year. Furthermore, the failure to address adequately the role of *Shari'a*, and
its relation to human rights safeguards, generated concerns that
conservative elements in the judiciary would be able to implement interpretations of Islam that might violate human rights
values. In late March President Karzai announced that the

presidential election was to be postponed until September owing to security concerns and delays in voter registration (only 1.5m. of an estimated 10.5m. eligible voters had been registered thus far). It was also agreed that the presidential and parliamentary elections would be held at the same time. Meanwhile, in the same month the Minister of Planning, Mohammad Mohaqqeq, reportedly resigned from his post; President Karzai appointed Ramazan Bashardost as his successor. Mohaqqeq claimed later that, rather than resigning, he had been dismissed. In July it was announced that the presidential election would be held on 9 October 2004. However, legislative elections were to be delayed until April–May 2005, owing to the ongoing unrest in the country.

Meanwhile, in March 2003 US-led forces launched 'Operation Valiant Strike', a major offensive to combat the regrouping of Taliban and al-Qa'ida fighters in southern Afghanistan. In early April, in response to an attack on US and Afghan forces by suspected Taliban members, US-led forces launched an assault on alleged remnants of the Taliban and al-Qa'ida in the Tor Ghar mountains of Afghanistan, close to the border with Pakistan. Attacks by suspected Islamist militants continued throughout the month. In early May the US Secretary of Defense, Donald Rumsfeld, announced that major combat operations had ended in Afghanistan and that US forces had begun to concentrate on the stabilization and reconstruction of the country. Despite this statement, the security situation remained fragile; in early June four members of the ISAF were killed and 31 injured in a suicide attack in Kabul. Later that month US-led forces launched a major assault on suspected Taliban and al-Qa'ida fighters along Afghanistan's border with Pakistan, in response to an increase in attacks on members of the Afghan Transitional Administration and the ISAF. The Taliban, reportedly bolstered by new volunteers from Pakistan and by funds from drugs-trafficking, continued their violent campaign; it was believed that at least 300 people had been killed in August–September. Humanitarian organizations were also affected by the increase in violence. In November a French refugee worker was shot dead in Ghazni, by suspected Taliban members. UNHCR announced that it would temporarily withdraw foreign staff from large parts of southern and eastern Afghanistan as a result. (In February 2004 two Afghan men were convicted of the murder of the French worker and sentenced to death. They were later granted permission to appeal against their convictions.) In the weeks preceding the Constitutional Loya Jirga, the Taliban increased their violent campaign against foreign aid workers and contractors and US and Afghan soldiers. In early December US forces launched 'Operation Avalanche' in southern and eastern Afghanistan against Taliban and al-Qa'ida members. The operation was condemned, however, after 15 Afghan children and two adults were killed in two separate miscalculated aerial attacks. In early January 2004 the ISAF assumed command of a Provincial Reconstruction Team (PRT) in Kunduz, as the pilot project for further expansion of the international security force. A new PRT was established in Jalalabad by US-led forces at the same time, bringing the total number of PRTs in Afghanistan to eight. The ISAF was expected to take over more PRTs in northern Afghanistan within the next few months, allowing the US-led coalition to concentrate more on the volatile southern and eastern parts of the country.

Throughout 2004 violence continued to affect significant areas of the country. In February five Afghan aid workers died following an ambush east of Kabul. In March the Minister of Civil Aviation and Tourism and son of Ismail Khan, Mirwais Sadiq, was killed in a reported grenade attack in Herat. Khan held the regional government commander, Gen. Zahir Nayebzada, responsible for his son's death, and violent clashes ensued between rival forces in the province. Nayebzada eventually fled, and Khan regained control of the city. President Karzai subsequently deployed forces of the ANA to Herat in an attempt to restore order. The level of provincial instability in the country was illustrated further in April, when fighters loyal to Gen. Dostam seized control of the city of Maymana, the capital of the northern province of Faryab, forcing the Governor of Faryab to flee, allegedly following a dispute over power-sharing in the region. Karzai reportedly sent soldiers into the city to stabilize the situation. Meanwhile, US troops continued to engage in operations against the Taliban. In May Taliban forces took control of the Mizan district of Zabul province, but were swiftly repelled. By the end of that month it was reported that 90 US soldiers had been killed in Afghanistan since the commencement of military action in the country. In the following month

the murder of 11 Chinese construction workers during an attack on a camp in the northern province of Kunduz, generally perceived to be one of the safer areas of the country, raised concerns regarding security for the forthcoming national elections. In the same month the killing of five Dutch workers from the international aid organization Médecins Sans Frontières (MSF), during an ambush of their vehicle in the province of Badghis, prompted MSF to suspend all its operations in Afghanistan. The organization subsequently announced that, after 24 years of aid work in the country, it had decided to withdraw completely from Afghanistan. MSF criticized the US-led coalition for putting aid workers at risk by failing to distinguish properly between humanitarian and military operations. Meanwhile, the Governor of Ghor, Ibrahim Malikzada, was ousted from his position following a violent power struggle between local militia commanders in the province. In an attempt to increase security in the country, and to ensure its expansion outside Kabul, NATO pledged to increase the size of the ISAF to 10,000, from 6,500. The Government expressed its concern that the additional forces would be deployed only in the north of the country, stressing that they were most urgently needed in the southern and eastern provinces.

Meanwhile, preparations for the holding of Afghanistan's first direct presidential election, due to be held in October 2004, continued. By the beginning of August, according to the UN, approximately 90% of those eligible to vote had registered to do so, despite reports of violence and intimidation towards staff and voters during the registration process. Later in that month it was announced that a total of 18 candidates had qualified to contest the presidential election, including one woman, Masooda Jalal. Interim President Hamid Karzai had formally announced his candidacy earlier in that month. Also in August a minor cabinet reorganization took place, in which Minister of Urban Development and Housing Gul Agha Sherzai and Minister of Public Works Abdullah Ali exchanged portfolios. Ahmed Moshashed was allocated the education portfolio, succeeding Yunus Qanooni, who had resigned in July in order to stand as a presidential candidate.

In September 2004, in an apparent attempt to assert his jurisdiction outside Kabul in advance of the election, President Karzai dismissed Ismail Khan, the powerful Governor of Herat province, and offered him the cabinet post of Minister of Mines and Industries. Khan's dismissal provoked rioting in the province as his supporters confronted US troops, reportedly resulting in the deaths of seven people and injuries to a further 60, including 15 US soldiers. Khan subsequently rejected the ministerial portfolio, and Mohammed Khairkhwa was appointed to succeed him as Governor of Herat. Shortly afterwards President Karzai survived an assassination attempt when a rocket narrowly missed the US military helicopter in which he was travelling on an official visit to the south-east of the country. The Taliban claimed responsibility for the attack. In the same month the UN Security Council adopted a resolution extending the mandate of the ISAF for one year.

On 9 October 2004 Afghanistan held its first direct presidential election. Despite some sporadic violence on the day of the election, no widespread disturbances were reported. Shortly after polling had begun, all 15 opposition candidates launched a boycott of the vote and demanded that it be abandoned, owing to alleged widespread electoral fraud. However, international observers announced in the following month that they had concluded, following an inquiry, that alleged irregularities during the poll were not considered significant enough to have altered the final result. Interim President Hamid Karzai was subsequently declared the winner, receiving 55.37% of the votes, sufficient to ensure that a second round of voting would not be necessary. Former Minister of Education Yunus Qanooni came second, with 16.28% of the votes, followed by Mohammad Mohaqqeq, with 11.66%, and Gen. Abdul Rashid Dostam, with 10.03%. A reported 83.66% of those registered to vote did so. Concerns were, however, raised by the regional nature of Karzai's victory, which seemed largely to have been secured by voters in the Pashtun-majority provinces, indicating that he had not succeeded in appealing to all ethnic groups. Meanwhile, the kidnapping of three foreign UN workers by armed militants in Kabul in late October raised fears that insurgents were adopting new tactics in their efforts to undermine democracy in the country. The kidnappers were reportedly members of the Jaish-e-Muslimeen (Army of Islam), a militant group. In a videotape released shortly after the kidnapping, the group threatened that the hostages would be killed unless its demands for the release of prisoners and the withdrawal of foreign troops from Afghanistan were met. However, the hostages were released unharmed in the following month, following a series of raids by US soldiers and Afghan security forces. It was later reported that the Afghan security personnel had killed one of the kidnappers during the raid and tortured another suspected kidnapper while in custody until he died.

In December 2004, following his inauguration, President Karzai announced the composition of his Cabinet. While Minister of Foreign Affairs Dr Abdullah Abdullah and Minister of Interior Affairs Ali Ahmad Jalali retained their portfolios, Marshal (formerly Gen.) Muhammad Qassim Fahim was replaced as Minister of Defence by Gen. Abdul Rahim Wardak. Hedayat Amin Arsala was allocated the commerce portfolio. Ismail Khan became Minister of Energy and Water, although several powerful regional commanders were not included in the new Cabinet, ostensibly owing to the fact that they did not satisfy a requirement that all cabinet ministers be educated to university level. Karzai was criticized for his failure to allocate more portfolios in the Pashtun-dominated Cabinet to other ethnic groups. In an attempt to address Afghanistan's continued problems with the widespread cultivation of opium, a Ministry of Anti-narcotics was created, headed by Habibullah Qaderi. According to the UN, in 2004 the total area under poppy cultivation had increased by 64% compared with the previous year, despite a government ban on cultivation and trafficking of the drug. Meanwhile, defeated presidential candidate Yunus Qanooni announced that he had decided to form a political party, New Afghanistan, to contest the 2005 legislative elections, which, it was announced in March 2005, would be held in September of that year.

On 22 December 2002 the Governments of Afghanistan, China, Iran, Pakistan, Tajikistan, Turkmenistan and Uzbekistan signed the Kabul Declaration on Good-Neighbourly Relations in which they pledged never again to interfere in each other's affairs. The agreement signalled a new era of regional co-operation, although, in reality, the situation was different. Afghan officials claimed that Iranian Revolutionary Guards were continuing to provide financial and military assistance to Ismail Khan; Russia was reportedly supporting Marshal Fahim and his army; and certain Saudis allegedly had resumed sending financial assistance to the remnants of the Taliban in Pakistan. In addition, the Uzbek President had provided Uzbek Gen. Dostam with his own bodyguards. Publicly, the Pakistani President supported Karzai and the USA's campaign against al-Qa'ida; however, at the same time Pakistan's Inter-Services Intelligence (ISI) was reportedly giving sanctuary to senior Taliban members and other anti-Government military commanders, such as Hekmatyar. In mid-February 2003 the Pakistani and Afghan military intelligence services held talks in Rome in an attempt to resolve deep-rooted differences. The Afghan delegation repeated its claims that the ISI was harbouring Islamist militants. The ISI, in turn, expressed its discontent at the Transitional Administration for granting India, Iran and Russia unrestricted movement around Afghanistan. The opening of Indian consulates in Jalalabad and Qandahar, close to the Afghan–Pakistani border, particularly irritated the ISI. Some two months later, during an official visit to Pakistan, President Karzai urged the Pakistani Government to assist in curbing the cross-border attacks by militant Islamists. Relations were strained when Pakistan delivered a formal protest to Afghanistan in June over the dumping of the bodies of some 21 Taliban fighters on its territory; the Afghan authorities were forced to take back the bodies after Pakistani border guards discovered that the dead were, in fact, not Pakistani, but Afghan citizens. One month later, in a seemingly well-planned operation, the Pakistani embassy in Afghanistan was stormed and raided by hundreds of Afghans in protest against alleged incursions by Pakistani border troops into Afghan territory. The crowds were dispersed by Afghan police; Karzai apologized for the incident to the Pakistani President and promised to pay compensation. The embassy was reopened almost two weeks later. In January 2004 the Pakistani Prime Minister paid his first ever official visit to Afghanistan; the two countries agreed to work together to combat cross-border infiltration.

Government

During 11–19 June 2002 an Emergency Loya Jirga, comprising an estimated 1,650 delegates, 1,051 of whom were elected by tribal representatives, with the remaining seats allocated to such groups as women and business leaders, appointed a head of state and the principal staff of a broad-based, gender-sensitive

Transitional Authority. A new Constitution was adopted by a Constitutional Loya Jirga in early January 2004, after three weeks of intensive negotiations. The charter provided for a presidential system of government and a bicameral legislature. Direct presidential elections were held in October 2004, and the elected President was formally inaugurated in December. Parliamentary elections were scheduled to be held in September 2005.

Defence

Following the defeat of the Taliban in December 2001, an International Security Assistance Force (ISAF) was deployed in Kabul and at Bagram airbase to help maintain security in the area. In August 2003 the North Atlantic Treaty Organization (NATO) assumed command of the force, which in late 2004 consisted of over 8,500 members from 37 countries. The ISAF was also responsible for the training of the first battalion of the Afghan National Guard, which was operational in April 2003. US and French forces began training the first set of recruits for a new multi-ethnic Afghan National Army (ANA) in May 2003. In December President Karzai announced that the ANA would comprise 70,000 soldiers and ordered all private armies to disarm and merge into the ANA within one year. Four committees were established in January 2003 to accelerate the disarmament and army-building process. By October 2003 some 7,000 troops had completed their training. It was envisaged that the army would be supported by a border guard of 12,000. There was to be a paramilitary force, including police trained by Germany, numbering some 70,000.

Economic Affairs

In 2003/04, according to official estimates, Afghanistan's gross domestic product (GDP), excluding the illegal cultivation of poppies and production of drugs, was US $4,585m. This implied a per head GDP of $199. During 1990–2003, it was estimated, the population increased at an average annual rate of 3.8%. According to IMF estimates, overall GDP increased by 29% in 2002/03 and by 16% in 2003/04. GDP was expected to rise by an estimated 16% in 2004/05.

Agriculture (including hunting, forestry and fishing), according to Asian Development Bank (ADB) estimates, contributed 48.5% of GDP in 2003/04. According to official figures, 69.6% of the economically active population were employed in the agricultural sector in 2002/03. Livestock plays an important role in the traditional Afghan economy and is normally a major source of income for the country's numerous nomadic groups. However, the total livestock population has been seriously depleted, owing to the many years of conflict and prolonged drought. In 2002/03 the sector benefited from greater rainfall and the increased availability and better quality of seeds and fertilizers. Cereal production was estimated to have increased by 83%, compared with the previous year, to 3.6m. metric tons. The production of fruits, vegetables and livestock products, such as dairy items, meat, wool and hides also increased in 2002/03. In that year dried fruit accounted for 40.5% of total exports. The agricultural sector experienced further growth in 2003/04, aided by increased rainfall, an expansion of the area under crop cultivation and the return of significant numbers of refugees to their lands; cereal production expanded by 50%, to 5.4m. tons, the level Afghanistan required to be self-sufficient. Wheat production was estimated at 4.4m. tons in 2003/04, a 62% increase in production compared with the previous year. However, expansion was not as significant as had been expected, owing to the ongoing drought in some regions of the country. In consequence of this drought, cereal production decreased by an estimated 25% during the first quarter of 2004/05, and was expected to record a full-year decline in production of some 10% compared with the previous year.The country would thus continue to be dependent on food assistance.

According to ADB estimates, the industrial sector (including mining, manufacturing, construction and power) contributed an estimated 19.4% of GDP in 2003/04 and employed an estimated 6.2% of the economically active population in 2002/03, according to official figures. The value of industrial output increased by 21.1% in 2002/03, according to official estimates, compared with the previous year.

Mining and quarrying, according to the ADB, contributed 0.2% of GDP in 2003/04 and employed about 1.5% of the settled labour force in 1979. Natural gas was the major mineral export (accounting for about 23.6% of total export earnings, according to the IMF, in 1988/89). Salt, hard coal, copper, lapis lazuli, emeralds, barytes and talc are also mined. In addition, Afghanistan has small reserves of petroleum and iron ore. In 1998 the Taliban had claimed that monthly revenue from the allegedly renascent mining sector in Afghanistan totalled US $3.5m. (including revenue from the recently revived steel-smelting plant in Baghlan province). The rehabilitation of the mining industry had begun in 2003/04.

Manufacturing, according to the ADB, contributed 14.0% of GDP in 2003/04 and employed about 10.9% of the settled labour force in 1979. Afghanistan's major manufacturing industries included food products, cotton textiles, chemical fertilizers, cement, leather and plastic goods. In 1999 only one of the four existing cement plants in Afghanistan and about 10% of the textile mills remained in operation (prior to the Soviet invasion in 1979 there were about 220 state-owned factories operating in Afghanistan). The traditional handicraft sector has better survived the devastating effects of war, however, and carpets, leather, embroidery and fur products continued to be produced.

Energy is derived principally from petroleum (which is imported from Iran and republics of the former USSR, notably Turkmenistan) and coal. Afghanistan was estimated to have some 73m. metric tons of coal reserves. In 2003 the ADB undertook a feasibility study into the possibility of constructing a pipeline to transport natural gas from the Dauletabad gas fields in Turkmenistan to markets in Afghanistan, Pakistan and, potentially, India. However, although a protocol concerning the pipeline was signed by the Governments of Afghanistan, Pakistan and Turkmenistan in December 2003, little further progress had been made by June 2004. The project had been proposed in 1996, but was postponed owing to political and security concerns until the establishment of the Interim Authority in 2001.

Services, according to ADB estimates, contributed 32.1% of GDP in 2003/04 and employed an estimated 24.2% of the economically active population in 2002/03, according to official figures. The value of the service sector's output increased by 39.5% in 2002/03 compared with the previous year, according to official estimates.

In 2003/04 there was a surplus of an estimated US $379m. on the current account of the balance of payments. In the same year a trade deficit of $2,058m. was recorded. In 2003/04 total exports (excluding opium-related exports) reached an estimated $1,700.8m., of which $1,255.0m. accounted for re-exports. Total imports, meanwhile, increased to an estimated $3,758.9m. in 2003/04. Exports were expected to reach $1,822.5m. in 2004/05, of which $1,180.2m. was projected to be in the form of re-exports; imports were forecast to increase to $4,134.1m. In 2002/03 the principal exports were carpets and dried fruit; the principal imports were machinery and equipment, and household items and medicine. In that year the principal market for exports was India (which purchased an estimated 27.4% of the total) and the principal source of imports was Japan (an estimated 43.0%). Another major trading partner was Pakistan. These official statistics do not, however, include illegal trade and smuggling. If the illegal revenue from the export of opium were included, a large trade surplus would be recorded for 2002/03. In 2000 a UN Development Programme/World Bank study estimated that out of total exports of $1,200m., about $1,000m. was unofficially exported. In March 2003 Afghanistan signed a new preferential trade agreement with India. Two months earlier India and Iran had agreed to improve the road network linking Afghanistan with the Chabahar port in Iran. Afghanistan began to open trade routes with Central Asia in late 2002; in August 2003 a memorandum of understanding was signed with Uzbekistan. Trade relations with Pakistan, the USA and the European Union also improved.

In the financial year ending 20 March 2005 there was a projected budgetary deficit of US $353m., which was expected to be covered by financial assistance. In 2000, according to UN figures, Afghanistan received $88.2m. in bilateral official development assistance and $52.7m. in multilateral official development assistance. In 2002/03 Afghanistan received $26.4m. in bilateral grants and $157.1m. in multilateral assistance (this did not include grants of $51.24m.). In 2003/04 donor grants and loans totalled an estimated $205m. Consumer prices in Kabul rose by an estimated average of 5.2% in 2002/03, compared with the previous year, and by an estimated 24.2% in 2003/04. They were projected to increase by 12.3% in 2004/05.

Afghanistan is a member of the Colombo Plan (see p. 373), which seeks to promote economic and social development in Asia and the Pacific, and the Economic Co-operation Organization (ECO, see p. 210). In April 2003 Afghanistan applied for membership to the World Trade Organization (see p. 357).

It is difficult to provide an accurate economic profile of Afghanistan, after more than 20 years of conflict, intermittent droughts and earthquakes and constant population movements. However, a data collection process has begun and more reliable statistics are becoming available, facilitated by the Afghan Transitional Administration's success from June 2002 in rebuilding government and financial institutions and restoring macroeconomic stability. In 2002 the Interim, and later Transitional, Administration began to address such problems as the severe food and fuel shortages, the lack of infrastructure and the difficulties posed by the return of millions of refugees to their ravaged farms and fields, often studded with mines or devastated by air-strikes. In early 2002 the Interim Authority devised a National Development Framework for the reconstruction programme, which focused on these challenges. It placed emphasis on allowing the private sector to lead Afghanistan's recovery and streamlining the public administration. In January international donors pledged US $4,500m. worth of aid over five years towards the reconstruction of Afghanistan, of which some $1,800m. had been disbursed by March 2003. The bulk of these funds, however, was dedicated to humanitarian assistance, and only a small proportion was invested in the country's reconstruction programmes. Nevertheless, by the end of 2003 a number of infrastructure projects, funded by international financial institutions and individual countries, were under way or had reached completion. From 2003 the economy showed strong signs of recovery, largely owing to the end of major conflict and prolonged drought, international financial assistance and the Transitional Administration's economic policies. A new currency was launched in late 2002 and a sound monetary policy has since been in place; consequently, the exchange rate has been largely stable. In 2003/04 the appreciation of the Afghani against the US dollar was indicative of growing domestic and international confidence in the new currency. Efforts to develop a modern banking sector commenced in 2003; the central bank was granted autonomy and in September the Government approved a law allowing foreign banks to open branches in Afghanistan. Reorganization and modernization of the central bank was ongoing in 2004–05, and by the end of 2004 seven new commercial banks had been granted licences to operate in the country, while three state-owned banks had gone into liquidation. Reconstruction of the education system was also under way; women were given equal employment rights, as well as access to education. In March 2004 international donors meeting in Berlin, Germany, pledged $4,400m. in aid for Afghanistan for that year, to be followed by $8,200m. in aid over the following three years. In June a 'core budget' was adopted, consolidating operational and most development expenditure for the first time. Expenditure of 69,000m. afghanis was projected for 2004/05, of which 38,000m. afghanis was allocated for development projects. The economy was expected to continue to grow in 2004/05. Several serious risks remained, however. First, while the formal economy was recovering, so too was the criminal economy. Despite the introduction of a ban in January 2002 on poppy cultivation and the processing, trafficking and abuse of opiates, the large-scale planting of poppies during the collapse of law and order in late 2001 had allowed Afghanistan to resume its place as the largest supplier of opium in the world, a position that it consolidated over the following years. In 2004 the area under poppy cultivation increased by 64% compared with the previous year. Opium production accounted for an estimated 40% of GDP in 2003/04. The opium trade, and the associated violence and corruption, posed a serious threat to the Afghan economy. However, it was hoped that the adoption of a National Drug Control Strategy in May 2003, intended to reduce opium production by 70% by 2008, and the creation of a Ministry of Anti-narcotics in December 2004, would achieve some success. The lack of security and limited rule of law also hampered Afghanistan's successful reconstruction, especially in the provinces. Furthermore, there were concerns that international financial assistance might decrease prematurely and that the political transition to an elected system of government could, in the short term, destabilize the reform process.

Education

The prolonged war resulted in a large-scale exodus of teachers, and some 3,600 school buildings were damaged or destroyed. In 1996/97 it was estimated that only about 600–650 primary and secondary schools were functioning.

Before the Taliban rose to power, primary education began at seven years of age and lasted for six years. Secondary education, beginning at 13 years of age, lasted for a further six years. As a proportion of the school-age population, the total enrolment at primary and secondary schools was equivalent to 36% (males 49%; females 22%) in 1995. Primary enrolment in that year was equivalent to an estimated 49% of children in the relevant age-group (boys 64%; girls 32%), while the enrolment ratio at general secondary schools was equivalent to 22% (boys 32%; girls 11%).

Higher education was disrupted by the departure of many teaching staff from Afghanistan during more than 20 years of civil war. In 1980 it was reported that up to 80% of university staff had fled their posts. In 1991 there were six institutions of higher education (including Kabul University, which was founded in 1932) in Afghanistan; a total of 17,000 students were enrolled in these institutions in that year.

Following their seizure of power in late September 1996, the Taliban banned education for girls over the age of eight, closed all the women's institutes of higher education and planned to draw up a new Islamic curriculum for boys' schools. In early 1998, however, there were still two co-educational universities functioning in Afghanistan (in areas not under Taliban control), one of which was situated in Bamian (with 300 students and 16 teachers). In mid-1998 the Taliban decided to close more than 100 private schools and numerous small, home-based vocational courses in Kabul, many of which were educating girls. According to Taliban figures, in September of that year 1,586,026 pupils were being educated by 59,792 teachers in 3,836 *madrassas* (mosque schools).

After the Taliban regime was defeated in late 2001, the Afghan Interim Administration, with the help of foreign governments and UN and humanitarian organizations, began to rehabilitate the education system. In March 2003 4.2m. boys and girls commenced a new academic year at some 7,000 schools around the country. The number of girls attending school increased by some 37% compared with the previous year, to approximately 1.2m. The boy-girl ratio in education in 2003/04 had returned to pre-Taliban levels. However, the attendance of girls at schools in parts of southern and eastern Afghanistan remained very low. In March 2004 5.5m. children reportedly sought enrolment; primary enrolment in 2003/04 was equivalent to an estimated 36% of children in the relevant age-group. The World Food Programme embarked on a food-for-education programme in 2002; organizations world-wide supplied educational material, and tents were provided as temporary classrooms. More than 27,000 teachers were involved in education in

20 provinces in July, 36% of whom were women. In 2004 UNICEF aimed to provide 4m. primary school children with access to high-quality education, especially girls and those living in remote areas. The organization also planned to rehabilitate 200 primary schools throughout Afghanistan and to ensure that every primary school in Afghanistan had a clean water point. The Afghan Ministry of Education, assisted by UNICEF, was also leading an initiative to establish community-based education, initially in six provinces, in order to provide basic educational opportunities for those with no access to formal schools. By December 2004 936 community classes had been created, attended by almost 50,000 children. The initiative was due to be extended into a further three provinces in 2005. Kabul University opened for men and women in March 2002. Some 24,000 students enrolled at the higher education level. Foreign universities as well as governments and non-governmental organizations donated books and teaching materials. Universities in at least five other provinces were being rehabilitated.

In January 2003 UNESCO and the Afghan Transitional Administration launched a major project to boost literacy rates throughout Afghanistan.

Public Holidays

The Afghan year 1384 runs from 21 March 2005 to 20 March 2006, and the year 1385 runs from 21 March 2006 to 20 March 2007.

2005: 21 January* (Id al-Adha, Feast of the Sacrifice), 1 February* (Arafat Day), 19 February* (Ashura, Martyrdom of Imam Husayn), 21 March (Nauroz: New Year's Day, Iranian calendar), 21 April* (Roze-Maulud, Birth of Prophet Muhammad), 28 April (Loss of the Muslim Nation), 1 May (Workers' Day), 19 August (Independence Day), 5 October* (first day of Ramadan), 4 November* (Id al-Fitr, end of Ramadan).

2006: 11 January* (Id al-Adha, Feast of the Sacrifice), 1 February* (Arafat Day), 9 February* (Ashura, Martyrdom of Imam Husayn), 21 March (Nauroz: New Year's Day, Iranian calendar), 11 April* (Roze-Maulud, Birth of Prophet Muhammad), 28 April (Loss of the Muslim Nation), 1 May (Workers' Day), 19 August (Independence Day), 24 September* (first day of Ramadan), 24 October* (Id al-Fitr, end of Ramadan).

* These holidays are dependent on the Islamic lunar calendar and may vary by one or two days from the dates given.

Weights and Measures

The metric system has been officially adopted but traditional weights are still used. One 'seer' equals 16 lb (7.3 kg).

Statistical Survey

Source (unless otherwise stated): Central Statistics Authority, Block 4, Macroraion, Kabul; tel. (93) 24883; Central Statistics Office, Ansar-i-Watt, Kabul; e-mail afghan_cso@yahoo.com; internet www.aims.org.af/cso.

Area and Population

AREA, POPULATION AND DENSITY

Area (sq km)	652,225*
Population (census results)	
23 June 1979†	
Males	6,712,377
Females	6,338,981
Total	13,051,358
Population (official estimate at September)‡	
2002	21,800,000
Density (per sq km) at September 2002	33.4

* 251,773 sq miles.

† Figures exclude nomadic population, estimated to total 2,500,000. The census data also exclude an adjustment for underenumeration, estimated to have been 5% for the urban population and 10% for the rural population.

‡ This data includes an estimate for nomadic population (1.5m in 2002), but takes no account of emigration by refugees. At the end of 2003 UNHCR estimated that the total Afghan refugee population numbered 2.1m., of whom 1.1m. were located in Pakistan and some 800,000 in Iran.

PROVINCES

(estimates, 2002, excluding nomad population)

	Area (sq km)	Population ('000)	Density (per sq km)	Capital
Kabul	4,462	3,314	742.7	Kabul
Kapisa	1,842	360	195.4	Mahmud-e-Iraqi
Parvan (Parwan) . .	9,584	726	75.8	Charikar
Wardak*	8,938	413	46.2	Maidanshahr
Loghar (Logar)* . .	3,880	292	75.3	Pul-i-Alam
Ghazni	22,915	931	40.6	Ghazni
Paktika	19,482	352	18.1	Sharan
Paktia (Paktya) . .	6,432	415	64.5	Gardez
Khost†	4,152	300	72.3	Khost
Nangarhar . . .	7,727	1,089	140.9	Jalalabad
Kunar (Kunarha) .	4,942	321	65.0	Asadabad
Laghman . . .	3,843	373	97.1	Mehter Lam
Nuristan (Nooristan)†	9,225	112	12.1	Nuristan
Badakhshan . . .	44,059	715	16.2	Faizabad
Takhar	12,333	750	60.8	Taloqan
Baghlan* . . .	21,118	745	35.3	Baghlan
Kunduz	8,040	820	102.0	Kunduz
Samangan . . .	11,262	378	33.6	Aybak
Balkh	17,249	869	50.4	Mazar-i-Sharif

— continued	Area (sq km)	Population ('000)	Density (per sq km)	Capital
Jawzjan (Juzjan) . .	11,798	441	37.4	Shiberghan
Sar-e Pol (Sar-e-Pul)‡	15,999	468	29.3	Sar-e Pol
Faryab	20,293	782	38.5	Maymana
Badghis . . .	20,591	301	14.6	Qaleh-ye-Now
Herat	54,778	1,182	21.6	Herat
Farah	48,471	338	7.0	Farah
Nimroz	41,005	149	3.6	Zaranj
Helmand . . .	58,584	745	12.7	Lashgar Gah
Qandahar (Kandahar)	54,022	886	16.4	Qandahar
Zabul	17,343	258	14.9	Qalat
Uruzgan (Urizan) .	30,784	627	20.4	Terin Kowt
Ghor	36,479	485	13.3	Chaghcharan
Bamian (Bamyan) .	14,175	356	25.1	Bamian
Total	645,807	20,291	31.4	

* By 1996 the capital of Loghar province had changed to Pul-i-Alam from Baraki Barak and the capital of Wardak province had moved to Maidanshahr from Kowt-i-Ashrow; it was reported that the capital of Baghlan province had moved to Pol-e-Khomri: this was yet to be confirmed.

† Nuristan province (formerly part of Kunar and Laghman provinces) and Khost province (formerly part of Paktia province) had been created by 1991 and 1995, respectively.

‡ Sar-e Pol province (formerly part of Balkh, Jawzjan and Samangan provinces) had been created by 1990.

PRINCIPAL TOWNS
(estimated population at March 1982)

Kabul (capital) . .	1,036,407	Kunduz	57,112
Qandahar . . .	191,345	Baghlan . . .	41,240
Herat	150,497	Maymana . . .	40,212
Mazar-i-Sharif . .	110,367	Pul-i-Khomri . .	32,695
Jalalabad	57,824	Ghazni	31,985

Estimated population at July 1988: Kabul 1,424,400; Qandahar 225,500; Herat 177,300; Mazar-i-Sharif 130,600 (Source: UN, *Demographic Yearbook*).

Mid-2003 (UN estimate, incl. suburbs): Kabul 2,955,880 (Source: UN, *World Urbanization Prospects: The 2003 Revision*).

BIRTHS AND DEATHS
(UN estimates, annual averages)

	1985–90	1990–95	1995–2000
Birth rate (per 1,000) . . .	49.1	48.0	47.7
Death rate (per 1,000)	23.8	22.5	22.3

Source: UN, *World Population Prospects: The 2002 Revision*.

2001: Birth rate (per 1,000) 48.0.

Expectation of life (WHO estimates, years at birth): 42.6 (males 41.9; females 43.4) in 2002 (Source: WHO, *World Health Report*).

ECONOMICALLY ACTIVE POPULATION*
(ISIC major divisions, '000 persons aged 15–59 years, year ending 20 March, estimates)

	2000/01	2001/02	2002/03
Agriculture, hunting, forestry and fishing	4,986.1	5,082.6	5,181.4
Mining, quarrying, manufacturing and utilities	348.6	355.3	362.2
Construction	94.9	96.7	98.6
Wholesale and retail trade . . .	490.4	499.9	509.6
Transport, storage and communications	163.1	166.3	169.5
Other services	1,083.6	1,104.5	1,126.0
Total	7,166.6	7,305.4	7,447.3

* Figures refer to settled population only.

Health and Welfare

KEY INDICATORS

Total fertility rate (children per woman, 2002)	6.8
Under-5 mortality rate (per 1,000 live births, 2003) . . .	257
HIV/AIDS (% of persons aged 15–49, 1994)	<0.01
Physicians (per 1,000 head, 1997)	0.11
Hospital beds (per 1,000 head, 1990)	0.25
Health expenditure (2001): US $ per head (PPP) . . .	34
Health expenditure (2001): % of GDP	5.2
Health expenditure (2001): public (% of total)	52.6
Access to water (% of persons, 2002)	13
Access to sanitation (% of persons, 2002)	8

For sources and definitions, see explanatory note on p. vi.

Agriculture

PRINCIPAL CROPS
('000 metric tons)

	2000	2001	2002
Wheat	1,469	1,598	2,686
Rice (paddy)	156	182	388
Barley	200*	200†	345
Maize	115*	160	298
Millet†	20	20	22
Potatoes†	230	235	240
Pulses†	50	50	50
Sesame seed*	23	23	23
Cottonseed*	37	37	37
Vegetables†	540	540	540
Watermelons†	90	90	90
Cantaloupes and other melons† .	22	25	22
Grapes	330*	365†	365†
Sugar cane†	38	38	38
Plums†	34	34	34
Apricots†	38	38	38
Other fruit†	551	586	586
Treenuts†	20	24	24

* Unofficial figure(s).
† FAO estimate(s).

Source: FAO, *Production Yearbook*.

LIVESTOCK
('000 head, year ending 30 September)

	2000	2001	2002
Horses*	104	104	104
Mules*	26	30	30
Asses*	920	920	920
Cattle	2,200*	2,000†	2,000*
Camels*	290	290	290
Sheep	12,000*	11,000†	11,000*
Goats	5,500*	5,000†	5,000*
Chickens (million)	7*	6†	6*

* FAO estimate(s).
† Unofficial estimate.

Source: FAO, *Production Yearbook*.

LIVESTOCK PRODUCTS

(FAO estimates, '000 metric tons)

	1999	2000	2001
Beef and veal	149	126	108
Mutton and lamb	112	96	88
Goat meat	35	32	30
Poultry meat	14	13	12
Other meat	12	13	12
Cows' milk	1,560	1,320	1,200
Sheep's milk	210	180	165
Goats' milk	135	100	91
Cheese	25	20	18
Butter and ghee	36	30	28
Hen eggs	18	18	18
Honey	3	3	3
Wool: greasy	18	17	14
Wool: scoured	10	9	8
Cattle hides	17	14	12
Sheepskins	18	15	14
Goatskins	7	6	6

2002: Figures as in 2001 (FAO estimates).

Source: FAO, *Production Yearbook*.

Forestry

ROUNDWOOD REMOVALS

(FAO estimates, '000 cubic metres, excl. bark)

	2001	2002	2003
Sawlogs, veneer logs and logs for sleepers*	856	856	856
Other industrial wood†	904	904	904
Fuel wood	1,314	1,351	1,388
Total	3,074	3,111	3,148

* Assumed to be unchanged from 1976.
† Assumed to be unchanged from 1999.

Source: FAO.

SAWNWOOD PRODUCTION

(FAO estimates, '000 cubic metres, incl. railway sleepers)

	1974	1975	1976
Coniferous (softwood)	360	310	380
Broadleaved (hardwood)	50	20	20
Total	410	330	400

1977–2003: Annual production as in 1976 (FAO estimates).

Source: FAO.

Fishing

(FAO estimates, metric tons, live weight)

	2000	2001	2002
Total catch (freshwater fishes)	1,000	800	900

Source: FAO.

Mining

(estimates, '000 metric tons, unless otherwise indicated)

	1999	2000	2001
Hard coal	190	190	185
Natural gas (million cu metres)*	3,000	3,000	3,000
Copper ore†	5	5	5
Salt (unrefined)	13	13	13
Gypsum (crude)	3	3	3

* Figures refer to gross output. Estimated marketed production was 2,500 million cubic metres per year in 1999–2001.
† Figures refer to metal content.

Source: US Geological Survey.

Industry

SELECTED PRODUCTS

(year ending 20 March, '000 metric tons, unless otherwise indicated)

	1986/87	1987/88	1988/89
Margarine	3.5	3.3	1.8
Vegetable oil	4	n.a.	n.a.
Wheat flour*	187	203	166
Wine ('000 hectolitres)*	289	304	194
Soft drinks ('000 hectolitres)	8,500	10,300	4,700
Woven cotton fabrics (million sq metres)	58.1	52.6	32.1
Woven woollen fabrics (million sq metres)	0.4	0.3	0.3
Footwear—excl. rubber ('000 pairs)*	613	701	607
Rubber footwear ('000 pairs)*	2,200	3,200	2,200
Nitrogenous fertilizers†	56	57	55
Cement	103	104	70
Electric energy (million kWh)*‡	1,171	1,257	1,109

* Production in calendar years 1986, 1987 and 1988.
† Production in year ending 30 June.
‡ Provisional.

Wheat flour ('000 metric tons): 1,832 in 1994; 2,029 in 1995; 2,145 in 1996.

Nitrogenous fertilizers (provisional, year ending 30 June, '000 metric tons): 49 in 1994/95; 50 in 1995/96; 50 in 1996/97; 5 in 1997/98; 5 in 1998/99; 5 in 1999/2000.

Cement (provisional, '000 metric tons): 116 in 1998; 120 in 1999; 120 in 2000.

Electric energy (year ending 20 March, million kWh): 503 in 2000/01; 490 in 2001/02; 557 in 2002/03.

Sources: UN, *Industrial Commodity Statistics Yearbook* and *Statistical Yearbook for Asia and the Pacific*, FAO, US Geological Survey and IMF.

Finance

CURRENCY AND EXCHANGE RATES

Monetary Units
100 puls (puli) = 2 krans = 1 afghani (Af).

Sterling, Dollar and Euro Equivalents (31 December 2004)
£1 sterling = 5,794.2 afghanis;
US $1 = 3,000.0 afghanis;
€1 = 4,086.3 afghanis;
10,000 afghanis = £1.73 = $3.33 = €2.45.

Exchange Rate: The foregoing information refers to the official exchange rate. The official rate was maintained at US $1 = 1,000 afghanis between 1 May 1995 and 30 April 1996. From 1 May 1996 a rate of US $1 = 3,000 afghanis was in operation. However, this rate was applicable to only a limited range of transactions. There was also a market-determined rate, which was US $1 = 34,000 afghanis in March 2002. A new afghani, equivalent to 1,000 of the old currency, was introduced in October 2002. In the following tables, data presented in terms of afghanis, have not been revised to take account of the introduction of the new currency.

OPERATING BUDGET

(million afghanis, year ending 20 March, unless otherwise indicated)

Revenue*	2003/04†	2004/05‡
Tax revenue	6,262.1	8,817.1
Taxes on income, profits and capital gains .	362.6	749.8
Taxes on international trade and transactions	5,368.6	7,167.3
Other taxes	530.9	900.0
Non-tax revenue	3,905.8	3,967.1
Total	10,167.9	12,783.9

Expenditure	2003/04†	2004/05‡
General public services	2,032.9	3,298.8
Defence	6,004.3	5,934.6
Public order and safety	5,148.3	6,721.0
Education	3,789.4	6,342.3
Health	1,067.4	1,262.9
Social protection	416.0	1,687.7
Housing and communal services	1,327.6	62.6
Recreation and culture	482.6	621.0
Economic affairs	1,882.9	4,401.1
Total	22,151.4	30,332.0

* Excluding donor assistance grants and loans (million afghanis): 10,469.6 (estimate) in 2003/04; 17,548.1 (projection) in 2004/05.
† Estimates, year ending 19 March.
‡ Projections.
2002/03 (estimates, million afghanis, year ending 20 March): Total revenue 5,864.5; Total expenditure 15,514.0.

Source: IMF, *Islamic State of Afghanistan: First Review Under the Staff-Monitored Program* (November 2004).

BANK OF AFGHANISTAN RESERVES

(US $ million at 31 December)*

	1989	1990	1991
IMF special drawing rights . .	10.63	9.02	6.67
Reserve position in IMF . . .	6.41	6.97	7.01
Foreign exchange	226.65	250.41	221.22
Total	243.69	266.40	234.89

IMF special drawing rights (US $ million at December): 4.37 in 1992; 2.76 in 1993; 1.40 in 1994; 0.59 in 2003 (no data available 1995–2002).

Reserve position in IMF (US $ million at December): 6.78 in 1992; 6.77 in 1993; 7.19 in 1994; 7.33 in 1995; 7.09 in 1996; 6.65 in 1997; 6.94 in 1998; 6.77 in 1999; 6.42 in 2000; 6.19 in 2001; 6.70 in 2002.

* Figures exclude gold reserves, totalling 965,000 troy ounces since 1980. Assuming a gold price of 12,850 afghanis per ounce, these reserves were officially valued at US $245.06 million in December of each year 1985–91.

Source: IMF, *International Financial Statistics*.

MONEY SUPPLY

(million afghanis at 21 December)

	1989	1990	1991
Currency outside banks . . .	222,720	311,929	454,750
Private-sector deposits at Bank of Afghanistan	12,838	13,928	19,368
Demand deposits at commercial banks	11,699	18,217	n.a.

Source: IMF, *International Financial Statistics*.

COST OF LIVING

(estimates, Consumer Price Index for Kabul, 20 March of each year unless otherwise indicated; base: previous year = 100))

	2002	2003	2004*
All items	56.6	152.3	110.3

* 19 March.

Source: IMF, *Islamic State of Afghanistan: First Review Under the Staff-Monitored Program* (November 2004).

NATIONAL ACCOUNTS

(US $ million at current prices, year ending 20 March unless otherwise indicated)

Expenditure on the Gross Domestic Product

	2002/03*	2003/04†	2004/05‡
Public consumption expenditure .	318	407	545
Private consumption expenditure .	4,344	5,031	5,589
Gross fixed capital formation . .	800	1,725	2,507
Total domestic expenditures .	5,462	7,163	8,641
Exports of goods and services . .	129	571	774
Less Imports of goods and services	1,542	3,149	3,613
Gross domestic product at market prices	4,048	4,585	5,802

* Estimates.
† Estimates, year ending 19 March.
‡ Projections.
Source: IMF, *Islamic State of Afghanistan: First Review Under the Staff-Monitored Program* (November 2004).

Gross Domestic Product by Economic Activity

	2001/02	2002/03	2003/04*
Agriculture, hunting, forestry and fishing	1,394	2,006	2,151
Mining and quarrying . . .		6	7
Manufacturing	516	606	620
Electricity, gas and water . .		2	5
Construction	166	194	230
Wholesale and retail trade, restaurants and hotels† . .	121	406	418
Transport, storage and communications	249	387	510
Public administration . . .	133	190	214
Other services, incl. finance .	39	n.a.	n.a.
Total	2,618	4,084	4,440

* Year ending 19 March.
† Residual item including data discrepancies.

Source: Asian Development Bank, *Key Indicators of Developing Asian and Pacific Countries*.

BALANCE OF PAYMENTS

(US $ million, year ending 20 March unless otherwise indicated)

	2002/03*	2003/04†	2004/05‡
Exports of goods§	1,248.3	1,700.8	1,822.5
Re-exports	971.5	1,225.0	1,180.2
Imports of goods	-2,407.6	-3,758.9	-4,134.1
Trade balance	-1,159.3	-2,058.0	-2,311.7
Exports of services	50.8	124.9	131.6
Imports of services	-195.9	-641.6	-660.2
Balance on goods and services	-1,304.4	-2,574.8	-2,840.2
Other income received	—	4.9	11.2
Other income paid	-1.1	-8.3	-9.7
Balance on goods, services and income	-1,305.5	-2,578.2	-2,838.7
Grants received	1,221.7	2,535.7	2,747.6
Current balance	-83.8	-42.4	-91.1
Capital financial account (net) .	144.0	145.9	242.0
Net errors and omissions . . .	95.1	275.5	—
Overall balance	155.3	379.0	150.9

* Estimates.
† Projections, year ending 19 March.
‡ Projections.
§ Excludes opium exports and flows associated with US Army and International Security Assistance Force activities.

Source: IMF, *Islamic State of Afghanistan: First Review Under the Staff-Monitored Program* (November 2004).

OFFICIAL DEVELOPMENT ASSISTANCE
(US $ million)

	1998	1999	2000
Bilateral	88.5	104.2	88.2
Multilateral	65.7	38.3	52.7
Total	154.2	142.5	140.9
Grants	154.3	140.9	140.9
Loans	-0.1	1.6	—
Per-capita assistance (US $)	7.4	6.7	6.5

Source: UN, *Statistical Yearbook for Asia and the Pacific.*

2002/03 (US $ million, excl. grants used for clearing debt arrears): Bilateral grants 26.4; Multilateral grants 157.1 (Source: IMF, *Islamic State of Afghanistan: 2003 Article IV Consultation—Staff Report; Public Information Notice on the Executive Board Discussion; and Statement by the Executive Director for the Islamic State of Afghanistan*).

External Trade

PRINCIPAL COMMODITIES
(US $ '000, year ending 20 March)

Imports c.i.f.*	2000/01	2001/02	2002/03†
Machinery and equipment	71,870	512,382	854,842
Chemical materials	3,865	39,728	172,679
Food	250,675	214,433	201,339
Fabrics, clothing and footwear	478,521	472,638	345,934
Household items and medicine	357,110	392,231	622,481
Total (incl. others)	1,175,896	1,696,525	2,322,609

Exports f.o.b.‡	2000/01	2001/02	2002/03†
Fresh fruits	8,403	4,269	5,587
Dried fruit	16,381	23,328	40,582
Animal skins	10,841	13,678	1,172
Wool	904	2,967	651
Carpets and rugs	99,571	21,503	47,474
Total (incl. others)	137,312	68,541	100,143

* Official recorded only; including re-exports (US $ million, estimates): 1,589 in 2001/02; 2,190 in 2002/03.
† Estimates.
‡ Official recorded only; excluding re-exports.

Source: IMF, *Islamic State of Afghanistan: Rebuilding a Macroeconomic Framework for Reconstruction and Growth* (September 2003).

PRINCIPAL TRADING PARTNERS
(US $ million, year ending 20 March)

Imports*	2000/01	2001/02	2002/03†
China, People's Republic	21.9	35.0	20.3
Germany	16.1	15.9	48.5
India	30.5	25.0	36.5
Japan	491.0	594.0	999.0
Kazakhstan	64.4	19.9	21.6
Kenya	47.2	52.1	56.5
Korea, Republic of	92.5	104.5	113.4
Pakistan	135.4	157.0	206.7
Singapore	6.6	2.8	1.5
Turkmenistan	41.8	46.2	50.1
Total (incl. others)	1,175.9	1,696.5	2,322.6

Exports‡	2000/01	2001/02	2002/03†
Belgium	16.9	4.4	3.3
Finland	1.0	6.3	9.0
Germany	5.1	6.6	5.5
India	8.0	10.0	27.4
Pakistan	52.0	26.0	26.0
Russia	4.9	2.5	3.5
United Arab Emirates	4.5	4.8	4.6
United Kingdom	11.6	0.8	0.4
USA	2.6	0.6	4.3
Total (incl. others)	137.3	68.5	100.1

* Figures refer to official recorded imports only and include re-exports (US $ million, estimates): 1,589 in 2001/02; 2,190 in 2002/03.
† Estimates.
‡ Excluding re-exports.

Source: IMF, *Islamic State of Afghanistan: Rebuilding a Macroeconomic Framework for Reconstruction and Growth* (September 2003).

Transport

ROAD TRAFFIC
('000 motor vehicles in use)

	1999	2000	2001
Passenger cars	5.4	6.2	8.6
Commercial vehicles	6.2	7.0	4.5

Source: UN, *Statistical Yearbook.*

Taxicabs (number in use): 33,507 in 2002 (Source: IMF, *Islamic State of Afghanistan: Rebuilding a Macroeconomic Framework for Reconstruction and Growth*).

CIVIL AVIATION
('000)

	1998	1999	2000
Kilometres flown	3,000	3,000	3,000
Passengers carried	53	140	150
Passenger-km	88,000	129,000	143,000
Freight ton-km	24,000	19,000	21,000

Source: UN, *Statistical Yearbook.*

Tourism

	1996	1997	1998
Tourist arrivals ('000)	4	4	4
Tourism receipts (US $ million)	1	1	1

Source: World Tourism Organization, *Yearbook of Tourism Statistics.*

Communications Media

	1995	1996	1997
Radio receivers ('000 in use) . .	2,400	2,550	2,750
Television receivers ('000 in use) .	200	250	270
Main telephone lines ('000 in use)*†	29	29	29
Daily newspapers:			
Number	15*	12	n.a.
Average circulation ('000 copies)	200*	113	n.a.

* Estimate(s).

† 1998–2001: Number of main telephone lines in use assumed to be unchanged.

2002: Telephones ('000 main lines in use) 33 (estimate); Mobile cellular telephones ('000 subscribers) 12; Internet users 1,000 (estimate).

Television receivers ('000 in use): 290 in 1998; 300 in 1999.

Sources: mainly UNESCO, *Statistical Yearbook* and UN, *Statistical Yearbook*.

Education

(1995/96)

	Institutions	Teachers	Pupils
Pre-primary	88	2,110	n.a.
Primary	2,146	21,869	1,312,200
Secondary*	n.a.	19,085	512,900
Higher	n.a.	n.a.	12,800

* Figures refer to general secondary education only, excluding vocational and teacher training.

Source: UN, *Statistical Yearbook for Asia and the Pacific*.

2001: Primary pupils 773,623; Secondary pupils 362,415 (Source: UN, *Statistical Yearbook*).

Adult literacy rate (UNESCO estimates): 36% in 2001 (Source: UN Development Programme, *Human Development Report*).

Directory

The Constitution

On 5 December 2001 28 Afghan leaders signed the Agreement on Provisional Arrangements in Afghanistan Pending the Re-establishment of Permanent Government Institutions (also known as the Bonn Agreement), stipulating a timetable for the creation of a permanent constitution and the holding of free national elections. In accordance with the agreement, Afghanistan temporarily reverted to the Constitution of 1964. A Transitional Authority, with the assistance of the UN, established a Constitutional Drafting Commission in November 2002 to draw up a new constitution. A new charter providing for a strongly presidential system following eventual elections by universal suffrage was approved by a Constitutional Loya Jirga (Grand National Council) in early January 2004.

The Government

On 11–19 June 2002 an Emergency Loya Jirga, comprising approximately 1,650 delegates, 1,051 of whom were elected by tribal representatives, and the remainder selected by aid organizations, universities and other civil society bodies to ensure diverse representation, convened. The Loya Jirga appointed a broad-based, gender-sensitive Transitional Authority and a Head of State. A democratic presidential election, based on the principles of the new Constitution, took place on 9 October 2004; legislative elections were expected to take place in September 2005.

HEAD OF STATE
(April 2005)

President: HAMID KARZAI (inaugurated as Chairman of Interim Authority 22 December 2001; elected as President of Transitional Authority by Loya Jirga 13 June 2002 and as President of Afghanistan by direct popular vote 9 October 2004).

Vice-Presidents: AHMAD ZIA MASOUD, KARIM KHALILI.

CABINET
(April 2005)

Minister of Commerce and Senior Presidential Adviser: HEDAYAT AMIN ARSALA.

Minister of Defence: Gen. ADBUL RAHIM WARDAK.

Minister of Foreign Affairs: Dr ABDULLAH ABDULLAH.

Minister of Finance: Prof. Dr ANWAR-UL-HAQ AHADY.

Minister of Interior Affairs: ALI AHMAD JALALI.

Minister of Economy: Dr MOHAMMAD FAHIM FARHANG.

Minister of Communications: AMIRZAI SANGIN.

Minister of Border and Tribal Affairs: MOHAMMAD KARIM BRAHWI.

Minister of Refugees: MOHAMMAD AZAM DADFAR.

Minister of Mines and Industries: MIR MOHAMMAD SEDIQ.

Minister of Energy and Water: ISMAIL KHAN.

Minister of Public Health: SAYED MOHAMMAD AMIN FATEMI.

Minister of Agriculture, Food and Livestock: OBAIDOLLAH RAMIN.

Minister of Justice: MOHAMMAD SARWAR DANESH.

Minister of Information and Culture: Dr SAYED MAKHDOOM RAHIN.

Minister of Haj and Religious Affairs: NEMATULLAH SHAHRANI.

Minister of Urban Development and Housing: MOHAMMAD YOSUF PASHTUN.

Minister of Public Works: SUHRAB ALI SAFARI.

Minister of Social and Labour Affairs: SAYED EKRAMODDIN MASUMI.

Minister of Martyrs and Disabled People: SEDIQA BALKHI.

Minister of Higher Education: AMIR SHAH HASANYAR.

Minister of Transport: SAYED ENAYATULLAH QASEMI.

Minister of Education: NOOR MOHAMMAD KARKIN.

Minister of Rural Rehabilitation and Development: HANIF ATMAR.

Minister of Women's Affairs: MASOODA JALAL.

Minister of Anti-narcotics: HABIBULLAH QADERI.

National Security Adviser: Dr ZALMAI RASSOUL.

Adviser on Youth Affairs: AMENA SAFI AFZALI.

MINISTRIES

Office of the Islamic Transitional State of Afghanistan: Kabul; internet www.afghanistangov.org.

Ministry of Agriculture, Food and Livestock: Jamal Mena, Kart-i-Sakhi, Kabul; tel. (20) 2500315; e-mail info@agriculture.gov.af; internet www.agriculture.gov.af.

Ministry of Anti-narcotics: Kabul.

Ministry of Border and Tribal Affairs: Shah Mahmud Ghazi Ave, Kabul; tel. (93) 21793.

Ministry of Commerce: Darulaman Wat, Kabul; tel. (20) 2290090; fax (20) 2290089; e-mail info@commerce.gov.af; internet www.commerce.gov.af.

Ministry of Communications: Mohammad Jan Khan Wat, Kabul; tel. (20) 2102655; fax (20) 290022; e-mail khalid.saleem@moc.gov.af; internet www.moc.gov.af.

Ministry of Defence: Darulaman Wat, Kabul; tel. (93) 41232.

Ministry of Economy: Kabul.

Ministry of Education: Mohammad Jan Khan Wat, Kabul; tel. and fax (20) 200000.

Ministry of Energy and Water: Kabul.

Ministry of Finance: Pashtunistan Wat, Kabul; tel. (20) 2102099; e-mail hasan@mof.gov.af; internet www.mof.gov.af.

Ministry of Foreign Affairs: Malak Azghar Rd, Kabul; tel. (20) 2100366; fax (866) 8909988; e-mail contact@afghanistan-mfa.net; internet www.afghanistan-mfa.net.

Ministry of Haj and Religious Affairs: Kabul.

Ministry of Higher Education: Jamal Mina, Kabul; tel. (93) 40041.

Ministry of Information and Culture: Mohammad Jan Khan Wat, Kabul; tel. and fax (20) 200000.

Ministry of Interior Affairs: Shar-i-Nau, Kabul; tel. (93) 32441.

Ministry of Justice: Shar Rahi Pashtunistan, Kabul; tel. (93) 23404.

Ministry of Martyrs and Disabled People: Kabul.

Ministry of Mines and Industries: Pashtunistan Watt, Kabul.

Ministry of Public Health: Micro-Rayon, Kabul; tel. (93) 40851.

Ministry of Public Works: Micro-Rayon 1, Kabul; tel. (20) 2301363; fax (20) 2301362.

Ministry of Refugees: Jungaluk, off Darlaman Rd, Kabul; e-mail afgmorr@afgmorr.com.

Ministry of Rural Rehabilitation and Development: Kabul; internet www.afghanistangov.org/mrrd.

Ministry of Social and Labour Affairs: Kabul.

Ministry of Transport: Ansari Wat, Kabul; tel. (93) 25541.

Ministry of Urban Development and Housing: Kabul.

Ministry of Women's Affairs: Kabul.

President and Legislature

PRESIDENT

Presidential Election, 9 October 2004

Candidates	Votes	% of votes
Hamid Karzai .	4,443,029	55.37
Younis Qanooni	1,306,503	16.28
Haji Mohammad Mohaqqeq	935,325	11.66
Abdul Rashid Dostam	804,861	10.03
Abdul Latif Pedram	110,160	1.37
Masooda Jalal	91,415	1.14
Syed Ishaq Gailani	80,081	1.00
Others	253,162	3.15
Total	**8,024,536**	**100.00**

LEGISLATURE

A Meli Shura (National Assembly) was established in 1987 to replace the Revolutionary Council. It was composed of two houses: the Wolasi Jirga (House of Representatives) and the Sena (Senate). However, following the downfall of Najibullah's regime in April 1992, an interim *mujahidin* Government took power in Kabul and both houses were dissolved. In September 1996 the Taliban took over Kabul and closed down the council. On assuming power, the regime adopted an Interim Council of Ministers to administer the country. After the Taliban regime collapsed in late 2001, an Interim Authority was installed. An Emergency Loya Jirga appointed a Transitional Authority six months later. In accordance with the new Constitution, which was ratified in January 2004, a Meli Shura was to be established following a general election. The election was scheduled to be held on 18 September 2005. The Meli Shura was to be composed of two houses: the Wolasi Jirga and the Meshrano Jirga (House of Elders).

Political Organizations

In September 2003 a new law allowing the formation of political parties was passed. By early 2005 the following parties were registered with the Ministry of Justice:

Afghan Mellat Party (Afghan Social Democratic Party): e-mail ajmal.mirranay@afghanmellat.com; internet www.afghanmellat.com; Pres. Dr ANWAR-UL-HAQ AHADY.

Afghan National Solidarity Movement: Kabul; Chair. Pir SAYED ISHAQ GAILANI.

Harakat-i Islami i Afghanistan (Islamic Movement of Afghanistan): Kabul; Leader SAYYED MOHAMMAD ALI JAWED.

Hizb-i Adalat-i Islami Afghanistan (Islamic Justice Party of Afghanistan): Kabul; f. 2004; Leader MOHAMMAD KABIR MARZBAN.

Hizb-i Afghanistan-i-Wahid (United Afghanistan Party): Kabul; Leader MOHAMMAD WASIL RAHIMI.

Hizb-i Hambastagi-yi Melli-yi Jawanan-i Afghanistan (National Solidarity Youth Party of Afghanistan): Kabul; f. 2004; Leader MOHAMMAD JAMIL KARZAI.

Hizb-i Harak-i-Islami Mardum-i Afghanistan (Islamic Movement Party of the People of Afghanistan): Kabul; f. 2004; Leader SYED HUSSAIN ANWARI.

Hizb-i Harakat-i-Melli Wahdat-i-Afghanistan (National Movement for the Unity of Afghanistan): Kabul; f. 2004; Chair. MOHAMMAD NADIR ATASH.

Hizb-i Isteqlal-i Islami-yi Afghanistan (Islamic Independence Party of Afghanistan): Kabul; f. 2004; Leader Dr GHULAM FAROOQ NAJRABI.

Hizb-i Jomhorikhahan (Republican Party of Afghanistan): Kabul; f. 2003; supporter of presidential system of government; Leader SEBGHATULLAH SANGAR; c. 35,000 mems.

Hizb-i Melli Afghanistan (National Party of Afghanistan): Kabul; Leader ABDUL RASHID ARYAN.

Hizb-i Muttahid-i Melli (Party of National Unity): Kabul; f. 2003 by members of the fmr communist People's Democratic Party of Afghanistan; proscribed until 2004; Leader ABDUL RASHID JALILI.

Hizb-i Rifah-i Mardum-i Afghanistan (Party of Welfare of the People of Afghanistan): Kabul; f. 2004; Leader MIAGUL WASIQ.

Hizb-i Sahadat-i Mardum-i-Afghanistan (Welfare Popular Party of Afghanistan): Kabul; Leader MOHAMMAD ZUBAIR FEROZE.

Hizb-i-Wahdat-i Islami Afghanistan (Islamic Unity Party of Afghanistan): Kabul; Leader MOHAMMAD KARIM KHALILI.

Hizb-i-Wahdat-i Islami Mardum-i Afghanistan (People's Islamic Unity Party of Afghanistan): Kabul; e-mail wahdat_magazine@yahoo.com; internet www.wahdat.org; represents Hazaras; advocate of equal rights, freedom and social justice; Leader USTAD Haji MOHAMMAD MOHAQIQ.

Junbesh-i Wahadat-i Melli (Afghan National Unity Movement): Kabul; f. 2003; royalist; Chair. Sultan MAHMOUD GHAZI.

Labour and Expansion Party of Afghanistan: Kabul; previously known as the National Reconciliation Party; Leader ZULFIQAR.

Mahaz-i-Melli-i-Islami (National Islamic Front): Pashtun; Leader Pir SAYED AHMAD GAILANI; Dep. Leader HAMED GAILANI; c. 15,000 supporters.

Majma'-i Milli Afghanistan (National Congress of Afghanistan): Kabul; f. 2004; Leader ABDUL LATIF PADRAM.

Movement for Democracy and Freedom in Afghanistan: Kabul; f. 2004; Leader JAVED KOHISTANI.

New Afghanistan: Kabul; f. 2005; Leader YOUNIS QANOONI.

Nizat-i Milli-i Afghanistan (National Movement of Afghanistan): Kabul; f. 2002; Leader AHMAD WALI MASOUD.

Party of National Unity of Muslim Tribes of Afghanistan: Kabul; Leader MOHAMMAD SHAH KHOGIANI.

Most of the following are unregistered political parties:

Hizb-i Islami Gulbuddin (Islamic Party Gulbuddin): e-mail info@hezb-e-islami.org; internet www.hezb-e-islami.org; Pashtun/Turkmen/Tajik; Leader GULBUDDIN HEKMATYAR; c. 50,000 supporters (estimate); based in Iran in 1998–99.

Hizb-i Islami Khalis (Islamic Party Khalis): Pashtun; Leader Maulvi MUHAMMAD YOUNIS KHALIS; c. 40,000 supporters.

Ittihad-i-Islami Bara i Azadi Afghanistan (Islamic Union for the Liberation of Afghanistan): Pashtun; Leader Prof. ABDUL RASUL SAYEF; Dep. Leader AHMAD SHAH AHMADZAY; c. 18,000 supporters.

Jamiat-i Islami (Islamic Society): internet www.jamiat.com; Turkmen/Uzbek/Tajik; Leaders Prof. BURHANUDDIN RABBANI, Marshal MUHAMMAD FAHIM; Sec.-Gen. ENAYATOLLAH SHADAB; c. 60,000 supporters.

Jebha-i-Nejat-i-Melli (National Liberation Front): Pashtun; Leader Prof. HAZRAT SIBGHATULLAH MOJADDEDI; Sec.-Gen. ZABIHOLLAH MOJADDEDI; c. 15,000 supporters.

Junbesh-i Melli-i Islami (National Islamic Movement): e-mail info@junbesh.com; internet www.junbesh.com; f. 1992; formed mainly from troops of former Northern Command of the Afghan army; predominantly Uzbek/Tajik/Turkmen/Ismaili and Hazara Shi'a; Leader SAYED NOORULLAH (acting); 65,000–150,000 supporters.

Renaissance Party of the People of Afghanistan: Kabul; f. 2003; Chair. SAYED ZAHER QAID OMULBELADI.

Taliban: internet www.taleban.com; emerged in 1994; Islamist fundamentalist; mainly Sunni Pashtuns; in power 1996–2001; largely disbanded; Leader Mullah MOHAMMAD OMAR.

Diplomatic Representation

EMBASSIES IN AFGHANISTAN

Bulgaria: Wazir Akbar Khan Mena, Kabul; tel. (93) 20683; Ambassador ANGEL URBETSOV.

Canada: House 256, St 15, Wazir Akbar Khan, Kabul; tel. (70) 294281; e-mail homcanadakabul@yahoo.com; Ambassador CHRISTOPHER ALEXANDER.

China, People's Republic: Sardar Shah Mahmoud Ghazi Wai, Kabul; tel. (93) 20446; Ambassador SUN YUXI.

Cuba: Shar Rahi Haji Yaqub, opp. Shar-i-Nau Park, Kabul; tel. (93) 30863.

Egypt: Kabul; Ambassador SHERIF RIHAN.

France: Shar-i-Nau, POB 62, Kabul; tel. (870) 682084815; Ambassador JEAN-PIERRE GUINHUT.

Germany: Wazir Akbar Khan Mena, POB 83, Kabul; tel. (20) 2101512; Ambassador Dr REINALD STECK.

India: Malalai Wat, Shar-i-Nau, Kabul; tel. (873) 763095560; fax (873) 763095561; e-mail embassy@indembassy-kabul.com; Ambassador RAKESH SOOD.

Indonesia: Malalai Wat, Shar-i-Nau, Kabul; tel. and fax (20) 2201066; e-mail kbrikbl@kbrikabul.go.id; Chargé d'affaires SUHASWOTO HIDYONINGRAT.

Iran: Shar-i-Nau, Kabul; tel. (93) 26255; Ambassador MOHAMMAD REZA BRAHIMI.

Italy: Great Masoud Rd, Kabul; tel. and fax (873) 763068371; e-mail ambasciata.kabul@esteri.it; Ambassador ETTORE FRANCESCO SEQUI.

Japan: St 15, Wazir Akbar Khan, Kabul; tel. (873) 762853777; fax (873) 761218272; Ambassador NORIHIRO OKUDA.

Kazakhstan: Kabul; Ambassador BAKHT SARGENOV.

Korea, Democratic People's Republic: Wazir Akbar Khan Mena, House 28, Sarak 'H' House 103, Kabul; tel. (93) 22161; Ambassador O IN YONG.

Korea, Republic: Wazir Akbar Khan, St 10, House 34, Kabul; tel. (873) 762728479; fax (873) 762728481; Ambassador PARK JOON-SOON.

Kuwait: Kabul; Chargé d'affaires NASEER AHMED NOOR.

Libya: 103 Wazir Akbar Khan, Kabul; tel. (20) 25948; fax (20) 290160.

Mongolia: Wazir Akbar Khan Mena, Sarak 'T' House 8714, Kabul; tel. (93) 22138.

Norway: Wazir Akbar Khan, St 15, Lane 4, Kabul; tel. (20) 2300899; e-mail emb.kabul@mfa.no; internet www.norway.org.af; Chargé d'affaires a.i. BJØRN JOHANNESSEN.

Pakistan: House 10, Nijat Watt Rd, Wazir Akbar Khan, Kabul; tel. (20) 20542; e-mail parepkbl@pes.comsats.net.pk; Ambassador MASOOD KHAN.

Poland: Gozargah St, POB 78, Kabul; tel. (93) 42461.

Russia: Darulaman Wat, Kabul; tel. (93) 41541; Ambassador ZAMIR KABULOV.

Saudi Arabia: Wazir Akbar Khan Mena, Kabul; tel. (93) 25260; Chargé d'affaires FAHD AL-QAHTANI.

Slovakia: Taimani Wat, Kala-i-Fatullah, Kabul; tel. (93) 32082.

Tajikistan: Vazir Akbarkhon, 10 Saraki St, Bldg 3, Kabul; tel. (873) 763010311; fax (873) 763010313; Ambassador FARHOD MAHKAMOV.

Turkey: Shar-i-Nau, Kabul; tel. (93) 20072; Ambassador BULENT TULUN.

Turkmenistan: Kabul; Ambassador AMANMAMMET YARANOV.

United Arab Emirates: Kabul; Ambassador ALI MUHAMMAD AL-SHAMSI.

United Kingdom: St 15, Roundabout Wazir Akbar Khan, POB 334, Kabul; tel. (93) 070102000; fax (93) 070102250; e-mail britishembassy.kabul@fco.gov.uk; internet www.britishembassy.gov.uk/afghanistan; Ambassador Dr ROSALIND MARSDEN.

USA: Great Masoud Rd, Kabul; tel. (20) 2300436; fax (20) 2301364; internet usembassy.state.gov/afghanistan; Ambassador (vacant).

Uzbekistan: House 14, St 13, Wazir Akbar Khan, Kabul; Ambassador ALISHER AHMADJONOV.

Viet Nam: 3 Nijat St, Wazir Akbar Khan Mena, Kabul; tel. (93) 26596.

Judicial System

After 23 years of civil war, which ended in December 2001 with the defeat of the Taliban, there no longer existed a functioning national judicial system. In accordance with the Bonn Agreement, Afghanistan temporarily reverted to the Constitution of 1964, which combined *Shari'a* with Western concepts of justice. A new Constitution was introduced in early 2004, which made no specific reference to the role of *Shari'a* but stated that Afghan laws should not contravene the main tenets of Islam. Following the inauguration of a directly elected President in December 2004, in January 2005 an interim Supreme Court was created, as required by the Constitution if a presidential election preceded legislative elections. The Court comprised nine members, including the Chief Justice.

Chief Justice: FAZUL HADI SHINWARI.

Religion

The official religion of Afghanistan is Islam. Muslims comprise 99% of the population, approximately 84% of them of the Sunni and the remainder of the Shi'ite sect. There are small minority groups of Hindus, Sikhs and Jews.

ISLAM

The High Council of Ulema and Clergy of Afghanistan: Kabul; f. 1980; 7,000 mems; Chair. Mawlawi ABDOL GHAFUR SENANI.

The Press

Many newspapers and periodicals stopped appearing on a regular basis or, in a large number of cases, ceased publication during the civil war. Following the defeat of the Taliban in late 2001, a number of newspapers and periodicals resumed publication or were established for the first time. In February 2002 the Media Law was amended, removing most restrictions on independent media. Newspapers and periodicals were required to obtain a licence under the legislation. By early 2005 more than 250 publications had been registered with the Ministry of Information and Culture.

PRINCIPAL DAILIES

Anis (Friendship): Ministry of Information and Culture, Mohammad Jan Khan Wat, Kabul; f. 1927; evening; independent; Dari, Uzbek and Pashto; state-owned; news and literary articles; Editor-in-Chief GHOLAM SAKHI MONIR; circ. 5,000.

Arman-e Melli: Kabul; f. 2002 by the Afghan Interim Authority; circ. 4,200.

Eradeh (Intention): Parwan Mina, Cinema Baharistan, House 95, Hajji Mir Ahmad St, Kabul; independent; Dari and Pashto; Editor-in-Chief Haji SYED DAUD.

Eslah: Kabul; state-owned; Dari.

Hewad (Homeland): Azadi Press Centre, Micro-rayon, Kabul; tel. (93) 22279; f. 1949; Pashto; state-owned; Dir AJRUDIN EGHBAL; circ. 5,000.

Ittefaq-e Islam: Herat; circ. 2,000.

Kabul Times: Azady Press Centre, Micro-rayon, POB 1560, Kabul; tel. (93) 61847; e-mail kabultimes@hotmail.com; f. 1962 as Kabul Times, renamed Kabul New Times in 1980; ceased publication in 2001; revived in 2002 under new management; English; state-owned; Editor-in-Chief ABDUL HAQ WALEH.

Shari'at: Kabul.

PERIODICALS

Aamu: Aria Press, Kabul; quarterly; research; circ. 1,000.

Amanat: House 3, Moslem St, Shar-i-Nau, POB 1158, Kabul; weekly; organ of Hindukosh News Agency; Editor-in-Chief SYED SHABIR ABIR.

Ambastagi: Aria Press, Kabul; weekly; circ. 1,000.

Anees: Kabul; weekly; govt-supported; Editor AHMAD ZIA SYAMAK.

Awa-e Naw: Herat; fortnightly; independent; circ. 2,000.

Ayina-e Zan (Women's Mirror): House 26, Park Northern Rd and Moslem Rd, Shar-i-Nau, Kabul; e-mail womensmirror@hotmail.com; f. 2002; weekly; women's; Dari, Pashto and English; Chief Editor SHUKRIA BAREKZAI; circ. 3,000.

Cinema: Kabul; f. 2003; monthly; entertainment and culture; Editor-in-Chief SIDDIQ BARMAK.

Farda (Tomorrow): POB 1758, Kabul; tel. (20) 2100199; fax (20) 2100699; e-mail farda-news@yahoo.com; weekly; Publr ABDUL GHAFUR AITEQAD; circ. 4,000.

Kabul Weekly: Afghan Media and Cultural Centre, Malik Ashgar Crossroads, POB 1831, Kabul; tel. (20) 2101589; e-mail kabulweekly@lycos.com; f. 1993; banned in 1997, revived in 2002; Dari, Pashto, English and French; weekly; independent; political, social and cultural issues; Editor-in-Chief FAHIM DASHTY; Sec. ABDUL AKBAR; circ. 8,000.

Killid (The Key): Kabul; weekly; current affairs; Editor MAHMOOD JAFFERY; circ. 20,000.

Malalai: Afghan Media and Cultural Centre, Malik Ashgar Cross-roads, Kabul; f. 2002; monthly; women's; Chief Editor JAMILA MUJAHID.

Mojahed: Kabul; weekly; Editor WAQIF HAKIMI.

Les Nouvelles de Kaboul (Kabul News): Afghan Media and Cultural Centre, Malik Ashgar Crossroads, Kabul; f. 2002; weekly; Dari, Pashto and French; French-owned; Editor OLIVIER PUECH; Owner and Dir SHAFIQA HABIBI.

Parvaz (Flight): Afghan Media and Cultural Centre, Malik Ashgar Crossroads, Kabul; e-mail roshanak@ainaworld.org; f. 2002; Dari and Pashto; every two months; children's; Editor MIRHASAMADEEN BRUMAND.

Payam-e-Mujahid (Holy Warrior's Message): Panjshir; internet www.payamemujahid.com; f. 1996; weekly; Dari and Pashto; sponsored by the Northern Alliance; Editor HAFIZ MANSOOR.

Roz (The Day): Kabul; f. 2002; monthly; women's; Dari, Pashto, French and English; Editor-in-Chief LAILOMA AHMADI.

Sabawoon: Afghan Media and Cultural Centre, Malik Ashgar Crossroads, Kabul; e-mail sabawoon_afg@hotmail.com; internet www.sabawoon.com; general interest; f. 1979; revived in 2002; monthly; Chief Editor LATIFA SAYEDI POPAL; circ. 6,000.

Seerat (Character): Afghan Media and Cultural Centre, Malik Ashgar Crossroads, Kabul; f. 2002; weekly; news; circ. 1,000; Chief Editor ABDUL RAHIM DEL.

Takhassos (Experts): Herat; monthly; Dari; published by Council of Professionals; Editor MOHAMMAD RAFIQ SHAHIR.

Zanbil-e-Gham: Afghan Media and Cultural Centre, Malik Ashgar Crossroads, Kabul; f. 1997; monthly; satirical; Editor OSMAN AKRAM; circ. 2,000.

NEWS AGENCIES

Afghan Islamic Press: Peshawar, North-West Frontier Province, Pakistan.

Ariana Press Agency: Kabul; f. 1987 in Dushanbe, Tajikistan; independent; publishes three newsletters.

Bakhtar News Agency (BNA): Ministry of Information and Culture, Mohammad Jan Khan Wat, Kabul; tel. and fax (20) 2101304; e-mail meenawee13@yahoo.com; f. 1939; government news agency; correspondents in 32 provinces; Dir-Gen. Sultan AHMAD BAHEEN.

Hindukosh News Agency (HNA): House 3, Moslem St, Shar-i-Nau, POB 1158, Kabul; f. 2002; independent; offices in Herat, Qandahar and Mazar-i-Sharif; Dir SYED NAJIBULLAH HASHIMI.

Pajhwok Afghan News: Kabul; internet www.pajhwak.com; f. 2004; independent; regional bureaux in Mazar-i-Sharif, Qandahar, Herat and Jalalabad.

PRESS ASSOCIATIONS

Afghanistan Women in Media Network: Afghan Media and Cultural Centre, Malik Ashgar Crossroads, Kabul; e-mail najibamaram@hotmail.com; f. 2002; association of female media staff; Pres. JAMILA MUJAHID; Vice-Pres. NAJIBA MARAM.

Publishers

Some of the following publishers were forced to close down during the Taliban regime. Since the fall of the Taliban, publishers have been slowly reopening, with the help of the UN and other international aid agencies and foreign publishing houses.

Afghan Book: POB 206, Kabul; f. 1969; books on various subjects, translations of foreign works on Afghanistan, books in English on Afghanistan and Dari language textbooks for foreigners; Man. Dir JAMILA AHANG.

Afghanistan Today Publishers: c/o The Kabul Times, Ansari Wat, POB 983, Kabul; tel. (93) 61847; publicity materials; answers enquiries about Afghanistan.

Ariana Press: Poli Jarkhi, Kabul; under the supervision of the Ministry of Information and Culture; Dir ABDUL KADER.

Azady (Freedom) Press: Ministry of Information and Culture, Mohammad Jan Khan Wat, Kabul; tel. (20) 2100113; under supervision of the Ministry of Information and Culture; Dir JAHAN YAR.

Balhaqi Book Publishing and Importing Institute: POB 2025, Kabul; tel. (93) 26818; f. 1971 by co-operation of the Government Printing House, Bakhtar News Agency and leading newspapers; publishers and importers of books; Pres. MUHAMMAD ANWAR NUMYALAI.

Beihagi Publishers: Azady Press Centre, Micro-rayon, Kabul; tel. (93) 63623; books on Afghan culture; also prints information related to the government and its plans; Dir SADIQ AYAR.

Book Publishing Institute: Herat; f. 1970 by co-operation of Government Printing House and citizens of Herat; books on literature, history and religion.

Book Publishing Institute: Qandahar; f. 1970; supervised by Government Printing House; mainly books in Pashto language.

Educational Publications: Ministry of Education, Mohammad Jan Khan Wat, Kabul; tel. and fax (20) 200000; textbooks for primary and secondary schools in the Pashto and Dari languages; also three monthly magazines in Pashto and in Dari.

Franklin Book Programs Inc: POB 332, Kabul.

Historical Society of Afghanistan: Kabul; tel. (93) 30370; f. 1931; mainly historical and cultural works and two quarterly magazines: *Afghanistan* (English and French), *Aryana* (Dari and Pashto); Pres. AHMAD ALI MOTAMEDI.

Institute of Geography: Kabul University, Kabul; geographical and related works.

International Center for Pashto Studies: Kabul; f. 1975 by the Afghan Govt with the assistance of UNESCO; research work on the Pashto language and literature and on the history and culture of the Pashto people; Pres. and Assoc. Chief Researcher J. K. HEKMATY; publs *Pashto* (quarterly).

Kabul University Press: Kabul; tel. (93) 42433; f. 1950; textbooks; two quarterly scientific journals in Dari and in English, etc.

Research Center for Linguistics and Literary Studies: Afghanistan Academy of Sciences, Akbar Khan Mena, Kabul; tel. (93) 26912; f. 1978; research on Afghan languages (incl. Pashto, Dari, Balochi and Uzbek) and Afghan folklore; Pres. Prof. MOHAMMED R. ELHAM; publs *Kabul* (Pashto), *Zeray* (Pashto weekly) and *Khurasan* (Dari).

GOVERNMENT PUBLISHING HOUSE

Government Printing House: Kabul; tel. (93) 26851; f. 1870; under supervision of the Ministry of Information and Culture; Dir SAID AHMAD RAHAA.

PUBLISHERS' ASSOCIATION

Afghan Libraries' and Publishers' Association: Chari Ansari, between Ansari Crossroads and Popo Lano Restaurant, Kabul.

Broadcasting and Communications

TELECOMMUNICATIONS

Afghan Wireless Communication Company (AWCC): Ministry of Communications Bldg, Mohammad Jan Khan Wat, Kabul; tel. and fax (93) 200000; e-mail info@afghanwireless.com; internet www.afghanwireless.com; f. 1999; jt venture between the Afghan Government and Telephone Systems International, Inc of the USA; reconstruction of Afghanistan's national and international telecommunications network; by June 2002 mobile and fixed-line telecommunications services covered Herat, Jalalabad, Kabul, Mazar-i-Sharif and Qandahar; the first centre providing internet services was opened in Kabul in July; CEO EHSAN BAYAT.

Roshan: Telecom Development Co Afghanistan Ltd, 461 Karta-e-Wali, Shash Darak, District 9, Kabul; tel. (79) 997333; internet www.roshan.af; f. 2002 by an international consortium comprising the Aga Khan Fund for Economic Development, French cos Monaco Telecom International and Alcatel, and US co MCT Corpn; provides mobile telecommunications services; CEO KARIM KHOJA.

BROADCASTING

The media were severely restricted by the militant Taliban regime (1996–2001): television was banned and Radio Afghanistan was renamed Radio Voice of Shari'a. The overthrow of the Taliban in November–December 2001 led to the liberation of the media. On 13 November Radio Afghanistan was revived in Kabul; music was broadcast for the first time in five years. A few days later Kabul TV was resurrected, and a woman was employed as its newsreader. By early 2005 there were 42 radio stations and eight private television stations broadcasting in Afghanistan.

Radio

Radio-Television Afghanistan: St 10, Lane 2, Wazir Akbar Khan, POB 544, Kabul; tel. (20) 2101086; e-mail rtakabul@hotmail.com; revived in 2001; programmes in Dari, Pashto, Turkmen and Uzbek; Dir-Gen. MOHAMMAD ESHAQ; Head of Radio GHULAM HASSAN HAZRATI.

Balkh Radio and TV: Mazar-i-Sharif; Pashto and Dari; Chair. ABDORRAB JAHED.

Radio Herat: Herat.

Radio Kabul: Ansari Wat, Kabul; tel. (20) 2101087; Dir GHULAM HASSAN HAZRATI.

Voice of Freedom: Kabul; f. 2002; broadcasts one hour a day in Dari and Pashto; German-funded.

Independent

Arman FM: POB 1045, Central Post Office, Kabul; tel. (70) 296723; e-mail info@arman.fm; internet www.arman.fm; f. 2003; Afghanistan's first ever privately owned independent FM radio station; broadcasts 24 hours a day of popular music and culture; Dir SAAD MOHSENI.

Radio Azad Afghan: Qandahar; f. 2004; broadcasts five hours daily; Dir ISMAIL TIMUR.

Radio Bamian: Bamian; f. 2003.

Radio Killid: Kabul; f. 2003 by Development and Humanitarian Services for Afghanistan; broadcasts 24 hours daily.

Radio Sahar: Herat; f. 2003; women's; broadcasts 90–120 mins daily; Dir HULAN KHATIBI.

Radio Sharq: Jalalabad; f. 2003; broadcasts 12 hours daily.

Radio Tiraj Mir: Pol-e-Khomri; f. 2003; broadcasts 16 hours daily.

Voice of Afghan Women: Kabul; f. 2003; relaunched in 2005 following closure owing to lack of funds; dedicated to interests of women; Dir JAMILA MUJAHID.

Television

Radio-Television Afghanistan: see Radio.

Balkh Radio and TV: see Radio.

Herat TV: Herat; state-owned.

Kabul TV: Kabul; revived in 2001; broadcasts four hours daily; Dir HUMAYUN RAWI.

TV Badakhshan: Faizabad; f. 1987 as Faizabad TV, name changed in 2000; Pashto and Dari.

Independent

Afghan TV: Kabul; f. 2004; broadcasts 18 hours daily; Man. AHMED SHAH AFGHANZAI.

Aina (Mirror): Shebarghan; f. 2003; broadcasts to Jawzjan, Sar-e Pol and Balkh provinces and to the bordering areas of Turkmenistan and Uzbekistan; Dir SYED ANWAR SADAT.

Tolo TV: Kabul; f. 2004; commercial station; broadcasts six hours daily.

Finance

(cap. = capital; auth. = authorized; p.u. = paid up; res = reserves; m. = million; brs = branches; amounts in afghanis unless otherwise stated)

BANKING

The banking sector was under reconstruction from 2002, following the collapse of the Taliban regime. In September 2003 the President approved a law allowing foreign banks to open branches in Afghanistan. By the end of 2004 11 foreign banks had opened branches in the country.

Central Bank

Da Afghanistan Bank (Central Bank of Afghanistan): Ibne Sina Wat, Kabul; tel. (93) 24075; f. 1939; main functions: banknote issue, modernize the banking system, re-establish banking relations with international banks, create a financial market system, foreign exchange regulation, govt and private depository; granted complete independence in September 2003; Gov. NUROLLAH DELAWARE; 84 brs.

Other Banks

Afghanistan International Bank: House 1608, behind Amani High School, Wazir Akbar Khan, POB 2074, Kabul; tel. and fax (20) 2103567; f. 2004; established and managed by the ING Institutional and Government Advisory Group (Netherlands) on behalf of a consortium of Afghan and US investors; 75% owned by Afghan nationals, 25% owned by Asian Development Bank; cap. US $10m. (March 2004); Chief Exec. JOHN HAYE.

Agricultural Development Bank (Agbank): Cineme Pamir Bldg, Jade Maiwand, POB 414, Kabul; tel. (93) 24459; f. 1954 as Agricultural and Handicraft Bank, renamed as above in 1969; makes available credits for farmers, co-operatives and agro-business; aid provided by IBRD and UNDP; nationalized in 1975; Chair. Prof. Dr ANWAR-UL-HAQ AHADY; 8 brs.

Banke Millie Afghan (Afghan National Bank): Jade Ibne Sina, POB 522, Kabul; tel. (20) 2100311; fax (20) 2101801; e-mail bankemillie_kabul@hotmail.com; f. 1933 as private bank, nationalized in 1976; Chair. HAMIDULLAH FAROOQI; Pres. Prof. Dr ABDUL QAYOUM ARIF; 19 brs in Afghanistan, 6 brs overseas.

Export Promotion Bank of Afghanistan: 24 Mohammad Jan Khan Wat, Kabul; tel. (93) 24447; f. 1976; provides financing for exports and export-orientated investments; state-owned; operations suspended under Taliban rule in 1996–2001; Pres. MOHAMMAD YAQUB NEDA; 3 brs.

Industrial Development Bank of Afghanistan: Shar-i-Nau, POB 14, Kabul; tel. (20) 2201637; f. 1973 as a private financial institution, nationalized in 1977; provides financing for industrial development; activities virtually ceased under Taliban rule in 1996–2001; Pres. G. GHAWSE HADAWI.

Mortgage and Construction Bank: Kabul; f. 1948 to finance residential and commercial construction; activities ceased in mid-1990s.

Pashtany Tejaraty Bank (Afghan Commercial Bank): Mohammad Jan Khan Wat, Kabul; tel. (20) 2100306; fax (20) 2102905; e-mail ptbank-af@yahoo.com; f. 1955 to provide short-term credits, forwarding facilities, opening letters of credit, purchase and sale of foreign exchange; nationalized in 1975; 14 brs in Afghanistan, 3 brs in Pakistan.

Foreign Commercial Banks

Aryan Bank (Iran): Kabul; f. 2004; Man. Dir MAJID FOTOUHI.

Habib Bank Ltd (Pakistan): Haji Yaqoob Sq., Shar-i-Nau, Kabul; tel. (20) 2200147; fax (20) 2200148; e-mail hblkblcm@hotmail.com; f. 2004; Country Man. MUSLIM UL-HAQ.

National Bank of Pakistan (Pakistan): House 2, St 10, Wazir Akbar Khan, Kabul; tel. (20) 2301660; fax (20) 2301659; internet www.nbp.com.pk; f. 2003; Gen. Man. SYED MEHMOOD UL-HASSAN.

Punjab National Bank (India): House 6, St 13, Wazir Akbar Khan, Kabul; tel. (20) 2301774; e-mail cmpnbkabul@rediffmail.com; f. 2004; Chief Man. SHRI S. K. MOHANTY.

Standard Chartered Bank (United Kingdom): House 10, St 10B, Wazir Akbar Khan, Kabul; tel. (216) 88840359; internet www .standardchartered.com/af; f. 2004; Country Man. JOHN JANES; 1 br.

INSURANCE

There was one national insurance company in the late 1990s:

Afghan National Insurance Co: National Insurance Bldg, Park, Shar-i-Nau, POB 329, Kabul; tel. (93) 33531; fax (762) 523846; f. 1964; mem. of Asian Reinsurance Corpn; marine, aviation, fire, motor and accident insurance; Pres. M. ABDULLAH MUDASIR; Claims Man. MEHRABUDDIN MATEEN.

Trade and Industry

GOVERNMENT AGENCIES

Export Promotion Department: Ministry of Commerce, Darulaman Wat, Kabul; tel. (873) 761885024; fax (873) 761885026; f. 1969; provides guidance for traders, collects and disseminates trade information, markets and performs quality control of export products.

High Commission for Combating Drugs: Kabul.

CHAMBERS OF COMMERCE AND INDUSTRY

Afghan Chamber of Commerce and Industry: Mohammad Jan Khan Wat, Kabul; tel. (93) 26796; fax (93) 2290089; e-mail acci2002@hotmail.com; internet www.afghanchamber.com; Head Mola MOHAMMAD DAUD ABED.

Federation of Afghan Chambers of Commerce and Industry: Darulaman Wat, Kabul; f. 1923; includes chambers of commerce and industry in Ghazni, Qandahar, Kabul, Herat, Mazar-i-Sharif, Fariab, Jawzjan, Kunduz, Jalalabad and Andkhoy.

INDUSTRIAL AND TRADE ASSOCIATIONS

Afghan Carpet Exporters' Guild: Darulaman Wat, POB 3159, Kabul; tel. (93) 41765; f. 1967; a non-profit-making, independent organization of carpet manufacturers and exporters; Pres. ZIAUDDIN ZIA; c. 1,000 mems.

Afghan Cart Company: Zerghona Maidan, Kabul; tel. (20) 2201309; fax (20) 290238; e-mail do_ik@yahoo.com; f. 1988; the largest export/import company in Afghanistan; imports electrical goods, machinery, metal, cars, etc.; exports raisins, medical herbs, wood, animal hides, etc; Pres. KABIR IMAQ.

Afghan Fruit Processing Co: Industrial Estate, Puli Charkhi, POB 261, Kabul; tel. (93) 65186; f. 1960; exports raisins, other dried fruits and nuts.

Afghan Raisin and Other Dried Fruits Institute: Sharara Wat, POB 3034, Kabul; tel. (93) 30463; exporters of dried fruits and nuts; Pres. NAJMUDDIN MUSLEH.

Afghan Wool Enterprises: Shar-i-Nau, Kabul; tel. (93) 31963.

Afghanistan Karakul Institute: Puli Charkhi, POB 506, Kabul; tel. (93) 61852; f. 1967; exporters of furs; Pres. G. M. BAHEER.

Afghanistan Plants Enterprise: Puli Charkhi, POB 122, Kabul; tel. (93) 31962; exports medicines, plants and spices.

Handicraft Promotion and Export Centre: Sharara Wat, POB 3089, Kabul; tel. (93) 32935; Dir MOMENA RANJBAR.

Parapamizad Co Ltd: Jadai Nader Pashtoon, Sidiq Omar Market, POB 1911, Kabul; tel. (93) 22116; export/import co; Propr PADSHAH SARBAZ.

TRADE UNIONS

Afghanistan Independent Journalists' Union (AIJU): Maiwand Press Club, Alam Ganj, Kabul; fax (20) 70285515; f. 2003; Chair. ABDULHAMID HAAMI.

Journalists' Union of Afghanistan: House 300, St 10, Wazir Akbar Khan, Kabul; f. 2003; Chair. SYED HAMED NOORI; Sec. Gen. ATIF MOCHADESEE; 350 mems.

National Union of Afghanistan Employees (NUAE): POB 756, Kabul; tel. (93) 23040; f. 1978 as Central Council of Afghanistan Trade Unions, to establish and develop the trade union movement, including the formation of councils and organizational cttees in the provinces; name changed in 1990; composed of seven vocational unions; 300,000 mems; Pres. A. HABIB HARDAMSHAID; Vice-Pres. ASAD KHAN NACEIRY.

Transport

RAILWAYS

There is no railway system currently operating in Afghanistan. Plans to build a rail line linking Pakistan, Afghanistan and Turkmenistan were under discussion in 2005.

ROADS

In 2001 there were an estimated 23,500 km of roads, of which more than 18,000 km were unpaved. All-weather highways link Kabul with Qandahar and Herat in the south and west, Jalalabad in the east and Mazar-i-Sharif and the Amu-Dar'ya river in the north. A massive reconstruction programme of the road system in Afghani-stan began in early 2002. The Salang Highway was rehabilitated, thus reconnecting Kabul with the north. In November the first of five bridges across the River Pyanj on the Tajik–Afghan border was reopened for use. By late 2004 the reconstruction of the important 482-km highway linking Kabul and Qandahar had been completed. Meanwhile, reconstruction of the 566-km highway linking Qandahar and Herat began in mid-2004.

In early 2005 Afghanistan, Iran and Uzbekistan signed an agreement concerning construction of a trans-Afghan transportation corridor, a 2,400-km road that would link the Uzbek city of Termez and the Iranian port of Bandar Abbas with Mazar-i-Sharif and Herat.

Afghan Container Transport Company Ltd: House 43, St 2, Left West of Charahe-Haji Yaqub, Shar-i-Nau, Kabul; tel. and fax (20) 2201392.

Afghan International Transport Company: Kabul.

Afghan Transit Company: Ghousy Market, Mohammad Jan Khan Wat, POB 530, Kabul; tel. (93) 22654.

AFSOTR: Kabul; resumed operations in 1998; transport co; 90 vehicles.

Land Transport Company: Khoshal Mena, Kabul; tel. (93) 20345; f. 1943; commercial transport within Afghanistan.

Milli Bus Enterprise: Ministry of Transport, Ansari Wat, Kabul; tel. (93) 25541; state-owned and -administered; 721 buses; Pres. Eng. AZIZ NAGHABAN.

Salang-Europe International Transport and Transit: Kabul; f. 1991 as joint Afghan/Soviet co; 500 vehicles.

INLAND WATERWAYS

There are 1,200 km of navigable inland waterways, including the Amu-Dar'ya (Oxus) river, which is capable of handling vessels of up to about 500 dwt. River ports on the Amu-Dar'ya are linked by road to Kabul.

CIVIL AVIATION

In early 2004 there were 22 airports in Afghanistan, including international airports at Kabul and Qandahar. Plans were under way to relocate the airport at Kabul.

Ariana Afghan Airlines: POB 76, Kabul; tel. (20) 2100351; fax (873) 762523846; e-mail flyariana@mail.com; internet www.flyariana.com; f. 1955; merged with Bakhtar Afghan Airlines Co Ltd in 1985; govt-owned; flights suspended in Nov. 1999–Jan. 2002, owing to UN sanctions; flights to India, Pakistan, Germany, the Middle East and Russia; Pres. Capt. JAHED AZIMI.

KamAir: 1205 Qalai Fatullah, POB 62, Kabul; tel. and fax (20) 2200108; internet www.flykamair.com; f. 2003; privately owned; domestic and regional flights.

Tourism

Afghanistan's potential tourism attractions include: Bamian, with its thousands of painted caves; Bandi Amir, with its suspended lakes; the Blue Mosque of Mazar; Herat, with its Grand Mosque and minarets; the towns of Qandahar and Girishk; Balkh (ancient Bactria), 'Mother of Cities', in the north; Bagram, Hadda and Surkh Kotal (of interest to archaeologists); and the high mountains of the Hindu Kush. Furthermore, ruins of a Buddhist city dating from the second century were discovered in July 2002 in southern Afghanistan. The restoration of cultural heritage, sponsored by UNESCO, began in 2002. In 1998 an estimated 4,000 tourists visited Afghanistan and receipts from tourism amounted to around US $1m.

Afghan Tourist Organization (ATO): Ansari Wat, Shar-i-Nau, Kabul; tel. (93) 30323; f. 1958; Pres. Dr HESSIAN UDDIN HAMRAH.

ALBANIA

Introductory Survey

Location, Climate, Language, Religion, Flag, Capital

The Republic of Albania lies in south-eastern Europe. It is bordered by Serbia and Montenegro (Montenegro to the north, and the province of Kosovo and Metohija—Kosovo, within Serbia, to the north-east), by the former Yugoslav republic of Macedonia to the east, by Greece to the south and by the Adriatic and Ionian Seas (parts of the Mediterranean Sea) to the west. The climate is Mediterranean throughout most of the country. The sea plays a moderating role, although frequent cyclones in the winter months make the weather unstable. The average temperature is 14°C (57°F) in the north-east and 18°C (64°F) in the south-west. The language is Albanian, the principal dialects being Gheg (north of the Shkumbini river) and Tosk (in the south). An official ban on religious worship was in effect between 1967 and 1990. Before 1946 Islam was the predominant faith, and there were small groups of Christians (mainly Roman Catholic in the north and Eastern Orthodox in the south). The national flag (proportions 5 by 7) is red, with a two-headed black eagle in the centre. The capital is Tirana (Tiranë).

Recent History

On 28 November 1912, after more than 400 years of Turkish rule, Albania declared its independence under a provisional Government. Although the country was occupied by Italy in 1914, its independence was re-established in 1920. Albania was declared a republic in 1925 and Ahmet Beg Zogu was elected President; proclaimed King Zog I in 1928, he reigned until he was forced into exile by the Italian occupation of Albania in April 1939. Albania was united with Italy for four years, before being occupied by German forces in 1943; the Germans withdrew one year later.

The communist-led National Liberation Front (NLF), established in 1941, was the most successful wartime resistance group and took power on 29 November 1944. Elections in December 1945 were contested by only communist candidates. The new regime was headed by Enver Hoxha, the leader of the Albanian Communist Party (ACP) since 1943. King Zog was declared deposed and the People's Republic of Albania was proclaimed on 11 January 1946. The ACP was renamed the Party of Labour of Albania (PLA) in 1948, the NLF having been succeeded by the Democratic Front of Albania (DFA) in 1945.

The communist regime developed close relations with Yugoslavia until the latter's expulsion from the Cominform (a Soviet-sponsored body co-ordinating the activities of European communist parties) in 1948. Albania, fearing Yugoslav expansionism, became a close ally of the USSR and joined the Moscow-based Council for Mutual Economic Assistance (CMEA) in 1949. Hoxha resigned as Head of Government in 1954, but retained effective national leadership as First Secretary of the PLA. Albania joined the Warsaw Treaty Organization (Warsaw Pact) in 1955, but relations with the USSR deteriorated when Soviet leaders attempted a *rapprochement* with Yugoslavia. The Albanian leadership declared its support for the People's Republic of China in the Sino–Soviet ideological dispute, prompting the USSR to suspend relations with Albania in 1961. Albania established increasingly close relations with China, ended participation in the CMEA in 1962 and withdrew from the Warsaw Pact in 1968. However, following the improvement of relations between China and the USA after 1972, and the death of Mao Zedong, the Chinese leader, in 1976, Sino-Albanian relations progressively deteriorated. In 1978 Albania declared its support for Viet Nam in its dispute with China, prompting the Chinese Government to suspend all economic and military co-operation with Albania.

A new Constitution was adopted in December 1976, and the country was renamed the People's Socialist Republic of Albania. In December 1981 Mehmet Shehu, the Chairman of the Council of Ministers (Prime Minister) since 1954, died as a result of a shooting incident. Although officially reported to have committed suicide, there were suggestions of a leadership struggle with Hoxha, and subsequent allegations that he had been executed. Following the death of Shehu, a new Government, headed

by Adil Çarçani, hitherto the First Deputy Chairman, was established. In November 1982 Ramiz Alia replaced Haxhi Lleshi as the Head of State, as President of the Presidium of the Kuvendi Popullor (People's Assembly). A number of former state and PLA officials were reportedly executed in September 1983.

Enver Hoxha died in April 1985, and was succeeded as First Secretary of the PLA by Alia. In March 1986 Hoxha's widow, Nexhmije, was elected to the chairmanship of the General Council of the DFA. Alia was re-elected as First Secretary of the PLA and as President of the Presidium of the Kuvendi Popullor in November 1986 and February 1987, respectively. In the latter month Adil Çarçani was reappointed Chairman of the Council of Ministers.

In November 1989, on the 45th anniversary of Albania's liberation from Nazi occupation, an amnesty for certain prisoners (including some political prisoners) was declared. From December a number of anti-Government demonstrations were reportedly staged, particularly in the northern town of Shkodër. In late January, while continuing to deny the reports of internal unrest, Alia announced proposals for limited political and economic reform, including the introduction of a system of multi-candidate elections (although the leading role of the PLA was to be maintained). The judicial system was reorganized, the number of capital offences considerably reduced, the practice of religion (which had been prohibited in 1967) was again to be tolerated, while Albanians were to be granted the right to foreign travel. Following renewed unrest in July, in which anti-Government demonstrators in Tirana were violently dispersed by the security forces, more than 5,000 Albanians took refuge in foreign embassies, and were subsequently granted permission to leave the country. Meanwhile, the membership of both the Council of Ministers and the Political Bureau of the PLA had been reorganized; a number of prominent anti-reformists were among those replaced. In late 1990 Alia announced proposals for more radical political reforms. In December it was announced that the establishment of independent political parties was to be permitted, prior to elections to the Kuvendi Popullor, scheduled for February 1991. In mid-December 1990, however, anti-Government demonstrators clashed with the security forces in several cities. Nexhmije Hoxha resigned from the chairmanship of the General Council of the DFA, and was replaced by Çarçani (who was, in turn, replaced in mid-1991).

On 20 February 1991, following widespread anti-Government demonstrations, Alia declared presidential rule. An eight-member Presidential Council was established, and a provisional Council of Ministers was appointed. Çarçani was replaced as Chairman of the Council of Ministers by Fatos Nano, a liberal economist, who had been appointed Deputy Chairman at the end of January. In late February the unrest finally ended. Meanwhile, following opposition pressure, the elections were postponed until the end of March 1991. In mid-March a general amnesty for all political prisoners was declared. The first round of the multi-party legislative elections took place on 31 March, with second and third ballots on 7 and 14 April, respectively. The PLA and affiliated organizations won 169 of the 250 seats, while the Democratic Party of Albania (DPA) secured 75 seats and the Democratic Union of the Greek Minority (OMONIA) obtained five seats. The victory of the PLA, amid allegations of electoral malpractice, prompted dismay in some urban areas, where support for the DPA had been strong. Widespread protests ensued, and in Shkodër security forces opened fire on demonstrators, killing four.

In late April 1991 an interim Constitution replaced that of 1976, pending the drafting of a new constitution. The country was renamed the Republic of Albania, and the post of executive President, to be elected by two-thirds of the votes cast in the Kuvendi Popullor, was created. Alia was subsequently elected to the new post, defeating the only other candidate, Namik Dokle, also of the PLA; all the opposition deputies abstained from voting. In early May Nano was reappointed Chairman of the Council of Ministers, and the Government was again reorganized. In accordance with the provisions of the interim Constitution, Alia resigned from the leadership of the PLA. In early

June 1991 the continuing general strike forced the resignation of Nano's administration. A Government of National Stability was subsequently formed, with Ylli Bufi (hitherto Minister of Food) as Chairman of the Council of Ministers. The coalition included representatives of the PLA, the DPA, the Albanian Republican Party (ARP), the Social Democratic Party (SDP) and the Agrarian Party (AP). Gramoz Pashko, a prominent member of the DPA, was appointed Deputy Chairman of the Council of Ministers and Minister of the Economy. At a party congress later in June, the PLA was renamed the Socialist Party of Albania (SPA). Further opposition strikes and demonstrations were staged in subsequent weeks. In early December the Chairman of the DPA, Sali Berisha, announced the withdrawal of the seven representatives of the party from the coalition Government. These withdrawals, which followed the expulsion of three ARP ministers who had criticized the administration, forced the resignation of Bufi's Government. Pending elections, Alia appointed an interim Government of non-party 'technocrats', under a new Prime Minister, Vilson Ahmeti (hitherto Minister of Food).

A new electoral law, approved by the legislature in early February 1992, reduced the number of deputies in the Assembly from 250 to 140. Under provisions that defined legitimate political parties, organizations that represented ethnic minorities, such as OMONIA, were prohibited from contesting the forthcoming general election, prompting widespread protests from the Greek minority. At the general election, conducted in two rounds on 22 and 29 March, the DPA secured 92 of the 140 seats, the SPA 38, the SDP seven, the Union for Human Rights Party (UHRP—supported by the minority Greek and Macedonian communities) two and the ARP one seat. According to official figures, 90% of the electorate participated. Following the defeat of the SPA, Alia resigned as President on 3 April. A few days later the new Kuvendi Popullor elected Berisha to the presidency. Berisha subsequently appointed a coalition Government dominated by the DPA (with 14 out of 16 ministerial portfolios), with Aleksander Meksi, a member of the DPA, as Prime Minister. The SDP and ARP were each allocated one ministerial portfolio. In July the DPA secured 43% of the total votes cast at multi-party local elections, compared with the 41% obtained by the SPA. In September divisions within the DPA resulted in the defection of a number of prominent party members, who formed a new political grouping, the Democratic Alliance Party (DAP).

During 1992 a number of former communist officials were detained, including Nexhmije Hoxha, who was arrested on charges of corruption. In February 1993 Ahmeti was placed under house arrest, following charges of corruption; further allegations concerning abuse of power resulted in the arrest of another former Prime Minister, Nano (by this time Chairman of the SPA), in July. Nexhmije Hoxha was imprisoned for nine years in January, having been convicted of embezzling state funds. (She was released in January 1997.) In August 1993 Alia was arrested on charges of abuse of power. Later that month Ahmeti was sentenced to two years' imprisonment. The trial of Nano commenced in April 1994, despite an international campaign on his behalf, organized by the SPA, and a European Parliament resolution appealing for his release. Nano was convicted of misappropriation of state funds during his premiership in 1991, and was sentenced to 12 years' imprisonment. In July 1994 Alia was sentenced to nine years' imprisonment for abuse of power and violating the rights of citizens. (In July 1995, following a court ruling, Alia was released.)

In October 1994 a draft Constitution was finally presented to Berisha, but failed to obtain the requisite two-thirds' majority approval in the Kuvendi Popullor, and was consequently submitted for endorsement at a national referendum. As a result of Berisha's personal campaign in support of the draft Constitution (which was to vest additional powers in the President, and reduce those of the legislature), the referendum was widely perceived as a vote of confidence in his leadership. At the referendum, which took place on 6 November, with the participation of 84.4% of the electorate, the draft Constitution was rejected by 53.9% of the voters, precipitating demands for a general election (on the grounds that the administration lacked a popular mandate). In early December Berisha effected an extensive reorganization of the Council of Ministers. On the following day the ARP, which held only one seat in the Kuvendi Popullor, withdrew from the governing coalition. The SDP split into two factions; of these, only a new grouping, known as the Union of Social Democrats, remained in the coalition. In March 1995 the Chairman of the DPA, Eduard Selami, who opposed

attempts to organize a further referendum on the draft Constitution, and who had accused Berisha of abuse of power, was removed from his post at an extraordinary party congress. Public discontent at a lack of improvement in economic conditions was demonstrated by a continued flow of illegal immigrants to Italy, which, in May, deployed troops along its coast in an attempt to stem the influx.

In June 1995 Ilir Hoxha, the son of Enver Hoxha, was convicted on charges of inciting hatred against elements of the population, after condemning leaders of the DPA in a newspaper interview. In September the Kuvendi Popullor adopted legislation prohibiting those in power under the former communist regime from holding public office until 2002 (thereby banning a large number of prospective candidates, including incumbent SPA deputies, from contesting legislative elections in 1996). In the same month the Minister of Justice dismissed three Supreme Court judges, owing to their alleged activities under the communist regime. The Chairman of the Supreme Court, Zef Brozi, challenged the Minister's authority to dismiss employees of the Court and refused to accept the decision. Following an ensuing ruling against Brozi by the Constitutional Court, he was dismissed by the Kuvendi Popullor. In response, the SPA deputies boycotted the legislature.

In November 1995 a parliamentary commission initiated an inquiry, following the discovery of a mass grave near the border town of Shkodër. Families of the deceased urged the prosecution service to initiate charges against former members of the communist regime, including Alia, who had allegedly been responsible for the killing by border guards of nationals attempting to flee the country in 1990–92. In that month the Kuvendi Popullor approved legislation requiring senior civil servants to be investigated for their activities under the communist regime. In December 14 prominent former members of the communist regime were arrested on charges of involvement in the execution, internment and deportation of citizens. (In May 1996 three of the former officials received death sentences, which were later commuted to terms of imprisonment, while the remaining defendants received custodial sentences.) In February Alia was detained on charges relating to the border incidents and the killing of demonstrators in Shkodër in April 1991.

The first round of the legislative elections took place on 26 May 1996; following alleged electoral irregularities, however, the principal opposition parties, including the SPA, the SDP and the DAP, withdrew from the poll and announced their rejection of the election results. A subsequent SPA demonstration held in protest at the alleged malpractice was violently dispersed by the security forces. The second round of the elections took place on 2 June; as a result of opposition demands for a boycott, only 59% of the electorate participated in the poll (compared with 89% in the first round). According to official results, the DPA secured 101 of the 115 directly elected seats (25 seats were to be allocated proportionately). However, international observers, who included representatives of the Organization for Security and Co-operation in Europe (OSCE, see p. 314), formerly the Conference on Security and Co-operation in Europe (CSCE), reported that widespread malpractice and intimidation of voters had been perpetrated, and urged the Government to conduct fresh elections, while SPA deputies staged a hunger strike in protest at the results. Berisha rejected the allegations, and agreed to conduct further elections in only 17 constituencies. The principal opposition parties continued their electoral boycott, demanding that further elections be held, under international supervision, in all constituencies. Consequently, the DPA won all the seats contested in the partial elections, held on 16 June, and secured a total of 122 of the 140 elective seats. The SPA won 10 of the remaining seats, while the UHRP and the ARP each secured three and the National Front two. (The SPA, however, refused to recognize the new legislature and boycotted its inaugural session.) In early July Meksi, who had been reappointed to the office of Prime Minister, formed a new Council of Ministers. In August 1996 the Government established a permanent Central Electoral Commission, prior to proposed local government elections; the main opposition parties subsequently nominated a number of representatives to the Commission. Despite continued division within the SPA, Nano (who remained in prison) was re-elected as Chairman at a party congress in late August. In the local government elections, which took place in two rounds in late October, the DPA secured the highest number of votes in 58 of the 65 municipalities and in 267 of the 305 communes. Although the OSCE had withdrawn its observers, after Berisha claimed that one of its members was biased against the DPA, monitors from the Council of Europe (see p. 199) declared that, despite some irregularities, the elections had been conducted fairly.

In January 1997 the collapse of several popular 'pyramid' financial investment schemes (which had offered high rates of interest), resulting in huge losses of individual savings, prompted violent anti-Government demonstrations, particularly in Tirana and the southern town of Vlorë. It was widely believed that members of the Government were associated with the pyramid schemes, which had allegedly financed widespread illegal activities. The Kuvendi Popullor subsequently adopted legislation prohibiting the schemes. However, the Government increased efforts to suppress the protests: large numbers of demonstrators were arrested and prominent opposition members were publicly assaulted by the security forces. At the end of January the Kuvendi Popullor granted Berisha emergency powers to restore order. It was reported that several people were killed in ensuing violent clashes between security forces and protesters. On 3 March, however, Berisha, whose mandate was due to expire in April, was re-elected unopposed by parliamentary deputies for a second five-year term (the SPA continued to boycott the Kuvendi Popullor).

Following an escalation in hostilities between insurgents (who seized armaments from military depots) and government troops in the south of the country, Berisha declared a state of emergency at the beginning of March 1997. However, insurgent groups gained control of the southern towns of Vlorë, Sarandë and Gjirokastër, and it was reported that large numbers of government forces had deserted or defected to join the rebels. Following negotiations with representatives of nine opposition parties, Berisha signed an agreement whereby an interim coalition government was to be installed, pending elections in June, and offered an amnesty to rebels who surrendered to the authorities. A former SPA mayor of the southern town of Gjirokastër, Bashkim Fino, was appointed to the office of Prime Minister. Berisha subsequently approved the formation of a Government of National Reconciliation, which included representatives of eight opposition parties. None the less, the insurgency continued, reaching the northern town of Tropojë and Tirana (where rebels seized the airport). All those detained in Tirana central prison, including Nano and Alia, were released; Berisha subsequently granted Nano an official pardon. Extreme hardship and concern that the fighting would escalate into widespread civil conflict prompted thousands of Albanians to flee to Italy, although later in March, Italian naval authorities were ordered to intercept boats transporting Albanian refugees, in an effort to halt the exodus.

By late March 1997 government forces had regained control of Tirana, although insurgent groups controlled the south of the country, while the north was largely held by paramilitary units loyal to Berisha. The Government of National Reconciliation requested military assistance in the restoration of civil order, and in late March Fino appealed to European Union (EU, see p. 217) for the establishment of a multinational force to supervise aid operations in Albania. At the end of March the UN Security Council endorsed an OSCE proposal that member states be authorized to contribute troops to the force. The 5,915-member Multinational Protection Force for Albania was established in April, with an official mission (known as Operation Alba) to facilitate the distribution of humanitarian assistance; the Italian contingent numbered 2,500, and the French 1,000, while Turkey, Greece, Spain, Romania, Austria and Denmark also contributed troops. The Force (which had a mandate to remain in the country for three months) was subsequently deployed in regions under government control in northern and central Albania. After negotiations between Italian forces and insurgents at Vlorë, the leader of the 'national committee for public salvation', Ekeren Osmani, announced that he would co-operate with the Italian troops.

At the beginning of April 1997 the SPA ended its boycott of the legislature, which subsequently voted to end press restrictions that had been imposed under the state of emergency in March. Later in April the National Council of the DPA endorsed Berisha's leadership of the party and removed a number of dissident members who had demanded his resignation. The son of King Zog I and claimant to the throne, Leka Zogu, returned to Albania in April, with the support of the pro-monarchist Legality Movement; the principal political parties had already agreed to conduct a referendum on the restoration of the monarchy. In May the Kuvendi Popullor adopted legislation regulating the operation of pyramid investment schemes. Later that month the

Kuvendi Popullor approved a proposal submitted by the DPA on the introduction of a new electoral system, in accordance with which the number of legislative deputies was to be increased from 140 to 155, of whom 40 were to be elected on the basis of proportional representation. Further elections were scheduled for 29 June. The SPA and its allied parties agreed to participate in the elections, after Berisha complied with the stipulation that the Central Electoral Commission be appointed by the interim Government (rather than by himself).

Election campaigning was marred by violence, including several bomb explosions in Tirana. Leaders of the DPA and SPA signed an agreement in Rome, Italy, pledging to abide by the results of the election. On 29 June 1997 the first round of voting in the legislative elections took place; a referendum on the restoration of the monarchy was conducted on the same day. Despite the presence of the Multinational Protection Force (the mandate of which had been extended to mid-August), three people were reportedly killed in violent incidents on polling day. A further ballot took place in 32 constituencies on 6 July. OSCE observers subsequently declared the electoral process to have been conducted satisfactorily. Later in July the Central Electoral Commission announced that the SPA had secured 101 seats in the Kuvendi Popullor, while the DPA had won 29 seats; the SPA and its allied parties (the SDP, the DAP, the AP and the UHRP) thereby secured the requisite two-thirds' majority for the approval of constitutional amendments that they had proposed earlier in the month. At the referendum, 66.7% of the electorate voted in favour of retaining a republic; at the end of August the Constitutional Court upheld the result, following a legal challenge by monarchists on the conduct of the vote. On 24 July, following Berisha's resignation as President, the Kuvendi Popullor elected the Secretary-General of the SPA, Rexhep Mejdani, to that position. Parliamentary deputies also voted to end the state of emergency imposed in March. The SPA proposed Nano to the office of Prime Minister, and a new Council of Ministers was appointed, which comprised representatives of the SPA and its allied parties, and retained Fino as Deputy Prime Minister. At the end of July the new Government's programme for the restoration of civil order and economic reconstruction received a legislative vote of confidence. The Kuvendi Popullor also voted in favour of auditing existing pyramid schemes and investigating those that had been dissolved, in an attempt to reimburse lost savings. In August the Government dispatched troops to the south of the country, in an effort to restore order in major towns that were under the control of rebel forces. It was subsequently announced that Vlorë had been recaptured and a number of rebel forces arrested; the Minister of the Interior ordered that all armaments looted during the unrest be surrendered to the authorities. By mid-August the Multinational Protection Force had left Albania, after the expiry of its mandate.

In September 1997 the Kuvendi Popullor established a parliamentary commission, which was to draft a new constitution, in accordance with the amendments proposed by the SPA. Later that month an SPA deputy shot and wounded a DPA deputy, Azem Hajdari, a prominent DPA official and close associate of Berisha, in the parliamentary building. Although the SPA deputy was subsequently charged with attempted murder, the DPA initiated a boycott of the legislature. In October Berisha was re-elected Chairman of the DPA. In the same month Alia and three other former senior officials were acquitted of genocide by a Tirana court (upholding a ruling of the Supreme Court), on the grounds that the charge did not exist under the penal legislation of the former communist Government.

Intermittent violent unrest continued in early 1998, with numerous minor bomb attacks. In February an armed revolt by civilians and disaffected members of the local security forces in Shkodër was suppressed by government troops. In March the DPA announced that it was to end its boycott of the Kuvendi Popullor, in order to express support within the legislature for ethnic Albanians in Kosovo and Metohija, Yugoslavia (now Serbia and Montenegro—see below). In early July a parliamentary commission into the unrest of 1997 recommended that several senior DPA officials, including Berisha, be charged in connection with the deployment of the armed forces to suppress the protests. Later in July 1998 Nano announced that the constitutional commission had presented a draft for approval by the Kuvendi Popullor in October, prior to its eventual endorsement by a national referendum.

In early September 1998 Hajdari was assassinated in Tirana. Berisha accused Nano of involvement in the killing, and the

DPA resumed its boycott of the legislature. The incident prompted violent protests by DPA supporters, who seized government offices and occupied the state television and radio buildings. Government security forces subsequently regained control of the capital, after clashes with protesters, in which about seven people were reported to have been killed. Although Berisha denied government claims that the uprising constituted a coup attempt, the Kuvendi Popullor voted to revoke Berisha's exemption (as a parliamentary deputy) from prosecution, thereby allowing him to be charged with attempting to overthrow the Government. An OSCE delegation, which mediated subsequent discussions between the political parties, condemned Berisha for inciting unrest, but also criticized Nano for the continued corruption within his administration. At the end of September the Minister of Public Order resigned, amid widespread criticism of the Government's failure to improve public security. Shortly afterwards Nano tendered his resignation, following a meeting of the SPA leadership, having failed to reach agreement with the government coalition on the composition of a new Council of Ministers. Mejdani subsequently requested that the Secretary-General of the SPA, Pandeli Majko, who had been nominated by the party to the office of Prime Minister, form a new government. In early October a new coalition Council of Ministers, headed by Majko, was installed. Later that month the Kuvendi Popullor approved the draft Constitution (with opposition deputies boycotting the vote). The new Constitution was submitted for endorsement at a national referendum, monitored by OSCE observers, on 22 November. The Government announced that 50.1% of the registered electorate had participated in the referendum, of whom 93.1% had voted in favour of adopting the draft. However, Berisha claimed that only 17% of the votes cast by a total of 35% of the electorate had been in favour of the new Constitution, and urged his supporters to stage further protests against the preliminary results of the referendum. The Government deployed additional security forces in Tirana in an effort to maintain public order. On 28 November Mejdani officially adopted the new Constitution, but Berisha subsequently announced that the DPA would continue to refuse to recognize it. In July 1999 a DPA congress voted in favour of ending the boycott of the legislature.

At an SPA party congress in September 1999 Nano (who had resigned from the party chairmanship in January) was re-elected to the post, narrowly defeating Majko. In October Majko (who, consequently, no longer had the support of the SPA legislative deputies) resigned as Prime Minister. Mejdani subsequently nominated Ilir Meta (hitherto Deputy Prime Minister), who was supported by Nano, as Prime Minister. Berisha announced that the DPA would boycott a parliamentary motion to approve Meta's new Council of Ministers, and that his supporters would stage mass protests, following the return of Nano to the SPA leadership. In early November the new Government was formally approved in the Kuvendi Popullor, despite the opposition boycott.

Local government elections took place in October 2000, following the preparation of a new voters' register, with assistance from the UN Development Programme (see p. 51). The first round of the elections, which took place on 1 October, was won by the SPA, with around 43% of the votes cast. The DPA (with around 34%) claimed that widespread electoral malpractice had been perpetrated and urged the party's supporters to boycott the second round. Nevertheless, OSCE observers, while reporting that irregularities had taken place, confirmed the results of the poll. On 15 October about 50% of the electorate participated in the second round of voting in a number of municipalities and communes where no candidates had obtained an absolute majority in the first round. Later that month the state electoral commission announced the official results, which indicated that the SPA had obtained control of a total of 252 communes and municipalities, compared with the 118 controlled by the DPA. However, DPA supporters subsequently staged a series of protests against the election results, which the party continued to refuse to recognize. In December, amid the continuing dispute over the local government elections, inter-party discussions over proposed amendments to electoral regulations commenced, prior to forthcoming elections to the Kuvendi Popullor. In February 2001 the DPA and the SPA reached agreement on the adoption of a new electoral code.

In April 2001 President Mejdani announced that the first ballot of the legislative elections would take place on 24 June, with a second round in early July. A number of opposition parties, led by the DPA, subsequently formed an electoral alliance, known as Union for Victory. The first round of the elections to the legislature (which was again reduced to number 140 deputies) took place as scheduled. Despite a number of minor violent incidents, the poll was judged by international observers to have been conducted satisfactorily. A second round took place on 8 July in 45 constituencies where no candidate had secured more than 50% of the votes cast. Ballots were repeated in four constituencies later in July, and in a further four in August, after opposition complaints of irregularities were upheld by the Constitutional Court. The Government subsequently announced that, according to provisional results, the SPA had retained its parliamentary majority. Berisha protested that the Government had perpetrated widespread fraud, and announced the decision of the Union for Victory to reject the election results and boycott the legislature. According to the final results, which were announced by the Central Electoral Commission on 21 August, the SPA won 73 of the 140 seats in the Kuvendi Popullor (considerably fewer than it had obtained in 1997), and the Union for Victory secured 46 seats.

Following Meta's re-appointment as Prime Minister, a reorganized Council of Ministers, nominated by President Mejdani, was approved in early September 2001. The new Government retained representatives of the SDP, notably the party Chairman, Skender Gjinushi, who was nominated to the post of Deputy Prime Minister and Minister of Labour and Social Affairs; the former Prime Minister, Pandeli Majko, became Minister of Defence. (Deputies belonging to the Union for Victory boycotted the new Kuvendi Popullor, which commenced sessions in early September, in continued protest at the outcome of the elections.) Following his inauguration, Meta announced that the country's rapid accession to the EU was to be a priority of the Government. A vote expressing confidence in the new Government, and its political and social programme, was adopted by 84 deputies in the Kuvendi Popullor (with six DAP representatives opposing the motion and the Union for Victory continuing to boycott the legislature).

In October 2001 the campaign by the Union for Victory to obtain international support for its allegations of malpractice in the legislative elections proved unsuccessful. OSCE observers maintained that the elections had been conducted successfully and urged the alliance to end its boycott of the Kuvendi Popullor. Later that month the Union for Victory agreed to enter the legislature, subject to several preconditions. In December severe division emerged within the SPA, after Nano publicly accused Meta's Government of engaging in corrupt practices. In that month the Minister of Finance and the Minister of the Public Economy and Privatization (both members of the SPA) agreed to resign from the Government, after being personally implicated in the corruption allegations. Subsequently, two further SPA members also resigned their ministerial portfolios. Later in December Berisha was re-elected to the leadership of the DPA. At the end of that month attempts by Meta to appoint new ministers to the four vacant posts in the Government proved unsuccessful, since his nominees were repeatedly rejected by supporters of Nano in the Kuvendi Popullor. On 29 January 2002 Meta tendered his resignation, after the two SPA factions failed to reach agreement on a government reorganization. Majko (a compromise candidate, who was supported by Meta) was nominated as the SPA's preferred candidate for Prime Minister, before being officially appointed to the office on 7 February. Following protracted negotiations between the two SPA factions and allied parties, the Kuvendi Popullor approved a new Council of Ministers on 22 February. Portfolios were divided between supporters of Nano and Meta, with Kastriot Islami, a former Deputy Prime Minister who was favoured by Nano, becoming Minister of Finance.

Following the establishment of the new, transitional Council of Ministers, deputies from the DPA-led Union for Victory decided to resume participation in the Kuvendi Popullor. As the end of Mejdani's term of office approached, it became apparent that Nano (who had announced his intention of contesting the presidency) would be unable to secure majority support in the legislature, owing to strong opposition from Berisha. Following prolonged negotiations between the SPA and the DPA, Alfred Moisiu, a retired general who had served in the Berisha administration, was selected as a compromise candidate (Albania's ambassador to the EU, Artur Kuko, who had been the initial preferred choice of the two parties, had declined to be nominated). He was elected by 97 of the 140 legislative deputies on 24 June 2002, and was inaugurated on 24 July. On the following day Majko resigned as Prime Minister. Moisiu subsequently appointed Nano to the premiership, and a new administration, again including members of both SPA factions, was approved at the end of the month, with Majko returning to his former post as Minister of Defence; Meta was allocated the office of Deputy Prime Minister and Minister of Foreign Affairs.

Despite the efforts towards reconciliation of the two SPA factions, prior to forthcoming local government elections, continuing differences culminated in Meta's resignation from his government office on 18 July 2003, citing authoritarian behaviour on the part of Nano. The Minister of State for Integration, an ally of Meta, also tendered his resignation. At the end of July Nano's nomination of a long-standing supporter, Marko Bello, as Minister of Foreign Affairs was rejected in the Kuvendi Popullor, owing to the opposition of Meta's faction.

The local government elections, conducted throughout Albania on 12 October 2003, were marred by a low rate of participation by the electorate, of less than 50%, and reports by OSCE observers of irregularities. Although the SPA claimed to have secured control of 36 of the country's 65 municipalities, the DPA immediately contested the results and accused the authorities of extensive malpractice. Later that month Nano removed the Minister of Public Order, Luan Rama, after he had reportedly assaulted the editor of a local television station that had been critical of the Government. Subsequent nominations by Nano to the posts of Minister of Foreign Affairs and Minister of Public Order were again rejected in the Kuvendi Popullor. Meta declared that his faction would continue to obstruct further appointments until Nano agreed to reorganize the Government, and the offices remained vacant. In early November, in an attempt to suppress dissent within the party, the SPA leadership adopted amendments to its statute, whereby public criticism of party decisions would be prohibited and the Chairman would automatically obtain the premiership. Following insistence by Moisiu that appointments be made to the vacant ministerial posts, Nano finally conceded the necessity of a government reorganization at the end of November, and commenced negotiations to secure the support of smaller parties within the Kuvendi Popullor. On 14 December, at the SPA annual congress, Nano was re-elected to the office of party Chairman, defeating a further two candidates (including Meta's preferred candidate, former President Mejdani). Later that month Nano signed agreements with the leaders of the SDP, the DAP, the AP, the UHRP, and the Social Democracy Party (PDS—which had been formed in April 2003 by a breakaway faction of the SDP, led by Paskal Milo), establishing the Coalition for Integration, which adopted the principal objective of supporting Albania's rapid accession to the EU and the North Atlantic Treaty Organization (NATO, see p. 301). With the additional votes of deputies belonging to the allied parties, a government reorganization by Nano, which included the appointment of a former parliamentary Speaker, Namik Dokle, as Deputy Prime Minister, and Kastriot Islami as Minister of Foreign Affairs, was approved by the Kuvendi Popullor on 29 December. Further municipal elections were conducted in parts of the country in December, after a court of appeal upheld DPA allegations and declared the results in a number of districts to be invalid; however, OSCE monitors reported further irregularities at some ballots.

In January 2004 the death of some 21 Albanians during an illegal attempt to reach Italy by sea prompted the declaration by Nano of a national day of mourning, and demands for an investigation into the incident by the opposition, which proposed a legislative motion of 'no confidence' in the Government; three local security officials were subsequently arrested on suspicion of complicity in the illicit trafficking of migrants. In February up to 20,000 people took part in demonstrations supported by the DPA in Tirana, accusing the Government of having failed to improve living standards and demanding the resignation of Prime Minister Nano. Concerns regarding independence of the press were raised in May, following the filing of a lawsuit against publisher Nikolle Lesi (the leader of the opposition Christian Democratic Party of Albania), whose *Koha Jonë* newspaper had accused Nano and his wife of corruption. In that month Zogu created a new political organization, the Movement for National Development (MND), that espoused monarchist principals, seeking to promote its leader as heir to the throne previously held by King Zog I. In June the approval by the Kuvendi Popullor of legislation on restitution and compensation of property (that sought to pay recompense to citizens whose property had been transferred to state ownership following the accession of the NLF to power in November 1944, with certain

exceptions) was described by the OSCE as representing a positive step towards economic and social stability, although there was difficulty in reaching consensus on some aspects of the new legislation, with President Moisiu demanding changes to certain articles. In July the Kuvendi Popullor approved further legislation, providing for the payment of compensation of former political prisoners. (The compensation proposed by the legislation was, however, widely criticized as inadequate.)

In September 2004 the ruling coalition was severely weakened by Meta's resignation from the SPA and his founding of a new political party, the Socialist Movement for Integration (SMI). Following continuing disputes with Prime Minister Nano, Meta stated that his intention was to create a third major political force, alongside the SPA and the DPA. Several SPA deputies joined the SMI, causing the SPA to lose its parliamentary majority, thereby increasing the SPA's dependence on its coalition partners. In October 2004, furthermore, plans were announced for the creation of a new party by a breakaway faction of the UHRP led by the deputies Kristo Goxhi and Ligoraq Karamelo. In November Lesi made further allegations against Nano, alleging that the Prime Minister had been involved in illegally supplying arms to ethnic Albanians in Kosovo in 1997. However, later in the month the Kuvendi Popullor rejected a proposal for an independent inquiry into the allegations.

The gradual relaxation of Albania's isolationist policies culminated in 1990, in a declaration of its intention to establish good relations with all countries, irrespective of their social system. Until 1990 Albania remained hostile to the USSR; in July of that year, however, Albania and the USSR formally agreed to restore diplomatic relations. Diplomatic relations between Albania and the USA were re-established in March 1991 (they had been suspended since 1946), and diplomatic links with the United Kingdom were restored in May. Albania was granted observer status at the 1990 CSCE summit meeting, and became a full member of the organization in June 1991. In May 1992 Albania and the European Community (now EU) signed a 10-year agreement on trade and co-operation. In June Albania, together with 10 other countries (including six of the former Soviet republics), signed a pact to establish the Black Sea Economic Co-operation (now the Organization of the Black Sea Economic Co-operation, see p. 325), which created a regional structure for economic co-operation. In December Albania was granted membership of the Organization of the Islamic Conference (OIC, see p. 327), and in the same month applied to join NATO (see p. 301), thus becoming the first former Warsaw Pact country formally to seek membership of the Western alliance. Albania joined NATO's 'Partnership for Peace' programme of military co-operation in April 1994. In July 1995 Albania was admitted to the Council of Europe, having agreed to adopt a new Constitution and to take measures to fulfil the Council's requirements concerning human rights. Prior to a NATO summit meeting in Prague, the Czech Republic, in November 2002, the Presidents of Albania, Croatia and the former Yugoslav republic of Macedonia (FYRM) agreed to adopt a common strategy for integration. Although those countries were not among the seven candidate nations invited at the summit to engage in accession discussions, NATO officials indicated that Albania's proposed entry would be considered in the future, subject to the implementation of further democratic and military reforms. At a NATO summit in İstanbul, Turkey, in June 2004, no date was set for the accession of Albania, Croatia and the FYRM, disappointing expectations. Negotiations on the signature of an initial Stabilization and Association Agreement with the EU, which officially commenced at the end of January 2003, were effectively suspended later in the year (see Economic Affairs). During 2004 EU officials reiterated the importance of judicial and legislative reforms, as well of reducing organized crime and of improving border monitoring, if significant progress towards EU membership was to be made. At the end of the year statements by the Government as well as by EU representatives indicated that the conduct of legislative elections in 2005 would be crucial in determining Albania's prospects for membership of the EU. During 2004 Albania also strengthened ties with the People's Republic of China, with the signing of seven agreements of co-operation by Nano and Chinese Premier Wen Jiabao in September.

Albania's relations with neighbouring Greece and Yugoslavia (now Serbia and Montenegro) have been strained. In August 1987 Greece formally ended the technical state of war with Albania that had been in existence since 1945. However, the status of the Greek minority in Albania, officially numbering some 59,000 at the 1989 census, but estimated to number some 300,000 by the Greek authorities, remained a sensitive issue. Relations between Albania and Greece deteriorated in 1993, owing to Greece's deportation of some 20,000 Albanian immigrants and to the alleged mistreatment of the Greek minority in southern Albania. Tensions were exacerbated further in April 1994, following a border incident in which two Albanian guards were killed by unidentified opponents; diplomatic expulsions ensued on both sides, and the border situation remained tense, with reports of minor skirmishes. In May six prominent members of the ethnic Greek organization, OMONIA, were arrested, following the alleged seizure by Albanian police of weapons and 'anti-constitutional' documents. Greece subsequently vetoed the provision of EU funds to Albania and increased deportations of illegal Albanian immigrants. In September five of the OMONIA detainees were convicted on charges including espionage and the illegal possession of weapons, and received custodial sentences. Following the verdict, Greece and Albania recalled their mutual ambassadors. In addition, the Greek Government submitted formal protests to the UN and the EU regarding Albania's perceived maltreatment of its ethnic Greek population and closed the Kakavija border crossing, which had hitherto been used by Albanian migrant workers. One of the OMONIA defendants was pardoned in December, after Greece withdrew its veto on EU aid to Albania in November. In February 1995 the four remaining OMONIA prisoners were released, allowing a subsequent improvement in bilateral relations. In June the Albanian Government approved a new education bill, which recognized the right of ethnic minorities to their own language and culture. In March 1996 the Greek President, Konstantinos Stefanopoulos, visited Albania, and a co-operation agreement was signed, apparently resolving outstanding issues of concern between the two nations. In August 1997 the Greek Government agreed to grant temporary work permits to illegal Albanian immigrants in Greece, in exchange for assistance from Albania in combating cross-border crime. In April 1998 the two countries signed a military co-operation agreement. A new border crossing between Albania and Greece was opened in May 1999. In February 2001 Albania and Greece signed an agreement on increased bilateral economic and financial co-operation. The Greek Government subsequently provided extensive credit to the Albanian authorities in a number of areas, and extended humanitarian aid during severe flooding in September 2002. In 2003 the fatal shooting of an illegal Albanian immigrant by Greek border guards led to widespread protests in Albania. In September 2004 an Albanian football fan was stabbed to death in Athens, the Greek capital, amid violent disorder. In the following month President Stefanopoulos again visited Albania and held talks with President Moisiu. Stefanopoulos expressed support for Albanian membership of NATO and the EU. He also held talks with OMONIA Chairman Jani Jani, although concerns regarding the protection of the rights of the Greek minority in Albania, as well as of Albanians living in Greece, continued to be expressed.

Relations with Yugoslavia deteriorated sharply in early 1989, when many ethnic Albanian demonstrators were killed during renewed unrest in the Yugoslav (Serbian) province of Kosovo (where the population was principally composed of ethnic Albanian Muslims). Kosovo (which was renamed Kosovo and Metohija in accordance with the new Serbian Constitution of September 1990, which also reduced the autonomy of the provincial authorities) remained a focus of political and ethnic tension, and the insurgency in southern Albania in early 1997 (see above) prompted concern among western European Governments that armaments seized by the rebels might also be used to support an insurrection by ethnic Albanians in Kosovo. In November Prime Minister Nano and the Yugoslav President, Slobodan Milošević, met in an effort to improve relations between Albania and the Federal Republic of Yugoslavia (FRY). However, the Albanian Government condemned increased Serbian military activity against the ethnic Albanian majority in Kosovo in early 1998 (see the chapter on Serbia and Montenegro). In April clashes were reported on the Albanian border with Kosovo between Serbian troops and suspected members of the paramilitary Kosovo Liberation Army (KLA). The Albanian administration initiated measures to prevent the illicit transportation of armaments from northern Albania to KLA forces in Kosovo. By mid-1998 some 10,000 ethnic Albanian refugees had fled to northern Albania, following continued Serbian military reprisals against the ethnic Albanian population in Kosovo.

In late March 1999, following the failure of diplomatic efforts to persuade Milošević to accede to NATO demands, NATO forces commenced an intensive aerial bombardment of the FRY. The Albanian Government expressed support for NATO military action, and allowed Albania's air and sea facilities to be used for NATO operations. Further Albanian troops were deployed on the northern border with Serbia in preparation for a possible Serbian retaliatory offensive. The atrocities committed by Yugoslav forces in Kosovo precipitated a mass exodus of ethnic Albanian refugees from the province. NATO troops (which later numbered about 8,000, and became known as AFOR) were dispatched to Albania to support humanitarian aid operations. The Government appealed for international financial assistance for the Kosovar refugee population, and requested a more rapid accession to NATO. In early April Yugoslav forces bombarded Albanian border villages during heavy fighting with the KLA in Kosovo, increasing international concern that a broader regional conflict might develop. Later that month Serbian troops advanced into Albanian territory, but were repelled by members of the Albanian armed forces. Meanwhile, the KLA had succeeded in establishing a supply route for the transportation of armaments from bases in northern Albania to Kosovo. Following the deployment of a NATO-led peace-keeping Kosovo Force (KFOR) in the province, under the terms of a peace agreement agreed with Milošević in June, about one-half of the refugees returned to Kosovo from Albania and the FYRM later that month. In September NATO announced that AFOR, which had been gradually withdrawing from the country, was to be replaced by a contingent to be known as Communications Zone West (COMMZ-W), which was mandated to maintain civil order in Albania and to support the KFOR mission in Kosovo. COMMZ-W (which was stationed in Durrës, under the command of KFOR) numbered some 1,200, principally Italian, forces. (In June 2002 COMMZ-W was officially dissolved, when a NATO headquarters was established at Tirana.) Following the removal from power of Milošević in September 2000, Albania and the FRY formally restored diplomatic relations in January 2001. Bilateral diplomatic relations were upgraded to ambassadorial level in September 2002. In December the principal Yugoslav airline resumed regular services to Albania (which had been suspended in 1981). In August 2003 a resolution adopted by the Serbian legislature, declaring Kosovo to be a permanent part of Serbia, was condemned by Nano. The President of Kosovo, Ibrahim Rugova, visited Albania in September 2004. In December Svetozar Marović, the President of the State Union of Serbia and Montenegro (as the FRY had become in the previous year), attended a regional summit on interethnic dialogue, held in Tirana.

In February 1993 Albania refused to accept an application by the FYRM for membership of the CSCE, and it was only in April that Albania officially recognized the existence of the republic as an independent state. Albania was concerned at the oppression of the large ethnic Albanian minority in the FYRM, who constituted about 21% of the population and the majority of whom were Muslims. Following the civil unrest in Albania in early 1997 (see above), a number of incursions into FYRM territory by armed groups of Albanian rebels were reported; in September two members of the FYRM's security forces were killed in a clash with Albanian citizens who had entered the country illegally. In October the Ministers of Defence of Albania and the FYRM signed an agreement providing for increased security at the joint border between the two countries.

The outbreak of conflict between government forces and ethnic Albanian rebels, known as the National Liberation Army (NLA), in the FYRM in February 2001 prompted large numbers of ethnic Albanian civilians to take refuge in Albania. Relations between Albania and the FYRM became strained, although the Albanian authorities maintained their opposition to the NLA's reported aim of creating a 'Greater Albania'. In August the FYRM Government and NLA leaders signed a peace agreement (which included constitutional amendments, adopted in November, according Albanian and other minority languages official status); however, the region remained unstable. In early September the Albanian ambassador to the FYRM was presented with a formal protest regarding the alleged involvement of Albanian nationals in rebel activities within the FYRM. Later that month the Albanian Government denied further claims by the FYRM that the NLA had established training bases in northern Albania. According to estimates by the office of the UN High Commissioner for Refugees, 7,626 refugees remained in Albania at the end of 2001. The replacement of the nationalist

Government in the FYRM at elections in September 2002 was widely perceived to favour prospects for regional stability. In January 2003 the Governments of Albania and the FYRM announced that they planned to strengthen economic co-operation, in an effort to advance their applications for EU membership (see above). Relations between the two countries continued to improve during that year, after the Albanian Government issued a statement in September condemning further extremist ethnic Albanian operations in the FYRM. In November the Ministries of Defence of Albania, Greece and the FYRM pledged to increase military co-operation to address the issues of illegal immigration and cross-border organized crime. In December the Albanian authorities signed an agreement with the Governments of Germany, Greece and Italy for the establishment of a centre at Vlorë, which was to co-ordinate regional efforts to combat trafficking in drugs and armaments. The Prime Minister of the FYRM, Vlado Buckovski, made an official visit to Albania in January 2005.

Government

Under the Constitution adopted in November 1998, legislative power is vested in the unicameral Kuvendi Popullor (People's Assembly). The Kuvendi Popullor, which is elected for a term of four years, comprises 140 deputies, of whom 100 are directly elected by a simple majority and the remainder on the basis of proportional representation. The President of the Republic is Head of State, and is elected by the Kuvendi Popullor for a term of five years. Executive authority is held by the Council of Ministers, which is led by the Prime Minister as Head of Government. The Prime Minister is appointed by the President and appoints a Council of Ministers, which is presented for approval to the Kuvendi Popullor. For the purposes of local government, Albania is divided into 12 counties (also called prefectures), 36 districts (*rrethe*), 65 municipalities and 305 communes. The representative organs of the basic units of local government are councils, which are elected by direct election for a period of three years. The Council of Ministers appoints a Prefect as its representative in each of the 12 counties.

Defence

In August 2004 the total strength of the Albanian armed forces was about 21,500; the army accounted for about 16,000, the air force for 3,500 and the navy for 2,000. Paramilitary forces comprised an internal security force, based in Tirana, and units in major towns, together with an estimated 500 border police. A programme of military reorganization, with assistance from European Governments and the USA, was scheduled for completion by 2010. Military service is compulsory and lasts for 12 months. From September 1999 a NATO contingent, known as Communications Zone West (COMMZ-W), numbering about 1,200, was deployed in Albania to maintain civil order in the country and support the NATO-led international Kosovo Force in the province of Kosovo and Metohija (Serbia). In June 2002 COMMZ-W was officially dissolved, when a NATO headquarters was established at Tirana. At the end of 2003 the headquarters comprised some 600 military and civilian personnel from Italy, Greece, Poland, Turkey and the USA. The budget for 2004 allocated some 10,700m. lekë to defence.

Economic Affairs

In 2003, according to World Bank estimates, Albania's gross national income (GNI), measured at average 2001–03 prices, was US $6,301.3m., equivalent to $1,740 per head (or $4,700 on an international purchasing-power parity basis). During 1990–2003, it was estimated, the population declined at an average annual rate of 0.3%, while gross domestic product (GDP) per head increased, in real terms, by an average of 2.7% per year. Overall GDP increased, in real terms, at an average annual rate of 2.4% in 1990–2003; growth was officially estimated at 3.4% in 2002 and at approximately 6% in 2003.

Agriculture (including forestry and fishing) contributed an estimated 26.0% of GDP in 2002. Some 58.2% of the labour force were engaged in the sector in 2003. An increasing degree of private enterprise was permitted from 1990, and agricultural land was subsequently redistributed to private ownership. The principal crops are wheat, sugar beet, maize, potatoes, barley and sorghum, and watermelons. Agricultural GDP increased at an average annual rate of 3.0%, in real terms, in 1990–2002; growth in the sector was officially estimated at 2.2% in 2001 and at 2.1% in 2002.

Industry (comprising mining, manufacturing, construction and utilities) accounted for an estimated 18.3% of GDP in 2002

and employed 13.3% of the labour force in 2003. Principal contributors to industrial output include mining, energy generation and food-processing. Construction has been the fastest-growing sector in recent years, contributing 7.8% of GDP in 2002. Industrial GDP declined at an average rate of 1.9% per year, in real terms, during 1990–2002; according to official estimates, the GDP of the sector increased by 7.0% in 2001, but declined by 7.9% in 2002.

Albania is one of the world's largest producers of chromite (chromium ore), possessing Europe's only significant reserves (an estimated 37m. metric tons of recoverable ore, constituting about 5% of total world deposits). The mining sector was centred on chromite and copper, following the closure of nickel and iron ore operations, together with more than one-half of the country's coal mines, in 1990. By 2001, however, chromite production had declined to 17,000 metric tons (compared with 587,000 tons in 1991), while output of copper also decreased significantly. Albania has petroleum resources and its own refining facilities, and there has been considerable foreign interest in the exploration of both onshore and offshore reserves since 1991. Proven reserves of petroleum were estimated at 165m. barrels in 2002.

The manufacturing sector contributed an estimated 9.8% of GDP in 2002. The sector is based largely on the processing of building materials, agricultural products, minerals and chemicals. Manufacturing GDP declined, in real terms, at an average annual rate of 7.9% during 1990–2002; the GDP of the sector increased by 6.3% in 2001 and declined by 4.5% in 2002, according to official estimates.

Hydroelectric generation accounted for some 98.7% of total electricity production in 2000. In 2003 imports of mineral fuels accounted for 8.6% of the value of total merchandise imports. An Albania–Macedonia–Bulgaria Oil Pipeline (AMBO) project, approved by the Albanian Government in December 2003, envisaged a 920-km pipeline, capable of transporting 750,000 barrels of petroleum per day, to connect the Bulgarian Black Sea port of Burgas with Vlorë and carry petroleum exports from Russia and the Caspian Sea region. In December 2004 the Albanian, FYRM and Bulgarian Governments signed an agreement enabling construction to commence. Work on the project was expected to begin in 2005 and be completed by 2009. The construction of a major thermal installation in Vlorë was expected to begin in mid-2005 and to be completed by 2008.

Services employed 28.5% of the labour force in 2003 and provided an estimated 55.7% of GDP in 2002. The combined GDP of the services sector increased, in real terms, by an average of 5.7% per year during 1990–2002; growth in the sector was 13.6% in 2001 and was officially estimated at 5.5% in 2002.

In 2003 Albania recorded a visible trade deficit of US $1,336.3m., and there was a deficit of $406.9m. on the current account of the balance of payments. In 2003 the principal source of imports (accounting for an estimated 33.5%) was Italy; other major suppliers were Greece and Turkey. Italy was also the principal market for exports (taking an estimated 74.9% of the total); Greece and Germany were also important purchasers. The principal exports in 2003 were miscellaneous manufactured articles (which accounted for 67.9% of the total). The main imports in that year were manufactured products, machinery and transport equipment, miscellaneous manufactured articles and food and live animals.

Albania's overall budget deficit in 2003 (including grants) was 30,904m. lekë (some 4.6% of GDP, representing a decline from 5.6% in 2002). At the end of 2002 Albania's total external debt was US $1,312m., of which $1,187m. was long-term public debt. In that year the cost of servicing the debt was equivalent to 3.4% of the value of exports of goods and services. In 1991–2002 the average annual rate of inflation was 29.0%; consumer prices increased by an estimated 2.3% in 2003 and by 2.2% in 2004. The rate of unemployment was estimated at 14.8% in the second quarter of 2004. In 2004 some sources estimated that over 35% of the Albanian labour force was working abroad.

Having reversed its long-standing policy of economic self-sufficiency, in 1991 Albania became a member of the World Bank, the IMF and the newly established European Bank for Reconstruction and Development (EBRD, see p. 212). In 1992 Albania became a founder member of the Black Sea Economic Co-operation group, known as the Organization of the Black Sea Economic Co-operation (see p. 325) from May 1999.

In 1992, in response to a serious economic crisis, a newly elected Government introduced an extensive programme of reforms, providing for the transfer to private ownership of farmland, state-owned companies and housing, and the abolition of price controls. A strict programme of high interest rates, reduced subsidies, banking reforms and trade liberalization was successful in reducing the budget deficit and stabilizing the currency. Nevertheless, illicit trade continued to account for a high proportion of revenue, and the country remained dependent on remittances from Albanian emigrants and foreign aid. Funding under the IMF's Poverty Reduction and Growth Facility (PRGF), which expired in July 2001, contributed to the restoration of high rates of growth, but poverty remained severe, particularly in rural areas. In early 2004 it was estimated that one-quarter of the Albanian population was still living in poverty. Albania's rapid accession to the European Union (EU) was a priority for the Government. The installation of a new President and the appointment of a new Council of Ministers in July 2002 eased political tension, and negotiations on the signature of an initial Stabilization and Association Agreement with the EU commenced in January 2003. EU representatives emphasized the need for further electoral and legislative reform, as well as progress in reducing organized crime and corruption, before an Agreement could be signed. With the aim of improving regional economic co-operation and furthering conformity with EU norms, during 2002–03 Albania ratified free-trade agreements with Bosnia and Herzegovina, Bulgaria, Croatia, the former Yugoslav republic of Macedonia, Romania and Serbia and Montenegro. However, divisions within the ruling party and an accompanying lack of parliamentary consensus impeded administrative decisions and in the second half of 2003 resulted in the effective suspension of negotiations on the signature of the Stabilization and Association Agreement. In December 2003 a significant advancement in the privatization programme was achieved with the sale of the country's Savings Bank. In January 2004 the IMF approved a further disbursement of funds under the PRGF arrangement, following a review of Albania's overall economic and financial performance, which was declared, despite the delays in structural reforms, to be satisfactory. Positive developments in the Albanian economy included reduction of the budgetary deficit and of inflation rates.

During 2004 there was also some progress on privatization in the energy and telecommunications sectors. In October the Ministry of Finance announced that €25m. of EU funding was expected to be made available to Albania in 2005. In November 2004 the IMF estimated that GDP growth in that year would be similar to that achieved in 2003, at around 6%.

Education

Education in Albania is free and compulsory for children between the ages of six and 14 years. Approximately 41.3% of children aged three to six years (boys 39.6%; girls 43.1%) attended pre-primary schools in 1999/2000. In 2000/01 97.6% of children in the relevant age-group (males 97.7%; females 97.4%) were enrolled at primary schools, while 72.9% of children in the appropriate age-group (boys 72.9%; girls 75.0%) attended secondary schools. In 2003/04 a total of 36,244 students were enrolled at Albania's institutions of higher education. Spending on education in 2003 was equivalent to some 2.9% of GDP.

Public Holidays

2005: 1 January (New Year's Day), 11 January (Republic Day), 21 January* (Great Bayram, Feast of the Sacrifice), 25–28 March (Roman Catholic Easter), 1 May (International Labour Day), 2 May (Eastern Orthodox Easter), 4 November* (Small Bayram, end of Ramadan), 28 November (Independence and Liberation Day), 25 December (Christmas Day).

2006: 1 January (New Year's Day), 11 January (Republic Day and Great Bayram*, Feast of the Sacrifice), 14–17 April (Roman Catholic Easter), 24 April (Eastern Orthodox Easter), 1 May (International Labour Day), 24 October* (Small Bayram, end of Ramadan), 28 November (Independence and Liberation Day), 25 December (Christmas Day).

* These holidays are dependent on the Islamic lunar calendar and may vary by one or two days from the dates given.

Weights and Measures

The metric system is in force.

Statistical Survey

Sources (unless otherwise indicated): Institute of Statistics (Instituti i Statistikës), POB 8194, Tirana; tel. (4) 222411; fax (4) 228300; e-mail root@instat .gov.al; internet www.instat.gov.al; Bank of Albania (Banka e Shqipërisë), Sheshi Skënderbeu 1, Tirana; tel. (4) 222752; fax (4) 223558; e-mail public@ bankofalbania.org; internet www.bankofalbania.org.

Area and Population

AREA, POPULATION AND DENSITY

Area (sq km)	
Land	27,398
Inland water	1,350
Total	28,748*
Population (census results)	
2 April 1989	3,182,417
1 April 2001	
Males	1,530,443
Females	1,538,832
Total	3,069,275
Population (UN estimates at mid-year)†	
2001	3,122,000
2002	3,141,000
2003	3,166,000
Density (per sq km) at mid-2003‡	115.6

* 11,100 sq miles.
† Figures not revised to take account of 2001 census.
‡ Land area only.

Source: UN, *World Population Prospects: The 2002 Revision*.

Ethnic Groups (census of 2 April 1989): Albanian 3,117,601; Greek 58,758; Macedonian 4,697; Montenegrin, Serb, Croat, etc. 100; others 1,261.

COUNTIES (PREFECTURES)
(census of 1 April 2001)

County	Area (sq km)	Population	Density (per sq km)	Capital
Berat	1,799	193,020	107.4	Berat
Dibër	2,586	189,854	73.4	Peshkopi
Durrës	766	245,179	320.1	Durrës
Elbasan	3,199	362,736	113.4	Elbasan
Fier	1,890	382,544	202.4	Fier
Gjirokastër	2,884	112,831	39.1	Gjirokastër
Korçë	3,711	265,182	71.5	Korçë
Kukës	2,374	111,393	46.9	Kukës
Lezhë	1,619	159,182	98.3	Lezhë
Shkodër	3,562	256,473	72.0	Shkodër
Tiranë	1,652	597,899	361.9	Tiranë
Vlorë	2,706	192,982	71.3	Vlorë
Total	28,748	3,069,275	106.8	

PRINCIPAL TOWNS
(population at 2001 census, preliminary results)

Tiranë (Tirana, the capital)	343,078	Korçë (Koritsa)	55,130
Durrës (Durazzo)	99,546	Berat	40,112
Elbasan	87,797	Lushnjë	32,580
Shkodër (Scutari)	82,455	Kavajë	24,817
Vlorë (Vlonë or Valona)	77,691	Pogradec	23,843
Fier	56,297	Gjirokastër	20,630

BIRTHS, MARRIAGES AND DEATHS*

	Registered live births		Registered marriages		Registered deaths	
	Number	Rate (per 1,000)	Number	Rate (per 1,000)	Number	Rate (per 1,000)
1994 . .	72,179	22.5	27,895	8.7	18,342	5.7
1995 . .	72,081	22.2	26,989	8.3	18,060	5.6
1996 . .	68,358	20.8	27,690	8.4	17,600	5.4
1997 . .	61,739	18.6	24,122	7.3	18,237	5.5
1998 . .	60,139	17.9	27,871	8.3	18,250	5.4
1999 . .	57,948	17.2	27,254	8.1	16,720	5.0
2000 . .	50,077	14.7	25,820	7.6	16,421	4.8
2001 . .	52,715	15.4	25,717	8.4	15,813	4.6

* Rates are based on official population projections for 1 January each year, and have not been revised to take account of the results of the census of 1 April 2001.

Expectation of life (WHO estimates, years at birth): 70.4 (males 67.3; females 74.1) in 2002 (Source: WHO, *World Health Report*).

ECONOMICALLY ACTIVE POPULATION
('000, end of period)*

	2001	2002	2003
Agriculture, hunting, forestry and fishing	531	531	539
Mining and quarrying	8	7	7
Manufacturing	47	47	46
Electricity, gas and water . . .	16	16	14
Construction	56	56	56
Wholesale and retail trade . . .	67	67	68
Hotels and restaurants . . .	16	16	16
Transport, storage and communications	32	32	32
Education	50	49	49
Health	26	26	27
Other activities	71	71	72
Total employed	920	920	926
Registered unemployed	181	172	163
Total labour force	1,101	1,092	1,089
Males	674	668	665
Females	427	424	424

* Totals may not be equal to the sum of component parts, owing to rounding.

Health and Welfare

KEY INDICATORS

Total fertility rate (children per woman, 2002) . . .	2.3
Under-5 mortality rate (per 1,000 live births, 2003) . .	21
HIV/AIDS (% of persons aged 15–49, 1999)	<0.01
Physicians (per 1,000 head, 2000)	1.39
Hospital beds (per 1,000 head, 2000)	3.26
Health expenditure (2001): US $ per head (PPP) . . .	150
Health expenditure (2001): % of GDP	3.7
Health expenditure (2001): public (% of total)	64.6
Access to water (% of total population)	97
Access to sanitation (% of total population)	89
Human Development Index (2002): ranking	65
Human Development Index (2002): value	0.781

For sources and definitions, see explanatory note on p. vi.

Agriculture

PRINCIPAL CROPS
('000 metric tons)

	2001	2002	2003
Wheat and spelt	282.2	295.3	280.0
Barley	3.0	3.8	4.0
Maize	198.3	197.3	200.0
Rye	3.7	2.7	3.0
Oats	15.3	19.7	20.0
Potatoes	163.7	163.1	170.0
Sugar beet	38.5	39.2	40.0
Dry beans	22.1	24.5	26.0
Tree-nuts*	3.0	3.0	3.0
Olives	39.6	27.0	38.0
Sunflower seed	2.7	2.6	3.0
Tomatoes	170.9	162.0	165.0
Green beans	5.6	5.4	5.4*
Other vegetables	192.1†	200.2*	200.2*
Oranges	2.2*	2.5	2.5*
Apples	15.8	15.8	15.8*
Pears	3.5	3.5	3.5*
Cherries (incl. sour)*	15.1	14.3	14.3
Peaches and nectarines	6.1	4.0	4.0*
Plums	17.0	15.3	15.3*
Grapes	85.1	83.1	83.1*
Watermelons	277.0	293.0	293.0*
Figs	22.8	14.5	14.5*
Tobacco (leaves)	3.6	2.6	2.6*

* FAO estimate(s).
† Unofficial figure.

Source: FAO.

LIVESTOCK
('000 head, year ending September)

	2001	2002	2003
Horses	67	65*	65*
Mules	22†	22*	22*
Asses	105†	105*	105*
Cattle	708	690	700
Pigs	106	114	109
Sheep	1,906	1,844	1,800
Goats	1,027	929	1,025
Chickens	4,285	4,446	4,300*

* FAO estimate.
† Unofficial figure.

Source: FAO.

LIVESTOCK PRODUCTS
('000 metric tons)

	2001	2002	2003
Beef and veal	35.3*	37.6*	40.0
Mutton and lamb	12.3†	12.3	12.3
Goat meat	7.2	7.2	7.2
Pig meat*	7.8	8.6	8.6
Poultry meat	4.0	6.0	7.0
Cows' milk	840.0	878.0	895.0
Sheep's milk	72.0	69.0	70.0
Goats' milk	72.0	63.0	65.0
Cheese	10.3	12.6	12.7†
Hen eggs	24.0	24.4	25.8†
Wool: greasy	3.3	3.3	3.0
Cattle hides†	7.4	7.9	7.9
Sheep and lamb skins†	3.4	3.4	3.4

* Unofficial figure(s).
† FAO estimate(s).

Source: FAO.

Forestry

ROUNDWOOD REMOVALS
('000 cubic metres, excl. bark)

	2001	2002	2003
Sawlogs, veneer logs and logs for sleepers	65	68	62
Pulpwood	13	15	—
Fuel wood	187	222	221
Total	265	305	283

Source: FAO.

SAWNWOOD PRODUCTION
('000 cubic metres, incl. railway sleepers)

	2001	2002	2003
Coniferous (softwood)*	47	47	47
Broadleaved (hardwood)	150†	50†	50*
Total	197	97	97

* FAO estimate(s).
† Unofficial figure.
Source: FAO.

Fishing

(metric tons, live weight)

	2000	2001	2002
Capture	3,320	3,310	3,955
Common carp	230	300	260
Bleak	190	478	234
Crucian carp	65	326	260
Silver carp	140	101	129
Salmonoids	110	56	43
Common sole	41	14	195
European hake	330	380	200
Gilthead seabream	23	90	181
Bogue	220	120	150
Surmullets	140	170	97
Mullets	150	180	128
European pilchard (sardines)	45	123	90
Mediterranean mussel	n.a.	n.a.	350
Aquaculture	307	286	860
Mediterranean mussel	200	150	300
Rainbow trout	100	15	350
Gilthead seabream	n.a.	100	200
Total catch	3,627	3,596	4,815

Note: Figures exclude Sardinia coral (metric tons): 1.0 in 2000; 1.2 in 2001; 1.8 in 2002.

Source: FAO, *Yearbook of Fishery Statistics*.

Mining

('000 metric tons, unless otherwise indicated)

	1999	2000	2001
Lignite (brown coal)	28	21	16
Crude petroleum (gross production)	323	314	308
Natural gas (gross production, million cu metres)	14	11	11
Copper (metal content, metric tons)	900*	—	—
Chromium ore (gross weight)	79	57	55

* Estimate.
Sources: US Geological Survey.

Industry

SELECTED PRODUCTS
('000 metric tons, unless otherwise indicated)

	1999	2000	2001
Wheat flour	63	90	260
Wine ('000 hectolitres)	13	7	14
Cigarettes (million)	647	372	126
Veneer sheets ('000 cubic metres)*	—	37	37†
Plywood ('000 cubic metres)	3	—	—
Paper and paperboard*	1	3	3†
Soap	0.6	0.1	0.4
Motor spirit (petrol)	20	24	n.a.
Kerosene	38	58	n.a.
Gas-diesel (distillate fuel) oil	63	72	n.a.
Residual fuel oils	114.	63	n.a.
Petroleum bitumen (asphalt)‡	17	16	15
Cement‡	108	180	—
Ferro-chromium‡	28	13	12
Crude steel‡	16†	65†	94
Electric energy (million kWh)	5,745	4,943	n.a.

* Source: FAO.
† Estimate.
‡ Source: US Geological Survey.

Source (unless otherwise indicated): UN, *Industrial Commodity Statistics Yearbook*.

Finance

CURRENCY AND EXCHANGE RATES

Monetary Units
100 qindarka (qintars) = 1 new lek.

Sterling, Dollar and Euro Equivalents (29 October 2004)
£1 sterling = 181.944 lekë;
US $1 = 99.320 lekë;
€1 = 126.504 lekë;
1,000 lekë = £5.50 = $10.07 = €7.90.

Average Exchange Rate (lekë per US $)
2001   143.49
2002   140.16
2003   121.86

STATE BUDGET
(million lekë)

Revenue*	2001	2002	2003
Tax revenue	116,171	128,948	145,314
Turnover tax/value-added tax	41,148	46,113	50,625
Taxes on income and profits	18,522	20,895	22,505
Social security contributions	22,506	25,637	28,613
Import duties and export taxes	12,794	13,387	13,854
Excise taxes	9,544	9,324	12,258
Other revenue	19,310	21,528	19,219
Profit transfer from Bank of Albania	10,912	10,291	8,852
Income from budgetary institutions	4,383	6,302	6,095
Total	135,481	150,476	164,533

Expenditure†	2001	2002	2003
Current expenditure	142,656	154,582	167,730
Wages	32,942	33,438	35,741
Social security contributions .	8,268	8,504	8,997
Interest	25,505	24,762	29,824
Operational and maintenance .	23,237	20,524	22,156
Subsidies	7,811	6,243	5,112
Social security	36,073	40,168	44,785
Unemployment insurance . .	1,881	1,115	999
Social assistance	6,939	7,598	7,824
Capital expenditure (investment)	43,095	41,967	31,472
Total	185,751	196,549	199,202

* Excluding grants received (million lekë): 3,670 in 2001; 4,119 in 2002; 2,617 in 2003.
† Excluding lending minus repayments (million lekë): 0 in 2001; −556 in 2002; −1,148 in 2003.

Source: IMF, *Albania: Fourth Review Under the Three-Year Arrangement Under the Poverty Reduction and Growth Facility* (July 2004).

INTERNATIONAL RESERVES
(US $ million at 31 December)

	2001	2002	2003
Gold*	30.70	27.68	28.86
IMF special drawing rights . .	81.52	81.60	90.61
Reserve position in IMF . . .	4.22	4.56	4.99
Foreign exchange	654.17	752.62	913.83
Total	770.60	866.46	1,038.31

* Valued at market-related prices.
Source: IMF, *International Financial Statistics*.

MONEY SUPPLY
('000 million lekë at 31 December)

	2001	2002	2003
Currency outside banks . . .	119.08	130.78	125.19
Demand deposits at deposit money banks	23.94	21.90	19.54
Total money	143.03	152.67	144.73

Source: IMF, *International Financial Statistics*.

COST OF LIVING
(Consumer Price Index; base: December 2001 = 100)

	2001	2002	2003
Food and non-alcoholic beverages .	93.7	99.4	103.5
Alcoholic beverages and tobacco .	99.5	99.3	101.7
Clothing and footwear . . .	101.2	95.7	91.5
Rent, water, fuel and power . .	92.0	99.0	99.8
Fuel and power	89.2	99.8	104.3
Household goods and maintenance	101.5	99.0	98.8
Medical care	99.0	103.9	108.0
Transport	101.1	99.0	102.1
Communication	100.5	98.8	100.3
Recreation and culture	102.1	100.4	100.8
Education	97.4	106.6	115.6
All items (incl. others)	94.7	99.7	102.0

NATIONAL ACCOUNTS
(million lekë at current prices)
Expenditure on the Gross Domestic Product

	2000	2001	2002
Final consumption expenditure .	397,548	415,766	428,330
Households	350,038	359,016	363,864
Non-profit institutions serving households	490	700	800
General government	47,020	56,050	63,666
Gross fixed capital formation . .	112,958	151,327	145,920
Changes in inventories	125,983	141,553	209,787
Total domestic expenditure .	636,489	708,646	784,037
Exports of goods and services . .	93,453	107,524	122,044
Less Imports of goods and services	199,036	227,507	276,081
GDP in market prices . . .	530,906	588,663	630,000

Gross Domestic Product by Economic Activity

	2000	2001	2002
Agriculture, hunting and forestry .	137,448	143,068	146,361
Industry	58,089	59,272	59,196
Mining and quarrying . . .	4,092	4,615	4,135
Manufacturing	53,997	54,657	55,060
Construction	31,603	45,288	43,929
Wholesale and retail trade, hotels and restaurants	102,915	105,739	122,664
Transport	40,479	49,161	45,549
Post and communications . . .	9,762	16,240	18,698
Other services	110,046	128,065	145,272
Sub-total	490,342	546,833	581,669
Less Financial intermediation services indirectly measured .	18,508	17,926	19,328
Gross value added in basic prices	471,834	528,907	562,341
Taxes on products	63,936	67,166	73,711
Less Subsidies on products . . .	4,863	7,410	6,052
GDP in market prices . . .	530,906	588,663	630,000

BALANCE OF PAYMENTS
(US $ million)

	2001	2002	2003
Exports of goods f.o.b.	304.5	330.2	447.2
Imports of goods f.o.b.	−1,331.6	−1,485.4	−1,783.5
Trade balance	−1,027.1	−1,155.1	−1,336.3
Exports of services	534.3	585.0	719.7
Imports of services	−444.1	−590.2	−802.6
Balance on goods and services	−936.9	−1,160.3	−1,419.2
Other income received	162.5	148.3	194.8
Other income paid	−13.5	−20.6	−24.4
Balance on goods, services and income	−787.9	−1,032.6	−1,248.8
Current transfers received . . .	647.5	683.7	924.2
Current transfers paid	−76.9	−58.6	−82.3
Current balance	−217.3	−407.5	−406.9
Capital account (net)	117.7	121.2	157.0
Direct investment from abroad .	207.3	135.0	178.0
Portfolio investment assets . .	−23.5	−36.8	−22.5
Other investment assets . . .	−197.2	−2.7	−71.6
Other investment liabilities . .	123.4	118.0	116.7
Net errors and omissions . . .	136.3	108.5	147.4
Overall balance	146.7	35.6	98.1

Source: IMF, *International Financial Statistics*.

External Trade

PRINCIPAL COMMODITIES
(million lekë)

Imports c.i.f.	2001	2002	2003
Food and live animals	26,949	31,652	32,613
Beverages and tobacco	6,805	7,827	8,256
Mineral fuels and lubricants . .	18,839	19,034	19,421
Chemical products	12,710	14,724	16,593
Manufactured products . . .	45,343	51,963	56,965
Machinery and transport equipment	46,304	44,901	48,870
Miscellaneous manufactured articles	27,972	34,055	36,485
Total (incl. others)	190,155	210,368	225,983

Exports f.o.b.	2001	2002	2003
Food and live animals . . .	1,610	2,077	2,314
Crude materials	3,310	4,280	4,732
Manufactured products . . .	5,575	5,535	6,892
Machinery and transport equipment	1,500	1,311	1,933
Miscellaneous manufactured articles	30,059	32,251	37,008
Total (incl. others)	44,096	47,490	54,487

PRINCIPAL TRADING PARTNERS
(million lekë*)

Imports c.i.f.	2001	2002	2003
Austria	1,547	2,675	3,646
Bulgaria	3,771	3,997	4,963
Croatia	2,428	4,527	3,458
Finland	3,908	701	368
France	1,760	2,321	2,447
Germany	11,150	11,804	12,777
Greece	48,946	45,679	45,287
Italy	60,737	72,601	75,640
Macedonia, former Yugoslav republic	2,192	2,318	1,901
Romania	1,722	2,211	1,849
Russia	2,437	5,454	6,387
Slovenia	2,102	2,560	3,233
Spain	2,323	2,900	3,870
Turkey	11,590	12,796	14,830
United Kingdom	6,743	6,457	5,460
Ukraine	2,039	2,543	5,656
USA	2,048	3,588	2,248
Total (incl. others)	190,155	210,368	225,983

Exports f.o.b.	2001	2002	2003
Austria	105	105	675
Germany	2,415	2,561	1,857
Greece	5,712	5,986	6,980
Italy	31,145	34,362	40,811
Macedonia, former Yugoslav republic	1,021	695	372
Serbia and Montenegro . . .	1,370	1,049	1,284
Turkey	444	477	451
Switzerland	643	75	161
USA	289	760	277
Total (incl. others)	44,095	47,490	54,487

* Imports by country of origin; exports by country of destination.

Transport

RAILWAYS
(traffic)

	1999	2000	2001
Passengers carried ('000) . . .	2,270	2,381	2,676
Passenger-km (million)	121	125	138
Freight carried ('000 metric tons) .	361	412	258
Freight ton-km (million) . . .	27	28	19

ROAD TRAFFIC
(motor vehicles in use at 31 December)

	1999	2000	2001
Passenger cars	92,252	114,532	133,533
Buses and coaches	12,306	16,806	20,813
Lorries and vans	35,266	43,301	49,600
Road tractors	1,860	2,274	2,721
Motorcycles and mopeds . . .	3,214	3,808	3,447

SHIPPING

Merchant Fleet
(registered at 31 December)

	2001	2002	2003
Number of vessels	33	74	83
Displacement ('000 gross registered tons)	25.2	48.7	70.0

Source: Lloyd's Register-Fairplay, *World Fleet Statistics*.

International Sea-borne Freight Traffic
('000 metric tons)

	1998	1999	2000
Goods loaded	108	120	132
Goods unloaded	1,536	2,040	2,424

2001 ('000 metric tons): Goods loaded 132 (Source: UN, *Monthly Bulletin of Statistics*).

CIVIL AVIATION
(traffic on scheduled services)

	1999	2000	2001
Passengers ('000):			
arrivals	173	195	220
departures	184	214	237
Freight (metric tons):			
loaded	95	141	174
unloaded	800	948	1,215

Tourism

FOREIGN TOURIST ARRIVALS BY COUNTRY OF ORIGIN*

	1999	2000	2001
Germany	11,761	11,978	13,255
Greece	13,717	28,374	28,022
Italy	41,067	40,734	46,715
Macedonia, former Yugoslav republic	63,498	72,646	68,755
Turkey	8,226	8,889	9,446
United Kingdom	4,653	10,676	15,572
USA	10,087	12,695	12,234
Yugoslavia	155,914	93,297	109,042
Total (incl. others)	358,481	317,149	342,908

* Figures refer to arrivals at frontiers of visitors from abroad, and include same-day visitors.

Source: World Tourism Organization, *Yearbook of Tourism Statistics*.

Tourism receipts (US $ million): 389 in 2000; 446 in 2001; 487 in 2002 (Source: World Tourism Organization).

Communications Media

	2001	2002	2003
Telephones ('000 main lines in use)	197.5	220.0	255.0
Mobile cellular telephones ('000 subscribers)	392.6	851.0	1,100.0
Personal computers ('000 in use)	30	36	n.a.
Internet users ('000)	10	12	30

Television receivers ('000 in use): 480 in 2000.

Radio receivers ('000 in use): 810 in 1997.

Facsimile machines ('000 in use): 18.3 in 1999.

Book production (1991): 381 titles (including 18 pamphlets).

Daily newspapers (1996): 5; Average circulation ('000 copies) 116.

Sources: UN, *Statistical Yearbook*; UNESCO, *Statistical Yearbook*; International Telecommunication Union.

Education

(2003/04)

	Institutions	Teachers	Students
Pre-primary	1,678	3,543	75,755
Primary	1,721	26,208	491,541
Secondary:			
general	309	4,625	96,637
vocational	53	1,508	21,724
Higher education*	11	3,997	36,244

* Figures include those enrolled at distance-learning institutions.

Source: Ministry of Education, Tirana.

Adult literacy rate (UNESCO estimates): 98.7% (males 98.3%; females 99.2%) in 2002 (Source: UN Development Programme, *Human Development Report*).

Directory

The Constitution

In October 1998 the Kuvendi Popullor (People's Assembly) approved a new Constitution, which had been drafted by a parliamentary commission. The Constitution was endorsed at a national referendum on 22 November, and was officially adopted on 28 November.

GENERAL PROVISIONS

Albania is a parliamentary republic. The Republic of Albania is a unitary state, with a system of government based on the separation and balancing of legislative, executive and judicial powers. Sovereignty is exercised by the people through their elected representatives. The Republic of Albania recognizes and protects the national rights of people who live outside the country's borders. Political parties are created freely, and are required to conform with democratic principles. The Republic of Albania does not have an official religion, and guarantees equality of religious communities. The economic system of the Republic of Albania is based on a market economy, and on freedom of economic activity, as well as on private and public property. The armed forces ensure the independence of the country, and protect its territorial integrity and constitutional order. Local government in the Republic of Albania is exercised according to the principle of decentralization of public power. The fundamental political, economic and social rights and freedoms of Albanian citizens are guaranteed under the Constitution.

LEGISLATURE

The Kuvendi Popullor comprises at least 140 deputies, and is elected for a term of four years. One hundred deputies are elected directly in single-member constituencies, while parties receiving more than 3% of votes cast nationally are allocated further deputies in proportion to the number of votes won. The Council of Ministers, every deputy and 20,000 voters each have the right to propose legislation. The Kuvendi Popullor makes decisions by a majority of votes, when more than one-half of the deputies are present. The 25-member Council of the Assembly is elected by the members of the Kuvendi Popullor at the beginning of the first session. The Council of the Assembly reviews preliminary draft laws, and gives opinions on specific issues.

PRESIDENT

The President of the Republic is the Head of State and represents the unity of the people. A candidate for President is proposed to the Kuvendi Popullor by a group of not less than 20 deputies. The President is elected by secret ballot by a majority of three-fifths of the members of the Kuvendi Popullor for a term of five years.

COUNCIL OF MINISTERS

The Council of Ministers comprises the Prime Minister, Deputy Prime Minister and ministers. The President of the Republic nominates as Prime Minister the candidate presented by the party or coalition of parties that has the majority of seats in the Kuvendi Popullor. The Prime Minister, within 40 days of his appointment, forms a Council of Ministers, which is presented for approval to the Kuvendi Popullor.

LOCAL GOVERNMENT

The units of local government are communes, districts, municipalities, and counties. The representative organs of the basic units of local government are councils, which are elected by general direct elections for a period of three years. The executive organ of a municipality or commune is the Chairman. The Council of Ministers appoints a Prefect in every county as its representative.

JUDICIARY

Judicial power is exercised by the High Court, as well as by the Courts of Appeal and the Courts of First Instance. The Chairman and members of the High Court are appointed by the President of the Republic, with the approval of the Kuvendi Popullor, for a term of seven years. Other judges are appointed by the President upon the proposal of a High Council of Justice. The High Council of Justice comprises the Chairman of the High Court, the Minister of Justice, three members elected by the Kuvendi Popullor for a term of five years, and nine judges who are elected by a national judicial conference. The Constitutional Court arbitrates on constitutional issues, and determines the conformity of proposed legislation with the Constitution. The Constitutional Court comprises nine members, who are appointed by the President, with the approval of the Kuvendi Popullor, for a term of nine years.

The Government

HEAD OF STATE

President of the Republic: ALFRED MOISIU (elected 24 June 2002; took office 24 July 2002).

COUNCIL OF MINISTERS
(April 2005)

A coalition of the Socialist Party of Albania (SPA), the Social Democratic Party of Albania (SDP) and the Union for Human Rights Party (UHRP).

Prime Minister: FATOS NANO (SPA).

Deputy Prime Minister: NAMIK DOKLE (SPA).

Minister of Foreign Affairs: KASTRIOT ISLAMI (SPA).

Minister of European Integration: ERMELINDA MEKSI (SPA).

Minister of Defence: PANDELI MAJKO (SPA).

Minister of Public Order: IGLI TOSKA (SPA).

Minister of Justice: FATMIR XHAFA (SPA).

Minister of Transport and Telecommunications: SPARTAK POÇI (SPA).

Minister of Finance: ARBEN MALAJ (SPA).

Minister of Education and Science: LUAN MEMUSHI (SPA).

Minister of Culture, Youth and Sports: BLENDI KLOSI (SPA).

Minister of Local Government and Decentralization: BEN BLUSHI (SPA).

Minister of the Environment: ETHEM RUKA (SPA).

Minister of Agriculture and Food: Agron Duka (SPA).

Minister of the Economy: Anastas Angjeli (SPA).

Minister of Health: Leonard Solis (UHRP).

Minister of Industry and Energy: Viktor Doda (SPA).

Minister of Labour and Social Affairs: Engjëll Bejtaj (SDP).

Minister of Territorial Adjustment and Tourism: Bashkim Fino (SPA).

Minister of State at the Office of the Prime Minister: Marko Bello (SPA).

MINISTRIES

Office of the President: Tirana; internet www.president.al.

Office of the Council of Ministers: Bulevardi Dëshmorët e Kombit, Tirana; tel. (4) 229980; fax (4) 234818; e-mail info@km.gov.al; internet www.keshilliministrave.al.

Ministry of Agriculture and Food: Sheshi Skenderbej 2, Tirana; tel. (4) 232796; fax (4) 227924; e-mail marsela_a@hotmail.com; internet www.mbu.gov.al.

Ministry of Culture, Youth and Sports: Ministria e Kulturës, Bulevardi Dëshmorët e Kombit, Tirana; tel. (4) 223474; fax (4) 232488; e-mail kabkult@mkrs.gov.al; internet www.mkrs.gov.al.

Ministry of Defence: Ministria e Mbrojtjes, Bulevardi Dëshmorët e Kombit, Tirana; tel. and fax (4) 225726; e-mail kontakt@mod.gov.al; internet www.mod.gov.al.

Ministry of the Economy: Boulevard Zhan D'Ark, Tirana; tel. (4) 364633; fax (4) 364639; internet www.minek.gov.al.

Ministry of Education and Science: Ministria e Arsimit dhe Shkences, Rruga Durrësit 23, Tirana; tel. (4) 226307; fax (4) 232002; e-mail rspahia@mash.gov.al; internet www.mash.gov.al; f. 1912.

Ministry of the Environment: Rruga Durrësit 27, Tirana; tel. (4) 270630; fax (4) 270627; internet www.moe.gov.al.

Ministry of European Integration: Pallati i Kongreseve, Tirana; tel. and fax (4) 228645; internet www.mie.gov.al.

Ministry of Finance: Ministria e Financave, Bulevardi Dëshmorët e Kombit, Tirana; tel. (4) 226001; fax (4) 226111; e-mail secretary.minister@minfin.gov.al; internet www.minfin.gov.al.

Ministry of Foreign Affairs: Ministria e Punëve të Jashtme, Bulevardi Zhan D'Ark 6, Tirana; tel. (4) 229521; fax (4) 362084; e-mail dshtypi@abissnet.com.al; internet www.mfa.gov.al.

Ministry of Health: Ministria e Shendetesisë, Tirana; tel. and fax (4) 264632.

Ministry of Industry and Energy: Bulevardi Dëshmorët e Kombit, Tirana; tel. (4) 227617; fax (4) 234052; e-mail dpzh@abissnet.com.al; internet www.mepp.gov.al.

Ministry of Justice: Ministria e Drejtësisë, Bulevardi Dëshmorët e Kombit, Tirana; tel. (4) 224041; fax (4) 228359; e-mail ministidre@albaniaonline.net.

Ministry of Labour and Social Affairs: Ministria e Punës dhe Ndihmës Sociale, Rruga e Kavajes, Tirana; tel. (4) 240412; fax (4) 227779; e-mail molsa@icc-al.org; internet www.molsa.gov.al.

Ministry of Local Government and Decentralization: Bulevardi Dëshmorët e Kombit, Tirana; tel. (4) 233538.

Ministry of Public Order: Sheshti Skënderbej 3,, Tirana; tel. and fax (4) 224364; e-mail mrp@mpo.gov.al; internet www.mpo.gov.al.

Ministry of Territorial Adjustment and Tourism: Bulevardi Dëshmorët e Kombit, Tirana; tel. and fax (4) 227879; e-mail militar@albaniaonline.net.

Ministry of Transport and Telecommunications: Rruga Abdi Toptani 5, Tirana; tel. (4) 234674; fax (4) 232389; e-mail spmt@albmail.com; internet www.mtt.gov.al.

Legislature

Kuvendi Popullor
(People's Assembly)

Bulevardi Dëshmorët e Kombit 4, Tirana; tel. (4) 362003; fax (4) 227949; e-mail head-directory@parliament.al; internet www.parlament.al.

President: Servet Pellumbi.

General Election, 24 June and 8 July 2001

Party	% of votes	Seats
Socialist Party of Albania	41.5	73
Union for Victory*	36.8	46
Democratic Alternative	5.1	6
Social Democratic Party of Albania	3.6	4
Union for Human Rights Party	2.6	3
Agrarian Party	2.6	3
Democratic Alliance Party	2.5	3
Independents	—	2
Others	5.3	—
Total	**100.0**	**140**

*Alliance comprising the Democratic Party of Albania, the Legality Movement, the Liberal Party, the National Front and the Republican Party.

Political Organizations

Albanian Communist Party (Partia Komuniste Shqipëtare—PKSh): Tirana; fax (4) 233164; f. 1991; granted legal recognition 1998; Chair. Hysni Milloshi.

Albanian Conservative Party (Partia Konservatore Shqiptare): Tirana; Chair. Armando Ruco.

Albanian Ecological Party (Partia Ekologjike Shqiptare): Rruga Aleksander Moisiu 26, POB 135, Tirana; tel. (4) 222503; fax (4) 234413; f. 1991; environmental political party; Chair. Dr Namik Vehbi Fadile Hoti.

Albanian Green Party (Partia e Blertë Shqiptare—PBS): POB 749, Tirana; tel. and fax (4) 233309; e-mail arandmaci@hotmail.com; f. 1991; campaigns on environmental issues; Chair. Nevruz Maluka.

Albanian National Democratic Party (Partia Nacional Demokratike): Tirana; f. 1991; Chair. Fatmir Çekani.

Christian Democratic Party of Albania (CDPA) (Partia Demokristiane) (PDK): Rruga Dëshmorët e 4 Shkurtit, Tirana; tel. (4) 2240574; fax (4) 2233024; f. 1991; Leader Nikolle Lesi.

Democratic Alliance Party (DAP) (Partia Aleanca Demokratike): Tirana; f. 1992 by former members of the DPA; Chair. Neritan Çeka; Sec.-Gen. Edmond Dragoti.

Democratic Party of Albania (DPA) (Partia Demokratike e Shqipërisë—PDSh): Rruga Punetoret e Rilindjes; Tirana; tel. (4) 228091; fax (4) 223525; e-mail profsberisha@albaniaonline.net; e-mail pdsecretary@albmail.com; f. 1990; centre-right, pro-democracy, pro-market; contested the legislative elections of June–July 2001 as part of the Union for Victory alliance; Chair. Prof. Dr Sali Berisha; Sec.-Gen. Ridvan Bode.

Democratic Prosperity Party (Partia e Prosperitetit Demokratik): Tirana; f. 1991; Chair. Yzeir Fetahu.

Democratic Union of the Greek Minority (OMONIA) (Bashkimia Demokratik i Minoritet Grek): Tirana; f. 1991; Chair. Jani Jani.

Environmentalist Agrarian Party (AP) (Partia Agrare Ambjentaliste): Rruga Budi 6, Tirana; tel. and fax (4) 231904; e-mail lxhuveli@europe.com; f. 1991; Chair. Lufter Xhuveli.

Labour Party of Albania (LPA) (Partia e Punës e Shqipërisë—PPSh): Rruga Sotir Peci 24, Tirana; fax (4) 233164; internet www.ppsh.org; f. 2002 by merger; extreme left-wing; defines itself as successor to the former communist Party of Labour of Albania.

Legality Movement (Partia Lëvizja e Legalitetit—PLL): Tirana; f. 1992; monarchist; contested the 2001 legislative elections as mem. of the Union for Victory alliance; Chair. Guri Durollari.

Liberal Party (Partia Liberale): Tirana; f. 1991; contested the 2001 legislative elections as mem. of the Union for Victory alliance; Chair. Valter File.

Movement for National Development (MND) (Lëvizjes për Zhvillim Kombëtar) (LZhK): Tirana; f. 2004; monarchist; led by claimant to the throne; Leader Leka Zogu.

National Front (Balli Kombëtar): c/o Kuvendi Popullor, Tirana; e-mail informacion@ballikombetar.org; contested 2001 legislative elections as mem. of the Union for Victory alliance; Chair. Ekrem Spahia.

National Unity Party (Partia e Unitetit Kombëtar): Rruga Alqi Kondi, Tirana; tel. (4) 227498; fax (4) 223929; f. 1991; Chair. of Steering Cttee Idajet Beqiri.

New Democratic Party (Partia Demokrate e Re—PDR): Tirana; f. 2001 by fmr mems of the DPA; Leader Genc Pollo.

Reformed Democratic Party (Partia demokratike te Rinovuar): Tirana; split from the New Democratic Party; Leader DASHAMIR SHEHI.

Republican Party of Albania (Partia Republika e Shqipërisë): Tirana; contested the 2001 legislative elections as mem. of the Union for Victory alliance; Chair. FATMIR MEDIU.

Social Democracy Party (Partia Demokracia Sociale—PDS): Tirana; f. 2003 by breakaway faction of the SDP; Chair. PASKAL MILO.

Social Democratic Party of Albania (SDP) (Partia Social Demokratike e Shqipërisë—PSDSh): Rruga Asim Vokshi 26, Tirana; tel. (4) 226540; fax (4) 227417; f. 1991; advocates gradual economic reforms and social justice; Chair. SKENDER GJINUSHI.

Socialist Movement for Integration (SMI) (Levizja Socialiste per Integrim) (LSI): Bulevardi Zogu I 72, Tirana; fax (4) 270412; e-mail secretariat@lsi-al.org; internet www.lsi-al.org; f. Sept. 2004 by fmr mems of SPA; moderate socialist; Chair. ILIR META.

Socialist Party of Albania (SPA) (Partia Socialiste e Shqipërisë—PSSh): Tirana; tel. (4) 227409; fax (4) 227417; f. 1941 as Albanian Communist Party; renamed Party of Labour of Albania in 1948, adopted present name in 1991; now rejects Marxism-Leninism and claims commitment to democratic socialism and a market economy; Chair. FATOS NANO; Sec.-Gen. GRAMOZ RUCI; 110,000 mems.

Union for Human Rights Party (UHRP) (Partia Bashkimi për të Drejtat e Njeriut—PBDNj): Tirana; f. 1992; represents the Greek and Macedonian minorities; Leader VANGJEL DULE.

Diplomatic Representation

EMBASSIES IN ALBANIA

Austria: Rruga Frederik Shiroka, Tirana; tel. (4) 233157; fax (4) 233140; e-mail tirana-ob@bmaa.gv.al; Ambassador HORST-DIETER RENNAU.

Bulgaria: Rruga Skënderbeu 12, Tirana; tel. (4) 233155; fax (4) 232272; Ambassador BOBI NIKOLOV BOBEV.

China, People's Republic: Rruga Skënderbeu 57, Tirana; tel. (4) 232385; fax (4) 233159; e-mail chem@adanet.com.al; Ambassador TIAN CHANGCHUN.

Croatia: Rruga Abdyl Frashëri, Tirana; tel. (4) 228390; fax (4) 230578; Ambassador RADE MARELIĆ.

Czech Republic: Rruga Skënderbeu 4, Tirana; tel. (4) 234004; fax (4) 232159; e-mail tirana@embassy.mzv.cz; internet www.mzv.cz/tirana; Ambassador MIROSLAV ŠINDELÁŘ.

Denmark: Rruga Nikolla Tupe 1, POB 1743, Tirana; tel. (4) 257422; fax (4) 257420; e-mail tiaamb@um.dk; internet www.um.dk; Chargé d'affaires FINN THEILGAARD.

Egypt: Rruga Skënderbeu 43, Tirana; tel. (4) 233022; fax (4) 232295; Ambassador MUHAMMAD A. SALAMA.

France: Rruga Skënderbeu 14, Tirana; tel. (4) 234250; fax (4) 233763; e-mail ambcrtir@mail.adanet.com.al; Ambassador FRANÇOISE BOUROLLEAU.

Germany: Rruga Skënderbeu 8, Tirana; tel. (4) 274505; fax (4) 233497; e-mail german.embassy@icc.al.eu.org; Ambassador HANS-PETER ANNEN.

Greece: Rruga Frederik Shiroka 3, Tirana; tel. (4) 234290; fax (4) 234443; e-mail grembtir@albnet.net; Ambassador PANDELIS KARKABASIS.

Holy See: Rruga e Durrësit 13, POB 8355, Tirana; tel. (4) 233516; fax (4) 232001; e-mail nunap-al@icc-al.org; Apostolic Nuncio Most Rev. GIOVANNI BULAITIS (Titular Archbishop of Narona).

Hungary: Rruga Skënderbeu 16, Tirana; tel. (4) 232238; fax (4) 233211; Ambassador SÁNDOR SZABÓ.

Iran: Rruga Mustafa Matohiti 20, Tirana; tel. (4) 227869; fax (4) 230409; Ambassador GHOLAMREZA HADDADI.

Italy: Rruga Lek Dukagjini, Tirana; tel. (4) 234045; fax (4) 234276; e-mail segreteria@ambitalia-tirana.com; internet www.ambitalia-tirana.com; Ambassador ATTILIO MASSIMO IANNUCCI.

Libya: Rruga Dëshmorët e 4 Shkurtit 48, Tirana; tel. (4) 228101; fax (4) 232098; Chargé d'affaires MAULOUD O. A. ALHAMUDI.

Macedonia, former Yugoslav republic: Rruga Lek Dukagjini, Vila 2; tel. (4) 233036; fax (4) 232514; Ambassador ELEONORA KARANFILOVSKA.

Netherlands: Rruga Asim Zeneli 10, Tirana; tel. (4) 240848; fax (4) 232723; e-mail tir@minbuza.nl; internet www.netherlandsembassytirana.com; Ambassador SWEDER VAN VOORST.

Norway: Sky Tower, Rruga Dëshmorët e 4 Shkurtit 5; tel. and fax (4) 257035; Chargé d'affaires SIGURD VALVATNE.

Poland: Rruga e Durrësit 123, Tirana; tel. (4) 234190; fax (4) 233464; Ambassador ARTUR TOMASZEWSKI.

Romania: Rruga Themistokli, Gjermeni 2, Tirana; tel. (4) 256071; fax (4) 256072; e-mail roemb@adanet.co.al; Ambassador CONSTANTIN EREMIA.

Russia: Rruga Asim Zeneli 5, Tirana; tel. (4) 256040; fax (4) 256046; Ambassador VLADIMIR N. TOKIN.

Saudi Arabia: Bulevardi Dëshmorët e Kombit; tel. (4) 248307; fax (4) 229982; Ambassador ABDULLAH S. ALHAMDAN.

Serbia and Montenegro: Skënderbeu Bldg 8/3–II, Tirana; tel. (4) 223042; fax (4) 232089; e-mail ambatira@icc-al.org; Ambassador MARKO CANAJ.

Switzerland: Rruga e Elbasanit 81, Tirana; tel. (4) 234890; fax (4) 234889; e-mail swissemb@adanet.com.al; Ambassador ERICH PIRCHER.

Turkey: Rruga Konferenca e Kavajes 31, Tirana; tel. (4) 233399; fax (4) 232719; e-mail turkemb@interalb.al; Ambassador SUPHAN ERKULA.

United Kingdom: Rruga Skënderbeu 12, Tirana; tel. (4) 234973; fax (4) 247697; e-mail tiran@fco.gov.uk; internet www.uk.al; Ambassador RICHARD JONES.

USA: Rruga Elbasanit 103, Tirana; tel. (4) 247285; fax (4) 232222; e-mail wm_tirana@pd.state.gov; internet www.usemb-tirana.rpo.at; Ambassador MARCIE RIES.

Judicial System

The judicial structure comprises the High Court, the Courts of Appeal and the Courts of First Instance. The Chairman and members of the High Court are appointed by the President of the Republic, with the approval of the legislature, for a term of seven years. Other judges are appointed by the President upon the proposal of a High Council of Justice. The High Council of Justice comprises the Chairman of the High Court, the Minister of Justice, three members elected by the legislature for a term of five years, and nine judges of all levels who are elected by a national judicial conference. The Constitutional Court arbitrates on constitutional issues, and determines, *inter alia*, the conformity of proposed legislation with the Constitution. It is empowered to prohibit the activities of political organizations on constitutional grounds, and also formulates legislation regarding the election of the President of the Republic. The Constitutional Court comprises nine members, who are appointed by the President, with the approval of the legislature, for a term of nine years.

Supreme Court (Gjykata e Larte): Tirana; e-mail supremecourt@albaniaonline.net; internet www.gjykataelarte.gov.al; Chief Justice THIMJO KONDI.

Constitutional Court: e-mail kujtim.osmani@gjk.gov.al; internet www.gjk.gov.al; Pres. Dr GJERGJ SAULI.

Religion

All religious institutions were closed by the Government in 1967 and the practice of religion was prohibited. In May 1990, however, the prohibition on religious activities was revoked, religious services were permitted and, from 1991, mosques and churches began to be reopened. Under the Constitution of November 1998, Albania is a secular state, which observes freedom of religious belief. On the basis of declared affiliation in 1945, it is estimated that some 70% of the population are of Muslim background (mainly Sunni or adherents of the liberal Bektashi order), 20% Eastern Orthodox Christian (mainly in the south) and some 10% Roman Catholic Christian (mainly in the north).

ISLAM

Albanian Islamic Community (Bashkesia Islame e Shqipërisë): Rruga Puntoret e Rilindjes, Tirana; e-mail icalb@yahoo.com; f. 1991; Chair. HAFIZ H. SABRI KOÇI; Grand Mufti of Albania HAFIZ SELIM STAFA.

Bektashi Sect

World Council of Elders of the Bektashis: Tirana; f. 1991; Chair. RESHAT BABA BARDHI.

CHRISTIANITY

The Eastern Orthodox Church

Orthodox Autocephalous Church of Albania (Kisha Orthodhokse Autoqefale të Shqipërisë): Rruga Kavaja 151, Tirana; tel. (4) 234117; fax (4) 232109; e-mail orthchal@ocual.tirana.al; the Albanian Orthodox Church was proclaimed autocephalous at the Congress of Berat in 1922, its status was approved in 1929 and it was recognized by the Ecumenical Patriarchate in Istanbul (Constantinople), Turkey, in 1936; Archbishop ANASTAS JANNOULATOS.

The Roman Catholic Church

Many Roman Catholic churches have been reopened since 1990, and in September 1991 diplomatic relations were restored with the Holy See. Albania comprises two archdioceses, four dioceses and one apostolic administration. At 31 December 2002 there were an estimated 521,214 adherents in the country.

Bishops' Conference: Rruga Don Bosco, Tirana; tel. and fax (4) 247159; e-mail cealbania@albnet.net; Pres. Most Rev. ANGELO MASSAFRA (Metropolitan Archbishop of Shkodër).

Archbishop of Durrës-Tirana: Most Rev. RROK K. MIRDITA, Arqipeshkvia, Bulevard Zhan d'Ark, Tirana; tel. (4) 232082; fax (4) 230727; e-mail arq@icc.al.org.

Archbishop of Shkodër: Most Rev. ANGELO MASSAFRA, Kryeipeshkëvi, Sheshi Gijon Pali II, Shkodër; tel. (22) 42744; fax (22) 43673.

The Press

Until 1991 the Press was controlled by the Party of Labour of Albania, now the Socialist Party of Albania (SPA), and adhered to a strongly Marxist-Leninist line. From 1991 many new periodicals and newspapers were established by the newly emerging independent political organizations. In 2000 there were some 12 daily newspapers and 18 principal weekly periodicals in publication. The total daily circulation of all newspapers declined to less than 50,000 in 2000, compared with 65,000 in 1999.

PRINCIPAL DAILIES

Albanian Daily News: Rruga Hile Mosi, 5, Tirana; tel. and fax (4) 227639; e-mail adn@icc.al.eu.org; internet www.albaniannews.com; f. 1995; in English, online edition updated daily, printed weekly newspaper; Editor ARBEN LESKAJ.

Biznesi (Business): Rruga Don Bosko, Vilat e Reja, POB 2423, Tirana; tel. (4) 251422; fax (4) 233526; e-mail kontakt@biznesi.com.al; internet www.biznesi.com.al; Editor-in-Chief GJERGJ EREBARA.

Ekonomia: Bulevardi Zhan D'Ark, Tirana; tel. (4) 250766; fax (4) 250767; e-mail gazekonomia@albaniaonline.com.

Gazeta Shqiptare: Rruga e Dibres 370, Tirana; tel. (4) 262646; fax (4) 263885; e-mail gazesh@katamail.com.

Gazeta Tema: Zayed Business Center, Rruga Sulejman Delvina, Tirana; tel. and fax (4) 425107; e-mail gazetatema@albmail.com; internet www.gazetatema.net; Editor-in-Chief MERO BAZE.

Koha Jonë (Our Time): Rruga Sami Frasheri, Pallatet e Aviacionit, Tirana; tel. and fax (4) 247004; e-mail redakskj@kohajone.com; internet www.kohajone.com; f. 1991; independent; Editor-in-Chief EDI LESI; circ. 400,000.

Korrieri: Rruga Dervish Hima Nr 1, Tirane; tel. (4) 233574; fax (4) 233575; internet www.korrieri.com; Editor-in-Chief ALFRED PEZA.

Republika: Sami Frasheri, Pallatet e Aviacionit, Tirana; tel. and fax (4) 25988; e-mail republika@albaniaonline.net; internet www.pages.albaniaonline.net/republika; organ of the Republican Party; Editor-in-Chief YLLI RAKIPI.

Rilindja Demokratike (Democratic Revival): Rruga Punetoret e Rindjes 16, Tirana; tel. (4) 232355; fax (4) 232357; e-mail gazetard@albaniaonline.net; internet www.rilindjademokratike.com; f. 1991; organ of the DPA; Editor-in-Chief ASTRIT PATOZI; circ. 50,000.

Shekulli (Century): Rruga Don Bosko, Vilat e Reja, Tirana; tel. (4) 233572; fax (4) 233526; e-mail kryeredaktori@shekulli.com.al; internet www.shekulli.com.al; independent; national and international politics, economics, culture; Editor-in-Chief ROBERT RAKIPLLARI.

Tema: Rruga Xhorxhi Martini 10; tel. (4) 251069; fax (4) 251073; e-mail tema@albaniaonline.net.

Zëri i Popullit (The Voice of the People): Bulevardi Zhan D'Ark, Tirana; tel. (4) 222192; fax (4) 227813; e-mail zeri@zeripopullit.com; internet www.zeripopullit.com; f. 1942; daily, except Mon.; organ of the SPA; Editor-in-Chief ERION BRACE; circ. 105,000.

PERIODICALS

Agrovizion: Rruga d'Istria, Tirana: tel. (4) 226147; f. 1992; 2 a week; agricultural economic policies, new technology in farming, advice for farmers; circ. 3,000.

Albanian Observer: Rruga Perlat Rexhepi Pall. 9, Shkurtit 1, Tirana; tel. and fax (4) 227419.

Bashkimi Kombëtar: Bulevardi Zhan D'Ark, Tirana; tel. (4) 228110; f. 1943; Editor-in-Chief QEMAL SAKAJEVA; circ. 30,000.

Blic: Rruga Fortuzi 44, Tirana; tel. (4) 234319; e-mail blici@juno.com; weekly; politics, information and culture; Editor ILIR YZEIRI.

Ditet Tona: Rruga Margaret Tutulani, Pall. 23, Shkurtit 1, Tirana; tel. (4) 230585.

Drita (The Light): Rruga Konferenca e Pezës 4, Tirana; tel. (4) 227036; f. 1960; weekly; publ. by Union of Writers and Artists of Albania; Editor-in-Chief BRISEIDA MEMA; circ. 31,000.

Fatosi (The Valiant): Tirana; tel. (4) 223024; f. 1959; fortnightly; literary and artistic magazine for children; Editor-in-Chief XHEVAT BEQARAJ; circ. 21,200.

Gazeta Ballkan: Rruga e Durresit, Lagjja 61, Tirane; tel. and fax (4) 229954; e-mail ballkanus@yahoo.com; internet www.ballkan.com; Editor-in-Chief ZAMIR ALUSHI.

Hosteni (The Goad): Tirana; f. 1945; fortnightly; political review of humour and satire; publ. by the Union of Journalists; Editor-in-Chief NIKO NIKOLLA.

The Hour of Albania: Rruga Dëshmorët e 4 Shkurtit, Tirana; tel. (4) 242042; fax (4) 234024; weekly; organ of the Christian Democratic Party of Albania; Editor-in-Chief Dr FAIK LAMA; circ. 3,000.

Identity: Rruga Daut Boriçi 874, Shköder; tel. (22) 41229; e-mail irsh@albnet.net.

Intervista: Rruga e Dibres 133, Tirana; tel. (4) 233164.

Klan: Rruga Myslym Shyri 8/1, Tirana; tel. (4) 240304; fax (4) 234424; e-mail redaksia@revistaklan.com; internet www.revistaklan.com; f. 1997.

Kombi (The Nation): Rruga Alqi Kondi, Tirana; tel. (4) 227498; fax (4) 223929; f. 1991; 2 a week; organ of the Party of National Unity; circ. 15,000.

Mbrojtja (The Defence): Bulevardi Dëshmorët e Kombit, Tirana; tel. (4) 226701; fax (4) 225726; e-mail tanct@al.pims.org; f. 1931; every 2 months; publ. by the Ministry of Defence; Editor-in-Chief ELMAZ LECI; circ. 1,500.

Official Gazette of the Republic of Albania: Kuvendi Popullore, Tirana; tel. (4) 228668; fax (4) 227949; f. 1945; occasional government review.

Panorama: Rruga Jordan Misja, prapa Shkollës Harry Fultz, Pallati 1, Kati i II-të, Tiranë; tel. (4) 273207; fax (4) 273206; e-mail gazetapanorama@hotmail.com; internet www.panorama.com.al; Editor-in-Chief ROLAND QAFOKU.

Pasqyra (The Mirror): Bulevardi Zogu I, Pall. A. Kelmendi, Tirana; tel. (4) 222956; fax (4) 229169; e-mail marketingu@pasqyra.com; internet www.pasqyra.com; f. 1991 to replace *Puna* (Labour); f. 1945; weekly; organ of the Confederation of Albanian Trade Unions; Editor-in-Chief XHAFER SHATRI.

Progresi (Progress): Rruga Budi 6, Tirana; tel. (4) 227481; fax (4) 227481; f. 1991; 2 a week; organ of the Agrarian Party.

Revista Pedagogjike: Naim Frashëri St 37, Tirana; fax (4) 256441; f. 1945; quarterly; organ of the Institute of Pedagogical Studies; educational development, psychology, didactic; Editor BUJAR BASKA; circ. 4,000.

Shëndeti (Health): M. Duri 2, Tirana; tel. (4) 227803; fax (4) 227803; f. 1949; monthly; publ. by the National Directorate of Health Education; issues of health and welfare, personal health care; Editors-in-Chief KORNELIA GJATA, AGIM XHUMARI.

Sindikalisti (Trade Unionists): Tirana; f. 1991; newspaper; organ of the Union of Independent Trade Unions of Albania; Editor-in-Chief VANGJEL KOZMAI.

Spektër: Rruga Don Bosko, Vilat e Reja, Tirana; tel. and fax (4) 251425; e-mail spekter@abissnet.com.al; internet www.spekter.com.al; f. 1991; 2 a month; general interest, illustrated; Editor-in-Chief ESTELA ZIU.

Sporti Shqiptar (Albanian Sports): Rruga e Kavajës 23, Sheshi Ataturk, 2908 Tirana; tel. and fax (4) 220237; internet www.sportishqiptar.com.al; f. 1935; 3 a week; national and international sports; Publisher KOÇO KOKËDHIMA; circ. 10,000.

Tregtia e Jashtme Popullore (Albanian Foreign Trade): Rruga Konferenca e Pezës 6, Tirana; tel. (4) 222934; f. 1961; 6 a year; in English and French; organ of the Albanian Chamber of Commerce; Editor AGIM KORBI.

Tribuna e Gazetarit (The Journalist's Tribune): Tirana; 6 a year; publ. by the Union of Journalists of Albania; Editor NAZMI QAMILI.

Ushtria (Army): Bulevardi Dëshmorët e Kombit, Tirana; tel. (4) 224350; fax (4) 225726; f. 1945; weekly; publ. by the Ministry of Defence; Editor-in-Chief BARDHYL GOSNISHTI; circ. 3,200.

NEWS AGENCIES

Albanian Independent News Agency: Rruga 4 Dëshmorët Vila 80, Tirana; tel. (4) 241721; fax (4) 230094; e-mail aina@abissnet.com.al; e-mail tirfaxnews@icc-al.org; Dir ZENEL CELIKU.

Albanian Telegraphic Agency (ATA): Bulevardi Zhan D'Ark 23, Tirana; tel. (4) 222929; fax (4) 234230; e-mail hola@ata.tirana.al; internet www.ata-al.net; f. 1929; domestic and foreign news; brs in provincial towns and in Kosovo (Serbia and Montenegro); Dir-Gen. FRROK CUPI.

Foreign Bureau

Agence France Presse: Rruga Muhamet Gjollesha, Pall. 69, Ap. 28, Tirana; tel. and fax (4) 227426.

PRESS ASSOCIATIONS

Albanian Media Institute: Rruga Gjin Bue Shpata 8, Tirana; tel. and fax (4) 229800; e-mail info@institutemedia.org.

Union of Journalists of Albania (Bashkimi i Gazetarëve të Shqipërisë): Tirana; tel. (4) 228020; f. 1949; Chair. MARASH HAJATI; Sec.-Gen. YMER MINXHOZI.

Publishers

Agjensia Qëndrore e Tregtimit të Librit Artistik dhe Shkencor (Central Agency of the Artistic and Scientific Book Trade): Tirana; tel. and fax (4) 227246.

Botime të Akademisë së Shkencave të RSH: Tirana; publishing house of the Albanian Academy of Sciences.

Botime të Universitetit Bujqësor te Tiranës: Kamzë, Tirana; publishing house of the Agricultural University of Tirana.

Botime të Shtëpisë Botuese 8 Nëntori: Tirana; tel. (4) 228064; f. 1972; books on Albania and other countries, political and social sciences, translations of Albanian works into foreign languages, technical and scientific books, illustrated albums, etc.; Dir XHEMAL DINI.

Dituria Publishing House: Rruga Dervish Hima 32, Tirana; tel. and fax (4) 225882; f. 1991; dictionaries, calendars, encyclopedias, social sciences, biographies, fiction and non-fiction; Gen. Dir PETRIT YMERI.

Drejtoria e Informacionit Agro-Ushqimor (Agriculture and Food Information Directory): Rruga S. Kosturi, Tirana; tel. (4) 226147; f. 1970; publishes various agricultural periodicals; Gen. Dir Prof. AGO NEZHA.

Fan Noli: Tirana; tel. (4) 242739; f. 1991; Albanian and foreign literature.

Shtëpia Botuese e Librit Shkollor: Tirana; tel. (4) 222331; f. 1967; educational books; Dir SHPËTIM BOZDO.

Shtëpia Botuese 'Libri Universitar': Rruga Dora d'Istria, Tirana; tel. (4) 225659; fax (4) 229268; f. 1988; publishes university textbooks on science, medicine, engineering, geography, history, literature, foreign languages, economics, etc.; Dir MUSTAFA FEZGA.

Shtëpia Botuese e Lidhjes së Shkrimtarëve: Konferenca e Pezës 4, Tirana; tel. (4) 222691; fax (4) 225912; f. 1990; artistic and documentary literature; Dir ZIJA ÇELA.

Shtëpia Botuese Naim Frashëri: Tirana; tel. (4) 227906; f. 1947; fiction, poetry, drama, criticism, children's literature, translations; Dir GAQO BUSHAKA.

Broadcasting and Communications

TELECOMMUNICATIONS

State Department of Posts and Telecommunications: Rruga Myslym Shyri 42, Tirana; tel. (4) 227204; fax (4) 233772; e-mail kote@dshpt.tirana.al; Gen. Dir HYDAJET KOPANI; Man. Dir FREDERIK KOTE.

Albanian Mobile Communications (AMC): Rruga Gjergi Legisi, Laprake, Tirana; tel. (4) 234915; fax (4) 235157; e-mail agreva@amc.al; f. 1996; fmrly state-owned, bought by a Greek/Norwegian con-sortium in 2000; operates mobile-telephone network; Man. Dir STEFANOS OKTAPODAS.

Albanian Telecom (Telekomi Shqiptar): Rruga Myslym Shyri 42, Tirana; tel. (4) 232169; fax (4) 233323; e-mail infocenter@atnet.com.al; internet www.atnet.com.al; scheduled for privatization; Dir-Gen. DHIMITRAQ RAFTI.

BROADCASTING

In 1991 state broadcasting was removed from political control and made subordinate to the Parliamentary Commission for the Media. By the end of 2000 the National Council of Radio and Television had licensed two national television stations, 45 local television stations, one national radio station and 31 local radio stations.

Regulatory Authority

National Council of Radio and Television (NCRT): Rruga Abdi Toptani, Tirana; tel. (4) 233326; fax (4) 226287; e-mail scela@kkrt.gov.al; internet www.kkrt.gov.al; f. 1998; Chair. SEFEDIN CELA.

Radio

Radio Televizioni Shqiptare: Rruga Ismail Qemali 11, Tirana; tel. (4) 228310; fax (4) 227745; e-mail dushiulp@yahoo.com; internet www.rtsh.sil.al; f. 1938 as Radio Tirana; two channels of domestic services (19 and five hours daily) and a third channel covering international broadcasting (two services in Albanian and seven in foreign languages); Chair. KASTRIST CAUSBI; Dir-Gen. EDUARD MAZI; Dir of Radio MARTIN LEKA.

Kontakt Radio: Rruga Muhamet Gjollesha, Kati i9, Tirana; tel. (4) 249474; fax (4) 257602; e-mail radiokontakt@albaniaonline.net; internet www.radiokontakt.com; independent radio station; commenced broadcasts Oct. 1997; Dir AGRON BALA.

Radio Klan: Rruga Myslim Shyri 8/1, Tirana; tel. (4) 240304; e-mail klan@albnet.net.

Top Albania Radio: International Centre of Culture, Bulevardi Dëshmorët e Kombit, Tirana; tel. (4) 247492; fax (4) 247493; e-mail topalbaniaradio@albaniaonline.net; internet www.pages.albaniaonline.net/topalbaniaradio.

Television

Radio Televizioni Shqiptare: Rruga Ismail Qemali 11, Tirana; tel. (4) 256056; fax (4) 256058; f. 1960; broadcasts range of television programmes; Chair. KASTRIST CAUSBI; Dir-Gen. EDUARD MAZI; Dir of Television VENA ISAK.

Alba Television: International Centre of Culture, Bulevardi Dëshmorët e Kombit, Tirana; tel. and fax (4) 234142; e-mail albatv@albaniaonline.net; internet www.pages.albaniaonline.net/albatv; private television station; Dir PAULIN SHKJEZI.

Albanian Satellite Television (ALSAT): Rruga Siri Kodra, Tirana; tel. and fax (4) 271738; e-mail info@alsat.tv; internet www.tvalsat.com; news satellite broadcasting in Albanian; from mid-2003 programmes also broadcast by local TV stations in Albania, the former Yugoslav republic of Macedonia and Kosovo (Serbia and Montenegro).

Shijak TV: Rruga Kavajes, Sheshi Ataturk, Tirana; tel. and fax (4) 247135; e-mail shijaktv01@albaniaonline.net; internet www.shijaktv.com; Pres. GËZIM ISMAILI.

Teutar Televizion: Tirana; e-mail teutartv@albaniaonline.net; internet www.teutartv.com.

Finance

(cap. = capital; dep. = deposits; res = reserves; m. = million; brs = branches; amounts in lekë, unless otherwise stated)

BANKING

Central Bank

Bank of Albania (Banka e Shqipërisë): Sheshi Skënderbej 1, Tirana; tel. (4) 222152; fax (4) 223558; e-mail public@bankofalbania.org; internet www.bankofalbania.org; f. 1992; cap. 750m., res 5,311m., dep. 41,211m. (Dec. 2003); Gov. ARDIAN FULLANI; 5 brs.

Other Banks

American Bank of Albania (Banka Amerikanë e Shqipërisë): Rruga Ismail Qemali 27, POB 8319, Tirana; tel. (4) 248753; fax (4) 248762; e-mail americanbank@ambankalb.com; internet www.ambankalb.com; f. 1998; owned by Albanian-American Enterprise Fund USA; cap. US $15m., res $1.4m., dep. $269.3m. (2003); Chair. MICHAEL GRANOFF; Pres. and Chief Exec. LORENZO RONCARI.

Italian-Albanian Bank (Banka Italo Shqiptare/Banco Italo Alba-nese): Rruga e Barrikadave, Tirana; tel. (4) 233965; fax (4) 235700; e-mail biatia@adanet.com.al; internet www.bia.com.al; f. 1993; cap. US $15.5m., res $1.5m., dep. $157.3m.; Pres. ADRIANA BERBERI; Chair. GIOVANNI BOGANI.

National Commercial Bank of Albania (Banka Kombëtare Treg-tare): Bulevardi Zhan D'Ark, Tirana; tel. (4) 250955; fax (4) 250960; e-mail bkt@bkt.com.al; internet www.bkt.com.al; f. 1993 by merger; privatized in 2000; cap. US $14.6m., res $0.4m., dep. $330.0m. (Dec. 2003); Chair. ILHAN NEBIOGLU; 30 brs.

ProCredit Bank (Albania): Rruga Sami Frasheri, POB 2395, Tirana; tel. (4) 271272; fax (4) 271276; e-mail info@procreditbank .com.al; internet www.procreditbank.com.al; f. 1996 as Foundation for Enterprise Finance and Development; name changed 1999; cap. 700.0m., res 91.9m., dep. 11,089.1m. (Dec. 2003); Gen. Man. EM-MANUEL DECAMPS; 9 brs.

Raiffeisen Bank: Rruga Kavajes 12, Tirana; e-mail info@raiffeisen .al; internet www.raiffeisen.al; f. 1991; fmrly Savings Bank of Albania; acquired by Raiffeisen Zentralbank Österreich AG (Aus-tria) in Dec. 2003; Chief Exec. STEVEN GRUNERUD; 37 brs.

Tirana Bank SA: Bulevardi Zogu I 55/1, Tirana; tel. (4) 233441; fax (4) 247140; e-mail tiranabank@icc.al.eu.org; f. 1996; cap. 1,018.6m., res 123.1m., dep. 21,242.9m. (Dec. 2002); Chair. MIHALIS KOLAKIDIS.

United Bank of Albania: Dëshmorët e Kombit 8, POB 128, Tirana; tel. (4) 227408; fax (4) 228460; e-mail uba@albaniaonline.net; f. 1994; joint venture; res $2.1m., dep. $20.5m. (2004); fmrly Arab-Albanian Islamic Bank, present name adopted 2003; Chair. SOL-AIMAN ELKHEREIJI; Gen. Dir WAHEED ALAUI; 3 brs.

INSURANCE

Agjensia Shqiptare e Garancisë (ASHG): Rruga Ismail Qemali 34, Tirana; tel. (4) 247048; fax (4) 247047; e-mail aga@aga-al.com; internet www.aga-al.com.

Insurance Institute of Albania (Instituti i Sigurimeve të Shqip-ërisë): Bulevardi Marcel Cachin, Tirana; tel. (4) 234170; fax (4) 223838; e-mail info@insig.com.al; internet www.insig.com.al; f. 1991; all types of insurance; Gen. Dir QEMAL DISHA; 12 brs.

Sigal: Bulevardi i Zogu I 1, Tirana; tel. and fax (4) 250220; e-mail info@sigal.com.al; internet www.albanianinsurance.com.

STOCK EXCHANGE

Tirana Stock Exchange (Bursa e Tiranes): Rruga Kavayes, pranë Bankës së Kursimeve, Kutia Postare 274/1, Tirana; tel. (4) 271849; fax (4) 271850; e-mail tseinfo@abcom-al.com; internet www.tse.com .al; f. 1996; Gen. Dir ELVIN MEKA.

Trade and Industry

PRIVATIZATION AGENCY

National Agency for Privatization (NAP): Tirana; tel. and fax (4) 227933; govt agency under the control of the Council of Ministers; prepares and proposes the legal framework concerning privatization procedures and implementation; Dir NIKO GLOZHENI.

SUPERVISORY ORGANIZATIONS

Albanian Securities Commission (ASC): Bulevardi Dëshmorët e 4 Shkürtit 6, POB 8363, Tirana; tel. and fax (4) 228260; e-mail asc@ asc.gov.al; internet www.asc.gov.al; Chair. FATOS RECA; Exec. Dir ELISABETA GJONI.

Albkontroll: Rruga Skënderbeu 45, Durrës; tel. (52) 23377; fax (52) 22791; f. 1962; brs throughout Albania; independent control body for inspection of goods for import and export, means of transport, etc.; Gen. Man. DILAVER MEZINI; 15 brs.

State Supreme Audit Control (Kontrolli I Larte I Shtetit): Region Eurosai, Tirana; tel. and fax (4) 232491; e-mail klsh@adn.net.al; internet www.klsh.org.al; Pres. ROBERT CEKU.

DEVELOPMENT ORGANIZATIONS

Albanian Centre for Economic Research: Rruga Frasheri 24, POB 2934, Tirana; tel. and fax (4) 225021; e-mail zefi@qske.tirana .al; internet www.arc.online.bq/ngos/albanian/acer.html; Pres. ZEF PREÇI.

Albanian Centre for Foreign Investment Promotion: Bule-vardi Zhan D'Ark, Tirana; tel. (4) 228439; internet www.ipanet.net.

Albanian Development Fund: Rruga Durrësi, Tirana; tel. and fax (4) 2234885; e-mail eneida@a-d-f.org; Exec. Dir MAKS MITROJORGJI.

Albanian Economy Development Agency (AEDA): Bulevardi Zhan D'Ark, Tirana; tel. (4) 230133; fax (4) 228439; e-mail xhepa@ cpfi.tirana.al; internet www.aeda.gov.al; f. 1993; govt agency to promote foreign investment in Albania and to provide practical support to foreign investors; publishes *Ekonomia*; Chair. SELAMI XHEPA.

Business in Albania: Lagja Luigi Gurakuqi, Palliti 73, Elbasen; tel. and fax (54) 58994; e-mail gmaksuti@yahoo.com; provision of information on commerce and business in Albania; market research; Pres. TOM LODGE.

Enterprise Restructuring Agency (Agjensia e Ristrukturimit te Ndermarrjeve): Rruga e Durrësit 83, Tirana; tel. (4) 227878; fax (4) 225730; govt agency established to assist state-owned enterprises to become privately owned by offering enterprise sector surveys, stra-tegic plans and consultations; provides technical assistance; Dir ADRIATIK BANKJA.

Foreign Investors' Association of Albania: Tirana Business Centre, Suite 20, Bulevardi Zogu I-re, Tirana; tel. (4) 256296; fax (4) 256291; e-mail fiaalb@albaniaonline.net; internet www.fiaalbania .org.

International Research And Exchange Board: Rruga Him Kolli 45, Tirana; tel. (4) 247543; fax (4) 247544; e-mail promedia@irex .tirana.al; internet www.irex.org.

Trade and Investment Promotion Support: Bulevardi Zhan D'Ark, Tirana; tel. and fax (4) 262067; e-mail besnik@tips.tirana.al; internet www.tips.eu.org/albania.

CHAMBERS OF COMMERCE

Union of Chambers of Commerce and Industry of Albania: Rruga Kavajes 6, Tirana; tel. and fax (4) 222934; f. 1958; Pres. ANTON LEKA.

Durrës Chamber of Commerce: Durrës; f. 1988; promotes trade with southern Italy.

Gjirokastër Chamber of Commerce: Gjirokastër; f. 1988; pro-motes trade with Greek border area.

Korçë Chamber of Commerce and Industry: Bulevardi Repub-lika, Korçë; tel. and fax (82) 42457; e-mail dhtiko@icc.al.eu.org; internet www.albchamber.org; f. 1995.

Shkodër Chamber of Commerce: Shkodër; promotes trade with Yugoslav border area.

Tirana Chamber of Commerce and Industry: Rruga Kavajes 6, Tirana; tel. (4) 232448; fax (4) 229779; e-mail ccitr@abissnet.com.al; internet www.cci.gov.al; f. 1926; Chair. LUAN BREGASI.

There are also chambers of commerce in Kukës, Peshkopi, Pogradec, Sarandë and Vlorë.

UTILITIES

Electricity

State Electricity Corporation of Albania (Korporata Elektroe-nergjetikc Shqiptare—KESH): Biloky 'Vasil Shanto', Tirana; tel. (4) 228434; fax (4) 232046; e-mail kesh@icc.al.eu.org; state corpn for the generation, transmission, distribution and export of electrical energy; govt-controlled; scheduled for reorganization, prior to transfer to private ownership; Chair. BASHKIM QATIPI; Gen. Dir Dr NAKO HOBDARI.

TRADE UNIONS

Until 1991 independent trade-union activities were prohibited, the official trade unions being represented in every work and production centre. During 1991, however, independent unions were established. The most important of these was the Union of Independent Trade Unions of Albania. Other unions were established for workers in various sectors of the economy.

Confederation of Albanian Trade Unions (Konfederata e Sindi-katave të Shqipërisë—KSSh): Bulevardi Zogu I, Pall. A. Kelmendi, Tirana; tel. (4) 222956; fax (4) 229169; e-mail kssh@icc.al.eu.org; f. 1991 to replace the official Central Council of Albanian Trade Unions; f. 1945; includes 13 trade union federations representing workers in different sectors of the economy; Chair. of Man. Council KASTRIOT MUÇO.

Union of Independent Trade Unions of Albania (Bashkimi i Sindikatave të Pavarura të Shqipërisë—BSPSh): Tirana; f. 1991; Chair. (vacant).

Agricultural Trade Union Federation (Federata Sindikale e Bujqesise): Tirana; f. 1991; Leaders ALFRED GJOMO, NAZMI QOKU.

Free and Independent Miners' Union (Sindikata e Lire dhe e Pavarur e Minatoreve): Tirana; f. 1991; Chair. GEZIM KALAJA.

Trade Union Federation of Employees and Pensioners of Albania: Bulevardi Dëshmorët e Kombit, Tirana; tel. (4) 229169; Chair. PETRAQ TAPIA.

Union of Oil Industry Workers: Tirana; seceded from the Confederation of Albanian Trade Unions in 1991; represents workers in the petroleum and natural gas industry; Chair. MENPOR XHEMALI.

Transport

RAILWAYS

In 1994 there were approximately 720 km of railway track, with lines linking Tirana–Vlorë–Durrës, Durrës–Kavajë–Rrogozhinë–Elbasan–Librazhd–Prenjas–Pogradec, Rrogozhinë–Lushnjë–Fier–Ballsh, Milot–Rrëshen, Vlorë–Laç–Lezhë–Shkodër and Selenicë–Vlorë. There are also standard-gauge lines between Fier and Selenicë and between Fier and Vlorë. In 2000 projects were under way to rehabilitate the Rrogozhinë–Vlorë and Fier–Ballsh railway lines. The 50-km international freight link between Shkodër and Podgorica, Montenegro (Serbia and Montenegro), reopened in 2003, after a 10-year suspension of service.

Albanian Railways: Rruga Skënderbeg, Durrës; tel. and fax (52) 22037; internet www.pages.albaniaonline.net/hsh; Dir-Gen. L. BURNACI.

ROADS

In 2001 the road network comprised an estimated 18,000 km of classified roads, including 3,220 km of main roads and 4,300 km of secondary roads; 39% of the total network was paved. All regions are linked by the road network, but many roads in mountainous districts are unsuitable for motor transport. In December 2002 a 23.5-km road, linking Greece with southern Albania, was opened. In 2003 the Albanian Government secured financing from the World Bank, the European Investment Bank and the European Bank for Reconstruction and Development for a number of road-maintenance projects. An essential component of government strategy for the development of the national road network in 2003–05 was the construction of a 175-km road, connecting the principal port of Durrës with the north-eastern town of Kukës, and Priština, the capital of the province of Kosovo and Metohija (Serbia and Montenegro). Several roads improving links with neighbouring borders and access to coastal tourist regions were also to be constructed.

SHIPPING

At December 2003 Albania's merchant fleet had 83 vessels, with a total displacement of 70,000 grt. The chief ports are those in Durrës, Vlorë, Sarandë and Shëngjin. In 1996 the port of Himare, which was closed in 1991, was reopened. Ferry services have been established between Durrës and three Italian ports (Trieste, Bari and Ancona) and between Sarandë and the Greek island of Corfu. Services also connect Vlorë with the Italian ports of Bari and Brindisi. The World Bank, the European Union and the Organization of the Petroleum Exporting Countries (OPEC) Fund For International Development have financed projects to improve existing port facilities.

Adetare Shipping Agency Ltd: Durrës; tel. (52) 23883; fax (52) 23666.

Albanian State Shipping Enterprise: Durrës; tel. (52) 22233; fax (52) 229111.

CIVIL AVIATION

There is a small international airport at Rinas, 25 km from Tirana. Reconstruction of the airport was undertaken in the late 1990s. On average, 900,000 metric tons of goods were carried by air each year. A civil and military airport was constructed at Pish Poro, 29 km from Vlorë, under an agreement between Albania and Italy. The construction of a second international airport (Zayed International Airport) at the north-eastern town of Kukës, with funding from the Government of the United Arab Emirates, was expected to be completed by the end of 2005.

General Directorate of Civil Aviation: Rruga e Kavajes, Perballe Xhamise, POB 205, Tirana; tel. and fax (4) 223969; e-mail dpac2@albanet.net.

Ada Air: Rruga Kemal Stafa 262, Tirana; tel. (4) 256111; fax (4) 226245; e-mail contact@adaair.com; internet www.adaair.com; f. 1991; operates passenger and cargo flights to Greece, Italy, Serbia and Montenegro and Switzerland; Pres. MARSEL SKENDO; Gen. Dir ILIR ZEKA.

Albanian Airlines SHPK: Rruga Mine Peza 2, Tirana; tel. and fax (4) 228461; e-mail tiadplvasita@msmail.com; f. 1992; acquired in 1995 by Aviation World Mak (Kuwait), and assumed present name; scheduled services to Germany, Italy and Turkey; Pres. FIKRY ABDUL WAHHAB; Man. Dir ASHRAF HASHEM.

Tourism

In 2001 there were some 342,908 international tourist arrivals. In 2002 receipts from tourism totalled US $487m., compared with $211m. in 1999. The main tourist centres include Tirana, Durrës, Sarandë, Shkodër and Pogradec. The Roman amphitheatre at Durrës is one of the largest in Europe. The ancient towns of Apollonia and Butrint are important archaeological sites, and there are many other towns of historic interest. However, expansion of the tourist industry has been limited by the inadequacy of Albania's infrastructure and a lack of foreign investment in the development of new facilities. Regional instability, particularly during the NATO air offensive against Yugoslavia (Serbia and Montenegro) in early 1999, also inhibited tourist activity.

Albturist: Bulevardi Dëshmorët e Kombit, Hotel Dhajti, Tirana; tel. (4) 251849; fax (4) 234359; e-mail albturist.t.a.@albnet.net; brs in main towns and all tourist centres; 28 hotels throughout the country; Dir-Gen. BESNIK PELLUMBI.

Committee for Development and Tourism: Bulevardi Dëshmorët e Kombit 8, Tirana; tel. (4) 258323; fax (4) 258322; e-mail arskenderi@albaniaonline.com; govt body.

ALGERIA

Introductory Survey

Location, Climate, Language, Religion, Flag, Capital

The Democratic and People's Republic of Algeria lies in north Africa, with the Mediterranean Sea to the north, Mali and Niger to the south, Tunisia and Libya to the east, and Morocco and Mauritania to the west. The climate on the Mediterranean coast is temperate, becoming more extreme in the Atlas mountains immediately to the south. Further south is part of the Sahara, a hot and arid desert. Temperatures in Algiers, on the coast, are generally between 9°C (48°F) and 29°C (84°F), while in the interior they may exceed 50°C (122°F). Arabic is the official language, but French is widely used. Tamazight, the principal language of Algeria's Berber community, was granted 'national' status in 2002. Islam is the state religion, and almost all Algerians are Muslims. The national flag (proportions 2 by 3) has two equal vertical stripes, of green and white, with a red crescent moon and a five-pointed red star superimposed in the centre. The capital is Algiers (el-Djezaïr).

Recent History

Algeria was conquered by French forces in the 1830s and annexed by France in 1842. The territory was colonized with French settlers, and many French citizens became permanent residents. Unlike most of France's overseas possessions, Algeria was not formally a colony but was 'attached' to metropolitan France. However, the indigenous Muslim majority were denied equal rights, and political and economic power within Algeria was largely held by the settler minority.

On 1 November 1954 the principal Algerian nationalist movement, the Front de libération nationale (FLN), began a war for national independence, in the course of which about 1m. Muslims were killed or wounded. The French Government agreed to a cease-fire in March 1962, and independence was declared on 3 July 1962. In August the Algerian provisional Government transferred its functions to the Political Bureau of the FLN, and in September a National Constituent Assembly was elected (from a single list of FLN candidates) and a Republic proclaimed. A new Government was formed, with Ahmed Ben Bella, founder of the FLN, as Prime Minister.

A draft Constitution, providing for a presidential regime with the FLN as the sole party, was adopted in August 1963, and approved by popular referendum in September. Ben Bella was elected President, although real power remained with the bureaucracy and the army. In June 1965 the Minister of Defence, Col Houari Boumedienne, deposed Ben Bella in a bloodless coup and took control of the country as President of a Council of the Revolution, composed chiefly of army officers.

Boumedienne encountered considerable opposition from left-wing members of the FLN, but from 1971 the Government was confident enough to adopt a more active social policy. In 1975 Boumedienne announced a series of measures to consolidate the regime and enhance his personal power, including the drafting of a National Charter and a new Constitution, and the holding of elections for a President and National People's Assembly. The National Charter, which enshrined both the creation of a socialist system and the maintenance of Islam as the state religion, and a new Constitution (incorporating the principles of the Charter) were approved at referendums held in June and November 1976, respectively, and in December Boumedienne was elected President unopposed. The new formal structure of power was completed in February 1977 by the election of FLN members to the National People's Assembly.

President Boumedienne died in December 1978, and the eight-member Council of the Revolution took over the Government. In January 1979 the FLN adopted a new party structure, electing a Central Committee that was envisaged as the highest policy-making body both of the party and of the nation as a whole. The Committee's choice of Col Ben Djedid Chadli, commander of Oran military district, as the sole presidential candidate (having been named as party Secretary-General) was endorsed by a referendum in February. Unlike Boumedienne, Chadli appointed a Prime Minister, Col Muhammad Abd al-Ghani, anticipating constitutional changes approved by the National People's Assembly in June, which included the obliga-

tory appointment of a premier. In mid-1980 the FLN authorized Chadli to form a smaller Political Bureau, with more limited responsibilities, thereby increasing the power of the President.

At a presidential election held in January 1984 Chadli's candidature was endorsed by 95.4% of the electorate. Chadli subsequently appointed Abd al-Hamid Brahimi as Prime Minister. In 1985 Chadli initiated a public debate on Boumedienne's National Charter, resulting in the adoption of a new National Charter at a special FLN Congress in December. The revised Charter, which emphasized a state ideology based on the twin principles of socialism and Islam while encouraging the development of private enterprise, was approved by a referendum in January 1986. In July 1987 the National People's Assembly adopted legislation to permit the formation of local organizations without prior government approval: a ban remained, however, on associations that were deemed to oppose the policies of the Charter or to threaten national security.

During the second half of the 1980s opposition to the Government was increasingly manifest. In 1985 22 Berber cultural and human rights activists were imprisoned after being convicted of belonging to illegal organizations. In 1987 several leading activists of an Islamist group were killed by security forces, and some 200 of the group's members were given prison sentences. From mid-1988 severe unemployment, high prices and shortages of essential supplies (resulting from economic austerity measures imposed in 1987 in response to a decline in world petroleum prices) provoked a series of strikes, and in early October rioting erupted in Algiers, spreading to Oran and Annaba. Chadli imposed a six-day state of emergency, and also proposed constitutional amendments that would allow non-FLN candidates to participate in elections and make the Prime Minister answerable to the National People's Assembly (rather than to the President). The reforms were approved by a referendum in November. In December Chadli was elected President for a third term of office, obtaining 81% of the votes cast.

In February 1989 a new Constitution, signifying the end of the one-party socialist state, was approved by referendum. The formation of political associations outside the FLN was henceforth permitted, while the armed forces were no longer allocated a role in the development of socialism. The executive, legislative and judicial functions of the State were separated and made subject to the supervision of a Constitutional Council. In July legislation permitting the formation of political parties entered force (although these were still required to be licensed by the Government): by mid-1991 a total of 47 political parties had been registered, including a radical Islamist group, the Front islamique du salut (FIS), the Mouvement pour la démocratie en Algérie (MDA), which had been founded by Ben Bella in 1984, the Parti d'avant-garde socialiste (renamed Ettahaddi in 1993), the Parti social-démocrate (PSD) and the Berber Rassemblement pour la culture et la démocratie (RCD). Other legislation adopted in July 1989 further reduced state control of the economy, allowed the expansion of investment by foreign companies, and ended the state monopoly of the press (although the principal newspapers remained under FLN control). Nevertheless, strikes and riots persisted during 1989. In September Chadli appointed Mouloud Hamrouche, hitherto a senior official in the presidential office, as Prime Minister.

At local elections held in June 1990 the principal Islamist party, the FIS, received some 55% of total votes cast, while the FLN obtained about 32%. In July, following disagreement within the FLN concerning the pace of economic and political reform, the Prime Minister and four other ministers resigned from the party's Political Bureau. In a reorganization of the Council of Ministers in the same month the defence portfolio was separated from the presidency for the first time since 1965. Also in July 1990 Chadli acceded to the demands of the FIS for an early general election, announcing that polling would take place in early 1991. In December 1990 the National People's Assembly adopted a law whereby after 1997 Arabic would be Algeria's only official language and the use of French and Berber in schools and in official transactions would be punishable offences. More than 100,000 people demonstrated in Algiers against political and religious intolerance.

In April 1991 Chadli declared that Algeria's first multi-party general election would take place in late June. The FIS argued that a presidential election should be held simultaneously with, or shortly after, the general election, and in May organized an indefinite general strike and demonstrations to demand Chadli's resignation and changes in the electoral laws. Violent confrontations in June between Islamist activists and the security forces prompted Chadli to declare a state of emergency and postpone the general election; he also announced that he had accepted the resignation of the Prime Minister and his Government. The former Minister of Foreign Affairs, Sid-Ahmad Ghozali, was appointed premier, and he subsequently nominated a Council of Ministers consisting mainly of political independents.

Meanwhile, the FLN and the FIS reached a compromise whereby the strike was abandoned and legislative and presidential elections were to be held before the end of 1991. In July, however, army units arrested some 700 Islamists and occupied the headquarters of the FIS. Among those arrested were the President of the FIS, Abbasi Madani, who had threatened to launch a *jihad* ('holy war') if the state of emergency was not ended, and the party's Vice-President, Ali Belhadj; both were charged with armed conspiracy against the State. The state of emergency was revoked in late September.

In October 1991, following revisions to the electoral code, Chadli formally announced that the first round of the multi-party general election to the newly enlarged 430-seat legislature would take place on 26 December, with a second round (in those constituencies where no candidate had secured an overall majority) scheduled for 16 January 1992. In all, 231 seats were won outright at the first round: the FIS took 188 seats (with 47.5% of the votes cast), the Front des forces socialistes (FFS) 25, the FLN just 15, and independents three. The FLN alleged widespread intimidation and electoral malpractice on the part of the FIS. On 11 January Chadli resigned as President, announcing that he had (one week earlier) dissolved the National People's Assembly. The following day the High Security Council (comprising the Prime Minister, three generals and two senior ministers) cancelled the second round of legislative voting, at which the FIS had been expected to consolidate its first-round victory, and on 14 January a five-member High Council of State (HCS) was appointed to act as a collegiate presidency until, at the latest, the expiry of Chadli's term of office in December 1993. The HCS was to be chaired by Muhammad Boudiaf, a veteran of the war of independence, but its most influential figure was believed to be Maj.-Gen. Khaled Nezzar, the Minister of Defence. The other members of the HCS were Ali Haroun (the Minister of Human Rights), Sheikh Tejini Haddam (the Rector of the Grand Mosque in Paris, France) and Ali Kafi (President of the war veterans' association, the Organisation nationale des moudjahidine—ONM). The constitutional legality of the HCS was disputed by all the political parties, including the FLN, while the FIS deputies who had been elected in December 1991 formed a 'shadow' assembly.

In February 1992 the HCS declared a 12-month state of emergency and detention centres were opened in the Sahara; the FIS, which was officially dissolved by the Government in March, claimed that 150 people had been killed, and as many as 30,000 detained, since the military-sponsored take-over. In April Boudiaf, as Chairman of the HCS, announced the creation of a 60-member National Consultative Council (NCC), which was to meet each month in the building of the suspended Assembly, although it was to have no legislative powers. In June Boudiaf promised a constitutional review, the dissolution of the FLN and a presidential election. Moreover, despite continuing violence, he ordered the release from detention of 2,000 FIS militants.

On 29 June 1992 Boudiaf was assassinated while making a speech in Annaba. The HCS ordered an immediate inquiry into the assassination, for which the FIS denied all responsibility. Ali Kafi succeeded Boudiaf as Chairman of the HCS, and Redha Malek, the Chairman of the NCC, was appointed as a new member of the HCS. In early July Ghozali resigned in order to enable Kafi to appoint his own Prime Minister. He was replaced by Belaid Abd es-Salam, who had directed Algeria's post-independence petroleum and gas policy. Abd es-Salam appointed a new Council of Ministers later in the month.

In late July 1992 Madani and Belhadj were sentenced to 12 years' imprisonment for conspiracy against the State. Violent protests erupted in Algiers and quickly spread to other cities. Despite appeals by Abd es-Salam for a multi-party dialogue in an attempt to end civil strife, the Government attracted widespread criticism for reinforcing its emergency powers to repress any person or organization whose activities were deemed to represent a threat to stability.

Political manoeuvring and attempts at reconciliation continued against a background of escalating violence throughout the country. In February 1993 the state of emergency was renewed for an indefinite period. In June the HCS appealed for a 'general mobilization' against terrorism, although in the same month Abd es-Salam expressed his willingness to open a dialogue with the militants. None the less, violence continued unabated, with terrorist attacks increasingly targeting not only political officials but also prominent intellectual and civilian figures. In June the HCS announced that it would dissolve itself at the end of December, asserting that a modern democracy and free market economy would be created within three years of that date.

In July 1993 a retired general, Liamine Zéroual, succeeded Maj.-Gen. Nezzar as Minister of Defence, although Nezzar retained his post within the HCS. In August Redha Malek, who similarly remained a member of the HCS, was appointed to replace Abd es-Salam as Prime Minister. Malek, who appointed a new Council of Ministers in September, stated that the resolute stance against terrorism would be maintained, and rejected the possibility of dialogue with its perpetrators. In October the HCS appointed an eight-member National Dialogue Commission (NDC), which was charged with the preparation of a political conference to organize the transition to an elected and democratic form of government. In December it was announced that the HCS would not be disbanded until a new presidential body had been elected at the NDC conference in January 1994. However, all the main political parties (with the exception of the moderate Islamist Hamas) boycotted the conference. Liamine Zéroual (who retained the defence portfolio in the Council of Ministers) was inaugurated as President on 31 January for a three-year term, on the apparent recommendation of senior members of the military.

In February 1994 two senior members of the FIS, Ali Djeddi and Abdelkader Boukhamkham, were released from prison, and rumours circulated that divisions had occurred within the military as a result of contacts made by high-ranking members of the regime, including Zéroual, with imprisoned Islamist leaders. Malek resigned as Prime Minister in April and was replaced by Mokdad Sifi, hitherto Minister of Equipment. In May the President inaugurated a National Transition Council (NTC), an interim legislature of 200 appointed members, the aim of which was to provide a forum for debate pending legislative elections. Except for Hamas, most of the 21 parties that agreed to participate in the NTC were virtually unknown, and the 22 seats that were allocated to other major parties remained vacant.

It remained unclear whether the FIS actively supported the most prominent and radical Islamist militant group, the Groupe islamique armé (GIA) in its frequent attacks on members of the security forces, local government and the judiciary, as well as prominent public figures, intellectuals, journalists and ordinary civilians. In March 1994 an attack by Islamist militants on the high-security Tazoult prison, near Batna, resulted in the release of more than 1,000 political prisoners. Certain towns were virtually controlled by Islamist activists, and the deaths of a number of foreign nationals led several countries to advise their citizens to leave Algeria. In response to the rise in violence, the security forces intensified their campaign against armed Islamist groups, resorting to air attacks, punitive raids, torture and psychological warfare, and killing thousands of militants.

In August 1994 members of the FLN, the Parti du renouveau algérien (PRA), the MDA, Nahdah and Hamas engaged in what was termed a national dialogue with the Government; the meetings were boycotted, however, by Ettahaddi, the FFS and the RCD. At further negotiations held in early September discussion focused on two letters sent to the President by Abbasi Madani, purportedly offering a 'truce'. Madani and Belhadj were released from prison in mid-September and placed under house arrest; however, the FIS did not participate in the next round of national dialogue later that month, declaring that negotiations could take place only after the granting of a general amnesty, the rehabilitation of the FIS and the repeal of the state of emergency. The GIA threatened reprisals if the FIS entered into dialogue with the regime, and intensified its campaign of violence against secular society by targeting educational institutions. In addition to the upheaval caused by Islamist violence, the Berber RCD urged a boycott of the start of the school year, and in September Berber activists in the Kabyle region organized a general strike in protest at the exclusion of the Berber language, Tamazight, from the syllabus and at the prospect of the FIS entering the national dialogue. In May 1995 the RCD welcomed the establishment of a government body to oversee the teaching of Tamazight in schools and universities (commencing in October) and to promote its use in the official media.

In October 1994 Zéroual announced that a presidential election would be held before the end of 1995. However, the FIS and other opponents of the Algerian regime condemned the proposed organization of an election in the context of the ongoing civil conflict. In November 1994 representatives of several major Algerian parties, including the FIS, the FLN, the FFS and the MDA, attended a two-day conference in Rome, Italy, organized by the Sant' Egidio Roman Catholic community to foster discussion about the crisis in Algeria. The ensuing Sant' Egidio pact, endorsed by all the participants at a meeting in Rome in January 1995, rejected the use of violence to achieve or maintain power, and urged the Algerian regime to repeal the state of emergency and thereby facilitate negotiations between all parties. However, the pact was dismissed as a 'non-event' by the Government. In April Zéroual resumed discussions with the legalized opposition parties in preparation for the presidential election. Talks with the FLN and the FFS quickly collapsed, however, as both rejected the prospect of participating in an election from which the FIS was excluded. Subsequent dialogue between the Government and the FIS also proved unsuccessful.

Some 40 candidates announced their intention to contest the presidential election, the first round of which was scheduled for 16 November 1995, but only four were confirmed as having attained the required number of signatures (an electoral decree issued by the Government in May, and promulgated by the NTC in July, stipulated that presidential candidates must obtain the endorsement of 75,000 signatures from at least 25 provinces in order to qualify). Despite an appeal by the FLN, the FFS and the FIS for voters to boycott the election, official figures showed that some 75% of the electorate participated in the poll, in which Zéroual secured an outright victory, with 61.0% of the valid votes cast. Zéroual was inaugurated for a five-year term on 27 November. Shortly afterwards the Government announced the closure of the last of seven detention centres opened since 1992, thereby releasing some 650 prisoners, many of whom were Islamist sympathizers. In late December 1995 Ahmed Ouyahia, a career diplomat, replaced Sifi as Prime Minister. Ouyahia's Government, named in early January 1996, included two members of Hamas and a dissident leader of the FIS.

In April 1996, in an attempt to foster national reconciliation, Zéroual held bilateral discussions with more than 50 influential individuals, including leaders of trade unions and opposition groups; the FIS was not invited to participate. In the following month Zéroual announced his intention to hold legislative elections in early 1997. In addition, he proposed that a referendum be held, prior to the elections, on amendments to the Constitution: these included measures to increase the powers of the President while limiting his tenure to a maximum of two consecutive mandates; the creation of a Council of the Nation as a second parliamentary chamber (one-third of whose members would be chosen by the President); the establishment of a State Council (to regulate the administrative judiciary) and a High State Court; and, significantly, a ban on political parties that were based on religion, language, gender or regional differences. It was also suggested that the electoral law be revised to allow for a system of full proportional representation. Several opposition parties reiterated their demands that the Government resume negotiations with the FIS, and argued that constitutional reform should be undertaken only after legislative elections. Some 1,000 delegates, including representatives of the FLN, Nahdah and Hamas, attended a government-sponsored conference on national concord held in September 1996. The conference was boycotted by the FFS, the RCD, Ettahaddi and the MDA. Zéroual subsequently withdrew his offer to include members of opposition parties in an expanded Council of Ministers and NTC. The proposed constitutional amendments were promulgated in December, having been approved by some 86% of the voters at a referendum held in November.

In January 1997 the Secretary-General of the FLN-affiliated Union Générale des Travailleurs Algériens (UGTA), Abd al-Hak Benhamouda, was shot dead in Algiers. Although an Islamist group claimed responsibility for the assassination, there was

speculation that it may have been perpetrated by opponents within the regime. In February Zéroual announced that elections to the National People's Assembly would take place in late May or early June. Shortly afterwards the NTC adopted restrictive legislation concerning political parties in accordance with the amended Constitution; new electoral legislation replacing the majority system with proportional representation was also adopted. Later in February Abdelkader Bensalah, the President of the NTC, formed a centrist grouping, the Rassemblement national démocratique (RND). The RND received support from a wide range of organizations, including trade unions, anti-Islamist groups and the influential war veterans' ONM, and was closely linked with Zéroual and the Government. Several other political parties emerged in the months that followed, while certain existing parties changed their names to comply with the new legislation. Notably, Hamas became the Mouvement de la société pour la paix (MSP).

Some 39 political parties contested the elections to the National People's Assembly, held on 5 June 1997, although the FIS and Ettahaddi urged a boycott of the polls. As the preliminary results of the elections began to emerge, opposition leaders complained of irregularities during the electoral process, and accused officials of manipulating the results in favour of the RND. International observers were critical of the conduct of the elections, and commented that the rate of voter participation (officially estimated at 65.5% of the electorate) seemed unrealistically high. According to the final official results, the RND won 156 of the Assembly's 380 seats, followed by the MSP (69) and the FLN (62); Nahdah took 34 seats, the FFS 20, and the RCD 19. President Zéroual asked Ahmed Ouyahia to form a new Government, and later in June Ouyahia announced a new Council of Ministers, comprising members of the RND, the FLN and the MSP.

Following the RND's success at regional and municipal elections held in October 1997, the party's political dominance was consolidated with the appointment of the Council of the Nation in late December. Of the Council's 96 seats indirectly elected by regional and municipal authorities, 80 were won by the RND, 10 by the FLN, four by the FFS and two by the MSP; President Zéroual appointed the remaining 48 members. In the following month the authorities disbanded some 30 political groupings, including Ettahaddi and the PSD, for failing to satisfy the legal requirements concerning political associations.

There were violent protests in the Kabyle region in June 1998 following the assassination of Lounes Matoub, a popular Berber singer and an outspoken critic of both the Government and the fundamentalist Islamist movement. There were further protests in July when controversial legislation on the compulsory use of the Arabic language in public life (see above) came into effect. Berber activists in the Kabyle fiercely opposed the 'arabization' policy, demanding the recognition of Tamazight as an official language.

In September 1998 President Zéroual announced that a presidential election would be held before March 1999, nearly two years ahead of schedule. There was considerable speculation that the announcement had been prompted primarily by a power struggle within the regime between the faction loyal to the President and figures close to Lt-Gen. Muhammad Lamari, the Chief of Staff of the Army. Zéroual declared at the end of October 1998 that the presidential election would be postponed until April 1999 to allow political parties to prepare their campaigns. In December 1998 Ouyahia resigned; he was replaced as premier by Smail Hamdani, a widely respected senior politician and former diplomat.

A total of 47 candidates registered to contest the presidential election; however, the Constitutional Council declared only seven eligible to stand. Although the senior generals had decided not to nominate a member of the armed forces for the presidency, there was widespread cynicism regarding the military's assurances of its neutrality, and Abdelaziz Bouteflika was believed to have the support of the military establishment. Bouteflika also enjoyed the support of the four main political parties as well as that of the UGTA.

On the eve of the election, which took place on 15 April 1999, Bouteflika's six rivals withdrew their candidacies after Zéroual refused to postpone the poll following allegations of massive electoral fraud in favour of Bouteflika. Voting papers were, nevertheless, distributed for all seven candidates, and no official boycott of the election was organized. The credibility of the poll was, however, seriously diminished, and Bouteflika announced that he would accept the presidency only if there were both a high rate of voter participation and a large majority in his favour. According to official results, Bouteflika won 73.8% of the votes cast (his closest rival, Ahmed Taleb Ibrahimi, a former Minister of Foreign Affairs who was now supported by the outlawed FIS, secured 12.5%). However, this figure, together with the estimated official turn-out of more than 60%, was immediately disputed by his opponents, who maintained that only 23.3% of the registered electorate had participated, and that Bouteflika had received only 28% of the votes cast, compared with 20% for Ibrahimi. At his inauguration, on 27 April, Bouteflika emphasized the need for national reconciliation to end the civil conflict in Algeria, but pledged to continue the military campaign against terrorists and reaffirmed that the FIS would not be legalized.

Following clandestine negotiations between the Government and representatives of the FIS, in June 1999 the Armée islamique du salut (AIS, the armed wing of the FIS) announced the permanent cessation of its armed struggle against the Government. President Bouteflika's plans for a national reconciliation initiative were incorporated in a Law on Civil Concord, promulgated in July, whereby there was to be an amnesty for members of armed Islamist groups who surrendered within a six-month deadline and who were not implicated in mass killings, rape or bomb attacks on public places. The legislation was approved by 98.6% of those who voted (85% of the electorate) in a national referendum in September. Meanwhile, Bouteflika exhibited unprecedented candour, admitting in August that the civil conflict of the past seven years had resulted in the deaths of at least 100,000 people (hitherto the authorities had put the number of deaths at 30,000).

Abdelkader Hachani, the most senior member of the FIS at liberty, was assassinated in Algiers in November 1999. Hachani was believed to have been involved in a secret political dialogue between the Government and the FIS. Although a member of the principal GIA faction was subsequently arrested and charged with the murder, several of Hachani's relatives claimed that the security forces, which had reportedly kept the FIS official under surveillance following his release from detention, had perpetrated the assassination.

Bouteflika finally named his Council of Ministers in December 1999. Led by Ahmed Benbitour, a former Minister of Finance, the new Government comprised members of the FLN, the MSP, Nahdah, the RCD, the Alliance nationale républicaine (ANR), the RND and the PRA, all of which had supported Bouteflika's presidential campaign. In February 2000 Bouteflika announced extensive changes to the military high command, which included the replacement of the commanders of four of the country's six military regions.

In early January 2000, following discussions between representatives of the Government, the army and the AIS, an agreement was reached whereby the AIS pledged to disband in return for the restoration of full civil and political rights to its former members. It was estimated that some 1,500–3,000 rebels were to be granted a full pardon under the agreement, some of whom were to be temporarily enlisted in an auxiliary unit to assist the security forces in apprehending members of the GIA and of a breakaway group from the GIA, the Groupe salafiste pour la prédication et le combat (GSPC, or Da'wa wal Djihad). In mid-January, following the expiry of the amnesty period specified under the Law on Civil Concord, the armed forces launched a concerted assault on rebel strongholds in the north-east and south-west of the country, in an attempt to eliminate remaining anti-Government factions. It was officially stated at this time that 80% of members of armed groups had surrendered. Meanwhile, the Government estimated that around 600 people (many of them civilians) had been killed between July 1999 and January 2000, mostly in incidents connected to the GIA and the GSPC.

The conflict between militant Islamist groups and the armed forces persisted following the expiry of the deadline for amnesty under the Law on Civil Concord; thousands of Islamist fighters remained at large. In July 2000 an article in the daily *Le Jeune Indépendant*, citing unofficial sources, claimed that some 1,100 civilians and an estimated 2,000 terrorists had been killed in Algeria since the expiry of the general amnesty in January. However, following visits to Algeria in mid-2000 (the first by human rights organizations to be permitted by the Algerian authorities for some years), both Amnesty International and the Fédération internationale des ligues des droits de l'Homme (FIDH) reported that there had been a significant decline in violence and a clear improvement in the country's human rights

situation, although concern was expressed about the fate of an estimated 22,000 missing persons who had disappeared since 1992.

In August 2000 Benbitour resigned the premiership and was replaced by Ali Benflis, a former Minister of Justice who had directed Bouteflika's presidential campaign. The composition of the new Government remained largely unchanged. At indirect elections in December 2000 for one-half of the 96 elective members of the Council of the Nation, the RND retained its comfortable majority, although its total number of seats was reduced from 80 to 74.

A sharp escalation in violence at the end of 2000 added weight to the arguments of those who believed that the amnesty under the Civil Concord had done little to quell unrest. Among more than 200 deaths recorded among Islamist fighters, government forces and civilians during the first three weeks of Ramadan were those of 16 pupils and their warden at a technical college in Médéa, who in mid-December were massacred in their dormitory by armed gunmen. The first killings of foreigners for almost two years were reported in early January 2001, when four Russian expatriate workers were killed in the Annaba region, and at least 190 deaths were reported as a result of continuing violence in that month. Meanwhile, there were persistent rumours of tensions between Bouteflika, the military high command and those parties opposed to any appeasement with militant fundamentalists.

Violence continued unabated throughout 2001, with regular reports of incidents involving Islamists, the security forces and civilians resulting in large numbers of deaths on all sides. Reports in the Algerian press indicated that during April more than 150 people had been killed in attacks involving armed Islamist groups and that over 1,000 people, including more than 400 Islamists, had been killed since the beginning of the year. In June at least 110 people, including 40 members of the security forces, were killed by armed Islamists, and a renewed upsurge in violence during the holy month of Ramadan resulted in the deaths of some 50 people.

In May 2001 the National People's Assembly approved amendments to the penal code whereby authors of articles judged defamatory could be sentenced to up to three years' imprisonment and fines of AD 100,000, while fines to a maximum of AD 5m. could be imposed for offending the Head of State. Later that month 21 independent dailies cancelled their editions and more than 1,000 journalists marched in Algiers in protest against the new laws. Also in late May Bouteflika effected an extensive reorganization of the Council of Ministers.

Violent clashes broke out in mid-April 2001 between protesters and security forces in several villages in the Kabyle following the death of a secondary school student (who had been apprehended for allegedly committing an assault during a robbery) in police custody at Beni Douala near the regional capital, Tizi Ouzou. Thousands of local inhabitants joined demonstrations, demanding a full inquiry into the incident and the withdrawal of paramilitary gendarmes from the Kabyle. Tensions were further fuelled by anger among Kabyles at the poor social and economic conditions in the region. Days after the student was killed the situation was further inflamed when three young Kabyles were assaulted by gendarmes near Béjaïa. The incidents coincided with demonstrations traditionally held to mark the anniversary of the so-called 'Berber Spring' protests of 1980, when Berber activism for cultural and linguistic rights had first taken form, and although the two major political parties in the Kabyle—the FFS and the RCD—appealed for calm, violence rapidly escalated throughout the area; as many as 80 people had reportedly died by the end of the month. In a televised address, Bouteflika announced the creation of a national commission of inquiry, to be headed by Mohand Issad, a lawyer originating from the Kabyle, to investigate recent events in the region. Bouteflika also indicated that he planned revisions to the Constitution that would address the status of Tamazight, and revealed his intention to adopt a proposal making instruction in the Berber language compulsory in Tamazight-speaking areas. Furthermore, he accused unnamed groups both inside and outside the country of inciting extremism. Bouteflika's speech was strongly criticized by the main political groupings in the Kabyle, and the RCD withdrew from the coalition Government.

In early May 2001 an FFS-organized demonstration in Algiers, attended by some 10,000–30,000 people, proceeded peacefully; however, rallies in several Berber towns and villages were dispersed by riot police using tear gas. Later in May rioting again intensified in the Kabyle. In one protest, some 500,000

Berbers marched through the streets of Tizi Ouzou. Bouteflika again addressed the nation, urging rigorous sanctions against those who had instigated the violence. In early June security forces dispersed a demonstration in Algiers by 3,000 Berbers, and a demonstration in Algiers the following week, organized by the Coordination des aarchs, dairas et communes (CADC—also known as the Coordination des comités de villages Kabyles), and which attracted more than 500,000 people, degenerated into violence after the protesters' intended route towards the presidential palace was blocked by security forces. Hundreds of protesters were injured and two journalists were killed as a result of the clashes. After further violent demonstrations in the Kabyle in mid-June, Prime Minister Benflis appeared on television to appeal for calm and all protests in Algiers were prohibited.

By the end of June 2001 unrest had spread beyond the Kabyle to the Aurès region, as well as to Annaba and to Biskra in the south of the country. Official reports stated that 56 people had been killed, and 1,300 injured, since the violence first erupted. Despite repeated calls in the independent press for his resignation, Bouteflika declared that he would not relinquish the presidency and again urged rioters not to participate in what he termed an external plot to undermine the security of the country. In late July the Issad commission issued its preliminary report into the events in the Kabyle, in which it attached the blame for the rioting to the gendarmerie, maintaining that gendarmes had adopted a 'shoot-to-kill' policy and had acted in an illegal manner. However, the report failed to name those responsible for ordering the gendarmes' actions, and the commission complained of attempts, apparently on the part of vested interests within the security forces, to obstruct its investigations.

In August 2001 security forces blocked roads in order to prevent a large number of Berbers from marching on the capital, where they intended to present a list of 15 demands at the presidential palace. This 'El-Kseur platform' (named after the Kabyle town in which it had been drawn up) notably requested the granting of official status to Tamazight without the holding of a referendum; the removal of all paramilitary gendarmes from the Kabyle; the annulment of legal proceedings against demonstrators; and the trial by civilian courts of all those who had ordered or perpetrated crimes and their dismissal from the security forces or the civil service.

In September 2001 President Bouteflika formally invited Berber community and tribal leaders, known as the *Aarouch*, to present their demands for social and political change, and designated premier Benflis to act as interlocutor between the authorities and the Berbers. Relations between the two sides were, however, complicated by divisions within the Berber movement, as some Berber leaders were unwilling to enter into any negotiations with the Government. The more radical *Aarouch*, angered by the prevention of three previous attempts to present the El-Kseur platform to Bouteflika, rejected the President's offer and announced their intention to proceed with a rally planned for 5 October in the capital. Nevertheless, official reports claimed that a meeting took place on 3 October between Benflis and moderate *Aarouch*, at which Benflis informed them that the President had decided to grant Tamazight the status of a national language in a forthcoming constitutional amendment. Ongoing dialogue between moderate Berber representatives and the Government resulted in the adoption, in January 2002, of a series of resolutions, including proposals for the establishment of a special ministerial council to implement the creation of decentralized government councils in the Kabyle at *wilaya* level. The Kabyles' demand that the gendarmerie be withdrawn from their region was, however, dismissed by Bouteflika as 'inconceivable'. The more radical Berber leaders voiced their disapproval of the resolutions, stating that the El-Kseur platform was non-negotiable, and again insisted that the gendarmerie be withdrawn from the Kabyle.

Meanwhile, in December 2001 the final report of the Issad commission had been published, confirming the initial findings that the gendarmerie had been to blame for the repression in the Kabyle, and also expressing deep pessimism about the immediate future of the region. Emphasizing the increasing authority of the military throughout the country since 1992, the report stated that the responsibilities of the civil and military authorities had become blurred and denounced the subtle slide from 'a state of emergency to a state of siege'. Issad also condemned the military's widespread abuse of its powers and the laws of the country.

In a televised address in early March 2002 Bouteflika officially announced that Tamazight would be recognized as a national language without, as had initially been intended, the issue being put to a national referendum. Accordingly, on 7 April the National People's Assembly voted almost unanimously in favour of amending the Constitution to grant Tamazight the status of a national language. Nevertheless, Kabyle leaders urged a boycott of the forthcoming legislative elections, due to take place on 30 May, and unrest continued in the region, which was brought to a standstill by a series of strikes.

A total of 23 parties contested elections to the newly enlarged National People's Assembly held on 30 May 2002, although the polls were boycotted by the FFS and the RCD. According to official results, the FLN won 199 of the 389 available seats (compared with 64 in the outgoing, 380-member legislature), while the RND suffered a significant loss of support, with its parliamentary representation reduced from 155 seats to just 47. Sheikh Abdallah Djaballah's Mouvement de la réforme nationale (MRN) took 43 seats, the MSP 38 (compared with 69 in 1997) and the Parti des travailleurs 21. Independent candidates secured a total of 30 seats. The overall credibility of the election was, however, undermined by a low rate of voter participation: only 46.2% of the country's 18m. eligible voters cast their ballot. Voter abstention was particularly high in the Kabyle, with participation rates in Béjaïa and Tizi Ouzou recorded at just 2.6% and 1.8%, respectively. The FFS and the RCD demanded an annulment of the results, claiming that real voter turn-out had reached no more than 15%–20%.

Following the elections Bouteflika reappointed Ali Benflis as Prime Minister, and in mid-June 2002 Benflis named a new, 39-member coalition Government, in which the majority of the key figures from the outgoing administration retained their posts. The most notable promotion was that of Muhammad Terbeche, hitherto Minister-delegate to the Minister of Finance, in charge of the Budget, who replaced Mourad Medelci as Minister of Finance. Former Prime Minister Ahmed Ouyahia was appointed Minister of State, Personal Representative of the President of the Republic. The new Government included five women, among them an outspoken campaigner for women's rights, Khalida Toumi-Messaoudi, who was appointed Minister for Communications and Culture, and Government Spokesperson.

In early July 2002, upon the 40th anniversary of independence from French rule, some 50 people were killed in a bomb attack in Larba, to the south of Algiers; this brought the total number of conflict-related deaths since the beginning of the year to more than 800. The attack came just days after the army Chief of Staff, Lt-Gen. Lamari, had declared that the Government had won its campaign against the Islamist guerrillas. Some 150 people were estimated to have died in ongoing violence during July; certain sources reported that GIA leader Rachid Abou Tourab had been killed, along with 15 other GIA militants, during a raid by security forces in the Tamezguida forest, south of the capital. (Tourab's predecessor, Antar Zouabri, had been killed by security forces in February.) A further 40 Islamists were killed in early August.

Prior to local elections in mid-October 2002, Bouteflika pardoned about 60 detainees who had been sentenced for public order offences following the unrest in the Kabyle in 2001. The persistance of divisions within the Berber movement was highlighted when the RCD, supported by the CADC, announced that it would again boycott the polls. This was in direct contrast to the FFS, which was to present candidates in 40 of the country's 48 *wilayat*, maintaining that these would provide ordinary Kabyles with the possibility of attaining some form of political representation. At the elections the FLN won 668 of the 1,541 communes and thus secured control of 43 *wilayat*, although there were violent clashes in the Kabyle where demonstrators attempted to prevent voting from taking place. Voter turn-out was again low, particularly in the Kabyle.

There was a further escalation of violence in early January 2003 after some 60 people, including at least 43 soldiers, were killed in an ambush by GSPC fighters near Batna. Although Algerian officials maintained that fewer than 1,000 Islamist rebels remained in the country, there were continued reports of attacks on civilians and security forces by the GIA and the GSPC throughout the first months of the year.

At the FLN party congress, held in mid-March 2003, evidence of a serious rift between Benflis and Bouteflika emerged when Benflis announced his opposition to a number of Bouteflika's economic policies and withdrew the party's support for the

President. Furthermore, it was rumoured that Benflis intended to stand as a candidate in the presidential election scheduled for April 2004. Benflis, who was re-elected Secretary-General of the FLN for a further five-year term, was also granted considerably increased powers, including the right to appoint senior party officials and to call extraordinary party congresses. In early May 2003 Bouteflika dismissed Benflis as Prime Minister, reportedly owing to 'far-reaching divergencies' between the two men. The former Prime Minister, Ahmed Ouyahia, was subsequently appointed to succeed Benflis. Ouyahia announced a new coalition Government shortly afterwards, in which the majority of portfolios remained unchanged, although Terbeche was replaced as Minister of Finance by Abdellatif Benachenhou.

In early July 2003 the two leaders of the proscribed FIS, Abassi Madani and Ali Belhadj, were released from house arrest and imprisonment, respectively, after completing their 12-year sentences for conspiracy against the State. However, upon their release both men were issued with court orders prohibiting them from engaging in any political activity; holding meetings; establishing a political, cultural, charitable or religious association; participating in any political party; or becoming a member or supporter of any other association. They were also barred from voting or standing as candidates in any election.

The Government announced in late July 2003 that it had agreed to reintroduce the use of Tamazight into Algeria's educational system, thereby fulfilling one of the demands of the El-Kseur platform. Ouyahia had, in May, urged local Berber leaders in the Kabyle to negotiate with the authorities to bring an end to the violence in the region following a series of protest marches and a general strike in the previous month, and in early June several senior members of the CADC had been released. Bouteflika remained eager to resolve the ongoing crisis in the Kabyle, and in late August the Algerian Government granted more than €23m. in 'overdue' development aid to the region. In early January 2004 lengthy negotiations took place between the *Aarouch* and the Government, following which the Government pledged to acquiesce to five of the six points deemed by the *Aarouch* to be 'prerequisites' before any further talks relating to the El-Kseur platform could take place; these included the release of all remaining prisoners and the annulment of legal proceedings against demonstrators detained during the riots of April 2001. The sixth point, regarding the dissolution of municipal and regional councils elected in the Kabyle in October 2002 (when there was a widespread voter boycott), was settled in late January 2004 when the Government agreed to remove any councillors who had been elected illegally in the contested polls. Days later the Algerian authorities released a further five Berber leaders who had been imprisoned for their role in the rioting, and Ouyahia stated that the meetings had provided a 'fundamental turning point' in the process between the two sides. However, the negotiations collapsed following the Government's assertion that the status of Tamazight should be decided in a national referendum, and further unrest ensued in the Kabyle, while the FFS declared that it would not participate in the forthcoming presidential election. It was announced in mid-January 2005 that, following a new round of talks, the Government and the *Aarouch* had reached an agreement regarding implementation of the El-Kseur platform. Later that month two joint committees were established to implement and monitor the agreement.

Meanwhile, in early September 2003 Bouteflika effected a reorganization of the Council of Ministers, in which he dismissed a number of FLN ministers who had indicated their support for Benflis's presidential campaign. During late 2003 relations between Bouteflika and Benflis continued to deteriorate and in early October the remaining FLN ministers, who had pledged their support for Benflis, withdrew from the coalition Government. The following day, at an extraordinary congress of the FLN (which took place despite attempts by a number of party members opposed to Benflis to have the meeting prohibited), 1,375 of the 1,500 members present approved Benflis's candidature, thus confirming him as the party's representative at the 2004 presidential election. Bouteflika immediately carried out a further reshuffle of the Council of Ministers, appointing new ministers to the seven posts vacated by the Benflis loyalists.

In late December 2003 the administrative chamber of the Algiers Court suspended all activities of the FLN after the pro-Bouteflika faction of the party lodged a complaint maintaining that the party congress held in April had been held illegally and that the results of the congress were 'null and void'. The party's

bank accounts were frozen and its headquarters and provincial offices were closed down. The decision was condemned by Benflis and in early January 2004 numerous FLN members protested against the decision outside the National People's Assembly. On 12 January a group of 11 leading politicians, including Benflis and four other former heads of government, signed a statement demanding the formation of an interim government ahead of the presidential election, citing the lack of impartiality in the current Government, and an independent body to oversee the polls. Prime Minister Ouyahia (whose party, the RND, had already declared its support for President Bouteflika were he to stand for re-election) responded to the communiqué by affirming that he had no intention of stepping down and pledging that the Government would organize a free and fair presidential election in the early part of the year. He also dismissed claims that the Government was restricting other political parties' access to state television and radio coverage.

Meanwhile, indirect elections took place on 30 December 2003 to renew 46 members of the Council of the Nation. (As a result of the unrest in the Kabyle, members for two constituencies in that region were to be selected at a later date.) The RND won 17 seats, while the (pro-Benflis) FLN obtained 11 seats, the Corrective Movement of the FLN 10, the MSP four, and the MRN and independents secured two seats each. One-half of the presidential appointees to the Council were also replaced.

During 2003 violent incidents in Algeria declined markedly; in that year, according to official figures, fewer than 900 people were killed as a result of violence involving Islamists and the security forces, compared with some 1,400 in 2002 and almost 1,900 in 2001. The Government attributed the decline in the number of attacks to the increased efficiency of the security forces, who had successfully dismantled many of the terrorists' support networks, and to divisions within the Islamist groups. It was claimed that the GIA, whose leader, Rachid Abou Tourab, was apparently captured in November 2003 (despite reports of his death in July 2002), had been reduced to just 30 members, while internal divisions had reportedly caused a split in the GSPC, with three separate factions of the group operating in the country.

In a statement made by the Chief of Staff, Lt-Gen. Muhammad Lamari, in early January 2004, the army, long considered a major power in Algerian politics, declared its neutrality in the forthcoming presidential election. Lamari warned, however, that the military would not be able to remain neutral were the stability of the nation to come under threat. Some analysts argued that the decision not to intervene in political affairs was prompted both by the army's determination that Algeria should join NATO and by pressure from Western countries, in particular the USA.

In early February 2004 Bouteflika announced that the presidential election would take place on 8 April. Having declared that a committee would be established to ensure the fairness and transparency of the election, he also invited representatives of international organizations to observe the electoral process. A fortnight later Bouteflika announced his intention to run for a second term as President. Although more than 40 candidates put forward applications to contest the poll, only six obtained the requisite 75,000 signatures from more than one-half of the country's 48 provinces. Bouteflika was joined in the presidential race by Ali Benflis, Secretary-General of the FLN; Sheikh Abdallah Djaballah, leader of the Islamist MRN; Saïd Saâdi, President of the RCD; Louiza Hanoune, head of the Parti des travailleurs; and Fawzi Rebaïne, Secretary-General of the small nationalist party Ahd 54. Prior to the presidential election, there were increased allegations of fraudulent behaviour on the part of Bouteflika, who was accused of monopolizing state media and of using state funds to set his re-election campaign in motion before the electoral race had officially begun. The President dismissed these claims by insisting that the media remained unbiased and emphasizing that the elections would be monitored by neutral observers.

On 8 April 2004 Bouteflika was decisively re-elected for a second term of office. He received 85.0% of the valid votes cast, while his nearest rival, Benflis, took 6.4%. Djaballah secured 5.0%, Saâdi 1.9%, Hanoune 1.0% and Rebaïne 0.6%. The rate of turn-out by eligible voters was reported to be 58.1%, although this rate was estimated to be as low as 18% in the Kabyle. Bouteflika's rivals immediately accused the President of electoral malpractice; however, international observers declared the election to have been representative of popular will and free from any vote-rigging. Both Benflis and Saâdi boycotted Bouteflika's inauguration ceremony on 19 April, at which he vouched to resolve the Berber crisis and to improve the rights of women by readdressing the controversial family code of 1984. He also emphasized his commitment to his campaign for 'true national reconciliation'. Ahmed Ouyahia resigned as Prime Minister, as required under the Constitution, and was immediately reinstated and given the task of forming a new government. On 26 April 2004 Ouyahia named his new Council of Ministers, which retained most of the senior ministers from the previous administration. The new Government consisted principally of FLN members and non-partisan supporters of Bouteflika, with a few representatives from the RND and the MSP. Meanwhile, Benflis resigned as Secretary-General of the FLN. At an FLN congress held in early February 2005 the Minister of State for Foreign Affairs, Abdelaziz Belkhadem, was elected to the post of Secretary-General and President Bouteflika was elected honorary President of the party.

In early June 2004 the President of the National People's Assembly, Karim Younès, resigned, stating that he had made the decision to leave office very soon after Bouteflika's re-election but had not wanted to disrupt the Government directly after the election. At the end of the month Younès was replaced by Amar Saidani of the FLN. In early August the Chief of Staff of the Army, Lt-Gen. Muhammad Lamari, resigned on the grounds of ill health, although there was considerable speculation that his departure from the military might also signal the final withdrawal of the army from the political sphere. Lamari was replaced by the Commander of the Land Force, Gen. Salah Ahmed Gaid.

Meanwhile, violence between the GSPC and the Algerian military began to escalate, particularly in the Kabyle region. In early March 2004 it was reported that fighting had occurred between the Chadian military and a faction of the GSPC led by the group's second-in-command, Amari Saifi, resulting in the deaths of more than 40 militants. Saifi was wanted in Algeria and abroad for various crimes, including the kidnapping in 2003 of a group of 32 European tourists (see below) and the killing of 43 Algerian soldiers. It was announced in October 2004 that Saifi had been taken into Algerian custody, having been intercepted by Libyan authorities on the Chadian–Libyan border. Meanwhile, in mid-June 2004 Nabil Sahraoui, the GSPC's leader since October 2003, was reportedly killed by the Algerian military (who were conducting a 'vast anti-terrorist operation' in the Kabyle) during a gun battle that also killed four of his senior aides, including the man widely viewed as his successor, Abdi Abdelaziz. The army subsequently announced that it had 'completely neutralized' the leadership of the GSPC and had seized many of its weapons and documents. Shortly after the announcement of Sahraoui's death, an explosion at the Hamma power station near Algiers injured 11 people. The Government declared the explosion to be accidental; however, the GSPC later claimed responsibility and warned that further attacks would ensue. In September 2004 Sahraoui was replaced as leader of the GSPC by Abu Musab Abd al-Wadud. Despite earlier reports regarding the fate of GIA leader Rachid Abou Tourab (see above), a message purporting to be from him was posted on an Islamist website in January 2005. Meanwhile, the Algerian authorities announced that the GIA had been virtually destroyed following a military campaign during the latter part of 2004, in which they claimed to have killed one of the group's leaders and to have made several important arrests.

Throughout 2004 the relationship between the national press and the Algerian authorities worsened, particularly during the run-up to the presidential election. The majority of the principal daily newspapers were highly critical of Bouteflika's re-election campaign and his overwhelming victory. In mid-June the editor of the Algerian daily *Le Matin*, Muhammad Benchicou, was gaoled for two years, having been convicted of violating foreign exchange laws. In July the Government refused to print *Le Matin* until all unpaid bills had been settled, and the newspaper went out of circulation. The newspaper had been a particularly outspoken source of criticism of Bouteflika during his election campaign, and in February Benchicou had published a book openly attacking the President. The international press freedom group Reporters sans frontières condemned Benchicou's imprisonment as an attempt to curb the independent Algerian press. These restrictions were extended to the international media when, in June, the Government suspended the activities of the Arabic television channel Al-Jazeera in Algeria following the broadcast of a programme in which critics of the Bouteflika

administration denounced the President's national reconciliation policy and the actions of several Algerian generals.

In August 2004 a bill to improve women's rights was drawn up by the commission in charge of revising the family code, which had been established in October 2003. The new legislation was approved by the Government and sent for review by the Council of Ministers, despite fierce opposition from Islamist groups who considered that it went against the teachings of the Koran. The reform would make it illegal for a man to divorce his wife without stating clear grounds, and would allow a woman to receive financial support from her husband once they were divorced. Moreover, women would not have to ask permission from a male relative in order to marry.

During the late 1970s and early 1980s the protracted struggle in Western Sahara embittered Algeria's relations with France, which supported the claims of Morocco. Algeria also criticized French military intervention elsewhere in Africa, while further grievances were the trade imbalance in favour of the former colonial power, recurrent disputes over the price of Algerian exports of gas to France, and the French Government's determination to reduce the number of Algerians residing in France. The Algerian military take-over in January 1992 was welcomed by the French Government, and French economic and political support for the Algerian regime increased in early 1993, following the appointment of Edouard Balladur as Prime Minister of France. Alleged Islamist militants residing in France continued to be prosecuted, and in August 1994, following the killing of five French embassy employees in Algiers, 26 suspected Algerian extremists were interned in northern France; 20 of them were subsequently expelled to Burkina Faso. In September the French embassy in Algiers confirmed that entry visas would be issued to Algerians only in exceptional cases. By November the number of French nationals killed by Islamist militants in Algeria had reached 21 and the French Government urged its citizens to leave Algeria. An Air France aircraft was hijacked at Algiers airport in December by members of the GIA, resulting in the deaths of three passengers and, later, in the killing of the hijackers by French security forces when the aircraft landed in France. A series of arrests made in early 1995 by French police in an attempt to dismantle support networks for Islamist militants in Algeria and Tunisia did not prevent an intensification of the GIA campaign of violence in France. The GIA claimed responsibility for numerous bomb attacks across France between July and November, in which seven people were killed and more than 160 injured. In July 1996 Hervé de Charette, the French Minister of Foreign Affairs, made the first ministerial-level visit to Algeria for three years. However, the success of the visit was marred by the assassination, in August, of the French Roman Catholic Bishop of Oran only hours after meeting de Charette. In December four people were killed as a result of a bomb explosion on a passenger train in Paris, prompting speculation that the GIA had resumed its campaign of violence in France. The French authorities subsequently arrested numerous suspected Islamist activists. In early 1998 a French court sentenced 36 Islamist militants to terms of imprisonment of up to 10 years for providing logistical support for the bomb attacks in France in 1995. A further 138 people stood trial in France in September 1998, accused of criminal association with Algerian terrorists.

In June 1999 the French National Assembly voted unanimously to abandon the official claim that the eight-year struggle between Algerian nationalists and French troops, which began in November 1954, had been no more than 'an operation for keeping order' and thus admitted that France had indeed fought in the Algerian war of independence. An apparent improvement in relations between Algeria and France was further signalled by a meeting in September 1999 between Bouteflika and the French President, Jacques Chirac, in New York (the first meeting between the leaders of the two countries since 1992). In November the President of the French Senate met Bouteflika in Algiers, and in January 2000 Algeria's Minister of Foreign Affairs, Youcef Yousfi, made the first official visit to France by an Algerian government member for six years. In mid-June Bouteflika made a full state visit to France—the first of its kind by an Algerian Head of State—during which he addressed the French National Assembly and held talks with both Chirac and the French Prime Minister, Lionel Jospin. Although the visit produced few tangible results, it was regarded as a success and an important step towards ending the diplomatic isolation imposed on Algeria following the military take-over in 1992.

Algeria's relations with France were placed under strain from late 2000 by a series of much-publicized revelations, mainly regarding occurrences during the war of independence. In November of that year Gen. Jacques Massu, who had commanded French troops during the Battle of Algiers in 1957, asserted in an interview with the French daily *Le Monde* that France should admit and condemn the use of torture by its forces during the conflict. In February 2001 the French Ministers of the Interior and of Defence held talks with their Algerian counterparts in Algiers. The meetings were, however, overshadowed by the recent publication of allegations of Algerian army involvement in the torture and massacre of civilians since 1992 (see above). In his book *Services spéciaux Algérie 1955–57: Mon témoignage sur la torture*, published in May, a retired French general, Paul Aussaresses, admitted that he had, with the full knowledge and support of the French Government, personally tortured and killed 24 Algerian prisoners during the war of independence. In January 2002 Aussaresses, who had been deprived of his military rank, was convicted of 'apologizing for war crimes' and fined €7,500. Meanwhile, in August 2001 eight 'harkis'—Algerian Muslims who had served in the French army prior to independence—filed a formal complaint against the French Government for crimes and complicity in crimes against humanity. As many as 130,000 harkis were estimated to have been murdered by FLN troops following France's withdrawal from Algeria in 1962. In September 2001 President Chirac unveiled a plaque in Paris to commemorate those who were killed, and acknowledged his country's failure to halt the reprisals against the harkis. In November 2003 it was announced that Pierre Messmer, the French Minister of the Armed Forces during the latter stages of the war of independence, would face charges of committing 'crimes against humanity' for his role in the decision not to allow the harkis to settle in France.

Relations between the two countries improved markedly during 2002, and in late July Algeria's Minister of State for Foreign Affairs visited Paris for talks with his French counterpart. Prime Minister Benflis visited Paris in January 2003 and in early March Jacques Chirac became the first French President to make a full state visit to Algeria since the former colony's independence in 1962; Bouteflika and Chirac signed the 'Declaration of Algiers', whereby both countries pledged to rebuild bilateral relations by holding annual meetings of their heads of state as well as twice-yearly talks between the two countries' ministers responsible for foreign affairs. The agreement was intended to initiate an 'exceptional partnership' between the two countries. In June 2003 Air France resumed flights to Algeria, which had been suspended since the hijacking of one of its aircraft in December 1994 (see above). President Chirac's official visit was repaid in August 2004 when Bouteflika held talks with the French President in France to mark the 60th anniversary of the Algerian landings in Provence, which opened up a new front against the Nazi German occupiers.

During the 1980s Algeria attempted to achieve a closer relationship with the other countries of the Maghreb region (Libya, Mauritania, Morocco and Tunisia). The Maghreb Fraternity and Co-operation Treaty, signed by Algeria and Tunisia in March 1983 and by Mauritania in December of that year, established a basis for the creation of the long-discussed 'Great Arab Maghreb'. Relations with Morocco, however, continued to be affected by the dispute over Western Sahara. In May 1988 Algeria and Morocco restored diplomatic relations (severed in 1976) at ambassadorial level. Meeting in Algiers in June, the five Heads of State of the Maghreb countries announced the formation of a Maghreb commission to examine areas of regional integration. In February 1989 the leaders signed a treaty establishing the Union du Maghreb arabe (UMA, see p. 376), with the aim of encouraging economic co-operation and eventually establishing a full customs union. The Algerian army's intervention in January 1992 to prevent victory by the FIS in the general election provoked relief, among the Maghreb countries, in Tunisia and Morocco that the establishment of a neighbouring fundamentalist state had been pre-empted.

Morocco imposed entry visas on Algerian nationals in August 1994, following the murder of two Spanish tourists in Morocco, allegedly by Algerian Islamist extremists. Algeria reciprocated by closing the border between the two countries and imposing entry visas on Moroccan nationals. Tensions eased slightly in September when Algeria announced the appointment of a new ambassador to Morocco, and in early 1995 negotiations commenced on the development of bilateral co-operation. However,

in December King Hassan of Morocco expressed his disapproval at Algeria's alleged continuing support for the independence of Western Sahara, and demanded that UMA activities be suspended. A UMA summit meeting, scheduled for later that month, was subsequently postponed. Indications of an improvement in relations were apparently enhanced in August 1998, when the Algerian and Moroccan Prime Ministers held talks. Following his accession to the presidency in April 1999, Bouteflika initially attempted further to improve bilateral relations during a visit to the Moroccan capital to attend the funeral of the Moroccan King, Hassan II. However, the *rapprochement* was halted in August, on the day when the imminent reopening of the common border was announced, by the massacre by the GIA of 29 civilians in the border region of Bechar. Bouteflika's public allegation that Morocco was providing sanctuary for the perpetrators of the attack extended to accusations of drugs-trafficking and arms-dealing on the Algerian border. In September Bouteflika accused both Morocco and Tunisia of acting against the interests of the UMA by negotiating separate agreements with the European Union (EU, see p. 217).

In February 2000 Algeria and Morocco both expressed their desire to improve bilateral relations, and in April Bouteflika met with the new Moroccan ruler, King Muhammad VI, at the Africa-EU summit held in Cairo, Egypt. The two leaders agreed to establish joint committees in an attempt to reduce the number of violent incidents on their mutual border, and joint military security operations began in May. In mid-March 2001 a meeting in Algiers of the UMA's council of ministers responsible for foreign affairs ended acrimoniously following disagreements between Moroccan and Algerian delegations. Relations between the two countries were further strained after Algeria announced its opposition to UN proposals for a settlement to the Western Sahara issue, as Algeria believed that the plans unduly favoured Morocco and would inevitably lead to the formal integration of the disputed territory into Morocco. (For further details, see the chapter on Morocco.) A UMA summit meeting scheduled to be held in Algiers in late December 2003 was postponed just days before it was due to take place following Morocco's announcement that King Muhammad's place at the summit was to be taken by its Minister of Foreign Affairs and amid reports that representatives from Libya and Mauritania would also not attend. In July 2004 talks between the Moroccan Minister of the Interior, Al Mustapha Sahel, and the Algerian Minister of State for the Interior and Local Authorities, Noureddine Yazid Zerhouni, recommenced in Algeria. The discussions, which were centred on the future of Western Sahara, were also attended by senior representatives of both France and Spain. However, Morocco remained opposed to the UN proposals, stating that they would place its sovereignty at risk. The ongoing differences between Morocco and Algeria led to the eventual breakdown of the talks, although in November King Muhammad reiterated his determination to resolve the continuing conflict over the territory.

In December 1996 the EU and Algeria began negotiations on Algeria's participation in a Euro-Mediterranean free-trade zone. In November 1999 an EU delegation visited Algiers, and negotiations on a trade partnership agreement resumed in April 2000. In January 2001 the President of the European Commission, Romano Prodi, visited Algeria, where he signed the financing protocols for a number of joint projects. In December negotiations for the EU-Algeria Euro-Mediterranean Association Agreement were concluded, and both parties formally signed the agreement in April 2002. It was ratified by the European Parliament in October of that year, and, following ratification by the requisite EU member states, was scheduled to enter effect on 1 July 2005.

The Algerian Government was swift to condemn the suicide attacks on New York and Washington, DC, on 11 September 2001, for which the USA held the al-Qa'ida (Base) organization of Osama bin Laden responsible, and to offer assistance for the USA's proposed 'coalition against terror'. Later that month the Algerian authorities handed the US authorities a list containing the profiles of some 350 Islamist militants it believed had links to bin Laden and al-Qa'ida. In November President Bouteflika visited Washington, where he met with President George W. Bush and reiterated his support for the US-led campaign. Algeria continued to assist the USA with anti-terrorist operations, and in September 2002 Algerian security forces killed a senior al-Qa'ida operative, who was alleged to be liaising with the GSPC, in a raid near Batna. In December the US Administration announced that it had for the first time agreed to sell weaponry and other military equipment to Algeria as part of the USA's policy of intensifying security co-operation with Algeria. In December 2003 the US Secretary of State, Colin Powell, visited Algeria for talks with President Bouteflika at which he praised Algeria's co-operation in the 'war on terror' and the strength of US-Algerian relations.

In March 2003 four Algerians were sentenced to terms of imprisonment ranging from 10 to 12 years by a court in Frankfurt, Germany, after being convicted of conspiracy to commit murder, conspiracy to plant a bomb and of weapons violations. The four men had been arrested in December 2000 in Strasbourg, France, where, it was alleged, they had intended to detonate a series of bombs. Meanwhile, in January 2003 five Algerians were arrested in London, United Kingdom, and charged with being 'concerned in the development or production of a chemical weapon' and with having materials 'connected with the commission, preparation or instigation of an act of terrorism'. A number of Algerians were also detained following a series of police raids across the United Kingdom later that month, and in April two Algerians were sentenced to 11 years' imprisonment for 'entering a funding arrangement for the purposes of terrorism'. In July another Algerian was gaoled for four years after being convicted of raising funds for al-Qa'ida.

During February and March 2003 32 European tourists, including 16 Germans and 10 Austrians, disappeared in the Algerian Sahara. The Algerian authorities refused to confirm allegations that the tourists had been kidnapped by a terrorist group with close links to the GSPC, although some reports maintained that they had been taken as hostages to be exchanged for Islamist militants imprisoned in Europe. In late April a senior Algerian army official stated that all 32 were alive but that they were being held by members of the GSPC outside the town of Illizi, close to the Libyan border. In early May government sources confirmed that talks were ongoing with the captors, and in late May 17 of the hostages were forcibly freed when Algerian special forces stormed the Islamists' hideout, reportedly killing at least nine of the kidnappers. In July it was claimed that the remaining 15 hostages had been moved to Mali; however, later that month one of the German hostages died from heatstroke. In mid-August a Malian presidential spokesman announced that all 14 hostages had been released from captivity and that a 'major and positive role' in their release had been played by Libya's Qaddafi International Association for Charitable Organizations, which had apparently paid €5m. to the kidnappers. Libyan diplomats, however, denied that any ransom had been paid and there were also unconfirmed reports that Germany had paid the hostage-takers between €4m. and €15m. to secure the release of the prisoners. Meanwhile, the German Chancellor, Gerhard Schröder, stated that German security forces would join Malian and Algerian troops in their search for the hostage-takers.

Government

Under the 1976 Constitution (with modifications adopted by the National People's Assembly in June 1979 and with further amendments approved by popular referendum in November 1988, February 1989 and November 1996), Algeria is a multi-party state, with parties subject to approval by the Ministry of the Interior and Local Authorities. The Head of State is the President of the Republic, who is elected by universal adult suffrage for a five-year term, renewable once. The President presides over a Council of Ministers and a High Security Council. The President must appoint a Prime Minister as Head of Government, who appoints a Council of Ministers. The bicameral legislature consists of the 389-member National People's Assembly and the 144-member Council of the Nation. The members of the National People's Assembly are elected by universal, direct, secret suffrage for a five-year term. Two-thirds of the members of the Council of the Nation are elected by indirect, secret suffrage from regional and municipal authorities; the remainder are appointed by the President of the Republic. The Council's term in office is six years; one-half of its members are replaced every three years. Both the Head of Government and the parliamentary chambers may initiate legislation. Legislation must be deliberated upon respectively by the National People's Assembly and the Council of the Nation before promulgation. The country is divided into 48 departments (*wilayat*), which are, in turn, sub-divided into communes. Each *wilaya* and commune has an elected assembly.

Defence

In August 2004 the estimated strength of the armed forces was 127,500 (including some 75,000 conscripts), comprising an army of 110,000, a navy of about 7,500 and an air force of 10,000. The defence budget for 2004 was estimated at AD 201,000m. Military service is compulsory for 18 months. There are paramilitary forces of about 181,200, controlled by the Ministry of Defence and the Directorate of National Security, and an estimated 100,000 self-defence militia and communal guards.

Economic Affairs

In 2003, according to estimates by the World Bank, Algeria's gross national income (GNI), measured at average 2001–03 prices, was US $62,790m., equivalent to $1,890 per head (or $5,940 on an international purchasing-power parity basis). During 1990–2003, it was estimated, the population increased at an average annual rate of 1.9%, while gross domestic product (GDP) per head increased, in real terms, by an average of 0.5% per year. Overall GDP increased, in real terms, at an average annual rate of 2.3% in 1990–2003; it grew by 4.1% in 2002 and by 6.8% in 2003.

Agriculture (including forestry and fishing) contributed 11.1% of GDP in 2003, and employed an estimated 23.6% of the labour force in that year. Domestic production of food crops is insufficient to meet the country's requirements. The principal crops are wheat, barley, potatoes and tomatoes. Dates are Algeria's principal non-hydrocarbon export; olives, citrus fruits and grapes are also grown, and wine has been an important export since the French colonial era. During 1990–2003 agricultural GDP increased at an average annual rate of 4.5%. Agricultural GDP declined by 1.3% in 2002, but increased by 12.0% in 2003.

Industry (including mining, manufacturing, construction and power) contributed 64.6% of GDP in 2003, and engaged 24.3% of the employed population in 2001. During 1990–2003 industrial GDP increased at an average annual rate of 2.0%. Industrial GDP increased by 4.7% in 2002 and by 6.0% in 2003.

The mining sector provides almost all of Algeria's export earnings, although it engaged only 1.6% of the employed population in 1987. Petroleum and natural gas, which together contributed 35.1% of GDP in 2002, are overwhelmingly Algeria's principal exports, providing 96.8% of total export earnings in 2002. Algeria's proven reserves of petroleum were 11,300m. barrels at the end of 2003, sufficient to maintain output at that year's levels—which averaged 1.86m. barrels per day (b/d)—for almost 17 years. With effect from March 2005 Algeria's production quota within the Organization of the Petroleum Exporting Countries (OPEC, see p. 331) was 878,000 b/d. Proven reserves of natural gas at the end of 2003 totalled 4,520,000m. cu m, sustainable at that year's production level (totalling 82,800m. cu m) for more than 54 years. Algeria currently transports natural gas through two pipelines—one to Spain and Portugal via Morocco, and the other to Italy and Slovenia via Tunisia. Substantial reserves of iron ore, phosphates, barite (barytes), lead, zinc, mercury, salt, marble and industrial minerals are also mined, and the exploitation of gold reserves commenced in 2001. The GDP of the hydrocarbons sector increased by 6.1% in 1999 and by an estimated 4.9% in 2000, while that of other mining activities declined by 3.0% in 1999 but expanded by some 6.5% in 2000.

Manufacturing engaged 12.2% of the employed population in 1987, and provided 8.3% of GDP in 2003. Measured by gross value of output, the principal branches of manufacturing in 1996 were food products, beverages and tobacco (which accounted for 52.3% of the total), metals, metal products, machinery and transport and scientific equipment (14.7%), non-metallic mineral products (10.2%), chemical, petroleum, coal, rubber and plastic products (8.6%), wood, paper and products (6.4%) and textiles and clothing (5.9%). During 1990–2003 the GDP of the manufacturing sector declined at an average annual rate of 1.4%. However, manufacturing GDP increased by 5.3% in 2002 and by 3.3% in 2003.

Energy is derived principally from natural gas (which contributed 96.8% of total electricity output in 2001). Algeria is a net exporter of fuels, with imports of energy products comprising only an estimated 1.1% of the value of merchandise imports in 2002.

Services engaged 54.7% of the employed labour force in 2001, and provided 24.4% of GDP in 2003. During 1990–2003 the combined GDP of the service sectors increased at an average annual rate of 2.7%. Services GDP increased by 4.5% in 2002 and by 8.3% in 2003.

In 2002 Algeria recorded a visible trade surplus of US $6,700m., while there was a surplus of US $4,360m. on the current account of the balance of payments. France was the principal source of imports in 2000 (providing 23.6% of the total); other important suppliers were the USA, Italy and Germany. Italy was the principal market for exports (20.1%) in that year; other major purchasers were the USA, France, Spain, the Netherlands, Brazil and Turkey. The principal exports in 2000 were, overwhelmingly, mineral fuels, lubricants, etc.; other exports included vegetables, tobacco, hides and dates. The principal imports in that year were machinery and transport equipment, food and live animals, and basic manufactures.

In 2001 Algeria recorded an overall budget surplus of AD 131,000m., equivalent to 3.1% of GDP. Algeria's total external debt at the end of 2002 amounted to US $22,800m., of which $21,255m. was long-term public debt. In 2001 the cost of debt-servicing was equivalent to 19.5% of the value of exports of goods and services. The annual rate of inflation averaged 14.2% in 1990–2002. Consumer prices increased by an average of 2.2% in 2002 and by 3.5% in 2003. According to official estimates, some 23.7% of the labour force were unemployed in September 2003.

Algeria is a member of the Union of the Arab Maghreb (UMA, see p. 376), which aims to promote economic integration of member states, and also of OPEC. A Euro-Mediterranean Association Agreement between Algeria and the European Union, signed in April 2002, was scheduled to enter effect on 1 July 2005.

Despite the persistent high levels of unemployment and poverty in the country, Algeria's economy showed continuing signs of improvement during 2004. Foreign debt had been reduced to one-third of the level witnessed 10 years previously, and in June foreign-exchange reserves stood at US $36,000m. Algeria remained a leading exporter of liquified natural gas, exporting 60,000m. cu m per year, chiefly to Europe. The Algerian Government had, in 2002, announced its intention further to develop natural gas production facilities and to more than double the export levels of that commodity to 85,000m. cu m per year by 2010, while plans to increase Algeria's oil production capacity from some 1.3m. b/d at the end of 2003—already substantially in excess of agreed OPEC quotas—to 1.5m b/d by 2005 were apparently on target. Algeria benefited greatly in 2004 from very high international oil prices, but many analysts commented that in order to maintain its high level of GDP growth (6.8% in 2003), the country would need to introduce further privatization of state-controlled companies to attract foreign investment. Nevertheless, progress was evident in the banking, energy, transport and telecommunications sectors; the latter, in particular, benefited from the acquisition of the third Global Standard for Mobiles (GSM) licence by Kuwait's National Mobile Telecommunications Co at a cost of $421m. In April 2004 Siemens (Germany) and Ericsson (Sweden) were awarded the contracts to complete the first phase of Algeria's GSM network. Although the country reportedly experienced a decrease in its trade surplus from some $10,800m. in 2003 to $5,600m. in 2004, Algeria's macroeconomic position remained strong. The budget deficit

was expected to widen further in 2005, owing to an anticipated levelling of world oil prices, but this was not expected to be significantly detrimental to the economy. Towards the end of 2004 President Bouteflika pledged to invest $50,000m. in rebuilding the country's impoverished infrastructure, and consequently to reduce unemployment and improve the population's standard of living. In December the Minister of Finance, Abdellatif Benachenhou, announced plans to privatize certain industrial sectors, including the state-run cement works and Algérie Télécom.

Education

Education, in the national language (Arabic), is officially compulsory for nine years between six and 15 years of age. Primary education begins at the age of six and lasts for six years. Secondary education begins at 12 years of age and lasts for up to six years (comprising two cycles of three years each). In 1996 the total enrolment at primary and secondary schools was equivalent to 86% of the school-age population (90% of boys; 82% of girls). Enrolment at primary schools in that year included 94% of children in the relevant age-group (97% of boys; 91% of girls), while enrolment at secondary schools included 56% of children in the relevant age-group (58% of boys; 54% of girls). In mid-2003 the Government agreed to permit the use of the Berber language, Tamazight, as a language of instruction in Algerian schools. Some 12.5% of total planned expenditure in the 1997 administrative budget was allocated to education and training. Priority is being given to teacher-training, to the development of technical and scientific teaching programmes, and to adult literacy and training schemes. In addition to the 10 universities, there are seven other *centres universitaires* and a number of technical colleges. In 1995/96 a total of 347,410 students were enrolled in higher education.

Public Holidays

2005: 1 January (New Year), 21 January* (Id al-Adha, Feast of the Sacrifice), 10 February* (Islamic New Year), 19 February* (Ashoura), 21 April* (Mouloud, Birth of Muhammad), 1 May (Labour Day), 19 June (Ben Bella's Overthrow), 5 July (Independence Day), 2 September* (Leilat al-Meiraj, Ascension of Muhammad), 5 October* (Ramadan begins), 1 November (Anniversary of the Revolution), 4 November* (Id al-Fitr, end of Ramadan).

2006: 1 January (New Year), 11 January* (Id al-Adha, Feast of the Sacrifice), 31 January* (Islamic New Year), 9 February* (Ashoura), 11 April* (Mouloud, Birth of Muhammad), 1 May (Labour Day), 19 June (Ben Bella's Overthrow), 5 July (Independence Day), 22 August* (Leilat al-Meiraj, Ascension of Muhammad), 24 September* (Ramadan begins), 24 October* (Id al-Fitr, end of Ramadan), 1 November (Anniversary of the Revolution).

*These holidays are dependent on the Islamic lunar calendar and may differ by one or two days from the dates given.

Weights and Measures

The metric system is in force.

Statistical Survey

Source (unless otherwise stated): Office National des Statistiques, 8 rue des Moussebilines, BP 202, Algiers; tel. (21) 63-99-74; fax (21) 63-79-55; e-mail ons@ons.dz; internet www.ons.dz.

Area and Population

AREA, POPULATION AND DENSITY

Area (sq km)	2,381,741*
Population (census results)†	
20 April 1987	23,038,942
25 June 1998	
Males	14,698,589
Females	14,402,278
Total‡	29,100,867
Population (official estimates at mid-year)	
2001	30,836,000
2002	31,357,000
2003	31,848,000
Density (per sq km) at mid-2003	13.4

* 919,595 sq miles.
† Excluding Algerian nationals residing abroad, numbering an estimated 828,000 at 1 January 1978.
‡ Excluding 171,476 Sahrawi refugees in camps.

POPULATION BY WILAYA (ADMINISTRATIVE DISTRICT)
(1998 census)

	Area (sq km)	Population	Density (per sq km)
Adrar	439,700	311,615	0.7
Aïn Defla	4,897	660,342	134.9
Aïn Témouchent	2,379	327,331	137.6
Algiers (el-Djezaïr)	273	2,562,428	9,386.2
Annaba	1,439	557,818	387.6
Batna	12,192	962,623	79.0
el-Bayadh	78,870	168,789	2.1
Béchar	162,200	225,546	1.4
Béjaïa	3,268	856,840	262.2
Biskra (Beskra)	20,986	575,858	27.4
Blida (el-Boulaïda)	1,696	784,283	462.4
Borj Bou Arreridj	4,115	555,402	135.0
Bouira	4,439	629,560	141.8
Boumerdes	1,591	647,389	406.9
Chlef (ech-Cheliff)	4,795	858,695	179.1
Constantine (Qacentina)	2,187	810,914	370.8
Djelfa	66,415	797,706	12.0
Ghardaïa	86,105	300,516	3.5
Guelma	4,101	430,000	104.9
Illizi	285,000	34,108	0.1
Jijel	2,577	573,208	222.4
Khenchela	9,811	327,917	33.4
Laghouat	25,057	317,125	12.7
Mascara (Mouaskar)	5,941	676,192	113.8
Médéa (Lemdiyya)	8,866	802,078	90.5
Mila	9,375	674,480	71.9
Mostaganem	2,175	631,057	290.1
M'Sila	18,718	805,519	43.0
Naâma	29,950	127,314	4.3
Oran (Ouahran)	2,121	1,213,839	572.3
Ouargla	211,980	445,619	2.1
el-Oued	54,573	504,401	9.2
Oum el-Bouaghi	6,768	519,170	76.7
Relizane (Ghilizane)	4,870	642,205	131.9
Saïda	6,764	279,526	41.3
Sétif	6,504	1,311,413	201.6
Sidi-bel-Abbès	9,096	525,632	57.8
Skikda	4,026	786,154	195.3
Souk Ahras	4,541	367,455	80.9

— continued	Area (sq km)	Population	Density (per sq km)
Tamanrasset (Tamanghest)	556,200	137,175	0.3
el-Tarf	3,339	352,588	105.6
Tébessa	14,227	549,066	38.6
Tiaret	20,673	725,853	35.1
Tindouf	159,000	27,060	0.2
Tipaza	2,166	506,053	233.6
Tissemsilt	3,152	264,240	83.8
Tizi Ouzou	3,568	1,108,708	310.7
Tlemcen	9,061	842,053	92.9
Total	2,381,741	29,100,867	12.2

PRINCIPAL TOWNS
(population at 1998 census)

Algiers (el-Djezaïr, capital)	1,519,570	Tébessa (Tbessa)	153,246
Oran (Ouahran)	655,852	Blida (el-Boulaïda)	153,083
Constantine (Qacentina)	462,187	Skikda	152,335
Batna	242,514	Béjaïa	147,076
Annaba	215,083	Tiaret (Tihert)	145,332
Sétif (Stif)	211,859	Chlef	133,874
Sidi-bel-Abbès	180,260	el-Buni	133,471
Biskra (Beskra)	170,956	Béchar	131,010
Djelfa	154,265		

Mid-2003 (UN estimate, incl. suburbs): Algiers 3,059,643 (Source: UN, *World Urbanization Prospects: The 2003 Revision*).

BIRTHS, MARRIAGES AND DEATHS*

	Registered live births†		Registered marriages		Registered deaths†	
	Number	Rate (per 1,000)	Number	Rate (per 1,000)	Number	Rate (per 1,000)
1995	711,000	25.3	152,786	5.5	180,000	6.4
1996	654,000	22.9	156,870	5.5	172,000	6.0
1997	654,000	22.5	157,831	5.4	178,000	6.1
1998	607,000	20.6	158,298	5.4	144,000	4.9
1999	594,000	19.8	163,126	5.5	141,000	4.7
2000	589,000	19.4	177,548	5.8	140,000	4.6
2001	619,000	20.0	194,273	6.3	141,000	4.5
2002	617,000	19.7	218,620	7.0	138,000	4.4

* Figures refer to the Algerian population only, and include adjustment for underenumeration.
† Excluding live-born infants dying before registration of birth.

Expectation of life (WHO estimates, years at birth): 69.4 (males 67.5; females 71.2) in 2002 (Source: WHO, *World Health Report*).

ECONOMICALLY ACTIVE POPULATION
(1987 census)*

	Males	Females	Total
Agriculture, hunting, forestry and fishing	714,947	9,753	724,699
Mining and quarrying	64,685	3,142	67,825
Manufacturing	471,471	40,632	512,105
Electricity, gas and water . . .	40,196	1,579	41,775
Construction	677,211	12,372	689,586
Trade, restaurants and hotels . .	376,590	14,399	390,990
Transport, storage and communications	207,314	9,029	216,343
Financing, insurance, real estate and business services . . .	125,426	17,751	143,178
Community, social and personal services	945,560	234,803	1,180,364
Activities not adequately defined .	149,241	83,718	232,959
Total employed	**3,772,641**	**427,183**	**4,199,824**
Unemployed	1,076,018	65,260	1,141,278
Total labour force	**4,848,659**	**492,443**	**5,341,102**

* Employment data relate to persons aged 6 years and over; those for unemployment relate to persons aged 16 to 64 years. Estimates have been made independently, so the totals may not be the sum of the component parts.

2000 (sample survey, '000 persons aged 15 years and over, July–September): Agriculture, hunting, forestry and fishing 898.0; Mining and quarrying, manufacturing, electricity, gas and water 720.9; Construction 669.8; Trade, restaurants and hotels 731.4; Government services 1,773.2; Other services 932.6; Total employed 5,725.9 (males 5,028.2, females 697.7); Unemployed 2,427.7 (males 2,132.7, females 295.0); Total labour force 8,153.6 (males 7,160.9, females 992.7).

2001 (sample survey, '000 persons aged 15 years and over, July–September): Agriculture, hunting, forestry and fishing 1,312.1; Mining and quarrying, manufacturing, electricity, gas and water 861.1; Construction 650.0; Services 3,405.6; Total employed 6,228.8; Unemployed 2,339.4 (males 1,934.9, females 404.5); Total labour force 8,568.2 (Source: ILO).

2003 (sample survey, '000 persons aged 15 years and over, July–September): Total employed 6,684.1 (males 5,751.0, females 933.0); Unemployed 2,078.3 (males 1,759.9, females 318.3); Total labour force 8,762.3 (males 7,510.9, females 1,251.3).

Health and Welfare

KEY INDICATORS

Total fertility rate (children per woman, 2002)	2.8
Under-5 mortality rate (per 1,000 live births, 2003) . . .	41
HIV/AIDS (% of persons aged 15–49, 2003)	0.10
Physicians (per 1,000 head, 1998)	1
Hospital beds (per 1,000 head, 1998)	2.1
Health expenditure (2001): US $ per head (PPP)	169
Health expenditure (2001): % of GDP	4.1
Health expenditure (2001): public (% of total)	75.0
Access to water (% of persons, 2002)	87
Access to sanitation (% of persons, 2002)	92
Human Development Index (2002): ranking	108
Human Development Index (2002): value	0.704

For sources and definitions, see explanatory note on p. vi.

Agriculture

PRINCIPAL CROPS
('000 metric tons)

	2001	2002	2003
Wheat	2,039	1,502	2,970*
Barley	575	416	1,220*
Oats	44	33	35†
Potatoes	967	1,333	1,300†
Broad beans, dry	21	23	20†
Chick-peas	12	15	15†
Almonds	25	32	32†
Olives	200	300†	300†
Rapeseed	29*	27*	27†
Cabbages	24	25	25†
Artichokes	35	34	35†
Tomatoes	831	815	820†
Cauliflowers	40	48	45†
Pumpkins, squash and gourds . .	88	101	100†
Cucumbers and gherkins . . .	59	68	68†
Aubergines (Eggplants)	32	43	42†
Chillies and green peppers . . .	160	168	165†
Dry onions	428	448	450†
Garlic	33	36	36†
Green beans	30	30†	30†
Green peas	63	66	65†
Green broad beans	125	135	135†
Carrots	156	159	158†
Other vegetables	288	290	290†
Oranges	327	362	360†
Tangerines, mandarins, clementines and satsumas . .	110	117	115†
Lemons and limes	32	39	38†
Apples	105	121	120†
Pears	92	110	110†
Apricots	68	74	70†
Peaches and nectarines	58	66	65†
Plums	25	30	30†
Grapes	196	234	230†
Watermelons	464	465†	465†
Figs	41	61	60†
Dates	437	418	420†
Other fruits	51	71	68†
Pimento and allspice†	8	8	8
Tobacco (leaves)	8	6	6†

* Unofficial figure.
† FAO estimate(s).

Source: FAO.

LIVESTOCK
('000 head, year ending September)

	2001	2002	2003
Sheep	17,299	17,300	17,300
Goats	3,129	3,200	3,200
Cattle	1,613	1,572	1,540
Horses	43	44	44
Mules	43	43	43
Asses	170	170	170
Camels	245	245	245
Chickens (million)	110	120	125

* FAO estimate.

Source: FAO.

LIVESTOCK PRODUCTS
('000 metric tons)

	2001	2002*	2003
Beef and veal	105	116	121
Mutton and lamb*	165	165	165
Goat meat*	12	12	12
Poultry meat*	231	244	244
Rabbit meat*	7	7	7
Other meat*	4	4	4
Cows' milk*	1,310	1,135	1,160
Sheep's milk*	200	200	200
Goats' milk*	155	155	155
Poultry eggs	108	110	110*
Honey	2	2	2*
Wool: greasy	18	19	19*
Wool: scoured*	12	12	12
Cattle hides*	12	12	12
Sheepskins*	24	24	24
Goatskins*	2	2	2

* FAO estimate(s).

Source: FAO.

Forestry

ROUNDWOOD REMOVALS
(FAO estimates, '000 cubic metres, excl. bark)

	2001	2002	2003
Sawlogs, veneer logs and logs for			
sleepers	13	13	13
Pulpwood	26	26	26
Other industrial wood . . .	182	182	182
Fuel wood	7,188	7,305	7,424
Total	7,409	7,526	7,645

Sawnwood production (FAO estimates, '000 cubic metres, incl. railway sleepers): 13 per year in 1975–2003.

Source: FAO.

Fishing

('000 metric tons, live weight)

	2000	2001	2002
Capture	113.2	133.6	134.3
Bogue	4.1	4.1	4.7
Jack and horse mackerels . .	7.7	8.2	7.1
Sardinellas	20.4	33.7	24.5
European pilchard (sardine) . .	47.7	59.0	72.5
European anchovy . . .	5.7	6.1	2.2
Crustaceans and molluscs . .	4.2	3.2	3.0
Aquaculture*	0.4	0.5	0.5
Total catch*	113.5	134.1	134.8

* FAO estimates.

Source: FAO.

Mining

('000 metric tons, unless otherwise indicated)

	2000	2001	2002*
Crude petroleum ('000 barrels) .	476,288	464,600	499,890
Natural gas (million cu m)† . .	139,499	140,740	139,998
Iron ore (gross weight) . . .	1,645	1,291	1,202
Lead concentrates (metric tons)‡ .	818	891	1,105
Zinc concentrates (metric tons)‡	10,452	10,693	8,576
Mercury (metric tons)‡	216	320	307
Phosphate rock§	877	939	740
Barite (Barytes)	52	43	52
Salt (unrefined)	182	195	233
Gypsum (crude)	1,341	281	322

* Provisional or estimated data.

† Figures refer to gross volume. Production on a dry basis (in million cu m) was: 100,092 in 2000; 102,332 in 2001; 101,557 in 2002.

‡ Figures refer to the metal content of ores or concentrates.

§ Figures refer to gross weight. The estimated phosphoric acid content (in '000 metric tons) was 265 in 2000; 280 in 2001; 230 in 2002.

Source: US Geological Survey.

Industry

SELECTED PRODUCTS
('000 metric tons, unless otherwise indicated)

	1999	2000	2001
Olive oil (crude)*	57	30	46†
Refined sugar	48	51	49
Wine*	42	42	42†
Beer ('000 hectolitres) . . .	383	453	435
Soft drinks ('000 hectolitres) . .	315	200	229
Footwear—excl. rubber ('000 pairs)	1,529	1,222	1,214
Nitrogenous fertilizers (a)‡ . . .	54	78	n.a.
Phosphate fertilizers (b)‡ . . .	201	212	254
Naphthas†	3,686	3,908	n.a.
Motor spirit (petrol)	2,472	2,106	n.a.
Kerosene†	300	280	n.a.
Jet fuel†	1,315	1,571	n.a.
Gas-diesel (distillate fuel) oils . .	6,452	6,008	n.a.
Residual fuel oils	5,683	5,526	n.a.
Lubricating oils	111	110	n.a.
Petroleum bitumen (asphalt) . .	186	250	n.a.
Liquefied petroleum gas:			
from natural gas plants . .	8,768	8,768	n.a.
from petroleum refineries . .	580	545	n.a.
Cement	7,685	8,406	8,710
Pig-iron for steel-making§ . . .	1,100	1,250	1,250
Crude steel (ingots)§	758	842†	850†
Zinc—unwrought	24.9	19.3	16.5
Refrigerators for household use			
('000)	181	117	64
Telephones (million)	151	172	57
Television receivers ('000) . . .	173	194	245
Buses and coaches—assembled			
(number)	529	255	199
Lorries—assembled (number) . .	1,583	1,719	2,811
Electric energy (million kWh) . .	24,654	24,654	n.a.

* Data from FAO.

† Provisional or estimated figure(s).

‡ Production in terms of (a) nitrogen or (b) phosphoric acid.

§ Data from the US Geological Survey.

Source: mainly UN, *Industrial Commodity Statistics Yearbook*.

2002 ('000 metric tons): Olive oil (estimate) 46; Wine (estimate) 42; Pig–iron for steel making 1,250; Crude steel (ingots) 1,090 (Sources: FAO; US Geological Survey).

Finance

CURRENCY AND EXCHANGE RATES

Monetary Units
100 centimes = 1 Algerian dinar (AD).

Sterling, Dollar and Euro Equivalents (31 December 2004)
£1 sterling = 140.25 dinars;
US $1 = 72.61 dinars;
€1 = 98.91 dinars;
1,000 Algerian dinars = £7.13 = $13.77 = €10.11

Average Exchange Rate (dinars per US $)
2002   79.682
2003   77.395
2004   72.061

BUDGET
('000 million AD)*

Revenue†	2000	2001	2002
Hydrocarbon revenue	1,213.2	1,001.4	1,007.9
SONATRACH dividends . .	40.0	45.0	65.0
Other revenue	364.9	462.0	595.1
Tax revenue	349.5	398.2	482.9
Taxes on income and profits .	82.0	98.5	112.2
Wage income taxes . . .	34.9	45.5	52.7
Taxes on goods and services .	165.0	179.2	233.4
Customs duties	86.3	103.7	128.4
Registration and stamps . .	16.2	16.8	18.9
Non-tax revenue	15.4	63.8	112.2
Total	**1,578.1**	**1,463.4**	**1,603.0**

Expenditure‡	2000	2001	2002
Current expenditure . . .	856.2	963.6	1,097.6
Personnel expenditure . . .	289.6	324.0	346.2
War veterans' pensions . .	57.7	54.4	73.8
Material and supplies . . .	54.6	46.3	68.5
Public services	92.0	114.6	137.6
Hospitals	33.0	41.4	49.2
Current transfers	200.0	276.8	334.3
Family allowances . . .	29.0	25.9	38.1
Public works and social			
assistance	16.2	1.2	2.4
Food subsidies	0.5	0.2	0.5
Agricultural price support .	5.8	23.5	38.1
Housing	8.6	26.4	14.5
Interest payments . . .	162.3	147.5	137.2
Capital expenditure	321.9	357.4	452.9
Total	**1,178.1**	**1,321.0**	**1,550.5**

* Figures refer to operations of the central Government, excluding special accounts. The balance (revenue less expenditure) on such accounts (in '000 million AD) was: −0.7 in 2000; −20.0 in 2001; −11.2 in 2002.
† Excluding grants received ('000 million AD): 0.0 in 2000; 15.6 in 2001; 0.2 in 2002.
‡ Excluding net lending by the Treasury ('000 million AD): 0.5 in 2000; −6.5 in 2001; 30.9 in 2002.

Source: IMF, *Algeria: Selected Issues and Statistical Appendix* (February 2004).

2003 ('000 million AD): Total revenue 1,966.6 (Hydrocarbons 1,350.0); Total expenditure 1,752.7 (Source: Banque d'Algérie).

CENTRAL BANK RESERVES
(US $ million at 31 December)

	2001	2002	2003
Gold*	246	266	290
IMF special drawing rights . .	11	14	57
Reserve position in IMF . .	107	116	126
Foreign exchange	17,963	23,108	32,942
Total	**18,327**	**23,504**	**33,415**

* Valued at SDR 35 per troy ounce.

Source: IMF, *International Financial Statistics*.

MONEY SUPPLY
('000 million AD at 31 December)

	2000	2001	2003*
Currency outside banks . . .	484.95	577.34	781.34
Demand deposits at deposit money			
banks	460.26	551.88	719.59
Checking deposits at post office .	89.09	97.00	117.19
Private sector demand deposits at			
treasury	7.07	9.44	12.94
Total money (incl. others) . .	**1,044.02**	**1,237.38**	**1,634.50**

* Figures for 2002 are not available.

Source: IMF, *International Financial Statistics*.

COST OF LIVING
(Consumer Price Index; base: 2000 = 100)

	2001	2002	2003
Foodstuffs	104.4	106.2	111.0
Clothing	104.5	107.4	109.3
Rent (incl. fuel and light) . . .	101.8	102.0	104.8
All items (incl. others)	**103.5**	**105.8**	**109.5**

Source: ILO.

NATIONAL ACCOUNTS

National Income and Product
(million AD at current prices)

	1998	1999	2000
Compensation of employees . .	785,838.1	846,679.2	882,826.4
Operating surplus	1,289,716.7	1,544,284.9	2,085,199.8
Domestic factor incomes .	**2,075,554.8**	**2,390,964.1**	**2,968,026.2**
Consumption of fixed capital .	218,993.4	262,852.8	357,371.6
Gross domestic product			
(GDP) at factor cost . .	**2,294,548.2**	**2,653,816.9**	**3,325,397.8**
Indirect taxes, *less* subsidies .	515,576.2	561,308.2	753,277.5
GDP in purchasers' values	**2,810,124.4**	**3,215,125.1**	**4,078,675.3**
Factor income received from			
abroad	25,958.0	19,920.2	37,700.8
Less Factor income paid abroad	140,715.5	167,254.2	211,390.2
Gross national product . .	**2,695,366.9**	**3,067,791.1**	**3,904,985.9**
Less Consumption of fixed capital	218,993.4	262,852.8	357,371.6
National income in market			
prices . .	**2,476,373.5**	**2,804,938.3**	**3,547,614.3**
Other current transfers from			
abroad	97,071.0	101,473.8	106,247.8
Less Other current transfers paid			
abroad	3,152.6	3,423.8	29,201.3
National disposable income .	**2,570,291.9**	**2,902,988.3**	**3,624,660.8**

Expenditure on the Gross Domestic Product
('000 million AD at current prices)

	2001	2002	2003
Government final consumption			
expenditure	625	683	758
Private final consumption			
expenditure	1,848	1,972	2,109
Increase in stocks	184	253	308
Gross fixed capital formation . .	966	1,102	1,219
Total domestic expenditure .	**3,622**	**4,010**	**4,394**
Exports of goods and services . .	1,551	1,588	1,989
Less Imports of goods and services	931	1,142	1,259
GDP in purchasers' values . .	**4,242**	**4,455**	**5,124**

Gross Domestic Product by Economic Activity
('000 million AD at current prices)

	2000	2001	2002
Agriculture, forestry and fishing .	346	412	415
Hydrocarbons	1,616	1,444	1,461
Industry (excl. hydrocarbons) . .	335	314	408
Construction and public works .	832	957	1,034
Government services . . .	250	284	290
Non-government services . . .	424	472	520
Statistical discrepancy	45	75	37
Sub-total	3,849	3,958	4,165
Import taxes and duties . . .	250	284	290
GDP in purchasers' values . .	4,099	4,242	4,455

* Extraction and processing of petroleum and natural gas, including related services and public works.

Source: IMF, *Algeria: Selected Issues and Statistical Appendix* (February 2004).

BALANCE OF PAYMENTS
(US $ million)

	2000	2001	2002
Exports of goods f.o.b.	21,650	19,090	18,710
Imports of goods f.o.b.	−9,350	−9,480	−12,010
Trade balance	12,300	9,610	6,700
Exports of services	910	910	1,300
Imports of services	−2,360	−2,440	−2,480
Balance on goods and services	10,850	8,080	5,520
Other income received . . .	380	850	680
Other income paid	−2,880	−2,540	−2,910
Balance on goods, services and income	8,350	6,390	3,290
Transfers (net)	790	670	1,070
Current balance	9,140	7,060	4,360
Direct investment (net)	420	1,180	970
Official capital (net)	−1,960	−1,990	−1,320
Short-term capital and net errors and omissions	−30	−60	−360
Overall balance	7,570	6,190	3,650

Source: IMF, *Selected Issues and Statistical Appendix* (February 2004).

External Trade

Note: Data exclude military goods. Exports include stores and bunkers for foreign ships and aircraft.

PRINCIPAL COMMODITIES
(distribution by SITC, US $ million)

Imports c.i.f.	1998	1999	2000
Food and live animals . . .	2,438.3	2,222.1	2,363.7
Dairy products and birds' eggs .	481.8	437.9	429.6
Milk and cream	411.1	365.9	373.9
Cereals and cereal preparations .	1,025.9	908.4	1,090.7
Wheat and meslin (unmilled) .	691.2	660.8	803.9
Crude materials (inedible) except fuels	273.2	263.4	263.1
Animal and vegetable oils, fats and waxes	312.9	230.5	174.5
Chemicals and related products	1,051.0	1,073.7	1,042.9
Medicinal and pharmaceutical products	503.8	534.8	466.4
Medicaments (incl. veterinary) .	468.9	499.9	428.9
Basic manufactures . . .	1,681.8	1,666.6	1,598.1
Iron and steel	594.5	654.2	566.4
Tubes, pipes and fittings . . .	191.5	301.7	169.1
Machinery and transport equipment	3,040.2	3,034.9	3,144.9
Power-generating machinery and equipment	296.4	255.2	266.2
Machinery specialized for particular industries . . .	325.2	342.1	418.4

Imports c.i.f.— *continued*	1998	1999	2000
General industrial machinery, equipment and parts	800.7	859.6	729.7
Electrical machinery, apparatus, etc.	748.7	705.5	402.3
Telecommunications, sound recording and reproducing equipment	192.1	217.5	298.1
Road vehicles and parts* . . .	648.8	666.1	604.6
Other transport equipment . .	59.3	32.3	275.3
Miscellaneous manufactured articles	422.7	459.6	397.5
Total (incl. others)	9,403.4	9,161.9	9,152.1

* Excluding tyres, engines and electrical parts.

Exports f.o.b.	1998	1999	2000
Mineral fuels, lubricants, etc. .	9,544.0	12,167.2	21,609.8
Petroleum, petroleum products, etc.	5,502.1	6,940.0	12,591.0
Crude petroleum oils, etc. . .	4,084.2	4,975.1	9,254.4
Refined petroleum products . .	1,340.4	1,882.6	3,146.1
Gas oils (distillate fuels) . .	378.6	515.6	727.8
Residual fuel oils	390.9	596.3	1,120.3
Gas (natural and manufactured) .	4,041.8	5,227.2	9,061.9
Liquefied petroleum gases . .	2,791.0	2,888.1	5,735.4
Petroleum gases, etc., in the gaseous state	1,250.8	2,339.2	3,281.5
Total (incl. others)	9,838.6	12,525.3	22,031.3

Source: UN, *International Trade Statistics Yearbook*.

2001 (US $ million): Total imports c.i.f. 9,482 (Food 2,346, Energy 97, Raw materials 445, Semi–finished articles 1,747, Agricultural equipment 154, Industrial equipment 3,293, Consumer goods 1,400); Total exports f.o.b. 19,091 (Food 30, Energy 18,531 (*of which* Crude petroleum 3,994), Raw materials 39, Semi–finished articles 413, Agricultural equipment 22, Industrial equipment 42, Consumer goods 14) (Source: IMF, *Selected Issues and Statistical Appendix*—February 2004).

2002 (US $ million): Total imports c.i.f. 12,010 (Food 2,572, Energy 132, Raw materials 490, Semi–finished articles 2,186, Agricultural equipment 139, Industrial equipment 4,146, Consumer goods 1,649, Direct investment 'en nature' 696); Total exports f.o.b. 18,700 (Food 35, Energy 18,109 (*of which* Crude petroleum 5,056), Raw materials 56, Semi–finished articles 403, Agricultural equipment 20, Industrial equipment 50, Consumer goods 27) (Source: IMF, *Selected Issues and Statistical Appendix*—February 2004).

PRINCIPAL TRADING PARTNERS
(US $ million)*

Imports c.i.f.	1998	1999	2000
Argentina	87.9	122.8	75.4
Austria	102.1	108.2	115.6
Belgium†	247.8	192.9	238.7
Brazil	57.7	104.8	56.3
Canada	523.2	385.8	349.9
China, People's Republic . . .	211.7	229.5	212.7
Côte d'Ivoire	105.2	77.4	92.2
Finland	81.5	97.4	96.6
France (incl. Monaco) . . .	2,241.3	2,086.1	2,159.4
Germany	645.1	678.7	709.6
Italy	845.8	907.4	811.1
Japan	205.7	356.6	273.1
Korea, Republic	209.4	308.8	185.5
Mexico	28.1	104.4	116.4
Netherlands	189.1	164.0	175.2
Russia	122.5	135.7	273.0
Spain	547.3	507.6	546.1
Sweden	105.0	75.4	55.6
Switzerland-Liechtenstein . . .	105.3	107.8	110.4
Syria	135.8	65.4	25.9
Turkey	410.8	337.6	286.2
Ukraine	75.2	122.7	138.5
United Kingdom	250.4	218.6	210.1
USA	991.7	769.7	1,045.1
Total (incl. others)	9,403.4	9,161.9	9,152.1

Exports f.o.b.	1998	1999	2000
Belgium†	420.8	327.4	659.0
Brazil	632.2	964.0	1,502.7
Canada	358.9	405.0	779.7
France (incl. Monaco)	1,675.9	1,719.1	2,920.0
Germany	166.7	198.4	732.7
Italy	1,841.6	2,942.2	4,425.0
Netherlands	806.8	1,021.3	1,657.7
Portugal	61.5	154.0	249.5
Spain	960.3	1,329.0	2,329.1
Turkey	579.3	605.3	1,332.1
United Kingdom	258.4	233.2	647.7
USA	1,520.0	1,755.1	3,424.8
Total (incl. others)	9,838.6	12,525.3	22,031.3

* Imports by country of production; exports by country of last consignment.
† Figures for 1998 include trade with Luxembourg.

Source: UN, *International Trade Statistics Yearbook*.

Transport

RAILWAYS
(traffic)

	1999	2000	2001
Passengers carried ('000) . . .	32,027	n.a.	n.a.
Freight carried ('000 metric tons) .	7,842	n.a.	n.a.
Passenger-km (million)	1,069	1,142	981
Freight ton-km (million) . . .	2,033	1,980	1,990

Source: mostly UN, *Statistical Yearbook*.

2001 ('000 passenger journeys): 28,800 (Source: Railway Gazette).

ROAD TRAFFIC
(motor vehicles in use at 31 December)

	2000	2001	2002
Passenger cars	1,692,148	1,708,373	1,739,286
Lorries	296,145	298,125	300,171
Vans	609,617	612,523	615,663
Buses and coaches	42,791	44,323	46,136
Motorcycles	9,198	9,245	9,258

SHIPPING

Merchant Fleet
(registered at 31 December)

	2001	2002	2003
Number of vessels	143	141	137
Total displacement ('000 grt) . .	963.9	936.1	872.0

Source: Lloyd's Register-Fairplay, *World Fleet Statistics*.

International Sea-borne Freight Traffic
('000 metric tons)

	1997	1998	1999
Goods loaded	74,300	75,500	77,900
Goods unloaded	15,200	16,000	16,600

Note: Figures are rounded to the nearest 100,000 metric tons.

CIVIL AVIATION
(traffic on scheduled services)

	1999	2000	2001
Kilometres flown (million) . . .	32	34	42
Passengers carried ('000) . . .	2,937	2,997	3,419
Passenger-km (million)	2,991	3,051	3,501
Total ton-km (million)	286	287	338

Source: UN, *Statistical Yearbook*.

Tourism

FOREIGN TOURIST ARRIVALS BY COUNTRY OF ORIGIN*

	2000	2001	2002
France	64,839	70,880	96,626
Germany	4,784	6,440	8,182
Italy	7,158	8,260	9,763
Libya	4,851	6,983	7,671
Mali	8,857	9,244	11,387
Morocco	3,805	3,485	3,849
Spain	7,048	4,585	5,468
Tunisia	32,481	33,607	47,704
Total (incl. others)	175,538	196,259	251,145

* Excluding arrivals of Algerian nationals resident abroad: 690,446 in 2000; 705,187 in 2001; 736,915 in 2002.

Tourism receipts (US $ million): 96 in 2000; 100 in 2001; 133 in 2002.

Source: World Tourism Organization.

Communications Media

	2001	2002	2003
Telephones ('000 main lines in use)	1,880.0	1,880.0	2,199.6
Mobile cellular telephones (subscribers)	100	400	1,447
Personal computers ('000 in use)	220	242	n.a.
Internet users ('000)	200	500	n.a.

1997: Radio receivers ('000 in use): 7,100; Facsimile machines (number in use) 7,000.

1998: Daily newspapers 24 (average circulation 796,000 copies); Non-daily newspapers 82 (average circulation 909,000 copies); Periodicals 106.

1999: Book production (titles) 133 (excl. pamphlets).

2001: Television receivers ('000 in use): 3,500.

Sources: UNESCO, *Statistical Yearbook*; UN, *Statistical Yearbook*; International Telecommunication Union.

Education

(2002/03, unless otherwise indicated)

	Institutions	Teachers	Pupils
Pre-primary*	n.a.	1,333	33,503
Primary	16,714	167,529	4,612,574
Secondary	4,980	162,076	3,282,068
Higher (incl. post-graduate) . .	55	57,747	624,364

* 1996/97.

Sources: UNESCO, *Statistical Yearbook*, and Ministère de l'Education nationale.

1998/99 (Pre-primary and primary): 15,729 institutions; 170,562 teachers; 4,843,313 pupils.

Adult literacy rate (UNESCO estimates): 68.9% (males 78.0%; females 59.6%) in 2002 (Source: UN Development Programme, *Human Development Report*).

Directory

The Constitution

A new Constitution for the Democratic and People's Republic of Algeria, approved by popular referendum, was promulgated on 22 November 1976. The Constitution was amended by the National People's Assembly on 30 June 1979. Further amendments were approved by referendum on 3 November 1988, on 23 February 1989, and on 28 November 1996. On 8 April 2002 the National People's Assembly approved an amendment, which granted Tamazight, the principal language spoken by the Berber population of the country, the status of a national language. The main provisions of the Constitution, as amended, are summarized below:

The preamble recalls that Algeria owes its independence to a war of liberation which led to the creation of a modern sovereign state, guaranteeing social justice, equality and liberty for all. It emphasizes Algeria's Islamic, Arab and Amazigh (Berber) heritage, and stresses that, as an Arab Mediterranean and African country, it forms an integral part of the Great Arab Maghreb.

FUNDAMENTAL PRINCIPLES OF THE ORGANIZATION OF ALGERIAN SOCIETY

The Republic

Algeria is a popular, democratic state. Islam is the state religion and Arabic and Tamazight are the official national languages.

The People

National sovereignty resides in the people and is exercised through its elected representatives. The institutions of the State consolidate national unity and protect the fundamental rights of its citizens. The exploitation of one individual by another is forbidden.

The State

The State is exclusively at the service of the people. Those holding positions of responsibility must live solely on their salaries and may not, directly or by the agency of others, engage in any remunerative activity.

Fundamental Freedoms and the Rights of Man and the Citizen

Fundamental rights and freedoms are guaranteed. All discrimination on grounds of sex, race or belief is forbidden. Law cannot operate retrospectively, and a person is presumed innocent until proved guilty. Victims of judicial error shall receive compensation from the State.

The State guarantees the inviolability of the home, of private life and of the person. The State also guarantees the secrecy of correspondence, the freedom of conscience and opinion, freedom of intellectual, artistic and scientific creation, and freedom of expression and assembly.

The State guarantees the right to form political associations (on condition that they are not based on differences in religion, language, race, gender or region), to join a trade union, the right to strike, the right to work, to protection, to security, to health, to leisure, to education, etc. It also guarantees the right to leave the national territory, within the limits set by law.

Duties of Citizens

Every citizen must respect the Constitution, and must protect public property and safeguard national independence. The law sanctions the duty of parents to educate and protect their children, as well as the duty of children to help and support their parents. Every citizen must contribute towards public expenditure through the payment of taxes.

The National Popular Army

The army safeguards national independence and sovereignty.

Principles of Foreign Policy

Algeria subscribes to the principles and objectives of the UN. It advocates international co-operation, the development of friendly relations between states, on the basis of equality and mutual interest, and non-interference in the internal affairs of states.

POWER AND ITS ORGANIZATION

The Executive

The President of the Republic is Head of State, Head of the Armed Forces and responsible for national defence. He must be of Algerian origin, a Muslim and more than 40 years old. He is elected by universal, secret, direct suffrage. His mandate is for five years, and is renewable once. The President embodies the unity of the nation. The President presides over meetings of the Council of Ministers. He decides and conducts foreign policy and appoints the Head of Government, who is responsible to the National People's Assembly. The Head of Government must appoint a Council of Ministers. He drafts, co-ordinates and implements his government's programme, which he must present to the Assembly for ratification. Should the Assembly reject the programme, the Head of Government and the Council of Ministers resign, and the President appoints a new Head of Government. Should the newly appointed Head of Government's programme be rejected by the Assembly, the President dissolves the Assembly, and a general election is held. Should the President be unable to perform his functions, owing to a long and serious illness, the President of the Council of the Nation assumes the office for a maximum period of 45 days (subject to the approval of a two-thirds' majority in the National People's Assembly and the Council of the Nation). If the President is still unable to perform his functions after 45 days, the Presidency is declared vacant by the Constitutional Council. Should the Presidency fall vacant, the President of the Council of the Nation temporarily assumes the office and organizes presidential elections within 60 days. He may not himself be a candidate in the election. The President presides over a High Security Council which advises on all matters affecting national security.

The Legislature

The legislature consists of the Assemblée Populaire Nationale (National People's Assembly) and the Conseil de la Nation (Council of the Nation, which was established by constitutional amendments approved by national referendum in November 1996). The members of the lower chamber, the National People's Assembly, are elected by universal, direct, secret suffrage for a five-year term. Two-thirds of the members of the upper chamber, the Council of the Nation, are elected by indirect, secret suffrage from regional and municipal authorities; the remainder are appointed by the President of the Republic. The Council's term in office is six years; one-half of its members are replaced every three years. The deputies enjoy parliamentary immunity. The legislature sits for two ordinary sessions per year, each of not less than four months' duration. The commissions of the legislature are in permanent session. The two parliamentary chambers may be summoned to meet for an extraordinary session on the request of the President of the Republic, or of the Head of Government, or of two-thirds of the members of the National People's Assembly. Both the Head of Government and the parliamentary chambers may initiate legislation. Legislation must be deliberated upon respectively by the National People's Assembly and the Council of the Nation before promulgation. Any text passed by the Assembly must be approved by three-quarters of the members of the Council in order to become legislation.

The Judiciary

Judges obey only the law. They defend society and fundamental freedoms. The right of the accused to a defence is guaranteed. The Supreme Court regulates the activities of courts and tribunals, and the State Council regulates the administrative judiciary. The Higher Court of the Magistrature is presided over by the President of the Republic; the Minister of Justice is Vice-President of the Court. All magistrates are answerable to the Higher Court for the manner in which they fulfil their functions. The High State Court is empowered to judge the President of the Republic in cases of high treason, and the Head of Government for crimes and offences.

The Constitutional Council

The Constitutional Council is responsible for ensuring that the Constitution is respected, and that referendums, the election of the President of the Republic and legislative elections are conducted in accordance with the law. The Constitutional Council comprises nine members, of whom three are appointed by the President of the Republic, two elected by the National People's Assembly, two elected by the Council of the Nation, one elected by the Supreme Court and one elected by the State Council. The Council's term in office is six years; the President of the Council is appointed for a six-year term and one-half of the remaining members are replaced every three years.

The High Islamic Council

The High Islamic Council is an advisory body on matters relating to Islam. The Council comprises 15 members and its President is appointed by the President of the Republic.

Constitutional Revision

The Constitution can be revised on the initiative of the President of the Republic (subject to approval by the National People's Assembly and by three-quarters of the members of the Council of the Nation), and must be approved by national referendum. Should the Constitutional Council decide that a draft constitutional amendment does not in any way affect the general principles governing Algerian society, it may permit the President of the Republic to promulgate the amendment directly (without submitting it to referendum) if it has been approved by three-quarters of the members of both parliamentary chambers. Three-quarters of the members of both parliamentary chambers, in a joint sitting, may propose a constitutional amendment to the President of the Republic who may submit it to referendum. The basic principles of the Constitution may not be revised.

The Government

HEAD OF STATE

President and Minister of Defence: ABDELAZIZ BOUTEFLIKA (inaugurated 27 April 1999; re-elected 8 April 2004).

COUNCIL OF MINISTERS
(April 2005)

Prime Minister: AHMED OUYAHIA.

Minister of State for the Interior and Local Authorities: NOUREDDINE YAZID ZERHOUNI.

Minister of State for Foreign Affairs: ABDELAZIZ BELKHADEM.

Minister of Justice and Attorney-General: TAYEB BELAIZ.

Minister of Commerce: NOUREDDINE BOUKROUH.

Minister of Energy and Mines: Prof. CHAKIB KHELIL.

Minister of Religious Affairs and Endowments: Prof. BOUABDELLAH GHLAMALLAH.

Minister of War Veterans: MUHAMMAD CHERIF ABBAS.

Minister of Town Planning and the Environment: Dr CHERIF RAHMANI.

Minister of Transport: MUHAMMAD MAGHLAOUI.

Minister of Youth and Sports: ABDELAZIZ ZIARI.

Minister of Agriculture and Rural Development: Dr SAÏD BERKAT.

Minister of Tourism: MUHAMMAD SEGHIR KARA.

Minister of Public Works: Dr AMAR GHOUL.

Minister of Health, Population and Hospital Reform: MOURAD REDJIMI.

Minister of Finance: ABDELLATIF BENACHENHOU.

Minister of Culture: KHALIDA TOUMI-MESSAOUDI.

Minister of Communications: BOUDJEMAÂ HAÏCHOUR.

Minister of Water Resources: ABDELMALEK SELLAL.

Minister of Small and Medium-sized Enterprises and Handicrafts: MUSTAPHA BENDADA.

Minister of National Education: Prof. BOUBEKEUR BENBOUZID.

Minister of Higher Education and Scientific Research: Dr RACHID HARROUBIA.

Minister of Postal Services, Telecommunications and Information Technology: AMAR TOU.

Minister of Vocational Training: Dr HEDI KHALDI.

Minister of Housing and Urban Development: MUHAMMAD NADIR HAMIMID.

Minister of Industry: EL-HACHEMI DJAABOUB.

Minister of Labour and Social Security: TAYEB LOUH.

Minister of Employment and National Solidarity: DJAMEL OULD ABBES.

Minister in charge of Relations with Parliament: MAHMOUD KHOUDRI.

Minister of Fishing and Fisheries Resources: Dr SMAIL MIMOUNE.

Minister-delegate to the Minister of State for Foreign Affairs, in charge of Maghreb and African Affairs: ABDELKADER MESSAHEL.

Minister-delegate to the Minister of State for the Interior and Local Authorities, responsible for Local Authorities: DAHO OULD KABLIA.

Minister-delegate to the Prime Minister, in charge of Family and Women's Affairs: NOUARA SAADIA DJAFFAR.

Minister-delegate to the Prime Minister, in charge of the Algerian Expatriate Community: SAKINA MESSADI.

Minister-delegate to the Prime Minister, in charge of Participation and Investment Promotion: YAHIA HAMLAOUI.

Minister-delegate to the Minister of Town Planning and the Environment, in charge of Cities: ABDERRACHID BOUKERZAZA.

Minister-delegate to the Minister of Agriculture and Rural Development, in charge of Rural Development: Dr RACHID BENAISSA.

Minister-delegate to the Minister of Higher Education and Scientific Research, in charge of Scientific Research: SOUAD BENDJABALLAH.

Minister-delegate to the Minister of Finance, responsible for Financial Reform: KARIM DJOUDI.

MINISTRIES

Office of the President: Présidence de la République, el-Mouradia, Algiers; tel. (21) 69-15-15; fax (21) 69-15-95; internet www.el-mouradia.dz.

Office of the Prime Minister: rue Docteur Saâdane, Algiers; tel. (21) 73-23-40; fax (21) 71-79-27.

Ministry of Agriculture and Rural Development: 4 route des Quatre Canons, Algiers; tel. (21) 71-17-12; fax (21) 61-57-39; internet www.miniagri-algeria.org.

Ministry of Commerce: rue Docteur Saâdane, Algiers; tel. (21) 73-23-40; fax (21) 73-54-18; internet www.cnrc.org.dz.

Ministry of Communications and Culture: Palais de la Culture, Les Annassers, BP 100, Kouba, Algiers; tel. (21) 29-12-28; fax (21) 29-20-89; e-mail info@mcc.gov.dz; internet www.mcc.gov.dz.

Ministry of Defence: Les Tagarins, el-Biar, Algiers; tel. (21) 71-15-15; fax (21) 64-67-26.

Ministry of Employment and National Solidarity: Route nationale 1, Les Vergers, BP 31, Bir Khadem, Algiers; tel. (21) 44-99-46; fax (21) 44-97-26; e-mail cellulemassn@massn.gov.dz; internet www.massn.gov.dz.

Ministry of Energy and Mines: 80 ave Ahmed Ghermoul, Algiers; tel. (21) 65-22-22; fax (21) 65-19-04; e-mail info@mem-algeria.org; internet www.mem-algeria.org.

Ministry of Finance: Immeuble Maurétania, place du Pérou, Algiers; tel. (21) 71-13-66; fax (21) 73-42-76; e-mail algeriafinance@multimania.com; internet www.finance-algeria.org.

Ministry of Fishing and Fisheries Resources: Route des Quatre Canons, Algiers; tel. (21) 43-39-51; fax (21) 43-31-68; e-mail sg@mpeche.gov.dz; internet www.mpeche.gov.dz.

Ministry of Foreign Affairs: place Mohamed Seddik Benyahia, el-Mouradia, Algiers; tel. (21) 69-23-33; fax (21) 69-21-61; internet www.mae.dz.

Ministry of Health, Population and Hospital Reform: 125 rue Abd ar-Rahmane Laâla, el-Madania, Algiers; tel. (21) 27-29-00; fax (21) 27-96-41; e-mail msmin@sante.dz; internet www.sante.dz.

Ministry of Higher Education and Scientific Research: 11 rue Doudou Mokhtar, Algiers; tel. (21) 91-23-23; fax (21) 91-21-13; e-mail webmaster@mesrs.dz; internet www.mesrs.dz.

Ministry of Housing and Urban Development: 135 rue Didouche Mourad, Algiers; tel. (21) 74-07-22; fax (21) 74-53-83; e-mail mhabitat@wissal.dz; internet www.mhu.gov.dz.

Ministry of Industry: Immeuble le Colisée, 4 rue Ahmed Bey, Algiers; tel. (21) 60-11-44; fax (21) 69-32-35; e-mail info@mir-algeria.org; internet www.mir-algeria.org.

Ministry of the Interior and Local Authorities: 18 rue Docteur Saâdane, Algiers; tel. (21) 73-23-40; fax (21) 73-43-67.

Ministry of Justice: 8 place Bir Hakem, el-Biar, Algiers; tel. (21) 92-41-83; fax (21) 92-25-60.

Ministry of Labour and Social Security: 40–44 blvd Mohamed Belouizdad, Algiers; tel. (21) 65-99-99; fax (21) 66-26-08; e-mail mtps@wissal.dz; internet www.mtss.gov.dz.

Ministry of National Education: 8 ave de Pékin, Algiers; tel. (21) 60-67-57; fax (21) 60-57-82; e-mail men@meducation.edu.dz; internet www.meducation.edu.dz.

Ministry of Participation and Investment Promotion: Chemin Ibn Badis el-Mouiz, El-Biar, Algiers; tel. (21) 92-98-85; fax (21) 92-17-55; internet www.mpcr-dz.com.

Ministry of Postal Services, Telecommunications and Information Technology: 4 blvd Krim Belkacem, Algiers; tel. (21) 71-12-20; fax (21) 71-92-71; internet www.barid.dz.

Ministry of Public Works: Algiers.

Ministry of Religious Affairs and Endowments: 4 rue de Timgad, Hydra, Algiers; tel. (21) 60-85-55; fax (21) 60-09-36.

Ministry of Small and Medium-sized Enterprises and Handicrafts: Immeuble le Colisée, 4 rue Ahmed Bey, Algiers; tel. (21) 69-73-63; fax (21) 23-00-94; internet www.pmepmi-dz.com.

Ministry of Tourism: 7 rue des Frères Ziata, el-Mouradia, 16000 Algiers; tel. (21) 60-33-55; fax (21) 59-13-15; internet www.mta.gov .dz.

Ministry of Town Planning and the Environment: rue des Quatre Canons, Bab-el-Oued, Algiers; tel. (21) 43-28-77; fax (21) 43-28-55; e-mail deeai@ifrance.com.

Ministry of Transport: 119 rue Didouche Mourad, Algiers; tel. (21) 74-06-99; fax (21) 74-33-95.

Ministry of Vocational Training: Algiers; e-mail abada@mfep .gov.dz; internet www.mfp.gov.dz.

Ministry of War Veterans: 2 ave du Lt. Med Benarfa, el-Biar, Algiers; tel. (21) 92-23-55; fax (21) 92-35-16.

Ministry of Water Resources: BP 86, Ex Grand Séminaire, Algiers; tel. (21) 68-95-00; fax (21) 58-63-64.

Ministry of Youth and Sports: 3 rue Mohamed Belouizdad, place du 1er mai, Algiers; tel. (21) 65-55-55; fax (21) 68-41-71; e-mail mjsalgerie@mjs-dz.org; internet www.mjs.dz.

President and Legislature

PRESIDENT

Presidential Election, 8 April 2004

Candidate	Votes	% of votes
Abdelaziz Bouteflika	8,651,723	84.99
Ali Benflis	653,951	6.42
Sheikh Abdallah Djaballah	511,526	5.02
Saïd Saâdi	197,111	1.94
Louiza Hanoune	101,630	1.00
Fawzi Rebaïne	63,761	0.63
Total*	10,179,702	100.00

* Excluding 329,075 invalid votes.

LEGISLATURE

National People's Assembly

President: AMAR SAIDANI.

General Election, 30 May 2002

	Votes	% of votes	Seats
Front de libération nationale (FLN)	2,618,003	35.28	199
Rassemblement national démocratique (RND)	610,461	8.23	47
Mouvement de la réforme nationale (MRN)	705,319	9.50	43
Mouvement de la société pour la paix (MSP)	523,464	7.05	38
Parti des travailleurs (PT)	246,770	3.33	21
Front national algérien	113,700	1.53	8
Nahdah	48,132	0.65	1
Parti du renouveau algérien (PRA)	19,873	0.27	1
Mouvement de l'entente nationale (MEN)	14,465	0.19	1
Independents	365,594	4.93	30
Others	2,155,056	29.04	—
Total	7,420,867	100.00	389

Council of the Nation

President: ABDELKADER BENSALAH.

Elections, 25 December 1997 and 30 December 2000*

	Seats*
Rassemblement national démocratique (RND)	74
Front de libération nationale (FLN)	15
Front des forces socialistes (FFS)	4
Mouvement de la société pour la paix (MSP)	3
Appointed by the President†	48
Total	144

* Deputies of the Council of the Nation serve a six-year term; one-half of its members are replaced every three years. Elected representatives are selected by indirect, secret suffrage from regional and municipal authorities.

† Appointed on 4 January 2001 and 8 January 2004.

Note: Elections took place on 30 December 2003 to renew 46 members of the Council of the Nation. (The two seats reserved for deputies from the Kabyle region were to be filled at a later date.) The seats were allocated accordingly: RND 17, FLN 11, Corrective Movement of the FLN 10, MSP four, MRN two and independents two. One-half of the presidential appointees to the Council were also replaced.

Political Organizations

Until 1989 the FLN was the only legal party in Algeria. The February 1989 amendments to the Constitution permitted the formation of other political associations, with some restrictions. The right to establish political parties was guaranteed by constitutional amendments in November 1996; however, political associations based on differences in religion, language, race, gender or region were proscribed. Some 23 political parties contested the legislative elections that took place in May 2002. The most important political organizations are listed below.

Ahd 54 (Oath 54): 53 rue Larbi Ben M'Hedi, Algiers; tel. (21) 73-61-37; fax (21) 71-16-79; e-mail info@ahd54.org; internet www.ahd54 .org; f. 1991; small nationalist party; Sec.-Gen. ALI FAWZI REBAÏNE.

Alliance nationale républicaine (ANR): Algiers; f. 1995; anti-Islamist; Leader REDHA MALEK.

Congrès national algérien: Algiers; f. 1999; Leader ABDELKADER BELHAYE.

Front démocratique: Algiers; f. 1999; unauthorized; Leader SID-AHMED GHOZALI.

Front des forces socialistes (FFS): 56 ave Souidani Boudjemaâ, 16032 Hydra, Algiers; tel. (21) 69-41-41; fax (21) 48-45-54; internet www.ffs-dz.org; f. 1963; revived 1989; seeks greater autonomy for Berber-dominated regions and official recognition of the Berber language; Leader HOCINE AÏT AHMED; Sec.-Gen. MOUSTAFA BOUHADEF.

Front islamique du salut (FIS): Algiers; fax (21) 69-72-66; e-mail info@fisweb.org; internet www.fisweb.org; f. 1989; aims to emphasize the importance of Islam in political and social life; formally dissolved by the Algiers Court of Appeal in March 1992; Leader ABBASI MADANI.

Front de libération nationale (FLN): 7 rue du Stade, Hydra, Algiers; tel. (21) 69-42-96; fax (21) 69-43-41; e-mail pfln@wissal.dz; internet www.pfln.org.dz; f. 1954; sole legal party until 1989; socialist in outlook, the party is organized into a Secretariat, a Political Bureau, a Central Committee, Federations, Kasmas and cells; under the aegis of the FLN are various mass political organizations, including the Union Nationale de la Jeunesse Algérienne (UNJA) and the Union Nationale des Femmes Algériennes (UNFA); Sec.-Gen. ABDELAZIZ BELKHADEM; Pres. ABDELAZIZ BOUTEFLIKA.

Front national algérien (FNA): Algiers; f. 1999; advocates eradication of poverty and supports the Govt's peace initiative; Pres. MOUSSA TOUATI.

Front national de renouvellement (FNR): Algiers; Leader ZINEDINE CHERIFI.

Mouvement algérien pour la justice et le développement (MAJD): Villa Laibi, Lot Kapiot No. 5, Bouzaréah, Algiers; tel. (21) 60-58-00; fax (21) 78-78-72; f. 1990; reformist party supporting policies of fmr Pres. Boumedienne; Leader MOULAY HABIB.

Mouvement pour l'autonomie de la Kabylie (MAK): f. 2001; advocates independence for the Kabylie region; Leader FERHAT MEHENNI.

Mouvement pour la démocratie et la citoyenneté (MDC): Tizi-Ouzou; f. 1997 by dissident members of the FFS; Leader SAÏD KHELIL.

Mouvement démocratique et social (MDS): Algiers; internet www.mds.pol.dz; f. 1998 by fmr mems of Ettahaddi; left-wing party; 4,000 mems; Sec.-Gen. HACHEMI CHERIF.

Mouvement pour la liberté: Algiers; f. 1999 in opposition to Pres. Bouteflika; Leader MOULOUD HAMROUCHE.

Mouvement de la réforme nationale (MRN) (al-Islah): Algiers; f. 1998; radical Islamist party; Leader Sheikh ABDALLAH DJABALLAH.

Mouvement de la société pour la paix (MSP): 163 Hassiba Ben Bouali, Algiers; e-mail bureau@hms-algeria.net; internet www .hms-algeria.net; f. as Hamas; adopted current name in 1997; moderate Islamic party, favouring the gradual introduction of an Islamic state; Pres. ABOU DJERRA SOLTANI.

Nahdah: Algiers; fundamentalist Islamist group; Sec.-Gen. HABIB ADAMI.

Parti démocratique progressif (PDR): Algiers; f. 1990 as a legal party; Leader SACI MABROUK.

Parti national pour la solidarité et le développement (PNSD): BP 110, Staouéli, Algiers; tel. and fax (21) 39-40-42; e-mail cherif_taleb@yahoo.fr; f. 1989 as Parti social démocrate; Leader MOHAMED CHERIF TALEB.

Parti du renouveau algérien (PRA): Algiers; tel. (21) 56-62-78; Sec.-Gen. YACINE TERKMANE; Leader NOUREDDINE BOUKROUH.

Parti républicain progressif (PRP): 10 rue Ouahrani Abou-Mediêne, Cité Seddikia, Oran; tel. (41) 35-79-36; f. 1990 as a legal party; Sec.-Gen. SLIMANE CHERIF.

Parti des travailleurs (PT): Algiers; workers' party; Leader LOUISA HANOUNE.

Rassemblement pour la concorde nationale: Algiers; f. 2001 to support the policies of President Bouteflika; Chair. SID AHMED ABACHI.

Rassemblement pour la culture et la démocratie (RCD): 40 rue Muhammad Chabane, el-Biar, Algiers; tel. (21) 92-50-76; fax (21) 92-51-01; internet www.rcd-algerie.org; f. 1989; secular party; advocates inclusion of Berber traditions into the Algerian identity; Pres. SAÏD SAÂDI.

Rassemblement national démocratique (RND): Cité des Asphodèles, BP 10, Ben Aknoun, Algiers; tel. (21) 91-64-10; fax (21) 91-47-40; e-mail rnd@rnd-dz.org; internet www.rnd-dz.org; f. 1997; centrist party; Sec.-Gen. AHMED OUYAHIA.

Union pour la démocratie et les libertés (UDL): Algiers; f. 1997; Leader ABDELKRIM SEDDIKI.

Wafa wa al-Adl (Wafa): Algiers; f. 1999; unauthorized; Leader AHMED TALEB IBRAHIMI.

The following groups are in armed conflict with the Government:

Da'wa wal Djihad—Groupe salafiste pour la prédication et le combat (GSPC): f. 1998; breakaway group from the GIA; particularly active in the east of Algiers and in the Kabyle; responds to preaching by Ali Belhadj, the second most prominent member of the proscribed FIS; reportedly split into several factions; Leader ABU MUSAB ABD AL-WADUD.

Groupe islamique armé (GIA): was the most prominent and radical Islamist militant group in the mid-1990s, but has reportedly split into several factions which do not all adhere to one leader; Leader (vacant).

Diplomatic Representation

EMBASSIES IN ALGERIA

Angola: 14 rue Marie Curie, el-Biar, Algiers; tel. (21) 92-54-41; fax (21) 79-74-41; Ambassador JOSÉ CÉSAR AUGUSTO.

Argentina: 7 rue Hamami, 16000 Algiers; tel. (21) 71-86-83; fax (21) 64-38-43; e-mail emargentin@djazair-connect.com; Ambassador JORGE ALBERTO RAFAEL VEHILS.

Austria: 17 chemin Abd al-Kader Gadouche, 16035 Hydra, Algiers; tel. (21) 69-10-86; fax (21) 69-12-32; e-mail algier-ob@bmaa.gov.at; Ambassador THOMAS MICHAEL BAIER.

Belgium: 22 chemin Youcef Tayebi, el-Biar, Algiers; tel. (21) 92-24-46; fax (21) 92-50-36; Ambassador DIRK LETTENS.

Benin: 36 Lot du Stade, Birkhadem, Algiers; tel. (21) 56-52-71; Ambassador LEONARD ADJIN.

Brazil: BP 246, 55 chemin Cheikh Bachir El-Ibrahimi, el-Biar, Algiers; tel. (21) 92–21–22; fax (21) 92–41–25; e-mail brasilia@mail .wissal.dz; Ambassador SÉRGIO THOMPSON-FLORES.

Bulgaria: 13 blvd Col Bougara, Algiers; tel. (21) 23-00-14; fax (21) 23-05-33; Ambassador PETER GRADEV.

Burkina Faso: 23 Lot el-Feth, Poirson, el-Biar, BP 212 Didouche Mourad, Algiers; tel. (21) 92-33-39; fax (21) 92-73-90; e-mail abfalger@yahoo.fr; Ambassador MAMADOU SERME.

Cameroon: 26 chemin Cheikh Bachir El-Ibrahimi, 16011 el-Biar, Algiers; tel. (21) 92-11-24; fax (21) 92-11-25; e-mail ambacam_alger@ yahoo.fr; Chargé d'affaires JEAN MISSOUP.

Canada: 18 rue Mustapha Khalef, Ben Aknoun, BP 48, 16000 Alger-Gare, Algiers; tel. (21) 91-49-51; fax (21) 91-49-73; e-mail alger@ dfait-maeci.go.ca; Ambassador ROBERT PECK.

Chad: Villa No. 18, Cité DNC, chemin Ahmed Kara, Hydra, Algiers; tel. (21) 69-26-62; fax (21) 69-26-63; Ambassador El-Hadj MAHAMOUD ADJI.

Chile: Rue F. les Crêtes N° 8, Hydra, Algiers; tel. (21) 48-31-63 ; fax (21) 60-71-85; e-mail embchile@gecos.net; Ambassador ARIEL ULLOA AZOCAR JUVENAL.

China, People's Republic: 34 blvd des Martyrs, Algiers; tel. (21) 69-27-24; fax (21) 69-29-62; Ambassador WANG WANGSHENG.

Congo, Democratic Republic: Algiers; tel. (21) 59-12-27; Ambassador IKAKI BOMELE MOLINGO.

Congo, Republic: 111 Parc Ben Omar, Kouba, Algiers; tel. (21) 58-68-00; Ambassador PIERRE N'GAKA.

Côte d'Ivoire: Immeuble 'Le Bosquet', Le Paradou, BP 260 Hydra, Algiers; tel. (21) 69-23-78; fax (21) 69-30-32; e-mail acialg@yahoo.fr; Ambassador LARGATON GILBERT OUATTARA.

Cuba: 22 rue Larbi Alik, Hydra, Algiers; tel. (21) 69-21-48; fax (21) 69-32-81; e-mail ambcuba@gecos.net; Ambassador ROBERTO BLANCO DOMÍNGUEZ.

Czech Republic: BP 358, Villa Koudia, 3 chemin Ziryab, Alger-Gare; Algiers; tel. (21) 23-00-56; fax (21) 23-01-03; e-mail algiers@ embassy.mzv.cz; internet www.mzv.cz/algiers; Ambassador JAROMÍR MAREK.

Denmark: 12 ave Emile Marquis, Lot Djenane el-Malik, 16035 Hydra, BP 384, 16000 Alger-Gare, Algiers; tel. (21) 54-82-28; fax (21) 69-29-09; e-mail algamb@um.dk; Ambassador BO ERIC WEBER.

Egypt: BP 297, 8 chemin Abd al-Kader Gadouche, 16300 Hydra, Algiers; tel. (21) 60-16-73; fax (21) 60-29-52; Ambassador IBRAHIM YOUSSRI.

Finland: BP 256, 16035 Hydra, Algiers; tel. (21) 69-29-25; fax (21) 69-16-37; e-mail finamb@wissal.dz.

France: chemin Abd al-Kader Gadouche, Hydra, Algiers; tel. (21) 69-24-88; fax (21) 69-13-69; internet www.ambafrance-dz.org; Chargé d'affaires a.i. HUBERT COLIN DE VERDIÈRE.

Gabon: BP 125, Rostomia, 21 rue Hadj Ahmed Mohamed, Hydra, Algiers; tel. (21) 69-24-00; fax (21) 60-25-46; Ambassador YVES ONGOLLO.

Germany: BP 664, Alger-Gare, 165 chemin Sfindja, Algiers; tel. (21) 74-19-56; fax (21) 74-05-21; e-mail info@allemagne-dj.org; Ambassador HANS PETER SCHIFF.

Ghana: 62 rue des Frères Benali Abdellah, Hydra, Algiers; tel. (21) 60-64-44; fax (21) 69-28-56; Ambassador GEORGE A. O. KUGBLENU.

Greece: 60 blvd Col Bougara, Algiers; tel. (21) 92-34-91; fax (21) 69-16-55; Ambassador IOANNIS DRAKOULARAKOS.

Guinea: 43 blvd Central Saïd Hamdine, Hydra, Algiers; tel. (21) 69-20-66; fax (21) 69-34-68; Ambassador MAMADY CONDÉ.

Guinea-Bissau: 17 rue Ahmad Kara, BP 32, Colonne Volrol, Hydra, Algiers; tel. (21) 60-01-51; fax (21) 60-97-25; Ambassador JOSÉ PEREIRA BATISTA.

Holy See: 1 rue Noureddine Mekiri, 16021 Bologhine, Algiers (Apostolic Nunciature); tel. (21) 95-45-20; fax (21) 95-40-95; e-mail nuntiusalger@hotmail.com; Apostolic Nuncio Most Rev. THOMAS YEH SHENG-NAN (Titular Archbishop of Leptis Magna).

Hungary: BP 68, 18 ave des Frères Oughlis, el-Mouradia, Algiers; tel. (21) 69-79-75; fax (21) 69-81-86; e-mail huembalg@yahoo.com; Chargé d'affaires LÁSZLÓ SZABÓ.

India: 14 rue des Abassides, BP 108, el-Biar, 16030 Algiers; tel. (21) 92-70-11; fax (21) 92-32-88; e-mail indemb@wissal.dz; Ambassador (vacant).

Indonesia: BP 62, 16 chemin Abd al-Kader Gadouche, 16070 el-Mouradia, Algiers; tel. (21) 69-20-11; fax (21) 69-39-31; Ambassador LILLAHI GRAHANA SIDHARTA.

Iraq: 4 rue Abri Arezki, Hydra, Algiers; tel. (21) 69-31-25; fax (21) 69-10-97.

Italy: 18 rue Muhammad Ouidir Amellal, 16030 el-Biar, Algiers; tel. (21) 92-23-30; fax (21) 92-59-86; e-mail ambitalgeri@ambitalgeri.org; internet www.ambitalgeri.org; Ambassador ROMUALDO BETTINI.

Japan: 1 chemin el-Bakri, el-Biar, Algiers; tel. (21) 91-20-04; fax (21) 91-20-46; Ambassador URABE AKIRA.

Jordan: 47 rue Ammani Belkalem, Hydra, Algiers; tel. (21) 60-20-31; e-mail jordan@wissal.dz; Ambassador ABDULLAH EL-AYYAM.

Korea, Democratic People's Republic: Algiers; tel. (21) 62-39-27; Ambassador PAK HO IL.

Korea, Republic: BP 92, 17 chemin Abd al-Kader Gadouche, Hydra, Algiers; tel. (21) 69-36-20; fax (21) 69-16-03; Ambassador HEUNG-SIK CHOI.

Kuwait: chemin Abd al-Kader Gadouche, Hydra, Algiers; tel. (21) 59-31-57; Ambassador SHAMLAN ABD-AL-AZIZ MUHAMMAD AR-RUMI.

Lebanon: 9 rue Kaïd Ahmad, el-Biar, Algiers; tel. (21) 78-20-94; Ambassador SALHAD NASRI.

Libya: 15 chemin Cheikh Bachir Ibrahimi, Algiers; tel. (21) 92-15-02; fax (21) 92-46-87; Ambassador ABDEL-MOULA EL-GHADHBANE.

Madagascar: 22 rue Abd al-Kader Aouis, 16090 Bologhine, BP 65, Algiers; tel. (21) 95-03-89; fax (21) 95-17-76; Chargé d'affaires BAKO RAJERISONINA.

Mali: Villa 15, Cité DNC/ANP, chemin Ahmed Kara, Hydra, Algiers; tel. (21) 69-13-51; fax (21) 69-20-82; Ambassador MAHAMADOU MAG-ASSOUBA.

Mauritania: 107 Lot Baranès, Aire de France, Bouzaréah, Algiers; tel. (21) 79-21-39; fax (21) 78-42-74; Ambassador MOHAMED LEMINE OULD MOHAMED VAL dit ISSELMOU BABAMINE.

Mexico: BP 329, 25 chemin el-Bakri (ex Mackley), Ben Aknoun, 16306 Algiers; tel. (21) 91-46-00; fax (21) 91-46-01; e-mail ambassade-mexique@edomex.com; Ambassador CARLOS FERRER ARGOTE.

Morocco: 8 rue des Cèdres, el-Mouradia, Algiers; tel. (21) 69-14-08; fax (21) 69-29-00; Ambassador ABDERRAZAK DOGHMI.

Netherlands: BP 72, el-Biar, Algiers; tel. (21) 92-28-28; fax (21) 92-37-70; e-mail alg@minbuza.nl; Ambassador H. J. W. M. REVIS.

Niger: 54 rue Vercors Rostamia, Bouzaréah, Algiers; tel. (21) 78-89-21; fax (21) 78-97-13; Ambassador MOUSSA SANGARE.

Nigeria: BP 629, 27 bis rue Blaise Pascal, Algiers; tel. (21) 69-18-49; fax (21) 69-11-75; Ambassador ALIYU MOHAMMED.

Oman: BP 201, 53 rue Djamel Eddine, El Afghani, Bouzaréah, Algiers; tel. (21) 94-13-10; fax (21) 94-13-75; Ambassador HELLAL AS-SIYABI.

Pakistan: BP 404, 62A Djenane el-Malik, Le Pardou, Hydra, Algiers; tel. (21) 69-37-81; fax (21) 69-22-12; e-mail parepalgiers@gwissal.dz; Ambassador M. ASLAM RIZVI.

Poland: 37 ave Mustafa Ali Khodja, el-Biar, Algiers; tel. (21) 92-25-53; fax (21) 92-14-35; e-mail lupina@wissal.dz; Ambassador ANDRZEJ MICHAŁ LUPINA.

Portugal: 4 rue Mohamed Khoudi, el-Biar, Algiers; tel. (21) 92-53-13; fax (21) 92-54-14; e-mail portemdz@hotmail.com; Ambassador EDUARDO FARINHA FERNANDES.

Qatar: BP 118, 7 chemin Doudou Mokhtar, Algiers; tel. (21) 92-28-56; fax (21) 92-24-15; Ambassador HUSSAIN ALI ED-DOUSRI.

Romania: 24 rue Abri Arezki, Hydra, Algiers; tel. (21) 60-08-71; fax (21) 69-36-42; Ambassador DUMITRU OLARU.

Russia: 7 chemin du Prince d'Annam, el-Biar, Algiers; tel. (21) 92-31-39; fax (21) 92-28-82; Ambassador ALEKSANDR ADSENYONOK.

Saudi Arabia: 62 rue Med. Drafini, chemin de la Madeleine, Hydra, Algiers; tel. (21) 60-35-18; Ambassador HASAN FAQQI.

Senegal: BP 379, Alger-Gare, 1 chemin Mahmoud Drarnine, Hydra, Algiers; tel. (21) 54-90-90; fax (21) 54-90-94; Ambassador SAÏDOU NOUROU BA.

Serbia and Montenegro: BP 561, 7 rue des Frères Ben-hafid, Hydra, Algiers; tel. (21) 69-12-18; fax (21) 69-34-72; e-mail yuga@wissal.dz; Chargé d'affaires a.i. JOVAN DASIĆ.

Slovakia: BP 84, 7 chemin du Ziryab, Didouche Mourad, 16006 Algiers; tel. (21) 23-01-31; fax (21) 23-00-51; e-mail amb.slovaque.alger@centrum.sk; Chargé d'affaires a.i. Dr JÁN DÖMÖK.

South Africa: Sofitel Hotel, 172 rue Hassuba Ben Bouali, Algiers; tel. (21) 68-52-10; fax (21) 66-21-04.

Spain: 46 bis, rue Mohamed Chabane, BP 142, el-Biar, Algiers; tel. (21) 92-27-13; fax (21) 92-27-19; e-mail ambespdz@mail.mae.es; Ambassador JUAN BATISTA LENA.

Sudan: Algiers; tel. (21) 56-66-23; fax (21) 69-30-19; Ambassador YOUCEF FADUL AHMED.

Sweden: rue Olof Palme, Nouveau Paradou, Hydra, Algiers; tel. (21) 54-83-33; fax (21) 54-83-34; e-mail ambassaden.alger@foreign.ministry.se; Ambassador PER SALAND.

Switzerland: BP 443, Paradou, 2 rue Numéro 3, 16035 Hydra, Algiers; tel. (21) 60-04-22; fax (21) 60-98-54; Ambassador MICHEL GOTTRET.

Syria: Domaine Tamzali, 11 chemin Abd al-Kader Gadouche, Hydra, Algiers; tel. (21) 91-20-26; fax (21) 91-20-30; Ambassador HAMMADI SAID.

Tunisia: 11 rue du Bois de Boulogne, el-Mouradia, Algiers; tel. (21) 60-13-88; fax (21) 69-23-16; Ambassador MOHAMED EL FADHAL KHALIL.

Turkey: Villa dar el Ouard, chemin de la Rochelle, blvd Col Bougara, Algiers; tel. (21) 23-00-04; fax (21) 23-01-12; e-mail cezayir.be@mfa.gov.tr; Ambassador ERCÜMEND AHMET ENÇ.

Ukraine: 199 rue des Frères Belhafid, Hydra, Algiers; tel. (21) 69-13-87; fax (21) 69-48-48; e-mail ekambas@gecos.net; Ambassador MYKHAILO DASHKEVYCH.

United Arab Emirates: BP 165, Alger-Gare, 14 rue Muhammad Drarini, Hydra, Algiers; tel. (21) 69-25-74; fax (21) 69-37-70; Ambassador HAMAD SAÏD AZ-ZAABI.

United Kingdom: 7ème étage, Hotel Hilton International Alger, Pins Maritimes, Palais des Expositions, el-Muhammadia, Algiers; tel. (21) 23-00-68; fax (21) 23-00-67; internet www.britishembassy.gov.uk/algeria; Ambassador ANDREW TESORIERE (designate).

USA: BP 549, 4 chemin Cheikh Bachir Ibrahimi, 16000 Alger-Gare, Algiers; tel. (21) 60-11-86; fax (21) 60-39-79; e-mail amembalg@ist.cerist.dz; Ambassador RICHARD W. ERDMAN.

Venezuela: BP 297, 3 impasse Ahmed Kara, Algiers; tel. (21) 69-38-46; fax (21) 69-35-55; Ambassador EDUARDO SOTO ALVAREZ.

Viet Nam: 30 rue de Chenoua, Hydra, Algiers; tel. (21) 69-27-52; fax (21) 69-37-78; Ambassador TRAN XUAN MAN.

Yemen: 18 Muhammad Drarini, Hydra, Algiers; tel. (21) 54-89-50; fax (21) 54-87-40; Ambassador HAMED MUHAMMAD OBADI.

Judicial System

The highest court of justice is the Supreme Court (Cour suprême) in Algiers, established in 1963, which is served by 150 judges. Justice is exercised through 183 courts (tribunaux) and 31 appeal courts (cours d'appel), grouped on a regional basis. New legislation, promulgated in March 1997, provided for the eventual establishment of 214 courts and 48 appeal courts. The Cour des comptes was established in 1979. Algeria adopted a penal code in 1966, retaining the death penalty. In February 1993 three special courts were established to try suspects accused of terrorist offences; however, the courts were abolished in February 1995. Constitutional amendments introduced in November 1996 provided for the establishment of a High State Court (empowered to judge the President of the Republic in cases of high treason, and the Head of Government for crimes and offences), and a State Council to regulate the administrative judiciary. In addition, a Conflicts Tribunal has been established to adjudicate in disputes between the Supreme Court and the State Council.

Supreme Court
ave du 11 décembre 1960, Ben Aknoun, Algiers; tel. and fax (21) 92-44-89.

President of Supreme Court: MUHAMMAD ZAGHLOUL BOUTERENE.

Attorney-General: TAYEB BELAIZ.

Religion

ISLAM

Islam is the official religion, and the vast majority of Algerians are Muslims.

High Islamic Council
16 rue du 11 décembre 1960, Ben-Aknoun, 16030 Algiers; tel. (21) 91-54-10; e-mail hci@hci.dz; internet www.hci.dz.

President of the High Islamic Council: (vacant).

CHRISTIANITY

The European inhabitants, and a few Arabs, are generally Christians, mostly Roman Catholics.

The Roman Catholic Church

Algeria comprises one archdiocese and three dioceses (including one directly responsible to the Holy See). In December 2002 there were an estimated 4,203 adherents in the country.

Archbishop of Algiers: Most Rev. HENRI TEISSIER, 22 Chemin d'Hydra, 16030 El Biar, Algiers; tel. (21) 92-56-67; fax (21) 92-55-76; e-mail evechealger@yahoo.fr.

Protestant Church

Protestant Church of Algeria: 31 rue Reda Houhou, 16110 Alger-HBB, Algiers; tel. and fax (21) 71-62-38; e-mail egliprot@hotmail.com; 12 parishes; 3,000 mems; Pastor Dr HUGH G. JOHNSON.

The Press

DAILIES

L'Authentique: Algiers; tel. (21) 67-06-42; fax (21) 67-06-42; internet www.authentique-dz.com; French.

Ach-Cha'ab (The People): 1 place Maurice Audin, Algiers; tel. (21) 73-94-91; e-mail ech-chaab@ech-chaab.com; internet www.ech-chaab.com; f. 1962; FLN journal in Arabic; Dir KAMEL AVACHE; circ. 24,000.

La Dépêche de Kabylie: f. 2002; Dir AMARA BENYOUNES.

Al-Djeza'ir El-Ghad (Algeria of Tomorrow): Algiers; f. 1999; Arabic; Editor MUSTAPHA HACINI.

Echourouk El Yaoumi: Algiers; f. 2000; Arabic.

El-Djazair News: Algiers; f. 2003; Man. Dir H'MIDA AYACHI.

L'Expression, Le Quotidien: Maison de la Presse, Kouba, Algiers; tel. (21) 23-37-97; fax (21) 23-25-80; e-mail direction@lexpressiondz.com; internet www.lexpressiondz.com; f. 2000; French; Editor AHMED FATTANI; circ. 70,000.

El Fedjr: Algiers; tel. (21) 73-76-78; internet www.al-fadjr.com; f. 2000; Arabic.

Horizons: 20 rue de la Liberté, Algiers; tel. (21) 73-47-25; fax (21) 73-61-34; e-mail admin@horizons-dz.com; internet www.horizons-dz.com; f. 1985; evening; French; circ. 35,000.

Le Jeune Indépendant: 1 rue Bachir-Attar, place du 1er mai, 16016 Algiers; tel. (21) 67-07-48; fax (21) 67-07-46; e-mail redaction@jeune-independant.com; internet www.jeune-independant.com; f. 1990; French; circ. 60,000; Dir CHAFIK ABDI.

Al-Joumhouria (The Republic): 6 rue Bensenouci Hamida, Oran; f. 1963; Arabic; Editor BOUKHALFA BENAMEUR; circ. 20,000.

Le Journal: Algiers; f. 1992; French.

El Khabar: Maison de Presse 'Abdelkader Safir', 2 rue Farid Zouioueche, Kouba, Algiers; tel. (21) 49-53-91; fax (21) 49-53-90; e-mail admin@elkhabar.com; internet www.elkhabar.com; f. 1990; Arabic; Dir-Gen. ALI DJERRI; circ. 450,000.

Liberté: 37 rue Larbi Ben M'Hidi, BP 178, Alger-Gare, Algiers; tel. (21) 69-25-88; fax (21) 69-35-46; e-mail webmaster@liberte-algeria.com; internet www.liberte-algerie.com; French; independent; Dir-Gen. ABROUS OUTOUDERT; Editor FARID ALILET; circ. 20,000.

Al-Massa: Maison de la Presse, Abd al-Kader Safir, Kouba, Algiers; tel. (21) 59-54-19; fax (21) 59-64-57; e-mail info@el-massa.com; internet www.el-massa.com; f. 1977; evening; Arabic; circ. 45,000.

Le Matin: Maison de la Presse, 1 rue Bachir Attar, 16016 Algiers; tel. (21) 66-07-08; fax (21) 66-20-97; e-mail info@lematin-dz.com; internet www.lematin-dz.com; French; Dir MUHAMMAD BENCHICOU; publication suspended since mid-2004.

El-Moudjahid (The Fighter): 20 rue de la Liberté, Algiers; tel. (21) 73-70-81; fax (21) 73-90-43; e-mail redchef@elmoudjahid-dz.com; internet www.elmoudjahid-dz.com; f. 1965; govt journal in French and Arabic; Dir ADBELMAJID CHERBAL; circ. 392,000.

An-Nasr (The Victory): BP 388, Zone Industrielle, La Palma, Constantine; tel. (31) 93-92-16; f. 1963; Arabic; Editor ABDALLAH GUETTAT; circ. 340,000.

La Nouvelle République: Algiers; tel. and fax (21) 67-10-44; e-mail contact@lanouvellerepublique.com; internet www.lanouvellerepublique.com; French.

Ouest Tribune: Oran; e-mail redact@ouest-tribune.com; internet www.ouest-tribune.com; French.

Le Quotidien d'Oran: 63 ave de l'ANP, BP 110, Oran; tel. (41) 32-63-09; fax (41) 32-51-36; internet www.quotidien-oran.com; French.

Le Soir d'Algérie: 1 rue Bachir Attar, place du 1er mai, Algiers; tel. (21) 67-06-58; fax (21) 67-06-56; e-mail info@lesoirdalgerie.com; internet www.lesoirdalgerie.com; f. 1990; evening; independent information journal in French; Editors ZOUBIR SOUISSI, MAAMAR FARRAH; circ. 80,000.

La Tribune: Algiers; tel. (21) 68-54-21; e-mail latribune@latribune-online.com; internet www.latribune-online.com; f. 1994; current affairs journal in French; Editor BAYA GACEMI.

El Watan: Maison de la Presse, 1 rue Bachir Attar, 16016 Algiers; tel. (21) 68-21-83; fax (21) 68-21-87; e-mail admin@elwatan.com; internet www.elwatan.com; French; Dir OMAR BELHOUCHET.

El-Youm: 1 rue Bachir Attar, place du 1er mai, Algiers; tel. (21) 67-39-37; fax (21) 67-39-49; e-mail info@el-youm.com; internet www.el-youm.com; Arabic; circ. 54,000.

WEEKLIES

Algérie Actualité: 2 rue Jacques Cartier, 16000 Algiers; tel. (21) 63-54-20; f. 1965; French; Dir KAMEL BELKACEM; circ. 250,000.

Al-Hadef (The Goal): Constantine; tel. (21) 93-92-16; f. 1972; sports; French; Editor-in-Chief LARBI MOHAMED ABBOUD; circ. 110,000.

Libre Algérie: Algiers; French; organ of the FFS.

La Nation: 33 rue Larbi Ben M'hidi, Algiers; f. 1993; French; Editor SALIMA GHEZALI; circ. 35,000.

Révolution Africaine: Algiers; tel. (21) 59-77-91; fax (21) 59-77-92; current affairs journal in French; socialist; Dir FERRAH ABDELLALI; circ. 50,000.

El Wadjh al-Akhar (The Other Face): Algiers; Arabic.

OTHER PERIODICALS

Al-Acala: 4 rue Timgad, Hydra, Algiers; tel. (21) 60-85-55; fax (21) 60-09-36; f. 1970; published by the Ministry of Religious Affairs and Endowments; fortnightly; Editor MUHAMMAD AL-MAHDI.

Algérie Médicale: Algiers; f. 1964; publ. of Union médicale algérienne; 2 a year; circ. 3,000.

Alouan (Colours): 119 rue Didouche Mourad, Algiers; f. 1973; cultural review; monthly; Arabic.

Bibliographie de l'Algérie: Bibliothèque Nationale d'Algérie, BP 127, Hamma el-Annasser, 16000 Algiers; tel. (21) 67-18-67; fax (21) 67-29-99; f. 1963; lists books, theses, pamphlets and periodicals published in Algeria; 2 a year; Arabic and French; Dir-Gen. MOHAMED AÏSSA OUMOUSSA.

Ach-Cha'ab ath-Thakafi (Cultural People): Algiers; f. 1972; cultural monthly; Arabic.

Ach-Chabab (Youth): Algiers; journal of the UNJA; bi-monthly; French and Arabic.

Al-Djeich (The Army): Office de l'Armée Nationale Populaire, Algiers; f. 1963; monthly; Algerian army review; Arabic and French; circ. 10,000.

Journal Officiel de la République Algérienne Démocratique et Populaire: BP 376, Saint-Charles, Les Vergers, Bir Mourad Rais, Algiers; tel. (21) 54-35-06; fax (21) 54-35-12; f. 1962; French and Arabic.

Nouvelles Economiques: 6 blvd Amilcar Cabral, Algiers; f. 1969; publ. of Institut Algérien du Commerce Extérieur; monthly; French and Arabic.

Révolution et Travail: Maison du Peuple, 1 rue Abdelkader Benbarek, place du 1er mai, Algiers; tel. (21) 66-73-53; journal of UGTA (central trade union) with Arabic and French editions; monthly; Editor-in-Chief RACHIB AÏT ALI.

Revue Algérienne du Travail: Algiers; f. 1964; labour publication; quarterly; French.

Ath-Thakafa (Culture): 2 place Cheikh ben Badis, Algiers; tel. (21) 62-20-73; f. 1971; every 2 months; cultural review; Editor-in-Chief CHEBOUB OTHMANE; circ. 10,000.

NEWS AGENCIES

Agence Algérienne d'Information: Maison de la Presse Tahar Djaout, 1 rue Bachir Attar, place du 1er mai, Algiers; tel. (21) 67-52-34; fax (21) 67-07-32; e-mail redaction@aai-online.com; internet www.aai-online.com; f. 1999; Dir FILALI HOURIA.

Algérie Presse Service (APS): BP 444, 58 ave des Frères Bouadou, Bir Mourad Rais, 16300 Algiers; tel. (21) 56-44-44; fax (21) 56-16-08; e-mail aps@wissal.dz; internet www.aps.dz; f. 1961; provides news reports in Arabic, English and French.

Foreign Bureaux

Agence France-Presse (AFP): 6 rue Abd al-Karim el-Khettabi, Algiers; tel. (21) 72-16-54; fax (21) 72-14-89; Chief MARC PONDAVEN.

Agencia EFE (Spain): 4 ave Pasteur, 15000 Algiers; tel. (21) 71-85-59; fax (21) 74-04-56; Chief MANUEL OSTOS LÓPEZ.

Agenzia Nazionale Stampa Associata (ANSA) (Italy): 4 ave Pasteur, Algiers; tel. (21) 63-73-14; fax (21) 61-25-84; Rep. CARLO DI RENZO.

Associated Press (AP) (USA): BP 769, 4 ave Pasteur, Algiers; tel. (21) 63-59-41; fax (21) 63-59-42; Rep. RACHID KHIARI.

Informatsionnoye Telegrafnoye Agentstvo Rossii—Telegrafnoye Agentstvo Suverennykh Stran (ITAR—TASS) (Russia): 21 rue de Boulogne, Algiers; Chief Konstantin Dudarev.

Rossiiskoye Informatsionnoye Agentstvo—Novosti (RIA—Novosti) (Russia): Algiers; Chief Officer Yurii S. Bagdasarov.

Xinhua (New China) News Agency (People's Republic of China): 32 rue de Carthage, Hydra, Algiers; tel. and fax (21) 69-27-12; Chief Wang Lianzhi.

Wikalat al-Maghreb al-Arabi (Morocco), the Middle East News Agency (Egypt) and Reuters (UK) are also represented.

Publishers

Entreprise Nationale du Livre (ENAL): 3 blvd Zirout Youcef, BP 49, Algiers; tel. and fax (21) 73-58-41; f. 1966 as Société Nationale d'Edition et de Diffusion, name changed 1983; publishes books of all types, and imports, exports and distributes printed material, stationery, school and office supplies; Pres. and Dir-Gen. Hassan Bendif.

Office des Publications Universitaires: 1 place Centrale de Ben Aknoun, Algiers; tel. (21) 78-87-18; publishes university textbooks.

Broadcasting and Communications

TELECOMMUNICATIONS

New legislation approved by the National People's Assembly in August 2000 removed the state's monopoly over the telecommunications sector and redefined its role to that of a supervisory authority. Under the legislation an independent regulator for the sector was created, and both the fixed-line and mobile sectors were opened to foreign competition.

Algérie Télécom: Route Nationale 5, Cinq Maisons Muhammadia, El-Harrech, Algiers; tel. (21) 82-38-38; fax (21) 82-38-39; e-mail at@postelecom.dz; internet www.postelecom.dz; f. 2001 to manage and develop telecommunications infrastructure; privatization pending.

Autorité de Régulation de la Poste et des Télécommunications (ARPT): 1 blvd Col Krim Belkacem, 16008 Algiers; e-mail arpt@postelecom.dz; internet www.arpt.dz; f. 2001; Dir-Gen. Ahmad Gaceb.

Djezzy GSM: Orascom Telecom Algérie, Algiers; tel. (21) 54-00-53; e-mail souheila.battou@otalgerie.com; internet www.otalgerie.com; f. 2002; operates mobile cellular telephone network; Group Chair. Naguib Sawiris.

Entreprise Nationale des Télécommunications (ENTC): 1 ave du 1er novembre, Tlemcen; tel. (43) 20-76-71; fax (43) 26-39-51; f. 1978; national telecommunications org; jt venture with Sweden; Dir-Gen. Sibawaghi Saker.

BROADCASTING

Radio

Arabic Network: transmitters at Adrar, Aïn Beïda, Algiers, Béchar, Béni Abbès, Djanet, El Goléa, Ghardaia, Hassi Messaoud, In Aménas, In Salah, Laghouat, Les Trembles, Ouargla, Reggane, Tamanrasset, Timimoun, Tindouf.

French Network: transmitters at Algiers, Constantine, Oran and Tipaza.

Kabyle Network: transmitter at Algiers.

Radiodiffusion Algérienne: 21 blvd des Martyrs, Algiers; tel. (21) 69-12-81; fax (21) 23-08-23; e-mail info@algerian-radio.dz; internet www.algerian-radio.dz; govt-controlled; Dir-Gen. Abdelkader Lalmi.

Television

The principal transmitters are at Algiers, Batna, Sidi-Bel-Abbès, Constantine, Souk-Ahras and Tlemcen. Television plays a major role in the national education programme.

Télévision Algérienne (ENTV): 21 blvd des Martyrs, Algiers; tel. (21) 60-23-00; fax (21) 60-19-22; internet www.entv.dz; Dir-Gen. Hamraoui Habib Chawki.

Finance

(cap. = capital; res = reserves; dep. = deposits; brs = branches; m. = million; amounts in Algerian dinars)

BANKING

Central Bank

Banque d'Algérie: Immeuble Joly, 38 ave Franklin Roosevelt, 16000 Algiers; tel. (21) 23-00-23; fax (21) 23-03-71; e-mail ba@bank-of-algeria.dz; internet www.bank-of-algeria.dz; f. 1963 as Banque Centrale d'Algérie; present name adopted 1990; cap. 40m.; res 35,497.0m. (Apr. 2004); dep. 744,395.0m. (March 2004); bank of issue; Gov. Muhammad Laksaci; Sec.-Gen. Hallime Driss Boughida; 50 brs.

Nationalized Banks

Banque Al-Baraka d'Algérie: Haï Bouteldja Houidef, Villa no. 1, Ben Aknoun, Algiers; tel. (21) 91-64-50; fax (21) 91-64-57; e-mail info@albaraka-bank.com; internet www.albaraka-bank.com; f. 1991; cap. and res 2,177.2m., dep. 25,709.1m. (Dec. 2003); Algeria's first Islamic financial institution; owned by the Jeddah-based Al-Baraka Investment and Development Co (50%) and the local Banque de l'Agriculture et du Développement Rural (BADR) (50%); Chair. Adnane Ahmad Youcef; Gen. Man. Muhammad Seddik Hafid.

Banque Extérieure d'Algérie (BEA): 3 rue Docteur Lucien Raynaud, 16000 Algiers; tel. (21) 23-92-78; fax (21) 23-92-67; e-mail dircom@bea.dz; internet www.bea.dz; f. 1967; cap. 5,600m., res 12,417m., dep. 362,283m. (Dec. 1999); chiefly concerned with energy and maritime transport sectors; Chair. Muhammad Terbeche; Dir-Gen. Hocine Hannachi; 81 brs.

Banque du Maghreb Arabe pour l'Investissement et le Commerce: 7 rue de Bois, Hydra, Algiers; tel. (21) 59-07-60; fax (21) 59-02-30; owned by the Algerian Govt (50%) and the Libyan Govt (50%); Pres. M. Hakiki; Dir-Gen. Ibrahim al-Bishary.

Banque Nationale d'Algérie (BNA): 8 blvd Ernesto Ché Guévara, 16000 Algiers; tel. (21) 71-55-64; fax (21) 71-24-24; e-mail dg-bna@bna.com.dz; internet www.bna.com.dz; f. 1966; cap. 8,000m., res 4,624m., dep. 338,818m. (Dec. 2001); specializes in industry, transport and trade sectors; Chair. and Man. Dir Mourad Chikhi; 163 brs.

Crédit Populaire d'Algérie (CPA): BP 1031, 2 blvd Col Amirouche, 16000 Algiers; tel. (21) 63-56-84; fax (21) 63-57-13; e-mail cpadmc@gecos.net; internet www.cpa-bank.com; f. 1966; cap. 21,600m., total assets 342,045m. (Dec. 2000); specializes in light industry, construction and tourism; partial privatization pending; Chair. El Hachemi Meghaoui; Dir-Gen. Ferhat Saouili; 121 brs.

Development Banks

Banque de l'Agriculture et du Développement Rural (BADR): 17 blvd Col Amirouche, 16000 Algiers; tel. (21) 63-49-22; fax (21) 63-51-46; internet www.badr.dz; f. 1982; cap. 33,000m., res 1,719m., dep. 414,338m. (Dec. 2002); finance for the agricultural sector; Chair. and Man. Dir Farouk Bouyakoub; 270 brs.

Banque Algérienne de Développement (BAD): Lot Mont-Froid, Zonka, Birkhadem, BP 36, 13336 Algiers; tel. (21) 55-22-89; fax (21) 55-48-63; e-mail bad@ist.cerist.dz; f. 1963; cap. 100m., total assets 152,082.0m. (Dec. 1999); a public establishment with fiscal sovereignty; aims to contribute to Algerian economic devt through long-term investment programmes; Chair. and Dir-Gen. Sadek Alilat; 4 brs.

Banque de Développement Local (BDL): 5 rue Gaci Amar, Staouéli, Algiers; tel. (21) 39-37-55; fax (21) 39-37-57; f. 1985; regional devt bank; cap. 7,140m., dep. 108,708m. (2000); Pres. and Dir-Gen. Amar Daoudi; 15 brs.

Caisse Nationale d'Epargne et de Prévoyance (CNEP): 42 blvd Khélifa Boukhalfa, Algiers; tel. (21) 71-33-53; fax (21) 71-41-31; f. 1964; total assets 206,915.8m. (Dec. 1992); savings and housing bank; Pres. and Dir-Gen. Abdelkrim Naas.

Private Banks

Arab Algérie Leasing: Algiers; f. 2001.

Banque Commerciale et Industrielle d'Algérie (BCIA): 4 chemin Doudou Mokhtar, Ben Aknoun, 16030 Algiers; tel. (21) 91-30-06; fax (21) 91-17-13; internet www.bciabank.com; f. 1998; cap. and res 804.8m., dep. 6,161.0m.; Pres. Ahmed Kherroubi; Chair. Muhammad Ali Kherroubi; Gen. Man. Badreddine Kherroubi.

BNP Paribas El-Djazair: 10 rue Abou Nouass, Hydra, Algiers; tel. (21) 60-39-42; fax (21) 60-39-29; f. 2001; cap 500m.; Chair. Fathi Mestiri; Man. Dir Jean-François Chazu.

EFG Hermes SPA: Algiers; f. 2000.

El-Khalifa Bank: 61 Lot Ben Haddadi, Dar Diaf, Chéraga, 16800 Algiers; tel. (21) 36-97-70; fax (21) 36-98-04; e-mail ek_bank@ist .cerist.dz; internet www.elkhalifbank.com; f. 1998; cap. 125m., total assets 11,659.4m. (Dec. 1999); placed in administration in 2003; Pres. RAFIK ABDELMOUMENE KHELIFA.

El-Mouna Bank: 22 rue Boudjellad Ahmad Hai el-Moudjahidine, Oran; tel. (41) 41-15-90; fax (41) 41-18-08; f. 1998; cap. 260m.; Pres. AHMED BENSADOUN.

Al-Rayan Algerian Bank: 29 rue Ahmad Kara, Bir Mourad Rais, Algiers; tel. (21) 44-99-00; fax (21) 44-96-40; e-mail info@ alrayan-bank.com; internet www.alrayan-bank.com; f. 2000; cap. 1,700m., dep. 2,500m.; Chair. HAZIM EL KARAKI; Dir-Gen. MADJID DASSOU; 5 brs.

Trust Bank: Algiers; f. 2001.

Union Bank: 5 bis chemin Mackley, el-Biar, 16030 Algiers; tel. (21) 91-45-49; fax (21) 91-45-48; internet www.ub-alger.com; f. 1995; cap. 250m., total assets 1,591m. (Dec. 1997); principal shareholder Brahim Hadjas; Pres. SELIM BENATA.

Foreign Banks

Arab Banking Corpn (Bahrain): 54 ave des Trois Frères Bouaddou, BP 367, Bir Mourad Rais, Algiers; tel. (21) 54-15-15; fax (21) 54-16-04; e-mail abc.general_management@arabbanking.com .dz; internet www.arabbanking.dz; f. 1998; cap. 2,670.0m., res 376.4m., dep. 16,325.7m. (Dec. 2002); Chair. ABDULAMAGID BREISH; Dir-Gen. REIDHA SLIMANE TALEB.

Natexis Algérie (France): 62 chemin Muhammad Drareni, 16035 Hydra, Algiers; tel. (21) 54-91-85; fax (21) 54-91-99; e-mail hocine .mouffok@dz.nxbp.com; f. 1999; owned by Natexis Banques Populaires; Man. Dir HOCINE MOUFFOK.

STOCK EXCHANGE
The Algiers Stock Exchange began trading in July 1999.

Commission d'Organisation et de Surveillance des Opérations de Bourse (COSOB): Algiers; tel. (21) 71-27-25; fax (21) 71-21-98; e-mail infos@cosob.com.dz; internet www.cosob.com.dz; Chair. BELKACEM IRATNI; Gen. Sec. ABDELHAKIM BERRAH.

INSURANCE
Insurance is a state monopoly; however, in 1997 regulations were drafted to permit private companies to enter the Algerian insurance market.

Caisse Nationale de Mutualité Agricole: 24 blvd Victor Hugo, Algiers; tel. (21) 73-46-31; fax (21) 73-34-79; f. 1972; Dir-Gen. YAHIA CHERIF BRAHIM; 47 brs.

Cie Algérienne d'Assurance et de Réassurance (CAAR): 48 rue Didouche Mourad, 16000 Algiers; tel. (21) 72-71-90; fax (21) 72-71-97; e-mail caaralg@caar.com.dz; internet www.caar.com.dz; f. 1963 as a public corpn; partial privatization pending; Pres. ALI DJENDI.

Cie Centrale de Réassurance (CCR): Lot No 1, Saïd Hamdine, Bir Mourad Rais, 16409 Algiers; tel. (21) 54-69-33; fax (21) 54-74-99; e-mail ccr@wissal.dz; internet www.ccr-dz.com; f. 1973; general; Pres. and Dir-Gen. DJAMEL-EDDINE CHOUAÏB CHOUITER.

Société Nationale d'Assurances (SNA): 5 blvd Ernesto Ché Guévara, Algiers; tel. (21) 71-47-60; fax (21) 71-22-16; f. 1963; state-sponsored co; Pres. KACI AISSA SLIMANE; Chair. and Gen. Man. LATROUS AMARQ.

Trust Algeria Assurances-Réassurance: 70 chemin Larbi Allik, Hydra, Algiers; tel. (21) 54-89-00; fax (21) 54-71-36; e-mail trustalgeria@ifrance.com; internet www.trust-algeriainfo.com; f. 1987; 60% owned by Trust Insurance Co (Bahrain), 17.5% owned by CAAR; Gen. Man. HORRI MUHAMMAD BOUZIANE.

Trade and Industry

GOVERNMENT AGENCIES

Centre Algérien pour la Promotion des Investissements (CALPI): Algiers; f. 1994 to promote investment; offices in the 48 administrative districts.

Conseil National des Participations de L'Etat (CNPE): Algiers; supervises state holdings; participants include the Prime Minister and reps of 16 govt ministries; Sec.-Gen. AHMED EL-ANTRI TIBAOUI.

DEVELOPMENT ORGANIZATIONS

Agence Nationale pour l'Aménagement du Territoire (ANAT): 30 ave Muhammad Fellah, Algiers; tel. (21) 58-48-12; fax (21) 68-85-03; f. 1980; Pres. and Dir-Gen. KOUIDER DJEBLI.

Engineering Environment Consult (EEC): BP 395, Alger-Gare, 50 rue Khélifa Boukhalfa, Algiers; tel. (21) 23-64-86; fax (21) 23-72-49; e-mail eec@wissal.dz; internet www.eec.com; f. 1982; Dir-Gen. MUHAMMAD BENTIR.

Institut National de la Production et du Développement Industriel (INPED): 126 rue Didouche Mourad, Boumerdès; tel. (21) 41-52-50.

Office Algérien de Promotion du Commerce Extérieur (PROMEX): RN 5, Muhammadia, Algiers; tel. (21) 52-20-82; fax (21) 52-11-26; e-mail promex@wissal.dz; internet www.promex.com .dz.

Office National de Recherche Géologique et Minière (ORGM): BP 102, Cité Ibn Khaldoun, 35000 Boumerdès; tel. (24) 81-75-99; fax (24) 81-83-79; e-mail orgm@wissal.dz; internet www.orgm .dz; f. 1992; mining, cartography, geophysical exploration.

CHAMBERS OF COMMERCE

Chambre Française de Commerce et d'Industrie en Algérie (CFCIA): Villa Clarac, 3 rue des Cèdres, 16070 Algiers; tel. (21) 48-08-00; fax (21) 60-95-09; e-mail cfcia@cfcia.org; internet www.cfcia .org; f. 1965; Pres. MICHEL DE CAFFARELLI; Dir JEAN-FRANÇOIS HEUGAS.

Chambre Algérienne de Commerce et d'Industrie (CACI): BP 100, Palais Consulaire, 6 blvd Amilcar Cabral C.P., 16003 Algiers; tel. (21) 96-66-66; fax (21) 96-70-70; e-mail caci@wissal.dz; internet www.caci.com.dz; f. 1980; Dir-Gen. MUHAMMAD CHAMI.

INDUSTRIAL AND TRADE ASSOCIATIONS

Centre d'Etudes et de Services Technologiques de l'Industrie des matériaux de Construction: Cité Ibn Khaldoun, BP 93, 35000 Boumerdès; tel. (24) 81-67-78; fax (24) 81-72-98; e-mail cetim@wissal.dz; f. 1982; Pres. and Dir-Gen. A. ADJTOUTAH.

Centre National des Textiles et Cuirs (CNTC): BP 65, route du Marché, Boumerdès; tel. (21) 81-13-23; fax (21) 81-13-57.

Entreprise Nationale de Développement des Industries Alimentaires (ENIAL): RN 5, 16110 Bab Ezzouar, Algiers; tel. (21) 76-21-06; fax (21) 75-77-65; f. 1982; Dir-Gen. ARESKI LAKABI.

Entreprise Nationale de Développement des Industries Manufacturières (ENEDIM): 22 rue des Fusillés, El Anasser, Algiers; tel. (21) 68-13-43; fax (21) 67-55-26; f. 1983; Dir-Gen. FODIL.

Institut National Algérien de la Propriété Industrielle (INAPI): 42 rue Larbi Ben M'hidi, 16000 Algiers; tel. (21) 73-01-42; fax (21) 73-55-81; e-mail info@inapi.org; internet www.inapi.org; f. 1973; Dir-Gen. M. BOUHNIK AMOR.

Institut National Algérien du Commerce Extérieur (COMEX): 6 blvd Anatole-France, Algiers; tel. (21) 62-70-44; Dir-Gen. SAAD ZERHOUNI.

Institut National des Industries Manufacturières (INIM): 35000 Boumerdès; tel. (21) 81-62-71; fax (21) 82-56-62; f. 1973; Dir-Gen. HOCINE HASSISSI.

Société d'Etudes et de Réalisation pour la Construction Industrialisée du Logement (SERCIL): BP 51, 3 ave Col Driant, 55102 Verdun, France; tel. 29-86-27-26; fax 29-86-20-51; e-mail sercil@wanadoo.fr; Dir JEAN MOULET.

State Trading Organizations

Since 1970 all international trading has been carried out by state organizations, of which the following are the most important:

Entreprise Nationale d'Approvisionnement en Bois et Dérivés (ENAB): BP 166, Alger-Gare, 2 blvd Muhammad V, Algiers; tel. (21) 63-75-35; fax (21) 63-77-17; e-mail info@enab-dz .com; internet www.enab-dz.com; import and distribution of wood and derivatives and other building materials; Dirs OMAR BENOU-NICHE, OMAR SADAOUI, SMAÏL AR-ROBRINI.

Entreprise Nationale d'Approvisionnement en Outillage et Produits de Quincaillerie Générale (ENAOQ): 5 rue Amar Semaous, Hussein-Dey, Algiers; tel. (21) 23-31-83; fax (21) 47-83-33; tools and general hardware; Dir-Gen. SMATI BAHIDJ FARID.

Entreprise Nationale d'Approvisionnements en Produits Alimentaires (ENAPAL): Algiers; tel. (21) 76-10-11; f. 1983; monopoly of import, export and bulk trade in basic foodstuffs; brs in more than 40 towns; Chair. LAID SABRI; Man. Dir BRAHIM DOUAOURI.

Entreprise Nationale d'Approvisionnement et de Régulation en Fruits et Légumes (ENAFLA): BP 42, 12 ave des Trois Frères Bouadou, Bir Mourad Rais, Algiers; tel. (21) 54-10-10; fax (21) 56-79-59; f. 1983; division of the Ministry of Commerce; fruit and vegetable marketing, production and export; Man. Dir REDHA KHELEF.

Entreprise Nationale de Commerce: 6–9 rue Belhaffat-Ghazali, Hussein-Dey, Algiers; tel. (21) 77-43-20; Dir-Gen. MUHAMMAD LAÏD BELARBIA.

Office Algérien Interprofessionel des Céréales (OAIC): 5 rue Ferhat-Boussaad, Algiers; tel. (21) 73-26-01; fax (21) 73-22-11; f. 1962; monopoly of trade in wheat, rice, maize, barley and products derived from these cereals; Gen. Man. LAÏD TALAMALI.

Office National de la Commercialisation des Produits Viti-Vinicoles (ONCV): 112 Quai-Sud, Algiers; tel. (21) 73-72-75; fax (21) 73-72-97; e-mail info@oncv-dz.com; internet www.oncv-dz.com; f. 1968; monopoly of importing and exporting products of the wine industry; Man. Dir SAÏD MEBARKI.

Société des Emballages Fer Blanc et Fûts: BP 245, Kouba, Route de Baraki, Gué de Constantine, Algiers; tel. (21) 89-94-23; fax (21) 83-05-29; e-mail sid_266@caramail.com; Dir-Gen. MOURAD BELHADJ.

UTILITIES

Commission de Régulation de l'Electricité et du Gaz: Algiers; f. 2002; regulatory authority.

Société Algérienne de l'Electricité et du Gaz (Sonelgaz Spa): 2 blvd Col Krim Belkacem, Algiers; tel. (21) 72-31-00; fax (21) 71-31-61; internet www.sonelgaz.dz; f. 1969; production, distribution and transportation of electricity and transportation and distribution of natural gas; Chair. and CEO NOUREDDINE BOUTARFA.

Electricity

Entreprise de Travaux d'Electrification (KAHRIF): Villa Malwall, Ain d'Heb, Médéa; tel. (25) 50-26-96; fax (25) 58-31-14; e-mail kahrif@ixiissal.dz; f. 1982; study of electrical infrastructure; Pres. and Dir-Gen. HOCINE RAHMANI.

Gas

Entreprise Nationale de Production et de Distribution des Gaz Industriels (ENGI): 23 route de l'ALN, 16040 Hussein-Dey, Algiers; tel. (21) 49-85-99; fax (21) 49-71-94; e-mail boucherit@usa.net; internet www.gaz-ind.com; f. 1972; production and distribution of gas; Gen. Man. LAHOCINE BOUCHERIT.

Water

Agence Nationale de l'Eau Potable et Industrielle et de l'Assainissement (AGEP): rue Chemseddine Hafid-Kouba, 16000 Algiers; tel. (21) 28-30-96; fax (21) 28-30-33; f. 1985; state water co.

STATE HYDROCARBONS COMPANIES

Société Nationale pour la Recherche, la Production, le Transport, la Transformation et la Commercialisation des Hydrocarbures (SONATRACH): 10 rue du Sahara, Hydra, Algiers; tel. (21) 54-70-00; fax (21) 54-77-00; e-mail sonatrach@sonatrach.dz; internet www.sonatrach-dz.com; f. 1963; exploration, exploitation, transport and marketing of petroleum, natural gas and their products; Chair. MUHAMMAD MEZIANE; Vice-Pres ALI HACHED (Marketing), ABDELHADI ZERGUINE (Transport), BACHIR ACHOUR (Liquefaction).

Since 1980 the following associated companies have shared SONATRACH's functions:

Entreprise Nationale de Canalisation (ENAC): Muhammadia, rue Benyoucef Khattab, El Harrach, Algiers; tel. (21) 53-85-49; fax (21) 53-85-53; piping; Dir-Gen. RACHID HAMADOU.

Entreprise Nationale d'Engineering Pétrolier (ENEP): 2 blvd Muhammad V, Algiers; tel. (21) 64-08-37; fax (21) 63-71-83; design and construction for petroleum-processing industry; Gen. Man. MUSTAPHA MEKIDECHE.

Entreprise Nationale de Forage (ENAFOR): BP 211, 30500 Hassi Messaoud, Algiers; tel. (21) 73-71-35; fax (21) 73-22-60; drilling; Dir-Gen. ABD AR-RACHID ROUABAH.

Entreprise Nationale des Grands Travaux Pétroliers (ENGTP): BP 09, Zone industrielle, Reghaïa, Boumerdès; tel. (24) 80-06-80; fax (24) 85-14-70; f. 1980; major industrial projects; Dir-Gen. B. DRIAD.

Entreprise Nationale des Services aux Puits (ENSP): BP 83, 30500 Hassi Messaoud, Ouargla; tel. (29) 73-73-33; fax (29) 73-82-01; e-mail info@enspgroup.com; internet www.enspgroup.com; f. 1970; oil-well services; Dir-Gen. ABDELHAK ZIADA.

Entreprise Nationale des Travaux aux Puits (ENTP): BP 206, 30500 Hassi Messaoud, Ouargla; tel. (29) 73-87-78; fax (29) 73-84-06; f. 1981; oil-well construction; Dir-Gen. ABD AL-AZIZ KRISSAT.

Groupe Industriel des Plastiques & Caoutchoucs: BP 452–453, Zone industrielle, 19000 Sétif; tel. (36) 90-75-45; fax (36) 93-05-65; e-mail grenpc@wissal.dz; internet www.grenpc.com; f. 1967; production and marketing of rubber and plastics products; Dir-Gen. BELKACEM SAMAI.

Société Nationale de Commercialisation et de Distribution des Produits Pétroliers (NAFTAL, SpA): BP 73, route des Dûnes, Chéraga, Algiers; tel. (21) 38-13-13; fax (21) 38-19-19; e-mail nas-div-bp@wissal.dz; internet www.naftal.dz; f. 1987; international marketing and distribution of petroleum products; Gen. Man. NOUREDDINE CHEROUATI.

Société Nationale de Génie Civil et Bâtiments (CGB): BP 23, route de Corso, Boudouaou, Algiers; tel. (21) 84-65-26; fax (21) 84-60-09; civil engineering; Dir-Gen. ABD AL-HAMID ZERGUINE.

TRADE UNIONS

Union Générale des Travailleurs Algériens (UGTA): Maison du Peuple, place du 1er mai, Algiers; tel. (21) 65-07-36; e-mail relex_ugta@hotmail.com; f. 1956; Sec.-Gen. ABDELMADJID SIDI SAID.

There are 10 national 'professional sectors' affiliated to the UGTA:

Secteur Alimentation, Commerce et Tourisme (Food, Commerce and Tourist Industry Workers): Gen. Sec. ABD AL-KADER GHRIBLI.

Secteur Bois, Bâtiments et Travaux Publics (Building Trades Workers): Gen. Sec. LAIFA LATRECHE.

Secteur Education et Formation Professionnelle (Teachers): Gen. Sec. SAÏDI BEN GANA.

Secteur Energie et Pétrochimie (Energy and Petrochemical Workers): Gen. Sec. ALI BELHOUCHET.

Secteur Finances (Financial Workers): Gen. Sec. MUHAMMAD ZAAF.

Secteur Information, Formation et Culture (Information, Training and Culture).

Secteur Industries Légères (Light Industry): Gen. Sec. ABD AL-KADER MALKI.

Secteur Industries Lourdes (Heavy Industry).

Secteur Santé et Sécurité Sociale (Health and Social Security Workers): Gen. Sec. ABD AL-AZIZ DJEFFAL.

Secteur Transports et Télécommunications (Transport and Telecommunications Workers): Gen. Sec. EL-HACHEMI BEN MOUHOUB.

Al-Haraka al-Islamiyah lil-Ummal al-Jazarivia (Islamic Movement for Algerian Workers): Tlemcen; f. 1990; based on teachings of Islamic faith and affiliated to the FIS.

Ittahad as-Sahafiyin al-Jaza'iriyin (Algerian Journalists Union): Algiers; f. 2001.

Union Nationale des Paysans Algériens (UNPA): f. 1973; 700,000 mems; Sec.-Gen. AÏSSA NEDJEM.

Transport

RAILWAYS

Entreprise Métro d'Alger: 4 chemin de Wilaya 13, Kouba, Algiers; tel. (21) 28-94-64; fax (21) 28-01-83; construction of a 26.5-km metro railway line began in 1991; initial 12.5-km section (16 stations) scheduled to open in two stages, starting in 2006; Dir-Gen. A. MERKEBI.

Infrafer (Entreprise Publique Economique de Réalisation des Infrastructures Ferroviaires): BP 208, 35300 Rouiba; tel. (21) 85-64-13; fax (21) 85-59-05; e-mail mkt_com2002@yahoo.fr; internet www.infrafer.com; f. 1987; responsible for construction and maintenance of track; Man. Dir SAIDI HASSANE.

Société Nationale des Transports Ferroviaires (SNTF): 21–23 blvd Muhammad V, Algiers; tel. (21) 71-15-10; fax (21) 63–32–98; e-mail dg-sntf@sntf.dz; internet www.sntf.dz; f. 1976 to replace Société Nationale des Chemins de Fer Algériens; 5,090 km of track, of which 289 km are electrified; daily passenger services from Algiers to the principal provincial cities and services to Tunisia and Morocco; Dir-Gen. ABD AL-ADIM BENALLEGUE.

ROADS

In 1996 there were an estimated 104,000 km of roads and tracks, of which 640 km were motorways, 25,200 km were main roads and 23,900 km were secondary roads. The French administration built a good road system (partly for military purposes), which, since independence, has been allowed to deteriorate in places. New roads have been built linking the Sahara oil fields with the coast, and the Trans-Sahara highway is a major project. In 1996 it was estimated that the cost of renovating the national road system would amount to US $4,124m.

Société Nationale des Transports Routiers (SNTR): 27 rue des Trois Frères Bouadou, Bir Mourad Rais, Algiers; tel. (21) 54-06-00; fax (21) 54-05-35; e-mail dg-sntr@sntr-groupe.com; internet www.sntr-groupe.com; f. 1967; goods transport by road; maintainance of industrial vehicles; Pres. and Dir-Gen. ABDALLAH BENMAAROUF.

Société Nationale des Transports des Voyageurs (SNTV): Algiers; tel. (21) 66-00-52; f. 1967; holds monopoly of long-distance passenger transport by road; Man. Dir M. DIB.

SHIPPING

Algiers is the main port, with anchorage of between 23 m and 29 m in the Bay of Algiers, and anchorage for the largest vessels in Agha Bay. The port has a total quay length of 8,380 m and is expected to be able to handle 250,000 containers per year by 2005. There are also important ports at Annaba, Arzew, Béjaia, Djidjelli, Ghazaouet, Mostaganem, Oran, Skikda and Ténès. Petroleum and liquefied gas are exported through Arzew, Béjaia and Skikda. Algerian crude petroleum is also exported through the Tunisian port of La Skhirra. In December 2003 Algeria's merchant fleet totalled 137 vessels, with an aggregate displacement of 872,028 grt.

Cie Algéro-Libyenne de Transports Maritimes (CALTRAM): 19 rue des Trois Frères Bouadou, Bir Mourad Rais, Algiers; tel. (21) 57-17-00; fax (21) 54-21-04; e-mail caltram@wissal.dz; f. 1974; Man. Dir A. KERAMANE.

Entreprise Nationale de Réparation Navale (ERENAV): quai no. 12, Algiers; tel. (21) 42-37-83; fax (21) 42-30-39; internet www.erenav.com.dz; f. 1987; ship repairs; Pres. and Dir-Gen. REGAINIA GHAZI.

Entreprise Nationale de Transport Maritime de Voyageurs—Algérie Ferries (ENTMV): BP 467, 5–6 rue Jawharlal Nehru, 16001 Algiers; tel. (21) 74-04-85; fax (21) 64-88-76; e-mail entmv@algerieferries.com; f. 1987 as part of restructuring of SNTM-CNAN; responsible for passenger transport; operates car ferry services between Algiers, Annaba, Skikda, Alicante (Spain), Marseille (France) and Oran; Dir-Gen. BOUDJEMA CHERIET.

Entreprise Portuaire d'Alger (EPAL): BP 16, 2 rue d'Angkor, Alger-Gare, Algiers; tel. (21) 71-54-39; fax (21) 71-54-52; e-mail portalg@ist.cerist.dz; internet www.portalger.com.dz; f. 1982; responsible for management and growth of port facilities and sea pilotage; Dir-Gen. ALI FERRAH.

Entreprise Portuaire d'Annaba (EPAN): BP 1232, Môle Cigogne-Quai nord, Annaba; tel. (38) 86-31-31; fax (38) 86-54-15; e-mail epan@annaba-port.com; internet www.annaba-port.com; Man. Dir DJILANI SALHI.

Entreprise Portuaire d'Arzew (EPA): BP 46, 7 rue Larbi Tebessi, Arzew; tel. (41) 37-24-91; fax (41) 47-49-90; Man. Dir CHAIB OUMER.

Entreprise Portuaire de Béjaia (EPB): 13 ave des Frères Amrani, BP 94, 06000 Béjaia; tel. (34) 21-18-07; fax (34) 22-03-46; e-mail portbj@wissal.dz; internet www.portdebejaia.com.dz; Pres. and Dir-Gen. A. BOUMESILLA.

Entreprise Portuaire de Djen-Djen (EPJ): BP 87,18000 Jijel; tel. (34) 44-65-64; fax (34) 44-52-60; e-mail epjdjendjen@wissal.dz; internet www.djendjen-port.com.dz; f. 1984; Pres. and CEO MUHAMMAD ATMANE.

Entreprise Portuaire de Ghazaouet (EPG): BP 217, 13400 Ghazaouet; tel. (43) 32-32-37; fax (43) 32-32-55; e-mail contact@portdeghazaouet.com; internet www.portdeghazaouet.com; f. 1982; Gen. Man. ABDELMALEK BRAHIM.

Entreprise Portuaire de Mostaganem (EPM): BP 131, quai du Port, Mostaganem; tel. (45) 21-14-11; fax (45) 21-78-05; Dir-Gen. M. LAKEHAL.

Entreprise Portuaire d'Oran (EPO): 1 rue du 20 août, 31000 Oran; tel. (41) 33-24-41; fax (41) 33-24-98; e-mail webmaster@oran-port.com; internet www.oran-port.com; Chair. and Dir Gen. M. S. LOUHIBI.

Entreprise Portuaire de Skikda (EPS): BP 65, 46 ave Rezki Rahal, Skikda; tel. (38) 75-68-50; fax (38) 75-20-15; e-mail info@skikda-port.com; internet skikda-port.com; Man. Dir M. LEMRABET.

Entreprise Portuaire de Ténès (EPT): BP 18, 02200 Ténès; tel. (27) 76-65-89; fax (27) 76-61-77; e-mail caporttenes@yahoo.fr; Man. Dir K. EL-HAMRI.

NAFTAL Division Aviation Marine: BP 70, Aéroport Houari Boumedienne, Dar-el-Beïda, Algiers; tel. (21) 50-95-50; fax (21) 50-67-09; e-mail avm@ist.cerist.dz; Dir MESNOUS NOUREDDINE.

Société Générale Maritime (GEMA): 2 rue J. Nehru, Algiers; tel. (21) 74-73-00; fax (21) 74-76-73; e-mail gemasie@gema-groupe.com; internet www.gema-groupe.com; f. 1987 as part of restructuring of SNTM-CNAN; shipping, ship-handling and forwarding; Dir-Gen. BELKADI BOUALEM.

Société Nationale de Transport Maritime et Cie Nationale Algérienne de Navigation (SNTM-CNAN): BP 280, 2 quai no. 9, Nouvelle Gare Maritime, Algiers; tel. (21) 71-14-78; fax (21) 73-02-33; f. 1963; state-owned co which owns and operates fleet of freight ships; rep. office in Marseille (France) and rep. agencies in Antwerp (Belgium), Valencia (Spain) and the principal ports in many other countries; Gen. Man. ABDELHAMID KARA.

Société Nationale de Transports Maritimes des Hydrocarbures et des Produits Chimiques (SNTM-HYPROC): BP 60, Arzew, 31200 Oran; tel. (41) 47-48-55; fax (41) 47-34-45; e-mail hyproc@hyproc.com; internet www.hyproc.com; f. 1982; Pres. and Dir-Gen. MUSTAPHA ZENASNI.

CIVIL AVIATION

Algeria's principal international airport, Houari Boumedienne, is situated 20 km from Algiers. At Constantine, Annaba, Tlemcen and Oran there are also airports that meet international requirements. There are, in addition, 65 aerodromes, of which 20 are public, and a further 135 airstrips connected with the petroleum industry.

Air Algérie (Entreprise Nationale d'Exploitation des Services Aériens): BP 858, 1 place Maurice Audin, Immeuble el-Djazair, Algiers; tel. (21) 74-24-28; fax (21) 61-05-53; e-mail contact@airalgerie.dz; internet www.airalgerie.dz; f. 1953 by merger; state-owned from 1972; partial privatization pending; internal services and extensive services to Europe, North and West Africa, and the Middle East; Chair. and Dir-Gen. TAYEB BENOUIS; Sec.-Gen. NOUREDDINE BEZAOUCHA.

Desert Aviation Co: Touggourt; f. 1999; private co; internal flights; Exec. Dir CHOKRI MIAADI.

Ecoair International: 12 rue Branly, El Mouradia, Algiers; tel. (21) 69-82-00; f. 1998; private co operating domestic and international passenger flights to Europe and North Africa.

Saharan Airlines: BP 65 Cité Ezzahra, Touggourt; tel. (29) 68-31-91; fax (29) 68-13-12; e-mail shddz@yahoo.fr; f. 1999; domestic and international passenger services; CEO MIADI CHOUKRI.

Tassili Airlines: blvd Mustapha Ben Boulaid, 301 Hassi Messaoud; tel. (29) 73-84-25; fax (29) 73-84-24; f. 1997; jt venture between SONATRACH and Air Algérie; domestic passenger services.

Tourism

Algeria's tourist attractions include the Mediterranean coast, the Atlas mountains and the desert. In 2002 a total of 988,060 tourists visited Algeria, compared with 901,446 in 2001. Receipts from tourism totalled US $133m. in 2002.

Agence Nationale de Développement Touristique (ANDT): BP 151, Sidi Fredj Staoueli, Algiers; tourism promotion; Dir-Gen. ABDELKRIM BOUCETTA.

Office National du Tourisme (ONT): 2 rue Ismail Kerrar, Algiers; tel. (21) 71-30-60; fax (21) 71-30-59; e-mail ont@wissal.dz; internet www.ont.dz; f. 1988; state institution; oversees tourism promotion policy; Dir-Gen. ABDELAADI TIR.

ONAT-TOUR (Opérateur National Algérien de Tourisme): 126 bis A, rue Didouche Mourod, 16000 Algiers; tel. (21) 74-44-48; fax (21) 74-32-14; e-mail onat@onat-dz.com; internet www.onat-dz.com; f. 1962; Dir-Gen. BELKACEMI HAMMOUCHE.

Société de Développement de l'Industrie Touristique en Algérie (SODITAL): 72 rue Asselah Hocine, Algiers; f. 1989; Dir-Gen. NOUREDDINE SALHI.

Touring Club d'Algérie (TCA): 30 rue Hassène Benaâmane, Les Vergers, Bir Mourad Raïs, Algiers; tel. (21) 54-13-13; fax (21) 44-68-29; f. 1963; Pres. ABDERRAHMANE ABDEDAIM.

ANDORRA

Introductory Survey

Location, Climate, Language, Religion, Flag, Capital

The Principality of Andorra lies in the eastern Pyrenees, bounded by France and Spain, and is situated roughly midway between Barcelona and Toulouse. The climate is alpine, with much snow in winter and a warm summer. The official language is Catalan, but French and Spanish are also widely spoken. Most of the inhabitants profess Christianity, and about 94% are Roman Catholics. The civil flag (proportions 2 by 3) has three equal vertical stripes, of blue, yellow and red. The state flag has, in addition, the state coat of arms (a quartered shield above the motto *Virtus unita fortior*) in the centre of the yellow stripe. The capital is Andorra la Vella.

Recent History

Owing to the lack of distinction between the authority of the Consell General (General Council) of Andorra and the Co-Princes (Coprínceps—the President of France and the Spanish Bishop of Urgel) who have ruled the country since 1278, the Andorrans encountered many difficulties in their attempts to gain international status for their country and control over its essential services.

Until 1970 the franchise was granted only to third-generation Andorran males who were more than 25 years of age. Thereafter, women, persons aged between 21 and 25, and second-generation Andorrans were allowed to vote in elections to the Consell General. In 1977 the franchise was extended to include all first-generation Andorrans of foreign parentage who were aged 28 and over. The electorate remained small, however, when compared with the size of the population, and Andorra's foreign residents increased their demands for political and nationality rights. In December 2003 foreign residents comprised 63.3% of the total population. Immigration is on a quota system, being restricted primarily to French and Spanish nationals intending to work in Andorra.

Prior to 1993, political parties were not directly represented in the Consell General, but there were loose groupings with liberal and conservative sympathies. The country's only political organization, the Partit Democràtic d'Andorra (Andorran Democratic Party—PDA), was technically illegal, and in the 1981 elections to the Consell General the party urged its supporters to cast blank votes.

In 1980, during discussions on institutional reform, representatives of the Co-Princes and the Consell General agreed that an executive council should be formed, and that a referendum should be held on changes to the electoral system. In early 1981 the Co-Princes formally requested the Consell General to prepare plans for reform, in accordance with these proposals. Following the December elections to the Consell General, in January 1982 the new legislature elected Oscar Ribas Reig as Head of Government (Cap de Govern). Ribas Reig appointed an executive of six ministers, who expressed their determination to provide Andorra with a written constitution. The formation of the executive body, known as the Govern, constituted the separation of powers between an executive and a legislature, and represented an important step towards institutional reform.

Severe storm damage in November 1982, and the general effects of the world-wide economic recession, led to a controversial vote by the Consell General, in August 1983, in favour of the introduction of income tax, in an effort to alleviate Andorra's budgetary deficit and to provide the Government with extra revenue for development projects. Subsequent government proposals for an indirect tax on bank deposits, hotel rooms and property sales encountered strong opposition from financial and tourism concerns, and prompted the resignation of the Government in April 1984. Josep Pintat Solans, a local business executive, was elected unopposed by the Consell General as Head of Government in May. In August, however, the Ministers of Finance and of Industry, Commerce and Agriculture resigned, following disagreements concerning the failure to implement economic reforms (including the introduction of income tax).

At the December 1985 elections to the Consell General the electorate was increased by about 27%, as a result of the newly introduced lower minimum voting age of 18 years. The Council re-elected Pintat Solans as Head of Government in January 1986, when he won the support of 27 of its 28 members.

In September 1986 President François Mitterrand of France and the Bishop of Urgel, Dr Joan Martí Alanís (respectively the French and Spanish Co-Princes), met in Andorra to discuss the principality's status in relation to the European Community (EC—now known as the European Union—EU, see p. 217), as well as the question of free exchange of goods between the members of the EC and Andorra, following Spain's admission to the Community in January of that year.

In April 1987 the Consejo Sindical Interregional Pirineos-Mediterráneo, a collective of French and Spanish trade unions, in conjunction with the Andorran Asociación de Residentes Andorranos, began to claim rights, including those of freedom of expression and association and the right to strike, on behalf of 20,000 of its members who were employed as immigrant workers in Andorra.

Further proposals for institutional reforms were approved by the Consell General in October 1987. The transfer to the Andorran Government of responsibility for such matters as public order was proposed, while the authority of the Co-Princes in the administration of justice was recognized. The drafting of a constitution for Andorra was also envisaged. The implementation of the reforms was, however, dependent on the agreement of the Co-Princes.

Municipal elections were held in December 1987, at which 80% of the electorate voted; however, the number of citizens eligible to vote represented only 13% of Andorra's total population. For the first time, the election campaign involved the convening of meetings and the use of the media, in addition to traditional canvassing. Although Andorra then had no political parties as such, four of the seven seats were won by candidates promoting a conservative stance.

In April 1988 Andorra enacted legislation recognizing the Universal Declaration of Human Rights, adopted by the UN General Assembly in 1948. In June 1988 the first Andorran trade union was established by two French union confederations and by the Spanish Unión General de Trabajadores. (There were about 26,000 salaried workers in Andorra at this time, 90% of whom were of French or Spanish origin.) In the following month, however, the Consell General rejected the formation of the union, as it did not recognize workers' right of association and prohibited the existence of any union.

Elections to the Consell General took place in December 1989, at which more than 80% of the electorate participated. In January 1990 the new Council elected the reformist Ribas Reig as Head of Government, with the support of 22 members. In June the Council voted unanimously to establish a special commission to draft a constitution. The proposed document was to promulgate popular sovereignty and to limit the role of the Co-Princes. In April 1991 representatives of the Co-Princes agreed to recognize popular sovereignty in Andorra and to permit the drafting of a constitution, which would be subject to approval by referendum. In September, however, Ribas Reig was threatened with a vote of 'no confidence' by traditionalist members of the Council. There followed a period of political impasse, during which no official budget was authorized for the principality. In January 1992, following small, but unprecedented, public demonstrations in protest against the political deadlock, Ribas Reig and the Consell General resigned. A general election took place in April, at which 82% of the electorate voted. However, the result was inconclusive, necessitating a second round of voting one week later, following which supporters of Ribas Reig controlled 17 of the 28 seats. Accordingly, Ribas Reig was re-elected as Head of Government.

At a referendum held in March 1993, in which 75.7% of the electorate participated, 74.2% of those who voted approved the draft Constitution. The document was signed by the Co-Princes in April, and was promulgated on 4 May. Under its provisions, the Co-Princes remained as Heads of State, but with greatly reduced powers, while Andorran nationals were afforded full sovereignty and (together with foreigners who had lived in

Andorra for at least 20 years) were authorized to form and to join political parties and trade unions. The Constitution provided for the establishment of an independent judiciary, and permitted the principality to formulate its own foreign policy and to join international organizations. The Co-Princes were to retain a right of veto over treaties with France and Spain that affected Andorra's borders or security.

The first general election under the terms of the new Constitution took place on 12 December 1993. One of the constitutional provisions was the implementation of a new system of partial proportional representation—one-half of the Consell General's 28 members were directly elected from a single national constituency by a system of proportional representation, the remainder being elected by Andorra's seven parishes (two for each parish). Ribas Reig's Agrupament Nacional Democràtic (National Democratic Grouping—AND), the successor to the PDA, secured eight seats, while Nova Democràcia (New Democracy—ND) and the Unió Liberal (Liberal Union—UL) each won five seats. Some 80.8% of the electorate participated in the election. In January 1994 Ribas Reig was re-elected Head of Government, supported by the AND and the ND, together with the two representatives of the Iniciatíva Democràtica Nacional (National Democratic Initiative—IDN). Ribas Reig announced that it would be a priority of his administration to restore economic growth by means of financial reforms and infrastructural development. Opposition to Ribas Reig's proposed budget and tax legislation, however, led in November to the adoption of a motion of 'no confidence' in the Government. Ribas Reig immediately submitted his resignation; Marc Forné Molné, the leader of the UL, was subsequently elected Head of Government, and was inaugurated in late December.

Forné Molné's Government lacked an overall majority in the Consell General; however, the support of councillors from regional political organizations enabled the Government to adopt more than 30 acts (between December 1994 and July 1996), including controversial legislation regarding foreign nationals (see Economic Affairs). After being censured twice in one year by the Consell General, Forné Molné was obliged to announce that an early general election would be held at the beginning of 1997. Elections to the Council took place in February 1997, at which 81.6% of the registered electorate participated. The UL won an overall majority of seats (18 of 28); six seats were secured by the AND, while the ND and the IDN won two seats each. In April Forné Molné announced the formation of a new, expanded Government. The UL was subsequently renamed the Partit Liberal d'Andorra (Andorran Liberal Party—PLA). In 2000 the AND split into two parties—the Partit Socialdemocràta (Social Democratic Party—PS) and the Partit Democràta (Democratic Party—PD).

Elections to the Consell General took place on 4 March 2001, at which 81.6% of the registered electorate participated; however, the number of citizens eligible to vote represented only 20.7% of Andorra's total population. The PLA won 15 of 28 seats, six seats were secured by the PS, the PD took five seats and the two remaining seats went to independent candidates. Forné Molné was re-elected Head of Government by the Council. On 9 April Forné Molné announced the composition of his new Government, which comprised few changes from the outgoing administration.

In late October 2002 the Government encountered controversy when it unexpectedly closed a waste incinerator in Lime Rosselló amid revelations that the plant had been emitting 1,000 times the amount of dioxins permitted by EU regulations. The Government had previously resisted demands from the opposition and ecological groups for the closure of the plant. Although Spain agreed temporarily to dispose of waste produced by the principality, in early November the Government approved a law permitting the construction of a new incinerator in Andorra. However, this did not prevent Forné Molné facing widespread public discontent at the lack of government transparency regarding the matter.

In May 2003 Joan Enric Vives i Sicilia succeeded Joan Martí Alanis as the Bishop of Urgel and therefore as *ex officio* Episcopal Co-Prince of Andorra.

In February 2005 Forné Molné announced that legislative elections would take place in April. Forné Molné had previously announced that he would not seek a new term of office and the PLA in September 2004 had selected the former Minister of Foreign Affairs, Albert Pintat, as their candidate for Head of Government. The PS, which was led by Jaume Bartumeu Cassany, signed a co-operation agreement in December 2004 with two other opposition parties, the Renovació Democràtica (Democratic Renovation) and the Grup d'Unió Parroquial Independents (Group of United Parish Independents—GUPI) to contest the forthcoming election. A new grouping, an ecological party founded in early 2004, Els Verds d'Andorra (the Andorran Greens), were also contesting the election. The elections took place, as scheduled, on 24 April 2005; 80.4% of the electorate participated. The PLA won 14 seats, while the PS secured 12 and a coalition of two smaller parties, the Centre Demòcrata Andorrà (Andorran Democratic Centre) and Segle 21 (21st Century), won two seats. Since no party had won an absolute majority, Albert Pintat was expected to form a coalition government.

Following the referendum of March 1993, Andorra formally applied for membership of the Council of Europe (see p. 199), gaining entry in October 1994. In June 1993 the Andorran Government signed a treaty of co-operation with France and Spain, which explicitly recognized the sovereignty of Andorra. In the following month Andorra became the 184th member of the UN. In late 1993 France and Spain each established an embassy in Andorra la Vella, and Andorra subsequently opened embassies in Paris and Madrid. In September 1997 Jacques Chirac made his first official visit to Andorra in his capacity as President of France. In 2003 Forné Molné announced plans for Andorra to join the EU within 15 years. In April 2004 a co-operation agreement was finally agreed with the EU after two years of negotiation, and in June the Charter of Fundamental Social Rights of Workers (commonly known as the Social Charter) was ratified by the Consell General; however certain articles of the Charter, relating to employment rights, were omitted.

Government

Andorra is a co-principality, under the suzerainty of the President of France and the Spanish Bishop of Urgel. However, since May 1993, when the Constitution of the Principality of Andorra was promulgated, these positions have been almost purely honorary.

The Consell General (General Council) currently comprises 28 councillors (although the number can be between 28 and 42), who are elected by universal suffrage for a four-year period. Two councillors are directly elected by each of the seven parishes of Andorra, and the remainder are elected from a single national constituency by a system of proportional representation. At its opening session the Council elects as its head the Speaker (Síndic General) and the Deputy Speaker (Subsíndic General), who cease to be members of the Council on their election. The Consell General elects the Head of Government (Cap de Govern), who, in turn, appoints ministers to the executive body, the Govern.

Andorra is divided into seven parishes, each of which is administered by a Communal Council. Communal councillors are elected for a four-year term by direct universal suffrage. At its opening session each Communal Council elects two consuls, who preside over it.

Defence

Andorra has no defence budget.

Economic Affairs

In 2000 Andorra's national revenue totalled an estimated US $1,275m., equivalent to $19,368 per head. Traditionally an agricultural country, Andorra's principal crop is tobacco; livestock-rearing, particularly sheep, is also of importance. However, the agricultural sector (including forestry and hunting) accounted for only 0.3% of total employment in 2003, and Andorra is dependent on imports of foodstuffs to satisfy domestic requirements.

Industry in Andorra includes the manufacture of cigars and cigarettes, together with the production of textiles, leather goods, wood products and processed foodstuffs. In addition to forested timber, natural resources include iron, lead, alum and stone. Including manufacturing, construction and the production and distribution of electricity, industry provided 19.3% of total employment in 2003.

The country's hydroelectric power plant supplies only about one-quarter of domestic needs, and Andorra is dependent on imports of electricity and other fuels from France and Spain. In 2002 fuel imports accounted for 4.5% of total merchandise imports. In early 2003 the Spanish electricity group Endesa reached an agreement with the Andorran authorities to supply one-half of Andorra's electricity requirements until 2008. Andorra's total electricity consumption in 2003 amounted to 492.4m. kWh.

After 1945 Andorra's economy expanded rapidly, as a result of the co-principality's development as a retail centre for numerous European and overseas consumer goods, owing to favourable excise conditions. The development of facilities for winter sports also helped to make tourism an important feature of the modern Andorran economy. The services sector engaged 80.4% of the employed labour force in 2003. The trade in low-duty consumer items and tourism are Andorra's most important sources of revenue. An estimated 3.1m. tourists and 8.5m. excursionists (mostly from Spain and France) visited Andorra in 2003; the hotel industry engaged 13.7% of the employed labour force in that year. The absence of income tax and other forms of direct taxation, in addition to the laws on secrecy governing the country's banks, favoured the development of Andorra as a 'tax haven'. The banking sector makes a significant contribution to the economy.

Andorra's external trade is dominated by the import of consumer goods destined for sale, with low rates of duty, to visitors. In 2003 imports were valued at €1,337.1m. and exports at €79.0m. Spain and France are Andorra's principal trading partners, respectively providing 54.1% and 25.6% of imports and taking 55.7% and 19.2% of exports in 2003. The European Union (EU, see p. 217) as a whole provided 93.7% of imports and received 95.7% of exports in that year.

In 2001 Andorra recorded a budgetary deficit of €15.3m. In the absence of direct taxation, the Government derives its revenue from levies on imports and on financial institutions, indirect taxes on petrol and other items, stamp duty and the sale of postage stamps. There is no recorded unemployment in Andorra: the restricted size of the indigenous labour force necessitates high levels of immigration. The annual rate of inflation was 3.4% in 2002 and 2.9% in 2003.

In March 1990 Andorra approved a trade agreement with the European Community (EC, now European Union—EU) which was effective from July 1991, allowing for the establishment of a customs union with the EC and enabling Andorran companies to sell non-agricultural goods to the EU market without being subject to the external tariffs levied on third countries. Andorra benefits from duty-free transit for goods imported via EU countries. The final text of a co-operation agreement was confirmed between Andorra and the EU on 30 April 2004 following two years of negotiations. The agreement would be signed by the two parties when the process of translating it into all EU languages was complete. In 2003 the Prime Minister, Marc Forné Molné, announced that Andorra wished to join the EU within 15 years. In October 1997 Andorra's request to commence negotiations for membership of the World Trade Organization (WTO, see p. 357) was approved by the WTO General Council.

Notable impediments to growth in Andorra include the narrow economic base and the inability of the agricultural, energy and manufacturing sectors to fulfil domestic needs. As part of a series of initiatives to establish Andorra as a major financial centre, a law regulating financial services was approved in 1993. In the following year legislation was approved requiring banks to invest as much as 4% of their clients' deposits in a fund intended to alleviate the public debt (there had been a succession of annual budgetary deficits in the 1980s and early 1990s). Controversial legislation was adopted in 1996 to allow certain foreign nationals to become 'nominal residents' (individuals who, for the purposes of avoiding taxation, establish their financial base in Andorra), on condition that they pay an annual levy of some 1m. pesetas, in addition to a deposit. The practice of granting this status (without the levy) was suspended in 1992; however, in the mid-1990s those already accorded nominal residency were estimated to contribute 90% of Andorra's bank deposits. Concerns were expressed regarding the Andorran banking sector, following the publication in January 1993 of a report by the French Government, which stated that Andorra was being used for 'money laundering' (the passage of profits from criminal activities through the banking system in order to legitimize them). In mid-2000, under its initiative to abolish 'harmful tax practices', the Organisation for Economic Co-operation and Development (OECD, see p. 307) identified a number of jurisdictions as 'tax havens' lacking financial transparency, and urged these to amend their national financial legislation.

Many of the countries and territories identified agreed to follow a timetable for reform, with the aim of eliminating such practices by the end of 2005. Others at least entered into dialogue with OECD. A few did neither and were designated by OECD as 'unco-operative tax havens'. In April 2002 OECD listed Andorra as one of seven states that remained 'unco-operative tax havens', which could be subject to financial sanctions by member states if non-compliance continued for a further year. In 2003 the (IMF, see p. 111) recommended that the Andorran Government afford more power to local financial regulatory bodies to inspect banking activities, and that the Institut Nacional Andorrà de Finances co-operate more closely with the Bank of Spain. In November 2004 the EU signed an agreement with Andorra on the taxation of savings income. Under the agreement savings income, in the form of interest payments made in Andorra to residents of the EU, were to be subject to a withholding tax. The agreement, which was to come into effect in Andorra on 1 July 2005, included a joint declaration of intent under which Andorra would negotiate on a bilateral basis with the EU its removal from the OECD list of unco-operative tax havens. Andorra also signed an undertaking to introduce the concept of tax fraud as a criminal offence. Also as a result of the progress towards a savings taxation agreement, in October 2004 representatives of Andorra, France, Spain and the EU discussed the introduction of country-specific euro coins in Andorra. Although the euro had been the sole legal tender in Andorra since February 2002, Andorrans had hitherto used euros minted for France and Spain. Euro coins with an individual design for Andorra were expected to enter into circulation in late 2005. In February 2005 Andorra accepted an invitation (also extended to the other four remaining countries on the OECD list of unco-operative havens, Liberia, Liechtenstein, the Marshall Islands and Monaco) to participate as an observer at the OECD Global Forum on Taxation, which was to be held in November 2005 as part of the initiative to abolish harmful tax practices.

Education

Education is compulsory for children of between six and 16 years of age, and is provided free of charge by Catalan-, French- and Spanish-language schools. (Children educated under the French or Spanish state systems are required to study some Catalan.) Six years of primary education are followed by four years of secondary schooling. University education is undertaken abroad, although there are two centres for vocational training in Andorra—the Andorran University School of Nursing and the National School of Computer Studies. In 1999/2000 there were a total of 9,276 pupils attending Andorra's 34 schools. Of these, 2,180 were under the Andorran education system (where Catalan is the teaching medium), 3,586 were attending French-speaking schools and 3,510 were being educated under the Spanish system (secular and congregational). In 2001/02 1,434 students were in higher education—377 students were studying in Andorra, 248 in France and 796 in Spain. The 2003 budget allocated €45.5m. (16.8% of total projected expenditure) to education.

Public Holidays

2005: 1 January (New Year's Day), 6 January (Epiphany), 14 March (Constitution Day), 25 March (Good Friday), 28 March (Easter Monday), 2 May (for Labour Day), 16 May (Whit Monday), 15 August (Assumption), 8 September (National Holiday), 1 November (All Saints' Day), 8 December (Immaculate Conception), 25 December (Christmas), 26 December (St Stephen's Day).

2006: 1 January (New Year's Day), 6 January (Epiphany), 13 March (for Constitution Day), 14 April (Good Friday), 17 April (Easter Monday), 1 May (Labour Day), 5 June (Whit Monday), 15 August (Assumption), 8 September (National Holiday), 1 November (All Saints' Day), 8 December (Immaculate Conception), 25 December (Christmas), 26 December (St Stephen's Day).

Each Parish also holds its own annual festival, which is taken as a public holiday, usually lasting for three days, in July, August or September.

Weights and Measures

The metric system is in force.

Statistical Survey

Source (unless otherwise stated): Servei d'Estudis, Ministeri de Finances, Carrer Dr Vilanova 13, Edif. Davi, Esc. C5è, Andorra la Vella AD500; tel. 865345; fax 867898; e-mail servest@andorra.ad; internet www.estadistica.ad.

AREA AND POPULATION

Area: 467.76 sq km (180.6 sq miles).

Population: 46,166 at census of 12 July 1989; 72,320 (males 37,582, females 34,738), comprising: Andorrans 26,506, Spanish 27,680, Portuguese 8,311, French 4,718 and others 5,015 at 31 December 2003.

Density (31 December 2003): 154.6 per sq km.

Parishes (population at 31 December 2003): Andorra la Vella (capital) 22,035; Escaldes-Engordany 16,402; Encamp 11,832; Sant Julià de Lòria 8,313; La Massana 7,264; Canillo 3,707; Ordino 2,767.

Births, Marriages and Deaths (2003): Registered live births 721; Registered marriages 187; Registered deaths 221.

Expectation of Life (WHO estimates, years at birth): 80.3 (males 76.8; females 83.7) in 2002. Source: WHO, *World Health Report*.

Employment (2003): Agriculture, forestry and hunting 134; Industry 7,591 (Construction 5,862, Manufacturing 1,573, Production and distribution of electricity 156); Services 31,649 (Repair and sale of motor vehicles 11,087, Hotels 5,393, Real estate 3,334, Administration 3,620, Finance and insurance 1,455, Transport and storage 1,496, Other services 5,264); *Total* 39,374.

HEALTH AND WELFARE

Key Indicators

Total Fertility Rate (children per woman, 2002): 1.3.

Under-5 Mortality Rate (per 1,000 live births, 2003): 7.

Physicians (per 1,000 head, 1998): 2.53.

Health Expenditure (2001): US $ per head (PPP): 1,821.

Health Expenditure (2001): % of GDP: 5.7.

Health Expenditure (2001): public (% of total): 71.0.

Access to Water (% of persons, 2002): 100.

Access to Sanitation (% of persons, 2002): 100.
For sources and definitions, see explanatory note on p. vi.

AGRICULTURE

Principal Crop (metric tons, 2002): Tobacco 318.6.

Livestock (head, 2002/03): Cattle 1,428; Sheep 2,807; Horses 830; Goats 459.

FINANCE

Currency and Exchange Rates: 100 cent = 1 euro. *Sterling and Dollar Equivalents* (31 December 2004): £1 sterling = 1.4180 euros; US $1 = 0.7342 euros; 100 euros = £70.52 = US $136.21. *Average Exchange Rate* (euros per US dollar): 1.0626 in 2002; 0.8860 in 2003; 0.8054 in 2004. Note: French and Spanish currencies were formerly in use. From the introduction of the euro, with French and Spanish participation, on 1 January 1999, fixed exchange rates of €1 = 6.55957 francs and €1 = 166.386 pesetas were in operation. Euro notes and coins were introduced on 1 January 2002. The euro and local currencies circulated alongside each other until 17 February (francs) and 28 February (pesetas), after which the euro became the sole legal tender.

Budget (€ million, 2004): *Revenue:* Indirect taxes 211.7; Property income 24.2; Other taxes and income 19.4; Assets 0.1; Liabilities 34.4; Total 289.8. *Expenditure:* Current expenditure 147.4 (Personnel emoluments 61.4, Goods and services 35.7, Interest payments 4.8, Current transfers 45.6); Capital expenditure 142.3 (Fixed capital investment 100.3, Capital transfers 42.0); Assets 0.2; Liabilities 0.0; Total 289.8.

Cost of Living (2002; consumer price index base: 2001 = 100): Food, beverages and tobacco 105.3; Clothing and footwear 101.1; Utilities 103.1; Health 102.6; Transport 103.3; Education 106.2; Hotels and restaurants 107.6; *All items* 103.4.

EXTERNAL TRADE

Principal Commodities (€ million, 2003): *Imports:* Live animals and animal products 62.5; Prepared foodstuffs, beverages, spirits and vinegar, tobacco and manufactured substitutes 168.2; Mineral products 71.6; Products of chemical or allied industries 136.8; Textiles and textile articles 118.7; Base metals and articles thereof 49.8; Machinery and electrical equipment 256.7; Vehicles, aircraft, vessels and associated transport equipment 138.8; Optical, photographic, cinematographic, precision and medical instruments, etc. 69.0; Furniture, bed linen, etc., lighting devices 75.1; Total (incl. others) 1,337.1. *Exports:* Prepared foodstuffs, beverages, spirits and vinegar, tobacco and manufactured substitutes 4.8; Products of chemical or allied industries 6.3; Paper and paperboard and articles thereof 2.4; Textiles and textile articles 3.8; Machinery and mechanical appliances; electrical equipment; sound and television apparatus 17.5; Vehicles, aircraft, vessels and associated transport equipment 17.6; Optical, photographic, cinematographic, precision and medical instruments, etc. 11.1; Furniture, bed linen, etc., lighting devices 3.5; Total (incl. others) 79.0.

Principal Trading Partners (US $ million, 2003): *Imports c.i.f.:* France 342.9; Germany 72.2; Italy 46.0; Netherlands 15.9; Spain 723.2; United Kingdom 25.4; Total (incl. others) 1,337.1. *Exports f.o.b.:* Benelux countries 2.4; France 15.7; Germany 9.8; Italy 0.6; Portugal 2.0, Spain 44.0; Total (incl. others) 79.0.

TRANSPORT

Road Traffic (registered motor vehicles, 2003): Total 63,616. *1996:* Passenger cars 35,358; Commercial vehicles 4,238.

TOURISM

Tourist Arrivals (2003): Spanish 6,479,066; French 4,765,015; Others 356,590; Total 11,600,671 (Visitors staying at least one night 3,137,738, Excursionists 8,462,933).

COMMUNICATIONS MEDIA

Radio Receivers (1997): 16,000 in use.

Television Receivers (2000): 36,000 in use (Source: UNESCO).

Daily Newspapers (2004): 2 titles published.

Telephones (main lines in use, 2003): 35,171.

Facsimile Machines (number in use, 1998): 5,000 (Source: UN, *Statistical Yearbook*).

Mobile Cellular Telephones (subscribers, 2003): 32,199.

Internet Users (2000): 7,000.
Source: partly International Telecommunication Union.

EDUCATION

Pre-primary Enrolment (1999/2000): Andorran schools 665; French schools 807; Spanish schools* 678.

Primary and Secondary Enrolment (1999/2000): Andorran schools 1,229; French schools 2,136; Spanish schools* 2,143.

Non-university Higher Education Enrolment (1999/2000): 1,845.

University Enrolment (2001/02): Andorra 377; Other countries 1,057; Total 1,434.
*Including congregational schools.
Source: partly Department of Education, Youth and Sports.

Directory

The Constitution

The Constitution of the Principality of Andorra came into force on 4 May 1993, having been approved by the Andorran people in a referendum on 14 March. The official name of the independent state is Principat d'Andorra. The Constitution asserts that Andorra is 'a Democratic and Social independent state abiding by the Rule of Law', defines the fundamental rights, freedoms and obligations of Andorran citizens and delineates the functions and competences of the organs of state.

In accordance with Andorran tradition, the Co-Princes (Coprínceps), respectively the Bishop of Urgel and the President of the French Republic, are titular Heads of State.

The legislature is the Consell General (General Council) which comprises between 28 and 42 members. Two members of the Consell General are elected to represent each of Andorra's seven parishes (Parròquies), and one-half are elected from a single national constituency by a system of proportional representation; members are elected to the Consell General for four years (or until the dissolution of the Consell General). Elections are on the basis of direct universal adult suffrage. The ruling organ of the Consell General is the Sindicatura, headed by a Speaker (Síndic General).

The Govern (the executive organ of state) is directed by the Head of Government (Cap de Govern), who is elected by the Consell General (and formally appointed by the Co-Princes) and who must command the support of the majority of the legislature's members. The Head of Government nominates government ministers, who may not at the same time be members of the Consell General. The Head of Government is restricted to two consecutive full terms of office.

The Constitution defines the composition and powers of the judiciary, the highest organ of which is the Higher Court of Justice (Consell Superior de Justícia).

The Constitution defines the functions of the communal councils (Comuns), which are the organs of representation and administration of the parishes.

Revision of the Constitution shall require the approval of two-thirds of the members of the Consell General and ratification by a referendum. The Consell General is advised on constitutional matters by the Institució del Raonador del Ciutadà, an independent institution established in 1998, responsible for the application of the Constitution.

The Constitutional Court is the supreme interpreter of the Constitution. Its decisions are binding for public authorities and for individuals.

The Government

HEADS OF STATE

Episcopal Co-Prince: JOAN ENRIC VIVES I SICILIA (Bishop of Urgel).
French Co-Prince: JACQUES CHIRAC (President of France).

GOVERN
(March 2005)

Legislative elections took place on 24 April 2005; it was anticipated that a new coalition government, to be headed by Albert Pintat of the PLA, would take office in May 2005.

Cap de Govern (Head of Government): MARC FORNÉ MOLNÉ.
Minister of Presidency and Tourism: ENRIC PUJAL ARENY.
Minister of Finance: MIREIA MAESTRE CORTADELLA.
Minister of Foreign Affairs: JULI MINOVES TRIQUELL.
Minister of Justice and the Interior: JOSEP MARIA CABANES DALMAU.
Minister of the Economy: MIQUEL ALVAREZ MARFANY.
Minister of Agriculture and the Environment: OLGA ADELLACH COMA.
Minister of Education, Culture, Youth and Sports: XAVIER MONTANÉ ATERO.
Minister of Territorial Development: JORDI SERRA MALLEU.
Minister of Health and Welfare: MÒNICA CODINA TORT.

MINISTRIES

Office of the Head of Government: Govern d'Andorra, Carrer Prat de la Creu 62–64, Andorra la Vella AD500; tel. 875700; fax 822882; internet www.govern.ad.

Ministry of Agriculture and the Environment: Carrer Dr Vilanova 13, Edif. Davi, Esc. C3r, Andorra la Vella AD500; tel. 875707; fax 869833; e-mail mediambient@andorra.ad; internet www.mediambient.ad.

Ministry of the Economy: Govern d'Andorra, Edif. Administratiu, Carrer Prat de la Creu 62–64, Andorra la Vella AD500; tel. 875700; fax 861519.

Ministry of Education, Culture, Youth and Sports: Avinguda Rocafort, Edif. Molí 21–23, Sant Julià de Lòria AD600; tel. 866585; fax 861229.

Ministry of Finance: Carrer Prat de la Creu 62–64, Andorra la Vella AD500; tel. 875700; fax 860962; internet www.finances.ad.

Ministry of Foreign Affairs: Carrer Prat de la Creu 62–64, Andorra la Vella AD500; tel. 875700; fax 869559; e-mail exteriors.gov@andorra.ad.

Ministry of Health and Welfare: Avinguda Príncep Benlloch 30, 4°, Andorra la Vella AD500; tel. 860345; fax 829347; e-mail min.sanitat@andorra.ad; internet www.salutibenestar.ad.

Ministry of Justice and the Interior: Carrer Ciutat de Sabadell, Escaldes-Engordany AD700; tel. 872080; fax 869250.

Ministry of Territorial Development: Carrer Prat de la Creu 62–64, Andorra la Vella AD500; tel. 875701; fax 861313; e-mail mot.gov@andorra.ad.

Ministry of Presidency and Tourism: Carrer Prat de la Creu 62–64, Andorra la Vella AD500; tel. 875702; fax 860184; e-mail turisme@andorra.ad; internet www.andorra.ad.

Legislature

CONSELL GENERAL
(General Council)

Consell General: Casa de la Vall, Andorra la Vella AD500; tel. 877877; fax 869863; e-mail consell_general@parlament.ad; internet www.consell.ad.

Síndic General (Speaker): FRANCESC ARENY CASAL (PLA).
Subsíndic General (Deputy Speaker): JOSEP ANGEL MORTÉS PONS.

General Election, 24 April 2005

Party	Votes cast	Seats
Partit Liberal d'Andorra	5,100	14
Partit Socialdemocràta	4,711	12
Centre Demòcrata Andorrà/Segle 21	1,360	2
Renovació Democràtica	772	0
Els Verds d'Andorra	433	0
Total	**12,376**	**28**

Political Organizations

The establishment of political parties was sanctioned under the Constitution that was promulgated in May 1993.

Centre Demòcrata Andorrà (CDA) (Andorran Democratic Centre): Edif. El Pico, Avinguda del Fener 15–17, 1° C, Andorra la Vella AD500; tel. 805777; fax 805779; e-mail cda@myp.ad; internet www.centredemocrateandorra.com; f. 2000 as Partit Demòcrata (PT); name changed as above in 2003; Pres. JOSEP MARIA COSAN.

Iniciatíva Democràtica Nacional (IDN) (National Democratic Initiative): Plaça Rebés 1, 2°, Andorra la Vella AD500; tel. 866406; fax 866306; e-mail idn@andorra.ad; f. 1993; Leader VICENÇ MATEU ZAMORA.

Partit Liberal d'Andorra (PLA) (Andorran Liberal Party): C. Babot Camp 13, 2°, Andorra la Vella AD500; tel. 807715; fax 869728; e-mail pla@pla.ad; internet www.partitliberal.ad; f. 1992 as Unió Liberal; Leader MARC FORNÉ MOLNÉ; Parliamentary Leader ALBERT PINTAT.

Partit Socialdemòcrata (PS) (Social Democratic Party): Carrer Verge del Pilar 5, 3°, Andorra la Vella AD500; tel. 805262; fax 821746; e-mail ps@andorra.ad; internet www.psa.ad; name changed from Nova Democràcia in 2000; formed alliance with the RD and GUPI in Dec. 2004 to contest 2005 elections; Pres. Mariona González Reolit; Sec. Francesc Casals Pantebre; Parliamentary Leader Jaume Bartumeu Cassany.

Renovació Democràtica (RD) (Democratic Renovation): Andorra la Vella AD500; e-mail infopartit@renovaciodemocratica.com; internet www.renovaciodemocratica.com; formed alliance with the PS and GUPI in Dec. 2004 to contest 2005 elections.

Els Verds d'Andorra (The Andorran Greens): Carrer de l'Aigüeta 10, entresòl, Andorra la Vella AD500; e-mail social@andorraverds.com; internet www.andorraverds.com; f. 2004; Pres. Isabel Lozano.

Other parties are the Bloc d'Acció Política (Bloc of Political Action), Democràcia Andorrana (Andorran Democracy), Grup d'Opinió Liberal (Group of Liberal Opinion), Iniciatíva Andorrana d'Escaldes-Engordany (Andorran Initiative of Escaldes-Engordany), Partit Unió Laurediana (Lauredian Union), Segle 21 (21st Century) and Unió Democràtica Andorrana (Andorran Democratic Union). There is also a grouping of independents, the Grup d'Unió Parroquial Independents (Group of United Parish Independents—GUPI).

Diplomatic Representation

EMBASSIES IN ANDORRA

France: Carrer de la Sobrevia 7, POB 155, Andorra la Vella AD500; tel. 736700; fax 736731; e-mail ambassade.de.franca@andorra.ad; internet www.ambafrance-ad.org; Ambassador Jean-Jacques Gaillarde.

Portugal: Carrer Prat de la Creu 59-65, Andorra la Vella AD500; tel. 805305; fax 869555; e-mail mail@cgand.dgaccp.pt; Ambassador Nuno António Ribeiro de Bessa Lopes.

Spain: Carrer Prat de la Creu 34, Andorra la Vella AD500; tel. 800030; fax 868500; e-mail embaspad@correo.mae.es; Ambassador César González Palacios.

Judicial System

The 1993 Constitution guarantees the independence of the judiciary.
Judicial power is vested, in the first instance, in the Magistrates' Courts (Batllia) and in the Judges' Tribunal (Tribunal de Batlles), the criminal-law courts (Tribunal de Corts) and the Higher Court of Justice (Tribunal Superior de la Justícia). The judiciary is represented, directed and administered by the Higher Council of Justice (Consell Superior de la Justícia), whose five members are appointed for single terms of six years. Final jurisdiction, in constitutional matters, is vested in the Constitutional Court (Tribunal Constitucional), whose four members hold office for no more than two consecutive eight-year terms.

The Press

7 DIES: Avinguda Riberaygua 39, Andorra la Vella AD500; tel. 863700; fax 863800; weekly; local issues; Catalan; Pres. Marc Vila Amigó; Dir Rosa Mari Sorribes; circ. 28,000.

Butlletí Oficial de Principat d'Andorra: Avinguda Santa Coloma 91, Andorra la Vella AD500; tel. 724400; e-mail administrador_bopa@govern.ad; internet www.bopa.ad; official govt gazette; weekly.

Diari d'Andorra: Avinguda Riberaygua 39, Andorra la Vella AD500; tel. 877477; fax 863802; e-mail redaccio@diariandorra.ad; internet www.diariandorra.ad; f. 1991; daily; local issues; Catalan; Pres. Marc Vila Amigó; Dir Ignasi Planell; circ. 3,500.

Informacions: Avinguda Riberaygua 39, Andorra la Vella AD500; tel. 863700; fax 863800; weekly.

Món Diplomatic: Avinguda Santa Coloma 36, Andorra la Vella AD500; tel. (972) 330344; fax (872) 031000; e-mail redaccio@mondiplomatic.com; internet www.mondiplomatic.com; Catalan edition of Le Monde Diplomatique; monthly.

El Periòdic d'Andorra: Parc de la Mola 10, Torre Caldea, Escaldes-Engordany AD700; tel. 736200; fax 736210; e-mail redaccio@andorra.elperiodico.com; internet www.elperiodico.es/andorra; daily; local issues; Catalan; Dir Josep Anton Rossell Pujol.

Broadcasting and Communications

TELECOMMUNICATIONS

Servei de Telecomunicacions d'Andorra (STA): Carrer Mossen Lluis Pujol 8–14, Santa Coloma AD500; tel. 875105; fax 725003; e-mail webmaster@sta.ad; internet www.sta.ad; provides national and international telecommunications services; Dir Xavier Palacios-Albacar.

BROADCASTING

In 2003 there were six radio stations in Andorra. In 2004 two television stations were active in Andorra, and it was possible to receive broadcasts from television stations in neighbouring countries. Digital television broadcasts began in October 2004.

Radio

Ràdio i Televisió d'Andorra, SA—Ràdio Nacional Andorra (RTVA): Baixada del Molí 24, Andorra la Vella AD500; tel. 873777; fax 863242; e-mail rtvasa@andorra.ad; internet www.rtvasa.ad; f. 1991; Andorran-owned commercial public broadcasting service; two stations: Ràdio Andorra and Andorra Música; Dir Enric Castellet Pifarré.

Ràdio Valira: Carrer de Parnal 2, Escaldes-Engordany AD700; tel. 829600; fax 828273; e-mail radiovalira@radiovalira.ad; internet www.radiovalira.com; f. 1985; public commercial broadcasting service; Dirs Gualberto Osorio, José Rabada.

Television

Ràdio i Televisió d'Andorra, SA—Andorra Televisió (RTVA): Baixada del Molí 24, Andorra la Vella AD500; tel. 873777; fax 864232; e-mail rtvasa@andorra.ad; internet www.rtvasa.ad; f. 1995 as an Andorran-owned commercial public broadcasting service; Dir Enric Castellet Pifarré.

Antena 7: Avinguda les Escoles 16, Escaldes-Engordany AD700; tel. 824433; fax 826088; private co.; in 1987 began to transmit one hour of Andorran-interest programmes from the Spanish side of the border.

Finance

(cap. = capital; res = reserves; dep. = deposits; m. = million; brs = branches; amounts in euros—€)

PRINCIPAL BANKS

Andorra Banc Agricol Reig, SA (Andbanc): Carrer Manuel Cerqueda i Escaler 6, Escaldes-Engordany AD700; tel. 873333; fax 868905; e-mail atclient@andbanc.com; internet andbanc.com; f. 2001 by merger of Banca Reig and Banc Agricol i Comercial d'Andorra; cap. €68.1m., res €253.3m., dep. €1,208.2m. (Dec. 2003); Chair. Manel Cerquerda; Gen. Man. Jaume Sabater; 12 brs.

Banc Internacional d'Andorra SA: Avinguda Meritxell 96, Andorra la Vella AD500; tel. 884488; fax 884499; e-mail bibm@bibm.ad; internet www.bibm.ad; f. 1958; 51% owned by Banco Bilbao Vizcaya Argentaria (Spain); cap. €42.4m., res €165.7m., dep. €1,873.4m. (Dec. 2003); Chair. Jordi Aristot Mora; Chief Exec. Joan Quera Font; 4 brs.

Banca Mora SA: Avinguda Meritxell 96, Andorra la Vella; tel. 884488; fax 884499; e-mail bibm@bibm.ad; internet www.bibm.ad; f. 1952; subsidiary of Banc Internacional d'Andorra SA; cap. €30.1m., res €64.3m., dep. €912.4m. (Dec. 2003); Chair. Francesc Mora Sagués; Dir Jordi Aristot Mora; 7 brs.

Banca Privada d'Andorra SA: POB 25, Avinguda Carlemany 119, Escaldes-Engordany AD700; tel. 873500; fax 873517; e-mail bpa@bpa.ad; internet www.bpa.ad; f. 1962 as Banca Cassany SA; name changed to above in 1994; cap. €33.0m., res €17.1m., dep. €722.7m. (Dec. 2003); Pres. Hinigi Cierco y Garcia; Gen. Man. Joan Pau Miquel Prats; 3 brs.

BancSabadell d'Andorra: Avinguda del Fener 7, Andorra la Vella AD500; tel. 735600; fax 735650; e-mail info@bsa.ad; internet www.bsa.ad; cap. €30.1m., res €-6.5m., dep. €336.1m. (Dec. 2003); Chair. Robert Cassany i Vila; Gen. Man. Miquel Alabern.

CaixaBank SA: POB 77F-2003E; Plaça Rebés 3, Andorra la Vella AD500; tel. 874874; fax 829003; e-mail info@caixabank.ad; internet www.caixabank.ad; f. 1997; cap. €30m., res €71.5m., dep. €965.0m. (Dec. 2003); Chair. Pere Roquet; Gen. Man. Pere Campistol.

Crèdit Andorrà: Avinguda Meritxell 80, Andorra la Vella AD500; tel. 888001; fax 888601; e-mail ca@creditandorra.ad; internet www.creditandorra.ad; f. 1955; cap. €70.0m., res €345.3m., dep.

€2,401.5m. (Dec. 2003); Chair. ANTONI PINTAT; CEO JOSEP PERALBA; 16 brs.

BANKING ASSOCIATION

Associació de Bancs Andorrans (ABA): Carrer Ciutat de Consuegra 16, Edif. L'Illa, Escala A-2°, Andorra la Vella AD500; tel. 807110; fax 866847; e-mail aba@andorra.ad; Dir ANTONI Armengol.

Trade and Industry

CHAMBER OF COMMERCE

Cambra de Comerç, Indústria i Serveis d'Andorra: Carrer Prat de la Creu 8, Edif. Le Mans, Despatx 204–205, Andorra la Vella AD500; tel. 863232; fax 863233; e-mail ccis@andorra.ad; internet www.ccis.ad; Pres. FRANCESC PALLAS VILADOMAT.

UTILITIES

Electricity

Forces Elèctriques d'Andorra (FEDA): Avinguda de la Barta s/n, Encamp AD200; tel. 739100; fax 739119; e-mail feda@feda.ad; internet www.feda.ad; f. 1988; imports, generates and distributes electricity; Pres. MIREIRA MAESTRE CORTADELLA; Dir-Gen. RAMON CEREZA PEREZ.

Mútua Elèctrica Sant Julià de Lòria: Avinguda Francesc Cairat, Sant Julià de Lòria AD600; tel. 841180; fax 843322; regional electricity distributor.

Sercensa: Avinguda Copríncep Francés 1, Encamp AD200; tel. 832103; fax 833007; regional electricity distributor.

TRADE UNIONS

Sindical de Treballadors d'Andorra: Andorra la Vella AD500.

Unió Sindical d'Andorra (USdA): Andorra la Vella AD500.

Transport

RAILWAYS

In 2001 construction began on a 40,000m.-peseta overhead train system, which was expected to alleviate traffic problems in Andorra la Vella. The 8 km line was to link Sant Julià de Lòria and Escaldes-Engordany to the capital. The link was scheduled for completion by 2008. Until then, the nearest stations are Ax-les-Thermes, L'Hospitalet and La Tour de Carol, in France (with trains from Toulouse and Perpignan), and Puigcerdá, in Spain, on the line from Barcelona. There is a connecting bus service from all four stations to Andorra.

ROADS

A good road connects the Spanish and French frontiers, passing through Andorra la Vella. In 1996 there were 279 national roads, 198 of which were tarmacked. The Envalira tunnel, between Andorra and France, was opened in September 2002. Construction of a tunnel linking La Massana to Encamp was put out to tender in late 2004. Work on the La Massana–Escaldes tunnel was scheduled to be finished by the end of 2005. In late 2004 there were plans to construct a by-pass around Sant Julià de Lòria.

CIVIL AVIATION

In 2005 the Seo d'Urgel-Andorra airport, located in Spanish territory 10 km from the border, was under redevelopment as a one-runway international airport for Andorra. Plans were under discussion for a helicopter link between Andorra and Barcelona.

Tourism

Andorra has attractive mountain scenery, and winter sports facilities are available at five skiing centres. In 2001 the Government announced plans to promote Andorra as a winter sports destination. In 2004 there were 177 ski slopes available. Tourists are also attracted by Andorra's duty-free shopping facilities. In 2003 there were 964 hotels and hostels in Andorra, and 13 campsites. Around 3.1m. tourists visited Andorra in 2003, as well as 8.5m. excursionists, mainly from Spain and France. In 2004 the valley of Madriu was declared a UNESCO World Heritage Site.

Ministry of Presidency and Tourism: Carrer Prat de la Creu 62–64, Andorra la Vella AD500; tel. 875702; fax 860184; e-mail turisme@andorra.ad; internet www.andorra.ad.

Sindicat d'Iniciatíva Oficina de Turisme: Carrer Dr Vilanova, Andorra la Vella AD500; tel. 820214; fax 825823; e-mail sindicatdiniciativa@andorra.ad; Dir ROSER JORDANA.

Ski Andorra: Avinguda Tarragona 58-70, Desptax 14, Andorra la Vella AD500; tel. 805200; fax 865910; e-mail skiandorra@skiandorra.ad; internet www.skiandorra.ad; association of ski stations; Dir MARTA ROTÉS.

Unió Hotelera d'Andorra (Hotel Association of Andorra): Antic Carrer Major 18, Andorra la Vella AD500; tel. 820602; fax 861539; e-mail info@uha.ad; internet www.uha.ad; Pres. CARLES FLINCH FONT.

Each parish has its own tourist office.

ANGOLA

Introductory Survey

Location, Climate, Language, Religion, Flag, Capital

The Republic of Angola lies on the west coast of Africa. The province of Cabinda is separated from the rest of the country by the estuary of the River Congo and territory of the Democratic Republic of the Congo (DRC—formerly Zaire), with the Republic of the Congo lying to its north. Angola is bordered by the DRC to the north, Zambia to the east and Namibia to the south. The climate is tropical, locally tempered by altitude. There are two distinct seasons (wet and dry) but little seasonal variation in temperature. It is very hot and rainy in the coastal lowlands but temperatures are lower inland. The official language is Portuguese, but African languages (the most widely spoken being Umbundo, Lunda, Kikongo, Chokwe and Kwanyama) are also in common use. Much of the population follows traditional African beliefs, although a majority profess to be Christians, mainly Roman Catholics. The flag (proportions 2 by 3) has two equal horizontal stripes, of red and black; superimposed in the centre, in gold, are a five-pointed star, half a cog-wheel and a machete. A new flag was proposed by the Constitutional Commission in August 2003, but had not been ratified by early 2005. The capital is Luanda.

Recent History

Formerly a Portuguese colony, Angola became an overseas province in 1951. African nationalist groups began to form in the 1950s and 1960s, including the Movimento Popular de Libertação de Angola (MPLA) in 1956, the Frente Nacional de Libertação de Angola (FNLA) in 1962 and the União Nacional para a Independência Total de Angola (UNITA) in 1966. Severe repression followed an unsuccessful nationalist rebellion in 1961, but, after a new wave of fighting in 1966, nationalist guerrilla groups were able to establish military and political control in large parts of eastern Angola and to press westward. Following the April 1974 *coup d'état* in Portugal, Angola's right to independence was recognized and it was agreed that Angola would become independent in November 1975.

In January 1975 a transitional Government was established, comprising representatives of the MPLA, the FNLA, UNITA and the Portuguese Government. However, from March political differences led to violent clashes between the MPLA and the FNLA. By the second half of 1975 control of Angola was effectively divided between the three major nationalist groups, each aided by foreign powers. The MPLA (which held the capital) was supported by the USSR and Cuba, the FNLA by Zaire and Western powers (including the USA), while UNITA was backed by South African forces. The FNLA and UNITA formed a united front to fight the MPLA.

The Portuguese Government proclaimed Angola independent from 11 November 1975, transferring sovereignty to 'the Angolan people' rather than to any of the liberation movements. The MPLA proclaimed the People's Republic of Angola in Luanda under the presidency of Dr Agostinho Neto. The FNLA and UNITA proclaimed the Democratic People's Republic of Angola, based in Nova Lisboa (renamed Huambo). By the end of February 1976, however, the MPLA, aided by Cuban technical and military expertise, had effectively gained control of the whole country.

In May 1977 an abortive coup, led by Nito Alves (a former minister), resulted in a purge of state and party officials. In December the MPLA was renamed the Movimento Popular de Libertação de Angola—Partido do Trabalho (MPLA—PT), but further divisions became evident in December 1978, when President Neto abolished the post of Prime Minister and ousted several other ministers.

Neto died in September 1979, and José Eduardo dos Santos, hitherto the Minister of Planning, was elected party leader and President by the MPLA—PT Central Committee. Dos Santos continued to encourage strong links with the Soviet bloc and led campaigns to eliminate corruption and inefficiency. Elections to the National People's Assembly (Assembléia Popular Nacional), which replaced the Council of the Revolution (Conselho da Revolução), were first held in 1980. Fresh elections, due to be held in 1983, were postponed until 1986, owing to political and military problems.

The MPLA—PT Government's recovery programme was continually hindered by security problems. Although the FNLA reportedly surrendered to the Government in 1984, UNITA conducted sustained and disruptive guerrilla activities, mainly in southern and central Angola, throughout the 1980s. In addition, forces from South Africa, which was providing UNITA with considerable military aid, made numerous armed incursions over the Angolan border with Namibia, ostensibly in pursuit of guerrilla forces belonging to the South West Africa People's Organisation (SWAPO), which was supported by the Angolan Government. Although the Government's military campaign against UNITA appeared to be increasingly successful during 1985, the rebels' position was strengthened in 1986, when US military aid began to arrive. (The US Government continued to provide covert military aid to UNITA until 1990.) Nevertheless, UNITA was excluded from a series of major peace negotiations, between Angola, Cuba and South Africa (with the unofficial mediation of the USA), which commenced in May 1988. By July the participants had agreed to a document containing the principles for a peace settlement that provided for independence for Namibia, the discontinuation of South African military support for UNITA and the withdrawal of Cuban troops from Angola. In July and August Dr Jonas Savimbi, the President of UNITA, travelled to the USA and to several European and African capitals to seek support for UNITA's demands to be included in the negotiations. Although movement for a negotiated settlement between the MPLA—PT Government and UNITA gathered momentum, UNITA's position became vulnerable in August, when a cease-fire between Angola and South Africa was declared, and South African troops were withdrawn from Angola. UNITA refused to adhere to the cease-fire. Following the conclusion of the New York accords on Angola and Namibia in December, the US Government renewed its commitment to the rebels. In accordance with the accords, the UN Security Council established the UN Angola Verification Mission (UNAVEM) to verify the phased withdrawal of Cuban troops from Angola, which was completed in May 1991.

In February 1989 the Angolan Government offered a 12-month amnesty to UNITA members. UNITA, restating its aim of entering into a transitional coalition government with the MPLA—PT as a prelude to multi-party elections, responded by launching an offensive against government targets. In June dos Santos and Savimbi attended a conference at Gbadolite, Zaire, convened by the Zairean President, Mobutu Sese Seko, who succeeded in mediating a peace agreement between the Angolan Government and UNITA, in accordance with which a cease-fire came into effect on 24 June. However, the terms of the accord were interpreted differently by each party, and in August Savimbi announced a resumption of hostilities.

In October 1989, following a meeting with President George Bush of the USA, Savimbi agreed to resume peace talks with the Angolan Government, with Mobutu acting as mediator. In December dos Santos proposed a peace plan that envisaged some political reform, but did not include provisions for a multi-party political system; the plan was rejected by UNITA.

In July 1990 the Central Committee of the MPLA—PT announced that the Government would allow Angola to 'evolve towards a multi-party system'. In October the Central Committee proposed a general programme of reform, including the replacement of the party's official Marxist-Leninist ideology with a commitment to 'democratic socialism', the legalization of political parties, the transformation of the army from a party institution to a state institution, the introduction of a market economy, a revision of the Constitution and the holding of multi-party elections in 1994, following a population census. These proposals were formally approved by the MPLA—PT in December. However, the Government and UNITA continued to disagree over the timing of elections and the status of UNITA pending the elections.

In March 1991 the Assembléia Popular approved legislation permitting the formation of political parties. On 1 May the

Government and UNITA concluded a peace agreement in Estoril, Portugal, which provided for a cease-fire from 15 May, to be monitored by a joint political and military commission, with representatives from the MPLA—PT, UNITA, the UN, Portugal, the USA and the USSR. A new national army of 50,000 men was to be established, comprising equal numbers of government and UNITA soldiers. Free and democratic elections were to be held by the end of 1992. On 31 May the Government and UNITA signed a formal agreement in Lisbon, Portugal, ratifying the Estoril agreement. The UN Security Council agreed to establish UNAVEM II, with a mandate to ensure implementation of the peace accord. In July the Standing Commission of the Assembléia Popular approved a new amnesty law, under the terms of which amnesty would be granted for all crimes against state security as well as for military and common law offences committed before 31 May 1991.

A reshuffle of the Council of Ministers in July 1991 included the appointment of Fernando José França van-Dúnem to the post of Prime Minister, thus reintroducing the premiership to the Government. Supreme executive power remained, however, with the President.

In September 1991 Savimbi returned to Luanda for the first time since the civil war began in 1975, and UNITA headquarters were transferred to the capital from Jamba in October. In the following month dos Santos announced that legislative and presidential elections were to take place in September 1992. In January 1992, on the recommendation of the joint political and military commission, a monitoring task group was established to oversee the implementation of the peace agreement. The creation of the group, which included members of the Government, UNITA and UNAVEM II, followed growing concern over the reported decline in the number of government and UNITA troops in confinement areas and the reoccupation of territory by UNITA forces.

Representatives of the Government and 26 political parties met in Luanda in January 1992 to discuss the transition to multi-party democracy. UNITA boycotted the meeting, but in February held talks with the Government, at which it was agreed that the elections would be conducted on the basis of proportional representation, with the President elected for a five-year term, renewable for a maximum of three terms. The legislature would be a national assembly, elected for a four-year term. In April the Assembléia Popular adopted electoral legislation incorporating these decisions and providing for the creation of a National Assembly (Assembléia Nacional) comprising 223 members (90 to be elected in 18 provincial constituencies and the remainder from national lists).

In April 1992 the Supreme Court approved UNITA's registration as a political party. In May the MPLA—PT voted to enlarge the membership of the Central Committee to include prominent dissidents who had returned to the party. The Central Committee recommended that the party's membership be further expanded with a view to broadening the party's support base. During the congress the delegates also voted to remove the suffix Partido do Trabalho (Party of Labour or Workers' Party) from the organization's official name. In August the legislature approved a further revision of the Constitution, removing the remnants of the country's former Marxist ideology, and deleting the words 'People's' and 'Popular' from the Constitution and from the names of official institutions. The name of the country was changed from the People's Republic of Angola to the Republic of Angola.

Increased tension and outbreaks of violence in the period preceding the general election seriously threatened to disrupt the electoral process. In early September 1992 in Cabinda province, the enclave that provides most of Angola's petroleum revenue, secessionist groups, notably the Frente de Libertação do Enclave de Cabinda (FLEC), intensified attacks on government troops. On 27 September the government Forças Armadas Populares de Libertação de Angola (FAPLA) and the UNITA forces were formally disbanded, and the new national army, the Forças Armadas de Angola (FAA), was established. However, the process of training and incorporating FAPLA and UNITA troops into the new 50,000-strong national army had been hindered by delays in the demobilization programme and fewer than 10,000 soldiers were ready to be sworn in as members of the FAA.

Presidential and legislative elections were held, as scheduled, on 29 and 30 September 1992. When preliminary results indicated victory for the MPLA in the elections to the new Assembléia Nacional, Savimbi accused the Government of electoral fraud, withdrew his troops from the FAA, and demanded the suspension of the official announcement of the election results until an inquiry into the alleged irregularities had been conducted. A second round of the presidential election was required to be held between dos Santos and Savimbi, as neither candidate had secured 50% of the votes cast in the first round. Savimbi, who had retreated to the UNITA-dominated province of Huambo, agreed to participate in this second round on the condition that it be conducted by the UN, while the Government insisted that the election should not take place until UNITA had satisfied the conditions of the Estoril peace agreement by transferring its troops to assembly points or to the FAA.

Following the announcement, on 17 October 1992, of the official results of the elections, which the UN had declared to have been free and fair, violence broke out between MPLA and UNITA supporters in the cities of Luanda and Huambo. By the end of October hostilities had spread throughout Angola, with the majority of UNITA's demobilized soldiers returning to arms. On 20 November, following negotiations with UN diplomats, Savimbi agreed to abide by the results of the September elections, although he maintained that the ballot had been fraudulent. Subsequently dos Santos announced that the Assembléia Nacional would be inaugurated on 26 November. On that day delegations from the Government and UNITA issued a joint communiqué, declaring full acceptance of the validity of the May 1991 Estoril peace agreement and the intention to implement immediately a nation-wide cease-fire. However, UNITA's 70 elected deputies failed to attend the inauguration of the Assembléia. On 27 November dos Santos announced the appointment of Marcolino José Carlos Moco, the Secretary-General of the MPLA, as Prime Minister. At the end of November, in violation of the recently signed accord, hostilities broke out in the north of the country. On 2 December a new Council of Ministers was announced, including minor ministerial positions for members of the FNLA and three other parties. In addition, one full and four deputy ministerial posts were reserved for UNITA, which was allowed one week to join the Government. UNITA subsequently nominated a number of its officials to the reserved posts. According to a statement by the Prime Minister, however, the appointment of UNITA officials to the Government was entirely dependent upon the implementation of the Estoril peace agreement.

In 1993–94 the UN continued its efforts to negotiate a permanent peace accord between the Government and UNITA. Meanwhile, civil war, in which both sides claimed military gains and suffered heavy losses, continued. In May 1993 the US President, Bill Clinton, announced that the USA was to recognize the Angolan Government. In September, following reports of an intensification of UNITA activity, the UN imposed an arms and petroleum embargo against the rebels, the 'freezing' of UNITA's foreign assets, and the expulsion of its representatives from Western capitals. However, in November UNITA agreed to withdraw its forces to UN-monitored confinement areas. In response, the UN agreed to delay the imposition of further sanctions against UNITA.

As a consequence of negotiations in Lusaka, Zambia, by 10 December 1993 an agreement had reportedly been reached between UNITA and the Government on issues concerning the demobilization and confinement of UNITA troops, the surrender of UNITA weapons to the UN, and the integration of UNITA generals into the FAA, prompting the UN again to postpone additional sanctions against the rebels. The Lusaka talks resumed in January 1994, and agreement was reached on the formation, under UN supervision, of a national police force of 26,700 members, of which UNITA was to provide 5,500. Further talks culminated in the signing, on 17 February, of a document on national reconciliation. Acceptance of the September 1992 election results by both sides was also reaffirmed. However, progress at the Lusaka peace talks slowed as discussions advanced to the issue of UNITA's participation in government. Negotiations on the distribution of ministerial posts appeared to have reached an impasse in March 1994, although in May agreement was reached on the second round of the presidential election between dos Santos and Savimbi. Further talks, concerning UNITA's representation in the Council of Ministers and the status of Savimbi, reached a stalemate in May. Talks continued in Lusaka in late June, culminating in the signing of an 18-point document on national reconciliation.

In July 1994 President Nelson Mandela of South Africa hosted discussions in Pretoria between the Presidents of Angola, Mozambique and Zaire. The discussions concentrated on allegations of Zairean support for UNITA and resulted in the re-establishment of a joint defence and security commission between Angola and Zaire, with the aim of curbing the supply of armaments to the rebels. In August UNITA acceded to government insistence that its officials be permitted to participate in government institutions only after the total demilitarization of the movement, and an 11-point procedural accord, enabling discussions on full reconciliation, was signed.

In September 1994 UNITA reportedly accepted a proposal for the allocation to UNITA of government positions that included some 170 posts in central and local administration, but excluded the governorship of Huambo. At the end of that month, following successive extensions, the UN Security Council further extended the mandate of UNAVEM II until 31 October. Talks continued throughout October, concentrating on the issue of Savimbi's security and the replacement of the joint political and military commission with a new joint commission, which was to be chaired by the UN Secretary-General's special representative and was to comprise representatives of the Government and UNITA and observers from the USA, Russia and Portugal. A peace accord was finally initialled on 31 October and formally signed on 20 November. However, hostilities continued beyond 22 November, when a permanent cease-fire was to have come into force, notably in Huambo and in Bié province.

In January 1995 a meeting took place at Chipipa, in Huambo province, between the Chief of General Staff of the FAA and his UNITA counterpart, at which agreement was reached on an immediate cessation of hostilities nation-wide. Nevertheless, the fighting continued. In February 1995 the UN Security Council adopted a resolution creating UNAVEM III. However, the deployment of the new peace-keeping mission remained conditional on the cessation of hostilities and the disengagement of government and UNITA forces.

In May 1995 dos Santos and Savimbi met in Lusaka for direct talks, which concluded with the ratification of the Lusaka peace accord. Savimbi recognized the status of dos Santos as President of Angola and pledged his full co-operation in the reconstruction of the nation. The two leaders agreed to accelerate the consolidation of the cease-fire, to create conditions for the deployment of UNAVEM III, to expedite the integration of UNITA troops into the FAA, and to establish a government of unity based on the provisions of the Lusaka accord (subsequent to the demobilization of the UNITA forces). Dos Santos requested that Savimbi immediately nominate the UNITA appointees to the new government.

In June 1995 the MPLA proposed a revision of the Constitution to create two new posts of Vice-President, of which one was to be offered to Savimbi, conditional upon the prior disbanding of UNITA forces. The other vice-presidency was to be assumed by van-Dúnem, the President of the Assembléia Nacional. Later that month Savimbi, who had publicly expressed his intention to accept the vice-presidency, declared the war in Angola to be at an end and appealed to neighbouring nations to prevent the traffic of arms to the country. In July the Assembléia approved the creation of the two new vice-presidential positions, and the UN announced that the deployment of UNAVEM III personnel would be completed by the end of August. In September 1995 the joint commission expressed concern at continuing violations of the cease-fire. However, in the following month, figures issued by UNAVEM III revealed that recorded cease-fire violations had decreased by approximately 50% between July and September.

The cantonment of UNITA forces began officially in November 1995. However, continued hostilities were reported that month, including confrontations in the diamond-producing areas of the north-east and in Cabinda. In December, following concerted military operations by government forces in Zaire province, UNITA suspended the confinement of its troops. In an effort to promote confidence in the peace process in advance of discussions to be conducted that month with US President Clinton, dos Santos introduced a number of conciliatory measures, including the withdrawal of government troops from positions seized in Zaire province, and the confinement of the paramilitary Rapid Intervention Force. In January 1996 UNITA resumed the process of confining its troops. By early February, however, only some 8,200 UNITA troops had been cantoned, prompting the UN Security Council to renew the mandate of UNAVEM III.

In March 1996 discussions between dos Santos and Savimbi, conducted in Libreville, Gabon, resulted in agreement on the establishment of a government of national unity, in accordance with the provisions of the Lusaka accord. Savimbi proposed the UNITA governmental nominees, while dos Santos formally invited Savimbi to assume the vice-presidency. (Later in March, however, Savimbi demanded the appointment of other opposition members to the government of national unity, most notably the President of the FNLA, Holden Roberto.) Agreement was also reached in Libreville on the formation of a unified national army, which, it was envisaged, would be concluded in June. In subsequent talks it was agreed that 18 UNITA generals would be appointed to command posts in the new, unified FAA. It was also established that 26,300 of UNITA's total force of some 62,000 would be integrated into the FAA. In May agreement was reached on a programme to integrate UNITA troops into the FAA. During that month Savimbi introduced further conditions for his acceptance of the vice-presidency and expressed his intention to retain control of diamond-producing areas in north-eastern Angola. In mid-May the Government and a Cabinda secessionist faction, FLEC—Forças Armadas Cabindesas (FLEC—FAC), signed an agreement outlining the principles of a cease-fire. However, following renewed fighting later that month between government troops and the secessionists, the leader of FLEC—FAC, N'zita Henriques Tiago, declared that a definitive cease-fire would only follow the withdrawal of the FAA from Cabinda. A separate cease-fire had been signed with FLEC—Renovada (FLEC—R) in September 1995.

In mid-1996 public protest at deteriorating economic conditions and the high level of corruption within the state apparatus placed increasing political pressure on dos Santos, who responded in June with the dismissal of the administration. Moco was succeeded as Prime Minister by van-Dúnem. In August, following its party congress, UNITA issued a communiqué declining the appointment of Savimbi to the position of national Vice-President. UNITA did not propose the appointment of another of its officials to the post.

In November 1996 the Assembléia Nacional adopted a constitutional revision extending its mandate, which was due to expire that month, for a period of between two and four years, pending the establishment of suitable conditions for the conduct of free and fair elections. In April 1997 an agreement was reached to accord Savimbi the special status of official 'leader of the opposition'. Following the arrival of the full contingent of UNITA deputies and government nominees in Luanda, on 11 April the new Government of National Unity and Reconciliation was inaugurated, despite reports from UN sources of the existence of a residual UNITA force in central and north-eastern Angola. As envisaged, UNITA assumed a number of ministerial and deputy ministerial portfolios. Ten minor political parties were also represented in the Government.

In May 1997 the Angolan Government officially recognized the new Government of Laurent-Désiré Kabila in the Democratic Republic of the Congo (DRC, formerly Zaire). The Angolan Government had actively supported Kabila's rebels during the civil war in Zaire, while UNITA, which relied on Zaire as a conduit for exporting diamonds and importing arms, had reportedly sent some 2,000 troops to support President Mobutu. In the light of the defeat of UNITA's main ally, the Government subsequently launched a military offensive on UNITA strongholds in the north-eastern provinces of Lunda-Sul and Lunda-Norte.

On 30 June 1997 the UN Security Council unanimously approved the discontinuation of UNAVEM III and its replacement by a scaled-down observer mission, the UN Observer Mission in Angola (MONUA), with a seven-month mandate to oversee the implementation of the remaining provisions of the Lusaka accord. In late July the UN condemned UNITA's failure to adhere to the Lusaka accord and threatened to impose further sanctions on the movement, including travel restrictions, if it did not take irreversible steps towards fulfilling its obligations. A deadline of 15 August was set by which date UNITA was to give a full account of its military strength and to allow for the disarmament of its troops and the extension of state administration into those areas under its control. UNITA failed to meet the requirements stipulated by the UN, which on 28 August unanimously adopted new sanctions. However, the implementation of the resolution was delayed until 30 September, and at the end of August UNITA announced that it intended to comply with the UN's demands. In September the restoration of state administration proceeded in several districts and, despite unsatisfactory progress in the demobilization of UNITA's residual force, was sufficient to prompt the UN

Security Council, at the end of that month, to postpone the implementation of the sanctions for a further 30 days.

In July 1997 government delegations from Angola and the Republic of the Congo met in Cabinda to discuss the security situation along the border between the Angolan exclave and the Congo, following armed clashes between Angolan soldiers and FLEC separatists apparently operating from Congolese territory. The talks resulted in proposals to strengthen border security, including the establishment of a joint police force, comprising representatives from both countries and the UN High Commissioner for Refugees. However, in October it became evident that FAA troops were actively supporting the former Marxist ruler of the Congo, Gen. Denis Sassou-Nguesso, in his attempts to overthrow the Government of President Pascal Lissouba. Angola's involvement had been prompted by attacks on Cabinda by FLEC and UNITA forces operating from bases in the Congo provided by Lissouba. In mid-October Sassou-Nguesso's Cobra militia, with Angolan assistance, succeeded in securing his return to power in the Congo.

On 31 October 1997, as a result of UNITA's continued failure to meet its obligations under the peace accord, the UN Security Council finally ordered the implementation of additional sanctions against the movement. In November UNITA expressed its intention to continue to pursue a peaceful settlement, and during the ensuing months ceded further territory to state administration, including the important Cuango valley diamond mines in Lunda-Norte province.

In January 1998 a new schedule was agreed for the implementation of the Lusaka protocol. In early March UNITA announced the disbandment of its remaining forces, following which it received official recognition as a legally constituted party. Later that month the Government implemented the special status agreed for Savimbi, and legislation was adopted allowing him to retain a 400-strong personal guard. However, allegations persisted of preparations by UNITA for a resumption of hostilities. By June fighting had spread to 14 of the country's 18 provinces, displacing some 150,000 people. In July many members of UNITA were reported to have left Luanda, and a meeting of the joint commission had to be postponed owing to the temporary absence of UNITA's chief representative. In August UNITA accused the observer countries in the joint commission (Portugal, Russia and the USA) of bias in the Government's favour and declared that it would no longer negotiate with them. On 31 August the Government suspended UNITA's government and parliamentary representatives from office.

On 2 September 1998 a group of five UNITA moderates, who were based in the capital and led by the suspended Minister of Hotels and Tourism, Jorge Alicerces Valentim, issued a manifesto declaring the suspension of Savimbi and the introduction of an interim UNITA leadership, pending a general congress of the party. Although the group, which styled itself UNITA—Renovada (UNITA—R), commanded very limited support among UNITA's leaders in Luanda, the Government welcomed the development, recognizing UNITA—R as the sole and legitimate representative of UNITA in negotiations concerning the implementation of the Lusaka peace process. The UN Security Council continued to seek a dialogue between dos Santos and Savimbi as the only solution to the conflict. In late September the Government revoked the suspension of UNITA's representatives in the Government and legislature, but dismissed UNITA's Minister of Geology and Mines, Marcos Samondo. In October the Assembléia Nacional revoked Savimbi's special status. In that month UNITA—R failed to impose its candidate to lead the UNITA parliamentary group when Abel Chivukuvuku was overwhelmingly re-elected as its Chairman. Chivukuvuku, while no longer claiming allegiance to Savimbi, was opposed to UNITA—R and subsequently formed his own wing of UNITA.

In November 1998, following increasingly frequent outbreaks of fighting, the UN Security Council demanded that UNITA withdraw immediately from territories that it had reoccupied through military action and complete the demilitarization of its troops. The military situation deteriorated considerably in December, prompting the Government to approve the introduction of compulsory military service.

In January 1999, in an effort to address the prevailing military and economic crisis, dos Santos assumed the role of Prime Minister, and in the same month UNITA—R conducted its first congress in Luanda, at which Eugénio N'Golo 'Manuvakola' was elected leader of the faction. In February the UN Security Council voted unanimously to end MONUA's mandate and withdraw its operatives by 20 March, on the grounds that

conditions had deteriorated to such an extent that UN personnel were no longer able to function. In October the UN and the Government formally agreed on the establishment of a 30-member 'follow-up' mission, the UN Office in Angola (UNOA), which was to focus on issues concerning humanitarian assistance and human rights.

In October 1999, following a large-scale offensive by the FAA in northern, eastern and central Angola, the Government claimed to have made considerable gains, including the capture of UNITA's headquarters in Andulo and Bailundo. While UNITA denied that the towns had fallen to the Government, there were reports that Savimbi had fled the area. In a letter to the Government received in late October, Savimbi warned that UNITA troops were approaching the capital and called for dialogue towards a 'national pact'. The Government, however, dismissed the possibility of further talks, demanding instead the full implementation of the Lusaka protocol.

During 1999 the UN increased its efforts to impose sanctions on UNITA, with the appointment of Canada's ambassador to the UN, Robert Fowler, as Chairman of the UN Sanctions Committee. In July the UN financed an investigation into UNITA's funding of its war effort, the source of its armaments and the inefficacy of the sanctions imposed against it. A UN report published in June disclosed the contravention of UN sanctions by a number of African heads of state, including the Presidents of Togo and Burkina Faso, who were apparently involved in the trading of arms for UNITA-mined diamonds. (Togo subsequently banned all sales of Angolan diamonds, except those bearing a certificate of origin.) In October 1999 the South African diamond company De Beers, which controls the majority of the international trade in diamonds, announced that it had placed a world-wide embargo on the purchase of all diamonds from Angola, except those whose acquisition was already under contract. The Angolan Government also attempted to stem the flow of illegal diamonds by introducing a strict regime of stone certification. In March 2000 a number of African leaders, as well as individuals in Belgium and Bulgaria, were criticized in a UN report for allegedly violating sanctions that had been imposed on UNITA following the discovery of the trade in illegally mined diamonds. In response, the Angolan Government announced the establishment of a state-owned company, the Sociedade de Comercialização de Diamantes, which was to be responsible for centralizing and regulating the country's diamond trade. All marketing was transferred to the newly created Angolan Selling Corporation. In December the UN Angola Sanctions Committee issued a further report on the smuggling of UNITA diamonds, which confirmed that sanctions had failed to prevent the movement's involvement in the diamond trade, and accused several countries of supporting the illegal trade.

At the end of June 2000 the Angolan Government and UNITA representatives were reported to have held secret talks on the possible means of achieving peace in Angola. The conference was attended by the Angolan Deputy Minister of Foreign Affairs, George Chicoti, by 'Manuvakola' from UNITA—R and by Chivukuvuku from UNITA. Furthermore, in August the Angolan Chief of Staff of the Armed Forces, Gen. João de Matos, announced that Savimbi would no longer be prosecuted for his failure to uphold the cease-fire imposed following the 1992 elections. However, he also stated that, although a position would be made available in the Assembléia Nacional for Savimbi, he would not be offered the vice-presidency.

In October 2000 UNITA put forward a 12-point peace plan, including proposals for the formation of a 'broad consensus government' and the depoliticization of the armed forces, the police and public administration. The plan was rejected by the Government. Nevertheless, UNITA reiterated its desire to negotiate with the Angolan Government, on condition that the current Portuguese, US and Russian observers be replaced by Angolan nationals, that the sanctions imposed on UNITA in 1993 be revoked, and that the second round of the 1992 presidential election be held. In November, however, UNITA admitted responsibility for shooting down an aircraft, allegedly carrying diamonds stolen from UNITA territory. Moreover, UNITA rejected an amnesty for all perpetrators of war crimes, which was declared by dos Santos in a speech marking the 25th anniversary of Angola's independence. Nevertheless, in December the Assembléia Nacional approved draft amnesty legislation, which had been proposed by the MPLA as a direct response to appeals for reconciliation in Angola.

In June 2001, following an alleged declaration by Savimbi that UNITA forces had been conclusively defeated by the FAA, the Minister of Industry, Joaquim Duarte da Costa David, announced that the civil war had effectively ended. Nevertheless, sporadic fighting between both factions persisted throughout mid-2001, and in mid-June the Minister of Defence, Gen. Kundi Paihama, stated that civil war was the only means of securing peace in Angola. In August UNITA carried out an attack on a train in the government-controlled province of Cuanza Norte that was allegedly carrying munitions, although this was denied by the Government; the attack, in which some 260 people were killed, cast further doubts on both sides' commitment to peace.

In September 2001 the Roman Catholic Church and civil movements in Angola launched an appeal for peace, calling for a cease-fire and the resumption of dialogue between the Government, UNITA and opposition parties. This appeal was supported by a coalition of 35 opposition parties, the Partidos da Oposição Civil, which advocated the establishment of a transitional government, to rule until such time as elections were held. In November dos Santos declared the civil war to be almost ended, on the grounds that UNITA had only a small number of troops remaining at its disposal.

On 22 February 2002 Savimbi was killed during an ambush by FAA soldiers in Moxico province. He was replaced as UNITA President by António Dembo; however, in early March it was reported that he, too, had died, possibly through FAA action, which the Government denied, or as a result of acute diabetes. On 13 March the Government halted military offensives against UNITA, and on 30 March, following talks between the Government and UNITA's Chief-of-Staff, Gen. Abreu 'Kamorteiro' Muengo, both parties signed a memorandum of understanding, aimed at ending the civil war. On 4 April a cease-fire agreement was ratified, in which UNITA accepted the Lusaka protocol and agreed to the cantonment of its soldiers. Some 5,000 UNITA soldiers were to be integrated into the FAA, and UNITA representatives were to take up positions in central, provincial and local government.

By the end of July 2002 some 85,000 UNITA soldiers and an estimated 300,000 family members had registered in quartering camps, amid severe food shortages, but only 30,000 light arms had been turned over to the Government. Nevertheless, in early August UNITA announced that its military wing had been disbanded, following the integration of its soldiers into the FAA. Also in August, the UN Security Council established the UN Mission in Angola (UNMA) to succeed UNOA until 15 February 2003. On 23 August 2002 the Government and UNITA set a 45-day deadline for the full implementation of the Lusaka protocol, which was to be monitored by a UN-led joint commission, comprising representatives of the Government, UNITA and observer countries (Portugal, Russia and the USA). In October the inauguration of a new national political commission for UNITA, including former members of UNITA—R, marked the official reunification of the party; Gen. Paulo Lukamba 'Gato' was confirmed as interim leader of the party, pending a full congress.

In September 2002 João Lourenço, the Secretary-General of the MPLA, admitted the possibility of limited autonomy for Cabinda, but ruled out independence. Meanwhile, fighting continued in Cabinda between FAA troops and FLEC—FAC rebels. An FAA offensive took FLEC—FAC headquarters in Kungo-Shonzo, in the municipality of Buco-Zau, in late October, and in December the FAA claimed that it had also seized FLEC—R's main base. During February 2003 FLEC—R and FLEC—FAC forces in Cabinda were actively dispersed by the FAA, and 7,000 captured civilians were freed. Action against the Cabinda rebels was strengthened by a security pact between Angola, the Republic of the Congo and the DRC, which had been signed in January.

The FAA maintained forces in Cabinda throughout 2003, and by the middle of that year it was believed that, with the exception of some pockets of resistance in the north, the province had been pacified. FLEC—FAC continued to state that it was prepared to negotiate a peace agreement based on a level of autonomy for Cabinda within Angola, and in August the Government declared that it was willing to reopen negotiations on that basis. The Government repeatedly denied claims by human rights and church groups that FAA soldiers had been responsible for human rights abuses in Cabinda. At the end of November the demobilization of former FLEC—FAC fighters began. In September 2004 the merger was announced of FLEC—FAC and FLEC—R. The new grouping, which adopted the name FLEC, was led by N'Zita Henriques Tiago, while

António Bento Bembe, previously the President of FLEC—R, became Secretary-General of the movement. A political wing, calling itself FLEC—Conselho Superior Alargado (FLEC—CSA), with the stated aim of achieving independence through political means, was subsequently established under the leadership of Liberal Nuno.

Meanwhile, in October 2002 the UN Development Programme reported that Angola was threatened with an 'extremely serious humanitarian crisis' as a result of the civil war, which had caused severe damage to political and economic structures and displaced some 4.3m. people. On 11 November, to mark the celebration of Angola's first peacetime Independence Day, UNITA declared its intention to accelerate the approval of new policies designed to aid the economy. Meanwhile, President dos Santos inaugurated several programmes for urban regeneration. The joint commission responsible for supervising the implementation of the Lusaka protocol was dissolved in late November, to be replaced by a joint UNITA-Government mechanism.

In early December 2002 Fernando (Nando) da Piedade Dias dos Santos, hitherto Minister of the Interior, was appointed as Prime Minister, a post that President dos Santos had himself held since January 1999. The Council of Ministers was subsequently reshuffled, with the inclusion of the four UNITA representatives. Shortly afterwards the UN Security Council voted to lift all remaining sanctions on UNITA, having previously removed travel restrictions on officials of the former rebel group. Meanwhile, a Constitutional Commission (which had been established by the Assembléia Nacional in 1998) was considering proposals for a new draft constitution. Agreement was reached on a major point of contention in January 2003, when the Commission decided that the President of the Republic would remain Head of Government, as favoured by MPLA deputies; UNITA had advocated the devolvement of executive power to the Prime Minister. In mid-February UNMA withdrew from Angola, as scheduled. Later that month the Government announced that five of the 35 quartering camps had been closed, with the resettlement of 22,643 former UNITA fighters and 70,694 civilians.

In June 2003 Isaías Samakuva was elected President of UNITA at the party congress. UNITA affirmed its intention to remain an active part of the Government until the next presidential and legislative elections, which were expected to be held in 2005 or 2006. In October 2003, in Luanda, more than 1,000 people reportedly participated in the first authorized anti-Government protests since peace was declared. The protesters, organized by a coalition of small opposition parties, demanded that elections be held in 2004. At the fifth MPLA congress, which took place in December 2003, President dos Santos was re-elected unopposed as Chairman of the party.

The demobilization of former UNITA soldiers continued throughout 2003. The Government closed the quartering camps in June, and by November around 80,000 soldiers, along with their families, had been demobilized. A number of difficulties arose regarding the economic reintegration of former combatants, principally owing to a lack of funds. Notably, the authorities struggled to provide soldiers with the agricultural equipment and financial assistance that they had been promised under the 2002 memorandum of understanding.

In January 2004 the Constitutional Commission was presented with a draft constitution and in mid-2004 the Government, which had identified 14 'key tasks' it wished to accomplish before calling concurrent legislative and presidential elections—including constitutional reform and the compiling of an electoral register— stated that polls would not take place until late 2006. A government report estimated that the cost of holding legislative and presidential elections would amount to US $430m., however, this figure was disputed by UNITA, which believed the sum required would be far greater. The report also recommended that a minimum period of one year be allowed in order to prepare for the elections, however, several opposition parties, including UNITA, insisted that elections could take place in 2005 without constitutional reform and withdrew from the Commission in May 2004 in protest at the perceived lack of progress towards elections. In September the opposition parties rejoined the Commission, which was dissolved in November after a draft constitutional bill had been presented to the Assembléia Nacional. Opposition parties strongly criticized the closure of the Commission. Also in November President dos Santos indicated that a presidential election could be delayed until one year after legislative elections. In December it was announced that a governmental commission to be chaired by the Minister of Territorial Administration, Virgílio Fontes Pereira, and charged with the task of preparing for the elections, had been created.

Meanwhile, in early July 2004 the leader of the opposition Partido Democrático para o Progresso—Aliança Nacional de Angola (PDP—ANA), Mfulupinga Lindo Victor, was shot dead in Luanda. The PDP—ANA blamed the MPLA for the killing and UNITA officials subsequently alleged that the MPLA had carried out a number of attacks on its members. Human rights organizations active in Angola confirmed that there had been an apparent rise in politically motivated violence

During late 2004 President dos Santos effected a series of minor reorganizations of the Council of Ministers and appointed several new Provincial Governors. Most notably, in mid-December the Minister of Justice, Paulo Tjipilika, was dismissed and replaced by Manuel da Costa Aragão, hitherto his deputy, while Joaquim António Carlos dos Reis succeeded António van Dúnem as the Secretary of the Council of Ministers.

Between late 2002 and late 2003 the Angolan Government and the office of the UN High Commissioner for Refugees (UNHCR) established separate tripartite commissions with Zambia, the DRC, Namibia, Botswana, the Republic of the Congo and South Africa, with the aim of facilitating the repatriation of Angolan refugees from these countries. In early 2003 there were an estimated 470,000 Angolan refugees in the region, including 210,000 in Zambia, 192,000 in the DRC and 24,000 in Namibia. By November around 200,000 of these had been repatriated by UNHCR or had returned without assistance. However, significant problems remained for returning refugees, notably the presence of landmines, a lack of infrastructure and social services in rural areas, and disputes over land rights. In November 2003 the Council of Ministers approved draft legislation on land possession, which was adopted by the Assembléia Nacional in August 2004. Non-governmental organizations had earlier expressed concern over the effect of the legislation on the urban and rural poor. In December 2004 UNHCR announced that 50,000 refugees, from a target of 90,000, had returned to Angola in that year. The lack of funds and infrastructural problems continued to hinder the refugees' return. In total, since 2002, more than 279,000 refugees had returned to Angola by late 2004, however, it was estimated that 167,000 Angolans remained in neighbouring countries. In late 2004 internal health authorities stated that there were just 13,700 officially recorded cases of HIV/AIDS in Angola, although it was believed that up to 1m. Angolans were infected.

Following the internal uprising in August 1998 against the Kabila regime in the DRC, the Angolan Government moved swiftly to provide Kabila with military support against the rebels. In September the number of FAA troops in the DRC was estimated at 5,000. In October, as the conflict escalated in the east of the DRC, Angola, in alliance with Namibia and Zimbabwe, stated that it would continue supporting Kabila until the rebels were defeated. Following the assassination of Kabila in January 2001, the Angolan Government announced its intention to allow its troops stationed in the DRC to remain there until further notice; moreover, several thousand additional Angolan troops were moved into that country later in January. However, by the end of October 2002 Angola, Namibia and Zimbabwe had completed the withdrawal of their troops from the DRC. Between December 2003 and August 2004 the Angolan authorities were reported to have expelled an estimated 120,000 illegal diamond workers, mostly from the DRC, from northern Angola.

Relations with Zambia became tense during 1999, following persistent allegations that it was actively supporting UNITA. It was further alleged that senior ministers in the Zambian Government had been personally involved in contravening sanctions. In June, following co-operation talks between the respective governments, an agreement was signed putting aside past disputes. In May 2000 the Zambian Minister of Defence accused the FAA of carrying out raids in Zambian territory; the allegations were denied by Angola. However, both countries subsequently agreed to increase cross-border co-operation, and Zambian government officials confirmed that UNITA rebels would not be allowed to undertake any military incursions into Angola from Zambian territory. Meanwhile, clashes reportedly took place along the Namibian border with Angola, during which UNITA rebels were killed or arrested by the Namibian security forces.

In 2000 a French judicial inquiry was instigated into alleged arms-trafficking to Angola by a French company, Brenco Inter-

national, and a French businessman, Pierre Falcone. The company, along with a number of prominent French politicians, was alleged to have engaged in money-laundering and the unauthorized sales of arms worth some US $600m. to the dos Santos Government in 1993–94. Falcone was placed under provisional detention in France in December 2000, but was released after one year, the maximum term allowed for temporary detention. French and Swiss investigations into the sale of weapons to Angola, as well as the settlement of the country's debt to Russia, continued during 2005. Meanwhile, Falcone's appointment, in June 2003, as a plenipotentiary minister at the Angolan permanent delegation to UNESCO, entitling him to diplomatic immunity, provoked considerable international controversy and condemnation from Angolan opposition parties and civil society organizations.

In July 1996 Angola was among the five lusophone African countries that, together with Portugal and Brazil, formed the Comunidade dos Países de Língua Portuguesa (see p. 383), a Portuguese-speaking commonwealth seeking to achieve collective benefits from co-operation in technical, cultural and social matters. In 2004 Angola joined the African Peer Review Mechanism, a group designed to monitor economic and political development.

Government

In March 1991 and in the first half of 1992 the Government of the Movimento Popular de Libertação de Angola—Partido do Trabalho (MPLA—PT) introduced a series of far-reaching amendments to the 1975 Constitution, providing for the establishment of a multi-party democracy (hitherto, no other political parties, apart from the ruling MPLA—PT, had been permitted). According to the amendments, legislative power was to be vested in the National Assembly (Assembléia Nacional), with 223 members elected for four years on the basis of proportional representation. Executive power was to be held by the President, who was to be directly elected for a term of five years (renewable for a maximum of three terms). As Head of State and Commander-in-Chief of the armed forces, the President was to govern with the assistance of an appointed Council of Ministers. Proposals for a new constitution were under consideration in early 2005.

For the purposes of local government, the country is divided into 18 provinces, each administered by an appointed Governor.

Legislative elections, held in September 1992, resulted in victory for the MPLA. However, in the presidential election, which was held at the same time, the MPLA's candidate and incumbent President, José Eduardo dos Santos, narrowly failed to secure the 50% of the votes necessary to be elected President. Following a resumption of hostilities between UNITA and government forces, the conduct of a second round of the presidential election was held in abeyance, with dos Santos remaining in the presidency. In accordance with the terms of the Lusaka peace accord of November 1994, in April 1997 a new Government of National Unity and Reconciliation was inaugurated in which UNITA held four portfolios. However, following a resumption of hostilities, in August 1998 UNITA's government representatives were suspended from office. In 2004 the Government proposed that legislative elections be held in late 2006, and it seemed likely that a presidential poll would take place one year later.

Defence

In accordance with the peace agreement concluded by the Government and the União Nacional para a Independência Total de Angola (UNITA) in May 1991 (see Recent History), a new 50,000-strong national army, the Forças Armadas de Angola (FAA), was established, comprising equal numbers of government forces, the Forças Armadas Populares de Libertação de Angola, and UNITA soldiers. Following elections in 1992, UNITA withdrew its troops from the FAA, alleging electoral fraud on the part of the Movimento Popular de Libertação de Angola, and hostilities resumed. After the signing of the Lusaka peace accord in November 1994, preparations for the confinement and demobilization of troops, and the integration of the UNITA contingent into the FAA, resumed. In 1995 the Government and UNITA reached agreement on the enlargement of the FAA to comprise a total of 90,000 troops, and discussions began concerning the potential formation of a fourth, non-combatant branch of the FAA, which would engage in public works projects. In mid-1997 the Government estimated that a residual UNITA force numbered some 25,000–30,000 troops, while UNITA claimed to have retained a force of only 2,963 'police'. In March

1998 UNITA issued a declaration announcing the complete demobilization of its forces. However, evidence of the existence of a large UNITA force became apparent with the escalation of widespread hostilities in Angola from mid-1998. Following the ratification of a peace agreement between UNITA and the Government in April 2002, some 5,000 former UNITA soldiers were incorporated into the FAA in mid-2002, and by November 2003 around 80,000 former combatants had been demobilized and were to be reintegrated into civilian life. In August 2004 the FAA had an estimated total strength of 108,400: army 100,000, navy 2,400 and air force 6,000. In addition, there was a paramilitary force numbering an estimated 10,000. The defence budget for 2005 was 171,124m. kwanza, or 17.7% of total expenditure. It was estimated that FLEC had a total strength of 600.

Economic Affairs

In 2003, according to estimates by the World Bank, Angola's gross national income (GNI), measured at average 2001–03 prices, was US $10,728m., equivalent to $740 per head (or $1,890 per head on an international purchasing-power parity basis). During 1990–2003, it was estimated, Angola's population increased at an average annual rate of 2.9%, while gross domestic product (GDP) per head declined, in real terms, by an average of 0.6% per year. Overall GDP increased, in real terms, at an average annual rate of 2.3% in 1990–2003; growth in 2003 was 4.5%.

Agriculture, forestry and fishing contributed an estimated 7.9% of GDP in 2003. An estimated 71.3% of the total working population were employed in the agricultural sector in 2002. Coffee is the principal cash crop. The main subsistence crops are cassava, maize, sweet potatoes, sugar cane and bananas. Severe food shortages following a period of drought in late 2000 worsened in 2001, owing to continued low levels of agricultural productivity. During 1990–2003, according to the World Bank, agricultural GDP increased at an average annual rate of 0.3%, and by 6.0% in 2003.

Industry (including mining, manufacturing, construction and power) provided an estimated 61.4% of GDP in 2003, and employed an estimated 10.5% of the labour force in 1991. According to the World Bank, industrial GDP increased, in real terms, at an average annual rate of 4.3% in 1990–2003; growth in industrial GDP was 4.4% in 2003.

Mining contributed an estimated 54.3% of GDP in 2003. Petroleum production (including liquefied petroleum gas) accounted for an estimated 49.6% of GDP in that year. Angola's principal mineral exports are petroleum and diamonds. In addition, there are reserves of iron ore, copper, lead, zinc, gold, manganese, phosphates, salt and uranium.

The manufacturing sector provided an estimated 3.7% of GDP in 2003. The principal branch of manufacturing is petroleum refining. Other manufacturing activities include food-processing, brewing, textiles and construction materials. According to the World Bank, the GDP of the manufacturing sector increased at an average annual rate of 1.4% in 1990–2003; growth in manufacturing GDP was 4.9% in 2003.

Energy is derived mainly from hydroelectric power, which, according to the World Bank, provided 63.2% of Angola's electricity production in 2001, while petroleum accounted for 36.8%. Angola's power potential exceeds its requirements.

Services accounted for an estimated 30.7% of GDP in 2003, and engaged an estimated 20.1% of the labour force in 1991. In real terms, the GDP of the services sector declined at an average annual rate of 0.8% in 1990–2003. However, services GDP increased by 4.2% in 2003.

In 2001 Angola recorded an estimated visible trade surplus of US $3,355m., while there was an estimated deficit of $1,431m. on the current account of the balance of payments. In 2002, according to estimates, the principal source of imports (15.4%) was Portugal; other major suppliers were the USA (11.2%) and South Africa (9.9%). In that year the principal market for exports, according to estimates, was the USA (42.0%); the People's Republic of China and Taiwan were also significant purchasers of Angola's exports. The principal exports in 2002 were crude petroleum, accounting for 90.5% of total export earnings, and diamonds (7.6%). The principal imports in 1985 were foodstuffs, transport equipment, electrical equipment and base metals. In 2003 petroleum exports amounted to US $8,546m.

In 2004 the projected budget anticipated a deficit of 53,782m. kwanza, excluding changes in payment arrears of 13,242m. kwanza. Angola's total external debt at the end of 2002 was US $10,134m., of which $8,883m. was long-term public debt. In that year the cost of debt-servicing was equivalent to 10.0% of the value of exports of goods and services. The average annual rate of inflation was 218.7% in 2000–2003. Consumer prices increased by an average of 108.9% in 2002 and of 98.2% in 2003.

Angola is a member of both the Common Market for Eastern and Southern Africa (see p. 179) and the Southern African Development Community (see p. 345), which was formed with the aim of reducing the economic dependence of southern African states on South Africa.

From independence, exploitation of Angola's extensive mineral reserves, hydroelectric potential and abundant fertile land was severely impaired by internal conflict, as well as an acute shortage of skilled personnel. Following the ratification of a cease-fire agreement in April 2002, Angola's prospects depended greatly on a resolution of the civil strife, the reintegration of the displaced population and the rehabilitation of the country's devastated infrastructure. Despite civil conflict, the development of the petroleum sector continued apace in the late 1990s and early 2000s, although much petroleum revenue was used to finance the Government's military expenditure. In late 2003 total national output of crude petroleum was more than 1m. barrels per day (b/d) and production was projected to reach some 2m. b/d by 2009. In 2003 Angola received US $1,400m. in foreign direct investment, mainly in the petroleum sector, however, this was a decline of 12.5% compared with the previous year. In early 2004 it was claimed that, according to IMF figures, the Angolan Government had failed to account for some $4,220m. of total petroleum revenues of $17,800m. between 1997 and 2002, equivalent to some 9% of GDP annually. The Minister of Finance, José Pedro de Morais, denounced the figures, estimating the financial discrepancy in 1997–2002 at $674m., which he attributed to known deficiencies in the budgetary system and the financial management of the public sector. It was hoped that Angola's participation in the IMF's general data dissemination system, from February 2004, would improve the accuracy of its national statistics system. In September 2004 de Morais announced the creation of a reserve fund to manage the surplus in tax revenues, estimated at $275m. in the first half of the year, which was generated by a rise in crude petroleum prices. Angola, which is sub-Saharan Africa's second largest petroleum producer, is also the fourth largest diamond producer in the world, in terms of revenue, and earnings from that sector totalled some $788m. in 2003. The budget for 2005 was projected to balance at 956,000m. kwanza with the petroleum sector expected to provide 66.7% of total revenue. Furthermore, it was anticipated that inflation in 2005 would be reduced to just 15%, and that GDP would increase by 16%. Following an Article IV consultation with the IMF in mid-2004, and a visit to Angola by IMF officials later in the year, it appeared likely that progress would be made towards a new Poverty Reduction and Growth Facility in 2005, which would further support the Government's efforts to rebuild the country's damaged infrastructure and combat poverty.

Education

Education is officially compulsory for eight years, between seven and 15 years of age, and is provided free of charge by the Government. Primary education begins at six years of age and lasts for four years. Secondary education, beginning at the age of 10, lasts for up to seven years, comprising a first cycle of four years and a second of three years. As a proportion of the school-age population, the total enrolment at primary and secondary schools was 45% in 1991. According to UNESCO estimates, enrolment at primary schools in 2000/01 included 37% of children in the relevant age-group (boys 39%; girls 35%), while secondary enrolment was equivalent to 18% of children in the relevant age-group (boys 19%; girls 16%). In 1997/98 the Agostinho Neto university, in Luanda, at that time the country's only university, had 8,337 students. In November 2002 the Government announced plans for the construction of seven provincial universities, five science and technology institutes, three medical schools and a nutrition research centre. Much education is now conducted in vernacular languages rather than Portuguese. In 2004 the Government recruited 29,000 new teachers, to be trained by the UN Children's Fund (UNICEF). The 1999 budget allocated an estimated 430m. kwanza (4.8% of total expenditure) to education.

Public Holidays

2005: 1 January (New Year's Day), 4 January (Martyrs' Day), 4 February (Anniversary of the outbreak of the armed struggle against Portuguese colonialism), 8 February (Carnival Day), 8 March (International Women's Day), 25 March (Good Friday), 27 March (Victory Day)*, 4 April (Peace and National Reconciliation Day), 14 April (Youth Day)*, 1 May (Workers' Day), 25 May (Africa Day), 1 June (International Children's Day), 1 August (Armed Forces' Day)*, 17 September (National Hero's Day, birthday of Dr Agostinho Neto), 2 November (All Souls' Day), 11 November (Independence Day), 1 December (Pioneers' Day)*, 10 December (Foundation of the MPLA Day)*, 25 December (Christmas Day and Family Day).

2006: 1 January (New Year's Day), 4 January (Martyrs' Day), 4 February (Anniversary of the outbreak of the armed struggle against Portuguese colonialism), 28 February (Carnival Day), 8 March (International Women's Day), 27 March (Victory Day)*, 4 April (Peace and National Reconciliation Day), 14 April (Good

Friday and Youth Day)*, 1 May (Workers' Day), 25 May (Africa Day), 1 June (International Children's Day), 1 August (Armed Forces' Day)*, 17 September (National Hero's Day, birthday of Dr Agostinho Neto), 2 November (All Souls' Day), 11 November (Independence Day), 1 December (Pioneers' Day)*, 10 December (Foundation of the MPLA Day)*, 25 December (Christmas Day and Family Day).

* Although not officially recognized as public holidays, these days are popularly treated as such.

Weights and Measures

The metric system is in force.

Statistical Survey

Source (unless otherwise stated): Instituto Nacional de Estatística, Avda Ho Chi Minh, CP 1215, Luanda; tel. (2) 322776; e-mail ine@angonet.gn.apc.org.

Area and Population

AREA, POPULATION AND DENSITY

Area (sq km)	1,246,700*
Population (census results)	
30 December 1960	4,480,719
15 December 1970	
Males	2,943,974
Females	2,702,192
Total	5,646,166
Population (UN estimates at mid-year)	
2001	12,768,000
2002	13,184,000
2003	13,625,000
Density (per sq km) at mid-2003	10.9

* 481,354 sq miles.

DISTRIBUTION OF POPULATION BY PROVINCE
(provisional estimates, mid-1995)

	Area (sq km)	Population	Density (per sq km)
Luanda	2,418	2,002,000	828.0
Huambo	34,274	1,687,000	49.2
Bié	70,314	1,246,000	17.7
Malanje	87,246	975,000	11.2
Huíla	75,002	948,000	12.6
Uíge	58,698	948,000	16.2
Benguela	31,788	702,000	22.1
Cuanza-Sul . . .	55,660	688,000	12.4
Cuanza-Norte . .	24,110	412,000	17.1
Moxico	223,023	349,000	1.6
Lunda-Norte	102,783	311,000	3.0
Zaire	40,130	247,000	6.2
Cunene	88,342	245,000	2.8
Cabinda	7,270	185,000	25.4
Bengo	31,371	184,000	5.9
Lunda-Sul	56,985	160,000	2.8
Cuando-Cubango . .	199,049	137,000	0.7
Namibe	58,137	135,000	2.3
Total	1,246,600	11,561,000	9.3

PRINCIPAL TOWNS
(population at 1970 census)

Luanda (capital) .	480,613	Benguela	40,996
Huambo (Nova Lisboa)	61,885	Lubango (Sá da Bandeira) . . .	31,674
Lobito	59,258	Malanje	31,559

Source: Direcção dos Serviços de Estatística.

Mid-2003 (UN estimate, incl. suburbs): Luanda 2,622,976 (Source: UN, *World Urbanization Prospects: The 2003 Revision*).

BIRTHS AND DEATHS
(UN estimates, annual averages)

	1985–90	1990–95	1995–2000
Birth rate (per 1,000)	52.1	52.1	52.2
Death rate (per 1,000)	25.1	24.7	24.0

Source: UN, *World Population Prospects: The 2002 Revision*.

Expectation of life (WHO estimates, years at birth): 39.9 (males 37.9; females 42.0) in 2002 (Source: WHO, *World Health Report*).

ECONOMICALLY ACTIVE POPULATION
(estimates, '000 persons, 1991)

	Males	Females	Total
Agriculture, etc.	1,518	1,374	2,892
Industry	405	33	438
Services	644	192	836
Total labour force	2,567	1,599	4,166

Source: UN Economic Commission for Africa, *African Statistical Yearbook*.

1996 (official estimates, '000 persons): Total employed 475,214 (males 363,646, females 111,569) (Source: ILO).

Mid-2003 (estimates in '000): Agriculture, etc. 4,406; Total (incl. others) 6,202 (Source: FAO).

Health and Welfare

KEY INDICATORS

Total fertility rate (children per woman, 2002)	7.2
Under-5 mortality rate (per 1,000 live births, 2003)	260
HIV/AIDS (% of persons aged 15–49, 2003)	3.9
Physicians (per 1,000 head, 1997)	0.08
Hospital beds (per 1,000 head, 1990)	1.29
Health expenditure (2001): US $ per head (PPP)	70
Health expenditure (2001): % of GDP	4.4
Health expenditure (2001): public (% of total)	63.1
Access to water (% of persons, 2002)	50
Access to sanitation (% of persons, 2002)	30
Human Development Index (2002): ranking	166
Human Development Index (2002): value	0.381

For sources and definitions, see explanatory note on p. vi.

Agriculture

PRINCIPAL CROPS
('000 metric tons)

	2001	2002	2003
Wheat*	4	4	4
Rice (paddy)†	16	16	16
Maize	429	426	545
Millet	148	119	97
Potatoes†	27	27	27
Sweet potatoes	353	423	438
Cassava (Manioc)	5,394	5,620	5,699
Sugar cane†	360	360	360
Dry beans	89	58	66
Groundnuts (in shell)	27	30	30†
Sunflower seed†	11	11	11
Oil palm fruit†	280	280	280
Cottonseed†	5.6	5.6	5.6
Tomatoes†	13	13	13
Onions and shallots (green)† . .	13	13	13
Other vegetables†	245	245	245
Bananas†	300	300	300
Citrus fruit†	78	78	78
Pineapples†	40	40	40
Other fruits (excl. melons)† . .	32	32	32
Coffee (green)	3*	1*	1†

* Unofficial figure(s).
† FAO estimate(s).
Source: FAO.

LIVESTOCK
(FAO estimates, '000 head, year ending September)

	2001	2002	2003
Cattle	4,100	4,150	4,150
Pigs	800	780	780
Sheep	350	340	340
Goats	2,150	2,050	2,050
Chickens	6,800	6,800	6,800

Source: FAO.

LIVESTOCK PRODUCTS
(FAO estimates, '000 metric tons)

	2000	2001	2002
Beef and veal	85.0	85.0	85.0
Goat meat	9.7	9.7	9.2
Pig meat	28.6	28.6	27.9
Chicken meat	7.7	7.7	7.7
Game meat	7.5	7.5	7.5
Mutton and lamb	1.3	1.3	1.3
Cows' milk	195.0	195.0	195.0
Cheese	1.2	1.2	1.2
Hen eggs	4.3	4.3	4.3
Honey	23.0	23.0	23.0
Beeswax	2.3	2.3	2.3
Cattle hides	10.6	10.8	11.0

2003: Figures assumed to be unchanged from 2002 (FAO estimates).
Source: FAO.

Forestry

ROUNDWOOD REMOVALS
('000 cubic metres, excluding bark, FAO estimates)

	2001	2002	2002
Sawlogs, veneer logs and logs for sleepers*	66	66	66
Other industrial wood	1,050	1,050	1,050
Fuel wood	3,241	3,320	3,402
Total	4,357	4,436	4,518

* Annual output assumed to be unchanged since 1990.
Source: FAO.

SAWNWOOD PRODUCTION
('000 cubic metres, including railway sleepers, FAO estimates)

	1983	1984	1985
Total	6	2	5

1986–2003: Annual production as in 1985 (FAO estimates).
Source: FAO.

Fishing

('000 metric tons, live weight)

	2000	2001	2002
Freshwater fishes*	6.0	6.0	6.0
West African croakers	8.0	8.7	29.9
Dentex	13.8	16.1	8.9
Cunene horse mackerel	53.2	40.9	43.3
Sardinellas	108.2	57.9	28.5
Total catch (incl. others) . . .	238.4	252.5	260.8

* FAO estimates.
Source: FAO.

Mining

('000 metric tons, unless otherwise indicated)

	2000	2001	2002
Crude petroleum*	36,900	36,600	44,600
Natural gas (million cu metres) .	11,613†	11,027†	n.a.
Salt (unrefined)	30	30	30
Diamonds ('000 carats):‡			
industrial	431	516	502
gem	3,882	4,644	4,520

* Data from BP, *Statistical Review of World Energy, 2004*.
† Reported figure.
‡ Reported figures, based on estimates of 90% of production at gem grade and 10% of production at industrial grade.
Source: mainly US Geological Survey.

2003 ('000 metric tons): Crude petroleum 43,600 (Source: BP, *Statistical Review of World Energy, 2004*).

Industry

SELECTED PRODUCTS
('000 metric tons, unless otherwise indicated)

	1998	1999	2000
Frozen fish	56.8	41.5	41.6
Wheat flour	46.0	57.5	69.0
Maize flour	113.8	n.a.	n.a.
Yam flour	260.0	n.a.	n.a.
Bread	70.0	87.5	105.0
Beer ('000 hectolitres)	1,297.3	1,609.4	1,931.3
Jet fuels	284.8	338.5	320.7
Motor spirit (petrol)	101.7	128.1	111.4
Kerosene	28.3	30.4	30.2
Distillate fuel oils	445.7	493.0	468.4
Residual fuel oils	662.8	646.8	595.3
Butane gas	28.5	30.5	29.6
Cement	194.5	206.7	200.6

Source: IMF, *Angola: Selected Issues and Statistical Appendix* (September 2003).

2002 (FAO estimates, '000 hectolitres, unless otherwise indicated): Beer of barley 1,050.0; Beer of maize 238.7; Beer of millet 535.3; Palm oil ('000 metric tons) 58 (official estimate) (Source: FAO).

2003 (FAO estimates, '000 hectolitres, unless otherwise indicated): Beer of barley 950.0; Beer of maize 290.4; Beer of millet 434.9; Palm oil ('000 metric tons) 58 (Source: FAO).

Finance

CURRENCY AND EXCHANGE RATES

Monetary Units
100 lwei = 1 kwanza.

Sterling, Dollar and Euro Equivalents (31 December 2004)
£1 sterling = 167.422 kwanza;
US $1 = 86.684 kwanza;
€1 = 118.073 kwanza;
1,000 kwanza = £5.97 = $11.54 = €8.47.

Average Exchange Rate (kwanza per US $)
2002   43.530
2003   74.606
2004   83.570

Note: In April 1994 the introduction of a new method of setting exchange rates resulted in an effective devaluation of the new kwanza, to US $1 = 68,297 new kwanza, and provided for an end to the system of multiple exchange rates. Further substantial devaluations followed, and in July 1995 a 'readjusted' kwanza, equivalent to 1,000 new kwanza, was introduced. The currency, however, continued to depreciate. Between July 1997 and June 1998 a fixed official rate of US $1 = 262,376 readjusted kwanza was in operation. In May 1999 the Central Bank announced its decision to abolish the existing dual currency exchange rate system. In December 1999 the readjusted kwanza was replaced by a new currency, the kwanza, equivalent to 1m. readjusted kwanza.

BUDGET
(million kwanza)

Revenue	2002	2003	2004*
Tax revenue	188,733	352,340	462,850
Petroleum	146,385	286,007	360,791
Income tax	12,405		
Tax on goods and services .	14,614	66,333	102,059
Taxes on foreign trade . . .	10,571		
Other taxes	4,759		
Non-tax revenue	1,978	2,982	10,597
Total	**190,711**	**355,321**	**473,448**

Expenditure†	2002	2003	2004*
Current	191,775	324,549	427,479
Personnel‡	53,078	138,986	221,044
Goods and services . . .	94,495	114,102	135,602
Interest payments . . .	19,587	21,223	19,526
Transfers	24,615	50,237	51,306
Capital	34,153	80,471	99,751
Total	**225,928**	**405,021**	**527,230**

* Projected figures.
† Excluding changes in payment arrears (million kwanza): 37,325 in 2002; 11,192 in 2003; 13,242 in 2004.
‡ Including wages and salaries of defence and public order personnel.

Source: Ministry of Finance.

INTERNATIONAL RESERVES
(US $ million at 31 December)

	2001	2002	2003
IMF special drawing rights . .	0.17	0.19	0.14
Foreign exchange	731.69	375.35	633.99
Total	**731.87**	**375.55**	**634.20**

Source: IMF, *International Financial Statistics.*

MONEY SUPPLY
(million kwanza at 31 December)

	2001	2002	2003
Currency outside banks . . .	8,215.3	20,878.5	35,406.9
Demand deposits at banking institutions	5,449.5	10,961.0	34,444.8
Total (incl. others)	**14,298.7**	**33,459.2**	**69,888.2**

Source: IMF, *International Financial Statistics.*

COST OF LIVING
(Consumer Price Index for Luanda at December; base: 1994 average = 100)

	1999	2000	2001
Food	3,551.1	11,211.2	22,494.2
Clothing	5,189.4	21,449.2	45,733.9
Rent, fuel and light	28,392.7	157,756.4	434,224.6
All items (incl. others)	**5,083.6**	**18,723.6**	**40,456.1**

Source: IMF, *Angola: Selected Issues and Statistical Appendix* (September 2003).

All items (Consumer Price Index for Luanda at December; base: 2001 = 100): 205.6 in 2002; 363.0 in 2003 (Source: Banco Nacional de Angola).

NATIONAL ACCOUNTS

Expenditure on the Gross Domestic Product
(US $ million at current prices)

	2000	2001	2002
Government final consumption expenditure	3,880.6	3,122.9	2,847.7
Private final consumption expenditure	2,128.4	3,034.6	3,994.2
Gross fixed capital formation . }	472.1	3,274.1	3,625.8
Increase in stocks . . . . . }			
Total domestic expenditure .	**6,481.1**	**9,431.6**	**10,467.7**
Exports of goods and services .	8,257.6	6,736.8	8,607.4
Less Imports of goods and services	5,880.2	6,696.9	7,826.5
GDP in purchasers' values (market prices)	**8,858.5**	**9,471.5**	**11,248.5**
GDP at constant 1995 prices .	6,877.4	7,095.1	8,180.7

Source: African Development Bank.

Gross Domestic Product by Economic Activity
(estimates, million kwanza at current prices)

	2001	2002	2003
Agriculture, forestry and fishing	16,077	37,661	79,579
Mining	113,055	235,820	549,284
Petroleum and gas	100,916	209,347	501,530
Manufacturing	7,634	17,566	37,063
Electricity and water	79	181	376
Construction	7,124	16,375	34,713
Trade	30,442	67,094	154,772
Other services	18,385	50,332	155,832
Sub-total	**192,798**	**425,029**	**1,011,620**
Import duties	4,313	8,524	25,421
GDP at market prices . . .	**197,111**	**433,553**	**1,037,040**

Source: Banco Nacional de Angola.

BALANCE OF PAYMENTS
(US $ million)

	2000	2001	2002
Exports of goods f.o.b.	7,920.7	6,534.3	8,327.9
Imports of goods f.o.b.	−3,039.5	−3,179.2	−3,760.1
Trade balance	4,881.2	3,355.1	4,567.8
Exports of services	267.3	202.5	206.8
Imports of services	−2,699.5	−3,518.1	−3,322.0
Balance on goods and services	2,449.0	39.5	1,452.6
Other income received . . .	34.4	23.0	17.7
Other income paid	−1,715.2	−1,584.0	−1,652.3
Balance on goods, services and income	768.2	−1,521.5	−182.1
Current transfers received . . .	123.5	208.3	142.3
Current transfers paid	−96.0	−117.8	−110.3
Current balance	795.7	−1,430.9	−150.1
Direct investment abroad . . .	—	—	−28.7
Direct investment from abroad .	878.6	2,145.5	1,672.1
Investment assets	−702.1	−516.6	−1,321.0
Investment liabilities . . .	−622.1	−678.9	−679.1
Net errors and omissions . . .	−50.6	−308.6	150.5
Overall balance	317.8	−785.6	−356.3

Source: IMF, *International Financial Statistics.*

External Trade

SELECTED COMMODITIES

Imports (million kwanza)	1983	1984	1985
Animal products	1,315	1,226	1,084
Vegetable products	2,158	3,099	2,284
Fats and oils	946	1,006	1,196
Food and beverages	2,400	1,949	1,892
Industrial chemical products . .	1,859	1,419	1,702
Plastic materials	431	704	454
Textiles	1,612	1,816	1,451
Base metals	1,985	3,730	2,385
Electrical equipment . . .	3,296	2,879	2,571
Transport equipment . . .	2,762	2,240	3,123
Total (incl. others)	20,197	21,370	19,694

Exports (US $ million)	2000	2001	2002*
Crude petroleum	6,951	5,690	7,561
Gas (per barrel)	25.0	18.0	n.a.
Diamonds	739	689	638
Coffee	908.3	687.0	n.a.
Total (incl. others)	7,921	6,534	8,359

* Estimates.

Total imports (US $ million): 2,477 in 1997; 2,079 in 1998; 3,109 in 1999; 3,040 in 2000; 3,179 in 2001; 3,709 (estimate) in 2002.

Source: Banco Nacional de Angola.

Exports (US $ million): Crude petroleum 8,546 in 2003 (Source: Ministry of Finance).

PRINCIPAL TRADING PARTNERS
(percentage of total trade)*

Imports c.i.f.	1997	1998	1999
Brazil	4.0	6.0	5.1
China, People's Repub.	1.4	1.8	1.3
France	5.8	5.8	8.2
Germany	2.3	2.4	1.7
Italy	2.7	3.7	4.5
Netherlands	4.6	5.1	3.6
Portugal	22.4	20.3	18.8
South Africa	9.2	9.7	11.9
Spain	8.5	4.9	5.9
United Kingdom	6.4	3.4	6.2
USA	13.6	17.6	14.6

Exports f.o.b.	1997	1998	1999
China, People's Repub.	13.2	4.0	8.2
France	3.9	2.9	2.1
Germany	0.7	1.7	2.4
Italy	0.4	1.4	1.4
Portugal	1.0	0.6	0.5
Spain	1.9	0.8	0.6
Taiwan	1.7	8.2	7.7
USA	64.9	63.8	59.5

2000: *Imports:* Portugal 17.1; South Africa 15.6; USA 11.0. *Exports:* Portugal 0.6; USA 44.6.

2001: *Imports:* Portugal 14.6; South Africa 10.0; USA 9.0. *Exports:* Portugal 1.7; USA 47.9.

2002 (estimates): *Imports:* Portugal 15.4; South Africa 9.9; USA 11.2. *Exports:* Portugal 0.8; USA 42.0.

* Data are compiled on the basis of reporting by Angola's trading partners.

Source: IMF, *Direction of Trade Statistics.*

Transport

GOODS TRANSPORT
(million metric tons)

	1999	2000	2001
Road	2,500.0	5,727.3	4,708.6
Railway	123.2	179.8	242.6
Water	2,009.0	5,981.0	3,045.6

Source: IRF, *World Road Statistics.*

PASSENGER TRANSPORT
(million passenger–km)

	1999	2000	2001
Road	73,644.9	111,455.7	166,044.7
Railway	3,467.3	3,194.9	3,722.3

Source: IRF, *World Road Statistics.*

ROAD TRAFFIC
(estimates, motor vehicles in use at 31 December)

	1999	2000	2001
Passenger cars	107,100	117,200	117,200
Lorries and vans	110,500	118,300	118,300
Total	217,600	235,500	235,500

Source: UN, *Statistical Yearbook.*

SHIPPING

Merchant Fleet
(registered at 31 December)

	2001	2002	2003
Number of vessels	123	124	122
Total displacement (grt) . . .	63,141	55,125	44,811

Source: Lloyd's Register-Fairplay, *World Fleet Statistics.*

International Sea-borne Freight Traffic
(estimates, '000 metric tons)

	1989	1990	1991
Goods loaded	19,980	21,102	23,288
Goods unloaded	1,235	1,242	1,261

Source: UN Economic Commission for Africa, *African Statistical Yearbook.*

CIVIL AVIATION
(traffic on scheduled services)

	1999	2000	2001
Kilometres flown (million) . . .	7	6	5
Passengers carried ('000) . . .	531	235	193
Passenger-km (million)	597	619	465
Total ton-km (million)	92	116	92

Source: UN, *Statistical Yearbook*.

Tourism

FOREIGN TOURIST ARRIVALS

Country of origin	2000	2001	2002
Belgium	597	1,303	2,162
Brazil	3,272	3,789	6,859
France	4,577	9,134	12,125
Germany	359	525	2,272
Italy	935	1,007	2,431
Philippines	1,175	1,963	1,034
Portugal	15,601	12,687	17,182
Russia	1,243	1,726	1,748
South Africa	3,774	6,880	9,674
Spain	1,361	1,569	2,005
United Kingdom	3,648	5,432	6,828
USA	3,013	3,924	5,409
Total (incl. others)	50,765	67,379	90,532

Tourism receipts (US $ million): 13 in 1999; 18 in 2000; 22 in 2001.

Source: World Tourism Organization.

Communications Media

	2001	2002	2003
Telephones ('000 main lines in use)	80.0	85.0	96.3
Mobile cellular telephones ('000 subscribers)	86.5	130.0	n.a.
Personal computers ('000 in use) .	17	27	n.a.
Internet users ('000)	60	41	41

Source: International Telecommunication Union.

Radio receivers ('000 in use, 1999): 840 (Source: UN, *Statistical Yearbook*).

Daily newspapers (1996): 5 (average circulation 128,000 copies) (Source: UNESCO, *Statistical Yearbook*).

Book production (1995): 22 titles (all books) (Source: UNESCO, *Statistical Yearbook*).

Education

(1997/98)

	Teachers	Pupils
Pre-primary	n.a.	214,867*
Primary	31,062†	1,342,116
Secondary:		
general	5,138‡	267,399
teacher training	280§	10,772*
vocational	286‡	12,116*
Higher	776	8,337

* Figure for school year 1991/92.
† Figure for school year 1990/91.
‡ Figure for school year 1989/90.
§ Figure for school year 1987/88.

Source: mainly UNESCO, Institute for Statistics.

Adult literacy rate (UNESCO estimates): 41.7% (males 55.6%; females 28.5%) in 1990 (Source: UNESCO, *Statistical Yearbook*).

Directory

The Constitution

The MPLA regime adopted an independence Constitution for Angola in November 1975. It was amended in October 1976, September 1980, March 1991, April and August 1992, and November 1996. The main provisions of the 1975 Constitution, as amended, are summarized below:

BASIC PRINCIPLES

The Republic of Angola shall be a sovereign and independent state whose prime objective shall be to build a free and democratic society of peace, justice and social progress. It shall be a democratic state based on the rule of law, founded on national unity, the dignity of human beings, pluralism of expression and political organization, respecting and guaranteeing the basic rights and freedoms of persons, whether as individuals or as members of organized social groups. Sovereignty shall be vested in the people, which shall exercise political power through periodic universal suffrage.

The Republic of Angola shall be a unitary and indivisible state. Economic, social and cultural solidarity shall be promoted between all the Republic's regions for the common development of the entire nation and the elimination of regionalism and tribalism.

Religion

The Republic shall be a secular state and there shall be complete separation of the State and religious institutions. All religions shall be respected.

The Economy

The economic system shall be based on the coexistence of diverse forms of property—public, private, mixed, co-operative and family—and all shall enjoy equal protection. The State shall protect foreign investment and foreign property, in accordance with the law. The fiscal system shall aim to satisfy the economic, social and administrative needs of the State and to ensure a fair distribution of income and wealth. Taxes may be created and abolished only by law, which shall determine applicability, rates, tax benefits and guarantees for taxpayers.

Education

The Republic shall vigorously combat illiteracy and obscurantism and shall promote the development of education and of a true national culture.

FUNDAMENTAL RIGHTS AND DUTIES

The State shall respect and protect the human person and human dignity. All citizens shall be equal before the law. They shall be subject to the same duties, without any distinction based on colour, race, ethnic group, sex, place of birth, religion, level of education, or economic or social status.

All citizens aged 18 years and over, other than those legally deprived of political and civil rights, shall have the right and duty to take an active part in public life, to vote and be elected to any state organ, and to discharge their mandates with full dedication to the cause of the Angolan nation. The law shall establish limitations in respect of non-political allegiance of soldiers on active service, judges and police forces, as well as the electoral incapacity of soldiers on active service and police forces.

Freedom of expression, of assembly, of demonstration, of association and of all other forms of expression shall be guaranteed. Groupings whose aims or activities are contrary to the constitutional order and penal laws, or that, even indirectly, pursue political objectives through organizations of a military, paramilitary or militarized nature shall be forbidden. Every citizen has the right to a defence if accused of a crime. Individual freedoms are guaranteed. Freedom of conscience and belief shall be inviolable. Work shall be the right and duty of all citizens. The State shall promote measures necessary to ensure the right of citizens to medical and health care, as well as assistance in childhood, motherhood, disability, old age, etc. It shall also promote access to education, culture and sports for all citizens.

STATE ORGANS

President of the Republic

The President of the Republic shall be the Head of State, Head of Government and Commander-in-Chief of the Angolan armed forces. The President of the Republic shall be elected directly by a secret universal ballot and shall have the following powers:

- to appoint and dismiss the Prime Minister, Ministers and other government officials determined by law;

- to appoint the judges of the Supreme Court;

- to preside over the Council of Ministers;

- to declare war and make peace, following authorization by the Assembléia Nacional;

- to sign, promulgate and publish the laws of the Assembléia Nacional, government decrees and statutory decrees;

- to preside over the National Defence Council;

- to decree a state of siege or state of emergency;

- to announce the holding of general elections;

- to issue pardons and commute sentences;

- to perform all other duties provided for in the Constitution.

Assembléia Nacional

The Assembléia Nacional is the supreme state legislative body, to which the Government is responsible. The Assembléia shall be composed of 223 deputies, elected for a term of four years. The Assembléia shall convene in ordinary session twice yearly and in special session on the initiative of the President of the Assembléia, the Standing Commission of the Assembléia or of no less than one-third of its deputies. The Standing Commission shall be the organ of the Assembléia that represents and assumes its powers between sessions.

Government

The Government shall comprise the President of the Republic, the ministers and the secretaries of state, and other members whom the law shall indicate, and shall have the following functions:

- to organize and direct the implementation of state domestic and foreign policy, in accordance with decision of the Assembléia Nacional and its Standing Commission;

- to ensure national defence, the maintenance of internal order and security, and the protection of the rights of citizens;

- to prepare the draft National Plan and General State Budget for approval by the Assembléia Nacional, and to organize, direct and control their execution.

The Council of Ministers shall be answerable to the Assembléia Nacional. In the exercise of its powers, the Council of Ministers shall issue decrees and resolutions.

Judiciary

The organization, composition and competence of the courts shall be established by law. Judges shall be independent in the discharge of their functions.

Local State Organs

The organs of state power at provincial level shall be the Provincial Assemblies and their executive bodies. The Provincial Assemblies shall work in close co-operation with social organizations and rely on the initiative and broad participation of citizens. The Provincial Assemblies shall elect commissions of deputies to perform permanent or specific tasks. The executive organs of Provincial Assemblies shall be the Provincial Governments, which shall be led by the Provincial Governors. The Provincial Governors shall be answerable to the President of the Republic, the Council of Ministers and the Provincial Assemblies.

National Defence

The State shall ensure national defence. The National Defence Council shall be presided over by the President of the Republic, and its composition shall be determined by law. The Angolan armed forces, as a state institution, shall be permanent, regular and non-partisan. Defence of the country shall be the right and the highest indeclinable duty of every citizen. Military service shall be compulsory. The forms in which it is fulfilled shall be defined by the law.

The Government

HEAD OF STATE

President: José Eduardo dos Santos (assumed office 21 September 1979).

COUNCIL OF MINISTERS
(April 2005)

Prime Minister: Fernando (Nando) da Piedade Dias dos Santos.

Deputy Prime Minister: Aguinaldo Jaime.

Minister of National Defence: Gen. Kundi Paihama.

Minister of the Interior: Osvaldo de Jesus Serra van-Dúnem.

Minister of Foreign Affairs: João Bernardo de Miranda.

Minister of Justice: Manuel da Costa Aragão.

Minister of Territorial Administration: Virgílio Ferreira Fontes Pereira.

Minister of Planning: Ana Afonso Dias Lourenço.

Minister of Finance: José Pedro de Morais.

Minister of Petroleum: Desidério da Graça Veríssimo da Costa.

Minister of Fisheries: Salomão Luheto Xirimbimbi.

Minister of Industry: Joaquim Duarte da Costa David.

Minister of Agriculture and Rural Development: Gilberto Buta Lutukuta.

Minister of Geology and Mines: Manuel António Africano Neto.

Minister of Public Administration, Labour and Social Security: Dr António Domingos Pitra da Costa Neto.

Minister of Health: Sebastião Sapuile Veloso.

Minister of Education: António Burity da Silva Neto.

Minister of Culture: Boaventura Cardoso.

Minister of Science and Technology: João Baptista Ngandajina.

Minister of Transport: André Luís Brandão.

Minister of Posts and Telecommunications: Licínio Tavares Ribeiro.

Minister of Family and the Promotion of Women: Cândida Celeste da Silva.

Minister of Former Combatants and War Veterans: Pedro José van-Dúnem.

Minister of Youth and Sports: José Marcos Barrica.

Minister of Public Works: Francisco Higino Carneiro.

Minister of Commerce: Joaquim Ekuma Muafumua.

Minister of Hotels and Tourism: Eduardo Jonatão Chingunji.

Minister of Social Assistance and Reintegration: João Baptista Kussumua.

Minister of Social Communication: Manuel António Rabelais.

Minister of Energy and Water: José Maria Botelho de Vasconcelos.

Minister of Urban Affairs and the Environment: Diakumpuna Sita José.

Ministers in the Office of the Presidency

Secretary of the Council of Ministers: Joaquim António Carlos dos Reis.

Minister in the Presidency and Head of the Civil House: Americo Maria de Morais Garcia.

Civil Affairs: José da Costa de Silva Leitão.

Military Affairs: Manuel Helder Dias.

General Secretariat: José Mateus de Adelino Peixoto.

MINISTRIES

Office of the President: Protocolo de Estado, Futungo de Belas, Luanda; tel. (2) 370150; fax (2) 370366.

Office of the Prime Minister: Luanda.

Office of the Deputy Prime Minister: Luanda; tel. (2) 371032; fax (2) 370842; e-mail ministro.adj1m@netangola.com.

Ministry of Agriculture and Rural Development: Avda Comandante Gika 2, CP 527, Luanda; tel. (2) 322694; fax (2) 323217; e-mail gabminander@netangola.com.

Ministry of Commerce: Largo 4 de Fevereiro, Palácio de Vidro, CP 1242, Luanda; tel. (2) 310626; fax (2) 370804; e-mail gab.min.com@ebonet.net.

Ministry of Culture: Avda Comandante Gika, Luanda; tel. and fax (2) 323979; e-mail mincultura@mincultura.gv.ao.

Ministry of Education: Avda Comandante Gika, CP 1281, Luanda; tel. (2) 320653; fax (2) 321592.

Ministry of Energy and Water: Avda 4 de Fevereiro 105, CP 2229, Luanda; tel. (2) 393681; fax (2) 298687.

Ministry of the Family and the Promotion of Women: Largo 4 de Fevereiro, Palácio de Vidro, Luanda; tel. and fax (2) 311728; e-mail phildelgado@netangola.com; internet minfam.netangola.com.

Ministry of Finance: Avda 4 de Fevereiro 127, CP 592, Luanda; tel. and fax (2) 332122; e-mail gm@minfin.gv.ao; internet www.minfin.gv.ao.

Ministry of Fisheries: Avda 4 de Fevereiro 30, Edif. Atlântico, CP 83, Luanda; tel. (2) 311420; fax (2) 310199; e-mail geral@angola-minpescas.com; internet www.angola-minpescas.com.

Ministry of Foreign Affairs: Rua Major Kanhangulo, Luanda; tel. (2) 397490; fax (2) 393246; e-mail webdesigner@mirex.ebonet.net.

Ministry of Former Combatants and War Veterans: Avda Comandante Gika 2, CP 3828, Luanda; tel. (2) 330876; fax 320876.

Ministry of Geology and Mines: Avda Comandante Gika, CP 1260, Luanda; tel. (2) 322766; fax (2) 321655; e-mail min.geominas@ebonet.net.

Ministry of Health: Rua 17 de Setembro, CP 1201, Luanda; tel. and fax (2) 338052.

Ministry of Hotels and Tourism: Largo 4 de Fevereiro, Palácio de Vidro, Luanda; tel. (2) 310899; fax (2) 310629.

Ministry of Industry: Rua Cerqueira Lukoki 25, CP 594, Luanda; tel. (2) 390728; fax (2) 392400; e-mail gmi@ebonet.net; internet www.mind-angola.com.

Ministry of the Interior: Avda 4 de Fevereiro 204, CP 2723, Luanda; tel. (2) 391049; fax (2) 395133.

Ministry of Justice: Rua 17 de Setembro, CP 2250, Luanda; tel. and fax (2) 339914; e-mail minijus20@hotmail.com.

Ministry of National Defence: Rua 17 de Settembro, Luanda; tel. (2) 337530; fax (2) 334276; e-mail minden1@ebonet.net.

Ministry of Petroleum: Avda 4 de Fevereiro 105, CP 1279, Luanda; tel. and fax (2) 385847.

Ministry of Planning: Largo do Palácio do Povo, Cidade Alta, Luanda; tel. (2) 390188; fax (2) 339586; e-mail lourenco@compuserve.com.

Ministry of Posts and Telecommunications: Rua Major Kanhangulo, Luanda; tel. (2) 311004; fax (2) 330776; e-mail sg_mct@snet.co.ao.

Ministry of Public Administration, Labour and Social Security: Rua do 1° Congresso do MPLA 5, Luanda; tel. (2) 338940; fax (2) 399507; e-mail mapess@ebonet.net; internet www.mapess.gv.ao.

Ministry of Public Works: Rua Frederich Engels 92, Luanda; tel. (2) 336715; fax (2) 392539.

Ministry of Science and Technology: Ilha do Cabo, Luanda; tel. and fax (2) 309794; e-mail dgmk@ebonet.com.

Ministry of Social Communication: Avda Comandante Valódia, 1°–2° andares, CP 2608, Luanda; tel. and fax (2) 443495; e-mail mcs@netangola.com.

Ministry of Social Assistance and Reintegration: Avda Hoji Ya Henda 117, CP 102, Luanda; tel. (2) 341460; fax (2) 342988.

Ministry of Territorial Administration: Avda Comandante Gika 8, Luanda; tel. (2) 321729; fax (2) 323272.

Ministry of Transport: Avda 4 de Fevereiro 42, CP 1250-C, Luanda; tel. (2) 311303; fax (2) 311582.

Ministry of Urban Affairs and the Environment: Luanda; tel. (2) 336717.

Ministry of Youth and Sports: Avda Comandante Valódia 229, 4° andar, Luanda; tel. (2) 321117; fax (2) 321118.

PROVINCIAL GOVERNORS
(April 2005)

All Provincial Governors are *ex officio* members of the Government.

Bengo: JORGE INOCENCIO DOMBOLO.

Benguela: DUMILDE DAS CHAGAS SIMÕES RANGEL.

Bié: JOSÉ AMARO TATI.

Cabinda: JOSÉ ANÍBAL LOPES ROCHA.

Cuando-Cubango: JORGE BIWANGO.

Cuanza-Norte: HENRIQUE ANDRE JÚNIOR.

Cuanza-Sul: SERAFIM MARIA DO PRADO.

Cunene: PEDRO MUTINDE.

Huambo: PAULO KASSOMA.

Huíla: FRANCISCO JOSÉ RAMOS DA CRUZ.

Luanda: JOB CASTELO CAPAPINHA.

Lunda-Norte: MANUEL FRANCISCO GOMES MAIATO.

Lunda-Sul: FRANCISCO TSCHIWISSA.

Malanje: CRISTOVÃO DA CUNHA.

Moxico: JOÃO ERNESTO DOS SANTOS.

Namibe: ÁLVARO MANUEL DE BOAVIDA NETO.

Uíge: ANTÓNIO BENTO KANGULO.

Zaire: PEDRO SEBASTIÃO.

President and Legislature

PRESIDENT*

Presidential Election, 29 and 30 September 1992

	Votes	% of votes
José Eduardo dos Santos (MPLA)	1,953,335	49.57
Dr Jonas Malheiro Savimbi (UNITA)	1,579,298	40.07
António Alberto Neto (PDA)	85,249	2.16
Holden Roberto (FNLA)	83,135	2.11
Honorato Lando (PDLA)	75,789	1.92
Luís dos Passos (PRD)	59,121	1.47
Bengui Pedro João (PSD)	38,243	0.97
Simão Cacete (FPD)	26,385	0.67
Daniel Júlio Chipenda (Independent)	20,646	0.52
Anália de Victória Pereira (PLD)	11,475	0.29
Rui de Victória Pereira (PRA)	9,208	0.23
Total	3,940,884	100.00

*Under the terms of the electoral law, a second round of the presidential election was required to take place in order to determine which of the two leading candidates from the first round would be elected. A resumption of hostilities between UNITA and government forces prevented a second round from taking place. The electoral process was to resume only when the provisions of the Estoril peace agreement, concluded in May 1991, had been fulfilled. However, provision in the Lusaka peace accord of November 1994 for the second round of the presidential election was not pursued.

ASSEMBLÉIA NACIONAL

Assembléia Nacional: CP 1204, Luanda; tel. (2) 334021; fax (2) 331118; e-mail assembleianacional@parlamento.ebonet.net; internet www.parlamento.ao.

President: ROBERTO DE ALMEIDA.

General Election, 29 and 30 September 1992

	Votes	% of votes	Seats†
MPLA	2,124,126	53.74	129
UNITA	1,347,636	34.10	70
FNLA	94,742	2.40	5
PLD	94,269	2.39	3
PRS	89,875	2.27	6
PRD	35,293	0.89	1
AD Coalition	34,166	0.86	1
PSD	33,088	0.84	1
PAJOCA	13,924	0.35	1
FDA	12,038	0.30	1
PDP—ANA	10,620	0.27	1
PNDA	10,281	0.26	1
CNDA	10,237	0.26	—
PSDA	19,217	0.26	—
PAI	9,007	0.23	—

— continued	Votes	% of votes	Seats†
PDLA	8,025	0.20	—
PDA	8,014	0.20	—
PRA	6,719	0.17	—
Total	3,952,277	100.00	220

† According to the Constitution, the total number of seats in the Assembléia Nacional is 223. On the decision of the National Electoral Council, however, elections to fill three seats reserved for Angolans resident abroad were abandoned.

Political Organizations

In 2004 there were 126 registered political parties.

Aliança Democrática de Angola: Leader SIMBA DA COSTA.

Angolan Democratic Coalition (AD Coalition): Pres. EVIDOR QUIELA (acting).

Convenção Nacional Democrata de Angola (CNDA): Leader PAULINO PINTO JOÃO.

Frente para a Democracia (FpD): Sec.-Gen. LUIS FERNANDES DO NASCIMENTO.

Frente de Libertação do Enclave de Cabinda (FLEC): f. 1963; comprises several factions, claiming total forces of c. 5,000 guerrillas, seeking the secession of Cabinda province; in September 2004 the Frente de Libertação do Enclave de Cabinda—Forças Armadas Cabindesas (FLEC—FAC) and the Frente de Libertação do Enclave de Cabinda—Renovada (FLEC—R) merged under the above name; Leader N'ZITA HENRIQUES TIAGO; Gen.-Sec. ANTÓNIO BENTO BEMBE.

Frente de Libertação do Enclave do Cabinda—Conselho Superior Alargado (FLEC—CSA): f. 2004; political wing of FLEC; supports Cabindan independance through negotiation; Leader LIBERAL NUNO.

Frente Nacional de Libertação de Angola (FNLA): Avda Hoji Va Henda (ex Avda do Brasil) 91/306, CP 151, Luanda; tel. and fax (2) 344638; e-mail fnla@fnla-angola.org; internet www.fnla-angola.org; f. 1962; Pres. ALVARO HOLDEN ROBERTO; Sec.-Gen. NGOLA KABANGU.

Movimento de Defesa dos Interesses de Angola—Partido de Consciência Nacional (MDIA—PCN) (Movement for the Defence of Angolan Interests—National Conscience Party): f. 1991; Pres. FILIPE PINTO SUAMINA; Sec.-Gen. AFONSO MAYTUKA.

Movimento Popular de Libertação de Angola (MPLA) (People's Movement for the Liberation of Angola): Luanda; e-mail mpla@ebonet.net; internet www2.ebonet.net/MPLA; f. 1956; in 1961–74 conducted guerrilla operations against Portuguese rule; governing party since 1975; known as Movimento Popular de Libertação de Angola—Partido do Trabalho (MPLA—PT) (People's Movement for the Liberation of Angola—Workers' Party) 1977–92; in Dec. 1990 replaced Marxist-Leninist ideology with commitment to 'democratic socialism'; absorbed the Fórum Democrático Angolano (FDA) in 2002; Chair. JOSÉ EDUARDO DOS SANTOS; Sec.-Gen. JULIÃO MATEUS PAULO.

Partido de Aliança de Juventude, Operários e Camponêses de Angola (PAJOCA) (Angolan Youth, Workers' and Peasants' Alliance Party): Pres. ALEXANDRE SEBASTIÃO ANDRÉ.

Partido Angolano Independente (PAI): Leader ADRIANO PARREIRA.

Partido de Apoio Democrático e Progreso de Angola (PADEPA): Luanda; f. 1995; Chair. JOSÉ CARLOS LEITÃO.

Partido Democrático Angolano (PDA): Leader ANTÓNIO ALBERTO NETO.

Partido Democrático Liberal de Angola (PDLA): Leader HONORATO LANDO.

Partido Democrático para o Progresso—Aliança Nacional de Angola (PDP—ANA): Interim Leader and Pres. SEDIANGANI MBIMBI.

Partido Democrático para o Progresso Social (PDPS): founded by members of the PRS; Pres. PAULO LUSENQUENY.

Partido Liberal Democrático (PLD): Rua Manuel Fernando Caldeira 3c, andar, Esquerda Município de Ingombotas, CP 10199, Luanda; tel. (2) 396968; fax (2) 395966; e-mail pld@ebonet.net; internet www.pld.ebonet.net; Leader ANÁLIA DE VICTÓRIA PEREIRA.

Partido Nacional Democrata de Angola (PNDA): Sec.-Gen. PEDRO JOÃO ANTÓNIO.

Partido Reformador de Angola (PRA): Leader RUI DE VICTÓRIA PEREIRA.

Partido Renovador Democrático (PRD): Leader LUÍS DOS PASSOS.

Partido Renovador Social (PRS): Pres. EDUARDO KWANGANA; Sec.-Gen. JOAO BAPTISTA NGANDAJINA.

Partido Social Democrata (PSD): Leader BENGUI PEDRO JOÃO.

Partido Social Democrata de Angola (PSDA): Leader ANDRÉ MILTON KILANDONOCO.

União Democrática Nacional de Angola (UDNA): 14/15 Largo Teixeira de Pascoais, Vila Alice, Luanda; internet www.democratafrica.org/angola/udna.html; f. 1980s as underground movement; recognized by Supreme Court in 1994; Pres. FRANCISCO J. PEDRO KIZADILAMBA.

União Nacional para a Independência Total de Angola (UNITA): f. 1966 to secure independence from Portugal; later received Portuguese support to oppose the MPLA; UNITA and the Frente Nacional de Libertação de Angola conducted guerrilla campaign against the MPLA Govt with aid from some Western countries, 1975–76; supported by South Africa until 1984 and in 1987–88, and by USA after 1986; obtained legal status in March 1998, but hostilities between govt and UNITA forces resumed later that year; signed cease-fire agreement with the MPLA Govt in April 2002; joined the Govt in Dec. 2002; support drawn mainly from Ovimbundu ethnic group; Pres. ISAÍAS SAMAKUVA.

There is also a coalition of parties, the Partidos de Oposicão Civil (POC).

Diplomatic Representation

EMBASSIES IN ANGOLA

Algeria: Edif. Siccal Rainha Ginga, CP 1389, Luanda; tel. (2) 332881; fax (2) 334785; e-mail ambalg@netangola.com; Ambassador HANAFI OUSSEDIK.

Belgium: Avda 4 de Fevereiro 93, 3° andar, CP 1203, Luanda; tel. (2) 336437; fax (2) 336438; e-mail luanda@diplobel.org; Ambassador MICHEL VANTROYEN.

Brazil: Avda Houari Boumedienne 132, CP 5428, Luanda; tel. (2) 441307; fax (2) 444913; e-mail emb.bras@ebonet.net; Ambassador PAULO DYRCEU PINHEIRO.

Bulgaria: Rua Fernão Mendes Pinto 35, Bairro Alvalade, CP 2260, Luanda; tel. (2) 324213; fax (2) 321010; e-mail bulgemb@ebonet.net; Ambassador ELENKO ANDREEV.

Cape Verde: Rua Oliveira Martins 3, Luanda ; tel. (2) 321765; fax (2) 320832 ; Ambassador JOSÉ LUÍS JESUS.

China, People's Republic: Rua Houari Boumedienne 196, Miramar, Luanda; tel. (2) 341683; fax (2) 344185; e-mail shiguan@netangola.com; Ambassador ZHANG BEISAN.

Congo, Democratic Republic: Rua Cesario Verde 24, Luanda; tel. (2) 361953; Ambassador MUNDINDI DIDI KILENGO.

Congo, Republic: Rua 4 de Fevereiro 3, Luanda; Ambassador ANATOLE KHONDO.

Côte d'Ivoire: Rua Eng° Armindo de Andrade 75, Miramar, CP 432, Luanda; tel. (2) 440878; fax (2) 440907; e-mail aciao@ambaci-angola.org; Ambassador TATRET ANNE GNAHOURET.

Cuba: Rua Che Guevara 42, Bairro Ingombotas, Luanda; tel. (2) 339165; Ambassador NOEMI MENDOZA.

Czech Republic: Rua Companhia de Jesus 43/45, Miramar, Luanda; tel. and fax (2) 430646; Ambassador ROBERTO KOPESKE.

Egypt: Rua Comandante Stona 247, CP 3704, Luanda; tel. (2) 321590; fax (2) 323285; e-mail embegipto@ebonet.net; Ambassador BELAL ABD EL-WAHED EL-MASRY.

Equatorial Guinea: Luanda; Ambassador Gen. EUSTAQUIO NZENG ESONO.

France: Rua Reverendo Pedro Agostinho Neto 31–33, CP 584, Luanda; tel. (2) 334841; fax (2) 391949; e-mail cad.luanda-amb@diplomatie.gouv.fr; Ambassador GUY AZAÏS.

Gabon: Avda 4 de Fevereiro 95, Luanda; tel. (2) 372614; Ambassador RAPHAËL NKASSA-NZOGHO.

Germany: Avda 4 de Fevereiro 120, CP 1295, Luanda; tel. and fax (2) 334516; e-mail germanembassy.luanda@netangola.com; Ambassador Dr KLAUS-CHRISTIAN KRAEMER.

Ghana: Rua Cirilo da Conceição e Silva 5, 1A, CP 1012, Luanda; tel. (2) 338239; fax (2) 338235; Ambassador KODJO ASIMENG WADEE.

Guinea: Luanda.

Holy See: Rua Luther King 123, CP 1030, Luanda; tel. (2) 330532; fax (2) 332378; e-mail nunc.nuncio@multitel.co.ao; Apostolic Nuncio Most Rev. GIOVANNI ANGELO BECCIU (Titular Archbishop of Roselle).

India: Rua Marques das Minas 18A, Macalusso, CP 6040, Luanda; tel. (2) 392281; fax (2) 371094; e-mail indembluanda@ebonet.net; Ambassador RAVI MOHAN AGGARWAL.

Israel: Edif., Rainha Ginga, 11° andar, Rua Rainha Ginga, Luanda; tel. (2) 395295; fax (2) 396366; e-mail info@luanda.mfa.gov.il; Ambassador BAHIJ MANSOUR.

Italy: Rua Americo Boavida 49/51, Ingombota, CP 6220, Luanda; tel. (2) 331245; fax (2) 333743; e-mail ambasciata.luanda@esteri.it; Ambassador ALFREDO BASTIANELLI.

Japan: Rua Armindo de Andrade 183/185, Bairro Miramar, Luanda; tel. (2) 442007; fax (2) 449888; Chargé d'affaires HIROAKI SANO.

Mali: Rua Padre Manuel Pombo 81, Maianga, Luanda; e-mail ambamali@netangola.com; Ambassador FAROUK CAMARA.

Morocco: Rua Rainha Ginga, Edif. Siccal, 10° andar, Luanda; tel. (2) 393708; fax (2) 338847; Ambassador ABDELLAH AIT EL HAJ.

Mozambique: Luanda; tel. (2) 330811; Ambassador ANTÓNIO MATOSE.

Namibia: Rua dos Cocqueiros 37, CP 953, Luanda; tel. (2) 395483; fax (2) 339234; e-mail embnam@netangola.com; Ambassador LINE-EKELA MBOTI.

Netherlands: Edif. Secil, Avda 4 de Fevereiro 42–6/10, CP 3624, Luanda; tel. (2) 310686; fax (2) 310966; e-mail lua@minbuza.nl; internet www.angolanda.com; Ambassador J. E. VAN DEN BERG.

Nigeria: Rua Houari Boumedienne 120, CP 479, Luanda; tel. (2) 340084; Ambassador ADAMU UMA.

Norway: Rua de Banguela 117, Bairro Patrice Lumumba, CP 3835, Luanda; tel. (2) 449936; fax (2) 446248; e-mail emb.luanda@mfa.no; internet www.noruega.ao; Ambassador ARILD R. ØYEN.

Poland: Rua Comandante N'zaji 21–23, CP 1340, Luanda; tel. (2) 323088; fax (2) 323086; Ambassador EUGENIUSZ RZEWUSKI.

Portugal: Avda de Portugal 50, CP 1346, Luanda; tel. (2) 333027; fax (2) 390392; Ambassador FRANCISCO XAVIER ESTEVES.

Romania: Ramalho Ortigão 30, Alvalade, Luanda; tel. and fax (2) 321076; e-mail ambromania@ebonet.net; Chargé d'affaires a.i. FLO-RICĂ BARBU.

Russia: Rua Houari Boumedienne 170, CP 3141, Luanda; tel. (2) 445028; fax (2) 445320; e-mail rusemb@netangola.com; Ambassador ANDREI KEMARSKY.

São Tomé and Príncipe: Rua Armindo de Andrade 173–175, Luanda; tel. (2) 345677; Ambassador ARMINDO BRITO FERNANDES.

Serbia and Montenegro: Rua Comandante Nzagi 25-27, Alvalade, CP 3278, Luanda; tel. (2) 321421; fax (2) 321724; e-mail yugoemb@snet.co.ao; Chargé d'affaires a.i. DRAGAN S. VUJNOVIC.

South Africa: Rua Kwamme Nkrumah 31, Largo da Maianga, Ed. Maianga 1–2° andar, CP 6212, Luanda; tel. (2) 330593; fax (2) 398730; e-mail saemb.and@netangola.com; internet www.sambangola.info; Ambassador T. S. MSIMANGA.

Spain: Avda 4 de Fevereiro 95, 1° andar, CP 3061, Luanda; tel. (2) 391166; fax (2) 332884; e-mail embespao@mail.mae.es; Ambassador MANUEL PRADAS ROMANÍ.

Sweden: Rua Garcia Neto 9, CP 1130, Miramar, Luanda; tel. (2) 440424; fax (2) 443460; e-mail ambassaden.luanda@foreign.ministry.se; Ambassador ANDERS HAGELBERG.

United Kingdom: Rua Diogo Cão 4, CP 1244, Luanda; tel. (2) 334583; fax (2) 333331; e-mail postmaster.luanda@fco.gov.uk; internet www.britishembassy.gov.uk/angola; Ambassador RALPH PUBLICOVER.

USA: Rua Houari Boumedienne 32, Miramar, CP 6468, Luanda; tel. (2) 445481; fax (2) 446924; e-mail econusembassyluanda@yahoo.com; Ambassador CYNTHIA G. EFIRD.

Viet Nam: Rua Comandante N'zaji 66–68, CP 75, Luanda; tel. (2) 323388; Ambassador NGUYEN HUY LOI.

Zambia: Rua Rei Katyavala 106–108, CP 1496, Luanda; tel. (2) 331145; Ambassador FRANCISCO XAVIER MUSSONDA.

Zimbabwe: Edif. Secil, Avda 4 de Fevereiro 42, CP 428, Luanda; tel. (2) 310125; fax (2) 311528; e-mail embzimbabwe@ebonet.net; Ambassador JAMES MANZOU.

Judicial System

There is a Supreme Court and Court of Appeal in Luanda. There are also civil, criminal and military courts.

Supreme Court: Rua 17 de Setembro, Luanda; fax (2) 335411; Pres. Dr CRISTIANO ANDRÉ.

Office of the Attorney-General: Rua 17 de Setembro, Luanda; tel. (2) 333171; fax (2) 333172; Attorney-General AUGUSTO DA COSTA CARNEIRO.

Religion

In 1998 it was estimated that 47% of the population followed indigenous beliefs, with 53% professing to be Christians, mainly Roman Catholic. There is a small Muslim community, which comprises less than 1% of the population.

CHRISTIANITY

Conselho de Igrejas Cristãs em Angola (CICA) (Council of Christian Churches in Angola): Rua Amílcar Cabral 182, 1° andar, CP 1659, Luanda; tel. (2) 330415; fax (2) 393746; f. 1977 as Conselho Angolano de Igrejas Evangélicas; 14 mem. churches; five assoc. mems; one observer; Pres. Rev. ALVARO RODRIGUES; Gen. Sec. Rev. LUÍS NGUIMBI.

Protestant Churches

Evangelical Congregational Church in Angola (Igreja Evangélica Congregacional em Angola—IECA): CP 1552, Luanda; tel. (2) 355108; fax (2) 350868; e-mail ieca.luanda@angonet.org; f. 1880; 350,000 mems; Gen. Sec. Rev. Dr JOSÉ BELO CHIPENDA.

Evangelical Pentecostal Church of Angola (Missão Evangélica Pentecostal de Angola): CP 219, Porto Amboim; 13,600 mems; Sec. Rev. JOSÉ DOMINGOS CAETANO.

United Evangelical Church of Angola (Igreja Evangélica Unida de Angola): CP 122, Uíge; 11,000 mems; Gen. Sec. Rev. A. L. DOMINGOS.

Other active denominations include the African Apostolic Church, the Church of Apostolic Faith in Angola, the Church of Our Lord Jesus Christ in the World, the Evangelical Baptist Church, the Evangelical Church in Angola, the Evangelical Church of the Apostles of Jerusalem, the Evangelical Reformed Church of Angola, the Kimbanguist Church in Angola, the Maná Church and the United Methodist Church.

The Roman Catholic Church

Angola comprises three archdioceses and 13 dioceses. At 31 December 2002 there were 9,519,000 adherents in the country, equivalent to 44.1% of the population.

Bishops' Conference

Conferência Episcopal de Angola e São Tomé (CEAST), CP 3579, Luanda; tel. (2) 443686; fax (2) 445504; e-mail ceast@snet.co.ao. f. 1967; Pres. Most Rev. DAMIÃO ANTÓNIO FRANKLIN (Archbishop of Luanda).

Archbishop of Huambo: Most Rev. JOSÉ DE QUEIRÓS ALVES, Arcebispado, CP 10, Huambo; tel. (41) 20130; fax (41) 20133.

Archbishop of Luanda: Most Rev. DAMIÃO ANTÓNIO FRANKLIN, Arcebispado, Largo do Palácio 9, CP 87, 1230-C, Luanda; tel. (2) 331481; fax (2) 334433; e-mail spastoral@snct.co.ao.

Archbishop of Lubango: Most Rev. ZACARIAS KAMWENHO, Arcebispado, CP 231, Lubango; tel. and fax (61) 20405; e-mail arquidiocese.lubango@netangola.com.

The Press

A free press was reinstituted in 1991, after 15 years of government control. In 2004 there were seven privately-owned newspapers in Angola.

DAILIES

Diário da República: CP 1306, Luanda; official govt bulletin.

O Jornal de Angola: Rua Rainha Ginga 18-24, CP 1312, Luanda; tel. (2) 338928; fax (2) 333342; internet www.jornaldeangola.com; f. 1975; state owned; Dir-Gen. LUÍS FERNANDO; mornings and Sun.; circ. 41,000.

PERIODICALS

Actual: Vila Alice, Rua Fernando Pessoa 103, CP 6959, Luanda; tel. and fax (2) 332116; e-mail actuals@hotmail.com; f. 2003; weekly; Editor JOAQUIM ALVES.

Agora: Rua Commandante Valódia 59, 2° andar, CP 24 Luanda; tel. and fax (2) 344680; e-mail agora-as@ebonet.net; f. 1996; weekly; Dir AGUIAR DOS SANTOS.

Angolense: Rua Cónego Manuel das Neves 83ʙ, Luanda; tel. (2) 341501; fax (2) 340549; e-mail angolense@netangola.com; f. 1998; weekly; Dir Américo Gonçalves.

O Apostolado: Rua Comandante Bula 118, Luanda; tel. (2) 432641; fax (2) 440628; e-mail direccao@apostolado.info; internet www .apostolado.info; current and religious affairs; Dir Aristides Nieva.

A Capital: Luanda; f. 2003; weekly; Dir Francisco Tandala.

Comércio Actualidade: Rua da Missão 81, CP 6375, Luanda; tel. (2) 334060; fax (2) 392216; e-mail actualidade@ebonet.net; f. 1993; weekly; Editor Victor Aleixo.

Eme: Luanda; tel. (2) 321130; f. 1996; fortnightly; MPLA publ.; Dir Fernando Fati.

Folha 8: Rua Conselheiro Júlio de Vilhena 24, 5° andar, CP 6527, Luanda; tel. (2) 391943; fax (2) 392289; e-mail folha8@ebonet.net; f. 1994; two a week; Dir William Tonet.

Gráfica Popular: Luanda; state owned.

Independente: Rua Gracia da Horta 9, Luanda; tel. and fax (2) 343968; weekly; Dir Pedro Narciso.

Jornal de Benguela: CP 17, Benguela; two a week.

Jornal de Desportos: Rua Rainha Ginga 18–24, CP 1312, Luanda; tel. (2) 335531; fax (2) 335481; e-mail jornaldosdesportos@hotmail .com; internet www.jornaldosdesportos.com; f. 1994; bi-weekly; Dir Policarpo da Rosa; Editor-in-chief Fontes Pereira; circ. 5,000.

Lavra & Oficina: CP 2767-C, Luanda; tel. (2) 322421; fax (2) 323205; e-mail uea@uea-angola.org; internet www.uea-angola.org; f. 1975; journal of the União dos Escritores Angolanos (Union of Angolan Writers); monthly; circ. 5,000.

A Palavra: Luanda; f. 2003; weekly.

Semanario Angolense: Luanda; e-mail editor@ semanarioangolense.com; internet www.semanarioangolense.net; f. 2003; current affairs; Dir Felizberto Graça Campos; weekly.

Tempos Novos: Avda Combatentes 244, 2° andar, CP 16088, Luanda; tel. (2) 349534; fax (2) 349534.

NEWS AGENCIES

Agência Angola Press (ANGOP): Rua Rei Katyavala 120, CP 2181, Luanda; tel. and fax (2) 447342; internet www .angolapress-angop.ao; f. 1975; Dir-Gen. Manuel da Conceiçao.

Centro de Imprensa Anibal de Melo (CIAM): Rua Cequeira Lokoki 124, CP 2805 Luanda; tel. (2) 393341; fax (2) 393445; government press centre.

Foreign Bureaux

Agence France-Presse (AFP): CIAM, Rua Cequeira Lokoki 124, CP 2805 Luanda; tel. (2) 3979033; Bureau Chief Manuela Teixeira.

Agência Lusa de Informação (Portugal): Luanda; Bureau Chief Miguel Souto.

Informatsionnoye Telegrafnoye Agentstvo Rossii—Telegrafnoye Agentstvo Suverennykh Stran (ITAR—TASS) (Russia): Rua Marechal Tito 75, CP 3209, Luanda; tel. (2) 342524; Correspondent Vladimir Borisovich Buyanov.

Inter Press Service (IPS) (Italy): CIAM, Rua Cerqueira Lukoki 124, CP 2805 Luanda; tel. (2) 334895; fax (2) 393445; Correspondent Chris Simpson.

Prensa Latina (Cuba): Rua D. Miguel de Melo 92-2, Luanda; tel. (2) 336804; e-mail prela-ang@elebonet.net; Chief Correspondent Rafael Contreras.

Reuters (UK): CIAM, Rua Cerqueira Lukoki 124, CP 2805 Luanda; tel. (2) 334895; fax (2) 393445; Correspondent Cristina Muller.

Rossiyskoye Informatsionnoye Agentstvo—Novosti (RIA—Novosti) (Russia): Luanda; Chief Officer Vladislav Z. Komarov.

Xinhua (New China) News Agency (People's Republic of China): Rua Karl Marx 57-3, andar E, Bairro das Ingombotas, Zona 4, Luanda; tel. (2) 332415; Correspondent Zhao Xiaozhong.

Publishers

Cha de Caxinde: Avda do 1° Congresso do MPLA 20-24, CP 5958 Luanda; tel. (2) 336020; fax (2) 332876; e-mail chacaxinde@ebonet .net; f. 1999; Dir Jaques Arlindo dos Santos.

Editorial Kilombelombe: Luanda; Dir Mateus Volódia.

Editorial Nzila: Rua Comandante Valódia 1, ao Largo do Kinaxixi, Luanda; tel. (2) 447137; e-mail edinzila@hotmail.com.

Nova Editorial Angolana, SARL: CP 1225, Luanda; f. 1935; general and educational; Man. Dir Pombo Fernandes.

Offsetográfica Gráfica Industrial Lda: CP 911, Benguela; tel. 32568; f. 1966; Man. Fernando Martins.

Ponto Um Indústria Gráfica: Rua Sebastião Desta Vez 55, Luanda; tel. (2) 344550; fax (2) 349424.

GOVERNMENT PUBLISHING HOUSE

Imprensa Nacional, UEE: CP 1306, Luanda; f. 1845; Gen. Man. Dr António Duarte de Almeida e Carmo.

Broadcasting and Communications

TELECOMMUNICATIONS

Angola Telecom: Rua Guilherme P. Inglês 43, 6° andar, CP 625 Luanda; tel. (2) 331032; fax (2) 391688; e-mail info@angolatelecom .com; internet www.angolatelecom.com; state telecommunications co.

Movicel Telecomunicações Lda: Luanda; f. 2002; mobile cellular telephone operator; Chair. Manuel Avelino; Exec.-Dir Francisco Basilio.

Mundo StarTel: Luanda; 44% owned by Telecom Namibia.

UNITEL Sarl: Luanda; f. 1998; 25% owned by Portugal Telecom; private mobile telephone operator; Dir Luciano Ferreira da Costa.

Regulatory Authority

Instituto Angolano das Comunicações (INACOM): Avda de Portugal 92, 7° andar, CP 1459 Luanda; ; tel. (2) 338352; fax (2) 339356; e-mail incom.dg@netangola.com; internet www.inacom.og .ao; f. 1999; monitoring and regulatory authority; Dir-Gen. João Beirào.

BROADCASTING

Radio

A decree on the regulation of radio broadcasting was approved in 1997. Since that time private operators have reportedly experienced difficulty in gaining permission to broadcast, however, four private stations were operating in Luanda in 2004.

Rádio Nacional de Angola: Rua Comandante Gika, CP 1329, Luanda; tel. (2) 320192; fax (2) 324647; e-mail rna.dg@netangola .com; internet www.rna.ao; state controlled; operates Canal A, Radio 5, Radio FM Stereo, Radio Luanda and Radio N'gola; broadcasts in Portuguese, English, French, Spanish and vernacular languages (Chokwe, Kikongo, Kimbundu, Kwanyama, Fiote, Ngangela, Luvale, Songu, Umbundu); Dir-Gen. (vacant).

Luanda Antena Comercial (LAC): Praceta Luther King 5, CP 3521, Luanda; tel. (2) 394989; fax (2) 396229; e-mail lac@ebonet.net; internet www.ebonet.net/lac; popular music.

Radio CEFOJOR: Luanda; f. 2003; commercial station.

Rádio Ecclésia—Emissora Católica de Angola: Rua Comandante Bula 118, São Paulo, CP 3579, Luanda; tel. (2) 443041; fax (2) 443093; e-mail recclesia@recclesia.org; internet www.recclesia.org; f. 1955; broadcasts mainly restricted to Luanda; coverage of politics and current affairs; Dir-Gen. António Jaca.

Radio Escola: Luanda; educational.

Rádio Morena Comercial Lda: Rua Comandante Kassanji, CP 537 Benguela; tel. (73) 32525; fax (73) 34242.

The Voice of America (internet www.ebonet.net/voa) also broadcasts from Luanda.

Television

Televisão Pública de Angola (TPA): Rua Ho Chi Minh, CP 2604, Luanda; tel. (2) 320025; fax (2) 391091; e-mail tpa.angola@netangola .com; internet www.tpa.ao; f. 1975; state-controlled; 2 channels; Man. Dir Carlos Cunha.

Finance

(cap. = capital; res = reserves; dep. = deposits; m. = million; brs = branches; amounts in kwanza (equivalent to 1m. readjusted kwanza), unless otherwise indicated)

BANKING

All banks were nationalized in 1975. In 1995 the Government authorized the formation of private banks.

Central Bank

Banco Nacional de Angola: Avda 4 de Fevereiro 151, CP 1298, Luanda; tel. and fax (2) 333717; e-mail bna.crib@bna.ao; internet www.bna.ao; f. 1976; bank of issue; cap. 5.0m., res 1.0m., dep. 63.8m. (1997); Gov. AMADEU MAURÍCIO; 6 brs.

Commercial Banks

Banco Comercial Angolano (BCA): Avda Comandante Valódia 83A, CP 6900, Luanda; tel. (2) 349548; fax (2) 349516; e-mail bca@snet.co.ao; f. 1997; 50% owned by Absa; cap. 0.9m., res 347.4m., dep. 1,799.3m. (Dec. 2002); Pres. Dr BENVINDO RAFAEL PITRA; 4 brs.

Banco Fomento Angola—BFA: Rua Amílcar Cabral 58, Luanda; tel. (2) 638930; fax (2) 638925; e-mail grupomkt@bf.co.ao; internet www.bfa.ao; f. 1993 as Banco Fomento Exterior; name changed to above in 2001; 100% owned by Banco BPI, SA, Portugal; cap. 2,984.3m., res 943.6m., dep. 49,165.9m. (Dec. 2003); Pres. ARTUR SANTOS SILVA; CEO FERNANDO ULRICH; 30 brs.

Banco de Poupança e Crédito (BPC): Largo Saydi Mingas, CP 1343, Luanda; tel. and fax (2) 372529; e-mail bpc@bpc.ao; internet www.bpc.ao; f. 1956 as Banco Comercial de Angola; 100% state-owned; cap. 811.6m., res 1,659.3m., dep. 36,499.0m. (Dec. 2003); Chair. PAIXÃO ANTÓNIO JÚNIOR; brs throughout Angola.

Banco Regional do Keve SARL: Rua Rainha Ginga 77, 1804 Luanda; tel. (2) 394100; fax (2) 395101; e-mail servicoscentrais@bankeve.com; internet www.bankeve.com; f. 2003; Pres. AMILCAR AZEVEDO DA SILVA.

Banco Sol: Rua Rei Katyavala 110–112, Maculusso, Zona 8, Imgombota, CP 814, Luanda; tel. (2) 440215; fax (2) 440226; e-mail banco.sol@ebonet.net; internet www.bancosol.co.ao; f. 2001; Pres. SEBASTIÃO BASTOS LAVRADOR.

Caixa de Crédito Agro-Pecuario e Pescas (CCAPP): Rua Rainha Ginga 83, Luanda; tel. (2) 392749; fax (2) 392225; f. 1991; assumed commercial operations of Banco Nacional de Angola in 1996.

Development Bank

Banco de Comércio e Indústria SARL: Rua Rainha Ginga, Largo do Atlético 79/83, POB 1395, Luanda; tel. (2) 333684; fax (2) 334924; e-mail falfredo@bci.ebonet.net; internet www.angola.org/bci; f. 1991; 91% state-owned; privatization pending in 2004; provides loans to businesses in all sectors; cap. US $9.5m., res $34.4m., dep. $247.3m. (Dec. 2002); Chair. GENEROSO HERMENEGILDO GASPAR DE ALMEIDA; 5 brs.

Investment Bank

Banco Africano de Investimentos SARL (BAI): Rua Major Kanhangulo 34, CP 6022, Luanda; tel. (2) 335749; fax (2) 335486; e-mail baisede@bancobai.co.ao; internet www.bancobai.co.ao; f. 1997; 37.5% interest owned by Angolan shareholders; cap. 6.5m., res 2,612.6m., dep. 29,706.8m. (Dec. 2002); Pres. Dr MÁRIO ABÍLIO PALHARES; 15 brs.

Foreign Banks

Banco Comercial Português—Atlântico SA: Largo Rainha Ginga 6/8, CP 5726, Luanda; tel. (2) 330985; fax (2) 397397; e-mail nazaredang-bcp@nexus.ao; Gen. Man. NAZARÉ DANG.

Banco Espírito Santo Angola SARL: Rua Guilherme Pereira Inglês 43–1, Largo das Ingombotas, Luanda; tel. (2) 333722; fax (2) 333465; f. 2002; 99.96% owned by Banco Espírito Santo SA, Lisbon; cap. 209.8m., res 269.3m., dep. 3,159.2m. (Dec. 2002); Chair Dr ÁLVARO SOBRINHO; Gen. Mans Dr CARLOS SILVA, Dr HELDER BATAGLIA.

Banco Totta de Angola SARL: Avda 4 de Fevereiro 99, CP 1231, Luanda; tel. and fax (2) 332729; fax (2) 333233; e-mail tottango@ebonete.net; 99.98% owned by Banco Santander Totta; cap. €15.3m., res €5.0m., dep. €146.7m.; Man. Dir Dr MÁRIO NELSON MAXIMINO; 7 brs.

NovoBanco: Rua N'Dunduma 253, Município Sambizanga, Luanda; tel. and fax (2) 430105; f. 2004; Pres. KOEN WASMUS; Dir BARBARA SAGET.

INSURANCE

AAA Seguros, SARL: Rua Major Kanhagulo 10, CP 440, Luanda; tel. (2) 370722; fax (2) 372100; e-mail saovicente@aaa.co.ao; all classes; Pres. Dr SÃO VICENTE.

Empresa Nacional de Seguros e Resseguros de Angola (ENSA), UEE: Avda 4 de Fevereiro 93, CP 5778, Luanda; tel. (2) 332990; fax (2) 332946; e-mail ensaio@ebonet.net; f. 1978; state-owned; Del. Admin. BERNARDO L. MAKOMBE.

Trade and Industry

GOVERNMENT AGENCIES

Agência Nacional para o Investimento Privado (ANIP): internet www.investinangola.org; agency advising on investing in Angola.

Corpo de Segurança de Diamantes-CSD: Luanda; f. 2004; security agency monitoring diamond mining sector.

Gabinete de Obras Especiais: Luanda; Dir MANUEL FERREIRA CLEMENTE JÚNIOR.

Gabinete de Reconstrução Nacional: Luanda; f. 2004; monitors economic and social reconstruction programmes; Dir MANUEL HELDER VIEIRA DIAS JÚNIOR.

Gabinete de Redimensionamento Empresarial: Rua Cerqueira Lukoki 25, 9° andar, CP 594, Luanda; tel. (2) 390496; fax (2) 393381; privatization agency.

Instituto de Desenvolvimento Agrário: Rua Commandante Gika, CP 2109, Luanda; tel. and fax (2) 323651; e-mail ida.canga@netangola.com; promotes agricultural development; Dir Eng. AFONSO PEDRO CANGA.

Instituto de Desenvolvimento Industrial de Angola (IDIA): Luanda; tel. (2) 395296; fax (2) 338492; e-mail idiadg@netangola.com; f. 1995; promotes industrial development; Dir KIALA NGONE GABRIELE.

Instituto de Investimento Estrangeiro: Rua Cerqueira Lukoki, 25, 9° andar, Luanda; tel. (2) 333727; fax (2) 393381; foreign investment agency.

Instituto Nacional de Cereais (INCER): Avda 4 de Fevereiro 101, CP 1105, Luanda; tel. and fax (2) 331611; promotes cereal crops; Dir-Gen. ESTEVÃO MIGUEL DE CARVALHO.

CHAMBER OF COMMERCE

Angolan Chamber of Commerce and Industry: Largo do Kinaxixi 14, 1° andar, CP 92, Luanda; tel. (2) 444506; fax (2) 444629; e-mail ccira@ebonet.net; internet www.ccia.ebonet.net; Pres. ANTÓNIO JOÃO DOS SANTOS.

INDUSTRIAL AND TRADE ASSOCIATIONS

Associação Comercial de Benguela: Rua Sacadura Cabral 104, CP 347, Benguela; tel. (72) 32441; fax (72) 33022; e-mail acbenguela@netangola.com; internet netangola.com/acb; f. 1907.

Associação Comercial e Industrial da Ilha de Luanda—ACIL: Largo do Kinaxixi 9, Luanda; tel. (2) 341866; fax (2) 349677; Pres. PEDRO GODHINO DOMINGOS.

Associação Comercial e Industrial de Luanda (ACOMIL): Largo do Kinaxixi 14–30, Luanda; tel. (2) 335728; Pres. JOÃO ADÃO ANTÓNIO TIGRE.

Associação Comercial de Luanda (ASCANGOLA): Edif. Palácio de Comércio, 1° andar, CP 1275, Luanda ; tel. (2) 332453.

Associação Industrial de Angola: Rua Manuel Fernando Caldeira 6, Luanda; tel. (2) 330624; Vice-Pres. AURELIO CABENDA.

Associação de Mulheres Empresariarias: Largo do Kinaxixi 14, 3° andar, Luanda; tel. (2) 346742; fax (2) 343088; f. 1990; association of business women; Sec-Gen. HENRIQUETA DE CARVALHO.

STATE TRADING ORGANIZATIONS

Angomédica, UEE: Rua do Sanatório, Bairro Palanca, CP 2698, Luanda; tel. (2) 363765; fax (2) 362336; f. 1981 to import pharmaceutical goods; Gen. Dir Dr FÁTIMA SAIUNDO.

Angolan Selling Corporation (ASCORP): Rua Tipografia Mama Tita, Edif. Soleil B, CP 3978, Ingombotas, Luanda; tel. (2) 396465; fax (2) 397615; e-mail ascorpadmin@ebonet.net; f. 1999; 51% state-owned diamond-trading co; Pres. NOE BALTAZAR.

Direcção dos Serviços de Comércio (Dept of Trade): Largo Diogo Cão, CP 1337, Luanda; f. 1970; brs throughout Angola.

Epmel, UEE: Rua Karl Marx 35–37, Luanda; tel. (2) 330943; industrial agricultural machinery.

Exportang, UEE: Rua dos Enganos 1A, CP 1000, Luanda; tel. (2) 332363; co-ordinates exports.

Importang, UEE: Calçada do Município 10, CP 1003, Luanda; tel. (2) 337994; f. 1977; co-ordinates majority of imports; Dir-Gen. SIMÃO DIOGO DA CRUZ.

Maquimport, UEE: Rua Rainha Ginga 152, CP 2975, Luanda; tel. (2) 339044; f. 1981 to import office equipment.

Mecanang, UEE: Rua dos Enganos, 1°–7° andar, CP 1347, Luanda; tel. (2) 390644; f. 1981 to import agricultural and construction machinery, tools and spare parts.

Sociedade de Comercialização de Diamantes de Angola, SARL (SODIAM): Rua Manuel Fernando Caldeira 6B-1, Luanda; tel. (2) 370217; fax (2) 370423; e-mail sodiama@hotmail.com; internet www.sodiam-angola.com; f. 2000; diamond trading organization.

STATE INDUSTRIAL ENTERPRISES

Bricomil: Rua Massano Amorim 79, Chicala, Luanda; tel. (2) 343895; fax (2) 342533; f. 1986; 55% state-owned; privatization planned; civil construction; 650 employees.

Companhia do Açúcar de Angola: Rua Direita 77, Luanda; production of sugar.

Companhia Geral dos Algodões de Angola (COTONANG): Avda da Boavista, Luanda; production of cotton textiles.

Empresa Abastecimento Técnico Material (EMATEC), UEE: Largo Rainha Ginga 3, CP 2952, Luanda; tel. (2) 338891; technical and material suppliers to the Ministry of National Defence.

Empresa Açucareira Centro (OSUKA), UEE.

Empresa de Construção de Edificações (CONSTROI), UEE: Rua Amilcar Cabral 167, 1° andar, Luanda; tel. (2) 333930; construction.

Empresa de Obras Especiais (EMPROE): Rua Ngola Kiluange 183–185, Luanda; tel. (2) 382142; fax (2) 382143; building and civil engineering.

Empresa de Pesca de Angola (PESCANGOLA), UEE: Luanda; f. 1981; state fishing enterprise, responsible to the Ministry of Fisheries.

Empresa de Rebenefício e Exportação do Café de Angola (CAFANGOL), UEE: Rua Robert Shields 4/6, CP 342, Luanda; tel. (2) 337916; fax (2) 332840; e-mail cafangol@nexus.ao; f. 1983; nat. coffee-processing and trade org; Dir-Gen. ALVARO FARIA.

Empresa de Tecidos de Angola (TEXTANG), UEE: Rua N'gola Kiluanji-Kazenga, CP 5404, Luanda; tel. (2) 381134; production of textiles.

Empresa dos Tabacos de Angola: CP 1238, Luanda; tel. (2) 336995; fax (2) 336921; manufacture of tobacco products; Gen. Man. K. BITTENCOURT.

Empresa Nacional de Cimento (ENCIME), UEE: CP 157, Lobito; tel. (711) 2325; cement production.

Empresa Nacional de Comercialização e Distribuição de Produtos Agrícolas (ENCODIPA): Luanda; central marketing agency for agricultural produce; numerous brs throughout Angola.

Empresa Nacional de Diamantes de Angola (ENDIAMA), UEE: Rua Major Kanhangulo 100, CP 1247, Luanda; tel. (2) 330377; fax (2) 337276; e-mail endiama@endiama-angola.com; internet www .endiama-angola.com; f. 1981; commenced operations 1986; diamond mining; a number of subsidiary companies undergoing privatization; Pres. Dr MANUEL ARNALDO DE SOUSA CALADO.

Empresa Nacional de Ferro de Angola (FERRANGOL): Rua João de Barros 26, CP 2692, Luanda; tel. (2) 373800; iron production; Dir ARMANDO DE SOUSA.

Empresa Nacional de Manutenção (MANUTECNICA), UEE: Rua 7, Avda do Cazenga 10, CP 3508, Luanda; tel. (2) 383646; assembly of machines and specialized equipment for industry.

Geotécnica Unidad Económica Estatal: Rua Angola Kilmanse 389/393, Luanda; tel. (2) 381795; fax (2) 382730; f. 1978 for surveying and excavation; Man. P. M. M. ELVINO, Jr; 500 employees.

Siderurgia Nacional, UEE: Rua Farol Lagostas, Luanda; tel. (2) 383587; f. 1963; nationalized 1980; undergoing rehabilitation in 2005; scheduled for privatization; steelworks and rolling mill plant.

Sociedade Nacional de Combustíveis de Angola (SONANGOL): Rua 1° Congreso do MPLA 8–16, CP 1316 Luanda; tel. (2) 334448; fax (2) 3919782; f. 1976 for exploration, production and refining of crude petroleum, and marketing and distribution of petroleum products; sole concessionary in Angola, supervises on- and offshore operations of foreign petroleum cos; 11 subsidiaries, including shipping companies; holds majority interest in jt ventures with Cabinda Gulf Oil Co (Cabgoc), Fina Petróleos de Angola and Texaco Petróleos de Angola; CEO MANUEL VICENTE.

UTILITIES

Electricity

Empresa Nacional de Construções Eléctricas (ENCEL), UEE: Rua Comandante Che Guevara 185/7, CP 5230, Luanda; tel. (2)

446712; fax (2) 446759; e-mail encel@encel.co.ao; f. 1982; electricity generation; Dir.-Gen. DANIEL SIMAS.

Empresa Nacional de Electricidade (ENE), EP: Prédio Geominas, 6°–7° andar, CP 772, Luanda; tel. (2) 321529; fax (2) 323433; e-mail ene-pdg@netangola.com; f. 1980; production and distribution of electricity; Pres. and Dir-Gen. Eng. EDUARDO GOMES NELUMBA.

Water

Empresa Provincial de Água de Luanda (EPAL): Rua Frederich Engels 3, CP 1387, Luanda; tel. (2) 335001; fax (2) 330380; e-mail epalsdg@sney.co.ao; state-owned; Dir DIÓGENES OLIVEIRA.

TRADE UNIONS

Angolan General Independent and Free Trade Union Confederation: Chair. MANUEL DIFUILA.

Sindicato dos Jornalistas Angolanos (SJA): Rua Francisco Távora 8, 1° andar, CP 2140 Luanda ; tel. (2) 331969; fax (2) 332420; e-mail sja@netangola.com; f. 1992; Pres. AVELINO MIGUEL; Gen. Sec. LUISA ROGÉRIO; 1,253 mems in 2003.

Sindicato Nacional de Professores (Sinprof): Rua da Missão 71, 4° andar, Luanda; tel. (2) 371780; e-mail sinprof@angonet.org; teachers' union; Gen. Sec. MIGUEL JOÃO FILHO.

União Nacional de Trabalhadores Angolanos (UNTA) (National Union of Angolan Workers): Avda 4 de Fevereiro 210, CP 28, Luanda; tel. (2) 334670; fax (2) 393590; e-mail untadis@ netangola.com; f. 1960; Pres. MANUEL AUGUSTO VIAGE; c. 160,000 mems.

Transport

The transport infrastructure was severely dislocated by the civil war that ended in 2002.

RAILWAYS

There are three main railway lines in Angola, the Benguela railway, which runs from the coast to the Zambian border, the Luanda–Malange line, and the Moçamedes line, which connects Namibe and Cuando-Cubango. In 2004 only 850 km out of a total of almost 3,000 km of track was operational. A plan introduced in late 2004 to rehabilitate and extend the rail network was expected to take 11 years and to cost US $4,000m.

Direcção Nacional dos Caminhos de Ferro: Rua Major Kanhangulo, CP 1250, Luanda; tel. (2) 370091; f. 1975; nat. network operating four fmrly independent systems covering 2,952 track-km; Dir JULIO BANGO.

Amboim Railway: Porto Amboim; f. 1922; 123 track-km; Dir A. GUIA.

Benguela Railway (Caminho de Ferro de Benguela—Empresa Pública): Praça 11 Novembro 3, CP 32, Lobito; tel. (72) 22645; fax (72) 25133; e-mail cfbeng@ebonet.net; f. 1903; line completed 1928; owned by Govt of Angola; line carrying passenger and freight traffic from the port of Lobito across Angola, via Huambo and Luena, to the border of the Democratic Republic of the Congo (fmrly Zaire); 1,301 track-km; guerrilla operations by UNITA suspended all international traffic from 1975, with only irregular services from Lobito to Huambo being operated; the rehabilitation of the railway was a priority of a 10-year programme, planned by the Southern African Development Co-ordination Conference (SADCC), now the Southern African Development Community—SADC), to develop the 'Lobito corridor'; from 2001 rehabilitation of the line was under Government control; in 2004 a consortium from China (People's Republic) agreed to rehabilitate the line to DR Congo; Pres. Dr GUILHERME PRATAS; Dir-Gen. DANIEL QUIPAXE.

Luanda Railway (Empresa de Caminho de Ferro de Luanda, UEE): CP 1250-C, Luanda; tel. (2) 370061; f. 1886; serves an iron-, cotton- and sisal-producing region between Luanda and Malanje; 536 track-km; Man. A. ÁLVARO AGANTE.

Moçamedes Railway: CP 130, Lubango; f. 1905; main line from Namibe to Menongue, via Lubango; br. lines to Chibia and iron ore mines at Cassinga; 899 track-km; Gen. Man. J. SALVADOR.

ROADS

In 2001 Angola had 51,429 km of roads, of which 7,944 km were main roads and 5,278 km were secondary roads. About 10.4% of roads were paved. In 1997 the state-owned road construction and maintenance company, the Instituto de Estradas de Angola, reported that 80% of the country's road network was in disrepair and that the cost of rebuilding the roads and bridges damaged during the civil conflict would total some US $4,000m.

Direcção Nacional dos Transportes Rodoviarias: Rua Rainha Ginga 74, 1° andar, Luanda; tel. (2) 339390.

Instituto de Estradas de Angola (INEA): Rua Amílcar Cabral 35, 3° andar, CP 5667, Luanda; tel. (2) 332828; fax (2) 335754.

SHIPPING

The main harbours are at Lobito, Luanda and Namibe. The first phase of a 10-year SADCC (now SADC) programme to develop the 'Lobito corridor', for which funds were pledged in January 1989, was to include the rehabilitation of the ports of Lobito and Benguela.

Direcção Nacional da Marinha Mercante e Portos: Rua Rainha Ginga 74, 4° andar, Luanda; tel. (2) 332032.

Agenang, UEE: Rua Engracia Fragoso, 47–49, Luanda; tel. (2) 336380; fax (2) 334392; state shipping co; scheduled for privatization.

Cabotang—Cabotagem Nacional Angolana, UEE: Avda 4 de Fevereiro 83A, Luanda; tel. (2) 373133; operates off the coasts of Angola and Mozambique; Dir-Gen. João Octavio van-Dúnem.

Empresa Portuária do Lobito, UEE: Avda da Independência, CP 16, Lobito; tel. (722) 2718; fax (722) 2719; e-mail webmasters@ eplobito.com; internet www.eplobito.com; long-distance sea transport; Gen. Man. José Carlos Gomes.

Empresa Portuária de Moçâmedes—Namibe, UEE: Rua Pedro Benje 10A and 10C, CP 49, Namibe; tel. (64) 60643; long-distance sea transport; Dir Humberto de Ataide Dias.

Orey Angola, Lda: Largo 4 de Fevereiro 3, 3° andar, CP 583, Luanda; tel. (2) 310290; fax (2) 310882; e-mail acarmona@oreylad .ebonet.net; internet www.orey.com/angola; international shipping, especially to Portugal; Dir Commdt A. Carmona e Costa.

Sécil Marítima SARL, UEE: Avda 4 de Fevereiro 42, 1° andar, CP 5910, Luanda; tel. (2) 310950.

CIVIL AVIATION

Angola's airport system is well-developed, but suffered some damage in the later years of the civil war. During 2004–05 airports at Luanda, Lobito, Soyo, Namibe, Saurimo, Uíge, Huambo and Bié were undergoing rehabilitation.

Direcção Nacional da Aviação Civil: Rua Frederick Engels 92, 6° andar, CP 569 Luanda; tel. (2) 339412.

TAAG—Linhas Aéreas de Angola: Rua da Missão 123, CP 79, Luanda; tel. (2) 332338; fax (2) 390396; e-mail taagangola@aol.com; f. 1938; internal scheduled passenger and cargo services, and services from Luanda to destinations within Africa and to Europe and South America; Chair. Júlio Sampaio Almeida; Pres. and CEO Mateus Neto.

Angola Air Charter: Aeroporto Internacional 4 de Fevereiro, CP 3010, Luanda; tel. (2) 321290; fax (2) 320105; e-mail aacharter@ independente.net; f. 1992; subsidiary of TAAG; CEO A. de Matos.

Air Nacoia: Rua Comandante Che Guevara 67, 1° andar, Luanda; tel. and fax (2) 395477; f. 1993; Pres. Salvador Silva.

SONAIR: Aeroporto Internacional 4 de Fevereiro, Luanda; tel. (2) 633502; fax (2) 321572; e-mail support.sonair@sonangol.co.ao; internet www.sonairsarl.com; f. 1998; subsidiary of SONANGOL; operates direct flights between Luanda and Houston, Texas, USA; Pres. of the Council of Administration Dr António dos Santos Domingos.

Transafrik International: 4th February International Airport, Luanda; tel. (2) 353714; fax (2) 354183; e-mail enquiries@transafrik .com; internet www.transafrik.com; f. 1986; operates contract cargo services mainly within Africa; Man. Dir Erich F. Koch; Gen. Man. Pimental Araujo.

Tourism

Angola's tourism industry is undeveloped as a result of the years of civil war, although its potential for development is great. Tourist arrivals, which totalled 67,739 in 2001, currently remain predominantly business-related.

National Tourist Agency: Palácio de Vidro, CP 1240, Luanda; tel. (2) 372750.

ANTARCTICA

Source: Scientific Committee on Antarctic Research, Scott Polar Research Institute, Lensfield Rd, Cambridge, CB2 1ER, United Kingdom; tel. (1223) 362061; fax (1223) 336549; e-mail info@scar.org; internet www.scar.org.

The Continent of Antarctica is estimated to cover 13,661,000 sq km. There are no indigenous inhabitants, but a number of permanent research stations have been established. W. S. Bruce, of the Scottish National Antarctic Expedition (1902–04), established a meteorological station on Laurie Island, South Orkney Islands, in 1903. After the expedition, this was transferred to the Argentine authorities (the British Government having declined to operate the station), who have maintained the observatory since 1904 (see Orcadas, below). The next permanent stations were established in 1944 by the United Kingdom, and then subsequently by other countries.

Tourism, which consists almost exclusively of 'eco-cruises', is promoted by the International Association of Antarctica Tour Operators (IAATO). The number of tourists visiting Antarctica totalled 27,537 in 2003/04 (compared with 4,800 in 1991), including 19,771 landed passengers. The dramatic increase in tourist numbers led to expressions of concern in the early 2000s regarding the environmental impact of the industry on the region. In 2003 the Antarctic and Southern Ocean Coalition, a consortium of 240 non-governmental organizations, appealed for quotas to be introduced to control tourist numbers and protect the continent's fragile environment.

Wintering Stations

(The following list includes wintering stations south of latitude 60° occupied during austral winter 2004)

	Latitude	Longitude
ARGENTINA		
Belgrano II, Bertrab Nunatak, Luitpold Coast	77° 52′ S	34° 37′ W
Esperanza, Hope Bay	63° 23′ S	56° 59′ W
Jubany, King George Island	62° 14′ S	58° 39′ W
Marambio, Seymour Island	64° 14′ S	56° 39′ W
Orcadas, Laurie Island	60° 44′ S	44° 44′ W
San Martín, Barry Island	68° 07′ S	67° 06′ W
AUSTRALIA		
Casey, Vincennes Bay, Budd Coast	66° 17′ S	110° 31′ E
Davis, Ingrid Christensen Coast	68° 34′ S	77° 58′ E
Mawson, Mac. Robertson Land	67° 36′ S	62° 52′ E
BRAZIL		
Comandante Ferraz, King George Island	62° 05′ S	58° 23′ W
CHILE		
Capitán Arturo Prat, Greenwich Island.	62° 30′ S	59° 41′ W
General Bernardo O'Higgins, Cape Legoupil	63° 19′ S	57° 54′ W
Presidente Eduardo Frei, King George Island	62° 12′ S	58° 57′ W
Escudero, King George Island	62° 12′ S	58° 57′ W
PEOPLE'S REPUBLIC OF CHINA		
Chang Cheng (Great Wall), King George Island	62° 12′ S	58° 57′ W
Zhongshan, Princess Elizabeth Land	69° 22′ S	76° 23′ E
FRANCE*		
Dumont d'Urville, Terre Adélie	66° 39′ S	140° 00′ E
GERMANY		
Neumayer, Ekstrømisen	70° 38′ S	08° 15′ W
INDIA		
Maitri, Schirmacheroasen	70° 45′ S	11° 44′ E
JAPAN		
Syowa, Ongul	69° 00′ S	39° 35′ E
REPUBLIC OF KOREA		
King Sejong, King George Island	62° 13′ S	58° 47′ W
NEW ZEALAND		
Scott Base, Ross Island	77° 51′ S	166° 45′ E
POLAND		
Arctowski, King George Island	62° 09′ S	58° 28′ W
RUSSIA		
Bellingshausen, King George Island	62° 11′ S	58° 57′ W
Mirnyy, Queen Mary Land	66° 33′ S	93° 00′ E
Molodezhnaya, Enderby Land	67° 40′ S	45° 51′ E
Novolazarevskaya, Prinsesse Astrid Kyst	70° 46′ S	11° 51′ E
Progress, Princess Elizabeth Land	69° 22′ S	76° 23′ E
Vostok, East Antarctica	78° 28′ S	106° 48′ E

	Latitude	Longitude
SOUTH AFRICA		
SANAE, Vesleskarvet	71° 40′ S	02° 49′ W
UKRAINE		
Vernadsky, Argentine Islands	65° 14′ S	64° 15′ W
UNITED KINGDOM		
Halley, Brunt Ice Shelf, Caird Coast	75° 34′ S	26° 32′ W
Rothera, Adelaide Island	67° 34′ S	68° 07′ W
USA		
McMurdo, Ross Island	77° 50′ S	166° 40′ E
Palmer, Anvers Island	64° 46′ S	64° 03′ W
Amundsen-Scott	South Pole†	
URUGUAY		
Artigas, King George Island	62° 11′ S	58° 54′ W

* The Concordia research station (at Dome C—75° 06′ S 123° 23′ E), a joint venture with Italy, was officially opened for for winter operation in February 2005.

† The precise co-ordinates of the location of this station are: 89° 59′ 51″ S, 139° 16′ 22″ E.

Territorial Claims

Territory	Claimant State
Antártida Argentina	Argentina
Australian Antarctic Territory	Australia
British Antarctic Territory	United Kingdom
Dronning Maud Land	Norway
Ross Dependency	New Zealand
Terre Adélie	France
Territorio Chileno Antártico	Chile

These claims are not recognized by the USA or Russia. No formal claims have been made in the sector of Antarctica between 90° W and 150° W.

See also Article 4 of the Antarctic Treaty, below.

Research

Scientific Committee on Antarctic Research (SCAR) of the **International Council for Science (ICSU):** Secretariat: Scott Polar Research Institute, Lensfield Rd, Cambridge, CB2 1ER, United Kingdom; tel. (1223) 362061; fax (1223) 336549; e-mail info@scar.org; internet www.scar.org; f. 1958 to initiate, promote and co-ordinate scientific research in the Antarctic, and to provide scientific advice to the Antarctic Treaty System; 26 full mems; six assoc. mems

President: Prof Dr Jörn Thiede (Germany).

Vice-Presidents: Prof. Hideki Shimamura (Japan), Prof. Dr Jerónimo L. Lopez-Martínez (Spain), Dr Clive Howard-Williams (New Zealand), Prof. Mahlon C. Kennicutt, II (USA).

Executive Director: Dr Colin P. Summerhayes.

Executive Secretary: Dr Peter D. Clarkson.

The Antarctic Treaty

The Treaty (summarized below) was signed in Washington, DC, on 1 December 1959 by the 12 nations co-operating in the Antarctic during the International Geophysical Year, and entered into force on 23 June 1961. The Treaty made provision for a review of its terms, 30 years after ratification; however, no signatory to the Treaty has requested such a review. The permanent Antarctic Treaty Secretariat was formally established, with its headquarters in Buenos Aires, Argentina, in September 2004.

Article 1. Antarctica shall be used for peaceful purposes only.

Article 2. On freedom of scientific investigation and co-operation.

Article 3. On exchange of information and personnel.

Article 4. i. Nothing contained in the present Treaty shall be interpreted as:

(a) a renunciation by any Contracting Party of previously asserted rights of or claims to territorial sovereignty in Antarctica;

(b) a renunciation or diminution by any Contracting Party of any basis of claim to territorial sovereignty in Antarctica which it may have whether as a result of its activities or those of its nationals in Antarctica, or otherwise;

(c) prejudicing the position of any Contracting Party as regards its recognition or non-recognition of any other State's right of or claim or basis of claim to territorial sovereignty in Antarctica.

Article 4. ii. No acts or activities taking place while the present Treaty is in force shall constitute a basis for asserting, supporting or denying a claim to territorial sovereignty in Antarctica or create any rights of sovereignty in Antarctica. No new claim, or enlargement of an existing claim, to territorial sovereignty in Antarctica shall be asserted while the present Treaty is in force.

Article 5. Any nuclear explosions in Antarctica and the disposal there of radioactive waste material shall be prohibited.

Article 6. On geographical limits and rights on high seas.

Article 7. On designation of observers and notification of stations and expeditions.

Article 8. On jurisdiction over observers and scientists.

Article 9. On consultative meetings.

Articles 10–14. On upholding, interpreting, amending, notifying and depositing the Treaty.

ORIGINAL SIGNATORIES

Argentina	France	South Africa
Australia	Japan	USSR (former)
Belgium	New Zealand	United Kingdom
Chile	Norway	USA

ACCEDING STATES

Austria, Brazil, Bulgaria, Canada, the People's Republic of China, Colombia, Cuba, the Czech Republic, Denmark, Ecuador, Finland, Germany, Greece, Guatemala, Hungary, India, Italy, the Democratic People's Republic of Korea, the Republic of Korea, the Netherlands, Papua New Guinea, Peru, Poland, Romania, Slovakia, Spain, Sweden, Switzerland, Turkey, Ukraine, Uruguay, Venezuela.

Brazil, Bulgaria, the People's Republic of China, Ecuador, Finland, Germany, India, Italy, the Republic of Korea, the Netherlands, Peru, Poland, Spain, Sweden and Uruguay have achieved consultative status under the Treaty, by virtue of their scientific activity in Antarctica.

Antarctic Treaty Secretariat: Leandro N. Alem 884, 4° 1001 Buenos Aires; tel. (11) 5169-1500; fax (11) 5169-1513; e-mail secret@ats.org.ar; internet www.ats.org.ar; Exec. Sec. JOHANNES HUBER.

ANTARCTIC TREATY CONSULTATIVE MEETINGS

Meetings of representatives from all the original signatory nations of the Antarctic Treaty and acceding nations accorded consultative status (27 in 2004), are held annually (with occasional exceptions) to discuss scientific, environmental and political matters. The 28th meeting was scheduled to be held in Stockholm, Sweden, on 6–17 June 2005.

To coincide with the 50th anniversary of International Geophysical Year, March 2007–March 2008 was designated International Polar Year. This date also represented the 125th and 75th anniversaries of the previous two International Polar Years (held in 1882–83 and 1957–58 respectively). By early 2005 some 12 countries had established National Committees to co-ordinate scientific activities for International Polar Year and a further seven were in the process of doing so.

Among the numerous measures that have been agreed and implemented by the Consultative Parties are several designed to protect the Antarctic environment and wildlife. These include Agreed Measures for the Conservation of Antarctic Flora and Fauna, the designation of Specially Protected Areas and Sites of Special Scientific Interest, a Convention for the Conservation of Antarctic Seals, and a Convention on the Conservation of Antarctic Marine Living Resources.

A Convention on the Regulation of Antarctic Mineral Resource Activities (the Wellington Convention) was adopted in June 1988 and was opened for signature in November. To enter into force, the Wellington Convention required the ratification of 16 of the then 22 Consultative Parties. However, France and Australia opposed the Convention, which would permit mineral exploitation (under stringent international controls) in Antarctica, and proposed the creation of an Antarctic wilderness reserve. An agreement was reached at the October 1989 Consultative Meeting whereby two extraordinary meetings were to be convened in 1990, one to discuss the protection of the environment and the other to discuss the issue of liability for environmental damage within the framework of the Wellington Convention. In September 1990 the Government of New Zealand,

which had played a major role in drafting the Wellington Convention, reversed its policy, stating that it was no longer willing to ratify the Convention. At the same time, it introduced legislation in the New Zealand House of Representatives to ban all mining and prospecting activities from its territories in Antarctica. At the special meeting held in Chile in November–December 1990, the Consultative Parties failed to reach an agreement regarding the protection of Antarctica's environment, although a draft protocol was approved that included provisions for elaborating the issue of liability for environmental damage. This formed the basis for a further meeting in Madrid, Spain, in April 1991. France, Australia and 16 other countries supported a permanent ban on mining, whereas the USA, the United Kingdom, Japan, Germany and four others were in favour of a moratorium. Subsequently, however, Japan and Germany transferred their allegiance to the Australian-French initiative, exerting considerable pressure on the USA and the United Kingdom. Agreement was eventually reached on a ban on mining activity for 50 years, and mechanisms for a review of the ban after 50 years, or before if all Parties agree. This agreement is embodied in Article 7 of the Protocol on Environmental Protection to the Antarctic Treaty, which was adopted by the original signatory nations in October 1991. By late 1997 the Protocol had been ratified by all 26 of the then Consultative Parties, and it entered into force on 14 January 1998. Thus there can be mining in the Antarctic only with the consent of all the present Consultative Parties, and even then only when a regulatory regime is in place. The first four annexes to the Protocol, providing for environmental impact assessment, conservation of fauna and flora, waste disposal, and monitoring of marine pollution, entered into force with the Protocol, but the fifth annex, on area protection, agreed after the adoption of the Protocol, has yet to take effect. A sixth annex on environmental liability is under negotiation. At the 22nd Consultative Meeting, held in Tromsø, Norway, in May 1998, the Committee for Environmental Protection (CEP) was established, under the provisions of the Protocol on Environmental Protection. The CEP meets at the location of the annual Antarctic Treaty Consultative Meeting.

At a meeting of the International Whaling Commission (see p. 366) held in Mexico in May 1994, it was agreed to establish a whale sanctuary around Antarctica below 40° S. The sanctuary, which was expected to protect about 80% of the world's remaining whales from commercial hunting, came into effect in December.

In late 1998 the New Zealand Government reported that the largest recorded hole in the ozone layer, covering more than 27m. sq km, had formed over Antarctica. In late 1999, however, the US National Aeronautics and Space Administration (NASA) reported that the ozone hole had decreased in size to 25.4m. sq km. In July 2001 the World Meteorological Organization (see p. 136) reported that record low ozone levels were recorded in 1999–2000.

Substantial calving from ice shelves along the Antarctic Peninsula has fuelled speculation that this may be attributable to climate warming. In early 1995 the Larsen A ice shelf lost 1,300 sq km, and in 1998 the Larsen B and Wilkins ice shelves together lost 3,000 sq km. These calvings represented a much greater rate of loss than had been predicted. The B15 iceberg, which was the largest in the world (measuring 11,000 sq km) when it calved from the Ross ice shelf in 2000, also split into smaller bergs in October 2003. Moreover, in March 2002 the Larsen B ice shelf, which had a surface area of 3,250 sq km and was 200 m thick, collapsed and fragmented into small icebergs. Scientists expressed alarm at the speed of the disintegration of Larsen B, which took place in a period of less than one month. Climate records from the Antarctic Peninsula show an increase in average temperatures of some 3°C during the period 1951–2000 and a 40% thinning of the ice in the Arctic Ocean between 1970 and 2000. Scientists revealed new evidence of global warming in 2003, derived from studies of sea ice distribution around the poles. This ice, which has little direct impact on global temperatures and sea levels, is believed to be responsible for the movement of global ocean currents, which ensure that land masses are kept at certain temperatures. Moreover, studies published by US scientists in September 2004 reported evidence of glaciers thinning at twice the rate recorded in the mid-1990s, prompting fears that the west Antarctic ice sheet (which contained sufficient ice to raise sea levels by six metres) could become destabilized. It was also claimed that following the collapse of an ice shelf, nearby inland glaciers flow up to eight times more quickly into the ocean (this had been shown to have occurred after the disintegration of Larsen B) causing sea levels to rise more rapidly than had previously been thought.

Committee for Environmental Protection (CEP): e-mail cep@cep.aq; internet www.cep.aq; Chair. Dr TONY PRESS (2003–05).

ANTIGUA AND BARBUDA

Introductory Survey

Location, Climate, Language, Religion, Flag, Capital

The country comprises three islands: Antigua (280 sq km—108 sq miles), Barbuda (161 sq km—62 sq miles) and the uninhabited rocky islet of Redonda (1.6 sq km—0.6 sq mile). They lie along the outer edge of the Leeward Islands chain in the West Indies. Barbuda is the most northerly (40 km—25 miles north of Antigua), and Redonda is 40 km south-west of Antigua. The French island of Guadeloupe lies to the south of the country, the United Kingdom Overseas Territory of Montserrat to the south-west and Saint Christopher and Nevis to the west. The climate is tropical, although tempered by constant sea breezes and the trade winds, and the mean annual rainfall of 1,000 mm (40 ins) is slight for the region. The temperature averages 27°C (81°F), but can rise to 33°C (93°F) during the hot season between May and October. English is the official language, but an English patois is commonly used. The majority of the inhabitants profess Christianity, and are mainly adherents of the Anglican Communion. The national flag consists of an inverted triangle centred on a red field; the triangle is divided horizontally into three unequal bands, of black, blue and white, with the black stripe bearing a symbol of the rising sun in gold. The capital is St John's, on Antigua.

Recent History

The British colonized Antigua in the 17th century. The island of Barbuda, formerly a slave stud farm for the Codrington family, was annexed to the territory in 1860. Until December 1959 Antigua and other nearby British territories were administered, under a federal system, as the Leeward Islands. The first elections under universal adult suffrage were held in 1951. The colony participated in the West Indies Federation, which was formed in January 1958 but dissolved in May 1962.

Attempts to form a smaller East Caribbean Federation failed, and most of the eligible colonies subsequently became Associated States in an arrangement that gave them full internal self-government while the United Kingdom retained responsibility for defence and foreign affairs. Antigua attained associated status in February 1967. A House of Representatives replaced the Legislative Council, the Administrator became Governor and the Chief Minister was restyled Premier.

In the first general election under associated status, held in February 1971, the Progressive Labour Movement (PLM) ousted the Antigua Labour Party (ALP), which had held power since 1946, by winning 13 of the 17 seats in the House of Representatives. George Walter, leader of the PLM, replaced Vere C. Bird, Sr, as Premier. However, a general election in February 1976 was won by the ALP, with 11 seats, while the seat representing Barbuda was won by an independent. Vere Bird, the ALP's leader, again became Premier, while Lester Bird, one of his sons, became Deputy Premier.

In 1975 the Associated States agreed to seek independence separately. In the 1976 elections the PLM campaigned for early independence while the ALP opposed it. In September 1978, however, the ALP Government declared that the economic foundation for independence had been laid, and a premature general election was held in April 1980, when the ALP won 13 of the 17 seats. There was strong opposition in Barbuda to gaining independence as part of Antigua, and at local elections in March 1981 the Barbuda People's Movement (BPM), which continued to campaign for secession from Antigua, won all the seats on the Barbuda Council. However, the territory finally became independent, as Antigua and Barbuda, on 1 November 1981, remaining within the Commonwealth. The grievances of the Barbudans concerning control of land and devolution of power were unresolved, although the ALP Government had conceded a certain degree of internal autonomy to the Barbuda Council. The Governor, Sir Wilfred Jacobs, became Governor-General, while the Premier, Vere Bird, Sr, became the country's first Prime Minister.

Following disagreements within the opposition PLM, George Walter formed his own political party, the United People's Movement (UPM), in 1982. In April 1984, at the first general election since independence, divisions within the opposition allowed the ALP to win all of the 16 seats that it contested. The remaining seat, representing Barbuda, was retained by an unopposed independent (who subsequently formed the Barbuda National Party—BNP). A new opposition party, the National Democratic Party (NDP), was formed in Antigua in 1985. In April 1986 it merged with the UPM to form the United National Democratic Party (UNDP). Dr Ivor Heath, who had led the NDP, was elected leader of the new party.

In November 1986 controversy surrounding a rehabilitation scheme at the international airport on Antigua led to an official inquiry, which concluded that Vere Bird, Jr (a senior minister and the eldest son of the Prime Minister), had acted inappropriately by awarding part of the contract to a company with which he was personally involved. The affair divided the ALP, with eight ministers (including Lester Bird, the Deputy Prime Minister) demanding the resignation of Vere Bird, Jr, and Prime Minister Bird refusing to dismiss him. The rifts within the ALP and the Bird family continued into 1988, when new allegations of corruption implicated Lester Bird. At a general election in March 1989 the ALP remained the ruling party by retaining 15 of the 16 seats that it had held previously. The UNDP won more than 30% of the total votes, but only one seat. The Barbuda seat was won by the BPM.

In April 1990 the Government of Antigua and Barbuda received a diplomatic note of protest from the Government of Colombia regarding the sale of weapons to the Medellín cartel of drugs-traffickers in Colombia. The weapons had originally been sold by Israel to Antigua and Barbuda, but, contrary to regulation, were then immediately shipped on to Colombia in April 1989. The communication from the Colombian Government implicated Vere Bird, Jr, and the Prime Minister eventually agreed to establish a judicial inquiry. In October 1990 the Chamber of Commerce recommended the resignation of the Government. In the following month a news agency obtained a copy of the unpublished report of the inquiry, which accused Antigua and Barbuda of having become 'engulfed in corruption'. In addition, the report revealed the activities of a number of British mercenaries on Antigua, involved in the training of paramilitary forces employed by Colombian drugs-trafficking organizations. Also in November, acting upon the recommendations of the report, the Government of Antigua and Barbuda dismissed Vere Bird, Jr, and banned him for life from holding office in the Government. The head of the defence force, Col Clyde Walker, was also dismissed.

Discontent within the ALP (including dissatisfaction with the leadership of Vere Bird, Sr), provoked a serious political crisis in early 1991. The Minister of Finance, John St Luce, resigned in February, after claiming that the Prime Minister ignored his proposals for a restructuring of government. A subsequent cabinet reshuffle (in which Lester Bird lost his deputy premiership) provoked the immediate resignation of three ministers. In September, however, Lester Bird and John St Luce accepted invitations from the Prime Minister to rejoin the Cabinet.

In early 1992 further reports of corruption involving Vere Bird, Sr, provoked public unrest and demands for his resignation. In April the Antigua Caribbean Liberation Movement, the PLM and the UNDP consolidated their opposition to the Government by merging to form the United Progressive Party (UPP). In May Vere Bird, Sr, was re-elected ALP leader. In August further controversy arose when proposed anti-corruption legislation (which had been recommended following the Colombian arms scandal in 1991) was withdrawn as a result of legal intervention by the Prime Minister.

On 10 June 1993 James (later Sir James) Carlisle took office as Governor-General, replacing Sir Wilfred Jacobs. In September the ALP convened in order to hold further leadership elections. As a result of the vote, Lester Bird became leader of the party, while Vere Bird, Jr, was elected as Chairman.

At a general election in March 1994 the ALP remained the ruling party, although with a reduced majority, having secured 11 seats; the UPP won five and the BPM retained the Barbuda seat. Following the election, Lester Bird assumed the premiership. Despite some criticism, the election was generally thought to have been free and fair.

In February 1995 an ALP activist, Leonard Aaron, was charged with threatening to murder Tim Hector, editor of an opposition newspaper, *The Outlet*. It was reported that Hector's house had been burgled on several occasions, when material containing allegedly incriminating information relating to members of the Government had been stolen. Aaron was subsequently released, following the intervention of the Prime Minister. In May the Prime Minister's brother, Ivor Bird, was arrested following an incident in which he collected luggage at V. C. Bird International Airport from a Barbadian citizen from Venezuela, which contained 12 kg of cocaine. *The Outlet* claimed that such an exchange had occurred on at least three previous occasions. Ivor Bird's subsequent release from police custody, upon payment of a fine of EC $200,000, attracted considerable criticism. In an attempt to improve the country's worsening reputation as a centre for drugs-trafficking, the Government proposed legislation in 1996 which aimed to curb the illegal drugs trade. In the same year Wrenford Ferrance, a former financial controller at the Organisation of Eastern Caribbean States (OECS, see p. 384), was appointed to the newly-created position of Special Adviser to the Government on money-laundering and on the control of illicit drugs. However, a report published by the US Government in early 1998 found Antigua and Barbuda to be 'of primary concern' with regard to both of these illegal activities.

In May 1996 Vere Bird, Jr, who had been declared unfit for public office following a judicial inquiry in 1990 (see above), was controversially appointed to the post of Special Adviser to the Prime Minister. In September Molwyn Joseph resigned as Minister of Finance over allegations that he had used his position in order to evade the payment of customs duties on the import of a vintage motor car. His resignation followed an opposition protest, at which the UPP leader, Baldwin Spencer, and seven other party members, including Tim Hector, were arrested (charges brought against them were later dismissed). A further demonstration took place at the end of the month, when some 10,000 people demanded a full inquiry into the affair and an early general election. In early December 1997, however, Joseph was reinstated in the Cabinet, assuming the new post of Minister of Planning, Implementation and the Environment; the opposition vehemently condemned the appointment.

In March 1997 the opposition BPM defeated the ALP's ally, the New Barbuda Development Movement, in elections to the Barbuda Council, winning all five of the contested seats and thus gaining control of all the seats in the nine-member Council. In the same month the High Court upheld a constitutional motion presented by Baldwin Spencer seeking the right of expression for the opposition on state-owned radio and television (denied during the electoral campaign in March 1994). In May and June the UPP boycotted sittings of the House of Representatives (the first legislative boycotts in the country's history) during a parliamentary debate on a proposed US $300m. tourism development on Guiana Island, which was to be constructed by a Malaysian company. The opposition claimed that the Prime Minister had failed to publish the proposals for public discussion prior to the parliamentary debate and that the 2,000-room hotel project would have adverse effects on the island's ecology. The project was, none the less, endorsed by the legislature. In September Spencer applied to the High Court to have the hotel project agreement declared illegal and unconstitutional. However, his objections were overruled by the High Court in November, and a subsequent appeal, made to the Eastern Caribbean Court of Appeal, was also dismissed in April 1998. (The Prime Minister had rejected demands for a referendum on the controversial scheme in October 1997.) However, the Guiana Island project continued to provoke controversy. In December 1997 Vere Bird, Jr, was slightly wounded in a shooting incident on the same day as the Government agreed terms for the compulsory resettlement of the island's sole occupants, Cyril 'Taffy' Bufton and his wife. Bufton was subsequently charged with attempted murder, but was acquitted in October 1998. The UPP denied government allegations of its involvement in the attack.

Meanwhile, in August 1997 *The Outlet* published further allegations regarding government-supported drugs-trafficking, including a claim that a Colombian drug cartel had contributed US $1m. to the ALP's election campaign in 1994. In response, Prime Minister Lester Bird obtained a High Court injunction in early September prohibiting the newspaper from publishing

further material relating to the allegations. In November the printing presses of *The Outlet* were destroyed by fire, two days after the newspaper's editor, Tim Hector, had publicly alleged that a large consignment of 'sophisticated' weaponry had entered Antigua. The Government denied allegations that it was responsible for the fire, and stated that a shipment of 'basic' arms had been imported for police use.

At a general election held on 9 March 1999, the ALP increased its representation in the 17-seat House of Representatives from 11 to 12, at the expense of the UPP, which secured four seats; the BPM retained its single seat. Following the election, Lester Bird was reappointed Prime Minister, and a new Cabinet was duly appointed, which again controversially included Vere Bird, Jr, as Minister of Agriculture, Lands and Fisheries. Independent observers declared the election to have been free, although they expressed reservations concerning its fairness, owing to the ALP's large-scale expenditure and use of the media during its electoral campaign.

Also in March 1999 the US Government published a report which claimed that recent Antiguan financial legislation had weakened regulations concerning money-laundering and increased the secrecy surrounding 'offshore' banks. It also advised US banks to scrutinize all financial dealings with Antigua and Barbuda, which was described as a potential 'haven for money-laundering activities'. In April the United Kingdom issued a similar financial advisory to its banks. In response, in July Antigua became the first Eastern Caribbean country to bring into force a treaty with the USA on extradition and mutual legal assistance. Furthermore, in September the Government established an independent body, the International Financial Sector Regulatory Body, to regulate 'offshore' banking. In November the authorities uncovered a significant money-laundering operation, run by a former Ukrainian prime minister. Although in 2000 Antigua and Barbuda's financial system was criticized by the Organisation for Economic Co-operation and Development (OECD, see p. 307) and by the Financial Action Task Force (FATF, see p. 377), in 2001 the FATF recognized the state as a 'fully co-operative jurisdiction against money laundering'. Furthermore, by July the country had satisfied the United Kingdom that its financial institutions no longer needed special attention and had conformed to the FATF rules on harmful tax practices and in the following month the US Treasury withdrew its financial advisory notice. In December the Government signed a tax information exchange agreement with the USA. Negotiations for a similar agreement with Australia and New Zealand were concluded in January 2004. In 2003 the Government strongly criticized OECD and the FATF for protecting the financial regimes of powerful states at the expense of smaller nations and for usurping the 'role of international organizations such as the World Trade Organization (WTO, see p. 357) in global governance'.

In January 2000 the Government established a commission, chaired by Sir Fred Philips, a former Governor of Saint Christopher and Nevis, to review the Constitution. The commission was to examine the role of the Government, political parties and non-governmental organizations, and was to focus on the maintenance of democracy and accountability. In addition, increased tensions between Antigua and Barbuda, and the latter's demands for autonomy, meant that constitutional change was a much discussed issue throughout 2001. The commission's recommendations, reported in February 2002, included the replacement of the Queen as head of state with a President chosen by the majority party in Parliament, and amalgamation of the Senate and House of Representatives into a unicameral legislature, as well as a bill of rights and integrity legislation.

In May 2001 Dr Errol Cort, the Attorney-General, George 'Bacchanal' Walker, the Leader of Government Business in the Senate, and Bernard Percival, the former Minister of Health and head of the state-run Medical Benefits Scheme (MBS), were dismissed from their posts after the publication of a forensic audit into alleged fraud in the MBS. Although there was no evidence that either minister was involved in financial malpractice, Prime Minister Bird stated that both had shown a 'lapse of good judgement' regarding payments made to the Scheme. In the following month, bowing to pressure from non-governmental organizations and the general public, Bird announced that an independent Commission of Inquiry into the funding and practices of the MBS would be held. The Inquiry opened in December and, in late July 2002, recommended that a special prosecutor be appointed to examine charges against 12 people, including two former health ministers, implicated in abusing the scheme. The Inquiry also recommended the conversion of the MBS into a health insurance scheme run by an independent body, and stressed that the Government should not interfere with the scheme's operation. In April, following fraud allegations arising from the Inquiry, the Minister of Trade, Industry and Business Development, Hilroy Humphreys, resigned. The trade portfolio was passed to the Minister of Planning, Implementation and Public Service Affairs, Gaston Brown. In November the British Broadcasting Corporation (BBC) paid the Prime Minister libel damages of £50,000 over radio news reports relating to the MBS.

Also in April 2002 a further public dispute emerged, which prompted the Prime Minister to initiate a libel suit against leading members of the UPP, including Baldwin Spencer, as well as against an independent newspaper and radio station and a 15-year old girl. In early June the Prime Minister abandoned an initial attempt to obtain a court injunction against further repetition of the allegations, paying costs of EC $26,000 to his opponents. The libel case was scheduled to open in February 2003, but Bird dropped the suit against the newspaper and radio journalists before proceedings began. The case against the 15-year old girl continued, however, although she in turn initiated civil proceedings against the Prime Minister, before dropping the case in October.

In May 2002 an ALP Member of Parliament, Sherfield Bowen, called for the Prime Minister and his Chief of Staff to resign, to allow an independent investigation of allegations made against both of them. In September a demonstration organized by the UPP reportedly attracted several thousand marchers demanding the immediate resignation of the Prime Minister and a general election within six months. Also in September Robin Yearwood was appointed to the post of Deputy Prime Minister. The Prime Minister acknowledged that Yearwood, who continued to hold the position of Minister of Public Utilities, Aviation, Transport and Housing, was promoted in order to improve discipline within the Government following a series of corruption scandals, most notably that relating to the MBS.

In June 2003 Senator Asot Michael, the Minister of State in the Office of the Prime Minister with responsibility for Finance, resigned following accusations that he wielded more power in the ALP administration than was suitable for a non-elected politician. Michael's departure prompted Bird to affect a cabinet reorganization, which included the appointment of Longford Jeremy as Minister of Home Affairs, Information, Local Government and Youth Empowerment. Earlier in the same month Jeremy, along with four other deputies, had resigned the ALP whip for a short period after criticizing Bird's leadership. In November a UPP request for a motion of 'no confidence' in two government ministers, Molwyn Joseph and Gaston Brown, was denied by the Speaker; the opposition party alleged that both men received substantial sums of money from Allen Stanford, a US businessman and Chairman of the Bank of Antigua, during the negotiation of a real-estate transaction between the Government and the bank.

At a general election held on 23 March 2004 the UPP, led by Baldwin Spencer, secured 12 out of the 17 parliamentary seats, thereby removing from government the ALP, which had held power since 1976. The ALP, which had been weakened by personal allegations surrounding Lester Bird and by a damaging contraction in the crucial tourism sector, secured only four seats. An extremely high voter turn-out—91.2% of the electorate, compared with 63.6% in the 1999 ballot—was interpreted as a strong indication of public resentment towards the Bird regime. The election in the remaining constituency, that of Barbuda, resulted in a tie between the incumbent BPM and a newly formed party, the Barbuda People's Movement for Change; since neither candidate favoured a recount of the ballots, the island's electorate voted again on 20 April. Trevor Walker, the candidate of the Barbuda People's Movement, was duly elected by a narrow margin. In advance of the general election a completely new electoral register was, with the assistance of the Electoral Office of Jamaica, prepared for the first time since 1975. Elimination of deceased and non-resident names reduced the list by more than one-fifth, while voters were issued with identity cards including a photograph and fingerprint, decreasing the risk that illegitimate votes would be cast.

Spencer was sworn in as Prime Minister on 24 March 2004; his first Cabinet included Colin Derrick, who had failed to win a parliamentary seat and was subsequently appointed to the Senate, as head of the new Ministry of Social Transformation. Shortly after its removal from government, Bird's regime was

again embroiled in controversy when Spencer ordered an investigation into accusations that the out-going Prime Minister had illegally removed documents from state offices; Bird insisted he had only removed personal items and described the ensuing police search of his house as a 'witch hunt'. Meanwhile, in Barbuda, the island's Council was deadlocked from 3 April 2003 when each party gained four seats at local elections; this impasse was expected to be resolved by the courts in 2005.

In January 2005 Spencer announced a small cabinet reshuffle; appointing new Ministers of State in three ministries and transferring extra responsibilities to himself. With the cabinet now numbering 16, the changes attracted some criticism from those who remembered Spencer's earlier promises to reduce the size of the Government's payroll; however, the Prime Minister argued the reorganization would improve his administration's efficiency, particularly in terms of combating corruption and international crime.

In foreign relations the ALP Government follows a policy of non-alignment, although the country has strong links with the USA. In September 2003 Antigua and Barbuda became the 67th country to agree to grant immunity from prosecutions before the International Criminal Court (ICC) to US nationals accused of war crimes. In July the US Administration had rescinded military aid to several Caribbean nations, including Antigua and Barbuda, following their failure to agree to US terms over the ICC. In September 2001 the Government established diplomatic relations with Libya, after that country announced a US $1m. aid package to Antigua. Antigua and Barbuda is also a member of the CARICOM (see p. 172). In November 2003 the People's Republic of China granted Antigua US $12m. loan, a large part of which was to fund the construction of a new sports stadium for the 2007 Cricket World Cup.

Government

Antigua and Barbuda is a constitutional monarchy. Executive power is vested in the British sovereign, as Head of State, and exercised by the Governor-General, who represents the sovereign locally and is appointed on the advice of the Antiguan Prime Minister. Legislative power is vested in Parliament, comprising the sovereign, a 17-member Senate and a 17-member House of Representatives. Members of the House are elected from single-member constituencies for up to five years by universal adult suffrage. The Senate is composed of 11 members (of whom one must be an inhabitant of Barbuda) appointed on the advice of the Prime Minister, four appointed on the advice of the Leader of the Opposition, one appointed at the discretion of the Governor-General and one appointed on the advice of the Barbuda Council. Government is effectively by the Cabinet. The Governor-General appoints the Prime Minister and, on the latter's recommendation, selects the other ministers. The Prime Minister must be able to command the support of a majority of the House, to which the Cabinet is responsible. The Barbuda Council has nine seats, with partial elections held every two years.

In December 2000 a Commonwealth review of the administration of Barbuda recommended the maintenance of the existing constitutional relationship between Barbuda and Antigua.

Defence

There is a small defence force of 170 men (army 125, navy 45). The US Government leases two military bases on Antigua. Antigua and Barbuda participates in the US-sponsored Regional Security System. The defence budget in 2004 was estimated at EC $12.0m.

Economic Affairs

In 2003, according to estimates by the World Bank, Antigua and Barbuda's gross national income (GNI), measured at average 2001–2003 prices, was US $716m., equivalent to $9,160 per head (or $9,590 per head on an international purchasing-power parity basis). During 1990–2003, it was estimated, the population increased at an average rate of 1.6% per year, while gross domestic product (GDP) per head increased, in real terms, by an average of 1.5% per year. Overall GDP increased, in real terms, at an average annual rate of 3.1% in 1990–2003. According to the Eastern Caribbean Central Bank (ECCB), real GDP increased by an estimated 5.5% in 2003.

Agriculture (including forestry and fishing) engaged 23.5% of the active labour force in 2003, according to estimates by the UN's Food and Agriculture Organization. The sector contributed an estimated 3.5% of GDP in 2003. According to the ECCB, agricultural GDP increased, in real terms, between 1990 and 2003 at an average rate of 1.4% per year. The agricultural sector increased, in real terms, by 1.0% in 2002 and by 2.5% in 2003. The principal crops are cucumbers, pumpkins, sweet potatoes, mangoes, coconuts, limes, melons and the speciality 'Antigua Black' pineapple. In 2000 the Ministry of Agriculture, Lands and Fisheries announced a programme to encourage farmers to increase production. Lobster, shrimp and crab farms are in operation, and further projects to develop the fishing industry were undertaken in the 1990s.

Industry (comprising mining, manufacturing, construction and utilities) employed 18.9% of the active labour force in 1991 and provided an estimated 19.5% of GDP in 2003. The principal industrial activity is construction, accounting for 11.6% of total employment in 1991. Industrial GDP increased, in real terms, at an average rate of 4.1% per year during 1990–2003. It rose by 3.4% in 2002 and by 4.8% in 2003.

Mining and quarrying employed only 0.2% of the active labour force in 1991 and contributed an estimated 2.1% of GDP in 2003. The real GDP of the mining sector increased at an average rate of 3.0% per year during 1990–2003. It rose by 2.0% in 2002 and by 5.5% in 2003.

The manufacturing sector consists of some light industries producing garments, paper, paint, furniture, food and beverage products, and the assembly of household appliances and electrical components for export. Manufacturing contributed an estimated 2.1% of GDP in 2003, when construction provided 13.1%. In real terms, the GDP of the manufacturing sector increased at an average rate of 1.0% per year during 1990–2003. Manufacturing GDP increased by 3.2% in 2002 and by 5.3% in 2003. Over the same period construction growth was 3.4% and 6.7%, respectively.

Most of the country's energy production is derived from imported fuel. Imports of mineral fuels, lubricants and related materials accounted for 10.5% of total imports in 1999.

Services provided 70.2% of employment in 1991 and an estimated 77.0% of GDP in 2003. The combined GDP of the service sectors increased, in real terms, at an average rate of 3.5% per year during 1990–2003. It rose by 2.8% in 2002 and by 5.5% in 2003. Tourism is the main economic activity, providing approximately 35% of employment in 1991, and accounting (directly and indirectly) for some 60% of GDP in the mid-1990s. By 1998 the industry showed significant signs of recovery, following the severe effects of 'Hurricane Luis' (despite suffering a minor setback in September, when 'Hurricane Georges' resulted in the closure of several hotels). Visitor arrivals increased from 470,975 in 1995 to 651,797 in 2000, decreasing hugely in 2001 and 2002 before recovering slightly in 2003, to an estimated 613,753; expenditure by tourists reached US $290.5m. in 2000, before decreasing to $272.1m. in 2001 and $273.8m. in 2002. According to preliminary figures, tourism receipts increased to $299.9m. in 2003. The real GDP of the hotels and restaurants sector decreased by 7.8% in 2001, but increased slightly in 2002 (by 2.1%) and considerably in 2003 (by 10.2%). Most stop-over tourists are from Europe (44.6% in 2003), the USA (30.4%), Canada (4.0%) and other Caribbean countries (20.4%). The decrease in tourists from the North American mainland following the terrorist attacks in the USA in September 2001 had an adverse affect on the sector; in 2001 tourist arrivals decreased to 193,176, compared with 206,871 in 2000. The sector recovered slightly in 2002 when 198,085 tourist arrivals were recorded, although there was an estimated decrease of 23.6% in the number of cruise-ship passengers. The number of cruise-ship passengers increased to 383,834 in 2003, something approaching the level of 2001, and 212,557 stop-over tourists holidayed on the islands in 2003, the greatest number since 1999. An independent body, the International Financial Sector Regulatory Body, was established in 1999 to regulate the 'offshore' financial services sector, operations of which in Antigua and Barbuda had hitherto been the subject of adverse international scrutiny (see Recent History). In 2001 the Financial Action Task Force (FATF, see p. 377) recognized Antigua and Barbuda as a 'fully co-operative jurisdiction against money-laundering'. In November 2004 there were 16 licensed 'offshore' banks registered in the country.

Antigua and Barbuda recorded a visible trade deficit in 2003 of EC $835.5m. and a deficit of EC $64.6m. on the current account of the balance of payments. The country's principal trading partners are the other members of the Caribbean Community and Common Market (CARICOM, see p. 172), the USA, the United Kingdom and Canada. In 1999 the USA provided 49.4% of total imports and was also the most important market for exports (mainly re-exports).

In 2003 there was an estimated budgetary deficit of EC $165.8m. In 2003 debt-servicing costs accounted for some 8.9% of the value of exports of goods and services. By the end of that year total external debt amounted to US $520.9m. The annual average rate of inflation was 2.3% in 1993–2001. Consumer prices rose by 1.1% in 2002 and by 3.4% in 2003. The rate of unemployment in 2001 was reported to be 8.1% of the labour force.

Antigua and Barbuda is a member of CARICOM, the Organisation of Eastern Caribbean States (OECS), the Organization of American States (see p. 319), and is a signatory of the Cotonou Agreement (the successor agreement to Lomé Conventions) with the European Union (EU, see p. 217). Antigua and Barbuda is also a member of the Eastern Caribbean Securities Exchange (based in Saint Christopher and Nevis), established in 2001.

The economy of Antigua and Barbuda is dominated by tourism, despite some efforts at diversification—for example the development of 'offshore' financial services. A decline in the rate of economic expansion in 2001 (to 1.5%) was principally attributable to the weak performance of the tourism sector and a slowdown in the growth of industrial sector. A recovery in 2002 and 2003, when growth was estimated at 2.1% and 5.5%, respectively, reflected in part the resilience of tourism revenue to the regional downturn in the sector. The economy also gained momentum from a buoyant construction industry in 2003, which expanded by 6.7%. Despite concerns that the tourism sector would decline in the latter part of 2004, the IMF forecast continued growth, of 4.1%, for that year, notably because of an improved fiscal regime and the expected continued expansion of the construction sector. This afforded optimism that the improved economic situation would allow the Government to address the issue of the country's very large external debt, responsibility for which the IMF apportioned to 'years of fiscal mismanagement'. In view of this, in December 2004 the legislature approved new taxation measures for the 2005 budget.

Education

Education is compulsory for 11 years between five and 16 years of age. Primary education begins at the age of five and normally lasts for seven years. Secondary education, beginning at 12 years of age, lasts for five years, comprising a first cycle of three years and a second cycle of two years. In 2000/01 there were 55 primary and 14 secondary schools; the majority of schools are administered by the Government. In the same year some 10,427 primary school pupils and 5,794 secondary school pupils were enrolled. Teacher-training and technical training are available at the Antigua State College in St John's. An extra-mural department of the University of the West Indies offers several foundation courses leading to higher study at branches elsewhere. In November 2002 the EU agreed to provide funding for tertiary education worth EC $2.6m. Current government expenditure on education in 1993/94 was projected at $37.1m., equivalent to 12.8% of total budgetary expenditure.

Public Holidays

2005: 1 January (New Year's Day), 25 March (Good Friday), 28 March (Easter Monday), 2 May (Labour Day), 16 May (Whit Monday), 11 June (Queen's Official Birthday), 4 July (Vere Cornwall Bird, Sr Day), 1–2 August (Carnival), 1 November (Independence Day), 25–26 December (Christmas).

2006: 1 January (New Year's Day), 14 April (Good Friday), 17 April (Easter Monday), 1 May (Labour Day), 5 June (Whit Monday), 10 June (Queen's Official Birthday), 3 July (Vere Cornwall Bird, Sr Day), 7–8 August (Carnival), 1 November (Independence Day), 25–26 December (Christmas).

Weights and Measures

The imperial system is in use, but a metrication programme is being introduced.

Statistical Survey

Source (unless otherwise stated): Ministry of Finance, Economic Development and Planning, Govt Office Complex, Parliament Dr., St John's; tel. 462-5015; fax 462-4860; e-mail budget@candw.ag.

AREA AND POPULATION

Area: 441.6 sq km (170.5 sq miles).

Population: 62,922 at census of 28 May 1991; 77,426 (provisional result, males 37,002, females 40,424) at census of 28 May 2001. *Mid-2002* (estimate): 76,500 (Source: Caribbean Development Bank, *Social and Economic Indicators*).

Density (mid-2002): 173.2 per sq km.

Principal Town: St John's (capital), population 22,342 at 1991 census. *Mid-2003* (UN estimate, incl. suburbs): St John's 27,516 (Source: UN, *World Urbanization Prospects: The 2003 Revision*).

Births, Marriages and Deaths (registrations, 2001): Live births 1,366 (birth rate 18.04 per 1,000); Marriages 1,784 (marriage rate 23.55 per 1,000); Deaths 457 (death rate 6.03 per 1,000).

Expectation of Life (WHO estimates, years at birth): 71.4 (males 69.0; females 73.9) in 2002. Source: WHO, *World Health Report*.

Employment (persons aged 15 years and over, census of 28 May 1991): Agriculture, forestry and fishing 1,040; Mining and quarrying 64; Manufacturing 1,444; Electricity, gas and water 435; Construction 3,109; Trade, restaurants and hotels 8,524; Transport, storage and communications 2,395; Finance, insurance, real estate and business services 1,454; Community, social and personal services 6,406; Activities not adequately defined 1,882; Total employed 26,753 (males 14,564, females 12,189) (Source: ILO). *2001:* Total active labour force 46,440. *Mid-2003* (estimates in '000): Agriculture, etc. 8; Total labour force 34 (Source: FAO).

HEALTH AND WELFARE

Key Indicators

Total Fertility Rate (children per woman, 2002): 1.6.

Under-5 Mortality Rate (per 1,000 live births, 2003): 12.

Physicians (per 1,000 head, 1996): 1.14.

Hospital Beds (per 1,000 head, 1998): 3.88.

Health Expenditure (2001): US $ per head (PPP): 614.

Health Expenditure (2001): % of GDP: 5.6.

Health Expenditure (2001): public (% of total): 60.9.

Access to Water (% of persons, 2002): 91.

Access to Sanitation (% of persons, 2002): 95.

Human Development Index (2002): ranking: 55.

Human Development Index (2002): value: 0.800.
For sources and definitions, see explanatory note on p. vi.

AGRICULTURE, ETC.

Principal Crops (FAO estimates, '000 metric tons, 2003): Vegetables 2.2; Melons 0.8; Mangoes 1.4; Other fruits 8.5. Source: FAO.

Livestock (FAO estimates, '000 head, year ending September 2003): Asses 1.6; Cattle 14.0; Pigs 5.5; Sheep 18.6; Goats 35.5; Poultry 100. Source: FAO.

Livestock Products (FAO estimates, '000 metric tons, 2003): Beef and veal 0.5; Cows' milk 5.4. Source: FAO.

Fishing (metric tons, live weight, 2002): Groupers and seabasses 364; Snappers and jobfishes 348; Grunts and sweetlips 259; Parrotfishes 252; Surgeonfishes 237; Caribbean spiny lobster 276; Total catch (incl. others) 2,374. Source: FAO.

INDUSTRY

Production (estimates, 1988): Rum 4,000 hectolitres; Wines and vodka 2,000 hectolitres; Electric energy (estimate, 2000) 99m. kWh. Source: UN, *Industrial Commodity Statistics Yearbook*.

FINANCE

Currency and Exchange Rates: 100 cents = 1 Eastern Caribbean dollar (EC $). *Sterling, US Dollar and Euro Equivalents* (31 December 2004): £1 sterling = EC $5.215; US $1 = EC $2.700; €1 = EC $3.678; EC $100 = £19.18 = US $37.04 = €27.19. *Exchange rate*: Fixed at US $1 = EC $2.700 since July 1976.

Budget (EC $ million, preliminary, 2003): *Revenue:* Tax revenue 381.5 (Taxes on income and profits 62.6, Taxes on Property 11.1, Taxes on domestic goods and services 75.4, Taxes on international transactions 232.4); Other current revenue 44.4; Capital revenue 1.1; Total 427.0, excluding grants received (3.2). *Expenditure:* Current expenditure 514.8 (Personal emoluments 250.1, Employment contributions 32.5, Other goods and services 89.1, Interest payments 92.3, Transfers and subsidies 50.8); Capital expenditure and net lending 81.2; Total 596.0. Source: IMF, *Antigua and Barbuda: Statistical Appendix* (November 2004).

International Reserves (US $ million at 31 December 2003): IMF special drawing rights 0.01; Foreign exchange 113.75; Total 113.76. Source: IMF, *International Financial Statistics*.

Money Supply (EC $ million at 31 December 2003): Currency outside banks 98.86; Demand deposits at deposit money banks 301.33; Total money (incl. others) 400.20. Source: IMF, *International Financial Statistics*.

Cost of Living (Consumer Price Index; base: 2000 = 100): 98.7 in 2001; 99.8 in 2002; 103.2 in 2003. Source: IMF, *Antigua and Barbuda: Statistical Appendix* (November 2004).

Expenditure on the Gross Domestic Product (preliminary, EC $ million at current prices, 2003): Government final consumption expenditure 525.74; Private final consumption expenditure 657.51; Gross capital formation 1,055.61; *Total domestic expenditure* 2,238.86; Exports of goods and services 1,281.77; *Less* Imports of goods and services 1,465.71; *GDP in purchasers' values* 2,054.92. Source: Eastern Caribbean Central Bank.

Gross Domestic Product by Economic Activity (preliminary, EC $ million at current prices, 2003): Agriculture, hunting, forestry and fishing 65.16; Mining and quarrying 29.81; Manufacturing 40.10; Electricity and water 50.59; Construction 243.85; Trade 175.50; Restaurants and hotels 173.43; Transport and communications 348.41; Finance, insurance, real estate and business services 291.86; Government services 322.03; Other community, social and personal services 126.69; *Sub-total* 1,867.43; *Less* Imputed bank service charges 120.25; *GDP at factor cost* 1,747.18. Source: Eastern Caribbean Central Bank.

Balance of Payments (preliminary, EC $ million, 2003): Exports of goods f.o.b. 129.38; Imports of goods f.o.b. –964.86; *Trade balance* –835.48; Exports of services 1,152.39; Imports of services –500.33; *Balance on goods and services* –183.94; Other income received 34.60; Other income paid –129.47; *Balance on goods, services and income* –278.81; Current transfers received 64.13; Current transfers paid –49.92; *Current account* –264.60; Capital account (net) 18.51; Direct investment from abroad (net) 255.44; Portfolio investment assets –0.16; Other investment assets (net) 10.78; Net errors and omissions 50.66; *Overall balance* 70.63. Source: Eastern Caribbean Central Bank.

EXTERNAL TRADE

Total Trade (EC $ million): *Imports f.o.b.:* 913.4 in 2000; 847.2 in 2001; 887.0 in 2002 (preliminary figure). *Exports f.o.b.:* 44.1 in 2000; 46.1 in 2001; 47.0 in 2002 (preliminary figure). Source: Eastern Caribbean Central Bank, *Report and Statement of Accounts*.

Principal Commodities (US $ million, 1999): *Imports:* Food and live animals 61.5 (Meat and meat preparations 12.3, Vegetables and fruit 14.1); Beverages and tobacco 14.6 (Beverages 13.5); Crude materials (inedible) except fuels 11.4; Mineral fuels, lubricants, etc. 37.4 (Refined petroleum products 34.7); Chemicals and related products 21.8; Basic manufactures 54.8; Machinery and transport equipment 114.7 (Telecommunications and sound equipment 16.6, Road vehicles 52.9); Miscellaneous manufactured articles 38.1. Total (incl. others) 356.0. *Exports:* Food and live animals 0.6; Crude materials (inedible) except fuels 0.5; Chemicals and related products 1.7 (Pigments, paints, varnishes, etc. 1.2); Basic manufactures 3.0 (Textiles, yarn, fabrics, made-up articles, etc. 0.7, Iron and steel 1.4); Machinery and transport equipment 5.9 (General industrial machinery and equipment 0.6, Telecommunications and sound equipment 1.8, Road vehicles 1.1); Miscellaneous manufactured articles 2.7 (Photographic equipment, optical goods and watches, etc. 0.8); Total (incl. others) 15.0. Source: UN, *International Trade Statistics Yearbook*.

Principal Trading Partners (US $ million, 1999): *Imports:* Barbados 6.7; Canada 9.4; Japan 36.2; Korea, Republic 5.1; Netherlands Antilles 19.6; Saint Vincent and the Grenadines 4.6; Trinidad and Tobago 21.4; United Kingdom 22.3; USA 176.1; Venezuela 14.7; Total (incl. others) 356.0. *Exports:* Anguilla 0.2; Barbados 0.5; British Virgin Islands 0.2; Canada 0.2; Dominica 1.0; France 1.1; Germany 0.2; Grenada 0.2; Jamaica 0.9; Montserrat 2.0; Netherlands Antilles 0.5; Saint Christopher and Nevis 1.7; Saint Lucia 0.8; Saint Vincent and the Grenadines 0.3; Trinidad and Tobago 0.8; United Kingdom 1.1; USA 3.2; Total (incl. others) 15.0. Source: UN, *International Trade Statistics Yearbook.*

TRANSPORT

Road Traffic (registered vehicles, 1998): Passenger motor cars and commercial vehicles 24,000. Source: UN, *Statistical Yearbook.*

Shipping (international freight traffic, '000 metric tons, 1990): Goods loaded 28; Goods unloaded 113 (Source: UN, *Monthly Bulletin of Statistics). Merchant Fleet* (registered at 31 December): 950 vessels (total displacement 6,004,650 grt) in 2003 (Source: Lloyd's Register-Fairplay, *World Fleet Statistics*).

Civil Aviation (traffic on scheduled services, 1999): Kilometres flown (million) 11; Passengers carried ('000) 1,371; Passenger-km (million) 276; Total ton-km (million) 26. Source: UN, *Statistical Yearbook.*

TOURISM

Tourist Arrivals: 193,176 in 2001; 198,085 in 2002; 212,557 in 2003 (preliminary figure). Source: IMF, *Antigua and Barbuda: Statistical Appendix* (November 2004).

Visitor Expenditure (US $ million): 272.1 in 2001; 273.8 in 2002; 299.9 in 2003 (preliminary figure). Source: IMF, *Antigua and Barbuda: Statistical Appendix* (November 2004).

COMMUNICATIONS MEDIA

Radio Receivers (1997): 36,000 in use*.

Television Receivers (1999): 33,000 in use*.

Telephones (2001): 37,300 main lines in use†.

Facsimile Machines (year ending 31 March 1997): 850 in use‡.

Mobile Telephones (2001): 25,000 subscribers†.

Internet Users (2000): 5,000†.

Daily Newspapers (2003): 2.

Non-daily Newspapers (1996): 4*.

* Source: UNESCO, *Statistical Yearbook.*
† Source: International Telecommunication Union.
‡ Source: UN, *Statistical Yearbook.*

EDUCATION

Pre-primary (1983): 21 schools; 23 teachers; 677 pupils.

Primary (2000/01): 55 schools; 525 teachers; 10,427 students.

Secondary (2000/01): 14 schools; 361 teachers; 5,794 students.

Special (2000/01): 2 schools; 15 teachers; 61 students.

Tertiary (1986): 2 colleges; 631 students.

Adult Literacy Rate: 86.6% in 2000 (Source: Organization of Eastern Caribbean States).

Directory

The Constitution

The Constitution, which came into force at the independence of Antigua and Barbuda on 1 November 1981, states that Antigua and Barbuda is a 'unitary sovereign democratic state'. The main provisions of the Constitution are summarized below

FUNDAMENTAL RIGHTS AND FREEDOMS

Regardless of race, place of origin, political opinion, colour, creed or sex, but subject to respect for the rights and freedoms of others and for the public interest, every person in Antigua and Barbuda is entitled to the rights of life, liberty, security of the person, the enjoyment of property and the protection of the law. Freedom of movement, of conscience, of expression (including freedom of the press), of peaceful assembly and association is guaranteed and the inviolability of family life, personal privacy, home and other property is maintained. Protection is afforded from discrimination on the grounds of race, sex, etc., and from slavery, forced labour, torture and inhuman treatment.

THE GOVERNOR-GENERAL

The British sovereign, as Monarch of Antigua and Barbuda, is the Head of State and is represented by a Governor-General of local citizenship.

PARLIAMENT

Parliament consists of the Monarch, a 17-member Senate and the House of Representatives composed of 17 elected members. Senators are appointed by the Governor-General: 11 on the advice of the Prime Minister (one of whom must be an inhabitant of Barbuda), four on the advice of the Leader of the Opposition, one at his own discretion and one on the advice of the Barbuda Council. The Barbuda Council is the principal organ of local government in that island, whose membership and functions are determined by Parliament. The life of Parliament is five years.

Each constituency returns one Representative to the House who is directly elected in accordance with the Constitution.

The Attorney-General, if not otherwise a member of the House, is an ex-officio member but does not have the right to vote.

Every citizen over the age of 18 is eligible to vote.

Parliament may alter any of the provisions of the Constitution.

THE EXECUTIVE

Executive authority is vested in the Monarch and exercisable by the Governor-General. The Governor-General appoints as Prime Minister that member of the House who, in the Governor-General's view, is best able to command the support of the majority of the members of the House, and other ministers on the advice of the Prime Minister. The Governor-General may remove the Prime Minister from office if a resolution of no confidence is passed by the House and the Prime Minister does not either resign or advise the Governor-General to dissolve Parliament within seven days.

The Cabinet consists of the Prime Minister and other ministers and the Attorney-General.

The Leader of the Opposition is appointed by the Governor-General as that member of the House who, in the Governor-General's view, is best able to command the support of a majority of members of the House who do not support the Government.

CITIZENSHIP

All persons born in Antigua and Barbuda before independence who, immediately prior to independence, were citizens of the United Kingdom and Colonies automatically become citizens of Antigua and Barbuda. All persons born outside the country with a parent or grandparent possessing citizenship of Antigua and Barbuda automatically acquire citizenship as do those born in the country after independence. Provision is made for the acquisition of citizenship by those to whom it would not automatically be granted.

The Government

Monarch: HM Queen ELIZABETH II (succeeded to the throne 6 February 1952).

Governor-General: Sir JAMES BEETHOVEN CARLISLE (took office 10 June 1993).

CABINET
(March 2005)

Prime Minister and Minister of Foreign Affairs, International Transportation, Trade, National Security, Telecommunications, Broadcasting, Information, Labour, Public Administration, Ecclesiastics and Barbuda Affairs: BALDWIN SPENCER.

Deputy Prime Minister and Minister of Public Works: WIL-MOTH DANIEL.

Minister of Finance, Economic Development and Planning: Dr ERROL CORT.

Attorney-General: JUSTIN SIMON.

Minister of Justice and Legal Affairs: COLIN DERRICK.

Minister of Health, Youth Affairs and Sports: JOHN MAGINLEY.

Minister of Tourism: HAROLD LOVELL.

Minister of Education, Human Development and Culture: BERTRAND JOSEPH.

Minister of Agriculture, Lands, Marine Resources and the Environment: CHARLESWORTH SAMUEL.

Minister of Housing, Culture and Social Transformation: HILSON BAPTISTE.

Minister of State in the Ministry of Agriculture, Lands, Marine Resources and the Environment: Sen. JOANNE MASSIAH.

Minister of State in the Ministry of Health, Youth Affairs and Sport, with Responsibility for Youth Affairs and Sport: WINSTON WILLIAMS.

Minister of State in the Ministry of Housing, Culture and Social Transformation, with Responsibility for Culture: ELESTON ADAMS.

Minister of State in the Office of the Prime Minister, Responsible for Public Administration: JACQUI QUINN-LEANDRO.

Minister of State in the Office of the Prime Minister, Responsible for Telecommunications, Broadcasting and Information: Dr EDMOND MANSOOR.

Minister of State with Responsibility for Barbuda Affairs: TREVOR WALKER.

MINISTRIES

Office of the Prime Minister: Queen Elizabeth Highway, St John's; tel. 462-4956; fax 462-3225; e-mail cora.richards@antigua.gov.ag; internet www.antigua.gov.ag.

Ministry of Agriculture, Lands, Marine Resources and the Environment: Queen Elizabeth Highway, St John's; tel. 462-1543; fax 462-6104.

Ministry of Barbuda Affairs: Govt Office Complex, Parliament Dr., St John's.

Ministry of Ecclesiastics: Govt Office Complex, Parliament Dr., St John's.

Ministry of Education, Human Development and Culture: Govt Office Complex, Queen Elizabeth Highway, St John's; tel. 462-4959; fax 462-4970; e-mail doristeen.etinoff@ab.gov.ag.

Ministry of Finance, Economic Development and Planning: Govt Office Complex, Parliament Dr., St John's; tel. 462-5015; fax 462-4260; e-mail budget@candw.ag.

Ministry of Foreign Affairs: Queen Elizabeth Highway, St John's; tel. 462-1052; fax 462-2482; e-mail minforeign@candw.ag; internet www.antiguabarbuda.net/external.

Ministry of Health: St John's St, St John's; tel. 462-1600; fax 462-5003.

Ministry of Housing, Culture and Social Transformation: St John's.

Ministry of Information: St John's.

Ministry of International Transportation: St John's St, St John's; tel. 462-0894; fax 462-1529.

Ministry of Justice and Legal Affairs, and Office of the Attorney-General: Hadeed Bldg, Redcliffe St, St John's; tel. 462-6037; fax 562-1879; e-mail legalaffairs@candw.ag; internet www.antiguabarbuda.net/ag.

Ministry of Labour: Govt Office Complex, Queen Elizabeth's Highway, St John's; tel. 462-3331; fax 462-1595.

Ministry of National Security: Govt Office Complex, Parliament Dr., St John's.

Ministry of Public Administration: St John's.

Ministry of Public Works: St John's.

Ministry of Tourism: Queen Elizabeth Highway, St John's; tel. 462-4625; fax 462-2836; e-mail mintourenv@candw.ag.

Ministry of Trade: Redcliffe St, St John's; tel. 462-1543; fax 462-5003.

Ministry of Youth Affairs and Sports: St John's.

Legislature

PARLIAMENT

Senate

President: Dr EDMOND MANSOOR.
There are 17 nominated members.

House of Representatives

Speaker: D. GISELLE ISAAC.
Ex-Officio Member: The Attorney-General.
Clerk: SYLVIA WALKER.

General Election, 23 March 2004*

Party	Votes cast	%	Seats
United Progressive Party . . .	21,892	55.2	12
Antigua Labour Party	16,544	41.7	4
Barbuda People's Movement . .	408	1.0	1
Barbuda People's Movement for Change	394	1.0	—
Independents and rejected ballots	391	0.9	—
Total	39,629	100.0	17

* The table reflects the final election results after a re-run ballot on 20 April 2004 in the constituency of Barbuda following a tie between the Barbuda People's Movement and the Barbuda People's Movement for Change.

Political Organizations

Antigua Freedom Party (AFP): St John's; f. 2003.

Antigua Labour Party (ALP): St Mary's St, POB 948, St John's; tel. 462-2235; f. 1968; Leader LESTER BRYANT BIRD; Chair. VERE BIRD, Jr.

Barbuda People's Movement (BPM): Codrington; campaigns for separate status for Barbuda; Parliamentary Leader THOMAS HILBOURNE FRANK; Chair. FABIAN JONES.

Barbuda People's Movement for Change (BPMC): Codrington; f. 2004; effectively replaced Organisation for National Reconstruction, which was f. 1983 and re-f. 1988 as Barbuda Independence Movement; advocates self-government for Barbuda; Pres. ARTHUR SHABAZZ-NIBBS.

Democratic People's Party (DPP): St John's; f. 2003; Leader SHERFIELD BOWEN.

First Christian Democratic Movement (FCDM): St John's; f. 2003; Leader EGBERT JOSEPH.

National Labour Party (NLP): St John's; f. 2003.

National Movement for Change (NMC): St John's; f. 2002; Leader ALISTAIR THOMAS.

New Barbuda Development Movement: Codrington; linked with the Antigua Labour Party.

Organisation for National Development: Upper St Mary St, St John's; f. 2003 by breakaway faction of the United Progressive Party; Sec.-Gen. VALERIE SAMUEL.

United Progressive Party (UPP): Nevis St, St John's; tel. 462-1818; fax 462-5937; e-mail upp@candw.ag; f. 1992, by merger of the Antigua Caribbean Liberation Movement (f. 1979), the Progressive Labour Movement (f. 1970) and the United National Democratic Party (f. 1986); Leader BALDWIN SPENCER; Dep. Leader WILMOTH DANIEL; Chair. LEON SYMISTER.

Diplomatic Representation

EMBASSIES AND HIGH COMMISSION IN ANTIGUA AND BARBUDA

China, People's Republic: Cedar Valley, POB 1446, St John's; tel. 562-0176; fax 462-6425; e-mail chinaemb_ag@mfa.gov.cn; Ambassador REN XIAOPING.

United Kingdom: British High Commission, Price Waterhouse Coopers Centre, 11 Old Parham Rd, POB 483, St John's; tel. 462-0008; fax 562-2124; e-mail britishc@candw.ag; High Commissioner JOHN WHITE (resident in Barbados).

Venezuela: Cross and Redcliffe Sts, POB 1201, St John's; tel. 462-1574; fax 462-1570; e-mail embaveneantigua@yahoo.es; Ambassador José Laurencio Silva Méndez.

Judicial System

Justice is administered by the Eastern Caribbean Supreme Court, based in Saint Lucia, which consists of a High Court of Justice and a Court of Appeal. One of the Court's Puisne Judges is resident in and responsible for Antigua and Barbuda, and presides over the Court of Summary Jurisdiction on the islands. There are also Magistrates' Courts for lesser cases.

Chief Justice: Dennis Byron.

Solicitor-General: Lebrecht Hesse.

Attorney-General: Justin Simon.

Religion

The majority of the inhabitants profess Christianity, and the largest denomination is the Church in the Province of the West Indies (Anglican Communion).

CHRISTIANITY

Antigua Christian Council: POB 863, St John's; tel. 462-0261; f. 1964; five mem. churches; Pres. Rt Rev. Donald J. Reece (Roman Catholic Bishop of St John's-Basseterre); Exec. Sec. Edris Roberts.

The Anglican Communion

Anglicans in Antigua and Barbuda are adherents of the Church in the Province of the West Indies. The diocese of the North Eastern Caribbean and Aruba comprises 12 islands: Antigua, Saint Christopher (St Kitts), Nevis, Anguilla, Barbuda, Montserrat, Dominica, Saba, St Martin/St Maarten, Aruba, St Bartholomew and St Eustatius; the total number of Anglicans is about 60,000. The See City is St John's, Antigua.

Bishop of the North Eastern Caribbean and Aruba: Rt Rev. Leroy Errol Brooks, Bishop's Lodge, POB 23, St John's; tel. 462-0151; fax 462-2090; e-mail dioceseneca@candw.ag.

The Roman Catholic Church

The diocese of St John's-Basseterre, suffragan to the archdiocese of Castries (Saint Lucia), includes Anguilla, Antigua and Barbuda, the British Virgin Islands, Montserrat and Saint Christopher and Nevis. At 31 December 2002 there were an estimated 15,322 adherents in the diocese. The Bishop participates in the Antilles Episcopal Conference (whose Secretariat is based in Port of Spain, Trinidad).

Bishop of St John's-Basseterre: Rt Rev. Donald James Reece, Chancery Offices, POB 836, St John's; tel. 461-1135; fax 462-2383; e-mail djr@candw.ag.

Other Christian Churches

Antigua Baptist Association: POB 277, St John's; tel. 462-1254; Pres. Ivor Charles.

Methodist Church: c/o POB 863, St John's; Superintendent Rev. Eloy Christopher.

St John's Evangelical Lutheran Church: Woods Centre, POB W77, St John's; tel. 462-2896; e-mail lutheran@candw.ag; Pastor M. Henrich, Pastor J. Sternhagen, Pastor T. Satorius.

There are also Pentecostal, Seventh-day Adventist, Moravian, Nazarene, Salvation Army and Wesleyan Holiness places of worship.

The Press

Antigua Sun: 15 Pavilion Dr., Coolidge, POB W263, St John's; tel. 480-5960; fax 480-5968; e-mail editor@antiguasun.com; internet www.antiguasun.com; twice weekly; published by Sun Printing and Publishing Ltd; Editor and Business Man. Patrick Henry.

Business Expressions: POB 774, St John's; tel. 462-0743; fax 462-4575; e-mail chamcom@candw.ag; monthly; organ of the Antigua and Barbuda Chamber of Commerce and Industry Ltd.

Daily Observer: Fort Rd, POB 1318, St John's; fax 462-5561; internet www.antiguaobserver.com; independent; Publr Samuel Derrick; Editor Winston A. Derrick; circ. 4,000.

The Nation's Voice: Public Information Division, Church St and Independence Ave, POB 590, St John's; tel. 462-0090; weekly.

National Informer: St John's; weekly.

The Outlet: Marble Hill Rd, McKinnons, POB 493, St John's; tel. 462-4410; fax 462-0438; e-mail outletpublishers@yahoo.com; f. 1975; weekly; publ. by the Antigua Caribbean Liberation Movement (founder member of the United Progressive Party in 1992); Editor Conrad Luke; circ. 5,000.

The Worker's Voice: Emancipation Hall, 46 North St, POB 3, St John's; tel. 462-0090; f. 1943; twice weekly; official organ of the Antigua Labour Party and the Antigua Trades and Labour Union; Editor Noel Thomas; circ. 6,000.

Publishers

Antigua Printing and Publishing Ltd: POB 670, St John's; tel. 462-1265; fax 462-6200.

Wadadli Productions Ltd: POB 571, St John's; tel. 462-4489.

Broadcasting and Communications

TELECOMMUNICATIONS

Most telephone services are provided by the Antigua Public Utilities Authority (see Trade and Industry).

Antigua Public Utilities Authority Personal Communications Services (APUA PCS): St John's; internet www.apuatel.com; f. 2000; digital mobile cellular telephone network; Man. Julian Wilkins.

Cable & Wireless (Antigua and Barbuda) Ltd: 42–44 St Mary's St, POB 65, St John's; tel. 480-4000; fax 480-4200; internet www.cwantigua.com; owned by Cable & Wireless PLC (United Kingdom).

RADIO

ABS Radio: POB 590, St John's; tel. 462-3602; internet www.cmattcomm.com/abs.htm; f. 1956; subsidiary of Antigua and Barbuda Broadcasting Service (see Television); Programme Man. D. L. Payne.

Caribbean Radio Lighthouse: POB 1057, St John's; tel. 462-1454; fax 462-7420; e-mail lighthouse@candw.ag; internet www.radiolighthouse.org; f. 1975; religious broadcasts; operated by Baptist Int. Mission Inc (USA); Dir Curtis L. Waite.

Caribbean Relay Co Ltd: POB 1203, St John's; tel. 462-0994; fax 462-0487; e-mail cm-crc@candw.ag; jtly operated by British Broadcasting Corpn and Deutsche Welle.

Observer Radio: f. 2001; independently-owned station; Gen. Man. Winston A. Derrick.

Radio ZDK: Grenville Radio Ltd, POB 1100, St John's; tel. 462-1100; f. 1970; commercial; Programme Dir Ivor Bird; CEO E. Philip.

Sun FM Radio: St John's; commercial.

TELEVISION

Antigua and Barbuda Broadcasting Service (ABS): Directorate of Broadcasting and Public Information, POB 590, St John's; tel. 462-0010; fax 462-4442; scheduled for privatization; Dir-Gen. Hollis Henry; CEO Denis Leandro.

ABS Television: POB 1280, St John's; tel. 462-0010; fax 462-1622; f. 1964; Programme Man. James Tanny Rose.

CTV Entertainment Systems: 25 Long St, St John's; tel. 462-0346; fax 462-4211; cable television co; transmits 33 channels of US television 24 hours per day to subscribers; Programme Dir K. Bird.

Finance

(cap. = capital; res = reserves; dep. = deposits; m. = millions; brs = branches)

BANKING

The Eastern Caribbean Central Bank, based in Saint Christopher, is the central issuing and monetary authority for Antigua and Barbuda.

Antigua Barbuda Investment Bank Ltd: High St and Corn Alley, POB 1679, St John's; tel. 480-2700; fax 480-2750; e-mail abib@abifinancial.com; internet www.abifinancial.com; f. 1990; three subsidiaries: Antigua Overseas Bank Ltd, ABI Trust Ltd and AOB Holdings Ltd; cap. EC $11.7m., res EC $8.4m., dep. EC $447.2m. (Sept. 2003); Chair. Eustace Francis; Man. Dir McAllister Abbott.

Directory

Antigua Commercial Bank: St Mary's and Thames Sts, POB 95, St John's; tel. 462-1217; fax 462-1220; f. 1955; auth. cap. EC $5m.; Man. JOHN BENJAMIN; 2 brs.

Antigua and Barbuda Development Bank: 27 St Mary's St, POB 1279, St John's; tel. 462-0838; fax 462-0839; f. 1974; Man. S. ALEX OSBORNE.

Bank of Antigua: 10 Pavilion Dr., POB 315, Coolidge; tel. 462-4282; fax 462-4718; internet www.bankofantigua.com; f. 1981; total assets EC $340m. (Dec. 2003); Chair. ALLEN STANFORD; 2 brs.

Swiss American National Bank of Antigua Ltd: High St, POB 1302, St John's; tel. 462-4460; fax 462-0274; f. 1983; cap. US $1.0m., res US $2.1m., dep. US $31.9m. (Dec. 1993); Gen. Man. JOSEPH D. DaSILVA; 3 brs.

Foreign Banks

Bank of Nova Scotia (Canada): High St, POB 342, St John's; tel. 480-1500; fax 480-1554; Man. LEN WRIGHT.

Banque R Supervielle et Fils SA: Suite 4, Mezzanine Floor, Woods Centre, Friars Hill Rd, POB W1267, St John's; tel. 562-3876; fax 562-3877; e-mail brs@candw.ag; internet www.brs-britishwi .com; f. 1996; cap. US $5.0m., res US $0.8m., dep. US $14.5m. (Dec. 2001).

FirstCaribbean International Bank Ltd: St John's; internet www.firstcaribbeanbank.com; adopted present name in 2002 following merger of Caribbean operations of CIBC and Barclays Bank PLC; Exec. Chair. MICHAEL MANSOOR; CEO CHARLES PINK.

RBTT Bank Caribbean Ltd (Trinidad and Tobago): 45 High St, POB 1324, St John's; tel. 462-4217; fax 462-8575; e-mail hollings@ candw.ag; Country Man. KATHRYNE ARMSTRONG-HOLLINGSWORTH.

Royal Bank of Canada: High and Market Sts, POB 252, St John's; tel. 480-1151; fax 480-1190; offers a trustee service.

At the beginning of 2004 there were 16 registered 'offshore' banks in Antigua and Barbuda.

Regulatory Body

Financial Services Regulatory Commission (FSRC): Patrick Michael Bldg, Lower Nevis St, POB 2674, St John's; fmrly known as International Financial Sector Regulatory Authority, adopted current name in 2002; Chair. LEBRECHT HESSE; Admin. LEROY KING.

STOCK EXCHANGE

Eastern Caribbean Securities Exchange: e-mail info@ ecseonline.com; internet www.ecseonline.com; based in Basseterre, Saint Christopher and Nevis; f. 2001; regional securities market designed to facilitate the buying and selling of financial products for the eight member territories—Anguilla, Antigua and Barbuda, Dominica, Grenada, Montserrat, Saint Christopher and Nevis, Saint Lucia and Saint Vincent and the Grenadines; Gen. Man. BALJIT VOHRA.

INSURANCE

Several foreign companies have offices in Antigua. Local insurance companies include the following:

General Insurance Co Ltd: Upper Redcliffe St, POB 340, St John's; tel. 462-2346; fax 462-4482.

Sentinel Insurance Co Ltd: Coolidge, POB 207, St John's; tel. 462-4603.

State Insurance Corpn: Redcliffe St, POB 290, St John's; tel. 462-0110; fax 462-2649; f. 1977; Chair. Dr VINCENT RICHARDS; Gen. Man. ROLSTON BARTHLEY.

Trade and Industry

DEVELOPMENT ORGANIZATIONS

Barbuda Development Agency: St John's; economic development projects for Barbuda.

Development Control Authority: St John's; internet www .antiguagov.com/dca.

Industrial Development Board: Newgate St, St John's; tel. 462-1038; fax 462-1033; f. 1984 to stimulate investment in local industries.

St John's Development Corporation: Heritage Quay, POB 1473, St John's; tel. 462-2776; fax 462-3931; e-mail stjohnsdevcorp@candw .ag; internet www.firstyellow.com/stjohnsdev; f. 1986; manages the Heritage Quay Duty Free Shopping Complex, Vendors' Mall, Public Market and Cultural and Exhibition Complex.

CHAMBER OF COMMERCE

Antigua and Barbuda Chamber of Commerce and Industry Ltd: Cnr of North and Popeshead Sts, POB 774, St John's; tel. 462-0743; fax 462-4575; e-mail chamcom@candw.ag; f. 1944 as Antigua Chamber of Commerce Ltd; name changed as above in 1991, following the collapse of the Antigua and Barbuda Manufacturers' Asscn; Pres. CLARVIS JOSEPH; Exec. Dir HOLLY PETERS.

INDUSTRIAL AND TRADE ASSOCIATIONS

Antigua Cotton Growers' Association: Dunbars, St John's; tel. 462-4962; Chair. FRANCIS HENRY; Sec. PETER BLANCHETTE.

Antigua Fisheries Corpn: St John's; e-mail fisheries@candw.ag; partly funded by the Antigua and Barbuda Development Bank; aims to help local fishermen.

Antigua Sugar Industry Corpn: Gunthorpes, POB 899, St George's; tel. 462-0653.

Private Sector Organization of Antigua and Barbuda: St John's.

EMPLOYERS' ORGANIZATION

Antigua Employers' Federation: Upper High Street, POB 298, St John's; tel. 462-0449; fax 462-0449; e-mail aempfed@candw.ag; f. 1950; 117 mems; Chair. PEDRO CORBIN; Exec. Sec. HENDERSON BASS.

UTILITIES

Antigua Public Utilities Authority (APUA): St Mary's St, POB 416, St John's; tel. 480-7000; fax 462-2782; generation, transmission and distribution of electricity; internal telecommunications; collection, treatment, storage and distribution of water; Gen. Man. PETER BENJAMIN.

Caribbean Power Ltd: supplies Barbuda with water and electricity services.

TRADE UNIONS

Antigua and Barbuda Meteorological Officers Association: c/o V. C. Bird International Airport, Gabatco, POB 1051, St John's; tel. and fax 462-4606; Pres. LEONARD JOSIAH.

Antigua and Barbuda Public Service Association (ABPSA): POB 1285, St John's; tel. 463-6427; fax 461-5821; e-mail abpsa@ candw.ag; Pres. JAMES SPENCER; Gen. Sec. ELLOY DE FREITAS; 550 mems.

Antigua and Barbuda Union of Teachers: c/o Ministry of Education, Human Development and Culture, Church St, St John's; tel. 462-4959; Pres. COLIN GREENE; Sec. FOSTER ROBERTS.

Antigua Trades and Labour Union (ATLU): 46 North St, POB 3, St John's; tel. 462-0090; fax 462-4056; e-mail atandlu@candw.ag; f. 1939; affiliated to the Antigua Labour Party; Pres. WIGLEY GEORGE; Gen. Sec. NATALIE PAYNE; about 10,000 mems.

Antigua Workers' Union (AWU): Freedom Hall, Newgate St, POB 940, St John's; tel. 462-2005; fax 462-5220; e-mail awu@candw.ag; f. 1967 following split with ATLU; not affiliated to any party; Pres. MAURICE CHRISTIAN; Gen. Sec. KEITHLYN SMITH; 10,000 mems.

Transport

ROADS

There are 384 km (239 miles) of main roads and 781 km (485 miles) of secondary dry-weather roads.

SHIPPING

The main harbour is the St John's Deep Water Harbour. It is used by cruise ships and a number of foreign shipping lines. There are regular cargo and passenger services internationally and regionally. At Falmouth, on the south side of Antigua, is a former Royal Navy dockyard in English Harbour. The harbour is now used by yachts and private pleasure craft.

Antigua and Barbuda Port Authority: Deep Water Harbour, POB 1052, St John's; tel. 462-4243; fax 462-2510; f. 1968; responsible to Ministry of Finance, Economic Development and Planning; Chair. LLEWELLYN SMITH; Port Man. LEROY ADAMS.

Joseph, Vernon, Toy Contractors Ltd: Nut Grove St, St John's.

Parenzio Shipping Co Ltd: Nevis St, St John's.

Vernon Edwards Shipping Co: Thames St, POB 82, St John's; tel. 462-2034; fax 462-2035; e-mail vedwards@candw.ag; cargo service to and from San Juan, Puerto Rico.

The West Indies Oil Co Ltd: Friars Hill Rd, POB 230, St John's; tel. 462-0140; fax 462-0543; e-mail wiocfs@candw.ag.

CIVIL AVIATION

Antigua's V. C. Bird (formerly Coolidge) International Airport, 9 km (5.6 miles) north-east of St John's, is modern and accommodates jet-engined aircraft. There is a small airstrip at Codrington on Barbuda. Antigua and Barbuda Airlines, a nominal company, controls international routes, but services to Europe and North America are operated by American Airlines (USA), Continental Airlines (USA), Lufthansa (Germany) and Air Canada. Antigua and Barbuda is a shareholder in, and the headquarters of, the regional airline, LIAT. Other regional services are operated by BWIA (Trinidad and Tobago) and Air BVI (British Virgin Islands).

LIAT (1974) Ltd: POB 819, V. C. Bird Int. Airport, St John's; tel. 480-5600; fax 480-5625; e-mail li.sales.mrkting@candw.ag; internet www.liatairline.com; f. 1956 as Leeward Islands Air Transport Services, jointly-owned by 11 regional Govts; privatized in 1995; shares are held by the Govts of Antigua and Barbuda, Montserrat, Grenada, Barbados, Trinidad and Tobago, Jamaica, Guyana, Dominica, Saint Lucia, Saint Vincent and the Grenadines and Saint Christopher and Nevis (30.8%), BWIA (29.2%), LIAT employees (13.3%) and private investors (26.7%); scheduled passenger and cargo services to 19 destinations in the Caribbean; charter flights are also undertaken; Chair. WILBUR HARRIGAN; CEO GARRY CULLEN.

Carib Aviation Ltd: V. C. Bird Int. Airport; tel. 462-3147; fax 462-3125; e-mail caribav@candw.ag; charter co; operates regional services.

Caribbean Star Airlines: Coolidge Industrial Estate, Airport Rd, POB 1628W, St George; f. 2000; operates regional services; Pres. and CEO PAUL MOREIRA.

Tourism

Tourism is the country's main industry. Antigua offers a reputed 365 beaches, an annual international sailing regatta and Carnival week, and the historic Nelson's Dockyard in English Harbour (a national park since 1985). Barbuda is less developed, but is noted for its beauty, wildlife and beaches of pink sand. In 1986 the Government established the St John's Development Corporation to oversee the redevelopment of the capital as a commercial duty-free centre, with extra cruise-ship facilities. In 2003 there were 212,557 stop-over visitors and 383,834 cruise-ship passengers. In the same year 30.4% of stop-over visitors came from the USA and expenditure by all visitors totalled an estimated US \$299.9m.

Antigua and Barbuda Department of Tourism: c/o Ministry of Tourism, Queen Elizabeth Highway, POB 363, St John's; tel. 462-0029; fax 462-2483; e-mail deptourism@antigua.gov.ag; internet www.antigua-barbuda.org; Dir-Gen. SHIRLENE NIBBS.

Antigua Hotels and Tourist Association (AHTA): Island House, Newgate St, POB 454, St John's; tel. 462-3703; fax 462-3702; e-mail ahta@candw.ag; internet www.antiguahotels.org; Chair. ANDREW V. MICHELIN; Exec. Dir CYNTHIA G. SIMON.

ARGENTINA

Introductory Survey

Location, Climate, Language, Religion, Flag, Capital

The Argentine Republic occupies almost the whole of South America south of the Tropic of Capricorn and east of the Andes. It has a long Atlantic coastline stretching from Uruguay and the River Plate to Tierra del Fuego. To the west lie Chile and the Andes mountains, while to the north are Bolivia, Paraguay and Brazil. Argentina also claims the Falkland Islands (known in Argentina as the Islas Malvinas), South Georgia, the South Sandwich Islands and part of Antarctica. The climate varies from sub-tropical in the Chaco region of the north to sub-arctic in Patagonia, generally with moderate summer rainfall. Temperatures in Buenos Aires are usually between 5°C (41°F) and 29°C (84°F). The language is Spanish. The great majority of the population profess Christianity: about 92% are Roman Catholics and about 2% Protestants. The national flag (proportions 14 by 9) has three equal horizontal stripes, of light blue (celeste), above white, above light blue. The state flag (proportions 1 by 2) has the same design with, in addition, a gold 'Sun of May' in the centre of the white stripe. The capital is Buenos Aires.

Recent History

During the greater part of the 20th century, government in Argentina tended to alternate between military and civilian rule. In 1930 Hipólito Yrigoyen, a member of the reformist Unión Cívica Radical (UCR), who in 1916 had become Argentina's first President to be freely elected by popular vote, was overthrown by an army coup, and the country's first military regime was established. Civilian rule was restored in 1932, only to be supplanted by further military intervention in 1943. A leading figure in the new military regime, Col (later Lt-Gen.) Juan Domingo Perón Sosa, won a presidential election in 1946. As President, he established the Peronista party in 1948 and pursued a policy of extreme nationalism and social improvement, aided by his second wife, Eva ('Evita') Duarte de Perón, whose popularity (particularly among industrial workers and their families) greatly enhanced his position and contributed to his re-election as President in 1951. In 1954, however, his promotion of secularization and the legalization of divorce brought him into conflict with the Roman Catholic Church. In September 1955 President Perón was deposed by a revolt of the armed forces. He went into exile, eventually settling in Spain, from where he continued to direct the Peronist movement.

Following the overthrow of Perón, Argentina entered another lengthy period of political instability. Political control continued to pass between civilian (mainly Radical) and military regimes during the late 1950s and the 1960s. This period was also characterized by increasing guerrilla activity, particularly by the Montoneros, a group of left-wing Peronist sympathizers, and urban guerrillas intensified their activities in 1971 and 1972.

Congressional and presidential elections were conducted in March 1973. The Frente Justicialista de Liberación, a Peronist coalition, secured control of the Congreso Nacional (National Congress), while the presidential election was won by the party's candidate, Dr Héctor Cámpora, who assumed office in May. However, Cámpora resigned in July, to enable Gen. Perón, who had returned to Argentina in June, to contest a fresh presidential election. In September Perón was returned to power, with more than 60% of the votes. He took office in October, with his third wife, María Estela ('Isabelita') Martínez de Perón, as Vice-President.

Gen. Perón died in July 1974 and was succeeded as President by his widow. The Government's economic austerity programme and the soaring rate of inflation led to widespread strike action, dissension among industrial workers, and demands for the resignation of 'Isabelita' Perón. In March 1976 the armed forces, led by Gen. Jorge Videla (Commander of the Army), overthrew the President and installed a three-man junta: Gen. Videla was sworn in as President. The junta made substantial alterations to the Constitution, dissolved the Congreso Nacional, suspended all political and trade union activity and removed most government officials from their posts. Several hundred people were arrested, while 'Isabelita' Perón was detained and later went into exile.

The military regime launched a successful, although ferocious, offensive against left-wing guerrillas and opposition forces. The imprisonment, torture and murder of suspected left-wing activists by the armed forces provoked domestic and international protests. Repression eased in 1978, after all armed opposition had been eliminated.

In March 1981 Gen. Roberto Viola, a former member of the junta, succeeded President Videla and made known his intention to extend dialogue with political parties as a prelude to an eventual return to democracy. Owing to ill health, he was replaced in December by Lt-Gen. Leopoldo Galtieri, the Commander-in-Chief of the Army, who attempted to cultivate popular support by continuing the process of political liberalization initiated by his predecessor.

In April 1982, in order to distract attention from an increasingly unstable domestic situation, and following unsuccessful negotiations with the United Kingdom in February over Argentina's long-standing sovereignty claim, President Galtieri ordered the invasion of the Falkland Islands (Islas Malvinas) (see chapter on the Falkland Islands, q.v.). The United Kingdom recovered the islands after a short conflict, in the course of which about 750 Argentine lives were lost. Argentine forces surrendered in June 1982, but no formal cessation of hostilities was declared until October 1989. Humiliated by the defeat, Galtieri was forced to resign, and the members of the junta were replaced. The army, under the control of Lt-Gen. Cristino Nicolaides, installed a retired general, Reynaldo Bignone, as President in July 1982. The armed forces were held responsible for the disastrous economic situation, and the transfer of power to a civilian government was accelerated. Moreover, in 1983 a Military Commission of Inquiry into the Falklands conflict concluded in its report that the main responsibility for Argentina's defeat lay with members of the former junta, who were recommended for trial. Galtieri was sentenced to imprisonment, while several other officers were put on trial for corruption, murder and insulting the honour of the armed forces. Meanwhile, in August 1983 the regime approved the Ley de Pacificación Nacional, an amnesty law which granted retrospective immunity to the police, the armed forces and others for political crimes that had been committed over the previous 10 years.

In February 1983 the Government announced that general and presidential elections would be held on 30 October. At the elections, the UCR defeated the Peronist Partido Justicialista (PJ), attracting the votes of many former Peronist supporters. The UCR won 317 of the 600 seats in the presidential electoral college, and 129 of the 254 seats in the Cámara de Diputados (Chamber of Deputies), although the PJ won a narrow majority of provincial governorships. Dr Raúl Alfonsín, the UCR candidate, took office as President on 10 December. President Alfonsín promptly announced a radical reform of the armed forces, which led to the immediate retirement of more than one-half of the military high command. In addition, he repealed the Ley de Pacificación Nacional and ordered the court martial of the first three military juntas to rule Argentina after the 1976 coup, for offences including abduction, torture and murder. Public opposition to the former military regime was reinforced by the discovery and exhumation of hundreds of bodies from unmarked graves throughout the country. (It was believed that 15,000–30,000 people 'disappeared' during the so-called 'dirty war' between the former military regime and its opponents in 1976–83.) In December the Government announced the formation of the National Commission on the Disappearance of Persons to investigate the events of the 'dirty war'. The trial of the former leaders began in April 1985. Several hundred prosecution witnesses gave testimonies which revealed the systematic atrocities and the campaign of terror perpetrated by the former military leaders. In December four of the accused were acquitted, but sentences were imposed on the remaining five, including sentences of life imprisonment for Gen. Videla and Adm. Eduardo Massera. The court martial of the members of the junta that had held power during the Falklands conflict was conducted concurrently with the trial of the former military leaders. In May 1986 all three members of the junta were found guilty of negligence and received prison sentences, including a term of 12 years for Galtieri.

In late 1986 the Government sought approval for the Punto Final ('Full Stop') Law, whereby civil and military courts were to begin new judicial proceedings against members of the armed forces accused of violations of human rights, within a 60-day period ending on 22 February 1987. The pre-emptive nature of the legislation provoked widespread popular opposition but was, nevertheless, approved by the Congreso Nacional in December 1986. However, in May 1987, following a series of minor rebellions at army garrisons throughout the country, the Government announced new legislation, known as the Obediencia Debida ('Due Obedience') law, whereby an amnesty was to be declared for all but senior ranks of the police and armed forces. Therefore, under the new law, of the 350–370 officers hitherto due to be prosecuted for alleged violations of human rights, only 30–50 senior officers were now to be tried. The legislation provoked great controversy, and was considered to be a decisive factor in the significant gains made by the PJ at gubernatorial and legislative elections conducted in September.

In January 1989 the army quickly repelled an attack by 40 left-wing activists on a military base at La Tablada, in which 39 lives were lost. Many of the guerrilla band were identified as members of the Movimiento Todos por la Patria.

In the campaign for the May 1989 elections, Carlos Saúl Menem headed the Frente Justicialista de Unidad Popular (FREJUPO) electoral alliance, comprising his own PJ grouping, the Partido Demócrata Cristiano (PDC) and the Partido Intransigente (PI). On 14 May the Peronists were guaranteed a return to power, having secured, together with the two other members of the FREJUPO alliance, 48.5% of the votes cast in the presidential election and 310 of the 600 seats in the electoral college. The Peronists were also victorious in the election for 127 seats (one-half of the total) in the Cámara de Diputados, winning 45% of the votes and 66 seats, in contrast to the 29% (41 seats) obtained by the UCR. The failure of attempts by the retiring and incoming administrations to collaborate, and the reluctance of the Alfonsín administration to continue in office with the prospect of further economic embarrassment, left the nation in a political vacuum. Although Menem was scheduled to take office as President on 10 December 1989, the worsening economic situation compelled Alfonsín to resign five months early, and Menem assumed the presidency on 8 July.

In early 1990 the Minister of the Economy, Antonio Erman González, introduced a comprehensive plan for economic readjustment, incorporating the expansion of existing plans for the transfer to private ownership of many state-owned companies, the rationalization of government-controlled bodies, and the restructuring of the nation's financial systems. In August Erman González appointed himself head of the Central Bank and assumed almost total control of the country's financial structure. Public disaffection with the Government's economic policy was widespread. Failure to contain the threat of hyperinflation led to a loss in purchasing power, and small-scale food riots and looting became more frequent. The Government's rationalization programme proved unpopular with public-sector employees, and resulted in industrial action and demonstrations, organized from within the sector with the support of trade unions, political opposition parties and human rights groups. In January 1991 Erman González was forced to resign from the Government following a sudden spectacular decline in the value of the austral in relation to the US dollar. He was succeeded as Minister of the Economy by Domingo Cavallo.

In October 1989 the Government issued decrees whereby 210 officers, NCOs and soldiers who had been involved in the 'dirty war', the governing junta during the Falklands conflict (including Gen. Galtieri) and leaders of three recent military uprisings (including Lt-Col Rico and Col Seineldín) were pardoned. Widespread public concern at the apparent impunity of military personnel further increased after a second round of presidential pardons was announced in late December 1990. More than 40,000 demonstrators gathered in Buenos Aires to protest against the release of former military leaders, including Gen. Videla, Gen. Viola and Adm. Massera. Critics and political opponents dismissed President Menem's claims that such action was essential for the effective 'reconciliation' of the Argentine people.

In the first two rounds of voting in gubernatorial and congressional elections, the Peronists were unexpectedly successful, wresting the governorship of San Juan from the provincial Bloquista party in August 1991, and securing control of nine of

the 12 contested provinces (including the crucial province of Buenos Aires) in September. The third and fourth rounds of voting, in October and December, respectively, proved less successful for the PJ. Overall, however, the Peronists secured control of 14 of the 24 contested territories and increased their congressional representation by seven seats, compared with a five-seat reduction in the congressional representation of the UCR.

The success of the Peronist campaign was widely attributed to the popularity of the Minister of the Economy, Domingo Cavallo. Economic measures implemented by Cavallo included the abolition of index-linked wage increases and, most dramatically, the implementation of the 'Convertibility Plan', which linked the austral to the US dollar, at a fixed rate of exchange. This initiative soon achieved considerable success in reducing inflation, and impressed international finance organizations sufficiently to secure the negotiation of substantial loan agreements. In October 1991 the President issued a comprehensive decree ordering the removal of almost all of the remaining bureaucratic apparatus of state regulation of the economy, and in November the Government announced plans to accelerate the transfer to private ownership of the remaining public-sector concerns. Continuing economic success in 1992 helped to secure agreements for the renegotiation of repayment of outstanding debts with the Government's leading creditor banks and with the 'Paris Club' of Western creditor governments. However, in November the Confederación General del Trabajo (CGT—General Confederation of Labour) organized a one-day general strike, in protest at the Government's continuing economic austerity programme. The strike was precipitated by revelations that senior government officials were to receive pay increases of as much as 200%.

Meanwhile, President Menem sought to consolidate his own position and to increase the popularity of his party in the months preceding legislative elections scheduled for 3 October 1993, at which the Peronists hoped to make significant gains in order to facilitate Menem's wish to effect a constitutional amendment that would allow him to pursue a second, consecutive presidential term. The elections to renew 127 seats in the Cámara de Diputados were won convincingly by the ruling PJ party, with 42.3% of the votes, while the UCR obtained 30% of the votes.

An unexpected development in November 1993 was the return to political prominence of former President Alfonsín. While UCR opposition to Menem's presidential ambitions had remained vociferous, several opposition leaders, notably Alfonsín, feared that the UCR would be excluded from negotiations on constitutional reform, should the unorthodox political manoeuvring of the Peronists, largely orchestrated by the President of the Senado (Senate), Menem's brother Eduardo, succeed in propelling the reform proposal through the legislature. Alfonsín, also anxious to avoid another humiliating defeat for the UCR at a national referendum which Menem had elected to organize in late 1993 on the question of constitutional reform, entered into a dialogue with the President, which resulted in a declaration, in November, that a framework for constitutional reform had been negotiated, apparently in return for Menem's postponement of the referendum and acceptance of modified reform proposals. In December the UCR national convention endorsed the terms of the agreement, which included the possibility of re-election of the President for one consecutive term, a reduction in the presidential term (to four years), the abolition of the presidential electoral college, the delegation of some presidential powers to a Chief of Cabinet, an increase in the number of seats in the Senado and a reduction in the length of the mandate of all senators, a reform of the procedure for judicial appointments, the removal of religious stipulations from the terms of eligibility for presidential candidates, and the abolition of the President's power to appoint the mayor of the federal capital. The need for constitutional reform was approved by the Congreso later in the month, and Menem immediately declared his intention to seek re-election in 1995.

Elections to the Constituent Assembly took place in April 1994. While the Peronists won the largest share of the vote, they failed to secure an absolute majority in the Assembly. The UCR won only 19.9% of the votes, while a centre-left coalition, Frente Grande, emerged unexpectedly as the third political force (with 12.5% of the votes), having campaigned against institutionalized corruption. The Assembly was inaugurated in May, and in August a new Constitution was duly promulgated. An electoral timetable was also established, with presidential, legislative and provincial elections all scheduled for May 1995. In December 1994 the Senado approved the new electoral code providing for the direct election of a president and a vice-president and for a second round of voting for the first- and second-placed candidates in the event of a closely contested election.

Menem's campaign for re-election concentrated on the economic success of his previous administration and, despite the increasingly precarious condition of the economy, was sufficiently successful to secure 49.9% of the votes at the presidential election of 14 May 1995, thereby avoiding a second ballot. José Octavio Bordón, the candidate of the Frente del País Solidario (Frepaso—a centre-left alliance of socialist, communist, Christian Democrat and dissident Peronist groups) was second with 29.3% of the votes, ahead of the UCR candidate, Horacio Massaccesi, who received 17.0% of the votes. The Peronists were also successful in nine of the 14 gubernatorial contests; however, Frepaso won the largest share of the 130 contested seats in the Cámara de Diputados at legislative elections conducted concurrently, and significantly increased its representation in the Senado (as did the Peronists), largely at the expense of the UCR. Menem was inaugurated as President for a four-year term on 8 July. The Peronists performed well at gubernatorial elections conducted in late 1995, but suffered an unexpected defeat at senatorial elections in the capital in October at which the Peronist candidate was beaten into third place by the Frepaso and UCR candidates, respectively.

Meanwhile, the Government's ongoing programme of economic austerity continued to provoke violent opposition, particularly from the public sector, where redundancies and a 'freeze' on salaries had been imposed in many provinces. However, in August 1994 a 12-month moratorium on appointments in the public sector was announced, as were plans to privatize several more state enterprises. In March 1995 the Government presented an economic consolidation programme aimed at protecting the Argentine currency against devaluation and supporting the ailing banking sector, which had been adversely affected by the financial crisis in Mexico in late 1994. Subsequent austerity measures adopted by provincial governments, together with a dramatic increase in the rate of unemployment, provoked widespread social unrest in the city of Córdoba and in the province of Río Negro in 1995.

In June 1996 the Government suffered a serious political defeat when a UCR candidate, Fernando de la Rúa, won almost 40% of the votes cast in the first direct elections for the Mayor of the Federal District of Buenos Aires; a Frepaso candidate secured 26.5% of the votes, while the incumbent Peronist Mayor, Jorge Domínguez, received only 18% of the ballot. The PJ also fared badly in concurrent elections to the 60-member Constituent Assembly (which was charged with drafting a constitution for the newly autonomous Federal District of Buenos Aires); Frepaso candidates secured 25 seats, the UCR 19, the PJ 11 and the recently formed Nueva Dirigencia (ND, led by a former Peronist, Gustavo Béliz) five. In July the Government was again undermined by the resignations of Rodolfo Barra, the Minister of Justice, and that of Oscar Camilión, the Minister of Defence, whose parliamentary immunity was to be removed to allow investigations in connection with the illegal sale of armaments to Ecuador and Croatia. More significant was the dismissal of Cavallo from the post of Minister of the Economy, following months of bitter dispute with the President and other cabinet members. Roque Fernández, hitherto President of the Central Bank, assumed the economy portfolio. Cavallo became increasingly vociferous in his attacks against the integrity of certain cabinet members, and, in October, as Menem launched a well-publicized campaign against corruption after the discovery of wide-scale malpractice within the customs service, he accused the Government of having links with organized crime.

Industrial unrest continued during 1996, and in August and September general strikes, organized by the CGT, the Congreso de los Trabajadores Argentinos (CTA) and the Movimiento de Trabajadores Argentinos (MTA), received widespread support. None the less, in the latter month taxation and austerity measures secured congressional approval, albeit with significant amendments. In October relations between the Government and the trade unions deteriorated, following the submission to the Congreso of controversial labour-reform legislation. In December, owing to the slow pace at which debate on the bill was progressing in the legislature, President Menem introduced part of the reforms by decree. Although three decrees were signed, radically altering labour contracts, in January 1997 a court declared that they were unconstitutional.

The popularity of the PJ was undermined further by an upsurge in social and industrial unrest during 1997, which was primarily the result of widespread discontent with proposed labour reforms, reductions in public expenditure and the high level of unemployment. In May violent protests erupted across Argentina as police clashed with thousands of demonstrators who had occupied government buildings and blockaded roads and bridges. In July some 30,000 people demonstrated in the capital to protest at the high level of unemployment, then estimated at more than 17%. A general strike in August, organized by the MTA and the CTA, was only partially observed.

In March 1997 Cavallo founded his own political party, Acción por la República (AR), and in July he and Béliz of the ND formed an alliance to contest the forthcoming congressional elections. In the following month the leaders of Frepaso and the UCR confirmed that they had agreed to an electoral pact, known as the Alianza por el Trabajo, la Justicia y la Educación (ATJE), in order to present joint lists in certain constituencies, notably in the province of Buenos Aires, and to remain in alliance subsequently.

At the mid-term congressional elections, held in October 1997, the UCR and Frepaso (in both separate and joint lists) won 45.6% of the votes and 61 of the 127 seats contested, in contrast to the 36.3% (51 seats) obtained by the PJ; of the remaining 15 seats, three were secured by AR—ND. The PJ thus lost its overall majority in the Cámara de Diputados (its total number of seats being reduced to 118), while the UCR and Frepaso together increased their representation to 110 seats. More significant was the PJ's poor performance in the critical constituency of the province of Buenos Aires, where it received only 41.3% of the votes, compared with the ATJE's 48.3%.

Preparations for the 1999 presidential election gained momentum in April 1998 with the UCR's selection of Fernando de la Rúa as the party's candidate. In a nation-wide primary in November, de la Rúa was elected as the ATJE presidential candidate, defeating Graciela Fernández Meijide, the highly regarded Frepaso nominee. In December Carlos 'Chacho' Alvarez of Frepaso was formally nominated as de la Rúa's running mate, while Fernández Meijide was to contest the governorship of Buenos Aires. In July President Menem abandoned a controversial campaign to amend the Constitution in order to allow him to contest the presidency for a third consecutive term of office. The campaign was vociferously opposed by the leading PJ contender, Eduardo Alberto Duhalde, who had threatened to hold a provincial plebiscite on the issue. Duhalde's main rival for the PJ presidential nomination was Ramón 'Palito' Ortega, a former Governor of Tucumán, who had been appointed Secretary of Social Development in April. The popularity of the PJ remained low, not least because of the corruption scandals that had beset the Menem administration. An agreement reached by Duhalde and Ortega to run jointly in the PJ presidential primary seemed to restore some unity to the party, although it was apparent that Menem had not entirely abandoned the idea of a re-election bid. In March 1999, however, the Supreme Court rejected appeals for Menem to be allowed to stand in the October elections.

In June 1999 Duhalde officially received the PJ presidential nomination after the only other contender, Adolfo Rodríguez Saá, the Governor of San Luis, withdrew from the contest. Duhalde's candidacy was publicly endorsed by Menem. Meanwhile, social unrest escalated in several provinces, as economic recession led to rising levels of unemployment and non-payment of public-sector salaries. At the presidential election, conducted on 24 October, de la Rúa (with 48.5% of the votes) defeated Duhalde (who secured 38.1%), thereby ending 10 years of Menem's Peronist rule. The ATJE also performed well in concurrent elections to renew 130 of the 257 seats in the Cámara de Diputados, winning 63 seats, while the PJ secured 50 seats and Cavallo's AR won nine. The ATJE's total number of seats in the Cámara increased to 127—only two short of an absolute majority—in contrast to the PJ, whose representation was reduced to 101 seats. However, in gubernatorial elections held on the same day, the ATJE candidate, Graciela Fernández Meijide, failed to secure the critical province of Buenos Aires, where Carlos Ruckauf, the outgoing Vice-President, was elected. As a result of the elections the PJ controlled 14 of the 24 provincial administrations, while the ATJE held only six. De la Rúa took office as President on 10 December, with Carlos Alvarez as his Vice-President. Later that month the new Congreso Nacional approved an austerity budget that reduced public expenditure by US $1,400m., as well as a major tax-reform programme and a federal revenue-sharing scheme.

In April 2000 the Senado approved a controversial major revision of employment law. The legislation met with public criticism and led to mass demonstrations by public-sector workers and, subsequently, to two 24-hour national strikes organized by the CGT. Later that year the Government came under intense pressure after it was alleged that some senators had received bribes from government officials to pass the employment legislation. (The affair was the subject of renewed investigation in late 2003.) In September the Senado voted to end the immunity that protected law-makers, judges and government ministers from criminal investigation in order to allow an inquiry into the corruption allegations. The political crisis intensified on 6 October when Alvarez resigned as Vice-President, one day after a cabinet reorganization, in which two ministers implicated in the bribery scandal were not removed. One of these, former labour minister Alberto Flamarique, who was appointed Presidential Chief of Staff in the reshuffle, resigned later the same day. The other, Fernando de Santibáñez, head of the state intelligence service (SIDE), resigned in late October. Earlier that month the President of the Senado, José Genoud, also resigned after he too was implicated in the bribery allegations.

The economic situation continued to deteriorate in 2000 and 2001. In November 2000 thousands of unemployed workers blocked roads throughout the country to demand jobs, welfare programmes and improvements in standards of living. In the same month the country was paralysed by a 36-hour national strike, organized in response to the Government's proposed introduction of an IMF-backed economic recovery package that included a five-year freeze on federal and provincial spending. Additional measures included a reform of the pension system and an increase in the female retirement age. In December the Congreso approved the reforms and, later in the month, the IMF agreed a package, worth an estimated US $20,000m., to meet Argentina's external debt obligations for 2001.

The resignation of the Minister of the Economy, José Luis Machinea, precipitated another political crisis in March 2001. The announcement by his successor, Ricardo López Murphy, of major reductions in public expenditure, resulted in several ministerial resignations. As a consequence, in late March a second reshuffle occurred, in which the most notable appointee was Domingo Cavallo as the new Minister of the Economy. In June Cavallo announced a series of measures designed to ease the country's financial situation. The most controversial of these was the introduction of a complex trade tariff system that created multiple exchange rates (based on the average of a euro and a US dollar); this was, in effect, a devaluation of the peso for external trade, although the dollar peg remained in operation for domestic transactions. As Argentina's debt crisis intensified and fears of a default increased, a further emergency package, the seventh in 19 months, was unveiled in July. A policy of 'zero-deficit' was announced, whereby neither the federal Government nor any province would be allowed to spend more than it collected in taxes. In order to achieve this, state salaries and pensions were to be reduced by 13%. Despite mass protests and a one-day national strike, the measures were granted congressional approval at the end of July. Nevertheless, the economic situation continued to deteriorate throughout 2001. There were protests against the austerity measures in August and following the introduction of one-year bonds, known as 'patacones', as payment to 160,000 public-sector workers. Meanwhile, the Government encountered difficulties in effecting economic policies: negotiations with the opposition Peronists, who controlled the majority of Argentina's provincial governments, on lower monthly tax transfers (essential to achieving a 'zero-deficit') were repeatedly stalled in late 2001.

The impoverished state of the economy contributed to the ATJE's poor performance in the legislative elections, held in October 2001. The PJ won control of the Cámara de Diputados, with 37.4% of the votes cast, and increased its representation in the lower house to 116 seats overall. In comparison, the ATJE obtained 23.1% of the votes cast and 88 seats (UCR 71 seats; Frepaso 17). In the Senado, which for the first time was directly elected by popular vote, the PJ increased its majority, winning 40 seats and 40.0% of the ballot, while the ATJE secured 23.3% of the vote and 25 seats (UCR 24 seats; Frepaso one seat). The elections were marred by a high percentage of spoiled ballots (21.1%—in some provinces the number of spoiled ballots was

higher than that for the winning candidate) and a high rate of abstention, about 28%, in a country where voting is obligatory.

In December 2001, as the economic situation deteriorated and the possibility of a default on the country's debt increased considerably, owing to the IMF's refusal to disburse more funds to Argentina, the Government introduced restrictions on bank account withdrawals and appropriated private pension funds. These measures proved to be extremely unpopular and resulted in two days of rioting and demonstrations nation-wide, in which at least 27 people died. On 20 December Cavallo resigned as Minister of the Economy and, following further rioting on the same day, President de la Rúa submitted his resignation. The newly appointed President of the Senado, Ramón Puerta, became acting President of the Republic, but was succeeded two days later by the Peronist Adolfo Rodríguez Saá. He, in turn, resigned one week later after protests against his proposed economic reforms (including the introduction of a new currency and the suspension of debt repayments) resulted in further unrest. On 1 January 2002 the former Peronist presidential candidate and recently elected Senator for the Province of Buenos Aires, Eduardo Alberto Duhalde, was elected President by the Congreso Nacional; he took office the following day. He was Argentina's fifth President in less than two weeks. (The President of the Cámara de Diputados, Eduardo Camaño, was acting President from 31 December 2001 to 2 January 2002 following the resignation of Puerta as President of the Senado.) On 3 January Argentina officially defaulted on its loan repayments, reportedly the largest ever debt default, and on 6 January the Senado gave authorization to the Government to set the exchange rate, thus officially ending the 10-year-old-parity between the US dollar and the peso. In January 2003 the Government initiated the compulsory conversion to pesos of US dollar bank deposits in order to prevent capital flight. This process of 'pesofication' led to many lawsuits (known as *amparos*) being brought by depositors against their banks (and other financial institutions) in an attempt to recover their losses. However, in October 2004 the Supreme Court ruled that the 'pesofication' was not unconstitutional, thereby effectively ruling against future *amparos*.

Nevertheless, in February 2002 the Supreme Court had ruled (by a margin of six to three) that the restrictions imposed on bank withdrawals (the 'corralito') were unconstitutional. Some accounts were freed from the restrictions but, in order to forestall the complete collapse of the financial system, the Government imposed a six-month ban on legal challenges to the remainder of the bank withdrawal regime. Numerous bank holidays were also decreed to prevent another run on the banks and a further devaluation of the currency. A constitutional crisis ensued as the Congreso initiated impeachment proceedings against the unpopular Supreme Court Justices (see below). Later that month the Government signed a new tax-sharing pact with the provincial Governors, linking the monthly amount distributed to the provinces to tax collections, as recommended by the IMF. However, in late April Jorge Remes Lenicov resigned as Minister of the Economy, following the Senado's refusal to support an emergency plan to exchange 'frozen' bank deposits for government bonds, despite an uncompromising message from the IMF that no further help would be available unless drastic reforms were forthcoming. He was replaced by Roberto Lavagna (the sixth Argentine economy minister in 12 months).

Meanwhile, the economy achieved mixed progress during 2002. While the number of deposits in Argentine banks increased, indicating a healthier economy, Argentina still defaulted on an US $805m. loan instalment that was owed to the World Bank in November, thus jeopardizing Argentina's last remaining source of external finance. The situation was aggravated by disagreements between the Minister of the Economy and the President of the Central Bank over the 'corralito' restrictions. Public anger against the Government and at the state of the economy did not subside, and in June two people were killed and dozens more injured when protesters demanding jobs and food clashed with the police. The following day thousands of anti-Government protesters marched in front of the Congreso building, and teachers and public-sector workers went on strike.

In the latter half of 2002 congressional efforts to impeach the Supreme Court Justices for incompetence were repeatedly frustrated. The Cámara de Diputados failed to achieve quorum to begin the impeachment debate on five occasions but, in October, and after calls from the IMF for political consensus between the judiciary and the legislature, the impeachment bid was voted down in the Cámara. Nevertheless, later that month one Supreme Court judge resigned. Contentious decisions taken by the Supreme Court included ruling against the 'corralito', pay and pensions reductions for public-sector workers and public utility price increases.

In July 2002 President Duhalde announced that presidential elections would take place six months earlier than planned, on 30 March 2003, and that a new administration would take office on 25 May. It was hoped that this move would reduce political pressures on the Government during its ongoing negotiations with the IMF. In November, following negotiations between the Government, legislators and provincial Governors, agreement was reached to postpone the presidential elections until 27 April 2003. Internal rivalries within the ruling PJ, most notably between Duhalde (who supported the candidacy of the Santa Cruz Governor, Néstor Carlos Kirchner) and former President Carlos Menem, resulted in a bitter argument regarding the election of a Peronist candidate. Eventually, in late January 2003, the PJ congress voted to allow all three Peronist aspirants (namely Menem, Kirchner and Adolfo Rodríguez Saá) to contest the presidential election, despite a court order (obtained by Menem) ordering that a primary election be held.

Former President Menem had been the subject of a number of scandals in 2001 and 2002. In June 2001 he was arrested on charges of illegal arms-trafficking during his terms in office, and in July was formally charged with selling arms to Croatia (in violation of international embargoes in the early 1990s) and Ecuador (at a time when Argentina was a guarantor of a peace treaty ending a border conflict between Ecuador and Peru, and was thus obliged to remain neutral). In November, however, the Supreme Court dismissed the charges against Menem and he was released from house arrest. In the previous month two Swiss bank accounts belonging to Menem had been 'frozen' pending an investigation into the origins of the funds. In August 2002 it was alleged that Menem had accepted a payment of US \$10m. to suppress evidence of Iranian involvement in a bomb attack on a Jewish social centre in Buenos Aires in 1994, which had resulted in 86 fatalities. Both Menem and the Iranian Government vigorously refuted the allegations. Menem declared that the money was compensation that he had been awarded for his imprisonment during the military dictatorship. He accused the Duhalde Peronist faction of attempting to sabotage his bid for a third presidential term. In August 2003 Menem was finally cleared of involvement in the arms-trafficking scandal. In December 2004 Menem returned to Argentina from self-imposed exile in Chile after charges of financial impropriety against him were dropped. On his return he announced his intention to stand in the presidential election scheduled for 2007.

In October 2004 the judges investigating the 1994 bomb attack issued a final report acquitting all Argentine suspects, owing to lack of evidence. However, the report severely criticized failures and procedural irregularities by the Menem administration, the judiciary, the intelligence services and federal judge Juan José Galeano, who had led the original investigation. Criminal investigations were subsequently initiated against Galeano, Carlos Corach (Minister of the Interior under Menem) and Hugo Anzorreguy (the former head of the Argentine intelligence service). In February 2005 Galeano was suspended for six months by the Supreme Council of Magistrates (by 16 votes to one). Furthermore, in that month the special unit of the Attorney-General's office investigating the bomb attack accused Menem of obstructing inquiries into the possible role of Argentine nationals.

Presidential elections were held on 27 April 2003. Menem obtained the largest share of the popular vote, with 24.34% of the votes cast, followed by Néstor Kirchner (representing the Frente para la Victoria faction of the PJ), with 21.99% of the ballot. Kirchner, who as Governor of Santa Cruz province had attracted recognition for his apparent probity and sound financial management, was the favoured candidate of outgoing President Duhalde. Ricardo López Murphy of the Movimiento Federal para Recrear el Crecimiento alliance, a former UCR Minister of Defence and (briefly) the economy minister under President de la Rúa, came third, with 16.35% of the ballot. The third Peronist candidate, former President Adolfo Rodríguez Sáa, representing the Frente Movimiento Popular/Partido Unión y Libertad alliance, attracted 14.12% of the votes. He was narrowly defeated by Elisa Carrió of the Alternativa por una República de Iguales, who won 14.15% of the votes cast. As no candidate had secured the majority of votes required by the Constitution, a run-off ballot between the two leading candidates was scheduled for 18 May. However, faced with the very likely possibility of a decisive protest vote against him, on 14 May Menem withdrew his candidacy from the election. Kirchner was thus elected by default. He was sworn in as President on 25 May.

Upon taking office, the new President faced the problem of strengthening his relatively weak popular mandate (he had been elected with less than 22% of the popular vote), in order to fulfil his electoral pledges to address Argentina's severe social and economic problems. In his inauguration speech, Kirchner pledged to put the needs of the Argentine people before the demands of the IMF. He immediately announced a series of popular measures, which included the replacement of several high-ranking military and police commanders, the opening of an investigation into allegedly corrupt practices by several Supreme Court Justices (which prompted the resignation of the President of the Supreme Court in June) and increases in pensions and minimum wages. He also announced a programme of investment in infrastructure, particularly housing, intended to lower the high unemployment rate. Kirchner's new Cabinet included five ministers with previous government experience; most notably, Roberto Lavagna, the Minister of the Economy in the previous administration, retained his post. Lavagna had been widely credited with averting hyperinflation and a possible collapse in the financial system in 2002.

President Kirchner's increasing popularity in 2003 successfully translated into significant gains for the PJ in the legislative elections that were held during the latter half of the year, which resulted in a working majority for the PJ and its allies in both the Cámara de Diputados and the Senado (of 127 and 41 seats, respectively). Gubernatorial elections, also held during the second half of the year, further consolidated Kirchner's position; by December the PJ controlled 16 of the country's 24 provinces (including the Federal District of Buenos Aires and the National Territory of Tierra del Fuego). Moreover, the corruption inquiry within the Supreme Court resulted in the removal of four Justices, including the Court's President, Julio Nazareno, all of whom were considered to be hostile to the new President. However, a fifth Justice and ally of Kirchner, Antonio Boggiano, was charged with misconduct in October 2004. This impeachment process prompted the Kirchner Government to consider a radical reform of the Supreme Court with a view to reducing its size and remit.

Meanwhile, in September 2003, the Kirchner administration was able to exploit popular hostility towards the IMF, as well as the scale of the Fund's exposure to Argentina's debt burden, in order to force an exceptionally favourable new international financing arrangement (see Economic Affairs).

Notwithstanding President Kirchner's pledges to improve social provisions, from 2003 frequent demonstrations against high levels of crime and unemployment continued to cause disruption in Buenos Aires and other cities. Loosely rganized groups of protesters, known as *piqueteros*, became increasingly radical during this period, erecting roadblocks and occupying both private and public institutions to demand jobs, redistribution of money and an end to a perceived culture of impunity. In April 2004 the federal Government announced a three-year anti-crime initiative; however, the plan failed to quell popular protests throughout the year.

Despite public expressions of regret (in 1995 and 2004) by the heads of the navy, the army and the air force for crimes committed by the armed forces during 1976–83, issues concerning the 'dirty war' remained politically sensitive in the early 21st century. In January 1998 Alfredo Astiz, a notorious former naval captain, was deprived of his rank and pension after he defended the elimination of political opponents during the dictatorship. In the following month the Swiss authorities revealed that they had discovered a number of Swiss bank accounts belonging to former Argentine military officials, including Astiz and Antonio Domingo Bussi, then Governor of Tucumán. It was rumoured that the accounts contained funds stolen by the military regime from Argentines who had been detained or 'disappeared'. In July 2001 Astiz was arrested at the request of an Italian court on the grounds of his involvement in the murder of three Italian citizens during the 'dirty war'. He was released the following month. In late 2004 Astiz also remained the subject of extradition requests by the French and Swedish Governments, although in June José Juan Bautista Pampuro, the Minister of Defence, had expressed his opposition to Astiz being judged abroad. In November 2004 an internal investigation of the US-based Riggs Bank implicated the Argentine navy in money-laundering. In March 2003 the Congreso approved legislation repealing the Punto Final and Obediencia Debida laws (adopted in 1986 and 1987, respectively); however, the new legislation was not retrospective and would not affect those who had already received an amnesty. In June Gen. Videla was arrested in connection with the abduction and illegal adoption of children whose parents had 'disappeared' during the dictatorship. As many as 300 infants born in special holding centres during the 'dirty war' were believed to have been abducted by the military and police. In late 2003 further arrests were made in connection with the alleged kidnappings, including that of former President Reynaldo Bignone, former army chief Lt-Gen. Cristino Nicolaides and former navy chief Vice-Adm. Rubén Oscar Franco. In March 2004 two former police officials were convicted of facilitating the illegal adoption of one such infant in a case that was seen to set a precedent for further possible prosecutions. In April 2000 a mass grave was discovered in Lomas de Zamora, containing the remains of about 90 victims of the 'dirty war'. In July 2001 Videla was arrested, pending an inquiry into his role in 'Plan Condor', an alleged scheme among right-wing dictators in Argentina, Chile, Uruguay and Bolivia to eradicate leftist political opponents living in exile during the 1970s. In September he was ordered to stand trial for the abduction of 72 foreigners who were taken as part of 'Plan Condor'. In July 2002 former dictator Gen. Galtieri was arrested, along with at least 30 others, on charges relating to the kidnapping and murder of opponents during the 'dirty war'. Specifically, the charges concerned the torture and murder of 20 members of the Montoneros guerrilla group in 1980. In September he was imprisoned, along with 24 other former military officers, pending trial. (Galtieri remained under house arrest until his death in January 2003.) In October 2004 the Supreme Court ruled that the state should pay compensation to Susana Yofre de Vaca Nervaja, who fled Argentina after her husband and son were killed by military personnel during the 'dirty war', as exile of this nature was equivalent to illegal detention. This ruling was widely expected to set a precedent for claims for compensation to be brought by others, thought to number between 10,000 and 50,000, who also fled Argentina during the years of military rule.

In 1996 a criminal investigation was begun in Spain regarding the torture, disappearance and killing of several hundred Spanish citizens in Argentina during 1976–83. A parallel investigation was initiated into the abduction of 54 children of Spanish victims during this period. In October 1997 Adolfo Scilingo, a former Argentine military official, was arrested in Madrid after admitting to his involvement in the 'dirty war'. However, he later retracted his confession, claiming it was given under duress, and contested the jurisdiction of the Spanish courts in this affair. His appeal was rejected in November 2004 and in April 2005 Scilingo was convicted of crimes against humanity, including the torture and murder of 30 prisoners; he was sentenced to 640 years' imprisonment. The Argentine Government expressed its approval of the verdict. During 1997 a Spanish High Court judge issued international arrest warrants for several other Argentine officers, including Adm. Massera and Gen. Galtieri. Following further investigations, in November 1999 international arrest warrants on charges of genocide, terrorism and torture were issued for 98 of those accused. In December the Spanish magistrate Baltasar Garzón issued international arrest warrants for 49 people, including former military presidents Videla and Galtieri, effectively confining them to Argentine territory. However, in January 2000 a federal judge refused to extradite them.

In July 2003 President Kirchner revoked a decree, issued by President de la Rúa in 2001, which had prevented the extradition of Argentine citizens suspected of human rights violations. Courts in Spain, France, Germany and Sweden have all since sought the extradition of former Argentine military personnel for crimes—including murder—committed against their citizens. In the following month the Senado approved legislation that would allow the annulment of the Punto Final and Obediencia Debida laws, and ratified a UN Convention that ostensibly removed all constitutional limitations on human rights prosecutions. In August 2004 the Supreme Court ruled, in reference to the assassination in Buenos Aires in 1974 of Carlos Prats (the former head of the Chilean army) and his wife, that crimes against humanity have no statutory limitations. This ruling was widely understood to be a step towards the annulment of the Punto Final and Obediencia Debida laws, as approved by the

Congreso, thereby opening the way for further prosecutions for abuses committed under military rule.

In May 1985 a treaty was formally ratified by representatives of the Argentine and Chilean Governments, concluding the territorial dispute over three small islands in the Beagle Channel, south of Tierra del Fuego. The islands were awarded to Chile, while Argentine rights to petroleum and other minerals in the disputed waters were guaranteed. In August 1991 Argentina and Chile reached a settlement regarding claims to territory in the Antarctic region; however, the sovereignty of the territory remained under dispute, necessitating the signing of an additional protocol in late 1996. In December 1998 the Presidents of the two countries signed a new agreement on the border demarcation of the contested 'continental glaciers' territory in the Antarctic region (despite the 1991 treaty); the accord became effective in June 1999 following ratification by the Argentine and Chilean legislatures. Meanwhile, the two countries' navies held joint exercises for the first time in August 1998. In February 1999, during a meeting held in Ushuaia, southern Argentina, President Menem and the Chilean President, Eduardo Frei Ruiz-Tagle, signed a significant defence agreement and issued a joint declaration on both countries' commitment to the consolidation of their friendship.

Relations between the two countries were strained in mid-2004, however, following President Kirchner's decision to reduce exports of gas to Chile by some 25% in order to meet a critical shortfall in stocks for domestic consumption. The Chilean Government claimed that this violated an agreement signed in 1995. In September tensions between the two countries were exacerbated following the appointment of Ignacio Walker Prieto as the Chilean Minister of Foreign Affairs in September. In a newspaper editorial prior to his appointment Walker had criticized both President Kirchner for opportunism and Peronism in general for displaying 'authoritarian' and 'fascistic' traits.

Full diplomatic relations were restored with the United Kingdom in February 1990, following senior-level negotiations in Madrid, Spain. The improvement in relations between Argentina and the United Kingdom prompted the European Community (now European Union, see p. 217) to sign a new five-year trade and co-operation agreement with Argentina in April. In November Argentina and the United Kingdom concluded an agreement for the joint administration of a comprehensive protection programme for the lucrative South Atlantic fishing region. Subsequent agreements to regulate fishing in the area were made in 1992 and 1993. A diplomatic accord, signed in September 1991, significantly reduced military restrictions in the region, which the United Kingdom had imposed on Argentina following the Falklands conflict. The question of sovereignty over the disputed islands was not resolved. The results of preliminary seismic investigations (published in late 1993), which indicated rich petroleum deposits in the region, were expected further to complicate future negotiations. Although a comprehensive agreement on exploration was signed by both countries in New York, USA, in September 1995, negotiations on fishing rights in the region remained tense. In 1996 the Argentine Government suggested, for the first time, that it might consider shared sovereignty of the Falkland Islands with the United Kingdom. The proposal was firmly rejected by the British Government and by the Falkland Islanders, who reiterated their commitment to persuading the UN Special Political and Decolonization Committee to adopt a clause allowing the Islanders the right to self-determination. Anglo-Argentine relations improved in November 1996 when Lt-Gen. Martín Balza, the Chief of Staff of the Argentine Army, became the first high-ranking Argentine military official to visit the United Kingdom since 1982. Relations between Argentina and the United Kingdom were consolidated further in January 1997 when the two countries agreed to resume negotiations on a long-term fisheries accord. Moreover, in October 1998 President Menem made an official visit to the United Kingdom, during which he held talks with the British Prime Minister, Tony Blair, on issues including the arms embargo, defence, trade and investment. Notably, Menem paid tribute to the British servicemen who died during the 1982 conflict, while he also appealed for an 'imaginative' solution to the Falkland Islands sovereignty issue. Earlier in 1998 relations with the United Kingdom had been strained by the presentation of draft legislation to the Argentine Congress on the imposition of sanctions on petroleum companies and fishing vessels operating in Falkland Island waters without Argentine authorization. In late 1998 the United Kingdom partially lifted its arms embargo against Argentina. In May

1999 formal negotiations were held between the British and Argentine Governments and members of the Falkland Islands' legislature. Following further talks in July, an agreement was reached providing for an end to the ban on Argentine citizens visiting the Falkland Islands and for the restoration of air links between the islands and South America, with stopovers in Argentina to be introduced from October. In September Argentine and British government officials reached an understanding on co-operation against illegal fishing in the South Atlantic, and naval forces from both countries held joint exercises in the region in November. In August 2001 Tony Blair became the first British Prime Minister to make an official visit to Argentina; however, the issue of the sovereignty of the Falkland Islands was not discussed. Despite President Kirchner's reiterated commitment to the issue upon taking office in May 2003, and at a meeting in London with Blair in July, none the less, there was little progress on the Islands' sovereignty by late 2004.

In March 1991 the Presidents of Argentina, Brazil, Paraguay and Uruguay signed the Asunción treaty in Paraguay, thereby confirming their commitment to the creation of a Southern Common Market, Mercosur (Mercado Común del Sur, see p. 349). Mercosur duly came into effect on 1 January 1995. While a complete common external tariff was not expected until 2006, customs barriers on 80%–85% of mutually exchanged goods were removed immediately. The effects of economic recession and the devaluation of the Brazilian currency in January 1999 provoked a series of trade disputes within Mercosur during that year, particularly between Argentina and Brazil, the two largest members. However, a document, known as the 'Buenos Aires Consensus', signed in 2003 by President Kirchner and his Brazilian counterpart, Luiz Inácio (Lula) da Silva, agreed to study the creation of common institutions for resolving trade disputes, in addition to the eventual establishment of a Mercosur legislature.

In late 1997, following a visit to Argentina by the then US President, Bill Clinton, the US Congress declared Argentina a 'special non-NATO ally', affording the country privileged access to US surplus defence supplies and certain military funding. Chile and Brazil criticized the granting of the special status, claiming it would lead to a regional imbalance. In January 1999, during a visit by President Menem to Washington, DC, a number of US-Argentine defence agreements were signed, which aimed to enhance military co-operation between the two countries. In September 2003, however, the USA protested at Argentina's membership of the so-called 'G-20' group of developing nations at the Ministerial Conference of the World Trade Organization meeting in Cancún, Mexico.

Government

For administrative purposes Argentina comprises 1,617 municipalities located in 22 provinces, the Federal District of Buenos Aires, and the National Territory of Tierra del Fuego.

Legislative power is vested in the bicameral Congress (Congreso): the Chamber of Deputies (Cámara de Diputados) has 257 members, elected by universal adult suffrage for a term of four years (with approximately one-half of the seats renewable every two years); the Senate (Senado) has 72 members, with three members drawn from each of the 22 provinces, the Federal District of Buenos Aires and the National Territory of Tierra del Fuego. Senators are elected for a six-year term (with one-third of the seats renewable every two years). In 2001, however, the entire Senate was renewed. The President is directly elected for a four-year term, renewable once. Each province has its own elected Governor and legislature, concerned with all matters not delegated to the federal Government.

Defence

Conscription was ended on 1 April 1995. The total strength of the regular armed forces in August 2004 was 71,400, comprising a 41,400-strong army, a 17,500-strong navy and an air force of 12,500 men. There were also paramilitary forces numbering 31,240 men. The defence budget for 2004 put defence expenditure at 4,800m. new pesos.

Economic Affairs

In 2003, according to estimates by the World Bank, Argentina's gross national income (GNI), measured at average 2001–2003 prices, was US $122,310m., equivalent to $3,650 per head (or $10,920 on an international purchasing-power parity basis). During 1990–2003, it was estimated, Argentina's population increased at an average rate of 1.3% per year, while gross domestic product (GDP) per head increased, in real terms, by an average of 1.6% per year. Overall GDP increased, in real terms, at an average annual rate of 2.9% in 1990–2003. Real GDP increased by 8.7% in 2003.

Agriculture (including forestry and fishing) contributed an estimated 11.0% of GDP in 2003, and, in mid-2002, employed an estimated 9.3% of the labour force. The principal cash crops are wheat, maize, sorghum and soybeans. Beef production is also important. During 1990–2003 agricultural GDP increased at an average annual rate of 2.8%. The GDP of the sector declined by 2.3% in 2002, but increased by an estimated 6.9% % in 2003.

Industry (including mining, manufacturing, construction and power) engaged 18.4% of the employed labour force in 2001 and provided an estimated 34.7% of GDP in 2003. During 1990–2003 industrial GDP increased, in real terms, at an estimated average rate of 2.4%. Sectoral GDP decreased by 13.8% in 2002, but increased by an estimated 16.5% in 2003.

Mining contributed an estimated 5.8% of GDP in 2003, and employed 0.3% of the working population in 2001. Argentina has substantial deposits of petroleum and natural gas, as well as steam coal and lignite. The GDP of the mining sector increased, in real terms, at an average rate of 3.8% per year during 1993–2003; estimated growth of 3.7% was recorded in 2003.

Manufacturing contributed an estimated 23.9% of GDP in 2003, and employed 11.4% of the working population in 2001. During 1993–2003 manufacturing GDP decreased, in real terms, at an estimated average annual rate of 0.3%. Manufacturing GDP decreased by an estimated 11% in 2002, but increased by an estimated 16.0% in 2003.

Energy is derived principally from natural gas, responsible for the production of 46.7% of total primary energy consumption in 2001. However, in early 2004 a critical shortage in the gas supply prompted the Government of President Néstor Carlos Kirchner to reduce the voltage in the national grid, ration gas supplies to various corporations and reduce exports of gas. Hydroelectricity produced 41.4% of Argentina's total energy requirements in 2001, while the country's two nuclear power-stations produced 7.8%. In 2003 imports of mineral fuels comprised an estimated 3.4% of the country's total imports.

Services engaged 69.3% of the employed labour force in 2001 and accounted for an estimated 54.3% of GDP in 2003. The combined GDP of the service sectors increased, in real terms, at an estimated average rate of 2.6% per year during 1990–2003; sectoral GDP decreased by 9.2% in 2002, and but increased by an estimated 4.2% in 2003.

In 2003 Argentina recorded a visible trade surplus of US $16,277m., and there was a surplus of $7,838m. on the current account of the balance of payments. In 2001 (according to provisional figures) the principal source of imports (26%) was Brazil, followed by the USA (19%). Brazil was also the principal recipient of exports, accounting for 24% of total exports in that year. Other major trading partners in 2001 were the People's Republic of China, Chile and Spain. In late 2004 President Kirchner and the Chinese President, Hu Jintao, signed a joint statement of intent to increase bilateral economic co-operation. The principal exports in 2003 were mineral products, animal feed and food-industry residues and waste, and animal and vegetable oils and fats. The principal imports were nuclear reactors and mechanical appliances, organic chemicals and electrical machinery.

In 2001 there was a budget deficit of 8,919.5m. new Argentine pesos, equivalent to 3.3% of GDP. Argentina's total external debt was US $132,314m. at the end of 2002, of which $74,661m. was long-term public debt. In that year the total cost of debt-servicing was equivalent to 18.3% of revenue from exports of goods and services. The annual rate of inflation averaged 4.8% in 1992–2003; following deflation of 1.0% in 2001, consumer prices increased in 2002 and 2003, by 25.8% and 13.5%, respectively. According to the 2001 census, the national unemployment rate was 28.5%, equivalent to some 4.4m. people. In 2002 the unemployment rate fell to 17.5%.

During 1986–90 Argentina signed a series of integration treaties with neighbouring Latin American countries, aimed at increasing bilateral trade and establishing the basis for a Latin American economic community. Argentina is a member of ALADI (see p. 289) and of Mercosur (see p. 349). In December 2004 Argentina was one of 12 countries that were signatories to the agreement, signed in Cusco, Peru, creating the South American Community of Nations (Comunidad Sudamericana de Naciones), intended to promote greater regional economic integration, due to become operational by 2007.

Economic growth in Argentina in the 1980s was hampered primarily by massive external debt obligations, limited access to financial aid and a scarcity of raw materials. The success of new economic measures introduced by the Government in the early 1990s, drastically reduced inflation and helped to secure international agreements to reschedule debt repayments and the disbursement of loans. From mid-1998, however, both the trade and budget deficits began to widen, as international prices for certain commodities fell, adversely affecting exports. Exports declined further in 1999 following the devaluation of the Brazilian currency in January, and the economy entered recession. Further decreases in the price of commodity exports, as well as an uncompetitive US dollar (to which the peso was tied) and higher international interest rates, increased the debt burden. In spite of a US $40,000m. loan from the IMF and an effective devaluation of the peso for foreign trade, throughout 2001 the economic situation worsened. Faced with declining tax revenues, the Government failed to secure any further IMF funding, and in January 2002 a major default on the country's sovereign debt (estimated at $155,000m.) and a 30% devaluation of the peso inevitably ensued. The de la Rúa administration collapsed, initiating a period of political, civil and economic turmoil. GDP contracted by 10.9% in 2002. In November of that year the Government of Eduardo Duhalde announced its intention to default on payment obligations to the World Bank and the Inter-American Development Bank (IDB), in the absence of a new agreement with the IMF. Both institutions ceased to disburse funds with immediate effect. In January 2003 a new $6,700m. stand-by agreement was reached with the IMF, after the Government agreed to repay creditor institutions from its international reserves. The deal also established economic performance targets upon which disbursement would be conditional. In August 2003 the stand-by agreement expired and in the following month Argentina failed to repay US $2,900m. owed to the IMF. However, the day after what was effectively the largest default in the Fund's history, the IMF extended a new, three-year deal to the Argentine Government. In return, the Government of President Néstor Kirchner agreed to implement some IMF-recommended austerity measures, such as a 'freeze' on public-sector salaries, tax reform, and reform of provincial government finances. In March 2004 the IMF agreed to release a further US $3,100m. in loans, after the Government agreed to continue negotiations with private-sector creditors. None the less, President Kirchner remained reluctant to honour international obligations at the expense of Argentina's fragile social stability. Furthermore, negotiations with the IMF were suspended in mid-2004 after the Government refused to accede to the Fund's demand that Argentina increase its fiscal surplus.

In November the Government announced plans to convert some $40,000m. of its defaulted, privately held debt (estimated at some $82,000m.) into bonds to appease creditors. Economic growth of about 7% was predicted for 2004. Much of this improvement was owing to record agricultural production, and the devalued currency's positive impact on export levels. Nevertheless, concerns remained that such a level of economic growth was unsustainable without increased foreign investment, which would largely depend on reducing the country's enormous debt burden and allowing increases in utility tariffs (to which President Néstor Kirchner remained opposed in early 2005).

Education

Education from pre-school to university level is available free of charge. Education is officially compulsory for all children at primary level, between the ages of six and 14 years. Secondary education lasts for between five and seven years, depending on the type of course: the normal certificate of education (bachillerato) course lasts for five years, whereas a course leading to a technical or agricultural bachillerato lasts for six years. Technical education is supervised by the Consejo Nacional de Educación Técnica. The total enrolment at primary and secondary schools in 1996 was estimated at 99.4% and 67.2% of the school-age population, respectively. Non-university higher education, usually leading to a teaching qualification, is for three or four years, while university courses last for four years or more. There are 36 state universities and 48 private universities. Government expenditure on education, culture, science and technology in 2001 was 2,632.4m. new pesos (5.7% of total public expenditure).

Public Holidays

2005: 1 January (New Year's Day), 25 March (Good Friday), 4 April (for Veterans' Day and Tribute to the Fallen of the Falkland (Malvinas) War), 1 May (Labour Day), 25 May (Anniversary of the 1810 Revolution), 20 June (Flag Day), 9 July (Independence Day), 15 August (Death of Gen. José de San Martín), 10 October (for Columbus Day), 8 December (Immaculate Conception), 25 December (Christmas).

2006: 1 January (New Year's Day), 3 April (for Veterans' Day and Tribute to the Fallen of the Falkland (Malvinas) War), 14 April (Good Friday), 1 May (Labour Day), 25 May (Anniversary of the 1810 Revolution), 19 June (for Flag Day), 9 July (Independence Day), 21 August (Death of Gen. José de San Martín), 16 October (for Columbus Day), 8 December (Immaculate Conception), 25 December (Christmas).

Weights and Measures

The metric system is in force.

Statistical Survey

Sources (unless otherwise stated): Instituto Nacional de Estadística y Censos, Avda Julio A. Roca 609, 1067 Buenos Aires; tel. (11) 4349-9200; fax (11) 4349-9601; e-mail ces@indec.mecon.gov.ar; internet www.indec.mecon.ar; and Banco Central de la República Argentina, Reconquista 266, 1003 Buenos Aires; tel. (11) 4348-3955; fax (11) 4334-5712; e-mail sistema@bcra.gov.ar; internet www.bcra.gov.ar.

Area and Population

AREA, POPULATION AND DENSITY

Area (sq km)	2,780,403*
Population (census results)†	
15 May 1991	32,615,528
17–18 November 2001	
Males	17,659,072
Females	18,601,058
Total	36,260,130
Population (official estimates at mid-year)	
2002	37,515,632
2003	37,869,730
2004	38,226,051
Density (per sq km) at mid-2004	13.7

* 1,073,519 sq miles. The figure excludes the Falkland Islands (Islas Malvinas) and Antarctic territory claimed by Argentina.
† Figures exclude adjustment for underenumeration, estimated to have been 0.9% at the 1991 census.

PROVINCES
(2001 census)

	Area (sq km)	Population	Density (per sq km)	Capital
Buenos Aires—				
Federal District	203	2,776,138	13,679.6	
Buenos Aires—				
Province . . .	307,571	13,827,203	45.0	La Plata
Catamarca . .	102,602	334,568	3.3	San Fernando del Valle de Catamarca
Chaco . . .	99,633	984,446	9.9	Resistencia
Chubut . . .	224,686	413,237	1.8	Rawson
Córdoba . . .	165,321	3,066,801	18.6	Córdoba
Corrientes . .	88,199	930,991	10.6	Corrientes
Entre Ríos . .	78,781	1,158,147	14.7	Paraná
Formosa . . .	72,066	486,559	6.8	Formosa
Jujuy	53,219	611,888	11.5	San Salvador de Jujuy
La Pampa . .	143,440	299,294	2.1	Santa Rosa
La Rioja . . .	89,680	289,983	3.2	La Rioja
Mendoza . . .	148,827	1,579,651	10.6	Mendoza
Misiones . . .	29,801	965,522	32.4	Posadas

— continued	Area (sq km)	Density Population (per sq km)		Capital
Neuquén . . .	94,078	474,155	5.0	Neuquén
Río Negro . . .	203,013	552,822	2.7	Viedma
Salta . . .	155,488	1,079,051	6.9	Salta
San Juan . . .	89,651	620,023	6.9	San Juan
San Luis . . .	76,748	367,933	4.8	San Luis
Santa Cruz . .	243,943	196,958	0.8	Río Gallegos
Santa Fe . .	133,007	3,000,701	22.6	Santa Fe
Santiago del Estero	136,351	804,457	5.9	Santiago del Estero
Tucumán . . .	22,524	1,338,523	59.4	San Miguel de Tucumán
Territory				
Tierra del Fuego .	21,571	101,079	4.7	Ushuaia
Total . . .	2,780,403	36,260,130	13.0	Buenos Aires

PRINCIPAL TOWNS
(population at 2001 census)*

Buenos Aires (capital) . . .	2,776,138	Malvinas Argentinas† . .	290,691
Córdoba	1,267,521	Berazategui† . .	287,913
La Matanza† . .	1,255,288	Bahía Blanca† . .	284,776
Rosario . . .	908,163	Resistencia . .	274,490
Lomas de Zamora† .	591,345	Vicente López† . .	274,082
La Plata†	574,369	San Miguel† . .	253,086
General Pueyrredón†	564,056	Posadas	252,981
San Miguel de Tucumán . . .	527,150	Esteban Echeverría†	243,974
Quilmes†	518,788	Paraná	235,967
Almirante Brown† .	515,556	Pilar†	232,463
Merlo†	469,985	San Salvador de Jujuy	231,229
Salta	462,051	Santiago del Estero .	230,614
Lanús†	453,082	José C. Paz† . . .	230,208
General San Martín†	403,107	Guaymallén . . .	223,365
Moreno†	380,503	Neuquén	201,868
Santa Fe	368,668	Formosa	198,074
Florencio Varela† .	348,970	Godoy Cruz . . .	182,563
Tres de Febrero† .	336,467	Escobar†	178,155
Avellaneda† . . .	328,980	Hurlingham† . . .	172,245
Corrientes . . .	314,546	Las Heras . . .	169,248
Morón†	309,380	Ituzaingó	158,121
Tigre†	301,223	San Luis	153,322
San Isidro† . . .	291,505	San Fernando† . .	151,131

* In each case the figure refers to the city proper. At the 2001 census the population of the Buenos Aires agglomeration was 13,827,203.
† Settlement within the Province of Buenos Aires.

Mid-2003 (UN estimate, incl. suburbs): Buenos Aires 13,047,115 (Source: UN, *World Urbanization Prospects: The 2003 Revision*).

BIRTHS, MARRIAGES AND DEATHS

	Registered live births		Registered deaths	
	Number	Rate (per 1,000)	Number	Rate (per 1,000)
1995 . . .	658,735	18.9	268,997	7.7
1996 . . .	675,437	19.2	268,715	7.6
1997 . . .	692,357	19.4	270,910	7.6
1998 . . .	683,301	18.9	280,180	7.8
1999 . . .	686,748	18.8	289,543	7.9
2000 . . .	701,878	19.0	277,148	7.5
2001 . . .	683,495	18.2	285,941	7.6
2002 . . .	694,684	18.3	291,190	7.7

Marriages: 130,553 (marriage rate 3.5 per 1,000) in 2001.
Source: mainly UN, *Demographic Yearbook* and *Population and Vital Statistics Report*.

Expectation of life (WHO estimates, years at birth): 74.4 (males 70.8; females 78.1) in 2002 (Source: WHO, *World Health Report*).

ECONOMICALLY ACTIVE POPULATION
(persons aged 14 years and over, census of November 2001)

	Males	Females	Total
Agriculture, hunting and forestry .	805,293	92,228	897,521
Fishing	11,843	1,632	13,475
Mining and quarrying	35,068	2,911	37,979
Manufacturing	966,056	279,488	1,245,544
Electricity, gas and water . . .	76,428	13,737	90,165
Construction	621,598	16,968	638,566
Wholesale and retail trade; repair of motor vehicles, motorcycles and personal and household goods	1,287,017	624,364	1,911,381
Hotels and restaurants	168,929	132,755	301,684
Transport, storage and communication	629,188	88,385	717,573
Financial intermediation . . .	111,717	74,796	186,513
Real estate, renting and business activities	456,005	255,746	711,751
Public administration and defence; compulsory social security . .	649,790	319,490	969,280
Education	200,538	730,387	930,925
Health and social work	197,282	394,824	592,106
Other community, social and personal services	266,782	186,202	452,984
Private households with employed persons	85,213	701,219	786,432
Extra-territorial organizations and bodies	1,084	917	2,001
Activities not adequately described	243,200	184,107	427,307
Total employed	6,813,031	4,100,156	10,913,187
Unemployed	2,212,776	2,138,820	4,351,596
Total labour force	9,025,807	6,238,976	15,264,783

Health and Welfare

KEY INDICATORS

Total fertility rate (children per woman, 2002)	2.5
Under-5 mortality rate (per 1,000 live births, 2003) . . .	20
HIV (% of persons aged 15–49, 2003)	0.7
Physicians (per 1,000 head, 1995)	2.68
Hospital beds (per 1,000 head, 1996)	3.29
Health expenditure (2001): US $ per head (PPP)	1,130
Health expenditure (2001): % of GDP	9.5
Health expenditure (2001): public (% of total)	53.4
Access to water (% of persons, 2000)	79
Access to sanitation (% of persons, 2000)	85
Human Development Index (2002): ranking	34
Human Development Index (2002): value	0.853

For sources and definitions, see explanatory note on p. vi.

Agriculture

PRINCIPAL CROPS
('000 metric tons)

	2001	2002	2003
Wheat	15,428	12,300	14,530
Rice (paddy)	859	713	718
Barley	573	570*	549
Maize	15,365	15,000	15,040
Rye	81	80	37
Oats	645	500	348
Sorghum	2,909	2,847	2,685
Potatoes	2,505	2,133	2,150*
Sweet potatoes	309	310*	315*
Cassava (Manioc)*	165	165	170
Sugar cane*	19,050	19,250	19,250
Dry beans	263	278	216
Soybeans (Soya beans)	26,864	30,180	34,800
Groundnuts (in shell)	563	517	314
Olives*	90	93	95
Cottonseed	257†	104	111†
Sunflower seed	3,043	3,843	3,714
Artichokes*	85	86	88
Tomatoes	648	668	670*
Pumpkins, squash and gourds	291	291*	295*
Chillies and green peppers*	122	123	125
Dry onions	576	642	645*
Garlic	135	126	127*
Carrots*	220	225	230
Other vegetables*	640	645	648
Watermelons*	125	126	126
Cantaloupes and other melons	78	79*	79*
Bananas*	175	180	180
Oranges	918	767	687
Tangerines, mandarins, clementines and satsumas	501	464	381
Lemons and limes	1,218	1,313	1,236
Grapefruit and pomelos	199	205	184
Apples	1,429	1,157	1,307
Pears	585	537	639
Peaches and nectarines	258	212	256
Plums	106	106	151
Grapes	2,244	2,360	2,370*
Tea (made)	63	63	64
Mate	310	285	285
Tobacco (leaves)	98	125	118
Cotton (lint)	167†	62	65†

* FAO estimate(s).
† Unofficial estimate.

Source: FAO.

LIVESTOCK
('000 head, year ending September)

	2001	2002	2003
Horses*	3,600	3,650	3,655
Mules*	180	180	185
Asses*	95	95	98
Cattle	48,851	48,100	50,869†
Pigs*	4,200	4,250	4,300
Sheep	13,500*	12,400	12,450*
Goats	3,387	4,000	4,200
Chickens*	110,000	110,500	110,700
Ducks*	2,300	2,350	2,355
Geese*	130	135	140
Turkeys*	2,800	2,850	2,900

* FAO estimate(s).
† Unofficial figure.

Source: FAO.

LIVESTOCK PRODUCTS
('000 metric tons)

	2001	2002	2003
Beef and veal	2,461	2,493	2,621
Mutton and lamb*	50	50	52
Pig meat	198	165	150
Horse meat*	55	56	56
Poultry meat	993	742	781
Cows' milk	9,769	8,793	8,197
Butter†	53	55	55
Cheese†	420	370	350
Hen eggs	302	255	263
Honey	80	83	75
Wool: greasy	56	65	72
Cattle hides (fresh)*	348	345	375
Sheepskins (fresh)*	24	23	23

* FAO estimates.
† Unofficial figures.

Source: FAO.

Forestry

ROUNDWOOD REMOVALS
('000 cubic metres, excl. bark)

	1999	2000	2001
Sawlogs, veneer logs and logs for sleepers	3,547	2,091	2,274
Pulpwood	2,944	3,794	2,962
Other industrial wood	161	120	99
Fuel wood	3,950	3,965	3,972
Total	10,602	9,970	9,307

2002–2003: Production as in 2001 (FAO estimates).

Source: FAO.

SAWNWOOD PRODUCTION
('000 cubic metres, incl. railway sleepers)

	1999	2000	2001
Coniferous (softwood)	686	619	1,630
Broadleaved (hardwood)	722	202	500
Total	1,408	821	2,130

2002–2003: Production as in 2001 (FAO estimates).

Source: FAO.

Fishing

('000 metric tons, live weight)

	2000	2001	2002
Capture*	913.6	931.7	945.8
Southern blue whiting	61.3	54.3	42.5
Argentine hake	193.7	249.5	358.9
Patagonian grenadier	123.7	111.9	98.7
Argentine red shrimp	37.1	78.9	51.4
Patagonean scallop	36.5	39.0	51.0
Argentine shortfin squid	279.0	230.3	177.3
Aquaculture	1.8	1.3	1.5
Total catch	915.4	933.1	947.3

* FAO estimates.
Note: The data exclude aquatic plants (metric tons, capture only): 3 in 2000. Also excluded are aquatic mammals, recorded by number rather than by weight. The number of toothed whales caught was 490 in 2000; 197 in 2001; 217 in 2002.

Source: FAO.

Mining

('000 metric tons, unless otherwise indicated)

	2000	2001	2002
Crude petroleum ('000 42-gallon barrels)	280,944	284,204	275,366
Natural gas (million cu metres) .	44,870	45,910	45,770
Lead ore*	14.1	12.3	12.0
Zinc ore*	34.9	39.7	37.3
Silver ore (kilograms)*	78,271	152,802	125,868
Copper ore*	145.2	191.7	204.0
Gold ore (kilograms)*	25,954	30,630	32,486

* Figures refer to the metal content of ores and concentrates.
Source: US Geological Survey.

Industry

SELECTED PRODUCTS
('000 metric tons, unless otherwise indicated)

	2001	2002	2003
Wheat flour	3,537	3,550	3,793
Beer (sales, '000 hectolitres) . .	12,390	11,990	12,600
Wine (sales, '000 hectolitres) . .	12,036	11,986	12,291
Cigarettes (million units) . .	1,739	1,812	1,990
Paper	1,229	1,208	1,394
Aluminium	248	269	272
Rubber tyres for motor vehicles ('000)	8,037	9,093	9,758
Portland cement	5,545	3,910	5,217
Urea	934	1,120	1,300
Ammonia (estimates)	732	771	884
Motor spirit (petrol, '000 cu metres)	30,241	29,040	30,405
Passenger cars ('000 units) . .	170	111	109
Washing machines ('000 units, estimates)	295	162	357
Home refrigerators ('000 units, estimates)	246	162	138

Electric energy (million kWh): 89,014 in 2000 (Source: UN, *Industrial Commodity Statistics Yearbook*).

Finance

CURRENCY AND EXCHANGE RATES

Monetary Units
100 centavos = 1 nuevo peso argentino (new Argentine peso).

Sterling, Dollar and Euro Equivalents (31 December 2004)
£1 sterling = 5.7150 new pesos;
US $1 = 2.9590 new pesos;
€1 = 4.0305 new pesos;
100 new pesos = £17.50 = $33.80 = €24.81.

Average Exchange Rate (new pesos per US $)
2002   3.0633
2003   2.9006
2004   2.9233

Note: From April 1996 to December 2001 the official exchange rate was fixed at US $1 = 99.95 centavos. In January 2002 the Government abandoned this exchange rate and devalued the peso: initially there was a fixed official exchange rate of US $1 = 1.40 new pesos for trade and financial transactions, while a free market rate was applicable to other transactions. In February, however, a unified 'floating' exchange rate system, with the rate to be determined by market conditions, was introduced.

BUDGET
(million new pesos)*

Revenue	1999	2000	2001
Tax revenue	35,387.8	36,785.4	33,511.1
Taxes on income and profits .	6,434.5	6,866.2	6,655.2
Social security contributions . .	9,654.9	9,437.5	8,455.4
Taxes on property	541.8	1,284.2	3,432.8
Taxes on goods and services . .	16,497.6	17,179.1	13,337.4
Taxes on international trade and transactions	2,210.6	1,971.7	1,586.1
Other current revenue	4,330.0	3,507.8	3,508.5
Property income	1,510.0	1,461.4	1,460.3
Fees and charges	2,601.4	1,772.8	1,750.9
Capital revenue	47.4	52.8	74.3
Total	**39,765.2**	**40,346.0**	**37,093.9**

Expenditure†	1999	2000	2001
General public services . . .	5,118.7	4,422.5	4,028.6
Defence	2,044.2	1,907.1	1,757.6
Public order and safety	1,458.3	1,448.3	1,386.2
Education	3,023.4	3,029.7	2,632.4
Health	1,045.5	904.4	818.7
Social security and welfare . .	23,280.3	23,369.0	22,009.2
Housing and community amenities	900.5	1,015.3	752.4
Recreational, cultural and religious affairs and services . . .	114.5	100.1	65.0
Economic affairs and services . .	2,806.3	2,264.8	2,172.4
Transport and communications .	1,503.5	1,251.2	1,145.1
Other expenditures	8,324.5	9,798.6	10,433.6
Sub-total	**48,116.2**	**48,259.8**	**46,056.1**
Adjustment	−59.6	−35.1	−42.7
Total	**48,056.6**	**48,224.7**	**46,013.4**
Current‡	44,986.3	45,332.6	43,548.1
Capital	3,070.3	2,892.1	2,465.3

* Budget figures refer to the consolidated accounts of the central Government.
† Excluding lending minus repayments (million new pesos): −111.8 in 1999; −1,410.7 in 2000; −44.1 in 2001.
‡ Including interest payments (million new pesos): 8,200.6 in 1999; 9,617.7 in 2000; 10,170.0 in 2001.
Source: IMF, *Government Finance Statistics Yearbook*.

2000 (execution of national budget, million new pesos): Current revenue 57,047 (tax revenues 50,983, non-tax revenues 6,063); Capital resources 462; *Total revenue* 57,508. Current expenditure 60,534 (consumption 9,243, interest on debts 9,666, current transfers 41,608, operational deficit of state enterprises 18); Capital expenditure 3,043 (real investment 480, capital transfers 2,528, financial investment 36); *Total expenditure* 63,577 (Source: Oficina Nacional de Presupuesto, Secretaría de Hacienda, Ministerio de Economía).

2001 (execution of national budget, million new pesos): Current revenue 50,557 (tax revenues 45,810, non-tax revenues 4,730, operational surplus of state enterprises 16); Capital resources 242; *Total revenue* 50,799. Current expenditure 62,027 (consumption 8,961, interest on debts 11,201, current transfers 41,865); Capital expenditure 2,511 (real investment 3,644, capital transfers 2,107, financial investment 41); *Total expenditure* 64,538 (Source: Oficina Nacional de Presupuesto, Secretaría de Hacienda, Ministerio de Economía).

2002 (execution of national budget, provisional, million new pesos): Current revenue 56,743 (tax revenues 51,950, non-tax revenues 4,793); Capital resources 202; *Total revenue* 56,945. Current expenditure 59,145 (consumption 9,464, interest on debts 8,071, current transfers 41,470, operational deficit of state enterprises 140); Capital expenditure 2,898 (real investment 511, capital transfers 2,344, financial investment 43); *Total expenditure* 62,043 (Source: Oficina Nacional de Presupuesto, Secretaría de Hacienda, Ministerio de Economía).

INTERNATIONAL RESERVES
(US $ million at 31 December)

	2001	2002	2003
Gold*	3	3	4
IMF special drawing rights . .	11	94	1,008
Foreign exchange	14,542	10,395	13,145
Total	**14,556**	**10,492**	**14,157**

* National valuation.
Source: IMF, *International Financial Statistics*.

MONEY SUPPLY
(million new pesos at 31 December)

	2001	2002	2003
Currency outside banks . . .	9,081	16,430	26,649
Demand deposits at commercial banks	6,763	11,843	16,292
Total money	15,844	28,273	42,940

Source: IMF, *International Financial Statistics*.

COST OF LIVING
(Consumer Price Index for Buenos Aires metropolitan area; annual averages; base: 1999 = 100)

	2001	2002	2003
Food and beverages	97.2	130.8	155.9
Clothing	92.6	125.7	152.9
Housing	99.2	105.8	114.3
All items (incl. others)	98.8	124.3	141.1

NATIONAL ACCOUNTS
(million new pesos at current prices)

National Income and Product

	2001	2002	2003*
Gross domestic product (GDP) at market prices . . .	268,697	312,580	375,909
Net primary income from abroad .	−7,744	−19,402	−22,429
Gross national income (GNI) .	260,953	293,178	353,480
Net current transfers . . .	281	1,311	1,319
Gross national disposable income	261,234	294,490	354,799

* Preliminary figures.

Expenditure on the Gross Domestic Product

	2001	2002	2003
Final consumption expenditure .	223,201	231,727	281,044
Households*	185,164	193,482	238,047
General government	38,037	38,245	42,997
Gross capital formation . . .	41,953	34,311	54,690
Gross fixed capital formation .	38,099	37,387	56,913
Changes in inventories . . .	3,854	−3,076	−2,223
Total domestic expenditure .	265,154	266,038	335,734
Exports of goods and services . .	30,977	86,552	93,878
Less Imports of goods and services	27,434	40,010	53,381
Gross domestic product (GDP) in market prices	268,697	312,580	376,232
GDP at constant 1993 prices .	263,997	235,236	255,751

* Including non-profit institutions serving households (NPISHs).

Source: IMF, *International Financial Statistics*.

Gross Domestic Product by Economic Activity

	2001	2002	2003*
Agriculture, hunting and forestry .	11,565	30,482	37,267
Fishing	711	1,422	1,558
Mining and quarrying	6,657	18,674	20,528
Manufacturing	43,242	63,603	84,530
Electricity, gas and water supply	6,332	5,352	6,127
Construction	11,597	7,888	11,531
Wholesale and retail trade . . .	32,831	33,691	41,183
Hotels and restaurants . . .	7,309	6,681	8,232
Transport, storage and communications	22,873	23,116	29,975
Financial intermediation . . .	13,762	16,457	13,683
Real estate, renting and business activities	42,697	39,885	42,195
Public administration and defence†	17,117	16,867	18,846
Education, health and social work	24,052	22,717	24,263
Other community, social and personal service activities‡ . .	14,232	11,807	13,455
Sub-total	254,976	298,641	353,375
Value-added tax	16,233	16,468	22,022
Import duties	1,575	1,308	2,289
Less Imputed bank service charge	4,087	3,837	1,774
GDP in market prices . . .	268,697	312,580	375,909

* Preliminary figures.
† Including extra-territorial organizations and bodies.
‡ Including private households with employed persons.

BALANCE OF PAYMENTS
(US $ million)

	2001	2002	2003
Exports of goods f.o.b.	26,543	25,709	29,566
Imports of goods f.o.b.	−19,158	−8,473	13,119
Trade balance	7,385	17,236	16,447
Exports of services	4,440	3,039	3,989
Imports of services	−8,384	−4,697	−5,530
Balance on goods and services	3,441	15,578	14,906
Other income received	5,358	3,052	3,197
Other income paid	−13,083	−10,061	−10,866
Balance on goods, services and income	−4,283	8,569	7,237
Current transfers received . .	838	761	892
Current transfers paid . . .	−407	−189	−290
Current balance	−3,853	9,142	7,838
Capital account (net)	157	406	70
Direct investment abroad . . .	−161	627	−774
Direct investment from abroad .	2,166	1,093	1,020
Portfolio investment assets . .	212	477	−95
Portfolio investment liabilities .	−9,715	−6,886	−8,064
Other investment assets . . .	−1,907	−8,896	−4,448
Other investment liabilities . .	−5,566	−10,364	−4,539
Net errors and omissions . .	−2,737	−1,929	−1,729
Overall balance	−21,405	−16,331	−10,720

Source: IMF, *International Financial Statistics*.

External Trade

PRINCIPAL COMMODITIES
(US $ million)

Imports c.i.f.	2001	2002	2003*
Mineral fuels, mineral oils and products of their distillation .	798	426	478
Organic chemicals	1,322	987	1,291
Pharmaceutical products . . .	639	393	475
Plastics and articles thereof . .	1,036	544	861
Nuclear reactors, boilers, machinery and mechanical appliances	3,521	1,281	2,273
Electrical machinery and equipment and parts; sound and television apparatus, parts and accessories	2,562	598	1,104
Vehicles other than railway or tramway rolling-stock, and parts and accessories	1,877	722	1,520
Total (incl. others)	20,320	8,990	13,833

Exports f.o.b.	2001	2002	2003*
Fish, crustaceans, molluscs, etc. .	939	711	868
Cereals	2,448	2,127	2,307
Oil seeds and oleaginous fruits; miscellaneous grains, seeds and fruit; industrial or medicinal plants; straw and fodder . .	1,401	1,288	1,993
Animal or vegetable fats, oils and waxes	1,637	2,087	2,832
Residues and waste from food industries; prepared animal fodder	2,628	2,790	3,500
Mineral fuels, mineral oils and products of their distillation . .	4,475	4,419	5,120
Raw hides and skins (other than furskins) and leather	803	685	712
Plastics	629	642	696
Nuclear reactors, boilers, machinery and mechanical appliances	797	684	641
Vehicles other than railway or tramway rolling-stock, and parts and accessories	1,978	1,603	1,428
Total (incl. others)	26,543	25,651	29,566

* Provisional figures.

PRINCIPAL TRADING PARTNERS
(US $ million)*

Imports c.i.f.	1999	2000	2001
Belgium	259.2	205.1	168.3
Brazil†	5,599.0	6,181.1	5,277.8
Canada	290.1	287.8	201.5
Chile†	638.5	571.2	505.7
China, People's Republic . .	992.1	1,060.2	1,066.3
France (incl. Monaco) . . .	1,774.3	926.6	737.3
Germany	1,409.4	1,205.1	1,051.9
Italy (incl. San Marino) . .	1,354.7	963.7	839.4
Japan	1,068.4	954.8	767.3
Korea, Republic	563.8	493.0	409.5
Mexico	490.7	547.9	437.4
Paraguay	304.1	287.4	302.8
Spain	999.9	846.0	712.4
Sweden	311.7	303.2	174.0
Switzerland	294.9	221.7	187.0
Taiwan	299.3	278.8	230.3
United Kingdom	542.6	426.8	407.3
USA	4,996.2	4,456.2	3,781.2
Uruguay†	395.8	413.0	329.0
Total (incl. others)	25,508.0	23,851.5	20,321.1

Exports f.o.b.	1999	2000	2001
Belgium	309.6	311.0	291.4
Bolivia	321.3	266.4	265.3
Brazil†	5,689.6	6,991.3	6,205.6
Canada	239.3	283.1	223.7
Chile†	1,869.0	2,670.6	2,851.7
China, People's Republic . .	507.9	796.2	1,122.6
Egypt	386.3	348.8	345.3
France (incl. Monaco) . . .	349.5	536.9	258.1
Germany	629.1	608.4	463.8
India	436.8	442.5	440.4
Iran	155.3	348.5	417.9
Italy (incl. San Marino) . . .	688.7	731.9	852.2
Japan	527.5	398.8	364.1
Korea, Republic	181.3	165.5	396.4
Malaysia	221.1	242.8	293.5
Mexico	281.6	325.7	484.3
Netherlands	1,013.0	745.9	798.6
Paraguay	563.1	592.2	498.8
Peru	212.7	293.4	394.0
South Africa	308.5	n.a.	n.a.
Spain	962.0	914.7	1,099.5
Thailand	169.7	187.9	304.2
United Kingdom	263.4	261.5	292.0
USA	2,628.3	3,110.8	2,900.1
Uruguay†	818.6	818.3	743.6
Venezuela	247.0	217.6	234.5
Total (incl. others)	23,332.7	26,409.7	26,610.1

* Imports by country of origin; exports by country of destination.
† Including free-trade zones.

Transport

RAILWAYS
(traffic)

	2000	2001	2002
Passengers carried (million) . .	478	432	355
Freight carried ('000 tons) . .	16,265	16,960	17,469
Passenger-km (million) . . .	8,939	7,975	6,586
Freight ton-km (million) . . .	8,696	8,989	9,444

2003: Passengers carried (million) 378; Freight carried ('000 tons) 20,544.

ROAD TRAFFIC
(motor vehicles in use)

	1996	1997	1998
Passenger cars	4,783,908	4,901,265	5,047,630
Buses and coaches	38,434	40,191	43,232
Lorries and vans	1,248,527	1,332,344	1,453,335
Motorcycles and mopeds . . .	35,640	n.a.	n.a.

Source: International Road Federation, *World Road Statistics.*

SHIPPING

Merchant Fleet
(registered at 31 December)

	2001	2002	2003
Number of vessels	478	481	497
Total displacement ('000 grt) . .	421.6	422.9	433.9

Source: Lloyd's Register-Fairplay, *World Fleet Statistics.*

International Sea-borne Freight Traffic
('000 metric tons)

	1996	1997	1998
Goods loaded	52,068	58,512	69,372
Goods unloaded	16,728	19,116	19,536

Source: UN, *Monthly Bulletin of Statistics.*

Total maritime freight handled ('000 metric tons): 118,965 in 2000; 125,685 in 2001; 112,944 in 2002 (Source: Dirección Nacional de Puertos y Vías Navegables).

CIVIL AVIATION
(traffic on scheduled services)

	1999	2000	2001
Kilometres flown (million) . .	170	160	107
Passengers carried ('000) . .	9,192	8,904	5,809
Passenger-km (million) . . .	14,024	15,535	8,330
Total ton-km (million)	1,559	1,751	883

Source: UN, *Statistical Yearbook*.

Tourism

TOURIST ARRIVALS BY REGION
('000)

	2000	2001	2002
Europe	354.1	370.9	323.7
USA and Canada	252.4	179.8	152.6
South America:			
Bolivia	95.1	113.2	119.1
Brazil	451.4	333.0	345.0
Chile	571.3	520.3	749.0
Paraguay	499.8	469.2	518.3
Uruguay	488.0	392.5	363.0
Total (incl. others)*	2,909.5	2,620.4	2,820.0

* Excluding nationals residing abroad.

Tourism receipts (US $ million): 2,813 in 1999; 2,817 in 2000; 2,547 in 2001 (Source: World Tourism Statistics).

Communications Media

	2000	2001	2002
Television receivers ('000 in use) .	11,500	11,800	n.a.
Telephones ('000 main lines in use)	7,894.2	8,108.0	8,009.4
Mobile cellular telephones ('000			
subscribers)	6,050.0	6,974.9	6,500.0
Personal computers ('000 in use) .	2,560	2,000	3,000
Internet users ('000)	2,600	3,000	4,100

Radio receivers ('000 in use): 24,300 in 1997.

Facsimile machines (estimate, '000 in use): 87 in 1998.

Book production: 13,148 titles in 2001.

Daily newspapers: 34 in 1998.

Sources: mainly UNESCO, *Statistical Yearbook*, and International Telecommunication Union.

Education

(2000)

	Institutions	Students	Teachers
Pre-primary	16,000	1,246,597	78,386
Primary	22,283	4,668,006	306,210
Secondary	21,114	3,419,901	182,863
Universities*	36	1,196,581	117,596
Colleges of higher education . .	1,754	440,164	12,825

* 2001 figures for state universities only.

Source: former Ministerio de Cultura y Educación.

Adult literacy rate (UNESCO estimates): 97.0% (males 97.0%; females 97.0%) in 2002 (Source: UN Development Programme, *Human Development Report*).

Directory

The Constitution

The return to civilian rule in 1983 represented a return to the principles of the 1853 Constitution, with some changes in electoral details. In August 1994 a new Constitution was approved, which contained 19 new articles, 40 amendments to existing articles and the addition of a chapter on New Rights and Guarantees. The Constitution is summarized below:

DECLARATIONS, RIGHTS AND GUARANTEES

Each province has the right to exercise its own administration of justice, municipal system and primary education. The Roman Catholic religion, being the faith of the majority of the nation, shall enjoy state protection; freedom of religious belief is guaranteed to all other denominations. The prior ethnical existence of indigenous peoples and their rights, as well as the common ownership of lands they traditionally occupy, are recognized. All inhabitants of the country have the right to work and exercise any legal trade; to petition the authorities; to leave or enter the Argentine territory; to use or dispose of their properties; to associate for a peaceable or useful purpose; to teach and acquire education, and to express freely their opinion in the press without censorship. The State does not admit any prerogative of blood, birth, privilege or titles of nobility. Equality is the basis of all duties and public offices. No citizens may be detained, except for reasons and in the manner prescribed by the law; or sentenced other than by virtue of a law existing prior to the offence and by decision of the competent tribunal after the hearing and defence of the person concerned. Private residence, property and correspondence are inviolable. No one may enter the home of a citizen or carry out any search in it without his consent, unless by a warrant from the competent authority; no one may suffer expropriation, except in case of public necessity and provided that the appropriate compensation has been paid in accordance with the provisions of the laws. In no case may the penalty of confiscation of property be imposed.

LEGISLATIVE POWER

Legislative power is vested in the bicameral Congreso (Congress), comprising the Cámara de Diputados (Chamber of Deputies) and the Senado (Senate). The Chamber of Deputies has 257 directly elected members, chosen for four years and eligible for re-election; approximately one-half of the membership of the Chamber shall be renewed every two years. Until October 1995 the Senate had 48 members, chosen by provincial legislatures for a nine-year term, with one-third of the seats renewable every three years. Since October 1995 elections have provided for a third senator, elected by provincial legislatures. In 2001 the entire Senate was renewed; one-third of the Senate was to be renewed every two years from 2003.

The powers of Congress include regulating foreign trade; fixing import and export duties; levying taxes for a specified time whenever the defence, common safety or general welfare of the State so requires; contracting loans on the nation's credit; regulating the internal and external debt and the currency system of the country; fixing the budget and facilitating the prosperity and welfare of the nation. Congress must approve required and urgent decrees and delegated legislation. Congress also approves or rejects treaties, authorizes the Executive to declare war or make peace, and establishes the strength of the Armed Forces in peace and war.

EXECUTIVE POWER

Executive power is vested in the President, who is the supreme head of the nation and controls the general administration of the country. The President issues the instructions and rulings necessary for the execution of the laws of the country, and himself takes part in drawing up and promulgating those laws. The President appoints, with the approval of the Senate, the judges of the Supreme Court and all other competent tribunals, ambassadors, civil servants, members of the judiciary and senior officers of the Armed Forces and bishops. The President may also appoint and remove, without reference to another body, his cabinet ministers. The President is Commander-in-Chief of all the Armed Forces. The President and

Vice-President are elected directly for a four-year term, renewable only once.

JUDICIAL POWER

Judicial power is exercised by the Supreme Court and all other competent tribunals. The Supreme Court is responsible for the internal administration of all tribunals. In April 1990 the number of Supreme Court judges was increased from five to nine.

PROVINCIAL GOVERNMENT

The 22 provinces, the Federal District of Buenos Aires and the National Territory of Tierra del Fuego retain all the power not delegated to the Federal Government. They are governed by their own institutions and elect their own governors, legislators and officials.

The Government

HEAD OF STATE

President of the Republic: NÉSTOR CARLOS KIRCHNER (took office 25 May 2003).

CABINET
(March 2005)

Cabinet Chief: ALBERTO FERNÁNDEZ.

General Secretary to the Presidency: OSCAR PARRILLI.

Minister of the Interior: ANÍBAL DOMINGO FERNÁNDEZ.

Minister of Foreign Affairs, International Trade and Worship: RAFAEL BIELSA.

Minister of Education, Science and Technology: DANIEL FERNANDO FILMUS.

Minister of Defence: JOSÉ JUAN BAUTISTA PAMPURO.

Minister of the Economy: ROBERTO LAVAGNA.

Minister of Labour, Employment and Social Security: CARLOS TOMADA.

Minister of Planning, Public Investment and Services: JULIO MIGUEL DE VIDO.

Minister of Health and the Environment: Dr GINÉS MARIO GONZÁLEZ GARCÍA.

Minister of Justice, Security and Human Rights: HORACIO ROSATTI.

Minister of Social Development: Dr ALICIA MARGARITA KIRCHNER DE MERCADO.

MINISTRIES

General Secretariat to the Presidency: Balcarce 50, 1064 Buenos Aires; tel. (11) 4344-3662; fax (11) 4344-3789; e-mail secgral@presidencia.net.ar.

Ministry of Defence: Azopardo 250, 1328 Buenos Aires; tel. (11) 4346-8800; e-mail mindef@mindef.gov.ar; internet www.mindef.gov.ar.

Ministry of the Economy: Hipólito Yrigoyen 250, 1310 Buenos Aires; tel. (11) 4349-5000; e-mail ministrosecpriv@mecon.gov.ar; internet www.mecon.gov.ar.

Ministry of Education, Science and Technology: Pizzurno 935, 1020 Buenos Aires; tel. (11) 4129-1000; e-mail info@me.gov.ar; internet www.me.gov.ar.

Ministry of Foreign Affairs, International Trade and Worship: Esmeralda 1212, 1007 Buenos Aires; tel. (11) 4819-7000; e-mail web@mrecic.gov.ar; internet www.mrecic.gov.ar.

Ministry of Health and the Environment: 9 de Julio 1925, 1332 Buenos Aires; tel. (11) 4381-8911; fax (11) 4381-2182; e-mail consultas@msal.gov.ar; internet www.msal.gov.ar.

Ministry of the Interior: Balcarce 50, 1064 Buenos Aires; tel. (11) 446-9841; fax (11) 4331-6376; e-mail secretariaprivada@mininterior.gov.ar; internet www.mininterior.gov.ar.

Ministry of Justice, Security and Human Rights: Sarmiento 329, 1041 Buenos Aires; tel. (11) 4328-3015; internet www.jus.gov.ar.

Ministry of Labour, Employment and Social Security: Leandro N. Alem 650, 1001 Buenos Aires; tel. (11) 4311-2913; fax (11) 4312-7860; e-mail consultas@trabajo.gov.ar; internet www.trabajo.gov.ar.

Ministry of Planning, Public Investment and Services: Buenos Aires.

Ministry of Social Development: Avda 9 de Julio 1925, 14°, 1332 Buenos Aires; tel. (11) 4379-3648; e-mail desarrollosocial@desarrollosocial.gov.ar; internet www.desarrollosocial.gov.ar.

President and Legislature

PRESIDENT

Election, First Round, 27 April 2003*

Candidates	Votes	% of votes cast
Carlos Saúl Menem (PJ)	4,677,213	24.34
Néstor Carlos Kirchner (PJ)	4,227,141	21.99
Ricardo López Murphy (MFRC†) . .	3,142,848	16.35
Elisa M. A. Carrió (ARI)	2,720,143	14.15
Adolfo Rodríguez Sáa (PJ)	2,714,760	14.12
Others	1,737,982	9.04
Total‡	19,220,087	100.00

* A second round of voting between the two leading candidates, Carlos Menem and Néstor Kirchner, was scheduled to be held on 18 May 2003; however, on 14 May Menem withdrew his candidacy from the ballot. The presidency was thus won by default by Kirchner.

† The Movimiento Federal para Recrear el Crecimiento, an electoral alliance comprising the Partido Recrear para el Crecimiento and several provincial parties.

‡ Excluding 535,082 invalid votes.

CONGRESO

Cámara de Diputados
(Chamber of Deputies)

President: EDUARDO OSCAR CAMAÑO.

The Chamber has 257 members, who hold office for a four-year term, with approximately one-half of the seats renewable every two years.

Distribution of Seats by Party, December 2004

	Seats
Partido Justicialista (PJ)	129
Unión Cívica Radical (UCR)	45
Alternativa por una República de Iguales (ARI) . .	11
Frente del Movimiento Popular	7
Partido Socialista	6
Frepaso (Frente País Solidario)	5
Autodeterminación y Libertad	4
Frente Popular Bonaerense (Frepobo)	4
Movimiento Popular Neuquino	4
Fuerza Republicana	3
Partido Unidad Federalista (PaUFe)	3
Compromiso para el Cambio	2
Frente Cívico y Social	2
Frente Nuevo	2
Fuerza Portena	2
Nuevo Buenos Aires	2
Renovador de Salta	2
Other parties	21
Vacant	3
Total	**257**

Senado
(Senate)

President: DANIEL OSVALDO SCIOLI.

The Senate has 72 directly elected members, three from each province. One-third of these seats are renewable every two years.

Distribution of Seats*, December 2004

	Seats
Partido Justicialista (PJ)	40
Unión Cívica Radical (UCR)	15
Frente Cívico y Social de Catamarca	2
Fuerza Republicana	2
Movimiento Popular Neuquino	2
Cruzada Renovadora de San Juan	1
Frente Cívico Jujeño	1
Frente Grande	1
Frepaso (Frente País Solidario)	1
Justicialista 17 de Octubre	1
Partido Socialista	1
Radical Independiente	1
Radical Rionegrino	1
Renovador de Salta	1
Vecinalista-Partido Nuevo	1
Vacant	1
Total	**72**

*The table shows the number of seats by legislative bloc.

PROVINCIAL ADMINISTRATORS
(March 2005)

Mayor of the Federal District of Buenos Aires: ANÍBAL IBARRA.

Governor of the Province of Buenos Aires: Dr FELIPE SOLÁ.

Governor of the Province of Catamarca: Dr EDUARDO BRIZUELA DEL MORAL.

Governor of the Province of Chaco: Dr ROY NIKISCH.

Governor of the Province of Chubut: Dr MARIO DAS NEVES.

Governor of the Province of Córdoba: Dr JOSÉ MANUEL DE LA SOTA.

Governor of the Province of Corrientes: Dr HORACIO RICARDO COLOMBI.

Governor of the Province of Entre Ríos: Dr JORGE PEDRO BUSTI.

Governor of the Province of Formosa: Dr GILDO INSFRÁN.

Governor of the Province of Jujuy: Dr EDUARDO FELLNER.

Governor of the Province of La Pampa: Dr CARLOS VERNA.

Governor of the Province of La Rioja: Dr ANGEL EDUARDO MAZA.

Governor of the Province of Mendoza: JULIO CÉSAR CLETO COBOS.

Governor of the Province of Misiones: CARLOS EDUARDO ROVIRA.

Governor of the Province of Neuquén: JORGE OMAR SOBISCH.

Governor of the Province of Río Negro: Dr MIGUEL SAIZ.

Governor of the Province of Salta: Dr JUAN CARLOS ROMERO.

Governor of the Province of San Juan: Dr JOSÉ LUIS GIOJA.

Governor of the Province of San Luis: Dr ALBERTO RODRÍGUEZ SÁA.

Governor of the Province of Santa Cruz: SERGIO ACEVEDO.

Governor of the Province of Santa Fe: Dr JORGE OBEID.

Governor of the Province of Santiago del Estero: GERARDO ZAMORA.

Governor of the Province of Tucumán: JOSÉ JORGE ALPEROVICH.

Governor of the Territory of Tierra del Fuego: Dr MARIO JORGE COLAZO.

Political Organizations

Acción por la República (AR): Buenos Aires; e-mail accionrepublica@geocities.com; internet www.ar-partido.com.ar; f. 1997; right-wing; Pres. CÉSAR ALBRISI; Sec.-Gen. ALFREDO CASTAÑÓN.

Alternativa por una República de Iguales (ARI): Buenos Aires; e-mail ; internet www.ari.org.ar; f. 2001; progressive party; Leader ELISA CARRIÓ.

Corriente Patria Libre: Humberto Iº 542, Buenos Aires; tel. (11) 4307-3724; e-mail sitio@patrialibre.org.ar; internet www.patrialibre.org.ar/local.htm; f. 1987; nationalist and left-wing.

Frente para el Cambio: Buenos Aires; Leader ALICIA CASTRO.

Frepaso (Frente País Solidario): Buenos Aires; tel. (11) 4370-7100; e-mail frepaso@sion.com; internet www.frepaso.org.ar; f. 1994; centre-left coalition of socialist, communist and Christian Democrat groups; Leader CARLOS ALVAREZ.

Movimiento por la Dignidad y la Independencia (Modin): Buenos Aires; e-mail modin@causa.zzn.com; internet www.geocities.com/CapitolHill/Parliament/9268/modin.htm; f. 1991; right-wing; Leader Col ALDO RICO.

Movimiento de Integración y Desarrollo (MID): Buenos Aires; e-mail midinterior@mid.org.ar; internet http://www.mid.org.ar/; f. 1963; Leader CARLOS ZAFFORE; 145,000 mems.

Movimiento al Socialismo (MAS): Chile 1362, 1098 Buenos Aires; tel. (11) 4381-2718; fax (11) 4381-2976; e-mail masarg@arnet.com.ar; internet www.mas.org.ar; Leaders RUBÉN VISCONTI, LUIS ZAMORA; 55,000 mems.

Nueva Dirigencia (ND): Buenos Aires; internet www.nuevadirigencia.org.ar; f. 1996; centre-right; Leader GUSTAVO BÉLIZ.

Partido Comunista de Argentina: Buenos Aires; e-mail central@pca.org.ar; internet www.pca.org.ar; f. 1918; Leader PATRICIO ECHEGARAY; Sec.-Gen. ATHOS FAVA; 76,000 mems.

Partido Demócrata Cristiano (PDC): Combate de los Pozos 1055, 1222 Buenos Aires; tel. (11) 4305-1229; fax (11) 4306-8242; e-mail democracia_cristiana@fibertel.com.ar; internet www.pdca.org.ar; f. 1954; Leader ROBERTO PABLO MEYER; 85,000 mems.

Partido Demócrata Progresista (PDP): Chile 1934, 1227 Buenos Aires; internet www.demoprogresista.org.ar; Gen. Sec. Dr ALBERTO NATALE; c. 100,000 mems.

Partido Federal: Buenos Aires; internet www.federal.org.ar; f. 1973; Pres. Dr MARTÍN BORELLI.

Partido Intransigente: Buenos Aires; e-mail nacional@pi.org.ar; internet www.pi.org.ar; f. 1957; left-wing; Leaders Dr OSCAR ALENDE, LISANDRO VIALE; Sec. MARIANO LORENCES; 90,000 mems.

Partido Justicialista (PJ): Buenos Aires; internet www.pj.org.ar; Peronist party; f. 1945; Pres. EDUARDO FELLNER; Leader ALBERTO FERNÁNDEZ; 3m. mems; three factions within party contested the 2003 presidential elections.

    Frente por la Libertad/Unión del Centro Democrático: Presidential Candidate CARLOS SAÚL MENEM.

    Frente del Movimiento Popular/Partido Unión y Libertad: Presidential Candidate ADOLFO RODRÍGUEZ SÁA.

    Frente para la Victoria: Presidential Candidate NÉSTOR CARLOS KIRCHNER.

Partido Memoria y Movilización Social: Buenos Aires; f. 2003; left-wing; mem. of the Mesa Coordinadora para un Nuevo Proyecto Nacional; Pres. EDUARDO LUIS DUHALDE.

Partido Nacional de Centro: Buenos Aires; f. 1980; conservative; Leader RAÚL RIVANERA CARLES.

Partido Nuevo Triunfo (PNT): Buenos Aires; e-mail pnt@libreopinion.com; internet pnt.libreopinion.com; f. 1990 as Partido de los Trabajadores; illegal extremist right-wing group; Pres. ALEJANDRO CARLOS BIONDINI; Vice-Pres. JORGE CASÓLIBA.

Partido Obrero: Ayacucho 444, Buenos Aires; tel. (11) 4953-3824; fax (11) 4953-7164; internet www.po.org.ar; f. 1982; Trotskyist; Leaders JORGE ALTAMIRA, CHRISTIAN RATH; 61,000 mems.

Partido Popular Cristiano (PPC): Entre Ríos; internet www.partidopopularcris.com.ar; Leader JOSÉ ANTONIO ALLENDE.

Partido Recrear para el Crecimiento (RECREAR): Buenos Aires; internet www.recrearargentina.org; contested 2003 elections as Movimiento Federal para Recrear el Crecimiento, in alliance with several provincial parties; Pres. RICARDO LÓPEZ MURPHY; Vice-Pres. JOSÉ MARÍA LLADÓS; Sec. RICARDO URQUIZA.

Partido de la Revolución Democrática (PRD): Buenos Aires; internet www.bonassoprd.com.ar; f. 2001; left-wing; mem. of the Mesa Coordinadora para un Nuevo Proyecto Nacional; Leader MIGUEL BONASSO.

Partido Socialista: Buenos Aires; f. 2003, following merger of the Partido Socialista Democrático and the Partido Socialista Popular.

Partido Socialista Auténtico: Sarandi 56, Buenos Aires; tel. and fax (11) 4952-3103; e-mail psacomitenacional@espeedy.com.ar; internet webs.psa.org.ar; f. 1896; Sec.-Gen. MARIO MAZZITELLI.

Partido Unidad Federalista (PaUFe): Buenos Aires; e-mail mlisa@unidadfederalista.org.ar; internet www.paufe.org.ar; Leader LUIS ABELARDO PATTI.

Polo Social: Echeverría 441, 1878 Quilmes, Buenos Aires; tel. and fax (11) 4253-0971; e-mail polosocial@cscom.com.ar; internet polosocial.agruparnos.com.ar; f. 1999; mem. of the Mesa Coordinadora para un Nuevo Proyecto Nacional; Leader FRANCISCO ('BARBA') GUTIÉRREZ.

Unión del Centro Democrático (UCeDé): Buenos Aires; f. 1980 as coalition of eight minor political organizations; Leader CARLOS CASTELLANI.

Unión Cívica Radical (UCR): Alsina 1786, 1088 Buenos Aires; tel. and fax (11) 4375-2000; e-mail info@ucr.org.ar; internet www.ucr.org.ar; moderate; f. 1890; Pres. ANGEL ROZAS; Sec.-Gen. GERARDO MORALES; 2.9m. mems.

Unión para la Nueva Mayoría: Buenos Aires; f. 1986; centre-right; Leader JOSÉ ANTONIO ROMERO FERIS.

The following political parties and groupings also contested the 2003 legislative elections: Alianza Nuevo Espacio Entrerriano, Autodeterminación y Libertad, Compromiso para el Cambio, Cruzada Renovadora de San Juan, Demócrata Mendoza, Demócrata Progresista, FISCAL—Mendoza, Frente Alternativa Pampeana, Frente Cívico Jujeño, Frente Cívico y Social de Catamarca, Frente Grande, Frente Nuevo, Frente Popular Bonaerense (Frepobo), Frente Renovador, Frente de Unidad Provincial, Fuerza Porteña, Fuerza Republicana, Izquierda Unida, Movimiento Multisectorial de Trabajo y la Autodeterminación, Movimiento Popular Neuquino, Nuevo Buenos Aires, Proyecto Corrientes, Radical Independiente, Radical Rionegrino, Renovador de Salta, Unión por la Argentina and Vecinalista-Partido Nuevo.

OTHER ORGANIZATIONS

Asociación Madres de Plaza de Mayo: Hipólito Yrigoyen 1584, 1089 Buenos Aires; tel. (11) 4383-0377 ; fax (11) 4954-0381; e-mail madres@satlink.com; internet www.madres.org; f. 1979; formed by mothers of those who 'disappeared' during the years of military rule, it has since become a broad-based grouping with revolutionary socialist aims; Founder and Leader HEBE MARÍA PASTOR DE BONAFINI.

Mesa Coordinadora para un Nuevo Proyecto Nacional: Buenos Aires; f. Oct. 2004; umbrella org. comprising various left-wing parties and *piquetero* groupings, including.

Federación de Tierra y Vivienda (FTV): e-mail ftv@cta.org.ar; moderate grouping; Leader LUIS D'ELIA.

Frente Transversal Nacional y Popular: Leader EDGARDO DEPETRI.

Movimiento Barrios de Pie: moderate grouping; Leader JORGE CEBALLOS.

Movimiento de Trabajadores Desocupados 'Evita' (MTD Evita): Leader EMILIO PÉRSICO.

Partido Memoria y Movilización Social: see Political Organizations.

Partido de la Revolución Democrática (PRD): see Political Organizations.

Polo Social: see Political Organizations.

Other *piquetero* groupings include:

Bloque Piquetero Nacional.

Corriente Clasista y Combativa (CCC): e-mail info@cccargentina.org.ar; internet www.cccargentina.org.ar; radical grouping; Leader CARLOS 'PERRO' SANTILLÁN.

Movimiento Independientes de Jubilados y Descocupados (MIJD): radical grouping; Leader RAÚL CASTELLS.

Movimiento Social de Trabajadores Teresa Rodríguez: Leguizamón 2570, Mar de Plata; tel. (223) 487-9931; e-mail noticias@elteresa.org.ar; internet www.elteresa.org.ar; f. 1996, Movimiento de Trabajadores Desocupados; adopted present name in 1997; extreme left-wing.

Movimiento de Trabajadores Desocupados 'Aníbal Verón' (MTD Aníbal Verón): tel. (11) 15-5489-1374.

Movimiento sin Trabajo—Teresa Vive (MST—TV): radical grouping; Leader GUSTAVO GIMÉNEZ.

Polo Obero: Leader NÉSTOR PITROLA.

Diplomatic Representation

EMBASSIES IN ARGENTINA

Albania: Avda del Libertador 946, 4°, 1001 Buenos Aires; tel. (11) 4812-8366; fax (11) 4815-2512; e-mail ambasada.bue@fibertel.com.ar; Ambassador EDMOND TRAKO.

Algeria: Montevideo 1889, 1021 Buenos Aires; tel. (11) 4815-1271; fax (11) 4815-8837; e-mail argelia@peoples.com.ar; Ambassador NOURREDINE AYADI.

Angola: Buenos Aires; Ambassador FERNANDO DITO.

Armenia: Avda Roque S. Peña 570, 3°, 1035 Buenos Aires; tel. (11) 4816-8710; fax (11) 4812-2803; e-mail armenia@fibertel.com.ar; Ambassador ARA AIVAZIAN.

Australia: Villanueva 1400, 1426 Buenos Aires; tel. (11) 4779-3500; fax (11) 4779-3585; e-mail info.bageneral@dfat.gov.au; internet www.argentina.embassy.gov.au; Ambassador SHARYN MINAHAN.

Austria: French 3671, 1425 Buenos Aires; tel. (11) 4802-1400; fax (11) 4805-4016; e-mail botschaft@austria.org.ar; internet www.austria.org.ar; Ambassador GUDRUN GRAF.

Belarus: Cazadores 2166, 1428 Buenos Aires; tel. (11) 4788-9394; fax (11) 4788-2322; e-mail argentina@belembassy.org; Ambassador VADIM IVANOVICH LAZERKO.

Belgium: Defensa 113, 8°, 1065 Buenos Aires; tel. (11) 4331-0066; fax (11) 4311-0814; e-mail buenosaires@diplobel.org; internet www.diplobel.org/argentina; Ambassador KOENRAAD ROUVROY.

Bolivia: Avda Corrientes 545, 2°, 1043 Buenos Aires; tel. (11) 4394-6042; fax (11) 5217-1070; Ambassador ARTURO LIEBERS BALDIVIESO.

Bosnia and Herzegovina: Miñones 2445, Buenos Aires; tel. (11) 4896-0284; fax (11) 4896-0351; Ambassador DUŠKO LADAN.

Brazil: Cerrito 1350, 1010 Buenos Aires; tel. (11) 4515-2400; fax (11) 4515-2401; e-mail embras@embrasil.org.ar; internet www.brasil.org.ar; Ambassador MAURO VIEIRA.

Bulgaria: Mariscal A. J. de Sucre 1568, 1428 Buenos Aires; tel. (11) 4781-8644; fax (11) 4786-6273; e-mail embular@sinectis.com.ar; internet www.sinectis.com.ar/u/embular; Ambassador ATRANAS I. BUDEV.

Canada: Tagle 2828, 1425 Buenos Aires; tel. (11) 4808-1000; fax (11) 4808-1111; internet www.dfait-maeci.gc.ca/bairs; e-mail bairs-webmail@dfait-maeci.gc.ca; Ambassador YVES GAGNON.

Chile: Tagle 2762, 1425 Buenos Aires; tel. (11) 4802-7020; fax (11) 4804-5927; e-mail data@embajadadechile.com.ar; internet www.embajadadechile.com.ar; Ambassador LUIS MAIRA AGUIRRE.

China, People's Republic: Avda Crisólogo Larralde 5349, 1431 Buenos Aires; tel. (11) 4543-8862; fax (11) 4545-1141; Ambassador KE XIAOGANG.

Colombia: Carlos Pellegrini 1363, 3°, 1010 Buenos Aires; tel. (11) 4325-0258; fax (11) 4322-9370; e-mail ebaires@minrelext.gov.co ; internet www.embajadacolombia.int.ar; Ambassador RODRIGO ERNESTO HOLGUÍN LOURIDO.

Congo, Democratic Republic: Callao 322, 2°, Buenos Aires; tel. (11) 4373-7565; fax (11) 4374-9865; Chargé d'affaires a.i. YEMBA LOHAKA.

Costa Rica: Avda Santa Fe 1460, 3°I, 2023 Buenos Aires; tel. (11) 4815-0072; fax (11) 4814-1660; e-mail embarica@ifibertel.com.ar; Ambassador EDUARDO FRANCISCO OTOYA BOULANGER.

Croatia: Gorostiaga 2104, 1426 Buenos Aires; tel. (11) 4777-6409; fax (11) 4777-9159; e-mail embajadadecroacia@velocom.com.ar; Ambassador RIKARD ROSSETTI.

Cuba: Virrey del Pino 1810, 1426 Buenos Aires; tel. (11) 4782-9049; fax (11) 4786-7713; e-mail embcuba@arnet.com.ar; Ambassador ALEJANDRO GONZÁLEZ GALIANO.

Czech Republic: Junín 1461, 1113 Buenos Aires; tel. (11) 4807-3107; fax (11) 4807-3109; e-mail buenosaires@embassy.mzv.cz; internet www.mfa.cz/buenosaires; Ambassador FRANTIŠEK PADĚLEK.

Dominican Republic: Avda Santa Fe 830, 7°, 1059 Buenos Aires; tel. (11) 4312-9378; fax (11) 4894-2078; Ambassador RAFAEL CALVENTI.

Ecuador: Presidente Quintana 585, 9° y 10°, 1129 Buenos Aires; tel. (11) 4804-0073; fax (11) 4804-0074; e-mail embecuador@embecuador.com.ar; Ambassador Dr JOSÉ RAFAEL SERRANO HERRERA.

Egypt: Virrey del Pino 3140, 1426 Buenos Aires; tel. (11) 4553-3311; fax (11) 4553-0067; e-mail embegypt@fibertel.com.ar; Ambassador HAZEM MOHAMED TAHER ELSAED.

El Salvador: Esmeralda 1066, 7°, 1059 Buenos Aires; tel. (11) 4311-1864; fax (11) 4314-7628; Ambassador RAFAEL ALFONSO QUIÑÓNEZ MEZA.

Finland: Avda Santa Fe 846, 5°, 1059 Buenos Aires; tel. (11) 4312-0600; fax (11) 4312-0670; e-mail sanomat.bue@formin.fi; internet www.finembue.com.ar; Ambassador RISTO KAARLO VELTHEIM.

France: Cerrito 1399, 1010 Buenos Aires; tel. (11) 4515-2930; fax (11) 4515-0120; e-mail ambafr@abaconet.com.ar; internet www.embafrancia-argentina.org; Ambassador FRANCIS LOTT.

Germany: Villanueva 1055, 1426 Buenos Aires; tel. (11) 4778-2500; fax (11) 4778-2550; e-mail administracion@embajada-alemana.org.ar; internet www.embajada-alemana.org.ar; Ambassador Dr ROLF SCHUMACHER.

Greece: Arenales 1658, 1061 Buenos Aires; tel. (11) 4811-4811; fax (11) 4816-2600; e-mail gremb.bay@mfa.gr; Ambassador COGEVINAS ALEXIOS.

Guatemala: Avda Santa Fe 830, 5°, 1059 Buenos Aires; tel. (11) 4313-9160; fax (11) 4313-9181; e-mail embargentina@minex.gob.gt; Ambassador (vacant).

Haiti: Avda Figueroa Alcorta 3297, 1425 Buenos Aires; tel. (11) 4802-0211; fax (11) 4802-3984; e-mail embahaiti@interar.com.ar; Ambassador JEAN-VICTOR GENEUS.

Holy See: Avda Alvear 1605, 1014 Buenos Aires; tel. (11) 4813-9697; fax (11) 4815-4097; Apostolic Nuncio Most Rev. ADRIANO BERNARDINI (Titular Archbishop of Faleri).

Honduras: Avda Libertador 1146, 1112 Buenos Aires; tel. (11) 4804-6181; fax (11) 4804-3222; e-mail honduras@ciudad.com.ar; Ambassador NAPOLEÓN ALVAREZ ALVARADO.

India: Córdoba 950, 4°, 1054 Buenos Aires; tel. (11) 4393-4001; fax (11) 4393-4063; e-mail indemb@indembarg.org.ar; internet www.indembarg.org.ar; Ambassador RINZING WANGDI.

Indonesia: Mariscal Ramón Castilla 2901, 1425 Buenos Aires; tel. (11) 4807-2211; fax (11) 4802-4448; e-mail emindo@tournet.com.ar; internet www.indonesianembassy.org.ar; Ambassador MAX PANGEMANAN.

Iran: Avda Figueroa Alcorta 3229, 1425 Buenos Aires; tel. (11) 4802-1470; fax (11) 4805-4409; Chargé d'affaires a.i. MUHAMMAD ALI TABATABAEI HASAN.

Ireland: Avda del Libertador 1068, 6°, 1112 Buenos Aires; tel. (11) 5787-0801; fax (11) 5787-0802; e-mail info@irlanda.org.ar; internet www.irlanda.org.ar; Ambassador MÁIRTÍN Ó FAININ.

Israel: Avda de Mayo 701, 10°, 1084 Buenos Aires; tel. (11) 4338-2500; internet www.israel-embassy.org.ar/embajada.html; Ambassador RAFAEL ELDAD.

Italy: Billinghurst 2577, 1425 Buenos Aires; tel. (11) 4802-0071; fax (11) 4804-4914; e-mail ambitalia@ambitalia-bsas.org.ar; internet www.ambitalia-bsas.org.ar; Ambassador ROBERTO NIGIDO.

Japan: Bouchard 547, 17°, 1106 Buenos Aires; tel. (11) 4318-8200; fax (11) 4318-8210; e-mail taishikan@japan.org.ar; internet www.ar.emb-japan.go.jp; Ambassador SHINYA NAGAI.

Korea, Republic: Avda del Libertador 2395, 1425 Buenos Aires; tel. (11)4802-8865; fax (11) 4803-6993 ; e-mail argentina@mofat.go.kr; internet www.embcorea.org.ar; Ambassador YANG-BOO CHOE.

Kuwait: Uruguay 739, 1015 Buenos Aires; tel. (11) 4374-7202; fax (11) 4374-8718; e-mail kuwait@microstar.com.ar; internet www.kuwait.com.ar; Ambassador ALI HUSSAIN AS-SAMMAK.

Lebanon: Avda del Libertador 2354, 1425 Buenos Aires; tel. (11) 4802-4492; fax (11) 4802-2909; e-mail embajada@ellibano.com.ar; Ambassador HICHAM SALIM HAMDAN.

Libya: 3 de Febrero 1358/62, 1426 Buenos Aires; tel. (11) 4788-3760; fax (11) 4784-9895; Chargé d'affaires a.i. Dr ALI Y. GUIMA BEN GUIMA.

Malaysia: Villanueva 1040-1048, 1062 Buenos Aires; tel. (11) 4776-0504; e-mail mwbaires@cvtci.com.ar; Ambassador Dato MOHD ROZE'RADZI ABDUL RAHMAN.

Mexico: Arcos 1650, Belgrano, 1426 Buenos Aires; tel. (11) 4789-8800; fax (11) 4789-8836; internet www.embamex.int.ar; Chargé d'affaires a.i. EDUARDO MARTÍNEZ CURIEL.

Netherlands: Edif. Porteño II, Olga Cossenttini 831, 3°, 1107 Buenos Aires; tel. (11) 4338-0050 ; fax (11) 4338-0060; e-mail bue@minbuza.nl; internet www.embajadaholanda.int.ar; Ambassador ROBERT JAN VAN HOUTUM.

New Zealand: Carlos Pellegrine 1427, 5°, 1010; Buenos Aires; tel. (11) 4328-0747; fax (11) 4328-0757; e-mail kiwiargentina@datamarkets.com.ar; internet www.nzembassy.com/argentina; Ambassador CARL ROBINSON WORKER.

Nicaragua: Callao 1564, 1°, Of. A, 1024 Buenos Aires; tel. (11) 4807-0260; fax (11) 4806-1221; e-mail embanic@fibertel.com.ar; Ambassador SILVIO AVILEZ GALLO.

Nigeria: Juez Estrada 2746, 1425 Buenos Aires; tel. (11) 4808-9245; fax (11) 4807-6423; Ambassador ANTHONY ADEYEMI SEKUDO.

Norway: Esmeralda 909, 3°B, 1007 Buenos Aires; tel. (11) 4312-2204; fax (11) 4315-2831; e-mail emb.buenosaires@mfa.no; internet www.noruega.org.ar; Ambassador GUNNAR H. LINDEMAN.

Pakistan: Gorostiaga 2176, 1426 Buenos Aires; tel. (11) 4775-1294; fax (11) 4776-1186; e-mail parepbaires@sinectis.com.ar; Ambassador MOHAMMAD NISAR.

Panama: Avda Santa Fe 1461, 1°, 1060 Buenos Aires; tel. (11) 4811-1254; fax (11) 4814-0450; e-mail epar@fibertel.com.ar; internet www.embajadadepanama.com.ar; Ambassador MANUEL ORESTES NIETO.

Paraguay: Avda Las Heras 2545, 1425 Buenos Aires; tel. (11) 4802-3826; fax (11) 4801-0657; Ambassador (vacant).

Peru: Avda del Libertador 1720, 1425 Buenos Aires; tel. (11) 4802-2000; fax (11) 4802-5887; e-mail embperu@arnet.com.ar; Ambassador Dr MARTÍN BELAÚNDE MOREYRA.

Philippines: Mariscal Ramón Castilla 3075/3085, 1425 Buenos Aires; tel. (11) 4807-3334 ; fax (11) 4804-1595; e-mail phba@peoples.com.ar; Ambassador GEORGE B. REYES.

Poland: Alejandro M. de Aguado 2870, 1425 Buenos Aires; tel. (11) 4802-9681; fax (11) 4802-9683; e-mail polemb@datamarkets.com.ar; Ambassador SLAWOMIR RATAJSKI.

Portugal: Maipú 942, 17°, 1340 Buenos Aires; tel. (11) 4312-0187; fax (11) 4311-2586; Ambassador ANTONIO CARLOS CARVALHO DE ALMEIDA RIVERO.

Romania: Arroyo 962-970, 1007 Buenos Aires; tel. and fax (11) 4326-5888; fax 4322-2630; e-mail embarombue@rumania.org.ar; internet www.roemb.com.ar; Ambassador ALEXANDRU VICTOR MICULA.

Russia: Rodríguez Peña 1741, 1021 Buenos Aires; tel. (11) 4813-1552; fax (11) 4812-1794; Ambassador YEVGENII M. ASTAKHOV.

Saudi Arabia: Alejandro M. de Aguado 2881, 1425 Buenos Aires; tel. (11) 4802-3375; fax (11) 4806-1581; e-mail embasaudita@fibertel.com.ar; internet www.embajadasaudi.org; Ambassador ADNAN BIN ABDULLAH BAGHDADI.

Serbia and Montenegro: Marcelo T. de Alvear 1705, 1060 Buenos Aires; tel. (11) 4812-9133; fax (11) 4812-1070; e-mail yuembaires@ciudad.com.ar; Ambassador IVAN SAVELJIĆ.

Slovakia: Avda Figueroa Alcorta 3240, 1425 Buenos Aires; tel. (11) 4801-3917; fax (11) 4801-4654; e-mail embsl@fibertel.com.ar; Ambassador VLADIMIR GRACZ.

Slovenia: Santa Fe 846, 6°, 1059 Buenos Aires; tel. (11) 4894-0621; fax (11) 4312-8410; e-mail vba@mzz-dkp.gov.si; Ambassador BOJAN GROBOVŠEK.

South Africa: Marcelo T. de Alvear 590, 8°, 1058 Buenos Aires; tel. (11) 4317-2900; fax (11) 4317-2951; e-mail embasa@ciudad.com.ar; internet www.sudafrica.org.ar; Ambassador Prof. MLUNGIS WASHINGTON MAKALIMA.

Spain: Mariscal Ramón Castilla 2720, 1425 Buenos Aires; tel. (11) 4802-6031; fax (11) 4802-0719; Ambassador CARMELO ANGULO BARTUREN.

Sweden: Casilla 3599, Correo Central 1000, Buenos Aires; tel. (11) 4329-0800; fax (11) 4342-1697; e-mail ambassaden.buenos-aires@foreign.ministery.ce; Ambassador MADELEINE STRÖJE-WILKENS.

Switzerland: Avda Santa Fe 846, 10°, 1059 Buenos Aires; tel. (11) 4311-6491; fax (11) 4313-2998; e-mail vertretung@bue.rep.admin.ch; internet www.eda.admin.ch/buenosaires_emb/s/home.html; Ambassador DANIEL VON MURALT.

Syria: Calloa 956, 1023 Buenos Aires; tel. (11) 4813-2113; fax (11) 4814-3211; Ambassador RIYAD SNEIH.

Thailand: Federico Lacroze 2158, 1426 Buenos Aires; tel. (11) 4774-4415; fax (11) 4773-2447; e-mail thaiembargen@fibertel.com.ar; Ambassador ASIPHOL CHABCHITRCHAIDOL.

Tunisia: Ciudad de la Paz 3086, 1429 Buenos Aires; tel. (11) 4544-2618; fax (11) 4545-6369; e-mail atbuenosaires@infovia.com.ar; Ambassador HAMIDA MRABET LABIDI.

Turkey: 11 de Setiembre 1382, 1426 Buenos Aires; tel. (11) 4788-3239; fax (11) 4784-9179; e-mail turquia@fibertel.com.ar; Ambassador SUKRU TUFAN.

Ukraine: Lafinur 3057, 1425 Buenos Aires; tel. (11) 4552-0657; fax (11) 4552-6771; e-mail embucra@embucra.com.ar; internet www.embucra.com.ar; Ambassador OLEKSANDR NYKONENKO.

United Kingdom: Dr Luis Agote 2412, 1425 Buenos Aires; tel. (11) 4808-2200; fax (11) 4808-2274; e-mail askinformation.baires@fco.gov.uk; internet www.britain.org.ar; Ambassador Dr JOHN HUGHES.

USA: Avda Colombia 4300, 1425 Buenos Aires; tel. (11) 5777-4533; fax (11) 5777-4240; internet buenosaires.usembassy.gov; Ambassador LINO GUTIÉRREZ.

Uruguay: Avda Las Heras 1907, 1128 Buenos Aires; tel. (11) 4803-6030; fax (11) 4807-3050; e-mail webmaster@embajadauruguay.com; internet www.embajadadeluruguay.com.ar; Ambassador ALBERTO C. VOLONTÉ BERRO.

Venezuela: Virrey Loreto 2035, 1428 Buenos Aires; tel. (11) 4788-4944; fax (11) 4784-4311; e-mail embaven@arnet.com.ar; internet www.la-embajada.com.ar; Ambassador FREDDY BALZÁN MORREL.

Viet Nam: 11 de Septiembre 1442, 1426 Buenos Aires; tel. (11) 4783-1802; fax (11) 4782-0078; e-mail sovnartn@teletel.com.ar; Ambassador DIEN NGUYEN NGOC.

Judicial System

SUPREME COURT

Corte Suprema

Talcahuano 550, 4°, 1013 Buenos Aires; tel. (11) 4370-4600; fax (11) 440-2270; e-mail albinogomez@cjsn.gov.ar; internet www.csjn.gov .ar.

The nine members of the Supreme Court are appointed by the President, with the agreement of at least two-thirds of the Senate. Members are dismissed by impeachment.

President: ENRIQUE SANTIAGO PETRACCHI.

Vice-President: AUGUSTO CÉSAR BELLUSCIO.

Justices: EUGENIO RAÚL ZAFFARONI, AUGUSTO CÉSAR BELLUSCIO, ENRIQUE SANTIAGO PETRACCHI, ANTONIO BOGGIANO, RICARDO LORENZETTI, JUAN CARLOS MAQUEDA, CARLOS S. FAYT, ELENA I. HIGHTON DE NOLASCO, one vacancy.

OTHER COURTS

Judges of the lower, national or further lower courts are appointed by the President, with the agreement of the Senate, and are dismissed by impeachment. From 1999, however, judges were to retire on reaching 75 years of age.

The Federal Court of Appeal in Buenos Aires has three courts: civil and commercial, criminal, and administrative. There are six other courts of appeal in Buenos Aires: civil, commercial, criminal, peace, labour, and penal-economic. There are also federal appeal courts in: La Plata, Bahía Blanca, Paraná, Rosario, Córdoba, Mendoza, Tucumán and Resistencia. In August 1994, following constitutional amendments, the Office of the Attorney-General was established as an independent entity and a Council of Magistrates was envisaged. In December 1997 the Senate adopted legislation to create the Council.

The provincial courts each have their own Supreme Court and a system of subsidiary courts. They deal with cases originating within and confined to the provinces.

Attorney-General: ESTEBÁN RIGHI.

Religion

CHRISTIANITY

Some 92% of the population are nominally Roman Catholics and about 2% belong to other Christian denominations.

Federación Argentina de Iglesias Evangélicas (Argentine Federation of Evangelical Churches): José María Moreno 873, 1424 Buenos Aires; tel. and fax (11) 4922-5356; e-mail presidencia@faie .com.ar; internet www.faie.org.ar; f. 1938; 29 mem. churches; Pres. Rev. EMILIO MONTI (Methodist Evangelical Church); Exec. Sec. Rev. FLORENCIA HIMITIAN.

The Roman Catholic Church

Argentina comprises 14 archdioceses, 50 dioceses (including one each for Uniate Catholics of the Ukrainian rite, of the Maronite rite and of the Armenian rite) and three territorial prelatures. The Archbishop of Buenos Aires is also the Ordinary for Catholics of Oriental rites, and the Bishop of San Gregorio de Narek en Buenos Aires is also the Apostolic Exarch of Latin America and Mexico for Catholics of the Armenian rite.

Bishops' Conference: Conferencia Episcopal Argentina, Suipacha 1034, 1008 Buenos Aires; tel. (11) 4328-0993; fax (11) 4328-9570; e-mail seccea@cea.org.ar; internet www.cea.org.ar; f. 1959; Pres. Mgr EDUARDO VICENTE MIRÁS (Archbishop of Rosario).

Armenian Rite

Bishop of San Gregorio de Narek en Buenos Aires: VARTAN WALDIR BOGHOSSIAN, Charcas 3529, 1425 Buenos Aires; tel. (11) 4824-1613; fax (11) 4827-1975; e-mail exarmal@pcn.net; internet fast.to/ exarcado.

Latin Rite

Archbishop of Bahía Blanca: GUILLERMO JOSÉ GARLATTI, Avda Colón 164, 8000 Bahía Blanca; tel. (291) 455-0707; fax (291) 452-2070; e-mail arzobispado@bblanca.com.ar.

Archbishop of Buenos Aires: Cardinal JORGE BERGOGLIO, Rivadavia 415, 1002 Buenos Aires; tel. (11) 4343-0812; fax (11) 4334-8373; e-mail arzobispado@arzbaires.org.ar.

Archbishop of Córdoba: CARLOS JOSÉ NÁÑEZ, Hipólito Irigoyen 98, 5000 Córdoba; tel. (351) 422-1015; fax (351) 422-1015; e-mail cararzcba@arnet.com.ar.

Archbishop of Corrientes: DOMINGO SALVADOR CASTAGNA, 9 de Julio 1543, 3400 Corrientes; tel. and fax (3783) 422436; e-mail arzctes@ arnet.com.ar.

Archbishop of La Plata: HÉCTOR AGUER, Calle 14, 1009, 1900 La Plata; tel. (221) 425-1656; e-mail cancillerialp@infovia.com.ar; internet www.arzolap.org.ar.

Archbishop of Mendoza: JOSÉ MARÍA ARANCIBIA, Catamarca 98, 5500 Mendoza; tel. (261) 423-3862; fax (261) 429-5415; e-mail arzobispadomza@supernet.com.ar.

Archbishop of Mercedes-Luján: RUBÉN HÉCTOR DI MONTE, Calle 22, No 745, 6600 Mercedes, Buenos Aires; tel. (2324) 432-412; fax (2324) 432-104; e-mail arzomerce@yahoo.com.

Archbishop of Paraná: MARIO LUIS BAUTISTA MAULIÓN, Monte Caseros 77, 3100 Paraná; tel. (343) 431-1440; fax (343) 423-0372; e-mail arzparan@satlink.com.ar.

Archbishop of Resistencia: CARMELO JUAN GIAQUINTA, Bartolomé Mitre 363, Casilla 35, 3500 Resistencia; tel. and fax (3722) 441908; fax (3722) 434573; e-mail arzobrcia@lared.com.ar.

Archbishop of Rosario: EDUARDO VICENTE MIRÁS, Córdoba 1677, 2000 Rosario; tel. (341) 425-1298; fax (341) 425-1207; e-mail arzobros@lidernet.com.ar; internet www.delrosario.org.ar.

Archbishop of Salta: MARIO ANTONIO CARGNELLO, España 596, 4400 Salta; tel. (387) 421-4306; fax (387) 421-3101; e-mail arzobisposalta@infovia.com.ar.

Archbishop of San Juan de Cuyo: ALFONSO ROGELIO DELGADO EVERS, Bartolomé Mitre 250 Oeste, 5400 San Juan de Cuyo; tel. (264) 422-2578; fax (264) 427-3530; e-mail arzobispadosanjuan@infovia .com.ar.

Archbishop of Santa Fe de la Vera Cruz: JOSÉ MARÍA ARANCEDO, Avda General López 2720, 3000 Santa Fe; tel. (342) 459-1780; fax (342) 459-4491; e-mail curia@arquisantafe.org.ar.

Archbishop of Tucumán: LUIS HÉCTOR VILLALBA, Avda Sarmiento 895, 4000 San Miguel de Tucumán; tel. (381) 422-6345; fax (381) 431-0617; e-mail arztuc@arnet.com.ar.

Maronite Rite

Bishop of San Charbel en Buenos Aires: CHARBEL MERHI, Eparquía Maronita, Paraguay 834, 1057 Buenos Aires; tel. (11) 4311-7299; fax (11) 4312-8348; e-mail mcharbel@hotmail.com.

Ukrainian Rite

Bishop of Santa María del Patrocinio en Buenos Aires: Rt Rev. MIGUEL MYKYCEJ, Ramón L. Falcón 3950, Casilla 28, 1407 Buenos Aires; tel. (11) 4671-4192; fax (11) 4671-7265; e-mail pekrov@ciudad .com.ar.

The Anglican Communion

The Iglesia Anglicana del Cono Sur de América (Anglican Church of the Southern Cone of America) was formally inaugurated in Buenos Aires in April 1983. The Church comprises seven dioceses: Argentina, Northern Argentina, Chile, Paraguay, Peru, Bolivia and Uruguay. The Primate is the Bishop of Argentina.

Bishop of Argentina: Rt Rev. GREGORY VENABLES, 25 de Mayo 282, 1002 Buenos Aires; Casilla 4293, Correo Central 1000, Buenos Aires; tel. (11) 4342-4618; fax (11) 4331-0234; e-mail diocesisanglibue@arnet.com.ar.

Bishop of Northern Argentina: Rt Rev. MAURICE SINCLAIR, Casilla 187, 4400 Salta; tel. (387) 431-1718; fax (387) 431-2622; e-mail sinclair@salnet.com.ar; jurisdiction extends to Jujuy, Salta, Tucumán, Catamarca, Santiago del Estero, Formosa and Chaco.

Protestant Churches

Convención Evangélica Bautista Argentina (Baptist Evangelical Convention): Virrey Liniers 42, 1174 Buenos Aires; tel. and fax (11) 4864-2711; e-mail ceba@sion.com; f. 1909; Pres. CARLOS A. CARAMUTTI.

Iglesia Evangélica Congregacionalista (Evangelical Congregational Church): Perón 525, 3100 Paraná; tel. (43) 21-6172; f. 1924; 100 congregations, 8,000 mems, 24,000 adherents; Supt Rev. REYNOLDO HORSTT.

Iglesia Evangélica Luterana Argentina (Evangelical Lutheran Church of Argentina): Ing. Silveyra 1639-41, 1607 Villa Adelina, Buenos Aires; tel. (11) 4766-7948; fax (11) 4766-7948; f. 1905; 30,000 mems; Pres. WALDOMIRO MAILI.

Iglesia Evangélica del Río de la Plata (Evangelical Church of the River Plate): Mariscal Sucre 2855, 1428 DVY Buenos Aires; tel. (11) 4787-0436; fax (11) 4787-0335; e-mail presidente@ierp.org.ar; f. 1899; 25,000 mems; Pres. FEDERICO HUGO SCHÄFER.

Iglesia Evangélica Metodista Argentina (Methodist Church of Argentina): Rivadavia 4044, 3°, 1205 Buenos Aires; tel. (11) 4982-

3712; fax (11) 4981-0885; e-mail iema@iema.com.ar; internet www
.iema.com.ar; f. 1836; 6,040 mems, 9,000 adherents, seven regional
superintendents; Bishop Aldo M. Etchegoyen; Exec. Sec.-Gen.
Daniel A. Favaro.

JUDAISM

Delegación de Asociaciones Israelitas Argentinas (DAIA)
(Delegation of Argentine Jewish Associations): Pasteur 633, 7°, 1028
Buenos Aires; tel. and fax (11) 4378-3200; e-mail daia@daia.org.ar;
internet news.daia.org.ar; f. 1935; there are about 250,000 Jews in
Argentina, mostly in Buenos Aires; Pres. Dr Gilbert Lewi; Sec.-Gen.
Dr Julio Toker.

The Press

PRINCIPAL DAILIES

Buenos Aires

Ambito Financiero: Avda Paseo Colón 1196, 1063 Buenos Aires;
tel. (11) 4349-1500; fax (11) 4349-1505; e-mail correo@ambito.com
.ar; internet www.ambitoweb.com.ar; f. 1976; morning (Mon.–Fri.);
business; Dir Julio A. Ramos; circ. 115,000.

Buenos Aires Herald: Azopardo 455, 1107 Buenos Aires; tel. (11)
4342-1535; fax (11) 4334-7917; e-mail info@buenosairesherald.com;
internet www.buenosairesherald.com; f. 1876; English; morning;
independent; Editor-in-Chief Andrew Graham-Yooll; circ. 20,000.

Boletín Oficial de la República Argentina: Suipacha 767, 1008
Buenos Aires; tel. (11) 4322-3982; fax (11) 4322-3982; internet www
.boletinoficial.gov.ar; f. 1893; morning (Mon.–Fri.); official records
publication; Dir Jorge Eduardo Feijóo; circ. 15,000.

Clarín: Piedras 1743, 1140 Buenos Aires; tel. (11) 4309-7500; fax
(11) 4309-7559; internet www.clarin.com; f. 1945; morning; independent; Dir Ernestina L. Herrera de Noble; circ. 616,000 (daily),
1.0m. (Sunday).

Crónica: Avda Juan de Garay 40, 1063 Buenos Aires; tel. (11) 4361-
1001; fax (11) 4361-4237; f. 1963; morning and evening; Dirs Mario
Alberto Fernández (morning), Ricardo Gangeme (evening); circ.
330,000 (morning), 190,000 (evening), 450,000 (Sunday).

El Cronista: Honduras 5663, 1414 Buenos Aires; tel. (11) 4778-
6789; fax (11) 4778-6727; e-mail cronista@sadei.org.ar; f. 1908;
morning; Dir Néstor Scibona; circ. 65,000.

Diario Popular: Beguiristain 142, 1872 Sarandí, Avellaneda,
Buenos Aires; tel. (11) 4204-2778; fax (11) 4205-2376; f. 1974;
morning; Dir Alberto Albertengo; circ. 145,000.

La Gaceta: Beguiristain 182, 1870 Avellaneda, Buenos Aires; Dir
Ricardo West Ocampo; circ. 35,000.

La Nación: Bouchard 551, 1106 Buenos Aires; tel. (11) 4319-1600;
fax (11) 4319-1969; e-mail cescribano@lanacion.com.ar; internet
www.lanacion.com.ar; f. 1870; morning; independent; Dir Bartolomé
Mitre; circ. 184,000.

Página 12: Avda Belgrano 671, 1092 Buenos Aires; tel. (11) 6772-
4400; fax (11) 4334-2335; e-mail lectores@pagina12.com.ar; internet
www.pagina12.com.ar; f. 1987; morning; independent; Dir Ernesto
Tiffemberg; Editor Fernando Sokolowicz; circ. 280,000.

La Prensa: Azopardo 715, 1107 Buenos Aires; tel. (11) 4349-1000;
fax (11) 4349-1025; e-mail laprensa@interlink.com; internet www
.interlink.com.ar/laprensa; f. 1869; morning; independent; Dir Florencio Aldrey Iglesias; circ. 100,000.

La Razón: Río Cuarto 1242, 1168 Buenos Aires; tel. and fax (11)
4309-6000; e-mail larazon@arnet.com.ar; internet www.larazon.com
.ar; f. 1992; evening; Dir Oscar Magdalena; circ. 62,000.

El Sol: Hipólito Yrigoyen 122, Quilmes, 1878 Buenos Aires; tel. and
fax (11) 4257-6325; e-mail autalan@elsolquilmes.com.ar; internet
www.elsolquilmes.com.ar; f. 1927; Dir Luis Angel Autalán; circ.
25,000.

Tiempo Argentino: Buenos Aires; tel. (11) 428-1929; Editor Dr
Tomás Leona; circ. 75,000.

PRINCIPAL PROVINCIAL DAILIES

Catamarca

El Ancasti: Sarmiento 526, 1°, 4700 Catamarca; tel. and fax (3833)
431385; e-mail ancasti@satlink.com; f. 1988; morning; Dir Roque
Eduardo Molas; circ. 8,000.

Chaco

Norte: Carlos Pellegrini 744, 3500 Resistencia; tel. (3722) 428204;
fax (3722) 426047; f. 1968; Dir Miguel A. Fernández; circ. 14,000.

Chubut

Crónica: Impresora Patagónica, Namuncurá 122, 9000 Comodoro
Rivadavia; tel. (297) 447-1200; fax (297) 447-1780; f. 1962; morning;
Dir Dr Diego Joaquín Zamit; circ. 15,000.

Córdoba

Comercio y Justicia: Mariano Moreno 378, 5000 Córdoba; tel. and
fax (351) 422-0040; e-mail redaccion@comercioyjusticia.info; f. 1939;
morning; economic and legal news with periodic supplements on
architecture and administration; Pres. Eduardo Pogrobinki; Dir
Javier Alberto de Pascuale; circ. 5,800.

La Voz del Interior: Monseñor P. Cabrera 6080, 5008 Córdoba; tel.
(351) 4757000; fax (351) 4757247; e-mail lavoz@lavozdelinterior.com
.ar; internet www.lavozdelinterior.com.ar; f. 1904; morning; independent; Dir Dr Carlos Hugo Jornet; circ. 68,000.

Corrientes

El Litoral: Hipólito Yrigoyen 990, 3400 Corrientes; tel. and fax
(3783) 422227; internet www.corrientes.com.ar/el-litoral; f. 1960;
morning; Dir Carlos A. Romero Feris; circ. 25,000.

El Territorio: Avda Quaranta 4307, 3300 Posadas; tel. and fax
(3752) 452100; e-mail elterritorio@elterritorio.com.ar; internet www
.territoriodigital.com.ar; f. 1925; Dir Gonzalo Peltzer; circ. 22,000
(Mon.–Fri.), 28,000 (Sunday).

Entre Ríos

El Diario: Buenos Aires y Urquiza, 3100 Paraná; tel. (343) 423-
1000; fax (343) 431-9104; e-mail saer@satlink.com; internet www
.eldiario.com.ar; f. 1914; morning; Dir Dr Luis F. Etchevehere; circ.
25,000.

El Heraldo: Quintana 42, 3200 Concordia; tel. (345) 421-5304; fax
(345) 421-1397; e-mail heraldo@infovia.com.ar; internet www
.elheraldo.com.ar; f. 1915; evening; Editor Dr Carlos Liebermann;
circ. 10,000.

Mendoza

Los Andes: Avda San Martín 1049, 5500 Mendoza; tel. (261) 449-
1280; fax (261) 449-1217; e-mail havila@losandes.com.ar; internet
www.losandes.com.ar; f. 1982; morning; Dir Gerardo Heidel; circ.
60,000.

Provincia de Buenos Aires

El Atlántico: Bolívar 2975, 7600 Mar del Plata; tel. (223) 435462; f.
1938; morning; Dir Oscar Alberto Gastiarena; circ. 20,000.

La Capital: Avda Champagnat 2551, 7600 Mar del Plata; tel. (223)
478-8490; fax (223) 478-1038; e-mail diario@lacapitalnet.com.ar;
internet www.lacapitalnet.com.ar; f. 1905; Dir Florencio Aldrey
Iglesias; circ. 32,000.

El Día: Avda A. Diagonal 80, 817-21, 1900 La Plata; tel. (221) 425-
0101; fax (221) 423-2996; e-mail redaccion@eldia.com; f. 1884;
morning; independent; Dir Raúl E. Kraiselburd; circ. 54,868.

Ecos Diarios: Calle 62, No 2486, 7630 Necochea; tel. (2262) 430754;
fax (2262) 424114; e-mail ecosdiar@satlink.com; internet www
.ecosdiarios.com; f. 1921; morning; independent; Dir Guillermo
Ignacio; circ. 6,000.

La Nueva Provincia: Rodríguez 55, 8000 Bahía Blanca; tel. (291)
459-0000; fax (291) 459-0001; e-mail info@lanueva.com; internet
www.lanueva.com.ar; f. 1898; morning; independent; Dir Diana
Julio de Massot; circ. 22,000 (Mon.–Fri.), 30,000 (Sunday).

La Voz del Pueblo: Avda San Martín 991, 7500 Tres Arroyos; tel.
(2983) 430680; fax (2938) 430682; e-mail redaccion@lavozdelpueblo
.com.ar; f. 1902; morning; independent; Dir Alberto Jorge Maciel;
circ. 8,500.

Río Negro

Río Negro: 9 de Julio 733, 8332, Gen. Roca, Río Negro; tel. (2941)
439300; fax (2941) 430517; e-mail comentario@rionegro.com.ar;
internet www.rionegro.com.ar; f. 1912; morning; Editor Nélida Raj-
neri de Gamba.

Salta

El Tribuno: Avda Ex Combatientes de Malvinas 3890, 4400 Salta;
tel. (387) 424-0000; fax (387) 424-1382; e-mail redaccion@eltribuno
.com.ar; internet www.eltribuno.com.ar; f. 1949; morning; Dir Roberto Eduardo Romero; circ. 25,000.

San Juan

Diario de Cuyo: Mendoza 380 Sur, 5400 San Juan; tel. (264) 429-0038; fax (264) 429-0063; e-mail fbmontes@infovia.com.ar; f. 1947; morning; independent; Dir Francisco B. Montes; circ. 20,000.

San Luis

El Diario de La República: Lafinur 924, 5700 San Luis; tel. and fax (2623) 422037; e-mail paynesa@infovia.com.ar; internet www.eldiariodelarepublica.com; f. 1966; Dir-Gen. Feliciana Rodríguez Saa; circ. 12,000.

Santa Fe

La Capital: Sarmiento 763, 2000 Rosario; tel. (341) 420-1100; fax (341) 420-1114; e-mail elagos@lacapital.com.ar; f. 1867; morning; independent; Dir Carlos María Lagos; circ. 65,000.

El Litoral: Avda 25 de Mayo 3536, 3000 Santa Fe; tel. (342) 450-2500; fax (342) 450-2530; e-mail litoral@litoral.com.ar; internet www.litoral.com.ar; f. 1918; morning; independent; Dir Gustavo Vittori; circ. 37,000.

Santiago del Estero

El Liberal: Libertad 263, 4200 Santiago del Estero; tel. (385) 422-4400; fax (385) 422-4538; e-mail liberal@teletel.com.ar; internet www.sdnet.com.ar; f. 1898; morning; Exec. Dir José Luis Castiglione; Editorial Dir Dr Julio César Castiglione; circ. 20,000.

Tucumán

La Gaceta: Mendoza 654, 4000 San Miguel de Tucumán; tel. (381) 431-1111; fax (381) 431-1597; e-mail redaccion@lagaceta.com.ar; internet www.lagaceta.com.ar; f. 1912; morning; independent; Dir Alberto García Hamilton; circ. 70,000.

WEEKLY NEWSPAPER

El Informador Público: Uruguay 252, 3°F, 1015 Buenos Aires; tel. (11) 4476-3551; fax (11) 4342-2628; f. 1986.

PERIODICALS

Aeroespacio: Avda Dorrego 4019, Buenos Aires; tel. and fax (11) 4514-1561; fax (11) 4514-1662; e-mail info@aeroespacio.com.ar; internet www.aeroespacio.com.ar; f. 1940; every 2 months; aeronautics; Dir Jorge A. Cuadros; circ. 24,000.

Billiken: Azopardo 579, 1307 Buenos Aires; tel. (11) 4346-0107; fax (11) 4343-7040; e-mail artebilliken@atlantida.com.ar; f. 1919; weekly; children's magazine; Dir Juan Carlos Porras; circ. 240,000.

Casas y Jardines: Sarmiento 643, 1382 Buenos Aires; tel. (11) 445-1793; f. 1932; every 2 months; houses and gardens; publ. by Editorial Contémpora SRL; Dir Norberto M. Muzio.

Chacra y Campo Moderno: Editorial Atlántida, SA, Azopardo 579, 1307 Buenos Aires; tel. (11) 4331-4591; fax (11) 4331-3272; f. 1930; monthly; farm and country magazine; Dir Constancio C. Vigil; circ. 35,000.

Claudia: Avda Córdoba 1345, 12°, Buenos Aires; tel. (11) 442-3275; fax (11) 4814-3948; f. 1957; monthly; women's magazine; Dir Ana Torrejón; circ. 150,000.

El Economista: Avda Córdoba 632, 2°, 1054 Buenos Aires; tel. (11) 4322-7360; fax (11) 4322-8157; f. 1951; weekly; financial; Dir Dr D. Radonjic; circ. 37,800.

Fotografía Universal: Buenos Aires; monthly; circ. 39,500.

Gente: Azopardo 579, 3°, 1307 Buenos Aires; tel. (11) 433-4591; f. 1965; weekly; general; Dir Jorge de Luján Gutiérrez; circ. 133,000.

El Gráfico: Paseo Colón 505, 2°, 1063 Buenos Aires; tel. (11) 5235-5100; fax (11) 5235-5137; e-mail elgrafico@elgrafico.com.ar; internet www.elgrafico.com.ar; f. 1919; weekly; sport; Editor Martin Mazur; circ. 127,000.

Guía Latinoamericana de Transportes: Florida 8287, esq. Portinari, 1669 Del Viso (Ptdo de Pilar), Provincia de Buenos Aires; tel. (11) 4320-7004; fax (11) 4307-1956; f. 1968; every 2 months; travel information and timetables; Editor Dr Armando Schlecker Hirsch; circ. 7,500.

Humor: Venezuela 842, 1095 Buenos Aires; tel. (11) 4334-5400; fax (11) 411-2700; f. 1978; every 2 weeks; satirical revue; Editor Andrés Cascioli; circ. 180,000.

Legislación Argentina: Talcahuano 650, 1013 Buenos Aires; tel. (11) 4371-0528; e-mail jurispru@lvd.com.ar; f. 1958; weekly; law; Dir Ricardo Estévez Boero; circ. 15,000.

Mercado: Rivadavia 877, 2°, 1002 Buenos Aires; tel. (11) 4346-9400; fax (11) 4343-7880; e-mail mdiez@mercado.com.ar; internet www.mercado.com.ar; f. 1969; monthly; business; Dir Miguel Angel Diez; circ. 28,000.

Mundo Israelita: Pueyrredón 538, 1°B, 1032 Buenos Aires; tel. (11) 4961-7999; fax (11) 4961-0763; f. 1923; weekly; Editor Dr José Kestelman; circ. 15,000.

Nuestra Arquitectura: Sarmiento 643, 5°, 1382 Buenos Aires; tel. (11) 445-1793; f. 1929; every 2 months; architecture; publ. by Editorial Contémpora SRL; Dir Norberto M. Muzio.

Para Ti: Azopardo 579, 1307 Buenos Aires; tel. (11) 4331-4591; fax (11) 4331-3272; internet www.parati.com.ar; f. 1922; weekly; women's interest; Dir Aníbal C. Vigil; circ. 104,000.

Pensamiento Económico: Avda Leandro N. Alem 36, 1003 Buenos Aires; tel. (11) 4331-8051; fax (11) 4331-8055; e-mail cac@cac.com.ar; internet www.cac.com.ar; f. 1925; quarterly; review of Cámara Argentina de Comercio; Dir Dr Carlos L. P. Antonucci.

La Prensa Médica Argentina: Junín 845, 1113 Buenos Aires; tel. (11) 4961-9793; fax (11) 4961-9494; e-mail presmedarg@hotmail.com; f. 1914; monthly; medical; Editor Dr P. A. López; circ. 8,000.

Prensa Obrera: Ayacucho 444, Buenos Aires; tel. (11) 4953-3824; fax (11) 4953-7164; f. 1982; weekly; publication of Partido Obrero; circ. 16,000.

La Semana: Sarmiento 1113, 1041 Buenos Aires; tel. (11) 435-2552; general; Editor Daniel Pliner.

La Semana Médica: Arenales 3574, 1425 Buenos Aires; tel. (11) 4824-5673; f. 1894; monthly; Dir Dr Eduardo F. Mele; circ. 7,000.

Siete Días Ilustrados: Avda Leandro N. Alem 896, 1001 Buenos Aires; tel. (11) 432-6010; f. 1967; weekly; general; Dir Ricardo Cámara; circ. 110,000.

Técnica e Industria: Buenos Aires; tel. (11) 446-3193; f. 1922; monthly; technology and industry; Dir E. R. Fedele; circ. 5,000.

Visión: French 2820, 2°A, 1425 Buenos Aires; tel. (11) 4825-1258; fax (11) 4827-1004; f. 1950; fortnightly; Latin American affairs, politics; Editor Luis Vidal Rucabado.

Vosotras: Avda Leandro N. Alem 896, 3°, 1001 Buenos Aires; tel. (11) 432-6010; f. 1935; women's weekly; Dir Abel Zanotto; circ. 33,000; monthly supplements:

Labores: circ. 130,000.

Modas: circ. 70,000.

NEWS AGENCIES

Agencia TELAM, SA: Bolívar 531, 1066 Buenos Aires; tel. (11) 4339-0330; fax (11) 4339-0353; e-mail telam@telam.com.ar; internet www.telam.com.ar; Dir Armando Vidal.

Diarios y Noticias (DYN): Avda Julio A. Roca 636, 8°, 1067 Buenos Aires; tel. (11) 4342-3040; fax (11) 4342-3043; e-mail info@dyn.com.ar; internet www.dyn.com.ar; f. 1982; Editorial Dir Carmen Coiro.

Noticias Argentinas, SA (NA): Suipacha 570, 3°B, 1008 Buenos Aires; tel. (11) 4394-7522; fax (11) 4394-7648; e-mail infogral@noticiasargentinas.com; internet www.noticiasargentinas.com; f. 1973; Dir Luis Fernando Torres.

Foreign Bureaux

Agence France-Presse (AFP): Avda Corrientes 456, 4°, Of. 41–42, 1366 Buenos Aires; tel. (11) 4394-8169; fax (11) 4393-9912; e-mail afp-baires@tournet.com.ar; internet www.afp.com; Bureau Chief Frédéric Garlan.

Agencia EFE (Spain): Avda Moreau de Justo 1720, 1°, 1107 Buenos Aires; tel. (11) 4312-5721; fax (11) 4815-8691; e-mail efebas@ciudad.com; Bureau Chief Agustín de Gracia.

Agenzia Nazionale Stampa Associata (ANSA) (Italy): San Martín 320, 6°, 1004 Buenos Aires; tel. (11) 4394-7568; fax (11) 4394-5214; e-mail ansabaires@infovia.com.ar; Bureau Chief Antonio Cavallari.

Associated Press (AP) (USA): Avda Leandro N. Alem 712, 4°, 1001 Buenos Aires; tel. (11) 4311-0081; fax (11) 4311-0083; e-mail bcormier@ap.org; Bureau Chief William Cormier.

Deutsche Presse-Agentur (dpa) (Germany): Buenos Aires; tel. (11) 4311-5311; e-mail msvgroth@ba.net; Bureau Chief Dr Hendrik Groth.

Informatsionnoye Telegrafnoye Agentstvo Rossii—Telegrafnoye Agentstvo Suverennykh Stran (ITAR—TASS) (Russia): Avda Córdoba 652, 11°E, 1054 Buenos Aires; tel. (11) 4392-2044; Dir Isidoro Gilbert.

Inter Press Service (IPS) (Italy): Buenos Aires; tel. (11) 4394-0829; Bureau Chief Ramón M. Gorriarán; Correspondent Gustavo Capdevilla.

Magyar Távirati Iroda (MTI) (Hungary): Marcelo T. de Alvear 624, 3° 16, 1058 Buenos Aires; tel. (11) 4312-9596; Correspondent ENDRE SIMÓ.

Prensa Latina (Cuba): Buenos Aires; tel. (11) 4394-0565; e-mail prela@teletel.com.ar; Correspondent VÍCTOR CARRIBA.

Reuters (United Kingdom): Avda Eduardo Madero 940, 25°, 1106 Buenos Aires; tel. (11) 4318-0600; fax (11) 4318-0698; Dir CARLOS PÍA MANGIONE.

Xinhua (New China) News Agency (People's Republic of China): Tucumán 540, 14°, Apto D, 1049 Buenos Aires; tel. (11) 4313-9755; Bureau Chief JU QINGDONG.

The following are also represented: Central News Agency (Taiwan), Interpress (Poland), Jiji Press (Japan).

PRESS ASSOCIATION

Asociación de Entidades Periodísticas Argentinas (ADEPA): Chacabuco 314, 3°, 1069 Buenos Aires; tel. and fax (11) 4331-1500; e-mail adepa@adepa.org.ar; internet www.adepa.org.ar; f. 1962; Pres. LAURO F. LAINO.

Publishers

Aguilar, Altea, Taurus, Alfaguara, SA de Ediciones: Avda Leandro N. Alem 720, 1001 Buenos Aires; tel. (11) 4119-5000; fax (11) 4119-5021; e-mail info@alfaguara.com.ar; internet www .alfaguara.com.ar; f. 1946; general, literature, children's books; Pres. ESTEBAN FERNÁNDEZ ROSADO; Gen. Man. DAVID DELGADO DE ROBLES.

Aique: Valentín Gómez 3530, Buenos Aires; tel. and fax (11) 4865-5152; e-mail editorial@aique.com.ar; internet www.aique.com.ar; f. 1976; division of Aique Grupo Editor, SA.

Amorrortu Editores, SA: Paraguay 1225, 7°, 1057 Buenos Aires; tel. (11) 4816-5812; fax (11) 4816-3321; e-mail info@ amorrortueditores.com; internet www.amorrortueditores.com; f. 1967; academic, social sciences and humanities; Man. Dir HORACIO DE AMORRORTU.

Az Editora, SA: Paraguay 2351, 1121 Buenos Aires; tel. (11) 961-4036; fax (11) 961-0089; e-mail info@az-editora.com.ar; internet www.az-editora.com.ar; f. 1976; educational, social sciences and medicine; Pres. DANTE OMAR VILLALBA.

Biblioteca Nacional de Maestros: c/o Ministerio de Educación, Ciencia y Tecnología, Pizzurno 935, planta baja, 1020 Buenos Aires; tel. (11) 4129-1272; fax (11) 4129-1268; e-mail gperrone@me.gov.ar; internet www.bnm.me.gov.ar; f. 1884; Dir GRACIELA PERRONE.

Carlos Lohlé, SA: Tacuarí 1516, 1139 Buenos Aires; tel. (11) 4427-9969; f. 1953; philosophy, religion, belles-lettres; Dir FRANCISCO M. LOHLÉ.

Club de Lectores: Avda de Mayo 624, 1084 Buenos Aires; tel. (11) 4342-6251; f. 1938; non-fiction; Man. Dir MERCEDES FONTENLA.

Cosmopolita, SRL: Piedras 744, 1070 Buenos Aires; tel. (11) 4361-8925; fax (11) 4361-8049; f. 1940; science and technology; Man. Dir RUTH F. DE RAPP.

Crecer Creando Editorial: Avda Callao 1225, 14° B, CP 1023, Buenos Aires; tel. and fax (11) 4812-4586; e-mail info@crecercreando .com.ar; internet www.crecercreando.com.ar; educational.

De Los Cuatro Vientos Editorial: Avda Balcarce 1053, Local 2, CP 1064, Buenos Aires; tel. and fax (11) 4300-0924; e-mail info@ deloscuatrovientos.com.ar; internet www.deloscuatrovientos.com .ar; Dir and Editor PABLO ALBORNOZ.

Depalma, SA: Talcahuano 494, 1013 Buenos Aires; tel. (11) 4371-7306; fax (11) 4371-6913; e-mail info@ed-depalma.com; internet www.ed-depalma.com; f. 1944; periodicals and books covering law, politics, sociology, philosophy, history and economics; Man. Dir ROBERTO SUARDIAZ.

Edicial, SA: Rivadavia 739, 1002 Buenos Aires; tel. (11) 4342-8481; fax (11) 4343-1151; e-mail edicial@ssdnet.com.ar; internet www .ssdnet.com.ar/edicial; f. 1931; education; Man. Dir J. A. MUSSET.

Ediciones Atril: Hortiguera 1411, Buenos Aires; tel. (11) 4924-3003; e-mail atril@interlink.com.ar.

Ediciones La Aurora: José María Moreno 873, 1°, 1424 Buenos Aires; tel. and fax (11) 4922-5356; f. 1925; general, religion, spirituality, theology, philosophy, psychology, history, semiology, linguistics; Dir Dr HUGO O. ORTEGA.

Ediciones de la Flor SRL: Avda Gorriti 3695, CP 1172, Buenos Aires; fax (11) 4963-5616; e-mail edic-flor@datamarkets.com.ar; internet www.edicionesdelaflor.com.ar; f. 1966; fiction, poetry, theatre, juvenile, humour and scholarly; Co-Dirs ANA MARÍA T. MILER, DANIEL DIVINSKY.

Ediciones Librerías Fausto: Avda Corrientes 1316, 1043 Buenos Aires; tel. (11) 4476-4919; fax (11) 4476-3914; f. 1943; fiction and non-fiction; Man. RAFAEL ZORRILLA.

Ediciones Macchi, SA: Alsina 1535/37, 1088 Buenos Aires; tel. (11) 446-2506; fax (11) 446-0594; e-mail info@macchi.com.ar; internet www.macchi.com; f. 1947; economic sciences; Pres. RAÚL LUIS MACCHI; Dir JULIO ALBERTO MENDONÇA.

Ediciones Nueva Visión, SAIC: Tucumán 3748, 1189 Buenos Aires; tel. (11) 4864-5050; fax (11) 4863-5980; e-mail ednuevavision@ciudad.com.ar; f. 1954; psychology, education, social sciences, linguistics; Man. Dir HAYDÉE P. DE GIACONE.

Ediciones del Signo: Julián Alvarez 2844, 1° A, CP 1425, Buenos Aires; tel. (11) 4861-3181; fax (11) 3462-5031; e-mail info@ edicionesdelsigno.com.ar; internet www.edicionesdelsigno.com.ar; f. 1995; philosophy, psychoanalysis, politics and scholarly.

Editorial Abril, SA: Moreno 1617, 1093 Buenos Aires; tel. (11) 4331-0112; f. 1961; fiction, non-fiction, children's books, textbooks; Dir ROBERTO M. ARES.

Editorial Acme, SA: Santa Magdalena 635, 1277 Buenos Aires; tel. (11) 4328-1508; f. 1949; general fiction, children's books, agriculture, textbooks; Man. Dir EMILIO I. GONZÁLEZ.

Editorial Albatros, SACI: Torres Las Plazas, J. Salguero 2745, 5°, 1425 Buenos Aires; tel. (11) 4807-2030; fax (11) 4807-2010; e-mail info@albatros.com.ar; internet www.albatros.com.ar; f. 1945; technical, non-fiction, social sciences, sport, children's books, medicine and agriculture; Pres. ANDREA INÉS CANEVARO.

Editorial Argenta Sarlep SA: Avda Corrientes 1250, 3°, Of. F, Buenos Aires; tel. and fax (11) 4382-9085; e-mail argenta@millic.com .ar; internet www.editorialargenta.com; f. 1970; literature, poetry, theatre and reference.

Editorial Bonum: Avda Corrientes 6687, CP 1427, Buenos Aires; tel. and fax (11) 4554-1414; e-mail ventas@editorialbonum.com.ar; internet www.editorialbonum.com.ar; f. 1960; religious, educational and self-help.

Editorial Don Bosco: Avda Don Bosco 4069, CP 1206, Buenos Aires; tel. (11) 4883-0111; fax (11) 4883-0115; e-mail administracion@edb.com.ar; internet www.edb.com.ar; f. 1993; religious and educational; Gen. Man. GERARDO BENTANCOUR.

Editorial Catálogos SRL: Avda Independencia, 1860, CP 1225, Buenos Aires; tel. and fax (11) 4381-5708; e-mail catalogos@ciudad .com.ar; internet www.catalogossrl.com.ar; religion, literature, academic, general interest and self-help.

Editorial Claretiana: Lima 1360, 1138 Buenos Aires; tel. (11) 427-9250; fax (11) 427-4015; e-mail editorial@editorialclaretiana.com.ar; internet www.editorialclaretiana.com.ar; f. 1956; Catholicism; Man. Dir DOMINGO ANGEL GRILLIA.

Editorial Claridad, SA: Viamonte 1730, 1°, 1055 Buenos Aires; tel. (11) 4371-5546; fax (11) 4375-1659; e-mail editorial@heliasta.com .ar; internet www.heliasta.com.ar; f. 1922; literature, biographies, social science, politics, reference, dictionaries; Pres. Dra ANA MARÍA CABANELLAS.

Editorial Columba, SA: Sarmiento 1889, 5°, 1044 Buenos Aires; tel. (11) 445-4297; f. 1953; classics in translation, 20th century; Man. Dir CLAUDIO A. COLUMBA.

Editorial Contémpora, SRL: Sarmiento 643, 5°, 1382 Buenos Aires; tel. (11) 445-1793; architecture, town-planning, interior decoration and gardening; Dir NORBERTO C. MUZIO.

Editorial Difusión, SA: Sarandi 1065–67, Buenos Aires; tel. (11) 4941-0088; f. 1937; literature, philosophy, religion, education, textbooks, children's books; Dir DOMINGO PALOMBELLA.

Editorial Errepar: Paraná 725, CP 1017, Buenos Aires; tel. (11) 4370-8025; fax (11) 4383-2202; e-mail clientes@errepar.com; internet www.errepar.com; legal texts.

Editorial Glem, SACIF: Avda Caseros 2056, 1264 Buenos Aires; tel. (11) 426-6641; f. 1933; psychology, technology; Pres. JOSÉ ALFREDO TUCCI.

Editorial Grupo Cero: Mansilla 2686, planta baja 2, CP 1425, Buenos Aires; tel. (11) 4328-0614; internet www.editorialgrupocero .com; fiction, poetry and psychoanalysis.

Editorial Guadalupe: Mansilla 3865, 1425 Buenos Aires; tel. (11) 4826-8587; fax (11) 4823-6672; e-mail ventas@editorialguadalupe .com.ar; internet www.editorialguadalupe.com.ar; f. 1895; social sciences, religion, anthropology, children's books, and pedagogy; Man. Dir LORENZO GOYENECHE.

Editorial Heliasta, SRL: Viamonte 1730, 1°, 1055 Buenos Aires; tel. (11) 4371-5546; fax (11) 4375-1659; e-mail editorial@heliasta .com.ar; internet www.heliasta.com.ar; f. 1944; literature, biography, dictionaries, legal; Pres. Dra ANA MARÍA CABANELLAS.

Editorial Hispano-Americana, SA (HASA): Alsina 731, 1087 Buenos Aires; tel. (11) 4331-5051; f. 1934; science and technology; Pres. Prof. HÉCTOR OSCAR ALGARRA.

Editorial Inter-Médica, SAICI: Junín 917, 1°, 1113 Buenos Aires; tel. (11) 4961-9234; fax (11) 4961-5572; e-mail info@inter-medica.com.ar; internet www.inter-medica.com.ar; f. 1959; medicine and veterinary; Pres. SONIA MODYEIEVSKY.

Editorial Inter-Vet, SA: Avda de los Constituyentes 3141, Buenos Aires; tel. (11) 451-2382; f. 1987; veterinary; Pres. JORGE MODYEIEVSKY.

Editorial Juris: Moreno 1580, 2000 Rosario; tel. (341) 426-7301; fax ; e-mail editorialjuris@arnet.com.ar; internet www.editorialjuris.com; f. 1952; legal texts.

Editorial Kier, SACIFI: Avda Santa Fe 1260, 1059 Buenos Aires; tel. (11) 4811-0507; fax (11) 4811-3395; e-mail info@kier.com.ar; internet www.kier.com.ar; f. 1907; Eastern doctrines and religions, astrology, parapsychology, tarot, I Ching, occultism, cabbala, freemasonry and natural medicine; Pres. HÉCTOR S. PIBERNUS; Mans SERGIO PIBERNUS, OSVALDO PIBERNUS.

Editorial Losada, SA: Moreno 3362/64, 1209 Buenos Aires; tel. (11) 4373-4006; fax (11) 4375-5001; e-mail administra@editoriallosada.com; f. 1938; general; Pres. JOSÉ JUAN FERNÁNDEZ REGUERA.

Editorial Médica Panamericana, SA: Marcelo T. de Alvear 2145, 1122 Buenos Aires; tel. (11) 4821-5520; fax (11) 4825-5006; e-mail info@medicapanamericana.com.ar; internet www.medicapanamericana.com.ar; f. 1962; medicine and health sciences; Pres. HUGO BRIK.

Editorial Mercosur: Dean Funes 923/25, CP 1231, Buenos Aires; tel. (11) 4822-4615; e-mail info@editorialmercosr.com; internet www.editorialmercosur.com; self-help and general interest.

Editorial del Nuevo Extremo: Juncal 4651, CP 1425, Buenos Aires; tel. (11) 4773-3228; fax (11) 473-8445; e-mail editorial@delnuevoextremo.com; internet www.delnuevoextremo.com; general interest.

Editorial Plus Ultra, SA: Callao 575, 1022 Buenos Aires; tel. (11) 4374-2953; f. 1964; literature, history, textbooks, law, economics, politics, sociology, pedagogy, children's books; Man. Editors RAFAEL ROMÁN, LORENZO MARENGO.

Editorial Santillana: Buenos Aires; f. 1960; education; Pres. JESÚS DE POLANCO GUTIÉRREZ.

Editorial Sigmar, SACI: Belgrano 1580, 7°, 1093 Buenos Aires; tel. (11) 4383-3045; fax (11) 4383-5633; e-mail editorial@sigmar.com.ar; f. 1941; children's books; Man. Dir ROBERTO CHWAT.

Editorial Sopena Argentina, SACI e I: Maza 2138, 1240 Buenos Aires; tel. (11) 4912-2383; fax (11) 4912-2383; f. 1918; dictionaries, classics, chess, health, politics, history, children's books; Dir MARTA A. J. OLSEN.

Editorial Stella: Viamonte 1984, 1056 Buenos Aires; tel. (11) 4374-0346; fax (11) 4374-8719; e-mail admin@editorialstella.com.ar; internet www.editorialstella.com.ar; general non-fiction and textbooks; owned by Asociación Educacionista Argentina.

Editorial Sudamericana, SA: Humberto 545, 1°, 1103 Buenos Aires; tel. (11) 4300-5400; fax (11) 4362-7364; e-mail info@edsudamericana.com.ar; internet www.edsudamericana.com.ar; f. 1939; general fiction and non-fiction; Gen. Man. OLAF HANTEL.

Editorial Troquel, SA: Pichincha 967, 1219 Buenos Aires; tel. (11) 4941-7943; e-mail troquel@ba.net; f. 1954; general literature and textbooks; Pres. GUSTAVO A. RESSIA.

Editorial Zeus SRL: Rosario; tel. (341) 449-5585; fax (341) 425-4259; e-mail editorialzeus@citynet.net.ar; internet www.editorial-zeus.com.ar; legal texts; Editor and Dir GUSTAVO L. CAVIGLIA.

Emecé Editores, SA: Alsina 2062, 1090 Buenos Aires; tel. (11) 4954-0105; fax (11) 4953-4200; f. 1939; fiction, non-fiction, biographies, history, art, essays; Pres. ALFREDO DEL CARRIL.

Espasa Calpe Argentina, SA: Avda Independencia 1668, 1100 Buenos Aires; tel. (11) 4382-4043; fax (11) 4383-3793; f. 1937; literature, science, dictionaries; publ. *Colección Austral*; Dir GUILLERMO SCHAVELZON.

EUDEBA (Editorial Universitaria de Buenos Aires): Rivadavia 1573, 1033 Buenos Aires; tel. (11) 4383-8025; fax (11) 4383-2202; e-mail eudeba@eudeba.com.ar; internet www.eudeba.com.ar; f. 1958; university text books and general interest publications; Pres. Dr LUIS YANES.

Fabril Editora, SA: Buenos Aires; tel. (11) 4421-3601; f. 1958; non-fiction, science, arts, education and reference; Editorial Man. ANDRÉS ALFONSO BRAVO; Business Man. RÓMULO AYERZA.

Galerna: Lambaré 893, CP 1185, Buenos Aires; tel. (11) 4867-1661; fax (11) 4862-5031; e-mail contacto@galerna.net; internet www.galernalibros.com; fiction, theatre, poetry and scholarly.

Gram Editora: Cochabamba 1652, CP 1148, Buenos Aires; tel. (11) 4304-4833; fax (11) 4304-5692; e-mail grameditora@infovia.com.ar; internet www.grameditora.com.ar; catholic.

Gránica Editorial: Lavalle 1634, 3°G, CP1048, Buenos Aires; tel. (11) 4374-1456; fax (11) 4373-0669; e-mail granica.ar@granicaeditor.com; internet www.granica.com; juvenile and fiction.

Kapelusz Editora, SA: San José 831, 1076 Buenos Aires; tel. (11) 4342-7400; fax (11) 4331-8020; e-mail empresa@kapelusz.com.ar; internet www.kapelusz.com.ar; f. 1905; textbooks, psychology, pedagogy, children's books; Vice-Pres. RAFAEL PASCUAL ROBIES.

Plaza y Janés, SA: Buenos Aires; tel. (11) 4486-6769; popular fiction and non-fiction; Man. Dir JORGE PÉREZ.

Schapire Editor, SRL: Uruguay 1249, 1016 Buenos Aires; tel. (11) 4812-0765; fax (11) 4815-0369; f. 1941; music, art, theatre, sociology, history, fiction; Dir MIGUEL SCHAPIRE DALMAT.

PUBLISHERS' ASSOCIATION

Cámara Argentina de Publicaciones: Reconquista 1011, 6°, 1003 Buenos Aires; tel. (11) 4311-6855; f. 1970; Pres. AGUSTÍN DOS SANTOS; Man. LUIS FRANCISCO HOULIN.

Broadcasting and Communications

Secretaría de Comunicaciones: Sarmiento 151, 4°, 1000 Buenos Aires; tel. (11) 4318-9410; fax (11) 4318-9432; internet www.secom.gov.ar; co-ordinates 30 stations and the international service; Sec. MARIO GUILLERMO MORENO.

Subsecretaría de Planificación y Gestión Tecnológica: Sarmiento 151, 4°, 1000 Buenos Aires; tel. (11) 4347-9970; Under-Sec. Ing. ALEJANDRA CABALLERO.

Subsecretaría de Radiocomunicaciones: Sarmiento 151, 4°, 1000 Buenos Aires; tel. (11) 4311-5909.

Subsecretaría de Telecomunicaciones: Sarmiento 151, 4°, 1000 Buenos Aires; tel. (11) 4311-5909.

Comité Federal de Radiodifusión (COMFER): Suipacha 765, 9°, 1008 Buenos Aires; tel. (11) 4320-4900; fax (11) 4394-6866; e-mail mlagier@comfer.gov.ar; internet www.comfer.gov.ar; f. 1972; controls various technical aspects of broadcasting and transmission of programmes; Insp. JULIO DONATO BÁRBARO.

TELECOMMUNICATIONS

Cámara de Informática y Comunicaciones de la República Argentina (CICOMRA): Avda Córdoba 744, 2°, 1054 Buenos Aires; tel. (11) 4325-8839; fax (11) 4325-9604; e-mail cicomra@starnet.net.ar; internet www.cicomra.org.ar; f. 1985; Pres. MIGUEL BERUTO.

Comisión Nacional de Comunicaciones (CNC): Perú 103, 9°, 1067 Buenos Aires; tel. (11) 4347-9242; fax (11) 4347-9244; internet www.cnc.gov.ar; f. 1996; Pres. Dr ROBERTO CATALÁN; Insp. FULVIO MARIO MADARO.

Cía Ericsson SACI: Güemes 676, 1°, 1638 Vicente López PCIA, Buenos Aires; tel. (11) 4319-5500; fax (11) 4315-0629; e-mail infocom@cea.ericsson.se; internet www.ericsson.com.ar; Dir-Gen. Ing. ROLANDO ZUBIRÁN.

Movicom BellSouth: Ingeniero Enrique Butty 240, 1001 Buenos Aires; tel. (11) 5321-0000; fax (11) 4321-0334; e-mail rree@movi.com.ar; internet www.movi.com.ar; telecommunications services, including cellular telephones, trunking, paging and wireless access to the internet; acquired by Telefónica Móviles in Jan. 2005; Pres. Lic. MAURICIO E. WIOR.

Telcosur, SA: Calle Don Bosco 3672, 5°, CP 1206, Buenos Aires; tel. (11) 4865-9060; e-mail telcosur@tgs.com.ar; internet www.telcosur.com.ar; f. 1998; 99% owned by Transportador de Gas del Sur (TGS); Operations Man. EDUARDO VIGILANTE.

Telecom Argentina: Alicia Moreau de Justo 50, 1107 Buenos Aires; tel. (11) 4968-4000; fax (11) 4968-1420; e-mail inversores@intersrv.telecom.com.ar; internet www.telecom.com.ar; provision of telecommunication services in the north of Argentina; Pres. CÉSAR ALIERTA IZUEL.

Telefónica de Argentina, SA (TASA): Tucumán 1, 17°, 1049 Buenos Aires; tel. (11) 4345-5772; fax (11) 4345-5771; e-mail gabello@telefonica.com.ar; internet www.telefonica.com.ar; subsidiary of Telefónica (Spain); provision of telecommunication services in the south of Argentina; Pres. MARIO EDUARDO VÁSQUEZ.

Unifón: Corrientes 655, 1043 Buenos Aires; tel. (11) 4130-4000; internet www.unifon.com.ar; 98% owned by Telefónicas Móviles, SA (Spain); operates mobile telephone network.

RADIO

There are three privately owned stations in Buenos Aires and 72 in the interior. There are also 37 state-controlled stations, four provincial, three municipal and three university stations. The principal ones are Radio Antártida, Radio Argentina, Radio Belgrano, Radio Ciudad de Buenos Aires, Radio Excelsior, Radio Mitre, Radio El Mundo, Radio Nacional, Radio del Plata, Radio Rivadavia and Radio Splendid, all in Buenos Aires.

Radio Nacional Argentina (RNA): Maipú 555, 1006 Buenos Aires; tel. (11) 4325-4590; fax (11) 4325-4313; e-mail secretariansor@sion.com; internet www.radionacional.com.ar; five radio stations: Nacional; Nacional Folklórica; Nacional Clásica; Nacional Faro; and RAE (q.v.); Exec. Dir MONA MONCALVILLO.

Radiodifusión Argentina al Exterior (RAE): Maipú 555, 1006 Buenos Aires; tel. (11) 4325-6368; fax (11) 4325-9433; e-mail rae@radionacional.gov.ar; f. 1958; broadcasts in seven languages to all areas of the world; Dir MARCELA CAMPOS.

Asociación de Radiodifusoras Privadas Argentinas (ARPA): Juan D. Perón 1561, 8°, 1037 Buenos Aires; tel. (11) 4382-4412; f. 1958; an association of all but three of the privately owned commercial stations; Pres. DOMINGO F. L. ELÍAS.

TELEVISION

There are 42 television channels, of which 29 are privately owned and 15 are owned by provincial and national authorities. The national television network is regulated by the Comité Federal de Radiodifusión (see above).

The following are some of the more important television stations in Argentina: Argentina Televisora Color LS82 Canal 7, LS83 (Canal 9 Libertad), LV80 Telenueva, LU81 Teledifusora Bahiense SA, LV81 Canal 12 Telecor SACI, Dicor Difusión Córdoba, LV80 TV Canal 10 Universidad Nacional Córdoba, and LU82 TV Mar del Plata SA.

Asociación de Teleradiodifusoras Argentinas (ATA): Avda Córdoba 323, 6°, 1054 Buenos Aires; tel. (11) 4312-4208; fax (11) 4315-4681; e-mail info@ata.org.ar; internet www.ata.org.ar; f. 1959; asscn of 21 private television channels; Pres. CARLOS FONTAN BALESTRA; Sec. JORGE RENDO.

América: Fitzroy 1650, Buenos Aires; internet www.america2.com.ar; Programme Man. LILIANA PARODI.

Canal 13: Lima 1261, 1147 Buenos Aires; tel. (11) 4305-0013; fax (11) 4307-0315; e-mail prensa@artear.com; internet www.canal13.com.ar; f. 1989; leased to a private concession in 1992; Programme Man. ADRIÁN SUAR.

LS82 TV Canal 7: Avda Figueroa Alcorta 2977, 1425 Buenos Aires; tel. (11) 4802-6001; fax (11) 4802-9878; e-mail info@canal7argentina.com.ar; internet www.canal7argentina.com.ar; state-controlled channel; Controller RICARDO PALACIO; Dir of News ANA DE SKALON; Dir of Drama LEONARDO BECHINI.

LS83 TV Canal 9: Dorrego 1708, Buenos Aires; tel. (11) 777-2321; fax (11) 777-9620; e-mail noticias@azultv.com; internet www.infobae.com/canal9/interiores/home.php; f. 1960; private channel; Dir-Gen. DANIEL HADAD; Gen. Man. SANDRO SCARAMELLI.

Telefé (Canal 11): Pavón 2444, 1248 Buenos Aires; tel. (11) 4941-9549; fax (11) 4942-6773; e-mail prensa@telefe.com; internet www.telefe.com.ar; private channel; Programme Man. CLAUDIO VILLARRUEL.

Finance

(cap. = capital; res = reserves; dep. = deposits; m. = million; amounts in nuevos pesos argentinos—$, unless otherwise stated)

BANKING

In September 2001 there were two public banks, 11 municipal banks, 33 domestic private banks, 39 foreign private banks and two co-operative banks.

Central Bank

Banco Central de la República Argentina: Reconquista 266, 1003 Buenos Aires; tel. (11) 4348-3500; fax (11) 4348-3955; e-mail sistema@bcra.gov.ar; internet www.bcra.gov.ar; f. 1935 as a central reserve bank; it has the right of note issue; all capital is held by the state; cap. and res $3,837.5m., dep. $992.3m. (Dec. 1999); Pres. MARTÍN REDRADO.

Government-owned Commercial Banks

Banco de la Ciudad de Buenos Aires: Florida 302, 1313 Buenos Aires; tel. (11) 4329-8600; fax (11) 4112-098; e-mail bcdad39@sminter.com.ar; internet www.bancociudad.com.ar; municipal bank; f. 1878; cap. $169.5m., res $654.3m., dep. $4,463.0m. (Dec. 2002); Chair. ROBERTO J. FELETTI; Gen. Man. HUGO HARLEY ARBARELLO; 42 brs.

Banco de Inversión y Commercio Exterior, SA (BICE): 25 de Mayo 526, 1002 Buenos Aires; tel. (11) 4317-6900; fax (11) 4311-5596; e-mail info@bice.com.ar; internet www.bice.com.ar; f. 1991; cap. $489.2m., res $17.8m., dep. $121.8m. (Dec. 2000); Pres.and Chair. Dr ARNALDO MÁXIMO BOCCO; Vice-Pres. JOSÉ ALBERTO SPOSATO.

Banco de la Nación Argentina: Bartolomé Mitre 326, 1036 Buenos Aires; tel. (11) 4347-6000; fax (11) 4347-6316; e-mail gerencia@bna.com.ar; internet www.bna.com.ar; f. 1891; national bank; dep. $18,766.0m. (Dec. 2002); Chair. HORACIO E. PERICOLI; Gen. Man. JUAN CARLOS FÁBREGA; 645 brs.

Banco de la Pampa SEM: Carlos Pellegrini 255, 6300 Santa Rosa; tel. (2954) 433008; fax (2954) 433196; e-mail cexterior@blp.com.ar; internet www.blp.com.ar; f. 1958; cap. $8.8m., res $153.2m., dep. $656.2m. (June 2002); Pres. LUIS E. ROLDÁN; Gen. Man. OSWALDO LUIS DADONE; 112 brs.

Banco de la Provincia de Buenos Aires: Avda San Martín 137, 1597 Buenos Aires; tel. (11) 4347-0000; fax (11) 4347-0229; e-mail gsaldana@bpba.com.ar; internet www.bpba.com; f. 1822; provincial govt-owned bank; cap. $1,250.0m., res $244,137m., dep. $9,918,116m. (Sept. 2003); Pres. JORGE EMILIO SARGHINI; Gen. Man. JAVIER ARTACHO; 370 brs.

Banco de la Provincia de Córdoba: San Jerónimo 166, 5000 Córdoba; tel. (351) 420-7200; fax (351) 422-9718; f. 1873; provincial bank; cap. $47.6m., res $142.8m., dep. $1,036.1m. (Dec. 1994); Pres. LUIS ENRIQUE GRUNHAUT; 150 brs.

Banco de la Provincia del Neuquén: Avda Argentina 41/45, 8300 Neuquén; tel. (299) 4496618; fax (299) 4496622; internet www.bpn.com.ar; f. 1960; dep. $232.8m., total assets $388.6m. (March 1995); Pres. FÉLIX RACCO; Vice-Pres. CARLOS ALBERTO SANDOVAL; 22 brs.

Banco Social de Córdoba: 27 de Abril 185, 1°, 5000 Córdoba; tel. (351) 422-3367; dep. $187.3m., total assets $677.3m. (June 1995); Pres. Dr JAIME POMPAS.

Banco de Tierra del Fuego: Maipú 897, 9410 Ushuaia; tel. (2901) 441600; fax (2901) 441601; e-mail entradas@bancotdf.com.ar; internet www.bancotdf.com.ar; national bank; cap. and res $21.8m., dep. $54.2m. (June 1992); Pres. GUSTAVO LOFIEGO; Gen. Man. MIGUEL LANDERRECHE; 4 brs.

Nuevo Banco de la Rioja, SA: Rivadavia 702, CP 5300, 5300 La Rioja; tel. (3822) 430575; fax (3822) 430618; f. 1994; provincial bank; Pres. ELIAS SAHAD; Gen. Man. CLAUDIA L. DE BRIGIDO; 2 brs.

Nuevo Banco de Santa Fe, SA: 25 de Mayo, 3000 Santa Fe, Rosario; tel. (342) 429-4200; fax (342) 455-4543; e-mail contactobc@bancobsf.com.ar; internet www.bancobsf.com.ar; f. 1847 as Banco Provincial de Santa Fe, adopted current name in 1998; provincial bank; cap. $60.0m., res $31.1m., dep. $643.5m. (Dec. 1998); Chair. JOSÉ ENRIQUE ROHM; Exec. Dir MARCELO MUIÑO; 103 brs.

Private Commercial Banks

Banco BI Creditanstalt, SA: Bouchard 547, 24° y 25°, 1106 Buenos Aires; tel. (11) 4319-8277; fax (11) 4319-8296; e-mail bicreditanstalt.com.ar; internet www.bicreditanstalt.com.ar; f. 1971 as Banco Interfinanzas, name changed as above in 1997; cap. and res $126,689m., dep. $749.7m. (Dec. 2002); Pres. Dr MIGUEL ANGEL ANGELINO; Gen. Man. RICARDO RIVERO HAEDO.

Banco CMF, SA: Macacha Güemes 555, Puerto Madero, 1106 Buenos Aires; tel. (11) 4318-6800; fax (11) 4318-6812; f. 1978 as Corporación Metropolitana de Finanzas, SA, adopted current name in 1999; cap. $49.0m., res $111.2m., dep. $254.0m. (Dec. 2002); Pres. JOSÉ P. BENEGAS LYNCH.

Banco COMAFI: Avda Roque Sáenz Peña 660, 1035 Buenos Aires; tel. (11) 4347-0400; fax (11) 4347-0404; e-mail contactenos@comafi.com.ar; internet www.comafi.com.ar; f. 1984; assumed control of 65% of Scotiabank Quilmes in April 2002; total assets US $410.1m. (June 2001); Pres. GUILLERMO CERVIÑO; Vice-Pres. EDUARDO MASCHWITZ.

Banco Comercial Israelita, SA: Bartolomé Mitre 702, 2000 Rosario; tel. (341) 420-0557; fax (341) 420-0517; f. 1921; cap. $4.3m., res $20.5m., dep. $232.0m. (June 1998); Pres. Ing. DAVID ZCARNY; 4 brs.

Banco de Corrientes: 9 de Julio 1099, esq. San Juan, 3400 Corrientes; tel. (3783) 479300; fax (3783) 479283; internet www.elbancodecorrientes.com.ar; f. 1951 as Banco de la República de Corrientes; adopted current name in 1993, after transfer to private ownership; cap. and res $38.5m., dep. $126.7m. (June 1995); Pres. Alejandro Retegui; 33 brs.

Banco Finansur, SA: Avda Corrientes 400, 1043 Buenos Aires; tel. (11) 4324-3400; fax (11) 4322-4687; e-mail bafin@bancofinansur.com .ar; f. 1973 as Finansur Compañía Financiera, SA; adopted current name in 1993; Pres. Jorge Sánchez Córdova; 5 brs.

Banco de Galicia y Buenos Aires SA: Juan D. Perón 407, Casilla 86, 1038 Buenos Aires; tel. (11) 4394-7080; fax (11) 4393-1603; e-mail bancogalicia@bancogalicia.com.ar; internet www .bancogalicia.com.ar; f. 1905; cap. $468.7m., res $2,244.3m., dep. $19,004.7m. (Dec. 2002); Pres. Juan Martín Etchegoyhen; CEO Eduardo Arrobas; 281 brs.

Banco Macro Bansud, SA: Sarmiento 447, 1041 Buenos Aires; tel. (11) 5222-6500; fax (11) 5222-6624; e-mail international@ macrobansud.com.ar; internet www.bansud.com; f. 1995 as Banco Bansud after merger of Banesto Banco Shaw, SA, and Banco del Sud, SA; adopted current name in 2002 following merger with Banco Macro (f. 1988); cap. $64.4m., res $1,132.0m., dep. $1,056.3m. (Dec. 2002); Pres. Jorge Horacio Brito; 149 brs.

Banco Mariva, SA: Sarmiento 500, 1041 Buenos Aires; tel. (11) 4321-2200; fax (11) 4321-2222; e-mail info@mariva.com.ar; internet www.mariva.com.ar; f. 1980; cap. $30.0m., res $10.0m., dep. $206.3m. (Dec. 1994); Pres. Ricardo May.

Banco Patagonia Sudameris Argentina, SA: Juan D. Perón 500, 1038 Buenos Aires; tel. (11) 4132-6055; fax (11) 4132-6059; e-mail international@patagoniasudameris.com.ar; internet www .patagoniasudameris.com.ar; f. 1912 as Banco Sudameris; adopted current name in 2003 following merger with Banco Patagonia; cap. $89.0m., res $11.5m., dep. $977.2m. (Dec. 1998); Chair. José María Dagnino Pastore.

Banco Regional de Cuyo, SA: Avda San Martín 841, 5500 Mendoza; tel. (261) 449-8800; fax (261) 449-8801; internet www .bancoregional.com.ar; f. 1961; Pres. and Gen. Man. José Federico López; 12 brs.

Banco Río de la Plata, SA: Bartolomé Mitre 480, 1036 Buenos Aires; tel. (11) 4341-1000; fax (11) 4342-8962; internet www .bancorio.com.ar; f. 1908; cap. $346.7m., res $1,988.9m., dep. $13,008.2m. (Dec. 2002); Pres. José Luis Enrique Cristofani; 266 brs.

Banco de San Juan: Rivadavia 86, 5400 San Juan; tel. (264) 429-1000; fax (264) 421-4126; internet www.bancosanjuan.com.ar; f. 1943; 25% owned by provincial govt of San Juan; 75% privately owned; Pres. Enrique Eskenazi; Gen. Man. Raúl Riobó; 8 brs.

Banco Santiago del Estero: Avda Belgrano 529 Sur, 4200 Santiago del Estero; tel. (385) 422-2300; e-mail info@bse.com.ar; internet www.bse.com.ar; dep. $69.9m., total assets $101.6m. (Jan. 1995); Pres. Américo Daher.

Banco de Valores, SA: Sarmiento 310, 1041 Buenos Aires; tel. (11) 4323-6900; fax (11) 4334-1731; e-mail info@banval.sba.com.ar; internet www.bancodevalores.com; f. 1978; cap. $10.0m., res $40.5m., dep. $142.2m. (Dec. 2002); Pres. Julio A. Macchi; 1 br.

Banex: San Martín 136, 1004 Buenos Aires; tel. (11) 4340-3000; fax (11) 4334-4402; e-mail infobcra@banex.com.ar; internet www.banex .com.ar; f. 1998 by merger of Exprinter Banco with Banco San Luis, SA; cap. $29.1m., res $18.8m., dep. $196.6m. (Dec. 1999); Pres. Julio Patricio Supervielle; Gen. Man. Gabriel Coqueugniot; 49 brs.

HSBC Bank Argentina, SA: Avda de Mayo 701, 27°, 1084 Buenos Aires; tel. (11) 4344-3333; fax (11) 4334-6679; internet www.hsbc .com.ar; f. 1978 as Banco Roberts, SA; name changed to HSBC Banco Roberts, SA, in 1998; adopted current name in 1999; cap. $512.4m., res $1,068.4m., dep. $5,694.3m. (June 2003); Chair. and CEO Michael Smith; 68 brs.

Nuevo Banco de Entre Ríos SA: Monte Caseros 128, 3100 Paraná; tel. (343) 423-1200; fax (343) 421-1221; e-mail exterior .cambios@nuevobersa.com.ar; internet www.nuevobersa.com.ar; f. 1935; provincial bank; transferred to private ownership in 1995; cap. $20.4m., dep. $624.5m. (Dec. 2002); Pres. Ricardo Matías Taddeo; 73 brs.

Nuevo Banco Industrial de Azul, SA: Avda Córdoba 675, 1054 Buenos Aires; tel. (11) 4311-4666; fax (11) 4315-8113; e-mail info@ bancoazul.com; internet www.bancoazul.com; f. 1971; Pres. and Gen. Man. Alberto Meta; 2 brs.

Nuevo Banco Suquía, SA: 25 de Mayo 160, 5000 Córdoba; tel. (351) 420-0200; fax (351) 420-0443; internet www.bancosuquia.com .ar; f. 1961 as Banco del Suquía, SA; adopted current name in 1998; dep. $2,051.0m. (June 2000); Pres. José P. Porta; Gen. Man. Raúl Fernández; 100 brs.

Co-operative Bank

Banco Credicoop Cooperativo Ltdo: Reconquista 484, 1003 Buenos Aires; tel. (11) 4320-5000; fax (11) 4324-5891; e-mail credicoop@bancocredicoop.coop; internet www.credicoop.com.ar; f.

1979; cap. $0.7m., res $546.5m., dep. $2,324.9m. (June 2003); Pres. Raúl Guelman; Gen. Man. Carlos Heller; 227 brs.

Foreign Banks

ABN Amro Bank NV (Netherlands): Florida 361, Casilla 171, 1005 Buenos Aires; tel. (11) 4320-0600; fax (11) 4322-0839; f. 1914; cap. and res $37.7m., dep. $94.5m. (June 1992); Gen. Man. César A. Deymonnaz; 7 brs.

Banca Nazionale del Lavoro, SA (BNL) (Italy): Florida 40, 1005 Buenos Aires; tel. (11) 4323-4400; fax (11) 4323-4689; internet www .bnl.com.ar; cap. $272m., dep. $2,306m. (June 1999); took over Banco de Italia y Río de la Plata in 1987; Pres. Ademaro Lanzara; Gen. Man. Niccolo Pandolfiu; 136 brs.

Banco do Brasil, SA (Brazil): Sarmiento 487, Casilla 2684, 1041 Buenos Aires; tel. (11) 4394-0939; fax (11) 4394-9577; f. 1960; cap. and res $33.9m., dep. $2.0m. (June 1992); Gen. Man. Hélio Testoni.

Banco do Estado de São Paulo (Brazil): Tucumán 821, Casilla 2177, 1049 Buenos Aires; tel. (11) 4325-9533; fax (11) 4325-9527; cap. and res $11.7m., dep. $6.7m. (June 1992); Gen. Man. Carlos Alberto Bergamasco.

Banco Europeo para América Latina (BEAL), SA: Juan D. Perón 338, 1038 Buenos Aires; tel. (11) 4331-6544; fax (11) 4331-2010; e-mail bealbsa@interprov.com; f. 1914; cap. and res $60m., dep. $121m. (Nov. 1996); Gen. Mans Jean Pierre Smeets, Klaus Krüger.

Banco Itaú, SA (Brazil): 25 de Mayo 476, 2°, 1002 Buenos Aires; tel. (11) 4325-6698; fax (11) 4394-1057; internet www.itau.com.ar; fmrly Banco Itaú Argentina, SA, renamed as above following purchase of Banco del Buen Ayre, SA, in May 1998; cap. and res $20.2m., dep. $1.2m. (June 1992); Pres. Olavo Egydio Setubal; 78 brs.

Banco Société Générale, SA (France): Reconquista 330, 1003 Buenos Aires; tel. (11) 4329-8000; fax (11) 4329-8080; e-mail info@ar .socgen.com; internet www.ar.socgen.com.ar; f. 1887 as Banco Supervielle de Buenos Aires, SA, adopted current name in 2000; cap. $50.5m., res $56.8m., dep. $820.6m. (Dec. 2001); Chair. and Gen. Man. Marc-Emmanuel Vives; 64 brs.

Bank of Tokyo-Mitsubishi, Ltd (Japan): Avda Corrientes 420, 1043 Buenos Aires; tel. (11) 4348-2001; fax (11) 4322-6607; f. 1956; cap. and res $20m., dep. $81m. (Sept. 1994); Gen. Man. Kazuo Omi.

BankBoston NA (USA): Florida 99, 1005 Buenos Aires; tel. (11) 4346-2000; fax (11) 4346-3200; f. 1784; cap. $456.8m., dep. $4,012m., total assets $8,677m. (Sept. 1998); Pres. Ing. Manuel Sacerdote; 139 brs.

Banque Nationale de Paris, SA (France): 25 de Mayo 471, 1002 Buenos Aires; tel. (11) 4318-0318; fax (11) 4311-1368; f. 1981; cap. and res $29.4m., dep. $86.7m. (June 1992); Gen. Man. Chislain de Beaucé.

BBVA Banco Francés, SA: Reconquista 199, 1003 Buenos Aires; tel. (11) 4346-4000; fax (11) 4346-4320; internet www.bancofrances .com; f. 1886 as Banco Francés del Río de la Plata, SA; changed name to Banco Francés, SA, in 1998 following merger with Banco de Crédito Argentino; adopted current name in 2000; cap. $368.1m., res $2,543.3m., dep. US $10,654.1m. (Dec. 2002); Chair. Gervásio Collar Zavaleta; CEO and Gen. Man. Antonio Martinez-Jorquera; 308 brs.

Chase Manhattan Bank (USA): Arenales 707, 5°, 1061 Buenos Aires; tel. (11) 4319-2400; fax (11) 4319-2416; f. 1904; cap. and res $46.3m., dep. $12,387m. (Sept. 1992); Gen. Man. Marcelo Podestá.

Citibank, NA (USA): Colón 58, Bahía Blanca, 8000 Buenos Aires; tel. (11) 4331-8281; f. 1914; cap. and res $172.8m., dep. $660.8m. (June 1992); Pres. Ricardo Angles; Vice-Pres. Guillermo Stanley; 16 brs.

Deutsche Bank, SA (Germany): Tucumán 1, 14°, 1049 Buenos Aires; tel. (11) 4590-2800; fax (11) 4590-2882; f. 1998; cap. $125.5m., res $182.6m., dep. $197.1m. (Dec. 2002); Pres. Patricio Eduardo Kelly; 47 brs.

Lloyds Bank (Bank of London and South America) Ltd (United Kingdom): Tronador 4890, 13°, Casilla 128, 1003 Buenos Aires; tel. (11) 4546-9000; fax (11) 4321-4789; f. 1862; subsidiary of Lloyds Bank TSB Group; cap. and res $108.1m., dep. $583.4m. (Sept. 1997); Gen. Man. for Argentina N. Hubbard; 31 brs.

Morgan Guaranty Trust Co of New York (USA): Avda Corrientes 411, 1043 Buenos Aires; tel. and fax (11) 4325-8046; cap. and res $29.1m., dep. $11.6m. (June 1992); Gen. Man. José McLoughlin.

Republic National Bank of New York (USA): Bartolomé Mitre 343, 1036 Buenos Aires; tel. (11) 4343-0161; fax (11) 4331-6064; cap. and res $17.2m., dep. $13.6m. (March 1994); Gen. Man. Alberto Muchnick.

Bankers' Associations

Asociación de Bancos del Interior de la República Argentina (ABIRA): Avda Corrientes 538, 4°, 1043 Buenos Aires; tel. (11) 4394-3439; fax (11) 4394-5682; f. 1956; Pres. Dr Jorge Federico Christensen; Dir Raúl Passano; 30 mems.

Asociación de Bancos Públicos y Privados de la República Argentina (ABAPPRA): Florida 470, 1°, 1005 Buenos Aires; tel. (11) 4322-6321; fax (11) 4322-6721; e-mail info@abappra.com.ar; internet www.abappra.com; f. 1959; Pres. Enrique Olivera; Man. Luis B. Bucafusco; 31 mems.

Federación de Bancos Cooperativos de la República Argentina (FEBANCOOP): Maipú 374, 9°/10°, 1006 Buenos Aires; tel. (11) 4394-9949; f. 1973; Pres. Omar C. Trillo; Exec. Sec. Juan Carlos Romano; 32 mems.

STOCK EXCHANGES

Mercado de Valores de Buenos Aires, SA: 25 de Mayo 367, 8°–10°, 1002 Buenos Aires; tel. (11) 4313-6021; fax (11) 4313-4472; e-mail merval@merval.sba.com.ar; internet www.merval.sba.com.ar; f. 1929; Pres. Héctor J. Bacqué.

There are also stock exchanges at Córdoba, Rosario, Mendoza and La Plata.

Supervisory Authority

Comisión Nacional de Valores (CNV): 25 de Mayo 175, 1002 Buenos Aires; tel. (11) 4342-4607; fax (11) 4331-0639; e-mail webadm@cnv.gov.ar; internet www.cnv.gob.ar; monitors capital markets; Pres. Guillermo Harteneck.

INSURANCE

In March 2001 there were 222 insurance companies operating in Argentina, of which 121 were general insurance companies. The following is a list of those offering all classes or a specialized service.

Supervisory Authority

Superintendencia de Seguros de la Nación: Avda Julio A. Roca 721, 5°, 1067 Buenos Aires; tel. (11) 4331-8733; fax (11) 4331-9821; f. 1938; Supt Dr Ignacio Warnes.

Major Companies

La Agrícola, SA: Buenos Aires; tel. (11) 4394-5031; f. 1905; associated co La Regional; all classes; Pres. Luis R. Marco; First Vice-Pres. Justo J. de Corral.

Aseguradora de Créditos y Garantías, SA: Avda Corrientes 415, 4°, 1043 Buenos Aires; tel. (11) 4394-4037; fax (11) 4394-0320; e-mail acgtias@infovia.com.ar; internet www.acg.com.ar; f. 1965; Pres. William A. Franke; CEO Horacio G. Scapparone.

Aseguradora de Río Negro y Neuquén: Avda Alem 503, Cipolletti, Río Negro; tel. (299) 477-2725; fax (299) 477-0321; f. 1960; all classes; Gen. Man. Ernesto López.

Aseguradores de Cauciones, SA: Paraguay 580, 1057 Buenos Aires; tel. (11) 4318-3700; fax (11) 4318-3799; e-mail directorio@caucion.com.ar; internet www.caucion.com.ar; f. 1968; all classes; Pres. José de Vedia.

Aseguradores Industriales, SA: Juan D. Perón 650, 6°, 1038 Buenos Aires; tel. (11) 4326-8881; fax (11) 4326-3742; f. 1961; all classes; Exec. Dir Luis Esteban Loforte.

La Austral: Buenos Aires; tel. (11) 442-9881; fax (11) 4953-4459; f. 1942; all classes; Pres. Rodolfo H. Taylor.

Colón, Cía de Seguros Generales, SA: San Martín 548–550, 1004 Buenos Aires; tel. (11) 4320-3800; fax (11) 4320-3802; f. 1962; all classes; Gen. Man. L. D. Stsck.

Columbia, SA de Seguros: Juan D. Perón 690, 1038 Buenos Aires; tel. (11) 4325-0208; fax (11) 4326-1392; f. 1918; all classes; Pres. Marta Blanco; Gen. Man. Horacio H. Petrillo.

El Comercio, Cía de Seguros a Prima Fija, SA: Avda Corrientes 415, 3° y 5°, 1043 Buenos Aires; tel. (11) 4394-1300; fax (11) 4393-1311; internet www.bristolgroup.com.ar; f. 1889; all classes; Pres. Horacio Scapparone; Vice-Pres. Eduardo Martelli.

Cía Argentina de Seguros de Créditos a la Exportación, SA: Corrientes 345, 7°, 1043 Buenos Aires; tel. (11) 4313-3048; fax (11) 4313-2919; f. 1967; covers credit and extraordinary and political risks for Argentine exports; Pres. Luis Orcoyen; Gen. Man. Dr Mariano A. García Galisteo.

Cía Aseguradora Argentina, SA: Avda Roque S. Peña 555, 1035 Buenos Aires; tel. (11) 430-1571; fax (11) 430-5973; f. 1918; all classes; Man. Guido Luttini; Vice-Pres. Alberto Fraguio.

La Continental, Cía de Seguros Generales SA: Avda Corrientes 655, 1043 Buenos Aires; tel. (11) 4393-8051; fax (11) 4325-7101; f. 1912; all classes; Pres. Raúl Mascarenhas.

La Franco-Argentina, SA: Buenos Aires; tel. (11) 430-3091; f. 1896; all classes; Pres. Dr Guillermo Moreno Hueyo; Gen. Man. Dra Haydée Guzian de Ramírez.

Hermes, SA: Edif. Hermes, Bartolomé Mitre 754/60, 1036 Buenos Aires; tel. (11) 4331-4506; fax (11) 4343-5552; e-mail hermes@mbox.servicenet.com.ar; f. 1926; all classes; Pres. Dionisio Katopodis; Gen. Man. Francisco Martín Zabalo.

India, Cía de Seguros Generales SA: Avda Roque S. Peña 728/36, 1035 Buenos Aires; tel. (11) 4328-6001; fax (11) 4328-5602; f. 1950; all classes; Pres. Alfredo Juan Priesse; Vice-Pres. Dr Raúl Alberto Guardia.

Instituto Italo-Argentino de Seguros Generales, SA: Avda Roque S. Peña 890, 1035 Buenos Aires; tel. (11) 4320-9200; fax (11) 4320-9229; f. 1920; all classes; Pres. Alejandro A. Soldati.

La Meridional, Cía Argentina de Seguros SA: Juan D. Perón 646, 1038 Buenos Aires; tel. (11) 4909-7000; fax (11) 4909-7274; e-mail meridi@starnet.net.ar; f. 1949; life and general; Pres. Guillermo V. Lascano Quintana; Gen. Man. Peter Hammer.

Plus Ultra, Cía Argentina de Seguros, SA: San Martín 548–50, 1004 Buenos Aires; tel. (11) 4393-5069; f. 1956; all classes; Gen. Man. L. D. Stsck.

La Primera, SA: Blvd Villegas y Oro, Trenque Lauquén, Prov. Buenos Aires; tel. (11) 4393-8125; all classes; Pres. Enrique Raúl U. Bottini; Man. Dr Rodolfo Raúl D'Onofrio.

La Rectora, SA: Avda Corrientes 848, 1043 Buenos Aires; tel. (11) 4394-6081; fax (11) 4394-3251; f. 1951; all classes; Pres. Pedro Pascual Megna; Gen. Man. Antonio López Bueno.

La República Cía Argentina de Seguros Generales, SA: San Martín 627/29, 1374 Buenos Aires; tel. (11) 4314-1000; fax (11) 4318-8778; e-mail ccastell@republica.com.ar; f. 1928; group life and general; Pres. José T. Guzman Dumas; Gen. Man. Eduardo Escriña.

Sud América Terrestre y Marítima Cía de Seguros Generales, SA: Florida 15, 2°, Galería Florida 1, 1005 Buenos Aires; tel. (11) 4340-5100; fax (11) 4340-5380; f. 1919; all classes; Pres. Ema Sánchez de Larragoiti; Vice-Pres. Alain Hombreux.

La Unión Gremial, SA: Mitre 665/99, 2000 Rosario, Santa Fe; tel. (341) 426-2900; fax (341) 425-9802; f. 1908; general; Gen. Man. Eduardo Ignacio Llobet.

La Universal: Buenos Aires; tel. (11) 442-9881; fax (11) 4953-4459; f. 1905; all classes; Pres. Rodolfo H. Taylor.

Zurich-Iguazú Cía de Seguros, SA: San Martín 442, 1004 Buenos Aires; tel. (11) 4329-0400; fax (11) 4322-4688; f. 1947; all classes; Pres. Ramón Santamarina.

Reinsurance

Instituto Nacional de Reaseguros: Avda Julio A. Roca 694, 1067 Buenos Aires; tel. (11) 4334-0084; fax (11) 4334-5588; f. 1947; reinsurance in all branches; Pres. and Man. Reinaldo A. Castro.

Insurance Associations

Asociación Argentina de Cías de Seguros (AACS): 25 de Mayo 565, 2°, 1002 Buenos Aires; tel. (11) 4312-7790; fax (11) 4312-6300; e-mail secret@aacsra.org.ar; internet www.aacsra.org.ar; f. 1894; 32 mems; Pres. Roberto F. E. Sollitto.

Asociación de Entidades Aseguradoras Privadas de la República Argentina (EAPRA): Esmeralda 684, 4°, 1007 Buenos Aires; tel. (11) 4393-2268; fax (11) 4393-2283; f. 1875; asscn of 12 foreign insurance cos operating in Argentina; Pres. Dr Piero Zuppelli; Sec. Bernardo von der Goltz.

Trade and Industry

GOVERNMENT AGENCIES

Agencia de Desarrollo de Inversiones: Avda Pte Julio A. Roca 651, 5°, Sector 20, CP 1067, Buenos Aires; tel. (11) 4349-3442; fax (11) 4349-3453; e-mail adi@mecon.gov.ar; internet www.inversiones.gov.ar; promotion of investment in Argentina; supervised by the Secretaría de Industria, Comercio y de la Pequeña y Mediana Empresa.

Cámara de Exportadores de la República Argentina: Avda Roque S. Peña 740, 1°, 1035 Buenos Aires; tel. (11) 4394-4351; fax (11) 4328-1003; e-mail contacto@cera.org.ar; internet www.cera.org.ar; f. 1943 to promote exports; 700 mems; Pres. Dr Enrique S. Mantilla.

Consejo Federal de Inversiones: San Martín 871, 1004 Buenos Aires; tel. (11) 4313-5557; fax (11) 4315-1639; e-mail cfi@cfired.org.ar; internet www.cfired.org.ar; federal board to co-ordinate domestic and foreign investment and provide technological aid for the provinces; f. 1959; Sec.-Gen. Ing. JUAN JOSÉ CIÁCERA.

Dirección de Forestación (DF): Avda Paseo Colón 982, anexo jardín, 1063 Buenos Aires; tel. (11) 4349-2124; fax (11) 4349-2102; e-mail bfores@mecon.gov.ar; assumed the responsibilities of the national forestry commission (Instituto Forestal Nacional—IFONA) in 1991, following its dissolution; supervised by the Secretaría de Agricultura, Ganadería, Pesca y Alimentación; maintains the Centro de Documentación e Información Forestal; Library Man. NILDA E. FERNÁNDEZ.

Instituto de Desarrollo Económico y Social (IDES): Araoz 2838, 1425 Buenos Aires; tel. (11) 4804-4949; fax (11) 4804-5856; e-mail ides@ides.org.ar; internet www.ides.org.ar; f. 1960; investigation into social sciences and promotion of social and economic devt; 700 mems; Pres. ADRIANA MARSHALL; Sec. LUIS BECCARIA.

Oficina Nacional de Control Comercial Agropecuario (ONCCA): Avda Paseo Colón 922, Buenos Aires; tel. (11) 4349-2034; fax (11) 4349-2005; e-mail infooncca@sagpya.minproduccion.gov.ar; oversees the agricultural sector; supervised by the Secretaría de Agricultura, Ganadería, Pesca y Alimentación.

Organismo Nacional de Administración de Bienes (ONABE): 1302 Avda J. M. Ramos Mejia, 3°, Of. 300, CP 1104, Buenos Aires; tel. (11) 4318-3458; responsible for overseeing privatization of state property.

Secretaría de Agricultura, Ganadería, Pesca y Alimentación: Avda Paseo Colón 922, 1°, Of. 146, 1063 Buenos Aires; tel. (11) 4349-2000; fax (11) 4349-2292; e-mail comunica@sagpya.minproduccion.gov.ar; internet www.sagpya.mecon.gov.ar; f. 1871; undertakes regulatory, promotional, advisory and administrative responsibilities on behalf of the meat, livestock, agriculture and fisheries industries; Sec. MIGUEL SANTIAGO CAMPOS.

Sindicatura General de Empresas Públicas: Lavalle 1429, 1048 Buenos Aires; tel. (11) 449-5415; fax (11) 4476-4054; f. 1978 to exercise external control over wholly or partly owned public enterprises; Pres. ALBERTO R. ABAD.

DEVELOPMENT ORGANIZATIONS

Instituto Argentino del Petróleo y Gas: Maipú 645, 3°, 1006 Buenos Aires; tel. (11) 4325-8008; fax (11) 4393-5494; e-mail informa@iapg.org.ar; internet www.iapg.org.ar; f. 1958; established to promote the devt of petroleum exploration and exploitation; Pres. Ing. JORGE OSCAR FERIOLI.

Secretario de Programación Económica: Hipólito Yrigoyen 250, 8°, Of. 819, Buenos Aires; tel. (11) 4349-5710; fax (11) 4349-5714; f. 1961 to formulate national long-term devt plans; Sec. Dr JUAN JOSÉ LACH.

Sociedad Rural Argentina: Florida 460, 1005 Buenos Aires; tel. (11) 4324-4700; fax (11) 4324-4774; e-mail prensa@ruralarg.com.ar; internet www.ruralarg.org.ar; f. 1866; private org. to promote the devt of agriculture; Pres. Dr LUCIANO MIGUENS; 9,400 mems.

CHAMBERS OF COMMERCE

Cámara Argentina de Comercio: Avda Leandro N. Alem 36, 1003 Buenos Aires; tel. (11) 5300-9000; fax (11) 5300-9058; e-mail gerencia@cac.com.ar; internet www.cac.com.ar; f. 1924; Pres. CARLOS RAÚL DE LA VEGA.

Cámara de Comercio, Industria y Producción de la República Argentina: Florida 1, 4°, 1005 Buenos Aires; tel. (11) 4331-0813; fax (11) 4331-9116; f. 1913; Pres. JOSÉ CHEDIEK; Vice-Pres Dr FAUSTINO S. DIÉGUEZ, Dr JORGE M. MAZALAN; 1,500 mems.

Cámara de Comercio Exterior de Rosario: Avda Córdoba 1868, 2000 Rosario, Santa Fe; tel. and fax (341) 425-7147; e-mail ccer@commerce.com.ar; internet www.commerce.com.ar; f. 1958; deals with imports and exports; Pres. JUAN CARLOS RETAMERO; Vice-Pres. EDUARDO C. SALVATIERRA; 150 mems.

Cámara de Comercio de los Estados Unidos en la República Argentina (AMCAM): Viamonte 1133, 8°, 1053 Buenos Aires; tel. (11) 4371-4500; fax (11) 4371-8100; e-mail amcham@amchamar.com.ar; internet www.amchamar.com.ar; f. 1918; US Chamber of Commerce; Mem. Man. GONZALO LERGA.

Similar chambers are located in most of the larger centres and there are many other foreign chambers of commerce.

INDUSTRIAL AND TRADE ASSOCIATIONS

Asociación de Importadores y Exportadores de la República Argentina: Avda Belgrano 124, 1°, 1092 Buenos Aires; tel. (11) 4342-0010; fax (11) 4342-1312; e-mail aiera@aiera.org.ar; internet www.aiera.org.ar; f. 1966; Pres. HÉCTOR MARCELO VIDAL; Man. ADRIANO DE FINA.

Asociación de Industriales Textiles Argentinos: Buenos Aires; tel. (11) 4373-2256; fax (11) 4373-2351; f. 1945; textile industry; Pres. BERNARDO ABRAMOVICH; 250 mems.

Asociación de Industrias Argentinas de Carnes: Buenos Aires; tel. (11) 4322-5244; meat industry; refrigerated and canned beef and mutton; Pres. JORGE BORSELLA.

Asociación Vitivinícola Argentina: Güemes 4464, 1425 Buenos Aires; tel. (11) 4774-3370; f. 1904; wine industry; Pres. LUCIANO COTUMACCIO; Man. Lic. MARIO J. GIORDANO.

Cámara de Sociedades Anónimas: Libertad 1340, POB 1016, Buenos Aires; tel. (11) 4000-7399; fax (11) 4000-7399; e-mail camsocanon@camsocanon.com; internet www.camsocanon.com; Pres. Dr ALFONSO DE LA FERRERE; Man. CARLOS ALBERTO PERRONE.

Centro de Exportadores de Cereales: Bouchard 454, 7°, 1106 Buenos Aires; tel. (11) 4311-1697; fax (11) 4312-6924; f. 1943; grain exporters; Pres. RAÚL S. LOEH.

Confederaciones Rurales Argentinas: México 628, 2°, 1097 Buenos Aires; tel. (11) 4261-1501; Pres. ARTURO J. NAVARRO.

Coordinadora de Actividades Mercantiles Empresarias: Buenos Aires; Pres. OSVALDO CORNIDE.

Federación Agraria Argentina (FAA): e-mail comunicacion@faa.com.ar; internet www.faa.com.ar; f. 1912; oversees the interests of small and medium-sized grain producers; Pres. EDUARDO BUZZI.

Federación Lanera Argentina: Avda Paseo Colón 823, 5°, 1063 Buenos Aires; tel. (11) 4300-7661; fax (11) 4361-6517; e-mail info@flasite.com; internet www.flasite.com; f. 1929; wool industry; Pres. RICHARD VON GERSTENBERG; Sec. JULIO AISENSTEIN; 80 mems.

EMPLOYERS' ORGANIZATION

Unión Industrial Argentina (UIA): Avda Leandro N. Alem 1067, 11°, 1001 Buenos Aires; tel. (11) 4313-4474; fax (11) 4313-2413; e-mail uia@uia.org.ar; internet www.uia.org.ar; f. 1887; re-established in 1974 with the fusion of the Confederación Industrial Argentina (CINA) and the Confederación General de la Industria; following the dissolution of the CINA in 1977, the UIA was formed in 1979; asscn of manufacturers, representing industrial corpns; Pres. ALBERTO ALVAREZ GAIANI; Sec. JUAN CARLOS SACCO.

UTILITIES

Regulatory Authorities

Energía Argentina, SA (ENARSA): Neuquén; f. 2004; state-owned; Dir EXEQUIEL ESPINOSA.

Ente Nacional Regulador de la Electricidad (ENRE): Avda Eduardo Madero 1020, 10°, 1106 Buenos Aires; tel. (11) 4314-5805; fax (11) 4314-5416; internet www.enre.gov.ar; Vice-Pres. Ing. RICARDO MARTÍNEZ LEONE.

Ente Nacional Regulador del Gas (ENARGAS): Suipacha 636, 10°, 1008 Buenos Aires; tel. (11) 4325-9292; fax (11) 4348-0550; internet www.enargas.gov.ar; Pres. Ing. HECTOR ENRIQUE FORMICA.

Electricity

CAPEX: Melo 630, Vicente López, 1638 Buenos Aires; tel. (11) 4796-6000; e-mail info@capex.com.ar; internet www.capex.com.ar; f. 1988; electricity generation; Chair. ENRIQUE GÖTZ; Vice-Chair. ALEJANDRO GÖTZ.

Central Costanera, SA (CECCO): Avda España 3301, 1107 Buenos Aires; tel. (11) 4307-3040; fax (11) 4307-1706; generation, transmission, distribution and sale of thermal electric energy; Chair. JAIME BAUZÁ BAUZÁ.

Central Puerto, SA (CEPU): Avda Tomás Edison 2701, 1104 Buenos Aires; tel. (11) 4317-5000; fax (11) 4317-5099; electricity generating co; CEO ANTONIO BÜCHI BUĆ.

Comisión Nacional de Energía Atómica (CNEA): Avda del Libertador 8250, 1429 Buenos Aires; tel. (11) 4704-1384; fax (11) 4704-1176; e-mail freijo@cnea.edu.ar; internet www.cnea.gov.ar; f. 1950; scheduled for transfer to private ownership; nuclear energy science and technology; Pres. JOSÉ PABLO ABRIATA.

Comisión Técnica Mixta de Salto Grande (CTMSG): Avda Leandro N. Alem 449, 1003 Buenos Aires; operates Salto Grande hydroelectric station, which has an installed capacity of 650 MW; joint Argentine-Uruguayan project.

Dirección de Energía de la Provincia de Buenos Aires: Calle 55, No. 570, La Reja, 1900 Buenos Aires; tel. (11) 4415-000; fax (11) 4216-124; f. 1957; electricity co for province of Buenos Aires; Dir AGUSTÍN NÚÑEZ.

Empresa Distribuidora y Comercializadora Norte, SA (EDENOR): Azopardo 1025, 1107 Buenos Aires; tel. (11) 4348-2121; fax (11) 4334-0805; e-mail ofitel@edenor.com.ar; internet www .edenor.com.ar; distribution of electricity; Pres. FERNANDO PONASSO.

Empresa Distribuidora Sur, SA (EDESUR): San José, 140, 1076 Buenos Aires; tel. (11) 4381-8981; fax (11) 4383-3699; internet www .edesur.com.ar; f. 1992; distribution of electricity; Gen. Man. JOSÉ MARÍA HIDALGO.

Entidad Binacional Yacyretá: Avda Eduardo Madero 942, 21°– 22°, 1106 Buenos Aires; tel. (11) 4510-7500; e-mail rrpp@eby.org.ar; internet www.eby.org.ar; operates the hydroelectric dam at Yacyretá on the Paraná river; owned jointly by Argentina and Paraguay; completed in 1998, it is one of the world's largest hydro-electric complexes, consisting of 20 generators with a total generating capacity of 2,700 MW; Exec. Dir OSCAR ALFREDO THOMAS.

Hidronor Ingenieria y Servicios, SA (HISSA): Hipólito Yrigoyen 1530, 6°, 1089 Buenos Aires; tel. and fax (11) 4382-6316; e-mail info@hidronor.com; internet www.hidronor.com.ar; fmrly HIDRONOR, SA, the largest producer of electricity in Argentina; responsible for developing the hydroelectric potential of the Limay and neighbouring rivers; Pres. CARLOS ALBERTO ROCCA; transferred to private ownership in 1992 and divided into the following companies.

Central Hidroeléctrica Alicurá, SA: Avda Leandro N. Alem 712, 7°, 1001 Buenos Aires.

Central Hidroeléctrica Cerros Colorados, SA: Avda Leandro N. Alem 690, 12°, 1001 Buenos Aires.

Central Hidroeléctrica El Chocón, SA: Suipacha 268, 9°, Of. A, Buenos Aires.

Hidroeléctrica Piedra del Aguila, SA: Avda Tomás Edison 1251, 1104 Buenos Aires; tel. (11) 4315-2586; fax (11) 4317-5174; Pres. Dr URIEL FEDERICO O'FARRELL; Gen. Man. IGNACIO J. ROSNER.

Transener, SA: Avda Paseo Colón 728, 6°, 1063 Buenos Aires; tel. (11) 4342-6925; fax (11) 4342-7147; energy transmission co.

Petrobrás Energía, SA: Maipú 1, 22°, 1084 Buenos Aires; tel. (11) 4344-6000; fax (11) 4331-8369; internet www.petrobrasenergia.com; f. 1946 as Pérez Compañc, SA; petroleum interests acquired by Petrobrás of Brazil in 2003; operates the hydroelectric dam at Pichi Picún Leufu; Chair. JORGE GREGORIO PÉREZ COMPANC.

Gas

Asociación de Distribuidores de Gas (ADIGAS): Diagonal Norte 740, 5°B, Buenos Aires; tel. (11) 4393-8294; e-mail consultas@ adigas.com.ar; internet www.adigas.com.ar; f. 1993 to represent newly privatized gas companies; Gen. Man. CARLOS ALBERTO ALFARO.

Distribuidora de Gas del Centro, SA: Avda Hipólito Yrigoyen 475, 5000 Córdoba; tel. (351) 4688-100; fax (351) 4681-568; state-owned co; distributes natural gas.

Gas Natural Ban, SA: Isabel la Católica 939, 1269 Buenos Aires; tel. (11) 4303-1380; internet www.gasnaturalban.com.ar; f. 1992; distribution of natural gas; Gen. Man. ANTONI PERIS MINGOT.

Metrogás, SA: Gregorio Aráoz de Lamadrid 1360, Buenos Aires; tel. (11) 4309-1434; fax (11) 4309-1025; f. 1992; gas distribution; Chair. RICK LYNN WADDELL; Dir LUIS AGUSTO DOMENECH.

Transportadora de Gas del Norte, SA: Don Bosco 3672, 3°, 1206 Buenos Aires; tel. (11) 4959-2000; fax (11) 4959-2242; internet www .tgn.com.ar; f. 1992; distributes natural gas; Gen. Man. FREDDY CAMEO.

Transportadora de Gas del Sur, SA (TGS): Don Bosco 3672, 5°, 1206 Buenos Aires; tel. (11) 4865-9050; fax (11) 4865-9059; e-mail totgs@tgs.com.ar; internet www.tgs.com.ar; processing and transport of natural gas; f. 1992; Gen. Dir EDUARDO OJEA QUINTANA.

Water

Aguas Argentinas: Buenos Aires; internet www.aguasargentinas .com.ar; distribution of water in Buenos Aires; privatized in 1993; Dir-Gen. JEAN-LOUIS CHAUSSADE.

TRADE UNIONS

Central de los Trabajadores Argentinos (CTA): Avda Independencia 766, 1099 Buenos Aires; tel. (11) 4307-3829; e-mail internacional@cta.org.ar; internet www.cta.org.ar; dissident trade union confederation; Gen. Sec. VÍCTOR DE GENNARO; Int. Sec. PEDRO WASIEJKO.

Confederación General del Trabajo (CGT) (General Confederation of Labour): Azopardo 802, CP 1107, Buenos Aires; tel. (11) 4343-1883 ; e-mail secgral@cgtra.org.ar; internet www.cgtra.org.ar;

f. 1984; Peronist; represents approx. 90% of Argentina's 1,100 trade unions; Sec.-Gen. HUGO MOYANO.

Movimiento de Trabajadores Argentinos (MTA): Buenos Aires; dissident trade union confederation.

Transport

Comisión Nacional de Regulación del Transporte (CNRT): Maipú 88, 1084, Buenos Aires; tel. (11) 4819-3000; e-mail msenet@ mecon.gov.ar; internet www.cnrt.gov.ar; regulates domestic and international transport services.

Secretaría de Obras Públicas y Transporte: Hipólito Yrigoyen 250, 12°, 1310 Buenos Aires; tel. (11) 4349-7254; fax (11) 4349-7201; Sec. Ing. ARMANDO GUIBERT.

Secretaría de Transporte Metropolitano y de Larga Distancia: Hipólito Yrigoyen 250, 12°, 1310 Buenos Aires; tel. (11) 4349-7162; fax (11) 4349-7146; Under-Sec. Dr ARMANDO CANOSA.

Secretaría de Transporte Aero-Comercial: Hipólito Yrigoyen 250, 12°, 1310 Buenos Aires; tel. (11) 4349-7203; fax (11) 4349-7206; Under-Sec. FERMÍN ALARCIA.

Dirección de Estudios y Proyectos: Hipólito Yrigoyen 250, 12°, 1310 Buenos Aires; tel. (11) 4349-7127; fax (11) 4349-7128; Dir Ing. JOSÉ LUIS JAGODNIK.

RAILWAYS

Lines: General Belgrano (narrow-gauge), General Roca, General Bartolomé Mitre, General San Martín, Domingo Faustino Sarmiento (all wide-gauge), General Urquiza (medium-gauge) and Línea Metropolitana, which controls the railways of Buenos Aires and its suburbs. There are direct rail links with the Bolivian Railways network to Santa Cruz de la Sierra and La Paz; with Chile, through the Las Cuevas–Caracoles tunnel (across the Andes) and between Salta and Antofagasta; with Brazil, across the Paso de los Libres and Uruguayana bridge; with Paraguay (between Posadas and Encarnación by ferry-boat); and with Uruguay (between Concordia and Salto). In 2002 there were 34,463 km of tracks. In the Buenos Aires commuter area 270.4 km of wide-gauge track and 52 km of medium gauge track are electrified.

Plans for the eventual total privatization of Ferrocarriles Argentinos (FA) were initiated in 1991, with the transfer to private ownership of the Rosario–Bahía Blanca grain line and with the reallocation of responsibility for services in Buenos Aires to the newly created Ferrocarriles Metropolitanos, prior to its privatization.

In 1993 central government funding for the FA was suspended and responsibility for existing intercity passenger routes was devolved to respective provincial governments. However, owing to lack of resources, few provinces have successfully assumed the operation of services, and many trains have been suspended. At the same time, long-distance freight services were sold as six separate 30-year concessions (including lines and rolling stock) to private operators. By late 1996 all freight services had been transferred to private management, with the exception of Ferrocarril Belgrano Cargas, SA, which was in the process of undergoing privatization. In the mid-1990s the FA was replaced by Ente Nacional Administrador de los Bienes Ferroviaros (Enabief), which assumed responsibility for railway infrastructure and the rolling stock not already sold off. The Buenos Aires commuter system was divided into eight concerns (one of which incorporates the underground railway system) and was offered for sale to private operators as 10- or 20-year (subsidized) concessions. The railway network is currently regulated by the Comisión Nacional de Regulación del Transporte (CNRT—see above).

Ente Nacional de Administración de Bienes Ferroviarios (ENABIEF): Avda Raqmos Mejía 1302, 6°, Buenos Aires; tel. (11) 4318-3594.

Ferrocarriles Metropolitanos, SA (FEMESA): Bartolomé Mitre 2815, Buenos Aires; tel. (11) 4865-4135; fax (11) 4861-8757; f. 1991 to assume responsibility for services in the capital; 820 km of track; Pres. MATÍAS ORDÓÑEZ; concessions to operate services have been awarded to the following companies.

Ferrovías: Avda Ramos Mejía 1430, 1104 Buenos Aires; tel. (11) 4314-1444; fax (11) 3311-1181; operates northern commuter line in Buenos Aires; Pres. B. G. ROMERO.

Metropolitano: Avda Santa Fe 4636, 1425 Buenos Aires; tel. (11) 4778-5800; fax (11) 4778-5878; e-mail eltren@metropolitano.co.ar; f. 1993; operates three commuter lines; Pres. J. C. LOUSTAU BIDAUT.

Metrovías (MV): Bartolomé Mitre 3342, 1201 Buenos Aires; tel. (11) 4959-6800; fax (11) 4866-3037; e-mail info@metrovias.com.ar; internet www.metrovias.com.ar; f. 1994; operates subway (Subterráneos de Buenos Aires, q.v.) and two commuter lines; Pres. A. VERRA.

Trenes de Buenos Aires, SA (TBA): Avda Ramos Mejia 1358, 1104 Buenos Aires; tel. (11) 4317-4400; fax (11) 4317-4409; e-mail prensa@tbanet.com.ar; took over operations of two commuter lines from state in 1995; Pres. S. C. CIRIGLIANO.

Cámara de Industriales Ferroviarios: Alsina 1609, 1°, Buenos Aires; tel. (11) 4371-5571; private org. to promote the devt of Argentine railway industries; Pres. Ing. ANA MARÍA GUIBAUDI.

The following consortia were awarded 30-year concessions to operate rail services, in the 1990s:

Ferrobaires (Unidad Ejecutora del Programa Ferroviario Provincial) (UEPFP): General Hornos 11, 4°, 1084 Buenos Aires; tel. (11) 4305-5174; fax (11) 4305-5933; f. 1993; operates long-distance passenger services; Pres. G. CRESPO.

Ferrocarril Buenos Aires al Pacífico/San Martín (BAP): Avda Santa Fe 4636, 3°, Buenos Aires; tel. (11) 4778-2486; fax (11) 4778-2493; operates services on much of the San Martín line, and on 706 km of the Sarmiento line; 6,106 km of track; bought by Brazil's América Latina Logística, SA, in 1999; Pres. N. SILVA.

Ferrocarril Belgrano Cargas, SA (FCGB): Maipú 88, 1084 Buenos Aires; tel. (11) 4343-7220; fax (11) 4343-7229; f. 1993; scheduled for privatization in Aug. 2004; operates freight services; 7,300 km of track and 120 locomotives; Pres. Dr IGNACIO A. LUDVEÑA.

Ferrocarril Mesopotámico General Urquiza (FMGU): Avda Santa Fe 4636, 3°, 1425 Buenos Aires; tel. (11) 4778-2425; fax (11) 4778-2493; operates freight services on the Urquiza lines; 2,272 km of track; bought by Brazil's América Latina Logística, SA, in 1999; Pres. N. SILVA.

Ferroexpreso Pampeano (FEPSA): Bouchard 680, 9°, 1106 Buenos Aires; tel. (11) 4318-4900; fax (11) 4510-4945; operates services on the Rosario–Bahía Blanca grain lines; 5,193 km of track; Pres. H. MASOERO.

Ferrosur Roca (FR): Bouchard 680, 8°, 1106 Buenos Aires; tel. (11) 4319-3900; fax (11) 4319-3901; e-mail ferrosur@impsat1.com.ar; operator of freight services on the Roca lines since 1993; 3,000 km of track; Gen. Man. SERGIO DO REGO.

Nuevo Central Argentino (NCA): Avda Alberdi 50, 2000 Rosario; tel. (341) 437-6561; fax (341) 439-2377; operates freight services on the Bartolomé Mitre lines since 1993; 5,011 km of track; Pres. M. ACEVEDO.

Buenos Aires also has an underground railway system:

Subterráneos de Buenos Aires: Bartolomé Mitre 3342, 1201 Buenos Aires; tel. (11) 4862-6844; fax (11) 4864-0633; f. 1913; became completely state-owned in 1951; fmrly controlled by the Municipalidad de la Ciudad de Buenos Aires; responsibility for operations was transferred, in 1993, to a private consortium (Metrovías) with a 20-year concession; five underground lines totalling 36.5 km, 63 stations, and a 7.4 km light rail line with 13 stations, which was inaugurated in 1987; Pres. A. VERRA.

ROADS

In 2002 there were 215,434 km of roads, of which 29.5% were paved. Four branches of the Pan-American highway run from Buenos Aires to the borders of Chile, Bolivia, Paraguay and Brazil. In 1996 9,932 km of main roads were under private management. Construction work on a 41-km bridge across the River Plate (linking Punta Lara in Argentina with Colonia del Sacramento in Uruguay) was scheduled to begin in the late 1990s; however, by 2005 the agreement with Uruguay to build the bridge still had not been ratified by the Congreso.

Dirección Nacional de Vialidad: Avda Julio A. Roca 378, Buenos Aires; tel. (11) 4343-2838; fax (11) 4343-7292; controlled by the Secretaría de Transportes; Gen. Man. Ing. ELIO VERGARA.

Asociación Argentina de Empresarios Transporte Automotor (AAETA): Bernardo de Irigoyen 330, 6°, 1072 Buenos Aires; e-mail aaeta@sei.com.ar; internet www.aaeta.org.ar; f. 1941; Pres. JUAN CARLOS VÁZQUEZ.

Federación Argentina de Entidades Empresarias de Auto-transporte de Cargas (FADEEAC): Avda 25 de Mayo 1370, 3°, 1372 Buenos Aires; tel. (11) 4383-3635; fax (11) 4383-7870; e-mail fadeeac@fadeeac.org.ar; Pres. LUIS A. MORALES.

There are several international passenger and freight services, including:

Autobuses Sudamericanos, SA: Buenos Aires; tel. (11) 4307-1956; fax (11) 4307-1956; f. 1928; international bus services; car and bus rentals; charter bus services; Pres. ARMANDO SCHLECKER HIRSCH; Gen. Man. MIGUEL ANGEL RUGGIERO.

INLAND WATERWAYS

There is considerable traffic in coastal and river shipping, mainly carrying petroleum and its derivatives.

Dirección Nacional de Construcciones Portuarias y Vías Navegables: Avda España 221, 4°, Buenos Aires; tel. (11) 4361-5964; responsible for the maintenance and improvement of waterways and dredging operations; Dir Ing. ENRIQUE CASALS DE ALBA.

SHIPPING

There are more than 100 ports, of which the most important are Buenos Aires, Quequén and Bahía Blanca. There are specialized terminals at Ensenada, Comodoro Rivadavia, San Lorenzo and Campana (petroleum); Bahía Blanca, Rosario, Santa Fe, Villa Concepción, Mar del Plata and Quequén cereals); and San Nicolas and San Fernando (raw and construction materials). In 2003 Argentina's merchant fleet totalled 497 vessels, with a combined aggregate displacement of 433,909 grt.

Administración General de Puertos: Avda Ing. Huergo 431, 1°, Buenos Aires; tel. (11) 4343-2425; fax (11) 4331-0298; e-mail institucionales@puertobuenosaires.gov.ar; internet www.puertobuenosaires.gov.ar; f. 1956; state enterprise for direction, administration and exploitation of all national sea- and river-ports; scheduled for transfer to private ownership; Gen. Sec. Dr CARLOS FERRARI.

Capitanía General del Puerto: Avda Julio A. Roca 734, 2°, 1067 Buenos Aires; tel. (11) 434-9784; f. 1967; co-ordination of port operations; Port Capt. Capt. PEDRO TARAMASCO.

Administración General de Puertos (Santa Fe): Duque 1 Cabacera, Santa Fe; tel. (42) 41732.

Consorcio de Gestión del Puerto de Bahía Blanca: Avda Dr Mario M. Guido s/n, 8103 Provincia de Buenos Aires; tel. (91) 57-3213; Pres. JOSÉ E. CONTE; Sec.-Gen. CLAUDIO MARCELO CONTE.

Terminales Portuarias Argentinas: Buenos Aires; operates one of five recently privatized cargo and container terminals in the port of Buenos Aires.

Terminales Río de la Plata: Buenos Aires; operates one of five recently privatized cargo and container terminals in the port of Buenos Aires.

Empresa Líneas Marítimas Argentinas, SA (ELMA): Avda Corrientes 389, 1327 Buenos Aires; tel. (11) 4312-9245; fax (11) 4311-7954; f. 1941 as state-owned org.; transferred to private ownership in 1994; operates vessels to northern Europe, the Mediterranean, west and east coasts of Canada and the USA, Gulf of Mexico, Caribbean ports, Brazil, Pacific ports of Central and South America, Far East, northern and southern Africa and the Near East; Pres. PABLO DOMINGO DE ZORZI.

Other private shipping companies operating on coastal and overseas routes include:

Antártida Pesquera Industrial: Moreno 1270, 5°, 1091 Buenos Aires; tel. (11) 4381-0167; fax (11) 4381-0519; Pres. J. M. S. MIRANDA; Man. Dir J. R. S. MIRANDA.

Astramar Cía Argentina de Navegación, SAC: Buenos Aires; tel. (11) 4311-3678; fax (11) 4311-7534; Pres. ENRIQUE W. REDDIG.

Bottacchi SA de Navegación: Buenos Aires; tel. (11) 4392-7411; fax (11) 411-1280; Pres. ÁNGEL L. M. BOTTACCHI.

Maruba S. en C. por Argentina: Maipú 535, 7°, 1006 Buenos Aires; tel. (11) 4322-7173; fax (11) 4322-3353; Chartering Man. R. J. DICKIN.

Yacimientos Petrolíferos Fiscales (YPF): Avda Roque S. Peña 777, 1364 Buenos Aires; tel. (11) 446-7271; privatization finalized in 1993; Pres. NELLS LEÓN.

CIVIL AVIATION

Argentina has 10 international airports (Aeroparque Jorge Newbery, Córdoba, Corrientes, El Plumerillo, Ezeiza, Jujuy, Resistencia, Río Gallegos, Salta and San Carlos de Bariloche). Ezeiza, 35 km from Buenos Aires, is one of the most important air terminals in Latin America. More than 30 airports were scheduled for transfer to private ownership.

Aerolíneas Argentinas: Bouchard 547, 9°, 1106 Buenos Aires; tel. (11) 4317-3000; fax (11) 4320-2116; internet www.aerolineas.com.ar; f. 1950; transfer to private ownership initiated in 1990; 97.9% stake acquired by the Spanish company AirComet Marsans in 2001; services to North and Central America, Europe, the Far East, New Zealand, South Africa and destinations throughout South America; the internal network covers the whole country; passengers, mail and freight are carried; Pres. ANTONIO MATA.

Austral Líneas Aéreas (ALA): Corrientes 485, 9°, 1398, Buenos Aires; tel. (11) 4317-3600; fax (11) 4317-3777; internet www

.austral.com.ar; f. 1971; domestic flights linking 27 cities in Argentina; Pres. MANUEL CASERO.

Aerovip: Ricardo Rojas 401, 5°, Buenos Aires; tel. (11) 4312-6954; fax (11) 4312-7080; f. 1999; domestic scheduled and charter flights.

Air Plus Argentina: Juncal 858, 3°c, Buenos Aires; tel. (11) 4393-9935; fax (11) 4328-3609; f. 1999; charter flights between Argentina and the USA; Pres. LUIS LÚPORI; Gen. Man. MIGUEL MAGGI.

Líneas Aéreas del Estado (LADE): Perú 710, 1068 Buenos Aires; tel. (11) 4361-7071; fax (11) 4362-4899; e-mail director@lade.com.ar; f. 1940; Dir GUILLERMO JOSÉ TESTONI.

Líneas Aéreas Federales, SA (LAFSA): Buenos Aires; f. 2003; founded following the suspension of operations of Líneas Aéreas Privadas Argentinas and Dinar Líneas Aéreas; co-operation accord signed with Southern Winds Líneas Aéreas in September 2003 (annulled by the Government in February 2005); signed a co-operation accord with Línea Aérea Nacional de Chile in March 2005, with a view to the creation of Línea Aérea Nacional de Argentina in mid-2005.

Southern Winds Líneas Aéreas: Quaglia 262, Local 13, Buenos Aires; internet www.fly-sw.com; f. 1996; co-operation accord signed with Líneas Aéreas Federales, SA in Sept. 2003 (annulled by the Govt in Feb. 2005); Pres. JUAN MAGGIO.

Transporte Aéreo Costa Atlántica (TACA): Bernardo de Yrigoyen 1370, 1°, Ofs 25–26, 1138 Buenos Aires; tel. (11) 4307-1956; fax (11) 4307-8899; f. 1956; domestic and international passenger and freight services between Argentina and Bolivia, Brazil and the USA; Pres. Dr ARMANDO SCHLECKER HIRSCH.

Transportes Aéreos Neuquén: Diagonal 25 de Mayo 180, 8300 Neuquén; tel. (299) 4423076; fax (299) 4488926; e-mail tancentr@satlink.com.ar; domestic routes; Pres. JOSÉ CHALÉN; Gen. Man. PATROCINIO VALVERDE MORAIS.

Valls Líneas Aéreas: Río Grande, Tierra del Fuego; f. 1995; operates three routes between destinations in southern Argentina, Chile and the South Atlantic islands.

Tourism

Argentina's superb tourist attractions include the Andes mountains, the lake district centred on Bariloche (where there is a National Park), Patagonia, the Atlantic beaches and Mar del Plata, the Iguazú falls, the Pampas and Tierra del Fuego. Tourist arrivals in Argentina in 2004 totalled an estimated 2.4m. In that year tourism receipts were an estimated US $2,500m.

Secretaría de Turismo de la Nación: Suipacha 1111, 20°, 1368 Buenos Aires; tel. (11) 4312-5611; fax (11) 4313-6834; e-mail info@turismo.gov.ar; internet www.sectur.gov.ar; Sec. CARLOS ENRIQUE MEYER.

Asociación Argentina de Agencias de Viajes y Turismo (AAAVYT): Viamonte 640, 10°, 1053 Buenos Aires; tel. (11) 4325-4691; fax (11) 4322-9641; e-mail secretaria@aaavyt.org.ar; internet www.aaavyt.org.ar; f. 1951; Pres. TOMÁS PATRICIO RYAN; Gen. Man. GERARDO BELIO.

ARMENIA

Introductory Survey

Location, Climate, Language, Religion, Flag, Capital

The Republic of Armenia is situated in south-west Transcaucasia, on the north-eastern border of Turkey. Its other borders are with Iran to the south, Azerbaijan to the east, and Georgia to the north. The Naxçıvan (Nakhchivan) Autonomous Republic, an Azerbaijani territory, is situated to the south, separated from the remainder of Azerbaijan by Armenian territory. The climate is typically continental: dry, with wide temperature variations. Winters are cold, the average January temperature in Yerevan being –3°C (26°F), but summers can be very warm, with August temperatures averaging 25°C (77°F), although high altitude moderates the heat in much of the country. Precipitation is low in the Yerevan area (annual average 322 mm), but much higher in the mountains. The official language is Armenian, the sole member of a distinct Indo-European language group. It is written in the Armenian script. Kurdish is used in broadcasting and publishing for some 56,000 Kurds inhabiting Armenia. Most of the population are adherents of Christianity, the largest denomination being the Armenian Apostolic Church. There are also Russian Orthodox, Protestant, Islamic and Yazidi communities. The national flag (approximate proportions 2 by 3) consists of three equal horizontal stripes, of red, blue and orange. The capital is Yerevan.

Recent History

Although Armenia was an important power in ancient times, and formed the first Christian state, around AD 300, for much of its history it was ruled by foreign states. In 1639 Armenia was partitioned, with the larger, western part being annexed by the Osmanlı (Ottoman) Empire and the eastern region becoming part of the Persian Empire. In 1828, after a period of Russo–Persian conflict, eastern Armenia was ceded to the Russian Empire by the Treaty of Turkmanchai. At the beginning of the 20th century Armenians living in western, or Anatolian, Armenia, under Ottoman rule, were subject to increasing persecution by the Turks. As a result of brutal massacres and deportations (particularly in 1915), the Anatolian lands were largely emptied of their Armenian population, and it was estimated that during 1915–22 some 1.5m. Armenians perished. After the collapse of Russian imperial power in 1917, Russian Armenia joined the anti-Bolshevik Transcaucasian Federation, which included Georgia and Azerbaijan. This collapsed when threatened by Turkish forces, and on 28 May 1918 Armenia was proclaimed an independent state. Without Russian protection, however, the newly formed republic was almost defenceless against Turkish expansionism and was forced to cede territory around Kars to the Turks. Armenia was recognized as an independent state by the Allied Powers and by Turkey in the Treaty of Sèvres, signed on 10 August 1920. However, the rejection of the Treaty by the new Turkish ruler, Mustafa Kemal, left Armenia vulnerable to renewed Turkish threats. In September Turkish troops attacked Armenia, but they were prevented from establishing full control over the country by the invasion of Armenia, from the east, by Russian Bolshevik troops, and the founding, on 29 November, of a Soviet Republic of Armenia. In December 1922 the republic became a member, together with Georgia and Azerbaijan, of the Transcaucasian Soviet Federative Socialist Republic (TSFSR), which, in turn, became a constituent republic of the USSR. In 1936 the TSFSR was dissolved, and the Armenian Soviet Socialist Republic (SSR) formed as a full union republic of the USSR.

The Soviet Armenian authorities implemented a policy of forced modernization, expanding communications and introducing industrial plants. Literacy and education were also improved. A programme to collectivize agriculture, initiated on a voluntary basis in 1928, was enforced in 1930 and many thousands of peasants who opposed it were deported. Thousands more Armenians were executed or imprisoned during the Stalinist purges of the late 1930s. During the Second World War (1939–45), Armenia avoided occupation by German forces, despite their invasion of the USSR in June 1941. Consequently, the republic provided an essential source of labour for the Soviet economy, and as many as 600,000 Armenians served in the Soviet armies (of whom an estimated 350,000 were killed). In the immediate post-war period the Soviet Government gave priority to developing the industrial sector in Armenia, while expanding the agricultural collectivization programme. In the late 1940s an estimated 150,000 Armenians of the diaspora returned to the republic.

The Soviet leader Mikhail Gorbachev's policies of *perestroika* (restructuring) and *glasnost* (openness), introduced following his accession to power in 1985, had little initial impact in Armenia. The first manifestations of the new policies were campaigns against corruption in the higher echelons of the Communist Party of Armenia (CPA). The most significant of the historical and ethnic concerns discussed from late 1987 was the status of Nagornyi Karabakh (known as Artsakh in Armenian), an autonomous oblast (region) within neighbouring Azerbaijan, largely populated by Armenians, control of which had been ceded to Azerbaijan in 1921 (see the chapter on Azerbaijan). In February 1988 up to 1m. people took part in demonstrations in Yerevan, the Armenian capital, organized by a group of Yerevan intellectuals, known as the Karabakh Committee, to support demands from Armenian inhabitants of Nagornyi Karabakh for the incorporation of the territory into the Armenian SSR. In response to increased unrest within Armenia, many Azeris began to leave the republic. Reports of ill-treatment of Azeris in Armenia and Nagornyi Karabakh led to anti-Armenian riots in Sumgait, Azerbaijan, in late February, in which 26 Armenians died. This event provoked further Armenian anger, which was compounded by the decision of the Presidium of the USSR's Supreme Soviet (legislature) that Nagornyi Karabakh should remain under Azerbaijani jurisdiction. The inability of the local authorities to control ongoing unrest led to the dismissal, in May, of the First Secretary (leader) of the CPA. In December, however, the issue of Nagornyi Karabakh was temporarily subordinated to the problem of overcoming the effects of a severe earthquake, which had struck northern Armenia. Some 25,000 people were reported to have been killed and many thousands more were made homeless. Following the earthquake members of the (outlawed) Karabakh Committee were arrested, ostensibly for interfering in relief work. They were released in May 1989, after huge demonstrations took place, protesting against their continued internment. Meanwhile, in January the Soviet Government had formed a Special Administration Committee (SAC) of the Council of Ministers to preside over Nagornyi Karabakh, although the enclave remained under formal Azerbaijani jurisdiction. In September Azerbaijan announced the closure of its borders with Armenia, and prohibited trade with the republic, seriously affecting the reconstruction programme required in Armenia after the 1988 earthquake. In November the SAC was disbanded, and Azerbaijan resumed control over Nagornyi Karabakh. This prompted the Armenian Supreme Soviet to declare the territory part of a 'unified Armenian Republic'. Following a declaration, in January 1990, by the USSR Supreme Soviet that this measure was unconstitutional, the Armenian legislature attributed to itself the power to veto any legislation approved by the central authorities.

The increasing disillusionment with the Soviet Government was apparently responsible for the low level of participation in the elections to the Armenian Supreme Soviet, which took place in May–July 1990. The Armenian Pan-National Movement (APNM), the successor to the Karabakh Committee, was the largest single party, with some 35% of the seats in the legislature. Supported by other non-communist groups, Levon Ter-Petrossian, a leader of the APNM was elected to the chairmanship of the Supreme Soviet. Vazgen Manukian, also an APNM leader, was appointed Prime Minister. On 23 August the legislature adopted a declaration of sovereignty, including a claim to the right to maintain armed forces and a demand for international recognition that the Turkish massacres of Armenians in 1915 constituted genocide. The Armenian SSR was renamed the Republic of Armenia. The new Government began to establish political and commercial links with the Armenian diaspora, and several prominent exiles returned to the republic.

The Armenian Government refused to enter into the negotiations between Soviet republics on a new treaty of union, which took place in late 1990 and early 1991, and officially boycotted the referendum on the renewal of the USSR, which was held in March 1991 in nine republics. Instead, the legislature decided to conduct a referendum on Armenian secession from the USSR, to be held in September. In late April there was an escalation of tension in Nagornyi Karabakh. The Armenian Government continued to deny any direct involvement in the violence, claiming that the attacks were outside its control, being organized by units of the ethnic Armenian 'Nagornyi Karabakh self-defence forces'. However, the Azerbaijani republican authorities countered that Armenia was, in fact, playing an aggressive role in the conflict. Meanwhile, Armenia suggested that the Soviet leadership was supporting Azerbaijan, following the latter's agreement to sign the new union treaty, and punishing Armenia for its moves towards independence and for its nationalization of CPA property.

The attempted coup in the Soviet and Russian capital, Moscow, in August 1991 provided further support for those advocating Armenian independence. According to the official results of the referendum called by the republican authorities, held on 21 September, 99.3% of those participating (some 94.4% of the electorate) supported Armenia's reconstitution as 'an independent, democratic state outside the Union'. On 23 September, instead of conforming to the Soviet law on secession (which had been adopted in April and provided for a transitional period of at least five years before full independence could be achieved), the Supreme Soviet declared Armenia to be, thenceforth, a fully independent state. Meanwhile, in early September a congress of the CPA voted to dissolve the party.

The independence declaration was followed, on 16 October 1991, by an election to the post of President of the Republic. Six candidates participated in the poll, which was won by Ter-Petrossian (with some 87% of the votes cast). The Armenian leadership joined the Commonwealth of Independent States (CIS, see p. 189), signing the founding Almaty (Alma-Ata) Declaration on 21 December. In early 1992 Armenia was admitted to the Conference on Security and Co-operation in Europe (CSCE—now the Organization for Security and Co-operation in Europe—OSCE, see p. 314), and the UN.

In 1992 economic conditions deteriorated, and there were widespread shortages of foodstuffs and fuel. The situation was exacerbated not only by the continuing conflict in Nagornyi Karabakh (see below), but also by fighting in neighbouring Georgia (which impeded supplies to Armenia), and the closure of borders with Azerbaijan. Compounding the economic crisis was an influx of refugees from Nagornyi Karabakh and elsewhere in Azerbaijan. There were also increasing indications of public dissatisfaction with the Ter-Petrossian administration, and in mid-August 1992 and in February 1993 mass rallies were staged in Yerevan to demand the President's resignation. Earlier in February 1993 Ter-Petrossian had dismissed the Prime Minister, Khosrov Haroutunian, following disagreements over economic and social policy, and a new Council of Ministers was subsequently announced, headed by Hrant Bagratian, who was widely regarded as an economic reformist. However, the economic crisis intensified, partly as a result of Turkey, Azerbaijan's ally, closing its borders with Armenia and imposing economic sanctions against the country in April 1993, and hundreds of thousands of Armenians were reported to have emigrated. In the latter half of 1994 thousands of people participated in frequent anti-Government protests, organized by an association of opposition groups, known as the Union of Civic Accord. The assassination in December of a former mayor of Yerevan prompted the Government to effect a number of measures that it described as aimed at eliminating terrorism, the most radical of which was the suspension of the leading opposition party, the Armenian Revolutionary Federation (ARF, or Dashnaktsutiun, which had formed the Government of independent Armenia in 1918–20).

Armenia's first post-Soviet legislative elections were held in July 1995. Thirteen parties and organizations contested the 190 seats of the new Azgayin Zhogov (National Assembly) under a mixed system of voting (with 150 seats to be filled by majority voting and 40 by proportional representation on the basis of party lists). Nine parties, including the ARF, were barred from participation. The Republican bloc (an alliance of six groups, led by the APNM) won a majority of the seats in the assembly (119), and 45 independent candidates were elected. Eight seats were won by the Shamiram Women's Party, while the revived CPA

secured seven. In late July Ter-Petrossian appointed a new Government, in which Bagratian remained as Prime Minister. A referendum on a new Armenian constitution was held simultaneously with the general election. Of the 56% of the electorate who participated in the plebiscite, some 68% voted in favour of the Constitution, which granted wide-ranging executive authority to the President and provided for a smaller, 131-member Azgayin Zhogov (to comprise 75 deputies elected by majority vote through single-mandate constituencies, and 56 elected on the basis of party lists) with effect from the next general election.

A presidential election was held on 22 September 1996. Ter-Petrossian was the candidate of the Republican bloc, while five opposition parties united to support Vazgen Manukian, the Chairman of the National Democratic Union (NDU). Although preliminary results indicated that Ter-Petrossian had been re-elected, the opposition made allegations of widespread electoral malpractice, and thousands staged protest rallies in Yerevan, to demand the President's resignation. International observers reported serious irregularities in the electoral proceedings. On 25 September supporters of Manukian stormed the Azgayin Zhogov, injuring, among others, the Chairman and his deputy. A temporary ban on rallies was consequently imposed, and large numbers of opposition supporters were arrested. According to the final election results, Ter-Petrossian received 51.8% of the votes cast, and Manukian secured 41.3% (although he received significantly more votes than Ter-Petrossian in Yerevan). Bagratian resigned as Prime Minister, reportedly in response to opposition to his programme of economic reforms, in November; he was replaced by Armen Sarkissian. The latter resigned in March 1997 on grounds of ill health, and was succeeded as Prime Minister by Robert Kocharian, hitherto the 'President' of the self-styled 'Republic of Nagornyi Karabakh', in what was regarded as an attempt by Ter-Petrossian to reduce pressure from nationalist opposition parties.

Following the resignation of Ter-Petrossian on 3 February 1998, owing to government controversy over his support of an OSCE plan for a progressive settlement in Nagornyi Karabakh (see below), a presidential election was held on 16 and 30 March. In the second round of voting, Kocharian, the acting President, secured victory over the former CPA leader, Karen Demirchian, obtaining 59.5% of the votes cast, and was inaugurated as President on 9 April. On the following day Kocharian appointed Armen Darbinian, the erstwhile Minister of Finance and the Economy, as Prime Minister. In early May Kocharian legalized the ARF, and appointed two members of the party, including its leader, Vahan Hovhanissian, to positions in the Government (an ARF member had also been included in the Government on its appointment the previous month).

In February 1999 the legislature, under threat of dissolution, endorsed a petition by the Prosecutor-General for permission to arrest the Chairman of the APNM and former Minister of the Interior, Vano Siradeghian (thereby removing his parliamentary immunity), who was alleged to have been involved in a number of politically motivated murders in the mid-1990s .(Siradeghian was arrested in May 1999; following the commencement of his trial, in January 2000, he fled the country in April). Also in February 1999 the commander of Armenia's interior ministry troops, Maj.-Gen. Artsrun Makarian, had been found shot dead, prompting speculation that he had been killed to prevent him from giving evidence against Siradeghian.

In the election to the Azgayin Zhogov, held on 30 May 1999, the Unity bloc (Miasnutiun), an alliance of the Republican Party of Armenia (RPA) and the People's Party of Armenia (PPA), won 55 of 131 elective seats; 32 independent candidates were elected. The CPA secured 11 seats and the ARF obtained nine. On 11 June 1999 Darbinian (who became Minister of the Economy) was replaced as Prime Minister by Vazgen Sarkissian, the unofficial leader of the RPA and hitherto Minister of Defence. Meanwhile, Demirchian, by this time head of the PPA, was elected as legislative Chairman.

On 27 October 1999 five gunmen entered the Azgayin Zhogov, killing eight people, including Prime Minister Sarkissian, Demirchian and his two deputies, and a cabinet minister. The gunmen, who claimed no political affiliation, announced that they were seeking revenge against the 'corrupt political élite'. On their surrender the assailants were charged with murder and terrorist offences. (Their trial commenced in February 2001.) In the aftermath of the attack, the Ministers of the Interior and of National Security tendered their resignations. At the beginning of November 1999 Armen Khachatrian of the PPA was elected Chairman of the legislature. Aram Sarkissian, the younger brother of the murdered premier, and a political novice, was subsequently appointed Prime Minister, on the recommendation of members of the Unity bloc. However, in May 2000 Kocharian dismissed the Prime Minister, appointing Andranik Markarian, the leader of the RPA, as his successor, prior to the implementation of a cabinet reshuffle.

The PPA left the Unity bloc in September 2001, following conflict between the RPA and PPA factions. In late October the PPA, together with Republic (Hanrapetutiun—founded by former members of the RPA and the Yerkrapah Union of Volunteers in early 2001) and the National Unity Party, organized a rally to demand the impeachment of the President, whom they accused, *inter alia*, of precipitating a socio-economic crisis in the country, acting in contravention of the Constitution and condoning terrorism. Meanwhile, in mid-September Gagik Pogossian, an aide to the Prime Minister, was killed as a result of a bomb attack; he had been involved in the investigation of fraud and corruption.

In April 2002 thousands of people participated in protests against the closure of the independent television station, A1+, which opposition parties claimed to be politically motivated, and further demands were made for the President's resignation. In the same month legislation was adopted abolishing the death penalty, although the new law was not to apply to those found guilty of perpetrating terrorist or paedophile offences prior to its introduction, including the parliamentary killings of October 1999. In September 2002, however, the Council of Europe (see p. 199) threatened Armenia with expulsion from the organization, unless it agreed to the unconditional abolition of capital punishment by June 2003. In September of that year the Government finally ratified a complete ban on capital punishment.

Meanwhile, in August 2002 legislation was approved increasing the number of deputies elected by majority vote through single-mandate constituencies to 56 (it had been reduced to 37 as part of electoral reform enacted in December 2000); opposition deputies argued that the amendment would serve to benefit the governing RPA in the legislative elections due to be held in May 2003. The composition of the Central Electoral Commission was also reorganized, with three of its nine members henceforth to be presidential appointments. In mid-December 2002 the Ministry of Internal Affairs and the Ministry of National Security were restructured as non-ministerial institutions, and renamed the Police of the Republic of Armenia and the National Security Service. Although the respective former ministers remained part of the Government, some observers interpreted the measure as reinforcing legislation passed earlier in the year, which had increased presidential control over the country's security framework.

The Azgayin Zhogov failed to reconvene in early February 2003, following a one-month recess, owing to the lack of a quorum, prompting opposition deputies to claim that the pro-Government majority was seeking deliberately to stall debate until after the presidential election. Nine candidates participated in the election, held on 19 February. Kocharian received 49.5% of the votes cast, fewer than the 50% required to secure an outright victory. In the second round, held on 5 March, Kocharian was re-elected as President with 67.5% of the votes cast, defeating Stepan Demirchian (the son of the murdered parliamentary Chairman), the candidate of the PPA. Monitors from both the OSCE and the Council of Europe recorded irregularities in electoral procedure, and thousands of people took part in protests against the results, which were, none the less, declared valid by the Constitutional Court in mid-April. Legislative proceedings were further impeded after the presidential election owing to a boycott of parliamentary sessions by opposition deputies.

Legislative elections were held on 25 May 2003, in which the pro-presidential RPA won 32 seats, the Law-Governed Country Party of Armenia received 18 seats, the Justice (Artarutiun) bloc (led by Demirchian, and comprising the Armenian Democratic Party, the National Democratic Party, the People's Party of Armenia and the Union of National Democrats) secured 15 seats, the ARF obtained 11 and the National Unity Party secured nine. However, once again both international observers and opposition parties reported incidences of electoral malpractice. A referendum on proposed constitutional amendments, held simultaneously with the elections, failed to attract the support of the requisite one-third of registered voters. On 11 June the RPA, the Law-Governed Country Party and the ARF formed a coalition Government, again led by Andranik Mar-

karian. Many RPA cabinet members retained their portfolios from the previous Government, while the two junior coalition parties were each awarded three ministerial portfolios. The Chairman of the Law-Governed Country Party, Artur Baghdasarian, was appointed Chairman of the Azgayin Zhogov. Members of both the Justice bloc and the National Unity Party boycotted parliamentary sessions until September, in protest at the results of the election.

In November 2003 Armen Sarkissian, brother of the murdered premier Vazgen Sarkissian and former premier Aram Sarkissian (by this time leader of the opposition Armenian Democratic Party), was sentenced to 15 years' imprisonment, after being found guilty of organizing the contract killing of Tigran Naghdalian, the Chairman of the board of Armenian Public Television and Radio, in December 2002. Sarkissian continued to deny the charge, claiming it to have been politically motivated, in an attempt to discredit the Armenian Democratic Party prior to the legislative elections. In December 2003 six men were sentenced to life imprisonment for their involvement in the attack on the Azgayin Zhogov in October 1999 (one other defendant was imprisoned for 14 years).

The legislative boycott by the parties of the Justice bloc and the National Unity Party was resumed from February 2004 following the refusal of the Azgayin Zhoghov to debate constitutional amendments allowing for a referendum of confidence in the President. In April demonstrations, organized by those parties boycotting the legislature, began in Yerevan in protest against the conduct of the presidential election of 2003 and to demand Kocharian's resignation. These demonstrations continued until their voluntary disbandment in June; demonstrators had been, at times, forcibly dispersed and arrested by the security forces, invoking denunciation from international sources. Two of the Law-Governed Country's three ministerial representatives left office in 2004; in April Tamara Poghossian was dismissed as Minister of Culture and Youth Affairs. She was subsequently replaced by Hovik Hoveian, while Ara Aramian resigned as Minister of Urban Planning, following the arrest of his son; he was succeeded by Aram Haroutunuian. Although the remaining minister of that party, Sergo Yeritsian, Minister of Education and Science was also linked with allegations of bribery in relation to university admissions, he remained in office.

The question of proposed constitutional reform (in association with which the Government had committed itself, in negotiations with the Council of Europe, to holding a constitutional referendum, no later than mid-2005) remained a contentious topic, both within the legislature and Government. Among the principal areas of disagreement were the proportion of deputies that were to be elected by proportional representation, and the extent to which presidential powers should be strengthened.

The proclamation of Armenia's independence in September 1991 led to an escalation of hostilities in the disputed oblast of Nagornyi Karabakh in Azerbaijan. In that month the territory declared itself an independent republic, and violence intensified following the dissolution of the USSR in December. In January 1992 the President of Azerbaijan, Ayaz Mutalibov, placed the region under direct presidential rule; in the same month Azerbaijani forces surrounded and attacked Stepanakert (Xanxandi—Khankendi in Azerbaijani), the capital of Nagornyi Karabakh, while the Armenians laid siege to Shushi (Şuşa), a town with a mainly Azerbaijani population. In May the Nagornyi Karabakh self-defence forces (which the Armenian Government continued to claim were operating without its military support) captured Shushi, thereby gaining complete control of the enclave and ending the bombardment of Stepanakert. With the capture of the strategically-important Lachin (Laçin) valley, the ethnic Armenian militia succeeded in opening a 'corridor' within Azerbaijan between Nagornyi Karabakh with Armenia.

In June 1992 Azerbaijani forces launched a sustained counter-offensive in Nagornyi Karabakh, recapturing villages both inside and around the enclave, and expelling several thousand inhabitants, thus exacerbating the already urgent refugee crisis. In August Azerbaijani forces resumed the bombardment of Stepanakert. In response to the escalation of attacks and ensuing military gains by Azerbaijani forces, the Nagornyi Karabakh legislature declared a state of martial law, and a state defence committee, in close alignment with the Ter-Petrossian administration of Armenia, replaced the territory's Government.

In early 1993 ethnic Armenian forces undertook a series of successful offensives in and around Nagornyi Karabakh. With the capture of the Kelbajar district of Azerbaijan in April 1993, a second, lengthier, corridor, linking the territory with Armenia, was formed, and ethnic Armenians effectively secured control of all Azerbaijani territory between Kelbajar in the north and Lachin in the south. Many thousands of Azeris fled or were expelled from their homes. The Armenian position was further strengthened by the growing political turmoil in Azerbaijan in mid-1993 (q.v.), and by late June Armenian forces had secured full control of Nagornyi Karabakh. The Armenian seizure of Azerbaijani territory prompted widespread international condemnation, particularly by Turkey and Iran, the latter fearing a massive influx of refugees from south-western Azerbaijan. UN Security Council Resolutions 822 and 853, demanding the withdrawal of occupying and local Armenian forces from Azerbaijan, went unheeded; hostilities reintensified, and more than 20% of Azerbaijan's total territory was reported to have been captured by the Nagornyi Karabakh Armenian forces, who had extended their operations as far south as the Azerbaijan–Iran border; Azerbaijani forces recaptured some territory in a counter-offensive launched in December. In February 1994 it was reported that as many as 18,000 people had been killed since 1988, with a further 25,000 wounded. The number of displaced Azeris was believed to have exceeded 1m.

A series of fragile cease-fire agreements was reached in early 1994, and in May, following protracted mediation by the CSCE and Russia, a new cease-fire agreement was signed by the Ministers of Defence of Armenia and Azerbaijan and representatives of Nagornyi Karabakh. The agreement was formalized in July. Ter-Petrossian held talks with the President of Azerbaijan, Heydar Aliyev, in Moscow, in September. Although agreement was reached on some key provisions of a future peace treaty, Aliyev stated that his willingness to negotiate such an accord depended on the unconditional withdrawal of Armenian forces from occupied Azerbaijani territory. Negotiations were held at regular intervals throughout 1995 under the aegis of the 'Minsk Group' of the OSCE, although only limited progress towards a political settlement was made. Nevertheless, only sporadic violations of the cease-fire were reported, and in May the three sides carried out a large-scale exchange of prisoners of war. Direct discussions between Armenia and Azerbaijan, which were held in conjunction with the OSCE negotiations, were initiated in December.

Elections to the post of president of Nagornyi Karabakh, held in November 1996, were condemned by Azerbaijan and criticized by the Minsk Group as a hindrance to the peace process. Robert Kocharian, the incumbent, was re-elected with some 86% of the votes cast. In December Ter-Petrossian and Aliyev attended an OSCE summit meeting in Lisbon, Portugal. Following demands by Azerbaijan, the OSCE Chairman issued a statement recommending three principles that would form the basis of a future political settlement in the enclave: the territorial integrity of Armenia and Azerbaijan; the legal status of Nagornyi Karabakh, which would be granted broad autonomy within Azerbaijan; and security guarantees for the population of Nagornyi Karabakh. Armenia, however, refused to accept the terms of the statement.

Relations between Armenia and Azerbaijan deteriorated in early 1997, with mutual accusations of the stockpiling of weapons in preparation for the renewal of military conflict in Nagornyi Karabakh. Fresh elections to the post of president of Nagornyi Karabakh in September, which were scheduled following the appointment of Kocharian as Prime Minister of Armenia, were won by Arkadii Ghukassian, with some 90% of the votes cast, but were criticized by the international community. Ghukassian reportedly rejected the OSCE peace settlement on the grounds that the proposals presupposed Azerbaijan's sovereignty over the enclave. A subsequent statement by President Ter-Petrossian that Nagornyi Karabakh could hope neither to gain full independence, nor to be united with Armenia, appeared to indicate a significant change in policy, but the President's moderate approach to the crisis, which provoked much government disapproval, led to his resignation in early February 1998. His replacement, Kocharian, who was born in Nagornyi Karabakh, was expected to adopt a more nationalist stance towards the situation in the disputed enclave, although in late November the Armenian Government accepted new proposals put forward by the Minsk Group for a settlement of the conflict, which were based on the principle of a 'common state'. They were, however, rejected by Azerbaijan. Following an escalation in hostilities in mid-1999, each side accused the other of attempting to abrogate the 1994 cease-fire agreement. In

March 2000 Ghukassian sustained serious injuries following an attack by gunmen in Stepanakert. The former Minister of Defence of Nagornyi Karabakh, Samuel Babaian, was subsequently sentenced to 14 years' imprisonment in February 2001 (he was, however, released under an amnesty in September 2004). Ghukassian was re-elected in August 2002, with some 88.4% of the votes. Meanwhile, despite several meetings between the Armenian and Azerbaijani Presidents in 1999–2002, no substantive progress was made towards reaching a final resolution of the Nagornyi Karabakh conflict. Direct negotiations did not take place in 2003, and there were concerns that the Azerbaijani President elected in October of that year, İlham Aliyev, might prove less open to negotiation, although interaction was resumed in 2004. In January 2005 the Parliamentary Assembly of the Council of Europe approved a controversial resolution on Nagornyi Karabakh, expressing concern at the large-scale ethnic expulsion and creation of mono-ethnic areas which resulted from the conflict, which were described as resembling 'the terrible concept of ethnic cleansing'; the resolution clearly stated the unacceptability of Armenian occupation of Azerbaijani territory.

In April 1997 the Armenian legislature ratified a treaty that allowed Russia to maintain military bases in Armenia for a period of 25 years. The ties between Russia and Armenia were reinforced by a declaration of alliance and co-operation, and a number of bilateral agreements were concluded in September 2000. A further, 10-year economic co-operation agreement was signed in September 2001, during a visit to Armenia by the Russian President, Vladimir Putin. Armenia's relations with Georgia were generally cordial in the post-Soviet period, particularly during the presidency of Eduard Shevardnadze (1995–2003), while the recently elected President of Georgia, Mikheil Saakashvili, visited Armenia in March 2004, reaffirming the stability of relations between the two countries. Meanwhile, relations with Turkey (which controlled large areas of historic Armenia, including Mount Ararat, regarded as a national symbol by many Armenians) remained uneasy, particularly following the closure of its borders with Armenia in 1993. Moreover, Turkey refused to allow the demarcation of its border with Armenia, owing to the presence of Russian border guards in that country. In September 2001 the first meeting of a Turkish-Armenian Reconciliation Commission (TARC), composed of members from both countries, was held in İstanbul, Turkey; at a second meeting, held in New York, USA, it was agreed to ask the New York-based International Centre for Transitional Justice to establish whether the Turkish massacre of Armenians in 1915–22 had constituted 'genocide'. In February 2003 it was reported that the International Centre for Transitional Justice had concluded that the massacres of 1915–22 could be interpreted as genocide, according to international criteria. (The TARC was officially dissolved in April 2004.) In December 2004, following an appeal from President Kocharian, the European Parliament issued a statement that Turkey should recognize that genocide against Armenians had taken place in 1915, and open its borders, as part of a non-binding resolution on the initiation of Turkey's negotiations for eventual EU membership. However, the Armenian Government's campaign to secure recognition of the killings in 1915 as 'genocide' and the continuing conflict with Azerbaijan over Nagornyi Karabakh remained serious obstacles to the development of closer relations. Armenia generally enjoyed cordial relations with Iran, with a permanent bridge between the two countries being opened in 1995. (During the Soviet period there had been no crossing point on the Armenian–Iranian border). In September 2004 President Hojatoleslam Dr Sayed Muhammad Khatami of Iran made a long-postponed official visit to Armenia, signing seven bilateral agreements with President Kocharian, which *inter alia*, were to promote enhanced co-operation in energy and transport.

In June 2000 the Parliamentary Assembly of the Council of Europe voted to admit both Armenia and Azerbaijan to that organization; they became full members in January 2001. In June 2004 Armenia, Azerbaijan and Georgia were included in the EU's new European Neighbourhood Policy.

Government

Under the Constitution of 1995, the President of the Republic is Head of State and Supreme Commander-in-Chief of the armed forces, but also holds broad executive powers. The President is directly elected for a term of five years (and for no more than two consecutive terms of office). The President appoints the Prime Minister and, on the latter's recommendation, the members of the Government. Legislative power is vested in the 131-member Azgayin Zhogov (National Assembly), which is elected for a four-year term by universal adult suffrage. For administrative purposes, Armenia is divided into 11 regions (*marzer*), including the capital, Yerevan. The regions are subdivided into communities (*hamaynker*).

Defence

Following the dissolution of the USSR in December 1991, Armenia became a member of the Commonwealth of Independent States (CIS, see p. 189) and its Collective Security Treaty. In April 2003 the Collective Security Treaty Organization (CSTO) was inaugurated as the successor to the CIS collective security system, with the participation of Armenia, Belarus, Kazakhstan, Kyrgyzstan, Russia and Tajikistan. After 1991 Armenia began to establish its own armed forces, which numbered some 44,874 in August 2004, including an army of 41,714 and an air force of 3,160. Military service is compulsory and lasts for two years (a draft law was adopted in December 2002, however, providing for a 42-month alternative, civilian service). There is also a paramilitary force of an estimated 1,000. In August 2004 there were approximately 3,500 Russian troops stationed on Armenian territory. In October 1994 Armenia joined the North Atlantic Treaty Organization's (NATO) 'Partnership for Peace' (see p. 303) programme of military co-operation. The budget for 2004 allocated an estimated US $89m. to defence. The budget for 2004 provided for an increase in defence expenditure of some 19%.

Economic Affairs

In 2003, according to estimates by the World Bank, Armenia's gross national income (GNI), measured at average 2001–03 prices, was US $2,919m., equivalent to $950 per head (or $3,770 on an international purchasing-power parity basis). During 1990–2003, it was estimated, the population decreased at an average rate of 1.1% per year, while gross domestic product (GDP) per head decreased, in real terms, by an annual average of 0.7%. Over the same period, Armenia's overall GDP decreased, in real terms, by an average of 0.3% annually. However, real GDP increased by 12.9% in 2002 and, according to official figures, GDP increased by 13.9% in 2003.

According to the World Bank, agriculture and forestry contributed 24.1% of GDP in 2003 and, according to official figures, employed 46.0% of the working population in 2003. (However, FAO estimated the proportion of the working population employed in agriculture at just 11.7% in that year.) The principal crops are potatoes and other vegetables, cereals and fruit, primarily grapes. Private farms accounted for some 98% of agricultural production by 1998. During 1990–2003, according to estimates by the World Bank, agricultural GDP increased, in real terms, at an average annual rate of 1.3%. The GDP of the sector increased by 4.4% in 2002 and by 2.6% in 2003. Further growth was expected in 2004, owing to improvements in the irrigation infrastructure and good weather conditions.

According to the World Bank, in 2003 industry (including mining, manufacturing, construction and power) contributed 37.7% of GDP. The sector employed 29.1% of the working population in 2003, according to official figures. World Bank estimates indicated that during 1990–2003 real industrial GDP declined by an average of 5.8% annually. However, the GDP of the sector increased by 20.4% in 2002 and by 14.5% in 2003.

The mining sector has not yet been extensively developed. Copper, molybdenum, gold, silver and iron are extracted on a small scale, and there are reserves of lead and zinc. There are also substantial, but largely unexploited, reserves of mineral salt, calcium oxide and carbon. Production of gold decreased significantly in the 1990s, but the Government hoped to encourage a recovery in the industry, following the conclusion of an agreement with a Canadian company to develop new extraction facilities, the first of which went into production in 1998. In December 2003 the Government approved a three-year programme for the stimulation of diamond production in Armenia. According to official figures, mining represented 10.9% of total industrial production in 2003.

In 2003, according to the World Bank, the manufacturing sector provided 21.8% of Armenia's GDP. According to IMF figures, in 2001 the principal branches of manufacturing, measured by gross value of output, were food-processing and beverages (accounting for 55.0% of the total), base metals and fabricated metal (12.4%), and jewellery and related articles (8.4%). According to the World Bank, during 1990–2003 the GDP of the manufacturing sector declined, in real terms, at an

average annual rate of 3.0%. However, real sectoral GDP increased by 14.2% in 2002 and by 6% in 2003.

Armenia is heavily dependent on imported energy, much of which is supplied by Russia (petroleum and derivatives) and Turkmenistan (natural gas). In May 2004 an agreement was concluded on the construction of a 141-km natural gas pipeline to connect the pipeline networks of Armenia and Iran, to provide Armenia with supplies of Iranian natural gas. It is thought probable that Armenia has significant reserves of petroleum and natural gas, although these remain undeveloped. By July 1999 Armenia had a surplus of electricity, some of which was exported to Georgia; a new high-voltage electricity line opened between the two countries in December 2000, and two high-voltage lines were subsequently opened to permit exports of electric energy to Iran. In September 1999 Armenia signed an initial agreement with the European Union (EU, see p. 217), providing for the closure of the country's sole nuclear power station, at Medzamor, by 2004. However, the Government subsequently claimed that the station could be operated safely for a longer period of time, following extensive renovation, and it sought international resources for the development of adequate alternative energy facilities; in the mean time the EU and the USA funded enhanced safety measures to permit the continuing use of the station. (In 2003 Armenia transferred responsibility for the financial management of the plant to Russia, in return for the settlement of its fuel arrears.) The construction of some 15 small hydroelectric power stations was initiated in 2004, and the construction of joint Armenian-Iranian hydroelectric plants on the River Araks was proposed in the mid-2000s. In 2003 nuclear power contributed 36.3% of the country's electricity supply, thermoelectric power produced 27.7% and hydroelectric power provided 36.0% of the total. Imports of mineral fuels comprised 1.4% of the value of merchandise imports in 2003 (compared with 20.2% in 2000).

The services sector contributed 38.2% of GDP in 2003, according to the World Bank, and official figures indicated that the sector (including utilities) engaged 24.9% of the employed labour force in 2003. According to the World Bank, during 1990–2003 the GDP of the sector declined by an average of 3.4% annually, in real terms. However, real services GDP increased by 9.2% in 2002 and by 28% in 2003.

In 2003 Armenia recorded a visible trade deficit of US $434.1m., while the deficit on the current account of the balance of payments was $190.6m. In 2003 the principal source of imports, according to official statistics, was Russia, which provided 15.9% of the total; other main sources were Belgium (10.1%), Israel (9.7%), the USA (8.7%), the United Kingdom (6.5%). In the same year Israel was the main market for exports, accounting for 20.8% of the total. Other important purchasers were Belgium (18.1%), Russia 13.8%), the USA (8.2%) and Germany (6.5%). The principal exports in 2003 were precious and semi-precious stones (in particular, diamonds), precious metals, imitation jewellery and coins; base metals; prepared foodstuffs, beverages and tobacco; mineral products; textiles; and machinery and electrical equipment. The principal imports in that year were pearls, precious and semi-precious stones, precious metals, imitation jewellery and coins; mineral products; machinery and electrical equipment; prepared foodstuffs, beverages and tobacco; vehicles, aircraft and transport equipment; chemicals and base metals.

In 2003, there was a budgetary deficit of 20,663m. drams (equivalent to 1.3% of GDP). At the end of 2002 Armenia's total external debt was US $1,149m. (equivalent to 46.8% of GNI), of which $941m. was long-term public debt. In that year the cost of debt-servicing was equivalent to 8.8% of the value of exports of goods and services. Inflation increased at an average annual rate of 46.2% in 1994–2003. Consumer prices increased by 4.7% in 2003, according to official figures, and by 7.4% in 2004. At the end of November 2004 an estimated 110,400 people were officially registered as unemployed, giving an unemployment rate of 9.0%.

Armenia is a member of the IMF, the World Bank and the European Bank for Reconstruction and Development (EBRD, see p. 212), and it is also a member of the Organization of the Black Sea Economic Co-operation (BSEC, see p. 325). In February 2003 Armenia became a member of the World Trade Organization (WTO, see p. 357).

The collapse of the Soviet central planning system, together with the effects of the earthquake in 1988 and of the conflict in Nagornyi Karabakh, exacerbated an already critical economic situation in Armenia. The closure by Azerbaijan and by Turkey of those countries' borders with Armenia resulted in widespread shortages and a decline in industrial production in Armenia. A wide-ranging programme of reforms, including price liberalization and the promotion of privatization, was initiated in the early 1990s, and the first signs of economic recovery were observed by 1994. By 2001 Armenia had recorded a significant improvement in economic performance. In 2002 economic growth of more than 12% was recorded, and GDP increased further in 2003, according to official figures. A significant reduction in the fiscal deficit was also recorded in 2002. However, one-half of the population continued to subsist below the World Bank's national poverty level and the unemployment rate remained high. Moreover, export trade remained severely hampered by the lack of transport links with Azerbaijan and Turkey. It was anticipated, however, that Armenia's membership of the WTO from February 2003 would be of substantial benefit to the economy in the long term; an increase in trade volumes could already be observed by the end of the year. Reform was implemented in the energy sector in 2003, with the privatization of two electricity-production plants. In August the Government adopted a poverty reduction plan, supported by the World Bank, which aimed to reduce the percentage of the population living in poverty to 19% by 2015. Further reform of the energy sector took place, with the privatization and restructuring of the electricity purchase and distribution systems. In 2004 Armenia was one of 16 countries to become eligible for the new US Millennium Challenge Account aid programme. In November the IMF approved the disbursement of the final tranche of funding under its Poverty Reduction and Growth Facility (PRGF), approved in May 2001, following a review of Armenia's macroeconomic and financial situation. Although the overall performance of the economy was commended, the IMF emphasized the need to reform tax-collection methods to enable increased social spending and relieve the country's dependence on external financing to support the budgetary deficit; to increase fiscal transparency; to strengthen the banking system; and to improve the business environment by combating widespread corruption. None the less, an 'Index of Economic Freedom' conducted in 2004 by the US-based Heritage Foundation and the *Wall Street Journal* and published in the following year described Armenia as the only 'mostly free' economy among the CIS states at that time.

Education

Education is free and compulsory at primary and secondary levels. Until the early 1990s the general education system conformed to that of the Soviet system, but extensive changes were subsequently introduced, with greater emphasis placed on Armenian history and culture. Primary education usually began at seven years of age and lasted for four years. Secondary education, beginning at 11 years of age, comprised a first cycle of four years and a second of two years. In 2001/02, however, Armenia introduced an 11-year system of schooling. In 2003 total enrolment at pre-school establishments was equivalent to 19.1% of the relevant age-group. In 1999 primary enrolment was equivalent to 86% of children in the relevant age-group, and the comparable ratio for secondary enrolment was 88%. Most instruction in higher institutions is in Armenian, although Russian is widely taught as a second language. In 2003/04 98.9% of students in general education schools were taught in Armenian, and 0.8% were mainly taught in Russian. Current expenditure on education and science from the state budget was 34,849m. drams in 2003 (11.1% of overall budgetary expenditure).

Public Holidays

2005: 1–2 January (New Year), 6 January (Christmas), 8 March (Women's Day), 24 April (Armenian Genocide Commemoration Day), 29 April–1 May (Easter), 9 May (Victory Day), 28 May (Declaration of the First Armenian Republic Day), 5 July (Constitution Day), 21 September (Independence Day), 7 December (Day of Remembrance of the 1988 Earthquake), 31 December (New Year's Eve).

2006: 1–2 January (New Year), 6 January (Christmas), 8 March (Women's Day), 21–23 April (Easter), 24 April (Armenian Genocide Commemoration Day), 9 May (Victory Day), 28 May (Declaration of the First Armenian Republic Day), 5 July (Constitution Day), 21 September (Independence Day), 7 December (Day of Remembrance of the 1988 Earthquake), 31 December (New Year's Eve).

Weights and Measures

The metric system is in force.

Statistical Survey

Principal source: National Statistical Service of the Republic of Armenia, 375010 Yerevan, Republic Sq., Government House 3; tel. (1) 52-42-13; fax (1) 52-19-21; e-mail armstat@sci.am; internet www.armstat.am.

Area and Population

AREA, POPULATION AND DENSITY

Area (sq km)	29,743*
Population (census results)†	
12 January 1989	3,287,677
10 October 2001	
Males	1,407,220
Females	1,595,374
Total	3,002,594
Population (official estimates at 1 January)‡	
2002	3,212,900
2003	3,210,300
2004	3,212,200
Density (per sq km) at 1 January 2004	108.0

* 11,484 sq miles.

† Figures refer to *de facto* populations, although the methodology for calculating the relationship between *de jure* and *de facto* populations was amended for the 2001 census, and later figures are, therefore, not strictly comparable with those for 1989.

‡ Figures include persons temporarily absent (475,200 at 1 January 1999).

POPULATION BY ETHNIC GROUP*
(permanent inhabitants, 1989 census)

	%
Armenian	93.3
Azerbaijani	2.6
Kurdish	1.7
Russian	1.5
Others	0.9
Total	**100.0**

* According to official declaration of nationality.

MARZER (PROVINCES)
(1 January 2001)

Marz (Province)	Area (sq km)*	Estimated Population†	Density (per sq km)	Capital
Yerevan City .	227	1,246,100	5,489.4	Yerevan
Aragatsotn . .	2,753	168,100	61.1	Ashtarak
Ararat . . .	2,096	311,400	148.6	Artashat
Armavir . . .	1,242	323,300	260.3	Armavir
Gegharkunik .	5,348	278,600	67.8	Gavar
Kotaik . . .	2,089	328,900	157.4	Hrazdan
Lori	3,789	392,300	103.5	Vanadzor
Shirak . . .	2,681	3621,400	134.8	Gyumri
Syunik . . .	4,506	164,000	36.4	Kapan
Tavush . . .	2,704	156,500	57.9	Ijevan
Vayots Dzor .	2,308	69,400	30.1	Yeghegnadzor
Total . . .	29,743	3,800,000	127.8	

* Including inland water, totalling 1,278 sq km.
† Provisional figures, including persons temporarily absent from the country.

PRINCIPAL TOWNS
(estimated population at 1 January 2001)

Yerevan (capital)	.	1,246,100	Vagarshapat
			(Echmiadzin) . . 65,700
Gyumri*		210,100	Hrazdan (Razdan) . 63,400
Vanadzor† . . .		170,800	Abovian 60,600

* Known as Leninakan between 1924 and 1991.
† Known as Kirovakan between 1935 and 1992.

Mid-2003 (UN estimate, incl. suburbs): Yerevan 1,079,054 (Source: UN, *World Urbanization Prospects: The 2003 Revision*).

BIRTHS, MARRIAGES AND DEATHS*

	Registered live births		Registered marriages		Registered deaths	
	Number	Rate (per 1,000)	Number	Rate (per 1,000)	Number	Rate (per 1,000)
1996 . .	48,134	12.8	14,234	3.8	24,936	6.6
1997 . .	43,929	11.6	12,521	3.3	23,985	6.3
1998 . .	39,366	10.4	11,365	3.0	23,210	6.1
1999 . .	36,502	9.6	12,459	3.3	24,087	6.3
2000 . .	34,276	9.0	10,986	2.9	24,025	6.3
2001 . .	32,065	10.0	12,302	3.8	24,003	7.5
2002 . .	32,200†	10.1	13,682	4.3	25,500†	8.0
2003 . .	35,800†	11.2	15,463	4.8	26,000†	8.1

* Rates for 1996–2000 are calculated from unrevised population estimates.
† Figures are rounded.

Expectation of life (WHO estimates, years at birth): 70.0 (males 67.0; females 73.0) in 2002 (Source: WHO, *World Health Report*).

ECONOMICALLY ACTIVE POPULATION
(annual averages, '000 persons)

	2001	2002	2003
Agriculture and Forestry . . .	570.0	500.8	509.0
Industry*	169.6	143.1	138.8
Construction	41.2	36.1	37.2
Transport and communications .	44.2	40.2	41.8
Trade and catering	110.5	99.6	105.0
Housing, public utilities and personal services	37.0	30.2	32.6
Health and social welfare . .	79.3	66.9	60.3
Education, culture and art . .	155.2	138.3	132.2
Science and scientific services . .	14.6	13.2	12.3
Finance and insurance	6.7	5.2	5.0
Public administration	25.2	23.8	25.0
Other activities	11.4	9.0	8.4
Total employed	1,264.9	1,106.4	1,107.6
Registered unemployed	146.8	133.7	124.8
Total labour force	1,411.7	1,240.1	1,232.4

* Principally mining, manufacturing, electricity, gas and water.

Health and Welfare

KEY INDICATORS

Total fertility rate (children per woman, 2002)	1.2
Under-five mortality rate (per 1,000 live births, 2003) . .	33
HIV (% of persons aged 15–49, 2003)	0.1
Physicians (per 1,000 head, 2001)	2.86
Hospital beds (per 1,000 head, 2001)	4.25
Health expenditure (2001): US $ per head (PPP) . . .	273
Health expenditure (2001): % of GDP	7.8
Health expenditure (2001): public (% of total)	41.2
Access to water (% of persons, 2002)	92
Access to sanitation (% of persons, 2002)	84
Human Development Index (2002): ranking	82
Human Development Index (2002): value	0.754

For sources and definitions, see explanatory note on p. vi.

Agriculture

PRINCIPAL CROPS
('000 metric tons)

	2001	2002	2003
Wheat	245.6	289.2	221.0
Barley	107.5	109.5	68.3
Maize	9.9	12.2	15.2
Other cereals*	4.4	4.8	5.5
Potatoes	363.8	374.3	507.5
Pulses*	3.4	3.4	4.8
Cabbages	80.4	82.7	97.5
Tomatoes	158.3	170.0	225.6
Cauliflowers	3.8	3.6	4.9
Cucumbers and gherkins* . . .	39.1	42.0	45.0
Dry onions	33.0	37.3	33.5
Garlic	6.7	5.1	6.5
Carrots	14.1	12.4	11.8
Other vegetables*	120.7	113.2	145.0
Watermelons†	54.8	89.7	115.4
Apples	35.4	35.2	45.0*
Pears	9.8	9.0	11.0*
Apricots	10.8	5.0	6.2*
Peaches and nectarines	16.0	10.5	13.0*
Plums	10.5	10.0	12.0*
Grapes	116.5	104.0	81.6

* Unofficial figure(s).
† Including melons, pumpkins and squash.

Source: FAO.

LIVESTOCK
('000 head, year ending September)

	2001	2002	2003
Horses	11	12	12
Asses*	3	3	3
Cattle	485	497	536
Pigs	69	98	111
Sheep	497	546	552
Goats	43	46	50
Rabbits*	5	5	5
Chickens†	3,850	3,000	3,400
Turkeys†	125	120	205

* FAO estimates.
† Unofficial figure(s).

Source: FAO.

LIVESTOCK PRODUCTS
('000 metric tons)

	2001	2002	2003
Beef and veal	29	30	30
Mutton and lamb	7	6	6
Pig meat	9	10	12
Poultry meat	4	4	5
Cows' milk	453	475	498†
Sheep's milk	10	12	13†
Cheese*	3	3	3
Hen eggs†	25	27	28
Wool: greasy	1	1	1
Wool: scoured*	1	1	1

* FAO estimates.
† Unofficial figure(s).

Source: FAO.

Forestry

ROUNDWOOD REMOVALS
('000 cubic metres, excluding bark)

	2001	2002	2003
Sawlogs, veneer logs and logs for sleepers	7	8	10
Fuel wood	42	46	57
Total	49	54	67

Source: FAO.

Fishing

(metric tons, live weight)

	2000	2001	2002
Capture	1,133	866	465
Crucian carp	38	32	54
Trouts	186	180	167
Whitefishes	881	632	202
Aquaculture	893	1,331	1,020
Common carp	372	511	305
Silver carp	51	312	327
Trouts	439	465	347
Total catch	2,026	2,197	1,485

Source: FAO.

Mining

	1999	2000	2001
Copper concentrates (metric tons)*†	9,600	7,231‡	7,056
Molybdenum concentrates (metric tons)*	2,800‡	6,044	5,770
Silver ores (kg)*†	1,200	1,300	1,300
Gold ores (kg)*†	400	400	400
Salt ('000 metric tons)	27	30	29

* Figures refer to the metal content of ores and concentrates.
† Estimated production.
‡ Reported figure.

Source: US Geological Survey.

Industry

SELECTED PRODUCTS
('000 metric tons, unless otherwise indicated)

	2001	2002	2003
Wheat flour	114	110*	132
Wine ('000 hectolitres)	64	40*	21
Beer ('000 hectolitres)	100	71	73
Mineral water ('000 hectolitres)	197	n.a.	n.a.
Soft drinks ('000 hectolitres)	274	268*	341
Cigarettes (million)	1,623	2,815	3,222
Wool yarn—pure and mixed (metric tons)	34	53	99
Cotton yarn—pure and mixed (metric tons)	60	224	86
Woven cotton fabrics ('000 sq metres)	148	574*	348
Woven woollen fabrics ('000 sq metres)	28	38	48
Carpets ('000 sq metres)	18	16*	29
Cement	275*	355	384
Electric energy (million kWh)	5,745	5,519	5,501

* Estimated figure.

Finance

CURRENCY AND EXCHANGE RATES

Monetary Units
100 louma = 1 dram.

Sterling, Dollar and Euro Equivalents (31 December 2004)
£1 sterling = 938.3 drams;
US $1 = 485.8 drams;
€1 = 661.8 drams;
1,000 drams = £1.066 = $2.058 = €1.511.

Average Exchange Rate (drams per US $)
2002   573.35
2003   578.76
2004   533.45

Note: The dram was introduced on 22 November 1993, replacing the Russian (formerly Soviet) rouble at a conversion rate of 1 dram = 200 roubles. The initial exchange rate was set at US $1 = 14.3 drams, but by the end of the year the rate was $1 = 75 drams. After the introduction of the dram, Russian currency continued to circulate in Armenia. The rouble had been withdrawn from circulation by March 1994.

STATE BUDGET
(million drams)

Revenue	2001	2002	2003
Tax revenue	154,892	185,437	212,233
Value-added tax	79,521	95,006	107,769
Excises	31,016	35,334	39,104
Enterprise profits tax	16,316	17,429	17,627
Income tax	11,219	12,478	16,781
Customs duties	9,794	9,692	10,724
Fixed payments	4,431	6,365	8,009
Other taxes	2,596	9,133	12,219
Government duty	13,917	13,182	15,214
Non-tax incomes	13,874	10,915	10,865
Other revenue	10,895	18,784	53,724
Total	193,578	228,318	292,035

Expenditure*	2001	2002	2003
Current expenditure	188,572	219,370	222,296
Wages	19,837	20,560	13,736
Interest	14,816	15,740	11,398
Subsidies	6,540	8,176	14,523
Current transfers	42,089	47,346	41,752
Goods and services	105,290	127,548	140,887
Capital expenditure	39,773	34,193	83,803
Total	228,345	253,563	306,100

* Excluding lending minus repayments (million drams): 16,036 in 2001; 10,349 in 2002; 6,598 in 2003.

INTERNATIONAL RESERVES
(US $ million at 31 December)

	2001	2002	2003
Gold*	12.41	15.68	—
IMF special drawing rights . .	10.24	30.10	18.83
Foreign exchange	310.58	394.92	491.36
Total	333.23	440.70	510.19

* National valuation.

Source: IMF, *International Financial Statistics*.

MONEY SUPPLY
(million drams at 31 December)

	2001	2002	2003
Currency outside banks . . .	65,037	88,553	91,997
Demand deposits at commercial banks	12,073	26,400	30,618
Total money (incl. others) . .	77,297	115,307	123,272

Source: IMF, *International Financial Statistics*.

COST OF LIVING
(Consumer Price Index; base: 2000 = 100)

	2001	2002	2003
Food (incl. non-alcoholic beverages)	104.7	107.0	114.4
Electricity, gas and other fuels .	99.8	99.9	102.1
Clothing (incl. footwear) . . .	98.9	101.3	102.7
Rent	100.1	100.6	100.7
All items (incl. others)	103.1	104.2	109.2

Source: ILO.

NATIONAL ACCOUNTS
(million drams at current prices)

Expenditure on the Gross Domestic Product

	2001	2002	2003
Government final consumption expenditure	132,708	136,071	166,602
Private final consumption expenditure	1,100,035	1,213,754	1,364,945
Increase in stocks	24,304	7,839	8,510
Gross fixed capital formation . .	208,025	287,369	392,096
Total domestic expenditure .	1,465,072	1,645,033	1,932,153
Exports of goods and services . .	299,477	399,975	516,878
Less Imports of goods and services	542,653	634,733	807,827
Sub-total	1,221,896	1,410,275	1,641,204
Statistical discrepancy* . . .	−46,020	−47,803	−17,867
GDP in purchasers' values . .	1,175,877	1,362,472	1,623,336

* Referring to the difference between the sum of the expenditure components and official estimates of GDP, compiled from the production approach.

Source: IMF, *International Financial Statistics*.

Gross Domestic Product by Economic Activity

	1999	2000	2001
Agriculture and hunting . . .	266,600	238,900	294,160
Industry*	216,500	236,600	245,775
Construction	82,000	105,900	125,751
Wholesale and retail trade; repair of motor vehicles; motorcycles and personal and household goods; hotels and restaurants .	89,000	95,500	115,770
Transport, storage and communications	74,800	74,700	87,810
Financial intermediation; real estate, renting and business activities	59,200	59,500	59,895
Public administration and defence; compulsory social security . .	33,800	34,100	39,476
Education; health and social work; other community, social and personal service activities . .	99,500	106,700	110,640
Sub-total	921,400	951,800	1,079,277
Less financial intermediation services indirectly measured .	17,900	12,600	17,559
Gross value added in basic prices	903,500	939,200	1,061,718
Taxes, *less* subsidies on products .	83,900	94,200	113,768
GDP in purchasers' values . .	987,400	1,033,300	1,175,487

* Comprising mining and quarrying, manufacturing, electricity, gas and water.

Source: UN, *National Accounts Statistics*.

BALANCE OF PAYMENTS
(US $ million)

	2001	2002	2003
Exports of goods f.o.b.	353.1	513.8	696.1
Imports of goods f.o.b.	−773.3	−882.5	−1,130.2
Trade balance	−420.2	−368.8	−434.1
Exports of services	186.5	183.8	207.4
Imports of services	−204.3	−224.5	−275.7
Balance on goods and services	−438.0	−409.5	−502.4
Other income received	103.1	136.6	164.9
Other income paid	−39.6	−48.4	−71.5
Balance on goods, services and income	−374.5	−321.3	−409.1
Current transfers received . . .	200.8	199.7	245.0
Current transfers paid	−26.8	−26.3	−26.5
Current balance	−200.5	−147.9	−190.6
Capital account (net)	30.1	68.1	89.9
Direct investment abroad . . .	—	—	−0.4
Direct investment from abroad .	69.9	110.7	120.9
Portfolio investment assets . .	−5.8	3.4	0.1
Portfolio investment liabilities .	−0.1	−1.9	0.2
Other investment assets . . .	−18.2	−88.6	−63.6
Other investment liabilities . .	131.1	123.3	117.6
Net errors and omissions . . .	12.1	−3.2	−1.7
Overall balance	18.6	63.9	72.4

Source: IMF, *International Financial Statistics*.

External Trade

PRINCIPAL COMMODITIES
(US $ '000)

Imports c.i.f.	2001	2002	2003
Live animals and animal products	30,816	27,678	32,822
Meat and edible meat offal	20,940	19,083	22,369
Vegetable products	85,151	74,394	75,002
Cereals	48,170	49,259	49,181
Prepared foodstuffs; beverages, spirits and vinegar; tobacco and manufactured substitutes	66,889	79,328	93,306
Tobacco and manufactured tobacco substitutes	29,923	30,114	35,168
Mineral products	188,191	171,413	179,484
Mineral fuels, mineral oils and products of their distillation; bituminous substances; mineral waxes	187,201	170,236	178,582
Products of chemical or allied industries	65,135	62,808	78,382
Pharmaceutical products	28,945	24,058	38,128
Textiles and textile articles	35,963	36,085	39,753
Natural or cultured pearls, precious or semi-precious stones, precious metals and articles thereof; imitation jewellery; coins	106,771	213,471	333,080
Base metals and articles thereof	36,056	55,692	76,723
Machinery and mechanical appliances; electrical equipment; sound and television apparatus	88,366	103,375	133,755
Nuclear reactors, boilers, machinery and mechanical appliances; parts thereof	48,529	52,974	80,082
Electrical machinery, equipment and parts; sound and television apparatus, and parts and accessories	39,836	50,401	53,673
Vehicles, aircraft, vessels and associated transport equipment	25,897	39,867	78,476
Vehicles other than railway or tramway rolling-stock, and parts and accessories thereof	24,619	39,001	76,067
Optical, photographic, measuring and medical instruments and apparatus; clocks and watches; musical instruments	26,953	20,487	34,202
Total (incl. others)	877,434	987,156	1,279,486

Exports f.o.b.	2001	2002	2003
Prepared foodstuffs; beverages, spirits and vinegar; tobacco and manufactured substitutes	47,978	54,779	72,196
Beverages, spirits and vinegar	39,119	44,930	60,105
Mineral products	37,885	42,124	50,308
Ores, slag and ash	20,493	28,242	38,051
Mineral fuels, mineral oils and products of their distillation; bituminous substances; mineral waxes	17,158	13,431	11,006
Plastics, rubber and articles thereof	13,068	6,320	4,807
Rubber and articles thereof	12,405	5,290	3,982
Textiles and textile articles	24,288	28,627	31,242
Non-knitted clothing and accessories	15,543	16,731	18,412
Natural or cultured pearls, precious or semi-precious stones, precious metals and articles thereof; imitation jewellery; coins	122,848	258,328	350,708
Base metals and articles thereof	43,445	44,778	90,401
Iron and steel	9,582	11,629	17,570
Copper and articles thereof	12,882	11,664	14,465
Aluminium and articles thereof	17,865	17,704	53,472
Machinery and mechanical appliances; electrical equipment; sound and television apparatus	28,474	21,435	20,124
Nuclear reactors, boilers, machinery and mechanical appliances; parts thereof	15,081	9,667	10,590
Electrical machinery, equipment and parts; sound and television apparatus, and parts and accessories	13,394	11,768	9,534
Total (incl. others)	341,836	505,160	685,599

PRINCIPAL TRADING PARTNERS
(US $ '000)

Imports c.i.f.	2001	2002	2003
Belgium	41,783	91,108	129,142
Bulgaria	6,424	49,496	13,209
China, People's Republic	7,811	10,128	8,657
Cyprus	8,204	2,457	15,040
France	12,048	12,196	15,455
Georgia	18,503	31,470	32,961
Germany	33,962	42,861	43,762
Greece	13,579	12,186	30,415
Iran	78,121	62,615	70,187
Israel	27,593	82,696	123,660
Italy	29,635	36,630	36,240
Luxembourg	6,626	10,692	27,682
Netherlands	6,958	10,080	10,701
Panama	19,331	n.a.	n.a.
Russia	173,648	192,898	203,374
Switzerland	26,516	10,267	53,029
Turkey	33,756	38,232	36,732
Turkmenistan	796	24,976	61
Ukraine	22,102	45,736	34,618
United Arab Emirates	47,422	42,947	60,471
United Kingdom	91,225	28,240	83,261
USA	84,153	52,722	111,248
Total (incl. others)	877,434	987,156	1,279,486

Exports f.o.b.	2001	2002	2003
Belgium	46,489	92,273	123,833
Georgia	12,413	16,607	18,674
Germany	11,122	28,164	44,419
Iran	31,870	31,469	22,479
Israel	33,391	87,713	142,347
Italy	6,065	11,698	19,315
Netherlands	1,264	11,218	21,908
Russia	60,501	64,634	94,418
Switzerland	8,937	7,758	32,699
Ukraine	10,983	8,091	6,992
United Arab Emirates	7,277	14,198	16,609
United Kingdom	20,116	51,091	42,567
USA	52,268	46,238	56,105
Total (incl. others)	341,836	505,160	685,599

Transport

RAILWAYS
(traffic)

	2001	2002	2003
Passenger journeys ('000) . . .	1,165.7	1,300.0*	1,100.0*
Passenger-km (million)	48.2	48.4	41.2
Freight carried ('000 metric tons)	1,398.0	2,019.3	2,125.5
Freight ton-km (million) . . .	343.5	451.8	529.2

* Rounded figure.

CIVIL AVIATION
(traffic)

	2001	2002	2003
Passengers carried ('000) . . .	769	900*	900*
Passengers-km (million) . . .	725.1	753.9	719.2
Freight carried ('000 metric tons) .	11.4	8.4	8.8
Cargo ton-kilometres ('000) . .	9.1	5.5	5.5

* Rounded figure.

Tourism

ARRIVALS BY NATIONALITY

	1999	2000	2001
Argentina	365	404	6,359
Brazil	29	41	4,119
Canada	462	725	8,867
CIS countries*	16,326	15,000	24,342
France	3,046	3,724	6,898
Germany	1,195	1,209	3,624
Greece	847	954	1,739
Iran	4,653	8,573	17,772
Lebanon	1,406	1,574	7,036
Turkey	823	427	710
United Kingdom	919	1,021	1,554
USA	5,151	6,804	21,314
Total (incl. others)	40,745	45,222	123,262

* Comprising Azerbaijan, Belarus, Georgia, Kazakhstan, Kyrgyzstan, Moldova, Russia, Tajikistan, Turkmenistan, Ukraine and Uzbekistan.

Tourism receipts (US $ million): 45 in 2000; 65 in 2001; 63 in 2002.

Sources: World Tourism Organization, *Yearbook of Tourism Statistics*.

Tourist arrivals: 162,089 in 2002.

Communications Media

	2001	2002	2003
Telephones ('000 main lines in use)	531.5	542.8	562.6
Mobile cellular telephones ('000 subscribers)	25.5	71.9	114.4
Personal computers ('000 in use)	35	60	n.a.
Internet users ('000)	50	60	200
Book production:*			
titles	893	809	1,025
copies ('000)	945	375	660
Newspapers:			
titles	82	97	120
total circulation ('000 copies) .	308	304	325
Periodicals:			
titles	64	69	77
total circulation ('000 copies) .	272	273	309

* Including brochures.

2000: Television receivers ('000 in use) 860.

Source: partly International Telecommunication Union.

Education

(2003/04, unless otherwise indicated)

	Institutions	Teachers	Students
Pre-primary (incl. private schools)	699*	7,585†	46,900*
General	1,439	46,000	498,500
Gymnasia and lyceums .	37	n.a.	11,800
Vocational	56‡	n.a.	5,100‡
Other specialized schools .	81	3,386	28,600
State higher schools (incl. universities)	20	6,628	55,900

* December 2003.
† 1998/99.
‡ 2000/01.

Adult literacy rate (estimates based on census data): 99.4% (males 99.7%; females 99.2%) in 2002 (Source: UN Development Programme, *Human Development Report*).

Directory

The Constitution

The Constitution was approved by some 68% of the electorate in a national referendum, held on 5 July 1995. It replaced the amended Soviet Constitution of 1978. The following is a summary of the Constitution's main provisions:

GENERAL PROVISIONS OF CONSTITUTIONAL ORDER

The Republic of Armenia is an independent democratic state; its sovereignty is vested in the people, who execute their authority through free elections, referendums and local self-government institutions and officials, as defined by the Constitution. Referendums, as well as elections of the President of the Republic, the Azgayin Zhoghov (National Assembly) and local self-government bodies, are carried out on the basis of universal, equal, direct suffrage by secret ballot. Through the Constitution and legislation, the State ensures the protection of human rights and freedoms, in accordance with the principles and norms of international law. A multi-party political system is guaranteed. The establishment of political parties is a free process, but the activities of political parties must not contravene the Constitution and the law. The right to property is recognized and protected. Armenia conducts its foreign policy based on the norms of international law, seeking to establish neighbourly and mutually beneficial relations with all countries. The State ensures the protection of the environment, and historical and cultural monuments, as well as cultural values. The official language is Armenian.

FUNDAMENTAL HUMAN AND CIVIL RIGHTS AND FREEDOMS

The acquisition and loss of citizenship are prescribed by law. A citizen of the Republic of Armenia may not be simultaneously a citizen of another country. The rights, liberties and duties of citizens of Armenia, regardless of nationality, race, sex, language, creed, political or other convictions, social origin, property and other status, are guaranteed. No one shall be subject to torture or cruel treatment. Every citizen has the right to freedom of movement and residence within the republic, as well as the right to leave the republic. Every citizen has the right to freedom of thought, speech, conscience and religion. The right to establish or join associations, trade unions, political organizations, etc., is guaranteed, as is the right to strike for protection of economic, social and labour interests. Citizens of the republic who have attained 18 years of age are entitled to participate in state government through their directly elected representatives or by expression of free will.

Every citizen has the right to social insurance in the event of old age, disability, sickness, widowhood, unemployment, etc. Every citizen has the right to education. Education is provided free at elementary and secondary state educational institutions. Citizens belonging to national minorities have the right to preserve their traditions and to develop their language and culture. Everyone charged with a penal offence has the right to be presumed innocent until proved guilty. The advocacy of national, racial and religious hatred, and the propagation of violence and war, are prohibited.

THE PRESIDENT OF THE REPUBLIC

The President of the Republic of Armenia ensures the observance of the Constitution and the effective operation of the legislative, executive and juridical authorities. The President is the guarantor of the independence, territorial integrity and security of the republic. He/she is elected by citizens of the republic for a period of five years. Any person who has the right to participate in elections, has attained the age of 35 years, and has been a resident citizen of Armenia for the preceding 10 years is eligible for election to the office of President. No person may be elected to the office for more than two successive terms.

The President signs and promulgates laws adopted by the Azgayin Zhoghov, or returns draft legislation to the Azgayin Zhoghov for reconsideration; may dismiss the Azgayin Zhoghov and declare special elections to it, after consultation with the Prime Minister and the Chairman of the Azgayin Zhoghov; appoints and dismisses the Prime Minister; appoints and dismisses the members of the Government, upon the recommendation of the Prime Minister; appoints civil service officials; establishes deliberation bodies; represents Armenia in international relations, co-ordinates foreign policy, concludes international treaties, signs international treaties ratified by the Azgayin Zhoghov, and ratifies agreements between governments; appoints and recalls diplomatic representatives of Armenia to foreign countries and international organizations, and receives the credentials of diplomatic representatives of foreign countries; appoints the Procurator-General, as nominated by the Prime Min-

ister; appoints members and the Chairman of the Constitutional Court; is the Supreme Commander-in-Chief of the Armed Forces; takes decisions on the use of the Armed Forces; grants titles of honour; and grants amnesties to convicts.

THE AZGAYIN ZHOGHOV

Legislative power in the Republic of Armenia is executed by the Azgayin Zhoghov. The Azgayin Zhoghov comprises 131 deputies, elected for a four-year term. Any person who has attained the age of 25 years and has been a permanent resident and citizen of Armenia for the preceding five years is eligible to be elected a deputy.

The Azgayin Zhoghov deliberates and enacts laws; has the power to express a vote of 'no confidence' in the Government; confirms the state budget, as proposed by the Government; supervises the implementation of the state budget; elects its Chairman (Speaker) and two Deputy Chairmen; appoints the Chairman and Deputy Chairman of the Central Bank, upon the nomination of the President; and appoints members of the Constitutional Court.

At the suggestion of the President of the Republic, the Azgayin Zhoghov declares amnesties; ratifies or declares invalid international treaties; and declares war. Upon the recommendation of the Government, the Azgayin Zhoghov confirms the territorial and administrative divisions of the republic.

THE GOVERNMENT

Executive power is realized by the Government of the Republic of Armenia, which is composed of the Prime Minister and the Ministers. The Prime Minister is appointed by the President; upon the recommendation of the Prime Minister, the President appoints the remaining Ministers. The Prime Minister directs the current activities of the Government and co-ordinates the activities of the Ministers.

The Government presents the programme of its activities to the Azgayin Zhoghov for approval; presents the draft state budget to the Azgayin Zhoghov for confirmation, ensures implementation of the budget and presents a report on its implementation to the Azgayin Zhoghov; manages state property; ensures the implementation of state fiscal, loan and tax policies; ensures the implementation of state policy in the spheres of science, education, culture, health care, social security and environmental protection; ensures the implementation of defence, national security and foreign policies; and takes measures to strengthen adherence to the laws, to ensure the rights and freedoms of citizens, and to protect public order and the property of citizens.

JUDICIAL POWER

The courts of general competence are the tribunal courts of first instance, the review courts and the courts of appeal. There are also economic, military and other courts. The guarantor of the independence of judicial bodies is the President of the Republic. He or she is the Head of the Council of Justice. The Minister of Justice and the Procurator-General are the Deputy Heads of the Council of Justice. Fourteen members appointed by the President of the Republic for a period of five years are included in the Council. The Constitutional Court is composed of nine members, of whom the Azgayin Zhoghov appoints five and the President of the Republic appoints four. The Constitutional Court, *inter alia* , determines whether decisions of the Azgayin Zhoghov, decrees and orders of the President, and resolutions of the Government correspond to the Constitution; decides, prior to ratification of an international treaty, whether the obligations created in it correspond to the Constitution; resolves disputes relating to referendums and results of presidential and legislative elections; and decides on the suspension or prohibition of the activity of a political party. The highest court of appeal is the Court of Cassation, the members of which are appointed by the President of the Republic, for life.

TERRITORIAL ADMINISTRATION AND LOCAL SELF-GOVERNMENT

The administrative territorial units of the Republic of Armenia are regions (Marzer) and communities. Regions are comprised of rural and urban communities. Local self-government takes place in the communities. Bodies of local self-government, community elders and the community head (city mayor or head of village) are elected for a three-year period to administer community property and solve issues of community significance. State government is exercised in the Marzer. The Government appoints and dismisses regional governors, who carry out the Government's regional policy and co-ordinate the performance of regional services by state executive bodies. The city of Yerevan has the status of a Marz.

The Government

HEAD OF STATE

President: ROBERT KOCHARIAN (acting from 3 February 1998, elected 30 March 1998, inaugurated 9 April 1998; re-elected 5 March 2003, inaugurated 9 April 2003).

GOVERNMENT
(March 2005)

A coalition of the Republican Party of Armenia (RPA), the Armenian Revolutionary Federation (ARF) and the Law-Governed Country Party of Armenia (OY).

Prime Minister: ANDRANIK MARKARIAN.

Minister of Foreign Affairs: VARDAN OSKANIAN.

Minister of Defence: SERGE SARKISSIAN.

Minister of Finance and the Economy: VARDAN KHACHATRIAN.

Minister of Justice: DAVID HAROUTUNIAN.

Minister of Energy: ARMEN MOVSISSIAN.

Minister of Regional Administration and the Co-ordination of Infrastructure: HOVIK ABRAHAMIAN.

Minister of Urban Planning: ARAM HAROUTUNIAN.

Minister of Employment and Social Issues: AGHVAN VARDANIAN.

Minister of Health: NORAIR DAVIDIAN.

Minister of Agriculture: DAVID LOKIAN.

Minister of Nature Protection: VARDAN AYVAZIAN.

Minister of Trade and Economic Development: KAREN CHSHMARITIAN.

Minister of Education and Science: SERGO YERITSIAN.

Minister of Culture and Youth Affairs: HOVIK HOVEIAN.

Minister of Transport and Communications: ANDRANIK MANUKIAN.

Minister and Chief of Staff: MANUK TOPUZIAN.

MINISTRIES

Office of the President: 375077 Yerevan, Marshal Baghramian St 26; tel. (1) 52-02-04; fax (1) 52-15-51; internet www.president.am.

Office of the Prime Minister: 375010 Yerevan, Republic Sq. 1, Govt House; tel. (1) 52-03-60; fax (1) 15-10-35; internet www.gov.am/am/gov/premier.

Ministry of Agriculture: 375010 Yerevan, Nalbandian St 48; tel. (1) 52-46-41; fax (1) 15-10-86; internet www.minagro.am.

Ministry of Culture and Youth Affairs: 375010 Yerevan, Govt House 3; tel. (1) 52-93-49; fax (1) 52-39-22; e-mail mcya@web.am.

Ministry of Defence: Yerevan, Proshian Settlement, G. Shaush St 60; tel. (1) 28-94-52; fax (1) 28-16-74.

Ministry of Education and Science: 375010 Yerevan, Movses Khorenatsi St 13; tel. (1) 52-66-02; fax (1) 58-04-03; internet www.edu.am/mes.

Ministry of Employment and Social Issues: 375025 Yerevan, Terian St 69; tel. (1) 52-68-31; fax (1) 15-19-20; internet www.mss.am.

Ministry of Energy: 375010 Yerevan, Republic Sq., Govt House 2; tel. (1) 52-19-64; fax (1) 52-63-65; e-mail minenergy@minenergy.am; internet www.minenergy.am.

Ministry of Finance and the Economy: 375010 Yerevan, Melik-Adamian St 1; tel. (1) 52-70-82; fax (1) 52-37-45; e-mail staff@mf.gov.am; internet mfe.gov.am.

Ministry of Foreign Affairs: 375010 Yerevan, Republic Sq., Govt House 2; tel. (1) 54-40-41; fax (1) 54-39-25; e-mail info@armeniaforeignministry.com; internet www.armeniaforeignministry.am.

Ministry of Health: 375001 Yerevan, Tumanian St 8; tel. (1) 58-24-13; fax (1) 15-10-97; internet www.armhealth.am.

Ministry of Justice: 375010 Yerevan, Vazgen Sarkissian St 3; tel. and fax (1) 58-21-57; e-mail justice@justice.am.

Ministry of Nature Protection: 375010 Yerevan, Republic Sq., Government Bldg 3; tel. (1) 52-10-99; fax (1) 58-54-69; e-mail interdpt@rambler.ru; internet www.mnpiac.am.

Ministry of Regional Administration and the Co-ordination of Infrastructure: 375010 Yerevan, Republic Sq., Govt Bldg 1; tel. (1) 52-52-74.

Ministry of Trade and Economic Development: 375008 Yerevan, Hanrapetoutioun St 5; tel. (1) 52-61-34; fax (1) 15-16-75; internet www.minted.am.

Ministry of Transport and Communications: 375010 Yerevan, Nalbandian St 28; tel. (1) 52-38-62; fax (1) 54-59-79; e-mail traceca@arminco.am; internet www.mtc.am.

Ministry of Urban Planning: 375010 Yerevan, Republic Sq., Govt House; tel. (1) 58-90-80; fax (1) 52-32-00.

President and Legislature

PRESIDENT

Presidential Election, First Ballot, 19 February 2003

Candidates	Votes	% of votes
Robert Kocharian	700,808	49.48
Stepan Demirchian	399,757	28.22
Artashes Geghamian	250,145	17.66
Others	65,647	4.63
Total	1,416,357*	100.00

*Excluding invalid votes and votes against all candidates.

Second Ballot, 5 March 2003

Candidates	% of votes
Robert Kocharian	67.48
Stepan Demirchian	32.52
Total*	100.00

*The total number of valid votes cast (excluding those against both candidates) was 1,536,098.

General Election, 25 May 2003

	Party lists		
Parties and blocs	% of votes	Seats	Total seats
Republican Party of Armenia . .	23.6	23	32
Law-Governed Country Party of Armenia	13.0	12	18
Justice bloc*	13.6	14	15
Armenian Revolutionary Federation	11.5	11	11
National Unity Party	8.9	9	9
United Labour Party	5.7	6	6
Independents and others . .	24.0	0	37
Total (incl. others)	100.0	75	131†

*A coalition of the Armenian Democratic Party, the National Democratic Party, the People's Party of Armenia and the Union of National Democrats.

†Results were annulled in three constituencies; the subsequent by-elections, which were held in June, were won by a member of the Law-Governed Country Party of Armenia, a member of the Republican Party of Armenia and an independent candidate.

LEGISLATURE

Azgayin Zhoghov
(National Assembly)

375095 Yerevan, Marshal Baghramian St 19; tel. (1) 58-82-25; fax (1) 52-98-26; internet www.parliament.am.

Chairman: ARTUR BAGHDASARIAN.

Political Organizations

Following the approval of new legislation in November 2002, all political parties were required to re-register with the Ministry of Justice. By December 2003 47 parties had been re-registered, eight parties had been denied registration and two parties had been founded in accordance with the new legislation.

Armenian Christian Democratic Union (HDQM): Yerevan; tel. (1) 52-62-49; e-mail pride@freenet.am; f. 1990; Chair. KHOSROV HAROUTUNIAN.

Armenian Democratic Party: Yerevan, Koriun St 14; tel. (1) 52-52-73; f. 1992 by elements of Communist Party of Armenia; contested the parliamentary election of 2003 as part of the Justice (Artarutiun) bloc; Chair. ARAM SARKISSIAN.

Armenian Liberal Democratic Party (Ramgavar Azatagan—HRAK): 375009 Yerevan, Koriun St 19A; tel. and fax (1) 52-64-03; e-mail hrak@arminco.com; internet adl.hayway.org; f. 1991; joined the Union of Social Democratic Forces in 2000; centre-right; Co-Chair. HARUTIUN ARAKELIAN, ARMEN STEPANIAN, MEKHAK GEVORGIAN; 10,400 mems.

Armenian Pan-National Movement (APNM) (Haiots Hamazgaien Sharjoum–HHSh): 375019 Yerevan, Khanjian St 27; tel. (1) 57-04-70; f. 1989; Pres. LEVON TER-PETROSSIAN; Chair. ALEKSANDR ARZUMANIAN.

Armenian Revolutionary Federation (ARF) (Hai Heghapokhakan Dashnaktsutiun): 375010 Yerevan, Mher Mkrtchyan St 30; tel. (1) 52-15-02; fax (1) 52-04-26; e-mail info@arf.am; internet www.arfd.am; f. 1890; formed the ruling party in independent Armenia, 1918–20; prohibited under Soviet rule, but continued its activities in other countries; permitted to operate legally in Armenia from 1991; suspended in December 1994; legally reinstated 1998; 40,000 mems; Chair. RUBEN HAGOBIAN, VAHAN HOVHANISSIAN.

Communist Party of Armenia (CPA) (HHK): Yerevan, Marshal Baghramian St 10; tel. (1) 56-79-33; fax (1) 53-38-55; f. 1920; dissolved 1991, relegalized 1992; c. 50,000 mems; Chair. RUBEN TOVMASSIAN.

Dignified Future Party (Arzhanapativ Apaga): 375025 Yerevan, 1st Lane, Koryuni St 11/1A; tel. (1) 52-31-24; fax (1) 54-29-96; f. 2004; Leader LYUDMILA HAROUTUNIAN.

Law-Governed Country Party of Armenia (Orinats Yerkir—OY): Yerevan; tel. (1) 52-69-39; f. 1998; centrist; also known as the Rule of Law Party and the Legal State Party; absorbed the People's Democratic Party of Armenia in Nov. 2003; Head ARTUR BAGHDASARIAN; 41,000 mems.

Mighty Fatherland (Hzor Hayrenik): 375010 Yerevan, Tigran Metsi Ave 9; tel. (1) 52-92-15; fax (1) 52-25-45; e-mail hzor_hayrenik@xter.net; f. 1997; Chair. VARDAN VARAPETIAN; 11,500 mems.

National Democratic Party: Yerevan, Abovian St 12; tel. and fax (1) 56-31-88; e-mail adjm@arminco.com; f. 2001 following the division of the National Democratic Union; contested the 2003 parliamentary election as part of the Justice (Artarutiun) bloc; Leader SHAVARSH KOCHARIAN.

National Unity Party (Azgayin Miabanutiun): c/o Azgayin Zhoghov, 375095 Yerevan, Marshal Baghramian St 19; tel. (1) 58-01-37; f. 1998; Chair. ARTASHES GEGHAMIAN.

New Times Party (Nor Zhamanakner): 375001 Yerevan, Tumanyan St 8; tel. (1) 56-83-17; fax (1) 56-83-39; e-mail nor_jamanakner@yahoo.com; f. 2003; Chair. ARAM KARAPETIAN.

People's Party of Armenia (PPA) (HzhK): Yerevan; f. 1998; contested the general election of May 2003 as part of the Justice (Artarutiun) bloc; Leader STEPAN DEMIRCHIAN.

Republic (Hanrapetutiun): 375002 Yerevan, Mashtotsi Ave. 37/30; tel. (1) 53-86-34; e-mail republic@arminco.com; internet www.hanrapetutyun.am; f. 2001 by members of the Yerkrapah Union of Volunteers and fmr members of the Republican Party of Armenia; Leader ARAM SARKISSIAN.

Republican Party of Armenia (Haiastani Hanrapetakan Kusaktsutiun—RPA) (HHK): 375010 Yerevan, Melik-Adamian St 2; tel. (1) 58-00-31; fax (1) 50-12-59; e-mail hhk@hhk.am; internet www.hhk.am; f. 1990; Chair. ANDRANIK MARKARIAN.

Union of National Democrats: Yerevan; f. 2001 following a split in the National Democratic Union; contested the general election of May 2003 as part of the Justice (Artarutiun) bloc; Leader ARSHAK SADOIAN.

Union for National Self-Determination (UNS): 375013 Yerevan, Grigor Lusavorichi St 15; tel. (1) 52-55-38; Chair. PARUIR HAIRIKIAN.

Union of Rightist Forces: Yerevan; f. 2000 as an alliance of the Hazatutiun (Freedom) Party, the 21st Century Party (Democratic National Party), the Liberal Democratic Party and the Armat (Root) Party.

Union of Socialist Forces: Yerevan; f. 1997; left-wing; Leader ASHOT MANUCHARIAN.

United Communist Party of Armenia: Yerevan; f. 2003 by the merger of seven pro-communist parties, including the Renewed Communist Party of Armenia, the Party of Intellectuals, the Communist Party of the Working People and the United Progressive Communist; First Sec. YURI MANUKIAN.

United Labour Party (MAK): Yerevan; tel. (9) 42-55-04; f. 2002; Chair. GURGEN ARSENIAN.

Diplomatic Representation

EMBASSIES IN ARMENIA

Belarus: 375009 Yerevan, Abovian St 23–6; tel. (1) 59-73-09; fax (1) 56-70-18; e-mail armenia@arminco.com; Ambassador MARINA DOLGOPOLOVA.

Bulgaria: Yerevan, Nor Aresh, Sofia St 16; tel. (1) 45-82-33; fax (1) 45-46-02; e-mail bularm@arminco.com; Ambassador STEFAN DIMITROV.

China, People's Republic: Yerevan, Marshal Baghramian St 12; tel. (1) 56-00-67; fax (1) 54-57-61; e-mail chiemb@mbox.amilink.net; Ambassador ZUO XUELIANG.

France: 375015 Yerevan, Grigor Lusavorichi St 8; tel. (1) 56-11-03; fax (1) 56-98-31; e-mail secretar@ambafran.am; internet www.ambafran.am; Ambassador HENRI CUNY.

Georgia: Yerevan, Arami St 42; tel. (1) 56-43-57; fax (1) 56-41-83; e-mail georgia@arminco.com; Ambassador REVAZ GACHECHILADZE.

Germany: 375025 Yerevan, Charents St 29; tel. (1) 52-32-79; fax (1) 52-47-81; e-mail info@eriw.diplo.de; internet www.eriwan.diplo.de; Ambassador Dr HEIKE PEITSCH.

Greece: Yerevan, Proshian St 12; tel. (1) 53-00-51; fax (1) 53-00-49; e-mail grembarm@arminco.com; Ambassador ANTONIOS VLAVIANOS.

India: 375019 Yerevan, Dzorapi St 50/2; tel. (1) 53-91-73; fax (1) 53-39-84; e-mail hoc@embassyofindia.am; internet www.indianembassy.am; Ambassador DEEPAK VOHRA.

Iran: Yerevan, Budaghian St 1; tel. (1) 28-04-57; fax (1) 23-00-52; e-mail info@iranembassy.am; internet www.iranembassy.am; Ambassador ALIREZA HAGHIGHIAN.

Italy: 375010 Yerevan, Italiayi St 5; tel. (1) 54-23-35; fax (1) 54-23-41; e-mail ambitaly@arminco.com; Ambassador MARCO CLEMENTE.

Lebanon: 375010 Yerevan, Vardanants St 7; tel. (1) 52-65-40; fax (1) 52-69-90; e-mail libarm@arminco.com; Ambassador TONY BADAWI.

Poland: Yerevan, Hanrapetoutioun St 44A; tel. (1) 54-24-93; fax (1) 54-24-98; e-mail polemb@arminco.com; Ambassador VIKTOR ROSS.

Romania: Yerevan, Barbusse St 15; tel. (1) 27-53-32; fax (1) 22-75-47; e-mail ambrom@netsys.am; Ambassador NICOLAE IORDACHE.

Russia: 375015 Yerevan, Grigor Lusavorichi St 13A; tel. (1) 56-74-27; fax (1) 56-71-97; e-mail rossia@arminco.com; internet www.armenia.mid.ru; Ambassador NIKOLAI PAVLOV.

Syria: 375019 Yerevan, Marshal Baghramian St 14; tel. (1) 52-40-28; fax (1) 52-52-19; e-mail syria.am@intertel.am; Ambassador Dr GHASSAN RESLAN.

Turkmenistan: Yerevan, Kievian St 19; tel. (1) 22-10-29; fax (1) 22-21-32; e-mail serdar@arminco.com; Chargé d'affaires a.i. SERDAR DURDIYEV.

Ukraine: 375033 Yerevan, Arabkir St 29/5/1; tel. (1) 22-97-27; fax (1) 25-13-83; e-mail ukremb@arminco.com; Ambassador VOLODOMYR M. TYAGLO.

United Kingdom: Yerevan, Charents St 28; tel. (1) 26-43-01; fax (1) 26-43-18; e-mail enquiries.yerevan@fco.gov.uk; internet www.britishembassy.am; Ambassador THORDA ABBOTT-WATT.

USA: Yerevan, Marshal Baghramian St 18; tel. (1) 52-46-61; fax (1) 52-08-00; e-mail usinfo@arminco.com; internet www.usa.am/index.html; Ambassador JOHN EVANS.

Judicial System

A new judicial and legal system came into force in January 1999. The Supreme Court was replaced as the highest court of appeal by the Court of Cassation, and Appellate Courts were to operate in the place of People's Courts. Members of the Court of Cassation were to be appointed by the President, for life.

Constitutional Court

375019 Yerevan, Marshal Baghramian St 10; tel. (1) 58-81-40; fax (1) 52-99-91; e-mail armlaw@concourt.am; internet www.concourt.am.

f. 1996; Chair. GAGIK HAROUTUNIAN.

Chairman of the Court of Cassation: HANRIK DANIELIAN.

Prosecutor-General: AGHVAN HOVSEPPIAN.

Religion

The major religion is Christianity. The Armenian Apostolic Church is the leading denomination and was widely identified with the movement for national independence. There are also Russian Orthodox and Islamic communities, although the latter lost adherents as a result of the departure of large numbers of Muslim Azeris from the republic. Most Kurds are also adherents of Islam, although some are Yazidis. In 2002 51 religious organizations were registered in Armenia, after legislative amendments were adopted, which increased the number of adherents required for registration from 50 to 200. (The Jehovah's Witness community was estimated to number 12,000, but failed to qualify for registration as its statutes were deemed to be in contravention of the Constitution.)

GOVERNMENT AGENCY

Council for the Affairs of the Armenian Church: 375001 Yerevan, Abovian St 3; tel. (1) 56-46-34; fax (1) 56-41-81.

Religious Council: Yerevan; f. 2002 as a consultative council, to advise the Government on religious affairs; was to comprise representatives of the Government, the Office of the Prosecutor-General, the Armenian Apostolic Church, and the Catholic and Protestant Churches.

CHRISTIANITY

Armenian Apostolic Church: Vagharshapat, Monastery of St Etchmiadzin; tel. (1) 28-57-37; fax (1) 15-10-77; e-mail holysee@etchmiadzin.am; internet www.holyetchmiadzin.am; nine dioceses in Armenia, four in other ex-Soviet republics and 25 dioceses and bishoprics in the rest of the world; 7m. members world-wide; 15 monasteries and three theological seminaries in Armenia; Supreme Patriarch KAREKIN II (Catholicos of All Armenians).

The Roman Catholic Church

Armenian Rite

Armenian Catholics in Eastern Europe are under the jurisdiction of an Ordinary (equivalent to a bishop with direct authority). At 31 December 2002 there were an estimated 220,000 adherents within this jurisdiction.

Ordinary: Most Rev. NERSES DER-NERSESSIAN (Titular Archbishop of Sebaste), Gyumri, Atarbekian St 82; tel. (41) 22-115; fax (41) 34-959; e-mail armorda@shirak.am.

Latin Rite

The Apostolic Administrator of the Caucasus is the Apostolic Nuncio (Ambassador of the Holy See) to Georgia, Armenia and Azerbaijan, who is resident in Tbilisi, Georgia.

JUDAISM

Although there is a long history of Jewish settlement in Armenia, the majority of Jews living in Armenia emigrated to Israel following the dissolution of the USSR. In the early 2000s the Jewish community was believed to number around 1,000, and was located principally in Yerevan, although there were also small Jewish communities in Sevan and Vanadzor.

Mordechay Navi Jewish Religious Community of Armenia: 375018 Yerevan, Nar-Dosi St 23; tel. (1) 57-16-77; fax (1) 55-41-32; e-mail burger_mc@rambler.ru; Chief Rabbi of Armenia GERSH MEIR BURSHTEIN; Chair. of the Jewish Community in Armenia RIMMA VARJAPETYAN.

The Press

PRINCIPAL NEWSPAPERS

In 2003 120 newspaper titles were published in Armenia, 107 of which were in Armenian. Those listed below are in Armenian except where otherwise stated.

Ankakhutiun (Independence): 375013 Yerevan, Grigor Lusavorichi St 15; tel. (1) 58-18-64; daily; organ of the Union for National Self-Determination; Editor PARUIR HAIRIKIAN.

Aravot: 375023 Yerevan, Arshakuniats Ave 2, 15th Floor; tel. (1) 56-89-68; fax (1) 52-87-52; e-mail news@aravot.am; internet www.aravot.am; daily; Editor A. ABRAMIAN; circ. 5,000.

Azg (The Nation): 375010 Yerevan, Hanrapetoutioun St 47; tel. (1) 52-16-35; fax (1) 56-28-63; e-mail azg2@arminco.com; internet www.azg.am; f. 1990; Editor HAGOP AVETIKIAN; circ. 3,000.

Bravo: Yerevan, Abovian St 12, Hotel Yerevan; tel. (1) 55-44-05; weekly; Editor K. KAZARIAN.

Delovoi Ekspress (Business Express): 375051 Yerevan, N. Zarian St 22, 2nd Floor; tel. (1) 25-26-83; fax (1) 25-90-23; e-mail editor@express.am; internet www.express.am; f. 1992; weekly; economic; in Russian; Editor E. NAGDALIAN.

Epokha (Epoch): 375023 Yerevan, Arshakuniats Ave 2; f. 1938; fmrly *Komsomolets (Young Communist)*; weekly; in Russian; organ of the Youth League of Armenia; Editor V. S. GRIGORIAN.

Golos Armenii (The Voice of Armenia): 375023 Yerevan, Arshakuniats Sq. 2, 7th Floor; tel. (1) 52-77-23; fax (1) 52-89-08; e-mail gonline@press.arminco.com; internet www.golos.am; f. 1934 as *Kommunist*; 3 a week; in Russian; Editor F. NAKHSHKARIAN.

Grakan Tert (Literary Paper): 375019 Yerevan, Marshal Baghramian St 3; tel. (1) 52-05-94; f. 1932; weekly; organ of the Union of Writers; Editor ZAVEN HOVHANISSIAN.

Haiastan Hanrapetutiun (Republic of Armenia): Yerevan; tel. (1) 52-69-74; fax (1) 54-86-11; e-mail hh@press.aic.net; daily; Editor TIGRAN FARMANIAN; circ. 6,000.

Haik (Armenia): Yerevan; tel. (1) 52-77-01; e-mail root@hayk.arminco.com; weekly; organ of the Armenian Pan-National Movement; Editor V. DAVTIAN; circ. 30,000.

Haiots Ashkhar: Yerevan, Tumanian St 38; tel. (1) 53-32-11; fax (1) 53-88-65; e-mail hayashkh@armnico.com; f. 1997; Editor G. MKRTCHIAN; circ. 3,500.

Haykakan Zhamanak: Yerevan, 37; tel. (1) 58-11-75; e-mail nikol@arminco.com; internet www.hzh.am; Editor-in-Chief NIKOL PASHINIAN; circ. 6,000.

Hazatamart (The Battle for Freedom): 375070 Yerevan, Zavarian 181; organ of the Armenian Revolutionary Federation (ARF); Editor M. MIKAYELIAN.

Marzakan Haiastan: 375023 Yerevan, Arshakuniats Ave 5; tel. and fax (1) 52-62-41; f. 1956; weekly; sports; Editor S. MOURADIAN; circ. 3,000.

Molorak: 375023 Yerevan, Arshakuniats Ave 5; tel. (1) 52-62-12; daily; Editor H. GHAGHRINIAN.

Vozny (Hedgehog): 375023 Yerevan, Arshakuniats Ave 2, 12th Floor; tel. (1) 52-63-83; f. 1954; Editor A. SAHAKIAN.

Yerevanian Orer (Yerevan Days): Yerevan; Editor M. AIRAPETIAN.

Yerokoian Yerevan (Evening Yerevan): 375023 Yerevan, Arshakuniats Ave 2, 10th Floor; tel. (1) 52-97-52; weekly; organ of Yerevan City Council; Editor N. YENGIBARIAN.

Yeter: Yerevan, A. Manukian St 5; tel. (1) 55-34-13; fax (1) 55-17-13; e-mail editor@eter.am; internet www.eter.am; weekly; independent; television and radio programming information; Editor G. KAZARIAN.

Zroutsakits: 375023 Yerevan, Arshakuniats Ave 2, 2nd Floor; tel. (1) 52-84-30; weekly; Editor M. MIRIDJANIAN.

PRINCIPAL PERIODICALS

In 2003 77 periodicals were published, of which 51 were in Armenian.

Aroghchapautiun (Health): 376001 Yerevan, Tumanian St 8; tel. (1) 52-35-73; e-mail mharut@dmc.am; f. 1956; quarterly; journal of the Ministry of Health; Editor M. A. MURADIAN; circ. 2,000–5,000.

Arvest (Art): 375001 Yerevan, Tumanian St 5; f. 1932; monthly; publ. by the Ministry of Culture and Youth Affairs; Editor G. A. AZAKELIAN.

Ayb-Fe: Yerevan; tel. 58-54-27; e-mail oratert@a1plus.am; internet www.a1plus.am; weekly.

Chorord Ishkhanutiun/Chetvertaya Vlast (The Fourth Estate): Yerevan, Abovian St 12, Rm 105, Hotel Yerevan 105; tel. (1) 52-02-12; e-mail chiog@arminco.com; internet www.chi.am; monthly; in Armenian and Russian; Editor SHOGHER MATEVOSSIAN.

Ekonomika (Economics): Yerevan, Vardanants St 2; tel. (1) 52-27-95; f. 1957; monthly; government organ; Editor R. H. SHAKHKULIAN; circ. 1,500–2,000.

Garoun (Spring): 375015 Yerevan, Grigor Lusavorichi St 15; tel. (1) 56-29-56; e-mail garoun@garoun.am; f. 1967; monthly; independent; fiction, poetry and socio-political issues; Editor V. S. AYOUZIAN; circ. 1,500.

Gitutyun ev Tekhnika (Science and Technology): 375048 Yerevan, Komitasa Ave 49/3; tel. (1) 23-37-27; e-mail giteknik@rambler.ru; f. 1963; monthly; journal of the Research Institute of Scientific-Technical Information and of Technological and Economic Research; Dir S. AGAJANIAN; Editor H. R. KHACHATRIAN; circ. 1,000.

Hanrapetakan: Yerevan, Melik–Adamian St 2; tel. (1) 58-00-31; fax (1) 50-12-59; internet www.hhk.am; f. 1991; organ of the Republican Party of Armenia; monthly.

Iravunk: 375002 Yerevan, Yeznik Koghbatsu St 50A; tel. (1) 53-27-30; fax (1) 53-41-92; e-mail info@iravunk.com; internet www.iravunk.com; f. 1989; weekly; Editor HAIK BABUKHANIAN; circ. 45,000.

Literaturnaya Armeniya (Literary Armenia): 375019 Yerevan, Marshal Baghramian St 3; tel. (1) 56-36-57; f. 1958; monthly; journal of the Union of Writers; fiction; in Russian; Editor A. M. NALBANDIAN.

Nork: Yerevan; f. 1934; fmrly *Sovetakan Grakanutyun* (Soviet Literature); monthly; journal of the Union of Writers; fiction; Russian; Editor R. G. OVSEPIAN.

Novoye Vremya (New Time): 375023 Yerevan, Arshakuniats Ave 2, 3rd Floor; tel. (1) 52-69-46; fax (1) 52-73-62; e-mail nvremya@arminco.com; internet www.nv.am; f. 1992; 3 a week; in Russian; Editor R. A. SATIAN; circ. 5,000.

Veratsnvats Haiastan (Reborn Armenia): Yerevan; f. 1945; monthly; journal of the Armenian Committee for Cultural Relations with Compatriots Abroad; fiction; Editor V. A. DAVITIAN.

Yerevan Times: 375009 Yerevan, Isaahakian St 28, 3rd Floor; tel. (1) 52-82-70; fax (1) 15-17-38; e-mail yertime@armpress.arminco.com; weekly; in English; Editor T. HAKOBIAN.

Yerkir (Country): 375010 Yerevan, Hanrapetoutioun St 30; tel. (1) 52-15-01; fax (1) 52-04-26; e-mail erkir@arminco.com; internet www.yerkir.am; f. 1991; weekly; organ of the ARF; also published in Lebanon; Editor-in-Chief SPARTAK SEYRANIAN; circ. 2,500.

NEWS AGENCIES

Arka News Agency: 375010 Yerevan, Pavstos Byuzand St 1/3; tel. (1) 52-21-52; fax (1) 52-40-80; e-mail arka@arminco.com; internet www.arka.am; f. 1996; economic, financial and political news; Russian and English.

Armenpress (Armenian News Agency): 375009 Yerevan, Isaahakian St 28, 4th Floor; tel. (1) 52-67-02; fax (1) 52-57-98; e-mail contact@armenpress.am; internet www.armenpress.am; f. 1922 as state information agency, transformed into state joint-stock company in 1997; Armenian, English and Russian; Dir H. ZORIAN.

Arminfo: 375009 Yerevan, Isaahakian St 28, 2nd Floor; tel. (1) 52-20-34; fax (1) 54-31-72; e-mail news@arminfo.am; internet www.arminfo.am; f. 1991 as Snark; name changed as above in 2001; Dir EMMANUIL MKRTCHIAN; Editor ALEKSANDR AVANISOV.

Mediamax (Armenian Press Agency): Yerevan, Marshal Baghramian St 31A; tel. (1) 22-87-86; fax (1) 27-11-56; e-mail media@arminco.com; internet www.mediamax.am; Dir ARA TADEVOSIAN; Editor-in-Chief DAVID ALAVERDIAN.

PRESS ASSOCIATION

Union of Journalists of Armenia: Yerevan, Pushkin St 3A; tel. (1) 56-12-76; fax (1) 56-14-47; e-mail www@internews.am; f. 1959; Dir ASTGHIK GEVORGIAN.

Publishers

Academy of Sciences Publishing House: 375019 Yerevan, Marshal Baghramian St 24G; Dir KH. H. BARSEGHIAN.

Arevik Publishing House: 375009 Yerevan, Terian St 91; tel. (1) 52-45-61; fax (1) 52-05-36; e-mail arevick@netsys.am; internet www.arevik.am; f. 1986; political, scientific, fiction for children, textbooks; Pres. DAVID HOVHANNES; Exec. Dir ASTGHIK STEPANIAN.

Hayastan (Armenia Publishing House): 375009 Yerevan, Isaahakian St 28; tel. (1) 52-85-20; e-mail nunjan@hragir.aua.am; f. 1921; political and fiction; Dir VAHAGN SARKISSIAN.

Haikakan Hanragitaran Hratarakchutioun (Armenian Encyclopaedia Publishing House): 375001 Yerevan, Tumanian St 17; tel. (1) 52-43-41; fax (1) 52-06-67; e-mail encyclop@sci.am; internet www.encyclopedia.am; f. 1967; encyclopedias and other reference books; Editor H. M. AIVAZIAN.

Louys Publishing Co: 375009 Yerevan, Isaahakian St 28; tel. (1) 52-53-13; fax (1) 56-55-07; e-mail louys@arminco.com; f. 1955; textbooks; Dir H. Z. HAROUTUNIAN.

Miva-Pres Publishing House: 375009 Yerevan, Isahaakian St 28/21; tel. (1) 52-65-00; e-mail miva@noyan-tapan.am; translations of Armenian and world literature; Dir MICHAEL STEPANIAN.

Nairi: 375009 Yerevan, Terian St 91; tel. and fax (1) 56-58-54; e-mail nairi_hrat@rambler.ru; f. 1991; fiction, science, translations and reference; Pres. HRACHIA TAMRAZIAN.

Noyan Tapan (Noah's Ark) Publishing House: 375009 Yerevan, Isahaakian St 28; tel. (1) 56-59-65; e-mail contact@noyan-tapan.am; internet www.nt.am; legal and medical; Gen. Dir TIGRAN HAROUTIU-NIAN.

Tigran Mets (Tigran the Great) Publishing House: 375023 Yerevan, Arshakuniats St 2; tel. (1) 52-70-56; e-mail tigranmets2002@yahoo.com; fiction, poetry, science and children's books; Dir VREJ MARKOSSIAN.

Yerevan State University Publishing House: 375028 Yerevan, Aleks Manukian St 1; tel. (1) 55-28-84; e-mail pr-int@ysu.am; text-books and reference books, history, literary criticism, science and fiction; Dir PERCH STEPANIAN.

PUBLISHERS' ASSOCIATION

National Book Chamber of Armenia: 375009 Yerevan, G. Kochar St 21; tel. (1) 52-75-95; e-mail grapalat@arminco.com; internet book-chamber.am; f. 1922; centre of national bibliography, bibliographical information and statistics, and central depositary of publications.

National Union of Armenian Publishers: 375009 Yerevan, Isahaakian St 28; tel. (1) 56-31-57; fax (1) 56-55-07; e-mail gam@arminco.com; internet www.magic.am/nuap; f. 1999; Pres. SOS MOV-SISSIAN.

Broadcasting and Communications

TELECOMMUNICATIONS

Armenia Telephone Co (ArmenTel): Yerevan, Azatutiun Ave 24; tel. (1) 54-91-00; fax (1) 28-98-88; internet www.armentel.com; f. 1995 by the Government and TransWorld Telecom (USA); transferred to private ownership in 1998; 10% state-owned, 90% owned by OTE Hellenic Telecommunications Organization (Greece); restructuring of monopoly pending; Chief Exec. VASILIOS FETSIS; Chair. GEORGIOS VASILAKIS; 7,159 employees (Dec. 2001).

BROADCASTING

National Commission on Television and Radio (NCTR): 375000 Yerevan; tel. (1) 53-78-48; e-mail nctr@tvradio.am; internet www.tvradio.am; Dir GRIGOR AMALIAN.

Radio

Armenian Public Radio: 375025 Yerevan, Alex Manoogian St 5; tel. (1) 55-33-43; fax (1) 55-46-00; e-mail president@mediaconcern.am; internet www.armradio.am; state jt-stock co; three programmes; domestic broadcasts in Armenian, Russian and Kurdish; external broadcasts in Armenian, Russian, Kurdish, Azerbaijani, Arabic, English, French, German, Spanish and Farsi; Dir-Gen. ARMEN AMIRIAN.

Television

Armenian Public Television: 375047 Yerevan, Hovsepian St 26; tel. (1) 56-95-74; fax (1) 56-24-60; internet www.armtv.com; state jt-stock co; Chair. of Council ALEKSAN HAROUTUNIAN; Exec. Dir ARMEN ARZUMANIAN.

Finance

(cap. = capital; res = reserves; dep. = deposits; m. = million; brs = branches; amounts in drams, unless otherwise stated)

BANKING

Central Bank

Central Bank of the Republic of Armenia: 375010 Yerevan, V. Sarkissian St 6; tel. (1) 58-38-41; fax (1) 52-38-52; e-mail mcba@cba.am; internet www.cba.am; f. 1993; state-owned; cap. 100.0m., res 21,938.3m., dep. 46,640.4m. (Dec. 2002); Chair. Dr TIGRAN SARKIS-SIAN.

Commercial Banks

At the end of 2003 there were 20 banks (with 232 branches) in operation in Armenia. Some of the most influential of these are listed below:

Agricultural Co-operative Bank of Armenia: 375009 Yerevan, Byron St 1; tel. (1) 56-85-58; fax (1) 54-34-85; e-mail acba@arminco.com; internet www.acba.am; f. 1996; cap. 1,252.6m., res 3,476.2m., dep. 11,947.3m. (Dec. 2003); Gen. Man. STEPAN GISHIAN.

Ardshininvestbank (ASHIB): 375015 Yerevan, Grigor Lusavroichi St 13; tel. (1) 52-85-13; fax (1) 56-74-86; e-mail office@ashib.am; internet www.ashib.am; f. 2003 on the basis of Ardshinbank; partially acquired the assets of Armagrobank in December 2003; 80% owned by Rasco Armenia, 20% owned by Business Investments Centre Ltd; cap. 2,946.3m., res 70.1m., dep. 26,033.3m. (Dec. 2004); Chair. of Bd ARAM ANDREASSIAN; 50 brs.

Armenian Development Bank: 375015 Yerevan, Paronian St 21/1; tel. (1) 53-88-41; fax (1) 53-32-33; e-mail info@armdb.com;

internet www.armdb.com; f. 1990; cap. US $4.3m., res $0.8m., dep. $14.8m. (2002); Chair. ALEKSANDR GRIGORIAN.

Armenian Economy Development Bank (Armeconombank): 375002 Yerevan, Amirian St 23/1; tel. (1) 56-33-32; fax (1) 53-89-04; e-mail bank@aeb.am; internet www.aeb.am; jt-stock co; corporate banking; cap. 1,500m., res 116.3m., dep. 12,787.8m. (Dec. 2002); Chair. of Bd SARIBEK SUKIASSIAN; Chief Exec. ASHOT OSSIPIAN; 23 brs.

Armenian Import-Export Bank (Armimpexbank): 375010 Yerevan, Vazgen Sarkissian St 2; tel. (1) 58-99-06; fax (1) 56-59-58; e-mail office@impexbank.am; internet www.impexbank.am; f. 1992 by reorganization of Armenian br. of the Vneshekonombank of the former USSR; 93.1% owned by CIE (United Kingdom); cap. 2,000m., res 427.9m., dep. 11,221.4m. (Dec. 2003); Chair. of Bd LEVON BARKHUDARIAN; Chief Exec. ARA ALEXANIAN; 5 brs.

Arminvestbank: 375010 Yerevan, Vardanants St 13; tel. (1) 52-39-29; fax (1) 54-58-35; e-mail ibank@dolphin.am; f. 1992; cap. US $2.7m., res $0.7m., dep. $9.8m. (Dec. 2004); Chair. of Bd VAROUZHAN AMIRAGHIAN.

Artsakhbank: 375028 Yerevan, Kievian St 3; tel. (1) 27-77-19; fax (1) 27-77-49; e-mail artsakhbank@ktsurf.net; internet www.artsakhbank.am; f. 1996; cap. 1,467.7m., res 151.5m., dep. 7,908m. (Jan. 2005); Chair.of Bd of Dirs HRATCH KAPRIELIAN; Chair. of Bd KAMO NERSISSIAN; 12 brs.

Bank Mellat: 375010 Yerevan, Amirian St 6, POB 24; tel. (1) 58-17-91; fax (1) 54-08-85; e-mail mellat@mellatbank.am; internet www.mellatbank.am; f. 1995; wholly owned by Bank Mellat (Iran); cap. and res 1,001.0m., dep. 6,418.4m. (Dec. 1999); cap. US $5.1m. (Jan. 2005); Chair.and Gen. Man. MORTEZA BEHESHTIROUY.

Converse Bank: 375010 Yerevan, Vazgen Sarkissian St 26; tel. (1) 56-92-48; fax (1) 54-09-20; e-mail post@conversebank.com; internet www.conversebank.com; f. 1994; reorganized in 1997; 48.72% owned by Hudsotrade (Cyprus); cap. 1,233.1m., res 371.28m., dep. 21,553.4m. (Dec. 2003); Pres. KHORI MODALAL; Chair. SMBAT NASIBIAN; 5 brs.

HSBC Bank of Armenia: 375010 Yerevan, Vazgen Sarkissian St 9; tel. (1) 56-32-29; fax (1) 52-70-78; e-mail hsbc@arminco.com; internet www.hsbc.com; f. 1996; 70% owned by HSBC Europe BV (Netherlands), 30% owned by Wings Establishment (Liechtenstein); cap. 2,438m., res 3m., dep. 61,537.8m. (Dec. 2003); Chief Exec. NICK D. GILMOUR; 2 brs.

InecoBank: 375001 Yerevan, Tumanian St 17; tel. (1) 56-37-25; fax (1) 54-51-66; e-mail inecobank@inecobank.am; internet www.inecobank.am; f. 1996; 43.9% owned by Avetis Baloyan; cap. 1,059.7m., res 40.4m., dep 5,502.6m. (Dec. 2003); Chair. AVETIS BALOYAN.

Prometey Bank: 375010 Yerevan, Hanrapetoutioun St 44/2; tel. (1) 56-20-36; fax (1) 54-57-19; e-mail intoperations@prometeybank.am; internet www.prometeybank.am; f. 1990; present name adopted 2001; cap. 2,773.9m. (Dec. 2003), res 52.1m., dep. 1,745.9m. (Dec. 2003); Chair. of Bd EMIL SOGHOMONIAN.

Unibank: 375001 Yerevan, Amirian St 12; tel. (1) 53-98-70; fax (1) 53-30-52; e-mail unibank@unibank.am; internet www.unibank.am; f. 2001; Russian-owned; cap. US $5m., dep. $8m. (2003); Exec. Dir VARDAN G. ATAIAN; Chair. GAGIK T. ZAKARIAN; 5 brs.

Savings Bank

Armsavingsbank (Armsberbank): 375010 Yerevan, Nalbandian St 46; tel. (1) 58-04-51; fax (1) 56-55-78; e-mail headoffice@asb.am; internet www.asb.am; f. 1923; 70.0% owned by Vneshtorgbank (Russia); cap. 444.4m., res 138.6m., dep. 3,320.1m. (Nov. 1998); Chair. of Bd ALEXANDER VARTANOV; 101 brs.

Banking Union

Union of Banks of Armenia: 375009 Yerevan, Koriun St 19A; tel. (1) 52-77-31; fax (1) 56-75-86; e-mail uba@xter.net; internet www.bank.am; f. 1995; oversees banking activity; Pres. SAMVEL CHZMACHIAN; Exec. Dir VLADIMIR BADALIAN.

COMMODITY AND STOCK EXCHANGES

Armenian Stock Exchange (Armex): Yerevan, Mher Mkrtchian St 5B, 6th Floor; tel. (1) 54-33-21; fax (1) 55-33-24; e-mail info@armex.am; internet www.armex.am; f. 2001; Man. Dir A. G. MELIKYAN.

Gyumri Stock Exchange: 375504 Gyumri, Abovian St 244; tel. (41) 2-31-09; fax (41) 2-10-23; f. 1995; Dir SISAK MCHITARIAN.

Yerevan Adamand Commodity and Raw Materials Exchange: 375010 Yerevan, Agatagegosa St 6/1; tel. (1) 56-31-15; fax (1) 56-52-28; e-mail ycre@cornet.am; internet www.yercomex.am; f. 1990; Dir GRIGOR VARDIKIAN.

Yerevan Stock Exchange: 375010 Yerevan, Hanrapetoutioun St 5; tel. (1) 52-32-01; fax (1) 15-15-48; internet www.yse.am; f. 1993; Pres. Dr SEDRAK SEDRAKIAN.

INSURANCE

In 2003 there were 22 licensed insurance companies in Armenia.

Arajin Apahovagrakan: 375025 Yerevan, Charents St 1, 4th Floor; tel. (1) 57-51-18; fax (1) 55-94-73; e-mail info@arajin.am; internet www.arajin.am; f. 1995; general non-life insurance; Exec. Dir PAYLAK GHUKASSIAN.

Armenian Financial Insurance Co (AFIC): 375010 Yerevan, Hanrapetoutioun St 5; tel. (1) 52-77-93; fax (1) 15-15-48; e-mail imamik@yse.armenia.su; f. 1996; Exec. Man. LEVON MAMIKONIAN.

Asco-Pro Insurance Co: 375010 Yerevan, Amirian St 5, apt 3; tel. (1) 53-93-70; fax (1) 53-93-72; e-mail info@asco-pro.am; internet www.asco-pro.am; Dir SERGEY A. MEKIK–YOLCHIAN.

Resolution Consultants: 375001 Yerevan, Moskovian St 31; tel. and fax (1) 55-79-37; e-mail recon@arminco.com; internet www.recon.am; f. 2000; insurance and reinsurance; Pres. JONATHAN STARK.

State Insurance Armenia: Yerevan, Zeytun, Karapet Ulnetsu St 31; tel. and fax (1) 24-94-83; e-mail petap@netsys.am; Russian-Armenian joint venture; Man. Dir V. H AVETISSIAN.

Trade and Industry

GOVERNMENT AGENCY

Armenian Development Agency (ADA): 375025 Yerevan, Charents St 17; tel. and fax (1) 54-22-72; e-mail info@ada.am; internet www.ada.am; f. 1998; foreign investment and export development; Gen. Dir Dr VAHAGN MOVSISSIAN.

CHAMBER OF COMMERCE

Chamber of Commerce and Industry of the Republic of Armenia: 375010 Yerevan, Khanjian St 11; tel. (1) 56-01-84; fax (1) 58-78-71; e-mail armcci@arminco.com; internet www.armcci.am; f. 1959; Chair. MARTIN SARKISSIAN.

EMPLOYERS' ORGANIZATIONS

Armenian Business Small and Medium Entrepreneurship Association: 375010 Yerevan, Republic Sq, House of Unions 43; tel. (1) 56-31-50; fax (1) 56-02-29; e-mail invest@arminco.com; f. 1991; includes the Institute of Business Development and Human Resources, FOBIX Business Consulting Centre, the Electronic Business Agency and the Bankruptcy Protection Foundation; Pres. SEYRAN AVAGHAIN.

Armenian Union of Manufacturers and Businessmen (Employers) of Armenia—UMB(E)A: 375010 Yerevan, Agatanghegos St 5; tel. and fax (1) 56-29-21; e-mail umba@arminco.com; internet www.umba.am; f. 1996; Chair. ARSEN KHAZARIAN.

Association for Foreign Investment and Co-operation (AFIC): 375010 Yerevan, Tigran Mets Ave 4; tel. and fax (1) 56-01-94; e-mail afic@arminco.com; internet www.afic.am; f. 1998; Chair. ANDRANIK ALEXANIAN.

Centre of Small and Medium Entrepreneurship: 375025 Yerevan, Norqi-Ayginer 257B; tel. (1) 52-44-72; fax (1) 54-88-81; e-mail consult@freenet.am; f. 1998; non-governmental organization; formerly Union of Small-sized Enterprises; Pres. KNARIK MALKHASIAN.

UTILITIES

Public Services Regulatory Commission of Armenia (PSRC): Yerevan, Sarian St 22; tel. (1) 52-25-22; fax (1) 52-55-63; e-mail rcnm@rcnm.am; internet www.rcnm.am; f. 1997; formerly the Energy Commission of Armenia; Chair. ROBERT NAZARIAN.

Electricity

Electricity Networks of Armenia (ArmElNet—ENA): Yerevan; tel. (1) 54-00-28; internet www.ena.am; f. 2002; wholly-owned by Midland Resources Holding Ltd (Channel Islands, United Kingdom); national electricity distributor comprising the four former regional electricity networks; Gen. Dir EUGENE GLADUNCHIK.

High Voltage Electric Networks (HV Networks): Yerevan; f. 2003; comprises nine regions; Dir SAHAK ABRAHAMIAN.

International Energy Corpn: Yerevan; f. 2003; wholly owned by Inter RAO EES, a subsidiary of Unified Energy System of Russia; manages Hrazdan Thermal Power Plant, Sevan-Hrazdan Hydroelectric Power Plant cascade and Armenian Nuclear Power Plant ; Gen. Dir MICHAEL MANTROV.

Armenian Nuclear Power Plant (ANPP) Co: 377766 Medzamor, Armavir; tel. (1) 28-18-80; fax (1) 28-06-69; e-mail anpp@lx2.yerphi.am; WWER-440 (V–270) pressurized water-reactor, with a 407.5 MW operating capacity; management transferred to Unified Energy System of Russia in Sept. 2003; Gen. Dir GAGIK MARKOSIAN.

Operator of Electrical Energy System: Yerevan; f. 2003; assumed part of the function of former state monopoly Armenergo.

Gas

ArmRosGazProm—ARG: 375091 Yerevan, Tbilisian St 43; tel. (1) 29-48-10; fax (1) 29-47-28; e-mail inbox@armrusgasprom.am; internet www.armrusgasprom.am; f. 1997; Armenian-Russian joint-stock co; 45% state-owned, 45% owned by Gazprom (Russia); sole natural gas producer in Armenia; Exec. Dir KAREN KARAPETIAN.

Water

Yerevan Water and Sewer: Yerevan; provides water and sewerage services to Yerevan municipality; state-operated.

TRADE UNIONS

At 1 January 2002 159 trade-union organizations were registered with the Ministry of Justice.

Confederation of Trade Unions of Armenia: 375010 Yerevan, Vazgen Sarkissian St 26; tel. (1) 58-36-82; fax (1) 54-33-82; e-mail boris@xar.am; Chair. MARTIN HAROUTUNIAN.

National Union of Farmers: Yerevan, Sebastia St 3A; tel. and fax (1) 74-40-05; e-mail fam2002@infocom.am; f. 1998; Pres. VANIK SOGHOMONIAN.

Union of Merchants of Armenia: 375037 Yerevan, Azatutiun Ave 1/1; tel. (1) 25-28-54; fax (1) 25-91-76; e-mail merchants@netsys.am; f. 1993; Pres. TSOLVARD GEVORGIAN.

Transport

RAILWAYS

In 2003 there were 711 km of railway track in Armenia. There are international lines to Iran and Georgia; the closure lines to Azerbaijan and Turkey remained closed in 2005. In November 2004 it was agreed that rail transport between Russia and Armenia would be restored in 2005, with the co-operation of Georgia; the restoration of the Kavkaz (Russia)—Poti (Georgia) ferry route, with its railway facility, in January 2005 was also expected to greatly enhance the speed of cargo transport across the region.

Armenia Railways: 375005 Yerevan, Tigran Mets St 50; tel. (1) 52-04-28; e-mail arway@mbox.amilink.net; Pres. ARARAT KHRIMIAN.

Metropolitan Railway

An initial 10-km route, with nine stations, opened in Yerevan in 1981, and a further branch opened in 1996. In 2002 the total length was 13.4 km with ten stations. A second line was planned, and proposals envisaged the installation of a 47-km network.

Yerevan Metro: 375033 Yerevan, Marshal Baghramian St 76; tel. (1) 27-45-43; fax (1) 27-24-60; e-mail papiev@netsys.am; f. 1981; Gen. Dir. VAHAGN HAKOPIAN.

ROADS

In 2000 there were an estimated 15,918 km of roads in Armenia (including 7,527 km of motorways, 3,360 km of highways and 4,167 km of secondary roads); 96.3% of roads were paved. As a result of the closure, in 1989 and 1993 respectively, of Azerbaijan's and Turkey's borders with Armenia, the Kajaran highway linking Armenia with Iran emerged as Armenia's most important international road connection; in December 1995 a permanent road bridge over the Araks (Aras) river was opened.

CIVIL AVIATION

Zvartnots International Airport, 15 km west of Yerevan, is the main national airport; there are also international airports in Shirak and Yerebuni.

Civil Aviation Department: 375042 Yerevan, Zvartnots International Airport; tel. (1) 28-57-68; fax (1) 15-11-23; internet www.aviation.am; Dir HOVHANNES YERITSIAN.

Armavia: 375025 Yerevan, Alek Manukian St 9, AUA Business Centre; tel. (1) 51-22-29; fax (1) 51-22-43; e-mail info@u8.am; internet www.u8.am; f. 1996; privately owned; operates flights to destinations in Europe, the Commonwealth of Independent States and the Middle East.

Armenian International Airways (AIA): 375042 Yerevan, Zvartnots International Airport; tel. and fax (1) 28-76-37; e-mail aa@armenianairways.com; internet www.armenianairways.am; f. 2002; privately owned; flies to Europe and the Middle East; Man. Dir VERSAND HAKOBIAN.

Yerevan-Avia: 375010 Yerevan, Busand St 1–3 ; tel. (1) 58-01-21; fax (1) 56-75-11; e-mail eravia@netsys.am; internet www.yer-avia.am; f. 1992; international cargo services; Chief Exec. ARSEN ASLANIAN.

Tourism

Prior to secession from the USSR in 1991, Armenia attracted a number of tourists from the other Soviet republics. Following its independence, however, tourism severely declined, although by the late 1990s some European firms were beginning to introduce tours to the country. According to the World Tourism Organization, tourism receipts increased from about US $5m. in 1995 to $7m. in 1997. Receipts, according to the World Bank, increased rapidly thereafter, reaching $27m. in 1999, $45m. in 2000 and $63m. in 2002. Armenia received an estimated 162,089 tourist arrivals in 2002. The major tourist attractions were the capital, Yerevan; Artashat, an early trading centre on the 'Silk Road'; and medieval monasteries. There was, however, little accommodation available outside the capital.

Directorate of Trade, Tourism and Services: Ministry of Trade and Economic Development, 375008 Yerevan, Hanrapetoutioun St 5; tel. (1) 58-94-94; fax (1) 56-61-23; e-mail garnikn@yahoo.com; Dir ARTAK DAVTIAN.

Armenian Tourism Association (ATA): 375010 Yerevan, Amirian St 27; tel. (1) 53-45-01; fax (1) 52-25-83; e-mail ata@tourismarmenia.com; f. 1997; non-governmental business association; Chair. ARTUR VOSKANIAN.

Armenian Tourism Development Agency: 375010 Yerevan, Nalbandian St 3; tel. (1) 57-80-01; fax (1) 54-23-03; e-mail help@armeniainfo.com; internet www.armeniainfo.am; Dir NINA HOVNANIAN.

AUSTRALIA

Introductory Survey

Location, Climate, Language, Religion, Flag, Capital

The Commonwealth of Australia occupies the whole of the island continent of Australia, lying between the Indian and Pacific Oceans, and its offshore islands, principally Tasmania to the south-east. Australia's nearest neighbour is Papua New Guinea, to the north. In the summer (November–February) there are tropical monsoons in the northern part of the continent (except for the Queensland coast), but the winters (July–August) are dry. Both the north-west and north-east coasts are liable to experience tropical cyclones between December and April. In the southern half of the country, winter is the wet season; rainfall decreases rapidly inland. Very high temperatures, sometimes exceeding 50°C (122°F), are experienced during the summer months over the arid interior and for some distance to the south, as well as during the pre-monsoon months in the north. The official language is English; 170 indigenous languages are spoken by Aboriginal and Torres Strait Islander peoples. At the census of 2001 68.0% of the population professed Christianity (of whom 26.6% were Roman Catholic and 20.7% Anglican). The national flag (proportions 1 by 2) is blue, with a representation of the United Kingdom flag in the upper hoist, a large seven-pointed white star in the lower hoist and five smaller white stars, in the form of the Southern Cross constellation, in the fly. The capital, Canberra, lies in one of two enclaves of federal territory known as the Australian Capital Territory (ACT).

Recent History

Since the end of the Second World War in 1945, Australia has played an important role in Asian affairs, and has strengthened its political and economic ties with Indonesia and the other countries of South-East Asia, and with Japan. The country co-operates more closely than formerly with the USA (in the context of ANZUS, see p. 382), and has given much aid to Asian and Pacific countries.

At the election of December 1949 the ruling Australian Labor Party (ALP) was defeated by the Liberal Party, in coalition with the Country Party. In January 1966 Sir Robert Menzies resigned after 16 years as Prime Minister, and was succeeded by Harold Holt, who was returned to office at elections in December of that year. However, Holt died in December 1967. His successor, Senator John Gorton, took office in January 1968 but resigned, after losing a vote of confidence, in March 1971. William McMahon was Prime Minister from March 1971 until December 1972, when, after 23 years in office, the Liberal-Country Party coalition was defeated at a general election for the House of Representatives. The ALP, led by Gough Whitlam, won 67 of the 125 seats in the lower chamber. Following a conflict between the Whitlam Government and the Senate, both Houses of Parliament were dissolved in April 1974, and a general election was held in May. The ALP was returned to power, although with a reduced majority in the House of Representatives. However, the Government failed to gain a majority in the Senate, and in October 1975 the Opposition in the Senate obstructed legislative approval of budget proposals. The Government was not willing to consent to a general election over the issue, but in November the Governor-General, Sir John Kerr, intervened and took the unprecedented step of dismissing the Government. A caretaker Ministry was installed under Malcolm Fraser, the Liberal leader, who formed a coalition Government with the Country Party. This coalition gained large majorities in both Houses of Parliament at a general election in December 1975, but the majorities were progressively reduced at general elections in December 1977 and October 1980.

Fraser's coalition Government was defeated by the ALP at a general election in March 1983. Robert (Bob) Hawke, who had replaced William (Bill) Hayden as Labor leader in the previous month, became the new Prime Minister and immediately organized a meeting of representatives of government, employers and trade unions to reach agreement on a prices and incomes policy (the 'Accord') that would allow economic recovery. Hawke called a general election for December 1984, 15 months earlier than necessary, and the ALP was returned to power with a reduced majority in the House of Representatives. The opposition coali-

tion between the Liberal Party and the National Party (formerly known as the Country Party) collapsed in April 1987, when 12 National Party MPs withdrew from the agreement and formed the New National Party (led by the right-wing Sir Johannes Bjelke-Petersen, the Premier of Queensland), while the remaining 14 National Party MPs continued to support their leader, Ian Sinclair, who wished to remain within the alliance. Parliament was dissolved in June, in preparation for an early general election in July. The election campaign was dominated by economic issues. The ALP was returned to office with an increased majority, securing 86 of the 148 seats in the House of Representatives. The Liberal and National Parties announced the renewal of the opposition alliance in August. Four months later, Bjelke-Petersen was forced to resign as Premier of Queensland, under pressure from National Party officials.

During 1988 the Hawke Government suffered several defeats at by-elections, seemingly as a result of a decline in living standards and an unpopular policy of wage restraint. The ALP narrowly retained power at state elections in Victoria, but was defeated in New South Wales, where it had held power for 12 years. In May 1989 the leader of the Liberal Party, John Howard, was replaced by Andrew Peacock, and Charles Blunt succeeded Ian Sinclair as leader of the National Party. In July a commission of inquiry into alleged corruption in Queensland published its report. The Fitzgerald report documented several instances of official corruption and electoral malpractice by the Queensland Government, particularly during the administration of Bjelke-Petersen. Following the publication of the report, support for the National Party within Queensland declined once more, and in December the ALP defeated the National Party in the state election (the first time that it had defeated the National Party in Queensland since 1957). By the end of 1991 four former members of the Queensland Cabinet and the former chief of the state's police force had received custodial sentences. The trial of Bjelke-Petersen, initially on charges of perjury and corruption but subsequently of perjury alone, resulted in dismissal of the case, when the jury failed to reach a verdict.

In February 1990 Hawke announced that a general election for the House of Representatives and for 40 of the 76 seats in the Senate was to be held on 24 March. The Government's position in the period preceding the election had been strengthened by the ALP's victory in Queensland in December 1989, the removal of an unpopular Labor leadership in Western Australia and its replacement by the first female Premier, Dr Carmen Lawrence, and by the support that it secured from environmental groups as a result of its espousal of 'green' issues. Although the opposition parties won the majority of the first-preference votes in the election for the House of Representatives, the endorsement of the environmental groups delivered a block of second-preference votes to the ALP, which was consequently returned to power, albeit with a reduced majority, securing 78 of the 148 seats. Following its defeat, Peacock immediately resigned as leader of the Liberal Party and was replaced by Dr John Hewson, a former professor of economics. Blunt lost his seat in the election and was succeeded as leader of the National Party by Timothy Fischer.

In September 1990, at a meeting of senior ALP members, government proposals to initiate a controversial programme of privatization were endorsed, effectively ending almost 100 years of the ALP's stance against private ownership. In October plans for constitutional and structural reform were approved in principle by the leaders of the six state and two territory governments. The proposed reforms envisaged the creation of national standards in regulations and services. They also aimed to alleviate the financial dependence of the states and territories on the Federal Government. These suggested reforms, however, encountered strong opposition from sections of the public services, the trade unions and the business community. In July 1991 the leaders of the federal and state Governments finally agreed to reforms in the country's systems of marketing, transport, trade and taxation, with the aim of creating a single national economy from 1992.

In April 1991, as a result of preliminary investigations by a Royal Commission into the financial dealings of the Labor Government of Western Australia in the 1980s, Brian Burke, the former state Premier, resigned as Australia's ambassador to Ireland and the Holy See. Owing to the alleged irregularities, more than $A1,000m. of public funds were believed to have been lost. In May the Premier of New South Wales called a state election, 10 months earlier than was necessary, in an attempt to take advantage of the problems of Labor administrations at federal and state level. However, the Liberal-National Party Government lost its overall majority and was able to retain power only with the support of independent members of the state legislature.

In June 1991, following months of divisions within the ALP, Hawke narrowly defeated a challenge to his leadership from Paul Keating, the Deputy Prime Minister and Treasurer, who accused the Prime Minister of reneging on a promise to resign in his favour before the next general election. This cast doubt on Hawke's credibility, as he had assured Parliament and the public in 1990 that he would continue as leader for the whole of the parliamentary term. Following his defeat, Keating resigned. In December Hawke dismissed John Kerin, Keating's replacement as Treasurer, following a series of political and economic crises. Hawke called another leadership election, but, on this occasion, he was defeated by Keating, who accordingly became Prime Minister. A major reorganization of the Cabinet followed. John Dawkins, a staunch supporter of Keating, was appointed Treasurer.

Following the ALP's defeat in state elections in Tasmania, the party encountered further embarrassment in April 1992, when a by-election in Melbourne to fill the parliamentary seat vacated by Bob Hawke was won by a local football club coach, standing as an independent candidate. In May the Prime Minister suffered another set-back, when Graham Richardson, the Minister for Transport and Communications, resigned, owing to his implication in a scandal involving a relative who was alleged to have participated in an illegal scheme whereby Taiwanese investors were able to secure US residency rights via the Marshall Islands. Meanwhile, Brian Burke, the former Premier of Western Australia, had been arrested. It was alleged that, during his term of office, he had misappropriated more than $A17,000 from a parliamentary expense account. In October 1992 the conclusions of the inquiry into the ALP's alleged involvement in corrupt practices in Western Australia were released. The Royal Commission was highly critical of the improper transactions between successive governments of Western Australia and business entrepreneurs. The conduct of Brian Burke drew particular criticism. In July 1994 Burke received a prison sentence of two years upon conviction on four charges of fraud; he was released in February 1995, but was sentenced to three years' imprisonment in February 1997 for the theft of $A122,000 from ALP funds. Furthermore, in February 1995 Ray O'Connor, Premier of Western Australia between 1982 and 1983, received a prison sentence of 18 months, having been found guilty of the theft in 1984 of $A25,000, intended as a donation to the Liberal Party. He was released in August 1995.

In September 1992 John Bannon became the seventh state Premier since 1982 to leave office in disgrace. The resignation of the ALP Premier of South Australia was due to a scandal relating to attempts to offset the heavy financial losses incurred by the State Bank of South Australia. At state elections in Queensland in mid-September, the ALP administration of Wayne Goss was returned to power. In the following month, however, the ruling ALP was defeated in state elections in Victoria. Furthermore, in November a new financial scandal emerged: the federal Treasurer was alleged to have suppressed information pertaining to the former ALP Government of Victoria, which, in a clandestine manner prior to the state elections, was believed to have exceeded its borrowing limits.

By late 1992, therefore, the ALP's prospects of being returned to office at the forthcoming general election appeared to have been seriously damaged. Proposals for radical tax and economic reforms that were advocated by the federal opposition leader, Dr John Hewson, attracted much attention. At state elections in Western Australia in February 1993, the incumbent Labor Government was defeated. Dr Carmen Lawrence was replaced as Premier by Richard Court of the Liberal-National coalition.

Nevertheless, at the general election, held on 13 March 1993, the ALP was unexpectedly returned to office for a fifth consecutive term, having secured 80 of the 147 seats in the House of Representatives. In January 1994 the Government was embarrassed by the resignation of the Minister of Industry, Technology and Regional Development, Alan Griffiths, as a result of allegations that public funds and ALP resources had been misappropriated in order to meet the private business debts incurred by his Melbourne sandwich shop. In the following month Ros Kelly, the Minister for Environment, Sport and Territories and close associate of the Prime Minister, yielded to pressure to resign, owing to a scandal relating to the alleged use of community sports grants to attempt to influence voters in vulnerable ALP-held constituencies prior to the 1993 general election. In May 1994 Dr John Hewson was replaced as leader of the Liberal Party by Alexander Downer, a supporter of the monarchy. Downer was therefore expected to lead the campaign against Paul Keating's proposal that Australia become a republic (see below). In January 1995, however, Downer resigned. The party leadership was resumed by John Howard, also a monarchist.

At state elections in New South Wales in March 1995 the ALP defeated the ruling Liberal-National coalition. Robert (Bob) Carr was appointed Premier. At a federal by-election in Canberra, however, the ALP suffered a serious reverse when, for the first time in 15 years, the seat fell to the Liberal Party. In July, at state elections in Queensland, the ALP Government of Wayne Goss was narrowly returned to office, only to be ousted following a by-election defeat in February 1996. In June 1995, meanwhile, the Deputy Prime Minister, Brian Howe, who intended to retire at the next general election, announced his resignation from the Cabinet. He was replaced by the Minister for Finance, Kim Beazley.

At the general election held on 2 March 1996 the Liberal-National coalition achieved a decisive victory, securing a total of 94 of the 148 seats in the House of Representatives. The ALP won only 49 seats. In the Senate the minor parties and independent members retained the balance of power. John Howard of the Liberal Party became Prime Minister, and immediately promised to give priority to the issues of industrial relations, the transfer to partial private ownership of the state telecommunications company, Telstra, and to expanding relations with Asia. The leader of the National Party, Tim Fischer, was appointed Deputy Prime Minister and Minister for Trade. Paul Keating was replaced as leader of the ALP by Kim Beazley.

In August 1996, in an unprecedented display of violence, demonstrators protesting against proposed budget cuts stormed the Parliament building in Canberra. Clashes between the police and the protesters resulted in many injuries. Meanwhile, fears for Australia's tradition of racial tolerance continued to grow. In October Pauline Hanson, a newly elected independent member of the House of Representatives, aroused much controversy when, in a speech envisaging 'civil war', she reiterated her demands for the ending of immigration from Asia and for the elimination of special funding for Aboriginal people. The Prime Minister attracted criticism for his failure to issue a direct denunciation of the views of Pauline Hanson, a former member of the Liberal Party. In March 1997 the One Nation party was established by Pauline Hanson and rapidly attracted support. In subsequent months, however, large protests against her policies took place in Perth, Melbourne and Canberra. Meanwhile, after his initial weak response, the Prime Minister condemned the views of the founder of One Nation. In August, as fears for Australian revenue from Asian investment, trade and tourism grew, the Government issued a document on foreign policy, in which Pauline Hanson's views were strongly repudiated and in which Australia's commitment to racial equality was reiterated. In November former Prime Ministers Keating, Hawke and Whitlam published a statement denouncing Pauline Hanson.

In early 1998 the long-standing tension between the National Farmers' Federation and the powerful Maritime Union of Australia (MUA) developed into a bitter dispute over trade unionists' rights when farmers established their own non-unionized stevedoring operation in Melbourne to handle their exports, in protest at high dockside costs and alleged inefficiency. The confrontation escalated in April, when Patrick Stevedores, a major cargo-handling company based in Sydney, dismissed its entire unionized work-force of 1,400 dockers, with the intention of replacing them with secretly-trained contract workers. As part of its campaign to break the MUA monopoly (the offensive being supported by the Government), Patrick Stevedores drafted in hundreds of security guards to its 14 terminals around Australia, in an operation to lock out the dockers. The Federal Court, however, subsequently ruled that Patrick Stevedores had acted illegally and ordered the company to reinstate the 1,400 trade unionists. Following the rejection of an appeal to the High Court by Patrick Stevedores and the return to work of the dockers in May, the Prime Minister nevertheless pledged to press ahead with waterfront reform. Although the majority of Australians appeared to support the reform of labour practices in the country's ports, the Government's handling of the dispute had attracted much criticism.

Meanwhile, in December 1997 the New One Nation Party was established by former supporters of Pauline Hanson, who had apparently become disillusioned with her autocratic style of leadership. In June 1998, at state elections in Queensland, One Nation won 23% of first-preference votes, thus unexpectedly securing 11 of the 89 seats in the legislature and leading to renewed concern among tourism and business leaders. In August it was announced that an early general election was to be held in October. As the campaign commenced, former Prime Ministers Whitlam, Fraser, Hawke and Keating signed an open letter urging citizens not to support racist candidates at the forthcoming election.

At the election, conducted on 3 October 1998, the Liberal-National coalition was narrowly returned to office, winning a total of 80 of the 148 seats in the House of Representatives. The ALP increased its representation to 67 seats. Contrary to expectations, the One Nation party failed to win any representation in the lower house, the controversial Pauline Hanson losing her Queensland seat. (The one seat secured by One Nation in the Senate was subsequently subjected to a legal challenge, owing to the candidate's apparent failure to meet citizenship requirements—see below.) In a referendum held on the same day, the electorate of the Northern Territory unexpectedly rejected a proposal for the territory's elevation to full statehood. In mid-October the Prime Minister announced the composition of his new Cabinet; most senior ministers retained their portfolios. Changes included the establishment of a special portfolio (transport and regional services) to focus on rural issues, in response to the ruling coalition's poor electoral performance in rural areas.

In February 1999 Pauline Hanson was re-elected leader of One Nation, despite a series of defections, including the departure from the party of several of the 11 One Nation members of the Queensland legislature. At state elections in New South Wales in March, at which the ALP was returned to power, One Nation won two seats in the 42-member upper chamber. In June a court ruled that the One Nation Senator was ineligible to occupy her seat in the federal upper house, owing to her failure to renounce her British citizenship prior to the general election. She was subsequently replaced by another member of One Nation. In January 2000 police officers in Queensland and New South Wales raided premises belonging to One Nation, seizing hundreds of documents relating to the party's membership and its financial structure. In April the Queensland Electoral Commission ruled that the party had been fraudulently registered by the falsification of significant sections of its 200-name membership list, in order to qualify for public funding in Queensland. Consequently, the party was ordered to repay some $A0.5m. of state funds which it had received. As the sole signatory on the registration papers, Pauline Hanson found herself personally responsible for the repayment. Hanson repaid the funds after a successful appeal for public donations, and she re-registered the One Nation party in January 2001 to contest the forthcoming Queensland state elections (see below).

Following state elections in Victoria in September 1999, the Liberal-National Premier, Jeffrey Kennett, was replaced by Stephen Bracks of the ALP. The defeat of the Liberal-National coalition was regarded as a set-back to the Federal Government's programme of economic reform, the transfer of public utilities to the private sector having been particularly unpopular among the voters of Victoria.

In September 2000 Australia hosted the Olympic Games in Sydney. The event was widely perceived as having been successful and of particular benefit to the local economy. However, the fact that security forces were given emergency powers to shoot on sight anyone thought likely to pose a threat to security at the Games caused some controversy, with civil rights groups expressing concern that the draconian anti-terrorist measures might persist after the conclusion of the event. In the same month a series of violent confrontations occurred between demonstrators and security personnel in Melbourne at a three-day summit meeting of the World Economic Forum. The demonstrators, several of whom were injured in the clashes, were protesting against capitalism and economic globalization.

A marked increase in illegal immigration during 1999 and 2000 prompted the introduction of new legislation empowering Australian police to board vessels in international waters. In 1999 almost 2,000 illegal immigrants were intercepted by the authorities and transferred to detention centres in Australia, while many others were believed to have died in the attempt to enter the country. In April 2000 more than 250 people, mostly from Iran and Iraq, died when their three boats sank in rough seas while trying to enter Australia illegally. The issue of alleged maltreatment of illegal immigrants captured in Australia was highlighted by a series of protests at a privately-run detention centre in Woomera, South Australia. Moreover, in November the Government ordered an inquiry into allegations that children at the centre had been subjected to systematic sexual abuse. Campaigners, who had repeatedly appealed for more humane treatment of illegal immigrants, claimed that the Government had suppressed evidence of abuse at Woomera and other detention centres.

Australia's handling of immigration problems provoked international condemnation in August 2001 when the Prime Minister refused to admit 433 refugees, stranded on an overcrowded Norwegian cargo ship off Christmas Island, onto the Australian mainland. The Government, faced with a high court challenge, swiftly enacted new legislation empowering the navy to prevent migrants coming ashore and excluding remote Australian island territories from the definition of official landfall. The situation was eventually resolved when New Zealand, Nauru and Papua New Guinea agreed to accommodate the asylum-seekers whilst their applications were processed. In the interim, however, traffic in illegal immigrants attempting to reach Australia's outlying territories—the majority via Indonesia—continued to increase; according to government figures, 1,823 'boat people' departed for Australia in September and October 2001. The Government proposed its so-called 'Pacific solution', whereby neighbouring South Pacific nations could agree to host asylum-seekers during their processing on a continuing basis in exchange for substantial aid. Nauru signed an agreement to take up to 1,200 refugees at any one time, whilst Papua New Guinea prevaricated on the possibility of accommodating a further 1,000 people. Concerns about Australia's immigration policy again focused on the Woomera detention centre in January 2002, when 259 detainees began a hunger strike in protest at poor living conditions there and at the long delays in the processing of their applications; 64 inmates had stitched together their lips. Neville Roach, the Chairman of the Council for Multicultural Australia, resigned in protest. In February the Australian Government announced that a representative of the UN High Commissioner for Human Rights and other observers would be permitted to inspect the camp between May and August.

A state election in Western Australia in February 2001 resulted in defeat for the governing Liberal-National coalition and the replacement of Premier Richard Court by the state's Labor leader, Geoffrey Gallop. Ongoing anxieties regarding illegal immigration were reflected in the unexpected success of One Nation, which secured almost 10% of votes at the poll. At the state election in Queensland in the same month, the ALP Government, led by Peter Beattie, was decisively re-elected. One Nation garnered 9% of the total votes.

A federal election took place on 10 November 2001. The Liberal-National coalition won 82 of the 150 seats in the House of Representatives, thus narrowly securing a third consecutive term of office. Despite its successes at state and territorial elections in Western Australia and the Northern Territory earlier in the year, the ALP, winning 65, took two fewer seats than at the previous federal election. Many political commentators attributed the coalition's apparent reversal of fortune to Howard's controversial handling of immigration issues, which had led to a surge in his popularity. Kim Beazley resigned as leader of the ALP and was replaced by Simon Crean, formerly the Shadow Treasurer. One Nation won no seats in either the House of Representatives or the Senate. (In December Pauline Hanson resigned as leader of One Nation to concentrate on contesting charges of electoral fraud brought against her in July 2001.)

John Howard announced the composition of his third Ministry in late November 2001, appointing six new cabinet ministers. Changes included the incorporation of the Department of Reconciliation and Aboriginal and Torres Strait Islander Affairs into the new portfolio of Immigration and Multicultural and Indigenous Affairs. The Department of Industry, Science and

Resources became that of Industry, Tourism and Resources, emphasizing the tourism sector's growing importance to the Australian economy. Wilson Tuckey was appointed Minister for Regional Services, Territories and Local Government, despite being the subject of a police investigation into issues associated with the charter of aircraft in Western Australia. At a state election in South Australia in February 2002, the ruling Liberal-National coalition was defeated. Michael Rann of the ALP was appointed Premier.

In mid-February 2002 the leader of the ALP accused the Prime Minister of having lied during the previous year's election campaign to boost his coalition's chances of victory, after it emerged that government claims that refugees in a ship intercepted by the Australian navy had thrown their children into the sea were false. John Howard, nevertheless, withstood a censure motion introduced in the House of Representatives. In mid-March the Prime Minister requested Senator Bill Heffernan to resign from his post as parliamentary secretary after he issued false allegations about Justice Michael Kirby in an attempt to ruin the judge's career. Senator Natasha Stott Despoja, leader of the Australian Democrats, resigned in August; she was replaced by Andrew Bartlett two months later. In late November the ruling ALP, led by Stephen Bracks, won a state election in Victoria. The Labor Government in New South Wales was re-elected in March 2003 for an unprecedented third term; Bob Carr was reappointed Premier. Meanwhile, in February the Senate passed a 'no confidence' motion in Howard over the Government's unilateral decision to deploy troops to the Middle East in preparation for a possible US-led military campaign to remove the regime of Saddam Hussain in Iraq. Although it had no legal impact, the motion—the first to be carried against a government in 102 years—was considered symbolic. Public demonstrations against Australia's anticipated involvement in the war took place throughout the month. In mid-March the Minister for Foreign Affairs announced that, owing to the Government's commitment to the US-led military campaign against Iraq (which began two days later), all Iraqi diplomatic staff would be expelled from the country with effect from 23 March. Public support for Howard rose substantially from May, largely owing to the apparent swift end to the conflict in Iraq and the absence of Australian casualties. In July, however, a former UN weapons inspector, Richard Butler, claimed that the Government had misled the public about Iraq's programme to develop weapons of mass destruction and demanded the Prime Minister's resignation. Howard denied this accusation; nevertheless, the ALP initiated a parliamentary inquiry on the Government's decision to participate in the war in Iraq. A former senior intelligence analyst, who had resigned in protest over Australia's involvement in the conflict, informed the inquiry in August that the Government had exaggerated and fabricated intelligence used to justify the case for war. Howard denied the allegations at a press conference. Meanwhile, in July Australia committed 870 troops to assist in the rehabilitation of Iraq.

Protesters against the Government's mandatory detention of all asylum-seekers stormed the Woomera detention centre in late March 2002. Most of the approximately 50 asylum-seekers who managed to escape were recaptured; about 11, however, disappeared into the desert. In April riots took place at detention centres in Curtin and Port Hedland, Western Australia. In late May the Government offered financial incentives to almost 1,000 Afghan asylum-seekers in detention centres throughout Australia and Nauru of $A2,000 each (with a limit of $A10,000 per family) if they returned to Afghanistan. The Government gave the detainees 28 days (from the day their asylum review process ended) to decide whether to accept the offer, which also included counselling, air fares and vocational training. International aid agencies criticized the scheme, stating that Afghanistan was not stable enough for asylum-seekers to return. By mid-July only 76 Afghans had accepted the offer. Concerns about the alleged maltreatment of asylum-seekers were raised again after supporters helped 34 detainees to escape from Woomera detention centre in late June. At the same time more than 120 inmates began a hunger strike in protest at poor living conditions and at the long delays in the processing of their applications. In the mean time, Australia's controversial efforts to deter refugees appeared to have been effective: the number of 'boat people' seeking asylum in Australia had declined significantly. In early December the Minister for Immigration and Multicultural and Indigenous Affairs, Philip Ruddock, announced plans to expand a programme to allow women and children asylum-seekers to live in the community rather than in

the detention camps. The authorities employed tighter security measures at detention centres following riots at Woomera, Baxter, Port Hedland and on Christmas Island in late December.

In mid-March 2003 Ruddock announced that Woomera detention centre would be closed down in mid-April, for reasons of cost. Families faced being separated after it was agreed that fathers and husbands would be moved to the Baxter detention centre near Port Augusta, while women and children would have to continue to live in the community in Woomera. The Government, however, stated that discussions to establish a residential housing programme for women and children at Port Augusta would continue. Several days later it was announced that the Christmas Island detention centre would also be closed. In mid-April the Federal Court issued a ruling that the Government had no right to detain asylum-seekers indefinitely prior to deportation, even if the asylum-seeker had been refused permission to enter another country. The case was related to a Palestinian asylum-seeker who had been detained at the Woomera detention centre for eight months, after being denied refugee status, because Israel had initially refused to allow his repatriation. The Court had previously twice ordered the release of the asylum-seeker while awaiting deportation (he was later deported in September 2002), and on each occasion the Government appealed. The Court's rejection of the latest appeal represented a set-back to the Government's policy of detaining asylum-seekers; nevertheless, anxious to avoid a precedent that could affect the detention of hundreds of other asylum-seekers, Ruddock announced that the Government would seek an appeal at the High Court. In mid-August 2003 the High Court upheld the ruling and rebuked the Government for wasting its time. Nearly two weeks later the Family Court ordered the Government to release from custody five children who had been detained as illegal immigrants since January 2002. In October 2003 an eight-year-old Iranian asylum-seeker launched a lawsuit against the Government, claiming that he had suffered severe mental health problems caused by his detention in the Woomera centre. In the same month a government report was issued stating that 90% of the 'boat people' who had arrived in Australia's migration zone between July 1999 and June 2002 had eventually gained asylum. This figure challenged the Government's claim that the majority of asylum-seekers were economic migrants and not genuine refugees. The Government's immigration policy came under heavy criticism again in November 2003 when, in response to the arrival of an Indonesian boat carrying 14 Turkish Kurdish asylum-seekers at Melville Island, the Government immediately separated the island and 4,000 other small islands from the Australian migration zone. It then ordered an Australian warship to tow the boat to the Indonesian island of Yamdena. The UN High Commissioner for Refugees stated that Australia's exclusion of the islands was 'meaningless', since its obligations as a signatory to the UN refugee convention applied to its entire territory. The Indonesian Government insisted that its agreement to the Kurds' expulsion had neither been requested nor given. In May 2004 Australia's Human Rights and Equal Opportunities Commission issued a report describing the country's immigration detention system as 'cruel, inhumane and degrading', and urged the Government to release all child detainees within a month. In July, in a relaxation of the immigration policy, it was announced that some 9,500 asylum-seekers who had been released from detention centres since 1999 on temporary protection visas (renewable every three years) would henceforth be entitled to apply for permanent settlement in Australia.

In mid-May 2002 the Government expressed its regret for the 'suffering and injustice' experienced by some 3,500 child migrants taken from British children's homes after the Second World War. The migrants, many of whom suffered serious physical, psychological and sexual abuse after being sent to Australia, were offered a $A3.8m. reparation package, mainly to assist them to trace their families. In June Roman Catholic Archbishop George Pell came under pressure to resign after he publicly admitted to offering compensation payments to the family of two girls who had been sexually abused by a priest. Pell denied claims that the payments included secrecy clauses; however, a lawyer representing the Church later confirmed that confidentiality terms were attached to the payments, adding that bishops appeared to have been unaware of the conditions. Some two months later Pell faced an inquiry into allegations that as a trainee priest in 1961 he had sexually abused a boy. Pell denied the allegations, but agreed to step down temporarily during the investigations. The inquiry cleared Pell of the allegations in mid-October.

In early June 2003 John Howard ended months of speculation by announcing that he intended to seek a fourth term in office. In mid-June the leader of the ALP, Simon Crean, won a leadership challenge mounted against him by his predecessor, Kim Beazley. Crean, however, failed to reunite his party and improve his popularity within the ALP, and in late November he resigned as leader of the opposition party. In early December the republican Mark Latham won the ALP leadership election, narrowly defeating Kim Beazley by 47 votes to 45. Meanwhile, in mid-August Richard Butler was appointed Governor of Tasmania, replacing Sir Guy Green. In the same month Pauline Hanson was convicted of electoral fraud by a court in Brisbane and sentenced to a three-year prison term; her conviction, however, was overturned by an appeals court in November. In late September a major reorganization of the Cabinet was announced, following the resignation of Richard Alston, the Minister for Communications, Information Technology and the Arts. Changes included the transfer of the controversial Minister for Immigration and Multicultural and Indigenous Affairs, Phillip Ruddock, to the post of Attorney-General; Senator Amanda Vanstone was allocated the immigration portfolio. In early December the leader of the Australian Democrats Party, Senator Andrew Bartlett, publicly apologized for swearing at and assaulting another senator during a drunken argument and temporarily relinquished his post. The party's deputy leader, Lyn Allison, was appointed acting leader for the duration of Andrew Bartlett's leave. At a state election in Queensland in February 2004, the ruling ALP was re-elected for a third term; Peter Beattie was reappointed Premier. In mid-February riots broke out in the predominantly Aboriginal district of Redfern in Sydney in protest against the death of an Aboriginal youth in an apparent cycling accident. At least four people were arrested and more than 30 police officers were injured during Sydney's worst violence in several years; three separate inquiries into the death of the youth and into the riots were launched the following day. (In August the New South Wales state coroner described the youth's death as a 'freak accident'.) In March the Premier of Tasmania, James Bacon, resigned owing to ill health; he was replaced by Paul Lennon, the former Deputy Premier.

In early March 2004 the parliamentary committee on intelligence on Iraq's weapons of mass destruction published its report, largely exonerating the Government of manipulating the intelligence used to justify Australia's involvement in the military campaign in Iraq. On the recommendation of the committee, the Prime Minister ordered an independent inquiry into the performance of the intelligence agencies in the period leading up to the war. At the end of that month the House of Representatives adopted a resolution opposing 'artificial deadlines' for the withdrawal of Australian troops from Iraq, after Mark Latham announced that if an ALP government were elected, he would withdraw Australian troops by Christmas. In July the report of the independent inquiry into the intelligence services judged that there had been an overall serious failure of intelligence relating to Iraq's alleged weapons of mass destruction, but that the Australian agencies' assessment of the available material had been more measured than that of their counterparts in the United Kingdom and the USA.

In April 2004 Prime Minister Howard announced controversial government plans to abolish the elected Aboriginal and Torres Strait Islander Commission (ATSIC), claiming that it had failed to improve conditions for the indigenous community since commencing operations in 1990. In response, the first national party for Aboriginal people, Your Voice, was launched in May. Legislation to dismantle ATSIC was approved by the House of Representatives in June, but the Senate ordered an inquiry into the proposal. In the mean time, ATSIC's budget was transferred to government departments in July 2004, and in December a new government-appointed advisory body on Aboriginal affairs, the 14-member National Indigenous Council, held its first meeting. In March 2005, following a report by the Senate committee, legislation was passed abolishing ATSIC.

In June 2004 the Anglican Archbishop of Adelaide, the Most Rev. Ian George, resigned after an independent inquiry reported that his diocese had mishandled more than 200 claims of sexual abuse by the clergy over a 50-year period. John Howard effected a minor government reorganization in July, replacing two ministers who had announced their intention to retire at the next federal election. In late August the Prime Minister announced that the election was to be held on 9 October. In the same month

Richard Butler stood down as Governor of Tasmania, following threats from the state opposition to withdraw its support for him, after four senior members of his staff tendered their resignations; he was replaced by William Cox, hitherto Chief Justice of Tasmania. Meanwhile, an issue that had caused controversy at the federal election of 2001 resurfaced, when Mike Scrafton, a former government adviser, revealed that he had told Prime Minister Howard, prior to the election, that government claims that refugees in a ship intercepted by the Australian navy had thrown their children overboard (see above) were unsubstantiated. The Senate established an inquiry into Scrafton's allegations at the end of August 2004.

The Liberal-National coalition increased its majority in the House of Representatives at the federal election on 9 October 2004, securing 86 of the 150 seats, and gained an outright majority in the Senate. Prime Minister John Howard was thus returned to office for a fourth consecutive term. The ALP won 60 seats in the lower chamber, five fewer than at the 2001 election, surprising many political analysts, who had predicted a much closer result. The coalition's victory was widely attributed to the continued strong performance of the economy under Howard's Government. In December Senator Lyn Allison replaced Senator Andrew Bartlett as leader of the Australian Democrats Party, following the party's poor performance in the elections to the Senate, at which it had lost four of the eight seats previously held. In the same month the Senate committee investigating Mike Scrafton's claims concluded that his evidence was credible and clearly implied that the Prime Minister had misled the public over the so-called 'children overboard' affair in the period leading up to the 2001 election. However, the two Liberal senators on the five-member committee rejected these findings.

On 12 October 2002 88 Australians were killed in a bomb explosion in a night-club on the Indonesian island of Bali. The Islamist militant group Jemaah Islamiah was held principally responsible for the attack, which killed more than 200 people in total. The Australian Government proscribed the organization, which was suspected of having links with the al-Qa'ida (Base) network, and successfully led a campaign to have Jemaah Islamiah listed as a terrorist organization by the UN. In an attempt to prevent retaliatory attacks against Muslims in Australia, the Prime Minister publicly declared that Islam was not responsible for the attack. However, a mosque and an Islamic school in Sydney were attacked in mid-October, prompting the Premier of New South Wales, Bob Carr, to establish a community harmony reference group to ease tensions. In early November the Government was accused of harassing Muslims, following a series of high-profile armed raids on the homes of Indonesian-born Muslims suspected of having connections with Jemaah Islamiah. Although the authorities denied the accusations, the raids antagonized the Muslim community and adversely affected relations with Indonesia. In mid-November Jack Roche, a British-born Australian, was charged with devising bomb attacks on the Israeli embassy in Canberra and the Israeli consulate in Sydney. Roche, a Muslim convert, who had earlier admitted to having met Osama bin Laden, the Saudi-born leader of al-Qa'ida, and Riduan Isamuddin, the suspected operations chief of Jemaah Islamiah, denied the charges. Having changed his plea to guilty, in late May 2004 Roche was convicted of plotting to attack the embassy, and was sentenced to nine years' imprisonment. Meanwhile, in late 2002 the number of reported attacks against Australian Muslims increased. In late March 2003 the Attorney-General announced a ban, effective immediately, on the Iraqi Kurdish Sunni Islamist fundamentalist group Ansar al-Islam. It was announced in mid-April that the Government had banned six more militant Islamist groups. In May the Government decided to create a new counter-terrorist unit from the country's volunteer military reserve force. One month later the Senate approved anti-terrorism legislation giving significant new powers to the Australian Security Intelligence Organization, including the power to detain suspects for up to seven days without charge. Opponents expressed concerns that the draconian law allowed the detaining and questioning of people even if they were not thought to have committed a crime. At the same time, it was reported that the Minister for Foreign Affairs, Alexander Downer, had been warned by intelligence agencies that Bali was a potential terrorist target four months before the bomb attack in October 2002; Downer denied that he had received any specific intelligence warning of an attack in Bali. In early February 2004 Australia and Indonesia co-hosted an anti-terrorism conference held on Bali, during which it was announced that a regional counter-terrorism centre would be established in the Indonesian capital, Jakarta. A bomb exploded outside the Australian embassy in Jakarta in September, killing at least nine people, mostly Indonesians, and injuring more than 180 others. Jemaah Islamiah was suspected of being responsible for the attack.

In March 1986, meanwhile, Australia's constitutional links with the United Kingdom were reduced by the Australia Act, which abolished the British Parliament's residual legislative, executive and judicial controls over Australian state law. In February 1992, shortly after a visit by Queen Elizabeth II, Paul Keating caused a furore by accusing the United Kingdom of abandoning Australia to the Japanese threat during the Second World War. Following a visit to the United Kingdom in September 1993, Keating announced that Australia was to become a republic by the year 2001, subject to approval by referendum. Sir William Deane succeeded William Hayden as Governor-General in February 1996, the former's term of office being scheduled to expire at the end of the year 2000. Although John Howard personally favoured the retention of the monarchy, in 1996 the new Prime Minister announced plans for a constitutional convention, prior to the holding of a referendum on the issue if necessary. In an unexpected development in January 1997, the Deputy Prime Minister put forward proposals for the removal from the Constitution of all references to the monarch and for the transfer of the Queen's functions to Australia's Chief Justice.

Voluntary postal voting to select, from among 609 candidates, 76 delegates who were to attend the constitutional convention (scheduled for February 1998) commenced in November 1997. The complex system of preferential voting, however, appeared to give rise to much confusion, particularly in New South Wales where a total of 174 candidates were contesting 20 places at the forthcoming convention. In addition to the official groupings, the Australian Republican Movement (ARM) and Australians for a Constitutional Monarchy (ACM), numerous other republican and monarchist, as well as individual, candidates were standing for election. Only 42.6% of registered voters were reported to have returned their ballot papers, the participation rate in New South Wales being only 39.9%. In February 1998, following nine days of debate, a majority of the 152 delegates (a further 76 having been appointed by the Government) endorsed proposals to adopt a republican system and to replace the British monarch as Head of State. Although the Constitutional Convention was dominated by republicans, delegates were divided over the method of election of a future head of state.

In December 1998 it was confirmed that a referendum on the republican issue would be held in late 1999. In August 1999 the Federal Parliament gave approval to the wording of the question to be posed to the electorate, which was to be asked if support was forthcoming for an 'act to alter the Constitution to establish the Commonwealth of Australia as a republic with the Queen and Governor-General being replaced by a President appointed by a two-thirds' majority of the members of the Commonwealth Parliament'. At the referendum, conducted on 6 November 1999, 55% of voters favoured the retention of the monarchy. Moreover, some 61% of voters expressed opposition to a proposal to include a preamble to the Constitution, recognizing Aborigines as 'the nation's first people'. Although the result was regarded as a victory for Howard, who had campaigned for the retention of the monarchy, many observers interpreted the result as a rejection of the particular republican system offered, opinion polls having indicated that more than two-thirds of Australians would support the introduction of a republican system of government if the President were to be directly elected. Howard extended Sir William Deane's tenure as Governor-General by six months, allowing Deane to participate in an official capacity in the events commemorating Australia's centenary of Federation.

In April 2001 the Anglican Archbishop of Brisbane, Peter Hollingworth, was named as Deane's successor; he was sworn in in June. In February 2002, as the Queen commenced a golden jubilee visit to Australia, the Governor-General refused to yield to pressure to resign over claims that he had deliberately concealed alleged cases of child abuse by the clergy in Queensland. The Prime Minister rejected calls to dismiss the Governor-General. On 11 May 2003 Hollingworth temporarily relinquished his post, pending the investigation of rape allegations against him. Sir Guy Green, the Governor of Tasmania, was appointed acting Governor-General. Hollingworth strongly denied the charge against him, which dated back to the 1960s. The woman accusing him of rape committed suicide in April, and

on 23 May the case was dismissed at the request of her family. Although the Prime Minister continued to show support for Hollingworth, the Governor-General had lost the confidence of opposition parties, church leaders, child welfare campaigners, several senior government ministers and the public. On 25 May Hollingworth succumbed to mounting pressure and resigned. Some four weeks later the former Governor of Western Australia, Maj.-Gen. Michael Jeffery, was named as the country's new Governor-General; he was sworn into office on 11 August.

In December 2003 the High Court ruled that long-term British residents without Australian citizenship who commit a crime in Australia could be deported to the United Kingdom. The judgment overturned the special status held by British residents, according to which they did not have to take Australian citizenship, and declared that any non-citizen who had arrived in the country after 26 January 1949 would henceforth be considered a foreign alien for immigration purposes. The ruling marked a further weakening of the relations between Australia and the United Kingdom.

In May 1987 Australia and the United Kingdom began a joint operation to ascertain the extent of plutonium contamination resulting from British nuclear weapons testing at Maralinga in South Australia between 1956 and 1963. Many Australians were highly critical of the United Kingdom's apparent disregard for the environmental consequences of the tests and of the British authorities' failure to make adequate arrangements to protect the local Aboriginal people, who were now campaigning for a thorough decontamination of their traditional lands. In June 1993 Australia announced its acceptance of $A45m. in compensation from the British Government for the cost of the decontamination. In December 1994 the displaced Aboriginal people and the Federal Government reached agreement on a compensation settlement of $A13.5m., to be spent on health, employment and infrastructural projects. In January 1999, furthermore, it was announced that the Australian and British Governments were to conduct separate inquiries into research linking the nuclear tests to the numerous cases of a rare form of cancer in servicemen who had witnessed the explosions. In March 2000 it was announced that a joint decontamination programme effected by the British and Australian Governments had been completed. However, the Australian Government issued a report in May 2000 stating that, despite the removal of 300,000 cu m of plutonium-contaminated topsoil during the operation, some 120 sq km of the territory were still considered too contaminated for permanent habitation, permitting only limited access. In March 2003, furthermore, the former head of the Maralinga Rehabilitation Committee declared the decontamination operation to have been a failure. In mid-September 2002 the Government's nuclear safety body authorized the construction in 2005 of a new nuclear research reactor in Sydney to replace an existing reactor.

The sensitive issue of Aboriginal land rights was addressed by the Government in August 1985, when it formulated proposals for legislation that would give Aboriginal people inalienable freehold title to national parks, vacant Crown land and former Aboriginal reserves, in spite of widespread opposition from state governments (which had previously been responsible for their own land policies), from mining companies and from the Aboriginal people themselves, who were angered by the Government's withdrawal of its earlier support for the Aboriginal right to veto mineral exploitation. In October 1985 Ayers Rock (Uluru), in the Northern Territory, was officially transferred to the Mutijulu Aboriginal community, on condition that continuing access to the rock (the main inland tourist attraction) be guaranteed. In 1986, however, the Government abandoned its pledge to impose such federal legislation on unwilling state governments, and this led to further protests from Aboriginal leaders. In June 1991 the Government imposed a permanent ban on mining at an historical Aboriginal site in the Northern Territory.

An important precedent was established in June 1992, when the High Court overruled the concept of *terra nullius* (unoccupied land) by recognizing the existence of land titles that predated European settlement in 1788 in cases where a close association with the land in question had been continued; however, land titles legally acquired since 1788 were to remain intact. As a result of the 'Mabo' decision of 1992 (named after the Aboriginal claimant, Eddie Mabo), in December 1993 Parliament approved the Native Title Act, historic legislation granting Aboriginal people the right to claim title to their traditional lands. Despite the Prime Minister's personal involvement in the issue, the legislation aroused much controversy, particularly in Western Australia (vast areas of the state being vacant Crown land), where rival legislation to replace native title rights with lesser rights to traditional land usage, such as access for ceremonial purposes only, had been enacted. In March 1995 the High Court declared the Native Title Act to be valid, rejecting as unconstitutional Western Australia's own legislation. The ruling was expected to have widespread implications for the mining industry.

In October 1996, following protracted delays in the development of a valuable zinc mine in Queensland owing to Aboriginal land claims, the Howard Government announced proposals to amend the Native Title Act to permit federal ministers to overrule Aboriginal concerns if a project of 'major economic benefit' to Australia were threatened. Other proposed amendments included the simplification of the process of negotiation between potential developers and Aboriginal claimants. In December the Larrakia people of the Northern Territory presented a claim under the Native Title Act. The area in question incorporated the city of Darwin and was thus the first such claim to encompass a provincial capital. The claim reached the Federal Court in September 2002. Meanwhile, in October 1996 the federal High Court upheld an appeal by two Aboriginal communities in Queensland (including the Wik people of Cape York) against an earlier ruling that prevented them from submitting a claim to land leased by the state Government to cattle and sheep farmers. The Court's decision, known as the Wik judgment, was expected to encourage similar challenges to 'pastoral' leases, which covered 40% of Australia. Vociferous protests from farmers, who were strongly opposed to the co-existence of native title and pastoral leases, followed.

In April 1997 the first native title deed to be granted on mainland Australia was awarded to the Dunghutti people of New South Wales. In the same month the Prime Minister announced the introduction of legislation to clarify the issue of land tenure; a 10-point plan was to be drawn up in consultation with state governments and with representatives of the Aboriginal community. In September the Government introduced the Wik Native Title Bill, which was subsequently passed by the House of Representatives. In November, however, the Senate questioned the constitutional validity of the proposed legislation, whereby pastoralists' rights and activities would prevail over, but not extinguish (as had been assumed), the Aboriginal people's rights to native title. In December the Government refused to accept the Senate's proposed amendments to the legislation, thus raising the possibility of an early general election dominated by Aboriginal issues. In April 1998 the Senate rejected the legislation for a second time. Finally, in July, following a protracted and acrimonious debate, the Senate narrowly approved the Native Title Amendment Bill, thereby restricting the Aboriginal people's rights to claim access to Crown land leased to farmers. The passage of the controversial legislation was immediately denounced by Aboriginal leaders, who threatened to enlist international support for their cause. In the same month, however, the federal court of Darwin granted communal (but not exclusive or commercial) native title to the waters and sea-bed around Croker Island in the Northern Territory to five Aboriginal groups. With about 140 similar claims over Australian waters pending, the historic ruling represented the first recognition of native title rights over the sea. However, the area's traditional owners launched an appeal against the decision, insisting on the commercial right to negotiate on fishing and pearling activities. In March 1999, in a conciliatory gesture that settled a land claim case outstanding since 1845, the Tasmanian Government relinquished the site of a mission station at Wybellena, where 200 Aboriginal people had been forcibly resettled; most had subsequently died of disease and maltreatment. The land rights movement suffered a set-back in August 2002 when the High Court in Canberra rejected a claim by the Miriuwung-Gajerrong people to territory in Western Australia and the Northern Territory that contained the Argyle diamond mine owned by the Anglo-Australian mining company Rio Tinto. The decision to give precedence to mining and petroleum leases over Aboriginal land rights appeared to reverse earlier court rulings that supported the land rights movement. In September, however, Rio Tinto offered to close the Jabiluka uranium mine in the Northern Territory following opposition to the project from the indigenous Mirrar people (the owners of the land) and environmental groups. The Mirrar people welcomed the proposal; the Government of the Northern Territory approved a plan to fill in the mine in August

2003. Meanwhile, in September 2002 the state Government of Western Australia agreed to return about 13.7m. ha of land to the Martu people. In December the Australian High Court rejected the Aboriginal Yorta Yorta people's claim to territory along the River Murray on the border of Victoria and New South Wales.

In November 1987 an official commission of inquiry into the cause of the high death rate among Aboriginal prisoners recommended immediate government action, and in July 1988 it was announced that 108 cases remained to be investigated. In August 1988 a UN report accused Australia of violating international human rights in its treatment of the Aboriginal people. In November the Government announced an inquiry into its Aboriginal Affairs Department, following accusations from the opposition coalition of nepotism and misuse of funds. The commission of inquiry published its first official report in February 1989. Following the report's recommendations, the Government announced the creation of a $A10m. programme to combat the high death rate among Aboriginal prisoners. In October an unofficial study indicated that Aboriginal people, although accounting for only 1% of the total population of Australia, comprised more than 20% of persons in prison. In May 1991 the report of the Royal Commission into Aboriginal Deaths in Custody was published, after three years of investigation. The report outlined evidence of racial prejudice in the police force and included more than 300 recommendations for changes in policies relating to Aboriginal people, aimed at improving relations between the racial groups of Australia and granting Aboriginal people greater self-determination and access to land ownership. In June Parliament established a Council for Aboriginal Reconciliation. In March 1992, Aboriginal deaths in custody having continued, radical plans for judicial, economic and social reforms, aimed at improving the lives of Aboriginal people, were announced. The Government made an immediate allocation of $A150m.; a total of $A500m. was to be made available over the next 10 years. In February 1993 the human rights organization Amnesty International issued a highly critical report on the prison conditions of Aboriginal people. In March 1996 Amnesty International claimed that Australia had made little progress with regard to its treatment of Aboriginal prisoners. In March 2000 the UN Committee on Elimination of Racial Discrimination issued a report denouncing Australia's treatment of its indigenous people. The report was particularly critical of the mandatory prison sentences for minor property offences in force in the Northern Territory and Western Australia, which appeared to target juvenile Aborigines. In July a legal case was initiated against the Australian Government accusing it of breaching the human rights of Aboriginal people with these harsh mandatory sentencing laws. In August 2001 the Australian Bureau of Statistics published its biannual survey of indigenous health, based on 1997–99 figures. It found the average life expectancy of Aboriginal men and women to be, respectively, 20 and 19 years less than that of other Australians. The Government claimed that $A220m. was being spent on Aboriginal health services in that year, to be increased to $A260m. by 2004. In November 2004 the death of an Aboriginal man in police custody prompted rioting by some 300 people on Palm Island, off the coast of Queensland, one of the country's largest Aboriginal communities; police reinforcements were dispatched to quell the disturbance, and an investigation into the death was promised.

In July 1996 the Roman Catholic Church issued an apology for its role in the forcible removal from their parents of tens of thousands of Aboriginal children, in a controversial practice of placement in white foster homes, where many were abused. This policy of assimilation had continued until the late 1960s. In August 1996 the new Governor-General, Sir William Deane, urged all state parliaments to affirm their support for reconciliation with the Aboriginal people. The legislature of South Australia was the first to do so, in November. In May 1997 the publication of the findings of a two-year inquiry into the removal of as many as 100,000 Aboriginal children from their families had profound political repercussions. The author of the report, a distinguished former judge and President of the Human Rights and Equal Opportunities Commission, urged the Government to issue a formal apology to the 'stolen generation'. At a conference on reconciliation at the end of the month, the Prime Minister made an unexpected personal apology. The Government, however, repudiated the commission's assertion that the policy of assimilation had been tantamount to genocide and rejected recommendations that compensation be paid to victims. In

December the Government reaffirmed that it would not issue a formal apology to the 'stolen generation'. A $63m. programme to help reunite divided Aboriginal families was nevertheless announced. In February 1998 the Anglican Church apologized unreservedly for its part in the removal of Aboriginal children from their families. In May 2000, when 250,000 citizens took part in a march across Sydney Harbour Bridge, the Prime Minister refused to involve himself fully in the campaign for reconciliation between white and Aboriginal Australia, and ruled out any notion of a treaty. Two separate UN reports, released in March and July 2000, were highly critical of Australia's treatment of the Aboriginal population. The findings of the UN Committee on Elimination of Racial Discrimination (see above), and subsequently of the UN Human Rights Committee, were strongly rejected by the Australian Government. In August 2000, at the conclusion of a test case brought in the Northern Territory by two members of the 'stolen generation', who hoped to win compensation for the trauma occasioned by their removal from their families, the Federal Court ruled that the Government was not obliged to pay punitive damages to the two Aboriginal claimants, on the grounds of insufficient evidence. As many as 30,000 similar cases had been pending. In December some 300,000 people took part in demonstrations in Melbourne and Perth in support of reconciliation between the white and indigenous communities, and the Prime Minister was subject to renewed pressure to apologize for the treatment of Aboriginal people by white settlers. A Senate committee recommended issuing an apology to the 'stolen generation' and establishing a reparations tribunal to deal with compensation claims. However, the Government strongly rejected the recommendations. In August 2001, at a human rights conference in Sydney, various indigenous and legal groups finalized a new proposal for a reparations tribunal; again the Government rejected it, insisting that its own $60m. programme of practical assistance was sufficient. In November 2001 Pope John Paul II apologized to Australia's Aboriginal community for what he called the 'shameful injustices' of the past, asking for forgiveness for the Roman Catholic Church's role in forcibly removing Aboriginal children from their families.

In foreign affairs, the Hawke and Keating Governments placed greater emphasis on links with South-East Asia. This policy was continued by John Howard, who took office in 1996, pledging to expand relations with Asia. In January 1989 Hawke proposed the creation of an Asia-Pacific Economic Co-operation forum (APEC, see p. 155) to facilitate the exchange of services, tourism and direct foreign investment in the region. The inaugural APEC conference took place in Canberra in November 1989.

Australian relations with Indonesia, which had been strained since the Indonesian annexation of the former Portuguese colony of East Timor in 1976, improved in August 1985, when Hawke made a statement recognizing Indonesian sovereignty over the territory, but subsequently deteriorated, following the publication in a Sydney newspaper, in April 1986, of an article containing allegations of corruption against the Indonesian President, Gen. Suharto. Relations between Australia and Indonesia improved in December 1989, when they signed an accord regarding joint exploration for petroleum and gas reserves in the Timor Gap, an area of sea forming a disputed boundary between the two countries. Portugal, however, withdrew its ambassador from Canberra in protest, and in February 1991 instituted proceedings against Australia at the International Court of Justice. In June 1995 the Court refused to invalidate the exploration treaty. In April 1992 Paul Keating's visit to Indonesia, the new Prime Minister's first official overseas trip, aroused controversy, owing to the repercussions of the massacre of unarmed civilians in East Timor by Indonesian troops in November 1991. In July 1995, owing to strong opposition in Australia, Indonesia was obliged to withdraw the appointment as ambassador to Canberra of Lt-Gen. (retd) Herman Mantiri, a former Chief of the General Staff of the Armed Forces and an apparent supporter of the November 1991 Dili massacre. Nevertheless, in December 1995 Australia and Indonesia unexpectedly signed a joint security treaty. In March 1996 a new Indonesian ambassador took up his appointment in Canberra, and in September, following a visit to Jakarta by John Howard, Indonesia accepted Australia's ambassador-designate.

Meanwhile, the investigation into the deaths of six Australia-based journalists (including two Britons) in East Timor in 1975 had been reopened, and in June 1996 a government report concluded that they had been murdered by Indonesian soldiers.

In October 1996, as Canberra continued to fail to denounce the Suharto Government's violations of human rights, Australian senators from all parties urged the Government to withdraw its recognition of Indonesian sovereignty over East Timor. In March 1997 Australia and Indonesia signed a treaty defining their seabed and 'economic zone' boundaries. The political unrest in Indonesia in early 1998, culminating in President Suharto's replacement in May, caused deep concern in Australia. In August the International Commission of Jurists, the Geneva-based human rights organization, reported that five of the six journalists had been murdered in an East Timorese village in October 1975 in an attempt to conceal the invasion of the territory, while the sixth man was killed in Dili in December of that year. Furthermore, it was claimed that the Australian embassy in Jakarta had been aware of the forthcoming invasion of East Timor but had failed to give adequate warning to the journalists. In October 1998, as newly-emerging evidence continued to suggest that the truth had been suppressed and as interest in the matter was renewed in the United Kingdom, the Indonesian Government declared that it would not open an inquiry into the deaths of the two British journalists, maintaining that they and their colleagues had been killed in cross-fire. Australia, however, announced that its judicial inquiry was to be reopened. Government documents declassified in late 2000 proved conclusively that Australian officials had prior knowledge of Indonesia's plans to invade East Timor.

In January 1999, in a significant shift in its policy, Australia announced that henceforth it would support eventual self-determination for East Timor. (Australia had been the only developed nation to recognize Indonesia's annexation of the territory.) In late January, furthermore, Australia welcomed the Indonesian Government's declaration of its willingness to consider the possibility of full independence, if proposals for autonomy were rejected by the East Timorese people. During 1999, however, Australia became increasingly concerned at the deteriorating security situation in East Timor. The announcement of the result of the referendum on the future of East Timor, held in late August, at which the territory's people voted overwhelmingly in favour of independence (see the chapter on Timor-Leste) led to a rapid escalation of the violence. As pro-Jakarta militias embarked upon a campaign of murder and arson against innocent civilians, most of whom were forced to flee their homes, thousands of refugees were airlifted to safety in northern Australia. With a commitment of 4,500 troops in its largest operation since the Viet Nam War, Australia took a leading role in the deployment of a multinational peace-keeping force, the first contingent of which landed in East Timor on 20 September 1999. Several Asian countries, however, in particular Malaysia and Thailand, along with Indonesia itself (which earlier in the month had suspended its security pact with Australia), were critical of Australia's bias towards pro-independence groups and of the country's apparent aggressive approach to its role in the operation, which some observers considered would have been more appropriately led by the Association of South East Asian Nations (ASEAN). A deterioration in relations between the two countries led President Abdurrahman Wahid of Indonesia to postpone an official visit to Australia in mid-2000. A series of postponements or cancellations of ministerial meetings followed.

In a further demonstration of anti-Australian feeling, Canberra's ambassador to Indonesia was assaulted by a pro-Jakarta mob in Makassar, Sulawesi, in November 2000. In the same month the Australian Government agreed to help create an East Timor defence force, contributing some US $26m. over five years and providing training for police officers and border guards. Abdurrahman Wahid made a long-postponed official visit to Australia in June 2001, the first Indonesian President to do so in 26 years. In turn, John Howard was the first foreign leader to meet the next President of Indonesia, Megawati Sukarnoputri, when he visited the country in August. He affirmed that Australia would encourage the international community's support for Indonesia. However, the increasing numbers of immigrants, the majority from the Middle East, attempting to enter Australia by boat via Indonesia during 2000–01 proved contentious. Indonesia disclaimed responsibility for the many boatloads of asylum-seekers on the grounds that they had entered Indonesia illegally. The situation prompted senior-level talks between Australian and Indonesian officials in September 2001 which, however, failed to resolve the problem. Discussions resumed in November, when the Indonesian Minister of Foreign Relations visited Canberra. At an international forum on the issue of people-smuggling in February 2002, delegates agreed to pursue a 12-month programme, which included imposing stricter law enforcement and better information and intelligence-sharing, to combat smuggling and illegal immigration. In late February officials from Australia, Indonesia and Timor-Leste (formerly East Timor) held the first ever trilateral talks on future co-operation issues in Denpasar, on the Indonesian island of Bali. In September three Indonesians were convicted of attempting to smuggle 'illegal immigrants' into Australia in October 2001; they were sentenced to five years' imprisonment. Relations between Australia and Indonesia were strained as a result of Australia's treatment of Indonesian-born Muslims suspected of having links with the banned Islamist militant organization, Jemaah Islamiah, in the aftermath of the bomb attack on Bali in October 2002 (see above).

In mid-December 2002 Timor-Leste's Parliament ratified a treaty with Australia on production, profit-sharing and royalty and tax distribution from oil and gas reserves. In August 2003 Australia and Timor-Leste signed a memorandum of understanding to collaborate in combating terrorism. Australia's relations with Timor-Leste, however, were made difficult by disagreements over the maritime boundaries in the Timor Sea. Preliminary sea boundary talks between the two countries took place in November. The Prime Minister of Timor-Leste accused Australia of deliberately stalling negotiations after the latter refused to set a schedule for their completion. Australia stated that all its resources were being applied to other boundary discussions and that the dialogue with Timor-Leste might take decades. Little progress was made at the first round of negotiations, which took place in Dili in April 2004, with Australia rejecting appeals to submit the dispute to international arbitration. However, in August the Australian Minister for Foreign Affairs and his Timorese counterpart announced that they hoped to agree on a settlement framework by the end of 2004, following a warning from the Australian company Woodside Petroleum that if the dispute was not resolved by the end of the year, its gas project in the Timor Sea would not proceed. Talks on the maritime boundaries resumed in September and continued in October, but reached an impasse at the end of that month, and in January 2005, in the absence of any agreement, Woodside confirmed that it was halting development of the gas project.

A crisis in Australia's relations with Malaysia arose in late 1993, when Paul Keating described the Malaysian Prime Minister as a 'recalcitrant' for his failure to attend the APEC summit meeting in Seattle, USA, in November. Relations subsequently improved, however, manifest in such initiatives as the Malaysia-Australia Dialogue (MAD), established in 1995 to encourage the long-term bilateral relationship at government-to-government level in education, business, the media and other sectors. In January 1996 Keating paid the first official visit to Malaysia by an Australian Prime Minister since 1984 and the ministerial-level Joint Trade Committee (JTC) talks were inaugurated. These led to the signing of a new trade and investment agreement, which took effect in January 1998. During 1999 Australia was critical of the continued detention and the trials of Anwar Ibrahim, the former Deputy Prime Minister and Minister of Finance (see the chapter on Malaysia). In early October 2002 the Australian Minister for Foreign Affairs met Myanma government officials and Myanma opposition leader Aung Sang Suu Kyi for discussions, during the first visit to Myanmar by an Australian minister for nearly 20 years. The Howard Government's more aggressive stance towards South-East Asia in late 2002 led to a deterioration in relations with the region. In early December the Prime Minister stated that he would be prepared to conduct pre-emptive strikes on militant organizations in neighbouring countries suspected of planning terrorist attacks on Australia. Malaysia warned Australia that any incursion into Malaysia would be considered as an act of war. Australia's increasingly interventionist stance towards its neighbours, in particular Solomon Islands and Papua New Guinea (see below), in 2003 encouraged Asian leaders to view the country more and more as a 'deputy' of the USA. In March 2003 Australia and the Philippines signed an agreement on increased bilateral co-operation to counter international terrorism. Australia's relations with Malaysia appeared to improve following the succession of Abdullah Ahmad Badawi to the premiership of that country in October 2003. In June 2004, during a visit to Malaysia by the Australian Minister for Foreign Affairs, Alexander Downer, agreement was reached to hold formal annual talks between the two countries'

foreign ministers and separate regular consultations between senior security officials. At the same time Prime Minister Badawi accepted an invitation to make a state visit to Australia, expected to take place in 2005, which would be the first by a Malaysian leader in more than 20 years. However, the Malaysian Government dismissed a plan announced by John Howard in September 2004 to establish specialist counter-terrorist centres in South-East Asia and Australia, complaining that it had not been consulted about the proposal. In the previous month the Indonesian Government had expressed concern at Australia's decision to pursue a programme to arm its fighter aircraft with a cruise missile system costing $A450m. In November, at a summit meeting of ASEAN leaders in Vientiane, Laos, Prime Minister Howard, together with his ASEAN and New Zealand counterparts, announced that negotiations would commence on a free-trade agreement between Australia, ASEAN and New Zealand in early 2005. However, in December 2004 Australia provoked further tension with neighbouring countries when it proposed the creation of a coastal security zone extending five times as far as its territorial waters. Under this counter-terrorist measure, which came into effect in March 2005, all ships entering the 1,000-nautical mile zone would be monitored, with Australian naval and customs ships given powers to intercept and board all vessels suspected of constituting a terrorist threat.

Australia's relations with the People's Republic of China, meanwhile, continued to be strained by the issue of China's nuclear-testing programme, and deteriorated further in September 1996 when the Dalai Lama, the exiled spiritual leader of Tibet, was received in Sydney by the Prime Minister. In March 1997, however, the Australian Prime Minister began a six-day official visit to China, where he had discussions with Premier Li Peng. In July 1999, during a visit to Beijing by the Australian Minister of Foreign Affairs, Australia endorsed China's bid for membership of the World Trade Organization (WTO). The two countries also signed a bilateral trade pact. In September, however, President Jiang Zemin's visit to Australia was disrupted by pro-Tibet and Taiwan activists. Political and economic relations with China improved in the early 2000s, partly owing to Australia's refraining from criticizing China's human rights record. During President Hu Jintao's visit to Australia in October 2003 Australia agreed to supply China with liquified natural gas for a period of 25 years. Australia's relations with Japan were strained in the late 1990s by a fishing dispute relating to the latter's failure to curb its catches of the endangered southern bluefin tuna, as agreed in a treaty of 1993, of which New Zealand was also a signatory. In August 1999, however, an international tribunal ruled in favour of Australia and New Zealand.

In May 2000 diplomatic relations between Australia and the Democratic People's Republic of Korea, which had been severed in 1975, were restored. Discussions between the two nations, initiated by the North Korean Government in April 1999, had been dominated by the International Atomic Energy Agency's concerns over nuclear facilities and long-range missile testing. The Australian Minister of Foreign Affairs paid an official two-day visit to Pyongyang in November 2000. He confirmed that six North Korean officials were expected to participate in a nuclear-safeguards training course in Australia. An Australian trade mission organized by Austrade, Australia's trade and investment promotion agency, visited North Korea in December; discussions were held with North Korean officials regarding problems in the country's energy sector. Australia and North Korea agreed to establish, within two years, embassies in their respective capitals when North Korea's Minister of Foreign Affairs paid Australia a reciprocal visit in June 2001. Furthermore, a Memorandum of Understanding was signed to facilitate co-operation between Australian and North Korean scientists in agricultural research, including the participation of North Korean scientists in research programmes and on-the-job training activities in Australian research institutes. Plans to open an embassy in North Korea were deferred in late 2002, however, owing to North Korea's efforts to reactivate its nuclear weapons programme.

The viability of the ANZUS military pact, which was signed in 1951, linking Australia, New Zealand and the USA, was disputed by the US Government following the New Zealand Government's declaration, in July 1984, that vessels which were believed to be powered by nuclear energy, or to be carrying nuclear weapons, would be barred from the country's ports. Hawke did not support the New Zealand initiative, and Australia continued to participate with the USA in joint military exercises from which New Zealand had been excluded. However, the Hawke Government declined directly to endorse the US action against New Zealand, and in 1986 stated that Australia regarded its 'obligations to New Zealand as constant and undiminishing'. In September 1990 Australia and New Zealand signed an agreement to establish a joint venture to construct as many as 12 naval frigates to patrol the South Pacific. In February 1994 the USA announced its decision to resume senior-level contacts with New Zealand. In July 1996 Australia and the USA upgraded their defence alliance. In 1999 Australia's trading relations with the USA were strained by the latter's imposition of tariffs on imports of Australian lamb. In October Australia urged that the dispute be settled by means of a WTO panel; in December 2000 the WTO upheld the complaint, ruling that the tariffs violated global trade rules. Meanwhile, in July 2000 the US Secretary of Defense made an official visit to Australia, following which he re-emphasized the importance of bilateral defence ties; and the Ministers for Foreign Affairs and Defence participated in the Australia-US Leadership Dialogue in Washington, DC. In September 2001 Prime Minister John Howard condemned the terrorist attacks suffered by the USA and promised Australia's full support for the offensive in Afghanistan. In 2002 John Howard expressed his support for the USA's 'war on terror' and in early 2003 deployed some 2,000 troops to the Middle East in preparation for the US-led military campaign to oust the regime of Saddam Hussain in Iraq, which commenced in March. During a visit to Australia by US President George W. Bush in October, the US leader thanked and commended Australia for its support for the war in Iraq and the 'war on terror' during an address in Parliament. Two senators from the Green Party were expelled from the chamber for heckling President Bush, while an estimated 5,000 anti-Bush protesters held a demonstration outside the Parliament building. Relations between Australia and the USA were further strengthened in 2004 with the conclusion of a free-trade agreement, which entered into force in January 2005.

Owing to Australian opposition to French test explosions of nuclear weapons at Mururoa Atoll (French Polynesia) in the South Pacific Ocean, a ban on uranium sales to France was introduced in 1983. However, in August 1986 the Government announced its decision to resume uranium exports. In December Australia ratified a treaty declaring the South Pacific area a nuclear-free zone. France's decision, in April 1992, to suspend its nuclear-testing programme was welcomed by Australia. In June 1995, however, the French President's announcement that the programme was to be resumed provoked outrage throughout the Pacific region. The Australian ambassador to France was recalled, and the French consulate in Perth was destroyed in an arson attack. Further widespread protests followed the first of the new series of tests in September. Australia's relations with the United Kingdom were strained by the British Government's refusal to join the condemnation of France's policy. The final test was conducted in January 1996. On an official visit to Paris in September, the Australian Minister for Foreign Affairs adopted a conciliatory stance (which drew much criticism from anti-nuclear groups). A ban on new contracts for the supply of uranium to France, imposed in September 1995, was removed in October 1996. Meanwhile, Australia remained committed to achieving the elimination of all nuclear testing. In August, following a veto of the draft text by India and Iran at the UN Conference on Disarmament in Geneva, Switzerland, Australia took the initiative in leading an international effort to secure the passage of the Comprehensive Test Ban Treaty. In an unusual procedure, the Treaty was referred to the UN General Assembly, which voted overwhelmingly in its favour in September.

Relations with neighbouring Pacific island states were strained in mid-1997. In July Australia was embarrassed by the unauthorized publication of a secret official document in which certain regional politicians were described as corrupt and incompetent. At a meeting of the South Pacific Forum (now Pacific Islands Forum) in September, the member countries failed to reach agreement on a common policy regarding mandatory targets for the reduction of emissions of the so-called 'greenhouse gases'. The low-lying nation of Tuvalu was particularly critical of Australia's refusal to compromise, the Australian Prime Minister declaring that the Pacific islands' concerns over rising sea levels were exaggerated. In July 2001 Australia declined Tuvalu's request to take in more Tuvaluan nationals. The Australian Government, committed to its 'Pacific

solution', nevertheless made a verbal request of shelter for some of its many asylum-seekers to Tuvalu in November.

Australia's relations with Papua New Guinea were strained in early 1997 as a result of the latter's decision to engage the services of a group of mercenaries in the Government's operations against secessionists on the island of Bougainville. Fearing for the stability of the South Pacific region, the Australian Prime Minister denounced the use of foreign forces as unacceptable. In January 1998 a permanent cease-fire agreement between the Papua New Guinea Government and the Bougainville secessionists, which was to take effect in April, was signed in New Zealand. Australia reaffirmed its commitment to the provision of a peace-monitoring force. Since 1998 both Canberra and Townsville, in Queensland, had provided a neutral platform for rounds of negotiations regarding Bougainville's secession, and in August 2001 the Minister for Foreign Affairs, Alexander Downer, signed the Bougainville Peace Agreement as a witness. In October the Government concluded a deal with Papua New Guinea for it to house 223 asylum-seekers in exchange for $A1m. In December 2003 the Australian Government announced its intention to send around 300 police officers and civil servants to Papua New Guinea as part of a five-year operation to assist in the fight against crime and corruption. In July 2004 the National Parliament of Papua New Guinea approved legislation allowing the deployment of the Australian police officers and officials; the first contingent of police officers arrived in Bougainville in September, with the remainder expected to be in place by March 2005.

Australia played a leading role in the events following a coup in Solomon Islands, which took place in June 2000. The Australian navy dispatched a warship to assist in the evacuation of Australian and other nationals from the islands, while a similar ship anchored off shore served as a venue for negotiations between the two warring ethnic militias. The Australian Minister for Foreign Affairs led an international delegation with the aim of facilitating discussions between the factions. In October a peace agreement was signed in Townsville, which ended the two-year conflict; it was qualified and complemented by the Marau Peace Agreement, signed in February 2001. The Australian Government subsequently led an International Peace Monitoring Team, in an attempt to ensure continued stability in the islands. In September Australia contributed $A1.6m. towards financing democratic elections, and technical support was provided by the Australian Electoral Commission. In July 2003 an Australian-led regional peace-keeping force was deployed in Solomon Islands to restore law and order, leading many to believe that Australia was establishing itself as the 'neighbourhood policeman' in Asia. The force was welcomed by the inhabitants of the islands, and at the end of the year the operation was judged to have been a success.

The Australian Government intervened in the severe financial crisis experienced by Nauru in 2004, agreeing, in May, to provide a senior Treasury officer and finance department officials to assist in reorganizing the island's finances and a police commissioner and officers to help maintain law and order.

Government

Australia comprises six states and three territories. Executive power is vested in the British monarch and exercised by the monarch's appointed representative, the Governor-General, who normally acts on the advice of the Federal Executive Council (the Ministry), led by the Prime Minister. The Governor-General appoints the Prime Minister and, on the latter's recommendation, other Ministers.

Legislative power is vested in the Federal Parliament. This consists of the monarch, represented by the Governor-General, and two chambers elected by universal adult suffrage (voting is compulsory). The Senate has 76 members (12 from each state and two each from the Northern Territory and the Australian Capital Territory), who are elected by a system of proportional representation for six years when representing a state, with half the seats renewable every three years, and for a term of three years when representing a territory. The House of Representatives has 150 members, elected for three years (subject to dissolution) from single-member constituencies. The Federal Executive Council is responsible to Parliament.

Each state has a Governor, representing the monarch, and its own legislative, executive and judicial system. The state governments are essentially autonomous, but certain powers are placed under the jurisdiction of the Federal Government. All states except Queensland have an upper house (the Legislative Council) and a lower house (the Legislative Assembly or House of Assembly). The chief ministers of the states are known as Premiers, as distinct from the Federal Prime Minister. The Northern Territory (self-governing since 1978) and the Australian Capital Territory (self-governing since 1988) have unicameral legislatures, and each has a government led by a Chief Minister. The Jervis Bay Territory is not self-governing.

Defence

Australia's defence policy is based on collective security, and it is a member of the British Commonwealth Strategic Reserve and of ANZUS, with New Zealand and the USA. Australia also participates in the Five-Power Defence Arrangements, with New Zealand, Malaysia, Singapore and the United Kingdom. In August 2004 Australia's armed forces numbered 51,800 (army 25,300, navy 12,850, air force 13,650). Defence expenditure for 2003/04 was budgeted at $A12,937m. Service in the armed forces is voluntary. In September 1999 Australia committed 4,500 troops to the peace-keeping operation in East Timor (now Timor-Leste), where 259 remained, including three observers, in August 2004. In October 2001 Australia committed 1,550 Australian servicemen and women to the International Coalition against Terrorism. In support of peace-keeping efforts, some 850 Australian troops were stationed in Iraq in August 2004. In the same month about 530 Australian military personnel remained in Solomon Islands. In February 2004 the Minister for Defence announced that the defence budget would be more than doubled over the following three years and that spending would be increased to $A50,000m. over a period of 10 years.

Economic Affairs

In 2003, according to estimates by the World Bank, Australia's gross national income (GNI), measured at average 2001–03 prices, was US $503,163m., equivalent to US $21,650 per head (or US $28,290 per head on an international purchasing-power parity basis). During 1990–2003, it was estimated, the population increased at an average annual rate of1.2%, while gross domestic product (GDP) per head increased, in real terms, by an average of 2.2%. Overall GDP increased, in real terms, at an average annual rate of 3.4% in 1990–2003. GDP expanded by 2.7% in 2002 and by 2.4% in 2003.

Agriculture (including forestry, hunting and fishing) contributed 3.1% of GDP in 2002/03. The sector engaged 3.9% of the employed labour force in 2003. The principal crops are wheat, fruit, sugar and cotton. Australia is the world's leading producer of wool. Export earnings from greasy wool, however, decreased from$A2,482m. in 2002 to $A1,790m. in 2003, reflecting a substantial decline in international prices for the commodity. The export of wine is of increasing importance, rising from 10m. litres in 1986 to 584m. litres in 2003/04, when the value of wine exports reached $A2,500m. Australia thus remainedthe world's fourth largest wine exporter. Meat production is also important. Beef is Australia's leading meat export, although this accounted for only about 3% of total export revenue in the year to March 2004. Between 1990 and 2001 agricultural GDP increased at an average annual rate of 2.8%. In 2000 it decreased by 0.5% compared with the previous year, but expanded by 2.3% in 2001. In 2002 agricultural production was severely affected by one of Australia's worst droughts in 100 years. According to FAO, total agricultural output declined by 16.4% and the production of crops decreased by 55.9% in this year. Wheat production declined from 24.9m. metric tons in 2001 to less than 10.1m. tons in 2002, before recovering to 24.9m. tons in 2003. By late October 2002 some 40,000 employees of the agricultural sector had lost their jobs, and in January 2003 Australia was forced to import grain for the first time since 1995. Water shortages also adversely affected the dairy industry. The recurrent problem of bush fires was exacerbated from late 2001 by the prolonged drought. Although there was some rainfall in mid-2003, water restrictions continued to constrain both agricultural producers and town dwellers in 2004.

Industry (comprising mining, manufacturing, construction and utilities) employed 21.0% of the working population in 2003, and provided 26.0% of GDP in 2002/03. Industrial GDP increased at an average rate of 2.4% per year between 1990 and 2001, declining by 1.0% in 2000, before expanding by 3.8% in 2001. Compared with the previous year, industrial output rose by 2.9% in 2002 but by only 0.3% in 2003.

The mining sector employed 0.8% of the working population in 2003, and contributed 5.0% of GDP in 2002/03. Australia is one of the world's leading exporters of coal. Earnings from coal and related products in 2002/03 reached $11,946m., accounting for 10.3% of total export receipts in that year. The other principal

minerals extracted are iron ore, gold, silver, magnesite, petroleum and natural gas. Bauxite, zinc, copper, titanium, nickel, tin, lead, zirconium and diamonds are also mined. Between 1989/90 and 1996/97 the GDP of the mining sector increased at an average annual rate of 2.9%. Compared with the previous year, mining GDP rose by 9.8% in 1999/2000.

Manufacturing contributed 11.9% of GDP in 2002/03. The sector employed 11.4% of the working population in 2003. Measured by the value of sales, the principal branches of manufacturing in 2000/01 were food, beverages and tobacco (22.1%), equipment and machinery (20.2%), petroleum, coal and chemical products (17.3%), metal products (16.6%), printing, publishing and recording (6.2%) and wood and paper products (6.2%). The manufacturing sector's GDP grew at an average annual rate of 2.0% between 1990 and 2001, increasing by 2.7% in 2000 and by 3.0% in 2001. Compared with the previous year, in 2002 the manufacturing sector's GDP grew by 4.2%.

Energy is derived principally from petroleum, natural gas and coal. Production of petroleum, however, declined from 33,320m. litres in 2002/03 to 27,876m. litres in 2003/04. Imports of crude petroleum and bituminous oils accounted for only 5.9% of total import costs in 2002/03. The production of black coal increased from 348.9m. tons in 2002/03 to 362.2m. tons in 2003/04.

The services sector provided 71.0% of GDP in 2002/03, and engaged 75.0% of the employed labour force in 2003. The tourism industry has become a major source of foreign-exchange earnings. The number of visitor arrivals, however, decreased from 4.8m. in 2002 to 4.7m. in 2003. Tourism revenuedeclined from $A17,080m. in 2001/02 to $A16,666m. in 2002/03. It was estimated that in 2002 the tourism sector contributed 4.3% of GDP and accounted for 6.0% of total employment. The GDP of the services sector increased at an average annual rate of 4.1% between 1990 and 2001, rising by 3.3% in 2000 and by 4.1% in 2001.

In 2003 Australia recorded a visible trade deficit of US $15,254m., and there was a deficit of US $30,544m. on the current account of the balance of payments. In the year ending 30 June 2003 the principal source of imports was the USA (which supplied 16.9%), followed by Japan (12.3%) and the People's Republic of China (10.4%). Japan was the principal market for exports in that year (purchasing 19.0%), followed by the USA (9.1%). Other major trading partners are the Republic of Korea, New Zealand, the United Kingdom, Germany, Singapore and Taiwan. The principal exports in 2002/03 included coal, crude petroleum, non-monetary gold and iron ore. The principal imports were passenger motor vehicles, crude petroleum, aircraft and parts and also computing equipment.

In the 2004/05 financial year a budgetary surplus of about $A2,400m. was originally forecast, but in September 2004 the projected surplus was revised upwards, to $A5,300m. In mid-2003 Australia's net external debt was equivalent to 47.8% of annual GDP, standingat $A358,965m., of which $A349,836m. was incurred by the private sector. An estimated average of 5.6% of the labour force were unemployed in 2004. The annual rate of inflation averaged 2.5% in 1990–2002. Consumer prices rose by 2.7% in 2003 and by 2.6% in 2004.

Australia is a member of the UN Economic and Social Commission for Asia and the Pacific (ESCAP, see p. 31), the Asian Development Bank (ADB, see p. 159), the Pacific Islands Forum (see p. 339), the Pacific Community (see p. 337) and the Colombo Plan (see p. 373). In 1989 Australia played a major role in the creation of the Asia-Pacific Economic Co-operation group (APEC, see p. 155), which aimed to stimulate economic development in the region. Australia is also a member of the Organisation for Economic Co-operation and Development (OECD, see p. 307), of the Cairns Group (see p. 423) and of the International Grains Council (see p. 370).

Upon taking office in March 1996, the Howard Government confirmed its determination to achieve fiscal balance. Although a deficit was recorded in 2001/02, the budget returned to surplus in 2002/03. One of the principal aims of the administration's programme was the transfer to the private sector of Telstra, the state-owned telecommunications company. The first sale of the company's assets took place in November 1997, with a second disposal being effected in October 1999. Following Howard's re-election for a fourth consecutive term in October 2004, legislation providing for the completion of the privatization of Telstra was expected to receive approval in 2005. It was anticipated that the sale of the Government's remaining 51.8% stake in the telecommunications operator would raise revenue of as much as $A30,000m.The introduction in July 2000 of a controversial goods-and-services tax (GST), levied at a general rate of 10%, had an initial inflationary impact on the economy, but the rate of inflation subsequently declined, and consumer confidence remained high. By the end of 2001 the Reserve Bank of Australia's rate of interest had been reduced to its lowest level for 28 years, standing at 4.25%. Interest rates were increased in November 2003, however, to 5.0% and again in December of that year to 5.25%, in an attempt to control rising property prices and consumer debt. Interest rates then remained unchanged until March 2005, when they were raised to 5.5%. Employment experienced positive growth, and the rate of unemployment decreased in 2002. The trend in employment growth continued in 2003–04, with the rate of unemployment declining to a 26-year low of 5.3% in October 2004. The 2002/03 budget introduced tax relief schemes for families, as well as increasing expenditure on defence, protecting Australia's borders, and improving domestic security, health, care of the aged and welfare reform. The 2003/04 budget incorporated further personal income tax reductions, increased spending on defence, education, health, and research and development in the industrial sector, and allocated drought relief for rural Australia. The budget for 2004/05 included concessions for families with children, while making further adjustments to the structure of personal taxation rates. The economy continued to expand steadily, despite the effects on the agricultural sector of protracted drought, compounded by external factors such as the repercussions of the terrorist attacks on Bali in October 2002, the outbreak of Severe Acute Respiratory Syndrome (SARS) in East Asia in early 2003 and the military campaign in Iraq, all of which adversely affected the tourism industry, in particular. The tourism sector, however, was showing signs of recovery by late 2003. After a period of weakness in 2000–01, the value of the Australian currency against the US dollar subsequently increased, rising by more than 16% in 2003 and by almost 12% in 2004. Having more than doubled between 2001 and 2002, the current-account deficit on the balance of payments increased by more than 80% in 2003. As exports declined in the second half of 2004, the current-account deficit was reported to have reached a record $A29,400m. in that year, giving rise to some concern. By late 2004 economic growth had begun to decelerate, with growth for the year estimated to have reached only 1.5%. Furthermore, shortages of labour skills in certain areas were beginning to emerge. Following 13 years of uninterrupted growth, fears that the Australian economy might be approaching the limits of its capacity were increasingly being expressed.

Education

Education is the responsibility of each of the states and the Federal Government. It is compulsory for all children from the ages of six to 15 years (16 in South Australia and Tasmania) and is free of charge. In most states and territories primary education generally begins with a preparatory year commencing at five years of age, followed by six or seven years of schooling. Secondary education, beginning at the age of 12, usually lasts for five or six years. As a proportion of children in the relevant age-groups, the enrolment ratios in 2000/01 were 95.7% in primary schools and 89.7% in secondary schools. In 2002 there were 1,932,600 children enrolled in primary schools (of whom 28.0% attended non-government schools, the majority being Catholic institutions) and 1,382,300 in secondary schools (with 36.6% at non-government schools). Special services have been developed to fulfil the requirements of children living in the remote 'outback' areas, notably Schools of the Air, using two-way receiver sets. A system of one-teacher schools and correspondence schools also helps to satisfy these needs. In 2003 there were 48 publicly-funded institutions of higher education. In the same year students totalled 830,058. Most courses last from three to six years. Public expenditure on education in the financial year 2003/04 was $A13,398m.

Public Holidays*

2005: 3 January (for New Year's Day, except New South Wales and Victoria), 26 January (Australia Day), 25–28 March (Easter), 25 April (Anzac Day), 13 June (Queen's Official Birthday, except Western Australia), 26–27 December (for Christmas Day, Boxing Day).

2006: 2 January (for New Year's Day), 26 January (Australia Day), 14–17 April (Easter), 25 April (Anzac Day), 12 June (Queen's Official Birthday, except Western Australia), 25–26 December (Christmas Day, Boxing Day).

*National holidays only. Some states observe these holidays on different days. There are also numerous individual state holidays.

Weights and Measures

The metric system is in force.

Statistical Survey

Source (unless otherwise stated): Australian Bureau of Statistics, POB 10, Belconnen, ACT 2616; tel. (2) 6252-7983; fax (2) 6251-6009; internet www.abs .gov.au.

Area and Population

AREA, POPULATION AND DENSITY

Area (sq km)	7,692,024*
Population (census results)†	
6 August 1996	17,892,423
7 August 2001	
Males	9,362,021
Females	9,610,329
Total	18,972,350
Population (official estimates at mid-year)†	
2001	19,485,300
2002	19,662,800
2003‡	19,881,500
Density (per sq km) at mid-2003	2.6

* 2,969,907 sq miles.

† Census results exclude, and estimates include, an adjustment for under-enumeration, estimated to have been 1.9% in 1991. Estimates also exclude overseas visitors in Australia and include Australian residents temporarily overseas. The estimates shown above have been revised to take account of the August 2001 census result.

‡ Provisional figure.

STATES AND TERRITORIES
(census results, 7 August 2001)

	Area (sq km)	Population	Density (per sq km)
New South Wales (NSW) .	800,642	6,371,745	8.0
Victoria	227,416	4,644,950	20.4
Queensland	1,730,648	3,655,139	2.1
South Australia	983,482	1,467,261	1.5
Western Australia	2,529,875	1,851,252	0.7
Tasmania	68,401	456,652	6.7
Northern Territory . . .	1,349,129	210,664	0.2
Australian Capital Territory (ACT)	2,358	311,947	132.3
Jervis Bay Territory . . .	73	611	8.4
Total	**7,692,024**	**18,972,350***	**2.5**

* Includes populations of Christmas Island (1,508) and the Cocos (Keeling) Islands (621).

PRINCIPAL TOWNS
(estimated population at 30 June 2002)*

Canberra (national capital)	321,400	Wollongong	272,100
Sydney (capital of NSW)	4,170,900	Hobart (capital of Tasmania)	198,000
Melbourne (capital of Victoria)	3,524,100	Sunshine Coast	191,900
Brisbane (capital of Queensland)	1,689,100	Geelong	161,700
Perth (capital of W Australia)	1,114,300	Townsville	137,400
Adelaide (capital of S Australia)	1,114,300	Cairns	114,500
Newcastle	497,500	Toowoomba	111,400
Gold Coast-Tweed	439,700	Darwin (capital of N Territory)	107,400

* Figures refer to metropolitan areas, each of which normally comprises a municipality and contiguous urban areas.

BIRTHS, MARRIAGES AND DEATHS*

	Registered live births		Registered marriages		Registered deaths	
	Number	Rate (per 1,000)	Number	Rate (per 1,000)	Number	Rate (per 1,000)
1994	258,051	14.5	111,174	6.2	126,692	7.1
1995	256,190	14.2	109,386	6.1	125,133	6.9
1996	253,834	13.9	106,103	5.8	128,719	7.0
1997	251,842	13.6	106,735	5.8	129,350	7.0
1998	249,616	13.3	110,598	5.9	127,202	6.8
1999	248,870	13.1	114,316	6.0	128,102	6.8
2000	249,636	13.0	113,429	5.9	128,291	6.7
2001	246,394	12.6	103,130	5.3	128,544	6.6

* Data are tabulated by year of registration rather than by year of occurrence.

Expectation of life (WHO estimates, years at birth): 80.4 (males 77.9; females 83.0) in 2002 (Source: WHO, *World Health Report*).

IMMIGRATION AND EMIGRATION
(year ending 30 June)*

	2000/01	2001/02	2002/03
Permanent immigrants	107,366	88,900	93,914
Permanent emigrants	46,521	48,241	50,463

* Figures refer to persons intending to settle in Australia, or Australian residents intending to settle abroad.

Source: Department of Immigration and Multicultural and Indigenous Affairs, Belconnen.

ECONOMICALLY ACTIVE POPULATION
(annual averages, '000 persons aged 15 years and over, excluding armed forces)

	2001	2002	2003
Agriculture, hunting and forestry	418.7	394.3	354.8
Fishing	18.8	17.6	17.9
Mining and quarrying	66.9	69.9	75.5
Manufacturing	1,092.0	1,103.8	1,082.2
Electricity, gas and water	67.5	67.1	75.3
Construction	667.5	700.1	755.4
Wholesale and retail trade; repair of motor vehicles, motorcycles and personal and household goods	1,771.4	1,836.5	1,898.1
Hotels and restaurants	458.2	457.1	464.9
Transport, storage and communications	597.0	569.8	599.6
Financial intermediation	345.7	342.8	347.4
Real estate, renting and business activities	1,078.4	1,091.7	1,139.1
Public administration and defence; compulsory social security	479.8	522.9	552.0
Education	633.9	655.7	681.7
Health and social work	898.6	933.2	931.5
Other community, social and personal service activities	456.2	473.6	474.5
Private households with employed persons	5.1	6.0	3.2
Extra-territorial organizations and bodies	1.9	1.5	1.2
Not classified by economic activity	5.4	4.4	4.9
Total employed	9,063.0	9,248.0	9,459.2

Source: ILO.

Health and Welfare

KEY INDICATORS

Total fertility rate (children per woman, 2002)	1.7
Under-5 mortality rate (per 1,000 live births, 2003)	6
HIV/AIDS (% of persons aged 15–49, 2003)	0.1
Physicians (per 1,000 head, 2001)	2.5
Hospital beds (per 1,000 head, 1999)	7.9
Health expenditure (2001): US $ per head (PPP)	2,532
Health expenditure (2001): % of GDP	9.2
Health expenditure (2001): public (% of total)	67.9
Access to water (% of persons, 2002)	100
Access to sanitation (% of persons, 2002)	100
Human Development Index (2002): ranking	3
Human Development Index (2002): value	0.946

For sources and definitions, see explanatory note on p. vi.

Agriculture

PRINCIPAL CROPS
('000 metric tons)

	2001	2002	2003
Wheat	24,854	10,059	24,920
Rice (paddy)	1,643	1,192	438
Barley	8,280	3,713	8,525
Maize	345	457	310
Oats	1,434	926	1,520
Millet	55*	55*	54
Sorghum	1,935	2,021	1,541
Triticale (wheat-rye hybrid)	860	269	675
Potatoes	1,302	1,333	1,200
Sugar cane	31,228	32,260	37,968
Dry beans	50	39	50*
Dry broad beans	350	108	283
Dry peas	512	178	407
Chick-peas	258	136	178
Lentils	266	67	207
Lupins	1,215	716	953
Soybeans (Soya beans)	49	63	18
Sunflower seed	77	70	25
Rapeseed	1,756	871	1,622
Cottonseed	1,054	546	480
Cabbages	81	76	80*
Lettuce	153	135	122
Tomatoes	556	425	364
Cauliflower	122	133	128
Pumpkins, squash and gourds	109	96	93
Dry onions	222	283	229
Green peas	58	62	48†
Carrots	321	331	306
Other fresh vegetables*	268	276	269
Watermelons	106	100	111
Cantaloupes and other melons	92	74	64
Bananas	358	313	265
Oranges	550	451	599
Tangerines, mandarins, clementines and satsumas	79	78	98
Apples	325	321	326
Pears	169	145	136
Peaches and nectarines	108	117	127
Grapes	1,546	1,754	1,497
Pineapples	120	119	105
Cotton (lint)	745	386	339

* FAO estimate(s).
† Unofficial figure.

Source: FAO.

LIVESTOCK
('000 head at 30 June)

	2001	2002	2003
Horses*	220	220	220
Cattle	27,721	27,870	26,664
Pigs	2,748	2,940	2,770
Sheep	110,900	106,200	99,300
Goats*	295	400	420
Chickens	90,973	85,002	90,000*
Ducks*	540	540	540
Turkeys*	1,400	1,400	1,400

* FAO estimate(s).

Source: FAO.

LIVESTOCK PRODUCTS
('000 metric tons)

	2001	2002	2003
Beef and veal	2,119	2,028	2,073
Mutton and lamb	715	644	597
Goat meat*	10.6	13.8	14.3
Pig meat	365.2	395.5	420.0
Horse meat*	21.3	21.3	21.3
Chicken meat	619.4	667.5	689.8
Duck meat*	9	9	9
Turkey meat*	25.9	25.9	25.9

— *continued*	2001	2002	2003
Cows' milk	10,872	11,620	10,646
Butter	172	178	149
Cheese	376	431	368
Hen eggs†	141	140	152
Honey*	21.5	22.0	22.5
Wool: greasy	657	607	545
Wool: scoured†	416	395	354
Cattle hides (fresh)*	254	243	248
Sheepskins (fresh)*	165.7	149.7	137.4

* FAO estimates.
† Unofficial figures.
Note: Figures for meat and milk refer to the 12 months ending 30 June of the year stated.

Source: FAO.

Forestry

ROUNDWOOD REMOVALS
('000 cubic metres, excl. bark)

	2001	2002	2003
Sawlogs, veneer logs and logs for sleepers	10,727	11,054	12,764
Pulpwood	12,691	11,142	13,047
Other industrial wood	935	906	923
Fuel wood*	6,707	3,082	3,092
Total	**31,060**	**26,184**	**29,826**

* FAO estimates.
Source: FAO.

SAWNWOOD PRODUCTION
('000 cubic metres, incl. railway sleepers)

	2001	2002	2003
Coniferous (softwood)	2,351	3,011	2,986
Broadleaved (hardwood)	1,174	1,108	1,063
Total	**3,525**	**4,119**	**4,049**

Source: FAO.

Fishing

('000 metric tons, live weight, year ending 30 June)

	1999/2000	2000/01	2001/02
Capture	190.1	194.4	194.2
Blue grenadier	9.5	7.6	9.2
Clupeoids	5.6	8.6	14.6
Australian spiny lobster	14.6	11.6	17.7
Penaeus shrimps	20.3	23.8	22.4
Scallops	12.0	9.2	5.7
Aquaculture	31.7	35.4	38.8
Atlantic salmon	10.9	12.7	14.4
Total catch	**221.8**	**229.8**	**233.0**

Note: Figures exclude aquatic plants ('000 metric tons, capture only): 13.7 in 1999/2000; 13.5 in 2000/01; 9.9 in 2001/02. Also excluded are crocodiles, recorded by number rather than by weight. The number of estuarine crocodiles caught was: 13,296 in 1999/2000; 11,849 in 2000/01; 7,205 in 2001/02. The number of Australian crocodiles caught was: 10 in 1999/2000; 0 in 2000/01; 2 in 2001/02. Also excluded are whales, recorded by number rather than weight. The number of Baleen whales caught was: 2 in 1999/2000; 10 in 2000/01; 1 in 2001/02. The number of toothed whales caught was: 25 in 1999/2000; 24 in 2000/01; 30 in 2001/02. Also excluded are pearl oyster shells (metric tons): 240 in 1999/2000; 190 in 2000/01; 220 in 2001/02.

Source: FAO.

Mining

(year ending 30 June, '000 metric tons, unless otherwise indicated)

	2001/02	2002/03	2003/04
Black coal	344,440	348,920	362,220
Brown coal*	67,400	67,830	67,400
Crude petroleum (million litres)	36,100	33,320	27,876
Natural gas (million cu metres)	32,136	33,162	33,267
Iron ore: gross weight*	185,302	198,062	220,683
Iron ore: metal content*	115,027	123,055	136,925
Copper ore*†	876	883	800
Nickel ore*†	205	183	185
Bauxite: gross weight	53,949	54,472	56,316
Bauxite: alumina content	169,676	19,921	20,516
Lead ore*†	744	695	677
Zinc ore*†	1,490	1,529	1,355
Tin ore (metric tons)*†	8,173	6,222	1,465
Manganese ore (metallurgical): gross weight*	1,850	2,472	3,062
Manganese ore (metallurgical): metal content*	994	1,127	1,171
Chromite	133‡	n.a.	n.a.
Ilmenite*	1,843	2,069	1,925
Leucoxene	34	43	57
Rutile*	207	208	154
Tantalum and niobium (Columbium) concentrates (metric tons)§	3,100‡	n.a.	n.a.
Zirconium concentrates*	389	458	451
Antimony ore (metric tons)†	1,200*‡	n.a.	n.a.
Cobalt ore (metric tons)†	6,600	n.a.	n.a.
Silver (metric tons)*†	2,106	1,905	2,056
Uranium (metric tons)†	6,753	7,855	8,089
Gold (metric tons)*†	265	278	262
Limestone	15,740	18,100	n.a.
Bentonite and bentonitic clay	200*‡	n.a.	n.a.
Kaolin and ball clay	230*‡	n.a.	n.a.
Brick clay and shale	8,000*‡	n.a.	n.a.
Magnesite	602	449	554
Phosphate rock‖	2,025*‡	n.a.	n.a.
Barite (Barytes)	20*‡	n.a.	n.a.
Salt (unrefined)*¶	9,213	10,438	10,698
Gypsum (crude)*	4,088	3,664	n.a.
Talc (metric tons)	160,741	165,980	n.a.
Pyrophyllite (metric tons)	868	n.a.	n.a.
Diamonds ('000 carats, unsorted)	30,676	32,006	24,310

* Estimated production.
† Figures refer to the metal content of ores and concentrates.
‡ Figure refers to January–December 2002 (Source: US Geological Survey).
§ The estimated metal content (in metric tons) was: Niobium (Columbium) 290 in 2002; Tantalum 940 in 2002.
‖ Figures refer to the gross weight of concentrates. The phosphoric acid (P$_2$O$_5$) content (in '000 metric tons) was 482 in 2002.
¶ Excludes production in Victoria.

Source (unless otherwise indicated): Australian Bureau of Agricultural and Resource Economics, *Australian Mineral Statistics* and *Australian Commodity Statistics*.

Industry

SELECTED PRODUCTS

(year ending 30 June, '000 metric tons, unless otherwise indicated)

	2001/02	2002/03	2003/04
Pig-iron	6,169	6,634	6,624
Raw steel	8,311	9,399	9,445
Aluminium—unwrought*	1,809	1,855	1,877
Copper—unwrought*	561	537	458
Lead—unwrought*	275	267	247
Zinc—unwrought*	572	570	502
Tin—unwrought (metric tons)*	829	708	553
Motor spirit (petrol—million litres)	18,000	17,984	17,375
Fuel oil (million litres)	1,684	1,441	1,105
Diesel-automotive oil (million litres)	13,064	13,335	12,544
Aviation turbine fuel (million litres)	5,390	5,149	4,964
Clay bricks (million)	1,514	n.a.	n.a.
Electricity (million kWh)	201,141	n.a.	n.a.
Cement	7,236	n.a.	n.a.
Concrete—ready-mixed ('000 cu m)	19,447	n.a.	n.a.
Newsprint	398	412	n.a.
Beer (million litres)	1,744	n.a.	n.a.
Unfortified wine (million litres)	1,151	n.a.	n.a.
Tobacco and cigarettes (metric tons)	18,367	n.a.	n.a.

* Primary refined metal only.

Source: mainly Australian Bureau of Agricultural and Resource Economics, *Australian Mineral Statistics*, *Australian Commodity Statistics* and *Energy in Australia*.

2000/01 ('000 metric tons, unless otherwise indicated): Woven cotton fabrics (incl. towelling, '000 sq metres) 39,000; Woven woollen fabrics (incl. blanketing, '000 sq metres) 4,000; Wheat flour 2,077 (Source: UN, *Industrial Commodity Statistics Yearbook*).

Finance

CURRENCY AND EXCHANGE RATES

Monetary Units
100 cents = 1 Australian dollar ($A).

Sterling, US Dollar and Euro Equivalents (31 December 2004)
£1 sterling = $A2.4793;
US $1 = $A1.2837;
€1 = $A1.7485;
$A100 = £40.33 = US $77.90 = €57.19.

Average Exchange Rate (Australian dollars per US $)
2002   1.8406
2003   1.5419
2004   1.3598

COMMONWEALTH GOVERNMENT BUDGET

($A million, year ending 30 June)

Revenue	2001/02	2002/03	2003/04
Tax revenue	149,848	163,055	175,058
Direct taxes	119,032	131,278	142,067
Individuals	86,422	91,303	98,779
Companies	27,133	33,365	36,337
Indirect taxes, etc.	25,634	27,255	27,692
Non-tax revenue	12,540	11,958	12,501
Total	162,388	175,014	187,559

Expenditure	2001/02	2002/03	2003/04
Defence	12,017	13,307	12,937
Education	11,761	12,109	13,398
Health	27,614	29,400	31,771
Social security and welfare	69,081	71,263	80,103
Economic services	12,974	12,646	14,223
General public services	12,097	12,956	13,234
Public-debt interest	4,995	4,629	4,001
Total (incl. others)	166,482	169,247	181,238

Source: Reserve Bank of Australia, *Bulletin*.

OFFICIAL RESERVES
(US $ million at 31 December)

	2001	2002	2003
Gold*	709	878	1,070
IMF special drawing rights . . .	109	136	170
Reserve position in IMF . . .	1,412	1,934	2,053
Foreign exchange	16,434	18,618	29,966
Total	18,664	21,567	33,259

* Valued at market-related prices.

Source: IMF, *International Financial Statistics*.

MONEY SUPPLY
($A million at 31 December)

	2001	2002	2003
Currency outside banks . . .	28,471	29,703	31,470
Demand deposits at trading and savings banks	138,456	180,177	200,008
Total money (incl. others) . .	167,126	210,120	231,553

Note: Data for 2002 and 2003 are collated in accordance with a revised reporting system and are not strictly comparable with data for 2001.
Source: IMF, *International Financial Statistics*.

COST OF LIVING
(Consumer Price Index*; base 2000 = 100)

	2001	2002	2003
Food	106.5	110.4	114.4
Electricity, gas and other fuels† .	105.6	110.0	n.a.
Clothing	102.3	103.6	n.a.
Rent‡	104.8	108.2	n.a.
All items (incl. others)	104.4	107.6	110.5

* Weighted average of eight capital cities.
† Including water and sewerage.
‡ Including expenditure on maintenance and repairs of dwellings; excluding mortgage interest charges and including house purchase and utilities.

Source: ILO.

NATIONAL ACCOUNTS
($A million, current prices, year ending 30 June)

National Income and Product

	2000/01	2001/02	2002/03
Compensation of employees . .	321,023	337,398	359,189
Gross operating surplus . . .	209,500	225,319	244,014
Gross mixed income	55,538	64,965	61,896
Total factor incomes	586,061	627,682	665,099
Taxes, less subsidies, on production and imports	82,365	85,547	93,048
GDP in market prices . . .	668,426	713,229	758,147
Net primary incomes from abroad	−18,702	−19,300	−21,469
Gross national income . . .	649,724	693,929	736,678
Current taxes on income, wealth, etc.	1,100	1,002	965
Other current transfers (net) . .	−1,068	−1,019	−1,179
Gross disposable income . .	649,756	693,912	736,464

Expenditure on the Gross Domestic Product

	2000/01	2001/02	2002/03
Government final consumption expenditure	119,970	127,325	136,848
Private final consumption expenditure	401,472	424,829	453,202
Gross fixed capital formation . .	145,361	161,937	184,802
Change in inventories	1,064	510	2,173
Total domestic expenditure .	667,867	714,601	777,026
Exports of goods and services . .	153,763	153,200	148,293
Less Imports of goods and services	153,205	154,573	167,169
GDP in market prices . . .	668,426	713,229	758,147
GDP at constant 2002/03 prices	707,140	734,575	758,147

Gross Domestic Product by Economic Activity

	2000/01	2001/02	2002/03
Agriculture, hunting, forestry and fishing	23,044	27,330	21,164
Mining and quarrying	34,051	33,820	34,271
Manufacturing	73,025	76,707	82,462
Electricity, gas and water . . .	15,479	16,096	16,961
Construction	33,875	39,608	45,668
Wholesale and retail trade . . .	66,253	72,127	78,685
Hotels and restaurants	14,877	14,915	15,456
Transport, storage and communications	51,198	53,963	57,740
Finance and insurance	46,991	52,626	57,963
Property and business activities .	73,392	75,441	79,391
Ownership of dwellings	57,924	61,415	63,860
Public administration and defence.	24,894	27,512	29,634
Education	29,729	31,130	33,144
Health and community services .	38,348	41,163	43,957
Cultural and recreational services	11,887	12,470	13,160
Personal and other services . .	14,799	16,023	17,494
Gross value added at basic prices	609,766	652,346	691,010
Taxes, less subsidies, on products .	58,660	60,883	67,137
GDP in market prices . . .	668,426	713,229	758,147

BALANCE OF PAYMENTS
(US $ million)

	2001	2002	2003
Exports of goods f.o.b.	63,676	65,099	70,540
Imports of goods f.o.b.	−61,890	−70,530	−85,852
Trade balance	1,786	−5,431	−15,312
Exports of services	16,698	17,906	21,143
Imports of services	−16,948	−18,107	−21,497
Balance on goods and services	1,536	−5,632	−15,667
Other income received	8,196	8,523	9,963
Other income paid	−18,065	−19,552	−24,513
Balance on goods, services and income	−8,333	−16,662	−30,217
Current transfers received . . .	2,242	2,310	2,767
Current transfers paid	−2,221	−2,373	−2,927
Current balance	−8,312	−16,726	−30,377
Capital account (net)	591	443	736
Direct investment abroad . . .	−12,077	−7,816	−15,515
Direct investment from abroad .	4,621	15,570	6,851
Portfolio investment assets . .	−10,306	−16,651	−7,969
Portfolio investment liabilities .	21,041	18,186	49,285
Financial derivatives assets . .	161	3,048	7,688
Financial derivatives liabilities .	453	−2,848	−7,282
Other investment assets . . .	891	−3,511	−6,219
Other investment liabilities . .	4,280	11,055	9,084
Net errors and omissions . . .	−246	−629	595
Overall balance	1,096	122	6,877

Source: IMF, *International Financial Statistics*.

External Trade

PRINCIPAL COMMODITIES
(distribution by SITC, $A million, year ending 30 June)

Imports f.o.b.	2001/02	2002/03
Food and live animals	4,613	5,107
Mineral fuels, lubricants, etc.	9,030	10,598
Petroleum and bituminous oils, crude	6,785	7,812
Chemicals and related products	14,635	15,025
Medicaments (incl. veterinary)	4,002	4,241
Basic manufactures	14,819	16,074
Machinery and transport equipment	53,654	60,640
Automatic data-processing machines and units thereof, magnetic, optical readers; data transcribers and processors	5,028	4,871
Miscellaneous telecommunications equipment and parts, and accessories of radio, television, etc.	4,507	4,239
Motor vehicles principally designed for transport of persons (excl. public transport, incl. racing cars)	8,955	10,283
Aircraft and associated equipment; spacecraft (incl. satellites and launch vehicles) and parts thereof	3,060	5,481
Miscellaneous manufactured articles	17,416	18,716
Total (incl. others)	119,649	133,131

Exports f.o.b.	2001/02	2002/03
Food and live animals	22,380	18,374
Meat of bovine animals, fresh, chilled or frozen	4,333	3,906
Wheat (incl. spelt) and meslin, unmilled	4,527	3,036
Crude materials (inedible) except fuels	22,448	21,429
Iron ore and concentrates	5,160	5,328
Aluminium ores and concentrates (incl. alumina)*		
Mineral fuels, lubricants, etc.	25,130	23,807
Coal, not agglomerated	13,403	11,946
Petroleum and bituminous oils, crude	5,963	5,881
Chemicals and related products	5,293	5,099
Basic manufactures	13,572	12,597
Machinery and transport equipment	14,160	13,528
Miscellaneous manufactured articles	4,483	4,413
Aluminium	4,412	4,059
Non-monetary gold (excl. gold ores and concentrates)	5,129	5,584
Total (incl. others)	121,108	115,442

* Excludes commodities subject to a confidentiality restriction. Such commodities are included in the total.

PRINCIPAL TRADING PARTNERS
($A million, year ending 30 June)

Imports f.o.b.	2000/01	2001/02	2002/03
Canada	1,869	1,607	1,755
China, People's Republic	9,881	11,275	13,792
France	2,478	2,691	3,781
Germany	6,172	6,732	7,953
Hong Kong	1,362	1,410	1,234
Indonesia	3,330	4,010	4,600
Ireland	1,140	1,469	1,607
Italy	3,257	3,410	4,149
Japan	15,371	15,461	16,335
Korea, Republic	4,710	4,722	4,753
Malaysia	4,177	3,857	4,262
New Zealand	4,565	4,740	5,019
Papua New Guinea	1,457	1,124	1,502
Saudi Arabia	1,634	1,026	1,284
Singapore	3,898	3,972	4,370
Sweden	1,624	1,625	1,810
Switzerland	1,171	1,302	1,230
Taiwan	3,327	3,312	3,401
Thailand	2,780	2,886	3,469
United Kingdom	6,321	6,219	5,770
USA	22,351	21,488	22,496
Viet Nam	2,431	1,855	2,503
Total (incl. others)	118,317	119,649	133,131

Exports f.o.b.	2000/01	2001/02	2002/03
Canada	1,768	1,900	1,816
China, People's Republic	6,846	7,816	8,793
France	1,079	1,343	1,171
Germany	1,490	1,349	1,579
Hong Kong	3,904	3,996	3,215
India	2,086	2,524	2,577
Indonesia	3,119	3,194	2,908
Italy	2,100	2,165	1,861
Japan	23,479	22,796	21,738
Korea, Republic	9,209	9,818	9,116
Malaysia	2,506	2,519	2,147
Netherlands	1,738	1,522	1,364
New Zealand	6,872	7,669	8,120
Philippines	1,501	1,252	1,091
Saudi Arabia	2,196	2,598	1,990
Singapore	6,009	4,936	4,655
South Africa	1,301	1,341	1,313
Taiwan	5,894	4,828	4,314
Thailand	2,222	2,291	2,479
United Kingdom	4,653	5,199	7,236
USA	11,654	12,008	10,369
Total (incl. others)	119,539	121,108	114,442

Transport

RAILWAYS
(traffic)*

	1997/98	1998/99	1999/2000
Passengers carried (million) . .	587.7	595.2	629.2
Freight carried (millon metric tons)	487.5	492.0	508.0
Freight ton-km ('000 million) . .	125.2	127.4	134.2

* Traffic on government railways only.

Freight ton-km ('000 million, government railways only): 139.7 in 2000/01; 134.1 in 2001/02 (Source: UN, *Statistical Yearbook*).

ROAD TRAFFIC
('000 vehicles registered at 31 March)

	2002	2003	2004
Passenger vehicles	10,137	10,366	10,629
Light commercial vehicles . . .	1,820	1,880	1,952
Trucks	425	470*	484*
Buses	70	70	71
Motorcycles	371	377	396

* Including camper vans, previously classified as passenger vehicles.

SHIPPING

Merchant Fleet
(registered at 31 December)

	2001	2002	2003
Number of vessels	622	624	643
Total displacement ('000 grt) . .	1,887.8	1,861.3	1,905.8

Source: Lloyd's Register-Fairplay, *World Fleet Statistics*.

International Sea-borne Traffic
('000 metric tons, year ending 30 June)

	2000/01	2001/02	2002/03
Goods loaded	496,204	506,317	540,570
Goods unloaded	54,579	58,041	62,459

CIVIL AVIATION
(traffic)*

	1997	1998	1999
International services:			
Passenger arrivals . . .	7,090,979	7,153,514	7,540,535
Passenger departures . .	7,010,931	7,084,655	7,442,226
Freight carried (metric tons) .	649,371	631,908	680,458
Mail carried (metric tons) . .	21,975	23,437	25,316
Domestic services†:			
Passengers carried . . .	23,375,317	23,574,788	24,375,906
Passenger-km ('000) . . .	26,357,069	26,774,140	27,842,795
Freight and mail carried (metric tons)	190,680	192,770	192,326

* Includes Christmas Island and Norfolk Island.
† Year ending 30 June.

2001/02 ('000, year ending 30 June): International passenger arrivals 8,254.1; International passenger departures 8,194.9.

Tourism

VISITOR ARRIVALS BY COUNTRY OF ORIGIN*

	2000	2001	2002
China, People's Republic . . .	120,259	157,955	190,016
Germany	143,273	147,613	134,806
Hong Kong	154,079	154,149	150,943
Indonesia	98,106	97,877	89,432
Japan	720,973	673,577	715,458
Korea, Republic	157,375	175,587	189,729
Malaysia	152,074	149,415	158,990
New Zealand	817,024	814,874	790,068
Singapore	285,729	296,007	286,852
Taiwan	134,349	110,070	97,429
United Kingdom	579,751	615,634	640,782
USA	488,105	446,443	434,470
Total (incl. others)	4,931,336	4,855,669	4,841,152

* Visitors intending to stay for less than one year.

Receipts from tourism ($A million): 17,000 in 1999; 19,800 in 2000; 15,344 in 2001 (estimate).

Source: Australian Tourist Commission, Sydney.

Communications Media

	2001	2002	2003
Television receivers ('000 in use) .	14,168	n.a.	n.a.
Telephones ('000 main lines in use)	10,485	10,905	10,815
Mobile cellular telephones ('000 subscribers)	11,132	12,575	14,347
Personal computers ('000 in use) .	10,000	11,100	n.a.
Internet users ('000)	7,700	9,472	11,300

Source: International Telecommunication Union.

Radio receivers ('000 in use, 1997): 25,500 (Source: UNESCO, *Statistical Yearbook*).

Facsimile machines ('000 in use, 1997): 900 (Source: UN, *Statistical Yearbook*).

Book production (1994): 10,835 titles (Source: UNESCO, *Statistical Yearbook*).

Newspapers (1996): 65 dailies (estimated combined circulation 5,370,000); 98 non-dailies (circulation 383,000) (Source: UNESCO, *Statistical Yearbook*).

Education

(August 2003)

	Institu- tions	Teaching staff*	Students
Government schools	6,930	154,872	
Non-government schools . . .	2,677	74,704	} 3,318,620†
Higher educational institutions‡	48§	78,189	830,058

* Full-time teaching staff and full-time equivalent of part-time teaching staff.
† Primary and secondary students. In 2002 the total was comprised of 1,932,600 primary and 1,382,300 secondary students.
‡ March 2004 (Source: Department of Education, Science and Training).
§ Public institutions only.

Directory

The Constitution

The Federal Constitution was adopted on 9 July 1900 and came into force on 1 January 1901. Its main provisions are summarized below:

PARLIAMENT

The legislative power of the Commonwealth of Australia is vested in a Federal Parliament, consisting of HM the Queen (represented by the Governor-General), a Senate and a House of Representatives. The Governor-General may appoint such times for holding the sessions of the Parliament as he or she thinks fit, and may also from time to time, by proclamation or otherwise, prorogue the Parliament, and may in like manner dissolve the House of Representatives. By convention, these powers are exercised on the advice of the Prime Minister. After any general election Parliament must be summoned to meet not later than 30 days after the day appointed for the return of the writs.

AUSTRALIA *Directory*

THE SENATE

The Senate is composed of 12 senators from each state, two senators representing the Australian Capital Territory and two representing the Northern Territory. The senators are directly chosen by the people of the state or territory, voting in each case as one electorate, and are elected by proportional representation. Senators representing a state have a six-year term and retire by rotation, one-half from each state on 30 June of each third year. The term of a senator representing a territory is limited to three years. In the case of a state, if a senator vacates his or her seat before the expiration of the term of service, the houses of parliament of the state for which the senator was chosen shall, in joint session, choose a person to hold the place until the expiration of the term or until the election of a successor. If the state parliament is not in session, the Governor of the state, acting on the advice of the state's executive council, may appoint a senator to hold office until parliament reassembles, or until a new senator is elected.

The Senate may proceed to the dispatch of business notwithstanding the failure of any state to provide for its representation in the Senate.

THE HOUSE OF REPRESENTATIVES

In accordance with the Australian Constitution, the total number of members of the House of Representatives must be as nearly as practicable double that of the Senate. The number in each state is in proportion to population, but under the Constitution must be at least five. The House of Representatives is composed of 150 members, including two members for the Australian Capital Territory and two members for the Northern Territory.

Members are elected by universal adult suffrage and voting is compulsory. Only Australian citizens are eligible to vote in Australian elections. British subjects, if they are not Australian citizens or already on the rolls, have to take out Australian citizenship before thay can enrol and before they can vote.

Members are chosen by the electors of their respective electorates by the preferential voting system.

The duration of the Parliament is limited to three years.

To be nominated for election to the House of Representatives, a candidate must be 18 years of age or over, an Australian citizen, and entitled to vote at the election or qualified to become an elector.

THE EXECUTIVE GOVERNMENT

The executive power of the Federal Government is vested in the Queen, and is exercisable by the Governor-General, advised by an Executive Council of Ministers of State, known as the Federal Executive Council. These ministers are, or must become within three months, members of the Federal Parliament.

The Australian Constitution is construed as subject to the principles of responsible government and the Governor-General acts on the advice of the ministers in relation to most matters.

THE JUDICIAL POWER

See Judicial System, below.

THE STATES

The Australian Constitution safeguards the Constitution of each state by providing that it shall continue as at the establishment of the Commonwealth, except as altered in accordance with its own provisions. The legislative power of the Federal Parliament is limited in the main to those matters that are listed in section 51 of the Constitution, while the states possess, as well as concurrent powers in those matters, residual legislative powers enabling them to legislate in any way for 'the peace, order and good Government' of their respective territories. When a state law is inconsistent with a law of the Commonwealth, the latter prevails, and the former is invalid to the extent of the inconsistency.

The states may not, without the consent of the Commonwealth, raise or maintain naval or military forces, or impose taxes on any property belonging to the Commonwealth of Australia, nor may the Commonwealth tax state property. The states may not coin money.

The Federal Parliament may not enact any law for establishing any religion or for prohibiting the exercise of any religion, and no religious test may be imposed as a qualification for any office under the Commonwealth.

The Commonwealth of Australia is charged with protecting every state against invasion, and, on the application of a state executive government, against domestic violence.

Provision is made under the Constitution for the admission of new states and for the establishment of new states within the Commonwealth of Australia.

ALTERATION OF THE CONSTITUTION

Proposed laws for the amendment of the Constitution must be passed by an absolute majority in both Houses of the Federal Parliament, and not less than two or more than six months after its passage through both Houses the proposed law must be submitted in each state to the qualified electors.

In the event of one House twice refusing to pass a proposed amendment that has already received an absolute majority in the other House, the Governor-General may, notwithstanding such refusal, submit the proposed amendment to the electors. By convention, the Governor-General acts on the advice of the Prime Minister. If in a majority of the states a majority of the electors voting approve the proposed law and if a majority of all the electors voting also approve, it shall be presented to the Governor-General for Royal Assent.

No alteration diminishing the proportionate representation of any state in either House of the Federal Parliament, or the minimum number of representatives of a state in the House of Representatives, or increasing, diminishing or altering the limits of the state, or in any way affecting the provisions of the Constitution in relation thereto, shall become law unless the majority of the electors voting in that state approve the proposed law.

STATES AND TERRITORIES

New South Wales

The state's executive power is vested in the Governor, appointed by the Crown, who is assisted by an Executive Council composed of cabinet ministers.

The state's legislative power is vested in a bicameral Parliament, composed of the Legislative Council and the Legislative Assembly. The Legislative Council consists of 42 members directly elected for the duration of two parliaments (i.e. eight years), 21 members retiring every four years. The Legislative Assembly consists of 93 members and sits for four years.

Victoria

The state's legislative power is vested in a bicameral Parliament: the Upper House, or Legislative Council, of 44 members, elected for two terms of the Legislative Assembly; and the Lower House, or Legislative Assembly, of 88 members, elected for a minimum of three and maximum of four years. One-half of the members of the Council retires every three–four years.

In the exercise of the executive power the Governor is assisted by a cabinet of responsible ministers. Not more than six members of the Council and not more than 17 members of the Assembly may occupy salaried office at any one time.

The state has 88 electoral districts, each returning one member, and 22 electoral provinces, each returning two Council members.

Queensland

The state's executive power is vested in the Governor, appointed by the Crown, who is assisted by an Executive Council composed of Ministers. The state's legislative power is vested in the Parliament comprising the Legislative Assembly (composed of 89 members who are elected at least every three years to represent 89 electoral districts) and the Governor, who assents to bills passed by the Assembly. The state's Constitution anticipates that Ministers are also members of the Legislative Assembly and provides that up to 18 members of the Assembly can be appointed Ministers.

South Australia

The state's Constitution vests the legislative power in a Parliament elected by the people and consisting of a Legislative Council and a House of Assembly. The Council is composed of 22 members, one-half of whom retire every three years. Their places are filled by new members elected under a system of proportional representation, with the whole state as a single electorate. The executive has no authority to dissolve this body, except in circumstances warranting a double dissolution.

The 47 members of the House of Assembly are elected for four years from 45 electoral districts.

The executive power is vested in a Governor, appointed by the Crown, and an Executive Council consisting of 10 responsible ministers.

Western Australia

The state's administration is vested in the Governor, a Legislative Council and a Legislative Assembly.

The Legislative Council consists of 34 members, two of the six electoral regions returning seven members on a proportional representation basis, and four regions returning five members. Election is for a term of four years.

The Legislative Assembly consists of 57 members, elected for four years, each representing one electorate.

Tasmania

The state's executive authority is vested in a Governor, appointed by the Crown, who acts upon the advice of his premier and ministers, who are elected members of either the Legislative Council or the

House of Assembly.

Tasmanian House of Assembly.

House of Assembly. The Council consists of 15 members who sit for six years, retiring in rotation. The House of Assembly has 25 members elected for four years.

Northern Territory

On 1 July 1978 the Northern Territory was established as a body politic with executive authority for specified functions of government. Most functions of the Federal Government were transferred to the Territory Government in 1978 and 1979, major exceptions being Aboriginal affairs and uranium mining.

The Territory Parliament consists of a single house, the Legislative Assembly, with 25 members. The first Parliament stayed in office for three years. As from the election held in August 1980, members are elected for a term of four years.

The office of Administrator continues. The Northern Territory (Self-Government) Act provides for the appointment of an Administrator by the Governor-General charged with the duty of administering the Territory. In respect of matters transferred to the Territory Government, the Administrator acts with the advice of the Territory Executive Council; in respect of matters retained by the Commonwealth, the Administrator acts on Commonwealth advice.

Australian Capital Territory

On 29 November 1988 the Australian Capital Territory (ACT) was established as a body politic. The ACT Government has executive authority for specified functions, although a number of these were to be retained by the Federal Government for a brief period during which transfer arrangements were to be finalized.

The ACT Parliament consists of a single house, the Legislative Assembly, with 17 members. The first election was held in March 1989. Members are elected for a term of three years.

The Federal Government retains control of some of the land in the ACT for the purpose of maintaining the Seat of Government and the national capital plan.

Jervis Bay Territory

Following the attainment of self-government by the ACT (see above), the Jervis Bay Territory, which had formed part of the ACT since 1915, remained a separate Commonwealth Territory, administered by the then Department of the Arts, Sport, the Environment and Territories. The area is governed in accordance with the Jervis Bay Territory Administration Ordinance, issued by the Governor-General on 17 December 1990.

The Government

Head of State: HM Queen ELIZABETH II (succeeded to the throne 6 February 1952).

Governor-General: Maj.-Gen. MICHAEL JEFFERY (assumed office 11 August 2003).

THE MINISTRY
(April 2005)

Cabinet Ministers

Prime Minister: JOHN HOWARD.

Deputy Prime Minister and Minister for Transport and Regional Services: JOHN ANDERSON.

Minister for Foreign Affairs: ALEXANDER DOWNER.

Treasurer: PETER COSTELLO.

Minister for Trade: MARK VAILE.

Minister for Defence and Leader of the Government in the Senate: Senator ROBERT HILL.

Minister for Communications, Information Technology and the Arts: Senator HELEN COONAN.

Minister for Employment and Workplace Relations: KEVIN ANDREWS.

Minister for Education, Science and Training: Dr BRENDAN NELSON.

Minister for Health and Ageing and Leader of the House: TONY ABBOTT.

Minister for Industry, Tourism and Resources: IAN MACFARLANE.

Minister for the Environment and Heritage: Senator IAN CAMPBELL.

Minister for Finance and Administration, and Deputy Leader of the Government in the Senate: Senator NICHOLAS MINCHIN.

Minister for Family and Community Services, and Minister Assisting the Prime Minister for the Status of Women: KAY PATTERSON.

Minister for Agriculture, Fisheries and Forestry: WARREN TRUSS.

Minister for Immigration and Multicultural and Indigenous Affairs and Minister assisting the Prime Minister for Reconciliation: Senator AMANDA VANSTONE.

Attorney-General: PHILIP RUDDOCK.

Other Ministers

Minister for Local Government, Territories and Roads: JIM LLOYD.

Minister for Revenue and Assistant Treasurer: MAL BROUGH.

Minister for Human Services: JOE HOCKEY.

Minister for Fisheries, Forestry and Conservation: Senator IAN MACDONALD.

Minister for Citizenship and Multicultural Affairs and Deputy Leader of the House: PETER McGAURAN.

Minister for Small Business and Tourism: FRAN BAILEY.

Minister for Veterans' Affairs: DE-ANNE KELLY.

Minister for Ageing: JULIE BISHOP.

Special Minister of State: Senator ERIC ABETZ.

Minister for Justice and Customs: Senator CHRISTOPHER ELLISON.

Minister for the Arts and Sport: Senator ROD KEMP.

Minister for Workplace Participation: PETER DUTTON.

Minister for Vocational and Technical Education: GARY HARDGRAVE.

DEPARTMENTS

Department of the Prime Minister and Cabinet: 3–5 National Circuit, Barton, ACT 2600; tel. (2) 6271-5111; fax (2) 6271-5414; internet www.dpmc.gov.au.

Department of Agriculture, Fisheries and Forestry: Edmund Barton Bldg, Broughton St, Barton, GPOB 858, Canberra, ACT 2601; tel. (2) 6272-3933; fax (2) 6272-3008; internet www.affa.gov.au.

Attorney-General's Department: Robert Garran Offices, Barton, ACT 2600; tel. (2) 6250-6666; fax (2) 6250-5900; internet www.law.gov.au.

Department of Communications, Information Technology and the Arts: GPOB 2154, Canberra, ACT 2601; tel. (2) 6271-1000; fax (2) 6271-1901; internet www.dcita.gov.au.

Department of Defence: Russell Offices, Russell Drive, Campbell, Canberra, ACT 2600; tel. (2) 6265-9111; e-mail webmaster@cbr.defence.gov.au; internet www.defence.gov.au.

Department of Education, Science and Training: GPOB 9880, Canberra, ACT 2601; tel. (2) 6240-8111; fax (2) 6240-8571; e-mail library@dest.gov.au; internet www.dest.gov.au.

Department of Employment and Workplace Relations: GPOB 9879, Canberra, ACT 2601; tel. (2) 6121-6000; fax (2) 6121-7542; e-mail webmaster@dewr.gov.au; internet www.dewr.gov.au.

Department of the Environment and Heritage: GPOB 787, Canberra, ACT 2601; tel. (2) 6274-1111; fax (2) 6274-1123; internet www.ea.gov.au.

Department of Family and Community Services: Library and Information Research Service, Box 7788, Canberra Mail Centre, ACT 2610; tel. (2) 6244-6385; fax (2) 6244-7919; e-mail library.research@facs.gov.au; internet www.facs.gov.au.

Department of Finance and Administration: John Gorton Bldg, King Edward Tce, Parkes, ACT 2600; tel. (2) 6263-2222; fax (2) 6273-3021; internet www.dofa.gov.au.

Department of Foreign Affairs and Trade: R. G. Casey Bldg, John McEwan Cres., Barton, ACT 0221; tel. (2) 6261-1111; fax (2) 6261-3111; internet www.dfat.gov.au.

Department of Health and Ageing: GPOB 9848, Canberra, ACT 2601; tel. (2) 6289-1555; fax (2) 6281-6946; internet www.health.gov.au.

Department of Immigration and Multicultural and Indigenous Affairs: POB 25, Chan St, Belconnen, ACT 2616; tel. (2) 6264-1111; fax (2) 6264-2670; internet www.immi.gov.au.

Department of Industry, Tourism and Resources: GPOB 9839, Canberra, ACT 2601; tel. (2) 6213-6000; fax (2) 6213-7000; e-mail customerrelation@industry.gov.au; internet www.industry.gov.au.

Department of Transport and Regional Services: GPOB 594, Canberra, ACT 2601; tel. (2) 6274-7111; fax (2) 6257-2505; e-mail publicaffairs@dotrs.gov.au; internet www.dotrs.gov.au.

Department of the Treasury: Langton Crescent, Parkes, ACT 2600; tel. (2) 6263-2111; fax (2) 6273-2614; internet www.treasury.gov.au.

Department of Veterans' Affairs: POB 21, Woden, ACT 2606; tel. (2) 6289-1111; fax (2) 6289-6025; internet www.dva.gov.au.

Legislature

FEDERAL PARLIAMENT

Senate

President: PAUL CALVERT.

Election, 9 October 2004

Party	Seats*
Liberal-National Coalition	39
Australian Labor Party	28
Australian Democrats Party	4
Greens	4
Family First	1
Total	76

* The election was for 36 of the 72 seats held by state senators and for all four senators representing the Northern Territory and the Australian Capital Territory (See The Constitution).

House of Representatives

Speaker: DAVID HAWKER.

Election, 9 October 2004

Party	Seats
Liberal Party of Australia	74
Australian Labor Party	60
National Party of Australia	12
Independents	3
Other	1
Total	150

State and Territory Governments

(April 2005)

NEW SOUTH WALES

Governor: MARIE BASHIR, Level 3, Chief Secretary's Bldg, 121 Macquarie St, Sydney, NSW 2000; tel. (2) 9242-4200; fax (2) 9242-4266; internet www.nsw.gov.au.

Premier: ROBERT (BOB) J. CARR (Labor), Level 40, Governor Macquarie Tower, 1 Farrer Place, Sydney, NSW 2000; tel. (2) 9228-5239; fax (2) 9228-3935; e-mail bob.carr@nsw.gov.au.

VICTORIA

Governor: JOHN LANDY, Government House, Melbourne, Vic 3004; tel. (3) 9655-4211; fax (3) 9654-8430; internet www.governor.vic.gov.au.

Premier: STEPHEN P. BRACKS (Labor), 1 Treasury Place, Vic 3000; internet www.premier.vic.gov.au.

QUEENSLAND

Governor: QUENTIN BRYCE, Government House, Brisbane, Qld 4001; tel. (7) 3858-5700; fax (7) 3858-5701; e-mail govhouse@govhouse.qld.gov.au; internet www.govhouse.qld.gov.au.

Premier: PETER D. BEATTIE (Labor), Executive Bldg, 100 George St, Brisbane, Qld 4002; tel. (7) 3224-2111; fax (7) 3229-2990; internet www.premiers.qld.gov.au.

SOUTH AUSTRALIA

Governor: MARJORIE JACKSON-NELSON, Government House, North Terrace, Adelaide, SA 5000; tel. (8) 8203-9800; fax (8) 8203-9899; e-mail govthsesa@saugov.sa.gov.au; internet www.sa.gov.au.

Premier: MICHAEL (MIKE) RANN (Labor), 200 Victoria Square, Adelaide, SA 5001; tel. and fax (8) 8463-3166; e-mail premier@saugov.sa.gov.au; internet www.ministers.sa.gov.au.

WESTERN AUSTRALIA

Governor: Lt-Gen. JOHN MURRAY SANDERSON, Government House, Perth, WA 6000; tel. (8) 9429-9199; fax (8) 9325-4476; e-mail enquiries@govhouse.wa.gov.au; internet www.wa.gov.au.

Premier: GEOFFREY GALLOP (Labor), 24th Floor, 197 St George's Terrace, Perth, WA 6000; tel. (8) 9222-9888; fax (8) 9322-1213; e-mail wa-government@mpc.wa.gov.au; internet www.premier.wa.gov.au.

TASMANIA

Governor: WILLIAM JOHN ELLIS COX, Government House, Hobart, Tas 7000; tel. (3) 6234-2611; fax (3) 6234-2556; internet www.tas.gov.au.

Premier: PAUL LENNON (Labor), GPOB 123B, Hobart, Tas 7001; tel. (3) 6233-3464; fax (3) 6234-1572; e-mail premier@dpac.tas.gov.au; internet www.premier.tas.gov.au.

NORTHERN TERRITORY

Administrator: TED EGAN, GPOB 497, Darwin, NT 0801; tel. (8) 8999-7103; fax (8) 8981-5521; e-mail governmenthouse.darwin@nt.gov.au; internet www.nt.gov.au/administrator.

Chief Minister: CLARE MARTIN (Labor), GPOB 3146, Darwin, NT 0801; tel. (8) 8901-4000; fax (8) 8901-4099; e-mail chiefminister.nt@nt.gov.au; internet www.nt.gov.au/ministers.

AUSTRALIAN CAPITAL TERRITORY

Chief Minister: JONATHAN STANHOPE (Labor), Legislative Assembly Bldg, Civic Square, London Circuit, Canberra, ACT 2601; tel. (2) 6205-0104; fax (2) 6205-0399; e-mail canberraconnect@.act.gov.au; internet www.act.gov.au.

Political Organizations

Australians for Constitutional Monarchy (ACM): GPOB 9841, Sydney, NSW 2001; tel. (2) 9231-2200; fax (2) 9231-2359; e-mail acmhq@norepublic.com.au; internet www.norepublic.com.au; f. 1992; also known as No Republic; Exec. Dir KERRY JONES.

Australian Democrats Party: Kingston, POB 1059, Canberra, ACT 2602; tel. (2) 6273-1059; e-mail inquiries@democrats.org.au; internet www.democrats.org.au; f. 1977; comprises the fmr Liberal Movement and the Australia Party; Fed. Parl. Leader Senator LYN ALLISON; Nat. Pres. NINA BURRIDGE.

Australian Greens: GPOB 1108, Canberra, ACT 2601; e-mail frontdesk@greens.org.au; internet www.greens.org.au; f. 1992; Leader Senator BOB BROWN.

Australian Labor Party (ALP): Centenary House, 19 National Circuit, Barton, ACT 2600; tel. (2) 6120-0800; fax (2) 6120-0801; e-mail info@alp.com; internet www.alp.com; f. 1891; advocates social democracy; trade unions form part of its structure; Fed. Parl. Leader KIM BEAZLEY; Nat. Pres. CARMEN LAWRENCE; Nat. Sec. TIM GARTRELL.

Australian Republican Movement (ARM): POB A870, Sydney South, NSW 1235; tel. (2) 9267-8022; fax (2) 9267-8155; e-mail republic@republic.org.au; internet www.republic.org.au; Chair. Prof. JOHN WARHURST; Nat. Dir ALLISON HENRY.

Communist Party of Australia: 74 Buckingham St, Surry Hills, NSW 2010; tel. (2) 9699-8844; fax (2) 9699-9833; e-mail cpa@cpa.org.au; internet www.cpa.org.au; f. 1971; fmrly Socialist Party; advocates public ownership of the means of production, working-class political power; Pres. Dr H. MIDDLETON; Gen. Sec. P. SYMON.

Family First: c/o The Senate, Canberra; supports family values.

Liberal Party of Australia: Federal Secretariat, cnr Blackall and Macquarie Sts, Barton, ACT 2600; tel. (2) 6273-2564; fax (2) 6273-1534; e-mail admin2@liberal.org.au; internet www.liberal.org.au; f. 1944; advocates private enterprise, social justice, individual liberty and initiative; committed to national development, prosperity and security; Fed. Dir BRIAN LOUGHNANE; Fed. Parl. Leader JOHN HOWARD.

National Party of Australia: John McEwen House, National Circuit, Barton, ACT 2600; tel. (2) 6273-3822; fax (2) 6273-1745; e-mail federal.nationals@nationals.org.au; internet www.nationals.org.au; f. 1916 as the Country Party of Australia; adopted present name in 1982; advocates balanced national development based on free enterprise, with special emphasis on the needs of people outside the major metropolitan areas; Fed. Pres. HELEN DICKIE; Fed. Parl. Leader JOHN ANDERSON; Fed. Dir ANDREW HALL.

One Nation: GPOB 812, Ipswich, Qld 4304; e-mail pauline@onenation.com.au; internet www.onenation.com.au; f. 1997; opposes globalization, high immigration and special funding for Aboriginal people, advocates public ownership of major services; Pres. (vacant); Vice-Pres. JOHN FISHER.

Your Voice: POB 1245, Collingwood, Vic 3066; e-mail vote1richardfrankland@yourvoice.org.au; internet www.yourvoice.org.au; f. 2004; represents the interests of Aboriginal people; Co-founder RICHARD FRANKLAND.

Diplomatic Representation

EMBASSIES AND HIGH COMMISSIONS IN AUSTRALIA

Afghanistan: POB 155, Deakin West, ACT 2600; tel. (2) 6282-7311; fax (2) 6282-7322; e-mail ambassador@afghanembassy.net; internet www.afghanembassy.net; Ambassador MAHMOUD SAIKAL.

Algeria: 9 Terrigal Crescent, O'Malley, ACT 2606; Ambassador KAMERZAMANE BELRAMOUL.

Argentina: POB 4835, Kingston, ACT 2604; tel. (2) 6273-9111; fax (2) 6273-0500; e-mail info@argentina.org.au; internet www.argentina.org.au; Ambassador NÉSTOR E. STANCANELLI.

Austria: POB 3375, Manuka, ACT 2603; tel. (2) 6295-1533; fax (2) 6239-6751; e-mail austria@bigpond.net.au; internet www.austriaemb.org.au/; Ambassador Dr HANS DEMEL.

Bangladesh: POB 5, Red Hill, ACT 2603; tel. (2) 6290-0511; fax (2) 6290-0544; e-mail bdoot.canberra@cyberone.com.au; internet www.bangladoot-canberra.org; High Commissioner ASHRAF-UD-DOULA.

Belgium: 19 Arkana St, Yarralumla, ACT 2600; tel. (2) 6273-2501; fax (2) 6273-3392; e-mail canberra@diplobel.org; Ambassador LUK DARRAS.

Bosnia and Herzegovina: 5 Beale Crescent, Deakin, ACT 2600; tel. (2) 6232-4646; fax (2) 6232-5554; e-mail embaucbr@webone.com.au; internet www.bosnia.webone.com.au; Ambassador Dr ZDRAVKO TODOROVIĆ.

Botswana: 52 Culgoa Circuit, O'Malley, ACT 2606; tel. (2) 6290-7500; fax (2) 6286-2566; High Commissioner MOLOSIWA SELEPENG.

Brazil: GPOB 1540, Canberra, ACT 2601; tel. (2) 6273-2372; fax (2) 6273-2375; e-mail brazil@connect.net.au; internet brazil.org.au; Ambassador FREDERICO CEZAR DE ARAUJO.

Brunei: 10 Beale Crescent, Deakin, ACT 2603; tel. (2) 6285-4500; fax (2) 6285-4545; High Commissioner Pengiran Datin Hajah MASRAINAH Pengiran AHMAD.

Bulgaria: 33 Culgoa Circuit, O'Malley, ACT 2606; tel. (2) 6286-9711; fax (2) 6286-9600; e-mail bulgem@bigpond.net.au; Ambassador Dr LUBOMIR TODOROV.

Cambodia: 5 Canterbury Crescent, Deakin, ACT 2600; tel. (2) 6273-1259; fax (2) 6273-1053; e-mail cambodianembassy@ozemail.net.au; internet www.embassyofcambodia.org.nz/au.htm; Ambassador MEAS KIM HENG.

Canada: Commonwealth Ave, Canberra, ACT 2600; tel. (2) 6270-4000; fax (2) 6273-3285; e-mail cnbra@international.gc.ca; internet www.canada.org.au; High Commissioner GASTON BARBAN (acting).

Chile: POB 69, Red Hill, ACT 2603; tel. (2) 6286-2430; fax (2) 6286-1289; e-mail chilemb@embachile-australia.com; internet www.embachile-australia.com; Ambassador FERNANDO SCHMIDT.

China, People's Republic: 15 Coronation Drive, Yarralumla, ACT 2600; tel. (2) 6273-4780; fax (2) 6273-4878; Ambassador FU YING.

Colombia: Colombia House, Level 2, 101 Northbourne Ave, Turner, ACT 2612; tel. (2) 6257-2027; fax (2) 6257-1448; e-mail emaustralia@iprimus.com.au; internet www.embacol.org.au; Ambassador FRANCISCO J. SIERRA ARANGO.

Croatia: 14 Jindalee Crescent, O'Malley, ACT 2606; tel. (2) 6286-6988; fax (2) 6286-3544; e-mail croemb@bigpond.net.au; Ambassador Dr MLADEN IBLER.

Cyprus: 30 Beale Crescent, Deakin, ACT 2600; tel. (2) 6281-0832; fax (2) 6281-0860; e-mail info@cyprus.org.au; internet www.cyprus.org.au; High Commissioner ACHILLEAS ANTONIADES.

Czech Republic: 8 Culgoa Circuit, O'Malley, ACT 2606; tel. (2) 6290-1386; fax (2) 6290-0006; e-mail canberra@embassy.mzv.cz; internet www.mzv.cz/canberra; Ambassador KAREL PAZOUREK.

Ecuador: 6 Pindari Crescent, O'Malley, ACT 2606; tel. (2) 6286-4021; fax (2) 6286-1231; e-mail embecu@bigpond.net.au; Chargé d'affaires Dr CUTY GARCÍA.

Egypt: 1 Darwin Ave, Yarralumla, ACT 2600; tel. (2) 6273-4437; fax (2) 6273-4279; Ambassador MOHAMED M. TAWFIK.

Eritrea: 16 Bulwarra Close, O'Malley, ACT 2606; tel. (2) 6290-1991; fax (2) 6286-8902; e-mail embassy_of_eritrea@bigpond.com; Ambassador ASMEROM ABRAHA MA'ASHIO.

Fiji: POB 159, Deakin West, ACT 2600; tel. (2) 6260-5115; fax (2) 6260-5105; e-mail fhc@cyberone.com.au; High Commissioner JIOJI KONROTE.

Finland: 12 Darwin Ave, Yarralumla, ACT 2600; tel. (2) 6273-3800; fax (2) 6273-3603; e-mail finland@austarmetro.com.au; internet www.finland.org.au; Ambassador ANNELI PUURA-MÄRKÄLÄ.

France: 6 Perth Ave, Yarralumla, ACT 2600; tel. (2) 6216-0100; fax (2) 6216-0127; e-mail ambassade@ambafrance-au.org; internet www.ambafrance-au.org; Ambassador PATRICK HÉNAULT.

Germany: 119 Empire Circuit, Yarralumla, ACT 2600; tel. (2) 6270-1911; fax (2) 6270-1951; e-mail info@germanembassy.org.au; internet www.germanembassy-canberra.com; Ambassador Dr KLAUS-PETER KLAIBER.

Greece: 9 Turrana St, Yarralumla, ACT 2600; tel. (2) 6273-3011; fax (2) 6273-2620; e-mail greekemb@greekembassy-au.org; Ambassador FOTIOS-JEAN XYDAS.

Holy See: POB 3633, Manuka, ACT 2603 (Apostolic Nunciature); tel. (2) 6295-3876; Apostolic Nuncio Most Rev. AMBROSE DE PAOLI (Titular Archbishop of Lares).

Hungary: 17 Beale Crescent, Deakin, ACT 2600; tel. (2) 6282-3226; fax (2) 6285-3012; e-mail hungcbr@ozemail.com.au; internet www.hunconsydney.com; Ambassador LAJOS FODOR.

India: 3–5 Moonah Place, Yarralumla, ACT 2600; tel. (2) 6273-3999; fax (2) 6273-1308; e-mail hciisi@bigpond.com.au; internet www.hcindia-au.org; High Commissioner P. P. SHUKLA.

Indonesia: 8 Darwin Ave, Yarralumla, ACT 2600; tel. (2) 6273-8600; fax (2) 6250-6017; e-mail embindo@cyberone.com.au; Ambassador IMRON COTAN.

Iran: POB 705, Mawson, ACT 2607; tel. (2) 6290-2427; fax (2) 6290-2431; e-mail general@embassyiran.org.au; internet www.embassyiran.org.au; Ambassador Dr HAMID ABOUTALEBI.

Iraq: 48 Culgoa Circuit, O'Malley, ACT 2606; tel. (2) 6286-9952; e-mail cnbemb@iraqmofa.net; Ambassador GHANIM T. AL-SHIBLI.

Ireland: 20 Arkana St, Yarralumla, ACT 2600; tel. (2) 6273-3022; fax (2) 6273-3741; e-mail irishemb@cyberone.com.au; Ambassador DECLAN M. KELLY.

Israel: 6 Turrana St, Yarralumla, ACT 2600; tel. (2) 6273-1309; tel. 62224; fax (2) 6273-4273; e-mail israelembassy@israemb.org; internet www.mfa.gov.il; Ambassador NAFTALI TAMIR.

Italy: 12 Grey St, Deakin, ACT 2600; tel. (2) 6273-3333; fax (2) 6273-4223; e-mail embassy@ambitalia.org.au; internet www.ambitalia.org.au; Ambassador DINO VOLPICELLI.

Japan: 112 Empire Circuit, Yarralumla, ACT 2600; tel. (2) 6273-3244; fax (2) 6273-1848; e-mail embofjpn@ozemail.com.au; internet www.japan.org.au; Ambassador HIDEAKI UEDA.

Jordan: 20 Roebuck St, Red Hill, ACT 2603; tel. (2) 6295-9951; fax (2) 6239-7236; Ambassador SAMIR MASARWEH.

Kenya: GPOB 1990, Canberra, ACT 2601; tel. (2) 6247-4788; fax (2) 6257-6613; e-mail kenrep@austarmetro.com.au; High Commissioner JOHN L. LANYASUNYA.

Korea, Democratic People's Republic: 57 Culgoa Circuit, O'Malley, ACT 2606; tel. (2) 6286-4770; fax (2) 6286-4795; e-mail dprkembassy@hotmail.com; Ambassador CHON JAE HONG.

Korea, Republic: 113 Empire Circuit, Yarralumla, ACT 2600; tel. (2) 6270-4100; fax (2) 6273-4839; e-mail embassy-au@mofat.go.kr; internet www.korea.org.au; Ambassador CHO SANG-HOON.

Kuwait: 5 Callemonda Rise, O'Malley, ACT 2606; tel. (2) 6286-7777; fax (2) 6286-3733; internet www.kuwaitemb-australia.com; Ambassador NASSER AL-MUZAYYAN.

Laos: 1 Dalman Crescent, O'Malley, ACT 2606; tel. (2) 6286-4595; fax (2) 6290-1910; e-mail clao1@cyberone.com.au; Ambassador KHENTHONG NUANTHOSING.

Lebanon: 27 Endeavour St, Red Hill, ACT 2603; tel. (2) 6295-7378; fax (2) 6239-7024; e-mail lebanemb@tpg.com.au; internet www.lebanemb.org.au; Ambassador MICHEL BITAR.

Macedonia, former Yugoslav republic: Perpetual Bldg, Suite 2:05, 10 Rudd St, Canberra, ACT 2601; tel. (2) 6249-8000; fax (2) 6249-8088; Ambassador VIKTOR GABER.

Malaysia: 7 Perth Ave, Yarralumla, ACT 2600; tel. (2) 6273-1543; fax (2) 6273-2496; e-mail malcanberra@netspeed.com.au; High Commissioner HUSSIN BIN NAYAN.

Malta: 38 Culgoa Circuit, O'Malley, ACT 2606; tel. (2) 6290-1724; fax (2) 6290-2453; e-mail maltahighcommission.canberra@gov.mt; High Commissioner Dr IVAN FSADNI.

Mauritius: 2 Beale Crescent, Deakin, ACT 2600; tel. (2) 6281-1203; fax (2) 6282-3235; e-mail mhccan@cyberone.com.au; High Commissioner JANE JOUANIS.

Mexico: 14 Perth Ave, Yarralumla, ACT 2600; tel. (2) 6273-3963; fax (2) 6273-1190; e-mail embamex@mexico.org.au; internet www.embassyofmexicoinaustralia.org; Ambassador MARTHA ORTHIS DE ROSAS.

Myanmar: 22 Arkana St, Yarralumla, ACT 2600; tel. (2) 6273-3811; fax (2) 6273-4357; Ambassador U SOE WIN.

Netherlands: 120 Empire Circuit, Yarralumla, ACT 2600; tel. (2) 6220-9400; fax (2) 6273-3206; e-mail can@minbuza.nl; internet www.netherlands.org.au; Ambassador H. H. M. SONDAAL.

New Zealand: Commonwealth Ave, Canberra, ACT 2600; tel. (2) 6270-4211; fax (2) 6273-3194; e-mail nzhccba@austarmetro.com.au; internet www.nzembassy.com/australia; High Commissioner KATE LACKEY.

Nigeria: POB 241, Civic Square, ACT 2608; tel. (2) 6282-7411; fax (2) 6282-8471; e-mail chancery@nigeria-can.org.au; internet www.nigeria-can.org.au; High Commissioner Dr ICHA EMMANUEL ITUMA.

Norway: 17 Hunter St, Yarralumla, ACT 2600; tel. (2) 6273-3444; fax (2) 6273-3669; e-mail emb.canberra@mfa.no; internet www.canberra.mfa.no; Ambassador LARS A. WENSELL.

Pakistan: POB 684, Mawson, ACT 2607; tel. (2) 6290-1676; fax (2) 6290-1073; e-mail parepcanberra@actonline.com.au; High Commissioner BABAR W. MALIK.

Papua New Guinea: POB E432, Queen Victoria Terrace, Kingston, ACT 2604; tel. (2) 6273-3322; fax (2) 6273-3732; High Commissioner RENAGI R. LOHIA.

Peru: POB 106, Red Hill, ACT 2603; tel. (2) 6286-9507; fax (2) 6286-7490; e-mail embassy@embaperu.org.au; internet www.embaperu.org.au; Ambassador MARTHA TOLEDO-OCAMPO.

Philippines: 1 Moonah Place, Yarralumla, Canberra, ACT 2600; tel. (2) 6273-2535; fax (2) 6273-3984; e-mail cbrpe@philembassy.au.com; internet www.philembassy.au.com; Ambassador CRISTINA GARCIA ORTEGA.

Poland: 7 Turrana St, Yarralumla, ACT 2600; tel. (2) 6273-1208; fax (2) 6273-3184; e-mail polish.embassy@tpg.com.au; internet www.poland.org.au; Ambassador JERZY WIECŁAW.

Portugal: 23 Culgoa Circuit, O'Malley, ACT 2606; tel. (2) 6290-1733; fax (2) 6290-1957; e-mail embport@internode.on.net; Ambassador Dr ANTONIO J. MENDES.

Romania: 4 Dalman Crescent, O'Malley, ACT 2606; tel. (2) 6286-2343; fax (2) 6286-2433; e-mail roembcbr@cyberone.com.au; internet www.roembau.org.au; Ambassador ANCA VISAN.

Russia: 78 Canberra Ave, Griffith, ACT 2603; tel. (2) 6295-9033; fax (2) 6295-1847; e-mail rusembassy@lightningpl.net.au; Ambassador LEONID MOISEEV.

Samoa: POB 3274, Manuka, ACT 2603; tel. (2) 6286-5505; fax (2) 6286-5678; e-mail samoahcaussi@netspeed.com.au; High Commissioner Leiataua Dr KILIFOTI S. ETEUATI.

Saudi Arabia: POB 63, Garran, ACT 2605; tel. (2) 6282-6999; fax (2) 6282-8911; e-mail saudiemb@hotmail.com; Chargé d'affaires a.i. ABDULLAH A. AL-QORDI.

Serbia and Montenegro: POB 728, Mawson, ACT 2607; tel. (2) 6290-2630; fax (2) 6290-2631; e-mail yuembau@ozemail.com.au; Ambassador MILIVOJE GLISIC.

Singapore: 17 Forster Crescent, Yarralumla, ACT 2600; tel. (2) 6273-3944; fax (2) 6273-9823; e-mail singapore_hc@bigpond.com; internet www.mfa.gov.sg/canberra; High Commissioner JOSEPH K. H. KOH.

Slovakia: 47 Culgoa Circuit, O'Malley, ACT 2606; tel. (2) 6290-1516; fax (2) 6290-1755; e-mail embassy@slovakemb-aust.org; internet www.slovakemb-aust.org; Ambassador Dr PETER PROCHÁCKA.

Slovenia: POB 284, Civic Square, Canberra, ACT 2608; tel. (2) 6243-4830; fax (2) 6243-4827; e-mail vca@mzz-dkp.gov.si; internet slovenia.webone.com.au; Chargé d'affaires BOJAN BERTONCELJ.

Solomon Islands: POB 256, Deakin West, ACT 2600; tel. (2) 6282-7030; fax (2) 6282-7040; e-mail info@solomon.emb.gov.au; High Commissioner MILNER TOZAKA.

South Africa: cnr State Circle and Rhodes Place, Yarralumla, ACT 2600; tel. (2) 6273-2424; fax (2) 6273-3543; e-mail info@rsa.emb.gov.au; internet www.rsa.emb.gov.au; High Commissioner ANTHONY MONGALO.

Spain: POB 9076, Deakin, ACT 2600; tel. (2) 6273-3555; fax (2) 6273-3918; e-mail embespau@mail.mae.es; internet www.embaspain.com; Ambassador JOSÉ RAMÓN BARANAÑO.

Sri Lanka: 35 Empire Circuit, Forrest, ACT 2603; tel. (2) 6239-7041; fax (2) 6239-6166; e-mail slhc@atrax.net.au; internet slhccanberra.webjump.com; High Commissioner Maj.-Gen. JANAKA PERERA.

Sweden: 5 Turrana St, Yarralumla, ACT 2600; tel. (2) 6270-2700; fax (2) 6270-2755; e-mail sweden@austarmetro.com.au; Ambassador KARIN EHNBOM-PALMQUIST.

Switzerland: 7 Melbourne Ave, Forrest, ACT 2603; tel. (2) 6273-3977; fax (2) 6273-3428; e-mail vertretung@can.rep.admin.ch; Ambassador CHRISTIAN MÜHLETHALER.

Syria: 41 Culgoa Circuit, O'Malley, ACT 2606; tel. (2) 6286-5235; fax (2) 6286-5253; internet www.syrianembassyaustralia.org; Ambassador TAMAM SOULIMAN.

Thailand: 111 Empire Circuit, Yarralumla, ACT 2600; tel. (2) 6273-1149; fax (2) 6273-1518; e-mail rtecanberra@mfa.go.th; Ambassador SUCHITRA HIRANPRUECK.

Timor-Leste: 25 Blaxland Crescent, Griffith, ACT 2603; tel. (2) 6260-8800; fax (2) 6239-7682; e-mail TL_Emb.Canberra@bigpond.com; Ambassador JORGE DA CONCEICAO TEME.

Turkey: 60 Mugga Way, Red Hill, ACT 2603; tel. (2) 6295-0227; fax (2) 6239-6592; e-mail turkembs@bigpond.net.au; internet www.turkishembassy.org.au; Ambassador TANSU OKANDAN.

Uganda: 7 Dunoon St, O'Malley, ACT 2606; tel. (2) 6286-1234; fax (2) 6286-1243; High Commissioner Dr CHRISTOPHER JAMES LUKABYO.

Ukraine: Level 12, St George Centre, 60 Marcus Clarke St, Canberra, ACT 2601; tel. (2) 6230-5789; fax (2) 6230-7298; e-mail ukremb@bigpond.com; internet www.ukremb.info; Ambassador Dr OLEXANDR MISCHENKO.

United Arab Emirates: 36 Culgoa Circuit, O'Malley, ACT 2606; tel. (2) 6286-8802; fax (2) 6286-8804; e-mail uaeembassy@bigpond.com; internet www.users.bigpond.com/uaeembassy; Ambassador Dr SAEED MOHAMMED AL-SHAMSI.

United Kingdom: Commonwealth Ave, Canberra, ACT 2600; tel. (2) 6270-6666; fax (2) 6273-3236; e-mail BHC.Canberra@uk.emb.gov.au; internet www.uk.emb.gov.au; High Commissioner Sir ALASTAIR GOODLAD.

USA: Moonah Place, Yarralumla, ACT 2600; tel. (2) 6214-5600; fax (2) 6214-5970; internet usembassy-australia.state.gov; Ambassador J. THOMAS SCHIEFFER.

Uruguay: POB 5058, Kingston, ACT 2604; tel. (2) 6273-9100; fax (2) 6273-9099; e-mail urucan@iimetro.com.au; Ambassador PEDRO MÓ AMARO.

Venezuela: 7 Culgoa Circuit, O'Malley, ACT 2606; tel. (2) 6290-2968; fax (2) 6290-2911; e-mail embaustralia@venezuela-emb-org.au; internet www.venezuela-emb.org.au; Ambassador LUIS VELÁSQUEZ.

Viet Nam: 6 Timbarra Crescent, O'Malley, ACT 2606; tel. (2) 6286-6059; fax (2) 6286-4534; e-mail vnembassy@webone.com.au; internet www.au.vnembassy.org; Ambassador LE XUAN LIEU.

Zimbabwe: 11 Culgoa Circuit, O'Malley, ACT 2606; tel. (2) 6286-2700; fax (2) 6290-1680; e-mail zimbabwe1@austarmetro.com.au; Ambassador FLORENCE L. CHITAURO.

Judicial System

The judicial power of the Commonwealth of Australia is vested in the High Court of Australia, in such other Federal Courts as the Federal Parliament creates, and in such other courts as it invests with Federal jurisdiction.

The High Court consists of a Chief Justice and six other Justices, each of whom is appointed by the Governor-General in Council, and has both original and appellate jurisdiction.

The High Court's original jurisdiction extends to all matters arising under any treaty, affecting representatives of other countries, in which the Commonwealth of Australia or its representative is a party, between states or between residents of different states or between a state and a resident of another state, and in which a writ of mandamus, or prohibition, or an injunction is sought against an officer of the Commonwealth of Australia. It also extends to matters arising under the Australian Constitution or involving its interpretation, and to many matters arising under Commonwealth laws.

The High Court's appellate jurisdiction has, since June 1984, been discretionary. Appeals from the Federal Court, the Family Court and the Supreme Courts of the states and of the territories may now be brought only if special leave is granted, in the event of a legal question that is of general public importance being involved, or of there being differences of opinion between intermediate appellate courts as to the state of the law.

Legislation enacted by the Federal Parliament in 1976 substantially changed the exercise of Federal and Territory judicial power, and, by creating the Federal Court of Australia in February 1977, enabled the High Court of Australia to give greater attention to its primary function as interpreter of the Australian Constitution. The Federal Court of Australia has assumed, in two divisions, the jurisdiction previously exercised by the Australian Industrial Court and the Federal Court of Bankruptcy and was additionally given jurisdiction in trade practices and in the developing field of administrative law. In 1987 the Federal Court of Australia acquired jurisdiction in federal taxation matters and certain intellectual property matters. In 1991 the Court's jurisdiction was expanded to include civil proceedings arising under Corporations Law. Jurisdiction has also been conferred on the Federal Court of Australia, subject to a number of exceptions, in matters in which a writ of mandamus, or prohibition, or an injunction is sought against an officer of the Commonwealth of Australia. The Court also hears appeals from the Court constituted by a single Judge, from the Supreme Courts of the territories, and in certain specific matters from State Courts, other than a Full Court of the Supreme Court of a state, exercising Federal jurisdiction.

In March 1986 all remaining categories of appeal from Australian courts to the Queen's Privy Council in the United Kingdom were abolished by the Australia Act.

FEDERAL COURTS

High Court of Australia

POB 6309, Kingston, Canberra, ACT 2604; tel. (2) 6270-6811; fax (2) 6270-6868; internet www.hcourt.gov.au.

Chief Justice: ANTHONY MURRAY GLEESON.

Justices: MICHAEL HUDSON MCHUGH, WILLIAM MONTAGUE CHARLES GUMMOW, MICHAEL DONALD KIRBY, KENNETH MADISON HAYNE, IAN DAVID FRANCIS CALLINAN, JOHN DYSON HEYDON.

Federal Court of Australia

Chief Justice: MICHAEL ERIC JOHN BLACK.
In 2003 there were 46 other judges.

Family Court of Australia

Chief Justice: ALISTAIR BOTHWICK NICHOLSON.
In 2003 there were 50 other judges.

NEW SOUTH WALES

Supreme Court

Chief Justice: JAMES JACOB SPIGELMAN.
President: KEITH MASON.
Chief Judge in Equity: PETER WOLSTENHOME YOUNG.
Chief Judge at Common Law: JAMES ROLAND TOMSON WOOD.

VICTORIA

Supreme Court

Chief Justice: MARILYN WARREN.
President of the Court of Appeal: JOHN SPENCE WINNEKE.

QUEENSLAND

Supreme Court

Chief Justice: PAUL DE JERSEY.
President of the Court of Appeal: MARGARET MCMURDO.
Senior Judge Administrator, Trial Division: MARTIN PATRICK MOYNIHAN.

Central District (Rockhampton)

Resident Judge: PETER RICHARD DUTNEY.

Northern District (Townsville)

Resident Judge: KEIRAN ANTHONY CULLINANE.

Far Northern District (Cairns)

Resident Judge: STANLEY GRAHAM JONES.

SOUTH AUSTRALIA

Supreme Court

Chief Justice: JOHN JEREMY DOYLE.

WESTERN AUSTRALIA

Supreme Court

Chief Justice: DAVID KINGSLEY MALCOLM.

TASMANIA

Supreme Court

Chief Justice: PETER UNDERWOOD.

AUSTRALIAN CAPITAL TERRITORY

Supreme Court

Chief Justice: JOHN HIGGINS.

NORTHERN TERRITORY

Supreme Court

Chief Justice: BRIAN FRANK MARTIN.

Religion

CHRISTIANITY

According to the provisional results of the population census of August 2001, Christians numbered 12,764,342.

National Council of Churches in Australia: Locked Bag 199, Sydney, NSW 1230; tel. (2) 9299-2215; fax (2) 9262-4514; e-mail info@ncca.org.au; internet www.ncca.org.au; f. 1946; 16 mem. churches; Pres. Rev. Prof. JAMES HAIRE; Gen. Sec. Rev. JOHN HENDERSON.

The Anglican Communion

The constitution of the Church of England in Australia, which rendered the church an autonomous member of the Anglican Communion, came into force in January 1962. The body was renamed the Anglican Church of Australia in August 1981. The Church comprises five provinces (together containing 22 dioceses) and the extra-provincial diocese of Tasmania. At the 2001 population census there were an estimated 3,881,162 adherents.

National Office of the Anglican Church

General Synod Office, Box Q190, QVB PO, Sydney, NSW 1230; tel. (2) 9265-1525; fax (2) 9264-6552; e-mail gsoffice@anglican.org.au; internet www.anglican.org.au.

Gen. Sec. Rev. Dr B. N. KAYE.

Archbishop of Adelaide and Metropolitan of South Australia: Ven. JOHN COLLAS (acting), Bishop's Court, 45 Palmer Place, North Adelaide, SA 5006; fax (8) 8305-9399; internet www.anglicare-sa.org.au.

Archbishop of Brisbane and Metropolitan of Queensland: Most Rev. Dr PHILLIP JOHN ASPINALL, Bishopsbourne, GPOB 421, Brisbane, Qld 4001; tel. (7) 3835-2218; fax (7) 3832-5030; e-mail archbishop@anglicanbrisbane.org.au; internet www.anglicanbrisbane.gil.com.au.

Archbishop of Melbourne and Metropolitan of Victoria: Most Rev. PETER R. WATSON, Bishopscourt, 120 Clarendon St, East Melbourne, Vic 3002; tel. (3) 9653-4220; fax (3) 9650-2184; e-mail archbishop@melbourne.anglican.com.au.

Archbishop of Perth and Metropolitan of Western Australia, Primate of Australia: Most Rev. Dr PETER F. CARNLEY, GPOB W2067, Perth, WA 6846; tel. (8) 9325-7455; fax (8) 9325-6741; e-mail abcsuite@perth.anglican.org; internet www.perth.anglican.org.

Also has jurisdiction over Christmas Island and the Cocos (Keeling) Islands.

Archbishop of Sydney and Metropolitan of New South Wales: Most Rev. Dr PETER F. JENSEN, POB Q190, QVB PO, Sydney, NSW 1230; tel. (2) 9265-1521; fax (2) 9265-1504; e-mail archbishop@sydney.anglican.asn.au; internet www.sydney.anglican.asn.au.

The Roman Catholic Church

Australia comprises five metropolitan archdioceses, two archdioceses directly responsible to the Holy See and 24 dioceses, including one diocese each for Catholics of the Maronite and Melkite rites, and one military ordinariate. At 31 December 2002 there were an estimated 5.2m. adherents in the country.

Australian Catholic Bishops' Conference

GPOB 368, Canberra, ACT 2601; tel. (2) 6201-9845; fax (2) 6247-6083; e-mail gensec@catholic.org.au; internet www.catholic.org.au. f. 1979; Pres. Most Rev. Francis Patrick Carroll (Archbishop of Canberra and Goulburn); Sec. Rev. Brian Lucas.

Archbishop of Adelaide: Most Rev. Philip Wilson, GPOB 1364, Adelaide, South Australia 5001; tel. (8) 8210-8108; fax (8) 8223-2307; e-mail cco@adelaide.catholic.org.au.

Archbishop of Brisbane: Most Rev. John A. Bathersby, POB 936, New Farm, Brisbane, Qld 4005; tel. (7) 3131-5500; fax (7) 3358-1357; e-mail archbishop@bne.catholic.net.au.

Archbishop of Canberra and Goulburn: Most Rev. Francis Patrick Carroll, GPOB 89, Canberra, ACT 2601; tel. (2) 6248-6411; fax (2) 6247-9636; e-mail archbish@cg.catholic.org.au.

Archbishop of Hobart: Most Rev. Adrian Doyle, GPOB 62, Hobart, Tas 7001; tel. (3) 6225-1920; fax (3) 6225-3865; e-mail archbishop.hobart@cdftas.com; internet www.hobart.catholic.org.au.

Archbishop of Melbourne: Most Rev. Denis Hart, GPOB 146, East Melbourne, Vic 3002; tel. (3) 9926-5613; fax (3) 9926-5698; e-mail archbishop@melbourne.catholic.org.au.

Archbishop of Perth: Most Rev. Barry J. Hickey, Catholic Church Office, 25 Victoria Ave, Perth, WA 6000; tel. (8) 9223-1351; fax (8) 9221-1716; e-mail archsec@perthcatholic.org.au; internet www.perthcatholic.org.au/.

Archbishop of Sydney: Cardinal George Pell, St Mary's Cathedral, Sydney, NSW 2000; tel. (2) 9390-5100; fax (2) 9261-0045; e-mail chancery@ado.syd.catholic.org.au.

Orthodox Churches

Greek Orthodox Archdiocese of Australia: 242 Cleveland St, Redfern, Sydney, NSW 2016; tel. (2) 9698-5066; fax (2) 9698-5368; f. 1924; 700,000 mems; Primate His Eminence Archbishop Stylianos. The Antiochian, Coptic, Romanian, Serbian and Syrian Orthodox Churches are also represented.

Other Christian Churches

Baptist Union of Australia: POB 377, Hawthorn, Vic 3122; tel. (3) 9810-7800; fax (3) 9810-1041; e-mail bua@baptist.org.au; internet www.baptist.org.au; f. 1926; 64,159 mems; 883 churches; Nat. Pres. Gwyn Milne; Nat. Sec. Naomi McConnell.

Churches of Christ in Australia: POB 55, Helensburgh, NSW 2508; tel. (2) 4294-1913; fax (2) 4294-1914; e-mail bobsmith@ozemail.com.au; internet www.churchesofchrist.org.au; 36,000 mems; Pres. Rev. Peter Overton; Co-ordinator Rev. Robert Smith.

Lutheran Church of Australia: National Office, 197 Archer St, North Adelaide, SA 5006; tel. (8) 8267-7300; fax (8) 8267-7310; e-mail president@lca.org.au; internet www.lca.org.au; f. 1966; 75,000 mems; Pres. Rev. M. P. Semmler.

United Pentecostal Church of Australia: GPOB 1434, Springwood, Qld 4127; tel. (7) 3806-1817; fax (7) 3806-0029; e-mail homemissions@powerup.com.au; internet www.upca.org.au; 174,720 adherents in 1996.

Uniting Church in Australia: POB A2266, Sydney South, NSW 1235; tel. (2) 8267-4202; fax (2) 8267-4222; e-mail assysec@nat.uca.org.au; internet nat.uca.org.au; f. 1977 with the union of Methodist, Presbyterian and Congregational Churches; third largest Christian denomination in Australia; 1.4m. mems; Pres. Rev. Dr Dean Drayton; Gen. Sec. Rev. Terence Corkin.

JUDAISM

The Jewish community numbered an estimated 83,993 at the census of August 2001.

Great Synagogue: 166 Castlereagh St, Sydney, NSW; tel. (2) 9267-2477; fax (2) 9264-8871; e-mail admin@greatsynagogue.org.au; internet www.greatsynagogue.org.au; f. 1828; Sr Rabbi Jeremy Lawrence.

OTHER FAITHS

According to the August 2001 census, Buddhists numbered an estimated 357,813, Muslims 281,578 and Hindus 95,473.

The Press

The total circulation of Australia's daily newspapers is very high, but in the remoter parts of the country weekly papers are even more popular. Most of Australia's newspapers are published in sparsely populated rural areas where the demand for local news is strong.

The only newspapers that may fairly claim a national circulation are the dailies *The Australian* and *Australian Financial Review*, and the weekly magazines *The Bulletin, Time Australia* and *Business Review Weekly*, the circulation of most newspapers being almost entirely confined to the state in which each is produced.

ACP Publishing Pty Ltd: 54–58 Park St, Sydney, NSW 1028; tel. (2) 9282-8000; fax (2) 9264-4541; internet www.acp.com.au; publishes *Australian Women's Weekly, The Bulletin with Newsweek, Cleo, Cosmopolitan, Woman's Day, Dolly, Belle, Wheels, Motor* and more than 60 other magazines; Chief Exec. John Alexander.

APN News and Media Ltd: Level 4, 100 William St, Sydney, NSW 2011; tel. (2) 9333-4999; fax (2) 9333-4900; e-mail info@apn.com.au; internet www.apn.com.au; Chair. James J. Parkinson; Chief Exec. Brendan M. A. Hopkins.

John Fairfax Holdings Ltd: POB 506, Sydney, NSW 2001; tel. (2) 9282-2833; fax (2) 9282-3133; e-mail rvictor@mail.fairfax.com.au; internet www.fairfax.com.au; f. 1987; Chair. Dean Wills; Chief Exec. Frederick G. Hilmer; publs include *The Sydney Morning Herald, The Australian Financial Review* and *Sun-Herald* (Sydney), *The Age* and *BRW Publications* (Melbourne); also provides online and interactive services.

The Herald and Weekly Times Ltd: POB 14999, Melbourne MC, Vic 8001; tel. (3) 9292-2000; fax (3) 9292-2002; e-mail newspapers@hwt.newsltd.com.au; internet www.heraldsun.news.com.au; acquired by News Ltd in 1987; Chair. Janet Calvert-Jones; Man. Dir Julian Clarke; publs include *Herald Sun, Sunday Herald Sun, The Weekly Times, MX.*

News Corporation: 2 Holt St, Surry Hills, Sydney, NSW 2010; tel. (2) 9288-3000; fax (2) 9288-2300; internet www.newscorp.com; Chair. and CEO K. Rupert Murdoch; controls *The Australian* and *The Weekend Australian* (national), *Daily Telegraph, Sunday Telegraph* (Sydney), *The Herald Sun* and *Sunday Herald Sun* (Victoria), *Northern Territory News* (Darwin), *Sunday Times* (Perth), *Townsville Bulletin, Courier Mail, Sunday Mail* (Queensland), *The Mercury* (Tasmania), *The Advertiser, Sunday Mail* (South Australia).

Rural Press Ltd: 159 Bells Line of Road, North Richmond, NSW 2754; tel. (2) 4570-4444; fax (2) 4570-4663; e-mail coysec@ruralpress.com; internet www.ruralpress.com; Chair. John B. Fairfax; Man. Dir B. K. McCarthy.

West Australian Newspapers Holdings Ltd: Newspaper House, 50 Hasler Rd, Osborne Park, WA 6017; tel. (8) 9482-3111; fax (8) 9482-9080; Chair. W. G. Kent; Man. Dir I. F. Law.

Other newspaper publishers include Federal Capital Press (K. Stokes).

NEWSPAPERS

Australian Capital Territory

The Canberra Times: POB 7155, Canberra Mail Centre, ACT 2610; tel. (2) 6280-2122; fax (2) 6280-2282; internet www.canberratimes.com; f. 1926; daily and Sun.; morning; Editor-in-Chief Jack Waterford; circ. 38,694 (Mon.–Fri.), 72,080 (Sat.), 39,075 (Sun.).

New South Wales

Dailies

The Australian: News Ltd, 2 Holt St, POB 4245, Surry Hills, NSW 2010; tel. (2) 9288-3000; fax (2) 9288-3077; f. 1964; edited in Sydney, simultaneous edns in Sydney, Melbourne, Perth, Townsville, Adelaide and Brisbane; Editor-in-Chief David Armstrong; Editor Campbell Reid; circ. 122,500 (Mon.–Fri.); *The Weekend Australian* (Sat.) 311,000.

Australian Financial Review: 201 Sussex St, GPOB 506, Sydney, NSW 2000; tel. (2) 9282-2512; fax (2) 9282-3137; f. 1951; distributed nationally; Publr/Editor-in-Chief Michael Gill; Editor Glen Burge; circ. 92,500 (Mon.–Fri.), 92,000 (Sat.).

The Daily Telegraph: 2 Holt St, Surry Hills, NSW 2010; tel. (2) 9288-3000; fax (2) 9288-2300; f. 1879; merged in 1990 with Daily Mirror (f. 1941); 24-hour tabloid; CEO Lachlan Murdoch; circ. 442,000.

The Manly Daily: 26 Sydney Rd, Manly, NSW 2095; tel. (2) 9977-3333; fax (2) 9977-2831; e-mail manlydailynews@cng.newsltd.com.au; f. 1906; Tue.–Sat.; Editor Steve Stickney; circ. 89,326.

The Newcastle Herald: 28–30 Bolton St, Newcastle, NSW 2300; tel. (2) 4979-5000; fax (2) 4979-5888; e-mail ntlinfo@newcastle.fairfax.com.au; f. 1858; morning; 6 a week; Editor Rod Quinn; circ. 54,006.

The Sydney Morning Herald: 201 Sussex St, GPOB 506, Sydney, NSW 2001; tel. (2) 9282-2822; fax (2) 9282-3253; internet www.smh

.com.au; f. 1831; morning; Editor-in-Chief and Publr ALAN REVELL; circ. 231,508 (Mon.–Fri.), 400,000 (Sat.).

Weeklies

Bankstown Canterbury Torch: 47 Allingham St, Condell Park, NSW 2200; tel. (2) 9795-0000; fax (2) 9795-0096; e-mail trevor@torchpublishing.com.au; internet www.torchpublishing.com.au; f. 1920; Wed.; owned by Torch Publishing Co Pty Ltd; Editor MARK KIRKLAND; circ. 90,066.

Northern District Times: 79 Rowe St, Eastwood, NSW 2122; tel. (2) 9858-1766; fax (2) 9804-6901; f. 1921; Wed.; Editor D. BARTOK; circ. 55,302.

The Parramatta Advertiser: 142 Macquarie St, Parramatta, NSW 2150; tel. (2) 9689-5370; fax (2) 9689-5353; Wed.; Editor LES POBJIE; circ. 96,809.

St George and Sutherland Shire Leader: 182 Forest Rd, Hurstville, NSW 2220; tel. (2) 9598-3999; fax (2) 9598-3987; f. 1960; Tue. and Thur.; Editor PETER ALLEN; circ. 143,595.

Sun-Herald: GPOB 506, Sydney, NSW 2001; tel. (2) 9282-1679; fax (2) 9282-2151; e-mail shnews@mail.fairfax.com.au; internet www.sunherald.com.au; f. 1953; Sun.; Editor PHILIP McLEAN; circ. 580,000.

Sunday Telegraph: 2 Holt St, Surry Hills, NSW 2010; tel. (2) 9288-3000; fax (2) 9288-3311; f. 1938; Editor JENI COOPER; circ. 720,000.

Northern Territory

Daily

Northern Territory News: Printers Place, POB 1300, Darwin, NT 0801; tel. (8) 8944-9900; fax (8) 8981-6045; f. 1952; Mon.–Sat.; Gen. Man. D. KENNEDY; circ. 24,470.

Weekly

Sunday Territorian: Printers Place, GPOB 1300, Darwin, NT 0801; tel. (8) 8944-9900; fax (8) 8981-6045; Sun.; Editor DAVID COREN; circ. 26,437.

Queensland

Daily

Courier-Mail: 41 Campbell St, Bowen Hills, Brisbane, Qld 4006; tel. (7) 3252-6011; fax (7) 3252-6696; f. 1933; morning; Editor DAVID FAGAN; circ. 208,902 (Mon.–Fri.), 332,335 (Sat.).

Weekly

Sunday Mail: 41 Campbell St, Bowen Hills, GPOB 130, Brisbane, Qld 4006; tel. (7) 3666-8000; fax (7) 3666-6787; e-mail smletters@qnp.news; internet www.thesundaymail.com.au; f. 1953; Editor MICHAEL PRAIN; circ. 611,298.

South Australia

Daily

The Advertiser: 121 King William St, Adelaide, SA 5001; tel. (8) 8206-2220; fax (8) 8206-3669; e-mail tiser@adv.newsltd.com.au; f. 1858; morning; Editor MELVIN MANSELL; circ. 203,440 (Mon.–Fri.), 274,045 (Sat.).

Weekly

Sunday Mail: 9th Floor, 121 King William St, GPOB 339, Adelaide, SA 5000; tel. (8) 8206-2000; fax (8) 8206-3646; e-mail gardnerp@adv.newsltd.com.au; internet www.theadvertiser.news.com.au/archive; f. 1912; Editor PHILLIP GARDNER; circ. 331,755.

Tasmania

Dailies

The Advocate: POB 63, Burnie, Tas 7320; tel. (3) 6440-7409; fax (3) 6440-7345; e-mail letters@theadvocate.com.au; internet www.theadvocate.com.au; f. 1890; morning; Editor PETER DWYER; circ. 25,623.

Examiner: 71–75 Paterson St, POB 99, Launceston, Tas 7250; tel. (3) 6336-7111; fax (3) 6334-7328; e-mail mail@examiner.com.au; internet www.examiner.com.au/examiner/; f. 1842; morning; independent; Editor D. SOUTHWELL; circ. 38,721.

Mercury: 91–93 Macquarie St, Hobart, Tas 7000; tel. (3) 6230-0622; fax (3) 6230-0711; e-mail mercury.news@dbl.newsltd.com.au; internet www.themercury.news.com.au; f. 1854; morning; Man. Dir REX GARDNER; Editor GARRY BAILEY; circ. 52,931.

Weeklies

Sunday Examiner: 71–75 Paterson St, Launceston, Tas 7250; tel. (3) 6336-7111; fax (3) 6334-7328; e-mail mail@examiner.com.au; f. 1924; Editor D. SOUTHWELL; circ. 42,000.

Sunday Tasmanian: 91–93 Macquarie St, Hobart, Tas 7000; tel. (3) 6230-0622; fax (3) 6230-0711; e-mail e-mailsuntas.news@dbl.newsltd.com.au; f. 1984; morning; Man. Dir REX GARDNER; Editor IAN McCAUSLAND; circ. 58,325.

Victoria

Dailies

The Age: 250 Spencer St (cnr Lonsdale St), Melbourne, Vic 3000; tel. (3) 9600-4211; fax (3) 9601-2598; e-mail newsdesk@theage.fairfax.com.au; internet www.theage.com.au; f. 1854; independent; morning, incl. Sun.; Editor-in-Chief MICHAEL GAWENDA; circ. 197,000 (Mon.–Fri.), 308,000 (Sat.), 191,000 (Sun.).

Herald Sun: HWT Tower, 40 City Rd, Southbank, Vic 3006; tel. (3) 9292-2000; fax (3) 9292-2112; e-mail news@heraldsun.com.au; internet www.heraldsun.news.com.au; f. 1840; Editor-in-Chief PETER BLUNDEN; circ. 553,100.

Weeklies

Progress Press: 360 Burwood Rd, Hawthorn, Vic 3122; tel. (3) 9818-0555; fax (3) 9818-0029; e-mail editor@ldr.newsltd.com.au; f. 1960; Tue.; Editor LYNNE KINSEY; circ. 74,829.

Sunday Herald Sun: HWT Tower, 40 City Rd, Southbank, Vic 3006; tel. (3) 9292-2962; fax (3) 9292-2080; e-mail sundayhs@heraldsun.com.au; internet www.sundayheraldsun.com.au; f. 1991; Editor ALAN HOWE; circ. 600,000.

Western Australia

Daily

The West Australian: POB D162, Perth, WA 6840; tel. (8) 9482-3111; fax (8) 9482-9080; e-mail editor@wanews.com.au; internet www.thewest.com.au; f. 1833; morning; Editor BRIAN ROGERS; circ. 214,000 (Mon.–Fri.), 386,000 (Sat.).

Weekly

Sunday Times: 34 Stirling St, Perth, WA 6000; tel. (8) 9326-8326; fax (8) 9326-8316; e-mail editorial@sundaytimes.newsltd.com.au; internet www.sundaytimes.news.com.au; f. 1897; Man. Dir DAVID MAGUIRE; Editor BRETT McCARTHY; circ. 346,014.

PRINCIPAL PERIODICALS

Weeklies and Fortnightlies

The Bulletin: 54 Park St, Sydney, NSW 2000; tel. (2) 9282-8227; fax (2) 9267-4359; e-mail cclegg@acp.com.au; f. 1880; Wed.; Editor-in-Chief GARRY LINNELL; circ. 70,000.

Business Review Weekly: Level 2, 469 La Trobe St, Melbourne, Vic 3000; tel. (3) 9603-3888; fax (3) 9670-4328; e-mail brwonline@brw.fairfax.com.au; internet www.brw.com.au; f. 1981; Man. Editor TONY FEATHERSTONE; circ. 75,166.

Computerworld Australia: POB 295, St Leonards, NSW 1590; tel. (2) 9901-0709; e-mail sandra_rossi@idg.com.au; internet www.computerworld.com.au; weekly; information technology news; Editor SANDRA ROSSI.

The Countryman: GPOB D162, Perth, WA 6840; tel. (8) 9482-3327; fax (8) 9482-3314; e-mail countryman@wanews.com.au; f. 1885; Thur.; farming; Editor CAMERON MORSE; circ. 10,500.

The Medical Journal of Australia: Locked Bag 3030, Strawberry Hills, NSW 2012; tel. (2) 9562-6666; fax (2) 9562-6699; e-mail medjaust@ampco.com.au; internet www.mja.com.au; f. 1914; fortnightly; Editor Dr MARTIN VAN DER WEYDEN; circ. 27,318.

New Idea: 35–51 Mitchell St, McMahons Point, NSW 2060; tel. (2) 9464-3200; fax (2) 9464-3203; e-mail newidea@pacpubs.com.au; weekly; women's; Editor JENNI GILBERT; circ. 471,000.

News Weekly: POB 186, North Melbourne, Vic 3051; tel. (3) 9326-5757; fax (3) 9328-2877; e-mail freedom@connexus.net.au; f. 1943; publ. by National Civic Council; fortnightly; Sat.; political, social, educational and trade union affairs; Editor PETER WESTMORE; circ. 12,000.

People: 54 Park St, Sydney, NSW 2000; tel. (2) 9282-8743; fax (2) 9267-4365; e-mail sbutler-white@acp.com.au; weekly; Editor SIMON BUTLER-WHITE; circ. 70,000.

Picture: GPOB 5201, Sydney, NSW 2001; tel. (2) 9288-9686; fax (2) 9267-4372; e-mail picture@acp.com.au; weekly; men's; Editor TOM FOSTER; circ. 110,000.

Queensland Country Life: cnr Finucane Rd and Delaney St, Ormiston, Qld 4160; tel. (7) 3826-8200; fax (7) 3821-1236; e-mail editorial.qcl@ruralpress.com; internet www.queenslandcountrylife .com; f. 1935; Thur.; Editor MARK PHELPS; Gen. Man. JOHN WARLTERS; circ. 32,976.

Stock and Land: 10 Sydenham St, Moonee Ponds, Vic 3039; tel. (3) 9287-0900; fax (3) 9370-5622; e-mail stockandland@ruralpress.com; internet www.stockandland.com; f. 1914; weekly; agricultural and rural news; Editor SUSAN MCNAIR; circ. 12,303.

That's Life!: 35–51 Mitchell St, McMahons Point, NSW 2060; tel. (2) 9464-3300; fax (2) 9464-3480; e-mail thatslife@pacpubs.com.au; f. 1994; weekly; features; Editor SANDY MCPHIE; circ. 465,500 (incl. New Zealand).

Time Australia Magazine: GPOB 3873, Sydney, NSW 2001; tel. (2) 9925-2646; fax (2) 9954-0828; e-mail time.letters@time.com.au; internet www.time.com.au; Editor STEVE WATERSON; circ. 111,000.

TV Week: 54 Park St, Sydney, NSW 2000; tel. (2) 9288-9611; fax (2) 9283-4849; e-mail tvweek@acp.com.au; internet www.tvweek .ninemsn.com.au; f. 1957; Wed.; colour national; Editor EMMA NOLAN; circ. 364,044.

The Weekly Times: POB 14999, Melbourne City MC, Vic 8001; tel. (3) 9292-2000; fax (3) 9292-2697; e-mail wtimes@theweeklytimes .com.au; internet www.theweeklytimes.com.au; f. 1869; farming, regional issues, country life; Wed.; Editor PETER FLAHERTY; circ. 78,900.

Woman's Day: POB 5245, Sydney, NSW 2001; tel. (2) 9282-8000; fax (2) 9267-4360; e-mail womansday@acp.com.au; weekly; circulates throughout Australia and NZ; Editor ALANA HOUSE; circ. 765,170.

Monthlies and Others

Architectural Product News: Architecture Media Pty Ltd, Level 3, 4 Princes St, Port Melbourne, Vic 3207; tel. (3) 9646-4760; fax (3) 9646-4918; e-mail apn@archmedia.com.au; internet www .architecturemedia.com; 6 a year; Editorial Dir SUE HARRIS; circ. 25,063.

Architecture Australia: Architecture Media Pty Ltd, Level 3, 4 Princes St, Port Melbourne, Vic 3207; tel. (3) 9646-4760; fax (3) 9646-4918; e-mail aa@archmedia.com.au; internet www .architecturemedia.com; f. 1904; 6 a year; Editor JUSTINE CLARK; circ. 14,999.

Artichoke: Architecture Media Pty Ltd, Level 3, 4 Princes St, Port Melbourne, Vic 3207; tel. (3) 9646-4760; fax (3) 9646-4918; e-mail artichoke@archmedia.com.au; internet www.architecturemedia .com; 4 a year; Editorial Dir SUE HARRIS; circ. 7,166.

Australian Hi-Fi: POB 5555, St Leonards, NSW 1590; tel. (2) 9901-6100; fax (2) 9901-6198; e-mail hifi@horwitz.com.au; f. 1970; every 2 months; consumer tests on hi-fi and home theatre equipment; Editor GREG BORROWMAN; circ. 11,800.

Australian Home Beautiful: 35–51 Mitchell St, McMahons Point, NSW 2060; tel. (2) 9464-3218; fax (2) 9464-3263; e-mail homebeaut@ pacpubs.com.au; internet www.homebeautiful.com.au; f. 1925; monthly; Editor ANDREA JONES; circ. 83,808.

Australian House and Garden: 54 Park St, Sydney, NSW 2000; tel. (2) 9282-8456; fax (2) 9267-4912; e-mail h&g@acp.com.au; f. 1948; monthly; design, decorating, renovating, gardens, food and travel; Editor ANNY FRIIS; circ. 110,000.

Australian Journal of Mining: Informa Australia Pty Ltd, Level 2, 120 Sussex St, Sydney, NSW 2000; e-mail charles.macdonald@ informa.com.au; internet www.theajmonline.com; f. 1986; bimonthly; mining and exploration throughout Australia and South Pacific; Editor CHARLES MCDONALD; circ. 6,771.

Australian Journal of Pharmacy: Suite F2, 1–15 Barr St, Balmain, NSW 2041; tel. (2) 9818-7800; fax (2) 9818-7811; internet appco.com.au; f. 1886; monthly; journal of the associated pharmaceutical orgs; Publ. DAVID WESTON; circ. 6,443.

Australian Law Journal: 100 Harris St, Pyrmont, NSW 2009; tel. (2) 8587-7000; fax (2) 8587-7104; f. 1927; monthly; Editor Justice P. W. YOUNG; circ 4,500.

Australian Photography: POB 606, Sydney, NSW 2001; tel. (2) 9281-2333; fax (2) 9281-2750; e-mail robertkeeley@yaffa.com.au; monthly; Editor ROBERT KEELEY; circ. 9,010.

The Australian Women's Weekly: 54–56 Park St, Sydney, NSW 2000; tel. (2) 9282-8000; fax (2) 9267-4459; e-mail womensweekly@ acp.com.au; internet www.ninemsn.com.au/aww; f. 1933; monthly; Editor DEBORAH THOMAS; circ. 701,088.

Belle: 54 Park St, Sydney, NSW 2000; tel. (2) 9282-8000; fax (2) 9267-8037; e-mail belle@acp.com.au; f. 1975; every 2 months; Editor ERIC MATTHEWS; circ. 44,663.

Better Homes and Gardens: 35–51 Mitchell St, McMahon's Point, NSW 2060; e-mail joanne.haig@pacificmags.com.au; internet www .bhg.com.au; f. 1978; 13 a year; Editor JULIA ZAETTA; circ. 266,742.

Cleo: 54 Park St, Sydney, NSW 2000; tel. (2) 9282-8617; fax (2) 9267-4368; internet cleo.ninemsn.com.au/cleo; f. 1972; women's monthly; Editor DEBORAH THOMAS; circ. 263,353.

Commercial Photography: GPOB 606, Sydney, NSW 1041; tel. (2) 9281-2333; fax (2) 9281-2750; e-mail yaffa@flex.com.au; every 2 months; journal of the Professional Photographers Asscn of Australia and Photographic Industry Marketing Asscn of Australia; Editor SAIMA MOREL; circ. 3,835.

Cosmopolitan: 54 Park St, Sydney, NSW 2000; tel. (2) 9282-8039; fax (2) 9267-4457; e-mail cosmo@acp.com.au; internet www .cosmopolitan.com.au; f. 1973; monthly; Editor MIA FREEDMAN; circ. 209,347.

Dolly: 54–58 Park St, Sydney, NSW 1028; tel. (2) 9282-8437; fax (2) 9267-4911; e-mail dolly@ninemsn.com.au; internet www.ninemsn .com.au/dolly; f. 1970; monthly; for young women; Editor VIRGINIA KNIGHT; circ. 177,268.

Ecos: CSIRO, POB 1139, Collingwood, Vic 3066; tel. (3) 9662-7500; fax (3) 9662-7555; internet www.publish.csiro.au/ecos; f. 1974; every two months; sustainability magazine covering emerging topics and research in Australia and the Asia-Pacific region; Editor JAMES PORTEOUS; circ. 8,000.

Electronics Australia: POB 199, Alexandria, NSW 1435; tel. (2) 9353-0620; fax (2) 9353-0613; e-mail electaus@fpc.com.au; internet www.electronicsaustralia.com.au; f. 1922; monthly; technical, radio, television, microcomputers, hi-fi and electronics; Editor GRAHAM CATTLEY; circ. 20,900.

Elle: 54 Park St, Sydney, NSW 2000; tel. (2) 9282-8790; fax (2) 9267-4375; f. 1990; monthly; Editor MARINA GO; circ. 68,154.

Family Circle: Pacific Magazines, 35–51 Mitchell St, McMahons Point, NSW 2060; tel. (2) 9464-3471; fax (2) 9464-3506; e-mail familycircle@pacificmags.com.au; 13 a year; circ. 100,000.

Gardening Australia: POB 199, Alexandria, NSW 1435; tel. (2) 9353-6666; fax (2) 9317-4615; e-mail gardeningaustralia@fpcliving .com.au; internet www.gardeningaustralia.com.au; f. 1991; monthly; Editor BRODEE MYERS-COOKE; circ. 87,000.

Houses: Architecture Media Pty Ltd, Level 3, 4 Princes St, Port Melbourne, Vic 3207; tel. (3) 9646-4760; fax (3) 9646-4918; e-mail houses@archmedia.com.au; internet www.architecturemedia.com; f. 1989; 4 a year; Editor JULIE DILLAN; Man. Editor SUE HARRIS; circ. 25,246.

HQ: 54 Park St, Sydney, NSW 1028; tel. (2) 9282-8260; fax (2) 9267-3616; e-mail hq@publishing.acp.com.au; internet www.hq.ninemsn .com.au; f. 1989; every 2 months; Publr JOHN ALEXANDER; Editor KATHY BAIL; circ. 32,837.

Manufacturers' Monthly: Level 1/28, Riddell Parade, Elsternwick, Vic 3185; tel. (3) 9245-7777; fax (3) 9245-7750; f. 1961; Editor GREG VIDEON; circ. 15,188.

Modern Boating: The Federal Publishing Co Pty Ltd, Unit 2, 160 Bourke Rd, Alexandria, NSW 2015; tel. (2) 9353-6666; fax (2) 9353-0935; e-mail imacrae@fpc.com.au; internet www.modernboating .com.au; f. 1965; every 2 months; Editor IAN MACRAE; circ. 11,000.

Motor: Locked Bag 12, Oakleigh, Vic 3166; tel. (3) 9567-4200; fax (3) 9563-4554; e-mail motor@acpaction.com.au; f. 1954; monthly; Editor GED BULMER; circ. 41,414.

New Woman: EMAP Australia, Level 6, 187 Thomas St, Haymarket, NSW 2000; tel. (2) 9581-9400; fax (2) 9581-9570; internet www.newwoman.com.au; monthly; Editor SUE WHEELER; circ. 85,539.

The Open Road: L27, 388 George St, Sydney, NSW 2000; tel. (2) 8222-2185; fax (2) 8222-2176; e-mail open.road@mynrma.com.au; internet www.theopenroad.com.au; f. 1927; every 2 months; journal of National Roads and Motorists' Asscn (NRMA); Editor STEVE FRASER; circ. 1,555,917.

Personal Investor: Level 2, 469 La Trobe St, Melbourne, Vic 3000; tel. (3) 9603-3888; fax (3) 9670-4328; e-mail pieditor@brw.fairfax .com.au; internet www.personalinvestor.com.au; monthly; Editor ROBIN BOWERMAN; circ. 61,016.

Reader's Digest: 26–32 Waterloo St, Surry Hills, NSW 2010; tel. (2) 9690-6111; fax (2) 9690-6211; e-mail editors.au@readersdigest .com; internet www.readersdigest.au.com; monthly; Editor-in-Chief BRUCE HEILBUTH; circ. 332,382.

Street Machine: Locked Bag 756, Epping, NSW 2121; tel. (2) 9868-4832; fax (2) 9869-7390; e-mail streetmachine@acpaction.com.au; Editor MARK OASTLER; circ. 55,000.

TV Hits: Private Bag 9900, North Sydney, NSW 2059; tel. (2) 9464-3300; fax (2) 9464-3508; f. 1988; monthly; circ. 114,509.

TV Soap: 55 Chandos St, St Leonards, NSW 2065; tel. (2) 9901-6100; fax (2) 9901-6166; f. 1983; monthly; Editor BEN MITCHELL; circ. 103,000.

Vogue Australia: 180 Bourke Rd, Alexandria, NSW 2015; tel. (2) 9353-6666; fax (2) 9353-6699; e-mail vogue@vogue.com.au; internet www.vogue.com.au; f. 1959; monthly; fashion; Editor KIRSTIE CLEMENTS; circ. 54,705.

Wheels: GPOB 4088, Sydney, NSW 2001; tel. (2) 9263-9732; fax (2) 9263-9702; internet www.wheelsmag.com.au; f. 1953; monthly; international motoring magazine; circ. 68,155.

Wildlife Research: CSIRO Publishing, 150 Oxford St, POB 1139, Collingwood, Vic 3066; tel. (3) 9662-7629; fax (3) 9662-7611; e-mail publishing.wr@csiro.au; internet www.publish.csiro.au/nid/144.htm; f. 1974; 6 a year; Man. Editor C. M. MYERS; circ. 1,000.

Your Garden: 35–51 Mitchell St, McMahons Point, NSW 2060; tel. (2) 9464-3586; fax (2) 9464-3487; e-mail yg@pacpubs.com.au; internet www.yourgarden.com.au; monthly; Editor MAREE TREDINNICK; circ. 60,246.

NEWS AGENCIES

AAP: Locked Bag 21, Grosvenor Place, Sydney, NSW 2000; tel. (2) 9322-8000; fax (2) 9322-8888; e-mail info@aap.com.au; internet www.aap.com.au; f. 1983; owned by major daily newspapers of Australia; Chair. MICHAEL GILL; CEO CLIVE MARSHALL.

Foreign Bureaux

Agence France-Presse (AFP): 7th Floor, 259 George St, Sydney, NSW 2000; tel. (2) 9251-1544; fax (2) 9251-5230; e-mail afpsyd@afp.com; internet www.afp.com; Bureau Chief DAVID MILLIKIN.

Agenzia Nazionale Stampa Associata (ANSA) (Italy): Suite 4, 2 Grosvenor St, Bondi Junction, NSW 2022; tel. (2) 9369-1427; fax (2) 9369-4351; e-mail ansasyd@ozemail.com.au; internet www.ansa.it; Bureau Chief CLAUDIO MARCELLO.

Deutsche Presse-Agentur (dpa) (Germany): 36 Heath St, Mona Vale, NSW 2103; tel. (2) 9979-8253; fax (2) 9997-3154; e-mail hofman@zip.com.au; Correspondent ALEXANDER HOFMAN.

Jiji Press (Australia) Pty Ltd (Japan): GPOB 2584, Sydney, NSW 2001; tel. (2) 9230-0020; fax (2) 9230-0024; e-mail jijiaust@bigpond.com; Bureau Chief NOBOTUSHI KOBAYASHI.

Kyodo News Service (Japan): Level 7, 9 Lang St, Sydney, NSW 2000; tel. (2) 9251-5240; fax (2) 9251-4980; e-mail ishii.masato@kyodonews.jp; Bureau Chief MASATO ISHII.

Reuters Australia Pty Ltd: Level 30, 60 Margaret St, Sydney, NSW 2031; e-mail Sydney.newsroom@reuters.com; internet www.reuters.com; Bureau Chief PHIL SMITH.

Xinhua (New China) News Agency (People's Republic of China): 50 Russell St, Hackett, Canberra, ACT 2602; tel. (2) 6248-6369; fax (2) 6257-7633; e-mail xinhua@webone.com.au; Chief Correspondent MI LIGONG.

The Central News Agency (Taiwan) and the New Zealand Press Association are represented in Sydney, and Antara (Indonesia) is represented in Canberra.

PRESS ASSOCIATIONS

Australian Press Council: Suite 10.02, 117 York St, Sydney, NSW 2000; tel. (2) 9261-1930; fax (2) 9267-6826; e-mail info@presscouncil.org.au; internet www.presscouncil.org.au; Chair. Prof. KEN McKINNON.

Community Newspapers of Australia Pty Ltd: POB 234, Auburn, NSW 1835; tel. (2) 8789-7300; fax (2) 8789-7387; e-mail robyn@printnet.com.au; Fed. Pres. JULIE UPSON; Sec. ROBYN BAKER.

Country Press Association of SA Incorporated: 198 Greenhill Rd, Eastwood, SA 5063; tel. (8) 8373-6533; fax (8) 8373-6544; e-mail sacp@iweb.net.au; internet www.cpasa.ans.au; f. 1912; represents South Australian country newspapers; Pres. T. McAULIFFE; Exec. Dir M. S. MANUEL.

Country Press Australia: POB Q182, QVB PO, Sydney, NSW 1230; tel. (2) 9299-4658; fax (2) 9299-1892; f. 1906; Exec. Dir D. J. SOMMERLAD; 420 mems.

Queensland Country Press Association: POB 103, Paddington, Qld 4064; tel. (7) 3356-0033; Pres. M. HODGSON; Sec. N. D. McLARY.

Tasmanian Press Association Pty Ltd: 71–75 Paterson St, Launceston, Tas 7250; tel. (3) 6336-7111; Sec. TOM O'MEARA.

Victorian Country Press Association Ltd: 113 Rosslyn St, West Melbourne, Vic 3003; tel. (3) 9320-8900; fax (3) 9328-1916; e-mail vcpa@vcpa.com.au; internet www.vcpa.com.au; f. 1910; Pres. G. KELLY; Exec. Dir J. E. RAY; 110 mems.

Publishers

Allen and Unwin Pty Ltd: 83 Alexander St, Crows Nest, NSW 2065; tel. (2) 8425-0100; fax (2) 9906-2218; e-mail info@allenandunwin.com; internet www.allenandunwin.com; fiction, trade, academic, children's; Man. Dir PATRICK A. GALLAGHER.

Australasian Medical Publishing Co Pty Ltd: Level 2, 26–32 Pyrmont Bridge Road, Pyrmont, NSW 2009; tel. (2) 9562-6666; fax (2) 9562-6600; e-mail ampco@ampco.com.au; internet www.ampco.com.au; f. 1913; scientific, medical and educational; CEO Dr MARTIN VAN DER WEYDEN.

Cambridge University Press (Australia): 10 477 Williamstown Rd, PB 31, Port Melbourne, Vic 3207; tel. (3) 8671-1400; fax (3) 9676-9966; e-mail customerservice@cambridge.edu.au; internet www.cambridge.edu.au; scholarly and educational; Dir SANDRA McCOMB.

Commonwealth Scientific and Industrial Research Organisation (CSIRO Publishing): 150 Oxford St, POB 1139, Collingwood, Vic 3066; tel. (3) 9662-7500; fax (3) 9662-7555; e-mail publishing@csiro.au; internet www.publish.csiro.au; f. 1926; scientific and technical journals, books, magazines, videos, CD-ROMs; Gen. Man. P. W. REEKIE.

Doubleday Australia Pty Ltd: 91 Mars Rd, Lane Cove, NSW 2066; tel. (2) 9911-1400; fax (2) 9427-6973; educational, trade, non-fiction, Australiana; Man. Dir COLIN JONES.

Elsevier Australia (a division of Reed International Books Australia Pty Ltd): 30–52 Smidmore St, Marrickville, NSW 2204; tel. (2) 9517-8999; fax (2) 9517-2249; e-mail service@elsevier.com.au; internet www.elsevier.com.au; health sciences, science and medicine; Man. Dir FERGUS HALL.

Encyclopaedia Britannica Australia Ltd: Level 1, 90 Mount St, North Sydney, NSW 2060; tel. (2) 9923-5600; fax (2) 9929-3758; e-mail sales@britannica.com.au; internet www.britannica.com.au; reference, education, art, science and commerce; Man. Dir DAVID CAMPBELL.

Harcourt Education Australia: POB 460, Port Melbourne, Vic 3207; tel. (3) 9245-7111; fax (3) 9245-7333; e-mail admin@harcourteducation.com.au; internet www.hi.com.au; primary, secondary and tertiary educational; division of Reed International; Man. Dir DAVID O'BRIEN.

Harlequin Enterprises (Australia) Pty Ltd: Unit 2, 3 Gibbes St, Chatswood, NSW 2067; tel. (2) 9415-9200; fax (2) 9415-9292; internet www.eHarlequin.com.au; Man. Dir MICHELLE LAFOREST.

Hyland House Publishing Pty Ltd: POB 122, Flemington, Vic 3031; tel. and fax (3) 9376-4461; e-mail hyland3@netspace.net.au; f. 1976; trade, general, gardening, pet care, Aboriginal, Asian-Pacific public policy, fiction; Rep. MICHAEL SCHOO.

Lansdowne Publishing: Level 1, 18 Argyle St, The Rocks, NSW 2000; tel. (2) 9240-9222; fax (2) 9241-4818; e-mail steven@lanspub.com.au; cookery, gardening, health, history, pet care; Chief Exec. STEVEN MORRIS.

LexisNexis: Tower 2, 475 Victoria Ave, Chatswood, NSW 2067; tel. (2) 9422-2222; fax (2) 9422-2444; internet www.lexisnexis.com.au; f. 1910; div. of Reed International Books Australia Pty Ltd; legal and commercial; Man. Dir MAX PIPER.

Lothian Books: Level 5, 132 Albert Rd, South Melbourne, Vic 3205; tel. (3) 9694-4900; fax (3) 9645-0705; e-mail books@lothian.com.au; internet www.lothian.com.au; f. 1888; gardening, health, sport, business, New Age, Buddhism, self-help, general non-fiction, young adult fiction and children's picture books; Man. Dir PETER LOTHIAN.

McGraw-Hill Australia Pty Ltd: Level 2, 82 Waterloo Rd, North Ryde, NSW 2113; tel. (2) 9900-1800; fax (2) 9878-8640; e-mail cservice_sydney@mcgraw-hill.com; internet www.mcgraw-hill.com.au; educational, professional and technical; Man. Dir MURRAY ST LEGER.

Melbourne University Publishing Ltd: 187 Grattan St, Carlton, Vic 3053; tel. (3) 9342-0300; fax (3) 9342-0399; e-mail mup-info@unimelb.edu.au; internet www.mup.com.au; f. 1922; scholarly non-fiction, Australian history and biography; CEO and Publr LOUISE ADLER.

Murdoch Books: GPOB 4115, Sydney, NSW 2001; tel. (2) 8220-2000; fax (2) 8220-2558; e-mail dideem@murdochbooks.com.au; cooking, gardening, DIY, craft, gift, general leisure and lifestyle; CEO JULIET ROGERS; Publr KAY SCARLETT.

National Library of Australia: Parkes Place, Canberra, ACT 2600; tel. (2) 6262-1111; fax (2) 6273-4493; e-mail serialorders@nla.gov.au; internet www.nla.gov.au; f. 1960; national bibliographic service, etc.; Publications Dir PAUL HETHERINGTON.

Nelson Thomson Learning: 102 Dodds St, South Melbourne, Vic 3205; tel. (3) 9685-4111; fax (3) 9685-4199; e-mail customerservice@

nelson.com.au; internet www.nelsonitp.com; educational; Man. Dir G. J. Browne.

Oxford University Press: 253 Normanby Rd, South Melbourne, Vic 3205; tel. (3) 9934-9123; fax (3) 9934-9100; f. 1908; general non-fiction and educational; Man. Dir Marek Palka.

Pan Macmillan Australia Pty Ltd: Level 18, St Martin's Tower, 31 Market St, Sydney, NSW 2000; tel. (2) 9285-9100; fax (2) 9285-9190; e-mail pansyd@macmillan.com.au; general, reference, children's, fiction, non-fiction; Chair. R. Gibb.

Pearson Education Australia Pty Ltd: 95 Coventry St, South Melbourne, Vic 3205; tel. (3) 9697-0666; fax (3) 9699-2041; e-mail longman.sales@pearsoned.com.au; internet www.pearsoned.com.au; f. 1957; mainly educational, academic, computer, some general; Man. Dir David Barnett.

Penguin Group (Australia): POB 701, Hawthorn, Vic 3122; tel. (3) 9811-2400; fax (3) 9811-2620; internet www.penguin.com.au; f. 1946; general; Man. Dir Gabrielle Coyne; Publishing Dir Robert Sessions.

Random House Australia Pty Ltd: 20 Alfred St, Milsons Point, NSW 2061; tel. (2) 9954-9966; fax (2) 9954-4562; e-mail random@randomhouse.com.au; internet www.randomhouse.com.au; fiction, non-fiction and children's; Man. Dir Margaret Seale.

Reader's Digest (Australia) Pty Ltd: POB 4353, Sydney, NSW 2000; tel. (2) 9690-6111; fax (2) 9699-8165; general; Man. Dir William B. Toohey.

Scholastic Australia Pty Ltd: Railway Crescent, Lisarow, POB 579, Gosford, NSW 2250; tel. (2) 4328-3555; fax (2) 4323-3827; internet www.scholastic.com.au; f. 1968; educational and children's; Man. Dir Ken Jolly.

Schwartz Publishing (Victoria) Pty Ltd: 45 Flinders Lane, Melbourne, Vic 3000; tel. (3) 9654-2000; fax (3) 9650-5418; fiction, non-fiction; Dir Morry Schwartz.

Simon and Schuster (Australia) Pty Ltd: Suite 2, Lower Ground Floor, 14–16 Suakin St, Pymble, NSW 2073; tel. (2) 9983-6600; fax (2) 9988-4317; internet www.simonsays.com.au; non-fiction incl. anthropology, cooking, gardening, house and home, craft, parenting, health, history, travel, biography, motivation and management; Man. Dir and Publr Jon Attenborough.

Thames and Hudson (Australia) Pty Ltd: 11 Central Boulevard, Portside Business Park, Fishermans Bend, Vic 3207; tel. (3) 9646-7788; fax (3) 9646-8790; e-mail enquiries@thaust.com.au; internet www.thamesandhudson.com; art, history, archaeology, architecture, photography, design, fashion, textiles, lifestyle; Man. Dir Peter Shaw.

Thomson Legal & Regulatory, Australia: Level 5, 100 Harris St, Pyrmont, NSW 2009; tel. (2) 8587-7000; fax (2) 8587-7100; e-mail support@thomson.com.au; internet www.thomson.com.au; legal, professional, tax and accounting; Man. Dir Jackie Rhodes.

Thorpe-Bowker: C3, 85 Turner St, POB 101, Port Melbourne, Vic 3207; tel. (3) 8645-0300; fax (3) 8645-0333; e-mail customer.service@thorpe.com.au; internet www.thorpe.com.au; bibliographic, library and book trade reference; Gen. Man. Richard Siegersma.

Time Life Australia Pty Ltd: Level 12, 33 Berry St, North Sydney, NSW 2060; tel. (2) 8925-3800; fax (2) 9957-4227; general and educational; Man. Dir Robert Hardy.

UNSW Press Ltd: University of New South Wales, Sydney, NSW 2052; tel. (2) 9664-0999; fax (2) 9664-5420; e-mail info.press@unsw.edu.au; f. 1961; scholarly, general and tertiary texts; Man. Dir Dr Robin Derricourt.

University of Queensland Press: POB 6042, St Lucia, Qld 4067; tel. (7) 3365-2127; fax (7) 3365-7579; e-mail uqp@uqp.uq.edu.au; internet www.uqp.uq.edu.au; f. 1948; scholarly and general cultural interest, incl. Black Australian writers, adult and children's fiction; Gen. Man. Greg Bain.

University of Western Australia Press: 35 Stirling Highway, Crawley, WA 6009; tel. (8) 6488-3670; fax (8) 6488-1027; e-mail uwap@cyllene.uwa.edu.au; internet www.uwapress.uwa.edu.au; f. 1935; natural history, history, literary studies, Australiana, children's, general non-fiction; Dir Dr Jenny Gregory.

John Wiley & Sons Australia, Ltd: POB 1226, Milton, Qld 4064; tel. (7) 3859-9755; fax (7) 3859-9715; e-mail brisbane@johnwiley.com.au; internet www.johnwiley.com.au; f. 1954; educational, reference and trade; Man. Dir Peter Donoughue.

GOVERNMENT PUBLISHING HOUSE

AusInfo: GPOB 1920, Canberra, ACT 2601; tel. (2) 6275-3442; fax (2) 6275-3682; internet www.ausinfo.gov.au; f. 1970; fmrly Australian Govt Publishing Service; Asst Sec. Michelle Kinnane.

PUBLISHERS' ASSOCIATION

Australian Publishers Association Ltd: 60/89 Jones St, Ultimo, NSW 2007; tel. (2) 9281-9788; fax (2) 9281-1073; e-mail apa@publishers.asn.au; internet www.publishers.asn.au; f. 1948; 115 mems; Pres. Peter Field; Chief Exec. Susan Bridge.

Broadcasting and Communications

TELECOMMUNICATIONS

By July 2004, 101 licensed telecommunications carriers were in operation.

AAPT Ltd: AAPT Centre, 9 Lang St, Sydney, NSW 2000; tel. (2) 9377-7000; fax (2) 9377-7133; internet www.aapt.com.au; f. 1991; long-distance telecommunications carrier; Chair C. L. Casey; CEO and Man. Dir L. Williams.

Matrix Telecommunications Services: 1st Floor, 24 Artamon Rd, Willoughby, NSW 2068; tel. (2) 9290-4111; fax (2) 9262-2574; f. 1985; mobile communication services; Chair. Mark Carnegie; Pres. and CEO Joseph Yang.

One.Tel Ltd: Level 28, 9 Castlereagh St, Sydney, NSW 2000; tel. (2) 9777-8111; fax (2) 9777-8199; internet www.onetel.com.au; telecommunication services; Chair. John Greaves.

Optus Ltd: POB 1, North Sydney, NSW 2059; tel. (2) 9342-7800; fax (2) 9342-7100; internet www.optus.com.au; f. 1992; division of Singapore Telecommunications Ltd; general and mobile telecommunications, data and internet services, pay-TV; Chair. Sir Ralph Robins; Chief Exec. Paul O'Sullivan.

Telstra Corpn Ltd: Level 14, 231 Elizabeth St, Sydney, NSW 2000; tel. (2) 9287-4677; fax (2) 9287-5869; internet www.telstra.com.au; general and mobile telecommunication services; Man. Dir and Chief Exec. Ziggy Switkowski.

Vodafone Australia Ltd: Tower A, 799 Pacific Highway, Chatswood, NSW 2067; tel. (2) 9415-7000; fax (2) 9878-7788; internet www.vodafone.com.au; mobile telecommunication services.

Regulatory Authority

Australian Communications Authority (ACA): POB 13112, Law Courts, Vic 8010; tel. (3) 9963-6800; fax (3) 9963-6899; e-mail candinfo@aca.gov.au; internet www.aca.gov.au; f. 1997; Commonwealth regulator for telecommunications and radiocommunications; Chair. Bob Horton (acting).

BROADCASTING

Many programmes are provided by the non-commercial statutory corporation, the Australian Broadcasting Corporation (ABC). Commercial radio and television services are provided by stations operated by companies under licences granted and renewed by the Australian Broadcasting Authority (ABA). They rely for their income on the broadcasting of advertisements. In mid-2004 there were about 256 commercial radio stations in operation, and 48 commercial television stations.

In 1997 there were an estimated 25.5m. radio receivers. The number of television receivers in use totalled 14,168,000 in 2001.

Australian Broadcasting Corporation (ABC): 700 Harris St, Ultimo, POB 9994, Sydney, NSW 2001; tel. (2) 9333-1500 (radio); fax (2) 8333-2603 (radio), (2) 9950-3050 (television); e-mail comments@your.abc.net.au; internet www.abc.net.au; f. 1932 as Australian Broadcasting Commission; became corporation in 1983; one national television network operating on about 700 transmitters, one international television service broadcasting via satellite to Asia and the Pacific and six radio networks operating on more than 6,000 transmitters; Chair. Donald McDonald; Man. Dir Russell Balding.

> **Radio Australia:** international service broadcast by short wave and satellite in English, Indonesian, Standard Chinese, Khmer, Tok Pisin and Vietnamese.

Radio

Commercial Radio Australia Ltd: Level 5, 88 Foveaux St, Surry Hills, NSW 2010; tel. (2) 9281-6577; fax (2) 9281-6599; e-mail mail@commercialradio.com.au; internet www.commercialradio.com.au; f. 1930; represents the interests of Australia's commercial radio broadcasters; CEO Joan Warner.

Major Commercial Broadcasting Station Licensees

5AD Broadcasting Co Pty Ltd: 201 Tynte St, Nth Adelaide, SA 5006; tel. (8) 8300-1000; fax (8) 8300-1020; internet www.5adfm.com.au; also operates 5DN and Mix102.3; Gen. Man. Graeme Tucker.

Associated Communications Enterprises (ACE) Radio Broadcasters Pty Ltd: POB 7515, Melbourne, Vic 3004; tel. (3) 9645-9877; fax (3) 9645-9886; operates six stations; Man. Dir S. EVERETT.

Austereo Pty Ltd: Ground Level, 180 St Kilda Rd, St Kilda, Vic 3182; tel. (3) 9230-1051; fax (3) 9593-9007; e-mail pharvie@austereo.com.au; internet www.austereo.com.au; operates 14 stations; Exec. Chair. PETER HARVIE.

Australian Radio Network Pty Ltd: Level 8, 99 Mount St, North Sydney, NSW 2060; tel. (2) 9464-1000; fax (2) 9464-1010; operates nine stations; CEO NEIL MOUNT.

Australian Regional Broadcasters: 1 June Rd, Gooseberry Hill, WA 6076; tel. (8) 9472-8900; fax (8) 9472-8911; operates three stations; Man. Dir NICK RINGROSE.

Bass Radio: 109 York St, Launceston, Tas 7250; tel. (3) 6331-4844; fax (3) 6334-5858; operates five radio stations and part of RG Capital Radio; Man. DAVE HILL; Contact MATT RUSSELL.

Capital Radio: 28 Sharp St, Cooma, NSW 2630; tel. (2) 6452-1521; fax (2) 6452-1006; operates four stations; Man. Dir KEVIN BLYTON.

DMG Regional Radio Pty Ltd: Level 5, 33 Saunders St, Pyrmont, NSW 2009; tel. (2) 9564-9888; fax (2) 9564-9867; e-mail sydoff@dmgradio.com.au; internet www.dmgradio.com.au; operates 59 stations; Group Mans STEVE HIRST (Western Group), SEAN RYAN (Northern Group), GARRY LEDDIN (Southern Group); Gen. Man. ROB GAMBLE.

Grant Broadcasting: 63 Minimbah Rd, Northbridge, NSW 2063; tel. (2) 9958-7301; fax (2) 9958-6906; operates seven stations; Gen. Man. JANET CAMERON.

Greater Cairns Radio Ltd: Virginia House, Abbott St, Cairns, Qld 4870; tel. (7) 4050-0800; fax (7) 4051-8060; e-mail cnssales@dmgradio.com.au; Gen. Man. J. ELLER.

Macquarie Radio Network Pty Ltd: POB 4290, Sydney, NSW 2001; tel. (2) 9269-0646; fax (2) 9287-2772; operates 2GB and 2CH; CEO GEORGE BUSCHMAN.

Moree Broadcasting and Development Company Ltd: 87–89 Balo St, Moree, NSW 2400; tel. (2) 6752-1155; fax (2) 6752-2601; operates two stations; Man. KEN BIRCH.

Radio 2SM Gold 1269: 8 Jones Bay Rd, Pyrmont, NSW 2009; tel. (2) 9922-1269; e-mail info@2sm.com.au; internet www.2sm.com.au; f. 1931; CEO and Chair. C. M. MURPHY.

RadioWest Hot FM: POB 10067, Kalgoorlie, WA 6430; tel. (8) 9021-2666; fax (8) 9091-2209; e-mail radio6KG@gold.net.au; f. 1931.

Regional Broadcasters (Australia) Pty: McDowal St, Roma, Qld 4455; tel. (7) 4622-1800; fax (7) 4622-3697; Chair. G. MCVEAN.

RG Capital Radio Pty Ltd: Level 2, Seabank Bldg, 12–14 Marine Parade, Southport, Qld 4215; tel. (7) 5591-5000; fax (7) 5591-2869; operates 34 stations; Man. Dir RHYS HOLLERAN.

Rural Press Ltd: Cnr Pine Mt Rd and Hill St, Raymonds Hill, Qld 4305; tel. (7) 3201-6000; fax (7) 3812-3060; internet www.rpl.com.au; f. 1911; operates five stations; Gen. Man. RICHARD BURNS.

SEA FM Pty Ltd: POB 5910, Gold Coast Mail Centre, Bundall, Qld 4217; tel. (7) 5591-5000; fax (7) 5591-6080; operates 28 stations; Man. Dir RHYS HOLLERAN.

Southern Cross Broadcasting (Australia) Ltd: see under Television.

Supernetwork Radio Pty Ltd: POB 97, Coolangatta, Qld 4225; tel. (7) 5524-4497; fax (7) 5554-3970; operates 15 stations; Chair. W. CARALIS.

Tamworth Radio Development Company Pty Ltd: POB 497, Tamworth, NSW 2340; tel. (2) 6765-7055; fax (2) 6765-2762; operates five stations; Man. W. A. MORRISON.

Tasmanian Broadcasting Network (TBN): POB 665G, Launceston, Tas 7250; tel. (3) 6431-2555; fax (3) 6431-3188; operates three stations; Chair. K. FINDLAY.

Wesgo Ltd: POB 234, Seven Hills, NSW 2147; tel. (2) 9831-7611; fax (2) 9831-2001; operates eight stations; CEO G. W. RICE.

Television

Free TV Australia (CTVA): 44 Avenue Rd, Mosman, NSW 2088; tel. (2) 8968-7100; fax (2) 9969-3520; e-mail contact@freetvaust.com.au; internet www.freetvaust.com.au; f. 1960; fmrly Commercial Television Australia; represents all commercial free-to-air broadcasters in Australia; Chair. JOHN MCALPINE; CEO JULIE FLYNN.

Commercial Television Station Licensees

Amalgamated Television Services Pty Ltd: Mobbs Lane, Epping, NSW 2121; tel. (2) 9877-7777; fax (2) 9877-7888; f. 1956; originating station for Seven Network TV programming; Exec. Chair. KERRY STOKES.

Australian Capital Television Pty Ltd (Southern Cross Ten): Private Bag 10, Dickson, ACT 2602; tel. (2) 6242-2400; fax (2) 6241-7230; e-mail reception@southerncrossnsw.com.au; f. 1962; Gen. Man. ERIC PASCOE.

Broken Hill Television Ltd: POB 472, Rocky Hill, Broken Hill, NSW 2880; tel. (8) 8087-6013; fax (8) 8087-8492; internet www.centralonline.com.au; f. 1968; operates one station; Chair. PETER STORROCK; Chief Exec. D. WESTON.

Channel 9 South Australia Pty Ltd: 202 Tynte St, North Adelaide 5006; tel. (8) 8267-0111; fax (8) 8267-3996; f. 1959; Gen. Man. M. COLSON.

Channel Seven Adelaide Pty Ltd: 45–49 Park Terrace, Gilberton, SA 5081; tel. (8) 8342-7777; fax (8) 8342-7717; f. 1965; mem. of Seven Network; Man. Dir MAX WALTERS.

Channel Seven Brisbane Pty Ltd: GPOB 604, Brisbane, Qld 4001; tel. (7) 3369-7777; fax (7) 3368-2970; f. 1959; operates one station; mem. of Seven Network; Man. Dir L. M. RILEY.

Channel Seven Melbourne Pty Ltd: 119 Wells St, Southbank, Vic 3006; tel. (3) 9697-7777; fax (3) 9697-7888; e-mail daspinall@seven.com.au; f. 1956; operates one station; Chair. KERRY STOKES; Man. Dir DAVID ASPINALL.

Channel Seven Perth Pty Ltd: POB 77, Tuart Hill, WA 6939; tel. (8) 9344-0777; fax (8) 9344-0670; f. 1959; Chair. C. S. WHARTON.

General Television Corporation Pty Ltd: 22–46 Bendigo St, POB 100, Richmond, Vic 3121; tel. (3) 9429-0201; fax (3) 9429-3670; internet www.nine.msn.com.au; f. 1957; operates one station; Man. Dir GRAEME YARWOOD.

Golden West Network: POB 5090, Geraldton, WA 6531; tel. (8) 9921-4422; fax (8) 9921-8096.

Golden West Network Pty Ltd: POB 1062, West Perth, WA 6872; tel. (8) 9481-0050; fax (8) 9321-2470; f. 1967; operates three stations (SSW10, VEW and WAW); Gen. Man. W. FENWICK.

Imparja Television Pty Ltd: POB 52, Alice Springs, NT 0871; tel. (8) 8950-1411; fax (8) 8953-0322; e-mail imparja@imparja.com.au; internet www.imparja.com.au; CEO ALISTAIR FEEHAN.

Independent Broadcasters of Australia Pty Ltd: POB 285, Sydney, NSW 2001; tel. (2) 9264-9144; fax (2) 9264-6334; fmrly Regional Television Australia Pty Ltd; Chair. GRAEME J. GILBERTSON; Sec. JEFF EATHER.

Mt Isa Television Pty Ltd: 110 Canooweal St, Mt Isa, Qld 4825; tel. (7) 4743-8888; fax (7) 4743-9803; f. 1971; operates one station; Station Man. LYALL GREY.

NBN Ltd: Mosbri Crescent, POB 750L, Newcastle, NSW 2300; tel. (2) 4929-2933; fax (2) 4926-2936; f. 1962; operates one station; Man. Dir DENIS LEDBURY.

Network Ten Ltd: GPOB 10, Sydney, NSW 2001; tel. (2) 9650-1010; fax (2) 9650-1170; operates Australian TV network and commercial stations in Sydney, Melbourne, Brisbane, Perth and Adelaide; CEO JOHN MCALPINE.

Nine Network Australia Pty Ltd: POB 27, Willoughby, NSW 2068; tel. (2) 9906-9999; fax (2) 9958-2279; internet www.ninemsn.com.au; f. 1956; division of Publishing and Broadcasting Ltd; operates three stations: TCN Channel Nine Pty Ltd (Sydney), Queensland Television Ltd (Brisbane) and General Television Corporation Ltd (Melbourne); CEO DAVID LECKIE.

Northern Rivers Television Pty Ltd: Peterson Rd, Locked Bag 1000, Coffs Harbour, NSW 2450; tel. (2) 6652-2777; fax (2) 6652-3034; f. 1965; CEO GARRY DRAFFIN.

Prime Television Group: Level 6, 1 Pacific Highway, North Sydney, NSW 2060; tel. (2) 9965-7700; fax (2) 9965-7729; e-mail primetv@primetv.com.au; internet www.primetv.com.au; Chair. PAUL RAMSAY; CEO BRENT HARMAN.

Prime Television (Northern) Pty Ltd: POB 2077, Elermore Vale, NSW 2287; tel. (2) 4952-0500; fax (2) 4952-0502; internet www.primetv.com.au; Gen. Man. BRAD JONES.

Prime Television (Southern) Pty Ltd: POB 465, Orange, NSW 2800; tel. (2) 6361-6888; fax (2) 6363-1889; Gen. Man. D. EDWARDS.

Prime Television (Victoria) Pty Ltd: Sunraysia Highway, Ballarat, Vic 3350; tel. (3) 5337-1777; fax (3) 5337-1700; e-mail primetv.ballarat@primetv.com.au; Gen. Man. CRAIG WHITFIELD.

Queensland Television Ltd: GPOB 72, Brisbane, Qld 4001; tel. (7) 3214-9999; fax (7) 3369-3512; f. 1959; operates one station; Gen. Man. IAN R. MÜLLER.

Seven Network Ltd: Level 13, 1 Pacific Highway, North Sydney, NSW 2060; tel. (2) 9967-7903; fax (2) 9967-7972; internet www.seven.com.au; owns Amalgamated Television Services Pty Ltd (Sydney), Brisbane TV Ltd (Brisbane), HSV Channel 7 Pty Ltd

(Melbourne), South Australian Telecasters Ltd (Adelaide) and TVW Enterprises Ltd (Perth); Exec. Chair. KERRY STOKES.

Seven Queensland: 140–142 Horton Parade, Maroochydore, Qld 4558; tel. (7) 5430-1777; fax (7) 5430-1767; f. 1965; fmrly Sunshine Television Network Ltd.

Southern Cross Broadcasting (Australia) Ltd: 41–49 Bank St, South Melbourne, Vic 3205; tel. (3) 9243-2100; fax (3) 9690-0937; internet www.scbnetwork.com.au; f. 1932; operates four TV and four radio stations; Man. Dir A. E. BELL.

Southern Cross Television (TNT9) Pty Ltd: Watchorn St, Launceston, Tas 7250; tel. (3) 6344-0202; fax (3) 6343-0340; f. 1962; operates one station; Gen. Man. BRUCE ABRAHAM.

Special Broadcasting Service (SBS): Locked Bag 028, Crows Nest, NSW 1585; tel. (2) 9430-2828; fax (2) 9430-3700; e-mail sbs .com.au; internet www.sbs.com.au; f. 1980; national multi-cultural broadcaster of TV and radio; Man. Dir NIGEL MILAN.

Spencer Gulf Telecasters Ltd: POB 305, Port Pirie, SA 5540; tel. (8) 8632-2555; fax (8) 8633-0984; e-mail dweston@centralonline.com .au; internet www.centralonline.com.au; f. 1968; operates two stations; Chair. P. M. STURROCK; Chief Exec. D. WESTON.

Swan Television & Radio Broadcasters Pty Ltd: POB 99, Tuart Hill, WA 6939; tel. (8) 9449-9999; fax (8) 9449-9900; Gen. Man. P. BOWEN.

Telecasters Australia Ltd: Level 8, 1 Elizabeth Plaza, North Sydney, NSW 2060; tel. (2) 9922-1011; fax (2) 9922-1033; internet www.telecasters.com.au; operates commercial TV services of TEN Queensland, TEN Northern NSW, Seven Central and Seven Darwin.

Territory Television Pty Ltd: POB 1764, Darwin, NT 0801; tel. (8) 8981-8888; fax (8) 8981-6802; f. 1971; operates one station; Gen. Man. A. G. BRUYN.

WIN Television Griffith Pty Ltd: 161 Remembrance Driveway, Griffith, NSW 2680; tel. (2) 6962-4500; fax (2) 6962-0979; e-mail mtntv@ozemail.com.au; fmrly MTN Television; Man. Dir RAY GAMBLE.

WIN Television Loxton SA Pty Ltd: Murray Bridge Rd, POB 471, Loxton, SA 5333; tel. (8) 8584-6891; fax (8) 8584-5062; f. 1976; operates one station; Exec. Chair. E. H. URLWIN; Gen. Man. W. L. MUDGE.

WIN Television Mildura Pty Ltd: 18 Deakin Ave, Mildura, Vic 3500; tel. (3) 5023-0204; fax (3) 5022-1179; f. 1965; Chair. JOHN RUSHTON; Man. NOEL W. HISCOCK.

WIN Television NSW Network: Television Ave, Mt St Thomas, Locked Bag 8800, South Coast Mail Centre, NSW 2521; tel. (2) 4223-4199; fax (2) 4227-3682; internet www.wintv.com.au; f. 1962; Man. Dir K. KINGSTON; CEO JOHN RUSHTON.

WIN Television Qld Pty Ltd: POB 568 Rockhampton, Qld 4700; tel. (7) 4930-4499; fax (7) 4930-4490; Station Man. R. HOCKEY.

WIN Television Tas Pty Ltd: 52 New Town Rd, Hobart, Tas 7008; tel. (3) 6228-8999; fax (3) 6228-8991; e-mail wintas.com.au; internet www.wintv.com.au; f. 1959; Gen. Man. GREG RAYMENT.

WIN Television Vic Pty Ltd: POB 464, Ballarat, Vic 3353; tel. (3) 5320-1366; fax (3) 5333-1598; internet www.winnet.com.au; f. 1961; operates five stations; Gen. Man. MICHAEL TAYLOR.

Satellite, Cable and Digital Television

Digital television became available in metropolitan areas in January 2001 and was to be available in all major regional areas by 2004.

Austar United Communications: Level 29, AAP Centre, 259 George St, Sydney, NSW 2000; tel. (2) 9251-6999; fax (2) 9251-6136; e-mail austar@austarunited.com.au; internet www.austarunited .com.au; began operations in 1995; 459,819 subscribers (June 2004); CEO JOHN C. PORTER.

Australia Television: international satellite service; broadcasts to more than 30 countries and territories in Asia and the Pacific.

Foxtel: Foxtel Television Centre, Pyrmont, Sydney; internet www .foxtel.com.au; owned by the News Corpn, Telstra Corpn and PBL; 800,100 subscribers (Aug. 2002).

Optus Vision: Tower B, Level 15, 16 Zenith Centre, 821–841 Pacific Highway, Chatswood, NSW 2067; commenced cable services on 11 channels in 1995; 210,000 subscribers (March 1999).

Regulatory Authority

Australian Broadcasting Authority: POB Q500, QVB PO, NSW 1230; tel. (2) 9334-7700; fax (2) 9334-7799; e-mail info@aba.gov.au; internet www.aba.gov.au; regulates radio and TV broadcasting, and internet content; Chair. LYN MADDOCK (acting).

Finance

(cap. = capital; p.u. = paid up; res = reserves; dep. = deposits; m. = million; brs = branches; amounts in Australian dollars)

Radical reforms of the financial sector were introduced in 1998. The banking system was opened up to greater competition. The licensing and regulation of deposit-taking institutions was supervised by the new Australian Prudential Regulation Authority, while consumer protection was the responsibility of the Australian Corporations and Financial Services Commission.

Australian Prudential Regulation Authority (APRA): GPOB 9836, Sydney, NSW 2000; tel. (2) 9210-3000; fax (2) 9210-3411; e-mail aprainfo@apra.gov.au; internet www.apra.gov.au; f. 1998; responsible for regulation of banks, insurance cos, superannuation funds, credit unions, building societies and friendly societies; Chair. Dr JOHN LAKER.

BANKING

Central Bank

Reserve Bank of Australia: GPOB 3947, Sydney, NSW 2001; tel. (2) 9551-8111; fax (2) 9551-8000; e-mail rbainfo@rba.gov.au; internet www.rba.gov.au; f. 1911; responsible for monetary policy, financial system stability, payment system development; cap. 40m., res 10,816m., dep. 18,126m. (June 2004), total assets 66,593m., notes on issue 32,172m. (June 2003); Gov. IAN MACFARLANE.

Development Bank

Rabobank Australia Ltd: GPOB 4577, 7th Floor, 115 Pitt St, Sydney, NSW 2000; tel. (2) 9234-4200; fax (2) 9221-6218; e-mail sydney.enquiry@rabobank.com; internet www.rabobank.com.au; f. 1978 as Primary Industry Bank of Australia Ltd; name changed as above 2003; cap. 123.2m., res 2.5m.; Chair. H. G. GENTIS, JAMES GRAHAM; 219 brs.

Trading Banks

ABN AMRO Australia Ltd: Level 29, ABN AMRO Tower, 88 Phillip St, Sydney, NSW 2000; tel. (2) 8259-5000; fax (2) 8259-5444; internet www.abnamro.com.au; f. 1971; cap. 70m., res 590,000 (Dec. 2000); CEO ANGUS JAMES.

Arab Bank Australia Ltd: GPOB N645, Grosvenor Place, 200 George St, Sydney, NSW 2000; tel. (2) 9377-8900; fax (2) 9221-5428; internet www.arabbank.com.au; cap. 55.0m., dep. 859.2m. (Dec. 2003); Chair. ABDEL-HAMID SHOMAN; Man. Dir JAMES WAKIM.

Australia and New Zealand Banking Group Ltd: 100 Queen St, 6th Floor, GPOB 537E, Melbourne, Vic 3000; tel. (3) 9273-5555; fax (3) 9658-2484; internet www.anz.com; f. 1835; present name adopted in 1970; cap. 6,387m., res 180m., dep. 130,961m. (2003); Chair. C. B. GOODE; CEO JOHN MCFARLANE; 748 domestic brs, 204 overseas brs.

Bank of America Australia Ltd: Level 63, MLC Centre, 19–29 Martin Place, Sydney, NSW 2000; tel. (2) 9931-4200; fax (2) 9221-1023; f. 1964; cap. 150.3m. (Dec. 1998); Man. Dir JOHN LILES.

Bank of Melbourne: 360 Collins St, Melbourne, Vic 3000; tel. (3) 9608-3222; fax (3) 9608-3700; division of Westpac Banking Corpn; f. 1989; cap. 752m., dep. 8,706m. (1997); Chair. CHRIS STEWART; CEO MATTHEW SLATTER; 129 brs.

Bank of Queensland Ltd: 229 Elizabeth St, POB 898, Brisbane, Qld 4001; tel. (7) 3212-3333; fax (7) 3212-3399; internet www.boq .com.au; f. 1874; cap. 321.9m., res 0.2m., dep. 6,114.2m. (Aug. 2004); Chair. NEIL ROBERTS; Man Dir. DAVID P. LIDDY; 137 brs.

Bank of Tokyo-Mitsubishi (Australia) Ltd: Level 26, Gateway, 1 Macquarie Place, Sydney, NSW 2000; tel. (2) 9296-1111; fax (2) 9247-4266; e-mail btmacorp@btma.com.au; f. 1985; cap. 152.9m., res 33,000m., dep. 1,910.8m. (Dec. 2000); Chair. R. NICOLSON; Man. Dir H. KOJIMA.

Bank of Western Australia Ltd (BankWest): Level 7, BankWest Tower, 108 St George's Terrace, POB E237, Perth, WA 6001; tel. (8) 9449-7000; fax (8) 9449-7050; e-mail finmkts@bankwest.com.au; internet www.bankwest.com.au; f. 1895 as Agricultural Bank of Western Australia, 1945 as Rural and Industries Bank of Western Australia; present name adopted in 1994; cap. 872.3m., res 300,000, dep. 16,436.9m. (Dec. 2002); Chair. IAN C. R. MACKENZIE; Man. Dir RODGER MCARTHUR; 87 brs.

Bankers' Trust Australia Ltd: GPOB H4, Australia Sq., Sydney, NSW 2000; tel. (2) 9259-3555; fax (2) 9259-9800; internet www.btal .com.au; f. 1986; cap. 273.3m., dep. 6,266.8m. (Dec. 1997); Man. Dir R. A. FERGUSON; 5 brs.

Bendigo Bank Ltd: 2nd Floor, Fountain Court, Bendigo, Vic 3550; tel. (3) 5433-9339; fax (3) 5433-9690; internet www.bendigobank .com.au; f. 1995; cap. 463.6m., res 1.1m., dep. 8,336.8m. (June 2003); Chair. RICHARD A. GUY; Man. Dir ROBERT G. HUNT; 268 brs.

The Chase Manhattan Bank: GPOB 9816, Sydney, NSW 2001; tel. (2) 9250-4111; fax (2) 9250-4554; internet www.chase.com; Man. Dir W. SCOTT REID.

Citibank Pty Ltd: GPOB 40, Sydney, NSW 2000; tel. (2) 8225-0000; fax (2) 9239-9110; internet www.citibank.com.au; f. 1954; cap. 457m., res 1m., dep. 5,619m. (Dec. 1998); CEO (Australasia) AHMED FAHOUR; Man. Dir LES MATHESON.

Commonwealth Bank of Australia: Level 7, 48 Martin Place, Sydney, NSW 1155; tel. (2) 9378-2000; fax (2) 9378-3317; internet www.commbank.com.au; f. 1912; merged with Colonial Ltd in 2000; cap. 13,365.0m., res 3,850.0m., dep. 172,373.0m. (June 2003); Chair. J. T. RALPH; CEO and Man. Dir D. V. MURRAY; more than 1,200 brs world-wide.

HSBC Bank Australia Ltd: Level 32, HSBC Centre, 580 George St, Sydney, NSW 2000; tel. (2) 9006-5888; fax (2) 9006-5440; e-mail pr@hsbc.com.au; internet www.hsbc.com.au; f. 1985; fmrly Hongkong Bank of Australia; cap. 641.0m., dep. 12,006.1m. (Dec. 2003), res 3.4m. (Dec. 2002); Chair D. J. SAY; CEO STUART DAVIS; 24 brs.

ING Bank (Australia) Ltd: Level 13, 140 Sussex St, Sydney, NSW 2000; tel. (2) 9028-4000; fax (2) 9028-4708; f. 1994; cap. 60m., res 1.3m., dep. 1,015.4m. (Dec. 1998); Gen. Man. JULIE BROWN.

Macquarie Bank Ltd: 1 Martin Place, Sydney, NSW 2000; tel. (2) 8232-3333; fax (2) 8232-3350; internet www.macquarie.com.au; f. 1969 as Hill Samuel Australia Ltd; present name adopted in 1985; cap. 1,382m., res 391m., dep. 32,926m. (March 2004); Chair. DAVID S. CLARKE; Man. Dir ALLAN E. MOSS; 4 brs.

National Australia Bank Ltd: 500 Bourke St, Melbourne, Vic 3000; tel. (3) 8641-3500; fax (3) 8641-4912; internet www.national .com.au; f. 1858; cap. 9,728m., res 893m., dep. 309,210m. (Sept. 2003); Chair. MARK RAYNER; Man. Dir and Chief Exec. JOHN STEWART; 2,349 brs.

N. M. Rothschild & Sons (Australia) Ltd: Level 16, 1 O'Connell St, Sydney, NSW 2000; tel. (2) 9323-2000; fax (2) 9323-2323; internet www.rothschild.com.au; f. 1967 as International Pacific Corpn; cap. 170.0m., res 1m., dep. 1,135.2m. (March 2003); Chair. PAUL ISHERWOOD; Chief Exec. RICHARD MARTIN; 3 brs.

SG Australia Ltd: Level 21, 400 George St, Sydney, NSW 2000; tel. (2) 9210-8000; fax (2) 9235-3941; internet www.au.sg-ib.com; f. 1981; fmrly Société Générale Australia Ltd; cap. 21.5m., res 208m., dep. 5,656m. (Dec. 1999); CEO MICHEL L. MACAGNO.

St George Bank Ltd: Locked Bag 1, St George House, 4–16 Montgomery St, Kogarah, NSW 2217; tel. (2) 9952-1311; fax (2) 9952-1000; e-mail stgeorge@stgeorge.com.au; internet www .stgeorge.com.au; f. 1937 as building society; cap. 3,485m., res 114m., dep. 45,713m. (Sept. 2003); Chair. F. J. CONROY; CEO and Man. Dir GAIL KELLY; 409 brs.

Standard Chartered Bank Australia Ltd: Level 11, 345 George St, Sydney, NSW 2000; tel. (2) 9232-9333; fax (2) 9232-9345; f. 1986; cap. 226.2m., dep. 667.8m. (Dec. 1999); Chair. RICHARD NETTLETON; CEO EUGENE ELLIS.

Toronto Dominion Australia Ltd: Level 34, Rialto South Tower, 525 Collins St, Melbourne, Vic 3000; tel. (3) 9993-1344; fax (3) 9614-0083; internet www.tdbank.ca; f. 1970; cap. 191.5m., res 6.0m., dep. 3,435.4m. (Oct. 1997); Man. Dir STEVE FRYER.

Westpac Banking Corporation: 60 Martin Place, Sydney, NSW 2000; tel. (2) 9226-3311; fax (2) 9226-4128; e-mail westpac@westpac .com.au; internet www.westpac.com.au; f. 1817; cap. 4,443m., res 2,179m., dep. 162,872m. (Sept. 2003); Chair. L. A. DAVIS; Man. Dir DAVID MORGAN; 812 domestic brs, 200 brs in New Zealand, 57 other brs.

Foreign Banks

Bank of China (People's Republic of China): 39–41 York St, Sydney, NSW 2000; tel. (2) 9267-5188; fax (2) 9262-1794; e-mail bocsyd@bigpond.com.au; Gen. Man. GAO JI LU.

Bank of New Zealand: 9th Floor, BNZ House, 333–339 George St, Sydney, NSW 2000; tel. (2) 9290-6666; fax (2) 9290-3414; Chief Operating Officer G. ARMBRUSTER.

BNP Paribas (France): POB 269, Sydney, NSW 2001; tel. (2) 9216-8633; fax (2) 9619-6104; e-mail finance@au.bnpparibas.com; internet www.bnpparibas.com.au; CEO FRANÇOIS CRISTOFARI; 4 brs.

Deutsche Bank AG (Germany): GPOB 7033, Sydney, NSW 1170; tel. (2) 9258-1234; fax (2) 9241-2565; internet www.australia.db .com; CEO CHUM DARVALL.

STOCK EXCHANGE

Australian Stock Exchange Ltd (ASX): Level 9, 20 Bridge St, Sydney, NSW 2000; tel. (2) 9227-0000; fax (2) 9227-0885; e-mail info@asx.com.au; internet www.asx.com.au; f. 1987 by merger of the stock exchanges in Sydney, Adelaide, Brisbane, Hobart, Melbourne

and Perth, to replace the fmr Australian Associated Stock Exchanges; demutualized and listed Oct. 1998; Chair. MAURICE NEWMAN; Man. Dir and CEO TONY D'ALOISIO.

Supervisory Body

Australian Securities and Investments Commission (ASIC): GPOB 9827, Sydney, NSW 2001; tel. (2) 9111-2000; fax (2) 9911-2333; e-mail infoline@asic.gov.au; internet www.asic.gov.au; f. 1990; corporations and financial products regulator; Chair. JEFFREY LUCY.

PRINCIPAL INSURANCE COMPANIES

Allianz Australia Ltd: 2 Market St, Sydney, NSW 2000; tel. (2) 9390-6222; fax (2) 9390-6425; internet www.allianz.com.au; f. 1914; workers' compensation; fire, general accident, motor and marine; Chair. J. S. CURTIS; Man. Dir T. TOWELL.

AMP Ltd: AMP Bldg, 33 Alfred St, Sydney, NSW 2000; tel. (2) 9257-5000; fax (2) 9257-7886; internet www.amp.com.au; f. 1849; fmrly Australian Mutual Provident Society; life insurance; Chair. PETER WILLCOX; CEO ANDREW MOHL.

Australian Guarantee Corpn Ltd: 130 Phillip St, Sydney, NSW 2000; tel. (2) 9234-1122; fax (2) 9234-1225; f. 1925; Chair. J. A. UHRIG; Man. Dir R. THOMAS.

Australian Unity General Insurance Ltd: 114 Albert Rd, South Melbourne, Vic 3205; tel. (3) 9697-0219; fax (3) 9690-5556; e-mail webmaster@austunity.com.au; internet www.austunity.com.au; f. 1948; Chair. LEON HICKEY; Chief Exec. M. W. SIBREE.

Aviva Australia Holdings Ltd: GPOB 2567W, 509 St Kilda Rd, Melbourne 3001; tel. (3) 9829-8989; fax (3) 9820-1534; internet www .avivagroup.com.au; f. 2000 as CGNU following merger of CGU and Norwich Union, renamed as above in 2003; CEO ALLAN GRIFFITHS.

Catholic Church Insurances Ltd: 324 St Kilda Rd, Melbourne, Vic 3004; tel. (3) 9934-3000; fax (3) 9934-3460; internet www .ccinsurances.com.au; f. 1911; Chair. Most Rev. KEVIN MANNING (Bishop of Parramatta); Gen. Man. PETER RUSH.

The Copenhagen Reinsurance Co Ltd: 60 Margaret St, Sydney, NSW 2000; tel. (2) 9247-7266; fax (2) 9235-3320; e-mail david .kennedy@copre.com; internet www.copre.com; reinsurance; Gen. Man. DAVID KENNEDY.

FAI Insurances Ltd: FAI Insurance Group, 333 Kent St, Sydney, NSW 1026; tel. (2) 9274-9000; fax (2) 9274-9900; internet www.fai .com.au; f. 1953; Chair. JOHN LANDERER; CEO RODNEY ADLER.

General Reinsurance Australia Ltd: Level 24, 123 Pitt St, Sydney, NSW 2000; tel. (2) 8236-6100; fax (2) 9222-1500; f. 1961; reinsurance, fire, accident, marine; Chair. F. A. McDONALD; Man. Dir D. W. BRADFORD.

GIO Australia Holdings Ltd: Level 39, Governor Phillip Tower, 1 Farrer Place, Sydney, NSW 2000; tel. (2) 9255-8090; fax (2) 9251-2079; e-mail emailus@gio.com.au; internet www.gio.com.au; f. 1926; CEO PETER CORRIGAN.

Guild Insurance Ltd: Guild House, 40 Burwood Rd, Hawthorn, Vic 3122; tel. (3) 9810-9820; fax (3) 9819-5670; internet www.guildifs .com.au/insurance; f. 1963; Gen. Man. DAVID BROWN.

HIH Insurance Ltd: AMP Centre, 50 Bridge St, Sydney, NSW 2000; tel. (2) 9650-2000; fax (2) 9650-2030; internet www.hih.com .au; f. 1968; Chair. G. A. COHEN; CEO R. R. WILLIAMS.

Lumley General Insurance Ltd: Lumley House, 309 Kent St, Sydney, NSW 1230; tel. (2) 9248-1111; fax (2) 9248-1122; e-mail general@lumley.com.au; Man. Dir D. M. MATCHAM.

The National Mutual Life Association of Australasia Ltd: 447 Collins St, Melbourne, Vic 3000; tel. (3) 9618-4920; fax (3) 9616-3445; e-mail investor.relations@axa.com.au; internet www.axa.com .au; f. 1869; life insurance, superannuation, income protection; Chair. R. H. ALLERT; Group CEO A. L. OWEN.

NRMA Insurance Ltd: 151 Clarence St, Sydney, NSW 2000; tel. (2) 9292-9222; fax (2) 9292-8472; internet www.nrma.com.au; f. 1926; CEO IAN BROWN (acting).

NZI Insurance Australia Ltd: 9th Floor, 10 Spring St, Sydney, NSW 2000; tel. (2) 9551-5000; fax (2) 9551-5865; Man. Dir H. D. SMITH.

QBE Insurance Group Ltd: 82 Pitt St, Sydney, NSW 2000; tel. (2) 9375-4444; fax (2) 9235-3166; internet www.qbe.com; f. 1886; general insurance; Chair. E. J. CLONEY; Man. Dir F. M. O'HALLORAN.

RAC Insurance Pty Ltd: 228 Adelaide Terrace, Perth, WA 6000; tel. (8) 9421-4444; fax (8) 9421-4593; f. 1947; Gen. Man. TONY CARTER.

RACQ Insurance: POB 4, Springwood, Qld 4127; tel. (7) 3361-2444; fax (7) 3841-2995; e-mail inorris@racqi.com.au; internet www .racqinsurance.com.au; f. 1971; CEO I. W. NORRIS.

RACV: 550 Princes Highway, Noble Park, Vic 3174; tel. (3) 9790-2211; fax (3) 9790-3091.

RSA Insurance Australia Ltd: 465 Victoria Ave, Chatswood, NSW 2067; tel. (2) 9978-9000; fax (2) 9978-9807; fire, accident and marine insurance; Gen. Man. E. KULK.

Suncorp-Metway Ltd: Level 18, 36 Wickham Tce, Brisbane, Qld 4000; tel. (7) 3835-5355; fax (7) 3836-1190; e-mail direct@suncorp.co.au; internet www.suncorp.com.au; f. 1996; Man. Dir STEVE JONES.

Swiss Re Australia Ltd: 363 George St, Sydney, NSW 2000; tel. (2) 8295-9500; fax (2) 8295-9804; f. 1962; Head of Australia and New Zealand operations KEITH SCOTT.

Wesfarmers Federation Insurance Ltd: 184 Railway Parade, Bassendean, WA 6054; tel. (8) 9273-5770; fax (8) 9273-5290; e-mail mel.rom@wfi.wesfarmers.com.au; internet www.wfi.com.au; Gen. Man. R. J. BUCKLEY.

Westpac Life Ltd: 35 Pitt St, Sydney, NSW 2000; tel. (2) 9220-4768; f. 1986; CEO DAVID WHITE.

World Marine & General Insurances Ltd: 600 Bourke St, Melbourne, Vic 3000; tel. (3) 9609-3333; fax (3) 9609-3634; f. 1961; Chair. G. W. MCGREGOR; Man. Dir A. E. REYNOLDS.

Zurich Financial Services Australia Ltd: 5 Blue St, North Sydney, NSW 2060; tel. (2) 9391-1111; fax (2) 9922-4630; e-mail client.service@zurich.com.au; internet www.zurich.com.au; CEO TOM BROWN; Chair. NANCY MILNE.

Insurance Associations

Australian Insurance Association: 54 Marcus Clarke St, Canberra City ACT; tel. (2) 6249-7666; f. 1968; Pres. RAYMOND JONES; Exec. Sec. P. M. MURPHY.

Australian and New Zealand Institute of Insurance and Finance: Level 17, 31 Queen St, Melbourne, Vic 3000; tel. (3) 9629-4021; fax (3) 9629-4204; e-mail ceo@theinstitute.com.au; internet www.theinstitute.com.au; f. 1919; Pres. JOHN RICHARDSON; CEO JOAN FITZPATRICK; 11,984 mems.

Insurance Council of Australia Ltd: Level 3, 56 Pitt St, Sydney, NSW 2000; tel. (2) 9253-5100; fax (2) 9253-5111; internet www.ica.com.au; f. 1975; CEO ALAN MASON.

Investment and Financial Services Association (IFSA): Level 24, 44 Market St, Sydney, NSW 2000; tel. (2) 9299-3022; fax (2) 9299-3198; e-mail ifsa@ifsa.com.au; internet www.ifsa.com.au; f. 1997 following merger of Australian Investment Managers' Association, Investment Funds Association and Life, Investment and Superannuation Association of Australia Inc; non-profit organization; Chair. Dr DOUG MCTAGGART; CEO RICHARD GILBERT.

Trade and Industry

GOVERNMENT AGENCY

Austrade: GPOB 5301, Sydney, NSW 2001; tel. (2) 9390-2000; fax (2) 9390-2024; e-mail info@austrade.gov.au; internet www.austrade.gov.au; f. 1931; export promotion agency; Chair. ROSS ADLER; Man. Dir PETER O'BYRNE.

CHAMBERS OF COMMERCE

Australian Chamber of Commerce and Industry (ACCI): POB E14, Kingston, ACT 2604; tel. (2) 6273-2311; fax (2) 6273-3286; e-mail acci@acci.asn.au; internet www.acci.asn.au; Pres. Dr JOHN KENIRY; CEO MARK PATERSON.

Chamber of Commerce and Industry of Western Australia (CCIWA): POB 6209, East Perth, WA 6892; tel. (8) 9365-7555; fax (8) 9365-7550; e-mail info@cciwa.com; internet www.cciwa.com; f. 1890; 6,000 mems; Chief Exec. JOHN LANGOULANT; Pres. Dr BRIAN HEWITT.

Commerce Queensland: Industry House, 375 Wickham Terrace, Brisbane, Qld 4000; tel. (7) 3842-2244; fax (7) 3832-3195; e-mail info@commerceqld.com.au; internet www.commerceqld.com.au; f. 1868; operates World Trade Centre, Brisbane; 5,500 mems; CEO ANDREW CRAIG.

South Australian Employers' Chamber of Commerce and Industry Inc: Enterprise House, 136 Greenhill Road, Unley, SA 5061; tel. (8) 8300-0000; fax (8) 8300-0001; e-mail enquiries@business-sa.com; internet www.business-sa.com; f. 1839; 4,700 mems; CEO P. VAUGHAN.

State Chamber of Commerce (New South Wales): Level 12, 83 Clarence St, Sydney, NSW 2000; tel. (2) 9350-8100; fax (2) 9350-8197; e-mail trade@thechamber.com.au; internet www.thechamber.com.au; f. 1825; offers advice to and represents over 70,000 businesses; Chief Exec. MARGY OSMOND.

Tasmanian Chamber of Commerce and Industry: GPOB 793H, Hobart, Tas 7001; tel. (3) 6234-5933; fax (3) 6231-1278; CEO TIM ABEY.

Victorian Employers' Chamber of Commerce and Industry: Industry House, 486 Albert St, Melbourne, Vic 3002; tel. (3) 8662-5333; fax (3) 8662-5462; e-mail vecci@vecci.org.au; internet www.vecci.org.au; f. 1885; CEO NEIL COULSON.

AGRICULTURAL, INDUSTRIAL AND TRADE ASSOCIATIONS

Australian Business Ltd: Locked Bag 938, North Sydney, NSW 2059; tel. (2) 9458-7500; fax (2) 9923-1166; e-mail member.services@australianbusiness.com.au; internet www.australianbusiness.com.au; f. 1885; fmrly Chamber of Manufactures of NSW; CEO MARK BETHWAITE.

Australian Manufacturers' Export Council: POB E14, Queen Victoria Terrace, ACT 2600; tel. (2) 6273-2311; fax (2) 6273-3196; f. 1955; Exec. Dir G. CHALKER.

Australian Wine and Brandy Corporation (AWBC): POB 2733, Kent Town Business Centre, Kent Town, SA 5071; tel. (8) 8228-2000; fax (8) 8228-2022; e-mail awbc@awbc.com.au; internet www.awbc.com.au; Chief Exec. SAM TOTLEY.

Australian Wool Services Ltd: Wool House, 369 Royal Parade, Parkville, Vic 3052; tel. (3) 9341-9111; fax (3) 9341-9273; internet www.woolmark.com; f. 2001 following the privatization of the Australian Wool Research and Promotion Organisation; operates two subsidiaries: Australian Wool Innovation and The Woolmark Company, which is responsible for commercial development; Chair. TREVOR FLUGGE.

AWB Ltd: Ceres House, 528 Lonsdale St, Melbourne, Vic 3000; tel. (3) 9209-2000; fax (3) 9670-2782; e-mail awb@awb.com.au; internet www.awb.com.au; f. 1939; fmrly Australian Wheat Board; national and international marketing of grain, financing and marketing of wheat and other grains for growers; 12 mems; Chair. BRENDAN STEWART; CEO ANDREW LINDBERG.

Business Council of Australia: GPOB 1472N, Melbourne, Vic 3001; tel. (3) 8664-2664; fax (3) 8664-2666; e-mail info@bca.com.au; internet www.bca.com.au; public policy research and advocacy; governing council comprises chief execs of Australia's major cos; Pres. STAN WALLIS; Chair. HUGH MORGAN.

Cotton Australia: Level 2, 490 Crown St, Surry Hills, NSW 2010; tel. (2) 9360-8500; fax (2) 9360-8555; e-mail talktous@cottonaustralia.com.au; internet www.cottonaustralia.com.au; Chair. CHARLES WILSON.

Meat and Livestock Australia: Level 1, 165 Walker St, North Sydney, NSW 2060; tel. 1800-023-100; fax (2) 9463-9393; internet www.mla.com.au; producer-owned co; represents, promotes, protects and furthers interests of industry in both the marketing of meat and livestock and industry-based research and devt activities; Chair. DAVID CROMBIE.

National Farmers' Federation: POB E10, Kingston, ACT 2604; tel. (2) 6273-3855; fax (2) 6273-2331; e-mail nff@nff.org.au; internet www.nff.org.au; Pres. PETER CORISH; CEO BEN FARGHER.

Natural Resources Management Ministerial Council (NRMC): Dept of Agriculture, Fisheries and Forestry—Australia, Barton, Canberra, ACT 2600; tel. (2) 6272-5216; fax (2) 6272-4772; internet www.mincos.gov.au; f. 2002 to replace the Agricultural and Resource Management Council of Australia and New Zealand to promote the conservation and sustainable use of Australia's natural resources; mems comprising the Commonwealth/state/territory and New Zealand ministers responsible for environment, water and natural resources.

Primary Industries Ministerial Council (PIMC): Dept of Agriculture, Fisheries and Forestry, Barton, Canberra, ACT 2600; tel. (2) 6272-5216; fax (2) 6272-4772; e-mail pimc@mincos.gov.au; internet www.mincos.gov.au; f. 2002 to develop and promote sustainable, innovative and profitable agriculture, fisheries, food and forestry industries; mems comprising the state/territory and New Zealand ministers responsible for agriculture, fisheries, food and forestry.

Trade Policy Advisory Council (TPAC): c/o Dept of Foreign Affairs and Trade, R. G. Casey Bldg, John McEwen Cres., Barton, ACT 0221; tel. (2) 6261-2910; fax (2) 6261-1385; e-mail tpac@dfat.gov.au; internet www.dfat.gov.au/trade/opening_doors/tpac.html; advises the Minister for Trade on business and investment issues; Chair. GEOFF ALLEN.

WoolProducers: POB E10, Kingston, Canberra, ACT 2604; tel. (2) 6273-2531; fax (2) 6273-1120; e-mail woolproducers@nff.org.au; internet www.woolproducers.com; fmrly Wool Council Australia; comprises 20 mems; represents wool-growers in dealings with the Federal Govt and industry; Pres. SIMON CAMPBELL.

EMPLOYERS' ORGANIZATIONS

Australian Co-operative Foods Ltd: 433 Victoria St, Wetherill Park, NSW 2164; tel. (2) 4821-1391; e-mail exports@dairyfarmers .com.au; f. 1900; Man. Dir A. R. TOOTH.

Australian Industry Group: 51 Walker St, North Sydney, NSW 2060; tel. (2) 9466-5566; fax (2) 9466-5599; e-mail louisep@aignsw .aigroup.asn.au; internet www.aigroup.asn.au; f. 1998 through merger of MTIA and ACM; 11,500 mems; Nat. Pres. G. J. ASHTON; CEO ROBERT N. HERBERT.

Australian Meat Industry Council: 25–27 Albany St, Crows Nest, NSW 2065; POB 1208, Crows Nest, NSW 1585; tel. (2) 9086-2200; fax (2) 9086-2201; e-mail admin@amic.org.au; internet www .amic.org.au; f. 1928; Chair. GARY HARDWICK; CEO KEVIN COTTRILL.

NSW Farmers' Association: GPOB 1068, Sydney, NSW 2001; tel. (2) 8251-1700; fax (2) 8251-1750; e-mail emailus@nswfarmers.org .au; internet www.nswfarmers.org.au; f. 1978; CEO JONATHAN MCKEOWN; Pres. MAL PETERS.

UTILITIES

Australian Institute of Energy: POB 268, Toukley, NSW 2263; tel. 1800-629-945; fax (2) 4393-1114; e-mail aie@tpgi.com.au; internet www.aie.org.au.

Australian Water Association: POB 388, Artarmon, NSW 1570; tel. (2) 9413-1288; fax (2) 9413-1047; e-mail info@awa.asn.au; internet www.awa.asn.au; f. 1962; c. 4,000 mems; CEO CHRIS DAVIS.

Electricity Supply Association of Australia: GPOB 1823Q, Melbourne, Vic 3001; tel. (2) 9670-0188; fax (2) 9670-1069; internet www .esaa.com.au; CEO BRAD PAGE.

Electricity Companies

Actew AGL: GPOB 366, Canberra, ACT 2601; tel. (2) 6248-3111; e-mail webmaster@actewagl.com.au; internet www.actewagl.com .au; f. 2000 by amalgamation of ACTEW Corpn Ltd and AGL; supplier of electricity, gas, water and wastewater services; Chief Exec. PAUL PERKINS.

Delta Electricity: POB Q863, QVB PO, NSW 1230; tel. (2) 9285-2700; fax (2) 9285-2777; internet www.de.com.au; f. 1996; Chief Exec. JIM HENNESS.

ENERGEX: GPOB 1461, Brisbane, Qld 4001; tel. (7) 3407-4000; fax (7) 3407-4609; e-mail enquiries@energex.com.au; internet www .energex.com.au; spans Queensland and New South Wales; CEO GREG MADDOCK.

EnergyAustralia: 145 Newcastle Rd, Wallsend, NSW 2287; tel. (2) 4951-9346; fax (2) 4951-9351; e-mail energy@energy.com.au; internet www.energy.com.au; supplies customers in NSW; CEO PETER HEADLEY; Man. Dir PAUL BROAD.

Ergon Energy: POB 107, Albert St, Brisbane, Qld 4002; tel. (7) 3228-8222; fax (7) 3228-8118; internet www.ergon.com.au; national retailer of electricity.

Generation Victoria Corpn—Ecogen Energy: 5th Floor, 416 Collins St, Melbourne, Vic 3000; tel. (3) 9679-4600; fax (3) 9679-4619; internet www.ecogen-energy.com.au/; f. 1994; CEO GERRY BASTEN.

Great Southern Energy: Level 1, Citilink Plaza, Morriset St, Queanbeyan, NSW 2620; tel. (2) 6214-9600; fax (2) 6214-9860; e-mail mail@gsenergy.com.au; internet www.gsenergy.com.au; state-owned electricity and gas distributor; Chair. BRUCE RODELY.

Power and Water Corpn: Energy House, 18–20 Cavenagh St, Darwin, NT 0800; tel. 1800-245-092; fax (8) 8924-7730; e-mail customerservice@powerwater.com.au; internet www.powerwater .com.au; state-owned; supplier of electricity, water and sewerage services in NT; Man. Dir KIM WOOD; Chair. NEIL PHILIP.

Powercor Australia Ltd: 40 Market St, Melbourne, Vic 3000; tel. (3) 9683-4444; fax (3) 9683-4499; e-mail info@powercor.com.au; internet www.powercor.com.au; Chair. WILLIAM SHURNIAK; CEO C. T. WAN.

Snowy Mountains Hydro-electric Authority: POB 332, Cooma, NSW 2630; tel. (2) 6452-1777; fax (2) 6452-3794; e-mail info@ snowyhydro.com.au; internet www.snowyhydro.com.au.

United Energy Ltd: Level 13, 101 Collins St, Melbourne, Vic 3000; fax (3) 9222-8588; e-mail info@mail.ue.com.au; internet www.ue .com.au; f. 1994 following division of State Electricity Commission of Victoria; transferred to private sector; distributor of electricity and gas.

Western Power Corpn: GPOB L921, Perth, WA 6842; tel. (8) 9326-4911; fax (8) 9326-4595; e-mail info@wpcorp.com.au; internet www .wpcorp.com.au; f. 1995; principal supplier of electricity in WA; Chair. HECTOR STEBBINS (acting); Man. Dir DAVID EISZELE.

Gas Companies

AlintaGas: GPOB W2030, Perth, WA 6846; internet www.alintagas .com.au; f. 1995; CEO ROBERT BROWNING.

Allgas Energy Ltd: 150 Charlotte St, Brisbane, Qld 4000; tel. (7) 3404-1822; fax (7) 3404-1821; e-mail corporate@allgas.com.au; internet www.allgas.com.au; f. 1885; Chief Exec. TOM BLOXSOM.

Australian Gas Light Co: AGL Centre, Corner Pacific Highway and Walker St, North Sydney, NSW 2060; tel. (2) 9922-0101; fax (2) 9957-3671; e-mail aglmail@agl.com.au; internet www.agl.com.au; f. 1837; Chair. M. J. PHILLIPS; Man. Dir. GREG MARTIN.

Envestra: 10th Floor, 81 Flinders St, Adelaide, SA 5000; tel. (8) 8227-1500; fax (8) 8277-1511; e-mail des.petherick@envestra.com .au; internet www.envestra.com.au; f. 1997 by merger of South Australian Gas Co, Gas Corpn of Queensland and Centre Gas Pty Ltd; purchased Victorian Gas Network in 1999; Chair. J. G. ALLPASS; Man. Dir I. B. LITTLE.

Epic Energy: GPOB 657, Brisbane, Qld 4001; tel. (7) 6200-1600; fax (7) 3218-1650; internet www.epicenergy.com.au; f. 1996; privately-owned gas transmission co; CEO SUE ORTENSTONE.

Origin Energy: GPOB 5376, Sydney, NSW 2001; tel. (2) 9220-6400; fax (2) 9235-1661; internet www.originenergy.com.au; Man. Dir GRANT KING.

TXU: Locked Bag 14060, Melbourne, Vic 8001; tel. (3) 133-466; fax (3) 9299-2777; e-mail enq@txu.com.au; internet www.txu.com.au.

Water Companies

Actew AGL: see Electricity, above.

Melbourne Water Corpn: 100 Wellington Parade, East Melbourne, Vic 3002; tel. (3) 9235-7100; fax (3) 9235-7200; state-owned; Man. Dir BRIAN BAYLEY.

Power and Water Corpn: see Electricity, above.

South Australian Water Corpn: 77 Grenfell St, Adelaide, SA 5000; tel. (8) 8204-1000; fax (8) 8204-1048; internet www.sawater .com.au; state-owned; Chief Exec. ANNE HOWE.

South East Water Ltd: POB 1382, Moorabbin, Vic 3189; tel. (3) 9552-3000; fax (3) 9552-3001; e-mail info@sewl.com.au; internet www.sewl.com.au; f. 1995; state-owned; Man. Dir DENNIS CAVAGNA.

Sydney Water Corpn: Ground Floor, 115–23 Bathurst St, Sydney NSW 2000; internet www.sydneywater.com.au; state-owned; Man. Dir GREG ROBINSON; Chair. GABRIELLE KIBBLE.

Water Corpn: 629 Newcastle St, Leederville, WA 6007; tel. (8) 9420-2420; fax (8) 9420-3200; e-mail webmaster@watercorporation .com.au; internet www.watercorporation.com.au; state-owned; Man. Dir Dr JIM GILL.

Yarra Valley Water Ltd: Lucknow St, Mitcham, Vic 3132; tel. (3) 9874-2122; fax (3) 9872-1353; e-mail enquiry@yvw.com.au; internet www.yvw.com.au; f. 1995; state-owned; Man. Dir TONY KELLY.

TRADE UNIONS

Australian Council of Trade Unions (ACTU): Level 2, 393 Swanston St, Melbourne, Vic 3000; tel. (3) 9663-5266; fax (3) 9663-4051; e-mail mailbox@actu.asn.au; internet www.actu.asn.au; f. 1927; br. in each state, generally known as a Trades and Labour Council; 46 affiliated trade unions; Pres. SHARAN BURROW; Sec. GREGORY COMBET.

Principal Affiliated Unions

Ansett Pilots Association (APA): POB 415, Essendon, Vic 3040; tel. (3) 9325-4233; fax (3) 9375-7405; e-mail secretary@apa.asn.au; internet www.apa.asn.au; Pres. HENRY OTTO; Sec. JOHN DOGGETT.

Association of Professional Engineers, Scientists & Managers, Australia (APESMA): POB 1272L, Melbourne, Vic 3001; tel. (3) 9695-8800; fax (3) 9696-9312; e-mail info@apesma.asn.au; internet www.apesma.asn.au; Nat. Pres. BARRY TONKIN; Nat. Sec. TIM GRIFFIN; 24,000 mems.

Australasian Meat Industry Employees' Union (AMIEU): Level 1, 39 Lytton Rd, East Brisbane, Qld 4169; tel. (7) 3217-3766; fax (7) 3217-4462; e-mail admin@amieuqld.asn.au; internet www .amieu.asn.au; Fed. Pres. ROSS RICHARDSON; Fed. Sec. T. R. HANNAN; 20,484 mems.

Australian Airline Flight Engineers Association (AAEA): Essendon, Vic 3040; f. 1984; Fed. Pres. JEFF SEABURN; Fed. Sec. RON HARE.

Australian Collieries Staff Association (ACSA): POB 21, Merewether, NSW 2291; tel. (2) 4963-5656; fax (2) 4963-3425; e-mail acsa@acsa.org.au; internet www.acsa.org.au; Gen. Pres. MICK BURGESS; Gen. Sec. WENDY CLEWS.

Australian Education Union (AEU): Ground Floor, 120 Clarendon St, Southbank, Vic 3006; tel. (3) 9693-1800; fax (3) 9693-1805; e-mail aeu@aeufederal.org.au; internet www.aeufederal.org.au; f. 1984; Fed. Pres. Patricia Byrne; Fed. Sec. Robert Durbridge; 164,642 mems.

Australian Manufacturing Workers' Union (AMWU): POB 160, Granville, NSW 2142; tel. (2) 9897-9133; fax (2) 9897-9274; e-mail amwu2@amwu.asn.au; internet www.amwu.asn.au; Nat. Pres. Julius Roe; Nat. Sec. Doug Cameron; 170,000 mems.

Australian Services Union (ASU): Ground Floor, 116 Queensberry St, Carlton South, Vic 3053; tel. (3) 9342-1400; fax (3) 9342-1499; e-mail asunatm@asu.asn.au; internet www.asu.asn.au; f. 1885; amalgamated in present form in 1993; Nat. Sec. Paul Slape; 140,000 mems.

Australian Workers' Union (AWU): 685 Spencer St, West Melbourne, Vic 3003; tel. (3) 8327-0888; fax (3) 8327-0899; e-mail awu@alphalink.net.au; internet www.awu.net.au; f. 1886; Nat. Pres. Bill Ludwig; Nat. Sec. Bill Shorten; 135,000 mems.

Communications, Electrical, Electronic, Energy, Information, Postal, Plumbing and Allied Services Union of Australia (CEPU): Suite 701, Level 7, 1 Rosebery Ave, Rosebery, NSW 2018; tel. (2) 9663-3699; fax (2) 9663-5599; e-mail edno@nat.cepu.asn.au; internet www.cepu.asn.au; Nat Pres. Brian Baulk; Nat. Sec. Peter Tighe; 180,000 mems.

Community and Public Sector Union (CPSU): Level 5, 191–199 Thomas St, Haymarket, NSW 2000; tel. (2) 9334-9200; fax (2) 8204-6902; e-mail cpsu@cpsu.org; internet www.cpsu.org; Nat. Pres. Matthew Reynolds; Nat. Sec. Wendy Caird; 200,000 mems.

Construction, Forestry, Mining and Energy Union (CFMEU): Box Q235, QVB PO, Sydney, NSW 1230; tel. (2) 9267-3393; fax (2) 9267-2460; internet www.cfmeu.asn.au; f. 1992 by amalgamation; Pres. Trevor Smith; Sec. John Maitland; 120,000 mems.

Finance Sector Union of Australia (FSU): GPOB 9893, 341 Queen St, Melbourne, Vic 3001; tel. (3) 9261-5300; fax (3) 9670-2950; e-mail fsuinfo@fsunion.org.au; internet www.fsunion.org.au; f. 1991; Nat. Pres. Joy Buckland; Nat. Sec. Anthony Beck; 61,000 mems.

Health Services Union of Australia (HSUA): Level 2, 106–108 Victoria St, Carlton, Vic 3053; tel. (3) 9341-3328; fax (3) 9341-3329; e-mail hsu@hsu.net.au; internet www.hsu.net.au; Nat. Pres. Michael Williamson; Nat. Sec. Craig Thomson; 90,000 mems.

Independent Education Union of Australia (IEU): POB 1301, South Melbourne, Vic 3205; tel. (3) 9254-1830; fax (3) 9254-1835; e-mail ieu@ieu.org.au; internet www.ieu.org.au; Fed. Sec. Lynne Rolley; Fed. Pres. Richard Shearman; 45,000 mems.

Liquor, Hospitality and Miscellaneous Union (LHMU): Locked Bag 9, Haymarket, NSW 1240; tel. (2) 8204-7200; fax (2) 9281-4480; e-mail lhmu@lhmu.org.au; internet www.lhmu.org.au; f. 1992; Nat. Pres. Helen Creed; Nat. Sec. Jeff Lawrence; 132,400 mems.

Maritime Union of Australia (MUA): 2nd Floor, 365 Sussex St, Sydney, NSW 2000; tel. (2) 9267-9134; fax (2) 9261-3481; e-mail muano@mua.org.au; internet www.mua.org.au; f. 1993; Nat. Sec. Paddy Crumlin; 10,012 mems.

Media, Entertainment & Arts Alliance (MEAA): POB 723, Strawberry Hills, NSW 2012; tel. (2) 9333-0999; fax (2) 9333-0933; e-mail mail@alliance.org.au; internet www.alliance.org.au; Fed. Sec. Christopher Warren; 30,000 mems.

National Union of Workers (NUW): POB 343, North Melbourne, Vic 3051; tel. (3) 9287-1850; fax (3) 9287-1818; e-mail nuwnat@nuw.org.au; internet www.nuw.org.au; Gen. Sec. Charles Donnelly; Gen. Pres. Doug Stevens; 100,000 mems.

Rail, Tram and Bus Union (RTBU): 83–89 Renwick St, Redfern, NSW 2016; tel. (2) 9310-3966; fax (2) 9319-2096; e-mail rtbu@rtbu-nat.abn.au; internet www.rtbu-nat.asn.au; Nat. Pres. R. Hayden; Nat. Sec. Roger Jowett; 35,000 mems.

Shop, Distributive & Allied Employees Association (SDA): 5th Floor, 53 Queen St, Melbourne, Vic 3000; tel. (3) 9629-2299; fax (3) 9629-2646; e-mail sdanat@c031.aone.net.au; internet www.sda.org.au; f. 1908; Nat. Pres. Don Farrell; Nat. Sec. Joe de Bruyn; 214,029 mems.

Textile, Clothing and Footwear Union of Australia (TCFUA): Ground Floor, 28 Anglo Rd, Campsie, NSW 2194; tel. (2) 9789-4188; fax (2) 9789-6510; e-mail tcfua@tcfua.org.au; f. 1919; Pres. Barry Tubner; Nat. Sec. Tony Woolgar; 21,354 mems.

Transport Workers' Union of Australia (TWU): St Kilda Rd, POB 7419, Vic 8004; tel. (3) 8645-3333; fax (3) 9676-2669; e-mail twu@twu.com.au; internet www.twu.com.au; Fed. Pres. Hughie Williams; Fed. Sec. John Allan; 82,000 mems.

Transport

Australian Transport Council: POB 594, Canberra, ACT 2601; tel. (2) 6274-7851; fax (2) 6274-7703; e-mail atc@dotars.gov.au; internet www.atcouncil.gov.au; f. 1993; mems include: Federal Minister for Transport and Regional Services, State, Territory and New Zealand Ministers responsible for transport; Sec. D. Jones.

State Transit Authority of New South Wales: 219–241 Cleveland St, Strawberry Hills, NSW 2010; tel. (2) 9245-5777; e-mail info@sydneybuses.nsw.gov.au; internet www.sta.nsw.gov.au; operates government buses and ferries in Sydney and Newcastle metropolitan areas; Chair. David Herlihy; CEO John Stott.

TransAdelaide (South Australia): GPOB 2351, Adelaide, SA 5001; tel. (8) 8218-2200; fax (8) 8218-4399; e-mail info@transadelaide.sa.gov.au; internet www.transadelaide.com.au; f. 1994; fmrly State Transport Authority; operates metropolitan train, bus, tram and Busway services; Gen. Man. Sue Filby.

RAILWAYS

In June 2001 there were 39,844 km of railways in Australia (including tram and light rail track). In September 2003 the construction of a 1,400-km railway between Alice Springs and Darwin was completed. The rail link was to be used principally for transporting freight.

Pacific National: Locked Bag 90, Parramatta, NSW 2124; tel. (2) 9893-2500; fax (2) 9893-2501; e-mail communication@pacificnational.com.au; internet www.pacificnational.com.au; freight; fmrly National Rail Corporation Ltd; CEO Stephen O'Donnell.

QR (Queensland Rail): POB 1429, Brisbane, Qld 4001; tel. (7) 3235-2180; fax (7) 3235-1799; internet www.qr.com.au; f. 1863; passenger commuter and long-distance services, freight and logistic services, track access and rail-specific expert services; CEO Bob Scheuber.

RailCorp: POB K349, Haymarket, NSW 1238; tel. (2) 8202-2000; fax (2) 8202-2111; internet www.railcorp.info; f. 1980; responsible for passenger rail and associated coach services in NSW; Chief Exec. Vince Graham.

Victorian Rail Track (VicTrack): Level 17, 589 Collins St, Melbourne, Vic 3000; tel. (3) 9619-8850; fax (3) 9619-8851; e-mail victrack@victrack.com.au; internet www.victrack.com.au; f. 1997; Chair. Dr Thomas W. Quirk; Chief Exec. John Sutton.

Western Australian Government Railways (Westrail): POB 8125, Perth 6849, WA; tel. (8) 9326-2000; fax (8) 9326-2500; internet www.wagr.wa.gov.au; statutory authority competing in the freight, passenger and related transport markets in southern WA; operates 1,029 main line route-km of track; Commr Reece Waldock (acting).

ROADS

In June 2001 there were 808,294 km of roads open for general traffic. In 1996 this included 1,000 km of freeways, a further 103 km of toll roads, 45,889 km of highways, 77,045 km of arterial and major roads and 30,596 of secondary tourist and other roads. Local roads in urban areas account for 93,677 km of the network and those in rural localities for 537,278 km.

Austroads Inc: POB K659, Haymarket, NSW 2000; tel. (2) 9264-7088; fax (2) 9264-1657; e-mail austroads@austroads.com.au; internet www.austroads.com.au; f. 1989; asscn of road transport and traffic authorities.

SHIPPING

In December 2003 the Australian merchant fleet comprised 643 vessels, with a total displacement of 1,905,778 grt.

Adsteam Marine Ltd: Level 22, Plaza 2, 500 Oxford St, Bondi Junction, NSW 2022; tel. (2) 9369-9200; fax (2) 9369-9288; e-mail info@adsteam.com.au; internet www.adsteam.com.au; f. 1875; fmrly Adelaide Steamship Co; Man. Dir and Chief Exec. John Moller.

ANL Ltd (Australian National Line): GPOB 2238T, Melbourne, Vic 3004; tel. (3) 9257-0613; fax (3) 9257-0517; e-mail anl@anl.com.au; f. 1956; shipping agents; coastal and overseas container shipping and coastal bulk shipping; container management services; overseas container services to Hong Kong, Taiwan, the Philippines, Korea, Singapore, Malaysia, Thailand, Indonesia and Japan; extensive transhipment services; Chair. E. G. Anson; Man. Dir Malcolm Turnbull.

BHP Transport Pty Ltd: 27th Level, 600 Bourke St, POB 86A, Melbourne, Vic 3001; tel. (3) 9609-3333; fax (3) 9609-2400; Chair. D. Argus; Man. Dir P. Andersen.

William Holyman and Sons Pty Ltd: No. 3 Berth, Bell Bay, Tas 7253; tel. (3) 6382-2383; fax (3) 6382-3391; coastal services; Chair. R. J. Hoy.

CIVIL AVIATION

Eastern Australia Airlines: POB 538, Mascot, Sydney, NSW 2020; tel. (2) 9691-2333; fax (2) 9693-2715; internet www.qantas .com.au; subsidiary of Qantas; domestic flights; Gen. Man. ASHLEY KILROY.

Impulse Airlines: Eleventh St, Sydney Kingsford-Smith Airport, Mascot, NSW 2020; tel. (2) 9317-5400; fax (2) 9317-3440; e-mail info@impulseairlines.com.au; internet www.impulseairlines.com .au; f. 1992; domestic services; Chief Exec./Chair. GERRY MCGOWAN; Exec. Dir SUE MCGOWAN.

Jetstar Airways Pty Ltd: Tullamarine, POB 1503, Melbourne, Vic 3043; tel. (3) 8341-4901; internet www.jetstar.com.au; f. 2004; owned by Qantas Airways Ltd; low-cost domestic passenger service; Chief Exec. ALAN JOYCE.

National Jet Systems: Adelaide Airport, 28 James Schofield Drive SA 5000; tel. (8) 8238-7200; fax (8) 8238-7238; internet www .nationaljet.com.au; f. 1989; domestic services; Man. Dir DANIELA MARSILLI; Group Gen. Man. Commdr ROBERT BIRKS.

Qantas Airways Ltd: Qantas Centre, 203 Coward St, Mascot, NSW 2020; tel. (2) 9691-3636; fax (2) 9691-3339; internet www.qantas .com.au; f. 1920 as Queensland and Northern Territory Aerial Services; Australian Govt became sole owner in 1947; merged with Australian Airlines in Sept. 1992; British Airways purchased 25% in March 1993; remaining 75% transferred to private sector in 1995; services throughout Australia and to 34 countries, including destinations in Europe, Africa, the USA, Canada, South America, Asia, the Pacific and New Zealand; Chair. MARGARET JACKSON; CEO GEOFF DIXON.

Spirit Airlines: Level 9, 580 St Kilda Rd, Melbourne, Vic 3004; fax (3) 9510-4095; e-mail info@spiritairlines.com.au; internet www .spiritairlines.com.au/; f. 1998; domestic services; CEO MIKE DIXON.

Sunstate Airlines: Lobby 3, Level 3, 153 Campbell St, Bowen Hills, Qld 4006; tel. (7) 3308-9022; fax (7) 3308-9088; e-mail edalessio@ qantas.com.au; f. 1982; wholly owned by Qantas; operates passenger services within Queensland and to Newcastle (NSW) and Lord Howe Island; Gen. Man. ELSA D'ALESSIO.

Virgin Blue: Centenary Place, Level 7, 100 Wickham St, Brisbane, Qld; tel. (7) 3295-3000; e-mail customercare@virginblue.com.au; internet www.virginblue.com.au; domestic services; CEO BRETT GODFREY.

Tourism

The main attractions are the cosmopolitan cities, the Great Barrier Reef, the Blue Mountains, water sports and also winter sports in the Australian Alps, notably the Snowy Mountains. The town of Alice Springs, the Aboriginal culture and the sandstone monolith of Ayers Rock (Uluru) are among the attractions of the desert interior. Much of Australia's wildlife is unique to the country. Australia received 5,215,000 foreign visitors in 2004. The majority of visitors came from New Zealand, Japan, the United Kingdom and the USA. Receipts totalled US $8,087m. in 2002. The 2000 Olympic Games were held in Sydney in September.

Tourism Australia: GPOB 2721, Sydney, NSW 2001; tel. (2) 9360-1111; fax (2) 9331-6469; e-mail corpaffairs@tourism.australia.com; internet www.tourism.australia.com; f. 2004; government authority responsible for marketing of international and domestic tourism; Chair. TIM FISCHER; Man. Dir SCOTT MORRISON.

AUSTRALIAN EXTERNAL TERRITORIES

CHRISTMAS ISLAND

Introduction

Christmas Island lies 360 km south of Java Head (Indonesia) in the Indian Ocean. The nearest point on the Australian coast is North West Cape, 1,408 km to the south-east. Christmas Island has no indigenous population. The population was 1,508 at the 2001 census (compared with 1,906 in 1996), comprising mainly ethnic Chinese (some 70%), but there were large minorities of Malays (about 10%) and Europeans (about 20%). A variety of languages are spoken (more than 60% of the population spoke a language other than English in 2001), but English is the official language. The predominant religious affiliation is Buddhist (55% in 1991). The principal settlement and only anchorage is Flying Fish Cove.

Following annexation by the United Kingdom in 1888, Christmas Island was incorporated for administrative purposes with the Straits Settlements (now Singapore and part of Malaysia) in 1900. Japanese forces occupied the island from March 1942 until the end of the Second World War, and in 1946 Christmas Island became a dependency of Singapore. Administration was transferred to the United Kingdom on 1 January 1958, pending final transfer to Australia, effected on 1 October 1958. The Australian Government appointed Official Representatives to the Territory until 1968, when new legislation provided for an Administrator, appointed by the Governor-General. Responsibility for administration lies with the Minister for Regional Services, Territories and Local Government. In 1980 an Advisory Council was established for the Administrator to consult. In 1984 the Christmas Island Services Corporation was created to perform those functions that are normally the responsibility of municipal government. This body was placed under the direction of the Christmas Island Assembly, the first elections to which took place in September 1985. Nine members were elected for one-year terms. In November 1987 the Assembly was dissolved, and the Administrator empowered to perform its functions. The Corporation was superseded by the Christmas Island Shire Council in 1992.

In May 1994 an unofficial referendum on the island's status was held concurrently with local government elections. At the poll, sponsored by the Union of Christmas Island Workers, the islanders rejected an option to secede from Australia, but more than 85% of voters favoured increased local government control. The referendum was prompted, in part, by the Australian Government's plans to abolish the island's duty-free status (which had become a considerable source of revenue).

Since 1981 all residents of the island have been eligible to acquire Australian citizenship. In 1984 the Australian Government extended social security, health and education benefits to the island, and enfranchised Australian citizens resident there. Full income-tax liability was introduced in the late 1980s.

During the late 1990s an increasing number of illegal immigrants travelling to Australia landed on Christmas Island. In January 2001 Australian government officials denied claims by Christmas Islanders that some 86 illegal immigrants who had arrived at the island from the Middle East via Indonesia were being detained in inhumane conditions. Local people claimed that the detainees were sleeping on concrete floors and were being denied adequate food and medical care. International attention was focused on Christmas Island in August 2001 when the *MV Tampa*, a Norwegian container ship carrying 433 refugees whom it had rescued from a sinking Indonesian fishing boat, was refused permission to land on the island. As the humanitarian crisis escalated, the Australian Government's steadfast refusal to admit the mostly Afghan refugees prompted international condemnation and led to a serious diplomatic dispute between Australia and Norway. The office of the United Nations High Commissioner for Refugees (UNHCR) and the International Organization for Migration (IOM) expressed grave concern at the situation. Hundreds of Christmas Island residents attended a rally urging the Australian Government to reconsider its uncompromising stance. In September the refugees were transferred (via Papua New

Guinea and New Zealand) to Nauru, where their applications for asylum were to be processed. In the same month the Senate in Canberra approved new legislation, which excised Christmas Island and other outlying territories from Australia's official migration zone. The new legislation also imposed stricter criteria for the processing of asylum-seekers and the removal of their right to recourse to the Australian court system. Meanwhile, increasing numbers of asylum-seekers continued to attempt to reach Christmas Island via Indonesia. Among the many controversial incidents that occurred in the waters of Christmas Island in September–December 2001 was that of 186 Iraqis who jumped into the sea when ordered to leave Australian waters in October. They were temporarily housed on Christmas Island before being transferred to Nauru. According to Australian Immigration Department figures, 146 asylum-seekers were turned away from Christmas Island and Ashmore Reef in December 2001. In January 2002 211 asylum-seekers remained on Christmas Island awaiting transferral. In March the Government announced plans to establish a permanent detention centre on the island, the construction of which was expected to cost more than $A150m. The Government was thus preparing to accommodate an anticipated total of 18,000 illegal immigrants who were expected to arrive at Christmas Island during 2002–06. However, plans to scale down the project were announced in February 2003. In July of that year a boat carrying 53 asylum-seekers from Viet Nam was intercepted in Australian waters (the first such vessel to be found in the region since 2001), and its passengers were transferred to Christmas Island. The construction of the detention centre was to begin in February 2005, by which time the estimated cost had increased to $A336m. for an 800-bed facility. Speculation among certain observers that the Australian Government intended to use the completed centre as a military base for US forces was dismissed by official sources.

In January 2005 the President of the island's Chamber of Commerce offered to provide refuge on Christmas Island for up to 1,500 victims of the recent tsunami in the Indian Ocean. It was suggested that, as Christmas Island had numerous unused buildings, including the defunct casino resort, plentiful supplies of clean water and strong links with South-East Asia, it would be an ideal haven for the victims, and would also be beneficial to the local economy. The Australian Government, however, did not support the proposals.

The economy has been based on the recovery of phosphates. During the year ending 30 June 1984 about 463,000 metric tons were exported to Australia, 332,000 tons to New Zealand and 341,000 tons to other countries. Reserves were estimated to be sufficient to enable production to be maintained until the mid-1990s. In November 1987 the Australian Government announced the closure of the phosphate mine, owing to industrial unrest, and mining activity ceased in December. In 1990, however, the Government allowed private operators to recommence phosphate extraction, subject to certain conditions such as the preservation of the rainforest. A total of 220,000 metric tons of phosphates were produced in 1995. In 2001 the mine employed some 180 workers. The owner of the mine, Phosphate Resources Ltd (trading as Christmas Island Phosphates), was thus the island's largest employer. A total of 570,000 metric tons of phosphate dust were exported in 2001/02, and phosphate exports were worth $A43.8m. in 1997/98. A new 21-year lease, drawn up by the Government and Phosphate Resources Ltd, took effect in February 1998. The agreement incorporated environmental safeguards and provided for a conservation levy, based on the tonnage of phosphate shipped, which was to finance a programme of rainforest rehabilitation.

The services sector engaged 65% of the employed labour force, according to the census of 2001. In that year the rate of unemployment was 8% of the workforce. Efforts have been made to develop the island's considerable potential for tourism. In 1989, in an attempt to protect the natural environment and many rare species of flora and fauna (including the Abbott's Booby and the Christmas frigate bird), the National Park was extended to cover some 70% of the island. A hotel and casino complex, covering 47 ha of land, was opened in November 1993. In 1994 revenue from the development totalled $A500m. A 50-room extension to the complex was constructed in 1995. In early 1997, however, fears for the nascent industry were expressed, following the decision by Ansett Australia to discontinue its twice-weekly air service to the island from September of that year. Despite the subsequent commencement of a weekly flight from Perth, Australia, operated by National Jet Systems, the complex was closed down in April 1998 and some 350 employees were made redundant. In July the resort's casino licence was cancelled and a liquidator was appointed to realize the complex's assets. The closure of the resort had serious economic and social repercussions for the island. An audit of tourist accommodation, conducted in May 2000, counted approximately 140 beds on the island. Only 60 visitors arrived on the island from overseas in 2001, according to official Australian figures. In August 2004 South Korean investors, willing to spend $A30m. on reopening the casino complex, met the Australian Minister for Territories. However, despite the strong support of a majority of islanders, who believed that the resort would regenerate the tourist industry and provide much-needed revenue, the Australian Government stated its opposition to the proposal. The decision prompted some islanders to protest outside the Australian administration offices.

Between 1992 and 1999 the Australian Government invested an estimated $A110m. in the development of Christmas Island's infrastructure as part of the Christmas Island Rebuilding Programme. The main areas of expenditure under this programme were a new hospital, the upgrading of ports facilities, school extensions, the construction of housing, power, water supply and sewerage, and the repair and construction of roads. In 2000 further improvements to marine facilities and water supply were carried out, in addition to the construction of new housing to relocate islanders away from a major rockfall risk area. In mid-2001 the Australian Government pledged a total of more than $A50m. for further developments including improvements to the airport and the road network, as well as an alternative port. The proposed additional port was to be constructed on the east coast of the island, allowing for the handling of sea freight and the launching of emergency vessels at times when the existing port at Flying Fish Cove is closed owing to north-west swells. These closures, which most commonly occur between December and March, had resulted in inflated costs for shipping companies and inconvenience for Christmas Islanders. The new port was expected to be built by 2005. The Australian Government announced in April 2004 that it would provide $A2.5m. to fund a new mobile telephone network for the Territory. It was hoped that enhanced communications would facilitate new business prospects for the island. The cost of the island's imports from Australia increased from $A13m. in 1998/99 to $A17m. in 1999/2000 and declined to $A16m. in 2000/01, when the Territory's exports to that country earned $A7m. In 1998/99 imports from New Zealand cost $NZ9m. Christmas Island purchased no imports from New Zealand in 2000/01, but exports to that country in the same year were worth $NZ4m. An estimated 7.5% of the island's population were unemployed in 1996.

Proposals for the development of a communications satellite launching facility on the island were under consideration in 1998. An assessment of the environmental impact was subsequently undertaken, and the scheme received government approval in May 2000. Following an agreement between the Governments of Australia and Russia in May 2001, preparations for the establishment of a space control centre on Christmas Island commenced. Australia and Russia were to contribute up to US $100m. towards the project, the total cost of which was expected to be US $425m. The Christmas Island site was to be developed by the Asia Pacific Space Centre, an Australian company. Construction began in November 2001, with the first rocket launch being planned for 2004. The space centre was expected to become the world's first wholly privately-owned land-based launch facility, with an operational lifespan of 15–20 years. Asia Pacific planned to launch 10–12 satellites annually by 2005. Although the project would create many employment opportunities on the island (an estimated 400 new jobs during construction and 550 during operation) and lead to substantial infrastructural improvements, environmentalists continued to express concern.

Statistical Survey

AREA AND POPULATION

Area: 136.7 sq km (52.8 sq miles).

Population: 1,906 (males 1,023, females 883) at census of 30 June 1996; 1,508 (males 850, females 658) at census of 7 August 2001; 1,506 (official estimate) at August 2002. Source: mainly UN, *Demographic Yearbook*.

Density (2002): 11.2 per sq km.

Country of Birth (2001 census): Australia 690; Malaysia 515; Singapore 52; United Kingdom 51; New Zealand 18; Indonesia 13.

Religion (2001 census, declared adherence): Buddhism 490; Christianity 338 (Roman Catholicism 140; Anglicanism 99; Uniting Church 45); Islam 298.

Births and Deaths (1985): Registered live births 36 (birth rate 15.8 per 1,000); Registered deaths 2.

Economically Active Population (persons aged 15 years and over, excl. overseas visitors, 2001 census): Agriculture, forestry and fishing 3; Mining 127; Manufacturing 9; Electricity, gas and water 21; Construction 71; Wholesale and retail trade, restaurants and hotels 100; Transport, storage and communications 44; Financing, insurance, real estate and business services 42; Government administration and defence 75; Community, social and personal services 148; Activities not stated or not adequately defined 29; *Total employed* 669 (males 442, females 227); Unemployed 59 (males 35, females 24); *Total labour force* 727 (males 482, females 245).

MINING

Natural Phosphates (official estimates, '000 metric tons): 285 in 1994; 220 in 1995.

FINANCE

Currency and Exchange Rates: Australian currency is used.

EXTERNAL TRADE

Principal Trading Partners (phosphate exports, '000 metric tons, year ending 30 June 1984)): Australia 463; New Zealand 332; Total (incl. others) 1,136.

2000/01 ($A million): *Imports:* Australia 16. *Exports:* Australia 7. Source: Australian Bureau of Statistics, *Year Book Australia*.

2000/01 ($NZ million): *Exports:* New Zealand 4. Source: Ministry of Foreign Affairs and Trade, New Zealand.

TRANSPORT

International Sea-borne Shipping (estimated freight traffic, '000 metric tons, 1990): Goods loaded 1,290; Goods unloaded 68. Source: UN, *Monthly Bulletin of Statistics*.

TOURISM

Visitor Arrivals and Departures by Air: 14,513 in 1996; 3,895 in 1997; 2,712 in 1998. Source: *Year Book Australia*.

COMMUNICATIONS MEDIA

Radio Receivers (1997): 1,000 in use.

Television Receivers (1997): 600 in use.

Personal Computers (home users, 2001 census): 506.

Internet Users (2001 census): 464.

EDUCATION

Pre-primary (2002): 37 pupils.

Primary (2002): 217 pupils.

Secondary (2002): 124 pupils.
Source: Education Department of Western Australia.

Directory

The Government

The Administrator, appointed by the Governor-General of Australia and responsible to the Minister for Regional Services, Territories and Local Government, is the senior government representative on the island.

Administrator: Evan Williams.

Administration Headquarters: POB 868, Christmas Island 6798, Indian Ocean; tel. (8) 9164-7901; fax (8) 9164-8524.

Shire of Christmas Island: George Fam Centre, POB 863, Christmas Island 6798, Indian Ocean; tel. (8) 9164-8300; fax (8) 9164-8304; e-mail chew@shire.cx; Community Services Man. Chew Boon Beng; Pres Gordon Thomson.

Judicial System

The judicial system comprises the Supreme Court, District Court, Magistrate's Court and Children's Court.

Supreme Court

c/o Govt Offices, Christmas Island 6798, Indian Ocean; tel. (8) 9164-7911; fax (8) 9164-8530.

Judges (non-resident): Robert Sheraton French, Malcolm Cameron Lee.

Managing Registrar: Jeffery Low, Govt Offices, Christmas Island 6798, Indian Ocean; tel. (8) 9164-7911; fax (8) 9164-8530.

Religion

According to official figures, in 1997 some 36% of Christmas Island residents were Buddhists, 25% were Muslims, and 18% were Christians. Within the Christian churches, Christmas Island lies in the jurisdiction of both the Anglican and Roman Catholic Archbishops of Perth, in Western Australia.

The Press

The Islander: Shire of Christmas Island, George Fam Centre, POB 863, Christmas Island 6798, Indian Ocean; tel. (8) 9164-8300; fax (8) 9164-8304; e-mail chong@shire.gov.cx; newsletter; fortnightly; Editor M. G. Chong.

Broadcasting and Communications

BROADCASTING

Radio

Christmas Island Community Radio Service: f. 1967; operated by the Administration since 1991; daily broadcasting service by Radio VLU-2 on 1422 KHz and 102 MHz FM, in English, Malay, Cantonese and Mandarin; Station Man. William Taylor.

Christmas Island Radio VLU2–FM: POB 474, Christmas Island 6798, Indian Ocean; tel. (8) 9164-8316; fax (8) 9164-8315; daily broadcasts on 102.1FM and 105.3FM in English, Malay, Cantonese and Mandarin; Chair. and Station Man. Tony Smith.

Television

Christmas Island Television: POB AAA, Christmas Island 6798, Indian Ocean.

Finance

BANKING

Commercial Bank

Westpac Banking Corpn (Australia): Flying Fish Cove, Christmas Island, Indian Ocean; tel. (8) 9164-8221; fax (8) 9164-8241.

Trade and Industry

In April 2001 there were 67 small businesses in operation.

Administration of Christmas Island: POB 868, Christmas Island 6798, Indian Ocean; tel. (8) 9164-7901; fax (8) 9164-8524; operates power, airport, seaport, health services, public housing, local courts; Dir of Finance Jeffery Tan.

Christmas Island Chamber of Commerce: Christmas Island 6798, Indian Ocean; tel. (8) 9164-8249; Pres. Don O'Donnell; Vice-Pres. Phillip Oakley.

Shire of Christmas Island: George Fam Centre, POB 863, Christmas Island 6798, Indian Ocean; tel. (8) 9164-8300; fax (8) 9164-8304; e-mail soci@iocomm.com.au; f. 1992 by Territories Law Reform Act to replace Christmas Island Services Corpn; provides local govt services; manages tourism and economic development; Pres. David McLane; CEO David Price.

Union of Christmas Island Workers (UCIW): Poon Saan Rd, POB 84, Christmas Island 6798, Indian Ocean; tel. (8) 9164-8471; fax (8) 9164-8470; e-mail uciw@pulau.cx; fmrly represented phosphate workers; Pres. Foo Kee Heng; Gen. Sec. Gordon Thomson; 800 mems.

Transport

There are good roads in the developed areas. National Jet Systems operate a twice-weekly flight from Perth, via the Cocos (Keeling) Islands, and a private Christmas Island-based charter company operates services to Jakarta, Indonesia. In 1998 arrivals and departures by air in Christmas Island totalled 2,712 (compared with 3,895 in the previous year). The Australian National Line (ANL) operates ships to the Australian mainland. Cargo vessels from Fremantle deliver supplies to the island every four to six weeks. The Joint Island Supply System, established in 1989, provides a shipping service for Christmas Island and the Cocos Islands. The only anchorage is at Flying Fish Cove.

Tourism

Tourism is a growing sector of the island's economy. Visitors are attracted by the unique flora and fauna, as well as the excellent conditions for scuba-diving and game-fishing. In 2000 there were approximately 90 hotel rooms on the island.

Christmas Island Tourism Association/Christmas Island Visitor Information Centre: POB 63, Christmas Island 6798, Indian Ocean; tel. (8) 9164-8382; fax (8) 9164-8080; e-mail cita@christmas.net.au; internet www.christmas.net.au.

Christmas Island Tours and Travel: Christmas Island 6798, Indian Ocean; tel. (8) 9164-7168; fax (8) 9164-7169; e-mail xch@citravel.com.au; Dir Tan Sim Kiat.

Island Bound Travel: tel. (8) 9381-3644; fax (8) 9381 2030; e-mail info@islandbound.com.au.

Parks Australia: POB 867, Christmas Island 6798, Indian Ocean; tel. (8) 9164-8700; fax (8) 9164-8755; internet www.deh.gov.au/pa.

COCOS (KEELING) ISLANDS

Introduction

The Cocos (Keeling) Islands are 27 in number and lie 2,768 km north-west of Perth, in the Indian Ocean. The islands, with a combined area of 14 sq km (5.4 sq miles), form two low-lying coral atolls, densely covered with coconut palms. The climate is equable, with temperatures varying from 21°C (69°F) to 32°C (88°F), and rainfall of 2,000 mm per year. In 1981 some 58% of the population were of the Cocos Malay community, and 26% were Europeans. The Cocos Malays are descendants of the

people brought to the islands by Alexander Hare and of labourers who were subsequently introduced by the Clunies-Ross family (see below). English is the official language, but Cocos Malay and Malay are also widely spoken. Most of the inhabitants are Muslims (56.8% in 1981). Home Island, which had a population of 446 in mid-1992, is where the Cocos Malay community is based. The only other inhabited island is West Island, with a population of 147 in mid-1992 and where most of the European community lives, the administration is based and the airport is located. The West Island population is comprised mainly of the mainland-based employees of various government departments and their families. The total population of the islands was 621 at the census of both 1998 and August 2001. According to official estimates, the total was 629 in 2004.

The islands were uninhabited when discovered by Capt. William Keeling, of the British East India Company, in 1609, and the first settlement was not established until 1826, by Alexander Hare. The islands were declared a British possession in 1857 and came successively under the authority of the Governors of Ceylon (now Sri Lanka), from 1878, and the Straits Settlements (now Singapore and part of Malaysia), from 1886. Also in 1886 the British Crown granted all land on the islands above the high-water mark to John Clunies-Ross and his heirs and successors in perpetuity. In 1946, when the islands became a dependency of the Colony of Singapore, a resident administrator, responsible to the Governor of Singapore, was appointed. Administration of the islands was transferred to the Commonwealth of Australia on 23 November 1955. The agent of the Australian Government was known as the Official Representative until 1975, when an Administrator was appointed. The Minister for Regional Services, Territories and Local Government is responsible for the governance of the islands. The Territory is part of the Northern Territory Electoral District.

In June 1977 the Australian Government announced new policies concerning the islands, which resulted in its purchase from John Clunies-Ross of the whole of his interests in the islands, with the exception of his residence and associated buildings. The purchase for $A6.5m. took effect on 1 September 1978. An attempt by the Australian Government to acquire Clunies-Ross' remaining property was deemed by the Australian High Court in October 1984 to be unconstitutional.

In July 1979 the Cocos (Keeling) Islands Council was established, with a wide range of functions in the Home Island village area (which the Government transferred to the Council on trust for the benefit of the Cocos Malay community) and, from September 1984, in the greater part of the rest of the Territory.

On 6 April 1984 a referendum to decide the future political status of the islands was held by the Australian Government, with UN observers present. A large majority voted in favour of integration with Australia. As a result, the islanders were to acquire the rights, privileges and obligations of all Australian citizens. In July 1992 the Cocos (Keeling) Islands Council was replaced by the Cocos (Keeling) Islands Shire Council, comprised of seven members and modelled on the local government and state law of Western Australia. The first Shire Council was elected in 1993. The Clunies-Ross family was declared bankrupt in mid-1993, following unsuccessful investment in a shipping venture, and the Australian Government took possession of its property.

In September 2001, following an increase in the numbers of illegal immigrants reaching Australian waters (see the section on Christmas Island), legislation was enacted removing the Cocos Islands and other territories from Australia's official migration zone. In October of that year the Australian Government sent contingency supplies to the islands as a precaution, should it be necessary to accommodate more asylum-seekers. This development provoked concern among many Cocos residents that the former quarantine station used as a detention centre might become a permanent asylum-processing facility under the order of the Australian Government. In December 123 Sri Lankan and Vietnamese asylum-seekers were housed at the station, which was built to accommodate only 40. They were transferred to Christmas Island in February 2002. The Government admitted that the establishment of an asylum-processing facility on Cocos might become necessary.

Although local fishing is good, some livestock is kept, and domestic gardens provide vegetables, bananas and papayas (pawpaws), the islands are not self-sufficient, and other foodstuffs, fuels and consumer items are imported from mainland Australia. Coconuts, grown throughout the islands, are the sole cash crop: total output was an estimated 7,600 metric tons in 2003. In 2001/02 the Administration and the Shire provided support for a study investigating the potential economic benefits of various coconut products, including the production of high-quality carbon from coconut kernels and the manufacture of furniture from coconut palm wood. A clam farm was established in 2000. A Cocos postal service (including a philatelic bureau) came into operation in September 1979, and revenue from the service is used for the benefit of the community. In early 2000

the islands' internet domain name suffix, '.cc', was sold to Clear Channel, a US radio group, thus providing additional revenue. The conversion of a disused quarantine station into a business centre was under consideration in the early 2000s. In October 2003 a ship carrying 52,000 Australian sheep was diverted to the Cocos Islands, having been refused entry in Saudi Arabia, where inspectors claimed to have found high levels of disease among the animals. Many islanders expressed concern over the arrangement and the Territory's lack of facilities to deal with the situation. The islands have a small tourist industry. During August, September and October 2003 there were a total of 76 non-resident arrivals, of whom 28 were travelling on business and 19 were visiting relatives. Some controversy arose in July 2004 when it was revealed that the Australian Government had drawn up plans to develop a resort on Cocos Islands without undertaking any consultation with the islanders.

The cost of the islands' imports from Australia increased from $A5m. in 1999/2000 to $A11m. in 2000/01. Exports to Australia totalled $A2m. in 1996/97, but by 2002 the Cocos Islands no longer exported any goods or produce. The Grants Commission estimated that the Australian Government's net funding of the Territory amounted to some $A18m. in 1999. In 2000/01 the Cocos Administration expended approximately $A9m. An estimated 19% of the total labour force was unemployed in 2001, 60% of whom were under the age of 30. The Shire Council and the Co-operative Society were the principal employers.

Primary education is provided at the schools on Home and West Islands. Secondary education is provided to the age of 16 years on West Island. A bursary scheme enables Cocos Malay children to continue their education on the Australian mainland.

Statistical Survey

AREA AND POPULATION

Area: 14.1 sq km (5.4 sq miles).

Population: 655 (males 338, females 317) at census of 30 June 1996; 621 (males 334, females 287) at census of 7 August 2001; 629 (official estimate) in 2004.

Density (2004): 44.6 per sq km.

Country of Birth (2001 census): Australia 528; Malaysia 26; United Kingdom 12.

Religion (2001 census, declared adherence): Islam 409; Christianity 90 (Anglicanism 34; Roman Catholicism 23).

Births and Deaths (1986): Registered live births 12 (birth rate 19.8 per 1,000); Registered deaths 2.

Economically Active Population (persons aged 15 years and over, excl. overseas visitors, 2001 census): Agriculture, forestry and fishing 3; Mining 3; Manufacturing 6; Electricity, gas and water 7; Construction 24; Wholesale and retail trade, restaurants and hotels 32; Transport, storage and communications 26; Financing, insurance, real estate and business services 32; Government administration and defence 32; Community, social and personal services 47; Activities not stated or not adequately defined 18; *Total employed* 230.

AGRICULTURE

Production (FAO estimates, metric tons, 2003): Coconuts 7,600; Copra 1,000. Source: FAO.

FINANCE

Currency and Exchange Rates: Australian currency is used.

EXTERNAL TRADE

Principal Commodities (metric tons, year ending 30 June 1985): *Exports*: Coconuts 202. *Imports*: Most requirements come from Australia. The trade deficit is offset by philatelic sales and Australian federal grants and subsidies. *2000/01* ($A '000, imports from Australia): 11,000.
Source: *Year Book Australia*.

COMMUNICATIONS MEDIA

Radio Receivers (1992): 300 in use.

Personal Computers (home users, 2001 census): 142.

Internet Users (2001 census): 171.

EDUCATION

Pre-primary (2002): 23 pupils.

Primary (2002): 84 pupils.

Secondary (2002): 31 pupils.

Teaching Staff (2004): 18.

Source: Education Department of Western Australia.

Directory

The Government

The Administrator, appointed by the Governor-General of Australia and responsible to the Minister for Regional Services, Territories and Local Government, is the senior government representative in the islands.

Administrator: EVAN WILLIAMS (non-resident).

Administrative Offices: POB 1093, West Island, Cocos (Keeling) Islands 6799, Indian Ocean; tel. (8) 9162-6615; fax (8) 9162-6697.

Cocos (Keeling) Islands Shire Council: POB 1094, Home Island, Cocos (Keeling) Islands 6799, Indian Ocean; tel. (8) 9162-6649; fax (8) 9162-6668; e-mail info@shire.cc; f. 1992 by Territories Law Reform Act; Pres. RONALD GRANT; CEO BOB JARVIS.

Judicial System

Supreme Court, Cocos (Keeling) Islands: West Island Police Station, Cocos (Keeling) Islands 6799, Indian Ocean; tel. (8) 9162-6615; fax (8) 9162-6697; Judge ROBERT SHERATON FRENCH; Additional Judge MALCOLM CAMERON LEE.

Magistrates' Court, Cocos (Keeling) Islands

Special Magistrate (vacant).

Managing Registrar: ROBYN JENKINS, Cocos (Keeling) Islands 6799, Indian Ocean; tel. (8) 9162-6615; fax (8) 9162-6697.

Religion

According to the census of 1981, of the 555 residents, 314 (some 57%) were Muslims and 124 (22%) Christians. The majority of Muslims live on Home Island, while most Christians are West Island residents. The Cocos Islands lie within both the Anglican and the Roman Catholic archdioceses of Perth (Western Australia).

Broadcasting and Communications

BROADCASTING

Radio

Radio VKW Cocos: POB 33, Cocos (Keeling) Islands 6799, Indian Ocean; tel. (8) 9162-6666; e-mail vkw@kampong.cc; non-commercial; daily broadcasting service in Cocos Malay and English; 200 listeners; Station Man. CATHERINE CLUNIES-ROSS.

Television

A television service, broadcasting Indonesian, Malaysian and Australian satellite television programmes and videotapes of Australian television programmes, began operating on an intermittent basis in September 1992.

Industry

Cocos (Keeling) Islands Co-operative Society Ltd: POB 1058, Home Island, Cocos (Keeling) Islands 6799, Indian Ocean; tel. (8) 9162-6703; fax (8) 9162-6764; f. 1979; conducts the business enterprises of the Cocos Islanders; activities include boat construction and repairs, copra and coconut production, sail-making, stevedoring and airport operation; owns and operates a supermarket and tourist accommodation; Chair. MOHAMMED SAID BIN CHONGKIN; Gen. Man. RONALD TAYLOR.

Transport

National Jet Systems operate a twice-weekly service from Perth, via Christmas Island, for passengers, supplies and mail to and from the airport on West Island. Cargo vessels from Singapore and Perth deliver supplies, at intervals of four to six weeks.

Cocos Trader: Cocos (Keeling) Islands 6799, Indian Ocean; tel. (8) 9162-6612; fax (8) 9162-6568; e-mail manpower@kampong.cc; shipping agent.

Tourism

Cocos Island Tourism Association: Admiralty House, POB 30, Cocos (Keeling) Islands 6799, Indian Ocean; tel. (8) 9162-6790; fax (8) 9162-6696; e-mail info@cocos-tourism.cc; internet www.cocos-tourism.cc.

NORFOLK ISLAND

Introductory Survey

Location, Climate, Language, Religion, Capital

Norfolk Island lies off the eastern coast of Australia, about 1,400 km east of Brisbane, to the south of New Caledonia and 640 km north of New Zealand. The Territory also comprises uninhabited Phillip Island and Nepean Island, 7 km and 1 km south of the main island respectively. Norfolk Island is hilly and fertile, with a coastline of cliffs and an area of 34.6 sq km (13.3 sq miles). It is about 8 km long and 4.8 km wide. The climate is mild and subtropical, and the average annual rainfall is 1,350 mm, most of which occurs between May and August. The resident population, which numbered 1,772 in August 1996, consists of 'islanders' (descendants of the mutineers from HMS *Bounty*, evacuated from Pitcairn Island, who numbered 683 in 1996) and 'mainlanders' (originally from Australia, New Zealand or the United Kingdom). English is the official language, but a local Polynesian dialect (related to Pitcairnese) is also spoken. Most of the population (70.4% at the 1996 census) adhere to the Christian religion. The capital of the Territory is Kingston.

Recent History

The island was uninhabited when discovered in 1774 by a British expedition, led by Capt. James Cook. Norfolk Island was used as a penal settlement from 1788 to 1814 and again from 1825 to 1855, when it was abandoned. In 1856 it was resettled by 194 emigrants from Pitcairn Island, which had become overpopulated. Norfolk Island was administered as a separate colony until 1897, when it became a dependency of New South Wales. In 1913 control was transferred to the Australian Government. Norfolk Island has a continuing dispute with the Australian Government concerning the island's status as a territory of the Commonwealth of Australia. There have been successive assertions of Norfolk Island's right to self-determination, as a distinct colony.

Under the Norfolk Island Act 1979, Norfolk Island is progressing to responsible legislative and executive government, enabling the Territory to administer its own affairs to the greatest practicable extent. Wide powers are exercised by the nine-member Legislative Assembly and by the Executive Council, comprising the executive members of the Legislative Assembly who have ministerial-type responsibilities. The Act preserves the Australian Government's responsibility for Norfolk Island as a territory under its authority, with the Minister for Regional Services, Territories and Local Government as the responsible minister. The Act indicated that consideration would be given within five years to an extension of the powers of the Legislative Assembly and the political and administrative institutions of Norfolk Island. In 1985 legislative and executive responsibility was assumed by the Norfolk Island Government for public works and services, civil defence, betting and gaming, territorial archives and matters relating to the exercise of executive authority. In 1988 further amendments empowered the Legislative Assembly to select a Norfolk Island government auditor (territorial accounts were previously audited by the Commonwealth Auditor-General). The office of Chief Minister was replaced by that of the President of the Legislative Assembly. David Ernest Buffett was reappointed to this post following the May 1992 general election. A lack of consensus among members of the Executive Council on several major issues prompted early legislative elections in April 1994. The newly-elected seventh Legislative Assembly was significant in having three female members. Following elections in April 1997, in which 22 candidates contested the nine seats, George Smith was appointed President (subsequently reverting to the title of Chief Minister) of the eighth Legislative Assembly. At legislative elections in February 2000 three new members were elected to the Assembly, and Ronald Nobbs was subsequently appointed Chief Minister. Geoffrey Gardner, hitherto Minister for Health, replaced Nobbs as Chief Minister following the elections of November 2001. The incoming Assembly included four new members.

In December 1991 the population of Norfolk Island overwhelmingly rejected a proposal, made by the Australian Government, to include the island in the Australian federal electorate. The outcome of the poll led the Australian Government, in June 1992, to announce that it had abandoned the plan. Similarly, in late 1996 a proposal by the Australian Government to combine Norfolk Island's population with that of Canberra for record-keeping purposes was strongly opposed by the islanders.

In late 1997 the Legislative Assembly debated the issue of increased self-determination for the island. Pro-independence supporters argued that the Territory could generate sufficient income by exploiting gas- and oilfields in the island's exclusive economic zone.

In August 1998 a referendum proposing that the Norfolk Island electoral system be integrated more closely with that of mainland Australia (initiated in Canberra by the Minister for Regional Development, Territories and Local Government) was rejected by 78% of the Territory's electorate. A similar referendum in May 1999 was opposed by 73% of voters.

Frustration with the Australian Government's perceived reluctance to facilitate the transfer of greater powers to the Territory (as outlined in the Norfolk Island Act of 1979, see above) led the island's Legislative Assembly in mid-1999 to vote by seven members to one in favour of full internal self-government. Negotiations regarding the administration of crown land on the island, which continued in 2000, were seen as indicative of the islanders' determination to pursue greater independence from Australia.

In April 2002 a hotel worker from Sydney, Australia, was murdered. This was the first murder to occur on Norfolk Island in more than 150 years. As part of its investigation, the police force took fingerprints of the entire adult population in August. The Australian authorities stated in April 2003 that they were no closer to solving the crime and in July announced that they had contacted more than 400 Australian and New Zealand nationals, who were visiting Norfolk Island at the time of the murder, to request fingerprints. In March 2004 the reward for information about the murder was tripled, and in May a further inquest was launched.

At a referendum held in August 2002 almost two-thirds of those who participated voted not to allow the operation of mobile telephones on the island. Furthermore, in March 2004 the Territory approved legislation to grant a monopoly on satellite internet connections to the government-owned Norfolk Telecom. The legislation, which was expected to put the Territory's private internet service provider, Norfolk Island Data Services, out of business, was criticized by the Australian Government.

The inhabitants of Norfolk Island were profoundly shocked when Deputy Chief Minister and long-standing political figure Ivens Buffett was shot dead in his office in mid-July 2004. A local man was arrested at the scene of the crime, although no motive was immediately apparent for the killing. It was subsequently revealed that the suspect was the politician's son.

A total of 14 candidates contested the legislative election held on 20 October 2004. Geoffrey Gardner, the Chief Minister, regained his seat in the nine-member Legislative Assembly, as did Speaker David Buffett. Two long-serving members, however, were defeated in the poll.

Legislation was approved in late March 2003 to amend the requirements to vote in Norfolk Island elections. Under the new system Australian, New Zealand and British citizens were to be allowed to vote after a residency period of 12 months (reduced from 900 days). The amendments, which followed a series of occasionally acrimonious discussions with the Australian Government, provoked concern among islanders who feared that succumbing to Australian pressure to reform the Norfolk Island Act would result in the effective removal of authority over electoral matters from island control. Moreover, a report by an Australian parliamentary committee published in July 2003 was critical of Norfolk Island's Government and public services. Many residents believed the report constituted a further attempt by Australia to undermine their autonomy. The Chief Minister refuted the committee's claims stating that he would refuse any offers of financial assistance from Canberra or any attempts to introduce income tax in return for access to services from the mainland. A further report by the Australian Government published later in the year alleged that officials on the island used intimidation to achieve political and financial gain and recommended that Norfolk Island's elections, government and financial matters should be overseen by Canberra.

Economic Affairs

Despite the island's natural fertility, agriculture is no longer the principal economic activity. Agriculture and quarrying accounted for only 5.3% of all paid employment in 2001. About 400 ha of land are arable. The main crops are Kentia palm seed, cereals, vegetables and fruit. Cattle and pigs are farmed for domestic consumption. Development of a fisheries industry is restricted by the lack of a harbour. Some flowers and plants are grown commercially. The administration is increasing the area devoted to Norfolk Island pine and hardwoods. Seed and seedlings of the Norfolk Island pine are exported. Potential oil- and gas-bearing sites in the island's waters may provide a possible future source of revenue. A re-export industry has been developed to serve the island's tourist industry. In early 1999 the Norfolk Island Legislative Assembly announced plans to seek assistance from the Australian Government to establish an offshore financial centre on the island. The Government is the most important employer, and there were 151 public sector workers in June 2003.

In 2000/01 imports from Australia cost $A19m. (compared with almost $A23m. in the previous year). In 1998/99 exports to Australia earned $A1m. In 1999/2000 imports from New Zealand totalled $A9.3m. (compared with $A9.0m. in the previous year). In 2000/01 the total cost of imports reached $A41.3m. (compared with $A59.1m. in 1999/2000), while revenue from exports amounted to $A2.7m.(compared with almost $A2.8m. in the previous year) The authorities receive revenue from customs duties (some $A3.9m., equivalent to 34.3% of total revenue in 2000/01), mail order services and the sale of postage stamps, but tourism is the island's main industry. In 2002/03 there were 37,671 tourist arrivals on the island, and in 2001 some 28.4% of the employed labour force were engaged in tourism and recreation. In 1985 and 1986 the Governments of Australia and Norfolk Island jointly established the 465-ha Norfolk Island National Park. This was to protect the remaining native forest, which is the habitat of several unique species of flora (including the largest fern in the world) and fauna (such as the Norfolk Island green parrot, the guavabird and the boobook owl). Conservation efforts include the development of Phillip Island as a nature reserve.

Education

Education is free and compulsory for all children between the ages of six and 15. Pupils attend the government school from infant to secondary level. A total of 187 pupils were enrolled at infant and primary levels and 118 at secondary levels in 2002/03. Students wishing to follow higher education in Australia are eligible for bursaries and scholarships. The budgetary allocation for education was $A2.12m. in 2002/03 (of which $A1.93m. was recurrent expenditure).

Weights and Measures

The metric system is in force.

Statistical Survey

Source: The Administration of Norfolk Island, Administration Offices, Kingston, Norfolk Island 2899; tel. 22001; fax 23177; internet www.norfolk.gov.nf.

AREA AND POPULATION

Area: 34.6 sq km (13.3 sq miles).

Population: 2,181, including 409 visitors, at census of 6 August 1996; 2,601 (males 1,257, females 1,344), including 564 visitors, at census of 7 August 2001.

Density (2001): 75.2 per sq km.

Births, Marriages and Deaths (2002/03): Live births 13; Marriages 35; Deaths 10.

Economically Active Population (persons aged 15 years and over, 2001 census): 1,609 (males 849, females 760).

FINANCE

Currency and Exchange Rates: Australian currency is used.

Budget (year ending 30 June 2003): Revenue $A23,251,781; Expenditure $A19,440,903.

EXTERNAL TRADE

2000/01 (year ending 30 June): *Imports:* $A41,260,213, mainly from Australia and New Zealand. *Exports:* $A2,708,120.

Trade with Australia ($A million, 2000/01): *Imports* 19.

Trade with New Zealand ($NZ million, 2000/01): *Imports* 6.7; *Exports* 0.04.

TOURISM

Visitors (year ending 30 June): 40,221 in 2000/01; 33,619 in 2001/02; 37,671 in 2002/03.

COMMUNICATIONS MEDIA

Radio Receivers (1996): 2,500 in use.

Television Receivers (1996): 1,200 in use.

Telephones (2002/03): 2,374 main lines in use.

Internet Users (2002/03): 494.

Non-daily Newspaper (2002): 1 (estimated circulation 1,400).

EDUCATION

Institution (2003): 1 state school incorporating infant, primary and secondary levels.

Teachers (2002/03): 22.

Students (1999/2000): Infants 79; Primary 116; Secondary 119.

Directory

The Constitution

The Norfolk Island Act 1979 constitutes the administration of the Territory as a body politic and provides for a responsible legislative and executive system, enabling it to administer its own affairs to the greatest practicable extent. The preamble of the Act states that it is the intention of the Australian Parliament to consider the further extension of powers.

The Act provides for an Administrator, appointed by the Australian Government, who shall administer the government of Norfolk Island as a territory under the authority of the Commonwealth of Australia. The Administrator is required to act on the advice of the Executive Council or the responsible Commonwealth Minister in those matters specified as within their competence. Every proposed law passed by the Legislative Assembly must be effected by the assent of the Administrator, who may grant or withhold that assent, reserve the proposed law for the Governor-General's pleasure or recommend amendments.

The Act provides for the Legislative Assembly and the Executive Council, comprising the executive members of the Assembly who have ministerial-type responsibilities. The nine members of the Legislative Assembly are elected for a term of not more than three years under a cumulative method of voting: each elector is entitled

to as many votes (all of equal value) as there are vacancies, but may not give more than four votes to any one candidate. The nine candidates who receive the most votes are declared elected.

The Government

The Administrator, who is the senior representative of the Commonwealth Government, is appointed by the Governor-General of Australia and is responsible to the Minister for Regional Services, Territories and Local Government. A form of responsible legislative and executive government was extended to the island in 1979, as outlined above.

Administrator: Grant Tambling (assumed office November 2003).

EXECUTIVE COUNCIL
(April 2005)

Chief Minister and Minister for Intergovernment Relations: Geoffrey R. Gardner.

Minister for Finance: Vicky Jack.

Minister for Tourism and Community Services: John Brown.

Minister for Land and the Environment: Ronald Nobbs.

MINISTRIES

All Ministries are located at: Old Military Barracks, Quality Row, Kingston, Norfolk Island 2899; tel. 22003; fax 23378; e-mail executives@assembly.gov.nf.

GOVERNMENT OFFICES

Office of the Administrator: POB 201, New Military Barracks, Norfolk Island 2899; tel. 22152; fax 22681.

Administration of Norfolk Island: Administration Offices, Kingston, Norfolk Island 2899; tel. 22001; fax 23177; e-mail records@admin.gov.nf; internet www.norfolkisland.gov.nf; all govt depts; CEO (vacant).

Legislature

LEGISLATIVE ASSEMBLY

Nine candidates are elected for not more than three years. The most recent general election was held on 20 October 2004.

Speaker: David E. Buffett.

Deputy Speaker: to be appointed.

Other Members: Ronald C. Nobbs, Geoffrey R. Gardner, Neville C. Christian, Timothy J. Sheridan, Lorraine C. Boudan, Timothy J. Brown, Vicky Jack, John T. Brown.

Judicial System

Supreme Court of Norfolk Island

Kingston.
Appeals lie to the Federal Court of Australia.

Chief Magistrate: Ron Cahill.

Judges: Mark Samuel Weinberg (Chief Justice), Murray Rutledge Wilcox, Susan Mary Kiefel.

Religion

The majority of the population professes Christianity (66.6%, according to the census of 2001), with the principal denominations being the Church of England (34.9%), the Catholic Church (11.7%) and the Uniting Church (11.2%).

The Press

Norfolk Island Government Gazette: Kingston, Norfolk Island 2899; tel. 22001; fax 23177; internet www.info.gov.nf/gazette; weekly.

Norfolk Islander: Greenways Press, POB 150, Norfolk Island 2899; tel. 22159; fax 22948; e-mail news@islander.nf; f. 1965; weekly; Co-Editors Tom Lloyd, Tim Lloyd; circ. 1,350.

Broadcasting and Communications

TELECOMMUNICATIONS

Norfolk Telecom: New Cascade Rd, Kingston; internet www .telecom.gov.nf; Man. Kim Davies.

BROADCASTING

Radio

Norfolk Island Broadcasting Service: New Cascade Rd, POB 456, Norfolk Island 2899; tel. 22137; fax 23298; e-mail 2niradio@ni .net.nf; govt-owned; non-commercial; broadcasts 112 hours per week; relays television and radio programmes from Australia; Broadcast Man. ROGER NEWMAN.

Radio VL2NI: New Cascade Rd, POB 456, Norfolk Island 2899; tel. 22137; fax 23298; e-mail 2niradio@ni.net.nf; internet www.users.nf/ nfradio/.

Television

Norfolk Island Broadcasting Service: see Radio.

Norfolk Island Television Service: f. 1987; govt-owned; relays programmes of Australian Broadcasting Corpn, Special Broadcasting Service Corpn and Central Seven TV by satellite.

TV Norfolk (TVN): locally operated service featuring programmes of local events and information for tourists.

Finance

BANKING

Commonwealth Bank of Australia (Australia): Taylors Rd, Norfolk Island 2899; tel. 22144; fax 22805.

Westpac Banking Corpn Savings Bank Ltd (Australia): Burnt Pine, Norfolk Island 2899; tel. 22120; fax 22808.

Trade

Norfolk Island Chamber of Commerce Inc: POB 370, Norfolk Island 2899; tel. 22317; fax 23221; e-mail photopress@ni.net.nf; f. 1966; affiliated to the Australian Chamber of Commerce; 60 mems; Pres. GARY ROBERTSON; Sec. MARK McGUIRE.

Norfolk Island Gaming Authority: POB 882, Norfolk Island 2899; tel. 22002; fax 22205; e-mail secgameauth@norfolk.net.nf; internet www.gamingauthority.nlk.nf; Dir KEVIN LEYSHON.

Transport

ROADS

There are about 100 km of roads, including 85 km of sealed road.

SHIPPING

Norfolk Island is served by the three shipping lines, Neptune Shipping, Pacific Direct Line and Roslyndale Shipping Company Pty Ltd. A small tanker from Nouméa (New Caledonia) delivers petroleum products to the island and another from Australia delivers liquid propane gas.

CIVIL AVIATION

Norfolk Island has one airport, with two runways (of 1,900 m and 1,550 m), capable of taking medium-sized jet-engined aircraft. Air New Zealand operates a twice-weekly direct service between Christchurch and Norfolk Island (via Auckland). Charter flights from Lord Howe Island and occasionally from New Caledonia also serve the island. The cessation of scheduled services from Australia by Ansett Australia in 1997 had an adverse effect on the island's important tourist industry. As a consequence, Norfolk Jet Express was established to provide a weekly service to Australia. In February 1999 Air Nauru began to operate a weekly charter flight service to Norfolk Island from Sydney, under contract with Norfolk Jet Express. In mid-2002 services from Brisbane and Sydney were also being provided by Alliance Airlines. The latter were increased to three times per week in September 2003.

Tourism

Visitor arrivals totalled 37,671 in 2002/03, of whom some 81% came from Australia, with most of the remainder travelling from New Zealand. In that year tourist accommodation totalled 1,551 beds.

Norfolk Island Visitors Information Centre: Taylors Rd, Burnt Pine, POB 211, Norfolk Island 2899; tel. 22147; fax 23109; e-mail info@norfolkisland.com.au; internet www.norfolkisland.com.au; Gen. Man. BRUCE WALKER.

Other Territories

Territory of Ashmore and Cartier Islands

The Ashmore Islands (known as West, Middle and East Islands) and Cartier Island are situated in the Timor Sea, about 850 km and 790 km west of Darwin respectively. The Ashmore Islands cover some 93 ha of land and Cartier Island covers 0.4 ha. The islands are small and uninhabited, consisting of sand and coral, surrounded by shoals and reefs. Grass is the main vegetation. Maximum elevation is about 2.5 m above sea-level. The islands abound in birdlife, sea-cucumbers (*bêches-de-mer*) and, seasonally, turtles.

The United Kingdom took formal possession of the Ashmore Islands in 1878, and Cartier Island was annexed in 1909. The islands were placed under the authority of the Commonwealth of Australia in 1931. They were annexed to, and deemed to form part of, the Northern Territory of Australia in 1938. On 1 July 1978 the Australian Government assumed direct responsibility for the administration of the islands, which rests with a parliamentary secretary appointed by the Minister for Regional Services, Territories and Local Government. Periodic visits are made to the islands by the Royal Australian Navy and aircraft of the Royal Australian Air Force, and the Civil Coastal Surveillance Service makes aerial surveys of the islands and neighbouring waters. The oilfields of Jabiru and Challis are located in waters adjacent to the Territory.

In August 1983 Ashmore Reef was declared a national nature reserve. An agreement between Australia and Indonesia permits Indonesian traditional fishermen to continue fishing in the territorial waters and to land on West Island to obtain supplies of fresh water. In 1985 the Australian Government extended the laws of the Northern Territory to apply in Ashmore and Cartier, and decided to contract a vessel to be stationed at Ashmore Reef during the Indonesian fishing season (March–November) to monitor the fishermen.

During 2000–01 increasing numbers of refugees and asylum-seekers attempted to land at Ashmore Reef, hoping to gain residency in Australia. The majority had travelled from the Middle East via Indonesia, where the illegal transport of people was widespread. Consequently, in late 2000 a vessel with the capacity to transport up to 150 people was chartered to ferry unauthorized arrivals to the Australian mainland. In September 2001 the Australian Government introduced an item of legislation to Parliament excising Ashmore Reef and other outlying territories from Australia's migration zone. However, in March 2004 a group of nine women and six men, believed to be seeking asylum in Australia, were discovered on Ashmore Reef. A government spokesperson reiterated the Territory's exclusion from Australia's migration zone, stating that this would preclude the group from seeking any form of residency in the country.

Australian Antarctic Territory

The Australian Antarctic Territory was established by Order in Council in February 1933 and proclaimed in August 1936, subsequent to the Australian Antarctic Territory Acceptance Act (1933). It consists of the portion of Antarctica (divided by the French territory of Terre Adélie) lying between 45°E and 136°E, and between 142°E and 160°E. The Australian Antarctic Division (AAD) of the Department of the Environment, Sport and Territories (subsequently renamed the Department of the Environment and Heritage) was established in 1948 as a permanent agency, and to administer and provide support for the Australian National Antarctic Research Expeditions (ANARE), which maintains three permanent scientific stations (Mawson, Davis and Casey) in the Territory. The area of the Territory is estimated to be 5,896,500 sq km (2,276,650 sq miles), and there are no permanent inhabitants, although there is a permanent presence of scientific personnel. Environmentalists expressed alarm at proposals in the late 1990s to encourage tourism in the Territory, which, they claimed, could damage the area's sensitive ecology. In November 2001 an international team of scientists commenced Australia's largest ever scientific expedition, to gather data on the influence of the Southern Ocean on the world's climate and the global carbon cycle. In January 2002 Australia attempted to expel Japanese whaling ships from the 200-nautical-mile exclusive economic zone it claimed to be under the jurisdiction of the Australian Antarctic Territory. The Government allocated $A102.3m. to its Antarctic Programme in 2002/03. The Territory is administered by the Antarctic Division of the Department of the Environment and Heritage. Australia is a signatory to the Antarctic Treaty (see p. 529)

Coral Sea Islands Territory

The Coral Sea Islands became a Territory of the Commonwealth of Australia under the Coral Sea Islands Act of 1969. The Territory lies east of Queensland, between the Great Barrier Reef and longitude 156° 06'E, and between latitude 12°S and 24°S, and comprises several islands and reefs. The islands are composed largely of sand and coral, and have no permanent fresh water supply, but some have a cover of grass and scrub. The area has been known as a notorious hazard to shipping since the 19th century, the danger of the reefs being compounded by shifting sand cays and occasional tropical cyclones. The Coral Sea Islands have been acquired by Australia by numerous acts of sovereignty since the early years of the 20th century.

Spread over a sea area of approximately 780,000 sq km (300,000 sq miles), all the islands and reefs in the Territory are very small, totalling only a few sq km of land area. They include Cato Island, Chilcott Islet in the Coringa Group, and the Willis Group. In 1997 the Coral Sea Islands Act was amended to include Elizabeth and Middleton Reefs. A meteorological station, operated by the Commonwealth Bureau of Meteorology and with a staff of four, has provided a service on one of the Willis Group since 1921. The other islands are uninhabited. There are eight automatic weather stations (on Cato Island, Flinders Reef, Frederick Reef, Holmes Reef, Lihou Reef, Creal Reef, Marion Reef and Gannet Cay) and several navigation aids distributed throughout the Territory.

The Act constituting the Territory did not establish an administration on the islands, but provides means of controlling the activities of those who visit them. The Lihou Reef and Coringa-Herald National Nature Reserves were established in 1982 to provide protection for the wide variety of terrestrial and marine wildlife, which include rare species of birds and sea turtles (one of which is the largest, and among the most endangered, of the world's species of sea turtle). The Australian Government has concluded agreements for the protection of endangered and migratory birds with Japan and the People's Republic of China. The Governor-General of Australia is empowered to make ordinances for the peace, order and good government of the Territory and, by ordinance, the laws of the Australian Capital Territory apply. The Supreme Court and Court of Petty Sessions of Norfolk Island have jurisdiction in the Territory. The Territory is administered by a parliamentary secretary appointed by the Minister for Local Government, Territories and Roads. The area is visited regularly by the Royal Australian Navy.

Territory of Heard Island and the McDonald Islands

These islands are situated about 4,000 km (2,500 miles) south-west of Perth, Western Australia. The Territory, consisting of Heard Island, Shag Island (8 km north of Heard) and the McDonald Islands, is almost entirely covered in ice and has a total area of 369 sq km (142 sq miles). Sovereignty was transferred from the United Kingdom to the Commonwealth of Australia on 26 December 1947, following the establishment of a scientific research station on Heard Island (which functioned until March 1955). The islands are administered by the Antarctic Division of the Australian Department of the Environment and Heritage. There are no permanent inhabitants. However, in 1991 evidence emerged of a Polynesian community on Heard Island some 700 years before the territory's discovery by European explorers. The island is of considerable scientific interest, as it is believed to be one of the few Antarctic habitats uncontaminated by introduced organisms. Heard Island is about 44 km long and 20 km wide and possesses an active volcano, named Big Ben. In January 1991 an international team of scientists travelled to Heard Island to conduct research involving the transmission of sound waves, beneath the surface of the ocean, in order to monitor any evidence of the 'greenhouse effect' (melting of polar ice and the rise in sea-level as a consequence of pollution). The pulses of sound, which travel at a speed largely influenced by temperature, were to be received at various places around the world, with international co-operation. Heard Island was chosen for the experiment because of its unique location, from which direct paths to the five principal oceans extend. The McDonald Islands, with an area of about 1 sq km (0.4 sq miles), lie some 42 km west of Heard Island. Only two successful landings by boat have been recorded since the discovery of the McDonald Islands in the late 19th century. In late 1997 Heard Island and the McDonald Islands were accorded World Heritage status by UNESCO in recognition of their outstanding universal significance as a natural landmark.

In 1999 concern was expressed that stocks of the Patagonian toothfish in the waters around the islands were becoming depleted as a result of over-exploitation, mainly by illegal operators. (The popularity of the fish in Japan and the USA, where it is known as Chilean sea bass, increased significantly during the early 2000s.) This problem was highlighted in August 2003 when a Uruguayan fishing vessel was seized, following a 20-day pursuit over 7,400 km by Australian, South African and British patrol boats. The trawler had been fishing illegally in waters near Heard and McDonald and had a full cargo of Patagonian toothfish worth some US $1.5m. Experts feared that, if poaching continued at current rates, the species would become extinct by 2007. In response to this situation, the Australian Government announced in December 2003 that it was to send an ice-breaking patrol vessel with deck-mounted machine guns to police the waters around Heard and McDonald Islands. It was hoped that this action might serve to deter illegal fishing activity in the area, much of which was believed to involve international criminal organizations.

In 2001 the Australian Government's Antarctic Division conducted a five-month scientific expedition to Heard Island. It claimed that glacial cover had retreated by 12% since 1947 as a result of global warming. In October 2002 the Australian Government declared the establishment of the Heard Island and McDonald Islands Marine Reserve. Covering 6.5m. ha, the marine reserve was to be the largest in the world, strengthening existing conservation measures and imposing an official ban on all fishing and petroleum and mineral exploitation. Among the many species of plant, bird and mammal to be protected by the reserve were the southern elephant seal, the sub-Antarctic fur seal and two species of albatross. Limited scientific research and environmental monitoring were to be allowed in the Marine Reserve.

AUSTRIA

Introductory Survey

Location, Climate, Language, Religion, Flag, Capital

The Republic of Austria lies in central Europe, bordered by Switzerland and Liechtenstein to the west, by Germany and the Czech Republic to the north, by Hungary and Slovakia to the east, and by Italy and Slovenia to the south. The mean annual temperature lies between 7°C and 9°C (45°F and 48°F). The population is 99% German-speaking, with small Croat- and Slovene-speaking minorities. The majority of the inhabitants profess Christianity: about 72% are Roman Catholics and about 5% are Protestants. The national flag (proportions 2 by 3) consists of three equal horizontal stripes, of red, white and red. The state flag has, in addition, the coat of arms (a small shield, with horizontal stripes of red separated by a white stripe, superimposed on a black eagle, wearing a golden crown and holding a sickle and a hammer in its feet, with a broken chain between its legs) in the centre. The capital is Vienna (Wien).

Recent History

Austria was formerly the centre of the Austrian (later Austro-Hungarian) Empire, which comprised a large part of central Europe. The Empire, under the Habsburg dynasty, was dissolved in 1918, at the end of the First World War, and Austria proper became a republic. The first post-war Council of Ministers was a coalition led by Dr Karl Renner, who remained Chancellor until 1920, when a new Constitution introduced a federal form of government. Many of Austria's inhabitants favoured union with Germany, but this was forbidden by the post-war peace treaties. In March 1938, however, Austria was occupied by Nazi Germany's armed forces and incorporated into the German Reich, led by the Austrian-born Adolf Hitler.

After Hitler's defeat in Austria, a provisional Government, under Dr Renner, was established in April 1945. In July, following Germany's surrender to the Allied forces, Austria was divided into four zones, occupied respectively by forces of the USA, the USSR, the United Kingdom and France. At the first post-war elections to the 165-seat Nationalrat (National Council), held in November 1945, the conservative Österreichische Volkspartei (ÖVP, Austrian People's Party) won 85 seats and the Sozialistische Partei Österreichs (SPÖ, Socialist Party of Austria) secured 76. The two parties formed a coalition Government. In December Dr Renner became the first Federal President of the second Austrian Republic, holding office until his death in December 1950. However, it was not until May 1955 that the four powers signed a State Treaty with Austria, ending the occupation and recognizing Austrian independence, effective from 27 July; occupation forces left in October.

More than 20 years of coalition government came to an end in April 1966 with the formation of a Council of Ministers by the ÖVP alone. Dr Josef Klaus, the Federal Chancellor since April 1964, remained in office. The SPÖ achieved a relative majority in the March 1970 general election and formed a minority Government, with Dr Bruno Kreisky (a former Minister of Foreign Affairs, who had been party leader since 1967) as Chancellor. In April 1971 the incumbent President, Franz Jonas of the SPÖ, was re-elected, defeating the ÖVP candidate, Dr Kurt Waldheim, a former Minister of Foreign Affairs (who subsequently served two five-year terms as UN Secretary-General, beginning in January 1972). The SPÖ won an absolute majority of seats in the Nationalrat at general elections in October 1971 (when the number of seats was increased from 165 to 183) and October 1975. President Jonas died in April 1974, and the subsequent presidential election, held in June, was won by Dr Rudolf Kirchschläger, who had been the Minister of Foreign Affairs since 1970. He was re-elected for a second six-year term in 1980.

In November 1978 a government proposal to commission Austria's first nuclear power plant was defeated in a national referendum. Despite expectations that Chancellor Kreisky would resign, he received the full support of the SPÖ and emerged in an apparently even stronger position. At the general election in May 1979 the SPÖ increased its majority in the Nationalrat. The general election of April 1983, however, marked the end of the 13-year era of one-party government: the SPÖ lost its absolute majority in the Nationalrat and Kreisky, unwilling to participate in a coalition, resigned as Chancellor. The reduction in the SPÖ's representation was partly attributed to the emergence of two environmentalist 'Green' parties, both founded in 1982. The two parties together received more than 3% of the total votes cast, but failed to win any seats. Kreisky's successor, Dr Fred Sinowatz (the former Vice-Chancellor and Minister of Education), took office in May, leading a coalition of the SPÖ and the right-of-centre Freiheitliche Partei Österreichs (FPÖ, Freedom Party of Austria). The new Government continued the social welfare policy that had been pursued by its predecessor, in addition to maintaining Austria's foreign policy of 'active neutrality'.

A presidential election was held in May 1986 to choose a successor to Kirchschläger. The SPÖ candidate was Dr Kurt Steyrer (the Minister of Health and Environment), while Dr Waldheim stood as an independent candidate, although with the support of the ÖVP. The campaign was dominated by allegations that Waldheim, a former officer in the army of Nazi Germany, had been implicated in atrocities committed by the Nazis in the Balkans during 1942–45; the ensuing controversy divided the country and brought unexpected international attention to the election. Waldheim won a run-off ballot in June 1986, with 54% of the votes cast. The defeat of the SPÖ presidential candidate led Chancellor Sinowatz and four of his ministers to resign. Dr Franz Vranitzky, hitherto the Minister of Finance, became the new Chancellor. In September the FPÖ elected a controversial new leader, Dr Jörg Haider, who represented the far right wing of his party. This precipitated the end of the partnership between the SPÖ and the FPÖ, and the general election for the Nationalrat, scheduled for April 1987, was brought forward to November 1986. No party won an absolute majority: the SPÖ took 80 seats, the ÖVP 77, the FPÖ 18 and an alliance of three Green parties eight. Following several weeks of negotiations, a 'grand coalition' of the SPÖ and the ÖVP, with Vranitzky as Chancellor, was formed in January 1987.

Waldheim's election to the presidency was controversial both domestically and internationally, and Austria's relations with Israel and the USA, in particular, were severely strained. In February 1988 a specially appointed international commission of historians concluded that Waldheim must have been aware of the atrocities that had been committed. Waldheim refused to resign, but in June 1991 he announced that he would not seek a second presidential term.

At the general election held in October 1990 the SPÖ retained its position as the largest single party, increasing its number of seats in the Nationalrat by one, to 81 of the 183 seats, while the ÖVP obtained only 60 seats, a decline of 17; the FPÖ increased its representation by 15 seats, to 33. The FPÖ's success was attributed, in large part, to its support for restrictions on immigration, especially from eastern Europe. The Grüne Alternative Liste (GAL, Green Alternative List), an informal electoral alliance comprising Die Grüne Alternative (The Green Alternative) and the Vereinte Grüne Österreichs (United Green Party of Austria), increased Green representation by one seat, to nine. In December, following several weeks of negotiations, the SPÖ and the ÖVP formed a new coalition Government, again led by Vranitzky.

A congress of the SPÖ held in June 1991 voted to revert to the party's original name, the Sozialdemokratische Partei Österreichs (SPÖ, Social-Democratic Party of Austria). In the same month the FPÖ leader, Dr Haider, was dismissed as Governor of Carinthia (Kärnten) after publicly praising Hitler's employment policies. In December the Nationalrat approved government legislation whereby Austria became the only country in Europe able to reject asylum requests from individuals without identity papers. Following the imprisonment, in January 1992, of a prominent right-wing activist for demanding the restoration of the Nazi party, and the subsequent fire-bombing of a refugee hostel by neo-Nazis in northern Austria, the Nationalrat voted unanimously in February to amend anti-Nazi legislation. The minimum prison sentence for Nazi agitation was reduced from five years to one year (in order to increase the number of

634   www.europaworld.com

successful prosecutions) and denial of the Nazi Holocaust was made a criminal offence.

At the presidential election held in April 1992 the two main candidates were Dr Rudolf Streicher (hitherto the Minister of Public Economy and Transport), for the SPÖ, and Dr Thomas Klestil (a former ambassador to the USA), representing the ÖVP. No candidate achieved the required 50% of the vote at the first ballot, but in the second run-off ballot, held in May, Klestil received almost 57% of the votes cast; he assumed the presidency in July.

In January 1993 the FPÖ organized a national petition seeking to require the Nationalrat to debate the introduction of legislation that would halt immigration into Austria and impose stricter controls on foreign residents in the country (the estimated number of whom had increased from 350,000 to 600,000 since 1989). Although the petition was signed by 7.4% of the electorate (417,000 signatures, compared with the constitutional requirement of 100,000 to force parliamentary debate), the result was considered disappointing by the FPÖ. The initiative was strongly opposed by a broad coalition of politicians, church leaders and intellectuals. In February 1993 five FPÖ deputies in the Nationalrat left the party, partly in protest at the petition on immigration, and formed a new political organization, the Liberales Forum (LiF, Liberal Forum), under the leadership of Dr Heide Schmidt, hitherto the Vice-President of the FPÖ. In December four campaigners for tolerance towards immigrant and refugee communities, including the Mayor of Vienna, were injured by letter-bombs. In March 1999 a lone right-wing extremist was sentenced to life imprisonment, having been found guilty of perpetrating these and other bomb attacks during the 1990s against members and supporters of ethnic minorities, including an assault in February 1995 that killed four gypsies.

In late 1993 an ongoing debate over Austria's future in Europe intensified when the European Union (EU, see p. 217) set a deadline of 1 March 1994 by which time the conditions of Austria's entry into the Union (pending a national referendum) were to be agreed. Austria strongly defended its right to preserve its neutrality, to uphold higher environmental standards and to impose restrictions on the transit of road-freight traffic through the Austrian Alps. Eventually a number of compromises were reached, including an extension of the existing limit on lorry transit traffic until 2001. At the ensuing national referendum on the terms of Austria's membership of the EU, held in June 1994, some two-thirds of voters (66.4%) supported Austria's entry into the Union. Following the referendum Austria announced plans to sign NATO's Partnership for Peace programme (see p. 303). Austria was formally admitted to the EU on 1 January 1995. Observer status at Western European Union (see p. 352) was subsequently granted.

At the general election held in October 1994 the ruling coalition lost its two-thirds' majority in the Nationalrat. The SPÖ obtained 66 of the 183 seats in the legislature (winning 35% of the votes cast), the ÖVP took 52 seats (with 28% of the votes cast), and the FPÖ (which had campaigned against Austria's accession to the EU) increased its share of the votes cast by 6%, to 23%, securing 42 seats. Die Grünen (the Greens) and the LiF also made gains, winning 13 and 10 seats respectively. The success of the FPÖ's populist campaign, which had concentrated on countering corruption and immigration and had advocated referendum-based rather than parliamentary-based governance, unsettled the Austrian political establishment after years of relative consensus. At the end of November, following protracted negotiations, the SPÖ and ÖVP finally agreed to form a new coalition Government, with Vranitzky remaining as Chancellor.

The new SPÖ-ÖVP coalition was beleaguered by disagreements, mainly concerning differences in approach to the urgent need to reduce the annual budgetary deficit in compliance with Austria's commitment, as a member of the EU, to future Economic and Monetary Union (EMU). In early 1995 five ministers, including the Vice-Chancellor, Dr Erhard Busek, resigned. Busek was simultaneously replaced as Chairman of the ÖVP by Dr Wolfgang Schüssel. In October a deepening rift between the SPÖ and ÖVP regarding the means of curtailing the 1996 budgetary deficit proved irreconcilable, culminating in the collapse of the coalition. Consequently a new general election was held in December 1995. The SPÖ improved upon its disappointing performance at the previous election, receiving 38.1% of the votes cast and winning 71 of the 183 seats in the Nationalrat. The ÖVP secured 28.3% of the votes cast (obtaining 53

seats), the FPÖ (which had been restyled Die Freiheitlichen in January 1995) 21.9% (40 seats), the LiF 5.5% (10 seats) and the Greens 4.8% (nine seats). In early March 1996, following lengthy negotiations, the SPÖ and ÖVP agreed an economic programme and formed a new coalition Government, with Vranitzky remaining as Chancellor. However, in mid-January 1997 Vranitzky unexpectedly resigned from the chancellorship. Viktor Klima, the Minister of Finance, was appointed as his successor, both as Chancellor and as Chairman of the SPÖ, and the Council of Ministers was reorganized.

In March 1998, following months of debate, the Government announced that Austria would not apply to join NATO, and would thereby preserve its traditional neutrality (as favoured by the SPÖ, but opposed by the ÖVP). Nevertheless, in early April 1999 Austria, in conjunction with the three other officially neutral EU member states, signed an EU declaration stating that the ongoing bombing of Serbia by NATO forces was 'both necessary and warranted' (although regrettable). During the 1990s, in its capacity as a participant of NATO's Partnership for Peace programme (which it had joined in 1995), Austria contributed to peace-keeping operations in Bosnia and Herzegovina, authorized by the UN Security Council and effectively carried out under NATO command. Austria also provided substantial humanitarian aid to the thousands of refugees who suffered as a consequence of the wars and ethnic conflicts in the Balkans. In the aftermath of the terrorist attacks on the USA in September 2001, Chancellor Schüssel stated, in early November, that Austria might consider abandoning its policy of neutrality and joining NATO at some time in the future. In early 2003, however, in the period immediately preceding the US-led military action to oust the regime of Saddam Hussein in Iraq, Austria refused permission for US fighter aircraft to fly over Austrian territory unless the action received UN authorization (which was ultimately not forthcoming).

At the presidential election held in April 1998 Klestil was re-elected emphatically, winning 63.5% of the votes cast. The FPÖ made significant gains at regional elections in March 1999, becoming the dominant party in Dr Haider's home province of Carinthia; Haider was subsequently elected Governor of Carinthia (having previously been dismissed from that post in 1991—see above). The general election held in October 1999 resulted in unprecedented success for the FPÖ, which, by a narrow margin of 415 votes, took second place ahead of the ÖVP. The SPÖ won 65 of the 183 seats in the Nationalrat (with 33.2% of the votes cast), while the FPÖ and ÖVP both secured 52 seats (each with 26.9% of the votes cast). The Greens took 14 seats (7.4%). The FPÖ had campaigned on a programme that included a halt to immigration, the obstruction of the projected eastwards expansion of the EU, the radical deregulation of the business sector and the introduction of a uniform low rate of income tax and of hugely increased child allowances for Austrian citizens. Dr Haider appeared to have inflamed popular fears that the planned admission to the EU of Austria's eastern neighbours would flood the domestic market with cheap labour, thereby causing the level of unemployment to rise. During the FPÖ campaign Haider allegedly revived nationalist terminology previously employed by the Nazi regime; nevertheless, he consistently denied embracing neo-Nazi ideology. The election result was most widely regarded as a protest against the 12-year old 'grand' SPÖ-ÖVP coalition, which had acquired a reputation for unwieldy bureaucracy and for sanctioning politically-motivated appointments to public companies.

Following the election, protracted negotiations took place with a view to forming a new administration. In late January 2000, after a failed attempt to reconstruct the SPÖ-ÖVP coalition, the SPÖ announced that it would not attempt to form a minority government. At the beginning of February President Klestil reluctantly presided over the inauguration of an ÖVP-FPÖ coalition Government, with the ÖVP leader, Dr Schüssel, as Chancellor. Dr Haider elected not to participate directly in the new administration, which included an FPÖ Vice-Chancellor, Dr Susanne Riess-Passer, and five FPÖ ministers (including those responsible for finance, justice and defence). Although the new coalition had committed itself to respecting human rights and had adopted a relatively moderate political programme, the participation in government of the FPÖ provoked strong opposition both within Austria and abroad. Israel and the USA immediately recalled their ambassadors from Vienna, pending a reassessment of bilateral relations, while Austria's 14 fellow EU member states each suspended bilateral political co-operation, maintaining diplomatic relations at a 'technical' level, pending the removal of the FPÖ from the coalition. In late February Dr Haider announced that he was to resign as leader of the FPÖ, stating that he would concentrate instead on his position as Governor of Carinthia; few people, however, doubted that he would remain the *de facto* leader of the party.

In February 2000 Klima resigned as Chairman of the SPÖ and was replaced by Dr Alfred Gusenbauer. In April Gusenbauer apologized on behalf of his party for decades of political opportunism and acknowledged that the SPÖ had erred in embracing and promoting former Nazis after the Second World War in its efforts to become Austria's most powerful political force. He later established a commission of independent historians to investigate the matter. The commission reported in January 2005 that the SPÖ had actively recruited former Nazis in order to help them reintegrate into society, as had the ÖVP. The report noted that, while the Nazi holocaust against the Jews had stripped Austria of many professionals (thereby necessitating, to some extent, the parties' efforts at recruitment), the SPÖ ought to have made greater attempts at bringing back exiles following the war and differentiated between those who were 'merely Nazi party members' and those who used their Nazi membership to act in a criminal fashion. Gusenbauer's initiative was expected to put pressure on the coalition Government to launch similar projects, but officials from both constituent parties claimed they had already dealt with the issue and had no plans to follow suit. However, in June 2000 Ernest Windholz, the newly elected head of the FPÖ in Lower Austria (Niederösterreich), provoked controversy by using a Nazi-era slogan to honour long-serving members of his party. The incident was thought to have harmed Austria's chances of having the diplomatic sanctions (see above) lifted at a forthcoming EU summit meeting, the last such meeting before the rotating EU presidency was to be assumed by France, which had pressed for the introduction of the sanctions following the FPÖ's accession to power. Prospects improved, however, at the end of June when Chancellor Schüssel agreed to the nomination by the President of the Court of Human Rights of a three-person EU delegation to examine the Austrian Government's commitment to common European values (with particular regard to the rights of minority groups, immigrants and refugees and to the political philosophy of the FPÖ). Following the publication of the delegation's report, the 14 members of the EU were to reassess the necessity for sanctions. The Austrian Government warned that the continuation of sanctions could affect EU decisions on constitutional reform and the accession of new member states. The delegation visited Austria in late July, and issued its report in September. The delegation recommended that the sanctions be lifted on the grounds that they were counter-productive and tended to generate increased nationalist sentiment. Although the EU report did criticize the xenophobic tendencies of the FPÖ, it confirmed that Austria's treatment of minorities was superior to that of many other member states and that incidences of violence against foreigners were less frequent in Austria than in other EU countries. The report also criticized the FPÖ for trivializing Nazism and threatening press freedom by using libel suits to silence criticism. Concurrently, economic analysts reported that upholding the sanctions against Austria could adversely affect the euro, which had reached a record low against the US dollar. As a result, the EU lifted its sanctions in September, but at the same time warned that it would continue to monitor closely the influence of the FPÖ, and Dr Haider, upon government policies.

Shortly after the lifting of EU sanctions in September 2000, Dr Haider attended a reunion of veterans of the Third Reich where he made a speech in which he praised those gathered as good citizens and reiterated comments that survivors of the Second World War had been maligned. He also demanded justice for German and Austrian citizens who had lost property after the war. Haider provoked further criticism when he spent more than 1m. Schilling on the restoration of Nazi frescoes, previously housed in the Carinthian parliament building, for display in a museum.

The end of 2000 was a troubled time for the FPÖ, whose influence and popularity (which had, rather perversely, benefited from the temporary imposition of EU sanctions) was beginning to wane. The party fared badly in regional elections in Styria (Steiermark) and Burgenland; the decline in support was widely attributed to the FPÖ losing its appeal as a 'protest party' upon entering into government. In November the Minister of Science and Transport, Michael Schmid, resigned from the coalition Government, citing the FPÖ's poor electoral perform-

ance in Styria. He was the third FPÖ minister to resign since the formation of the Government in February, prompting accusations that the party was unfit to govern. Schmid subsequently resigned from the FPÖ after refusing to pay one-half of his government pension into a party fund. Poor electoral results, instability and repeated indiscretions linking the party with Nazism were, however, overshadowed by the emergence of a major political scandal. In October a number of senior members of the FPÖ (including the Minister of Justice, Dr Dieter Böhmdorfer) were accused of using illicitly obtained police files to discredit opponents, including the former Minister of Finance, Caspar Einem. Böhmdorfer rejected calls from the opposition and the judges' union to resign, and in October survived a vote of 'no confidence', the third such vote in his short ministerial career. By November the number of FPÖ members under investigation had risen to 67 and 11 police-officers were suspended in connection with the scandal.

In March 2001 the FPÖ performed poorly in local elections in Vienna, and in May the German Federal Chancellor, Gerhard Schröder, refused to meet with any members of the FPÖ during an official visit to Austria. Also in May the head of Vienna's Jewish community, Dr Ariel Muzicant, won a lawsuit against Dr Haider, barring him from repeating comments in which he branded Muzicant as dirty and mocked his first name (also the name of a household detergent). After the ruling, Muzicant stated that he would seek to establish whether Dr Haider could be found guilty of anti-Semitism. Days earlier the World Jewish Congress had strongly criticized the FPÖ for its anti-Semitism and racism, including the adoption of Nazi slogans, and had alleged that anti-Semitism had increased in Austria since the entry of the FPÖ into government.

In early May 2001 Böhmdorfer presented draft legislation under which journalists would face prosecution and up to six months' imprisonment for divulging information drawn from judicial inquiries. The proposed legislation was strongly condemned by journalists' unions as an attack on press freedom.

In late September 2001, purportedly as part of a plan to combat international terrorism following the devastating terrorist attacks in the USA, Dr Haider asserted that refugees from continents other than Europe seeking asylum within the EU should no longer be granted residence in Europe while their requests were being processed. The FPÖ's parliamentary leadership supported Dr Haider's standpoint. The FPÖ also suggested the introduction of 'biometric' identification methods (namely, fingerprinting), a fortnightly 'control' of all asylum-seekers and the immediate expulsion of any foreigners suspected of being involved in criminal activities. Furthermore, the FPÖ proposed the introduction of a so-called *Integrationsvertrag* ('integration contract') for immigrant workers and their families, including those who were already living in the country. Under this contract immigrants would be obliged to attend, and pass, 'integration' courses in German language and citizenship; those who did not comply within four years would have their social security benefits gradually reduced, and, in extreme cases, would face expulsion from the country. The controversial propositions provoked fierce criticism from political leaders and human rights groups both within Austria and throughout the EU. Despite initial reservations, in early October the ÖVP endorsed the FPÖ's recommendations regarding asylum-seekers and immigrants (with the exception of the proposal to deny asylum-seekers the right of temporary residence). Despite strong opposition from the SPÖ and the Greens, the proposed measures, including the introduction of the 'integration contract', were approved by the legislature and came into force on 1 January 2003. Moreover, in late 2001 the Minister of the Interior, Dr Ernst Strasser, announced that it would no longer be possible to claim asylum through Austria's consulates overseas; Austria had been the only EU country to offer this facility.

The ÖVP-FPÖ coalition was characterized by periods of drive and reform intermittently supplanted by bouts of internecine strife. It was an internal power struggle within the FPÖ that, in early September 2002, led to the resignation of a number of moderate FPÖ ministers, including the Vice-Chancellor and party Chairwoman, Dr Susanne Riess-Passer. Hitherto, Schüssel had succeeded in persuading these moderate FPÖ ministers to eschew the more extremist elements of their party's credo, while himself adopting some of the FPÖ's more reasonable policies. Haider, believing that his party's influence was thus being undermined, had reverted to populist tactics in an effort to restore the FPÖ's perceived credentials as an 'anti-establishment' party. In February he had lost the support of many Austrians and had been severely criticized by the opposition for making an unofficial visit to the Iraqi President, Saddam Hussain, in Baghdad. Haider's renewed bouts of invective against foreigners, the EU and even against Schüssel himself, did nothing to improve his political standing or that of the FPÖ. With this increasing instability in his party's junior coalition partner, Schüssel had little option but to dissolve the legislature on 20 September pending an early general election. On the same day Mathias Reichhold was elected as the new Chairman of the FPÖ, following Haider's refusal to stand for the post. When Reichhold resigned from the leadership of the FPÖ later that year owing to ill health, he was replaced by a staunch ally of Haider, Herbert Haupt.

At the general election, which was held on 24 November 2002, the ÖVP received 42.3% of the votes cast, securing 79 of the 183 seats in the legislature (the party's largest single share of the votes in more than 30 years), mainly at the expense of the FPÖ, which obtained only 10.0% of the votes cast (18 seats), compared with 26.9% in 1999. The SPÖ received 36.5% of the votes cast (69 seats) and the Greens 9.5% (17 seats). Although the ÖVP was the party with the largest representation in the legislature, it did not have a sufficient number of seats to form a majority government. The Greens, many of whom were still mistrustful of Schüssel after his earlier co-operation with Haider, had already ruled out any coalition agreement with the ÖVP; many members of the SPÖ, too, were unwilling to form a coalition with the ÖVP in which their party would be the junior partner; finally, the FPÖ, much weakened and still riven by factional infighting, was initially no longer viewed as a suitable coalition partner. Such were the difficulties facing Schüssel that by mid-February 2003 he had still not managed to form a new government. At the end of the month, however, and with some apparent reluctance, Schüssel invited the FPÖ to form another coalition administration with the ÖVP; a new Council of Ministers was sworn in on 28 February. The new Government notably included only three ministers from the FPÖ, compared with five in the previous administration.

On 6 May 2003 the Österreichischer Gewerkschaftsbund (ÖGB—Austrian Trade Union Federation) called a one-day general strike (the first such strike in Austria for some 50 years) in protest at proposed reforms to the pension system, under which the retirement age would be increased to 65 years with some pension benefits reduced by more than 30%. It was estimated that some 1.4m. people (about one-quarter of Austria's workforce) participated in the strike. A second one-day strike (observed by around 1m. workers) was held in early June, and the ÖGB promised further action unless the Government abandoned its plans for pension reform. Confronted by such large-scale opposition, the Government was forced to concede some significant modifications of its original proposals.

The FPÖ suffered heavy losses in regional elections held in September 2003, with the Greens, for the first time, receiving more votes than the right-wing party. The following month the Chairman of the FPÖ, Herbert Haupt, resigned from his post as Vice-Chancellor (he was replaced by Hubert Gorbach of the FPÖ, who was the incumbent Minister of Transport, Innovation and Technology), while retaining his position as Minister of Social Security, Generations and Consumer Protection. Haupt was reported to have been under pressure to resign from Haider and was widely believed to have lost the support of his party over what it perceived as his poor media performance. Haupt was to remain as the nominal leader of the FPÖ until the holding of party elections in 2004, but under the supervision of the party's new Managing Chairwoman, Haider's sister, Ursula Haubner. Many observers viewed the latter's appointment as evidence that Haider had again assumed control of the FPÖ. In March 2004 local elections were held in Carinthia (Haider's traditional stronghold); forecasts of an SPÖ victory were confounded when the FPÖ won 42.4% of the votes cast, compared with 38.4% for the SPÖ and only 11.6% for the ÖVP. Haider, therefore, retained the governorship of his home province. Notably, the FPÖ secured Haider's re-election with the help of the SPÖ, which in return gained influence in the state Government. In previous years the FPÖ had relied on the ÖVP for such support. Moreover, in supporting Haider, the SPÖ had broken a self-imposed prohibition on working with the FPÖ which had stood since 1986, when Haider was first appointed to the party leadership. The FPÖ performed poorly in elections in other provinces in March 2004, however, losing half its support in Salzburg, where the SPÖ won a majority for the first time in 50 years, supplanting the incumbent ÖVP administration.

In late October 2003 the Nationalrat approved amendments to Austria's asylum legislation that would, according to the Government, speed up the asylum process; the Office of the UN High Commissioner for Refugees, however, described the controversial amendments as 'among the most restrictive pieces of legislation' within the EU, whilst other critics claimed that the revised legislation was in breach of the Geneva Convention and the Austrian Constitution. The changes included measures such as deporting some asylum-seekers while their appeals were under review, demanding full statements from asylum-seekers within 72 hours of their arrival in Austria, and medically certifying cases involving traumatized people. According to government figures, in 2002 Austria received more asylum-seekers per head of the population than any other EU member state, amounting to a total of some 39,000 cases. Of these, so the Government claimed, around 85% were in fact 'economic migrants' and not genuine asylum-seekers.

A presidential election was held on 25 April 2004, at which Dr Heinz Fischer of the SPÖ received 52.4% of the votes cast and Dr Benita Ferrero-Waldner of the ÖVP received 47.6%. It was widely held that the result of the election reflected growing public dissatisfaction with the governing ÖVP-FPÖ coalition. On 5 July the incumbent President, Dr Thomas Klestil, suffered a heart attack from which he did not recover; he died the following day, just two days before the end of his term of office. Chancellor Schüssel temporarily assumed charge of Dr Klestil's duties until 8 July, when Dr Fischer was sworn in as the new President.

On 13 June 2004 Austria participated in elections to the European Parliament, in which the FPÖ performed very poorly, losing four of its five seats. A week later Böhmdorfer resigned as Minister of Justice and was replaced by Karin Miklautsch (also of the FPÖ). At a special conference held by the FPÖ in Linz on 3 July Ursula Haubner was elected unopposed as the party's new Chairwoman, with 79% of the votes cast. Other allies of Haider were appointed to key positions within the party.

In October 2004 Ursula Plassnik was appointed as Minister of Foreign Affairs, to replace Dr Benita Ferrero-Waldner, who had left to assume the post of European Commissioner for External Relations and European Neighbourhood Policy. In December Liese Prokop was appointed Minister of the Interior; her predecessor, Dr Ernst Strasser, had resigned earlier that month to move into the private sector.

As a result of the continuing decline in support for his party, Haider and several prominent FPÖ members split from the party in April 2005 to form Bündnis Zukunft Österreich (BZÖ—Alliance for Austria's Future). All of the FPÖ government ministers and several FPÖ members of parliament defected to the BZÖ. (The ministers retained their posts, while the members of parliament remained members of the FPÖ parliamentary grouping.) Haider was elected as leader of the BZÖ at its founding conference in Salzburg.

On 30 June 2003 the Österreich-Konvent (Austrian Convention) was inaugurated to discuss and draw up proposals for the reform of the Austrian State and Constitution. Austria had not had a new constitution since 1920, despite having passed through the Second World War and the creation of a new Republic in 1955. The 1920 Constitution had been amended more than 80 times, however, and, by 2004, consisted of more than 1,000 constitutional provisions and was thus somewhat confusing. In January 2005 the Convention published its proposals for a new constitution; a public debate was to precede their consideration by Parliament. The proposals outlined a new division of jurisdictions between federal government and the provinces, and proposed reducing the age of franchise for referendums and municipal votes to 16 years (whilst maintaining it at 18 years for legislative elections). The draft document listed fundamental social rights, but did not grant the opposition its request for the right to carry out parliamentary investigations on its own initiative. The proposed constitution would require a two-thirds' majority in Parliament to become law.

During the late 1990s a number of lawsuits were filed by US interests against several Austrian banks, which were accused of having profited during the Second World War from handling stolen Jewish assets. In November 1999 Bank Austria AG agreed to pay US $33m. as compensation to Holocaust survivors and, furthermore, to establish a humanitarian fund to assist survivors resident in Austria. Similar lawsuits were also filed against the Government, and in February 2000 Chancellor Schüssel appointed a former President of Bank Austria AG, Maria Schaumayer, as the co-ordinator in charge of Nazi-era compensation claims. In July the legislature approved the establishment of a €438m. fund, which was to be financed by unspecified contributions from the Government and from Austrian businesses (that had profited from slave labour), to compensate an estimated 150,000 concentration camp inmates, who had been forced into slave labour by the Nazis. However, doubts subsequently arose as to whether Austrian businesses would agree to pay for their share of the compensation fund. Another potential problem facing the settlement of the slave-labourers' claims was that 'class-action' lawyers were threatening not to drop their claims unless the agreement contained a firm commitment to a similarly extensive solution for the restitution of Jewish property. In January 2001, however, Austria signed an agreement with the USA to pay US $500m. to compensate Jews for property lost when the Nazis took power, in return for the dismissal of survivors' lawsuits. The agreement, which allowed for the first payments to take place in March/April, was strongly criticized by Haider.

The Heads of Government of Austria, Hungary and Slovakia met on several occasions during the late 1990s in order to pursue co-operation on security and economic issues. In September 1999, however, Austria threatened to hinder Slovakia's entry into the EU, in protest at the alleged inadequacy of that country's nuclear safety standards. There were protests in the latter half of 2000 against the proposed activation of a Soviet-designed nuclear power installation at Temelín in the Czech Republic, 48 km from the border with Austria; both Austria and Germany claimed that the power plant was dangerously flawed. Despite a blockade of the Austro-Czech border staged by Austrian environmentalist protesters and despite pressure from the Austrian Government, which suspended imports of Czech electricity, the nuclear power plant commenced production in early October, after receiving authorization from the Czech nuclear safety office. Border protests were resumed, and, following negotiations between the Austrian and Czech authorities, an agreement was signed by the two countries in December under which the plant was not to operate at commercial capacity until a full evaluation of its safety and environmental impact had been completed by a joint Austro-Czech safety body under the supervision of the European Commission. In August 2001 the Czech authorities maintained that a report issued by the European Commission demonstrated the safety of the plant, and immediately commenced its reconnection with the national power network; this move met with strong criticism from the Austrian Government, which, together with the German authorities, continued to express concern over the safety of the plant. Later that year Chancellor Schüssel threatened to veto the Czech Republic's accession to the EU unless the matter were satisfactorily resolved, on the grounds that the nuclear installation had failed to meet minimum safety requirements. Further safety issues were subsequently agreed, however, and in April 2003 the Temelín installation commenced production at full capacity for an 18-month trial period, prior to entering into commercial operations by the end of 2004. In late 2003 the Austrian Government vehemently criticized alleged proposals by the Czech authorities to build two new reactor units at the Temelín power plant (with construction reportedly to commence in 2009). Relations between Austria and the Czech Republic were further marred by the latter's refusal to abolish the so-called Beneš Decrees—legislation enacted at the end of the Second World War, providing for the expulsion of about 2.5m. ethnic Sudeten Germans from the Czech Republic without recourse to compensation. Austria repeatedly threatened to block the Czech Republic's anticipated accession to the EU in 2004 unless the Decrees were annulled; the EU authorities, however, did not regard their abolition as a prerequisite for entry, and Austria did not carry out its threats. Following the Czech Republic's accession to the EU in May 2004, relations between the two countries improved somewhat. The Czech Prime Minister, Stanislav Gross, visited Vienna in September 2004 and Chancellor Schüssel visited Prague in January 2005.

Government

Austria is a federal republic, divided into nine provinces, each with its own provincial assembly and government. Legislative power is held by the bicameral Parliament (Parlament). The first chamber, the Nationalrat (National Council), has 183 members, elected by universal, direct adult suffrage for four years (subject to dissolution) on the basis of proportional representation. The second chamber, the Bundesrat (Federal Council), has 62 members, elected for varying terms by the provincial assemblies. The Federal Assembly (Bundesversammlung—a joint meeting of the Nationalrat and the Bundesrat) is convened for certain matters of special importance, for example to witness the swearing-in of the Federal President. The Federal President, elected by popular vote for six years, is the Head of State, and normally acts on the advice of the Council of Ministers, which is led by the Federal Chancellor, and which is responsible to the Nationalrat.

Defence

After the ratification of the State Treaty in 1955, Austria declared its permanent neutrality. To protect its independence, the armed forces were instituted. In 1995 Austria joined NATO's Partnership for Peace programme, but reaffirmed its neutrality in March 1998, having evaluated and discounted the possibility of becoming a full member of NATO. Military service is compulsory and normally consists of seven months' initial training, followed by a maximum of 30 days' reservist training over eight years (officers, non-commissioned officers and specialists undergo 60–90 days' of additional training); alternatively, military service may entail eight months' training, with no further reservist training. In August 2004 the total armed forces numbered some 35,000 (including an estimated 10,200 conscripts). The air force (numbering 6,000, of whom 3,000 were conscripts) is an integral part of the army. Total reserves in August 2004 numbered 75,000, compared with 100,700 in August 1999 and 200,000 in June 1992. The defence budget for 2004 amounted to an estimated €2,200m.

Economic Affairs

In 2003, according to estimates by the World Bank, Austria's gross national income (GNI), measured at average 2001–03 prices, was US $248,429m., equivalent to $26,720 per head (or $29,610 per head on an international purchasing-power parity basis). During 1990–2003 the population grew at an estimated average rate of only 0.3% per year, while gross domestic product (GDP) per head increased, in real terms, at an average annual rate of 1.7%. Overall GDP grew, in real terms, at an average annual rate of 1.9% in 1990–2003; growth was 1.1% in 2002 and 0.7% in 2003.

The contribution of agriculture (including hunting, forestry and fishing) to GDP was 2.0% in 2003. In that year, according to the ILO, some 5.6% of the employed labour force were engaged in the agricultural sector. Austrian farms produce more than 90% of the country's food requirements, and surplus dairy products are exported. The principal crops are wheat, barley, maize and sugar beet. The GDP of the agricultural sector increased, in real terms, at an average annual rate of 2.8% in 1990–2002; it declined by 0.7% in 2001 and by 0.1% in 2002.

Industry (including mining and quarrying, manufacturing, construction and power) contributed 30.5% of GDP in 2003; according to the ILO, the sector engaged 29.3% of the employed labour force in that year. Industrial GDP increased, in real terms, at an average annual rate of 2.4% in 1990–2002; it declined by 0.1% in 2001 and increased by 1.0% in 2002.

In 2003 mining and quarrying contributed 0.5% of GDP; according to the ILO, the sector employed 0.2% of the employed labour force in that year. The most important indigenous mineral resource is iron ore (1.9m. metric tons, with an iron content of 31%, were mined in 2002). Austria also has deposits of petroleum, lignite, magnesite, lead and some copper. The GDP of the mining sector declined, in real terms, at an average rate of 2.6% per year during 1990–99; it declined by 2.7% in 1998, but increased by 4.4% in 1999.

Manufacturing contributed 19.9% of GDP in 2003; according to the ILO, the sector engaged 19.3% of the employed labour force in that year. Measured by the value of output, the principal branches of manufacturing in 1998 were metals and metal products (accounting for 13.9% of the total), electrical machinery and telecommunications equipment (13.0%), food products (10.2%), wood and paper products (9.4%), and non-electrical machinery (9.2%). The production of non-metallic mineral products, beverages, chemicals and road vehicles are also important activities. The GDP of the manufacturing sector increased, in real terms, at an average annual rate of 2.6% during 1990–2001; it grew by 6.5% in 2000 and by 1.2% in 2001.

Hydroelectric power resources provide the major domestic source of energy, accounting for 67.0% of total electricity production in 2001, followed by gas (13.6%), coal (12.7%) and petroleum (3.2%). Austria is heavily dependent on imports of energy, mainly from eastern Europe. Net imports of energy for commercial use were equivalent to 71% of the total in 1997.

Imports of mineral fuels and lubricants (including electrical current) accounted for 8.0% of the total cost of imports in 2003.

The services sector contributed 67.5% of GDP in 2003; according to the ILO, the sector engaged 65.1% of the employed labour force in that year. Tourism has traditionally been a leading source of revenue, providing receipts of €11,237m. in 2002. The GDP of the services sector increased, in real terms, at an average annual rate of 2.0% in 1990–2002; it grew by 0.9% in 2001 and by 1.0% in 2002.

In 2003, according to the IMF, Austria recorded a visible trade surplus of US $1,440m., while the current account of the balance of payments showed a deficit of $1,363m. Much of Austria's trade is conducted with other member countries of the European Union (EU, see p. 217), which accounted for 65.2% of Austria's imports and 59.8% of exports in 2003. In that year the principal source of imports (41.0%) was Germany; other major suppliers were Italy (7.0%), Switzerland (4.1%) and France (3.9%). Germany was also the principal market for exports (31.8%); other significant purchasers were Italy (9.0%), the USA (5.2%) and Switzerland (5.2%). The principal exports in 2003 were machinery and transport equipment (accounting for 42.1% of total export revenue) and basic manufactures (22.4%). The principal imports were also machinery and transport equipment (particularly road vehicles and electrical machinery) and basic manufactures (accounting, respectively, for 39.5% and 15.9% of total import costs).

The federal budget for 2003 produced a deficit of €3,498m., equivalent to 1.5% of GDP. The central Government's debt was 1,623,361m. Schilling at 31 December 1999, equivalent to 59.9% of annual GDP; this ratio had risen to 68% by 2003. The average annual rate of inflation was 2.0% in 1992–2003. Consumer prices increased by 2.7% in 2001, by 1.8% in 2002 and by 1.3% in 2003. In 2003 some 4.4% of the labour force were unemployed.

Austria joined the EU in January 1995. The country is also a member of the Organisation for Economic Co-operation and Development (OECD, see p. 307).

Following the enlargement of the EU in May 2004 Austria found itself once again at the heart of Europe. Of its main trading partners, Germany, to the north, was underperforming, while, to the south, Italy too was languishing and, to the west, Switzerland's growth was fragile. In contrast, trade with the east had become one of the main engines of Austria's economic growth: after four decades facing an 'iron curtain' and, since 1989, a region of potential instability on its eastern border, Austria now abuts stable democracies and some of the EU's fastest growing economies. Trade with these countries—in particular the Czech Republic, Hungary, Poland, Slovenia and Slovakia—had been increasing steadily since the mid-1990s and accounted for 14.3% of imports and 18.4% of exports in 2003. What is more, Austria accounted for some 10% of foreign-owned assets in almost all of the EU accession countries; in Slovenia this figure was as high as almost 40%. This factor was expected to help offset the anticipated rise in imports from Austria's eastern neighbours following their accession to the EU. It was also foreseen that Austria would benefit from increased competition as a result of the EU enlargement; one tangible result of this was the reduction in Austria's corporate tax rate from 34% to 25% in 2005. This was expected to contribute to a rise in the rate of GDP growth from 2.0% in 2004 to 2.5% in 2005, although this projected increase was forecast to be susceptible to a rise in the price of petroleum. One of Austria's biggest economic challenges in the early 2000s was to reduce its ratio of public debt to GDP, which stood at 65% in 2004, above the 60% target set out in the Maastricht Treaty. In order to achieve this Austria needed to achieve budgetary surpluses, but continued low deficits were forecast: the budgetary deficit was expected to increase from 1.1% of GDP in 2003 to 1.4% in 2004. While this was less than the 3% allowed under the EU's Stability and Growth Pact, the Minister of Finance, Karl-Heinz Grasser, did not expect to deliver a balanced budget until 2008. Short-term steps taken in an attempt to balance the budget had also endangered long-term priorities, such as research and development spending. More stringent restraints on expenditure were required in order to allow for the tax reforms to which the authorities were committed. Austria had one of the highest tax burdens in EU in the early 2000s: around 43% of total GDP was taken by the State in the form of taxes and levies, with labour taxation and non-wage labour levies being unusually high. Luckily for Austria, labour costs in Germany and Switzerland were significantly higher. That Austria had a more flexible labour market, in industry if not in services, than either Germany or Switzerland was also an advantage, although scope for improvements remained. Additionally, while labour costs in the new EU countries to the east were significantly lower than in Austria, this was paired with weak productivity; Austria thus remained competitive.

Education

The central controlling body is the Federal Ministry of Education, Science and Cultural Affairs. Provincial boards (Landesschulräte) supervise school education in each of the nine federal provinces. Budgetary expenditure on education in 2004 was forecast at €5,720m. (equivalent to 9.1% of total spending).

Education is free and compulsory between the ages of six and 15 years. In 1999/2000 enrolment at pre-primary level was equivalent to 81.4% of those in the relevant age-group, enrolment at primary level in 2000/01 included 91.0% of children in the relevant age-group (males 90.4%; females 91.5%), and enrolment at secondary level in 2000/01 included an estimated 88.5% of children in the relevant age-group (males 88.9%; females 88.1%). Children undergo four years' primary education at a Volksschule, after which they choose between two principal forms of secondary education. This may be a Hauptschule, which, after four years, may be followed by one of a variety of schools offering technical, vocational and other specialized training, some of which provide a qualification for university. Alternatively, secondary education may be obtained in an Allgemeinbildende höhere Schule, which provides an eight-year general education covering a wide range of subjects, culminating in the Reifeprüfung or Matura. This gives access to all Austrian universities. In addition, all Austrian citizens over the age of 24, and with professional experience, may attend certain university courses in connection with their professional career or trade.

Opportunities for further education exist at six universities as well as 13 colleges of technology, all of which have university status, and schools of art and music. Institutes of adult education (Volkshochschulen) are found in all provinces, as are other centres operated by public authorities, church organizations and the Austrian Trade Union Federation. In 2000/01 enrolment at tertiary level was equivalent to 57.7% of those in the relevant age-group (males 53.9%; females 61.7%).

Public Holidays

2005: 1 January (New Year's Day), 6 January (Epiphany), 28 March (Easter Monday), 1 May (Labour Day), 5 May (Ascension Day), 16 May (Whit Monday), 26 May (Corpus Christi), 15 August (Assumption), 26 October (National Holiday), 1 November (All Saints' Day), 8 December (Immaculate Conception), 25 December (Christmas Day), 26 December (St Stephen's Day).

2006: 1 January (New Year's Day), 6 January (Epiphany), 17 April (Easter Monday), 1 May (Labour Day), 25 May (Ascension Day), 5 June (Whit Monday), 15 June (Corpus Christi), 15 August (Assumption), 26 October (National Holiday), 1 November (All Saints' Day), 8 December (Immaculate Conception), 25 December (Christmas Day), 26 December (St Stephen's Day).

Weights and Measures

The metric system is in force.

Statistical Survey

Sources (unless otherwise stated): Statistik Austria, Hintere Zollamtsstr. 2ʙ, 1033 Vienna; tel. (1) 711-28-76-55; fax (1) 711-28-77-28; e-mail info@statistik
.gv.at; internet www.statistik.at; Austrian National Bank, Postfach 61, Otto-Wagner-Pl. 3, 1090 Vienna; tel. (1) 404-20-0; fax (1) 404-20-66-96; e-mail
oenb.info@oenb.co.at; internet www.oenb.at.

Area and Population

AREA, POPULATION AND DENSITY

Area (sq km)		83,871*
Population (census results)†		
15 May 1991		7,795,786
15 May 2001		
Males		3,889,189
Females		4,143,737
Total		8,032,926
Population (official estimates at mid-year)		
2001		8,043,046
2002		8,083,797
2003		8,117,754
Density (per sq km) at mid-2003		96.8

* 32,383 sq miles.
† Figures include all foreign workers.

PROVINCES
(official estimates at mid-2003)

	Area (sq km)*	Population	Density (per sq km)	Capital (with population)†
Burgenland . . .	3,965.5	276,419	69.7	Eisenstadt (11,334)
Kärnten (Carinthia) .	9,536.0	559,440	58.7	Klagenfurt (90,141)
Niederösterreich (Lower Austria) .	19,177.8	1,552,848	81.0	Sankt Pölten (49,121)
Oberösterreich (Upper Austria) .	11,981.7	1,387,086	115.8	Linz (183,504)
Salzburg	7,154.2	521,238	72.9	Salzburg (142,662)
Steiermark (Styria) .	16,391.9	1,190,574	72.6	Graz (226,244)
Tirol (Tyrol) . . .	12,647.7	683,317	54.0	Innsbruck (113,392)
Vorarlberg . . .	2,601.5	356,590	137.1	Bregenz (121,123)
Wien (Vienna) . .	414.7	1,590,242	3,834.7	—
Total	83,871.0	8,117,754	96.8	—

* According to the reorganization of Länder boundaries in 2002.
† At census of 15 May 2001.

PRINCIPAL TOWNS
(population at census of 15 May 2001)

Wien (Vienna, the capital) . . .	1,550,123	Klagenfurt . . .	90,141
Graz	226,244	Villach	57,497
Linz	183,504	Wels	56,478
Salzburg . . .	142,662	Sankt Pölten . . .	49,121
Innsbruck . . .	113,392	Dornbirn	42,301

Mid-2003 (UN estimate, incl. suburbs)): Vienna 2,178,674 (Source: UN, *World Urbanization Prospects: The 2003 Revision*).

BIRTHS, MARRIAGES AND DEATHS*

	Registered live births Number	Rate (per 1,000)	Registered marriages Number	Rate (per 1,000)	Registered deaths Number	Rate (per 1,000)
1996	88,809	10.9	42,298	5.2	80,790	9.9
1997	84,045	10.4	41,394	5.1	79,432	9.8
1998	81,233	10.1	39,143	4.8	78,339	9.7
1999	78,138	9.7	39,485	4.9	78,200	9.7
2000	78,268	9.7	39,228	4.8	76,780	9.5
2001	75,458	9.3	34,213	4.2	74,767	9.2
2002	78,399	9.7	36,570	4.5	76,131	9.5
2003	76,944	9.5	37,195	4.6	77,209	9.5

* Rates prior to 2001 are based on unrevised population estimates.

Expectation of life (WHO estimates, years at birth): 79.4 (males 76.4; females 82.2) in 2002 (Source: WHO, *World Health Report*).

IMMIGRATION AND EMIGRATION

Immigrants from:	2001	2002	2003
Bosnia and Herzegovina . . .	6,586	4,078	4,823
Croatia	5,455	3,152	2,896
Germany	15,810	9,403	12,239
Hungary	3,398	2,337	2,595
Italy	2,260	1,386	1,460
Poland	3,679	2,514	2,974
Romania	2,455	4,222	5,176
Russia	924	1,579	3,447
Serbia and Montenegro . . .	6,392	8,914	9,520
Slovakia	2,506	2,246	2,330
Turkey	8,156	10,626	9,982
Europe (other)	26,589	19,038	21,213
Africa	3,837	4,083	4,333
USA	1,930	1,250	1,473
Americas (other)	2,411	1,923	1,977
Asia	8,888	10,425	10,551
Oceania	612	329	355
Stateless, undeclared or unknown	81*	32,890	23,929
Total	89,928	113,165	113,554

Emigrants to:	2001	2002	2003
Bosnia and Herzegovina . . .	4,795	1,568	1,969
Croatia	4,478	1,604	1,964
Czech Republic	1,598	630	837
Germany	14,162	3,605	4,422
Hungary	2,871	1,279	1,752
Italy	1,946	735	852
Poland	3,297	1,538	1,904
Romania	1,580	4,158	2,435
Serbia and Montenegro . . .	5,098	2,982	4,041
Slovakia	1,818	1,066	1,329
Switzerland	2,894	552	612
Turkey	3,885	1,934	2,482
United Kingdom	1,863	529	668
Europe (other)	8,878	1,229	5,635
Africa	2,092	1,516	5,065
USA	3,354	888	934
Americas (other)	1,712	631	909
Asia	5,529	3,632	4,732
Oceania	707	245	242
Stateless, undeclared or unknown	97*	49,337	37,250
Statistical discrepancy	—	—	−2,777
Total	72,654	79,658	77,257

* Unknown only.

ECONOMICALLY ACTIVE POPULATION*
('000 persons aged 15 years and over)

	2001	2002	2003
Agriculture, hunting and forestry	215.1	214.6	210.1
Fishing	0.1	0.7	0.8
Mining and quarrying	9.5	8.3	6.1
Manufacturing	746.3	747.1	734.3
Electricity, gas and water supply .	31.5	35.2	34.8
Construction	339.5	338.0	338.6
Wholesale and retail trade; repair of motor vehicles, motorcycles and personal and household goods	602.7	601.2	594.6
Hotels and restaurants	207.8	217.7	217.7
Transport, storage and communications	254.9	251.8	238.2
Financial intermediation . . .	132.4	132.8	131.8
Real estate, renting and business activities	293.2	303.4	308.1
Public administration and defence; compulsory social security . .	258.3	248.4	237.2
Education	224.5	230.1	230.7
Health and social work	310.6	327.3	327.7
Other community, social and personal service activities . .	156.0	162.2	169.4
Private households with employed persons	12.6	13.4	13.6
Extra-territorial organizations and bodies	4.6	3.5	4.6
Total employed	**3,799.6**	**3,835.7**	**3,798.4**
Unemployed	142.5	161.0	168.8
Statistical discrepancy	−1.8	—	0.1
Total labour force	**3,940.3**	**3,996.7**	**3,967.3**
Males	2,218.5	2,230.7	2,196.6
Females	1,721.6	1,766.0	1,770.7

* Yearly averages, based on the results of quarterly sample surveys. The figures include members of the armed forces, except conscripts not employed before their military service.

Source: ILO.

Health and Welfare

KEY INDICATORS

Total fertility rate (children per woman, 2002)	1.3
Under-5 mortality rate (per 1,000 live births, 2003) . . .	5
HIV/AIDS (% of persons aged 15–49, 2003)	0.3
Physicians (per 1,000 head, 2000)	3.1
Hospital beds (per 1,000 head, 2000)	8.6
Health expenditure (2001): US $ per head (PPP) . . .	2,259
Health expenditure (2001): % of GDP	8.0
Health expenditure (2001): public (% of total)	69.3
Access to water (% of persons, 2002)	100
Access to sanitation (% of persons, 2002)	100
Human Development Index (2002): ranking	14
Human Development Index (2002): value	0.934

For sources and definitions, see explanatory note on p. vi.

Agriculture

PRINCIPAL CROPS
('000 metric tons)

	2001	2002	2003
Wheat	1,508.3	1,434.2	1,191.4
Barley	1,012.4	861.4	882.3
Maize	1,771.1	1,666.6	1,452.1
Rye	213.5	171.1	132.8
Oats	128.3	116.9	128.5
Triticale (wheat-rye hybrid) . .	157.0	172.5	168.6
Potatoes	694.6	684.3	560.3
Sugar beet	2,773.5	3,043.4	2,585.4
Peas (dry)*	96.4	104.0	104.0
Sunflower seed	50.6	58.5	71.0
Rapeseed	146.5	128.6	88.0
Cabbages	107.7	118.0	92.2†
Lettuce	60.5	60.7	46.0†
Onions (dry)	95.7	117.1	103.4†
Carrots	65.0	71.3	72.6†
Other fresh vegetables* . . .	206.7	191.8	209.9
Apples	409.7	478.8	422.6
Pears	108.6	103.6	175.5
Plums	75.3	43.4	69.4
Grapes	328.9	351.0	341.5

* FAO estimates.
† Unofficial figure.

Source: FAO.

LIVESTOCK
('000 head at December)

	2001	2002	2003
Horses*	63.0	60.0	85.0
Cattle	2,155.4	2,118.5	2,066.9
Pigs	3,427.0	3,440.4	3,304.7
Sheep	357.9	320.5	304.4
Goats	69.6	59.5	57.8
Chickens	11,077	11,905	11,000*
Ducks*	95	95	95
Geese*	22	22	22
Turkeys	589	547	700*

* FAO estimate(s).

LIVESTOCK PRODUCTS
('000 metric tons)

	2001	2002	2003
Beef and veal	215.2	211.9	207.7
Mutton and lamb	7.2	7.0	7.1*
Pig meat*	613.8	653.3	662.9
Poultry meat	113.0	112.6	113.4
Cows' milk	3,299.6	3,292.2	3,229.9
Sheep's milk	7.6	7.0	7.0†
Goats' milk	16.5	17.2	16.5†
Cheese	163.1	169.2	185.7
Butter	36.9	33.3	33.2
Hen eggs	86.1	88.0	85.1
Honey	8.0	7.7	9.0†
Cattle hides (fresh)† . . .	22.3	23.0	23.1

* Unofficial figure(s).
† FAO estimate(s).

Source: FAO.

Forestry

ROUNDWOOD REMOVALS
('000 cubic metres, excl. bark)

	2001	2002	2003
Sawlogs, veneer logs and logs for sleepers	8,057	9,183	10,578
Pitprops (mine timber), pulpwood, and other industrial wood	2,505	2,627	3,141
Fuel wood	2,905	3,036	3,336
Total	13,467	14,846	17,055

Source: FAO.

SAWNWOOD PRODUCTION
('000 cubic metres, incl. railway sleepers)

	2001	2002	2003
Coniferous (softwood)	10,011	10,191	10,263
Broadleaved (hardwood)	216	224	210
Total	10,227	10,415	10,473

Source: FAO.

Fishing

(metric tons, live weight)

	2000	2001	2002
Capture	439	362	350
Freshwater fishes	439	362	350
Aquaculture	2,847	2,393	2,333
Common carp	620	385	303
Rainbow trout	1,950	1,735	1,738
Brook trout	162	188	188
Total catch	3,286	2,755	2,683

Source: FAO.

Mining

('000 metric tons, unless otherwise indicated)

	2000	2001	2002
Brown coal (incl. lignite)	1,254.6	1,194.0	1,411.8
Crude petroleum	1,056.2	1,050.4	1,032.2
Iron ore:			
gross weight	1,859.4	1,843.3	1,941.8
metal content*	586	581	600
Magnesite (crude)	725.8	680.5	728.2
Tungsten, concentrate (metric tons)*†	1,600‡	1,273	1,400
Gypsum and anhydrite (crude)	946.0	929.2	969.2
Kaolin	118.5	89.6	50.9
Basalt	4,933.2	4,689.8	4,533.1
Dolomite	7,152.2	6,172.0	5,839.7
Limestone and marble	23,823.5	23,799.7	24,884.1
Quartz and quartzite*	372	402	400
Natural gas (million cu metres)	1,804.7	1,954.4	2,014.6

* Data from the US Geological Survey.
† Figures refer to metal content.
‡ Estimated production.

Industry

SELECTED PRODUCTS
('000 metric tons, unless otherwise indicated)

	1999	2000	2001
Wheat flour	293	291	278
Raw sugar*	545	447	447
Wine ('000 hectolitres)	246	224	229
Beer ('000 hectolitres)	8,884	8,725	8,528
Woven cotton fabrics—pure and mixed (million sq metres)	74	58	62
Woven woollen fabrics—pure and mixed (million sq metres)	13	15	n.a.
Mechanical wood pulp	369	390	376
Chemical and semi-chemical wood pulp	1,319	1,370	1,352
Newsprint	394	384	383
Other printing and writing paper	2,067	2,186	2,081
Other paper and paperboard	1,681	1,815	1,786
Motor spirit (petrol)	2,140	1,819	n.a.
Jet fuel	508	544	n.a.
Distillate fuel oils	3,687	3,724	n.a.
Residual fuel oils	1,338	1,002	n.a.
Cement†	3,817	3,799	3,863
Crude steel†	5,213	5,725	5,887
Refined copper—unwrought ('000 metric tons): secondary†	n.a.	79	69
Passenger motor cars (number)	123,586	115,979	131,098
Motorcycles, etc. (number)	21,647	29,208	40,088
Electric energy (million kWh)	66,113	69,483	n.a.

* Provisional figures.
† Data from the US Geological Survey.

Construction (new dwellings completed, number): 59,447 in 1999.

Manufactured gas (production of blast-furnace gas and coke-oven gas, terajoules): 30,076 in 1998.

Sources: mainly Austrian Central Statistical Office, Vienna; FAO, *Yearbook of Forest Products*; UN, *Industrial Commodity Statistics Yearbook* and *Monthly Bulletin of Statistics*; International Road Federation, *World Road Statistics*.

Finance

CURRENCY AND EXCHANGE RATES

Monetary Units
100 cent = 1 euro (€).

Sterling and Dollar Equivalents (31 December 2004)
£1 sterling = 1.4180 euros;
US $1 = 0.7342 euros;
100 euros = £70.52 = $136.21.

Average Exchange Rate (euros per US $)
2002   1.0626
2003   0.8860
2004   0.8054

Note: The national currency was formerly the Schilling. From the introduction of the euro, with Austrian participation, on 1 January 1999, a fixed exchange rate of €1 = 13.7603 Schilling was in operation. Euro notes and coins were introduced on 1 January 2002. The euro and local currency circulated alongside each other until 28 February, after which the euro became the sole legal tender.

FEDERAL BUDGET
(€ million)

Revenue	2002	2003*	2004†
Total taxes and levies (net) . .	36,666	35,468	38,616
Gross tax revenue	54,951	53,498	57,618
Tax on wages and salaries .	16,219	16,944	17,300
Tax on assessed income . .	3,126	2,677	3,000
Withholding tax	1,663	1,410	1,730
Corporate income tax . . .	4,559	4,332	4,300
Turnover tax	17,639	16,472	19,000
Tobacco tax	1,297	1,329	1,350
Mineral oils tax	3,109	3,310	3,450
Car engine related insurance tax.	1,185	1,217	1,250
Other taxes and levies . . .	6,155	5,806	6,238
Transfers to provinces, municipalities, etc.	−16,176	−16,077	−16,602
Transfers to European Union	−2,108	−1,952	−2,400
Transfers from tax revenues	1,507	1,497	1,688
Social insurance contributions . .	7,331	7,473	7,952
Other revenue	13,924	13,454	10,980
Total	59,428	57,892	59,237

Expenditure‡	2002	2003*	2004†
Education	5,657	5,745	5,720
Research and development . . .	2,566	2,581	3,514
Art and culture	689	660	489
Health	792	871	841
Social welfare	18,206	18,882	18,598
Housing construction	1,807	1,805	1,810
Transport	6,726	6,579	7,118
Agriculture and forestry . . .	1,798	1,835	1,830
Industry and trade	874	761	1,199
Public-sector services	346	357	404
Private-sector services	179	232	219
Defence	1,624	1,721	1,702
Security and law enforcement . .	2,253	2,344	2,310
Other sovereign administration services	18,298	17,016	16,911
Total	61,818	61,390	62,667

* Provisional.

† Forecast.

‡ Excluding debt-servicing and currency swaps (including interest and charges, but excluding redemption payments) (€ million): 8,547 in 2002; 8,344 in 2003 (provisional); 8,329 in 2004 (forecast).

Note: Totals may not be equal to the sum of component parts, owing to rounding.

Source: Federal Ministry of Finance, Vienna.

NATIONAL BANK RESERVES
(US $ million at 31 December)

	2001	2002	2003
Gold*	3,089	3,499	4,259
IMF special drawing rights . .	233	185	181
Reserve position in IMF . . .	833	959	1,145
Foreign exchange	11,444	8,540	7,144
Total	15,599	13,183	12,729

* Valued at market prices.

Source: IMF, *International Financial Statistics*.

MONEY SUPPLY
(€ '000 million at 31 December)

	2001	2002	2003
Currency in circulation	10.69	11.01*	12.29*
Demand deposits at banking institutions	51.04	54.07	63.44

* Currency put into circulation by the Oesterreichische Nationalbank was (€ '000 million): 18.41 in 2002; 15.35 in 2003.

Source: IMF, *International Financial Statistics*.

COST OF LIVING
(Consumer Price Index; base: 2000 = 100)

	2001	2002	2003
Food and beverages	103.3	105.2	107.3
Tobacco	104.9	110.8	114.8
Rent (incl. maintenance and repairs)	102.9	104.8	106.2
Fuel and power	103.2	101.1	102.5
Household goods and furnishings .	101.4	103.4	105.1
Clothing and footwear	101.6	102.7	103.9
Miscellaneous household services .	102.3	105.7	106.8
Health	104.4	107.0	107.9
Education and leisure	102.4	105.8	107.0
Transport	101.9	102.8	103.6
All items	102.7	104.5	105.9

NATIONAL ACCOUNTS
(€ million at current prices)

National Income and Product

	2001	2002	2003
Compensation of employees . .	109,325	111,298	113,752
Gross operating surplus and mixed income	80,328	83,171	85,565
Taxes on production and imports, *less* subsidies	25,940	26,538	26,825
Gross domestic product (GDP) in market prices	215,593	221,008	226,142
Primary incomes received from abroad	14,235	14,755	14,640
Less Primary incomes paid abroad	19,407	18,305	18,058
Gross national income (GNI) .	210,421	217,458	222,725
Less Consumption of fixed capital	30,578	31,565	32,289
Net national income	179,843	185,893	190,436
Current transfers from abroad .	2,585	3,001	2,673
Less Current transfers paid abroad	3,446	4,890	4,866
Net national disposable income	178,982	184,004	188,243

Expenditure on the Gross Domestic Product

	2001	2002	2003
Final consumption expenditure .	161,807	163,897	167,555
Households	119,052	120,153	122,687
Non-profit institutes serving households	3,912	4,104	4,233
General government	38,842	39,639	40,635
Gross capital formation	48,348	46,511	49,503
Gross fixed capital formation .	47,374	45,939	48,648
Changes in inventories, and acquisitions (less disposals) of valuables	975	572	854
Total domestic expenditure .	210,155	210,408	217,058
Exports of goods and services . .	102,910	107,456	109,062
Less Imports of goods and services	97,759	96,421	100,110
Statistical discrepancy	288	−434	132
GDP in market prices . . .	215,593	221,008	226,142
GDP at constant 1995 prices .	198.5	201.2	202.5

Gross Domestic Product by Economic Activity

	2001	2002	2003
Agriculture, hunting, forestry and fishing	4,149	4,041	3,960
Mining and quarrying	831	913	919
Manufacturing	39,257	39,644	40,251
Electricity, gas and water	4,256	4,661	4,988
Construction	14,529	14,653	15,529
Wholesale and retail trade	25,624	25,975	26,309
Restaurants and hotels	8,283	8,827	9,281
Transport, storage and communications	13,927	14,503	15,335
Finance and insurance	10,377	11,098	10,730
Real estate and business services*	32,447	33,669	34,626
Public administration and defence	11,821	11,888	12,201
Other services	27,583	27,511	28,155
Sub-total	193,083	197,383	202,285
Taxes on products	25,781	26,655	26,929
Less Subsidies on products	3,271	3,030	3,072
GDP in purchasers' values	215,593	221,008	226,142

* Including imputed rents of owner-occupied dwellings.

BALANCE OF PAYMENTS
(US $ million)

	2001	2002	2003
Exports of goods f.o.b.	66,900	73,667	89,619
Imports of goods f.o.b.	−68,169	−70,080	−88,479
Trade balance	−1,269	3,588	1,140
Exports of services	33,352	35,386	43,053
Imports of services	−31,437	−34,996	−41,391
Balance on goods and services	646	3,978	2,802
Other income received	12,031	13,816	16,169
Other income paid	−15,111	−15,406	−18,005
Balance on goods, services and income	−2,435	2,389	966
Current transfers received	3,267	3,815	4,382
Current transfers paid	−4,468	−5,639	−6,712
Current balance	−3,636	565	−1,363
Capital account (net)	−529	−378	−12
Direct investment abroad	−3,132	−5,745	−7,061
Direct investment from abroad	5,906	319	7,276
Portfolio investment assets	−10,955	−22,992	−18,414
Portfolio investment liabilities	16,699	18,490	22,992
Financial derivatives assets	−143	−495	−668
Financial derivatives liabilities	95	8	−77
Other investment assets	−8,680	11,978	−15,117
Other investment liabilities	2,005	−6,576	10,610
Net errors and omissions	482	2,803	−203
Overall balance	−1,888	−1,723	−2,036

Source: IMF, *International Financial Statistics.*

External Trade

Note: Austria's customs territory excludes Mittelberg im Kleinen Walsertal (in Vorarlberg) and Jungholz (in Tyrol). The figures also exclude trade in silver specie and monetary gold.

PRINCIPAL COMMODITIES
(distribution by SITC, € million)

Imports c.i.f.	2001	2002	2003
Food and live animals	3,937.1	4,029.5	4,202.5
Crude materials (inedible) except fuels	2,930.0	2,959.7	2,933.8
Mineral fuels, lubricants, etc. (incl. electric current)	5,500.3	5,730.7	6,453.2
Petroleum, petroleum products, etc.	3,277.4	3,262.3	3,526.2
Chemicals and related products	8,229.2	8,683.2	9,015.9
Medicinal and pharmaceutical products	2,639.7	3,090.8	2,920.7
Medicaments (including veterinary medicaments)	1,485.4	1,672.2	1,733.4

Imports c.i.f.— *continued*	2001	2002	2003
Basic manufactures	13,264.5	12,506.7	12,863.1
Paper, paperboard and manufactures	1,708.3	1,616.0	1,678.1
Iron and steel	1,777.2	1,705.7	1,864.1
Non-ferrous metals	1,872.9	1,675.9	1,687.4
Other metal manufactures	3,252.1	3,025.4	3,127.2
Machinery and transport equipment	31,612.2	30,019.8	32,003.7
Power-generating machinery and equipment	2,300.9	2,287.7	2,388.4
Machinery specialized for particular industries	2,298.1	2,156.7	2,362.7
General industrial machinery, equipment and parts	4,252.6	4,056.1	4,223.7
Office machines and automatic data-processing machines	2,658.6	2,593.3	2,550.6
Telecommunications and sound equipment	2,526.9	2,507.1	2,511.9
Other electrical machinery, apparatus, etc.	6,238.0	5,881.4	5,990.1
Road vehicles and parts (excl. tyres, engines and electrical parts)	9,021.9	8,643.0	9,221.3
Passenger motor cars (excl. buses)	4,098.0	4,040.0	4,748.3
Parts for cars, buses, lorries, etc.	3,108.9	2,952.9	2,579.6
Other transport equipment	1,622.4	1,384.0	2,011.4
Miscellaneous manufactured articles	12,430.8	12,184.3	12,377.1
Clothing and accessories (excl. footwear)	3,126.9	3,090.9	3,160.1
Total (incl. others)	78,691.6	77,104.4	80,993.3

Exports f.o.b.	2001	2002	2003
Food and live animals	2,803.3	3,074.5	3,323.1
Crude materials (inedible) except fuels	2,387.6	2,511.2	2,569.9
Mineral fuels, lubricants, etc. (incl. electric current)	1,451.6	1,840.0	2,011.2
Chemicals and related products	7,077.4	7,928.9	7,971.6
Medicinal and pharmaceutical products	2,296.6	3,041.4	2,954.1
Medicaments (including veterinary medicaments)	1,313.8	1,822.1	1,894.6
Basic manufactures	17,187.3	17,309.4	17,687.7
Paper, paperboard and manufactures	3,381.7	3,586.8	3,561.0
Paper and paperboard (not cut to size or shape)	2,352.4	2,438.3	2,408.0
Textile yarn, fabrics, made-up articles and related products	1,904.4	1,844.9	1,775.4
Iron and steel	3,182.4	3,133.1	3,380.9
Other metal manufactures	3,309.3	3,302.7	3,485.8
Machinery and transport equipment	32,137.5	33,068.9	33,233.8
Power-generating machinery and equipment	3,981.7	3,923.0	3,957.1
Internal combustion piston engines and parts	2,963.7	2,976.1	3,004.6
Machinery specialized for particular industries	4,041.2	4,131.2	4,239.3
General industrial machinery, equipment and parts	4,269.7	4,459.0	4,666.7
Telecommunications and sound equipment	2,378.0	2,172.1	1,818.1
Other electrical machinery, apparatus, etc.	6,519.6	6,592.7	6,588.5
Road vehicles and parts (excl. tyres, engines and electrical parts)	7,316.5	7,586.1	7,575.6
Passenger motor cars (excl. buses)	3,189.3	3,440.2	3,299.7
Parts for cars, buses, lorries, etc.	2,150.8	2,254.0	2,288.5
Miscellaneous manufactured articles	9,909.9	10,091.6	10,245.2
Total (incl. others)	74,251.5	77,400.4	78,902.6

PRINCIPAL TRADING PARTNERS
(€ million)*

Imports c.i.f.	2001	2002	2003
Belgium-Luxembourg . .	1,509.1	1,507.4	1,412.8
China, People's Republic . .	1,359.5	1,404.9	1,788.2
Czech Republic	2,118.9	2,235.8	2,631.4
Finland	789.3	741.2	747.6
France	3,198.1	2,980.6	3,145.6
Germany	31,901.1	31,085.5	33,190.0
Hungary	2,688.0	2,556.5	2,626.3
Italy	5,642.6	5,547.6	5,687.0
Japan	1,757.9	1,645.8	1,813.9
Netherlands	2,299.1	2,553.0	2,427.3
Poland	938.3	926.1	979.7
Russia	1,146.0	1,032.3	1,322.7
Slovakia	1,113.1	1,199.8	1,421.5
Spain	1,088.0	1,193.6	1,405.3
Sweden	1,041.7	994.3	1,062.0
Switzerland-Liechtenstein .	2,527.7	2,533.4	3,312.6
United Kingdom	2,081.3	2,016.6	1,851.5
USA	4,209.9	3,735.4	3,126.7
Total (incl. others) . . .	78,692.0	77,104.4	80,993.3

Exports f.o.b.	2001	2002	2003
Belgium-Luxembourg . .	1,448.9	1,366.1	1,260.1
China, People's Republic . .	844.5	1,170.2	888.5
Croatia	886.6	992.7	1,032.5
Czech Republic	2,151.3	2,247.5	2,410.7
France	3,391.1	3,427.4	3,509.8
Germany	24,160.0	24,779.8	25,090.5
Hungary	3,316.0	3,335.5	3,173.7
Italy	6,323.2	6,544.2	7,074.1
Japan	908.6	912.2	855.3
Netherlands	1,764.0	1,829.1	1,631.0
Poland	1,215.3	1,301.5	1,335.1
Russia	941.2	957.5	1,134.2
Slovakia	946.0	1,065.7	1,187.5
Slovenia	1,282.8	1,398.1	1,548.1
Spain	1,853.8	2,121.1	2,017.8
Sweden	845.2	836.3	883.5
Switzerland-Liechtenstein .	3,862.4	4,074.4	4,066.6
United Kingdom	3,467.0	3,608.0	3,484.2
USA	3,932.9	4,009.6	4,086.7
Total (incl. others) . . .	74,251.0	77,400.4	78,902.6

* Imports by country of production; exports by country of consumption.

Transport

RAILWAYS
(traffic, Federal Railways only)

	2001	2002	2003
Number of passengers carried ('000)	183,300	184,800	183,700
Freight net ton-km (millions) . .	17,387	n.a.	n.a.
Freight tons carried ('000) . . .	85,809	87,215	86,997

ROAD TRAFFIC
(motor vehicles in use at 31 December)

	2001	2002	2003
Passenger cars	4,182,027	3,987,093	4,054,308
Buses and coaches	9,902	9,179	9,231
Goods vehicles	331,394	319,981	326,087
Motorcycles	294,843	292,569	305,481
Mopeds and motor scooters . .	346,591	304,225	301,387

SHIPPING

Merchant Fleet
(registered at 31 December)

	2001	2002	2003
Number of vessels	8	6	7
Total displacement ('000 grt) . .	35.3	29.9	32.0

Source: Lloyd's Register-Fairplay, *World Fleet Statistics*.

International Freight Traffic on the Danube
('000 metric tons, excl. transit traffic)

	2001	2002	2003
Goods loaded	1,257.6	1,554.8	1,567.3
Goods unloaded	5,607.0	6,311.8	5,225.1

CIVIL AVIATION
(Austrian Airlines, '000)

	2000	2001	2002
Kilometres flown	70,411	66,316	129,649
Passenger ton-km	914,870	846,385	1,434,582
Cargo ton-km	284,533	252,406	396,021
Mail ton-km	11,635	12,539	28,099

Tourism

FOREIGN TOURIST ARRIVALS
(by country of origin)*

	2000	2001	2002†
Belgium	349,391	360,203	374,183
France	386,828	385,296	406,251
Germany	9,990,133	10,114,870	10,349,377
Italy	911,030	964,248	995,182
Netherlands	1,185,856	1,238,240	1,350,212
Switzerland-Liechtenstein .	736,877	778,596	817,382
United Kingdom	666,616	645,513	684,839
USA	781,455	639,271	512,384
Total (incl. others) . . .	17,982,204	18,180,079	18,610,925

* Arrivals at accommodation establishments.
† Source: World Tourism Organization, *Yearbook of Tourism Statistics*.

Receipts from tourism (US $ million): 9,931 in 2000; 10,118 in 2001; 11,237 in 2002 (Source: World Tourism Organization).

Communications Media

	2000	2001	2002
Radio licences issued . . .	2,755,126	2,808,948	2,897,864
Television licences issued . .	2,712,352	2,779,279	2,873,458
Telephones ('000 main lines in use)*	3,995	3,997	3,883
Mobile cellular telephones ('000 subscribers)*	6,117	6,566	6,760
Personal computers ('000 in use)*	2,270	2,730	3,013
Internet users ('000)*	2,700	2,600	3,340
Book titles produced . . .	20,283	20,192	25,358
Daily newspapers	16	16	15
Weekly newspapers	191	197	214
Other periodicals	2,783	2,788	2,792

* Source: International Telecommunication Union.

Facsimile machines ('000 in use): 210.0 in 1993; 240.0 in 1994; 284.7 in 1995 (Source: UN, *Statistical Yearbook*).

Telephones ('000 main lines in use): 3,881.0 in 2003 (Source: International Telecommunication Union).

Mobile cellular telephones ('000 subscribers): 7,094.5 in 2003 (Source: International Telecommunication Union).

Internet users ('000): 3,730.0 in 2003 (Source: International Telecommunication Union).

Education

(2002/03)

	Institutions	Staff	Students
Pre-primary	4,891	26,720	216,571
Primary	3,299	33,590	381,140
General secondary and upper primary	2,012	61,593	479,934
Compulsory vocational* . . .	176	4,664	130,597
Technical and vocational . . .	702	n.a.	66,797
Teacher training:			
second level	47	1,443	8,996
third level	35	2,674	13,664
Universities*	19	16,099	242,598
Tertiary vocational*	67	229	11,743

* 2001/02 figures.

Directory

The Constitution

The Austrian Constitution of 1920, as amended in 1929, was restored on 1 May 1945. Its main provisions, with subsequent amendments, are summarized below:

Austria is a democratic republic, having a Federal President (Bundespräsident), elected directly by the people, and a bicameral legislature, the Parliament (Parlament), consisting of the National Council (Nationalrat) and the Federal Council (Bundesrat). The republic is organized on the federal system, comprising the nine federal provinces (Bundesländer) of Burgenland, Carinthia (Kärnten), Lower Austria (Niederösterreich), Upper Austria (Oberösterreich), Salzburg, Styria (Steiermark), Tyrol (Tirol), Vorarlberg and Vienna (Wien). There is universal suffrage for men and women who are more than 18 years of age.

The Nationalrat consists of 183 members, elected by universal direct suffrage, according to a system of proportional representation. It functions for a maximum period of four years.

The Bundesrat represents the Bundesländer. Lower Austria sends 12 members, Vienna and Upper Austria 11 each, Styria 9, Tyrol five, Carinthia and Salzburg four each, and Burgenland and Vorarlberg three each, making 62 in total. The seats are divided between the parties according to the number of seats that they control in each Provincial Assembly (Landtag) and are held during the life of the provincial government (Landesregierung) that they represent. Each Land, in turn, provides the Chairman of the Bundesrat for six months.

The Federal Assembly (Bundesversammlung—a joint meeting of the Nationalrat and the Bundesrat) is convened for certain matters of special importance, for example to witness the swearing-in of the Federal President. It can also be convened to declare war or to demand a referendum on the deposition of the President, if demanded by the Nationalrat.

The Federal President, elected by popular vote, is the Head of State and holds office for a term of six years. The President is eligible for re-election only once in succession. Although invested with special emergency powers, the President normally acts on the authority of the Federal Government, which is responsible to the Nationalrat for governmental policy.

The Federal Government consists of the Federal Chancellor, the Vice-Chancellor and the other ministers and state secretaries, who may vary in number. The Chancellor is chosen by the President, usually from the party with the strongest representation in the newly elected Nationalrat, and the other ministers are then selected by the President on the advice of the Chancellor.

If the Nationalrat adopts an explicit motion expressing 'no confidence' in the Federal Government or individual members thereof, the Federal Government or the federal minister concerned is removed from office.

All new legislative proposals must be read and submitted to a vote in both chambers of the Parliament. A new draft law is presented first to the Nationalrat, where it usually has three readings, and secondly to the Bundesrat, where it can be delayed or vetoed.

The Constitution also provides for appeals by the Government to the electorate on specific points by means of referendum. If a petition supported by 100,000 electors or more is presented to the Government, the Government must submit it to the Nationalrat.

The Landtag exercises the same functions in each province as the Nationalrat does in the State. The members of the Landtag elect the Landesregierung, consisting of a provincial governor (Landeshauptmann) and his or her councillors (Landesräte). They are responsible to the Landtag.

The spheres of legal and administrative competence of both national and provincial governments are clearly defined. The Constitution distinguishes four groups:

1. Law-making and administration are the responsibility of the State: e.g. foreign affairs, justice and finance.

2. Law-making is the responsibility of the State, administration is the responsibility of the provinces: e.g. elections, population matters and road traffic.

3. The State formulates the rudiments of the law, the provinces enact the law and administer it: e.g. charity, rights of agricultural workers, land reform.

4. Law-making and administration are the responsibility of the provinces in all matters not expressly assigned to the State: e.g. municipal affairs.

On 30 June 2003 the Österreich-Konvent (Austrian Convention) was inaugurated to examine and amend the Constitution. The Convention published its proposals for a new draft constitution in January 2005; a public debate was to precede their consideration by Parliament. The proposed constitution would require a two-thirds' majority in Parliament to become law.

The Government

HEAD OF STATE

Federal President: Dr HEINZ FISCHER (sworn in 8 July 2004).

COUNCIL OF MINISTERS
(April 2005)

A coalition of Bündnis Zukunft Österreich (BZÖ) and the Österreichische Volkspartei (ÖVP).

Federal Chancellor: Dr WOLFGANG SCHÜSSEL (ÖVP).

Vice-Chancellor and Minister for Transport, Innovation and Technology: HUBERT GORBACH (BZÖ).

Minister for Economic Affairs and Labour: Dr Martin Bartenstein (ÖVP).

Minister for Foreign Affairs: Dr Ursula Plassnik (ÖVP).

Minister for Education, Science and Cultural Affairs: Elisabeth Gehrer (ÖVP).

Minister of Finance: Karl-Heinz Grasser (BZÖ).

Minister for Social Security, Generations and Consumer Protection: Herbert Haupt (BZÖ).

Minister of Justice: Karin Miklautsch (BZÖ).

Minister of Defence: Günther Platter (ÖVP).

Minister for Agriculture, Forestry, Environment and Water Management: Josef Pröll (ÖVP).

Minister for Health and Women: Maria Rauch-Kallat (ÖVP).

Minister of the Interior: Liese Prokop (ÖVP).

Secretaries of State in the Federal Chancellery: Franz Morak (ÖVP), Karl Schweitzer (BZÖ).

Secretary of State in the Ministry of Social Security, Generations and Consumer Protection: Ursula Haubner (BZÖ).

Secretary of State in the Ministry of Finance: Dr Alfred Finz (ÖVP).

Secretaries of State in the Ministry of Transport, Innovation and Technology: Helmut Kukacka (ÖVP), Eduard Mainoni (BZÖ).

Secretary of State in the Ministry of Health and Women's Issues: (vacant).

Note: Government chief whips, the leaders of the parliamentary parties and the respective directors of the parliamentary groups (Klubdirektoren) are also members of the Council of Ministers.

MINISTRIES

Office of the Federal President: Hofburg, Leopoldinischer Trakt, 1014 Vienna; tel. (1) 534-22; fax (1) 535-65-12; internet www.hofburg.at.

Office of the Federal Chancellor: Ballhauspl. 2, 1014 Vienna; tel. (1) 531-15-0; fax (1) 535-03-380; e-mail praesidium@bka.gv.at; internet www.bka.gv.at.

Ministry of Agriculture, Forestry, Environment and Water Management: Stubenring 1, 1012 Vienna; tel. (1) 711-00-0; fax (1) 711-00-21-40; e-mail office@lebensministerium.at; internet www.lebensministerium.at.

Ministry of Defence: Rossauer Lände 1, 1090 Vienna; tel. (1) 5200-21160; fax (1) 520-17111; e-mail buergerservice@bmlv.gv.at; internet www.bundesheer.at.

Ministry of Economic Affairs and Labour: Stubenring 1, 1011 Vienna; tel. (1) 711-00-0; fax (1) 713-79-95; e-mail service@bmwa.gv.at; internet www.bmwa.gv.at.

Ministry of Education, Science and Cultural Affairs: Minoritenpl. 5, 1014 Vienna; tel. (1) 531-20-00; fax (1) 531-20-30-99; e-mail ministerium@bmbwk.gv.at; internet www.bmbwk.gv.at.

Ministry of Finance: Himmelpfortgasse 4–8, 1015 Vienna; tel. (1) 514-33-0; fax (1) 512-78-69; internet www.bmf.gv.at.

Ministry of Foreign Affairs: Ballhauspl. 2, 1014 Vienna; tel. (1) 531-15-0; fax (1) 535-45-30; e-mail presse@bmaa.gv.at; internet www.bmaa.gv.at.

Ministry of Health and Women: Radetzkystr. 2, 1030 Vienna; tel. (1) 711-00-0; fax (1) 711-00-143-00; e-mail buergerservice@bmgf.gv.at; internet www.bmgf.gv.at.

Ministry of the Interior: Herrengasse 7, 1014 Vienna; tel. (1) 531-26-0; fax (1) 531-26-34-80; e-mail infomaster@bmi.gv.at; internet www.bmi.gv.at.

Ministry of Justice: Museumstr. 7, 1016 Vienna; tel. (1) 521-52-0; fax (1) 521-52-72-7; internet www.bmj.gv.at.

Ministry of Social Security, Generations and Consumer Protection: Stubenring 1, 1010 Vienna; tel. (1) 711-00; fax (1) 715-28-78; e-mail briefkasten@bmsg.gv.at; internet www.bmsg.gv.at.

Ministry of Transport, Innovation and Technology: Radetzkystr. 2, 1030 Vienna; tel. (1) 711-62-0; fax (1) 713-70-76; e-mail post@bmvit.gv.at; internet www.bmvit.gv.at.

President and Legislature

PRESIDENT

Presidential Election, 25 April 2004

Candidates		Votes	% of votes
Dr Heinz Fischer (SPÖ)	. . . . .	2,166,690	52.4
Dr Benita Ferrero-Waldner (ÖVP)	. . .	1,969,326	47.6
Total	. . . .	4,136,016	100.0

PARLIAMENT

Nationalrat
(National Council)

President of the Nationalrat: Prof. Dr Andreas Kohl.

General Election, 24 November 2002

Party	Votes	% of votes	Seats
Sozialdemokratische Partei Österreichs (SPÖ)	1,792,499	36.51	69
Österreichische Volkspartei (ÖVP) . .	2,076,833	42.30	79
Freiheitliche Partei Österreichs (FPÖ) . .	491,328	10.01	18
Die Grünen	464,980	9.47	17
Others	84,005	1.71	—
Total	4,909,645	100.00	183

Bundesrat
(Federal Council)
(January 2005)

President of the Bundesrat: Mag. Georg Pehm (January–June 2005).

Provinces	SPÖ	ÖVP	FPÖ	Die Grünen	Total seats
Burgenland	2	1	—	—	3
Carinthia (Kärnten) . .	2	—	2	—	4
Lower Austria (Niederösterreich) . .	4	7	—	1	12
Upper Austria (Oberösterreich) . . .	5	5	—	1	11
Salzburg	2	2	—	—	4
Styria (Steiermark) . .	3	5	1	—	9
Tyrol (Tirol)	1	3	—	1	5
Vorarlberg	1	2	—	—	3
Vienna (Wien) . . .	6	2	2	1	11
Total	26	27	5	4	62

Political Organizations

Bündnis Zukunft Österreich (BZÖ): Kärntner Ring 11–13/7/4 1010 Vienna; tel. (1) 512-04-04; fax (1) 512-04-04-21; e-mail info@bzoe.at; internet www.bzoe.at; f. 2005 by split from Freiheitliche Partei Österreichs (FPÖ); parliamentary representatives remain members of FPÖ parliamentary grouping; proponent of social market-economy, controlled immigration and protection of Austria's cultural identity; Leader Dr Jörg Haider; Parliamentary Spokesman Uwe Scheuch.

Freiheitliche Partei Österreichs (FPÖ/Die Freiheitlichen) (Freedom Party): Esslingasse 14–16, 1010 Vienna; tel. (1) 512-35-35; fax (1) 513-35-35-9; internet www.fpoe.at; f. 1955; partially succeeding the Verband der Unabhängigen (League of Independents, f. 1949); popularly known as Die Freiheitlichen; populist right-wing party advocating the participation of workers in management, stricter immigration controls and deregulation in the business sector; opposes Austria's membership of the EU; breakaway party, Bündnis Zukunft Österreichs (BZÖ), formed in 2005; Chair. (vacant); Vice-Chair. Heinz-Christian Stracher, Günther Steinkellner; Man. Chair. (vacant); Gen. Sec. (vacant).

Die Grünen (Greens): Lindengasse 40, 1071 Vienna; tel. (1) 521-25-0; fax (1) 526-91-10; e-mail bundesbuero@gruene.at; internet www.gruene.at; f. 1986; campaigns for environmental protection, peace and social justice; Chair. and Leader of Parliamentary Group Prof. Dr Alexander van der Bellen.

Kommunistische Partei Österreichs (KPÖ) (Communist Party of Austria): Weyringergasse 33/5, 1040 Vienna; tel. (1) 503-65-80; fax (1) 503-65-80-411; e-mail bundesvorstand@kpoe.at; internet www.kpoe.at; f. 1918; strongest in the industrial centres and trade unions; advocates a policy of strict neutrality and opposes Austria's membership of the EU; Chair. WALTER BAIER.

Liberales Forum (LiF) (Liberal Forum): Dürergasse 6/10, 1060 Vienna; tel. (1) 503-06-67; fax (1) 503-06-67-20; e-mail office@lif.at; internet www.lif.at; f. 1993 by fmr mems of Freiheitliche Partei Österreichs; Leader ALEXANDER ZACH.

Österreichische Volkspartei (ÖVP) (Austrian People's Party): Lichtenfelsgasse 7, 1010 Vienna; tel. (1) 401-26; fax (1) 401-26-32-9; e-mail email@oevp.at; internet www.oevp.at; f. 1945; Christian-Democratic party; advocates an ecologically orientated social market economy; Chair. Dr WOLFGANG SCHÜSSEL; Sec.-Gen. Dr REINHOLD LOPATKA.

Sozialdemokratische Partei Österreichs (SPÖ) (Social-Democratic Party of Austria): Löwelstr. 18, 1014 Vienna; tel. (1) 534-27-0; fax (1) 535-96-83; e-mail spoe@spoe.at; internet www.spoe.at; f. as the Social-Democratic Party in 1889, subsequently renamed the Socialist Party, reverted to its original name in 1991; advocates democratic socialism and Austria's permanent neutrality; 500,000 mems; Chair. Dr ALFRED GUSENBAUER; Secs ANDREA KUNTZL, DORIS BURES.

Die Unabhängigen (DU) (Independents): Gablenzgasse 11, 1015 Vienna; tel. (1) 981-40-202; fax (1) 981-40-99; e-mail service@ldu.at; f. 1999; Chair. RICHARD LUGNER.

Diplomatic Representation

EMBASSIES IN AUSTRIA

Afghanistan: Lackierergasse 8/9, 1090 Vienna; tel. (1) 524-78-06; fax (1) 524-78-07; e-mail afg.emb.vie@chello.at; internet www.embassyofafghanistan.com; Ambassador Dr ZIA U. NEZAM.

Albania: Prinz-Eugen-Str. 18/1/5, 1040 Vienna; tel. (1) 328-86-56; fax (1) 328-86-58; e-mail albemb.vie@chello.at; Ambassador Dr SHPRESA KURETA.

Algeria: Rudolfinergasse 18, 1190 Vienna; tel. (1) 369-88-53; fax (1) 369-88-56; e-mail office@dz_embassy_at.org; Ambassador TAOUS FEROUKHI.

Angola: Seilerstätte 15/10, 1010 Vienna; tel. (1) 718-74-88; fax (1) 718-74-86; e-mail embangola.vienna@embangola.at; Ambassador Dr FIDELINO LOY DE JESUS FIGUEIREDO.

Argentina: Goldschmiedgasse 2/1, 1010 Vienna; tel. (1) 533-84-63; fax (1) 533-87-97; e-mail argviena@hotmail.com; Ambassador ELSA DIANA ROSA KELLY.

Armenia: Neubaugasse 12–14/1/16, 1070 Vienna; tel. (1) 522-74-79; fax (1) 522-74-81; e-mail armenia@armembassy.at; internet www.armembassy.at; Ambassador Dr JIVIAN TABIBIAN.

Australia: Mattiellistr. 2, 1040 Vienna; tel. (1) 506-74-0; fax (1) 504-11-78; e-mail receptionist@dfat.gov.au; internet www.australian-embassy.at; Ambassador DEBORAH STOKES.

Azerbaijan: Hügelgasse 2, 1130 Vienna; tel. (1) 403-13-22; fax (1) 403-13-23; e-mail office@azembvienna.at; internet www.azembvienna.at; Chargé d'affaires a.i. PARVIZ SHAHBAZOV.

Belarus: Hüttelbergstr. 6, 1140 Vienna; tel. (1) 419-96-30-11; fax (1) 416-96-30-30; e-mail mail@byembassy.at; internet www.byembassy.at; Ambassador Prof. Dr VIKTAR GAISENAK.

Belgium: Wohllebengasse 6, 1040 Vienna; tel. (1) 502-07; fax (1) 502-07-22; e-mail vienna@diplobel.be; internet www.diplomatie.be/vienna; Ambassador PHILIPPE ANDRÉ J. M. H. G. NIEUWENHUYS.

Belize: Franz Josefs Kai 13/5/16, Postfach 982, 1011 Vienna; tel. (1) 533-76-63; fax (1) 533-81-14; e-mail belizeembassy@utanet.at; Ambassador ALEXANDER PILETSKY.

Bolivia: Waaggasse 10/4, 1040 Vienna; tel. (1) 587-46-75; fax (1) 586-68-80; e-mail embolaustria@of-viena.at; Ambassador Dr HORACIO BAZOBERRY OTERO.

Bosnia and Herzegovina: Tivoligasse 54, 1120 Vienna; tel. (1) 811-85-55; fax (1) 811-85-69; e-mail bihembassyvienna@diplomats.com; Ambassador AMIRA KAPETANOVIĆ.

Brazil: Lugeck 1/V/15, 1010 Vienna; tel. (1) 512-06-31; fax (1) 513-83-74; e-mail ausbrem@utanet.at; Ambassador CELSO MARCOS VIEIRA DE SOUZA.

Bulgaria: Schwindgasse 8, 1040 Vienna; tel. (1) 505-64-44; fax (1) 505-14-23; e-mail bulgembassy@eunet.at; internet www.botschaftbulgarien.at; Ambassador Dr ELENA KIRTCHEVA.

Burkina Faso: Prinz-Eugen-Str. 18/3A, 1040 Vienna; tel. (1) 503-82-64; fax (1) 503-82-64-20; e-mail s.r@abfvienne.at; internet www.abfvienne.at; Ambassador NOELLIE MARIE BÉATRICE DAMIBA.

Canada: Laurenzerberg 2/III, 1010 Vienna; tel. (1) 531-38-30-00; fax (1) 531-38-33-21; e-mail vienn@dfait-maeci.gc.ca; internet www.kanada.at; Ambassador INGRID MARIANNE HALL.

Cape Verde: Schwindgasse 20, 1040 Vienna; tel. (1) 503-87-27; fax (1) 503-87-29; e-mail embcviena@nnweb.at; Ambassador ALIRIO VICENTE SILVA.

Chile: Lugeck 1/3/10, 1010 Vienna; tel. (1) 512-92-08-0; fax (1) 512-92-08-33; e-mail echileat1@chello.at; Ambassador RAIMUNDO ALBERTO GONZALEZ ANINAT.

China, People's Republic: Metternichgasse 4, 1030 Vienna; tel. (1) 714-31-49-48; fax (1) 713-68-16; Ambassador YONGHUA LU.

Colombia: Stadiongasse 6–8/15, 1010 Vienna; tel. (1) 406-44-46; fax (1) 408-83-03; e-mail embcolviena@aon.at; internet www.embcol.or.at; Ambassador ROSSO JOSÉ SERRANO CADENA.

Costa Rica: Hadikgasse 32/3, 1140 Vienna; tel. (1) 804-05-37; fax (1) 804-05-37-2; e-mail embajadaaustria_costa.rica@chello.at; Ambassador ISABEL MONTERO DE LA CAMARA (resident in Switzerland).

Croatia: Heuberggasse 10, 1170 Vienna; tel. (1) 485-95-24; fax (1) 480-29-42; e-mail vlprhbec@reinprecht.at; Ambassador Prof. Dr ZORAN JAŠIĆ.

Cuba: Himmelhofgasse 40A–C, Postfach 36, 1130 Vienna; tel. (1) 877-81-98; fax (1) 877-81-98-30; e-mail secembajador@ecuaustria.jet2web.at; internet www.ecuaustria.jet2web.at; Ambassador JOSÉ RAMÓN CABANAS RODRIGUEZ.

Cyprus: Parkring 20, 1010 Vienna; tel. (1) 513-06-30; fax (1) 513-06-32; e-mail embassy2@cyprus.vienna.at; Ambassador STAVROS A. EPAMINONDAS.

Czech Republic: Penzingerstr. 11–13, 1140 Vienna; tel. (1) 894-21-25; fax (1) 894-12-00; e-mail vienna@embassy.mzv.cz; internet www.mzv.cz/vienna; Ambassador Dr RUDOLF JINDRAK.

Denmark: Führichgasse 6, 1015 Vienna; tel. (1) 512-79-04-0; fax (1) 513-81-20; e-mail vieamb@um.dk; internet www.daenischebotschaft.at; Ambassador TORBEN MAILAND CHRISTENSEN.

Ecuador: Goldschmiedgasse 10/2/24, 1010 Vienna; tel. (1) 535-32-08; fax (1) 535-08-97; e-mail mecaustria@chello.at; Ambassador BYRON MOREJON ALMEIDA.

Egypt: Hohe Warte 52, 1190 Vienna; tel. (1) 370-81-04; fax (1) 370-81-04-27; e-mail egyptembassyvienna@egyptembassyvienna.at; internet www.egyptembassyvienna.at; Ambassador RAMZY EZZELDIN RAMZY.

Estonia: Wohllebengasse 9/13, 1040 Vienna; tel. (1) 503-77-61; fax (1) 503-77-61-20; e-mail saatkond@estwien.at; Ambassador KATRIN SAARSALU.

Ethiopia: Wagramer Str. 14, 1223 Vienna; tel. (1) 710-21-68; fax (1) 710-21-71; e-mail ethiopia@eunet.at; Ambassador HALIMA MOHAMED FEGI.

Finland: Gonzagagasse 16, 1010 Vienna; tel. (1) 531-59-0; fax (1) 535-57-03; e-mail sanomat.wie@formin.fi; internet www.finlandembassy.at; Ambassador TOM CARL ERNST GRÖNBERG.

France: Technikerstr. 2, 1040 Vienna; tel. (1) 502-75-0; fax (1) 502-75-168; e-mail presse@ambafrvienne.at; internet www.ambafrance.at.org; Ambassador ALAIN CATTA.

Georgia: Marokkanergasse 16, 1030 Vienna; tel. (1) 710-36-11; fax (1) 710-36-10; e-mail georgia@magnet.at; Ambassador Prof. Dr GIORGI ARSENISHVILI.

Germany: Metternichgasse 3, 1030 Vienna; tel. (1) 711-54; fax (1) 713-83-66; e-mail diplo@deubowien.at; internet www.deubowien.at; Ambassador HANS-HENNING HORSTMANN.

Greece: Argentinierstr. 14, 1040 Vienna; tel. (1) 505-57-91; fax (1) 505-62-17; e-mail hellasemb@greekembassy.jet2web.at; Ambassador THEODOROS SOTIROPOULOS.

Guatemala: Landstr. Hauptstr. 21/Top 9, 1030 Vienna; tel. (1) 714-35-70; fax (1) 714-35-70-15; e-mail embaguate.viena@chello.at; Ambassador LUIS ALBERTO PADILLA MENÉNDEZ.

Holy See: Theresianumgasse 31, 1040 Vienna; tel. (1) 505-13-27; fax (1) 505-61-40; e-mail nuntius@nuntiatur.at; internet www.nuntiatur.at; Apostolic Nuncio Most Rev. Dr GEORG ZUR (Titular Archbishop of Sesta).

Hungary: Bankgasse 4–6, 1010 Vienna; tel. (1) 537-80-300; fax (1) 535-99-40; e-mail kom@huembvie.at; Ambassador Dr ISTVÁN HORVÁTH.

Iceland: Naglergasse 2/8, 1010 Vienna; tel. (1) 533-27-71; fax (1) 533-27-74; e-mail icedel.vienna@utn.stjr.is; internet www.iceland.org/at; Ambassador THORDUR ÆGIR OSKARSSON.

India: Opernring 1E, 4th Floor, 1010 Vienna; tel. (1) 505-86-66; fax (1) 505-95-19; internet www.indianembassy.at; Ambassador THETTALIL PARAMESWARAN PILLAI SREENIVASAN.

Indonesia: Gustav-Tschermak-Gasse 5–7, 1180 Vienna; tel. (1) 479-23-0; fax (1) 479-05-57; e-mail unitkom@kbriwina.at; Ambassador THOMAS AQUINO SAMODRA SRIWIDJAJA.

Iran: Jaurèsgasse 9, 1030 Vienna; tel. (1) 712-26-57; fax (1) 713-57-33; e-mail public@iranembassy-wien.at; Ambassador SEYED MOHSEN NABAVI.

Iraq: Johannesgasse 26, 1010 Vienna; tel. (1) 713-81-95; fax (1) 713-67-20; e-mail botschaft_von_irak@utanet.at; Chargé d'affaires a.i. BUSHRA A. HAMAD.

Ireland: Rotenturmstr. 16–18, 5th Floor, 1010 Vienna; tel. (1) 715-42-46; fax (1) 713-60-04; e-mail vienna@dfa.ie; Ambassador DAVID DONOGHUE.

Israel: Anton-Frank-Gasse 20, 1180 Vienna; tel. (1) 476-46-0; fax (1) 476-46-55-5; e-mail info-sec@vienna.mfa.gov.il; Ambassador AVRAHAM TOLEDO.

Italy: Rennweg 27, 1030 Vienna; tel. (1) 712-51-21; fax (1) 713-97-19; e-mail info@ambitaliavienna.org; internet www.ambitaliavienna.org; Ambassador Dr RAFFAELE BERLENGHI.

Japan: Hessgasse 6, 1010 Vienna; tel. (1) 531-92-0; fax (1) 532-05-90; e-mail gem@embjp.at; internet www.st.emb-japan.go.jp; Ambassador HIROSHI HASHIMOTO.

Jordan: Doblhoffgasse 3/2, 1010 Vienna; tel. (1) 405-10-25; fax (1) 405-10-31; e-mail jordanembassy@aon.at; internet www.jordanembassy.at; Ambassador Prof. Dr MUHYIEEDDEEN TOUQ.

Kazakhstan: Felix-Mottl-Str. 23, 1190 Vienna; tel. (1) 367-91-75; fax (1) 367-91-75-33; e-mail kazakhstan.emb.vienna@aon.at; Ambassador RAKHAT M. ALIYEV.

Kenya: Neulinggasse 29/8, 1030 Vienna; tel. (1) 712-39-19; fax (1) 712-39-22; e-mail kenyarep-vienna@aon.at; Ambassador JULIUS KIPLAGAT KANDIE.

Korea, Democratic People's Republic: Beckmanngasse 10–12, 1140 Vienna; tel. (1) 894-23-13; fax (1) 894-31-74; Ambassador KIM GWANG SOP.

Korea, Republic: Gregor-Mendel-Str. 25, 1180 Vienna; tel. (1) 478-19-91; fax (1) 478-10-13; e-mail mail@koreaemb.at; internet www.mofat.go.kr/austria; Ambassador CHANG BEOM CHO.

Kuwait: Universitätsstr. 5/2, 1010 Vienna; tel. (1) 405-56-46; fax (1) 405-564-639; e-mail kuwaitem@eunet.at; Ambassador FAWZI ABUL-AZIZ AL JASEM.

Kyrgyzstan: Invalidenstr. 3/8, 1030 Vienna; tel. (1) 535-03-79; fax (1) 535-03-79-13; e-mail kyrbot@mail.austria.eu.net; Ambassador Dr ZEINEP SHAIMERGUENOVA.

Latvia: Stefan Esders Pl. 4, 1190 Vienna; tel. (1) 403-31-12; fax (1) 403-311-227; e-mail embassy.austria@mfa.gov.lv; Ambassador ELITA KUZMA.

Lebanon: Oppolzergasse 6/3, 1010 Vienna; tel. (1) 533-88-21; fax (1) 533-49-84; e-mail ambassade.liban@vienna.telecom.at; Ambassador SAMIR CHAMMA.

Libya: Blaasstr. 33, 1190 Vienna; tel. (1) 367-76-39; fax (1) 367-76-01; Chargé d'affaires a.i. SOAD A. M. SHILLI.

Liechtenstein: Löwelstr. 8/7, 1010 Vienna; tel. (1) 535-92-11; fax (1) 535-92-114; e-mail info@vie.rep.llv.li; Ambassador Princess MARIA-PIA KOTHBAUER of Liechtenstein.

Lithuania: Löwengasse 47/4, 1030 Vienna; tel. (1) 718-54-67; fax (1) 718-54-69; e-mail chancery@mail.austria.eu.net; Ambassador Dr JONAS RUDALEVIČIUS.

Luxembourg: Sternwartestr. 81, 1180 Vienna; tel. (1) 478-21-42; fax (1) 478-21-44; e-mail vienne.amb@mae.etat.lu; Ambassador Dr PAUL FABER.

Macedonia, former Yugoslav republic: Maderstr. 1/10, 1040 Vienna; tel. (1) 524-87-56; fax (1) 524-87-53; e-mail macembassy@24on.cc; Chargé d'affaires a.i. VUKICA KRTOLICA-POPOVSKA.

Malaysia: Prinz-Eugen-Str. 18, 1040 Vienna; tel. (1) 505-10-42-0; fax (1) 505-79-42; e-mail mwvienna@utanet.at; Ambassador Dato HUSSEIN HANIFF.

Malta: Opernring 5/1, 1010 Vienna; tel. (1) 586-50-10; fax (1) 586-50-109; e-mail office@maltaembassy.at; Ambassador Dr WALTER BALZAN.

Mexico: Operngasse 21/10, 1040 Vienna; tel. (1) 310-73-83; fax (1) 310-73-87; e-mail embamex@embamex.or.at; Ambassador PATRICIA ESPINOSA CANTELLANO.

Moldova: Löwengasse 47/10, 1030 Vienna; tel. (1) 961-10-30; fax (1) 961-10-30-34; e-mail vienna@moldmission.at; Ambassador Dr NATALIA GHERMAN.

Mongolia: Teinfaltstr. 3/6, 1010 Vienna; tel. (1) 535-30-13; fax (1) 535-30-06; e-mail office@embassymon.at; Ambassador LUVSANDAGVA ENKHTAIVAN.

Morocco: Opernring 3–5/I/4, 1010 Vienna; tel. (1) 586-66-50; fax (1) 586-76-67; e-mail emb-pmissionvienna@morocco.at; Ambassador Dr OMAR ZNIBER.

Namibia: Strozzigasse 10/14, 1080 Vienna; tel. (1) 402-93-71; fax (1) 402-93-70; e-mail nam.emb.vienna@eunet.at; Ambassador HANNO BURKHARD RUMPF (resident in Germany).

Netherlands: Opernring 5/7, 1010 Vienna; tel. (1) 589-39; fax (1) 589-39-265; e-mail nlgovwen@eunet.at; internet www.netherlands-embassy.at; Ambassador JUSTUS JONATHAN DE VISSER.

Nicaragua: Ebendorferstr. 10/3/12, 1010 Vienna; tel. (1) 403-18-38; fax (1) 403-27-52; Chargé d'affaires a.i. CRISTOBAL GOMEZ RODRIGUEZ.

Nigeria: Postfach 183, Rennweg 25, 1030 Vienna; tel. (1) 712-66-85; fax (1) 714-14-02; e-mail he@nigeriaembassyvienna.com; internet www.nigeriaembassyvienna.com; Ambassador BIODUN OWOSENI.

Norway: Reisnerstr. 55–57, 1030 Vienna; tel. (1) 715-66-92; fax (1) 712-65-52; e-mail emb.vienna@mfa.no; internet www.norwegen.or.at; Ambassador ROLF TROLLE ANDERSEN.

Oman: Währingerstr. 2–4/24, 1090 Vienna; tel. (1) 310-86-43; fax (1) 310-72-68; e-mail embassy.oman@chello.at; Ambassador SALIM MOHAMMED MASOUD AR-RIYAMI.

Pakistan: Hofzeile 13, 1190 Vienna; tel. (1) 368-73-81; fax (1) 368-73-76; e-mail parepvienna@hotmail.com; Ambassador ALI SARWAR NAQVI.

Panama: Elisabethstr. 4–5/4/10, 1010 Vienna; tel. (1) 587-23-47; fax (1) 586-30-80; e-mail mail@empanvienna.co.at; Ambassador Dr JORGE ENRIQUE HALPHEN PÉREZ.

Paraguay: Prinz-Eugen-Str. 18/1/2/7, 1040 Vienna; tel. (1) 505-46-74; fax (1) 941-98-98; e-mail embaparvienna@chello.at; Ambassador Dr OSCAR CABELLO SARUBBI.

Peru: Gottfried-Keller-Gasse 2/35, 1030 Vienna; tel. (1) 713-43-77; fax (1) 712-77-04; e-mail embajada@embaperuaustria.at; internet www.embaperuaustria.at; Chargé d'affaires a.i. HUGO PORTUGAL.

Philippines: Laurenzerberg 2, 1010 Vienna; tel. (1) 533-24-01; fax (1) 533-24-01-24; e-mail office@philippine-embassy.at; internet www.philippine-embassy.at; Ambassador VICTOR G. GARCIA, III.

Poland: Hietzinger Hauptstr. 42C, 1130 Vienna; tel. (1) 870-15-00; fax (1) 870-15-222; e-mail sekretariat@botschaftrp.at; internet www.botschaftrp.at; Ambassador MAREK JEDRYS.

Portugal: Opernring 3/1, 1010 Vienna; tel. (1) 586-75-36; fax (1) 586-75-36-99; e-mail portugal@portembassy.at; internet www.portembassy.at; Ambassador Dr CARLOS NEVES FERREIRA.

Qatar: Währinger Str. 2–4/24–25, 1090 Vienna; tel. (1) 310-49-50; fax (1) 319-08-97; e-mail vertret.qatar@chello.at; Chargé d'affaires ABDULRAHMAN YOUSUF AL-MULLA.

Romania: Prinz-Eugen-Str. 60, 1040 Vienna; tel. (1) 505-32-27; fax (1) 504-14-62; e-mail ambromviena@ambrom.at; internet www.ambrom.at; Ambassador Dr TRAIAN CHEBELEU.

Russia: Reisnerstr. 45–47, 1030 Vienna; tel. (1) 712-12-29; fax (1) 712-33-88; e-mail rusemb@chello.at; internet www.austria.mid.ru; Ambassador ALEXANDR W. GOLOVIN.

San Marino: Getreidemarkt 12, 1010 Vienna; tel. (1) 586-21-80; fax (1) 586-22-35; e-mail pfk@pfk.at; Ambassador GIOVANNI VITO MARCUCCI.

Saudi Arabia: Formanekgasse 38, 1190 Vienna; tel. (1) 367-25-31; fax (1) 367-25-40; e-mail emb.saudiarabia.vienna@aon.at; Ambassador OMAR MUHAMMAD KURDI.

Serbia and Montenegro: Rennweg 3, 1030 Vienna; tel. (1) 713-25-95; fax (1) 713-25-97; e-mail ambasada@yugoslavia.at; internet www.yugoslavia.at; Ambassador MIHAJLO KOVAĆ.

Slovakia: Armbrustergasse 24, 1190 Vienna; tel. (1) 318-90-55-200; fax (1) 318-90-55-208; e-mail slovakembassy@vienna.mfa.sk; internet www.vienna.mfa.sk; Ambassador Prof. Dr JOZEF KLIMKO.

Slovenia: Nibelungengasse 13/3, 1010 Vienna; tel. (1) 586-13-09; fax (1) 586-12-65; e-mail vdu@mzz-dkp.gov.si; Ambassador Prof. Dr ERNEST PETRIČ.

South Africa: Sandgasse 33, 1190 Vienna; tel. (1) 320-64-93; fax (1) 320-64-93-51; e-mail saembvie@aon.at; internet www.southafrican-embassy.at; Ambassador Prof. ALFRED TOKOLLO MOLEAH.

Spain: Argentinierstr. 34, 1040 Vienna; tel. (1) 505-57-88; fax (1) 505-57-88-25; e-mail embespat@mail.mae.es; internet www.embesp-at.org; Ambassador RAIMUNDO PÉREZ-HERNÁNDEZ Y TORRA.

Sri Lanka: Rainergasse 1/2/5, 1040 Vienna; tel. (1) 503-79-88; fax (1) 503-79-93; e-mail embassy.srilanka@utanet.at; internet www.embassy.srilanka.at; Ambassador DAYANTHA LAKSIRI MENDIS.

Sudan: Reisnerstr. 29/5, 1030 Vienna; tel. (1) 710-23-43; fax (1) 710-23-46; e-mail botshcaft.d.rep.sudan@chello.at; internet www.members.chello.at/botschaft.d.rep.sudan; Ambassador YOUSIF SAEED MUHAMMAD AHMAD.

Sweden: Obere Donaustr. 49–51, Postfach 18, 1025 Vienna; tel. (1) 217-53-0; fax (1) 217-53-370; e-mail ambassaden.wien@foreign.ministry.se; Ambassador GABRIELLE LINDHOLM.

Switzerland: Prinz-Eugen-Str. 7, 1030 Vienna; tel. (1) 795-05-0; fax (1) 795-05-21; e-mail vertretung@vie.rep.admin.ch; internet www.eda.admin.ch/wien; Ambassador Dr JOHANN BUCHER.

Syria: Daffingerstr. 4, 1030 Vienna; tel. (1) 533-46-33; fax (1) 533-46-32; e-mail vienna_embassy@syrianembassy.jet2web.at; Ambassador SAFWAN GHANEM.

Tajikistan: Universitätsstr. 8/1A, 1090 Vienna; tel. and fax (1) 409-82-66; fax (1) 409-82-66-14; e-mail tajikembassy@chello.at; Ambassador ERKIN KASIMOV.

Thailand: Cottagegasse 48, 1180 Vienna; tel. (1) 478-33-35; fax (1) 478-29-07; e-mail thai.vn@embthai.telecom.at; Ambassador ADISAK PANUPONG.

Tunisia: Opernring 5/3, 1010 Vienna; tel. (1) 581-52-81; fax (1) 581-55-92; e-mail at.vienne@aon.at; Ambassador Prof. MOHAMED DAOUAS.

Turkey: Prinz-Eugen-Str. 40, 1040 Vienna; tel. (1) 505-73-38-0; fax (1) 505-36-60; e-mail tuerkische-botschat@chello.at; Ambassador A. MITHAT BALKAN.

Turkmenistan: Argentinierstr. 22/11/EG, 1040 Vienna; tel. (1) 503-64-70; fax (1) 503-64-73; e-mail turkmen.del.osce@chello.at; Ambassador VLADIMIR KADYROV.

Ukraine: Naaffgasse 23, 1180 Vienna; tel. (1) 479-71-72; fax (1) 479-71-72-47; e-mail ukremb@netway.at; internet www.ukremb.at; Ambassador Dr VOLODYMYR OHRYZKO.

United Arab Emirates: Peter-Jordan-Str. 66, 1190 Vienna; tel. (1) 368-14-55; fax (1) 368-44-85; Ambassador AHMAD RASHED AL DOSARI.

United Kingdom: Jaurèsgasse 12, 1030 Vienna; tel. (1) 716-13-0; fax (1) 716-13-29-99; e-mail info@britishembassy.at; internet www.britishembassy.at; Ambassador JOHN MALCOLM MACGREGOR.

USA: Boltzmanngasse 16, 1090 Vienna; tel. (1) 313-39-0; fax (1) 310-06-82; e-mail embassy@usembassy.at; internet www.usembassy.at; Ambassador WILLIAM LEE LYONS BROWN, Jr.

Uruguay: Palais Esterhazy, Wallnerstr. 4/3/17, 1010 Vienna; tel. (1) 535-66-36; fax (1) 535-66-18; e-mail uruvien@embuy.or.at; Ambassador JORGE PEREZ OTERMIN.

Uzbekistan: Poetzleinsdorferstr. 49, 1180 Vienna; tel. (1) 315-39-94; fax (1) 315-39-93; e-mail botschaft.usbekistan@aon.at; Chargé d'affaires a.i. ALISHER KAYUMOV.

Venezuela: Prinz-Eugen-Str. 72/1.OG/Steige 1/Top1.1, 1040 Vienna; tel. (1) 712-26-38; fax (1) 715-32-19; e-mail emba@venezuela-vienna.com; internet www.venezuela-vienna.com; Ambassador GUSTAVO ADOLFO MARQUEZ MARIN.

Viet Nam: Félix-Mottl-Str. 20, 1190 Vienna; tel. (1) 368-07-55; fax (1) 368-07-54; e-mail embassy.vietnam@aon.at; Ambassador TRUONG GIANG NGUYEN.

Yemen: Wasagasse 6/10, 1090 Vienna; tel. (1) 503-29-30; fax (1) 505-31-59; e-mail yemenembassy.vienna@aon.at; Ambassador ALI HAMEED SHARAF.

Zimbabwe: Strozzigasse 10/15, 1080 Vienna; tel. (1) 407-92-36; fax (1) 407-92-38; e-mail z.vien@chello.at; Ambassador G. T. MUTANDIRO.

Judicial System

The Austrian legal system is based on the principle of a division between legislative, administrative and judicial power. There are three supreme courts (Verfassungsgerichtshof, Verwaltungsgerichtshof and Oberster Gerichtshof). The judicial courts are organized into about 200 local courts (Bezirksgerichte), 17 provincial and district courts (Landes- und Kreisgerichte), and four higher provincial courts (Oberlandesgerichte) in Vienna, Graz, Innsbruck and Linz.

SUPREME ADMINISTRATIVE COURTS

Verfassungsgerichtshof (Constitutional Court): Judenpl. 11, 1010 Vienna; tel. (1) 531-22-0; fax (1) 531-22-499; e-mail vfgh@vfgh.gv.at; internet www.vfgh.gv.at; f. 1919; deals with matters affecting the Constitution, examines the legality of legislation and admini-

stration; Pres. Prof. Dr KARL KORINEK; Vice-Pres. Dr BRIGITTE BIERLEIN.

Verwaltungsgerichtshof (Administrative Court): Judenpl. 11, 1010 Vienna; tel. (1) 531-11; fax (1) 531-11-135; internet www.vwgh.gv.at; deals with matters affecting the legality of administration; Pres. Prof. Dr CLEMENS JABLONER; Vice-Pres. Prof. Dr WOLFGANG PESENDORFER.

SUPREME JUDICIAL COURT

Oberster Gerichtshof: Schmerlingpl. 10–11, 1016 Vienna; tel. (1) 521-52; fax (1) 521-52-37-10; e-mail ogh.praesidium@justiz.gv.at; internet www.ris.bka.gv.at/jus; Pres. Dr JOHANN RZESZUT; Vice-Pres Prof. Dr KONRAD BRUSTBAUER, Prof. Dr BIRGIT LANGER.

Religion

CHRISTIANITY

Ökumenischer Rat der Kirchen in Österreich (Ecumenical Council of Churches in Austria): Severin Schreibner-Gasse 3, 1180 Vienna; tel. (1) 479-15-23-300; fax (1) 479-15-23-330; internet www.kirchen.at; f. 1958; 14 mem. Churches, 11 observers; Hon. Pres. Mother Superior Prof. CHRISTINE GLEIXNER (Roman Catholic Church); Vice-Pres. Bishop Mag. HERWIG STURM (Protestant Church of the Augsburg Confession), Bishop ANBA GABRIEL (Coptic Orthodox Church); Secretary Mag. ERIKA TUPPY (Protestant Church of the Helvetic Confession).

The Roman Catholic Church

Austria comprises two archdioceses, seven dioceses and the territorial abbacy of Wettingen-Mehrerau (directly responsible to the Holy See). The Archbishop of Vienna is also the Ordinary for Catholics of the Byzantine rite in Austria (totalling an estimated 5,000). At 31 December 2003 there were an estimated 5,751,872 adherents (about 72% of the population).

Bishops' Conference

Österreichische Bischofskonferenz, Wollzeile 2, 1010 Vienna; tel. (1) 516-11-32-80; fax (1) 516-11-34-36; e-mail sekretariat@bischofskonferenz.at; internet www.bischofskonferenz.at; f. 1849; Pres. Cardinal Dr CHRISTOPH SCHÖNBORN (Archbishop of Vienna); Gen. Sec. Mgr Dr ÄGIDIUS ZSIFKOVICS.

Archbishop of Salzburg: Most Rev. Dr ALOIS KOTHGASSER, Postfach 62, Kapitelpl. 2, 5020 Salzburg; tel. (662) 80-47-1100; fax (662) 80-47-1109; e-mail salzburg@ordinariat.kirchen.net; internet www.kirchen.net.

Archbishop of Vienna: Cardinal Dr CHRISTOPH SCHÖNBORN, Wollzeile 2, 1010 Vienna; tel. (1) 515-52-0; fax (1) 515-52-37-28; internet www.stephanscom.at.

Orthodox Churches

The Armenian Apostolic Church and the Bulgarian, Coptic, Greek, Romanian, Russian, Serbian and Syrian Orthodox Churches are active in Austria.

The Anglican Communion

Within the Church of England, Austria forms part of the diocese of Gibraltar in Europe. The Bishop is resident in London, United Kingdom.

Archdeacon of the Eastern Archdeaconry: Ven. JEREMY PEAKE, Thugutstr. 2/12, 1020 Vienna; tel. and fax (1) 663-92-09-264.

Protestant Churches

Bund der Baptistengemeinden in Österreich (Fed. of Baptist Communities): Krummgasse 7/4, 1030 Vienna; tel. (1) 713-68-28; fax (1) 713-68-28-11; Pres. ANITA IVANOVITS.

Evangelische Kirche Augsburgischen Bekenntnisses in Österreich (Protestant Church of the Augsburgian Confession): Severin-Schreiber-Gasse 3, 1180 Vienna; tel. (1) 479-15-23; fax (1) 479-15-23-110; e-mail bischof@evang.at; internet www.evang.at; 327,743 mems; Bishop Mag. HERWIG STURM.

Evangelische Kirche HB (Helvetischen Bekenntnisses) (Protestant Church of the Helvetic Confession): Dorotheergasse 16, 1010 Vienna; tel. (1) 513-65-64; fax (1) 512-44-90; e-mail kirche-hb@evang.at; 13,994 mems (2002); Landessuperintendent Hofrat Pfarrer Mag. WOLFRAM NAUMANN.

Evangelisch-methodistische Kirche (United Methodist Church): Sechshauser Str. 56, 1150 Vienna; tel. (1) 604-53-47; fax (1) 897-58-76; e-mail info@emk.at; internet www.emk.at; Superintendent LOTHAR PÖLL.

Other Christian Churches

Altkatholische Kirche Österreichs (Old Catholic Church in Austria): Schottenring 17, 1010 Vienna; tel. (1) 317-83-94; fax (1) 317-83-94-9; e-mail bischof.heitz@altkatholiken.at; internet www.altkatholiken.at; c. 18,000 mems; Bishop BERNHARD HEITZ.

ISLAM

There are about 350,000 Muslims in Austria.

Islamische Glaubensgemeinschaft in Österreich: Bernardgasse 5, 1070 Vienna; tel. (1) 526-31-22; e-mail info@derislam.at; internet www.derislam.at.

JUDAISM

There are five Jewish communities in Austria, the largest of which is in Vienna. At the end of 2004 there were 6,890 Jews in Vienna, and a combined total of 400 in Graz, Innsbruck, Linz and Salzburg.

Israelitische Kultusgemeinde Graz (Jewish Community in Graz): David Herzözpl. 1, 8020 Graz; tel. (316) 712-46-8; fax (316) 720-43-3; e-mail office@ikg-graz.at; internet www.ikg-graz.at.

Israelitische Kultusgemeinde Innsbruck (Jewish Community in Innsbruck): Sillgasse 15, 6020 Innsbruck; tel. (512) 586-89-2; e-mail office@ikg-innsbruck.at; internet www.ikg-innsbruck.at.

Israelitische Kultusgemeinde Salzburg (Jewish Community in Salzburg): Lasserstr. 8, 5020 Salzburg; tel. (662) 872-22-8; e-mail office@ikg-salzburg.at; internet www.ikg-salzburg.at.

Israelitische Kultusgemeinde Wien (Jewish Community in Vienna): Seitenstettengasse 4, 1010 Vienna; tel. (1) 531-04-0; fax (1) 531-04-109; e-mail office@ikg-wien.at; internet www.ikg-wien.at; Pres. Dr ARIEL MUZICANT.

The Press

Austria's first newspaper was published in 1605. The *Wiener Zeitung*, founded in 1703, is the world's oldest daily newspaper. Restrictions on press freedom are permissible only within the framework of Article 10 (2) of the European Convention on Human Rights.

The Austrian Press Council (Presserat), founded in 1961, supervises the activities of the press. Vienna is the focus of newspaper and periodical publishing, although there is also a strong press in some provinces. The three highest circulation dailies are the *Neue Kronen-Zeitung*, the *Kurier* and the *Kleine Zeitung* (Graz).

In 2002 there were 15 daily newspapers and 214 weekly newspapers in Austria; 2,792 other periodicals were active in that year.

PRINCIPAL DAILIES

Bregenz

Neue Vorarlberger Tageszeitung: Arlbergstr. 117, 6901 Bregenz; tel. (5574) 40-90; fax (5574) 40-93-00; f. 1972; morning; independent; Editor (vacant); circ. 20,136.

Vorarlberger Nachrichten: Gutenbergstr. 1, 6858 Schwarzach; tel. (5572) 501-0; fax (5572) 501-227; internet www.medienhaus.at; morning; Editor EUGEN A. RUSS; circ. 76,000.

Graz

Kleine Zeitung: Schönaugasse 64, 8011 Graz; tel. (316) 87-50; fax (316) 87-54-03-4; internet www.kleine.co.at; f. 1904; independent; Chief Editor Dr ERWIN ZANKEL; circ. 177,050.

Innsbruck

Tiroler Tageszeitung: Ing.-Etzel-Str. 30, 6020 Innsbruck; tel. (512) 53-54-0; fax (512) 57-59-24; e-mail redaktion@tt.com; internet www.tirol.com/tt; morning; independent; Chief Editor CLAUS REITAN; circ. 112,690.

Klagenfurt

Kärntner Tageszeitung: Viktringer Ring 28, 9020 Klagenfurt; tel. (463) 58-66-0; fax (463) 58-66-32-1; f. 1946; morning except Monday; Socialist; Chief Editor Dr HELLWIG VALENTIN.

Kleine Zeitung: Funderstr. 1A, 9020 Klagenfurt; tel. (463) 200-58-00; fax (463) 56-50-0; independent; Editor Dr HORST PIRKER; circ. 99,380.

Linz

Neues Volksblatt: Hafenstr. 1–3, 4010 Linz; tel. (732) 76-06-0; fax (732) 77-92-42; e-mail volksblatt@volksblatt.at; internet www.volksblatt.at; f. 1869; organ of Austrian People's Party; Chief Editor Dr FRANZ ROHRHOFER.

Oberösterreichische Nachrichten: Promenade 23, 4010 Linz; tel. (732) 78-05-41-0; fax (732) 78-05-329; e-mail redaktion@oon.at; internet www.nachrichten.at; f. 1865; morning; independent; Chief Editor Mag. GERALD WANDBLAUER; circ. 123,470.

Salzburg

Salzburger Nachrichten: Karolingerstr. 40, 5021 Salzburg; tel. (662) 83-73-0; fax (662) 83-73-39-9; e-mail marketing@salzburg.com; internet www.salzburg.com; f. 1945; morning; independent; Editor-in-Chief RONALD BARAZON; circ. 99,123.

Salzburger Volkszeitung: Bergstr. 12, 5020 Salzburg; tel. (662) 87-94-91; fax (662) 87-94-91-13; e-mail redaktion@svz.at; organ of Austrian People's Party; Editor HELMUT MÖDLHAMMER; circ. weekdays 12,030.

Vienna

Kurier: Lindengasse 52, 1072 Vienna; tel. (1) 521-00; fax (1) 521-00-22-63; e-mail leser@kurier.at; internet www2.kurier.at; f. 1954; independent; Chief Editor PETER RABL; circ. weekdays 334,204, Sunday 545,700.

Neue Kronen-Zeitung: Muthgasse 2, 1190 Vienna; tel. (1) 360-10; fax (1) 369-83-85; internet www.krone.at; f. 1900; independent; Editor HANS DICHAND; circ. weekdays 510,226, Sunday 751,296.

Die Presse: Parkring 12A, 1015 Vienna; tel. (1) 514-14; fax (1) 514-14-368; e-mail chefredaktion@diepresse.com; internet www.diepresse.com; f. 1848; morning; independent; Editor-in-Chief ANDREAS UNTERBERGER; circ. Mon.–Wed. 104,000, Thur.–Fri. 116,000, Sat. 150,000.

Der Standard: Herrengasse 19–21, 1014 Vienna; tel. (1) 531-70; fax (1) 531-70-13-1; e-mail documentation@derstandard.at; internet www.derstandard.at; f. 1988; independent; Editors-in-Chief OSCAR BRONNER, Dr GERFRIED SPERL; circ. 85,945.

Wiener Zeitung: Wiedner Gürtel 10, 1040 Vienna; tel. (1) 206-99-0; fax (1) 206-99-433; e-mail redaktion@wienerzeitung.at; internet www.wienerzeitung.at; f. 1703; morning; official govt paper; Editors PETER BOCHSKAN, HANZ FAHNLER; circ. 20,020.

PRINCIPAL WEEKLIES

Blickpunkt: E.-Bodem-Gasse 6, 6020 Innsbruck; tel. (512) 32-00; fax (512) 32-01-20; Editor OTTO STEIXNER.

Die Furche: Lobkowitzpl. 1, 1010 Vienna; tel. (1) 512-52-61; fax (1) 512-82-15; e-mail furche@furche.at; internet www.furche.at; f. 1945; Catholic; Editor Dr GOTTFRIED MOIK.

Die Ganze Woche: Heiligenstaedter Str. 121, 1190 Vienna; tel. (1) 291-60-0; fax (1) 291-60-73; e-mail redaktion@dgw.at; internet www.ganzewoche.at; f. 1985; circ. 400,000.

IW-Internationale Wirtschaft: Nikolsdorfer Gasse 7–11, 1051 Vienna; tel. (1) 546-64-346; fax (1) 546-64-342; economics; Editor NIKOLAUS GERSTMAYER; circ. 13,430.

Kärntner Nachrichten: Stauderpl. 5, 9020 Klagenfurt; tel. (463) 511515; fax (463) 511515-51; e-mail office@abc-werbeagentur.at; f. 1954; Editors ARMIN KORDESCH, HELMUT PRASCH; circ. 17,500.

Die Neue Wirtschaft: Nikolsdorfer Gasse 7–11, 1051 Vienna; tel. (1) 546-64-24-7; fax (1) 546-64-34-7; economics; circ. 25,650.

Neue Wochenschau: J. N. Bergerstr. 2, 7210 Mattersburg; tel. and fax (2622) 67-47-3; e-mail redaktion@wochenschau.at; internet www.wochenschau.at; f. 1908; Editor HELMUT WALTER; circ. 128,500.

NFZ (Neue Freie Zeitung): Postfach 81, 1013 Vienna; Esslinggasse 14–16, 1010 Vienna; tel. (1) 512-35-35-311; fax (1) 512-35-35-412; e-mail redaktion.nfz@fpoe.at; organ of Freedom Party; Chief Editor MICHAEL A. RICHTER; circ. 70,000.

Niederösterreichische Nachrichten: Gutenbergstr. 12, 3100 St Pölten; tel. (2742) 80-20; fax (2742) 80-21-48-0; e-mail chefredaktion@noen.at; internet www.noen.at; Editor HARALD KNABL; circ. 158,972.

Oberösterreichische Rundschau: Hafenstr. 1–3, 4010 Linz; tel. (732) 76-16-0; fax (732) 76-16-302; Editor-in-Chief Dr JOSEF ERTL; circ. 284,650.

Präsent: Exlgasse 20, 6020 Innsbruck; tel. (512) 22-33; fax (512) 22-33-50-1; f. 1892; independent Catholic; Chief Editor PAUL MVIGG.

Samstag: Faradaygasse 6, 1030 Vienna; tel. (1) 795-94-13-5; e-mail samstag@heroldwien.at; f. 1951; weekly; independent; Chief Editor GERLINDE KOLANDA; circ. 41,000.

Tiroler Bauernzeitung: Brixner Str. 1, 6021 Innsbruck; tel. (512) 59-90-00; fax (1) 59-90-03-1; publ. by Tiroler Bauernbund; Chief Dir GEORG KEUSCHNIGG; circ. 23,000.

Volksstimme: Lichteinsteinstr. 123/20, 1090 Vienna; tel. (1) 503-68-28; fax (1) 503-66-38; e-mail redaktion@volksstimme.at; internet www.volksstimme.at; f. 1994; Chief Editor WALTER BAIER.

POPULAR PERIODICALS

Agrar Post: Schulstr. 64, 2103 Langenzersdorf; tel. (2244) 46-47; f. 1924; monthly; agriculture.

Austria-Ski: Olympiastr. 10, 6020 Innsbruck; tel. (512) 335-01-0; fax (512) 361-99-8; 6 a year; official journal of Austrian Skiing Asscn; Editor JOSEF SCHMID.

Auto Touring: Tauchnergasse 5, 3400 Klosterneuburg; tel. (2243) 404-0; fax (2243) 404-27-21; e-mail autotouring.redaktion@oeamtc .at; monthly; official journal of the Austrian Automobile Organization; Editor-in-Chief ELISABETH PECHMANN; circ. 1,240,000.

Frauenblatt: Faradaygasse 6, 1032 Vienna; tel. (1) 795-94-13-5; e-mail samstag@heroldwien.at; women's weekly; Editor KURT MARKARITZER; circ. 22,300.

Die Neue Sportzeitung: Linke Wienzeile 40, 1060 Vienna; tel. (1) 585-57-57-0; fax (1) 585-57-57-411; e-mail redaktion@sportzeitung .at; internet www.sportzeitung.at; f. 1949; weekly sports illustrated; Editor HORST HÖTSCH; circ. 28,330.

News: Praterstr. 31, 1020 Vienna; tel. (1) 213-12-0; fax (1) 213-12-30-0; weekly; illustrated; Editor WOLFGANG FELLNER; circ. 342,244.

Profil: Lindengasse 52, 1070 Vienna; tel. (1) 534-70-0; fax (1) 535-32-50; e-mail redaktion@profil.at; internet www.profil.at; f. 1970; weekly; political, general; independent; circ. 100,000.

RZ (Wochenschau): Lilienbrumgasse 7–9, 1020 Vienna; tel. (1) 993-99-0; fax (1) 993-99-10-11; e-mail info@rizit.at; internet www.rizit .at; f. 1936; weekly illustrated; Chief Editor PAUL WEISS.

Trend: Marc-Aurel-Str. 10–12, 1010 Vienna; tel. (1) 534-70; e-mail redaktion@trend.at; internet www.trend.at; monthly; economics.

TV Media: Taborstr. 1–3, 1020 Vienna; tel. (1) 213-120; weekly; illustrated; Editor WOLFGANG MAIER; circ. 297,888.

Vídeňské svobodné listy: Margaretenpl. 7/2, 1050 Vienna; tel. (1) 587-83-08; fortnightly for Czech and Slovak communities in Austria; Editor HEINRICH DRAZDIL.

Welt der Frau: Lustenauerstr. 21, 4020 Linz; tel. (732) 77-00-01-11; fax (732) 77-00-01-24; internet www.welt-der-frau.at; women's monthly magazine; circ. 67,073.

Wiener: Lifestyle Zeitschriften Verlag GmbH, Davidgasse 79, 1100 Vienna; tel. (1) 601-17-249; fax (1) 601-17-350; e-mail wiener@ lifestylezv.at; 10 a year; Chief Editor PETER MOSSER; circ. 85,000.

SPECIALIST PERIODICALS

Eurocity: Leberstr. 122, 1110 Vienna; tel. (1) 740-95-46-4; fax (1) 740-95-49-1; e-mail karp.zv@bohmann.at; internet www.eurocity.at; f. 1928; every 2 months; Editor-in-Chief GEORG KARP; circ. 70,000.

Itm Praktiker: ZB-Verlag, Marochallpl. 23/1/21, 1125 Vienna; tel. (1) 804-04-74; fax (1) 804-44-39; technical hobbies; Chief Editor GERHARD K. BUCHBERGER; circ. 18,800.

Juristische Blätter (mit Beilage 'Wirtschaftsrechtliche Blätter'): Springer Verlag, Sachsenpl. 4, 1201 Vienna; tel. (1) 330-24-15-0; fax (1) 330-24-26; internet www.springer.at/jbl; f. 1872; monthly; nine editors.

Die Landwirtschaft: Wiener Str. 64, 3100 St Pölten; tel. (2742) 259-93-00; e-mail presse@lk-noe.at; internet www.lk-noe.at; f. 1923; monthly; agriculture and forestry; owned and publ. by Österreichischer Agrarverlag; Editor GERD RITTENAUER.

Liberale Zeichen: Dürergasse 6/10, 1060 Vienna; tel. (1) 503-06-67; fax (1) 503-06-67-20; e-mail office@lif.at; internet www.lif.at; 4 a year; organ of Liberal Forum.

Literatur und Kritik: Otto-Müller-Verlag, Ernest-Thun-Str. 11, 5020 Salzburg; tel. (662) 88-19-74; fax (662) 87-23-87; e-mail luk@ omvs.at; internet www.omvs.at; f. 1966; 5 a year; Austrian and European literature and criticism; Editor KARL-MARKUS GAUSS.

Monatshefte für Chemie: Sachsenpl. 4–6, 1201 Vienna; tel. (1) 330-24-15-0; fax (1) 330-24-26; e-mail journals@springer.at; internet www.springer.at/mochem; f. 1880; monthly; chemistry; Man. Editor H. FALK.

Oeffentliche Sicherheit: Postfach 100, Herrengasse 7, 1014 Vienna; tel. (1) 531-26-2307; fax (1) 531-26-2701; e-mail sicherheit@ mail.bmi.gv.at; internet www.bmi.gv.at/oeffentlsicherheit; 6 a year; published by the Ministry of the Interior; circ. 15,000.

Österreichische Ärztezeitung: Nibelungengasse 13, 1010 Vienna; tel. (1) 512-44-86; fax (1) 512-44-86-24; e-mail presse .verlags@oak.at; f. 1945; 20 a year; organ of the Austrian Medical Board; Editor MARTIN STICKLER.

Österreichische Ingenieur- und Architekten-Zeitschrift (ÖIAZ): Eschenbachgasse 9, 1010 Vienna; tel. (1) 587-35-36-0; fax (1) 587-35-36-5; e-mail office@oiav.at; internet www.oiav.at; f. 1849; 6 a year; Editor Dr GEORG WIDTMANN; circ. 3,000.

Österreichische Monatshefte: Lichtenfelsgasse 7, 1010 Vienna; tel. (1) 401-26-53-2; f. 1945; monthly; organ of Austrian People's Party; Editor GERHARD WILFLINGER.

Österreichische Musikzeitschrift: Hegelgasse 13, 1010 Vienna; tel. (1) 512-68-69; fax (1) 512-68-69-9; e-mail order@musikzeit.at; internet internet www.musikzeit.at; f. 1946; monthly; Editor Dr M. DIEDERICHS-LAFITE; circ. 5,000.

Reichsbund-Aktuell mit SPORT: Laudongasse 16, 1080 Vienna; tel. and fax (1) 405-54-06; e-mail info@amateurfussball.at; internet www.amateurfussball.at; f. 1917; monthly; Catholic; organ of Reichsbund, Bewegung für christliche Gesellschaftspolitik und Sport; Editor WALTER RAMING; circ. 12,000.

Welt der Arbeit: Altmannsdorferstr. 154–156, 1230 Vienna; tel. (1) 662-32-96; socialist industrial journal; Editor WALTER KRATZER; circ 64,350.

Wiener Klinische Wochenschrift: Sachsenpl. 4–6, 1201 Vienna; tel. (1) 330-24-15; fax (1) 330-24-26; e-mail journals@springer.at; internet www.springer.at/wkw; f. 1888; medical bi-weekly; Editors W. DRUML, H. SINZINGER.

Die Zukunft: Löwelstr. 18, 1014 Vienna; tel. (1) 534-27-280; fax (1) 534-27-282; monthly; organ of Social-Democratic Party of Austria; Editor ALBRECHT K. KONECNY; circ. 15,000.

NEWS AGENCIES

APA (Austria Presse-Agentur): Internationales Pressezentrum (IPZ), Gunoldstr. 14, 1190 Vienna; tel. (1) 360-60-0; fax (1) 360-60-30-99; e-mail marketing@apa.at; internet www.apa.at; f. 1946; co-operative agency of the Austrian Newspapers and Broadcasting Co (private co); 37 mems; Man. Dir Dr WOLFGANG VYSLOZIL; Chief Editor WOLFGANG MAYR.

Foreign Bureaux

Agence France-Presse (AFP) (France): Ares Tower, 17th Floor, Donau City Str. 11, 1220 Vienna; tel. (1) 269-63–00; fax (1) 269-63-00-20; e-mail robert.koch@afp.com; Bureau Chief JEAN-MICHEL STOULLIG.

Agenzia Nazionale Stampa Associata (ANSA) (Italy): IPZ, Gunoldstr. 14, 1199 Vienna; tel. (1) 368-13-00; fax (1) 368-79-35; e-mail ansa.vienna@chello.at; Bureau Chief GAETANO STELLACCI.

Associated Press (AP) (USA): IPZ, Gunoldstr. 14, 1199 Vienna; tel. (1) 368-41-56; fax (1) 369-15-58; Bureau Chief ROBERT REID.

Central News Agency (CNA) (Taiwan): Vienna; tel. (1) 799-17-02; fax (1) 798-45-98; Bureau Chief OU CHUN-LIN.

Česká tisková kancelář (ČTK) (Czech Republic): Penzingerstr. 114/206, 1140 Vienna; tel. and fax (1) 439-21-8.

Deutsche Presse-Agentur (dpa) (Germany): IPZ, Gunoldstr. 14, 1199 Vienna; tel. (1) 368-21-58; fax (1) 369-85-49.

Informatsionnoye Telegrafnoye Agentstvo Rossii– Telegrafnoye Agentstvo Suverennykh Stran (ITAR—TASS) (Russia): Grosse Neugasse 28, 1040 Vienna; tel. (1) 810-43-1; fax (1) 566-53-6; Correspondent ALEKSANDR S. KUZMIN.

Jiji Tsushin (Japan): IPZ, Gunoldstr. 14, 1199 Vienna; tel. (1) 369-17-97; fax (1) 369-10-52; Bureau Chief NOBUYUKI SATO.

Kyodo Tsushin (Japan): IPZ, Gunoldstr. 14/130, 1199 Vienna; tel. (1) 368-15-20; fax (1) 369-92-52-2; e-mail kyodowien@apanet.at; internet www.kyodo.co.jp; Bureau Chief MASATOSHI NAGATA.

Magyar Távirati Iroda (MTI) (Hungary): Peter-Jordan Str. 120/4, 1190 Vienna; tel. and fax (1) 479-43-96; e-mail tivadar.keller@lycos .at; Correspondent KELLER TIVADAR.

Reuters (UK): Börsegasse 11, 1010 Vienna; tel. (1) 531-12-0; fax (1) 531-12-5; e-mail marketing@reuters.at; internet www.reuters.at; Bureau Chief MARCUS KABEL.

Xinhua (New China) News Agency (People's Republic of China): Reisnerstr. 15/8, 1030 Vienna; tel. (1) 713-41-40; fax (1) 714-14-57; Chief Correspondent YANG HUANQIN.

PRESS ASSOCIATIONS

Österreichischer Zeitschriften- und Fachmedien-Verband (Asscn of Periodical Publrs): Renngasse 12/6, 1010 Vienna; tel. and fax (1) 319-70-01; e-mail oezv@oezv.or.at; internet www.oezv.or.at; f. 1946; 160 mems; Pres. Dr RUDOLF BOHMANN; Man. Dir Dr WOLFGANG BRANDSTETTER.

Verband Österreichischer Zeitungen (Newspaper Asscn of Austria): Wipplingerstr. 15, 4. Stock, TOP 19, Postfach 144, 1013

Vienna; tel. (1) 533-79-79-0; fax (1) 533-79-79-422; e-mail gs@voez
.at; internet www.voez.at; f. 1946; mems include 16 daily and most
weekly newspapers; Pres. Mag. Franz Ivan; Sec.-Gen. Dr Walter
Schaffelhofer.

Publishers

Akademische Druck- und Verlagsanstalt: Postfach 598, Auer-
sperggasse 12, 8010 Graz; tel. (316) 36-44; fax (316) 36-44-24; e-mail
info@adeva.com; internet www.adeva.com; f. 1949; scholarly
reprints and new works, facsimile editions of Codices, fine art
facsimile editions; Man. Dr Hubert C. Konrad.

Betz, Annette, Verlag GmbH: Alser Str. 24, 1091 Vienna; tel. (1)
404-44-0; fax (1) 404-44-5; internet www.annettebetz.com; f. 1962;
Man. Dir Dr Johanna Rachinger.

Böhlau Verlag GmbH & Co KG: Sachsenpl. 4–6, 1201 Vienna; tel.
(1) 330-24-27; fax (1) 330-24-32; e-mail boehlau@boehlau.at; internet
www.boehlau.at; f. 1947; history, law, philology, the arts, sociology;
Dir Dr Peter Rauch.

Bohmann Fachbuch im Verlag Jugend & Volk: Universitätsstr.
11, 1010 Vienna; tel. (1) 407-27-07; fax (1) 407-27-07-22; e-mail
verlag@jugendvolk.at; internet www.jugendvolk.at; f. 1936; trade,
technical and educational books.

Christian Brandstätter, Verlag und Edition: Schwarzen-
bergstr. 5, 1010 Vienna; tel. (1) 512-15-43-233; fax (1) 512-15-43-231;
e-mail cbv@oebv.co.at; f. 1982; art books; Chair. Dr Christian Brandstätter.

**Wilhelm Braumüller Universitäts Verlagsbuchhandlungs,
GmbH:** Servitengasse 5, 1092 Vienna; tel. (1) 319-11-59; fax (1) 310-
28-05; e-mail office@braumueller.at; internet www.braumueller.at;
f. 1783; politics, law, ethnology, literature and theatre, linguistics,
history, journalism, sociology, philosophy, psychology, communications; university publrs; Dirs Brigitte Pfeifer, Konstanze Weber.

Czernin Verlag GmbH: Piaristengasse 1, 1080 Vienna; tel. (1) 512-
01-32; fax (1) 512-01-32-15; e-mail office@czernin-verlag.com;
internet www.czernin-verlag.com.

Franz Deuticke Verlagsgesellschaft mbH: Hegelgasse 21, 1010
Vienna; tel. (1) 512-15-44-281; fax (1) 512-15-44-289; e-mail info@
deuticke.at; internet www.deuticke.at; f. 1878; culture, literature,
non-fiction; Dirs Dr Robert Sedlaczek, Dr Martina Schmidt.

Ludwig Doblinger Musikhaus-Musikverlag: Dorotheergasse
10, 1010 Vienna; tel. (1) 515-03-0; fax (1) 515-03-51; e-mail music@
doblinger.at; internet www.doblinger.at; f. 1876; music; Dir Helmuth
Pany.

Freytag-Berndt und Artaria KG Kartographische Anstalt:
Brunnerstr. 69, 1231 Vienna; tel. (1) 869-90-90; fax (1) 869-88-55;
e-mail sales@freytag-berndt.at; internet www.freytag-berndt.at; f.
1879; 1770—Artaria; geography, maps and atlases; Chair. Dr Christian Halbwachs.

Jugend and Volk GmbH: Universitätsstr. 11, 1016 Vienna; tel. (1)
407-27-07; fax (1) 407-27-07-22; e-mail verlag@jugendvolk.at;
internet www.jugendvolk.at; f. 1921; pedagogics, textbooks.

Kunstverlag Wolfrum: Augustinerstr. 10, 1010 Vienna; tel. (1)
512-53-98-0; fax (1) 512-53-98-57; e-mail wolfrum@utanet.at; f.
1919; art; Dir Hubert Wolfrum.

Leykam Verlag: Stempfergasse 3, 8011 Graz; tel. (316) 80-76; fax
(316) 80-76-39; f. 1585; art, literature, academic, law; Dir Dr Klaus
Brunner.

LexisNexis Verlag ARD ORAC GmbH & Co KG: Graben 17,
1010 Vienna; tel. (1) 534-52-0; fax (1) 534-52-14-1; e-mail verlag@
lexisnexis.at; internet www.lexisnexis.at; f. 1946; legal books, periodicals and online databases; CEO Peter J. Davies; Dir Dr Dietrich
Scherf.

Linde Verlag Wien: Scheydgasse 24, 1211 Vienna; tel. (1) 278-05-
26; fax (1) 278-05-26-23; e-mail office@lindeverlag.at; internet www
.lindeverlag.at; f. 1925; business; Man. Dir Andreas Jentzsch.

Manz'sche Verlags- und Universitätsbuchhandlung GmbH:
Kohlmarkt 16, 1014 Vienna; tel. (1) 531-61-0; fax (1) 531-61-181;
e-mail verlag@manz.at; internet www.manz.at; f. 1849; law, tax and
economic sciences; textbooks and school-books; Chief Execs Dr Kri-
stin Hanusch-Linser, Lucas Schneider-Manns-Au.

Wilhelm Maudrich: Spitalgasse 21a, 1096 Vienna; tel. (1) 408-58-
92; fax (1) 408-50-80; e-mail medbook@maudrich.com; internet www
.maudrich.com; f. 1909; medical; Man. Dir Gerhard Grois.

Molden Verlag GmbH: Stadiongasse 6–8, 1010 Vienna; tel. (1)
403-94-09; fax (1) 402-17-55.

**Niederösterreichisches Pressehaus Druck– und Verlagsge-
sellschaft mbH** (Residenz Verlag): Gaisbergstr. 6, 5025 Salzburg;

tel. (662) 64-19-86; fax (662) 64-35-48; e-mail info@residenzverlag
.at; internet www.residenzverlag.at; f. 1956; Dir Harald Knabl.

Otto Müller Verlag: Ernest-Thun-Str. 11, 5020 Salzburg; tel. (662)
88-19-74; fax (662) 87-23-87; e-mail info@omvs.at; internet www
.omvs.at; f. 1937; general; Man. Arno Kleibel.

Öbv & hpt Verlagsgesellschaft mbH: Frankgasse 4, 1090
Vienna; tel. (1) 401-36; fax (1) 401-36-185; e-mail office@oebvhpt.at.

Pinguin Verlag Pawlowski GmbH: Lindenbühelweg 2, 6021
Innsbruck; tel. (512) 28-11-83; fax (512) 29-32-43; f. 1945; illustrated
books; Dir Olaf Pawlowski.

Anton Schroll & Co: Spengergasse 37, 1051 Vienna; tel. (1) 544-56-
41; fax (1) 544-56-41-66; f. 1884; also in Munich; art; Man. F. Geyer.

Springer-Verlag GmbH: Sachsenpl. 4–6, 1201 Vienna; tel. (1) 330-
24-15; fax (1) 330-24-26; e-mail springer@springer.at; internet www
.springer.at; f. 1924; medicine, science, technology, law, sociology,
economics, architecture, art, periodicals; Man. Dir Rudolf Siegle.

Leopold Stocker Verlag: Hofgasse 5, 8011 Graz; tel. (316) 82-16-
36; fax (316) 83-56-12; f. 1917; history, nature, hunting, fiction,
agriculture, textbooks; Dir Wolfgang Dvorak-Stocker.

Carl Ueberreuter Verlag: Alserstr. 24, 1091 Vienna; tel. (1) 404-
44-0; fax (1) 404-44-5; e-mail office@vcu.ueberreuter.com; internet
www.ueberreuter.at; non-fiction, children's; Chief Exec. Johanna
Rachinger.

Universal Edition: Brucknerstr. 6, 1040 Vienna; tel. (1) 337-23-0;
fax (1) 337-23-40-0; e-mail office@universaledition.com; internet
www.universaledition.com; f. 1901; music; Dir Dr J. Juranek; Dir.
Marion von Hartlieb.

Urban & Schwarzenberg GmbH: Frankgasse 4, 1096 Vienna; tel.
(1) 405-27-31; fax (1) 405-27-24-41; e-mail kundenservice@urban.at;
f. 1866; science, medicine; Dir (vacant).

Verlag Kerle im Verlag Herder & Co: Wollzeile 33, 1010 Vienna;
tel. (1) 512-14-13; fax (1) 512-14-13-60; f. 1886; children's books,
juvenile.

Verlag Kremayr & Scheriau: Ungargasse 45/13, 1030 Vienna; tel.
(1) 713-87-70-0; fax (1) 713-87-70-20; f. 1951; non-fiction, history.

Verlag Oldenbourg: Neulinggasse 26/12, 1030 Vienna; tel. (1) 712-
62-58; fax (1) 712-62-58-19; e-mail gala@oldenbourg.co.at; f. 1959;
Dir Dr Thomas Cornides.

Verlag Styria: Schönaugasse 64, 8011 Graz; tel. (316) 80-63-0; fax
(316) 80-63-70-04; e-mail office@styriapichler.at; f. 1869; biographies, theology, religion, philosophy; Man. Dir Dietmar Sternad.

Verlagsanstalt Tyrolia GmbH: Postfach 220, Exlgasse 20, 6020
Innsbruck; tel. (512) 22-33-202; fax (512) 22-33-206; e-mail
buchverlag@tyrolia.at; internet www.tyrolia.at; f. 1888; geography,
history, science, children's, religion, fiction; Chair. Dr Gottfried
Kompatscher.

Verlagsbuchhandlung Brüder Hollinek und Co GmbH: Lui-
senstr. 20, 3002 Purkersdorf; tel. and fax (2231) 673-65; f. 1872;
science, law and administration, printing, reference works, dictionaries; Dir Richard Hollinek.

Paul Zsolnay Verlag GmbH: Prinz-Eugen-Str. 30, 1041 Vienna;
tel. (1) 505-76-61; fax (1) 505-76-61-10; e-mail info@zsolnay.at;
internet www.zsolnay.at; f. 1923; fiction, non-fiction; Dirs Michael
Krüger, Stephan D. Joss.

GOVERNMENT PUBLISHING HOUSE

Verlag Österreich GmbH (Austrian Publishing House): Kandl-
gasse 21, 1070 Vienna; tel. (1) 610-77-0; fax (1) 610-77-419; e-mail
office@verlagoesterreich.at; internet www.verlagoesterreich.at; f.
1804; law, CD-ROMs.

PUBLISHERS' ASSOCIATION

Hauptverband des Österreichischen Buchhandels (Asscn of
Austrian Publrs and Booksellers): Grünangergasse 4, 1010 Vienna;
tel. (1) 512-15-35; fax (1) 512-84-82; e-mail sekretariat@hvb.at;
internet www.buecher.at; f. 1859; Pres. Dr Alexander Potyka; 605
mems.

Broadcasting and Communications

REGULATORY BODY

Rundfunk und Telekom Regulierungs GmbH: Mariahilferstr.
77–79, 1060 Vienna; tel. (1) 580-58-0; fax (1) 580-58-91-91; e-mail
rtr@rtr.at; internet www.rtr.at; f. 1997 as Telekom-Control GmbH;
regulatory body for the broadcasting and telecommunications sector.

TELECOMMUNICATIONS

Telekom Austria AG: Lassallestr. 9, 1020 Vienna; tel. and fax (1) 590-59-1-0; e-mail kundenservice@telekom.at; internet www .telekom.at; f. 1998; Dir-Gen. HEINZ SUNDT.

Connect Austria Gesellschaft für Telekommunikation GmbH: Brunnerstr. 52, 1210 Vienna; tel. (1) 277-28-0; internet www.connectaustria.at; Chair. FRANZ GEIGER.

Max.mobil Telekommunikation Service GmbH: Kelsenstr. 5–7, 1030 Vienna; tel. (1) 795-85-0; fax (1) 795-85-53-2; internet www .maxmobil.at; Chair. Dr STEPHAN HUXOLD.

Mobilkom Austria AG & Co KG: Obere Donaustr. 29, 1020 Vienna; tel. (1) 331-61-0; internet www.mobilkom.at.

Tele.ring Telekom Service GmbH & Co KG: Hainburgerstr. 33, 1030 Vienna; tel. (1) 931-01-20; e-mail info@telering.co.at; internet www.telering.at; wholly owned by Western Wireless International (USA).

RADIO AND TELEVISION

The state-owned Österreichischer Rundfunk (ORF) provides three national and nine regional radio channels, as well as an overseas service. The ORF also has two terrestrial television channels, and operates a satellite station in conjunction with German and Swiss companies. While the ORF retains a monopoly over television broadcasting in Austria, the provision of radio services was liberalized in 1998, when a number of commercial radio stations were launched.

Digital radio is available in Vienna. The channels available are Ö1 (classical music), Radio Wien (local station), Ö3 (popular music) and FM4. An estimated 19% of Austria's population receives Digital Audio Broadcast (DAB) coverage. ORF has established two DAB transmitters in Tyrol under a trial licence, covering the Inn valley between Kufstein and the Brenner mountain. There is continuous coverage between south Germany and northern Italy. Ö1, the regional station, Ö3 and FM4 are available.

Österreichischer Rundfunk (ORF) (Austrian Broadcasting Company): Würzburggasse 30, 1136 Vienna; tel. (1) 87878-0; fax (1) 878-78-12250; e-mail kundendienst@orf.at; internet www.orf.at; f. 1924; state-owned; Dir-Gen. Dr MONIKA LINDNER; Dirs Dr REINHARD DRAXLER (Television), KURT RAMMERSTORFER (Radio).

Private and Commercial Television Operators

ATV Privat-TV Services AG: Aspernbrückengasse 2, 1020 Vienna; tel. (1) 21364; internet atvplus.at; f. 2003; private, commercial channel.

Premiere Fernsehen GmbH: Kreitnergasse 5, 1163 Vienna; internet www.premiere-austria.at; f. 2003; satellite operator offering films, sport and adult programming; wholly owned by Premiere Fernsehen GmbH & Co KG (Germany).

Other channels available nationally through cable and satellite include Blue Movie 1, Blue Movie 2, Eurotic TV , Fashion TV, Gotv, INXTC TV, K-TV, Kabel Woche, Pro7 Austria, Raceon TV, Sat1 Österreich, TV 6, TW1 and X-Plus TV.

Finance

(cap. = capital; res = reserves; dep. = deposits; m. = million; brs = branches; amounts in euros)

BANKS

Banks in Austria, apart from the National Bank, belong to one of five categories. The first category comprises banks that are organized as corporations (i.e. joint-stock and private banks), and special-purpose credit institutions; the second category comprises savings banks; and the third category comprises co-operative banks. Co-operative banks include rural credit co-operatives (Raiffeisenbanken) and industrial credit co-operatives (Volksbanken). The remaining two categories comprise the mortgage banks of the various Austrian Länder, and the building societies. The majority of Austrian banks (with the exception of the building societies) operate on the basis of universal banking, although certain categories have specialized. Banking operations are governed by the Banking Act of 1993 (Bankwesengesetz–BWG).

Central Bank

Oesterreichische Nationalbank (Austrian National Bank): Postfach 61, Otto-Wagner-Pl. 3, 1090 Vienna; tel. (1) 404-20; fax (1) 404-20-66-99; e-mail oenb.info@oenb.co.at; internet www.oenb.at; f. 1922; 50% state-owned; cap. €12m., res €4,201m., dep. €7,789m. (Dec. 2003); Pres. HERBERT SCHIMETSCHEK; Gov. Dr KLAUS LIEBSCHER; 8 brs.

Commercial Banks

Adria Bank AG: Gonzagagasse 16, 1010 Vienna; tel. (1) 514-09-0; fax (1) 514-09-43; e-mail headoffice@adriabank.at; internet www .adriabank.at; f. 1980; cap. €9,447m., res €19,282m., dep. €178,508m. (Dec. 2003); Chair. EVA KRAPFENBAUER.

Alpenbank AG: Kaiserjägerstr. 9, 6020 Innsbruck; tel. (512) 599-77; fax (512) 562-01-5; e-mail private-banking@alpenbank.at; internet www.alpenbank.at; f. 1983 as Save Rössler Bank AG; present name adopted 1991; 58.75% owned by Raiffeisen-Landesbank Tirol AG (Innsbruck), 32.75% owned by Raiffeisen Landesbank Südtirol AG (Bolzano, Italy), 4.9993% owned by Hauck & Aufhäuser Privatbankiers KGaA (Frankfurt a.M., Germany), 3.5% owned by Bankhaus Carl Spängler & Co AG (Salzburg); cap. €10m., res €1m., dep. €54m. (Dec. 2003); Gen. Mans Mag. MARTIN STERZINGER, Mag. ANDREAS HALLER, Dr HEIDI VEROCAL-DÖNZ.

Anglo Irish Bank (Austria) AG: Postfach 306, Rathausstr. 20, 1011 Vienna; tel. (1) 406-61-61-0; fax (1) 405-81-42; f. 1890 as Bankhaus Rosenfeld; present name adopted 1995; acquired Crédit Lyonnais Bank (Austria) AG 1998; wholly owned by Anglo Irish Bank Corpn PLC (Dublin, Ireland); cap. €7m., res €49m., dep. €797m. (Dec. 2003); Chair. and CEO DESMOND O'HOULIHAN.

Arab Bank (Austria) AG: Postfach 100, Seilerstätte 11, 1010 Vienna; tel. (1) 513-42-42-0; fax (1) 513-42-40-9; e-mail arabbank@ arabbank.at; f. 1987; wholly owned by Arab Holding Co BV (Netherlands); cap. €7m., res €5m., dep. €144m. (Dec. 2003); Chair., Supervisory Bd ABDUL MAJEED SHMOAN; Dir-Gen, and Chair., Executive Bd AZZAM NAJJAR.

Bank Austria Creditanstalt AG: Am Hof 2, 1010 Vienna; tel. (0) 505050; fax (0) 5050556149; e-mail info@ba-ca.com; internet www .ba-ca.com; f. 1991 as Bank Austria AG by merger of Österreichische Länderbank and Zentralsparkasse und Kommerzialbank; merged with HypoVereinsbank AG of Germany in mid-2001; present name adopted 2002; cap. €1,069m., res €2,598m., dep. €110,356m. (Dec. 2003); Pres. and Group CEO GERHARD RANDA; Chair. Bd of Man. Dirs ERICH HAMPEL; 381 brs.

> **Bank Austria Creditanstalt International AG:** Am Hof 2, 1010 Vienna; tel. (1) 536-36-0; fax (1) 536-36-61-0; e-mail info@at .bacai.com; f. 1998; through merger of international business of Bank Austria AG (see above) with Creditanstalt AG (f. 1855); wholly owned by Bank Austria AG.

Bank für Arbeit und Wirtschaft AG (BAWAG): Seitzergasse 2–4, 1010 Vienna; tel. (1) 534-53-0; fax (1) 534-53-2840; e-mail bawag@ bawag.com; internet www.bawag.com; f. 1947; present name adopted 1963; purchased PSK, the state-owned postal bank in Aug. 2000; wholly owned by Österreichischer Gewerkschaftsbund; cap. €125m., res €913m., dep. €35,824m. (Dec. 2002); Chair. and CEO HELMUT ELSNER; 155 brs.

Bank Gutmann AG: Schwarzenbergpl. 16, 1010 Vienna; tel. (1) 502-20-0; fax (1) 502-201-99; e-mail info@gutmann.at; internet www .gutmann.at; f. 1970 as Bank Gebrüd AG, present name adopted 1995; 83% owned by Gutmann Holding AG, 17% owned by partners; cap. €12m., res €13m., dep. €339m. (Dec. 2003); Gen. Man. Dr RUDOLF F. STAHL.

Bank Vontobel Österreich AG: Rathauspl. 4, 5024 Salzburg; tel. (662) 810-40; fax (662) 810-47; e-mail vontobel@salzburg.co.at; f. 1885 as Bankhaus Berger & Co AG; name changed to Vontobel Bank AG 1998; present name adopted 2000; 99.24% owned by Vontobel Holding AG (Zürich, Switzerland), 0.76% owned by Pellegrinus Holding AG; cap. €10m., res €6m., dep. €143m. (Dec. 2002); Chair., Exec. Bd Dr ROLAND HENGARTNER.

Bank Winter und Co AG: Singerstr. 10, 1011 Vienna; tel. (1) 515-04-0; fax (1) 515-04-21-3; e-mail contact@bankwinter.com; internet www.bankwinter.com; f. 1892; re-established 1959; 75% owned by HSBC Republic Trust Services (Suisse) AG as trustees, 25% owned by trust in favour of Stern-Moskovics family; cap. €35m., res €78m., dep. €1,701m. (June 2003); Chair. and CEO THOMAS MOSKOVICS; 1 br.

Bankhaus Schelhammer und Schattera AG: Postfach 618, 1011 Vienna; Goldschmiedgasse 3, 1010 Vienna; tel. (1) 534-34; fax (1) 534-34-65; e-mail bank.office@schelhammer.at; internet www .schelhammer.at; f. 1832; cap. €36.1m., res €20.8m., dep. €433.6m. (Dec. 2003); Chair. Dr HEINZ BURGMANN; 1 br.

Capital Bank-Grawe Gruppe AG: Burgring 16, 8010 Graz; tel. (316) 807-20; fax (316) 807-23-90; e-mail office@capitalbank.at; internet www.capitalbank.at; f. 1922 as Gewerbe- und Handelsbank; present name adopted 2001; wholly owned by Grazer Wechselseitige Versicherung AG (Graz); cap. €10m., res €56m., dep. €120m. (Dec. 2003); CEO CHRISTIAN JAUK.

DenizBank AG: Postfach 85, 1015 Vienna; Kärntner Ring 12, 1010 Vienna; tel. (1) 503-93-96-0; fax (1) 503-93-96-133; e-mail service@ denizbank.at; internet www.denizbank.at; f. 1996 as ESBANK AG; present name adopted 2003; wholly owned by DenizBank AS

(Turkey); cap. €7m., res €16m., dep. €306m. (Dec. 2003); Chair., Supervisory Bd HAKAN ATES; Gen. Man. Dr ISMAIL ERGENER.

Donau-Bank AG: Postfach 1451, Parkring 6, 1011 Vienna; tel. (1) 515-35; fax (1) 515-35-29-7; e-mail general@donau-bank.at; internet www.donau-bank.at; f. 1974; 85% owned by Bank for Foreign Trade (Russia), 15% owned by Central Bank of the Russian Federation; cap. €73m., res €205m., dep. €527m. (Dec. 2003); Chair. and Gen. Dir ANDREI E. TCHETYRKIN.

Investkredit Bank AG: Renngasse 10, 1010 Vienna; tel. (1) 531-35-0; fax (1) 531-35-98-3; e-mail invest@investkredit.at; internet www.investkredit.at; cap. €46m., res €265m., dep. €15,011m. (Dec. 2003); Pres. Prof. Dr GEISERICH E. TICHY; Chair. Dr WILFRIED STADLER.

Kathrein und Co Privatgeschäftsbank AG: Postfach 174, Wipplingerstr. 25, 1013 Vienna; tel. (1) 534-51-0; fax (1) 534-51-221; e-mail privatgeschaeftsbank.ag@kathrein.at; internet www .kathrein.at; f. 1924; 100% owned by Raiffeisen Zentralbank Österreich AG; Chair. Dr CHRISTOPH KRAUS; Dir Dr CLAUDIO CANTELE.

Meinl Bank AG: Postfach 99, Bauernmarkt 2, 1015 Vienna; tel. (1) 531-88; fax (1) 531-88-44; e-mail servicecentre@meinlbank.com; internet www.meinlbank.com; f. 1922; cap. €9m., res €32m., dep. €493m. (Dec. 2003); Chair., Supervisory Bd Dr WALTER JAKOBLJEVICH; Chair., Management Bd JULIUS MEINL; 2 brs.

Österreichische Verkehrskreditbank AG: Auerspergstr. 17, 1080 Vienna; tel. (1) 405-76-48; fax (1) 405-76-48-18; e-mail vst-sekretariat@verkehrskreditbank.at; internet www .verkehrskreditbank.at; f. 1969; wholly owned by Bank für Arbeit und Wirtschaft AG (Vienna); cap. €4m., res €9m., dep. €364m. (Dec. 2003); Pres. STEPHAN KOREN; CEO MANFRED SOOS; Chair. ALEXANDER WIDDER.

Schoellerbank AG: Renngasse 1–3, 1010 Vienna; tel. (1) 534-71-0; fax (1) 534-71-635; e-mail info@schoellerbank.at; internet www .schoellerbank.at; f. 1998 by merger of Schoellerbank AG (f. 1833) and Salzburger Kredit-und Wechsel-Bank AG (f. 1922); wholly owned by Bank Austria Creditanstalt AG (Vienna); cap. €20m., res €70m., dep. €1,429m. (Dec. 2003); Chair. JÜRGEN DANZMAYR.

VakifBank International (Wien) AG: Kärntner Ring 17, 1010 Vienna; tel. (1) 512-35-20; fax (1) 512-35-20-22; e-mail office@ vakifbank.at; internet www.vakifbank.at; f. 1999 as Vakifbank International (Wien) AG; present name adopted 2002; 90% owned by Türkiye Vakifar Bankasi TAO (Kavaklidere, Turkey), 10% owned by Pension Fund of Turkiye Vakifar Bankasi TAO; cap. €16m., res €10m., dep. €161m. (Dec. 2003); Pres. A. AHMET KACAR.

Zveza Bank RZZOJ (Bank und Revisionsverband rGmbH): Postfach 465, Paulitschgasse 5–7, 9010 Klagenfurt; tel. (463) 512-36-5; fax (463) 512-36-51-9; e-mail office@zvezabank.co.at; internet www.zvezabank.co.at; f. 1921 as Zveza Koroških zadrug/Verband Kärntner Genossenschaften; integrated into Austria Raiffeisen Asscn 1921; in 1949 name changed to Zveza slovenskih zadrug v Celovcu/Verband slowenischer Genossenschaften in Klagenfurt; present name adopted 1996; 55 mems, of which seven are credit cooperatives; cap. €7m., res €5m., dep. €188m. (Dec. 2003); Chair. Dr LUDWIG DRUML; Gen. Mans RUDOLF URBAN, JOSEF LANG.

Regional Banks

Allgemeine Sparkasse Oberösterreich Bank AG: Postfach 92, Promenade 11–13, 4041 Linz; tel. (0) 50100-40000; fax (0) 50100-458011; e-mail intl.division@sparkasse-ooe.at; internet www .sparkasse-ooe.at; f. 1849; cap. €57m., res €270m., dep. €6,918m. (Dec. 2003); Chair. Dr MARKUS LIMBERGER; 132 brs.

Bank für Kärnten und Steiermark AG: St. Veiter Ring 43, 9020 Klagenfurt; tel. (463) 58-58; fax (463) 58-58-94-3; e-mail bks@bks.at; internet www.bks.at; f. 1922; cap. €50m., res €159m., dep. €3,532m. (Dec. 2003); Pres. Dr HEINRICH TREICHL; 6 brs.

Bank für Tirol und Vorarlberg AG: Langer Weg 11, 6020 Innsbruck; tel. (512) 53-33-0; fax (512) 533-31-408; e-mail btv@btv.at; internet www.btv.at; f. 1904; cap. €50m., res €244m., dep. €5,435m. (Dec. 2003); Chair. PETER GAUGG; 37 brs.

Bankhaus Carl Spängler und Co AG: Postfach 41, 5024 Salzburg; Schwarzstr. 1, 5020 Salzburg; tel. (662) 86-86; fax (662) 86-86-15-8; e-mail bankhaus@spaengler.co.at; internet www.spaengler.co .at; f. 1828; cap. €11m., res €26m., dep. €570m. (Dec. 2003); Gen. Man. HEINRICH SPÄNGLER; 10 brs.

Bankhaus Krentschker und Co AG: Am Eisernen Tor 3, 8010 Graz; tel. (316) 80-30-0; fax (316) 80-30-94-9; e-mail mail@ krentschker.at; internet www.krentschker.at; f. 1924; 92.58% owned by Die Steiermärkische Bank und Sparkassen AG (Graz), 7.34% owned by Kärntner Sparkasse AG (Klagenfurt), 0.08% owned by private shareholders; cap. €14m., res €31m., dep. €918m. (Dec. 2003); Chair. Dr JÖRG BRUCKBAUER; 3 brs.

Hypo Alpe-Adria-Bank AG: Postfach 517, Alpen-Adria-Pl. 1, 9020 Klagenfurt; tel. (0) 502020; fax (0) 502023000; e-mail austria@

hypo-alpe-adria.com; internet www.hypo-alpe-adria.com; f. 1896 as Kärntner Landes- und Hypothekenbank AG; present name adopted 1999; cap. €34m., res €197m., dep. €9,610m. (Dec. 2003); Mans Mag. GERT XANDER, Mag. ANDREA MALLER; 200 brs.

Hypo Alpe-Adria-Bank International AG: Alpen Adria Pl. 1, 9020 Klagenfurt; tel. (0) 502020; fax (0) 502023000; e-mail international@hypo-alpe-adria.com; internet www.hypo-alpe-adria .com; f. 2004; from split of Hypo Alpe-Adria-Bank AG; operates in Bosnia and Herzegovina, Croatia, Italy, Liechtenstein, Serbia and Montenegro, and Slovenia; 52% owned by Kärntner Landes- und Hypothekenbank Holding (Klagenfurt), 48% owned by Grazer Wechselseitige Versicherungs AG (Graz); cap. €34m., res €344m., dep. €11,489m. (Dec. 2003); Chair., Management Bd Dr WOLFGANG KULTERER.

Hypo Tirol Bank AG: Postfach 524, Meranerstr. 8, 6020 Innsbruck; tel. (512) 59-11-0; fax (512) 59-11-21-21; e-mail office@ hypotirol.at; internet www.hypotirol.at; f. 1901 as Landes-Hypothekenbank Tirol AG, present name adopted 2000; cap. €18m., res €232m., dep. €7,301m. (Dec. 2003); Pres. Dr JOHANN GRUBER; 23 brs.

Niederösterreichische Landesbank-Hypothekenbank AG: Kremsergasse 20, 3100 St Pölten; tel. (2742) 49-20; fax (2742) 49-20-14-44; e-mail hypobank@hypobank.co.at; internet www.hypobank .co.at; f. 1889; cap. €38m., res €146m., dep. €4,776m. (Dec. 2003); Pres. and Chair. HERBERT FICHTA; Gen. Man. WERNER SCHMITZER; 26 brs.

Oberbank AG: Hauptpl. 10–11, 4020 Linz; tel. (732) 78-02-0; fax (732) 78-58-04; e-mail office@oberbank.at; internet www.oberbank .at; f. 1869 as Bank für Oberösterreich und Salzburg; present name adopted 1998; cap. €70m., res €408m., dep. €9,383m. (Dec. 2003); Chair. Dr FRANZ GASSELSBERGER; 101 brs and sub-brs.

Oberösterreichische Landesbank AG: Landstr. 38, 4020 Linz; tel. (70) 76-39-0; fax (70) 76-39-20-5; e-mail managementservice@ hypo-ooe.at; internet www.hypo.at; f. 1891; cap. €70m., res €166m., dep. €4,702m. (Dec. 2003); Pres. Dr WOLFGANG STAMPFL; Chair. and Gen. Man. Dr ANDREAS MITTERLEHNER; 16 brs.

Salzburger Landes-Hypothekenbank AG: Postfach 136, Residenzpl. 7, 5010 Salzburg; tel. (662) 804-60; fax (662) 804-65-69-2; e-mail office@hypobank.sbg.at; internet www.hypobank.sbg.at; f. 1909 as bank of the Government of Salzburg; present name adopted 1992; 50.02% owned by Hypo Holding GmbH (Linz), 25% owned by Oberösterreichische Landesbank AG (Linz), 14.97% owned by Raiffeisenlandesbank Oberösterreich AG (Linz), 10% owned by Salzburger Landesholding; cap. €15m., res €73m., dep. €3,015m. (Dec. 2003); Gen. Man. Dr REINHARD SALHOFER; 24 brs.

Die Steiermärkische Bank und Sparkassen AG: Postfach 844, Sparkassenpl. 4, 8011 Graz; tel. (316) 80-33-0; fax (316) 80-33-30; e-mail international@bank-styria.co.at; internet www.bank-styria .co.at; f. 1825 as Steyermärkischer Spar-Casse Graz; present name adopted 1992; cap. €55m., res €377m., dep. €6,178m. (Dec. 2002); CEO JOSEPH KASSLER; Dirs Dr HEINZ HOFER, AUGUST JOST, Dr GERHARD FABISCH; 122 brs.

Tiroler Sparkasse-Bankaktiengesellschaft Innsbruck: Sparkassenpl. 1, 6020 Innsbruck; tel. (512) 59-10-2; fax (512) 59-10-45-00; f. 1822 as Sparkasse der Stadt Innsbruck; present name adopted 1990, following merger in 1975; incorporated Bank der Tiroler Sparkasse in Jungholz AG by merger in 2002; 48.93% owned by Erste Bank der Österreichischen Sparkassen AG (Vienna), 48.51% owned by AVS Beteiligungs GmbH (Innsbruck), 1% owned by Anteilsverwaltungssparkasse (Innsbruck); cap. €66m., res €91m., dep. €3,039m. (Dec. 2003); Pres. ANDREAS TREICHL; 49 brs.

Volkskreditbank AG: Postfach 116, Rudigierstr. 5–7, Pfarrpl. 12 und Domgasse 12 , 4010 Linz; tel. (732) 76-37-0; fax (732) 76-37-29-0; e-mail international@vkb-bank.at; internet www.vkb-bank.at; f. 1872; cap. €30m., res €197m., dep. €1,313m. (Dec. 2003); Chair., Supervisory Bd JOHANNES BRANDL; Chair, Management Bd Dr GERNOT KRENNER; 45 brs.

Vorarlberger Landes- und Hypothekenbank AG: Hypo-Passage 1, 6900 Bregenz; tel. (5574) 414-0; fax (5574) 414-45-7; e-mail info@hypovbg.at; internet www.hypovbg.at; f. 1899 as Hypothekenbank des Landes Vorarlberg; name changed to Vorarlberger Landes- und Hypothekenbank 1990; status changed as above 1996; cap. €24m., res €287m., dep. €6,152m. (Dec. 2003); Chair. Dr KURT RUPP; 25 brs.

Specialized Banks

Kommunalkredit Austria AG: Türkenstr. 9, 1092 Vienna; tel. (1) 316-31-0; fax (1) 316-31-50-0; e-mail kommunal@kommunalkredit .at; internet www.kommunalkredit.at; f. 1958; 50.78% owned by Investkredit Bank AG (Vienna), 49% owned by Dexia Crédit Local SA (Paris), 0.22% owned by Austrian Asscn of Municipalities; dep. €9,263m., total assets €9,756m. (Dec. 2003); Chair., Supervisory Bd ALFRED REITER; CEO and Chair., Executive Bd Dr REINHARD PLATZER.

Oesterreichische Kontrollbank AG: Postfach 70, Am Hof 4 & Strauchgasse 3, 1011 Vienna; tel. (1) 531-27-0; fax (1) 531-27-5698; e-mail public.relations@oekb.at; internet www.oekb.at; f. 1946; administration of guarantees, export financing, stock exchange clearing, organization and administration of domestic bond issues, central depository for securities and settlement of off-floor transactions, money market operations; cap. €130m., res €83m., dep. €744m. (Dec. 2003); Mans Dr JOHANNES ATTEMS, Dr RUDOLF SCHOLTEN.

Privatinvest Bank AG: Postfach 16, Griesgasse 11, 5010 Salzburg; tel. (662) 80-48-0; fax (662) 80-48-33-3; e-mail piag@piag.at; internet www.privatinvestbank.com; 74% owned by Reuschel & Co Finanz Service GmbH, 26% owned by Salzburger Sparkasse Bank AG (Salzburg); f. 1885 as Bankhaus Daghofer & Co AG; present name adopted 1990; cap. €6m., res €5m., dep. and bonds €143m. (Dec. 2003); Chair. HANS-WERNER ZESCHKY.

Savings Banks

Dornbirner Sparkasse Bank AG: Postfach 199, Bahnhofstr. 2, 6850 Dornbirn; tel. (5572) 381-10; fax (5572) 381-14; e-mail service@dornbirn.sparkasse.at; internet www.dornbirn.sparkasse.at; cap. €10m., res €135m., dep. €1,728m. (Dec. 2003); Chair. WOLFGANG RÜMMELE; 15 brs.

Erste Bank der österreichischen Sparkassen AG (Erste Bank) (First Austrian Savings Bank): Postfach 162, Graben 21, 1010 Vienna; tel. (1) 531-00-0; fax (1) 531-00-22-72; e-mail service.center@erstebank.at; internet www.erstebank.at; f. 1819; present name adopted 1997; dep. €107,487m., total assets €128,575m. (Dec. 2003); Chair. and CEO ANDREAS TREICHL; 279 brs.

Kärntner Sparkasse AG: Neuer Pl. 14, 9020 Klagenfurt; tel. (463) 588-80; fax (463) 588-82-91; e-mail info@kaerntnersparkasse.co.at; internet www.kaerntnersparkasse.at; f. 1835; 75% owned by private foundation Die Kärntner Sparkasse AG, 25% owned by Erste Bank der Östereichischen Sparkassen AG (Vienna); dep. €2,441m., total assets €2,787m. (Dec. 2003); Pres. Dr HANS KOSTWEIN; Chair. and Gen. Man. ALOIS HOCHEGGER; 49 brs.

Salzburger Sparkasse Bank AG: Postfach 5000, Alter Markt 3, 5021 Salzburg; tel. (662) 80-40-0; fax (662) 80-40-81; internet www.salzburger-sparkasse.co.at; f. 1855 as Salzburger Sparkasse; present name adopted 1991; absorbed ALPHA-Beteiligungs GmbH in 1997; 98.69% owned by Erste Bank der österreichischen Sparkassen AG (Vienna); cap. €34m., res €143m., dep. €3,521m. (Dec. 2003); Gen. Man. WALTER SCHWIMBERSKY; 79 brs.

Sparkasse der Stadt Bludenz: Postfach 19, Sparkassepl. 1, 6700 Bludenz; tel. (5552) 636-81; fax (5552) 636-81-4; e-mail sparkasse.bludenz@telecom.at; internet www.bludenz.sparkasse.at; f. 1892 as Bludenzer Spar- und Vorschussverein; present name adopted 1939; guaranteed by town of Bludenz; res €28m., dep. €398m. (Dec. 2003); Pres. Bürgermeister Dr OTHMAR KRAFT; Chair. and Man. Dir Mag. WILLI BURTSCHER.

Co-operative Banks

Österreichische Volksbanken-AG: Peregringasse 3, 1090 Vienna; tel. (1) 313-40-37-89; fax (1) 313-40-31-70; e-mail info@oevag.volksbank.at; internet www.oevag.volksbank.at; f. 1922; cap. and res €833m., dep. and bonds €19,087m., total assets €21,562m. (Dec. 2003); Chair. and CEO FRANZ PINKL; 85 brs.

Raiffeisen Centrobank AG: Postfach 272, Tegetthoffstr. 1, 1015 Vienna; tel. (1) 515-20-0; fax (1) 513-43-96; e-mail general@centrobank.com; internet www.centrobank.com; f. 1973; 99.99% owned by Raiffeisen Zentralbank Österreich AG (Vienna), 0.01% owned by Raiffeisen-Invest-Gesellschaft mbH (Vienna); cap. €48m., res €18m., dep. €425m. (Dec. 2003); Chair. Dr GERHARD VOGT.

Raiffeisen Zentralbank Österreich AG (RZB-Austria): Am Stadtpark 9, 1030 Vienna; tel. (1) 717-07-0; fax (1) 717-07-17-15; internet www.rzb.at; f. 1927; dep. €47,919m., total assets €56,051m. (Dec. 2003); central institute of the Austrian Raiffeisen banking group; Chair. Supervisory Bd Dr CHRISTIAN KONRAD; Chair. Bd of Management Dr WALTER ROTHENSTEINER.

Raiffeisen-Landesbank Tirol AG (RLB Tirol AG): Adamgasse 1–7, 6020 Innsbruck; tel. (512) 530-50; fax (512) 530-52-229; e-mail andrea.zankl@rbgt.raiffeisen.at; internet www.rlb-tirol.at; f. 1894; cap. €80m., res €195m., dep. €4,735m. (Dec. 2003); Chair. REINHARD MAYR; 21 brs.

Raiffeisenlandesbank Kärnten-Rechenzentrum und Revisionsverband rGmbH: St-Veiter-Ring 53, 9020 Klagenfurt; tel. (463) 581-52-7-0; fax (463) 581-53-6; internet www.raiffeisen.at/ktn; cap. €5m., res €75m., dep. €1,846m. (Dec. 2003); Chair. Dr KLAUS PEKAREK; 48 brs.

Raiffeisenlandesbank Niederösterreich-Wien AG: Friedrich-Wilhelm-Raiffeisen-Pl. 1, Raiffeisenhaus, 1020 Vienna; tel. (1) 21-13-60; fax (1) 21-13-62-22-3; e-mail info@rlb-noe.raiffeisen.at;

internet www.rlbnoew.at; f. 1898; cap. €199m., res €348m., dep. €9,738m. (Dec. 2003); Chair. Dr CHRISTIAN KONRAD.

Raiffeisenlandesbank Oberösterreich AG: Postfach 455, Europapl. 1A, 4021 Linz; tel. (732) 6596-3150; fax (732) 6596-3155; e-mail cb@rlbooe.at; internet www.rlbooe.at; f. 1900; cap. €100m., res €472m., dep. €13,990m. (Dec. 2003); Chair. Dr LUDWIG SCHARINGER; 21 brs.

Raiffeisenlandesbank Steiermark rGmbH: Kaiserfeldgasse 5–7, 8010 Graz; tel. (316) 80-36-0; fax (316) 80-36-24-37; e-mail info.rlb-stmk@rlb-stmk.raiffeisen.at; internet www.raiffeisen.at/rlb-steiermark; f. 1927; cap. €96m., res €318m., dep. €4,983m. (Dec. 2003); Chair. Bd of Management Dr GEORG DOPPELHOFER.

Raiffeisenlandesbank Vorarlberg Waren-und Revisions Verband rGmbH: Rheinstr. 11, 6900 Bregenz; tel. (5574) 4050; fax (5574) 405-333; internet www.vol.at/raiffeisen; cap. €25m., res €85m., dep. €2,593m. (Dec. 2003); Chair. Dr KARL WALTLE; Dirs KARLHEINZ WAIBEL, WILFRIED HOPFNER.

Raiffeisenverband Salzburg rGmbH: Postfach 6, Schwarzstr. 13–15, 5024 Salzburg; tel. (662) 8886-0; fax (662) 888-65-97; e-mail friedrich.buchmueller@rvs.at; internet www.salzburg.raiffeisen.at; f. 1905; present name adopted 1949; cap. €44m., res €173m., dep. €4,071m. (Dec. 2003); Chair. MANFRED HOLZTRATTNER.

Welser Volksbank rGmbH: Postfach 234, Pfarrgasse 5, 4601 Wels; tel. (7242) 495; fax (7242) 495-97; e-mail office@welser.volksbank.at; internet www.welser.volksbank.at; f. 1912 as Welser Handels- und Gewerbekasse rGmbH; present name adopted 1971; 12,494 shareholders (2003); cap. €2m., res €21m., dep. €248m. (Dec. 2003); Chair. Mag. Dr JOSEF STEINBÖCK; Gen. Man. HANS MAYR.

Bankers' Organization

Verband österreichischer Banken und Bankiers (Asscn of Austrian Banks and Bankers): Postfach 132, Börsegasse 11, 1013 Vienna; tel. (1) 535-17-71; fax (1) 535-17-71/38; e-mail voebb@voebb.at; internet www.voebb.at; f. 1945; Pres. Dr STEPHAN KOREN; Gen. Sec. MARIO GEYER; 59 mems and 21 extraordinary mems.

STOCK EXCHANGES

Wiener Börse (Vienna Stock Exchange): Postfach 192, Strauchagasse 1–3, 1014 Vienna; tel. (1) 531-65-0; fax (1) 532-97-40; e-mail communications@vienna-stock-exchange.at; internet www.wbag.at; f. 1771; 50% state-owned; two sections: Stock Exchange, Commodity Exchange; Pres. GERHARD REIDLINGER; Gen. Sec. Dr ULRICH KAMP.

Österreichische Termin- und Optionenbörse (Austrian Futures and Options Exchange): Postfach 192, Walluerstr. 8, 1014 Vienna; tel. (1) 531-65-0; fax (1) 532-97-40; f. 1991 by appointment to the Vienna Stock Exchange, provides a fully automated screen-based trading system, the Austrian Traded Index (ATX), and acts as clearing house for options and futures; trades futures on the Austrian index and options on 17 Austrian stocks listed on the Vienna Stock Exchange; CEOs Dr ERICK OBERSTEINER, Dr STEFAN ZAPOTOCKY.

INSURANCE COMPANIES

Allgemeine Rechtsschutz Versicherungs-AG (ARAG): Favoritenstr. 36, 1041 Vienna; tel. (1) 531-02-0; fax (1) 531-02-1923; e-mail info@arag.at; internet www.arag.at; Man. Dr HERBERT KITTINGER.

Allianz Elementar Lebensversicherung-AG: Hietzinger Kai 101–105, 1130 Vienna; tel. (1) 878-07-0; fax (1) 878-07-27-03; e-mail office@allianz.at; internet www.allianz.at; life insurance; Chair., Supervisory Bd Dr GERHARD RUPPRECHT; Chair., Management Bd Dr WOLFRAM LITTICH.

Allianz Elementar Versicherungs-AG: Hietzinger Kai 101–105, 1130 Vienna; tel. (1) 878-07-0; fax (1) 878-07-53-90; e-mail office@allianz.at; internet www.allianz.co.at; f. 1860; all classes except life insurance; Chair., Supervisory Bd Dr REINER HAGEMANN; Chair., Management Bd Dr WOLFRAM LITTICH.

AXA Nordstern Colonia Versicherungs-AG: Uraniastr. 2, 1010 Vienna; tel. (1) 711-50-0; fax (1) 711-50-212; e-mail kundendienst@axa-versicherung.at; internet www.axa-versicherung.at; Gen. Man. DAVID FURTWÄNGLER.

Donau Allgemeine Versicherungs-AG: Schottenring 15, 1010 Vienna; tel. (1) 313-11; fax (1) 310-77-51; e-mail donau@donauversicherung.at; internet www.donauversicherung.at; f. 1867; all classes; Gen. Man. HANS RAUWAUF.

Generali Versicherung AG: Landskrongasse 1–3, 1011 Vienna; tel. (1) 534-01; fax (1) 534-01-12-26; e-mail headoffice@generali.at; internet www.generali.co.at; f. 1882 as Erste Österreichische Allgemeine Unfall-Versicherungs-Gesellschaft; Gen. Man. Dr HANS PEER.

Grazer Wechselseitige Versicherung: Herrengasse 18–20, 8011 Graz; tel. (316) 80-37-0; fax (316) 80-37-41-4; f. 1828; all classes; Gen. Man. Dr OTHMAR EDERER.

Interunfall Versicherungs-AG: Tegetthoffstr. 7, 1011 Vienna; tel. (1) 514-03-0; fax (1) 514-03-4590; e-mail z-v@interunfall.at; internet www.interunfall.at; all classes (incl. reinsurance); Man. Dr HANS PEER.

Raiffeisen-Versicherung AG: Untere Donaustr. 25, 1021 Vienna; tel. (1) 211-19-0; fax (1) 211-19-11-34; e-mail kommunikation@raiffeisen-versicherung.at; internet www.raiffeisen-versicherung.at; Dir Dr PETER EICHLER.

Salzburger Landes-Versicherung AG: Auersperstr. 9, 5021 Salzburg; tel. (662) 899-98-0; fax (662) 889-98-109; e-mail sekretariat@slv.co.at; internet www.slv.co.at; Gen. Man. Dr JOSEF GLASER.

Sparkassen Versicherung AG: Wipplingerstr. 36–38, 1011 Vienna; tel. (1) 313-81-0; fax (1) 313-81-300; e-mail sag@s-versicherung.co.at; internet www.s-versicherung.co.at; Gen. Man. Dr MICHAEL HARRER.

Uniqa Versicherungen AG: Praterstr. 1–7, 1021 Vienna; tel. (1) 211-11-0; fax (1) 214-33-36; e-mail kommunikation@uniqa.at; internet www.uniqa.at; present name adopted 1999, fmrly Versicherungsanstalt der österreichischen Bundesländer Versicherungs-AG; Chair. Dr KONSTANTIN KLIEN.

Wiener Städtische Allgemeine Versicherung AG: Schottenring 30, Ringturm, 1010 Vienna; tel. (1) 531-39-0; fax (1) 535-34-37; e-mail mail-us@wr.staedtische.co.at; internet www.staedtische.co.at; f. 1824; all classes; CEO Dr SIEGFRIED SELLITSCH.

Wüstenrot Versicherungs-AG: Alpenstr. 61, 5033 Salzburg; tel. (662) 6386-0; fax (662) 6386-623; e-mail versicherung@wuestenrot.at; internet www.wuestenrot.at; Gen. Man. HELMUT GEIER.

Zürich Versicherungs AG: Schwarzenbergpl. 15, 1015 Vienna; tel. (1) 501-25-0; fax (1) 505-04-85; internet www.zuerich.at; f. 1910; all classes; Gen. Man. RUDOLF KRAFT.

Insurance Organization

Verband der Versicherungsunternehmen Österreichs (Asscn of Austrian Insurance Cos): Schwarzenbergpl. 7, 1030 Vienna; tel. (1) 711-56-0; fax (1) 711-56-27-0; e-mail versver@ibm.net; internet www.vvo.at; f. 1945; Pres. Dr ALEXANDER HOYOS; Gen. Sec. HERBERT RETTER; 86 mems.

Trade and Industry

GOVERNMENT AGENCIES

Austrian Business Agency (ABA): Opernring 3, 1010 Vienna; fax (1) 586-86-59; e-mail office@aba.gv.at; internet www.aba.gv.at; Man. Dir RENÉ SIEGL.

Österreichische Industrieholding AG (ÖIAG): Postfach 99, Kantgasse 1, 1015 Vienna; tel. (1) 711-14-0; fax (1) 711-14-37-8; f. 1970; Mans. KARL HOLLWEGER, Dr ERICH BECKER.

CHAMBERS OF COMMERCE

All Austrian enterprises must by law be members of the Economic Chambers. The Federal Economic Chamber promotes international contacts and represents the economic interests of trade and industry on a federal level. Its Foreign Trade Organization includes about 90 offices abroad.

Wirtschaftskammer Österreich (Austrian Federal Economic Chamber): Wiedner Hauptstr. 63, 1045 Vienna; tel. (0) 590900; fax (0) 590900-250; e-mail callcenter@wko.at; internet www.wko.at; f. 1946; seven divisions: Crafts and Trades, Industry, Commerce, Bank and Insurance, Transport and Communications, Tourism and Leisure, Industry, Information and Consulting; these divisions are subdivided into branch asscns; Regional Economic Chambers with divisions and branch asscns in each of the nine Austrian provinces; Pres. CHRISTOPH LEITL; Sec.-Gen. CHRISTIAN DOMANY; c. 330,000 mems.

INDUSTRIAL AND TRADE ASSOCIATIONS

Wirtschaftskammer Österreich—Bundessparte Industrie: Wiedner Hauptstr. 63, 1045 Vienna; tel. (0) 590900-3420; fax (0) 590900-273; e-mail bsi@wko.at; internet www.wko.at; f. 1896 as Zentralverband der Industrie Österreichs (Central Fed. of Austrian Industry), merged into present org. 1947; Chair. Dr WERNER TESSMAR-PFOHL; Dir WOLFGANG DAMIANISCH; comprises the following industrial feds:

Fachverband der Audiovisions-und Filmindustrie Österreichs (Film): Postfach 327, Wiedner Hauptstr. 63, 1045 Vienna;

tel. (0) 590900-3010; fax (0) 590900-276; e-mail krenmayr@fafo.at; internet www.fafo.at; Chair. MICHAEL WOLKENSTEIN; 2,500 mems.

Fachverband der Bekleidungsindustrie (Clothing): Schwarzenbergpl. 4, 1030 Vienna; tel. (1) 712-12-96; fax (1) 713-92-04; e-mail pitnik@fashion-industry.at; internet www.fashion-industry.at; Chair. WOLFGANG SIMA; Dir FRANZ J. PITNIK; 240 mems.

Fachverband der Bergwerke und Eisenerzeugenden Industrie (Mining and Steel Production): Wiedner Hauptstr. 3, 1045 Vienna; tel. (1) 512-46-01; fax (1) 512-46-01-20; e-mail fvil@wkoesk.wk.or.at; internet www.wko.at/bergbau-stahl; Dir HERBERT BARDACH; Sec. Ing. HERMANN PRINZ; 39 mems.

Fachverband der Chemischen Industrie (Chemicals): Postfach 325, Wiedner Hauptstr. 63, 1045 Vienna; tel. (1) 501-05-280; fax (1) 502-06-28-0; e-mail office@fcio.wko.at; internet www.fcio.at; Pres. Dr WOLFGANG FRANK; Gen. Dir Dr WOLFGANG EICKHOFF; 530 mems.

Fachverband der Elektro- und Elektronikindustrie Oesterreichs (Electrical): Mariahilfer Str. 37–39, 1060 Vienna; tel. (1) 588-39-0; fax (1) 586-69-71; e-mail info@feei.at; internet www.feei.at; Pres. ALBERT HOCHLEITNER; Man. Dir LOTHAR ROITNER; 350 mems.

Fachverband der Fahrzeugindustrie (Vehicles): Wiedner Hauptstr. 63, 1045 Vienna; tel. (0) 590900-4800; fax (0) 590900-289; e-mail kfz@wko.at; internet www.wko.at/fahrzeuge; Pres. BRUNO KRAINZ; Gen. Sec. WALTER LINSZBAUER; 200 mems.

Fachverband der Gas- und Wärmeversorgungsunternehmungen (Gas and Heating): Schubertring 14, 1010 Vienna; tel. (1) 513-15-88-0; fax (1) 513-15-88-25; e-mail office@gaswaerme.at; internet www.gaswaerme.at; Gen. Dir Dr KARL SKYBA.

Fachverband der Giessereiindustrie (Foundries): Postfach 339, Wiedner Hauptstr. 63, 1045 Vienna; tel. (0) 590900-3463; fax (0) 590900-279; e-mail giesserei@wko.at; Chair. MICHAEL ZIMMERMANN; Dir ADOLF KERBL; 60 mems.

Fachverband der Glasindustrie (Glass): Wiedner Hauptstr. 63, 1045 Vienna; tel. (0) 590900-3448; fax (0) 590900-281; e-mail office@fvglas.at; Chair. RUDOLF SCHRAML; Dir ALEXANDER KRISSMANEK; 50 mems.

Fachverband der Holzindustrie (Wood): Postfach 123, Schwarzenbergpl. 4, 1037 Vienna; tel. (1) 712-26-01-0; fax (1) 712-26-01-19; e-mail office@saege.at; internet www.holzindustrie.at; f. 1947 as Fachverband der Sägeindustrie Österreichs; present name adopted 2000; Chair. Dr ERICH WIESNER; Dir Dr GERHARD ALTRICHTER; 1,800 mems.

Fachverband der Ledererzeugenden Industrie (Leather Production): Postfach 312, Wiedner Hauptstr. 63, 1045 Vienna 4; tel. (0) 590900-3453; fax (0) 590900-278; e-mail fvleder@wko.at; internet www.leather-industry.at; f. 1945; Chair. HELMUT SCHMIDT; Dir PETER KOVACS; 8 mems.

Fachverband der Lederverarbeitenden Industrie (Leather Processing): Postfach 313, Wiedner Hauptstr. 63, 1045 Vienna; tel. (0) 590900-3453; fax (0) 590900-278; e-mail fvleder@wko.at; internet www.shoes-leather.at; f. 1945; Chair. JOSEPH LORENZ; Dir PETER KOVACS; 45 mems.

Fachverband der Maschinen- und Stahlbauindustrie (Machinery and Steel Construction): Wiedner Hauptstr. 63, 1045 Vienna; tel. (1) 502-25; fax (1) 505-10-20; e-mail machinen@fms.at; internet www.fms.at; Pres. Dr CLEMENS MALINA-ALTZINGER; Dir JOHANN ZODER; 850 mems.

Fachverband der Metallwarenindustrie Österreichs (Metal Goods): Postfach 335, Wiedner Hauptstr. 63, 1045 Vienna; tel. (1) 501-05; fax (1) 505-09-28; internet www.fmwi.at; f. 1908; Chair. Ing. WOLFGANG WELSER; Gen. Man. Dr WOLFGANG LOCKER; 800 mems.

Fachverband der NE-Metallindustrie Österreichs (Austrian Non-Ferrous Metals Federation): Postfach 338, Wiedner Hauptstr. 63, 1045 Vienna; tel. (0) 590900-3309; fax (0) 590900-3378; e-mail nemetall@wko.at; f. 1946; Chair. GERHARD ESCHNER; Dir HERBERT BADRACH; 69 mems.

Fachverband der Mineralölindustrie (Petroleum): Wiedner Hauptstr. 63, 1045 Vienna; tel. (0) 590900-4892; fax (0) 590900-4895; e-mail office@oil-gas.at; internet www.oil-gas.at; f. 1947; Gen. Dirs Dr WOLFGANG RUDDENSDORFER, Dr CRISTOPH CAPEK; 21 mems.

Fachverband der Nahrungs- und Genussmittelindustrie (Provisions): Zaunergasse 1–3, 1030 Vienna; tel. (1) 712-21-21; fax (1) 713-18-02; e-mail fiaa@dielebensmittel.at; internet dielebensmittel.at; Chair. Dr RUDOLF KOBATSCH; Dir Dr MICHAEL BLASS; 280 mems.

Fachverband der Papier und Pappe verarbeitenden Industrie (Paper and Board Processing): Brucknerstr. 8, 1041 Vienna; tel. (1) 505-53-82-0; fax (1) 505-90-18; e-mail ppv@ppv.at; internet www.ppv.at; Chair. GUSTAV GLÖCKLER; 134 mems.

Fachverband der Papierindustrie (Paper): Gumpendorferstr. 6, 1061 Vienna; tel. (1) 588-86-0; fax (1) 588-86-22-2; e-mail austropapier@austropapier.at; internet www.austropapier.at; Chair. Dr VEIT SORGER; Dir Dr GEROLF OTTAWA; 30 mems.

Fachverband der Stein- und keramischen Industrie (Stone and Ceramics): Postfach 329, Wiedner Hauptstr. 63, 1045 Vienna; tel. (0) 590900-3531; fax (1) 505-62-40; e-mail steine@wko.at; internet www.baustoffindustrie.at; f. 1946; Chair. Dr CARL HENN-RICH; Pres. Dr ERHARD SCHASCHL; 400 mems.

Fachverband der Textilindustrie (Textiles): Rudolfspl. 12, 1013 Vienna; tel. (1) 533-37-26-0; fax (1) 533-37-26-40; e-mail fvtextil@fvtextil.wk.or.at; internet www.textilindustrie.at; Pres. Dr PETER PFNEISL; Dir Dr WOLFGANG ZEYRINGER; 265 mems.

Geschäftsstelle Bau (Building): Schaumburgergasse 20/8, 1010 Vienna; tel. (1) 718-37-37; e-mail office@bau.or.at; internet www.bau.or.at; formerly Fachverband der Bauindustrie; Dir Mag. MANFRED KATZENSCHLAGER; 150 mems.

UTILITIES

Electricity

Burgenländische Elektrizitätswirtschafts-AG: Kasemenstr. 9, 7001 Eisenstadt; tel. (2682) 900-01-02-1; fax (2682) 900-01-91-0; e-mail guenther.ofner@bewag.co.at; Chair. Dr GÜNTHER OFNER.

Energie-Versorgung-Niederösterreich AG (EVN): Johann-Steinboeck-Str. 1, 2344 Maria Enzersdorf; tel. (2742) 80-00; fax (2742) 80-03-60; Chair. Dr RUDOLF GRUBER.

Kärntner Elektrizitäts-AG: Arnulfpl. 2, 9020 Klagenfurt; tel. (463) 52-50; fax (463) 52-51-59-6; Chair. Dr GÜNTHER BRESITZ.

Oberösterreichische Kraftwerke AG: Böhmerwaldstr. 3, 4020 Linz; tel. (732) 65-93-0; fax (732) 65-93-36-00; Chair. Dr LEOPOLD WINDTNER.

Österreichische Elektrizitätswirtschafts-AG: Am Hof 6A, 1010 Vienna; tel. (1) 531-13-0; fax (1) 531-13-41-91; e-mail info@pol.verbund.co.at; internet www.verbund.co.at/verbund; federal electricity authority; operates national grid, wholesales electricity to the nine regional operators; Dir HANS HAIDER.

Salzburg AG für Energie, Verkehr und Telekommunikation: Bayerhamerstr. 16, 5021 Salzburg; tel. (662) 88-84-0; fax (662) 88-84-17-0; e-mail offic@salzburg-ag.at; internet www.salzburg-ag.at.

Steirische Wasserkraft- und Elektrizitäts-AG: Leonhardgurtel 10, 8011 Graz; tel. (316) 3870; fax (316) 387290; Chair. Dr OSWIN KOIS.

Tiroler Wasserkraftwerke AG: Landhauspl., 6010 Innsbruck; tel. (512) 50-60; fax (512) 50-62-12-6; Chair. Dr HELMUT MAYR.

Vorarlberger Kraftwerke AG: Weidachstr. 6, 6900 Bregenz; tel. (5574) 601-0; fax (5574) 601-50-0; e-mail energie@vkw.at; internet www.vkw.at; Chair. Dr LEO WAGNER, Dr OTTO WAIBEL.

WienStrom GmbH: Mariannegasse 4, 1095 Vienna; tel. (1) 400-43-00-00; fax (1) 400-43-00-99; e-mail vavra@wienstrom.co.at; internet www.wienstrom.co.at; f. 1902; Chair. HELMUT KASTL.

Gas

BEGAS (Burgenländische Erdgasversorgungs AG): Kasernenstr. 10, 7000 Eisenstadt; tel. (2682) 709-0; fax (2682) 709-174; internet www.begas.at; Chair. RUDOLF SIMANDL, REINHARD SCHWEIFER.

Oberösterreichische Ferngas-AG: Neubauzeile 99, 4030 Linz; tel. (732) 38-83; fax (732) 37-72-19; Chair. MAX DOBRUCKT.

Steirische Ferngas-AG: Gaslaternenweg 4, 8041 Graz; tel. (316) 476-0; fax (316) 476-28-000; e-mail info@steirische.ferngas.at; internet www.steirische.ferngas.at; Chair. DOMINIQUE BAYEN, PETER KÖBERL, MAX PÖLZL.

Water

Österreichischer Wasser- und Abfallwirtschaftsverband (ÖWAV) (Austrian Water and Waste Management Asscn): Marc-Aurel-Str. 5, 1010 Vienna; tel. (1) 535-57-20-0; fax (1) 535-40-64; e-mail buero@oewav.at; internet www.oewav.at.

TRADE UNIONS

Österreichischer Gewerkschaftsbund (ÖGB) (Austrian Trade Union Fed.): Hohenstaufengasse 10–12, 1010 Vienna; tel. (1) 534-44; fax (1) 534-44-20-4; e-mail oegb@oegb.or.at; internet www.oegb.or.at; non-party union org. with voluntary membership; f. 1945; org. affiliated with ICFTU and the European Trade Union Confederation

(ETUC); Pres. FRIEDRICH VERZETNITSCH; Exec. Sec. ROSWITHA BACHNER; 1,428,409 mems (Sept. 2001); comprises the following 13 trade unions.

Gewerkschaft Agrar-Nahrung-Genuss (Agricultural, Food, Beverage and Tobacco Workers): Albertgasse 35, 1081 Vienna; tel. (1) 401-49; fax (1) 401-49-20; e-mail ang@ang.oegb.or.at; Chair. Dr LEOPOLD SIMPERL.

Gewerkschaft Bau-Holz (Building Workers and Woodworkers): Ebendorferstr. 7, 1010 Vienna; tel. (1) 401-47; fax (1) 401-47-314; e-mail sonja.schmid@gbh.oegb.or.at; Chair. JOHANN DRIEMER; 171,000 mems (1997).

Gewerkschaft der Chemiearbeiter (Chemical Workers): Stumpergasse 60, 1060 Vienna; tel. (1) 597-15-01; fax (1) 597-21-01-23; Chair. WILHELM BECK; 51,172 mems (1993).

Gewerkschaft Druck, Journalismus und Papier (Printing, Journalism and Paper Trade Workers): Postfach 91, Seidengasse 15–17, 1070 Vienna; tel. (1) 523-82-31; fax (1) 523-81-32-28; e-mail gewdu@netway.at; f. 1842; Chair. FRANZ BITTNER; 18,023 mems (1999).

Gewerkschaft der Eisenbahner (Railwaymen): Margaretenstr. 166, 1051 Vienna; tel. (1) 546-41-50-0; fax (1) 546-41-50-4; e-mail gde@gde.oegb.or.at; Chair. WILHELM HABERZETTL; 100,000 mems (2000).

Gewerkschaft der Gemeindebediensteten (Municipal Employees): Maria-Theresien-Str. 11, 1090 Vienna; tel. (1) 313-16-0; fax (1) 313-16-7701; e-mail gdg@gdg.oegb.or.at; internet www.gdg.at; Chair. RUDOLF HUNDSTORFER; 171,978 mems (2003).

Gewerkschaft Handel, Transport, Verkehr (Workers in Commerce and Transport): Teinfaltstr. 7, 1010 Vienna; tel. (1) 534-54; fax (1) 534-54-32-5; f. 1904; Chair. WILLIBALD STEINKELLNER.

Gewerkschaft Hotel, Gastgewerbe, Persönlicher Dienst (Hotel and Restaurant Workers): Hohenstaufengasse 10, 1013 Vienna; tel. (1) 534-44; fax (1) 534-44-50-5; e-mail hgpd@hgpd.oegb.or.at; f. 1906; Chair. RUDOLF KASKE; 48,697 mems (2003).

Gewerkschaft Kunst, Medien, Sport, freie Berufe (Musicians, Actors, Artists, Journalists, etc.): Maria-Theresien-Str. 11, 1090 Vienna; tel. (1) 313-16; fax (1) 313-16-77-00; e-mail sekretariat@kmsfb.oegb.or.at; f. 1945; Chair. PETER PAUL SKREPEK; Sec.-Gen. Dr HERBERT STEGMÜLLER; 11,603 mems (2003).

Gewerkschaft Metall-Textil (Metal Workers, Miners and Power Supply Workers and Textile, Leather and Garment Industry Workers): Plösslgasse 15, 1041 Vienna; tel. (1) 501-46-0; fax (1) 501-46-13-30-0; e-mail international@metaller.at; internet www.metaller.at; following merger of Gewerkschaft Metall-Bergbau-Energie (f. 1890) and Gewerkschaft Textil, Bekleidung, Leder (f. 1945); Chair. RUDOLF NÜRNBERGER; 202,725 mems (2004).

Gewerkschaft Öffentlicher Dienst (Public Employees): Teinfaltstr. 7, 1010 Vienna; tel. (1) 534-54-0; fax (1) 534-54-207; e-mail goed@goed.at; internet www.goed.at; f. 1945; Chair. FRITZ NEUGEBAUER; Gen. Secs Dr MANFRED MÖGELE, REGINA BAUER-ALBRECHT, ERICH RUDOLF; 230,000 mems (2002).

Gewerkschaft der Post- und Fernmeldebediensteten (Postal and Telegraph Workers): Postfach 343, Biberstr. 5, 1010 Vienna; tel. (1) 512-55-11; fax (1) 512-55-11/52; e-mail gpf@gpf.oegb.or.at; Chair. GERHARD FRITZ; 66,756 mems (2003).

Gewerkschaft der Privatangestellten (Commercial, Clerical and Technical Employees): Deutschmeisterpl. 2, 1013 Vienna; tel. and fax (1) 313-93; e-mail gpa@gpa.at; internet www.gpa.at; Chair. HANS SALLMUTTER; 301,046 mems (1997).

Bundesfraktion Christlicher Gewerkschafter im Österreichischen Gewerkschaftsbund (FCG) (Christian Trade Unionists' Section of the Austrian Trade Union Fed.): Hohenstaufengasse 12, 1010 Vienna; tel. (1) 534-44-269; e-mail stefan.stoeger@fcg.at; internet www.fcg.at; organized in Christian Trade Unionists' Sections of the above 13 trade unions; affiliated to WCL; Sec.-Gen. Mag. STEFAN STOEGER.

Transport

RAILWAYS

Österreichische Bundesbahnen (ÖBB—Austrian Federal Railways) operates more than 90% of all the railway routes in Austria. In 2002 there were 6,579 km of track, of which ÖBB operated 5,648 km; all main lines were electrified.

Österreichische Bundesbahnen (ÖBB) (Austrian Federal Railways): Head Office: Elisabethstr. 9, 1010 Vienna; tel. (1) 930-00-0; fax (1) 930-00-25010; e-mail stab.kom@kom.oebb.at; internet www.oebb.at; CEO and Chair. Bd of Management RÜDIGER VORM WALDE.

Innsbruck Divisional Management: Claudiastr. 2, 6020 Innsbruck; tel. (512) 50-33-00-0; fax (512) 50-35-00-5; Dir JOHANN LINDENBERGER.

Linz Divisional Management: Bahnhofstr. 3, 4021 Linz; tel. (732) 69-09-0; fax (732) 69-09-18-33; Dir HELMUTH AFLENZER; Vice-Dir KLAUS SEEBACHER.

Vienna Divisional Management: Nordbahnstr. 50, 1020 Vienna; tel. (1) 580-05-00-00; fax (1) 580-02-56-01; Dir FRANZ POLZER.

Villach Divisional Management: 10-Oktober-Str. 20, 9501 Villach; tel. (4242) 20-20-32-00; fax (4242) 20-20-32-29; e-mail willibald.schicho@gv.oebb.at; internet www.railcargo.at; Dir WILLIBALD SCHICHO.

Other railway companies include: Achenseebahn AG, AG der Wiener Lokalbahnen, Graz-Köflacher Eisenbahn- und Bergbau GmbH, Lokalbahn, Montafonerbahn AG, Raab-Oedenburg-Ebenfurter Eisenbahn, Salzburger Stadtwerke AG-Verkehrsbetriebe, Steiermärkische Lokalbahnen, Stern & Hafferl Verkehrs GmbH, Zillertaler Verkehrsbetriebe AG.

ROADS

At 1 January 2002 Austria had 133,636 km of classified roads, of which 1,645 km were modern motorways, 10,334 km main roads, 23,657 km secondary roads and 98,000 km other roads.

INLAND WATERWAYS

The Danube (Donau) is Austria's only navigable river. It enters Austria from Germany at Passau and flows into Slovakia near Hainburg. The length of the Austrian section of the river is 351 km. Danube barges carry up to 1,800 metric tons, but loading depends on the water level, which varies considerably throughout the year. Cargoes are chiefly petroleum and derivatives, coal, coke, iron ore, iron, steel, timber and grain. The Rhine-Main-Danube Canal opened in 1992. A passenger service is maintained on the Upper Danube and between Vienna and the Black Sea. Passenger services are also provided on Bodensee (Lake Constance) and Wolfgangsee by Austrian Federal Railways, and on all the larger Austrian lakes.

CIVIL AVIATION

The main international airport is located at Schwechat, near Vienna. There are also international flights from Graz, Innsbruck, Klagenfurt, Linz and Salzburg, and internal flights between these cities.

Principal Airlines

Austrian Airlines (Österreichische Luftverkehrs AG): Fontanastr. 1, 1107 Vienna; tel. (1) 517-66; fax (1) 688-55-05; e-mail public.relations@aua.com; internet www.aua.com; f. 1957; 39.7% state-owned; serves 116 cities in 64 countries world-wide; Chair. RAINER WIELTSCH; Pres. VAGN SÖRENSEN.

Austrian Airtransport (AAT): Postfach 50, Fontanastr. 1, 1107 Vienna; tel. (1) 688-16-91; fax (1) 688-11-91; f. 1964; 80% owned by Austrian Airlines, from which it leases most of its aircraft; operates scheduled and charter flights for passengers and cargo, and tour services; Man. Dir Dr HERBERT KOSCHIER.

Lauda Air Luftfahrt AG: Postfach 56, Lauda Air Bldg, 1300 Vienna-Schwechat; tel. (1) 7000-0; fax (1) 7000-790-15; e-mail office@laudaair.com; internet www.laudaair.com; f. 1979; became a scheduled carrier 1987; 47% owned by Austrian Airlines; operates scheduled passenger services and charter flights to Europe, Australia, the Far East and the USA; Chair. FERDINAND SCHMIDT.

Tiroler Luftfahrt GmbH (Tyrolean Airways): Postfach 98, Fürstenweg 176, 6026 Innsbruck; tel. (512) 22-22-0; fax (512) 28-66-46; e-mail pressestelle@tyrolean.at; internet www.aua.com; f. 1978 as Aircraft Innsbruck; adopted present name 1980; operates scheduled services and charter flights within Austria and to other European countries; Pres. and Chief Exec. (vacant); Man. Dir JOHANN MESSNER.

Tourism

Tourism plays an important part in the Austrian economy. Following a decline in the number of foreign visitors and the consequent decrease in tourism receipts during the mid-1990s, the sector showed signs of recovery in the late 1990s and early 2000s. In 2002 Austria received 18.6m. foreign visitors at accommodation establishments (compared with 18.2m. in 2001) and receipts from the tourism sector rose by 11.1% to reach €11,237m. The country's mountain scenery attracts visitors in both summer and winter, while Vienna and Salzburg, hosts to a number of internationally-renowned arts festivals, are important cultural centres.

Österreich Werbung (Austrian National Tourist Office): Margaretenstr. 1, 1040 Vienna; tel. (1) 588-66-0; fax (1) 588-66-20; internet www.austria.info; f. 1955.

AZERBAIJAN

Introductory Survey

Location, Climate, Language, Religion, Flag, Capital

The Azerbaijan Republic is situated in eastern Transcaucasia, on the western coast of the Caspian Sea. To the south it borders Iran, to the west Armenia, to the north-west Georgia, and to the north the Republic of Dagestan, in Russia. The Naxçivan (Nakh-chivan) Autonomous Republic is part of Azerbaijan, although it is separated from the rest of Azerbaijan by Armenian territory. Azerbaijan also includes the territory of the former Nagorno-Karabakh Autonomous Oblast (Nagornyi Karabakh), which is largely populated by Armenians. The Kura plain has a dry, temperate climate with an average July temperature of 27°C (80°F) and an average January temperature of 1°C (34°F). Average annual rainfall on the lowlands is 200 mm–300 mm, but the Lankaran (Lenkoran) plain normally receives between 1,000 mm and 1,750 mm. The official language is Azerbaijani, one of the South Turkic group of languages. Religious adherence corresponds largely to ethnic origins: almost all ethnic Azerbaijanis are Muslims, some 70% being Shi'ite and 30% Sunni. There are also Christian communities, mainly representatives of the Russian Orthodox and Armenian Apostolic denominations. The national flag (proportions 1 by 2) consists of three equal horizontal stripes, of pale blue, red and green, with a white crescent moon framing a white eight-pointed star on the central red stripe. The capital is Baku (Bakı).

Recent History

An independent state in ancient times, Azerbaijan was dominated for much of its subsequent history by foreign powers. Under the Treaty of Turkmanchai of 1828, Azerbaijan was divided between Persia (now Iran) and Russia. During the latter half of the 19th century petroleum was discovered in Azerbaijan, and by 1900 the region had become one of the world's leading petroleum producers. Immigrant Slavs began to dominate Baku and other urban areas.

After the October Revolution of 1917 in Russia, there was a short period of pro-Bolshevik rule in Baku before a nationalist Government took power and established an independent state on 28 May 1918, with Ganca (Gyanja—formerly Elisavetpol, but renamed Kirovabad in 1935) as the capital. Independent Azerbaijan was occupied by troops of both the Allied and Central Powers; after their withdrawal, it was invaded by the Red Army in April 1920, and on 28 April a Soviet Republic of Azerbaijan was established. In December 1922 the republic became a member of the Transcaucasian Soviet Federative Socialist Republic (TSFSR), a constituent republic of the newly formed USSR. The TSFSR was disbanded in 1936, and Azerbaijan became a full union republic, the Azerbaijan Soviet Socialist Republic (SSR).

Following the Soviet seizure of power in 1920, many nationalist and religious leaders and activists were persecuted or killed. In 1930–31 forced collectivization of agriculture led to peasant uprisings, which were suppressed by Soviet troops. The purges of 1937–38, under the Soviet leader, Stalin (Iosif V. Dzhugashvili), involved the execution or imprisonment of many prominent members of the Communist Party of Azerbaijan (CPA). In 1945 the Soviet Government attempted to unite the Azerbaijani population of northern Iran with the Azerbaijan SSR, by providing military support for a local 'puppet' government in Iran; Soviet troops were forced to withdraw from Iran in the following year by US-British opposition.

In 1982 Heydar Aliyev, First Secretary of the CPA since 1969, was promoted to First Deputy Chairman of the USSR Council of Ministers, based in the Russian and Soviet capital, Moscow, while retaining his republican office; he remained an influential figure at all-Union level until his dismissal from the Politburo in October 1987, amid popular dissatisfaction at widespread corruption within Azerbaijan. Unlike most Soviet republics, Azerbaijan had an annual trade surplus with the rest of the USSR, and yet its income per head was the lowest outside Central Asia. Public grievances over economic mismanagement and the privileges enjoyed by the party leadership were expressed at demonstrations in November 1988, when protesters occupied the main square in Baku for 10 days, before being dispersed by troops.

The initial impetus, however, for the demonstrations was the debate on the status of Nagornyi Karabakh (a nominally autonomous oblast—region—within Azerbaijan—known as Artsakh in Armenian) and Naxçivan (an exclave of Azerbaijan, with the status of Autonomous Republic, separated from metropolitan Azerbaijan by Armenia). Both territories were claimed by Armenia, on historical grounds, and Nagornyi Karabakh had a majority of Armenians, who are distinguished from ethnic Azerbaijanis (Azeris) by both language and religion, among its population. Naxçivan, despite the apparent surrender of Azerbaijan's claims to the territory in 1920, never became part of Soviet Armenia, and Azerbaijani jurisdiction over the territory had been guaranteed by the Soviet-Turkish Treaty of March 1921. (The 45%–50% of the republic's population that had been ethnically Armenian in 1919 had declined to less than 5% by 1989.) Nagornyi Karabakh had been a disputed territory during the period of Armenian and Azerbaijani independence (1918–20), but in June 1921 the Bolshevik Bureau for Caucasian Affairs (Kavburo) voted to unite Nagornyi Karabakh with Armenia. However, shortly afterwards, following an intervention by Iosif Dzhugashvili (Stalin), the decision was reversed. In 1923 the territory was declared an autonomous oblast within Azerbaijan. There were attempts to challenge Azerbaijani jurisdiction over the region, including two petitions by the inhabitants of Nagornyi Karabakh in the 1960s, but they were strongly opposed by the Soviet and Azerbaijani authorities.

Conflict over the territory re-emerged in February 1988, when the Nagornyi Karabakh regional soviet (council) requested the Armenian and Azerbaijani Supreme Soviets to agree to the transfer of the territory to Armenia. The Soviet and Azerbaijani authorities rejected the request, thus provoking huge demonstrations by Armenians in both Nagornyi Karabakh and in Yerevan, the capital of Armenia. Azeris began leaving Armenia, and reports that refugees had been attacked led to three days of anti-Armenian violence in the Azerbaijani town of Sumqayıt (Sumgait). According to official figures, 32 people died, 26 of whom were Armenians. Disturbances over the issue of Nagornyi Karabakh continued, leading to a large-scale exodus of refugees from both Armenia and Azerbaijan. In January 1989, in an attempt to end the tension, the Soviet Government suspended the activities of the local authorities in Nagornyi Karabakh and established a Special Administration Committee (SAC), responsible to the USSR Council of Ministers. Although it was stressed that the region would formally retain its status as an autonomous oblast within Azerbaijan, the decision was widely viewed by Azerbaijanis as an infringement of the country's territorial integrity. This imposition of 'direct rule' from Moscow and the dispatch of some 5,000 Soviet troops did little to reduce tensions within Nagornyi Karabakh, where ethnic Armenians went on strike from May until September.

In mid-1989 the nationalist Popular Front of Azerbaijan (PFA) was established. Following sporadic strikes and demonstrations throughout August, the PFA organized a national strike in early September and demanded discussion on the issue of sovereignty, the situation in Nagornyi Karabakh, the release of political prisoners and official recognition of the PFA. After one week, the Azerbaijan Supreme Soviet (Supreme Majlis or Supreme Council) agreed to concessions to the PFA, including official recognition. On 23 September the republican Supreme Soviet adopted a 'Constitutional Law on the Sovereignty of the Azerbaijan SSR', effectively a declaration of sovereignty. The conflict with Armenia continued, and Azerbaijan closed its borders and prohibited all trade with Armenia. In November the Soviet Government transferred control of Nagornyi Karabakh from the SAC to an Organizing Committee, dominated by Azeris. The Armenian Supreme Soviet denounced this decision and declared Nagornyi Karabakh to be part of a 'unified Armenian republic', prompting further outbreaks of violence in Nagornyi Karabakh and along the Armenian–Azerbaijani border. Growing unrest within Azerbaijan, exacerbated by the influx of refugees from Armenia, was directed both at the local communist regime and at ethnic Armenians.

In January 1990 radical members of the PFA led assaults on CPA and government buildings in Baku and other towns. Border posts were attacked on the Soviet–Iranian border, and nationalist activists seized CPA buildings in Naxçıvan. Meanwhile, renewed violence against Armenians, with some 60 people killed in rioting in Baku, led to a hasty evacuation of the remaining non-Azeris from the city. On 19 January a state of emergency was declared in Azerbaijan, and Soviet troops were ordered into Baku, where the PFA was in control. According to official reports, 131 people were killed, and some 700 wounded, during the Soviet intervention. The inability of the CPA to ensure stability in the republic led to the dismissal of Abdul Vezirov as First Secretary of the party; he was replaced by Ayaz Mutalibov.

Despite the arrest of leading members of the PFA and the outlawing of other nationalist organizations, continuing unrest caused the scheduled election to the republic's Supreme Soviet to be postponed until September–October, and the continuing state of emergency, which prohibited large public meetings, severely disrupted campaigning by the opposition. When the new Supreme Soviet convened in February 1991, some 80% of its deputies were members of the CPA. The small group of opposition deputies united as the Democratic Bloc of Azerbaijan.

Unlike the other Caucasian republics (Armenia and Georgia), Azerbaijan declared a willingness to sign a new Union Treaty and participated in the all-Union referendum on the preservation of the USSR, which took place in March 1991. Official results of the referendum demonstrated a qualified support for the preservation of the USSR, with 75.1% of the electorate participating, of whom 93.3% voted for a 'renewed federation'. In Naxçıvan, however, only some 20% of eligible voters approved the proposal.

In August 1991, following the attempted seizure of power in Moscow by the conservative communist 'State Committee for the State of Emergency', Mutalibov issued a statement that appeared to demonstrate support for the coup. Despite denials that he had supported the coup leaders, large demonstrations took place, demanding his resignation; the declaration of Azerbaijan's independence; the repeal of the state of emergency; and the postponement of the presidential election, scheduled for 8 September. The opposition was supported by Heydar Aliyev, by this time Chairman of the Supreme Majlis (legislature) of Naxçıvan. Mutalibov responded by ending the state of emergency and resigning as First Secretary of the CPA; on 30 August the Azerbaijani Supreme Soviet voted to 'restore the independent status of Azerbaijan'. The election to the presidency proceeded, although it was boycotted by the opposition, with the result that Mutalibov was the only candidate. According to official results, he won 84% of the total votes cast. At a congress of the CPA, held later in September, it was agreed to dissolve the party.

Independence was formally declared on 18 October 1991. Following the adoption of legislation allowing for the creation of national armed forces, Azerbaijani units began to take control of the Soviet Army's military facilities in the republic. However, Azerbaijan did join the Commonwealth of Independent States (CIS, see p. 189), signing the Almaty (Alma-Ata) Declaration on 21 December.

Following the dissolution of the USSR, hostilities intensified in Nagornyi Karabakh. In March 1992 President Mutalibov resigned, owing to military reverses by Azeri forces. He was replaced, on an interim basis, by Yagub Mamedov, the Chairman of the Milli Majlis, or National Assembly (which had replaced the Supreme Majlis following its suspension in late 1991), pending a presidential election in June. However, further military reverses, including the occupation of Azerbaijani territory between Nagornyi Karabakh and Armenia by ethnic Armenian forces, and the consequent expulsion from these areas of Azeris, prompted the Majlis to reinstate Mutalibov as President in May. His immediate declaration of a state of emergency and the cancellation of the forthcoming presidential election outraged the PFA, which organized a large-scale protest rally in Baku. The demonstrators occupied both the Majlis building and the presidential palace, and succeeded in deposing Mutalibov, who subsequently took refuge in Russia. The PFA's effective takeover was consolidated in June, when the party's leader, Abulfaz Elchibey, was elected President of Azerbaijan by direct popular vote, defeating four other candidates by a substantial margin. Meanwhile, the Government had to contend with a steadily deteriorating economic situation. Severe shortages of food and fuel were reported throughout the country, and the Government's failure to provide adequate support for an esti-

mated 500,000 refugees prompted protests in Baku from mid-1992.

The military defeats and continuing economic decline severely undermined the Government and led to divisions within the PFA in early 1993. In June a rebel army, led by Col Surat Husseinov (the former Azerbaijani military commander in Nagornyi Karabakh), seized the city of Ganca and advanced towards Baku, with the apparent intention of deposing Elchibey. In an attempt to bolster his leadership, Elchibey summoned Heydar Aliyev to the capital, and in mid-June Aliyev was elected Chairman of the legislature. Following Elchibey's subsequent flight from the capital, Aliyev announced that he had assumed the powers of the presidency. There ensued what appeared to be a power struggle between Aliyev and Husseinov, following the bloodless capture of Baku by the rebel forces. However, in late June virtually all presidential powers were transferred, on an acting basis, to Aliyev by the Milli Majlis (which had voted to impeach Elchibey), and Husseinov was appointed Prime Minister, with control over the security services. A referendum of confidence in Elchibey (who had taken refuge in Naxçıvan and still laid claim to the presidency) was held in late August 1993; of the 92% of the electorate that participated, 97.5% voted against him. The Milli Majlis endorsed the result and announced the holding of a direct presidential election, which took place on 3 October. Aliyev was elected President of Azerbaijan, with 98.8% of the votes cast. In the months preceding the election there was an escalation of opposition harassment, particularly of the PFA, which boycotted the election in protest.

The domestic political situation remained tense during 1994. Opponents of President Aliyev and his New Azerbaijan Party (NAP) were subject to increasing harassment, and their media activities were severely restricted. In February over 40 PFA members were arrested at a regional party conference, and in March more than 100 people were arrested at the PFA headquarters in Baku; it was claimed that the organization had been planning to overthrow the Government. The signature, in May, of a cease-fire agreement in Nagornyi Karabakh (see below) led to further unrest in Azerbaijan, and large-scale anti-Government demonstrations were organized by the PFA in Baku in May and September.

A new political crisis arose in September 1994 when the Deputy Chairman of the Milli Majlis and Aliyev's security chief were assassinated; three members of the special militia (known as OPON) attached to the Ministry of Internal Affairs were subsequently arrested. In early October some 100 OPON troops, led by Rovshan Javadov, stormed the office of the Procurator-General, taking him and his officials hostage and securing the release of the three OPON members in custody. Aliyev described the incident as an attempted coup and declared a state of emergency in Baku and Ganca.

In the immediate aftermath of these events, other forces mutinied in Baku and elsewhere in Azerbaijan. In Ganca, rebel forces occupied government and strategic buildings, although troops loyal to Aliyev quickly re-established control. Despite Husseinov's assurances of allegiance to Aliyev, he was dismissed as Prime Minister, and replaced, on an acting basis, by Fuad Kuliyev. However, Aliyev stated that he would head the Government for the immediate future, and initiated a series of purges of senior members of the Government and the armed forces. In mid-October 1994 the Milli Majlis voted unanimously to remove Husseinov's parliamentary immunity from prosecution, so that he could be arrested on charges of treason (he was, however, believed to have fled to Russia).

Further political turmoil arose in March 1995, following a decree by the Government to disband the OPON militia (which had remained under the control of Javadov). OPON forces seized government and police buildings in Baku and in north-western Azerbaijan, and many casualties were reported, as government forces clashed with the OPON units. The rebellion was crushed when government troops stormed the OPON headquarters near Baku; Javadov and many of his men were killed, and some 160 rebels were arrested. Aliyev accused former President Elchibey and Surat Husseinov of collusion in the attempted coup. Subsequently, the PFA was also accused of involvement, and the party was banned. In early April Aliyev extended the state of emergency in Baku until June, although that in Ganca was lifted. In May Kuliyev was confirmed as Prime Minister, although unrest continued in subsequent months.

Elections to the new, 125-member Milli Majlis took place, as scheduled, on 12 November 1995. Of Azerbaijan's 31 officially registered parties, only eight were permitted to participate; of these, only two were opposition parties—the PFA (recently relegalized) and the National Independence Party (NIP). Almost 600 nominally independent candidates were barred from participation. The elections were held under a mixed system of voting: 25 seats were to be filled by proportional representation on the basis of party lists and the remaining 100 by majority voting in single-member constituencies. These included the constituencies within Nagornyi Karabakh and of the other territories occupied by ethnic Armenian forces (refugees from those regions voted in areas under Azerbaijani control, in anticipation of the eventual restoration of the country's territorial integrity). The results demonstrated widespread support for Aliyev's NAP, which won 19 of the 25 party-list seats (with the PFA and the NIP receiving three seats each). The NAP and independent candidates supporting Aliyev won an overwhelming majority of single-constituency seats. Of the remaining 28 seats in the Majlis, 27 were filled at 'run-off' elections held in late November 1995 and in February 1996, and one seat remained vacant. Some international observers declared that the elections had not been free and fair and that 'serious electoral violations' had occurred. Concurrently with the election of the Milli Majlis, Azerbaijan's new Constitution was approved by an overwhelming majority of the electorate (officially, 91.9%) in a national referendum. The Constitution provided for a secular state, headed by the President, who was accorded wide-ranging executive powers.

In early 1996 supporters of Husseinov and Elchibey received lengthy custodial sentences for their involvement in the alleged coup attempts of October 1994 and March 1995. In February 1996 two former government members were sentenced to death on charges of treason and several others were sentenced to death on conspiracy charges in the following months. Former President Mutalibov, whom Aliyev had accused of conspiring with Javadov, was arrested in Russia in April. However the Russian authorities refused to extradite him, on the grounds of insufficient evidence. Repressive measures against the opposition continued, with the seizure by the police of the PFA headquarters in April 1996. Several members of the party were later arrested. In July Fuad Kuliyev resigned from the office of Prime Minister, officially on grounds of ill health, after he was accused by Aliyev of hindering the process of reform; Artur Rasizade, hitherto first Deputy Prime Minister, was appointed Prime Minister, initially in an acting capacity. In September the Chairman of the Milli Majlis, Rasul Kuliyev, who had been criticized by the NAP, resigned. Murtuz Aleskerov, a staunch supporter of Aliyev, was elected in his place.

In January 1997 the authorities released details of an abortive coup in October 1996, which had reportedly been organized by, among others, Mutalibov and Surat Husseinov. Charges were subsequently brought against some 40 alleged conspirators; in early 1997 many people received prison sentences for their part in the attempted coups of October 1994 and March 1995. Husseinov was extradited from Russia in March 1997, and he was sentenced to life imprisonment in February 1999, but received a presidential pardon in March 2004.

In January 1998 the Azerbaijani authorities accused Rasul Kuliyev (who was resident in the USA) of organizing a conspiracy to depose President Aliyev. In April Kuliyev, who denied the accusations, was charged *in absentia* with alleged abuses of power while Chairman of the Milli Majlis. (Further charges were brought against him in October 2000.) In May 1998 legislation was passed creating a 24-member Central Electoral Commission, 12 members of which were to be directly appointed by the President, and 12 by the legislature. A law regarding presidential elections was approved in June, which required candidates to collect 50,000 signatures to stand, and set a minimum level of voter participation of 50%, although this was reduced to 25% in July. The opposition protested that the law favoured Aliyev's re-election, and launched a series of demonstrations to demand the cancellation of the election, which was scheduled to be held in October. In mid-September police and demonstrators clashed violently in Baku, resulting in a number of arrests. Subsequent demonstrations were conducted peacefully, following the imposition of new restrictions on public protests.

The presidential election was held, as planned, on 11 October 1998; according to official results, Heydar Aliyev was re-elected with 77.6% of the votes cast. Five other candidates contested the election, which was criticized by the Organization for Security and Co-operation in Europe (OSCE, see p. 314) and the Council of Europe (see p. 199) for failing to meet international democratic standards. Unrest continued, owing to the opposition's

dissatisfaction with the validity of the results. In late October the majority of government ministers, including Prime Minister Rasizade, were reconfirmed in their positions by President Aliyev. In late December the Milli Majlis approved a revised Constitution for Naxçıvan, which defined the enclave as an 'autonomous state' within Azerbaijan. The amended Constitution had earlier been endorsed by the Naxçıvan legislature, the Ali Majlis (Supreme Assembly).

In the first half of 1999 Aliyev's poor health caused fears of instability and reports circulated that he was preparing his son İlham (the Vice-Chairman of the State Oil Company of the Azerbaijan Republic—SOCAR) to assume the presidency. Meanwhile, in April parliamentarians of the Democratic Congress, which comprised a total of 17 deputies, including those of the PFA and the Civic Solidarity Party (CSP), began a boycott of the Milli Majlis, owing to conflict over draft legislation on municipal elections. The boycott was ended in late June following negotiations with the Government, and Azerbaijan's first municipal elections since independence were held in December, thereby fulfilling a prerequisite for membership of the Council of Europe. However, mass electoral violations were observed and repeat elections were subsequently held in those constituencies where the results had been deemed invalid.

In April 2000 a demonstration, attended by up to 20,000 people, was organized by the Democratic Congress, which demanded the introduction of measures to ensure that the legislative elections due to be held in November would be free and fair. Many arrests were made, and the security forces were accused of using excessive force. The death, in August, of Elchibey prompted divisions to emerge within the PFA, which divided into traditionalist and reformist factions; the Central Electoral Commission recognized only the reformist wing, led by Ali Kerimli. In September the Central Electoral Commission refused to register eight opposition parties. Although the Commission's decision was revoked, following strong criticism from the US Government, a number of political parties decided to boycott the legislative elections, which they condemned as undemocratic. The Democratic Congress was forced to restructure in October, when five parties, including the reformist branch of the PFA, withdrew.

The legislative elections, held, as scheduled, on 5 November 2000, were condemned by the OSCE for the falsification of results and intimidatory practices, and country-wide protests followed. Of the 25 seats filled by proportional representation, 17 were obtained by the NAP and four by the PFA, while the CPA and the CSP each secured two seats in the legislature. Of the 99 seats contested in single-mandate constituencies, 62 were obtained by the NAP and 26 by independent candidates. The election results were invalidated in 11 constituencies; repeat elections were held on 7 January 2001. Ultimately, the reformist faction of the PFA reversed an earlier decision to reject the legitimacy of the legislature and took up its seats in the Milli Majlis, as did the CSP. Divisions within the NAP became increasingly evident during 2001, with the emergence of a faction known as the '91st' group, the members of which were largely excluded from the party's political council, following a party congress held in November. Aliyev was re-elected as Chairman of the NAP and İlham Aliyev was elected to the newly established post of First Deputy Chairman. In June 2002 President Aliyev confirmed his intention to stand for re-election in 2003.

On 24 August 2002 a referendum was held to seek approval for 39 proposed amendments to the Constitution, among the most notable of which were proposals for executive power to be transferred to the (presidentially appointed) prime minister, rather than the elected chairman of the Milli Majlis, in the event of the president's inability to govern; and for the outcome of the presidential election to be determined by a straightforward majority of the votes cast, rather than the existing pre-requisite of two-thirds. According to the official results of the plebiscite, 96% of votes (cast by 84% of the electorate) were in favour of the constitutional amendments, although demonstrations followed, after reports by both opposition parties and observers from the OSCE and the USA of fraud and procedural violations. The amendments were subsequently approved by the Council of Europe, but large-scale protest rallies took place from September, to demand: the annulment of the results of the referendum; the holding of free and fair elections; and the resignation of President Aliyev. A number of opposition members were arrested. Following a protest rally against repression of the media, held in December, the Editor-in-Chief of the leading opposition newspaper, *Yeni Müsavat*, and 11 other journalists began a hunger strike, in protest at legal action against the publication by representatives of the Government, and alleged physical assaults on its staff. Large-scale protest demonstrations demanding Aliyev's resignation continued into early 2003.

In April 2003 President Aliyev collapsed while delivering a televised speech, and in subsequent months he reportedly travelled to Turkey and the USA for medical treatment. In May opposition demonstrations took place to demand the President's resignation. Eventually, on 4 August an emergency session of the Milli Majlis approved İlham Aliyev's appointment as Prime Minister (which, under the constitutional amendments approved in 2002, enabled him to assume executive power). Two days later Artur Rasizade assumed the premiership, on an acting basis, to allow İlham Aliyev to campaign for the presidential election, scheduled to take place in October. In early October it was announced that Heydar Aliyev was formally to withdraw his candidacy, in favour of his son. Meanwhile, opposition demonstrations in September had resulted in violent clashes with the security forces.

The fractured opposition failed to consolidate support in favour of one principal candidate, and İlham Aliyev secured 79.5% of the votes cast in the presidential election, held on 15 October 2003. The second-placed candidate, the Chairman of the Müsavat (Equality) party, İsa Qambar, obtained only 12.1% of the votes cast, according to official results. However, both international observers and opposition parties reported widespread electoral malpractice. The opposition subsequently refused to recognize the validity of the election results and opposition protests, led by Müsavat, were violently repressed by the authorities; there were reports of a number of deaths. Many protesters were arrested and press restrictions were imposed, prompting international condemnation of the deteriorating human rights situation. İlham Aliyev was inaugurated as President at the end of October. The nomination of Rasizade as Prime Minister was approved by the Milli Majlis on 4 November, and the majority of ministers in the previous administration were subsequently reappointed to the Government. Heydar Aliyev's death was announced in mid-December.

In the months following his election as President, İlham Aliyev implemented measures that were regarded as seeking to consolidate his position, including the announcement of new appointments to several senior government posts. In February 2004 Aliyev dismissed Nadir Akhmedov as Minister of Communications, replacing him with Ali Abbasov. In April Aliyev appointed a career diplomat, Elmar Mammedyarov, as Minister of Foreign Affairs, and in July dismissed Namik Abbasov as Minister of National Security, a position Abbasov had held for some 10 years, amid speculation that Abbasov might have represented a potential rival for power. Irshad Aliyev was replaced as Minister of Agriculture and Produce by Ismet Aliyev in October, allegedly in response to the impounding of several Azerbaijani vessels, following the failure of the ministry to repay its debts to Turkey.

In January 2004 the Milli Majlis endorsed the European Social Charter on Human Rights. However, in June 2004 international controversy arose in response to the withdrawal of the registration of an Islamic community in Baku, the forced replacement of its leader and its eviction from a mosque, allegedly on the grounds of religious extremism. In October seven prominent opposition activists, who had been detained on charges of inciting violence following the presidential election in 2003, were sentenced to between two and one-half and five years' imprisonment. Those sentenced included: the Chairman of the People's Party of Azerbaijan, Panah Husseinov; the Chairman of the Ümid (Hope) Party, Iqbal Agazade; the General Secretary of the Democratic Party of Azerbaijan; and three Deputy Chairmen of Müsavat, including Rauf Arifoglu, also Editor-in-Chief of the leading opposition newspaper, *Yeni Müsavat*. (The newspaper was subsequently forced to suspend publication owing to the financial constraints imposed by court fines and the impounding of its bank accounts; however, publication was resumed in 2005.) In January 2005 a further 10 people, residents of the eastern village of Nardaran (where anti-government protests had been severely repressed in mid-2002), also received custodial sentences for participation in post-election protests, although many of the sentences were suspended; by this time some 50 people had received custodial sentences on charges connected with the post-election protests.

Municipal elections held on 17 December 2004 did not meet democratic norms, according to the OSCE. The NAP won 64.7%

of seats and independent candidates received 31.1%. Three of the four largest opposition parties boycotted the poll in protest at obstacles to campaigning and pressure exerted by the authorities prior to the ballot; NIP was the only major opposition party to participate; however, its popular leader Etibar Mamedov resigned soon after the election and the party remained without a headquarters, since its eviction in 2001. A legislative election was due to take place in late 2005, although it appeared unlikely that the opposition would be able to achieve any significant increase in representation. The apparent murder, in Baku in early March, of a prominent opposition journalist, Elmar Huseinov, the Editor-in-Chief of the Russian-language periodical, *Monitor*, prompted renewed concerns about the rule of law in Azerbaijan.

At the time of the disintegration of the USSR in late 1991, the leadership of Nagornyi Karabakh declared the enclave to be an independent republic. Azerbaijan refused to accept the territory's attempts to secede, and in January 1992 Nagornyi Karabakh was placed under direct presidential rule. International efforts to negotiate a peace settlement foundered, owing to Azerbaijan's insistence that the conflict was a domestic problem. Military successes by the ethnic Armenian forces of Nagornyi Karabakh in early 1992 culminated in the creation, in May, of a 'corridor' through Azerbaijani territory around Laçin, linking Nagornyi Karabakh with Armenia. Despite a successful Azerbaijani counter-offensive in late 1992, ethnic Armenian forces were able to open a second corridor in early 1993, eventually obtaining control of the regions of Azerbaijan between Nagornyi Karabakh and Armenia. By August some 20% of Azerbaijan's territory had been seized by ethnic Armenian units. The ethnic Armenian military gains prompted alarm among the Azeri population, and large numbers of refugees fled the occupied territories. Although it did not directly accuse Armenia itself of aggression, the UN Security Council adopted a series of resolutions demanding an immediate cease-fire and the withdrawal of all occupying units from Azerbaijan. There were also strong protests by Turkey and Iran, both of which mobilized troops in regions bordering Armenia and Azerbaijan in September. In December Azerbaijani forces launched a new counter-offensive in Nagornyi Karabakh, recapturing some areas that had been lost to Armenian control, although suffering heavy casualties. Meanwhile, international efforts to halt the conflict continued, led by the 'Minsk Group' of the Conference on Security and Co-operation in Europe (CSCE—later OSCE). In early 1994 it was estimated that, since the conflict began in 1988, some 18,000 people had been killed and a further 25,000 had been wounded. The number of Azeri refugees was believed to have exceeded 1m.

In early May 1994 a major breakthrough was achieved, with Azerbaijan's signature of the so-called Bishkek Protocol, which had been adopted several days previously at a meeting of the CIS Inter-Parliamentary Assembly, with the approval of representatives of both Armenia and the self-styled 'Republic of Nagornyi Karabakh'. On 8 May the Nagornyi Karabakh leadership ordered its forces to cease hostilities, in accordance with the Protocol. Although isolated violations were subsequently reported, the cease-fire remained in force. In the latter half of the year efforts were made to co-ordinate the separate peace proposals of the CSCE Minsk Group and Russia. However, Azerbaijan refused either to negotiate a peace settlement or to discuss the future status of Nagornyi Karabakh until Armenian forces were withdrawn entirely from occupied Azerbaijani territory and Azeri refugees had returned to their homes. In May 1995 the exchange of prisoners of war and other hostages was commenced. In April–June a new, 33-seat legislature was elected in Nagornyi Karabakh (replacing the 81-member Supreme Soviet). Robert Kocharian, hitherto Chairman of the State Defence Committee, was appointed to the new office of an executive presidency. An election to the (internationally unrecognized) office of president of Nagornyi Karabakh was held in November 1996, when Kocharian was elected with more than 85% of votes cast. In December Aliyev and President Levon Ter-Petrossian of Armenia attended a summit meeting of the OSCE, in Lisbon, Portugal. Following demands by Azerbaijan, a statement was released by the OSCE Chairman, recommending three principles that would form the basis of a political settlement to the conflict: the territorial integrity of Armenia and Azerbaijan; legal status for Nagornyi Karabakh, which would be granted self-determination within Azerbaijan; and security guarantees for the population of Nagornyi Karabakh. However, Armenia refused to accept the terms of the statement.

Relations between Azerbaijan and Armenia deteriorated in February 1997, when Azerbaijan condemned the provision of weapons to Armenia by several countries, including Russia, as a violation of the Conventional Forces in Europe (CFE) Treaty. Armenia retaliated by accusing Azerbaijan of preparing for a military offensive against Nagornyi Karabakh. Negotiations under the auspices of the OSCE resumed in April, but later that month a series of clashes, which left many people killed or wounded, occurred on the Armenian–Azerbaijani border. In May 1997 a draft peace settlement for the disputed territory was presented by the Minsk Group. Although the proposals were initially rejected, a revised plan, issued in July, received the qualified support of President Aliyev. The proposals provided for a stage-by-stage settlement of the conflict: Nagornyi Karabakh would receive autonomous status within Azerbaijan, and the withdrawal of ethnic Armenian forces from the enclave was to be followed by the deployment of OSCE peace-keeping troops, which would guarantee freedom of movement through the Laçin corridor linking Armenia with Nagornyi Karabakh. The appointment of Robert Kocharian, hitherto 'President' of Nagornyi Karabakh, as Prime Minister of Armenia in March, and the proposed presidential election in Nagornyi Karabakh, scheduled for September, were severely criticized by Aliyev; the Azerbaijani authorities also expressed concern at the conclusion of a partnership treaty between Armenia and Russia, fearing that a strengthening of relations between the two countries was a hindrance to the peace process.

The election of Arkadii Ghukassian to the post of President of Nagornyi Karabakh in September 1997 threatened to hamper further progress on reaching a settlement, owing to his outright dismissal of the OSCE proposals; it was reported later in that month, however, that both Azerbaijan and Armenia had accepted the revised plan drawn up by the Minsk Group. In addition, in an apparently significant change in policy, President Ter-Petrossian of Armenia publicly admitted that Nagornyi Karabakh could expect neither to gain full independence, nor to be united with Armenia. Ter-Petrossian's cautious and moderate approach to the Nagornyi Karabakh crisis provoked much disapproval in Armenia and led to the President's resignation in early February 1998. His replacement, Kocharian, was expected to adopt a more nationalistic stance. In late November the Armenian Government announced that, despite some reservations, it officially accepted the latest proposals put forward by the Minsk Group, which were based on the principle of a 'common state' (comprising Azerbaijan and Nagornyi Karabakh). The Azerbaijani Government, however, rejected the proposals, claiming that they threatened the territorial integrity of Azerbaijan.

An escalation in hostilities in mid-1999 prompted mutual accusations by Azerbaijan and Armenia that the other was attempting to abrogate the 1994 cease-fire agreement. Presidents Kocharian and Aliyev met on several occasions in the latter half of 1999, but no substantive progress was made. Following an assassination attempt against Ghukassian in late March 2000, the former Minister of Defence of Nagornyi Karabakh, Samuel Babaian, was charged with organizing the attack, as part of a purported coup. (He was sentenced to 14 years' imprisonment in February 2001, but subsequently released.) Legislative elections were held in Nagornyi Karabakh on 18 June 2000, in which the pro-presidential Democratic Artsakh Party secured 13 seats in the 33-seat legislature. On 11 August 2002 Ghukassian was re-elected President of Nagornyi Karabakh, receiving 88.4% of the votes cast. Meanwhile, direct negotiations between the Armenian and Azerbaijani Presidents continued in 1999–2002, but little progress was made towards reaching a final solution to the crisis. No further talks took place in 2003, and indications in late 2003 that the newly elected Azerbaijani President, İlham Aliyev, while supporting a peaceful resolution of the conflict, reserved the right to use military pressure appeared unlikely to hasten a diplomatic solution. Talks were resumed in 2004, but in September NATO was compelled to cancel 'Partnership for Peace' (see p. 303) military exercises scheduled to be held in Azerbaijan, following the Government's refusal to issue the Armenian delegation with visas and public demonstrations against their presence.

In 2004 the Azerbaijani Government began to appeal to international organizations other than the Minsk Group to act with regard to the occupation of Azerbaijani territory: in November the country successfully requested that 'the situation on occupied lands of Azerbaijan' be included for debate on the agenda of the General Assembly of the United Nations. How-

ever, the debate was adjourned indefinitely following an appeal from representatives of the countries comprising the Minsk Group, who claimed that such a debate would impair the mediation effort. In January 2005 the OSCE agreed to a request by Azerbaijan that it monitor settlements in the region, in which Azerbaijan claimed some 23,000 ethnic Armenians had been settled by the Armenian authorities, and to report on its findings. On 25 January the Parliamentary Assembly of the Council of Europe adopted a report describing the occupation of Azerbaijani territory by Armenian forces as a 'grave violation' and stating that the conflict had led to 'ethnic expulsion and the creation of mono-ethnic areas that resemble the terrible concept of ethnic cleansing'; however, the resolution also stated that Azerbaijani leaders should establish contacts unconditionally with the leaders of the secessionist region (which they had hitherto refused to do) and refrain from any use of force. The resolution suggested, furthermore, that should the Minsk Group fail to resolve the situation, then a submission to the International Court of Justice should be considered.

Although it signed the Almaty Declaration in December 1991, in October 1992 the Milli Majlis voted overwhelmingly against further participation in the CIS. However, with the overthrow of the nationalist PFA Government and the accession to power of Heydar Aliyev, the country's position regarding the CIS was reversed, and in September 1993 Azerbaijan was formally admitted to full membership of the body. None the less, Azerbaijan did not renew its membership of the CIS Collective Security Treaty in 1999, because of the continued occupation of Nagornyi Karabakh by Armenian troops, and in protest against Russia's continuing supply of armaments to Armenia. However, a visit to Azerbaijan by the Russian President, Vladimir Putin, in January 2001, and the signature of a number of co-operation agreements, appeared to signal a new stage in relations between the two countries. A reciprocal visit to Russia by President Heydar Aliyev took place in January 2002, at which a 10-year economic co-operation plan was agreed. Furthermore, in late September a bilateral agreement was signed on the delimitation of the Caspian Sea, according to which the seabed would be divided into national sectors, and the surface be used in common. A similar agreement had already been reached with Kazakhstan, and a trilateral agreement was signed in mid-May 2003. Although in November Azerbaijan expressed concern at new Russian-Armenian plans for defence co-operation, in February 2004 the newly elected President of Azerbaijan, İlham Aliyev, paid an official visit to Russia, during which the so-called Moscow Declaration was signed, reaffirming bilateral agreements signed in 1997 and 2001; a further trip followed in early 2005.

The strengthening of relations with Turkey, which had been cultivated by successive leaderships following independence in 1991, continued under the presidencies of both Heydar and İlham Aliyev. Throughout the conflict over Nagornyi Karabakh, Azerbaijan was supported by Turkey, which provided humanitarian and other aid and reinforced Armenia's international isolation by closing its borders with Armenia and prohibiting trade with the country. An intergovernmental agreement in support of the construction of a pipeline to connect the Azerbaijani petroleum fields near Baku to the Turkish port of Ceyhan via Tbilisi, Georgia, was signed in October 1998 (see Economic Affairs), and a further agreement was signed by the Azerbaijani Government with SOCAR and a number of petroleum companies in October 2000. (However, there was speculation that Turkey might come under pressure to exercise greater diplomatic co-operation with Armenia, owing to its status as a candidate for European Union—EU (see p. 217) membership, thus potentially jeopardizing the consistency of its long-term allegiance with Azerbaijan.) The large Azeri minority in neighbouring Iran (numbering an estimated 20m.) was regarded as a potential source of tension. Nevertheless, official relations between Iran and Azerbaijan remained amicable, and bilateral trade increased significantly in the 1990s. Relations deteriorated in 1999, however, following Azerbaijani allegations, which were denied by Iran, that Iranian spies had been operating in Azerbaijan to supply Armenia with military intelligence and that Islamist guerrillas had been trained in Iran as part of a plot against the Azerbaijani Government. Tensions also arose over the status of the Caspian Sea, together with Azerbaijan's increasing involvement with international petroleum companies. In July 2001 an Iranian military patrol boat ordered Azerbaijani survey vessels leased by the company BP (of the United Kingdom) to leave the disputed Sharg-Araz-Alov

(Alborz) area of the Sea. As a result, BP suspended its petroleum-exploration operations in the southern Caspian, pending a resolution of the dispute. In May 2002 President Heydar Aliyev paid an official visit to Iran, signing a number of accords on bilateral co-operation, which were expected significantly to stimulate trade. A further agreement on economic co-operation was signed in October, which included plans for the construction of a pipeline to carry natural gas from Iran to Naxçivan, and for improved transit links and customs procedures between the two countries. In November 2003, in Tehran, Iran, representatives of Azerbaijan, Iran, Kazakhstan, Russia and Turkmenistan signed a UN-sponsored framework Convention for the Protection of the Marine Environment of the Caspian Sea, which sought to alleviate environmental damage in the Caspian Sea region. In August 2004 President Hojatoleslam Dr Sayed Muhammad Khatami of Iran visited Azerbaijan, signing 10 bilateral accords and committing to further energy co-operation with Naxçivan. President İlham Aliyev made a reciprocal visit to Iran in January 2005, where he signed further agreements and obtained permission for the establishment of an Azerbaijani consulate in the city of Tabriz in Iran, which had previously been denied by the Iranian authorities. International observers judged the improvement in relations to be based on strategic diplomacy and the consolidation of allegiances by Iran, in response to increasingly belligerent statements against Iran made by senior members of the US administration, particularly in response to Iran's alleged illicit development of nuclear weapons and its support for militant Islamist groups internationally.

Azerbaijan's relations with the USA developed significantly in the mid-1990s, and in July 1997 President Heydar Aliyev visited the USA. A bilateral agreement on military co-operation was signed, and four contracts between SOCAR and US petroleum companies to develop offshore oilfields in the Caspian Sea were also concluded. New contracts for the development of the petroleum industry, worth US $10m., were signed during a visit to Washington, DC, USA, by Aliyev in April 1999. The USA also expressed its support for the proposed pipeline to carry petroleum from Baku to Ceyhan (see Economic Affairs), and a financial agreement on its construction was signed in Washington in April 2000. Following the initiation in late 2001 of US-led military action to combat global terrorism, the US Administration agreed to halt the provision of financial assistance to separatists in Nagornyi Karabakh and commit funds to Azerbaijan, through the temporary suspension of Amendment 907 to the Freedom Support Act of 1992 (establishing a foreign assistance programme to the countries of the former USSR), which prevented the donation of aid to Azerbaijan while that country's closure of the Armenian border remained in place. The waiver was renewed in January 2003. In January 2004 a co-operation agreement was signed between Azerbaijan and the USA, which aimed to prevent the proliferation of weapons of mass destruction, and according to which the USA was to grant funds of $10m. to Azerbaijan for the strengthening of border security.

In March 1992 Azerbaijan was admitted to the UN; it subsequently became a member of the CSCE. In April 1996, together with Armenia and Georgia, Azerbaijan signed a co-operation agreement with the EU. Azerbaijan joined the North Atlantic Treaty Organization's (NATO) 'Partnership for Peace' programme in May 1994, and was awarded observer status at the Alliance in June 1999. In January 2001 the country was inaugurated as a full member of the Council of Europe (as was Armenia).

Government

Under the Constitution of November 1995, the President of the Azerbaijan Republic is Head of State and Commander-in-Chief of the armed forces. The President, who is directly elected for a five-year term of office, holds supreme executive authority in conjunction with the Cabinet of Ministers, which is appointed by the President and is headed by the Prime Minister. Supreme legislative power is vested in the 125-member Milli Majlis (National Assembly), which is directly elected (under a mixed system of voting) for a five-year term. Azerbaijan is divided into 74 administrative districts (rajons) and an autonomous republic, the exclave of Naxçivan. By early 2005 central Government control did not extend to the former autonomous oblast (region) of Nagornyi Karabakh and seven rajons located between Nagornyi Karabakh and Armenia.

Defence

After gaining independence in 1991, Azerbaijan began the formation of national armed forces. In August 2004 these numbered 66,490: an army of 56,840, a navy of 1,750 and an air force of 7,900. The Ministry of Internal Affairs controls a militia of some 10,000 and a border guard of an estimated 5,000. Military service lasts for 17 months (but may be extended for ground forces). As a member of the Commonwealth of Independent States (CIS, see p. 189), Azerbaijan's naval forces operate under CIS (Russian) control. In May 1994 Azerbaijan became the 15th country to join NATO's 'Partnership for Peace' (see p. 303) programme of military co-operation. The 2004 budget allocated an estimated US $156m. to defence.

Economic Affairs

In 2003, according to World Bank estimates, Azerbaijan's gross national income (GNI), measured at average 2001–03 prices, was US $6,682m., equivalent to $810 per head (or $3,380 per head on an international purchasing-power parity basis). During 1990–2003, it was estimated, the population increased at an average rate of 1.1% per year, while gross domestic product (GDP) per head decreased from 1992–2003, in real terms, at an average annual rate of 0.7%. Overall GDP increased, in real terms, at an average annual rate of 0.3% in 1992–2003. Real GDP increased by 10.6% in 2002 and by 11.2% in 2003.

Agriculture (including fishing) contributed 14.1% of GDP in 2003, when some 40.0% of the working population were employed in the sector. The principal crops are grain, apples, watermelons and other fruit, vegetables and cotton. By mid-1999 some 80% of state-owned agriculture had passed into private ownership, and by the end of 2001 all collective farms had been privatized. During 1992–2003, according to World Bank estimates, agricultural GDP increased, in real terms, at an average annual rate of 0.4%. Real agricultural GDP increased by 6.4% in both 2002 and 2003.

Industry (including mining, manufacturing, construction and power) contributed 53.7% of GDP in 2003. In that year, according to official sources, 11.5% of the working population were employed in the sector. According to the World Bank, during 1992–2003 industrial GDP increased, in real terms, by an annual average of 1.5%, although real sectoral GDP increased by an estimated 24.9% in 2002 and by 5.6% in 2003. Those sectors associated with the petroleum industry, such as construction, have tended to experience steady growth, whereas non-petroleum-based industries have demonstrated a significant decline.

Mining accounted for 30.8% of GDP in 2003, when the sector employed 1.1% of the working population. Azerbaijan is richly endowed with mineral resources, the most important of which is petroleum. The country's known reserves of petroleum were estimated to total 1,000m. metric tons at the end of 2003, mainly located in offshore fields in the Caspian Sea and production in that year was estimated to amount to 15.5m. tons. In September 1994 the Azerbaijani Government and a consortium of international petroleum companies, the Azerbaijan International Operating Company (AIOC), concluded an agreement to develop the offshore oilfields. By 2000 the State Oil Company of the Azerbaijan Republic (SOCAR) had signed more than 20 production-sharing agreements with international partners, largely for the exploration of new fields. Production of 'early' oil began in October 1997 and accounted for a 50% increase in overall petroleum extraction over the following two years. The petroleum was transported to the Russian Black Sea port of Novorossiisk (Krasnodar Krai), via Chechnya, although technical problems with the pipeline and the conflict in Chechnya caused regular closures; a new section of the pipeline, avoiding Chechnya, was completed in March 2000. A further pipeline, transporting petroleum from Baku to the Georgian port of Supsa, opened in April 1999. In October 2000 the Government of Azerbaijan signed an agreement with SOCAR and a consortium of petroleum companies on the construction of a pipeline from Baku, via Tbilisi (Georgia), to Ceyhan in Turkey. Construction work on what became known as the BTC pipeline commenced in April 2003 and was expected to conclude in the first half of 2005, in spite of an increase in estimated construction costs (to some US $4,000,000m.). Azerbaijan also has substantial reserves of natural gas, most of which are located offshore; however, owing to a lack of suitable infrastructure, Azerbaijan is a net importer of gas. In 1999 a gasfield was discovered at Shah Deniz in the Caspian Sea, with reserves estimated at more than 600,000m. cu m, and the construction was under way of a gas pipeline to transport natural gas to Erzurum (Turkey), via Tbilisi, running parallel with the BTC pipeline. This new South Caucasus Pipeline was scheduled for completion in 2006, with an initial anticipated capacity of 1,500m. cu m per year; both original budgetary estimates and gas reserve estimates increased (by some 25% and some 20% respectively) during the construction process. Other minerals extracted include gold, silver, iron ore, copper concentrates, alunite (alum-stone), iron pyrites, barytes, cobalt and molybdenum.

Manufacturing accounted for some 8.6% of GDP in 2003, when it employed 4.5% of the population. In 2002 the principal branches of manufacturing, measured by gross value of output, were food products, beverages and tobacco (50.3%), refined petroleum products (accounting for 30.2% of the total), and chemicals and fibres (7.0%). The GDP of the sector declined, in real terms, at an annual average rate of 14.6% in 1992–1999. However, sectoral GDP increased by 8.5% in 2001 and by 5.0% in 2002.

In 2001 only 28.4% of Azerbaijan's supply of primary energy was provided by petroleum and petroleum products, although in 2000 72.6% of electricity generation had been derived from petroleum, while natural gas accounted for 19.2% of production in 2000, but for 64.8% in 2001 and the remainder was provided by hydroelectric stations. In 2004 Azerbaijan participated in an agreement with Iran and Russia on the synchronization and parallel operation of their national power grids from March 2006, following the necessary construction work. Fuels accounted for 13.6% of merchandise imports in 2003.

In 2003 the services sector provided an estimated 32.2% of GDP and accounted for 48.4% of employment. During 1992–2003 the GDP of the services sector declined, in real terms, at an average annual rate of 0.3%. Real sectoral GDP decreased by an estimated 5.8% in 2002 and increased by 15.6% in 2003.

In 2003 Azerbaijan recorded a visible trade deficit of US $98.5m., and there was a deficit of $2,020.9m. on the current account of the balance of payments. In that year the principal source of imports was Russia (14.6%). Other major sources of imports were the United Kingdom (10.9%), Turkey (7.4%), Kazakhstan (9.0%), Turkmenistan (7.2%) and Germany (6.5%). France, Kazakhstan and the USA were also important purchasers. The main market for exports was Italy (51.9%). Other important purchasers were France (8.1%), Russia (5.7%) and Israel (5.3%). The principal exports in 2003 were mineral products (accounting for 86.0% of the total). The principal imports were machinery and electrical equipment (26.1%), base metals (19.0%), mineral products (13.6%), vehicles and transport equipment (12.7%) and vegetable products (5.6%).

Azerbaijan's budgetary deficit for 2003 was some 41,100m. manats (equivalent to some 0.1% of GDP). At the end of 2002 the country's total external debt was estimated to be US $1,398m., of which $964m. was long-term public debt. The cost of debt-servicing in that year was equivalent to 6.5% of the value of exports of goods and services. Inflation increased by an average of 137.4% per year during 1991–2002. Consumer prices increased by an average of 1,664.5% in 1994, but the rate of inflation declined to 19.8% in 1996, and deflation was recorded in 1998–99. The average annual rate of inflation was 1.5% in 2001 and 2.8% in 2002. Some 54,365 people were registered as unemployed in 2003, although the actual rate of unemployment was thought to be much higher.

Azerbaijan is a member of the IMF and the World Bank. It has also joined the Islamic Development Bank (see p. 287), the European Bank for Reconstruction and Development (EBRD, see p. 212), the Economic Co-operation Organization (ECO, see p. 210) and the Black Sea Economic Co-operation group (now known as the Organization of the Black Sea Economic Co-operation, see p. 325). In February 2000 Azerbaijan became a member of the Asian Development Bank (see p. 159).

The dissolution of the USSR in 1991, the conflict in Nagornyi Karabakh and the disruption of trade routes through Armenia, Georgia and Chechnya all caused significant economic problems in Azerbaijan. However, owing to its enormous mineral wealth, Azerbaijan's prospects for eventual economic prosperity were considered to be favourable. Agreements were concluded with international consortiums from the mid-1990s, and the development of export routes for the country's petroleum and natural gas reserves was expected greatly to improve Azerbaijan's economic situation. The Government's stabilization and reform programme, adopted in early 1995, had achieved considerable success by 1998, and confidence in the manat was rapidly restored after the adverse impact of the Russian financial crisis

of 1998. In 1999 the State Oil Fund of Azerbaijan (SOFAZ) was established for the management of petroleum- and gas-related revenue, and a new Ministry of Fuel and Energy was established in 2001, to assume some regulatory responsibility for the petroleum sector. The disbursement of funding under the IMF's Poverty Reduction and Growth Facility (PRGF–approved in July 2001) was suspended in 2002, owing to the Government's failure to comply with IMF recommendations. However, lending resumed in 2003. A major concern was the economy's vulnerability to fluctuations in world petroleum prices, together with the need to alleviate security risks associated with the BTC pipeline. In April 2004 the IMF issued a formal warning over the continued slow pace of reforms by the Government and again threatened to withhold a scheduled disbursement of PRGF funding. Largely as a result of this pressure, towards the end of 2004 Azerbaijan implemented a long-term petroleum-revenue management strategy intended to stimulate sustained growth and reduce poverty and underemployment in the non-petroleum sector, and passed legislation on structural reform of the banking sector. However, the privatization of the country's two largest banks, another principal requirement for continued funding, remained uncompleted. Consumer prices faced significant increases in 2004 and 2005; food prices escalated as a result of the closure of the Russian border with Azerbaijan in August 2004, in order to combat smuggling and terrorism, and energy prices were raised sharply following a reduction in state subsidy in November. Further growth in the rate of inflation was anticipated in the mid-2000s, partly as a result of continued foreign direct investment and a projected increase of energy exports. Further economic growth was forecast for 2005, with a projected increase in petroleum production (particularly from the Azeri–Chirag–Deepwater Guneshli oilfields) expected to offset the current-account deficit.

Education

In the early 1990s the education system was reorganized, as part of overall economic and political reforms. Education is officially compulsory between the ages of six and 17 years. Primary education begins at six years of age and lasts for four years. Secondary education, beginning at the age of 10, comprises a first cycle of five years and a second cycle of two years. In 2003 19.9% of children in the relevant age-group attended pre-primary schools. In 1999/2000 total net enrolment at primary schools was equivalent to 91% of the school-age population. Enrolment at secondary schools was equivalent to 78% in 1998/99. Almost all secondary schools use Azerbaijani as the medium of instruction, although some 6% use Russian. There are 27 state-supported institutions of higher education and 15 private universities; courses of study for full-time students last between four and five years. Higher education institutes include Baku State University, which specializes in the sciences, and the State Petroleum Academy, which trains engineers for the petroleum industry. In 2003/04 there were 121,535 students enrolled in institutes of higher education. Government expenditure on education was estimated at 1,170,500m. manats in 2003 (representing 18.9% of total state expenditure).

Public Holidays

2005: 1 January (New Year), 20 January (Martyrs' Day), 8 March (International Women's Day), 20–21 March (Novruz Bayrami, Festival of Spring), 9 May (Victory Day), 28 May (Republic Day), 15 June (Day of Liberation of the Azerbaijani People), 26 June (Day of the Foundation of the Army), 9 October (Day of the Armed Services), 18 October (Day of Statehood), 4 November* (Ramazan Bayramy, end of Ramadan), 12 November (Constitution Day), 17 November (Day of National Revival), 31 December (Day of Azerbaijani Solidarity World-wide).

2006: 1 January (New Year), 20 January (Martyrs' Day), 8 March (International Women's Day), 22 March (Novruz Bayrami, Festival of Spring), 9 May (Victory Day), 28 May (Republic Day), 15 June (Day of Liberation of the Azerbaijani People), 26 June (Day of the Foundation of the Army), 9 October (Day of the Armed Services), 18 October (Day of Statehood), 24 October* (Ramazan Bayramy, end of Ramadan), 12 November (Constitution Day), 17 November (Day of National Revival), 31 December (Day of Azerbaijani Solidarity World-wide).

*These holidays are dependent on the Islamic lunar calendar and may vary by one or two days from the dates given.

Weights and Measures

The metric system is in force.

Statistical Survey

Source (unless otherwise stated): State Statistical Committee of Azerbaijan Republic, 1136 Baku, Inshaatchilar St; tel. (12) 438-64-98; fax (12) 438-24-42; e-mail ssc@azstat.org; internet www.azstat.org.

Area and Population

AREA, POPULATION AND DENSITY

Area (sq km)	86,600*
Population (census results)†	
12 January 1989	7,021,178
27 January 1999	
Males	3,883,155
Females	4,070,283
Total	7,953,438
Population (official estimates at 1 January)	
2002	8,141,400
2003	8,202,500
2004	8,265,700
Density (per sq km) at 1 January 2004	95.4

* 33,400 sq miles.

† Figures refer to *de jure* population. The *de facto* total at the 1989 census was 7,037,867.

ETHNIC GROUPS

(permanent inhabitants, 1999 census)

	Number ('000)	%
Azeri	7,205.5	90.6
Lazs (Lezghi)	178.0	2.2
Russian	141.7	1.8
Armenian	120.7	1.5
Talish	76.8	1.0
Avar	50.9	0.6
Turkish	43.4	0.5
Others	136.4	1.7
Total	**7,953.4**	**100.0**

AUTONOMOUS REPUBLIC

Republic	Area (sq km)	Population (estimate at 1 January 2003)	Population density (per sq km)
Naxçıvan (Nakhchivan) .	5,500	367,100	66.7

PRINCIPAL TOWNS

(estimated population at 1 January 2003)

Bakı (Baku, the capital)	1,828,800	Naxçıvan (Nakhchivan) . .	64,400
Ganca (Gyanja) * .	301,700	Şaki (Sheki) . . .	61,900
Sumqayıt (Sumgait)	262,400	Xankandi (Khankendi— Stepanakert) . .	52,900
Mingaçevir (Mingechaur) . .	94,900	Lankaran . . .	48,400
Ali-Bayramlı . . .	69,200	Ağdam (Agdam) . .	38,200

* Known as Kirovabad between 1935 and 1989.

BIRTHS, MARRIAGES AND DEATHS

	Registered live births		Registered marriages		Registered deaths	
	Number	Rate (per 1,000)	Number	Rate (per 1,000)	Number	Rate (per 1,000)
1996	129,247	16.9	38,572	5.1	48,242	6.3
1997	132,052	17.1	46,999	6.1	46,962	6.1
1998	123,996	15.9	40,851	5.2	46,299	5.9
1999	117,539	14.9	37,382	4.8	46,295	5.9
2000	116,994	14.8	39,611	5.0	46,701	5.9
2001	110,356	13.8	41,861	5.2	45,284	5.7
2002	110,715	13.8	41,661	5.2	46,522	5.8
2003	113,467	14.0	56,091	6.9	49,001	6.0

Expectation of life (WHO estimates, years at birth): 65.8 (males 63.0; females 68.6) in 2002 (Source: WHO, *World Health Report*).

ECONOMICALLY ACTIVE POPULATION

(ISIC major divisions, annual average, '000 persons)

	2001	2002	2003
Agriculture, hunting and forestry	1,482.0	1,495.0	1,497.0
Fishing	2.3	2.5	2.8
Mining and quarrying	42.1	42.2	42.3
Manufacturing	163.9	169.5	169.9
Electricity, gas and water supply	41.0	39.9	39.8
Construction	155.0	178.0	180.0
Wholesale and retail trade; repair of motor vehicles, motorcycles and household goods . . .	659.5	611.9	618.3
Hotels and restaurants	11.0	11.3	11.8
Transport, storage and communications	167.5	169.8	178.5
Financial intermediation . . .	13.0	13.2	13.0
Real estate, renting and business activities	97.0	97.2	97.5
Public administration and defence; compulsory social security . .	267.3	265.3	265.0
Education	318.0	329.9	330.0
Health and social work	170.0	173.6	173.8
Other community, social and personal service activities . .	125.0	126.7	126.8
Extra-territorial organizations and bodies	0.4	0.5	0.5
Total employed	**3,715.0**	**3,726.5**	**3,747.0**
Unemployed	48.4	51.0	54.4
Total labour force	**3,763.4**	**3,777.5**	**3,801.4**

Health and Welfare

KEY INDICATORS

Total fertility rate (children per woman, 2002) . . .	2.1
Under-five mortality rate (per 1,000 live births, 2003) . .	91
HIV (% of persons aged 15–49, 2003)	<0.10
Physicians (per 1,000 head, 2001)	3.59
Hospital beds (per 1,000 head, 2001)	8.51
Health expenditure (2001): US $ per head (PPP)	48
Health expenditure (2001): % of GDP	1.6
Health expenditure (2001): public (% of total)	66.9
Human Development Index (2002): ranking	91
Human Development Index (2002): value	0.746

For sources and definitions, see explanatory note on p. vi.

Agriculture

PRINCIPAL CROPS
('000 metric tons)

	2001	2002	2003
Wheat	1,493.7	1,692.8	1,509.6
Rice (paddy)	18.4	16.6	15.6
Barley	327.0	295.2	324.3
Maize	116.7	128.0	143.1
Potatoes	605.8	694.9	769.0
Sugar beet	41.3	115.8	128.9
Pulses	14.3	15.0	14.7
Hazelnuts	15.9	16.1	19.9
Other nuts	12.9	12.4	13.2
Cottonseed	55.9	53.1	60.8
Cabbages	81.1	89.7	96.6
Tomatoes	402.5	411.7	421.5
Cucumbers and gherkins* . . .	96.0	102.0	115.0
Dry onions	115.5	119.5	145.3
Garlic	17.8	16.4	17.9
Other vegetables*	203.5	235.4	249.9
Watermelons†	290.9	330.3	356.7
Oranges*	38.0	40.0	45.0
Apples*	304.2	287.0	300.0
Pears	31.5	32.9	36.0*
Apricots	13.3	12.8	15.0*
Peaches and nectarines* . . .	36.0	38.0	42.0
Plums	18.5	17.4	20.0*
Grapes	68.1	62.0	65.0
Other fruits*	55.9	88.8	151.9
Tobacco (leaves)	12.7	3.3	4.7
Cotton (lint)	27.7	27.3	38.8

* Unofficial figure(s).
† Including melons, pumpkins and squash.

Source: FAO.

LIVESTOCK
('000 head, year ending September)

	2001	2002	2003
Horses	64	66	68
Asses	38	39	38*
Cattle	1,723	1,794	1,872
Buffaloes	299	304	306
Pigs	19	17	20
Sheep	5,553	6,003	6,392
Goats	533	556	594
Chickens†	14,298	14,891	16,623
Turkeys†	443	460	515

* FAO estimate.
† Unofficial figure(s).

Source: FAO.

LIVESTOCK PRODUCTS
('000 metric tons)

	2001	2002	2003
Beef and veal . . .	57.1	62.6	67.5
Mutton and lamb . . .	36.7	37.6	40.5
Pig meat	1.1	1.3	1.3
Poultry meat	19.1	23.1	25.0
Cows' milk	1,054.9	1,099.7	1,144.4†
Cheese	11.0	11.4*	10.8*
Butter	5.0	4.8*	5.2*
Hen eggs	31.1	31.4	37.6
Wool: greasy	11.6	11.8	12.1
Wool: scoured	7.0	7.1	7.2
Cattle hides (fresh)* . . .	9.6	10.6	11.4
Sheepskins (fresh)*	4.1	4.5	4.8

* FAO estimate(s).
† Unofficial figure.

Source: FAO.

Forestry

ROUNDWOOD REMOVALS
('000 cubic metres, excl. bark)

	1998	1999	2000
Sawlogs, veneer logs and logs for sleepers*	3,200	3,200	3,500
Pulpwood*	3,200	3,200	3,500
Other industrial wood	—	—	100*
Fuel wood*	6,200	6,200	6,400
Total	12,600	12,600	13,500

* Unofficial figure(s).

2001–03: Production as in 2000 (FAO estimates).

Source: FAO.

Fishing

(metric tons, live weight)

	2000	2001	2002
Capture	18,797	10,893	11,334
Azov sea sprat	18,520	10,389	10,950
Aquaculture	120	170	168
Total catch	18,917	11,063	11,502

Source: FAO.

Mining

	2001	2002	2003
Crude petroleum ('000 metric tons)	14,909	15,333	15,378
Natural gas (million cu metres) .	5,535	5,144	5,128

Source: Asian Development Bank, *Key Indicators of Developing Asian and Pacific Countries.*

Industry

SELECTED PRODUCTS
('000 metric tons, unless otherwise indicated)

	1999	2000	2001
Wheat flour	52	234	370
Wine ('000 hectolitres)	47	77	76
Beer ('000 hectolitres)	69	71	116
Mineral water ('000 hectolitres) . .	16	21	30
Soft drinks ('000 hectolitres) . . .	326	478	2,171
Cigarettes	416	2,362	6,808
Wool yarn—pure and mixed (metric tons)	100	—	—
Cotton yarn—pure and mixed (metric tons)	900	700	2,000
Woven cotton fabrics ('000 metres)	1,000	1,000	3,000
Woollen woven fabrics ('000 sq metres)	100	—	n.a.
Leather footwear ('000 pairs) . .	54	122	220
Cement	171	251	523
Sulphuric acid	26	52	10
Caustic soda (Sodium hydroxide) .	21	30	27
Bricks (million)	10	10	12
Electric energy (million kWh) . .	18,177	18,699	18,970

— continued	1999	2000	2001
Jet fuels	631	580	n.a.
Motor spirit (petrol)	353	357	598
Kerosene	58	175	624
Gas-diesel (distillate fuel) oil . .	1,895	1,957	1,562
Lubricants	45	229	n.a.
Residual fuel oil (Mazout) . . .	3,871	4,072	2,648

Source: mostly UN, *Industrial Commodity Statistics Yearbook*.

2002 ('000 metric tons, unless otherwise indicated): Cement 847.7; Motor spirit (petrol) 610.5; Kerosene 649.7; Gas-diesel (distillate fuel) oil 1,593.5; Residual fuel oil (Mazout) 2,568.8; Finished cotton fabrics ('000 sq m) 2,926.

2003 ('000 metric tons, unless otherwise indicated): Cement 1,012.5; Motor spirit (petrol) 714.1; Kerosene 654.2; Gas-diesel (distillate fuel) oil 1,638.2; Residual fuel oil (Mazout) 2,469; Finished cotton fabrics ('000 sq m) 693.

Finance

CURRENCY AND EXCHANGE RATES

Monetary Units
100 gopik = 1 Azerbaijani manat.

Sterling, Dollar and Euro Equivalents (31 December 2004)
£1 sterling = 9,469.7 manats;
US $1 = 4,903.0 manats;
€1 = 6,678.4 manats;
10,000 manats = £1.056 = $2.040 = €1.497.

Average Exchange Rate (Azerbaijani manats per US $)
2002   4,860.8
2003   4,910.7
2004   4,913.5

Note: The Azerbaijani manat was introduced in August 1992, initially to circulate alongside the Russian (formerly Soviet) rouble, with an exchange rate of 1 manat = 10 roubles. In December 1993 Azerbaijan left the rouble zone, and the manat became the country's sole currency.

STATE BUDGET
('000 million manats)

Revenue	2001	2002	2003
Tax revenue	3,597.7	4,234.3	5,055.8
Value-added tax	1,266.4	1,674.4	2,048.6
Excises	554.6	433.3	335.2
Taxes on profits	588.2	739.1	891.5
Tax on rents	237.5	250.1	283.5
Taxes on income	473.6	548.3	752.1
Taxes on international trade and transactions	299.6	376.0	463.5
Taxes on land	52.1	44.0	56.6
Other	125.7	169.0	224.8
Non-tax revenue	326.3	316.9	1,076.1
Total	**3,924.0**	**4,551.2**	**6,131.9**

Expenditure	2001	2002	2003
Finance of national economy . .	512.2	685.0	1,214.5
Finance of social and cultural activities	2,650.5	2,993.4	3,569.4
Education	931.1	956.2	1,170.0
Culture, mass media and sport .	109.9	116.6	159.9
Health	210.1	224.1	276.6
Social security and welfare funds	730.7	951.1	1,070.0
Law-enforcement bodies . . .	427.4	472.8	603.4
Expenses of state administration bodies	241.3	272.6	289.5
Other purposes	874.8	980.4	1,389.1
Total	**4,037.5**	**4,658.8**	**6,173.0**

INTERNATIONAL RESERVES
(US $ million at 31 December)

	2001	2002	2003
IMF special drawing rights . .	2.49	0.70	18.03
Reserve position in IMF . . .	0.01	0.01	0.01
Foreign exchange	894.20	720.80	802.80
Total	**896.70**	**721.51**	**820.84**

Source: IMF, *International Financial Statistics*.

MONEY SUPPLY
('000 million manats at 31 December)

	2001	2002	2003
Currency outside banks . . .	1,468.99	1,668.73	2,040.88
Demand deposits at commercial banks	218.73	292.74	458.18
Total money (incl. others) . .	**1,693.10**	**1,967.27**	**2,499.09**

Source: IMF, *International Financial Statistics*.

COST OF LIVING
(Consumer Price Index; base: 1993 = 100)

	2000	2001	2002
Food	9,853.0	10,117.3	10,489.5
Fuel	304,403.6	303,981.8	303,981.8
Clothing	4,331.6	4,386.8	4,556.8
All items (incl. others)	**10,365.9**	**10,526.3**	**10,817.9**

Source: ILO.

NATIONAL ACCOUNTS
('000 million manats at current prices)

Expenditure on the Gross Domestic Product

	2001	2002	2003
Government final consumption expenditure	1,385.3	2,070.1	2,095.0
Private final consumption expenditure	18,512.2	20,756.5	22,959.2
Increase in stocks	−622.2	150.5	133.4
Gross fixed capital formation . .	6,081.3	10,330.3	17,809.5
Total domestic expenditure .	**25,356.6**	**33,307.4**	**42,997.1**
Exports of goods and services . .	11,029.9	12,963.9	14,066.2
Less Imports of goods and services	9,917.8	15,170.9	21,608.9
Statistical discrepancy	—	−788.1	−401.0
GDP in purchasers' values . .	**26,468.7**	**30,312.3**	**35,053.4**

Source: Asian Development Bank, *Key Indicators of Developing Asian and Pacific Countries.*

Gross Domestic Product by Economic Activity

	2001	2002	2003
Agriculture and fishing	3,943.0	4,230.0	4,605.2
Mining	7,880.3	8,756.2	10,032.8
Manufacturing	1,730.8	2,252.6	2,819.4
Electricity, gas and water . . .	387.4	341.4	399.6
Construction	1,553.6	2,640.0	4,250.4
Trade	2,072.7	2,385.2	2,742.6
Transport and communications	2,694.7	2,369.3	2,544.3
Finance	325.4	313.2	324.2
Public administration	712.0	1,002.6	1,034.0
Other	3,186.1	3,590.5	3,861.6
GDP at factor cost	**24,486.0**	**27,881.0**	**32,614.1**
Indirect taxes *less* subsidies . .	2,091.9	2,431.3	2,439.3
GDP in purchasers' values . .	**26,578.0**	**30,312.3**	**35,053.4**

Source: Asian Development Bank, *Key Indicators of Developing Asian and Pacific Countries.*

BALANCE OF PAYMENTS
(US $ million)

	2001	2002	2003
Exports of goods f.o.b.	2,078.9	2,304.9	2,624.6
Imports of goods f.o.b.	−1,465.1	−1,823.3	−2,723.1
Trade balance	613.9	481.6	−98.5
Exports of services	289.8	362.1	432.0
Imports of services	−664.9	−1,297.7	−2,046.5
Balance on goods and services	238.8	−454.0	−1,713.0
Other income received	41.5	37.1	52.6
Other income paid	−408.7	−421.8	−494.7
Balance on goods, services and income	−128.4	−838.7	−2,155.0
Current transfers received	176.5	228.2	225.1
Current transfers paid	−99.9	−157.9	−90.9
Current balance	−51.8	−768.4	−2,020.9
Capital account (net)	—	−28.7	−23.1
Direct investment abroad	—	−325.6	−933.3
Direct investment from abroad	226.5	1,392.4	3,285.0
Portfolio investment assets	—	0.4	—
Other investment assets	−394.0	−302.9	−169.2
Other investment liabilities	293.5	154.4	97.2
Net errors and omissions	−0.9	−87.4	−111.8
Overall balance	73.4	34.2	123.8

Source: IMF, *International Financial Statistics*.

External Trade

PRINCIPAL COMMODITIES
(US $ million)

Imports c.i.f.	2001	2002	2003
Vegetable products	116.8	106.1	146.2
Prepared foodstuffs, beverages, spirits and vinegar; tobacco and manufactured substitutes	69.7	84.0	101.9
Mineral products	248.0	324.7	356.1
Products of chemical or allied industries	68.7	83.0	110.2
Base metals and articles thereof	132.1	281.1	498.8
Machinery and mechanical appliances; electrical equipment; sound and television apparatus	353.8	395.9	685.0
Vehicles, aircraft, vessels and associated transportation equipment	198.6	123.5	332.9
Total (incl. others)	1,430.9	1,665.6	2,626.2

Exports f.o.b.	2001	2002	2003
Mineral products	2,113.6	1,927.4	2,229.5
Total (incl. others)	2,314.2	2,167.5	2,592.0

PRINCIPAL TRADING PARTNERS
(US $ million)

Imports c.i.f.	2001	2002	2003
China, People's Repub.	42.0	51.0	92.4
France	26.1	118.1	155.6
Germany	72.8	83.5	169.9
India	15.1	19.4	35.4
Iran	55.4	57.9	50.6
Italy	24.7	26.4	74.0
Japan	66.7	48.4	101.8
Kazakhstan	99.5	149.8	138.4
Malaysia	2.4	4.2	100.3
Netherlands	13.4	15.9	44.0
Norway	3.6	20.2	33.6
Russia	153.0	280.9	383.8
Singapore	3.1	34.6	n.a.
Sweden	13.9	5.6	40.9
Switzerland	18.2	21.0	n.a.
Turkey	148.2	156.2	195.1
Turkmenistan	135.2	119.8	188.4
Ukraine	39.3	80.0	118.7
United Arab Emirates	18.7	19.2	26.5
United Kingdom	54.0	85.2	286.5
USA	230.9	98.7	132.6
Total (incl. others)	1,237.3	1,665.3	2,625.2

Exports f.o.b.	2001	2002	2003
Croatia	24.3	7.3	61.1
France	66.5	166.3	209.7
Georgia	103.2	80.8	111.5
Germany	12.9	28.8	7.3
Greece	50.8	54.1	71.4
Iceland	85.9	n.a.	n.a.
Iran	9.1	29.9	49.1
Israel	164.1	154.1	138.1
Italy	1,324.1	1,082.7	1,345.9
Malta	8.7	30.2	n.a.
Norway	1.8	1.0	34.4
Romania	9.0	28.4	n.a.
Russia	77.5	95.7	148.1
Spain	101.8	104.0	43.3
Switzerland	7.7	20.4	n.a.
Tajikistan	12.1	28.0	34.4
Turkey	67.4	83.4	107.0
United Kingdom	35.4	9.1	7.7
USA	13.6	52.0	63.9
Total (incl. others)	1,757.1	2,167.5	2,592.0

Transport

RAILWAYS

	2001	2002	2003
Passengers carried ('000)	4,646	4,442	4,695
Passenger-km (million)	537	584	636
Freight carried (million metric tons)	15.4	17.5	19.7
Freight ton-km (million)	6,141	6,980	7,696

ROAD TRAFFIC
(vehicles in use at 31 December)

	2001	2002	2003
Passenger cars	342,958	350,559	370,439
Buses	17,275	17,422	18,781
Lorries and vans	77,142	76,928	77,019
Motorcycles and mopeds	6,719	8,278	7,313

SHIPPING

Merchant Fleet
(registered at 31 December)

	2001	2002	2003
Number of vessels	283	285	288
Total displacement ('000 grt) . .	641.2	633.2	638.0

Source: Lloyd's Register-Fairplay, *World Fleet Statistics*.

International Sea-borne Freight Traffic
('000 metric tons)

	1997	1998	1999
Goods loaded	7,128	7,812	7,176

Source: UN, *Monthly Bulletin of Statistics*.

Sea-borne imports ('000 metric tons): 5,118 in 2000; 7,029 in 2001; 7,853.4 in 2002.

Sea-borne exports ('000 metric tons): 703 in 2000; 996.3 in 2001; 1,057.3 in 2002.

CIVIL AVIATION
(traffic on scheduled services)

	2001	2002	2003
Kilometres flown (million) . . .	9	n.a.	n.a.
Passengers carried ('000) . . .	701	732	870
Passenger-km (million)	827	884	1,112
Total ton-km (million)	76	84	75

Tourism

FOREIGN TOURIST ARRIVALS

Country of residence	2001	2002	2003
CIS countries*	263,780	288,428	628,299
Iran	321,882	284,570	267,796
Turkey	8,493	11,082	14,589
Total (incl. others)	766,992	793,345	1,066,290

* Comprising Armenia, Belarus, Georgia, Kazakhstan, Kyrgyzstan, Moldova, Russia, Tajikistan, Turkmenistan, Ukraine and Uzbekistan.

Tourism receipts (US $ million): 63 in 2000; 43 in 2001; 51 in 2002 (Sources: World Tourism Organization).

Communications Media

	2000	2001	2002
Television receivers ('000 in use)	2,000	n.a.	n.a.
Telephones ('000 main lines in use)	801.2	864.8	923.8
Mobile cellular telephones ('000 subscribers)	420.4	730.0	870.0
Internet users ('000)	12	25	300
Book production (including pamphlets): titles	400	n.a.	n.a.
Newspapers and magazines (million copies)	20.7	17.9	n.a.

1994: Facsimile machines (number in use) 2,500.

1996: Daily newspapers (number) 6; Non-daily newspapers (number) 251.

Sources: UN, *Statistical Yearbook*, UNESCO, *Statistical Yearbook*, and International Telecommunication Union.

Education

(2003/04, unless otherwise indicated)

	Institutions	Teachers	Students
Pre-primary*	1,777	11,181†	110,800‡
General (primary and secondary) .	4,565	171,725	1,689,676
Specialized secondary education institutions	60	6,547	53,964
Higher	42	13,032	121,535

* Figures for state institutions only.
† 2002/03.
‡ Figures are rounded to the nearest 100 students.

Adult literacy rate (UNESCO estimates): 99.6% (males 99.7%; females 99.5%) in 1995 (Source: UNESCO, *Statistical Yearbook*).

Directory

The Constitution

A new Constitution was endorsed by 91.9% of the registered electorate in a national referendum, held on 12 November 1995. The following is a summary of the Constitution's main provisions, including amendments to the status of Naxçıvan (Nakhchivan) approved by the Milli Majlis (National Assembly) in December 1998:

GENERAL PROVISIONS

The Azerbaijan Republic is a democratic, secular and unitary state. State power is vested in the people, who implement their sovereign right through referendums and their directly elected representatives. No individual or organization has the right to usurp the power of the people. State power is exercised on the principle of the division of powers between the legislature, the executive and the judiciary. The supreme aim of the state is to ensure human and civil rights and freedoms. The territory of the Azerbaijan Republic is inviolable and indivisible. Azerbaijan conducts its foreign policy on the basis of universally accepted international law. The state is committed to a market economic system and to freedom of entrepreneurial activity. Three types of ownership—state, private and municipal—are recognized; natural resources belong to the Azerbaijan Republic. The state promotes the development of art, culture, education, medical care and science, and defends historical, material and spiritual values. All religions are equal by law; the spread of religions that contradict the principles of humanity is prohibited. The state language is Azerbaijani, although the republic guarantees the free use of other languages. The capital is Baku (Bakı).

MAJOR RIGHTS, FREEDOMS AND RESPONSIBILITIES

Every citizen has inviolable, undeniable and inalienable rights and freedoms. Every person is equal before the law and the courts, regardless of sex, race, nationality, religion, origin, property and other status, and political or other convictions. Every person has the right to life. Any person charged with a penal offence is considered innocent until proven guilty. Capital punishment as an extreme measure of punishment, while still in force, can be applied for grave crimes. Every person has the right to freedom of thought, speech, conscience and religion. Everyone has the right to protect their national and ethnic affiliation. No one is to be subject to torture or the degradation of human dignity. The mass media are free, and censorship is prohibited. Every person has the right to freedom of movement and residence within the republic, and the right to leave the republic. The right to assemble publicly is guaranteed, and every person has the right to establish a political party, trade union or other organization; the activity of unions that seek to overthrow state power is prohibited. Citizens of the Azerbaijan Republic have the right to participate in the political life of society and the state, and the right to elect and to be elected to government bodies, and to participate in referendums. Every person has the right to health protection and medical aid, and the right to social security in old age, sickness, disability, unemployment, etc. The state guarantees the right to free secondary education.

THE LEGISLATURE

The supreme legislative body is the 125-member Milli Majlis. Deputies are elected by universal, equal, free, direct suffrage, and by secret ballot, for a five-year term. Any citizen who has reached the age of 25 years is eligible for election, with the exception of those possessing dual citizenship, those performing state service, and those otherwise engaged in paid work, unless employed in the creative, scientific and education sectors. The instigation of criminal proceedings against a deputy, and his or her detention or arrest, are only permitted on the decision of the Milli Majlis, on the basis of a recommendation by the Prosecutor-General. The Milli Majlis passes legislation, constitutional laws and resolutions; ratifies or denunciates treaties, agreements and conventions; ratifies the state budget; gives consent to declare war, on the recommendation of the President of the Republic; confirms administrative and territorial divisions; and declares amnesties. Upon the nomination of the President, the Milli Majlis is authorized to approve the appointment of the Prime Minister and the Prosecutor-General; appoint and dismiss members of the Constitutional Court and Supreme Court; and appoint and dismiss the Chairperson of the National Bank. It also has the power to express a vote of 'no confidence' in the Government; to call a referendum; to initiate impeachment proceedings against the President, on the recommendation of the Constitutional Court; and to introduce draft legislation and other issues for parliamentary discussion.

EXECUTIVE POWER

The President, who is directly elected for a term of five years, is Head of State and Commander-in-Chief of the Armed Forces. Executive power is held by the President, who acts as guarantor of the independence and territorial integrity of the republic. Any university graduate aged 35 years or over, who has the right to vote, has been a resident of the republic for the preceding 10 years, has never been tried for a major crime, and who is exclusively a citizen of the Azerbaijan Republic, is eligible for election to the office of President. The President appoints and dismisses the Cabinet of Ministers, headed by the Prime Minister, which is the highest executive body.

The President calls legislative elections; concludes international treaties and agreements, and submits them to the Milli Majlis for ratification; signs laws or returns draft legislation to the Milli Majlis for reconsideration; proposes candidates for the Constitutional Court, the Supreme Court and the Economic Court, and nominates the Prosecutor-General and the Chairman of the National Bank; appoints and recalls diplomatic representatives of Azerbaijan to foreign countries and international organizations, and receives the credentials of diplomatic representatives; may declare a state of emergency or martial law; and grants titles of honour.

The President enjoys immunity from prosecution during his or her period in office. In the event that the President commits a grave crime, he may be removed from office on the recommendation of the Supreme Court and the Constitutional Court, and with the approval of the Milli Majlis.

THE JUDICIARY

Judicial power is implemented only by the courts. Judges are independent and are subordinate only to the Constitution and the law; they are immune from prosecution. Trials are held in public, except in specialized circumstances.

The Constitutional Court is composed of nine members, appointed by the Milli Majlis on the recommendation of the President. It determines, among other things, whether presidential decrees, resolutions of the Milli Majlis and of the Cabinet of Ministers, laws of the Naxçivan Autonomous Republic, and international treaties correspond to the Constitution; and decides on the prohibition of the activities of political parties. The Supreme Court is the highest judicial body in administrative, civil and criminal cases; the Economic Court is the highest legal body in considering economic disputes.

THE NAXÇIVAN AUTONOMOUS REPUBLIC

The Naxçivan Autonomous Republic forms an autonomous state that is an inalienable part of the Azerbaijan Republic. It has its own Constitution, which must not contravene the Constitution and laws of Azerbaijan. Legislative power in Naxçivan is vested in the 45-member Ali Majlis (Supreme Assembly), which serves a five-year term, and executive power is vested in the Cabinet of Ministers. The Ali Majlis elects a Chairman from among its members, as the highest official in the Republic of Naxçivan. The Ali Majlis is responsible for the budget, the approval of economic and social programmes; and the approval of the Cabinet of Ministers. The Ali Majlis may dismiss its Chairman and express 'no confidence' in the Cabinet of Ministers. Justice is administered by the courts of the Republic of Naxçivan.

LOCAL SELF-GOVERNMENT

Local government in rural areas and towns, villages and settlements is exercised by elected municipalities.

RIGHTS AND LAW

The Constitution has supreme legal force. Amendments and additions may only be introduced following a referendum.

The Government

HEAD OF STATE

President: İLHAM HEYDAR OĞLU ALIYEV (inaugurated 31 October 2003).

CABINET OF MINISTERS
(April 2005)

Prime Minister: ARTUR TAHIR OĞLU RASIZADE.

First Deputy Prime Ministers: ABBAS AYDIN OĞLU ABBASOV, YAGUB ABDULLA OĞLU AYYUBOV.

Deputy Prime Ministers: ELCHIN ILYAS OĞLU EFENDIYEV, ABID QOCA OĞLU SHARIFOV, ALI SAMIL OĞLU HASANOV.

Minister of Public Health: ALI BINNET OĞLU INSANOV.

Minister of Foreign Affairs: ELMAR MAHARRAM OĞLU MAMMEDYAROV.

Minister of Agriculture and Produce: ISMET ALIYEV.

Minister of Internal Affairs: Col RAMIL IDRIS OĞLU USUBOV.

Minister of Culture: POLAD OĞLU BUL-BUL.

Minister of Education: MISIR CUMAYIL OĞLU MARDANOV.

Minister of Communications and Information Technology: ALI MAMMAD OĞLU ABBASOV.

Minister of Finance: AVAZ AKBAR OĞLU ALEKPEROV.

Minister of Justice: FIKRET FARRUKH OĞLU MAMMADOV.

Minister of Labour and Social Protection: ALI TEYMUR OĞLU NAGIYEV.

Minister of National Security: Lt-Gen. ELDAR AKHMED OĞLU MAKHMUDOV.

Minister of Defence: Col-Gen. SAFAR AKHUNDBALA OĞLU ABIYEV.

Minister of Industry and Energy: MAJID KARIMOV.

Minister of Taxes: FAZIL MAMEDOV.

Minister of Youth, Sport and Tourism: ABULFAZ MURSAL OĞLU KARAYEV.

Minister of Economic Development: FARKHAD SOKHRAT OĞLU ALIYEV.

Minister of Ecology and Natural Resources: HUSSEIN BAGHIROV.

Minister of Transport: ZIYA MAMMEDOV.

MINISTRIES

Office of the President: 1066 Baku, İstiklal küç. 19; tel. (12) 492-17-26; fax (12) 492-35-43; e-mail office@apparat.gov.az; internet www.president.az.

Office of the Prime Minister: 1066 Baku, Lermontov küç. 63; tel. (12) 492-66-23; fax (12) 492-91-79.

Ministry of Agriculture and Produce: 1016 Baku, Azadliq meydani 1; tel. (12) 493-53-55.

Ministry of Communications and Information Technology: 1000 Baku, Azarbaycan pr. 33; tel. (12) 493-00-04; fax (12) 498-79-12; e-mail mincom@mincom.gov.az; internet www.mincom.gov.az.

Ministry of Culture: 1016 Baku, Azadliq meydani 1; tel. (12) 493-43-98; fax (12) 493-56-05; e-mail mugam@culture.gov.az.

Ministry of Defence: 1139 Baku, Azarbaycan pr.; tel. (12) 439-41-89; fax (12) 492-92-50.

Ministry of Ecology and Natural Resources: 1073 Baku, Bahram Agayev küç. 100A; tel. (12) 492-59-07; fax (12) 439-84-32; internet eco.gov.az.

Ministry of Economic Development: 1001 Baku, Niyazi küç. 23; tel. (12) 490-24-30; fax (12) 490-24-08; e-mail office@economy.gov.az; internet economy.gov.az.

Ministry of Education: 1008 Baku, Xatai pr. 49; tel. (12) 496-06-47; fax (12) 496-34-83; e-mail office@min.edu.az; internet www.min.edu.az.

Ministry of Finance: 1022 Baku, Samed Vurghun küç. 83; tel. (12) 493-30-12; fax (12) 498-79-69; e-mail office@maliyye.gov.az; internet maliyye.gov.az.

Ministry of Foreign Affairs: 1009 Baku, S. Qurbanov küç. 4; tel. (12) 492-96-92; fax (12) 498-84-80; e-mail secretariat@mfa.gov.az; internet www.mfa.gov.az.

Ministry of Industry and Energy: 1000 Baku, Hasanbek Zardabi küç. 88; tel. (12) 447-05-84; fax (12) 431-90-05; e-mail mfe@azdata .net.

Ministry of Internal Affairs: 1005 Baku, Gusi Hajiyev küç. 7; tel. (12) 492-57-54; fax (12) 498-22-85.

Ministry of Justice: 1000 Baku, İnşaatçılar pr. 1; tel. (12) 430-01-16; fax (12) 430-09-81; e-mail contact@justice.gov.az; internet www .justice.gov.az.

Ministry of Labour and Social Protection: 1000 Baku, Uzeyir Hajibeyov küç. 40; tel. (12) 493-05-42; fax (12) 493-94-72; e-mail mlspp@mlspp.gov.az; internet www.mlspp.gov.az.

Ministry of National Security: 1602 Baku, Parlament pr. 2; tel. (12) 495-07-63; fax (12) 495-04-91.

Ministry of Public Health: 1014 Baku, Kicik Deniz küç. 4; tel. (12) 493-29-77; fax (12) 493-07-11; e-mail moh@alexd.baku.az.az; internet www.mednet.az.

Ministry of Taxes: 1073 Baku, Landau küç. 16; tel. (12) 497-06-11; fax (12) 498-54-07; e-mail info@taxes.gov.az; internet www.taxes .gov.az.

Ministry of Transport: 1010 Baku, Uzeyir Hajibeyov küç. 72/4; tel. (12) 498-50-87.

Ministry of Youth, Sport and Tourism: 1072 Baku, Olympiya küç. 4; tel. (12) 465-64-42; fax (12) 465-64-38; e-mail myst@myst.gov .az; internet www.myst.gov.az.

President and Legislature

PRESIDENT

Presidential Election, 15 October 2003

Candidates	Votes	% of votes
İlham Aliyev (New Azerbaijan Party) . .	2,438,787	79.53
İsa Qambar (Müsavat—Equality—Party) .	372,385	12.14
Lala Şövket Hacıyev (Independent) . . .	100,558	3.28
Ehtibar Mammadov (Azerbaijan National Independence Party)	82,401	2.69
Others	72,270	2.36
Total	**3,066,401**	**100.00**

LEGISLATURE

Milli Majlis
(National Assembly)

1152 Baku, Parliament pr. 1; tel. (12) 439-97-50; fax (12) 493-49-43; e-mail azmm@meclis.gov.az; internet www.meclis.gov.az.

Chairman: MURTUZ ALESKEROV.

General Election, 5 November 2000*

Parties and blocs	Single-member constituency seats	Party-list seats	Total seats
New Azerbaijan Party	62	16	78
Independents	26	—	26
Popular Front of Azerbaijan . .	2	4	6
Civic Solidarity Party	—	3	3
Communist Party of Azerbaijan .	—	2	2
Others	9	—	9
Vacant†	1	—	1
Total	**100**	**25**	**125**

* Election results in 11 districts were annulled by the Constitutional Court and the Central Electoral Commission following confirmed irregularities. Fresh elections were held in these districts on 7 January 2001.

† No elections were held in the Xankandi-Xocalı-Xocavand constituency, located within the former autonomous oblast of Nagornyi Karabakh, which remained outside central government control.

Political Organizations

Adalat (Justice) Party: 1000 Baku, Nasimi rajon, Ceyhun Hacıbayli küç. 2; tel. (12) 440-85-23; f. 2001; Leader İLYAS İSMAYILOV; 21,000 mems.

Alliance in the Name of Azerbaijan Party (Azarbaycan Namina Alyans Partiyası—DvIA): 1001 Baku, Muktarov küç. 9/7; tel. (50) 214-49-37; f. 1994; supports adminstration of İlham Aliyev; participated in the formation of the Solidarity and Trust alliance in advance of legislative elections, scheduled to be held in late 2005; Leader ABUTALYB SAMADOV; Chair. of Co-ordinating Council Gen. ILGAR GASYMOV.

Ana Vatan (Fatherland) Party (Ana Vatan Partiyası): 1000 Baku, M. Gardashlary küç. 14; tel. (12) 493-82-92; supports administration of İlham Aliyev; represents interests of Naxçivan Autonomous Republic in Azerbaijan; Leader FAZAIL AGAMALIYEV.

Azerbaijan Communist Party (CPA) (Azarbaycan Kommunist Partiyası—AKP): 1000 Baku; tel. (12) 494-89-37; disbanded Sept. 1991, re-established Nov. 1993; Chair. RAMIZ AHMADOV.

Azerbaijan Democratic Independence Party (Azerbaijani Demokratik İstiqlal Partiyası): 1000 Baku; tel. (12) 467-45-16; Chair. LEYLA YUNUSOVA; Leader VAGIT KERIMOV.

Azerbaijan Democratic Party (Azarbaycan Demokrat Partiyası): 1000 Baku, Nasimi Rajon, Alişraf Alizada küç. 13; tel. (12) 496-07-22; internet www.gouliev.com; f. 1994; unregistered; Chair. RASUL BAYRAM oğlu QULIYEV; Gen. Sec. AKIF RAHIM oğlu ŞAHBAZOV (acting).

Azerbaijan Islamic Party (Azarbaycan İslam Partiyası—AİP): 1000 Baku; tel. (12) 491-86-45; fax (12) 491-83-88; e-mail AIP@azer .net; internet www.islaminsesi.org.az; f. 1992; forms part of the Union of Pro-Azerbaijanist Forces; Chair. Hacı HACIAĞA NURI.

Azerbaijan Liberal Party of Azerbaijan (Azarbaycan Liberal Partiyası): 1000 Baku, Azarbaycan pr.; tel. (12) 498-00-95; f. 1995; pro-Russian; Exec. Chair. AVAZ TAMIRKHAN.

Azerbaijan National Democratic Party (Azarbaycan Milli Demokrat Partiyası): 1000 Baku; tel. (12) 494-89-37; nationalist; fmrly associated with the prohibited Boz Gurd (Grey Wolves) militia; Leader İSKANDAR MEJID oğlu HAMIDOV.

Azerbaijan National Independence Party—AMIP (Azarbaycan Milli İstiqlal Partiyası): 1000 Baku, Nasimi rajon, Mirqasımov küç. 4; tel. (12) 441-53-09; e-mail nipa@azeri.com; internet www.amip .info; f. 1992; centre-right, supports liberalization of the economy and strengthening of democratic institutions; opposed to administration of İlham Aliyev; Chair. ALI ALIYEV.

Azerbaijan Popular Front Party (PFA) (Azarbaycan Xalq Cabhasi Partiyası—AXCP): 1152 Baku, Milli Majlis, Mehti Hussein küç. 2; tel. (12) 498-07-94; internet www.axcp.org; f. 1989; divided into reformist and conservative factions; the reformist faction was registered for the legislative election held in Nov. 2000, while the conservative faction entered into co-operation with Msavat; in Jan. 2002 the conservative faction of the PFA joined the United Opposition Movement, comprising a total of 25 parties; Chair. (reformist) ALI KERIMLI; Chair. (traditionalist) MURMAHMUD FATTAYEV.

Azerbaijan Popular Party (Azarbaycan Xalq Partiyası): Baku; f. 1998; Chair. PANAH HUSSEINOV (in prison).

Azerbaijan Social Democratic Party (Azarbaycan Sosial Demokrat Partiyası—ASDP): 1014 Baku, 28 May küç. 3/11; tel. (12) 493-33-78; fax (12) 498-79-03; e-mail asdp@bakililar.az; f. 1989; agreed merger with the Civic Unity Party in 2003; Co-Chair. ARAZ ALIZADEH, AYAZ MUTALIBOV; 5,672 mems (2002).

Civic Solidarity Party (Vatandaş Hamrayliyi Partiyası): 1000 Baku, Sabayıl rajon, Abdülkarim Alizada küç. 9; tel. (12) 493-71-45; f. 1992; Chair. SABIR RÜSTAMXANLI.

Müsavat (Equality) Party (Müsavat Partiyası): 1000 Baku, Darnagül qasabasi 30/97; tel. (12) 447-46-57; fax (12) 448-23-84; e-mail ilkin@turgut.baku.az; f. 1992 as revival of party founded in 1911 and in exile from 1920; joined the United Opposition Movement in 2002; several senior members imprisoned in 2004; Chair. İSA QAMBAR; Gen. Sec. VURGUN EYYUB.

Namus (Dignity) Party (Namus Partiyası): 1000 Baku; f. 1999; Chair. TOĞRUL İBRAHIMLI.

National Congress Party: 1000 Baku; f. 1997 by mems of Müsavat; Chair. IHTIYAR SHIRINOV.

New Azerbaijan Party (NAP) (Yeni Azarbaycan Partiyası—YAP): 1000 Baku, Bülbül pr. 13; tel. (12) 493-42-76; fax (12) 498-03-22; e-mail yap@bakinter.net; internet www.yap.org.az; f. 1992; Chair. İLHAM ALIYEV.

Popular Freedom Party (Xalq Azadlıq Partiyası): 1000 Baku, Khagani küç. 22; tel. (12) 498-31-45; Chair. YUNUS OGUZ.

Progress Party (Taraqqi Partiyası): 1000 Baku; Chair. Çıngız Damiroğlu.

Reformist Communist Party of Azerbaijan (CPA-2): 1000 Baku; tel. (12) 494-89-37; f. 1998 as Communist Party of Azerbaijan 2; name changed 2001; supports administration of İlham Aliyev; Chair. Firudin Hasanov.

Social Justice Party (Sotsial Adalat Partiyası): 1000 Baku; Leader Matlab Mutallimov.

Ümid (Hope) Party: 1000 Baku, İlqar Xalifov küç. 19/29; tel. (12) 496-65-48; f. 1993; socialist; Chair. Iqbal Agazade (in prison); Leader Abulfar Ahmadov; 5,000 mems (1998).

United Azerbaijan Popular Front Party (Bütöv Azarbaycan Xalq Cabhasi Partiyası) (BAXCP): 1000 Baku, 12-ci aşırım küç. 70A; tel. (12) 492-96-23; fax (12) 461-29-42; e-mail qudrat@hasanquliyev.com; internet www.hasanquliyev.com; f. 2003 by fmr mems of reformist wing of Azerbaijan Popular Front Party (q.v.); Leader Qüdrat Hasanquliyev.

Diplomatic Representation

EMBASSIES IN AZERBAIJAN

Bulgaria: 1000 Baku, Etibar Gudjayev küç. 13; tel. (12) 441-43-81; fax (12) 440-81-82; e-mail yuksel@bulgaria.embassy.in-baku.com; Ambassador Ivan Palchev.

China, People's Republic: 1000 Baku, S. Ragimov küç. 183; tel. (12) 498-62-57; fax (12) 498-00-10; e-mail chinaemb@azeurotel.com; Ambassador Zhang Xiyun.

Egypt: 1000 Baku, Hasan Aliyev küç. 7/15; tel. (12) 498-79-06; fax (12) 498-79-54; e-mail emb.egypt@azeuro.net; Ambassador Youssef Ahmed Ebrahim Al-Sharkawy.

France: 1000 Baku, Rasul Rza küç. 7, POB 36; tel. (12) 492-89-77; fax (12) 498-92-53; e-mail ambafranbakou@azerin.com; Ambassador Roland Blatmann.

Georgia: 1000 Baku, Asaf Zeynalli küç. 24; tel. (12) 497-45-58; fax (12) 497-45-61; e-mail emb@georgian.baku.az; Ambassador Zurab Gumberidze.

Germany: 1005 Baku, Mamedaliyev küç. 15 ,POB 28; tel. (12) 498-78-19; fax (12) 498-54-19; e-mail post@bakudiplo.org; Ambassador Detlef Lingemann.

Greece: 1004 Baku, Icheri Şeher, Kichik Gala küç. 86/88; tel. (12) 492-46-80; fax (12) 492-48-35; e-mail greekemb@azeurotel.com; Ambassador Dimidis Temistokles.

India: 1069 Baku, Narimanov rajon, Oktay Karimov Stküç. 31/39; tel. (12) 447-41-86; fax (12) 447-25-72; e-mail eibaku@adanet.az; Ambassador Jyoti Swarup Pande.

Iran: 1000 Baku, B. Sadarov küç. 4; tel. (12) 492-64-53; fax (12) 498-07-33; e-mail iranemb@azerin.com; Ambassador Afshar Suleymani.

Iraq: 1000 Baku, Khagani küç. 9; tel. (12) 498-14-47; fax (12) 498-14-37; e-mail iraqyia@azeri.com; Ambassador Omar Ismayil.

Israel: 1033 Baku, Izmir küç., Hyatt Complex, 7th Floor; tel. (12) 490-78-81; fax (12) 490-78-92; e-mail israelembassy@azdata.net; Ambassador Eitan Na'eh.

Italy: 1004 Baku, Kichik Gala küç. 44; tel. (12) 497-51-33; fax (12) 497-52-02; e-mail ambbaku@azeuro.net; internet www.ambitalbaku.com; Ambassador Margherita Costa.

Japan: 1033 Baku, Izmir küç., Hyatt Tower 3, 5th Floor; tel. (12) 490-78-18; fax (12) 490-78-20; e-mail japan@emb.baku.az; Ambassador Tadakhiru Abe.

Kazakhstan: 1000 Baku, Hasan Aliyev küç. 82; tel. (12) 465-62-48; fax (12) 465-62-49; e-mail embassyk@azdata.net; Ambassador Andar Shukputov.

Libya: 1000 Baku, H. Javid pr. 520/20; tel. (12) 493-23-65; fax (12) 498-12-47; e-mail libiya@streamteach.net.az; Ambassador Mustafa Shahtur.

Norway: 1000 Baku, Nizami küç. 340, ISR Plaza; tel. (12) 497-43-25; fax (12) 497-37-98; e-mail emb.baku@mfa.no; internet www.norway.az; Ambassador Steinar Gil.

Pakistan: 1000 Baku, Atatürk pr. 30; tel. (12) 490-68-39; fax (12) 490-68-41; e-mail parepbaku@artel.net.az; Ambassador Muhammad Hafiz.

Poland: 1000 Baku, Icheri Şeher, Kichik Gala küç. 2; tel. (12) 492-01-14; fax (12) 492-02-14; e-mail embpol@azeurotel.com; internet www.embpol.azeurotel.com; Ambassador Marcin Nawrot.

Romania: 1069 Baku, Tariverdiyev küç. 9A; tel. (12) 462-04-29; fax (12) 440-77-00; e-mail rom_amb_baku@azdata.net; Ambassador Nikolai Ureke.

Russia: 1022 Baku, Bakixanov küç. 17; tel. (12) 498-60-16; fax (12) 497-36-08; e-mail embrus@embrus.baku.az; internet www.embrus-az.com; Chargé d'affaires a.i. Petr Burdikin.

Saudi Arabia: 1000 Baku, S. Dadashov küç. 44/2; tel. (12) 497-23-05; fax (12) 497-23-02; e-mail najdiahbaku@azereurotel.com; Ambassador Ali Hasan Jafar.

Turkey: 1000 Baku, Xagani küç. 27; tel. (12) 498-81-33; fax (12) 498-83-49; e-mail bakube@azeronline.com; Ambassador Turan Morali.

Ukraine: 1069 Baku, Y. Vezirov küç. 49; tel. and fax (12) 498-27-42; e-mail ukremb@azeurotel.com; Ambassador Anatoliy Yurchenko.

United Kingdom: 1010 Baku, Xagani küç. 45; tel. (12) 497-51-88; fax (12) 497-24-74; e-mail office@britemb.baku.az; internet www.britishembassy.az; Ambassador Dr Laurence Bristow.

USA: 1007 Baku, Azadlıq pr. 83; tel. (12) 498-03-36; fax (12) 498-37-55; internet www.usembassybaku.org; Ambassador Reno Harnish.

Uzbekistan: 1000 Baku, Atatürk pr. 46; tel. (12) 497-25-49; fax (12) 497-25-48; e-mail embuzb@azeronline.com; Ambassador Ismatilla Ergashev.

Judicial System

The judicial system in Azerbaijan is implemented by the following courts: regional (municipal) courts; the Court on Grave Crimes; the Military Court on Grave Crimes; local economical courts; the Economic Court on Disputes arising from International Agreements; the Supreme Court of Naxçıvan Autonomous Republic; the Court of Appeal; the Economic Court; the Supreme Court.

Supreme Court
(Azarbaycan Respublikasi Ali Mahkamasi)
1601 Baku, Z. Xalilov küç. 540; tel. (12) 493-18-37; fax (12) 493-11-68; e-mail sudaba_hasanova@supremecourt.gov.az; internet www.supremecourt.gov.az.

the highest judicial body in civil, criminal, administrative and other cases, referring to the activity of the general courts; judges are nominated by the President of the Republic and confirmed in office by the Milli Majlis.

President: Südaba Camşid qızı Hasanova.

Prosecutor-General: Zakir Bekir oğlu Garalov.

Constitutional Court
(Azarbaycan Republikasi Konstitusiya Mahkamasi)
1005 Baku, Genjler meydani 1; tel. (12) 492-88-41; fax (12) 492-97-66; e-mail inter.dept@constitutional-court-az.org; internet www.constitutional-court-az.org.

f. 1998; comprises a Chairman and eight judges, who are nominated by the President and confirmed in office by the Milli Majlis for a term of office of 15 years. Only the President, the Milli Majlis, the Cabinet of Ministers, the Procurator-General, the Supreme Court and the legislature of the Naxçıvan Autonomous Republic are permitted to submit cases to the Constitutional Court.

Chairman: Farhad Sahib oğlu Abdullayev.

Religion

ISLAM

The majority (some 70%) of Azerbaijanis are Shi'ite Muslims; most of the remainder are Sunni (Hanafi school). In 1944 the Soviet authorities established a Spiritual Board of Muslims of the Caucasus, with spiritual jurisdiction over the Muslims of Armenia, Georgia and Azerbaijan. The Chairman of the Board, which is based in Baku, is normally a Shi'ite, while the Deputy Chairman is usually a Sunni. The severe restrictions on religious activity during the Soviet period were liberalized following Azerbaijani independence in 1991.

Spiritual Board of Muslims of the Caucasus: 1000 Baku; Chair. Sheikh ul-Islam Haci Allashukur Pashezade.

CHRISTIANITY

The Roman Catholic Church

The Church is represented in Azerbaijan by a Mission, established in October 2000. There were an estimated 200 adherents at 31 December 2002.

Superior: Rev. Jozef Daniel Pravda, 1069 Baku, Teimur Aliyev küç. 69B/1; tel. (12) 462-36-15; fax (12) 462-22-55; e-mail parish@catol.baku.az.

The Russian Orthodox Church (Moscow Patriarchate)

Bishop of Baku and the Caspian Region: ALEKSANDR, 1010 Baku, Ş. Azizbekova küç. 205; tel. (12) 440-43-52; fax (12) 440-04-43; e-mail baku@eparchia.ru.

The Press

In 1996 there were 257 newspaper titles, and in 1995 49 periodicals were officially registered in Azerbaijan.

PRINCIPAL NEWSPAPERS

In Azerbaijani, except where otherwise stated.

525-ci Qazet/525–ya Gazeta/525 Qazet: 1033 Baku, Ş. Mustafayev küç. 27/121; tel. (12) 466-67-98; fax (12) 466-25-20; e-mail 525@azdata.net; internet www.525ci.com; f. 1992; 5 a week; in Azerbaijani, English and Russian; Editor-in-Chief RASHAD MAJID.

Ayna/Zerkalo (Mirror): 1138 Baku, Sharifzadeh küç. 1; tel. and fax (12) 497-71-23; e-mail gazeta@zerkalo.az; internet www.ayna.az; internet www.zerkalo.az; f. 1990; daily; independent; Azerbaijani and Russian edns; Editor-in-Chief ELCIN SIXLINSKI; circ. 4,500 (daily).

Azadliq (Liberty): 1000 Baku, Xagani küç. 33; tel. (12) 498-90-81; fax (12) 498-78-18; e-mail mail@azadliq.com; internet www.azadliq.az; f. 1989; weekly; independent; organ of the Azerbaijan Popular Front; in Azerbaijani and Russian; Editor-in-Chief GANIMAT ZAKHIDOV.

Azarbaycan/Azerbaijan: 1073 Baku, Matbuat pr. 529/4; tel. (12) 438-20-87; fax (12) 439-43-23; e-mail azerbaijan_newspaper@azdata.net; internet www.azerbaijan.news.az; f. 1991; 5 a week; publ. by the Milli Majlis; in Azerbaijani and Russian; Editor-in-Chief BAKHTIYAR SADIGOV; circ. 10,242 (Azerbaijani), 3,040 (Russian).

Azernews: 1002 Baku, S. Askerova küç. 85; tel. (12) 494-93-73; fax (12) 495-85-37; e-mail azernews@azeurotel.com; internet www.azernews.net; f. 1997; weekly; in Azerbaijani, Russian and English; in association with AssA-Irada news agency; Editor-in-Chief FAZIL ABBASOV; circ. 5,000–6,000.

Bakı Xabar (Baku News): 1000 Baku; e-mail baku-xeber@azdata.net; internet www.baku-xeber.com; newspaper of the Azerbaijan Democratic Party; Editor-in-Chief AYDIN GULIEV.

Bakinskii Rabochii (The Baku Worker): 1146 Baku, Matbuat pr. 529; tel. (12) 438-00-29; e-mail bakrab@azerin.com; internet www.br.az; f. 1906; 5 a week; govt newspaper; in Russian; Editor I. VEKILOVA; circ. 4,776.

Baku Today/Xabar Xetti: 1000 Baku, A. Guliyev küç. 133/23; tel. and fax (12) 498-68-69; e-mail editor@bakutoday.net; internet www.bakutoday.net; internet www.xeber.net; English and Azerbaijani edns; Editor-in-Chief MAHIR İSKENDER; circ. 1,500–3,000 daily.

Baku Sun: 1073 Baku, İnşaatçılar pr. 2/42; tel. and fax (12) 497-55-31; e-mail editor@bakusun.baku.az; internet www.bakusun.az; f. 1998; weekly; in English; free of charge; Editor VALENTINA HUBER.

Bizim Asr: 1141 Baku, A. Alekperov küç. 83/23; tel. (12) 497-88-99; fax (12) 497-88-98; e-mail bizim_asr@media-az.com; internet bizimasr.media-az.com; f. 1999.

Echo: 1138 Baku, Sharifzadeh küç. 1; tel. (12) 497-51-74; fax (12) 447-41-50; e-mail gazeta@echo-az.com; internet www.echo-az.com; daily; Editor-in-Chief RAUF TALISHINSKY; circ. 10,000.

Ekspress (The Express): 1000 Baku, Xagani küç. 20в/43; tel. (12) 498-08-63; e-mail express@azeronline.com; internet www.express.com.az; Editor QAZANFAR BAYRAMOV.

İstiqlal (Independence): 1014 Baku, 28 May küç. 3–11; tel. (12) 493-33-78; fax (12) 498-75-55; e-mail istiklal@ngonet.baku.az; 4 a month; organ of the Azerbaijan Social Democratic Party; Editor ZARDUSHT ALIZADEH; circ. 5,000.

Millat: 1000 Baku, Rasul Rza küç. 6; organ of the National Independence Party.

Molodezh Azerbaidzhana (Youth of Azerbaijan): 1146 Baku, Matbuat pr. 529; tel. (12) 439-00-51; f. 1919; weekly; in Russian; Editor V. YEFENDIYEV; circ. 7,000.

Respublika (Republic): 1146 Baku, Matbuat pr. 529; tel. (12) 438-01-14; fax (12) 438-01-31; e-mail resp@azdata.net; internet www.respublica.news.az; f. 1996; daily; govt newspaper; Editor-in-Chief T. AHMADOV; circ. 5,500.

Sharg (The East): 1000 Baku, Matbuat pr. 529; tel. (12) 447-37-80; fax (12) 439-00-79.

Xalq Qazetı (Popular Gazette): 1000 Baku, Bül-Bül pr. 18; tel. (12) 493-02-80; fax (12) 498-85-29; e-mail webmaster@xalqqazeti.com; internet www.xalqqazeti.com; f. 1919; fmrly *Kommunist*; 6 a week; organ of the office of the President; Editor HASAN HASANOV.

Yezhednevniye Novosti (The Daily News): 1000 Baku, Terlan Aliyarbekov küç. 43; tel. and fax (12) 492-12-24; e-mail alpha@azeri.com; internet www.alpha.azeri.com; in Russian; Editor EMIL ASADOV; circ. 14,000.

Yeni Azerbaijan (A New Azerbaijan): 1000 Baku; tel. (12) 439-82-27; fax (12) 497-53-04; internet www.yeniazerbaycan.com; f. 1993; weekly; organ of the New Azerbaijan Party; Editor ALGYSH MUSAYEV; circ. 2,493.

Yeni Müsavat (A New Equality): 1000 Baku; tel. (12) 498-00-61; e-mail ymusavat@azeronline.com; independent; pro-opposition; Editor-in-Chief AZAR AYHAN (acting).

Yeni Yuzil (A New Century): 1000 Baku; f. 2001 by the founder of Azadliq (q.v.); Editor-in-Chief GUNDUZ TAHIRLI.

PRINCIPAL PERIODICALS

Adabiyat (Literature): 1146 Baku, Matbuat pr. 529; tel. (12) 439-50-37; organ of the Union of Writers of Azerbaijan.

Azarbajcan: 1000 Baku; tel. (12) 492-59-63; f. 1923; monthly; publ. by the Union of Writers of Azerbaijan; recent works by Azerbaijani authors; Editor-in-Chief YUSIF SAMEDOĞLU.

Azarbajcan Gadyny (Azerbaijan Woman): 1000 Baku; f. 1923; monthly; illustrated; Editor H. M. HASILOVA.

Caspian Business News (CBN): 1000 Baku, Icheri Şeher, Magomayev küç. 4; tel. (12) 497-07-43; fax (12) 497-07-62; e-mail office@cbnmail.com; internet www.caspianbusinessnews.com; f. 2000; weekly; in English.

Dialog (Dialogue): 1000 Baku; f. 1989; fortnightly; in Azerbaijani and Russian; Editor R. A. ALEKPEROV.

Iki Sahil: 1025 Baku, A. Akhundov 22; tel. (12) 90-49-89; internet www.ikisahil.com; f. 1965; weekly; organ of the New Baku Oil-Refining Plant; Editor-in-Chief V. RAHIMZADEH; circ. 2,815.

Kend Khayaty (Country Life): 1000 Baku; f. 1952; monthly; journal of the Ministry of Agriculture and Produce; in Azerbaijani and Russian; Editor D. A. DAMIRLI.

Kirpi (Hedgehog): 1046 Baku, Matbuat pr. 529; tel. (12) 432-18-18; f. 1952; fortnightly; satirical; Editor A. M. AIVAZOV.

Literaturnyi Azerbaijan (Literary Azerbaijan): 1001 Baku, Khagani küç. 25; tel. (12) 493-51-00; e-mail sima@azeri.com; f. 1931; monthly; journal of the Union of Writers of Azerbaijan; fiction; in Russian; Editor-in-Chief M. F. VEKILOV.

Monitor: 1000 Baku, Islam Seferli küç. 54; tel. (12) 494-88-37; fax (12) 493-93-96; e-mail monitor-week@mail.ru; f. 2002; independent; Editor-in-Chief (vacant).

Ulus (The Nation): 1000 Baku; tel. (12) 492-27-43; internet www.ulus-az.com; 2 a week; Editor TOFIK DADASHEV.

Vyshka—Oil (Oil derrick): 1073 Baku, Matbuat pr. 529; tel. and fax (12) 439-96-97; e-mail medina@vyshka.com; internet vyshka.com; f. 1928; weekly; independent social-political newspaper; in Russian; Editor M. E. GASANOVA.

NEWS AGENCIES

ANIK 'Bilik Dunyasi': 1000 Baku, D. Alievoli küç. 241/22; tel. (12) 493-55-61; fax (12) 498-18-41.

AssA-Irada: 1002 Baku, S. Askerova küç. 85; tel. (12) 494-93-73; fax (12) 495-85-37; e-mail azernews@azeurotel.com; internet www.azernews.net; f. 1991; in Azerbaijani, English and Russian.

Azadinform Information Agency: 1000 Baku, F. Amirov küç. 1; tel. (12) 498-48-59; fax (12) 498-47-60; e-mail azadinform@azerin.com; internet www.azadinform.baku-az.com; f. 1998; independent information agency; Chief Editor ASEF HAJIYEV.

AzartAc—Azarbaycan Dövlat Teleqraf Agentlıyı (Azerbaijan State Telegraph Agency): 1000 Baku, Bül-Bül pr. 18; tel. (12) 493-59-29; fax (12) 493-62-65; e-mail azertac@azdata.net; internet www.azertag.net; f. 1920; provides information in Azerbaijani, Russian and English; Dir-Gen. ASLAN ASLANOV.

Baku Telegraph: 1000 Baku, Azarbaycan pr. 41; tel. (12) 493-61-42; fax (12) 498-55-25; f. 1932; Dir SABIRA AGARZAEVA.

Media-Press: 1141 Baku, A. Alekperov küç. 83/23; tel. (12) 497-07-05; fax (12) 497-88-98; e-mail news@mediapress.media-az.com; internet mediapress.media-az.com; f. 1999; owned by Media Holding; independent; Gen. Dir VUGAR GARADAGLY.

Olaylar İnformasiya Agentliyi: 1000 Baku, B. Safaroğlu St 536; tel. (12) 439-62-44; internet www.olaylar.net; also produces newspaper.

Sharg News Agency: 1001 Baku, Mirza Shafi küç. 6; tel. (12) 492-69-80; fax (12) 492-46-23; e-mail sharg@azeri.com; f. 1994; Correspondent K. MUSTAFAYEVA.

Trend Information-Analytical Agency: 1601 Baku, Fizuli St 69; tel. (12) 497-31-72; fax (12) 497-30-89; e-mail infotrend@azdata.net; internet www.trend-az.com; f. 1995; in Azerbaijan, Russian and English; Dir-Gen. INGILAB AKHMEDOV.

Turan İnformasıya Agentlıyı: 1000 Baku, Xagani küç. 33; tel. (12) 498-42-26; fax (12) 498-38-17; e-mail turan@azdata.net; internet www.turaninfo.com; f. 1990; independent news agency; Azerbaijani, English and Russian; Dir MEHMAN ALIYEV.

Foreign Bureaux

Agence France-Presse (AFP): 1000 Baku, Zargar Palan 128; tel. and fax (12) 447-07-18.

Anadolu Ajansı (Turkey): 1000 Baku, Bül-Bül pr. 18; tel. (12) 493-05-96; fax (12) 493-06-63; e-mail baku@anadoluajansi.com.tr.

Interfax-Azerbaijan: 1000 Baku; tel. (12) 497-35-07; fax (12) 497-42-94; e-mail office1@interfax.baku.az; f. 2002; founded by the Interfax Group (Russia) and AzPetrol Azerbaijani Petroleum Co.

PRESS ASSOCIATIONS

Azerbaijan Journalists' Confederation (AJK): 1000 Baku, Xagani küç. 33; tel. (50) 335-27-95; fax (12) 498-78-18; e-mail hasret@akjib.org; internet www.akjib.org; f. 2002; 14 member organizations; Gen. Sec. AZER H. HASRET.

Press Council: 1010 Baku, Nizami küç. 121/11; tel. and fax (12) 498-27-48; e-mail info@presscouncil.az; internet www.presscouncil.az; f. 2003; mediates disputes between the media and the authorities; acts as a self-regulatory body for the print media; Chair. AFLATUN AMASHOV.

Publishers

Azarbaycan Ensiklopediyasy (Azerbaijan Encyclopedia): 1004 Baku, Boyuk Gala küç. 41; tel. (12) 492-87-11; fax (12) 492-77-83; e-mail azenciklop@ctc.net.az; f. 1965; encyclopedias and dictionaries; Gen. Dir I. O. VELIYEV.

Azarneshr State Publishing House: 1005 Baku, Gusi Hajiyev küç. 4; tel. (12) 492-50-15; f. 1924; Dir A. MUSTAFAZADE; Editor-in-Chief A. KUSEINZADE.

Elm Azerbaijani Academy of Sciences Publishing House: 1000 Baku; scientific books and journals.

Gyanjlik (Youth): 1005 Baku, Gusi Hajiyev küç. 4; books for children and young people; Dir E. T. ALIYEV.

Ishyg (Light): 1601 Baku, Gogol küç. 6; illustrated publs; Dir G. N. ISMAILOV.

Maarif State Educational Publishing House: 1111 Baku, A. Mageramov küç. 4; tel. and fax (12) 431-58-27; f. 1959; Dir ABAS ALI GIZI ALIYEVA SEVDA.

Madani-maarif Ishi (Education and Culture): 1073 Baku, Matbuat pr. 529; tel. (12) 432-79-17; Editor-in-Chief ALOVSAT ATAMALY OĞLU BASHIROV.

Medeniyyat (Culture) Publishing House: 1146 Baku, Matbuat pr. 146; tel. (12) 432-98-38; Dir SHAKMAR AKPER OĞLU AKPERZADE.

Sada: 1004 Baku, Boyuk Gala küç. 28; tel. (12) 492-75-64; fax (12) 492-98-43; reference.

Shur: 1000 Baku; tel. (12) 492-93-72; f. 1992; Dir GASHAM ISA OĞLU ISABEYLI.

Yazychy (Writer) Publishing House: 1005 Baku, Natavan meydani 1; fiction; Dir F. M. MELIKOV.

Broadcasting and Communications

TELECOMMUNICATIONS

Azercell Telecom: 1139 Baku, Tbilisi pr. 61A; tel. (12) 496-70-07; fax (12) 430-05-68; internet www.azercell.com; f. 1996; joint-venture co between the Ministry of Communications and Information Technology and Fintur Holdings B.V. (Netherlands); Gen. Dir ESRA TAN.

AzEuroTel: 1001 Baku, B. Sardarov küç. 1; tel. (12) 492-65-00; fax (12) 497-01-01; e-mail aet@azeurotel.com; internet www.azeurotel.com; f. 1995 as jt venture between Ministry of Communications, LUKoil Europe (Russia); digital, wireless, trunk, satellite telecommunications; Gen. Dir NURI AGAMIRZA AKHMEDOV.

AzTelecom Production Management: 1000 Baku, Tbilisi pr.; tel. (12) 430-26-02; fax (12) 493-17-87; e-mail aztelecom@azerin.com; national monopoly fixed-line telecommunications operator; f. 1992;

owned by the Ministry of Communications and Information Technology; privatization pending; Dir NAZIM CAFAROV.

Bakcell: 1000 Baku, U. Hajibeyov küç. 24; tel. (12) 498-94-44; fax (12) 498-92-55; e-mail bakcell@bakcell.com; internet www.bakcell.com; f. 1994; mobile telecommunications service provider; wholly owned by GTIB (Israel); Gen. Man. HAIM MAIMON.

RADIO AND TELEVISION

National Television and Radio Council: 1000 Baku; f. 2003; regulatory body, comprising nine members, six of whom are presidential appointees; Chair. NUSHIRAVAN MAGERRAMOV.

Radio and Television Company of Azerbaijan: 1011 Baku, Mehti Hussein küç. 1; tel. (12) 492-72-53; fax (12) 439-54-52; f. 1956; state-owned; Dir NIZAMI MANAF OĞLU KHUDIYEV.

Azerbaijan National Television: tel. (12) 439-77-72; fax (12) 497-20-20; internet www.aztv.az; f. 1956; programmes in Azerbaijani, English and Russian; two channels.

Azerbaijan State Radio: tel. (12) 492-87-68; fax (12) 439-72-48; f. 1926; broadcasts in Azerbaijani, Arabic, English and Turkish; two channels and one international broadcasting studio; Head MOVLUD SULEIMAN.

ANS Independent Broadcasting and Media Co (Azerbaijan News Service): 1073 Baku, Matbuat pr. 28/11; tel. (12) 497-72-67; fax (12) 498-94-98; e-mail ans@ans.az; internet www.ans.az; f. 1999; independent; broadcasts ANS-TV (f. 1990) and NAS-CHM Radio (f. 1994); Pres. VAHID MUSTAFAYEV.

Lider TV and Radio: 1141 Baku, A. Alekperov küç. 83/23; tel. (12) 497-88-99; fax (12) 497-87-77; e-mail mail@media-az.com; internet www.lidertv.com; f. 2000; owned by Media Holding.

Space TV and Radio: 1073 Baku, H. Javid pr. 8; tel. (12) 433-00-66; fax (12) 492-76-65; e-mail info@space-az.com; internet www.space-az.com; f. 1997 (radio broadcasts commenced in 2001); Chair. ETIBAR ADIL BABAYEV.

Finance

(cap. = capital; res = reserves; dep. = deposits; m. = million; brs = branches; amounts in manats, unless otherwise stated)

BANKING

Central Bank

National Bank of Azerbaijan: 1014 Baku, R. Behbutov küç. 32; tel. (12) 493-11-22; fax (12) 493-55-41; e-mail mail@nba.az; internet www.nba.az; f. 1992; central bank and supervisory authority; cap. 27,992m., res 397,413m., dep. 1,030,064m. (Dec. 2003); Chair. ELMAN RUSTAMOV.

State-owned Banks

BUSBank United Universal Bank (BUSBank): 1014 Baku, Fizuli küç. 71; tel. (12) 493-66-30; fax (12) 493-79-05; e-mail office@busbank.az; internet www.busbank.az; f. 2000 by merger; largest state-owned bank; Chair. RAUF RZAYEV; 87 brs.

International Bank of Azerbaijan: 1005 Baku, Nizami küç. 67; tel. (12) 493-00-91; fax (12) 493-40-91; e-mail ibar@ibar.az; internet www.ibar.az; f. 1992 to succeed br. of USSR Vneshekonombank; 50.2% owned by the Ministry of Finance, 7.36% owned by employees; carries out all banking services; cap. 34,110m., res 3,823m., dep. 1,952,347m. (Dec. 2002); Chair. of Bd JAHANGIR F. HAJIYEV; 36 brs.

Other Banks

At 1 January 2004 there were 46 banks operating in Azerbaijan, including two state-owned banks and 17 banks backed by foreign capital.

Azalbank: 1000 Baku, Nizami küç. 86; tel. (12) 498-20-42; fax (12) 498-97-01; e-mail post@azalbank.info; f. 1993; joint-stock bank; Chair. of Bd TEYMUR MAMEDOV; 14 brs.

Azardamiryolbank (Azerdemiryolbank): 1008 Baku, Qarabağ küç. 31; tel. (12) 440-24-29; fax (12) 496-09-77; e-mail damir@azerdemiryolbank.az; internet www.azerdemiryolbank.com; f. 1992; operates mainly in transport sector; cap. 16,799.0m., dep. 91,046.0m. (Dec. 2003); Chair. of Bd ROMAN AMIRDJANOV; 18 brs.

Azer-Turk Azerbaijan-Turkish Commercial Bank: 1005 Baku, Islam Seferli küç. 5; tel. (12) 497-43-16; fax (12) 498-37-02; e-mail atb@azerturkbank.biz; internet www.azerturkbank.biz; f. 1995; 46% owned by Türkiye Cumhuriyeti Ziraat Bankasi AS (Turkey); 46% owned by Agrarkredit; cap. 15,962.9m., res 4,350.3m., dep. 69,223.6m. (Jan. 2005); Chair. MAMMAD MUSAYEV; Gen. Man. MEHMET SAMI ACAROZMEN.

Azerigazbank: 1073 Baku, Landau küç. 16; tel. (12) 497-50-17; fax (12) 498-96-15; e-mail azerigazbank@azerigazbank.com; internet www.azerigazbank.com; f. 1992; joint-stock investment bank; cap. 19,000m., dep. 77,480.2m. (Dec. 2003); Chair. AZER F. MOVSUMOV; 5 brs.

Bank of Baku: 1000 Baku, Atatürk pr. 40/42; tel. (12) 447-00-55; fax (12) 498-82-78; e-mail root@bankofbaku.com; internet www .bankofbaku.com; f. 1994; 48% owned by NAB DIS Tiscarat; cap. 17,421m., dep. 80,713m. (Dec. 2004); Chair. of Bd SHAHRAM OROMI.

Capital Investment Bank: 1001 Baku, Azarbaycan pr. 3; tel. (12) 493-49-49; fax (12) 493-84-50; e-mail cibank@azersun.com; internet www.azersun.com/cibank.htm; f. 1996; privately owned; Pres. ABDULBARI GOOZAL; Gen. Man. HASSAN BERGSADI.

Günay Bank: 1095 Baku, Rasul Rza küç. 4/6; tel. (12) 498-04-55; fax (12) 498-14-39; e-mail gunaybank@azerin.com; internet www .gunaybank.com; f. 1992; cap. 16,600m., res 2,589.4m., dep. 41,472.5m. (Dec. 2003); Pres. AHAD SHIRINOV; Gen. Man. SHAKIR ABDULLAYEV; 1 br.

Ilkbank: 1052 Baku, Aga Neymatulla küç. 63/65; tel. (12) 465-65-12; fax (12) 465-80-01; e-mail office@ilkbank.baku.az; internet www .ilkbank.az; f. 1992; acquired BillurBank in 1997; 35.3% owned by AzPetrol Oil Co; 22.5% owned by AzerTrans; 22.4% owned by Rafik Aliyev; 19.8% owned by AzInvest; cap. 12,679.6m., res 235.1m., dep. 50,188.7m. (Dec. 2003); Chair. of Bd CHINGIZ MEKHTIYEV.

NBC Bank: 1055 Baku, İstiklal küç 27; tel. (12) 492-72-43; fax (12) 492-78-12; e-mail nbcbank@baku-az.net; f. 1992 as Ruzubank; in 2003 was renamed as above; commercial bank; Chair. S. AKHMEDOV.

Rabitabank: 1001 Baku, B. Sardarov küç. 1; tel. (12) 492-57-61; fax (12) 492-61-57; e-mail rb@rabitabank.com; f. 1993; joint-stock commercial bank; operates mainly in telecommunications sector; cap. 14,240.5m., res 3,121.0m., dep. 54,253.0m. (Dec. 2003); Chair.of Council ZAKIR NURIYEV; 9 brs.

Unibank Commercial Bank: 1022 Baku, Raşid Behbudov küç. 57; tel. (12) 498-22-44; fax (12) 498-09-53; e-mail bank@unibank.az; internet www.unibank.az; f. 2002 by merger; cap. 25,000m., res 808m., dep. 52,468m. (Dec. 2003); Chair. and Chief Exec. FAIG HUSSEINOV.

United Credit Bank: 1025 Baku, N. Rafiyev küç. 49; tel. (12) 490-06-41; e-mail ucb@ucb.baku.az; internet www.ucb.az; f. 1996; Chair. of Bd AZAD ISKENDEROV.

Association

Azerbaijan Association of Banks: 1001 Baku, B. Sardarov küç. 1; tel. (12) 497-58-29; fax (12) 497-15-15; e-mail bank_assoc@azeurotel .com; f. 1990; co-ordinates banking activity; Pres. ZAKIR NURIYEV; 47 mems.

Stock Exchange

Baku Stock Exchange (Bakı Fond Birjasi): 1070 Baku, Bül-Bül pr. 19; tel. (12) 498-85-22; fax (12) 493-77-93; e-mail info@bse.az; internet www.bse.az; f. 2001; Pres. SALIM KRIMAN.

INSURANCE

In January 2002 there were 38 insurance companies operating in Azerbaijan.

AZAL-siğorta: 1000 Baku, Khagan küç. 1/4; tel. (12) 498-39-50; fax (12) 498-38-02; e-mail azalsigorta@azalsigorta.com; Dir NIYAZI IMANOV.

Azergarant: 1001 Baku, H. Aslanov küç. 115/18; tel. (12) 493-81-65; fax (12) 493-81-02; e-mail azergarant@azdata.net; f. 1993; Pres. Dr ALEKPER MAMEDOV; Gen. Dir FAIG HUSSEINOV.

Azersiğorta: 1014 Baku, Füzuli 69; tel. (12) 495-95-64; fax (12) 495-94-69; e-mail azersigorta@azeuro.net; Dir MEMMED MEMMEDOV.

Günay Anadolu Siğorta: 1005 Baku, Terlan Aliyarbekov küç. 3; tel. (12) 498-13-56; fax (12) 498-13-60; e-mail office@gunaysigorta .in-baku.com; internet insurancegunayanadolu.com; f. 1992; Gen. Man. ALOVSET GOJAYEV.

International Insurance Co (Beynalxalq Siğorta Şirkati—BSŞ): 1065 Baku, J. Jabbarli küç., IIC Bldg; tel. (12) 499-22-02; fax (12) 499-22-12; e-mail iic@iic.az; internet www.iic.az; f. 2002; universal insurance co; wholly-owned subsidiary of the International Bank of Azerbaijan; Dir ELKHAN AHMED OĞLU GARIBLI.

MBask Insurance Co: 1095 Baku, Azi Aslanov küç. 90/9; tel. (12) 498-91-90; fax (12) 498-10-62; f. 1992; 30% owned by the European Bank for Reconstruction and Development (United Kingdom); 12 brs; Chair. of Bd of Dirs JAMIL MALIKOV.

MOST Insurance Co: 1073 Baku, H. Javid pr. 15/21; tel. (12) 497-37-60; fax (12) 433-08-58; e-mail most@mostinsurance.com; Dir KAMAL MIRSAHIB OĞLU IBRAHIMOV.

Trade and Industry

CHAMBER OF COMMERCE

Chamber of Commerce and Industry: 1601 Baku, İstiklal küç 31/33; tel. (12) 492-89-12; fax (12) 498-93-24; e-mail expo@chamber .baku.az; Pres. SULEYMAN BAYRAM OĞLU TATLIYEV.

INDUSTRIAL AND TRADE ASSOCIATIONS

National Confederation of Entrepreneurs' (Employers') Organizations of Azerbaijan (Azarbaycan Respublikasi Sahib-karlar—İşagötüranlar—Taşkilatları Milli Konfederasiyasi—ASK): 1002 Baku, S. Askerova küç 85; tel. (12) 494-90-16; fax (12) 494-99-76; e-mail aazerenterprise@artel.net.az; internet www.ask.org.az; f. 1999; Pres. ALEKPER MAMEDOV.

UTILITIES

Electricity

Azerenerji: 1005 Baku, A. Alizade küç. 10; tel. (12) 493-73-58; fax (12) 498-55-23; e-mail azener@azener.in-baku.com; internet www .azener.in-baku.com; state-owned jt-stock co; power generation and transmission company; Pres. ETIBAR S. PIRVERDIYEV.

AliBayramlıelektrikşebeke: 1800 Ali Bayramlı; f. 2001; comprises the Azerbaijani electricity network's southern zone; managed by Bakı Yüksakgarginlikli Elektroavadanliq (BYGEA—Baku High Voltage Electrical Equipment Co).

Barmek-Azerbaijan Electricşebeke (Barmek-zerbaijan Electricity Network): 1000 Baku, Kazumzada 20; tel. (12) 440-44-04; fax (12) 440-22-26; e-mail barmek@barmek.az; internet www.barmek .az; f. 2001 as Bakielektrikşebeke open joint stock co; following the restructuring of the distribution assets of Azerenerji into five regional orgs; managed by Barmek Holding AS (Turkey); subsequently renamed as above.

Barmek-Azerbaijan Sumqayıt Elektrikshebeke (Sumqayıtelektrikshebeke): 5000 Sumqayıt; tel. (164) 298-88; fax (164) 296-18; f. 2001; covering the northern zone of the Azerbaijani electricity distribution network; managed by Barmek Holding AS (Turkey).

Bayva-Enerji: 2000 Ganca, Ruzigar Gasimov küç. 10; tel. and fax (22) 56-97-40; e-mail bayva-qerbenerji@mail.ru; internet www .bayva.org; f. 2002 as Ganjaelektrikşebeke; comprising the Azerbaijani electricity distribution network's western zone; managed by Bakı Yüksakgarginlikli Elektroavadanliq (BYGEA—Baku High Voltage Electrical Equipment); Gen. Dir RAMIZ AGAMALIYEV.

Naxçıvan Electrikşebeke: 7000 Naxçıvan; f. 2001; state-owned open joint-stock co; one of the five transmission and distribution area networks into which the national grid was divided; approximately 60% of electricity imported from Iran.

Gas

AzeriGaz: 1025 Baku, Yusif Safarov küç. 23; tel. (12) 490-42-52; fax (12) 490-42-55; e-mail azer_bayramov@azerigaz.com; f. 1992; transport, distribution, sale, compression and storage of natural gas; Chair. ALIKHAN MELIKHOV; 13,000 employees.

STATE HYDROCARBONS COMPANIES

Azerbaijan International Operating Co (AIOC): 1003 Baku, Neftchilar pr. 2, Villa Petrolea; tel. (12) 491-21-02; fax (12) 475-96-02; e-mail bayatltf@bp.com; f. 1994 as a consortium of: SOCAR (q.v.); British Petroleum (United Kingdom); Devon Energy, ExxonMobil and Unocal (USA); Itochu and Inpex (Japan); Statoil (Norway); Türkiye Petrolleri (Turkey); and the Delta Hess alliance (Saudi Arabia–USA); exploration and development of offshore petroleum reserves; Pres. DAVID WOODWARD.

State Committee for Geology and Mineral Resources of Azerbaijan: 1073 Baku, Bakhram Agayev küç. 100A; tel. (12) 438-04-31; fax (12) 439-84-32; f. 1932; prospecting, research and surveys; Chair. ISLAM TAGIEV.

State Oil Co of the Azerbaijan Republic (SOCAR): 370004 Baku, Neftchilar pr. 73; tel. (12) 492-07-45; fax (12) 497-11-67; e-mail akhmedo@aiocaz.com; f. 1992; production and exploration activities, oversees refining and capital construction; owns Azerneftyag and Azerneftyanayag refineries; Pres. NATIK ALIYEV; Exec. Dir SAMIR RAUF OĞLU SHARIFOV; 67,000 employees.

TRADE UNIONS

Confederation of Azerbaijan Trade Unions (AHIK): 1000 Baku, Genjler meydani 3; tel. and fax (12) 492-72-68; e-mail ahik@azerin .com; Chair. SATTAR MEHBALIYEV.

Trade Union of Oil and Gas Industry Workers: 1033 Baku, Aga Neymatulla küç. 39; tel. (12) 467-69-53; fax (12) 447-15-85; e-mail oilunion@online.az; f. 1906; 161 local orgs in the petroleum and gas sectors; 67,900 mems (2003); Chair. JAHANGIR ALIYEV.

Transport

RAILWAYS

In 2003 there were 2,122 km of railway track, of which 1,270 km were electrified. The overwhelming majority of total freight traffic is carried by the railways. Railways connect Baku with Tbilisi (Georgia), Makhachkala (Dagestan, Russia) and Yerevan (Armenia). In 1997 passenger rail services between Moscow and Baku were resumed, and a service to Kiev (Ukraine) was inaugurated. The rail link between metropolitan Azerbaijan and the Naxçıvan Autonomous Republic runs through Armenia, but is currently disrupted, owing to Azerbaijan's economic blockade of Armenia. From Naxçıvan an international line links Azerbaijan with Tabriz (Iran). There is an underground railway in Baku; initially comprising two lines (total length 38.5 km), with 20 stations.

Azerbaijani Railways (AZ): 1010 Baku, Dilara Aliyeva küç. 230; tel. (12) 498-44-67; fax (12) 498-85-47; e-mail info@addy.gov.az; f. 1992; First Dep. Pres. and Chief Eng. M. M. MEHTIYEV.

Baku Metro: 1602 Baku, H. Javid pr. 33A; tel. (12) 490-00-00; fax (12) 497-53-96; f. 1967; Gen. Man. T. AKHMEDOV.

ROADS

In 2002 the total length of roads in Azerbaijan was 25,0127 km, of which 6,928 km were main roads; 92.4% of the road network was paved.

SHIPPING

Shipping services on the Caspian Sea link Baku with Astrakhan (Russia), Türkmenbaşi (formerly Krasnovodsk—Turkmenistan) and the Iranian ports of Bandar Anzali and Bandar Nowshar. At 31 December 2003 the Azerbaijani merchant fleet comprised 288 vessels, with a combined displacement of 637,994 grt.

Baku Sea Port: 1010 Baku, U. Hajibeyov küç. 72; tel. (12) 493-67-74; fax (12) 493-36-72; e-mail port@sea.baku.az; internet www.bakuport.com.

Shipowning Company

Caspian Shipping Company (Caspar): 1005 Baku, Mammademin Rasulzade küç. 5; tel. (12) 493-20-58; fax (12) 493-53-39; e-mail gkmp@caspar.baku.az; internet www.caspar.baku.az; transports crude petroleum and petroleum products; operates cargo and passenger ferries; fleet of 69 vessels; Pres. A. A. BASHIROV.

CIVIL AVIATION

There are five airports in Azerbaijan, of which Baku is the largest. A new air terminal was commissioned for the Bina-Baku airport in 1999; the airport was named after Heydar Aliyev in 2003. Naxçıvan also has its own airport.

Civil Aviation Administration: 1000 Baku, Azadliq pr. 11; tel. (12) 493-44-34; fax (12) 498-52-37; e-mail azal_coordpt@azerin.com; Chief Inspector İLHAM G. AMIROV.

Azerbaijan Airlines (AZAL) (Azerbaijan Hava Yollari): 1000 Baku, Azadliq pr. 11; tel. (12) 493-44-34; fax (12) 498-52-37; e-mail azal@azal.baku.az; f. 1992; formerly Azalavia; state airline operating scheduled and charter passenger and cargo services to Africa, the CIS, Europe, South-East Asia and the Middle East; Gen. Dir JAHANGIR ASKEROV.

IMAIR Airlines: 1000 Baku, Hazi Aslanov küç. 115; tel. (12) 493-41-71; fax (12) 493-27-77; e-mail root@imair.com; internet www.imair.com; f. 1995; independent airline operating international regular passenger and charter passenger and cargo services, mainly within the CIS region; Pres. FIZOULI ALEKPEROV.

Turan Air: 1022 Baku, Terlan Mardanov küç 102; tel. (12) 498-94-31; fax (12) 498-94-34; e-mail root@turan-air.com; internet www.turan-air.com; f. 1994; operates scheduled and charter passenger and cargo services, mainly within the former USSR.

Tourism

Tourism is not widely developed. However, there are resorts on the Caspian Sea, including the Ganjlik international tourist centre, on the Apsheron Peninsula, near Baku, which has four hotels as well as camping facilities. There were 1,066,290 tourist arrivals in 2003.

Council for Foreign Tourism: 1007 Baku, Neftchilar pr. 65; tel. (12) 492-87-13; fax (12) 492-98-41; e-mail tourism@myst.co-az.net; dept of the Ministry of Youth, Sport and Tourism; Head Deputy Minister TEYMUR MEHDIYEV.

THE BAHAMAS

Introductory Survey

Location, Climate, Language, Religion, Flag, Capital

The Commonwealth of the Bahamas consists of about 700 islands and more than 2,000 cays and rocks, extending from east of the Florida coast of the USA to just north of Cuba and Haiti, in the West Indies. The main islands are New Providence, Grand Bahama, Andros, Eleuthera and Great Abaco. Almost 70% of the population reside on the island of New Providence. The remaining members of the group are known as the 'Family Islands'. A total of 29 of the islands are inhabited. The climate is mild and sub-tropical, with average temperatures of about 30°C (86°F) in summer and 20°C (68°F) in winter. The average annual rainfall is about 1,000 mm (39 ins). The official language is English. Most of the inhabitants profess Christianity, the largest denominations being the Anglican, Baptist, Roman Catholic and Methodist Churches. The national flag (proportions 1 by 2) comprises three equal horizontal stripes, of blue, gold and blue, with a black triangle at the hoist, extending across one-half of the width. The capital is Nassau, on the island of New Providence.

Recent History

A former British colonial territory, the Bahamas attained internal self-government in January 1964, although the parliamentary system dates back to 1729. The first elections under universal adult suffrage were held in January 1967 for an enlarged House of Assembly. The Progressive Liberal Party (PLP), supported mainly by Bahamians of African origin and led by Lynden (later Sir Lynden) Pindling, won 18 of the 38 seats, as did the ruling United Bahamian Party (UBP), dominated by those of European origin. With the support of another member, the PLP formed a Government and Pindling became Premier (he was restyled Prime Minister in September 1968). At the next elections, in April 1968, the PLP won 29 seats and the UBP only seven.

Following a constitutional conference in September 1968, the Bahamas Government was given increased responsibility for internal security, external affairs and defence in May 1969. In the elections of September 1972, which were dominated by the issue of independence, the PLP maintained its majority. Following a constitutional conference in December 1972, the Bahamas became an independent nation, within the Commonwealth, on 10 July 1973. Pindling remained Prime Minister. The PLP increased its majority in the elections of July 1977 and was again returned to power in the June 1982 elections, with 32 of the 43 seats in the enlarged House of Assembly. The remaining 11 seats were won by the Free National Movement (FNM), which had reunited for the elections after splitting into several factions over the previous five years.

Trading in illicit drugs, mainly for the US market, has become a major problem for the country, since many of the small islands and cays are used by drugs-traffickers in their smuggling activities. In 1983 allegations of widespread corruption, and the abuse of Bahamian bank secrecy laws by drugs-traffickers and US tax evaders, led Pindling to appoint a Royal Commission to investigate thoroughly the drugs trade in the Bahamas. The Commission's hearings revealed the extent to which money deriving from this trade had permeated Bahamian social and economic affairs. Evidence presented to the Commission led to the resignation, in October 1984, of two cabinet ministers, and by November 1985 a total of 51 suspects had been indicted, including the assistant police commissioner. The Commission also revealed that Pindling had received several million dollars in gifts and loans from business executives, although it found no evidence of a link to the drugs trade. After unsuccessfully demanding Pindling's resignation, the Deputy Prime Minister, Arthur Hanna, resigned, and two other ministers, Perry Christie and Hubert Ingraham, were dismissed.

Although the issue of the illegal drugs trade and of drugs-related corruption within the Government dominated the general election campaign, the PLP was returned to power for a fifth consecutive term in June 1987, winning 31 of the 49 seats in the enlarged House of Assembly. The FNM won 16 seats, while the remaining two seats were secured by Christie and Ingraham as independents.

In February 1988 new claims of official corruption were made at the trial in Florida, USA, of a leading Colombian drugs-trafficker. Pindling and the Deputy Prime Minister were alleged to have accepted bribes, but this was vehemently denied. In March 1990 the Minister of Agriculture, Trade and Industry, Ervin Knowles, resigned, following allegations of nepotism and the misuse of public funds. He was replaced by Christie, who rejoined the PLP. The other independent member, Ingraham, subsequently joined the FNM and became its leader in May, upon the death of Sir Cecil Wallace-Whitfield.

Campaigning for the August 1992 general election was disrupted by industrial unrest in the country's telephone and electricity companies, and by the continuing problems of the state airline, Bahamasair. Despite predictions of a PLP victory, the FNM won the election, securing 33 seats, while Pindling's party won the remaining 16. Ingraham replaced Pindling as Prime Minister, and announced a programme of measures aimed at increasing the accountability of government ministers, combating corruption and revitalizing the economy. Acknowledging responsibility for his party's defeat in the election, Pindling resigned as leader of the PLP, but, at the party's annual convention in January 1993, he agreed to continue in office.

A marked increase in violent crime in parts of New Providence led the Government to announce the creation, in March 1995, of a special police unit to tackle the problem. Meanwhile, the trade in illegal drugs remained widespread in the country, and in late 1995 several local business leaders, as well as close relatives of a member of Parliament, were arrested in connection with a large seizure of cocaine. In October of that year the Prime Minister introduced further legislation that aimed to prevent the abuse of Bahamian banks by drugs-traffickers, and thus improve the reputation of the country's financial sector, particularly in the USA.

At a general election held in March 1997 the FNM won 34 of the 40 seats in a reduced House of Assembly, and the PLP six. The FNM's overwhelming victory in the election was attributed both to the Prime Minister's success in reversing the economic decline and the involvement of the PLP in various financial scandals. Most notably, Pindling was implicated in February in the findings of a public inquiry (instituted in 1993) to investigate alleged corruption and misappropriation of funds in the three principal state corporations. Following the election, Pindling, who had retained his seat in the House of Assembly, resigned as leader of the PLP and was replaced by Christie. The PLP was further damaged in January 2000 by the resignation of its deputy leader, Bernard Nottage, who subsequently formed a rival party, the Coalition for Democratic Reform.

Violent crime continued to be of major concern to Bahamians. In April 1998 the Government signed a convention drawn up by the Organization of American States (OAS, see p. 319) to ban illegal guns, amid a disturbing increase in gun-related crime. In September 1998, following the murders of several tourists, the Prime Minister increased security in tourist areas, and announced plans to limit the right of appeal against death sentences (the sentences of 17 prisoners had been commuted in January). The hanging in October of two convicted murderers caused controversy, despite growing public demand for execution as a deterrent against crime. The Government had rejected a last-minute plea for clemency from the European Union, on the grounds that both men had appeals pending at the Inter-American Commission on Human Rights (IACHR, see p. 320). In August 1999 the Bahamian authorities were strongly criticized by human rights groups after they announced their intention to execute another two convicted murderers who had also submitted petitions to the IACHR. Despite attempts to reduce levels of crime, the murder rate reached a high of 72 in 2000. Although there was a marked decrease in 2001, to 43, the number of murders increased again in 2002, to 52. In 2002 the murder rate remained static at 50, although 2004 witnessed a decrease in the number of people murdered, to 40.

In 2000 the Bahamas was listed by the Financial Action Task Force (FATF, see p. 377) as a non-co-operative jurisdiction, and by the Organisation for Economic Co-operation and Development (OECD, see p. 307) as a tax 'haven'. The Bahamas also received the lowest grade of bank supervision in a report by the Financial Stability Forum, a group of international regulators, and remained classified as a 'Country of Primary Concern' in the US International Narcotics Control Strategy Report, partly because of its banking secrecy laws and the size of its 'offshore' financial sector. The Government responded by establishing, in October 2000, a Financial Intelligence Unit and by adopting legislation intended to encourage transparency in the sector. As a result, in August 2001 the FATF removed the Bahamas from its 'blacklist'. In January 2002 an agreement to share information on tax matters with the USA was signed, while in March OECD accepted the Bahamas' commitment to improve the transparency of its financial sector. In 2004 the FATF announced that it intended to re-evaluate the Bahamas' financial sector.

In November 2001 the Governor-General, Orville Turnquest, resigned after seven years in office. Dame Ivy Dumont, the Bahamas' first female Governor-General, succeeded him.

At the general election held on 2 May 2002 the PLP unexpectedly secured an overwhelming victory over the FNM, winning 29 of the 40 seats (with 50.8% of the vote) in the House of Assembly. The FNM retained seven seats (with 41.1% of the ballot). Independent candidates won the remaining four seats. The tourism minister and FNM leader-designate, Tommy Turnquest, failed to retain his seat, as did several other outgoing ministers. Notable appointments to Perry Christie's Cabinet included those of Allyson Maynard-Gibson to the newly created post of Minister of Financial Services and Investments and James Smith, the former Governor of the Central Bank, as Minister of State in the Ministry of Finance. The new Government pledged the establishment of a national health-insurance system, as well as constitutional reform; commissions were subsequently established to develop detailed proposals with regard to these commitments. A commission on health insurance reported in May 2004, although its recommendations had not been implemented by early 2005.

The Bahamas' traditionally close relationship with the USA was strained during the 1990s by the increasingly uncompromising attitude of the US authorities towards bank secrecy laws and drugs-smuggling in the islands. The USA and the Bahamas collaborated in a series of operations to intercept drugs-traffickers, and in 1998 the USA commended the Bahamian authorities for their efforts to curb this illegal trade. However, there were reports that the detection by surveillance equipment in the Bahamas of fewer suspected drugs transhipments during 2001 than in 2000 was in part attributable to the withdrawal of some US detection and monitoring aircraft following the suicide attacks on the USA in September 2001. In late 2002 the relationship worsened after the then US ambassador to the Bahamas, J. Richard Blankenship, asserted that the judicial system did not penalize drugs-traffickers severely enough and urged a thorough reform of the Royal Bahamian Defence Force. A report published in March 2004 by the US Department of State suggested that 12% of cocaine imports to the USA were transhipped through the Jamaica-Cuba-Bahamas corridor. Relations with the USA, however, improved in July after the Bahamian Government amended the country's extradition laws to give the state increased rights of appeal against the release of a suspect by the courts. (Of some 50 recent US extradition requests, 35 had been rejected by Bahamian courts.) Meanwhile, in the same month a new maritime agreement was signed with the USA. Cocaine seizures amounted to 4.0 metric tons in 2003.

Meanwhile, relations with the Bahamas' other neighbours, Haiti and Cuba, were strained by the influx of large numbers of illegal immigrants from both countries. In June 1998 the Bahamian Government agreed to inform Cuba of the arrival of illegal Cuban immigrants within 72 hours of their discovery, while Cuba agreed to their repatriation within 15 days. In 1995–2003 more than 35,000 Haitian illegal migrants and refugees were deported from the Bahamas, with a peak figure of 7,589 in 2001. In November 2003 the human rights organization Amnesty International released a report that criticized prison conditions in the Bahamas and accused the country of mistreating asylum-seekers from Cuba and Haiti; the Christie Government countered that the report was 'unbalanced'.

Government

Legislative power is vested in the bicameral Parliament. The Senate has 16 members, of whom nine are appointed by the Governor-General on the advice of the Prime Minister, four by the Leader of the Opposition and three after consultation with the Prime Minister. The House of Assembly has 40 members, elected for five years (subject to dissolution) by universal adult suffrage. Executive power is vested in the British monarch, represented by a Governor-General, who is appointed on the Prime Minister's recommendation and who acts, in almost all matters, on the advice of the Cabinet. The Governor-General appoints the Prime Minister and, on the latter's recommendation, selects the other ministers. The Cabinet is responsible to the House of Assembly.

Defence

The Royal Bahamian Defence Force, a paramilitary coastguard, is the only security force in the Bahamas, and numbered 860 (including 70 women) in August 2004. Defence expenditure in 2004 was budgeted at B $30m.

Economic Affairs

In 2002, according to estimates by the World Bank, the Bahamas' gross national income (GNI), measured at average 2000–02 prices, was US $4,837m., equivalent to US $15,110 per head (or US $16,140 per head on an international purchasing-power parity basis). During 1990–2003, it was estimated, the population increased at an average annual rate of 1.7%. In 1990–2002 gross domestic product (GDP) per head decreased, in real terms, by an annual average of 0.2%. Overall GDP increased, in real terms, at an average rate of 1.5% per year in 1990–2002; real GDP decreased by 2.0% in 2001, but increased by 0.7% in 2002.

Agriculture, hunting, forestry and fishing, which together accounted for only 3.8% of GDP in 1995 and engaged an estimated 4.0% of the employed labour force in 1999, were developed by the Government in the 1990s in an attempt to reduce dependence on imports (80% of food supplies were imported in the 1980s). In 1998, however, agricultural production accounted for only 1.0% of total land area. By the late 1990s, according to official estimates, agriculture contributed less than 3% of GDP. An increase in some areas of agricultural output has, none the less, resulted in the export of certain crops, particularly of cucumbers, tomatoes, pineapples, papayas, avocados, mangoes, limes and other citrus fruits. The development of commercial fishing has concentrated on conchs and crustaceans. In 2000 exports of Caribbean spiny lobster (crawfish) provided 26.5% of domestic export earnings, and accounted for 97.6% of the fishing total. There is also some exploitation of pine forests in the northern Bahamas. According to government estimates, 'Hurricane Frances', which struck the Bahamas in August 2004, caused damage to the agricultural sector equivalent to B $45m.

Industry (comprising mining, manufacturing, construction and utilities) employed an estimated 16.6% of the working population in 1999 (construction accounted for 11.4%) and provided 11.0% of GDP in 1995.

Mining and manufacturing together contributed only 4.0% of GDP in 1995. Mining provided an estimated 1.2% of employment, and manufacturing 4.1%, in 1999. The islands' principal mineral resources are aragonite (which provided 8.1% of domestic export earnings in 2000) and salt. In late 2002 the Government granted a licence to an international oil company to explore for petroleum in Bahamian waters.

The manufacturing sector alone contributed some 10% of GDP in 1982, since when it has declined, owing to the closure, in 1985, of the country's petroleum refinery. The principal branches of manufacturing were beverages, chemicals and printing and publishing. Exports of rum accounted for 5.9% of domestic export earnings in 2000. The construction sector experienced much activity in the latter part of the 20th century, owing to the construction of hotels and tourist complexes and harbour developments.

Most of the energy requirements of the Bahamas are fulfilled by the petroleum that Venezuela and, particularly, Mexico provide under the San José Agreement (originally negotiated in 1980), which commits both the petroleum producers to selling subsidized supplies, on favourable terms, to the developing countries of the region. Excluding transhipments of petroleum, imports of mineral fuels accounted for 12.7% of total imports in 2001. In December 2004 the Government gave approval to a US company to construct the islands' first liquefied petroleum gas terminal. The plant was expected to become operational in 2007.

Service industries constitute the principal sectors of the economy, providing 85.2% of GDP in 1995 and about 78.9% of total employment in 1999. In 1999 an international container transhipment facility was completed at Freeport, Grand Bahama; it was to act as an intercontinental hub port serving North America, the Caribbean and South America. Petroleum transhipment on Grand Bahama remains an important activity. At the end of 2003 a total of 1,297 vessels were registered under the Bahamian flag. With a combined displacement of 34.8m. grt, the fleet was the third largest in the world. Banking is the second most important economic activity in the Bahamas and there is a large 'offshore' financial sector. In May 2000 a stock exchange, where it was planned to develop trading in global depository receipts for overseas companies, became operational; by 2005 it was trading the shares of 19 local companies. Despite increasing competition, the Bahamas continues to be the principal tourist destination of the Caribbean. Tourism is the predominant sector of the economy, directly accounting for 15% of GDP in 1998 and employing some 30% of the working population. In 2003 estimated travel receipts covered 109% of the cost of goods imported. In 2002 81.0% of stop-over visitors were from the USA, although attempts are being made to attract visitors from other countries and improve air access to resorts. Visitor arrivals increased from 4.21m. in 2002 to 4.40m. in 2003. Receipts from tourism also increased; from B $1,650m. in 2000 to $1,782m. in 2003. The Bahamas receives more cruise-ship arrivals annually than any other Caribbean destination.

In 2003 the Bahamas recorded a visible trade deficit of US $1,204.7m., and there was a deficit of $429.8m. on the current account of the balance of payments. The USA is the principal trading partner of the Bahamas, providing 85.8% total imports and taking 77.5% of exports in 2001. The principal exports in 2001 were basic manufactures (23.3% of total imports), machinery and transport equipment (22.6%) and mineral fuels and lubricants (12.7%). In that year the principal imports were chemicals (25.9% of total imports), food and live animals (21.4%) and mineral fuels and lubricants (18.2%).

In 2003 there was a budgetary deficit of B $207.7m. At 31 December 2002 the external debt of the central Government was some $96.0m.; the cost of servicing foreign-currency debt in that year was $74.1m., equivalent to 8.3% of current revenue. The debt-service ratio in 2002 was equivalent to 5.2% of the value of goods and services. The annual rate of inflation averaged 1.9% in 1997–2003; consumer prices increased by 3.0% in 2003. The rate of unemployment stood at some 8% of the labour force in 2001.

The Bahamas is a member of the Caribbean Community and Common Market (CARICOM, see p. 172) and the Organization of American States (OAS, see p. 319), the Association of Caribbean States (see p. 372) and is a signatory of the Cotonou Agreement (see p. 262) with the European Union. The Government applied for membership of the World Trade Organization (see p. 357) in 2004.

Economic expansion through foreign investment has continued to be restricted in the past decade by fears of widespread corruption and instability (caused by the activities of illegal drugs-trafficking networks in the islands), although investor confidence was reported to have increased since the 1990s. In spite of measures, taken from 1989, to combat corruption in the financial sector and thus improve the reputation of the country's economic institutions, in 2000 the Bahamas was listed by the Financial Action Task Force (FATF, see p. 377) as a non-co-operative jurisdiction and by the Organisation for Economic Co-operation and Development (OECD, see p. 307) as a tax 'haven'. Following the introduction of further legislation in late 2000, in 2001 the FATF removed the country from its 'blacklist', and OECD followed suit in March 2002. However, legal challenges were initiated against various aspects of the new financial legislation in late 2001 and early 2002, and the incoming Progressive Liberal Party (PLP) Government, elected in May 2002, pledged to review the recent financial legislation. The divestment of the state electricity company and of the loss-making Bahamasair Holdings was expected during the PLP administration, although plans remained at a preliminary stage in early 2005. The liberalization of the telecommunications sector was also pending. A reduction in revenues in the tourism sector (in large part attributable to the consequences for the sector of the US-led military campaign to oust the regime of Saddam Hussein in Iraq) led the Prime Minister in July 2003 to abandon an agreed wage increase for 24,000 public servants in order to protect the fiscal position. In late 2003 the Government announced its intention to reform the fiscal regime: in particular, the country's dependence on customs and excise taxes and stamp duties, incompatible with future regional and international trade agreements, was to be reduced; the loss was expected to be offset by the introduction of value-added tax. Economic growth, negative in 2001 and negligible in 2002, was estimated to have remained subdued in 2003, at around 1%, although an increase in tourism revenue, stimulated by the recovering US market, helped to improve the growth rate to around 3% in 2004 and was expected to provide a further boost for the economy in 2005. The positive economic outlook was, however, compromised by the arrival of 'Hurricane Frances' in late August 2004, which was estimated to have caused up to B $200m.-worth of damage to the islands.

Education

Education is compulsory between the ages of five and 16 years, and is provided free of charge in government schools. There are several private and denominational schools. Primary education begins at five years of age and lasts for six years. Secondary education, beginning at the age of 11, also lasts for six years and is divided into two equal cycles. In 2000 98% of children in the relevant age-group were enrolled at primary level. In the same year 89% of children in the relevant age-group were enrolled at secondary level. The University of the West Indies has an extra-mural department in Nassau, offering degree courses in hotel management and tourism. The Bahamas Hotel Training College was established in 1992. The Bahamas Law School, part of the University of the West Indies, opened in 1998. Technical, teacher-training and professional qualifications can be obtained at the two campuses of the College of the Bahamas.

Government expenditure on education in 2004/05 was budgeted at B $201.8m. (or 17.1% of total spending from the General Budget).

Public Holidays

2005: 1 January (New Year's Day), 25 March (Good Friday), 28 March (Easter Monday), 16 May (Whit Monday), 3 June (Labour Day), 10 July (Independence Day), 1 August (Emancipation Day), 12 October (Discovery Day/Columbus Day), 25–26 December (Christmas).

2006: 1 January (New Year's Day), 14 April (Good Friday), 17 April (Easter Monday), 2 June (Labour Day), 5 June (Whit Monday), 10 July (Independence Day), 7 August (Emancipation Day), 12 October (Discovery Day/Columbus Day), 25–26 December (Christmas).

Weights and Measures

The imperial system is used.

Statistical Survey

Source (unless otherwise stated): Central Bank of the Bahamas, Frederick St, POB N-4868, Nassau; tel. 322-2193; fax 322-4321; e-mail cbob@centralbankbahamas.com; internet www.centralbankbahamas.com.

AREA AND POPULATION

Area: 13,939 sq km (5,382 sq miles).

Population: 255,095 at census of 2 May 1990; 303,611 (males 147,778, females 155,833) at census of 1 May 2000; 311,900 at mid-2002. *By Island* (1990): New Providence 172,196 (including the capital, Nassau); Grand Bahama 40,898; Andros 8,187; Eleuthera 10,586. Source: partly Caribbean Development Bank, *Social and Economic Indicators*.

Density (mid-2002): 22.9 per sq km.

Principal Town (population, UN estimate, incl. suburbs): Nassau (capital) 222,163 in mid-2003. Source: UN, *World Urbanization Prospects: The 2003 Revision*.

Births, Marriages and Deaths (1999, unless otherwise indicated): Registered live births 6,367 (birth rate 21.4 per 1,000); Registered marriages (1996) 2,628 (marriage rate 9.3 per 1,000); Registered deaths 1,567 (death rate 5.3 per 1,000). *2000:* Crude birth rate 17.4 per 1,000; Crude death rate 5.3 per 1,000. *2001:* Total live births 5,353; Total deaths 1,609. Sources: UN, *Demographic Yearbook, Population and Vital Statistics Report,* and Caribbean Development Bank, *Social and Economic Indicators.*

Expectation of Life (WHO estimates, years at birth): 72.1 (males 69.0; females 75.2) in 2002. Source: WHO, *World Health Report.*

Economically Active Population (sample survey, persons aged 15 years and over, excl. armed forces, April 1999): Agriculture, hunting, forestry and fishing 5,835; Mining, quarrying, electricity, gas and water 1,745; Manufacturing 5,910; Construction 16,540; Wholesale and retail trade 19,955; Hotels and restaurants 23,300; Transport, storage and communications 10,305; Finance, insurance, real estate and business services 13,350; Community, social and personal services 47,780; Activities not adequately defined 630; *Total employed* 145,350 (males 77,245, females 68,105); Unemployed 12,290 (males 4,955, females 7,335); *Total labour force* 157,640 (males, 82,200, females 75,440) (Source: ILO Caribbean Office). *2002* (figures rounded to nearest 10 persons): Total employed 152,690 (males 78,410, females 74,280); Unemployed 15,290 (males 7,560, females 7,730); Total labour force 167,980 (males 85,970, females 82,010).

HEALTH AND WELFARE

Key Indicators

Total Fertility Rate (children per woman, 2002): 2.3.

Under-5 Mortality Rate (per 1,000 live births, 2003): 14.

HIV/AIDS (% of persons aged 15–49, 2003): 3.0.

Physicians (per 1,000 head, 1996): 1.52.

Hospital Beds (per 1,000 head, 1996): 3.94.

Health Expenditure (2001): US $ per head (PPP): 1,220.

Health Expenditure (2001): % of GDP: 5.7.

Health Expenditure (2001): public (% of total): 57.0.

Access to Water (% of persons, 2002): 97.

Access to Sanitation (% of persons, 2002): 100.

Human Development Index (2002): ranking: 51.

Human Development Index (2002): value: 0.815.
For sources and definitions, see explanatory note on p. vi.

AGRICULTURE, ETC.

Principal Crops (FAO estimates, '000 metric tons, 2003): Roots and tubers 1.0; Sugar cane 55.5; Tomatoes 4.0; Other vegetables 19.7; Bananas 3.4; Lemons and limes 8.5; Grapefruit and pomelos 12.5; Other fruits 3.6. Source: FAO.

Livestock (FAO estimates, '000 head, year ending September 2003): Cattle 0.7; Pigs 5.0; Sheep 6.5; Goats 14.0; Poultry 2,975. Source: FAO.

Livestock Products (FAO estimates, '000 metric tons, 2003): Chicken meat 8.0; Cows' milk 0.7; Goats' milk 1.0; Hen eggs 0.9. Source: FAO.

Forestry (FAO estimates, '000 cubic metres, 2003): *Roundwood Removals (excl. bark):* Sawlogs and veneer logs 17 (output assumed to be unchanged since 1992); *Sawnwood Production (incl. railway sleepers):* Coniferous (softwood) 1 (output assumed to be unchanged since 1970). Source: FAO.

Fishing (metric tons, live weight, 2002, estimates): Capture 9,300 (Nassau grouper 280; Snappers 780; Caribbean spiny lobster 7,050; Stromboid conchs 650); Aquaculture 13; *Total catch* 9,313. Source: FAO.

MINING

Production (estimates, '000 metric tons, 2001): Unrefined salt 900; Aragonite 1,200. Source: US Geological Survey.

INDUSTRY

Production (estimate, million kWh, 2002): Electric energy 1,826.

FINANCE

Currency and Exchange Rates: 100 cents = 1 Bahamian dollar (B $). *Sterling, US Dollar and Euro Equivalents* (31 December 2004): £1 sterling = B $1.9314; US $1 = B $1.0000; €1 = B $1.3621; B $100 = £51.78 = US $100.00 = €73.42. *Exchange Rate:* Since February 1970 the official exchange rate, applicable to most transactions, has been US $1 = B $1, i.e. the Bahamian dollar has been at par with the US dollar. There is also an investment currency rate, applicable to certain capital transactions between residents and non-residents and to direct investments outside the Bahamas. Since 1987 this exchange rate has been fixed at US $1 = B $1.225.

General Budget (preliminary, B $ million, 2002): *Revenue:* Taxation 796.0 (Taxes on international trade and transactions 506.6; Taxes on tourism 88.2; Taxes on property 76.6; Taxes on companies 61.2); Other current revenue 89.7; Total 885.6. *Expenditure:* Wages and salaries 475.5; Goods and services 227.4; Interest payments 100.8; Subsidies and transfers 91.4; Capital expenditure and net lending 131.1; Total 1,026.2 (Source: IMF, *Bahamas: Statistical Appendix* (July 2003)). *2003* (preliminary, B $ million): Total revenue and grants 901.8; Total expenditure (excl. net lending, 43.1) 1,046.5 (Current expenditure 962.7, Capital expenditure 83.8). *2004* (approved estimates, B $ million): Total revenue and grants 991.5; Total expenditure (excl. net lending, 25.9) 1,088.6 (Current expenditure 968.9, Capital expenditure 119.7).

International Reserves (US $ million at 31 December 2003): Reserve position in IMF 9.3; Foreign exchange 481.8; Total 491.1. Source: IMF, *International Financial Statistics.*

Money Supply (B $ million at 31 December 2003): Currency outside banks 160; Demand deposits at deposit money banks 714; Total money (incl. others) 884. Source: IMF, *International Financial Statistics.*

Cost of Living (consumer price index; base: 2000 = 100): 102.0 in 2001; 104.3 in 2002; 107.4 in 2003. Source: IMF, *International Financial Statistics.*

Gross Domestic Product (estimates, B $ million at current prices): 4,950 in 2001; 5,050 in 2002; 5,260 in 2003. Source: Caribbean Development Bank, *Social and Economic Indicators.*

Expenditure on the Gross Domestic Product (B $ million at current prices, 1995): Government final consumption expenditure 483.9; Private final consumption expenditure 2,077.4; Increase in stocks 13.8; Gross fixed capital formation 698.5; *Total domestic expenditure* 3,273.6; Exports of goods and services 1,680.1; *Less* Imports of goods and services 1,819.6; Statistical discrepancy –64.7; *GDP in purchasers' values* 3,069.4. Source: IMF, *International Financial Statistics.*

Gross Domestic Product by Economic Activity (B $ million at current prices, 1995): Agriculture, hunting, forestry and fishing 100; Manufacturing (incl. mining and quarrying) 106; Electricity, gas and water 116; Construction 71; Trade, restaurants and hotels 705; Transport, storage and communications 295; Finance, insurance, real estate and business services 599; Government services 210; Other community, social and personal services 454; *Sub-total* 2,656; Statistical discrepancy 65; Taxes, less subsidies, on products 503; *Less* Imputed bank service charges 423; Import duties 268; *GDP in purchasers' values* 3,069. Source: UN, *National Accounts Statistics.*

Balance of Payments (US $ million, 2003): Exports of goods f.o.b. 424.8; Imports of goods f.o.b. –1,629.5; *Trade balance* –1,204.7; Exports of services 1,979.9; Imports of services –1,079.5; *Balance on goods and services* –304.3; Other income received 48.4; Other income paid –211.5; *Balance on goods, services and income* –467.4; Current transfers received 48.8; Current transfers paid –11.2; *Current balance* –429.8; Capital account (net) –37.4; Direct investment from abroad (net) 145.0; Other investment assets 46,576.8; Other investment liabilities –46,462.1; Net errors and omissions 317.5; *Overall balance* 110.0. Source: IMF, *International Financial Statistics.*

EXTERNAL TRADE

Principal Commodities (US $ million, 2001): *Imports c.i.f.:* Food and live animals 298.1 (Meat and preparations 78.3); Mineral fuels, lubricants, etc. 301.2 (Refined petroleum products, etc. 278.3); Chemicals 146.8; Basic manufactures 551.4 (Non-metallic mineral manufactures 297.7); Machinery and transport equipment 536.1 (General industrial machinery and equipment 105.0; Road vehicles 151.8); Miscellaneous manufactured articles 385.9 (Articles of apparel and clothing accessories 143.2); Total (incl. others) 2,370.1. *Exports f.o.b.:* Food and live animals 80.8 (Fish, crustacean and molluscs, and preparations thereof 72.1); Beverages and tobacco 40.8 (Alcoholic beverages 39.6); Crude materials (inedible) except fuels 27.8; Refined petroleum products 68.8; Chemicals 97.8 (Organic chemicals 14.4; Artificial resins and plastic materials, and cellulose esters, etc. 71.7); Machinery and transport equipment 45.5

(General industrial machinery and equipment 14.2); Total (incl. others) 378.2.

Principal Trading Partners (US $ million, 2001): *Imports c.i.f.:* USA 2,032.5; Venezuela 107.9; Total (incl. others) 2,370.1. *Exports f.o.b.:* France 21.5; Germany 14.5; Spain 12.5; United Kingdom 12.0; USA 293.1; Total (incl. others) 378.2.
Source: UN, *International Trade Statistics Yearbook.*

TRANSPORT

Road Traffic (vehicles in use, 1998): 67,400 passenger cars; 16,800 commercial vehicles. Source: Auto and Truck International (Illinois), *World Automotive Market Report.*

Shipping: *Merchant fleet* (displacement, '000 grt at 31 December): 33,386 in 2001; 35,798 in 2002; 34,752 in 2003 (Source: Lloyd's Register-Fairplay, *World Fleet Statistics*). *International sea-borne freight traffic* (estimates, '000 metric tons, 1990): Goods loaded 5,920; Goods unloaded 5,705 (Source: UN, *Monthly Bulletin of Statistics*).

Civil Aviation (2001): Kilometres flown (million) 7; Passengers carried ('000) 1,626; Passenger-km (million) 391; Total ton-km of freight (million) 48. Source: UN, *Statistical Yearbook.*

TOURISM

Visitor Arrivals ('000): 3,979.9 (1,428.2 by air, 2,551.7 by sea) in 2001; 4,205.0 (1,402.9 by air, 2,802.1 by sea) in 2002; 4,398.8 (1,428.6 by air, 2,970.2 by sea) in 2003. Source: Caribbean Development Bank, *Social and Economic Indicators.*

Tourism Receipts (B $ million): 1,649.7 in 2001; 1,762.6 in 2002; 1,782.0 in 2003.

COMMUNICATIONS MEDIA

Radio Receivers (1997): 215,000 in use.

Television Receivers (1999): 73,000 in use.

Telephones (2001): 123,300 main lines in use.

Facsimile Machines (1996): 500 in use.

Mobile Cellular Telephones (2001): 60,600 subscribers.

Internet Users (2001): 16,900.

Daily Newspapers (1996): 3 titles (total circulation 28,000 copies).
Sources: UN, *Statistical Yearbook*; UNESCO, *Statistical Yearbook*; International Telecommunication Union.

EDUCATION

Pre-primary (1996/97): 20 schools; 76 teachers; 1,094 pupils.

Primary (1996/97): 113 schools; 1,792 teachers; 42,839 pupils (2001).

Secondary: 37 junior/senior high schools (1990); 2,097 teachers (1996/97); 23,401 students (2001).

Tertiary (1987): 249 teachers; 5,305 students. In 2002 there were 3,463 students registered at the College of the Bahamas.
Sources: UNESCO, *Statistical Yearbook*; UN, Economic Commission for Latin America and the Caribbean, *Statistical Yearbook*; Caribbean Development Bank, *Social and Economic Indicators 2001.*

Adult Literacy Rate (UNESCO estimates): 95.5% (males 94.6%; females 96.3%) in 2002. Source: UN Development Programme, *Human Development Report.*

Directory

The Constitution

A representative House of Assembly was first established in 1729, although universal adult suffrage was not introduced until 1962. A new Constitution for the Commonwealth of the Bahamas came into force at independence, on 10 July 1973. The main provisions of the Constitution are summarized below.

Parliament consists of a Governor-General (representing the British monarch, who is Head of State), a nominated Senate and an elected House of Assembly. The Governor-General appoints the Prime Minister and, on the latter's recommendation, the remainder of the Cabinet. Apart from the Prime Minister, the Cabinet has no fewer than eight other ministers, of whom one is the Attorney-General. The Governor-General also appoints a Leader of the Opposition.

The Senate (upper house) consists of 16 members, of whom nine are appointed by the Governor-General on the advice of the Prime Minister, four on the advice of the Leader of the Opposition and three on the Prime Minister's advice after consultation with the Leader of the Opposition. The House of Assembly (lower house) has 40 members. A Constituencies Commission reviews numbers and boundaries at intervals of not more than five years and can recommend alterations for approval of the House. The life of Parliament is limited to a maximum of five years.

The Constitution provides for a Supreme Court and a Court of Appeal.

The Government

HEAD OF STATE

Monarch: HM Queen Elizabeth II (succeeded to the throne 6 February 1952).
Governor-General: Dame Ivy Dumont (took office 1 January 2002).

THE CABINET
(March 2005)

Prime Minister and Minister of Finance: Perry G. Christie.

Deputy Prime Minister and Minister of National Security: Cynthia A. Pratt.

Attorney-General and Minister of Justice and of Education: Alfred M. Sears.

Minister of Agriculture, Fisheries and Local Government: V. Alfred Gray.

Minister of Financial Services and Investments: Allyson Maynard-Gibson.

Minister of Foreign Affairs and Public Service: Frederick A. Mitchell.

Minister of Health and Environmental Services: Dr Marcus C. Bethel.

Minister of Housing and National Insurance: D. Shane Gibson.

Minister of Labour and Immigration: Vincent A. Peet.

Minister of Public Works and Utilities: Bradley B. Roberts.

Minister of Social Services and Community Development: Melanie S. Griffin.

Minister of Tourism: Obediah 'Obie' H. Wilchcombe.

Minister of Trade and Industry: Leslie O. Miller.

Minister of Transport and Aviation: Glennys M. E. Hanna-Martin.

Minister of Youth, Sports and Culture: Neville W. Wisdom.

Minister of State in the Ministry of Finance: Sen. James H. Smith.

MINISTRIES

Attorney-General's Office and Ministry of Justice: Post Office Bldg, East Hill St, POB N-3007, Nassau; tel. 322-1141; fax 356-4179.

Office of the Prime Minister: Sir Cecil V. Wallace-Whitfield Centre, West Bay St, POB CB-10980, Nassau; tel. 327-5826; fax 327-5806; e-mail info@opm.gov.bs; internet www.opm.gov.bs.

Office of the Deputy Prime Minister: Churchill Bldg, Bay St, POB N-3217, Nassau; tel. 356-6792; fax 356-6087.

Ministry of Agriculture, Fisheries and Local Government: Levy Bldg, East Bay St, POB N-3028, Nassau; tel. 325-7502; fax 322-1767.

Ministry of Education: Collins House, Shirley St, POB N-3913, Nassau; tel. 322-8140; fax 322-8491.

Ministry of Finance: Cecil V. Wallace-Whitfield Centre, West Bay St, POB N-3017, Nassau; tel. 327-1530; fax 327-1618; internet www.bahamas.gov.bs/finance.

Ministry of Financial Services and Investments: Sir Cecil V. Wallace-Whitfield Centre, West Bay St, POB CB-10980, Nassau; tel. 327-5826; fax 327-5806.

Ministry of Foreign Affairs and Public Service: East Hill St, POB N-3746, Nassau; tel. 322-7624; fax 328-8212; e-mail mfabahamas@batelnet.bs.

Ministry of Health and Environmental Services: Royal Victoria Gardens, Shirley St, POB N-3730, Nassau; tel. 322-7425; fax 322-7788.

Ministry of Housing and National Insurance: National Insurance Bldg, Baillou Rd, POB N-7508, Nassau; tel. 502-1500; fax 323-3048.

Ministry of Labour and Immigration: Post Office Bldg, East Hill St, POB N-3008, Nassau; tel. 323-7814; fax 325-1920.

Ministry of National Security: Churchill Bldg, Bay St, POB N-3217, Nassau; tel. 356-6792; fax 356-6087.

Ministry of Social Services and Community Development: Frederick House, Frederick St, POB N-3206, Nassau; tel. 356-0765; fax 323-3883.

Ministry of Public Works and Utilities: John F. Kennedy Dr., POB N-8156, Nassau; tel. 322-4830; fax 326-7344.

Ministry of Tourism: British Colonial Hilton Hotel, Bay St, POB N-3701, Nassau; tel. 322-7500; fax 328-0945; e-mail tourism@bahamas.com; internet www.bahamas.com.

Ministry of Trade and Industry: Manx Bldg, West Bay St, POB N-4849, Nassau; tel. 328-2700; fax 328-1324.

Ministry of Transport and Aviation: Pilot House Complex, POB N-10114, Nassau; tel. 394-0445; fax 394-5920.

Ministry of Youth, Sports and Culture: 7th Floor, Post Office Bldg, East Hill St, POB N-4891, Nassau; tel. 322-6250; fax 322-6546.

Legislature

PARLIAMENT

Senate

President: Sharon R. Wilson.

There are 16 nominated members.

House of Assembly

Speaker: Oswald Ingraham.

The House has 40 members.

General Election, 2 May 2002

Party	Seats
Progressive Liberal Party (PLP)	29
Free National Movement (FNM)	7
Independents	4
Total	**40**

Political Organizations

Bahamas Freedom Alliance (BFA): Nassau; formed Coalition Plus Labour alliance with CDR and PLM to contest 2002 legislative elections; Leader D. Halston Moultrie.

Coalition for Democratic Reform (CDR): Nassau; f. 2000; centrist; formed Coalition Plus Labour alliance with BFA and PLM to contest 2002 legislative elections; Leader Bernard Nottage.

Free National Movement (FNM): Mackey St, POB N-10713, Nassau; tel. 393-7853; fax 393-7914; e-mail fnm@coralwave.com; internet www.freenationalmovement.org; f. 1972; Leader Orville Alton Thompson (Tommy) Turnquest; Chair. Carl W. Bethel.

People's Labour Movement (PLM): Nassau; formed Coalition Plus Labour alliance with BFA and CDR to contest 2002 legislative elections.

Progressive Liberal Party (PLP): Sir Lynden Pindling Centre, PLP House, Farrington House, POB N-547, Nassau; tel. 325-5492; fax 328-0808; e-mail eightmr@bahamiansfirst.com; internet www.progressiveliberalparty.com; f. 1953; centrist party; Leader Perry G. Christie; Chair. Raynard S. Rigby.

Diplomatic Representation

EMBASSIES AND HIGH COMMISSION IN THE BAHAMAS

China, People's Republic: 3 Orchard Terrace, Village Rd, POB SS-6389, Nassau; tel. 393-1415; fax 393-0733; e-mail chinemb@batel.net; Ambassador Li Yuanming.

Haiti: Sears House, Shirley St, POB N-666, Nassau; tel. 326-0325; fax 322-7712; Chargé d'affaires Joseph J. Etienne.

United Kingdom: Ansbacher Bldg, 3rd Floor, East St, POB N-7516, Nassau; tel. 325-7471; fax 323-3871; e-mail bhcnassau@fco.gov.uk; internet www.britishhighcommission.gov.uk/bahamas; High Commissioner Roderick Gemmell.

USA: Mosmar Bldg, Queen St, POB N-8197, Nassau; tel. 322-1181; fax 328-7838; e-mail embnas@state.gov; internet nassau.usembassy.gov; Ambassador John D. Rood.

Judicial System

The Judicial Committee of the Privy Council (based in the United Kingdom), the Bahamas Court of Appeal, the Supreme Court and the Magistrates' Courts are the main courts of the Bahamian judicial system.

All courts have both a criminal and civil jurisdiction. The Magistrates' Courts are presided over by professionally qualified Stipendiary and Circuit Magistrates in New Providence and Grand Bahama, and by Island Administrators sitting as Magistrates in the Family Islands.

Whereas all magistrates are empowered to try offences that may be tried summarily, a Stipendiary and Circuit Magistrate may, with the consent of the accused, also try certain less serious indictable offences. The jurisdiction of magistrates is, however, limited by law.

The Supreme Court consists of the Chief Justice, two Senior Justices and six Justices. The Supreme Court also sits in Freeport, with two Justices.

Appeals in almost all matters lie from the Supreme Court to the Court of Appeal, with further appeal in certain instances to the Judicial Committee of the Privy Council.

Supreme Court of the Bahamas
Parliament Sq., POB N-8167, Nassau; tel. 322-3315; fax 323-6895. Chief Justice Sir Burton Hall.

Court of Appeal: POB N-8167, Nassau; tel. 322-3315; fax 325-6895; Pres. Dame Joan Sawyer.

Magistrates' Courts: POB N-421, Nassau; tel. 325-4573; fax 323-1446; 15 magistrates and a circuit magistrate.

Registrar of the Supreme Court: Estelle G. Gray Evans, POB N-167, Nassau; tel. 322-4348; fax 325-6895; e-mail estelleevans@bahamas.gov.bs.

Attorney-General: Alfred M. Sears.

Office of the Attorney-General: 3rd Floor, Post Office Bldg, East Hill St, POB N-3007, Nassau; tel. 322-1141; fax 356-4179; Dir of Legal Affairs Rhonda Bain; Dir of Public Prosecutions Bernard Turner.

Registrar-General: Elizabeth E. M. Thompson, 50 Shirley St, POB N-532, Nassau; tel. 322-3316; fax 322-5553; e-mail registra@batelnet.bs.

Religion

Most of the population profess Christianity, but there are also small communities of Jews and Muslims.

CHRISTIANITY

According to the census of 1990, there were 79,465 Baptists (31.2% of the population), 40,894 Roman Catholics (16.0%) and 40,881 Anglicans (16.0%). Other important denominations include the Pentecostal Church (5.5%), the Church of Christ (5.0%) and the Methodists (4.8%).

Bahamas Christian Council: POB N-3101, Nassau; tel. 326-7114; f. 1948; 27 mem. churches; Pres. Rev. William Thompson.

The Roman Catholic Church

The Bahamas comprises the single archdiocese of Nassau. At 31 December 2002 there were an estimated 41,077 adherents in the Bahamas. The Archbishop participates in the Antilles Episcopal Conference (whose Secretariat is based in Port of Spain, Trinidad). The Turks and Caicos Islands are also under the jurisdiction of the Archbishop of Nassau.

Archbishop of Nassau: Most Rev. LAWRENCE ALOYSIUS BURKE, The Hermitage, West St, POB N-8187, Nassau; tel. 322-8919; fax 322-2599; e-mail rcchancery@batelnet.bs.

The Anglican Communion

Anglicans in the Bahamas are adherents of the Church in the Province of the West Indies. The diocese also includes the Turks and Caicos Islands.

Archbishop of the West Indies, and Bishop of Nassau and the Bahamas: Most Rev. DREXEL GOMEZ, Bishop's Lodge, POB N-7107, Nassau; tel. 322-3015; fax 322-7943.

Other Christian Churches

Bahamas Conference of the Methodist Church: POB SS-5103, Nassau; tel. 393-3726; fax 393-8135; e-mail bcmc@bahamas.net.bs; Pres. KENRIS L. CAREY.

Bahamas Conference of Seventh-day Adventists: Harrold Rd, POB N-356, Nassau; tel. 341-4021; fax 341-4088; internet www.bahamasconference.org.

Bahamas Evangelical Church Association: Carmichael Rd, POB N-1224, Nassau; tel. 362-1024.

Greek Orthodox Church: Church of the Annunciation, West St, POB N-823, Nassau; tel. 322-4382; f. 1928; part of the Archdiocese of North and South America, based in New York (USA); Priest Rev. THEOPHANIS KULYVAS.

Methodist Church Conference in the Bahamas (MCCA): POB N-3702, Nassau; tel. 373-1888; Conference Pres. Rev. LIVINGSTON MALCOLM.

Other denominations include African Methodist Episcopal, the Assemblies of Brethren, Christian Science, the Jehovah's Witnesses, the Salvation Army, Pentecostal, Presbyterian, Baptist, Lutheran and Assembly of God churches.

OTHER RELIGIONS

Bahá'í Faith

Bahá'í National Spiritual Assembly: Arianna House, Dunmore Lane, Nassau; tel. 326-0607; e-mail nsabaha@mail.com.

Islam

There is a small community of Muslims in the Bahamas.

Islaamic Centre: Carmichael Rd, POB N-10711, Nassau; tel. 341-6612.

Islaamic Centre Jamaat Ul-Islam: 13 Davies St, Oakes Field, POB N-10711, Nassau; tel. 325-0413.

Judaism

Most of the Bahamian Jewish community are based on Grand Bahama.

Bahamas Jewish Congregation Synagogue: POB CB-11003, Cable Beach Shopping Centre, Nassau; tel. 327-2064.

The Press

NEWSPAPERS

The Bahama Journal: Media House, POB N-8610, Nassau; tel. 325-3082; fax 356-7256; internet www.jonesbahamas.com; daily; circ. 5,000.

The Freeport News: Cedar St, POB F-40007, Freeport; tel. 352-8321; fax 352-3449; internet freeport.nassauguardian.net; f. 1961; daily; Gen. Man. DORLAN COLLIE; Editor ROBYN ADDERLEY; circ. 6,000.

The Nassau Guardian: 4 Carter St, Oakes Field, POB N-3011, Nassau; tel. 302-2300; fax 328-8943; e-mail editor@nasguard.com; internet www.thenassauguardian.com; f. 1844; daily; CEO CHARLES CARTER; Man. Editor ANTHONY CAPRON; circ. 12,277.

The Punch: POB N-4081, Nassau; tel. 322-7112; fax 323-5268; twice weekly; Editor IVAN JOHNSON; circ. 25,000.

The Tribune: Shirley St, POB N-3207, Nassau; tel. 322-1986; fax 328-2398; e-mail tribune@100jamz.com; f. 1903; daily; Publr and Editor EILEEN DUPUCH CARRON; circ. 13,500.

PERIODICALS

The Bahamas Financial Digest: Miramar House, Bay and Christie Sts, POB N-4271, Nassau; tel. 356-2981; fax 356-7118; e-mail michael.symonette@batelnet.bs; f. 1973; 4 a year; business and investment; Publr and Editor MICHAEL A. SYMONETTE; circ. 15,890.

Bahamas Tourist News: Bayparl Bldg, Parliament St, POB N-4855, Nassau; tel. 322-4528; fax 322-4527; e-mail starpub@batelnet .bs; f. 1962; monthly; Editor BOBBY BOWER; circ. 371,000 (annually).

Nassau City Magazine: Miramar House, Bay and Christie Sts, POB N-4824, Nassau; tel. 356-2981; fax 326-2849.

Official Gazette: c/o Cabinet Office, POB N-7147, Nassau; tel. 322-2805; weekly; publ. by the Cabinet Office.

What's On Magazine: Woodes Rogers Wharf, POB CB-11713, Nassau; tel. 323-2323; fax 322-3428; e-mail info@whatsonbahamas .com; internet www.whatsonbahamas.com; monthly; Publr NEIL ABERLE.

Publishers

Bahamas Free Press Ltd: POB CB-13309, Nassau; tel. 323-8961.

Etienne Dupuch Jr Publications Ltd: 51 Hawthorne Rd, POB N-7513, Nassau; tel. 323-5665; fax 323-5728; e-mail dupuch@ bahamasnet.com; internet www.dupuch.com; f. 1959; publishes *Bahamas Handbook, Trailblazer* maps, *What To Do* magazines, *Welcome Bahamas, Tadpole* (educational colouring book) series and *Dining and Entertainment Guide*; Dirs ETIENNE DUPUCH, Jr, S. P. DUPUCH.

Media Enterprises Ltd: 31 Shirley Park Ave, POB N-9240, Nassau; tel. 325-8210; fax 325-8065; e-mail info@bahamasmedia .com; internet www.bahamasmedia.com; Pres. and Gen. Man. LARRY SMITH; Publishing Dir NEIL E. SEALEY.

Printing Tours and Publishing: Miramar House, Bay and Christie Sts, POB N-4846, Nassau; tel. 356-2981; fax 356-7118.

Sacha de Frisching Publishing: POB N-7776, Nassau; tel. 362-6230; fax 362-6274; children's books.

Star Publishers Ltd: POB N-4855, Nassau; tel. 322-3724; fax 322-4537; e-mail starpub@bahamas.net.bs; internet www.supermaps .com.

Broadcasting and Communications

TELECOMMUNICATIONS

The telecommunications sector was in the process of being opened to private participation in 2005.

Bahamas Telecommunications Co (BTC): POB N-3048, John F. Kennedy Dr., Nassau; tel. 302-7000; fax 326-7474; e-mail info@ batelnet.bs; internet www.batelnet.bs; f. 1966; fmrly known as BaTelCo; state-owned; intended sale of 49% stake to private investors failed in 2003; privatization remained pending in 2005; Chair. RENO BROWN; Gen. Man. MICHAEL SYMONETTE.

Cable Bahamas Ltd: POB CB-13050, Nassau; tel. 356-2200; fax 356-8997; e-mail info@cablebahamas.com; internet www .cablebahamas.com; f. 1995; provides cable television and internet services; Pres. RICHARD PARDY.

BROADCASTING

Radio

Broadcasting Corporation of the Bahamas: 3rd Terrace, POB N-1347, Centreville, New Providence; tel. 322-4623; fax 322-6598; f. 1936; govt-owned; operates the ZNS radio and television network; Chair. MICHAEL D. SMITH; Gen. Man. ANTHONY FOSTER.

> **Radio Bahamas:** internet www.univox.com/radio/zns.html; f. 1936; broadcasts 24 hours per day on four stations: the main Radio Bahamas ZNS1, Radio New Providence ZNS2, which are both based in Nassau, Radio Power 104.5 FM, and the Northern Service (ZNS3—Freeport); f. 1973; Station Man. ANTHONY FORSTER; Programme Man. TANYA PINDER.

Cool 96 FM: POB F-40773, Freeport, Grand Bahama; tel. 353-7440; fax 352-8709.

Love 97 FM: Bahamas Media House, East St North, POB N-3909, Nassau; tel. 356-2555; fax 356-2555; e-mail twilliams@ jonescommunications.com; internet www.love97fm.com.

More 95.9 FM: POB CR-54245, Nassau; tel. 361-2447; fax 361-2448; e-mail morefm94.9@batelnet.bs.

Tribune Radio Ltd (One Hundred JAMZ): Shirley and Deveaux St, POB N-3207, Nassau; tel. 328-4771; fax 356-5343; e-mail michelle@ 100jamz.com; internet www.100jamz.com; Gen. Man. STEPHEN HAUGHEY; Programme Dir ERIC WARD.

Television

Broadcasting Corporation of the Bahamas: see Radio.

Bahamas Television: f. 1977; broadcasts for Nassau, New Providence and the Central Bahamas; transmitting power of 50,000 watts; full colour; Programme Man. CARL BETHEL.

US television programmes and some satellite programmes can be received. Most islands have a cable-television service.

Finance

The Bahamas developed into one of the world's foremost financial centres (there are no corporation, income, capital gains or withholding taxes or estate duty), and finance has become a significant feature of the economy. At 31 December 2003 there were 284 banks and trust companies operating in the Bahamas; 169 banks and trust companies had a physical presence in the islands.

BANKING

(cap. = capital; res = reserves; dep. = deposits; m. = million; brs = branches)

Central Bank

The Central Bank of the Bahamas: Frederick St, POB N-4868, Nassau; tel. 322-2193; fax 322-4321; e-mail cbob@centralbankbahamas.com; internet www.centralbankbahamas.com; f. 1973; bank of issue; cap. B \$3.0m., res B \$92.2m., dep. B \$273.4m. (Dec. 2003); Gov. and Chair. JULIAN W. FRANCIS; Dep. Gov. WENDY M. CRAIGG.

Development Bank

The Bahamas Development Bank: Cable Beach, West Bay St, POB N-3034, Nassau; tel. 327-5780; fax 327-5047; e-mail info@bahamasdevelopmentbank.com; internet www.bahamasdevelopmentbank.com; f. 1978 to fund approved projects and channel funds into appropriate investments; Chair. K. NEVILLE ADDERLEY; Man. Dir GEORGE E. RODGERS; 2 brs.

Principal Bahamian-based Banks

Bank of the Bahamas International: Claughton House, Shirley St, POB N-7118, Nassau; tel. 326-2560; fax 325-2762; f. 1970 as Bank of Montreal (Bahamas and Caribbean); name changed as above in 2002; jtly-owned by Govt and Euro Canadian Bank; 50% owned by Govt, 50% owned by c. 4,000 Bahamian shareholders; cap. B \$12.0m., res B \$9.0m., dep. B \$294.8m. (June 2003); Chair. HUGH G. SANDS; Man. Dir PAUL MCWEENEY; 10 brs.

Commonwealth Bank Ltd: 610 Bay St, POB SS-5541, Nassau; tel. 394-7373; fax 394-5807; e-mail cbinquiry@combankltd.com; internet www.combankltd.com; f. 1960; total assets B \$17m. (Dec. 2002); Pres., CEO and Dir WILLIAM BATEMAN SANDS, Jr; 9 brs.

Principal Foreign Banks

Banque Privée Edmond de Rothschild Ltd (Switzerland): 51 Frederick St, POB N-1136, Nassau; tel. 328-8121; fax 328-8115; internet www.lcf-rothschild.com; f. 1997; cap. 67.4m. Swiss francs, res 4.2m. Swiss francs, dep. 7.0m. Swiss francs (Dec. 2002); Chair. ROBERT MISRAHI; Dir CLAUDE MESSULAM.

BNP Paribas (Bahamas) Ltd: Beaumont House, 3rd Floor, Bay St, POB N-4883, Nassau; tel. 326-5935; fax 326-5871; internet www.bnpgroup.com; Man. Dir ANDRÉ LAMOTHE.

BSI Overseas (Bahamas) Ltd (Italy): Bayside Executive Park, West Bay St, POB N-7130, Nassau; tel. 702-1200; fax 702-1250; f. 1990; wholly-owned subsidiary of BSI AG (Switzerland); cap. US \$10.0m., res US \$66.1m., dep. US \$1,103.4m. (Dec. 2001); Chair. RETO KESSLER; Man. Dir MARTIN HUTTER.

Canadian Imperial Bank of Commerce (CIBC) (Canada): 4th Floor, 308 East Bay St, POB N-8329, Nassau; tel. 393-4710; fax 393-4280; internet www.cibc.com; Area Man. TERRY HILTS; 9 brs.

Citibank NA (USA): 4th Floor, Citibank Bldg, Thompson Blvd, Oakes Field, POB N-8158, Nassau; tel. 302-8859; fax 302-8625; internet www.citibank.com; Gen. Man. ALISON JOHNSTON; 2 brs.

Credit Suisse (Bahamas) Ltd (Switzerland): 4th Floor, Bahamas Financial Centre, Shirley and Charlotte Sts, POB N-4928, Nassau; tel. 356-8100; fax 356-6589; f. 1968; subsidiary of Credit Suisse Zurich; portfolio and asset management, 'offshore' company management, trustee services; cap. US \$12.0m., res US \$20.0m., dep. US \$500.7m. (Dec. 1997); CEO and Man. Dir EUGEN SCHAEFLI; Chair. JOACHIM STRÄHLE.

Eni International Bank Ltd: 1st Floor, British American Insurance House, Marlborough St, POB SS-6377, Nassau; tel. 322-1928;

fax 323-8600; e-mail eib-info@enibank.eni.it; cap. US \$50.0m., dep. US \$260.0m., total assets US \$324.3m. (Dec. 2003); Pres., Chair. and Man. Dir PAOLO CARCMOSINO.

FirstCaribbean International Bank Ltd: Charlotte House, Shirley St, POB N-3221, Nassau; tel. 325-7384; fax 322-8267; internet www.firstcaribbeaninternational.com; f. 2002 following merger of Caribbean operations of Barclays Bank PLC and CIBC; Exec. Chair. MICHAEL MANSOOR; CEO CHARLES PINK.

Guaranty Trust Bank Ltd: Lyford Manor Ltd, Lyford Cay, POB N-4918, Nassau; tel. 362-7200; fax 362-7210; e-mail guaranty@gtblbah.com; f. 1962; cap. US \$18.0m., res US \$0.1m., dep. US \$106.1m. (Jan. 2004); Chair. Sir WILLIAM C. ALLEN; Man. Dir JAMES P. COYLE.

HSBC Private Banking (Bahamas) Ltd (Switzerland): 3rd Floor, Maritime House, Frederick St, POB N-10441, Nassau; tel. 328-8644; fax 328-8600; e-mail hfccfint@bahamas.net.bs; f. 1971 as Handelsfina Int., name changed as above in 2002; cap. US \$5.0m., res US \$15.5m., dep. US \$581.3m. (Dec. 1999); Chair. MARC DE GUILLEBON; CEO JEAN-JACQUES SALOMON.

National Bank of Canada (International) Ltd: Ground Floor, Goodman's Bay Corporate Centre, POB N-3015, Nassau; tel. 502-8100; fax 323-8600; e-mail info@nbclintl.com; f. 1978; 100% owned by Natcan Holdings International Ltd; cap. US \$20.0m., dep. US \$156.2m., total assets US \$537.6m. (Oct. 2002); Pres. and Man. Dir JACQUES LATENDRESSE.

Overseas Union Bank and Trust (Bahamas) Ltd (Switzerland): 250 Bay St, POB N-8184, Nassau; tel. 322-2476; fax 323-8771; f. 1980; cap. US \$5.0m., res US \$6.2m., dep. US \$97.9m. (Dec. 1997); Chair. Dr CARLO SGANZINI; Gen. Man. URS FREI.

Pictet Bank and Trust Ltd (Switzerland): Building No. 1, Bayside Executive Park, West Bay St and Blake Rd, POB N-4837, Nassau; tel. 302-2222; fax 327-6610; e-mail pbtbah@bahamas.net.bs; internet www.pictet.com; f. 1978; cap. US \$1.0m., res US \$10.0m., dep. US \$126.2m. (Dec. 1995); Chair. CHRISTIAN MALLET; Pres. and Man. YVES LOURDIN.

Private Investment Bank Ltd: Devonshire House, Queen St, POB N-3918, Nassau; tel. 302-5950; fax 302-5970; f. 1984 as Bank Worms and Co International Ltd; renamed in 1990, 1996 and 1998; in 2000 merged with Geneva Private Bank and Trust (Bahamas) Ltd; cap. US \$3.0m., res US \$12.0m., dep. US \$151.3m. (Dec. 2003); Chair. and Dir FRANÇOIS ROUGE.

Royal Bank of Canada Ltd (Canada): 4th Floor, Royal Bank House, East Hill St, POB N-7549, Nassau; tel. 356-8500; fax 328-7145; internet www.royalbank.com; f. 1869; Chair. ALLAN TAYLOR; Vice-Pres. MICHAEL F. PHELAN; 16 brs.

Scotiabank (Bahamas) Ltd (Canada): Scotiabank Bldg, Rawson Sq., POB N-7518, Nassau; tel. 356-1400; fax 322-7989; e-mail scotiabank@batelnet.bs; internet www.scotiabank.com; Man. Dir ANTHONY C. ALLEN; Pres. BRUCE BIRMINGHAM; 18 brs.

SG Hambros Bank and Trust (Bahamas) Ltd (United Kingdom): SG Hambros Bldg, West Bay St, POB N-7788, Nassau; tel. 302-5000; fax 326-6709; e-mail dominique.lefevre@sghambros.com; internet www.sghambros.com; f. 1936, above name adopted in 1998; cap. B \$2.0m., res B \$10.3m., dep. B \$461.3m. (Dec. 2003); Chair. WARWICK NEWBURY; Man. Dir DOMINIQUE LEFEVRE.

UBS (Bahamas) Ltd (Switzerland): UBS House, East Bay St, POB N-7757, Nassau; tel. 394-9300; fax 394-9333; internet www.ubs.com/bahamas; f. 1968 as Swiss Bank Corpn (Overseas) Ltd, name changed as above 1998; cap. US \$4.0m., dep. US \$420.2m. (Dec. 1997); Chair. MARTIN LIECHTI; CEO ERIC TSCHIRREN.

Principal Bahamian Trust Companies

Ansbacher (Bahamas) Ltd: Ansbacher House, Bank Lane, POB N-7768, Nassau; tel. 322-1161; fax 326-5020; e-mail info@ansbacher.bs; internet www.ansbacher.com; incorporated 1957 as Bahamas International Trust Co Ltd, name changed 1994; cap. B \$1.0m., res B \$9.7m., dep. B \$190.3m. (Sept. 1998); Man. Dir IAN D. TOWELL.

Bank of Nova Scotia International Ltd: Scotiabank Bldg, Rawson Sq., POB N-7545, Nassau; tel. 356-1517; fax 328-8473; e-mail bahamas@scotiatrust.com; internet www.scotiabank.com; wholly owned by the Bank of Nova Scotia; Vice-Pres. and Gen. Man. STEPHEN J. GRAINGER.

Chase Manhattan Trust Corpn: Shirley and Charlotte Sts, POB N-3708, Nassau; tel. 356-1305; fax 325-1706; Gen. Man. KEN BROWN; 4 brs.

Leadenhall Bank and Trust Co Ltd: IBM Bldg, East Bay and Church Sts, POB N-1965, Nassau; tel. 325-5508; fax 328-7030; e-mail drounce@leadentrust.com; f. 1976; Man. Dir DAVID J. ROUNCE.

Oceanic Bank and Trust: POB AP-59203, Nassau; tel. 502-8822; fax 502-8840; f. 1969; Man. Dir BRUCE BELL.

Winterbotham Trust Co Ltd: Bolam House, King and George Sts, POB N-3026, Nassau; tel. 356-5454; fax 356-9432; e-mail nassau@winterbotham.com; internet www.winterbotham.com; cap. US $3.8m.; CEO Geoffrey Hooper; 2 brs.

Bankers' Organizations

Association of International Banks and Trust Companies in the Bahamas: POB N-7880, Nassau; tel. 356-3898; Chair. Andrew Law.

Bahamas Financial Services Board (BFSB): 4th Floor, Euro-Canadian Centre, POB N-1764, Nassau; e-mail info@bsfb-bahamas.com; internet www.bfsb-bahamas.com; f. 1998; jt govt/private initiative responsible for overseas marketing of financial services; CEO and Exec. Dir Wendy C. Warren; Chair. Michael Paton.

Bahamas Institute of Bankers: Royal Palm Mall, Mackey St, POB N-3202, Nassau; tel. 393-0456; fax 394-3503; Pres. Kim Bodie.

STOCK EXCHANGE

Bahamas International Securities Exchange (BISX): British Colonial Centre of Commerce, 1 Bay St, POB EE-15672, Nassau; e-mail info@bisxbahamas.com; internet www.bisxbahamas.com; f. 2000; 19 local companies listed at January 2005; Chair. Ian Fair; CEO Keith Davies (acting).

INSURANCE

The leading British and a number of US, Canadian and Caribbean companies have agents in Nassau and Freeport. Local insurance companies include the following:

Allied Bahamas Insurance Co Ltd: 93 Collins Ave, POB N-1216, Nassau; tel. 326-5439; fax 356-5472; general, aviation and marine.

Bahamas First General Insurance Co Ltd: 93 Collins Ave, POB N-1216, Nassau; tel. 326-5439; fax 326-5472; Man. Dir Patrick G. W. Ward.

Colina Insurance Co Ltd: 12 Village Rd, POB N-4728, Nassau; tel. 393-2224; fax 393-1710; Colina Insurance Co merged with Global Life Assurance Bahamas in July 2002; operates under above name.

Commonwealth General Insurance Co Ltd: POB N-4200, Nassau; tel. 322-8210; fax 322-5277; Man. Dir Albert Archer.

Family Guardian Insurance Co Ltd (FamGuard): East Bay St, POB SS-6232, Nassau; tel. 393-1023; fax 394-1631; f. 1965.

Royal and Sun Alliance Insurance (Bahamas) Ltd: POB N-4391, Nassau; tel. 328-7888; fax 325-3151; Gen. Man. Steven Watson.

Security and General Insurance Co Ltd: POB N-3540, Nassau; tel. 326-7100; fax 325-0948; Gen. Man. Mark Shirra.

Summit Insurance Co Ltd: POB SS-19028, Nassau; tel. 394-2351; fax 394-2353; Gen. Man. Colin Jones.

Association

Bahamas General Insurance Association: POB N-860, Nassau; tel. 323-2596; fax 328-4354; e-mail bgia@bahamas.net.bs; Co-ordinator Robin B. Hardy.

Trade and Industry

DEVELOPMENT ORGANIZATIONS

Bahamas Agricultural and Industrial Corpn (BAIC): Levy Bldg, East Bay St, POB N-4940, Nassau; tel. 322-3740; fax 322-2133; internet www.bahamasb2b.com/baic; f. 1981 as an amalgamation of Bahamas Development Corpn and Bahamas Agricultural Corpn for the promotion of greater co-operation between tourism and other sectors of the economy through the development of small and medium-sized enterprises; Exec. Chair. Alvin Smith.

Bahamas Financial Services Board (BFSB): see Finance, Bankers' Organizations.

Bahamas Investment Authority: Cecil V. Wallace-Whitfield Centre, POB CB-10980, Nassau; tel. 327-5970; fax 327-5907; e-mail info@opm.gov.bs; internet www.opm.gov.bs/bia.php; Deputy Dir Philip Miller.

Bahamas Light Industries Development Council: POB SS-5599, Nassau; tel. 394-1907; Pres. Leslie Miller.

Nassau Paradise Island Promotion Board: Dean's Lane, Fort Charlotte, POB N-7799, Nassau; tel. 322-8381; fax 325-8998; f. 1970; Chair. George R. Myers; Sec. Michael C. Reckley; 30 mems.

CHAMBER OF COMMERCE

Bahamas Chamber of Commerce: Shirley St and Collins Ave, POB N-665, Nassau; tel. 322-2145; fax 322-4649; internet www.bahamasb2b.com/bahamaschamber; f. 1935 to promote, foster and protect trade, industry and commerce; Pres. D. Neil McKinney; 450 mems.

EMPLOYERS' ASSOCIATIONS

Bahamas Association of Land Surveyors: POB N-10147, Nassau; tel. 322-4569; Pres. Donald Thompson; Vice-Pres. Godfrey Humes; 30 mems.

Bahamas Boatmen's Association: POB ES-5212, Nassau; f. 1974; Pres. and Sec. Frederick Gomez.

Bahamas Contractors' Association: POB N-8170, Nassau; Chair. Godfrey E. Lightbourn; Sec. Robert E. Myers.

Bahamas Employers' Confederation: POB N-166, Nassau; tel. 328-5719; fax 322-4649; f. 1963; Pres. Brian Nutt.

Bahamas Hotel Employers' Association: SG Hambros Bldg, West Bay St, POB N-7799, Nassau; tel. 322-2262; fax 502-4221; e-mail bhea4mcr@hotmail.com; f. 1958; Pres. J. Barrie Farrington; Exec. Vice-Pres. Michael C. Reckley; 16 mems.

Bahamas Institute of Chartered Accountants: Star Plaza, Mackey St, POB N-7037, Nassau; tel. 394-3439; fax 394-3629; f. 1971; Pres. L. Edgar Moxey.

Bahamas Institute of Professional Engineers: Nassau; tel. 322-3356; fax 323-8503; Pres. Anthony Dean.

Bahamas Motor Dealers' Association: POB N-3919, Nassau; tel. 328-7671; fax 328-1922; Pres. Harry Roberts.

Bahamas Real Estate Association: Bahamas Chamber Bldg, POB N-8860, Nassau; tel. 325-4942; fax 322-4649; Pres. Patrick Strachan.

UTILITIES

Electricity

Bahamas Electricity Corpn (BEC): Big Pond and Tucker Rds, POB N-7509, Nassau; tel. 325-4101; fax 323-6852; internet www.bahamaselectricity.com; f. 1956; state-owned; transfer to private ownership pending in 2005; provides 70% of the islands' power-generating capacity; Chair. Al Jarrett; Gen. Man. Bradley S. Roberts.

Freeport Power Co Ltd: Mercantile Bldg, Cedar St, POB F-888, Freeport; tel. 352-6611; f. 1962; privately owned; Pres. Albert J. Miller.

Gas

Caribbean Gas Storage and Terminal Ltd: POB N-9665, Nassau; tel. 327-5587; fax 362-5006; e-mail info@caribbeangas.com; internet www.caribbeangas.com; f. 1992; Man. Dir Peter T. Newell.

Tropigas: Nassau; tel. 322-2404.

Water

Bahamas Water and Sewerage Corpn (WSC): 87 Thompson Blvd, POB N-3905, Nassau; tel. 302-5500; fax 328-3896; e-mail wscomplaints@wsc.com.bs; internet www.wsc.com.bs; f. 1960; Chair. Abraham Butler.

TRADE UNIONS

All Bahamian unions are members of one of the following:

Commonwealth of the Bahamas Trade Union Congress: Congress House, 3 Warwick St, POB CB-10992, Nassau; tel. 394-6301; fax 394-7401; e-mail tuc@bahamas.net.bs; Pres. Obie Ferguson Jr; 12,500 mems.

National Congress of Trade Unions: Horseshoe Dr., POB GT-2887, Nassau; tel. 356-7459; fax 356-7457; Pres. Leroy (Duke) Hanna; Gen. Sec. Kingsley L. Black; 20,000 mems.

The main unions are as follows:

Bahamas Airport, Airline and Allied Workers' Union: Workers' House, Harold Rd, POB N-3364, Nassau; tel. 323-4491; fax 323-7086; f. 1958; Pres. Franklyn Carter; Gen. Sec. Patricia Tynes; 550 mems.

Bahamas Brewery, Distillers Union: POB N-838, Nassau; tel. 362-1412; fax 362-1415; f. 1968; Pres. Joseph Moss; Gen. Sec. Rafael Holmes; 140 mems.

Bahamas Communications and Public Officers' Union: Farrington Rd, POB N-3190, Nassau; tel. 322-1537; fax 323-8719; e-mail prebcpou@batelnet.bs; f. 1973; Pres. D. Shane Gibson; Sec.-Gen. Robert A. Farquharson; 2,100 mems.

Bahamas Doctors' Union: Nassau; Pres. Dr EUGENE NEWERY; Gen. Sec. GEORGE SHERMAN.

Bahamas Electrical Workers' Union: East West Highway, POB GT-2535, Nassau; tel. 393-1838; fax 356-7383; Pres. CHARLES ROLLE; Gen. Sec. PATRICIA JOHNSON.

Bahamas Hotel Catering and Allied Workers' Union: Harold Rd, POB GT-2514, Nassau; tel. 323-5933; fax 325-6546; f. 1958; Pres. PATRICK BAIN; Gen. Sec. LEO DOUGLAS; 6,500 mems.

Bahamas Maritime Port and Allied Workers' Union: Prince George Docks, POB FF-6501, Nassau; tel. 322-2049; fax 322-5445; Pres. FREDERICK N. RODGERS; Sec.-Gen. LEON WALLACE.

Bahamas Musicians' and Entertainers' Union: Horseshoe Dr., POB N-880, Nassau; tel. 322-3734; fax 323-3537; f. 1958; Pres. LEROY (DUKE) HANNA; Gen. Sec. PORTIA NOTTAGE; 410 mems.

Bahamas Public Services Union: Wulff Rd, POB N-4692, Nassau; tel. 325-0038; fax 323-5287; f. 1959; Pres. WILLIAM McDONALD; Sec.-Gen. SYNIDA DORSETT; 4,247 mems.

Bahamas Taxi-Cab Union: Nassau St, POB N-1077, Nassau; tel. 323-5818; fax 326-2919; Pres. FELTON COX; Gen. Sec. ROSCOE WEECH.

Bahamas Union of Teachers: 104 Bethel Ave, Stapledon Gardens, POB N-3482, Nassau; tel. 323-4491; fax 323-7086; f. 1945; Pres. KINGSLEY L. BLACK; Sec.-Gen. HELLENA O. CARTWRIGHT; 2,600 mems.

Bahamas Utility Services and Allied Workers' Union: Nassau; Pres. HUEDLEY MOSS.

Eastside Stevedores' Union: POB N-2167, Nassau; tel. 322-4069; fax 364-7437; f. 1972; Pres. CURTIS TURNQUEST; Gen. Sec. TREVOR CAREY.

Grand Bahama Construction, Refinery, Maintenance and Allied Workers' Union: 33A Kipling Bldg, POB 42397, Freeport; tel. 352-2476; fax 351-7009; f. 1971; Pres. NEVILLE SIMMONS; Gen. Sec. MCKINLEY JONES.

United Brotherhood of Longshoremen's Union: Wulff Rd, POB N-7317, Nassau; f. 1959; Pres. JOSEPH McKINNEY; Gen. Sec. DEGLANVILLE PANZA; 157 mems.

Transport

ROADS

There are about 966 km (600 miles) of roads in New Providence and 1,368 km (850 miles) in the Family Islands, mainly on Grand Bahama, Cat Island, Eleuthera, Exuma and Long Island. In 1999 57.4% of roads were paved.

SHIPPING

The principal seaport is at Nassau (New Providence), which can accommodate the very largest cruise ships. Passenger arrivals exceed 2m. annually. The other main ports are at Freeport (Grand Bahama), where a container terminal opened in 1997, and Matthew Town (Inagua). There are also modern berthing facilities for cruise ships at Potters Cay (New Providence), Governor's Harbour (Eleuthera), Morgan's Bluff (North Andros) and George Town (Exuma).

The Bahamas converted to free-flag status in 1976. The fleet's aggregate displacement was 34,751,748 grt in December 2003 (the third largest national fleet in the world).

There is a weekly cargo and passenger service to all the Family Islands.

Bahamas Maritime Authority: POB N-4679, Nassau; tel. 323-3130; fax 323-2119; internet www.bahamasmaritime.com; e-mail nassau@bahamasmaritime.com; f. 1995; promotes ship registration and co-ordinates maritime administration.

Freeport Harbour Co Ltd: POB F-42465, Freeport; tel. 352-9651; fax 352-6888; e-mail fhcol@batelnet.bs; Gen. Man. MICHAEL J. POWER.

Nassau Port Authority: Prince George Wharf, POB N-8175, Nassau; tel. 326-7354; fax 322-5545; e-mail aja@batelnet.bs; regulates principal port of the Bahamas; Port Dir ANTHONY ALLENS.

Principal Shipping Companies

Bahamas Fast Ferries: Bahamas Ferry Services Ltd, POB N-3709, Nassau; tel. 323-2166; fax 322-8185; e-mail info@ bahamasferries.com; internet www.bahamasferries.com; services Spanish Wells, Harbour Island, Current Island and Governors Harbour in Eleuthera, Morgan's Bluff and Fresh Creek in Andros and George Town in Exuma; Chair. CRAIG R. SYMONETTE.

Cavalier Shipping: Arawak Cay, POB N-8170, New Providence; tel. 328-3035.

Dockendale Shipping Co Ltd: Dockendale House, West Bay St, POB N-10455, Nassau; tel. 325-0448; fax 328-1542; e-mail dockship@dockendale.com; f. 1973; ship management; Man. Dir L. J. FERNANDES; Tech. Dir K. VALLURI.

Eleuthera Express Shipping Co: POB N-4201, Nassau.

Grand Master Shipping Co: POB N-4208, Nassau.

Grenville Ventures Ltd: 43 Elizabeth Ave, POB CB-13022, Nassau.

HJH Trading Co Ltd: POB N-4402, Nassau; tel. 392-3939; fax 392-1828.

Gladstone Patton: POB SS-5178, Nassau.

Pioneer Shipping Ltd: Union Wharf, POB N-3044, Nassau; tel. 325-7889; fax 325-2214.

Teekay Shipping Corporation: TK House, Bayside Executive Park, West Bay St & Blake Rd, POB AP-59212, Nassau; tel. 502-8820; fax 502-8840; internet www.teekay.com; petroleum transporting; Chair. C. SEAN DAY; Pres. and CEO BJORN MOLLER.

Tropical Shipping Co Ltd: POB N-8183, Nassau; tel. 322-1012; fax 323-7566.

United Shipping Co Ltd: POB F-42552, Freeport; tel. 352-9315; fax 352-4034; e-mail info@unitedship.com; internet www.unitedship.com.

CIVIL AVIATION

Nassau International Airport (15 km—9 miles—outside the capital) and Freeport International Airport (5 km—3 miles—outside the city, on Grand Bahama) are the main terminals for international and internal services. There are also important airports at West End (Grand Bahama) and Rock Sound (Eleuthera) and some 50 smaller airports and landing strips throughout the islands. A $30m. airport improvement programme was completed in 2004.

Bahamasair Holdings Ltd: Coral Harbour Rd, POB N-4881, Nassau; tel. 377-8451; fax 377-7409; e-mail astuart@bahamasair.com; internet www.bahamasair.com; f. 1973; state-owned, scheduled for privatization by Sept. 2005; scheduled services between Nassau, Freeport, destinations within the USA and 20 locations within the Family Islands; Chair. ANTHONY MILLER; Man. Dir PAT ROLLE (acting).

Tourism

The mild climate and beautiful beaches attract many tourists. In 2003 tourist arrivals increased by 1.8%, compared with the previous year, to some 1,428,600 (excluding 2,970,200 visitors by sea). The majority of stop-over arrivals (85% in 2001) were from the USA. Receipts from the tourism industry stood at B $1,782m. in 2003. In September 1999 there were 223 hotels in the country, with a total of 14,080 rooms.

Ministry of Tourism: British Colonial Hilton Hotel, Bay St, POB N-3701, Nassau; tel. 322-7500; fax 328-0945; e-mail tourism@ bahamas.com; internet www.bahamas.com; Dir-Gen. VINCENT VANDERPOOL-WALLACE.

Bahamas Hotel Association: Dean's Lane, Fort Charlotte, POB N-7799, Nassau; tel. 322-8381; fax 326-5346; e-mail bhainfo@ batelnet.bs; Pres. JEREMY MacVEAN COX; Exec. Vice-Pres. BASIL H. SMITH.

Bahamas Tourism and Development Authority: POB N-4740, Nassau; tel. 326-0992; fax 323-0993; e-mail linkages@batelnet.bs; f. 1995; Exec. Dir FRANK J. COMITO.

Hotel Corporation of the Bahamas: West Bay St, POB N-9520, Nassau; tel. 327-8395; fax 327-6978; Chair. GEOFFREY JOHNSTONE; Chief Exec. WARREN ROLLE.

BAHRAIN

Introductory Survey

Location, Climate, Language, Religion, Flag, Capital

The Kingdom of Bahrain consists of a group of some 36 islands, situated midway along the Persian (Arabian) Gulf, approximately 24 km (15 miles) from the east coast of Saudi Arabia (to which it is linked by a causeway), and 28 km from the west coast of Qatar. The construction of a causeway linking eastern Bahrain to Qatar (the Friendship Bridge) is planned. There are six principal islands in the archipelago, the largest of these being Bahrain itself, which is about 50 km long, and between 13 km and 25 km wide. To the north-east of Bahrain island, and linked to it by a causeway and road, lies Muharraq island, which is approximately 6 km long. Another causeway links Bahrain island with Sitra island. The climate is temperate from December to the end of March, with temperatures ranging from 19°C to 25°C, but becomes very hot and humid during the summer months. In August and September temperatures can rise to 40°C. The official language is Arabic, but English is also widely spoken. More than 80% of Bahraini citizens are Muslims, divided into two sects: Shi'ites (almost 60%) and Sunnis (more than 40%). Non-Bahrainis comprised 37.6% of the total population at the census of April 2001. The national flag (proportions 3 by 5) is red, with a vertical white stripe at the hoist, the two colours being separated by a serrated line forming five white triangles. The capital is Manama, on Bahrain island.

Recent History

Bahrain, a traditional Arab monarchy, became a British Protected State in the 19th century. Under this arrangement, government was shared between the ruling Sheikh and his British adviser. Following a series of territorial disputes in the 19th century, Persia (now Iran) made renewed claims to Bahrain in 1928. This disagreement remained unresolved until May 1970, when Iran accepted the findings of a UN-commissioned report showing that the inhabitants of Bahrain overwhelmingly favoured complete independence, rather than union with Iran.

Sheikh Sulman bin Hamad al-Khalifa, who became ruler of Bahrain in 1942, was succeeded upon his death in November 1961 by his eldest son, Sheikh Isa bin Sulman al-Khalifa. Extensive administrative and political reforms were implemented in January 1970, when a supreme executive authority, the 12-member Council of State, was established, representing the first formal derogation of the ruler's powers. Sheikh Khalifa bin Sulman al-Khalifa, the ruler's eldest brother, was appointed President of the Council.

Meanwhile, in January 1968 the United Kingdom had announced its intention to withdraw British military forces from the area by 1971. In March 1968 Bahrain joined the nearby territories of Qatar and the Trucial States (now the United Arab Emirates—UAE), which were also under British protection, in the Federation of Arab Emirates. It was intended that the Federation should become fully independent, but the interests of Bahrain and Qatar proved to be incompatible with those of the smaller sheikhdoms, and both seceded from the Federation. Bahrain thus became a separate independent state on 15 August 1971, when a new treaty of friendship was signed with the United Kingdom. Sheikh Isa took the title of Amir, while the Council of State became the Cabinet, with Sheikh Khalifa as Prime Minister. A Constituent Assembly, convened in December 1972, formulated a new Constitution providing for a National Assembly to be comprised of 14 cabinet ministers and 30 elected members. The Constitution came into force on 6 December 1973, and elections to the new Assembly were conducted the following day. In the absence of political parties, candidates sought election as independents. In August 1975 the Prime Minister submitted his resignation, complaining that the National Assembly was obstructing the Government's initiatives for new legislation, particularly regarding national security. However, Sheikh Khalifa was reappointed and, at his request, the Assembly was dissolved by Amiri decree. New elections were to be held following minor changes to the Constitution and to the electoral law, but there were few subsequent signs that the National Assembly would be reconvened. With no elected legislative body, the ruling family continued to exercise near-abso-

lute power. On 16 January 1993 a 30-member Consultative Council (Majlis ash-Shoura)—appointed by the ruling authorities and comprising a large number of business executives and some members of the old National Assembly—held its inaugural meeting. The Council was to act in a purely advisory capacity, with no legislative powers.

In March 1981 Bahrain was one of the six founder members of the Co-operation Council for the Arab States of the Gulf (or Gulf Co-operation Council—GCC, see p. 193), which was established in order to co-ordinate defence strategy and to promote freer trade and co-operative economic protection among Gulf states.

For many years there have been indications of tension between Shi'ite Muslims, who form a slender majority in Bahrain (and many of whom are of Iranian descent), and the dominant Sunni Muslims, to which sect the ruling family belongs. During the 1980s two plots to overthrow the Government, one of which was alleged to have had Iranian support, were uncovered, as was a plan to sabotage Bahrain's petroleum installations, in which Iran was also alleged to be implicated. In December 1993 the human rights organization Amnesty International published a report criticizing the Bahraini Government's treatment of Shi'ite Muslims, some of whom had been forcibly exiled. In March 1994, apparently in response to this criticism, the Amir issued a decree pardoning 64 Bahrainis who had been in exile since the 1980s and permitting them to return to Bahrain. In December 1994, however, Sheikh Ali Salman Ahmad Salman, a Muslim cleric, was arrested following his criticism of the Government and his public appeal for reform, particularly the restoration of the National Assembly. Widespread rioting ensued throughout Bahrain, especially in Shi'ite districts, and large-scale demonstrations were held in Manama in support of Sheikh Salman's demands and to petition for his release. Civil unrest continued despite the Amir's pledge to extend the powers of the Consultative Council; 12 people died and some 2,500 demonstrators were arrested in clashes with the security forces during December and in early January 1995. Sheikh Salman was deported in January and sought asylum in the United Kingdom (a request that was finally granted in July 1998). The unprecedented scale of the protests was widely attributed to a marked deterioration in socio-economic conditions in Bahrain, and in particular to a high level of unemployment.

There were further anti-Government demonstrations in Shi'ite districts in March and April 1995, following a police search of the property of an influential Shi'ite cleric, Sheikh Abd al-Amir al-Jamri, who was subsequently placed under house arrest and later imprisoned. In May and July several people received custodial sentences for damaging public installations, and one Bahraini was sentenced to death for the murder of a police-officer in March. In June, in an apparent attempt to appease Shi'ite opposition leaders, the Prime Minister announced the first major cabinet reshuffle for 20 years, although the strategic portfolios of the interior, defence, foreign affairs and of finance and national economy remained unchanged.

In August 1995 the Government initiated talks with Shi'ite opposition leaders in an effort to foster reconciliation. In the same month the Amir issued a decree pardoning 150 people detained since the unrest. However, a report issued by Amnesty International in September indicated that as many as 1,500 demonstrators remained in detention in Bahrain, and that two prisoners had died in police custody following torture. Talks between the Government and opposition leaders collapsed in mid-September, but more than 40 political prisoners, among them Sheikh al-Jamri, were none the less released later in the month. In late October al-Jamri and six other opposition figures began a hunger strike in protest at the Government's refusal to concede to their demands, which included the release of all political prisoners and the restoration of the National Assembly. In early November, following a large demonstration to mark the end of the hunger strike, the Government announced that it would take 'necessary action' to prevent future 'illegal' gatherings. In December the Amir declared an amnesty for nearly 150 prisoners, most of whom had been arrested during the recent disturbances. There were large-scale demonstrations in late December and in early January 1996, in protest at the heavy deployment of security forces in Shi'ite districts and at the closure of two mosques. Opposition activists strongly criticized the use of tear gas and plastic bullets to disperse protesters, and also suggested that Saudi Arabian and Indian security officers had been dispatched to reinforce the Bahrain police. In mid-January eight opposition leaders, including Sheikh al-Jamri, were arrested on charges of inciting unrest. In February Ahmad ash-Shamlan, a noted lawyer and writer, became the first prominent Sunni to be detained in connection with the disturbances, following his distribution of a statement accusing the Government of authoritarianism. A number of bomb explosions in February and early March culminated in an arson attack on a restaurant in Sitra, in which seven Bangladeshi workers died. Also in March jurisdiction with regard to a number of criminal offences was transferred from ordinary courts to the High Court of Appeal, acting in the capacity of State Security Court. This move effectively accelerated court proceedings, while removing the right of appeal and limiting the role of the defence. In late March Isa Ahmad Hassan Qambar was executed by firing squad, having been condemned to death for killing a police-officer during the unrest of March 1995 (see above). The execution—the first to take place in Bahrain since 1977—provoked mass protests by Bahrainis, while international human rights organizations challenged the validity of Qambar's confession and trial.

Civil disturbances continued during 1996, and tensions were exacerbated by the Government's announcement, in April, of the creation of a Higher Council of Islamic Affairs (to be appointed by the Prime Minister and headed by the Minister of Justice and Islamic Affairs) to supervise all religious activity (including that of the Shi'ite community) in Bahrain. In June, however, the Amir sought to appease the demands of opposition reformers by announcing the future expansion of the Consultative Council from 30 to 40 members: a new 40-member Council was duly appointed by the Amir in September. In July the State Security Court imposed death sentences on three of the eight Bahrainis convicted of the arson attack in Sitra, while four men were sentenced to life imprisonment. Although the death sentences provoked widespread domestic protests and international criticism, resulting in an appeal being permitted against the ruling, in October the Court of Cassation ruled that it had no jurisdiction to overturn the verdict. Towards the end of the year government plans to close a number of Shi'ite mosques resulted in further riots.

As unrest continued into early 1997, there were rumours of division within the ruling family concerning the use of force in response to the crisis. In January a National Guard was created, to provide support for the Bahrain Defence Force and the security forces of the Ministry of the Interior. The Amir's son, Hamad, was appointed to command the new force, prompting speculation that its primary duty would be to protect the ruling family. In March a week of anti-Government protests marked the first anniversary of the execution of Isa Ahmad Hassan Qambar. It was reported that since the outbreak of civil unrest at the end of 1994 some 28 people had been killed and 220 imprisoned in connection with the protests. In July and August 1997 two human rights groups produced reports criticizing the Bahrain police for allegedly making arbitrary arrests, using torture, and arresting children as young as seven years of age. The Government rejected these reports, claiming that they were based on dishonest sources. It did, however, appear to respond to the allegations when, in November, the trial *in absentia* of eight prominent exiled activists (including Sheikh Ali Salman) on charges including the attempted overthrow of the regime resulted in the imposition of prison sentences of between five and 15 years. Although the activists claimed not to have been summoned to stand trial, their sentences were considered lenient in view of the severity of their alleged offences. Furthermore, during 1997 publishing restrictions were relaxed, and in December the Amir announced plans to enlarge further the Consultative Council and to allow greater media coverage of its activities. In February 1998 opposition groups welcomed the appointment of Khalid bin Muhammad al-Khalifa as the new head of the State Security Investigation Directorate (in place of a long-serving British national) and urged the continuing 'Bahrainization' of the security apparatus as a precondition for the initiation of dialogue between the regime and the opposition.

Sheikh Isa died on 6 March 1999. He was succeeded as Amir by his son, Crown Prince Sheikh Hamad bin Isa al-Khalifa, hitherto Commander-in-Chief of the Bahrain Defence Force and the National Guard; Sheikh Hamad's eldest son, Sheikh Salman bin Hamad al-Khalifa, became Crown Prince and also assumed his father's military command. Initially, opposition groups welcomed Sheikh Hamad's accession, which raised expectations of political change. In his first months in office Sheikh Hamad permitted Shi'ites to join the armed forces, allowed an investigation by Amnesty International into alleged brutality by the Sunni security forces, and released more than 300 Shi'ite prisoners being held on security-related charges. However, the opposition claimed that 1,200–1,500 political prisoners remained in detention, and Sheikh Hamad was regarded as having failed to initiate prompt negotiations to end political unrest. At the end of May he announced a limited cabinet reorganization in which three new ministers were appointed, including the former Governor of the Bahrain Monetary Agency, Abdullah bin Hassan Saif, as Minister of Finance and National Economy. Despite evident tension in relations between the new Amir and the uncompromising Sheikh Khalifa, the Prime Minister retained his position. In July Sheikh al-Jamri, who was brought to trial in February, having been detained since 1996 under the terms of the 1974 Decree Law on State Security Measures (which allowed the imprisonment of suspects without trial for a period of up to three years), was sentenced to 10 years' imprisonment for espionage and inciting anti-Government unrest; a substantial fine was also imposed. Following intense international pressure Sheikh Hamad granted al-Jamri an official pardon the following day, although he remained effectively under house arrest. In August 1999 Bahrain's longest serving political prisoner, As-Sayed Jafar al-Alawi, was released from detention, having served 18 years of a 25-year prison sentence imposed in 1981 for plotting against the Government. In November–December 1999 the Amir ordered the release of some 345 detainees. In October, meanwhile, Sheikh Hamad issued a decree ordering the Consultative Council to establish a human rights committee. None the less, Amnesty International asserted in November 2000 that while the human rights situation in Bahrain had improved since 1998 (among the advances cited by the organization was the ratification, in March 1998, of the UN Convention against Torture and Other Cruel, Inhuman or Degrading Treatment or Punishment), the mechanisms that had facilitated past human rights violations remained in place.

In May 2000 the Prime Minister stated that municipal elections, on the basis of universal suffrage, would be held in early 2001 and that parliamentary elections would take place in 2004. At the end of September 2000 four women, as well as a number of non-Muslims, were appointed for the first time to the Consultative Council. The Amir announced in late November that a 46-member Supreme National Committee (SNC) had been formed to prepare a National Action Charter (NAC), which would outline the further evolution of Bahrain's political system. Among the SNC's recommendations, submitted in late December, were that there should be a transition from an emirate to a constitutional monarchy, comprising a directly elected bicameral parliament (with women permitted both to vote and to seek election), a consultative chamber that would be appointed by the Government from all sections of society, and an independent judiciary. Critics of the Bahrain regime dismissed the proposed transition to a monarchy as a pretext for the continuation of autocratic rule. Meanwhile, a Supreme Council for Economic Development (subsequently restyled the Economic Development Board) was established in April, under the chairmanship of the Prime Minister.

The new Charter was submitted for approval in a national referendum held on 14–15 February 2001 (at which Bahraini women were permitted to vote for the first time), and was duly endorsed by 98.4% of participating voters. Two committees were formed by Sheikh Hamad later that month. The tasks of the first committee, the Committee for the Activation of the National Charter, headed by the Crown Prince, were to implement the NAC and to define the respective roles of the legislature and the monarchy. The second committee, chaired by the Minister of Justice and Islamic Affairs, was required to oversee amendments to the Constitution. The Decree Law on State Security Measures and the State Security Court were both abolished at this time. Prior to the referendum all political prisoners, including the Shi'ite cleric Sheikh al-Jamri, were reportedly released by the Amir. Moreover, following the removal of travel restrictions for members of the opposition, by March 2001 at least 100 political exiles had returned to Bahrain, among them Sheikh Ali Salman, the Muslim cleric deported in 1995. Also in March 2001, prior to a visit by representatives of Amnesty International, the Government granted a licence to the independent Bahrain Human Rights Society. A government reorganization was effected in April. Although the key portfolios remained unaltered, several ministries were restructured and five new ministers were appointed to the Cabinet. The formation of a Supreme Council for Women in Bahrain, to be chaired by the wife of the Amir, was announced in August.

On 14 February 2002 Sheikh Hamad announced the establishment of a constitutional monarchy in Bahrain, proclaiming himself King. The new monarch approved the amendments to the Constitution outlined in the NAC and dissolved the Consultative Council. Municipal elections were held on 9 May (with run-off voting one week later); however, female candidates—for the first time permitted to stand for public office—failed to win any seats on the five new regional councils.

Meanwhile, it was announced that Bahrain's first legislative elections for 27 years would take place, earlier than had previously been indicated, on 24 October 2002. In preparation for the elections, in late June the Government approved a draft electoral law. The new legislation was criticized by opposition groups on the grounds that it barred all trade unions and overtly political organizations from participating in the ballot; in September, however, King Hamad removed restrictions on campaigning by political groups. Opposition activists expressed strong concern, furthermore, that the unelected Consultative Council would have the same rights as the elected House of Representatives in the bicameral parliament, and stated that they would boycott the polls. Meanwhile, in early July the King ordered the establishment of an independent financial auditing court, with far-reaching powers to monitor state spending. Later in that month the creation of a Constitutional Court was also approved by the Government: this became operational in April 2005. Meanwhile, legislation allowing the establishment of independent trade unions was enacted in late September.

At the elections to the House of Representatives held on 24 October 2002, 21 of the 40 seats were won by independents and 'moderate' Sunni candidates, with the remaining 19 seats taken by more radical Islamists. The rate of participation by voters was recorded as 53.2% of the registered electorate. Reformists expressed their view that the newly elected legislature would not reflect the structure of Bahraini society, since a large proportion of the Shi'ite majority had boycotted the elections and female candidates had failed to win any seats (there had been eight women among a total of 174 candidates). Opposition groups, both leftist and Islamist, also complained that international human rights groups had not been permitted to monitor the elections. Moreover, there was considerable criticism of the policy of political naturalization adopted by the Amir (whereby Sunnis from the Eastern Province of Saudi Arabia were granted full voting rights), which was interpreted as a deliberate attempt to reduce the size of the Shi'ite majority. On 17 November the new Consultative Council, headed by Dr Faisal Radhi al-Mousawi, hitherto Minister of Health, was sworn in by the King: the new body comprised 40 appointed members, including four women. Earlier in the same month King Hamad named an expanded Cabinet, in which Dr Khalil bin Ibrahim Hassan succeeded al-Mousawi as Minister of Health. Other notable changes included the appointment of two Shi'ites, Dr Majid bin Hassan al-Alawi and Sheikh Jawad bin Salem al-Oraid, as Minister of Labour and Social Affairs and Minister of Justice, respectively. In addition, for the first time two deputy prime ministers were appointed: Sheikh Abdullah bin Khalid al-Khalifa, who also held the position of Minister of Islamic Affairs, and Sheikh Muhammad bin Mubarak al-Khalifa, who retained the foreign affairs portfolio. The legislation permitting the establishment of independent trade unions was ratified in November and in January 2004 the General Federation of Bahrain Workers' Unions, which represents some 40 trade unions, was founded; the King also, in late 2002, declared 1 May, international Labour Day, as an official holiday.

In late August 2003 a hunger strike by more than 200 inmates at a prison in southern Bahrain, in protest at their alleged ill-treatment, ended following successful negotiations involving the Ministry of the Interior, members of the House of Representatives and human rights organizations. In January 2004 17 members of parliament applied for permission to question three cabinet ministers, including the Minister of Finance and National Economy, Abdullah Saif, about alleged irregularities

in the administration of two pension funds—the first such request since the establishment of the House of Representatives in 2002. The Speaker, Khalifa adh-Dhahrani, urged MPs to withdraw the request and claimed that the move was unjustified. King Hamad, however, expressed his support for a parliamentary investigation into the alleged mismanagement. In September 2004 the Bahraini authorities closed down the Bahrain Centre for Human Rights, an independent grouping authorized by the Government, and arrested its director, Abd al-Hadi al-Khawaja, for criticizing Bahrain's economic policies and human rights record and for calling for the removal of the Prime Minister. International observers (including Amnesty International) condemned the decision and accused Bahrain of taking a backward step in terms of human rights reform. Later in the same month King Hamad warned his regime's critics not to abuse the country's 'openness and freedoms'; however, in November he ordered the release of al-Khawaja and 13 other people who had publicly demonstrated their support for the activist.

In April 2004 Dr Nada Haffadh replaced Dr Khalil Hassan as the Minister of Health, thereby becoming Bahrain's first female cabinet minister. In late May King Hamad dismissed the long-serving Minister of the Interior, Sheikh Muhammad bin Khalifa al-Khalifa, following clashes between Bahraini police and mainly Shi'ite protesters who were demonstrating against US military operations in two Shi'ite holy cities in Iraq. Maj.-Gen. Sheikh Rashid bin Abdullah bin Ahmad al-Khalifa was named as his successor. A further reorganization of the Government was effected in mid-January 2005, in which two new cabinet members were appointed: Dr Fatima al-Blushi became Bahrain's second female minister when she secured the social affairs portfolio, and Sheikh Ahmad bin Muhammad al-Khalifa was given the post of Minister of Finance and National Economy (replacing Saif, who had been questioned in parliament in 2004 in connection with the pension fund controversy). In addition, the Ministries of Industry and Commerce were merged under the control of Dr Hassan bin Abdullah Fakhro and new appointments were made to the Ministries of Justice, of Information and to the position of Minister of State for Cabinet Affairs. The representation of the royal family in the Cabinet was unaffected by the changes.

Although relations between Bahrain and Iran were upgraded to ambassadorial level in late 1990, the situation between the two countries began to deteriorate in the mid-1990s. While there was sufficient evidence to suggest largely domestic motivation for the recent increase in popular disaffection, the Bahraini authorities continued to imply that the disturbances were fomented by Iranian-backed militant Shi'ite fundamentalists seeking to destabilize the country. These allegations were frequently dismissed by Iran. In June 1996 the Bahraini Government announced that it had uncovered details of a plot, initiated in 1993 with support from fundamentalist Shi'ite groups in Iran, to oust the Government and ruling family in Bahrain and replace them with a pro-Iranian administration. It was claimed that a previously unknown Shi'ite group, Hezbollah Bahrain, had been established and financed by Iran's Revolutionary Guard. Young Bahraini Shi'ites were alleged to have received military training in Iran and at guerrilla bases in Lebanon, in preparation for a terrorist offensive in Bahrain, which had culminated in the unrest of the previous 18 months. Within days of the Government's announcement more than 50 Bahrainis had been arrested in connection with the alleged plot. Many of the detainees, including six who made televised confessions, admitted membership of Hezbollah Bahrain. The Iranian authorities denied any involvement in the planned insurrection, but bilateral relations were severely undermined by the unprecedented directness of the Bahrain Government's accusations; the two countries' respective ambassadors were withdrawn, and diplomatic relations were downgraded. During June 1996 more than 30 Bahrainis received prison sentences of between one and 13 years—for offences connected to the disturbances—from the State Security Court (and were therefore denied the right of appeal). In March 1997 59 Bahraini Shi'ites accused of belonging to Hezbollah Bahrain were brought to trial; similar charges had been made against a further 22 Shi'ites who, according to the Bahrain Government, were to be tried *in absentia*. The State Security Court sentenced 37 of the defendants to terms of imprisonment ranging from three to 15 years, and acquitted the others. There was a period of *détente* in relations between most countries of the GCC and Iran following the election of Muhammad Khatami to the Iranian presidency in

May of that year, and in December 1999 relations at ambassadorial level were formally restored between Bahrain and Iran. In March 2000 the Ministers of Foreign Affairs of the two countries met in Manama to discuss regional security as well as political and economic co-operation; a bilateral economic commission held its first meeting in that month. In early 2001 it was announced that Shi'ite Muslims of Iranian descent and whose families had lived in Bahrain for several generations were to be granted full Bahraini citizenship.

In common with other Gulf states, Bahrain consistently expressed support for Iraq at the time of the Iran–Iraq War (1980–88). However, following the Iraqi invasion of Kuwait in August 1990, Bahrain firmly supported the implementation of UN economic sanctions against Iraq and permitted the stationing of US troops and combat aircraft in Bahrain. (Military co-operation with the USA had been close for many years.) In June 1991, following the liberation of Kuwait in February, it was confirmed that Bahrain would remain a regional support base for the USA, and later in the year the two countries signed a defence co-operation agreement. In January 1994 Bahrain signed further accords of military co-operation with the USA and the United Kingdom. Relations with Iraq remained strained, and in October hopes of improved relations receded when Iraqi forces were again deployed in the Iraq–Kuwait border area. In response, Bahrain deployed combat aircraft and naval units to join GCC and US forces in the defence of Kuwait. In late 1995 Bahrain agreed to the temporary deployment on its territory of US fighter aircraft, in order to deter any possible military threat from Iraq. In February 1998 Bahrain strongly advocated a diplomatic solution to the ongoing dispute between Iraq and the UN weapons inspectors (see the chapter on Iraq), and refused to allow US military aircraft to launch attacks on Iraq from Bahraini bases. In June, as part of a wider US effort to reduce its military presence in the region, US military aircraft were withdrawn from Bahrain. In December a further US-led military campaign against Iraq was supported by the Bahraini authorities (the operation was centred in Manama, where the US Fifth Fleet is based), although Bahrain refrained from any public endorsement of the air-strikes. In August 1999 it was reported that Bahrain desired a further reduction of the US military presence in Bahrain, particularly that of the Fifth Fleet.

Bahrain joined the other GCC states in condemning the suicide attacks on New York and Washington, DC, on 11 September 2001, and pledged to co-operate with the USA's attempts to forge an international 'coalition against terror', notably by 'freezing' the financial assets of individuals or organizations allegedly linked to the fundamentalist Islamist al-Qa'ida (Base) network of Osama bin Laden, held by the USA to be principally responsible for the attacks. Nevertheless, in the aftermath of the suicide attacks, small demonstrations and 'bomb-scare' telephone calls to US companies based in Bahrain indicated renewed antipathy towards the USA in some quarters. As in the other Gulf states, there was concern in Bahrain that US-led military action, which began in Afghanistan in early October, should not be directed against any Muslim target in the Middle East. As the momentum towards a US-led military campaign to oust the regime of Saddam Hussein in Iraq grew, anti-war riots became increasingly frequent in Bahrain, and in February 2003 police opened fire on a 2,000-strong violent demonstration outside the US embassy in Manama. Although King Hamad expressed hope that a diplomatic solution to the crisis could be found, Bahrain announced that it would contribute a frigate and an unspecified number of troops to the defence of Kuwait from possible Iraqi retaliation should the US-led campaign proceed. In March the Bahrain Government lent its support to an appeal by the UAE for Saddam Hussein to go into exile in order to save his country from the consequences of the US pursuit of 'regime change', and offered him asylum in Bahrain. Following the commencement, later in March, of US-led military action in Iraq, in April Bahrain ordered the expulsion of an Iraqi diplomat who was alleged to be linked to an explosion outside the Fifth Fleet base. Sporadic violent incidents and threats, believed to be related to the continued presence of the US military in Bahrain, continued throughout 2003–04. In October 2003 five officers were injured when a petrol bomb was thrown at a police vehicle, and in December the US Government asserted that it had received a 'specific' threat that a terrorist attack was planned for the Christmas period. In April 2004 Bahrain's first Formula One motor-racing Grand Prix, which the British Foreign and Commonwealth Office had warned was a potential terrorist target,

passed without reported incident. In early 2005 the ongoing contention between the USA and Iran over the latter's nuclear programme (see the chapter on Iran) was regarded in some quarters as a potential threat to Bahrain's security, and there was speculation that the issue could foster further domestic resentment towards the Bahraini Government's hosting of the US base: in the event of conflict, the US Fifth Fleet base in Bahrain was considered likely to be a priority target for Iranian military action.

In April 1986 Qatari military forces raided the island of Fasht ad-Dibal, which had been artificially constructed on a coral reef (submerged at high tide), situated midway between Bahrain and Qatar; both countries claimed sovereignty over the island. Following GCC mediation, in May the two Governments agreed to destroy the island. Other areas of dispute between the two states were Zubarah (which was part of Bahraini territory until the early 20th century), in mainland Qatar, and the Hawar islands, the region of which is believed to contain potentially valuable reserves of petroleum and natural gas. In July 1991 Qatar instituted proceedings at the International Court of Justice (ICJ) in The Hague, Netherlands, regarding the issue of the Hawar islands (in 1939 a British judgment had awarded sovereignty of the islands to Bahrain), Fasht ad-Dibal and Qit'at Jaradah (over which the British Government had recognized Bahrain's 'sovereign rights' in 1947), together with the delimitation of the maritime border between Qatar and Bahrain. The question of sovereignty was further confused in April 1992, when the Government of Qatar issued a decree redefining its maritime borders to include territorial waters claimed by Bahrain, and tensions were exacerbated by Qatar's persistent rejection of Bahrain's insistence that the two countries should seek joint recourse to the ICJ. Moreover, Bahrain had reportedly attempted to widen the issue to include its claim to the Zubarah region. Qatar applied unilaterally to the Court, and in February 1995 the ICJ ruled that it was competent to adjudicate in the dispute. Relations between Bahrain and Qatar deteriorated following the Bahrain Government's decision, in September, to construct a tourist resort on the Hawar islands, and remained tense subsequently, with the Bahraini Government advocating a regional solution to the dispute in preference to ICJ jurisdiction.

In December 1996 Bahrain boycotted the GCC annual summit convened in Doha, Qatar, at which it was decided to establish a quadripartite committee (comprising those GCC members not involved in the dispute) to facilitate a solution. The committee reportedly made some progress, and following senior-level ministerial meetings between Bahrain and Qatar in London, United Kingdom, and in Manama in early 1997, it was announced that diplomatic relations at ambassadorial level were to be established between the two countries. Qatar, however, was alone in nominating its diplomatic representative shortly afterwards. Regional efforts failed to find a solution to the territorial dispute, and the announcement of Bahraini construction plans on the Hawar islands (which, in addition to the opening of an hotel in mid-1997, included a housing complex and a causeway linking the islands to Bahrain) did little to further bilateral relations. Bahrain emphasized that it would disregard any ruling on the issue by the ICJ, and also dismissed as a forgery a series of documents, submitted to the ICJ by the Qatar Government, supporting the Qatari claim. Qatar subsequently agreed to withdraw the documents from evidence. At the end of 1999 the Amir of Qatar made his first official visit to Manama, during which it was agreed that a joint committee, headed by the Crown Princes of Bahrain and Qatar, would be established to encourage bilateral co-operation. Qatar also agreed to withdraw its petition from the ICJ in the event of the joint committee's reaching a solution to the territorial disputes. Senior-level contacts were furthered in January 2000, upon the first visit of the new Amir of Bahrain, Sheikh Hamad, to Qatar, and the two countries agreed to hasten the opening of embassies in Manama and Doha. In February, following the first meeting of the Bahrain-Qatar Supreme Joint Committee, it was announced that the possibility of constructing a causeway (the Friendship Bridge) to link the two states was to be investigated; Qatar officially named its ambassador to Bahrain on the same day. In May, however, Bahrain unilaterally suspended the Supreme Joint Committee pending the ruling of the ICJ. Hearings by the Court began later that month and were completed by the end of June. A verdict was issued in March 2001, whereby Bahrain was found to have sovereignty over the Hawar islands and Qit'at Jaradah, while Qatar held sovereignty over Zubarah, Janan island and the low-tide elevation of Fasht ad-Dibal; the Court drew a single maritime boundary between the two states. Both Bahrain and Qatar accepted the ICJ ruling. Later in March, following a high-profile visit by Sheikh Hamad to Doha, the two sides announced that meetings of the Supreme Joint Committee would resume. From early 2002 international oil companies were invited to submit bids to drill for oil and gas off the Hawar islands, which Sheikh Hamad also intended to transform into a major tourist resort. Approval for the construction of the causeway linking Bahrain to Qatar was finally given in May 2004; the project was expected to cost some US $2,000m. and international companies were invited to present bids in late 2004.

Following an unusually short period of negotiations, in September 2004 Bahrain signed a free-trade agreement with the USA, to be implemented following US congressional approval (expected in 2005). In response, the Saudi Government, which claimed that the accord contravened the GCC's external tariff agreement (a view disputed by Bahrain), in January 2005 threatened to impose customs duties on foreign goods imported duty-free through GCC countries, a move that would affect US goods imported to Bahrain under the bilateral agreement. In December 2004 Crown Prince Abdullah of Saudi Arabia had failed to attend the GCC annual summit in Manama, a decision that for some commentators symbolized growing Saudi disapproval of the burgeoning relationship between Bahrain and the USA, and, in particular, indicated the seriousness of the dispute over the free-trade agreement.

Government

A National Action Charter, drafted in late 2000 by a Supreme National Committee and approved in a national referendum held in February 2001, recommended the transition from an emirate to a constitutional monarchy. The Amir proclaimed himself King in February 2002. Subsequently, a bicameral legislature, comprising a directly elected legislative body and an appointed consultative chamber, was instituted. Elections to a 40-member House of Representatives took place in October 2002, and a new Consultative Council (Majlis ash-Shoura), comprising 40 appointed members, was sworn in by the King in November of that year.

Defence

Military service is voluntary. In August 2004 the active Bahrain Defence Force consisted of 11,200 men (8,500 army, 1,200 navy, 1,500 air force). There were also paramilitary forces of an estimated 10,160 men (9,000 police, some 900 national guard, 260 coastguard). The defence budget for 2004 was estimated at BD 180m. (excluding procurement).

Economic Affairs

In 2002, according to estimates by the World Bank, Bahrain's gross national income (GNI), measured at average 2000–02 prices, was US $7,241.8m., equivalent to $11,260 per head (or $16,170 per head on an international purchasing-power parity basis). During 1990–2003, it was estimated, the population increased at an average annual rate of 2.7%, while gross domestic product (GDP) per head increased, in real terms, by an average of 2.5% per year during 1990–2002. Overall GDP increased, in real terms, at an average annual rate of 5.0% per year in 1990–2002; growth was an estimated 5.1% in 2002 and about 6.8% in 2003.

Agriculture (including hunting, forestry and fishing) engaged 0.9% of the labour force in 2001, and contributed an estimated 0.6% of GDP in 2003. The principal crops are dates, tomatoes, onions and cabbages. Livestock production is also important. Agricultural GDP increased at an average annual rate of 2.2% in 1993–2002. The GDP of the sector increased by 8.8% in 2003.

Industry (comprising mining, manufacturing, construction and utilities) engaged 54.5% of the employed labour force in 2001, and provided some 38.6% of GDP in 2003. During 1993–2002 industrial GDP increased by an average of 4.4% per year; growth of the sector was 4.8% in 2003.

Mining and quarrying engaged 0.2% of the employed labour force in 2001, and contributed an estimated 23.4% of GDP in 2003. The major mining activities are the exploitation of petroleum and natural gas, which in 2003 accounted for 23.1% of GDP. At the beginning of 2003 Bahrain's proven published reserves of crude petroleum were estimated to be only 100m. barrels. Including production from the Abu Saafa oilfield, situated between Bahrain and Saudi Arabia, all revenues from which have since 1996 been allocated to Bahrain, production for the whole of 2000 averaged 102,000 b/d. Bahrain's reserves of natural gas at the end of 2003 were put at 90,000m. cu m, sufficient to maintain production (at 2003 levels) for 8.8 years. Mining GDP increased by an annual average of 4.6% in 1993–2002. The sector's GDP increased by 1.9% in 2003.

In 2001 manufacturing engaged 25.6% of the employed labour force, and the sector provided an estimated 10.4% of GDP in 2003. Important industries include the petroleum refinery at Sitra, aluminium (Bahrain is the region's largest producer) and aluminium-related enterprises, shipbuilding, iron and steel, and chemicals. Since the mid-1980s the Government has encouraged the development of light industry. During 1993–2002 manufacturing GDP increased at an average annual rate of 4.4%; the sector's GDP increased by 6.3% in 2003.

Industrial expansion has resulted in energy demand that threatens to exceed the country's 1,800-MW total installed generating capacity, particularly as not all of the installed capacity is operational, owing to the advanced age of a number of stations. (It was reported in 2004 that energy demands were increasing by more than 6% per year.) An agreement was signed in July 2004 with Tractebel of Belgium to run the Al-Ezzal independent power project from April 2006; the project was intended to increase the country's generating capacity to some 2,800 MW by mid-2007.

The services sector engaged 44.6% of the employed labour force in 2001, and contributed some 60.8% of GDP in 2003. The financial services industry, notably the operation of 'offshore' banking units (OBUs), is a major source of Bahrain's prosperity. In early 2005 there were 53 registered OBUs. Bahrain has developed as a principal centre for Islamic banking and other financial services. In January 2002 Bahrain became the first country to publish a full set of regulations, including requirements in terms of capital adequacy, risk management, asset quality, liquidity management and corporate governance, for its Islamic banking sector. The first International Islamic Financial Market, with a liquidity management centre and Islamic ratings agency based in Bahrain, was inaugurated in August. In October the Government launched the Bahrain Financial Harbour project, at a cost of some US $1,300m., whereby the Manama port area was to be redeveloped in order to provide a home for the 'offshore' financial sector and to protect Bahrain's status as the leading financial centre in the Gulf. Completion of the project was anticipated by 2007, although extra land was set aside for additional construction. During 1993–2002 the services sector showed an average GDP increase of 3.4% per year. The GDP of the sector increased by 9.3% in 2003.

In 2003 Bahrain recorded a visible trade surplus of US $1,610.5m., but there was a deficit of $68.4m. on the current account of the balance of payments. In 2002 the principal sources of non-petroleum imports were Japan (accounting for 9.5% of the total), Saudi Arabia (8.8%), Germany, Australia, the USA and the United Kingdom. Saudi Arabia provided most of Bahrain's petroleum imports (and accounted for 50.8% of all imports in 1990). The USA was the principal customer for Bahrain's non-petroleum exports (25.9% of the total) in 2002; other important markets were Saudi Arabia (17.2%) and Taiwan (9.3%). The principal exports are petroleum, petroleum products and aluminium. Sales of petroleum and petroleum products provided 70.4% of total export earnings in 2002. The principal import is crude petroleum (for domestic refining), accounting for 35.8% of total imports in 2002. The main category of non-petroleum imports (22.5% in 2002) is machinery and mechanical appliances, electrical, sound and television equipment.

In 2004 there was an anticipated budgetary deficit of BD 383m. (equivalent to about 11% of GDP). Consumer prices decreased at an average annual rate of 0.2% in 1997–2002; however, inflation was recorded of 0.2% in 2001 and 1.2% in 2002. An estimated 58.9% of the labour force were expatriates in 2002. The official rate of unemployment was 5.6% in late 2001, but unofficial sources estimated unemployment to be in excess of 15% in 2003.

Bahrain is a member of the Co-operation Council for the Arab States of the Gulf (Gulf Co-operation Council—GCC, see p. 193). The GCC's six members established a unified regional customs tariff in January 2003, and agreed to create a single market and currency no later than January 2010. The country is also a member of the Organization of Arab Petroleum Exporting Countries (OAPEC), see p. 324, the Arab Monetary Fund (see p. 153) and the Islamic Development Bank (see p. 287).

In recognition of the fact that Bahrain's reserves of petroleum and natural gas are nearing exhaustion, the Government has introduced measures both to diversify the country's industrial base and to attract wider foreign investment: non-petroleum exports reportedly increased by 125% between 1992 and 2001, although petroleum and related products still accounted for more than two-thirds of total export earnings in 2002. During the past decade the Government has continued to encourage greater participation of the private sector in economic development, and has adopted a gradual approach to the privatization of state enterprises (excluding the petroleum sector). Following the foundation of the Telecommunications Regulatory Authority in 2002, in April 2003 the Government ended the monopoly of the state-owned Bahrain Telecommunications Company (BATELCO) over the rapidly expanding mobile phone services market by granting, to MTC Vodafone Bahrain, a second GSM (Global System for Mobile Communications) licence. In January 2004 the Government announced plans further to liberalize the telecommunications sector by inviting applications for new licences in four areas of the industry, including public access mobile radio and paging. In addition, the Cabinet approved the privatization of electricity production in December 2003. In early 2005 Bahrain approved a proposal to establish a private company to acquire the Government's shares in tourism projects in the kingdom; the divestment of shares in BATELCO and Aluminium Bahrain was also expected from 2005. Several important construction developments made progress in the early years of the 21st century, as Bahrain's economy remained buoyant. Among several large-scale tourism projects initiated was a scheme to develop infrastructure on the Hawar islands, following the settlement of Bahrain's long-standing territorial dispute with Qatar. Furthermore, following the signing in 2002 of a six-year agreement between the Bahrain Government and the sport's governing body, Bahrain hosted its first Formula One motor-racing Grand Prix in April 2004. Meanwhile, investor confidence was enhanced by moves towards political liberalization. Despite the continued fear of regional instability linked to the US-led military involvement in Iraq from 2003, GDP growth, stimulated by an increase in government spending, was expected to remain at around 7% per year in 2004 and 2005. It was anticipated that the implementation of a free-trade agreement with the USA (expected in 2005) would provide a further boost to economic growth. In mid-2004 the IMF commended the progress of the economy, but warned that job-creation for Bahraini nationals was the greatest economic challenge facing the country.

Education

Although education is not compulsory, it is provided free of charge up to the secondary level. The education system is composed of three different stages: primary and intermediate schooling, which together form 'basic education', and secondary schooling. Primary education lasts from six to 11 years of age; it is divided into two cycles, each comprising three years. Intermediate education lasts for three years, between the ages of 12 and 14. Entry to secondary education, which comprises three years between the ages of 15 and 17, is conditional on obtaining the Intermediate School Certificate or its equivalent. Students choose to follow one of the following curriculums: general (science or literary), commercial, technical or vocational. Private and religious education are also available. The University of Bahrain, established by Amiri decree in 1986, comprises five colleges: the College of Engineering, the College of Arts, the College of Science, the College of Education and the College of Business Administration. About 13,528 students were enrolled at the University in 2001/02. The Arabian Gulf University (AGU), funded by seven Arab governments, also provides higher education. The AGU comprises two colleges: the College of Medicine and Medical Sciences and the College of Graduate Studies, which together enrolled some 659 students in 2001/02. The University campus was due to be completed by the end of 2006, and will accommodate 5,000 students. In 1996 enrolment at primary, intermediate and secondary levels was 97.8% (males 97.6%; females 97.9%), 96.0% (males 96.4%; females 95.5%) and 95.0% (males 90.2%; females 99.9%), respectively, of the relevant age-groups. Budget forecasts for 2004/05 allocated BD 125.4m. (14.6% of total government expenditure) to education.

Public Holidays

2005: 1 January (New Year's Day), 21 January* (Id al-Adha, Feast of the Sacrifice), 10 February* (Muharram, Islamic New Year), 19 February* (Ashoura), 21 April* (Mouloud, Birth of the Prophet), 1 May (Labour Day), 4 November* (Id al-Fitr, end of Ramadan), 16 December (National Day).

2006: 1 January (New Year's Day), 11 January* (Id al-Adha, Feast of the Sacrifice), 31 January* (Muharram, Islamic New Year), 9 February* (Ashoura), 11 April* (Mouloud, Birth of the Prophet), 1 May (Labour Day), 24 October* (Id al-Fitr, end of Ramadan), 16 December (National Day).

*These holidays are dependent on the Islamic lunar calendar and may vary by one or two days from the dates given.

Weights and Measures

The metric system is being introduced.

Statistical Survey

Sources (unless otherwise stated): Central Statistics Organization, POB 5835, Manama; tel. 17725725; fax 17728989; e-mail cso@bahrain.gov.bh; Bahrain Monetary Agency, POB 27, Bldg 96, Block 317, Rd 1702, Manama; tel. 17547777; fax 17531115; e-mail info@bma.gov.bh; internet www.bma.gov.bh; Ministry of Finance and National Economy, POB 333, Diplomatic Area, Manama; tel. 17530800; fax 17532713; e-mail mofne@batelco.com.bh; internet www.mofne.gov.bh.

AREA AND POPULATION

Area: 717.5 sq km (277.0 sq miles).

Population: 508,037 at census of 16 November 1991; 650,604 (males 373,649, females 276,955), comprising 405,667 Bahrainis (males 204,623, females 201,044) and 244,937 non-Bahraini nationals (males 169,026, females 75,911), at census of 7 April 2001; 689,418 (estimate) at December 2003.

Density (December 2003): 960.9 per sq km.

Principal Towns (populations at 2001 census): Manama (capital) 153,395; Muharraq 91,939; Rifa'a 79,985; Hamad Town 52,718; Jidd Hafs 52,450. *Mid-2003* (UN estimate, incl. suburbs): Manama 138,643 (Source: UN, *World Urbanization Prospects: The 2003 Revision*).

Births, Marriages and Deaths (2002): Registered live births 13,576 (birth rate 20.2 per 1,000); Registered marriages 4,909 (marriage rate 7.3 per 1,000); Registered deaths 2,035 (death rate 3.0 per 1,000).

Expectation of Life (WHO estimates, years at birth): 73.2 (males 72.1; females 74.5) in 2002. Source: WHO, *World Health Report*.

Economically Active Population (persons aged 15 years and over, economic activity covered by social welfare system only, 2001): Agriculture, hunting, forestry and fishing 1,439; Mining and quarrying 283; Manufacturing 43,134; Electricity, gas and water 3,465; Construction 44,899; Trade, restaurants and hotels 34,683; Transport, storage and communications 10,322; Financing, insurance, real estate and business services 8,774; Community, social and personal services 21,339; Activities not adequately defined 656; *Total employed* 168,994 (males 147,683, females 21,311) comprising 56,165 Bahrainis (males 42,781, females 13,384) and 112,829 non-Bahraini nationals (males 104,902, females 7,927).

Total Labour Force (persons aged 15 years and over, census of 2001): Total Bahrainis employed 110,987 (males 84,920, females 26,067); Total non-Bahrainis employed 180,391 (males 146,604, females 33,787); *Total employed* 291,378. Total Bahraini labour force (incl. unemployed) 127,123 (males 94,354, females 32,769); Total non-Bahraini labour force (incl. unemployed) 181,220 (males 147,123, females 34,097); *Total labour force* 308,343. *2002* (estimates): Total labour force 319,000 (Bahrainis 131,000, non-Bahrainis 188,000).

HEALTH AND WELFARE

Key Indicators

Total Fertility Rate (children per woman, 2002): 2.7.

Under-5 Mortality Rate (per 1,000 live births, 2003): 15.

HIV/AIDS (% of persons aged 15–49, 2003): 0.2.

Physicians (per 1,000 head, 2002): 1.53.

Hospital Beds (per 1,000 head, 2002): 2.7.

Health Expenditure (2001): US $ per head (PPP): 664.

Health Expenditure (2001): % of GDP: 4.1.

Health Expenditure (2001): public (% of total): 69.0.

Human Development Index (2002): ranking: 40.

Human Development Index (2002): value: 0.843.
For sources and definitions, see explanatory note on p. vi.

AGRICULTURE, ETC.

Principal Crops (FAO estimates, '000 metric tons, 2003): Tomatoes 2.1; Dry onions 1.3; Other vegetables (incl. melons) 5.0; Lemons and limes 1.0; Dates 17.0; Other fruits 4.1. Source: FAO.

Livestock (FAO estimates, '000 head, year ending September 2003): Cattle 15.0; Sheep 17.5; Goats 16.0. Source: FAO.

Livestock Products (FAO estimates, '000 metric tons, 2003): Beef and veal 1.4; Mutton and lamb 7.4; Goat meat 1.5; Poultry meat 5.6; Cows' milk 14.0; Hen eggs 2.0. Source: FAO.

Fishing (metric tons, live weight, 2002): Capture 11,204 (Groupers 725; Emperors 1,675; Porgies and seabreams 488; Spinefeet 2,009; Carangids 470; Portunus swimcrabs 2,828; Penaeus shrimps 1,401); Aquaculture 3; *Total catch* 11,207. Source: FAO.

MINING

Production (estimates, 2003): Crude petroleum 13,720,000 barrels; Natural gas 9,500 million cubic metres. Source: US Geological Survey.

INDUSTRY

Production ('000 barrels, 2003, unless otherwise indicated): Liquefied petroleum gas 350; Naphtha 1,600; Motor spirit (Gasoline) 7,000; Kerosene and jet fuel 21,000; Distillate fuel oil 20,000; Residual fuel oil 29,000; Petroleum bitumen (asphalt, 2000) 1,078; Electric energy 7,278 million kWh (2002); Aluminium (unwrought) 531,991 metric tons. Source: mostly US Geological Survey.

FINANCE

Currency and Exchange Rates: 1,000 fils = 1 Bahraini dinar (BD). *Sterling, Dollar and Euro Equivalents* (31 December 2004): £1 sterling = 726.2 fils; US $1 = 376.0 fils; €1 = 512.2 fils; 100 Bahraini dinars = £137.70 = $265.96 = €195.25. *Exchange Rate:* Fixed at US $1 = 376.0 fils (BD 1 = $2.6596) since November 1980.

Budget (BD million, 2001): *Revenue:* Taxation 215.0 (Taxes on income and profits 44.4, Social security contributions 76.5, Domestic taxes on goods and services 19.0, Import duties 57.3); Entrepreneurial and property income 716.3; Other current revenue 37.5; Capital revenue 0.5; Total 969.3, excl. grants from abroad (37.6). *Expenditure:* General public services 243.6; Defence 125.9; Public order and safety 101.3; Education 110.2; Health 64.4; Social security and welfare 62.4; Housing and community amenities 30.3; Recreational, cultural and religious affairs and services 4.4; Economic affairs and services 32.5 (Transport and communications 22.5); Interest payments 51.6; Total 826.6 (Current 653.8, Capital 172.8) (Source: IMF, *Government Finance Statistics Yearbook*). *2002* (forecasts, BD million): Revenue 675; Expenditure 835. *2003* (forecasts, BD million): Revenue 797; Expenditure 1,159. *2004* (forecasts, BD million): Revenue 806; Expenditure 1,189.

International Reserves (US $ million at 31 December 2003): Gold (valued at $44 per troy oz) 6.6; IMF special drawing rights 1.0; Reserve position in IMF 103.6; Foreign exchange 1,673.8; Total 1,785.0. Source: IMF, *International Financial Statistics*.

Money Supply (BD million at 31 December 2003): Currency outside banks 155.8; Demand deposits at commercial banks 665.6; Total money 821.4. Source: IMF, *International Financial Statistics*.

Cost of Living (Consumer Price Index; base: 1995 = 100): 99.6 in 2000; 99.8 in 2001; 101.0 in 2002. Source: IMF, *International Financial Statistics*.

Expenditure on the Gross Domestic Product (provisional, BD million, 2003): Government final consumption expenditure 672.34; Private final consumption expenditure 1,479.69; Increase in stocks 114.01; Gross fixed capital formation 699.84; *Total domestic expenditure* 2,965.88; Exports of goods and services 2,883.30; *Less* Imports of goods and services 2,237.20; *GDP in purchasers' values* 3,611.98.

Gross Domestic Product by Economic Activity (provisional, BD million at current prices, 2003): Agriculture, hunting, forestry and fishing 22.54; Mining and quarrying 910.45; Manufacturing 403.65; Electricity and water 49.55; Construction 139.05; Trade 304.11; Restaurants and hotels 65.32; Transport, storage and communications 262.63; Finance and insurance 711.27; Real estate and business services 320.59; Government services 360.40; Other community, social and personal services 343.77; *Sub-total* 3,893.30; *Less* Imputed bank service charge 331.21; *GDP at factor cost* 3,562.10; Import duties 49.86; *GDP in purchasers' values* 3,611.98.

Balance of Payments (US $ million, 2003): Exports of goods f.o.b. 6,689.8; Imports of goods f.o.b. –5,079.3; *Trade balance* 1,610.5; Exports of services 1,067.8; Imports of services –870.8; *Balance on goods and services* 1,807.6; Other income received 1,206.7; Other income paid –1,742.7; *Balance on goods, services and income* 1,271.6; Current transfers (net) –1,340.0; *Current balance* –68.4; Capital account (net) 50.0; Direct investment abroad –741.4; Direct investment from abroad 516.7; Portfolio investment assets –3,064.4; Portfolio investment liabilities 688.4; Other investment assets – 20,786.6; Other investment liabilities 23,134.3; Net errors and omissions 314.9; *Overall balance* 43.7. Source: IMF, *International Financial Statistics*.

EXTERNAL TRADE

Total Trade (BD million): *Imports c.i.f.:* 1,619.0 in 2001; 1,874.5 in 2002; 1,923.7 in 2003. *Exports:* 2,096.9 in 2001; 2,175.4 in 2002; 2,393.0 in 2003. Source: IMF, *International Financial Statistics*.

Principal Commodities (BD million, 2002): *Imports c.i.f.:* Live animals and animal products 54.1; Vegetable products 63.9; Prepared foodstuffs; beverages, spirits and vinegar; tobacco and manufactured substitutes 84.2; Mineral products 71.0; Products of chemical or allied industries 150.2; Plastics, rubber and articles thereof 37.7; Wood and articles thereof 16.5; Paper and paper products 20.8; Textiles and textile articles 95.9; Articles of stone, plaster, cement, asbestos, mica, etc.; ceramic products; glass and glassware 33.7; Base metals and articles thereof 86.8; Machinery and mechanical appliances; electrical equipment; sound and television apparatus 282.4; Vehicles, aircraft, vessels and associated transport equipment 166.2; Miscellaneous manufactured articles 34.3; Total (incl. others) 1,252.5. *Exports f.o.b.:* Prepared foodstuffs; beverages, spirits and vinegar; tobacco and manufactured substitutes 7.8; Mineral products 74.2; Products of chemical or allied industries 41.1 (Organic chemicals 15.7, Fertilizers 25.4); Plastic and plastic products 9.9; Paper and paper products 11.0; Cotton 29.6; Articles of clothing and accessories 134.0; Nuclear reactors, boilers, machinery and mechanical goods 13.1; Total (incl. others) 657.1, excl. re-exports (27.8). Note: Figures exclude trade in petroleum (BD million): Imports 699.1; Exports 1,562.6.

Principal Trading Partners (BD million, 2002): *Imports c.i.f.:* Australia 101.1; Belgium 18.0; Brazil 32.3; China, People's Repub. 61.4; France 51.5; Germany 105.4; India 50.9; Italy 48.7; Japan 118.8; Korea, Repub. 32.6; Malaysia 17.3; Netherlands 20.3; Pakistan 16.9; Saudi Arabia 109.9; Spain 15.7; Switzerland 31.5; Thailand 15.3; United Arab Emirates 52.5; United Kingdom 71.1; USA 81.9; Total (incl. others) 1,252.5. *Exports f.o.b.:* Algeria 9.8; Australia 7.2; China, People's Repub. 12.2; India 20.2; Indonesia 12.3; Iran 15.9; Italy 19.3; Japan 25.4; Korea, Repub. 15.9; Kuwait 13.2; Libya 10.8; Malaysia 11.3; Netherlands 13.9; Qatar 22.2; Saudi Arabia 112.9; Taiwan 60.9; Thailand 7.5; United Arab Emirates 28.5; USA 170.5; Total (incl. others) 657.1. Note: Figures exclude trade in petroleum.

TRANSPORT

Road Traffic (motor vehicles in use, 2002): Passenger cars 206,544; Buses and coaches 5,017; Lorries and vans 35,281; Motor cycles and mopeds 2,279 (Source: International Road Federation, *World Road Statistics*).

Shipping (international sea-borne freight traffic, '000 metric tons, 1990): *Goods Loaded:* Dry cargo 1,145; Petroleum products 12,140. *Goods Unloaded:* Dry cargo 3,380; Petroleum products 132 (Source: UN, *Monthly Bulletin of Statistics*). *Merchant Fleet* (31 December 2003): Registered vessels 120; Total displacement 276,065 grt (Source: Lloyd's Register-Fairplay, *World Fleet Statistics*).

Civil Aviation (2001): Kilometres flown (million) 28; Passengers carried ('000) 1,250; Passenger-km (million) 3,076; Total ton-km (million) 525. Figures include an apportionment (equivalent to one-quarter) of the traffic of Gulf Air, a multinational airline with its headquarters in Bahrain. Source: UN, *Statistical Yearbook.*

TOURISM

Tourist Arrivals (2002): 4,830,943*.

Tourist Receipts (2002): US \$741m.

*Figure refers to arrivals at frontiers of visitors from abroad (excluding Bahraini nationals residing abroad).
Source: World Tourism Organization.

COMMUNICATIONS MEDIA

Radio Receivers ('000 in use, 1997): 338.

Television Receivers ('000 in use, 2000): 275.

Telephones ('000 main lines in use, 2003): 185.8.

Facsimile Machines (2002): 4,514 in use.

Mobile Cellular Telephones ('000 subscribers, 2003): 443.1.

Personal Computers ('000 in use, 2002): 107.

Internet Users ('000, 2003): 195.7.

Book Production (1996, titles, first editions only): 40.

Daily Newspapers (1996): 4 (circulation 67,000 copies).

Non-daily Newspapers (1993): 5 (circulation 17,000 copies).

Other Periodicals (1993): 26 (circulation 73,000 copies).
Source: mainly UNESCO, *Statistical Yearbook,* and International Telecommunication Union.

EDUCATION

Pre-primary: 90 schools (1996/97); 449 teachers (1995/96); 12,308 pupils (1996/97) (Source: UNESCO, *Statistical Yearbook*).

Primary (2000/01): 62,917 pupils* (males 31,374, females 31,543).

Intermediate (2000/01): 28,972 pupils* (males 14,211, females 14,761).

General Secondary (2000/01): 11,974 pupils (males 3,941, females 8,033).

Commercial Secondary (2000/01): 7,870 pupils (males 3,622, females 4,248).

Technical Secondary (2000/01): 2,566 pupils.

Vocational Secondary (2000/01): 956 pupils.

*Figures refer to government schools only and exclude pupils of religious education.
Source: Ministry of Education.

Adult Literacy Rate (UNESCO estimates): 88.5% (males 91.5%; females 84.2%) in 2002. Source: UN Development Programme, *Human Development Report.*

Directory

The Constitution

A 108-article Constitution was ratified in June 1973. It states that 'all citizens shall be equal before the law' and guarantees freedom of speech, of the press, of conscience and of religious beliefs. Other provisions include the outlawing of the compulsory repatriation of political refugees. The Constitution also states that the country's financial comptroller should be responsible to the legislature and not to the Government, and allows for national trade unions 'for legally justified causes and on peaceful lines'. Compulsory free primary education and free medical care are also laid down in the Constitution. The Constitution, which came into force on 6 December 1973, also provided for a National Assembly, composed of 14 members of the Cabinet and 30 members elected by popular vote, although this was dissolved in August 1975.

A National Action Charter was approved in a nation-wide referendum held on 14–15 February 2001. The Charter had been prepared by a Supreme National Committee, created by Amiri decree in late 2000 with the task of outlining the future evolution of Bahrain's political system. Principal among the Committee's recommendations were that there should be a transition from an emirate to a constitutional monarchy (the Amir proclaimed himself King on 14 February 2002), with a bicameral parliament (comprising a directly elected legislature and an appointed consultative chamber). Bahraini women were to be permitted for the first time to hold public office and to vote in elections. Direct elections to the 40-member House of Representatives took place on 24 October 2002, and the new Consultative Council (Majlis ash-Shoura), also comprising 40 members, was appointed by the King on 17 November. Members of both chambers are appointed for terms of four years. Members of the lower house are required to be Bahraini nationals of at least 30 years of age, while those of the appointed chamber—who must also be Bahraini citizens—are to be aged at least 35.

The Government

HEAD OF STATE

King: HM Sheikh HAMAD BIN ISA AL-KHALIFA (acceded as Amir 6 March 1999; proclaimed King 14 February 2002).

Crown Prince and Commander-in-Chief of Bahrain Defence Force: Sheikh SALMAN BIN HAMAD AL-KHALIFA.

CABINET
(April 2005)

Prime Minister: Sheikh KHALIFA BIN SALMAN AL-KHALIFA.

Deputy Prime Minister and Minister of Islamic Affairs: Sheikh ABDULLAH BIN KHALID AL-KHALIFA.

Deputy Prime Minister and Minister of Foreign Affairs: Sheikh MUHAMMAD BIN MUBARAK AL-KHALIFA.

Minister of the Interior: Maj.-Gen. Sheikh RASHID BIN ABDULLAH BIN AHMAD AL-KHALIFA.

Minister of Transport: Sheikh ALI BIN KHALIFA AL-KHALIFA.

Minister of Justice: MUHAMMAD ALI SITRI.

Minister of the Prime Minister's Court: Sheikh KHALID BIN ABDULLAH AL-KHALIFA.

Minister of Municipalities and Agriculture: Dr ALI SALEH AS-SALEH.

Minister of Public Works and Housing: FAHMI BIN ALI AL-JOUDER.

Minister of Finance and National Economy: Sheikh AHMAD BIN MUHAMMAD AL-KHALIFA.

Minister of Defence: Maj.-Gen. Sheikh KHALIFA BIN AHMAD AL-KHALIFA.

Minister of Information and Minister of State for Foreign Affairs: MUHAMMAD ABD AL-GHAFFAR.

Minister of Oil: Sheikh ISA BIN ALI AL-KHALIFA.

Minister of Commerce and Industry: Dr HASSAN BIN ABDULLAH FAKHRO.

Minister of Education: Dr MAJID BIN ALI AN-NO'AIMI.

Minister of Health: Dr NADA HAFFADH.

Minister of Electricity and Water: Sheikh ABDULLAH BIN SALMAN AL-KHALIFA.

Minister of Labour: Dr MAJID BIN HASSAN AL-ALAWI.

Minister of Social Affairs: Dr FATIMA AL-BLUSHI.

Minister of State for Consultative Council and House of Representatives Affairs: Brig.-Gen. ABD AL-AZIZ MUHAMMAD AL-FADHIL.

Minister of State for Cabinet Affairs: ABD AL-HUSSAIN BIN ALI MIRZA.

MINISTRIES

Royal Court: POB 555, Riffa Palace, Manama; tel. 17666666; fax 17663070.

Office of the Prime Minister: POB 1000, Government House, Government Rd, Manama; tel. 17253361; fax 17533033.

Ministry of Cabinet Affairs: POB 26613, Manama; tel. 17223366.

Ministry of Commerce: POB 5479, Diplomatic Area, Manama; tel. 17531531; fax 17534547; e-mail drmansoor@commerce.gov.bh; internet www.commerce.gov.bh.

Ministry of Defence: POB 245, West Rifa'a; tel. 17653333; fax 17663923.

Ministry of Education: POB 43, Isa Town; tel. 17873333; fax 17687866; e-mail info@batelco.com.bh; internet www.education.gov.bh.

Ministry of Electricity and Water: POB 2, Manama; tel. 17533133; fax 17533035.

Ministry of Finance and National Economy: POB 333, Diplomatic Area, Manama; tel. 17530800; fax 17532713; e-mail mofne@batelco.com.bh; internet www.mofne.gov.bh.

Ministry of Foreign Affairs: POB 547, Government House, Government Rd, Manama; tel. 17227555; fax 17212603.

Ministry of Health: POB 12, Sheikh Sulman Rd, Manama; tel. 17255555; fax 17252569; e-mail webmaster@health.gov.bh; internet www.moh.gov.bh.

Ministry of Industry: POB 10908, Manama; tel. 17291511; fax 17290157; e-mail industry@industry.gov.bh; internet www.industry.gov.bh.

Ministry of Information: POB 572, Manama; tel. 17781111; fax 17682777; e-mail brtcnews@batelco.com.bh; internet www.bna.bh.

Ministry of the Interior: POB 13, Police Fort Compound, Manama; tel. 17272111; fax 17262169.

Ministry of Islamic Affairs: POB 450, Diplomatic Area, Manama; tel. 17531333; fax 17536343; internet www.moia.gov.bh.

Ministry of Justice: POB 450, Diplomatic Area, Manama; tel. 175313333; fax 17536343.

Ministry of Labour: POB 32333, Isa Town; tel. 17687800; fax 17686954; e-mail jamalq@bah-molsa.com; internet www.bah-molsa.com.

Ministry of Municipalities and Agriculture: POB 26909, Manama; tel. 17293693; fax 17293694.

Ministry of Oil: POB 1435, Manama; tel. 17291511; fax 17293007.

Ministry of Public Works and Housing: POB 5, Muharraq Causeway Rd, Manama; tel. 17535222; fax 17533095.

Ministry of Social Affairs: Manama.

Ministry of Transport: POB 10325, Diplomatic Area, Manama; tel. 17534534; fax 17534041; internet www.transportation.gov.bh.

Legislature

The National Assembly provided for in the 1973 Constitution was dissolved in August 1975. Among the recommendations of the National Action Charter, approved in a referendum in February 2001, was that there should be a bicameral parliament, comprising a directly elected legislature and an appointed consultative chamber. Elections to a 40-member legislature (House of Representatives) were subsequently held on 24 October 2002; 21 seats were taken by independent candidates, with the remaining 19 seats taken by Islamist candidates. On 17 November a new 40-seat Consultative Council (Majlis ash-Shoura) was also established, with members appointed by the King.

Political Organizations

Political parties are still prohibited in Bahrain. However, several political and civic societies (many of which were previously in exile) are now active in the country, and a number of new groups have been established since 2001. Restrictions on campaigning by political groups were revoked prior to the elections to the new House of Representatives, held in October 2002, although the principal opposition organizations boycotted the polls.

Diplomatic Representation

EMBASSIES IN BAHRAIN

Algeria: POB 26402, Villa 579, Rd 3622, Adliya, Manama; tel. 17713669; fax 17713662; e-mail abdemyh@hotmail.com; Ambassador MUHAMMAD MELLOUH.

Bangladesh: POB 26718, House 2280, Rd 2757, Area 327, Adliya, Manama; tel. 17714717; fax 17710031; e-mail bangla@batelco.com.bh; Chargé d'affaires KHANDAKAR ABDUS SATAR.

Brunei: Manama; Chargé d'affaires Haji MULOK BIN Haji JUMAT.

Bulgaria: Manama; Ambassador ANGEL MANTCHEV.

China, People's Republic: POB 3150, Bldg 158, Rd 382, Juffair Ave, Block 341, Manama; tel. 17723800; fax 17727304; Ambassador YANG HONGLIN.

Egypt: POB 818, Adliya, Manama; tel. 17720005; fax 17721518; e-mail egyembbh@batelco.com.bh; internet www.geocities.com/egyptemb; Ambassador AZMI KHALIFA.

France: POB 11134, Rd 1901, Bldg 51, Block 319, Diplomatic Area, Manama; tel. 17298600; fax 17298637; e-mail consulfr@batelco.com.bh; Ambassador MALIKA BERAK.

Germany: POB 10306, Al-Hasan Bldg, Sheikh Hamad Causeway, Manama; e-mail zreg@manam.diplo.de; tel. 17530210; fax 17536282; Ambassador ROLAND HERRMANN.

India: POB 26106, Bldg 182, Rd 2608, Area 326, Adliya, Manama; tel. 17712785; fax 17715527; e-mail indemb@batelco.com.bh; internet www.indianembassy-bah.com; Ambassador Dr BALKRISHNA SHETTY.

Iran: POB 26365, Entrance 1034, Rd 3221, Area 332, Mahooz, Manama; tel. 17722400; fax 17722101; Ambassador MUHAMMAD FARAZMAND.

Iraq: POB 26477, Ar-Raqib Bldg, No. 17, Rd 2001, Comp 320, King Faysal Ave, Manama; tel. 17741472; fax 17720756.

Italy: PO Box 397, Manama; tel. 17252424; Ambassador ANGELO LA MARTE.

Japan: POB 23720, 55 Salmaniya Ave, Manama Tower 327, Manama; tel. 17716565; fax 17715059; e-mail embjap@batelco.com.bh; Ambassador TAKAO NATSUME.

Jordan: POB 5242, Villa 43, Rd 915, Area 309, Hoora, Manama; tel. 17291109; fax 17291980; e-mail jordemb@batelco.com.bh; Ambassador LUAY MUHAMMAD ALKHASHMAN.

Kuwait: POB 786, Rd 1703, Diplomatic Area, Manama; tel. 17534040; fax 17530278; Ambassador JASSIM MUBARAK AL-MUBARAKI.

Lebanon: POB 32474, Manama; tel. 17786994; fax 17784998; Ambassador MUHAMMAD SHAKEEB AL-HAIJAR.

Libya: Manama; Chargé d'affaires EL-MEHDI SALEH EL-MEJRBI.

Morocco: POB 26229, Manama; tel. 17740566; fax 17740178; Ambassador ABDELKADER ZAOUI.

New Zealand: Manama; Ambassador JAMES ALEXANDER HOWELL.

Oman: POB 26414, Bldg 37, Rd 1901, Diplomatic Area, Manama; tel. 17293663; fax 17293540; Ambassador SALIM ALI OMAR BAYAQOOB.

Pakistan: POB 563, Bldg 261, Rd 2807, Block 328, Segeiya, Manama; tel. 17244113; fax 17255960; e-mail parep@batelco.com.bh; Chargé d'affaires NISARULLAH BALUCH.

Philippines: POB 26681, Manama; tel. 17250990; fax 17258583; e-mail manamape@batelco.com.bh; Ambassador EDWARDO PABLO M. MAGLAYA.

Qatar: Manama; Ambassador Sheikh ABDULLAH BIN THAMIR ATH-THANI.

Russia: POB 26612, House 877, Rd 3119, Block 331, Zinj, Manama; tel. 17725222; fax 17725921; e-mail rusemb@batelco.com.bh; Ambassador YURII ANTONOV.

Saudi Arabia: POB 1085, Bldg 82, Rd 1702, Block 317, Diplomatic Area, Manama; tel. 17537722; fax 17533261; Ambassador Dr ABDULLAH BIN IBRAHIM EL-KUWAIZ.

Sudan: POB 5438, Villa 690, Rd 1219, Block 312, Manama; tel. 17252558; fax 17252594; e-mail sudanimanama@hotmail.com; Ambassador (vacant).

Syria: Villa 867, Rd 3315, Block 333, Malhouze, Manama; tel. 17722484; fax 17740380; e-mail syremb@batelco.com.bh; Ambassador SULEIMAN ADEL SARRA.

Thailand: Manama; Ambassador WIDHYA BHOOLSUWAN.

Tunisia: POB 26911, House 54, Rd 3601, Area 336, Manama; tel. 17714149; fax 17715702; e-mail atmanama@batelco.bh; Ambassador MUHAMMAD AOUITI.

Turkey: POB 10821, 5th Floor, Sehl Centre, Bldg 81, Rd 1702, Area 317, Manama; tel. 17533448; fax 17536557; e-mail tcbahrbe@batelco.com.bh; Ambassador HILAL BASKAL.

Ukraine: Manama; Ambassador I. V. TYMOFYEYEV.

United Arab Emirates: POB 26505, Manama; tel. 17723737; fax 17727343; Ambassador SULTAN AL-QARTASI AN-NUAIMI.

United Kingdom: POB 114, 21 Government Ave, Area 306, Manama; tel. 17534404; fax 17536109; e-mail britemb@batelco.com.bh; internet www.ukembassy.gov.bh; Ambassador ROBIN LAMB.

USA: POB 26431, Bldg 979, Rd 3119, Block 331, Zinj, Manama; tel. 17242700; fax 17272594; e-mail consularmanama@state.gov; internet www.usembassy.gov.bh; Ambassador RONALD E. NEUMANN.

Yemen: POB 26193, House 1048, Rd 1730, Area 517, Saar; tel. 17277072; fax 17262358; Ambassador Ali Abdullah al-Bujayri.

Zimbabwe: Manama; Ambassador Issa Nyathi.

Judicial System

Since the termination of British legal jurisdiction in 1971, intensive work has been undertaken on the legislative requirements of Bahrain. The Criminal Law is at present contained in various Codes, Ordinances and Regulations. All nationalities are subject to the jurisdiction of the Bahraini courts, which guarantee equality before the law irrespective of nationality or creed. The 1974 Decree Law on State Security Measures and the State Security Court were both abolished in February 2001. A Constitutional Court, consisting of seven members appointed by the King, became operational in April 2005.

Directorate of Courts: POB 450, Government House, Government Rd, Manama; tel. 17531333.

Religion

At the April 2001 census the population was 650,604, distributed as follows: Muslims 528,393; Christians 58,315; others 63,896.

ISLAM

Muslims are divided between the Sunni and Shi'ite sects. The ruling family is Sunni, although the majority of the Muslim population (estimated at almost 60%) are Shi'ite.

CHRISTIANITY

The Anglican Communion

Within the Episcopal Church in Jerusalem and the Middle East, Bahrain forms part of the diocese of Cyprus and the Gulf. There are two Anglican churches in Bahrain: St Christopher's Cathedral in Manama and the Community Church in Awali. The congregations are entirely expatriate. The Bishop in Cyprus and the Gulf is resident in Cyprus, while the Archdeacon in the Gulf is resident in Qatar.

Provost: Very Rev. Keith W. T. W. Johnson, St Christopher's Cathedral, POB 36, Al-Mutanabi Ave, Manama; tel. 17253866; fax 17246436; e-mail decani@batelco.com.bh; internet www.stchcathedral.org.bh.

Roman Catholic Church

A small number of adherents, mainly expatriates, form part of the Apostolic Vicariate of Arabia. The Vicar Apostolic is resident in the United Arab Emirates.

The Press

DAILIES

Akhbar al-Khaleej (Gulf News): POB 5300, Manama; tel. 17620111; fax 17624312; e-mail editor@akhbar-alkhaleej.com; internet www.aaknews.com; f. 1976; Arabic; Chair. and Editor-in-Chief Anwar Abd ar-Rahman; circ. 42,000.

Al-Ayam (The Days): POB 3232, Manama; tel. 17727111; fax 17729009; e-mail alayam@batelco.com.bh; internet www.alayam.com; f. 1989; Arabic; publ. by Al-Ayam Establishment for Press and Publications; Editor-in-Chief Isa ash-Shalji; circ. 21,000.

Bahrain Tribune: POB 3232, Manama; tel. 17827111; fax 17827222; e-mail tribune@batelco.com.bh; internet www.bahraintribune.com; f. 1997; English; Editor-in-Chief Jalil Omar; circ. 12,500.

Gulf Daily News: POB 5300, Manama; tel. 17620222; fax 17622141; e-mail gdnl@batelco.com.bh; internet www.gulf-daily-news.com; f. 1978; English; Chair. Anwar Abd ar-Rahman; Editor-in-Chief George Williams; circ. 50,000.

Khaleej Times: POB 26707, City Centre Bldg, Suite 403, 4th Floor, Government Ave, Manama; tel. 17213911; fax 17211819; f. 1978; English; circ. 72,565.

WEEKLIES

Al-Adhwaa' (Lights): POB 250, Old Exhibition Rd, Manama; tel. 17290942; fax 17293166; f. 1965; Arabic; publ. by Arab Printing and Publishing House; Chair. Raid Mahmoud al-Mardi; Editor-in-Chief Muhammad Qassim Shirawi; circ. 7,000.

Al-Bahrain ath-Thaqafia: POB 2199, Manama; tel. 17290210; fax 17292678; e-mail aqaqeel@batelco.com.bh; internet www.al-thaqafia.com; Arabic; publ. by the Ministry of Information; Editor Mai bint Muhammad al-Khalifa.

BAPCO News: Bahrain Refinery, Sitra; tel. 17755049; fax 17755047; e-mail kathleen_croes@bapco.net.bh; bi-weekly; English and Arabic; publ. by the Bahrain Petroleum Co BSC; Editors Kathleen Croes, Khalid F. Mehmas; circ. 4,000.

Gulf Economic Monitor: POB 224, Exhibition Ave, Manama; tel. 17293131; fax 17293400; e-mail hilalmag@tradearabia.net; internet www.tradearabia.com; English; publ. by Al-Hilal Publishing and Marketing Group; Man. Dir Ronnie Middleton.

Huna al-Bahrain (Here is Bahrain): POB 26005, Isa Town; tel. 17731888; fax 17681292; f. 1957; Arabic; publ. by the Ministry of Information; Editor Hamad al-Mannai; circ. 3,000.

Al-Mawakif (Attitudes): POB 1083, Manama; tel. 17231231; fax 17271720; f. 1973; Arabic; general interest; Editor-in-Chief Mansoor M. Radhi; circ. 6,000.

Oil and Gas News: POB 224, Bldg 149, Exhibition Ave, Manama; tel. 17293131; fax 17293400; e-mail hilalmag@batelco.com.bh; f. 1983; English; publ. by Al-Hilal Publishing and Marketing Co; Editor-in-Chief Clive Jacques; circ. 5,000.

Sada al-Usbou (Weekly Echo): POB 549, Manama; tel. 17291234; fax 17290507; f. 1969; Arabic; Owner and Editor-in-Chief Ali Abdullah Sayyar; circ. 40,000 (in various Gulf states).

OTHER PERIODICALS

Arab Agriculture: POB 10131, Manama; tel. 17213900; fax 17211765; e-mail fanar@batelco.com.bh; f. 1984; annually; English and Arabic; publ. by Fanar Publishing WLL; Editor-in-Chief Abd al-Wahed Alwani; circ. 12,650.

Arab World Agribusiness: POB 10131, Manama; tel. 17213900; fax 17211765; e-mail fanar@batelco.com.bh; f. 1985; nine per year; English and Arabic; publ. by Fanar Publishing WLL; Editor-in-Chief Abd al-Wahed Alwani; circ. 18,005.

Bahrain This Month: POB 20461, Manama; tel. 17813777; fax 17813700; e-mail redhouse@batelco.com.bh; internet www.bahrainthismonth.com; f. 1997; monthly; English; Publ. Dir George F. Middleton; Editorial Dir Richard Moore; circ. 10,000.

Discover Bahrain: POB 10704, Manama; tel. 17534587; fax 17531296; f. 1988; English; publ. by G. and B. Media Ltd; Publr and Editor Robert Graham.

Gulf Construction: POB 224, Exhibition Ave, Manama; tel. 17293131; fax 17293400; e-mail editor@gulfconstructiononline.com; internet www.gulfconstructionworldwide.com; f. 1980; monthly; English; publ. by Al-Hilal Publishing and Marketing Group; Editor Bina Prabhu Goveas; circ. 26,539.

Gulf Industry: POB 224, Manama; tel. 17293131; fax 17293400; e-mail salvador.almeida@tradearabia.net; English; journal of industry and transport; publ. By Al-Hilal Publishing and Marketing Group; Editor Salvador Almeida.

Gulf Panorama: POB 3232, Manama; tel. 17727111; fax 17727552; f. 1983; monthly; Arabic; Editor Ibrahim Bashmi; circ. 10,000.

Al-Hayat at-Tijariya (Commerce Review): POB 248, Manama; tel. 17229555; fax 17224985; e-mail bahcci@batelco.com.bh; monthly; English and Arabic; publ. by Bahrain Chamber of Commerce and Industry; Editor Khalil Yousuf; circ. 7,500.

Al-Hidayah (Guidance): POB 450, Manama; tel. 17727100; fax 17729819; f. 1978; monthly; Arabic; publ. by Ministry of Islamic Affairs; Editor-in-Chief Abd ar-Rahman bin Muhammad Rashid al-Khalifa; circ. 5,000.

Middle East Expatriate: POB 224, Manama; tel. 17293131; fax 17292400; e-mail info@middleeastexpatonline.com; internet www.middleeastexpatonline.com; monthly; English; publ. by Al-Hilal Publishing and Marketing Group; Editor Babu Kalyanpur; circ. 16,816.

Al-Mohandis (The Engineer): POB 835, Manama; e-mail mohandis@batelco.com.bh; internet www.mohandis.org; f. 1972; quarterly; Arabic and English; publ. by Bahrain Society of Engineers; Editor Isa Ali Janahi.

Al-Musafir al-Arabi (Arab Traveller): POB 10131, Manama; tel. 17213900; fax 17211765; e-mail fanar@batelco.com.bh; f. 1984; six per year; Arabic; publ. by Fanar Publishing WLL; Editor-in-Chief Abd al-Wahed Alwani; circ. 34,640.

Profile: POB 10243, Manama; tel. 17291110; fax 17294655; f. 1992; monthly; English; publ. by Bahrain Market Promotions; Editor Isa Khalifa al-Khalifa.

Al-Quwwa (The Force): POB 245, Manama; tel. 17291331; fax 17659596; f. 1977; monthly; Arabic; publ. by Bahrain Defence Force; Editor-in-Chief Maj. AHMAD MAHMOUD AS-SUWAIDI.

Travel and Tourism News Middle East: POB 224, Exhibition Ave, Manama; tel. 17293131; fax 17293400; e-mail hilalmag@ tradearabia.net; internet www.ttnonline.com; f. 1983; monthly; English; travel trade; publ. by Al-Hilal Publishing and Marketing Group; Editorial Man. KAMLESHKUMAR DESAI; circ. 6,621.

NEWS AGENCIES

Bahrain News Agency (BNA): Ministry of Information, POB 572, Manama; tel. 17689044; fax 17683825; e-mail news@bahrain.gov .bh; internet www.bna.bh; f. 2001 to cover local and foreign news; replaced Gulf News Agency as national news agency.

Gulf News Agency (GNA): POB 5421, Manama; tel. 17689044; fax 17683825; e-mail brtcnews@batelco.com.bh; internet www.bna.bh; f. 1978; transmits news to the Gulf region in Arabic and English; broadcasts on the same frequency as the BNA, the national news agency; Chief Editor KHALID ABDULLAH AZ-ZAYANI.

Foreign Bureaux

Agence France-Presse (AFP): POB 5890, Kanoo Tower, Phase 3, Tijaar Ave, Manama; tel. and fax 17403446; Dir JEAN-PIERRE PERRIN.

Associated Press (AP) (USA): POB 26940, Mannai Bldg, Manama; tel. 17530101; fax 17530249.

Deutsche Presse-Agentur (dpa) (Germany): POB 26695, Manama; tel. 17716655; fax 17714119.

Reuters (United Kingdom): POB 1030, UGB Bldg, 6th Floor, Diplomatic Area, Manama; tel. 17536111; fax 17536192; Bureau Man. KENNETH WEST.

PRESS ASSOCIATION

Bahrain Journalists' Association (BJA): Manama; f. 2000; Pres. ISA ASH-SHAIJI; 250 mems.

Publishers

Arab Communicators: POB 551, 6th Floor, Almoayyed Bldg, Government Ave, Manama; tel. 17534664; fax 17531837; f. 1981; publrs of annual Bahrain Business Directory; Dirs AHMAD A. FAKHRI, HAMAD A. ABUL.

Fanar Publishing WLL: POB 10131, Manama; tel. 17213900; fax 17211765; e-mail fanar@batelco.com.bh.

Gulf Advertising: POB 5518, Manama; tel. 17226262; fax 17228660; e-mail gulfad@batelco.com.bh; f. 1974; advertising and marketing communications; Chair. and Man. Dir KHAMIS AL-MUQLA.

Al-Hilal Publishing and Marketing Group: POB 224, Exhibition Ave, Manama; tel. 17293131; fax 17293400; e-mail hilalpmg@ tradearabia.net; internet www.tradearabia.com; f. 1977; specialist magazines and newspapers of commercial interest; Chair. A. M. ABD AR-RAHMAN; Man. Dir RONNIE MIDDLETON.

Manama Publishing Co WLL: POB 1013, Manama; tel. 17213223; fax 17211548.

Al-Masirah Journalism, Printing and Publishing House: POB 5981, Manama; tel. 17258882; fax 17276178; e-mail almasera@ batelco.com.bh.

Tele-Gulf Directory Publications, WLL: POB 2738, 3rd Floor, Bahrain Tower, Manama; tel. 17213301; fax 17210503; e-mail telegulf@batelco.com.bh; f. 1977; publrs of annual *Gulf Directory* and *Arab Banking and Finance*.

GOVERNMENT PUBLISHING HOUSE

Directorate of Publications: POB 26005, Manama; tel. 17689077; Dir MUHAMMAD AL-KHOZAI.

Broadcasting and Communications

TELECOMMUNICATIONS

Regulatory Authority

Telecommunications Regulatory Authority (TRA): POB 10353, Manama; tel. 17540120; fax 17532125; e-mail contact@tra .org.bh; internet www.tra.org.bh; f. 2002; Chair. and Dir-Gen. ANDREAS AVGOUSTI.

Principal Operators

Bahrain Telecommunications Co BSC (BATELCO): POB 14, Manama; tel. 17884557; fax 17611898; e-mail batelco@btc.com.bh; internet www.batelco.com.bh; f. 1981; cap. BD 100m.; 80% owned by Government of Bahrain, financial institutions and public of Bahrain, 20% by Cable and Wireless PLC (United Kingdom); launched mobile cellular telecommunications service, Sim Sim, in 1999; Chair. HASSAN ALI JUMA; CEO TONY HART.

MTC Vodafone Bahrain: Manama; internet www.mtc-vodafone .com.bh; f. 2003; 60% owned by Mobile Telecommunications Co (Kuwait), 40% by Bahraini Govt.

BROADCASTING

Radio

Bahrain Radio and Television Corpn: POB 702, Manama; tel. 17686000; fax 17681544; e-mail ceobrtc@batelco.com.bh; internet www.bahraintv.com; f. 1955; state-owned and -operated enterprise; two 10-kW transmitters; programmes are in Arabic and English, and include news, drama and discussions; Dir of Broadcasting ABD AR-RAHMAN ABDULLAH.

Radio Bahrain: POB 702, Manama; tel. 17871585; fax 17780911; e-mail skhalid@bahrainradio.com; f. 1977; commercial radio station in English language; Head of Station SALAH KHALID.

Television

Bahrain Radio and Television Corpn: POB 1075, Manama; tel. 17686000; fax 17681544; e-mail ceobrtc@batelco.bh; internet www .gna.gov.bh/brtc/bah-tv.html; commenced colour broadcasting in 1973; broadcasts on five channels, of which the main Arabic and the main English channel accept advertising; covers Bahrain, eastern Saudi Arabia, Qatar and the UAE; an Amiri decree in early 1993 established the independence of the Corpn, which was to be controlled by a committee; Dir H. AL-UMRAN.

Finance

(cap. = capital; res = reserves; dep. = deposits; m. = millions; brs = branches; amounts in Bahraini dinars unless otherwise stated)

BANKING

Central Bank

Bahrain Monetary Agency (BMA): POB 27, Bldg 96, Block 317, Rd 1702, Manama; tel. 17547777; fax 17531115; e-mail info@bma .gov.bh; internet www.bma.gov.bh; f. 1973; in operation from January 1975; controls issue of currency, regulates exchange control and credit policy, organization and control of banking and insurance systems, bank credit and stock exchange; cap. 200.0m., res 150.1m., dep. 308.8m. (Dec. 2003); Gov. RASHID MUHAMMAD AL-MARAJ.

Locally-incorporated Commercial Banks

Ahli United Bank BSC (AUB): POB 2424, 120 Government Ave, Manama; tel. 17221700; fax 17220552; e-mail info@ahliunited.com; internet www.ahliunited.com; f. 2001 by merger of Al-Ahli Commercial Bank and Commercial Bank of Bahrain; cap. US $650.0m., res US $286.1m., dep. US $4,593.2m. (Dec. 2003); Chair. FAHAD AR-RAJAAN; Gen. Man. ADEL AL-LABBAN; 14 brs.

Bahrain Islamic Bank BSC: POB 5240, As-Salam Tower, Diplomatic Area, Manama; tel. 17546111; fax 17535808; e-mail bahisl@ batelco.com.bh; internet www.bahisl.com.bh; f. 1979; cap. 23.0m., res 16.3m., dep. 188.4m. (Dec. 2003); Chair. MOHD ABDULLAH AZ-ZAMIL; CEO ADNAN A. YOUSUF; Gen. Man. ABDULLAH ABOLFATIH; 8 brs.

Bahrain Saudi Bank BSC (BSB): POB 1159, As-Saddah Bldg, Government Ave, Manama; tel. 17211010; fax 17210989; e-mail bsbbahr@batelco.com.bh; internet www.bahrainisaudibank.com; f. 1983; licensed as a full commercial bank; cap. 20.0m., res 9.9m., dep. 184.5m. (Dec. 2002); Chair. Sheikh FAHAD M. AL-ATHEL; CEO KHALID S. SHAHEEN; 6 brs.

Bank of Bahrain and Kuwait BSC (BBK): POB 597, 43 Government Ave, Manama 309; tel. 17223388; fax 17229822; e-mail bbkp@ bbkonline.com; internet www.bbkonline.com.bh; f. 1971; cap. 56.9m., res 43.1m., dep. 1,148.3m. (Dec. 2003); Chair. HASSAN KHALIFA AL-JALAHMA; Gen. Man. and CEO MURAD ALI MURAD; 20 brs.

National Bank of Bahrain BSC (NBB): POB 106, Government Ave, Manama; tel. 17228800; fax 17228998; e-mail nbb@nbbonline .com; internet www.nbbonline.com; f. 1957; 49% govt-owned; cap. 45.0m., res 108.0m., dep. 1,059.7m. (Dec. 2003); Chair. ABDULLAH ALI KANOO; Gen. Man. ABD AR-RAZAK A. HASSAN; 25 brs.

Shamil Bank of Bahrain EC (SBB): POB 3005, Chamber of Commerce Bldg, King Faysal Rd, Manama; tel. 17227040; fax 17224872; e-mail alshamil@shamilbank.com.bh; internet www .shamilbank.com.bh; f. 1982 as Massraf Faysal Al-Islami of Bahrain EC, renamed Faysal Islamic Bank of Bahrain in 1987 and as above in 2000; cap. US $230.0m., res US $24.0m., dep. US $126.1m. (Dec. 2002); Chair. MUHAMMAD AL-FAISAL AS-SAUD; CEO SAEED AL-MARTAN; 3 brs.

Foreign Commercial Banks

Arab Bank PLC (Jordan): POB 395, Government Rd, Manama; tel. 17229988; fax 17210443; internet www.arabbank.com; f. 1960; Chair. ABD AL-MAJEED SHOMAN; 3 brs.

Bank Melli Iran: POB 785, Government Rd, Manama; tel. 17229910; fax 17224402; e-mail bmibah@batelco.com.bh; f. 1970; Gen. Man. MUHAMMAD TAGHI TAVAKULI; 2 brs.

Bank Saderat Iran: POB 825, 106 Government Rd, Manama; tel. 17210003; fax 17210398; f. 1974; Man. MUHAMMAD JAVAD NASSIRI; 1 br.

Citibank NA (USA): POB 548, Bab al-Bahrain Bldg, Government Rd, Manama; tel. 17223344; fax 17211323; internet www.citibank .com/bahrain; f. 1969; Gen. Man. MUHAMMAD ASH-SHROOGI; 1 br.

Habib Bank Ltd (Pakistan): POB 566, Government Ave, Manama; tel. 17224746; fax 17224749; e-mail maziz@batelco.com.bh; f. 1941; Exec. Vice-Pres. and Gen. Man. ASHRAF BIDIWALA; 3 brs.

HSBC Bank Middle East (United Kingdom): POB 57, 93 Al-Khalifa Ave, Manama 304; tel. 17224555; fax 17226822; e-mail hsbcmnm@batelco.com.bh; internet www.banking.middleeast.hsbc .com; f. 1944; CEO SALEH AL-KOWARY; 4 brs.

Rafidain Bank (Iraq): POB 607, Heaya House Bldg, Government Rd, Manama; tel. 17275796; fax 17255656; f. 1969; Man. IBTISAM NAJEM ABOUD; 1 br.

Standard Chartered Bank (United Kingdom): POB 29, Government Rd, Manama; tel. 17223636; fax 17225001; internet www .standardchartered.com/bh/index.html; f. 1920; Man. PETER RAW-LINGS; 5 brs.

United Bank Ltd (Pakistan): POB 546, Government Rd, Manama; tel. 17224030; fax 17224099; e-mail ublbah@batelco.com.bh; f. 1969; Gen. Man. M. A. RAUF; 3 brs.

Specialized Financial Institutions

Bahrain Development Bank (BDB): POB 20501, Manama; tel. 17537007; fax 17534005; e-mail info@bdb-bh.com; internet www .bdb-bh.com; f. 1992; invests in manufacturing, agribusiness and services; cap. 10.0m., res 0.3m., total assets 31.9m. (Dec. 2003); Chair. Sheikh IBRAHIM BIN KHALIFA AL-KHALIFA; Gen. Man. NEDHAL S. AL-AUJAN.

The Housing Bank: POB 5370, Diplomatic Area, Manama; tel. 17534443; fax 17533437; f. 1979; provides housing loans for Bahraini citizens and finances construction of commercial properties.; Chair. Sheikh KHALID BIN ABDULLAH BIN KHALID AL-KHALIFA; Gen. Man. ISA SULTAN ADH-DHAWADI; one br.

'Offshore' Banking Units

Bahrain has been encouraging the establishment of 'offshore' banking units (OBUs) since 1975. An OBU is not permitted to provide local banking services, but is allowed to accept deposits from governments and large financial organizations in the area and make medium-term loans for local and regional capital projects. In early 2005 there were 53 OBUs in operation in Bahrain.

Allied Banking Corporation (Philippines): POB 20493, Bahrain Tower, 11th Floor, Govt Ave, Manama; tel. 17224707; fax 17210506; e-mail ally3540@batelco.com.bh; f. 1980; Chair. LUCIO C. TAN; Gen. Man. RAMON R. LANDINGIN.

Alubaf Arab International Bank EC: POB 11529, Sheraton Tower 13F, Manama; tel. 17531212; fax 17540094; f. 1982; cap. US $50.0m., res US $0.6m., dep. US $4.6m. (Dec. 2001); Chair. RASHID AZ-ZAYANI.

Arab Bank PLC (Jordan): POB 813, Manama; tel. 17549000; fax 17541116; e-mail arabbank@batelco.com.bh; f. 1930; Senior Vice-Pres. and Man. HANI FADAYEL.

Arab Banking Corporation BSC: POB 5698, ABC Tower, Diplomatic Area, Manama; tel. 17543000; fax 17533062; e-mail webmaster@arabbanking.com; internet www.arabbanking.com; f. 1980; cap. US $1,000m., res US $374m., dep. US $24,789m. (Dec. 2003); Chair. MUHAMMAD LAYAS; Pres. and CEO GHAZI ABD AL-JAWAD.

Arab Investment Co SAA. (Saudi Arabia): POB 5559, Bldg 2309, Rd 2830, As-Seef District 428, Manama; tel. 17588888; fax 17588885; e-mail taic@taicobu.com; Dir-Gen. Dr SALEH AL-HUMAIDAN.

Bahrain International Bank EC: POB 5016, 15th Floor, As-Salam Tower, Government Ave, Manama; tel. 17538777; fax 17535141; internet www.dilmun.com; f. 1982; cap. US $182.1m., res US $14.4m., dep. US $441.5m. (Dec. 2001); Chair. and CEO FAISAL YOUSUF AL-MARZOUK; CEO ROBIN MCILVENNY; 1 br.

Bank of Tokyo-Mitsubishi Ltd (Japan): POB 5850, Government Ave, Manama; tel. 17227518; fax 17225013; Regional and Gen. Man. KAN SATOH.

BNP Paribas (France): POB 5253, UGB Bldg, 10th Floor, Diplomatic Area, Manama; tel. 17531152; fax 17531237; e-mail jean-christophe.durand@mideastbnpparibas.com; Regional Man. JEAN-CHRISTOPHE DURAND.

Gulf International Bank BSC (GIB): POB 1017, Ad-Duwali Bldg, 3 Palace Ave, Manama; tel. 17534000; fax 17522633; e-mail info@ gibbah.com; internet www.gibonline.com; cap. US $1,000m., res US $262.7m., dep. US $10,448.4m. (June 2004); Chair. Sheikh IBRAHIM BIN KHALIFA AL-KHALIFA; CEO Dr KHALID AL-FAYEZ.

Korea Exchange Bank (Repub. of Korea): POB 5767, Manama; tel. 17229333; fax 17225327; e-mail kebbn002@batelco.com.bh; Gen. Man. JONG-HO YOON.

Mashreq Bank PSC (UAE): POB 20654, Manama Centre, Govt Ave, Manama; tel. 17211241; fax 17213516; Branch Man. ADEL AL-MANNAI.

Muslim Commercial Bank Ltd (Pakistan): POB 10164, Dipl. Area, Manama; tel. 17533306; fax 17533308; e-mail mcbobubh@ batelco.com.bh; Gen. Man. FAQIR EIAZ ASGHER.

National Bank of Abu Dhabi (UAE): POB 5886, Manama 304; tel. 17214450; fax 17210086.

National Bank of Kuwait SAK: POB 5290, Bahrain BMB Centre, Dipl. Area, Manama; tel. 17532225; fax 17530658; e-mail nbkbah@ batelco.com.bh; Gen. Man. ALI Y. FARDAN.

Standard Chartered Bank PLC (United Kingdom): POB 29, Manama; tel. 17223636; fax 17225001; CEO RUPERT KEELEY.

State Bank of India: POB 5466, Bahrain Tower, Govt Ave, Manama; tel. 17224956; fax 17224692; e-mail sbigen@batelco.com .bh; CEO ASHWINI KUMAR SHARMA.

Woori Bank (Repub. of Korea): POB 1151, Government Rd, Manama; tel. 17223503; fax 17224429; e-mail bahrain@wooribank .com; internet www.wooribank.com; formerly Hanvit Bank; Gen. Man. OK YOUNG KANG.

Yapi ve Kredi Bankasi AS (Turkey): POB 10615, c/o Bahrain Development Bank, Dipl. Area, Manama; tel. 17530313; fax 17530311; Dir TURAN UNGOR.

Investment Banks

Al-Baraka Islamic Bank BSC (EC): POB 1882, Diplomatic Area, Manama; tel. 17535300; fax 17533993; e-mail baraka@batelco.com .bh; internet www.barakaonline.com; f. 1984 as Al-Baraka Islamic Investment Bank BSC (EC), current name adopted in 1998; cap. US $50.0m., res US $9.9m., dep. US $307.3m. (Dec. 2003); Chair. MAHMOOD JAMEEL HASSOUBAH; Gen. Man. SALAH AHMAD ZAINDABEDIN; 7 brs.

Bahrain Middle East Bank EC (BMB Investment Bank): POB 797, BMB Centre, Diplomatic Area, Manama; tel. 17532345; fax 17530526; e-mail corpcom@bmb.com.bh; internet www.bmb.com.bh; formerly Bahrain Middle East Bank EC; cap. US $90.8m., res US $–47.6m., dep. US $353.2m. (Dec. 2001); Chair. Sheikh ALI JARRAH AS-SABAH; CEO ALBERT I. KITTANEH.

Investcorp Bank BSC: POB 5340, Investcorp House, Diplomatic Area, Manama; tel. 17532000; fax 17530816; e-mail info@investcorp .com; internet www.investcorp.com; f. 1982 as Arabian Investment Banking Corpn (Investcorp) EC, current name adopted in 1990; cap. US $400.0m., res US $33.4m., dep. US $827.9m. (June 2003); Pres. and CEO NEMIR A. KIRDAR; Chair. ABD AR-RAHMAN SALIM AL-ATEEQI.

Nomura Investment Banking (Middle East) EC: POB 26893, 7th Floor, BMB Centre, Diplomatic Area, Manama; tel. 17530531; fax 17530365; f. 1982; cap. US $25m., res US $93.4m., dep. US $11.5m. (Dec. 2002); Chair. TAKUMI SHIBATA.

TAIB Bank EC: POB 20485, Sehl Centre, 81 Rd 1702, Diplomatic Area, Manama 317; tel. 17533334; fax 17533174; e-mail taib@taib .com; internet www.taib.com; f. 1979 as Trans-Arabian Investment Bank EC, current name adopted in 1994; cap. US $97.4m., res US $27.4m., dep. US $259.9m. (Dec. 2002); Chair. ABD AR-RAHMAN AL-JERAISY; Vice-Chair. and CEO IQBAL G. MAMDANI.

United Gulf Bank (BSC) EC: POB 5964, UGB Tower, Diplomatic Area, Manama; tel. 17533233; fax 17533137; e-mail ugbbah@batelco .com.bh; internet www.ugbbh.com; f. 1980; cap. US $200.0m., res US $21.4m., dep. US $835.1m. (Dec. 2002); Chair. FAISAL HAMAD M. AL-AYYAR; CEO WILLIAM KHOURI.

Other investment banks operating in Bahrain include the following: ABC Islamic Bank EC, Al-Amin Bank (BSC) EC, Amex (Middle East) EC, Arab Financial Services Co EC, Bahrain Investment Bank BSC, Capital Union EC, Daiwa Securities SMBC Europe Ltd (Middle East), First Islamic Investment Bank EC, Gulf Finance House (BSC) EC, Investors Bank EC, Al-Khaleej Islamic Investment Bank (BSC) EC, Merrill Lynch Int. Bank Ltd, Société General Asset Management Bahrain EC.

STOCK EXCHANGE

Bahrain Stock Exchange (BSE): POB 3203, Manama; tel. 17261260; fax 17256362; e-mail info@bahrainstock.com; internet www.bahrainstock.com; f. 1989; 48 listed companies at Dec. 2004; linked to Muscat Securities Market (Oman) in 1995, and to Amman Financial Market (Jordan) in 1996; Dir-Gen. Sheikh AHMAD BIN MUHAMMAD AL-KHALIFA.

INSURANCE

Abdullah Yousuf Fakhro Corpn: POB 39, Government Ave, Manama; tel. 17275000; fax 17256999; e-mail aybc@fakhro.com; internet www.fakhro.com; f. 1988; general; Man. Dir ADEL FAKHRO.

Al-Ahlia Insurance Co BSC: POB 5282, 4th Floor, Chamber of Commerce Bldg, King Faysal Rd, Manama; tel. 17225860; fax 17224870; e-mail alahlia@alahlia.com; internet www.alahlia.com; f. 1976; Chair. ABDULLATIF MUHAMMAD SHARIF AR-RAYES; Gen. Man. YAHYA NOORUDDIN.

Arab Insurance Group BSC (ARIG): POB 26992, Arig House, Diplomatic Area, Manama; tel. 17544444; fax 17531155; e-mail info@arig.com.bh; internet www.arig.com.bh; f. 1980; owned by Govts of Kuwait, Libya and the UAE (49.5%), and other shareholders; reinsurance and insurance; Chair. KHALID ALI AL-BUSTANI; CEO UDO KRUEGER.

Arab International Insurance Co EC (AIIC): POB 10135, Manama; tel. 17295935; fax 17294059; f. 1981; non-life reinsurance; Chair. and Man. Dir Sheikh KHALID J. AS-SABAH.

Bahrain Kuwait Insurance Co BSC: POB 10166, Diplomatic Area, Manama; tel. 17542222; fax 17530799; e-mail bkicbah@ batelco.com.bh; internet www.bkic.com; f. 1975; CEO IBRAHIM SHARIF AR-RAYES; Gen. Man. GOPINATH RAO.

Bahrain National Holding Co BSC (BNH): POB 843, Manama; tel. 17228877; fax 17224385; e-mail bnh@bnhgroup.com; internet www.bnhgroup.com; f. 1998 by merger of Bahrain Insurance Co and National Insurance Co; all classes including life insurance; Chair. QASSIM MUHAMMAD FAKHRO; CEO MAHMOUD AS-SOUFI.

Gulf Union Insurance and Reinsurance Co: POB 10949, Ground Floor, Manama Centre, Manama; tel. 17215622; fax 17215421; e-mail guirco@batelco.com.bh; internet www .gulfunion-bah.com; Chair. Sheikh IBRAHIM BIN HAMAD AL-KHALIFA.

Trade and Industry

GOVERNMENT AGENCIES

Economic Development Board (EDB): POB 11299, Manama; tel. 17583311; fax 17583322; e-mail edb@bahrainedb.com; internet www .bahrainedb.com; f. 2000; assumed duties of Bahrain Promotions and Marketing Board (f. 1993) and Supreme Council for Economic Development (f. 2000) in 2001; provides national focus for Bahraini marketing initiatives; attracts inward investment; encourages development and expansion of Bahraini exports; Chair. Sheikh SALMAN BIN HAMAD AL-KHALIFA; CEO JAMAL ALI AL-HAZEEM.

Supreme Oil Council: Manama; formulates Bahrain's petroleum policy; Chair. Sheikh KHALIFA BIN SALMAN AL-KHALIFA.

CHAMBER OF COMMERCE

Bahrain Chamber of Commerce and Industry: POB 248, Manama; tel. 17229555; fax 17224985; e-mail bahcci@batelco.com .bh; f. 1939; 7,300 mems (1996); Chair. KHALID MUHAMMAD KANOO; Sec.-Gen. JASSIM MUHAMMAD ASH-SHATTI.

STATE HYDROCARBONS COMPANIES

Bahrain National Gas Co BSC (BANAGAS): POB 29099, Rifa'a; tel. 17756222; fax 17756991; e-mail bng@banagas.com.bh; internet www.banagas.com.bh; f. 1979; responsible for extraction, processing and sale of hydrocarbon liquids from associated gas derived from onshore Bahraini fields; ownership is 75% Government of Bahrain, 12.5% Caltex and 12.5% Arab Petroleum Investments Corpn (API-CORP); produced 202,955 metric tons of LPG and 189,803 tons of naphtha in 1996; Chair. Sheikh HAMAD BIN IBRAHIM AL-KHALIFA; Gen. Man. Dr Sheikh MUHAMMAD BIN KHALIFA AL-KHALIFA.

Bahrain Petroleum Co BSC (BAPCO): POB 25555, Awali; tel. 17704040; fax 17704070; e-mail info@bapco.net; f. 2000 by merger of Bahrain National Oil Co (f. 1976) and Bahrain Petroleum Co (f. 1980); fully integrated co responsible for exploration, drilling and production of oil and gas; supply of gas to power-generating plants and industries, refining crude oil, international marketing of crude oil and refined petroleum products, supply and sale of aviation fuel at Bahrain International Airport, and local distribution and marketing of petroleum products; Chair. Sheikh ISA BIN ALI AL-KHALIFA (Minister of Oil); Pres. and Man. Dir MUSTAFA AS-SAYED.

Gulf Petrochemical Industries Co BSC (GPIC): POB 26730, Manama; tel. 17731777; fax 17731047; e-mail gpic@gpic.com.bh; internet www.gpic.com.bh; f. 1979 as a joint venture between the Governments of Bahrain, Kuwait and Saudi Arabia, each with one-third equity participation; a petrochemical complex at Sitra, inaugurated in 1981; produces 1,200 metric tons of both methanol and ammonia per day (1990); Chair. Sheikh ISA BIN ALI AL-KHALIFA.

UTILITIES

Ministry of Electricity and Water: see Ministries, above; provides electricity and water throughout Bahrain; privatization of the Ministry's assets was pending in 2005; privatization of electricity production was approved in late Dec. 2003.

Electricity

Directorate of Electricity: POB 2, King Faysal Rd, Manama; tel. 17533133; supplies domestic and industrial power and street lighting.

Water

Directorate of Water Supply: POB 326, Manama; tel. 17727009; responsible for water supply to all areas except Awali.

TRADE UNIONS

In November 2002 legislation was ratified to permit the establishment of independent trade unions.

General Federation of Bahrain Workers' Unions (GFBWU): Manama; f. 2004; Chair. ABD AL-GHAFFAR ABD AL-HUSSAIN.

Transport

RAILWAYS

There are no railways in Bahrain.

ROADS

In 2002 Bahrain had 3,459 km of roads, including 428 km of highways, main or national roads, 474 km of secondary or regional roads and 1,827 km of other roads; about 78.9% of roads were paved. A modern network of dual highways is being developed, and a 25-km causeway link with Saudi Arabia was opened in 1986. A three-lane dual carriageway links the causeway to Manama. Other causeways link Bahrain with Muharraq island and with Sitra island. In 2003 the construction of the Sheikh Khalifa bin Sulman Causeway, linking Hidd on Muharraq island with the port of Mina Salman, was completed. A second, 2.5-km Manama-to-Muharraq causeway was opened in early 1997. Approval for the construction of a causeway (the Friendship Bridge) linking eastern Bahrain with Qatar was given in May 2004; the project was likely to cost some US $2,000m.

Directorate of Roads: POB 5, Manama; tel. 17545555; fax 17532565; responsible for traffic engineering and planning, traffic control and safety, bridges, road design, maintenance and construction supervision; Dir WALEED Y. AS-SAIE.

SHIPPING

Numerous shipping services link Bahrain and the Gulf with Europe, the USA, Pakistan, India, the Far East and Australia.

The deep-water harbour of Mina Salman was opened in 1962; it has 13 conventional berths, two container terminals (one of which has a 400-m quay—permitting two 180-m container ships to be handled simultaneously) and a roll-on roll-off berth. Two nearby slipways can accommodate vessels of up to 1,016 metric tons and 73 m in length, and services are available for ship repairs afloat. During 2000 906 vessels called at Mina Salman, and in that year the port handled 1,954,396 tons of cargo.

In 1999 work began on the construction of a new port and industrial zone at Hidd, on Muharraq island. The port, Mina Khalifa bin Salman, which was scheduled to become operational in mid–2006 (at an estimated cost of US $330m.), was to have an annual handling capacity of 234,000 TEUs and to include a general cargo berth and two container berths with roll-on roll-off facilities. Plans for the privatization of Mina Khalifa bin Salman and Mina Salman were under development in 2005.

Directorate of Customs and Ports: (Customs) POB 15, Manama; tel. 17725333; fax 17727556; e-mail customs@batelco.com.bh; internet www.bahraincustoms.com.bh; (Ports) POB 453, Manama; tel. 17725555; fax 17729709; internet www.bahrainports.com.bh; responsible for customs, ports and free-zone activities; Pres. of Customs and Ports EID ABDULLAH YOUSUF; Dir-Gen. of Ports SALEH ABDULLAH AL-MUSALLAM; Dir-Gen. of Customs ALI IBRAHIM AL-MAHMEED; Dir–Gen. of Free Zones IBRAHIM HASSAN SALMAN.

Arab Shipbuilding and Repair Yard Co (ASRY): POB 50110, Hidd; tel. 17671111; fax 17670236; e-mail asryco@batelco.com.bh; internet www.asry.net; f. 1974 by OAPEC members; 500,000-ton dry dock opened 1977; two floating docks in operation since 1992; repaired 132 ships in 2004; Chair. EID ABDULLAH YOUSUF; CEO MUHAMMAD M. AL-KHATEEB.

Principal Shipping Agents

Bahrain Enterprises Co Ltd: POB 2661, Manama; tel. 17731224.

Dilmun Shipping Co Ltd EC: POB 11664, Manama; tel. 17534530; fax 17531287; e-mail dilmunbh@batelco.com.bh; Chair. Capt. PHILIP G. CARR.

The Gulf Agency Co (Bahrain) WLL: POB 412, Manama; tel. 827927; fax 17827928; e-mail bahrain.ops@gulfagencycompany.com; internet www.gulfagencycompany.com.com; f. 1957; Man. Dir Capt. BJORN SVANHOLM.

Al-Jazeera Shipping Co WLL: POB 302, Manama; tel. 17728837; fax 17728217; Dir ALI HASSAN MAHMOUD.

Abdullah Ahmad Nass: POB 669, Manama; tel. 17725522; fax 17728184; e-mail nassbah@batelco.com.bh; f. 1963; Chair. ABDULLAH AHMAD NASS; Man. Dir SAMIR ABDULLAH NASS.

Ash-Sharif Group: POB 1322, Manama; tel. 17530535; fax 17537637; e-mail general@bahragents.com; Dirs ALI ABD AR-RASOOL ASH-SHARIF, KHALID ABD AR-RASOOL ASH-SHARIF.

UCO Marine Contracting WLL: POB 1074, Manama; tel. 17730816; fax 17732131; e-mail ucomarin@batelco.com.bh; Man. Dirs BADER A. KAIKSOW, HASSAN AS-SABAH, ALI AL-MUSALAM.

Yusuf bin Ahmad Kanoo: POB 45, Al-Khalifa Ave, Manama; tel. 17220800; fax 17229122; e-mail kanoomgt@batelco.com.bh; internet www.kanoogroup.com; f. 1890; air and shipping cargo services, commercial and holiday services; Chair. and CEO ABDULLAH ALI KANOO.

CIVIL AVIATION

Bahrain International Airport (BIA) has a first-class runway, capable of taking the largest aircraft in use. In 2003, according to preliminary estimates, there were 58,100 commercial flights to and from the airport, and some 4.3m. passengers were carried. Extension work to the airport's main terminal building was undertaken during the 1990s, in order to increase the airport's cargo-handling facilities. A project to expand the existing passenger terminal, at a cost of some US $157m., was under way in early 2005; it was hoped to increase the annual passenger capacity of BIA to 15m. by 2010.

Department of Civil Aviation Affairs: POB 586, Bahrain International Airport, Muharraq; tel. 321000; fax 325757; e-mail caainfo@bahrainairport.com; internet www.bahrainairport.com; Under-Sec. IBRAHIM ABDULLAH AL-HAMER.

Gulf Air Co GSC (Gulf Air): POB 138, Manama; tel. 17322200; fax 17338033; e-mail gfpr@batelco.com.bh; internet www.gulfairco.com; f. 1950; jointly owned by Govts of Bahrain, Oman and Abu Dhabi (part of the United Arab Emirates) since 1974; services to the Middle East, South-East Asia, the Far East, Australia, Africa and Europe; Chair. Sheikh HAMDAN BIN MUBARAK AN-NAHYAN (UAE); Pres. and CEO JAMES HOGAN.

Tourism

There are several archaeological sites of importance in Bahrain, which is the site of the ancient trading civilization of Dilmun. There is a wide selection of hotels and restaurants, and a new national museum opened in 1989. The Government is currently promoting Bahrain as a destination for sports and leisure activities. In 2002 Bahrain received 4.8m. foreign visitors (excluding Bahraini nationals residing abroad). Income from tourism totalled US $741m. in that year.

Bahrain Tourism Co (BTC): POB 5831, Manama; tel. 17530530; fax 17530867; e-mail btc@alseyaha.com; internet www.alseyaha.com; Chair. MUHAMMAD YOUSUF JALAL.

Tourism Affairs: Ministry of Information, POB 26613, Manama; tel. 17201203; fax 17229787; e-mail btour@bahraintourism.com; internet www.bahraintourism.com; Asst Under-Sec. for Tourism Dr KADHIM RAJAB.

BANGLADESH

Introductory Survey

Location, Climate, Language, Religion, Flag, Capital

The People's Republic of Bangladesh lies in southern Asia, surrounded by Indian territory except for a short south-eastern frontier with Myanmar (formerly Burma) and a southern coast fronting the Bay of Bengal. The country has a tropical monsoon climate and suffers from periodic cyclones. The average temperature is 19°C (67°F) from October to March, rising to 29°C (84°F) between May and September. The average annual rainfall in Dhaka is 188 cm (74 ins), of which about three-quarters occurs between June and September. About 95% of the population speak Bengali, the state language, while the remainder mostly use tribal dialects. More than 85% of the people are Muslims, Islam being the state religion, and there are small minorities of Hindus, Buddhists and Christians. The national flag (proportions 3 by 5) is dark green, with a red disc slightly off-centre towards the hoist. The capital is Dhaka (Dacca).

Recent History

Present-day Bangladesh was formerly East Pakistan, one of the five provinces into which Pakistan was divided at its initial creation, when Britain's former Indian Empire was partitioned in August 1947. East Pakistan and the four western provinces were separated by about 1,000 miles (1,600 km) of Indian territory. East Pakistan was created from the former Indian province of East Bengal and the Sylhet district of Assam. Although the East was more populous, government was based in West Pakistan. Dissatisfaction in East Pakistan at its dependence on a remote central government flared up in 1952, when Urdu was declared Pakistan's official language. Bengali, the main language of East Pakistan, was finally admitted as the joint official language in 1954, and in 1955 Pakistan was reorganized into two wings, east and west, with equal representation in the central legislative assembly. However, discontent continued in the eastern wing, particularly as the region was under-represented in the administration and armed forces, and received a disproportionately small share of Pakistan's development expenditure. The leading political party in East Pakistan was the Awami League (AL), led by Sheikh Mujibur (Mujib) Rahman, who demanded autonomy for the East. A general election in December 1970 gave the AL an overwhelming victory in the East, and thus a majority in Pakistan's National Assembly. Sheikh Mujib should therefore have been appointed Prime Minister, but Pakistan's President, Gen. Yahya Khan, would not accept this, and negotiations on a possible constitutional compromise broke down. The convening of the new National Assembly was postponed indefinitely in March 1971, leading to violent protests in East Pakistan. The AL decided that the province should unilaterally secede from Pakistan, and on 26 March Sheikh Mujib proclaimed the independence of the People's Republic of Bangladesh ('Bengal Nation').

Civil war immediately broke out. President Yahya Khan outlawed the AL and arrested its leaders. By April 1971 the Pakistan army dominated the eastern province. In August Sheikh Mujib was secretly put on trial in West Pakistan. Resistance continued, however, from the Liberation Army of East Bengal (the Mukhti Bahini), which launched a major offensive in November. As a result of the conflict, an estimated 9.5m. refugees crossed into India. On 4 December India declared war on Pakistan, with Indian forces intervening in support of the Mukhti Bahini. Pakistan surrendered on 16 December, and Bangladesh became independent. Pakistan was thus confined to its former western wing. In January 1972 Sheikh Mujib was freed by Pakistan's new President, Zulfiqar Ali Bhutto, and became Prime Minister of Bangladesh. Under a provisional Constitution, Bangladesh was declared to be a secular state and a parliamentary democracy. The new nation quickly achieved international recognition, causing Pakistan to withdraw from the Commonwealth in January 1972. Bangladesh joined the Commonwealth in April. The members who had been elected from the former East Pakistan for the Pakistan National Assembly and the Provincial Assembly in December 1970 formed the Bangladesh Constituent Assembly. A new Constitution was approved by this Assembly in November 1972 and

came into effect in December. A general election for the country's first Jatiya Sangsad (Parliament) was held in March 1973. The AL received 73% of the total votes and won 292 of the 300 directly elective seats in the legislature. Bangladesh was finally recognized by Pakistan in February 1974. Internal stability, however, was threatened by opposition groups which resorted to terrorism and included extremists such as Islamist fundamentalists and Maoists. In December a state of emergency was declared and constitutional rights were suspended. In January 1975 parliamentary government was replaced by a presidential form of government. Sheikh Mujib became President, assuming absolute power, and created the Bangladesh Peasants' and Workers' Awami League. In February Bangladesh became a one-party state.

In August 1975 Sheikh Mujib and his family were assassinated in a right-wing coup, led by a group of Islamist army officers. Khandakar Mushtaq Ahmed, the former Minister of Commerce, was installed as President; martial law was declared, and political parties were banned. A counter-coup on 3 November brought to power Brig. Khalid Musharaf, the pro-Indian commander of the Dhaka garrison, who was appointed Chief of Army Staff; on 7 November a third coup overthrew Brig. Musharaf's brief regime, and power was assumed jointly by the three service chiefs, under a non-political President, Abusadet Mohammed Sayem, the Chief Justice of the Supreme Court. A neutral non-party Government was formed, in which the reinstated Chief of Army Staff, Major-Gen. Ziaur Rahman (Gen. Zia), took precedence over his colleagues. Political parties were legalized again in July 1976.

An early return to representative government was promised, but in November 1976 elections were postponed indefinitely and, in a major shift of power, Gen. Zia took over the role of Chief Martial Law Administrator from President Sayem, assuming the presidency also in April 1977. He amended the Constitution, making Islam, instead of secularism, its first basic principle. In a national referendum held in May 99% of voters affirmed their confidence in President Zia's policies, and in June 1978 the country's first direct presidential election resulted in a clear victory for Zia, who formed a Council of Ministers to replace his Council of Advisers. Parliamentary elections followed in February 1979: in an attempt to persuade opposition parties to participate in the elections, Zia met some of their demands by repealing 'all undemocratic provisions' of the 1974 constitutional amendment, releasing political prisoners and withdrawing press censorship. Consequently, 29 parties contested the elections, in which Zia's Bangladesh Nationalist Party (BNP) received 49% of the total votes and won 207 of the 300 contested seats in the Jatiya Sangsad. In April 1979 a new Prime Minister was appointed, and martial law was repealed. The state of emergency was revoked in November.

Political instability recurred, however, when Gen. Zia was assassinated on 30 May 1981 during an attempted military coup, allegedly led by Maj.-Gen. Mohammad Abdul Manzur, an army divisional commander who was himself later killed in unclear circumstances. The Vice-President, Justice Abdus Sattar, assumed the role of acting President, but was confronted by strikes and demonstrations in protest against the execution of several officers who had been involved in the coup, and by pressure from opposition parties to reschedule the date of the presidential election. As the only person acceptable to the different groups within the BNP, Sattar was none the less nominated as the party's presidential candidate, and secured an overwhelming victory at the November election. President Sattar announced his intention of continuing the policies of the late Gen. Zia. He found it increasingly difficult, however, to retain civilian control over the country, and in January 1982 formed a National Security Council, which included military personnel, led by the Chief of Army Staff, Lt-Gen. Hossain Mohammad Ershad. On 24 March Gen. Ershad seized power in a bloodless coup, claiming that political corruption and economic mismanagement had become intolerable. The country was placed under martial law, with Ershad as Chief Martial Law Administrator (redesignated Prime Minister in October), aided by a mainly military Council of Advisers. Ershad nominated a retired judge, Justice Abul Chowdhury, as President. Political activities were banned, and several former ministers were later tried and imprisoned on charges of corruption.

Although the Government's economic policies achieved some success and gained a measure of popular support for Ershad, there were increasing demands in 1983 for a return to democratic government. The two principal opposition groups that emerged were an eight-party alliance headed by the AL under Sheikh Hasina Wajed (daughter of the late Sheikh Mujib), and a seven-party group led by the BNP under former President Sattar (who died in 1985) and Begum Khaleda Zia (widow of Gen. Zia). In September 1983 the two groups formed an alliance, the Movement for the Restoration of Democracy (MRD), and jointly issued demands for an end to martial law, for the release of political prisoners and for the holding of parliamentary elections before any other polls. In November the resumption of political activity was permitted, and it was announced that a series of local elections between December 1983 and March 1984 were to precede a presidential and parliamentary elections later in the year. A new political party, the Jana Dal (People's Party), was formed in November 1983 to support Ershad as a presidential candidate. Following demonstrations demanding civilian government, the ban on political activity was reimposed at the beginning of December, only two weeks after it had been rescinded, and leading political figures were detained. On 11 December Ershad declared himself President.

Strikes and political demonstrations occurred frequently during 1984. Local elections, planned for March, were postponed, as the opposition objected to their taking place prior to the presidential and parliamentary elections, on the grounds that Ershad was trying to strengthen his power-base. The presidential and parliamentary elections, scheduled for May, were also postponed until December, in response to persistent opposition demands for the repeal of martial law and for the formation of an interim neutral government to oversee a fair election. In October an offer by Ershad to repeal martial law if the opposition would participate in the elections was met with an appeal for a campaign of civil disobedience, which led to the indefinite postponement of the elections.

In January 1985 it was announced that parliamentary elections would be held in April, to be preceded by a partial relaxation of martial law: the Constitution was to be fully restored after the elections. The announcement was followed by the formation of a new Council of Ministers, composed entirely of military officers and excluding all members of the Jana Dal, in response to demands by the opposition parties for a neutral government during the pre-election period. Once more, the opposition threatened to boycott the elections, as President Ershad would not relinquish power to an interim government, and in March the elections were abandoned and political activity was again banned. This was immediately followed by a referendum, held in support of the presidency, in which Ershad reportedly received 94% of the total votes. Local elections were held in May, without the participation of the opposition, following which Ershad claimed that 85% of the elected council chairmen were his supporters, although not necessarily of his party. In September a new five-party political alliance, the National Front (comprising the Jana Dal, the United People's Party, the Gonotantrik Party, the Bangladesh Muslim League and a breakaway section of the BNP), was established to promote government policies.

In January 1986 the 10-month ban on political activity was ended. The five components of the National Front formally became a single pro-Government entity, named the Jatiya Dal (National Party). In March President Ershad announced that parliamentary elections were to be held (under martial law) at the end of April. He relaxed martial law, however, by removing all army commanders from important civil posts and by abolishing more than 150 military courts and the martial law offices. These concessions fulfilled some of the opposition's demands, and candidates from the AL alliance (including Sheikh Hasina Wajed herself), the Jamaat-e-Islami Bangladesh and other smaller opposition parties thus participated in the parliamentary elections—which eventually proceeded in May. However, the BNP alliance, led by Begum Khaleda Zia, boycotted the polls, which were characterized by allegations of extensive fraud, violence and intimidation. The Jatiya Dal won 153 of the 300 directly elective seats in the Jatiya Sangsad. In addition, 30 seats reserved for women were filled by nominees of the Jatiya Dal. In July a mainly civilian Council of Ministers was sworn in.

Mizanur Rahman Chowdhury, former General Secretary of the Jatiya Dal, was appointed Prime Minister.

In order to be eligible to stand as a candidate in the forthcoming presidential election, Ershad retired as Chief of Army Staff in August 1986, while remaining Chief Martial Law Administrator and Commander-in-Chief of the Armed Forces. In early September Ershad officially joined the Jatiya Dal, whereupon he was elected as Chairman of the party and nominated as its presidential candidate. The presidential election, held in October, was boycotted by both the BNP and the AL, and resulted in an overwhelming victory for Ershad over his 11 opponents.

In November 1986 the Jatiya Sangsad approved indemnity legislation, effectively legitimizing the military regime's actions since March 1982. Ershad repealed martial law and restored the 1972 Constitution. The opposition alliances criticized the indemnity law, stating that they would continue to campaign for the dissolution of the Jatiya Sangsad and the overthrow of the Ershad Government. In December 1986, in an attempt to curb increasing dissent, President Ershad formed a new Council of Ministers, including four AL members of the legislature. The Minister of Justice, Justice A. K. M. Nurul Islam, was appointed Vice-President.

Opposition groups continued to organize anti-Government strikes and demonstrations during 1987, often with the support of trade unions and student groups. In July the Jatiya Sangsad approved a bill enabling army representatives to participate alongside elected representatives in the district councils. The adoption of this controversial legislation provoked widespread and often violent strikes and demonstrations, organized by the opposition groups, which perceived the measure as an attempt by the President to entrench military involvement in the governing of the country despite the ending of martial law in November 1986. Owing to the intensity of public opposition, President Ershad was forced to withdraw the legislation in August 1987 and return it to the Jatiya Sangsad for reconsideration. In November, in a renewed effort to oust President Ershad, opposition groups combined forces and organized further protests. Thousands of activists were detained, but demonstrations and strikes continued. In an attempt to forestall another general strike, President Ershad declared a nation-wide state of emergency on 27 November, suspending political activity and civil rights and banning all anti-Government protests. Disturbances persisted, despite the imposition of curfews on the main towns. In December, as about 6,000 activists remained in detention, opposition parties in the Jatiya Sangsad announced that their representatives intended to resign their seats. After 12 opposition members had withdrawn and the 73 AL members had agreed to do likewise, President Ershad dissolved the Jatiya Sangsad. In January 1988 the President announced that parliamentary elections would be held on 28 February, but leaders of the main opposition parties declared their intention to boycott the proposed poll while Ershad remained in office. Local elections, held throughout Bangladesh in February, were not boycotted by the opposition but were marred by serious outbreaks of violence. The parliamentary elections (postponed until 3 March) were also characterized by widespread violence, as well as by alleged fraud and malpractice. The opposition's appeal for a boycott of the polls was widely heeded, with the actual level of participation by the electorate appearing to have been considerably lower than the Government's estimate of 50%. As expected, the Jatiya Dal won a large majority of the seats.

A radical reshuffle of the Council of Ministers later in March 1988 included the appointment of a new Prime Minister, Moudud Ahmed, a long-time political ally of Ershad and hitherto the Minister of Industry and a Deputy Prime Minister, in place of Mizanur Rahman Chowdhury. In response to an abatement in the opposition's anti-Government campaign, Ershad repealed the state of emergency in April. Despite strong condemnation by the political opposition and sections of the public, a constitutional amendment establishing Islam as Bangladesh's state religion was approved by an overall majority in the Jatiya Sangsad in June. By early September, however, political events had been completely overshadowed by new monsoon floods, which began in August and proved to be the most severe in the area's recorded history. Bangladesh suffered further flooding in December 1988 and January 1989, following a devastating cyclone in late November. At the end of 1988 the Government established a national Disaster Prevention Council.

In July 1989 the Jatiya Sangsad approved legislation limiting the tenure of the presidency to two electoral terms of five years each and creating the post of a directly elected Vice-President (an appointment hitherto in the gift of the President). In August Ershad appointed Moudud Ahmed as Vice-President to replace Justice A. K. M. Nurul Islam, who was dismissed following charges of inefficiency. Kazi Zafar Ahmed, formerly the Minister of Information and a Deputy Prime Minister, was in turn promoted to the post of Prime Minister. Local elections held in March 1990 were officially boycotted by the opposition parties, although many members participated on an individual basis. In April Ershad announced that he would present himself as a candidate in the presidential election, which was scheduled for mid-1991.

Opposition groups, with the support of thousands of students, co-operated to intensify their anti-Government campaign in late 1990. On 27 November President Ershad proclaimed a nation-wide state of emergency for the second time in three years, suspending civil rights, imposing strict press censorship and enforcing an indefinite curfew throughout the country. On the following day, however, army units were summoned to impose order in the capital as thousands of protesters defied the curfew and attacked police. Under increasing pressure from the opposition groups, Ershad resigned on 4 December and declared that parliamentary elections would be held before the presidential election; the state of emergency was revoked, and the Jatiya Sangsad was dissolved. Following his nomination by the opposition, Justice Shahabuddin Ahmed, the Chief Justice of the Supreme Court, was appointed Vice-President. He assumed the responsibilities of acting President and was appointed to lead a neutral interim Government pending fresh parliamentary elections. Shahabuddin Ahmed undertook a comprehensive reorganization of personnel in financial institutions, local government and the civil service in an effort to remove Ershad's appointees from important posts. The opposition parties welcomed these developments and abandoned their protest campaigns. They also demanded that Ershad be tried for alleged corruption and abuse of power. Ershad was placed under house arrest, and was later sentenced to 20 years' imprisonment for illegal possession of firearms and other offences. (In June 1995 the former President was acquitted of illegally possessing firearms, and his sentence was halved. In the following month, however, Ershad was sentenced to a further three years' imprisonment for criminal misconduct.)

The BNP alliance won an overall majority at parliamentary elections held in February 1991. Following discussions with the Jamaat-e-Islami, as a result of which the BNP was ensured a small working majority in the Jatiya Sangsad, Begum Khaleda Zia assumed office as Prime Minister. In May the Government was faced with the immense problems created by a devastating cyclone, which caused the deaths of as many as 250,000 people and wrought massive economic damage. In August the Jatiya Sangsad approved a constitutional amendment ending 16 years of presidential rule and restoring the Prime Minister as executive leader (under the previous system, both the Prime Minister and the Council of Ministers had been responsible to the President). The amendment, which was approved by national referendum in the following month, reduced the role of the President, who was now to be elected by the Jatiya Sangsad for a five-year term, to that of a titular Head of State. Accordingly, a new President was elected by the Jatiya Sangsad in October. The successful candidate was the BNP nominee, former Speaker of the Jatiya Sangsad Abdur Rahman Biswas. In September the BNP had secured an absolute majority in the Jatiya Sangsad as a result of the party's success in a number of by-elections. In November, despite strong protest from the opposition parties, the Government abolished the *upazilla* (sub-district) system of rural administration, introduced by Ershad in 1982. Henceforth, all public functions at *upazilla* level were to be performed through executive orders of the central Government, pending the introduction of a new system of rural administration. To this end, the Government established a special committee to review all aspects of local government.

In early 1992 measures to transfer public-sector industries to private ownership and to curb endemic labour unrest led to strong political resistance from the opposition. In August the Government defeated a parliamentary motion of 'no confidence' introduced by the AL. The opposition accused the Government of failing to curb the increasing lawlessness in the country, notably amongst university students. Anti-terrorism measures introduced in November were, however, widely criticized as being excessively harsh and undemocratic. Subsequently, the opposition parties sank their differences in pursuit of a common

demand that the general election due in 1996 be held under the auspices of a neutral, caretaker government.

From late 1993 and into 1994 mass anti-Government demonstrations were organized by the opposition, which initiated a boycott of parliamentary proceedings in February 1994. The number of strikes and violent protests staged by the opposition multiplied in the latter half of the year, and culminated in the resignation of all the opposition members from the Jatiya Sangsad in December. In spite of the political chaos, compounded by the holding of further general strikes by the opposition, the Prime Minister pledged to use her party's parliamentary majority to maintain constitutional government.

The opposition co-ordinated further nation-wide strikes in September–October 1995, which were, at times, marked by outbreaks of violence. In response to the intensification of the anti-Government campaign, and in an attempt to break the political impasse caused by the refusal of the opposition parties to take part in forthcoming by-elections, the Jatiya Sangsad was dissolved in November at the request of the Prime Minister, pending the holding of a general election in early 1996. Despite opposition demands for a neutral interim government to oversee the election, the President requested that Begum Khaleda Zia's administration continue in office in an acting capacity. All of the main opposition parties boycotted the general election, which was held in mid-February, and independent monitors estimated the turn-out at only about 10%–15% of the registered electorate. Of the 207 legislative seats declared by the end of February, the BNP had won 205 (a partial repoll had been ordered in most of the 93 remaining constituencies where violence had disrupted the electoral process). The opposition refused to recognize the legitimacy of the polls, and announced the launch of a 'non-co-operation' movement against the Government. Renewed street protests rendered the country virtually ungovernable, and Begum Khaleda Zia eventually agreed to the holding of fresh elections under neutral auspices. The Prime Minister and her Government duly resigned on 30 March, and the Jatiya Sangsad was dissolved. President Biswas appointed former Chief Justice Muhammad Habibur Rahman as acting Prime Minister, and requested that a fresh general election be held, under the auspices of an interim neutral government, within three months. At the general election, held on 12 June, the AL won 146 of the 300 elective seats in the Jatiya Sangsad, the BNP 116, the Jatiya Dal 32 and the Jamaat-e-Islami three. An understanding was rapidly reached between the AL and the Jatiya Dal, the latter's major interest being the release of Ershad, who had secured a legislative seat from within prison. (The former President was released on bail in January 1997.) Sheikh Hasina Wajed was sworn in as Prime Minister on 23 June 1996.

On 23 July 1996 the AL's presidential nominee, retired Chief Justice and former acting President Shahabuddin Ahmed, was elected unopposed as Bangladesh's Head of State. In early September the AL won eight of the 15 seats contested in by-elections; this result gave the AL, which was also allocated 27 of the 30 nominated women's parliamentary seats in July, an absolute majority in the Jatiya Sangsad.

On assuming power, Sheikh Hasina Wajed had vowed to bring to justice those responsible for the assassination of her father, Sheikh Mujibur Rahman, in 1975. In November 1996 the Jatiya Sangsad voted unanimously to repeal the indemnity law enacted in 1975 to protect the perpetrators of the military coup in that year; the BNP and the Jamaat-e-Islami, however, boycotted the vote. The trial of 19 people accused of direct involvement in Sheikh Mujib's assassination began in March 1997, with 14 of the defendants being tried *in absentia*.

Agitation persisted throughout 1997. In addition to the disruption caused by a series of strikes and demonstrations organized by the BNP in conjunction with Islamist and right-wing groups (which frequently led to violent clashes between demonstrators and police), the efficacy of the Jatiya Sangsad was undermined by several boycotts of parliamentary proceedings organized by BNP deputies. In mid-1998 the opposition organized public demonstrations in protest at problems of law and order and at power failures. The BNP's foremost demand was the holding of fresh elections, reiterating the AL's earlier campaign. The AL, however, strengthened its position through a series of by-election victories. Thus the departure of the Jatiya Dal from the coalition in March had little effect on the ruling party's hold on power. In June and August Begum Khaleda Zia was charged with corruption and abuse of power, allegedly perpetrated during her tenure as premier (the charges were later dismissed as politically motivated). In August 1998 the

Government appealed for international aid following devastating floods (the worst since 1988), which caused more than 1,500 deaths and infrastructural damage estimated at about US $220m.

In September 1998 the controversial feminist writer Taslima Nasreen was reported to have secretly returned to Bangladesh after four years in self-imposed exile. (Nasreen, whose allegedly anti-Islamic public stance and statements had made her the target of a campaign of vilification by fundamentalist Islamist groups in Bangladesh, had—with the apparent complicity of government officials—fled the country in August 1994 and been granted refuge in Sweden, shortly after a warrant had been issued for her arrest on blasphemy-related charges.) On her return, a fresh warrant for the writer's arrest on charges of blasphemy was issued by a Dhaka court. Islamist extremists organized street protests, reiterating their demand for Nasreen's immediate arrest and execution. In November 1998 Nasreen voluntarily surrendered herself before the High Court in Dhaka, where she was granted bail. In January 1999 the author again left Bangladesh for Sweden, following renewed death threats from Islamist extremists. The sale of her third novel was authorized in Bangladesh in 2001; however, her fourth book was banned by the Bangladeshi authorities in August 2002. In October a court outside Dhaka sentenced Nasreen *in absentia* to one year's imprisonment on charges of blasphemy.

Also in September 1998 three former government ministers, including the former Deputy Prime Minister, Shah Moazzem Hossain, and a prominent member of the BNP, K. M. Obaidur Rahman, were arrested in connection with the murder in 1975 of four former government ministers, who were shot dead in Dhaka two months after the assassination of Bangladesh's founder, Sheikh Mujib. In October 2000 they were indicted on charges of murder. Of a total of 22 defendants, 14 had fled the country. In November 1998 a Dhaka court sentenced to death 15 of the 19 people accused of Mujib's assassination, acquitting the others. Only four of those convicted, however, were in custody in Bangladesh; the 11 others remained fugitives abroad. In April 2000 the Chief Justice established a two-judge bench to review the sentences. In December, after a 64-day appeal hearing and High Court review of the sentences, the two judges confirmed the death sentence against 10 of the accused, but announced a split verdict on the sentences of five defendants. The case was referred to another court, which sentenced 12 of those accused to death and acquitted the remaining three defendants. Those convicted appealed to the Supreme Court against their sentences. In October 2004, following a significant delay, 15 defendants were convicted of the murders of the four former government ministers in 1975. Three former junior army officers were sentenced to death, while the remaining 12 defendants were sentenced to life imprisonment. Five other defendants—four politicians and an army officer—were acquitted. All three of those awarded the death sentence remained fugitives abroad, as did nine of those sentenced to life in prison, and all were among those convicted of the murder of Sheikh Mujib and his family. The AL subsequently announced its displeasure at the acquittal of the four politicians.

The BNP organized a three-day, nation-wide general strike in November 1998, in protest at alleged government repression. At least two people were killed and many injured when the police clashed with protesters in Dhaka (the tension was exacerbated by the BNP's disapproval of the death sentences imposed on Mujib's assassins). The Government, in response, accused the opposition of disrupting vital post-flood rehabilitation work. In late December the opposition was strengthened by a decision by the BNP and the Jamaat-e-Islami to accept Ershad and the Jatiya Dal in the anti-Government movement without any condition.

Unrest continued throughout the latter half of 1999 and into 2000. The opposition parties boycotted parliamentary proceedings from January 2000, and persisted in their demands for the holding of early elections. The situation remained tense, despite the efforts of influential business leaders to negotiate an arrangement between the Prime Minister and the opposition parties. Street demonstrations resumed in February. The announcement in the same month of the introduction of the controversial Public Safety Act, which permitted detention without trial for up to 90 days, provoked a three-day nation-wide strike. The opposition parties suspended their boycott of the Jatiya Sangsad in June in order to avoid disqualification (which would take effect after an absence of 90 working days from the

legislature without the Speaker's approval). However, following accusations that the Government was conspiring to change the Constitution, opposition members promptly resumed their boycott, claiming that they were not allowed to address the legislature (an allegation denied by the Speaker).

In August 2000 the High Court in Dhaka reduced the sentence imposed by a lower court on Ershad to five years' imprisonment, and stipulated the payment of a fine of 54m. taka and the confiscation of a property, the Janata Tower, for misappropriating funds during his tenure of power between 1983 and 1990. In accordance with the Constitution, Ershad was deprived of his parliamentary seat. Following an appeal in November, and shortly after Ershad had begun his term of imprisonment, the Supreme Court reduced the sentence to three years and seven months; the former President was released on bail in April 2001, owing to illness. In May 2002 Ershad was sentenced to six months' imprisonment for attempting to influence the proceedings in a corruption case. In early September 2000 the opposition leader, Begum Khaleda Zia, was accused by the anti-corruption unit of financial irregularities.

Intermittent opposition-led strikes in early 2001 caused serious disruption and adversely affected the economy. Discontent with the Government was often manifested violently: in mid-June, for example, 22 people were killed as a result of a bomb explosion at a local office of the AL. It was alleged that militant Islamist groups were involved, although none claimed responsibility.

In June 2001 Sheikh Hasina Wajed became the first Prime Minister in the history of Bangladesh to complete a five-year term of office. In mid-July the Government resigned, and the Jatiya Sangsad was dissolved in order to allow an interim neutral administration to prepare for a general election, to be held within three months. The interim administration was established shortly afterwards under the leadership of former Chief Justice Latifur Rehman. The election campaign was reportedly the most violent in the country's history, and Rehman ordered the deployment of more than 50,000 troops to curb the violence.

The general election proceeded on 1 October 2001, although voting was postponed in several constituencies owing to violence. The AL claimed that voting had been manipulated as it became clear that the opposition alliance, led by the BNP, had won an overwhelming majority of the 300 directly elective seats in the Jatiya Sangsad; however, international monitors declared the poll to be free and fair. Immediately after the election the BNP leader, Begum Khaleda Zia, asserted, in an apparent effort to allay national and international concerns regarding the presence of two fundamentalist Islamist parties in the four-party alliance, that Bangladesh would not become an Islamic state. Following elections on 9 October in 15 of those constituencies where voting had been delayed, the BNP-led alliance controlled a total of 214 of the directly elective seats, the AL 62 and the Jatiya Dal 14; two smaller parties held one seat each, and independents a total of six. Meanwhile, the AL, refusing to accept the election results, boycotted the ceremony at which newly elected members of the legislature were sworn in. On 10 October Begum Khaleda Zia was sworn in as Prime Minister, and a new Cabinet was appointed the following day. At the end of October newly elected members of Parliament representing the opposition AL took the oath of office, but refused to join the opening session of the Jatiya Sangsad, in continuing protest against what they considered a rigged election; the opposition party also condemned violence allegedly perpetrated by the BNP-led alliance against AL members and religious minority groups, stating that it would not attend the Jatiya Sangsad until the Government demonstrated a greater commitment to curb the alleged violence. Reports of attacks, particularly against the Hindu minority, increased markedly after the victory of the BNP-led coalition. Hindus either sought refuge in AL offices or fled the country to neighbouring India. The Government admitted that some of the assertions were true, while dismissing reports of widespread attacks as overstated, and announced that an investigation would be conducted into alleged violent acts against religious minorities and into reports that Hindus had left the country. In May 2002 the human rights organization Amnesty International issued a report stating that the Bangladeshi Government had failed to take effective measures to curb attacks allegedly perpetrated by supporters of the BNP-led coalition, before, during and after the October 2001 election, against the Hindu community, other minorities and women. The report also claimed that the police had failed to protect the

minorities and that custodial torture by members of the police
and armed forces had taken place during and after the general
election. The Government rejected the charges; while admitting
to some of the incidents, the BNP-led coalition held its political
opponents responsible for the criminal acts. In the mean time,
the Goverment had not provided any information regarding an
official investigation into the alleged attacks. In August 2002
the Chief of the Hindu Unity Council warned that unless
demands for the restoration of a secular Constitution, as originally devised immediately after Bangladesh's independence,
were met, Hindus would remain 'second-class citizens' in the
country.

Meanwhile, elections took place on 12 November 2001 in the
remaining two constituencies where voting had not taken place
in October. On the same day Prof. A. Q. M. Badrudozza Chowdhury, a former Minister of Foreign Affairs, was declared President after his only nominated opponent, Mohammad Rowshan
Ali, withdrew. Prof. Chowdhury immediately resigned from the
BNP, and was sworn into office two days later. The AL (which
had refused to participate in the presidential election) boycotted
the oath-taking ceremony. In December the Jatiya Sangsad
repealed the Father of the Nation Family Security Act. The
Security Act, which had been approved in June under the AL
administration, guaranteed lifelong security for Sheikh Hasina
Wajed and her sister, the daughters of Sheikh Mujib (the 'father
of the nation' according to the AL), because several convicted
assassins of the latter remained at large; however, the Act was
strongly criticized by the BNP, which considered its own
founder, Gen. Zia, to be the 'father of the nation'. In March 2002
the AL demonstrated against the repealing of the Father of the
Nation's Portrait Display and Preservation Act, which made it
mandatory for government officials to display portraits of
Sheikh Mujib in their offices.

AL members of Parliament continued their boycott of the
Jatiya Sangsad until June 2002. The party also refused to take
part in civic elections in April and carried out a policy of
agitation, organizing a series of strikes in protest against higher
taxes, crime and rises in fuel prices. In response to the opposition's campaign, the Government filed two corruption charges
against Sheikh Hasina Wajed and other AL members in
December 2001, in relation to an arms contract with Russia
signed in 1999.

In mid-June 2002 the President yielded to pressure from the
BNP to resign from office after he failed to visit Gen. Zia's grave
on the anniversary of the latter's assassination. The resignation
was considered unconstitutional by many observers. Some two
days later Begum Khaleda Zia appointed her son, Tarique
Rahman, to the post of Secretary-General of the BNP,
prompting claims that the Prime Minister intended eventually
to relinquish power to Rahman. In early September the BNP
candidate, Iajuddin Ahmed, was declared President by the
Election Commission after it was established that the nomination papers of the two other candidates were invalid. In May
2003 Begum Khaleda Zia conducted a government reorganization, which led to the resignations of three ministers and four
ministers of state.

In late September 2002 bomb explosions in the south-western
town of Satkhira occurred, killing at least 10 people and seriously injuring 150. Islamist militant groups were suspected to
have carried out the attack, although none claimed responsibility. In mid-October the Government launched a campaign to
curb crime; some 40,000 members of the armed forces had been
enlisted to assist the police. The AL claimed that the Government was using this campaign as a guise for the harassment of
opposition members. By the end of the month almost 3,500
people had been arrested, including two former AL ministers.
Concerns were raised over the unusually high number of people
who had died in army custody. In early January the Government
approved a law granting the armed forces legal immunity for
any actions carried out during the three-month operation
against crime. A number of journalists were also detained
during the campaign. Meanwhile, in December 2002 bomb
explosions at four cinemas in the town of Mymensingh occurred,
killing at least 18 people and injuring some 300. The Prime
Minister rejected suggestions that the Islamist militant al-
Qa'ida (Base) organization was involved in the attack. However,
it was claimed that Bangladeshi Islamist militant groups had
collaborated with South-East Asian Islamist groups connected
with al-Qa'ida since 1999. In mid-February 2003 the Government proscribed the activities of the militant Islamist organization Shahadat-e-Al-Hikma. In January–March almost 50

people were killed and 6,000 injured in violent attacks during
staggered local elections. In late August two senior members of
the AL were shot dead in Khulna, provoking a general strike in
Dhaka by demonstrators demanding an end to lawlessness. A
report published by the Bureau of Human Rights Bangladesh in
September stated that 2,974 people had been killed in separate
violent incidents throughout Bangladesh between January and
September.

Unrest continued throughout the latter half of 2003. In
November the UN Development Programme and the Bangladeshi Government jointly produced a preliminary report on the
country's 100,000-strong police force. The report stated that the
deep-rooted problems of corruption, inadequate pay, low morale
and understaffing within the force were adversely affecting
Bangladesh's social and economic conditions. In January 2004 a
bomb explosion at the Muslim Hazrat Shah Jalal shrine in
Sylhet killed five people.

In late March 2004 the Minister of Commerce, Amir Khosru
Mahmud Chowdhury, resigned citing personal reasons. The
Minister of State for Foreign Affairs also resigned; he was
immediately appointed as adviser in the Ministry of Foreign
Affairs, with the status of Minister of State. A. K. M. Chowdhury's resignation led to a minor government reorganization, in
which the Minister of Home Affairs, Air Vice-Marshal Altaf
Hossain Chowdhury (retd), was appointed Minister of Commerce and Lutfuzzaman Babar was designated Minister of State
for Home Affairs.

In May 2004 a grenade attack at the Hazrat Shah Jalal shrine
resulted in the deaths of three people and injuries to at least a
further 100, including the British High Commissioner to Bangladesh, Anwar Chowdhury. By the end of that month 109
people had been arrested in connection with the attack. Meanwhile, Ahsanullah Master, an AL legislator, was shot dead in his
constituency. While the AL accused the Government of having
ordered the attack, the Government blamed factional fighting
within the AL. Also in May the Jatiya Sangsad approved a bill
of constitutional amendments (comprising the 14th Amendment
to the Constitution) that made provision for the existing 300-
member legislature to be enlarged to 345 members—45 seats
were to be reserved for women. The AL and most other opposition parties boycotted the vote, on the grounds that the seats for
women would be awarded on a proportional representation
basis, rather than by direct election. In the same month a minor
cabinet reorganization took place, in which four ministries were
merged and eight portfolios reallocated. In June the AL
announced the end of the parliamentary boycott that it had
initiated one year previously, following the return of several AL
legislators to the Jatiya Sangsad in the previous month in
tribute to Ahsanullah Master.

In August 2004 another grenade attack on an AL rally in
Dhaka resulted in the deaths of 20 people, including the President of the AL women's wing, Ivy Rahman. AL leader Sheikh
Hasina Wajed was slightly injured. Widespread rioting subsequently occurred in Dhaka and 13 other towns in Bangladesh,
and the AL called a series of general strikes in protest. Later in
that month a previously unknown group, Hikmatul Zihad,
claimed responsibility for the attack. In January 2005 an explosion at an AL rally in Habiganj, in the north-east of the country,
killed five AL activists, including Shah Kibria, a former Minister
of Finance.

Meanwhile, in mid-2004 severe flooding affected some two-
thirds of the country, resulting in the deaths of an estimated 628
people by the beginning of August. At the end of July Prime
Minister Begum Khaleda Zia finally appealed for international
aid, having maintained until then that government resources
would be sufficient to deal with the crisis. In mid-September
flooding in the capital, Dhaka, was so extensive that government offices, businesses and the stock exchange had to be closed
for several days.

In foreign affairs, Bangladesh has traditionally maintained a
policy of non-alignment. Relations with Pakistan improved in
1976: ambassadors were exchanged, and trade, postal and telecommunication links were resumed. In September 1991 Pakistan finally agreed to initiate a process of phased repatriation
and rehabilitation of some 250,000 Bihari Muslims (who supported Pakistan in Bangladesh's war of liberation in 1971) still
remaining in refugee camps in Bangladesh. The first group of
Bihari refugees returned to Pakistan from Bangladesh in January 1993, but the implementation of the repatriation process
has since been very slow. Relations with Pakistan deteriorated
in September 2000 when, at the UN Millennium Summit in New

York, USA, the Prime Minister Sheikh Hasina Wajed condemned Pakistan's military leadership, ostensibly as part of a general request for the UN to take action against undemocratic changes of government. A diplomatic row ensued over who was responsible for the events during Bangladesh's war of liberation, culminating in the withdrawal of the Pakistani Deputy High Commissioner to Bangladesh. In late July 2002 Pakistani President Pervez Musharraf paid a visit to Bangladesh, during which he expressed regret for the atrocities committed by Pakistani troops during the 1971 war.

Relations with India have been strained over the questions of cross-border terrorism (especially around the area of the Chittagong Hill Tracts, where Buddhist tribal rebels, the Shanti Bahini, waged a lengthy guerrilla campaign against the Bangladeshi police and Bengali settlers—see below) and of the Farrakka barrage, which was constructed by India on the Ganga river in 1975, so depriving Bangladesh of water for irrigation and river transport during the dry season. In December 1996, however, Indo-Bangladesh relations were given a major boost following the signing of an historic 30-year water-sharing agreement. In January 1997 the Indian Prime Minister paid an official visit to Bangladesh, the first Indian premier to do so for 20 years. In June 1999, during a visit to Dhaka by the Indian Prime Minister, Atal Bihari Vajpayee, to celebrate the inauguration of the first direct passenger bus service between Bangladesh and India, Vajpayee promised Bangladesh greater access to Indian markets and announced that India would give its neighbour US \$50m. in credits over three years to help develop its transport and industrial infrastructure. In August the Bangladeshi Government was criticized by the opposition for its approval of proposals to permit the transhipment of Indian goods through Bangladesh to the north-eastern states of India by Bangladeshi transport companies (see above). In October 2003 Bangladesh and India signed another water-sharing agreement.

In June 1992 the Indian Government, under the provisions of an accord signed with Bangladesh in 1974, formally leased the Tin Bigha Corridor (a small strip of land covering an area of only 1.5 ha) to Bangladesh for 999 years. India maintained sovereignty over the corridor, but the lease gave Bangladesh access to its enclaves of Dahagram and Angarpota. In September 1997 India granted Nepal a transit route through a 60-km corridor in the Indian territory joining Nepal and Bangladesh, thus facilitating trade between those two countries. Despite the 1992 border agreement between Bangladesh and India, the issue of territorial rights to pockets of land or enclaves along the irregular border remained a source of dispute, and occasional efforts to resolve this problem failed to prevent intermittent clashes between border guards. The worst fighting between the two countries since 1976 took place in April 2001 on the Bangladeshi border with the Indian state of Meghalaya. Some 16 members of the Indian Border Security Forces and three members of the Bangladesh Rifles were killed. The situation was brought under control, and the two sides entered border negotiations in June and July, as a result of which two joint working groups were established to review the undemarcated section of the border.

Relations with India deteriorated in November 2002 as a result of accusations by India's Deputy Prime Minister and Minister of Home Affairs, Lal Krishna Advani, that al-Qa'ida had increased its activities in Bangladesh since the BNP-led coalition's assumption of power in October 2001. Advani also claimed that Bangladesh was covertly assisting al-Qa'ida and Pakistan's Inter-Services Intelligence Agency, and was providing refuge for Indian separatist groups. The Bangladeshi Government strongly denied the allegations. In January 2003 the Indian Government announced plans to deport some 16m. Bangladeshis who it claimed were working and living in India illegally, because they were perceived to be a security threat. The Bangladeshi Government rejected the claim as groundless. In mid-February the Bangladeshi Minister of Foreign Affairs visited India to discuss the issue of illegal immigration; India expressed dismay at the outcome of the negotiations. Meanwhile, the number of people stranded between the countries' borders increased. In September 2004 senior Bangladeshi and Indian officials held talks in Dhaka concerning water-sharing and security issues. Some progress was made in resolving the issue of water-sharing between the two countries, and an agreement was reached to co-ordinate border patrols by security forces in both countries. However, Bangladesh continued to deny the existence of Indian separatist groups within its borders. In the following month members of the two countries'

border patrols exchanged fire when a dispute occurred as several Bangladeshis attempted to cross illegally into India. The Indian Government again claimed that a significant number of Indian insurgent groups had established bases in Bangladesh, an allegation emphatically denied by the Bangladeshi Government. Relations continued to be strained into 2005.

In 1989 the Government attempted to suppress the Shanti Bahini insurgency in the Chittagong Hill Tracts by introducing concessions providing limited autonomy to the region in the form of three new semi-autonomous hill districts. Voting to elect councils for the districts took place relatively peacefully in June, despite attempts at disruption by the Shanti Bahini, who continued to demand total autonomy for the Chakma tribals. The powers vested in the councils were designed to give the tribals sufficient authority to regulate any further influx of Bengali settlers to the districts (the chief complaint of the tribals since Bengalis were settled in the Chittagong Hill Tracts, as plantation workers and clerks, by the British administration in the 19th century). Despite these concessions, violence continued unabated, and refugees continued to flee across the border into India (the number of refugees living in camps in Tripura reached about 56,000). In May 1992 Bangladesh and India negotiated an agreement intended to facilitate the refugees' return. However, the refugees, fearing persecution by the Bangladesh security forces, proved reluctant to repatriate. Following the conclusion of a successful round of negotiations in early 1994, the process of phased repatriation commenced, although by August only about 2,000 refugees had returned. In December 1997 the Bangladeshi Government signed a peace agreement with the political wing of the Shanti Bahini ending the insurgency in the Chittagong Hill Tracts. The treaty offered the rebels a general amnesty in return for the surrender of their weapons and gave the tribal people greater powers of self-governance through the establishment of three new elected district councils (to control the area's land management and policing) and a regional council (the chairman of which was to enjoy the rank of a state minister). The peace agreement, which was strongly criticized by the opposition for representing a 'sell-out' of the area to India and a threat to Bangladesh's sovereignty, was expected to accelerate the process of repatriating the remaining refugees from Tripura (who totalled about 31,000 at the end of December 1997). By the end of 2000 most of the Chakma refugees had been repatriated, the district and regional councils were in operation, and a land commission had been established. In early 2001 a tribal group in Tripura threatened forcibly to repatriate remaining refugees if India failed to deport them. In June it was reported that rioting in the Chittagong area had caused a new flow of refugees to Tripura. Following the accession to power of the BNP-led alliance in October, there were reports of thousands of members of Buddhist, Christian and Hindu minorities fleeing to Tripura. In May 2003 the Chakma tribal people held nation-wide demonstrations protesting against discrimination by Bengalis and the apparent reneging on the 1997 peace agreement. In December 2003 and January 2004 protesters in the south-eastern Hill Tracts succeeded in cutting off the region from the rest of the country as they demanded the full implementation of the 1997 agreement.

Bangladesh security forces were put on alert in late 2000, as tension along the border with Myanmar increased following reports that Myanmar was laying land-mines and that Myanma troops had been deployed in the border area. In January 2001 border guards exchanged fire, amid rising tension over a controversial dam project on the Naaf river, which Bangladesh claimed would cause flooding in its territory; the shooting took place after work began in Myanmar on the construction of an embankment. The Myanma authorities agreed to suspend the project. Shortly afterwards Myanmar alleged that Bangladesh had violated the two countries' 1979 border agreement by cultivating shrimps in the area, an accusation denied by the Bangladeshi Government. Border negotiations took place subsequently, but collapsed after the Myanma authorities refused to sign the minutes. In early February 2001, however, Myanmar agreed permanently to halt construction of the dam. The official visit of the Myanma ruler, Gen. Than Shwe, to Bangladesh in December 2002 indicated an improvement in relations. Meanwhile, some 250,000 Rohingyas had fled Myanmar's Northern Rakhine state in 1991–92. Myanmar had in August 1997 suspended a programme of voluntary repatriations agreed by the Bangladeshi and Myanma authorities in 1992, under which about 230,000 refugees had returned to Myanmar, although smaller-scale repatriations had resumed in late 1998 following intervention by the office of the UN High Commissioner for Refugees (UNHCR). According to UNHCR data, 16,000 of the Rohingyas remaining in Bangladesh were considered by the Government of Myanmar to be ineligible for repatriation, since they had not been authorized for return prior to August 1997, and 5,000 were unwilling to return owing to protection concerns; however, the Bangladeshi Government continued to favour repatriation of the refugees. In January 2002 the World Food Programme launched an appeal for US $2.1m. in assistance for 21,500 Myanma Rohingya Muslim refugees who remained in two camps in south-eastern Bangladesh.

In September 2001 Bangladesh's interim administration agreed, with the support of the AL and BNP, to offer the USA use of Bangladeshi airspace and ports in the event of military action against Afghanistan, where the Taliban leadership was believed to be harbouring Osama bin Laden and al-Qa'ida—held principally responsible by the USA for that month's suicide attacks against New York and Washington, DC. However, the US-led military campaign to oust the regime of Saddam Hussein in Iraq from March 2003 provoked anti-US and anti-British demonstrations in Dhaka at the end of March and during April. In June 2004 US Secretary of Defense Donald Rumsfeld visited Bangladesh and held talks with Prime Minister Begum Khaleda Zia. There were protests against his visit, as it was believed that he intended to request that Bangladesh contribute troops to assist the US-led coalition in Iraq. The Bangladeshi Minister of Foreign Affairs stressed that Bangladesh would not send any troops to the country without a UN mandate.

In May 2003 the High Court in London, United Kingdom, ruled that a case brought against the British Geological Survey (BGS) on behalf of two Bangladeshis who had been diagnosed as suffering from arsenic poisoning should go ahead. The Bangladeshis alleged that the BGS had failed to detect the presence of arsenic in groundwater in the country during a survey in 1992. Hundreds of people had since fallen ill with arsenicosis after drinking the groundwater from deep tube wells constructed to provide an alternative to contaminated surface water. However, in February 2004 the British Court of Appeal dismissed the case, overturning the High Court's ruling on the matter.

Bangladesh is a member of the South Asian Association for Regional Co-operation (SAARC, see p. 343), formally constituted in 1985, with Bhutan, India, the Maldives, Nepal, Pakistan and Sri Lanka. Included in SAARC's charter are pledges of non-interference by members in each other's internal affairs and a joint effort to avoid 'contentious' issues whenever the association meets. The SAARC Preferential Trading Arrangement (SAPTA) was signed in April 1993 and came into effect in December 1995. At the 12th SAARC summit meeting held in Islamabad, Pakistan, in January 2004, members signed an agreement stipulating the establishment of a South Asian Free Trade Area (SAFTA) by 1 January 2006. An additional protocol on terrorism was also signed. Bangladesh was due to host the 13th SAARC summit meeting in 2005.

Government

The role of the President, who is elected by the Jatiya Sangsad (Parliament) for a five-year term, is essentially that of a titular Head of State. Executive power is held by the Prime Minister, who heads the Council of Ministers. The President appoints the Prime Minister and, on the latter's recommendation, other ministers. The Jatiya Sangsad comprises 345 members, 300 of whom are elected by universal suffrage: an additional 45 female members are appointed by the elective members. The Jatiya Sangsad serves a five-year term, subject to dissolution.

For purposes of local government, the country is divided into 64 administrative districts.

Defence

Military service is voluntary. In August 2004 the armed forces numbered 125,500: an army of 110,000, a navy of 9,000 and an air force of 6,500. The paramilitary forces totalled 63,200, and included the Bangladesh Rifles (border guard) of 38,000. Budget expenditure on defence was estimated at 39,000m. taka for 2004.

Economic Affairs

In 2003, according to estimates by the World Bank, Bangladesh's gross national income (GNI), measured at average 2001–03 prices, was US $54,323m., equivalent to $400 per head (or $1,870 per head on an international purchasing-power parity basis). During 1990–2003, it was estimated, the population increased at an average annual rate of 1.8%, while gross domestic product (GDP) per head increased, in real terms, by an average of 3.0% per year. Overall GDP increased at an average annual rate of 4.8% in 1990–2003. GDP grew by 5.2% in 2002/03 and by 5.5% in 2003/04. GDP was projected to increase by 5.1% in 2004/05.

Agriculture (including hunting, forestry and fishing) contributed an estimated 20.5% of total GDP in 2003/04. In 1999/2000 64.8% of the employed labour force were engaged in that sector. The principal sources of revenue in the agricultural sector are jute, tea, shrimps and fish. Raw jute and jute goods accounted for 4.3% of total export earnings in 2003/04. Despite severe flooding in 2000, Bangladesh achieved self-sufficiency in basic foods for the first time in 2000/01, mainly owing to increased rice production. The output of foodgrains declined in 2001/02; nevertheless, self-sufficiency in foodgrains was maintained. According to official figures, agricultural production grew by 2.7% in 2003/04, largely owing to the expansion of the area under high-yielding variety crops. However, it was feared that sectoral GDP would be adversely affected in 2004/05 by the consequences of severe flooding in July–September 2004. Agricultural GDP expanded at an average annual rate of 2.9% in 1990–2003.

Industry (including mining, manufacturing, power and construction) employed 10.7% of the working population in 1999/2000. The industrial sector contributed an estimated 26.7% of total GDP in 2003/04. During 1990–2003 industrial GDP increased at an average annual rate of 7.0%. According to official figures, growth in the industrial sector was 7.3% in 2002/03 and 7.7% in 2003/04.

Bangladesh's proven reserves of natural gas totalled 340,000m. cu m at the end of 2003. Production of natural gas increased from 11,400m. cu m in 2002 to 12,200m. cu m in 2003. It is envisaged that an exportable surplus of natural gas may eventually be produced. In November 2004 the US company Unocal signed an agreement with the state-owned Petrobangla corporation to develop the country's most extensive gas field, at Bibiyana. Bangladesh possesses substantial deposits of coal (estimated at more than 1,000m. metric tons), although difficulties of exploitation continue to make coal imports necessary, and petroleum.

Manufacturing contributed an estimated 16.0% of GDP in 2003/04. The sector employed 7.6% of the working population in 1999/2000. The principal branches of the manufacturing sector include textiles, food products, garments and chemicals. During 1990–2003 manufacturing GDP increased at an average annual rate of 6.7%. According to official figures, the GDP of the manufacturing sector grew by an estimated 7.4% in 2003/04.

Energy is derived principally from natural gas (which contributed 84.6% of total electricity output in 2001). Imports of petroleum products comprised 7.1% of the cost of total imports in 2003/04.

The services sector accounted for an estimated 52.7% of total GDP in 2003/04. In 1999/2000 24.5% of the employed labour force were engaged in the sector. The GDP of the services sector increased at an average annual rate of 4.9% during 1990–2003. According to official figures, the sector's GDP expanded by an estimated 5.9% in 2003/04.

In 2003, according to the IMF, Bangladesh recorded a visible trade deficit of US $2,421.1m., and there was a surplus of $182.5m. on the current account of the balance of payments. In 2003 the principal source of imports was India (which contributed 15.4% of the total), while the USA was the principal market for exports (accounting for 25.2% of the total). Other major trading partners were the People's Republic of China, Singapore, Germany and the United Kingdom. The principal exports in 2003/04 were ready-made garments (accounting for an estimated 46.5% of export revenue), knitwear and hosiery products, frozen shrimp and fish and raw jute and jute goods. The principal imports were capital goods (an estimated 26.4% of the total), textiles, petroleum products, and cotton.

In 2004/05 the overall budgetary deficit was projected to amount to the equivalent of 4.3% of GDP. Bangladesh's total external debt was US $17,037m. at the end of 2002, of which $16,445m. was long-term public debt. In that year the cost of debt-servicing was equivalent to 7.3% of total revenue from exports of goods and services. The annual rate of inflation averaged 5.0% in 1990–2003. Consumer prices increased by an average of 4.4% in 2002/03 and 5.8% in 2003/04. About 3.3% of the total labour force were unemployed in 1999/2000.

Bangladesh is a member of the UN Economic and Social Commission for Asia and the Pacific (ESCAP, see p. 31), of the

Asian Development Bank (ADB, see p. 159), of the South Asian Association for Regional Co-operation (SAARC, see p. 343) and of the Colombo Plan (see p. 373). Bangladesh is also a member of the International Jute Organization, which is based in Dhaka.

The problems of developing Bangladesh include widespread poverty, malnutrition and underemployment, combined with an increasing population and a poor resource base—this last meaning that the country is particularly vulnerable to adverse climatic conditions and to fluctuations in international prices for its export commodities. Despite the frequency of natural disasters, food security has improved somewhat in recent years, as have efforts to enhance production methods (notably through subsidies and the increased use of high-yielding variety crops), storage and distribution facilities. The birth rate has decreased considerably, owing to a successful nation-wide birth-control campaign. In the 1990s high rates of growth were achieved in exports of non-traditional items, particularly ready-made garments and knitwear. Furthermore, recent discoveries of huge reserves of natural gas appear to offer opportunities both in terms of domestic fuel self-sufficiency and, in the longer term, export potential. Nevertheless, the increasing fiscal deficit, exacerbated by the heavy losses incurred by state-owned enterprises, continues to cause concern, as does Bangladesh's heavy dependence on foreign aid: total disbursed aid in 2002/03 amounted to US $1,162m. In 2001/02 real GDP growth slowed to the lowest rate in six years, owing to a deceleration in all sectors of the economy. However, in the following year the economy regained momentum: exports and imports rose, the textile industry was showing signs of recovery and the wider trade deficit was more than offset by the increased level of remittances from Bangladeshis working abroad. The economy continued to expand in this way in 2003/04. The GDP growth rate of 5.5% for this year, however, was short of the 8% growth rate required for the country to meet its poverty-reduction target of 50% by 2010. In 2003 the Government agreed to follow a three-year IMF poverty-reduction programme in exchange for a loan of $500m. The Government also revealed a set of measures to curb corruption and improve tax collection; the fiscal deficit, however, was expected to grow as a result of costly economic reforms. The expiry of the World Trade Organization's Multi-fibre Arrangement (MFA) at the end of 2004 was expected to have a severe impact on Bangladesh's garment industry (Bangladesh has been a beneficiary of the MFA quotas limiting garments exports to developed countries). The rapid establishment of domestic yarn and fabric industries thus became increasingly important if Bangladesh was to compete with more advanced developing countries, such as China and India. Diversification of Bangladesh's export base was also necessary, in order to reduce the dependency on garment exports. In 2004 it was feared that increasing political violence would discourage foreign investment in Bangladesh; following a bomb attack on an opposition Awami League (AL) rally in August and subsequent violent protests, India's Tata Group announced that it intended to postpone its planned $2,000m. investment in the country. Ongoing general strikes, orchestrated by the political opposition, also proved economically damaging, as did severe flooding in mid-2004. It was hoped, however, that the formation of an independent Anti-Corruption Commission in November 2004 would improve the country's image abroad and lead to increased foreign investment in the long term. In January 2005 the Governments of Bangladesh, India and Myanmar announced that they had agreed, in principle, to co-operate on a gas pipeline and exploration project. It was intended that a pipeline would be constructed between Myanmar and India, passing through Bangladesh, which could receive as much as $125m. annually in transit and other fees from the agreement. The economy was not expected to meet the Government's target of 5.5% growth in GDP in 2004/05, owing primarily to the effects of flooding. However, growth of 5.1% was forecast.

Education

The Government provides free schooling for children of both sexes for eight years. Primary education, which is compulsory, begins at six years of age and lasts for five years. Secondary education, beginning at the age of 11, lasts for up to seven years, comprising a first cycle of five years and a second cycle of two further years. In 2000/01 an estimated 100% of children (100% of boys; 101% of girls) in the relevant age-group attended primary schools, while the enrolment ratio at secondary schools was 46% of children (45% of boys; 47% of girls) in the relevant age-group. Secondary schools and colleges in the private sector vastly outnumber government institutions. There are 13 state universities, including one for agriculture, one for Islamic studies and one for engineering. The Government launched an Open University Project in 1992 at an estimated cost of US $34.3m. The 2004/05 budget allocated 47,060m. taka to education and technology (equivalent to 13.8% of total government expenditure).

Public Holidays

2005: 1 January (New Year's Day), 21 January* (Id al-Adha, Feast of the Sacrifice), 10 February* (Muharram, Islamic New Year), 21 February (Shaheed Day and International Mother Language Day), 17 March (Birth of the Father of the Nation), 26 March (Independence Day), 14 April (Bengali New Year), 21 April* (Birth of the Prophet), 29 April* (Buddha Purnima), 1 May (May Day), 7 July (First Monday in July), 15 August (National Mourning Day), 20 August* (Janmashtami), 2 September (Shab-i Bharat, Ascension of the Prophet), 11 October* (Durga Puja), 4 November* (Id al-Fitr, end of Ramadan), 7 November (National Revolution Day), 16 December (Victory Day), 25 December (Christmas), 26 December (Boxing Day), 31 December (Bank Holiday).

2006: 1 January (New Year's Day), 11 January* (Id al-Adha, Feast of the Sacrifice), 31 January* (Muharram, Islamic New Year), 21 February (Shaheed Day and International Mother Language Day), 17 March (Birth of the Father of the Nation), 26 March (Independence Day), 11 April* (Birth of the Prophet), 14 April (Bengali New Year), 1 May (May Day), 13 May* (Buddha Purnima), 3 July (First Monday in July), 15 August (National Mourning Day), 16 August* (Janmashtami), 22 August* (Shab-i Bharat, Ascension of the Prophet), 29 September* (Durga Puja), 24 October* (Id al-Fitr, end of Ramadan), 7 November (National Revolution Day), 16 December (Victory Day), 25 December (Christmas), 26 December (Boxing Day), 31 December (Bank Holiday).

* Dates of certain religious holidays are subject to the sighting of the moon, and there are also optional holidays for different religious groups.

Weights and Measures

The imperial system of measures is in force, pending the introduction of the metric system. The following local units of weight are also used:

1 maund = 82.28 lb (37.29 kg).

1 seer = 2.057 lb (932 grams).

1 tola = 180 grains (11.66 grams).

Statistical Survey

Source (unless otherwise stated): Bangladesh Bureau of Statistics, Statistics Division, Ministry of Planning, E-27/A, Agargaon, Sher-e-bangla Nagar, Dhaka 1207; tel. (2) 9118045; fax (2) 9111064; e-mail ndbp@bangla.net; internet www.bbsgov.org.

Area and Population

AREA, POPULATION AND DENSITY

Area (sq km)	147,570*
Population (census results)	
11 March 1991†	111,455,185
22 January 2001‡	
Males	65,841,419
Females	63,405,814
Total	129,247,233
Population (UN estimates at mid-year)§	
2001	140,880,000
2002	143,809,000
2003	146,736,000
Density (per sq km) at mid-2003	994.3

* 56,977 sq miles.
† Including adjustment for underenumeration, estimated to have been 3.08%.
‡ Preliminary result; including adjustment for underenumeration, estimated to have been 4.95%.
§ Source: UN, *World Population Prospects: The 2002 Revision*. Figures do not take into account results of the 2001 census.

ADMINISTRATIVE DIVISIONS
(2001 census, preliminary figures)

Division	Area (sq km)	Population ('000)*	Density (per sq km)
Barisal	13,297	8,514	640.3
Chittagong	33,771	25,187	745.8
Dhaka	31,119	40,592	1,304.4
Khulna	22,274	15,185	681.7
Rajshahi	34,513	31,478	912.1
Sylhet	12,596	8,291	658.2
Total	147,570	129,247	875.8

* Including adjustments for net underenumeration.

PRINCIPAL TOWNS
(population at 1991 census)*

Dhaka (capital) . .	3,612,850	Comilla	135,313
Chittagong . . .	1,392,860	Nawabganj . . .	130,577
Khulna	663,340	Dinajpur	127,815
Rajshahi	294,056	Bogra	120,170
Narayanganj . .	276,549	Sylhet	114,300
Sitakunda . .	274,903	Brahmanbaria . .	109,032
Rangpur	191,398	Tangail	106,004
Mymensingh			
(Nasirabad) . .	188,713	Jamalpur	103,556
Barisal (Bakerganj) .	170,232	Pabna	103,277
Tongi (Tungi) . .	168,702	Naogaon	101,266
Jessore	139,710	Sirajganj	99,669

* Figures in each case refer to the city proper. The population of the largest urban agglomerations at the 1991 census was: Dhaka 6,487,459 (including Narayanganj and Tongi); Chittagong 2,079,968 (including Sitakunda); Khulna 921,365; Rajshahi 507,435; Mymensingh 273,350; Sylhet 225,541; Comilla 225,259; Rangpur 208,294; Barisal 202,746; Jessore 169,349; Bogra 161,155.

2001 (preliminary census figures, urban agglomerations): Dhaka 9,912,908 (including Narayanganj 230,294 and Tongi 281,928); Chittagong 3,202,710 (including Patiya 47,625); Khulna 1,227,239; Rajshahi 646,716.

Mid-2003 (UN estimate, incl. suburbs): Dhaka 11,560,211 (Source: UN, *World Urbanization Prospects: The 2003 Revision*).

BIRTHS, MARRIAGES AND DEATHS*

	Registered live births (rate per 1,000)	Registered deaths (rate per 1,000)
1990	32.8	11.4
1991	31.6	11.2
1992	30.8	11.0
1993	28.8	10.0
1994	27.8	9.0
1995	26.5	8.4
1996	25.6	8.1

* Registration is incomplete. According to UN estimates, the average annual rates per 1,000 were: Births 35.9 in 1990–95, 32.5 in 1995–2000; Deaths 11.4 in 1990–95, 9.8 in 1995–2000 (Source: UN, *World Population Prospects: The 2002 Revision*).

1997 (provisional): Registered live births 3,057,000 (birth rate 24.6 per 1,000); Registered deaths 958,000 (death rate 7.7 per 1,000) (Source: UN, *Population and Vital Statistics Report*).

Marriages: 1,181,000 in 1997 (Source: UN, *Demographic Yearbook*).

Expectation of life (WHO estimates, years at birth): 62.6 (males 62.6; females 62.6) in 2002 (Source: WHO, *World Health Report*).

ECONOMICALLY ACTIVE POPULATION*
(sample survey, '000 persons aged 15 years and over, year ending June 2000)

	Males	Females	Total
Agriculture, hunting, forestry and fishing	17,256	14,914	32,171
Mining and quarrying	107	188	295
Manufacturing	2,346	1,436	3,783
Electricity, gas and water . . .	116	18	134
Construction	999	100	1,099
Trade, restaurants and hotels . .	5,769	506	6,275
Transport, storage and communications	2,432	77	2,509
Financing, insurance, real estate and business services . . .	357	46	403
Community, social and personal services	1,243	1,726	2,969
Activities not adequately defined .	1,744	384	2,126
Total employed	32,369	19,395	51,764
Unemployed	1,083	666	1,750
Total labour force	33,452	20,061	53,514

* Figures exclude members of the armed forces.
Note: Totals may not be equal to sum of components, owing to rounding.

Source: ILO.

Mid-2003 (estimates in '000): Agriculture, etc. 39,466; Total labour force 74,834 (Source: FAO).

Health and Welfare

KEY INDICATORS

Total fertility rate (children per woman, 2002)	3.5
Under-five mortality rate (per 1,000 live births, 2003) . .	69
HIV/AIDS (% of persons aged 15–49, 2001)	<0.1
Physicians (per 1,000 head, 1997)	0.20
Hospital beds (per 1,000 head, 1994)	0.30
Health expenditure (2001): US $ per head (PPP)	58
Health expenditure (2001): % of GDP	3.5
Health expenditure (2001): public (% of total)	44.2
Access to water (% of persons, 2002)	75
Access to sanitation (% of persons, 2002)	48
Human Development Index (2002): ranking	138
Human Development Index (2002): value	0.509

For sources and definitions, see explanatory note on p. vi.

Agriculture

PRINCIPAL CROPS
('000 metric tons, year ending 30 June)

	2000/01	2001/02	2002/03
Wheat	1,673	1,606	1,507
Rice (paddy)	36,269	37,593	39,090
Millet*	57	57	57
Potatoes	3,216	2,994	3,386
Sweet potatoes	357	346	332
Sugar cane	6,742	6,502	6,838
Other sugar crops	300	278	298
Beans (dry)	53	49	48
Lentils	126	115	116
Other pulses	191	180	181
Groundnuts (in shell)	27	34	34
Areca nuts (betel)	47	51	51*
Coconuts	89	87*	88
Rapeseed	238	233	218
Sesame seed†	49	49	49
Linseed†	50	50	50
Cottonseed	30	24	30†
Cabbages	115	119	118
Lettuce	35	30	31
Spinach	27	27	28
Tomatoes	100	103	102
Cauliflower	79	82	84
Pumpkins, squash and gourds	206	200	213
Dry onions	127	150	153
Garlic	39	41	43
Beans (green)	50	51	50
Other vegetables	911	920	907
Cantaloupes and other melons	85	86	85
Mangoes	188	187	243
Pineapples	152	153	154
Bananas	606	654	650
Papayas	44	48	48
Other fruits and berries	417	424	456
Tea (made)	52	53†	57†
Tobacco (leaves)	37	38	40*
Pimento and allspice	141	136	137
Ginger	42	43	43
Other spices	48	48	48
Jute	859	800	792

* FAO estimate(s).
† Unofficial figure(s).
Source: FAO.

LIVESTOCK
(FAO estimates, '000 head, year ending September)

	2001	2002	2003
Cattle	24,100	24,300	24,500
Buffaloes	850	850	850
Sheep	1,143	1,194	1,260
Goats	34,400	36,900	34,500
Chickens	140,000	140,000	140,000
Ducks	11,700	11,500	13,000

Source: FAO.

LIVESTOCK PRODUCTS
('000 metric tons)

	2001	2002	2003
Beef and veal	174.4*	178.4*	180.0†
Buffalo meat	3.6*	3.6*	3.6†
Mutton and lamb	2.6*	2.8*	3.0†
Goat meat	129*	137*	130†
Chicken meat	98.5*	101.0*	102.0†
Duck meat	13.5*	14.0*	13.0†
Cows' milk†	784	791	797
Buffalo milk†	22.8	22.8	22.8
Sheep's milk†	22.8	23.8	25.1
Goats' milk†	1,320	1,416	1,328
Ghee*	17.0	17.5	17.9
Hen eggs†	133.5	134.5	134.5
Other poultry eggs†	26	26	26
Cattle and buffalo hides†	32.3	32.7	32.9
Goatskins†	38.8	41.6	41.8

* Unofficial figure(s).
† FAO estimate(s).
Source: FAO.

Forestry

ROUNDWOOD REMOVALS
('000 cubic metres, excl. bark)

	2001	2002	2003
Sawlogs, veneer logs and logs for sleepers*	174	174	174
Pulpwood	34	18	18
Other industrial wood	380†	63	90
Fuel wood†	27,799	27,763	27,728
Total	28,387	28,018	28,010

* Annual output assumed to be unchanged since 1996.
† FAO estimate(s).
Source: FAO.

SAWNWOOD PRODUCTION
('000 cubic metres, incl. railway sleepers)

	2001	2002	2003
Total (all broadleaved)	79*	255	388

* FAO estimate.
Source: FAO.

Fishing

('000 metric tons, live weight)

	2000	2001	2002
Capture	1,004.3	1,068.4	1,103.9
Freshwater fishes	591.3	613.9	620.2
Hilsa shad	219.5	229.7	220.6
Marine fishes	162.0	193.7	231.0
Aquaculture	657.1	712.6	786.6
Roho labeo	120.4	133.0	144.8
Catla	104.4	110.6	127.7
Silver carp	120.8	152.1	170.2
Penaeus shrimps	59.1	55.5	57.6
Total catch	1,661.4	1,781.1	1,890.5

Source: FAO.

Mining

(million cubic feet, year ending 30 June)

	1999/2000	2000/01	2001/02
Natural gas	332,389	373,372	391,530

Source: IMF, *Bangladesh: Statistical Appendix* (June 2003).

Industry

SELECTED PRODUCTS
('000 metric tons, unless otherwise indicated; year ending 30 June)

	2000/01	2001/02	2002/03
Refined sugar	96.3	204.3	177.4
Cigarettes (million)	20,120	20,344	20,418
Cotton yarn ('000 bales)* . . .	338	336	358
Woven cotton fabrics ('000 metres)	14,731	15,860	17,834
Jute fabrics†	325.6	319.4	312.1
Newsprint	11.2	3.0	n.a.
Other paper	40.0	37.4	30.3
Fertilizers	2,073.7	1,752.5	2,263.5

* 1 bale = 180 kg.
† Production of jute mills.

2003/04 ('000 metric tons): Paper (excl. newsprint) 28.9; Fertilizers 2,198.2.

Source: Bangladesh Bank.

Finance

CURRENCY AND EXCHANGE RATES

Monetary Units
100 poisha = 1 taka.

Sterling, Dollar and Euro Equivalents (31 December 2004)
£1 sterling = 117.318 taka;
US $1 = 60.742 taka;
€1 = 84.737 taka;
1,000 taka = £8.52 = $16.46 = €12.09.

Average Exchange Rate (taka per US $)
2002   57.888
2003   58.150
2004   59.513

BUDGET
(million taka, year ending 30 June)

Revenue	2002/03*	2003/04*	2004/05†
Taxation	249,500	283,000	336,400
Customs duties	58,750	73,000	89,030
Income and profit taxes . .	47,880	52,700	62,770
Excise duties	3,100	1,700	1,800
Value-added tax	124,610	140,050	164,250
Other revenue	61,700	71,000	76,600
Total	311,200	354,000	413,000

Expenditure	2002/03*	2003/04*	2004/05†
General public services . . .	40,590	45,770	71,060
Local government and rural development	6,330	8,110	10,190
Defence	34,060	37,780	38,660
Public order and safety . . .	19,470	21,940	24,120
Education and technology . . .	40,410	45,620	47,060
Health	13,340	14,970	16,520
Social security and welfare . .	9,410	13,140	16,550
Housing	3,690	4,720	5,240
Recreation, culture and religious affairs	3,150	3,900	3,520
Fuel and energy	90	90	100
Agriculture, forestry and fishing .	9,670	12,740	21,270
Industrial and economic services .	1,320	1,440	1,480
Transport and communications .	15,800	19,190	19,580
Interest payments	55,740	58,420	65,330
Gross current expenditure . .	253,070	287,830	340,680

* Revised figures.
† Forecasts.

Source: Ministry of Finance (Finance Division).

PUBLIC-SECTOR DEVELOPMENT EXPENDITURE
(million taka, year ending 30 June)

	2000/01*	2001/02*	2002/03†
Agriculture	9,000	8,000	8,527
Rural development	18,000	17,000	17,205
Water and flood control . . .	10,000	10,000	8,454
Industry	4,000	3,000	3,344
Power, scientific research and natural resources	30,000	25,000	28,451
Transport‡	26,000	32,000	34,862
Communications	5,000	7,000	8,707
Physical planning and housing .	12,000	12,000	12,135
Education	23,000	22,000	30,641
Health, population and family welfare	17,000	14,000	18,119
Social welfare§	2,000	2,000	2,981
Other sectoral	—	3,000	3,464
Total sectoral allocations . .	156,000	155,000	176,890
Block allocations	11,000	10,000	13,040
Food for Work	4,000	3,000	3,940
Technical assistance	5,000	5,000	—
Domestic self-financing	3,000	2,000	2,070
Total development expenditure	175,000‖	160,000‖	192,000

* IMF estimates, rounded to nearest 1,000m. taka.
† Forecasts.
‡ Includes Jamuna Bridge.
§ Includes employment.
‖ Total expenditure figures are based on revised budget estimates and may differ from the sum of sectoral components.

Sources: IMF, *Bangladesh: Statistical Appendix* (June 2003); Ministry of Finance (Economic Relations Division).

INTERNATIONAL RESERVES
(US $ million at 31 December)

	2001	2002	2003
Gold*	30.6	39.2	46.3
IMF special drawing rights . .	1.2	2.2	3.2
Reserve position in IMF . . .	0.2	0.3	0.3
Foreign exchange	1,273.6	1,680.7	2,574.4
Total	1,305.6	1,722.4	2,624.2

* Valued at market-related prices.

Source: IMF, *International Financial Statistics.*

MONEY SUPPLY
(million taka at 31 December)

	2001	2002	2003
Currency outside banks . . .	127,863	133,895	144,556
Demand deposits at deposit money banks*	114,572	120,705	129,272
Total money (incl. others) . .	242,437	254,717	274,021

* Comprises the scheduled banks plus the agricultural and industrial development banks.

Source: IMF, *International Financial Statistics.*

COST OF LIVING
(Consumer Price Index, year ending 30 June; base: 1995/96 = 100)

	2001/02	2002/03	2003/04
Food, beverages and tobacco . .	132.4	137.0	146.5
Rent, fuel and lighting	125.0	131.2	136.2
Household requisites	126.1	132.3	138.0
Clothing and footwear	124.6	130.6	136.3
Transport and communications .	144.4	159.5	170.8
All items (incl. others)	130.3	136.0	143.9

Source: Bangladesh Bank.

NATIONAL ACCOUNTS

Expenditure on the Gross Domestic Product
('000 million taka at current prices, year ending 30 June)

	2000/01	2001/02	2002/03
Government final consumption expenditure	114.3	136.6	149.0
Private final consumption expenditure	1,964.9	2,099.2	2,308.0
Gross capital formation	585.4	632.4	697.4
Statistical discrepancy	26.1	−5.8	17.5
Total domestic expenditure	2,690.6	2,862.4	3,171.9
Exports of goods and services	390.0	390.0	398.2
Less Imports of goods and services	545.1	520.4	565.2
GDP in purchasers' values	2,535.5	2,732.0	3,004.9
GDP at constant 1995/96 prices	2,157.4	2,252.6	2,372.6

Source: IMF, *International Financial Statistics*.

Gross Domestic Product by Economic Activity
(million taka at current prices, year ending 30 June)

	2001/02	2002/03	2003/04*
Agriculture and forestry	460,030	487,980	509,910
Fishing	138,970	142,590	149,660
Mining and quarrying	29,970	33,090	36,380
Manufacturing	418,050	458,130	515,010
Electricity, gas and water	36,400	39,890	44,330
Construction	211,590	230,160	260,630
Trade, hotels and restaurants	370,520	410,470	463,110
Transport, storage and communications	255,240	311,120	359,410
Financial, real estate and business services	282,020	303,960	327,250
Public administration and defence	71,170	77,830	84,930
Other services	361,290	403,510	458,190
Statistical discrepancy	—	—	870
Sub-total	2,635,250	2,898,730	3,209,680
Import duties	96,760	107,070	115,990
GDP in purchasers' values	2,732,010	3,005,800	3,325,670

* Provisional figures.

Source: Bangladesh Bank.

BALANCE OF PAYMENTS
(US $ million)

	2001	2002	2003
Exports of goods f.o.b.	6,084.7	6,102.4	6,928.2
Imports of goods f.o.b.	−8,133.4	−7,780.1	−9,349.3
Trade balance	−2,048.7	−1,677.8	−2,421.1
Exports of services	752.2	848.7	978.8
Imports of services	−1,521.5	−1,405.7	−1,710.4
Balance on goods and services	−2,818.0	−2,234.8	3,152.7
Other income received	76.6	56.8	55.7
Other income paid	−361.9	−322.0	−278.8
Balance on goods, services and income	−3,103.3	−2,500.1	−3,375.8
Current transfers received	2,572.8	3,245.4	3,565.0
Current transfers paid	−4.9	−6.0	−6.7
Current balance	−535.4	739.3	182.5
Capital account (net)	235.4	363.7	298.1
Direct investment abroad	n.a.	−2.7	−5.9
Direct investment from abroad	78.5	52.3	102.5
Portfolio investment assets	0.1	−1.2	—
Portfolio investment liabilities	−3.5	−1.4	1.6
Other investment assets	−433.8	−560.4	−557.9
Other investment liabilities	620.7	257.1	670.3
Net errors and omissions	−106.0	−349.3	196.0
Overall balance	−143.9	497.4	887.1

Source: IMF, *International Financial Statistics*.

FOREIGN AID DISBURSEMENTS
(US $ million, year ending 30 June)

	1999/2000	2000/01	2001/02
Bilateral donors	785	706	709
Canada	28	19	18
China, People's Republic	18	26	12
Denmark	29	5	29
France	1	6	20
Germany	21	43	21
India	4	20	7
Japan	390	316	287
Kuwait	8	36	12
Netherlands	28	19	1
Norway	19	17	9
Sweden	20	16	7
United Kingdom	61	53	21
USA	92	39	20
Multilateral donors	790	663	733
Asian Development Bank	283	236	182
International Development Association	354	299	323
European Union	5	32	80
International Fund for Agricultural Development	15	—	12
UN Development Programme	7	17	10
World Food Programme	68	1	30
UNICEF	27	49	46
Islamic Development Bank	16	16	23
Total aid disbursements	1,575	1,369	1,442

Source: IMF, *Bangladesh: Statistical Appendix* (June 2003).

External Trade

PRINCIPAL COMMODITIES
(US $ million, year ending 30 June)

Imports c.i.f.	2001/02	2002/03	2003/04
Edible oil	251	364	471
Petroleum products	481	620	770
Chemicals	335	353	406
Plastics, rubber and articles thereof	250	281	367
Cotton	312	393	583
Yarn	283	270	323
Textiles	1,063	1,106	1,295
Iron and steel	413	455	479
Capital goods	2,617	2,660	2,875
Total (incl. others)	8,540	9,658	10,903

Exports f.o.b.	2001/02	2002/03	2003/04
Raw jute	61	82	80
Jute goods (excl. carpets)	242	257	247
Leather and leather products	207	191	211
Frozen shrimp and fish	276	322	390
Ready-made garments	3,125	3,258	3,538
Knitwear and hosiery products	1,459	1,654	2,148
Total (incl. others)	5,986	6,548	7,603

Source: Bangladesh Bank.

PRINCIPAL TRADING PARTNERS
(US $ million)

Imports c.i.f.	2001	2002	2003
Australia	215	172	174
China, People's Republic	772	910	1,326
Hong Kong	462	422	471
India	1,195	1,146	1,444
Japan	721	595	611
Korea, Republic	404	341	358
Singapore	827	906	910
Thailand	180	163	263
United Kingdom	238	223	137
USA	265	234	247
Total (incl. others)	9,011	7,848	9,388

Exports f.o.b.	2001	2002	2003
Belgium	180	188	265
Canada	96	83	131
France	308	311	404
Germany	588	566	956
Hong Kong	101	101	80
Italy	263	216	251
Netherlands	251	208	279
Spain	88	104	188
United Kingdom	487	532	782
USA	1,697	1,504	1,765
Total (incl. others)	5,736	5,443	7,012

Source: Asian Development Bank, *Key Indicators of Developing Asian and Pacific Countries.*

Transport

RAILWAYS
(traffic, year ending 30 June)

	1995/96	1996/97	1997/98
Passenger-km (million)	3,333	3,754	3,855
Freight ton-km (million) . . .	689	782	804

Source: UN, *Statistical Yearbook.*

ROAD TRAFFIC
(motor vehicles in use at 31 December)

	1997	1998	1999*
Passenger cars	54,784	57,068	60,846
Buses and coaches	29,310	30,361	32,371
Lorries and vans	40,084	42,425	45,234
Road tractors	2,769	2,813	2,999
Motorcycles and mopeds . . .	125,259	145,259	147,205
Total	252,206	277,926	288,655

* Estimates.

Source: International Road Federation, *World Road Statistics.*

SHIPPING

Merchant Fleet
(registered at 31 December)

	2001	2002	2003
Number of vessels	317	325	327
Total displacement ('000 grt) . .	387.6	432.4	446.8

Source: Lloyd's Register-Fairplay, *World Fleet Statistics.*

International Sea-borne Freight Traffic
('000 metric tons, year ending 30 June)

	2000/01	2001/02	2002/03
Total goods loaded	888	888	996
Total goods unloaded	15,984	14,784	13,632

Source: UN, *Monthly Bulletin of Statistics.*

CIVIL AVIATION
(traffic on scheduled services)

	1999	2000	2001
Kilometres flown (million) . . .	21	25	27
Passengers carried ('000) . . .	1,215	1,331	1,450
Passenger-km (million)	3,515	3,988	4,395
Total ton-km (million)	545	632	599

Source: UN, *Statistical Yearbook.*

Tourism

TOURIST ARRIVALS BY COUNTRY OF NATIONALITY

	1999	2000	2001
Canada	2,461	2,723	5,484
China, People's Republic . . .	5,208	5,901	6,867
India	62,935	74,268	78,090
Japan	7,055	8,006	7,090
Korea, Republic	6,596	6,746	6,896
Malaysia	2,890	3,827	3,204
Nepal	4,733	4,481	4,280
Pakistan	7,894	10,637	7,010
United Kingdom	22,510	29,106	34,087
USA	9,557	11,924	13,394
Total (incl. others)	172,781	199,211	207,199

Source: World Tourism Organization, *Yearbook of Tourism Statistics.*

Tourism receipts (US $ million): 50 in 1999; 50 in 2000; 48 in 2001 (Source: World Bank, *World Development Indicators*).

Communications Media

	2001	2002	2003
Telephones ('000 main lines in use)	564.9	605.9	740.0
Mobile cellular telephones ('000 subscribers)*	520	1,075	1,365
Personal computers ('000 in use) .	250	450	1,050
Internet users ('000)	186	204	243

* Twelve months ending 30 June of year stated.

Radio receivers ('000 in use): 6,150 in 1997.

Television receivers ('000 in use): 2,200 in 2001.

Facsimile machines (number in use, year ending 30 June 1998, provisional): 75,000.

Newspapers (provisional, 1998): *Daily:* 233 titles with average circulation of 6,658,000. *Non-daily incl. periodicals:* 509 titles with average circulation of 9,256,000.

Books published: 483 titles in 1998.

Sources: mainly UNESCO, *Statistical Yearbook*; UN, *Statistical Yearbook*; International Telecommunication Union.

Education
(2000)

	Institutions	Teachers	Students
Primary schools*	66,235	250,990	17,627,000
Secondary schools	16,095	187,338	7,746,885
Universities (government)† . .	13	5,172	85,224

Technical institutes (2000): 138 institutions, 2,560 teachers, 44,832 students.

* 1997/98, provisional.
† Provisional figures.

Source: Ministry of Education.

Adult literacy rate (UNESCO estimates): 41.1% (males 50.3%; females 31.4%) in 2002 (Source: UN Development Programme, *Human Development Report*).

Directory

The Constitution

The members who were returned from East Pakistan (now Bangladesh) for the Pakistan National Assembly and the Provincial Assembly in the December 1970 elections formed the Bangladesh Constituent Assembly. A new Constitution for the People's Republic of Bangladesh was approved by this Assembly on 4 November 1972 and came into effect on 16 December 1972. Following the military coup of 24 March 1982, the Constitution was suspended, and the country was placed under martial law. On 10 November 1986 martial law was repealed and the suspended Constitution was revived. The main provisions of the Constitution, including amendments, are listed below.

SUMMARY

Fundamental Principles of State Policy

The Constitution was initially based on the fundamental principles of nationalism, socialism, democracy and secularism, but in 1977 an amendment replaced secularism with Islam. The amendment states that the country shall be guided by 'the principles of absolute trust and faith in the Almighty Allah, nationalism, democracy and socialism'. A further amendment in 1988 established Islam as the state religion. The Constitution aims to establish a society free from exploitation in which the rule of law, fundamental human rights and freedoms, justice and equality are to be secured for all citizens. A socialist economic system is to be established to ensure the attainment of a just and egalitarian society through state and co-operative ownership as well as private ownership within limits prescribed by law. A universal, free and compulsory system of education shall be established. In foreign policy the State shall endeavour to consolidate, preserve, and strengthen fraternal relations among Muslim countries based on Islamic solidarity.

Fundamental Rights

All citizens are equal before the law and have a right to its protection. Arbitrary arrest or detention, discrimination based on race, age, sex, birth, caste or religion, and forced labour are prohibited. Subject to law, public order and morality, every citizen has freedom of movement, of assembly and of association. Freedom of conscience, of speech, of the press and of religious worship are guaranteed.

GOVERNMENT

The President

The President is the constitutional Head of State and is elected by Parliament (Jatiya Sangsad) for a term of five years. He is eligible for re-election. The supreme control of the armed forces is vested in the President. He appoints the Prime Minister and other Ministers as well as the Chief Justice and other judges.

The Executive

Executive authority shall rest in the Prime Minister and shall be exercised by him either directly or through officers subordinate to him in accordance with the Constitution.

There shall be a Council of Ministers to aid and advise the Prime Minister.

The Legislature

Parliament (Jatiya Sangsad) is a unicameral legislature. It comprises 345 members, including 45 women members elected by the other members on the basis of proportional representation. Members of Parliament, other than the 45 women members, are directly elected on the basis of universal adult franchise from single territorial constituencies. Persons aged 18 and over are entitled to vote. The parliamentary term lasts for five years. War can be declared only with the assent of Parliament. In the case of actual or imminent invasion, the President may take whatever action he may consider appropriate.

THE JUDICIARY

The Judiciary comprises a Supreme Court with High Court and an Appellate Division. The Supreme Court consists of a Chief Justice and such other judges as may be appointed by the President. The High Court division has such original appellate and other jurisdiction and powers as are conferred on it by the Constitution and by other law. The Appellate Division has jurisdiction to determine appeals from decisions of the High Court division. Subordinate courts, in addition to the Supreme Court, have been established by law.

ELECTIONS

An Election Commission supervises elections, delimits constituencies and prepares electoral rolls. It consists of a Chief Election Commissioner and other Commissioners as may be appointed by the President. The Election Commission is independent in the exercise of its functions. Subject to the Constitution, Parliament may make provision as to elections where necessary.

The Government

HEAD OF STATE

President: Prof. Iajuddin Ahmed (took office 6 September 2002).

COUNCIL OF MINISTERS
(April 2005)

Prime Minister and Minister of the Armed Forces Division, of Defence, of the Cabinet Division, of Power, Energy and Mineral Resources, of Chittagong Hill Tracts Affairs, of the Primary and Mass Education Division, and of Establishment: Begum Khaleda Zia.

Minister of Foreign Affairs: M. Morshed Khan.

Minister of Local Government, Rural Development and Co-operatives: Abdul Mannan Bhuiyan.

Minister of Finance and of Planning: M. Saifur Rahman.

Minister of Education: Dr Osman Faruque.

Minister of Water Resources: Maj. (retd) Hafizuddin Ahmad.

Minister of Commerce: Air Vice-Marshal (retd) Altaf Hossain Chowdhury.

Minister of Industries: Matiur Rahman Nizami.

Minister of Post and Telecommunications: Mohammad Aminul Haque.

Minister of Information: M. Shamsul Islam.

Minister of Agriculture: M. K. Anwar.

Minister of Housing and Public Works: Mirza Abbas.

Minister of Law, Justice and Parliamentary Affairs: Moudud Ahmed.

Minister of Communications: Nazmul Huda.

Minister of Women and Children's Affairs: Khurshid Jahan Haque.

Minister of Health and Family Welfare: Dr Khandaker M. Hossain.

Minister of Social Welfare: Ali Ahsan Muhammad Mujahid.

Minister of Environment and Forests: Tariqul Islam.

Minister of Textiles and Jute: Shahjahan Siraj.

Minister of Food and Disaster Management: Kamal Ibne Yusuf Chowdhury.

Minister of Shipping: Lt-Col (retd) Akbar Hossain.

Minister of Science and Information and Communication Technology: Dr Abdul Moyeen Khan.

Minister of Fisheries and Livestock: Abdullah al-Noman.

Minister without Portfolio: Abdul Matin Chowdhury.

There are also 23 Ministers of State and four Deputy Ministers.

MINISTRIES

Prime Minister's Office: Old Sangsad Bhaban, Tejgaon, Dhaka 1215; tel. (2) 8155100; fax (2) 8113244; e-mail pm@pmo.gov.bd; internet www.pmo.gov.bd.

Ministry of Agriculture: Bangladesh Secretariat, Bhaban 4, 2nd 9-Storey Bldg, Dhaka; tel. (2) 832137; internet www.bangladesh.gov.bd/moa.

Ministry of Chittagong Hill Tracts Affairs: Dhaka; internet www.bangladesh.gov.bd/mochta.

Ministry of Civil Aviation and Tourism: Bangladesh Secretariat, Bhaban 6, 19th Floor, Dhaka 1000; tel. (2) 866485.

Ministry of Commerce: Bangladesh Secretariat, Bhaban 3, Dhaka 1000; tel. (2) 862826; fax (2) 865741.

Ministry of Communications: Bangladesh Secretariat, Bhaban 7, 1st 9-Storey Bldg, 8th Floor, Dhaka 1000; tel. (2) 868752; fax (2) 866636; internet www.moc.gov.bd.

Ministry of Cultural Affairs: Dhaka; tel. (2) 402133.

Ministry of Defence: Old High Court Bldg, Dhaka; tel. (2) 259082.

Ministry of Education: Bangladesh Secretariat, Bhaban 7, 17th–18th Floors, Dhaka 1000; tel. (2) 404162; e-mail moe1@bdcom.com; internet dns3.bd.com/iactive/moe/index.html.

Ministry of Environment and Forests: Dhaka; tel. (2) 7165436; e-mail admin1@moef.gov.bd; internet www.moef.gov.bd.

Ministry of Establishment: Dhaka; internet www.pacc-moe.gov.bd.

Ministry of Finance: Bangladesh Secretariat, Bhaban 7, 1st 9-Storey Bldg, 3rd Floor, Dhaka 1000; tel. (2) 8690202; fax (2) 865581; internet www.gobfinance.org.

Ministry of Fisheries and Livestock: Dhaka; tel. (2) 862430.

Ministry of Food and Disaster Management: Bangladesh Secretariat, Dhaka; e-mail mof@bttb.net.bd; internet www.mofdm.gov.bd.

Ministry of Foreign Affairs: Segunbagicha, Dhaka 1000; tel. (2) 9556020; fax (2) 9555283; e-mail info@mofabd.org; internet www.mofabd.org.

Ministry of Health and Family Welfare: Bangladesh Secretariat, Main Bldg, 3rd Floor, Dhaka; tel. (2) 832079.

Ministry of Home Affairs: Bangladesh Secretariat, School Bldg, 2nd and 3rd Floors, Dhaka; tel. (2) 404142.

Ministry of Housing and Public Works: Bangladesh Secretariat, Bhaban 5, Dhaka; tel. (2) 834494; fax (2) 861290.

Ministry of Industries: Shilpa Bhaban, 91 Motijheel C/A, Dhaka 1000; tel. (2) 9564250; fax (2) 860588.

Ministry of Information: Bangladesh Secretariat, 2nd 9-Storey Bldg, 8th Floor, Dhaka; tel. (2) 235111; fax (2) 834535; internet www.moi-gob.org.

Ministry of Labour and Employment: Bangladesh Secretariat, 1st 9-Storey Bldg, 4th Floor, Dhaka; tel. (2) 404106; fax (2) 813420.

Ministry of Land: Bangladesh Secretariat, Bhaban 4, 2nd 9-Storey Bldg, 3rd Floor, Dhaka.

Ministry of Local Government, Rural Development and Co-operatives: Bangladesh Secretariat, Bhaban 7, 1st 9-Storey Bldg, 6th Floor, Dhaka.

Ministry of Planning: Block No. 7, Sher-e-Bangla Nagar, Dhaka; tel. (2) 815142; fax (2) 822210.

Ministry of Post and Telecommunications: Bangladesh Secretariat, Bhaban 7, 6th Floor, Dhaka 1000; tel. (2) 864800; fax (2) 865775.

Ministry of Power, Energy and Mineral Resources: Bangladesh Secretariat, Bhaban 6, 1st Floor, Dhaka 1000; tel. (2) 865918; fax (2) 861110.

Ministry of Religious Affairs: Bangladesh Secretariat, Dhaka; tel. (2) 7165800; fax (2) 7165040.

Ministry of Science and Information and Communication Technology: Bangladesh Secretariat, Bhaban 6, Dhaka; tel. (2) 8616144; fax (2) 8619606; e-mail most@bangla.net; internet www.most-bd.org.

Ministry of Shipping: Bangladesh Secretariat, Bhaban 6, 8th Floor, Dhaka 1000; tel. (2) 861275.

Ministry of Social Welfare: Bangladesh Secretariat, Bhaban 6, New Bldg, Dhaka 1000; tel. (2) 7160452; fax (2) 7168969.

Ministry of Textiles and Jute: Bangladesh Secretariat, Bhaban 6, 7th Floor, Dhaka 1000; tel. (2) 8612250; fax (2) 8618766; e-mail jutebd@bangla.net; internet www.bangladesh.gov.bd/jute/jute_information.htm.

Ministry of Water Resources: Dhaka.

Ministry of Women and Children's Affairs: Bangladesh Secretariat, Bhaban 6, Dhaka 1000; tel. (2) 861012; fax (2) 837867.

Ministry of Youth and Sports: Dhaka; tel. (2) 407670.

President and Legislature

PRESIDENT

On 5 September 2002 the Bangladesh Nationalist Party's presidential candidate, Prof. Iajuddin Ahmed, was declared elected unopposed by the Election Commission as Bangladesh's new Head of State.

JATIYA SANGSAD
(Parliament)

Speaker: Jamiruddin Sircar.

General Election, 1 and 9 October 2001

	Seats
Bangladesh Jatiyatabadi Dal (Bangladesh Nationalist Party—BNP)	199*
Awami League (AL)	62
Jamaat-e-Islami Bangladesh	17
Jatiya Dal	14†
Jatiya Dal (Manju)	1
Bangladesh Krishak Sramik Party	1
Independents	6
Total	**300**

In addition to the 300 directly-elected members, a further 45 seats are reserved for women members.

* Includes six seats won by the Jatiya Dal (Naziur-Firoz) and the Islami Jatiya Oikya Jote.

† Includes several seats won by the Islami Jatiya Oikya Front.

Political Organizations

Bangladesh Awami League (AL): 23 Bangabandhu Ave, Dhaka; e-mail info@albd.org; internet www.albd.org; f. 1949; supports parliamentary democracy; advocates socialist economy, but with a private sector, and a secular state; pro-Indian; 28-member central executive committee, 15-member central advisory committee and a 13-member presidium; Pres. Sheikh Hasina Wajed; Gen.-Sec. Abdul Jalil; c. 1,025,000 mems.

Bangladesh Jatiya League: 500A Dhanmandi R/A, Rd 7, Dhaka; f. 1970 as Pakistan National League, renamed in 1972; supports parliamentary democracy; Leader Ataur Rahman Khan; c. 50,000 mems.

Bangladesh Jatiyatabadi Dal (Bangladesh Nationalist Party—BNP): Banani Office, House 23, Rd 13, Dhaka; tel. (2) 8819525; fax (2) 8813063; e-mail bnpbd@e-fsbd.net; internet www.bnpbd.com; f. 1978 by merger of groups supporting Ziaur Rahman, including Jatiyatabadi Gonotantrik Dal (Jagodal—Nationalist Democratic Party); right of centre; favours multi-party democracy and parliamentary system of govt; Chair. Begum Khaleda Zia; Sec.-Gen. Abdul Mannan Bhuiyan, Tarique Rahman.

Bangladesh Khelafat Andolon: 314/2 Lalbagh Kellar Morr, Dhaka 1211; tel. (2) 8612465; fax (2) 9881436; e-mail khelafat@cimabd.com; Supreme Leader Shah Ahmadullah Ashraf Ibn Hafezzee; Sec.-Gen. Maulana Muhammad Zafrullah Khan.

Bangladesh Krishak Sramik Party (Peasants' and Workers' Party): Sonargaon Bhavan, 99 South Kamalapur, Dhaka 1217; tel. (2) 834512; f. 1914; renamed 1953; supports parliamentary democracy, non-aligned foreign policy, welfare state, guarantee of fundamental rights for all religions and races, free market economy and non-proliferation of nuclear weapons; 15-mem. exec. council; Pres. A. S. M. Sulaiman; Sec.-Gen. Rasheed Khan Memon; c. 125,000 mems.

Bangladesh Muslim League: Dhaka; Sec.-Gen. Alhaj Mohammad Zamir Ali.

Bangladesh People's League: Dhaka; f. 1976; supports parliamentary democracy; Leader Garib Newaz; c. 75,000 mems.

Bikalpa Dhara Bangladesh: Dhaka; f. 2004; Pres. Prof. A. Q .M. Badruddoza Chowdhury.

Communist Party of Bangladesh: 'Mukti Vaban', 21/1, Purana Paltan, Dhaka 1000; tel. (2) 9558612; fax (2) 9552333; e-mail cpbdhaka@aitlbd.net; internet www.cpbdhaka.org; f. 1968 following split from Communist Party of Pakistan; Pres. Manzurul Ahasan Khan; Gen. Sec. Mujahidul Islam Selim; c. 22,000 mems.

Democratic League: 68 Jigatola, Dhaka 9; tel. (2) 507994; f. 1976; conservative; Leader Abdur Razzak.

Freedom Party: f. 1987; Islamic; Co-Chair. Lt-Col (retd) Said Faruq Rahman, Lt-Col (retd) Khandakar Abdur Rashid.

Gonoazadi League: 30 Banagran Lane, Dhaka.

Islami Jatiya Oikya Front: Dhaka.

Islami Jatiya Oikya Jote: Dhaka; mem. of the BNP-led alliance; Chair. Maulana Azizul Haq; Sec.-Gen. Mufti Fazlul Haq Amini.

Islamic Solidarity Movement: 84 East Tejturi Bazar, Tejgaon, Dhaka 1215; tel. (2) 325886; fmrly known as Islamic Democratic League; renamed as above in 1984; Chair. Hafiz Muhammad Habibur Rahman.

Jamaat-e-Islami Bangladesh: 505 Elephant Rd, Bara Magh-bazar, Dhaka 1217; tel. (2) 9331581; fax (2) 8312997; e-mail jibco@gtlbd.com; internet www.jamaat-e-islami.org; f. 1941; Islamist party striving to establish an Islamic state through the democratic process; mem. of the BNP-led alliance; Chair. MOTIUR RAHMAN NIZAMI; Sec.-Gen. ALI AHSAN MOHAMMAD MUJAHID.

Jatiya Dal (National Party): c/o Jatiya Sangsad, Dhaka; e-mail ershad@dhaka.agni.com; internet www.jatiyaparty.org; f. 1983 as Jana Dal; reorg. 1986, when the National Front (f. 1985), a five-party alliance of the Jana Dal, the United People's Party, the Gonotantrik Dal, the Bangladesh Muslim League and a breakaway section of the Bangladesh Nationalist Party, formally converted itself into a single pro-Ershad grouping; advocates nationalism, democracy, Islamic ideals and progress; Chair. Lt-Gen. HOSSAIN MOHAMMAD ERSHAD; Sec.-Gen. A. B. M. RUHUL AMIN HAWLADER; in April 1999 a group of dis-sidents, led by MIZANUR RAHMAN CHOWDHURY and ANWAR HUSSAIN MANJU, formed a rival faction; a rival faction, led by Kazi FIROZ RASHID, was also formed.

Jatiya Samajtantrik Dal (JSD—(S)) (National Socialist Party): 23 DIT Ave, Malibagh Choudhury Para, Dhaka; f. 1972; left-wing; Leader SHAJAHAN SIRAJ; c. 5,000 mems.

Jatiya Samajtantrik Dal (Rab): breakaway faction of JSD; Pres. A. S. M. ABDUR RAB; Gen. Sec. HASANUL HAQUE INU.

Jatiyo Gonotantrik Party (JAGPA): Purana Paltan, Dhaka; Jt Gen. Secs AZIZUR RAHMAN, SARDAR SHAHJAHAN.

Jatiyo Janata Party: Janata Bhaban, 47A Toyenbee Circular Rd, Dhaka 1000; tel. (2) 9667923; f. 1976; social democratic; Chair. NURUL ISLAM KHAN; Gen. Sec. MUJIBUR RAHMAN HERO; c. 35,000 mems.

National Awami Party—Bhashani–Mustaq (NAP): Dhaka; f. 1957; Maoist; Leader MUSTAQ AHMED; Gen. Sec. ABDUS SUBHANI.

National Awami Party—Muzaffar (NAP—M): 21 Dhanmandi Hawkers' Market, 1st Floor, Dhaka 5; f. 1957; reorg. 1967; Pres. MUZAFFAR AHMED; Sec.-Gen. PANKAJ BHATTACHARYA; c. 500,000 mems.

Parbattya Chattagram Jana Sanghati Samity: f. 1972; political wing of the Shanti Bahini; represents interests of Buddhist tribals in Chittagong Hill Tracts; Leader JATINDRA BODDHIPRIYA ('SHANTU') LARMA.

Samyabadi Dal: Dhaka; Marxist-Leninist; Leader DILIP BARUA.

Zaker Party: f. 1989; supports sovereignty and the introduction of an Islamic state system; Leader SYED HASMATULLAH; Mem. of the Presidium MUSTAFA AMIR FAISAL.

Diplomatic Representation

EMBASSIES AND HIGH COMMISSIONS IN BANGLADESH

Afghanistan: House CWN(C) 2A, 24 Gulshan Ave, Gulshan Model Town, Dhaka 1212; tel. (2) 9895994; fax (2) 9884767; e-mail afghanembassydhaka@yahoo.com; Ambassador AKMAL GHANI.

Australia: 184 Gulshan Ave, Gulshan Model Town, Dhaka 1212; tel. (2) 8813105; fax (2) 8811125; e-mail ahc.dhaka@dfat.gov.au; internet www.bangladesh.embassy.gov.au; High Commissioner LORRAINE BARKER.

Bhutan: House No. F5(SE), Gulshan Ave, Gulshan Model Town, Dhaka 1212; tel. (2) 886863; fax (2) 8813939; e-mail kutshab@bdmail.net; Ambassador Dasho JIGME TSHULTIM.

Brunei: House 26, Rd 6, Baridhara, Dhaka; tel. (2) 8819552; fax (2) 8819551; e-mail bruhcomm@citechco.net; High Commissioner Dato' Paduka Haji ABDUL MOKTI BIN Haji MOHAMMAD DAUD.

Canada: House 16A, Rd 48, Gulshan 2, Dhaka 1212; tel. (2) 9887091; fax (2) 8823043; e-mail dhaka@international.gc.ca; internet www.dfait-maeci.gc.ca/bangladesh; High Commissioner DAVID SPROULE.

China, People's Republic: Plots 2 and 4, Rd 3, Block 1, Baridhara, Dhaka; tel. (2) 8824862; fax (2) 8823004; e-mail chinaemb@bdmail.net; internet bd.china-embassy.org; Ambassador CHAI XI.

Denmark: House 1, Rd 51, Gulshan Model Town, POB 2056, Dhaka 1212; tel. (2) 8811799; fax (2) 8813638; e-mail dandhaka@mail.citechco.net; internet www.citechco.net/dandhaka; Ambassador NIELS SEVERIN MUNK.

Egypt: House NE(N) 9, Rd 90, Gulshan Model Town, Dhaka 1212; tel. (2) 882766; fax (2) 884883; Ambassador OSSAMA MOHAMED TAWFIK.

France: House 18, Rd 108, Gulshan Model Town, POB 22, Dhaka 1212; tel. (2) 8813812; Ambassador JACQUES COSTILHES.

Germany: 178 Gulshan Ave, Gulshan Model Town, POB 108, Dhaka 1212; tel. (2) 8853521; fax (2) 8853528; e-mail aadhaka@citech-bd.com; internet www.dhaka.diplo.de; Ambassador DIETRICH ANDREAS.

Holy See: United Nations Rd 2, Diplomatic Enclave, Baridhara Model Town, POB 6003, Dhaka 1212; tel. (2) 8822018; fax (2) 8823574; e-mail nuntius@dhaka.net; Apostolic Nuncio Most Rev. PAUL TSCHANG IN-NAM (Titular Archbishop of Amantia).

India: House 2, Rd 142, Gulshan-I, Dhaka; tel. (2) 8820243; fax (2) 8817487; internet www.hcidhaka.org; High Commissioner VEENA SIKRI.

Indonesia: CWS(A) 10, 75 Gulshan Ave, Gulshan Model Town, Dhaka 1212; tel. (2) 600131; fax (2) 885391; Ambassador MANSYUR MADLANGENG.

Iran: CWN(A), 12 Kamal Atatürk Ave, Gulshan Model Town, Dhaka 1212; tel. (2) 601432; Ambassador MOHAMMAD BEHESHTI MONFARED.

Italy: Plots 2 and 3, Rd 74/79, Gulshan Model Town, POB 6062, Dhaka 1212; tel. (2) 8822781; fax (2) 8822578; e-mail ambdhaka@dominox.net; internet dominox.com/italydhaka; Ambassador PIETRO BALLERO.

Japan: 5 and 7, Dutabash Rd, Baridhara, Dhaka; tel. (2) 8810087; fax (2) 8826737; Ambassador MATSUSHIRO HORIGUCHI.

Korea, Democratic People's Republic: House 6, Rd 7, Baridhara Model Town, Dhaka; tel. (2) 601250; Ambassador MUN SONG HO.

Korea, Republic: 4 Madani Ave, Diplomatic Enclave, Baridhara, Dhaka; tel. (2) 872088; fax (2) 883871; e-mail rokdhaka@bangla.net; Ambassador PARK SEONG-UNG.

Kuwait: Plot 39, Rd 23, Block J, Banani, Dhaka 13; tel. (2) 600233; Ambassador ABDULLAH AL-MASUD.

Libya: NE(D), 3A Gulshan Ave (N), Gulshan Model Town, Dhaka 1212; tel. (2) 600141; Chargé d'affaires LUFTI ALAMIN M. MUGHRABI.

Malaysia: House 19, Rd 6, Baridhara, Dhaka 1212; tel. (2) 8827759; fax (2) 8823115; e-mail mwdhaka@citech-bd.net; High Commissioner ASHARRY BIN SANI.

Morocco: House 44, United Nations Road, Baridhara, Dhaka; tel. (2) 8823176; fax (2) 8810028; Ambassador MOHAMMAD SEGROUCHNI.

Myanmar: NE(L) 3, Rd 84, Gulshan 2, Dhaka 1212; tel. (2) 600988; fax (2) 8823740; Ambassador U OHN THWIN.

Nepal: United Nations Rd, Rd 2, Diplomatic Enclave, Baridhara, Dhaka; tel. (2) 601790; fax (2) 8826401; e-mail rnedhaka@bdmail.net; Ambassador BHAGIRATH BASNET.

Netherlands: House 49, Rd 90, Gulshan Model Town, POB 166, Dhaka 1212; tel. (2) 8822715; fax (2) 8823326; e-mail nlgovdha@citech-bd.com; internet www.netherlandsembassydhaka.org; Ambassador KEES BEEMSTERBOER.

Nigeria: House 9, Rd 1, Baridhara, Dhaka; tel. (2) 8817944; fax (2) 8817989; High Commissioner ABDULLAHI MADAKI BAGE.

Norway: House 9, Rd 111, Gulshan, Dhaka 1212; tel. (2) 8823065; fax (2) 8823661; e-mail emb.dhaka@mfa.no; internet www.dhaka.mfa.no; Ambassador AUD LISE NORTHEIN.

Pakistan: House NE(C) 2, Rd 71, Gulshan Model Town, Dhaka 1212; tel. (2) 8825388; fax (2) 8823677; e-mail parepdka@bangla.net; High Commissioner MANZAR SHAFIQ.

Philippines: House 6, Rd 101, Gulshan 2, Dhaka 1212; tel. (2) 9881590; fax (2) 8822686; e-mail philemb1@citechco.net; Ambassador JOSE LINO B. GUERRERO.

Poland: House 12A, Rd 86, Gulshan 2, POB 6089, Dhaka 1212; tel. (2) 8825895; fax (2) 8827568; e-mail pl_dhaka@citech-bd.com; Chargé d'affaires a.i. ZBIGNIEW SMUGA.

Qatar: House 23, Rd 108, Gulshan Model Town, Dhaka 1212; tel. (2) 604477; Ambassador IBRAHIM MOHAMMAD A. AL-ABDULLA.

Russia: NE(J) 9, Rd 79, Gulshan Model Town, Dhaka 1212; tel. (2) 8828147; fax (2) 8823735; e-mail rusemb@citechco.net; Ambassador OLEG S. MALGINOV.

Saudi Arabia: House 12, Rd 92, Gulshan (North), Dhaka 1212; tel. (2) 889124; fax (2) 883616; Ambassador ABDULLAH MOHAMMAD AL-OBAID AL-NAMLA.

Sri Lanka: House NW 15, Rd 50, Gulshan Model Town, Dhaka 1212; tel. (2) 8822790; fax (2) 8823971; e-mail slhc@citechco.net; High Commissioner GAMINI SARATH MUNASINGHE.

Sweden: House 1, Rd 51, Gulshan, Dhaka 1212; tel. (2) 884761; fax (2) 883948; Ambassador BORJE MATTSON.

Thailand: House 14, Rd 11, Baridhara, Dhaka 1212; tel. (2) 8812795; fax (2) 8854280; e-mail thaidac@mfa.go.th; internet www.thaidac.com; Ambassador SUPHAT CHITRANUKROH.

Turkey: House 14A, Rd 62, Gulshan 2, Dhaka 1212; tel. (2) 8823536; fax (2) 8813297; e-mail dakkabe@citechco.net; Ambassador FERIT ERGIN.

United Arab Emirates: POB 6014, Dhaka 1212; tel. (2) 9882244; fax (2) 8823225; e-mail info@uaeembassydhaka.com; internet www .uaeembassydhaka.com; f. 1978; Ambassador KHALFAN BATTAL AL MANSOURI.

United Kingdom: United Nations Rd, Baridhara, POB 6079, Dhaka 1212; tel. (2) 8822705; fax (2) 8826181; e-mail ukcomsec@ bolonline.com; internet www.ukinbangladesh.org; High Commissioner ANWAR CHOWDHURY.

USA: Madani Ave, Baridhara, POB 323, Dhaka 1212; tel. (2) 8824700; fax (2) 8823744; e-mail ustc@bangla.net; internet www .usembassy-dhaka.org; Ambassador HARRY K. THOMAS, Jr.

Viet Nam: House 8, Rd 51, Gulshan 2, Dhaka 1212; tel. and fax (2) 8854051; e-mail vietnam@citech-bd.com; Ambassador NGO VAN HOA.

Judicial System

A judiciary, comprising a Supreme Court with High Court and Appellate Divisions, is in operation (see under Constitution).

Supreme Court

Dhaka 2; tel. (2) 433585.

Chief Justice: SYED J. R. MUDASIR HUSSAIN.

Attorney-General: Gen. A. J. MOHAMMAD ALI.

Deputy Attorney-General: A. M. FAROOQ.

Religion

The results of the 1991 census classified 88.3% of the population as Muslims, 10.5% as caste Hindus and scheduled castes, and the remainder as Buddhists, Christians and tribals.

Freedom of religious worship is guaranteed under the Constitution but, under the 1977 amendment to the Constitution, Islam was declared to be one of the nation's guiding principles and, under the 1988 amendment, Islam was established as the state religion.

BUDDHISM

World Fellowship of Buddhists Regional Centre: Dharmarajik Buddhist Monastery, Atish Dipanker Sarak, Basabo, Dhaka 1214; tel. (2) 7205665; fax (2) 7202503; e-mail drbb@bangla.net; internet www.dhammarajika.com; f. 1962; Pres. Ven. SUDDHANANDA MAHATHERO; Sec.-Gen. P. K. BARUYA.

CHRISTIANITY

Jatiyo Church Parishad (National Council of Churches): POB 220, Dhaka 1000; tel. (2) 9332869; fax (2) 8312996; e-mail nccb@ bangla.net; f. 1949 as East Pakistan Christian Council; four mem. churches; Pres. Dr SAJAL DEWAN; Gen. Sec. SUBODH ADHIKARY.

Church of Bangladesh—United Church

After Bangladesh achieved independence, the Diocese of Dacca (Dhaka) of the Church of Pakistan (f. 1970 by the union of Anglicans, Methodists, Presbyterians and Lutherans) became the autonomous Church of Bangladesh. In 2001 the Church had an estimated 14,000 members. In 1990 a second diocese, the Diocese of Kushtia, was established.

Bishop of Dhaka: Rt Rev. MICHAEL S. BAROI, St Thomas's Church, 54 Johnson Rd, Dhaka 1100; tel. (2) 7116546; fax (2) 7118218; e-mail cbdacdio@bangla.net.

Bishop of Kushtia: Rt Rev. PAUL SHISHIR SARKAR, Church of Bangladesh, 94 N.S. Rd, Thanapara, Kushtia; tel. (71) 3603.

The Roman Catholic Church

For ecclesiastical purposes, Bangladesh comprises one archdiocese and five dioceses. At 31 December 2002 there were an estimated 265,518 adherents in the country.

Catholic Bishops' Conference: Archbishop's House, 1 Kakrail Rd, Ramna, POB 3, Dhaka 1000; tel. (2) 9358247; fax (2) 8314993; e-mail archbp@bangla.net; f. 1978; Pres. Most Rev. MICHAEL ROZARIO (Archbishop of Dhaka).

Secretariat

CBCB Centre, 24c Asad Ave, Mohammadpur, Dhaka 1207; tel. and fax (2) 9127339; e-mail cbcbsec@bdcom.com.

Sec.-Gen. Rt Rev. THEOTONIUS GOMES (Titular Bishop of Zucchabar).

Archbishop of Dhaka: Most Rev. MICHAEL ROZARIO, Archbishop's House, 1 Kakrail Rd, Ramna, POB 3, Dhaka 1000; tel. (2) 8314384; e-mail secabdac@progetelbd.net.

Other Christian Churches

Bangladesh Baptist Sangha: 33 Senpara Parbatta, Mirpur 10, Dhaka 1216; tel. (2) 8012967; fax (2) 9005842; e-mail bbsangha@ bdmail.net; f. 1922; 35,150 mems (2004); Pres. Dr S. M. CHOWDHURY; Gen. Sec. Rev. ROBERT SARKAR.

In early 2002 there were about 51 denominational churches active in the country, including the Bogra Christian Church, the Evangelical Christian Church, the Garo Baptist Union, the Reformed Church of Bangladesh and the Sylhet Presbyterian Synod. The Baptist Sangha was the largest Protestant Church.

The Press

PRINCIPAL DAILIES

Bengali

Ajker Kagoj: Meena House, 116 Arjot Para, Dhaka 1215; tel. (2) 9138245; fax (2) 9139859; e-mail info@ajkerkagoj.com; internet www .ajkerkagoj.com; Editor KAZI SHAHED AHMED; circ. 9,139,848.

Azadi: 9 C.D.A. C/A, Momin Rd, Chittagong; tel. (31) 612380; e-mail azadi@globalctg.net; f. 1960; Editor Prof. MOHAMMAD KHALED; circ. 13,000.

Banglar Bani: 81 Motijheel C/A, Dhaka 1000; tel. (2) 9551173; e-mail bani@bangla.net; f. 1972; Editor Sheikh FAZLUL KARIM SALIM; circ. 20,000.

Daily Jugantor: 12/7, North Kamalpur, Dhaka 1217; tel. (2) 7102701; fax (2) 7101917; e-mail jugantor@gononet.com; internet www.jugantor.com; Editor GOLAM SARWAR.

Dainik Arthaneeti: Bangladesh Media Services Ltd, Biman Bhaban, 5th Floor, 100 Motijheel C/A, Dhaka 1000; tel. (2) 9667789; fax (2) 9555707; e-mail dartho@citecho.net.

Dainik Bhorer Kagoj: 8 Link Rd, Banglamotor, Dhaka; tel. (2) 8625502; fax (2) 8618802; e-mail bkagoj@gononet.com; Editor (vacant); circ. 50,000.

Dainik Birol: 26 R. K. Mission Rd, Motijheel C/A, Dhaka 1203; tel. (2) 7121620; fax (2) 8013721; Chair. of Editorial Bd ABDULLAH AL-NASER.

Dainik Inqilab: 2/1 Ramkrishna Mission Rd, Dhaka 1203; tel. (2) 9563162; fax (2) 9552881; e-mail inqilab@bttb.net; internet www .dailyinqilab.com; Editor A. M. M. BAHAUDDIN; circ. 180,025.

Dainik Ittefaq: 1 Ramkrishna Mission Rd, Dhaka 1203; tel. (2) 7122660; e-mail info@ittefaq.com; internet www.ittefaq.com; f. 1953; Editor RAHAT KHAN; circ. 200,000.

Dainik Jahan: 3/B Shehra Rd, Mymensingh; tel. (91) 5677; f. 1980; Editor MUHAMMAD HABIBUR RAHMAN SHEIKH; circ. 4,000.

Dainik Janakantha (Daily People's Voice): Globe Janakantha Shilpa Paribar, Janakantha Bhaban, Dhaka 1000; tel. (2) 9347780; fax (2) 9351317; e-mail janakantha@citechco.net; internet www .janakantha.net; f. 1993; Man. Editor TOAB KHAN; Exec. Editor BORHAN AHMED; circ. 100,000.

Dainik Janata: 24 Aminbagh, Shanti Nagar, Dhaka 1217; tel. (2) 400498; Editor Dr M. ASADUR RAHMAN.

Dainik Janmabhumi: 110/2 Islampur Rd, Khulna; tel. (41) 721280; fax (41) 724324; e-mail janmo@khulna.bangla.net; f. 1982; Editor (vacant); circ. 30,000.

Dainik Karatoa: Chalkjadu Rd, Bogra 5800; tel. (51) 63660; fax (51) 73057; e-mail abas@bttb.net.bd; f. 1976; Editor MOZAMMEL HAQUE LALU; circ. 44,000.

Dainik Khabar: 137 Shanti Nagar, Dhaka 1217; tel. (2) 406601; f. 1985; Editor MIZANUR RAHMAN MIZAN; circ. 18,000.

Dainik Millat: Dhaka; tel. (2) 242351; Editor CHOWDHURY MOHAMMAD FAROOQ.

Dainik Nava Avijan: Dhaka; tel. (2) 257516; Editor A. S. M. REZAUL HAQUE; circ. 15,000.

Dainik Patrika: 85 Elephant Rd, Maghbazar, Dhaka 1217; tel. (2) 415057; fax (2) 841575; e-mail patrika@citechco.net; Publr and Chief Editor MIA MUSA HOSSAIN; Editor M. FAISAL HASSAN HASSAN (acting).

Dainik Probaha: 3 KDA Ave, Khulna; tel. (41) 722552; f. 1977; Editor ASHRAF-UL-HAQUE; circ. 11,400.

Dainik Purbanchal: 38 Iqbal Nagar Mosque Lane, Khulna 9100; tel. (41) 22251; fax (41) 21432; f. 1974; Editor LIAQUAT ALI; circ. 42,000.

Dainik Rupashi Bangla: Abdur Rashid Rd, Natun Chowdhury Para, Bagicha Gaon, Comilla 3500; tel. (81) 76689; f. 1972; a weekly until 1979; Editor Prof. ABDUL WAHAB; circ. 10,000.

Dainik Sangram: 423 Elephant Rd, Baramaghbazar, Dhaka 1217; tel. (2) 9346448; fax (2) 9330579; e-mail dsangram@bttb.net; f. 1970; Chair. ALI AHSAN MUHAMMAD MUJAHID; Editor ABUL ASAD; circ. 50,000.

Dainik Sphulinga: Amin Villa, P-5 Housing Estate, Jessore 7401; tel. (421) 6433; f. 1971; Editor Mian ABDUS SATTAR; circ. 14,000.

Dainik Uttara: Bahadur Bazar, Dinajpur Town, Dinajpur; tel. (531) 4326; f. 1974; Editor Prof. MUHAMMAD MOHSIN; circ. 8,500.

Ganakantha: Dhaka; f. 1979; morning; Editor JAHANGIR KABIR CHOWDHURY; Exec. Editor SAIYED RABIUL KARIM; circ. 15,000.

Janabarta: 5 Babu Khan Rd, Khulna; tel. (41) 21075; f. 1974; Editor SYED SOHRAB ALI; circ. 4,000.

Jugabheri: Sylhet; tel. (821) 5461; f. 1931; Editor FAHMEEDA RASHEED CHOWDHURY; circ. 6,000.

Manav Jomeen (Human Land): Dhaka; f. 1998; tabloid.

Naya Bangla: 101 Momin Rd, Chittagong; tel. (31) 206247; f. 1978; Editor ABDULLAH AL-SAGIR; circ. 12,000.

Prothom Alo: C. A. Bhaban, 100 Kazi Nazrul Islam Ave, Kaiwan Bazar, Dhaka 1215; tel. (2) 8110081; fax (2) 9130496; e-mail info@prothom-alo.com; internet www.prothom-alo.net; Editor MATIUR RAHMAN.

Protidin: Ganeshtola, Dinajpur; tel. (531) 4555; f. 1980; Editor KHAIRUL ANAM; circ. 3,000.

Runner: Pyari Mohan Das Rd, Bejpara, Jessore; tel. (421) 6943; f. 1980; circ. 2,000.

Sangbad: 36 Purana Paltan, Dhaka 1000; tel. (2) 9558147; fax (2) 9562882; e-mail sangbad@bangla.net; f. 1952; Editor AHMADUL KABIR; circ. 71,050.

Swadhinata: Chittagong; tel. (31) 209644; f. 1972; Editor ABDULLAH AL-HARUN; circ. 4,000.

English

Bangladesh Observer: Observer House, 33 Toyenbee Circular Rd, Motijheel C/A, Dhaka 1000; tel. (2) 235105; e-mail observer@shapla.net; internet www.thebangladeshobserver.com; f. 1949; morning; Editor S. M. ALI; circ. 75,000.

The Bangladesh Today: 9 Motijheel C/A, Dhaka 1000; tel. (2) 9556254; fax (2) 9565257; e-mail editor@thebangladeshtoday.com; internet www.thebangladeshtoday.com; Editor-in-Chief M. ASAFUD-DOWLAH.

Daily Evening News: 26 R. K. Mission Rd, Motijheel C/A, Dhaka 1203; tel. (2) 7121619; fax (2) 8013721; Chair. of Editorial Bd ABDULLAH AL-NASER.

Daily Rupali: 28/A/3 Toyenbee Circular Rd, Dhaka 1000; tel. (2) 235542; fax (2) 9565558; e-mail network@bangla.net; Editor MAFUZUR RAHMAN MITA.

Daily Star: 19 Karwan Bazar, Dhaka 1215; tel. (2) 8124944; fax (2) 8125155; e-mail dseditor@gononet.com; internet www.dailystarnews.com; f. 1991; Publr and Editor MAHFUZ ANAM; circ. 30,000.

Daily Tribune: 38 Iqbal Nagar Mosque Lane, Khulna 9100; tel. (41) 21944; fax (41) 22251; f. 1978; morning; Editor FERDOUSI ALI; circ. 22,000.

Financial Express: 28/1 Toyenbee Circular Rd, 2nd Floor, POB 2526, Dhaka 1000; tel. (2) 9568154; fax (2) 9567049; e-mail tfe@bangla.net; internet www.financialexpress-bd.com; f. 1994; Editor MOAZZEM HOSSAIN.

The Independent: Beximco Media Complex, 32 Kazi Nazrul Islam Ave, Karwan Bazar, Dhaka 1215; tel. (2) 9129938; fax (2) 9127722; e-mail ind@gononet.com; internet www.independent-bangladesh.com; f. 1995; Editor MAHBUBUL ALAM.

New Age: Holiday Bldg, 30 Tejgaon Industrial Area, Dhaka 1208; tel. (2) 8114145; fax (2) 8112247; e-mail newage@bangla.net; internet www.newagebd.com; Editor and Publr ENAYETULLAH KHAN.

New Nation: 1 Ramkrishna Mission Rd, Dhaka 1203; tel. (2) 7122654; fax (2) 7122650; e-mail n.editor@link3.net; internet nation.ittefaq.com; f. 1981; Editor ALAMGIR MOHIUDDIN; circ. 15,000.

People's View: 102 Siraj-ud-Daulla Rd, Chittagong; tel. (31) 227403; f. 1969; Editor SABBIR ISLAM; circ. 3,000.

PERIODICALS

Bengali

Aachal: Dhaka; weekly; Editor FERDOUSI BEGUM.

Adhuna: 1/3 Block F, Lalmatia, Dhaka 1207; tel. (2) 812353; fax (2) 813095; e-mail adab@bdonline.com; f. 1974; quarterly; publ. by the Asscn of Devt Agencies in Bangladesh (ADAB); Exec. Editor MINAR MONSUR; circ. 10,000.

Ahmadi: 4 Bakshi Bazar Rd, Dhaka 1211; tel. (2) 7300808; fax (2) 7300925; e-mail amgb@bol-online.com; f. 1925; fortnightly; Editor-in-Chief M. A. S. MAHMOOD; Exec. Editor MOHAMMAD M. RAHMAN.

Alokpat: 166 Arambagh, Dhaka 1000; tel. (2) 413361; fax (2) 863060; fortnightly; Editor RABBANI JABBAR.

Amod: Chowdhury Para, Comilla 3500; tel. (81) 5193; f. 1955; weekly; Editor SHAMSUN NAHAR RABBI; circ. 6,000.

Begum: 66 Loyal St, Dhaka 1; tel. (2) 233789; f. 1947; women's illustrated weekly; Editor NURJAHAN BEGUM; circ. 25,000.

Chakra: 242A Nakhalpara, POB 2682, Dhaka 1215; tel. (2) 604568; social welfare weekly; Editor HUSNEARA AZIZ.

Chitra Desh: 24 Ramkrishna Mission Rd, Dhaka 1203; weekly; Editor HENA AKHTAR CHOWDHURY.

Chitrali: Observer House, 33 Toyenbee Circular Rd, Motijheel C/A, Dhaka 1000; tel. (2) 9550938; fax (2) 9562243; f. 1953; film weekly; Editor PRODIP KUMAR DEY; circ. 25,000.

Ekota: 15 Larmini St, Wari, Dhaka; tel. (2) 257854; f. 1970; weekly; Editor MATIUR RAHMAN; circ. 25,000.

Fashal: 28J Toyenbee Circular Rd, Motijheel C/A, Dhaka 1000; tel. (2) 233099; f. 1965; agricultural weekly; Chief Editor ERSHAD MAZUMDAR; circ. 8,000.

Ispat: Majampur, Kushtia; tel. (71) 3676; f. 1976; weekly; Editor WALIUR BARI CHOUDHURY; circ. 3,000.

Jaijaidin: 15 New Bailey Rd, Dhaka 1000; tel. (2) 8316448; fax (2) 9568598; e-mail jajadi@aitlbd.net; internet www.jaijaidin.com; f. 1984; weekly; Editor SHAFIK REHMAN; circ. 100,000.

Jhorna: 4/13 Block A, Lalmatia, Dhaka; tel. (2) 415239; Editor MUHAMMAD JAMIR ALI.

Kalantar: 87 Khanjahan Ali Rd, Khulna; tel. (41) 61424; f. 1971; weekly; Editor NOOR MOHAMMAD; circ. 12,000.

Kankan: Nawab Bari Rd, Bogra; tel. (51) 6424; f. 1974; weekly; Editor SUFIA KHATUN; circ. 6,000.

Kirajagat: National Sports Council, 62/63 Purana Paltan, Dhaka 1000; f. 1977; fortnightly; Editor MAHMUD HOSSAIN KHAN DULAL; circ. 10,000.

Kishore Bangla: Observer House, Motijheel C/A, Dhaka 1000; juvenile weekly; f. 1976; Editor RAFIQUL HAQUE; circ. 5,000.

Moha Nagar: 4 Dilkusha C/A, Dhaka 1000; tel. (2) 255282; Editor SYED MOTIUR RAHMAN.

Moshal: 4 Dilkusha C/A, Dhaka 1000; tel. (2) 231092; Editor MUHAMMAD ABUL HASNAT; circ. 3,000.

Muktibani: Toyenbee Circular Rd, Motijheel C/A, Dhaka 1000; tel. (2) 253712; f. 1972; weekly; Editor NIZAM UDDIN AHMED; circ. 35,000.

Natun Bangla: 44/2 Free School St Bylane, Hatirpool, Dhaka 1205; tel. (2) 866121; fax (2) 863794; e-mail mujib@bangla.net; f. 1971; weekly; Editor MUJIBUR RAHMAN.

Natun Katha: 31E Topkhana Rd, Dhaka; weekly; Editor HAJERA SULTANA; circ. 4,000.

Nipun: 520 Peyarabag, Magbazar, Dhaka 11007; tel. (2) 312156; monthly; Editor SHAJAHAN CHOWDHURY.

Parikrama: 65 Shanti Nagar, Dhaka; tel. (2) 415640; Editor MOMTAZ SULTANA.

Prohar: 35 Siddeswari Rd, Dhaka 1217; tel. (2) 404206; Editor MUJIBUL HUQ.

Protirodh: Dept of Answar and V.D.P. Khilgoan, Ministry of Home Affairs, School Bldg, 2nd and 3rd Floors, Bangladesh Secretariat, Dhaka; tel. (2) 405971; f. 1977; fortnightly; Editor ZAHANGIR HABIBULLAH; circ. 20,000.

Purbani: 1 Ramkrishna Mission Rd, Dhaka 1203; tel. (2) 256503; f. 1951; film weekly; Editor KHONDKER SHAHADAT HOSSAIN; circ. 22,000.

Robbar: 1 Ramkrishna Mission Rd, Dhaka; tel. (2) 256071; e-mail robbar@nation-online.com; internet www.robbar.com; f. 1978; weekly; Editor ABDUL HAFIZ; circ. 20,000.

Rokshena: 13B Avoy Das Lane, Tiktuli, Dhaka; tel. (2) 255117; Editor SYEDA AFSANA.

Sachitra Bangladesh: 112 Circuit House Rd, Dhaka 1000; tel. (2) 402129; f. 1979; fortnightly; Editor A. B. M. ABDUL MATIN; circ. 8,000.

Sachitra Sandhani: 68/2 Purana Paltan, Dhaka; tel. (2) 409680; f. 1978; weekly; Editor GAZI SHAHABUDDIN MAHMUD; circ. 13,000.

Sandip Bhabhan: 28/A/3 Toyenbee Circular Rd, Dhaka; tel. (2) 235542; fax (2) 9565558; e-mail network@bangla.net; weekly; Editor MAFUZUR RAHMAN MITA.

Shaptahik Ekhon: Dhaka; internet www.weeklyekhon.com; weekly; Editor ALTAUS SAMAD.

Shishu: Bangladesh Shishu Academy, Old High Court Compound, Dhaka 1000; tel. (2) 230317; f. 1977; children's monthly; Editor GOLAM KIBRIA; circ. 5,000.

Sonar Bangla: 423 Elephant Rd, Mogh Bazar, Dhaka 1217; tel. (2) 400637; f. 1961; Editor MUHAMMED QAMARUZZAMAN; circ. 25,000.

Swadesh: 19 B.B. Ave, Dhaka; tel. (2) 256946; weekly; Editor ZAKIUDDIN AHMED; circ. 8,000.

Tarokalok: Tarokalok Complex, 25/3 Green Rd, Dhaka 1205; tel. (2) 506583; fax (2) 864330; weekly; Editor AREFIN BADAL.

Tilotwoma: 14 Bangla Bazar, Dhaka; Editor ABDUL MANNAN.

English

ADAB News: 1/3, Block F, Lalmatia, Dhaka 1207; tel. (2) 327424; f. 1974; 6 a year; publ. by the Assen of Devt Agencies in Bangladesh (ADAB); Editor-in-Chief AZFAR HUSSAIN; circ. 10,000.

Bangladesh: 112 Circuit House Rd, Dhaka 1000; tel. (2) 402013; fortnightly; Editor A. B. M. ABDUL MATIN.

Bangladesh Gazette: Bangladesh Government Press, Tejgaon, Dhaka; f. 1947; name changed 1972; weekly; official notices; Editor M. HUDA.

Bangladesh Illustrated Weekly: Dhaka; tel. (2) 23358; Editor ATIQUZZAMAN KHAN; circ. 3,000.

Cinema: 81 Motijheel C/A, Dhaka 1000; Editor SHEIKH FAZLUR RAHMAN MARUF; circ. 11,000.

Detective: Polwell Bhaban, Naya Paltan, Dhaka 2; tel. (2) 402757; f. 1960; weekly; also publ. in Bengali; Editor SYED AMJAD HOSSAIN; circ. 3,000.

Dhaka Courier: Cosmos Centre, 69/1 New Circular Rd, Malibagh, Dhaka 1217; tel. (2) 408420; fax (2) 831942; e-mail cosmos@citecho .net; internet www.dhakacourier.net; weekly; Editor ENAYETULLAH KHAN; circ. 18,000.

Holiday: Holiday Bldg, 30 Tejgaon Industrial Area, Dhaka 1208; tel. (2) 9122950; fax (2) 9127927; e-mail holiday@bangla.net; internet www.weeklyholiday.net; f. 1965; weekly; independent; Editor-in-Chief ENAYETULLAH KHAN; circ. 18,000.

Motherland: Khanjahan Ali Rd, Khulna; tel. (41) 61685; f. 1974; weekly; Editor M. N. KHAN.

Tide: 56/57 Motijheel C/A, Dhaka; tel. (2) 259421; Editor ENAYET KARIM.

Voice from the North: Dinajpur Town, Dinajpur; tel. (531) 3256; f. 1981; weekly; Editor Prof. MUHAMMAD MOHSIN; circ. 5,000.

NEWS AGENCIES

Bangladesh Sangbad Sangstha (BSS) (Bangladesh News Agency): 68/2 Purana Paltan, Dhaka 1000; tel. (2) 9555036; fax (2) 9568970; e-mail bss@bssnews.net; internet www.bssnews.net; f. 1972; Man. Dir and Chief Editor MAHBUBUL ALAM; Gen. Man. D. P. BARUA.

Islamic News Society (INS): 24 RK Mission Rd, Motijheel C/A, Dhaka 1203; tel. (2) 7121619; fax (2) 8013721; Editor ABDULLAH AL-NASER.

United News of Bangladesh (UNB): Cosmos Centre, 69/1 New Circular Rd, Malibagh, Dhaka 1217; tel. (2) 9356220; fax (2) 9344556; e-mail unbnews@dhaka.net; internet www.unbnews.com; f. 1988; independent; Chair. AMANULLAH KHAN.

Foreign Bureaux

Agence France-Presse (AFP): Shilpa Bank Bldg, 5th Floor, 8 Rajuk Ave, nr Dhaka Stadium, Dhaka 1000; tel. (2) 9555701; fax (2) 9562007; e-mail helen.rowe@afp.com; Bureau Chief HELEN ROWE.

Associated Press (AP) (USA): 69/1 New Circular Rd, Dhaka 1217; tel. (2) 833717; e-mail apdha@citechco.net; Representative HASAN SAEED FARID HOSSAIN.

Inter Press Service (IPS) (Italy): c/o Bangladesh Sangbad Sangstha, 68/2 Purana Paltan, Dhaka 1000; tel. (2) 235036; Correspondent A. K. M. TABIBUL ISLAM.

Reuters Ltd (United Kingdom): POB 3993, Dhaka; tel. (2) 864088; fax (2) 832976; Bureau Chief ATIQUL ALAM.

PRESS ASSOCIATIONS

Bangladesh Press Council: Dhaka; f. 1974; established under an act of Parliament to preserve the freedom of the press and maintain and develop standards of newspapers and news agencies; Chair. Justice MOHAMED MOZAMMEL HAQ.

Bangladesh Sangbadpatra Karmachari Federation (Newspaper Employees' Fed.): Dhaka; tel. (2) 235065; f. 1972; Pres. RAFIQUL ISLAM; Sec.-Gen. MIR MOZAMMEL HOSSAIN.

Bangladesh Sangbadpatra Press Sramik Federation (Newspaper Press Workers' Federation): 1 Ramkrishna Mission Rd, Dhaka 1203; f. 1960; Pres. M. ABDUL KARIM; Sec.-Gen. BOZLUR RAHMAN MILON.

Dhaka Union of Journalists: National Press Club, Dhaka; f. 1947; Pres. ABEL KHAIR; Gen.-Sec. ABDUL KALAM AZAD.

Newspaper Owners' Association of Bangladesh: Dhaka; f. 2002; promotes interests of newspaper industry; Pres. MAHBUBUL ALAM; Vice-Pres. MATIUR RAHMAN.

Overseas Correspondents' Association of Bangladesh (OCAB): 18 Topkhana Rd, Dhaka 1000; e-mail naweed@bdonline .com; f. 1979; Pres. ZAGLUL A. CHOWDHURY; Gen. Sec. NADEEM QADIR; 60 mems.

Press Institute of Bangladesh: 3 Circuit House Rd, Dhaka 1000; tel. (2) 9330081; fax (2) 8317458; e-mail pib@bdonline.com; f. 1976; trains journalists, conducts research, operates a newspaper library and data bank; Dir-Gen. REZWAN SIDDIQUI.

Publishers

Academic Publishers: 2/7 Nawab-Habibullah Rd, Dhaka 1000; tel. (2) 507355; fax (2) 863060; f. 1982; social sciences and sociology; Jt Man. Dir HABIBUR RAHMAN.

Agamee Prakashani: 36 Bangla Bazar, Dhaka 1100; tel. (2) 7111332; fax (2) 7123945; e-mail agamee@bdonline.com; internet www.agameeprakashani-bd.com; f. 1986; fiction and academic; Chief Exec. OSMAN GANI.

Ahmed Publishing House: 7 Zindabahar 1st Lane, Dhaka 1; tel. (2) 36492; f. 1942; literature, history, science, religion, children's, maps and charts; Man. Dir KAMALUDDIN AHMED; Man. MESBAHUDDIN AHMED.

Ankur Prakashani: 38/4 Bangla Bazar, Dhaka 1100; tel. (2) 9564799; e-mail ankur@agnionline.com; f. 1986; academic and general.

Ashrafia Library: 4 Hakim Habibur Rahman Rd, Chawk Bazar, Dhaka 1000; Islamic religious books, texts, and reference works of Islamic institutions.

Asiatic Society of Bangladesh: 5 Old Secretariat Rd, Ramna, Dhaka; tel. (2) 9560500; f. 1952; periodicals on science, Bangla and humanities; Pres. Prof. WAKIL AHMED; Admin. Officer MD ABDUL AWAL MIAH.

Bangla Academy (National Academy of Arts and Letters of Bangladesh): Burdwan House, 3 Kazi Nazrul Islam Ave, Dhaka 1000; tel. (2) 8619577; fax (2) 8612352; e-mail bcademy@citechco .net; f. 1955; higher education textbooks in Bengali, books on language, literature and culture, language planning, popular science, drama, encyclopaedias, translations of world classics, dictionaries; Dir-Gen. Prof. MONSUR MUSA.

Bangladesh Books International Ltd: Ittefaq Bhaban, 1 Ramkrishna Mission Rd, POB 377, Dhaka 3; tel. (2) 256071; f. 1975; reference, academic, research, literary, children's in Bengali and English; Chair. MOINUL HOSSEIN; Man. Dir ABDUL HAFIZ.

Bangladesh Publishers: 45 Patuatully Rd, Dhaka 1100; tel. (2) 233135; f. 1952; textbooks for schools, colleges and universities, cultural books, journals, etc.; Dir MAYA RANI GHOSAL.

Gatidhara: 38/2-Ka Bangla Bazar, POB 2723, Dhaka 1100; tel. (2) 7118273; fax (2) 9134617; e-mail akter@aitlbd.net; f. 1988; academic, general and fiction; Publr and Chief Exec. SIKDER ABDUL BASHAR.

Gono Prakashani: House 14/E, Rd 6, Dhanmondhi R/A, Dhaka 1205; tel. (2) 8617208; fax (2) 8613567; e-mail gk@citechco.net; f. 1978; science and medicine; Man. Dir SHAFIQ KHAN; Editor BAZLUR RAHIM.

International Publications: 8 Baitul Mukarram, 1st Floor, GPOB 45, Dhaka 1000.

Muktadhara: 22 Payridas Rd, Dhaka 1100; tel. (2) 7111374; e-mail muktadhara1971@yahoo.com; f. 1971; educational and literary; Bengali and English; Dir JAHAR LAL SAHA; Man. Dir C. R. SAHA.

Mullick Brothers: 3/1 Bangla Bazar, Dhaka 1100; tel. (2) 232088; fax (2) 833983; educational.

Osmania Book Depot: 30/32 North Brook Hall Rd, Dhaka 1100.

Puthighar Ltd: 22 Pyaridas Rd, Dhaka 1100; tel. (2) 7111374; e-mail muktadhara1971@yahoo.com; f. 1951; educational; Bengali and English; Dir J. L. SAHA; Man. Dir C. R. SAHA.

Rahman Brothers: 5/1 Gopinath Datta, Kabiraj St, Babu Bazar, Dhaka; tel. (2) 282633; educational.

Royal Library: Ispahani Bldg, 31/32 P. K. Roy Rd, Bangla Bazar, Dhaka 1; tel. (2) 250863.

Shahitya Prakash: 51 Purana Paltan, Dhaka 1000; tel. (2) 9560485; fax (2) 9565506; f. 1970; Prin. Officer MOFIDUL HOQUE.

University Press Ltd: Red Crescent Bldg, 114 Motijheel C/A, POB 2611, Dhaka 1000; tel. (2) 9565444; fax (2) 9565443; e-mail upl@bttb .net.bd; internet www.uplbooks.com; f. 1975; educational, academic and general; Man. Dir MOHIUDDIN AHMED.

GOVERNMENT PUBLISHING HOUSES

Bangladesh Bureau of Statistics: Parishankhan Bhaban, E-27/A, Agargaon, Sher-e-Bangla Nagar, Dhaka 1207; tel. (2) 9133378; fax (2) 9111064; internet www.bbsgov.org; f. 1971; statistical year book and pocket book, censuses, surveys, agricultural year book, special reports, etc.; Jt Dir S. M. TAJUL ISLAM; Sec. BADIUR RAHMAN.

Bangladesh Government Press: Tejgaon, Dhaka 1209; tel. (2) 606316; f. 1972.

Department of Films and Publications: 112 Circuit House Rd, Dhaka 1000; tel. (2) 402263.

Press Information Department: Bhaban 6, Bangladesh Secretariat, Dhaka 1000; tel. (2) 400958.

PUBLISHERS' ASSOCIATIONS

Bangladesh Publishers' and Booksellers' Association: 3 Liaquat Ave, 3rd Floor, Dhaka 1; f. 1972; Pres. JANAB JAHANGIR MOHAMMED ADEL; 2,500 mems.

National Book Centre of Bangladesh: 67A Purana Paltan, Dhaka 1000; f. 1963 to promote the cause of 'more, better and cheaper books'; organizes book fairs, publs a monthly journal; Dir FAZLE RABBI.

Broadcasting and Communications

TELECOMMUNICATIONS

Bangladesh Telecommunication Regulatory Commission (BTRC): House 10, Rd 135, Gulshan 1, Dhaka 1212; tel. (2) 9893917; fax (2) 9890029; e-mail info@btrc.org.bd; internet www.btrc.org.bd; f. 2002; regulates the telecommunications sector; Chair. SYED MARGHUB MORSHED; Vice-Chair. F. Q. M. FAROOQ.

Bangladesh Telegraph and Telephone Board: Central Office, Telejogajog Bhaban, 37/E Eskaton Garden, Dhaka 1000; tel. (2) 8322661; fax (2) 832577; internet www.bttb.gov.bd; Chair. M. A. MANNAN CHOWDHURY; Dir (International) MD HASSANUZZAMAN.

Grameen Telecom: Dhaka; f. 1996 by Grameen Bank to expand cellular telephone service in rural areas; Head NAJMUL HUDA.

Pacific Bangladesh Telecom Ltd: Pacific Centre, 14 Mohakhali C/A, Dhaka 1212; tel. (2) 8822186; fax (2) 8823575; e-mail customerservice@citycell.com; internet www.citycell.org; Man. Dir FAISAL MORSHED KHAN.

Teletalk Bangladesh Ltd: Dhaka; f. 2004; govt-owned; controls mobile cellular telephone operations of Bangladesh Telegraph and Telephone Board.

BROADCASTING

Radio

Bangladesh Betar: NBA House, 121 Kazi Nazrul Islam Ave, Shahabag, Dhaka 1000; tel. (2) 865294; fax (2) 862021; e-mail dgradio@drik.bgd.toolnet.org; f. 1971; govt-controlled; regional stations at Dhaka, Chittagong, Khulna, Rajshahi, Rangpur, Sylhet, Rangamati and Thakurgaon broadcast a total of approximately 160 hours daily; transmitting centres at Lalmai and Rangamati; external service broadcasts 8 transmissions daily in Arabic, Bengali, English, Hindi, Nepalese and Urdu; Dir-Gen. M. I. CHOWDHURY; Dep. Dir-Gen. (Programmes) ASHFAQUR RAHMAN KHAN.

Television

ATN Bangla: WASA Bhaban, 1st Floor, 98 Kazi Nazrul Islam Ave, Kawran Bazar, Dhaka 1215; tel. (2) 8111207; fax (2) 8111876; e-mail info@atnbangla.tv; internet www.atnbangla.tv; f. 1997; private satellite channel; broadcasts in Bengali; Chair. MAHFUZUR RAHMAN.

Bangladesh Television (BTV): Television House, Rampura, Dhaka 1219; tel. (2) 866606; fax (2) 832927; f. 1964; govt-controlled; daily broadcasts on one channel from Dhaka station for 10 hours; transmissions also from nation-wide network of 14 relay stations; Dir-Gen. SAYED SALAHUDDIN ZAKI; Gen. Man. NAWAZISH ALI KHAN.

Channel-i: Impress Telefilm Ltd, 62/A, Shiddeshwari Rd, Dhaka 1217; tel. (2) 9332444; fax (2) 9338285; e-mail info@channel-i-tv.com; internet www.channel-i-tv.com; f. 1999; Dir SHYKH SERAJ.

NTV Bangladesh: BSEC Bhaban, 7th Floor, 102 Kazi Nazrul Islam Ave, Karwan Bazar, Dhaka 1215; tel. (2) 9143381; fax (2) 9143386; e-mail info@ntvbd.com; internet www.ntvbd.com; f. 2003; private satellite channel; Chair. M. ENAYETUR RAHMAN.

Finance

(cap. = capital; res = reserves; dep. = deposits; m. = million; brs = branches; amounts in taka)

BANKING

Central Bank

Bangladesh Bank: Motijheel C/A, POB 325, Dhaka 1000; tel. (2) 7126101; fax (2) 9566212; e-mail banglabank@bangla.net; internet www.bangladesh-bank.org; f. 1971; cap. 30m., res 26,678.4m., dep. 95,620.7m. (June 2003); Gov. Dr FAKHRUDDIN AHMED; 9 brs.

Nationalized Commercial Banks

Agrani Bank: 9D Dilkusha C/A, POB 531, Dhaka 1000; tel. (2) 9566160; fax (2) 9563662; e-mail agrani@agranibank.org; internet www.agranibank.org; f. 1972; 100% state-owned; cap. 2,484m., res 911m., dep. 117,427m. (Dec. 2003); Chair. M. FAZLUR RAHMAN; Man. Dir A. S. IMDADUL HAQUE; 872 brs.

Janata Bank: 110 Motijheel C/A, POB 468, Dhaka 1000; tel. (2) 9565041; fax (2) 9564644; e-mail id-obd@janatabank-bd.com; internet www.janatabank-bd.com; f. 1972; 100% state-owned; cap. 2,594m., res 574m., dep. 140,798m. (Dec. 2003); Chair. M. AYUBUR RAHMAN; Man. Dir S. M. AMINUR RAHMAN; 867 brs in Bangladesh, 4 brs in the UAE.

Rupali Bank Ltd: Rupali Bhaban, 34 Dilkusha C/A, POB 719, Dhaka 1000; tel. (2) 9554122; fax (2) 9564148; e-mail rblhocom@ bdcom.com; internet www.rupali-bank.com; f. 1972; 94% state-owned, 6% by public; cap. 1,250m., res 2,862.5m., dep. 39,637.8m. (Dec. 1999); Chair. MUFLEH R. OSMANY; Man. Dir ABUL HAMID MIAH; 508 brs in Bangladesh, 1 br. in Pakistan.

Sonali Bank: 35–44 Motijheel C/A, POB 3130, Dhaka 1000; tel. (2) 9550426; fax (2) 9561410; e-mail sbhoitd@bttb.net; internet www .sonalibankbd.com; f. 1972; 100% state-owned; cap. 3,272.2m., res 2,036.0m., dep. 170,960.7m. (Dec. 1999); Chair. MUHAMMED ALI; Man. Dir TAHMILUR RAHMAN; 1,313 brs in Bangladesh, 6 brs in United Kingdom and 2 brs in India.

Private Commercial Banks

Al-Arafah Islami Bank Ltd: Rahman Mansion, 161 Motijheel C/A, Dhaka; tel. (2) 9567819; fax (2) 9569351; e-mail arafah@bangla.net; f. 1995; 100% owned by 23 sponsors; cap. 720m., res 10m., dep. 852.0m. (Feb. 2004); Chair. A. Z. M. SHAMSUL ALAM; Man. Dir M. M. NURUL HAQUE.

Al-Baraka Bank Bangladesh Ltd: 60 Dilkusha C/A, Dhaka 1000; tel. (2) 9563768; fax (2) 9562768; e-mail alb@bdonline.com; f. 1987 on Islamic banking principles; 34.68% owned by Al-Baraka Group, Saudi Arabia, 5.78% by Islamic Development Bank, Jeddah, 45.91% by local sponsors, 5.75% by Bangladesh Govt, 7.8% by general public; cap. 259.6m., res 14.9m., dep. 4,898.1m. (June 1996); Chair. Dr SALEH J. MALAIKAH; Man. Dir ANOWAR AHMED; 33 brs.

Arab Bangladesh Bank Ltd: Head Office, BCIC Bhaban, 30–31 Dilkusha C/A, POB 3522, Dhaka 1000; tel. (2) 9560312; fax (2) 9564122; e-mail abbank@abbank.org; internet www.abbank.org; f. 1981; 99.3% owned by Bangladesh nationals and 0.7% by Bangladesh Govt; cap. 409.9m., res 592.1m., dep. 27,260m. (Dec. 2003); Chair. FAISAL MORSHED KHAN; Pres. and Man. Dir KAISER A. CHOWDHURY; 69 brs, 1 br. in India.

The City Bank Ltd: Jiban Bima Tower, 10 Dilkusha C/A, POB 3381, Dhaka 1000; tel. (2) 9565919; fax (2) 9562347; e-mail cbl@ citechco.net; internet www.thecitybank.com; f. 1983; 50% owned by sponsors and 50% by public; cap. 240.0m., res 413.7m., dep. 19,683.3m. (Dec. 2002); Chair. DEEN MOHAMMAD; Man. Dir ABBAS UDDIN AHMED; 76 brs.

Dhaka Bank Ltd: Biman Bhaban, 100 Motijheel C/A, Dhaka 1000; tel. (2) 9554514; fax (2) 9556584; e-mail dhakabnk@bdonline.com; internet www.dhakabank.com.bd; f. 1995; cap. 531.06m., res 520.01m., dep. 16,850.83m. (Dec. 2003); Chair. A. T. M. HAYATUZ-ZAMAN KHAN; Man. Dir SHAHED NOMAN; 20 brs.

Dutch-Bangla Bank Ltd: 3rd, 4th, 5th and 10th Floors, Sena Kalyan Bhaban, 195 Motijheel C/A, Dhaka 1000; tel. (2) 7176390; fax (2) 9561889; e-mail id@dutchbanglabank.com; internet www .dutchbanglabank.com; f. 1996; cap. 202.1m., res 264.2m., dep. 17,133.8m. (Dec. 2003); Chair. MOHAMMED SAHABUDDIN AHMED; Man. Dir MOHAMMED YEASIN ALI; 19 brs.

Eastern Bank Ltd: Jiban Bima Bhaban, 2nd Floor, 10 Dilkusha C/A, POB 896, Dhaka 1000; tel. (2) 9556360; fax (2) 9562364; e-mail ebank@bdcom.com; internet www.ebl-bd.com; f. 1992; appropriated assets and liabilities of fmr Bank of Credit and Commerce International (Overseas) Ltd; 83% owned by public, 17% owned by government and private commercial banks; cap. 828m., res 1,262.1m., dep. 14,802.4m. (Dec. 2003); Chair. M. GHAZIUL HAQUE; Man. Dir and CEO K. MAHMOOD SATTAR; 22 brs.

International Finance Investment and Commerce Bank Ltd (IFICB): BSB Bldg, 17th–19th Floors, 8 Motijheel C/A, Rajuk Ave, POB 2229, Dhaka 1000; tel. (2) 9563020; fax (2) 9562015; e-mail ificmd@citechco.net; internet www.ificbankbd.com; f. 1983; 40% state-owned; cap. 406.4m., res 513.8m., dep. 20,453.2m. (Dec. 2002); Chair. MANZURUL ISLAM; Man. Dir ATAUL HAQ; 62 brs in Bangladesh.

Islami Bank Bangladesh Ltd (IBBL): Head Office, Islami Bank Tower, 40 Dilkusha C/A, POB 233, Dhaka 1000; tel. (2) 9563040; fax (2) 9564532; e-mail ibbl@ncll.com; internet www.islamibankbd.com; f. 1983 on Islamic banking principles; cap. 3,000m. (June 2003), res 2,097.6m., dep. 47,555.5m. (June 2002); Chair. SHAH ABDUL HANNAN; Exec. Pres. and CEO ABDUR RAQUIB; 141 brs.

Mercantile Bank Ltd: 61 Dilkusha C/A, Dhaka 1000; tel. (2) 9559333; fax (2) 9561213; e-mail mbl@bol-online.com; internet www .mblbd.com; f. 1999; cap. 304.5m., res 287.6m., 14,681.8m. (Dec. 2002); Chair. MOHAMMED ABDUL JALIL; 20 brs.

National Bank Ltd: 18 Dilkusha C/A, POB 3424, Dhaka 1000; tel. (2) 9557045; fax (2) 9563953; e-mail nblid@bdonline.com; internet www.nblbd.com; f. 1983; 50% owned by sponsors and 50% by general public; cap. 430.3m., res 860.0m., dep. 27,575.5m. (June 2003); Chair. PARVEEN HAQUE SIKDER; Man. Dir MUSTAQUE AHMED; 76 brs.

National Credit and Commerce Bank Ltd: 7–8 Motijheel C/A, POB 2920, Dhaka 1000; tel. (2) 9561902; fax (2) 9566290; e-mail nccbl@bdmail.net; internet www.nccbank-bd.com; f. 1993; 50% owned by sponsors, 50% by general public; cap. 552.6m., res 391.4m., dep. 15,340.8m. (Dec. 2003); Chair. M. WAZHIULLAH BHUIYAN; Man. Dir M. AMINUZZAMAN; 32 brs.

ONE Bank Ltd: Zaman Court, 1st Floor, 45 Dilkusha C/A, Dhaka 1000; tel. (2) 9551799; fax (2) 9564870; e-mail onebnkid@bdcom.com; f. 1999; cap. 600.0m., res 188.1m., dep. 8,847m. (Dec. 2003); Chair. SAYEED HOSSAIN CHOWDHURY; Man. Dir SYED NURUL AMIN.

Prime Bank Ltd: Adamjee Court Annex Bldg No. 2, 119–20 Motijheel C/A, Dhaka 1000; tel. (2) 9567265; fax (2) 9567230; e-mail primebnk@bangla.net; internet www.prime-bank.com; f. 1995; cap. 700m., res 1,056.9m., dep. 21,659.1m. (Dec. 2003); Chair. MIZANUR RAHMAN BHUIYAN; Man. Dir SHAH MOHAMMED NURUL ALAM; 30 brs.

Pubali Bank Ltd: Pubali Bank Bhaban, 26 Dilkusha C/A, POB 853, Dhaka 1000; tel. (2) 9551614; fax (2) 9564009; e-mail pbltid@ bol-online.com; internet www.pubalibangla.com; f. 1959 as Eastern Mercantile Bank Ltd; name changed to Pubali Bank in 1972; 98.5% privately owned, 1.5% state-owned; cap. 200m., res 1,931.8m., dep. 36,173.1m. (Dec. 2003); Chair. EMADUDDIN AHMED CHAUDHURY; Man. Dir KHONDKAR IBRAHIM KHALED; 350 brs.

Social Investment Bank: 15 Dilkusha C/A, Dhaka 1000; tel. (2) 9559014; fax (2) 9559013; e-mail sibl@bdonline.com; internet www .siblbd.com; f. 1995; cap. 260.0m., res 631.0m., dep. 19,709.3m. (Dec. 2003); Chair. KAMALUDDIN AHMED; Man. Dir KAZI ANWARUL MAHBUB; 5 brs.

Southeast Bank Ltd: 1 Dilkusha C/A, 3rd Floor, Dhaka 1000; tel. (2) 9550081; fax (2) 9563102; e-mail seastbk@citechco.net; internet www.southeastbank-bangladesh.com; f. 1995; cap. 363m., res 517.3m., dep. 15,343.5m. (Dec. 2002); Chair. AZIM UDDIN AHMED; Pres. and Man. Dir SYED ABU NASER BUKHTEAR AHMED; 25 brs.

United Commercial Bank Ltd: Federation Bhaban, 4th–6th Floors, 60 Motijheel C/A, POB 2653, Dhaka 1000; tel. (2) 9568690; fax (2) 9560587; e-mail ucb@bangla.net; internet www.ucbl.com; f. 1983; 50% owned by sponsors, 45% by general public and 5% by Govt; cap. 230.2m., res 334.8m., dep. 10,102.0m. (Dec. 1999); Chair. ZAFAR AHMED CHOWDHURY; 79 brs.

Uttara Bank Ltd: 90 Motijheel C/A, POB 818, Dhaka 1000; tel. (2) 9551162; fax (2) 8613529; e-mail ublid@citecho.net; internet www .uttarabank-bd.com; f. 1965 as Eastern Banking Corpn Ltd; name changed to Uttara Bank in 1972 and to Uttara Bank Ltd in 1983; cap. 99.8m., res 1,204.9m., dep. 29,382.0m. (Dec. 2001); Chair. AZHARUL ISLAM; Man. Dir and CEO SHAMSUDDIN AHMED; 198 brs.

Foreign Commercial Banks

American Express Bank Ltd (USA): ALICO Bldg, 18–20 Motijheel C/A, POB 420, Dhaka 1000; tel. (2) 9561751; fax (2) 9561806; e-mail amexbd@gononet.com; res 537.5m., dep. 6,236.5m. (Dec. 1995); Chair. RICHARD HOLMES; Gen. Man. JOHN A. SMETANKA; 8 brs.

Citibank, NA (USA): Chamber Bldg, 122–124 Motijheel C/A, POB 1000, Dhaka 1000; tel. (2) 9550060; fax (2) 9562236; e-mail mamun

.rashid@citicorp.com; f. 1995; cap. 209.5m., res 5.5m., dep. 648.8m. (July 1996); Chair. JOHN S. REED; CEO MAMUN RASHID; 1 br.

Crédit Agricole Indosuez (France): 47 Motijheel C/A, POB 3490, Dhaka 1000; tel. (2) 9566566; fax (2) 9565707; e-mail cai@dhaka-bd .net; res 591m., dep. 5,302m. (Dec. 1997); Country Man. GERARD MARCHAND; Chief Operating Officer S. R. VATOVEY; 2 brs.

Habib Bank Ltd (Pakistan): 53 Motijheel C/A, POB 201, Dhaka 1000; tel. (2) 9563043; fax (2) 9561784; e-mail hbldhaka@bdonline .com; cap. 80.5m., res 14.3m., dep. 578.6m. (Dec. 1996); Country Man. GHAZANFAR ALI; 2 brs.

The Hongkong and Shanghai Banking Corpn Ltd (Hong Kong): Anchor Tower, 2nd Floor, 1/1B Sonargaon Rd, Dhaka 1205; tel. (2) 9660536; fax (2) 9660554; e-mail hsbc@hsbc.dhaka-bd.net; CEO for Bangladesh DAVID J. H. GRIFFITHS.

Standard Chartered Bank (United Kingdom): 2 Dilkusha C/A, Dhaka 1000; tel. (2) 9550181; fax (2) 9562332; e-mail badrul .ahshan@bd.com; internet www.standardchartered.com; cap. 215m., dep. 5,850m. (Dec. 1995); Chief Exec. (Bangladesh) DAVID MARTIN FLETCHER; 3 brs.

State Bank of India: 24–25 Dilkusha C/A, POB 981, Dhaka 1000; tel. (2) 9559935; fax (2) 9563991; e-mail sbibd@bangla.net; cap. 190.4m., dep. 557.1m. (March 1997); Chief Exec. for Bangladesh J. K. KANJILAL; 1 br.

Development Finance Organizations

Bangladesh House Building Finance Corpn (BHBFC): HBFC Bldg, 22 Purana Paltan, POB 2167, Dhaka 1000; tel. (2) 9562767; fax (2) 9561324; e-mail bhbfc@bangla.net; f. 1952; provides low-interest credit for residential house-building; 100% state-owned; cap. 972.9m. (Dec. 2003); Chair. A. S. ABDUL QADIR MAHMUD; Man. Dir Dr JADAB CHANDRA SAHA; 9 zonal offices, 13 regional offices and 2 camp offices.

Bangladesh Krishi Bank (BKB): 83–85 Motijheel C/A, POB 357, Dhaka 1000; tel. (2) 9558109; fax (2) 9553028; e-mail idbkb@citechco .net; internet www.krishibank.org.bd; f. 1961 as the Agricultural Development Bank of Pakistan, name changed as above in 1973; provides credit for agricultural and rural devt; also performs all kinds of banking; 100% state-owned; cap. 1,400m., res 820.4m., dep. 44,611m. (June 2002); Chair. Dr MUHAMMAD AHBAB AHMED; Man. Dir A. K. M. SAJEDUR RAHMAN; 930 brs.

Bangladesh Samabaya Bank Ltd (BSBL): 'Samabaya Sadan', 9D Motijheel C/A, POB 505, Dhaka 1000; tel. (2) 9564628; f. 1948; provides credit for agricultural co-operatives; cap. 31.6m., res 558m., dep. 22m. (June 1996); Chair. Dr ABDUL MOYEEN KHAN; Gen. Man. MD ABDUL WAHED.

Bangladesh Shilpa Bank (BSB) (Industrial Development Bank): Shipla Bank Bhaban, 8 Rajuk Ave, POB 975, Dhaka; tel. (2) 9555151; fax (2) 9562061; e-mail bsblink@citechco.net; f. 1972; fmrly Industrial Devt Bank; provides long- and short-term financing for industrial devt in the private and public sectors; also provides underwriting facilities and equity support; 51% state-owned; cap. 1,320.0m., res 957.5m., dep. 641.1m. (June 2003); Man. Dir M. ZIAUL HUQUE; Chair. Prof. ABU AHMED; 15 brs.

Bangladesh Shilpa Rin Sangstha (BSRS) (Industrial Loan Agency): BIWTC Bhaban, 5th Floor, 141–143 Motijheel C/A, Dhaka 1000; tel. (2) 9553546; fax (2) 9567057; f. 1972; 100% state-owned; cap. 700m., res 462.8m. (June 1996); Chair. Dr M. FARASHUDDIN; Man. Dir MOHAMMAD FARHAD HOSSAIN; 4 brs.

Bank of Small Industries and Commerce Bangladesh Ltd (BASIC Bank): Suite 601–602, Sena Kalyan Bhaban, 6th Floor, 195 Motijheel C/A, Dhaka 1000; tel. (2) 9564830; fax (2) 9564829; e-mail basicho@citechco.net; internet www.basicbankbd.com; f. 1988; 100% state-owned; cap. 300m., res 713m., dep. 10,698m. (Dec. 2002); Chair. A. M. AKHTER; Man. Dir MD SALEHUDDIN QUASEM; 19 brs.

Export-Import Bank of Bangladesh Ltd: Printers' Bldg, 5 Rajuk Ave, Motijheel C/A, Dhaka 1000; tel. (2) 9553925; fax (2) 9556988; e-mail eximho@bdonline.com; internet www.eximbd.com; f. 1999; cap. 313.9m., res 310.8m., dep. 15,243.0m. (Dec. 2003); Man. Dir MOHAMMAD LAKIOTULLAH; Chair. NAZRUL ISLAM MAZUMDER; 19 brs.

Grameen Bank: Head Office, Mirpur-2, POB 1216, Dhaka 1216; tel. (2) 801138; fax (2) 803559; e-mail grameen.bank@grameen.net; internet www.grameen.com; f. 1976; provides credit for the landless rural poor; 6.97% owned by Govt; cap. 258.1m., res 188.2m., dep. 6,063.2m. (Dec. 1998); Chair. REHMAN SOBHAN; Man. Dir Dr MUHAMMAD YUNUS; 1,140 brs.

Infrastructure Development Co Ltd (IDCOL): Dhaka; f. 1999; state-owned.

Investment Corpn of Bangladesh (ICB): BSB Bldg, 12th–15th Floors, 8 DIT Ave, POB 2058, Dhaka 1000; tel. (2) 9563455; fax (2) 9563313; e-mail icb@agni.com; internet www.icb.gov.bd; f. 1976; provides investment banking services; 27% owned by Govt; cap.

500.0m., res 691.1m. (June 2004); Chair. MUHAMMAD HASINUR RAHMAN; Man. Dir MUHAMMAD ZIAUL HAQUE KHONDKER; 7 brs.

Rajshahi Krishi Unnayan Bank: Sadharan Bima Bhaban, Kazihata, Greater Rd, Rajshahi 6000; tel. (721) 775848; fax (721) 775947; e-mail mdrakub@rajbd.com; f. 1987; 100% state-owned; cap. 980m., res 208.4m., dep. 2,622.7m. (June 1996); Chair. MD EMRAN ALI SARKAR; Man. Dir SHAHIDUL HAQ KHAN.

Banking Association

Bangladesh Association of Banks: Iqbal Centre, 12th Floor, 42 Kamal Atatürk Ave, Banani C/A, Dhaka 1213; tel. and fax (2) 8851015; e-mail bab@citechco.net; Chair. SYED MANZUR ELAHI.

STOCK EXCHANGES

Chittagong Stock Exchange: CSE Bldg, 1080 Sk Mujib Rd, Agrabad, Chittagong; tel. (31) 714100; fax (31) 714101; e-mail maroof@csebd.com; internet www.csebd.com; CEO WALI-UL-MAROOF MATIN.

Dhaka Stock Exchange Ltd: 9F Motijheel C/A, Dhaka 1000; tel. (2) 9564601; fax (2) 9564727; e-mail dse@bol-online.com; internet www.dsebd.org; f. 1954; 264 listed cos; Chair. AHMED IQBAL HASAN; CEO SALAHUDDIN AHMED KHAN.

Regulatory Authority

Bangladesh Securities and Exchange Commission: Jiban Bima Tower, 15th, 16th and 20th Floors, 10 Dilkusha C/A, Dhaka 1000; tel. (2) 9568101; fax (2) 9563721; e-mail secbd@bdmail.net; internet www.secbd.org; f. 1993; CEO Dr MIRZA AZIZUL ISLAM.

INSURANCE

Department of Insurance: 74 Motijheel C/A, Dhaka 1000; attached to Ministry of Commerce; supervises activities of domestic and foreign insurers; Controller of Insurance SHAMSUDDIN AHMAD.

Bangladesh Insurance Association: Rupali Bima Bhaban, 7th Floor, 7 Rajuk Ave, Dhaka 1000; tel. (2) 9557330; fax (2) 9562345; e-mail bia@bdcom.com; Chair. NASIR A. CHOWDHURY.

Bangladesh General Insurance Co Ltd: 42 Dilkusha C/A, Dhaka 1000; tel. (2) 9555073; fax (2) 9564212; e-mail bgic@citechco.net; Chair. and Man. Dir M. A. SAMAD.

Eastern Insurance Co Ltd: 44 Dilkusha C/A, Dhaka 1000; tel. (2) 9563033; fax (2) 9569735; e-mail eicl@spaninn.com; Chair. M. HAIDER CHOWDHURY.

Jiban Bima Corpn: 24 Motijheel C/A, POB 346, Dhaka 1000; tel. (2) 9552047; fax (2) 868112; state-owned; comprises 37 national life insurance cos; life insurance; Man. Dir A. K. M. MOSTAFIZUR RAHMAN.

Pioneer Insurance Co Ltd: Jiban Bima Bhaban, 10 Dilkusha C/A, Dhaka 1000; tel. (2) 9557674; fax (2) 9557676; e-mail biclho@bangla.net; Man. Dir R. N. DAS.

Pragati Insurance Ltd: Pragati Bhaban, 12th Floor, 20–21 Kawran Bazar, Dhaka 1215; tel. (2) 8117996; fax (2) 8122980; e-mail pilbima@bangla.net; Man. Dir A. K. M. RAFIQUL ISLAM.

Reliance Insurance Ltd: BSB Bldg, 8 Rajuk Ave, Dhaka 1000; tel. (2) 9560105; fax (2) 9562005; e-mail ril@bol-online.com; Man. Dir M. SHAMSUL ALAM.

Sadharan Bima Corpn: 33 Dilkusha C/A, Dhaka 1000; tel. (2) 9552070; fax (2) 9564197; e-mail sbc@bttb.net; state-owned; general insurance; Man. Dir AKHTAR AHMED.

Trade and Industry

GOVERNMENT AGENCIES

Board of Investment: Jiban Bima Tower, 19th Floor, 10 Dilkusha C/A, Dhaka 1000; tel. (2) 9563570; fax (2) 9562312; e-mail ec@boi.bdmail.net; internet www.boidb.org; f. 1989; Exec. Chair. MAHMUDUR RAHMAN; Dep. Dir LUTFUR RAHMAN BHUIYA.

Export Promotion Bureau: TCB Bhaban, 1st Floor, 1 Kawran Bazar, Dhaka 1215; tel. (2) 9144821; fax (2) 9119531; e-mail epb.bd@aitlbd.net; internet www.epb.gov.bd; f. 1972; attached to Ministry of Commerce; regional offices in Chittagong, Khulna and Rajshahi; brs in Comilla, Sylhet and Narayaganj; Dir-Gen. MUSTAFA MOHIUDDIN; Vice-Chair. Mir SHAHABUDDIN MOHAMMAD.

Petrobangla (Bangladesh Oil, Gas and Mineral Corporation): Petrocenter Bhaban, 3 Kawran Bazar C/A, POB 849, Dhaka 1215; tel. (2) 8114972; fax (2) 9120224; e-mail petchair@petrobangla.org; internet www.petrobangla.org; f. 1972; explores and develops gas, petroleum and mineral resources, manages Bangladesh Petroleum Exploration Co Ltd and Sylhet Gas Fields Ltd; Chair. S. R. OSMANI.

Planning Commission: Planning Commission Secretariat, G.O. Hostel, Sher-e-Bangla Nagar, Dhaka; f. 1972; govt agency responsible for all aspects of economic planning and development including the preparation of the five-year plans and annual development programmes (in conjunction with appropriate govt ministries), promotion of savings and investment, compilation of statistics and evaluation of development schemes and projects.

Privatization Board: Jiban Bima Tower, 14th Floor, 10 Dilkusha C/A, Dhaka 1000; tel. (2) 9563723; fax (2) 9563766; e-mail pb@bdonline.com; internet www.bangladeshonline.com/pb; f. 1993; Chair. KAZI ZAFRULLAH; Sec. A. M. M. NASIR UDDIN.

Trading Corpn of Bangladesh: TCB Bhavan, 1 Kawran Bazar, Dhaka 1215; tel. (2) 8111521; fax (2) 8113582; e-mail tcb@bdonline.com; f. 1972; imports, exports and markets goods through appointed dealers and agents; Chair. MOHAMMAD MATIUR RAHMAN KHAN; Sec. MOHAMMAD ZAKIR HOSSAIN.

DEVELOPMENT ORGANIZATIONS

Bangladesh Chemical Industries Corpn: BCIC Bhaban, 30–31 Dilkusha C/A, Dhaka; tel. (2) 955280; fax (2) 9564120; e-mail bciccomp@bangla.net; internet www.bangla.net/bcic; Chair. A. K. M. MOSHARRAF HOSSAIN.

Bangladesh Export Processing Zones Authority: 222 New Eskaton Rd, Dhaka 1000; tel. (2) 8312553; fax (2) 8314967; e-mail bepza@bdmail.net; internet www.bangladesh-epz.com; f. 1983 to plan, develop, operate and manage export processing zones (EPZs) in Bangladesh; in mid-2000 two state-owned EPZs (one in Chittagong and the other in Dhaka) were in operation, and another four EPZs were at the implementation stage; Exec. Chair. Brig M. A. B. SIDDIQUE TALUKDER.

Bangladesh Fisheries Development Corpn: 24–25 Dilkusha C/A, Dhaka 1000; tel. (2) 9552689; fax (2) 9563990; e-mail bfdc@citechco.net; f. 1964; under Ministry of Fisheries and Livestock; development and commercial activities; Chair. Brig.-Gen. (retd) CHOWDHURY KHALEQUZZAMAN; Sec. A. K. M. SHAHIDUL ISLAM.

Bangladesh Forest Industries Development Corpn: 73 Motijheel C/A, Dhaka; tel. (2) 9552010; fax (2) 9563990; Chair. M. ATIKULLAH.

Bangladesh Jute Mills Corpn: Adamjee Court, 115–120 Motijheel C/A, Dhaka 1000; tel. (2) 9558182; fax (2) 9567508; e-mail bjmc@bttb.net.bd; f. 1972; operates 32 jute mills; bags, carpet backing cloth, yarn, twine, tape, felt, floor covering, etc.; Chair. MOHAMMAD MUZIBUR RAHMAN.

Bangladesh Small and Cottage Industries Corpn (BSCIC): 137/138 Motijheel C/A, Dhaka 1000; tel. (2) 9565612; fax 9550704; e-mail cbscic@aitlbd.net; internet www.bscic-bd.org; f. 1957; Chair. MUHAMMAD SIRAJUDDIN.

Bangladesh Steel and Engineering Corpn (BSEC): BSEC Bhaban, 102 Kazi Nazrul Islam Ave, Dhaka 1215; tel. (2) 8114616; fax (2) 8112846; 16 industrial units; sales US $83m. (1994); cap. US $52m.; Chair. A. I. M. NAZMUL ALAM; Gen. Man. (Marketing) ASHRAFUL HAQ; 8,015 employees.

Bangladesh Sugar and Food Industries Corpn: Shilpa Bhaban, Motijheel C/A, Dhaka 1000; tel. (2) 258084; f. 1972; Chair. M. NEFAUR RAHMAN.

Bangladesh Textile Mills Corpn: 7–9 Bastra Bhaban, Kawran Bazar, Dhaka 1215; tel. (2) 8111088; fax (2) 814600; f. 1972; Chair. M. NURUNNABI CHOWDHURY.

CHAMBERS OF COMMERCE

Federation of Bangladesh Chambers of Commerce and Industry (FBCCI): Federation Bhaban, 60 Motijheel C/A, Dhaka 1000; tel. (2) 9560102; fax (2) 7176030; e-mail fbcci@bol-online.com; internet www.fbcci-bd.org; f. 1973; comprises 204 trade asscns and 76 chambers of commerce and industry; Pres. ABDUL AWAL MINTOO; Sec.-Gen. Col (retd) M. M. JAHANGIR.

Barisal Chamber of Commerce and Industry: Asad Mansion, 1st Floor, Sadar Rd, Barisal; tel. (431) 3984; Pres. Qazi ISRAIL HOSSAIN.

Bogra Chamber of Commerce and Industry: Chamber Bhaban, 2nd Floor, Kabi Nazrul Islam Rd, Jhawtola, Bogra 5800; tel. (51) 64138; fax (51) 66257; e-mail bccibgr@bttb.net.bd; f. 1963; Pres. Alhaj MOHAMMAD FAZLUR RAHMAN PAIKER; Sr Vice-Pres. Alhaj ABUL KALAM AZAD.

Chittagong Chamber of Commerce and Industry: Chamber House, Agrabad C/A, POB 481, Chittagong; tel. (31) 713366; fax (31) 710183; e-mail ccci@globalctg.net; f. 1959; 4,000 mems; Pres. AMIR HUMAYUN MAHMUD CHOWDHURY; Sec. OSMAN GANI CHOWDHURY.

Comilla Chamber of Commerce and Industry: Rammala Rd, Ranir Bazar, Comilla; tel. (81) 5444; Pres. AFZAL KHAN.

Dhaka Chamber of Commerce and Industry: Dhaka Chamber Bldg, 1st Floor, 65–66 Motijheel C/A, POB 2641, Dhaka 1000; tel. (2) 9552562; fax (2) 9560830; e-mail dcci@bangla.net; f. 1958; 5,000 mems; Pres. MATIUR RAHMAN; Sr Vice-Pres. AM MUBASH-SHAR.

Dinajpur Chamber of Commerce and Industry: Chamber Bhaban, Maldhapatty, Dinajpur 5200; tel. (531) 3189; Pres. KHAIRUL ANAM.

Faridpur Chamber of Commerce and Industry: Chamber House, Niltuly, Faridpur; tel. (631) 3530; Pres. KHANDOKER MOHSIN ALI.

Foreign Investors' Chamber of Commerce and Industry: 'Prime View', 7 Gulshan Ave, Gulshan 1, Dhaka 1212; tel. (2) 9892913; fax (2) 9893058; e-mail ficci@bangla.net; internet www .ficci.org.bd; f. 1963 as Agrabad Chamber of Commerce and Industry, name changed as above in 1987; Pres. MAHBUB JAMIL; Sec. JAHANGIR BIN ALAM.

Khulna Chamber of Commerce and Industry: 5 KDA C/A, Khulna; tel. (41) 24135; e-mail kcci@bttb.net.bd; f. 1934; Pres. S. M. NAZRUL ISLAM.

Kushtia Chamber of Commerce and Industry: 15, S Rd, Kushtia; tel. (71) 54068; e-mail kushcham@kushtia.com; Pres. MOHAMMAD MOZIBAR RAHMAN.

Metropolitan Chamber of Commerce and Industry: Chamber Bldg, 4th Floor, 122–124 Motijheel C/A, Dhaka 1000; tel. (2) 9565208; fax (2) 9565212; e-mail sg@citechco.net; internet www .mccibd.org; f. 1904; 310 mems; Sec.-Gen. C. K. HYDER.

Noakhali Chamber of Commerce and Industry: Noakhali Pourshara Bhaban, 2nd Floor, Maiydee Court, Noakhali; tel. (321) 5229; Pres. MOHAMMAD NAZIBUR RAHMAN.

Rajshahi Chamber of Commerce and Industry: Chamber Bhaban, Station Rd, PO Ghoramara, Rajshahi 6100; tel. (721) 772115; fax (721) 772412; f. 1960; 800 mems; Pres. MOHAMMAD LUTFAR RAHMAN.

Sylhet Chamber of Commerce and Industry: Chamber Bldg, Jail Rd, POB 97, Sylhet 3100; tel. (821) 714403; fax (821) 715210; e-mail scci@btsnet.net; Pres. MOHD SAFWAN CHOUDHURY.

INDUSTRIAL AND TRADE ASSOCIATIONS

Bangladesh Frozen Foods Exporters Association: 50/1 Inner Circular Rd, 2nd Floor, Shantinagar, Dhaka; tel. (2) 418720; fax (2) 837531; e-mail bffea@drik.dgd.toolnet.org; Pres. SALAHUDDIN AHMED.

Bangladesh Garment Manufacturers and Exporters Association: 7–9 Karwanbazar, BTMC Bhaban, Dhaka 1215; tel. (2) 8115597; fax (2) 8113951; e-mail bgmea@bgmea.agni.com; Pres. Qazi MONIRUZZAMAN; Vice-Pres. NURUL HAQ SIKDAR.

Bangladesh Jute Association: BJA Bldg, 77 Motijheel C/A, Dhaka; tel. (2) 9552916; fax (2) 9560137; Chair. M.A. MANNAN; Sec. S. H. PRODHAN.

Bangladesh Jute Exporters Association: Nahar Mansion, 2nd Floor, 150 Motijheel C/A, Dhaka 1000; tel. (2) 9561102.

Bangladesh Jute Goods Association: Nahar Mansion, 2nd Floor, 150 Motijheel C/A, Dhaka 1000; tel. (2) 253640; f. 1979; 17 mems; Chair. M. A. KASHEM; Haji MOHAMMAD ALI.

Bangladesh Jute Mills Association: Adamjee Court, 4th Floor, 115–120 Motijheel C/A, Dhaka 1000; tel. (2) 9560071; fax (2) 9566472; Chair. A. M. ZAHIRUDDIN KHAN.

Bangladesh Jute Spinners Association: 55 Purana Paltan, 3rd Floor, Dhaka 1000; tel. (2) 9551317; fax (2) 9562772; f. 1979; 50 mems; Chair. AHMED HOSSAIN; Sec. SHAHIDUL KARIM.

Bangladesh Tea Board: 171–172 Baizid Bostami Rd, Nasirabad, Chittagong; tel. (31) 682903; fax (31) 682863; e-mail btb@spnetctg .com; internet bdteaboard.com; f. 1951; regulates, controls and promotes the cultivation and marketing of tea, both in Bangladesh and abroad; Contact ALI OHIDUZ ZAMAN.

Bangladesh Textile Mills Association: Moon Mansion, 6th Floor, Block M, 12 Dilkusha C/A, Dhaka 1000; tel. (2) 9552799; fax 9563320; e-mail btma@citechco.net.

Bangladeshiyo Cha Sangsad (Tea Association of Bangladesh): 'Dar-e-Shahidi', 3rd Floor, 69 Agrabad C/A, POB 287, Chittagong 4100; tel. (31) 501009; f. 1952; Chair. QUAMRUL CHOWDHURY; Sec. G. S. DHAR.

UTILITIES

Electricity

Bangladesh Atomic Energy Commission (BAEC): 4 Kazi Nazrul Islam Ave, POB 158, Dhaka 1000; tel. (2) 502600; fax (2) 863051; f. 1964 as Atomic Energy Centre of the fmr Pakistan Atomic Energy Comm. in East Pakistan; reorg. 1973; operates an atomic energy research establishment and a 3-MW research nuclear reactor (inaugurated in January 1987) at Savar, an atomic energy centre at Dhaka, etc.; Chair. M. A. QUAIYUM; Sec. RAFIQUL ALAM.

Bangladesh Power Development Board: WAPDA Bldg, Motijheel C/A, Dhaka; tel. (2) 9562154; fax (2) 9564765; e-mail chpdb@ bol-online.com; internet www.bd-pdb.org; f. 1972; under Ministry of Power, Energy and Mineral Resources; generation, transmission and distribution of electricity; installed capacity 4,710 MW (2002); Chair. SYED ABDUL MAYEED.

Dhaka Electric Supply Authority: Bidyut Bhaban, 1 Nawab Abdul Gani Rd, Dhaka 1000; tel. (2) 9563520; fax (2) 9566699; f. 1991; under Ministry of Power, Energy and Mineral Resources; Chair. S. M. SHAMSUL ALAM.

Dhaka Electric Supply Co Ltd (DESCO): Dhaka; fax (2) 823140; f. 1997; Man. Dir SALEH AHMED.

Energy Regulatory Commission: Dhaka; f. 2004; regulates activities of power sector.

Power Grid Company of Bangladesh Ltd (PGCB): Red Crescent Concord Tower, 6th Floor, 17 Mohakhali C/A, Dhaka 1212; tel. and fax (2) 9888501; f. 1996; responsible for power transmission throughout Bangladesh; Sec. MOHAMMED SALIM.

Rural Electrification Board: Nikanja-2, Khilkhet, Dhaka 1229; tel. (2) 8916412; fax (2) 8916400; internet www.bangladesh.gov.bd/ reb; under Ministry of Power, Energy and Mineral Resources; Chair. ZIAUL ISLAM CHOWDHURY.

Water

Chittagong Water Supply and Sewerage Authority: Dampara, Chittagong; tel. (31) 621606; fax (31) 610465; f. 1963; govt corpn; Chair. SULTAN MAHMUD CHOWDHURY.

Dhaka Water Supply and Sewerage Authority: 98 Kazi Nazrul Islam Ave, Kawran Bazar, Dhaka 1215; tel. (2) 8116792; fax (2) 8112109; e-mail mddwasa@bangla.net; f. 1963; govt corpn; Man. Dir K. AZHARUL HAQ.

TRADE UNIONS

In 2001 only 4.3% of the non-agricultural labour force was unionized. There were about 4,200 registered unions, organized mainly on a sectoral or occupational basis. There were 23 national trade unions to represent workers at the national level.

Bangladesh Free Trade Union Congress (BFTUC): 6A 1–19 Mirpur, Dhaka 1216; tel. (2) 8017001; fax (2) 8015919; e-mail bftuc@ agni.com; Gen. Sec. M. R. CHOWDHURY; 115,000 mems.

Bangladesh Jatio Sramik League (BJSL): POB 2730, Dhaka; tel. (2) 282063; fax (2) 863470; 62,000 mems.

Transport

RAILWAYS

In July 2000 Bangladesh Railway and the Indian Railway Board signed an agreement to resume rail services on the Benapole–Petrapole route. The service opened fully in January 2001. In December regular rail services between Bangabandhu and Kolkata (Calcutta—India) resumed.

Bangladesh Railway: Rail Bhaban, 16 Abdul Ghani Rd, Dhaka 1000; tel. (2) 9561200; fax (2) 9563413; e-mail dg_rail@bangla.net; internet www.railway.gov.bd; f. 1862; supervised by the Ministry of Communications; divided into East and West Zones, with East Zone HQ at Chittagong (tel. (31) 843200; fax (31) 843215) and West Zone HQ at Rajshahi (tel. (721) 761576; fax (721) 761982); total length of 2,888.1 route km (2003); 459 stations; Dir-Gen. A. F. M. MUSTAFIZUR RAHMAN; Gen. Man. (East Zone) Sultan AHMED TALUKDER; Gen. Man. (West Zone) MD SAIFUR RAHMAN.

ROADS

In 1999 the total length of roads in use was 207,486 km (19,775 km of highways, 17,297 km of secondary roads and 170,413 km of other roads), of which 9.5% were paved. In 1992 the World Bank approved Bangladesh's US $700m. Jamuna Bridge Project. The construction of the 4.8-km bridge, which was, for the first time, to link the east and the west of the country with a railway and road network, was begun in early 1994. The bridge, which was renamed the Bangabandhu Jamuna Multipurpose Bridge, was officially opened in June 1998.

In June 1999 the first direct passenger bus service between Bangladesh (Dhaka) and India (Kolkata) was inaugurated.

Bangladesh Road Transport Corpn: Paribhaban, DIT Ave, Dhaka; f. 1961; state-owned; operates transport services, incl. truck division; transports govt food grain; Chair. AZMAN HOSSAIN CHOWD-HURY.

INLAND WATERWAYS

In Bangladesh there are some 8,433 km of navigable waterways, which transport 70% of total domestic and foreign cargo traffic and on which are located the main river ports of Dhaka, Narayanganj, Chandpur, Barisal and Khulna. A river steamer service connects these ports several times a week. Vessels of up to 175-m overall length can be navigated on the Karnaphuli river.

Bangladesh Inland Water Transport Corpn: 5 Dilkusha C/A, Dhaka 1000; tel. (2) 257092; f. 1972; 273 vessels (1986).

SHIPPING

The chief ports are Chittagong, where the construction of a second dry-dock is planned, and Chalna. A modern seaport is being developed at Mongla.

Atlas Shipping Lines Ltd: Atlas House, 7 Sk. Mujib Rd, Agrabad C/A, Chittagong 2; tel. (31) 504287; fax (31) 225520; Man. Dir S. U. CHOWDHURY; Gen. Man. M. KAMAL HAYAT.

Bangladesh Shipping Corpn: BSC Bhaban, Saltgola Rd, POB 641, Chittagong 4100; tel. (31) 713277; fax (31) 710506; e-mail bsc-ctg@spnetctg.com; f. 1972; maritime shipping; 15 vessels, 210,672 dwt capacity (1999); Chair. MOFAZZAL HOSSAIN CHOWDHURY MAYA; Man. Dir ZULFIQAR HAIDAR CHAUDHURY.

Bengal Shipping Line Ltd: Palm View, 100A Agrabad C/A, Chittagong 4100; tel. (31) 714800; fax (31) 710362; e-mail bsl@mkrgroup .com; Chair. MOHAMMED ABDUL AWWAL; Man. Dir MOHAMMED ABDUL MALEK.

Blue Ocean Lines Ltd: H.B.F.C. Bldg, 1st Floor, 1D Agrabad C/A, Agrabad, Chittagong; tel. (31) 501567; fax (31) 225415.

Broadway Shipping Line: Hafiz Estate, 65 Shiddeswari Rd, Dhaka; tel. (2) 404598; fax (2) 412254.

Chittagong Port Authority: POB 2013, Chittagong 4100; tel. (31) 505041; f. 1887; provides bunkering, ship repair, towage and lighterage facilities as well as provisions and drinking water supplies; Chair. MD SHAHADAT HUSSAIN.

Continental Liner Agencies: Facy Bldg, 3rd Floor, 87 Agrabad C/A, Chittagong; tel. (31) 721572; fax (31) 710965; Man. SAIFUL AHMED; Dir (Technical and Operations) Capt. MAHFUZUL ISLAM.

Nishan Shipping Lines Ltd: Monzoor Bldg, 1st Floor, 67 Agrabad C/A, Chittagong; tel. (31) 710855; fax (31) 710044; Dir Capt. A. K. M. ALAMGIR.

CIVIL AVIATION

There is an international airport at Dhaka (Zia International Airport), situated at Kurmitola, with the capacity to handle 5m. passengers annually. There are also airports at all major towns. In 1997 the civil aviation industry was deregulated to permit domestic competition to Biman Bangladesh Airlines.

Biman Bangladesh Airlines: Head Office, Balaka, Kurmitola, Dhaka 1229; tel. (2) 8917400; fax (2) 8913005; internet www .bimanair.com/; f. 1972; 100% state-owned; domestic services to seven major towns; international services to the Middle East, the Far East, Europe, and North America; Chair. Minister of Civil Aviation and Tourism; Man. Dir Air Cmmdre M. KHUSRUL ALAM.

GMG Airlines: ABC House, 9th Floor, 8 Kamal Atatürk Ave, Banani, Dhaka 1213; tel. (2) 8825845; fax (2) 8826115; e-mail gmgairlines@gmggroup.com; internet www.gmgairlines.com; f. 1997; private, domestic airline; Dir (Flight Operations) Capt. HABIBUR RAHMAN; Man. Dir SHAHAB SATTAR.

Tourism

Tourist attractions include the cities of Dhaka and Chittagong, Cox's Bazar—which has the world's longest beach (120 km)—on the Bay of Bengal, and Teknaf, at the southernmost point of Bangladesh. Tourist arrivals totalled 207,199 in 2001. Earnings from tourism reached US $48m. in the same year. The majority of visitors are from India, Japan, Pakistan, the United Kingdom and the USA.

Bangladesh Parjatan Corpn (National Tourism Organization): 233 Airport Rd, Tejgaon, Dhaka 1215; tel. (2) 8117855; fax (2) 8126501; e-mail bpcho@bangla.net; internet www .bangladeshtourism.org; f. 1972; there are four tourist information centres in Dhaka, and one each in Bogra, Chittagong, Cox's Bazar, Dinajpur, Khulna, Kuakata, Rangamati, Rangpur, Rajshahi and Sylhet; Chair. Dr MAHBUBUR RAHMAN; Man. (Public Relations Division) MOHAMMAD AHSAN ULLAH.

BARBADOS

Introductory Survey

Location, Climate, Language, Religion, Flag, Capital

Barbados is the most easterly of the Caribbean islands, lying about 320 km (200 miles) north-east of Trinidad. The island has a total area of 430 sq km (166 sq miles). There is a rainy season from July to November and the climate is tropical, tempered by constant sea winds, during the rest of the year. The mean annual temperature is about 26°C (78°F). Average annual rainfall varies from 1,250 mm (49 ins) on the coast, to 1,875 mm (74 ins) in the interior. The official language is English. Almost all of the inhabitants profess Christianity, but there are small groups of Hindus, Muslims and Jews. The largest denomination is the Anglican church, but about 90 other Christian sects are represented. The national flag (proportions 2 by 3) has three equal vertical stripes, of blue, gold and blue; superimposed on the centre of the gold band is the head of a black trident. The capital is Bridgetown.

Recent History

Barbados was formerly a British colony. The Barbados Labour Party (BLP) won a general election in 1951, when universal adult suffrage was introduced, and held office until 1961. Although the parliamentary system dates from 1639, ministerial government was not established until 1954, when the BLP's leader, Sir Grantley Adams, became the island's first Premier. He was subsequently Prime Minister of the West Indies Federation from January 1958 until its dissolution in May 1962.

Barbados achieved full internal self-government in October 1961. The Democratic Labour Party (DLP), formed in 1955 by dissident members of the BLP, won an election in December. The DLP's leader, Errol Barrow, became Premier, succeeding Dr Hugh Cummins of the BLP. When Barbados achieved independence on 30 November 1966, Barrow became the island's first Prime Minister, following another electoral victory by his party earlier in the month.

The DLP retained power in 1971, but in the general election of September 1976 the BLP, led by J. M. G. M. ('Tom') Adams (Sir Grantley's son), ended Barrow's 15-year rule. The BLP successfully campaigned against alleged government corruption, winning a large majority over the DLP. At a general election in June 1981 the BLP was returned to office with 17 of the 27 seats in the newly-enlarged House of Assembly. The DLP won the remainder of the seats. Adams died suddenly in March 1985 and was succeeded as Prime Minister by his deputy, Bernard St John, a former leader of the BLP.

At a general election in May 1986 the DLP won a decisive victory, receiving 59.4% of the total votes and winning 24 seats in the House of Assembly. Bernard St John and all except one of his cabinet ministers lost their seats, and Errol Barrow returned as Prime Minister after 10 years in opposition. In June it was announced that Barrow was to review Barbados' participation in the US-supported Regional Security System (RSS), the defence force that had been established soon after the US invasion of Grenada in October 1983. Under Adams Barbados was one of the countries whose troops had supported the invasion. In June 1987 Barrow died suddenly. He was succeeded by L. Erskine Sandiford (hitherto the Deputy Prime Minister), who pledged to continue Barrow's economic and social policies. In September 1987, however, the Minister of Finance, Dr Richard (Richie) Haynes, resigned, accusing Sandiford of failing to consult him over financial appointments. Sandiford assumed the finance portfolio, but acrimony over government policy continued to trouble the DLP. In February 1989 Haynes and three other members of Parliament resigned from the DLP and announced the formation of the National Democratic Party (NDP). Haynes was subsequently appointed as leader of the parliamentary opposition.

At a general election in January 1991 the DLP won 18 of the 28 seats in the enlarged House of Assembly, while the BLP secured the remaining 10. The creation of a Ministry of Justice and Public Safety by the new Government, and the reintroduction of flogging for convicted criminals reflected widespread concern over increased levels of violent crime on the island.

Moreover, as a result of serious economic problems, a series of austerity measures were proposed in September. However, the proposals resulted in public unrest, which continued in 1992, as large numbers of civil servants and agricultural workers were made redundant. In 1993 and 1994 the increasing unpopularity of Sandiford's premiership provoked continued demands for his resignation, culminating, in June 1994, in his narrow defeat in a parliamentary motion of confidence. At a general election on 6 September, the BLP won a decisive victory, securing 19 seats in the House of Assembly, compared with the DLP's eight and the NDP's one. Owen Arthur was subsequently appointed as Prime Minister.

In May 1995 Arthur announced the formation of a 10-member commission to advise the Government on possible reforms of the country's Constitution and political institutions. In July 1996 the commission was asked to consider, in particular, the continuing role of the British monarch as Head of State in Barbados. The commission's report, published in December 1998, recommended, as expected, the replacement of the British monarch with a ceremonial President. It also proposed changes in the composition of the Senate and the substitution of a jointly administered Caribbean Court of Justice for the existing highest judicial body, the Privy Council. In February 2001 Caribbean leaders agreed to establish such a court; following many delays, the court was inaugurated in April 2005.

In December 1996 the DLP retained a seat in a by-election. This development resulted in renewed pressure for the reunification of the DLP and the NDP, which together secured more votes (though fewer seats) than the BLP in the general election. In mid-1997 two prominent members of the NDP (including the influential General Secretary of the National Union of Public Workers, Joseph Goddard) rejoined the DLP. The NDP lost a further electoral candidate to the ruling BLP in November, and in September two candidates (one of whom subsequently joined the DLP) resigned from the BLP, attributing their decision to the Prime Minister's lack of control over the party. In September 1998 Hamilton Lashley, a prominent DLP member of the House of Assembly, accepted the post of consultant to the Prime Minister on matters of poverty alleviation. In October Lashley transferred political allegiance to the governing BLP.

The BLP received 64.8% of the total votes cast at the general election held in January 1999, taking 26 of the 28 seats in the House of Assembly; the two remaining seats were won by the DLP (the NDP did not contest the election). The heavy defeat for the DLP was largely attributed to the Government's recent successes in reviving the Barbadian economy, particularly in reducing unemployment. The Prime Minister announced an expanded 14-member Cabinet, including the new post of Minister of Social Transformation (to which Lashley was appointed), whose major concern was to be poverty alleviation.

In April 1999 Trafalgar Square, in the centre of Bridgetown, was renamed National Heroes Square, and the decision was made to replace the statue of the British Admiral Lord Horatio Nelson which stood there, with one of Errol Barrow, the country's first Prime Minister. These developments, which reinforced existing differences between Barbados' two main ethnic communities, were seen as evidence that the country was beginning its transformation into a republic, an aim set out by Arthur on the BLP's re-election. With the aim of resolving any growing divisions, the Government organized a day of national reconciliation in July, while a 13-member Committee for National Reconciliation was also established. In August 2000 Arthur announced that there would be a referendum on the replacement of the monarchy with a republic, a move that had the clear support of all political parties. A series of sharp political controversies in neighbouring Trinidad and Tobago over the constitutional powers of the President in 2000–02 led to an enhanced appreciation in Barbados of the need for careful consideration of the relationship between an elected Government and a ceremonial President. In early 2002 the Deputy Prime Minister and Minister of Foreign Affairs and Foreign Trade, Billie Miller, announced that new constitutional legislation would be drafted by the end of the year; however, the only change made was an amendment approved in September to override human rights judgments by the Privy Council, making it easier to make use of the death penalty.

A general election was held on 21 May 2003. The BLP conducted a strong electoral campaign that, notwithstanding the recent contraction of the tourism sector, emphasized the party's solid economic record. Some voters were reportedly concerned over allegations of serious mismanagement in the tourism sector (in particular, the Government's use of public money to pay off the debts of a financially troubled tourist resort—known as Gems of Barbados), waste disposal and other public-sector projects. None the less, Owen Arthur's BLP secured a third successive victory, attracting 55.8% of the votes cast, and securing 23 of the 30 seats in the enlarged House of Assembly. The DLP did, however increase its share of the popular vote to 44.1% (from 35.1% in 1999) and its parliamentary strength to seven, and the BLP retained four of its seats only by narrow margins. Clyde Mascoll, a former Central Bank economist, was appointed opposition leader, thereby potentially ending the DLP's long-running leadership dispute, which had adversely affected its election campaign, and allowing it to present itself as a more credible alternative. Arthur meanwhile appointed Mia Mottley, the Attorney-General and Minister of Home Affairs, as Deputy Prime Minister, making her a strong favourite as his eventual successor.

In June 2003 the Governor-General, appointed by the British monarch on the recommendation of Owen Arthur, announced that the Government intended to transform Barbados into a republic during the BLP's current five-year term in office. In February 2005 Arthur announced that a referendum on the issue would be held by the end of the year.

In late 1997 the Government established a committee to examine alternative methods of punishing offenders, following a report which found Barbados' only prison to be grossly overcrowded. In November 1998, owing to a recent significant increase in the number of violent crimes involving firearms, stricter penalties for unlawful possession of firearms were introduced. Amid a further escalation in violent crime and fears that the country's tourism industry might be affected, it was announced in October 1999 that an anti-firearms unit was to be established in the police force. In July 2001 the Inter-American Development Bank approved a US $8.75m. loan to help Barbados modernize and strengthen its justice and penal system. Furthermore, in September 2001 the Government announced plans to build a modern maximum-security prison, capable of housing 500 inmates. In November 2002 the Government established a National Commission on Law and Order to help develop a plan of action to combat the rising crime rate on the island.

The Governments of Barbados and Trinidad and Tobago agreed in late 1999 to draft a boundary delimitation treaty and to establish a negotiating mechanism to resolve trade disputes. The issue of boundary delimitation, however, remained unresolved, and in late January 2004 the Prime Minister of Trinidad and Tobago indicated he would refer the matter to the Caribbean Community and Common Market (CARICOM, see p. 172). Relations between the two countries worsened early in the following month after several Barbadian fishermen were arrested in Trinidad and Tobago's waters; in response, in early February Arthur called an emergency cabinet meeting, after which it was announced that sanctions would be imposed against Trinidad and Tobago manufacturers. Later that month Barbados referred the dispute for arbitration under the UN Convention on the Law of the Sea. In January 2005 the Barbados Government formed a committee to investigate whether a significant natural gas discovery off east Trinidad fell within Barbadian maritime territory. The Government of Trinidad and Tobago insisted the discovery was within its jurisdiction.

In late 1996 Barbados signed an agreement with the USA to co-operate with a regional initiative to combat the illegal drugs trade. The Government signed a similar agreement with the Organization of American States (OAS) in January 2005. In March 1998 Barbados began negotiations with the Organisation of Eastern Caribbean States (OECS, see p. 384) concerning the country's eventual membership of a confederation, and possible political union, of Eastern Caribbean states. Areas under discussion included health, education, diplomatic representation and the judiciary. A 14-member joint 'task force' had been appointed in February to discuss the possible incorporation of Barbados into the OECS. An inaugural meeting of the discussion group took place in April, when it was suggested that a working confederation could be instituted within 2–3 years.

Although monetary union was not to be a prior condition to membership, OECS spokesmen described the adoption of a single currency as highly desirable. In June 2000 Barbados officially declared its acceptance of the compulsory jurisdiction of the Inter-American Court of Human Rights (see p. 320), an institution of the OAS. Meanwhile, in 2005 Barbados was scheduled to join CARICOM's Caribbean Single Market and Economy (CSME). The CSME was to enshrine the free movement of good, services and labour throughout most of the CARICOM region, although most of the organization's members were not expected to join the new project until the end of 2005 at the earliest.

Government

Executive power is vested in the British monarch, represented by a Governor-General, who acts on the advice of the Cabinet. The Governor-General appoints the Prime Minister and, on the latter's recommendation, other members of the Cabinet. Legislative power is vested in the bicameral Parliament, comprising a Senate of 21 members, appointed by the Governor-General, and a House of Assembly with 30 members, elected by universal adult suffrage for five years (subject to dissolution) from single-member constituencies. The Cabinet is responsible to Parliament. In 1969 elected local government bodies were abolished in favour of a division into 11 parishes, all of which are administered by the central Government.

Defence

The Barbados Defence Force was established in 1978. The total strength of the Barbados armed forces in August 2004 was estimated at 610; the army consisted of 500 members and the navy (coastguard) 110. There was also a reserve force of 430. The defence budget for 2004 was estimated at Bds $26m.

Economic Affairs

In 2003, according to estimates by the World Bank, the island's gross national income (GNI), measured at average 2001–03 prices, was US $2,518m., equivalent to US $9,270 per head (or US $15,060 on an international purchasing-power parity basis). Between 1990 and 2003 the population increased at an average rate of 0.4% per year. Barbados' gross domestic product (GDP) per head, increased, in real terms, at an average rate of 0.6% per year during 1990–2003. Overall GDP increased, in real terms, at an average annual rate of 1.0% in 1990–2003. Real GDP decreased by 2.1% in 2002 and increased by1.6% in 2003.

Agriculture (including hunting, forestry and fishing) contributed 5.1% of GDP in 2003 and engaged an estimated 4.0% of the employed labour force in 2002. Sugar remains the main commodity export, earning US $21m. in 2003, when output was 36,000 metric tons (compared with $27m. and 58,000 tons in 2000). In 2003 sugar accounted for 9.2% of total exports, compared with 10.2% in 1999. Sea-island cotton, once the island's main export crop, was revived in the mid-1980s. The other principal crops, primarily for local consumption, are sweet potatoes, carrots, yams and other vegetables and fruit. Fishing was also developed in the late 20th century. The GDP of the agricultural sector declined, in real terms, at an average rate of 1.3% per year during 1990–2002. Agricultural GDP was estimated to have decreased by 3.6% in 2002 and by a further by 5.7% in 2003.

In 2003 industry accounted for an estimated 20.7% of GDP, and 18.8% of the working population were employed in all industrial activities (manufacturing, construction, quarrying and utilities) in 2002. In real terms, industrial GDP increased at an average rate of 1.1% annually in 1990–2002. Real industrial GDP rose by 1.0% in both 2002 and 2003.

Owing to fluctuations in international prices, the production of crude petroleum declined substantially from its peak in 1985, to 328,000 barrels in 1997. In late 1996 the Barbados National Oil Company signed a five-year agreement with a US company to intensify exploration activity, with the aim of increasing petroleum production from 1,000 barrels per day (b/d) to 10,000 b/d by 2001. As a result of an onshore drilling programme begun in 1997, production increased markedly, reaching 708,500 barrels in 1999; however, production fell thereafter and stood at 463,699 barrels in 2001. Production of natural gas decreased from 46.9m. cu m in 1998 to 35m. cu m in 2001. Imports of mineral fuels accounted for 11.1% of total imports in 2003. Mining and construction contributed 8.4% of GDP in 2003 and employed 10.3% of the working population in 2002.

Manufacturing contributed 8.2% of GDP in 2003 and employed 7.0% of the working population in 2002. Excluding sugar factories and refineries, the principal branches of manufacturing were chemical, petroleum, rubber and plastic products, food products and beverages and tobacco. Manufacturing GDP decreased, in real terms, at an average rate of 0.7% per year during 1990–2002; it remained at the same level in 2002 and 2003.

Service industries are the main sector of the economy, accounting for 74.2% of GDP in 2003 and 77.4% of employment in 2002. The combined GDP of the service sectors increased, in real terms, at an average rate of 0.7% per year during 1990–2002. In 2002 the sector grew by 0.7% and, in 2003, by 3.3%. Business and general services contributed 16.6% of GDP in 2003. The Government has encouraged the growth of 'offshore' financial facilities, particularly through the negotiation of double taxation agreements with other countries. At the end of 2003 there were 4,637 international business companies and at the end of 2001 2,981 foreign sales corporations were operating in the country. Barbados has an active anti-money-laundering regime, which was further strengthened by new legislation in 1998. Despite this, in May 2000 the Organisation for Economic Co-operation and Development (OECD, see p. 307) placed Barbados on a list of tax 'havens' that were likely to incur countermeasures from February 2002 if they failed to modify tax regimes in line with OECD requirements. However, Barbados avoided inclusion on a list of non-co-operating jurisdictions drawn up by the Financial Action Task Force on Money Laundering (see p. 377) in September 2001, and was removed from the OECD list in January 2002. Tourism made a direct contribution of an estimated 10.3% to GDP in 2002, and tourism with commerce employed 26.3% of the working population in that same year. Receipts from the tourist industry almost doubled between 1980 and 1988, and in 2003 totalled US $695.1m.. Partly because of the reduction in the number of US tourists following the terrorist attacks in the USA of September 2001 and partly owing to the US Government's 'war on terror' that commenced shortly afterwards, stop-over tourist arrivals decreased from 545,027 in 2000 to 497,899 in 2002, while cruise-ship passenger arrivals also decreased over the same period by 0.9%, to 523,253. By 2004, however, the number of stop-over tourist arrivals had recovered and reportedly increased to over 550,000 in that year—a record figure. In 2002 some 38.8% of stop-over arrivals were from the United Kingdom.

In 2003 Barbados recorded a visible trade deficit of US $801.4m., while there was a deficit of $169.4m. on the current account of the balance of payments. In 2002 the USA was both the principal source of imports (44.1%) and the largest single recipient of exports (13.7%). The United Kingdom accounted for 7.9% of imports and 9.9% of exports. Other major trading partners included the CARICOM (see below) countries, especially Trinidad and Tobago. The principal commodity exports in 2003 were sugar and molasses (9.2% of total exports), chemicals (8.3%) and rum (7.0%). The principal imports were food and beverages and fuels.

For the financial year ending 31 March 2004 there was an estimated total budgetary deficit of Bds $144m. At December 2003 the total external debt of Barbados was some US $712m.; the cost of foreign debt-servicing was equivalent to 7.3% of the value of current-account receipts. The average annual rate of inflation was 1.2% in 1997–2003. Consumer prices rose by an average of 0.1% in 2002 and by 1.7% in 2003. By the end of Dceember 2003 the official unemployment rate was 11.0%, compared with 9.4% at the end of 2000.

Barbados is a member of the Caribbean Community and Common Market (CARICOM, see p. 172), of the Inter-American Development Bank (IDB, see p. 268), of the Latin American Economic System (SELA, see p. 374) and of the Association of Caribbean States (see p. 372).

Political stability and consensus have contributed to the economic strengths of Barbados. Tourism dominates the economy but 'offshore' banking and sugar production are also important.

The sugar industry came under increased pressure to reform from the 1990s, particularly as further liberalization of international trade made the island's principal export less competitive. A phased liberalization of the telecommunications market commenced at the end of 2000; the commencement of the third phase—exposing the sector to full competition in the international telecommunications market—was anticipated in 2005. The proposed privatization of the Barbados National Bank and the Insurance Company of Barbados were also announced (the latter was transferred to the private sector in December 2000), and plans to partially privatize Grantley Adams International Airport and to restructure the ailing sugar industry were in progress in 2005. Following eight successive years of economic expansion, in 2001 a decrease in real GDP of 2.8% was recorded, and there was a further decrease of 2.1% in 2002. The economy emerged from recession in 2003, however, when growth of 1.6% was recorded; projected growth for 2004 was 2.5% and the Government budgeted for growth of around 3.0% in 2005. Following the 2001 terrorist attacks in the USA and the subsequent US-led military engagements in Afghanistan and Iraq, the Barbados tourist industry suffered a significant decrease in bookings. The sector, however, expanded in 2003 and tourists were reported to have holidayed in Barbados in record numbers in 2004. The projected 25% increase in the number of cruise-ship passengers and 8.8% increase in the number of stop-over visitors underpinned the economy's predicted sturdy performance in that year.

Education

Education is compulsory for 12 years, between five and 16 years of age. Primary education begins at the age of five and lasts for seven years. Secondary education, beginning at 12 years of age, lasts for five years. In 2002 enrolment of children in the primary age-group was 99.1% (males 99.8%, females 98.5%), and in the secondary-school age-group enrolment was 98% (males 97.4%, females 98.6%). Tuition at all government schools is free. In the same year enrolment at tertiary level was some 48% of the relevant age-group (males 38.5%; females 57.5%). In 1998 7,538 students were enrolled at universities or similar institutions. Degree courses in arts, law, education, natural sciences and social sciences are offered at the Cave Hill campus of the University of the West Indies. A two-year clinical-training programme for medical students is conducted by the School of Clinic Medicine and Research of the University, while an in-service training programme for teachers is provided by the School of Education. In 2002 80% of children aged three and four attended school. According to the 2002 budget address, government expenditure on education in 2002/03 would equal Bds $396m., representing 19.8% of total expenditure. A US $200m. programme for curriculum reform and the introduction of technology into education, Edutech 2000, was scheduled for completion by 2007.

Public Holidays

2005: 1 January (New Year's Day), 21 January (Errol Barrow Day), 25 March (Good Friday), 28 March (Easter Monday), 28 April (National Heroes' Day), 2 May (Labour Day), 16 May (Whit Monday), 1 August (Kadooment Day), 2 August (Emancipation Day), 30 November (Independence Day), 25–26 December (Christmas).

2006: 1 January (New Year's Day), 21 January (Errol Barrow Day), 14 April (Good Friday), 17 April (Easter Monday), 28 April (National Heroes' Day), 1 May (Labour Day), 5 June (Whit Monday), 1 August (Emancipation Day), 7 August (Kadooment Day), 30 November (Independence Day), 25–26 December (Christmas).

Weights and Measures

The metric system is used.

Statistical Survey

Sources (unless otherwise stated): Barbados Statistical Service, National Insurance Bldg, 3rd Floor, Fairchild St, Bridgetown; tel. 427-7841; fax 435-2198; e-mail barstats@caribsurf.com; internet www.bgis.gov.bb/stats; Central Bank of Barbados, Tom Adams Financial Centre, Spry St, POB 1016, Bridgetown; tel. 436-6870; fax 427-1431; e-mail cbb.libr@caribsurf.com; internet www.centralbank.org.bb.

AREA AND POPULATION

Area: 430 sq km (166 sq miles).

Population: 252,029 (males 119,665, females 132,364) at census of 12 May 1980; 257,082 (provisional) at census of 2 May 1990; 270,800 at mid-2002.

Density (mid-2002): 629.8 per sq km.

Ethnic Groups (*de jure* population, excl. persons resident in institutions, 1990 census): Black 228,683; White 8,022; Mixed race 5,886; Total (incl. others) 247,288.

Principal Town: Bridgetown (capital), population 5,928 at 1990 census. *Mid-2003* (UN estimate, incl. suburbs): Bridgetown 139,854 (Source: UN, *World Urbanization Prospects: The 2003 Revision*).

Births, Marriages and Deaths (provisional, 2000): Live births 3,762 (birth rate 14.1 per 1,000); Marriages (1997) 3,377 (marriage rate 12.7 per 1,000); Deaths 2,367 (death rate 8.8 per 1,000). Source: partly UN, *Population and Vital Statistics Report*.

Expectation of Life (WHO estimates, years at birth): 74.3 (males 70.5; females 77.9) in 2002. Source: WHO, *World Health Report*.

Economically Active Population (provisional and rounded figures, labour force sample survey, '000 persons aged 15 years and over, excl. armed forces, 2001): Agriculture, forestry and fishing 5.4; Manufacturing 9.2; Electricity, gas and water 2.0; Construction and quarrying 14.2; Wholesale and retail trade 18.9; Tourism 13.7; Transport, storage and communications 5.9; Financing, insurance, real estate and business services 10.4; Community, social and personal services 48.8; Activities not adequately defined 0.2; *Total employed* 128.7 (males 67.6, females 58.5); Unemployed 14.1 (males 6.1, females 7.5); *Total labour force* 142.8 (males 73.7, females 66.0) (Source: ILO Caribbean Office). *2002:* Total employed: 128.7; Unemployed 14.5; Total labour force 143.2 (Source: IMF, *Barbados: Statistical Appendix* (May 2004)).

HEALTH AND WELFARE

Key Indicators

Total Fertility Rate (children per woman, 2002): 1.5.

Under-5 Mortality Rate (per 1,000 live births, 2003): 13.

HIV/AIDS (% of persons aged 15–49, 2003): 1.5.

Physicians (per 1,000 head, 1995): 1.28.

Hospital Beds (per 1,000 head, 1996): 7.56.

Health Expenditure (2001): US $ per head (PPP): 940.

Health Expenditure (2001): % of GDP: 6.5.

Health Expenditure (2001): public (% of total): 66.3.

Access to Water (% of persons, 2002): 100.

Access to Sanitation (% of persons, 2002): 99.

Human Development Index (2002): ranking: 29.

Human Development Index (2002): value: 0.888.

For sources and definitions, see explanatory note on p. vi.

AGRICULTURE, ETC.

Principal Crops ('000 metric tons, 2003): Sweet potatoes 2.6; Yams 1.2; Other roots and tubers 0.6*; Sugar cane 364.6; Pulses 1.0*; Coconuts 1.7*; Cabbages 0.6; Tomatoes 1.2; Cucumbers 2.0; Chillies and peppers 1.3; String beans 0.9*; Carrots 1.0; Okra 1.5; Green corn 0.7*; Other vegetables 4.6*; Bananas 0.6*; Other fruits 3.0*.
* FAO estimate. Source: FAO.

Livestock (FAO estimates, '000 head, year ending September 2003): Horses 1.1; Mules 2.0; Asses 2.1; Cattle 13.5; Pigs 16.6; Sheep 27.0; Goats 5.0; Poultry 3,450. Source: FAO.

Livestock Products (FAO estimates, '000 metric tons, 2003): Beef and veal 0.4; Pig meat 2.2; Poultry meat 11.1; Cows' milk 7.0; Hen eggs 1.6. Source: FAO.

Forestry (FAO estimates, '000 cubic metres): Roundwood removals 5 in 2001; 5 in 2002; 5 in 2003. Source: FAO.

Fishing (metric tons, live weight, 2002): Total catch 2,500 (Yellowfin tuna 115; Flyingfishes 1,590; Common dolphinfish 553). Source: FAO.

MINING

Production (2001): Natural gas 35.0m. cu m; Crude petroleum 463,699 barrels.

INDUSTRY

Selected Products (2001): Raw sugar 36,325 metric tons (2003); Rum 12,000,000 litres; Beer 6,700,000 litres; Cigarettes (1995) 65m.; Batteries (official estimate, 1998) 17,165; Electric energy (estimate, 2000) 787m. kWh. Sources: partly UN, *Industrial Commodity Statistics Yearbook*, and IMF, *Barbados: Statistical Appendix* (May 2004).

FINANCE

Currency and Exchange Rates: 100 cents = 1 Barbados dollar (Bds $). *Sterling, US Dollar and Euro Equivalents* (31 December 2004): £1 sterling = Bds $3.8628; US $1 = Bds $2.0000; €1 = Bds $2.7242; Bds $100 = £25.89 = US $50.00 = €36.71. *Exchange Rate:* Fixed at US $1 = Bds $2.000 since 1986.

Budget (Bds $ million, year ending 31 March 2003): *Revenue:* Tax revenue 1,620.6 (Direct taxes 731.6, of which Personal income tax 358.3, Corporate taxes 220.3, Taxes on property 95.7; Indirect taxes 889.0, of which Value-added tax 494.5, Excises 114.2, Import duties 160.1, Other indirect taxes 106.9); Non-tax revenue 114.6; Total 1,735.2. *Expenditure:* Current 1,688.3 (Wages and salaries 683.6, Other goods and services 215.3, Interest payments 268.7, Transfers and subsidies 520.7); Capital (incl. net lending 2.8) 316.0; Total 2,004.3. Note: Budgetary data refer to current and capital budgets only and exclude operations of the National Insurance Fund and other central government units with their own budgets.

International Reserves (US $ million at 31 December 2003): IMF special drawing rights 0.01; Reserve position in IMF 7.46; Foreign exchange 730.47; Total 737.94. Source: IMF, *International Financial Statistics*.

Money Supply (Bds $ million at 31 December 2003): Currency outside banks 329.0; Demand deposits at commercial banks 1,211.7; Total money (incl. others) 1,543.0. Source: IMF, *International Financial Statistics*.

Cost of Living (Index of Retail Prices; base: 2000 = 100): 102.6 in 2001; 102.7 in 2002; 104.4 in 2003. Source: IMF, *International Financial Statistics*.

Expenditure on the Gross Domestic Product (Bds $ million at current prices, 2002): Total consumption expenditure 4,621.0; Gross fixed capital formation 835.4; *Total domestic expenditure* 5,456.4; Exports of goods and services 2,479.6; *Less* Imports of goods and services 2,739.5; *GDP in purchasers' values* 5,196.5. Source: UN, *National Accounts Statistics*.

Gross Domestic Product by Economic Activity (estimates, Bds $ million at current prices, 2001): Agriculture, hunting, forestry and fishing 199; Mining and quarrying 28; Manufacturing 256; Electricity, gas and water 146; Construction 243; Wholesale and retail trade 645; Hotels and restaurants 471; Transport, storage and communications 467; Finance, insurance, real estate and business services 798; Government services 758; Other community, social and personal services 211; *GDP at factor cost* 4,223; Indirect taxes, *less* subsidies 875; *GDP in purchasers' values* 5,098.

Balance of Payments (US $ million, 2003): Exports of goods f.o.b. 264.2; Imports of goods f.o.b. –1,065.6; *Trade balance* –801.4; Exports of services 1,165.5; Imports of services –518.8; *Balance on goods and services* –154.7; Other income received 75.1; Other income paid –182.0; *Balance on goods, services and income* –261.6; Current transfers received 126.5; Current transfers paid –34.3; *Current balance* –169.4; Direct investment abroad –0.5; Direct investment from abroad 58.3; Portfolio investment assets –22.9; Portfolio investment liabilities 84.1; Other investment assets –83.1; Other investment liabilities 166.5; Net errors and omissions 34.4; *Overall balance* 67.4. Source: IMF, *International Financial Statistics*.

EXTERNAL TRADE

Principal Commodities (preliminary, US $ million, 2003): *Imports c.i.f.:* Food and beverages 159; Motor cars 37; Fuels 114; Chemicals 52; Construction materials 74; Total (incl. others) 1,025. *Exports f.o.b.:* Sugar and molasses 21; Rum 16; Other food and beverages 21; Chemicals 19; Electrical components 12; Other manufactures 39; Total (incl. other exports and re-exports) 229. Source: IMF, *Barbados: Statistical Appendix* (May 2004).

Principal Trading Partners (US $ million, 2002): *Imports:* Brazil 16.7; Canada 37.1; China, People's Republic 26.6; Demark 10.0; France 19.1; Germany 17.8; Guyana 10.6; Italy 10.4; Japan 45.0; Mexico 10.4; Netherlands 18.6; New Zealand 11.5; Suriname 6.7; Switzerland 7.3; Trinidad and Tobago 116.2; United Kingdom 78.6; USA 439.8; Total (incl. others) 996.6. *Exports:* Antigua and Barbuda 7.2; Bahamas 2.1; Belize 2.5; Canada 4.5; Dominica 4.1; Grenada 6.7; Guyana 8.5; Jamaica 15.0; Saint Lucia 11.4; Saint Christopher and Nevis 5.5; Saint Vincent and the Grenadines 9.1; Spain 2.9; Suriname 5.3; Trinidad and Tobago 23.7; United Kingdom 25.7; USA 35.6; Total (incl. others) 259.3 (Source: UN, *International Trade Statistics Yearbook*). *2003* (preliminary, US $ million): Total imports 1,025; Total exports 229 (Source: IMF, *Barbados: Statistical Appendix* (May 2004)).

TRANSPORT

Road Traffic (motor vehicles in use, 2002): Private cars 81,648; Buses and coaches 736; Lorries and vans 6,962; Motor cycles and mopeds 1,856; Road tractors 921. Source: International Road Federation, *World Road Statistics*.

Shipping (estimated freight traffic, '000 metric tons, 1990): Goods loaded 206; Goods unloaded 538 (Source: UN, *Monthly Bulletin of Statistics*). *Total goods handled* ('000 metric tons, 1997): 1,095 (Source: Barbados Port Authority). *Merchant Fleet* (vessels registered at 31 December 2003): Number of vessels 68; Total displacement 467,653 grt (Source: Lloyd's Register-Fairplay, *World Fleet Statistics*).

Civil Aviation (1994): Aircraft movements 36,100; Freight loaded 5,052.3 metric tons; Freight unloaded 8,548.3 metric tons.

TOURISM

Tourist Arrivals ('000 persons): *Stop-overs:* 507.1 in 2001; 498.0 in 2002; 531.2 in 2003. *Cruise-ship Passengers:* 527.6 in 2001; 523.3 in 2002; 559.1 in 2003. Source: Caribbean Development Bank, *Social and Economic Indicators*.

Visitor Arrivals by Country ('000 persons, 2002): Canada 47; United Kingdom 193; USA 123; Total (incl. others) 498. Source: IMF, *Barbados: Statistical Appendix* (May 2004).

Tourism Receipts (estimates, US $ million): 697.2 in 2001; 657.9 in 2002; 695.1 in 2003. Source: Caribbean Development Bank, *Social and Economic Indicators*.

COMMUNICATIONS MEDIA

Radio Receivers (1999): 175,000 in use.

Television Receivers (2000): 83,000 in use.

Telephones (2001): 129,000 main lines in use.

Facsimile Machines (year ending 31 March 1997): 1,800 in use.

Mobile Cellular Telephones (2001): 53,100 subscribers.

Personal Computers (2001): 25,000 in use.

Internet Users (2001): 15,000.

Newspapers: *Daily* (1996): 2 (circulation 53,000). *Non-daily* (1990): 4 (estimated circulation 95,000).
Sources: partly UNESCO, *Statistical Yearbook*, UN, *Statistical Yearbook*, and International Telecommunication Union.

EDUCATION

Pre-primary (1995/96): 84 schools; 529 teachers; 4,689 pupils.

Primary (2002): 109 schools; 1,823 teachers; 29,502 pupils.

Secondary (2002): 32 schools; 1,389 teachers; 21,436 pupils.

Tertiary (2002): 4 schools; 339 teachers; 11,226 students.
Source: Ministry of Education, Youth Affairs and Sport.

Adult Literacy Rate (UNESCO estimates): 99.7% (males 99.7%; females 99.7%) in 2002. Source: UN Development Programme, *Human Development Report*.

Directory

The Constitution

The parliamentary system has been established since the 17th century, when the first Assembly sat, in 1639, and the Charter of Barbados was granted, in 1652. A new Constitution came into force on 30 November 1966, when Barbados became independent. Under its terms, protection is afforded to individuals from slavery and forced labour, from inhuman treatment, deprivation of property, arbitrary search and entry, and racial discrimination; freedom of conscience, of expression, assembly, and movement are guaranteed.

Executive power is nominally vested in the British monarch, as Head of State, represented in Barbados by a Governor-General, who appoints the Prime Minister and, on the advice of the Prime Minister, appoints other ministers and some senators.

The Cabinet consists of the Prime Minister, appointed by the Governor-General as being the person best able to command a majority in the House of Assembly, and not fewer than five other ministers. Provision is also made for a Privy Council, presided over by the Governor-General.

Parliament consists of the Governor-General and a bicameral legislature, comprising the Senate and the House of Assembly. The Senate has 21 members: 12 appointed by the Governor-General on the advice of the Prime Minister, two on the advice of the Leader of the Opposition and seven as representatives of such interests as the Governor-General considers appropriate. The House of Assembly has (since 2003) 30 members, elected by universal adult suffrage for a term of five years (subject to dissolution). The minimum voting age is 18 years.

The Constitution also provides for the establishment of Service Commissions for the Judicial and Legal Service, the Public Service, the Police Service and the Statutory Boards Service. These Commissions are exempt from legal investigation; they have executive powers relating to appointments, dismissals and disciplinary control of the services for which they are responsible.

The Government

HEAD OF STATE

Monarch: HM Queen Elizabeth II (succeeded to the throne 6 February 1952).

Governor-General: Sir Clifford Husbands (appointed 1 June 1996).

THE CABINET
(March 2005)

Prime Minister and Minister of Finance, Economic Affairs and the Civil Service: Owen S. Arthur.

Deputy Prime Minister, Attorney-General, Leader of Government Business in the House of Assembly and Minister of Home Affairs: Mia Amor Mottley.

Minister of Agriculture and Rural Development: Sen. Erskine Griffith.

Minister of Commerce, Consumer Affairs and Business Development: Sen. Lynette Eastmond.

Minister of Education, Youth Affairs and Sport: Reginald Farley.

Minister of Energy and Public Utilities: Anthony P. Wood.

Minister of Foreign Affairs and Foreign Trade: Sen. Billie A. Miller.

Minister of Health: Dr Jerome Walcott.

Minister of Housing, Lands and the Environment: Elizabeth Thompson.

Minister of Industry and International Business: Dale Marshall.

Minister of Labour and Social Security: Rawle C. Eastmond.

Minister of Public Works: Gline A. Clarke.

Minister of Social Transformation: HAMILTON F. LASHLEY.

Minister of Tourism and International Transport: NOEL A. LYNCH.

Minister of State in the Office of the Prime Minister and the Ministry for the Civil Service: Sen. JOHN WILLIAMS.

Minister of State in the Ministry of Foreign Affairs and Foreign Trade: KERRIE SYMONDS.

Minister of State in the Ministry of Education, Youth Affairs and Sport: CYNTHIA FORDE.

MINISTRIES

Office of the Prime Minister: Government Headquarters, Bay St, St Michael; tel. 436-6435; fax 436-9280; e-mail info@primeminister .gov.bb; internet www.primeminister.gov.bb.

Ministry of Agriculture and Rural Development: Graeme Hall, POB 505, Christ Church; tel. 428-4150; fax 420-8444; internet www .barbados.gov.bb/minagri.

Ministry for the Civil Service: Roebuck Plaza, 20–23 Roebuck St, Bridgetown; tel. 426-2390; fax 228-0093.

Ministry of Commerce, Consumer Affairs and Business Development: Government Headquarters, Bay St, St Michael; tel. 427-5270.

Ministry of Education, Youth Affairs and Sport: Elsie Payne Complex, Constitution Rd, Bridgetown; tel. 430-2700; fax 436-2411; e-mail mined1@caribsurf.com; internet www.edutech2000.gov.bb.

Ministry of Energy and Public Utilities: Government Headquarters, Bay St, St Michael.

Ministry of Finance and Economic Affairs: Government Headquarters, Bay St, St Michael; tel. 436-6435; fax 429-4032.

Ministry of Foreign Affairs and Foreign Trade: 1 Culloden Rd, St Michael; tel. 436-2990; fax 429-6652; e-mail barbados@foreign .gov.bb; internet www.foreign.gov.bb.

Ministry of Health: Jemmott's Lane, St Michael; tel. 426-5080; fax 426-5570.

Ministry of Home Affairs: General Post Office Bldg, Level 5, Cheapside, Bridgetown; tel. 228-8961; fax 437-3794; e-mail mha@ caribsurf.com.

Ministry of Housing, Lands and the Environment: National Housing Corpn Bldg, 'The Garden', Country Rd, St Michael; tel. 431-7800; fax 435-0174; e-mail nurses@gob.bb.

Ministry of Industry and International Business: The Business Centre, Upton, St Michael; tel. 430-2200; fax 429-6849; e-mail mtbbar@caribsurf.com.

Ministry of Labour and Social Security: Docklands Pl. and Cavans Lane, Bridgetown; tel. 427-7550; fax 426-8959; internet www.labour.gov.bb.

Ministry of Public Works: The Pine, St Michael; tel. 429-2191; fax 437-8133; internet www.publicworks.gov.bb.

Ministry of Social Transformation: Nicholas House, Broad St, Bridgetown; tel. 228-5878.

Ministry of Tourism and International Transport: Sherbourne Conference Centre, Two Mile Hill, St Michael; tel. 430-7500; fax 436-4828; e-mail barmot@sunbeach.net; internet www.barmot.gov.bb.

Office of the Attorney-General: Sir Frank Walcott Bldg, Culloden Rd, St Michael; tel. 431-7750; fax 228-5433; e-mail attygen@ caribsurf.com.bb.

Legislature

PARLIAMENT

Senate

President: Sir FRED GOLLOP.

There are 21 members.

House of Assembly

Speaker: ISHMAEL ROETT.

General Election, 21 May 2003

Party	% of votes	Seats
Barbados Labour Party (BLP) . .	55.8	23
Democratic Labour Party (DLP) . .	44.1	7
Total	100.0	30

Political Organizations

Barbados Labour Party: Grantley Adams House, 111 Roebuck St, Bridgetown; tel. 429-1990; e-mail hq@blp.org.bb; internet www.blp .org.bb; f. 1938; moderate social democrat; Leader and Chair. OWEN S. ARTHUR; Gen. Sec. WILLIAM DUGUID.

Democratic Labour Party (DLP): 'Kennington', George St, Belleville, St Michael; tel. 429-3104; fax 427-0548; e-mail dlp@sunbeach .net; internet www.dlpbarbados.org; f. 1955; Pres. Sen. FREUNDEL STUART; Leader CLYDE MASCOLL.

Diplomatic Representation

EMBASSIES AND HIGH COMMISSIONS IN BARBADOS

Brazil: Sunjet House, 3rd Floor, Fairchild St, Bridgetown; tel. 427-1735; fax 427-1744; e-mail brembarb@sunbeach.net; internet www .brazilbb.org; Ambassador ORLANDO GALVÊAS OLIVEIRA.

Canada: Bishops Court Hill, Pine Rd, POB 404, St Michael; tel. 429-3550; fax 429-3780; e-mail bdgtn@international.gc.ca; internet www .dfait-maeci.gc.ca/barbados; High Commissioner MICHAEL C. WELSH.

China, People's Republic: 17 Golf View Terrace, Rockley, Christ Church; tel. 435-6890; fax 435-8300; e-mail chineseembbds@ caribsurf.com; Ambassador YANG ZHIKUAN.

Costa Rica: Omega Bldg, Suite 4, 1st Floor, Dayreels Rd, Christ Church; tel. 431-0250; fax 431-0261; e-mail embc@sunbeach.net; Ambassador EMILIA SALAZAR BORBÓN.

Cuba: Palm View, Erdiston Dr., St Michael; tel. 435-2769; fax 435-2734; e-mail embajadadecuba@sunbeach.net; Ambassador JOSÉ JOAQUÍN ALVAREZ PORTELA.

United Kingdom: Lower Collymore Rock, POB 676, St Michael; tel. 430-7800; fax 430-7813; e-mail britishhcb@sunbeach.net; internet www.britishhighcommission.gov.uk/barbados; High Commissioner JOHN WHITE.

USA: Canadian Imperial Bank of Commerce Bldg, Broad St, POB 302, Bridgetown; tel. 436-4950; fax 429-5246; internet bridgetown .usembassy.gov; Ambassador MARY ELIZABETH KRAMER.

Venezuela: Hastings, Main Rd, Christ Church; tel. 435-7903; fax 435-7830; e-mail jesusmachin@sunbeach.net; Ambassador MARIA CORINA RUSSIAN FRONTADO.

Judicial System

Justice is administered by the Supreme Court of Judicature, which consists of a High Court and a Court of Appeal. Final appeal lies with the Judicial Committee of the Privy Council, in the United Kingdom. There are Magistrates' Courts for lesser offences, with appeal to the Court of Appeal.

Supreme Court: Judiciary Office, Coleridge St, Bridgetown; tel. 426-3461; fax 246-2405.

Chief Justice: Sir DAVID SIMMONS.

Justices of Appeal: G. C. R. MOE; ERROL DA COSTA CHASE; COLIN A. WILLIAMS.

Judges of the High Court: FREDERICK A. WATERMAN; MARIE A. MACCORMACK; E. GARVEY HUSBANDS; CARLISLE PAYNE; SHERMAN MOORE; LIONEL DACOSTA GREENIDGE.

Registrar of the Supreme Court: SANDRA MASON.

Office of the Attorney-General: Sir Frank Walcott Bldg, Culloden Rd, St Michael; tel. 431-7750; fax 228–5433; e-mail attygen@ caribsurf.com.bb; Dir of Public Prosecutions CHARLES LEACOCK; e-mail cbleacock@inaccs.com.bb.

Religion

More than 100 religious denominations and sects are represented in Barbados, but the vast majority of the population profess Christianity. About 40% of the total population were Anglican, while the Pentecostal (8%) and Methodist (7%) churches were next in importance. There are also small groups of Hindus, Muslims and Jews.

CHRISTIANITY

Barbados Christian Council

Caribbean Conference of Churches Bldg, George St and Collymore Rock, St Michael; tel. 426-6014.

The Anglican Communion

Anglicans in Barbados are adherents of the Church in the Province of the West Indies, comprising eight dioceses. The Archbishop of the Province is the Bishop of Nassau and the Bahamas, resident in Nassau, the Bahamas. In Barbados there is a Provincial Office (St George's Church, St George) and an Anglican Theological College (Codrington College, St John).

Bishop of Barbados: Rt Rev. RUFUS THEOPHILUS BROOME, Leland, Philip Dr., Pine Gardens, St Michael; fax 426-0871; e-mail mandeville@sunbeach.com.

The Roman Catholic Church

Barbados comprises a single diocese (formed in January 1990, when the diocese of Bridgetown-Kingstown was divided), which is suffragan to the archdiocese of Port of Spain (Trinidad and Tobago). At 31 December 2002 there were an estimated 10,750 adherents in the diocese. The Bishop participates in the Antilles Episcopal Conference (currently based in Port of Spain, Trinidad and Tobago).

Bishop of Bridgetown: Rt Rev. MALCOLM PATRICK GALT, St Patrick's Presbytery, Jemmott's Lane, POB 1223, Bridgetown; tel. 426-3510; fax 429-6198; e-mail rcbishopbgi@caribnet.com.

Other Churches

Baptist Churches of Barbados: National Baptist Convention, President Kennedy Dr., Bridgetown; tel. 429-2697.

Church of God (Caribbean Atlantic Assembly): St Michael's Plaza, St Michael's Row, POB 1, Bridgetown; tel. 427-5770; Pres. Rev. VICTOR BABB.

Church of Jesus Christ of Latter-Day Saints (Mormons)—West Indies Mission: Bridgetown; tel. 435-8595; fax 435-8278.

Church of the Nazarene: District Office, Eagle Hall, Bridgetown; tel. 425-1067.

Methodist Church: Bethel Church Office, Bay St, Bridgetown; tel. and fax 426-2223; e-mail methodist@caribsurf.com.

Moravian Church: Roebuck St, Bridgetown; tel. 426-2337; Superintendent Rev. ERROL CONNOR.

Seventh-day Adventists (East Caribbean Conference): Brydens Ave, Brittons Hill, POB 223, St Michael; tel. 429-7234; fax 429-8055; e-mail president@eastcarib.org; internet wwww.eastcarib.org; Pres. JAMES F. DANIEL.

Wesleyan Holiness Church: General Headquarters, Bank Hall; tel. 429-4864.

Other denominations include the Abundant Life Assembly, the African Orthodox Church, the Apostolic Church, the Assemblies of Brethren, the Berean Bible Brethren, the Bethel Evangelical Church, Christ is the Answer Family Church, the Church of God the Prophecy, the Ethiopian Orthodox Church, the Full Gospel Assembly, Love Gospel Assembly, the New Testament Church of God, the Pentecostal Assemblies of the West Indies, the People's Cathedral, the Salvation Army, Presbyterian congregations, the African Methodist Episcopal Church, the Mt Olive United Holy Church of America and Jehovah's Witnesses.

ISLAM

In 1996 there were an estimated 2,000 Muslims in Barbados.

Islamic Teaching Centre: Harts Gap, Hastings; tel. 427-0120.

JUDAISM

Jewish Community: Nidhe Israel and Shaara Tzedek Synagogue, Rockley New Rd, POB 651, Bridgetown; tel. 437-1290; fax 437-1303; Pres. RACHELLE ALTMAN; Sec. SHARON ORAN.

HINDUISM

At the census of 1980 there were 411 Hindus on the island.

Hindu Community: Hindu Temple, Roberts Complex, Government Hill, St Michael; tel. 434-4638.

The Press

Barbados Advocate: POB 230, St Michael; tel. 467-2000; fax 434-1000; e-mail news@barbadosadvocate.com; internet www.barbadosadvocate.com; f. 1895; daily; Editor (vacant); circ. 11,413.

The Broad Street Journal: Plantation Complex, St Lawrence Main Rd, Christ Church; tel. 420-6245; fax 420-5477; e-mail bsj@sunbeach.net; f. 1993; weekly; business; Editor RICHARD COSTAS.

The Nation: Nation House, Fontabelle, POB 1203, St Michael; tel. 430-5400; fax 427-6968; e-mail nationnews@sunbeach.net; internet www.nationnews.com; f. 1973; daily; also publishes the *Sun on*

Saturday, the *Sunday Sun* (q.v.) and the *Visitor* (a free publ. for tourists); Pres. and Editor-in-Chief HAROLD HOYTE; circ. 23,144 (weekday), 33,084 (weekend).

Official Gazette: Government Printing Office, Bay St, St Michael; tel. 436-6776; Mon. and Thur.

Sunday Advocate: POB 230, St Michael; tel. 467-2000; fax 434-1000; e-mail news@sunbeach.net; internet www.barbadosadvocate.com; f. 1895; Editor REUDON EVERSLEY; circ. 17,490.

The Sunday Sun: Nation House, Fontabelle, St Michael; tel. 430-5400; fax 427-6968; e-mail sundaysun@sunbeach.net; internet www.nationnews.com; f. 1977; Dir HAROLD HOYTE; circ. 48,824.

Weekend Investigator: POB 230, St Michael; tel. 434-2000; circ. 14,305.

NEWS AGENCIES

Caribbean Media Corporation (CMC): Unit 1B, Bldg 6A, Harbour Industrial Estate, St Michael; tel. 467-1000; fax 429-4355; e-mail admin@cananews.com; internet www.cananews.com; f. by merger of Caribbean News Agency (CANA) and Caribbean Broadcasting Union; COO GARY ALLEN.

Foreign Bureaux

Inter Press Service (IPS) (Italy): POB 697, Bridgetown; tel. 426-4474; Correspondent MARVA COSSY.

Xinhua (New China) News Agency (People's Republic of China): Christ Church; Chief Correspondent DING BAOZHONG.

Agence France-Presse (AFP) and Agencia EFE (Spain) are also represented.

Publishers

The Advocate Publishing Co Ltd: POB 230, St Michael; tel. 434-2000; fax 434-2020.

Business Tutors: POB 800, St Michael; tel. 428-5664; fax 429-4854; e-mail pchad@caribsurf.com; business, management, computers.

Carib Research and Publications Inc: POB 556, Bridgetown; tel. 438-0580; f. 1986; regional interests; CEO Dr FARLEY BRAITHWAITE.

Nation Publishing Co Ltd: Nation House, POB 1203, Fontabelle, St Michael; tel. 430-5400; fax 427-6968.

Broadcasting and Communications

TELECOMMUNICATIONS

Cable & Wireless (Barbados) Ltd: POB 32, Wildey, St Michael; tel. 292-6000; fax 427-5808; e-mail bdsinfo@caribsurf.com; internet www.candwbet.com.bb; f. 1984; fmrly Barbados External Telecommunications Ltd; became Cable & Wireless BET Ltd, which merged with Barbados Telephone Co Ltd (BARTEL), Cable & Wireless Caribbean Cellular and Cable & Wireless Information Systems in 2002; provides international telecommunications services; owned by Cable & Wireless PLC (United Kingdom); Chair. STEPHEN EMTAGE; Pres. DONALD AUSTIN; Gen. Man. VINCENT YEARWOOD.

Digicel Barbados Ltd: The Courtyard, Hastings, Christ Church; tel. 434-3444; fax 426-3444; e-mail customercare@digicelgroup.com; internet www.digicelbarbados.com; f. 2003; awarded licence to operate cellular telephone services in March 2003; owned by an Irish consortium; Dir RALPH 'BIZZY' WILLIAMS.

Sunbeach Communications: 'San Remo', Belmont, St Michael; tel. 430-1569; fax 228-6330; e-mail customerservice@sunbeach.net; internet www.sunbeach.net; f. 1995; awarded licence to operate cellular telephone services in March 2003; Man. Dir MICHAEL WAKLEY.

BROADCASTING

Radio

Barbados Broadcasting Service Ltd: Astoria St George, Bridgetown; tel. 437-9550; fax 437-9203; e-mail action@sunbeach.net; f. 1981; operates BBS FM and Faith FM (religious broadcasting).

Barbados Rediffusion Service Ltd: River Rd, Bridgetown; tel. 430-7300; fax 429-8093; f. 1935; public company; runs the commercial stations HOTT FM (f. 1998), Voice of Barbados (f. 1981) and YESS Ten-Four FM (f. 1988); Gen. Man. VIC FERNANDES.

Caribbean Broadcasting Corporation (CBC): The Pine, POB 900, Wildey, St Michael; tel. 429-2041; fax 429-4795; e-mail cbc@

caribsurf.com; internet www.cbcbarbados.bb; f. 1963; Chair. Folzo Brewster; operates three radio stations.

CBC Radio 900 AM: tel. 434-1900; f. 1963; spoken word and news.

Liberty 98.1 FM: tel. 429-5522; f. 1984; popular music.

Quality 100.7 FM: international and regional music, incl. folk, classical, etc.

Voice of Barbados 92.9 FM: Bridgetown; internet vob929.com; f. 1981; owned by the Starcom network; current affairs, sport, music.

Television

CBC TV: The Pine, POB 900, Wildey, St Michael; tel. 429-2041; fax 429-4795; e-mail cbc@caribsurf.com; internet www.cbcbarbados.bb; f. 1964; part of the Caribbean Broadcasting Corpn (q.v.); Channel Eight is the main national service, broadcasting 24 hours daily; a maximum of 115 digital subscription channels will be available through Multi-Choice Television; Gen. Man. Melba Smith; Programme Man. Hilda Cox.

Finance

At the end of 2003 there were 4,637 international business companies registered in Barbados, and there were 2,981 foreign sales corporations in December 2001. At July 2004 53 'offshore' banks were licensed.

BANKING

(cap. = capital; auth. = authorized; res = reserves; dep. = deposits; brs = branches; m. = million; amounts in Barbados dollars unless otherwise indicated)

Central Bank

Central Bank of Barbados: Tom Adams Financial Centre, Spry St, POB 1016, Bridgetown; tel. 436-6870; fax 427-9559; e-mail cbb.libr@caribsurf.com; internet www.centralbank.org.bb; f. 1972; bank of issue; cap. 2.0m., res 10.0m., dep. 690.2m. (July 2004); Gov. Marion V. Williams; Deputy Gov. Carlos A. Holder.

Commercial Banks

Caribbean Commercial Bank Ltd (CCB): Lower Broad St, POB 1007c, Bridgetown; tel. 431-2500; fax 431-2530; f. 1984; purchased by RBTT Financial Holdings, Trinidad and Tobago, in 2004; cap. 25.0m., res 6.0m., dep. 258.5m. (Dec. 2002); Chair. David C. Shorey; Pres. and CEO Mariano R. Browne; 4 brs.

FirstCaribbean International Bank Ltd: Warrens, POB 503, St Michael; tel. 367-2500; fax 424-8977; e-mail firstcaribbeanbank@firstcaribbeanbank.com; internet www.firstcaribbeanbank.com; f. 2002; previously known as CIBC West Indies Holdings, adopted present name following merger of CIBC West Indies and Caribbean operations of Barclays Bank PLC; cap. and res $1,898.1m., dep. $14,512.2m. (Oct. 2003); Chair. Michael K. Mansoor; CEO Charles Pink; 9 brs.

Mutual Bank of the Caribbean Inc: Trident House, Lower Broad St, Bridgetown; tel. 436-8335; fax 429-5734; 4 brs.

Regional Development Bank

Caribbean Development Bank: Wildey, POB 408, St Michael; tel. 431-1600; fax 426-7269; e-mail info@caribank.org; internet www.caribank.org; f. 1970; cap. US $155.7m., res US $14.1m., total assets US $756.2m. (Dec. 2003); Pres. Dr Compton Bourne.

National Bank

Barbados National Bank Inc (BNB): Independence Sq, POB 1002, Bridgetown; tel. 431-5700; fax 426-2606; internet www.bnbbarbados.com; f. 1978 by merger; cap. 48.0m., res 56.4m., dep. 1,161.7m. (Sept. 2003); partially privatized; Chair. Ronald F. D. Harford; Man. Dir and CEO Louis A. Greenidge; 6 brs.

Foreign Banks

Bank of Nova Scotia (Canada): Broad St, POB 202, Bridgetown; tel. 431-3000; fax 228-8574; e-mail peter.vanschie@scotiabank.com; f. 1956; Gen. Man. Peter F. van Schie; 6 brs.

Royal Bank of Canada: 2nd Floor, Bldg 2, Chelston Park, Collymore Rock, POB 986, St Michael; tel. 431-6680; fax 436-9675; e-mail roycorp@caribsurf.com; f. 1911; 1 br.

Trust Companies

Bank of Nova Scotia Trust Co (Caribbean) Ltd: Bank of Nova Scotia Bldg, Broad St, POB 1003b, Bridgetown; tel. 431-3120; fax 426-0969.

Barbados International Bank and Trust Co: Bissex House, Bissex, St Joseph; tel. 422-4629; fax 422-7994; e-mail bdosintlbank&trustco@caribsurf.com; f. 1981; Chair. Douglas Leese.

Clico Mortgage & Finance Corporation: C. L. Duprey Financial Centre, Walrond St, Bridgetown; tel. 431-4719; fax 426-6168; e-mail cmfc@sunbeach.net.

Concorde Bank Ltd: The Corporate Centre, Bush Hill, Bay St, POB 1161, St Michael; tel. 430-5320; fax 429-7996; e-mail concorde@sunbeach.net; f. 1987; cap. US $2.0m., res US $2.0m., dep. US 16.1m. (June 2003); Pres. Gerard Lussan; Man. Marina Corbin.

Ernst & Young Trust Corporation: Bay St, POB 261, St Michael; tel. 430-3900; fax 435-2079.

FirstCaribbean International Trust and Merchant Bank (Barbados) Ltd: Warren, St Michael; tel. 367-2324; fax 421-7178; internet www.firstcaribbeanbank.com; known as CIBC Trust and Merchant Bank until 2002.

Royal Bank of Canada Financial Corporation: 2nd Floor, Bldg 2, Chelston Park, Collymore Rock, POB 986, St Michael; tel. 431-6580; fax 429-3800; e-mail roycorp@caribsurf.com; Man. N. L. Smith.

St Michael Trust Corpn: c/o PriceWaterhouseCoopers, Collymore Rock, St Michael; tel. 436-7000; fax 429-3747; e-mail bb@fiscglobal.com; internet www.fiscglobal.com; f. 1987.

STOCK EXCHANGE

Barbados Stock Exchange (BSE): Carlisle House, 1st Floor, Hincks St, Bridgetown; tel. 436-9871; fax 429-8942; internet www.bse.com.bb; f. 1987 as the Securities Exchange of Barbados; in 1989 the Govts of Barbados, Trinidad and Tobago and Jamaica agreed to link exchanges; cross-trading began in April 1991; reincorporated in 2001; Gen. Man. Marlon Yarde.

INSURANCE

The leading British and a number of US and Canadian companies have agents in Barbados. At the end of 2002 there were 392 exempt insurance and insurance management companies were registered in the country. Local insurance companies include the following:

Barbados Fire & Commercial Insurance Co: Beckwith Pl., Broad St, POB 150, Bridgetown; tel. 431-2800; fax 426-0752; e-mail info@bfc-ins.com; internet www.bfc-ins.com; f. 1996 following merger of Barbados Commercial Insurance Co. Ltd and Barbados Fire and General Insurance Co; f. 1880; Man. Dir David A. Deane.

Insurance Corporation of Barbados (ICB): Roebuck St, Bridgetown; tel. 427-5590; fax 426-3393; e-mail icb@icbbarbados.com; internet www.icbbarbados.com; f. 1978; partially privatized in 2000; cap. Bds $3m.; Chair. Dr John Mayers; Man. Dir Wismar Greaves; Gen. Man. Monica Skinner.

Sagicor: Sagicor Financial Centre, Lower Collymore Rock, St Michael; tel. 467-7500; fax 436-8829; e-mail info@sagicor.com; internet www.sagicor.com; f. 1840 as Barbados Mutual Life Assurance Society (BMLAS), changed name as above in 2002 after acquiring majority ownership of Life of Barbados (LOB) Ltd; Chair. Colin G. Goddard; Pres. and CEO Dodridge D. Miller.

United Insurance Co Ltd: United Insurance Centre, Lower Broad St, POB 1215, Bridgetown; tel. 430-1900; fax 436-7573; e-mail united@caribsurf.com; f. 1976; Man. Dir Dave A. Blackman.

Insurance Association

Insurance Association of the Caribbean Inc: IAC Bldg, Collymore Rock, St Michael; tel. 427-5608; fax 427-7277; e-mail info@iac-caribbean.com; internet www.iac-caribbean.com; regional asscn; Dir (Barbados) Davis Browne.

Trade and Industry

GOVERNMENT AGENCY

Barbados Agricultural Management Co Ltd: Warrens, POB 719c, St Michael; tel. 425-0010; fax 425-0007; e-mail bamc@cariaccess.com; Chair. Lindsay Holder; Gen. Man. E. LeRoy Roach.

DEVELOPMENT ORGANIZATIONS

Barbados Agriculture Development and Marketing Corpn: Fairy Valley, Christ Church; tel. 428-0250; fax 428-0152; f. 1993 by merger; programme of diversification and land reforms; Chair. Tyrone Power; CEO E. LeRoy Roach.

Barbados Investment and Development Corpn: Pelican House, Princess Alice Highway, Bridgetown; tel. 427-5350; fax 426-7802; e-mail bidc@bidc.org; internet www.bidc.com; f. 1992 by merger; facilitates the devt of the industrial sector, especially in the areas of manufacturing, information technology and financial services; offers free consultancy to investors; provides factory space for lease or rent; administers the Fiscal Incentives Legislation; CEO ANTON NORRIS.

Department for International Development in the Caribbean: Chelsea House, Chelsea Rd, POB 167, St Michael; tel. 430-7900; fax 430-7959; division of the British Govt's Dept for Int. Devt.

CHAMBER OF COMMERCE

Barbados Chamber of Commerce and Industry: Nemwil House, 1st Floor, Lower Collymore Rock, POB 189, St Michael; tel. 426-2056; fax 429-2907; e-mail bdscham@caribsurf.com; internet www.bdscham.com; f. 1825; 200 mem. firms, 321 reps; Pres. MARK A. B. THOMPSON.

INDUSTRIAL AND TRADE ASSOCIATIONS

Barbados Agricultural Society: The Grotto, Beckles Rd, St Michael; tel. 436-6683; fax 435-0651; e-mail heshimu@sunbeach.net; Pres. TYRONE POWER.

Barbados Association of Medical Practitioners: BAMP Complex, Spring Garden, St Michael; tel. 429-7569; fax 435-2328; e-mail bamp@sunbeach.net; Pres. Dr MARGARET O'SHEA.

Barbados Association of Professional Engineers: POB 666, Bridgetown; tel. 425-6105; fax 425-6673; f. 1964; Pres. GLYNE BARKER; Sec. PATRICK CLARKE.

Barbados Hotel and Tourism Association: Fourth Ave, Belleville, St Michael; tel. 426-5041; fax 429-2845; e-mail bhta@maccs.com.bb; internet www.funbarbados.com/bhta; Pres. ALAN BANFIELD; First Vice-Pres. SUSAN SPRINGER.

Barbados Manufacturers' Association: Bldg 1, Pelican Industrial Park, St Michael; tel. 426-4474; fax 436-5182; e-mail bmex-products@sunbeach.net; internet www.bma.org.bb; f. 1964; Pres. PETER MILLER; Exec. Dir WENDELL CALLENDER; 100 mem. firms.

EMPLOYERS' ORGANIZATION

Barbados Employers' Confederation: Nemwil House, 1st Floor, Collymore Rock, St Michael; tel. 426-1574; fax 429-2907; e-mail bcon@sunbeach.net; internet www.barbadosemployers.com; f. 1956; Pres. Dr ASHWELL THOMAS; 235 mems (incl. associate mems).

UTILITIES

Electricity

Barbados Light and Power Co (BL & P): POB 142, Garrison Hill, St Michael; tel. 436-1800; fax 429-6000; f. 1911; electricity generator and distributor; operates three stations with a combined capacity of 209,500 kW; Chair. F. O. McCONNEY; Man. Dir ANDREW GITTENS.

Gas

Barbados National Oil Co Ltd (BNOCL): POB 175, Woodbourne, St Philip; tel. 423-0918; fax 423-0166; e-mail ronhewitt@bnocl.com; internet www.bnocl.com; f. 1979; extraction of petroleum and natural gas; state-owned, scheduled for privatization; Chair. HARCOURT LEWIS; Gen. Man. RONALD HEWITT; 166 employees.

National Petroleum Corporation (NPC): Wildey, St Michael; tel. 430-4020; fax 426-4326; gas production and distribution; Chair. Dr WILLIAM DUGUID; Gen. Man. KEN LINTON.

Water

Barbados Water Authority: The Pine, St Michael; tel. 426-4134; fax 426-4507; e-mail bwa@caribsurf.com; f. 1980; Gen. Man. DENNIS YEARWOOD.

TRADE UNIONS

Principal unions include:

Barbados Secondary Teachers' Union: Ryeburn, Eighth Ave, Belleville, St Michael; tel. and fax 429-7676; e-mail bstumail@caribsurf.com; f. 1949; Pres. PHIL PERRY; Gen. Sec. PATRICK FROST; 375 mems.

Barbados Union of Teachers: Merry Hill, Welches, POB 58, St Michael; tel. 427-8510; fax 426-9890; e-mail but4@hotmail.com; internet www.butbarbados.org; f. 1974; Pres. UNDENE WHITTAKER; Gen. Sec. HERBERT GITTENS; 1,800 mems.

Barbados Workers' Union (BWU): Solidarity House, Harmony Hall, POB 172, St Michael; tel. 426-3492; fax 436-6496; e-mail bwu@caribsurf.com; internet www.bwu-bb.org; f. 1941; operates a Labour College; Pres.-Gen. HUGH ARTHUR; Gen. Sec. Sir LEROY TROTMAN; 20,000 mems.

National Union of Public Workers: Dalkeith House, Dalkeith Rd, POB 174, St. Michael; tel. 426-1764; fax 436-1795; e-mail nupwbarbados@sunbeach.net; f. 1944; Pres. CECIL W. DRAKES; Gen. Sec. JOSEPH E. GODDARD; 6,000 mems.

Transport

ROADS

Ministry of Public Works: The Pine, St Michael; tel. 429-2191; fax 437-8133; internet www.publicworks.gov.bb; maintains a network of 1,600 km (994 miles) of roads, of which 1,578 km (981 miles) are paved; a US $40m. road-paving programme was announced in August 2001; Chief Tech. Officer C. H. ARCHER.

SHIPPING

Bridgetown harbour has berths for eight ships and simultaneous bunkering facilities for five. In October 2003 the Government announced a 10-year plan to expand the harbour, at an estimated cost of US $101m. The plan was to include the construction of a new sugar terminal and a new cruise-ship pier.

Barbados Port Authority: University Row, Bridgetown Harbour; tel. 430-4700; fax 429-5348; e-mail administrator@barbadosport.com; internet www.barbadosport.com; f. 1979; Chair. LARRY TATEM; Gen. Man. EVERTON WALTERS; Port Dir Capt. H. L. VAN SLUYTMAN.

Shipping Association of Barbados: 2nd Floor, Trident House, Broad St, Bridgetown; tel. 427-9860; fax 426-8392; e-mail shasba@caribsurf.com.

Principal Shipping Companies

Barbados Shipping and Trading Co Ltd (B. S. and T.): 1st Floor, The Auto Dome, Warrens, St Michael; tel. 417-5110; fax 417-5116; e-mail info@bsandtco.com; internet www.bsandtco.com; f. 1920; Chair. C. DAVID BYNOE; Man. Dir ALLAN C. FIELDS.

Bernuth Agencies: Bridgetown; tel. 431-3343.

Carlisle Shipping Ltd: Carlisle House, Bridgetown; tel. 430-4803.

DaCostas Ltd: Carlisle House, Hincks St, POB 103, Bridgetown; tel. 426-3451; fax 429-5445; shipping company; Man. Dir JOHN WILKINSON.

T. Geddes Grant Bros: White Park Rd, Bridgetown; tel. 431-3300.

Hassell, Eric and Son Ltd: Carlisle House, Hincks St, Bridgetown; tel. 436-6102; fax 429-3416; e-mail info@erichassell.com; internet www.erichassell.com; shipping agent, stevedoring contractor and cargo fowarder.

Maersk: James Fort Bldg, Hincks St, Bridgetown; tel. 430-4816.

Tropical Shipping Kensington: Fontabelle Rd, St Michael; tel. 426-9990; fax 426-7750; internet www.tropical.com.

CIVIL AVIATION

The principal airport is Grantley Adams International Airport, at Seawell, 18 km (11 miles) from Bridgetown. A US $100m. contract to build a new arrivals terminal was awarded in late 2001. The project was scheduled for completion by mid-2005.

Tourism

The natural attractions of the island consist chiefly of the warm climate and varied scenery. In addition, there are many facilities for outdoor sports of all kinds. Revenue from tourism increased from Bds $13m. in 1960 to some $1,423m. in 2000; the 2003 figure was slightly lower (about $1,390m.). The number of stop-over tourist arrivals was an estimated 531,211 in 2003, while the number of visiting cruise-ship passengers was 559,119. There were some 7,000 hotel rooms on the island in 2003.

Barbados Tourism Authority: Harbour Rd, POB 242, Bridgetown; tel. 427-2623; fax 426-4080; e-mail btainfo@barbados.org; internet www.barbados.org; f. 1993 to replace Barbados Board of Tourism; offices in London, New York, Los Angeles, Miami, Munich, Paris and Caracas; Chair. HUDSON HUSBANDS; Pres. and CEO STUART LANE.

BELARUS

Introductory Survey

Location, Climate, Language, Religion, Flag, Capital

The Republic of Belarus is a land-locked state in north-eastern Europe. It is bounded by Lithuania and Latvia to the north-west, by Ukraine to the south, by Russia to the east, and by Poland to the west. The climate is of a continental type, with an average January temperature, in Minsk, of –5°C (23°F) and an average for July of 19°C (67°F). Average annual precipitation is between 560 mm and 660 mm. The official languages of the republic are Belarusian and Russian. The major religion is Christianity—the Eastern Orthodox Church and Roman Catholic Church (of both the Latin and Byzantine rites) being the largest denominations. There are also small Muslim and Jewish communities. The national flag (proportions 1 by 2) consists of two unequal horizontal stripes, of red over light green, with a red-outlined white vertical stripe at the hoist, bearing in red a traditional embroidery pattern. The capital is Minsk (Miensk).

Recent History

Following periods of Lithuanian and Polish rule, Belarus became a part of the Russian Empire in the late 18th century. During the 19th century there was a growth of national consciousness in Belarus and, as a result of industrialization, significant migration from rural to urban areas. After the February Revolution of 1917 in Russia, Belarusian nationalists and socialists formed a rada (council), which sought a degree of autonomy from the Provisional Government in Petrograd (St Petersburg). In November, after the Bolsheviks had seized power in Petrograd, Red Army troops were dispatched to Minsk, and the rada was dissolved. However, the Bolsheviks were forced to withdraw by the invasion of the German army. The Treaty of Brest-Litovsk, signed in March 1918, assigned most of Belarus to Germany. On 25 March Belarusian nationalists convened to proclaim a Belarusian National Republic, but it achieved only limited autonomy. After the Germans had withdrawn, the Bolsheviks easily reoccupied Minsk, and the Belarusian Soviet Socialist Republic (BSSR) was declared on 1 January 1919.

In February 1919 the BSSR was merged with neighbouring Lithuania in a Lithuanian-Belarusian Soviet Republic (known as 'Litbel'). In April, however, Polish armed forces entered Lithuania and Belarus, and both were declared part of Poland. In July 1920 the Bolsheviks recaptured Minsk, and in August the BSSR was re-established; Lithuania became an independent state. However, the BSSR comprised only the eastern regions of the lands populated by Belarusians. Western territories were granted to Poland by the Treaty of Rīga, signed on 18 March 1921. The Treaty also assigned Belarus's easternmost regions to the Russian Federation, but they were returned to the BSSR in 1924 and 1926. Meanwhile, the BSSR, with Ukraine and Transcaucasia, had joined with Russia to establish the Union of Soviet Socialist Republics (USSR) in December 1922.

The Soviet leadership's New Economic Policy of 1921–28, which permitted some liberalization of the economy, brought a measure of prosperity, and there was significant cultural and linguistic development, with the use of the Belarusian language officially encouraged. This period ended in 1929 with the emergence of Stalin (Iosif V. Dzhugashvili) as the dominant figure in the USSR. In that year Stalin began a campaign to collectivize agriculture, which was strongly resisted by the peasantry, and many peasants were deported or imprisoned. The purges of the early 1930s were initially targeted against Belarusian nationalists and intellectuals, but by 1936–38 they had widened to include all sectors of the population.

After the invasion of Poland by German and Soviet forces in September 1939, the BSSR was enlarged by the inclusion of the lands that it had lost to Poland and Lithuania in 1921. Between 1941 and 1944 the BSSR was occupied by Nazi German forces; an estimated 2.2m. people died, including most of the republic's large Jewish population. At the Yalta conference, in February 1945, the Allies agreed to recognize the 'Curzon line' as the western border of the BSSR, thus endorsing the unification of western and eastern Belarus. As a result of the Soviet demand for increased voting strength in the UN, the Western powers permitted the BSSR (along with the Ukrainian SSR) to become a member of the UN in its own right.

The immediate post-war period was dominated by the need to rehabilitate the republic's infrastructure. The requirements of the reconstruction programme and the local labour shortage led to an increase in Russian immigration, thus discouraging use of the Belarusian language. During the 1960s and 1970s the process of 'russification' continued; there was a decline in the use of Belarusian in schools and in the media. The relative prosperity of the republic, however, effectively permitted the ruling Communist Party of Belarus (CPB) to resist implementing the economic and political reforms that were proposed by the Soviet leader, Mikhail Gorbachev, from 1985. By 1987, however, the press had become critical of the CPB's stance on cultural and ecological issues. Intellectuals and writers campaigned for the greater use of Belarusian in education. Campaigners also demanded more information about the consequences of the explosion of April 1986 at the Chornobyl (Chernobyl) nuclear power station in northern Ukraine, which had affected large areas of southern Belarus.

There was, however, little opportunity for overt political opposition. A Belarusian Popular Front (BPF) was established in October 1988, but the CPB severely restricted its activities and banned republican media reports about the new group. None the less, the BPF did have some success in the elections to the all-Union Congress of People's Deputies, which took place in March 1989, persuading voters to reject several leading officials of the CPB. In January 1990 a law was approved, declaring Belarusian to be the state language, effective from 1 September. The BPF was not officially permitted to participate in the elections to the Belarusian Supreme Council, which took place in March 1990. Instead, its members joined other pro-reform groups in a coalition known as the Belarusian Democratic Bloc (BDB). The BDB secured about one-quarter of the 310 seats that were decided by popular election; most of the remainder were won by CPB members loyal to the republican leadership. The opposition won most seats in the large cities, notably Gomel (Homiel) and Minsk, where Zyanon Paznyak, the leader of the BPF, was elected to the Supreme Soviet. When it first convened in May the BDB deputies immediately demanded the adoption of a declaration of sovereignty. The CPB initially opposed such a move, but on 27 July, apparently after consultations with the leadership of the Communist Party of the Soviet Union in Moscow, the capital of the Russian Federation and the USSR, a Declaration of State Sovereignty of the BSSR was adopted unanimously by the Belarusian Supreme Soviet. The declaration asserted the republic's right to maintain armed forces, to establish a national currency and to exercise full control over its domestic and foreign policies, and stated the republic's right to compensation for the damage caused by the nuclear accident at Chornobyl. The Belarusian Government appealed to the all-Union Government for a minimum of 17,000m. roubles to address the consequences of the disaster, but was offered only 3,000m. roubles in compensation.

The Belarusian Government took part in the negotiation of a new Treaty of Union. The all-Union referendum on the preservation of the USSR took place in the BSSR on 17 March 1991; of the 83% of the electorate who participated, 83% voted in favour of Gorbachev's proposals for a 'renewed federation of equal sovereign republics'.

On 10 April 1991 a general strike took place, and an estimated 100,000 people attended a demonstration in Minsk. The Government agreed to certain economic concessions, including high wage increases, but the strikers' political demands, including the resignation of the Belarusian Government and the depoliticization of republican institutions, were rejected. Some 200,000 workers were estimated to have taken part in a second general strike on 23 April, in protest at the legislature's refusal to reconvene. The CPB-dominated Supreme Council was eventually convened in May, although the authority of the CPB was threatened by increased internal dissent. In June 33 deputies joined the opposition as a 'Communists for Democracy' faction, led by Alyaksandr Lukashenka, the director of a state farm.

The Belarusian leadership did not strongly oppose the attempted *coup d'état*, led by conservative communist elements, in Moscow in August 1991. The Presidium of the Supreme Soviet released a neutral statement on the last day of the coup, but the Central Committee of the CPB declared its unequivocal support. Following the failure of the coup, Mikalay Dzemyantsei, the Chairman of the Supreme Soviet (republican head of state), was forced to resign; he was replaced by Stanislau Shushkevich, a centrist, pending an election to the office. In addition, the Supreme Soviet agreed to nationalize all CPB property, to prohibit the party's activities in law-enforcement agencies, and to suspend the CPB, pending an investigation into its role in the coup. On 25 August 1991 the legislature voted to grant constitutional status to the July 1990 Declaration of State Sovereignty, and declared the political and economic independence of Belarus.

On 19 September 1991 the Supreme Soviet voted to rename the BSSR the Republic of Belarus, and also elected Shushkevich as its Chairman. Shushkevich demonstrated his strong support for the continuation of some form of union by signing, in October, a treaty to establish an economic community and by agreeing, in November, to the first draft of the Treaty on the Union of Sovereign States. On 8 December Shushkevich, with the Russian and Ukrainian Presidents, signed the Minsk Agreement, establishing a Commonwealth of Independent States (CIS, see p. 189), which was to have its headquarters in Minsk. On 21 December the leaders of 11 former Soviet republics confirmed this decision by the Almaty (Alma-Ata) Declaration.

By comparison with other former Soviet republics, Belarus experienced relative stability in 1992, attributed to the country's more favourable social and economic policies, and to the comparatively homogenous nature of the population. In March 1993 the CPB formed, with 17 other parties and groups opposed to continued Belarusian independence, an informal coalition, the Popular Movement of Belarus. Divisions between the various branches of government became more pronounced during that year, and a major source of controversy was the drafting of a new Constitution. Shushkevich and the BPF strongly opposed the establishment of Belarus as a presidential republic; nevertheless, the new Constitution, which provided for a presidential system, was adopted in March 1994. A further point of dispute was whether Belarus should adopt closer relations with Russia and the CIS (as advocated by the Supreme Council). Shushkevich and the BPF were opposed to Belarus's signing the Collective Security Treaty concluded by six other CIS states in May 1992, on the grounds that this would contravene the Declaration of State Sovereignty, which defined Belarus as a neutral state, and lead to renewed Russian domination. None the less, in April 1993 the Supreme Council voted to authorize the signature of the Treaty, although Shushkevich delayed doing so. In July the legislature passed a vote of 'no confidence' in Shushkevich; he remained in office until a second vote of confidence, held in January 1994 (by which time he had signed the Treaty), voted overwhelmingly in favour of his dismissal. He was replaced by Mechislau Gryb. Meanwhile, in February 1993 the suspension on the CPB was lifted, and the party was re-established.

Allegations of corruption against the premier, Vyacheslau Kebich, and leading members of the Cabinet of Ministers, coupled with the worsening economic situation, culminated in a BPF-led general strike in Minsk in February 1994, which forced Gryb to bring forward the presidential election to mid-1994. Six candidates stood for election, including Kebich, Shushkevich, Paznyak and Lukashenka, head of the Supreme Council's anti-corruption committee since the previous year. In the first round of voting, held in late June, no candidate secured an overall majority, although Lukashenka, with 47% of the valid votes cast, led by a considerable margin. In the second ballot, contested by Lukashenka and Kebich and held on 10 July, Lukashenka received 85% of the votes cast, and he was inaugurated as the first President of Belarus on 20 July. Mikhail Chigir, an economic reformist, became Chairman of a new Cabinet of Ministers (Prime Minister).

In early 1995 there were repeated confrontations between Lukashenka and the Supreme Council over constitutional issues. In late January the Council voted for a second time to adopt legislation whereby the President could be removed by a two-thirds' quorum in the Council. In March Lukashenka announced that, simultaneously with the legislative election scheduled to take place in May, a referendum would be held on four policy questions. In early April, following the Council's rejection of all but one of the proposed questions (on closer

integration with Russia), Lukashenka threatened to dissolve the legislature. A number of opposition deputies (including Paznyak) were forcibly evicted from the Supreme Council building, where they had declared a hunger strike in protest at the referendum. Shortly after this action, deputies voted in favour of the inclusion in the referendum of the remaining three questions: to give the Russian language equal status with Belarusian as an official language; to abandon the state insignia and flag of independent Belarus in favour of a modified Soviet-era version; and to amend the Constitution in order to empower the President to suspend the Supreme Council in the event of unconstitutional acts. Some 65% of the electorate participated in the referendum, held on 14 May, at which all four questions received overwhelming popular support.

On the same day, Belarus's first post-Soviet legislative elections were held. However, owing to stringent electoral regulations, only 18 of the 260 seats in the Supreme Council were filled. A further 101 deputies were elected at 'run-off' elections held on 28 May 1995, but the necessary two-thirds' quorum was only achieved after two further rounds of voting, held on 29 November and 10 December, brought the total membership of the Supreme Council to 198. The CPB emerged with the largest number of seats in the new legislature (42), followed by the Agrarian Party (AP—33), the United Civic Party of Belarus and the Party of People's Accord. Independent candidates accounted for 95 seats. The BPF failed to win representation in the Council, as the 62 seats remaining vacant, largely owing to low electoral participation, were mostly in areas where the BPF commanded its strongest support. The Supreme Council held its inaugural session in early January 1996. Syamyon Sharetski, the leader of the AP, was appointed Chairman of the Council, replacing Gryb.

Despite strong opposition and protests against government proposals to sign a new union treaty with Russia, President Lukashenka and the Russian President, Boris Yeltsin, signed the Treaty on the Formation of a Community of Sovereign Republics (CSR) in Moscow on 2 April 1996. Although it did not establish a single state, the Treaty included extensive provisions covering military, economic and political co-operation. Following the Treaty's endorsement, confrontation between Lukashenka and the opposition parties increased. A warrant was issued in April for the arrest of Paznyak, who was accused of organizing the anti-union demonstrations; he fled the country and later applied for political asylum in the USA. Unauthorized rallies, organized by the opposition movement, were held in Minsk at the end of the month to commemorate the 10th anniversary of the disaster at the Chornobyl nuclear power station. The rallies, which the demonstrators used to express publicly their dissatisfaction with the Government and the formation of the CSR, were reportedly brutally dispersed by the police, and numerous arrests were made.

Lukashenka, seeking to enhance his powers, scheduled another national referendum for 24 November 1996 (with polling stations to be open from 9 November for those unable to vote on the later date), which was to consider, *inter alia*, proposed amendments to the 1994 Constitution. Elections for the remaining vacant seats in the Supreme Council were due to be held on the same day. Relations between Lukashenka and the Constitutional Court deteriorated in November, when the Court ruled that the approval of amendments to the Constitution would not be legally binding. The revocation of this decision by presidential decree provoked fierce criticism.

The referendum ballot papers contained seven questions, four of which were proposed by Lukashenka: that amendments be made to the Constitution to extend the President's term of office from 1999 to 2001, to enable the President to issue decrees that would carry legal force, and to grant him extensive powers of appointment both to the judiciary and to the envisaged bicameral National Assembly, which would replace the Supreme Council; that Belarusian Independence Day be moved from 27 July (the anniversary of the Declaration of State Sovereignty) to 3 July (the anniversary of the liberation from the Nazis); that there be an unrestricted right to purchase and sell land; and that the death penalty be abolished. The remaining three questions were submitted by the Supreme Council in an attempt to curtail the President's powers, and proposed that there be a significant reduction in the powers of the President (in effect, virtually abolishing the presidency); that the Supreme Council be allowed to elect heads of local administration (hitherto appointed by the President); and that state institutions be funded from the budget, instead of from a non-budgetary fund controlled by the President.

Despite the inclusion of questions concerning proposed constitutional changes, copies of the draft Constitution were not available to the public by the time that voting began. The Chairman of the Central Electoral Commission, Viktar Ganchar, stated that he would not approve the results of the voting, owing to this and other electoral violations, and was subsequently dismissed by Lukashenka. The crisis worsened in mid-November 1996, when Chigir resigned as Chairman of the Cabinet of Ministers, urging that the referendum be cancelled; he was replaced, initially in an acting capacity, by Syarhey Ling. Some 10,000 people attended an anti-Government rally in Minsk, protesting at the restrictions on their freedom of expression. Radio stations and newspapers came under renewed government pressure, and widespread violations of the law were reported by parliamentary electoral observers. The Organization for Security and Co-operation in Europe (OSCE, see p. 314) refused to send observers to monitor the referendum, and the Council of Europe (see p. 199) declared that the presidential draft of the amended Constitution did not comply with European standards. Meanwhile, 75 deputies in the Supreme Council submitted a motion to the Constitutional Court to begin impeachment proceedings against the President; although the Court had already found 17 decrees issued by Lukashenka to be unconstitutional, it was forced to abandon the motion, as deputies subsequently retracted their support.

The referendum results revealed considerable support for the President, but their accuracy was disputed. According to official figures, some 84% of the electorate took part, 70.5% of whom voted for the President's constitutional amendments; only 7.9% voted for those of the Supreme Council. The amended Constitution was published on 27 November 1996 and came into immediate effect.

Following the referendum, the Supreme Council divided into two factions. More than 100 deputies declared their support for Lukashenka, and adopted legislation abolishing the Supreme Council and establishing a 110-member Palata Predstaviteley (House of Representatives), which was to be the lower chamber of the new bicameral Natsionalnoye Sobraniye (National Assembly). Some 50 other deputies denounced the referendum as invalid and declared themselves to be the legitimate legislature. The Palata Predstaviteley convened shortly afterwards and elected Anatol Malafeyeu as its Chairman. Deputies were granted a four-year mandate, while the term of office of those opposed to the new legislature was curtailed to two months. Deputies elected in the by-elections held simultaneously with the referendum were denied registration. Legislation governing the formation of the upper house of the Natsionalnoye Sobraniye, the 64-member Soviet Respubliki (Council of the Republic), was approved by Lukashenka in early December 1996: eight members were appointed by the President and the remaining 56 were elected by regional councils. No deputies from the former Supreme Council participated in the new upper chamber, which convened for the first time in mid-January 1997, and elected Pavel Shypuk as its Chairman. Meanwhile, in protest at the constitutional amendments introduced by the referendum, the Chairman of the Constitutional Court, Valery Tsikhinya, and several other judges announced their resignations.

In January 1997 the Public Coalition Government-National Economic Council (PCG-NEC), a form of 'shadow' cabinet, was formed, chaired by Genadz Karpenka. Doubts about the legitimacy of the referendum were expressed by international organizations, including the Council of Europe, which suspended Belarus's 'guest status', and the Permanent Council of the Parliamentary Assembly of the OSCE, which recognized the right of a delegation from the former Supreme Council, rather than members of the Palata Predstaviteley, officially to represent Belarus at that organization.

The signing with Russia of the Treaty of Union, and initialling of the Charter of the Union on 2 April 1997, by Presidents Lukashenka and Yeltsin (see below) prompted an anti-Union demonstration in Minsk, which was forcibly suppressed by the police, resulting in many arrests. Charges of violating a presidential decree (which had entered into force in the previous month) restricting the right to demonstrate were subsequently brought against opposition members. Nevertheless, support for the union treaty appeared to be widespread, and some 15,000 people participated in a pro-Union rally in Minsk in mid-May. The Charter of the Union was signed in Moscow on 23 May. The

Treaty and Charter were ratified shortly afterwards by the respective legislatures, and came into effect in mid-June.

Negotiations mediated by the Council of Europe and the European Union (EU, see p. 217) to end the confrontation between the former Supreme Council and the new legislature began in June 1997, but collapsed in July, following disagreement over which constitution was to form the basis of the discussions. In November the opposition launched a petition movement, Charter 97, which called for greater democracy in Belarus and for presidential elections to be held in 1999 as demanded by the 1994 Constitution. A number of senior BPF members were arrested in April 1998 during an unauthorized rally to protest against the Treaty of Union. A further 30 demonstrators were arrested later in the month at a rally led by former members of the disbanded Supreme Council, urging Lukashenka's resignation for mismanaging the economy and destroying national culture; Lukashenka's campaign to institutionalize the use of the Russian language had successfully marginalized Belarusian, which had become widely associated with the opposition. In June legislation was approved that rendered defamation of the President an offence punishable by up to five years' imprisonment.

In November 1998 Lukashenka decreed the formation of a special economic committee, to be known as the National Headquarters, which was to supersede the Cabinet of Ministers in economic policy. A new law on local elections was approved by the Palata Predstaviteley in December, effectively banning those with a police record or fine from standing in the local elections that were to be held in April 1999, thereby excluding numerous opposition candidates. In the event, the opposition organized an electoral boycott, and the majority of the seats in the elections were each contested by a single candidate. International observers noted irregularities in the voting procedure, and the participation rate was believed to be much lower than the officially reported 66.9% of the electorate.

Meanwhile, in January 1999 the 'Central Electoral Commission' of the former Supreme Council scheduled a 'shadow' presidential election for 16 May. In March the Commission's Chairman, Ganchar, was arrested and charged with the offence of 'appointing oneself as an official', but was released after a 10-day hunger strike. Chigir was registered as a candidate for the election in March, but was arrested in April and charged with embezzlement and abuse of office (the embezzlement charges were later dropped), prompting speculation that his arrest was politically motivated. (In May 2000 Chigir received a three-year suspended sentence and a substantial fine). Following the death of Karpenka in April 1999, Gryb was elected Chairman of the PCG-NEC in November. In the event it proved impossible to organized fixed polling stations for the election, which was not recognized by the Government or by the international community. The election results were declared invalid later in the month, owing to alleged irregularities, despite a reported participation rate of 53%. In July Sharetski fled to Lithuania, anticipating his imminent arrest in Belarus, following his 'appointment' by the Supreme Council as acting President of the country (according to the 1994 Constitution Lukashenka's legitimate term of office expired in mid-July 1999).

In January 1999 Lukashenka had decreed that political parties, trade unions and other organizations were required to re-register by 1 July; those failing to do so were to be disbanded. By September only 17 of the 28 existing official parties had been re-registered. In late September supporters of the exiled BPF leader Zyanon Paznyak formed a breakaway faction, known as the Conservative Christian Party of the BPF, with Paznyak as Chairman. At the end of October Vintsuk Vyachorka was elected Chairman of the 'rump' BPF, which changed its name to BPF—'Revival' in December, in order to comply with legislation banning the use of certain words in the names of non-governmental organizations (NGOs). In early September OSCE-mediated negotiations commenced between the Government and the opposition, concerning the legislative elections to be held in 2000; however, further rounds of talks were subject to government-proposed postponements, and opposition frustration was such that when talks resumed in March 2000 its participation was much reduced. Although stricter security measures were implemented in 1999, and the independent press also came under greater scrutiny, the Government made a statement in August, in which it expressed its commitment to a number of measures to defend and improve human rights in Belarus. Meanwhile, however, a number of outspoken critics of the President disappeared in unexplained circumstances. In May a former Minister of the Interior and campaigner for Chigir, Yuriy Zakharenka, went missing. His disappearance was followed in subsequent months by those of: Tamara Vinnikava, a former head of the central bank, who had been under house arrest since January 1997; an independent publisher; and Ganchar. It was officially claimed that the four had voluntarily gone into hiding to attract attention to their political cause. In October 1999 15,000 people were estimated to have taken part in an anti-Government 'Freedom March' in Minsk (this constituted the largest opposition demonstration to have taken place in Belarus since April 1996).

In February 2000 Syarhey Ling resigned as Chairman of the Cabinet of Ministers, and was replaced by Uladzimir Yermoshin, hitherto the Governor of Minsk City. In that month opposition parties agreed to boycott the parliamentary elections due to take place in October, in protest at not having been consulted about the preparation of a new draft electoral code. This decision appeared to prompt increased repression of both the unofficial media and the opposition. The peaceful staging, in March, of a second Freedom March resulted in the prohibition of demonstrations in the centre of the capital. A further demonstration, to commemorate the creation of the Belarusian National Republic in 1918, which took place later that month, in contravention of the ban, was suppressed by the security forces and resulted in 272 arrests. Many of those detained were journalists and international observers, and Lukashenka subsequently issued an apology. In the following month the Minister of Internal Affairs, Yuriy Sivakow, resigned, ostensibly for health reasons.

A large-scale anti-election rally by opposition activists preceded the elections to the Natsionalnoye Sobraniye that took place on 15 October 2000. In this first round of voting 41 seats were filled and the results of voting were declared invalid in 13 constituencies. A second round of voting for the remaining 56 seats took place on 29 October. The OSCE denounced the elections as neither free nor fair. The official rate of participation, at 60.6%, was widely believed to have been exaggerated, and the international community refused to recognize the validity of the elections, in which nominally independent candidates were reported to have obtained an overwhelming majority of seats.

In late November 2000 Lukashenka made a number of changes to government and security-service personnel. Notably, Ural Latypaw, hitherto Deputy Prime Minister and Minister of Foreign Affairs, was appointed State Secretary of the Security Council; he was replaced by Mikhail Khvastow. The new appointments, which were allegedly linked to the lack of progress made in investigating the disappearance of public figures, resulted in a transfer of power from ethnic Belarusians to ethnic Russians. In February 2001 a further, minor reshuffle of the Cabinet of Ministers and of security officials took place.

In early January 2001 tax officials seized equipment from a publishing company that printed several major newspapers critical of the Government, prompting concern that the authorities intended further to suppress press freedoms ahead of the presidential election, due to take place in September. Meanwhile, Alyaksandr Chigir, a son of Mikhail Chigir, was arrested in February, and charged with selling stolen goods; the former premier claimed that the arrest was an attempt to discredit his candidacy for the presidency. (Alyaksandr Chigir was sentenced to seven years' imprisonment in March 2002.)

In mid-March 2001 President Lukashenka signed a decree imposing severe restrictions on the use of foreign financial assistance by both individuals and national organizations. The decree required all foreign aid to be officially registered, and prohibited the use of such aid for political campaigning or for the organization of strikes and rallies, prompting fears by opposition activists that the decree would prevent the deployment of observers at the presidential election, which was to have been funded by the OSCE. Repeat elections were held on 18 March and 1 April to fill the vacant seats remaining in the Palata Predstaviteley. The opposition held a third 'Freedom March' in Minsk on 25 March, at which a small number of arrests were made. In early May the five main opposition candidates for the presidency announced their intention to select a joint candidate. The candidates comprised: Mikhail Chigir; a former Chairman of the Regional Executive Committee of Grodno (Horadnia) Oblast, Syamyon Domash; the leader of the Party of Communists of Belarus, Syarhey Kalyakin; the Chairman of the Federation of Trade Unions of Belarus, Uladzimir Gancharyk; and a former Minister of Defence, Pavel Kazlovsky. In the same month

the opposition formed a new, popular movement, known as 'For a New Belarus', to support the candidacy of a democratic presidential candidate.

In June 2001 two former investigators at the Office of the Prosecutor-General, who had been granted asylum in the USA, claimed that senior government officials had organized the assassinations of political opponents to Lukashenka's regime, and alleged them to be responsible for the deaths of the missing opposition figures Ganchar and Zakharenka, as well as a cameraman for a Russian television channel, Dmitrii Zavadski, who had been missing since July 2000. The allegations were supported by Gancharyk, who revealed documents in mid-July 2001 that apparently linked the Prosecutor-General and former State Secretary of the Security Council, Viktar Sheyman, and the former Minister of Internal Affairs, Yuriy Sivakow, with the disappearance and presumed murder of Ganchar and Zakharenka. In late July the opposition selected Gancharyk as its candidate for the presidency; his election campaign focused on continuing allegations of the government-sanctioned assassination of opposition figures. In late August two state security agents released to the media a recorded testimony, in which they supported claims that Ganchar, together with a business associate, had been kidnapped and killed in September 1999 by a special police unit, attached to the Ministry of Internal Affairs. Meanwhile, media outlets came under increased pressure to withdraw their support for Gancharyk, as a number of police raids took place throughout the month.

The presidential election was held, as scheduled, on 9 September 2001, although a constitutional provision had permitted some voting to begin on 4 September. This provision was criticized by the opposition, which asserted that it made the election more difficult to monitor. Lukashenka was re-elected with 75.7% of the valid votes cast; Gancharyk received 15.7% of the votes; and the only other candidate, the leader of the Liberal Democratic Party of Belarus (LDPB), Syarhey Gaydukevich, received just 2.5%. The election was described as fundamentally flawed by the OSCE, and Gancharyk urged the public to protest against Lukashenka's victory; however, a popular uprising failed to materialize, and observers noted that voters, particularly in the rural areas where Lukashenka drew much of his support, feared that the election of a new, reformist leader might lead to increased economic hardship.

Following Lukashenka's inauguration on 20 September 2001, the Prime Minister, Uladzimir Yermoshin, tendered the resignation of his Government. Lukashenka subsequently reshuffled the Cabinet of Ministers, reducing the number of ministries to 28. In the same month, Latypaw was appointed to head the presidential administration; his former post as State Secretary of the Security Council was filled by Lt-Gen. Genadz Nyavyhlas. At the beginning of October Lukashenka nominated former Deputy Prime Minister Genadz Navitsky as premier, and the appointment was approved by the Palata Predstaviteley on 10 October. In late 2001 and early 2002 a number of state officials and managers of state enterprises were arrested, as part of an anti-corruption campaign initiated by the President. The opposition media claimed the arrests to be politically motivated, and linked them to criticism of Lukashenka's economic policies. Meanwhile, in late December 2001 Gancharyk resigned the chairmanship of the Federation of Trade Unions, citing differences with the Government. In July 2002 Lukashenka's position was strengthened when the Deputy Head of the Presidential Administration, Leanid Kozik, was elected Chairman of the Federation of Trade Unions. Kozik's appointment was expected to reverse the Federation's association with opposition forces.

Meanwhile, in March 2002 two former police officers were sentenced to life imprisonment, having been found guilty of kidnapping Zavadski. However, there were claims that the charges had been fabricated to divert attention from the involvement of more senior government officials. In May 2002 the first sentences were awarded to the state-enterprise officials arrested from late 2001, and in the following month three opposition journalists were given quasi-labour sentences after publishing articles criticizing Lukashenka. In July 2002 Mikhail Chigir was given a further three-year, suspended prison sentence, following his trial on charges of tax evasion; Chigir declared the case to have been politically motivated. In August two opposition newspapers were closed down and in September the Editor-in-Chief of the independent newspaper *Rabochy (The Worker)* was sentenced to two years' corrective labour, after accusing the President of having profited from illicit arms sales. In January 2003 six journalists were dismissed from the newspaper of the Trade Union Federation of Belarus, *Belaruski Chas (The Belarusian Hour)*, amid allegations of a political motivation; the newspaper's editor had already been dismissed. The Government also undertook dramatically to reduce the re-broadcast of Russian programmes, which were often critical of Lukashenka; to this end all radio and television companies were required to re-register by June 2003.

Fears over the future of religious freedom in Belarus were heightened from early October 2002, when the Natsionalnoye Sobraniye adopted a new law on religion, which imposed severe restrictions on the practice of minority faiths. The law prohibited meetings of fewer than 20 people and meetings in private homes, and banned those religious associations that had become active after 1982 from establishing missions and producing written material. All religious organizations were compelled to re-register and conform to the new regulations, which required religious literature to be submitted to the Government for state approval. Officially, the law, which came into effect on 16 November, was introduced to prevent the spread of cults, but, in practice, it was expected to serve to guarantee the dominance of the Belarusian Orthodox Church of the Moscow Patriarchate.

By late 2002 there were reports that President Lukashenka planned to schedule a referendum on proposed amendments to the Constitution, to allow him to stand for a third term of office in 2006. In January 2003 Yuriy Sivakow, the controversial former Minister of Internal Affairs, was appointed Minister of Sports and Tourism, and in March Syarhey Martynow was appointed as Minister of Foreign Affairs. Local elections were held in two rounds in March, amid opposition allegations of electoral irregularities. Many constituencies registered only one candidate for the ballot, and a substantial number of opposition candidates were reported to have been denied registration.

In July 2003 the President effected a significant cabinet reshuffle, dismissing premier Genadz Navitsky and three officials accused of failing to implement instructions concerning the agricultural sector, including Deputy Prime Minister Alyaksandr Papkow and the Minister of Agriculture and Food, Mikhail Rusy. The First Deputy Prime Minister, Syarhey Sidorsky, was appointed acting Prime Minister. In the same month Navitsky was elected to succeed the retiring Chairman of the Council of the Republic and Eduard Tovpenets replaced Uladzimir Symashka as Minister of Energy. In August new appointments were made to the education and information portfolios. In December Sidorsky was confirmed as Prime Minister, and a further reorganization of the Cabinet of Ministers took place. Notably, Mikalay Zaychenka became Minister of the Economy, Anatoly Rusetsky was appointed Minister of Industry and Vasil Dvoryaninovich became Minister of Agriculture and Food.

State repression of independent organizations and the media continued throughout 2003 and 2004, with the closure of several NGOs and efforts to prevent the publication and distribution of independent and satirical newspapers, such as *Belorusskaya Delovaya Gazeta (Belarusian Business Newspaper)* and *Navinki*; in addition, Russian television broadcasts were restricted and a Russian news bureau was closed. Meanwhile, in November 2003 an opposition alliance, known as the 'Five Plus' Popular Coalition, was formed by: the Belarusian Party of Labour; the Belarusian Social Democratic Assembly; BPF—Revival; the Party of Communists of Belarus; and the United Civic Party of Belarus. Other newly formed alliances included the 'Free Belarus' European Coalition, comprising: the Belarusian Social Democratic Party (National Hramada—Assembly); the 'Hope' Belarusian Party of Women; Charter 97 activists; and the Young Belarus bloc. In January 2004 the Five Plus alliance signed a co-operation agreement with the Belarusian Green Party and a number of NGOs, in advance of parliamentary elections, which were subsequently held on 17 October. The opposition presented at the time of the election thus consisted of three broad groupings: Five Plus; the European Coalition, favouring EU membership rather than federation with Russia; and a youth bloc, the Young Belarusians. No opposition candidates won seats in the election, which was the subject of intense scrutiny by international electoral observers; 96 nominally independent candidates were elected, the CPB obtained eight mandates, the AP three, and the LDPB one; repeat elections were held in two constituencies, in which no candidate had held an absolute majority of votes cast, on 31 October. In the constitutional referendum, held concurrently with the first round of elections, it was claimed, 77.3% of voters approved the amendment which would effectively clear the way for Lukashenko to seek an unprecedented third term in

office in 2006, on an official turnout of nearly 90%. An independent poll, however, claimed the 'yes' voters could have accounted for as little as 48.3% of the electorate, throwing the result into question. Controls on political parties had been gradually tightening since February 2004, and in August the abolition of the Belarusian Party of Labour was decreed by the Supreme Court, a move which attracted widespread criticism. The former Governor of Minsk City, a prominent opponent of the Government, Mikhail Marinich, was arrested in April 2004 on several charges, precipitating a number of incidents of unrest, including a strike in June by vendors, market traders and small business owners.

In January 2004 the Parliamentary Assembly of the Council of Europe published a preliminary report on the disappearances of Zakharenka, Ganchar, Zavidski and an associate of Ganchar, Anatol Krasouski. The report concluded that senior government officials, including Sheyman (who remained in position as Prosecutor-General) and Sivakow, may have been involved in co-ordinating the disappearances, and urged member states of the Council of Europe to exert political pressure on the Belarusian Government to prompt an independent investigation into the alleged murders. In the same month the families of the missing parties appealed to the State Security Committee to undertake a criminal investigation into the disappearances. In August Sivakow was banned by EU member states from entering Greece (in his capacity as Minister of Sports and Tourism he had planned to visit the summer Olympic Games) in a further attempt to pressure the regime into performing a full investigation.

Following the dissolution of the USSR in 1991, Belarus's closest relations continued to be with member states of the CIS, in particular neighbouring Russia. In April 1993 the Supreme Council authorized Shushkevich to signed the CIS Collective Security Treaty that had initially been established, between six member states in the previous year; Shushkevich eventually signed the treaty in late December, and accords on closer economic co-operation with CIS states followed. In April 1994 Belarus and Russia concluded an agreement on eventual monetary union. In March 1996 Belarus, Kazakhstan, Kyrgyzstan and Russia signed the Quadripartite Treaty, which envisaged a common market and a customs union between the four countries, as well as joint transport, energy and communications systems (Tajikistan signed the Treaty in 1998). In September 2003 Belarus, Kazakhstan, Russia and Ukraine signed a new agreement on the establishment of a common economic space. (However, the election of the reformist, Viktor Yushchenko, as President of Ukraine in December 2004, appeared likely to delay or prevent the implementation of these proposals) Meanwhile, in April 2003 Armenia, Belarus, Kazakhstan, Kyrgyzstan, Russia and Tajikistan had formally inaugurated the successor to the Collective Security Treaty, a new regional defence structure known as the Collective Security Treaty Organization.

In April 1996 Belarus and Russia concluded the far-reaching and controversial Treaty on the Formation of a Community of Sovereign Republics, providing for closer economic, political and military integration. On 2 April 1997 a further Treaty of Union was signed by Yeltsin and Lukashenka in Moscow, and a Charter of the Union, detailing the process of integration, was also initialled. The stated aim of the Union was the 'voluntary unification of the member states'. The Union's Parliamentary Assembly (provision for which had been made in the 1996 Treaty and which had convened in March) was to comprise 36 members from the legislature of each country. The Charter was submitted for nation-wide discussion in both countries, before being signed in Moscow on 23 May. Ratification of the documents by the respective legislatures took place in June, and the first official session of the Parliamentary Assembly followed shortly afterwards, with the Assembly adopting the anthem of the former USSR.

In November 1998 the Parliamentary Assembly of the Russia-Belarus Union voted for the creation of a unified parliament, to consist of two chambers. The upper chamber was to include deputies delegated by the legislatures of the two countries, and the lower chamber, comprising 25 Belarusian and 75 Russian deputies, was to be elected by direct universal suffrage. (However, it was unclear when the first elections to this polity would occur.) On 25 December, in Moscow, Presidents Lukashenka and Yeltsin signed an outline union accord. A draft treaty on unification was submitted for national discussion in October 1999. Lukashenka's hopes for the formation of a single state, which were much contested by the Belarusian opposition, were not shared by Russia, and the draft treaty did not fully satisfy the wishes of the Belarusian President. The signature of the treaty, which created a more formal union structure, officially known as the Union of the Russian Federation and Belarus, took place in Moscow on 8 December. The treaty was ratified in January 2000 and came into force on 26 January, when Lukashenka was appointed Chairman of the High State Council of the Union. Although progress towards a full union appeared to be advancing steadily, President Vladimir Putin of Russia remained more pragmatic than did Lukashenka, in particular in his attitude towards the formation of joint armed forces, a measure that the Belarusian President strongly favoured. On 30 November, during a CIS summit meeting in Minsk, an agreement on the introduction of a single currency was signed; the agreement, according to which the Russian rouble was to be adopted as the union currency from 1 January 2005 and a new currency was to be adopted three years later, was ratified by the Natsionalnoye Sobraniye in April 2001. In November the eventual merger of the air defence systems of Belarus and Russia was announced, and a draft constitution of the Russia-Belarus Union was made public.

During 2002, however, relations with Russia notably worsened, owing to disagreements over the nature of the planned union. In mid-March 2002 Belarus and Russia reached agreement on the harmonization of customs and tax laws and the removal of trade barriers, but in late June, at a meeting held in St Petersburg, Russia, Putin publicly criticized Lukashenka's union plans. Subsequently, in mid-August, at a summit meeting held in Moscow, Putin presented Lukashenka with a new unification plan, which effectively provided for the absorption of the seven administrative regions of Belarus (rather than Belarus as a country) into the Russian Federation; Lukashenka denounced the plan as unacceptable and as an insult to Belarus's sovereignty. Detailed negotiations on monetary union commenced in April 2003, and by June it had been agreed that although the two countries were to retain their own central banks, the Russian central bank was to supply Belarus with bank notes from 1 January 2005. However, the two countries' failure to sign a final agreement on the proposed single currency by the end of 2003, largely owing to demands by Lukashenka for the prior adoption of a constitutional act on the formation of the union state (together with guarantees of Belarusian independence), delayed its planned introduction indefinitely. Relations with Russia were also strained from 2003 by inconclusive negotiations over the settlement of Belarusian fuel arrears, together with plans by the Russian energy supplier Gazprom to increase gas prices, which eventually led to the repeated suspension of gas supplies from Russia in early 2004.

In June 1998 a diplomatic scandal resulted from the enforced eviction (for 'repairs'), of 22 diplomatic families from their residences outside Minsk. This violation of the Vienna Convention, guaranteeing the inviolability of diplomatic residences, led to the recall from Belarus of the ambassadors from EU countries, a number of other European states and the USA and Japan. Belarusian envoys were expelled from the EU in June, and in the following month Belarusian officials were barred from entering its member states. The ban was subsequently adopted by several other European countries and the USA. In December, however, Belarus agreed to provide compensation to those forced to relocate and Lukashenka gave assurances that, henceforth, he would comply with international agreements. All heads of diplomatic missions accredited to Belarus, with the exception of the US ambassador, returned to Minsk in January 1999. The EU ban on Belarusian officials entering its territory was repealed in February, and the US ambassador returned to Minsk in September. However, relations with the USA remained uneasy during 2000, and the USA urged the Belarusian opposition to boycott the legislative elections of October. The USA did not recognize the results of the presidential election, held in September 2001, and the US ambassador refused to attend Lukashenka's inauguration ceremony. From late 2001 the USA expressed increasing concern over the alleged illegal sale of arms to states accused of supporting terrorist activity. Notably, Belarus had developed close economic and military relations with Iraq, and was reported to have helped to upgrade Iraq's air defence systems, although the Belarusian Government denied having acted in contravention of UN sanctions. In March 2003 Lukashenka expressed criticism of the US-led military action in Iraq that had commenced in that month, but announced his willingness to improve relations with the USA.

International organizations, including the OSCE, had continued to recognize the former Supreme Council as the legitimate legislature of Belarus. An OSCE Advisory and Monitoring Group commenced operations in Minsk in February 1998, with the aim of encouraging democratization and monitoring human rights. The OSCE described the 2001 presidential election as flawed, but warned against the pursuit of a policy that might serve to strengthen Belarus's international isolation. Relations with the OSCE deteriorated severely during 2002, and all OSCE representatives in Belarus were compelled to leave when the authorities refused to renew their visas. In November 2002 the Czech Government denied an entry visa to President Lukashenka, thereby preventing him from attending a meeting of NATO's Euro-Atlantic Partnership Council in the capital, Prague. Fourteen EU member states subsequently agreed to impose a visa ban on Lukashenka and seven other senior Belarusian officials, and in late November the USA also prohibited Lukashenka from entering the country, in protest at his country's poor record on human rights and the expulsion of the OSCE Advisory and Monitoring Group. (The bans were not lifted until April 2003.) However, following negotiations between the Belarusian Government and the OSCE in December 2002, an agreement was reached, which provided for the establishment of a new OSCE mission in Belarus in January 2003. In late February the OSCE Parliamentary Assembly voted to recognize the legitimacy of the Natsionalnoye Sobraniye, despite a negative assessment of the country's democratic progress by an OSCE delegation. Meanwhile, in January 2004 the Council of Europe refused to renew Belarus's special guest status at that organization (suspended since January 1997), owing to its continued failure to observe European norms on democracy and human rights.

With the dissolution of the USSR in December 1991, Belarus effectively became a nuclear power, with approximately 80 SS-25 intercontinental ballistic missiles stationed on its territory. However, the Government described Belarus as a neutral and non-nuclear state, in accordance with the Declaration of State Sovereignty of July 1990. Accordingly, in May 1992 Belarus signed the Lisbon Protocol to the Treaty on the Non-Proliferation of Nuclear Weapons (see p. 93), under which it pledged to transfer all nuclear missiles to Russia by 1999. In February 1993 the Supreme Council ratified the first Strategic Arms' Reduction Treaty (START 1). Substantial amounts of financial and technical aid were pledged by the USA to help Belarus dismantle its nuclear arsenal. The last remaining nuclear warhead was transported to Russia in late 1996. In 1998 Belarus signed the International Convention on Nuclear Safety, adopted in June 1994 in Vienna.

In September 2000 Belarus became a permanent member of the Non-aligned Movement (see p. 384).

Government

Under the Constitution of March 1994, which was amended in November 1996, legislative power is vested in the bicameral Natsionalnoye Sobraniye (National Assembly). The lower chamber, the 110-member Palata Predstaviteley (House of Representatives), is elected by universal adult suffrage for a term of four years. The upper chamber, the Soviet Respubliki (Council of the Republic), comprises 64 members: 56 members elected by organs of local administration, and eight members appointed by the President. The President is the Head of State, and is elected by popular vote for five years. Executive authority is exercised by the Cabinet of Ministers, which is led by the Chairman (Prime Minister) and is responsible to the Natsionalnoye Sobraniye. For administrative purposes, Belarus is divided into six regions (*oblasts*) and the capital city of Minsk; the regions are divided into districts (*raions*).

Defence

In August 2004 the total strength of Belarus's armed forces was 72,940, comprising an army of 29,600, an air force and air defence forces of 18,170, as well as 25,170 in centrally controlled units and Ministry of Defence staff. There are also paramilitary forces, controlled by the Ministry of Internal Affairs, which number 110,000, including a border guard of 12,000. Military service is compulsory and lasts for between nine and 12 months. In October 1994 it was announced that two Russian non-nuclear military installations were to remain in Belarus. In late 2001 it was reported that the armed forces were to be reduced to 65,000 personnel, including 50,000 servicemen, by 2006. The budget for 2004 allocated 339,000m. readjusted roubles to defence. In January 1995 Belarus joined the North Atlantic Treaty Organization's (NATO) 'Partnership for Peace' (see p. 303) programme of military co-operation.

Economic Affairs

In 2003, according to estimates by the World Bank, Belarus's gross national income (GNI), measured at average 2001–03 prices, was US $17,492.8m., equivalent to $1,590 per head. In terms of purchasing-power parity, GNI in that year was equivalent to $6,010 per head. During 1990–2003 the population declined at an average annual rate of 0.2%, while gross domestic product (GDP) per head increased by an annual average of 0.5%, in real terms. Over the same period, overall GDP increased, in real terms, by an average of 0.2% annually. Real GDP increased by 4.7% in 2002 and by 6.8% in 2003.

Agriculture contributed 9.8% of GDP in 2003. In 2000 14.8% of the employed labour force were engaged in the sector, according to FAO estimates. The principal crops are potatoes, grain and sugar beet. Large areas of arable land (some 1.6m. ha) are still unused after being contaminated in 1986, following the accident at the Chornobyl nuclear power station in Ukraine. The Belarusian authorities have largely opposed private farming, and by 1999 collective and state farms still accounted for some 83% of agricultural land. However, private farms produced the majority of Belarus's potatoes, fruit and vegetables, as well as a significant proportion of total livestock-product output. In 1998, according to the IMF, 49.8% of total crop output was produced by the private sector. During 1993–2003, according to World Bank estimates, real agricultural GDP decreased at an average annual rate of 0.9%. Agricultural output increased, in real terms, by 3.1% in 2002 and by 7.8% in 2003.

Industry (comprising mining, manufacturing, construction and power) provided 37.1% of GDP in 2003, and engaged 34.7% of the employed labour force in 2000. According to the World Bank, industrial GDP decreased, in real terms, at an average annual rate of 3.0% during 1990–2001, while IMF figures for 2002 and 2003 show year-on-year real increases of 6.1% and 9.1% respectively.

Belarus has relatively few mineral resources, although there are small deposits of petroleum and natural gas, and important peat reserves. Peat extraction, however, was severely affected by the disaster at Chornobyl, since contaminated peat could not be burned. Belarus produced 50% of the former USSR's output of potash; annual output of around 4.5 metric tons was reported by 2001 Less than 0.5% the labour force were engaged in mining and quarrying at that time.

According to the World Bank, the manufacturing sector contributed an estimated 30.8% of GDP in 2002, and employed 26.5% of the labour force in 1994. Machine-building, power generation and chemicals are the principal branches of the sector. During 1990–2001 manufacturing GDP increased, in real terms, at an average annual rate of 0.6%, according to World Bank estimates. Overall sectoral GDP increased by 6.0% in 2002 and by 9.1% in 2003.

In 2001 much of Belarus's supply of energy was provided by natural gas (92.2%), with petroleum and petroleum products accounting for almost all of the remainder. In 2001, according to IMF figures, the country imported 89.5% of its crude-oil consumption, 99.2% of its natural gas consumption and 32.9% of its electricity consumption. Energy products comprised 25.8% of the total value of imports in 2002. There are two large petroleum refineries, at Novopolotsk and Mozyr. In 2000 Belarus's principal gas supplier, the Russian state-controlled company Gazprom, announced plans to construct two new natural gas pipelines across Belarus, in order to halt the alleged misappropriation of supplies from existing pipelines in Ukraine. However, from the latter half of the 1990s Gazprom repeatedly threatened to reduce gas supplies to Belarus, owing to that country's energy arrears, which continued to increase, despite subsidized gas prices (a concession viewed to result from the signature of the Russia-Belarus Union Treaty). In 2002 the Belarusian Government agreed to authorize the partial denationalization of the domestic natural gas importer, Beltransgaz, enabling Gazprom to acquire a stake in the company, in return for the partial settlement of Belarus's arrears. However, negotiations over the valuation of the company subsequently stalled, as did negotiations held in September 2003 between President Alyaksandr Lukashenka and President Vladimir Putin of Russia over Russian plans to introduce market prices for gas exports to Belarus. The failure to reach agreement on either issue eventually led Gazprom temporarily to suspend gas supplies to Belarus in early 2004. Gas consumption in Belarus has continued to show a steady increase, these difficulties notwithstanding, and cheap

energy prices remain a principle, and popular, aspect of Lukashenka's economic policy.

The services sector developed during the 1990s and early 2000s , providing 53.1% of GDP in 2003 and accounting for 50.5% of total employment in 2000. The sector is led by transport and communications and trade and catering, which accounted for 12.2% and 11.7% of GDP, respectively, in 2003. According to World Bank estimates, during 1990–2001 the GDP of the services sector increased, in real terms, at an average annual rate of 0.2%. Sectoral GDP decreased, by 1.1% in 2002 but increased by 2.0% in 2003.

In 2003 Belarus recorded a visible trade deficit of US $1,255.6m., and there was a deficit of US $527.4m. on the current account of the balance of payments. Trading partners outwith the Commonwealth of Independent States (CIS, see p. 189) accounted for 30.8% of Belarus's imports and 45.3% of its exports in 2002. However, the accession to the European Union of a number of neighbouring countries in May 2004 was expected to have a negative impact on Belarusian foreign trade, as they imposed additional border and trade controls. In 2002 Belarus's principal trading partner was Russia (which accounted for 65.1% of total imports and 49.6% of exports). Germany was also an important source of imports (accounting for 7.6% of the total), and Latvia and the United Kingdom were significant purchasers of exports (accounting for 6.5% and 6.2% of the total, respectively). In 2000 the principal exports were machinery and metalworking, petroleum and gas, chemical and petroleum products, and light manufactures. The principal imports were petroleum and gas, machinery and metalworking, chemical and petroleum products, and metallurgy.

The 2002 republican and local government budgets registered a deficit of 472,388m. roubles (equivalent to 1.8% of GDP). Preliminary budget figures for 2003 set out a deficit of 491,912m. roubles, or around 1.4% of GDP in that year. Belarus's total external debt was US $907.6m. at the end of 2002, of which $709.5m. was long-term public debt. In that year the cost of debt-servicing was equivalent to 2.1% of the value of exports of goods and services. During 1991–2002 consumer prices increased at an average rate of 286.0% per year. The average annual rate of inflation was 43.0% in 2002, 28.0% in 2003 and an estimated 14.4% in 2004. At the end of 2004 1.9% of the economically active population were registered as unemployed. However, the true rate of unemployment was believed to be far higher, as many people were unwilling to register, owing to the low level of official benefits.

Belarus joined the IMF and the World Bank in 1992. It also became a member of the European Bank for Reconstruction and Development (EBRD, see p. 212). Belarus is pursuing membership of the World Trade Organization (WTO, see p. 357), at which it holds observer status, although its failure to introduce market economic principles made the prospect of early accession unlikely; in 2003 the WTO suggested that Belarus synchronize its accession negotiations with those of Russia. The IMF closed its Belarus office in 2004.

Following the dissolution of the USSR, Belarus experienced serious economic problems and a severe contraction in output in all sectors. Belarus was slow to adopt economic reforms, and economic policy was influenced by the country's aim of eventual integration with Russia, as envisaged in a number of treaties and agreements signed from the mid-1990s, and the increasing international isolation of the regime of President Alyaksandr Lukashenka. In 2001 both the IMF and the World Bank resumed relations with Belarus, suspended since the mid-1990s (although the IMF resumed relations at an evaluative level only). Meanwhile, in April 2001 the legislature ratified a currency agreement with Russia, according to which the Russian rouble was to be adopted as the Belarusian currency from 2005, and a new single currency was to be introduced in 2008. However, by early 2005, there was no indication as to when, or whether, either of these measures would be implemented. None the less, President Lukashenka set ambitious economic targets for 2004, which envisaged economic growth of 10% and a 71% increase in the minimum wage, despite the potential inflationary consequences of such a development. In early 2004 the IMF praised the maintenance of economic growth in 2003 (when GDP increased by some 6.8%, in real terms, according to official figures), but warned that the Government's projections for 2004 were unrealistic. The annual rate of inflation was the highest in the region and there were problems within the industrial sector, where approximately 30% of enterprises were loss-making. The agricultural sector, in which almost 60% of enterprises recorded a loss in 2003, was also in need of urgent reform. In 2004 Lukashenka announced that bankrupt or unprofitable collective farms would be leased to private enterprises. The IMF emphasized the fact that foreign and private-sector investment was likely to remain limited while the so-called golden share regulation, which permitted any company in which the Government retained as little as one share to come under renewed state control (even if this had not been anticipated when the firm was initially privatized), remained in place. In fact, the golden share regulation was expanded further in early 2002.

Education

Education is officially compulsory for nine years. Generally, education lasts for 11 years, from six to 17 years of age. In 2001 the total enrolment at pre-primary level was equivalent to 70.8% of children in the relevant age group. Primary education usually begins at six years of age and lasts for four years (Grades 1–4). In 2001 the total enrolment at primary level was equivalent to 91.5% of the school-age population (males 91.8%; females 91.2%). Secondary education, beginning at the age of 10, lasts for a further seven years (Grades 5–11), comprising a first cycle of five years and a second of two years. In 2001 enrolment at Grades 5–9 was equivalent to 93.9% of those in the relevant age group (males 93.9%; females 93.9%). Enrolment at Grades 10–11 was equivalent to 54.6% of those aged 16–17 years, while a further 21% were enrolled at vocational schools. Enrolment at specialized institutions of secondary education was equivalent to 36.8% of those aged 18–23 years in 2001. From 1998 a transition began to be made towards introducing compulsory

education for 10 years and general education for 12 years. In 2001/02 27.7% of all pupils were taught in Belarusian, and 72.2% were taught in Russian (0.1% were taught in Polish). Higher education institutions include 26 universities, as well as nine academies, 15 institutes, five higher colleges, one higher technical school, and two theological seminaries. In 2001/02 301,753 students were enrolled in higher education (equivalent to 302 per 10,000 inhabitants). Research is co-ordinated by the National Academy of Sciences of Belarus. Budgetary expenditure on education by all levels of government was 2,343,119m. roubles (equivalent to 4.7% of GDP) in 2003, compared with 2.1% of GDP in 2001.

Public Holidays

2005: 1 January (New Year's Day), 7 January (Orthodox Christmas), 7–8 March (International Women's Day), 15 March (Constitution Day), 28 March (Catholic Easter), 1 May (Labour Day), 2 May (Orthodox Easter), 6 May (Radunitsa, Remembrance Day), 9 May (Victory Day), 11 May (State Flag Day), 3 July (Independence Day), 25 December (Catholic Christmas).

2006: 1 January (New Year's Day), 7 January (Orthodox Christmas), 8 March (International Women's Day), 15 March (Constitution Day), 16 April (Catholic Easter), 23 April (Orthodox Easter), 1 May (Labour Day), 6 May (Radunitsa, Remembrance Day), 9 May (Victory Day and State Flag Day), 3 July (Independence Day), 25 December (Catholic Christmas).

Weights and Measures

The metric system is in force.

Statistical Survey

Source: mainly Ministry of Statistics and Analysis, 220070 Minsk, pr. Partizanski 12; tel. (17) 249-42-78; fax (17) 249-22-04; e-mail minstat@mail.belpak .by; internet www.www.belstat.gov.by/homep/en/main.html.

Area and Population

AREA, POPULATION AND DENSITY

Area (sq km)	207,595*
Population (census results)†	
12 January 1989	10,151,806
16 February 1999	
Males	4,717,621
Females	5,327,616
Total	10,045,237
Population (official estimates at 1 January)	
2002	9,951,000
2003	9,899,000
2004	9,849,000
Density (per sq km) at 1 January 2004	45.7

* 80,153 sq miles.

† Figures refer to the *de jure* population. The *de facto* total was 10,199,709 in 1989.

POPULATION BY NATIONALITY

(1999 census)

	%
Belarusian	81
Russian	11
Polish	4
Ukrainian	2
Others	2
Total	**100**

PRINCIPAL TOWNS*

(estimated population at 1 January 2001)

Minsk (Miensk, capital)	1,699,100	Borisov (Barysau) .	150,900
Gomel (Homiel) . . .	480,000	Pinsk	131,100
Mogilev (Mahilioŭ) . .	360,600	Orsha (Vorsha) . .	124,000
Vitebsk (Viciebsk) . .	341,500	Mozyr (Mazyr) . .	110,700
Grodno (Horadnia) . .	307,100	Novopolotsk . . .	102,100
Brest (Bieraście)† . .	291,400	Soligorsk	101,900
Bobruysk (Babrujsk) .	221,400	Lida	100,000
Baranovichi			
(Baranavichy) . .	168,800		

* The Belarusian names of towns are given in parentheses after the more widely used Russian names, where they differ.

† Formerly Brest-Litovsk.

Mid-2003 (UN estimate, incl. suburbs): Minsk 1,704,866 (Source: UN, *World Urbanization Prospects: The 2003 Revision*).

BIRTHS, MARRIAGES AND DEATHS

	Registered live births		Registered marriages		Registered deaths	
	Number	Rate (per 1,000)	Number	Rate (per 1,000)	Number	Rate (per 1,000)
1994 . .	110,599	10.7	75,540	7.3	130,003	12.6
1995 . .	101,144	9.8	77,027	7.5	133,775	13.0
1996 . .	95,798	9.3	63,677	6.2	133,422	13.0
1997 . .	89,586	8.8	69,735	6.8	136,653	13.4
1998 . .	92,645	9.1	71,354	7.0	137,296	13.5
1999 . .	92,975	9.3	72,994	7.3	142,027	14.2
2000 . .	93,691	9.4	62,485	6.2	134,867	13.5
2001* . .	91,700	9.2	68,700	6.9	140,300	14.1

* Figures are provisional.

Expectation of life (WHO estimates, years at birth): 68.3 (males 62.6; females 74.3) in 2002.

EMPLOYMENT
(annual averages, '000 persons)

	1998	1999	2000
Agriculture	695.3	659.5	625.1
Forestry	28.7	29.7	32.5
Industry*	1,221.0	1,231.0	1,226.7
Construction	329.5	330.5	312.3
Trade and communications	321.4	323.5	318.3
Trade and public catering†	483.2	493.3	532.3
Housing, public utilities and personal services	193.4	202.5	208.1
Health care	262.0	266.1	269.9
Physical culture and social security	51.6	56.3	56.2
Education	454.5	460.6	463.7
Culture and arts	73.9	77.0	80.2
Science	43.7	43.9	42.2
Credit and insurance	53.2	55.7	58.4
Other activities	205.2	212.4	215.1
Total	4,416.6	4,442.0	4,441.0
Males	2,146.5	2,127.8	2,113.9
Females	2,270.1	2,314.2	2,327.1

* Comprising manufacturing (except printing and publishing), mining and quarrying, electricity, gas, logging and fishing.
† Including material and technical supply and procurement.

Unemployment ('000 persons registered at December): 95.8 (males 37.6, females 58.2) in 2000; 102.9 (males 40.8, females 62.1) in 2001; 130.5 (males 47.8, females 82.7) in 2002; 136.1 (males 46.1, females 90.0) in 2003.

2001 ('000 persons): Total employment (estimated annual average) 4,417.4 (Source: ILO).

2002 ('000 persons): Total employment (estimated annual average) 4,380.8 (Source: ILO).

2003 ('000 persons): Total labour force (estimated annual averages) 4,446 (males 2,075, females 2,371).

Health and Welfare

KEY INDICATORS

Total fertility rate (children per woman, 2002)	1.2
Under-5 mortality rate (per 1,000 live births, 2003)	17
HIV/AIDS (% of persons aged 15–49, 2001)	0.27
Physicians (per 1,000 head, 2001)	4.50
Hospital beds (per 1,000 head, 2001)	12.58
Health expenditure (2001): US $ per head (PPP)	464
Health expenditure (2001): % of GDP	5.6
Health expenditure (2001): public (% of total)	86.7
Access to water (% of persons, 2002)	100
Human Development Index (2002): ranking	62
Human Development Index (2002): value	0.790

For sources and definitions, see explanatory note on p. vi.

Agriculture

PRINCIPAL CROPS
('000 metric tons)

	2001	2002	2003
Wheat	1,050.0	1,017.0	787.0
Barley	1,750.0	1,681.2	1,590.0
Maize	15.7	30.0	52.0*
Rye	1,300.0	1,600.0	1,137.0
Oats	600.0	575.0	587.5
Buckwheat	12.0	7.0	20.0*
Triticale (wheat-rye hybrid)	198.0	798.0	878.5
Potatoes	7,767.6	7,420.7	8,649.0
Sugar beet	1,682.1	1,146.0	1,920.0
Dry beans	100.0	188.0	222.0*
Dry peas	127.0	91.0	109.5*
Walnuts†	12.0	12.0	12.0
Sunflower seed*	18.0	18.0	11.0
Rapeseed	65.0	60.0	54.0*
Linseed	15.0	13.8	15.0*
Cabbages*	538.0	545.0	845.0
Tomatoes*	130.0	120.0	150.0
Cucumbers and gherkins*	150.0	179.0	210.0
Dry onions*	70.0	73.0	80.0
Carrots*	171.0	200.0	310.0
Other vegetables	356.0	390.0	407.0*
Apples*	150.0	330.0	165.0
Pears*	10.0	74.6	34.6
Plums*	30.0	17.0	10.0
Sour cherries*	18.0	19.0	10.0
Cherries*	10.0	13.4	7.0
Other fruits and berries*	6.0	24.0	11.6
Flax fibre	31.5	26.0	26.0†

* Unofficial figure(s).
† FAO estimate(s).
Source: FAO.

LIVESTOCK
('000 head at 1 January)

	2001	2002	2003
Horses	217	209	202
Cattle	4,005	4,085	4,005
Pigs	3,431	3,373	3,329
Sheep	89	83	73
Goats	61	66	64
Chickens*	32,000	25,300	24,300

* FAO estimates.
Source: FAO.

LIVESTOCK PRODUCTS
('000 metric tons)

	2001	2002	2003
Beef and veal	283.0	226.5	216.9*
Mutton and lamb	2.7	1.8	2.5*
Pig meat	270.0	300.7	290.0*
Poultry meat	68.0	84.7	97.5
Other meat	6.0	3.2	3.6*
Cows' milk	4,834.1	4,772.5	4,683.0
Cheese	71.3	64.0	66.9†
Butter	65.9	65.1	62.0
Hen eggs*	174.0	162.5	156.4
Honey†	3.0	3.1	3.1
Cattle hides (fresh)†	31.2	26.0	24.3
Sheepskins (fresh)†	86.4	72.0	100.0

* Unofficial figure(s).
† FAO estimate(s).
Source: FAO.

Forestry

ROUNDWOOD REMOVALS
('000 cubic metres, excl. bark)

	2001	2002	2003
Sawlogs, veneer logs and logs for sleepers	3,650	3,900	2,304
Pulpwood	1,415	1,505	1,612
Other industrial wood	473	564	2,531
Fuel wood	947	978	1,097
Total	6,485	6,947	7,543

Source: FAO.

SAWNWOOD PRODUCTION
('000 cubic metres, incl. railway sleepers)

	2001	2002	2003
Coniferous (softwood) . . .	1,379	1,484	2,064
Broadleaved (hardwood) . . .	679	698	239
Total	2,058	2,182	2,304

Source: FAO.

Fishing

(metric tons, live weight)

	2000	2001	2002
Capture	553	943	5,575
Freshwater bream	27	198	403
Common carp	17	15	3,845
Aquaculture	6,716	4,666	6,825
Common carp	5,867	3,845	4,504
Crucian carp	396	268	1,595
Silver carp	358	459	261
Total catch	7,269	5,609	12,400

Source: FAO.

Mining

('000 metric tons, unless otherwise indicated)

	1999	2000	2001
Crude petroleum	1,840	1,851*	1,852
Natural gas (million cu metres) .	256	257	255
Peat: for fuel	3,090	3,786*	4,495
Peat: for agriculture†	100	100	100

* Reported figure.
† Estimates.

Source: US Geological Survey.

Industry

SELECTED PRODUCTS
('000 metric tons, unless otherwise indicated)

	1998	1999	2000
Refined sugar	476	501	565
Margarine	15.0	22.4	20.8
Wheat flour	1,153	1,134	924
Ethyl alcohol ('000 hectolitres) .	1,046	982	1,035
Wine ('000 hectolitres)	5,832	5,467	6,917
Beer ('000 hectolitres)	2,603.7	2,728.4	2,370.6
Mineral water ('000 hectolitres) .	1,082.5	1,453.4	1,532.5
Soft drinks ('000 hectolitres) . .	2,196.3	1,870.3	1,861.4
Cigarettes (million)	7,296	9,259	10,356
Cotton yarn (pure and mixed) . .	18.6	15.1	16.8
Flax yarn	17.4	16.6	10.2
Wool yarn (pure and mixed) . .	16.3	16.4	15.7
Woven cotton fabrics (million sq metres)	67.1	50.6	66.6
Woven woollen fabrics (million sq metres)	9.5	9.3	9.3
Linen fabrics (million sq metres) .	50.1	49.4	33.1
Woven fabrics of cellulosic fibres (million sq metres)	77.2	71.5	62.4
Carpets ('000 sq metres) . . .	8,145	9,155	8,744
Footwear (excluding rubber, '000 pairs)	16,223	16,538	15,388
Plywood ('000 cu metres) . . .	139	140	126
Paper	45	53	44
Paperboard	150	162	176
Benzene (Benzol)	16.7	23.4	51.7
Ethylene (Ethene)	108.1	115.4	114.7
Propylene (Propene)	70.5	74.2	70.7
Xylenes (Xylol)	—	7.5	38.0
Sulphuric acid (100%)	640	614	584
Nitrogenous fertilizers (a)[1] . .	559	615	597
Phosphate fertilizers (b)[1] . . .	130	120	87
Potash fertilizers (c)[1]	3,451	3,613	3,372
Non-cellulosic continuous fibres .	66.2	66.8	72.7
Cellulosic continuous filaments .	14.3	13.0	11.7
Soap	26.3	33.7	38.6
Rubber tyres ('000)[2]	2,324	2,263	2,440
Rubber footwear ('000 pairs) . .	5,036	4,797	3,348
Quicklime	684	663	586
Cement	2,035	1,998	1,847
Concrete blocks ('000 cu metres) .	2,130	1,759	1,752
Crude steel	1,412	1,449	1,623
Tractors ('000)	26.9	27.4	22.5
Refrigerators ('000)	802	802	812
Domestic washing machines ('000)	90.8	92.2	88.1
Television receivers ('000) . . .	468	516	532
Radio receivers ('000)	114	195	101
Lorries (number)	12,799	13,370	14,656
Motorcycles ('000)	20.4	24.4	36.6
Bicycles ('000)	452	508	586
Cameras ('000)	5	8	4
Watches ('000)	4,848	5,218	5,602
Electric energy (million kWh) . .	23,492	26,516	26,095

[1] Production in terms of (a) nitrogen; (b) phosphoric acid; or (c) potassium oxide.

[2] For lorries and farm vehicles.

2001 ('000 metric tons, unless otherwise indicated): Paper 51; Cement 1,803; Tractors ('000) 22.7; Electric energy (million kWh) 25,063.

2002 ('000 metric tons, unless otherwise indicated): Paper 54; Cement 2,171; Tractors ('000) 24.3; Electric energy (million kWh) 26,455.

2003 ('000 metric tons, unless otherwise indicated): Paper 64; Cement 2,472; Tractors ('000) 26.7; Electric energy (million kWh) 26,615.

Finance

CURRENCY AND EXCHANGE RATES

Monetary Units
100 kopeks = 1 readjusted Belarusian rouble (rubel).

Sterling, Dollar and Euro Equivalents (30 November 2004)
£1 sterling = 4,146.5 readjusted roubles;
US $1 = 2,174.0 readjusted roubles;
€1 = 2,890.3 readjusted roubles;
10,000 readjusted Belarusian roubles = £2.412 = $4.600 = €3.460.

Average Exchange Rate (readjusted Belarusian roubles per US $)
2001   1,390.000
2002   1,790.917
2003   2,051.270

Note: The Belarusian rouble was introduced in May 1992, initially as a coupon currency, to circulate alongside (and at par with) the Russian (formerly Soviet) rouble. The parity between Belarusian and Russian currencies was subsequently ended, and the Belarusian rouble was devalued. In August 1994 a new Belarusian rouble, equivalent to 10 old roubles, was introduced. On 1 January 1995 the Belarusian rouble became the sole national currency, while the circulation of Russian roubles ceased. On 1 January 2000 a readjusted Belarusian rouble, equivalent to 1,000 of the former units, was introduced.

STATE BUDGET
('000 million roubles)

Revenue	2001	2002	2003*
Tax revenue	4,389.1	6,263.4	9,333.6
Direct taxes on income and profits	1,315.9	1,684.5	2,369.0
Payroll taxes	154.5	220.4	273.2
Domestic taxes on goods and services	2,283.8	3,311.7	4,837.2
General sales, turnover or value-added taxes . . .	1,446.7	2,165.1	2,894.8
Excises	442.0	592.0	837.8
Property tax	237.4	390.5	728.8
Current non-tax revenue . . .	224.5	383.0	596.3
Capital revenue	59.0	449.2	51.5
Revenue of republic budgetary funds	908.3	1,275.5	1,886.2
Revenue of local budgetary funds .	124.7	194.7	287.4
Statistical discrepancy	29.5	−357.2	−0.8
Total†	5,734.6	8,208.6	12,154.2

Expenditure	2001	2002	2003
Republican and local administrations	168.1	251.6	381.5
Defence	183.8	259.9	376.9
Law, order and security . . .	333.3	461.0	654.1
Agriculture	146.4	178.8	520.3
Housing and communal services .	450.1	612.4	940.9
Emergency funds, Chornobyl .	228.7	307.0	376.4
Education	1,109.5	1,738.1	2,343.1
Health, sports and physical education	872.5	1,270.1	1,809.8
Servicing of state debt	124.9	154.2	175.7
Other	1,157.9	1,773.2	2,601.3
Capital investment	252.3	323.6	533.4
Expenditure of budgetary funds .	996.0	1,351.2	1,932.7
Total	6,023.5	8,681.1	12,646.1

* Preliminary figures.
† Excluding receipts from privatization and revenues from the Social Protection Fund.

Consolidated budget ('000 million roubles): *2001:* Revenue 7,713.5 (Tax revenue 6,368.0); Expenditure 8,039.0. *2002:* Revenue 11,194.0 (Tax revenue 9,248.6); Expenditure 11,672.7. *2003* (preliminary): Revenue 16,075.3 (Tax revenue 13,254.8); Expenditure 16,577.3.

Source: IMF, *Republic of Belarus: Statistical Appendix* (May 2004).

INTERNATIONAL RESERVES
(US $ million at 31 December)

	2001	2002	2003
IMF special drawing rights . .	0.40	0.26	0.03
Reserve position in IMF . . .	0.03	0.03	0.03
Foreign exchange	390.26	618.52	594.75
Total	390.68	618.81	594.81

Source: IMF, *International Financial Statistics.*

MONEY SUPPLY
(million roubles at 31 December)

	2001	2002	2003
Currency outside banks . . .	512,211	650,020	926,438
Demand deposits at deposit money banks	425,663	714,285	1,311,184
Total money (incl. others) . .	939,179	1,365,668	2,238,376

Source: IMF, *International Financial Statistics.*

COST OF LIVING
(Consumer price index; base: 1992 = 100)

	2000	2001	2002
Food (incl. beverages) . . .	13,945.7	21,871.1	30,381.1
Fuel and light	22,462.4	60,457.4	140,364.0
Clothing (incl. footwear) . . .	3,369.5	4,939.0	6,002.4
Rent	41,576.4	85,797.1	406,523.8
All items (incl. others)	11,094.6	17,877.8	25,490.2

Source: ILO.

NATIONAL ACCOUNTS
('000 million roubles at current prices)

Expenditure on the Gross Domestic Product

	2001	2002	2003
Government final consumption expenditure	3,701.3	5,496.7	7,674.4
Private final consumption expenditure	9,895.9	15,549.9	21,406.6
Increase in stocks	187.5	50.2	189.5
Gross fixed capital formation . .	3,893.0	5,746.4	8,484.7
Total domestic expenditure	17,677.7	26,843.2	37,755.2
Exports of goods and services . .	11,462.7	16,631.2	23,855.2
Less Imports of goods and services	12,072.3	17,610.6	25,280.9
Statistical discrepancy	105.1	274.5	−399.3
GDP in purchasers' values . .	17,173,2	26,138.2	35,930.2

Source: IMF, *International Financial Statistics.*

Gross Domestic Product by Economic Activity

	2001	2002	2003
Agriculture and forestry . . .	1,778	2,647	2,985
Industry*	4,474	6,647	9,180
Construction	1,007	1,528	2,151
Transport and communications .	1,975	2,710	3,735
Trade and catering	1,724	2,600	3,560
Material supply and procurement	189	226	287
Housing and public utilities . .	954	1,368	1,998
Health care	619	995	1,613
Education, culture and science .	1,086	1,698	2,151
Other	1,164	2,064	2,862
Gross value added in basic prices	14,969	22,483	30,522
Taxes, *less* subsidies on products .	2,205	3,655	5,408
GDP in purchasers' values . .	17,173	26,138	35,930

* Principally mining, manufacturing, electricity, gas and water.

Source: IMF, *Republic of Belarus: Statistical Appendix* (May 2004).

BALANCE OF PAYMENTS
(US $ million)

	2001	2002	2003
Exports of goods f.o.b.	7,334.1	7,964.7	10,072.9
Imports of goods f.o.b.	−8,140.8	−8,879.0	−11,328.5
Trade balance	−806.7	−914.3	−1,255.6
Exports of services	1,142.3	1,340.8	1,503.9
Imports of services	−841.3	−908.0	−943.7
Balance on goods and services	−505.7	−481.5	−686.4
Other income received . . .	20.8	25.7	27.0
Other income paid	−62.8	−72.4	−69.8
Balance on goods, services and income	−297.5	−493.1	−548.5
Current transfers received . . .	202.6	260.4	291.7
Current transfers paid	−48.5	−61.5	−97.1
Current balance	−394.4	−311.2	−527.4
Capital account (net)	56.3	52.7	68.9
Direct investment abroad . .	−0.3	206.2	−1.5
Direct investment from abroad .	95.8	247.1	171.8
Portfolio investment assets .	25.5	−2.4	0.8
Portfolio investment liabilities .	−45.4	−6.7	5.3
Other investment assets . . .	−139.2	−309.4	−61.0
Other investment liabilities . .	328.6	347.7	116.5
Net errors and omissions . .	−5.4	−126.9	145.3
Overall balance	−78.5	97.1	−81.4

Source: IMF, *International Financial Statistics.*

External Trade

PRINCIPAL COMMODITIES
(distribution by SITC, US $ million)

Imports c.i.f.	2000	2001	2002
Food and live animals . . .	818.5	724.6	716.8
Crude materials (inedible) except fuels	359.4	307.3	367.7
Mineral fuels, lubricants, etc. .	2,595.1	2,232.2	2,347.0
Petroleum, petroleum products, etc.	1,862.4	1,486.9	1,620.6
Crude petroleum oils, etc. . .	1,627.8	1,379.6	1,504.5
Gas, natural and manufactured .	565.3	576.4	567.9
Petroleum gases in the gaseous state	526.4	536.8	538.5
Chemicals and related products	978.8	890.1	918.9
Basic manufactures	1,616.6	1,609.8	1,679.3
Textile yarn, fabrics, etc. . . .	255.9	276.5	265.7
Iron and steel	579.5	558.6	559.3
Machinery and transport equipment	1,421.7	1,703.3	1,727.2
Machinery specialized for particular industries	238.8	241.3	246.1
General industrial machinery and equipment	232.6	285.0	332.6
Electric machinery, apparatus and appliances, etc.	281.3	319.7	355.7
Road vehicles	232.6	467.4	331.9
Miscellaneous manufactured articles	371.5	385.2	422.2
Total (incl. others)	8,492.4	8,140.8	8,979.9

Exports f.o.b.	2000	2001	2002
Food and live animals . . .	444.9	528.5	541.1
Crude materials (inedible) except fuels	307.0	301.7	369.5
Mineral fuels, lubricants, etc. .	1,453.2	1,325.5	1,625.4
Petroleum, petroleum products, etc.	1,436.5	1,315.0	1,606.1
Refined petroleum products . .	1,359.0	1,209.6	1,479.8
Chemicals and related products	942.7	1,000.3	960.2
Fertilizers, manufactured . . .	487.0	538.2	540.5
Potassium chloride	410.0	463.4	463.1
Basic manufactures	1,443.1	1,515.5	1,520.8
Textile yarn, fabrics, etc. . . .	405.2	396.6	380.8
Iron and steel	280.3	283.6	320.3
Machinery and transport equipment	1,755.6	1,856.2	1,853.3
Machinery specialized for particular industries	312.4	348.0	350.5
Electrical machinery, apparatus and appliances, etc.	325.8	358.8	389.5
Road vehicles	747.3	755.8	722.5
Lorries and special purposes motor vehicles	382.9	395.4	349.4
Motor vehicles for the transport of goods or materials . . .	350.1	380.8	331.5
Miscellaneous manufactured articles	749.4	823.9	814.1
Clothing and accessories (excl. footwear)	262.2	282.3	259.4
Total (incl. others)	7,331.1	7,484.6	8,097.8

Source: UN, *International Trade Statistics Yearbook.*

PRINCIPAL TRADING PARTNERS
(US $ million)

Imports c.i.f.	2000	2001	2002
Brazil	42.3	60.8	104.5
France	80.2	86.9	94.8
Germany	587.6	594.5	692.7
Italy	162.6	163.1	215.2
Lithuania	69.0	107.3	109.4
Poland	215.8	197.9	219.6
Russia	5,549.7	5,307.5	5,842.5
Sweden	35.1	58.9	99.3
Ukraine	340.6	277.4	290.7
USA	138.7	131.3	103.3
Total (incl. others)	8,492.4	8,140.8	8,979.9

Exports f.o.b.	2000	2001	2002
Brazil	65.9	76.7	89.4
Germany	231.7	241.0	348.0
Italy	76.1	85.4	130.1
Latvia	467.3	492.3	520.1
Lithuania	348.8	275.8	256.7
Netherlands	130.3	125.8	279.0
Poland	276.8	248.0	273.3
Russia	3,715.7	3,996.1	4,053.9
Ukraine	559.7	421.8	271.6
United Kingdom	95.9	222.9	493.7
Total (incl. others)	7,331.1	7,484.6	8,097.8

Source: UN, *International Trade Statistics Yearbook.*

Transport

RAILWAYS
(traffic)

	2001	2002	2003
Passenger-km (million) . . .	15,264	14,349	13,308
Freight ton-km (million) . . .	29,727	34,169	38,402

ROAD TRAFFIC
(motor vehicles in use at 31 December)

	1998	1999	2000
Passenger cars	1,279,208	1,356,611	1,448,491
Buses and coaches	8,768	8,452	8,273
Motorcycles and mopeds . . .	558,251	533,658	523,613

Source: partly IRF, *World Road Statistics*.

CIVIL AVIATION
(traffic on scheduled services)

	2001	2002	2003
Passenger-km (million)	546	553	564
Total ton-km (million)	28	37	34

Tourism

FOREIGN TOURIST ARRIVALS

Country of nationality	1999	2000	2001
Cyprus	1,887	1,101	1,375
Germany	5,354	5,669	4,952
Israel	4,724	3,723	882
Italy	1,812	1,463	1,642
Latvia	9,020	6,364	7,603
Lithuania	3,437	1,949	2,744
Poland	19,122	13,464	11,755
Russia	17,657	11,257	9,929
Ukraine	1,624	449	540
United Kingdom	3,983	6,197	8,915
USA	2,223	2,881	4,768
Total (incl. others)	75,440	59,676	61,033

Tourism receipts (US $ million): 12 in 1999; 93 in 2000; 82 in 2001.

Sources: World Tourism Organization.

Communications Media

	1998	1999	2000
Television receivers ('000 in use) .	3,300	3,400	3,500
Telephones ('000 main lines in use)	2,489.9	2,638.5	2,751.9
Facsimile machines (number in use)	19,472	23,847	26,925
Mobile cellular telephones (subscribers)	12,155	23,457	49,353
Internet users ('000)	7.5	50.0	180.0
Book production (incl. pamphlets):			
titles	6,073	6,064	7,686
copies ('000)	60,022	63,305	61,627
Daily newspapers:			
number	20	12	10
average circulation ('000) . .	1,559	1,094	1,101
Non-daily newspapers:			
number	560	578	600
average circulation ('000) . .	8,973	10,094	10,339
Other periodicals:			
number	318	331	354
average circulation ('000) . .	1,687	1,498	1,381

Radio receivers ('000 in use): 3,020 in 1997 (Source: UNESCO, *Statistical Yearbook*).

2001: Telephones ('000 main lines in use) 2,862.4; Mobile cellular telephones ('000 subscribers) 138.3; Internet users ('000) 430.3.

2002: Telephones ('000 main lines in use) 2,967.2; Mobile cellular telephones ('000 subscribers) 462.6; Internet users ('000) 808.7.

2003: Telephones ('000 main lines in use) 3,071.3; Mobile cellular telephones ('000 subscribers) 1,118.0; Internet users ('000) 1,391.9.

Source: partly International Telecommunication Union.

Education

(2001/02)

	Institutions	Teachers	Students
Pre-primary	4,423	52,524	390,812
Primary (Grades 1–4) . . . }	4,709	138,744	1,473,950
Secondary (Grades 5–11) . . }			
Vocational and technical . .	248	14,772	138,593
Specialized secondary . . .	156	12,748	155,352
Higher	58	21,684	301,753
Institutions offering post-graduate studies	377	9,000	570,000

Source: Ministry of Education, Minsk.

Adult literacy rate (UNESCO estimates): 99.7% (males 99.8%; females 99.6%) in 2002 (Source: UN Development Programme, *Human Development Report*).

Directory

The Constitution

A new Constitution came into effect on 30 March 1994. An amended version of the 1994 Constitution became effective on 27 November 1996, following a referendum held on 24 November. A constitutional referendum, held on 17 October 2004, removed the former two-term limit for presidential tenure. The following is a summary of its main provisions:

PRINCIPLES OF THE CONSTITUTIONAL SYSTEM

The Republic of Belarus is a unitary, democratic, social state based on the rule of law. The people are the sole source of state power and the repository of sovereignty in the Republic of Belarus. The people shall exercise their power directly through representative and other bodies in the forms and within the bounds specified by the Constitution. Democracy in the Republic of Belarus is exercised on the basis of diversity of political institutions, ideologies and opinions. State power in the Republic of Belarus is exercised on the principle of division of powers between the legislature, executive and judiciary, which are independent of one another. The Republic of Belarus is bound by the principle of supremacy of law; it recognizes the supremacy of the universally acknowledged principles of international law and ensures that its laws comply with such principles. Property may be the ownership of the State or private. The mineral wealth, waters and forests are the sole and exclusive property of the State. Land for agricultural use is the property of the State. All religions and creeds are equal before the law. The official languages of the Republic of Belarus are Belarusian and Russian. The Republic of Belarus aims to make its territory a neutral, nuclear-free state. The capital is Minsk (Miensk).

THE INDIVIDUAL, SOCIETY AND THE STATE

All persons are equal before the law and entitled without discrimination to equal protection of their rights and legitimate interests. Every person has the right to life. Until its abolition, the death penalty may be applied in accordance with the verdict of a court of law as an exceptional penalty for especially grave crimes. The State ensures the freedom, inviolability and dignity of the individual. No person may be subjected to torture or cruel, inhuman or humiliating treatment or punishment. Freedom of movement is guaranteed. Every person is guaranteed freedom of opinion and beliefs and their free expression. The right to assemble publicly is guaranteed, as is the right to form public associations, including trade unions. Citizens of the Republic of Belarus have the right to participate in the solution of state matters, both directly and through freely elected representatives; the right to vote freely and to be elected to state bodies on the basis of universal, equal, direct or indirect suffrage by secret ballot. The State shall create the conditions necessary for full employment. The right to health care is guaranteed, as is the right to social security in old age, in the event of illness, disability and in other instances. Each person has the right to housing and to education. Everyone has the right to preserve his or her ethnic affiliation, to use his or her native language and to choose the language of communication. Payment of statutory taxes and other levies is obligatory. Every person is guaranteed the protection of his or her rights and freedom by a competent, independent and impartial court of law, and every person has the right to legal assistance.

THE ELECTORAL SYSTEM AND REFERENDUMS

Elections and referendums are conducted by means of universal, free, equal and secret ballot. Citizens of the Republic of Belarus who have reached the age of 18 years are eligible to vote. Deputies are elected by direct ballot. Referendums may be held to resolve the most important issues of the State and society. National referendums may be called by the President of the Republic of Belarus, by the Natsionalnoye Sobraniye (National Assembly) or by no fewer than 450,000 citizens eligible to vote. Local referendums may be called by local representative bodies or on the recommendation of no less than 10% of the citizens who are eligible to vote and resident in the area concerned. Decisions adopted by referendum may be reversed or amended only by means of another referendum.

THE PRESIDENT

The President of the Republic of Belarus is Head of State, the guarantor of the Constitution of the Republic of Belarus, and of the rights and freedoms of its citizens. The President is elected for a term of five years by universal, free, equal, direct and secret ballot.

The President calls national referendums; calls elections to the Natsionalnoye Sobraniye and local representative bodies; dissolves the chambers of the Natsionalnoye Sobraniye, as determined by the Constitution; appoints six members to the Central Electoral Commission; forms, dissolves and reorganizes the Administration of the President, as well as other bodies of state administration; appoints the Chairman of the Cabinet of Ministers (Prime Minister) of the Republic of Belarus with the consent of the Palata Predstavitaley (House of Representatives); determines the structure of the Government, appoints and dismisses Ministers and other members of the Government, and considers the resignation of the Government; appoints, with the consent of the Soviet Respubliki (Council of the Republic), the Chairman of the Constitutional, Supreme and Economic Courts, the judges of the Supreme and Economic Courts, the Chairman of the Central Electoral Commission, the Prosecutor-General, the Chairman and members of the board of the National Bank, and dismisses the aforementioned, having notified the Soviet Respubliki; appoints six members of the Constitutional Court, and other judges of the Republic of Belarus; appoints and dismisses the Chairman of the State Supervisory Committee; reports to the people of the Republic of Belarus on the state of the nation and on domestic and foreign policy; may chair meetings of the Government of the Republic of Belarus; conducts negotiations and signs international treaties, appoints and recalls diplomatic representatives of the Republic of Belarus; in the event of a natural disaster, a catastrophe or unrest involving violence or the threat of violence that may endanger people's lives or jeopardize the territorial integrity of the State, declares a state of emergency; has the right to abolish acts of the Government and to suspend decisions of local councils of deputies; forms and heads the Security Council of the Republic of Belarus, and appoints and dismisses the Supreme State Secretary of the Security Council; is the Commander-in-Chief of the Armed Forces and appoints and dismisses the Supreme Command of the Armed Forces; imposes, in the event of military threat or attack, martial law in the Republic of Belarus; issues decrees and orders which are mandatory in the Republic of Belarus. In instances determined by the Constitution, the President may issue decrees which have the force of law. The President may be removed from office for acts of state treason and other grave crimes, by a decision of the Natsionalnoye Sobraniye.

THE NATSIONALNOYE SOBRANIYE

The Natsionalnoye Sobraniye (National Assembly) is a representative and legislative body of the Republic of Belarus, consisting of two chambers: the Palata Predstavitaley (House of Representatives) and the Soviet Respubliki (Council of the Republic). The term of the Natsionalnoye Sobraniye is four years. The Palata Predstavitaley comprises 110 deputies. Deputies are elected by universal, equal, free, direct suffrage and by secret ballot. The Soviet Respubliki is a chamber of territorial representation with 64 members, consisting of eight deputies from every region and from Minsk, elected by depu-

ties of local councils. Eight members of the chamber are appointed by the President. Any citizen who has reached the age of 21 years may become a deputy of the Palata Predstavitaley. Any citizen who has reached the age of 30 years, and who has been resident in the corresponding region for no less than five years, may become a member of the Soviet Respubliki. The chambers of the Natsionalnoye Sobraniye elect their Chairmen.

The Palata Predstavitaley considers draft laws concerning amendments and alterations to the Constitution; domestic and foreign policy; the military doctrine; ratification and denunciation of international treaties; the approval of the republican budget; the introduction of national taxes and levies; local self-government; the administration of justice; the declaration of war and the conclusion of peace; martial law and a state of emergency; and the interpretation of laws. The Palata Predstavitaley calls elections for the presidency; grants consent to the President concerning the appointment of the Chairman of the Cabinet of Ministers; accepts the resignation of the President; together with the Soviet Respubliki, takes the decision to remove the President from office.

The Soviet Respubliki approves or rejects draft laws adopted by the Palata Predstavitaley; consents to appointments made by the President; elects six judges of the Constitutional Court and six members of the Central Electoral Commission; considers charges of treason against the President; takes the decision to remove the President from office; considers presidential decrees on the introduction of a state of emergency, martial law, and general or partial mobilization.

Any proposed legislation is considered initially in the Palata Predstavitaley and then in the Soviet Respubliki. On the proposal of the President, the Palata Predstavitaley and the Soviet Respubliki may adopt a law, delegating to him legislative powers to issue decrees which have the power of a law. However, he may not issue decrees making alterations or addenda to the Constitution or to policy laws.

THE GOVERNMENT

Executive power in the Republic of Belarus is exercised by the Cabinet of Ministers. The Government is accountable to the President and responsible to the Natsionalnoye Sobraniye. The Chairman of the Cabinet of Ministers is appointed by the President with the consent of the Palata Predstavitaley. The Government of the Republic of Belarus formulates and implements domestic and foreign policy; submits the draft national budget to the President; and issues acts that have binding force.

THE JUDICIARY

Judicial authority in the Republic of Belarus is exercised by the courts. Justice is administered on the basis of adversarial proceedings and equality of the parties involved in the trial. Supervision of the constitutionality of enforceable enactments of the State is exercised by the Constitutional Court, which comprises 12 judges (six of whom are appointed by the President and six are elected by the Soviet Respubliki).

LOCAL GOVERNMENT

Citizens exercise local and self-government through local councils of deputies, executive and administrative bodies and other forms of direct participation in state and public affairs. Local councils of deputies are elected by citizens for a four-year term, and the heads of local executive and administrative bodies are appointed and dismissed by the President of the Republic of Belarus.

THE OFFICE OF THE PROSECUTOR-GENERAL AND THE STATE SUPERVISORY COMMITTEE

The Office of the Prosecutor-General exercises supervision over the implementation of the law. The Prosecutor-General is appointed by the President with the consent of the Soviet Respubliki, and is accountable to the President. The Supervisory Authority monitors the implementation of the national budget and the use of public property. The State Supervisory Committee is formed by the President, who appoints the Chairman.

APPLICATION OF THE CONSTITUTION AND THE PROCEDURE FOR AMENDING THE CONSTITUTION

The Constitution has supreme legal force. Amendments and supplements to the Constitution are considered by the chambers of the Natsionalnoye Sobraniye on the initiative of the President, or of no fewer than 150,000 citizens of the Republic of Belarus who are eligible to vote. The Constitution may be amended or supplemented via a referendum.

The Government

HEAD OF STATE

President: ALYAKSANDR R. LUKASHENKA (elected 10 July 1994; inaugurated 20 July; re-elected 9 September 2001; inaugurated 20 September).

COUNCIL OF MINISTERS
(April 2005)

Chairman (Prime Minister): SYARHEY S. SIDORSKY.

First Deputy Prime Minister: ULADZIMIR I. SEMASHKO.

Deputy Prime Ministers: IVAN M. BAMBIZA, VASIL B. DALHALYOW, ULADZIMIR N. DRAZHYN, ANDREY V. KOBYAKOW, VASIL I. HAPEYEW.

Deputy Prime Minister and Plentipotentary Representative of the President: VASIL B. DALHALYOU.

Minister of Agriculture and Food: LEANID V. RUSAK.

Minister of Architecture and Construction: GENADZ F. KURACHKIN.

Minister of Communication: ULADZIMIR I. GANCHARENKO.

Minister of Culture: LEANID P. HULYAKA.

Minister of Defence: Col-Gen. LEANID S. MALTSAW.

Minister of the Economy: MIKALAY P. ZAYCHENKA.

Minister of Education: ALYAKSANDR M. RADZKOW.

Minister for Emergency Situations: ENVER BARIYEV.

Minister of Energy: ALEKSANDR A. AHEYEU.

Minister of Finance: NIKOLAY P. KORBUT.

Minister of Foreign Affairs: SYARHEY N. MARTYNOW.

Minister of Forestry: PYOTR SYAMASHKA.

Minister of Health: LYDMILA A. PASTAYALKA.

Minister of Housing and Municipal Services: ULADZIMIR M. BELAKHVOSTOW.

Minister of Industry: ANATOLY M. RUSETSKY.

Minister of Information: ULADZIMIR U. RUSAKEVICH.

Minister of Internal Affairs: ULADZIMIR U. NAUMAU.

Minister of Justice: VIKTAR G. GOLOVANOU.

Minister of Labour and Social Protection: ANTONINA P. MOROVA.

Minister for Natural Resources and Environmental Protection: LYAVONTSY I. KHAROUZHYK.

Minister of Sports and Tourism: YURIY L. SIVAKOW.

Minister of Statistics and Analysis: ULADZIMIR I. ZINOVSKY.

Minister of Taxes and Revenue: HANNA K. DZEYKA.

Minister of Trade: (vacant).

Minister of Transport and Communications: MIKALAY I. BOROVOY.

Note: The following positions are also members of the Council of Ministers: Head of the Presidential Administration; President of the National Academy of Sciences; Chairman of the Management of the National Bank; and Chairmen of the following organizations: the Committee of State Control; the State Military-Industrial Committee; the Committee of State Security; the State Committee of Aviation; the Belarusian Republic Union of Consumer Societies; the State Committee of Border Troops; the State Committee of Science and Technology; and the State Customs Committee.

MINISTRIES

Office of the President: 220016 Minsk, vul. K. Marksa 38, Dom Urada; tel. (17) 222-60-06; internet www.president.gov.by.

Office of the Prime Minister and Deputy Prime Ministers: 220010 Minsk, vul. Savetskaya 11; tel. (17) 222-61-05; fax (17) 222-66-65.

Office of the Cabinet of Ministers: 220010 Minsk, pl. Nezalezhnasti, Dom Pravitelstva; tel. (17) 222-69-05; fax (17) 222-66-65; e-mail sm@mail.belpak.by; internet www.government.by.

Ministry of Agriculture and Food: 220050 Minsk, vul. Kirava 15; tel. (17) 227-37-51; fax (17) 227-42-96; e-mail kanc@mshp.minsk.by; internet mshp.minsk.by.

Ministry of Architecture and Construction: 220048 Minsk, vul. Myasnikova 39; tel. (17) 227-26-42; fax (17) 220-74-24; internet www2.main.gov.by.

Ministry of Communication: 220050 Minsk, pr. F. Skaryny 10; tel. (17) 227-38-61; fax (17) 226-08-48; e-mail mpt@belpak.by; internet www.mpt.gov.by.

Ministry of Culture: 220004 Minsk, pr. Masherava 11; tel. (17) 223-75-74; fax (17) 223-90-45.

Ministry of Defence: 220034 Minsk, vul. Kamunistychnaya 1; tel. (17) 239-23-79; fax (17) 289-19-74; internet www.mod.mil.by.

Ministry of the Economy: 220050 Minsk, vul. Bersona 14; tel. (17) 222-60-48; fax (17) 220-37-77; e-mail gen@plan.minsk.by; internet 194.158.197.134/ministry/economy.nsf.

Ministry of Education: 220010 Minsk, vul. Savetskaya 9; tel. (17) 227-47-36; fax (17) 220-84-83; e-mail root@minedu.unibel.by; internet www.minedu.unibel.by.

Ministry for Emergency Situations: 220050 Minsk, vul. Revolutsionnaya 5; tel. (17) 206-54-25; fax (17) 206-51-91; e-mail mcs@infonet.by; internet www.rescue01.gov.by.

Ministry of Energy: 220050 Minsk, vul. K. Marksa 14; tel. (17) 229-83-59; fax (17) 229-84-68.

Ministry of Finance: 220048 Minsk, vul. Savetskaya 7; tel. (17) 222-41-91; fax (17) 222-45-93; e-mail web_mf@open.by; internet ncpi.gov.by/minfin.

Ministry of Foreign Affairs: 220030 Minsk, vul. Lenina 19; tel. (17) 227-29-22; fax (17) 227-45-21; e-mail mail@mfabelar.gov.by; internet www.mfa.gov.by.

Ministry of Forestry: 220039 Minsk, vul. Chkalova 6; tel. (17) 224-47-05; fax (17) 224-41-83; e-mail info@komleshoz.org; internet www.komleshoz.org.

Ministry of Health: 220095 Minsk, vul. Myasnikova 39; tel. (17) 222-60-33; fax (17) 222-62-97.

Ministry of Housing and Municipal Services: 220050 Minsk, vul. Stankevicha 16; tel. (17) 220-31-85; fax (17) 220-87-08; internet 194.158.197.134/New_web/cis.nsf.

Ministry of Industry: 220033 Minsk, pr. Partizansky 2; tel. (17) 224-95-95; fax (17) 224-87-84; e-mail minproml@ntc3.niievm.minsk.by; internet 194.158.197.134/New_web/minprom.nsf.

Ministry of Information: 220048 Minsk, pr. Masherava 11; tel. (17) 223-92-31; fax (17) 223-34-35.

Ministry of Internal Affairs: 220050 Minsk, vul. Gorodskoy Val 4; tel. (17) 229-78-08; fax (17) 226-12-47; internet mvd-belarus.nsys.by.

Ministry of Justice: 220004 Minsk, vul. Kalektarnaya 10; tel. (17) 206-37-30; fax (17) 206-37-28; e-mail kanc@minjust.belpak.minsk.by; internet ncpi.gov.by/minjust.

Ministry of Labour and Social Protection: 220004 Minsk, pr. Masherava 23, kor. 2; tel. (17) 206-37-97; fax (17) 206-38-84; e-mail mintrud@mail.belpak.by; internet www.ssf.gov.by.

Ministry for Natural Resources and Environmental Protection: 220048 Minsk, vul. Kalektarnaya 10; tel. (17) 220-66-91; fax (17) 220-55-83; e-mail minproos@mail.belpak.by.

Ministry of Sports and Tourism: 220050 Minsk, vul. Kirava 8, kor. 2; tel. (17) 227-72-37; fax (17) 227-30-31; e-mail intersport@mst.by; internet www.mst.by.

Ministry of Statistics and Analysis: 220070 Minsk, Partizansky pr. 12; tel. (17) 249-42-78; fax (17) 249-22-04; e-mail minstat@mail.belpak.by; internet www.belstat.gov.by.

Ministry of Taxes and Revenue: 220010 Minsk, vul. Savetskaya 9; tel. (17) 222-49-92; fax (17) 222-64-50; e-mail gnk@mail.belpak.by; internet www.nalog.by.

Ministry of Trade: 220050 Minsk, vul. Kirava 8, kor. 1; tel. (17) 227-08-97; fax (17) 227-24-80.

Ministry of Transport and Communications: 220029 Minsk, vul. Chicherina 21; tel. (17) 234-11-52; fax (17) 239-42-26; e-mail mail@mintrans.by; internet www.mintrans.by.

President and Legislature

PRESIDENT

Presidential Election, 9 September 2001

Candidates	Votes	%
Alyaksandr Lukashenka	4,666,680	75.65
Uladzimir Gancharyk	965,261	15.65
Syarhey Gaydukevich	153,199	2.48
Invalid votes	383,947	6.22
Total	**6,169,087**	**100.00**

NATSIONALNOYE SOBRANIYE
(National Assembly)

Soviet Respubliki (Council of the Republic)
220010 Minsk, vul. Sovietskaya 11; tel. (17) 227-25-14; fax (17) 222-31-78; e-mail cr@sovrep.gov.by; internet www.sovrep.gov.by.

Chairman: Genadz V. Navitsky.

The Soviet Respubliki is the upper chamber of the legislature and comprises 64 deputies. Of the total, 56 deputies are elected by regional councils (eight each from the six oblasts and the city of Minsk) and eight deputies are appointed by the President of the Republic.

Palata Predstaviteley (House of Representatives)
220010 Minsk, vul. Sovietskaya 11; tel. (17) 227-25-14; fax (17) 222-31-78; e-mail vasko@belarus.minsk.by; internet house.gov.by.

Chairman: Uladzimir Kanaplyou.

General Election, 17 October 2004

Parties or groups	Number of seats
Independents	96
Communist Party of Belarus	8
Agrarian Party	3
Liberal Democratic Party of Belarus	1
Vacant*	2
Total	**110**

* Repeat elections were scheduled to be held in two constituencies, in which no candidate had received an absolute majority of votes cast, on 31 October 2004.

Political Organizations

Following the Government's imposition of stringent measures for re-registration in January 1999, in September of that year there were only 17 political parties officially registered with the Ministry of Justice (28 had previously been registered). Of these, several were reported to exist in name only, while a number of unregistered parties operated, but were not permitted to participate in elections.

Agrarian Party (AP) (Agrarnaya Partya): 220050 Minsk, vul. Kazintsa 86–2; tel. (17) 220-38-29; fax (17) 249-50-18; f. 1992; Leader Syamyon Sharetsky.

Belarusian Christian-Democratic Union (Belaruskaya Khrystsiyanska-Demakratychnaya Zluchnasts): 220065 Minsk, vul. Avakyana 38–59; tel. and fax (17) 229-67-56; e-mail p.p.silko@tut.by; f. 1991; nationalist, reformist; Leader Petr Silko.

Belarusian Green Party (Belaruskaya Partya Zyaleny): 246023 Gomel, vul. Brestskaya 6; tel. (23) 247-08-08; fax (23) 247-96-96; e-mail bpz@tut.by; f. 1994 as Belarusian Greenpeace Party, present name adopted 1999; Leaders Oleg Gromyko, Nick Lekunovich, Valentin Gromyko.

Belarusian National Front—'Revival' (Belaruski Narodny Front—'Adradzhenniye'): 220005 Minsk, vul. Varvašeni 8; tel. and fax (17) 284-50-12; e-mail pbnf@pbnf.org; internet www.pbnf.org; f. 1988; fmrly the Belarusian Popular Front, name changed as above Dec. 1999; anti-communist movement campaigning for democracy, genuine independence for Belarus and national and cultural revival; Chair. Vintsuk Vyachorka.

Belarusian National Party (Belaruskaya Natsiyanalnaya Partya): 220094 Minsk, vul. Plekhanava 32–198; tel. (17) 227-43-76; f. 1994; Leader Anatol Astapenka.

Belarusian Party of Labour (Belaruskaya Partya Pratsy): 220126 Minsk, pr. Masherava 21; tel. (17) 223-82-04; fax (17) 223-97-92; e-mail acmbel2@mail.belpak.by; f. 1993; liquidated by order of Supreme Court Aug. 2004; Leader Leanid Lemyashonak.

Belarusian Party of Women 'Hope' (Belaruskaya Partya Zhanchyn 'Nadzeya'): Minsk; tel. (17) 223-89-57; fax (17) 223-90-40; e-mail zmn@sfpb.belpak.minsk.by; f. 1994; Leader Valyantsina Matusevich.

Belarusian Patriotic Party (Belaruskaya Patryatychnaya Partya): Minsk; tel. (17) 220-27-57; f. 1994; Leader Anatol Barankevich.

Belarusian People's Patriotic Union (BNPS): Minsk; f. 1998; a pro-Lukashenka alliance supportive of further integration with Russia, comprising 30 left-wing and centrist organizations, incl. the CPB, the Belarusian Patriotic Party, the Liberal Democratic Party of Belarus, the White Rus Slavonic Council and the Union of Reserve Officers; Exec. Sec. Viktar Chykin.

Belarusian Popular Party (Belaruskaya Narodnaya Partya): 220050 Minsk, vul. K. Marksa 18; tel. (17) 227-89-52; fax (17) 227-13-30; e-mail imi@imibel.belpak.minsk.by; f. 1994; Leader Viktar Tereschenko.

Belarusian Republican Party (Belaruskaya Respublikanskaya Partya): 220100 Minsk, vul. Kulman 13–71; tel. (17) 234-07-49; f. 1994; Leaders Valery Artysheusky, Uladzimir Ramanau.

Belarusian Social-Democratic Hramada (Assembly) (Belaruskaya Satsyal-demakratychnaya Hramada): 220035 Minsk, vul. Drozda 8–52; tel. and fax (17) 226-74-37; e-mail bsdggramada@tut.by; f. 1998; Leader Anatol Lyawkovich.

Belarusian Social Democratic Party (National Hramada—Assembly) (Belaruskaya Satsyal-demakratychnaya Partya—Narodnaya Hramada): 220114 Minsk, pr. F. Skaryny 153/2/107; tel. and fax (17) 263-37-48; e-mail bsdp@tut.by; f. 1991; merged with Party of People's Accord 1996; centrist; pro-European; Chair. Mikalai Statkevich; c. 2,500 mems.

Belarusian Socialist Party (Belaruskaya Satsyalistychnaya Partya): Minsk; tel. (17) 229-37-38; f. 1994; aims for a civilized society, where rights and freedoms are guaranteed for all; Leader Mikhail Padgainy.

Communist Party of Belarus (CPB) (Kamunistychnaya Partya Belarusi): 220007 Minsk, vul. Varanyanskaga 52; tel. (17) 226-64-22; fax (17) 232-31-23; Leader Tatsyana Holubeva.

Conservative Christian Party of the Belarusian National Front (CCP/BPF): Minsk; tel. (17) 285-34-70; e-mail bpfs@narod.ru; internet www.bpfs.boom.ru; f. 1999 as a breakaway faction of the BNF; Chair. Zyanon Paznyak.

Liberal Democratic Party of Belarus (Liberalna-Demakratychnaya Partya Belarusi): 220005 Minsk, vul. Platonava 22, 12th Floor; tel. and fax (17) 231-63-31; e-mail ldpb@infonet.by; internet www.ldpb.net; f. 1994; advocates continued independence of Belarus, increased co-operation with other European countries and eventual membership of the European Union, and expansion of the private sector; Leader Syarhey Gaydukevich; approx. 50,000 mems (2004).

National Democratic Party of Belarus (Natsyanalna-Demakratychnaya Partya Belarusi): Minsk, vul. Labanka 97–140; tel. (17) 271-95-16; fax (17) 236-99-72; f. 1990; Leader Viktar Navumenka.

Party of Communists of Belarus (Partya Kamunistau Belaruskaya): 220005 Minsk, POB 194; tel. (17) 284-16-08; fax (17) 231-80-36; e-mail ck_pkb@anitex.by; f. 1991; First Sec. Syarhey Kalyakin.

Party of Freedom and Progress (PSP): Minsk; f. 2003; refused registration in March 2004; liberal; joined the Free Belarus coalition in Nov. 2004; Chair. Uladzimir Navasyad.

Republican Party of Labour and Justice (Respublikanskaya Partya Pratsy i Spravyadlivasti): 220004 Minsk, vul. Amuratarskaya 7; tel. (17) 223-93-21; fax (17) 223-86-41; f. 1993; Leader Anatol Nyatylkin.

Social-Democratic Party of Popular Accord (Satsial-Demakratychnaya Partya Narodnay Zgody): 220050 Minsk, vul. K. Marksa 10; tel. (29) 686-35-65; fax (23) 253-12-60; f. 1992; Leader Syarhey Ermak.

United Civic Party of Belarus (UCP) (Abyadnanaya Hramadzyanskaya Partya Belarusi): 220050 Minsk, vul. Kamsamolskaya 11, Office 216; tel. (17) 227-75-49; fax (17) 211-02-79; e-mail ucpb@ucpb.org; internet www.ucpb.org; f. 1990; liberal-conservative; Chair. Anatol U. Liabedzka.

Diplomatic Representation

EMBASSIES IN BELARUS

Armenia: 220050 Minsk, vul. Kirava 17; tel. (17) 227-51-53; fax (17) 227-23-39; e-mail armrep@cis.minsk.by; Ambassador Suren Haroutunian.

Bulgaria: 220000 Minsk, pl. Svoboda 11; tel. (17) 206-65-58; fax (17) 206-65-59; e-mail embassy@bulgaria.by; Chargé d'affaires a.i. Boyko Kosev Boev.

China, People's Republic: 220071 Minsk, vul. Berestyanskaya 22; tel. (17) 284-97-28; fax (17) 285-38-61; e-mail chinaemb_by@mfa.gov.cn; Ambassador Yu Zhenqi.

Cuba: 220005 Minsk, vul. Krasnozvezdnaia 13; tel. (17) 200-03-83; fax (17) 2200-23-45; e-mail embacuba@belsonet.net; Ambassador Félix León Carballo.

Czech Republic: 220030 Minsk, Muzykalny per. 1/2; tel. (17) 226-52-43; fax (17) 211-01-37; e-mail minsk@embassy.mzv.cz; internet www.mzv.cz/minsk; Chargé d'affaires Vladimír Ruml.

France: 220030 Minsk, pl. Svabody 11; tel. (17) 210-28-68; fax (17) 210-25-48; internet www.ambafrance-by.org; Ambassador Stéphane Chmelewsky.

Germany: 220034 Minsk, vul. Zakharava 26; tel. (17) 217-59-00; fax (17) 236-85-52; e-mail germanembassy@mail.belpak.by; internet www.germanembassy.org.by; Ambassador Dr Martin Hecker.

Greece: 220030 Minsk, vul. Engelsa 13, Hotel Oktyabrskaya 515; tel. (17) 227-27-60; fax (17) 226-08-05; Ambassador Panayotis Goumas.

Holy See: 220050 Minsk, vul. Valadarskaga 6, 3rd Floor; tel. (17) 289-15-84; fax (17) 289-15-17; e-mail nuntius@catholic.by; internet nunciature.catholic.by; Apostolic Nuncio Martin Vidović (Titular Archbishop of Nin).

India: 220090 Minsk, vul. Kaltsova 4, kor. 5; tel. (17) 262-93-99; fax (17) 262-97-99; e-mail indemb@mail.belpak.by; internet www .indembminsk.org; Ambassador Shri Tara Singh.

Iran: 220049 Minsk, vul. Suvorava 2; tel. (17) 207-66-99; fax (17) 207-61-99; Ambassador Abdulhamid Fekri.

Israel: 220033 Minsk, pr. Partizansky 6a; tel. (17) 230-44-44; fax (17) 210-52-70; Ambassador Zeev Ben Arie.

Italy: 220030 Minsk, vul. K. Marksa 37; tel. (17) 229-29-69; fax (17) 234-30-46; e-mail ambitminsk@belsonet.net; Ambassador Guglielmo Ardizzone.

Japan: 220004 Minsk, pr. Masherova 23, kor. 1, 8th Floor; tel. (17) 223-62-33; fax (17) 210-41-80; Chargé d'affaires a.i. Naotake Yamashita.

Kazakhstan: 220029 Minsk, vul. Kuibysheva 12; tel. (17) 234-99-37; fax (17) 234-96-50; e-mail kazemb@nsys.by; internet www .kazembassy.by; Ambassador Gaziz Aldamzharov.

Kyrgyzstan: 220002 Minsk, vul. Starovilenskaya 57; tel. (17) 234-91-17; fax (17) 234-16-02; e-mail manas@nsys.minsk.by; Ambassador Rysbek O. Kachkeyev.

Latvia: 220013 Minsk, vul. Doroshevicha 6a; tel. (17) 284-93-93; fax (17) 284-74-94; e-mail embassy.belarus@mfa.gov.lv; Ambassador Maira Mora.

Libya: Minsk, vul. Nyajdanavay 41; tel. (17) 268-66-01; fax (17) 234-70-88; Chargé d'affaires a.i. Abdalla al Magravi.

Lithuania: 220088 Minsk, vul. Zakharova 68; tel. (17) 285-24-48; fax (17) 285-33-37; e-mail embassy.lt@belsonet.net; internet amb .by@urm.lt; Ambassador Petras Vaitiekunas (designate).

Moldova: 220030 Minsk, vul. Belaruskaya 2; tel. (17) 289-14-41; fax (17) 289-11-47; e-mail emmdby@anitex.by; Ambassador Ilie Vancea.

Peru: 220082 Minsk, vul. Pritytskogo 34; tel. and fax (17) 216-91-14.

Poland: 220034 Minsk, vul. Rumyantsava 6; tel. (17) 288-21-14; fax (17) 236-49-92; e-mail ambminsk@nsys.by; internet embassypoland .nsys.by; Ambassador Tadeusz Pawlak.

Romania: 220035 Minsk, per. Moskvina 4; tel. (17) 223-80-97; fax (17) 210-40-85; e-mail romania@nsys.by; Chargé d'affaires a.i. Gheorghe Nicolae Pahonea.

Russia: 220002 Minsk, vul. Staravilenskaya 48; tel. (17) 250-36-66; fax (17) 250-36-64; e-mail karp@rusamb.belpak.minsk.by; internet www.belarus.mid.ru; Ambassador Aleksandr V. Blokhin.

Serbia and Montenegro: 220012 Minsk, vul. Razinskaya 66a; tel. (17) 226-34-92; fax (17) 226-34-95; e-mail jugoslav@anitex.by; Ambassador Srecko Djukic.

Tajikistan: 220050 Minsk, vul. Kirava 17; tel. (17) 222-76-13; fax (17) 227-76-13; e-mail tajikemb-belarus@rambler.ru; Ambassador Amirkhon Safarov.

Turkey: 220050 Minsk, vul. Valadarskaga 6, 4th Floor; tel. (17) 227-13-83; fax (17) 227-27-46; e-mail trembassy@forenet.by; Ambassador Birnur Fertekligil.

Turkmenistan: 220050 Minsk, vul. Kirava 17; tel. (17) 222-34-27; fax (17) 222-33-67; Ambassador Ilya Veldzhanov.

Ukraine: 220002 Minsk, vul. Staravilenskaya 51; tel. (17) 283-19-90; fax (17) 283-19-80; e-mail emb_by@mfa.gov.ua; Ambassador Petro Shapoval.

United Kingdom: 220030 Minsk, vul. K. Marksa 37; tel. (17) 210-59-20; fax (17) 229-23-06; e-mail britinfo@nsys.by; Ambassador Brian Bennett.

USA: 220002 Minsk, vul. Staravilenskaya 46; tel. (17) 210-12-83; fax (17) 234-78-53; e-mail webmaster@usembassy.minsk.by; internet www.usembassy.minsk.by; Ambassador George A. Krol.

Judicial System

Supreme Court: 220030 Minsk, vul. Lenina 28; tel. (17) 226-12-06; fax (17) 227-12-25; e-mail scjustrb@pmrb.gov.by; f. 1923; Chair. Valentin Sukalo.

Supreme Economic Court: 220050 Minsk, vul. Valadarskaga 8; tel. (17) 227-16-41; fax (17) 229-20-85; e-mail bxc@court.by; internet court.by/en; Chair. Viktar Kamyankow.

Office of the Prosecutor-General: 220050 Minsk, vul. Internatsionalnaya 22; tel. (17) 226-43-57; fax (17) 226-42-52; Prosecutor-General Pyotr Miklashevich.

Constitutional Court: 220016 Minsk, vul. K. Marksa 32; tel. and fax (17) 227-80-12; e-mail ksrb@user.unibel.by; internet ncpi.gov.by/ ConstSud; f. 1994; 12 mem. judges; Chair. Grygory Vasilevich.

Religion

CHRISTIAN

The major grouping is the Eastern Orthodox Church, but there are also an estimated 1.0m. adherents of the Roman Catholic Church. Of these, some 25% are ethnic Poles and there is a significant number of Catholics of the Eastern Rites.

The Eastern Orthodox Church

In 1990 Belarus was designated an exarchate of the Russian Orthodox Church (Moscow Patriarchate), known as the Belarusian Orthodox Church.

Belarusian Orthodox Church (Moscow Patriarchate): 220004 Minsk, vul. Osvobozhdeniya 10; tel. and fax (17) 223-25-05; e-mail orthobel@gin.by; 1,319 parishes, seven monasteries and 18 convents (2004); Metropolitan of Minsk and Slutsk, Patriarchal Exarch of All Belarus His Eminence Filaret (Vakhromeyev).

The Roman Catholic Church

Although five Roman Catholic dioceses, embracing 455 parishes, had officially existed since the Second World War, none of them had a bishop. In 1989 a major reorganization of the structure of the Roman Catholic Church in Belarus took place. The dioceses of Minsk and Mogilev (Mahiloŭ) were merged, to create an archdiocese, and two new dioceses were formed, in Grodno (Horadnia) and Pinsk. The Eastern-rite ('Uniate') Church was abolished in Belarus in 1839, but was re-established in the early 1990s. At 31 December 2002 the Roman Catholic Church had an estimated 1,037,000m. adherents in Belarus (about 10.0% of the population).

Latin Rite

Archdiocese of Minsk and Mogilev: 220030 Minsk, pl. Svabody 9; tel. (17) 239-17-50; fax (17) 226-17-53; e-mail info@catholic.by; internet catholic.by; Archbishop Cardinal Kazimierz Świątek.

Byzantine Rite

Belarusian Greek Catholic Church: 224014 Brest, vul. Dvornikova 63; tel. and fax (16) 224-74-82; e-mail bgkc_carkva@tut.by; Dean Protopresbyter Viktar Danilau.

Protestant Churches

Union of Evangelical Christian Baptists in the Republic of Belarus: 220093 Minsk, Puteprovodny per. 2, POB 108; tel. (17) 253-92-67; fax (17) 253-82-49; e-mail belUECB@tut.by; internet www.baptist.by; f. 1989; Pres. Nikolay Sinkovets.

ISLAM

There are small communities of Azeri and Tatar adherents of Islam. In 1994 the supreme administration of Muslims in Belarus, which had been abolished in 1939, was reconstituted. In mid-1998 there were some 4,000 Muslims and four mosques.

Muslim Society: 220004 Minsk, vul. Zaslavskaya 11, kor. 1, kv. 113; tel. (17) 226-86-43; f. 1991; Chair. Ali Halembek.

JUDAISM

Before Belarus was occupied by Nazi German forces, in 1941–44, there was a large Jewish community, notably in Minsk. There were some 142,000 Jews at the census of 1989, according to official declaration of nationality (ethnicity), but many have since emigrated.

Jewish Religious Society: 220030 Minsk, pr. F. Skaryny 44a.

The Press

According to official figures, in 2002 there were 740 newspapers, 351 magazines and other periodicals and four information agencies in Belarus; 12 titles were published in a language other than Belarusian or Russian (primarily English, Polish or Ukrainian). Most daily newspapers are government-owned.

PRINCIPAL DAILIES

In Russian, except where otherwise stated. The Russian-based newspapers *Argumenty i Fakty* and *Komosomolskaya Pravda* (in a special edition, *Komsomolskaya Pravda v Belorusii*), also maintain a high rate of circulation in the country.

Belaruskaya Niva (Belarusian Cornfield): 220013 Minsk, vul. B. Hmyalnitskaga 10A; tel. (17) 287-16-20; fax (17) 232-39-62; e-mail info@belniva.by; internet belniva.by; f. 1921; 5 a week; organ of the Cabinet of Ministers; in Belarusian and Russian; Editor E. SEMASHKO; circ. 34,021 (Aug. 2004).

Belorusskaya Delovaya Gazeta (BDG) (Belarusian Business Newspaper): 220039 Minsk, vul. Chekalova, d. 12, et. 4; tel. (17) 216-25-85; e-mail edit@bdg.unibel.by; internet www.bdg.by; f. 1992; 2 a week; business affairs; in Russian; suspended for three months in May 2003; subsequently printed in Smolensk, Russia; independent; Editor-in-Chief SVETLANA KALINKINA; circ. 11,000.

Narodnaya Hazeta (The People's Newspaper): 220013 Minsk, vul. B. Hmyalnitskaga 10A; tel. (17) 268-28-70; fax (17) 268-25-29; e-mail info@ng.press.net.by; f. 1990; 5–6 a week; in Belarusian and Russian; Editor-in-Chief M. SHIMANSKY; circ. 90,000 (2000).

Narodnaya Volya (People's Will): Minsk; f. 1995; daily; independent; 5 a week; in Belarusian and Russian; Editor-in-Chief IOSIF SEREDICH; circ. 55,000.

Respublika (Republic): 220013 Minsk, vul. B. Hmyalnitskaga 10A; tel. (17) 287-16-15; fax (17) 287-16-12; e-mail info@respublika.info; internet www.respublika.info; 5 a week; in Belarusian and Russian; Editor ANATOLI LEMIASHONOK; circ. 101,000 (2005).

Sovetskaya Belorussiya (Soviet Belarus): 220013 Minsk, vul. B. Hmyalnitskaga 10A; tel. and fax (17) 232-14-32; e-mail admin@sb .by; internet sb.by; 5 a week; Editor-in-Chief PAVEL YAKUBOVICH; circ. 400,000 (2004).

Vechernii Minsk (Evening Minsk): 220005 Minsk, pr. F. Skaryny 44; tel. (17) 284-50-44; fax (17) 288-28-35; e-mail vm@nsys.by; internet newsvm.com; f. 1967; Editor S. SVERKUNOU; circ. 40,000 (2004).

Znamya Yunosti (Banner of Youth): 220013 Minsk, vul. B. Hmyalnitskaga 10A; tel. and fax (17) 268-26-84; f. 1938; 5 a week; organ of the Cabinet of Ministers; Editor-in-Chief ELENA PHILIPTCHIK; circ. 9,000 (2000).

Zvyazda (Star): 220013 Minsk, vul. B. Hmyalnitskaga 10A; tel. (17) 268-29-19; fax (17) 268-27-79; f. 1917 as Zvezda; 5 a week; organ of the Cabinet of Ministers; in Belarusian; Editor ULADZIMIR B. NARKEVICH; circ. 90,000 (1998).

PRINCIPAL PERIODICALS

In Belarusian, except where otherwise stated.

Alesya: 220013 Minsk, pr. F. Skaryny 77; tel. and fax (17) 232-20-51; e-mail magalesya@mail.ru; f. 1924; monthly; Editor TAMARA BUNTO; circ. 10,500 (2003).

Belarus: 220005 Minsk, vul. Zakharava 19; tel. (17) 284-80-01; f. 1930; monthly; publ. by the State Publishing House; journal of the Union of Writers of Belarus and the Belarusian Society of Friendship and Cultural Links with Foreign Countries; fiction and political essays; in Belarusian, English and Russian; Editor-in-Chief A. A. SHABALIN.

Belaruskaya Krinitsa: 220065 Minsk, vul. Avakyana 38–59; tel. and fax (17) 229-67-56; e-mail bposdc@tut.by; internet www.bposdc .at.tut.by; f. 1991; monthly; journal of the Belarusian Public Organization of Social Development and Co-operation; Editor-in-Chief Dr PETER SILKO; circ. 5,000.

Chyrvonaya Zmena (The Red Rising Generation): 220013 Minsk, vul. B. Hmyalnitskaga 10A; tel. and fax (17) 232-21-03; e-mail czm@ mail.ru; f. 1921; weekly; Editor A. KARLUKIEVICH; circ. 5,000 (2000).

Gramadzyanin: Minsk; tel. (17) 229-08-34; fax (17) 272-95-05; publ. by the United Civic Party of Belarus.

Holas Radzimy (Voice of the Motherland): 220005 Minsk, pr. F. Skaryny 44; tel. (17) 288-12-80; fax (17) 288-17-82; e-mail golas_radzimy@tut.by; internet www.belarus21.by; f. 1955; weekly; articles of interest to Belarusians in other countries; Editor-in-Chief NATALIA SALUK.

Krynitsa (Spring): Minsk; tel. (17) 236-60-71; e-mail www .krynitsa@open.by; f. 1988; monthly; publ. by the state media

holding, Literatura i Mastatstva; literary and cultural; in Belarusian; Editor ALA KAPANELKA; circ. 2,100 (2001).

Kultura (Culture): 220029 Minsk, vul. Chicherina 1; tel. and fax (17) 289-34-66; e-mail kultura@tut.by; f. 1991; weekly; colour illustrated; incorporates *Mastatstva (Arts)*; Editor-in-Chief LUDMILA KRUSHINSKAYA; circ. 3,500 (2004).

Litaratura i Mastatstva (Literature and Arts): 220005 Minsk, vul. Zakharava 19; tel. (17) 284-84-61; f. 1932; weekly; Editor ALYAKSANDR PISMENKOV; circ. 5,000 (1998).

Maladosts (Youth): 220013 Minsk, vul. B. Hmyalnitskaga 10A; tel. (17) 268-27-54; f. 1953; monthly; publ. by the state media holding, Literatura i Mastatstva; novels, short stories, essays, translations, etc., for young people; Editor-in-Chief G. DALIDOVICH.

Narodnaya Asveta (People's Education): 220023 Minsk, vul. Makaenka 12; tel. (17) 264-62-68; f. 1924; publ. by the Ministry of Education; Editor-in-Chief N. I. KALESNIK.

Nasha Niva (Our Field): 220050 Minsk, a/s 537; tel. (17) 707-73-29; fax (29) 284-73-29; e-mail nn@promedia.by; internet www.nn.by; f. 1991; first founded in 1906; independent; weekly; Editor-in-Chief ANDREY DYNKO; circ. 3,500 a month (2004).

Navinki (News): Minsk; tel. www.navinki.net/portal; private; weekly; satirical; publication suspended for three months in June 2003 and again in Aug. 2004; Editor-in-Chief PAVLYUK KANAVALCHYK; circ. 3,000.

Neman (The River Nieman): 220005 Minsk, pr. F. Skaryny 39; tel. (17) 213-40-72; fax (17) 213-44-61; f. 1945; monthly; publ. by the state media holding, Literatura i Mastatstva; literary; fiction; in Russian; Editor-in-Chief A. ZHOUK.

Polymya (Flame): 220005 Minsk, vul. Zakharava 19; tel. (17) 284-80-12; f. 1922; monthly; publ. by the state media holding, Literatura i Mastatstva; literary; fiction; Editor-in-Chief S. I. ZAKONNIKOU.

Tovarisch (Comrade): 220005 Minsk, pr. F. Skaryny 46A; tel. (17) 202-08-14; fax (17) 231-80-36; e-mail ck_pkb@anitex.by; internet pkb.promedia.minsk.by; f. 1994; weekly newspaper of the Party of Communists of Belarus; Editor-in-Chief SYARGEY. V. VOZNYAK; circ. 6,000 (2001).

Vozhyk (Hedgehog): 220013 Minsk, pr. F. Skaryny 77; tel. and fax (17) 232-12-40; f. 1941; fortnightly; satirical; Editor-in-Chief MIKHAIL POZDNYAKOV; circ. 12,000 (1998).

Vyaselka (Rainbow): 220004 Minsk, vul. Kalektarnaya 10; tel. (17) 220-91-90; fax (17) 220-92-61; f. 1957; bi-annual; popular; for 5–10-year-olds; Editor-in-Chief V. S. LIPSKY.

PRESS ASSOCIATIONS

Belarusian Association of Journalists (Belaruskaya Asatsyyatsyya Zhurnalistau): 220030 Minsk, pl. Svabody 17/304; tel. (17) 226-70-98; fax (17) 223-63-66; e-mail baj@user.unibel.by; internet www .baj.unibel.by; f. 1995; Chair. ZHANNA LITVINA.

Belarusian Union of Journalists: 220005 Minsk, vul. Rumyantsava 3; tel. and fax (17) 236-51-95; 3,000 mems; Chair. L. EKEL.

NEWS AGENCIES

BelaPAN: tel. (17) 232-55-01; fax (17) 232-56-57; e-mail mail@ belapan.com; internet www.belapan.com; in Belarusian, English and Russian; independent, commercial information company.

BelTA (Belarusian News Agency): 220030 Minsk, vul. Kirava 26; tel. (17) 227-19-92; fax (17) 227-13-46; e-mail oper@belta.by; internet www.belta.by; f. 1918; Gen. Dir DMITRIY A. ZHUK.

FOREIGN BUREAU

Interfaks Zapad (Interfax-West) (Russia): 222050 Minsk, vul. Bersana 3; tel. (17) 222-42-75; fax (17) 222-42-76; e-mail infportal@ interfax.minsk.by; internet interfax.minsk.by; regional bureaux in Brest, Vitebsk, Gomel, Grodno and Mogilev.

Publishers

In 2000 there were 7,686 titles published in Belarus (62m. copies).

Belarus: 220600 Minsk, pr. F. Skaryny 79; tel. (17) 223-87-42; fax (17) 223-87-31; f. 1921; social, political, technical, medical and musical literature, fiction, children's, reference books, art reproductions, etc.; Dir MIKHALAY KAVALEVSKY; Editor-in-Chief ELENA ZAKONNIKOVA.

Belaruskaya Entsiklopediya (Belarusian Encyclopedia): 220072 Minsk, vul. Akademicheskaya 15A; tel. and fax (17) 284-17-67; e-mail belen@mail.belpak.by; f. 1967; encyclopedias, dictionaries, directories and scientific books; Editor-in-Chief G. P. PASHKOV.

Belaruskaya Navuka (Belarusian Science): 220141 Minsk, Star-oborisovsky trakt 40; tel. (17) 263-76-18; e-mail belnauka@infonet .by; f. 1924; scientific, technical, reference books, educational literature and fiction in Belarusian and Russian; Dir LUDMILA PIETROVA.

Belarusky Dom Druku (Belarusian Printing House): 220013 Minsk, pr. F. Skaryny 79; tel. (17) 268-27-03; fax (17) 231-67-74; e-mail dom.pechati@bdp.minsk.by; f. 1917; social, political, children's and fiction in Belarusian, Russian and other European languages; Dir ROMAN OLEINIK.

Belblankavyd: 220035 Minsk, vul. Timirazeva 2; tel. (17) 226-71-22; reference books in Belarusian and Russian; Dir VALENTINA MILOVANOVA.

Mastatskaya Litaratura (Literary Fiction): 220600 Minsk, pr. Masherava 11; tel. (17) 223-48-09; f. 1972; fiction in Belarusian and Russian; Dir GEORGE MARCHUK.

Narodnaya Asveta (People's Education): 220600 Minsk, pr. Masherava 11; tel. and fax (17) 223-61-84; e-mail igpna@asveta .belpak.minsk.by; f. 1951; scientific, educational, reference literature and fiction in Belarusian, Russian and other European languages; Dir IGAR N. LAPTSYONAK.

Vysheyshaya Shkola (Higher School): 220048 Minsk, pr. Masherava 11; tel. and fax (17) 223-54-15; e-mail vsh@solo.by; internet www.vsh.h1.ru; f. 1954; textbooks and science books for higher educational institutions; in Belarusian, Russian and other European languages; absorbed the Universitetskaye publishing house in 2002; Dir ANATOL A. ZHADAN; Editor-in-Chief TETYANA K. MAIBORODA.

Yunatstva (Youth): 220600 Minsk, pr. Masherava 11; tel. (17) 223-24-30; fax (17) 223-31-16; f. 1981; fiction and children's books; Dir ALYAKSANDR KOMAROVSKY.

Broadcasting and Communications

TELECOMMUNICATIONS

BelCel: 22005 Minsk, vul. Zolotaya Gorka 5; tel. (17) 276-01-00; fax (17) 276-03-33; e-mail belcel@belcel.by; internet www.belcel.com.by; f. 1993; 50% owned by Cable and Wireless (United Kingdom); mobile telecommunications services; Gen. Dir ARTEM H. ORANDZH; 23,000 subscribers (2003).

Beltelecom: 220030 Minsk, vul. Engelsa 6; tel. (17) 217-10-05; fax (17) 227-44-22; e-mail info@main.beltelecom.by; internet www .beltelecom.by; f. 1995; national telecommunications operator; Dir-Gen. NIKOLAY KRUKOVSKY.

MTS Belarus: 222043 Minsk, pr. F. Skaryny 95; tel. (17) 237-98-98; e-mail info@mts.by; internet www.company.mts.by; f. 2002; mobile cellular communications; 49% owned by Mobile TeleSystems (Russia); Dir-Gen. ANDREI B. RUMYANTSEV; 465,500 subscribers (2004).

Velcom: Minsk; tel. (17) 222-49-01; fax (17) 206-62-52; internet www.velcom.by; f. 1999; mobile cellular telecommunications; 950,000 subscribers (2004).

BROADCASTING

Television and Radio

The Russian channels 'Kultura', ORT—Public Russian Television (later Pervyi Kanal—First Channel) and RTR–TV (later Telekanal—Rossiya) had been widely viewed in Belarus; however, in 2003 their transmitter facilities were reallocated by the Government to regional television channels. By October 2003 NTV—Independent Television was the country's sole remaining Russian television channel.

National State Television and Radio Company of Belarus: 220807 Minsk, vul. A. Makayenka 9; tel. (17) 263-15-37; fax (17) 264-81-82; internet www.tvr.by; f. 1925; Chair. ULADZIMIR MATVYAYCHUK.

Belarusian Television: 220807 Minsk, vul. A. Makayenka 9; tel. (17) 233-45-01; fax (17) 264-81-82; f. 1956; Dir V. V. ISSAT.

Belarusian Radio: 220807 Minsk, vul. Chyrvonaya 4; tel. (17) 239-58-30; fax (17) 284-85-74; e-mail radio-minsk@tvr.by; internet www.tvr.by; Gen. Dir V. A. MARTYNOV.

ONT—Obshchenatsionalnoye Televideniye (Nationwide TV): Minsk; e-mail info@ont.by; internet www.ont.by; f. 2002; 51% state-owned; broadcasts nationwide; Chair. GRIGORIY L. KISEL.

TVS—Televizionnaya Veshchatelnaya Set (TBN—Television Broadcasting Network): 220072 Minsk, pr. F. Skaryny 15A; tel. (17) 284-10-86; fax (17) 284-10-86; e-mail tbn@promedia.by; internet www.data.minsk.by/tbn; f. 1995; comprises 16 private television cos in Belarus's largest cities and an advertising co.

Finance

(cap. = capital; dep. = deposits; res = reserves; m. = million; brs = branches; amounts in readjusted Belarusian roubles, unless otherwise indicated)

BANKING

At January 2003 there were 28 commercial banks registered in Belarus.

Central Bank

National Bank of the Republic of Belarus: 220008 Minsk, pr. F. Skaryny 20; tel. (17) 219-23-03; fax (17) 227-48-79; e-mail email@ nbrb.by; internet www.nbrb.by; f. 1990; cap. 60,000m., res 483,958m. (Jan. 2004), dep. 1,186,635.4m. (Dec. 2003); Chair. PYOTR P. PRAKAPOVICH; 6 brs.

Commercial Banks

Absolutbank: 220023 Minsk, pr. F. Skaryny 95, POB 9; tel. (17) 237-07-02; fax (17) 264-24-43; e-mail root@absolutbank.by; internet www.absolutbank.by; f. 1993; closed jt-stock co; cap. 10,000m. (Oct. 2003); Chair. BORIS G. CHEREDNIK; 2 brs.

Bank Moskva–Minsk (Moscow–Minsk Bank): 220002 Minsk, vul. Kommunisticheskaya 49; tel. (17) 288-63-01; fax (17) 288-63-02; e-mail mmb@mmbank.by; internet www.mmbank.by; f. 2000; wholly owned by Bank of Moscow (Russia); cap. US $1.8m., res $2.8m., dep. $36.6m. (Dec. 2003); Dir Dr ALEXANDER RAKOVETS; 3 brs.

Belagroprombank: 220073 Minsk, vul. Olshevskaga 24; tel. (17) 228-55-13; fax (17) 228-53-19; e-mail bapb@bapb.minsk.by; internet www.belapb.by; f. 1991; 98.93% state-owned; cap. 597,530.1m., res 114,038.9m., dep. 521,028.3m. (Dec. 2003); Chair. ALYAKSANDR A. GAVRUSHEV; 132 brs.

Belarusbank: 220050 Minsk, vul. Myasnikova 32; tel. (17) 220-18-31; fax (17) 226-47-50; e-mail info@belarusbank.minsk.by; internet www.belarusbank.minsk.by; f. 1995 following merger with Sberbank (Savings Bank; f. 1922); joint stock bank; cap. 300,478m., dep. 3,291,264m. (Dec. 2003); Chair. NADEZHDA A. YERMAKOVA; 147 brs.

Belarusian Bank for Industry and Construction (BelProm-StroiBank): 220071 Minsk, Blvd Lunacharskogo 6; tel. (17) 210-13-14; fax (17) 210-03-42; e-mail teletype@bpsb.by; internet www.bpsb .by; f. 1923; provides credit to enterprises undergoing privatization and conversion to civil production; 32% privately owned; cap. 25,180.1m., res 80,173.5m., dep. 617,575.8m. (Dec. 2003); Gen. Dir GALINA P. KUKHORENKO; 53 brs.

Belarusian Industrial Bank (Belarusskii industrialnyi bank): 220004 Minsk, vul. Melnikaite 8; tel. (17) 223-95-78; fax (17) 209-42-06; e-mail bib@bib.by; internet www.bib.by; f. 1991 as Profbank; name changed as above in 1999; jt-stock co; cap. €2,462.9m., res €0.5m., dep. €8,633.6m. (Mar. 2004); Chair. of Bd ANDREY KIREEV.

Belaruski Narodny Bank (Belarusian People's Bank): 220004 Minsk, vul. Tanka 1A; tel. and fax (17) 223-84-57; e-mail bnb@bnb .by; internet www.bnb.by; f. 1992; cap. 593.4m., res 3,610.1m., dep. 7,663.9m. (Dec. 2001); Chair. of Bd ANDREY S. TARATUKHIN; 1 br.

Belgazprombank: 220121 Minsk, vul. Pritytsky 60/2; tel. (17) 259-40-24; fax (17) 259-45-25; e-mail bank@belgazprombank.by; internet www.belgazprombank.by; f. 1990; present name adopted 1997; 33.91% owned by Gazprombank (Russia), 33.91% owned by OAO Gazprom (Russia), 23.50% owned by Beltransgaz, 8.63% owned by the Ministry of the Economy; joint stock bank; cap. 24,662m., res 7,756.6m., dep. 141,437.2m. (Dec. 2003); Chair. of Bd VIKTAR D. BABARIKO; 7 brs.

Belinvestbank—Belarusian Bank of Development and Reconstruction: 220002 Minsk, vul. Varvasheniy 81; tel. and fax (17) 289-35-22; e-mail corr@belinvestbank.by; internet www .belinvestbank.by; f. 2001 by merger; 41.74% owned by National Bank of the Republic of Belarus; cap. 94,618.2m., res 16,914.1m., dep. 595,458.1m. (Dec. 2003); Chair. of Bd ALYAKSANDR E. RUTKOVSKY; 49 brs.

Belvnesheconombank: 220050 Minsk, vul. Myasnikova 32; tel. (17) 238-12-15; fax (17) 226-48-09; e-mail office@bveb.minsk.by; internet www.bveb.by; f. 1991; 29.1% owned by National Space Bank (Russia), 25.3% by National Bank of the Republic of Belarus; cap. 177,438m., res 1,639m., dep. 451,554m. (Dec. 2003); Chair. of Bd GEORGIY YEGOROV; 26 brs.

Djembank: 220012 Minsk, vul. Surganava 28; tel. (17) 219-84-44; fax (17) 219-84-90; e-mail main@djem.com; internet www.djem.com; f. 1991; present name adopted 1995; cap. 28,170.4m., dep. 15,050.8m. (Jul. 2004); Gen. Dir ALEXANDER V. TATARINTSEV.

ITI Bank (International Trade and Investment Bank): 220030 Minsk, vul. Sovetskaya 12; tel. (17) 220-68-80; fax (17) 220-17-00; e-mail office@itibank.by; f. 1999; 40.9% owned by National Bank of the Republic of Belarus, 25.1% owned by Daltotrade Ltd (Cyprus), 15.1% owned by INVB Invest Vermogenserwaltungs-und Beteiti-gungs AG (Austria); cap. 38,692m., dep. 266,103m. (Dec. 2003); Chair. GENNADY ALEINIKOV; 4 brs.

MinskComplexBank: 220050 Minsk, vul. Miasnikova 40; tel. (17) 217-84-42; fax (17) 217-83-55; e-mail welcome@minskcomplexbank .com; internet www.minskcomplexbank.com; f. 1994; cap. US $4.5m., res $4.2m., dep. $27.7m. (Dec. 2001); Chair. of Council YURIY PREDCA.

Minski Tranzitnyi Bank (Minsk Transit Bank): 220033 Minsk, pr. Partizansky 6A; tel. (17) 213-29-00; fax (17) 213-29-09; e-mail cor@ mtb.minsk.by; internet www.mtb.by; f. 1994; 90.29% owned by Nachalo Veka, Minsk; cap. US $13.7m., res $2.3m., dep. $15.2m. (Jan. 2005); Chair. of Bd TAMARA I. ZHEVNYAK; 5 brs.

Paritetbank: 220090 Minsk, vul. Gamarnik 9/4; tel. (17) 228-32-50; fax (17) 228-32-48; e-mail info@paritetbank.by; f. 1974 (as a regional branch of Gosbank of the USSR); renamed Housing and Communal Bank (ZhilSotsBank) in 1989; renamed Bank Poisk in 1992; adopted current name in 2004; 90.58% owned by the National Bank of Belarus; cap. 13,478.8m., res 3,701.2m., dep. 9,948.9m. (Dec. 2003); Chair. of Bd NATALYA ALEKSEYEVNA ALEKSEYEVA; 4 brs.

Priorbank: 220002 Minsk, vul. V. Khoruzhey 31A; tel. (17) 289-90-87; fax (17) 289-91-91; e-mail root@priorbank.by; internet www .priorbank.by; f. 1989, present name since 1992; 61.3% owned by Raffeisen International Beteiligungs AG (Austria), 13.5% owned by the European Bank for Reconstruction and Development (United Kingdom); cap. $ US $33.7m., res $50.0m. (Jan. 2004), dep. $533.9m. (Dec. 2004); Chair. of Bd SERGEY A. KOSTYUCHENKO; 18 brs.

Slavneftebank: 220007 Minsk, vul. Fabritsius 8; tel. (17) 222-07-09; fax (17) 222-07-52; e-mail snb@snbank.by; internet www.snbank .by; f. 1996; 32.63% owned by Belneftechim, Minsk; 26.25% owned by Slavneft-M CJSC, Minsk; cap. US $16.9m., res $1.5m., dep. $66.9m. (Dec. 2004); Chair.of Supervisory Bd IVAN BAMBIZA; Chair. of Bd ULADZIMIR V. IVANOV; 6 brs.

Tekhnobank (Technobank): 220002 Minsk, vul. Krapotkina 44; tel. (17) 283-27-27; fax (17) 283-15-10; e-mail info@tb.by; internet www .tb.by; f. 1994; total assets 32,332m. (Jan. 2005); Chair. of Bd VIKTOR I. KHLOPITSKI; 2 brs.

Trastbank: 220035 Minsk, vul. Ignatenka 11; tel. and fax (17) 250-43-88; e-mail root@infobank.by; f. 1994; jt-stock co; 35% owned by Libyan Arab Foreign Bank (Libya), 33% owned by Technochimtrade; fmrly Infobank, present name adopted Feb. 2005; cap. 12,528.2m., res 14,845.7m., dep. 65,104.2m. (Dec. 2003); Chair. VIKTOR SHEVTSOV; 4 brs.

Zolotoi Taler GT Bank (Golden Taler Bank): 220035 Minsk, vul. Tatarskaya 3; tel. (17) 206-44-26; fax (17) 223-06-40; e-mail office@ gtbank.gtp.by; internet www.gtbank.gtp.by; f. 1994; owned by British and Belarusian interests; cap. 990.1m., res 3,235.9m., dep. 13,586.6m. (Jan. 2004); Chair. of Bd ALYAKSANDR A. ZHILINSKY; 2 brs.

BANKING ASSOCIATION

Association of Belarusian Banks: 220071 Minsk, vul. Smolyach-kova 9; tel. (17) 227-78-90; fax (17) 227-58-41; e-mail root@abbank .minsk.by; Chair. NIKOLAY POZNIAK.

COMMODITY AND STOCK EXCHANGES

Belagroprambirzha—Belorusskaya   Valyutno-Fondovaya Birzha (Belarusian Agro-Industrial Trade and Stock Exchange): 220108 Minsk, vul. Kazintsa 86, kor. 2; tel. (17) 277-07-26; fax (17) 277-01-37; f. 1991; trade in agricultural products, industrial goods, shares; 900 mems; Pres. ANATOL TIBOGANOU; Chair. of Bd ALYAKSANDR P. DECHTYAR.

Belarusian Currency and Stock Exchange: 220013 Minsk, vul. Surganova 48A; tel. (17) 209-41-03; fax (17) 209-41-10; e-mail bcse@ bcse.by; internet www.bcse.by; f. 1998; currency and securities exchange trading organization, depository, clearing and information activities; value of trade US $8,934.5m. (2004); Gen. Dir PAVEL TSEKHANOVICH.

Belarusian Universal Exchange (BUE): 220099 Minsk, vul. Kazintsa 4; tel. (17) 278-11-21; fax (17) 278-85-16; f. 1991; Pres. ULADZIMIR SHEPEL.

IINSURANCE

Belarusian Insurance Co: 220141 Minsk, vul. Zhodinskaya 1–4; tel. (17) 263-38-57; fax (17) 268-80-17; e-mail reklama@belinscosc .belpak.minsk.by; f. 1992; Dir-Gen. LEANID M. STATKEVICH.

Belgosstrakh (Belarusian Republican Unitary Insurance Co): 220036 Minsk, vul. K. Libknekht 70; tel. (17) 259-10-21; fax (17) 213-08-05; e-mail bgs@belsonet.net; internet www.belgosstrakh.by; Dir-Gen. VIKTAR I. SHOUST; 145 brs.

Belingosstrakh: 220050 Minsk, pr. Myasnikova 40; tel. (17) 223-58-78; fax (17) 217-84-19; e-mail bigs1@mail.belpak.by; internet www.belingosstrakh.by; f. 1992; non-life, property, vehicle and cargo insurance; Dir-Gen. ALYAKSANDR KHOMYAKOV.

GARIS: 220600 Minsk, vul. Myasnikova 32; tel. (17) 220-37-01.

Polis: 220087 Minsk, pr. Partizansky 81; tel. (17) 245-02-91; Dir DANUTA I. VORONOVICH.

SNAMI: 220040 Minsk, vul. Nekrasova 40A; tel. and fax (17) 231-63-86; f. 1991; Dir S. N. SHABALA.

Trade and Industry

CHAMBER OF COMMERCE

Belarusian Chamber of Commerce and Industry (Belorus-skaya Torgovo-promyshlennaya Palata): 220035 Minsk, pr. Masherava 14; tel. (17) 226-91-27; fax (17) 226-98-60; e-mail mbox@ cci.by; internet www.cci.by; f. 1952; brs in Brest, Gomel, Grodno, Mogilev and Vitebsk; Pres. ULADZIMIR N. BOBROV.

EMPLOYERS' ORGANIZATION

Belarusian Union of Entrepreneurs and Employers: 220004 Minsk, vul. Kalvaryskaya 1-608; tel. (17) 222-47-96; fax (17) 222-47-94; e-mail buee@nsys.by; f. 1990; Pres. GEORGY BADEY.

UTILITIES

Electricity

Belenergo/Belenerha (Belarusian Energy Co): 220677 Minsk, vul. K. Marksa 14; tel. (17) 229-84-64; fax (17) 227-41-81; e-mail econolinks@odu.energo.net.by; f. 1995; restructuring pending; gen-eration, transmission and distribution of electric power; includes six regional generation companies; Chair. SYARHEY BELY.

Institute of Nuclear Energy: 223061 Minsk, Sosny Settlement; tel. (17) 246-77-12.

Gas

Beltopgaz: 220002 Minsk, vul. V. Khoruzhey 3; tel. (17) 288-23-93; fax (17) 284-37-86; internet www.topgas.by; f. 1992; distributes natural gas to end-users.

Beltransgaz: 220040 Minsk, vul. Nekrasova 9; tel. (17) 266-01-01; fax (17) 266-16-78; legislation enabling privatization approved in Nov. 2002; imports natural gas; acts as holding co for regional transmission and storage enterprises; Dir DZMITRY M. KAZAKOU.

TRADE UNIONS

Automobile and Agricultural Machinery Workers' Union: Minsk; largest industrial trade union in Belarus; Leader ALYAKSANDR I. BUKHVOSTOU; 130,000 mems.

Belarusian Congress of Democratic Trade Unions (BCDTU): 220070 Minsk, pr. Partyzanski 12A, k. 7; tel. (17) 249-31-79; fax (17) 210-15-00; e-mail bcdtu@mail.ru; f. 1993; alliance of four inde-pendent trade unions; Pres. ALYAKSANDR YARASHUK; 15,000 mems.

> **Free Trade Union of Belarus:** 220005 Minsk, vul. Zakharova 24; tel. (17) 284-31-82; fax (17) 284-59-94; e-mail spb@user.unibel .by; internet www.praca.by; f. 1992; Chair. SYARHEY ANTONCHYK; Vice-Chair. NIKOLAY KANAH; 6,000 mems.

> **Independent Trade Union of Belarus:** 223710 Soligorsk, vul. Lenina 42; tel. and fax (17) 102-00-59; e-mail sol_sn@inbox.ru; f. 1991; Chair. VIKTAR BABAYED; Sec. NIKOLAY ZIMIN; 10,000 mems.

Belarusian Peasants' Union (Syalansky Sayuz): 220199 Minsk, vul. Brestskaya 64-327; tel. (17) 277-99-93; Chair. KASTUS YARMO-LENKA.

Federation of Trade Unions of Belarus: 220126 Minsk, pr. Masherova 21; tel. (17) 210-43-37; fax (17) 203-89-93; e-mail contact@fpb.by; internet www.fpb.by; f. 1990; Chair. LEANID P. KOZIK.

> **Belarusian Union of Industrial Workers:** f. 2003 by merger of nine principal state-organized industrial trade unions.

Union of Radio and Electronic Industry Workers: 220013 Minsk, vul. Kulman 4; tel. (17) 232-46-51; fax (17) 284-41-87; e-mail prof@anitex.by; internet rep.praca.by; f. 1990; Leader G. F. FEDY-NICH; 40,000 mems.

Transport

RAILWAYS

In 2000 the total length of railway lines in use was 5,512 km. Minsk is a major railway junction, situated on the east–west line between Moscow and Warsaw, and the north-west—south-east line linking Lithuania and Ukraine. There is an underground railway in Minsk, the Minsk Metro, which has two lines (total length 24.5 km), with 20 stations.

Belarusian State Railways (Belorusskaya Zheleznaya Doroga): 220745 Minsk, vul. Lenina 17; tel. (17) 225-44-00; fax (17) 227-56-48; internet www.rw.by; f. 1992; Pres. VLADIMIR ZHERELO.

ROADS

At 31 December 2001 the total length of roads in Belarus was 75,302 km (comprising 15,377 km of main roads and 59,925 km of secondary roads). Some 89.0% of the total network was hard-surfaced. In September 1999 it was estimated that more than 28,000 km of Belarus' road network was in need of repair.

CIVIL AVIATION

Minsk has two airports, one largely for international flights and one for domestic connections.

State Committee for Aviation: 220065 Minsk, vul. Aerodromnaya 4; tel. (17) 222-53-93; fax (17) 222-77-28; e-mail gka@ivcavia.com; internet www.ivcavia.com; Chair. FEDOR IVANOV.

Belavia Belarusian Airlines: 220004 Minsk, vul. Nemiga 14; tel. (17) 229-24-24; fax (17) 229-23-83; e-mail info@belavia.by; internet www.belavia.by; f. 1993 on basis of regional division of Aeroflot; state carrier in 1996; operates services in Europe and selected destinations in the CIS and the Middle East; Gen. Dir ANATOLY GUSAROV.

Gomelavia: 246011 Gomel, Gomel Airport; tel. (23) 253-53-58; fax (23) 253-02-00; e-mail gomelavia@ivcavia.com; f. 1944; state owned; includes Gomel Airport and Gomelavia Airlines; Dir ANATOLY KIRSANOV.

Tourism

Belintourist: 220004 Minsk, pr. Masherava 19; tel. (17) 226-98-40; fax (17) 203-11-43; e-mail marketing@belintourist.by; internet www.belintourist.by; f. 1992; state tourist org.; Dir-Gen. MARIA I. FILIPOVICH.

BELGIUM

Introductory Survey

Location, Climate, Language, Religion, Flag, Capital

The Kingdom of Belgium lies in north-western Europe, bounded to the north by the Netherlands, to the east by Luxembourg and Germany, to the south by France, and to the west by the North Sea. The climate is temperate. Temperatures in the capital, Brussels, are generally between 0°C (32°F) and 23°C (73°F). Flemish (closely related to Dutch), spoken in the north (Flanders), and French, spoken in the south (Wallonia), are the two main official languages. Brussels (which is situated in Flanders) has bilingual status. Nearly 60% of the population are Flemish-speaking, about 40% are French-speaking and less than 1% have German as their mother tongue. The majority of the inhabitants profess Christianity, and about four-fifths are Roman Catholics. The national flag (proportions 13 by 15) consists of three equal vertical stripes, of black, yellow and red.

Recent History

Since the Second World War, Belgium has promoted international co-operation in Europe. It is a founder member of many important international organizations, including the North Atlantic Treaty Organization (NATO, see p. 301), the Council of Europe (see p. 199), the European Union (EU, see p. 217) and the Benelux Economic Union (see p. 373).

In the latter half of the 20th century linguistic divisions were exacerbated by the political and economic polarization of Flemish-speaking Flanders in the north and francophone Wallonia in the south. The faster-growing and relatively prosperous population of Flanders has traditionally supported the conservative Flemish Christelijke Volkspartij (CVP—Christian People's Party) and the nationalist Volksunie—Vlaamse Vrije Democraten (VU—People's Union—Flemish Free Democrats), while Wallonia has traditionally been a stronghold of socialist political sympathies. Most major parties have both French and Flemish sections, as a result of a trend away from centralized administration towards greater regional control. Moderate constitutional reforms, introduced in 1971, were the first steps towards regional autonomy; in the following year further concessions were made, with the German-speaking community being represented in the Cabinet for the first time, and in 1973 linguistic parity was assured in central government. Provisional legislation, adopted in 1974, established separate Regional Councils and Ministerial Committees. The administrative status of Brussels remained contentious: the majority of the city's inhabitants are francophone, but the Flemish parties were, until the late 1980s, unwilling to grant the capital equal status with the other two regional bodies (see below).

In June 1977 the Prime Minister, Leo Tindemans, formed a coalition composed of the CVP and the francophone Parti Social Chrétien (PSC—Christian Social Party), which were collectively known as the Christian Democrats, the Socialists, the Front Démocratique des Francophones (FDF—French-speaking Democratic Front) and the VU. The Cabinet, in what became known as the Egmont Pact, proposed the abolition of the virtually defunct nine-province administration, and devolution of power from the central Government to create a federal Belgium, comprising three political and economic regions (Flanders, Wallonia and Brussels), and two linguistic communities. However, these proposals were not implemented. Tindemans resigned in October 1978 and the Minister of Defence, Paul Vanden Boeynants, was appointed Prime Minister in a transitional Government. Legislative elections in December caused little change to the distribution of seats in the Chamber of Representatives. Four successive Prime Minister-designates failed to form a new government, the main obstacle being the future status of Brussels. The six-month crisis was finally resolved when a new coalition Government was formed in April 1979 under Dr Wilfried Martens, the President of the CVP.

During 1980 the linguistic conflict worsened, sometimes involving violent incidents. Legislation was formulated, under the terms of which Flanders and Wallonia were to be administered by regional assemblies, with control of cultural matters, public health, roads, urban projects and 10% of the national budget, while Brussels was to retain its three-member executive.

Belgium suffered severe economic difficulties during the late 1970s and early 1980s, and internal disagreement over Martens' proposals for their resolution resulted in the formation of four successive coalition Governments between April 1979 and October 1980. Proposed austerity measures, including a 'freeze' on wages and reductions in public expenditure at a time of high unemployment, provoked demonstrations and lost Martens the support of the Socialist parties. Martens also encountered widespread criticism over plans to install NATO nuclear missiles in Belgium. In April 1981 a new Government was formed, comprising a coalition of the Christian Democrats and the Socialist parties and led by Mark Eyskens (of the CVP), hitherto Minister of Finance. However, lack of parliamentary support for his policies led to Eyskens' resignation in September. In December Martens formed a new centre-right Government, comprising the Christian Democrats and the two Liberal parties. In 1982 Parliament granted special powers for the implementation of economic austerity measures; these were effective until 1984, and similar powers were approved in March 1986. Opposition to reductions in public spending was vigorous, with public-sector trade unions undertaking damaging strike action throughout the 1980s.

In May 1985 a riot at a football match between English and Italian clubs at the Heysel Stadium in Brussels, which resulted in 39 deaths, precipitated demands for the resignation of the Minister of the Interior, Charles-Ferdinand Nothomb, over accusations of inefficient policing. In July the resignation, in connection with the issue, of six Liberal cabinet members (including the Deputy Prime Minister, Jean Gol) led to the collapse of the coalition. Martens offered the resignation of his Government, but this was 'suspended' by King Baudouin pending a general election, which was called for October. Meanwhile, however, controversy regarding educational reform provoked a dispute between the two main linguistic groups and caused the final dissolution of Parliament in September. The general election returned the Christian Democrats-Liberal alliance to power, and in November Martens formed his sixth Cabinet.

The Government collapsed in October 1987, as a result of continuing division between the French- and Flemish-speaking parties of the coalition. At the ensuing general election in December, the CVP sustained significant losses in Flanders, while the French-speaking Parti Socialiste (PS—Socialist Party) gained seats in Wallonia, and the Socialists became the largest overall grouping in the Chamber of Representatives. No party, however, had a clear mandate for power, and negotiations for a new coalition lasted 146 days. During this time, Martens assumed a caretaker role, while a series of mediators, appointed by the King, attempted to reach a compromise. In May 1988 Martens was sworn in at the head of his eighth administration, after agreement was finally reached by the French- and Flemish-speaking wings of both the Christian Democrats and Socialist parties and by the VU.

The five-party coalition agreement committed the new Government to a programme of further austerity measures, together with tax reforms and increased federalization. In August 1988 Parliament approved the first phase of the federalization plan, intended ultimately to lead to a constitutional amendment, whereby increased autonomy would be granted to the country's Communities and Regions in several areas of jurisdiction, including education and socio-economic policy. It was also agreed that Brussels would have its own Regional Council, with an executive responsible to it, giving the city equal status with Flanders and Wallonia. In January 1989 Parliament approved the second phase of the federalization programme, allocating the public funds necessary to give effect to the regional autonomy that had been approved in principle in August 1988. The federal Constitution formally came into effect in July 1989.

A brief constitutional crisis in 1990 provoked widespread demands for a review of the powers of the Monarch, as defined by the Constitution. In March proposals for the legalization of abortion (in strictly-controlled circumstances) completed their passage through Parliament. However, King Baudouin had previously stated that his religious convictions would render him unable to give royal assent to any such legislation. A compromise solution was reached in early April, whereby Article 82 of the Constitution, which makes provision for the Monarch's 'incapacity to rule', was invoked. Baudouin thus abdicated for 36 hours, during which time the new legislation was promulgated. A joint session of Parliament was then convened to declare the resumption of Baudouin's reign. However, the incident prompted considerable alarm within Belgium: it was widely perceived as setting a dangerous precedent for the reinterpretation of the Constitution.

The Government was weakened by the resignation of both VU ministers in September 1991 and by the resultant loss of its two-thirds' parliamentary majority, necessary for the implementation of the third stage of the federalization programme. Further linguistic conflict between the remaining coalition partners led to Martens' resignation as Prime Minister in October and the subsequent collapse of the Government. However, King Baudouin rejected the resignations of Martens and the Cabinet. The Government remained in office until the next general election, which took place in November. The results of the election reflected a significant decline in popular support for all five parties represented in the outgoing Government. The Socialist parties remained the largest overall grouping in the Chamber of Representatives, although they sustained the highest combined loss of seats (nine). Following the election, the political parties conducted protracted negotiations, during which Martens' interim Cabinet continued in office. In early March 1992 four of the five parties that had composed the previous Government, the CVP, the PSC, the Socialistische Partij (SP) and the PS (which together controlled 120 seats in the 212-member Chamber of Representatives), agreed to form a new administration; a leading member of the CVP, Jean-Luc Dehaene, was appointed Prime Minister. The new Government committed itself to the completion of the constitutional reforms that had been initiated under Martens' premiership. For several months, however, the coalition partners repeatedly failed to reach agreement, both on proposals for the implementation of the third stage of the federalization programme and on amendments to the 1993 budget. A compromise on both issues was eventually reached at the end of September 1992.

In July 1992 the Chamber of Representatives voted, by 146 to 33, in favour of ratifying the Treaty on European Union, agreed by the heads of government of member states of the European Community (now EU) at Maastricht, in the Netherlands, in December 1991. The Senate approved ratification in November 1992.

In February 1993 (in accordance with the constitutional reforms agreed in September 1992) Parliament voted to amend the Constitution to create a federal state of Belgium, comprising the largely autonomous regions of Flanders, Wallonia and (bilingual) Brussels. The three regions, and the country's three linguistic groups, were to be represented by the following directly-elected administrations: a combined administration for Flanders and the Flemish-speaking community, regional administrations for Wallonia and Brussels, and separate administrations for French- and German-speakers. The regional administrations were to assume sole responsibility for the environment, housing, transport and public works, while the language community administrations were to supervise education policy and culture. Legislation to implement the reforms was enacted in July 1993.

In July 1993 King Baudouin died; he was succeeded by his brother, hitherto Prince Albert of Liège, in August.

In January 1994 three government ministers who were members of the PS (including a Deputy Prime Minister, Guy Coëme) resigned from their posts, following allegations that they had been involved in a bribery scandal in connection with the award, in 1988, of a defence contract to an Italian helicopter company. The PS (the Walloon section of the party) was subsequently implicated in a similar scandal involving a French aviation company. In April 1996 Coëme and seven others were found guilty of fraud and abuse of public office. The scandal also led to the suicide in March 1995 of a retired Chief of Staff of the Air Force, the resignation in the same month of Frank Vandenbroucke, a Deputy Prime Minister and the Minister of Foreign Affairs, and the resignation of Willy Claes, a former Deputy Prime Minister and Minister of Foreign Affairs, as Secretary-General of NATO, and his eventual conviction in February 1999

on charges of corruption, fraud and forgery; he received a three-year suspended prison sentence.

At a general election held in May 1995 the ruling centre-left coalition retained significant support, securing a total of 82 seats in the Chamber of Representatives (membership of which had been reduced from 208 to 150), despite the ongoing investigation into allegedly illegal activities by officials of the two Socialist parties. The performance of the extreme right-wing Vlaams Blok (Flemish Bloc) was not as strong as had been anticipated (the party having performed well in the mid-1994 elections to the European Parliament): although the Vlaams Blok won nearly 28% of the votes cast in Antwerp, Belgium's second largest city, it received only 12% of the votes overall in Flanders. Elections to the regional assemblies took place concurrently with the national legislative elections. Following an unusually short period of negotiations, the CVP-PSC-PS-SP coalition was reformed and in mid-June a new Cabinet was appointed, with Dehaene remaining as Prime Minister. The Government introduced several strict economic austerity measures in late 1995; public-sector trade unions responded by organizing protest strike action. In April 1996 the Government, employers and trade unions agreed measures that aimed to reduce the high level of unemployment. The agreement was, however, short-lived, owing to the subsequent withdrawal of one of the main trade unions. In the following month Parliament granted the Dehaene administration special emergency powers to implement economic austerity measures by decree.

The latter half of 1996 was dominated by extreme public concern over allegations of endemic official corruption, following the discovery, in August, of an international paedophile network based in Belgium, and subsequent widespread speculation (fuelled by the arrests in early September of several police-officers) that this had received protection from the police force and from the judicial and political establishment. During September King Albert II promised a thorough investigation of the network and, in an unprecedented gesture, demanded a review of the judicial system. In October, however, allegations of a conspiracy to impede the progress of the investigation were prompted by the removal from the case of Jean-Marc Connerotte, a widely-respected senior investigating judge. The prevailing mood of national crisis was heightened by the arrests, during September, of Alain van der Biest of the PS (a former federal Minister of Pensions) and four others, on charges connected with the assassination in 1991 of a former Deputy Prime Minister, André Cools. It was alleged that PS colleagues had ordered Cools' murder, in order to prevent him from disclosing corruption within the party. In June 1998 a Tunisian court found two Tunisian citizens guilty of the murder; however, the background to the assassination remained unclear. Although the motive remained elusive, in December 2001 van der Biest, in addition to eight members of his entourage, was charged with murder for his part in the killing. However, van der Biest, still protesting his innocence, committed suicide in March 2002 before he could be tried. Six members of his entourage were convicted in January 2004 of organizing the assassination, and were sentenced to between five and 20 years' imprisonment.

Meanwhile, in March 1997 Guy Spitaels, a former Deputy Prime Minister and an erstwhile President of the PS, was indicted on bribery charges relating to the political scandals of 1994–95 (see above). In April 1997 a parliamentary committee investigating allegations of official corruption and mismanagement, issued a report that claimed that rivalry between the country's various police and judicial divisions often prevented their effective co-operation; it recommended the establishment of a single integrated national police force. However, the committee found little evidence that paedophile networks had received official protection. In February 1998 the Government announced that, in place of the recommended integrated national police force, efforts would be made to facilitate 'voluntary co-operation contracts' between the various law enforcement services.

In April 1998 Marc Dutroux, a convicted paedophile whose arrest in August 1996 on charges of child kidnapping and murder had prompted the ongoing scrutiny of Belgium's national institutions, briefly escaped from police custody. (In June 2000 Dutroux was sentenced to five years' imprisonment for his escape, but had not yet been tried for his role in the murder of at least two children.) The incident incited renewed public anger and precipitated the resignations of several high-ranking figures, including the commander of the national gendarmerie and the Ministers of the Interior and of Justice. A proposed vote of 'no confidence' in the Dehaene Government, also ensuing from Dutroux's escape, was defeated in the Chamber of Representatives. Dehaene immediately reaffirmed his commitment to restructuring the police and judiciary. However, in May 2002, the parents of one of Dutroux's alleged child victims declared a lack of confidence in the competence of the authorities and withdrew from the criminal investigation. Their principal complaint was the alleged obstruction of attempts to broaden the inquiry to include an investigation into allegations of Dutroux's involvement in a putative paedophile network that extended into the political and judicial establishment. The police completed their inquiry in August and Dutroux's trial began in March 2004. In June Dutroux was found guilty of the kidnapping, imprisonment and rape of six young girls and of three murders; he was sentenced to life imprisonment with no possibility of parole.

In mid-June 1998 a reorganization of the Cabinet included the appointment of a new (Socialist) Minister of Finance. In late September Louis Tobback, who had been appointed Deputy Prime Minister and Minister of the Interior in April, resigned, following protests at the death of a Nigerian woman during an attempt forcibly to deport her from Belgium. Four police-officers were subsequently convicted of involuntary manslaughter in December 2003, and the Government suspended the forced repatriation of asylum-seekers, pending further investigations.

Preparations for the general election scheduled to be held in mid-June 1999 were overshadowed by the public announcement in late May that animal feed contaminated with industrial oil containing dioxin (a carcinogenic chemical) had been supplied to farms throughout Belgium from a factory near Ghent. Following the announcement, many Belgian food products, particularly poultry and egg-based products, were withdrawn from sale in Belgium and elsewhere in Europe, while production was suspended at farms across Belgium. There was widespread public anger that, although veterinary inspectors had identified a problem as early as mid-March, it was not until May that the Ministry of Agriculture had suspended sales from the affected animal-feed suppliers, and had informed government officials in neighbouring countries. On 1 June Karel Pinxten, the Minister of Agriculture and Small and Medium-sized Enterprises, and Marcel Colla, the Minister of Consumer Affairs, Public Health and the Environment, who had been jointly blamed for the delay in informing the public of the contamination, resigned from their posts. In early June the EU announced that it was to demand the removal from sale, and subsequent destruction, of poultry, pork and cattle products from farms whose feed had been contaminated with dioxin. The Belgian Government subsequently introduced a total ban on the slaughter and transportation of all poultry, cattle and pigs until it could confirm which farms had received the affected feed. On 7 June Dehaene took the unprecedented step of halting his electoral campaign, and announced an official parliamentary inquiry into the contamination. On 10 June, in an apparent attempt to assuage farmers who were losing large amounts of income on a daily basis and demanding compensation, the Government announced that slaughtering and exports could resume at farms that had not received the contaminated feed, despite the lack of a definitive list of dioxin-free farms. This relaxation of the temporary ban on production contravened the advice of the European Commission, which had recommended that the ban should remain in place while there continued to be uncertainty about which farms had received the contaminated feed. It was alleged that the Government had believed that, for political reasons, it could not wait for the convening of the Commission's scientific and veterinary committee, whose meeting was scheduled to take place after the Belgian general election. Confusion, however, remained within Belgium as to the identification of the affected farms, and Belgian farmers blocked the roads into the country from France and the Netherlands, in an attempt to prevent agricultural imports. The Commission later announced that it was to initiate legal proceedings against the Belgian Government over its handling of the crisis, which had led to imports of European food products being banned by many non-European countries (including the USA). The Commission announced in June 2001 that it had dropped legal action against Belgium.

At the general election, which was held on 13 June 1999, the Christian Democrats suffered heavy losses, mainly at the hands of the Liberals and the ecologist parties. The Vlaams Blok also showed significant gains, winning more than 10% of the vote in many areas. The Vlaamse Liberalen en Demokraten—Partij

van de Burger (VLD—Flemish Liberals and Democrats—Citizens' Party) emerged as the largest single party with 23 seats in the 150-member Chamber of Representatives, while the ecologist parties, Anders Gaan Leven (Agalev) and the Ecologistes Confédérés pour l'Organisation des Luttes Originales (Ecolo), almost doubled their representation, to 20 seats, and the Vlaams Blok became the fifth largest party in the lower house with 15 seats. The CVP secured 22 seats and the PSC won 10 seats, while the Socialist parties obtained a combined total of 33 seats. The VLD also performed well in the elections to the Senate. The electoral defeat of the outgoing coalition was largely attributed to public dissatisfaction with the authorities' response to the dioxin crisis compounded by general disquiet over the earlier corruption and paedophile scandals. Dehaene, who had held the premiership for eight years, tendered his resignation on 14 June. The President of the VLD, Guy Verhofstadt, formed a new six-party coalition Government, comprising the VLD, the francophone Parti Réformateur Libéral (PRL), the two Socialist parties and the two ecologist parties, which was sworn in on 12 July. The new administration was of historic note in that it was the first Belgian Government in 40 years not to include the Christian Democrats, the first to include the ecologist parties, and the first to be headed by a Liberal Prime Minister since 1884.

Despite demonstrations staged by farmers (many of whom were reportedly on the brink of bankruptcy) in late June and in early July 1999, in protest at the authorities' handling of the dioxin crisis, the new Government announced that it was to add a further 400 farms to the list of 800 already forbidden to sell their produce. The Government also announced that it was to buy back and destroy some 80,000 metric tons of pork. In early August, in response to recommendations made by scientific advisers from the European Commission, the Belgian Government agreed to add beef to the list of livestock exports that were banned until definitively cleared of contamination. A few days later the Government promulgated a decree banning the export of food products containing more than 2% animal fat (except dairy products) that did not have a certificate guaranteeing their safety. The agricultural industry maintained that stringent procedures were required in order to regain consumer confidence and to avoid the imposition of a total ban on all Belgian agricultural exports by the EU.

In October 1999 the Government announced that legislation was to be introduced, aimed at reforming the procedure of applying for asylum. The new procedure was to take no longer than one month, including the appeals process, and those applicants not granted asylum were to be repatriated without delay. The Government also announced that all outstanding asylum applications would be processed within one year. In a temporary amnesty in January 2000 asylum-seekers resident in Belgium for five years and illegal immigrants resident in Belgium for six years were granted legal status. In November, in an attempt to address the growing number of asylum-seekers (which had increased from 35,778 in 1999 to more than 40,000 in 2000, many of whom were from Eastern Europe), the Government proposed the introduction of border controls to slow down the inflow of immigrants and an accelerated procedure for deporting those whose claims were without foundation.

The general popularity of the new Government was slightly undermined by the results of the local elections that took place in early October 2000. Although the government parties performed well, their achievements were overshadowed by the success of the Vlaams Blok, which had campaigned against immigration and in favour of independence for Flanders. The Vlaams Blok made significant advances in Flanders, particularly in Antwerp. It also performed well in Ghent and Mechelen, and most surprisingly in Brussels, where its share of the vote doubled in several districts, compared with the previous election. The Vlaams Blok remained unrepresented in any municipal government, owing to the refusal of any other party to co-operate with the group, but there were fears nevertheless that its extremist positions were altering political debate in Belgium. In September 2002 the Court of Appeal ruled that two human rights groups could begin legal proceedings seeking the dissolution of the Vlaams Blok, on the grounds that its xenophobic and racist views were in contravention of equal rights legislation.

In January 2001 the federal Cabinet approved a directive for the decriminalization, subject to parliamentary approval, of cannabis. The following October, the Senate approved legislation which enabled the legalization of euthanasia. In May

2002 the Chamber of Representatives endorsed a law that permitted adult patients suffering extreme physical or psychological pain resulting from an accident or terminal illness, to seek the right to die. Despite opposition from the Roman Catholic Church, the law was promulgated in September. Legislation providing for marriage between homosexual couples was approved by the Senate in November and by the Chamber of Representatives in January 2003; it awarded homosexual couples similar rights to heterosexual couples, with the notable exception of the right to adopt children.

In mid-August 2002 an agreement secured by the Minister of Foreign Affairs, Louis Michel, for the supply of 5,500 automatic rifles to the Government of Nepal caused divisions within the coalition Government. While Michel maintained that the sale would help the Nepalese administration counter Maoist rebel attempts to establish a communist dictatorship in the country, opponents led by Agalev claimed that the deal broke EU directives against the sale of weapons to countries engaged in civil war. On 26 August the Agalev Minister of Consumer Affairs, Health, and the Environment, Magda Aelvoet, resigned in protest at the deal; she was replaced by fellow Agalev member, Jef Tavernier. On 31 August the Government won a parliamentary vote of confidence by 87 votes to 38, although Verhofstadt was obliged to accede to a number of minor concessions concerning the deal to secure the support of all the coalition partners. The first consignment of weapons arrived in Nepal in January 2003. In July of that year the Nieuw-Vlaamse Alliantie (N-VA—New Flemish Alliance), a small nationalist party, filed a suit against Michel under controversial Belgian war crimes legislation (see below), accusing him of complicity with alleged atrocities committed by the Nepalese military against the Maoist rebels.

In late November 2002 the murder of a man of Moroccan origin, allegedly by a white man, provoked rioting in Antwerp; police arrested some 160 people of North African origin in the city. Among the detainees was Abu Jahjah, the leader of an Arab militant group, the Arab European League (AEL). Originally from Lebanon, Jahjah had previously fought for the Islamist extremist group, Hezbollah (Party of God) and rejected the assimilation of Arabs into Belgian society, demanding separate schools and the creation of self-governing Arab areas. He was subsequently charged with conspiracy to foment disorder. A week before the rioting began, members of the AEL had been pursuing police with video recorders to compile evidence of what they claimed was racist behaviour by the authorities. The Vlaams Blok demanded that the organization be banned. Also in November a Tunisian member of the Islamist Al-Qa'ida (Base) terrorist network, Nizar Trabelsi, confessed that he had planned a suicide attack on a US air force installation in eastern Belgium, which was believed to contain nuclear warheads. Although Belgium has no specific anti-terrorism laws, Trabelsi was sentenced in October 2003 to 10 years' imprisonment, following his conviction for attempting to destroy public property, possession of firearms and membership of a private militia. At the same time a further 17 Islamist militants were also convicted for related offences to terrorism, while five others were acquitted.

In December 2002 the Chamber of Representatives voted to close all seven nuclear power plants, which supplied about 57.8% of Belgian electricity requirements in 2001, by 2025. The legislation also provided incentives for the use of alternative energy sources.

In January 2003 Verhofstadt announced that a general election would take place a month earlier than scheduled, on 18 May. Verhofstadt was obliged to reorganize the Cabinet in early May, following the withdrawal of Ecolo from the six-party coalition Government. The Deputy Prime Minister and Minister of Mobility and Transport, Isabelle Durant, and the State Secretary for Energy and Sustainable Development, Olivier Deleuze, resigned after Durant had been deprived of responsibility for the transport portfolio following her refusal to implement a recently negotiated compromise on night flights over Brussels. The dispute over flight routes reflected Belgium's language divide, as the proposed route change would affect the predominantly French-speaking population of the city, whereas the previous arrangement caused greater disturbance to the Flemish-speaking residents. (Durant and Deleuze represented the French-speaking Ecolo, whereas Verhofstadt's VLD was Flemish-speaking.) The transport portfolio was allocated to the PS Deputy Prime Minister and Minister of Employment, Laurette Onkelinx, while responsibility for energy and sustainable

development was awarded to a PRL government official, Alain Zenner.

Belgium's international profile was raised in 2003 by its Government's public opposition to the USA's policy of a preemptive military attack against Iraq, owing to the alleged failure of Saddam Hussain's regime to disarm in compliance with a resolution by the UN. The Belgian position, which was shared by the French and German Governments, also created a crisis in NATO as the three countries used their veto to reject US-supported defensive aid to Turkey in preparation for a potential war with Iraq. France, Germany and Belgium argued that the timing was inappropriate and that military planning by NATO would undermine continuing diplomatic attempts to prevent a war with Iraq. While opposition from Germany and France was successfully circumvented, the Belgian Government, which was under considerable pressure from domestic anti-war public opinion prior to a general election, remained isolated. The issue was resolved by the inclusion of Belgian amendments to the agreement to provide military aid to Turkey, notably the addition of an explicit reference to the framework of the UN for the peaceful solution of the crisis.

At the general election on 18 May 2003, in which 91.63% of the electorate participated, the outgoing centre-left Liberal and Socialist coalition was returned to power. The ecologist parties suffered heavy losses, while the controversial Vlaams Blok achieved the best result in its 25-year history. The VLD won the highest proportion of the vote (15.4%) and secured 25 seats in the Chamber of Representatives, two more than in the previous administration. The PS received 13.0% of the vote and won an additional six seats, bringing them level with the VLD in the 150-member chamber. The Mouvement Réformateur (MR) coalition obtained 24 seats (11.4%), while the Flemish wing of the Socialist party (renamed the Sociaal Progressief Alternatief—SP.A—in 2001) in an alliance with the smaller Flemish regional party, Spirit, won 23 seats (14.9%). The Christian Democrats (restyled the Christen-Democratisch en Vlaams Partij—CD&V—in 2001) secured 21 seats, with 13.2% of the votes. The CD&V Chairman, Stefaan De Clerck, subsequently resigned and was replaced by Yves Leterme. The Vlaams Blok became the sixth largest party in the house, increasing its representation from 15 to 18 seats (11.6%). It gained 18% of the Flemish vote and one-third of the votes cast in Antwerp. The growing popularity of the party stimulated debate about the counter-productiveness of the 12-year agreement by the principal political parties to exclude the Vlaams Blok from mainstream politics. The ecologist parties Ecolo and Agalev (which was subsequently renamed Groen!), which had together won 20 seats in the 1999 election, were reduced to four representatives, obtaining just 5.6% of the total votes cast. The poor performance of the ecology parties was partly attributed to their prominent role in promoting unpopular legislation such as the early introduction of an EU-mandated ban on tobacco advertising, which led to the loss of Belgium's right to stage a Formula One motor racing event. (The new Government, which excluded the ecology parties, rescinded the early introduction of the ban in August 2003 in order to regain the right to host the annual event.) The VLD and the SP.A-Spirit coalition also performed well in the concurrent election to the Senate; each winning seven of the 40 directly elective seats. The CD&V and the PS each secured six seats, while the MR and the Vlaams Blok obtained five apiece.

On 28 May 2003 King Albert II asked Verhofstadt to form a new government. Two months of negotiations ensued between the Liberal and Socialist parties and led to the successful resolution of the issue of night flights (which had proven divisive prior to the election). When the talks were finalized Verhofstadt announced the composition of a new coalition Government. The new administration, comprising the VLD, the MR, the PS, the SP.A and Spirit, took office on 12 July. The Minister of Defence, André Flahaut, and the Minister of Foreign Affairs, Louis Michel, who were both outspoken critics of the US-led military campaign in Iraq to remove the regime of Saddam Hussain, retained their portfolios, as did the Minister of Finance, Didier Reynders, although the administration of 16 included nine new appointments. Verhofstadt's Government pledged to reduce personal income tax, to increase expenditure on health and justice, and to create 200,000 new jobs by 2007.

It was widely believed that the established parties' continued refusal to enter into coalition with the Vlaams Blok was counter-productive and, despite the Government's adoption of more stringent policies with regard to asylum-seekers, the popularity of the Vlaams Blok grew. In the European and regional elections concurrently held on 10 June 2004, the Vlaams Blok increased its representation in the European Parliament from two to three of Belgium's 24 seats and it became the second largest party in the 124-member Flemish Parliament (while the VLD was only the fourth largest), with a rise in the number of its seats from 22 to 32. Following the poor performance of the ruling coalition parties in the regional elections, Verhofstadt effected a wide-ranging cabinet reorganization (including five new appointments) later that month; the new administration was formally sworn in in July.

On 9 November 2004 the Supreme Court of Appeal found the Vlaams Blok guilty of promoting racial discrimination and ruled that freedom of speech should be curtailed in the interests of national security and to protect the rights of other people. The judgment upheld an earlier ruling made in April in a case brought by the government anti-racism agency. The Vlaams Blok was fined and lost access both to state funding and to television exposure, thus effectively forcing the party to disband. The organization had been prepared for the court's decision and consequently changed its statutes and renamed itself Vlaams Belang (Flemish Interest). In a bid to capitalize on its growing popularity, the organization announced plans to broaden its appeal; members had already voted, on 4 November, to moderate the party's policy on immigration.

From late 1988 Belgium's hitherto cordial relations with its former colonies underwent considerable strain. Proposals that Prime Minister Martens made in November 1988 regarding the relief of public and commercial debts owed to Belgium by Zaire (formerly the Belgian Congo, renamed the Democratic Republic of the Congo—DRC—in 1997) provoked allegations in the Belgian press of corruption within the Zairean Government and of the misappropriation of development aid. President Mobutu Sese Seko of Zaire responded by ordering the withdrawal of all Zairean state-owned businesses from Belgium and by demanding that all Zairean nationals resident in Belgium remove their assets from, and leave, their host country. In July 1989 the situation was apparently resolved following meetings between Martens and Mobutu, at which a new debt-servicing agreement was signed. However, relations again deteriorated when, in May 1990, the Mobutu regime refused to accede to demands for an international inquiry into the alleged massacre of as many as 150 students by the Zairean security forces. Mobutu accused Belgium of interfering in his country's internal affairs, and ordered the expulsion from Zaire of some 700 Belgian technical workers, together with the closure of three of Belgium's four consular offices. Following the collapse of public order in Zaire in September 1991, the Belgian Government dispatched 1,000 troops to Zaire for the protection of the estimated 11,000 Belgian nationals resident there. By the end of 1991 all the troops had been withdrawn and about 8,000 Belgian nationals had been evacuated. Prospects for the normalization of relations improved following the establishment of a transitional Government in Zaire in July 1992 and the removal of Zairean sanctions against Belgium. Relations deteriorated again, however, in January 1993, when, in response to rioting by troops loyal to President Mobutu, Belgium dispatched 520 troops to evacuate the remaining 3,000 Belgian nationals in Zaire. In October 1994 the Belgian Government pledged to resume humanitarian aid to Zaire. In August 1997, following the deposition of Mobutu's regime in May by the forces of Laurent-Désiré Kabila, it was announced that normal relations between Belgium and the DRC (as Zaire was now renamed) would be gradually restored.

In October 1990 the Martens Government dispatched 600 troops to protect some 1,600 Belgian nationals resident in Rwanda (part of the former Belgian territory of Ruanda-Urundi), when exiled opponents of the incumbent regime invaded that country. The Belgian Government insisted that the deployment was a purely humanitarian action, and stated that it would not agree to a request from the Rwandan Government for military assistance, citing unacceptable violations of human rights by the authorities. In late October a cease-fire agreement came into effect, and in early November Belgian forces were withdrawn from Rwanda. Nevertheless, the conflict in Rwanda continued during 1991–94. Following the signing of a peace accord in August 1993, some 420 Belgian troops were redeployed as part of a UN peace-keeping force; this was, however, unable to prevent an outbreak of extreme violence, beginning in April 1994, which resulted in the deaths of many hundreds of thousands of people. Following the execution of 10 Belgian troops in April, the Belgian Government withdrew its peace-keeping contingent. It also dispatched some 800 paratroopers to Rwanda to co-ordinate the evacuation of the estimated 1,500 Belgian expatriates remaining in the country, as well as other foreign nationals. In October 1998 three Belgian army officers were demoted, having been found negligent in not preventing the 10 troop fatalities in April 1994. The Belgian Ministries of Foreign Affairs and Defence rejected allegations, published in November 2003, of racist, aggressive and undisciplined behaviour by Belgian UN troops at the start of Rwanda's 1994 genocide. Verhofstadt denounced the author of the book, Gen. Romeo Dallaire, the Commander-in-Chief of the UN Assistance Mission for Rwanda from 1993–94, as unprofessional and noted that Dallaire had refused to testify before the Belgian Senate's Parliamentary Commission of Inquiry Regarding the Events in Rwanda, which took place in 1997–98.

The election of a new Government in Belgium in June 1999 led to an improvement in relations between Belgium and the DRC. The new Belgian Minister of Foreign Affairs, Louis Michel, was determined to develop a new strategy towards the central African countries with which Belgium had historical ties. Following the assassination of the DRC's President Kabila in January 2001, the Belgian Government intensified its attempts to relaunch the peace initiative in the region. During a visit to Belgium by the new DRC President, Kabila's son, Joseph, as part of a tour to meet those instrumental in the DRC peace efforts, the Belgian Prime Minister urged Kabila to commit to peace negotiations under the auspices of the UN. Michel also aimed to add an 'ethical' dimension to Belgian foreign policy. Initiatives that reflected this new approach included an apology made by Belgium in February 2002 for its role in the murder of the Belgian Congo's first Prime Minister, Patrice Lumumba, in 1961. Although a report had found no direct link between the killing and the Belgian Government, it did conclude that ministers at the time bore a 'moral responsibility' by failing to prevent it. In July 2002 the state-funded Royal Museum for Central Africa announced that it had commissioned a review of Belgium's colonial past. This followed allegations by a US author, Adam Hochschild, in his book published in translation in Belgium in 1999, that 10m. Congolese had been killed as a result of policies adopted during the colonial rule of King Leopold II (1885–1908). The investigators presented their findings in 2004 (which, although disputing the actual number of Congolese killed during King Leopold's rule, did not deny that many atrocities had indeed taken place), and an exhibition entitled 'Memory of Congo: The Colonial Era' was staged at the museum in Brussels in early 2005. Following a peace accord formalized in April 2003 and the installation in June of Joseph Kabila as leader of an interim DRC Government that was charged with staging the first democratic elections in the country since independence from Belgium in 1960, in October 2003 the Belgian Government announced its intention to double its aid to the DRC to €82m. in 2004. Kabila visited Belgium and met Verhofstadt in February 2004 as part of a European tour to secure investment in the DRC's devastated economy. Prior to Kabila's visit the Belgian Government announced that it would send military instructors to the DRC to train DRC troops in peace-keeping operations. The mission, which was expected to last from February to June, represented the first time that Belgium had sent troops to a former African colony since 1994. In October 2004, however, the Government of the DRC recalled its ambassador from Brussels, in protest at remarks made by the Belgian Minister of Foreign Affairs, Karel de Gucht, criticizing the DRC authorities for their alleged continuing corrupt practices and lack of democracy.

The Belgian Government co-hosted a donor conference in January 2004 for another of its former African colonies, Burundi (which had constituted part of the former Belgian territory of Ruanda-Urundi), whose Government had signed a power-sharing accord with rebels in November 2003. The Belgian administration pledged €35m. in aid to Burundi to support the transition to peace.

In September 2003 Prime Minister Verhofstadt announced that the Government was continuing with plans to open a new autonomous European military command headquarters near Brussels. The proposal, which was opposed by several EU states, notably the United Kingdom, had been put forward by Belgium, France, Germany and Luxembourg (the EU states most opposed to the US-led military campaign in Iraq) following a meeting in Brussels at the end of April. Verhofstadt claimed that the capacity to plan and execute European operations autonomously was essential and would complement NATO. The British Government, which feared that NATO would be undermined, reportedly proposed the creation of a European 'planning cell' based at the NATO headquarters in Mons, Belgium. The proposal was welcomed by Verhofstadt, although he regarded the establishment of such a cell as suitable for liaison purposes rather than as an alternative to a European military command headquarters.

In 2000 Belgium was criticized in a UN report on sanctions against diamonds used to fund anti-Government rebels in Angola for 'extremely lax controls and regulations governing the Antwerp market'. The new Government protested, however, that it had already agreed a certification scheme with Angola to ensure that it did not sell diamonds from rebel-held areas.

In June 2001 a Belgian court convicted four Rwandan nationals of war crimes for their role in the ethnic violence in Rwanda in 1994. The case was the first to be successfully conducted under legislation introduced in 1993, which endowed Belgian courts with universal jurisdiction in human rights cases. (Three of the four subsequently filed an appeal against their convictions.) In February 2002, however, the International Court of Justice (see p. 19) ruled that Belgium did not have the right to try suspects who were protected by diplomatic immunity. In mid-May 2002 the final hearing began in a Belgian appeals court for a case brought against the Israeli Prime Minister, Ariel Sharon, for war crimes allegedly committed against Palestinian refugees in Lebanon in 1982, when he was the Israeli Minister of Defence. However, in June judges ruled that the case could not be brought to trial since, according to the Belgian criminal code, alleged crimes committed outside the country required subjects to be on Belgian territory to be investigated and tried. Another human rights case, against President Laurent Gbagbo of Côte d'Ivoire, was similarly dismissed. In early February 2003, however, the Supreme Court reversed the earlier ruling regarding Sharon, but recognized his diplomatic immunity so that proceedings against him were inadmissible while he remained the Israeli premier. However, the court ruled that proceedings against members of the Israeli Defence Forces who had served as senior commanders during the conflict in Lebanon could begin. Israel responded by recalling its ambassador from Belgium.

The 1993 law also jeopardized relations with the USA. In May 2003 Gen. Tommy Franks, the retiring US commander in Iraq, was indicted under the legislation by a Belgian lawyer representing 19 Iraqis. Despite the fact that the case was ended the following week under new procedures introduced in April to prevent the legislation being used for politically motivated litigation, the US Government demanded the abolition of the legislation, dismissing previous modifications as inadequate. The US Secretary of Defense, Donald Rumsfeld, warned that US officials would be unable to attend meetings of NATO and threatened to withdraw US funding for a new NATO headquarters in Belgium. In July 2003 cases were initiated (and dismissed) against several other prominent US politicians, including the President, George W. Bush, Donald Rumsfeld and the Secretary of State, Colin Powell, as well as against the British Prime Minister, Tony Blair, for their roles in the military action in Afghanistan and Iraq. Legislation was passed in August that repealed the 1993 law and established a procedure for nullifying pending cases; it limited the jurisdiction of the law to cases involving Belgian citizens and long-term residents, and granted automatic legal immunity to all officials attending meetings at NATO and the EU. The repeal of the legislation was opposed by human rights organizations; in February 2004 a human rights group lodged an appeal demanding the partial annulment of the new legislation to eliminate alleged discrimination against the victims of genocide, war crimes and crimes against humanity.

Government

Belgium is a constitutional and hereditary monarchy, consisting of a federation of the largely autonomous regions of Brussels, Flanders and Wallonia and of the Flemish-, French- and German-speaking language communities. The central legislature consists of a bicameral Parliament (the Chamber of Representatives and the Senate). The Chamber has 150 members, all directly elected for a term of four years by universal adult suffrage, on the basis of proportional representation. The Senate has 71 normal members, of whom 40 are directly elected at intervals of four years, also by universal suffrage on the basis of proportional representation, 21 appointed by the legislative

bodies of the three language communities (see below), and 10 are co-opted by the elected members. In addition, children of the King are entitled to honorary membership of the Senate from 18 years of age and acquire voting rights at the age of 21. Members of both Houses serve for up to four years. Executive power, nominally vested in the King, is exercised by the Cabinet. The King appoints the Prime Minister and, on the latter's advice, other Ministers. The Cabinet is responsible to the Chamber of Representatives. The three regions and three linguistic communities are represented by the following directly-elected legislative administrations: a combined administration for Flanders and the Flemish-speaking community, regional administrations for Wallonia and Brussels, and separate administrations for French- and German-speakers. The regional administrations have sole responsibility for the environment, housing, transport and public works, while the language community administrations supervise education policy and culture. Under a constitutional amendment approved by the Chamber of Representatives in June 2001, the regions were also granted greater autonomy over taxation and public expenditure, agriculture, and policies regarding foreign aid and trade. In April 2002 a further set of reforms was agreed in principle. It was proposed that the Senate would become the assembly of the regions and communities and the Chamber of Representatives the sole federal representative body.

Defence

Belgium is a member of NATO. In August 2004 the total strength of the armed forces was 40,800 (including 1,800 in the Medical Service and 1,500 in Joint Service), comprising an army of 24,800, a navy of 2,450 and an air force of 10,250. The defence budget for 2004 was estimated at €2,700m. Compulsory military service was abolished in 1995. In 1996 the Belgian and Netherlands navies came under a joint operational command, based at Den Helder, the Netherlands. In November 2000 Belgium committed 1,000 troops to a proposed joint 60,000-strong EU rapid reaction force, which was to be ready and able to be deployed by 2003. The logistics of assembling this force proved problematic, however, and in November 2004 the EU defence ministers agreed to create 13 'battlegroups' (each numbering 1,000–1,500 men) by 2007, which could be deployed at short notice (within 10 days) to carry out peace-keeping activities at crisis points around the world.

Economic Affairs

In 2003, according to estimates by the World Bank, Belgium's gross national income (GNI), measured at average 2001–03 prices, was US $307,876m., equivalent to $25,820 per head (or $28,930 per head on an international purchasing-power parity basis). During 1990–2003, it was estimated, the population increased at an average annual rate of 0.3% per year, while gross domestic product (GDP) per head increased, in real terms, by an average of 1.6% per year. Overall GDP increased, in real terms, at an average annual rate of 1.9% during 1990–2002; it rose by 0.7% in 2002 and by 1.1% in 2003.

Agriculture (including hunting, forestry and fishing) contributed 1.3% of GDP in 2002 and engaged 0.9% of the employed labour force (in paid employment). The principal agricultural products are sugar beet, cereals and potatoes. Pig meat, beef and dairy products are also important. Exports of live animals and animal and vegetable products accounted for 7.6% of Belgium's total export revenue in 2002. The agricultural sector was adversely affected by the dioxin contamination scandal (see Recent History) in the late 1990s. According to World Bank estimates, agricultural GDP increased, in real terms, at an average annual rate of 3.8% in 1990–2002; it decreased by 4.0% in 2001 before increasing by 14.7% in the following year.

Industry (including mining and quarrying, manufacturing, power and construction) contributed 26.9% of GDP and engaged 23.9% of the paid labour force in 2002. According to World Bank estimates, real industrial GDP increased at an average rate of 1.5% per year in 1990–2002; it rose by 0.1% in 2001 and by 0.3% in 2002.

Belgium has few mineral resources, and the country's last coal mine closed in 1992. In 2001 extractive activities accounted for only 0.1% of GDP and engaged only 0.1% of the employed labour force. Belgium is, however, an important producer of copper, zinc and aluminium, smelted from imported ores. The sector's GDP declined at an average rate of 2.5% per year during 1995–99, although it increased by 0.7% in 1999.

According to World Bank estimates, manufacturing contributed 18.3% of GDP in 2001 and engaged 17.2% of the employed labour force in 2002. In 2001 the main branches of manufacturing, in terms of value added, were chemicals, chemical products and man-made fibres (accounting for 20.0% of the total), basic metals and fabricated metal products (13.6%) and food products (13.1%). According to World Bank estimates, during 1995–2001 manufacturing GDP increased at an average annual rate of 2.7%; it rose by 4.0% in 2000 and by 0.3% in 2001.

Belgium's seven nuclear reactors accounted for 55.5% of total electricity generation in 2003. A further 27.3% was produced by natural gas power stations and 12.9% by coal-fired stations. The country's dependence on imported petroleum and natural gas has increased since 1988, following the announcement by the Government in that year of the indefinite suspension of its nuclear programme and of the construction of a gas-powered generator. In December 2002 a bill was approved by the Chamber of Representatives to phase out the use of nuclear power by 2025, with the first nuclear power station scheduled to be closed in 2015. Imports of mineral fuels comprised an estimated 7.9% of the value of Belgium's total imports in 2002. The electricity market in Flanders was opened up to competition from July 2003, and the remainder of the electricity sector was scheduled for complete liberalization by mid-2007. According to an EU directive, the natural gas market was also scheduled to be fully liberalized by July 2007.

The services sector contributed 71.8% of GDP and engaged 74.7% of the employed labour force in 2002. The presence in Belgium of the offices of many international organizations and businesses is a significant source of revenue. In September 2000 Euronext was formed from the merger of the stock exchanges of Brussels (Brussels Exchanges), Amsterdam (Amsterdam Exchanges) and Paris (Paris Bourse). Tourism is an expanding industry in Belgium, and in 2003 an estimated 11.1m. foreign tourists visited the country. Tourism receipts totalled US $6,892m. in 2002 (including receipts from Luxembourg). According to World Bank estimates, the GDP of the services sector increased at an average annual rate of 1.8% in 1990–2002; it increased by 2.0% in 2001 and by 0.2% in 2002.

In 2003 Belgium recorded a visible trade surplus of US $7,165m., and there was a surplus of $9,365m. on the current account of the balance of payments. Belgium's principal source of imports in 2003 was the Netherlands (providing 19.4% of the total); other major suppliers were Germany (16.6%), France (14.5%) and the United Kingdom (8.7%). The principal markets for exports in that year were Germany and France (each accounting for 17.3% of the total); other major purchasers were the Netherlands (12.9%) and the United Kingdom (9.0%). The principal exports in 2002 were road vehicles, medicinal and pharmaceutical products, non-metallic mineral manufactures, and organic chemicals. The principal imports in that year were road vehicles, medicinal and pharmaceutical products, non-metallic mineral manufactures, and petroleum and related products.

In 2003 there was a budgetary surplus of €1,040.5m., equivalent to an estimated 0.4% of GDP. The country's total external debt was equivalent to 107.5% of GDP in 2001. The annual rate of inflation averaged 1.7% in 1997–2003. Consumer prices increased by an annual average of 1.7% in 2002 and by 1.5% in 2003. In 2003 8.0% of the labour force were unemployed.

Belgium is a member of the European Union (EU, see p. 217), including the European Monetary System (EMS, see p. 251), and of the Benelux Economic Union (see p. 373). Belgium is also a member of the European System of Central Banks (ESCB), which was inaugurated in 1998 under the auspices of the European Central Bank (see p. 229).

In the late 1990s Belgium successfully reduced its large budget deficit and chronic public-sector debt in order to qualify for the final stage of Economic and Monetary Union (EMU) within the EU. The reduction of the budget deficit to the equivalent of 0.9% of GDP and the level of public debt to 116.1% of GDP by 1999 (from 7% and 135%, respectively, in 1993) enabled Belgium to participate in the introduction of the European single currency, the euro, which came into effect on 1 January 1999 (in 11 participating countries). The first Verhofstadt administration, which presided over a period of growth in the economy, continued to reduce the budget deficit and public indebtedness, achieving the first budget surplus for 50 years (of 0.2%) in 2001. In June 2001 the Government attempted to address the imbalances in the performances of the regional economies in Belgium, granting greater fiscal control to the

regions (a long-held demand of the more affluent Flanders), with the discretion to raise or lower local taxes. Expenditure on health was unexpectedly high in 2004 and a tax amnesty on the repatriation of Belgian savings held abroad, which it was envisaged would fund reductions in income tax, was less effective than anticipated. Nevertheless, the Government's objective of a balanced budget for that year was achieved. However, the National Bank of Belgium predicted a budget deficit equivalent to 0.3% of GDP for 2005. Moreover, the IMF expressed concern that non-recurring measures, such as the timely assumption of Belgacom's pension liabilities in preparation for the partial divestment of the company's shares (the deal included a payment from Belgacom to the Government of €1,400m.), had thus far played a crucial role in returning a balanced budget, but would not strengthen the underlying fiscal position in the longer term. In anticipation of the associated health and welfare costs of the ageing population, the Government planned to achieve a budget surplus of 0.3% of GDP in 2007, rising to a surplus of 1.5% of GDP by 2011. Progress in job creation was considered essential for the long-term prospects of the economy, as social security and pension payments remained a serious burden on public finances. Preliminary estimates revealed that the economy grew by a robust 2.7% in 2004, fuelled by strong private consumption and international trade. This figure was substantially higher than the EU average of 2.1%. The National Bank of Belgium forecast more moderate growth, of 2.3%, in 2005. At 95.9% of GDP in 2004, public debt fell below 100% of GDP for the first time in 20 years, although this was still far above the 60% limit set by the EU Stability and Growth Pact.

Education

Legislation granting responsibility for the formulation of education policy to the administrations of the Flemish-, French- and German-speaking communities came into effect in 1993. Education may be provided by the Communities, by public authorities or by private interests. All educational establishments, whether official or 'free' (privately-organized), receive most of their funding from the Communities. Roman Catholic schools constitute the greatest number of 'free' establishments.

Full-time education in Belgium is compulsory between the ages of six and 16 years. Thereafter, pupils must remain in part-time education for a further two-year period. About 90% of infants attend state-financed nursery schools. Elementary education begins at six years of age and consists of three courses of two years each. Secondary education, beginning at the age of 12, lasts for six years and is divided into three two-year cycles or, in a few cases, two three-year cycles. According to UNESCO, enrolment at primary schools in 2000/01 included 100% of children in the relevant age-group, while the comparable ratio at secondary schools was 95.0% (males 94.6%; females 95.5%) in 1999/2000.

The requirement for university entrance is a pass in the 'examination of maturity', taken after the completion of secondary studies. Courses are divided into 2–3 years of general preparation followed by two to three years of specialization. The French Community controls four universities, while the Flemish Community controls three such institutions; in addition, there are 11 university centres or faculties (six French, five Flemish). In 2002/03 a total of 119,484 students were enrolled in university-level establishments. Non-university institutions of higher education provide arts education, technical training and teacher training; in 2002/03 a total of 178,903 students were enrolled in such institutions. In 1999/2000 enrolment at tertiary level was equivalent to 57.0% of those in the relevant age-group (males 53.5%; females 60.6%). A national study fund provides grants where necessary and almost 20% of students receive scholarships.

Expenditure on education by all levels of government was equivalent to 11.6% of total public expenditure in 1999/2000. The budget for education in 2002 was €4,571m.

Public Holidays

2005: 1 January (New Year's Day), 28 March (Easter Monday), 1 May (Labour Day), 5 May (Ascension Day), 16 May (Whit Monday), 11 July (Flemish-speaking Community), 21 July (Independence Day), 15 August (Assumption), 27 September (French-speaking Community), 1 November (All Saints' Day), 11 November (Armistice Day), 15 November (German-speaking Community), 25 December (Christmas Day).

2006: 1 January (New Year's Day), 17 April (Easter Monday), 1 May (Labour Day), 25 May (Ascension Day), 5 June (Whit Monday), 11 July (Flemish-speaking Community), 21 July (Independence Day), 15 August (Assumption), 27 September (French-speaking Community), 1 November (All Saints' Day), 11 November (Armistice Day), 15 November (German-speaking Community), 25 December (Christmas Day).

Weights and Measures

The metric system is in force.

Statistical Survey

Source: mainly Institut National de Statistique, 44 rue de Louvain, 1000 Brussels; tel. (2) 548-62-11; fax (2) 548-63-67; e-mail info@statbel.mineco.fgov.be; internet www.statbel.fgov.be.

Area and Population

AREA, POPULATION AND DENSITY

Area (sq km)	30,528*
Population (census results)†	
1 March 1981	9,848,647
1 March 1991	
Males	4,875,982
Females	5,102,699
Total	9,978,681
Population (official estimates at 1 January)†	
2002	10,309,725
2003	10,355,844
2004	10,396,421
Density (per sq km) at 1 January 2004	340.6

* 11,787 sq miles.
† Population is *de jure*.

PROVINCES
(1 January 2003)

	Area (sq km)	Population	Density (per sq km)	Capital (with population)
Flemish region . .	13,521	5,995,553	443.4	
Antwerp . . .	2,867	1,661,119	579.4	Antwerp (452,474)*
Brabant (Flemish)	2,106	1,027,839	488.1	Leuven (90,406)
Flanders (East) .	2,982	1,370,136	459.5	Ghent (228,016)
Flanders (West) .	3,144	1,133,931	360.7	Brugge (116,811)
Limburg . . .	2,422	802,528	331.3	Hasselt (68,931)
Walloon region . .	16,845	3,368,250	200.0	
Brabant (Walloon)	1,091	358,012	328.0	Wavre (31,725)
Hainaut . . .	3,786	1,281,706	338.5	Mons (91,078)
Liège	3,862	1,025,842	265.6	Liège (184,303)
Luxembourg .	4,440	252,295	56.8	Arlon (25,569)
Namur	3,666	450,395	122.9	Namur (105,705)
Brussels (capital) .	162	992,041	6,123.7	—
Total	30,528	10,355,844	339.2	—

* Including Deurne and other suburbs.

PRINCIPAL TOWNS
(population at 1 January 2004)

Bruxelles (Brussel, Brussels—capital)	992,041*	Leuven (Louvain) .	89,777
Antwerpen (Anvers, Antwerp) . . .	455,148†	Mechelen (Malines) .	76,981
Gent (Gand, Ghent)	229,344	Aalst (Alost) . . .	76,852
Charleroi	200,608	La Louvière . . .	76,784
Liège (Luik) . . .	185,488	Kortrijk (Courtrai) .	73,984
Brugge (Bruges) . .	117,025	Hasselt	69,127
Namur (Namen) . .	106,213	Sint-Niklaas (Saint-Nicolas) . . .	68,820
Mons (Bergen) . .	91,185	Oostende (Ostende, Ostend) . . .	68,273

* Including Schaerbeek (population 110,253), Anderlecht (92,755) and other suburbs.
† Including Deurne and other suburbs.

BIRTHS, MARRIAGES AND DEATHS

	Registered live births		Registered marriages*		Registered deaths†	
	Number	Rate (per 1,000)	Number	Rate (per 1,000)	Number	Rate (per 1,000)
1996 . .	115,214	11.3	50,552	5.0	104,140	10.3
1997 . .	115,864	11.4	47,759	4.7	103,802	10.2
1998 . .	114,276	11.2	44,393	4.4	104,583	10.3
1999 . .	113,469	11.1	44,171	4.3	104,904	10.2
2000 . .	114,883	11.2	45,123	4.4	104,903	10.2
2001 . .	114,014	11.1	42,110	4.1	103,447	10.1
2002 . .	111,225	10.8	40,434	3.9	105,642	10.2
2003 . .	112,149	10.8	41,805	4.0	107,039	10.3

* Including marriages among Belgian armed forces stationed outside the country and alien armed forces in Belgium, unless performed by local foreign authority.
† Including Belgian armed forces stationed outside the country, but excluding alien armed forces stationed in Belgium.

Expectation of life (WHO estimates, years at birth): 78.4 (males 75.2; females 81.5) in 2002 (Source: WHO, *World Health Report*).

ECONOMICALLY ACTIVE POPULATION*
('000 persons aged 15 and over)

	2001	2002	2003
Agriculture, hunting and forestry .	65.4	68.7	71.4
Fishing	0.8	0.6	0.6
Mining and quarrying	6.7	6.8	5.8
Manufacturing	756.2	737.2	714.3
Electricity, gas and water supply .	30.9	30.5	32.1
Construction	260.2	260.1	259.1
Wholesale and retail trade . . .	554.4	582.9	560.3
Hotels and restaurants	129.5	139.0	132.9
Transport, storage and communications	325.5	313.4	311.7
Financial intermediation . . .	161.3	156.9	154.5
Real estate, renting and business activities	358.4	369.7	382.4
Public administration and defence.	392.5	395.1	397.1
Education	348.4	339.1	351.0
Health and social work	470.2	494.1	518.6
Other community, social and personal service activities . .	160.1	153.8	160.4
Private households with employed persons	11.4	10.6	9.6
Extra-territorial organizations and bodies	19.1	11.2	8.7
Total employed	4,051.2	4,069.8	4,070.4
Unemployed	286.4	332.1	364.3
Total labour force	4,337.6	4,401.9	4,434.7
Males	2,494.2	2,507.2	2,510.0
Females	1,843.3	1,894.7	1,924.7

* Includes professional armed forces, but excludes compulsory military service.

Source: ILO.

Health and Welfare

KEY INDICATORS

Total fertility rate (children per woman, 2002)	1.7
Under-5 mortality rate (per 1,000 live births, 2003) . . .	5
HIV/AIDS (% of persons aged 15–49, 2003)	0.2
Physicians (per 1,000 head, 2000)	3.9
Hospital beds (per 1,000 head, 1997)	7.2
Health expenditure (2001): US $ per head (PPP)	2,481
Health expenditure (2001): % of GDP	8.9
Health expenditure (2001): public (% of total)	71.7
Human Development Index (2002): ranking	6
Human Development Index (2002): value	0.942

For sources and definitions, see explanatory note on p. vi.

Agriculture
(Figures include totals for Luxembourg)

PRINCIPAL CROPS
('000 metric tons)

	2001	2002	2003
Wheat	1,457	1,675	1,640
Barley	369	343	271
Maize	461	531	555
Oats	34	36	42
Triticale (wheat-rye hybrid) . .	33	50	47
Potatoes	2,564	2,909	2,522
Sugar beet	5,614	6,537	6,450
Rapeseed	18	18	17
Cabbages	110	113	150*
Lettuce	95	85	85*
Spinach	43	77	75*
Tomatoes	233	253	235*
Cauliflowers	81	86	86*
Leeks and other alliaceous vegetables	152	160*	160*
Beans (green)	96	97	62
Peas (green)	60	74	80
Carrots	172	231	230*
Mushrooms	41	43	43*
Chicory roots	600	607	693
Other vegetables	520	468*	466*
Apples	337	349	274
Pears	89	171	142
Strawberries	41	40	40*

* FAO estimate.

Source: FAO.

LIVESTOCK
('000 head, year ending September)

	2001	2002	2003
Horses	31	31	33
Cattle	3,038	2,891	2,778
Pigs	6,834	6,735	6,539
Sheep	156	146	146
Goats	21	25	26
Rabbits*	180	180	n.a.
Chickens	39	38	32
Ducks*	40	40	n.a.
Geese*	10	10	n.a.
Turkeys*	250	200	200

* FAO estimate(s).

Source: FAO.

LIVESTOCK PRODUCTS
('000 metric tons)

	2001	2002	2003
Beef and veal	285	305	275
Mutton and lamb	5	3	4†
Pig meat	1,062	1,041	1,050†
Horse meat	6	4	4†
Poultry meat	387*	407†	407†
Cows' milk	3,694	3,469	3,500†
Butter	102*	120†	120†
Cheese	62*	55†	55†
Hen eggs	184	177*	179*
Cattle hides†	26	29	27

* Unofficial figure.
† FAO estimate(s).

Source: FAO.

Forestry

ROUNDWOOD REMOVALS

('000 cubic metres, excluding bark)

	2001	2002	2003
Sawlogs, veneer logs and logs for sleepers	2,370†	2,575†	2,690
Pulpwood	1,095†	1,175†	1,325
Other industrial wood	200†	200†	200*
Fuel wood*	550	550	550
Total	4,215	4,500	4,765

* FAO estimate(s).
† Unofficial estimate.
Source: FAO.

SAWNWOOD PRODUCTION

('000 cubic metres, including railway sleepers)

	2001	2002	2003
Coniferous (softwood)	1,075*	975	1,000
Broadleaved (hardwood)	200	200	215
Total	1,275	1,175	1,215

* Unofficial estimate(s).
Source: FAO.

Fishing

('000 metric tons, live weight)

	2000	2001	2002
Capture	29.8	30.2	29.0
European plaice	9.1	8.5	7.0
Lemon sole	1.1	1.1	1.1
Common sole	4.5	5.0	5.1
Atlantic cod	3.7	3.2	3.5
Angler (Monk)	1.0	1.4	1.3
Rays	1.2	1.5	1.7
Aquaculture	1.9	1.6	1.6
Total catch	31.7	31.8	30.6

Source: FAO.

Mining

('000 metric tons, unless otherwise indicated)

	2000	2001	2002
Barite (Barytes)*	30	30	30
Dolomite	3,500	3,500	3,500
Kaolin*	300	300	300
Limestone	30,000	30,000	30,000
Petit granite—Belgian Bluestone ('000 cubic metres)	916,200	916,200	916,200

* Estimates.
Source: US Geological Survey.

Industry

SELECTED PRODUCTS

('000 metric tons, unless otherwise indicated)

	1998	1999	2000
Wheat flour[1]	1,332	1,417	1,271
Raw sugar	994	926	1,070
Margarine	305	299	315
Beer ('000 hectolitres)	14,663	15,057	15,471
Cigarettes (million)	17,519	14,713	n.a.
Cotton yarn—pure and mixed (metric tons)	20,375	22,221	23,482
Woven cotton fabrics—pure and mixed (metric tons)[2]	39,347	38,093	37,317
Flax yarn (metric tons)[3]	3,027	2,867	2,697
Wool yarn—pure and mixed (metric tons)	14,889	14,434	14,959
Woven woollen fabrics—pure and mixed (metric tons)[2]	3,051	3,023	2,644
Woven rayon and acetate fabrics—pure and mixed (metric tons)[4]	173	196	196
Mechanical wood pulp[5]	207	196[6]	196[6]
Chemical and semi-chemical wood pulp[5]	225	235	235
Newsprint[5]	105	124[6]	124[6]
Other paper and paperboard[5]	1,726	1,603[6]	1,603[6]
Sulphuric acid (100%)	627	683	742
Nitric acid (100%)	56	56.0	56
Jet fuels	2,067	2,030	2,230
Motor spirit (petrol)	6,431	6,035	5,311
Naptha	1,524	1,608	2,026
Kerosene	128	98	87
White spirit	157	202	202
Distillate fuel oils	12,447	11,749	12,501
Residual fuel oil	6,958	5,821	6,659
Petroleum bitumen (asphalt)	797	767	553
Liquefied petroleum gas	598	593	764
Coke-oven coke	3,400	3,400	3,400
Cement	9,875	9,249	8,601
Pig-iron[1]	8,619	8,436	8,472
Crude steel[7]	11,617	10,931	11,635
Refined copper—unwrought[7]	623	388	423
Refined lead—unwrought[7]	111.9	103.2	118.0
Zinc—unwrought[7]	205	232	252
Tin—unwrought (metric tons)[7]	2,500	8,100	8,500
Passenger motor cars ('000)[8]	975	934	923
Commercial motor vehicles ('000)[8]	98	84	110
Electric energy (million kWh)	79,492.4	84,465	93,899

2001 ('000 metric tons): Wheat flour 1,339; Raw sugar 913[9]; Pig-iron 8; Refined copper—unwrought 423; Refined lead—unwrought 96; Zinc—unwrought 255; Tin—unwrought 8; Manufactured gas 375 (Source: UN, *Industrial Commodity Statistics Yearbook* and US Geological Survey).

2002 ('000 metric tons): Pig-iron 8; Refined copper—unwrought 425; Refined lead—unwrought 95; Zinc—unwrought 260; Tin—unwrought 5; Manufactured gas 375 (Source: UN, *Industrial Commodity Statistics Yearbook* and US Geological Survey).

[1] Source: UN, *Industrial Commodity Statistics Yearbook*.
[2] Including blankets and carpets.
[3] Including yarn made from tow.
[4] Including fabrics of natural silk and blankets and carpets of cellulosic fibres.
[5] Data for 1998 include production in Luxembourg. Source: FAO, *Yearbook of Forest Products*.
[6] Unofficial or FAO estimate.
[7] Source: US Geological Survey.
[8] Assembled wholly or mainly from imported parts.
[9] Includes production in Luxembourg.

Finance

CURRENCY AND EXCHANGE RATES

Monetary Units

100 cent = 1 euro (€).

Sterling and Dollar Equivalents (31 December 2004)

£1 sterling = 1.4180 euros;

US $1 = 0.7342 euros;

100 euros = £70.52 = $136.21.

Average Exchange Rate (euros per US $)

2002   1.0626

2003   0.8860

2004   0.8054

Note: The national currency was formerly the Belgian franc. From the introduction of the euro, with Belgian participation, on 1 January 1999, a fixed exchange rate of €1 = 40.3399 Belgian francs was in operation. Euro notes and coins were introduced on 1 January 2002. The euro and local currency circulated alongside each other until 28 February, after which the euro became the sole legal tender.

FEDERAL BUDGET
(€ million)

Revenue	2001	2002	2003
Fiscal and parafiscal receipts . .	69,463.5	69,084.6	69,449.7
Direct taxes	41,825.9	41,944.6	41,473.8
Households	33,400.9	33,477.7	33,117.9
Corporations	8,188.5	8,190.0	8,010.2
Other	236.5	276.9	345.7
Indirect taxes	26,179.7	25,667.1	26,108.8
Actual social contributions . .	1,324.4	1,389.3	1,768.7
Taxes on capital	133.5	83.6	98.4
Imputed social contributions . .	1,803.4	1,837.1	1,760.3
Other current revenue	2,943.3	2,641.1	2,543.6
Capital revenue	334.0	72.2	5,020.5
Total	74,544.2	73,635.0	78,774.1

Expenditure	2001	2002	2003
Current expenditure excluding interest charges	58,779.4	58,205.3	61,735.5
Compensation of employees . .	6,916.1	7,010.3	7,165.1
Intermediate consumption and paid taxes	2,236.8	2,251.9	2,299.3
Subsidies to companies . . .	1,419.5	1,336.4	1,637.5
Social benefits	5,989.0	6,130.5	6,556.0
Other current transfers . . .	42,218.0	41,476.2	44,077.6
Interest charges	15,596.5	14,630.5	13,617.6
Capital expenditure	2,208.3	1,343.5	2,380.5
Gross fixed capital formation .	309.0	497.8	359.2
Other net acquisitions of non-financial assets	−410.6	−156.9	16.0
Capital transfers	2,309.9	10,02.6	2,005.3
Total	76,584.2	74,179.3	77,733.6

General budget (€ million): *Total revenue:* 126,875.5 in 2001; 131,363.8 in 2002; 138,285.4 in 2003. *Total expenditure:* 125,428.6 in 2001; 131,182.9 in 2002; 137,451.0 in 2003.

INTERNATIONAL RESERVES
(US $ million at 31 December)

	2001	2002	2003
Gold*	2,294	2,843	3,459
IMF special drawing rights . .	472	554	645
Reserve position in IMF . . .	2,051	2,392	2,693
Foreign exchange	8,743	8,909	7,651
Total	13,560	14,698	14,448

* Valued at market-related prices.

Source: IMF, *International Financial Statistics*.

MONEY SUPPLY
(€ million at 31 December)

	2001	2002	2003
Currency outside banks . . .	9,081	12,715*	14,877*
Demand deposits at commercial banks	61,397	62,067	69,449

* Currency put into circulation by the Banque Nationale de Belgique was €7,887m. in 2002 and €3,807m. in 2003.

Source: IMF, *International Financial Statistics*.

COST OF LIVING
(Consumer Price Index; base: 1990 = 100)

	1999	2000	2001
Food (incl. beverages)	109.3	110.2	114.9
Fuel and light	106.7	118.9	122.3
Clothing (incl. footwear) . . .	116.5	117.2	118.3
Rent	132.0	133.9	136.5
All items (incl. others)	119.5	122.5	125.6

All items (base: 2000 = 100): 102.5 in 2001; 104.2 in 2002; 105.8 in 2003 (Source: IMF, *International Financial Statistics*).

NATIONAL ACCOUNTS

National Income and Product
(€ million at current prices)

	1999	2000	2001
Compensation of employees . .	121,294.4	126,847.0	133,381.1
Operating surplus	52,032.1	54,454.5	52,803.4
Domestic factor incomes . .	173,326.5	181,301.5	186,184.5
Consumption of fixed capital . .	33,428.9	35,815.8	38,240.1
Gross domestic product (GDP) at factor cost	206,755.4	217,117.3	224,424.6
Indirect taxes	33,191.0	34,767.2	34,592.0
Less Subsidies	4,314.4	4,415.7	4,734.2
GDP in purchasers' values . .	235,632.0	247,468.8	254,282.4
Factor income received from abroad	30,060.5	34,241.8	40,027.6
Less Factor income paid abroad .	24,037.3	27,374.2	33,697.9
Subsidies received from abroad .	857.6	694.2	733.6
Less Indirect taxes paid abroad .	2,186.2	2,395.1	2,476.5
Gross national product (GNP) .	240,326.6	252,635.5	258,869.2
Less Consumption of fixed capital	33,428.9	35,815.8	38,240.1
National income in market prices	206,897.8	216,819.7	220,629.1
Other current transfers from abroad	3,071.4	3,344.0	3,631.8
Less Other current transfers paid abroad	5,529.5	5,660.0	5,801.3
National disposable income .	204,439.6	214,503.7	218,459.6

Source: Service Statistiques financières et économiques, Banque Nationale de Belgique.

Expenditure on the Gross Domestic Product
(€ million at current prices)

	2001	2002	2003*
Government final consumption expenditure	55,091	58,056	60,681
Private final consumption expenditure	138,565	141,514	146,571
Increase in stocks	−1,098	−593	222
Gross fixed capital formation . .	53,091	51,558	52,537
Total domestic expenditure .	245,649	250,535	260,011
Exports of goods and services . .	217,799	218,020	220,460
Less Imports of goods and services	209,648	208,545	212,316
GDP in purchasers' values . .	253,800	260,011	268,154

* Estimates.

Source: Service Statistiques financières et économiques, Banque Nationale de Belgique.

Gross Domestic Product by Economic Activity
(€ million at current prices)

	1999	2000	2001
Agriculture, hunting and forestry .	2,826.7	3,082.0	3,354.4
Fishing	59.8	52.4	59.4
Mining and quarrying	337.2	350.2	346.8
Manufacturing	41,437.8	43,400.9	43,174.2
Electricity, gas and water supply .	5,859.0	5,997.4	5,942.3
Construction	10,794.3	11,501.6	11,879.8
Wholesale and retail trade; repair of motor vehicles, motorcycles and personal and household goods	25,538.8	26,222.3	27,617.2
Hotels and restaurants	3,519.8	3,789.3	3,867.0
Transport, storage and communications	15,021.7	15,568.7	16,307.3
Financial intermediation . . .	14,254.5	13,431.9	12,814.3
Real estate, renting and business activities*	47,069.2	50,611.9	53,298.3
Public administration and defence; compulsory social security . .	17,324.3	17,948.6	18,701.2
Education	14,035.9	14,501.0	15,094.7
Health and social work	13,952.3	15,004.1	16,289.5
Other community, social and personal service activities . .	5,414.4	5,657.2	5,804.8
Private households with employed persons	1,162.0	1,199.8	1,265.0
Sub-total	218,607.7	228,319.3	235,816.2
Less Financial intermediation services indirectly measured .	−8,792.9	−8,304.6	−8,446.7
GDP at basic prices	209,814.8	220,014.7	227,369.4
Taxes on products	28,569.2	30,113.2	29,728.7
Less Subsidies on products . . .	2,752.0	2,659.1	2,815.7
GDP in purchasers' values . .	235,632.0	247,468.8	254,282.4

* Including imputed rents of owner-occupied dwellings.

Source: Service Statistiques financières et économiques, Banque Nationale de Belgique.

BALANCE OF PAYMENTS
(US $ million)

	2001*	2002	2003
Exports of goods f.o.b.	163,498	168,192	204,074
Imports of goods f.o.b.	−159,790	−159,459	−196,909
Trade balance	3,707	8,734	7,165
Exports of services	50,314	37,776	44,296
Imports of services	−43,316	−35,727	−42,318
Balance on goods and services	10,705	10,783	9,143
Other income received	78,906	35,845	37,174
Other income paid	−75,999	−29,003	−30,330
Balance on goods, services and income	13,612	17,625	15,987
Current transfers received . . .	7,316	5,288	6,229
Current transfers paid	−11,535	−9,608	−12,850
Current balance	9,392	13,305	9,365
Capital account (net)	26	−661	−968
Direct investment abroad . . .	−86,092	−11,442	−39,594
Direct investment from abroad .	73,635	13,772	31,091
Portfolio investment assets . .	−125,068	−5,007	−2,795
Portfolio investment liabilities .	140,588	19,683	5,196
Financial derivatives assets .	−5,089	−3,864	−6,717
Financial derivatives liabilities .	942	1,921	3,568
Other investment assets . . .	−70,053	−44,556	−76,605
Other investment liabilities .	62,158	15,636	69,511
Net errors and omissions . . .	3	1,181	6,224
Overall balance	1,442	−32	−1,723

* Data refer to the Belgium-Luxembourg Economic Union and exclude transactions between the two countries.

Source: IMF, *International Financial Statistics.*

External Trade

PRINCIPAL COMMODITIES
(distribution by SITC, € million)

Imports c.i.f.	2000	2001	2002
Food and live animals . . .	12,867.2	13,905.3	14,224.2
Crude materials (inedible) except fuels	7,503.0	6,709.2	6,870.7
Mineral fuels, lubricants, etc.	17,077.2	17,209.5	16,570.3
Petroleum, petroleum products, etc.	13,272.2	12,836.3	12,047.2
Chemicals and related products	31,426.6	35,620.5	50,081.2
Organic chemicals	9,250.4	10,679.9	11,991.3
Medicinal and pharmaceutical products	6,072.0	9,327.1	22,252.1
Basic manufactures	39,445.6	37,952.0	38,747.3
Non-metallic mineral manufactures	15,733.5	14,778.0	15,909.1
Machinery and transport equipment	60,367.4	63,137.7	59,253.3
General industrial machinery, equipment and parts	6,855.2	6,990.4	6,549.5
Office machines and automatic data-processing machines . .	5,971.9	6,187.7	5,597.9
Electrical machinery, apparatus, etc.	14,729.0	14,369.0	7,565.1
Road vehicles (incl. air-cushion vehicles) and parts* . .	22,417.7	24,871.3	25,112.1
Miscellaneous manufactured articles	20,627.4	21,440.1	20,745.5
Clothing and accessories (excl. footwear)	5,227.7	5,597.4	5,575.7
Total (incl. others)	192,194.9	199,491.5	209,720.7

Exports f.o.b.	2000	2001	2002
Food and live animals . . .	15,931.0	17,143.0	17,375.9
Mineral fuels, lubricants, etc.	9,699.2	8,532.6	9,932.5
Petroleum, petroleum products, etc.	8,419.3	7,662.0	7,979.1
Chemicals and related products	41,504.1	44,856.8	61,713.3
Organic chemicals	9,236.7	9,399.3	13,500.4
Medicinal and pharmaceutical products	7,419.8	10,450.7	23,083.7
Plastics in primary forms . .	9,351.0	9,345.5	9,487.6
Basic manufactures	48,090.4	46,101.5	47,438.6
Textile yarn, fabrics, etc. . . .	6,833.0	6,787.3	6,602.0
Non-metallic mineral manufactures	17,214.0	15,953.8	17,529.4
Iron and steel	8,617.5	7,959.6	8,019.4
Machinery and transport equipment	61,165.2	66,416.1	63,558.7
General industrial machinery, equipment and parts	6,675.7	6,857.5	6,163.9
Electrical machinery, apparatus, etc.	13,260.2	13,720.6	11,657.5
Road vehicles (incl. air-cushion vehicles) and parts*	26,834.5	31,213.6	31,631.2
Miscellaneous manufactured articles	19,390.5	20,867.6	20,870.6
Total (incl. others)	203,953.2	212,538.5	228,561.7

* Data on parts exclude tyres, engines and electrical parts.

PRINCIPAL TRADING PARTNERS
(€ million)*

Imports c.i.f.	2001	2002	2003
China, People's Repub.	4,315.7	4,746.5	3,409.7
France†	26,867.0	26,409.3	24,781.1
Germany	32,427.6	36,228.0	28,258.6
Ireland	5,592.2	14,722.9	2,267.8
Israel	2,160.7	2,216.7	1,554.5
Italy	8,519.9	6,999.2	5,889.8
Japan	5,713.2	6,642.9	5,231.4
Netherlands	34,139.4	33,115.5	33,070.9
Norway	2,185.9	1,658.4	1,885.7
Spain	3,894.7	3,889.4	3,840.2
Sweden	4,656.0	4,567.3	4,234.5
United Kingdom	15,496.6	15,645.9	14,864.1
USA	13,940.0	13,809.7	9,979.3
Total (incl. others)	199,491.6	209,721.2	170,634.7

Exports f.o.b.	2001	2002	2003
Austria	2,307.1	2,395.1	1,956.8
France†	36,955.8	37,320.4	31,080.5
Germany	38,526.2	42,606.5	31,166.4
India	3,017.4	4,083.4	3,804.8
Israel	3,071.1	3,083.2	2,256.2
Italy	12,266.0	12,398.2	9,953.5
Japan	2,197.4	2,225.2	1,590.3
Luxembourg	4,176.3	4,118.5	3,969.5
Netherlands	25,892.9	26,677.8	23,196.2
Spain	8,203.9	8,282.1	7,393.8
Sweden	2,959.5	3,138.9	2,713.3
Switzerland	3,067.8	2,865.7	2,422.1
United Kingdom	21,375.7	21,975.0	16,113.2
USA	11,823.8	17,781.3	8,459.7
Total (incl. others)	212,538.7	228,596.2	179,896.4

* Imports by country of production; exports by country of last consignment.
† Including trade with Overseas Departments (French Guiana, Guadeloupe, Martinique and Réunion).

Transport

RAILWAYS
(traffic)

	1999	2000	2001
Passenger journeys ('000)	147,291	153,300	160,300
Passenger-km (million)	6,737	7,732	8,038
Freight carried ('000 metric tons)	59,149	61,279	57,050
Freight ton-km (million)	7,287	7,674	7,080

2003: Passenger journeys ('000) 168,300; Passenger-km (million) 8,265; Freight carried ('000 metric tons) 55 732; Freight ton-km (million) 7,293.
Source: SNCB Railways.

ROAD TRAFFIC
(motor vehicles in use)

	2000	2001	2002
Passenger cars	4,678,376	4,739,850	4,787,359
Buses and coaches	14,722	14,676	14,769
Lorries and vans	502,979	526,334	540,637
Road tractors	45,452	46,302	46,789
Motorcycles and mopeds	277,838	293,630	305,510

Source: IRF, *World Road Statistics*.

SHIPPING
Merchant Fleet
(registered at 31 December)

	2001	2002	2003
Number of vessels	185	188	222
Displacement ('000 grt)	151.0	186.7	1,392.9

Source: Lloyd's Register-Fairplay, *World Fleet Statistics*.

International Sea-borne Freight Traffic
(estimates, '000 metric tons)

	2001	2002	2003
Goods loaded	422,700	439,860	419,388
Goods unloaded	436,932	447,108	427,032

Source: UN, *Monthly Bulletin of Statistics*.

CIVIL AVIATION
(traffic)

	1999	2000	2001
Kilometres flown (million)	219	216	186
Passengers carried ('000)	9,965	10,738	8,489
Passenger-km ('000)	17,692	19,379	15,320
Ton-km ('000)	2,218	2,921	2,356

Tourism

TOURIST ARRIVALS BY COUNTRY OF ORIGIN*

Country of residence	2001	2002	2003
France	835,130	908,619	940,628
Germany	782,586	815,476	780,911
Italy	205,581	223,372	231,085
Japan	140,057	154,138	114,452
Netherlands	1,656,978	1,681,501	1,746,093
Spain	179,863	215,316	214,992
United Kingdom	1,253,550	1,250,274	1,195,123
USA	325,971	301,286	274,906
Total (incl. others)	6,451,513	11,067,755	11,072,079

* Non-residents staying in accommodation establishments.

Tourism receipts (US $ million): 6,592 in 2000; 6,903 in 2001; 6,892 in 2002.

Source: World Tourism Organization, mainly *Yearbook of Tourism Statistics*.

Communications Media

	2000	2001	2002
Television receivers ('000 in use)	5,500	n.a.	n.a.
Telephones ('000 main lines in use)	5,060.9	5,074.0	5,132.4
Mobile cellular telephones ('000 subscribers)	5,577.0	7,690.0	8,135.5
Personal computers ('000 in use)	3,500	3,500	2,500
Internet users ('000)	2,000	2,881	3,400

Source: International Telecommunication Union.

Facsimile machines ('000 in use): 180 in 1995; 190 in 1996.
Radio receivers ('000 in use): 8,000 in 1995; 8,050 in 1996; 8,075 in 1997.
Daily newspapers: 30 in 1996 (circulation 1,625,000).
Sources: mainly UN, *Statistical Yearbook*; UNESCO, *Statistical Yearbook*.

Education
(2002/03)

	Institutions		Students	
	French	Flemish	French	Flemish
Pre-primary	1,843	2,398	161,025	238,143
Primary	1,936	2,660	324,238	431,209
Secondary	607	1,304	359,809	435,781
Non-university higher education	144	64	79,242	99,661
University level	10	8	62,645	56,839

Teachers (2002/03): *French:* Pre-primary and primary 33,654; Secondary 45,001; Higher education 11,973. *Flemish:* Pre-primary and primary 55,791; Secondary 67,486; Higher education 14,481.

Directory

The Constitution

The Belgian Constitution has been considerably modified by amendments since its creation in 1831. Belgium is a constitutional monarchy. The central legislature consists of a bicameral Parliament (the Chamber of Representatives—Chambre des Représentants/Kamer van Volksvertegenwoordigers and the Senate—Sénat/Senaat). In July 1993 the Constitution was amended to provide for a federation of the largely autonomous regions of Brussels, Flanders and Wallonia and of the Flemish-, French- and German-speaking language communities. Article 1 of the Constitution states 'Belgium is a federal state which consists of communities and regions'. The three regions and three linguistic groups are represented by the following directly-elected legislative bodies: a combined administration for Flanders and the Flemish-speaking community, regional administrations for Wallonia and Brussels, and separate community administrations for French- and German-speakers. Each body is elected for a term of four years. The regional administrations have sole responsibility for the local economy, the environment, housing, transport and public works, while the language community administrations supervise education policy and culture. In addition, in June 2001 a constitutional amendment was passed by Parliament granting the regions greater responsibility for taxation and public expenditure, agriculture, and issues relating to foreign aid and trade.

ELECTORAL SYSTEM

Members of Parliament must be at least 25 years of age, and they are elected by secret ballot according to a system of proportional representation. Suffrage is universal for citizens of 18 years or over, and voting is compulsory.

The Chamber of Representatives consists of 150 members, who are elected for four years unless the Chamber is dissolved before that time has elapsed. The Senate comprises 71 normal members, of whom 40 are directly elected, usually at intervals of four years, 21 are appointed by the legislative bodies of the three language communities (10 each from the Flemish- and French-speaking communities and one from the German-speaking community), and 10 are co-opted by the elected members. Children of the King are entitled to honorary membership of the Senate from 18 years of age and acquire voting rights at the age of 21.

THE CROWN

The King has the right to veto legislation, but, in practice, he does not exercise it. The King is nominally the supreme head of the executive, but, in fact, he exercises his control through the Council of Ministers, which is responsible for all acts of government to the Chamber of Representatives. According to the Constitution, the King appoints his own ministers, but in practice, since they are responsible to the Chamber of Representatives and need its confidence, they are generally the choice of the Representatives. Similarly, the royal initiative is in the control of the ministry.

LEGISLATION

Legislation is introduced either by the federal Government or the members in the two Houses, and as the party complexion of both Houses is generally almost the same, measures passed by the Chamber of Representatives are usually passed by the Senate. Each House elects its own President at the beginning of the session, who acts as an impartial Speaker, although he is a party nominee. The Houses elect their own committees, through which all legislation passes. They are so well organized that through them the Legislature has considerable power of control over the Council of Ministers. Nevertheless, according to the Constitution (Article 68), certain treaties must be communicated to the Chamber only as soon as the 'interest and safety of the State permit'. Further, the Government possesses an important power of dissolution which it uses; a most unusual feature is that it may be applied to either House separately or to both together (Article 71).

Revision of the Constitution is to be first settled by an ordinary majority vote of both Houses, specifying the article to be amended. The Houses are then automatically dissolved. The new Chambers thereupon determine the amendments to be made, with the provision that in each House the presence of two-thirds of the members is necessary for a quorum, and a two-thirds' majority of those voting is required.

The Government

HEAD OF STATE

King of the Belgians: HM King ALBERT II (succeeded to the throne 9 August 1993).

THE COUNCIL OF MINISTERS
(April 2005)

The coalition comprised the Vlaamse Liberalen en Demokraten—Partij van de Burger (VLD), the Mouvement Réformateur (MR—which included the Parti Réformateur Libéral—PRL), the Parti Socialiste (PS), the Sociaal Progressief Alternatief (SP.A) and Spirit.

Prime Minister: GUY VERHOFSTADT (VLD).

Deputy Prime Minister and Minister of Justice: LAURETTE ONKELINX (PS).

Deputy Prime Minister and Minister for the Budget and Public Enterprise: JOHAN VANDE LANOTTE (SP.A).

Deputy Prime Minister and Minister of the Interior: PATRICK DEWAEL (VLD).

Deputy Prime Minister and Minister of Finance: DIDIER REYNDERS (MR).

Minister of Foreign Affairs: KAREL DE GUCHT (VLD).

Minister of Defence: ANDRÉ FLAHAUT (PS).

Minister of Development Co-operation: ARMAND DE DECKER.

Minister of Social Affairs and Public Health: RUDY DEMOTTE (PS).

Minister for the Economy, Energy, Foreign Trade and Science Policy: MARC VERWILGHEN (VLD).

Minister of Transport: RENAAT LANDUYT.

Minister for the Civil Service, Social Integration, Urban Policy and Equal Opportunities: CHRISTIAN DUPONT.

Minister for the Self-employed and Agriculture: SABINE LARUELLE (MR).

Minister of Employment: FREYA VAN DEN BOSSCHE (SP.A).

Minister for the Environment and Pensions: BRUNO TOBBACK.

MINISTRIES

Office of the Prime Minister: 16 rue de la Loi, 1000 Brussels; tel. (2) 501-02-11; fax (2) 512-69-53; internet verhofstadt.fgov.be.

Ministry of the Budget and Public Enterprise: 180 rue Royale, 1000 Brussels; tel. (2) 210-19-11; fax (2) 217-33-28; e-mail info@johanvandelanotte.be; internet www.begroting.be.

Ministry of the Civil Service, Social Integration, Urban Policy and Equal Opportunities: Copernicus Building, 6th–7th Floors, 51 rue de la Loi, 1040 Brussels; tel. (2) 790-57-11; fax (2) 790-57-98; e-mail marie.arena@p-o.be; internet www.p-o.be.

Ministry of Defence: 8 rue Lambermont, 1000 Brussels; tel. (2) 550-28-11; fax (2) 550-29-19; e-mail cabinet@mod.mil.be; internet www.mil.be.

Ministry of the Economy, Energy and Science Policy: 23 square de Meeûs, 1000 Brussels; tel. (2) 506-51-11; fax (2) 513-29-54; internet mineco.fgov.be.

Ministry of Employment and Pensions: Maria-Theresiastraat 1–3, 1000 Brussels; tel. (2) 549-09-20; e-mail info@work.fed.be; internet www.freyaweb.be.

Ministry of the Environment, Consumer Protection and Sustainable Development: Quartier Esplanade, E13.03, 1010 Brussels; tel. (2) 214-43-21; e-mail fonctionnaire-information@health.fgov.be; internet www.health.fgov.be.

Ministry of Finance: 12 rue de la Loi, 1000 Brussels; tel. (2) 233-81-11; fax (2) 233-80-03; e-mail contact@ckfin.minfin.be; internet www.minfin.fgov.be.

Ministry of Foreign Affairs, Foreign Trade and Development Co-operation: 15 rue des Petits Carmes, 1000 Brussels; tel. (2) 501-81-11; fax (2) 511-63-85; e-mail info@diplobel.fed.be; internet www.diplomatie.be.

Ministry of the Interior: 60–62 rue Royale, 1000 Brussels; tel. (2) 504-85-11; fax (2) 504-85-00; e-mail patrick.dewael@ibz.fgov.be; internet www.ibz.be.

Ministry of Justice: rue de Commerce, 1040 Brussels; tel. (2) 233-51-11; fax (2) 230-10-67; internet www.just.fgov.be.

Ministry of Social Affairs and Public Health: 7 ave des Arts, 1210 Brussels; tel. (2) 220-20-11; fax (2) 220-20-67; e-mail cabinet .demotte@minsoc.fed.be.

Ministry of Transport and Social Economy: 104 rue d'Arlon, 1040 Brussels; tel. (2) 233-15-17; fax (2) 233-15-04; e-mail info@ mobilit.fgov.be ; internet www.mobilit.fgov.be.

Legislature

CHAMBRE DES REPRÉSENTANTS/KAMER VAN VOLKSVERTEGENWOORDIGERS
(Chamber of Representatives)

General Election, 18 May 2003

	Votes cast	% of votes	Seats
VLD	1,009,223	15.4	25
PS	855,992	13.0	25
MR	748,954	11.4	24
SP.A-Spirit	979,750	14.9	23
CD&V	870,749	13.2	21
Vlaams Blok	761,407	11.6	18
CDH	359,660	5.5	8
Ecolo	201,123	3.1	4
Nieuw-Vlaamse Alliantie	201,399	3.1	1
FN	—	2.0	1
Total (incl. others)	6,572,198	100.0	150

SÉNAT/SENAAT

General Election, 18 May 2003

	Votes cast	% of votes	Seats
SP.A-Spirit	1,013,560	15.5	7
VLD	1,007,868	15.4	7
PS	840,908	12.8	6
CD&V	832,849	12.7	6
MR	795,763	12.1	5
Vlaams Blok	741,940	11.3	5
CDH	362,708	5.5	2
Ecolo	208,868	3.2	1
FN	—	2.2	1
Total (incl. others)	6,551,519	100.0	40

In addition, the Senate has 21 members appointed by the legislative bodies of the three language communities and 10 members co-opted by the elected members. Children of the King are entitled to honorary membership of the Senate from 18 years of age and acquire voting rights at the age of 21.

Advisory Councils

Conseil Central de l'Economie/Centrale Raad voor het Bedrijfsleven: 17–21 ave de la Joyeuse entrée, 1040 Brussels; tel. (2) 233-88-11; fax (2) 233-89-12; e-mail mail@ccecrb.fgov.be; internet www.ccecrb.fgov.be; f. 1948; representative and consultative body; advises the authorities on economic issues; 50 mems; Pres. Baron ROBERT TOLLET.

Conseil d'Etat/Raad van Staat: 33 rue de la Science, 1040 Brussels; tel. (2) 234-96-11; e-mail info@raadvst-consetat.be; internet www.raadvst-consetat.be; f. 1946; advisory body on legislative and regulatory matters; supreme administrative court; hears complaints against the actions of the legislature; 38 mems; Pres. W. DEROOVER.

Regional and Community Administrations

Belgium is a federal state, and considerable power has been devolved to the regional administrations of Brussels, Wallonia and Flanders, and to the French-, German- and Flemish-speaking communities. The regional authorities have sole responsibility for the environment, housing, transport and public works, and for certain aspects of social welfare, while the community administrations are primarily responsible for cultural affairs and for education. In addition, in June 2001 Parliament granted the regions greater

responsibility for taxation and public expenditure, agriculture, and matters relating to foreign aid and trade. The administrations of Flanders and of the Flemish-speaking community are homologous.

REGION OF FLANDERS AND THE FLEMISH-SPEAKING COMMUNITY

Minister-President: YVES LETERME (CD&V).

Vlaams Parlement (Flemish Parliament): Leuvensweg 86, 1011 Brussels; tel. (2) 552-45-45; fax (2) 552-45-00; e-mail informatheek@ vlaamsparlement.be; internet www.vlaamsparlement.be; f. 1980; 124 mems.

Vlaamse Overheid (Flemish Authority): Boudewijnlaan 30, 1000 Brussels; tel. (2) 553-29-11; fax (2) 553-29-05; e-mail info@ vlaanderen.be; internet www.vlaanderen.be.

REGION OF WALLONIA

Minister-President: JEAN-CLAUDE VAN CAUWENBERGHE (PS).

Le Parlement Wallon (Walloon Parliament): 24 rue Saint-Nicolas, 5000 Namur; tel. (81) 23-10-36; fax (2) 23-12-20; e-mail presse@ parlement-wallon.be; internet www.parlement-wallon.be; elects Government of Wallonia; 75 mems.

Gouvernement Wallon (Walloon Government): 1 Place de la Wallonie, Bât 2, 5100 Namur; tel. (81) 33-31-60; fax (81) 33-31-66; e-mail vancau@gov.wallonie.be; internet www.wallonie.be; 9 mems.

REGION OF BRUSSELS-CAPITAL

Minister-President: CHARLES PICQUÉ (PS).

Parlement de la Région de Bruxelles-Capitale/Brussels Hoofdstedelijk Parlement (Parliament of the Region of Brussels-Capital): 1005 Brussels; tel. (2) 549-62-11; fax (2) 549-62-12; e-mail Parlement@parlbru.irisnet.be; internet www.parlbru.irisnet.be.

Gouvernement de la Région de Bruxelles-Capitale/Brusselse Hoofdstedelijke Regering (Government of Brussels-Capital): 7–9 rue Ducale, 1000 Brussels; tel. (2) 506-32-11; fax (2) 514-40-22; internet www.bruxelles.irisnet.be.

FRENCH-SPEAKING COMMUNITY

Minister-President: MARIE ARENA (PRL).

Parlement de la Communauté française de Belgique (Parliament of the French-speaking Community): 6 rue de la Loi, 1000 Brussels; tel. (2) 506-38-11; fax (2) 506-38-08; internet www.pcf.be; comprises the 75 mems of the Walloon Parliament and 19 French-speaking mems of the Council of the Region of Brussels-Capital; 94 mems.

Gouvernement de la Communauté française Wallonie-Bruxelles (Government of the French-speaking Community): 15–17 place Surlet de Chokier, 1000 Brussels; tel. (2) 227-32-11; fax (2) 227-33-53; internet www.gouvernement-francophone.be.

GERMAN-SPEAKING COMMUNITY

Minister-President: KARL-HEINZ LAMBERTZ (PS).

Rat der Deutschsprachigen Gemeinschaft Belgiens (Council of the German-speaking Community): 8 Kaperberg, 4700 Eupen; tel. (87) 59-07-20; fax (87) 59-07-30; e-mail info@dgparlament.be; internet www.dgparlament.be.

Regierung der Deutschsprachigen Gemeinschaft Belgiens (Government of the German-speaking Community): 32 Klötzerbahn, 4700 Eupen; tel. (87) 59-64-00; fax (87) 74-02-58; e-mail kab .lambertz@dgov.be; internet www.dglive.be; Pres. LUDWIG SIQUET.

Political Organizations

Le Centre Démocrate Humaniste (CDH) (Humanist Democrats): 41 rue des Deux-Eglises, 1000 Brussels; tel. (2) 238-01-11; fax (2) 238-01-29 ; e-mail info@lecdh.be; internet www.lecdh.be; f. 1945; founded as the Parti Social Chrétien/Christelijke Volkspartij (PSC/CVP), the PSC separated from the CVP by 1972, name changed as above in May 2002; Pres. JOËLLE MILQUET; Vice-Pres. MELCHIOR WATHELET.

Christen-Democratisch en Vlaams Partij (CD&V): 89 Wetstraat, 1040 Brussels; tel. (2) 238-38-11; fax (2) 230-43-60; e-mail inform@cdenv.be; internet www.cdenv.be; f. 1945; founded as Parti Social Chrétien/Christelijke Volkspartij (PSC/CVP), CVP separated from PSC by 1972, renamed as above in 2001; Chair. JO VANDEURZEN.

Ecologistes Confédérés pour l'Organisation des Luttes Originales (Ecolo) (Ecologist Party—French-speaking): ave de Marlagne 52, 5000 Namur; tel. (8) 122-78-71; fax (8) 123-06-03; e-mail ecolo.sf@ecolo.be; internet www.ecolo.be; Fed. Secs JEAN-MICHEL JAVAUX, ISABELLE DURANT, CLAUDE BROUIR.

Front National (FN): 12 clos du Parnasse, 1050 Brussels; tel. (2) 511-75-77; e-mail daniel.feret@frontnational.be; internet www .frontnational.be; f. 1985; extreme right-wing nationalist party; Pres. DANIEL FÉRET.

Groen! (Green!) (Ecologist Party—Flemish-speaking): Sergeant De Bruynestraat 78–82, 1070 Anderlecht; tel. (2) 219-19-19; fax (2) 223-10-90; e-mail info@groen.be ; internet www.groen.be; f. 1982; fmrly Anders Gaan Leven (Agalev), name changed as above in November 2003; Chair. VERA DUA.

Mouvement Réformateur (MR): 39 rue de Naples, 1050 Brussels; tel. (2) 500-35-43; fax (2) 500-35-42; e-mail mr@mr.be; internet www .mr.be; f. 2002; Pres. ANTOINE DUQUESNE.

Association of the following parties:

Front Démocratique des Francophones (FDF) (French-speaking Democratic Front): 127 chaussée de Charleroi, 1060 Brussels; tel. (2) 538-83-20; fax (2) 539-36-50; e-mail fdf@imaginet .be; internet www.fdf.be; f. 1964; aims to preserve the French character of Brussels; Pres. OLIVIER MAINGAIN; Sec.-Gen. CAROLINE PERSOONS.

Mouvement des Citoyens pour le Changement (MCC): 50 rue de la Vallée, 1000 Brussels; tel. (2) 642-29-99; fax (2) 642-29-90; e-mail info@lemcc.be; internet www.lemcc.be; Pres. NATHALIE DE T'SERCLAES.

Parti Réformateur Libéral (PRL) (Liberal Party—French-speaking wing): 41 rue de Naples, 1050 Brussels; tel. (2) 500-35-11; fax (2) 500-35-00; e-mail prl@prl.be; internet www.prl.be; f. 1846 as Parti Libéral; Pres. ANTOINE DUQUESNE; 50,000 mems.

Partei für Freiheit und Fortschritt (PFF) (German-speaking wing of PRL): 11A Kehrweg, 4700 Eupen; e-mail pff@skynet.be; internet www.pff.be; Pres. FERDEL SCHRÖDER.

Nieuw-Vlaamse Alliantie (N-VA) (New-Flemish Alliance): 12 Barrikadenplein, 1000 Brussels; tel. (2) 219-49-30; fax (2) 217-35-10; e-mail info@n-va.be; internet www.n-va.be; f. 1954 as Volksunie—Vlaamse Vrije Democraten, name changed, as above, 2001; Flemish nationalist party supporting national and European federalism; Chair. KOEN KENNIA; Sec. KRIS VAN DIJCK; 11,000 mems.

Partei der Deutschsprachigen Belgier (PJU-PDB) (Party of German-speaking Belgians): 6 Kaperberg, 4700 Eupen; tel. (87) 55-59-87; fax (87) 55-59-84; internet www.pju-pdb.be; f. 1971; promotes equality for the German-speaking minority; Pres. GERHARD PALM.

Parti Communiste (PC) (Communist Party): 162 rue du Midi, 1000 Brussels; tel. (2) 503-35-80; fax (2) 511-34-96; e-mail parti .communiste@skynet.be; f. 1921 as Parti Communiste de Belgique—Kommunistische Partij van België, name changed 1990; Pres. PIERRE BEAUVOIS; 5,000 mems.

Parti Humaniste de Belgique: 131 rue du Noyer, 1000 Brussels; tel. (2) 427-71-43; fax (2) 426-03-78; e-mail ph_hp_belgium@yahoo .fr; internet parti.humaniste.be; f. 1994; promotes social equality and human rights.

Parti Socialiste (PS) (Socialist Party—French-speaking wing): Maison du PS, 13 blvd de l'Empereur, 1000 Brussels; tel. (2) 548-32-11; fax (2) 548-33-80; e-mail secretariat@ps.be; internet www.ps.be; f. 1885 as the Parti Ouvrier Belge; split from the Flemish wing 1979; Pres. ELIO DI RUPO; Sec. JEAN-POL BARAS.

Partij van de Arbeid van België (PvdA)/Parti du Travail de Belgique (PTB) (Worker's Party of Belgium): 171 blvd M. Lemonnier, 1000 Brussels; tel. (2) 504-01-10; fax (2) 513-98-31; e-mail wpb@wpb.be; internet www.wpb.be; f. 1979; Marxist-Leninist; Chair. LUDO MARTENS.

Rassemblement Wallonie-France (RWF-RBF) (Wallonia-France Union): POB 19, 4910 Theux; e-mail rwf@rwf.be; internet www.rwf.be; f. 1999 by amalgamation of the Rassemblement Wallon (f. 1968), the Alliance Démocratique Wallonne and the Mouvement Wallon pour le Retour à la France; promotes the union of Wallonia with France; Pres. CLAUDE THAYSE.

Sociaal Progressief Alternatief (SP.A) (Socialist Party—Flemish wing): 105/37 Grasmarkt, 1000 Brussels; tel. (2) 552-02-00; fax (2) 552-02-55; e-mail info@s-p-a.be; internet www.s-p-a.be; f. 1885; fmrly Socialistische Partij, renamed as above in 2001; Chair. STEVE STEVAERT; Sec. ALAIN ANDRÉ.

Spirit (Sociaal, Progressief, Internationaal, Regionalistisch, Integraal-democratisch en Toekomstgericht): Woeringenstraat 19, 1000 Brussels; tel. (2) 513-20-63; fax (2) 512-85-75; e-mail info@meerspirit .be; internet www.meerspirit.be; Chair. GEERD LAMBERT.

Vlaams Belang (Flemish Interest): 8 Madouplein, bus 9, 1210 Brussels; tel. (2) 219-60-09; fax (2) 219-52-75; e-mail info@ vlaamsbelang.org; internet www.vlaamsbelang.org; f. 1979 as

Vlaams Blok as a breakaway party from the Volksunie; name changed as above Nov. 2004; advocates Flemish separatism and is anti-immigration; Chair. FRANK VANHECKE; Chief Officer LUK VAN NIEUWENHUYSEN.

Vlaamse Liberalen en Demokraten (VLD) (Flemish Liberals and Democrats—Liberal Party—Flemish-speaking wing): 34 Melsensstraat, 1000 Brussels; tel. (2) 549-00-20; fax (2) 512-60-25; e-mail vld@vld.be; internet www.vld.be; f. 1961 as Partij voor Vrijheid en Vooruitgang; name changed, as above, 1992; Pres. BART SOMERS; Sec.-Gen. SOFIE STAELRAEVE; 72,000 mems.

Diplomatic Representation

EMBASSIES IN BELGIUM

Afghanistan: 61 ave de Wolvendael, 1180 Uccle; tel. (2) 761-31-66; fax (2) 761-31-67; e-mail ambassade.afghanistan@skynet.be; Ambassador HOMAYOUN TANDAR.

Albania: 30 rue Tenbosch ,1000 Brussels; tel. (2) 640-34-45; fax (2) 640-31-77; e-mail amba.brux@skynet.be; Ambassador ARTUR KUKO.

Algeria: 207 ave Molière, 1060 Brussels; tel. (2) 343-50-78; fax (2) 343-51-68; internet www.algerian-embassy.be; Ambassador HALIM BENATTALLAH.

Andorra: 10 rue de la Montagne, 1000 Brussels; tel. (2) 513-28-06; fax (2) 513-07-41; e-mail meritxell.mateu@andorra.be; internet www .andorra.be; Ambassador MERITXELL MATEU.

Angola: 182 rue Franz Merjay, 1050 Brussels; tel. (2) 346-18-72; fax (2) 344-08-94; e-mail angola.embassy.brussels@skynet.be; Ambassador TOTO DIAKENZA SERAO.

Argentina: 225 ave Louise, bte 3, 1050 Brussels; tel. (2) 647-78-12; fax (2) 647-93-19; e-mail info@embargentina.be; Ambassador GUILLERMO MARCOS JACOVELLA.

Armenia: 157 rue Franz Merjay, 1050 Brussels; tel. (2) 348-44-00; fax (2) 348-44-01; e-mail armembel@tiscali.be; internet www .armenian-embassy.be; Ambassador VIGEN TCHITETCHIAN.

Australia: 6–8 rue Guimard, 1040 Brussels; tel. (2) 286-05-00; fax (2) 230-68-02; e-mail austemb.brussels@dfat.gov.au; internet www .austemb.be; Ambassador PETER GREY.

Austria: 5 place du Champs de Mars, BP 5, 1050 Brussels; tel. (2) 289-07-00; fax (2) 513-66-41; e-mail bruessel-ob@bmaa.gv.at; Ambassador FRANZ CEDE.

Azerbaijan: 464 ave Molière, 1050 Brussels; tel. (2) 345-26-60; fax (2) 345-91-58; e-mail embassy@azerbaijan.be; internet www .azerbaijan.be; Ambassador ARIF MAMEDOV.

Bangladesh: 29–31 rue Jacques Jordaens, 1000 Brussels; tel. (2) 640-55-00; fax (2) 646-59-98; e-mail bdootbrussels@freegates.be; Ambassador SYED MADUD ALI.

Barbados: 100 ave F. D. Roosevelt, 1050 Brussels; tel. (2) 732-17-37; fax (2) 732-32-66; e-mail brussels@foreign.gov.bb; internet www .foreign.gov.bb; Ambassador ERROL HUMPHREY.

Belarus: 192 ave Molière, 1050 Brussels; tel. (2) 340-02-70; fax (2) 340-02-87; e-mail embassy@belembassy.org.be; internet www .belembassy.org; Chargé d'affaires a.i. IGOR FISENKO.

Belize: 136 blvd Brand Witlock, 1200 Brussels; tel. (2) 732-62-04; fax (2) 732-62-46; e-mail embel.bru@pophost.eunet.be; Ambassador YVONNE HYDE.

Benin: 5 ave de l'Observatoire, 1180 Brussels; tel. (2) 374-91-92; fax (2) 375-83-26; e-mail ambassade.du.benin@skynet.be; Ambassador EULOGE HINVI.

Bolivia: 176 ave Louise, bte 6, 1050 Brussels; tel. (2) 627-00-10; fax (2) 647-47-82; e-mail embajada.bolivia@embolbrus.be; internet www .embolbrus.be; Chargé d'affaires a.i. ARTURO SUAREZ VARGAS.

Bosnia and Herzegovina: 34 rue Tenbosch, 1000 Brussels; tel. (2) 644-20-08; fax (2) 644-16-98; e-mail bh-mission-07@skynet.be; Ambassador ZDENKO MARTINOVIĆ.

Botswana: 169 ave de Tervueren, 1150 Brussels; tel. (2) 735-20-70; fax (2) 735-63-18; e-mail embasofbotswana@yahoo.co.uk; internet www.gov.bw; Ambassador SASARA CHASALA GEORGE.

Brazil: 350 ave Louise, bte 5, 1050 Brussels; tel. (2) 640-20-15; fax (2) 640-81-34; e-mail brasbruxelas@beon.be; Ambassador JERÓNIMO MOSCARDO.

Brunei: 238 ave F. D. Roosevelt, 1050 Brussels; tel. (2) 675-08-78; fax (2) 672-93-58; e-mail kedutaan-brunei.brussels@skynet.be; Ambassador Dato' YUSOFF HAMID.

Bulgaria: 58 ave de Hamoir, 1180 Brussels; tel. (2) 374-59-63; fax (2) 375-84-94; e-mail embassy@bulgaria.be; Ambassador EMIL VALEV.

Burkina Faso: 16 place Guy d'Arezzo, 1180 Brussels; tel. (2) 345-99-12; fax (2) 345-06-12; e-mail ambassade.burkina@skynet.be; internet www.ambassadeduburkina.be; Ambassador KADRÉ DÉSIRÉ OUEDRAOGO.

Burundi: 46 square Marie-Louise, 1000 Brussels; tel. (2) 230-45-35; fax (2) 230-78-83; e-mail ambassade.burundi@skynet.be; Ambassador FERDINAND NYABENDA.

Cameroon: 131–133 ave Brugmann, 1190 Brussels; tel. (2) 345-18-70; fax (2) 344-57-35; Ambassador ISABELLE BASSONG.

Canada: 2 ave de Tervueren, 1040 Brussels; tel. (2) 741-06-11; fax (2) 741-06-43; e-mail bru@dfait-maeci.gc.ca; internet www.dfait-maeci.gc.ca/brussels; Ambassador JOHN MCNEE.

Cape Verde: 29 ave Jeanne, 1050 Brussels; tel. (2) 646-62-70; fax (2) 646-33-85; e-mail emb.caboverde@skynet.be; Ambassador FERNANDO WAHNON FERREIRA.

Central African Republic: 416 blvd Lambermont, 1030 Brussels; tel. (2) 242-28-80; fax (2) 215-13-11; Ambassador ARMAND-GUY ZOUNGUERE-SOKAMBI.

Chad: 52 blvd Lambermont, 1030 Brussels; tel. (2) 215-19-75; fax (2) 216-35-26; e-mail ambassade.tchad@chello.be; Ambassador ABDERAHIM Y. NDIAYE.

Chile: 40 rue Montoyer, 1000 Brussels; tel. (2) 280-16-20; fax (2) 280-14-81; e-mail embachile.belgica@skynet.be; internet www.embachile.be; Ambassador RICARDO BRODSKY BAUDET.

China, People's Republic: 463 ave de Tervuren, 1160 Brussels; tel. (2) 771-14-97; fax (2) 779-28-95; internet www.chinaembassy-org.be; e-mail bangongshi@skynet.be; Ambassador ZHANG QIYUE.

Colombia: 96A ave F. D. Roosevelt, 1050 Brussels; tel. (2) 649-56-79; fax (2) 646-54-91; e-mail colombia@emcolbru.org; internet www.emcolbru.org; Ambassador NICHOLAS ECHAVARRIA MESA.

Congo, Democratic Republic: 30 rue Marie de Bourgogne, 1000 Brussels; tel. (2) 213-49-81; fax (2) 213-49-95; e-mail chefdemission@amba-rdcongo.be; internet www.amba-rdcongo.be; Ambassador JEAN PIERRE MUTAMBA TSHAMPANGA.

Congo, Republic: 16–18 ave F. D. Roosevelt, 1050 Brussels; tel. (2) 648-38-56; fax (2) 648-42-13; e-mail ambassade.congobrazza@skynet.be; Ambassador JACQUES OBIA.

Costa Rica: 489 ave Louise, bte 13, 1050 Brussels; tel. (2) 640-55-41; fax (2) 648-31-92; e-mail ambcrbel@coditel.net; Ambassador MARÍA SALVADORA ORTÍZ ORTÍZ.

Côte d'Ivoire: 234 ave F. D. Roosevelt, 1050 Brussels; tel. (2) 672-23-57; fax (2) 672-04-91; Ambassador MARIE GOSSET.

Croatia: ave Louise 425, 1050 Brussels; tel. (2) 639-20-36; fax (2) 512-03-38; e-mail croemb.bruxelles@mvp.kr; Ambassador LJERKA ALAJBEG.

Cuba: 77 rue Roberts-Jones, 1180 Brussels; tel. (2) 343-00-20; fax (2) 344-96-91; e-mail mision@embacuba.be; Ambassador RODRIGO MALMIERCA DIAZ.

Cyprus: 51 rue de la Vallée, 1000 Brussels; tel. (2) 650-06-10; fax (2) 650-06-20; e-mail ambassade.cyprus@skynet.be; Ambassador KALLIOPI AVRAAM.

Czech Republic: 154 ave Adolphe Buyl,1050 Brussels; tel. (2) 641-89-30; fax (2) 640-77-94; e-mail brussels@embassy.mzv.cz; internet www.mzv.cz/brussels; Ambassador JIŘÍ HAVLÍK.

Denmark: 73 rue d'Arlon, 1040 Brussels; tel. (2) 233-09-00; fax (2) 233-09-30; e-mail bruamb@um.dk; internet www.ambbruxelles.um.dk; Ambassador KARSTEN PETERSEN.

Djibouti: 204 ave F. D. Roosevelt, 1050 Brussels; tel. (2) 347-69-67; fax (2) 347-69-63; e-mail amb_djib@yahoo.fr; Ambassador MOHAMMED MOUSSA CHEHEM.

Dominican Republic: 12 ave Bel Air, 1180 Brussels; tel. (2) 346-49-35; fax (2) 346-51-52; Ambassador CLARA JOSELYN QUIÑONES DE LONGO.

Eastern Caribbean States: 42 rue de Livourne, 1000 Brussels; tel. (2) 534-26-11; fax (2) 539-40-09; e-mail ecs.embassies@skynet.be; internet www.caribisles.org; Ambassador GEORGE RANDOLPH EARLE BULLEN.

Ecuador: 363 ave Louise, 1050 Brussels; tel. (2) 644-30-50; fax (2) 644-28-13; e-mail equateur@skynet.be; Ambassador MENTOR VILLAGOMEZ.

Egypt: 19 ave de l'Uruguay, 1000 Brussels; tel. (2) 663-58-00; fax (2) 675-58-88; e-mail embassy.egypt@skynet.be; Ambassador MAHMOUD KAREM MAHMOUD.

El Salvador: 171 ave de Tervueren, 1150 Brussels; tel. (2) 733-04-85; fax (2) 735-02-11; Ambassador HÉCTOR GONZÁLEZ URRUTIA.

Equatorial Guinea: Jupiterlaan 17, 1190 Brussels; tel. (2) 346-25-09; fax (2) 346-33-09; Ambassador VICTORINO OBIANG MAYE.

Eritrea: Wolvendaellaan 15–17, 1180 Brussels; tel. (2) 374-44-34; fax (2) 372-07-30; e-mail andatw@hotmail.com; Ambassador ANDERBRHAN WELDEGIORGIS.

Estonia: 1 ave Isidore Gérard, 1160 Brussels; tel. (2) 770-71-93; fax (2) 779-28-17; e-mail saatkond@estemb.be; internet www.estemb.be; Ambassador MALLE TALVET.

Ethiopia: 231 ave de Tervueren, 1150 Brussels; tel. (2) 771-32-94; fax (2) 771-49-14; e-mail etebru@brutele.be; Ambassador BERHANE GEBRE-CHRISTOS.

Fiji: 92–94 square Plasky, 1030 Brussels; tel. (2) 736-90-50; fax (2) 736-14-58; e-mail info@fijiembassy.be; internet www.fijiembassy.be; Ambassador S. T. CAVUILATI.

Finland: 58 ave des Arts, 1000 Brussels; tel. (2) 287-12-12; fax (2) 287-12-00; e-mail sanomat.bry@formin.fi; internet www.formin.fi/english/ Ambassador ANTII SIERLA.

France: 65 rue Ducale, 1000 Brussels; tel. (2) 548-87-11; fax (2) 548-87-32; internet www.ambafrance-be.org; Ambassador JOËLLE BOURGOIS.

Gabon: 112 ave Winston Churchill, 1180 Brussels; tel. (2) 340-62-10; fax (2) 346-46-69; e-mail ambassadedugabon@brutele.be; Ambassador RENÉ MAKONGO.

Gambia: 126 ave F. D. Roosevelt, 1050 Brussels; tel. (2) 640-10-49; fax (2) 646-32-77; Ambassador YUSUPHA KAH.

Georgia: 58 ave Orban, 1150 Brussels; tel. (2) 761-11-91; fax (2) 761-11-99; e-mail mdgadc@skynet.be; Ambassador KONSTANTINE ZALDASTANISHVLI.

Germany: 190 ave de Tervueren, 1150 Brussels; tel. (2) 774-19-11; fax (2) 772-36-92; e-mail info@bruessel.diplo.de; internet www.bruessel.diplo.de; Ambassador PETER VON BUTLER.

Ghana: blvd Général Wahis, 1030 Brussels; tel. (2) 705-82-20; fax (2) 705-66-53; e-mail ghanaemb@chello.be; Ambassador KOBINA WUDU.

Greece: 10 rue des petits Carmes, 1000 Brussels; tel. (2) 545-55-00; fax (2) 545-55-85; e-mail ambagre@skynet.be; Ambassador IOANNIS CORANTIS.

Grenada: 123 Laekenstraat, 1000 Brussels; tel. (2) 223-73-03; fax (2) 223-73-07; e-mail embassyofgrenadabxl@skynet.be; Ambassador JOAN-MARIE COUTAIN.

Guatemala: 185 ave Winston Churchill, 1180 Brussels; tel. (2) 345-69-92; fax (2) 344-90-58; e-mail embbelgica@minex.gob.gt; Ambassador EDMOND MULET-LESIEUR.

Guinea: 108 blvd Auguste Reyers, 1030 Brussels; tel. (2) 771-01-26; fax (2) 762-60-36; Ambassador NABY MOUSSA SOUMAH.

Guinea-Bissau: 70 ave F. D. Roosevelt, 1050 Brussels; tel. (2) 647-13-51; fax (2) 640-43-12; Ambassador JOSÉ FRANCISCO DA COSTA.

Guyana: 12 ave du Brésil, 1000 Brussels; tel. (2) 675-62-16; fax (2) 675-55-98; e-mail embassy.guyana@skynet.be; Ambassador KENNETH F.S. KING.

Haiti: 139 chaussée de Charleroi, 1060 Brussels; tel. (2) 649-73-81; fax (2) 640-60-80; Ambassador MYRTO CELESTIN-SAUREL.

Holy See: 9 ave des Franciscains, 1150 Brussels (Apostolic Nunciature). tel. (2) 762-20-05; fax (2) 762-20-32; e-mail nonciature.apostolique.be@skynet.be; internet www.vatican.va; Apostolic Nuncio Most Rev. KARL-JOSEF RAUBER.

Honduras: 3 ave des Gaulois (5e étage), 1040 Brussels; tel. (2) 734-00-00; fax (2) 735-26-26; e-mail ambassade.Honduras@chello.be; Ambassador TEODOLINDA BANEGAS DE MAKRIS.

Hungary: 44 ave du Vert Chasseur, 1180 Brussels; tel. (2) 348-18-00; fax (2) 347-60-28; e-mail huembbxl@huembbxl.be; Ambassador FERENC ROBÁK.

Iceland: Rond Point Schuman 11, 1040 Brussels; tel. (2) 238-50-00; fax (2) 230-69-38; e-mail icemb.brussel@utn.stjr.is; internet www.iceland.org/be; Ambassador KJARTAN JÓHANNSSON.

India: 217 chaussée de Vleurgat, 1050 Brussels; tel. (2) 640-91-40; fax (2) 648-96-38; e-mail hoc@indembassy.be; internet www.indembassy.be; Ambassador R. M. ABHYANKAR.

Indonesia: 294 ave de Tervueren, 1150 Brussels; tel. (2) 771-20-14; fax (2) 771-22-91; e-mail kbribxl@brutele.be; Ambassador SULAIMAN ABDULMANAN.

Iran: 415 ave de Tervueren, 1150 Brussels; tel. (2) 762-37-45; fax (2) 762-39-15; e-mail eiri.bxl@skynet.be; Ambassador ABOLGHASEM DELFI.

Iraq: 23 ave des Aubépines, 1180 Brussels; tel. (2) 374-59-92; fax (2) 374-76-15; e-mail abassade.irak@skynet.be; Ambassador MOHAMMED AL-DOREKY.

Ireland: 50 rue Wiertz, 1050 Brussels; tel. (2) 235-66-76; fax (2) 235-66-71; e-mail embirl@online.be; Ambassador BRIAN NASON.

Israel: 40 ave de l'Observatoire, 1180 Brussels; tel. (2) 373-55-36; fax (2) 373-56-17; e-mail info@brussels.mfa.gov.il; Ambassador JEHUDI KINAR.

Italy: 28 rue Emile Claus, 1050 Brussels; tel. (2) 643-38-50; fax (2) 648-54-85; e-mail ambit.bxl.politico@ibm.net; internet www .ambitaliabruxelles.org; Ambassador MASSIMO MACCHIA.

Jamaica: 2 ave Palmerston, 1000 Brussels; tel. (2) 230-11-70; fax (2) 230-37-09; e-mail emb.jam.brussels@skynet.be; Ambassador EVADNE COYE.

Japan: 58 ave des Arts, bte 17/18, 1000 Brussels; tel. (2) 513-23-40; fax (2) 513-15-56; e-mail kobun1@amb-jpn.be; internet www.be .emb-japan.go.jp; Ambassador SHOHEI NAITO.

Jordan: 104 ave F. D. Roosevelt, 1050 Brussels; tel. (2) 640-77-55; fax (2) 640-27-96; e-mail jordan.embassy@skynet.be; Chargé d'aff- aires a.i. Dr MALEK TWAL.

Kazakhstan: 30 ave Van Bever, 1180 Brussels; tel. (2) 373-38-90; fax (2) 374-50-91; e-mail kazakstan.embassy@swing.be; Ambas- sador KONSTANTIN V. ZHIGALOV.

Kenya: 208 ave Winston Churchill, 1180 Brussels; tel. (2) 340-10- 40; fax (2) 340-10-50; e-mail kenyabrussels@yahoo.com; Ambassador MARX G. N. KAHENDE.

Korea, Republic: 173–175 chaussée de la Hulpe, 1170 Brussels; tel. (2) 662-57-77; fax (2) 675-52-21; e-mail eukorea@skynet.be; Ambassador OH HAENG-KYEOM.

Kuwait: 43 ave F. D. Roosevelt, 1050 Brussels; tel. (2) 647-79-50; fax (2) 646-12-98; e-mail embassy.kwt@skynet.be; Ambassador ABDULAZEEZ AL-SHARIKH.

Kyrgyzstan: 47 Abdijstraat, 1050 Brussels; tel. (2) 640-18-68; fax (2) 640-01-31; e-mail kyrgyz.embassy@skynet.be; Ambassador CHINGIZ T. AITMATOV.

Laos: 19–21 ave de la Brabançonne, 1000 Brussels; tel. (2) 740-09- 50; fax (2) 734-16-66.

Latvia: 158 ave Molière, 1050 Brussels; tel. (2) 344-16-82; fax (2) 344-74-78; e-mail embassy.belgium@mfa.gov.lv; Ambassador AIVARS GROZA.

Lebanon: 2 rue Guillaume Stocq, 1050 Brussels; tel. (2) 645-77-60; fax (2) 645-77-69; Ambassador JIHAD MORTADA.

Lesotho: 45 blvd Général Wahis, 1030 Brussels; tel. (2) 705-39-76; fax (2) 705-67-79; e-mail lesothobrussels@skynet.be; Ambassador M. A. MATLANYANE.

Libya: 28 ave Victoria, 1050 Brussels; tel. (2) 647-37-37; fax (2) 640- 90-76; e-mail be@yahoo.com; Sec. of People's Bureau HAMED AHMED ELHOUDERI.

Liechtenstein: 1 place du Congrès, 1000 Brussels; tel. (2) 229-39- 00; fax (2) 219-35-45; e-mail ambassade.liechtenstein@bbru.llv.li; Ambassador Prince NIKOLAUS VON LIECHTENSTEIN.

Lithuania: 48 rue Maurice Liétart, 1150 Brussels; tel. (2) 772-27- 50; fax (2) 772-17-01; e-mail lithembassy@pop.kpn.be; Ambassador AUDRIUS NAVIKAS.

Luxembourg: 75 ave de Cortenbergh, 1000 Brussels; tel. (2) 737- 56-00; fax (2) 737-56-10; e-mail secretariat@mae.etat.lu; Ambas- sador MARTINE SCHOMMER.

Macedonia, former Yugoslav republic: 209A ave Louise, 1050 Brussels; tel. (2) 734-56-87; fax (2) 732-07-17; e-mail ambassade .mk@skynet.be; Ambassador SAŠKO STEFKOV.

Madagascar: 276 ave de Tervueren, 1150 Brussels; tel. (2) 770-17- 26; fax (2) 772-37-31; e-mail beriziky.jean.omer@ ambassademadagascar.be; Ambassador JEAN OMER BERIZIKY.

Malawi: 15 rue de la Loi, 1040 Brussels; tel. (2) 231-09-80; fax (2) 231-10-66; Ambassador JULIE NANYONI MPHANDE.

Malaysia: 414A ave de Tervueren, 1150 Brussels; tel. (2) 776-03-40; e-mail mwbrusel@euronet.be; fax (2) 762-50-49; Ambassador Dato RIDZAM DEVA BIN ABDULLAH.

Mali: 487 ave Molière, 1050 Brussels; tel. (2) 345-74-32; fax (2) 344- 57-00; e-mail ambassade.mali@skynet.be; Ambassador IBRAHIM BOCAR.

Malta: 65–67 rue Belliard, 1040 Brussels; tel. (2) 343-01-95; fax (2) 343-01-06; e-mail tarcisio.zamnit@gov.mt; Ambassador TARCISIO ZAMNIT.

Mauritania: 6 ave de la Colombie, 1000 Brussels; tel. (2) 672-47-47; fax (2) 672-20-51; e-mail ambbxlmauritanie@yahoo.fr; Ambassador M. BA ALIOU IBRA DIT YELLÉ.

Mauritius: 68 rue des Bollandistes, 1040 Brussels; tel. (2) 733-99- 88; fax (2) 734-40-21; e-mail ambmaur@skynet.be; Ambassador SUTIAWAN GUNESSEE.

Mexico: 94 ave F. D. Roosevelt, 1050 Brussels; tel. (2) 629-07-77; fax (2) 644-08-19; e-mail embamexbelgica-ue@skynet.be; internet www .sre.gob.mx/belgica-ue; Ambassador MARÍA DE LOURDES DIECK ASSAD.

Moldova: Tenboschstraat 54, 1050 Brussels; tel. (2) 732-96-59; fax (2) 732-96-60; e-mail ambassademoldavie@brutele.be; Chargé d'aff- aires a.i. EMIL DRUC.

Monaco: 17 place Guy d'Arezzo, bte 7, 1180 Brussels; tel. (2) 347-49- 87; fax (2) 343-49-20; e-mail ambassade.monaco@skynet.be; Ambas- sador JEAN PASTORELLI.

Mongolia: 18 ave Besme, 1190 Brussels; tel. (2) 344-69-74; fax (2) 344-32-15; e-mail brussels.mn.embassy@chello.be; Ambassador ONON SODOV.

Morocco: 275 ave Louise, 1050 Brussels; tel. (2) 626-34-10; fax (2) 626-34-34; e-mail mission.maroc@skynet.be; Ambassador MENOVAR ALEM.

Mozambique: 97 blvd St-Michel, 1040 Brussels; tel. (2) 736-25-64; fax (2) 735-62-07; e-mail embamoc.bru@yahoo.com; Ambassador MARIA MANUELA LUCAS.

Namibia: 454 ave de Tervueren, 1150 Brussels; tel. (2) 771-14-10; fax (2) 771-96-89; e-mail nam.emb@brutele.be; Ambassador Prof. PETER KATJAVIVI.

Nepal: 210 ave Brugmann, 1050 Brussels; tel. (2) 346-26-58; fax (2) 344-13-61; e-mail rne.bru@skynet.be; Ambassador NARAYAN S. THAPA.

Netherlands: 48 ave Hermann Debroux, 1160 Brussels; tel. (2) 679- 17-11; fax (2) 679-17-75; e-mail bru@minbuza.nl; internet www .nederlandseambassade.be; Ambassador RUDOLF BEKINK.

New Zealand: square de Meeûs 1, 1000 Brussels; tel. (2) 512-10-40; fax (2) 513-48-56; e-mail nzemb.brussels@skynet.be; internet www .nzembassy.com/belgium; Ambassador WADE ARMSTRONG.

Nicaragua: 55 ave de Wolvendael, 1180 Brussels; tel. (2) 375-65-00; fax (2) 375-71-88; e-mail sky77706@skynet.be; Ambassador LESTER MEJÍA SOLÍS.

Niger: 78 ave F. D. Roosevelt, 1050 Brussels; tel. (2) 648-61-40; fax (2) 648-27-84; Ambassador ABDOU ABBARY.

Nigeria: 288 ave de Tervueren, 1150 Brussels; tel. (2) 762-52-00; fax (2) 762-37-63; Ambassador GABRIEL SAM AKUNWAFOR.

Norway: 17 rue Archimède (3e étage), 1000 Brussels; tel. (2) 646-07- 80; fax (2) 646-28-82; e-mail emb.brussels@mfa.no; internet www .norvege.be; Ambassador JOHN BJØRNEBYE.

Pakistan: 57 ave Delleur, 1170 Brussels; tel. (2) 673-80-07; fax (2) 675-83-94; e-mail parepbrussels@skynet.be; Ambassador SAEED KHALID.

Panama: 390–392 ave Louise, 1050 Brussels; tel. (2) 647-07-29; fax (2) 642-92-16; e-mail embajada.panama@skynet.be; Ambassador ROLANDO A. GUEVARA ALVARADO.

Papua New Guinea: 430 ave de Tervueren, 1150 Brussels; tel. (2) 779-06-09; fax (2) 772-70-88; e-mail kundu.brussels@skynet.be; Ambassador ISAAC B. LUPARI.

Paraguay: 475 ave Louise, BP 21, 1050 Brussels; tel. (2) 649-90-55; fax (2) 647-42-48; e-mail embapar@skynet.be; Ambassador EMILIO GIMÉNEZ FRANCO.

Peru: 179 ave de Tervueren, 1150 Brussels; tel. (2) 733-33-19; fax (2) 733-48-19; e-mail comunicaciones@embassy-of-peru.be; Ambas- sador JOSÉ URRUTIA.

Philippines: 297 ave Molière, 1050 Brussels; tel. (2) 340-33-77; fax (2) 345-64-25; e-mail brusselspe@brutele.be; Chargé d'affaires a.i. ANAMARIE A. MORALES.

Poland: 29 ave des Gaulois, 1040 Brussels; tel. (2) 739-01-51; fax (2) 736-18-81; e-mail polambbxl@skynet.be; internet www.polembassy .be; Ambassador IWO BYCZEWSKI.

Portugal: 55 ave de la Toison d'Or, 1060 Brussels; tel. (2) 533-07-00; fax (2) 539-07-73; e-mail portugal@skynet.be; Ambassador FRANCISCO PESSANHA DE QUEVEDO CRESPO.

Romania: 105 rue Gabrielle, 1180 Brussels; tel. (2) 345-26-80; fax (2) 346-23-45; e-mail secretariat@roumanieamb.be; Ambassador Dr ION JINGA.

Russia: 66 ave de Fré, 1180 Brussels; tel. (2) 374-34-00; fax (2) 374- 26-13; e-mail amrusbel@skynet.be; Ambassador SERGEI KISLYAK.

Rwanda: 1 ave des Fleurs, 1150 Brussels; tel. (2) 763-07-05; fax (2) 763-07-53; e-mail ambarwanda@skynet.be; internet www .ambarwanda.be; Ambassador EMMANUEL IMANZI KAYITANA.

Samoa: 123 ave F. D. Roosevelt, bte 14, 1050 Brussels; tel. (2) 660- 84-54; fax (2) 675-03-36; e-mail samoa.emb.bxl@skynet.be; Ambas- sador TAU'ILI'ILI UILI MEREDITH.

San Marino: 62 ave F. D. Roosevelt, 1050 Brussels; tel. (2) 644-22-24; fax (2) 644-20-57; e-mail ambrsm.bxl@coditel.net; Ambassador SAVINA ZAFFERANI.

São Tomé and Príncipe: 175 ave de Tervueren, 1150 Brussels; tel. (2) 734-89-66; fax (2) 734-88-15; e-mail ambassade.saotome@fri.be; Chargé d'affaires a.i. A. DE BRITO FERNANDES.

Saudi Arabia: 45 ave F. D. Roosevelt, 1050 Brussels; tel. (2) 649-20-44; fax (2) 647-24-92; Ambassador NASSER ASSAF HUSSEIN AL-ASSAF.

Senegal: 196 ave F. D. Roosevelt, 1050 Brussels; tel. (2) 673-00-97; fax (2) 675-04-60; e-mail senegal.ambassade@coditel.net; Ambassador SALOUM KANDE.

Serbia and Montenegro: 11 ave Emile de Mot, 1000 Brussels; tel. (2) 647-57-81; fax (2) 647-29-41; e-mail ambayougoslavie@skynet.be; Ambassador MILICA PEJANOVIĆ.

Sierra Leone: 410 ave de Tervueren, 1150 Brussels; tel. (2) 771-00-53; fax (2) 771-82-30; e-mail sierraleoneembassy-brussels@brutele.be; Ambassador FODE M. DABOR.

Singapore: 198 ave F. D. Roosevelt, 1050 Brussels; tel. (2) 660-29-79; fax (2) 660-86-85; e-mail amb.eu@singembbru.be; internet www.mfa.gov.sg/brussels; Ambassador WALTER WOON.

Slovakia: 195 ave Molière, 1050 Brussels; tel. (2) 346-40-45; fax (2) 346-63-85; e-mail ambassade.slovaque@skynet.be; Ambassador FRANTIŠEK LIPKA.

Slovenia: 179 ave Louise, 1050 Brussels; tel. (2) 646-90-99; fax (2) 646-36-67; e-mail vbr@mzz-dkp.gov.si; Ambassador BORUT TREKMAN.

Solomon Islands: 17 ave Edouard Lacomble, 1040 Brussels; tel. (2) 732-70-85; fax (2) 732-68-85; e-mail siembassy@compuserve.com; Ambassador ROBERT SISILO.

South Africa: 26 rue de la Loi, bus 7–8, 1040 Brussels; tel. (2) 285-44-00; fax (2) 285-44-02; e-mail embassy@southafrica.be; internet www.southafrica.be; Ambassador JERRY MATTHEWS MATJILA.

Spain: 19 rue de la Science, 1040 Brussels; tel. (2) 230-03-40; fax (2) 230-93-80; e-mail ambespbe@mail.mae.es; Ambassador MARÍA VICTORIA MORERA VILLUENDAS.

Sri Lanka: 27 rue Jules Lejeune, 1050 Brussels; tel. (2) 344-53-94; fax (2) 344-67-37; e-mail sri.lanka@euronet.be; Ambassador G. R. JAYASINGHE.

Sudan: 124 ave F. D. Roosevelt, 1050 Brussels; tel. (2) 647-94-94; fax (2) 648-34-99; e-mail sudanbx@yahoo.com; Ambassador ALI YOUSIF AHMED.

Suriname: 379 ave Louise, 1050 Brussels; tel. (2) 640-11-72; fax (2) 646-39-62; e-mail sur.amb.bru@online.be; Ambassador GERHARD O. HIWAT.

Swaziland: 188 ave Winston Churchill, 1180 Brussels; tel. (2) 347-47-71; fax (2) 347-46-23; Ambassador Dr THEMBAYENA ANNASTASIA DLAMINI.

Sweden: 3 rue de Luxembourg, 1000 Brussels; tel. (2) 289-57-60; fax (2) 289-57-90; e-mail ambassaden.bryssel@foreign.ministry.se; internet www.swedenembassy.be; Ambassador HERMAN AF TROLLE.

Switzerland: 26 rue de la Loi, bte 9, 1040 Brussels; tel. (2) 285-43-50; fax (2) 230-37-81; e-mail vertretung@bru.rep.admin.ch; internet www.eda.admin.ch/bruxelles; Ambassador ROBERT MAYOR.

Syria: 3 ave F. D. Roosevelt, 1050 Brussels; tel. (2) 648-01-35; fax (2) 646-40-18; e-mail ambsyrie@skynet.be; Ambassador Dr TOUJIK SALLOUM.

Tajikistan: 363–365 ave Louise, BP 14, 1050 Brussels; tel. (2) 640-69-33; fax (2) 649-01-95; e-mail tajemb-belgium@skynet.be; Ambassador SHARIF RAKHIMOV.

Tanzania: 363 ave Louise (7e étage), 1050 Brussels; tel. (2) 640-65-00; fax (2) 640-80-26; e-mail tanzania@skynet.be; Ambassador ALI ABEID KARUME.

Thailand: 2 square du Val de la Cambre, 1050 Brussels; tel. (2) 640-68-10; fax (2) 648-30-66; e-mail thaibxl@pophost.eunet.be; internet www.waw.be/rte-be; Ambassador DON PRAMUDWINAI.

Togo: 264 ave de Tervueren, 1150 Brussels; tel. (2) 770-55-63; fax (2) 771-50-75; e-mail ambassade.togo@skynet.be; Ambassador FOLLY-GLIDJITO AKAKPO.

Trinidad and Tobago: 14 ave de la Faisanderie, 1150 Brussels; tel. (2) 762-94-00; fax (2) 772-27-83; e-mail info@embtrinbago.be; Ambassador LEARIE ROUSSEAU.

Tunisia: 278 ave de Tervueren, 1150 Brussels; tel. (2) 771-73-95; fax (2) 771-94-33; e-mail amb.detunisie@brutele.be; Ambassador FETHI MERDASSI.

Turkey: 4 rue Montoyer, 1000 Brussels; tel. (2) 513-40-95; fax (2) 514-07-48; e-mail info@turkey.be; internet www.turkey.be; Ambassador ERKAN GEZER.

Turkmenistan: 106 ave F. D. Roosevelt, 1050 Brussels; tel. (2) 648-18-74; fax (2) 648-19-06; e-mail turkmenistan@skynet.be.

Uganda: 317 ave de Tervueren, 1150 Brussels; tel. (2) 762-58-25; fax (2) 763-04-38; e-mail ugembrus@brutele.be; Ambassador DEO K. RWABITA.

Ukraine: 30–32 ave Lancaster, 1180 Brussels; tel. (2) 379-21-00; fax (2) 379-21-79; e-mail embassy@ukraine.be; internet www.ukraine.be; Ambassador VOLODYMYR KHANDOGIY.

United Arab Emirates: 73 ave F. D. Roosevelt, 1050 Brussels; tel. (2) 640-60-00; fax (2) 646-24-73; e-mail emirates.bxl@infonie.be; Ambassador ABDULHADI AL-KHAJAH.

United Kingdom: 85 rue d'Arlon, 1040 Brussels; tel. (2) 287-62-11; fax (2) 287-63-60; e-mail info@britain.be; internet www.britishembassy.gov.uk/belgium; Ambassador RICHARD KINCHEN.

USA: 27 blvd du Régent, 1000 Brussels; tel. (2) 508-21-11; fax (2) 511-21-60; internet www.usinfo.be; Ambassador TOM C. KOROLOGOS.

Uruguay: 22 ave F. D. Roosevelt, 1050 Brussels; tel. (2) 640-11-69; fax (2) 648-29-09; e-mail uruemb@skynet.be; internet www.mrree.gub.uy; Ambassador ELBIO ROSSELLI.

Uzbekistan: 99 ave F. D. Roosevelt, 1050 Brussels; tel. (2) 672-88-44; fax (2) 672-39-46; e-mail embassy@uzbekistan.be; internet corporate.skynet.be/uzbekistan; Ambassador VLADIMIR NOROV.

Venezuela: 10 ave F. D. Roosevelt, 1050 Brussels; tel. (2) 639-03-40; fax (2) 647-88-20; e-mail embajada@venezuela-eu.org; Ambassador LUISA ROMERO.

Viet Nam: 1 blvd General Jacques, 1050 Brussels; tel. (2) 374-91-33; fax (2) 374-93-76; e-mail vnemb.brussels@skynet.be; Ambassador TON NU THI NINH.

Yemen: 114 ave F. D. Roosevelt, 1050 Brussels; tel. (2) 646-52-90; fax (2) 646-29-11; Ambassador A. K. AL-AGHBARI.

Zambia: 469 ave Molière, 1050 Brussels; tel. (2) 343-56-49; fax (2) 347-43-33; e-mail zambians_brussels@brutele.be; Ambassador IRENE M. KAMANGA.

Zimbabwe: 11 square Joséphine Charlotte, 1200 Brussels; tel. (2) 762-58-08; fax (2) 762-96-05; e-mail zimbrussels@skynet.be; Ambassador GIFT PUNUNGWE.

Judicial System

The independence of the judiciary is based on the constitutional division of power between the legislative, executive and judicial bodies, each of which acts independently. Judges are appointed by the crown for life, and cannot be removed except by judicial sentence. The judiciary is organized on four levels, from the judicial canton to the district, regional and national courts. The lowest courts are those of the Justices of the Peace and the Police Tribunals. Each district has one of each type of district court, including the Tribunals of the First Instance, Tribunals of Commerce, and Labour Tribunals, and there is a Court of Assizes in each province. There are Courts of Appeal and Labour Courts in each region. The highest courts are the national civil and criminal Courts of Appeal, Labour Courts and the Supreme Court of Justice. The Military Court of Appeal is in Brussels.

COUR DE CASSATION/HOF VAN CASSATIE
(Supreme Court of Justice)

First President: M. LAHOUSSE.

President: I. VEROUGSTRAETE.

Counsellors: D. BATSELÉ, R. BOES, C. PARMENTIER, P. ECHEMENT, CHR. STORCK, P. MATHIEU, C. MATRAY, S. VELU, E. WAUTERS, G. SUETENS-BOURGEOIS, G. LONDERS, E. DIRIX, STASSIJNS, A. FETTWEIS, G. DHAEYER, E. GOETHALS, P. MAFFEI, D. DEBRUYNE, J. DE CODT, F. CLOSE, D. PLAS, F. FISCHER, E. FETTWEIS, B. DEJEMEPPE, E. FORRIER L. HUYBRECHTS, J.-P. FRÈRE, L. VAN HOOGENBEMT.

Attorney-General: J. DU JARDIN.

First Advocate-General: J.-F. LECLERQ.

Advocates-General: X. DE RIEMAECKER, J. SPREUTELS, A. HENKES, R. LOOP, M. TIMPERMAN, M. DE SWAEFF, G. BRESSELEERS, A. DE RAEVE, G. DUBRULLE, P. DUINSLAEGER, TH. WERQUIN.

COURS D'APPEL/HOVEN VAN BEROEP
(Civil and Criminal High Courts)

Antwerp: First Pres. CHRISTIAN DE VEL, Attorney-Gen. CHRISTINE DEKKERS.

Brussels: First Pres. JACQUELINE COPPIN, Attorney-Gen. ANDRÉ VAN OUDENHOVE.

Ghent: First Pres. JEAN-PAUL DE GRAEF, Attorney-Gen. FRANK SCHINS.

Liège: First Pres. MICHEL JOACHIM, Attorney-Gen. ANNE THILY.

Mons: First Pres. CHRISTIAN JASSOGNE, Attorney-Gen. GASTON LADRIÈRE.

COURS DU TRAVAIL/ARBEIDSHOVEN
(Labour Courts)

Antwerp: First Pres. BEATRICE HOMANS.

Brussels: First Pres. FRANCIS VANDERVEEREN.

Ghent: First Pres. CHARLES VAN GREMBERGEN.

Liège: First Pres. JOËL HUBIN.

Mons: First Pres. CHARLES DELIGNE.

Religion

CHRISTIANITY

The Roman Catholic Church

Belgium comprises one archdiocese and seven dioceses. At 31 December 2002 there were an estimated 7,839,563 adherents (some 76.2% of the total population).

Bishops' Conference

Bisschoppenconferentie van België/Conférence Episcopale de Belgique, 1 rue Guimard, 1040 Brussels; tel. (2) 509-96-93; fax (2) 509-96-95; e-mail ce.belgica@catho.kerknet.be; internet www.kerknet.be.

f. 1981; Pres. Cardinal GODFRIED DANNEELS (Archbishop of Mechelen-Brussels).

Archbishop of Mechelen-Brussels: Cardinal GODFRIED DANNEELS, Aartsbisdom, 15 Wollemarkt, 2800 Mechelen; tel. (15) 21-65-01; fax (15) 20-94-85; e-mail aartsbisdom@kerknet.be; internet www.catho.be.

Protestant Churches

Church of England: Holy Trinity Pro-Cathedral, 29 rue Capitaine Crespel, 1050 Brussels; tel. (2) 511-71-83; fax (2) 511-10-28; e-mail admin@htbrussels.com; internet www.htbrussels.com; Rev. Canon NIGEL WALKER (Chaplain and Chancellor of the Pro-Cathedral of the Holy Trinity, Brussels).

Eglise Protestante Unie de Belgique (EPUB): 5 rue du Champ de Mars, 1050 Brussels; tel. and fax (2) 510-61-66; e-mail belpro@epub.be.be; internet www.protestanet.be; f. 1979; Pres. Rev. Dr GUY LIAGRE; Contact MICHEL DANDOY; 45,000 mems; publ. *Mosaïque* (monthly).

Lutheran Church of Belgium: ave de Mersch 10, 6700 Arlon; tel. (6) 323-27-90; f. 1964; 809 mems; Pres. Rev. JEAN LOUIS CORNEZ.

Mission Evangélique Belge: 158 blvd Lambermont, 1030 Brussels; tel. (2) 241-30-15; fax (2) 245-79-65; e-mail information@b-e-m.org; internet www.bez-meb.org; f. 1919; Dirs WILFRIED GOOSSENS, ERIC ZANDER; c. 12,000 mems.

Union of Baptists in Belgium (UBB): 85A Liebaertstraat, 8400 Ostend; tel. (59) 32-46-10; fax (59) 32-46-10; e-mail 106466.3510@compuserve.com; f. 1922 as Union of Protestant Baptists in Belgium; Pres. SAMUEL VERHAEGHE; Sec. EMMANUEL MUKWEGE.

The Orthodox Church

There are about 70,000 Greek and Russian Orthodox believers in Belgium.

Archbishop of Belgium (Ecumenical Patriarchate of Constantinople): Metropolitan PANTELEIMON, ave Charbo 71, 1030 Brussels; tel. (2) 736-52-78; fax (2) 735-32-64; e-mail Eglise.Orthodoxe@belgacom.net; internet www.eglise-orthodoxe.be.

Archbishop of Brussels and Belgium (Moscow Patriarchate): SIMON ISHUNIN, 29 rue des Chevaliers, Brussels 5; tel. and fax (2) 513-33-74; e-mail sergemodel@hotmail.com; internet users.skynet.be/archiepiscopia.

ISLAM

There are some 364,000 Muslims in Belgium and an estimated 380 mosques. In December 1998 the Belgian Islamic community elected an Islamic representative body.

Leader of the Islamic Community: Imam Prof. SALMAN AL-RAHDI.

JUDAISM

The Jewish population in Belgium is estimated at between 45,000 and 55,000.

Consistoire Central Israélite de Belgique (Central Council of the Jewish Communities of Belgium): 2 rue Joseph Dupont, 1000 Brussels; tel. (2) 512-21-90; fax (2) 512-35-78; e-mail consis@online.be; internet www.jewishcom.be; f. 1808; Chair. Prof. JULIEN KLENER; Sec.-Gen. MICHEL LAUB.

The Press

Article 25 of the Belgian Constitution states: 'The Press is free; no form of censorship may ever be instituted; no cautionary deposit may be demanded from writers, publishers or printers. When the author is known and is resident in Belgium, the publisher, printer or distributor may not be prosecuted.'

There were an estimated 30 general information dailies in 1996, with an estimated combined circulation of 1,625,000 copies per issue.

There is a trend towards concentration. The Rossel ('Le Soir') group and the Médiabel group control the majority of francophone newspapers, while the principal publisher of Flemish newspapers is the VUM ('De Standaard') group. The Roularta media group is an important publisher of regional newspapers and periodicals, and the Mediaxis group is an important magazine publisher.

PRINCIPAL DAILIES

Antwerp

Gazet van Antwerpen: 2 Katwilgweg, 2050 Antwerp; tel. (3) 210-02-10; fax (3) 219-40-41; e-mail gvaredactie@concentra.be; internet www.gva.be; f. 1891; Christian Democrat; Editor LUC RADEMAKERS; circ. 123,000.

De Lloyd/Le Lloyd: 18 Vleminckstraat, 2000 Antwerp; tel. (3) 234-05-50; fax (3) 234-25-93; e-mail info@lloyd.be; internet www.anlloyd.be; f. 1858; Flemish and French edns, with supplements in English; shipping, commerce, industry, finance; Dir GUY DUBOIS; Editor BERNARD VAN DEN BOSSCHE; circ. 10,600.

De Nieuwe Gazet: Brusselsesteenweg 347, 1730 Asse; tel. (3) 212-13-48; fax (3) 212-13-46; f. 1897; liberal; Chief Editor LUC VAN DER KELEN.

De Tijd: Franklin Bldg, 3 Posthoflei, 2600 Berchem; tel. (3) 286-02-11; fax (3) 286-02-10; e-mail contactcenter@tijd.be; internet www.tijd.be; f. 1968; economic and financial; Gen. Man. HANS MAERTENS; circ. 51,700.

Arlon

L'Avenir du Luxembourg: 38 rue des Déportés, 6700 Arlon; tel. (63) 23-10-20; fax (63) 23-42-89; e-mail infoal@verslavenir.be; f. 1897; 100% owned by Médiabel; Catholic; Chief Editor BERNARD MOTTET; circ. 117,175 (with *Vers l'Avenir, Le Courrier de l'Escaut, Le Jour, Le Courrier*).

Brussels

La Capitale: 120 rue Royale, 1000 Brussels; tel. (2) 225-54-52; fax (2) 225-59-17; e-mail redaction.generale@sudpresse.be; internet www.lacapitale.be; f. 1944; independent; fmrly La Lanterne; Chief Editor DIDIER HAMANN.

La Dernière Heure/Les Sports: 127 blvd Emile Jacqmain, 1000 Brussels; tel. (2) 211-28-88; fax (2) 211-28-70; e-mail dhbelgique@saipm.com; internet www.dhnet.be; f. 1906; independent Liberal; Dir FRANÇOIS LE HODEY; Chief Editor MICHEL MARTEAU; circ. 73,130.

L'Echo: 131 rue de Birmingham, 1070 Brussels; tel. (2) 526-55-11; fax (2) 526-55-26; e-mail redaction@echonet.be; internet www.lecho.be; f. 1881; economic and financial; Dir R. WATSON; Editor YVES CAVALIER; circ. 22,230.

Het Laatste Nieuws: 347 Brusselsesteenweg, 1730 Asse-Kobbegem; tel. (2) 454-22-11; fax (2) 454-28-22; e-mail redactie.hln@persgroep.be; internet www.hln.be; f. 1888; Flemish; independent; Dir-Gen. R. BERTELS; Editors JAAK SMEETS, PAUL DAENEN; circ. 306,279.

La Libre Belgique: 127 blvd Emile Jacqmain, 1000 Brussels; tel. (2) 211-27-77; fax (2) 211-28-32; e-mail llb.redaction@saipm.com; internet www.lalibre.be; f. 1884; European; independent; Chief Editor MICHEL KONEN; circ. 80,000 (with *La Libre Belgique—Gazette de Liège*).

De Morgen: 54 Brogniezstraat, 1070 Brussels; tel. (2) 556-68-11; fax (2) 520-35-15; e-mail info@demorgen.be; internet www.demorgen.be; Dir-Gen. WIM COESSENS; Editor RUDY COLLIER; circ. 35,000.

Het Nieuwsblad: 30 Gossetlaan, 1702 Groot Bijgaarden; tel. (2) 467-22-11; fax (2) 466-30-93; e-mail nieuwsblad@vum.be; internet www.vum.be; f. 1923; Dir-Gen. JO VAN CROONENBORCH; Chief Editors DIRK REMMERIE, FRANK BUYSE; circ. 320,000 (with *Het Volk* and *De Gentenaar*).

Le Soir: 120 rue Royale, 1000 Brussels; tel. (2) 225-54-32; fax (2) 225-59-10; e-mail journal@lesoir.be; internet www.lesoir.com; f. 1887; independent; Dir-Gen. DANIEL VAN WYLICK; Chief Editor BÉATRICE DELVAUX; circ. 178,569.

De Standaard: 28 Gossetlaan, 1702 Groot Bijgaarden; tel. (2) 467-22-11; fax (2) 467-26-96; e-mail standaard@vum.be; internet www.standaard.be; f. 1914; Dir-Gen. JO VAN CROONENBORCH; Chief Editor PETER VANDERMEERSCH; circ. 77,000.

Charleroi

La Nouvelle Gazette (Charleroi, La Louvière, Philippeville, Namur, Nivelles); La Province (Mons): 2 quai de Flandre, 6000 Charleroi; tel. (71) 27-64-11; fax (71) 27-65-67; e-mail redaction.generale@sudpresse.be; internet www.nouvellegazette.be; f. 1878; Man. Dir JEAN-CLAUDE FYON; Editor DIDIER HAMANN.

Le Rappel: rue de France 24, 5600 Philippeville; tel. (71) 66-69-49; fax (71) 66-86-50; e-mail infonam@verslavenir.be; f. 1900; Dir-Gen. BRUNO DE CARTIER D'YVES; Chief Editor BRUNO MALTER.

Eupen

Grenz-Echo: 8 Marktplatz, 4700 Eupen; tel. (87) 59-13-00; fax (87) 74-38-20; e-mail redaktion@grenzecho.be; internet www.grenzecho.be; f. 1927; German; independent Catholic; Dir A. KÜCHENBERG; Chief Editor GERARD CERMER; circ. 12,040.

Ghent

De Gentenaar: François Laurentplein 27, 9000 Ghent; tel. (9) 268-72-70; fax (9) 268-72-71; e-mail de.gentenaar@vum.be; internet www.gentenaar.be; f. 1879; Chief Editors DIRK REMMERIE, FRANK BUYSE; Co-ordinator ERIC DE KEYZER; circ. 366,665 (with *Het Nieuwsblad* and *De Standaard*).

Het Volk: Ghent; tel. (9) 265-61-11; fax (9) 225-35-27; e-mail hetvolkhoofdredactie@vum.be; internet www.hetvolk.be; f. 1891; Chief Editor DIRK REMMERIE; circ. 114,473.

Hasselt

Het Belang van Limburg: 10 Herckenrodesingel, 3500 Hasselt; tel. (11) 87-88-00; fax (11) 87-89-00; e-mail hbvlredactie@concentra.be; internet www.hbvl.be; f. 1879; Dir MARC VANGEEL; Editor IVO VANDEKERCKHOVE; circ. 114,056.

Liège

La Libre Belgique—Gazette de Liège: 26 blvd d'Avroy, 4000 Liège; tel. (4) 223-19-33; fax (4) 222-41-26; e-mail llb.redaction@saipm.com; internet www.lalibre.be; f. 1840; Dir-Gen. F. LE HODEY; Editor MICHEL KONEN; circ. 80,000 (with *La Libre Belgique—Brussels*).

La Meuse: place Cathédrale 16, 4000 Liège; tel. (4) 220-08-11; fax (4) 220-08-59; e-mail redliege.lameuse@sudpresse.be; internet www.lameuse.be; owned by Sud Presse; Editor LOUIS MARAITE.

Mons

La Province: 29 rue des Capucins, 7000 Mons; tel. (65) 31-71-51; fax (65) 33-84-77; e-mail redaction.generale@sudpresse.be; internet www.nouvellegazette.be; Dir JEAN-CLAUDE FYON; Editor DAVID FLAMENT.

Namur

Vers l'Avenir: 12 blvd Ernest Mélot, 5000 Namur; tel. (81) 24-88-11; fax (81) 22-60-24; e-mail infonam@verslavenir.be; f. 1918; 100% by Médiabel; Editors JEAN-FRANÇOIS PACCO, BRUNO MALTER; circ. 117,175 (with *L'Avenir du Luxembourg, Le Courrier de l'Escaut, Le Jour, Le Courrier*).

Tournai

Le Courrier de l'Escaut: 10 rue de Paris, 7500 Tournai; tel. (69) 88-96-20; fax (69) 88-96-61; e-mail infoce@verslavenir.be; f. 1829; 100% owned by Médiabel; Chief Editor JEAN-PIERRE DE ROUCK; circ. 117,175 (with *L'Avenir du Luxembourg, Vers l'Avenir, Le Jour, Le Courrier*).

Verviers

Le Jour/Le Courrier: 14 rue du Brou, 4800 Verviers; tel. (87) 32-20-70; fax (87) 31-67-40; e-mail infolj@verslavenir.be; f. 1894; 100% owned by Médiabel; Editor CLAUDE GILLET; circ. 117,175 (with *L'Avenir du Luxembourg, Le Courrier de l'Escaut, Vers l'Avenir*).

WEEKLIES

Atlas Weekblad: 89 Condédreef, 8500 Kortrijk; tel. (56) 26-10-10; fax (56) 21-35-93; e-mail atlas@atlasweekblad.be; internet www.atlasweekblad.be; classified advertising, regional news and sports.

Boer en Tuinder: 8 Minderbroedersstraat, 3000 Leuven; tel. (16) 24-21-60; fax (16) 24-21-68; internet www.boerenbond.be; f. 1891; agriculture and horticulture; circ. 30,000.

De Bond: 170 Langestraat, 1150 Brussels; tel. (2) 779-00-00; fax (2) 779-16-16; e-mail com@publicarto.be; internet www.publicarto.be; f. 1921; general interest; circ. 298,991 (2003).

Brugsch Handelsblad: 20 Sint-Jorisstraat, 8000 Brugge; tel. (50) 44-21-55; fax (50) 44-21-66; e-mail redactie.bhblad@roularta.be; internet www.kw.be; f. 1906; local news; includes *De Krant van West-Vlaanderen* as a supplement; Dir EDDY BROUCKAERT; Editor-in-Chief HEDWIG DACQUIN; circ. 40,000.

Ciné Télé Revue: 101 ave Reine Marie-Henriette, 1190 Brussels; tel. (2) 345-99-68; fax (2) 343-12-72; e-mail redaction@cinetelerevue.be; internet www.cinetelerevue.be; f. 1944 as Theatra Ciné Revue, current name adopted 1984; TV listings, celebrity news, family issues; circ. 2m.

European Voice: Résidence Palace, rue de la Loi 155, POB 6, 1040 Brussels; tel. (2) 540-90-90; fax (2) 540-90-71; e-mail info@europeanvoice.com; internet www.europeanvoice.com; f. 1995; EU policy-making, politics and business; Editor DANA SPINANT; circ. 16,388.

Femmes d'Aujourd'hui: 109 rue Neewald, 1200 Brussels; tel. (2) 776-28-53; fax (2) 776-23-99; e-mail editeur@femmesaujourdhui.be; internet www.femmesaujourdhui.com; f. 1933; women's magazine; Chief Editor ANOUK VAN GESTEL; circ. 124,443.

Flair: 82 Uitbreidingstraat, 2600 Berchem; tel. (3) 290-13-92; fax (3) 290-13-94; e-mail flairsec@flair.be; internet www.flair.be; Flemish; women's magazine; Chief Editor A. BROUCKMANS; circ. 157,955.

Humo: Telecomlaan 5–7, 1831 Diegem; tel. (2) 776-24-20; fax (2) 776-23-24; e-mail redactie@humo.be; internet www.humo.be; general weekly and TV and radio guide in Flemish; Chief Editor JÖRGEN OOSTERWAAL; circ. 277,863.

Joepie TV Plus: 2 Brandekensweg, 2627 Schelle; tel. (3) 880-84-65; fax (3) 844-61-52; e-mail redactie@joepie.be; internet www.joepie.be; f. 1973; Magnet Magazines; teenagers' interest; Dir-Gen. KOEN CLEMENT; Chief Editor ISABELLE VANDENBERGHE; circ. 76,540.

Kerk en Leven: 92 Halewijnlaan, 2050 Antwerp; tel. (3) 210-08-40; fax (3) 210-08-36; e-mail redactie.kerkleven@kerknet.be; internet www.kerknet.be; f. 1942; Catholic; five regional edns; circ. 620,000.

Knack: 50 Raketstraat, 1130 Brussels; tel. (2) 702-46-51; fax (2) 702-46-52; e-mail knack@knack.be; internet www.knack.be; f. 1971; news magazine; Dir and Chief Editor RIK VAN CAUWELAERT; circ. 140,000.

Kortrijks Handelsblad: 33 Meiboomlaan, 8800 Roeselare; tel. (51) 26-63-96; fax (51) 26-65-87; e-mail luc.demiddele@roularta.be; regional news; owned by Roularta Media Group; includes *De Krant van West-Vlaanderen* as a supplement; Chief Editor LUC DEMIDDELE.

De Krant van West-Vlaanderen: 33 Meiboomlaan, 8800 Roeselare; tel. (51) 26-61-11; fax (51) 26-65-87; e-mail redactie.kvwvl@roularta.be; internet www.kw.be; regional news and sport; owned by Roularta Media Group; 11 different edns; included as a supplement with titles *De Weekbode, Het Wekelijks Nieuws, De Zeewacht, Brugsch Handelsblad, Kortrijks Handelsblad*; Dir EDDY BROUCKAERT; Chief Editor JAN GHEYSEN; circ. 401,800.

Landbouwleven/Le Sillon Belge: 92 ave Léon Grosjean, 1140 Brussels; tel. (2) 730-33-00; fax (2) 726-91-34; e-mail erulu@landbouwleven.be; internet www.sillonbelge.be; f. 1952; agriculture; Gen. Dir P. CALLEBAUT; Editorial Man. ANDRÉ DE MOL; circ. 32,000.

Libelle : 82 Uitbreidingstraat, 2600 Berchem; tel. (3) 290-14-42; fax (3) 290-14-44; e-mail libelle@sanoma-magazines.be; internet www.libelle.be; f. 1945; Flemish; women's interest; Dir DIRK VAN DEN BOSSCHE; Chief Editor LILIANE SENEPART; circ. 261,675.

Le Soir Magazine: 120 rue Royale, 1000 Brussels; tel. (2) 225-55-55; fax (2) 225-59-11; e-mail redaction@lesoirmagazine.com; internet www.lesoir.be; f. 1928; independent illustrated; Dir-Gen. DANIEL VAN WYLICK; Chief Editor XAVIER BEGHIN; circ. 90,903.

Spirou/Robbedoes: 52 rue Jules Destrée, 6001 Marcinelle; tel. (71) 60-05-00; internet www.spirou.com; children's interest; Chief Editor T. H. TINCOT; circ. 80,000.

Sport/Foot Magazine and Sport/Voetbal Magazine: 50 Raketstraat, 1130 Brussels; tel. (2) 702-45-71; fax (2) 702-45-72; e-mail sportmagazine@roularta.be; internet www.sport.be/sportmagazine; Flemish and French; football; Chief Editors J. SYS, J. BAETE.

Story: 82 Uitbreidingstraat, 2600 Berchem; tel. (3) 290-15-13; fax (3) 290-15-14; e-mail story@sanoma-magazines.be; f. 1975; Flemish;

women's interest; Dir Dirk Van den Bossche; Publr Sandra De Preter; circ. 175,111.

De Streekkrant / De Weekkrant: 10 Herckenrodesingel, 3500 Hasselt; tel. (11) 87-83-70; fax (11) 87-85-09; e-mail philippe .belpaire@roularta.be; internet www.streekkrant.be; f. 1949; local news; circ. 2,832,220.

Télémoustique: Telecomlaan 5–7, 1831 Diegem; tel. (2) 776-25-20; fax (2) 776-23-17; e-mail telemoustique@sanoma-magazines.be.; internet www.telemoustique.be; f. 1924; radio and TV; Dir Jan Vandenwyngaerden; Editor Jean-Luc Cambier; circ. 170,000.

Télépro/Telepro: 31 rue Saint Remacle, 4800 Verviers; tel. (87) 30-87-31; fax (87) 31-35-37; e-mail courrier@telepromagazine.be; internet www.telepromagazine.be; f. 1954; TV listings; owned by Roularta Media Group; Dir Michel Huppertz; Chief Editor Guy Darrenougué; circ. 168,652.

TeVe-Blad: 82 Uitbreidingsstraat, 2600 Berchem; tel. (3) 290-14-81; fax (3) 290-14-82; e-mail teveblad@sanoma-magazines.be; f. 1981; TV listings; illustrated; Editor Geert Van Boxem; circ. 220,000.

Trends: Brussels Media Centre, rue de la Fusée, 50, POB 9, 1130 Brussels; tel. (2) 702-48-01; fax (2) 702-48-02; e-mail trends@ roularta.be; internet www.trends.be; economic analysis and business news; owned by Roularta Media Group; Dir Frans Crols; Chief Editors Johan Van Overtveld, Erik Bruyland; circ. 50,434.

TV7: 82 Uitbreidingsstraat, 2600 Berchem; tel. (3) 290-14-81; fax (3) 290-14-82; e-mail tvexpres@mediaxis.be; fmrly TV Ekspres, name changed as above 2004; Chief Editor Rob Jans; circ. 60,000.

Le Vif/L'Express: Roularta Media Group NV, Research Park, Zellik, De Haak, 1731 Zellik; tel. (2) 467-56-11; fax (2) 467-57-57; internet www.levif.be; f. 1971; current affairs; owned by Roularta Media Group; Dir-Gen. Patrick de Borchgrave; Chief Editors Jacques Gevers, Stéphane Renard; circ. 95,715.

De Weekbode: 33 Meiboomlaan, 8800 Roeselare; tel. (51) 26-61-11; fax (51) 26-65-87; regional news; owned by Roularta Media Group; includes *De Krant van West-Vlaanderen* as a supplement; Chief Editor Jan Gheysen.

Het Wekelijks Nieuws: Meiboomlaan 33, 8800 Roeselare; tel. (51) 26-65-55; fax (51) 26-55-87; e-mail herman.degryse@roularta.be; Christian news magazine; Editor Herman Degryse; circ. 56,000.

Het Wekelijks Nieuws Kust: Meiboomlaan 33, 8800 Roeselare; tel. (051) 26-62-60; fax (051) 26-65-87; e-mail sandra.rosseel@ roularta.be; internet www.kw.be; Furnes, Dixmude and Belgian West coast local news; owned by Roularta Media Group; includes *De Krant van West-Vlaanderen* as a supplement.

De Zeewacht: Meiboomlaan 33, 8800 Roeselare; tel. (51) 26-62-74; fax (51) 26-65-87; e-mail redactie.zeewacht@roularta.be; internet www.zeewacht.be; Ostend local news; owned by Roularta Media Group; includes *De Krant van West-Vlaanderen* as a supplement.

Zondag Nieuws: 2 Brandekensweg, 2627 Schelle; tel. (2) 220-22-11; fax (2) 217-98-46; f. 1958; general interest; circ. 48,101.

Zondagsblad: 22 Forelstraat, 9000 Ghent; tel. (9) 265-68-02; fax (9) 223-16-77; f. 1949; circ. 48,101.

SELECTED OTHER PERIODICALS

Alternative Libertaire: BP 3, 4000 Liège; e-mail alternative .libertaire@teledisnet.be; internet www.anarchie.be/AL; monthly; radical social criticism and debate.

Axelle: 170 Langestraat, 1150 Brussels; tel. (2) 799-00-00; fax (2) 799-16-16; e-mail com@publicarto.be; internet www.publicarto.be; f. 1917; monthly; women's interest; circ. 22,863 (2003).

Le Cri du Citoyen: BP 1607, 1000 Brussels 1; tel. and fax (2) 217-48-31; e-mail redaction@lecriducitoyen.com; internet www.chez .com/lecriducitoyen; social comment; 10 a year; Editor Francesco Paolo Catania.

Eigen Aard: Remylaan 4B, 3018 Wijgmaal-Leuven; tel. (2) 624-39-99; fax (2) 624-39-09; e-mail kvlv@kvlv.be; internet www.kvlv.be/ kvlv/eige_fra.htm; f. 1911; monthly; women's interest; circ. 127,627 (2004).

International Engineering News (IEN Europe): Potvlietlaan 5B, 2600 Antwerp; tel. (2) 285-33-77; fax (2) 285-33-35; e-mail p .alvenius@ien-online.com; internet www.ien-online.com; f. 1975; 11 a year; Man. Dir Orhan Erenberk; circ. 50,010.

Jet Limburg: 10 Herckenrodesingel, 3500 Hasselt; tel. (11) 87-84-85; fax (11) 87-84-84; e-mail jetinfo@concentra.be; internet www .jetmagazine.be; fortnightly; general interest; circ. 292,000.

Marie Claire: Neerveldstraat 109, 1200 Brussels; tel. (2) 776-22-11; fax (2) 776-23-99; e-mail marieclaire@sanoma-magazines.be; monthly; women's interest; Man. Dir Rosette Van Rossem; Editors Fabienne Willaert, Stéphanie Jottard; circ. 40,430.

Le Moniteur Belge/Belgisch Staatsblad: 40–42 rue de Louvain, 1000 Brussels; tel. (2) 552-22-11; fax (2) 511-01-84; internet moniteur.be; legislation and official documents; up to 5 a week.

Le Moniteur de l'Automobile: 56 ave Général Dumonceau, 1190 Brussels; tel. (2) 333-32-20; fax (2) 333-32-10; e-mail contact.mab@ lemoniteurautomobile.be; internet www.lemoniteurautomobile.be; fortnightly; motoring; Editors Etienne Visart, T. Verhelle; circ. 41,662.

Notre Temps/Onze Tijd: 33 rue de la Concorde, 1050 Brussels; tel. (2) 514-24-24; fax (2) 514-22-44; e-mail Redaction.NT@ bayard-presse.be; internet www.notretemps.com; senior citizens' interests; monthly; Dir Alain Cordier; circ. 96,672.

Sélection du Reader's Digest: 20 blvd Paepsem, 1070 Brussels; tel. (2) 526-81-85; fax (2) 526-81-89; e-mail service@readersdigest.be; internet www.rdb.be; f. 1947; monthly; general; Dir Gerard Visser; Chief Editor Oele Steenks; circ. 56,678.

Vrouw & Wereld: 170 Langestraat, 1150 Brussels; tel. (2) 799-00-00; fax (2) 799-16-16; e-mail com@publicarto.be; internet www .publicarto.be; f. 1920; monthly; women's interest; circ. 135,815 (2003).

NEWS AGENCIES

Agence Belga (Agence Télégraphique Belge de Presse SA)— Agentschap Belga (Belgisch Pers-telegraafagentschap NV): 8B rue F. Pelletier, 1030 Brussels; tel. (2) 743-23-11; fax (2) 735-18-74; e-mail redaction@belga.be; internet www.belga.be; f. 1920; largely owned by daily newspapers; Gen. Man. E. Hans; Editors-in-Chief Jean-Pierre Breulet, Marc Hollanders.

Agence Europe SA: 36 rue de la Gare, 1040 Brussels; tel. (2) 737-94-94; fax (2) 736-37-00; internet www.agenceurope.com; f. 1952; daily bulletin on EU activities.

Foreign Bureaux

Agence France-Presse (AFP): ave d'Auderghem 22–28, 1040 Brussels; tel. (2) 230-83-94; fax (2) 230-23-04; e-mail afp.bru@afp .com; internet www.afp.com; Dir Philippe Ries.

Agencia EFE (Spain): 1 blvd Charlemagne, bte 20, 1041 Brussels; tel. (2) 285-48-30; internet www.efe.com; Dir José Manuel Sanz Mingote.

Agenzia Nazionale Stampa Associata (ANSA) (Italy): 1 blvd Charlemagne, bte 7, 1040 Brussels; tel. (2) 230-81-92; fax (2) 230-60-82; internet www.ansa.it; Dir Luigi Mayer.

Algemeen Nederlands Persbureau (ANP) (Netherlands): 1 blvd International Press Centre ANP/IPC, Karel de Grotelaan 1, bte 6, 1041 Brussels; tel. (2) 230-11-88; fax (2) 231-18-04; internet www .anp.nl; Correspondents Ton van Lierop, Kees Pijnappels, Wilma van Meleren.

Anadolu Agency (Turkey): rue Louis Titz 27, 1040 Brussels; tel. (2) 732-50-76; fax (2) 732-50-77; e-mail bruksel@anadoluajansi.com.tr.

Česká Tisková Kancelář (ČTK) (Czech Republic): 2 rue des Egyptiens, bte 6, 1050 Brussels; tel. (2) 648-01-33; fax (2) 640-31-91; e-mail karol.bartak@skynet.be; internet www.ctk.cz; Correspondent M. Bartak.

DDP Nachrichtenagentur GmbH (ddp) (Germany): Brussels.

Deutsche Presse-Agentur (dpa) (Germany): 1 blvd Charlemagne, bte 17, 1041 Brussels; tel. (2) 230-36-91; fax (2) 230-98-96; e-mail dpa@dpa.be; internet www.dpa.de; Dir Thomas Spieker.

Informatsionnoye Telegrafnoye Agentstvo Rossii-Telegrafnoye Agentstvo Suverennykh Stran (ITAR-TASS) (Russia): 103 rue Général Lotz, bte 10, 1180 Brussels; tel. (2) 343-86-70; fax (2) 344-83-76; e-mail tassfoto@noos.fz; internet www.itar-tass.com; Correspondents Aleksandr Kondrashev, Mstislav Kondrashev.

Inter Press Service-Vlaanderen (IPS) (Italy): 21 Inquisitie-straat, 1000 Brussels; tel. (2) 732-69-16; fax (2) 735-20-89; e-mail ipseumed@ipsnews.net; internet www.ips.org; Dirs Peter Dhondt, Maarten Messiaen.

Jiji Tsushin (Jiji Press Ltd) (Japan): 1 blvd Charlemagne, bte 26, 1041 Brussels; tel. (2) 285-09-48; fax (2) 230-14-50; Dir Hiroshi Masuda.

Kyodo Tsushin (Kyodo News) (Japan): 1 blvd Charlemagne, bte 37, 1041 Brussels; tel. (2) 285-09-10; fax (2) 230-53-34; e-mail ono .keiichiro@kyodonews.jp; internet www.kyodo.co.jp; Dir Ohno Keiichiro.

Magyar Távirati Iroda Rt. (MTI) (Hungary): 41 rue Jean Chapelié, 1050 Brussels; tel. and fax (2) 343-75-35; internet hirek.mti.hu; Correspondents Jenö Erdész, Balázs László.

Reuters (United Kingdom): 61 rue de Trèves, 1040 Brussels; tel. (2) 287-66-11; fax (2) 230-55-40; internet www.reuters.com; Man. Dir Peter Kayer.

Rossiyskoye Informatsionnoye Agentstvo—Novosti (RIA—Novosti) (Russia): 74 rue du Merlo, 1180 Brussels; tel. (2) 332-24-35; fax (2) 332-17-29; e-mail novosti@skynet.be; internet www.rian.ru; Dir NIKOLAY VENEDIKTOV.

Xinhua (New China) News Agency (People's Republic of China): 32 square Ambiorix, Résidence le Pavois, bte 4, 1040 Brussels; tel. (2) 230-32-54; internet www.xinhua.org; Chief Correspondent LE ZUDE.

PRESS ASSOCIATIONS

Association belge des Editeurs de Journaux/Belgische Vereniging van de Dagbladuitgevers: 22 blvd Paepsem, bte 7, 1070 Brussels; tel. (2) 558-97-60; fax (2) 558-97-68; e-mail kris.destaercke@pressorg.be; f. 1964; 17 mems; Pres H. MAERTENS; Gen. Secs ALEX FORDYN (Flemish), MARGARET BORIBON (French).

Association générale des Journalistes professionnels de Belgique/Algemene Vereniging van de Beroepsjournalisten in België: Résidence Palace, Bloc C, rue de la Loi 155, 1040 Brussels; tel. (2) 235-22-60; fax (2) 235-22-72; e-mail info@ajp.be; internet www.agjpb.be; f. 1978 by merger; 4,000 mems; affiliated to IFJ (International Federation of Journalists); Pres. PHILIPPE LERUTH.

Association des Journalistes de la Presse Périodique/Vereniging van Journalisten van de Periodieke Pers: 54 rue Charles Martel, 1000 Brussels; tel. (2) 230-09-99; fax (2) 231-14-59; e-mail info@ajpp-vjpp.be; internet www.ajpp-vjpp.be; f. 1891; Pres. CLAUDE MUYLS.

Fédération Belge des Magazines/Federatie van de Belgische Magazines: 22/8 blvd Paepsemlaan, 1070 Brussels; tel. (2) 558-97-50; fax (2) 558-97-58; e-mail magazines@febelma.be; internet www.febelma.be; f. 1956; Pres. PATRICK DE BORCHGRAVE; Sec.-Gen. ALAIN LAMBRECHTS.

Principal Publishers

Acco CV: 153 Brusselsestraat, 3000 Leuven; tel. (1) 662-80-00; fax (1) 662-80-01; e-mail uitgeverij@acco.be; internet www.acco.be; f. 1960; general reference, scientific books, periodicals; Dir ROB BERREVOETS.

Uitgeverij Altiora Averbode NV (Publishing Dept): 1 Abdijstraat, bte 54, 3271 Averbode; tel. (1) 378-01-82; fax (1) 378-01-79; e-mail sabine.wouters@verbode.be; internet www.averbode.com; f. 1993; educational, religious; Business Unit Man. P. HERMANS.

De Boeck & Larcier SA: 39 rue des Minimes, 1000 Brussels; tel. (2) 548-07-11; fax (2) 513-90-09; e-mail deboeck.larcier@deboeck.be; internet www.deboeck.com; f. 1795; French imprints: De Boeck Education, De Boeck Université, Duculot, Estem, Larcier; Dutch imprints: Uitgeverij De Boeck, Uitgeverij Larcier; educational, scientific, academic, medical, legal; Chair. CHRISTIAN DE BOECK; Dirs BERNARD HOUDMONT, YANN DELALANDE.

Brepols Publishers NV: 67 Begijnhof, 2300 Turnhout; tel. (1) 444-80-20; fax (1) 442-89-19; e-mail info@brepols.net; internet www.brepols.net; f. 1796; humanities; Dir PAUL DE JONGH.

Etablissements Emile Bruylant: 67 rue de la Régence, 1000 Brussels; tel. (2) 512-98-45; fax (2) 511-72-02; e-mail info@bruylant.be; internet www.bruylant.be; f. 1838; law; Chief Man. Dir J. VANDEVELD.

Casterman SA: 132 rue Royale, bte 2, 1000 Brussels; tel. (2) 209-83-00; fax (2) 209-83-01; internet www.casterman.com; f. 1780; fiction, encyclopaedias, education, history, comic books and children's books; Man. Dir LOUIS DELAS.

Davidsfonds vzw: 79–81 Blijde Inkomststraat, 3000 Leuven; tel. (1) 631-06-00; fax (1) 631-06-08; e-mail uitgeverij@davidsfonds.be; internet www.davidsfonds.be; f. 1875; general, reference, textbooks; Dir KATRIEN DE VREESE.

Editions Dupuis SA: 52 rue Jules Destrée, 6001 Marcinelle; tel. (7) 160-50-00; fax (7) 160-05-99; internet www.dupuis.com; f. 1898; children's fiction, periodicals and comic books for children and adults, multimedia and audiovisual; Dir JEAN DENEUROSTIER.

Groupe Eramse: 2 place Baudouin, 5004 Bouge; tel. (8) 121-37-00; fax (8) 121-23-72; e-mail d2h@euronet.be; internet www.groupeerasme.be; f. 1979; imprints: Artel, D2H Didier Hatier-Hachette Education, Didier-Hatier, Érasme; school books; Dir I. PONET.

Halewijn NV: 92 Halewijnlaan, 2050 Antwerp; tel. (3) 210-08-11; fax (3) 210-08-36; e-mail Jo.Cornille@kerknet.be; f. 1953; general, periodicals; Dir-Gen. J. CORNILLE.

Editions Hemma SA: 106 rue de Chevron, 4987 Chevron; tel. (8) 643-01-01; fax (8) 643-36-40; e-mail hemma@hemma.be; internet www.hemma.be; f. 1956; juveniles, educational books and materials; Dir ALBERT HEMMERLIN.

Houtekiet NV: 33 Vrijheidstraat, 2000 Antwerp; tel. (3) 238-12-96; fax (3) 238-80-41; e-mail info@houtekiet.com; internet www.houtekiet.com; f. 1983; Dir LEO DE HAES.

Intersentia NV: Churchilllaan 108, 2900 Schoten, Antwerp; tel. (3) 680-15-50; fax (3) 658-71-21; e-mail mail@intersentia.be; internet www.intersentia.be; Publrs KRIS MOEREMANS, HANS KLUWER.

Die Keure NV: 108 Oude Gentweg, 8000 Brugge; tel. (5) 047-12-72; fax (5) 047-12-64; e-mail info@diekeure.be; internet www.diekeure.be; f. 1948; textbooks, law, political and social sciences; Dirs B. VANDENBUSSCHE (secondary schools), N. PAPPIJN (primary schools).

Uitgeverij De Klaproos: 4 Hostenstraat, 8670 Koksijde; tel. (5) 851-85-30; fax (5) 851-29-42; e-mail info@klaproos.be; internet www.klaproos.be; f. 1992; historical works; Dir SIEGFRIED DEBAEKE.

Uitgeverij Lannoo NV: 97 Kasteelstraat, 8700 Tielt; tel. (5) 142-42-11; fax (5) 140-11-52; e-mail lannoo@lannoo.be; internet www.lannoo.com; f. 1909; general, reference.

Editions du Lombard SA: 1–11 ave Paul-Henri Spaak, 1060 Brussels; tel. (2) 526-68-11; fax (2) 520-44-05; e-mail info@lombard.be; internet www.lombard.be; f. 1946; graphic novels; Gen. Man. FRANÇOIS PERNOT.

Manteau: 147A Belgiëlei, 2018 Antwerp; tel. (3) 285-72-26; fax (3) 285-72-99; e-mail info@standaarduitgeverij.be; internet www.standaarduitgeverij.be; f. 1932; literature; Publr WIM VERHEIJE; Dirs ERIC WILLEMS, JOHAN DE KONING.

Mercatorfonds: 85 Meir, 2000 Antwerp; tel. (3) 202-72-60; fax (3) 231-13-19; f. 1965; art, ethnography, literature, music, geography and history; Dir JAN MARTENS.

Peeters: 153 Bondgenotenlaan, 3000 Leuven; tel. (1) 623-51-70; fax (1) 622-85-00; e-mail peeters@peeters-leuven.be; internet www.peeters-leuven.be; f. 1856; academic; Dir P. PEETERS.

Uitgeverij Pelckmans NV: 222 Kapelsestraat, 2950 Kapellen; tel. (3) 664-53-20; fax (3) 655-02-63; e-mail everij@pelckmans.be; internet www.pelckmans.be; f. 1893 as De Nederlandsche Boekhandel, name changed (as above) 1988; school books, scientific, general; Dirs J. PELCKMANS, R. PELCKMANS.

Roularta Books: 33 Meiboomlaan, 8800 Roeselare; tel. (5) 126-66-80; fax (5) 126-69-67; e-mail roulartabooks@roularta.be; internet www.roulartabooks.be; f. 1988; owned by Roularta Media Group; Publr JAN INGELBEEN.

Snoeck-Ducaju en Zoon NV: 464 Begijnhoflaan, 9000 Ghent; tel. (9) 267-04-11; fax (9) 267-04-60; e-mail sdz@sdz.be; internet www.sdz.be; f. 1782; art books, travel guides; Pres. SERGE SNOECK.

Sanoma Magazines Belgium SA: Telecomlaan 5–7, 1831 Diegem; tel. (2) 776-22-11; fax (2) 776-23-99; e-mail info@sanoma-magazines.be; internet www.sanoma-magazines.be; periodicals; Dir DIRK VAN DEN BOSSCHE.

Standaard Uitgeverij NV: 147A Belgiëlei, 2018 Antwerp; tel. (3) 285-72-00; fax (3) 285-72-99; e-mail info@standaarduitgeverij.be; internet www.standaarduitgeverij.be; f. 1924; general, fiction, non-fiction, comics, dictionaries and professional literature; Dirs ERIC WILLEMS, JOHAN DE KONING, JOHAN VAN HULLE.

Vlaamse Uitgeversmaatschappij (VUM): 30 Gossetlaan, 1702 Groot-Bijgaarden; tel. (2) 467-22-11; internet www.vum.be; f. 1976; newspaper and magazine publishing group; Man. Dir JO VAN CROONENBORCH.

Wolters Kluwer Belgie NV: 30 Motstraat, 2800 Mechelen; tel. (1) 536-11-87; fax (1) 536-11-91; e-mail françois.bourgeois@wkb.be; internet www.wkb.be; law, business, scientific; Dir F. BOURGEOIS.

Wolters Plantyn: 32 Motstraat, 2800 Mechelen; tel. (1) 536-36-36; fax (1) 536-36-37; e-mail info@woltersplantyn.be; internet www.woltersplantyn.be; f. 1959; education; Dir ERIK TAMBORYN.

Yoyo Books: Hagelberg 25, 2250 Olen; tel. (1) 428-23-40; fax (1) 428-23-49; e-mail jo.dupre@yoyo-books; internet www.yoyo-books.co; imprints: Yoyo ECP, Allegrio; educational, cookery; Man. Dir JO DUPRÉ.

PUBLISHERS' ASSOCIATIONS

Association des Editeurs Belges (ADEB): 140 blvd Lambermont, 1030 Brussels; tel. (2) 241-65-80; fax (2) 216-71-31; e-mail adeb@adeb.be; internet www.adeb.irisnet.be; f. 1922; asscn of French-language book publrs; Dir BERNARD GÉRARD.

Vlaamse Uitgevers Vereniging: Hof ter Schrieklaan 19, 2600 Berchem, Antwerp; tel. (3) 281-53-61; fax (3) 281-67-62; e-mail hilde.van.laere@boek.be; internet www.vuv.be; asscn of Flemish-language book publrs; Dir HILDE VAN LAERE.

Broadcasting and Communications

TELECOMMUNICATIONS

In January 1998 the Belgian telecommunications sector was fully opened to private-sector competition. More than 300 private companies have subsequently registered as service providers.

Regulatory Authority

Institut Belge des Services Postaux et de Télécommunications (IBPT)/Belgisch Instituut voor Postdiensten en Telecommunicatie (BIPT): 14 ave de l'Astronomie, 1210 Brussels; tel. (2) 226-88-88; fax (2) 223-24-77; e-mail info@bipt.be; internet www.bipt.be; Administrator-Gen. ERIC VAN HEESVELDE.

Major Service Providers

BASE: 115 rue Colonel Bourg, 1140 Brussels; tel. (2) 728-42-00; fax (2) 728-42-01; e-mail help@base.be; internet www.base.be; mobile cellular telephone operator; subsidiary of Koninklijke KPN, Netherlands.

Belgacom: 27 blvd du Roi Albert II, 1030 Brussels; tel. (2) 202-41-11; fax (2) 203-65-93; e-mail about@belgacom.be; internet www.belgacom.be; 50% plus 1 share state owned, scheduled to increase to 51.6% following flotation in 2004; total service operator; Pres and CEO DIDIER BELLENS.

Belgacom Mobile SA (Proximus): rue du Progrès 55, 1210 Brussels; tel. (2) 205-40-00; fax (2) 205-40-40; internet company.proximus.be; 75% owned by Belgacom, 25% by Vodafone AirTouch; mobile cellular telephone operator; Man. Dir PHILIPPE VANDER PUTTEN.

BT (Worldwide) Ltd: Zaventem; tel. (2) 718-22-11; e-mail olivier.servais@bt.be; internet www.bt.be.

Cable & Wireless Belgium SA: 331–333 ave Louise, 1050 Brussels; tel. (2) 627-34-00; fax (2) 627-34-01; e-mail info.be@cw.com; internet www.cw.com.

Coditel S.A.: 26 rue des Deux Eglises, 1000 Bruxelles; tel. (2) 226-55-11; fax (2) 219-77-25; e-mail business-solutions@coditel.be; internet www.coditel.be; main cable operator in the Brussels region.

Esprit Telecom Belgium BV: Zaventem; tel. (2) 720-35-45; fax (2) 720-01-02; e-mail belgiuminfo@esprittele.com; internet www.esprittele.com; f. 1995.

Mobistar: 149 rue Colonel Bourg, 1140 Brussels; tel. (2) 745-71-11; fax (2) 745-70-00; internet www.mobistar.be; f. 1995; mobile cellular telephone and fixed-line operator; CEO BERNARD MOSCHENI.

Telenet Operaties NV: 4 Liersesteenweg, 2800 Mechelen; tel. (1) 533-30-00; fax 533-39-99; e-mail communicatie@telenet.be; internet www.telenet.be; f. 1996; telecommunications and cable service provider; CEO DUCO SICKINGHE.

KPN Belgium: 50 Medialaan, 1800 Vilvoorde; tel. (2) 275-33-11; fax (2) 275-33-33; internet www.eunet.be; formerly Unisource Belgium NV; Man. Dir PIERRE VERBRUGEN.

Versatel Belgium NV: 166 Koningin Astridlaan, 1780 Wemmel; e-mail serviceclientele@versatel.be; internet www.versatel.be; f. 1995.

WorldCom NV: Culliganlaan 2E, 1831 Diegem; tel. (2) 400-80-00; fax (2) 400-84-00; e-mail info-belgium-be@be.mci.com; internet www.worldcom.be; subsidiary of WorldCom.Inc; telecom operator.

STATE BROADCASTING ORGANIZATIONS

Flemish

Vlaamse Radio- en Televisieomroep NV (VRT): 52 Auguste Reyerslaan, 1043 Brussels; tel. (2) 741-31-11; fax (2) 734-93-51; e-mail info@vrt.be; internet www.vrt.be; f. 1998; shares held by Flemish Community; operates five radio stations and three television stations; Chair. GUY PEETERS; Vice-Chair. ANNELIES VAN CAUWELAERT; Man. Dir TONY MARY.

French

Radio-Télévision Belge de la Communauté Française (RTBF): 52 blvd Auguste Reyers, 1044 Brussels; tel. (2) 737-21-11; fax (2) 737-25-56; internet www.rtbf.be; operates five radio stations and three television stations; Admin.-Gen. JEAN-PAUL PHILIPPOT; Dir of Radio FRANCIS GOFFIN; Dir of Television ALAIN GERLACHE.

German

Belgisches Rundfunk- und Fernsehzentrum der Deutschsprachigen Gemeinschaft (BRF): 11 Kehrweg, 4700 Eupen; tel. (87) 59-11-11; fax (87) 59-11-09; e-mail info@brf.be; internet www.brf.be; Dir HANS ENGELS.

COMMERCIAL, CABLE AND PRIVATE BROADCASTING

Canal Plus Belgique: 656 chaussée de Louvain, 1030 Brussels; tel. (2) 730-02-11; fax (2) 730-03-79; internet www.canalplus.be; f. 1989; 42% owned by Canal Plus Europe; broadcasts to Brussels region and Wallonia.

Regionale TV Media: Research Park De Haak, 1731 Zellik, Brussels; tel. (2) 467-58-77; fax (2) 467-56-54; e-mail contact@rtvm.be; internet www.rtvm.be; group of 11 regional news broadcasters within Flanders; commercial.

RTL-TVI: 1 ave Ariane, 1200 Brussels; tel. (2) 778-68-11; fax (2) 778-68-12; internet nwww.rtl.be; fmrly Télévision Indépendante; owned by RTL Group, Luxembourg; commercial station; broadcasts in French.

Vlaamse Media Maatschappij: 1 Medialaan, 1800 Vilvoorde; tel. (2) 255-32-11; fax (2) 252-37-87; e-mail info@vtm.be; internet www.vtm.be; f. 1987; commercial; broadcasts in Flemish; Dir-Gen. PETER QUAGHEBEUR.

Finance

(cap. = capital; m. = million; res = reserves; dep. = deposits; brs = branches; amounts in euros, unless otherwise indicated)

BANKING

Commission bancaire, financière et des assurances /Commissie voor het Bank-, Financie- en Assurantiewezen: rue du Congrès 12–14, 1000 Brussels; tel. (2) 220-52-11; fax (2) 220-52-75; e-mail cpb@cbfa.be; internet www.cbfa.be; f. 1935; merged with Office de Contrôle des Assurances/Controledienst voor de Verzekeringen; to supervise the application of legislation relating to the legal status of credit institutions and to the public issue of securities, and insurance and mortgage cos, pension funds and insurance intermediaries; Chair. E. WYMEERSCH; CEOs P. PRAET, R. BONTE, M. DE WACHTER; Sec.-Gen. A. NIESTEN.

Central Bank

Banque Nationale de Belgique: 14 blvd de Berlaimont, 1000 Brussels; tel. (2) 221-21-11; fax (2) 221-31-01; e-mail info@nbb.be; internet www.nbb.be; f. 1850; bank of issue; cap. 10m., res 1,6936.4m., total assets 47,988.2m. (Dec. 2003); Gov. GUY QUADEN; Vice-Gov. LUC COENE; Dirs J.-P. PAUWELS, MARCIA DE WACHTER, JAN SMETS, JEAN HILGERS, FRANÇOISE MASAI, PETER PRAET; 2 brs.

Development Bank

Investeringsmaatschappij voor Vlaanderen (GIMV): 37 Karel Oomsstraat, 2018 Antwerp; tel. (3) 290-21-00; fax (3) 290-21-05; e-mail receptie@gimv.be; internet www.gimv.com; f. 1980; promotes creation, restructuring and expansion of private cos; cap. 220m. (2002); Chair. HERMAN DAEMS; CEO DIRK BOOGMANS.

Major Commercial Banks

ABN AMRO Bank NV: 53 Regentlaan, 1000 Brussels; tel. (2) 546-04-60; fax (2) 546-04-23; e-mail postbox@abnamro.be; internet www.abnamro.be; f. 1824; cap. 1,732.0m., res 11,315.0m., dep. 472,441.0m. (Dec. 2003); Chair. R. W. J. GROENINK; 7 brs.

Antwerpse Diamantbank NV/Banque Diamantaire Anversoise SA/Antwerp Diamond Bank NV: 54 Pelikaanstraat, 2018 Antwerp; tel. (3) 204-72-04; fax (3) 233-90-95; e-mail info@adia.be; f. 1934; cap. 34.4m., res 92.0m., dep. 1,669.9m. (Dec. 2003); Chair. JAN VANHEVEL; Man. Dir and Chair. of Exec. Cttee PAUL C. GORIS.

AXA Bank Belgium NV: 214 Grotesteenweg, 2600 Antwerp; tel. (3) 286-22-11; fax (3) 286-24-07; e-mail contact@axa-bank.be; internet www.axa.be; f. 1881 as ANHYP Bank NV, present name adopted 2000; cap. 6.2m., res 285.7m., dep 12,480.2m. (Dec. 2003); Chair. of Bd of Dirs ALFRED BOUCKAERT; Chair. of Exec. Cttee SERGE WIBAUT.

Banca Monte Paschi Belgio SA/NV: 24 rue Joseph II, 1000 Brussels; tel. (2) 220-72-11; fax (2) 218-83-91; e-mail info@montepaschi.be; internet www.montepaschi.be; f. 1947 as Banco di Roma (Belgique), name changed 1992; cap. 33.6m., res 6.9m., dep. 881.8m. (Dec. 2003); Pres. of Exec. Cttee and Man. Dir LUIGI MACCHIOLA.

Bank J. van Breda & Co NV: 295 Plantin en Moretuslei, 2140 Borgerhout; tel. (3) 217-51-11; fax (3) 235-37-84; e-mail info@bankvanbreda.be; internet www.bankvanbreda.be; f. 1930; cap. 17.5m., res 116.3m., dep. 1,7963m. (Dec. 2003); Gen. Man. CARLO HENRIKSEN; 42 brs.

Bank Brussels Lambert/Banque Brussels Lambert (BBL): 24 ave Marnix, 1000 Brussels; tel. (2) 547-21-11; fax (2) 547-38-44;

e-mail info@bbl.be; internet www.bbl.be; f. 1975; taken over by ING Bank NV (the Netherlands) Jan. 1998; cap. 850m., res 2,732.9m., dep. 116,309.7m. (Dec. 2001); Chair. of Bd MICHEL TILMANT; Pres. and CEO LUC VANDEWALLE; 953 brs.

Bank Degroof SA/Banque Degroof SA: 44 rue de l'Industrie, 1040 Brussels; tel. (2) 287-91-11; fax (2) 230-67-00; e-mail info@degroof.be; internet www.degroof.be; f. 1871; present name adopted 1998; cap. 39.8m., res 104.8m., dep. 2,178.8m. (Sept. 2003); CEO ALAIN SIAENS.

Banque Belgolaise SA/Belgolaise Bank: 1 Cantersteen, bte 807, 1000 Brussels; tel. (2) 551-72-11; fax (2) 551-75-15; e-mail belgolaise.brussels@belgolaise.com; internet www.belgolaise.com; f. 1960; wholly-owned by Fortis Bank since 2000; cap. 25.0m., res 59.1m., dep. 2,008.5m. (Dec. 2002); Chair. MARC YVES BLANPAIN; Vice-Chair. FILIP DIERCKX; 2 brs (Paris and London) and 13 affiliates in Africa.

Banque Delen NV/SA: 184 Jan van Rijswijcklaan, 2020 Antwerp; tel. (3) 244-55-66; fax (3) 216-04-91; e-mail info@delen.be; internet www.delen.be; f. 1928; cap. 40.0m., res 2.9m., dep. 614.0m. (Dec. 2002); Pres. JACQUES DELEN; Chair. JAN SUYKENS; 2 brs.

Banque Européenne pour l'Amérique Latine (BEAL) SA: 166 chaussée de la Hulpe, 1170 Brussels; tel. (2) 663-69-00; fax (2) 663-69-59; e-mail head-office_bealbrussels@bankbeal.com; internet www2.westlb.de/beal; f. 1974; cap. 80.0m., res 40.6m., dep. 3,122.0m. (Dec. 2001); Chair. ANDREAS SEIBERT; Man. Dirs PHILIP WYKES, HORST R. MAGIERA.

Byblos Bank Europe SA: 10B rue Montoyer, 1000 Brussels; tel. (2) 551-00-20; fax (2) 513-05-26; e-mail byblosbank.europe@byblosbankeur.com; internet www.byblosbank.com.lb; f. 1976; cap. 20.0m., res 8.7m., dep. 248.8m. (Dec. 2003); Chair. ALBERT S. NASSAR; Man. Dir and Pres. NAJAH L. SALEM.

CBC Banque SA: 5 Grand-Place, 1000 Brussels; tel. (2) 547-12-11; fax (2) 547-11-10; e-mail info@cbc.be; internet www2.cbc.be; f. 1958; name changed as above 1998; cap. 89.6m., res 302.6m., dep. 8.216m. (Dec. 2002); Chair. of Bd of Dirs Baron HUYGHEBAERT; Chair. of Exec. Cttee CHRISTIAN DELEU; 115 brs.

Citibank Belgium NV/SA: 263 blvd Général Jacques, 1050 Brussels; tel. (2) 626-51-11; fax (2) 626-55-84; internet www.citibank.be; f. 1919; present name adopted 1992; cap. 44.9m., res 11.0m., dep. 1,950.0m. (Dec. 2000); Gen. Man. JACK WRIGHT.

Crédit Agricole SA/Landbouwkrediet NV: 251 blvd Sylvain Dupuis, 1070 Brussels; tel. (2) 558-71-11; fax (2) 558-76-23; e-mail info@credit-agricole.be; f. 1937; cap. 206.6m., res 107.2m., dep. 5,002.4m. (Dec. 2003); Pres. LUC VERSELE.

Crédit Professionnel SA/Beroepskrediet NV: 6–9 ave des Arts, 1210 Brussels; tel. (2) 289-82-00; fax (2) 289-89-90; e-mail info@bkcp.be; internet www.bkcp.be; f. 1992 as Caisse Nationale de Crédit Professionnel SA; name changed as above 1997; cap. 56.3m., res 1.4m., dep. 2,120.9m. (Dec. 2002); Chair. of Supervisory Bd GUIDO VERHAEGEN; Chair. of Exec. Cttee THIERRY FAUT.

Delta Lloyd Bank NV: 23 ave de l'Astronomie, 1210 Brussels; tel. (2) 229–76-00; fax (2) 229-76-99; e-mail info@dlbank.be; internet www.dlbank.be; f. 1966; cap. 22.8m., res 10.9m., dep. 762.5m. (Dec. 1999); Pres. PIET VERBRUGGE.

Deutsche Bank SA/NV: 13 ave Marnix, 1000 Brussels; tel. (2) 551-65-11; fax (2) 551-66-66; internet www.deutschebank24.be; f. 1893 as Banque de Commerce SA (Handelsbank NV), renamed Crédit Lyonnais Belgium 1989, bought by Deutsche Bank 1999; cap. BF 6,587m., res BF 3,847m., dep. BF 406,231m. (Dec. 1997); Chair. RAINER NESKE; Chief Exec. YVES DELACOLLETTE; 26 brs.

Dexia Bank Belgium SA: 44 Pachécolaan, 1000 Brussels; tel. (2) 222-11-11; fax (2) 222-30-41; internet www.dexia.be; f. 1860 as Crédit Communal de Belgique SA, present name adopted 2000; cap. 924.1m., res 2,965.0m., dep. 129,379.0m. (Dec. 2003); Chair. AXEL MILLER.

Europabank NV: 170 Burgstraat, 9000 Ghent; tel. (9) 224-73-11; fax (9) 223-34-72; e-mail europabank@europabank.be; f. 1964; 99.9% owned by Landbouwkrediet NV; cap. 1.6m., res 46.2m., dep. 553.6m. (Dec. 2003); Pres. LUK OSTE; 27 brs.

Euroclear Bank SA: 1 blvd du Roi Albert II, 1210 Brussels; tel. (2) 224-12-11; fax (2) 224-40-45; internet www.euroclear.com; f. Dec. 2000; Euroclear Plc 97.4%; cap. 654.2m., res 1,115.6m., dep. 6,529.2m. (Dec. 2003); CEO PIERRE FRANCOTTE.

Fortis Bank NV/Fortis Banque SA: 3 Montagne du Parc, 1000 Brussels; tel. (2) 511-26-311; fax (2) 565-49-29; e-mail info@fortisbank.com; internet www.fortisbank.com; f. 1822; 1999 merger of Generale Bank/Générale de Banque and ASLK-CGER Bank/Banque with the Fortis Group; banking, insurance and investments; cap. 3,111.8m., res 7,131.0m., dep. 365,976.1m. (Dec. 2003); Chair. of Bd of Dirs ANTON VAN ROSSUM; Chair. of Exec. Cttee HERMAN VERWILST; 1,375 brs.

Goffin Bank NV (HBM Bank NV): 120 Verlorenbroodstraat, 9820 Merelbeke; tel. (9) 261-02-00; fax (9) 261-02-01; e-mail info@goffin.be; internet www.goffin.be; f. 1955; cap. 6.5m., res 1.1m., dep. 211.1m. (Dec. 2001); Pres. ANTOON VAN COILLIE; Chair. WALTER VANDERBREKEN.

ING Belgium SA/NV: ave Marnix, 1000 Brussels; tel. (2) 547-21-11; fax (2) 547-38-44; e-mail info@ing.be; internet www.ing.be; merged with Caisse Privée Banque SA/Private Kas Bank NV in May 2003; cap. 850.0m., res 2,554.1m., dep. 108,556.7m. (Dec. 2003); Chair. CEES MAAS.

KBC Bank NV: 2 Havenlaan, 1080 Brussels 8; tel. (2) 429-11-11; fax (2) 429-81-31; e-mail kbc.telecenter@kbc.be; internet www.kbc.be; f. 1935 as Kredietbank NV; merged with Bank von Roeselare NV and CERA Investment Bank NV in 1998; cap. and res 7,870.1m., dep. 171,805.5m. (Dec. 2003); Pres. A. BERGEN.

Keytrade Bank SA: 100 blvd de Souverain, 1170 Brussels; tel. (2) 679-90-00; fax (2) 679-90-01; e-mail info@keytradebank.com; internet www.keytradebank.com; f. July 2002 by merger of RealBank SA and VMS Keytrade.com, present name adopted Aug. 2002; Pres., CEO and Gen. Man. JEAN ZURSTRASSEN.

Parfibank SA: 40 blvd du Régent, 1000 Brussels; tel. (2) 513-90-20; fax (2) 512-73-20; e-mail parfibank@dexia.be; f. 1976 as Nippon European Bank SA, present name adopted 1996; cap. 75.0m., res 46.7m., dep. 1,048.1m. (Dec. 2003); Chair. CHRISTIAN PINTE; Man. Dir JACQUES JANSSENS.

Santander Benelux SA/NV: 227 rue de la Loi, 1040 Brussels; tel. (2) 286-54-11; fax (2) 230-09-40; f. 1914 as Société Hollandaise de Banque, name changed to Santander Central Hispano Benelux in 2001, present name adopted 2004; cap. 39.6m., res 0.7m., dep. 657.1m. (Dec. 2003); Man. Dir GUILLERMO SANZ MURAT.

Banking Association

Association Belge des Banques/Belgische Vereniging van Banken (ABB): 36 rue Ravenstein, 1000 Brussels; tel. (2) 507-68-11; fax (2) 512-58-61; e-mail abb-bvb@abb-bvb.be; internet www.abb-bvb.be; f. 1936; 137 mems; affiliated to Fédération des Entreprises de Belgique and Fédération Bancaire de l'UE; Pres. L. VANDEWALLE; CEO M. VERMAERKE.

STOCK EXCHANGE

In September 2000 Euronext was formed from the merger of the stock exchanges of Brussels (Brussels Exchanges), Amsterdam (Amsterdam Exchanges) and Paris (Paris Bourse).

Euronext Brussels: Palais de la Bourse, 1000 Brussels; tel. (2) 509-12-11; fax (2) 509-12-12; e-mail info@euronext.com; internet www.euronext.com; formed in 2000 by merger of Amsterdam, Paris and Brussels exchanges, and joined in 2002 by the Lisbon stock exchange and Euronext.liffe; CEO JOOST VAN DER DOES DE WILLEBOIS; Vice Pres. OLIVIER LEFEBVRE.

HOLDING COMPANY

SUEZ-TRACTEBEL: place du Trône 1, 1000 Brussels; tel. (2) 510–71–11; fax (2) 510-73-30; internet www.suez.be; f. 1822 as Société Générale de Belgique, merged with Tractebel and name changed as above in 2003; investment and holding co with substantial interests in energy and services; Pres. GÉRARD MESTRALLET; Dir JEAN-PIERRE HANSEN.

INSURANCE

Principal Insurance Companies

Aviabel, Compagnie Belge d'Assurances Aviation, SA: 10 ave Brugmann, 1060 Brussels; tel. (2) 349-12-11; fax (2) 349-12-99; e-mail insurance@aviabel.be; internet www.aviabel.be; f. 1935; aviation, insurance, reinsurance; Chair. P. GERVY; Gen. Man. J. VERWILGHEN.

AXA: 25 blvd du Souverain, 1170 Brussels; tel. (2) 678-61-11; fax (2) 678-93-40; e-mail elly.bens@axa.be; internet www.axa.be; f. 1853; member of the AXA group; all branches; Pres. Comte JEAN-PIERRE DE LAUNOIT; Man. Dir ALFRED BOUCKAERT.

Compagnie de Bruxelles 1821 SA d'Assurances: Brussels; tel. (2) 237-12-11; fax (2) 237-12-16; f. 1821; fire, life, general; Pres. C. BASECQ.

DVV Verzekeringen NV/Les AP Assurances SA: 6 ave Livingston, 1000 Brussels; tel. (2) 286-61-11; fax (2) 286-15-15; internet www.dvv.be; f. 1929; all branches; 82% owned by Artesia Banking Corporation.

Ethias: 24 rue des Croisiers, 4000 Liège; tel. (4) 220-31-11; fax (4) 220-30-05; e-mail info@ethias.be; internet www.ethias.be; f. 1919; fmrly Société Mutuelle des Administrations Publiques (SMAP), name changed as above in 2003; institutions, civil service employees, public administration and enterprises; CEO GUY BURTON.

Naviga-Mauretus SA: Frankrijkei 79, 2000 Antwerp; tel. (3) 247-35-11; fax (3) 247-35-90; e-mail info@naviga-mauretus.be; f. 2003 as a result of merger between Naviga, Mauretus, and Aachener & Münchener; marine insurance broker; Dirs HANS VERSTRAETE, BENOIT VERWILGHEN, ANNE MARIE SEEUWS, CHRIS BELIEN.

Euler Hermes SA/NV: 15 rue Montoyer, 1000 Brussels; tel. (2) 289-31-11; fax (2) 289-32-99; e-mail info.belgium@eulerhermes.com ; internet www.eulerhermes.com; f. 1929 as Compagnie Belge d'Assurance-Crédit; present name adopted 1998; credit insurance, reinsurance; CEO JEAN-LUC LOUIS.

Fortis AG: 53 blvd Emile Jacqmain, 1000 Brussels; tel. (2) 220-81-11; fax (2) 220-81-50; e-mail info@fortisag.be; internet www.fortisag.be; f. 1990; owned by the Fortis Group; CEO JOZEF DE MEY.

Generali Belgium SA: 149 ave Louise, 1050 Brussels; tel. (2) 403-81-11; fax (2) 403-88-99; e-mail generali_belgium@generali.be; internet www.generali.be; fire, accident, marine, life, reinsurance; Pres. G. BECKERS; Dir-Gen. T. DELVAUX.

KBC SA/NV: Waaistraat 6, 3000 Leuven; tel. (07) 815-21-53; fax (03) 283-29-50; e-mail kbc.telecenter@kbc.be; internet www.kbc.be; f. 1998; Chair. JAN HUYGHEBAERT.

Mercator & Noordstar NV: 302 Kortrijksesteen Weg, 9000 Ghent; tel. (9) 242-37-11; fax (9) 242-36-36; e-mail info@mercator.be; internet www.mercator.be; CEO JAN DE MEULDER.

Insurance Associations

Assuralia: 29 square de Meeûs, 1000 Brussels; tel. (2) 547-56-11; fax (2) 547-56-00; internet www.assuralia.be; f. 1921; affiliated to Fédération des Entreprises de Belgique; Pres. C. DESSEILLE; Man. Dir MICHEL BAECKER; 95 mems.

Fédération des Producteurs d'Assurances de Belgique (FEPRABEL): 40 ave Albert-Elisabeth, 1200 Brussels; tel. (2) 743-25-60; fax (2) 735-44-58; e-mail info@feprabel.be; internet www.feprabel.be; f. 1934; Pres. ANDRÉ LAMOTTE; 500 mems.

Trade and Industry

GOVERNMENT AGENCIES

Investeren in Vlaanderen—Flanders Foreign Investment Office: Regentlaan 40, 1000 Brussels; tel. (2) 227-53-11; fax (2) 227-53-10; e-mail flanders@ffio.be; internet www.ffio.com; f. 1988; promotes investment in Flanders; Man. Dir PASCAL WALRAVE.

Société de Développement de la Région de Bruxelles (SDRB): 6 rue Gabrielle Petit, 1080 Brussels; tel. (2) 422-51-11; fax (2) 422-51-12; e-mail info@brda.be; internet www.brda.be; f. 1974; promotes economic development in the capital; Chair. C. PAELINCK.

Société Régionale d'Investissement de Wallonie: 13 ave Destenay, 4000 Liège; tel. (4) 221-98-11; fax (4) 221-99-99; e-mail sriw@sriw.be; internet www.sriw.be; f. 1979; promotes private enterprise in Wallonia; Pres. JEAN-CLAUDE DEHOVRE.

PRINCIPAL CHAMBERS OF COMMERCE

There are chambers of commerce and industry in all major towns and industrial areas.

Voka—Kamer van Koophandel Antwerpen-Waasland: 12 Markgravestraat, 2000 Antwerp; tel. (3) 232-22-19; fax (3) 233-64-42; e-mail info@kvkaw.voka.be; internet www.kvkaw.voka.be; f. 1969; Pres. JOHN STOOP; Gen. Man. LUC LUWEL.

Chambre de Commerce et d'Industrie de Bruxelles: 500 ave Louise, 1050 Brussels; tel. (2) 648-50-02; fax (2) 640-93-28; e-mail yhuyghebaert@ccib.irisnet.be; internet www.portalccib.irisnet.be; f. 1875; Pres. YVAN HUYGHEBAERT; 3,000 mems.

Chambre de Commerce et d'Industrie de Liège: Palais des Congrès, 2 Esplanade de l'Europe, 4020 Liège; tel. (43) 43-92-92; fax (43) 43-92-67; e-mail info@ccilg.be; internet www.ccilg.be; f. 1866; Pres. JEAN PHILIPPE DESPONTIN.

INDUSTRIAL AND TRADE ASSOCIATIONS

Fédération des Entreprises de Belgique (Federation of Belgian Companies): 4 rue Ravenstein, 1000 Brussels; tel. (2) 515-08-11; fax (2) 515-09-99; e-mail red@vbo-feb.be; internet www.vbo-feb.be; f. 1895; federates all the main industrial and non-industrial asscns; Pres. KAREL BOONE; CEO TONY VANDEPUTTE; 35 full mems.

Agoria—Fédération Multisectorielle de l'Industrie Technologique (Multisector Federation for the Technology Industry): 80 blvd Auguste Reyers, 1030 Brussels; tel. (2) 706-78-00; fax (2) 706-78-01; e-mail info@agoria.be; internet www.agoria.be; f. 1946

as Fédération des Enterprises de l'Industrie des Fabrications Métalliques, Mécaniques, Electriques, Electroniques et de la Transformation des Matières Plastiques (FABRIMETAL), present name adopted 2000; more than 1,200 mem. cos; Pres. JOHN CORDIER; CEO PAUL SOETE.

ASBL Fédération des Carrières de Petit Granit—Pierre Bleue de Belgique (Limestone): 1 chemin de Carrières, 7063 Neufvilles; tel. (67) 34-68-00; fax (67) 34-68-01; f. 1948; Pres. F. GALER.

Association Belge des Banques/Belgische Vereniging van Banken (ABB): see Finance above.

Association des Fabricants de Pâtes, Papiers et Cartons de Belgique (COBELPA) (Paper): 306 Louizalaan, bus 11, 1050 Brussels; tel. (2) 646-64-50; fax (2) 646-82-97; e-mail general@cobelpa.be; internet www.cobelpa.be; f. 1940; Pres. PIERRE MACHARIS.

Brasseurs Belges (Breweries): Maison des Brasseurs, 10 Grand' Place, 1000 Brussels; tel. (2) 511-49-87; fax (2) 511-32-59; e-mail belgian.brewers@beerparadise.be; internet www.beerparadise.be; f. 1971; Pres. THEO VERLOET.

Confédération Nationale de la Construction (CNC) (Civil Engineering, Road and Building Contractors and Auxiliary Trades): 34–42 rue du Lombard, 1000 Brussels; tel. (2) 545-56-00; fax (2) 545-59-00; e-mail info@confederatiebouw.be; internet www.cnc.be; f. 1946; Pres. ROB LENAERS; 14,000 mems.

Confédération Professionnelle du Sucre et de ses Dérivés (Sugar): 182 ave de Tervueren, 1150 Brussels; tel. (2) 775-80-69; fax (2) 775-80-75; e-mail info@subel.be; f. 1938; mems: 10 groups, 66 cos; Pres. E. KESSELS; Dir-Gen. M. ROSIERS.

Fédération Belge de la Brique (Bricks): 13 rue des Poissonniers, bte 22, 1000 Brussels; tel. (2) 511-25-81; fax (2) 513-26-40; e-mail info@brique.be; internet www.brique.be; f. 1947; Pres. GILBERT DE BAERE.

Fédération Belge des Dragueurs de Gravier et de Sable (BELBAG-DRAGBEL) (Quarries): Rue Meier 12, 3640 Kinrooi; tel. (89) 56-73-45; fax (89) 56-45-42; f. 1967; Pres. CHARLES LECLUYSE.

Fédération Belge des Entreprises de la Transformation du Bois (FEBELBOIS) (Wood): 5 Hofter-Vleest, bte 1, 1070 Brussels; tel. (2) 556-25-55; fax (2) 556-25-70; e-mail dir@febehout.be; internet www.febelhout.be; Pres. GUSTAAF NEYT.

Fédération Belge des Industries Graphiques (FEBELGRA) (Graphic Industries): 20 rue Belliard, bte 16, 1040 Brussels; tel. (2) 512-36-38; fax (2) 513-56-76; e-mail info@febelgra.be; internet www.febelgra.be; f. 1978.

Fédération Belge des Industries de l'Habillement (Clothing): 24 rue Montoyer, 1040 Brussels; tel. (2) 238-10-11; fax (2) 230-10-10; e-mail roggeman@belgianfashion.be; internet www.belgianfashion.be; f. 1946; Pres. ALAIN CHAUVEHEID.

Fédération Belgo-Luxembourgeoise de l'Industrie du Tabac (FEDETAB) (Tobacco): 251 ave Louise, 1000 Brussels; tel. (2) 646-04-20; fax (2) 646-22-13; e-mail tobacco@fedetab.be; f. 1947; Pres. G. VANDERMARLIÈRE.

Fédération Charbonnière de Belgique (Coal): Brussels; tel. (2) 230-37-40; fax 230-88-50; f. 1909; Pres. YVES SLEUWAEGEN; Dir JOS VAN DEN BROECK.

Fédération d'Employeurs pour le Commerce International, le Transport et les Branches d'Activité Connexes (Employers' Federation of International Trade, Transport and Related Activities) (inc. Fédération Patronale des Ports Belges): 33 Brouwersvliet, bus 7, 2000 Antwerp; tel. (3) 221-99-90; fax (3) 221-99-09; e-mail cepa@cepa.be; f. 1937; Pres. MARINO VERMEERSCH; Dir RENÉ DE BROUWER.

Fédération de l'Industrie Alimentaire/Federatie Voedingsindustrie (FEVIA) (Food): 43 ave des Arts, bte 7, 1040 Brussels; tel. (2) 550-17-40; fax (2) 550-17-54; e-mail info@fevia.be; internet www.fevia.be; f. 1937; Pres. MICHEL DELBAERE; Dir-Gen. CHRIS MORIS.

Fédération de l'Industrie du Béton (FEBE) (Precast Concrete): 12 rue Volta, 1050 Brussels; tel. (2) 735-80-15; fax (2) 734-77-95; e-mail mail@febe.be; internet www.febe.be; f. 1936; Pres. J. FRANSSENS; Dir EDDY DANO.

Fédération des Industries Chimiques de Belgique (FEDICHEM) (Chemical Industries): 49 square Marie-Louise, 1000 Brussels; tel. (2) 238-97-11; fax (2) 231-13-01; e-mail postmaster@fedichem.be; internet www.fedichem.be; f. 1919; Pres. ANTOON DIEUSAERT; Man. Dir JEAN-MARIE BIOT.

Fédération de l'Industrie Cimentière Belge (FEBELCEM) (Cement): 8 rue Volta, 1050 Brussels; tel. (2) 645-52-11; fax (2)

640-06-70; e-mail febelcem@febelcem.be; internet www.febelcem .be; f. 1949; Pres. ANDRÉ JACQUEMART; Dir-Gen. JEAN-PIERRE JACOBS.

Fédération des Industries Extractives et Transformatrices de Roches non-Combustibles (FEDIEX) (Extraction and processing of non-fuel rocks): 8 rue Volta, B-1050 Brussels; tel. (2) 511-61-73; fax (2) 511-12-84; e-mail m.lerat@fediex.org; f. 1942 as Union des Producteurs Belges de Chaux, Calcaires, Dolomies et Produits Connexes, name changed (as above) 1990; co-operative society; CEO J.-P. JACOBS; Chair. D. MERTENS.

Fédération de l'Industrie du Gaz (FIGAZ) (Gas): 4 ave Palmerston, 1000 Brussels; tel. (2) 237-11-11; fax (2) 230-44-80; e-mail figaz@figaz.be; f. 1946; Pres. WALTER PEERAER; Sec. Gen. FERDINAND DE LICHTERVELDE.

Fédération de l'Industrie Textile Belge (FEBELTEX) (Textiles): 24 rue Montoyer, bte 1, 1000 Brussels; tel. (2) 287-08-11; e-mail info@febeltex.be; internet www.febeltex.be; f. 1945; Pres. PHILIPPE VLERICK; Dir-Gen. JEAN-FRANÇOIS QUIX; 500 mems.

Fédération des Industries Transformatrices de Papier et Carton (FETRA) (Paper and Cardboard): 715 chaussée de Waterloo, BP 25, 1180 Brussels; tel. (2) 344-19-62; fax (2) 344-86-61; f. 1976; Pres. PAUL PISSENS.

Fédération de l'Industrie du Verre (Glass): 89 ave Louise, 1050 Brussels; tel. (2) 542-61-20; fax (2) 542-61-21; e-mail info@vgi-fiv.be; internet www.vgi-fiv.be; f. 1947; Pres. O. DU BOUCHERON; Man. Dir ROLAND DERIDDER.

Fédération Pétrolière Belge (Petroleum): 39 ave des Arts, bte 2, 1040 Brussels; tel. (2) 508-30-00; fax (2) 511-05-91; e-mail fpb-bpf@petrolfed.be; internet www.petrolfed.be; f. 1926; Pres. G. ASSELMAN; Sec.-Gen. G. VAN DE WERVE.

Groupement des Sablières (Sand and Gravel): 49 Quellinstraat, 2018 Antwerp; tel. (3) 223-66-83; fax (3) 223-66-47; e-mail paul.de.nie@sibelco.be; f. 1937; Pres. A. SPECKAERT; Sec. PAUL DE NIE.

Groupement de la Sidérurgie (Iron and Steel): 5 ave Ariane, 1200 Brussels; tel. (2) 509-14-11; fax (2) 509-14-00; e-mail gsv@steelbel.be; internet www.steelbel.be; f. 1953; Pres. PAUL MATTHYS.

Industrie des Huiles Minérales de Belgique (IHMB—IMOB) (Mineral Oils): 49 square Marie-Louise, 1000 Brussels; tel. (2) 238-97-11; fax (2) 230-03-89; e-mail ihmb–imob@fedichem.be; internet www.fedichem.be/ihmb-imob; f. 1921; Pres. D. JONGERT; Sec. D. DE HEMPTINNE; 44 mems.

Union des Armateurs Belges (Shipowners): 33 Brouwersvliet, 2000 Antwerp; tel. (3) 232-72-32; fax (3) 231-39-97; e-mail info@brv.be; internet www.brv.be; Chair. NICOLAS SAVERYS; Man. Dir M. NUYTEMANS.

Union des Carrières et Scieries de Marbres de Belgique (UCSMB) (Marble): 8 Heideveld, 1654 Huizingen; tel. (2) 361-36-81; fax (2) 361-31-55; internet www.ucsmb.be; Pres. P. STONE.

Union Professionnelle des Producteurs de Fibres-Ciment (Fibre-Cement): 114 Aerschotstraat, 9100 Sint-Niklaas; tel. (3) 760-49-29; fax (3) 777-47-84; f. 1941; Pres. MARC VANDEN BOSCH; Sec. BERT TOCK.

Union de la Tannerie et de la Mégisserie Belges (UNITAN) (Tanning and Tawing): c/o 140 rue des Tanneurs, 7730 Estaimbourg; tel. (69) 36-23-23; fax (69) 36-23-10; f. 1962; Pres. BRUNO COLLE.

UTILITIES

Regulatory Authority

Commission de Régulation de l'Electricité et du Gaz (CREG): rue de l'Industrie 26-38, 1040 Bruxelles; tel. (2) 289-76-11; fax (2) 289-76-09; e-mail info@creg.be; internet www.creg.be; regulatory body for both gas and electricity markets; Pres. CHRISTINE VANDERVEEREN.

Electricity

Electrabel: 8 Regentlaan, 1000 Brussels; tel. (2) 518-61-11; fax (2) 518-64-00; internet www.electrabel.com; f. 1905; 50.01% owned by Suez-Tractebel; CEO JEAN-PIERRE HANSEN; generates and distributes electricity and natural gas.

SPE NV: rue Royale 55, POB 14, 1000 Brussels; tel. (2) 217-10-30; fax (2) 218-61-34; e-mail info@spe.be; internet www.energie.be; became a public company in 2000; builds, operates and maintains power plants; sells electricity to industrial customers and power distribution companies.

Gas

Distrigas: 10 rue de l'Industrie, 1000 Brussels; tel. (2) 557-31-11; fax (2) 557-31-12; e-mail info@distri.be; internet www.distrigas.be;

51.97% owned by Suez-Tractebel; supply and sale of natural gas; f. 2001; CEO ALAIN JANSSENS.

Fluxys: 31 Kunstlaan, 1040 Brussels; tel. (2) 282-78-33; fax (2) 282-71-50; internet www.fluxys.net; natural gas transportation services.

Luminus: Kempische Steenweg 299, 3500 Hasselt; tel. (78) 150-207; e-mail info@luminus.be; internet www.luminus.be.

Total Belgium: 93 rue du Commerce, 1040 Bruxelles; tel. (2) 288-99-33; fax (2) 288-32-60; e-mail gaznat.ventes@total.com; internet www.total.be.

Water

Société Wallonne des Eaux: 41 rue de la Concorde, 4800 Verviers; tel. (87) 34-28-11; fax (87) 34-28-00; e-mail relex@swde.be; internet www.swde.be; f. 1986; Dir-Gen. MARC DECONINCK; water production and distribution.

Vlaamse Maatschappij voor Watervoorziening: 73 Belliardstraat, 1040 Brussels; tel. (2) 238-94-11; fax (2) 230-97-98; e-mail info@vmw.be; internet www.vmw.be.

TRADE UNIONS

Confédération des Syndicats Chrétiens (ACV-CSC): 579 Haachtsesteenweg, POB 10, 1031 Brussels; tel. (2) 246-31-11; fax (2) 246-30-10; e-mail international@acv-csc.be; internet www.acv-csc .be; Pres. LUC CORTEBEECK; 16 affiliated unions with an estimated total membership of 1,652,854 (2000).

Affiliated unions:

ACV-CSC Textura (Textile and Clothing Workers): 27 Koning Albertlaan, 9000 Ghent; tel. (9) 222-57-01; fax (9) 220-45-59; e-mail acv.csc.textura@acv-csc.be; f. 1886; fmrly Centrale Chrétienne des Ouvriers de Textile et du Vêtement de Belgique; Pres. DIRK UYTTENHOVE; Gen. Secs JAN CALLAERT, REIN DE TREMERIE.

CSC Bâtiment et Industrie (Building and Industrial Workers): 31 rue de Trèves, 1040 Brussels; tel. (2) 285-02-11; fax (2) 230-74-43; e-mail bouw_industrie@acv-csc.be; internet www.cscbi.be; Pres. J. JACKERS; Sec.-Gen. ISABELLE PARENT; 235,000 mems.

Centrale Chrétienne de l'Alimentation et des Services (Food and Service Industries): 70 Kartuizersstraat, 1000 Brussels; tel. (2) 500-28-11; fax (2) 500-28-99; e-mail ccvd-ccas@acv-csc.be; internet www.acv-voeding-diensten.be; f. 1919; Pres. W. VIJVERMAN; Sec.-Gen. F. BOCKLANDT.

Centrale Chrétienne des Métallurgistes de Belgique (Metal Workers): 127 rue de Heembeek, 1120 Brussels; tel. (2) 244-99-11; fax (2) 244-99-90; e-mail ccmb@acv-csc.be; internet www .csc-metal.be; Pres. T. JANSSEN.

Centrale Chrétienne du Personnel de l'Enseignement Technique (Teachers in Technical Education): 16 rue de la Victoire, 1060 Brussels; tel. (2) 542-09-00; fax (2) 542-09-08; e-mail ccpet-uceo@acv-csc.be; Sec.-Gen. PROSPER BOULANGE; 8,500 mems (2001).

Centrale Chrétienne des Professeurs de l'Enseignement Moyen et Normal Libre (Lay Teachers in Secondary and Teacher-Training Institutions): 16 rue de la Victoire, 1060 Brussels; tel. (2) 543-68-00; fax (2) 543-68-10; e-mail cemnl@acv-csc.be; internet www.cemnl.be; Pres. WILLEM MILLER.

Centrale Chrétienne des Services Publics—Christelijke Centrale van de Openbare Diensten (Public-Service Workers): 31 rue de Trèves, bte 2, 1040 Brussels; tel. (2) 285-03-30; fax (2) 280-31-33; e-mail ccod@acv-csc.be; internet www.epsu.org; f. 1921; Pres. FILIP WIEERS; Sec.-Gen. GUY RASNEUR.

Centrale Nationale des Employés (CNE) (Private-Sector Workers): 46 rue Pépin, 5000 Namur; tel. (81) 22-02-22; fax (81) 22-50-47; internet www.cne-gnc.be; Sec.-Gen. RAYMOND COUMONT; 140,000 mems.

Christelijke Onderwijs Centrale (COC) (Teachers): 31–33 Trierstraat, 1040 Brussels; tel. (2) 285-04-40; fax (2) 230-28-83; e-mail coc.brussel@acv-csc.be; internet www.coc.be; f. 1993 as a result of a merger of the Flemish wings of three teachers' unions; Chair. ERIC DOLFEN; Gen. Sec. JOS VAN DER HOEVEN.

Christelijk Onderwijzersverbond van België (Schoolteachers): 203 Koningsstraat, 1210 Brussels; tel. (2) 227-41-11; fax (2) 219-47-61; e-mail cov@acv-csc.be; internet www.cov.be; f. 1893; Pres. G. BOURDEAUD'HUI; Sec.-Gen. R. MAES; 41,000 mems (1999).

CSC Energie-Chimie (Chemical and Energy Workers): 52 ave de Cortenbergh, 1000 Brussels; tel. (2) 739-45-45; e-mail a.depotter@acv-csc.be; internet www.csc-energie-chimie.be; f. 1912; Pres. A. DE POTTER; Gen. Sec. I. RODOMONTI; 63,155 mems (1993).

CSC—Transcom (Confédération des Syndicats Chrétiens) (Christian Trade Union Confederation; railway, post, telecommunications, water, transport, shipping, civil aviation, radio, television and cultural workers): Galerie Agora, 105 rue Marché aux Herbes, bte 40, 1000 Brussels; tel. (2) 549-07-60; fax (2) 512-95-91; e-mail acv-transcom@acv-csc.be; f. 1919; Pres. M. BOVY; Vice-Pres. P. BERTIN.

Fédération des Instituteurs Chrétiens (Schoolteachers): 16 rue de la Victoire, 1060 Brussels; tel. (2) 539-00-01; fax (2) 534-13-36; internet www.fic.be; f. 1893; publishes twice monthly periodical 'L'éducateur'; Sec.-Gen. R. DOHOGNE; 17,600 mems (2001).

Sporta-vsb (Sport): 70 Kaltuizersstraat, 1000 Brussels; tel. (2) 500-28-30; fax (2) 500-28-39; e-mail sporta@acv-csc.be; Nat. Sec. DIRK DE VOS.

Union Chrétienne des Membres du Personnel de l'Enseignement Officiel: 16 rue de la Victoire, 1060 Brussels; tel. (2) 542-09-00; fax (2) 542-09-08; e-mail ccpet-uceo@acv-csc.be; Sec.-Gen. P. BOULANGE.

Fédération Générale du Travail de Belgique (FGTB)/Algemeen Belgisch Vakverbond (ABVV): 42 rue Haute, 1000 Brussels; tel. (2) 506-82-11; fax (2) 506-82-29; e-mail xavier.verlouen@abvv.be; internet www.abvv.be; f. 1899; affiliated to ICFTU; Pres. ANDRÉ MORDANT (acting); Gen. Sec. XAVIER VERLOUEN (acting); an association of seven branch unions, three inter-regional organizations and 17 regional organizations with an estimated total membership of 1.2m.

Affiliated unions:

Belgische Transportarbeidersbond/Union Belge des Ouvriers du Transport (Belgian Transport Workers' Union): 66 Paardenmarkt, 2000 Antwerp; tel. (3) 224-34-11; fax (3) 224-34-49; f. 1913; Pres. IVAN VICTOR; 29,091 mems (2001).

La Centrale Générale/De Algemene Centrale (FGTB/ABVV) (Central Union, building, timber, glass, paper, chemicals and petroleum industries): 26–28 rue Haute, 1000 Brussels; tel. (2) 549-05-49; fax (2) 514-16-91; e-mail info@accg.be; internet www.accg.be; Pres. ALAIN CLAUWERT; Sec.-Gen. JACQUES MICHIELS; 338,000 mems (2003).

Centrale Générale des Services Publics/Algemene Centrale der Openbare Diensten (Public-Service Workers): Maison des Huit Heures, 9–11 place Fontainas, 1000 Brussels; tel. (2) 508-58-11; fax (2) 508-59-02; e-mail general@cgsp.be; internet www.acod.be; f. 1945; Pres. GUY BIAMONT; Vice-Pres. K. STESSENS.

Centrale de l'Industrie du Métal de Belgique/Centrale der Metaalindustrie van België (Metal Workers): 17 rue Jacques Jordaens, 1000 Brussels; tel. (2) 627-74-11; fax (2) 627-74-90; f. 1887; Pres. HERWIG JORISSEN; 185,570 mems (1993).

FGTB—Textile, Vêtement et Diamant/ABVV—Textiel, Kleding en Diamant (Textile, Clothing and Diamond Workers): 13 Barrierestraat, 8200 Brugge; tel. 050-72-95-70; fax 050-72-95-80; e-mail abvvtkd.fgtbtvd@glo.be; f. 1994; Pres. DONALD WITTEVRONGEL; 60,000 mems (1999).

Syndicat des Employés, Techniciens et Cadres de Belgique/Bond der Bedienden, Technici en Kaders van België (Employees, Technicians, Administrative Workers, Graphical and Paper Workers—SETCa / BBTK): 42 rue Haute, 1000 Brussels; tel. (2) 512-52-50; fax (2) 511-05-08; e-mail nationaal@setca-fgtb.be; internet www.bbtk.org; f. 1891; Pres. CHRISTIAN ROLAND; Vice-Pres. CARLOS POLENUS.

Syndicat des Travailleurs de l'Alimentation, Hôtellerie, Services/Centrale Voeding-Horeca-Diensten (Catering and Hotel Workers): 18 rue des Alexiens, 1000 Brussels; tel. (2) 512-97-00; fax (2) 512-53-68; e-mail jean.paschenkol@horval.be; internet www.horval.be; f. 1912; Pres. F. DE MEY; Nat. Sec. J. PASCHENKO.

Centrale Générale des Syndicats Libéraux de Belgique (CGSLB) (General Federation of Liberal Trade Unions of Belgium): 95 Koning Albertlaan, 9000 Ghent; tel. (9) 222-57-51; fax (9) 221-04-74; e-mail cgslb@cgslb.be; internet www.cgslb.be; f. 1891; Nat. Pres. GUY HAAZE; 240,000 mems.

Fédération Wallonne de l'Agriculture (FWA): 47 chaussée de Namur, 5030 Gembloux; tel. (81) 60-00-60; fax (81) 60-04-46; e-mail fwa@fwa.be; internet www.fwa.be; Pres. RENÉ LADOUCE; Sec.-Gen. J. P. CHAMPAGNE.

Landelijke Bediendencentrale-Nationaal Verbond voor Kaderpersoneel (LBC-NVK) (Employees): 5 Sudermanstraat, 2000 Antwerp; tel. (3) 220-87-11; fax (3) 220-87-33; e-mail lbc-nvk@acv-csc.be; internet www.lbc-nvk.be; f. 1912; Sec.-Gen. FERRE WYCKMANS; 290,000 mems (2004).

Nationale Unie der Openbare Diensten (NUOD)/Union Nationale des Services Publics (UNSP): 36 blvd Bischoffsheim, 1000 Brussels; tel. (2) 219-88-02; fax (2) 223-38-36; e-mail unsinues@swing.be; f. 1983; Pres. LUE MICHEL; Sec.-Gen. PHILIPPE LAMBERT.

Transport

RAILWAYS

The Belgian railway network is one of the densest in the world. The main lines are operated by the Société Nationale des Chemins de Fer Belges (SNCB) under lease from the State Transport Administration. Construction of the Belgian section of a high-speed railway network for northern Europe, which will eventually link Belgium, France, Germany, the Netherlands and the United Kingdom, is expected to be completed by 2005. A high-speed link between Brussels and Paris was completed in 1997.

Société Nationale des Chemins de Fer Belges/Nationale Maatschappij der Belgische Spoorwegen (SNCB/NMBS): 85 rue de France, 1060 Brussels; tel. (2) 526-37-79; fax (2) 526-37-76; internet www.sncb.be; f. 1926; 168.4m. passengers were carried in 2003; 3,521 km of lines, of which 2,927 km are electrified; Chair. ALAIN DENEEF; Man. Dir KAREL VINCK.

ROADS

In 2000 there were 1,726.7 km of motorways and some 12,600 km of other main or national roads. There were also 1,349 km of secondary or regional roads and an additional 132,540 km of minor roads.

Société Régionale Wallonne du Transport: 96 ave Gouverneur Bovesse, 5100 Namur; tel. (81) 32-27-11; fax (81) 32-27-10; e-mail jean-claude.phlypo@tec-wl.be; internet www.infotec.be; f. 1991; operates light railways, buses and trams; Dir-Gen. JEAN-CLAUDE PHLYPO.

Société des Transports Intercommunaux de Bruxelles: 15 ave de la Toison d'Or, 1050 Brussels; tel. (2) 515-20-00; fax (2) 515-32-84; e-mail flauscha@stib.irisnet.be; internet www.stib.be; operates a metro service, buses and trams; Dir-Gen. ALAIN FLAUSCH.

VVM-De Lijn: 1 Hendrik Consciencestraat, 2800 Mechelen; tel. (15) 44-07-11; fax (15) 44-07-09; internet www.delijn.be; f. 1991; public transport; Dir-Gen. INGRID LIETEN.

INLAND WATERWAYS

There are over 1,520 km of inland waterways in Belgium, of which 660 km are navigable rivers and 860 km are canals.

In 1989 waterways administration was divided between the Flemish region (1,055 km), the Walloon region (450 km) and the Brussels region (15 km):

Flemish region:

Departement Leefmilieu en Infrastructuur Administratie Waterwegen en Zeewezen: Graaf de Ferraris-Gebouw, 20 Koning Albertlaan, bte 5, 1000 Brussels; tel. (2) 553-77-11; fax (2) 553-77-05; e-mail awz@lin.vlaanderen.be; internet www.lin.vlaanderen.be; Dir-Gen. JAN STRUBBE.

Walloon region:

Direction Générale des Voies Hydrauliques: Centre administratif du MET, 8 blvd du Nord, 5000 Namur; tel. (81) 77-29-94; fax (81) 77-37-80; e-mail jlaurent@met.wallonie.be; internet voies-hydrauliques.wallonie.be; Dir-Gen. J. LAURENT.

Brussels region:

Haven van Brussel: 6 place des Armateurs, 1000 Brussels; tel. (2) 421-66-56; fax (2) 420-69-74; e-mail uxelles@port.irisnet.be; internet www.havenvanbrussel.irisnet.be; f. 1993; Chair. FABRICE CUMPS; Gen. Mans CHARLES HUYGENS, PAUL LELEU.

SHIPPING

The modernized port of Antwerp is the second biggest in Europe and handles about 80% of Belgian foreign trade by sea and inland waterways. It is also the largest railway port and has one of the largest petroleum refining complexes in Europe. Antwerp has 98 km of quayside and 17 dry docks. Other ports include Zeebrugge, Ostend, Ghent, Liège and Brussels.

Ahlers Logistic and Maritime Services: 139 Noorderlaan, 2030 Antwerp; tel. (3) 543-72-11; fax (3) 542-00-23; e-mail info@ahlers.com; internet www.ahlers.com; services to Finland, Poland, Latvia, Morocco; Man. Dir IVAN GEILENKOTTEN.

ESSO Belgium: POB 100, 2060 Antwerp; tel. (3) 543-31-11; fax (3) 543-34-95; internet www.esso.be; refining and marketing of petroleum products; Pres. REX W. TILLERSON.

De Keyser Thornton: Oude Leeuwenui 25/27, 2000 Antwerp; tel. (3) 205-31-00; fax (3) 205-31-32; e-mail info@multimodal.be; internet www.dekeyserthornton.com; f. 1853; shipping agency, forwarding and warehousing services; Pres. PHILIP VAN TILBURG.

Manuport Group: 59 Vosseschijnstraat, Haven 182, 2030 Antwerp; tel. (3) 204-93-00; fax (3) 204-93-01; e-mail info@

manuportgroup.com; internet www.manuportgroup.com; forwarding, customs clearance, liner and tramp agencies, chartering, Rhine and inland barging, multi-purpose bulk/bags fertilizer, minerals and agri-bulk terminal; Man. Dirs ALAIN AUDET, DIRK VERCRUYSSEN.

P&O North Sea Ferries Ltd: Leopold II Dam, 13, 8380 Zeebrugge; tel. (50) 54-34-11; fax (50) 54-68-35; internet www.ponsf.com; 9 ships; roll-on/roll-off ferry services between Zeebrugge, Hull and Middlesbrough; CEO ROBERT WOODS.

Total SA: 52 rue de l'Industrie, 1040 Brussels; tel. (2) 288-94-49; fax (2) 288-34-45; internet www.be.total.com; result of Petrofina's merger with Total in 1998 and Elf in 1999; integrated petroleum co active in exploration and production, transportation and petroleum refining, petrochemicals, etc., marketing of petroleum products and research; Vice-Chair. FRANÇOIS CORNELIS.

CIVIL AVIATION

The main international airport is at Brussels, with a direct train service from the air terminal. There are also international airports at Antwerp, Liège, Charleroi and Ostend. Following the collapse of the Belgian state airline, SABENA, in late 2001, the latter's regional subsidiary, Delta Air Transport, was reorganized as SN Brussels Airlines in February 2002.

SN Brussels Airlines: The Corporate Village, Da Vincilaan 9, 1935 Zaventem; tel. (2) 754-19-07; fax (2) 754-19-99; internet www.flysn.com; f. 1966; fmrly Delta Air Transport NV, reorganized under current name 2002; scheduled services within Europe and to Africa and the USA; CEO PETER DAVIES.

Virgin Express: Airport Bldg 116, 1820 Melsbroek; tel. (2) 752-05-11; fax (2) 752-05-06; internet www.virgin-express.com; f. 1991 as EuroBelgium Airlines, name changed as above 1996; 88.6% owned by Virgin Group Investments Ltd (UK); scheduled and charter services to European destinations; Chair DAVID HOARE; Man. Dir NEIL BURROWS.

Tourism

Belgium has several towns of rich historic and cultural interest, such as Antwerp, Bruges, Brussels, Durbuy, Ghent, Liège, Namur and Tournai. The country's seaside towns attract many visitors. The forest-covered Ardennes region is renowned for hill-walking and gastronomy. In 2003 tourist arrivals totalled an estimated 11.1m., and in 2002 receipts from tourism totalled US $6,892m.

Brussels Tourism (Bi-Tc): Hôtel de Ville, Grand-Place, 1000 Brussels; tel. (2) 513-89-40; fax (2) 513-83-20; e-mail info@brusselstourism.com; internet www.brusselstourism.com.

Office de Promotion du Tourisme Wallonie–Bruxelles: 61 rue Marché-aux-Herbes, 1000 Brussels; tel. (2) 504-03-90; fax (2) 513-69-50; e-mail info@opt.be; e-mail info@opt.be; internet www.belgique-tourisme.net; f. 1981; promotion of tourism in French-speaking Belgium; Dir-Gen. VIVIANE JACOBS.

Tourist Office for Flanders: 63 Grasmarkt, 1000 Brussels; tel. (2) 504-03-90; fax (2) 504-02-70; e-mail info@toerismvlaanderen.be; internet www.visitflanders.com; f. 1985; official promotion and policy body for tourism in Flemish region of Belgium; Gen. Commissioner WIM VANSEVEREN.

BELIZE

Introductory Survey

Location, Climate, Language, Religion, Flag, Capital

Belize lies on the Caribbean coast of Central America, with Mexico to the north-west and Guatemala to the south-west. The climate is sub-tropical, tempered by trade winds. The temperature averages 24°C (75°F) from November to January, and 27°C (81°F) from May to September. Annual rainfall ranges from 1,290 mm (51 ins) in the north to 4,450 mm (175 ins) in the south. The average annual rainfall in Belize City is 1,650 mm (65 ins). Belize is ethnically diverse, the population (according to the 2000 census) consisting of 49% Mestizos (Maya-Spanish), 25% Creoles (those of predominantly African descent), 11% Amerindian (mainly Maya), 6% Garifuna ('Black Caribs', descendants of those deported from the island of Saint Vincent in 1797) and communities of Asians, Portuguese, German Mennonites and others of European descent. English is the official language and an English Creole is widely understood. Spanish is the mother-tongue of some 15% of the population but is spoken by many others. There are also speakers of Garifuna (Carib), Maya and Ketchi, while the Mennonites speak a German dialect. Most of the population profess Christianity, with about 50% being Roman Catholics in 2002. The national flag (proportions usually 3 by 5) is dark blue, with narrow horizontal red stripes at the upper and lower edges; at the centre is a white disc containing the state coat of arms, bordered by an olive wreath. The capital is Belmopan.

Recent History

Belize, known as British Honduras until June 1973, was first colonized by British settlers (the 'Baymen') in the 17th century, but was not recognized as a British colony until 1862. In 1954 a new Constitution granted universal adult suffrage and provided for the creation of a legislative assembly. The territory's first general election, in April 1954, was won by the only party then organized, the People's United Party (PUP), led by George Price. The PUP won all subsequent elections until 1984. In 1961 Price was appointed First Minister under a new ministerial system of government. The colony was granted internal self-government in 1964, with the United Kingdom retaining responsibility for defence, external affairs and internal security. Following an election in 1965, Price became Premier and a bicameral legislature was introduced. In 1970 the capital of the territory was moved from Belize City to the newly-built town of Belmopan.

Much of the recent history of Belize has been dominated by the territorial dispute with Guatemala, particularly in the years prior to Belize's independence (see below). This was achieved on 21 September 1981, within the Commonwealth, and with Price becoming Prime Minister. However, the failure of the 1981 draft treaty with Guatemala, and the clash of opposing wings within the ruling party, undermined the dominance of the PUP. Internal disputes within the PUP intensified during 1983, although Price succeeded in keeping the factions together. However, at the general election held in December 1984 the PUP's 30 years of rule ended when the United Democratic Party (UDP) received 53% of the total votes and won 21 of the 28 seats in the enlarged House of Representatives. The UDP's leader, Manuel Esquivel, was appointed Prime Minister. The new Government pledged to revive Belize's economy through increased foreign investment.

A general election was held in September 1989. At the election the PUP obtained almost 51% of the total valid votes cast, and won 15 seats in the 28-member House of Representatives. The UDP received 49% of the votes and retained 13 seats, although one of their members subsequently joined the PUP. Price was again appointed Prime Minister.

The PUP called a general election in June 1993, 15 months before it was constitutionally due, following recent successes at local and by-elections. However, at the election the party secured only 13 seats in the House of Representatives, despite obtaining more than 51% of the votes. An alliance of the UDP and the National Alliance for Belizean Rights (NABR) received 48.7% of the votes but secured 16 seats (the total number of seats having been increased from 28 to 29). Esquivel was appointed Prime Minister. In November, at Esquivel's request,

Dame Minita Gordon, who had been the Governor-General since independence, resigned her position. She was replaced by Dr (later Sir) Colville Young, formerly President of the University College of Belize.

In June 1994 the sale of citizenship, of which many Hong Kong Chinese had taken advantage, was officially ended, following criticism that the system was open to abuse. However, a revised 'economic citizenship' programme, including mechanisms to prevent corruption, received government approval in early 1995. In June the Minister of Human Resources, Community and Youth Development, Culture and Women's Affairs, Phillip S. W. Goldson, was relieved of responsibility for immigration and nationality affairs, following allegations implicating him in the sale of false residence and visitor permits to nationals of the People's Republic of China and Taiwan. Reportedly some 5,000 such permits had been issued over the previous 12-month period, and the recipients then smuggled into the USA. In August the Judicial Committee of the Privy Council in the United Kingdom (the final court of appeal for Belize) issued stays of execution for two convicted murderers. The ruling, which came amid growing concern at rising crime in Belize, prompted widespread criticism of the British court, which was considered to be undermining the authority of the Belizean judiciary, and demands for a revision of the appeals system.

In mid-1996 the UDP established a bipartisan committee to discuss political reform. However, the committee made little progress and, in October 1997, PUP members withdrew from it. In the following month the PUP presented its own proposals for reform, which included the establishment of a republican form of government, with the Governor-General to be replaced by a president elected by the National Assembly. The PUP leader, Said Musa, pledged that, should his party gain power at the forthcoming general election, preliminary proposals for political reform would be introduced within 100 days of taking office. At the general election of August 1998 the PUP won an overwhelming victory, securing 26 of the 29 seats in the House of Representatives. The UDP obtained the remaining three seats. The result reflected popular discontent with the outgoing Government's structural-adjustment policies, including the introduction of value-added tax (VAT), which the PUP had pledged to repeal. The PUP had also promised to create 15,000 new jobs, to build 10,000 new houses and to reduce public utility tariffs. Following the defeat of his party, Esquivel, who had lost his seat in the House of Representatives, resigned as leader of the UDP. He was succeeded by Dean Barrow. On 1 September Said Musa was sworn in as Prime Minister.

In July 1999 Musa issued a statement rejecting allegations, published in the British press, that Michael Ashcroft, a businessman with dual British/Belizean nationality, who had extensive business and banking interests in Belize and was its ambassador to the UN, had used improper influence in Belizean affairs and was involved in money-laundering. In March 2000 Ashcroft resigned his UN post after receiving a life peerage in the British House of Lords. In the same year the British Government commissioned an investigation, by KPMG accountants, into Belize's financial system, including the regulation of the 'offshore' sector and the impact of tax concessions on the level of poverty. The British Government had previously suspended debt relief to Belize, pending the completion of the audit. However, following the conclusion of the investigation in late 2000, it requested that the inquiry be expanded to investigate public investment companies operating from Belize, including Ashcroft's Carlisle Holdings. In December 2001 it was announced that the Government had refused the United Kingdom's offer of £10m. of debt relief in exchange for a reform of its financial regime and an end to tax relief given to Carlisle Holdings and another company.

On 5 April 2000 Belize became the eighth country to ratify the Rome Statute of the International Criminal Court, which was to be established following its ratification by 60 states. On 14 February 2001, following legislative approval in November 2000, the leaders of 11 Caribbean countries, including Belize, signed an agreement to establish a Caribbean Court of Justice, based in Trinidad and Tobago. The Court was to replace the British Privy Council as the final court of appeal, and would allow the execution of convicted criminals. In August the Government announced that although it supported the foundation of the Caribbean Court of Justice, the British Privy Council would continue to handle final appeal cases in Belize. However, in August 2002 the Government announced its intention to ratify the agreement establishing the regional Court.

In late October 2002 the Attorney-General, Godfrey Smith, defended before a panel of the Inter-American Commission on Human Rights a proposed amendment to the Constitution that would prevent prisoners sentenced to death from appealing to the Privy Council in the United Kingdom. This followed a petition to the Commission by a group of prisoners who claimed that the amendment was incompatible with the Government's obligations to an Organization of American States (OAS) treaty on human rights. The proposed amendment would establish the Court of Appeals as the final court of appeal. It would also allow the National Assembly to approve either the establishment of a higher court of appeal or to declare the proposed Caribbean Court of Justice as the highest appellate court. The Attorney-General maintained that Belize had the right to legislate in its own domestic affairs. In July 2004 parliament approved legislation sanctioning Belize's membership of the Caribbean Court of Justice in its original jurisdiction. However, the Government failed to garner the three-quarters' majority required to amend the Constitution that would have allowed Belize to participate fully as part of the appellate jurisdiction. Thus, the Privy Council remained Belize's final court of appeal.

In October 2001 'Hurricane Iris' struck Belize, killing 19 tourists and causing an estimated US $250m.-worth of damage. Some 12,000 people were left homeless, crops were destroyed and the power and communications infrastructures were damaged. On 12 October the Minister of National Security and of Economic Development, Jorge Espat, resigned his post, after criticizing the Government. In an attempt to resolve the economic crisis and the damage resulting from the hurricane, Musa undertook a reorganization of the Cabinet. In January 2002 Assad Shoman, hitherto High Commissioner to the United Kingdom, assumed the foreign affairs, foreign trade and co-operation portfolio, held by Musa since October.

In February 2002 the policy of economic citizenship was formally abolished. However, a report produced in late July by the Ministry of Foreign Affairs substantiated claims that the immigration authorities had apparently continued the practice illegally until that month. As a result, the Director of Immigration, Paulino Castellano, was suspended and replaced by Col Peter Parchue. In early August Maxwell Samuels, hitherto Minister of Home Affairs, was appointed Minister of Public Utilities, Transport and Communications. Samuels' move precipitated a cabinet reorganization. At the same time, Musa announced that a Commission of Inquiry into the economic citizenship affair would ensue. In late November the Commission of Inquiry into the economic citizenship programme reported that while no person was granted Belizean citizenship under the programme following its annulment in February, over 1,000 applications were approved during the first seven months of 2002 and a number of irregularities had been detected.

In October 2002 a High Seas Fishing Act was approved by the Government. Under the Act, the activities of fishing boats operating under the Belizean flag would be monitored by satellite and licences were to be issued from July 2003. In 2001 the Government had been accused of allowing illegal fishing to be carried out by foreign vessels using the Belizean flag as a so-called 'flag of convenience'.

In its campaign for the March 2003 general election the PUP, which had repealed the unpopular VAT during its 1998–2003 administration, promised that, if re-elected, it would abolish sales tax on basic items and move towards the eradication of personal income tax. The party had also pledged to create 20,000 jobs, to build 5,000 affordable houses and to provide access to primary and secondary education for all children. In the election, which took place on 5 March, the PUP won 53.2% of valid votes cast and 22 seats in the House of Representatives, while the UDP secured 45.6% of votes cast and increased its legislative representation to seven seats (from three). Musa became the country's first Prime Minister to be sworn in for a second term in office. He subsequently formed a new Cabinet. In October, following the death of a PUP member of parliament, a by-election was held in the Cayo South constituency, which was won by the UDP candidate, increasing to eight that party's

representation in the lower house. In January 2004, in a stated attempt to bring about 'more effective management' of the Government, Musa announced a wide-ranging reallocation of cabinet portfolios.

In line with pre-election pledges, a number of measures were implemented in 2004 to improve security, including the inauguration of a Police Information Technology Unit, a Scenes of Crimes Technicians' Unit and a Legal Affairs Office. In addition, a project to construct hurricane shelters and a disaster preparedness system was scheduled for completion in May 2005. However, the PUP struggled to maintain popular support as protracted financial crises in the Development Finance Corporation and the Social Security Board forced the Government to reduce spending on social projects (see below). On 16 August 2004 seven cabinet ministers, including Deputy Prime Minister John Brinceño, resigned, reportedly owing to dissatisfaction with the financial policies of the Minister of Home Affairs and Finance, Ralph Fonseca. Following a cabinet reorganization, including three new appointments, the seven ministers returned to government two days later. Prime Minister Said Musa assumed the finance and defence portfolios, while Ralph Fonseca became Minister of Home Affairs and Investment.

An audit into the Social Security Board's (SSB) financial operations in 2004 found that it had made a series of unsecured loans, principally to the housing and tourism sectors and to the Development Finance Corporation (DFC), incurring substantial financial losses. Following a senate investigation, in December the SSB was prohibited from contracting new loans pending new investment policy guide-lines. In the same month it was announced that the DFC was to be dissolved. The Government affirmed that upon liquidation of the corporation's assets, priority would be given to the DFC's debt commitments to the SSB.

On 29 December 2004 Musa effected a further redistribution of government responsibilities, and reduced the overall composition of the Cabinet from 16 to 12 members. The Minister of Housing and of Transport, Cordel Hyde, submitted his resignation, while the Minister of Foreign Trade, Eamon Courtenay, and the high-profile Minister of Tourism, Culture and Enterprise, Mark Espat, who had overseen significant improvements in the tourism sector, were dismissed from their posts. Courtenay reportedly declined alternative posts within the Government and subsequently tendered his resignation to the Senate. The tourism portfolio was transferred to Godfrey Smith, who retained his position as Minister of Foreign Affairs (which now included foreign trade, national emergency management and information). The responsibilities of the Minister of Public Works, José Coye, were expanded to include public service and transport, and Coye also became Minister of State in the Ministry of Finance. Servulo Baeza, formerly responsible for agriculture, replaced Hyde as Minister of Housing, while Mike Espat was appointed Minister of Agriculture and Fisheries. The Minister of Health, Vildo Marin, took on the additional role of Minister of Energy and Communications.

The frontier with Guatemala was agreed by a convention in 1859 but this was declared invalid by Guatemala in 1940. Guatemalan claims to sovereignty of Belize date back to the middle of the 19th century and were written into Guatemala's Constitution in 1945. In November 1975 and July 1977 British troops and aircraft were sent to protect Belize from the threat of Guatemalan invasion, and a battalion of troops and a detachment of fighter aircraft remained in the territory. Negotiations between the United Kingdom and Guatemala began in 1977. In 1980 the United Kingdom warned that it might unilaterally grant independence to Belize if no settlement with Guatemala were forthcoming, and later that year the British Government finally excluded the possibility of any cession of land to Guatemala, although offering economic and financial concessions. In November the UN General Assembly overwhelmingly approved a resolution urging that Belize be granted independence (similar resolutions having been adopted in 1978 and 1979), and the United Kingdom decided to proceed with a schedule for independence. A tripartite conference in March 1981 appeared to produce a sound basis for a final settlement, with Guatemala accepting Belizean independence in exchange for access to the Caribbean Sea through Belize and the use of certain offshore cayes and their surrounding waters. A constitutional conference began in April. Further tripartite talks in May and July collapsed, however, as a result of renewed claims by Guatemala to Belizean land. With Belizean independence imminent, Guatemala made an unsuccessful appeal to the UN Security Council to intervene, severing diplomatic relations with the United

Kingdom and sealing its border with Belize on 7 September. However, on 21 September, as scheduled, Belize achieved independence. Guatemala alone refused to recognize Belize's new status, and during 1982 requested the reopening of negotiations with the United Kingdom, alleging that Belize was not legally independent. Tripartite talks in January 1983 collapsed when Belize rejected Guatemala's proposal that Belize should cede the southern part of the country. This claim was subsequently suspended. Belize is a member of the Caribbean Community and Common Market (CARICOM, see p. 172), whose summit conferences have consistently expressed support for Belize's territorial integrity against claims by Guatemala.

At independence the United Kingdom had agreed to leave troops as protection and for training of the Belize Defence Force 'for an appropriate time'. Discussions with Guatemala resumed in February 1985, with greater optimism shown by all three parties. In July the new draft Guatemalan Constitution omitted the previous unconditional claim to Belize, while Esquivel had previously acknowledged Guatemala's right of access to the Caribbean Sea, but no settlement was forthcoming. In December 1986, following the change from military to civilian government in Guatemala at the beginning of the year, the United Kingdom and Guatemala renewed full diplomatic relations. In March 1987 the first Guatemalan trade delegation since independence visited Belize, and in April renewed discussions were held between Guatemala, the United Kingdom and Belize (although Belize was still regarded by Guatemala as being only an observer at the meetings). Tripartite negotiations continued, and in May 1988 the formation of a permanent joint commission (which, in effect, entailed a recognition of the Belizean state by Guatemala) was announced.

In September 1991 Belize and Guatemala signed an accord under the terms of which Belize pledged to legislate to reduce its maritime boundaries and to allow Guatemala access to the Caribbean Sea and use of its port facilities. In return, President Jorge Serrano Elías of Guatemala officially announced his country's recognition of Belize as an independent state and established diplomatic relations. In January 1992 the Maritime Areas Bill was approved in the Belizean House of Representatives. The legislation, however, had caused serious divisions within the UDP, leading to the formation, in December 1991, of the Patriotic Alliance for Territorial Integrity (PATI) by certain members of the party to co-ordinate opposition to the bill. Further disagreement between PATI activists and the leaders of the UDP resulted in the expulsion or resignation of five UDP members (including two members of Parliament) in January 1992. In February these members formed a new organization, the NABR (see above), led by the former UDP Deputy Leader and Minister of Transport, Derek Aikman. In November 1992 the Guatemalan legislature voted to ratify Serrano's decision to recognize Belize. Serrano, however, indicated that the accord was not definitive and that Guatemala maintained its territorial claim over Belize.

In April 1993 Belize and Guatemala signed a non-aggression pact, affirming their intent to refrain from the threat or use of force against each other, and preventing either country from being used as a base for aggression against the other. Relations between the two countries were jeopardized when, in June, Guatemalan President Marco Vinicio Serrano was ousted. However, his successor, Ramiro de León Carpio, announced that Guatemala would continue to respect Belize's independence. In July the Belizean Prime Minister, Manuel Esquivel, reportedly suspended the September 1991 accord, which had been signed by the previous administration and had still not been formally ratified, stating that it involved too many concessions on the part of Belize and that the issue should be put to a referendum.

In January 1994 responsibility for the defence of Belize was transferred to the Belize Defence Force; all British troops were withdrawn by October, with the exception of some 180 troops who remained to organize training for jungle warfare.

In March 1994, in a letter to the UN Secretary-General, Guatemala formally reaffirmed its territorial claim to Belize, prompting the Belizean Minister of Foreign Affairs to seek talks with the British Government regarding assistance with national defence. Concern was also expressed by the Standing Committee of CARICOM Ministers of Foreign Affairs, which reaffirmed its support for Belizean sovereignty. In mid-1994 Esquivel accused Guatemala of employing destabilizing tactics against Belize by encouraging Guatemalans to occupy and settle in areas of Belizean forest. In September 1996 the Ministers of Foreign Affairs of Belize and Guatemala conducted preliminary talks in

New York, USA, concerning a resumption of negotiations on the territorial dispute. Further such discussions, involving representatives of the Governments and armed forces of both countries, were conducted in Miami, Florida, USA, in February 1997. In November 1998, at a meeting of ambassadors and officials of both countries, conducted in Miami, agreement was reached on the establishment of a joint commission to deal with immigration, cross-border traffic and respect for the rights of both countries' citizens.

In January 2000 Belizean security guards shot and killed a Guatemalan civilian in what was claimed to be an act of self-defence. In February Guatemalan forces captured three members of the Belizean border patrol, who later escaped; the men were assisted in their escape by the Belizean ambassador, who was expelled from Guatemala as a result. Bilateral talks resumed in May and in August a panel of negotiators was installed at the headquarters of the OAS. In November the two countries signed an agreement to initiate joint patrols of the unofficial common border and to hold quarterly meetings between operational commanders.

In June 2002 the Ministers of Foreign Affairs from both countries met to discuss the border dispute issue. The meeting was mediated by the OAS. Relations appeared to have improved further when Musa attended a ceremony in Guatemala City in late July, marking the twinning of Belmopan with the Guatemalan capital. At the same time, during a visit by Pope John Paul II to Guatemala, a member of the papal delegation, Cardinal Angelo Sodano, mediated in further talks. Following further, OAS-mediated, negotiations in August, in early September proposals were outlined for a solution to the dispute. These included the provision that Guatemala would recognize Belize's land boundary as laid out in the treaty of 1859 and the creation of a model settlement, complete with modern amenities, for peasants and landless farmers in the border area. Guatemalan farmers occupying land within the Belizean border were to have priority rights of residency on this settlement. There was also provision for the establishment of a Free Trade Agreement between the two countries and a Development Trust Fund, to be managed by the Inter-American Development Bank, with the money being used to alleviate poverty in the border region. In addition, Guatemala would be granted a 200 sq mile Exclusive Economic Zone in the Gulf of Honduras, although Belize and Honduras would retain fishing rights and 50% of any mineral resources discovered in the sea-bed. A Commission comprising Belize, Guatemala and Honduras would oversee the establishment and management of an Ecological Marine Park in coastal areas and a separate Tripartite Regional Fisheries Management Commission would manage fishing in the Gulf of Honduras. The details of the agreement were concluded on 30 September and the two countries agreed to hold simultaneous public referendums by the end of November. However, in early October, the Guatemalan legislature approved a resolution recommending the establishment of temporary military outposts on the Belizean border following the fatal shooting of a Guatemalan farmer in the border area and the alleged arrest of three Guatemalans by Belizean soldiers. In February 2003 the two countries signed a co-operation agreement. However, in September the Guatemalan Government announced that it planned to reject the OAS-proposed agreement. Delegations from the two countries met for further OAS-mediated negotiations in May 2004. Under discussion was the establishment of a Joint Commission that would explore means of promoting mutual confidence, such as a free trade agreement, a mutual legal assistance treaty and the joint promotion of tourism.

Government

Belize is a constitutional monarchy, with the British sovereign as Head of State. Executive authority is vested in the sovereign and is exercised by the Governor-General, who is appointed on the advice of the Prime Minister, must be of Belizean nationality, and acts, in almost all matters, on the advice of the Cabinet. The Governor-General is also advised by an appointed Belize Advisory Council. Legislative power is vested in the bicameral National Assembly, comprising a Senate (eight members appointed by the Governor-General) and a House of Representatives (29 members elected by universal adult suffrage for five years, subject to dissolution). The Governor-General appoints the Prime Minister and, on the latter's recommendation, other ministers. The Cabinet is responsible to the House of Representatives.

Defence

The Belize Defence Force was formed in 1978 and was based on a combination of the existing Police Special Force and the Belize Volunteer Guard. Military service is voluntary. Provision has been made for the establishment of National Service if necessary to supplement normal recruitment. In August 2004 the regular armed forces totalled an estimated 1,050, with some 700 militia reserves. In 1994 all British forces were withdrawn from Belize and in 2003 some 30 troops remained to organize training for jungle warfare. The defence budget for 2004 was an estimated BZ $38m.

Economic Affairs

In 2002, according to estimates by the World Bank, Belize's gross national income (GNI), measured at average 2000–02 prices, was US $828m., equivalent to US $3,190 per head (or $5,840 per head on an international purchasing-power parity basis). During 1990–2002 Belize's population grew at an average annual rate of 2.5%, while gross domestic product (GDP) per head increased, in real terms, at an average rate of 3.2%. Overall GDP increased, in real terms, at an average rate of 5.7% per year in 1990–2002; growth was 4.3% in 2002 and 9.4% in 2003.

Although 38% of the country is considered suitable for agriculture, only an estimated 6.7% of total area was used for agricultural purposes in 2001. Nevertheless, in 2003 agriculture, hunting, forestry and fishing employed an estimated 22.6% of the working population and contributed an estimated 15.9% of GDP. The principal cash crops are citrus fruits (citrus concentrates accounted for 20.4% of total domestic exports in 2003), sugar cane (sugar accounted for 19.2%) and bananas (an estimated 13.7%). Having recovered from hurricane damage in 2001, banana production increased by 70.1% in 2003, leading to an increase in banana export revenues of 57.6%. Improvements in field productivity were expected to contribute to a further increase in production in 2004, although export revenues were expected to be constrained by a decline in international prices. Citrus-juice production increased by 3.3% in 2002/03 (although exports declined by 2.4%), and further growth was predicted in 2003/04. Agricultural policy promotes the cultivation of crops for domestic consumption and the diversification of crops for export. Maize, red kidney beans and rice are the principal domestic food crops, and the development of crops, such as soybeans (soya beans), papayas, organic rice and cocoa is being encouraged. The country is largely self-sufficient in fresh meat and eggs. Belize has considerable timber reserves, particularly of tropical hardwoods, and the forestry sector is being developed. However, revenue from the forestry sector declined by 5.6% in 2003, owing to damage by the pine bark beetle, and to the introduction of a licensing system intended to limit the exploitation of mahogany, in accordance with the UN's Convention on International Trade in Endangered Species of Wild Fauna and Flora (CITES). The fishing sector increased by 111.0% in 2003, largely owing to an expansion in farmed shrimp production. In that year marine products were Belize's principal export earner, providing 28.7% of total domestic export revenue. The real GDP of the agricultural sector increased at an average annual rate of 5.3% during 1990–2002; real agricultural GDP increased by 0.9% in 2002 and by a dramatic 37.6% in 2003.

Industry (including mining, manufacturing, construction, water and electricity) employed 17.2% of the working population and contributed 17.6% of GDP in 2003. In that year mining and quarrying accounted for an estimated 0.6% of GDP and for only 0.4% of employment. Industrial GDP increased at an average annual rate of 4.1% during 1990–2002; real industrial GDP increased by 2.4% in 2002, but declined by 1.4% in 2003.

Manufacturing accounted for 9.2% of GDP and employed 7.6% of the working population in 2003. Dominant activities are the manufacture of clothing and the processing of agricultural products, particularly sugar cane (for sugar and rum). Manufacturing GDP increased at an average rate of 3.4% per year during 1990–2002; the sector increased by 1.5% in 2002 and by a further 3.1% in 2003.

Imports of fuels and lubricants accounted for an estimated 14.2% of the total cost of imports in 2003. Hydroelectric power was developed in the 1990s; in the late 1990s the Mollejón hydroelectric station, on the Macal River, began operations. Financed by the International Finance Corporation and the Caribbean Development Bank, the project attracted criticism over its cost and efficiency. In 2001 construction began of a controversial second hydroelectric dam at Chalillo on the Macal River; upon completion, the dam would be operated by its Canadian contractor before transfer to state ownership in 2031. The dam was expected to provide 5.3 MW of electricity annually and, according to the Government, would provide Belize's energy needs for 50 years. Environmentalist groups contended that the dam would destroy the habitat of some 40 species of rare animals and birds, including the endangered scarlet macaw. Following a protracted appeals process initiated in early 2002 by the Belize Alliance of Conservation Non-Government Organizations, in January 2004 the Privy Council in the United Kingdom ruled in favour of the Belizean Government's decision that construction of the dam should proceed. Completion was scheduled for mid-2005. In 2004 Hydro Maya Ltd signed a 15-year agreement to provide 2.8 MW of electricity annually to Belize Electricity Ltd. Construction of a hydroelectric dam on the Rio Grande River, to generate the required power, was scheduled for completion in 2006.

The services sector employed 59.9% of the working population and contributed 66.5% of GDP in 2003. Tourist development is concentrated on promoting 'eco-tourism', based on the attraction of Belize's natural environment, particularly its rainforests and the barrier reef, the second largest in the world. Tourist arrivals totalled 686,591 in 2003, a 52.3% increase compared with the previous year. The increase was mainly in the cruise-ship sector, where a cut in the passenger tax rate and the opening of new facilities prompted a rise in numbers of 79.9%. An air service to Montego Bay, Jamaica, operated by Air Jamaica, was inaugurated in 2002, but was suspended in 2003. The service, intended to transfer US passengers to Belize via Montego Bay, reportedly failed owing to competition from US Air. None the less, air arrivals rose by 19.7% in 2003. A new service to Atlanta, Georgia, USA, established by Delta Air Lines in 2004, also contributed to the increase in tourist arrivals. According to UN estimates, the GDP of the services sector increased, in real terms, at an average rate of 5.7% per year during 1990–2002; real sectoral GDP increased by 6.6% in 2002 and by 5.5% in 2003. Belize's 'offshore' financial centre opened in 1996 and by 2003 there were more than 25,000 registered 'offshore' companies.

In 2003 Belize recorded a trade deficit of BZ $418.6m. and a deficit of BZ $361.9m. on the current account of the balance of payments. In that year the principal source of imports was the USA (accounting for 42.2% of the total), followed by Mexico (7.9%) and the United Kingdom(3.2%). The USA was also the principal export market, accounting for 53.8% of total exports in 2001, followed by the United Kingdom (23.0%). The principal exports in 2003 were marine products (excluding aquarium fish, 28.7%), citrus concentrates (20.4%) and sugar (19.2%). The principal imports in that year were basic manufactures (19.4%), and machinery and transport equipment (18.0%).

For the financial year 2001/02 there was a budgetary deficit of BZ $174.8m, equivalent to 10.9% of GDP. Belize's total external debt was US $834.6m. in 2002, of which US $789.6m. was long-term public debt. In that year the cost of debt-servicing was equivalent to 36.5% of the value of exports of goods and services. The annual rate of inflation averaged 1.8% in 1990–2003. Consumer prices increased by 2.2% in 2002 and by 2.5% in 2003. In 2003 some 12.9% of the economically active population were unemployed. Many Belizeans, however, work abroad, and remittances to the country from such workers are an important source of income. Emigration, mainly to the USA, is offset by the number of immigrants and refugees from other Central American countries, particularly El Salvador.

Belize is a member of the Caribbean Community and Common Market (CARICOM, see p. 172), and in 1991 acceded to the Organization of American States (OAS, see p. 319). In September 1992 Belize was granted membership of the Inter-American Development Bank (IDB, see p. 268). Belize is also a member of the Central American Integration System (SICA, see p. 176). In 2001 Central American countries, including Belize, reached agreement with Mexico on regional integration through the 'Plan Puebla-Panamá', a series of joint projects intended to integrate the transport, industry and tourism of the countries involved. As a member of the Commonwealth, Belize enjoys low tariffson its exports to the European Union (EU) under the Cotonou Agreement (see p. 262), and tariff-free access to the USA under the Caribbean Basin Initiative.

In an attempt to improve the extremely weak fiscal position that it inherited on taking office in 1998, the Musa administration undertook a restructuring of the tax system, began a large-scale public investment programme, expanded market opportunities for bananas and increased investment in the tourism sector. As a result, GDP increased by 11.1% in 2000. Following extensive hurricane damage in 2000 and 2001, however, growth slowed to 5.1% in 2001 and to 4.3% in 2002. In November 2002 the IMF expressed concern at the country's current-account deficit, which was equivalent to an estimated 17.8% of GDP. It urged the Government to reduce the fiscal deficit to 5.0% of GDP in the 2002/03 financial year and advised against proposals for a government-subsidized national health service and affordable housing scheme. Nevertheless, in the months preceding the general election of March 2003, the incumbent PUP administration (which was subsequently returned to office) pledged to build a further 5,000 affordable houses, as well as to increase public-sector pay. GDP increased by 9.4% in 2003, fuelled mainly by growth in the tourism and fishing industries. However, public and publicly guaranteed debt reached 92% of GDP and the current account deficit widened to 18.3% of GDP. In April 2004 the IMF warned that stricter monetary policy was critical if an unmanageable deficit on the balance of payments was to be avoided. In response, the Government announced reductions in expenditure and further measures to refinance debt. The 2004/05 budget aimed to reduce the fiscal deficit to less than 3% of GDP, from an estimated 8.1% of GDP in 2003/04. Meanwhile, there were concerns regarding the impact on banana revenues following the ending of EU preferential markets for Caribbean bananas from 2001. From that year a transitional system, issuing licences according to historical trade patterns, was implemented, with a definitive tariff-only system to be in place by 1 January 2006. Furthermore, from 2005 EU preferential prices for sugar were also to be gradually eliminated. (In July 2004 it was announced that an initial reduction of 20% was to be implemented in 2005, with the full reduction scheduled to enter effect in 2007/08.)

Education

Education is compulsory for all children for a period of 10 years between the ages of five and 14 years. Primary education, beginning at five years of age and lasting for eight years, is provided free of charge, principally through subsidized denominational schools under government control. There were 62,074 pupils enrolled at 275 primary schools in 2003/04. Secondary education, beginning at the age of 13, lasts for four years. There were 15,344 students enrolled in 43 general secondary schools in 2003/04. In 1999 the combined enrolment in primary, secondary and tertiary education was an estimated 73% (males 73%; females 72%).

In 1998/99 there were 2,853 students enrolled in 12 other educational institutions, which included technical, vocational and teacher-training colleges. There is an extra-mural branch of the University of the West Indies in Belize. In 2000 the University of Belize was formed through the amalgamation of five higher education institutions, including the University College of Belize and Belize Technical College. Budgetary expenditure on education in the financial year 1997/98 was projected at BZ $74.2m., representing 20.5% of total spending by the central Government.

Public Holidays

2005: 1 January (New Year's Day), 7 March (for Baron Bliss Day), 25–28 March (Easter), 2 May (for Labour Day), 23 May (for Commonwealth Day), 10 September (St George's Caye Day), 21 September (Independence Day), 10 October (for Pan-American Day), 19 November (for Garifuna Settlement Day), 25–26 December (Christmas).

2006: 1 January (New Year's Day), 9 March (Baron Bliss Day), 14–17 April (Easter), 1 May (Labour Day), 22 May (for Commonwealth Day), 11 September (for St George's Caye Day), 21 September (Independence Day), 12 October (Pan-American Day), 20 November (for Garifuna Settlement Day), 25–26 December (Christmas).

Weights and Measures

Imperial weights and measures are used, but petrol and paraffin are measured in terms of the US gallon (3.785 litres).

Statistical Survey

Sources (unless otherwise stated): Central Statistical Office, Cnr Culvert Rd and Mountain View Blvd, Belmopan; tel. 822-2207; fax 822-3206; e-mail info@cso.gov.bz; internet www.cso.gov.bz; Central Bank of Belize, Gabourel Lane, POB 852, Belize City; tel. 223-6194; fax 223-6226; e-mail cenbank@btl.net; internet www.centralbank.org.bz.

AREA AND POPULATION

Area: 22,965 sq km (8,867 sq miles).

Population: 189,774 at census of 12 May 1991; 240,204 (males 121,278, females 118,926) at census of 12 May 2000; 282,600 at mid-2004 (official estimate).

Density (mid-2004): 12.3 per sq km.

Districts (official estimates at mid-2004, rounded figures): Belize 84,200; Cayo 63,900; Orange Walk 43,800; Corozal 35,000; Stann Creek 28,900; Toledo 26,800.

Principal Towns (official estimates at mid-2004, rounded figures): Belize City (former capital) 59,400; San Ignacio/Santa Elena 16,100; Orange Walk 15,000; Belmopan (capital) 12,300; Dangriga (fmrly Stann Creek) 10,400; Corozal 8,600; San Pedro 7,600; Benque Viejo 6,700; Punta Gorda 4,900.

Births, Marriages and Deaths (estimates, 2000): Registered live births 7,313 (birth rate 29.3 per 1,000); Registered marriages (1998) 1,374 (marriage rate 5.8 per 1,000); Registered deaths 1,543 (death rate 6.1 per 1,000). *2002* (provisional): Registered live births 7,356; Registered deaths 1,284. Sources: UN, *Demographic Yearbook*, and *Population and Vital Statistics Report*.

Expectation of Life (WHO estimates, years at birth): 69.7 (males 67.4; females 72.4) in 2002. Source: WHO, *World Health Report*.

Economically Active Population (2003): Agriculture 17,164; Forestry 864; Fishing 2,120; Mining and quarrying 360; Manufacturing 6,739; Electricity, gas and water 778; Construction 7,475; Wholesale and retail trade and repairs 14,687, Tourism (incl. restaurants and hotels) 9,400; Transport and communications 3,297; Financial intermediation 1,518; Real estate and renting 1,770; General government services 10,309; Community, social and personal services 10,779; Work abroad and in commercial free zone 1,676; Other 286; *Total employed* 89,222; Total unemployed 13,219; *Total labour force* 102,441. *April 2004* (labour force survey): Total employed 95,911

(Primary sector 19,566, Secondary sector 17,456, Services 58,889); Total unemployed 12,580; Total labour force 108,491.

HEALTH AND WELFARE

Key Indicators

Total Fertility Rate (children per woman, 2002): 3.2.

Under-5 Mortality Rate (per 1,000 live births, 2003): 39.

HIV/AIDS (% of persons aged 15–49, 2003): 2.4.

Physicians (per 1,000 head, 1996): 0.55.

Hospital Beds (per 1,000 head, 1996): 2.13.

Health Expenditure (2001): US $ per head (PPP): 278.

Health Expenditure (2001): % of GDP: 5.2.

Health Expenditure (2001): public (% of total): 45.1.

Access to Water (% of persons, 2002): 91.

Access to Sanitation (% of persons, 2002): 47.

Human Development Index (2002): ranking: 99.

Human Development Index (2002): value: 0.737.

For sources and definitions, see explanatory note on p. vi.

AGRICULTURE, ETC.

Principal Crops ('000 metric tons, 2003): Rice (paddy) 13.2; Maize 33.6; Sorghum 9.2; Sugar cane 1,073.2; Dry beans 5.0; Fresh vegetables 7.9 (FAO estimate); Bananas 73.5; Plantains 28.0 (FAO estimate); Oranges 165.5; Grapefruit and pomelos 39.2; Other fresh fruit 21.6 (FAO estimate). Source: FAO.

Livestock ('000 head, year ending September 2003): Horses 5; Mules 5; Cattle 58; Pigs 21; Sheep 5; Chickens 1,450 (FAO estimate). Source: FAO.

Livestock Products (FAO estimates, '000 metric tons, 2003): Beef and veal 2.2; Chicken meat 13.4; Pig meat 1.0; Cows' milk 3.8; Hen eggs 1.5. Source: FAO.

Forestry (1995): *Roundwood Removals* ('000 cubic metres, excl. bark): Sawlogs, veneer logs and logs for sleepers 62, Fuel wood 126, Total 188. *Sawnwood* ('000 cubic metres, incl. railway sleepers): Coniferous (softwood) 5, Broadleaved (hardwood) 30, Total 35. *1996–2003*: Annual production as in 1995 (FAO estimates). Source: FAO.

Fishing ('000 metric tons, live weight, 2002): Capture 24.8 (Sardinellas 5.0; European pilchard 2.0; European anchovy 5.0; Jack and horse mackerels 5.4; Chub mackerel 3.7; Caribbean spiny lobster 0.5; Stromboid conchs 1.4); Aquaculture 4.4 (Whiteleg shrimp 4.4); Total catch 29.2. Source: FAO.

INDUSTRY

Production (2001): Raw sugar 103,862 long tons; Molasses 34,291 long tons; Cigarettes 88 million; Beer 2,385,000 gallons; Batteries 5,397; Flour 26,122,000 lb; Fertilizers 23,749 short tons; Garments 1,507,000 items; Citrus concentrate 6,503,000 gallons; Soft drinks 1,346,000 cases. Source: IMF, *Belize: Statistical Appendix* (October 2002).

FINANCE

Currency and Exchange Rates: 100 cents = 1 Belizean dollar (BZ $). *Sterling, US Dollar and Euro Equivalents* (31 December 2004): £1 sterling = BZ $3.8628; US $1 = BZ $2.0000; €1 = BZ $2.7242; BZ $100 = £25.89= US $50.00 = €36.71. *Exchange rate*: Fixed at US $1 = BZ $2.000 since May 1976.

Budget (BZ $ million, year ending 31 March 2002): *Revenue*: Taxation 331.0 (Taxes on income, profits, etc. 77.0; Domestic taxes on goods and services 117.0; Import duties 134.2); Other current revenue 36.1; Capital revenue 10.4; Total 377.5, excl. grants (22.0). *Expenditure*: Current expenditure 326.2 (Wages and salaries 162.7, Pensions 23.6, Expenditure on goods and services 62.6, Interest payments 51.6, Subsidies and current transfers 25.7); Capital expenditure 263.3; Statistical discrepancy –15.2; Total 574.3. Source: IMF, *Belize: Statistical Appendix* (October 2002).

International Reserves (US $ million at 31 December 2003): IMF special drawing rights 2.32; Reserve position in the IMF 6.30; Foreign exchange 76.07; Total 84.68. Source: IMF, *International Financial Statistics*.

Money Supply (BZ $ million at 31 December 2003): Currency outside banks 103.27; Demand deposits at commercial banks 295.42; Total money (incl. others) 402.17. Source: IMF, *International Financial Statistics*.

Cost of Living (Consumer Price Index; base: 1990 = 100): All items 120.2 in 2001; 122.9 in 2002; 126.0 in 2003.

Expenditure on the Gross Domestic Product (BZ $ million at current prices, 2003): Government final consumption expenditure 284.3; Private final consumption expenditure 1,527.1; Increase in stocks 10.8; Gross fixed capital formation 394.6; *Gross domestic expenditure* 2,216.9; Exports of goods and services 1,101.2; *Less* Imports of goods and services 1,316.9; Statistical discrepancy–24.3; *GDP at market prices* 1,976.8.

Gross Domestic Product by Economic Activity (BZ $ million at current prices, 2003): Agriculture, forestry and fishing 279.4; Mining and quarrying 9.8; Manufacturing 161.3; Electricity and water 60.7; Construction 77.7; Wholesale and retail trade, restaurants and hotels 396.0; Transport, storage and communications 183.1; Financial intermediation 128.6; Real estate, renting and business services 137.9; Community, social and personal services 120.0; General government services 202.8; *Sub-total* 1,757.5; Taxes, less subsidies, on products 272.6; *Less* Imputed bank service charges 53.3; *GDP at market prices* 1,976.8; *GDP at constant 2000 prices* 1,989.8.

Balance of Payments (BZ $ million, 2003): Exports of goods f.o.b. (incl. re-exports) 632.6; Imports of goods f.o.b. –1,051.2; *Trade balance* –418.6; Exports of services 425.9; Imports of services –278.6; *Balance on goods and services* –271.3; Other income received 8.4; Other income paid –188.0; *Balance on goods, services and income* –450.9; Current transfers received 94.0; Current transfers paid –4.9; *Current balance* –361.9; Capital account (net) –96.1; Direct investment abroad –0.7; Direct investment from abroad 57.6; Portfolio investment assets –0.3; Portfolio investment liabilities 151.1; Financial derivatives assets 1.1; Other investment assets –17.1; Other investment liabilities 192.4; Net errors and omissions 13.8; *Overall balance* –60.1.

EXTERNAL TRADE

Principal Commodities (provisional, BZ $ million, 2003): *Imports c.i.f.*: Food and live animals 118.7; Fuels, lubricants, etc. 161.2 (incl. electricity 28.4); Chemicals and related products 82.5; Manufactured goods (materials) 128.7; Miscellaneous manufactured articles 102.5; Machinery and transport equipment 203.6; Commercial free zone 180.5; Export processing zone 130.5; Total (incl. others) 1,131.7. *Exports f.o.b.*: Marine products (excl. aquarium fish) 110.2; Sugar 73.8; Orange concentrate 66.2; Grapefruit concentrate 12.4; Bananas 52.6; Garments 31.4; Papaya 16.6; Total (incl. others) 384.6.

Principal Trading Partners (US $ million, 2001): *Imports c.i.f.*: Mexico 49.8; United Kingdom 11.9; USA 216.3; Total (incl. others) 450.5. *Exports f.o.b.* (excl. re-exports): United Kingdom 37.0; USA 86.6; Total (incl. others) 161.0. Source: IMF, *Belize: Statistical Appendix* (October 2002).

TRANSPORT

Road Traffic ('000 vehicles in use, 1998): Passenger cars 9,929; Buses and coaches 416; Lorries and vans 11,339; Motorcycles and mopeds 270 (Source: IRF, *World Road Statistics*). *2000* ('000 vehicles in use): Passenger cars 21.5; Commercial vehicles 3.9 (Source: UN, *Statistical Yearbook*).

Shipping (sea-borne freight traffic, '000 metric tons, 1996): Goods loaded 255.4; Goods unloaded 277.1. *Merchant Fleet* (vessels registered at 31 December 2003): Number of vessels 1,040; Total displacement 1,533,673 grt (Source: Lloyd's Register-Fairplay, *World Fleet Statistics*).

Civil Aviation (2001): Passenger arrivals 174,201. Source: IMF, *Belize: Statistical Appendix* (October 2002).

TOURISM

Tourist Arrivals: 218,503 (cruise-ship passengers 40,898, stop-over visitors 177,605) in 2001; 450,689 (cruise-ship passengers 271,737, stop-over visitors 178,952) in 2002; 686,591 (cruise-ship passengers 488,917, stop-over visitors 197,674) in 2003.

Tourism Receipts (US $ million): 120.5 in 2001; 132.8 in 2002; 156.2 in 2003.
Source: Belize Tourist Board.

COMMUNICATIONS MEDIA

Radio Receivers (1997): 133,000 in use*.

Television Receivers (2000): 44,000 in use†.

Telephones (2003): 33,300 main lines in use†.

Facsimile Machines (1996): 500 in use‡.

Mobile Cellular Telephones (2003): 60,400 subscribers†.

Personal Computers (2002): 35,000 in use†.

Internet Users (2002): 30,000†.

Book Production (1996): 107 titles*.

Non-daily Newspapers (1996): 6 (circulation 80,000)*.
* Source: UNESCO, *Statistical Yearbook*.
† Source: International Telecommunication Union.
‡ Source: UN, *Statistical Yearbook*.

EDUCATION

Pre-primary (2002/03): 103 schools, 214 teachers, 3,773 students.

Primary (2003/04): 275 schools, 2,618 teachers, 62,074 students.

Secondary (2003/04): 43 schools, 1,074 teachers, 15,344 students.

Higher (1997/98): 12 institutions, 228 teachers, 2,853 students. Source: Ministry of Education, Youth and Sports.

Adult Literacy Rate (UNESCO estimates): 76.9% (males 77.1%; females 76.7%) in 2002. Source: UN Development Programme, *Human Development Report*.

Directory

The Constitution

The Constitution came into effect at the independence of Belize on 21 September 1981. Its main provisions are summarized below:

FUNDAMENTAL RIGHTS AND FREEDOMS

Regardless of race, place of origin, political opinions, colour, creed or sex, but subject to respect for the rights and freedoms of others and for the public interest, every person in Belize is entitled to the rights of life, liberty, security of the person, and the protection of the law. Freedom of movement, of conscience, of expression, of assembly and association and the right to work are guaranteed and the inviolability of family life, personal privacy, home and other property and of human dignity is upheld. Protection is afforded from discrimination on the grounds of race, sex, etc., and from slavery, forced labour and inhuman treatment.

CITIZENSHIP

All persons born in Belize before independence who, immediately prior to independence, were citizens of the United Kingdom and Colonies automatically become citizens of Belize. All persons born outside the country having a husband, parent or grandparent in possession of Belizean citizenship automatically acquire citizenship, as do those born in the country after independence. Provision is made which permits persons who do not automatically become citizens of Belize to be registered as such. (Belizean citizenship was also offered, under the Belize Loans Act 1986, in exchange for interest-free loans of US $25,000 with a 10-year maturity. The scheme was officially ended in June 1994, following sustained criticism of alleged corruption on the part of officials. A revised economic citizenship programme, offering citizenship in return for a minimum investment of US $75,000, received government approval in early 1995, but was ended in 2002.)

THE GOVERNOR-GENERAL

The British monarch, as Head of State, is represented in Belize by a Governor-General, a Belizean national.

Belize Advisory Council

The Council consists of not less than six people 'of integrity and high national standing', appointed by the Governor-General for up to 10 years upon the advice of the Prime Minister. The Leader of the Opposition must concur with the appointment of two members and be consulted about the remainder. The Council exists to advise the Governor-General, particularly in the exercise of the prerogative of mercy, and to convene as a tribunal to consider the removal from office of certain senior public servants and judges.

THE EXECUTIVE

Executive authority is vested in the British monarch and exercised by the Governor-General. The Governor-General appoints as Prime Minister that member of the House of Representatives who, in the Governor-General's view, is best able to command the support of the majority of the members of the House, and appoints a Deputy Prime Minister and other Ministers on the advice of the Prime Minister. The Governor-General may remove the Prime Minister from office if a resolution of 'no confidence' is passed by the House and the Prime Minister does not, within seven days, either resign or advise the Governor-General to dissolve the National Assembly. The Cabinet consists of the Prime Minister and other Ministers.

The Leader of the Opposition is appointed by the Governor-General as that member of the House who, in the Governor-General's view, is best able to command the support of a majority of the members of the House who do not support the Government.

THE LEGISLATURE

The Legislature consists of a National Assembly comprising two chambers: the Senate, with eight nominated members; and the House of Representatives, with 29 elected members. The Assembly's normal term is five years. Senators are appointed by the Governor-General: five on the advice of the Prime Minister; two on the advice of the Leader of the Opposition or on the advice of persons selected by the Governor-General; and one after consultation with the Belize Advisory Council. If any person who is not a Senator is elected to be President of the Senate, he or she shall be an ex-officio Senator in addition to the eight nominees.

Each constituency returns one Representative to the House, who is directly elected in accordance with the Constitution.

If a person who is not a member of the House is elected to be Speaker of the House, he or she shall be an ex-officio member in addition to the 29 members directly elected. Every citizen older than 18 years is eligible to vote. The National Assembly may alter any of the provisions of the Constitution.

The Government

HEAD OF STATE

Sovereign: HM Queen ELIZABETH II (succeeded to the throne 6 February 1952).

Governor-General: Sir COLVILLE YOUNG (appointed 17 November 1993).

THE CABINET
(March 2005)

Prime Minister and Minister of Finance and of Defence: SAID MUSA.

Deputy Prime Minister and Minister of Natural Resources and the Environment and Minister of State in the Ministry of Finance: JOHN BRICEÑO.

Attorney-General and Minister of Education (Culture, Youth and Sports): FRANCIS FONSECA.

Minister of Home Affairs and Investment (Commercial Free Zones and Export Processing Zones): RALPH FONSECA.

Minister of Health and of Energy and Communications (including Commerce and Industry): VILDO MARIN.

Minister of Foreign Affairs (Foreign Trade, National Emergency Management and Information)and of Tourism: GODFREY SMITH.

Minister of the Public Service, of Public Works and Transport and Minister of State in the Ministry of Finance: JOSÉ COYE.

Minister of Local Government, Labour and Rural Development: MARCIAL MES.

Minister of Housing: SERVULO BAEZA.

Minister of Human Development: SYLVIA FLORES.

Minister of National Development: ASSAD SHOMAN.

Minister of Agriculture and Fisheries: MIKE ESPAT.

MINISTRIES

Office of the Prime Minister: New Administration Bldg, Belmopan; tel. 822-2346; fax 822-0071; e-mail primeminister@belize.gov.bz.

Ministry of Agriculture and Fisheries: 2nd Floor, West Block Bldg, Belmopan; tel. 822-2241; fax 822-2409; e-mail mafpaeu@btl.net.

Ministry of the Attorney-General: Belmopan; tel. 822-2504; fax 822-3390; e-mail atgenmin@btl.net.

Ministry of Education: West Block Bldg, Belmopan; tel. 822-2380; fax 822-3389.

Ministry of Finance: New Administration Bldg, Belmopan; tel. 822-2169; fax 822-3317; e-mail finsecmof@btl.net.

Ministry of Foreign Affairs, Defence and National Emergency Management: NEMO Bldg, POB 174, Belmopan; tel. 822-2167; fax 822-2854; e-mail belizemfa@btl.net; internet www.mfa.gov.bz.

Ministry of Foreign Trade: NEMO Bldg, POB 174, Belmopan; tel. 822-2167; fax 822-2854; e-mail belizemfa@btl.net; internet www.mfa.gov.bz.

Ministry of Health and the Environment: New Administration Bldg, Belmopan; tel. 822-2325; fax 822-2942.

Ministry of Home Affairs and Investment: New Administration Bldg, Belmopan; tel. 822-2218; fax 822-2195; e-mail investment@btl.net.

Ministry of Housing: East Block Bldg, Belmopan; tel. 822-2016; fax 822-3337.

Ministry of Human Development: West Block, Independence Hill, Belmopan; tel. 822-2161; fax 822-3175; e-mail mhd@btl.net.

Ministry of Local Government, Labour and Rural Development: New Administrative Bldg, Belmopan; tel. 822-2167; fax 822-2322; e-mail minmsillg@belize.gov.bz.

Ministry of Natural Resources, the Environment, Commerce and Industry: Market Sq., Belmopan; tel. 822-2226; fax 822-2333; e-mail info@mnrei.gov.bz; internet www.mnrei.gov.bz.

Ministry of Public Works, Transport, Communications and Energy: New Administration Bldg, Belmopan.

Ministry of Tourism: Constitution Dr., Belmopan; tel. 822-3393; fax 822-3815; e-mail tourismmdpt@btl.net.

Legislature

NATIONAL ASSEMBLY

The Senate

President: PHILIP ZUNIGA.

There are eight nominated members.

House of Representatives

Speaker: ELIZABETH ZABANEH.

Clerk: JESUS KEN.

General Election, 5 March 2003

	Votes cast	% of total	Seats
People's United Party (PUP) .	52,934	53.2	22
United Democratic Party (UDP)	45,415	45.6	7
Others	1,211	1.2	—
Total	**99,560**	**100.0**	**29**

Political Organizations

People's United Party (PUP): 3 Queen St, Belize City; tel. 223-2428; fax 223-3476; f. 1950; based on organized labour; merged with Christian Democratic Party in 1988; Leader SAID MUSA; Exec. Chair. EIDEN SALAZAR, Jr; Deputy Leaders MAXWELL SAMUELS, JOHN BRICEÑO.

United Democratic Party (UDP): South End Bel-China Bridge, POB 1898, Belize City; tel. 227-2576; fax 227-6441; e-mail unitedd@btl.net; internet www.udp.org.bz; f. 1974 by merger of People's Development Movement, Liberal Party and National Independence Party; conservative; Leader DEAN BARROW; Chair. DOUGLAS SINGH.

Diplomatic Representation

EMBASSIES AND HIGH COMMISSION IN BELIZE

China (Taiwan): 20 North Park St, POB 1020, Belize City; tel. 227-8744; fax 223-3082; e-mail embroc@btl.net; Ambassador CHARLES ERH-HUANG TSAI.

Costa Rica: 10 Unity Blvd, POB 288, Belmopan; tel. 822-1582; fax 822-1583; e-mail fborbon@btl.net; Ambassador FERNANDO BORBÓN.

Cuba: 6087 Manatee Dr., Buttonwood Bay, POB 1775, Belize City; tel. 223-5345; fax 223-1105; e-mail embacuba@btl.net; Ambassador REGALA CARIDAD DÍAZ HERNÁNDEZ.

El Salvador: 49 Nanche St, POB 215, Belmopan; tel. 823-3404; fax 823-3569; e-mail embasalva@btl.net; Ambassador MANUEL ANTONIO VÁSQUEZ MEZA.

Guatemala: 8 'A' St, King's Park, POB 1771, Belize City; tel. 233-3150; fax 235-3140; e-mail embbelice1@minex.gob.gt; Ambassador TÉLLEZ MIRALDA.

Honduras: 114 Bella Vista, POB 285, Belize City; tel. 224-5889; fax 223-0562; e-mail embahonbe@sre.hn; Ambassador JOSÉ RIGOBERTO ARRIAGA CHINCHILLA.

Mexico: 18 North Park St, POB 754, Belize City; tel. 223-0193; fax 227-8742; e-mail embamexbze@btl.net; internet www.sre.gob.mx/belice; Ambassador JOSÉ ARTURO TREJO NAVA.

Nicaragua: 124 Barrack Rd, Belize City; tel. and fax 223-2666; e-mail embanicbelize@btl.net; Ambassador JAVIER WILLIAMS SLATE.

United Kingdom: Embassy Sq., POB 91, Belmopan; tel. 822-2146; fax 822-2761; e-mail brithicom@btl.net; internet www.britishhighbze.com; High Commissioner ALAN JONES.

USA: 29 Gabourel Lane, POB 286, Belize City; tel. 227-7161; fax 223-0802; e-mail embbelize@state.gov; internet www.usembassy.state.gov/belize; Ambassador RUSSEL F. FREEMAN.

Venezuela: 19 Orchid Garden St, POB 49, Belmopan; tel. 822-2384; fax 822-2022; e-mail embaven@btl.net; Ambassador AMINTA GUACARAN TORREALBA.

Judicial System

Summary Jurisdiction Courts (criminal jurisdiction) and District Courts (civil jurisdiction), presided over by magistrates, are established in each of the six judicial districts. Summary Jurisdiction Courts have a wide jurisdiction in summary offences and a limited jurisdiction in indictable matters. Appeals lie to the Supreme Court, which has jurisdiction corresponding to the English High Court of Justice and where a jury system is in operation. From the Supreme Court further appeals lie to a Court of Appeal, established in 1967, which holds an average of four sessions per year. Final appeals are made to the Judicial Committee of the Privy Council in the United Kingdom.

Supreme Court: Supreme Court Bldg, Belize City; tel. 227-7256; fax 227-0181; e-mail chiefjustice@btl.net; internet www.belizelaw.org/supreme_court/chief_justice.html; Registrar MICHELLE ARANA; Chief Justice Dr ABDULAI OSMAN CONTEH.

Magistrate's Court: Paslow Bldg, Belize City; tel. 227-7164; Chief Magistrate HERBERT LORD.

Religion

CHRISTIANITY

Most of the population are Christian, the largest denomination being the Roman Catholic Church (an estimated 50% of the population in 2002). The other main groups were the Pentecostal (an estimated 7% in 2000), Anglican (5%), Seventh-day Adventist (5%), Methodist (4%) and Mennonite (4%) churches.

Belize Council of Churches: 149 Allenby St, POB 508, Belize City; tel. 227-7077; f. 1957 as Church World Service Committee, present name adopted 1984; nine mem. Churches, four assoc. bodies; Pres. Rev. LEROY FLOWERS; Gen. Sec. SADIE VERNON.

The Roman Catholic Church

Belize comprises the single diocese of Belize City-Belmopan, suffragan to the archdiocese of Kingston in Jamaica. At 31 December 2002 it was estimated that there were 132,940 adherents in the diocese. The Bishop participates in the Antilles Episcopal Conference (whose secretariat is based in Port of Spain, Trinidad and Tobago).

Bishop of Belize City-Belmopan: OSMOND PETER MARTIN, Bishop's House, 144 North Front St, POB 616, Belize City; tel. 227-2122; fax 223-1922; e-mail episkopos@btl.net.

The Anglican Communion

Anglicans in Belize belong to the Church in the Province of the West Indies, comprising eight dioceses. The Archbishop of the Province is the Bishop of the North Eastern Caribbean and Aruba, resident in St John's, Antigua and Barbuda.

Bishop of Belize: Rt Rev. SYLVESTRE DONATO ROMERO-PALMA, Bishopthorpe, 25 Southern Foreshore, POB 535, Belize City; tel. 227-3029; fax 227-6898; e-mail bzediocese@btl.net; internet www.belize.anglican.org.

Protestant Churches

Methodist Church in the Caribbean and the Americas (Belize/Honduras District) (MCCA): 88 Regent St, POB 212, Belize City; tel. 227-7173; fax 227-5870; f. 1824; c. 2,620 mems; District Pres. Rev. DAVID GOFF.

Mennonite Congregations in Belize: POB 427, Belize City; tel. 823-0137; fax 823-0101; f. 1958; an estimated 3,575 members live in eight Mennonite settlements, the largest of which is Altkolonier Mennotitengemeinde with 1,728 mems; Bishop AARON HARDER.

Other denominations active in the country include the Presbyterians, Baptists, Moravians, Jehovah's Witnesses, the Church of God, the Nazarene Church, the Assemblies of Brethren and the Salvation Army.

OTHER RELIGIONS

There are also small communities of Hindus (106, according to the census of 1980), Muslims (110 in 1980), Jews (92 in 1980) and Bahá'ís.

The Press

Amandala: Amandala Press, 3304 Partridge St, POB 15, Belize City; tel. 202-4476; fax 222-4702; e-mail editor@amandala.com.bz; internet www.amandala.com.bz; f. 1969; 2 a week; independent; Publr EVAN X. HYDE; Editor RUSSELL VELLOS; circ. 45,000.

Ambergris Today: San Pedro Town, Ambergris Caye; tel. 226-3462; e-mail ambertoday@btl.net; internet www.ambergristoday.com; weekly; independent; Editor DORIAN NUÑEZ.

The Belize Times: 3 Queen St, POB 506, Belize City; tel. 224-5757; fax 223-1940; e-mail belizetime@btl.net; internet www.belizetimes.bz; f. 1956; weekly; party political paper of PUP; Editor-in-Chief ANDREW STEINHAUER; circ. 6,000.

Belize Today: Belize Information Service, East Block, POB 60, Belmopan; tel. 822-2159; fax 822-3242; monthly; official; circ. 17,000.

Government Gazette: Print Belize, 1 Power Lane, Belmopan; tel. 822-0194; fax 822-3367; e-mail admin@printbze.bz; internet www.printbelize.bz; f. 1871; official; weekly; CEO LAWRENCE J. NICHOLAS.

The Guardian: Ebony St and Bel-China Bridge, POB 1898, Belize City; tel. 207-5346; fax 227-5343; e-mail info@guardian.bz; internet www.guardian.bz; weekly; party political paper of UDP; Editor JOHN AVERY; circ. 5,000.

The Reporter: 147 Allenby St, POB 707, Belize City; tel. 227-2503; fax 227-8278; e-mail editor@belizereporter.bz; internet www.reporter.bz; f. 1967; weekly; Editor ANN MARIE WILLIAMS; circ. 6,500.

The San Pedro Sun: POB 35, San Pedro Town, Ambergris Caye; fax 226-2905; e-mail sanpedrosun@btl.net; internet www.sanpedrosun.net; weekly; Editors RON SNIFFIN, TAMARA SNIFFIN.

NEWS AGENCY

Agencia EFE (Spain): c/o POB 506, Belize City; tel. 224-5757.

Publishers

Angelus Press Ltd: 10 Queen St, POB 1757, Belize; tel. 223-5777; fax 227-8825; e-mail angelgm@btl.net; Gen. Man. AMPARO M. NOBLE.

Cubola Productions: Montserrat Duran, 35 Elizabeth St, Benque, Viejo del Carmen; tel. 932-0853; fax 932-240; e-mail cubolabz@btl.net; internet www.belizebusiness.com/cubola.

Print Belize Ltd: 1 Power Lane, Belmopan; tel. 822-0194; fax 882-3367; e-mail admin@printbze.bz; internet www.printbelize.bz; f. 1871; responsible for printing, binding and engraving requirements of all govt depts and ministries; publications include annual govt estimates, govt magazines and the official Government Gazette.

Broadcasting and Communications

TELECOMMUNICATIONS

In September 2001 the Government announced that the telecommunications sector was to be liberalized.

Belize Telecommunications Ltd (BTL): Esquivel Telecom Centre, St Thomas St, POB 603, Belize City; tel. 223-2868; fax 223-1800; e-mail prdept@btl.net; internet www.btl.net; f. 1987; owned by Innovative Communication Corpn; taken over by the Govt in Feb. 2005; Chair. CARLA BARNET (acting).

Office of Telecommunications: Administration Complex, Mahogany St Extension, Belize City; tel. 222-4938; fax 222-4939; Dir CLIFFORD SLUSHER.

RADIO

Love FM: 33 Freetown Rd, Belize City; tel. 223-2098; fax 223-0529; e-mail lovefm@btl.net; internet www.lovefm.com; f. 1992; purchased Friends FM in 1998; Man. Dir RENE VILLANUEVA.

Radio Krem Ltd: 3304 Partridge St, POB 15, Belize City; tel. 227-5929; fax 227-4079; e-mail kremwub@hotmail.com; internet www.krem.bz; commercial; purchased Radio Belize in 1998; Man. EVA S. HYDE.

Other private radio stations broadcasting in Belize include: Estereo Amor, More FM, My Refuge Christian Radio, Radio 2000 and Voice of America.

TELEVISION

In 1986 the Belize Broadcasting Authority issued licences to eight television operators for 14 channels, which mainly retransmit US satellite programmes, thus placing television in Belize on a fully legal basis for the first time.

Baymen Broadcasting Network (CTV-Channel 9): 27 Baymen Ave, Belize City; tel. 224-4400; fax 223-1242; commercial; Man. MARIE HOARE.

Channel 5 Belize: POB 679, Belize City; tel. 227-3146; fax 227-4936; e-mail gbtv@btl.com; internet www.channel5belize.com; f. 1991.

Tropical Vision (Channel 7): 73 Albert St, Belize City; tel. 227-3988; fax 227-5602; e-mail tvseven@btl.net; internet 7newsbelize.com; commercial; Man. NESTOR VASQUEZ.

Finance

(cap. = capital; res = reserves; dep. = deposits; brs = branches; amounts in BZ $, unless otherwise indicated)

BANKING

Central Bank

Central Bank of Belize: Gabourel Lane, POB 852, Belize City; tel. 223-6194; fax 223-6226; e-mail cenbank@btl.net; internet www.centralbank.org.bz; f. 1982; cap. 10m., res 12.9m. (2004); Gov. SYDNEY CAMPBELL; Dir and Chair. JORGE MELITON AUIL.

Development Bank

Development Finance Corporation: Bliss Parade, Belmopan; tel. 822-2360; fax 822-3096; e-mail info@dfcbelize.org; internet www.dfcbelize.org; f. 1972; ceased to finance loans following a govt review in Dec. 2004; issued cap. 10m.; Chair. GLENN GODFREY; CEO TROY GABB; 5 brs.

Other Banks

Alliance Bank of Belize Ltd: 106 Princess Margaret Dr., POB 1988, Belize City; tel. 223-6783; fax 223-6785; e-mail alliance@btl.net; internet www.alliancebank.bz; f. 2001; dep. 6,876m., total assets 113.7m.; 3 brs.

Atlantic International Bank Ltd: Cnr Freetown Rd and Cleghorn St, POB 481, Belize City; tel. 223-3152; fax 223-3528; e-mail banking@atlabank.com; internet www.atlanticibl.com; f. 1971; offshore banking; dep. 161.0m., total assets 191.9m. (2001); Chair. Dr GUILLERMO BUESO; 8 brs.

Bank of Nova Scotia (Scotiabank) (Canada): Albert St, POB 708, Belize City; tel. 227-7027; fax 227-7416; e-mail bns.belize@scotiabank.com; Man.Dir PATRICK ANDREWS; 6 brs.

Barclays Bank PLC (United Kingdom): c/o First Caribbean Bank Ltd, 21 Albert St, POB 363, Belize City; tel. 227-7211; fax 227-8572; e-mail barclaysbz@btl.net; Man. TILVAN KING; 5 brs.

Belize Bank Ltd: 60 Market Sq., POB 364, Belize City; tel. 227-7132; fax 227-2712; e-mail bblbz@belizebank.com; internet www.belizebank.com; cap. $4.3m., res $5.9m., dep. $639.3m. (2003); Chair. Sir EDNEY CAIN; Senior Vice-Pres. LOUIS ANTHONY SWASEY; 12 brs.

Provident Bank and Trust of Belize: 35 Barrack Rd, POB 1867, Belize City; tel. 223-5698; fax 223-0368; e-mail services@providentbank.bz; internet www.providentbelize.com; f. 1998; cap. US $6.0m., res US $1.5m., dep. US $121.3m. (2003); Chair. JOY VERNON GODFREY; Pres. ALVARO ALAMINA.

There is also a government savings bank. In late 2001 the Government amended the exchange-control regulations to allow foreign-currency exchange bureaux.

INSURANCE

The insurance sector is regulated by the Office of the Supervisor of Insurance, part of the Ministry of Finance.

Atlantic Insurance Company Ltd: Atlantic Bank Bldg, 3rd Floor, Corner Cleghorn St and Freetown Rd, Belize City; tel. 223-2657; fax 223-2658; e-mail info@atlanticinsurancebz.com; internet www.atlanticinsurancebz.com; f. 1990; Chair. Dr GUILLERMO BUESO.

Belize Insurance Centre : 212 North Front St Belize City; tel. ; tel. 227-7310; fax 227-4803; e-mail info@belizeinsurance.com; internet www.belizeinsurance.com; insurance broker; Gen. Man. Cynthia Awe.

F & G Insurance: 6 Fort St, POB 438, Belize City; tel. 227-7493; fax 227-8617; e-mail fandg@btl.net; internet www.fandginsurance.com.

Regent Insurance Company Ltd: 81 North Front St, POB 661, Belize City; tel. 227-3744; fax 227-2022; e-mail regent@btl.net; internet www.regentinsurance.com; f. 1982; CEO Anthony Flynn.

Trade and Industry

STATUTORY BODIES

Banana Control Board: c/o Dept of Agriculture, West Block, Belmopan; management of banana industry; in 1989 it was decided to make it responsible to growers, not an independent executive.

Belize Marketing Board: 117 North Front St, POB 633, Belize City; tel. 227-7402; fax 227-7656; f. 1948 to encourage the growing of staple food crops; purchases crops at guaranteed prices, supervises processing, storing and marketing intelligence.

Belize Sugar Cane Board: 7 Second St South, Corozal Town; tel. 422-2005; fax 422-2672; f. 1960 to control the sugar industry and cane production; includes representatives of the Government, sugar manufacturers, cane farmers and the public sector.

Citrus Control Board: c/o Dept of Agriculture, West Block, Belmopan; tel. 822-2199; f. 1966; determines basic quota for each producer, fixes annual price of citrus.

DEVELOPMENT ORGANIZATIONS

Belize Reconstruction and Development Corporation: 1 Bliss Promenade, POB 92, Belize City; tel. 227-7424; e-mail recondev@btl.net; Gen. Man. Aloysius Palacio.

Belize Trade and Investment Development Service (BELTRAIDE): 14 Orchid Garden St, Belmopan; tel. 822-3737; fax 822-0595; e-mail beltraide@belizeinvest.org.bz; internet www.belizeinvest.org.bz; f. 1986 as a joint government and private-sector institution to encourage export and investment; Exec. Dir Lourdes Smith.

CHAMBERS OF COMMERCE

Belize British Chamber of Commerce (BBCC): Embassy Sq., Ring Rd, Cayo District, POB 91, Belmopan; tel. 822-2146; fax 822-2761; internet www.belizebritishchamber.com; Chair. Philip Osborne; Sec. Mike Hernandez, Jr.

Belize Chamber of Commerce and Industry: 63 Regent St, POB 291, Belize City; tel. 227-3148; fax 227-4984; e-mail bcci@btl.net; internet www.belize.org; f. 1920; Pres. Gilbert Canton; Gen. Man. Kevin Herrera; 300 mems.

EMPLOYERS' ASSOCIATIONS

Banana Growers' Association: Big Creek, Independence Village, Stann Creek District; tel. 622-001; fax 622-112; e-mail banana@btl.net.

Belize Cane Farmers' Association: 34 San Antonio Rd, Orange Walk; tel. 322-005; fax 323-171; f. 1959 to assist cane farmers and negotiate with the Sugar Board and manufacturers on their behalf; Chair. Pablo Tun; 16 district brs.

Belize Livestock Producers' Association: 47.5 miles Western Highway, POB 183, Belmopan; tel. 823-202; fax 823-886; e-mail blpa@btl.net; Chair. Pete Lizarraga.

Citrus Growers Association: Mile 9, Stann Creek Valley Rd, POB 7, Dangriga, Stann Creek District; tel. 522-3585; fax 522-2686; e-mail cga@belizecitrus.org; internet www.belizecitrus.org; f. 1966; CEO Bridget Cullerton.

UTILITIES

Electricity

Office of Electricity Supply: 44 Queen St, POB 1846, Belize City; tel. 222-4995; fax 222-4994; e-mail oes@btl.net; f. 1992; Dir-Gen. Herman Charlesworth.

Belize Electricity Co Ltd (BECOL): 115 Barrack Rd, POB 327, Belize City; tel. 227-0954; fax 223-0891; e-mail bel@btl.net; owned by Fortis Inc (Canada); operates Mollejón 25 MW hydroelectric plant, which supplies electricity to Belize Electricity Ltd (BEL—see below); Chair. Nestor Vasquez; Pres. and CEO Lynn Young.

Belize Electricity Ltd (BEL): 2.5 miles Northern Highway, POB 327, Belize City; tel. 227-0954; fax 223-0891; e-mail pr@bel.com.bz; internet www.bel.com.bz; fmrly Belize Electricity Board, changed name upon privatization in 1992; Govt held 51% of shares until 1999; 68% owned by Fortis Inc (Canada); Pres. and CEO Lynn R. Young; Vice-Pres. Derek Davis; Chair. Robert Usher.

Water

Belize Water Services Ltd: POB 150, Central American Blvd, Belize City; tel. 222-4757; fax 222-4759; e-mail bws_ceosec@btl.net; f. 1971 as Water and Sewerage Authority (WASA); changed name upon privatization in March 2001; 82.7% owned by Cascal, BV (United Kingdom/Netherlands); CEO Martin R. Greenhalgh.

TRADE UNIONS

National Trade Union Congress of Belize (NTUCB): POB 2359, Belize City; tel. 227-1596; fax 227-2864; e-mail ntucb@btl.net; Pres. Horris Patten; Gen. Sec. George Frazer.

Principal Unions

Belize Communications Workers' Union: POB 1291, Belize City; tel. 223-4809; fax 224-4090; e-mail bcwu@btl.net; Pres. Paul Perriott; Gen. Sec. Laurie Barrow.

Belize Energy Workers' Union: c/o Belize Electricity Ltd, 2.5 miles Northern Highway, POB 327, Belize City; tel. 227-0954; Pres. Colville Young; Gen. Sec. Floyd Herrera.

Belize National Teachers' Union: 10 Eve St, POB 382, Belize City; tel. 227-2857; fax 223-5233; e-mail bntu@btl.net; Pres. Anthony Fuentes; Gen. Sec. Lois Barber; 1,000 mems.

Belize Workers' Union: Tate St, Orange Walk Town; tel. 822-2327; Pres. Edwardo Meléndez.

Christian Workers' Union: 107b Cemetery Rd, POB 533, Belize City; tel. and fax 227-2150; e-mail cwu@btl.net; f. 1962; general; Pres. Antonio González; 1,000 mems.

Public Service Union of Belize: 2 Mayflower St, POB 458, Belmopan; tel. 822-0282; fax 822-0283; e-mail belizepsu@btl.net; f. 1922; public workers; Pres. Dylan Reneaw; Sec.-Gen. Francisco G. Zuniga; 1,600 mems.

United Banners Banana Workers' Union: Dangriga; f. 1995; Pres. Marciana Funez.

Transport

Department of Transport: Power Lane, Belmopan; tel. 822-2435; fax 822-3317; e-mail transcom@btl.net; Commissioner Phillip Brackett.

RAILWAYS

There are no railways in Belize.

ROADS

There are 2,710 km of roads, of which 2,210 km (1,600 km of gravel roads, 300 km of improved earth roads and 310 km of unimproved earth roads) are unpaved. In 2000 the World Bank approved a loan of US $13m. for road construction. In 2002 the European Union approved a grant of BZ $3.6m. towards the construction of a bridge over the New Sibun river. The Government was to provide BZ $1m. in funding and the project was expected to be completed by late 2004.

SHIPPING

There is a deep-water port at Belize City and a second port at Commerce Bight, near Dangriga (formerly Stann Creek), to the south of Belize City. There is a port for the export of bananas at Big Creek and additional ports at Corozal and Punta Gorda. Nine major shipping lines operate vessels calling at Belize City, including the Carol Line (consisting of Harrison, Hapag-Lloyd, Nedlloyd and CGM). A proposal to develop a cruise-ship port at Port Loyola at a cost of BZ $963.5m. was submitted to parliament in October 2004.

Belize Port Authority: Caesar Ridge Rd, POB 633, Belize City; tel. 227-2480; fax 227-2500; e-mail bzportauth@bpa.org.bz; f. 1980; Chair. Fred Hunter; CEO Lloyd Jones.

Marine & Services: 95 Albert St, POB 611, Belize City; tel. 227-2112; fax 227-5404; e-mail shipping@marineservices.bz; internet www.marineservices.bz; f. 1975; shipping and cargo services, cruise line agent; Gen. Man. José Gallego.

Port of Belize Ltd: Caesar Ridge Rd, POB 2674, Belize City; tel. 227-2439; fax 227-3571; e-mail portbz@btl.net; operates the main port facility; CEO Raineldo Guerrero; Deputy CEO Franzine A. Waight.

CIVIL AVIATION

Phillip S. W. Goldson International Airport, 14 km (9 miles) from Belize City, can accommodate medium-sized jet-engined aircraft. The runway was extended in 2000. There are 37 airstrips for light aircraft on internal flights near the major towns and offshore islands.

Belize Airports Authority (BAA): POB 1564, Belize City; e-mail aviation@btl.net; tel. 225-2045; fax 225-2439; e-mail bzeaa@btl.net; CEO PABLO ESPAT.

Maya Island Air: Municipal Airport, POB 458, Belize City; tel. 223-1403; fax 223-0576; e-mail mayair@btl.net; internet www.ambergriscaye.com/islandair; f. 1997 as merger between Maya Airways Ltd and Island Air; operated by Belize Air Group; internal services, centred on Belize City, and charter flights to neighbouring countries; Exec. Dir TREVOR ROE; Gen. Man. ROSITA MENZIES.

Tropic Air: San Pedro, POB 20, Ambergris Caye; tel. 226-5671; fax 226-2338; e-mail reservations@tropicair.com; internet www.tropicair.com; f. 1979; operates internal services and services to Guatemala; Chair. CELI McCORKLE; Man. Dir JOHN GREIF.

Tourism

The main tourist attractions are the beaches and the barrier reef, diving, fishing and the Mayan archaeological sites. There are nine major wildlife reserves (including the world's only reserves for the jaguar and for the red-footed booby), and government policy is to develop 'eco-tourism', based on the attractions of an unspoilt environment and Belize's natural history. The country's wildlife also includes howler monkeys and 500 species of birds, and its barrier reef is the second largest in the world. However, in May 2000 scientists reported that the high sea temperatures recorded in 1998, caused by the El Niño phenomenon and global warming, had resulted in extensive damage to the coral population. There were some 437 hotels in Belize in 2002. In 2003 there were an estimated 686,591 tourist arrivals and tourism receipts totalled an estimated US $156.2m. In February 1996 the Mundo Maya Agreement was ratified, according to which Belize, El Salvador, Guatemala, Honduras and Mexico would co-operate in the management of Mayan archaeological remains. In June 2000 the Inter-American Development Bank approved a loan of US $11m. towards the Government's tourism development plan.

Belize Tourism Board: Level 2, New Central Bank Bldg, POB 325, Gabourel Lane, Belize City; tel. 223-1913; fax 223-1943; e-mail info@travelbelize.org; internet www.travelbelize.org; f. 1964; fmrly Belize Tourist Bureau; eight mems; Chair. PATTY ARCEO; Dir TRACY TAEGAR.

Belize Tourism Industry Association (BTIA): 10 North Park St, POB 62, Belize City; tel. 227-5717; fax 227-8710; e-mail info@btia.org; internet www.btia.org; promoyes sustainable tourism; Exec. Dir ANDREW GODOY.

BENIN

Introductory Survey

Location, Climate, Language, Religion, Flag, Capital

The Republic of Benin is a narrow stretch of territory in West Africa. The country has an Atlantic coastline of about 100 km (60 miles), flanked by Nigeria to the east and Togo to the west; its northern borders are with Burkina Faso and Niger. Benin's climate is tropical, and is divided into three zones: the north has a rainy season between July and September, with a hot, dry season in October–April; the central region has periods of abundant rain in May–June and in October; and there is year-round precipitation in the south, the heaviest rains being in May–October. Average annual rainfall in Cotonou is 1,300 mm. French is the official language, but each of the indigenous ethnic groups has its own language. Bariba and Fulani are the major languages in the north, while Fon and Yoruba are widely spoken in the south. It is estimated that 35% of the people follow traditional beliefs and customs; about 35% are Christians, mainly Roman Catholics, and the majority of the remainder are Muslims. The national flag (proportions 2 by 3) has a vertical green stripe at the hoist, with equal horizontal stripes of yellow over red in the fly. The administrative capital is Porto-Novo, but most government offices and other state bodies are presently in the economic capital, Cotonou.

Recent History

Benin, called Dahomey until 1975, was formerly part of French West Africa. It became a self-governing republic within the French Community in December 1958, and an independent state on 1 August 1960. The early years of independence were characterized by chronic political instability and by periodic regional unrest, fuelled by long-standing rivalries between north and south.

Elections in December 1960 were won by the Parti dahoméen de l'unité, whose leader, Hubert Maga (a northerner), became the country's first President. In October 1963 Maga was deposed in a coup led by Col (later Gen.) Christophe Soglo, Chief of Staff of the Army. Soglo served as interim Head of State until January 1964, when Sourou-Migan Apithy, a southerner and former Vice-President, was elected President. Another southerner, Justin Ahomadegbé, became Prime Minister. In November 1965 Gen. Soglo forced Apithy and Ahomadegbé to resign. A provisional Government was formed, but a further military intervention, in December, resulted in Soglo again assuming power. In December 1967 industrial unrest precipitated another coup, led by Maj. (later Lt-Col) Maurice Kouandété. Lt-Col Alphonse Alley, hitherto Chief of Staff, became interim Head of State, and Kouandété Prime Minister.

A new Constitution, providing for a return to civilian rule, was approved by referendum in March 1968, and a presidential election followed in May. However, leading politicians, including all former Heads of State, who were banned from contesting the presidency, urged their supporters to boycott the election, and only about 26% of the electorate voted; the abstention rate reportedly reached 99% in northern regions. The election was declared void, and in June the military regime nominated Dr Emile-Derlin Zinsou as President. In December 1969 Zinsou was deposed by Lt-Col Kouandété, then Commander-in-Chief of the Army, and a three-member military Directoire assumed power. In March 1970 a presidential election was abandoned when counting revealed roughly equal support for the three main candidates—Ahomadegbé, Apithy and Maga—to whom the Directoire ceded power in May: it was intended that each member of this Presidential Council would act as Head of State, in rotation, for a two-year period. Maga was the first to hold this office and was succeeded in May 1972 by Ahomadegbé.

In October 1972 the civilian leadership was deposed by Maj. (later Brig.-Gen.) Mathieu Kérékou, Deputy Chief of Staff of the armed forces and a northerner. In September 1973 a Conseil national révolutionnaire (CNR), which was intended to ensure equal representation for the northern, central and southern regions of the country, was established. Strategic sectors and financial institutions were acquired by the State, under Kérékou's regime, which pursued Marxist-based policies. In late 1975 the Parti de la révolution populaire du Bénin (PRPB) was established as the sole party, and Dahomey was renamed the People's Republic of Benin.

In January 1977 an airborne attack on Cotonou, led by a French mercenary, Col Robert Denard, was repelled by the armed forces. In August the CNR adopted a *Loi fondamentale* decreeing new structures in government. Elections to a new 'supreme authority', the Assemblée nationale révolutionnaire (ANR), took place in November 1979, when a single list of 336 'People's Commissioners' was approved by 97.5% of voters. At the same time a Comité exécutif national (CEN) was established to replace the CNR. The PRPB designated Kérékou as the sole candidate for President of the Republic, and in February 1980 the ANR unanimously elected him to this office. In April 1981 it was announced that Ahomadegbé, Apithy and Maga, imprisoned following the coup of 1972, had been released from house arrest. A gradual moderation in Benin's domestic policies followed, and both the extreme left and the army, whose officers were by now outnumbered by civilians in the Government, gradually lost influence. At legislative elections in June 1984 the single list of People's Commissioners was approved by 98% of voters, and in July the ANR re-elected Kérékou, again the sole candidate, as President.

In January 1987 Kérékou resigned from the army to become a civilian Head of State. Chronic economic difficulties caused Benin to seek stronger ties with the West in the late 1980s. In June 1989 economic adjustment measures were agreed with the IMF and the World Bank, prompting fears of further austerity measures. At elections to the ANR in that month a relative decline in support for the single list of PRPB-approved candidates (which was endorsed by 89.6% of voters) was attributed to dissatisfaction with the economic situation, amid continuing labour and academic unrest. In August the ANR re-elected Kérékou (once again the sole candidate) as President. A reorganization of the CEN included the appointment of several advocates of reform. At the end of the year Kérékou yielded to domestic and international pressure, instituting radical political changes and abandoning Marxism-Leninism as the official state ideology.

In February 1990 delegates at a conference of the 'active forces of the nation' voted to abolish the *Loi fondamentale* and its institutions; all resolutions adopted by the conference were incorporated in a 'national charter' that was to form the basis of a new constitution. An Haut conseil de la République (HCR) was appointed to assume the functions of the ANR pending the appointment of a new legislature. Among the members of the HCR were former Presidents Ahomadegbé, Maga and Zinsou, all of whom had returned to Benin to lead opposition parties. Presidential and legislative elections, to be held in the context of a multi-party political system, were scheduled for early 1991. A former official of the World Bank (who had briefly been Minister of Finance and Economic Affairs in the mid-1960s), Nicéphore Soglo, was designated interim Prime Minister, and Kérékou subsequently relinquished the defence portfolio to Soglo. The conference also voted to change the country's name to the Republic of Benin.

In March 1990 an amnesty was announced for all political dissidents. The HCR was inaugurated, and Soglo appointed a transitional Government. Of the previous administration, only Kérékou remained in office. In May civilian administrators replaced the provincial military prefects, prior to an extensive restructuring of the armed forces. Legislation permitting the registration of political parties was promulgated in August.

A national referendum on the draft Constitution was conducted on 2 December 1990. Voters were asked to choose between two proposed documents, one of which incorporated a clause stipulating upper and lower age-limits for presidential candidates, and would therefore prevent the candidatures of Ahomadegbé, Maga and Zinsou. It was reported that 95.8% of those who voted approved one or other of the versions, with 79.7% of voters favouring the age-restriction clause.

Some 24 political parties contested the legislative elections on 17 February 1991. The largest grouping in the new 64-member Assemblée nationale was an alliance of three pro-Soglo parties, which secured 12 seats. Kérékou and Soglo were among 13 candidates at the first round of the presidential election on 10 March. Soglo, who won 36.2% of the total votes cast, received his greatest support in the south of the country, while Kérékou, who received 27.3% of the overall vote, was reported to have secured the support of more than 80% of voters in the north. Soglo and Kérékou proceeded to a second round of voting on 24 March, when Soglo was elected President, with 67.7% of the total votes cast. In late March, prior to its dissolution, the HCR granted Kérékou immunity from any legal proceedings connected with actions committed since the *coup d'état* of 1972.

Soglo was inaugurated as President on 4 April 1991, and shortly afterwards he relinquished the defence portfolio. Tensions between the executive and legislature, particularly over the Government's programme of economic reform, eased somewhat following the formation, in June, of a 34-member pro-Soglo parliamentary grouping, styled Le Renouveau.

In October 1992 15 deputies withdrew from Le Renouveau, alleging that Soglo was consistently excluding the legislature from the decision-making process. In July Soglo, who had previously asserted his political neutrality, had made public his membership of a political party, La renaissance du Bénin (RB), formed by his wife, Rosine Soglo, in 1992; he was appointed leader of the RB in July 1994.

In November 1994 the Assemblée nationale voted to establish an independent electoral supervisory body, the Commission électorale nationale autonome (CENA), despite resistance from Soglo, who also opposed a planned increase in the number of deputies from 64 to 83. Some 31 political organizations participated in the legislative elections, which took place on 28 March 1995. In mid-April the Constitutional Court annulled the results of voting for 13 seats on the grounds of irregularities. Following by-elections in May, the RB held 20 seats in the Assemblée nationale, and other supporters of Soglo 13. Opposition parties held 49 seats, the most prominent being the Parti du renouveau démocratique (PRD), with 19 seats, and the Front d'action pour le renouveau et le développement—Alafia (FARD—Alafia), with 10; the latter had attracted considerable support from Kérékou supporters in the north, although the former President had not actively campaigned in the election. In June 1995 Bruno Amoussou, the leader of the opposition Parti social-démocrate (PSD), was elected President of the Assemblée nationale. Later that month a new Government was formed.

The success of supporters of Kérékou at the legislative elections prompted speculation that Kérékou might again contest the presidency in 1996, and in January of that year he announced his candidature. While Soglo's economic policies had earned his administration the respect of the international financial community, there was internal disquiet that growth had been achieved at the expense of social concerns and that the regime had become increasingly authoritarian. Notably, in December 1995 the Assemblée nationale had voted to delay ratification of the third phase of Benin's structural adjustment programme, the most contentious element of which was the planned restructuring of the state company responsible for the distribution of petroleum products, the Société nationale de commercialisation des produits pétroliers (SONACOP). Deputies rejected ratification of a modified programme twice during January 1996, and also rejected the Government's draft budget for that year, prompting Soglo to implement the budget and adjustment programme by decree.

The first round of the presidential election, on 3 March 1996, was contested by seven candidates. Some 22.8% of the votes cast were invalidated by the Constitutional Court prior to the announcement of the official results, whereby Soglo secured 35.7% of the valid votes and Kérékou 33.9%, followed by the leader of the PRD, Adrien Houngbédji, (19.7%) and Amoussou (7.8%). The rate of participation by voters was 86.9%. Most of the defeated candidates quickly expressed their support for Kérékou, among them Houngbédji, who had, in 1975, been sentenced to death *in absentia* for his part in a plot to overthrow Kérékou's military regime. The second round of voting took place on 18 March. Several days later the Constitutional Court announced Kérékou's election, with 52.5% of the valid votes. Some 78.1% of those eligible had voted, and less than 3% of the votes had been disallowed. Kérékou won the support of a majority of voters in four of the country's six provinces, although Soglo performed strongly in Cotonou and in his native Zou province, in central Benin. Having sought authorization by the Constitutional Court for the appointment of a Prime Minister (provision for such a post is not stipulated in the Constitution), Kérékou named

Houngbédji as premier, while assuming personal responsibility for defence.

In September 1997 the Assemblée nationale approved an amnesty for electoral and media crimes and all acts seeking to undermine state security committed between January 1990 and June 1996. However, in October 1997 the Constitutional Court declared the amnesty legislation to be unconstitutional, on the grounds that the Government had failed to undertake the requisite consultations with the Supreme Court.

In early May 1998 Houngbédji resigned the premiership, apparently prompted by dissatisfaction at his exclusion from the drafting of the 1998 budget and by concern that an impending government reshuffle would result in a loss of influence for himself and the PRD. Later in the month Kérékou named a new Government in which there was no Prime Minister, the most senior minister being Pierre Osho (hitherto Minister of Foreign Affairs and Co-operation) as Minister-delegate to the Presidency, in charge of Defence and Relations with the Institutions.

Elections to the 83 seats in the Assemblée nationale, held on 30 March 1999, were contested by more than 2,900 candidates, representing 35 parties and alliances. International monitors reported that the elections had been conducted peacefully and democratically. Official results, issued by the CENA on 3 April and confirmed by the Constitutional Council one week later, indicated that the combined opposition parties had won a slender majority in the legislature, with 42 seats. The RB won the largest number of seats, with 27, principally in the south and centre (including eight of Cotonou's nine seats), while FARD—Alafia (10 seats), the PSD (nine seats) and other parties loyal to the President performed strongly in the north and west. The representation of the PRD was reduced to 11 seats. The rate of participation by voters was in excess of 70%. Houngbédji was elected Speaker of the new assembly, defeating Amoussou. In June Kérékou effected a government reshuffle, increasing the number of parties represented in the Council of Ministers from seven to 10, in an apparent effort to consolidate his support in the Assemblée nationale.

In January 2000 Kérékou imposed the annual budget by decree, after opposition deputies had rejected its provisions. In the same month members of the armed forces demonstrated in Cotonou against the non-payment of bonuses due to them for their service in West African peace-keeping missions; the Government later admitted that sums of money due to the troops had been misappropriated by senior military figures. In early 2000 Soglo and Houngbédji formed a new alliance of 10 opposition parties, which condemned the perceived corruption of the Kérékou administration, particularly in relation to the privatization of SONACOP.

In the period preceding the presidential election, scheduled for March 2001, Soglo was widely regarded as the sole credible challenger to Kérékou. Corruption became a leading issue, as allegations emerged of fraudulent behaviour by both Kérékou and Soglo involving large parastatal companies. Early results of the first round of the election, which was held on 4 March and contested by 17 candidates, indicated that Kérékou had gained the largest share of the vote, but had failed to secure an absolute majority; a second round, to be contested by Kérékou and Soglo, the second-placed candidate, was scheduled for 18 March. As campaigning proceeded, the Constitutional Court conducted a review of the election results declared by the CENA. Revised provisional results of the first round gave Kérékou 45.42% of the votes cast, Soglo 27.12%, Houngbédji 12.62% and Amoussou (who had originally been placed fifth) 8.59%. Following the declaration of the revised results, which indicated an increase in the electoral roll of some 300,000 and a participation rate of around 80%, Houngbédji endorsed the candidature of Soglo, while Amoussou encouraged his supporters to vote for Kérékou, who stated that he would form a broad-based government of national unity, if re-elected. Meanwhile, there were calls for a boycott of the second round of voting, owing to alleged irregularities in the conduct of the first round. Soglo appealed to the Constitutional Court to annul the disputed results, and to rerun the election, either in those constituencies, or on a nation-wide basis. On 16 March Soglo, having had his appeal rejected, withdrew his candidature. The Government postponed the second round of the election, which was thus to be contested by Kérékou and Houngbédji, firstly until 19 March and subsequently until 22 March. However, on 19 March Houngbédji also declared his dissatisfaction with the conduct of the election and withdrew from the second round. Consequently, Amoussou, who had previously declared his support for Kérékou, was now to challenge him for the presidency. Nine opposition members of the CENA resigned in protest at the conduct of the election, alleging that a small group close to both Kérékou and Amoussou had effectively manipulated the commission to their own ends. Voter participation in the second round of voting, duly held on 22 March was significantly lower than in the first round, at about 55%. Two days after polling the CENA announced that Kérékou had won 84.06% of the valid votes cast. Kérékou was declared President for a further term, despite allegations that the depleted CENA was not qualified to organize the election.

In May 2001 Kérékou announced the formation of a new Government, which included eight new appointees among the 21 ministers. Amoussou was reappointed to a senior position in the Council of Ministers, as Minister of State, responsible for the Co-ordination of Government Action, Future Planning and Development. In June the Assemblée nationale adopted legislation that granted amnesty to those who had committed various crimes during the period surrounding the presidential election. None the less, one of the stated priorities of the new administration was to combat corruption, and the Government announced the implementation of what it termed a strategic plan to that end. In July it was announced that proposed municipal elections, initially scheduled to be held in 2000, had been cancelled, as a result of overspending on the presidential election.

In August 2001 dissent within the RB became apparent, when 10 of the party's deputies, led by its Vice-Chairman, Nathaniel Bah, formed a separate grouping within the Assemblée nationale. Despite the expulsion of Bah from the RB in mid-August, his supporters announced his assumption of the party leadership (displacing Rosine Soglo) at an extraordinary congress in early September. In January 2002 a congress of the RB reinstated Rosine Soglo as the party Chairperson, although factionalism within the party persisted throughout 2002 and the first half of 2003.

Meanwhile, in February 2002 the President was again obliged to implement the state budget by decree, following the failure of the Assemblée nationale to adopt the proposed draft. In late 2001 and early 2002 up to 32,000 civil servants and workers, primarily in the health and education sectors, participated in a series of nation-wide strikes, in support of demands for higher salaries and the withdrawal of proposals to introduce promotion on grounds of merit within the public sector. (Sporadic industrial unrest, notably within the civil service, had occurred intermittently since the mid-1990s.) In early March 2002 the Government reached agreement with six of the seven trade unions that had organized the strikes; wage arrears were to be paid and an increase in civil servants' salaries granted, while the question of procedures for promotions was to be referred to the Assemblée nationale. Meanwhile, the appointment of Grégoire Laourou as Minister of Finance and the Economy in mid-February, following the resignation of his predecessor, Abdoulaye Bio Tchané, to take up a position at the IMF, was regarded as an indication of the President's commitment to sustained and pragmatic economic reform.

The delayed elections to 1,199 municipal and local seats were held in two rounds in December 2002 and January 2003, contested by some 5,700 candidates. Supporters of Kérékou, who had formed an electoral alliance known as the Union pour le Bénin du futur (UBF), in anticipation of legislative elections scheduled to be held in March 2003, were the most successful grouping overall. Nevertheless, and despite the continued existence of divisions within the party, the RB gained the majority of seats in Cotonou, where Nicéphore Soglo was elected mayor, while the PRD secured control of the municipality of Porto-Novo. Rosine Soglo was subsequently successful in consolidating her position as Chairperson of the RB, and Bah announced that he was to contest the legislative elections as a candidate of the pro-presidential Mouvement africain pour la démocratie et le progrès (MADEP), led by Séfou Fagbohoun, a business executive. Meanwhile, the UBF constituted itself as a unified party, led by Amoussou as Co-ordinator.

Following the legislative elections, which were held on 30 March 2003, a secure pro-presidential majority in the Assemblée nationale was formed for the first time since the introduction of multi-party elections in Benin. Pro-Kérékou parties and alliances won 52 of the 83 elective seats, and in mid-April the PRD, which had secured 11 seats, announced that it would, henceforth, also support the Government. The UBF emerged as the largest single party, with 31 seats, and the MADEP won nine seats. The representation of the RB, the largest party in the

outgoing assembly, was reduced from 27 to 15 seats. Eight other parties or alliances won representation in the elections, which were contested by 1,162 candidates, representing 14 political groups. It was reported that as many as one-half of the deputies elected to the new legislature had not served in the outgoing assembly. Among the new deputies elected was the President's son, Modeste Kérékou, who became the youngest member of the legislature. At the end of April Antoine Idji Kolawolé of the MADEP, hitherto Minister of Foreign Affairs and African Integration, was elected as President of the Assemblée nationale, defeating Rosine Soglo. The formation of a new Government was announced in mid-June 2003: Amoussou was appointed to the most senior ministerial post in the new Government, as Minister of State, responsible for Planning and Development; Osho was appointed as Minister of State, responsible for National Defence.

A major political concern during the second half of 2003 was the alleged involvement of senior police and judicial officials with international criminal gangs based in Benin. The activities of these gangs, who were reported to be principally involved in the smuggling of stolen motor cars, had, in mid-August, resulted in the closure of the Beninois–Nigerian border for six days (see below). In early September President Kérékou established a special commission to investigate alleged links between government officials and organized criminal groups. In late October, following the publication of a report by the commission, the Beninois authorities announced that several senior police and judicial officials had been dismissed. In early June 2004, in an unrelated major case of corruption, 37 civil servants from the judiciary and the Ministry of Finance and the Economy were sentenced to between 30 months' and five years' imprisonment for their involvement in the embezzlement of more than 8,000m. francs CFA from state funds between 1996 and 2000; 25 defendants received suspended sentences and a further 25 were acquitted. Of the country's nine lower courts, only one was not implicated in the scandal, in which 27 magistrates were among the accused. Later in June 2004 magistrates in Benin commenced a three-day strike in support of their demands for greater independence for the judiciary.

In February 2005 President Kérékou effected a major cabinet reshuffle, formulating what was widely expected to be the last Government of his presidency. Significantly, Amoussou was removed from the Government and was replaced as Minister of State, responsible for Planning and Development by Zul Kifl Salami (there was speculation that this move was intended to allow Amoussou to concentrate on preparing his candidacy for the presidential election in March 2006).

Benin has in recent years played an active role in efforts to co-ordinate regional peace-keeping and humanitarian assistance operations, contributing troops to peace-keeping operations undertaken by the Economic Community of West African States (see p. 205) in Guinea-Bissau from late 1998 until mid-1999, in Côte d'Ivoire from early 2003, and in Liberia from September 2003.

Benin maintains generally good relations with neighbouring countries and joined the Community of Sahel-Saharan States (see p. 373) in March 2002. None the less, in mid-2000 a long-term dispute between Benin and Niger, over the ownership of various small islands in the Niger river, erupted after Nigerien soldiers reportedly sabotaged the construction of a Beninois administrative building on Lété Island. Meetings between representatives of the two Governments and arbitration by the Organization of African Unity (now the African Union, see p. 144) failed to resolve the dispute, and in April 2002 the two countries officially ratified an agreement (signed in 2001) to refer the dispute to the International Court of Justice (ICJ) at The Hague, Netherlands, for arbitration. Benin and Niger filed confidential written arguments with the Court, and in November 2003 a five-member Chamber formed to consider the case held its first public sitting. Both countries subsequently submitted counter-arguments, and a third written pleading was submitted by both parties in December of that year. (In June the UN had awarded Benin and Niger US $350,000 each towards the cost of resolving their dispute.) The public hearings took place before the Chamber of the ICJ in March 2005, at which time both parties presented their final submissions. Meanwhile, in late 2004 Nigerien traders and haulage contractors boycotted Cotonou port in reaction to the shooting of two Nigerien citizens by Beninois gendarmes in the city in September. The boycott was ended in January 2005 following a visit to Niamey by the Beninois Minister of Foreign Affairs and African Integration,

Rogatien Biaou, during which he announced that the Beninois Government would compensate the victims' families.

Benin and Nigeria launched joint police patrols along their common border in August 2001. However, renewed concerns about cross-border crime, particularly the smuggling of petroleum and automobiles, resulted in the unilateral closure, by the Nigerian authorities, of the frontier in August 2003. Following a meeting between the Presidents of the two countries later in the month, the border was reopened, and the Beninois and Nigerian authorities announced a series of measures intended to enhance co-operation to combat cross-border crime. Tensions between the two countries were further eased by the extradition, in September, from Benin to Nigeria, of Hamani Tidjani, a Nigerien citizen resident in Cotonou, who was sought in Nigeria on suspicion of smuggling stolen motor cars, as well as for his alleged involvement in a suspected assassination attempt on a daughter of President Gen. Olusegun Obasanjo earlier in the year. Nevertheless, security around the common border was believed to have been the main focus of further discussions between Kérékou and Obasanjo in April 2004. In July it was reported that a joint commission had amicably resolved a dispute over the land and maritime boundary between Benin and Nigeria, and in January 2005 it was announced that joint border patrols were to resume.

Government

The Constitution of the Republic of Benin, which was approved in a national referendum on 2 December 1990, provides for a civilian, multi-party political system. Executive power is vested in the President of the Republic, who is elected by direct universal adult suffrage with a five-year mandate, renewable only once. The legislature is the 83-member Assemblée nationale, which is similarly elected, for a period of four years, by universal suffrage. The President of the Republic appoints the Council of Ministers, subject to formal parliamentary approval.

For the purposes of local administration, Benin is divided into 12 departments, each administered by a civilian prefect. These departments are further divided into a total of 77 communes.

Defence

In August 2004 the Beninois Armed Forces numbered an estimated 4,550 in active service (land army 4,300, navy about 100, air force 150). Paramilitary forces comprised a 2,500-strong gendarmerie. Military service is by selective conscription, and lasts for 18 months. The estimated defence budget for 2004 was 36,000m. francs CFA.

Economic Affairs

In 2003, according to estimates by the World Bank, Benin's gross national income (GNI), measured at average 2001–03 prices, was US $3,468m., equivalent to $440 per head (or $1,110 on an international purchasing-power parity basis). During 1990–2003, it was estimated, the population increased at an average annual rate of 2.8%, while gross domestic product (GDP) per head increased, in real terms, by an average of 2.1% per year. Overall GDP increased, in real terms, at an average annual rate of 5.0% in 1990–2003; growth in 2003 was 5.6%.

Agriculture (including forestry and fishing) contributed 35.7% of GDP in 2003. In 2003 an estimated 51.0% of the labour force were employed in the sector. The principal cash crops are cotton (exports of which accounted for an estimated 65.0% of total exports in 2001), oil palm and cashew nuts. Benin is normally self-sufficient in basic foods; the main subsistence crops are cassava, yams and maize. The World Bank estimated that agricultural GDP increased at an average annual rate of 5.7% in 1990–2003; growth in 2003 was 5.0%.

Industry (including mining, manufacturing, construction and power) contributed 14.3% of GDP in 2003,and engaged 10.4% of the employed labour force at the time of the 1992 census. According to the World Bank, industrial GDP increased at an average annual rate of 5.0% in 1990–2003; growth in 2003 was 5.5%.

Mining contributed only 0.2% of GDP in 2002, and engaged less than 0.1% of the employed labour force in 1992. Petroleum extraction at Sémé was terminated on the grounds of unprofitability in 1998, contributing to a 82.2% decline in mining GDP in the following year. However, a contract signed between Benin and the multinational Zetah Oil Company in October 1999 envisaged the exploitation of Sémé's remaining petroleum reserves, estimated at some 22m. barrels, and operations recommenced in 2000. Marble and limestone are also exploited commercially. There are also deposits of gold, phosphates, natural

gas, iron ore, silica sand, peat and chromium. The GDP of the mining sector declined at an average annual rate of 28.6% in 1994–2001; growth in mining GDP was negligible in 2001.

The manufacturing sector, which contributed 9.0% of GDP in 2003, engaged 7.8% of the employed labour force in 1992. The sector is based largely on the processing of primary products (principally cotton-ginning and oil-palm processing). Construction materials and some simple consumer goods are also produced for the domestic market. According to the World Bank, manufacturing GDP increased at an average annual rate of 6.1% in 1990–2003; growth in 2003 was 4.6%.

Benin is at present highly dependent on imports of electricity from Ghana (which supplied some 85% of total available production in 1996). It is envisaged that a hydroelectric installation on the Mono river, constructed and operated jointly with Togo, will reduce Benin's dependence on imported electricity, and a second such installation is under construction downstream. In 2001 hydroelectric sources were responsible for 2.3% of Benin's electricity production, while the remaining 97.7% was derived from petroleum. In 2000 the construction of a further electricity line, to run from Lagos, Nigeria, to Togo, through Benin, was proposed by the Governments of the three countries. A pipeline to supply natural gas from Nigeria to Benin, Togo and Ghana was expected to come on stream in 2005, three years later than initially planned. Imports of mineral fuels and lubricants accounted for 17.3% of the value of total imports in 2001.

The services sector contributed 50.0% of GDP in 2003, and engaged 31.8% of the employed labour force in 1992. The port of Cotonou is of considerable importance as an entrepôt for regional trade: re-exports comprised an estimated 38.5% of the value of total exports in 1997. According to the World Bank, the GDP of the services sector increased at an average annual rate of 4.4% in 1990–2003; growth in 2003 was 6.1%.

In 2003, according to the IMF, Benin recorded a visible trade deficit of an estimated US $385.3m., while there was a deficit of $295.9m. on the current account of the balance of payments. In 2001 the principal source of imports (23.0%) was France; other major sources were the People's Republic of China, Côte d'Ivoire, Ghana and Nigeria. The principal market for exports in that year was India (30.6%); other important purchasers were Ghana, Brazil, Indonesia and Nigeria. The principal exports in 2001 were raw cotton, cashew nuts and gold. The main imports in that year were refined petroleum products, textile yarn and fabrics, non-metallic mineral manufactures (principally cement), meat and meat preparations, road vehicles and parts, medicinal and pharmaceutical products, and cereals and cereal preparations.

In 2003, according to the IMF, Benin recorded an overall budget deficit of 95,500m. francs CFA, excluding grants received and net lending (equivalent to 4.7% of GDP). The country's total external debt at the end of 2002 was US $1,843m., of which $1,690m. was long-term public debt. In that year the cost of debt-servicing was equivalent to 9.7% of the value of exports of goods and services. The annual rate of inflation, which had been negligible prior to the 50% devaluation of the CFA franc in January 1994, increased to 38.5% in 1994, but slowed to an average of 3.5% per year in 1995–2002. The overall average annual rate of inflation between 1990 and 2003 was 5.7%. Consumer prices increased by 1.5% in 2003. About one-quarter of the urban labour force was estimated to be unemployed in 1997.

Benin is a member of the Economic Community of West African States (ECOWAS, see p. 205), of the West African organs of the Franc Zone (see p. 267), of the African Petroleum Producers' Association (APPA, see p. 369), of the Conseil de l'Entente (see p. 373) and of the Niger Basin Authority (see p. 375).

Benin has experienced considerable economic growth since the early 1990s. A three-year Enhanced Structural Adjustment Facility (ESAF) was agreed with the IMF in August 1996. The renewal of co-operation with the IMF ensured debt-relief measures, notably along concessionary terms by the 'Paris Club' of official creditors. The IMF suspended disbursements for several months in 1998, following delays in the privatization of several major state enterprises. In July 2000, as part of their initiative for heavily indebted poor countries (HIPCs), the IMF and the World Bank cancelled some US $460m. of Benin's debt and announced a further three-year enhanced HIPC programme for 2000–03. Also in that month the IMF approved funding of some $35.7m., under its Poverty Reduction and Growth Facility (PRGF, the successor to ESAF), in support of the Government's economic programme for 2000–03. (In July 2002 the IMF announced that the PRGF arrangement was to be extended until 2004, and additional debt relief, amounting to $5m., was also granted under the HIPC initiative.) However, proposed restructuring and divestiture programmes continued to be implemented only sporadically. Although the primary marketing of the important crop of seed cotton was transferred, in January 2001, from the parastatal Société Nationale pour la Promotion Agricole (SONAPRA) to the private sector, the privatization of SONAPRA itself, which began in mid-2003, proceeded slowly and sporadically in 2004, amid protests by workers and unions that the company was being sold for less than its true value. None the less, by the early 2000s the country's cotton sector was one of the most liberalized in western or central Africa. In the early 2000s programmes to open the water and electricity sectors to private-sector involvement were being developed; moreover, it was also intended that the telecommunications and postal operations of the Office des Postes et des Télécommunications be separated, with the former to be transferred to private management. The Government also implemented a series of measures to improve the regulation of state expenditure, including a number of civil service reforms, the first stages of which took effect from early 2003. GDP growth of 5.6% was recorded in 2003, and the Government forecast growth of 7.0% for 2004. However, an economic downturn in 2004, characterized by a sharp rise in maize prices and a fall in tax revenues, and variously attributed to low global cotton prices and internal corruption, resulted in growth of only 3% in that year, according to official figures released in December.

Education

The Constitution of Benin obliges the state to make a quality compulsory primary education available to all children. All public primary and secondary schools in Benin finance themselves through school fees. Primary education begins at six years of age and lasts for six years. Secondary education, beginning at 12 years of age, lasts for up to seven years, comprising a first cycle of four years and a second of three years. Primary enrolment in 1999/2000 included 70.3% of children in the appropriate age-group (males 83.2%; females 57.3%), according to

UNESCO estimates. Enrolment at secondary schools in that year included 17.4% of children in the appropriate age group (males 23.8%; females 11.0%). In the 1990s the Government sought to extend the provision of education. In 1993 girls in rural areas were exempted from school fees, and in 1999 the Government created a 500m. francs CFA fund to increase female enrolment. The Université Nationale du Bénin, at Cotonou, was founded in 1970 and had a student population of approximately 9,000 in 1999/2000. A second university, in Parakou, with a student capacity of approximately 3,000, opened in 2001. In 2001 public expenditure on education totalled 71,100m. francs CFA.

Public Holidays

2005: 1 January (New Year's Day), 10 January (Vodoun national holiday), 16 January (Martyrs' Day, anniversary of mercenary attack on Cotonou), 21 January* (Id al-Adha, Feast of the Sacrifice), 25 March (Good Friday), 28 March (Easter Monday), 1 April (Youth Day), 1 May (Workers' Day), 5 May (Ascension Day), 16 May (Whit Monday), 1 August (Independence Day), 15 August (Assumption), 26 October (Armed Forces Day), 1 November (All Saints' Day), 4 November* (Id al-Fitr, end of Ramadan), 30 November (National Day), 25 December (Christmas Day), 31 December (Harvest Day).

2006: 1 January (New Year's Day), 10 January (Vodoun national holiday), 11 January* (Id al-Adha, Feast of the Sacrifice), 16 January (Martyrs' Day, anniversary of mercenary attack on Cotonou), 1 April (Youth Day), 14 April (Good Friday), 17 April (Easter Monday), 1 May (Workers' Day), 25 May (Ascension Day), 5 June (Whit Monday), 1 August (Independence Day), 15 August (Assumption), 24 October* (Id al-Fitr, end of Ramadan), 26 October (Armed Forces Day), 1 November (All Saints' Day), 30 November (National Day), 25 December (Christmas Day), 31 December (Harvest Day).

*These holidays are dependent on the Islamic lunar calendar and may vary by one or two days from the dates given.

Weights and Measures

The metric system is in force.

Statistical Survey

Source (unless otherwise stated): Institut National de la Statistique et de l'Analyse Economique, BP 323, Cotonou; tel. and fax 30-82-46; e-mail insae@planben.intnet.bj.

Area and Population

AREA, POPULATION AND DENSITY

Area (sq km)	112,622*
Population (census results)	
15–29 February 1992	
Males	2,390,336
Females	2,525,219
Total	4,915,555
11 February 2002	6,752,569†
Population (UN estimates at mid-year)‡	
2001	6,387,000
2002	6,558,000
2003	6,736,000
Density (per sq km) at 11 February 2002	60.0†

* 43,484 sq miles.
† Provisional.
‡ Source: UN, *World Population Prospects: The 2002 Revision.*

ETHNIC GROUPS

1995 (percentages): Fon 25.2; Yoruba 13.2; Bariba 11.6; Gun 11.6; Somba 6.9; Aizo 4.2; Mina 2.8; Dendi 1.9; Others 22.6 (Source: La Francophonie).

PROVINCES
(1992 census)

Province	Area (sq km)*	Population	Capital	Population of capital
Atacora	31,200	649,308	Natitingou	57,173
Atlantique . . .	3,222	1,066,373	Cotonou	536,827
Borgou	51,000	827,925	Parakou	127,347
Mono	3,800	676,377	Lokossa	54,260
Ouémé	4,700	876,574	Porto-Novo	179,138
Zou	18,700	818,998	Abomey	66,595
Total	**112,622**	**4,915,555**		

* Figures are rounded.
Note: In July 1998 the six provinces listed above were replaced by 12 administrative departments: Alibori (area 25,683 sq km), Atacora (20,459 sq km), Atlantique (3,233 sq km), Borgou (25,310 sq km), Collines (13,561 sq km), Couffo (2,404 sq km), Donga (10,691 sq km), Littoral (79 sq km), Mono (1,396 sq km), Ouémé (2,835 sq km), Plateau (1,865 sq km) and Zou (5,106 sq km).

PRINCIPAL TOWNS
(Localities, 1992 census)

Cotonou	536,827	Natitingou	57,153
Porto-Novo (capital)	179,138	Djougou	49,769
Parakou	103,577	Save	45,403
Abomey	66,595	Bohicon	43,453

Source: Thomas Brinkoff, *City Population* (internet www.citypopulation.de).

Mid-2003 (UN estimate, incl. suburbs): Cotonou 827,754 (Source: UN, *World Urbanization Prospects: The 2003 Revision*).

BIRTHS AND DEATHS
(UN estimates, annual averages)

	1985–90	1990–95	1995–2000
Birth rate (per 1,000)	49.1	45.7	43.4
Death rate (per 1,000)	16.5	15.2	14.4

Source: UN, *World Population Prospects: The 2002 Revision*.

Expectation of life (WHO estimates, years at birth): 51.2 (males 50.1; females 52.4) in 2002 (Source: WHO, *World Health Report*).

ECONOMICALLY ACTIVE POPULATION
(persons aged 10 years and over, 1992 census)

	Males	Females	Total
Agriculture, hunting, forestry and fishing	780,469	367,277	1,147,746
Mining and quarrying	609	52	661
Manufacturing	93,157	67,249	160,406
Electricity, gas and water	1,152	24	1,176
Construction	50,959	696	51,655
Trade, restaurants and hotels	36,672	395,829	432,501
Transport, storage and communications	52,228	609	52,837
Finance, insurance, real estate and business services	2,705	401	3,106
Community, social and personal services	126,122	38,422	164,544
Activities not adequately defined	25,579	12,917	38,496
Total employed	1,169,652	883,476	2,053,128
Unemployed	26,475	5,843	32,318
Total labour force	1,196,127	889,319	2,085,446

Source: ILO, *Yearbook of Labour Statistics*.

Mid-2003 (estimates in '000): Agriculture, etc. 1,568; Total labour force 3,072 (Source: FAO).

Health and Welfare

KEY INDICATORS

Total fertility rate (children per woman, 2002)	5.7
Under-5 mortality rate (per 1,000 live births, 2003)	154
HIV/AIDS (% of persons aged 15–49, 2003)	1.9
Physicians (per 1,000 head, 1995)	0.06
Hospital beds (per 1,000 head, 1994)	0.23
Health expenditure (2001): US $ per head (PPP)	39
Health expenditure (2001): % of GDP	4.4
Health expenditure (2001): public (% of total)	46.9
Access to water (% of persons, 2002)	68
Access to sanitation (% of persons, 2002)	32
Human Development Index (2002): ranking	161
Human Development Index (2002): value	0.421

For sources and definitions, see explanatory note on p. vi.

Agriculture

PRINCIPAL CROPS
('000 metric tons)

	2001	2002	2003
Rice (paddy)	54.9	66.2	64.5
Maize	685.9	622.1	937.7
Millet	35.0	40.6	41.2
Sorghum	165.3	195.5	186.8
Sweet potatoes	57.0	74.5	70.5
Cassava (Manioc)	2,703.5	2,452.1	3,675.1
Yams	1,701.0	1,875.0	2,408.6
Sugar cane	73.4	65.4*	75.4
Dry beans	78.4	100.5	101.5
Pulses	15.7	18.3	22.6*
Cashew nuts†	40	40	40
Groundnuts (in shell)	125.4	146.2	125.0
Coconuts†	20	20	20
Oil palm fruit†	220	220	244
Karité nuts (Sheanuts)†	15	15	15
Cottonseed	216.1†	267.0†	230.0*
Tomatoes	117.6	141.3	167.3*
Chillies and green peppers	29.3	32.7	45.3*
Okra	58.1	68.6	85.3*
Other vegetables†	112.1	109.2	113.0
Pineapples	57.1	86.7	105.9*
Other fruit†	143	143	143
Cotton (lint)*	141.0	174.0	148.0
Pimento and allspice†	14	14	14

* Unofficial figure(s).
† FAO estimate(s).

Source: FAO.

LIVESTOCK
('000 head, year ending September)

	2001	2002	2003
Cattle	1,584	1,635	1,689
Sheep*	655	670	670
Goats*	1,250	1,270	1,300
Pigs	277	286	297
Poultry*	10,000	10,000	10,000

* FAO estimates.

Source: FAO.

LIVESTOCK PRODUCTS
(FAO estimates, '000 metric tons)

	2001	2002	2003
Beef and veal	19.2	19.8	20.4
Mutton and lamb	2.4	2.5	2.5
Goat meat	4.3	4.3	4.3
Pig meat	3.5	3.6	3.8
Poultry meat	11.6	11.6	11.6
Game meat	6.0	6.0	6.0
Cows' milk	24.7	25.5	26.3
Goats' milk	6.5	6.7	6.8
Poultry eggs	7.2	7.2	7.2
Cattle hides	3.1	3.2	3.3

Source: FAO.

Forestry

ROUNDWOOD REMOVALS

(FAO estimates, '000 cubic metres, excl. bark)

	2001	2002	2003
Sawlogs, veneer logs and logs for sleepers	35	35	35
Other industrial wood	297	297	297
Fuel wood	5,937	5,966	5,996
Total	6,269	6,298	6,328

Source: FAO.

SAWNWOOD PRODUCTION

('000 cubic metres, incl. railway sleepers)

	2001	2002	2003*
Total (all broadleaved)	32	46	46

* FAO estimate.
Source: FAO.

Fishing

('000 metric tons, live weight)

	2000	2001	2002
Capture			
Tilapias*	9.6	10.9	10.9
Black catfishes*	1.3	1.5	1.5
Torpedo-shaped catfishes* . .	1.3	1.5	1.5
Mullets	1.8*	2.1	2.1
Sardinellas	0.8*	1.4	1.5
Bonga shad	1.5*	1.7	1.7
Freshwater crustaceans* . .	4.2	4.7	4.7
Penaeus shrimps*	2.1	2.4	2.4
Aquaculture	—	—	0.0
Total catch (incl. others)* . . .	32.3	38.4	40.7

* FAO estimate(s).
Note: Figures exclude catches by Beninois canoes operating from outside the country.
Source: FAO.

Mining

	2000	2001	2002*
Gold (kg)	—	16	20
Crude petroleum ('000 barrels) .	365	365	—

* Estimates.
Source: US Geological Survey.

Industry

SELECTED PRODUCTS

('000 metric tons, unless otherwise indicated)

	2000	2001	2002
Cement*	250	250	250†
Beer of barley†	35.0	35.0	35.0
Beer of sorghum†	32.8	35.0	41.8
Salted, dried or smoked fish . .	2.0	2.0	n.a.
Palm oil†	15	15	15
Palm kernel oil	9.7‡	9.7‡	9.7†
Electric energy (million kWh) . .	56	56	n.a.

* Data from the US Geological Survey.
† Estimate(s).
‡ Unofficial figure.
Sources: mainly UN, *Industrial Commodity Statistics Yearbook*; FAO.

Finance

CURRENCY AND EXCHANGE RATES

Monetary Units
100 centimes = 1 franc de la Communauté financière africaine (CFA).

Sterling, Dollar and Euro Equivalents (31 December 2004)
£1 sterling = 930.1 francs CFA;
US $1 = 481.6 francs CFA;
€1 = 655.96 francs CFA;
10,000 francs CFA = £10.75 = $20.77 = €15.24.

Average Exchange Rate (francs CFA per US $)
2002   696.99
2003   581.20
2004   528.29

Note: An exchange rate of 1 French franc = 50 francs CFA, established in 1948, remained in force until January 1994, when the CFA franc was devalued by 50%, with the exchange rate adjusted to 1 French franc = 100 francs CFA. This relationship to French currency remained in effect with the introduction of the euro on 1 January 1999. From that date, accordingly, a fixed exchange rate of €1 = 655.957 francs CFA has been in operation.

BUDGET

('000 million francs CFA)

Revenue*	2001	2002	2003
Tax revenue	247.1	282.5	307.2
Taxes on international trade and transactions†	133.2	145.9	159.2
Non-tax revenue	33.9	35.7	35.7
Total	281.0	318.2	342.9

Expenditure‡	2001	2002	2003
Salaries	80.7	90.1	103.0
Pensions and scholarships . . .	20.5	21.5	25.7
Other expenditure and current transfers	101.1	132.2	152.6
Investment	135.3	120.7	144.8
Budgetary contribution . . .	55.4	54.5	71.4
Financed from abroad . . .	79.8	66.2	73.4
Interest due	15.2	15.5	12.3
External debt	13.5	14.3	11.3
Total	352.8	380.0	438.4

* Excluding grants received ('000 million francs CFA): 46.0 in 2001; 20.1 in 2002; 40.5 in 2003.
† Including value-added taxes on imports.
‡ Excluding net lending ('000 million francs CFA): 0.4 in 2001; 3.2 in 2002; −2.0 in 2003.
Source: IMF, *Benin: Statistical Appendix* (November 2004), *Benin: 2004 Article IV Consultation—Staff Report; Staff Statement; Public Information Notice on the Executive Board Discussion; and Statement by the Executive Director for Benin* (November 2004).

INTERNATIONAL RESERVES

(excluding gold, US $ million at 31 December)

	2001	2002	2003
IMF special drawing rights . .	0.4	0.1	0.2
Reserve position in IMF . . .	2.7	3.0	3.3
Foreign exchange	574.9	612.6	506.3
Total	578.0	615.7	509.8

Source: IMF, *International Financial Statistics*.

MONEY SUPPLY

('000 million francs CFA at 31 December)

	2001	2002	2003
Currency outside banks . . .	222.3	167.9	80.0
Demand deposits at deposit money banks	167.2	191.3	208.8
Checking deposits at post office .	9.6	7.3	7.4
Total money (incl. others) . .	401.8	367.3	297.3

Source: IMF, *International Financial Statistics*.

COST OF LIVING
(Consumer Price Index; base: 1996 = 100)

	2000	2001	2002
Food, beverages and tobacco . .	111.7	114.3	120.6
Clothing	109.0	108.7	110.6
Housing, water, electricity and gas	120.8	125.4	129.6
All items (incl. others)	114.7	119.2	122.1

Source: Banque centrale des états de l'Afrique de l'ouest.

All items (Consumer Price Index; base 2000=100): 104.0 in 2001; 106.6 in 2002; 108.2 in 2003 (Source: IMF, *International Financial Statistics*).

NATIONAL ACCOUNTS
('000 million francs CFA at current prices)
Expenditure on the Gross Domestic Product

	2000	2001	2002
Final consumption expenditure .	1,442.6	1,546.2	1,736.3
Households, incl. non-profit institutions serving households	1,305.7	1,400.3	1,569.6
General government . . .	136.9	145.9	166.7
Gross capital formation . .	313.5	345.2	393.3
Gross fixed capital formation .	302.8	333.7	380.3
Changes in inventories . .			
Acquisitions, less disposals, of valuables	10.7	11.5	13.0
Total domestic expenditure .	1,756.1	1,891.4	2,129.6
Exports of goods and services .	345.4	367.3	373.7
Less Imports of goods and services	496.1	520.4	544.1
GDP in market prices . . .	1,605.4	1,738.4	1,959.0
GDP at constant 1985 prices .	782.7	822.0	871.3

Source: IMF, *International Financial Statistics*.

Gross Domestic Product by Economic Activity

	2000	2001	2002
Agriculture, livestock, forestry, hunting and fishing	586.5	617.7	662.9
Mining and petroleum . . .	3.7	4.0	4.2
Manufacturing and handicrafts .	140.8	159.7	167.5
Water, gas and electricity . . .	14.3	16.6	20.1
Construction and public works .	64.2	70.7	75.4
Trade	292.7	318.0	376.6
Transport and communications .	122.1	139.8	167.8
Public administration	100.2	106.8	128.8
Other services	154.2	167.5	195.1
GDP at factor cost	1,478.6	1,600.7	1,798.3
Indirect taxes, *less* subsidies . .	126.8	137.8	160.8
GDP in purchasers' values . .	1,605.4	1,738.4	1,959.0
GDP at constant 1985 prices .	782.6	821.9	871.3

Source: mainly Banque centrale des états de l'Afrique de l'ouest.

BALANCE OF PAYMENTS
(US $ million)

	2001	2002	2003
Exports of goods f.o.b.	210.2	196.3	268.9
Imports of goods f.o.b.	−466.6	−509.5	−654.2
Trade balance	−256.4	−313.2	−385.3
Exports of services	146.7	175.7	220.4
Imports of services	−193.5	−217.0	−277.3
Balance on goods and services	−303.2	−354.5	−442.2
Income (net)	−21.4	−26.0	−25.9
Balance on goods, services and income	−324.6	−380.5	−468.1
Private unrequited transfers . .	81.1	79.6	97.2
Public unrequited transfers . .	83.8	58.9	75.0
Current balance	−159.7	−242.1	−295.9
Capital account (net) . . .	43.6	34.3	191.1
Medium- and long-term public capital	84.2	57.4	51.4

— *continued*	2001	2002	2003
Principal not yet due	—	—	−116.5*
Medium- and long-term private capital	35.7	12.7	32.4
Deposit money banks	−19.7	−4.3	64.5
Short-term capital	60.0	28.2	11.0
Net errors and omissions . . .	85.1	11.9	−8.3
Overall balance	129.0	−102.0	−70.4

* Stock of debt operation at completion point.

Source: IMF, *Benin: 2004 Article IV Consultation—Staff Report; Staff Statement; Public Information Notice on the Executive Board Discussion; and Statement by the Executive Director for Benin* (November 2004).

External Trade

PRINCIPAL COMMODITIES
(US $ million)

Imports c.i.f.	1999	2000	2001
Food and live animals . . .	133.7	106.9	111.8
Meat and preparations . . .	35.0	35.7	34.7
Meat and edible meat offal, fresh, chilled or frozen	34.8	35.5	34.4
Poultry, dead and edible offal, fresh, chilled or frozen . .	34.7	35.5	30.7
Cereals and cereal preparations .	37.6	24.6	30.2
Rice	22.0	11.9	15.7
Rice, semi-milled or milled (unbroken)	22.0	11.9	14.4
Crude materials (inedible) except fuels	50.5	34.1	35.8
Bulk textile waste, old clothing traded in bulk or in bales . . .	44.2	28.6	30.0
Mineral fuels, lubricants, etc. .	73.5	104.9	104.2
Petroleum, petroleum products, etc.	52.9	80.6	77.0
Petroleum products, refined . .	52.1	79.9	76.0
Electric current	20.0	23.1	25.6
Chemicals and related products	85.3	55.1	64.7
Medicinal and pharmaceutical products	23.0	20.4	31.4
Medicaments (incl. veterinary medicaments)	21.1	18.7	28.3
Fertilizers, manufactured . . .	26.9	10.3	12.1
Basic manufactures	161.3	122.5	147.1
Textile yarn, fabrics, etc. . .	80.0	56.1	63.2
Cotton fabrics, woven (not incl. narrow or special fabrics) . .	46.5	36.2	42.0
Cotton fabrics, woven, bleached, dyed or otherwise finished .	46.2	36.1	41.9
Woven fabrics with 85% or more of cotton, bleached, etc., finished	39.3	35.0	41.7
Fabrics, woven, of man-made fibres (not narrow or special fabrics)	30.8	17.0	17.9
Non-metallic mineral manufactures	26.9	30.0	36.9
Lime, cement and fabricated construction materials . . .	19.6	23.3	30.8
Cement	18.7	22.5	30.0
Machinery and transport equipment	129.5	82.4	97.7
Machinery specialized for particular industries	15.1	8.0	20.6
Electric machinery, apparatus and appliances, and parts	26.5	13.0	11.5
Road vehicles and parts* . . .	36.9	29.2	31.6
Passenger motor vehicles (excl. buses)	23.3	16.4	17.3
Miscellaneous manufactured articles	32.4	28.6	29.8
Total (incl. others)	691.0	547.1	601.9

* Excluding tyres, engines and electrical parts.

Exports f.o.b.	1999	2000	2001
Food and live animals . . .	17.7	22.4	28.1
Meat and edible meat offal, fresh,			
chilled or frozen	—	0.5	9.0
Vegetables and fruit	15.4	18.0	12.5
Fruit and nuts, fresh or dried .	15.4	17.6	12.0
Cashew nuts, fresh or dried .	15.1	17.4	11.1
Crude materials (inedible)			
except fuels	186.1	142.8	129.0
Oil seeds and oleaginous fruit . .	13.7	11.4	7.0
Cotton seeds	11.7	10.2	5.0
Raw cotton, excl. linters, not carded			
or combed	168.9	127.8	118.2
Basic manufactures	6.7	8.6	6.7
Gold, non-monetary, unwrought			
or semi-manufactured . . .	3.9	5.8	10.2
Total (incl. others)	225.6	188.4	181.8

Source: UN, *International Trade Statistics Yearbook.*

PRINCIPAL TRADING PARTNERS
(US $ million)

Imports c.i.f.	1999	2000	2001
Belgium	13.6	10.5	17.4
China, People's Repub.	42.8	29.6	48.0
Côte d'Ivoire	37.2	50.9	32.7
France (incl. Monaco) . . .	182.0	146.9	138.7
Germany	27.4	15.9	17.2
Ghana	22.3	26.7	29.4
Hong Kong	7.0	2.8	2.3
India	15.3	8.9	8.5
Indonesia	7.6	4.7	5.7
Italy	29.5	20.1	22.1
Japan	26.1	16.9	18.5
Korea, Repub.	5.3	3.0	6.3
Mauritania	4.6	7.6	2.7
Netherlands	40.3	32.2	23.2
Nigeria	4.1	10.2	29.3
Pakistan	5.6	5.5	2.0
Saudi Arabia	2.0	9.5	6.5
Senegal	17.1	12.5	11.7
Spain	25.0	16.1	13.5
Thailand	22.4	15.0	19.1
United Kingdom	32.3	18.2	20.9
USA	40.3	18.1	26.0
Total (incl. others)	691.0	547.1	601.9

Exports f.o.b.	1999	2000	2001
Bangladesh	9.7	7.2	2.0
Belgium	2.7	4.4	4.0
Brazil	41.0	16.8	10.4
China, People's Repub.	3.0	0.4	0.4
France (incl. Monaco) . . .	3.6	3.2	4.7
Germany	1.9	4.0	3.2
Ghana	2.2	4.9	10.7
India	32.4	59.8	55.7
Indonesia	20.7	9.4	10.2
Italy	9.3	12.0	8.3
Morocco	4.2	7.1	4.4
Niger	5.9	7.4	4.5
Nigeria	12.9	2.8	9.7
Pakistan	8.8	1.5	1.3
Portugal	5.5	2.3	1.8
Saudi Arabia	2.2	2.0	2.3
Spain	7.5	5.6	4.8
Switzerland-Liechtenstein . . .	4.9	2.6	1.5
Thailand	11.0	7.2	7.9
Turkey	5.8	8.9	3.7
United Kingdom	1.7	0.9	2.5
USA	8.8	1.0	0.1
Viet Nam	0.8	0.8	3.3
Total (incl. others)	225.6	188.4	181.8

Source: UN, *International Trade Statistics Yearbook.*

Transport

RAILWAYS
(traffic)

	1998	1999	2000
Passengers carried ('000) . . .	699.8	n.a.	n.a.
Passenger-km (million)	112.0	82.2	156.6
Freight ton-km (million) . . .	218.7	269.0	153.2

Source: mainly IMF, *Benin: Statistical Appendix* (August 2002).

ROAD TRAFFIC
(motor vehicles in use)

	1994	1995	1996
Passenger cars	26,507	30,346	37,772
Buses and coaches	353	405	504
Lorries and vans	5,301	6,069	7,554
Road tractors	2,192	2,404	2,620
Motorcycles and mopeds . . .	220,800	235,400	250,000

Source: IRF, *World Road Statistics.*

PASSENGER CARS ('000 in use): 7.3 in 1997; 7.3 in 1998 (Source: UN, *Statistical Yearbook*).

COMMERCIAL VEHICLES ('000 in use): 6.0 in 1997; 6.2 in 1998 (Source: UN, *Statistical Yearbook*).

SHIPPING

Merchant Fleet
(registered at 31 December)

	2001	2002	2003
Number of vessels	6	6	6
Total displacement ('000 grt) . .	1.0	1.0	1.0

Source: Lloyd's Register-Fairplay, *World Fleet Statistics.*

International Sea-borne Freight Traffic
(at Cotonou, including goods in transit, '000 metric tons)

	2001	2002	2003
Goods loaded	380.5	462.2	469.4
Goods in transit	6.5	5.6	8.6
Goods unloaded	2,929.3	3,007.7	3,808.9
Goods in transit	984.9	514.7	838.1

Source: IMF, *Benin: Statistical Appendix* (November 2004).

CIVIL AVIATION
(traffic on scheduled services, domestic and international)*

	1999	2000	2001
Kilometres flown (million) . . .	3	3	1
Passengers carried ('000) . . .	84	77	46
Passenger-km (million)	235	216	130
Total ton-km (million)	36	32	19

* Including an apportionment of the traffic of Air Afrique.

Source: UN, *Statistical Yearbook.*

Tourism

FOREIGN VISITORS BY COUNTRY OF ORIGIN*

	2000	2001†	2002†
Austria	8,262	8,000	5,000
Belgium	5,250	5,000	3,000
Burkina Faso	2,857	2,750	2,800
Cameroon	2,255	3,300	2,200
Côte d'Ivoire	7,814	7,700	7,600
France	19,388	18,800	10,000
Niger	4,320	4,300	4,310
Nigeria	15,277	15,200	15,250
Togo	4,696	4,600	4,650
USA	3,363	500	1,000
Total (incl. others)	96,146	87,555	72,288

* Arrivals of non-resident tourists at national borders.
† Component data are rounded to the nearest 100 persons.

Tourism receipts (US $ million): 77 in 2000; 73 in 2001; 60 in 2002.

Source: World Tourism Organization.

Communications Media

	2001	2002	2003
Telephones ('000 main lines in use)	59.3	62.7	66.5
Mobile cellular telephones ('000 subscribers)	125.0	218.8	236.2
Personal computers ('000 in use) .	11	15	26
Internet users ('000)	25	50	70

Facsimile machines (number in use, 1996): 1,064 (Source: International Telecommunication Union).

Television receivers ('000 in use, 2000): 272 (Source: UNESCO, *Statistical Yearbook*).

Radio receivers ('000 in use, 1999): 2,661 (Source: UNESCO, *Statistical Yearbook*).

Daily newspapers (1996): 1 (average circulation 12,000 copies) (Source: UNESCO, *Statistical Yearbook*).

Non-daily newspapers (1996): 4 (average circulation 66,000 copies) (Source: UNESCO, *Statistical Yearbook*).

Periodicals (1999): 106 (average circulation 110,000 copies) (Source: UNESCO, *Statistical Yearbook*).

Book production (first editions, 1994): 84 titles (42,000 copies) (Source: UNESCO, *Statistical Yearbook*).

Education

(1996/97)

	Institu-tions	Tea-chers	Students		
			Males	Females	Total
Pre-primary . .	283*	622	9,106	8,335	17,441
Primary† . .	4,178	17,710	557,802	374,622	932,424
Secondary . .	145‡	5,352	102,011	44,124	146,135
Tertiary† . .	n.a.	n.a.	15,034	3,719	18,753

* 1995/96.
† 1999/2000.
‡ 1993/94.

Source: UNESCO, *Statistical Yearbook* and Institute for Statistics.

1998/99: *Secondary:* 174,450 students; *Tertiary:* 16,284 students.

Adult literacy rate (UNESCO estimates): 39.8% (males 54.8%; females 25.5%) in 2002 (Source: UN Development Programme, *Human Development Report*).

Directory

The Constitution

A new Constitution was approved in a national referendum on 2 December 1990. Its main provisions are summarized below:

PREAMBLE

The Beninois People reaffirm their opposition to any political regime founded on arbitrariness, dictatorship, injustice and corruption, reassert their attachment to the principles of democracy and human rights, as defined in the United Nations Charter, the Universal Declaration of Human Rights and the African Charter of the Rights of Man and Peoples, proclaim their attachment to the cause of African Unity and solemnly adopt this new Constitution as the supreme Law of the State.

I. THE STATE AND SOVREIGNTY

Articles 1–6: The State of Benin is an independent, sovereign, secular, democratic Republic. The capital is Porto-Novo. The official language is French. The principle of the Republic is 'government of the People, by the People and for the People'. National sovereignty belongs to the People and is exercised through elected representatives and by referendums. Political parties operate freely, as determined by the Charter of Political Parties, and must respect the principles of national sovereignty, democracy, territorial integrity and the secular basis of the State. Suffrage is universal, equal and secret.

II. RIGHTS AND DUTIES OF THE INDIVIDUAL

Articles 7–40: The State is obliged to respect and protect the sacred and inviolable rights of the individual, and ensures equal access to health, education, culture, information, vocational training and employment. Primary education is compulsory. The State progressively assures the provision of free public education. Private schools are permitted. Torture and the use of cruel or degrading punishment are prohibited, and detention is subject to strict limitations. All persons have the right to property ownership, to freedom of conscience and expression. The State guarantees the freedoms of movement and association. All are equal before the law. The State recognizes the right to strike. Military service is compulsory.

III. THE EXECUTIVE

Articles 41–78: The President of the Republic is the Head of State. Candidates for the presidency must be of Beninois nationality by birth or have been naturalized for at least 10 years, and must be aged 40–70 years. The President is elected for a mandate of five years, renewable only once, by an absolute majority of votes cast. If no candidate receives an absolute majority, a second round is to be held between the two highest placed candidates. The Constitutional Court oversees the regularity of voting and announces the results. No President may serve more than two mandates.

The President of the Republic holds executive power. Following consultation with the Bureau of the Assemblée nationale, he names the members of the Government, who may not hold any parliamentary mandate. The President of the Republic chairs the Council of Ministers and has various defined powers of appointment.

The President of the Republic promulgates laws adopted by the Assemblée nationale, and may demand the resubmission of a law to the Assemblée nationale prior to its promulgation. In the event that the President of the Republic fails to promulgate a law, the Constitutional Court may, in certain circumstances, declare the law as binding.

After consultation with the President of the Assemblée nationale and the President of the Constitutional Court, the President of the Republic may call a referendum on matters pertaining to human rights, sub-regional or regional integration or the organization of public powers. The President of the Republic is the Supreme Chief of the Armed Forces.

The President of the Republic may delegate certain specified powers to ministers. The President of the Republic or any member of his Government may be called to account by the Assemblée nationale.

IV. THE LEGISLATURE

i. The Assemblée Nationale

Articles 79–93: Parliament exercises legislative power and controls the activities of the Government. Deputies of the Assemblée nationale, who must be civilians, are elected by direct universal suffrage for four years, and may be re-elected. The Assemblée nationale elects its President and a Bureau. Deputies enjoy various conditions of immunity from prosecution.

ii. Relations between the Assemblée Nationale and the Government

Articles 94–113: Members of the Government may attend sessions of the Assemblée nationale. Laws are approved by a simple majority, although organic laws require an absolute majority and approval by the Constitutional Court. The Assemblée nationale authorizes any declaration of war. States of siege and of emergency are declared in the Council of Ministers, although the Assemblée nationale must approve the extension of any such state beyond 15 days.

Deputies may, by a three-quarters' majority, decide to submit any question to referendum. If the Assemblée nationale has not approved a balanced budget by 31 December of any year, the measures foreseen by the finance law may be implemented by ordinance.

V. THE CONSTITUTIONAL COURT

Articles 114–124: The Constitutional Court is composed of seven members, of which four are named by the Bureau of the Assemblée nationale and three by the President of the Republic, each for a mandate of five years, renewable only once. The President of the Constitutional Court is elected by his peers for a period of five years and is a senior magistrate or lawyer. The decisions of the Constitutional Court are not subject to appeal.

VI. THE JUDICIARY

Articles 125–130: The judiciary is independent of the legislature and of the executive. It consists of the Supreme Court, and other courts and tribunals created in accordance with the Constitution. Judges may not be removed from office. The President of the Republic appoints magistrates and is the guarantor of the independence of the judiciary, assisted by the Higher Council of Magistrates, the composition, attributes, organization and function of which are fixed by an organic law.

i. The Supreme Court

Articles 131–134: The Supreme Court is the highest jurisdiction of the State in administrative and judicial matters, and with regard to the accounts of the State and to local elections. The decisions of the Court are not subject to appeal. The President of the Supreme Court is appointed for five years by the President of the Republic. The President of the Supreme Court may not be removed from office during his mandate, which is renewable only once.

ii. The High Court of Justice

Articles 135–138: The High Court of Justice comprises the members of the Constitutional Court (other than its President), six deputies of the Assemblée nationale and the President of the Supreme Court. The High Court of Justice elects a President from among its members and is competent to try the President of the Republic and members of the Government in cases of high treason, crimes committed during the exercise of their functions and plots against state security. In the event of an accusation of high treason or of contempt of the Assemblée nationale, and in certain other cases, the President of the Republic and members of the Government are to be suspended from their functions. In the case of being found guilty of such charges, they are dismissed from their responsibilities.

VII. THE ECONOMIC AND SOCIAL COUNCIL

Articles 139–141: The Economic and Social Council advises on proposed laws, ordinances or decrees that are submitted to it. Proposed laws of an economic or social nature must be submitted to the Council.

VIII. THE HIGH AUTHORITY FOR BROADCASTING AND COMMUNICATION

Articles 142–143: The High Authority for Broadcasting and Communication assures the freedom of the press and all other means of mass communication. It oversees the equitable access of political parties, associations and citizens to the official means of communication and information.

IX. INTERNATIONAL TREATIES AND ACCORDS

Articles 144–149: The President of the Republic negotiates and ratifies international treaties and accords. Peace treaties, those relating to international organization or territorial changes and to certain other matters must be ratified by law.

X. LOCAL AUTHORITIES

Articles 150–153: The local authorities of the Republic are created by law and are freely administered by elected councils. Their development is overseen by the State.

XI. ON REVISION

Articles 154–156: The initiative for the revision of the Constitution belongs jointly to the President of the Republic, after a decision has been taken in the Council of Ministers, and to the Assemblée nationale, given a majority vote of three-quarters of its members. A revision requires approval by referendum, unless it is supported by a majority of four-fifths of the members of the Assemblée nationale. The republican and secular basis of the State may not be the subject of any revision.

XII. TRANSITIONAL AND FINAL DISPOSITIONS

Articles 157–160: This new Constitution must be promulgated within eight days of its adoption by referendum. The President of the Republic must assume office and the Assemblée nationale convene by 1 April 1991. The Haut Conseil de la République and the transitional Government will continue to exercise their functions until the installation of the new institutions.

The Government

HEAD OF STATE

President: Gen. (retd) Mathieu Kérékou (took office 4 April 1996; re-elected 22 March 2001).

COUNCIL OF MINISTERS
(March 2005)

President: Gen. (retd) Mathieu Kérékou.

Minister of State, responsible for National Defence: Pierre Osho.

Minister of State, responsible for Planning and Development: Zul Kifl Salami.

Keeper of the Seals, Minister of Justice, Legislation and Human Rights: Dorothée Sossa.

Minister of Primary and Secondary Education: Rafiatou Karimou.

Minister of Mines, Energy and Water Resources: Kamarou Fassassi.

Minister of Higher Education and Scientific Research: Osséni K. Bagnan.

Minister of Foreign Affairs and African Integration: Rogatien Biaou.

Minister of Industry, Commerce and the Promotion of Employment: Massiyatou Latoundji Lauriano.

Minister responsible for Relations with the Institutions, Civil Society and Benin Nationals Abroad: Valentin Aditi Houdé.

Minister of Technical Education and Professional Training: Alain F. Adihou.

Minister of the Civil Service, Labour and Administrative Reform: Boubacar Arouna.

Minister of Agriculture, Stockbreeding and Fishing: Fatiou Akplogan.

Minister of Youth, Sport and Leisure: Jean-Baptiste Edayé.

Minister of Communication and the Promotion of New Technologies: Frédéric Dohou.

Minister of Finance and the Economy: Cosme Sèhlin.

Minister of the Interior, Security and Decentralization: Seïdou Mama Sika.

Minister of the Family, Social Protection and Solidarity: Léa D. Ahougbénou Hounkpé.

Minister of Public Health: Dorothée Akoko Kindé Gazard.

Minister of the Environment, Housing and Town Planning: Jules Codjo Assogba.

Minister of Public Works and Transport: CHRISTIANE JEANNE-MARIE OMICHESSAN TABÉLÉ.

Minister of Culture, Handicrafts and Tourism: ANTOINE DAYORI.

MINISTRIES

Office of the President: BP 1288, Cotonou; tel. 30-00-90; fax 30-06-36; internet www.gouv.bj.

Ministry of Agriculture, Stockbreeding and Fishing: 03 BP 2900, Cotonou; tel. 30-04-10; fax 30-03-26; e-mail sg@agriculture.gouv.bj; internet www.agriculture.gouv.bj.

Ministry of the Civil Service, Labour and Administrative Reform: BP 907, Cotonou; tel. 31-26-18; fax 31-06-29; e-mail sg@travail.gouv.bj; internet www.travail.gouv.bj.

Ministry of Communication and the Promotion of New Technologies: 01 BP 120, Cotonou; tel. 31-22-27; fax 31-59-31; e-mail sg@communication.gouv.bj; internet www.communication.gouv.bj.

Ministry of Culture, Handicrafts and Tourism: 01 BP 2037, Guincomey, Cotonou; tel. 30-70-10; fax 30-70-31; e-mail sg@tourisme.gouv.bj; internet www.tourisme.gouv.bj.

Ministry of the Environment, Housing and Town Planning: 01 BP 3621, Cotonou; tel. 31-55-96; fax 31-50-81; e-mail sg@environnement.gouv.bj; internet www.mehubenin.net.

Ministry of the Family, Social Protection and Solidarity: 01 BP 2802, Cotonou; tel. 31-67-08; fax 31-64-62; e-mail sg@famille.gouv.bj; internet www.famille.gouv.bj.

Ministry of Finance and the Economy: BP 302, Cotonou; tel. 30-02-81; fax 31-18-51; e-mail sg@finance.gouv.bj; internet www.finance.gouv.bj.

Ministry of Foreign Affairs and African Integration: Zone Résidentielle, route de l'Aéroport, 06 BP 318, Cotonou; tel. 30-04-00; fax 30-19-70; e-mail sg@etranger.gouv.bj; internet www.etranger.gouv.bj.

Ministry of Higher Education and Scientific Research: 01 BP 348, Cotonou; tel. 30-06-81; fax 30-57-95; e-mail sg@recherche.gouv.bj; internet www.recherche.gouv.bj.

Ministry of Industry, Trade and the Promotion of Employment: BP 363, Cotonou; tel. 30-76-46; fax 30-30-24; e-mail sg@commerce.gouv.bj; internet www.commerce.gouv.bj.

Ministry of the Interior, Security and Decentralization: BP 925, Cotonou; tel. 30-11-06; fax 30-01-59; e-mail sg@securite.gouv.bj; internet www.securite.gouv.bj.

Ministry of Justice, Legislation and Human Rights: BP 2493, Cotonou; tel. 30-08-90; fax 30-18-21; e-mail sg@justice.gouv.bj; internet www.justice.gouv.bj.

Ministry of Mining, Energy and Water Resources: 04 BP 1412, Cotonou; tel. 31-29-07; fax 31-35-46; e-mail sg@energie.gouv.bj; internet www.energie.gouv.bj.

Ministry of National Defence: BP 2493, Cotonou; tel. 30-08-90; fax 30–18–21; e-mail sg@defense.gouv.bj; internet www.defense.gouv.bj.

Ministry of Planning and Development: BP 342, Cotonou; tel. 30-00-30; fax 30-16-60; e-mail sg@planben.gouv.bj; internet www.planben.gouv.bj.

Ministry of Primary and Secondary Education: 01 BP 10, Porto-Novo; tel. 21-33-27; fax 21-50-11; e-mail sg@enseignement.gouv.bj; internet www.enseignement.gouv.bj.

Ministry of Public Health: Immeuble ex-MCAT, 01 BP 882, Cotonou; tel. 33-21-63; fax 33-04-62; e-mail sg@sante.gouv.bj; internet www.sante.gouv.bj.

Ministry of Public Works and Transport: BP 351, Cotonou; tel. 31-46-33; fax 31-06-17; e-mail sg@transport.gouv.bj; internet www.transport.gouv.bj.

Ministry of Relations with the Institutions, Civil Society and Benin Nationals Abroad: 01 BP 406, Cotonou; tel. 30-60-93; fax 30-78-94; e-mail sg@exterieur.gouv.bj; internet www.exterieur.gouv.bj.

Ministry of Technical Education and Professional Training: 10 BP 250, Cotonou; tel. and fax 30-56-15; e-mail sg@formation.gouv.bj; internet www.formation.gouv.bj.

Ministry of Youth, Sport and Leisure: 03 BP 2103, Cotonou; tel. 30-36-14; fax 38-21-26; e-mail sg@jeunesse.gouv.bj; internet www.jeunesse.gouv.bj.

President and Legislature

PRESIDENT

Presidential Election, First Ballot, 4 March 2001

Candidate	Votes	% of votes
Mathieu Kérékou (Ind.)	1,127,200	45.42
Nicéphore Soglo (RB)	672,927	27.12
Adrien Houngbédji (PRD)	313,186	12.62
Bruno Amoussou (PSD)*	213,136	8.59
Others	155,080	6.25
Total	**2,481,529**	**100.00**

* Parti social démocrate, which was absorbed into the Union pour le Bénin du futur in late 2002.

Second Ballot, 22 March 2001*

Candidate	Votes	% of votes
Mathieu Kérékou	1,286,465	84.06
Bruno Amoussou	244,032	15.94
Total	**1,530,497**	**100.00**

* Following the withdrawal of Nicéphore Soglo and Adrien Houngbédji, the second-round ballot took place, in accordance with the Constitution, between Bruno Amoussou and Mathieu Kérékou.

ASSEMBLÉE NATIONALE

Assemblée nationale: BP 371, Porto-Novo; tel. 21-22-19; fax 21-36-44; e-mail assemblee.benin@yahoo.fr; internet www.gouv.bj/institutions/assemblee/presentation.php.

President: ANTOINE IDJI KOLAWOLÉ.

General Election, 30 March 2003

Party	Seats
Union pour le Bénin du futur (UBF)	31
La renaissance du Bénin (RB)	15
Parti du renouveau démocratique (PRD)	11
Mouvement africain pour la démocratie et le progrès (MADEP)	9
Force clé	5
Alliance étoile	3
Alliance MDC-PS-CPP	2
La nouvelle alliance (LNA)	2
Alliance impulsion pour le progrès et la démocratie (Alliance IPD)	2
Alliance des forces du progrès (AFP)	1
Rassemblement pour la démocratie et le panafricanisme (RDP)	1
Mouvement pour le développement et la solidarité (MDS—Alodé Alomè)	1
Total	**83**

Advisory Council

Economic and Social Council (CES): ave Jean-Paul II, 08 BP 679, Cotonou; tel. 30-03-91; fax 30-03-13; e-mail dasoul@cma.inbox.as; internet www.ces.gouv.bj; f. 1994; 30 mems, representing the executive, legislature and 'all sections of the nation'; reviews all legislation relating to economic and social affairs; competent to advise on proposed economic and social legislation, as well as to recommend economic and social reforms; Pres. RAPHIOU TOUKOUROU.

Political Organizations

The registration of political parties commenced in August 1990. In mid-2002 there were more than 160 registered parties. The following parties and alliances secured representation in the legislative elections of March 2003:

Alliance étoile: f. 2002; opposes Govt of Pres. Kérékou; Leader SACCA LAFIA.

Union pour la démocratie et la solidarité nationale (UDS): BP 1761, Cotonou; tel. 31-38-69; Pres. SACCA LAFIA.

Les verts du Bénin—Parti écologiste du Bénin: 06 BP 1336, Cotonou; tel. and fax 35-19-47; Pres. TOUSSAINT HINVI; Sec. PIERRE AHOUANOZIN.

Alliance des forces du progrès (AFP): Assemblée nationale, BP 371, Porto-Novo; supports Pres. Kérékou; Leader Valentin Aditi Houdé.

Alliance impulsion pour le progrès et la démocratie (Alliance IPD): 04 BP 0812, Cotonou; tel. 33-11-45; f. 1999; supports Govt of Pres. Kérékou; Leaders Bertin Borna, Théophile Nata.

Alliance MDC-PS-CPP: Assemblée nationale, BP 371, Porto-Novo; Leader Damien Zinsou Modéran Alahassa.

  Congrès du peuple pour le progrès (CPP): quartier Houéyiho, villa 061, cité BCEAO, Cotonou; Leader Sédégnon Adande-Kinti.

  Mouvement pour le développement par la culture (MDC): Assemblée nationale, BP 371, Porto-Novo; Pres. Codjo Achodé.

  Parti du salut (PS): 06 BP 11, Cotonou; tel. 36-02-56; f. 1994; Leader Damien Modéran Zinsou Alahassa.

Force clé: Carré 315, Scoa Gbéto, 01 BP 1435, Cotonou; tel. 35-09-36; f. 2003 on basis of Mouvement pour une alternative du peuple; supports Pres. Kérékou; Leader Lazare Sehouéto.

Mouvement africain pour la démocratie et le progrès (MADEP): Assemblée nationale, BP 371, Porto-Novo; tel. 31-31-22; f. 1997; supports Pres. Kérékou; Leader El Hadj Séfou L. Fagbohoun.

Mouvement pour le développement et la solidarité (MDS—Alodé Alomè): Assemblée nationale, BP 371, Porto-Novo; Leader Sacca Moussédikou Fikara.

La nouvelle alliance (LNA): Assemblée nationale, BP 371, Porto-Novo; opposes Govt of Pres. Kérékou; Leader Soulé Dankoro.

Union pour le progrès et la démocratie (UPD—Gamèsu): Assemblée nationale, BP 371, Porto-Novo; f. 2002 by mems of fmr Parti social démocrate; Pres. Jean-Claude Hounkponou.

Parti du renouveau démocratique (PRD): BP 281, Cotonou; tel. 33-94-88; fax 33-94-89; f. 1990; Leader Adrien Houngbédji.

Rassemblement pour la démocratie et le panafricanisme (RDP): 03 BP 4073, Cotonou; tel. 32-02-83; f. 1995; Leaders Dominique O. Houngninou, Gilles Auguste Minontin.

La renaissance du Bénin (RB): BP 2205, Cotonou; tel. 31-40-89; f. 1992; Hon. Pres. Nicéphore Soglo; Chair. Rosine Vieyra Soglo.

Union pour le Bénin du futur (UBF): 04 BP 0772, Cotonou; tel. 33-12-23; e-mail amoussou@avu.org; f. 2002 by supporters of Pres. Kérékou; Co-ordinator Bruno Amoussou.

  Front d'action pour le renouveau, la démocratie et le développement—Alafia (FARD—Alafia): BP 925, Cotonou; tel. 33-34-10; f. 1994; Sec.-Gen. Daniel Tawéma.

Diplomatic Representation

EMBASSIES IN BENIN

China, People's Republic: 2 route de l'Aéroport, 01 BP 196, Cotonou; tel. 30-07-65; fax 30-08-41; e-mail prcbenin@serv.eit.bj; Ambassador Li Beifen.

Congo, Democratic Republic: Carré 221, Ayélawadjè, Cotonou; tel. 30-00-01.

Cuba: ave de la Marina, face Hôtel du Port, 01 BP 948, Cotonou; tel. 31-52-97; fax 31-65-91; Ambassador Gabriel Tiel Capote.

Denmark: Lot P7, Les Cocotiers, 04 BP 1223, Cotonou; tel. 30-38-62; fax 30-38-60; e-mail cooamb@um.dk; Ambassador Anders Serup Rasmussen.

Egypt: Lot G26, route de l'Aéroport, BP 1215, Cotonou; tel. 30-08-42; fax 30-14-25; Ambassador Amina Gomaa.

France: ave Jean-Paul II, BP 966, Cotonou; tel. 30-02-25; fax 30-07-57; e-mail ambafrance.cotonou@diplomatie.gouv.fr; internet www.ambafrance-bj.org; Ambassador Christian Daziano.

Germany: 7 ave Jean-Paul II, BP 504, Cotonou; tel. 31-29-67; fax 31-29-62; e-mail info@coto.diplo.de; Ambassador Dr Peter Wienand.

Ghana: route de l'Aéroport, Lot F, Les Cocotiers, BP 488, Cotonou; tel. 30-07-46; fax 30-03-45; e-mail ghaemb02@leland.bj; Ambassador Timothy Enyo Kwaku Amesimeku.

Holy See: blvd de France, quartier Awhouanléko/Djoméhountin, Zone des Ambassades, 08 BP 400, Cotonou; tel. 30-03-57; fax 30-03-10; internet noncia@intnet.bj; Apostolic Nuncio Pierre Nguyên Van Tot (Titular Bishop of Rusticiana).

Libya: Carré 36, Cotonou; tel. 30-04-52; fax 30-03-01; Ambassador Toufik Ashour Adam.

Netherlands: Port de Pêche, Immeuble RORO Shipping, 08 BP 0783, Cotonou; tel. 31-87-23; fax 31-87-22; e-mail cot@minbuza.nl; Chargé d'affaires Bram van Ojik.

Niger: derrière l'Hôtel de la Plage, BP 352, Cotonou; tel. 31-56-65; Ambassador Lompo Souleymane.

Nigeria: ave de France, Marina, BP 2019, Cotonou; tel. 30-11-42; fax 30–18–79; Ambassador Ezekeil O. Oladeji.

Russia: Zone résidentielle, ave de la Marina, face Hôtel du Port, BP 2013, Cotonou; tel. 31-28-34; fax 31-28-35; e-mail benamrus@leland.bj; internet www.benin.mid.ru; Ambassador Vladimir S. Timoshenko.

USA: Carré 125, rue Caporal Anani Bernard, 01 BP 2012, Cotonou; tel. 30-06-50; fax 30-06-70; internet usembassy.state.gov/benin; Ambassador Wayne E. Neill.

Judicial System

Constitutional Court: BP 2050, Cotonou; tel. 31-16-10; fax 31-37-12; e-mail cconstitut_sg@netcourrier.com; internet www.gouv.bj/institutions/cour_constitutionnelle/presentation.php; f. 1990; inaug. 1993; seven mems; four appointed by the Assemblée nationale, three by the President of the Republic; exercises highest jurisdiction in constitutional affairs; determines the constitutionality of legislation, oversees and proclaims results of national elections and referendums, responsible for protection of individual and public rights and obligations, charged with regulating functions of organs of state and authorities; Pres. Conceptia L.-Denis-Ouinsou; Sec.-Gen. Marcelline-Claire Gbeha Afouda.

High Court of Justice: Cotonou; internet www.gouv.bj/institutions/haute_cour/presentation.php; comprises the six members of the Constitutional Court (other than its President), six deputies of the Assemblée nationale and the First President of the Supreme Court; competent to try the President of the Republic and members of the Government in cases of high treason, crimes committed in, or at the time of, the exercise of their functions, and of plotting against state security; Pres. Clotilde Medegan Nougbode.

Supreme Court: Ganhi, 01 BP 330, Cotonou; tel. 31-50-47; fax 31-54-92; e-mail info@coursupreme.gouv.bj; internet www.gouv.bj/institutions/cour_supreme/presentation.php; f. 1960; highest juridical authority in administrative and judicial affairs and in matters of public accounts; competent in disputes relating to local elections; advises the executive on jurisdiction and administrative affairs; comprises a First President (appointed by the President of the Republic, after consultation with the President of the Assemblée nationale, senior magistrates and jurists), presidents of the component chambers, a public prosecutor, four assistant procurators-fiscal, counsellors and clerks; First Pres. Me Saliou Aboudou; Attorney-Gen. Nestor Dako; Pres. of the Judicial Chamber Edwige Boussari; Pres. of the Administrative Chamber Samson Dossoumon; Pres. of the Chamber of Accounts Firmin Djimenou; Chief Clerk Françoise Quenum.

Religion

At the time of the 1992 census it was estimated that some 35% of the population held animist beliefs; another 35% were Christians (mainly Roman Catholics) and the remainder were mostly Muslims. Religious and spiritual cults, which were discouraged under Kérékou's military regime, re-emerged as a prominent force in Beninois society during the 1990s.

CHRISTIANITY

The Roman Catholic Church

Benin comprises two archdioceses and eight dioceses. At 31 December 2002 there were an estimated 1.6m. Roman Catholics (about 24.0% of the population), mainly in the south of the country.

Bishops' Conference

Conférence Episcopale du Bénin, Archevêché, 01 BP 491, Cotonou; tel. 30-66-48; fax 30-07-07.

Pres. Most Rev. Nestor Assogba (Archbishop of Cotonou).

Archbishop of Cotonou: Most Rev. Nestor Assogba, Archevêché, 01 BP 491, Cotonou; fax 30-07-07; e-mail cotonou@cef.fr.

Archbishop of Parakou: Most Rev. Fidèle Agbatchi, Archevêché, BP 75, Parakou; tel. 61-02-54; fax 61-01-99; e-mail archeveche@borgou.net.

Protestant Church

There are an estimated 257 Protestant mission centres in Benin.

Eglise Protestante Méthodiste en République du Bénin: 54 ave Mgr Steinmetz, 01 BP 34, Cotonou; tel. 31-11-42; fax 31-25-20;

f. 1843; Pres. Rev. Dr Moïse Sagbohan; Sec. Rev. Mathieu D. Olodo; 95,827 mems (1996).

VODOUN

The origins of the traditional *vodoun* religion can be traced to the 14th century. Its influence is particularly strong in Latin America and the Caribbean, owing to the shipment of slaves from the West African region to the Americas in the 18th and 19th centuries.

Communauté Nationale du Culte Vodoun (CNCV): Ouidah; Pres. Adan Yossi Guédéhoungué.

ISLAM

Union Islamique du Bénin (UIB): Cotonou; Pres. Imam El Hadj Mohamed Amed Sanni.

BAHÁ'Í FAITH

National Spiritual Assembly: BP 1252, Cotonou.

The Press

In 2001 there were 18 daily newspapers and 37 periodicals published in Benin.

DAILIES

L'Araignée: siège du cyber DOPHIA, face Cité Houeyiho, 01 BP 1357, Cotonou; tel. 30-64-12; fax (44) 87-01-32-18-84; e-mail direction@laraignee.org; internet www.laraignee.org; f. 2001; online only; politics, public affairs, culture, society, sport; Dir of Publishing Félix Aniwanou Hounsa; Editor-in-Chief Willéandre Houngbédji.

L'Aurore: face Clinique Boni, 05 BP 464, Cotonou; tel. 33-70-43; Dir Patrick Adjamonsi; circ. 1,500.

Bénin-Presse Info: 01 BP 72, Cotonou; tel. 31-26-55; e-mail abpben@intnet.bj; internet www.gouv.bj/presse/abp/index.php; bulletin of Agence Bénin-Presse; Dir Yaovi Hounkponou; Editor-in-Chief Emmanuel K. Gbokou.

Les Echos du Jour: Carré 136, Sodjatimè, 08 BP 718, Cotonou; tel. 33-18-33; fax 33-17-06; e-mail echos@intnet.bj; internet www.lesechosdujour.info; independent; Dir Maurice Chabi; Editor-in-Chief Sébastien Dossa; circ. 3,000.

Fraternité: face Station Menontin, 05 BP 915, Cotonou; tel. 38-47-70; fax 38-47-71; e-mail fraternite@altern.org; internet www.webfirstplus.com/fraternite; Dir-Gen. Malick Seibou Gomina; Editor-in-Chief Brice U. Houssou.

L'Informateur: Etoile Rouge, Bâtiment Radio Star, Carré 1072c, 01 BP 5421, Cotonou; tel. and fax 32-66-39; f. 2001; Dir Clément Adéchian; Editor-in-Chief Brice Guèdè.

Le Matin: Carré 54, Tokpa Hoho, 06 BP 2217, Cotonou; tel. 31-10-80; fax 33-42-62; e-mail lematinonline@moncourrier.com; f. 1994; independent; Dir Moïse Dato; Editorial Dir Luc-Aimé Dansou.

Le Matinal: Carré 153–154, Atinkanmey, 06 BP 1989, Cotonou; tel. 31-49-20; fax 31-49-19; e-mail contact@lematinalonline.com; internet www.lematinalonline.com; f. 1997; daily print and online editions in French, weekly online summaries in English and German; Dir-Gen. Charles Toko; Editor-in-Chief Napoléon Maforikan; circ. 5,000.

La Nation: Cadjèhoun, 01 BP 1210, Cotonou; tel. 30-02-99; fax 30-34-63; e-mail onipben@yahoo.fr; internet www.gouv.bj/presse/lanation/index.php; f. 1990; official newspaper; Dir Akuété Assevi; Editor-in-Chief Léon Brathier; circ. 4,000.

La Nouvelle Tribune: Lot 1409, Houéyiho II, 09 BP 336, Cotonou; tel. 30-65-16; Editor-in-Chief Alain Assogba.

L'Oeil du Peuple: Carré 743, rue PTT, Gbégamey, 01 BP 5538, Cotonou; tel. 30-22-07; e-mail loeildupeuple@yahoo.fr; Dir Celestin Abissi; Editor-in-Chief Paul Agboyidou.

Le Point au Quotidien: 332 rue du Renouveau, 05 BP 934, Cotonou; tel. 91-69-45; fax 32-25-31; e-mail info@lepointauquotidien.com; internet www.lepointauquotidien.info; independent; Dir and Editor-in-Chief Fernando Hessou; circ. 2,000.

Le Républicain: Les Presses d'Afrique, Carré 630, Tanto, 05 BP 1230, Cotonou; tel. and fax 33-83-04; e-mail lerepublicain@lerepublicain.org; internet www.lerepublicain.org; independent; Editor-in-Chief Isidore Zinsou.

Le Soleil: Carré 850, Sikècodji, 02 BP 8187, Cotonou; tel. 32-69-96; Dir Maurille Gnansounou; Editor-in-Chief Matini Marcos.

La Tribune de la Capitale: Lot 03-46, Parcelle E, Houinmè, Maison Onifadé, Catchi, 01 BP 1463, Porto-Novo; tel. 22-55-69;

e-mail latribunedelacapitale@yahoo.fr; Dir. of Publication Seth Evariste Hodonou.

PERIODICALS

Afrique Identité: ave du Canada, Lot 1069 T, 02 BP 1215, Cotonou; Dir Angelo Ahouanmagma; Editorial Dir Serge Auguste Loko.

Agri-Culture: 03 BP 0380, Cotonou; tel. and fax 36-05-46; e-mail agriculture@uva.org; f. 1999; monthly; Editor-in-Chief Joachim Saï-zonou; circ. 1,000.

L'Autre Gazette: 02 BP 1537, Cotonou; tel. 32-59-97; e-mail collegi@beninweb.org; Editor-in-Chief Wilfried Ayibatin.

L'Avenir: Carré 911, 02 BP 8134, Cotonou; tel. 32-21-23; fortnightly; political analysis; Dir Claude Firmin Gangbe.

Bénin Hebdo: 03 BP 2332, Cotonou; tel. 92-24-09; Dir Sangaré Nouhoun; Editor-in-Chief Denis Chaumereuil.

Bénin Info: 06 BP 590, Cotonou; tel. 32-52-64; fortnightly; Dir Romain Toi.

Bénin Santé: 06 BP 1905, Cotonou; tel. 33-26-38; fax 33-18-23; fortnightly.

Le Canard du Golfe: Carré 240, Midombo, Akpakpa, 06 BP 59, Cotonou; tel. 32-72-33; e-mail lecanardugolfe@yahoo.fr; satirical; weekly; Dir. F. L. Tingbo; Editor-in-Chief Emmanuel Sotikon.

Le Continental: BP 4419, Cotonou; Editor-in-Chief Arnauld Houndete.

La Croix du Bénin: Centre Paul VI, 01 BP 105, Cotonou; tel. and fax 32-11-19; e-mail indcroix@intnet.bj; f. 1946; fortnightly; Roman Catholic; Dir Abbé André S. Quenum.

La Dernière Barque—Creuset de la Jeunesse Chrétienne Céleste: 06 BP 446, Cotonou; tel. 33-04-07; fax 33-42-14.

Emotion: 06 BP 1404, Cotonou; tel. 40-17-07; fax 32-50-83; e-mail emomagazine@yahoo.fr; f. 1998; monthly; cultural and social affairs; Dir of Publication and Editor-in-Chief Eric Sessinou Huannou; circ. 3,000.

L'Enjeu: 04 BP 0454, Cotonou; tel. 35-19-93; Editor-in-Chief Mathurin Assogba.

La Flamme: 01 BP 2582, Cotonou; tel. 30-69-03; Editor-in-Chief Philippe Noudjenoume.

La Gazette du Golfe: Immeuble La Gazette du Golfe, Carré 902e, Sikècodji, 03 BP 1624, Cotonou; tel. 32-68-44; fax 32-52-26; e-mail gazettedugolfe@serv.eit.bj; f. 1987; weekly; Dir Ismaël Y. Soumanou; Editor Marcus Boni Teiga; circ. 18,000 (nat. edn), 5,000 (international edn).

Le Gongonneur: 04 BP 1432, Cotonou; tel. 90-60-95; fax 35-04-22; e-mail dahoun@yahoo.com; Dir Mathias C. Sossou; Editor-in-Chief Pascaline Aphia Hounkanrin.

Le Héraut: 03 BP 3417, Cotonou; tel. 36-00-64; e-mail heraut@syfed.bj.refer.org; monthly; current affairs; analysis; produced by students at Université nationale du Bénin; Dir Geoffrey Gounou N'Goye; Editor-in-Chief Gabriel Dideh.

Initiatives: 01 BP 2093, Cotonou; tel. 31-22-61; fax 31-59-50; e-mail cepepe@firstnet1.com; 6 a year; journal of the Centre de Promotion et d'Encadrement des Petites et Moyennes Entreprises.

Journal Officiel de la République du Bénin: BP 59, Porto-Novo; tel. 21-39-77; f. 1890; present name adopted 1990; official govt bulletin; fortnightly; Dir Afize Désiré Adamo.

Labari: BP 816, Parakou; tel. and fax 61-69-10; f. 1997; weekly; Dir Dramane Ami-Toure; circ. 3,000.

La Lumière de l'Islam: Carré 163, 01 BP 4022, Cotonou; tel. and fax 31-34-59; monthly; Dir Mohamed Bachirou Soumanou.

Madame Afrique: Siège Mefort Inter Diffusion, c/1066, quartier Cadjehoun, 05 BP 1914, Cotonou; tel. 68-22-90; e-mail madafric@yahoo.fr; f. 2000; monthly; women's interest; Dir of Publication Bernard G. Zanklan.

Le Magazine de l'Entreprise: BP 850, Cotonou; tel. 30-80-79; fax 30-47-77; e-mail oliviergat@hotmail.com; f. 1999; monthly; business; Dir A. Victor Fakèye.

Nouvel Essor: Carré 497, Jéricho, 06 BP 1182, Cotonou; tel. 32-43-13; monthly; Editor-in-Chief Jean-Baptiste Hounkonnou.

Opérateur Économique: ave du Général de Gaulle, 01 BP 31, Cotonou; tel. 31-20-81; fax 31-22-99; monthly; published by Chambre de Commerce et d'Industrie du Bénin; Dir Wassi Mouftaou.

Le Perroquet: Carré 478, quartier Bar-Tito, 03 BP 880, Cotonou; tel. 32-18-54; e-mail perroquet@uva.org; internet www.leperroquet.fr.tc; f. 1995; two a month; independent; news and analysis; Dir Damien Houessou; Editor-in-Chief Septome Atchèkpe; circ. 4,000 (2004).

Le Piment: Carré 1965, Zogbo, 07 BP 0665, Cotonou; tel. 30-26-01; fax 31-25-81; 2 a month; independent; Editor-in-Chief JOACHIM GBOYOU.

Le Radical: 03 BP 0408, Cotonou; Dir ALASSANE BAWA.

Le Recadaire: 02 BP 308, Cotonou; tel. 22-60-11; e-mail lerecadaire@yahoo.com; Dir GUTEMBERT HOUNKANRIN.

La Région: Carré 1030, 05 BP 708, Cotonou; Editor-in-Chief ROMAIN CODJO.

La Réplique: BP 1087, Porto-Novo; tel. and fax 21-45-77; Dir EMILE ADECHINA; Editor-in-Chief JERÔME AKLAMAVO.

La Sirène: Carré 357, Sènadé, 01 BP 122, Cotonou; tel. 33-40-17; Dir ETIENNE HOUSSOU.

Le Télégramme: 06 BP 1519, Cotonou; tel. 33-04-18; fortnightly; Editor-in-Chief RENÉ NANA.

Le Temps: Kouhounou, 04 BP 43, Cotonou; tel. 30-55-06; 2 a month; Dir YAYA YOLOU; Editor-in-Chief GUY CONDÉ.

Le Tribune de l'Economie: BP 31, Cotonou; tel. 31-20-81; fax 31-32-99; monthly; Editor-in-Chief MOUFTAOU WASSI.

Press Association

Union des Journalistes de la Presse Privée du Bénin (UJPB): blvd de la République, près Cadmes Plus, 03 BP 383, Cotonou; tel. 32-52-73; e-mail ujpb@h2com.com; internet www.h2com.com/ujpb; f. 1992; asscn of independent journalists; Pres. AGAPIT N. MAFORIKAN.

NEWS AGENCIES

Agence Bénin-Presse (ABP): BP 72, Cotonou; tel. and fax 31-26-55; e-mail abpben@intnet.bj; f. 1961; national news agency; section of the Ministry of Communication and the Promotion of New Technologies; Dir YAOVI R. HOUNKPONOU.

Associated Press (USA) is also represented in Benin.

Publishers

AFRIDIC: 01 BP 269, 01 Porto-Novo; tel. 22-32-28; e-mail afridic@caramail.com; internet www.afrilivres.com/index.asp?navig=annuaire; f. 1996; poetry, essays, fiction; Dir ADJIBI JEAN-BAPTISTE.

Editions de l'ACACIA: 06 BP 1978, Cotonou; tel. 33-04-72; e-mail zoundin@yahoo.fr; f. 1989; fmrly Editions du Flamboyant; literary fiction, history, popular science; Dir OSCAR DE SOUZA.

Editions des Diasporas: 04 BP 792, Cotonou; e-mail camouro@yahoo.fr; internet www.afrilivres.com/index.asp?navig=annuaire; poetry, essays; Editor CAMILLE AMOURO.

Editions Ruisseaux d'Afrique: 04 BP 1154, Cotonou; tel. and fax 94-79-25; fax 30-31-86; e-mail ruisseau@leland.bj; internet www.afrilivres.com/index.asp?navig=annuaire; f. 1992; children's literature; Dir BÉATRICE GBADO.

Editions Souvenir: 01 BP 2589, Porto-Novo ; tel. 88-49-04; e-mail editsouvenir@voila.fr; internet www.afrilivres.com/index.asp?navig=annuaire; youth and adult literature; Dir. JEAN-BAPTISTE KUNDA LI FUMU'NSAMU.

Graphitec: 04 BP 825, Cotonou; tel. and fax 30-46-04; e-mail lewado@yahoo.com.

Imprimerie Notre Dame: BP 109, Cotonou; tel. 32-12-07; fax 32-11-19; e-mail lacroixbenin@excite.fr; f. 1974; Roman Catholic publications; Dir BARTHÉLÉMY ASSOGBA CAKPO.

Société Tunde: 06 BP 1925, Cotonou; tel. 30-15-68; fax 30-42-86; f. 1997; economics, management; Pres. BABATOUNDÉ RASAKI OLLOFINDJI.

Star Editions: 01 BP 367, Recette principale, Cotonou; tel. 94-66-28; fax 33-05-29; e-mail star_editions@yahoo.fr; internet www.afrilivres.com/index.asp?navig=annuaire; business, economics, science, poetry; Editor JOACHIM ADJOVI.

GOVERNMENT PUBLISHING HOUSE

Office National d'Edition, de Presse et d'Imprimerie (ONEPI): 01 BP 1210, Cotonou; tel. 30-02-99; fax 30-34-63; f. 1975; Dir-Gen. INNOCENT ADJAHO.

Broadcasting and Communications

TELECOMMUNICATIONS

Office des Postes et des Télécommunications (OPT): 01 BP 5959, Cotonou; tel. 31-38-43; fax 31-47-03; e-mail opt@intnet.bj; internet www.opt.bj; f. 1959; state-owned; separation of posts and telecommunications activities, and privatization of future Société Béninoise des Télécommunications (SOBETEL) proposed in early 2000s; Dir-Gen. SABI SOUMANOU SANNI.

Bell Bénin Communications (BBCOM): Cotonou; f. 2002; mobile cellular telephone operator; Chief Exec. ISSA SALIFOU.

Libercom: blvd Saint-Michel, face Hall des Arts et de la Culture, 01 BP 5959, Cotonou; tel. 31-68-01; fax 31-68-00; internet www.test.bj/libercom; f. 2000; mobile cellular telephone operator in Cotonou and Porto-Novo; jt venture between the OPT, Alcatel (France) and Titan Corpn (USA); 23,000 subscribers (2001).

Spacetel Bénin-BéninCell: 01 BP 5293, Cotonou; tel. 31-66-41; internet www.spacetelbenin.com; f. 2000; mobile cellular telephone operator in Cotonou, Porto-Novo and Parakou; affiliate of Spacetel (United Kingdom); 6,000 subscribers (2001).

Telecel Bénin: Cotonou; tel. 31-66-60; internet www.telecel.com; f. 2000; mobile cellular telephone operator in Cotonou, Porto-Novo, Abomey, Lokossa, additional regions of southern Benin and in Parakou; subsidiary of Atlantique Telecoms (Côte d'Ivoire); Dir-Gen. ERIC TRONEL; 130,000 subscribers (Jan. 2004).

BROADCASTING

Since 1997 the HAAC has issued licences to private radio and television stations.

Haute Autorité de l'Audiovisuel et de la Communication (HAAC): 01 BP 3567, Cotonou; tel. 31-17-45; fax 31-17-42; e-mail haac@planben.intnet.bj; internet www.gouv.bj/institutions/haac/presentation_top.php; f. 1992; Pres. TIMOTHÉE ADANLIN.

Radio

In early 2002 there were nine commercial radio stations, 17 non-commercial stations and five rural or local stations broadcasting in Benin.

Office de Radiodiffusion et de Télévision du Bénin (ORTB): 01 BP 366, Cotonou; tel. 30-46-19; fax 30-04-48; e-mail info@ortb.org; state-owned; radio programmes broadcast from Cotonou and Parakou in French, English and 18 local languages; Dir-Gen. JEAN N'TCHA; Dir FIDÈLE EDOH AYIKOUE.

Atlantic FM: 01 BP 366, Cotonou; tel. 30-20-41; Dir JOSEPH OGOUNCHI.

Radiodiffusion nationale du Benin: BP 366, Cotonou; tel. 30-10-96; f. 1953; Dir MOUFALIOU LIADY.

Radio Régionale de Parakou: BP 128, Parakou; tel. 61-07-73; Dir SÉNI SOUROU.

Bénin-Culture: BP 21, Association pour l'Institutionnalisation de la Mémoire et de la Pensée Intellectuelle Africaine, BP 21, Porto-Novo; tel. 22-28-83; Dir MAURILLE AGBOKOU.

Golfe FM-Magic Radio: 03 BP 1624, Cotonou; tel. 32-42-08; fax 32-52-26; e-mail golfefm@serv.eit.bj; internet www.eit.bj/golfefm.htm; Dir ISMAËL SOUMANOU.

Radio Afrique Espoir: Carré 123, 03 BP 203, Porto-Novo; tel. 21-34-55; fax 21-32-63; e-mail afespoir@intnet.bj; Dir RAMANOU KOUFER-IDJI.

Radio Carrefour: BP 440, Bohicon; tel. 51-16-03; fax 51-16-55; e-mail chrisdavak@yahoo.fr; f. 1999; production and broadcast of radio and television programmes; Dir-Gen. CHRISTOPHE DAVAKAN.

Radio FM-Ahémé: BP 66, Bopa, Mono; tel. 05-58-18; f. 1997; informative, cultural and civic education broadcasts; Dir AMBROISE COKOU MOUSSOU.

Radio Immaculée Conception: BP 88, Allada; tel. 36-80-97; operated by the Roman Catholic Church of Benin; broadcasts to Abomey, Allada, Bembéréke, Cotonou, Dassa-Zoume, Djougou and Parakou; Dir Fr ALFONSO BRUNO.

Radio Maranatha: 03 BP 4113, Cotonou; tel. and fax 32-58-82; e-mail maranatha.fm@serv.eit.bj; internet www.eit.to/RadioMaranatha.htm; operated by the Conseil des Eglises Protestantes Evangéliques du Bénin; Dir Rev. CLOVIS ALFRED KPADE.

Radio Planète: 02 BP 1528, Immeuble Master Soft, Cotonou; tel. 30-30-30; fax 30-24-51; e-mail janvier@planetefm.com; internet www.planetefm.com; Dir JANVIER YAHOUEDEHOU.

Radio Solidarité FM: BP 135, Djougou; tel. 80-11-29; fax 80-15-63; Dir DAOUDA TAKPARA.

La Voix de la Lama: 03 BP 3772, Cotonou; tel. 37-12-26; fax 37-13-67; e-mail voix_delalama@yahoo.fr; f. 1998; non-commercial FM station, broadcasting on 103.8 Mhz from Allada; Dir SÉRAPHINE DADY.

La Voix de l'Islam: 08 BP 134, Cotonou; tel. 31-11-34; fax 31-51-79; e-mail islamben@leland.bj; operated by the Communauté musulmane de Zongo; Dir El Hadj MAMAN YARO.

Radio Wêkê: 05 BP 436, Cotonou; tel. 21-38-40; fax 21-37-14; e-mail issabadarou@hotmail.com; Promoter Issa Badarou-Soulé.

Benin also receives broadcasts from Africa No. 1, the British Broadcasting Corporation World Service and Radio France International.

Television

ORTB: (see Radio); Dir of Television Pierette Amoussou.

ATVS: BP 7101, Cotonou; tel. 31-43-19; owned by African Television System-Sobiex; Dir Jacob Akinocho.

LC2—La Chaîne 2 (LC2): 05 BP 427, Cotonou; tel. 33-47-49; fax 33-46-75; e-mail lc2@intnet.bj; commenced broadcasts 1997; Pres. and Dir-Gen. Christian Lagnide; Dir-Gen. Nadine Lagnide.

Telco: 44 ave Delorme, 01 BP 1241, Cotonou; tel. 31-34-98; e-mail telco@serv.eit.bj; relays five international channels; Dir Joseph Jébara.

TV+ International/TV5: 01 BP 366, Cotonou; tel. 30-10-96; Dir Claude Karam.

Finance

(cap. = capital; res = reserves; dep. = deposits; m. = million; br. = branch; amounts in francs CFA)

BANKING

Central Bank

Banque Centrale des Etats de l'Afrique de l'Ouest (BCEAO): ave Jean-Paul II, BP 325, Cotonou; tel. 31-24-66; fax 31-24-65; e-mail akangni@bceao.int; internet www.bceao.int; HQ in Dakar, Senegal; f. 1962; bank of issue for the mem. states of the Union économique et monétaire ouest-africaine (UEMOA, comprising Benin, Burkina Faso, Côte d'Ivoire, Guinea-Bissau, Mali, Niger, Senegal and Togo); cap. and res 859,313m., total assets 5,671,675m. (Dec. 2002); Gov. Charles Konan Banny; Dir in Benin Idriss Lyassou Daouda; br. at Parakou.

Commercial Banks

Bank of Africa—Bénin (BOAB): ave Jean-Paul II, 08 BP 0879, Cotonou; tel. 31-32-28; fax 31-31-17; e-mail boa.dg@sobiex.bj; internet www.bkofafrica.net/benin.htm; f. 1990; 35.2% owned by African Financial Holding; cap. 7,000m., res. 11,636m., dep. 207,326m. (Feb. 2005); Dir-Gen. André Froissant; 11 brs.

Banque Internationale du Bénin (BIBE): carrefour des Trois Banques, ave Giran, 03 BP 2098, Jéricho, Cotonou; tel. 31-55-49; fax 31-23-65; e-mail bibe@intnet.bj; f. 1989; owned by Nigerian commercial interests; cap. 9,000m., dep. 48,577m.m.(Dec. 2002); Pres. Chief Dr Rufus Foluso Giwa; Man. Dir Jean-Paul K. Aiddo; 4 brs.

Continental Bank—Bénin (La Continentale): ave Jean-Paul II, carrefour des Trois Banques, 01 BP 2020, Cotonou; tel. 31-24-24; fax 31-51-77; e-mail contibk@intnet.bj; internet www.cbankbenin.com; f. 1993 to assume activities of Crédit Lyonnais Bénin; 43% state-owned; full transfer to private-sector ownership proposed for 2004; res 1,974m., dep. 23,230m., total assets 50,594m. (2005); Pres. Nicolas Adagbe; Gen. Man. Joseph Ayeh; 4 brs.

Diamond Bank Bénin: 308 rue du Révérend Père Colineau, 01 BP 955, Cotonou; tel. 31-79-27; fax 31-79-33; e-mail bao@diamondbank.com; majority owned by Diamond Bank (Nigeria); cap. and res 1,876m., total assets 13,468m. (Dec. 2002); Chair. Pascal Gabriel Dozie; Dir-Gen. Benjamin Oviosu; 2 brs.

Ecobank Bénin: rue Gouverneur Bayol, 01 BP 1280, Cotonou; tel. 31-40-23; fax 31-33-85; e-mail ecobnet@intnet.bj; internet www.ecobank.com; f. 1989; 78% owned by Ecobank Transnational Inc (operating under the auspices of the Economic Community of West African States); cap. 3,500m., res 5,869m., dep. 112,736m. (Dec. 2003); Pres., Chair. & Dir Gilbert Medje; Man. Dir Christophe Jocktane; 8 brs in Benin.

FINADEV: rue du Commandant Decoeur, 01 BP 6335, Cotonou; tel. 33-73-70; fax 31-31-02; e-mail info@finadev.org; internet www.finadev.org; f. 1998; 25% owned by Financial Bank Bénin, 25% owned by FMO (Netherlands), 25% owned by International Finance Corpn; cap. and res 1,000.0m., total assets 1,812.2m. (Dec. 2001); Dir-Gen. Patrick Lelong; 4 brs.

Financial Bank Bénin (FBB): Immeuble Adjibi, rue du Commandant Decoeur, 01 BP 2700, Cotonou; tel. 31-31-00; fax 31-31-02; e-mail fbbcti@leland.bj; f. 1996; 85% owned by Financial BC (Togo); cap. and res 3,161.7m., total assets 58,999.5m. (Dec. 2000); Pres. Rémy Baysset; Dir-Gen. Pierre Leclaire; 8 brs.

Société Générale de Banques au Bénin (SGBBE): ave Clozel, quartier Ganhi, 01 BP 585, Cotonou; tel. 31-83-00; fax 31-82-95; f.

2003; 70% owned by Groupe Société Générale (France); cap. 3.5m.; Pres. Axelle de Saint-Afrique.

Savings Bank

Caisse Nationale d'Epargne: Cadjèhoun, route Inter-Etat Cotonou-Lomé, Cotonou; tel. 30-18-35; fax 31-38-43; state-owned; cap. and res 736m., total assets 15,738m. (Dec. 1997); Pres. Marcellin Dossou Kpanou; Dir André H. Affedjou.

Credit Institutions

Crédit du Bénin: 08 BP 0936, Cotonou; tel. 31-30-02; fax 31-37-01; Man. Dir Gilbert Hounkpain.

Crédit Promotion Bénin: 03 BP 1672, Cotonou; tel. 31-31-44; fax 31-31-66; wholly owned by private investors; cap. 150m., total assets 409m. (Dec. 1998); Pres. Bernard Adikpeto; Man. Dir Dénis Oba Chabi.

Equipbail Bénin: blvd Jean-Paul II, 08 BP 0690, Cotonou; tel. 31-11-45; fax 31-46-58; e-mail equip.be@bkofafrica.com; internet www.bkofafrica.net/equipbail.htm; f. 1995; 78.7% owned by Bank of Africa—Bénin; cap. and res 717.2m., total assets 3,882.2m. (Dec. 2001); Pres. Paul Derreumaux.

Financial Institution

Caisse Autonome d'Amortissement du Bénin: BP 59, Cotonou; tel. 31-47-81; fax 31-53-56; manages state funds; Man. Dir Ibrahim Pedro-Boni.

STOCK EXCHANGE

Bourse Régionale des Valeurs Mobilières (BRVM): Antenne Nationale des Bourses du Bénin, Immeuble Chambre de Commerce et d'Industrie du Bénin, ave Charles de Gaulle, 01 BP 2985, Cotonou; tel. 31-21-26; fax 31-20-77; e-mail agnigla@brvm.org; internet www.brvm.org; f. 1998; national branch of BRVM (regional stock exchange based in Abidjan, Côte d'Ivoire, serving the member states of UEMOA); Man. in Benin Yvette Aissi Gnigla.

INSURANCE

A&C Bénin: Cotonou; all branches; Dir-Gen. Justin Herbert Agboton.

ASA Bénin: 01 BP 5508, Cotonou; tel. and fax 30-00-40; fmrly Société Nationale d'Assurance; Pres. Egouleti Montetcho.

Assurances et Réassurance du Golfe de Guinée (ARGG): 04 BP 0851, Cotonou; tel. 30-56-43; fax 30-55-55; non-life insurance and re-insurance; Man. Dir Colette Posset Tagnon.

Gras Savoye Bénin: Immeuble Aboki Hounkpehedji, 1er étage, ave Mgr Steinmetz, face de l'Immeuble Kougblenou, 01 BP 6901 RP Cotonou; tel. 31-69-22; fax 31-69-79; e-mail gsbenin@leland.bj; internet www.grassavoye.com; affiliated to Gras Savoye (France); Man. Guy Bihannic.

SOBAC: Carré 5, ave Delorme, 01 BP 544, Cotonou; tel. 31-67-35; fax 31-67-34; e-mail sobac@intnet.bj; affiliate of AGF (France).

Union Béninoise d'Assurance-Vie: 08 BP 0322, Cotonou; tel. 30-06-90; fax 30-07-69; e-mail uba@firstnet.bj; f. 1994; cap. 400m.; 51% owned by Union Africaine Vie (Côte d'Ivoire); Man. Dir Venance Amoussouga.

Trade and Industry

GOVERNMENT AGENCIES

Centre Béninois de la Recherche Scientifique et Technique (CBRST): 03 BP 1665, Cotonou; tel. 32-12-63; fax 32-36-71; e-mail cbrst@bow.intnet.bj; f. 1986; promotes scientific and technical research and training; 10 specialized research units; Dir-Gen. Prof. Théophile Zohoun.

Centre Béninois du Commerce Extérieur: place du Souvenir, BP 1254, Cotonou; tel. 30-13-20; fax 30-04-36; e-mail cbce@bow.intnet.bj; internet www.cbce.africa-web.org; f. 1988; provides information to export cos.

Centre de Promotion et de l'Artisanat: à côté du Hall des Arts et de la Culture, BP 2651, Cotonou; tel. and fax 30-34-91; e-mail cpa.info@netcourrier.com; f. 1987; Dir Jeanne-Marie Houessou.

Centre de Promotion et d'Encadrement des Petites et Moyennes Entreprises (CEPEPE): face à la Mairie de Xlacondji, BP 2093, Cotonou; tel. 31-44-47; e-mail cepepe@uva.org; f. 1989; promotes business and employment; offers credits and grants to small businesses; undertakes management training and recruitment; publishes bi-monthly journal, *Initiatives*; Dir-Gen. Théophile Capo-Chichi.

Cellule des Opérations de Dénationalisation (COD): 02 BP 8140, Cotonou; tel. 31-59-18; fax 31-23-15; Co-ordinator VICTORIN DOSSOU-SOGNON.

Institut National de Recherches Agricoles du Bénin (INRAB): 01 BP 884, Cotonou; tel. 30-02-64; fax 30-37-70; e-mail inrabdg4@ intnet.bj; internet www.bj.refer.org/benin_ct/rec/inrab/inrab.htm; f. 1992; undertakes research into agricultural improvements; publicizes advances in agriculture; Dir DAVID Y. ARODOKOUN.

Office Béninois de Recherches Géologiques et Minières (OBRGM): Ministry of Mining, Energy and Water Resources, 04 BP 1412, Cotonou; tel. 31-03-09; fax 31-41-20; e-mail nestorved@yahoo .fr; internet www.energie.gouv.bj/obrgm/index.htm; f. 1996 as govt agency responsible for mining policy, exploitation and research; Dir-Gen. NESTOR VEDOGBETON.

Office National d'Appui à la Sécurité Alimentaire (ONASA): 06 BP 2544, Cotonou; tel. 33-15-02; fax 33-02-93; e-mail onasamdr@ intnet.bj; f. 1992; distribution of cereals; Pres. IMAROU SALÉ; Dir-Gen. MOUSSA ASSOUMA.

Office National du Bois (ONAB): BP 1238, Cotonou; tel. 33-04-59; fax 33-39-83; e-mail onabdgle@intnet.bj; f. 1983; reorganized and partially privatized in 2002; forest development and management, manufacture and marketing of wood products; transfer of industrial activities to private ownership pending; Dir-Gen. PIERRE HOUAYE.

DEVELOPMENT ORGANIZATIONS

Agence Française de Développement (AFD): blvd de France, 01 BP 38, Cotonou; tel. 31-35-80; fax 31-20-18; e-mail adfcot@leland.bj; internet www.afd.fr; fmrly Caisse Française de Développement; Dir YVES TERRACOL.

Mission de Coopération et d'Action Culturelle (Mission Française d'Aide et de Coopération): BP 476, Cotonou; tel. 30-08-24; administers bilateral aid from France; Dir BERNARD HADJADJ.

SNV Bénin (Société Néerlandais de Développement): 01 BP 1048, carré 107, Zone Résidentielle, Rue du PNUD, Cotonou; tel. 31-31-42; fax 31-35-59; e-mail snvben@intnet.bj; internet www .snvbenin.org.

CHAMBER OF COMMERCE

Chambre de Commerce et d'Industrie du Bénin (CCIB): ave du Général de Gaulle, 01 BP 31, Cotonou; tel. 31-20-80; fax 31-32-99; e-mail ccib@bow.intnet.bj; internet www.ccib.bj; f. 1908; present name adopted 1962; Pres. ATAOU SOUFIANO; Vice-Pres. responsible for Trade SOULEY MAMAN YACOUBOU; Vice-Pres. responsible for Industry PATRICK NOYES; Vice-Pres. responsible for Services GRÂCE LAWANI; brs at Parakou (CCIB-Borgou-Allibori), Abomey (CCIB-Zou-Collines), Natitingou (CCIB-Atacora-Donga) and Porto-Novo (CCIB—Ouémé-Plateau).

EMPLOYERS' ORGANIZATIONS

Conseil National des Chargeurs du Bénin: 06 BP 2528, Cotonou; tel. 31-59-47; fax 31-59-07; e-mail cncb@intnet.bj; f. 1983; represents interests of shippers; Dir IDRISSOU TCHENEGNON.

Conseil National du Patronat du Bénin (CNP-Bénin): 01 BP 1260, Cotonou; tel. 30-74-06; fax 30-83-22; e-mail lucien.glele@ intnet.bj; f. 1984 as Organisation Nationale des Employeurs du Bénin; Pres. LUCIEN G. GLÈLÈ.

Fondation de l'Entrepreneurship du Bénin (FEB): place du Québec, 08 BP 1155, Cotonou; tel. 31-35-37; fax 31-37-26; e-mail fonda@intnet.bj; internet www.placequebec.org; non profit-making org.; encourages the devt of the private sector and of small- and medium-sized businesses; Dir PIERRE DOVONOU LOKOSSOU.

Syndicat des Commerçants Importateurs et Exportateurs du Bénin: Cotonou; Pres. M. BENCHIMOL.

Syndicat Interprofessionnel des Entreprises Industrielles du Bénin: Cotonou; Pres. M. DOUCET.

Syndicat National des Commerçants et Industriels Africains du Bénin (SYNACIB): BP 367, Cotonou; Pres. URBAIN DA SILVA.

UTILITIES

Communauté Electrique du Bénin (CEB): Vedoko, BP 537, Cotonou; tel. 30-06-75; f. 1968; jt venture between Benin and Togo to exploit energy resources in the two countries; Dir N'PO CYR KOUAGOU.

Société Béninoise d'Electricité et d'Eau (SBEE): 01 BP 2047, Cotonou; tel. 31-21-45; fax 31-50-28; f. 1973; state-owned; production and distribution of electricity and water; separation of electricity and water sectors pending in 2004, prior to proposed privatization of electricity operations; Man. Dir ROGER KOUESSI.

Société Nationale des Eaux du Bénin (SONEB): Cotonou; f. 2003 to assume water activities of Société Béninoise d'Electricité et d'Eau; Dir-Gen. ALASSANE BABA-MOUSSA.

TRADE UNIONS

Centrale des Organisations Syndicales Indépendantes (COSI): 04 BP 706, Cotonou; tel. 30-20-12; principally active in the health and education sectors; Sec.-Gen. JOSÉ DE SOUZA.

Centrale Syndicale des Travailleurs du Bénin (CSTB): 03 BP 0989, Cotonou; tel. 30-13-15; fax 33-26-01; actively opposes privatization and the influence of the international financial community; linked to the Parti Communiste du Bénin; Sec.-Gen. GASTON AZOUA.

Centrale des Syndicats Autonomes du Bénin (CSA—Bénin): 04 BP 1115, Cotonou; tel. 30-31-82; fax 30-04-48; principally active in private-sector enterprises; Sec.-Gen. GUILLAUME ATTIGBÉ.

Centrale des Syndicats du Secteur Privé et Informel du Bénin (CSPIB): 03 BP 2961, Cotonou; tel. 33-53-53.

Centrale des Syndicats Unis du Bénin (CSUB): Cotonou; tel. 33-10-27.

Confédération Générale des Travailleurs du Bénin (CGTB): 06 BP 2449, Cotonou; tel. and fax 33-50-07; principally active in public administration; Sec.-Gen. PASCAL TODJINOU; 33,275 mems (2002).

Union Nationale des Syndicats de Travailleurs du Bénin (UNSTB): 1 blvd Saint-Michel, BP 69, Recette Principale, Cotonou; tel. and fax 30-36-13; principally active in public administration; sole officially recognized trade union 1974–90; 40,000 members in 2005, of which 25,000 in the informal sector; Sec.-Gen. EMMANUEL ZOUNON.

Transport

In 1996 the World Bank approved a credit of US $40m., to be issued through the International Development Association, in support of a major programme of investment in Benin's transport network. The integrated programme aimed to enhance Benin's status as an entrepôt for regional trade, and also to boost domestic employment and, by improving the infrastructure and reducing transport costs, agricultural and manufacturing output.

RAILWAYS

In 1997 the network handled 311,400 metric tons of goods. In January 1999 the line between Cotonou and Porto-Novo was re-opened after nine years of closure.

Organisation Commune Bénin-Niger des Chemins de Fer et des Transports (OCBN): BP 16, Cotonou; tel. 31-28-57; fax 31-41-50; e-mail ocbn@intnet.bj; f. 1959; 50% owned by Govt of Benin, 50% by Govt of Niger; total of 579 track-km; main line runs for 438 km from Cotonou to Parakou in the interior; br. line runs westward via Ouidah to Segboroué (34 km); also line of 107 km from Cotonou via Porto-Novo to Pobé (near the Nigerian border); extension to the Republic of Niger proposed; Pres. ABDOU LABO; Man. Dir JOSEPH KETCHION.

ROADS

In 1999 there were 7,704 km of roads, including 1,405 km of paved roads and 2,019 km of classified roads.

Agence Générale de Transit et de Consignation (AGETRAC): blvd Maritime, BP 1933, Cotonou; tel. 31-32-22; fax 31-29-69; e-mail agetrac@leland.bj; f. 1967; goods transportation and warehousing.

Compagnie de Transit et de Consignation du Bénin (CTCB Express): Cotonou; f. 1986; Pres. SOULÉMAN KOURA ZOUMAROU.

SHIPPING

The main port is at Cotonou. In 2001 the port handled some 3,325,600 metric tons of goods.

Port Autonome de Cotonou (PAC): BP 927, Cotonou; tel. 31-28-90; fax 31-28-91; e-mail pac@leland.bj; f. 1965; state-owned port authority; private-sector involvement proposed for 2004; Dir-Gen. JÉRÔME HOUNSI DANDJINOU.

Association pour la Défense des Intérêts du Port de Cotonou (AIPC) (Communauté Portuaire du Bénin): Port Autonome de Cotonou; tel. 31-17-26; fax 31-28-91; f. 1993; promotes, develops and co-ordinates port activities at Cotonou; Pres. ISSA BADAROU-SOULÉ; Sec.-Gen. CAMILLE MÉDÉGAN.

Compagnie Béninoise de Navigation Maritime (COBENAM): Place Ganhi, 01 BP 2032, Cotonou; tel. 31-27-96; fax 31-09-78; e-mail cobenam@elodia.intnet.bj; f. 1974; 51% state-owned, 49% by Govt of

Algeria; Pres. ABDEL KADER ALLAL; Man. Dir ARMAND PRIVAT KANDIS-SOUNON.

Maersk Bénin: Centre Kodeih, ave Steinmetz, BP 2826, Cotonou; tel. 31-43-30; fax 31-15-83; e-mail coologmng@maersk-logistics.com; internet www.maersk-logistics.com/sw1059.asp; subsidiary of Maersk Sealand (Denmark); Dir AUGIS ROBERT.

SDV Bénin: route du Collège de l'Union, Akpakpa, 01 BP 433, Cotonou; tel. 31-21-19; fax 31-59-26; e-mail sdvbenin@bow.intnet.bj; f. 1986; affiliated to SDV Group (France); Pres. J. F. MIGNONNEAU; Dir-Gen. R. PH. RANJARD.

Société Béninoise d'Entreprises Maritimes (SBEM): BP 1733, Cotonou; tel. 31-23-57; fax 31-59-26; warehousing, storage and transportation; Dir RÉGIS TISSER.

Société Béninoise des Manutentions Portuaires (SOBEMAP): 35 blvd de la Marina, BP 35, Cotonou; tel. 31-41-45; fax 31-53-71; e-mail infos@sobemap.com; internet www.sobemap.com; f. 1969; state-owned; Dir-Gen. BERNARD AMOUSSOU-SOSSOU.

Société Béninoise Maritime (SOBEMAR): Carré 8, Cruintomé, 08 BP 0956, Cotonou; tel. 31-49-65; fax 31-67-72; e-mail sobemar@intnet.bj.

CIVIL AVIATION

The international airport at Cotonou (Cotonou-Cadjehoun) has a 2.4-km runway, and there are secondary airports at Parakou, Natitingou, Kandi and Abomey.

Aéro Bénin: Cotonou; f. 2002; regional flights.

Trans Air Bénin (TAB): Cotonou; f. 2000; regional flights; Dir BRICE KIKI.

Tourism

Benin's rich cultural diversity and its national parks and game reserves are the principal tourist attractions. About 72,000 tourists visited Benin in 2002. Receipts from tourism were estimated at US $60m. in that year

Direction de la Promotion et des Professions Touristiques: BP 2037, Cotonou; tel. 32-68-24; fax 32-68-23; e-mail dth@benintourism.com; internet www.benintourism.com.

BHUTAN

Introductory Survey

Location, Climate, Language, Religion, Flag, Capital

The Kingdom of Bhutan lies in the Himalaya range of mountains, with Tibet (the Xizang Autonomous Region), part of the People's Republic of China, to the north and India to the south. Average monthly temperature ranges from 4.4°C (40°F) in January to 17°C (62°F) in July. Rainfall is heavy, ranging from 150 cm (60 ins) to 300 cm (120 ins) per year. The official language is Dzongkha, spoken mainly in western Bhutan. Written Dzongkha is based on the Tibetan script. The state religion is Mahayana Buddhism, primarily the Drukpa school of the Kagyupa sect, although Nepalese settlers, who comprise about one-quarter of the country's total population, practise Hinduism. The Nepali-speaking Hindus dominate southern Bhutan and are referred to as southern Bhutanese. The national flag (proportions 2 by 3) is divided diagonally from the lower hoist to the upper fly, so forming two triangles, one orange and the other maroon, with a white dragon superimposed in the centre. The capital is Thimphu.

Recent History

The first hereditary King of Bhutan was installed in December 1907. An Anglo-Bhutanese Treaty, signed in 1910, placed Bhutan's foreign relations under the supervision of the Government of British India. After India became independent, this treaty was replaced in August 1949 by the Indo-Bhutan Treaty of Friendship, whereby Bhutan agrees to seek the advice of the Government of India with regard to its foreign relations but remains free to decide whether or not to accept such advice. King Jigme Dorji Wangchuck, installed in 1952, established the National Assembly (Tshogdu Chenmo) in 1953 and a Royal Advisory Council (Lodoi Tsokde) in 1965. He formed the country's first Council of Ministers (Lhengye Zhungtshog) in 1968. He died in 1972 and was succeeded by the Western-educated 16-year-old Crown Prince, Jigme Singye Wangchuck. The new King stated his wish to preserve the Indo-Bhutan Treaty and further to strengthen friendship with India. In 1979, however, during the Non-aligned Conference and later at the UN General Assembly, Bhutan voted in opposition to India, in favour of Chinese policy. In 1983 India and Bhutan signed a new trade agreement concerning overland trade with Bangladesh and Nepal. India raised no objection to Bhutan's decision to negotiate directly with the People's Republic of China over the Bhutan–China border, and discussions between Bhutan and China were begun in 1984 (see below).

When Chinese authority was established in Tibet (Xizang) in 1959, Bhutan granted asylum to more than 6,000 Tibetan refugees. As a result of the discovery that many refugees were allegedly engaged in spying and subversive activities, the Bhutanese Government decided in 1976 to disperse them in small groups, introducing a number of Bhutanese families into each settlement. In June 1979 the National Assembly approved a directive establishing the end of the year as a time-limit for the refugees to decide whether to acquire Bhutanese citizenship or accept repatriation to Tibet. By September 1985 most of the Tibetans had chosen Bhutanese citizenship, and the remainder were to be accepted by India. A revised Citizenship Act, adopted by the National Assembly in 1985, confirmed residence in Bhutan in 1958 as a fundamental basis for automatic citizenship (as provided for by the 1958 Nationality Act), but this was to be interpreted flexibly. Provision was also made for citizenship by registration for Nepalese immigrants who had resided in the country for at least 20 years (15 years if employed by the Government) and who could meet linguistic and other tests of commitment to the Bhutanese community.

The violent ethnic Nepalese agitation in India for a 'Gurkha homeland' in the Darjiling-Kalimpong region during the late 1980s and the populist movement in Nepal in 1988–90 (see the chapters on India and Nepal, respectively) spread into Bhutan in 1990. Ethnic unrest became apparent in that year when a campaign of intimidation and violence, directed by militant Nepalese against the authority of the Government in Thimphu, was initiated. In September thousands of southern Bhutanese villagers, and Nepalese who entered Bhutan from across the Indian border, organized demonstrations in border towns in southern Bhutan to protest against domination by the indigenous Buddhist Drukpa. The 'anti-nationals' (ngolops), as they were called by the Bhutanese authorities, demanded a greater role in the country's political and economic life and were bitterly opposed to official attempts to strengthen the Bhutanese sense of national identity through an increased emphasis on Tibetan-derived, rather than Nepalese, culture and religion (including a formal dress code, Dzongkha as the sole official language, etc.). Bhutanese officials, by contrast, viewed the southerners as recent arrivals who abused the hospitality of their hosts through acts of violence and the destruction of development infrastructure.

Most southern villagers are relatively recent arrivals from Nepal, and many of them have made substantial contributions to the development of the southern hills. The provision of free education and health care by the Bhutanese Government for many years attracted Nepalese who had been struggling to survive in their own country and who came to settle illegally in Bhutan. This population movement was largely ignored by local administrative officials, many of whom accepted incentives to disregard the illegal nature of the influx. The Government's policy of encouraging a sense of national identity, together with rigorous new procedures (introduced in 1988) to check citizenship registration, revealed the presence of thousands of illegal residents in southern Bhutan—many of whom had lived there for a decade or more, married local inhabitants and raised families. During the ethnic unrest in September 1990 the majority of southern villagers were coerced into participating in the demonstrations by groups of armed and uniformed young men (including many of Nepalese origin who were born in Bhutan). Many of these dissidents, including a large number of students and former members of the Royal Bhutan Army and of the police force, had fled Bhutan in 1989 and early 1990. In 1988–90 a large number of the dissidents resided in the tea gardens and villages adjoining southern Bhutan. Following the demonstrations that took place in Bhutan in September–October 1990, other ethnic Nepalese left Bhutan. In January 1991 some 234 persons, claiming to be Bhutanese refugees, reportedly arrived in the Jhapa district of eastern Nepal. In September, at the request of the Nepalese Government, the office of the UN High Commissioner for Refugees (UNHCR) inaugurated a relief programme providing food and shelter for more than 300 people in the *ad hoc* camps. By December the number of people staying in the camps had risen to about 6,000. This number was substantially augmented by landless and unemployed Nepalese, who had been expelled from Assam and other eastern states of India. The small and faction-ridden ethnic Nepalese Bhutan People's Party (BPP) purported to lead the agitation for 'democracy' but presented no clear set of objectives and attracted little support from within Bhutan itself. Schools and bridges became principal targets for arson and looting during 1990–92. Most of the schools in southern Bhutan were closed indefinitely from the end of September 1990, in response to threats to the lives of teachers and students' families, but the majority of pupils affected by these closures were provided with temporary places in schools in northern Bhutan. By mid-1995, despite the continuing security problems, some 74 schools and 89 health facilities had been reopened in the five southern districts.

Between 1988 and the end of 1999 King Jigme personally authorized the release of more than 1,700 militants captured by the authorities. The King asserted that, while he had an open mind regarding the question of the pace and extent of political reform (including a willingness to hold discussions with any discontented minority group), his Government could not tolerate pressures for change if based on intimidation and violence. Although several important leaders of the dissident movement remained in custody, the King stated that they would be released upon a return to normal conditions of law and order. On the one hand, some leaders of the BPP declared that they had no differences with the King, but with 'corrupt officials'; on the other hand, certain militants strongly condemned the King as their 'main enemy'.

A number of southern Bhutanese officials (including the Director-General of Power, Bhim Subba, and the Managing Director of the State Trading Corporation, R. B. Basnet) absconded in June 1991 (on the eve of the publication of departmental audits) and went directly to Nepal, where they reportedly sought political asylum on the grounds of repression and atrocities against southern Bhutanese. These accusations were refuted by the Government in Thimphu. The former Secretary-General of the BPP, D. K. Rai, was tried by the High Court in Thimphu in May 1992 and was sentenced to life imprisonment for terrorist acts; a further 35 defendants received lesser sentences. Teknath Rizal, who was alleged to be responsible for the ethnic unrest and who had been held in prison since November 1989, came to trial, and was sentenced to life imprisonment in November 1993, having been found guilty of offences against the Tsawa Sum ('the country, the King, and the people'). (Rizal, together with 40 other 'political prisoners', was pardoned by the King and released from prison in December 1999; he decided to remain in Thimphu.)

Violence continued in the disturbed areas of Samtse, Chhukha, Tsirang, Sarpang and Gelephu (then called Gelephug) throughout the early 1990s, and companies of trained militia volunteers were posted to these areas to relieve the forces of the regular army. The state Government of West Bengal in India, the territory of which abuts much of southern Bhutan, reaffirmed in 1991 and 1992 that its land would not be used as a base for any agitation against Bhutan.

In late 1991 and throughout 1992 several thousand legally settled villagers left southern Bhutan for the newly established refugee camps in eastern Nepal. The Bhutanese Government alleged that the villagers were being enticed or threatened to leave their homes by militants based outside Bhutan, in order to augment the population of the camps and gain international attention; the dissidents, by contrast, claimed that the Bhutanese Government was forcing the villagers to leave. The formation of the Bhutan National Democratic Party (BNDP), including members drawn from supporters of the BPP and with R. B. Basnet as its President, was announced in Kathmandu, Nepal, in February 1992. Incidents of ethnic violence, almost all of which involved infiltration from across the border by ethnic Nepalese who had been trained and dispatched from the camps in Nepal, reportedly diminished substantially in the first half of 1993, as talks continued between Bhutanese and Nepalese officials regarding proposals to resolve the issues at stake. The Nepalese Government steadfastly refused to consider any solution that did not include the resettlement in Bhutan of all ethnic Nepalese 'refugees' living in the camps (by November 1993 the number of alleged ethnic Nepalese refugees from Bhutan totalled about 85,000). This proposal was rejected by the Bhutanese Government, which maintained that the majority of the camp population merely claimed to be from Bhutan, had absconded from Bhutan (and thus forfeited their citizenship, according to Bhutan's citizenship laws), or had departed voluntarily after selling their properties and surrendering their citizenship papers and rights. The apparent deadlock was broken, however, when a joint statement was signed by the two countries' Ministers of Home Affairs in July, which committed each side to establishing a 'high-level committee' to work towards a settlement and, in particular, to fulfilling the following mandate prior to undertaking any other related activity: to determine the different categories of people claiming to have come from Bhutan in the refugee camps in eastern Nepal (which now numbered eight); and to specify the positions of the two Governments on each of these categories, which would provide the basis for the resolution of the problem. The two countries held their first ministerial-level meeting regarding the issue in Kathmandu in October, at which it was agreed that four categories would be established among the people in the refugee camps: '(i) bona fide Bhutanese who have been evicted forcefully; (ii) Bhutanese who emigrated; (iii) non-Bhutanese; and (iv) Bhutanese who have committed criminal acts' (henceforth referred to as Categories I, II, III and IV, respectively). Further meetings were held in 1994. Following the election of a new Government in Nepal in November of that year, however, little progress was made at joint ministerial meetings held in the first half of 1995. Nepal's communist Government demanded that all persons in the camps be accepted by Bhutan; the Bhutanese authorities, on the other hand, were prepared to accept only the unconditional return of any bona fide Bhutanese citizens who had left the country involuntarily. Nevertheless, diplomatic exchanges continued in the latter half of the year, despite serious political instability in Nepal.

In January 1996 the new Nepalese Prime Minister, Sher Bahadur Deuba, proposed a resumption of intergovernmental talks, this time at foreign minister level. King Jigme welcomed the proposal, but the seventh round of talks, which was held in April, resulted in demands by Nepal that exceeded the mandate drawn up by the joint ministerial committee in mid-1993. It was widely understood that the Nepalese Government had again reverted to a requisition that all persons in the camps be accepted by Bhutan, regardless of status. This demand remained unacceptable to the Bhutanese Government, which stated that the problem of the people in the camps would not have arisen if conditions (such as prospects of free food, shelter, health and education, and 'moral support' by the Nepalese authorities for all persons claiming to be Bhutanese refugees) had not been created when there were reportedly only 234 persons in Jhapa making such claims. In addition, the Bhutanese Government stated that even with such conditions attracting people to the refugee camps, a well-organized screening process would have prevented the sheer scale of ethnic Nepalese claiming to be Bhutanese refugees. (Until June 1993 no screening of claimants to refugee status had been enforced on the India–Nepal border.) In August 1996 a UNHCR delegation visited Bhutan at the invitation of the authorities, who provided detailed information pertaining to the camps. Talks at ministerial level were held in 1997, without any public communiqué. Following informal discussions during the summit meeting of the South Asian Association for Regional Co-operation (SAARC, see p. 343) in Colombo, Sri Lanka, in July 1998, the new Chairman of the Council of Ministers, Lyonpo Jigmi Y. Thinley, held talks with the Nepalese Prime Minister, G. P. Koirala; both leaders stated that their meeting had been 'very positive'. Thinley and Koirala agreed that bilateral negotiations would continue through their respective Ministers of Foreign Affairs on the issue of persons claiming refugee status in Nepal (who now numbered about 100,000). The 77th National Assembly session, which took place in June–August 1999, unanimously reiterated that the Bhutanese Government accepted full responsibility for any Bhutanese found to have been forcefully evicted (Category I—see above): such persons would be recognized and accepted as genuine refugees, while those responsible for their eviction would be punished. Category II persons who had voluntarily emigrated from the country would be dealt with according to the respective immigration and citizenship laws of Bhutan and Nepal; those classified as Category III 'must return to their own country'; and the repatriation of those in Category IV was to be conducted in accordance with the laws of the two countries. At the eighth round of joint ministerial negotiations between Bhutan and Nepal, which was held in Kathmandu in September, the Bhutanese Minister of Foreign Affairs agreed that some of those previously classified as voluntary emigrants (under Category II) might be reclassified as Category I (according to the Bhutanese Government, the number of people in this category totalled only about 3,000, while the Nepalese Government claimed that all of the camp dwellers had been compelled to leave Bhutan). In 1999 the Bhutanese Government was reported to have resettled people from the central and eastern hill regions of Bhutan in the southern areas of the country.

At the 10th round of joint ministerial negotiations, held in December 2000, the Bhutanese and Nepalese Ministers of Foreign Affairs agreed that nationality would be verified on the basis of the head of the refugee family for those over 25 years of age, and that refugees under 25 years of age would be verified on an individual basis. This important advance in bilateral negotiations signified a major concession by Bhutan, which had hitherto insisted that verification be conducted on an individual basis. By the end of January 2001 a Joint Verification Team (JVT), consisting of five officials each from the Nepalese and Bhutanese Governments, had concluded the inspection of the refugee camps. Verification of the nationality of 98,897 people claiming refugee status (including 13,000 minors born in the camp) began at the end of March, commencing with the Khudanabari camp. Despite criticisms in the Nepalese press that the pace was too slow, the minister argued that it was essential for both parties to maintain a credible verification process. The Assembly endorsed the ongoing verification process, and decided that any ensuing problems should be resolved first at the secretary level of the two Governments, or if necessary, at the ministerial level. At a meeting in early November the

Ministers of Foreign Affairs of Bhutan and Nepal were unable to harmonize the positions of their respective Governments with regard to the four categories (established in October 1993—see above) for the people in the camps. In late 2001 the verification of the Khudanabari camp had been completed; however, with the subsequent disagreements over harmonization, the process reached a standstill. Discussions continued to take place between Bhutanese and Nepalese officials, although progress was very slow.

In January 2003 Bhutan hosted the 12th ministerial joint committee (MJC), at which the two Governments finally harmonized their positions on each of the four categories. The 14th MJC in May resolved all the remaining issues in order to finalize the categorization process. Details of the results of the verification process at Khudanabari were published on 18 June: 74 families (293 people) were in Category I (forcefully evicted Bhutanese people); 2,182 families (8,595 people) were in Category II (Bhutanese who had emigrated); 817 families (2,948 people) were in Category III (non-Bhutanese people); and 85 families (347 people) in were in Category IV (Bhutanese who had committed criminal acts). The JVT allowed 14 days for appeals (which were to be rejected if not based on documentation), and was to submit its recommendation on the appeals to the 15th meeting of the MJC. Despite a new Nepalese Government from late May criticizing the agreements and several political parties in Nepal calling for the Nepalese Government to repudiate the deal, arrangements were being made to conduct the repatriation to Bhutan of most of the families in Category I by the end of 2003. The Minister of Home Affairs informed the 81st session of the National Assembly in mid-2003 that there were more than 55,000 non-national workers in Bhutan in 2003, all of whom would also like to claim Bhutanese citizenship, and stated that it was imperative that any persons returning to the country should be dealt with strictly according to the citizenship and immigration laws. He also claimed that the ultimate agenda of those who had left Bhutan and now resided in camps in Nepal was to bring into Bhutan a large number of non-Bhutanese people of Nepalese origin, take over the country's political power and government machinery, and provide themselves and other people of Nepalese origin with land and Bhutanese citizenship. The 15th MJC, held in Thimphu in October, was hailed as very successful by the leader of Nepal's delegation. It was agreed at the meeting that the JVT would return to Jhapa in November to review the remaining appeals from people in the Khudunabari camp and then begin verification of the Sanischare camp. The committee also decided that Bhutan would be fully responsible for any Category I persons, while Category II people could apply for either Bhutanese or Nepalese citizenship, in accordance with the respective laws. Any appeals by people in Category III were to be resolved by the end of January 2004. However, in December 2003 the Bhutanese members of the JVT, while explaining the remaining procedures to Sector A residents of the Khudanabari camp, were attacked by several thousand other camp members protesting against the terms and conditions of the agreement. The JVT members were subsequently withdrawn to Thimphu and talks between Bhutan and Nepal were suspended. In March 2004 Teknath Rizal, Chairman of the Human Rights Council of Bhutan, began a hunger strike in Nepal, with the intention of drawing international attention to the plight of the refugees. Rizal ended his strike in the following month after receiving assurances from the Nepalese Government that it would attempt to enlist the involvement of UNHCR and India in restarting the stalled repatriation process. In September Rizal led a Nepalese delegation to the headquarters of UNHCR in Geneva, Switzerland, in a further attempt to raise the international profile of the refugees. In the following month the US Assistant Secretary of State for Population, Refugees and Migration, Arthur Dewey, visited the area and held discussions on how to end the stalemate. However, in early 2005 it appeared unlikely that there would be any swift resumption of the registration process, mainly owing to political instability in Nepal.

A diminution in guerrilla violence in Bhutan from late 1995 coincided with the adoption of the 'peace march' tactic by persons claiming to be Bhutanese and seeking to travel from Nepal into Bhutan. These marches continued throughout 1996; a small group of marchers actually reached Phuentsholing in August and again in December before being forced to return to India (which maintained a neutral stance with regard to the refugee issue). Bhutan's Minister of Home Affairs asserted that those participating in the marches were not Bhutanese, but were non-

nationals and emigrants attempting to enter the country illegally. A number of isolated bombing incidents occurred in Bhutan during 1998–99, most notably in Thimphu's main stadium in November 1998, and were attributed by Bhutanese authorities to Nepalese militants.

In 1991 'Rongthong' Kinley Dorji (also styled Kuenley or Kunley), a former Bhutanese businessman accused of unpaid loans and of acts against the state, had absconded to Nepal and joined the anti-Government movement. In 1992 he established and became President of the Druk National Congress, claiming human rights violations in Bhutan. Following the signing of an extradition treaty between India and Bhutan in December, Kinley was arrested by the Indian authorities during a visit to Delhi in April 1997; he remained in detention until June 1998, when he was released on bail while his case was being examined by the Indian courts. Meanwhile, the extradition treaty was read to the 75th Assembly in July 1997, when demands for Kinley Dorji's return to Bhutan for trial were unanimously supported (as they were also at the 76th Assembly in 1998 and the 77th Assembly in 1999). At the same time the Assembly resolved that all relatives of alleged 'anti-national militants' in government service should be compulsorily retired as soon as possible. The 75th Assembly also discussed the intrusions into Bhutan's south-eastern border forests by Bodo and Maoist extremists from the neighbouring Indian state of Assam.

Important institutional changes were introduced in mid-1998, whereby King Jigme relinquished his role as head of government (while remaining Head of State) in favour of a smaller elected Council of Ministers, which was to enjoy full executive power under the leadership of a Chairman (elected by ministers, on a rotational basis, for a one-year term in office) who would be head of government. In June the King informed the members of the existing Council of Ministers that it was to be dissolved, and stated that he had issued a royal decree to the Speaker of the National Assembly, which was to be discussed at the forthcoming 76th session. In the decree the King stressed the necessity to promote greater popular participation in the decision-making process, to strengthen the Government's mandate, and to enhance the administration's transparency and efficiency with integral checks and balances. He stated that the Council of Ministers should now be restructured as an elected body 'vested with full executive powers', and he presented three key points: (i) all government ministers should henceforth be elected by the National Assembly, with the first election to take place during the 76th session; (ii) a decision should be taken on the exact role and responsibilities of the Council of Ministers; and (iii) the National Assembly should have a mechanism to move a vote of confidence in the King. King Jigme further advised that the Council of Ministers should henceforth consist of six elected ministers and all nine members of the Royal Advisory Council; ministers should be elected by secret ballot; candidates should be selected from those who had held senior government posts at the rank of secretary or above; and a candidate must secure a majority of the votes cast to be considered elected. The portfolios for the elected ministers were to be awarded by the King. A minister's term in office was to be five years, after which he would undergo a vote of confidence in the National Assembly (previously there had been no limit on the tenure of ministerial posts). All decisions adopted by the Council of Ministers were to be based on consensus, and, while the Council was to govern Bhutan with full executive powers, it was also to be obliged to keep the King fully informed on all matters concerning the security and sovereignty of the country. The procedures of the Council of Ministers were to be supervised by a Cabinet Secretary appointed by the Council. The 76th session of the National Assembly voted by secret ballot on six new ministerial nominees; all were successful, but all received some negative votes.

An act to regulate the Council of Ministers, which was framed by a committee comprising members of the Government, clergy and people's representatives of the 20 districts, was presented to the 77th session of the National Assembly in mid-1999 and was subjected to extensive discussion and amendment. The rules as finally endorsed explicitly specified that the King had full power to dissolve the Council of Ministers. Procedures for a confidence vote with regard to the King were also drafted by the aforementioned committee and presented to the 77th session of the National Assembly, where members unanimously expressed regret over (and opposition to) the draft and repeatedly requested that King Jigme withdraw the proposal. Following a further earnest plea by the King, however, a key draft provision that a confidence vote regarding the monarch should only be placed on the agenda of an assembly session if a minimum of 50% of the districts requested it, was amended to allow the initiative if supported by at least one-third of the assembly members. The 77th session also agreed that ministers should serve a maximum of two consecutive five-year terms.

At the 11th SAARC summit, held in Kathmandu in January 2002, the incumbent Chairman of the Council, Lyonpo Khandu Wangchuck, was referred to as 'Prime Minister' of Bhutan, a title that subsequently became accepted usage. In accordance with a decree issued by King Jigme in September 2001, a committee to draft a written constitution for Bhutan was inaugurated in late November and began functioning at the end of the year. The 39-member committee was chaired by the Chief Justice and included the Chairman and members of the Royal Advisory Council, five government representatives, the Speaker of the National Assembly, representatives from each of the 20 local districts and two lawyers from the High Court. It was agreed that, on completion, the draft would be subjected to extensive public comment and review before being presented to the Assembly for formal approval. In December 2002 the preliminary draft of the constitution was presented by the committee to King Jigme; the King subsequently referred the draft to the Prime Minister for further scrutiny, envisaging widespread public debate. However, by mid-2003 two further drafts had only been studied by the committee, King and Council of Ministers. In November 2004 King Jigme presented a fourth draft of the proposed constitution to the Council of Ministers for discussion; the draft was made available for public review in early 2005. Further reform of the National Assembly and the Royal Advisory Council was expected to continue alongside constitutional discussions.

The creation of four new ministerial positions was announced in June 2003, bringing the total number of ministers to 10. The former Ministry of Health and Education was divided into two ministries and the erstwhile Ministry of Communications was converted into the Ministry of Information and Communications and the Ministry of Works and Human Settlements. The Ministry of Labour and Human Resources was also created, incorporating the Central Statistical Office, the National Technical Training Authority and, amongst others, the Department of Employment and Labour. Under the government reorganization, the Ministry of Finance was to include the Planning Commission Secretariat; the Ministry of Agriculture was instructed to take over the land records and survey departments; and the Ministry of Education was to incorporate the UNESCO national commission and Dzongkha Development Commission. The Ministry of Home Affairs absorbed the National Commission of Cultural Affairs to become the Ministry of Home and Cultural Affairs. Subsequently, the six retiring ministers were reconfirmed in office and four new ministers were elected by the National Assembly. In August 2004 Minister of Trade and Industry Lyonpo Yeshey Zimba was appointed Chairman of the Council of Ministers. In October the Crown Prince, Dasho Jigme Khesar Namgyal, was formally installed as the Chhoetse Penlop (heir to the throne) at a ceremony held at the Trongsa Dzong Buddhist monastery. In December a ban on sales of tobacco throughout the kingdom came into effect, making Bhutan the first country in the world completely to prohibit the substance.

The activities of the militant 'anti-nationals' were unanimously condemned at the 76th session of the National Assembly in mid-1998, but the most pressing security issue was by then judged to be the perceived threat from the presence of Assamese tribal (Bodo) and Maoist (United Liberation Front of Assam—ULFA) militants, who had established military training bases in the jungle border regions of south-eastern Bhutan. Particular concern was expressed regarding the Indian military incursions into Bhutanese territory in an attempt to expel the militants. In mid-1999 the Minister of Home Affairs reported that talks with ULFA leaders (in November 1998 and May 1999) had elicited the response that members of the ULFA had been forced to enter Bhutanese territory in 1992, but that they were not ready to leave Bhutan for at least another 18 months. They asserted that they were determined to fight until independence for Assam was achieved, but offered to reduce their military presence in Bhutan. The Government of Bhutan reiterated to the ULFA leadership that its concern was at the very presence of any number of armed militants on Bhutanese soil. After detailed discussion, assembly members decided that all supplies of food and other essentials to the ULFA and National Democratic Front of Bodoland (NDFB) must be stopped, that any Bhutanese

who assisted the militants should be punished according to the National Security Act and that discussions should continue with the ULFA to seek a peaceful withdrawal of these forces from Bhutan. At the 78th session of the National Assembly in July 2000, members adopted a resolution stating that the problem should be solved through peaceful means, but that if negotiations failed military force should be used to evict the insurgents from Bhutanese territory. Supplies of rations had already been halted, and the police had taken action against Bhutanese citizens found to be helping the militants. Some groups of militants began to return to India. However, most ULFA and Bodo militants, who had hitherto refrained from carrying out violent activities in Bhutan, were angered by the decision. In December some 13 people were killed when members of the Bodo Liberation Tigers attacked a convoy of Bhutanese vehicles on the Bhutan–India border. The act was perceived as a warning to the Bhutanese Government not to shelter ULFA and NDFB militants. The Indian Government subsequently agreed to provide a military escort for Bhutanese vehicles travelling to Assam.

In mid-2001 the Minister of Home Affairs, addressing the 79th session of the National Assembly, reported that negotiations had been held with leaders of the NDFB in October 2000 and May 2001. During the talks NDFB leaders had responded to a demand for the removal of their camps by declaring their intention to leave Bhutan, but would not commit themselves to a deadline. Following three days of discussions in June, representatives of the ULFA agreed to seven points, including the removal of four of the nine military camps in Bhutan by December 2001 and the reduction in strength of the cadres in the remaining camps; further meetings were planned in order to find a solution to the issue of the remaining five camps. Members of the National Assembly were informed of the Government's preparations in the event of armed conflict with the militants: security had been strengthened, funds had been reserved for fuel supplies and medical support services, and contingency plans had been made to ensure the continued operation of the communications and transport systems. In addition, supplies of grains and other essential foods, sufficient to last for three to six months, were stored in towns throughout Bhutan. Disappointment and concern were expressed at the low level of volunteer recruitment. Districts were asked to send lists of volunteers to army headquarters; however, it was reported in mid-2002 that of the 1,410 men who had reported for training, only 24 wished to join the militia. Nevertheless, in mid-2003 members of the National Assembly were informed that some 4,558 persons had since volunteered and, of these, 667 volunteers (including 15 women) had been selected for a two-month training programme from mid-July.

On 31 December 2001 the army visited the four designated ULFA training camps and confirmed that these had been abandoned. Initially, however, the whereabouts of their militants was unknown. It was not possible immediately to ascertain whether the ULFA units had managed to leave Bhutan and, evading Indian military forces in Assam, reach their presumed goals of Bangladesh and Myanmar. At the same time there were concerns that the militants had repositioned their camps elsewhere in Bhutan. At the 80th session of the National Assembly in mid-2002 the Minister of Home Affairs confirmed that the ULFA had closed down a military training centre and three camps. The ULFA, however, had opened a new camp on a mountain ridge above the main Samdrup Jongkhar–Trashigang highway, raising the total number of camps remaining in Bhutan to six. In the mean time, the NDFB had three main camps and four mobile camps between Lhamoizingkha and Daifam. The Minister of Home Affairs also reported that the Government had only recently become aware that the Indian militant Kamtapur Liberation Organization (KLO) had established camps in Bhangtar dungkhag and near Piping in Lhamoizingkha dungkhag. The KLO armed militants were Rajbansi tribals of north Bengal, bordering Chhukha and Samtse dzongkhags, who were campaigning for separate statehood for the Kamtapuris.

The Minister for Home Affairs stressed that the presence of armed militants in Bhutan remained a grave threat. It appeared that no further negotiations could be held with the NDFB. The issue was further complicated by the presence of KLO militants. Following extensive discussions, the National Assembly endorsed three decisions proposed by the Council of Ministers: first, to hold negotiations with the Chairman and the military commander of the ULFA; second, the Government would not agree to participate in any more meetings on the reduction of ULFA camps but was prepared only to discuss the closure of the militants' main training camp and headquarters. Finally, if ULFA leaders refused to relocate their headquarters, there would be no option but to evict them physically. King Jigme informed the Assembly that it was important to hold talks with the ULFA and NDFB separately. Although the KLO was a new, relatively unknown group, the King warned that if the authorities had to resort to military action, they would have to deal with all three organizations. Little progress was achieved that year and in mid-2003 the Minister of Home Affairs, addressing the 81st session of the National Assembly, reported that the ULFA had increased the total number of camps inside Bhutan to eight, with an estimated 1,560 militants. The NDFB had eight camps, with about 740 militants. The KLO from West Bengal had three camps in Bhutan, with an estimated 430 militants in mid-2003. Following talks held in March with mid-level KLO leaders, the Government proposed entering dialogue with the Chairman of the organization in Thimphu before the 81st session of the Assembly commenced; the KLO, however, did not respond. At the Assembly session the Minister of Home Affairs stressed that military action would cause unimaginable suffering to the people, directly affecting more than 66,000 people in 304 villages in 10 districts. The Council of Ministers approved a contingency budget of up to Nu 2,000m. in the event of military action. In addition, two refugee camps and 12 transit camps were being prepared to accommodate the Bhutanese population that might be displaced. Many chimis (National Assembly members) proposed immediate military action. King Jigme informed the Assembly that India had given its assurance that the Indian army would not enter Bhutan without the permission of the Council of Ministers and the National Assembly. However, he observed, with reference to newspaper reports in India, that, as the Assembly had been holding similar discussions and passing similar resolutions every year since 1997 on the issue, it was natural that people in India would consider this discussion process as a ploy to avoid taking actions against the militants. He again stressed that, if the ULFA agreed to remove their central headquarters, other camps would subsequently close, and that, if the negotiations failed, military action would be aimed at all three militant groups. King Jigme visited India in mid-September 2003 to discuss mainly economic and defence issues. The Bhutanese Government subsequently made further efforts to seek a peaceful resolution of the issue of militants by directly addressing the three armed groups. The Government conducted negotiations with an ULFA delegation in October; however, the ULFA representatives insisted that their executive council would need to discuss the closure of the main camp (without which, it was stated, the others would not be viable) and that the leaders of the ULFA would visit in the first week of December to deliver their decision. According to a government statement on 13 December, however, the leaders had failed to appear. Negotiations with the NDFB in late November were also unsuccessful: the NDFB representatives stated that even if they removed their presence now, they would have to return and establish camps in other parts of Bhutan. The Ministry of Home Affairs thus concluded that 'given such an attitude, there is no scope for resolving the problem through dialogue', and it appeared that the Government would have to implement the decision of the 81st session of the National Assembly. Meanwhile, the KLO continued to fail to respond to any initiatives taken by the Bhutanese Government.

A 48-hour notice to leave Bhutan, issued to the militants by the Government on 13 December 2003, was unheeded. Therefore, on 15 December the Royal Bhutan Army simultaneously attacked most of the training camps, concentrating on the elimination of the general headquarters of the ULFA. By the end of the month the Government was able to report that all 30 camps had been captured and destroyed (14 of the camps belonged to the ULFA, the NDFB operated 11 camps and the KLO had five camps). Large quantities of armaments and ammunition were seized during the operation, including an anti-aircraft gun. In February 2004 the Chief of Staff of the Indian Army stated that the offensive had been highly successful, resulting in the deaths of at least 420 insurgents. In March it was reported that the Royal Bhutan Army had launched another offensive against the remaining militants. In September a bomb explosion in Gelephu killed two people and injured a further 27. Both those killed were of Indian nationality. The NDFB was believed to have been responsible for the attack. Meanwhile, 111 people in six courts in various locations

in Bhutan were convicted of aiding and abetting the NDFB, the ULFA and the KLO and sentenced to prison terms of various lengths. In November King Jigme paid an official visit to India, meeting with Prime Minister Manmohan Singh and various other Indian officials during his six-day stay.

Reflecting the increasing complexities of contemporary administration, the 77th Assembly also approved an unprecedented number of acts in mid-1999 to enhance the prevailing legal framework relating to telecommunications (providing for the creation of a state-owned public corporation, Bhutan Telecom, from the existing Telecommunications Division), the postal sector (enabling Bhutan Post to become an autonomous public-sector corporation), bankruptcy (giving a contemporary context for the rights and duties of borrowers and lenders), property (setting a legal framework for the management of loans, mortgages and related securities and financial services), legal deposit, municipalities (establishing legal authority for municipalities to enforce rules relating to urban development), and road safety. Further indications of the modernization of Bhutan were the inauguration of (limited) television and internet services in mid-1999, and the election of nine women to attend the 1999 session of the National Assembly (this number had increased to 11 and 16 by 2000 and 2001, respectively). Furthermore, the mid-2001 Assembly session for the first time elected a woman to the Royal Advisory Council. At the end of 2001 revised rules for geog (village block) and district development committees to create a legal basis for local autonomy in development issues (a fundamental issue under the Ninth Plan) were under discussion. The revisions were approved by the National Assembly at its 80th session in mid-2002. In accordance with the 1999 Municipal Act, residents of Thimphu elected members of the municipal council in late December 2001. The response to elections in late 2002, however, was indifferent. At the 81st session of the Assembly in mid-2003, a number of international treaties and conventions (including SAARC conventions) were ratified. The Royal Civil Service Commission (RCSC) was formally established as an autonomous body by the 81st National Assembly; the heads of the three branches of Government (the judiciary with 271 employees, the legislature with 39 employees; and the executive branch with 13,151 employees) would propose the members, functions, and responsibilities of the commission members, while appointment of the RCSC Chairman would be on the advice of the King. A National Judicial Commission was established in September, comprising the Chief Justice as Chairman, two justices of the High Court, the head of the Office of Legal Affairs and the Secretary of the National Assembly. The Commission's principal role was to professionalize further the appointment and tenure of judges in the court system. From November mobile cellular telephone services were provided for a limited number of towns and the major highways. It was expected that the services would be extended to all provincial capitals and much of the east–west highway by the end of 2005.

In mid-2001 the Council of Ministers decided to reduce the number of skilled expatriate workers from 50,000 to 25,000 with immediate effect, and aimed further to lower the number to 12,500 by the end of 2002. The decision was strongly criticized as unduly hasty by the Bhutan Chamber of Commerce and Industry, on the grounds that Bhutan's labour force was seasonal, owing to rural harvesting, and that the Bhutanese generally disparage manual labour. In October 2001 the Council of Ministers permitted the mining industry more time to reduce imported labour, but insisted that all firms and industries would have similar obligations from 2004.

Following the relaxation of many policies in the People's Republic of China from 1978, and anticipating improved relations between India and China, Bhutan moved cautiously to assert positions on regional and world affairs that took into account the views of India but were not necessarily identical to them. Discussions with China regarding the formal delineation and demarcation of Bhutan's northern border were begun in 1984, and substantive negotiations commenced in 1986. At the 12th round of talks, held in Beijing, China, in December 1998, the Ministers of Foreign Affairs of Bhutan and China signed an official interim agreement (the first agreement ever to be signed between the two countries) to maintain peace and tranquillity in the Bhutan–China border area and to observe the status quo of the border as it was prior to May 1959, pending a formal agreement on the border alignment. The disputed area, which was 1,128 sq km during the early rounds of bilateral talks, was subsequently reduced to 269 sq km in three areas in the north-west of Bhutan. Meanwhile, demarcation of Bhutan's southern border was agreed with India, except for small sectors in the middle zone (between Sarpang and Gelephu) and in the eastern zone of Arunachal Pradesh and the *de facto* China–India border. Following bilateral discussions in Thimphu in September 1999, the 14th round of 'satisfactory' border discussions took place in Beijing in November 2000, at which Bhutan extended the area of its claim beyond the boundary offered by the Chinese Government. The three sections under discussion were in the Doglam, Sinchulumba and Dramana areas. The negotiations continued in November 2001, following which the Chinese Deputy Minister of Foreign Affairs stated that the boundary question generally had been resolved, although relatively minor issues remained outstanding. The 16th round of talks was held in Beijing in October 2002 and was described by the Bhutanese delegation as 'yet another step towards a permanent solution'. Two delegations from Bhutan (a 'cultural' group and an 'officials' group) also visited China, in April and July 2001, respectively.

Bhutan became a member of the UN in 1971 and of the Non-aligned Movement in 1973.

Government

Bhutan's state system is a modified form of constitutional monarchy, hitherto without a formal, written constitutional document. In accordance with a decree by the King in September 2001, a 39-member special committee convened at the end of the year to draft a written constitution (see above). The system of government is unusual in that power is shared by the monarchy (assisted by the Royal Advisory Council—Lodoi Tsokde), the Council of Ministers (Lhengye Zhungtshog), the National Assembly (Tshogdu Chenmo) and the Head Abbot (Je Khempo) of Bhutan's 3,000–4,000 Buddhist monks.

Important institutional changes were introduced at the 76th session of the National Assembly in July 1998. In accordance with a royal decree, King Jigme relinquished his role as Head of Government (while remaining Head of State) in favour of an elected Council of Ministers, which was to enjoy full executive powers (although the King was to retain authority with regard to strategic security issues) and was to be headed by a Chairman (elected by ministers, on a rotational basis, for a one-year period), who would be Head of Government. The new Council of Ministers was subsequently elected by the National Assembly by secret ballot and the portfolios of the elected ministers were awarded by the King. The term in office of a minister was to be five years, after which he would be obliged to undergo a vote of confidence in the National Assembly. In 1999 the National Assembly agreed that ministers should serve a maximum of two consecutive five-year terms.

The National Assembly, which serves a three-year term, has 150 members, including 105 directly elected by adult suffrage; 10 seats in the Assembly are reserved for religious bodies, while the remainder are occupied by officials, ministers and members of the Royal Advisory Council.

There are 20 local districts (dzongkhags), each headed by a Dzongda (district officer, in charge of administration and law and order) and a Drangpon (magistrate, in charge of judicial matters, formerly known as a Thrimpon). Dzongdas are appointed by the Royal Civil Service Commission and are responsible to the Commission and the Ministry of Home Affairs. Drangpons are responsible to the High Court. The principal officers under the Dzongda are the Dzongda Wongma and the Dzongrab, responsible for locally administered development projects and fiscal matters, respectively. Seven of the districts are further sub-divided into sub-districts (dungkhags), and the lowest administrative unit in all districts is the block (geog) of several villages. There are Geog Yargye Tshogchungs (GYT—Geog Development Committees) in each of the geogs (of which there were 202 in January 2002). New rules governing GYTs and Dzongkhag Yargye Tshogchungs (DYTs—District Development Committees) were adopted by the National Assembly at its session in mid-2002, and in October secret ballots were held in all 202 geogs to re-elect gups (heads of geogs), who, under the new rules, were to chair the GYT meetings. Other GYT members number between eight and 31, depending on the size of the block, and include a mangmi (deputy gup) and tshogpas (village elders). Public meetings (zomdue) are held periodically, at the village level, to discuss local issues.

Defence

The strength of the Royal Bhutanese Army, which is under the direct command of the King, is officially said to number just over 6,000, and is based on voluntary recruitment. Army training facilities are provided by an Indian military training team. Although India is not directly responsible for the country's defence, the Indian Government has indicated that any act of aggression against Bhutan would be regarded as an act of aggression against India.

Economic Affairs

In 2003, according to estimates by the World Bank, Bhutan's gross national income (GNI), measured at average 2001–03 prices, was US $584m., equivalent to $660 per head. During 1990–2003, it was estimated, the population increased at an average annual rate of 2.9%, while gross domestic product (GDP) per head increased, in real terms, by an average of 2.6%. Overall GDP increased, in real terms, at an average annual rate of 6.5% in 1990–2003. Real GDP growth was estimated at 7.7% in 2002 and at 6.7% in 2003.

Agriculture (including livestock and forestry) contributed an estimated 32.7% of GDP in 2003. About 94% of the economically active population were employed in the sector in the early 2000s. The principal sources of revenue in the agricultural sector are apples, oranges and cardamom. Timber production is also important; about 60% of the total land area is covered by forest. Agricultural GDP increased, in real terms, at an average annual rate of 3.4% in 1990–2003; it increased by 2.6% in 2002 and by an estimated 4.1% in 2003.

Industry (including mining, manufacturing, utilities and construction) employed only about 0.9% of the labour force in 1990, but contributed an estimated 38.9% of GDP in 2003. Industrial GDP increased at an average annual rate of 9.8% in 1990–2003; growth in the sector was estimated at 17.9% in 2002 and at 7.3% in 2003.

Mining and quarrying contributed an estimated 1.9% of GDP in 2003. Calcium carbide is the principal mineral export (contributing 13.1% of total export revenue in 1998). Gypsum, coal, limestone, slate and dolomite are also mined. Mining GDP increased by an average rate of an estimated 10.8% per year in 1990–2003.

Manufacturing contributed an estimated 7.6% of GDP in 2003. The most important sector is cement production, and there is a calcium carbide plant and a ferro-alloy plant. Small-scale manufacturers produce, *inter alia*, textiles, soap, matches, candles and carpets. Manufacturing GDP increased at an average annual rate of an estimated 6.3% in 1990–2003; it increased by 0.3% in 2002 and by an estimated 10.1% in 2003.

Energy is derived principally from hydroelectric power. The Chhukha hydroelectric power (HEP) project, with a generating capacity of about 336 MW, provides electricity for domestic consumption and also for export to India. The Indian-financed Tala HEP project, scheduled for completion in 2005, is to have an installed capacity of 1,020 MW. Expenditure on the project (including the cost of repairing damage by floods in 2000) was expected to reach some Nu 36,000m. The Kurichhu power project, completed in 2003, exported 90% of its electricity to India in the same year. In 2002/03 exports of electricity provided 43.7% of total export revenue, while in 1999 the cost of imports of diesel oil and petroleum was equivalent to 10.4% of total import costs.

The services sector, which employed only about 3.4% of the labour force in 1981/82, contributed an estimated 28.4% of GDP in 2003. The tourism sector has become increasingly significant. In 2004 the total number of foreign visitors was 9,259, and in that year receipts from tourism totalled US $12.45m. The GDP of the services sector increased at an average annual rate of an estimated 6.5% in 1990–2003; sectoral GDP declined by 2.3% in 2002, before increasing by an estimated 7.8% in 2003.

In the financial year ending 30 June 2003, according to the Asian Development Bank (ADB), Bhutan recorded a visible trade deficit of US $75.9m., but there was a surplus of $61.3m. on the current account of the balance of payments. In 2002 the principal source of imports (an estimated 75.0%) was India, which was also the principal market for exports (an estimated 93.5%). The principal exports in 1999 were electricity, calcium carbide, cement and particle board. The principal imports in 1997 were telecommunications equipment, rice and diesel oil.

The 2004/05 budget envisaged a deficit of Nu 2,269.7m. (revenue Nu 11,352.0m., expenditure Nu 13,621.7m.). Bhutan's total external debt amounted to US $376.9m. at the end of 2002, all of which was long-term public debt. In that year the cost of debt-servicing was equivalent to 4.6% of the value of exports of goods and services. The average annual rate of inflation was 7.6% in 1990–2003. Consumer prices increased by an annual average of 2.5% in 2002 and 1.5% in 2003. By 2000 the rising level of unemployment was beginning to cause concern; an estimated 50,000 school-leavers were expected to join the labour force over the next five years.

Bhutan is a member of the UN Economic and Social Commission for Asia and the Pacific (ESCAP, see p. 31), of the Asian Development Bank (ADB, see p. 159), of the Colombo Plan (see p. 373) and of the South Asian Association for Regional Co-operation (SAARC, see p. 343), all of which seek to improve regional co-operation, particularly in economic development.

The Seventh Plan (1992–97) asserted seven main objectives: self-reliance, with emphasis on internal resource mobilization; sustainability, with emphasis on environmental protection; private-sector development; decentralization and popular participation; human resources' development; balanced development in all districts; and national security. The Eighth Plan (1997–2002) further refined the seven objectives of the Seventh Plan and explicitly added another: 'the preservation and promotion of cultural and traditional values'. The guiding goal was declared as the establishment of sustainability in development, while balancing achievements with the popular sense of contentment. Core areas were to be the further development of HEP, further industrialization, development of the infrastructure and social services, human resource development, and renewable natural resources. In June 2002 the Minister of Finance reported that actual expenditure on the Eighth Plan had reached around Nu 40,000m., some 33% more than the original planned outlay. Nevertheless, the overall resource deficit was limited to Nu 307.8m., owing to a substantial increase of Nu 7,580m. in domestic revenues to Nu 20,580m. The Ninth Plan, effective from July, consisted, unlike previous plans, of separate programmes and budget allocations for individual sectors and dzongkhags (local districts). The dzongkhag plans became geog-based through the devolution of powers to GYT members, under new rules approved by the National Assembly at its 80th session. The central Government, however, maintained financial control in order to ensure budgetary discipline. Expenditure during these five years was expected to reach Nu 70,000m. Domestic revenue, which was forecast to reach Nu 30,000m., and external resources, amounting to an estimated Nu 35,000m. (of which Nu 20,000m. was requested as assistance from India) were expected to cover the proposed outlay. GDP was forecast to grow at an average annual rate of 6%–7% in 2002–07.

The production of low-cost electricity by the Chhukha HEP project helped to stimulate growth in the industrial sector in the 1990s. It was hoped that, on completion, Bhutan's Kurichhu and Tala schemes would earn sufficient revenue for Bhutan to achieve economic self-reliance. In mid-2001 new legislation was enacted to reform the electricity supply industry and to develop and regulate the country's HEP resources; a Bhutan Electricity Authority was established. Multilateral investment in Bhutan's financial sector was agreed by the Government for the first time in September 1998, when the ADB and the US Citibank purchased shares in the Bhutan National Bank. Two important measures were implemented in 1999: a formal personal income tax (to be levied only on wealthier Bhutanese) was introduced, and the country was opened up to foreign investment (foreign investors were to be permitted up to 51% ownership in a joint venture), although the stock exchange remained closed to external investors. In 2004 Bhutan became a member of the BIMST–EC (Bay of Bengal Initiative for Multi-Sectoral Technical and Economic Co-operation) and a signatory to the group's free trade area. In the same year the country signed the Framework Agreement on the South Asia Free Trade Area (SAFTA), which was due to become operational on 1 January 2006. It was hoped that membership of these trade groupings would enable Bhutan to develop its export markets and transport infrastructure and to become more economically integrated into the region.

Education

Education is not compulsory. Pre-primary education usually lasts for one year. Primary education begins at six years of age and lasts for five years. Secondary education, beginning at the age of 12, lasts for a further five years, comprising three cycles. Virtually free education is available (nominal fees are demanded), but there are insufficient facilities to accommodate all school-age children. In order to accommodate additional children, community schools (established in 1989 as 'extended classrooms', but renamed as above in 1991) were set up as essentially one-teacher schools for basic primary classes, whence children were to be 'streamed' to other schools. In 1988 the total enrolment at primary schools was equivalent to an estimated 26% of children in the relevant age-group (31% of boys; 20% of girls), while the comparable ratio for secondary schools was only 5% (boys 7%; girls 2%). All schools are co-educational. English is the language of instruction and Dzongkha is a compulsory subject. Bhutan has no mission schools. By 2004 some 19 private schools had been established (the majority in Thimphu); these schools are under the supervision of the Department of Education. Owing to a shortage of qualified staff (despite the existence of two teacher-training institutes with a combined enrolment of 1,014 students in 2002), many Indian teachers are employed. In August 2004 the total number of enrolled pupils was 153,235, and the total number of teachers was 5,216. In 2004 there were more than 447 educational institutions under the supervision of the Department of Education, including 202 community schools, 90 primary schools, 77 lower secondary schools, 29 middle secondary schools, 16 higher secondary schools, one degree college and seven post-secondary institutions. A further three technical institutes are directly administered by the National Technical Training Authority. Some Bhutanese students were receiving higher education abroad. The 2001/02 budget allocated an estimated Nu 1,528.4m. (15.6% of total projected expenditure) to education. The 2004/05 budget allocated 16% of the total projected expenditure.

Public Holidays

2005 and 2006: The usual Buddhist holidays are observed, as well as three days for Thimphu Tsechu (September/October, in Thimphu district only), the Winter Solstice, the Birthday of the late third King Jigme Dorji Wangchuck (2 May), Coronation Day of HM Jigme Singye Wangchuck (2 June), the Anniversary of the death of the late third King (7 August), the Birthday of HM Jigme Singye Wangchuck (11–13 November), the movable Hindu feast of Dussehra and the National Day of Bhutan (17 December).

.

Weights and Measures

The metric system is in operation.

Statistical Survey

Source (unless otherwise stated): Royal Government of Bhutan, Thimphu.

Area and Population

AREA, POPULATION AND DENSITY

Area (sq km)	38,364*†
Population (official estimates)‡	
2002	670,299
2003	687,056
2004	704,233
Density (per sq km) in 2004	18.4

* 14,812 sq miles.

† In accordance with official adjustment recorded in Ninth Plan.

‡ These figures are much lower than former estimates. They are based on the 2000 estimate (638,000) and assume an annual population growth rate of 2.5%. It was previously reported that a census in 1969 enumerated a population of 931,514, and a 1980 census recorded a total of 1,165,000. On the basis of the latter figure, a mid-1988 population of 1,375,400 was projected. Other figures in this Survey are derived from the earlier, higher estimates of Bhutan's population.

POPULATION OF DISTRICTS*
(mid-1985 estimates, based on 1980 census)

Bumthang	23,842
Dagana	28,352
Gasa†	16,907
Gelephug	111,283
Ha	16,715
Lhuentse	39,635
Mongar	73,239
Paro	46,615
Pemagatshel	37,141
Punakha†	16,700
Samdrup Jongkhar	73,044
Samtse	172,109
Thimphu	58,660
Trashigang	177,718
Trongsa	26,017
Tsirang	108,807
Wangdue Phodrang	47,152
Zhemgang	44,516
Total population	**1,286,275**
Rural	1,119,452
Urban	167,823

* The above figures are approximate, and predate the creation of a new district, Chhukha, in 1987. Chhukha has an estimated total population of about 13,372 (based on the figure of 3,343 households, with an estimated average of four persons per household), who were formerly included in Samtse, Paro or Thimphu districts. The above figures also predate the creation of a further three new districts, Gasa (previously within Punakha), Trashi Yangtse (previously within Trashigang) and Sarpang (of which Gelephug—restyled as Gelephu in 1997—became a sub-district), in 1992.

† Gasa and Punakha were merged into a single district, which was to be known as Punakha, in 1987 (to be separated again in 1992).

PRINCIPAL TOWNS
(1997 estimates)

Thimphu (capital) .	45,000	Gelephu	12,500
Phuentsholing . .	45,000	Samdrup Jongkhar .	12,500

Source: Thomas Brinkhoff, *City Population* (internet www.citypopulation.de).

Mid-2003 (UN estimate, incl. suburbs): Thimphu 34,836 (Source: UN, *World Urbanization Prospects: The 2003 Revision*).

BIRTHS AND DEATHS
(UN estimates, annual averages)

	1985–90	1990–95	1995–2000
Birth rate (per 1,000)	40.9	38.4	36.0
Death rate (per 1,000)	14.4	11.4	9.8

Source: UN, *World Population Prospects: The 2002 Revision*.

Expectation of life (WHO estimates, years at birth): 61.3 (males 60.2; females 62.4) in 2002 (Source: WHO, *World Health Report*).

ECONOMICALLY ACTIVE POPULATION
(estimates, '000 persons, 1981/82)

Agriculture, etc.	613
Industry	6
Trade	9
Public services	22
Total	**650**

Mid-2003 (estimates in '000): Agriculture, etc. 1,023; Total labour force 1,093 (Source: FAO).

Health and Welfare

KEY INDICATORS

Total fertility rate (children per woman, 2002)	5.1
Under-5 mortality rate (per 1,000 live births, 2003) . . .	85
HIV/AIDS (% of persons aged 15–49, 2001)	<0.1
Physicians (per 1,000 head, 1995)	0.16
Hospital beds (per 1,000 head, 1994)	1.61
Health expenditure (2001): US $ per head (PPP)	64.0
Health expenditure (2001): % of GDP	3.9
Health expenditure (2001): public (% of total)	90.6
Access to water (% of persons, 2002)	62
Access to sanitation (% of persons, 2002)	70
Human Development Index (2002): ranking	134
Human Development Index (2002): value	0.536

For sources and definitions, see explanatory note on p. vi.

Agriculture

PRINCIPAL CROPS
('000 metric tons)

	2001	2002	2003
Rice (paddy)	40*	38	46†
Maize	60*	42	50
Other cereals*	15.3	13.1	12.0
Potatoes	27.0*	31.5	40.5
Other roots and tubers* . . .	21.8	21.8	21.8
Sugar cane*	12.8	12.8	12.8
Oranges	58.0*	37.3	36.3
Apples	6.0†	7.5	5.7
Nutmeg, mace and cardamom* . .	5.8	5.8	5.8
Other spices*	8.1	8.1	8.1

* FAO estimate(s).

† Unofficial figure.

Source: FAO.

LIVESTOCK
('000 head, year ending September)

	2001	2002	2003
Horses	28*	29*	28
Mules*	10	10	10
Asses*	18	18	18
Cattle	355*	355	372
Buffaloes	2*	2	2*
Pigs	41*	41	41
Sheep	26*	23	21*
Goats	38*	31	30*
Poultry	230*	231	220

* FAO estimate(s).

Source: FAO.

Yaks ('000 head): 35 in 1993; 39 in 1994 (provisional); 40 in 1995 (estimate) (Source: IMF, *Bhutan—Selected Issues* (February 1997)).

LIVESTOCK PRODUCTS
(FAO estimates, '000 metric tons)

	2001	2002	2003
Beef and veal	4.8	4.7	5.1
Pig meat	1.3	1.3	1.3
Cows' milk	41.1	41.1	41.1
Buffaloes' milk	0.4	0.3	0.3
Cattle hides (fresh)	1.0	1.0	1.1

Source: FAO.

Forestry

ROUNDWOOD REMOVALS
('000 cubic metres, excl. bark)

	2001	2002	2003
Sawlogs, veneer logs and logs for sleepers	64*	63	63
Other industrial wood*	70	70	70
Fuel wood*	4,284	4,348	4,413
Total	4,418*	4,480	4,546

* FAO estimate(s).

Source: FAO.

SAWNWOOD PRODUCTION
(FAO estimates, '000 cubic metres, incl. railway sleepers)

	1998	1999	2000
Coniferous (softwood)	12	15	21
Broadleaved (hardwood) . . .	6	7	10
Total	18	22	31

2001–03: Annual production as in 2000 (FAO estimates).

Source: FAO.

Fishing
(FAO estimates, metric tons, live weight)

	1999	2000	2001
Capture			
Freshwater fishes	300	300	300
Aquaculture			
Freshwater fishes	30	30	30
Total catch	330	330	330

2002 (FAO estimate, metric tons, live weight): Capture 300.

Source: FAO.

Mining
(estimates, metric tons, unless otherwise indicated)

	2001	2002	2003
Dolomite	265,000	270,000	270,000
Limestone	280,000	282,000	285,000
Gypsum	55,000	55,000	56,000
Coal	65,000	65,000	66,000
Marble chips (sq m)	4,000	4,000	4,000
Slate (sq m)	9,000	9,000	9,000
Quartzite	53,000	53,000	54,000
Talc	3,800	3,900	3,900

Source: US Geological Survey.

Iron ore (metric tons, official figure): 6,273 in 2000 (Source: Ministry of Trade and Industry).

Industry

GROSS SALES AND OUTPUT OF SELECTED INDUSTRIES
(million ngultrum)

	2001	2002	2003*
Penden Cement Authority . . .	763.9	814.3	896.1
Bhutan Ferro Alloys	579.0	643.2	658.1
Bhutan Fruit Products . . .	111.6	133.9	122.4
Army Welfare Project†	283.8	255.0	190.4
Bhutan Carbide and Chemicals .	675.9	707.5	703.4
Bhutan Board Products . . .	294.1	288.8	491.5
Eastern Bhutan Coal Company .	141.0	133.4	110.7
Druk Satair Corporation Ltd . .	98.3	106.0	118.4

* Provisional figures.
† Manufacturer of alcoholic beverages.

Source: Royal Monetary Authority of Bhutan.

Electric energy (million kWh, year ending 30 June): 1,972.2 in 1995/96; 1,838.4 in 1996/97; 1,800.0 in 1997/98 (Source: Department of Power, Royal Government of Bhutan).

Revenue from the Chhukha, Basochhu and Kurichhu Hydroelectric Projects (million ngultrum): 2,657.0 (Internal consumption 192.3, Exports 2,464.7) in 2002; 2,875.0 (Internal consumption 199.8; Exports 2,675.2) in 2003 (Source: Department of Power, Royal Government of Bhutan).

Finance

CURRENCY AND EXCHANGE RATES

Monetary Units
100 chetrum (Ch) = 1 ngultrum (Nu).

Sterling, Dollar and Euro Equivalents (31 December 2004)
£1 sterling = 88.170 ngultrum;
US $1 = 45.580 ngultrum;
€1 = 59.360 ngultrum;
1,000 ngultrum = £11.88 = $22.95 = €16.85.

Average Exchange Rate (ngultrum per US $)
2002   48.610
2003   46.583
2004   45.317

Note: The ngultrum is at par with the Indian rupee, which also circulates freely within Bhutan. The foregoing figures relate to the official rate of exchange, which is applicable to government-related transactions alone. Since April 1992 there has also been a market rate of exchange, which values foreign currencies approximately 20% higher than the official rate of exchange.

BUDGET
(million ngultrum, year ending 30 June)

Revenue	1999/2000	2000/01	2001/02*
Taxation	1,977.1	1,916.9	2,196.5
Taxes on income, profit and			
capital gains	1,056.7	1,257.6	1,232.9
Income tax	223.5	338.1	293.7
Corporation tax	833.2	919.5	939.2
Domestic taxes on goods and			
services	842.5	564.1	860.6
General sales, turnover or			
value-added tax	299.9	342.7	330.4
Excises	470.3	130.3	458.8
Taxes on international trade .	70.5	94.6	94.0
Import duties	57.9	78.3	78.3
Export duties	9.4	13.2	12.7
Other current revenue . . .	2,537.0	2,982.7	2,906.4
Entrepreneurial and property			
income	1,692.5	2,285.7	1,976.0
Administrative fees and charges,			
non-industrial and incidental			
sales	71.5	80.7	64.1
Other	773.0	616.3	866.3
Capital revenue	71.3	76.1	37.7
Grants	3,274.1	3,711.0	2,918.4
Total revenue and grants . .	7,859.5	8,686.7	8,059.0

Expenditure	1999/2000	2000/01	2001/02*
General public services . . .	1,787.0	2,466.6	2,149.9
Public order and safety . . .	453.6	474.6	486.1
Education	1,120.5	1,215.2	1,528.4
Health	768.3	804.0	1,000.2
Housing and community amenities	276.9	279.3	751.0
Recreational, cultural and religious			
affairs	69.5	113.9	172.2
Economic services	3,778.2	5,285.1	3,640.5
Fuel and energy	1,990.4	3,349.9	1,289.2
Agriculture, forestry, fishing and			
hunting	666.0	753.1	1,007.2
Mining and mineral resources,			
manufacturing and			
construction	42.7	24.2	28.9
Transportation and			
communication	1,029.9	1,084.0	1,216.8
Other purposes	80.2	77.8	85.4
Net lending	289.9	461.0	2.0
Total expenditure and net			
lending	8,624.1	11,177.5	9,815.7

* Provisional figures.

Source: IMF, *Government Finance Statistics Yearbook*.

2002/03 (million ngultrum, revised): *Revenue:* Domestic revenue 5,100.2; Other receipts 18.0; Grants 3,299.7; Project-tied loans 1,128.3; Total 9,546.3. *Expenditure:* Current expenditure 4,863.8; Capital expenditure 6,024.2; Net lending 73.6; Repayments 240.3; Total 11,201.9.

2003/04 (million ngultrum, revised): *Revenue:* Domestic revenue 5,948.2; Other receipts 947.6; Grants 1,824.0; Project-tied loans 2,632.2; Total 11,352.0. *Expenditure:* Current expenditure 5,569.1; Capital expenditure 6,332.1; Net lending 103.0; Repayments 475.4; Total 12,479.6.

2004/05 (million ngultrum, forecast): *Revenue:* Domestic revenue 5,801.7; Other receipts 1,175.2; Grants 1,894.0; Project-tied loans 2,481.1; Total 11,352.0. *Expenditure:* Current expenditure 5,968.7; Capital expenditure 7,158.3; Net lending 104.7; Repayments 390.0; Total 13,621.7.

FOREIGN EXCHANGE RESERVES
(at 30 June)

	2002	2003	2004
Indian rupee reserves (million			
Indian rupees)	3,663.9	3,330.2	4,362.8
Royal Monetary Authority . .	635.7	863.6	1,822.4
Bank of Bhutan	1,964.7	1,734.4	1,988.3
Bhutan National Bank . . .	1,063.6	732.1	552.1
Convertible currency reserves (US			
$ million)	240.5	301.7	287.2
Royal Monetary Authority* . .	202.6	244.4	248.9
Bank of Bhutan	18.4	39.6	31.3
Bhutan National Bank . . .	19.5	17.7	7.0

* Includes tranche position in the International Monetary Fund.

Source: Royal Monetary Authority of Bhutan.

MONEY SUPPLY
(million ngultrum at 31 December)

	2001	2002	2003
Currency outside banks* . . .	1,609.9	1,648.3	1,802.3
Demand deposits at the Bank of			
Bhutan	3,238.2	5,322.8	4,967.5
Total money (incl. others)† . .	16,312.7	20,252.8	20,233.9

* Including an estimate for Indian rupees.
† Including non-monetary deposits with the Royal Monetary Authority by financial institutions.

Source: Royal Monetary Authority of Bhutan.

COST OF LIVING
(Consumer Price Index at 31 December, excluding rent; base: 30 September 2003 = 100)

	2001	2002	2003
Food	98.0	99.9	101.4
Non-food items	94.4	97.0	102.3
All items	96.5	98.7	102.0*

* For 2003 the overall index was calculated on a different basis to previous years.

Source: National Statistical Bureau of the Planning Commission, Royal Government of Bhutan.

NATIONAL ACCOUNTS
(million ngultrum at current prices)

Expenditure on the Gross Domestic Product

	1998	1999	2000
Government final consumption			
expenditure	3,308	4,271	4,422
Private final consumption			
expenditure	9,322	10,067	11,329
Increase in stocks	45	108	49
Gross fixed capital formation . .	6,200	8,127	9,447
Total domestic expenditure .	18,875	22,573	25,247
Exports of goods and services . .	5,148	5,714	6,456
Less Imports of goods and services	7,686	9,164	10,004
GDP in purchasers' values . .	16,337	19,122	21,698

Source: IMF, *International Financial Statistics*.

Gross Domestic Product by Economic Activity

	2001*	2002*	2003†
Agriculture, forestry and livestock	8,471	9,371	10,595
Mining and quarrying	401	501	612
Manufacturing	1,973	2,038	2,445
Electricity	2,666	3,039	3,097
Construction	3,945	5,360	6,431
Trade, restaurants and hotels . .	1,627	1,579	1,768
Transport, storage and communications	2,232	2,329	2,772
Finance, insurance and real estate	1,601	1,801	2,089
Community, social and personal services	2,137	2,241	2,554
Sub-total	25,053	28,257	32,363
Less Imputed bank service charges	736	478	479
GDP at factor cost	24,317	27,779	31,884
GDP at constant 1980 factor cost	4,266	4,551	4,849

* Revised figures.
† Provisional figures.

Source: Royal Monetary Authority of Bhutan.

BALANCE OF PAYMENTS
(US $ million, year ending 30 June)

	2000/01	2001/02	2002/03
Merchandise exports f.o.b. . . .	99.5	103.6	112.8
Merchandise imports c.i.f. . . .	−196.3	−186.5	−188.6
Trade balance	−96.8	−82.9	−75.9
Services and transfers	88.8	76.7	137.1
Current balance	−8.0	−6.2	61.3
Grants and loans	30.8	59.0	94.5
Foreign direct investment . . .	—	2.1	2.5
Net errors and omissions . . .	−17.6	−29.2	−104.5
Overall balance	5.2	25.8	53.7

Source: Asian Development Bank, *Key Indicators of Developing Asian and Pacific Countries*.

OFFICIAL DEVELOPMENT ASSISTANCE
(US $ million)

	1998	1999	2000
Bilateral donors	39.8	52.1	33.3
Multilateral donors	16.0	14.7	20.0
Total	55.8	66.8	53.3
Grants	48.2	60.2	42.5
Loans	7.6	6.6	10.8
Per caput assistance (US $) . .	28.3	33.1	25.5

Source: UN, *Statistical Yearbook for Asia and the Pacific*.

External Trade

SELECTED COMMODITIES
(million ngultrum, provisional)

Imports c.i.f.	1995	1996	1997
Wood charcoal	n.a.	122.3	139.6
Telecommunications equipment .	n.a.	302.0	491.0
Beer	n.a.	66.0	86.3
Coal	n.a.	44.6	103.3
Diesel oil	136.1	138.8	163.2
Petroleum	64.0	67.4	73.0
Rice	217.3	209.1	215.3
Wheat	39.3	89.0	100.0
Vegetable fats and oils . . .	134.7	134.4	121.1
Cotton fabric	41.9	38.2	n.a.
Industrial machinery	142.0	77.5	54.3
Tyres for buses and trucks . .	37.5	34.5	n.a.
Iron and steel	115.4	109.6	117.0
Electricity	10.7	7.6	n.a.
Total (incl. others)	3,802.3	4,250.0	4,980.0

Exports f.o.b.	1995	1996	1997
Electricity	721.9	747.6	1,290.0
Calcium carbide	497.9	533.0	546.3
Cement	278.4	253.0	371.4
Particle board	329.1	286.0	329.0
Non-coniferous plywood . . .	32.8	2.2	n.a.
Sawn logs (hard)	71.8	79.1	78.1
Sawn timber (soft)	60.7	27.1	76.5
Cardamom	73.8	68.2	36.9
Wheat and flour	23.8	58.0	n.a.
Mixed fruit/vegetable juice . . .	119.5	86.7	7.8
Coal (bituminous)	n.a.	19.9	25.6
Rum	n.a.	65.0	58.8
Total (incl. others)	3,349.1	3,553.8	4,270.0

Exports (million ngultrum): *2001:* Electricity 2,072.0; Calcium carbide 571.3; Cement 413.0; Particle board 215.2. *2002:* Electricity 2,344.2; Calcium carbide 643.4; Cement 199.6; Particle board 120.7. *2003:* Electricity 2,603.5; Calcium carbide 520.7; Cement 356.4; Particle board 149.2 (Source: Asian Development Bank, *Key Indicators of Developing Asian and Pacific Countries*).

PRINCIPAL TRADING PARTNERS
(estimates, US $ million, year ending 30 June)

Imports c.i.f.	1998/99*	1999/2000	2000/01†
India	115.5	139.0	159.3
Other countries	46.8	46.0	56.0
Total	162.3	185.0	215.3

Exports f.o.b.	1998/99	1999/2000	2000/01†
India	98.2	108.0	106.0
Other countries	6.6	6.3	6.3
Total	104.8	114.3	112.3

* Revised figures.
† Preliminary estimates.

Source: Royal Monetary Authority of Bhutan.

Transport

ROAD TRAFFIC: At April 2003 there were 25,046 registered, roadworthy vehicles—10,574 light four-wheeled vehicles, 8,373 two-wheeled vehicles (motorcycles and scooters), 2,062 heavy vehicles (trucks, buses, bulldozers, etc.), 1,517 taxis and 730 others (Source: National Statistical Bureau, Ministry of Planning, Royal Government of Bhutan).

CIVIL AVIATION
(traffic on scheduled services)

	1999	2000	2001
Kilometres flown (million) . . .	1	1	1
Passengers carried ('000) . . .	31	34	35
Passenger-km (million)	41	47	47
Total ton-km (million)	4	4	4

Source: UN, *Statistical Yearbook*.

2002: Paying passengers 40,859; Revenue (million ngultrum, year ending 30 June) 393.

Source: National Statistical Bureau, Ministry of Planning, Royal Government of Bhutan.

Tourism

FOREIGN VISITORS BY COUNTRY OF ORIGIN*

	2001	2002	2003
Australia	138	214	165
Austria	128	92	152
France	287	192	288
Germany	414	346	496
Italy	192	177	331
Japan	1,038	892	952
Netherlands	180	197	176
Switzerland	170	164	177
Taiwan	44	40	90
United Kingdom	581	519	605
USA	2,149	1,913	1,806
Total (incl. others)	6,374	5,594	6,261

* Figures relate to tourists paying in convertible currency.

Receipts (US $ million): 9.2 in 2001; 7.4 in 2002; 8.3 in 2003.

Sources: Department of Tourism; World Tourism Organization.

Government hotel rooms: 560 in 1996; 560 in 1997; 560 in 1998 (provisional) (Source: IMF, *Bhutan—Statistical Annex* (July 1999)).

Communications Media

	2001	2002	2003
Telephone ('000 main lines in use)	17.6	19.6	25.2
Mobile cellular telephones ('000 subscribers)	—	—	8
Personal computers ('000 in use)	7	10	10
Internet users ('000)	5	10	15

Radio receivers ('000 in use): 37 in 1997.

Television receivers ('000 in use): 13.5 in 2000.

Facsimile machines ('000 in use): 1.5 in 1998.

Sources: International Telecommunication Union; UNESCO, *Statistical Yearbook*.

Education

(August 2004)

	Institutions	Teachers	Students
Community primary schools	202	707	24,533
Primary schools	90	752	26,508
Lower secondary schools	77	1,461	48,089
Middle secondary schools	29	729	20,775
Higher secondary schools	16	440	10,865
Private schools	19	287	5,218
Institutes	14	321	3,381
Non-formal education (NFE) centres	455	519	13,866

Source: Ministry of Education, Thimphu.

Adult literacy rate (UNESCO estimates): 42.2% (males 56.3%; females 28.2%) in 1995 (Source: UNESCO, *Statistical Yearbook*).

Directory

The Constitution

The Kingdom of Bhutan has no formal constitution. However, the state system is a modified form of constitutional monarchy. Written rules, which are changed periodically, govern procedures for the election of members of the Council of Ministers, the Royal Advisory Council and the Legislature, and define the duties and powers of those bodies. A special committee was convened in late 2001 to prepare a draft written constitution (Tsa-Thrim). A completed first draft was formally presented to King Jigme Singye Wangchuck in December 2002, who then passed the draft to the Prime Minister. Another draft was submitted to King Jigme in mid-2003 for further revisions. In November 2004 King Jigme submitted a 34-article fourth draft to the Council of Ministers; the document was made public for review and comment in March 2005. Subsidiary legislation will be enacted before a final draft is submitted to the National Assembly for discussion and formal approval.

The Government

HEAD OF STATE

Druk Gyalpo ('Dragon King'): HM JIGME SINGYE WANGCHUCK (succeeded to the throne in July 1972).

LODOI ZHUNGTSHOG
(Royal Advisory Council)
(April 2005)

The Royal Advisory Council (Lodoi Tsokde), established in 1965, comprises nine members: two monks representing the Central Monk Body (Dratshang) and District Monastic Body (Rabdeys), respectively, six people's representatives, and a Chairman (Kalyon) nominated by the King. Each geog (group of villages, known also as a block) within a dzongkhag (district) selects one representative, from whom the respective Dzongkhag Yargye Tshogchungs (DYTs—District Development Committees) each agree on one nomination to be forwarded to the National Assembly (Tshogdu Chenmo). From

these 20 nominees, the National Assembly, in turn, elects six persons to serve on the Royal Advisory Council as people's representatives for the whole country. The Council's principal task is to advise the Chairman of the Council of Ministers (Lhengye Zhungtshog), as head of government, and to supervise all aspects of administration. The Council is in permanent session, virtually as a government department, and acts, on a daily basis, as the *de facto* Standing Committee of the National Assembly. Representatives of the monastic bodies serve for one year, representatives of the people for three years, and the duration of the Chairman's term of office is at the discretion of the King. Representatives may be re-elected, but not for consecutive terms; they are all full members of the Council of Ministers.

Chairman (Kalyon): Dasho RINZIN GYELTSHEN.

Councillors: Dasho YESHEY DORJI*, Dasho D. B. SINCHAURI*, Dasho SANGAY WANGDI*, Dasho SIGAY DORJI*, Dasho ZEKO DORJI*, Dasho JANGCHUB DORJI*, Lopen TSHERING PENJOR†, Lopen RINZIN†.
* From November 2004 to November 2007.
† From November 2004 to November 2005.

LHENGYE ZHUNGTSHOG
(Council of Ministers)
(April 2005)

Prime Minister and Chairman (August 2004–July 2005) and Minister of Trade and Industry: Lyonpo YESHEY ZIMBA.

Minister of Agriculture: Lyonpo SANGYE NGEDUP DORJI.

Minister of Education: Lyonpo THINLEY GYAMTSHO.

Minister of Finance: Lyonpo WANGDI NORBU.

Minister of Foreign Affairs: Lyonpo KHANDU WANGCHUCK.

Minister of Health: Lyonpo JIGME SINGAY.

Minister of Home and Cultural Affairs: Lyonpo JIGMI YOZER THINLEY.

Minister of Information and Communications: Lyonpo LEKI DORJI.

Minister of Labour and Human Resources: Lyonpo UGYEN TSHERING.

Minister of Works and Human Settlements: Lyonpo KINZANG DORJI.

Cabinet Secretary: Dasho SHERUB TENZIN.

All members of the Royal Advisory Council are also members of the Council of Ministers.

MINISTRIES AND OTHER MAJOR GOVERNMENT BODIES

Ministry of Agriculture: POB 252, Thimphu; tel. (2) 322129; fax (2) 323153; internet www.moa.gov.bt.

Ministry of Education: Thimphu; tel. (2) 323825; fax (2) 326424; internet www.education.gov.bt.

Ministry of Finance: Tashichhodzong, POB 117, Thimphu; tel. (2) 322223; fax (2) 323154; internet www.mof.gov.bt; internet www.dop .gov.bt (Department of Planning).

Ministry of Foreign Affairs: Convention Centre, POB 103, Thimphu; tel. (2) 322781; fax (2) 322079.

Ministry of Health: Tashichhodzong, POB 726, Thimphu; tel. (2) 322502; fax (2) 323113; internet www.health.gov.bt.

Ministry of Home and Cultural Affairs: Tashichhodzong, POB 133, Thimphu; tel. (2) 322301; fax (2) 322214; internet www.ctf.gov .bt (Cultural Trust Fund); internet www.library.gov.bt (National Library).

Ministry of Information and Communications: Division of Information Technology, Old Bhutan Hotel, Thimphu; tel. (2) 322567; fax (2) 328154; e-mail dit@druknet.bt; internet www.dit.gov .bt.

Ministry of Labour and Human Resources: Old Protocol Office, Thimphu; tel. (2) 327125; fax (2) 327126; e-mail eboard@druknet.bt.

Ministry of Trade and Industry: Tashichhodzong, POB 141, Thimphu; tel. (2) 322211; fax (2) 323617; internet www.mti.gov.bt; internet www.tourism.gov.bt (Department of Tourism).

Ministry of Works and Human Settlements: Thimphu; tel. (2) 327451; fax (2) 323144.

National Environment Commission: Thimphu, POB 466; tel. (2) 323384; fax (2) 323385; e-mail rnrec@druknet.bt; internet www.nec .gov.bt; Hon. Dep. Minister Dasho NADO RINCHEN; Dir SONAM YANGLEY.

Office of the Royal Advisory Council: Tashichhodzong, POB 200, Thimphu; tel. (2) 312339; fax (2) 325343.

Royal Audit Authority: Thimphu; tel. (2) 322111; fax (2) 323491; internet www.raa.gov.bt; Auditor-Gen. Dasho KUNZANG WANGDI.

Cabinet Secretariat: Tashichhodzong, Thimphu; tel. (2) 321437; fax (2) 321438; e-mail cabinet@druknet.bt.

Legislature

TSHOGDU CHENMO

A National Assembly (Tshogdu Chenmo) was established in 1953. The Assembly has a three-year term and meets (in recent years) at least once a year (usually in June–July). However, to cope better with an increasing workload, twice-yearly sessions were resumed from 2005. The size of the membership is based, in part, on the population of the districts; although the size is, in principle, subject to periodic revision, in practice the basis for popular representation has remained unchanged since 1953. In 2005 the Assembly had 151 members, including the Speaker. Of this number, 100 were elected by direct popular consensus in the districts (formal voting is used, however, in the event of a deadlock); 10 of the 20 districts elected new public members (chimis) in November 2001, to replace those whose term of office had expired. (Not all of the chimis are elected simultaneously; there are, therefore, overlaps in tenure.) Six were members of the Royal Advisory Council (RAC), elected by secret ballot; the Chairman (Kalyon) of the RAC also sits in the Assembly. Ten seats were reserved for representatives of the Central and District Monk Bodies (of whom two sit as members of the RAC), one was reserved for a representative of industry (elected by the Bhutan Chamber of Commerce and Industry), and one place for a representative of the Thimphu municipality. The remainder were occupied by officials (including senior department secretaries, a representative of the Royal Bhutan Army and eight of the 20 Dzongdas or district officers) selected by the King in conjunction with the National Assembly Secretariat. The Assembly elects its own Speaker from among its members, for a three-year (renewable) term. The Speaker's Act of 2004 extended the length of a Speaker's term in office to five years (extendable to a second term) and ordered that the Speaker would, henceforth, be selected only by the elected members of the Assembly. Under the new agreement, the Speaker must also

be fluent in both Dzongkha and English and will have the status of cabinet minister. The Assembly enacts laws, advises on constitutional and political matters and debates all important issues. There is provision for a secret ballot on controversial issues, but, in practice, decisions are usually reached by consensus (the Speaker's Act of 2004 was voted on by secret ballot). Ministers (upon nomination by the King) and the six public members of the RAC (nominated by the districts) are chosen by the entire Assembly in a secret ballot. Both the RAC and the Council of Ministers are responsible to the Assembly.

Speaker: Dasho UGEN DORJE.

Political Organizations

Political parties are banned in Bhutan, in accordance with long-standing legislation. There are, however, a small number of anti-Government organizations, composed principally of Nepali-speaking former residents of Bhutan, which are based in Kathmandu, Nepal and New Delhi, India.

Bhutan Communist Party (Marxist-Leninist-Maoist): Nepal; f. 2003; Gen. Sec. VIKALPA.

Bhutan Gorkha Liberation Front: f. 2003; based in southern Bhutan.

Bhutan Gurkha National Liberation Front (BGNLF): Nepal; f. 1994; Sec.-Gen. R. P. SUBBA.

Bhutan National Democratic Party (BNDP): POB 3334, Kathmandu, Nepal; tel. 525682; f. 1992; also has offices in Delhi and Varanasi, India, and in Thapa, Nepal; Pres. R. B. BASNET; Gen. Secs Dr HARI P. ADHIKARI (Organization), D. N. S. DHAKAL (Planning and External Affairs).

Bhutan People's Party (BPP): Kathmandu, Nepal; f. 1990 as a successor to the People's Forum on Democratic Rights (f. 1989); advocates unconditional release of all political prisoners, judicial reform, freedom of religious practices, linguistic freedom, freedom of press, speech and expression, and equal rights for all ethnic groups; Pres. (vacant); Gen. Sec. R. K. CHETTRI.

Druk National Congress (DNC): D-18, 19th Floor, Amar Colony, Lajpat Nagar IV, New Delhi 110 024; tel. (11) 26276586; fax (11) 26291494; e-mail dnc@ndf.vsnl.net.in; internet www.bhutanandnc .com; f. 1992; claims to represent 'all the oppressed people of Bhutan'; Pres. 'RONGTHONG' KINLEY DORJI; Gen. Sec. RINJIN DORJI.

Human Rights Organization of Bhutan (HUROB): Patan Dhoka, POB 172, Lalitpur, Kathmandu, Nepal; tel. 525046; fax 526038; f. 1991; documents alleged human rights violations in Bhutan and co-ordinates welfare activities in eight refugee camps in Nepal for ethnic Nepalese claiming to be from Bhutan; Chair. S. B. SUBBA; Gen. Sec. OM DHUNGEL.

United Liberation People's Front: f. 1990; Leader BALARAM POUDYAL.

Diplomatic Representation

EMBASSIES IN BHUTAN

Bangladesh: POB 178, Upper Choubachu, Thimphu; tel. (2) 322539; fax (2) 322629; e-mail bdoot@druknet.bt; Ambassador MOHAMMAD ENAMUL KABIR.

India: India House, Lungtenzampa, Thimphu; tel. (2) 323162; fax (2) 323195; internet www.eoithimphu.org; Ambassador K. S. JASROTIA.

Judicial System

Bhutan has Civil and Criminal Codes, which are based on those laid down by the Shabdrung Ngawang Namgyal in the 17th century. An independent judicial authority was established in 1961, but law was mostly administered at the district level until 1968, when the High Court was set up. Existing laws were consolidated in 1982, although annual or biennial conferences of Drangpons (previously styled Thrimpons) are held to keep abreast of changing circumstances and to recommend (in the first instance, to the King) amendments to existing laws. Most legislation is sent by the Council of Ministers to the National Assembly for approval and enactment. A substantially revised Civil and Criminal Procedure Code was endorsed by the 79th National Assembly session in July 2001. In accordance with the law, a National Judicial Commission was established in September 2003. The principal role of the judicial board was to professionalize further the appointment and tenure of judges in the court system; the Chief

Justice was to preside over the Commission. A revised Penal Code was presented to the National Assembly in mid-2004.

Appeal Court: The Supreme Court of Appeal is the King.

High Court
(Thrimkhang Gongma)

Thimphu; tel. (2) 322344; fax (2) 322921.

Established 1968 to review appeals from Lower Courts, although some cases are heard at the first instance. The Full Bench is presided over by the Chief Justice. There are normally seven other judges (Drangpons), who are appointed by the King on the recommendation of the Chief Justice and who serve until their superannuation. Three judges form a quorum. Assistance to defendants is available through jabmis (certificated pleaders), whose responsibilities were formalized by the Jabmi Act in mid-2003. The operation of the legal system and proposed amendments are considered by regular meetings of all the judges and Drangpons (usually annually, or at least once every two years). Under the mid-1998 grant of governance to an elected Council of Ministers and pending the adoption of detailed regulations, proposed amendments are expected to be submitted to the Council of Ministers for consideration. Major changes to structure, administration and personnel were implemented from mid-2001.

Chief Justice: Lyonpo SONAM TOBGYE.

Judges (Drangpons) of the High Court: Dasho THINLEY YOEZER, Dasho PASANG TOBGYE, Dasho KARMA D. SHERPA, Dasho PHUB DORJI.

District Courts (Dzongkhag Thrimkhang): Each district has a court, headed by the drangpon (magistrate), which tries most cases. Appeals are made to the High Court, and less serious civil disputes may be settled by a gup or mandal (village headman) through written undertakings (genja) by the parties concerned.

All citizens have the right to make informal appeal for redress of grievances directly to the King, through the office of the gyalpoi zimpon (court chamberlain).

Office of Legal Affairs: tel. (2) 326889; fax (2) 324606; consists of a prosecution division, with civil and criminal sections, to indict offenders on behalf of the Government; and a legal services division, to assist in the drafting of laws and acts, advance Bhutan's interest internationally in accordance with public international laws, develop the legal profession, and create public awareness of laws and acts; Dir Dasho KUENLAY TSHERING.

Religion

The state religion is Mahayana Buddhism, but the southern Bhutanese are predominantly followers of Hinduism. Buddhism was introduced into Bhutan in the eighth century AD by the Indian saint Padmasambhava, known in Bhutan as Guru Rimpoche. In the 13th century Phajo Drugom Shigpo made the Drukpa school of Kagyupa Buddhism pre-eminent in Bhutan, and this sect is still supported by the dominant ethnic group, the Drukpas. The main monastic group, the Central Monastic Body (comprising about 1,600 monks in Thimphu and Punakha), led by an elected Head Abbot (Je Khenpo), is directly supported by the State and spends six months of the year at Tashichhodzong and at Punakha, respectively. A further 2,120 monks, who are members of the District Monastic Bodies, are sustained by the lay population. The Council for Ecclesiastical Affairs oversees all religious bodies. Monasteries (Gompas) and shrines (Lhakhangs) are numerous. Religious proselytizing, in any form, is illegal.

Council for Ecclesiastical Affairs (Dratshang Lhentshog): POB 254, Thimphu; tel. (2) 322754; fax (2) 323867; e-mail dratsang@ druknet.bt; f. 1984; replacing the Central Board for Monastic Studies, to oversee the national memorial chorten and all Buddhist meditational centres and schools of Buddhist studies, as well as the Central and District Monastic Bodies; daily affairs of the Council are run by the Central Monastic Secretariat; Chair. His Holiness the 70th Je Khenpo Trulku JIGME CHOEDRA; Sec. Dasho SANGAY WANGCHUCK; Dep. Sec. NGAWANG PHUNTSHO.

The Press

The Bhutan Review: Patan Dhoka, POB 172, Lalitpur, Kathmandu, Nepal; tel. 525046; fax 523819; f. 1993; monthly organ of the Human Rights Organization of Bhutan (HUROB); opposed to existing government policies.

Kuensel Corporation: POB 204, Thimphu; tel. (2) 322483; fax (2) 322975; internet www.kuenselonline.com; f. 1965 as a weekly govt bulletin; reorg. as a national weekly newspaper in 1986; became autonomous corporation in 1992 (previously under Dept of Informa-

tion), incorporating former Royal Government Press; in English, Dzongkha and Nepali; Man. Dir and Editor-in-Chief KINLEY DORJI; Editors TIKA RAM SHARMA (Nepali), PHUNTSO WANGDI (English), CHOKI DHENDUP (Dzongkha); circ. 280 (Nepali), 12,875 (English), 4,280 (Dzongkha).

Broadcasting and Communications

TELECOMMUNICATIONS

Bhutan Communications Authority: POB 1072, Thimphu; tel. (2) 321506; fax (2) 326909; e-mail bca@druknet.bt; internet www.bta .gov.bt; f. 2000; telecommunications regulatory body.

Bhutan Telecom Ltd: POB 134, Thimphu; tel. (2) 322678; fax (2) 324312; e-mail info@telecom.net.bt; internet www.telecom.net.bt; f. 2000; state-owned public corpn; regulation authority; agency for satellite telephones; Chair. Lyonpo LEKI DORJI; Exec. Dir Dasho SANGEY TENZING; Man. Dir THINLEY DORJI.

B-Mobile: c/o Bhutan Telecom, Drophenlam, POB 134, Thimphu; tel. (2) 320194; fax (2) 320193; e-mail mkto@telecom.net.bt; internet www.b-mobile.net.bt; f. 2002; offered mobile cellular telephone services from Nov. 2003; covered Thimphu and most of Paro by mid-2004; coverage to extend to all district centres and much of the East–West Highway by the end of 2005; subsidiary of Bhutan Telecom Ltd.

DrukNet: Bhutan Telecom, 2/28 Drophenlam, POB 134, Thimphu; tel. (2) 326998; fax (2) 328160; e-mail info@druknet.bt; internet www .druknet.bt; f. 1999; internet service provider; Head GANGA SHARMA.

BROADCASTING

Radio

In 1994 there were 52 radio stations for administrative communications. Of these, 34 were for internal communications (to which the public had access), and three were external stations serving Bhutan House at Kalimpong and the Bhutanese diplomatic missions in India and Bangladesh.

BBS Corporation (Bhutan Broadcasting Services): POB 101, Thimphu; tel. (2) 323071; fax (2) 323073; e-mail bbs@bbs.com.bt; internet www.bbs.com.bt; f. 1973 as Radio National Youth Association of Bhutan (NYAB); became autonomous corporation in 1992 (previously under Dept of Information); short-wave radio station broadcasting daily in Dzongkha, Sharchopkha, Nepali (Lhotsamkha) and English; a daily FM programme (for Thimphu only) began in 1987; simultaneous broadcasting in FM for western Bhutan and parts of central and southern Bhutan began in 2000; a one-hour daily television service for Thimphu was introduced in mid-1999 and later increased to two hours daily; Chair. Lyonpo LEKI DORJI; Exec. Dir KINGA SINGYE.

Television

In June 1999 the BBS Corporation started operating a television service (in Dzongkha and English) in Thimphu; the service was gradually to be expanded throughout the country. Broadcasts are limited to a few hours a day and consist of national news and documentaries about Bhutan. By March 2002, according to official figures, each of the two cable television operators was providing 45 channels.

Finance

(cap. = capital; auth. = authorized; p.u. = paid up; res = reserves; dep. = deposits; m. = million; brs = branches; amounts in ngultrum)

BANKING

Central Bank

Royal Monetary Authority (RMA): POB 154, Thimphu; tel. (2) 323111; fax (2) 322847; e-mail rmarsd@rma.org.bt; internet www .rma.org.bt; f. 1982; bank of issue; frames and implements official monetary policy, co-ordinates the activities of financial institutions and holds foreign-exchange deposits on behalf of the Govt; cap. 4.4m. (June 2004); Chair. Lyonpo WANGDI NORBU; Man. Dir DAW TENZIN.

Commercial Banks

Bank of Bhutan: POB 75, Phuentsholing; tel. (5) 252225; fax (5) 252641; e-mail bobho1@druknet.bt; f. 1968; 20% owned by the State Bank of India and 80% by the Govt of Bhutan; wholly managed by Govt of Bhutan from 1997; cap. 100m., res 817.3m., dep. 10,019.5m. (Dec. 2003); Dirs nominated by the Bhutan Govt: Chair. Lyonpo

WANGDI NORBU; Dirs Dasho KARMA DORJI, Dasho NIMA WANGDI, TSHERING DORJI; Dir nominated by the State Bank of India SUNIL PANT; 26 brs and 2 extension counters.

Bhutan National Bank (BNB): POB 439, Thimphu; tel. (2) 322767; fax (2) 323895; e-mail bnbpling@druknet.bt; internet www .bnb.com.bt; f. 1996; Bhutan's second commercial bank; partially privatized in 1998; 27.2% owned by Govt and 20.1% by Asian Development Bank; auth. cap. 200m., cap. p.u. 59.5m., res 269.0m., dep. 4,522.2m. (2002); Chair. Lyonpo KHANDU WANGCHUCK; Man. Dir KIPCHU TSHERING; 4 brs.

Development Bank

Bhutan Development Finance Corporation (BDFC): POB 256, Thimphu; tel. (2) 322579; fax (2) 323428; e-mail bdfc@druknet.bt; f. 1988; provides industrial loans and short- and medium-term agricultural loans; cap. p.u. 100m., loans 1,114m. (2003); Chair. Dasho WANGDI NORBU; Man. Dir KARMA RANGDOL.

STOCK EXCHANGE

Royal Securities Exchange of Bhutan Ltd (RSEB): POB 742, Thimphu; tel. (2) 323995; fax (2) 323849; e-mail rseb@druknet.bt; f. 1993; supervised by the Royal Monetary Authority; open to Bhutanese nationals only; 15 listed cos (2003); Chair. DAW TENZIN; CEO TASHI YEZER.

INSURANCE

Royal Insurance Corporation of Bhutan: POB 77, Phuentsholing; tel. (5) 252453; fax (5) 252640; e-mail ricb@druknet.bt; f. 1975; provides general and life insurance and credit investment services; Chair. Lyonpo YESHEY ZIMBA; Man. Dir LAMKEY TSHERING; 10 brs and development centres.

Trade and Industry

GOVERNMENT AGENCIES

Department of Planning: Convention Centre, POB 127, Thimphu; tel. (2) 325192; fax (2) 322928; e-mail administrator@dop.gov.bt; internet www.dop.gov.bt; f. 1971 as Planning Commission; replaced by Department of Planning in 2002; under Ministry of Finance; consists of 21 officials; proposes socio-economic policy guide-lines, issues directives for the formulation of development plans, ensures efficient and judicious allocation of resources, directs socio-economic research, studies and surveys, and appraises the Govt on the progress of development plans and programmes; Dir LAM DORJI.

Food Corporation of Bhutan (FCB): POB 80, Phuentsholing; tel. (5) 252241; fax (5) 252289; e-mail drukfood@druknet.bt; f. 1974; activities include procurement and distribution of food grains and other essential commodities through appointed Fair Price Shop Agents; marketing of surplus agricultural and horticultural produce through FCB-regulated market outlets; logistics concerning World Food Programme food aid; maintenance of buffer stocks to offset any emergency food shortages; maintenance of SAARC Food Security Reserve Stock; importing consumer goods from major Indian enterprises; exporting oranges and apples; Man. Dir SHERUB GYALTSHEN; 19 outlets and 100 Fair Price Shops.

Forestry Development Corporation: Thimphu; tel. (2) 323834; fax (2) 325585; Man. Dir NAMGAY WANGCHUK.

State Trading Corpn of Bhutan Ltd (STCB): POB 76, Phuentsholing; tel. (5) 252286; fax (5) 252619; e-mail stcbl@druknet.bt; manages imports and exports on behalf of the Govt; Chair. Dasho KARMA DORJEE; Man. Dir Dasho DORJI NAMGAY; brs in Thimphu (POB 272; tel. (2) 322953; fax (2) 323781; e-mail stcbthim@druknet.bt) and Kolkata (Calcutta), India.

CHAMBER OF COMMERCE

Bhutan Chamber of Commerce and Industry (BCCI): POB 147, Thimphu; tel. (2) 322742; fax (2) 323936; e-mail bcci@druknet .bt; internet www.bcci.com.bt; f. 1980; reorg. 1988; promotion of trade and industry and privatization, information dissemination, private-sector human resource development; 434 registered mems; 12-mem. technical advisory committee; 21-mem. district executive committee; Pres. Dasho UGYEN DORJI; Sec.-Gen. Dasho TSHERING DORJI.

UTILITIES

Electricity

Department of Energy: c/o Ministry of Trade and Industry, Tashichhodzong, POB 141, Thimphu; tel. (2) 322279; fax (2) 328278.

Basochhu Hydropower Corporation: Basochhu; tel. (2) 471021; fax (2) 471020; co-ordinates construction of dam and hydroelectric power-generating facilities.

Bhutan Power Corporation: Thimphu; tel. (2) 325095; fax (2) 322279; f. 2002; responsible for ensuring electricity supply for the whole country at an affordable cost by 2020 and for providing uninterrupted transmission access for export of surplus power; Man. Dir SONAM TSHERING.

Chhukha Hydropower Corporation: Phuentsholing; tel. (5) 252575; fax (5) 252582; f. 1991; state-owned; Chair. Lyonpo YESHEY ZIMBA; Man. Dir YESHEY WANGDI.

Kurichhu Project Authority: Gyelpozhing (Mongar); tel. (4) 744113; fax (4) 744130; e-mail kpa@druknet.bt; operates and maintains a 60-MW hydroelectric power-generating facility at Gyelpozhing; Chair. Lyonpo KHANDU WANGCHUCK; Man. Dir. CHHEWANG RINZIN.

Tala Hydroelectric Project Authority: POB 908, Tala; tel. (5) 253233; fax (5) 252841; e-mail mdthpa@druknet.bt; co-ordinates construction of dam and hydroelectric power-generating facilities; Man. Dir R. N. KHAZANCHI.

Water

Thimphu City Corporation (Water Supply Unit): POB 215, Thimphu; tel. (2) 324710; fax (2) 324315; f. 1982; under Ministry of Home and Cultural Affairs from mid-2003; responsible for water supply of Thimphu municipality; Head BHIMLAL DHUNGEL.

TRADE UNIONS

Under long-standing legislation, trade union activity is illegal in Bhutan.

Transport

ROADS AND TRACKS

In June 2003 there were 4,007 km of roads in Bhutan, of which 2,419 km were black-topped. Surfaced roads link the important border towns of Phuentsholing, Gelephu, Sarpang and Samdrup Jongkhar in southern Bhutan to towns in West Bengal and Assam in India. There is a shortage of road transport. Yaks, ponies and mules are still the chief means of transport on the rough mountain tracks. By 1990 most of the previously government-operated transport facilities (mainly buses and minibuses) on major and subsidiary routes had been transferred to private operators on the basis of seven-year contracts.

Road Safety and Transport Authority: Thimphu; tel. (2) 321282; fax (2) 321281; e-mail director_rsta@druknet.bt; f. 1995; under Ministry of Information and Communications; regulates all motor vehicle activities and surface transport services; Dir NIMA WANGDI.

Transport Corpn of Bhutan: Phuentsholing; tel. (5) 252476; f. 1982; subsidiary of Royal Insurance Corpn of Bhutan; operates direct coach service between Phuentsholing and Kolkata via Siliguri.

Other operators are Barma Travels (f. 1990), Dawa Transport (Propr SHERUB WANGCHUCK), Dhendup Travel Service (Phuentsholing; tel (5) 252437), Gyamtsho Transport, Gurung Transport Service, Namgay Transport, Nima Travels (Phuentsholing; tel. (5) 252384), and Rimpung Travels (Phuentsholing; tel. (5) 252354).

Lorries for transporting goods are operated by the private sector.

CIVIL AVIATION

There is an international airport at Paro. There are also some 30 helicopter landing pads, which are used, by arrangement with the Indian military and aviation authorities, solely by government officials. The Council of Ministers approved the operation of a domestic helicopter service to improve mobility and to promote tourism; by mid-2003 five domestic heliports had been surveyed and found acceptable, and preparations for the introduction of services were being finalized. In August 2002 an air service agreement was signed with Myanmar (formerly Burma) to resume air services to and from Yangon (Rangoon).

Department of Civil Aviation: c/o Ministry of Information and Communications, Woochu, Paro; tel. (8) 271347; fax (8) 271909; e-mail aviation@druknet.bt; Dir PHALA DORJI.

Druk-Air Corpn Ltd (Royal Bhutan Airlines): Head Office, Nemizampa, PO Paro; tel. (8) 271856; fax (8) 271861; e-mail drukair@ druknet.bt; internet www.drukair.com.bt; national airline; f. 1981; became fully operational in 1983; services from Paro to Delhi and Gaya in India, Myanmar, Nepal and Thailand; services to Bangladesh suspended in mid-December 2003 for security reasons; charter services also undertaken; Chair. Lyonpo Jigmi Y. Thinley; Man. Dir Sangay Tenzing.

Tourism

Bhutan was opened to tourism in 1975. In 2004 the total number of foreign visitors was 9,259, compared with 6,261 in 2003. Receipts from tourism in 2004 totalled US $12.45m., compared with $8.3m. in 2003. Tourists travel in organized 'package', cultural or trekking tours, or individually, accompanied by trained guides. Hotels have been constructed at Phuentsholing, Paro, Bumthang, Wangduephodrang and Thimphu, with lodges at Trongsa, Trashigang and Mongar. In addition, there are many small privately operated hotels and guest-houses. Plans for several foreign-managed commercial hotels, in the style of resorts, were under way in early 2005. The Government exercises close control over the development of tourism. In 1987 the National Assembly resolved that all monasteries, mountains and other holy places should be inaccessible to tourists from 1988 (this resolution is flexibly interpreted, however—e.g. Japanese Buddhist tour groups are permitted to visit 'closed' monasteries). In 1991 the Government began transferring the tourism industry to the private sector and licences were issued to new private tourism operators. Rules were introduced in 1995, asserting more stringent controls over private operators, through the Tourism Authority of Bhutan (TAB). In 1998 the Government's tourism policy was liberalized further. In 2001 the TAB was reorganized as the Department of Tourism, under the Ministry of Trade and Industry. The Government has identified and encouraged the industry's potential to grow and to provide significant employment opportunities. A levy of $10 per visitor contributed to a Tourist Development Fund, which, by the end of 2002, amounted to more than Nu 10m. An Association of Bhutan Travel Operators (ABTO) was established in 1998 to act as a forum for co-ordinating tourism issues among the travel agencies. ABTO also surveyed new trekking routes in Ha, following the opening of the district to tourists from mid-2001. At the end of 2003 more than 140 private travel agencies were registered in Bhutan (of which more than 80 had each brought in at least one foreign tourist during the calendar year).

Department of Tourism: POB 126, Thimphu; tel. (2) 323251; fax (2) 323695; e-mail tab@druknet.bt; internet www.tourism.gov.bt; f. 2001 to replace Tourism Authority of Bhutan; under regulatory authority of Ministry of Trade and Industry; exercises overall authority over tourism policy, pricing, hotel, restaurant and travel agency licensing, visa approvals, etc.; Dir-Gen. Lhatu Wangchuck.

Association of Bhutan Travel Operators: POB 938, Thimphu; tel. (2) 322862; fax (2) 325286; e-mail abto@druknet.bt; internet www.abto.org.bt; f. 1998 to provide forum for members' views and to unite, supervise and co-ordinate activities of members; Chair. Dasho Ugen Tsechup Dorji.

BOLIVIA

Introductory Survey

Location, Climate, Language, Religion, Flag, Capital

The Republic of Bolivia is a land-locked state in South America, bordered by Chile and Peru to the west, by Brazil to the north and east, and by Paraguay and Argentina to the south. The climate varies, according to altitude, from humid tropical conditions in the northern and eastern lowlands, which are less than 500 m (1,640 ft) above sea-level, to the cool and cold zones at altitudes of more than 3,500 m (about 11,500 ft) in the Andes mountains. The official languages are Spanish, Quechua and Aymará. Almost all of the inhabitants profess Christianity, and the great majority are adherents of the Roman Catholic Church. The national civil flag (proportions 2 by 3) has three equal horizontal stripes, of red, yellow and green. The state flag has, in addition, the national coat of arms in the centre of the yellow stripe. The legal capital is Sucre. The administrative capital and seat of government is La Paz.

Recent History

The Incas of Bolivia were conquered by Spain in 1538 and, although there were many revolts against Spanish rule, independence was not achieved until 1825. Bolivian history has been characterized by recurrent internal strife, resulting in a lengthy succession of presidents, and frequent territorial disputes with its neighbours, including the 1879–83 War of the Pacific between Bolivia, Peru and Chile, which resulted in the loss of Bolivia's coastline, and the Chaco Wars of 1928–30 and 1932–35 against Paraguay.

At a presidential election in May 1951 the largest share of the vote was won by Dr Víctor Paz Estenssoro, the candidate of the Movimiento Nacionalista Revolucionario (MNR), who had been living in Argentina since 1946. He was denied permission to return to Bolivia and contested the election *in absentia*. However, he failed to gain an absolute majority, and the incumbent President transferred power to a junta of army officers. This regime was itself overthrown in April 1952, when a popular uprising, supported by the MNR and a section of the armed forces, enabled Dr Paz Estenssoro to return from exile and assume the presidency. His Government, a coalition of the MNR and the Labour Party, committed itself to profound social revolution. The coalition nationalized the tin mines and introduced universal suffrage (the franchise had previously been limited to literate adults) and land reform. Dr Hernán Siles Zuazo, a leading figure in the 1952 revolution, was elected President for the 1956–60 term, and Dr Paz Estenssoro was again elected President in 1960. However, the powerful trade unions came into conflict with the Government, and in November 1964, following widespread strikes and disorder, President Paz Estenssoro was overthrown by the Vice-President, Gen. René Barrientos Ortuño, who was supported by the army. After serving with Gen. Alfredo Ovando Candía as Co-President under a military junta, Gen. Barrientos resigned in January 1966 to campaign for the presidency; he was elected in July 1966.

President Barrientos encountered strong opposition from left-wing groups, including mineworkers' unions. There was also a guerrilla uprising in south-eastern Bolivia, led by Dr Ernesto ('Che') Guevara, the Argentine-born revolutionary who had played a leading role in the Castro regime in Cuba. However, the insurgency was suppressed by government troops, with the help of US advisers, and guerrilla warfare ended in October 1967, when Guevara was captured and killed. (In July 1997 Guevara's remains, together with those of three of his comrades, were finally located and returned to Cuba.) In April 1969 President Barrientos was killed in an air crash and Dr Luis Adolfo Siles Salinas, the Vice-President, succeeded to the presidency. In September, however, President Siles Salinas was deposed by the armed forces, who reinstated Gen. Ovando. He was forced to resign in October 1970, when, after a power struggle between right-wing and left-wing army officers, Gen. Juan José Torres González, who had support from leftists, emerged as President, pledging support for agrarian reform and worker participation in management. A 'People's Assembly', formed by Marxist politicians, radical students and leaders of trade unions, was allowed to meet and demanded the introduction of extreme socialist measures, causing disquiet in right-wing circles. President Torres was deposed in August 1971 by Col (later Gen.) Hugo Bánzer Suárez, who drew support from the right-wing Falange Socialista Boliviana and a section of the MNR, as well as from the army. In June 1973 President Bánzer announced an imminent return to constitutional government, but elections were later postponed to June 1974. The MNR withdrew its support and entered into active opposition.

Following an attempted military coup in June 1974, all portfolios within the Cabinet were assigned to military personnel. After another failed coup attempt in November, President Bánzer declared that elections had been postponed indefinitely and that his military regime would retain power until at least 1980. All political and union activity was banned. Political and industrial unrest in 1976, however, led President Bánzer to announce that elections would be held in July 1978. Allegations of fraud rendered the elections void, but Gen. Juan Pereda Asbún, the armed forces candidate in the elections, staged a successful military coup. In November 1978 his right-wing Government was overthrown in another coup, led by Gen. David Padilla Aranciba, Commander-in-Chief of the Army, with the support of national left-wing elements.

Presidential and congressional elections were held in July 1979. The presidential poll resulted in almost equal support for two ex-Presidents, Dr Siles Zuazo (with 36.0% of the vote) and Dr Paz Estenssoro (with 35.9%), who were now leading rival factions of the MNR. The Congreso (Congress), which was convened in August to resolve the issue, failed to award a majority to either candidate. An interim Government was formed under Walter Guevara Arce, President of the the upper house of the Congreso, but this administration was overthrown on 1 November by a right-wing army officer, Col Alberto Natusch Busch. He withdrew 15 days later after failing to gain the support of the Congreso, which elected Dra Lidia Gueiler Tejada, President of the Cámara de Diputados (Chamber of Deputies, the lower congressional house), as interim Head of State pending presidential and congressional elections scheduled for June 1980.

The result of the 1980 presidential election was inconclusive, and in July, before the Congreso could meet to decide between the two main contenders (again Siles Zuazo and Paz Estenssoro), a military junta led by an army commander, Gen. Luis García Meza, staged a coup—the 189th in Bolivia's 154 years of independence. In August 1981 a military uprising forced Gen. García to resign. In September the junta transferred power to another army commander, Gen. Celso Torrelio Villa, who declared his intention to fight official corruption and to return the country to democracy within three years. Labour unrest, provoked by Bolivia's severe economic crisis, was appeased by restitution of trade-union and political rights, and a mainly civilian Cabinet was appointed in April 1982. Elections were scheduled for April 1983. The political liberalization disturbed the armed forces, who attempted to create a climate of violence, and President Torrelio resigned in July 1982, amid rumours of an impending coup. The junta installed the less moderate Gen. Guido Vildoso Calderón, the Army Chief of Staff, as President. Unable to resolve the worsening economic crisis or to control a general strike, in September the military regime announced that power would be handed over in October to the Congreso that had originally been elected in 1980. Dr Siles Zuazo, who had obtained most votes in both 1979 and 1980, was duly elected President by the Congreso, and was sworn in for a four-year term in October 1982.

President Siles Zuazo appointed a coalition Cabinet consisting of members of his own party, the Movimiento Nacionalista Revolucionario de Izquierda (MNRI), the Movimiento de la Izquierda Revolucionaria (MIR) and the Partido Comunista de Bolivia (PCB). Economic aid from the USA and Europe was resumed, but the Government found itself unable to fulfil the expectations that had been created by the return to democratic rule. The entire Cabinet resigned in August 1983, and the President appointed a Cabinet in which the number of portfolios that were held by the right-wing of the MNRI, the Partido Demócrata Cristiano (PDC) and independents was increased. The MIR joined forces with the MNR and with business interests in rejecting the Government's policy of complying with IMF conditions for assistance, which involved harsh economic measures. The Government lost its majority in the Congreso and was confronted by strikes and mass labour demonstrations. In November the opposition-dominated Cámara de Senadores (Senate) approved an increase of 100% in the minimum wage, in defiance of the Government's austerity measures. Following a 48-hour general strike, the whole Cabinet resigned once again in December, in anticipation of an opposition motion of censure; the ministers accused the Senado of planning a 'constitutional coup' and urged the formation of a government of 'national unity'. In January 1984 President Siles Zuazo appointed a new coalition Cabinet, including 13 members of the previous Government.

The new Cabinet's main priority was to reverse Bolivia's grave economic decline. However, constant industrial agitation by the trade-union confederation, the Central Obrera Boliviana (COB), coupled with rumours of an imminent coup, seriously undermined public confidence in the President. In June 1984 the country was again thrown into turmoil by the temporary abduction of President Siles Zuazo. Two former cabinet ministers and some 100 right-wing army officers were arrested in connection with the kidnapping, which was believed to have been supported by leading figures in the illicit drugs trade.

At elections in July 1985, amid reports of electoral malpractice and poor organization, the right-wing Acción Democrática Nacionalista (ADN), whose presidential candidate was Gen. Hugo Bánzer Suárez (the former dictator), received 28.6% of the votes cast, and the MNR obtained 26.4%, while the MIR was the leading left-wing party. At a further round of voting in the Congreso in August, an alliance between the MNR and the leading left-wing groups, including the MIR, enabled Dr Víctor Paz Estenssoro of the MNR to secure the presidency (which he had previously held in 1952–56 and 1960–64). The armed forces pledged their support for the new Government.

On taking office in August 1985, the new Government immediately introduced a very strict economic programme, designed to reduce inflation, which was estimated to have reached 14,173% in the year to August. The COB rejected the programme and called an indefinite general strike in September. The Government responded by declaring the strike illegal and by ordering a 90-day state of siege throughout Bolivia. Leading trade unionists were detained or banished, and thousands of strikers were arrested. The strike was called off in October, when union leaders agreed to hold talks with the Government. The conclusion of the strike was regarded as a considerable success for the new administration which, in spite of having achieved office with the assistance of left-wing parties, had subsequently found a greater ally in the right-wing ADN.

Throughout 1986 demonstrations and strikes were held by the COB in protest at the Government's austerity measures. Following a general strike in August, the Government imposed another 90-day state of siege. Social discontent persisted in 1987 and extensive unrest continued in 1988 (following a further increase in the price of petrol in February of that year), which culminated in April with a national hunger strike, called by the COB, to protest against the continuing austerity measures. These problems led to the resignation of the Cabinet in August, although all except four ministers were reappointed.

Presidential and congressional elections took place in May 1989. Of the votes cast in the presidential election, Gonzalo Sánchez de Lozada of the MNR obtained 23.1%, Gen. Hugo Bánzer Suárez of the ADN 22.7%, and Jaime Paz Zamora of the MIR 19.6%. As no candidate had gained the requisite absolute majority, responsibility for the choice of President passed to the newly-elected Congreso, which was to convene in August. Shortly before the second stage of the election, Bánzer withdrew his candidacy in order to support his former adversary, Paz Zamora. The 46 ADN and 41 MIR seats in the Congreso were sufficient to assure a majority vote for Paz Zamora, who assumed the presidency. A coalition Government of 'national unity', the Acuerdo Patriótico, was then formed. At the same time, a joint political council (with undefined powers), headed by Bánzer, was established.

From 1988 the Government increased its attempts to reduce the illegal production of coca. As a result, during 1989 clashes between the drugs-control troops, Unidad Móvil de Patrullaje Rural (UMOPAR), and drugs-traffickers intensified, particularly in the coca-processing region of northern Beni. By the middle of the year, however, it became clear that the Government had failed to attain the targets of its coca-eradication programme (begun in 1986 after the US Government had agreed to provide more than US $100m. in aid), having encountered staunch opposition from the powerful coca-growers' organizations. Paz Zamora was critical of the militaristic approach of the USA to coca eradication and emphasized the need for economic and social support. In May 1990, however, he accepted US $35m. in military aid from the USA. In late 1990 reaction to US involvement in Bolivia became increasingly violent. The left-wing Nestor Paz Zamora guerrilla group claimed responsibility for several bomb attacks, declaring that its actions were in response to the violation of Bolivia's political and territorial sovereignty by the USA.

In December 1989 a serious institutional conflict arose when the Government allowed a former Minister of the Interior, Migration and Justice, Col Luis Arce Gómez, to be taken to Miami, Florida (USA), to be tried on drugs-trafficking charges, despite the absence of a formal extradition treaty between Bolivia and the USA. Arce Gómez had been on trial in Bolivia since 1986, accused of violating human rights. His extradition, therefore, constituted a contravention of Bolivian law, which states that a Bolivian cannot be extradited while undergoing trial in Bolivia. Following an acrimonious conflict between the Government and the judiciary, the Congreso temporarily suspended eight of the 12 supreme court judges in late 1990. In retaliation, the court threatened to annul the 1989 elections. The conflict was resolved in early 1991 with the signing by the country's five main political parties of a pact affirming the independence of the Supreme Court. In January 1991 a federal jury in Miami found Arce Gómez guilty on two charges of drugs-trafficking, and he was sentenced to 30 years' imprisonment.

In March 1991 the reputation of the Government was seriously undermined when three of its senior officials were forced to resign amid allegations of corruption. Moreover, the appointment in February of Col Faustino Rico Toro as the new head of Bolivia's anti-drugs-trafficking force, La Fuerza Especial de Lucha Contra el Narcotráfico (FELCN) had provoked widespread outrage. In addition to his alleged connections with illegal drugs-traffickers, Rico was accused of having committed human rights abuses during his tenure as chief of army intelligence under the regime of Gen. Luis García Meza (1980–81). After considerable pressure from the USA (including the suspension of all military and economic aid), Rico resigned from his new position in early March. Later that month, following accusations by the USA linking them with illegal drugs-traffickers, the Minister of the Interior, Migration and Justice and the Chief of Police resigned from their posts, although both maintained their innocence. In July the Government announced a decree granting a period of amnesty, lasting 120 days, for drugs-traffickers to surrender voluntarily. A condition of the amnesty was that those giving themselves up confess their crimes and contribute effectively to the apprehension of other such criminals. In return, they were offered minimum prison sentences and the guarantee that they would not risk extradition to the USA. As many as seven of the country's most powerful drugs-traffickers were reported to have taken advantage of the amnesty.

Government plans to privatize state-owned enterprises, including the state mining corporation, COMIBOL, resulted in a series of strikes, organized by the COB, in late 1991 and early 1992. In July the COB called a further general strike, and in October, in what was regarded as a major reversal for the Government and a considerable victory for the mining union, Federación Sindical de Trabajadores Mineros de Bolivia (FSTMB), the Government suspended its programme of joint ventures between COMIBOL and private companies. Continued social unrest led to violent confrontation between protesters and troops throughout the country in early 1993, and the military occupation of La Paz in March of that year.

In April 1993 the Supreme Court found the former military dictator Gen. Luis García Meza guilty on 49 charges of murder, human rights abuses, corruption and fraud, and sentenced him, *in absentia*, to 30 years' imprisonment. Similar sentences were imposed on 14 of his collaborators. García Meza was arrested in Brazil in March 1994 and, following his extradition to Bolivia in October of that year, began his prison sentence in March 1995.

Presidential and congressional elections were held in June 1993. Sánchez de Lozada was the MNR's presidential candidate, while Bánzer Suárez was supported by both the ADN and the

MIR, as Paz Zamora was ineligible for re-election. In the presidential election no candidate secured the requisite absolute majority, so a congressional vote was scheduled to take place in August to decide between the two main contenders, Sánchez de Lozada and Bánzer. However, Bánzer withdrew from the contest, thereby leaving Sánchez de Lozada's candidacy unopposed. He was sworn in as President on 6 August. At legislative elections, conducted simultaneously, the MNR secured 69 of the 157 seats in the bicameral Congreso, while the ruling Acuerdo Patriótico coalition won only 43. The MNR subsequently concluded a pact with the Unión Cívica Solidaridad (UCS) and the Movimiento Bolivia Libre (MBL), thus securing a congressional majority.

Despite the new Government's stated intention to combat corruption in Bolivia's political and public life, evidence of fraudulent practice continued to feature widely in the country's affairs in 1994. In March former President Jaime Paz Zamora announced his retirement from political life following the presentation of a report by the FELCN to the Congreso alleging his co-operation with drugs-traffickers (However, his retirement proved short-lived: in January 1995 Paz Zamora announced his return to political life, while denying the allegations against him in the FELCN report.) In June the President of the Supreme Court and its third judge were found guilty of bribery by the Senado and were dismissed and banned from holding public office for 10 years. In the same month it was revealed that a large proportion of the US $20m. seized from drugs-traffickers between 1988 and 1993 had disappeared. Members of the FELCN, trustees from the Attorney-General's office and local government officials were implicated in the affair.

In early 1995 some 80,000 teachers across the country undertook a campaign of industrial action in opposition to a proposed programme of education reforms, which advocated the privatization of much of the education system and the restriction of teachers' rights to union membership. In response to a call by COB for an indefinite strike, and in an attempt to quell several weeks of civil unrest, the Government declared a state of siege for 90 days. Military units were deployed throughout the country, and 370 union leaders were arrested and banished to remote areas. However, protests continued nation-wide and the state of siege was extended by a further 90 days in July, owing to continued civil unrest, which had become particularly intense in the Chapare valley of Cochabamba, where, despite the introduction of a voluntary coca-eradication programme, UMOPAR forces had begun to occupy villages and to destroy coca plantations. Violent clashes between peasant farmers and UMOPAR personnel between July and September resulted in the arrest of almost 1,000 coca growers. Human rights organizations expressed alarm at the force with which UMOPAR was conducting its operations and at the number of peasants killed and injured in the campaign. In October the state of siege was revoked, and negotiations between the Government and the coca growers were undertaken, although the talks soon broke down.

Meanwhile, allegations implicating senior public officials in corruption and, particularly, the illegal drugs trade continued to emerge in 1995 and 1996. Four members of the FELCN, including the organization's second-in-command, Col Fernando Tarifa, were dismissed in September, following an investigation into their links with drugs-traffickers. A further 100 FELCN members were detained in November on drugs-related charges. Moreover, a serious political scandal erupted in October, following allegations that Guillermo Bedregal, the President of the Senado and a deputy leader of the MNR, had co-operated with leading drugs-traffickers. In early 1996 allegations concerning the abuse of the personal expenses system resulted in the resignation of 10 MNR members of the Congreso and the suspension of 12 others on criminal charges. Moreover, in March a supreme court judge who had presided over numerous cases involving drugs-related offences was arrested by the FELCN, after having been filmed accepting money from a defendant's relative.

Continued opposition to the Government's capitalization programme led to further industrial unrest and a general strike in early 1996. In April more than 100,000 transport workers undertook a series of strikes and demonstrations in protest at the sale of the Eastern Railway to a Chilean company. Riots in La Paz resulted in damage to Chilean-owned railway property, which prompted threats from the Chilean Government to withdraw its investment from Bolivia. During violent clashes with the police several protesters were injured and one was killed. The dispute ended later in the month, when the COB signed an agreement with the Government which provided for modest public-sector wage increases, but did not include concessions in the Government's plans to continue implementation of its capitalization policies.

The proposed introduction of an agrarian reform law led to a series of protests in September and October 1996 by indigenous and peasant groups who feared that their land rights would be undermined by measures contained in the proposed legislation. In October the leaders of several peasant farmers' groups began a hunger strike, while the COB called an indefinite general strike. Shortly afterwards Sánchez de Lozada agreed to hold discussions with representatives of some of the indigenous and peasant groups (although not with the COB) and subsequently secured their support for the law by making a number of significant concessions. The most important of these was the modification of the proposed role of the Agrarian Superintendency, such that it would not be authorized to rule on issues of land ownership. The law was approved by the Congreso later that month.

Dissatisfaction with the continued privatization of major industrial companies in Bolivia, particularly in the mining sector, resulted in further unrest in late 1996. In December a group of miners occupied a pit at Amayapampa in northern Potosí to protest at the actions of the mine's Canadian operators, who, they alleged, had failed to pay local taxes and had caused damage to the environment. When troops arrived at the site to remove the miners 10 protesters were killed and 50 others injured in ensuing violent clashes. The incident provoked outrage throughout the country and was the subject of an investigation by the Organization of American States' Inter-American Human Rights Commission in 1997.

Presidential elections were held on 1 June 1997. The MNR's candidate was Juan Carlos Durán (Sánchez de Lozada was ineligible for re-election), the MIR presented Paz Zamora, while Bánzer Suárez, in a fourth attempt to gain the presidency by democratic means, was the nominee of the ADN. In the event, Bánzer secured 22.3% of the total votes, Durán won 17.7% and Paz Zamora received 16.7%. At legislative elections held concurrently the ADN failed to secure a majority of seats; however, it subsequently formed a pact with the MIR, the UCS and Condepa to form a congressional majority. As a result, on 5 August Bánzer was elected President for a newly-extended term of five years with 118 congressional votes. The inclusion of the MIR in the coalition prompted concern among some observers, as it was feared that previous allegations of corruption and of involvement in the illegal drugs trade against the party and, in particular, against Paz Zamora (see above) would jeopardize the country's ability to attract international aid and investment.

In August 1997 the newly-elected Government signed a financial co-operation agreement with the USA for continued action to combat the illegal drugs trade. The agreement, which provided finance for the implementation of eradication programmes, was criticized for its emphasis on the suppression of coca cultivation rather than on the development of alternative crops. Nevertheless, many observers believed the policy to be ineffective, as, despite the provision of US finance worth US $500m. since 1990 to eradicate the crop, there had been no net reduction in coca production in Bolivia. There was also evidence that compensation payments given to coca growers for the destruction of their crops had been used to replant coca in more remote areas. Meanwhile, discontent with some of the new Government's economic policies, particularly an increase in petrol prices and taxes announced in November, prompted several COB-organized strikes in late 1997 and early 1998.

In February 1998 coca producers in the Cochabamba region announced their rejection of the Government's new anti-coca policy (the so-called 'Dignity Plan', which aimed to eradicate all illegal coca plantations by 2002), claiming that an agreement, signed in October 1997, to provide alternative development programmes had not been honoured. Violent clashes ensued when army and police personnel converged on the region in April to implement the eradication programme, and in the following month the Government temporarily suspended the measures.

More than 1,000 coca growers undertook a 800-km protest march from Chapare to La Paz in August 1998 to demand that the Government review its coca-eradication programme. The farmers denounced new measures, including the confiscation of land used for coca cultivation, the incarceration of new coca growers and the reduction, by more than 50%, of compensation rates paid to farmers who voluntarily ceased to grow coca. The

Government rejected the protesters' demands, reiterating its intention to eradicate more than 9,000 ha of the crop by the end of the year. Demonstrations and roadblocks by coca growers in La Paz and Cochabamba during September were disrupted by security forces, leading to violent confrontation in many cases. The relocation of the headquarters of the armed forces from La Paz to Cochabamba in 1999 was interpreted by some observers as a further measure to suppress the activities of the coca-growing community. The Government, however, denied that a process of militarization of the Cochabamba region was being implemented. In late 1998 it was announced that the 'Dignity Plan' was progressing successfully, with more than 11,500 ha of coca having been destroyed during that year. The Bolivian Government stated that funding for the programme had been received from the USA and the European Union (EU), but that a further US $300m. was required to develop alternative resources to replace revenue lost from the illegal sale of coca. In 1999 the amount of eradicated coca crops increased to 14,000 ha.

In mid-1999 a number of reforms of the judicial system were announced, including the appointment of a people's ombudsman, a constitutional tribunal and an independent judicial council. It was hoped that these measures, when implemented, would help to reduce levels of corruption, particularly with regard to the accountability of the police force. Bolivia's new penal code, which came into effect at the end of May 1999, was groundbreaking in that it formally incorporated into the country's legal system the customary law of indigenous Indian peoples.

In December 1999 a sharp increase in water charges in Cochabamba prompted violent demonstrations, which spread to other areas. Further violent protests in April 2000 led to the imposition of a state of emergency by the Government. In the same month a brief strike by the police, coinciding with a general strike in protest at the water charges, forced the Government to withdraw the measure, which had been intended to help the newly privatized water authority fund improvements in supply. The reverse in policy precipitated a cabinet reshuffle, which increased the representation of the ADN by one post at the expense of the MIR. The Government was put under further pressure in September when striking teachers demanding higher salaries were joined by peasants protesting against the Government's plan to tax water used for crop irrigation. As coca growers were already protesting against the Government's plans to restrict the cultivation of the coca leaf, the combination of roadblocks and demonstrations brought the country to a standstill. Violence ensued between the protesters and riot police, resulting in at least 10 fatalities. A settlement was achieved in October, whereby the teachers received bonus payments and the Government signed a 50-point agreement with the peasant farmers' union, which included a pledge to draft new agrarian reform legislation and to review the controversial water-privatization law. Later in the month the Government acceded to coca growers' demands for a halt to the construction of new military bases in the Chapare region; however, the process of coca eradication intensified. In December President Bánzer announced that most of the coca leaf in the Chapare region had been eradicated, with only 1,500 acres remaining. However, in September 2001 the Minister of the Interior, Leopoldo Fernández Ferreira, admitted that the success of the eradication programme had been exaggerated and that about 6,000 ha of coca plantations were yet to be destroyed in the Chapare valley.

In May 2001, following further protests against the Government's privatization and coca-eradication policies, a tentative agreement was reached in which seven commissions would be established, comprising representatives of government and civic opposition groups, to review government policy in areas such as agrarian reform, coca eradication and water privatization. Nevertheless, popular protests continued throughout the country. A new criminal code was introduced in June that allowed for trial by public jury and made provision for the creation of a prosecution service independent of the police force.

In early August 2001 President Bánzer resigned, owing to ill health. The Vice-President, Jorge Quiroga Ramírez, assumed the presidency on 6 August and immediately replaced 12 of the 16 members of the Government; almost one-half of the new Cabinet was not affiliated to any political party. The new Government's main stated aims were to stabilize the economy, implement anti-corruption measures and continue the dialogue with aggrieved peasants and indigenous groups. In that month the Government reached an agreement with the main peasant

farmers' union to implement a US $70m. rural development programme.

Presidential and legislative elections were held on 30 June 2002. The main contenders in the presidential contest were former President Sánchez de Lozada, again representing the MNR, Manfred Reyes Villa of the centre-right Nueva Fuerza Republicana (NFR) and Evo Morales, a coca-grower leader, representing the left-wing Movimiento al Socialismo—Instrumento Político por la Soberanía de los Pueblos (MAS). In the event, Sánchez de Lozada won the largest share of the ballot (22.5%). Morales, who opposed the Government's free-market economic policy and its coca-eradication programme, performed unexpectedly well, coming second with 20.9% of the votes cast. As no candidate had achieved an absolute majority, however, responsibility for choosing the new President again passed to the Congreso. On 4 August it voted to appoint Sánchez de Lozada to the presidency once more. The MNR also won the largest number of seats (47) in the concurrently held legislative elections, followed by the MAS with 35 seats, the MIR with 31 seats and the NFR with 27 seats.

Following his inauguration on 6 August 2002 Sánchez de Lozada formed a coalition Government comprising representatives of the MNR, the MIR, the UCS, the MBL and the ADN, although the new Cabinet was dominated by MNR and MIR members. The new President's priorities were to continue the coca-eradication policy of its predecessor and to bring about economic recovery, by implementing a public-works programme. Sánchez de Lozada also pledged to review the country's privatization programme. However, the ruling coalition was a fragile one; the MNR could not rely on the support of the other alliance parties in the Congreso. This, coupled with the strong performance of the opposition parties in the elections led the new administration to encounter sustained resistance to its proposed agenda.

In light of renewed pressure from the US Administration to intensify eradication efforts, in September 2002 the Government held talks with coca-growers' representatives, led by Morales. The USA had threatened to suspend preferential access to certain US markets, agreed under the Andean Trade Promotion and Drug Eradication Act, if Bolivia failed to meet the agreed eradication target of 9,000 ha of coca crops. The talks ended inconclusively, although the Government did agree to suspend eradication temporarily in the Chapare region; however, it remained committed to the programme in the long term. In October the USA published a report in which it was claimed that there were an estimated 24,400 ha of coca plantations in Bolivia in 2002, twice the agreed level, and that, contrary to government claims, new plantation rates exceeded eradication levels.

In response to the US study, the Government announced its intention to commission an independent survey of illegal coca plantations, as well as a review of legal cultivation levels (which stood at 12,000 ha in 2002). Peasant organizations insisted that eradication be suspended while the study was under way. In January 2003 coca growers staged roadblocks and demonstrations in protest at the Government's refusal to meet their demands. At the same time, about 5,000 pensioners marched from Patacamaya to La Paz in protest at legislation, approved in December 2002, which linked pensions to the consumer price index, rather than to the US dollar. Following two weeks of clashes with the police, in which 10 people were killed, in late January President Sánchez de Lozada and Evo Morales agreed to restart negotiations on coca eradication, as well as on trade issues and the privatization programme. However, a plan to increase the maximum area for the legal cultivation of coca prompted strong protests from the USA in March.

In February 2003 the Sánchez de Lozada administration's budget proposals increased popular dissatisfaction still further. Faced with a fiscal deficit of more than 8.6% of GDP, and under IMF pressure to secure new sources of revenue to finance a planned US $3,900m. public-works programme, the Government proposed increasing income tax rates. The new measure—known as an *impuestazo*, or 'tax shock'—drew widespread condemnation from representatives of middle- and lower-income groups, and prompted civil unrest. On 12 February, following the Government's dismissal of their 40% wage-increase demand, approximately 7,000 armed police officers joined civilian protests in central La Paz. During the ensuing confrontation with elements of the military 32 people were killed and President Sánchez de Lozada was forced to withdraw to safety. The riots prompted the resignation, on 19 February, of the entire Cabinet.

A new Government was appointed the following day. Seven ministers were reappointed to their previous posts and, in a measure intended to restore public confidence and reduce spending, President Sánchez de Lozada announced that the number of ministries would be reduced from 18 to 13.

In March 2003 the Government announced revised budget proposals, following extensive negotiations with opposition groups. It withdrew the proposal to increase income taxes that had prompted the previous month's riots, and pledged to increase public investment by 25%, in order to reduce unemployment. In spite of its effective abandonment of the IMF-approved budget measures, in early April the Government reached a stand-by agreement with the Fund, worth US $118m., the first tranche of which was disbursed in early July. Furthermore, in August the opposition NFR announced that it was to join the ruling coalition. A subsequent cabinet reshuffle in the same month allocated significant portfolios to representatives of that party.

From 2001 proposals to construct a natural gas pipeline from the southern department of Tarija to the Pacific had been met with public hostility. Opposition groups protested at the export of natural resources to Mexico and the USA. In March 2003 opposition to the project increased following the announcement by the international consortium overseeing the project that it favoured the Chilean port of Patillos as the location for the pipeline's export terminal. Patillos was on that part of the Pacific coastline Bolivia had lost to Chile in the late 19th century. Opposition groups accused the Government of putting foreign interests above domestic ones and also claimed that President Sánchez de Lozada had failed to fulfil economic pledges. Opposition continued to grow and in September there were strikes and roadblocks organized in protest.

In the following month, increasing civil unrest in El Alto, an industrial suburb of La Paz, culminated in military intervention, resulting in the deaths of some 36 people on 12 October 2003. The following day protests in La Paz fuelled by the events in El Alto resulted in further violent clashes with the army, and a further 13 deaths. The violent suppression of the protests prompted the resignation of the Vice-President, Carlos Mesa Gisbert, and the Minister of Economic Development, Jorge Torres, and the COB declared an indefinite general strike. On 15 October, in an attempt to restore order, the Government announced that it would hold a referendum on gas exports and would revise existing energy legislation. It also pledged to establish a constituent assembly to examine possible constitutional changes. Nevertheless, the civil unrest continued unabated and the death toll rose to an estimated 74. Two days later, on 17 October, the NFR withdrew from the governing coalition. On the same day, Sánchez de Lozada resigned as President and travelled to the USA. Congress approved erstwhile Vice-President Mesa to succeed him. Mesa was sworn in as President on 18 October.

Upon taking office, President Mesa appointed a Cabinet largely composed of independent technocrats, and notably restored the indigenous affairs portfolio abolished in February. The new President pledged to re-examine the contentious gas-export plan (suspended since 13 October 2003) and reiterated the previous administration's pledges to hold a referendum on the pipeline through Chile, to establish a constituent assembly, and to revise energy legislation. He also announced a plan to connect some 200,000 households in central Bolivia to the gas network. Opposition groups agreed to a 90-day truce while the new Government began to implement these new policies. In December the new President announced plans to reduce the coca-eradication programme, in order to strengthen efforts to eliminate cocaine production. Peasant and coca growers' leaders expressed cautious approval of this new policy, although the US Government announced its opposition. In September 2004 President Mesa announced a new anti-drugs strategy that would receive some US $969m. in funding over the following four years. Instead of forcible eradication, the focus of this strategy would be to encourage the cultivation of alternative crops. Accordingly, in November the Government signed an agreement with Evo Morales (in his capacity as leader of the coca growers) to suspend the programme of forcible eradication in the Chapare region. On 14 October the Congreso voted to prosecute former President Lozada and all members of his Government over the decision to deploy troops to quell the civil unrest prompted by the gas-export proposals in October 2003 in El Alto, which resulted in considerable loss of life. It was thought likely that Lozada, who remained in exile in February 2005, would even-

tually be tried *in absentia*, although in that month the Government admitted that several procedural errors in the indictment of the former President might lead to it being overturned.

In accordance with President Mesa's pledges on taking office, in July 2003 a referendum was held on energy policy. The electorate was asked the following questions: if it agreed with the abrogation of the hydrocarbons law that had been reintroduced by President Sánchez de Lozada; if state intervention in the oil and gas industry should be increased; if the state oil company, Yacimientos Petrolíferos Fiscales Bolivianos, should reclaim shares in privatized energy companies; if Bolivia's gas reserves should be used as a negotiating tool to regain access to the Pacific Ocean; and if reform of the energy sector under broadly left-wing principles should be allowed to proceed. All five of the Government's proposals were accepted but, despite this clear mandate for change, the resulting draft legislation caused great controversy over the following months and, consequently, during this time several revisions were made to the Government's legislative proposals. Specifically, there was disagreement as to whether extant contracts with energy-sector companies should be voided and rewritten to provide for greater state control and revenue. Although various congressional, popular and indigenous groups strongly supported such moves, several foreign companies (notably, BP and Repsol) and foreign government delegations acting in their interests (notably, those of the USA, Brazil, Spain and the United Kingdom) voiced their opposition to any proposals they considered illegal under international law. The Mesa Government gave assurances that contracts with foreign oil companies would not be rewritten without the companies' agreement.

Also in late 2004 a broad-based coalition that included politicians, employers and trade unions from Santa Cruz and the oil- and gas-producing department of Tarija, made increasingly vociferous demands for a referendum on greater regional autonomy or even full secession. This grouping was also opposed to an increased role of central government in the energy sector, fearing that this would deter foreign investment and increase corruption, inefficiency and political centralization. In furtherance of the aim for autonomy, a widely supported general strike was held in Santa Cruz and Tarija in November. The civil unrest continued in the following month, after the Government's announcement of significant increases in fuel prices were met with public protests across the country, particularly in Santa Cruz and El Alto, where people were also protesting against charges imposed by the local water company, Aguas de Illimani. In response to the growing public discontent, the Government agreed to cancel Aguas de Illimani's contract. Nevertheless, the COB called for President Mesa's resignation and announced that it was to organize an indefinite nation-wide general strike from 11 January 2005. Throughout early 2005 the country suffered severe disruption from roadblocks and other acts of civil disobedience by protesters demanding, *inter alia*, the immediate annulment of Aguas de Illimani's contract, a decrease in the price of fuel and a dramatic increase in government revenues from the hydrocarbon sector. In face of such public opposition, on 19 January President Mesa announced that the fuel increases would be reduced from 23% to 15%. However, this was not enough to appease the protesters in Santa Cruz; on 28 January a mass rally was held in the department, at which the Comité Cívico pro Santa Cruz declared Santa Cruz to be autonomous and announced that it was to establish a provincial interim government. On the same day President Mesa announced that provincial gubernatorial elections would be held on 12 June (departmental prefects were hitherto appointed by the President). However, this measure first required approval by referendum in order to be constitutional, and a constituent assembly was duly appointed. In early February, in an attempt to restore confidence in his Government (and following the resignation of two cabinet members from Santa Cruz), Mesa effected a wide-ranging reallocation of cabinet portfolios; notably, three ministers from Santa Cruz were included in the new Government. Nevertheless, anti-Government protests continued throughout the month and the President also faced opposition from the left-wing MAS, who accused him of surrendering to the Santa Cruz protesters' demands. Hoping to avoid the violence that resulted in his predecessor's departure from office, Mesa refused to deploy troops to disband the protests by force, pledging to end the unrest by 'constitutional means'. To this effect, on 8 March he submitted his resignation to the Congreso, declaring that he would only continue in office if a consensus could be reached that would end the disruption. The Congreso rejected Mesa's resignation after an agreement to achieve consensus had been signed by the major congressional blocs. On 16 March Evo Morales called for a temporary cessation of the roadblocks following the approval by the upper house of legislation that provided for a state royalty of 18% on hydrocarbons at the point of extraction and a further tax of 32%; Morales had initially favoured a royalty of 50%. To prevent further disruption, Mesa proposed that the presidential election, scheduled for June 2007, be held in September 2005. Although the Congreso rejected the proposal, Mesa announced his intention to remain in office for the duration of his term.

The issue of the participation of the Aymara, Quechua and Guaraní indigenous peoples in Bolivia's public life reached a critical phase in the early 21st century, following limited progress in the 1990s. Government decrees issued in 1990 acknowledging as Indian territory more than 1.6m. ha of tropical rainforest in northern Bolivia constituted an unprecedented act of recognition of Indian land rights. In September 2002 the Sánchez de Lozada administration announced a Land Reform Programme, under which some 1.2m. ha were to be bought by the Government and redistributed to some 11,000 landless families, at a cost of approximately US $2,500m. The Ministry for Peasants', Indigenous Peoples' and Ethnic Affairs, created in 2000, was abolished in February 2003 as part of the Government's cost-cutting programme, although it was re-established after President Mesa assumed power in October. Moreover, despite government claims that some 500,000 ha of land was available for redistribution, landless peasants continued to occupy farms illegally in late 2003 and throughout 2004. In August land owned by the multinational oil company BP was occupied until the Government agreed to accelerate the process of land redistribution. In early December there was an unprecedented level of indigenous political participation in municipal elections. In sharp contrast to the elections of 1999, in which candidates from just 18 parties stood, over 400 'citizen organizations' (mostly formed by local activist and indigenous groupings) fielded candidates. Preliminary results indicated that some 90% of constituencies were won by candidates from these new political groupings.

Bolivia's relations with Peru and Chile have been dominated by the long-standing issue of possible Bolivian access to the Pacific Ocean. An agreement with Peru, completed in 1993, granted Bolivia free access from its border town of Desaguadero to the Pacific port of Ilo, Peru, until 2091. In August 2004, following talks to further economic integration, the Presidents of Bolivia and Peru signed a declaration of intent to create a special zone in Ilo for the exportation of Bolivian gas. None the less, the President of the Cámara Boliviana de Hidrocarburos, Raúl Kieffer, expressed doubts over the practicality of the plan.

Bolivia's desire to regain sovereign access to the Pacific continued to impair relations with Chile, however. In March 1997 (and again in May) failure to reach agreement on this matter led to the suspension of talks which aimed to improve trade arrangements between the two countries. Relations deteriorated further in late 1997 when the Bolivian Government filed an official protest note to Chile regarding its failure to remove land-mines along the common border (planted during the 1970s). Although in mid-1999 Bolivia briefly renounced its demand of Chile for Pacific access in mid-1998, Chilean unwillingness to resume negotiations led to a return to diplomatic hostilities later that year. In November 2003 the new Bolivian Government of Carlos Mesa stated its commitment to obtaining sovereign access to the Pacific, prompting bilateral relations to deteriorate further. The Bolivian claim on Chile's Pacific coastline became a matter of greater regional concern in 2004 following the outspoken expressions of support from President Hugo Rafael Chávez Frías of Venezuela in November of the previous year; in January the Mesa Government announced it was withdrawing from trade agreement talks with Chile. Diplomatic interventions by Argentina and Brazil followed in an attempt to normalize relations between the countries concerned. The Chilean Government's decision in October to privatize the port of Arica elicited vehement objections from the Mesa administration, which feared this would adversely effect Bolivia's external trade, owing to significant increases in port tariffs (supposedly in contravention of the 1904 treaty that guaranteed duty-free passage of Bolivian goods through Arica). However, in the following month there were moves towards *rapprochement* at the Rio Group summit in Brazil after the Bolivian delegation notably omitted mention of its demand for sovereign access to the Pacific.

In 1992 Bolivia signed an agreement with Brazil for the construction of a 3,150-km pipeline to carry natural gas from Bolivia to southern Brazil. The outlines of the project, which was expected to cost US $1,800m. and was the largest of its kind in South America, were finalized, following considerable delay, in mid-1996. The pipeline (the first 1,970 km of which were completed in early 1999) transported an initial 3.7m. cu m of natural gas per day to Brazil, increasing to 30m. cu m by 2004, when the pipeline was due to reach full capacity.

In November 1994 an agreement to provide a waterway linking Bolivia with the Atlantic coast in Uruguay was concluded. However, by 2004 the controversial project, which involved dredging a deep-water channel in the Paraguay and Paraná Rivers, still had not begun, owing to Brazilian fears that the scheme would devastate a large, undeveloped area of ecological importance in south-western Brazil, known as the Pantanal.

Government

Legislative power is held by the bicameral Congreso Nacional (Congress), comprising a Cámara de Senadores (Senate), with 27 members and a Cámara de Diputados (Chamber of Deputies), comprising 130 members. Both houses are elected for a four-year term by universal adult suffrage. Executive power is vested in the President and the Cabinet, which is appointed by the President. The President is directly elected for five years. If no candidate gains an absolute majority of votes, the President is chosen by the Congreso. The country is divided, for administrative purposes, into nine departments, each of which is governed by a prefect.

Defence

Military service, for one year, is selective. In August 2004 the armed forces numbered 31,500 men (there were plans to increase this to 35,000), of whom the army had 25,000 (including 18,000 conscripts), the air force 3,000 and the navy 3,500. Expenditure on defence by the central Government in 2004 was an estimated 1,000m. bolivianos.

Economic Affairs

In 2003, according to World Bank estimates, Bolivia's gross national income (GNI), measured at average 2001–2003 prices, totalled US $7,722m., equivalent to about $890 per head (or $2,450 per head on an international purchasing-power parity basis). During 1990–2003, it was estimated, the population increased at an average annual rate of 2.4%, while gross domestic product (GDP) per head increased, in real terms, by an average of 0.9% per year. Bolivia's overall GDP increased, in real terms, at an average annual rate of 3.4% in 1990–2003; GDP increased by an estimated 2.5% in 2003.

Agriculture (including forestry and fishing) contributed 14.3% of GDP in 2003. In 2000 4.9% of the working population was employed in agriculture. Wood accounted for 2.6% of export earnings in 2003. The principal cash crops are soybeans (which accounted for 13.7% of export earnings in 2002), sugar, edible oils and coffee. Beef and hides are also important exports. In the period 1990–2003 agricultural GDP increased at an average annual rate of 2.8%; it rose by 0.6% in 2002 and by 3.0% in 2003.

Industry (including mining, manufacturing, construction and power) provided some 28.9% of GDP in 2003. In 2000 28.2% of the working population was employed in industry. In 1990–2003 industrial GDP increased at an average annual rate of 3.5%; it increased by 4.2% in 2002 and by 2.5% in 2003.

Mining (including petroleum exploration) contributed 8.4% of GDP in 2003 and employed about 1.7% of the working population in 2000. Investment in petroleum exploration totalled an estimated US $1m. in 2002, compared with $374m. in 1998. In 2002 nine foreign companies were involved in petroleum exploration in the country. Zinc, tin, silver, gold, lead and antimony are the major mineral exports. Tungsten and copper continue to be mined. Exports of zinc and tin earned an estimated $73.3m. and $123.4m., respectively, in 2003. In 1990–2003 the GDP of the mining sector increased at an estimated average annual rate of 3.0%; mining GDP increased by an estimated 3.6% in 2002 and by a further estimated 6.4% in 2003.

In 2003 manufacturing accounted for 14.3% of GDP and in 2000 some 15.3% of the working population was employed in the sector. The GDP of this sector increased during 1990–2003 at an average annual rate of 3.1%; it rose 2.2% in 2002 and by 0.9% in 2003.

Energy is derived principally from hydroelectricity and natural gas. In 2002 electricity generation totalled 3,695m. kWh, of which 59% was provided by hydroelectric plants. In 2002 production of crude petroleum totalled 11.3m. barrels, a slight decrease (of 0.8%) on the previous year. In 2003 imports of mineral products comprised an estimated 7.6% of total merchandise imports. Earnings from exports of petroleum accounted for an estimated 6.5% of the total in 2003. Exports of natural gas accounted for an estimated 26.1% of total export earnings in the same year. During the late 1990s several major new natural gas deposits were discovered, which significantly increased the country's total known reserves. In October 2003 a plan to export natural gas to the USA via the Chilean port of Patillos was suspended following public opposition (see Recent History). In mid-2004 proven reserves of natural gas were given at 27,600m. cu ft by the state oil company Yacimientos Petrolíferos Fiscales Bolivianos (YPFB). In October TotalFinaElf announced the discovery of a new gas field in the department of Chuquisaca, which geological surveys suggested would significantly increase Bolivia's natural gas reserves.

The services sector accounted for some 56.9% of GDPin 2003 and engaged 67.0% of the employed population in 2000. During the period 1990–2003 the GDP of this sector increased at an average annual rate of 3.6%; services GDP increased by 2.3% in 2002 and by 3.3% in 2003.

In 2003 Bolivia recorded a visible trade surplus of US $54.0m., and there was a surplus of $19.2m. on the current account of the balance of payments. In 2003 the main sources of imports were Brazil (20.4%), the USA (17.9%), Argentina (16.7%) and Chile (7.2%). Brazil, the USA, Colombia and Switzerland were the major recipients of Bolivian exports in 2003 (30.0%, 14.3%, 10.3% and 10.1%, respectively). The principal imports in that year included machinery, chemicals and chemical products and transport equipment. The principal legal exports were natural gas and prepared foodstuffs. However, it was estimated that a large proportion of Bolivia's export earnings came from the illegal trade in coca and its derivatives (mainly cocaine).

In 2001 Bolivia's overall budget deficit amounted to 3,561.7m. bolivianos (equivalent to 6.7% of GDP). Bolivia's total external debt at the end of 2002 was US $4,867m., of which $3,378m. was long-term public debt. The cost of debt-servicing in that year was equivalent to 25.3% of the total value of exports of goods and services. In 1990–2003 the average annual rate of inflation was 7.4%. Consumer prices increased by an average of 0.9% in 2002 and by 3.3% in 2003. In 2002 some 8.7% of the labour force in urban areas was unemployed.

In May 1991 Bolivia was one of five Andean Pact countries to sign the Caracas Declaration providing the foundation for a common market. In October 1992 Bolivia officially joined the Andean free-trade area, removing tariff barriers to imports from Colombia, Ecuador and Venezuela. Bolivia also agreed to sign a free-trade accord with Mexico in September 1994. In January 1997 a free-trade agreement with Mercosur (see p. 349), equivalent to associate membership of the organization, came into effect. In mid-1999 an agreement on the rationalization of their respective customs systems (thus moving closer to the formation of a regional free-trade area) was reached between Mercosur and the Andean Community (see p. 148); the two-year accord came into effect in August. Bolivia is a member of the Andean Community, and in 1989 the Andean Social Development Fund was established. The country is also a member of the Organization of American States (OAS, see p. 319), and of the Latin American Integration Association (ALADI, see p. 289). Bolivia became the 97th contracting party to GATT (which was superseded by the World Trade Organization, WTO (see p. 357), in 1995) in 1989. In December 2004 Bolivia was one of the founder signatories to the agreement signed in Cusco, Peru, creating the South American Community of Nations (Comunidad Sudamericana de Naciones), intended to promote greater regional economic integration, due to become operational by 2007.

The development of Bolivia's fossil fuels export sector was seen as crucial to economic growth in the early 21st century; a series of concessions for oil and natural gas projects were awarded in the late 1990s. In July 2001 an international consortium was formed in order to construct a pipeline, some 640 km in length, from the Margarita gasfield to the Chilean port of Patillos, for export to the USA. However, public opposition led to the project being suspended October 2003 (see Recent

History). The future of the pipeline, which had been forecast to increase Bolivia's GDP by an additional 1% per year, appeared uncertain in early 2005, particularly in view of the proposed gas-export project via the Peruvian port of Ilo (see Recent History).

The country's severe debt burden was a major factor inhibiting economic growth in the late 1990s, and in recognition of this in 1998 the World Bank and the IMF approved a debt-relief package worth US $760m. under the heavily indebted poor countries (HIPC) initiative. A further disbursement was allocated under HIPC in 2001. However, economic growth in the early years of the 21st century was impeded by social unrest (often linked to demands for increased public spending) and low international prices for Bolivian exports, while coca-eradication policies reduced incomes in the informal sector. Successive Governments committed themselves to the maintenance of IMF-sponsored fiscal economic policies, although overall growth rates remained modest in relation to the rate of population increase: GDP grew by 2.8% in 2002and by 2.5% in 2003; growth of 3.8% was forecast for 2004. Plans by the Government of President Sánchez de Lozada, which took office in mid-2002, to increase tax revenues to a sustainable level in order to qualify for international funding were abandoned in February 2003 following civil unrest. Despite this, in April the Government reached a stand-by agreement with the IMF, worth US $118m., and in early July some $15m. in loans was disbursed. The new Government of Carlos Mesa Gisbert, which took office in October 2003, pledged to reduce the fiscal deficit in order to qualify for further IMF funding. Official development assistance in that year was equivalent to an estimated 9.0% of GNI. In July 2004 the Government's proposals for greater state control of the country's oil and gas industry were approved in a referendum, but in early 2005 legislation to this end was still pending amid widespread disagreement and continuing civil unrest (see Recent History). Although successive US Administrations emphasized the importance of coca-eradication in eliminating cocaine production, in 2005 US aid was projected to increase to Bolivia following its renewed inclusion in the list of countries eligible for funding from the Millennium Challenge Corporation; this was in spite of the Mesa Government's suspension of some coca-eradication programmes in 2004 (see Recent History).

Education

Primary education, beginning at six years of age and lasting for eight years, is officially compulsory and is available free of charge. Secondary education, which is not compulsory, begins at 14 years of age and lasts for up to four years. In 1990 the total enrolment at primary and secondary schools was equivalent to 77% of the school-age population (81% of boys; 73% of girls). In that year enrolment at primary schools included an estimated 91% of children in the relevant age-group (95% of boys; 87% of girls), while the comparable ratio for secondary enrolment was only 29% (32% of boys; 27% of girls). There are eight state universities and two private universities. Expenditure on education by the Central Government in 2001 was 2,796.9m. bolivianos, representing 19.9% of total spending.

Public Holidays

2005: 1 January (New Year), 10 February (Oruro only), 25 March (Good Friday), 15 April (Tarija only), 1 May (Labour Day), 25 May (Sucre only), 26 May (Corpus Christi), 16 July (La Paz only), 6 August (Independence), 14 September (Cochabamba only), 24 September (Santa Cruz and Pando only), 1 October (Pando only), 1 November (All Saints' Day and Potosí), 10 November (Oruro only), 18 November (Beni only), 25 December (Christmas).

2006: 1 January (New Year), 10 February (Oruro only), 14 April (Good Friday), 15 April (Tarija only), 1 May (Labour Day), 25 May (Sucre only), 15 June (Corpus Christi), 16 July (La Paz only), 6 August (Independence), 14 September (Cochabamba only), 24 September (Santa Cruz and Pando only), 1 October (Pando only), 1 November (All Saints' Day and Potosí), 10 November (Oruro only), 18 November (Beni only), 25 December (Christmas).

Weights and Measures

The metric system is officially in force, but various old Spanish measures are also used.

Statistical Survey

Sources (unless otherwise indicated): Instituto Nacional de Estadística, José Carrasco 1391, Casilla 6129, La Paz; tel. (2) 222-2333; fax (2) 222-693; internet www.ine.gov.bo; Banco Central de Bolivia, Ayacucho esq. Mercado, Casilla 3118, La Paz; tel. (2) 240-9090; fax (2) 240-6614; e-mail bancocentraldebolivia@bcb.gov.bo; internet www.bcb.gov.bo.

Area and Population

AREA, POPULATION AND DENSITY

Area (sq km)
Land	1,084,391
Inland water	14,190
Total	1,098,581*

Population (census results)†
3 June 1992	6,420,792
5 September 2001	
Males	4,123,850
Females	4,150,475
Total	8,274,325

Population (official estimates at mid-year)
2003	9,024,922
2004	9,226,506
Density (per sq km) at mid-2004	8.5‡

* 424,164 sq miles.
† Figures exclude adjustment for underenumeration. This was estimated at 6.92% in 1992.
‡ Land area only.

DEPARTMENTS
(2001 census)

	Area (sq km)	Population	Density (per sq km)	Capital
Beni	213,564	362,521	1.7	Trinidad
Chuquisaca	51,524	531,522	10.3	Sucre
Cochabamba	55,631	1,455,711	26.2	Cochabamba
La Paz	133,985	2,350,466	17.5	La Paz
Oruro	53,588	391,870	7.3	Oruro
Pando	63,827	52,525	0.8	Cobija
Potosí	118,218	709,013	6.0	Potosí
Santa Cruz	370,621	2,029,471	5.5	Santa Cruz de la Sierra
Tarija	37,623	391,226	10.4	Tarija
Total	1,098,581	8,274,325	7.5	

PRINCIPAL TOWNS
(2001 census)

Santa Cruz de la Sierra	1,135,526	Oruro	215,660
La Paz (administrative capital)	793,293	Tarija	153,457
El Alto	649,958	Potosí	145,057
Cochabamba	517,024	Sacaba	117,100
Sucre (legal capital)	215,778	Quillacollo	104,206

BIRTHS AND DEATHS
(UN estimates, annual averages)

	1985–90	1990–95	1995–2000
Birth rate (per 1,000)	36.8	35.8	32.6
Death rate (per 1,000)	11.4	10.0	8.9

Source: UN, *World Population Prospects: The 2002 Revision*.

Expectation of life (WHO estimates, years at birth): 63.2 (males 61.8; females 64.7) in 2002 (Source: WHO, *World Health Report*).

ECONOMICALLY ACTIVE POPULATION
(labour force surveys, '000 persons aged 10 years and over, at November, urban areas only)

	1999	2000
Agriculture, hunting, forestry and fishing	77.4	102.7
Mining and quarrying	17.2	35.3
Manufacturing	370.5	320.1
Electricity, gas and water supply	5.5	15.9
Construction	176.5	218.9
Wholesale and retail trade; repair of motor vehicles, motorcycles and personal and household goods	542.5	536.1
Hotels and restaurants	126.8	124.4
Transport, storage and communications	173.0	144.3
Financial intermediation	17.5	20.0
Real estate, renting and business activities	71.7	95.8
Public administration and defence; compulsory social security	78.7	72.7
Education	135.6	132.8
Health and social work	63.2	48.8
Other community, social and personal service activities	76.6	98.8
Private households with employed persons	83.0	126.8
Extra-territorial organizations and bodies	1.2	2.8
Total employed	2,017.0	2,096.0
Unemployed	156.7	167.5
Total labour force	2,173.7	2,263.5
Males	1,204.6	1,248.1
Females	969.1	1,015.4

Source: ILO.

Mid-2003 (estimates in '000): Agriculture, etc. 1,588; Total labour force 3,662 (Source: FAO).

Health and Welfare

KEY INDICATORS

Total fertility rate (children per woman, 2002)	3.9
Under-5 mortality rate (per 1,000 live births, 2003)	66
HIV/AIDS (% of persons aged 15–49, 2003)	0.1
Physicians (per 1,000 head, 1997)	1.30
Hospital beds (per 1,000 head, 1996)	1.67
Health expenditure (2001): US $ per head (PPP)	125
Health expenditure (2001): % of GDP	5.3
Health expenditure (2001): public (% of total)	66.3
Access to water (% of persons, 2002)	85
Access to sanitation (% of persons, 2002)	45
Human Development Index (2002): ranking	114
Human Development Index (2002): value	0.681

For sources and definitions, see explanatory note on p. vi.

Agriculture

PRINCIPAL CROPS
('000 metric tons)

	2001	2002	2003
Wheat	117	118	89
Rice (paddy)	287	202	424
Barley	64	62	60
Maize	678	673	708
Sorghum	105	172	176
Potatoes	902	794	787
Cassava (Manioc)	517	393	392
Other roots and tubers* . . .	100	95	96
Sugar cane	3,859	4,735	4,872
Brazil nuts*	38	38	39
Chestnuts*	35	35	35
Soybeans (Soya beans)	834	1,298	1,550
Sunflower seeds	149	173	179
Cottonseed	48†	48*	48*
Tomatoes	138	117	135
Pumpkins, squash and gourds* .	110	111	112
Onions (dry)	49	49	49
Peas (green)	30	24	24
Broad beans (green)	66	60	59
Carrots	36	36	36
Green corn*	60	62	61
Other vegetables*	74	75	74
Watermelons	23	23	23
Bananas	688	624	627
Plantains*	187	188	185
Oranges	110	105	104
Tangerines, mandarins clementines and satsumas . .	62	58	58
Lemons and limes	64	64	64
Grapefruit and pomelos	29	29	29
Peaches and nectarines* . . .	37	37	37
Grapes	29	30	30
Pineapples	60	58	58
Papayas	23	23	23
Other fruits and berries . . .	51	51	52
Coffee (green)	25	25	25
Cotton (lint)	26†	26*	26*

* FAO estimate(s).
† Unofficial figure.
Source: FAO.

LIVESTOCK
('000 head, year ending September)

	2001	2002	2003
Horses*	322	323	323
Mules*	81	82	82
Asses*	631	632	635
Cattle	6,457	6,576	6,680
Pigs	2,851	2,851	2,925
Sheep	8,902	8,902	8,596
Goats*	1,500	1,501	1,501
Chickens*	74,000	74,500	75,000
Ducks*	280	280	295
Turkeys*	150	150	155

* FAO estimates.
Source: FAO.

LIVESTOCK PRODUCTS
('000 metric tons)

	2001	2002	2003
Beef and veal	160.9	164.6	168.2
Mutton and lamb	16.3	16.9	17.6
Goat meat*	5.8	5.8	5.8
Pig meat*	97.0	100.6	104.2
Poultry meat	129.0	136.0	136.0
Cows' milk	170.0	291.0	240.0*
Sheep's milk*	29.1	29.1	29.5
Goats' milk*	11.5	11.6	12.0
Cheese*	6.8	6.8	7.0
Hen eggs	38.7	38.7	38.7
Wool: greasy*	8.9	8.9	8.9
Cattle hides (fresh)*	19.6	19.9	20.4
Sheepskins (fresh)*	5.8	5.8	4.4

* FAO estimate(s).
Source: FAO.

Forestry

ROUNDWOOD REMOVALS
('000 cubic metres, excl. bark)

	2001	2002	2003
Sawlogs, veneer logs and logs for sleepers	559	544	544
Pulpwood	7,923	7,062	7,062
Other industrial wood	404	448	448
Fuel wood*	2,163	2,184	2,206
Total	11,049	10,238	10,260

* FAO estimates.
Source: FAO.

SAWNWOOD PRODUCTION
('000 cubic metres, incl. railway sleepers)

	2001	2002	2003
Total (all broadleaved)	308	299	347

Source: FAO.

Fishing

(metric tons, live weight)

	2000	2001	2002
Capture	6,106	5,940	5,800*
Freshwater fishes	4,911	4,900	4,853*
Rainbow trout	345	280	197
Silversides (sand smelts) . .	850	760	750*
Aquaculture	405	320	418
Rainbow trout	335	250	328
Total catch	6,511	6,260	6,218

* FAO estimate.
Note: Figures exclude crocodiles and alligators, recorded by number rather than by weight. The number of spectacled caimans caught was: n.a. in 2000; 28,170 in 2001; 31,021 in 2002.

Source: FAO, *Yearbook of Fishery Statistics*.

Mining

(metric tons, unless otherwise indicated; figures for metallic minerals refer to the metal content of ores)

	2000	2001	2002
Crude petroleum ('000 barrels) .	10,106	11,424	11,337
Natural gas (million cu feet) . .	127,044	186,276	226,740
Copper	110	18	120
Tin	12,503	12,039	13,210
Lead	9,523	9,090	9,268
Zinc	149,134	141,983	141,708
Tungsten (Wolfram)	495	671	474
Antimony	1,907	2,072	2,343
Silver	434	410	461
Gold (kg)	12,000	12,374	11,269

Source: IMF, *Bolivia: Selected Issues and Statistical Appendix* (August 2003).

Industry

SELECTED PRODUCTS
('000 metric tons, unless otherwise indicated)

	1999	2000	2001*
Flour	567	731	788
Cement	1,180	1,008	903
Refined sugar	294	311	333
Carbonated drinks ('000 hectolitres)	2,192	2,343	1,996
Beer ('000 hectolitres) . . .	1,797	1,509	1,586
Cigarettes (packets)	67,332	67,211	75,373
Alcohol ('000 litres)	26,412	30,981	29,099
Diesel oil ('000 barrels) . . .	3,063	2,727	2,923
Motor spirit (petrol) ('000 barrels)	4,176	3,852	3,439
Electric energy (million kWh) . .	3,881	3,498	3,529

* Provisional figures.

Source: partly UN, *Industrial Commodity Statistics Yearbook*.

2002: Electric energy: 3,695 million kWh (Source: IMF, *Bolivia: Selected Issues and Statistical Appendix*, August 2003).

Finance

CURRENCY AND EXCHANGE RATES

Monetary Units
100 centavos = 1 boliviano (B).

Sterling, Dollar and Euro Equivalents (31 December 2004)
£1 sterling = 15.548 bolivianos;
US $1 = 8.050 bolivianos;
€1 = 10.965 bolivianos;
1,000 bolivianos = £64.32 = $124.22 = €91.20.

Average Exchange Rate (bolivianos per US $)
2002   7.1700
2003   7.6592
2004   7.9363

BUDGET
(million bolivianos)*

Revenue†	1999	2000	2001
Taxation	6,749.2	7,276.1	7,302.6
Taxes on income, profits, etc. .	710.9	723.5	635.0
Social security contributions .	951.3	872.9	964.7
Taxes on property	641.9	697.8	703.2
Domestic taxes on goods and services	3,561.9	4,450.1	4,388.0
Value-added tax	2,206.8	2,315.0	2,331.2
Excises	1,345.7	2,123.5	2,045.4
Import duties	480.7	519.7	465.1
Other tax revenue	402.5	12.1	146.1
Other current revenue . . .	1,294.2	1,740.8	1,752.2
Capital revenue	594.9	261.8	113.3
Total	**8,638.3**	**9,278.7**	**9,168.1**

Expenditure‡	1999	2000	2001
General public services . . .	800.2	799.3	1,076.8
Defence	857.7	864.5	1,047.3
Public order and safety	767.9	939.3	1,013.8
Education	2,280.3	2,442.8	2,796.9
Health	426.0	1,287.0	1,397.9
Social security and welfare . .	2,793.5	2,588.2	2,905.6
Housing and community amenities	173.2	278.1	269.0
Recreational, cultural, and religious affairs and services .	38.3	42.5	42.5
Economic services	1,795.0	1,854.7	2,027.1
Fuel and energy	483.5	108.9	150.5
Agriculture, forestry, fishing and hunting	290.6	364.5	374.4
Transportation and communications	825.9	997.1	767.8
Other purposes	1,234.6	1,217.9	1,513.2
Total	**11,166.9**	**12,314.4**	**14,089.9**
Current§	9,395.7	10,184.5	12,117.3
Capital	1,771.2	2,129.9	1,972.6

* Budget figures refer to the consolidated accounts of the central Government, including government agencies and social security institutions.
† Excluding grants received (million bolivianos): 950.6 in 1999; 908.8 in 2000; 1,350.5 in 2001.
‡ Excluding lending minus repayments (million bolivianos): −473.7 in 1999; −397.0 in 2000; −9.6 in 2001.
§ Including interest payments (million bolivianos): 627.6 in 1999; 890.5 in 2000; 1,103.0 in 2001.

Source: IMF, *Government Finance Statistics Yearbook*.

INTERNATIONAL RESERVES
(US $ million at 31 December)

	2001	2002	2003
Gold*	259.6	316.4	379.4
IMF special drawing rights . .	34.3	37.2	40.3
Reserve position in IMF . . .	11.2	12.1	13.2
Foreign exchange	840.9	531.2	663.3
Total	**1,146.0**	**896.9**	**1,096.2**

* National valuation.

Source: IMF, *International Financial Statistics*.

MONEY SUPPLY
(million bolivianos at 31 December)

	2001	2002	2003
Currency outside banks . . .	2,422	2,707	3,231
Demand deposits at commercial banks	1,353	1,271	1,385
Total money (incl. others) . .	**4,743**	**4,725**	**5,636**

Source: IMF, *International Financial Statistics*.

COST OF LIVING
(Consumer Price Index for urban areas; base: 2000 = 100)

	2001	2002	2003
Food and beverages	100.6	99.7	103.2
Fuel and light	104.4	108.9	114.2
Clothing and footwear . . .	102.9	105.9	109.0
Rent	100.2	101.1	109.0
All items (incl. others) . . .	**101.6**	**102.5**	**105.9**

Source: ILO.

NATIONAL ACCOUNTS

Expenditure on the Gross Domestic Product
(million bolivianos at current prices)

	2001	2002	2003
Government final consumption expenditure	8,071	8,638	9,980
Private final consumption expenditure	40,475	41,840	44,389
Increase in stocks	−135	−642	−1,274
Gross fixed capital formation	7,687	8,885	7,971
Total domestic expenditure	56,099	58,722	61,066
Exports of goods and services	10,436	12,264	14,286
Less Imports of goods and services	13,525	15,052	15,101
GDP at market prices	53,010	55,933	60,252
GDP at constant 1990 prices	22,642	23,266	23,837

Source: IMF, *International Financial Statistics*.

Gross Domestic Product by Economic Activity
(million bolivianos at current prices)

	2001	2002	2003
Agriculture, hunting, forestry and fishing	7,019.0	7,115.3	7,803.0
Mining and quarrying	3,214.7	3,524.1	4,597.2
Manufacturing	7,003.6	7,297.1	7,802.1
Electricity, gas and water	1,622.8	1,706.6	1,830.1
Construction	1,539.9	1,831.5	1,580.6
Trade	3,776.1	3,951.6	4,199.5
Hotels and restaurants	1,691.7	1,794.4	1,835.0
Transport, storage and communications	6,240.1	6,652.6	7,111.1
Finance, insurance, real estate and business services	6,889.3	6,848.7	6,943.5
Government services	6,548.3	7,038.1	7,797.3
Other community, social and personal services	2,861.5	3,045.1	3,242.3
Sub-total	48,407.0	50,805.1	54,741.7
Value-added tax	6,867.8	7,267.3	7,713.6
Import duties			
Less Imputed bank charge	2,264.5	2,139.2	2,203.6
GDP in purchasers' values	53,010.3	55,933.1	60,251.7

BALANCE OF PAYMENTS
(US $ million)

	2001	2002	2003
Exports of goods f.o.b.	1,284.8	1,298.7	1,573.4
Imports of goods f.o.b.	−1,580.0	−1,639.0	−1,519.4
Trade balance	−295.2	−340.3	54.0
Exports of services	235.9	256.6	305.9
Imports of services	−399.4	−432.9	−485.5
Balance on goods and services	−458.7	−516.6	−125.6
Other income received	121.2	103.2	71.7
Other income paid	−332.5	−307.9	−373.4
Balance on goods, services and income	−670.1	−721.3	−427.4
Current transfers received	431.6	407.8	486.2
Current transfers paid	−35.5	−38.4	−39.9
Current balance	−274.0	−351.9	19.2
Direct investment abroad	−2.5	−2.5	−2.5
Direct investment from abroad	705.8	676.6	171.3
Portfolio investment assets	−23.0	−19.3	−68.4
Other investment assets	−166.7	−193.7	−177.6
Other investment liabilities	−72.9	188.7	283.2
Net errors and omissions	−202.7	−640.5	−279.5
Overall balance	−36.0	−342.7	−54.6

Source: IMF, *International Financial Statistics*.

External Trade

PRINCIPAL COMMODITIES
(distribution by SITC, US $ million)

Imports c.i.f.	2001	2002	2003
Vegetable products	145.9	144.6	130.2
Prepared foodstuffs (incl. beverages and tobacco)	78.8	71.1	78.7
Mineral fuels, lubricants, etc.	126.6	93.9	128.7
Chemicals and related products	238.9	223.1	241.0
Plastic and articles thereof	121.9	123.4	123.5
Wood and wood products	81.3	74.0	75.3
Textiles and textile products	100.3	79.4	78.9
Basic manufactures	157.9	269.4	161.9
Machinery and mechanical appliances (incl. electrical equipment and parts thereof)	409.5	447.0	350.6
Transport equipment	88.4	150.5	174.6
Total (incl. others)	1,708.3	1,832.0	1,684.6

Exports f.o.b.	2001	2002	2003
Vegetable products	63.8	73.5	105.7
Prepared foodstuffs (incl. beverages and tobacco)	220.1	240.8	253.3
Animal and vegetable oils, fats and waxes	108.6	116.6	129.4
Mineral fuels, lubricants, etc.	492.5	545.0	723.7
Wood and wood products	41.0	41.1	42.6
Textiles and textile products	42.6	33.0	52.6
Jewellery, goldsmiths' and silversmiths' wares, etc.	188.2	214.1	185.1
Basic manufactures	53.5	51.9	62.4
Total* (incl. others)	1,265.6	1,377.2	1,621.7

* Including re-exports (US $ million): 123.7 in 2001; 54.4 in 2002; 79.6 in 2003.

PRINCIPAL TRADING PARTNERS
(US $ million)

Imports c.i.f.	2001	2002	2003
Argentina	307.9	308.5	281.4
Brazil	276.4	392.5	343.4
Canada	19.8	12.6	7.0
Chile	144.8	126.1	122.0
China, People's Republic	86.3	95.9	84.6
Colombia	47.9	42.6	48.1
France	17.0	19.9	19.5
Germany	37.5	31.6	36.7
Italy	29.5	24.3	21.2
Japan	58.4	101.3	83.5
Korea, Republic	20.8	17.2	17.2
Mexico	37.8	32.9	34.7
Paraguay	23.0	18.1	16.7
Peru	107.9	95.0	104.4
Spain	26.8	24.3	23.6
Taiwan	20.8	15.2	7.0
USA	313.3	309.9	302.3
Venezuela	17.1	14.0	8.8
Total (incl. others)	1,708.3	1,832.0	1,684.6

Exports f.o.b.	2001	2002	2003
Argentina	67.5	27.9	56.3
Belgium	14.0	8.7	15.7
Brazil	289.2	336.6	495.7
Canada	20.2	7.8	6.1
Chile	30.3	32.8	43.5
Colombia	191.9	139.5	170.3
Germany	8.4	66.5	67.5
Italy	13.3	13.8	16.4
Japan	2.8	5.9	18.6
Mexico	8.3	19.9	21.0
Netherlands	16.0	13.4	13.4
Peru	67.5	74.1	83.7
Switzerland	176.5	214.9	165.9
United Kingdom	71.5	32.0	33.5
USA	187.8	193.0	235.3
Venezuela	98.2	175.4	155.4
Total* (incl. others)	1,352.9	1,376.9	1,650.7

* Including re-exports (US $ million): 123.7 in 2001; 54.4 in 2002; 79.6 in 2003.

Transport

RAILWAYS
(traffic)

	1999	2000	2001
Passenger-kilometres (million) .	271	259	267
Freight ton-kilometres (million) .	832	856	750

Source: UN, *Statistical Yearbook*.

ROAD TRAFFIC
(motor vehicles in use at 31 December)

	1999*	2000*	2001
Passenger cars	168,611	181,409	254,853
Buses	19,581	21,183	21,808
Lorries and vans	213,455	234,746	133,686
Tractors	804	944	n.a.
Motorcycles	25,917	27,897	27,626

* Estimates.
Source: IRF, *World Road Statistics*.

SHIPPING
Merchant Fleet
(registered at 31 December)

	2001	2002	2003
Number of vessels	78	96	136
Total displacement ('000 grt) . .	174.0	358.1	420.4

Source: Lloyd's Register-Fairplay, *World Fleet Statistics*.

CIVIL AVIATION
(traffic on scheduled services)

	1996	1997	1998
Kilometres flown (million) . .	24	28	28
Passengers carried ('000) . .	1,783	2,251	2,115
Passenger-km (million) . . .	1,634	2,143	2,179
Freight ton-km (million) . . .	223	274	273

Source: UN, *Statistical Yearbook*.

Tourism

ARRIVALS AT HOTELS
(regional capitals only, '000)

Country of origin	2000	2001	2002
Argentina	43.8	42.1	35.2
Brazil	24.3	24.0	26.2
Canada	7.9	7.8	8.2
Chile	22.4	23.2	21.9
France	21.0	24.5	26.7
Germany	23.6	23.4	21.7
Israel	10.0	9.2	10.6
Italy	7.7	7.6	7.9
Japan	7.0	7.2	7.0
Netherlands	13.9	12.9	12.2
Peru	50.2	52.6	59.7
Spain	9.6	9.5	10.9
Switzerland	9.7	10.4	9.2
United Kingdom	18.0	19.6	20.1
USA	44.2	37.9	38.5
Total (incl. others)	381.1	378.6	382.2

Source: World Tourism Organization, *Yearbook of Tourism Statistics*.

Total tourism receipts (US $ million): 160 in 2000; 156 in 2001; n.a. in 2002 (Source: World Tourism Organization).

Communications Media

	2001	2002	2003
Telephones ('000 main lines in use)	524.4	530.9	600.1
Mobile cellular telephones ('000 subscribers)	779.9	872.7	1,401.5
Personal computers ('000 in use)*	170	190	n.a.
Internet users ('000)*	180	270	n.a.

* Estimates.
Source: International Telecommunication Union.

Television receivers ('000): 990 in use in 2000 (Source: International Telecommunication Union).

Radio receivers ('000): 5,250 in use in 1997 (Source: UNESCO, *Statistical Yearbook*).

Daily newspapers: 18 in 1996 (average circulation 420,000 copies) (Source: UNESCO, *Statistical Yearbook*).

Education

(2001)

	Institutions	Teachers	Students
Pre-primary	2,294*	4,133	198,640
Primary	12,639†	66,339	1,666,150
Secondary	n.a.	16,507	398,360
Higher:			
state universities . . .	n.a.	7,738‡	212,594‡
private universities . .	n.a.	3,332§	48,817‖

* 1988.
† 1987.
‡ 2000.
§ 1998.
‖ Preliminary figure.

Source: partly UNESCO, *Statistical Yearbook*.

Adult literacy rate (census data): 86.7% (males 93.1%; females 80.7%) in 2002 (Source: UN Development Programme, *Human Development Report*).

Directory

The Constitution

Bolivia became an independent republic in 1825 and received its first Constitution in November 1826. Since that date a number of new Constitutions have been promulgated. Following the *coup d'état* of November 1964, the Constitution of 1947 was revived. Under its provisions, executive power is vested in the President, who chairs the Cabinet. According to the revised Constitution, the President is elected by direct suffrage for a five-year term (extended from four years in 1997) and is not eligible for immediate re-election. In the event of the President's death or failure to assume office, the Vice-President or, failing the Vice-President, the President of the Senate becomes interim Head of State.

The President has power to appoint members of the Cabinet and diplomatic representatives from a panel proposed by the Senate. The President is responsible for the conduct of foreign affairs and is also empowered to issue decrees, and initiate legislation by special messages to Congress.

The Congreso Nacional (Congress) consists of a 27-member Cámara de Senadores (Senate) and a 130-member Cámara de Diputados (Chamber of Deputies). The Congreso meets annually and its ordinary sessions last only 90 working days, which may be extended to 120. Each of the nine departments (La Paz, Chuquisaca, Oruro, Beni, Santa Cruz, Potosí, Tarija, Cochabamba and Pando), into which the country is divided for administrative purposes, elects three senators. Members of both houses are elected for five years.

The supreme administrative, political and military authority in each department is vested in a prefect appointed by the President. The sub-divisions of each department, known as provinces, are administered by sub-prefects. The provinces are further divided into cantons. There are 94 provinces and some 1,000 cantons. The capital of each department has its autonomous municipal council and controls its own revenue and expenditure.

Public order, education and roads are under national control.

A decree issued in July 1952 conferred the franchise on all persons who had reached the age of 21 years, whether literate or illiterate. Previously the franchise had been restricted to literate persons. (The voting age for married persons was lowered to 18 years at the 1989 elections.)

The Government

HEAD OF STATE

President: CARLOS MESA GISBERT (took office 18 October 2003).

THE CABINET
(April 2005)

Minister of Foreign Affairs and Worship: JUAN IGNACIO SILES DEL VALLE.

Minister of the Interior: Dr SAÚL LARA TORRICO.

Minister of National Defence: Gen. GONZALO ARREDONDO MILLÁN.

Minister of Finance: LUIS CARLOS JEMIO MOLLINEDO.

Minister of Sustainable Development and Planning: ERWIN AGUILERA ANTONEZ.

Minister of the Presidency: JOSÉ ANTONIO GALINDO NEDER.

Minister of Health and Sport: (vacant).

Minister of Labour: AUDALIA ZURITA ZELADA.

Minister of Education: MARÍA SOLEDAD QUIROGA.

Minister of Agriculture, Livestock and Rural Development: VÍCTOR BARRIOS ARANCIBIO.

Minister of Economic Development: WALTER KREIDLER.

Minister of Hydrocarbons and Energy: GUILLERMO TORRES ORÍAS.

Minister of Mines and Metallurgy: JORGE ESPINOZA MORALES.

Minister of Public Works and Services: RENÉ GÓMEZ-GARCÍA PALAU.

Minister without Portfolio responsible for Popular Participation: GLORIA ARDAYA SALINAS.

Minister without Portfolio responsible for Indigenous and Ethnic Peoples' Affairs: PEDRO TICONA CRUZ.

MINISTRIES

Ministry of Agriculture, Livestock and Rural Development: Avda Camacho 1471, La Paz.

Ministry of Economic Development: Edif. Palacio de Comunicaciones, Avda Mariscal Santa Cruz, La Paz; tel. (2) 237-7234; fax (2) 235-9955; e-mail contactos@desarrollo.gov.bo; internet www.desarrollo.gov.bo.

Ministry of Education: Casilla 6500, La Paz; tel. (2) 220-3576; fax (2) 220-3576; internet www.minedu.gov.bo.

Ministry of Finance: Edif. Palacio de Comunicaciones, Avda Mariscal Santa Cruz, La Paz; tel. (2) 237-7234; fax (2) 235-9955.

Ministry of Foreign Affairs and Worship: Calle Ingavi, esq. Junin, La Paz; tel. (2) 237-1150; fax (2) 237-1155; e-mail mreuno@rree.gov.bo; internet www.rree.gov.bo.

Ministry of Health and Sport: Plaza del Estudiante, La Paz; tel. (2) 237-1373; fax (2) 239-1590; e-mail minsalud@ceibo.entelnet.bo; internet www.sns.gov.bo.

Ministry of Hydrocarbons and Energy: La Paz.

Ministry of the Interior: Avda Arce 2409, esq. Belisario Salinas, La Paz; tel. (2) 237-0460; fax (2) 237-1334; e-mail mail@mingobierno.gov.bo; internet www.mingobierno.gov.bo.

Ministry of Labour: Calle Yanacocha, esq. Mercado, La Paz; tel. (2) 236-4164; fax (2) 237-1387; e-mail mintrabajo@unete.com; internet www.mintrabajo.gob.bo.

Ministry of Mines and Metallurgy: Avda Mariscal Santa Cruz, esq. Oruro Edif., Palacio de Telecomunicaciones, 12°, La Paz; tel. (2) 237-4050; fax (2) 239-2758.

Ministry of National Defence: Plaza Avaroa, esq. Pedro Salazar y 20 de Octubre 2502, La Paz; tel. (2) 232-0225; fax (2) 243-3153; e-mail comunicaciones@mindef.gov.bo; internet www.mindef.gov.bo.

Ministry of the Presidency: Palacio de Gobierno, Plaza Murillo, La Paz; tel. (2) 237-1082; fax (2) 237-1388.

Ministry of Public Works and Services: La Paz.

Ministry of Sustainable Development and Planning: Arce 2147, 4°, Casilla 12814, La Paz; tel. and fax (2) 231-0860; fax (2) 231-7320; e-mail sdnp@coord.rds.org.bo; internet www.rds.org.bo.

President and Legislature

PRESIDENT

At the presidential election that took place on 30 June 2002 the majority of votes were spread between five of the 11 candidates. Gonzalo ('Goni') Sánchez de Lozada of the Movimiento Nacionalista Revolucionario (MNR) obtained 22.49% of the votes cast, Evo Morales of the Movimiento al Socialismo (MAS) won 20.94%, Manfred Reyes Villa of the Nueva Fuerza Republicana (NFR) won 20.91%, Jaime Paz Zamora of the Movimiento de la Izquierda Revolucionaria (MIR) secured 16.31% and Felipe Quispe Huanca of Movimiento Indígena Pachakuti (MIP) won 6.09%. As no candidate obtained the requisite absolute majority, responsibility for the selection of the President passed to the new Congreso Nacional (National Congress), which, on 4 August 2002, voted, by 84 votes to 43, to appoint Goni Sánchez de Lozada to the presidency. On 18 October 2003, following Sánchez de Lozada's resignation, Carlos Mesa Gisbert (Vice-President until he had resigned on 13 October) was sworn in as President.

CONGRESO NACIONAL

President of the Cámara de Senadores: HORMANDO VACA DÍEZ.

President of the Cámara de Diputados: MARIO COSSÍO CORTEZ.

BOLIVIA *Directory*

General Election, 30 June 2002

Party	Cámara de Diputados	Cámara de Senadores
Movimiento Nacionalista Revolucionario (Histórico) (MNR)	36	11
Movimiento al Socialismo (MAS)	27	8
Movimiento de la Izquierda Revolucionaria (MIR)	26	5
Nueva Fuerza Republicana (NFR)	25	2
Movimientio Indígena Pachakuti (MIP)	7	—
Unión Cívica Solidaridad (UCS)	5	—
Acción Democrática Nacionalista (ADN)	4	1
Partido Socialista (PS)	1	—
Total	**130**	**27**

Political Organizations

Acción Democrática Nacionalista (ADN): Calle Uruguay 454, La Paz; tel. (2) 242-3067; fax (2) 242-3412; e-mail mvberteros@aol.com; internet www.bolivian.com/adn; f. 1979; right-wing; Leader MAURO BERTERO GUTIÉRREZ; Nat. Exec. Sec. JORGE LANDÍVAR.

Alianza de Renovación Boliviana (ARBOL): La Paz; f. 1993; conservative; Leader CASIANO ACALLE CHOQUE.

Bolivia Insurgente: La Paz; f. 1996; populist party; Leader MÓNICA MEDINA.

Comité Cívico pro Santa Cruz: Avda Cañada Strongest 70, CP 1801, Santa Cruz; tel. (3) 334-2777; fax (3) 334-1812; e-mail info@comiteprosantacruz.org; internet www.comiteprosantacruz.org; f. 1950; right-wing autonomist grouping; Pres. GERMÁN ANTELO; Vice-Pres. NINO GANDARILLA.

Comité Cívico de Tarija (CCT): Tarija; right-wing autonomist grouping; Pres. ROBERTO RUIZ.

Conciencia de Patria (Condepa): La Paz; f. 1988; populist party; Leader NICOLAS FELIPE VALDIVIA ALMANZA.

Frente Revolucionario de Izquierda (FRI): La Paz; left-wing; Leader OSCAR ZAMORA.

Frente Unidad Nacional (FUN): Cochabamba; f. 2003; left-wing; Leader SAMUEL DORIA MEDINA.

Movimiento Bolivariano: La Paz; f. 1999; Leader CRISTINA CORRALES.

Movimiento Bolivia Libre (MBL): Edif. Camiri, Of. 601, Calle Comercio 972, esq. Yanacocha, Casilla 10382, La Paz; tel. (2) 234-0257; fax (2) 239-2242; f. 1985; left-wing; breakaway faction of MIR; 60,000 mems; Leader FRANK BARRIOS.

Movimiento Indígena Pachakuti (MIP): indigenous movement; f. 2002; Leader FELIPE QUISPE HUANCA.

Movimiento de la Izquierda Revolucionaria (MIR): Avda América 119, 2°, La Paz; e-mail mir@ceibo.entelnet.bo; internet www.cibergallo.com; f. 1971; split into several factions in 1985; left-wing; 150,000 mems; Leader JAIME PAZ ZAMORA; Sec.-Gen. OSCAR EID FRANCO.

Movimiento sin Miedo: La Paz; f. 1999; left-wing; Leader JUAN DEL GRANADO.

Movimiento Nacionalista Revolucionario (Histórico) (MNR): Calle Nicolás Acosta 574, La Paz; tel. (2) 249-0748; fax (2) 249-0009; formerly part of the Movimiento Nacionalista Revolucionario (MNR, f. 1942); centre-right; Leader GONZALO SÁNCHEZ DE LOZADA; Sec.-Gen. CARLOS SÁNCHEZ BERZAIN; 165,000 mems.

Movimiento Revolucionario Túpac Katarí de Liberación (MRTKL): Avda Baptista 939, Casilla 9133, La Paz; tel. (2) 235-4784; f. 1978; peasant party; Leader VÍCTOR HUGO CÁRDENAS CONDE; Sec.-Gen. NORBERTO PÉREZ HIDALGO; 80,000 mems.

Movimiento al Socialismo—Instrumento Político por la Soberanía de los Pueblos (MAS): La Paz; e-mail webmaster@masbolivia.org; internet www.masbolivia.org; f. 1987; left-wing; Leader EVO MORALES.

Nueva Fuerza Republicana (NFR): Cochabamba; f. 1996; centre-right; Leader MANFRED REYES VILLA.

Partido Comunista de Bolivia (PCB): La Paz; f. 1950; Leader MARCOS DOMIC; First Sec. SIMÓN REYES RIVERA.

Partido Demócrata Cristiano (PDC): Casilla 4345, La Paz; f. 1954; Pres. BENJAMÍN MIGUEL HARB; Sec. ANTONIO CANELAS-GALATOIRE; 50,000 mems.

Partido Obrero Revolucionario (POR): Correo Central, La Paz; f. 1935; Trotskyist; Leader GUILLERMO LORA.

Partido Revolucionario de la Izquierda Nacionalista (PRIN): Calle Colón 693, La Paz; f. 1964; left-wing; Leader JUAN LECHIN OQUENDO.

Partido Socialista (PS): La Paz; f. 1987; Leader JERES JUSTINIANO.

Partido de Vanguardia Obrera: Plaza Venezuela 1452, La Paz; Leader FILEMÓN ESCOBAR.

Unión Cívica Solidaridad (UCS): Calle Mercado 1064, 6°, La Paz; tel. (2) 236-0297; fax (2) 237-2200; f. 1989; populist; 102,000 mems; Leader JOHNNY FERNÁNDEZ.

Vanguardia Revolucionaria 9 de Abril: Avda 6 de Agosto 2170, Casilla 5810, La Paz; tel. (2) 232-0311; fax (2) 239-1439; Leader Dr CARLOS SERRATE REICH.

Other parties include the Alianza Democrática Socialista and the Eje Patriótica.

Diplomatic Representation

EMBASSIES IN BOLIVIA

Argentina: Calle Aspiazú 497, CP 64, La Paz; tel. (2) 241-7737; fax (2) 242-2727; e-mail embarbol@caoba.entelnet.bo; Ambassador HORACIO ANTONIO MACEDO.

Belgium: Calle 9, No 6, Achumani, Casilla 2433, La Paz; tel. (2) 277-1430; fax (2) 279-1219; e-mail lapaz@diplobel.be; internet www.diplomatie.be/lapazes; Ambassador FRANK VAN DE CRAEN.

Brazil: Edif. Multicentro, Torre B, Avda Arce s/n, esq. Rosendo Gutierrez, Sopocachi, La Paz; tel. (2) 244-0202; fax (2) 244-0043; e-mail webmaster@brasil.org.bo; internet www.brasil.org.bo; Ambassador ANTONINO MENA-GONÇALVES.

China, People's Republic: Calle 1, Los Pinos 8532, Casilla 10005, La Paz; tel. (2) 279-3851; fax (2) 279-7121; e-mail emb-china@kolla.net; Ambassador ZHANG TUO.

Colombia: Calle 9, 7835 Calacoto; tel. (2) 271-2413; fax (2) 278-6510; e-mail emco@acelerate.com; Ambassador GUILLERMO ANTONIO VANEGAS SIERRA.

Costa Rica: Edif. San Miguel Arcángel 1420, 1°, Of. 102, Avda Montenegro en Calacoto, La Paz; tel. and fax (2) 279-8930; e-mail embcrbo@entelnet.bo; Ambassador DIDIER CARRANZA RODRÍGUEZ.

Cuba: Bajo Irpavi Avda Gobles 20, entre 13 y 14, La Paz; tel. (2) 272-1157; fax (2) 272-3419; e-mail embacuba@ceibo,entelnet.bo; Ambassador LUIS FELIPE VÁSQUEZ VÁSQUEZ.

Denmark: Edif. Fortaleza, Avda Arce 2799, esq. Cordero, 9°, Casilla 9860, La Paz; tel. (2) 243-2070; fax (2) 243-3150; e-mail lpbamb@um.dk; Ambassador MOGENS PEDERSEN.

Ecuador: Edif. Hermman, 14°, Plaza Venezuela 1440, Casilla 406, La Paz; tel. (2) 233-1588; fax (2) 231-9739; e-mail mecuabol@caoba.entelnet.bo; Ambassador MANUEL ROMERO CEVALLOS.

Egypt: Avda Ballivián 599, Casilla 2956, La Paz; tel. (2) 278-6511; fax (2) 278-4325; e-mail embegylp@ceibo.entelnet.bo; Ambassador NAGWA MOHAMED AFIFI.

France: Avda Hernando Silés 5390, esq. Calle 8, Obrajes, Casilla 717, La Paz; tel. (2) 214-9900; fax (2) 214-9904; e-mail information@ambafrance-bo.org; internet www.ambafrance-bo.org; Ambassador ANITA LIMIDO.

Germany: Avda Arce 2395, esq. Belisario Salinas, Casilla 5265, La Paz; tel. (2) 244-0066; fax (2) 244-1441; e-mail info@embajada-alemana-bolivia.org; internet www.embajada-alemana-bolivia.org; Ambassador Dr BERND SPROEDT.

Holy See: Avda Arce 2990, Casilla 136, La Paz; tel. (2) 243-1007; fax (2) 243-2120; e-mail nunapobol@acelerate.com; Apostolic Nuncio Most Rev. IVO SCAPOLO (Titular Archbishop of Tagaste).

Israel: Edif. Esperanza, 10°, Avda Mariscal Santa Cruz 2150, Casilla 1309, La Paz; tel. (2) 237-4329; fax (2) 239-1712; e-mail embisrael@acelerate.com; Ambassador MERON REUBEN.

Italy: Avda 6 de Agosto 2575, Casilla 626, La Paz; tel. (2) 243-4929; fax (2) 243-4975; e-mail ambitlap@ceibo.entelnet.bo; internet www.ambital.org.bo; Ambassador Dr MAURIZIO ZANINI.

Japan: Calle Rosendo Gutiérrez 497, Casilla 2725, La Paz; tel. (2) 237-3151; fax (2) 239-1052; e-mail embjapon@ceibo.entelnet.bo; Ambassador MITSUNORI SHIRAKAWA.

Korea, Republic: La Paz; Ambassador CHUNG JIN-HO.

Mexico: Sánchez Bustamante 509, Casilla 430, La Paz; tel. (2) 277-2133; fax (2) 277-6085; e-mail embamex@acelerate.com; internet

844

www.sre.gob.mx/bolivia; Ambassador José Antonio Zabalgoitia Trejo.

Netherlands: Edif. Hilda, 7°, Avda 6 de Agosto 2455, La Paz; tel. (2) 244-4040; fax (2) 244-3804; e-mail nllap@caoba.entelnet.bo; internet www.embholanda-bo.org; Ambassador Ronald C. J. Muyzert.

Panama: Calle 10, No 7853 de Colacoto, Casilla 678, La Paz; tel. (2) 278-7334; fax (2) 279-7290; e-mail empanbol@ceibo.entelnet.bo; Ambassador Augusto Luis Villarreal Amaranto.

Paraguay: Edif. Illimani II, 1°, Avda 6 de Agosto y Pedro Salazar, Casilla 882, La Paz; tel. (2) 243-3176; fax (2) 243-2201; e-mail embapar@acelerate.com; Ambassador Nimia Oviedo de Torales.

Peru: Calle F. Guachalla 300, Casilla 668, Sopocachi, La Paz; tel. (2) 244-1250; fax (2) 244-1240; e-mail embbol@caoba.entelnet.bo; Ambassador Luzmila Zanabria.

Russia: Calacoto, Avda Walter Guevara Arze 8129, La Paz; tel. (2) 278-6419; fax (2) 278-6531; e-mail embrusia@ceibo.entelnet.bo; Ambassador Vladimir L. Kulikov.

Spain: Avda 6 de Agosto 2827, Casilla 282, La Paz; tel. (2) 243-3518; fax (2) 211-3267; e-mail embespa@ceibo.entelnet.bo; Ambassador Juan Francisco Montalbán Carrasco.

Switzerland: Calle 13, esq. Avda 14 de Setiembre, Obrajes, Casilla 9356, La Paz; tel. (2) 275-1001; fax (2) 214-0885; e-mail vertretung@paz.rep.admin.ch; internet www.eda.admin.ch/lapaz; Chargé d'affaires a.i. Jacques Gremaud.

United Kingdom: Avda Sopocachi, Arce 2732, Casilla 694, La Paz; tel. (2) 243-3424; fax (2) 243-1073; e-mail ppa@megalink.com; internet www.britishembassy.gov.uk/bolivia; Ambassador William Baldie Sinton.

USA: Avda Arce 2780, Casilla 425, La Paz; tel. (2) 243-0251; fax (2) 243-3900; internet www.megalink.com/usemblapaz; Ambassador David N. Greenlee.

Uruguay: Edif. Monroy Velez, 7°, Calle 21 No 8350, Calacoto, La Paz, La Paz; tel. (2) 279-1482; fax (2) 212-9413; e-mail urulivia@acelerate.com; Ambassador Juan A. Pacheco Ramírez.

Venezuela: Edif. Illimani, 4°, Avda Arce, esq. Campos, Casilla 441, La Paz; tel. (2) 243-1365; fax (2) 243-2348; e-mail embvzla@acelerate.com; Chargé d'affaires María Eugenia Pérez Godoy.

Judicial System

SUPREME COURT

Corte Suprema

Calle Pilinco 352, Sucre; tel. (4) 645-1883; fax (4) 646-2696; e-mail csuprema@poderjudicial.gov.bo; internet www.poderjudicial.gov.bo.

Judicial power is vested in the Supreme Court. There are 12 members, appointed by Congress for a term of 10 years. The court is divided into four chambers of three justices each. Two chambers deal with civil cases, the third deals with criminal cases and the fourth deals with administrative, social and mining cases. The President of the Supreme Court presides over joint sessions of the courts and attends the joint sessions for cassation cases.

President of the Supreme Court: Eduardo Rodríguez Veltzé.

DISTRICT COURTS

There is a District Court sitting in each Department, and additional provincial and local courts to try minor cases.

ATTORNEY-GENERAL

In addition to the Attorney-General at Sucre (appointed by the President on the proposal of the Senate), there is a District Attorney in each Department as well as circuit judges.

Attorney-General: Dr Oscar Crespo Soliz.

Religion

The majority of the population are Roman Catholics; there were an estimated 7.4m. adherents at 31 December 2002, equivalent to 80.5% of the population. Religious freedom is guaranteed. There are a number of Bahá'ís and a small Jewish community, as well as various Protestant denominations, in Bolivia.

CHRISTIANITY

The Roman Catholic Church

Bolivia comprises four archdioceses, six dioceses, two Territorial Prelatures and five Apostolic Vicariates.

Bishops' Conference

Conferencia Episcopal Boliviana, Calle Potosí 814, Casilla 2309, La Paz; tel. (2) 240-6855; fax (2) 240-6941; e-mail asc@scbbs-bo.com. f. 1972; Pres. Cardinal Julio Terrazas Sandoval (Archbishop of Santa Cruz de la Sierra).

Archbishop of Cochabamba: Most Rev. Tito Solari, Avda Heroínas 152, esq. Zenteno Anaya, Casilla 129, Cochabamba; tel. (4) 425-6562; fax (4) 425-0522; e-mail arz_cbba@supernet.com.bo.

Archbishop of La Paz: Most Rev. Edmundo Luis Flavio Abastoflor Montero, Calle Ballivián 1277, Casilla 259, La Paz; tel. (2) 234-1920; fax (2) 239-1244; e-mail edabasto@caoba.entelnet.bo.

Archbishop of Santa Cruz de la Sierra: Cardinal Julio Terrazas Sandoval, Calle Ingavi 49, Casilla 25, Santa Cruz; tel. (3) 332-4286; fax (3) 333-0181; e-mail asc@scbbs-bo.com.

Archbishop of Sucre: Most Rev. Jesús Gervasio Pérez Rodríguez, Calle Bolívar 702, Casilla 205, Sucre; tel. (4) 645-1587; fax (4) 646-0336; e-mail arzsucre@mara.scr.entelnet.bo.

The Anglican Communion

Within the Iglesia Anglicana del Cono Sur de América (Anglican Church of the Southern Cone of America), Bolivia forms part of the diocese of Peru. The Bishop is resident in Lima, Peru.

Protestant Churches

Baptist Union of Bolivia: Casilla 2199, La Paz; tel. (2) 222-9538; Pres. Rev. Augusto Chuijo.

Convención Bautista Boliviana (Baptist Convention of Bolivia): Casilla 3147, Santa Cruz; tel. (3) 334-0717; fax (3) 334-0717; f. 1947; Pres. Eira Soruco de Flores.

Iglesia Evangélica Metodista en Bolivia (Evangelical Methodist Church in Bolivia): Casillas 356 y 8347, La Paz; tel. (2) 249-1628; fax (2) 249-1624; autonomous since 1969; 10,000 mems; Bishop Rev. Carlos Intipampa.

BAHÁ'Í FAITH

National Spiritual Assembly of the Bahá'ís of Bolivia: Casilla 1613, La Paz; tel. (2) 278-5058; fax (2) 278-2387; e-mail secretariat@bahai.org.bo; internet bahai.org.bo; mems resident in 5,161 localities.

The Press

DAILY NEWSPAPERS

Cochabamba

Opinión: General Acha 252, Casilla 287, Cochabamba; tel. (4) 425-4400; fax (4) 441-5121; e-mail opinion@opinion.com.bo; internet www.opinion.com.bo; f. 1985; Dir Edwin Tapia Frontanilla; Man. Graciela Méndez de Escobar.

Los Tiempos: Edif. Los Tiempos, Plaza Quintanilla-Norte, Casilla 525, Cochabamba; tel. (4) 425-4562; fax (4) 425-4577; e-mail lostiempos@lostiempos-bolivia.com; internet www.lostiempos.com; f. 1943; morning; independent; Dir Fernando Canelas; Man. Editor Alcides Flores Moncada; circ. 19,000.

La Paz

El Diario: Calle Loayza 118, Casilla 5, La Paz; tel. (2) 239-0900; fax (2) 236-3846; e-mail contacto@eldiario.net; internet www.eldiario.net; f. 1904; morning; conservative; Dir Jorge Carrasco Jahnsen; Man. Editor Mauricio Carrasco; circ. 55,000.

Jornada: Edif. Almirante Grau 672, Zona San Pedro, Casilla 1628, La Paz; tel. (2) 248-8163; fax (2) 248-7487; e-mail cartas@jornadanet.com; internet www.jornadanet.com; f. 1964; evening; independent; Dir David Ríos Aranda; circ. 11,500.

La Razón: Colinas de Santa Rita, Auquisamaña, Casilla 13100, La Paz; tel. (2) 227-1415; fax (2) 277-0908; e-mail larazon@la-razon.com; internet www.la-razon.com; f. 1990; Dir Juan Carlos Rocha Chavarría; Gen. Man. Gerardo Tórrez Ossio; circ. 35,000.

Oruro

El Expreso: Potosí 4921, esq. Villarroel, Oruro; f. 1973; morning; independent; right-wing; Dir Alberto Frontanilla Morales; circ. 1,000.

La Patria: Avda Camacho 1892, Casilla 48, Oruro; tel. (2) 525-0761; fax (2) 525-0781; f. 1919; morning; independent; Pres. Marcelo Mirralles Bová; Dir Enrique Miralles Bonnecarrere; circ. 6,000.

Potosí

El Siglo: Calle Linares 99, Casilla 389, Potosí; f. 1975; morning; Dir WILSON MENDIETA PACHECO; circ. 1,500.

Santa Cruz

El Deber: Avda El Trompillo 1144, Casilla 2144, Santa Cruz; tel. (3) 353-8000; fax (3) 353-9053; e-mail web@eldeber.com.bo; internet www.eldeber.com.bo; f. 1955; morning; independent; Dir Dr PEDRO RIVERO MERCADO; Man. Editor TUFFÍ ARÉ VÁZQUEZ; circ. 35,000.

La Estrella del Oriente: Calle Sucre 558, Casilla 736, Santa Cruz; tel. (3) 337-0707; fax (3) 337-0557; e-mail estrella@mitai.nrs.bolnet .bo; f. 1864; Pres. JORGE LANDÍVAR ROCA; Man. Editor TUFFI ARÉ.

El Mundo: Parque Industrial MZ-7, Casilla 1984, Santa Cruz; tel. (3) 346-4646; fax (3) 346-5057; e-mail redaccion@mail.elmundo.com .bo; internet www.elmundo.com.bo; f. 1979; morning; owned by Santa Cruz Industrialists' Asscn; Pres. WALTER PAREJAS MORENO; Dir JUAN JAVIER ZEBALLOS GUTIÉRREZ; circ. 15,000.

El Nuevo Día: Calle Independencia 470, Casilla 5344, Santa Cruz; tel. (3) 333-7474; fax (3) 336-0303; e-mail nuevodia@el-nuevodia .com; internet www.el-nuevodia.com; f. 1987; Dir NANCY EKLUND VDA DE GUTIÉRREZ; Man. Editor JORGE ORÍAS HERRERA.

Sucre

Correo del Sur: Sucre; internet correodelsur.net; f. 1987; Pres. GONZALO CANELAS TARDÍO; Gen. Man. JULIO AUZA ANGLARILL.

Trinidad

La Razón: Avda Bolívar 295, Casilla 166, Trinidad; tel. (3) 462-1377; f. 1972; Dir CARLOS VÉLEZ.

PERIODICALS

Actualidad Boliviana Confidencial (ABC): Fernando Guachalla 969, Casilla 648, La Paz; f. 1966; weekly; Dir HUGO GONZÁLEZ RIOJA; circ. 6,000.

Aquí: Casilla 10937, La Paz; tel. (2) 234-3524; fax (2) 235-2455; f. 1979; weekly; circ. 10,000.

Bolivia Libre: Edif. Esperanza, 5°, Avda Mariscal Santa Cruz 2150, Casilla 6500, La Paz; fortnightly; govt organ.

Carta Cruceña de Integración: Casilla 3531, Santa Cruz de la Sierra; weekly; Dirs HERNÁN LLANOVARCED A., JOHNNY LAZARTE J.

Comentarios Económicos de Actualidad (CEA): Casilla 312097, La Paz; tel. (2) 242-4766; fax (2) 242-4772; e-mail veceba@ caoba.entelnet.bo; f. 1983; fortnightly; articles and economic analyses; Editor GUIDO CESPEDES.

Información Política y Económica (IPE): Calle Comercio, Casilla 2484, La Paz; weekly; Dir GONZALO LÓPEZ MUÑOZ.

Informe R: La Paz; weekly; Editor SARA MONROY.

Notas: Edif. Mariscal de Ayacucho, 5°, Of. 501, Calle Loayza 233, Casilla 5782, La Paz; tel. (2) 233-5577; fax (2) 233-7607; e-mail anf@ ceibo.entelnet.bo; internet www.agenciadenoticiasfides.net; f. 1963; weekly; political and economic analysis; Editor JOSÉ GRAMUNT DE MORAGAS.

El Noticiero: Sucre; weekly; Dir DAVID CABEZAS; circ. 1,500.

Prensa Libre: Sucre; tel. (4) 646-2447; fax (4) 646-2768; e-mail prelibre@mara.scr.entelnet.bo; f. 1989; weekly; Dir JULIO PEMINTEL A.

Servicio de Información Confidencial (SIC): Elías Sagárnaga 274, Casilla 5035, La Paz; weekly; publ. by Asociación Nacional de Prensa; Dir JOSÉ CARRANZA.

Siglo XXI: La Paz; weekly.

Unión: Sucre; weekly; Dir JAIME MERILES.

Visión Boliviana: Calle Loayza 420, Casilla 2870, La Paz; 6 a year.

PRESS ASSOCIATIONS

Asociación Nacional de la Prensa: Avda 6 de Agosto 2170, Casilla 477, La Paz; tel. (2) 236-9916; Pres. Dr CARLOS SERRATE REICH.

Asociación de Periodistas de La Paz: Avda 6 de Agosto 2170, Casilla 477, La Paz; tel. (2) 236-9916; fax (2) 232-3701; f. 1929; Pres. MARIO MALDONADO VISCARRA; Vice-Pres. MARÍA EUGENIA VERASTEGUI A.

NEWS AGENCIES

Agencia de Noticias Fides (ANF): Edif. Mariscal de Ayacucho, 5°, Of. 501, Calle Loayza, Casilla 5782, La Paz; tel. (2) 236-5152; fax (2) 236-5153; e-mail anf@ceibo.entelnet.bo; internet www .agenciadenoticiasfides.net; f. 1963; owned by Roman Catholic Church; Dir JOSÉ GRAMUNT DE MORAGAS; Man. Editor WALTER PATIÑO.

Foreign Bureaux

Agencia EFE (Spain): Edif. Anibal Mz 01, Avda Sánchez Lima 2520, Casilla 7403, La Paz; tel. (2) 241-9222; fax (2) 241-8388; e-mail efebol@entelnet.bo; Bureau Chief ESTHER REBOLLO.

Agenzia Nazionale Stampa Associata (ANSA) (Italy): La Paz; tel. (2) 235-5521; fax (2) 236-8221; Correspondent RAÚL PENARANDA UNDURRAGA.

Associated Press (AP) (USA): Edif. Mariscal de Ayacucho, Of. 1209, Calle Loayza 273, Casilla 9569, La Paz; tel. (2) 220-1557; fax (2) 220-1558; e-mail varrington@ap.org; Correspondent VANESSA ARRINGTON.

Deutsche Presse-Agentur (dpa) (Germany): Edif. Esperanza, 9°, Of. 3, Av. Mariscal Santa Cruz 2150, Casilla 13885, La Paz; tel. (2) 235-2684; fax (2) 239-2488; Correspondent ROBERT BROCKMANN.

Informatsionnoye Telegrafnoye Agentstvo Rossii—Telegrafnoye Agentstvo Suverennykh Stran (ITAR—TASS) (Russia): Casilla 6839, San Miguel, Bloque 0–33, Casa 958, La Paz; tel. (2) 279-2108; Correspondent ELDAR ABDULLAEV.

Inter Press Service (IPS) (Italy): Edif. Esperanza, 6°, Of. 6, Casilla 4313, La Paz; tel. (2) 236-1227; Correspondent RONALD GREBE LÓPEZ.

Prensa Latina (Cuba): La Paz; tel. (2) 232-3479; Correspondent MANUEL ROBLES SOSA.

Reuters (United Kingdom): Edif. Loayza, 3°, Of. 301, Calle Loayza 349, Casilla 4057, La Paz; tel. (2) 235-1106; fax (2) 239-1366; Correspondent RENÉ VILLEGAS MONJE.

Rossiyskoye Informatsionnoye Agentstvo—Novosti (RIA—Novosti) (Russia): La Paz; tel. (2) 237-3857; Correspondent VLADIMIR RAMÍREZ.

Agence France-Presse and Telam (Argentina) are also represented.

Publishers

Ediciones Runa: Calle España 459, Cochabamba; tel. (4) 523-389; e-mail edicionesruna@yahoo.com; internet www.geocities.com/ edicionesruna/; f. 1968; juvenile, educational and scholarly.

Editora Khana Cruz SRL: Avda Camacho 1372, Casilla 5920, La Paz; tel. (2) 237-0263; Dir GLADIS ANDRADE.

Editora Lux: Edif. Esperanza, Avda Mariscal Santa Cruz, Casilla 1566, La Paz; tel. (2) 232-9102; fax (2) 234-3968; f. 1952; Dir FELICISIMO TARILONTE PÉREZ.

Editorial los Amigos del Libro: Avda Ayacucho 0-156, Casilla 450, Cochabamba; tel. (4) 450-4150; fax (4) 411-5128; e-mail amigol@ amigol.bo.net; e-mail gutten@amigol.bo.net; internet www .librosbolivia.com; f. 1945; general; Man. Dir WERNER GUTTENTAG; Gen. Man. INGRID GUTTENTAG.

Editorial Bruño: Loayza 167, Casilla 4809, La Paz; tel. (2) 233-1254; fax (2) 233-5043; e-mail brunol@caoba.entelnet.bo; f. 1964; Dir IGNACIO LOMAS.

Editorial Don Bosco: Avda 16 de Julio 1899, Casilla 4458, La Paz; tel. (2) 237-1449; fax (2) 236-2822; f. 1896; social sciences and literature; Dir GRAMAGLIA MAGLIANO.

Editorial Icthus: La Paz; tel. (2) 235-4007; f. 1967; general and textbooks; Man. Dir DANIEL AQUIZE.

Editorial Popular: Plaza Pérez Velasco 787, Casilla 4171, La Paz; tel. (2) 235-0701; f. 1935; textbooks, postcards, tourist guides, etc; Man. Dir GERMÁN VILLAMOR.

Editorial Puerta del Sol: Edif. Litoral Sub Suelo, Avda Mariscal Santa Cruz, La Paz; tel. (2) 236-0746; f. 1965; Man. Dir OSCAR CRESPO.

Empresa Editora Proinsa: Avda Saavedra 2055, Casilla 7181, La Paz; tel. (2) 222-7781; fax (2) 222-6671; f. 1974; school books; Dirs FLOREN SANABRIA G., CARLOS SANABRIA C.

Gisbert y Cía, SA: Calle Comercio 1270, Casilla 195, La Paz; tel. (2) 220-2626; fax (2) 220-2911; e-mail libgis@entelnet.bo; f. 1907; textbooks, history, law and general; Pres. JAVIER GISBERT; Promotions Man. MARÍA DEL CARMEN SCHULCZEWSKI; Admin. Man. ANTONIO SCHULCZEWSKI.

Ivar American: Calle Potosí 1375, Casilla 6016, La Paz; tel. (2) 236-1519; Man. Dir HÉCTOR IBÁÑEZ.

Librería Editorial Juventud: Plaza Murillo 519, Casilla 1489, La Paz; tel. (2) 240-6248; f. 1946; textbooks and general; Dir GUSTAVO URQUIZO MENDOZA.

Librería El Ateneo SRL: Calle Ballivián 1275, Casilla 7917, La Paz; tel. (2) 236-9925; fax (2) 239-1513; Dirs JUAN CHIRVECHES D., MIRIAN C. DE CHIRVECHES.

Librería Dismo Ltda: Calle Comercio 806, Casilla 988, La Paz; tel. (2) 240-6411; fax (2) 31-6545; e-mail dismo@caoba.entelnet.bo; Dir TERESA GONZÁLEZ DE ALVAREZ.

Librería La Paz: Calle Campos y Villegas, Edif. Artemis, Casilla 539, La Paz; tel. (2) 243-4927; fax (2) 243-5004; e-mail liblapaz@ceibo.entelnet.bo; f. 1900; Dirs EDUARDO BURGOS R., CARLOS BURGOS M.

Librería La Universal SRL: Calle Genaro Sanjines 538, Casilla 2888, La Paz; tel. (2) 234-2961; f. 1958; Man. Dir ROLANDO CONDORI.

Librería San Pablo: Calle Colón 627, Casilla 3152, La Paz; tel. (2) 232-6084; f. 1967; Man. Dir MARÍA DE JESÚS VALERIANO.

Santillana de Ediciones SA: Avda Arce 2333, La Paz; tel. (2) 441-122; fax (2) 442–208; internet www.santillanabo.com; f. ; Gen. Man. ANDRÉS CARDÓ.

PUBLISHERS' ASSOCIATION

Cámara Boliviana del Libro: Calle Capitán Ravelo 2116, Casilla 682, La Paz; tel. (2) 244-4239; fax (2) 244-1523; e-mail cabolib@ceibo.entelnet.bo; f. 1947; Pres. AMPARO LINARES; Vice-Pres. ERNESTO MARTÍNEZ; Gen. Man. ANA PATRICIA NAVARRO.

Broadcasting and Communications

TELECOMMUNICATIONS

Cámara Nacional de Medios de Comunicación: Casilla 2431, La Paz.

Empresa Nacional de Telecomunicaciones (ENTEL): Calle Federico Zuazo 1771, Casilla 4450, La Paz; tel. (2) 231-3030; fax (2) 239-1789; tel. contacto@entelsa.entelnet.bo; internet www.entel.bo; f. 1965; privatized in the Govt's capitalization programme in 1995; owned by Telecom Italia; Exec. Pres. MARIO FUMI.

Superintendencia de Telecomunicaciones: Calle 13, No 8260, Calacoto, La Paz; tel. (2) 277-2266; fax (2) 277-2299; e-mail supertel@ceibo.entelnet.bo; internet www.sittel.gov.bo; f. 1995; govt-controlled broadcasting authority; Supt RENÉ BUSTILLO PORTOCARRERO.

BROADCASTING

Radio

The majority of radio stations are commercial. Broadcasts are in Spanish, Aymará and Quechua. In 1999 there were 171 MW and LW radio stations and 73 FM stations, as well as 77 short-wave stations.

Asociación Boliviana de Radiodifusoras (ASBORA): Edif. Jazmin, 10°, Avda 20 de Octubre 2019, Casilla 5324, La Paz; tel. (2) 236-5154; fax (2) 236-3069; broadcasting authority; Pres. TERESA SANJINÉS L.; Vice-Pres. LUIS ANTONIO SERRANO.

Educación Radiofónica de Bolivia (ERBOL): Calle Ballivian 1323, 4°, Casilla 5946, La Paz; tel. (2) 235-4142; fax (2) 239-1985; asscn of 28 educational radio stations in Bolivia; Gen. Sec. RONALD GREBE LÓPEZ.

Radio Fides: La Paz; internet www.fides.com; network of 19 radio stations; Catholic; Dir EDUARDO PÉREZ IRIBARNE.

Radio Illimani: Avda Camacho 1485, 6°, La Paz; tel. (2) 220-0473; e-mail illimani@comunica.gov.bo; internet www.comunica.gov.bo/illimani; f. 1932 as Compañia Radio Boliviana; govt-owned.

Radio Panamerica: Edif. 16 de Julio, 9°, Of. 902, El Prado, La Paz; tel. (2) 233-4271; e-mail pana@panamericana-bolivia.com; internet www.panamericanabolivia.com; f. 1972; Dir DANIEL SÁNCHEZ.

Television

There were 48 television stations in 1999.

ATB Red Nacional (Canal 9): Avda Argentina 2057, Casilla 9285, La Paz; tel. and fax (2) 222-9922; internet www.atb.com.bo; f. 1985; privately owned television network.

Bolivisión (Canal 4): Santa Cruz; internet www.bolivisiontv.com; f. 1997; privately owned television network; Exec. Pres. Ing. ERNESTO ASBÚN GAZAUI; Gen. Man. Lic. JEANNETTE ARRÁZOLA RIVERO.

Empresa Nacional de Televisión Boliviana (Canal 7): Edif. La Urbana, 6° y 7°, Avda Camacho 1486, Casilla 900, La Paz; tel. (2) 237-6356; fax (2) 235-9753; f. 1969; govt network operating stations in La Paz, Oruro, Cochabamba, Potosí, Chuquisaca, Pando, Beni, Tarija and Santa Cruz; Gen. Man. MIGUEL N. MONTERO VACA.

Televisión Universitaria (Canal 13): Edif. 'Hoy', 12°–13°, Avda 6 de Agosto 2170, Casilla 13383, La Paz; tel. (2) 235-9297; fax (2) 235-9298; internet www.umsanet.edu.bo; f. 1980; educational programmes; stations in Oruro, Cochabamba, Potosí, Sucre, Tarija, Beni and Santa Cruz; Dir Lic. ROBERTO CUEVAS RAMÍREZ.

Unitel (Canal 9): Km 5, Carretera antigua a Cochabamba, Santa Cruz; tel. (3) 352-7686; fax (3) 352-7688; e-mail webmaster@unitel.com.bo; internet www.unitel.tv; f. 1997; privately owned television network; Gen. Man. Ing. JUAN ALBERTO ROJAS.

Finance

(cap. = capital; res = reserves; dep. = deposits; m. = million; brs = branches; amounts are in bolivianos, unless otherwise stated)

BANKING

Supervisory Authority

Superintendencia de Bancos y Entidades Financieras: Plaza Isabel la Católica 2507, Casilla 447, La Paz; tel. (2) 243-1919; fax (2) 243-0028; e-mail sbef@sbef.gov.bo; internet www.sbef.gov.bo; f. 1928; Supt Dr LUIS FERNANDO CALVO UNZUETA.

Central Bank

Banco Central de Bolivia: Avda Ayacucho, esq. Mercado, Casilla 3118, La Paz; tel. (2) 237-4151; fax (2) 239-2398; e-mail vmarquez@mail.bcb.gov.bo; internet www.bcb.gov.bo; f. 1911 as Banco de la Nación Boliviana, name changed as above in 1928; bank of issue; cap. 515.8m., res 4,438.6m., dep. 11,079.5m. (Dec. 2002); Pres. Dr JUAN ANTONIO MORALES ANAYA; Gen. Man. Lic. JAIME VALENCIA.

Commercial Banks

Banco Bisa SA: Avda 16 de Julio 1628, Casilla 1290, La Paz; tel. (2) 235-9471; fax (2) 239-2013; e-mail bancobisa@grupobisa.com; internet www.grupobisa.com; f. 1963; cap. 479.7m., res 165.3m., dep. 4,353.8m. (Dec. 2002); Pres. and CEO Ing. JULIÓ LEÓN PRADO.

Banco de Crédito de Bolivia, SA: Calle Colón, esq. Mercado 1308, Casilla 907, La Paz; tel. (2) 220-1154; fax (2) 223-2203; internet www.bancodecredito.com.bo; f. 1993 as Banco Popular, SA, name changed as above 1994; owned by Banco de Crédito del Perú; cap. 315.5m., res 109.1m., dep. 2,995.1m. (Dec. 2002); Chair. DIONISIO ROMERO SEMINARIO; Gen. Man. DAVID SAETTONE WATMOUGH; 6 brs.

Banco Económico SA-SCZ: Calle Ayacucho 166, Casilla 5603, Santa Cruz; tel. (3) 336-1177; fax (3) 336-1184; e-mail baneco@baneco.com.bo; f. 1990; dep. US $174.3m., cap. $20.99m., total assets US $240.7m. (Dec. 2003); Pres. LUIS PERROGÓN TOLEDO; Gen. Man. Ing. JUSTO YEPEZ KAKUDA; 14 brs.

Banco Ganadero SA-Santa Cruz: Calle 24 de Setiembre 110, Casilla 4492, Santa Cruz; tel. (3) 336-1616; fax (3) 333-2567; e-mail hkrutzfeldt@bancoganadero.co.bo; internet www.bancoganadero.com.bo; f. 1994; cap. and res 108.1m., dep. 1,078.1m. (Dec. 2000); Pres. FERNANDO MONASTERIO NIEME; Gen. Man. RONALD GUTIÉRREZ LÓPEZ.

Banco Mercantil, SA: Calle Ayacucho, esq. Mercado 295, Casilla 423, La Paz; tel. (2) 240-9040; fax (2) 240-9185; e-mail bercant@bancomercantil.com.bo; internet www.bancomercantil.com.bo; f. 1905; cap. and res 57.7m., dep. 457m. (Dec. 2003); Pres. EDUARDO QUINTANILLA; Exec. Vice-Pres. ÉMILIO UNZUETA ZEGARRA; 41 brs.

Banco Nacional de Bolivia: Avda Camacho, esq. Colón 1312, Casilla 360, La Paz; tel. (2) 311-139; fax (2) 334-723; e-mail info@bnb.com.bo; internet www.bnb-bol.com; f. 1871; cap. 261.0m., res 84.9m., dep. 3,853.7m. (Dec. 2004); Pres. GONZALO ARGANDOÑA; Gen. Man. PABLO BEDOYA; 9 brs.

Banco Santa Cruz, SA: Calle Junín 154, Casilla 865, Santa Cruz; tel. (3) 336-9911; fax (3) 335-0114; e-mail ggeneral@mail.bsc.com.bo; internet www.bsc.com.bo; f. 1965; 96% owned by Santander Central Hispano (Spain); Gen. Man. LISARDO PELAEZ ACERO; 19 brs.

Banco Solidario, SA (BancoSol): Calle Nicolás Acosta, esq. Cañada Strongest 289, Casilla 13176, La Paz; tel. (2) 248-6563; fax (2) 248-6533; e-mail info@bancosol.com.bo; internet www.bancosol.com.bo; f. 1992; Pres. HERBERT MÜLLER; Gen. Man. KURT KÖNIGSFEST.

Banco Unión, SA: Calle Libertad 156, Casilla 4057, Santa Cruz; tel. (3) 336-6869; fax (3) 334-0684; e-mail info@bancounion.com.bo; internet www.bancounion.com.bo; f. 1982; cap. US$40.9m., res US$3.1m., dep. US$307.1m. (Dec. 2002); Pres. Ing. ANDRÉS PETRICEVIC; Gen. Man. JULIAN SECO; 2 brs.

Foreign Banks

Banco ABN AMRO Real, SA (Netherlands): Avda 16 de Julio 1642, Casilla 10008, La Paz; tel. (2) 233-4477; fax (2) 233-5588; f. 1978 as Banco Real, name changed as above 2000; dep. US $8.3m., total assets US $17.5m. (Dec. 1997); Operations Man. JOSÉ PORFIRIO VASCONCELOS.

Banco do Brasil, SA: Avda 16 de Julio 1642, El Prado, La Paz; tel. (2) 231-0909; fax (2) 231-1788; e-mail lapaz@bb.com.br; f. 1961; Gen. Man. José Eneas Bueno Junior; 1 br.

Banco de la Nación Argentina: Junín 22, Plaza 24 de Setiembre, Santa Cruz; tel. (3) 334-3777; fax (2) 334-3729; e-mail eaira@bnasc .com.bo; internet www.bna.com.ar; f. 1891; Man. Esteban Salvador Aira; 1 br.

Banking Association

Asociación de Bancos Privados de Bolivia (ASOBAN): Edif. Cámara Nacional de Comercio, 15°, Avda Mariscal Santa Cruz, esq. Colombia 1392, Casilla 5822, La Paz; tel. (2) 237-6164; fax (2) 239-1093; e-mail info@asoban.bo; internet www.asoban.bo; f. 1957; Pres. Emilo Unzueta Zegarra; Vice-Pres Pablo Bedoya, Francisco Monasterios; 18 mems.

STOCK EXCHANGE

Supervisory Authorities

Superintendencia de Pensiones, Valores y Seguros: Calle Reyes Ortiz, esq. Federico Zuazo, Edif. Torres Gundlach Este, 3°, Casilla 6118, La Paz; tel. (2) 233-1212; fax (2) 233-0001; e-mail spvs@spvs.gov.bo; internet www.spvs.gov.bo; Supt Guillermo Aponte; Operations Dir Luis Tejada Ponce.

Bolsa Boliviana de Valores SA: Edif. Zambrana P.B., Calle Montevideo 142, Casilla 12521, La Paz; tel. (2) 244-3232; fax (2) 244-2308; e-mail info@bolsa-valores-bolivia.com; internet www .bolsa-valores-bolivia.com; f. 1989; Gen. Man. Lic. Armando Alvarez Arnal.

INSURANCE

Supervisory Authority

Superintendencia de Pensiones, Valores y Seguros: see above.

National Companies

Adriatica Seguros y Reaseguros, SA: Calle Libertad, esq. Cañoto 879, Casilla 1515, Santa Cruz; tel. (3) 336-6667; fax (3) 336-0600; e-mail elandivar@adriatica.com.bo; internet www.adriatica.com.bo; f. 1995; Pres. Antonio Olea Baudoin.

Alianza, Cía de Seguros y Reaseguros, SA: Avda 20 de Octubre 2680, esq. Campos, Zona San Jorge, Casilla 1043, La Paz; tel. (2) 243-2121; fax (2) 243-2713; e-mail info@alianzaseguros.com; f. 1991; Pres. Juan Manuel Peña Roca.

Alianza Vida Seguros y Reaseguros, SA: Avda Viedma 19, Casilla 7181, Santa Cruz; tel. (3) 337-5656; fax (3) 337-5666; e-mail alejandroy@alianzaseguros.com; f. 1999; Pres. Raúl Adler K; Gen. Man. Alejandro Ybarra Carrasco.

Bisa Seguros y Reaseguros, SA: Edif. San Pablo, 13°, Avda 16 de Julio 1479, Casilla 3669, La Paz; tel. (2) 235-2123; fax (2) 239-2500; e-mail bisaseguros@grupobisa.com; internet www.grupobisa.com; f. 1991; Pres. Julio Cesar León Prado.

La Boliviana Ciacruz de Seguros y Reaseguros, SA: Calle Colón, esq. Mercado 288, Casilla 628, La Paz; tel. (2) 220-3131; fax (2) 220-4087; e-mail rodrigo.bedoya@zurich.com; internet www .boliviana-ciacruz.com; f. 1946; owned by Zurich group; all classes; Pres. Gonzalo Bedoya Herrera; Gen. Man. Rodrigo Bedoya Diez de Medina.

Compañía de Seguros y Reaseguros Fortaleza, SA: Avda Virgen de Cotoca 2080, Casilla 1366, Santa Cruz; tel. (3) 348-7273; fax (3) 348-7273; e-mail nhinojosa@grupofortaleza.com.bo; Pres. Guido Hinojosa; Gen. Man. Nelson Hinojosa.

Credinform International SA de Seguros: Edif. Credinform, Calle Potosí, esq. Ayacucho 1220, Casilla 1724, La Paz; tel. (2) 231-5566; fax (2) 220-3917; e-mail maicobarragan@credinformsa.com; f. 1962; all classes; Pres. Dr Robín Barragán Peláez; Gen. Man. Miguel Angel Barragán Ibarguen.

Nacional Vida Seguros de Personas, SA: Edif. Sucumbé, Avda Gral. San Martín esq. Ricardo Jamies Freire, Casilla 4387, Santa Cruz; tel. (3) 333-6262; fax (3) 333-7969; e-mail nv_jlcamacho@cotas .com.bo; f. 1999; Pres. Carmen Seeghers de Zwahlen; Gen. Man. José Luis Camacho.

Seguros y Reaseguros Generales 24 de Septiembre, SA: Avda Ejercito Nacional 487, Santa Cruz; tel. (3) 354-8484; fax (3) 354-8484; e-mail seguros@caoba.entelnet.com.bo; f. 2001; Pres. Col. Roberto Foronda; Gen. Man. Josefina Soliz de Foronda.

Seguros Illimani, SA: Edif. Mariscal de Ayacucho, 10°, Calle Loayza 233, Casilla 133, La Paz; tel. (2) 220-3040; fax (2) 239-1149; e-mail sisalp@entelnet.bo; internet www.segurosillimani.com; f. 1979; all classes; Pres. Fernando Arce Grandchant.

Seguros Próvida, SA: Edif. San José, Avda 20 de Octubre 2524, Casilla 133, La Paz; tel. (2) 243-0300; fax (2) 243-0318; e-mail provida@segurosprovida.com.bo; f. 1999; Exec. Pres. Fernando Arce Grandchant; Gen. Man. Justino Avendaño.

La Vitalicia Seguros y Reaseguros de Vida, SA: Edif. Hoy, Avda 6 de Agosto 2860, Casilla 8424, La Paz; tel. (2) 212-5355; fax (2) 211-3480; e-mail aibanez@grupobisa.com; internet www.grupobisa.com/somosvitalicia.html; f. 1988; part of Grupo Bisa; Pres. Julio Cesar León Prado; Exec. Vice-Pres. Lic. Luis Alfonso Ibañez Montes.

There are also four foreign-owned insurance companies operating in Bolivia: American Life Insurance Co, American Home Assurance Co, United States Fire Insurance Co and International Health Insurance Danmarck.

Insurance Association

Asociación Boliviana de Aseguradores: Edif. Castilla, 5°, Of. 510, Calle Loayza, esq. Mercado 250, Casilla 4804, La Paz; tel. (2) 220-1014; fax (2) 220-1088; e-mail aba@ababolivia.org; internet www.ababolivia.org; f. 1962; Pres. Luis Alfonso Ibáñez Montes; Gen. Man. Carlos Baudoin Dávalos.

Trade and Industry

GOVERNMENT AGENCIES

Cámara Nacional de Exportadores (CAMEX): Avda Arce 2017, esq. Goitia, Casilla 12145, La Paz; tel. (2) 234-1220; fax (2) 236-1491; e-mail camex@caoba.entelnet.bo; internet www.camex-lpb.com; f. 1970; Pres. Luis Nemtala Yamin; Gen. Man. Jorge Adriazola Reimers.

Instituto Nacional de Inversiones (INI): Edif. Cristal, 10°, Calle Yanacocha, Casilla 4393, La Paz; tel. (2) 237-5730; fax (2) 236-7297; e-mail abeseg@kolla.net.bo; f. 1971; state institution for the promotion of new investments and the application of the Investment Law; Exec. Dir Ing. José Mario Fernández Irahola.

Sistema de Regulación Sectorial (SIRESE): Edif. Capitán Ravelo, 8°, Casilla 9647, La Paz; tel. (2) 244-4545; fax (2) 244-4017; e-mail sg@sirese.gov.bo; internet www.sirese.gov.bo; f. 1994; regulatory body for the formerly state-owned companies and utilities; oversees the general co-ordination and growth of the regulatory system and the work of its Superintendencies of Electricity, Hydrocarbons, Telecommunications, Transport and Water; Supt-Gen. Claude Besse Arze.

DEVELOPMENT ORGANIZATIONS

Consejo Nacional de Acreditación y Medición de la Calidad Educativa (CONAMED): La Paz; f. 1994; education quality board.

Consejo Nacional de Planificación (CONEPLAN): Edif. Banco Central de Bolivia, 26°, Calle Mercado, esq. Ayacucho, Casilla 3118, La Paz; tel. (2) 237-4151; fax (2) 235-3840; e-mail claves@mail.bcb .gov.bo; internet www.bcb.gov.bo; f. 1985.

Corporación de las Fuerzas Armadas para el Desarrollo Nacional (COFADENA): Avda 6 de Agosto 2649, Casilla 1015, La Paz; tel. (2) 237-7305; fax (2) 236-0900; f. 1972; industrial, agricultural and mining holding co and development org. owned by the Bolivian armed forces; Gen. Man. Col Juan Manuel Rosales.

Corporación Regional de Desarrollo de La Paz (CORDEPAZ): Avda Arce 2529, Edif. Santa Isabel, Casilla 6102, La Paz; tel. (2) 243-0313; fax (2) 243-2152; f. 1972; decentralized government institution to foster the development of the La Paz area; Pres. Lic. Ricardo Paz Ballivián; Gen. Man. Ing. Juan G. Carrasco R.

Instituto para el Desarrollo de la Pequeña Unidad Productiva: La Paz.

CHAMBERS OF COMMERCE

Cámara Nacional de Comercio: Edif. Cámara Nacional de Comercio, Avda Mariscal Santa Cruz 1392, 1° y 2°, Casilla 7, La Paz; tel. (2) 237-8606; fax (2) 239-1004; e-mail cnc@boliviacomercio.org .bo; internet www.boliviacomercio.org.bo; f. 1890; 30 brs and special brs; Pres. Guillermo Morales Fernández; Gen. Man. Rodrigo Agreda Gómez.

Cámara de Comercio de Oruro: Pasaje Guachalla s/n, Casilla 148, Oruro; tel. and fax (2) 525-0606; e-mail camacor@coteor.net.bo; f. 1895; Pres. Alvaro Cornejo Gazcón; Gen. Man. Luis Camacho Vargas.

Cámara Departamental de Industria y Comercio de Santa Cruz: Calle Suárez de Figueroa 127, esq. Saavedra, 3°, Casilla 180, Santa Cruz; tel. (3) 333-4555; fax (3) 334-2353; e-mail cainco@cainco .org.bo; internet www.cainco.org.bo; f. 1915; Pres. Zvonko Matkovic Fleig; Gen. Man. Lic. Oscar Ortiz Antelo.

Cámara Departamental de Comercio de Cochabamba: Calle Sucre E-0336, Casilla 493, Cochabamba; tel. (4) 425-7715; fax (4) 425-7717; e-mail camcom@pino.cbb.entelnet.bo; f. 1922; Pres. Ing. CARLOS OLMEDO Z.; Gen. Man. Lic. JUAN CARLOS AVILA S.

Cámara Departamental de Comercio e Industria de Potosí: Calle Matos 12, Casilla 159, Potosí; tel. (2) 622-2641; fax (2) 622-2641; Pres. JAVIER FLORES CASTRO; Gen. Man. WALTER ZAVALA AYLLON.

Cámara Departamental de Industria y Comercio de Chuquisaca: Calle España 64, Casilla 33, Sucre; tel. (4) 645-1194; fax (4) 645-1850; e-mail cicch@camara.scr.entelnet.bo; f. 1923; Pres. MARCO MIHAIC; Gen. Man. Lic. ALFREDO YÁÑEZ MERCADO.

Cámara Departamental de Comercio e Industria de Pando—Cobija: Plaza Germán Busch, Casilla 110, Cobija; tel. (3) 842-3139; fax (3) 842-2291; Pres. NEMESIO RAMÍREZ.

Cámara Departamental de Industria y Comercio de Tarija: Avda Bolívar 0413, esq. General Trigo, 1°, Casilla 74, Tarija; tel. (6) 642-2737; fax (6) 642-2737; e-mail metfess@olivo.tja.entelnet.bo; Pres. RENE SILBERMANN U.; Gen. Man. VÍCTOR FERNÁNDEZ ARAMAYO.

Cámara Departamental de Comercio de Beni: Casilla 96, Trinidad; tel. (3) 462-2365; fax (3) 462-1400; Pres. EDUARDO AVILA ALVERDI; Sec.-Gen. JOSÉ MAMERTO DURÁN.

Cámara de Exportadores de Santa Cruz (CADEX): Avda Velarde 131, Santa Cruz; tel. (3) 336-2030; fax (3) 332-1509; e-mail cadex@cadex.org; internet www.cadex.org; f. 1986; Gen. Man. JUAN MANUEL ARIAS CASTRO.

INDUSTRIAL AND TRADE ASSOCIATIONS

Asociación Nacional de Exportadores de Café (ANDEC): Calle Nicaragua 1638, Casilla 9770, La Paz; tel. (2) 224-4290; fax (2) 224-4561; e-mail andec@caoba.entelnet.bo; internet www.boliviancoffee.bo; controls the export, quality and marketing of coffee producers; Exec. Pres. CARMEN DONOSO DE ARAMAYO.

Cámara Agropecuaria del Oriente: 3 anillo interno zona Oeste, Casilla 116, Santa Cruz; tel. (3) 352-2200; fax (3) 352-2621; e-mail caosrz@bibosi.scz.entelnet.bo; f. 1964; agriculture and livestock association for eastern Bolivia; Pres. RICARDO FRERKING ORTIZ; Gen. Man. WALTER NÚÑEZ RODRÍGUEZ.

Cámara Agropecuaria de La Paz: Avda 16 de Julio 1525, Casilla 12521, La Paz; tel. (2) 239-2911; fax (2) 235-2308; Pres. ALBERTO DE OLIVA MAYA; Gen. Man. JUAN CARLOS ZAMORANO.

Cámara Boliviana de Hidrocarburos: Radial 17 1/2 y Sexto Anillo, Santa Cruz; tel. (3) 353-8799; fax (3) 357-7868; e-mail cbh@cbh.org.bo; internet www.cbh.org.bo; f. 1986; Pres. RAÚL KIEFFER.

Cámara Forestal de Bolivia: Prolongación Manuel Ignacio Salvatierra 1055, Casilla 346, Santa Cruz; tel. (3) 333-2699; fax (3) 333-1456; e-mail camaraforestal@cfb.org.bo; internet www.cfb.org.bo; f. 1969; represents the interests of the Bolivian timber industry; Pres. JUAN ABUAWAD CHAHUÁN; Gen. Man. Lic. ARTURO BOWLES OLHAGARAY.

Cámara Nacional de Industrias: Edif. Cámara Nacional de Comercio, 14°, Avda Mariscal Santa Cruz 1392, Casilla 611, La Paz; tel. (2) 237-4477; fax (2) 236-2766; e-mail cni@entelnel.bo; internet www.bolivia-industry.com; f. 1931; Pres. ROBERTO MUSTAFÁ; Man. GERARDO VELASCO T.

Cámara Nacional de Minería: Pasaje Bernardo Trigo 429, Casilla 2022, La Paz; tel. (2) 235-0623; f. 1953; mining institute; Pres. Ing. LUIS PRADO BARRIENTOS; Sec.-Gen. GERMÁN GORDILLO S.

Comité Boliviano de Productores de Antimonio: Edif. El Condor, Batallon Colorados 1404, 14°, Casilla 14451, La Paz; tel. (2) 244-2140; fax (2) 244-1653; f. 1978; controls the marketing, pricing and promotion policies of the antimony industry; Pres. MARIO MARISCAL MORALES; Sec.-Gen. Dr ALCIDES RODRÍGUEZ J.

Comité Boliviano del Café (COBOLCA): Calle Nicaragua 1638, Casilla 9770, La Paz; tel. (2) 222-3883; fax (2) 224-4591; e-mail cobolca@ceibo.entelnet.bo; controls the export, quality, marketing and growing policies of the coffee industry; Gen. Man. MAURICIO VILLARROEL.

EMPLOYERS' ASSOCIATIONS

Asociación Nacional de Mineros Medianos: Calle Pedro Salazar 600, esq. Presbítero Medina, Casilla 6190, La Paz; tel. and fax (2) 241-4123; e-mail anmm@caoba.entelnet.bo; f. 1939; asscn of 14 private medium-sized mining cos; Pres. Dr OSCAR BONIFAZ G.; Sec.-Gen. Dr HUGO URIONA.

Confederación de Empresarios Privados de Bolivia (CEPB): Calle Méndez Arcos 117, Plaza España, Zona Sopacachi, Casilla 4239, La Paz; tel. (2) 242–0999; fax (2) 242-1272; e-mail cepb@cepb.org.bo; internet www.cepb.org.bo; largest national employers' organization; Pres. ROBERTO MUSTAFÁ SCHNOR; Dir of Social and Institutional Affairs Lic. MAX GASTELÚ ZACONETA.

There are also employers' federations in Santa Cruz, Cochabamba, Oruro, Potosí, Beni and Tarija.

UTILITIES

Electricity

Superintendencia de Electricidad: Avda 16 de Julio 1571, La Paz; tel. (2) 231-2401; fax (2) 231-2393; e-mail superele@superele.gov.bo; internet www.superele.gov.bo; f. 1994; regulates the electricity sector; Superintendent ALEJANDRO NOWOTNY VERA; Gen. Sec. ROLANDO LÓPEZ.

Compañía Boliviana de Energía Eléctrica, SA (COBEE): Avda Hernando Siles 5635, Casilla 353, La Paz; tel. (2) 278-2474; fax (2) 278-5920; e-mail cobee@cobee.com; internet www.cobee.com; f. 1925; largest private power producer and distributor, serving the areas of La Paz and Oruro; generated 27.2% of Bolivia's total electricity output in 2002; mainly hydroelectric; Gen. Man. JULIO LEMAITRE SOLARES.

Compañía Eléctrica Central Bulo Bulo, SA (CECBB): Avda San Martín 1700, Equipetrol Norte, 6°, Santa Cruz; tel. (3) 346-0314; fax (3) 349-7800; e-mail carlosg@ipolbolivia.com.bo; f. 1999; generator co; 101.2 MW capacity in 2002; Gen. Man. RAMÓN BASCOPE PARADA.

Compañía Eléctrica Sucre, SA (CESSA): Calle Ayacucho 254, Sucre; tel. (4) 645-3126; fax (4) 646-0292; e-mail cessa@mara.scr.entelnet.bo; electricity distributor; Gen. Man. Ing. JOSÉ ANAVE LEÓN.

Cooperativa Rural De Electrificación Ltda (CRE): Avda Busch, esq. Honduras, Santa Cruz; tel. (3) 336-7777; fax (3) 336-9391; e-mail cre@cre.com.bo; internet www.cre.com.bo; electricity distributor; Gen. Man. Ing. LUIS FERNANDO AÑEZ PEREIRA.

Electropaz: Avda Illimani 1973, Miraflores, La Paz; tel. (2) 222-2200; fax (2) 222-3756; e-mail covideo@electropaz.com; internet www.electropaz.com; distributor serving La Paz area; Gen. Man. Ing. CARLOS PASTOR AREITI.

Empresa Corani, SA: Avda Oquendo 654, Edif. Las Torres Soler I, 9°, Cochabamba; tel. (4) 423-5444; fax (4) 411-5191; e-mail corani@corani.com; internet www.corani.com; generator co; 126 MW capacity in 2002; Gen. Man. Ing. JOSÉ LA FUENTE TAPIA.

Empresa Eléctrica Valle Hermoso, SA (EVH): Calle Tarija 1425, esq. Adela Zamudio, Cala Cala, Cochabamba; tel. (4) 428-6600; fax (4) 428-6838; e-mail vhermoso@pino.cbb.entelnet.bo; generator co; 347.41 MW capacity in 2002; Gen. Man. Ing. CARLOS QUEREJAZU ORTIZ.

Empresa de Generación Guaracachi, SA (EGSA): Avda Brasil y Tercer Anillo Interno s/n, Santa Cruz; tel. (3) 346-0314; fax (3) 346-5888; e-mail central@egsa-bol.com; internet www.egsa-bol.com; generator co; 347.41 MW capacity in 2002; Gen. Man. Ing. MAURICIO PERÓ DIEZ DE MEDINA.

Empresa de Luz y Fuerza Eléctrica Cochabamba, SA (ELFEC): Avda Heroínas 0686, Cochabamba; tel. (4) 425-9410; fax (4) 425-9427; e-mail sugerencias@elfec.com; internet www.elfec.com; electricty distributor; Gen. Man. Ing. JOSÉ D. TRONCOSO ESPARZA.

Empresa Nacional de Electricidad, SA (ENDE): Avda Balliván 503, esq. México, 7°, Casilla Correo 565, Cochabamba; tel. (4) 452-0322; fax (4) 452-0318; e-mail ende@pino.cbb.entelnet.bo; f. 1962; former state electricity company; privatized under the Govt's capitalization programme in 1995 and divided into three arms concerned with generation, transmission and distribution, respectively; Gen. Man. Dr ENRIQUE GÓMEZ D'ANGELO.

Gas

Numerous distributors of natural gas exist throughout the country, many of which are owned by the petroleum distributor, Yacimientos Petrolíferos Fiscales Bolivianos (YPFB).

Yacimientos Petrolíferos Fiscales Bolivianos (YPFB): Calle Bueno 185, Casilla 401, La Paz; tel. (2) 235-6540; fax (2) 239-2596; f. 1936; exploration, drilling, production, refining, transportation and distribution of petroleum; partially privatized in 1996; Pres. CARLOS D'ARLACH LEMA (acting); 4,900 employees.

Water

Aguas de Illimani, SA: Avda de las Américas 705, La Paz; tel. (2) 221-1181; fax (2) 221-2451; e-mail aguailli@datacom-bo.net; majority stake owned by Suez Group (France); supplies drinking water and sewerage in La Paz and El Alto; Govt commenced annulment of contract in late 2004; Man. ROBERTO BIANCHI.

CO-OPERATIVE

Instituto Nacional de Co-operativas (INALCO): Edif. Lotería Nacional, 4°, Avda Mariscal Santa Cruz y Cochabamba, La Paz; tel. (2) 237-4366; fax (2) 237-2104; e-mail inalcolp@ceibo.entelnet.bo; f. 1974; Pres. DAVID AYAVIRI.

TRADE UNIONS

Central Obrera Boliviana (COB): Edif. COB, Calle Pisagua 618, Casilla 6552, La Paz; tel. (2) 352-426; fax (2) 281-201; e-mail postmast@cob-bolivia.org; internet www.cob-bolivia.org; f. 1952; main union confederation; 800,000 mems; Exec. Sec. JAIME SOLARES QUINTANILLA; Pres. SATURNINO MALLCU; Sec.-Gen. LUIS CHOQUETICLLA VÉLIZ.

Affiliated unions:

Central Obrera Departamental de La Paz: Estación Central 284, La Paz; tel. (2) 235-2898; Exec. Sec. GENARO TORRICO.

Confederación Sindical Unica de los Trabajadores Campesinos de Bolivia (CSUTCB): Calle Sucre, esq. Yanacocha, La Paz; tel. (2) 236-9433; f. 1979; peasant farmers' union; Sec.-Gen. FELIPE QUISPE HUANCA.

Federación de Empleados de Industria Fabril: Edif. Fabril, 5°, Plaza de San Francisco, La Paz; tel. (2) 240-6799; fax (2) 240-7044; Exec. Sec. ALEX GÁLVEZ.

Federación Sindical de Trabajadores Mineros de Bolivia (FSTMB): Plaza Venezuela 1470, Casilla 14565, La Paz; tel. (2) 235-9656; fax (2) 248-4948; f. 1944; mineworkers' union; Leader MIGUEL ZUBIETA; Gen. Sec. EDGAR RAMÍREZ SANTIESTÉBAN; 27,000 mems.

Federación Sindical de Trabajadores Petroleros de Bolivia: Calle México 1504, La Paz; tel. (2) 235-1748; Exec. Sec. NEFTALYMENDOZA DURÁN.

Confederación General de Trabajadores Fabriles de Bolivia (CGTFB): Avda Armentia 452, Casilla 21590, La Paz; tel. (2) 237-1603; fax (2) 232-4302; e-mail dirabc@bo.net; f. 1951; manufacturing workers' union; Exec. Sec. ANGEL ASTURIZAGA; Gen. Sec. ROBERTO ENCINAS.

Transport

RAILWAYS

Empresa Nacional de Ferrocarriles (ENFE): Estación Central de Ferrocarriles, Plaza Zalles, Casilla 428, La Paz; tel. (2) 232-7401; fax (2) 239-2677; f. 1964; privatized under the Government's capitalization programme in 1995; administers most of the railways in Bolivia; holding co for unauctioned former state assets; total networks: 3,608 km (1999); Andina network: 2,274 km; Oriental (Eastern) network: 1,424 km; Pres. J. L. LANDÍVAR.

Empresa Ferrocarril Andino, SA: Casilla 4350, La Paz; tel. (2) 239-145; fax (2) 239-145; e-mail efasa@fca.com.bo; internet www.fca.com.bo; f. 1996; Gen. Man. EDUARDO MACLEAN AVAROA.

Empresa Ferroviaria Oriental, SA (FCOSA): Avda Montes Final s/n, Casilla 108, Santa Cruz; tel. (3) 346-3900; fax (3) 346-3920; e-mail fcosa@fcosa.com; internet www.fcosa.com; f. 1996; Gen. Man. JAIME VALENCIA.

There are plans to construct a railway line with Brazilian assistance, to link Cochabamba and Santa Cruz. There were also plans for the construction of a rail link between Santa Cruz and Mutún on the border with Brazil.

ROADS

In 2002 Bolivia had some 53,790 km of roads, of which an estimated 6.5% (3,496 km) were paved. Almost the entire road network is concentrated in the Altiplano region and the Andes valleys. A 560-km highway runs from Santa Cruz to Cochabamba, serving a colonization scheme on virgin lands around Santa Cruz. The Pan-American Highway, linking Argentina and Peru, crosses Bolivia from south to north-west. In 1997 the Government announced the construction of 1,844 km of new roads in the hope of improving Bolivia's connections with neighbouring countries.

INLAND WATERWAYS

By agreement with Paraguay in 1938 (confirmed in 1939), Bolivia has an outlet on the River Paraguay. This arrangement, together with navigation rights on the Paraná, gives Bolivia access to the River Plate and the sea. The River Paraguay is navigable for vessels of 12-ft draught for 288 km beyond Asunción, in Paraguay, and for smaller boats another 960 km to Corumbá in Brazil. In late 1994 plans were finalized to widen and deepen the River Paraguay, providing a waterway from Bolivia to the Atlantic coast in Uruguay. However, work on the project was delayed, owing largely to environmental concerns.

In 1974 Bolivia was granted free duty access to the Brazilian coastal ports of Belém and Santos and the inland ports of Corumbá and Port Velho. In 1976 Argentina granted Bolivia free-port facilities at Rosario on the River Paraná. In 1992 an agreement was signed with Peru, granting Bolivia access to (and the use, without customs formalities, of) the Pacific port of Ilo. Most of Bolivia's foreign trade is handled through the ports of Matarani (Peru), Antofagasta and Arica (Chile), Rosario and Buenos Aires (Argentina) and Santos (Brazil). An agreement between Bolivia and Chile to reform Bolivia's access arrangements to the port of Arica came into effect in January 1996.

Bolivia has over 14,000 km of navigable rivers, which connect most of Bolivia with the Amazon basin.

Bolivian River Navigation Company: f. 1958; services from Puerto Suárez to Buenos Aires (Argentina).

CIVIL AVIATION

Bolivia has 30 airports, including the two international airports at La Paz (El Alto) and Santa Cruz (Viru-Viru).

Dirección General de Aeronáutica Civil: Avda Mariscal Santa Cruz 1278, Casilla 9360; La Paz; tel. (2) 237-4142; e-mail dgacbol@ceibo-entelnet.bo; internet www.dgac.gov.bo; f. 1947; Dir-Gen. ORLANDO MONTOYA KOËSTER.

AeroSur: Calle Colón y Avda Irala 616, Casilla 3104, Santa Cruz; tel. (3) 336-4446; fax (3) 333-0666; e-mail aerosur@aerosur.com; internet www.aerosur.com; f. 1992 by merger of existing charter cos following deregulation; privately-owned; Pres. OSCAR ALCOCER; Gen. Man. FERNANDO PRUDENCIO.

Lloyd Aéreo Boliviano, SAM (LAB): Casilla 132, Aeropuerto 'Jorge Wilstermann', Cochabamba; tel. (4) 425-1270; fax (4) 425-0766; e-mail presidencia@labairlines.com.bo; internet www.labairlines.com; f. 1925; privatized under the Government's capitalization programme in 1995; jtly-owned by Bolivian Govt (48%), and private interests (52%); operates a network of scheduled services to 12 cities within Bolivia and to 21 international destinations in South America, Central America and the USA; Pres. Ing. ERNESTO ASBÚN; Gen. Man. JOSÉ RODRÍGUEZ.

Transportes Aéreos Bolivianos (TAB): Casilla 12237, La Paz; tel. (2) 237-8325; fax (2) 235-9660; f. 1977; regional scheduled and charter cargo services; Gen. Man. LUIS GUERECA PADILLA; Chair. CARLO APARICIO.

Transportes Aéreos Militares: Avda Montes 738, La Paz; tel. (2) 237-9286; internal passenger and cargo services; Dir-Gen. REMBERTO DURÁN.

Tourism

Bolivia's tourist attractions include Lake Titicaca, at 3,810 m (12,500 ft) above sea-level, pre-Incan ruins at Tiwanaku, Chacaltaya in the Andes mountains, which has the highest ski-run in the world, and the UNESCO World Cultural Heritage Sites of Potosí and Sucre. In 2002 382,185 foreign visitors arrived at hotels in Bolivian regional capitals. In 2001 receipts from tourism totalled US $156m. Tourists come mainly from South American countries, the USA and Europe.

Asociación Boliviana de Agencias de Viajes y Turismo: Edif. Litoral, Avda Mariscal Santa Cruz 1351, Casilla 3967, La Paz; f. 1984; Pres. EUGENIO MONROY VÉLEZ.

Viceministerio de Turismo: Avda Mariscal Santa Cruz, 16°, Casilla 1868, La Paz; tel. (2) 235-8312; fax (2) 237-4630; Vice-Minister of Tourism VÍCTOR HUGO ORDÓÑEZ.

BOSNIA AND HERZEGOVINA

Introductory Survey

Location, Climate, Language, Religion, Flag, Capital

Bosnia and Herzegovina is situated in south-eastern Europe. It is bounded by Croatia to the north west and south-west, and by Serbia and Montenegro to the east and southeast (Serbia to the east, Montenegro to the south-east). There is a short (20 km—12 miles) south-western coastline on the Adriatic Sea around the town of Neum, which borders an exclave of Croatia, including Dubrovnik, to the south-east, and Croatia proper to the north-west. Bosnia and Herzegovina is a largely mountainous territory with a continental climate and steady rainfall throughout the year; in areas nearer the coast, however, the climate is more Mediterranean. The official languages are Bosnian, Croatian and Serbian, all of which were formerly referred to as variants of Serbo-Croat. Bosnian and Croatian are written in the Latin script, while Serbian has traditionally been written in the Cyrillic script, but is sometimes also written in the Latin script. The Muslims (Bosniaks), the majority of whom belong to the Sunni sect, are the largest religious grouping in Bosnia and Herzegovina, comprising 43.7% of the population in 1991. Religious affiliation is roughly equated with ethnicity, the Serbs (31.4% of the population) belonging to the Serbian Orthodox Church and the Croats (17.3%) being members of the Roman Catholic Church. The national flag (proportions 1 by 2) consists of two unequal vertical sections of blue, separated by a yellow triangle, which is bordered on the left by a diagonal line of nine white five-pointed stars. The capital is Sarajevo.

Recent History

The provinces of Bosnia and Herzegovina formed part of the Turkish Osmanlı (Ottoman) Empire for almost 400 years, but, following the Congress of Berlin of 1878, were administered by the Habsburg Empire of Austria-Hungary, which formally annexed the territories in 1908. The population of the provinces was composed of a mixture of Orthodox Christian Serbs, Roman Catholic Croats and Muslims (Bosniaks—mainly Slavs who had converted to Islam during the Ottoman period). Serbian expansionist aims caused tension from the late 19th century, and in 1914, following the assassination of the heir to the Habsburg throne by a Bosnian Serb extremist in Sarajevo, Austria-Hungary declared war on Serbia, thereby precipitating the First World War. On 4 December 1918 the Kingdom of Serbs, Croats and Slovenes was proclaimed, when the Serbs and Croats agreed with other ethnic and communal groups to establish a common state under the Serbian monarchy. The provinces of Bosnia and Herzegovina formed part of the new kingdom. Bitter disputes ensued between Serbs and Croats (see the chapter on Croatia), however, and in 1929 King Alexandar imposed a dictatorship, formally renaming the country Yugoslavia ('land of the Southern Slavs') in October.

Although officially banned in 1921, the Communist Party of Yugoslavia (CPY) operated clandestinely, and in 1937 Josip Broz (Tito) became its General-Secretary. During the Second World War (1939–45) intense fighting took place between Croats and Serbs in Bosnia and Herzegovina, which was incorporated into a fascist Independent State of Croatia in 1941. From 1943, however, Tito's communist-led Partisan movement dominated most of Bosnia and Herzegovina. Following Tito's victory in 1945, Bosnia and Herzegovina became one of the six constituent republics of the Yugoslav federation. In the 1960s Tito sought to counter increasing tension between three principal ethnic groups of the Republic, as well as maintaining a balance of power between the various ethnic groups of the Socialist Federal Republic of Yugoslavia (SFRY—as the country was renamed in 1963). Slav Muslims were granted a distinct ethnic status (as 'Muslims'), as a nation of Yugoslavia, prior to the 1971 census. In that year a collective state presidency was established for Bosnia and Herzegovina, with a regular rotation of posts.

Communal affiliation proved to be a decisive factor in the elections held to the republican legislature, the Skupština Republike Bosne i Hercegovine (Assembly of the Republic of Bosnia and Herzegovina) in November–December 1990. The ruling League of Communists of Bosnia and Herzegovina was

ousted, and three main nationalist parties emerged as the largest parties in the Skupština: the principally Bosniak Party of Democratic Action (PDA), with 86 seats; the Serbian Democratic Party (SDP), with 72 seats; and the Croatian Democratic Union of Bosnia and Herzegovina (CDU—BH), an affiliate of the ruling party of Croatia, with 44 seats. The three nationalist parties also took all seven seats on the directly elected collective Presidency and formed a coalition administration for the republic. On 20 December they announced that Alija Izetbegović of the PDA (a former dissident, who had been imprisoned in 1946–49 and in 1983–88, following his publication of books calling for Islam to have a role in political life) was to be President of the Presidency, while members of the CDU—BH and the SDP were to be President of the Executive Council (Prime Minister) and President of the Skupština, respectively.

In 1991 the politics of Bosnia and Herzegovina were increasingly dominated by the Serb–Croat conflict. Following the declarations of independence by Slovenia and Croatia in June, Serb-dominated territories in Bosnia and Herzegovina declared their intent to remain within the Yugoslav federation (or in a 'Greater Serbia'). On 16 September a self-proclaimed 'Serb Autonomous Region' (SAR) of Bosnian Krajina was proclaimed, based in Banja Luka, the second largest city in Bosnia and Herzegovina; this SAR was formed on the basis of a Serb 'Community of Municipalities of Bosnian Krajina' that had been formed in April, and which had announced its unification with the neighbouring 'Serb Autonomous Region (SAR) of Krajina' in Croatia in June. The republican Government rejected these developments and declared the inviolability of the internal boundaries of the SFRY. Armed incidents contributed to the rising tension throughout mid-1991, and the formation of further SARs was proclaimed, amid accusations that Serb nationalist elements sought to establish a 'Greater Serbia', with the support of the Yugoslav People's Army (JNA). In October the JNA assumed effective control of the southern multi-ethnic city of Mostar, north-west of the predominately Bosnian Serb 'Old' Herzegovina.

In October 1991 both the republican Presidency (with the dissenting votes of the Bosnian Serb members) and the PDA proposed to the Skupština that the republic declare its independence. Later that month the Serb deputies rejected the resolution as a move towards secession from the SFRY, and subsequently withdrew from the chamber. On 15 October, however, the remaining parliamentarians approved a resolution declaring the sovereignty of Bosnia and Herzegovina. The SARs rejected the declaration of sovereignty and declared that, henceforth, only the federal laws and Constitution would apply on their territory. On 24 October the Serb deputies of the republican Skupština announced the formation of a Serb Narodna skupština (National Assembly), while further SARs were subsequently proclaimed in various regions of Bosnia and Herzegovina. On 9–10 November a referendum, organized by the Bosnian Serb Narodna skupština, indicated overwhelming support for remaining in a common Serb state. On 9 January the formation of a 'Serb Republic' (Republika Srpska) of Bosnia and Herzegovina', comprising Serb-held areas of the republic (about 65% of the total area), was proclaimed, headed by Dr Radovan Karadžić, the leader of the SDP and a prominent poet and psychiatrist. The republican Government immediately declared this secessionist republic, the headquarters of which were based in Banja Luka, to be illegal. (In August the designation of the unrecognized Bosnian Serb polity was changed to simply 'Republika Srpska'.) Meanwhile, in a republic-wide referendum on 29 February and 1 March 1992, boycotted by the overwhelming majority of the Bosnian Serb populace, 99.4% of the participating 63% of the electorate expressed support for the full independence of Bosnia and Herzegovina. Izetbegović immediately declared the republic's independence and omitted the word 'socialist' from the new state's official title.

Following the declaration of independence, renewed Serb–Muslim tension led to clashes in Sarajevo, the republican capital, and elsewhere. On 18 March 1992, following mediation by the European Community (EC, now European Union—EU, see

p. 217), the leaders of the Serb, Croat and Bosniak communities signed an agreement providing for the division of Bosnia and Herzegovina into three autonomous units. In April fighting between the Serbian-dominated JNA and Bosniak and Croatian forces intensified, particularly following the recognition of Bosnia and Herzegovina's independence by the EC and the USA on 7 April; Serbian troops besieged Sarajevo and launched frequent mortar attacks on the city from the surrounding mountains and hills. Meanwhile, Bosnian Serb fighters and irregular troops from Serbia conducted a campaign of 'ethnic cleansing' in the areas under Bosnian Serb control, initially in the north-east and north-west of Bosnia, with the intent of creating an ethnically homogenous territory, and systematically destroying Muslim and Roman Catholic places of worship. Early EC and UN efforts at mediation proved unsuccessful, and their respective peace monitors were withdrawn from Sarajevo in mid-May. Izetbegović requested foreign military intervention to support the republican Government, but the UN, while deploying a UN Protection Force (UNPROFOR) in Croatia, decided against the deployment of a peace-keeping force in the republic under prevailing conditions. On 20 May the Government of Bosnia and Herzegovina declared the JNA to be an 'occupying force' and announced the formation of a republican army. Two days later Bosnia and Herzegovina was admitted to the UN, concurrently with Croatia and Slovenia. On 30 May the UN imposed economic sanctions against the recently established Federal Republic of Yugoslavia (FRY—comprising solely the republics of Serbia and Montenegro), in response to its involvement in the conflict in Bosnia and Herzegovina. In early June, in an apparent effort to placate the UN, Serbian leaders in Belgrade (the FRY capital) ordered the Bosnian Serbs to end the siege of Sarajevo and to surrender Sarajevo airport to UN control.

The proclamation, on 3 July 1992, by ethnic Croats in Western Herzegovina and central Bosnia, of an autonomous 'Croat Community of Herzeg-Bosna' (Herzeg-Bosna), covering about 30% of the territory of Bosnia and Herzegovina and which was headed by Mate Boban, was immediately declared to be illegal by Izetbegović's Government. Despite their political differences, Izetbegović and President Franjo Tuđman of Croatia (a nationalist, who supported the establishment of Herzeg-Bosna) signed a co-operation agreement in late July. Under this accord, the Governments of Bosnia and Herzegovina and of Croatia formed a Joint Defence Committee in late September, and repeated demands that the UN end an armaments embargo (which had been imposed on the SFRY in September 1991, and which was subsequently determined to apply to all regions thereof, following the disintegration of the SFRY). However, hostilities erupted between Croats and Bosniaks in October, after several months of increasing tensions, and the towns of Mostar, Novi Travnik and Vitez were captured by Croat forces (the HVO). Mostar was subsequently proclaimed capital of 'Herzeg-Bosna, with the city effectively being split into Croat- and Bosniak-controlled zones; the Serb population of the city, which had accounted for about 20% of the population prior to the onset of conflict, had largely fled. In November the Croatian Government admitted for the first time that Croatian regular army units had been deployed in Bosnia and Herzegovina, and accordingly became a signatory to the latest cease-fire agreement in Bosnia and Herzegovina. In early December the UN Human Rights Commission declared that Bosnian Serbs were largely responsible for violations of human rights in Bosnia and Herzegovina. (Television broadcasts of concentration camps in Serb-held areas of the Bosnian Krajina, in which more than 1,500 Bosniaks were reported to have been killed, had provoked international outrage in August 1992.) Later in December the UN Security Council unanimously adopted a resolution condemning the atrocities, particularly the widespread rape of Bosniak women, and demanding access to all Serb detention camps.

In January 1993 the Co-Chairmen of the Geneva Peace Conference (a permanent forum for talks on the conflict, established in 1992), Lord (David) Owen (a former British Secretary of State for Foreign and Commonwealth Affairs) and Cyrus Vance (the UN mediator and a former US Secretary of State), visited Belgrade for talks with the newly re-elected President of Serbia, Slobodan Milošević. Their aim was to persuade him to convince the Bosnian Serbs to agree to a division of Bosnia and Herzegovina into 10 provinces (with three provinces allocated to each faction and Sarajevo as a province with special status). The peace plan was approved by Boban, and, in part, by Izetbegović, but was rejected by Karadžić, who insisted on the establishment

of an autonomous Serb state within the territory of Bosnia and Herzegovina. (The extent of territory allocated to Bosnian Croats by the plan considerably exceeded prior expectations, being disproportionately large compared with the share of the population constituted by Croats, a factor that was widely regarded as decisive in encouraging Croat aspirations to obtain control of further territory, and a subsequent intensification of hostilities between Croats and Bosniaks in central Bosnia.) In mid-January Milošević attended the peace talks in Geneva, Switzerland, for the first time. Karadžić, under pressure from Milošević and the President of the FRY, agreed to the constitutional proposals included in the plan and, subsequently, to the military arrangements. On 19–20 January the Bosnian Serb Narodna skupština, based at Pale, outside Sarajevo, voted to accept the general principles of the Vance-Owen plan. On 22 February the UN Security Council adopted a resolution providing for the establishment of an international court to try alleged war criminals for acts committed since 1991 in the territories formerly included in the SFRY. On 31 March the UN Security Council adopted a resolution permitting the taking of 'all necessary measures' by UN member states or regional organizations to enforce a 'no-fly zone' imposed (by another Security Council resolution) on the airspace of Bosnia and Herzegovina in October 1992. During March 1993, at further peace talks, Izetbegović agreed to both the military arrangements and the proposed territorial divisions included in the Vance-Owen plan. In April, however, the Bosnian Serb Narodna skupština rejected the territorial arrangements, incurring international disapproval (including that of Serbia, which had endorsed the plan under pressure from UN and EC sanctions). In early May Karadžić signed the Vance-Owen plan in Geneva, but two days later it was decisively rejected by the Bosnian Serb Narodna skupština.

In late May 1993 the USA, France, Russia, Spain and the United Kingdom signed a communiqué declaring that the arms embargo to the post-SFRY states would continue and that international armed forces would not intervene in the conflict; they proposed instead, with effect from 22 July, the creation of six designated 'safe areas' (Sarajevo, Bihać, Tuzla, Goražde, Srebrenica and Žepa), mostly in eastern Bosnia, in which disarmed Bosniaks (who, unlike the Bosnian Serbs and Croats, lacked substantial external military support) would be settled, with the intention that they would be safe from Serb attack in these locations. In early June a UN Security Council resolution permitted UNPROFOR to use force, including air power, in response to attacks against these 'safe areas'. (Earlier proposals, led by the USA, to permit the use of force against Bosnian Serb positions had not reached fruition, to a large extent owing to opposition by the France, Russia and the United Kingdom.) Later that month a joint Serb-Croat offensive began against the northern, predominately Bosniak, town of Maglaj. In July intense fighting between Croats and Bosniaks for the control of Mostar commenced. The city suffered severe damage over subsequent months, when all bridges between the predominately Croat West bank of the Neretva river, and the predominately Bosniak East bank, were destroyed. In mid-June new peace proposals were announced in Geneva by Lord Owen and Thorvald Stoltenberg (who had replaced Vance as the UN mediator in May), under which Bosnia and Herzegovina would become a confederation of three ethnically determined states. Izetbegović refused to discuss the tripartite division of Bosnia and boycotted the remainder of the Geneva talks, although other members of the Presidency continued discussions.

On 30 July 1993 the three factions reached a constitutional agreement in Geneva on the reconstruction of Bosnia and Herzegovina into a confederation of three states, styled the 'Union of Republics of Bosnia and Herzegovina', under a central government with powers limited to foreign policy and foreign trade. Under this agreement, Sarajevo would be placed under UN administration for a two-year transitional period. Despite this agreement and numerous negotiated cease-fires, fighting continued, and in early August the three Croat members of the Bosnian State Presidency (including the Prime Minister, Mile Akmadžić, who was consequently dismissed from that post) left the delegation to Geneva, in protest at Bosniak attacks on Croat populations, and instead joined the Croatian negotiators. On 28 August a 'Croat Republic of Herzeg-Bosna' was proclaimed by a Croat Assembly in Grude, which proceeded to accept the Owen-Stoltenberg plan on condition that the Serbs and Bosniaks also accepted it. On the same day the Bosnian Serb Narodna skupština also voted in favour of the plan. On 31 August, however, a session of the Skupština Republike Bosne i Hercegovine rejected the Geneva plan, while agreeing to use it as a basis for further peace negotiations.

On 10 September 1993 Fikret Abdić, a Bosniak member of the State Presidency and a factory director, announced the creation of an 'Autonomous Province of Western Bosnia' in the region around Bihać, in the extreme north-west, which, Abdić declared, was to form part of the 'Union of Republics of Bosnia and Herzegovina'. On 27 September Abdić was elected President by a 'Constituent Assembly' in Velika Kladusa. Abdić (who signed a peace agreement with representatives of the Bosnian Serbs, and reportedly assured Croat forces that his troops would not fight them), was subsequently dismissed from the State Presidency of Bosnia and Herzegovina. Izetbegović imposed martial law on the area and government forces attacked troops under Abdić's command.

In early February 1994 the apparent shelling of a Sarajevo market-place, killing at least 68 people and wounding 200 others, prompted the UN to threaten military intervention if Serb forces failed to cease their bombardment of the city. Following the issuing of an ultimatum by NATO, the Bosnian Serbs withdrew most of their heavy weaponry from a 20-km 'exclusion zone' around the city, which, however, remained effectively blockaded. Moreover, the exclusion zone was frequently violated. In late February NATO forces shot down four Serb aircraft near Banja Luka, which had violated the UN prohibition of non-humanitarian flights over Bosnia and Herzegovina. The incident represented the first aggressive military action taken by NATO since its establishment. None the less, Bosnian Serb forces continued to shell Maglaj throughout March, while several of the 'safe areas' were also bombarded. Following a cease-fire agreed by the republican Government and the authorities of Herzeg-Bosna in late February 1994, Haris Silajdžić (Prime Minister of the republican Government since late October 1993) and Kresimir Zubak (who had replaced Boban as the leader of Herzeg-Bosna) signed an agreement on 18 March, in Washington, DC, USA, providing for the creation of a Federation of Bosnia and Herzegovina on those territories controlled by Croats and Bosniaks, with power to be shared equally between the two groups. The federation government was to be responsible for defence, foreign affairs and the economy, while the offices of prime minister and president were to rotate annually between the two communities. A second 'preliminary' agreement was signed by Presidents Izetbegović and Tuđman, which provided for the eventual creation of a loose confederation of the Federation and Croatia. In late March the accords were approved by the Herzeg-Bosna Assembly, and the new Constitution was ratified by the Skupština Republike Bosne i Hercegovine. In April, in response to the continued shelling of the eastern 'safe area' of Goražde by Bosnian Serb forces, UN-sanctioned air strikes were launched by NATO aircraft on Serb ground positions. However, Serb forces captured Goražde later that month, prompting strong criticism from the Russian Government, which hitherto had been perceived as sympathetic towards the Serbs, but which now indicated that it would not oppose the use of force against them. Bosnian Serb forces withdrew from Goražde in late April. On 26 April a new negotiating forum, the 'Contact Group', comprising representatives from France, Germany, Russia, the United Kingdom and the USA, was established.

In late May 1994 the Ustavotvorna skupština Federacije Bosne i Hercegovine (Constituent Assembly of the Federation of Bosnia and Herzegovina) elected Zubak to the largely ceremonial post of President of the Federation at its inaugural meeting. Ejup Ganić, a Bosniak, was elected Vice-President of the Federation (he was concurrently a Vice-President of the collective Presidency of the Republic of Bosnia and Herzegovina) and Silajdžić was appointed Prime Minister of the Federation. A joint Government of the Federation and the Republic of Bosnia and Herzegovina, led by Silajdžić, was appointed in late June.

Following peace negotiations in Geneva in early June 1994, a one-month republic-wide cease-fire was declared. Repeated violations were reported by the end of the month, however, by which time Bosnian government forces had captured Serb-held areas of central Bosnia. The Contact Group presented new peace proposals in early July, according to which the Federation of Bosnia and Herzegovina would be granted 51% of the territory of Bosnia and Herzegovina, while the Bosnian Serbs would yield approximately one-third of the territory they controlled. Key sensitive areas, including Sarajevo, Srebrenica, Goražde and Brčko, would be placed under UN and EU administration. On 17

July Izetbegović and Tuđman endorsed the Contact Group plan, which was also approved by the Skupština Republike Bosne i Hercegovine. However, the proposed territorial division was rejected by the Bosnian Serb Narodna skupština. President Milošević of Serbia subsequently criticized Bosnian Serb opposition to the plan, and in early August the FRY announced the closure of its borders with Republika Srpska. On 5 August NATO air strikes (the first since April) were launched against Bosnian Serb targets, following Serb attacks against UN forces and the renewed shelling of Sarajevo. In late August 96% of participants of a referendum held in Republika Srpska reportedly voted to reject the Contact Group plan; this rejection was unanimously approved by the Bosnian Serb Narodna skupština on 1 September. Meanwhile, on 21 August the Bihać enclave, held by Abdić's forces, was captured by the government army of Bosnia and Herzegovina. In early December the Contact Group issued proposals based on the July peace plan, which indicated the possibility of confedaral links between a Bosnian Serb polity and the FRY. On 31 December the Republika Srpska authorities and the Government of the Republic of Bosnia and Herzegovina signed a four-month cease-fire agreement, to take effect from the following day. Both sides expressed their readiness to resume peace negotiations based on the revised Contact Group plan. The republic-wide cease-fire was generally observed during January 1995. However, intense fighting continued in the Bihać enclave between government forces and troops loyal to Abdić, who was supported by troops from the adjoining self-proclaimed 'Republic of Serbian Krajina' in Croatia. In February the USA refused to continue negotiations with Karadžić until the Bosnian Serb authorities accepted the Contact Group plan.

On 20 February 1995 representatives of the Bosnian Serbs and the Croatian Serbs signed a military pact, guaranteeing mutual assistance in the event of attack and providing for the establishment of a joint Supreme Defence Council. In early March, in response, a formal military alliance was announced between the armies of Croatia, the authorities of Herzeg-Bosna and the Government of the Republic of Bosnia and Herzegovina. On 8 April President Zubak of the Federation and Ejup Ganić, the Vice-President of both the Federation and of Bosnia and Herzegovina, signed an agreement in Bonn, Germany, on the implementation of federation principles, including the formation of unified police forces, local government and, eventually, armed forces. On 25 May, following a UN request in response to the continued bombardment of Sarajevo, NATO aircraft carried out strikes on Bosnian Serb ammunition depots. Within hours, Serb forces responded by shelling five of the six 'safe areas' and, following further NATO air strikes on 26 May, retaliated with a massive bombardment of Tuzla, which resulted in at least 70 deaths. Bosnian Serb troops subsequently disarmed and took hostage 222 UNPROFOR personnel in the Goražde 'safe area'. In early June defence ministers from NATO and other European states agreed on the creation of a 10,000-strong 'rapid reaction force' for Bosnia and Herzegovina, which was to operate under UN command from mid-July, with a mandate to provide 'enhanced protection' to UNPROFOR. The ongoing hostage crisis, led, however, to a withdrawal of UNPROFOR troops from Bosnian Serb territory around Sarajevo in mid-June. Although the UN denied that any deal had been reached with the Bosnian Serbs, the release of the remaining hostages coincided with the withdrawal of UNPROFOR from around the capital.

On 11 July 1995 the eastern 'safe area' of Srebrenica was captured by Bosnian Serb fighters, after Dutch UNPROFOR troops based in the town were taken hostage, despite NATO air strikes on Bosnian Serb tanks approaching the town. Following the capture of Srebrenica, an estimated 7,000–8,000 Muslim male civilians were massacred by Bosnian Serb forces, the largest atrocity to take place in Europe since the end of the Second World War.

Bihać was attacked on 20 July 1995, in a concerted effort by Bosnian Serbs, Croatian Serbs, and rebel Bosniaks, led by Abdić. The situation in Bihać prompted the signature of a military co-operation agreement between Izetbegović and Tuđman on 22 July. Croatian and Herzeg-Bosna troops subsequently launched attacks on Serb positions around Bihać, thereby blocking Serb supply routes into the Krajina enclave. Meanwhile, the 'safe area' of Žepa, near Srebrenica, was captured by Bosnian Serb troops on 25 July.

Croatian government forces invaded the Croatian Serb-held Krajina on 4 August 1995, and rapidly recaptured the entire enclave, prompting a massive exodus of Serb civilians from the region into Serb-held areas of Bosnia and Herzegovina and into

Serbia itself. On 6–7 August the siege of Bihać was ended by Bosnian government and Croatian troops. On 9 August a further peace initiative (devised by Richard Holbrooke, a US Assistant Secretary of State) was announced by the US Administration; the proposals, which were based on the Contact Group plan of 1994, none the less allowed the Bosnian Serb authorities to retain control of Srebrenica and Žepa. On 28 August an apparent mortar attack on a market in central Sarajevo, attributed to Bosnian Serb forces, resulted in at least 38 deaths. Two days later NATO responded by commencing a series of air strikes (known as 'Operation Deliberate Force') on Serb positions throughout Bosnia and Herzegovina, which continued until 14 September and had the effect of markedly reducing the territory controlled by Bosnian Serb forces.

On 8 September 1995 major progress in the peace process was achieved when, at a meeting in Geneva, chaired by the Contact Group, the Ministers of Foreign Affairs of the Republic of Bosnia and Herzegovina, Croatia and the FRY (the latter acting on behalf of the Bosnian Serbs) signed an agreement determining basic principles for a peace accord. These principles included the continuing existence of Bosnia and Herzegovina within its present borders, but the state was to comprise two administrative units, known as entities: the Federation of Bosnia and Herzegovina; and Republika Srpska, with each entity largely retaining its existing Constitution. In mid-September 'Operation Deliberate Force' was suspended, following the withdrawal of Bosnian Serb weaponry from the 'exclusion zone' around Sarajevo. Agreement on further basic principles for a peace accord was reached by the Ministers of Foreign Affairs of Bosnia and Herzegovina, Croatia and the FRY, meeting in New York, USA, on 26 September. Within the state parliament, Republika Srpska was to be apportioned one-third of the seats; the Federation was to control two-thirds of the seats (legislative decisions were only to be implemented, however, with the approval of at least one-third of the deputies of each entity). A collective presidency was also to be organized according to the one-third Serb to two-thirds Bosniak-Croat proportional division, with all decisions to be taken by majority vote. A 60-day cease-fire came into effect on 12 October; the UN simultaneously announced its intention to reduce the number of peace-keeping troops in the area.

On 1 November 1995 peace negotiations between the three warring parties in the conflict began in Dayton, Ohio, USA. A comprehensive peace agreement was reached on 21 November, when Izetbegović, Tuđman and Milošević (the latter representing both the FRY and the Bosnian Serbs) initialled a General Framework Agreement for Peace in Bosnia and Herzegovina, dividing the country between the Federation, with 51% of the territory, and the Republika Srpska, which would control 49% of the area, although the sovereignty of the state, which was henceforth to be known simply as Bosnia and Herzegovina, was to be maintained within its existing borders. Whereas the Government of Republika Srpska was to be highly centralized, with a directly elected presidency and no level of local government other than that of municipality, power in the Federation was largely devolved to 10 cantonal administrations, as well as to municipalities. The Federation was to have a bicameral legislature, whereas that of Republika Srpska was to be unicameral. The Dayton accords included provisions for a state government with a democratically elected collective presidency and a parliament, based in Sarajevo, and provisions for a single monetary system, central bank and other economic institutions. It also stipulated the right of all refugees and displaced persons to return to their homes and either to have seized property returned to them or to receive fair compensation. Of the former 'safe areas' in eastern Bosnia, only Goražde was to remain under the control of the Federation and was to be linked to Sarajevo via a federation-administered land corridor; several south-eastern suburbs of Sarajevo were to form part of Republika Srpska, although most regions of the city was to be in the Federation. No agreement was reached, however, regarding the width of the strategically important Posavina corridor, surrounded by Federation territory, connecting the northern sector of Republika Srpska (including the Bosnian Kraina) with the southern sector, as well as to Serbia, and control of the town and strategic riverport of Brčko, located at this point; the three sides agreed to place the issue under international arbitration. (In the meantime, Brčko was to be administered as part of Republika Srpska.) Under the Dayton agreement, UNPROFOR troops were to be replaced by an international, NATO-commanded, 60,000-strong Implementation Force (IFOR). The agreement

provided IFOR with a mandate to oversee the withdrawal of the warring parties from zones of separation and to monitor the agreed exchanges of territory. In all, estimates for the number of people killed in the conflict in Bosnia and Herzegovina ranged from 200,000–250,000, and some 2.7m. people were believed to have been displaced.

Following the initialling of the Dayton peace accords, the UN suspended the remaining economic sanctions against the FRY and voted to remove gradually the arms embargo against the post-SFRY states. At a conference on the implementation of the Dayton peace accords, held in London, United Kingdom, in early December, it was agreed that an Organization for Security and Co-operation in Europe (OSCE, see p. 314) mission would organize and monitor parliamentary elections in Bosnia and Herzegovina and that the Contact Group would be replaced by a Peace Implementation Council based in Brussels, Belgium. The former Swedish Prime Minister and EU envoy to the Bosnian peace talks, Carl Bildt, was appointed High Representative of the International Community in Bosnia and Herzegovina, with responsibility for the implementation of the civilian aspects of the Dayton agreement. On 14 December the Dayton peace agreement was formally signed by Izetbegović, Tuđman and Milošević and by President Bill Clinton of the USA and a number of European political leaders in Paris, France. The formal transfer of power from UNPROFOR to IFOR took place on 20 December.

In mid-December 1995 the Narodna skupština Republike Srpske elected a new Government, headed by Rajko Kasagić. On 30 January 1996 Hasan Muratović was elected by the state Assembly as Prime Minister of Bosnia and Herzegovina, following the resignation from the premiership of Silajdžić, apparently in protest at the increasing Bosniak nationalism of the ruling PDA; a new state Government was appointed on the same day. On 31 January the Ustavotvorna skupština Federacije Bosne i Hercegovine appointed a new federation Government, with Izudin Kapetanović as Prime Minister. In mid-February, in response to unrest in Mostar (where tensions between Croats and Bosniaks remained high) and isolated attacks elsewhere, an emergency summit meeting took place in Rome, Italy, during which Izetbegović, Tuđman and Milošević reaffirmed their adherence to the Dayton agreement. A joint Croat-Bosniak security patrol, accompanied by officers from the UN International Police Task Force (IPTF) and Western European Union (WEU), subsequently began operating in Mostar.

By the end of April 1996 substantial progress had been made in the implementation of the military aspects of the Dayton agreement. The former warring parties completed staged withdrawals from the IFOR-controlled zone of separation; agreement was reached, under the auspices of the OSCE, on the exchange of information on weaponry and the submission of arsenals to OSCE inspection; and the majority of prisoners of war were released. However, the exchange of territory between the two entities did not proceed as envisaged in the peace agreement. From mid-January there was a mass exodus of ethnic Serbs from the Bosnian Serb-held suburbs of Sarajevo that were to be transferred to the control of the Federation. The Republika Srpska authorities in Pale were criticized for using intimidation to coerce the Serb inhabitants of these districts to resettle in towns in eastern regions of Republika Srpska from which Muslims had been driven during the war. By late March only about 10% of the pre-war Serb population in Sarajevo remained.

In early April 1996 Bosniak and Croat leaders agreed on the formation of a federation-wide customs union, a single federation budget and a unitary banking system. In May further agreement was reached between the two sides, meeting in Washington, DC, on the merger of their armed forces and the return of refugees. The agreement on a unified federation army was the principal precondition for the implementation of a US-sponsored programme to train and equip the Federation's army in order to give it equal military capabilities to that of Republika Srpska's armed forces. Also in May Karadžić dismissed Kasagić, regarded as a relative moderate, as Prime Minister of Republika Srpska and appointed Gojko Kličković in his place; this appointment was endorsed by the Bosnian Serb Narodna Skupština. Karadžić had been indicted by the International Criminal Tribunal for the former Yugoslavia (ICTY, see p. 17), based in The Hague, Netherlands, for war crimes, notably responsibility for the massacre at Srebrenica in July 1995. His continued position as President (and that of Gen. Ratko Mladić as head of the armed forces) was in breach of the Dayton agreement, which prohibited indicted war criminals from holding public office. In response to international pressure, Karadžić announced the delegation of some of his powers to his deputy, Dr Biljana Plavšić. At a Peace Implementation Conference, held in Florence, Italy, in mid-June, it was agreed that elections to the entity and state parliaments, and to the presidency of Republika Srpska, would take place in September.

In mid-June 1996 ethnic Croats in Mostar announced a new Government of Herzeg-Bosna, in contravention of agreements that the autonomous state would be dissolved. At a summit meeting of the Presidents of Bosnia and Herzegovina, Croatia and Serbia, which was convened by the USA in Geneva in mid-August, Tuđman and Izetbegović agreed on the full establishment of federation institutions by the end of the month.

In late June 1996 western European countries issued an ultimatum to Karadžić to resign, on penalty of the reimposition of sanctions against Republika Srpska that had been suspended in April. In defiance of this, the SDP re-elected Karadžić as party leader. At the end of June Karadžić announced his temporary resignation and the appointment of Plavšić as the acting President of Republika Srpska. It was then confirmed that Karadžić would not contest the election to the presidency of Republika Srpska, and Plavšić was nominated as the SDP candidate. None the less, it was deemed unacceptable that Karadžić should retain the powerful position of party leader, and the OSCE mission to Bosnia and Herzegovina declared that the SDP would be excluded from the elections if Karadžić retained any party office. In mid-July the ICTY issued arrest warrants for Karadžić and Mladić and a few days later the USA dispatched Holbrooke to the region in an attempt to bring about Karadžić's removal. Following intensive negotiations with Milošević and Bosnian Serb leaders, Holbrooke secured Karadžić's resignation on 19 July, both from the presidency and as head of the SDP.

During the electoral campaign there were increasing reports of harassment and violence in both the Federation and Republika Srpska. In late August 1996 the OSCE announced that municipal elections were to be postponed, in response to evidence that the Republika Srpska authorities were forcibly registering displaced Serbs in formerly Muslim-dominated localities. This arose from a provision in the Dayton agreement permitting displaced persons to vote either in their former homes or in the place where they chose to settle. (In mid-October the OSCE changed the voting regulations, ruling that people could only vote in their places of residence prior to 1992.) National elections were held on 14 September 1996 to the state Presidency and legislature, the presidency and legislature of Republika Srpska, and the legislature and cantonal authorities of the Federation. At the elections to the state collective Presidency, Izetbegović won 80% of the Bosniak votes cast; Zubak (contesting the election as the candidate of the CDU—BH) 88% of the Croat votes; and Momčilo Krajišnik (of the SDP) 67% of the Serb votes. Having received the largest number of votes of the three winning presidential candidates, Izetbegović became Chairman of the Presidency. Both the Federation section of the Predstavnički dom (House of Representatives—the lower chamber of the bicameral Parlamentarna skupština Bosne i Hercegovine—Parliamentary Assembly of Bosnia and Herzegovina) and the Predstavnički dom Federacije (House of Representatives of the Federation), which replaced the Ustavotvorna skupština Federacije Bosne i Hercegovine and formed the lower chamber of a bicameral Parlament Federacije (Parliament of the Federation), alongside an indirectly elected Dom Naroda (House of Peoples), were dominated by the PDA and the CDU—BH. None the less, an alliance of social-democratic Bosniak and Croat parties, the Joint List of Bosnia and Herzegovina and the Party for Bosnia and Herzegovina (led by Silajdžić) won a significant number of votes in the elections to both the state and federation legislatures. Although the SDP secured a majority of votes in both the Serb section of the Predstavnički dom and in the Narodna skupština Republike Srpske (National Assembly of Republika Srpska—as the Narodna skupština was renamed), the PDA won about one-sixth of the votes cast within the entity. Plavšić was elected President of Republika Srpska, receiving 59% of the votes cast. Following the OSCE's endorsement of the election results, on 1 October 1996 the UN Security Council finally decided to remove sanctions against the FRY and Republika Srpska. A few days later Bosnia and Herzegovina and the FRY agreed to establish full diplomatic relations. The inauguration of the state Presidency took place on 5 October. The inaugural session of the bicameral Parlamentarna skupština (Parliamentary Assembly, comprising the Dom Naroda—House of

Peoples—and the Predstavnički dom) was postponed, owing to a boycott by the Serb deputies.

In November 1996 Plavšić announced that she had dismissed Gen. Mladić as Commander of the Serb armed forces, replacing him with Maj.-Gen. Pero Colić, although Mladić initially refused to accept his dismissal. In late 1996 and early 1997 acts of violence were reported in areas along the inter-entity boundary, with incidents reported over subsequent months in which Bosniaks seeking to reclaim their homes in territory apportioned to Republika Srpska were forcibly repulsed, while tensions between Croats and Bosniaks resulted in violence in Mostar.

Following a Peace Implementation Conference, held in London, it was announced, with effect from 20 December 1996, that IFOR would be replaced by a Stabilization Force (SFOR). In mid-December, after some delay, the Presidency appointed the two Co-Prime Ministers of the national Council of Ministers: Haris Silajdžić of the Party for Bosnia and Herzegovina and Boro Bosić of the SDP. One week later the Predstavnički dom Federacije elected Edhem Bičakčić as the federation Prime Minister, replacing Izudin Kapetanović. (On the previous day the dissolution of 'Herzeg-Bosna' was announced.) The national Council of Ministers was appointed by the Co-Prime Ministers and approved by the inaugural session of the Parlamentarna skupština, which was held on 3 January 1997. The Council of Ministers comprised Ministers for Foreign Affairs, for Foreign Trade and Economic Relations, and for Communications and Civilian Affairs. Each post had two Deputy Ministers, with each of the three ethnic groups holding an equal number of offices. In March 1997 Vladimir Soljić was elected to replace Kresimir Zubak as President of the Federation. (Soljić, in turn, was succeeded by the Vice-President, Dr Ejup Ganić, in December.)

On 28 February 1997 Krajišnik signed, on behalf of Republika Srpska, an agreement with the FRY to foster mutual economic co-operation and to collaborate on regional security. The accord was ratified by the Narodna skupština Republike Srpske in March, despite Plavšić's opposition. In June Bildt was replaced as High Representative by Carlos Westendorp. In July Plavšić announced the dissolution of the Narodna skupština, scheduling parliamentary elections for September; this measure followed the assembly's opposition to the suspension of the entity's Minister of Internal Affairs by Plavšić. Although this action was supported by both the UN and the OSCE, it was strongly criticized by Gojko Klicković, the Prime Minister of Republika Srpska, and a number of resolutions designed to undermine Plavšić were approved by the Narodna skupština. In mid-August the Constitutional Court ruled that Plavšić's decision to dissolve the legislature had been illegal: the Narodna skupština proceeded to vote to disregard future decrees by her. The delayed municipal elections took place in both entities on 13–14 September; when the three main nationalist parties, the PDA, the CDU—BH and the SDP, received the vast majority of the votes cast. In late September a constitutional crisis in Republika Srpska was averted, following a meeting in Belgrade hosted by Milošević and attended by Plavšić and Krajišnik. A joint statement was issued detailing an agreement, whereby elections to the Narodna skupština would take place in November, and presidential elections for both Republika Srpska and the Serb member of the collective Presidency on 7 December. Meanwhile, tensions between the two principal centres of administration centres in Republika Srpska—Pale, in the south, where the republic's legislature was based (and which was perceived as a centre of more extreme nationalist elements), and Banja Luka, in the north, where the presidential administration was based, were reported to undermine the coherence of the Republic's Government.

Elections to the Narodna skupština Republike Srpske were held on 22–23 November 1997, under the supervision of the OSCE. The SDP secured 24 seats (compared with 45 in 1996), but remained the largest party in the legislature. A newly formed electoral alliance, the Coalition for a Single and Democratic Bosnia and Herzegovina, which included the PDA and the Party for Bosnia and Herzegovina, secured 16 seats, while the Serb National Alliance (SNA—established by Plavšić in September, following her expulsion from the SDP in July) and the Serb Radical Party (SRP) each achieved 15 seats. At the inaugural session of the new Narodna skupština on 27 December, Plavšić nominated Mladen Ivanić, an economist with no political affiliation, to the office of prime minister. The nomination was immediately challenged by the leadership of the SDP, which insisted that as the largest party in the new Narodna skupština it should be empowered to propose a new prime minister and government. On 18 January 1998, following the failure of Ivanić's inter-party talks, Milorad Dodik, who was considered to be a 'moderate', secured sufficient parliamentary support to form a new government. Krajišnik condemned Dodik's appointment, who warned that it would result in the destabilization of Republika Srpska. At the end of January Dodik announced that government bodies were to be transferred from Pale to Banja Luka.

At a further Peace Implementation Conference, held in Sintra, Portugal, in May 1997, NATO stipulated deadlines for the approval by the entities of a number of laws on property and the establishment of common passports and citizenship across Bosnia and Herzegovina and, in addition, demanded a new list of ambassadors that represented all ethnic groups. In early July the EU announced the suspension of economic aid to Republika Srpska, owing to its failure to extradite suspected war criminals to the ICTY. Following the expiry on 1 August of the deadline for the submission of a new diplomatic list, the USA and the EU suspended recognition of Bosnia and Herzegovina's ambassadors. On 17 December the Parlamentarna skupština approved the law on passports, but failed to ratify the law on citizenship; on the following day Westendorp announced that the law on common citizenship would be imposed with effect from 1 January 1998. (An agreement had been signed earlier in the month by Krajišnik and the FRY Government, which accorded Bosnian Serbs citizenship of both Bosnia and Herzegovina and the FRY.) In June 1998 the UN Security Council officially voted in favour of extending the mandate of SFOR to remain in the country indefinitely, with six-monthly reviews.

In April 1998 the OSCE dissolved the municipal assembly of Srebreniča, in Republika Srpska, owing to its failure to assist in the resettlement of displaced Muslims in the town; a provisional executive council, headed by a senior OSCE official, was established to replace the assembly. In June Krajišnik criticized a motion by the Narodna skupština expressing 'no confidence' in its Speaker, Dragan Kalinić, and Deputy Speaker, Aleksa Buha, who had succeeded to the chairmanship of the SDP following the resignation of Karadžić in July 1996, subsequently resigned from that position, citing what he claimed to be interference in his leadership by Krajišnik; Kalinić was elected as the new Chairman of the SDP.

In September 1998 elections took place to a new state Presidency and legislature, for the presidency and legislature of Republika Srpska, and for the Predstavnički dom Federacije. Izetbegović was re-elected as the Bosniak member of the collective Presidency. The Chairman of the Socialist Party of Republika Srpska (SPRS, a member of the SNA-led Accord Coalition), Zivko Radišić, replaced Krajišnik, and the Chairman of the CDU—BH, Ante Jelavić, was elected as the Croat member of the Presidency. In the election to the presidency of Republika Srpska the Chairman of the SRP, Dr Nikola Poplasen (who represented a coalition of the SRP and the SDP), defeated Plavšić. The SDP retained 19 of the 83 seats in the Narodna skupština, while the Coalition for a Single and Democratic Bosnia and Herzegovina won 15 seats; the latter also secured 14 of the 42 seats in the Predstavnički dom and 68 of the 140 seats in the Predstavnički dom Federacije.

On 13 October 1998 the newly elected Presidency of Bosnia and Herzegovina was inaugurated. Radišić became Chairman of the Presidency, replacing Izetbegović; this position was henceforth to rotate between the elected representatives of each of the three principal communities every eight-months. Poplasen was inaugurated as President of Republika Srpska; he pledged to maintain good relations with western Governments and to comply with the Dayton agreement. The major parties represented in the Narodna skupština Republike Srpske subsequently conducted negotiations regarding the appointment of a new entity Council of Ministers. The Accord Coalition, which held 32 seats in the Narodna skupština, rejected Poplasen's nomination of Kalinić as Prime Minister, and supported the reappointment of Dodik to the post. In December the Parlament federacije re-elected Ganić as President (to which post he had been elected in December 1997) and a new federation Council of Ministers was established.

In January 1999 Poplasen nominated Brane Miljus, a member of the Alliance of Independent Social Democrats (AISD), as Prime Minister of Republika Srpska. The Accord Coalition objected to Miljus' candidacy, and Dodik (the leader of the AISD) announced his expulsion from the party. Later in January the Narodna skupština rejected Miljus' nomination to the office of Prime Minister.

In February 1999 Westendorp declared that supreme command of the armed forces of the two entities was to be transferred to the members of the collective state Presidency. However, the Republika Srpska Government contested the decision, and announced that Poplasen would remain Commander of the entity's armed forces, pending a ruling by the state Constitutional Court. In early March Poplasen proposed a motion in the Narodna skupština Republike Srpske, in an attempt to instigate Dodik's dismissal. Westendorp announced Poplasen's removal from office, on the grounds that he had exceeded his authority. In the same month international arbitrators ruled that Serb control of Brčko would end, and that the town would henceforth be governed jointly by Republika Srpska and the Federation, under international supervision. Dodik tendered his resignation (which he later withdrew) in protest at the announcement, and the Narodna skupština rejected both the ruling on Brčko and Westendorp's decision to remove Poplasen from office. (The Narodna skupština subsequently withdrew its opposition to Poplasen's dismissal, and Mirko Sarović, the incumbent Vice-President, provisionally assumed the presidential office.) In mid-April a new municipal government of Serbs, Bosniaks and Croats was elected in Brčko. (In March 2000, following the completion of the process of demilitarization, Brčko was established as a neutral district, and an Interim District Government, comprising representatives of the three ethnic groups, was established.)

In June 1999, in accordance with the Constitution, Jelavić became Chairman of the state Presidency, replacing Radišić. In the same month the UN Security Council voted to extend the mandate of SFOR and the principally civilian security force, the UN Mission in Bosnia and Herzegovina (UNMIBH), for a further year; NATO announced that the strength of the SFOR contingent was to be reduced to about 16,500. In July SFOR members arrested Radislav Brđanin, a former Bosnian Serb official (who had served as Deputy Prime Minister under Karadžić), following his indictment by the ICTY in connection with massacres of Bosniaks and Croats by Serb forces in 1992.

In August 1999 Wolfgang Petritsch, hitherto the Austrian ambassador to the FRY, succeeded Westendorp as High Representative in Bosnia. In September Plavšić was re-elected leader of the SNA at a party congress. In December Ivo Andrić-Luzanski (of the CDU—BH) assumed the Federation, in accordance with the one-year rotational mandate stipulated in the Constitution. In February 2000 Izetbegović replaced Jelavić as Chairman of the collective Presidency. Later in February the SPRS withdrew from the governing Accord Coalition of Republika Srpska, in protest at the dismissal in January of the SPRS Deputy Prime Minister, Tihomir Gligorić, by Dodik. In March a senior Bosnian Croat commander, Gen. Tihomir Blaskić, was sentenced by the ICTY to 45 years' imprisonment (the most severe sentence issued by the Tribunal) for war crimes perpetrated against Muslims in 1992–93. In early April 2000 Krajišnik was arrested in Pale by SFOR troops and extradited to the ICTY.

At municipal elections held on 8 April 2000 the SDP won control of 49 of the country's 145 municipal councils (mainly in Republika Srpska), while the CDU—BH secured 25 and the PDA 23; the multi-ethnic Social Democratic Party of Bosnia and Herzegovina (SDP BiH) made significant electoral gains in the Federation. In the same month the Predstavnički dom adopted legislation providing for the restructuring of the state Council of Ministers, which would henceforth comprise a Chairman (appointed by the collective Presidency for an eight-month term) and five ministers. In late May the federation Vice-President, Ejup Ganić, was expelled from the PDA, after failing to comply with the party's decision that he resign from his government office. In early June a new state Council of Ministers was appointed, after the Predstavnički dom confirmed the nomination of Spasoje Tusevljak (a non-party candidate) to the office of Chairman.

In September 2000 the Narodna skupština Republike Srpske adopted a motion, proposed by the SDP, expressing 'no confidence' in Dodik's administration. However, the Government submitted a legal challenge to the entity's Constitutional Court and announced that it would remain in office pending forthcoming legislative elections. In October Izetbegović retired from the collective state Presidency; Halid Genjac, a senior official of the PDA, replaced him as the Bosniak member of the Presidency, and the Serb representative, Zirko Radišić, became Chairman. A member of the CDU—BH, Martin Raguz, subsequently became Chairman of the Council of Ministers, replacing Tusevljak as Prime Minister.

On 11 November 2000 elections to the Predstavnički dom, the legislatures of both entities and to the presidency of Republika Srpska took place. The results of elections to the Predstavnički dom and the Predstavnički dom Federacije demonstrated a relative decline in support for the nationalist parties, and a growth in support for the SDP BiH. In elections to the 42-member Predstavnički dom the SDP BiH secured nine seats, the PDA eight seats, the SDP six seats and the CDU—BH five seats, while in the 140-member Predstavnički dom Federacije the PDA won 38 seats, the SDP BiH 37 seats, the CDU—BH 25 seats and the Party for Bosnia and Herzegovina 21 seats. The SDP secured 31 of the 83 seats in the Narodna skupština Republike Srpske, while the SPRS and the Party of Democratic Progress of Republika Srpska (PDP) each received 11 seats. Mirko Sarović, the SDP candidate who had reportedly been selected by Karadžić, was elected, with some 49.8% of votes cast, to the presidency of Republika Srpska, defeating Dodik. The SDP subsequently announced that it was to establish a parliamentary coalition with the PDP, the SPRS and the PDA, thereby securing a majority in the Narodna skupština.

In December 2000 Sarović designated Ivanić, who was now the leader of the PDP, as Prime Minister of Republika Srpska. In mid-January 2001 Ivanić formed the entity's first multi-ethnic Council of Ministers. However, the inclusion in the Council of Ministers of several SDP representatives proved controversial, following warnings by the USA that it might suspend financial aid to Republika Srpska if the SDP entered the Government. Ivanić subsequently requested that government members suspend party activities, and replaced the newly appointed Minister of Trade and Tourism (a prominent SDP member). In the same month Raguz was renominated as Chairman of the state Council of Ministers. Meanwhile, the SDP BiH had established parliamentary coalitions with a further nine non-nationalist parties (known as the Alliance for Change), which held 17 seats in the Predstavnički dom and 69 seats in the Predstavnički dom Federacije.

In January 2001 Plavšić surrendered to the ICTY, following her indictment in April 2000, but subsequently denied charges that she, together with other Bosnian Serb officials, had organized a campaign of genocide and deportation against Bosniaks and Croats between July 1991 and December 1992. In February 2001 three Bosnian Serbs were sentenced to terms of imprisonment by the ICTY for crimes against humanity perpetrated against Bosniak women in Foča in 1992 (the first case at the Tribunal concerning systematic rape and sexual enslavement). In the same month a former Herzeg-Bosna official received a custodial term of 25 years for authorizing crimes against humanity to be committed against Bosniaks in 1993–94.

In early February 2001 the Predstavnički dom rejected the nomination of Raguz to the office of Chairman of the Council of Ministers, owing to the opposition of the Alliance for Change deputies. The Presidency's subsequent designation of a member of the SDP BiH, Bozidar Matić, to the post, was endorsed, and on 22 February the Predstavnički dom approved a new state Council of Ministers, headed by Matić. On 28 February the Predstavnički dom Federacije elected a member of the SDP BiH, Karlo Filipović, as President of the Federation. In early March the federation legislature endorsed the nomination of Alija Behmen, a member of the SDP BiH, as Prime Minister, and a new Government, including members of the Alliance for Change, was approved. Meanwhile, in response to the rejection of Raguz's candidacy to the state premiership, a newly formed grouping of parties led by the CDU—BH, the self-styled 'Croat People's Assembly', declared self-government in three Croat-majority cantons, and voted to establish autonomous power structures. Petritsch subsequently dismissed Jelavić of the CDU—BH from the collective Presidency. Many Croat members of the armed forces and local officials declared support for the Croat People's Assembly, which announced that it intended to secede from the Federation. On 28 March the Predstavnički dom voted in favour of appointing Jozo Križanović of the SDP BiH as the new Croat member of the collective Presidency. (Beriz Belkić, a member of the Party for Bosnia and Herzegovina, replaced Halid Genjac.) Following negotiations with the federal authorities and international community officials, however, the Croat alliance agreed to end its boycott of state institutions in May.

In mid-June 2001 Križanović assumed the chairmanship of the collective Presidency for a period of eight months. Later in June Matić resigned from the office of Chairman of the Council of Ministers, following the rejection, by the Parlamentarna skupstina of proposed electoral legislation. On 7 July the state legislature accepted the nomination of Zlatko Lagumdzija, the leader of the SDP BiH and the hitherto Minister of Foreign Affairs, as the new Chairman of the Council of Ministers. (The legislation, which was regarded as bringing electoral practice more closely in alignment with norms prevailing in the EU, was finally approved by the Parlamentarna skupština in August.) In late July the Narodna skupština Republike Srpske provisionally approved legislation providing for the entity's co-operation with the ICTY, after the SDP withdrew its opposition to the proposals. (The new legislation, which required the Republika Srpska security forces actively to pursue and extradite war crimes suspects, was finally adopted in early October.) On 2 August a former senior Serb army officer, Radislav Krstić, received a sentence of 46 years for his responsibility for the massacre at Srebrenica in 1995, the first time that the Tribunal had succeeded in obtaining a conviction on charges of genocide. At the end of August 2001 the ICTY provisionally released Plavšić, pending her trial. In late September Gen. Sefer Halilović, a former Chief of Staff of the army of the Republic of Bosnia and Herzegovina surrendered to the ICTY. Halilović (who was the most senior Bosniak official to be indicted by the Tribunal) pleaded not guilty to charges relating to the killing of 62 Croat citizens by troops under his command in 1993. (Halilović's trial commenced at the ICTY in January 2005.)

In October 2001 the federation Minister of the Interior, Muhammad Besić, was forced to resign, after media ridicule of his statement that militant Islamists were planning to take refuge in Bosnia and Herzegovina, following the commencement of US-led military action in Afghanistan in that month. Also in October three former officials of Herzeg-Bosna, who had been sentenced in 2000 for involvement in the killing of more than 100 Bosniaks in 1993, succeeded in having their convictions overturned on appeal, and the custodial terms of a further two detainees were reduced. In early November 2001 five Bosnian Serbs received terms of imprisonment at the ICTY for participating in the torture and killing of prisoners at Omarska detention camp near Prijedor, in the Bosnian Kraijina, in 1992. Later that month Milošević (who had been extradited to the ICTY in June 2001 and had been charged with crimes against humanity relating to Croatia in 1991–92 and Kosovo and Metohija in 1999) was additionally indicted with perpetrating genocide in Bosnia and Herzegovina in 1992–95.

In March 2002 Dragen Mikerević was appointed to the rotating chairmanship of the state Council of Ministers. Later in March the leading political parties, under pressure from Petritsch, reached agreement on the adoption of constitutional reforms, which would ensure the representation of the three principal constituent peoples (Serb, Croat and Bosniak) at all levels of government throughout the country. The reforms were officially adopted in April. Notably, a 28-member Vijece Naroda (Council of Peoples—comprising eight Bosniaks, eight Croats, eight Serbs and four others) was established within the Narodna skupština Republike Srpske; among the duties of the Vijece would be the selection of the entity's delegates to the state Dom Naroda. In May Petritsch issued a ruling, providing for the adoption of judicial reforms, which would ensure the independent appointment of judges and prosecutors. On 27 May he announced the appointment of eight judges to a new Court of Bosnia and Herzegovina, which was to become the country's highest judicial organ. On the same day Sir Jeremy (Paddy) Ashdown, a British politician and former diplomat, officially replaced Petritsch as High Representative. (Ashdown was additionally appointed to a new position, as EU Special Representative for Bosnia and Herzegovina.) In June Ashdown dismissed the federation Deputy Prime Minister and Minister of Finance, Nikola Grabovac, and the Republika Srpska Minister of Finance, Milenko Vracar, tendered his resignation, following pressure from Ashdown (who had criticized official malpractice in both entities). At the end of that month the USA vetoed a further extension of the mandate of the UNMIBH, after failing to secure immunity from prosecution in the new International Criminal Court for US peace-keeping troops. The UN Security Council subsequently voted in favour of a provisional extension of the mandate. In early July the mandate of the UNMIBH was extended until the end of 2002, when responsibility for peace-keeping was to be transferred to the EU.

In September 2002 an organ of the Republika Srpska Government issued a report disputing the veracity of the Srebrenica massacre and claiming that only some 2,000 members of the republican armed forces had been killed (mainly in military operations) in the region. The report was strongly condemned as a fabrication by the Bosniak community and by Ashdown. In early October Plavšić agreed to plead guilty at the ICTY to one charge of crimes against humanity. The prosecution subsequently abandoned seven other charges, including one of genocide. Later that month a Bosnian Serb former official, Milan Simić (who had surrendered to the Tribunal in February 1998), was sentenced to five years' imprisonment on charges of having committed torture in 1992.

On 5 October 2002 elections were conducted to the state presidency, the presidency of Republika Srpska, the state and entity legislatures, and to cantonal assemblies within the Federation. In the three ballots to the state Presidency, the Chairman of the PDA, Sulejman Tihić, was elected the Bosniak member, with 37.3% of the votes cast, while Dragan Čović of the CDU—BH became the Croat member (with 61.5%) and Mirko Sarović of the SDP (35.5%) the Serb member. Dragan Cavić of the SDP secured the presidency of the Republika Srpska, with 40.1% of the votes cast. The SDP BiH-led alliance lost its majority in the Predstavnički dom following the polls, and the PDA became the largest single party, with 10 seats. The PDA also secured the highest number of seats (32) in the Predstavnički dom Federacije (which was reduced in size to 98 deputies), while the CDU—BH, contesting the elections in alliance with the Croatian Democratic Community, obtained 16 seats, while the SDP BiH and the Party for Bosnia and Herzegovina each obtained 15 seats. In the elections to the Narodna skupština Republike Srpske, the SDP remained the largest party, with 26 seats, while the AISD obtained 19. At the end of October both the Minister of Defence and the army Chief of the General Staff of the Republika Srpska resigned, after it emerged that an aviation company owned by the Republika Srpska authorities had exported military equipment to Iraq, in contravention of a UN armaments embargo (see the chapter on Iraq). The state Government subsequently imposed an indefinite ban on the export of all armaments and military equipment from Bosnia and Herzegovina.

At the end of November 2002 the Bosnian Serb former leader of a paramilitary group, Mitar Vasiljević, was sentenced to 20 years' imprisonment at the ICTY on two charges relating to atrocities perpetrated against Bosniaks in 1992–94. On 7 December 2002 Cavić nominated Mikerević, the Chairman of the Council of Ministers and Minister of European Integration in the state Government, and a member of the PDP, as Prime Minister of Republika Srpska. Also in December Ashdown introduced new legislation to strengthen the powers of the state Government: two new ministries, of security and justice, were to be established and the Prime Minister was henceforth to be appointed for a four-year term (replacing the system of rotation between the three ethnic representatives). The 14 Bosnian Serb delegates in the new Predstavnički dom boycotted its first session in protest at these amendments. At the end of 2002 the mandate of the UNMIBH officially expired, and the UN transferred responsibility for peace-keeping to an EU Police Mission, which was to supervise the reorganization and training of the country's security forces.

On 13 January 2003 the Predstavnički dom approved the appointment of Adnan Terzić, a member of the PDA, as state Chairman of the Council of Ministers and a new Council of Ministers was formed. Although this Government was dominated by the three main nationalist parties (the PDA, the CDU—BH and the SDP), representatives of the PDP and the Party for Bosnia and Herzegovina were also included to ensure a legislative majority. On 17 January the Narodna skupština Republike Srpske approved Mikerević's nomination as entity Prime Minister, and a new Government for the entity, which (in accordance with recently approved constitutional requirements) comprised eight Serb, five Bosniak and three Croat representatives. Later that month the Predstavnički dom Federacije elected a Croat, Niko Lozancić, to the presidency and, in an amendment to the entity's system of government, a Bosniak and a Serb to the office of joint Vice-President. The appointment of a new federation Government, under Ahmet Hadžipašić, was approved in mid-February.

On 27 February 2003 the ICTY sentenced Plavšić to 11 years' imprisonment on the charge of crimes against humanity. On 2 April Sarović resigned as the Bosnian Serb member of the collective state presidency, after being implicated in both the illicit exports to Iraq and alleged espionage activities by the Republika Srpska military. Ashdown (who had been expected to dismiss Sarović) announced the abolition of the Republika Srpska Supreme Military Council; command of the armed forces was transferred provisionally to the entity's President. He also removed all references of statehood from the Constitution of Republika Srpska. On 10 April the Predstavnički dom confirmed the nomination of Borislav Paravać, also a member of the SDP, to replace Sarović.

In early July 2003 Zeljko Mejakić, the Bosnian Serb commander of the Omarska detention camp (who had originally been indicted in 1995), was transferred to the ICTY, having finally surrendered to the authorities in Serbia. At the end of July a former mayor of Prijedor, Dr Milomir Stakić, was sentenced to life imprisonment by the ICTY (the first time that the Tribunal had imposed this verdict) for his leading involvement in the campaign of 'ethnic cleansing' of non-Serbs from the region (involving the killing of 1,500 and deportation of a further 20,000) in 1992–95. (He was, however, acquitted of genocide.) In October 2003 a former Bosnian Serb detention camp guard was sentenced to eight years' imprisonment by the ICTY, having been convicted of participating in the abuse of prisoners. At the end of October the international community pledged to finance the establishment of a new war crimes' court in Sarajevo, which would assume competence for a number of less important trials pending at the ICTY, enabling the Tribunal to complete operations in 2010, as scheduled. (The court was expected to commence operations in early 2005.)

In July 2003 a mass grave (the largest to be found) was uncovered near the north-eastern town of Zvornik, believed to contain the remains of some 700 Muslim males, who had been killed in the Srebreniča massacre and subsequently reburied by Bosnian Serb forces in an attempt to conceal evidence. In November a Banja Luka-based television station broadcast the results of an investigation by the Republika Srpska Government, conducted under pressure from Ashdown, into the Srebreniča massacre; the authorities conceded for the first time that Bosnian Serb forces had perpetrated the killings. During a state visit to Sarajevo in November Svetozar Marović, the President of Serbia and Montenegro (as the FRY became in February 2003), issued a formal apology for the atrocities committed against Bosnian civilians during the 1992–95 conflict, and urged reconciliation. However, tension between the two countries continued, owing to demands by Serb nationalists that Republika Srpska ultimately become part of Serbia, and the perceived complicity of the Serbian authorities in supporting Mladić (who was reported to be in hiding in that country).

In December 2003 a Bosnian Serb former army commander, Momir Nikolić, was sentenced at the ICTY to 27 years' imprisonment for his involvement in the Srebreniča massacre. Also in early December the first conviction relating exclusively to the siege of Sarajevo by Serb forces was imposed by the Tribunal on the commanding officer in 1992–94, Gen. Stanislav Galić, who was sentenced to 20 years' imprisonment. In the same month two Bosniak senior army officers (the first to appear before the ICTY) pleaded not guilty to charges relating to responsibility for the killing of some 200 Croat and Serb civilians in 1993.

In early January 2004, amid continuing pressure from the international community, SFOR, assisted by Republika Srpska military personnel for the first time, conducted a search operation in Pale, in an unsuccessful attempt to apprehend Karadžić. (The Chief Prosecutor at the ICTY, Carla Del Ponte, subsequently announced that he was believed to have taken refuge in Belgrade.) On 28 January 2004 Ashdown issued a decree, providing for the reunification of Mostar (divided between six Croat- and Bosniak-controlled municipalities since 1993) into a single administration, thereby fulfilling one of the preconditions for signature of a Stabilization and Association Agreement with the EU. In February 2004 Ashdown announced the dismissals of three security officials of Republika Srpska and the removal of Mirko Sarović from the presidium of the SDP, owing to suspicions of their complicity in attempts to prevent Karadžić's capture. The SDP refused to approve Sarović's dismissal and the party leader, Dragan Kalinić, subsequently resigned in protest at Ashdown's decision. In mid-March the Predstavnički dom approved the nomination of Nikola Radovanović of the SDP as the first state Minister of Defence (following the rejection, at the instigation of Ashdown, of two extreme nationalist candidates). At the end of the month the state Constitutional Court ruled that the renaming since 1992 of some 13 towns or municipalities in Republika Srpska with variants of the prefix 'Srpski' (Serbian) was unconstitutional; the Republika

Introductory Survey

Srpska authorities subsequently agreed to rename these districts, but emphasized that they regarded this as a temporary measure.

In early April 2004 a Republika Srpska security force unit accidentally killed a relative of two indicted war crime suspects in the eastern town of Višegrad; a special commander and several officers were subsequently dismissed. In mid-April Ashdown removed the Republika Srpska army Chief of Staff, who had failed to provide information required by a commission investigating the Srebreniča massacre. Also in April, in response to an appeal brought before the ICTY by Krstić, his sentence was reduced to 35 years, although the court confirmed that the killings at Srebreniča constituted an act of genocide. In June Ashdown dismissed 60 officials of Republika Srpska, including the Minister of the Interior and the legislative Chairman, who were reportedly implicated in the continued failure of the authorities to locate and apprehend Karadžić. At the end of July the ICTY reduced the 45-year sentence of Tihomir Blaskić, imposed in March 2000, to nine years, on appeal reversing most of the convictions against him on the grounds that he had not been responsible for atrocities perpetrated by forces under his command.

In July 2004 the Stari most (Old Bridge) at Mostar was officially reopened, in what was regarded as an important symbolic act of reconstruction. In August six former officials of Herzeg-Bosna, who had surrendered to the ICTY in early April, were provisionally released, pending their trial on charges of the forcible removal on non-Croats from the territory. At the beginning of September the ICTY sentenced Radislav Brđanin, Deputy Prime Minister of Republika Srpska in 1992, to 32 years' imprisonment for involvement in crimes committed against Croats and Muslims in the Krajina region, although he was cleared of charges of committing genocide.

In municipal elections, held on 2 October 2004, the PDA received the highest level of support in the Federation, while in Republika Srpska the SDP lost support to the AISD, which, notably. secured the mayoralty of Banja Luka. In early October Ljubiša Beara, a former head of intelligence of the Republika Srpska army charged with organizing the Srebreniča massacre, surrendered to security forces in Serbia and was extradited to the ICTY. In mid-October the commission established by the Republika Srpska authorities to investigate the Srebreniča massacre submitted a final report acknowledging that Bosnian Serb forces had, on that occasion, killed an estimated 7,800 Muslim males. On 11 November the Republika Srpska Government (which continued to attract strong criticism from the international community for failing to apprehend any war crime suspects believed to be hiding in their territory) issued an official apology for the Srebreniča massacre. Later that month Terzić tendered his resignation as state Prime Minister, after proposals for the adoption of a single-rate value-added tax (VAT) were rejected by the Predstavnički dom. However, in the event, his resignation was rejected by the governing parties, and the introduction of a single-rate VAT, which received the support of international financial institutions, was approved in the Dom Naroda.

On 22 November 2004 the UN Security Council approved a resolution authorizing the establishment of a new peacekeeping contingent under the command of the EU, and on 2 December SFOR officially transferred authority to the new 7,000-member EU Force (EUFOR), which incorporated many of the former members of the outgoing SFOR contingent. EUFOR was additionally mandated to assist Bosnia and Herzegovina in further progress towards European integration. Some 150 US members of the outgoing SFOR mission were to remain provisionally in the north-east of the country to assist in continuing efforts to arrest war crime suspects. (Meanwhile, at the end of November press reports disclosed that Mladić had received a regular pension from the Republika Srpska army until 2002.) In early December NATO rejected for the second time Bosnia and Herzegovina's application to join the 'Partnership for Peace' programme, largely in response to the failure of the Republika Srpska authorities to co-operate with the ICTY. Ashdown responded by announcing the acceleration of military reforms: the entity ministries of defence were to be abolished by 2005, earlier than previously envisaged, while three existing police and security agencies were to merge to form a single police force, which was to operate on the basis of multi-ethnic regional divisions, in several cases including territories from both entities. This police force was to be monitored by the state Minister of Security, while the state Minister of Defence was to organize

an investigation into alleged clandestine support for Mladić by elements of the Republika Srpska military. In addition, Ashdown removed nine Republika Srpska security officials accused of complicity in the evasion from arrest of war crime suspects, and the US Administration imposed travel restrictions on the leadership of the PDP and SDP. On 17 December Mikerević tendered his resignation as Prime Minister of Republika Srpska in protest at the dismissals, and leaders of the entity continued to express opposition to the abolition of the existing defence structures. The Minister of Foreign Affairs and leader of the PDP, Mladen Ivanić, announced his resignation, while other ministers of the state Government and Paravać (who had assumed the chairmanship of the collective presidency in October 2004, under the rotational system) also tendered their resignations. Later that month Dodik and the Minister of Finance of his former administration in Republika Srpska were charged with financial misconduct. On 8 January 2005, following inter-party discussions, Cavić nominated Pero Bukejlović, a member of the SDP who had served as Minister of Industry and Technology in the former Ivanić Government, as Prime Minister of Republika Srpska.

In January 2005 the former deputy commander of a Serb detention camp in the eastern town of Foča (previously referred to by the Republika Srpska authorities as Srbinje, 'Place of the Serbs'), Savo Todorović, surrendered to the Republika Srpska authorities (the first war crime suspect to do so, after the Government, under continued pressure from the international community, offered financial support to the families of fugitives who voluntarily co-operated with the ICTY). Todorović was extradited to the Tribunal, which had indicted him on 18 charges relating to atrocities perpetrated against prisoners. In the same month two Bosnian Serb former officers were convicted by the ICTY for their involvement in the Srebreniča massacre: Col Vidoje Blagojević received an 18-year sentence on a number of charges, including complicity in genocide, while the other defendant, Dragan Jokić, was sentenced to a term of nine years. On 15 February the Government nominated by Bukejlović was approved by 46 of the 83 deputies in the Narodna skupština Republike Srpske, thereby ending protracted inter-party deliberations. The new administration was dominated by the SDP, and, in accordance with the Republika Srpska Constitution, comprised eight Serbs, five Bosniaks and three Croats. Following a subsequent meeting of the four main parties represented in the state and entity Governments, Ivanić announced that the PDP was to remain in the state-level administration, and in March his resignation and those of the other state ministers were officially withdrawn. Later that month the Croat member of the state presidency, Dragan Čović, was charged with corruption during his former tenure as Federation Minister of Finance; he was removed from office by Ashdown on 29 March.

Government

In accordance with the General Framework Agreement for Peace in Bosnia and Herzegovina, signed in December 1995, Bosnia and Herzegovina is a single state, which consists of two autonomous political entities: the Federation of Bosnia and Herzegovina, principally comprising the Bosniak (Muslim)- and Croat-majority areas, and the Republika Srpska, principally comprising the Serb-majority area at that time. A civilian High Representative of the International Community in Bosnia and Herzegovina oversees government institutions and the implementation of the peace accords. The state Government of Bosnia and Herzegovina has a three-member collective presidency of one Bosniak, one Croat and one Serb. Members of the Presidency are directly elected for a term of four years, and are eligible to serve for only two consecutive terms. Chairmanship of the Presidency is rotated between the members every eight months. The bicameral Parlamentarna škupstina Bosne i Hercegovine (Parliamentary Assembly of Bosnia and Herzegovina) comprises the Dom Naroda (House of Peoples) and the Predstavnički dom (House of Representatives). The Predstavnički dom has 42 deputies, of whom 28 are directly elected from the Federation and 14 directly elected from Republika Srpska for a four-year term. The Dom Naroda has 15 deputies, of whom 10 are selected by the Federation legislature and five by the Republika Srpska legislature for a four-year term. The Presidency appoints a Chairman of the state Council of Ministers (subject to the approval of the Predstavnički dom), who subsequently appoints the other ministers.

The Federation of Bosnia and Herzegovina and the Serb Republic each retain an executive presidency, government and legislature. The bicameral Parlament Federacije (Parliament of the Federation) comprises a 98-member Predstavnički dom Federacije (House of Representatives of the Federation), which is directly elected for a four-year term, and a 58-member Dom Naroda Federacije (House of People of the Federation), comprising 17 Serb, 17 Bosniak, 17 Croat and seven other deputies, who are elected by the cantonal assemblies. The unicameral legislature of Republika Srpska, the Narodna skupština Republike Srpske (National Assembly of Republika Srpska), has 83 deputies, who are directly elected for a four-year term. The federation legislature elects a President and two joint Vice-Presidents, comprising one Bosniak, one Croat and one Serb, for a term of four years. The President and two Vice-Presidents of Republika Srpska are directly elected, for a four-year term. The Federation is divided into 10 cantons; each canton has an elected assembly and a President. The Federation comprises 84 and the Serb Republic 63 municipalities; in addition, the north-eastern town of Brčko was established as a neutral self-governing district in 2000, under the sovereignty of the state Government.

Defence

At August 2003 the two entities of Bosnia and Herzegovina maintained separate armed forces: Republika Srpska had an army of about 6,600 and the Federation an army of around 13,200. Under the terms of the Dayton agreement of 1995, the size of the armed forces of the two entities was restricted. In April 2003 the authorities announced further restructuring and reduction of the military, with the aim of establishing a unified defence command structure under a state-level Ministry of Defence (a principal requirement for the country's accession to the North Atlantic Treaty Organization's—NATO 'Partnership for Peace'—PfP (see p. 303) programme). Following the establishment of a state-level Ministry of Defence in March 2004, the armed forces' operational command structure was to be unified. In mid-2004 the state authorities announced that the Republika Srpska army had been reduced to number about 4,000 troops, and the Federation army to 8,000. In November the first state armed forces unit, comprising troops from the country's three constitutive ethnic groups, was established. In December, after NATO rejected Bosnia and Herzegovina's application to join the PfP programme for a second time, the High Representative announced that the entity ministries of defence were to be abolished in 2005 (thereby establishing a single state-level defence structure), and that the existing police and security agencies were to merge to form a single police force.

On 20 December 1995 power was formally transferred to an international, NATO-commanded, 60,000-strong 'Implementation Force' (IFOR), which was granted authority to oversee the implementation of the peace accord. In December 1996 IFOR was superseded by a Stabilization Force (SFOR), which initially comprised about 32,000 troops. At the end of 2002 the mandate of the UN Mission in Bosnia and Herzegovina (UNMIBH), established in 1995, was officially completed, and the UN transferred responsibility for peace-keeping to a European Union Police Mission (EUPM). The EUPM, which comprised 512 police officers, supported by 50 civilian monitors and 300 local staff, was to supervise the reorganization and training of the country's security forces. The number of SFOR personnel stationed in Bosnia and Herzegovina was reduced to about 7,000 by mid-2004. On 2 December of that year SFOR officially transferred authority to a EU Force (EUFOR), which had an initial mandate of one year. EUFOR was authorized to maintain peace, in co-operation with a permanent NATO presence of some 200 personnel based in Sarajevo, and to support the country's progress towards European integration. EUFOR comprised 7,000 personnel from 33 countries (including 11 non-EU states). Some 150 US members of the outgoing SFOR mission were to remain provisionally in the north-east of the country to assist in continuing efforts to arrest war crime suspects. The state Government allocated US $130m. to defence in 2002.

Economic Affairs

In 2003, according to World Bank estimates, Bosnia and Herzegovina's gross national income (GNI), measured at average 2001–03 prices, was US $7,296.1m., equivalent to $1,540 per head (or $6,320 on an international purchasing-power parity basis). During 1994–2003, it was estimated, the population of Bosnia and Herzegovina increased at an average annual rate of 1.4%, while gross domestic product (GDP) per head rose, in real terms, by an average of 16.8% per year. Overall GDP increased, in real terms, at an average annual rate of 18.5% in 1994–2003; real growth was 3.9% in 2002 and 3.5% in 2003.

Agriculture (including forestry and fishing) contributed an estimated 16.7% of GDP in 2003. In 2003 about 4.0% of the labour force were employed in the agricultural sector. The major agricultural products are tobacco and fruit, and the livestock sector is also significant. Imports of foodstuffs comprised 4.1% of total imports in 1997. According to World Bank estimates, the GDP of the agricultural sector increased, in real terms, by an annual average of 5.0% in 1994–2000. Total agricultural GDP, at current prices, increased from 1,114.2m. konvertibilna marka (KM or convertible marks) in 2001 to KM 1,143.6m. in 2002.

Industry (mining, manufacturing, utilities and construction) contributed an estimated 34.7% of GDP in Bosnia and Herzegovina in 2003. Some 47.5% of the labour force were employed in the industrial sector in 1990. According to World Bank estimates, industrial GDP increased, in real terms, by an annual average of 26.0% in 1994–2000. Total industrial GDP, at current prices, increased from KM 2,395.7m. in 2001 to KM 2,457.6m. in 2002.

The mining sector contributed 2.3% of GDP in 2002. Bosnia and Herzegovina possesses extensive mineral resources, including iron ore, lignite, copper, lead, zinc and gold. Total mining GDP, at current prices, increased from KM 208.6m. in 2001 to KM 221.0m. in 2002.

Manufacturing contributed 21.0% of GDP in 2003. The manufacturing sector is based largely on the processing of iron ore, non-ferrous metals, coal, and wood and paper products. Manufacturing GDP increased, in real terms, by an annual average of 17.2% in 1994–2000. Total manufacturing GDP, at current prices, increased from KM 1,073.5m. in 2001 to KM 1,162.0m. in 2002.

The civil conflict resulted in the destruction of much of the electric power system in Bosnia and Herzegovina. Prior to the conflict, the system comprised 13 hydroelectric installations and 12 coal- and lignite-fuelled thermal power installations. In 2001 50.7% of electricity production was derived from coal and 48.8% from hydroelectric power. Electric power accounted for 3.2% of total imports in 1997.

The services sector contributed an estimated 48.6% of GDP in 2003. According to World Bank estimates, the GDP of the services sector increased, in real terms, by an annual average of 35.9% in 1994–2000. Total services GDP, at current prices, increased from KM 5,092.1m. in 2001 to KM 5,840.6m. in 2002.

In 2003 Bosnia and Herzegovina recorded a visible trade deficit of US $3,945.6m., and there was a deficit of $2,038.1m. on the current account of the balance of payments. In 2003 the principal source of imports was Croatia (which accounted for 17.5% of total imports); other important suppliers were Germany, Italy, Slovenia, Serbia and Montenegro, Hungary and Austria. In that year the main market for exports was also Croatia (which accounted for 17.9% of total exports); other significant purchasers were Serbia and Montenegro, Germany, Italy, Slovenia and Switzerland. The principal exports in 2003 were basic manufactures (principally base metals, and wood and paper products), machinery and transport equipment (notably electrical machinery and equipment), miscellaneous manufactured articles and mineral fuels. The main imports in that year were machinery and transport equipment (particularly machinery and mechanical appliances), basic manufactures, food and live animals (notably prepared foodstuffs), mineral fuels and chemicals.

Bosnia and Herzegovina's overall budget deficit for 2002 was estimated at KM 489.0m., equivalent to 4.5% of GDP. The country's total external debt was estimated at US $2,515m. at the end of 2002 (of which $2,282m. was public debt), and the cost of debt-servicing was equivalent to about 7.0% of the value of exports of goods and services. Consumer prices, according to the IMF, declined by an average of 0.3% in 1998, and increased by 3.4% in 1999, by 5.0% in 2000, by 3.2% in 2001, and by 0.3% in 2002; the inflation rate was estimated at only 0.1% in 2003. The rate of unemployment was estimated at 20% in 2003.

Bosnia and Herzegovina became a member of the IMF in December 1995 and was admitted to the World Bank in April 1996. In July 1999 the first summit meeting of the Stability Pact for South-Eastern Europe took place in Bosnia and Herzegovina, with the aim of adopting a common strategy for regional stability.

The conflict in 1992–95 resulted in extensive damage to the economy. Following the signature of the Dayton peace agreement in December 1995, economic reconstruction commenced. An early priority of the reconstruction programme was the resolution of the considerable foreign debt that Bosnia and

Herzegovina had inherited from the Socialist Federal Republic of Yugoslavia. The new national currency, the Convertible Mark, fixed at par with the German Deutsche Mark (and subsequently linked to the euro), was officially introduced in June 1998. In October agreement was reached with the 'Paris Club' of creditor governments on the reduction of external debt. Following large inflows of foreign assistance, the economy rapidly recovered under the IMF-supported economic reconstruction and development programme, although unemployment remained high, and corruption and poor customs controls continued to contribute to a major loss of revenue. In addition, performance varied widely in each of the two entities, with higher rates of inflation generally being recorded in the Republika Srpska. A further stand-by arrangement was approved by the IMF in August 2002 (and subsequently extended until February 2004). During 2002 the High Representative imposed a series of economic regulations, with the ultimate aim of unifying principal sectors, such as telecommunications, banking, and tax and customs administration, throughout the country, as a prerequisite for eventual membership of the European Union (EU, see p. 217), and macroeconomic indicators, including GDP growth and the inflation rate, continued to improve steadily. The most significant progress was demonstrated by the return of large numbers of refugees and internally displaced civilians (estimated in early 2004 at 989,080 since the signing of the Dayton peace agreement), which was supported by foreign remittances. A further increase in GDP growth was recorded in 2004, and further growth was forecast in 2005–06, partially as a result of increased domestic and foreign investment. In September 2004 a conference of bilateral and multilateral donors pledged to assist in financing three-year development projects, particularly in the infrastructure and social welfare sectors. The proposed introduction of a single-rate value-added tax (VAT), which was expected to take effect from July 2005, caused considerable dissent within the state Government in late 2004 (see Recent History); a state Indirect Taxation Administration was established to supervise adoption of the new tax. However, discussions with the IMF over a new stand-by arrangement (which were conducted jointly by the entity Governments for the first time) failed, as a result of demands by the Governments for relaxed monetary targets and slower liberalization of trade terms. Despite progress in implementing reforms of the armed forces and intelligence services, the failure of the authorities, particularly of Republika Srpska, to co-operate fully with the International Criminal Tribunal for the former Yugoslavia was expected to impede any agreement with the EU on negotiations on the signature of a Stabilization and Association Agreement.

Education

A nine-year system of elementary education, free and compulsory for all children between the ages of six and 15 years, was introduced throughout Bosnia and Herzegovina in 2003/04, replacing the 'eight-year school' cycle. Various types of secondary education available to all who qualify include: general secondary schools (gymnasiums), where children may follow a four-year course to prepare them for university entrance; vocational schools; and technical schools. In 2002/03 some 363,072 were enrolled in 1,862 primary schools, and 169,497 pupils attended 301 secondary schools. In the Federation of Bosnia and Herzegovina in that year, 53,985 students attended higher education institutions. In 2004 higher education comprised seven universities (situated in Sarajevo, East Sarajevo, Banja Luka, Mostar—where there are two universities, Tuzla and Bihać) and six further institutions (four teaching and two art academies). In August 2003 officials at state, entity and local level signed an agreement to replace the country's three ethnically-based education systems with a single unified system. In 2004, however, some local authorities remained resistant to the unification of the education system.

Public Holidays

2005: 1 January (New Year), 6–7 January (Orthodox Christmas), 14–15 January (Orthodox New Year), 21 January* (Great Bayram, Feast of the Sacrifice), 27 January (Orthodox St Sava's Day), 1 March† (Independence Day), 25–28 March (Catholic Easter), 29 April–2 May (Orthodox Easter), 1–2 May (Labour Day), 15 August (Catholic Assumption), 1 November (Catholic All Saints' Day), 4 November* (Small Bayram, end of Ramadan), 25 November (National Statehood Day), 25 December (Catholic Christmas).

2006: 1–2 January (New Year), 6–7 January (Orthodox Christmas), 11 January* (Great Bayram, Feast of the Sacrifice), 14–15 January (Orthodox New Year), 27 January (Orthodox St Sava's Day), 1 March† (Independence Day), 14–17 April (Catholic Easter), 21–24 April (Orthodox Easter), 1 May (Labour Day), 15 August (Catholic Assumption), 24 October* (Small Bayram, end of Ramadan), 1 November (Catholic All Saints' Day), 25 November (National Statehood Day), 25 December (Catholic Christmas Day).

* These holidays are dependent on the Islamic lunar calendar and may vary by one or two days from the dates given.

† Celebrated in the Federation of Bosnia and Herzegovina only.

Weights and Measures

The metric system is in force.

Statistical Survey

Source (unless otherwise stated): Agencija za statistiku Bosne i Hercegovine, 71000 Sarajevo, Trg Bosne i Hercegovine 1; tel. and fax (33) 2206222; e-mail bhas@bih.net.ba; internet www.bhas.ba.

Area and Population

AREA, POPULATION AND DENSITY

Area (sq km)	51,129*
Population (census results)	
31 March 1981	4,124,008
31 March 1991	
Males	2,183,795
Females	2,193,238
Total	4,377,033
Population (UN estimates at mid-year)†	
2001	4,067,000
2002	4,126,000
2003	4,161,000
Density (per sq km) at mid-2003	81.4

* 19,741 sq miles.

† Source: UN, *World Population Prospects: The 2002 Revision*.

PRINCIPAL ETHNIC GROUPS

(1991 census, provisional, according to official declaration of nationality)

	Number	% of total population
Muslims	1,905,829	43.7
Serbs	1,369,258	31.4
Croats	755,892	17.3
Yugoslavs	239,845	5.5
Total (incl. others)	4,364,574	100.0

PRINCIPAL TOWNS
(population at 1991 census)

Sarajevo (capital)	416,497	Bihać	45,995
Banja Luka	143,079	Brčko	41,405
Zenica	96,027	Bijeljina	37,216
Tuzla	83,770	Prijedor	34,613
Mostar	75,865		

Source: Thomas Brinkhoff, *City Population* (internet www.citypopulation.de).

Mid-2003 (UN estimate, incl. suburbs)): Sarajevo 578,838 (Source: UN, *World Urbanization Prospects: The 2003 revision*).

BIRTHS, MARRIAGES AND DEATHS

	Registered live births		Registered marriages		Registered deaths	
	Number	Rate (per 1,000)	Number	Rate (per 1,000)	Number	Rate (per 1,000)
2000	39,563	9.9	21,897	5.5	30,482	7.7
2001	37,717	9.3	20,302	5.0	30,325	7.5
2002	36,485	8.8	20,766	5.0	30,831	7.5
2003	34,777	8.4	20,467	4.9	30,906	7.4

Expectation of life (WHO estimates, years at birth): 72.8 (males 69.3; females 76.4) in 2002 (Source: WHO, *World Health Report*).

EMPLOYMENT
(Federation, average for December)

	1997	1998	1999
Activities of the material sphere	173,857	204,117	217,000
Non-material services	113,723	131,945	127,345
Total	287,580	336,062	344,345

Source: IMF, *Bosnia and Herzegovina: Selected Issues and Statistical Appendix* (June 2000).

Total employed (Federation, at 31 December): 412,305 in 2000; 405,689 in 2001; 390,201 in 2002 (Source: Central Bank of Bosnia and Herzegovina).

Total employed (Republika Srpska, at 31 December): 228,834 in 2000; 219,954 in 2001; 234,713 in 2002 (Source: Central Bank of Bosnia and Herzegovina).

Unemployed (Federation, persons registered at 31 December): 261,773 in 2000, 269,004 in 2001; 290,715 in 2002 (Source: Central Bank of Bosnia and Herzegovina).

Unemployed (Republika Srpska, persons registered at 31 December): 153,264 in 2000; 147,749 in 2001; 144,790 in 2002 (Source: Central Bank of Bosnia and Herzegovina).

Health and Welfare

KEY INDICATORS

Total fertility rate (children per woman, 2002)	1.3
Under-5 mortality rate (per 1,000 live births, 2003)	17
HIV/AIDS (% of persons aged 15–49, 2001)	0.10
Physicians (per 1,000 head, 2001)	1.45
Hospital beds (per 1,000 head, 2001)	3.22
Health expenditure (2001): US $ per head (PPP)	268
Health expenditure (2001): % of GDP	7.5
Health expenditure (2001): public (% of total)	36.8
Access to water (% of persons, 2002)	98
Access to sanitation (% of persons, 2002)	93
Human Development Index (2002): ranking	66
Human Development Index (2002): value	0.781

For sources and definitions, see explanatory note on p. vi.

Agriculture

PRINCIPAL CROPS
('000 metric tons)

	2001	2002	2003
Wheat	255.2	272.3	159.7
Barley	55.5	61.2	40.0
Maize	770.6	903.2	545.1
Rye	9.6	11.1	6.9
Oats	47.1	59.9	50.0*
Potatoes	397.1	404.5	302.2
Dry beans	10.3	10.8	7.9
Soybeans (Soya beans)	3.8	6.7	4.9
Cabbages	73.7	85.6	71.1
Tomatoes	30.8	37.7	31.9
Chillies and green peppers	24.3	31.7	28.4
Dry onions	28.2	34.0	27.0
Garlic	6.0	8.4	5.9
Carrots	8.6	11.2	9.3
Other vegetables*	453.1	452.8	502.8
Watermelons	77.8	48.0*	19.5
Grapes	13.3*	17.6*	21.8
Apples	14.4	14.5*	40.6
Pears	8.1	8.1*	15.8
Plums	26.8	58.0*	88.3
Tobacco (leaves)	3.7	5.2	3.3

* FAO estimate(s).

Source: FAO.

LIVESTOCK
('000 head, year ending September)

	2001	2002	2003
Horses*	18	18	18
Cattle*	440	440	440
Pigs*	330	300	300
Sheep *	640	670	670
Chickens	4,740†	4,700*	4,700*
Ducks*	120	120	120
Geese*	150	150	150
Turkeys*	120	120	120

* FAO estimate(s).
† Unofficial figure.

Source: FAO.

LIVESTOCK PRODUCTS
('000 metric tons)

	2001	2002	2003
Beef and veal	13.0*	13.0†	13.0†
Mutton and lamb†	2.7	2.7	2.7
Pig meat†	11.0	10.0	8.2
Poultry meat†	8.4	8.4	8.4
Cows' milk†	500.0	460.0	460.0
Sheep's milk†	7.0	7.0	7.0
Cheese†	8.7	8.6	8.6
Hen eggs†	15.1	15.1	15.1
Cattle and buffalo hides†	2.4	2.4	2.4

* Unofficial figure.
† FAO estimate(s).

Source: FAO.

Forestry

ROUNDWOOD REMOVALS
('000 cubic metres, excluding bark)

	2001	2002	2003
Sawlogs, veneer logs and logs for sleepers	2,531	2,637	2,446
Pulpwood	141	133	141
Other industrial wood	286	304	293
Fuel wood	860	1,150	1,215
Total	3,818	4,224	4,095

Source: FAO.

SAWNWOOD PRODUCTION
('000 cubic metres, including railway sleepers)

	2001*	2002	2003
Coniferous (softwood) . . .	60	489	503
Broadleaved (hardwood) . . .	250	249	257
Total	310	738	760

* Unofficial figures.

Source: FAO.

Fishing

(FAO estimates, metric tons, live weight)

	2000	2001	2002
Total catch (capture, freshwater fish)	2,500	2,500	2,500

Source: FAO.

Mining

('000 metric tons)

	1999	2000	2001
Brown coal and lignite	1,800	1,900	1,900
Iron ore: metal content	35	36	36
Bauxite	75	75	75
Kaolin (crude)	3	3	3
Barite (Barytes) concentrate . .	2	2	2
Salt (unrefined)	50	50	50
Gypsum (crude)	30	30	30

Source: US Geological Survey.

Industry

SELECTED PRODUCTS
('000 metric tons, unless otherwise indicated)

	1990
Electric energy (million kWh)	14,632
Crude steel	1,421
Aluminium	89
Machines	16
Tractors (number)	34,000
Lorries (number)	16,000
Motor cars (number)	38,000
Cement	797
Paper and paperboard	281
Television receivers (number)	21,000

Electric energy (million kWh): 9,633 in 1998; 10,547 in 1999; 10,429 in 2000 (Source: UN, *Industrial Commodity Statistics Yearbook*).

Mineral manufactures (estimates, '000 metric tons): Crude steel 60 in 1999, 77 in 2000, 80 in 2001; Aluminium (primary and secondary) 70 in 1999, 95 in 2000, 100 in 2001; Cement 200 in 1997, 300 per year in 1998–2001 (Source: US Geological Survey).

Finance

CURRENCY AND EXCHANGE RATES

Monetary Units
100 pfeninga = 1 konvertibilna marka (KM or convertible marka).

Sterling, Dollar and Euro Equivalents (31 December 2004)
£1 sterling = KM 2.7733;
US $1 = KM 1.4359;
€1 = KM 1.9558;
KM 100 = £36.06 = $69.64 = €51.13.

Average Exchange Rate (KM per US $)
2002   2.0782
2003   1.7329
2004   1.5752

Note: The new Bosnia and Herzegovina dinar (BHD) was introduced in August 1994, with an official value fixed at 100 BHD = 1 Deutsche Mark (DM). The DM, the Croatian kuna and the Yugoslav dinar also circulated within Bosnia and Herzegovina. On 22 June 1998 the BHD was replaced by the KM, equivalent to 100 of the former units. The KM was thus at par with the DM. From the introduction of the euro, on 1 January 1999, the German currency had a fixed exchange rate of €1 = DM 1.95583.

BUDGET
(KM million*)

Revenue†	2001	2002	2003‡
Tax revenue	4,209.2	4,450.5	4,722.2
Indirect taxes	1,470.3	1,541.5	2,006.4
Trade taxes	840.0	990.2	697.6
Direct taxes	362.4	369.4	392.2
Social security contributions .	1,536.5	1,549.4	1,626.0
Other revenue (incl. grants) . .	446.7	554.1	551.2
Total	4,655.9	5,004.6	5,273.4

Expenditure	2001	2002	2003‡
Interest payments	129.3	129.7	80.0
Subsidies and transfers to non-public agents§	2,011.1	2,288.3	2,349.4
Other current expenditure . . .	2,571.6	2,723.0	2,734.6
Investment expenditure . . .	1,012.9	733.6	542.2
Total	5,724.9	5,874.6	5,706.2

* Figures represent a consolidation of the budgetary accounts of the central Government and the authorities in the Federation and (except for local and district administration) Republika Srpska.
† Excluding grants (KM million): 794.5 in 2001; 590.4 in 2002; 413.8 in 2003 (projected figure).
‡ Projected figures.
§ Excluding transfers by Federation Cantons .

Source: IMF, *Bosnia and Herzegovina: 2004 Article IV Consultation—Staff Report; Fourth Review Under the Stand-By Arrangement and Request for Waiver of Nonobservance of a Structural Performance Criterion—Staff Report; Staff Supplement; and Public Information Notice and Press Release on the Executive Board Discussion* (March 2004).

INTERNATIONAL RESERVES
(US $ million at 31 December)

	2001	2002	2003
IMF special drawing rights . .	6	3	3
Foreign exchange	1,215	1,318	1,792
Total	1,221	1,321	1,796

Source: IMF, *International Financial Statistics*.

MONEY SUPPLY
(KM million at 31 December)

	2001	2002	2003
Currency outside banks . .	1,674	1,734	1,601
Demand deposits at banks .	957	1,221	1,442
Total money (incl. others) .	2,790	3,154	3,289

Source: IMF, *International Financial Statistics*.

COST OF LIVING
(Retail Price Index; base: December 1995 = 100)

	2000	2001	2002
All items (Federation) . . .	101.2	101.7	99.8
All items (Republika Srpska) . .	113.6	106.5	101.7
All items (Bosnia and Herzegovina)	104.8	103.1	100.4

NATIONAL ACCOUNTS

Expenditure on the Gross Domestic Product
(US $ million at current prices)

	1996	1997	1998
Government final consumption expenditure . . . . . } Private final consumption expenditure . . . . . }	3,237	3,589	3,914
Increase in stocks . . . . . } Gross fixed capital formation . }	1,124	1,438	1,481
Total domestic expenditure .	4,361	5,027	5,396
Exports of goods and services .	658	1,002	1,367
Less Imports of goods and services	−2,278	−2,606	−2,864
GDP in purchasers' values	2,741	3,423	3,899

Source: IMF, *Bosnia and Herzegovina: Selected Issues and Statistical Appendix* (June 2000).

Gross Domestic Product by Economic Activity
(KM million at current prices)

	2000	2001	2002
Agriculture, hunting and forestry .	1,061.4	1,112.6	1,141.4
Fishing	2.6	1.6	2.2
Mining and quarrying	182.2	208.6	221.0
Manufacturing	1,014.0	1,073.5	1,162.0
Electricity, gas and water . . .	630.1	655.8	592.3
Construction	463.8	457.8	482.3
Wholesale and retail trade . . .	789.7	995.7	1,224.4
Hotels and restaurants . . .	188.9	202.9	239.0
Transport and communications .	804.3	947.7	1,045.0
Financial intermediation . . .	323.6	329.6	389.9
Real estate and business services .	197.2	199.9	222.0
Public administration and defence.	1,147.3	1,262.1	1,449.7
Education	501.9	505.0	554.6
Health and social welfare . . .	450.5	458.6	512.4
Other personal services	177.9	190.6	203.6
Sub-total	7,935.4	8,602.0	9,441.6
Less Imputed bank service charges	212.5	236.5	276.9
GDP at basic prices	7,723.0	8,365.5	9,164.7
Taxes, less subsidies, on products .	1,888.2	2,114.4	2,486.4
GDP in purchasers' values . .	9,611.2	10,480.0	11,651.1

BALANCE OF PAYMENTS
(estimates, US $ million)

	2001	2002	2003
Exports of goods f.o.b.	1,134.2	1,109.7	1,437.7
Imports of goods f.o.b.	−4,092.0	−4,449.4	−5,383.3
Trade balance	−2,957.8	−3,339.7	−3,945.6
Exports of services	376.2	475.5	621.2
Imports of services	−202.6	−288.8	−361.4
Balance on goods and services	−2,784.2	−3,153.0	−3,685.8
Other income received	396.3	350.8	356.4
Other income paid	−80.6	−86.5	−107.1
Balance on goods, services and income	−2,468.5	−2,888.7	−3,436.5
Current transfers received . . .	1,255.6	1,223.1	1,435.1
Current transfers paid	−3.9	−28.4	−36.7
Current balance	−1,216.8	−1,693.9	−2,038.1
Capital account (net)	382.9	392.0	474.4
Direct investment from abroad .	118.5	267.8	381.8
Other investment assets . . .	906.2	317.0	134.1
Other investment liabilities . .	−13.8	112.9	406.0
Net errors and omissions . . .	225.5	105.2	464.0
Overall balance	402.5	−499.0	−177.8

Source: IMF, *International Financial Statistics.*

External Trade

SELECTED COMMODITIES
(KM million*)

Imports	2003
Food and live animals	1,834.3
Vegetable products	438.0
Prepared foodstuffs	1,022.3
Mineral fuels, lubricants, etc.	856.3
Chemicals and related products	723.6
Basic manufactures	1,922.1
Plastics and rubber	373.6
Wood and wood products	336.3
Textiles and textile articles	268.5
Articles of stone, plaster, cement and asbestos .	315.3
Base metals and articles thereof	594.5
Machinery and transport equipment	2,003.1
Machinery and mechanical appliances	1,269.4
Transport equipment	619.7
Total (incl. others)	7,616.0

Exports	2003
Food and live animals	141.8
Prepared foodstuffs	86.1
Mineral fuels, lubricants, etc.	221.0
Basic manufactures	1,207.9
Wood and wood products	455.9
Textiles and textile articles	131.7
Base metals and articles thereof	498.3
Machinery and transport equipment	428.2
Electrical machinery and equipment	286.1
Transport equipment	104.2
Miscellaneous manufactured articles	272.4
Footwear	96.3
Total (incl. others)	2,319.5

* Figures from the Customs Administration of the Federation, the Customs Administration of Republika Srpska and the Customs Service of Brčko District, not including adjustments.
Source: Central Bank of Bosnia and Herzegovina, *Annual Report 2003.*

PRINCIPAL TRADING PARTNERS
(KM '000)

Imports	2001	2002	2003
Austria	416,642	463,792	358,726
Croatia	1,104,538	1,330,043	1,441,091
France	98,212	134,567	153,481
Germany	772,527	998,531	1,059,253
Hungary	411,652	491,428	510,496
Italy	957,233	789,764	772, 192
Slovenia	945,602	906,329	765,502
Switzerland	226,925	149,000	139,883
Yugoslavia	523,827	697,856	652,443
Total (incl. others)	7,331,430	8,168,124	8,223,336

Exports	2001	2002	2003
Austria	83,190	83,640	87,555
Croatia	247,278	313,266	422,670
France	24,256	41,723	24,553
Germany	328,378	262,698	362,817
Hungary	9,510	12,933	14,624
Italy	412,797	248,396	317,272
Slovenia	175,634	174,258	227,953
Switzerland	242,854	229,993	219,113
Yugoslavia	466,386	421,059	391,542
Total (incl. others)	2,255,526	2,099,203	2,362,849

Source: Central Bank of Bosnia and Herzegovina, *Annual Report 2001, 2002* and *2003*.

Transport

RAILWAYS
(traffic)

	2001	2002	2003
Passengers ('000 journeys)	1,296	1,128	1,090
Freight carried ('000 metric tons) .	5,400	6,600	6,799
Passenger-km (million)	48	48	55
Freight ton-km (million):	288	312	318

CIVIL AVIATION
(traffic on scheduled services)

	1999	2000	2001
Kilometres flown (million)	1	2	1
Passengers carried ('000)	60	69	65
Passenger-km (million)	42	48	44
Total ton-km (million)	5	6	6

Source: UN, *Statistical Yearbook*.

Tourism

FOREIGN TOURIST ARRIVALS BY COUNTRY OF ORIGIN
('000)*

Country of origin	2000	2001	2002
Austria	4	3	4
Croatia	30	22	24
Czech Republic	2	2	3
France	3	3	3
Germany	8	7	8
Italy	9	7	7
Slovenia	11	10	15
Turkey	4	2	2
United Kingdom	4	4	4
USA	9	7	7
Yugoslavia	51	42	46
Total (incl. others)	171	139	160

* Figures refer to arrivals at frontiers by visitors from abroad, and include same-day visitors.
Source: World Tourism Organization, *Yearbook of Tourism Statistics*.

Tourism receipts (US $ million): 97 in 2000; 101 in 2001; 112 in 2002 (Source: World Tourism Organization).

Communications Media

	2001	2002	2003
Telephones ('000 main lines in use)	847.0	902.8	938.0
Mobile cellular telephones ('000 subscribers)	444.7	748.8	1,050.0
Internet users ('000)	45.0	100.0	n.a.

Daily newspapers (government-controlled areas only): 2 (average circulation 520,000 copies) in 1995; 3 in 1996.

Non-daily newspapers (1992): 22 (average circulation 2,508,000 copies).

1997: Radio receivers ('000 in use) 940; Television receivers ('000 in use) 900.

Sources: UN, *Statistical Yearbook*; UNESCO, *Statistical Yearbook*; International Telecommunication Union.

Education

(2002/03*)

	Institu-tions	Teachers	Students Males	Students Females	Students Total
Pre-primary† .	123	n.a.	n.a.	n.a.	8,761
Primary . . .	1,862	20,874	186,039	177,033	363,072
Secondary . .	301	10,792	85,609	83,888	169,497
Higher† . . .	65	1,012	n.a.	n.a.	53,985

* Figures at end of academic year.
† Figures for Federation only.

Sources: partly Federation Institute of Statistics and Republika Srpska Institute of Statistics.

Adult literacy rate (UNESCO estimates): 94.6% (males 98.4%; females 91.1%) in 2002 (Source: UN Development Programme, *Human Development Report*).

Directory

The Constitution

The Constitution of Bosnia and Herzegovina was Annexe 4 to the General Framework Agreement for Peace in Bosnia and Herzegovina (known as the Dayton accords, after the town in Ohio, the USA, where negotiations took place in November 1995), signed in Paris, France, on 14 December 1995. Annexe 4 took effect as a constitu-tional act upon signature, superseding and amending the Constitution of the Republic of Bosnia and Herzegovina.

THE ENTITIES

Bosnia and Herzegovina comprises two 'entities': the Federation of Bosnia and Herzegovina and Republika Srpska, each of which has its own Government and institutions. According to the General

Framework Agreement, the two Entities were to exist under their existing Constitutions, which were to be amended to conform with the peace agreement. (In March 2000, following completion of a demilitarization process, the north-eastern Bosnian town of Brčko was established as a neutral district and placed under joint Serb, Croat and Bosniak authority, bringing to an end sole Serb control of the area.)

The Federation of Bosnia and Herzegovina

The Federation had been formed on 31 March 1994 on those territories controlled by the 'Croat Republic of Herzeg-Bosna' (proclaimed in August 1993) and by the Government of the Republic of Bosnia and Herzegovina. The federation Constitution provides for a balance of powers between Bosniak and Croat elements, with significant powers devolved to each of ten constituent cantons, based in: Bihać; Goražde; Livno; Mostar; Orašje; Sarajevo; Široki Brijeg; Travnik; Tuzla; and Zenica. The Prime Minister of the Federation has a greater executive role than the federation President; these two posts rotate between the two ethnic groups. There are also two Vice-Presidents. The federation legislature is bicameral, comprising a 98–member Predstavnički dom Federacije (House of Representatives of the Federation), which is directly elected for a four-year term, and a 51-member Dom Naroda Federacije (House of Peoples of the Federation), comprising 17 Bosniak, 17 Croat, 10 Serb and seven other deputies, who are elected by the cantonal assemblies.

Republika Srpska

A Republika Srpska of Bosnia and Herzegovina was proclaimed by the Bosnian Serb deputies of the Skupština Republike Bosne i Hercegovine (Assembly of the Republic of Bosnia and Herzegovina) on 27 March 1992, and subsequently comprised those territories within Bosnia and Herzegovina controlled by Serb forces. (The name was abbreviated to Republika Srpska in August 1992.) Its Constitution provides for an executive President (with two Vice-Presidents), a Government headed by a Prime Minister and a unicameral legislature, the Narodna Skupština Republike Srpske (National Assembly of Republika Srpska).

THE HIGH REPRESENTATIVE OF THE INTERNATIONAL COMMUNITY

The Office of a High Representative of the International Community, established by the Dayton Accords, is responsible for the civilian implementation of the terms of the peace settlement, and, as such, has the power to compel the entity governments to comply with the terms of the peace agreement and the state constitution. The High Representative also has the authority to dismiss members of the entity Governments and organizations that fail to uphold the terms of the peace agreement.

STATE CONSTITUTION OF BOSNIA AND HERZEGOVINA

The Preamble declares the basic, democratic principles of the country and its conformity with the principles of international law. The Bosniaks, Croats and Serbs are declared to be the constituent peoples (along with others) of Bosnia and Herzegovina.

Article I affirms the continuity of Bosnia and Herzegovina with the former Republic of Bosnia and Herzegovina, within its existing international boundaries, but with its internal structure modified. Bosnia and Herzegovina is a democratic state, consisting of two Entities, the Federation of Bosnia and Herzegovina and Republika Srpska (see above). The capital of the country, and of both Entities, is Sarajevo (although, in practice, most institutions and the Government of Republika Srpska are located in Banja Luka, while the government ministries of the Federation are shared between Sarajevo and Mostar). Citizenship is to exist both for Bosnia and Herzegovina and for the Entities.

Article II guarantees human rights and fundamental freedoms, and makes specific mention of the Human Rights Commission to be established under Annexe 6 of the General Framework Agreement. The provisions of a number of international agreements are assured and co-operation and access for the international war-crimes tribunal specified. The provisions of this Article, according to Article X, are incapable of diminution or elimination by any amendment to the Constitution.

The responsibilities of and relations between the Entities and the institutions of Bosnia and Herzegovina are dealt with in Article III. The institutions of Bosnia and Herzegovina are responsible for foreign policy (including trade and customs), overall financial policy, immigration and refugee issues, international and inter-entity law enforcement, common and international communications facilities, inter-entity transportation and air-traffic control. Any governmental functions or powers not reserved to the institutions of Bosnia and Herzegovina by this Constitution are reserved to the Entities, unless additional responsibilities are agreed between the Entities or as provided for in the General Framework Agreement (Annexes 5–8). The Entities may establish special, parallel relations with neighbouring states, provided this is consistent with the sovereignty and

territorial integrity of Bosnia and Herzegovina. The Constitution of Bosnia and Herzegovina has primacy over any inconsistent constitutional or legal provisions of the Entities.

Parlamentarna skupština Bosne i Hercegovine

Bosnia and Herzegovina has a bicameral legislature, known as the Parlamentarna skupština Bosne i Hercegovine (Parliamentary Assembly of Bosnia and Herzegovina). It consists of the Dom Naroda (House of Peoples) and the Predstavnički dom (House of Representatives). The Dom Naroda comprises 15 Members, five each from the Bosniaks, the Croats and the Serbs, who are elected for a term of four years. The Bosniak and Croat Delegates are selected by, respectively, the Bosniak and Croat Delegates to the Predstavnički dom Federacije, and the Serb Delegates by the Vijeće Naroda (Council of Peoples) of the Narodna skupština Republike Srpske.

The Predstavnički dom consists of 42 Members, of whom two-thirds are directly elected from the territory of the Federation and one-third from the territory of Republika Srpska. Deputies are elected for a term of four years.

The Parlamentarna skupština convenes in Sarajevo and each chamber rotates its chair between three members, one from each of the constituent peoples. The Parlamentarna skupština is responsible for: necessary legislation under the Constitution or to implement Presidency decisions; determining a budget for the institutions of Bosnia and Herzegovina; and deciding whether to ratify treaties.

The State Presidency

Article V concerns the state Presidency of Bosnia and Herzegovina. The office of the head of state consists of three Members: one Bosniak and one Croat, each directly elected from the Federation; and one Serb, directly elected from Republika Srpska. Members are elected for a term of four years and are restricted to two consecutive terms. Chairmanship of the Presidency is rotated between the Members every eight months. A Presidency decision, if declared to be destructive of a vital interest of an Entity, can be vetoed by a two-thirds' majority in the relevant body: the Narodna skupština Republike Srpske if the declaration was made by the Serb Member; or by the Bosniak or Croat Delegates in the federation Dom Naroda if the declaration was made by, respectively, the Bosniak or Croat Members. The Presidency is responsible for the foreign policy and international relations of Bosnia and Herzegovina. It is required to execute the decisions of the Parlamentarna skupština and to propose an annual central budget to that body, upon the recommendation of the Council of Ministers.

The Chairman of the Council of Ministers is nominated by the Presidency and confirmed in office by the Predstavnički dom. The Chairman of the Council of Ministers is required to be from a different constituent people than the Chairman of the Presidency. Other Ministers and Deputy Ministers are nominated by the Chairman of the Council of Ministers, and also approved by the Predstavnički dom. The Council of Ministers is responsible for carrying out the policies and decisions of Bosnia and Herzegovina and reporting to the Parlamentarna skupština. There are also guarantees that no more than two-thirds of Ministers be from the territory of the Federation, and Deputy Ministers are to be from a different constituent people to their Minister.

Each Member of the Presidency has, *ex officio*, civilian command authority over armed forces. Each Member is a member of a Standing Committee on Military Matters, appointed by the Presidency and responsible for co-ordinating the activities of armed forces in the country. The inviolability of each Entity to any armed force of the other is assured.

Other Institutions and Provisions

Article VI is on the Constitutional Court, which is to have nine members, four selected by the Predstavnički dom Federacije and two by the Narodna skupština Republike Srpske. The three remaining judges, at least initially, are to be selected by the President of the European Court of Human Rights. Judges usually serve until they are 70 years of age (unless they retire or are removed by the consensus of the other judges). The Constitutional Court of Bosnia and Herzegovina is to uphold the Constitution, to resolve the jurisdictions of the institutions of Bosnia and Herzegovina and the Entities, to ensure consistency with the Constitution and to guarantee the legal sovereignty and territorial integrity of the country. Its decisions are final and binding.

The Central Bank of Bosnia and Herzegovina is the sole authority for issuing currency and for monetary policy in Bosnia and Herzegovina. The Governing Body consists of five members, appointed by the Presidency for a term of six years, with a Governor selected by them from among their number.

Article VIII concerns the finances of Bosnia and Herzegovina and its institutions. Article IX concerns general provisions, notably forbidding anyone convicted or indicted by the International Criminal Tribunal for the former Yugoslavia from standing for or holding public office in Bosnia and Herzegovina. These provisions also guarantee the need for all public appointments to be generally representative of the peoples of Bosnia and Herzegovina. Amendments to the Constitution need a two-thirds majority of those present and voting in the Predstavnički dom. The penultimate Article XI is on transitional arrangements provided for in an annexe to the Constitution.

The Government

(April 2005)

HIGH REPRESENTATIVE OF THE INTERNATIONAL COMMUNITY IN BOSNIA AND HERZEGOVINA

Under the terms of the treaty and annexes of the General Framework Agreement for Peace in Bosnia and Herzegovina, signed in December 1995, the international community, as authorized by the UN Security Council, was to designate a civilian representative to oversee the implementation of the peace accords and the establishment of the institutions of the new order in Bosnia and Herzegovina.

High Representative of the International Community and Special Representative of the European Union to Bosnia and Herzegovina: Sir JEREMY (PADDY) ASHDOWN, 71000 Sarajevo, Emerika Bluma 1; tel. (33) 283500; fax (33) 283501; internet www.ohr.int.

STATE GOVERNMENT OF BOSNIA AND HERZEGOVINA

Presidency

The Dayton accords, which were signed into treaty in December 1995, provide for a three-member Presidency for the state, comprising one Bosniak (Muslim), one Croat and one Serb. The collective Presidency, which governs Bosnia and Herzegovina at state level, comprises a Chairman and a further two members, with the post of Chairman rotating every eight months between Bosniak, Croat and Serb representatives. The Presidency nominates a Chairman of the Council of Ministers (subject to the approval of the legislature), who appoints the other ministers.

Chairman of the Presidency: BORISLAV PARAVAĆ (Serbian Democratic Party of Bosnia and Herzegovina).

Member of the Presidency: SULEJMAN TIHIĆ (Party of Democratic Action).

Member of the Presidency: (vacant).

Council of Ministers
(April 2005)

A coalition of the Party of Democratic Action (PDA), the Party of Democratic Progress of Republika Srpska (PDP), the Croatian Democratic Union of Bosnia and Herzegovina (CDU), the Party for Bosnia and Herzegovina, and the Serbian Democratic Party (SDP).

Chairman: ADNAN TERZIĆ (PDA).

Minister of Defence: NIKOLA RADOVANOVIĆ (SDP).

Minister of Justice: SLOBODAN KOVAČ (SDP).

Minister of Foreign Affairs: MLADEN IVANIĆ (PDP).

Minister of Security: BARIŠA ČOLAK (CDU).

Minister of Civil Affairs: SAFET HALILOVIĆ (Party for Bosnia and Herzegovina).

Minister of Foreign Trade and Economic Relations: DRAGAN DOKO (CDU).

Minister of Human Rights and Refugees: MIRSAD KEBO (PDA).

Minister of Finance and the Treasury: LJERKA MARIĆ (CDU).

Minister of Communications and Transport: BRANKO DOKIĆ (PDP).

Ministries

Office of the Presidency: 71000 Sarajevo, Musala 5; tel. (33) 664941; fax (33) 472491; internet www.predsjednistvobih.ba.

Office of the Chairman of the Council of Ministers: 71000 Sarajevo, Vojvode Putnika 3; tel. (33) 211581; fax (33) 205347; e-mail cmpress@smartnet.ba; internet www.vijeceministara.gov.ba.

Ministry of Civil Affairs: 71000 Sarajevo, Vojvode Putnika 3; tel. (33) 786822; fax (33) 786944; internet www.mcp.gov.ba.

Ministry of Communications and Transport: 71000 Sarajevo.

Ministry of Defence: 71000 Sarajevo, Hamdije Kreševljakovica 98; tel. (33) 263180; fax (33) 206094.

Ministry of Finance and the Treasury: 71000 Sarajevo, trg Bosne i Hercegovine 1; tel. (33) 205345; fax (33) 471822; e-mail trezorbih@trezorbih.gov.ba; internet www.trezorbih.gov.ba.

Ministry of Foreign Affairs: 71000 Sarajevo, Musala 2; tel. (33) 281100; fax (33) 472188; e-mail info@mvp.gov.ba; internet www.mvp.gov.ba.

Ministry of Foreign Trade and Economic Relations: 71000 Sarajevo, Musala 9; tel. (33) 663863; fax (33) 655060; internet www.mvteo.gov.ba.

Ministry of Human Rights and Refugees: 71000 Sarajevo, trg Bosne i Hercegovine 1; tel. (33) 206673; fax (33) 206140; e-mail kabmin@mhrr.gov.ba; internet www.mhrr.gov.ba.

Ministry of Justice: 71000 Sarajevo, trg Bosne i Hercegovine 1; tel. (33) 223501; fax (33) 223504; e-mail kontakt@mpr.gov.ba; internet www.mpr.gov.ba.

Ministry of Security: 71000 Sarajevo, trg Bosne i Hercegovine 1; tel. (33) 213623; fax (33) 213628; e-mail bdautbasic@smartnet.ba.

Presidency and Legislature

STATE PRESIDENCY

Election, 5 October 2002

	Votes	% of votes
Bosniak Candidates		
Sulejman Tihić (Party of Democratic Action)	192,661	37.29
Haris Silajdžić (Party for Bosnia and Herzegovina)	179,726	34.79
Alija Behmen (Social Democratic Party of Bosnia and Herzegovina)	90,434	17.51
Fikret Abdić (Democratic People's Union)	21,164	4.10
Others	32,625	6.31
Total	516,610	100.00
Croat Candidates		
Dragan Čović (Croatian Democratic Union of Bosnia and Herzegovina/Croatian Christian Democratic Union)	114,606	61.52
Mladen Ivanković-Lijanović (Economic Bloc HDU-For Progress)	32,411	17.40
Mijo Anić (New Croatian Initiative)	16,345	8.77
Stjepan Kljuić (Republican Party)	9,413	5.05
Others	13,516	7.26
Total	186,291	100.00
Serb Candidates		
Mirko Sarović (Serbian Democratic Party of Bosnia and Herzegovina)*	180,212	35.52
Nebojsa Radmanović (Alliance of Independent Social Democrats)	101,119	19.93
Ognjen Tadić (Serb Radical Party of Republika Srpska)	44,262	8.72
Desnica Radivojević (Party of Democratic Action)	41,667	8.21
Ranko Bakić (Party of the Social Democratic Centre)	41,228	8.13
Mirko Banjac (Alliance of National Rebirth	23,238	4.58
Grahovac Mladen (Social Democratic Party of Bosnia and Herzegovina)	22,852	4.50
Others	52,836	10.41
Total	507,414	100.00
Total votes cast for all candidates	1,210,315	n.a.

*MIRKO SAROVIĆ was obliged to resign as the Serb member of the collective presidency in April 2003; he was replaced by the nominee of the national legislature, BORISLAV PARAVAĆ.

PARLAMENTARNA SKUPŠTINA BOSNE I HERCEGOVINE
(Parliamentary Assembly of Bosnia and Herzegovina)

The Parlamentarna skupština Bosne i Hercegovine (Parliamentary Assembly of Bosnia and Herzegovina) comprises two chambers, the Dom Naroda (House of Peoples) and the Predstavnički dom (House of Representatives).

Dom Naroda
(House of Peoples)

71000 Sarajevo, Trg Bosne i Hercegovine 1; tel. (33) 284440; fax (33) 233480; e-mail goran.milojevic@psbih.org; internet www.parlament.ba/bos/dn/index.php.

There are 15 deputies in the Dom Naroda (House of Peoples), of whom 10 are elected by the Dom Narodna Federacije (House of Peoples of the Federation) and five by the Vijece Naroda (Council of Peoples) of the Narodna skupština Republike Srpske (National Assembly of Republika Srpska).

Speaker: GORAN MILOJEVIĆ.

Predstavnički dom
(House of Representatives)

71000 Sarajevo, Trg Bosne i Hercegovine 1; tel. (33) 666585; fax (33) 233480; e-mail martin.raguz@psbih.org; internet www.parlament .ba/bos/pd/index.php.

The Predstavnički dom has 42 deputies directly elected for a four-year term, of whom 28 are elected from the Federation and 14 from Republika Srpska.

Speaker: MARTIN RAGUŽ.

General Election, 5 October 2002

Party	% of votes	Seats
Party of Democratic Action	21.9	10
Serbian Democratic Party of Bosnia and Herzegovina	14.0	5
Party for Bosnia and Herzegovina . .	10.5	6
Social Democratic Party of Bosnia and Herzegovina	10.4	4
Alliance of Independent Social Democrats .	9.8	3
Croatian Democratic Community/Croatian Christian Democratic Union—Bosnia and Herzegovina	9.5	5
Party of Democratic Progress of Republika Srpska	4.6	2
Socialist Party of Republika Srpska . .	1.9	1
Bosnian Party	1.5	1
Others	15.9	5
Total	100.0	42

The Entities of Bosnia and Herzegovina

GOVERNMENT OF THE FEDERATION OF BOSNIA AND HERZEGOVINA

Following an agreement reached in Washington, DC, the USA, by representatives of the Republic of Bosnia and Herzegovina and the 'Croat Republic of Herzeg-Bosna' (declared on 28 August 1993), the Federation of Bosnia and Herzegovina was formed on 31 March 1994. The Federation was reorganized as one of the two constituent entities of Bosnia and Herzegovina in the peace agreements of 1995.

President: NIKO LOZANCIĆ (Croatian Democratic Community).

Vice-Presidents: SAHBAZ DZIKANOVIĆ (Party for Bosnia and Herzegovina), DEZNICA RADIVOJEVIĆ (Party of Democratic Action).

Government
(April 2005)

Prime Minister: Dr AHMET HADŽIPAŠIĆ.

Deputy Prime Minister and Minister of Finance: DRAGAN VRANKIĆ.

Deputy Prime Minister and Minister of Culture and Sports: GAVRILO GRAHOVAC.

Minister of Defence: MIROSLAV NIKOLIĆ.

Minister of Internal Affairs: MEVLUDIN HALILOVIĆ.

Minister of Justice: BORJANA KRIŠTO.

Minister of Energy, Mining and Industry: Dr IZET ŽIGIĆ.

Minister of Transport and Communications: NEDŽAC BRANKOVIĆ.

Minister of Labour and Social Policy: RADOVAN VIGNJEVIĆ.

Minister of Displaced Persons and Refugees: EDIN MUŠIĆ.

Minister of War Veterans and the Disabled: IBRAHIM NADAREVIĆ.

Minister of Health: TOMO LUČIĆ.

Minister of Education and Science : Dr ZIJAD PAŠIĆ.

Minister of Trade: MAID LJUBOVIĆ.

Minister of Urban Planning and the Environment: RAMIZ MEHMEDAGIĆ.

Minister of Agriculture, Water Management and Forestry: MARINKO BOŽIĆ.

Minister of Development, Entrepreneurship and Crafts: MLADEN ČABRILO.

Ministries

Office of the President: 71000 Sarajevo; tel. and fax (33) 472618; e-mail info@fbihvlada.gov.ba; internet www.fbihvlada.gov.ba.

Office of the Prime Minister: 71000 Sarajevo, Alipašina 41; tel. (33) 663649; fax (33) 444718; e-mail kabprem@fbihvlada.gov.ba.

Ministry of Agriculture, Water Management and Forestry: 71000 Sarajevo, Titova 15; tel. (33) 443338; fax (33) 663659; e-mail info@fmpvs.gov.ba; internet www.fmpvs.gov.ba.

Ministry of Defence: 71000 Sarajevo, Hamdije Kreševljakovića 98; tel. (33) 650677; fax (33) 663785; e-mail cabmod@bih.net.ba.

Ministry of Development, Entrepreneurship and Crafts: 88000 Mostar, Zgrada Vlade FBiHEr, Dr A.Starčevića bb; tel. (36) 320896; fax (36) 320897; e-mail fmrpo@tel.net.ba.

Ministry of Displaced Persons and Refugees: 71000 Sarajevo, Alipašina 41; tel. (33) 663977; fax (33) 204552; e-mail fmsa_ras@ fbihvlada.gov.ba.

Ministry of Education and Science: 71000 Sarajevo, Obala Maka Dizdara 2; tel. (33) 663691; fax (33) 664381; e-mail fmonks@bih.net .ba.

Ministry of Energy, Mining and Industry: 88000 Mostar, Adema Buća 34; tel. (36) 580020; fax (36) 580015; e-mail fmeri-mo@ bih.net.ba.

Ministry of Finance: 71000 Sarajevo, Mehmeda Spahe 5; tel. (33) 203147; fax (33) 203152; e-mail fmf.kab@bih.net.ba; internet www .fmf.gov.ba.

Ministry of Health: 71000 Sarajevo, Titova 9; tel. and fax (33) 664245; e-mail moh@bih.net.ba.

Ministry of Internal Affairs: 71000 Sarajevo, Mehmeda Spahe 7; tel. (33) 664904; fax (33) 472593.

Ministry of Justice: 71000 Sarajevo, Valtera Perica 15; tel. and fax (33) 213155; e-mail mirjanab@pris.gov.ba.

Ministry of Labour and Social Policy: 71000 Sarajevo, Vilsonovo šetalište 10; tel. (33) 661782; fax (33) 661783; e-mail fmsa@fbihvlada .gov.ba.

Ministry of Trade: 88000 Mostar, Kneza Domagoja 12; tel. (36) 310148; fax (36) 318684.

Ministry of Transport and Communications: 88000 Mostar, Ivana Krndelja b.b.; tel. (36) 550025; fax (36) 550024; internet www .fmpik.gov.ba.

Ministry of Urban Planning and the Environment: 71000 Sarajevo, Marsala Tita 9A; tel. and fax (33) 473124; e-mail fmpuio@ fbihvlada.gov.ba.

Ministry of Veterans and the Disabled of the War of Liberation: 71000 Sarajevo, Alipašina 41; tel. (33) 212932; fax (33) 209333; e-mail kabinet@bih.net.ba; internet www.fmbi.gov.ba.

PARLAMENT FEDERACIJE

The bicameral Parlament Federacije (Parliament of the Federation) comprises the Dom Naroda Federacije (House of Peoples of the Federation) and the Predstavnički dom Federacije (House of Representatives of the Federation).

Dom Naroda Federacije
(House of Peoples of the Federation)

Sarajevo; tel. (33) 203246; fax (33) 205547; e-mail izmirhadziavdic@ parlamentfbih.gov.ba; internet www.parlamentfbih.gov.ba.

The 51-member Dom Naroda Federacije, comprises 17 Bosniak, 17 Croat, 10 Serb and seven other deputies, who are elected by the cantonal assemblies.

Speaker: SLAVKO MATIĆ.

Predstavnički dom Federacije
(House of Representatives of the Federation)

71000 Sarajevo; internet www.parlamentfbih.gov.ba.

The 98 deputies of the Predstavnički dom Federacije are directly elected for a four-year term.

Speaker: Sefić Dzaferović.

General Election, 5 October 2002

Party	Votes	% of votes	Seats
Party of Democratic Action . . .	234,923	32.7	32
Croatian Democratic Community/Croatian Christian Democratic Union—Bosnia and Herzegovina	113,197	15.8	16
Social Democratic Party of Bosnia and Herzegovina	111,668	15.6	15
Party for Bosnia and Herzegovina	109,843	15.3	15
Bosnian Party	20,188	2.8	3
Pensioners' Party of Bosnia and Herzegovina	16,583	2.3	2
National Democratic Union . . .	16,363	2.3	2
Economic Bloc HDU-For Progress	14,130	2.0	2
New Croatian Initiative	13,967	2.0	2
Others	67,230	9.2	9
Total	**718,092**	**100.0**	**98**

GOVERNMENT OF REPUBLIKA SRPSKA

On 9 January 1992 the 'Republika Srpska of Bosnia and Herzegovina' was proclaimed. It was immediately declared illegal by the President of the State Presidency. The Republic comprised Serb-held areas of Bosnia and Herzegovina, including the 'Serb Autonomous Regions' of Eastern and Old Herzegovina, the Bosnian Krajina, Romanija and Northern Bosnia. (In August 1992 the self-styled republic changed its name to Republika Srpska.) According to the peace treaty of December 1995, Republika Srpska constituted one of the two territorial entities comprising Bosnia and Herzegovina, with 49% of the country's area. It retained its own executive presidency, government and parliament (henceforth known as the Narodna Skupština Republika Srpska—the National Assembly of Republika Srpska).

President: Dragan Čavić (Serbian Democratic Party).

Vice-President: Adil Osmanović (Party of Democratic Action).

Vice-President: Ivan Tomljenović (Serbian Democratic Party).

Government
(April 2005)

Prime Minister: Pero Bukejlović.

Minister of Finance: Svetlana Cenić.

Minister of Internal Affairs: Darko Matijasević.

Minister of Defence: Milovan Stanković.

Minister of Justice: Dzerard Selman.

Minister of Administration and Local Government: Zdenka Abazagić.

Minister of the Economy, Energy and Development: Miladin Gligorić.

Minister of Foreign Economic Relations and Co-ordination: Jasmin Seferović.

Minister of Labour and the Protection of War Veterans: Miodrag Deretić.

Minister of Trade and Tourism: Boris Gaspar.

Minister of Transport and Communications: Dragoje Lajić.

Minister of Agriculture, Water Resources and Forestry: Goran Perković.

Minister of Urban Planning, Housing and the Environment: Muhamed Lisić.

Minister of Education and Culture: Milovan Pecelj.

Minister of Refugees and Displaced Persons: Jasmin Samardzić.

Minister of Health and Social Welfare: Ivo Komljenović.

Minister of Science and Technology: Fuad Turalić.

Ministries

Office of the President: 78000 Banja Luka, Vuka Karadžica 4; tel. (51) 212407; internet www.predsjednikrs.net.

Office of the Prime Minister: 78000 Banja Luka, Vuka Karadžica 4; tel. (51) 331333; fax (51) 331366; e-mail kabinet@vladars.net; internet www.vladars.net.

Ministry of Administration and Local Government: 78000 Banja Luka, Vuka Karadžica 4; tel. (51) 331680; fax (51) 331681; e-mail muls@muls.vladars.net.

Ministry of Agriculture, Water Resources and Forestry: 78000 Banja Luka, Vuka Karadžica 4; tel. (51) 331634; fax (51) 331631; e-mail mps@mps.vladars.net.

Ministry of Defence: 78000 Banja Luka, Bana Lazarevića 15; tel. (51) 218823; fax (51) 300243; e-mail mo@mo.vladars.net.

Ministry of the Economy, Energy and Development: 78000 Banja Luka, Vuka Karadžica 4; tel. (51) 331710; fax (51) 331702; e-mail mer@mer.vladars.net.

Ministry of Education and Culture: 78000 Banja Luka, Vuka Karadžica 4; tel. (51) 331424; fax (51) 331423; e-mail mp@mp.vladars.net.

Ministry of Finance: 78000 Banja Luka, Vuka Karadžica 4; tel. (51) 331350; fax (51) 331351; e-mail dcutkovic@mf.vladars.net.

Ministry of Foreign Economic Relations and Co-ordination: 78000 Banja Luka, Vuka Karadžica 4; tel. (51) 331430; fax (51) 331436; e-mail meoi@meoi.vladars.net.

Ministry of Health and Social Welfare: 78000 Banja Luka, Vuka Karadžica 4; tel. (51) 331600; fax (51) 331601; e-mail mzsz@mzsz.vladars.net.

Ministry of Internal Affairs: 78000 Banja Luka, Jug Bogdana 108; tel. (51) 331106; fax (51) 331206; e-mail mup@mup.vladars.net.

Ministry of Justice: 78000 Banja Luka, Vuka Karadžica 4; tel. (51) 331582; fax (51) 331594; e-mail mpr@mpr.vladars.net.

Ministry of Labour and the Protection of War Veterans: 78000 Banja Luka, Vuka Karadžica 4; tel. (51) 331651; fax (51) 331652; e-mail mpb@mpb.vladars.net.

Ministry of Refugees and Displaced Persons: 78000 Banja Luka, Vuka Karadžica 4; tel. (51) 331470; fax (51) 331471; e-mail mirl@mirl.vladars.net.

Ministry of Science and Technology: 78000 Banja Luka, Vuka Karadžica 4; tel. (51) 331542; fax (51) 331548; e-mail mnk@mnk.vladars.net; internet www.vladars.net.

Ministry of Trade and Tourism: 78000 Banja Luka, Vuka Karadžica 4; tel. (51) 331523; fax (51) 331499; e-mail mtt@mtt.vladars.net.

Ministry of Transport and Communications: 78000 Banja Luka, Vuka Karadžica 4; tel. (51) 331611; fax (51) 331612; e-mail msv@msv.vladars.net.

Ministry of Urban Planning, Housing and the Environment: 78000 Banja Luka, trg Srpskih Junaka 4; tel. (51) 215511; fax (51) 215548; e-mail mgr@mgr.vladars.net.

PRESIDENT OF REPUBLIKA SRPSKA

Election, 5 October 2002

Candidate	Votes	% of votes
Dragan Čavić (Serbian Democratic Party) .	183,121	35.9
Milan Jelić (Alliance of Independent Social Democrats)	112,612	22.1
Dragan Mikerivić (Party of Democratic Progress of Republika Srpska)	39,978	7.8
Adil Osmanović (Party of Democratic Action)	34,129	6.7
Petar Cokić (Socialist Party of Republika Srpska)	27,137	5.3
Others	113,286	22.2
Total	**510,263**	**100.0**

Narodna skupština Republike Srpske
(National Assembly of Republika Srpska)
78000 Banja Luka, ul. Vuka Karažića 2; tel. (51) 301099; fax (51) 301087; internet www.narodnaskupstinars.net.

Speaker: Dušan Stojičić.

Election, 5 October 2002

Party	Votes	% of votes	Seats*
Serbian Democratic Party of Bosnia and Herzegovina	159,164	31.2	26
Alliance of Independent Social Democrats	111,226	21.8	19
Party of Democratic Progress of Republika Srpska	54,756	10.7	9
Party of Democratic Action	36,212	7.1	6
Serbian Radical Party of Republika Srpska	22,396	4.4	4
Socialist Party of Republika Srpska	21,502	4.2	3
Democratic People's League	29,375	4.0	3
Party for Bosnia and Herzegovina	18,624	3.7	4
Social Democratic Party of Bosnia and Herzegovina	17,227	3.4	3
Others	39,895	6.5	6
Total	510,377	100.0	83

*About three-quarters of deputies are elected in multi-seat constituencies, with the remainder selected through compensatory lists.

Political Organizations

Alliance of Independent Social Democrats (AISD) (Savez nezavisnih socijaldemokrata—SNSD): 78000 Banja Luka, Petra Kočića 5; tel. (51) 318492; fax (51) 318495; e-mail snsd@inecco.net; internet www.snsd.org; Chair. MILORAD DODIK; Sec.-Gen. IGOR RADOJIČIĆ.

Bosnian Party (Bosanska Stranka—BOSS): 75000 Tuzla, Stari Grad 9; tel. and fax (35) 251035; e-mail boss.bh@delta.com.ba; internet www.trazim.com/BOSS/BOSS.htm; socialist, supports policies of former Yugoslav leader Josep Broz (Tito); Chair. MIRNES AJANOVIĆ.

Civic Democratic Party (Građanska Demokratska Stranka): 71000 Sarajevo, Maršala Tita 9A; tel. (33) 213435; fax (33) 266630; e-mail ibrosa@bih.net.ba; Chair. IBRAHIM SPAHIĆ.

Croatian Christian Democratic Union—Bosnia and Herzegovina (Hrvatska Kršćanska Demokratska Unija—Bosne i Hercegovine): 80240 Tomislavgrad, Kulina bana bb; tel. and fax (80) 352051; e-mail hkdubih@tel.net.ba; Pres. MIJO IVANČIĆ-LONIĆ.

Croatian Democratic Union of Bosnia and Herzegovina (CDU—BH) (Hrvatska Demokratska Zajednica Bosne i Hercegovine—HDZ BiH): 88000 Mostar, Kneza Domagoja b.b.; tel. (36) 310701; fax (36) 315024; e-mail hdzbih@hdzbih.org; internet www .hdzbih.org; f. 1990; affiliate of the CDU in Croatia; adopted new party statute July 2000; Croat nationalist party; Chair. BARIŠA ČOLAK; Gen.-Sec. VLATKO MEDUGORAC.

Croatian Peasants' Party of Bosnia and Herzegovina (Hrvatska Seljacka Stranka BiH): 71000 Sarajevo, Radićeva 4; tel. and fax (33) 441987; e-mail info@hssbih.co.ba; internet www.hssbih .co.ba; affiliated to Croatian Peasants' Party in Croatia; Chair. ILIJA ŠIMIĆ.

Democratic National Alliance (Demokratski Narodni Savez): 78000 Banja Luka, Aleja Svetog Save 20; tel. (51) 219020; fax (51) 219033; internet www.dnsrs.org; f. 2000 by fmr mems of the Serb National Alliance; Chair. Dr MARKO PAVIĆ.

Democratic Party of Republika Srpska (Demokratska Stranka Republike Srpske): 76300 Bijeljina, Kneza Miloša 26; tel. and fax (55) 201951; e-mail dsrs@bn.rstel.net; Pres. DRAGOMIR DUMIĆ.

Liberal Democratic Party (LDP) (Liberalno Demokratska Stranka): 71000 Sarajevo, Maršala Tita 9A; tel. and fax (33) 664540; e-mail centrala@liberali.ba; internet www.liberali.ba; f. 2000 by merger of Liberal Party of Bosnia and Herzegovina and the Liberal Bosniak Organization; Chair. RASIM KADIĆ.

National Democratic Union (Narodna Demokratska Zajednica—NDZ): 77230 Velika Kladuša, Sulejmana Topića 7; tel. and fax (77) 770407; e-mail dnzbih@bih.net.ba; f. 1996; Chair. FIKRET ABDIĆ.

New Croatian Initiative (Nova Hrvatska Inicijativa): 71000 Sarajevo, Sime Milutinovića 2/II; tel. (33) 214602; fax (33) 214603; e-mail nhi@nhi.ba; f. 1998 by fmr mems of the Croatian Democratic Union of Bosnia and Herzegovina; Chair. KREŠIMIR ZUBAK.

Party for Bosnia and Herzegovina (Stranka za Bosnu i Hercegovinu): 71000 Sarajevo, Maršala Tita 9A; tel. and fax (33) 214417; e-mail zabih@zabih.ba; internet www.zabih.ba; f. 1996; integrationist; member of the Coalition for a Single and Democratic Bosnia electoral alliance; Pres. Prof. Dr SAFET HALILOVIĆ.

Party of Democratic Action (PDA) (Stranka Demokratske Akcije—SDA): 71000 Sarajevo, Mehmeda Spahe 14; tel. (33) 472192;

fax (33) 650429; e-mail centrala@sda.ba; internet www.sda.ba; f. 1990; supports admission of Bosnia and Herezegovina to the European Union and formation of a Republic of Bosnia and Herzegovina as decentralized state composed of multi-ethnic regions, with Bosniaks, Croats and Serbs as members of a common Bosnian nation; Chair. SULEJMAN TIHIĆ; Sec.-Gen. MIRSAD CEMAN.

Party of Democratic Progress of Republika Srpska (PDP) (Partija Demokratskog Progresa Republike Srpske): 78000 Banja Luka, Majke Marije i Braće Mažar 52; tel. (51) 218078; fax (51) 218115; e-mail pdp@blic.net; internet www.pdp-rs.org; f. 1999; moderate, supports equal rights for all ethnic groups, supports closer cooperation of Republika Srpska with the European Union; Chair. MLADEN IVANIĆ.

Party of Independent Social Democrats of Republika Srpska (Stranka Nezavisnih Socijaldemokrata Republike Srpske): 78000 Banja Luka; f. breakaway faction of the Alliance of Independent Social Democrats; Leader BRANE MILJUS.

Pensioners' Party of the Federation of Bosnia and Herzegovina (Stranka Penzionera Federacije BiH): 71000 Sarajevo, Obala Kulina bana 1/1; tel. and fax (33) 667997; Chair. HUSEIN VOJNIKOVIĆ.

Pensioners' Party of Republika Srpska (Penzionerska Stranka Republike Srpske): 78000 Banja Luka, Grčka 19; tel. (51) 301212; fax (51) 214789; Chair. STOJAN BOGOSAVAC.

Radical Party of Republika Srpska (Radikalna Stranka Republike Srpske): 79101 Prijedor, Srpskih velikana b.b.; tel. and fax (52) 213428; e-mail goran-b@inecco.net; extreme Serb nationalist; Chair. GORAN ZMIJANJAC.

Republican Party of Bosnia and Herzegovina (Republikanska Stranka BiH): 71000 Sarajevo, Maršala Tita 9; tel. (33) 664525; fax (33) 664987; e-mail republ94@bih.net.ba; internet www .republikanci.ba; integrationist; Chair. STJEPAN KLJUIĆ.

Serbian Democratic Party of Bosnia and Herzegovina (SDP) (Srpska Demokratska Stranka Bosne i Hercegovine—SDS BiH): 78000 Banja Luka, Kralja Petra I Karađorđevića; tel. (51) 212738; fax (51) 217640; f. 1990; allied to SDP of Croatia; Serb nationalist party; Chair. DRAGAN ČAVIĆ (acting).

Serbian Radical Party of Republika Srpska (Srpska Radikalna Stranka Republike Srpske—SRS): 78000 Banja Luka, Vidovdanska 53; tel. (51) 219428; radical Serb nationalist, supports the notion of a 'Greater Serbia'; Chair. RADISLAV KANJERIĆ.

Social Democratic Party of Bosnia and Herzegovina (Socijaldemokratska Partija BiH—SDP BiH): 71000 Sarajevo, Alipašina 41; tel. (33) 664044; fax (33) 644042; e-mail generalni.sekretar@sdp-bih .org.ba; internet www.sdp-bih.org.ba; Chair. Dr ZLATKO LAGUMDŽIJA; Sec.-Gen. KARLO FILIPOVIĆ.

Social Democratic Union of Bosnia and Herzegovina (Socijaldemokratski savez BiH): 71000 Sarajevo; f. 2002 by fmr mems of Party for Bosnia and Herzegovina; Chair. MIRO LAZOVIĆ.

Socialist Party of Republika Srpska (Socijalistička Partija Republike Srpske—SPRS): 78000 Banja Luka, Kralja Petra I Karađorđevića 103/1; tel. (51) 215301; fax (51) 215336; e-mail sprs@ inecco.net; f. 1993; br. of the Socialist Party of Serbia; Chair. ŽIVKO RADIŠIĆ.

Youth Party of Bosnia and Herzegovina (Stranka Mladih BiH): 78000 Banja Luka, Vida Nježića 36; tel. (51) 379780; fax 379781; e-mail contact@strankamladih.org; internet www.strankamladih .com; Chair. MILAN BAŠTINAC.

Diplomatic Representation

EMBASSIES IN BOSNIA AND HERZEGOVINA

Austria: 71000 Sarajevo, Džidžikovac 7; tel. (33) 279400; fax (33) 668339; e-mail obsaraje@obsaraje.bmaa.gv.at; Ambassador GERHARD JANDL.

Bulgaria: Sarajevo, Trampina 14/11; tel. (33) 668191; fax (33) 668182; Ambassador LJUBČO BUDINOV TROHAROV.

Canada: Sarajevo, Grbavicka 4/II; tel. (33) 222033; fax (33) 222044; Ambassador SHELLEY WHITING.

China, People's Republic: Sarajevo, Braće Begića 17; tel. (33) 215102; fax (33) 215108; Ambassador LI SHUYUAN.

Croatia: 71000 Sarajevo, Mehmeda Spahe 20; tel. (33) 444330; fax (33) 472434; Ambassador Dr JOSIP VRBOSIĆ.

Czech Republic: 71000 Sarajevo, Franjevačka 19; tel. (33) 447525; fax (33) 447526; e-mail embassy@embassy.mzv.cz; internet www .mzv.cz/wwwo/defaultform.asp?idj=2&amb=69; Ambassador ALOIS BUCHT.

Denmark: 71000 Sarajevo, Splitska 9; tel. (33) 665901; fax (33) 665902; e-mail sijamb@um.dk; internet www.danishembassy.ba; Ambassador JOHANNES DAHL-HANSEN.

Egypt: Sarajevo, Nurudina Gackića 58; tel. (33) 666498; fax (33) 666499; e-mail eg.em.sa@bih.net.ba; Ambassador MUHAMMAD NOUR ELDIN NASRAT.

France: 71000 Sarajevo, Kapetanović Ljubušaka 18; tel. (33) 668149; fax (33) 668103; e-mail france-1@bih.net.ba; internet www .ambafrance.com.ba; Ambassador HENRI ZIPPER DE FABIANI.

Germany: 71000 Sarajevo, ul. Buka 11-13; tel. (33) 275000; fax (33) 652978; e-mail debosara@bih.net.ba; Ambassador FREIHERR VON KIT-TLITZ UND OTTENDORF.

Greece: Sarajevo, Obala Maka Dizdara I; tel. (33) 203516; fax (33) 203512; e-mail greekemb@bih.net.ba; Ambassador MIHAIL KOUKAKIS.

Guinea-Bissau: 71000 Sarajevo, Zmaja od Bosne 6, Hotel Holiday Inn; tel. (33) 288805; Ambassador DESIDERIUS OSTROGON DA COSTA.

Holy See: Pehlivanuša 9, 71000 Sarajevo, Nadbiskupa Josipa Sta-dlera 5; tel. (33) 207847; fax (33) 207863; e-mail nunbosnia@lsinter .net; Apostolic Nuncio Mgr GIUSEPPE LEANZA.

Hungary: 71000 Sarajevo, Hasana Bibera 53; tel. (33) 205302; fax (33) 268930; e-mail kommunikacio@hung-emb.com.ba; internet www.hungemb.ba; Ambassador ISTVÁN VARGA.

Iran: 71000 Sarajevo, Obala Maka Dizdara 6; tel. (33) 650210; fax (33) 663910; e-mail iries1@bih.net.ba; Ambassador SEYED MAHMOUD TABAEE ZAVAREH.

Italy: 71000 Sarajevo, Čekaluša 39; tel. (33) 218022; fax (33) 659368; e-mail ambsara@bih.net.ba; Ambassador ALESSANDRO FALLA-VOLLITO.

Japan: 71000 Sarajevo, Mula Mustafe Bašeskije 2; tel. (33) 209580; fax (33) 209583; Ambassador ITARU UMEZU.

Libya: 71000 Sarajevo, Tahtali sokak 17; tel. (33) 657534; fax (33) 663620; Head of People's Bureau IBRAHIM ALI TAGIURI.

Macedonia, former Yugoslav republic: 71000 Sarajevo, Emerika Bluma 23; tel. and fax (33) 206004; Chargé d'affaires a.i. MIHAILO TRPKOSKI.

Malaysia: 71000 Sarajevo, Trnovska 6; tel. (33) 201578; fax (33) 667713; e-mail malsrjevo@bih.net.ba; Ambassador RAMLAN BIN IBRAHIM.

Malta: 71000 Sarajevo, Mula Mustafe Bašeskije 12; tel. and fax (33) 668632; e-mail lor.tac@tiscalinet.it; Ambassador Dr LORENZO TAC-CHELLA.

Netherlands: 71000 Sarajevo, Obala Kulina Bana 4/2; tel. (33) 668422; fax (33) 668423; e-mail nlgovsar@bih.net.ba; internet www .netherlandsembassy.ba; Ambassador ROBERT BOSSCHER.

Norway: 71000 Sarajevo, Ferhadija 20; tel. (33) 666373; fax (33) 666505; e-mail emb.sarajevo@mfa.no; internet www.norveska.ba; Ambassador HENRIK OFSTAD.

Pakistan: 71000 Sarajevo, Emerika Bluma 17; tel. (33) 211836; fax (33) 211837; e-mail parep@bih.net.ba; Ambassador SHIREEN MOIZ.

Poland: 71000 Sarajevo, Emerika Bluma 27; tel. (33) 201142; fax (33) 233796; Ambassador Dr LESZEK HENSEL.

Romania: 71000 Sarajevo, Tahtali sokak 13–15; tel. (33) 207447; fax (33) 668940; e-mail rumunska@bih.net.ba; Ambassador PETRE CATRINCIUC.

Russia: 71000 Sarajevo, Urjan Dedina 93–95; tel. (33) 668147; fax (33) 668148; Ambassador ALEXANDER S. GRISHCHENKO.

Saudi Arabia: 71000 Sarajevo, Koševo 44; tel. (33) 211861; fax (33) 211744; Ambassador FAHD BIN ABD AL-MUHSIN AZ-ZEIDA.

Serbia and Montenegro: 71000 Sarajevo, Obala Maka Dizdara 3A; tel. (33) 260080; fax (33) 221469; e-mail yugoamba@bih.net.ba; Ambassador STANIMIR VUKIĆEVIĆ.

Slovakia: 71000 Sarajevo, Skopljanska 7; tel. (33) 716440; fax 716410; Ambassador MIROSLAV MOJŽITA.

Slovenia: 71000 Sarajevo, Bendbaša 7; tel. (33) 271260; fax (33) 271270; Ambassador TADEJ LABERNIK.

Spain: 71000 Sarajevo, Čekaluša 16; tel. (33) 278560; fax (33) 208758; Ambassador RAFAEL VALLE GARAGORRI.

Sweden: 71000 Sarajevo, Ferhadija 20; tel. (33) 276030; fax (33) 276060; e-mail ambassaden.sarajevo@foreign.ministry.se; Ambas-sador ANDREAS MÖLLANDER.

Switzerland: 71000 Sarajevo, Josipa Štadlera 15; tel. (33) 275850; fax (33) 570120; e-mail vertretung@sar.rep.admin.ch; Ambassador URS BREITER.

Turkey: 71000 Sarajevo, Hamdije Kreševljakovića 5; tel. and fax (33) 472437; e-mail turksa@bih.net.ba; Ambassador SINA BAYDUR.

United Kingdom: 71000 Sarajevo, Tina Ujevića 8; tel. (33) 444429; fax (33) 666131; e-mail britemb@bih.net.ba; internet www .britishembassy.ba; Ambassador MATTHEW JOHN RYCROFT.

USA: 71000 Sarajevo, Alipašina 43; tel. (33) 445700; fax (33) 659722; e-mail bhopa@state.gov; internet www.sarajevo.usembassy.gov; Ambassador DOUGLAS L. MCELHANEY.

Judicial System

The Constitutional Court of Bosnia and Herzegovina has three international judges (selected by the President of the European Court of Human Rights) and six national judges (of whom four are elected by the Predstavnički dom Federacije and two by the Narodna skupština Republike Srpske). The Constitutional Court has com-petence regarding constitutional matters in both entities, but there are separate judicial systems in the Federation and in Republika Srpska. The judicial system of each entity comprises a Constitu-tional Court, a Supreme Court and local district courts. The Court of Bosnia and Herzegovina, which was officially inaugurated on 27 January 2003, represents the country's highest judicial organ. The eight judges of the Court were appointed by the High Representative of the International Community. A High Judicial and Prosecutorial Council, to regulate the conduct of the judiciary, and to oversee appointments and dismissals of judges and prosecutors, was estab-lished in May 2004. In early June the High Representative appointed 13 national and three international members to the Council.

Court of Bosnia and Herzegovina: Sarajevo; inaugurated Jan. 2003; state-level court and highest judicial organ; comprises eight judges and four prosecutors; Pres. MARTIN RAGUZ.

Constitutional Court of Bosnia and Herzegovina: 71000 Sar-ajevo, Reisa Dzemaludina Causevića 6/III; tel. and fax (33) 663784; e-mail dusan.kalember@ccbh.ba; internet www.ustavnisud.ba; f. 1997; nine mems, incl. four judges; elected for a five-year term; assumed role of fmr Human Rights Chamber in Dec. 2003; Pres. MATO TADIĆ; Sec.-Gen. DUSAN KALEMBER.

FEDERATION OF BOSNIA AND HERZEGOVINA

Constitutional Court of the Federation of Bosnia and Herze-govina: 71000 Sarajevo, Valtera Perića 15; tel. (33) 251650; fax (33) 251651.

Supreme Court of the Federation of Bosnia and Herzegovina: 71000 Sarajevo, Valtera Perića 15; tel. (33) 664751; fax (33) 553754; e-mail vrh.sud@bih.net.ba; internet www.vsfbih.ba; four chambers; Pres. AMIR JAGANJAĆ.

Office of the Federation Prosecutor: 71000 Sarajevo, Valtera Perića 11; tel. (33) 214990; Prosecutor SULJO BABIĆ.

REPUBLIKA SRPSKA

Constitutional Court of Republika Srpska: 78000 Banja Luka, Kralja Alfonsa 11; tel. and fax (51) 301218; e-mail contact@ ustavnisud.org; internet www.ustavnisud.org; eight mems; Pres. RAJKO KUZMANOVIĆ; Sec. MIODRAG SIMOVIĆ.

Supreme Court of Republika Srpska: 78000 Banja Luka; tel. (51) 211690; Pres. JOVO ROSIĆ.

Office of the Republican Prosecutor of Republika Srpska: 78000 Banja Luka, Kralja Petra I Karađorđevića 12; tel. (51) 218827; fax (51) 218834; e-mail rjt@inecco.net; internet www.tuzilastvo-rs .org; Prosecutor AMOR BUKIĆ.

Religion

Bosnia and Herzegovina has a diversity of religious allegiances, although as a result of the conflict of 1992–95, members of the various religious groupings have tended to live in separate regions of Bosnia and Herzegovina. There was widespread destruction of reli-gious monuments and places of worship during the conflict, partic-ularly of mosques and other Islamic sites in the territories that formed Republika Srpska, while the destruction of Roman Catholic and Serbian Orthodox Churches also occurred in several regions of the country. The dominant single religion is Islam. The Reis-ul-ulema, the head of the Muslims in the territory comprising the former Yugoslavia, is resident in Sarajevo. Most of the Muslims are ethnic Muslims or Bosniaks (Slavs who converted to Islam under the Ottomans). There are, however, some ethnic Albanian and Turkish Muslims. Virtually all are adherents of the Sunni persuasion. Approximately one-half of the inhabitants are Christian, but these are divided between the Serbian Orthodox Church and the Roman Catholic Church. There is a small Jewish community; since 1966, however, there has been no rabbi in the community. In June 1997 an agreement to establish an inter-religious council was signed by the leaders of the Roman Catholic, Serbian Orthodox, Jewish and Islamic communities.

ISLAM

Islamic Community of Bosnia and Herzegovina: 71000 Sarajevo, Isa-bega Ishakovica 2; tel. (33) 239404; fax (33) 441573; Reis-ul-ulema Dr MUSTAFA EFENDI CERIĆ.

CHRISTIANITY

The Serbian Orthodox Church

Metropolitan of Dabrobosna: NICOLAJ (MRDA), 71000 Sarajevo, Zelenih Beretki 3; tel. and fax (71) 210518; e-mail info@ mitropolijadabrobosanska.org; internet www .mitropolijadabrobosanska.org.

The Roman Catholic Church

For ecclesiastical purposes, Bosnia and Herzegovina comprises one archdiocese and three dioceses. At 31 December 2002 adherents of the Roman Catholic Church represented about 15.8% of the total population.

Bishops' Conference

71000 Sarajevo, Kaptol 7; tel. (33) 208878; fax (33) 472429; e-mail mata.zovkic@lsinter.com; internet www.vrhbosanska-nadbiskupija .com.

f. 1995; Pres. Rt Rev. FRANJO KOMARICA (Bishop of Banja Luka).

Archbishop of Vrhbosna-Sarajevo: Cardinal VINKO PULJIĆ, 71000 Sarajevo, Kaptol 7; tel. (33) 472430; fax (33) 472429.

JUDAISM

Jewish Community of Bosnia and Herzegovina: 71000 Sarajevo, Hamdije Kreševljekoviće 59; tel. (33) 663472; fax (33) 663473; e-mail jakob_99@yahoo.com; Pres. JAKOB FINCI.

The Press

In 2004 five daily newspapers and several principal weekly, or bi-weekly, newspapers were published.

PRINCIPAL DAILIES

Dnevni Avaz (Daily Herald): 71000 Sarajevo, Džemala Bijedića 185; tel. (33) 281393; fax (33) 281414; e-mail webmaster@avaz.ba; internet www.avaz.ba; f. 1995; Editor-in-Chief SAMIR MUSLIĆ; circ. 15,700 (2001).

Dnevni List (Daily News): 88000 Mostar, Ante Starčevića 56; tel. (36) 313370; e-mail national-holding@tel.net.ba; internet www .dnevni-list.ba.

Glas Srpske (Voice of Republika Srpska): 78000 Banja Luka; fmrly *Glas Srpski*; Editor-in-Chief TOMO MARIĆ; Deputy Editor-in-Chief NIKOLA GUZIJAN.

Jutarnje Novine (Morning News): Sarajevo; e-mail irfan_ljevakovic@jutarnje.ba; internet www.jutarnje,ba; fmrly Vecernje Novine (Evening News); Dir IRFAN LJEVAKOVIĆ; circ. 10,000 (2001).

Nezavisne novine (The Independent): 78000 Banja Luka, Krajiških brigada 8; tel. (51) 331800; fax (51) 331810; e-mail desk@ nezavisne.com; internet www.nezavisne.com; f. 1995; Editor-in-Chief DRAGAN JERINIĆ; circ. 7,500 (2001).

Oslobođenje (Liberation): 71000 Sarajevo, Džemala Bijedića 185; tel. (33) 467723; fax (33) 4680504; e-mail info@oslobodjenje.com.ba; internet www.oslobodjenje.com.ba; f. 1943; morning; Editor-in-Chief SENKA KURTOVIĆ; circ. 15,700 (2001).

WEEKLY NEWSPAPERS

Dani (Days): 71000 Sarajevo, Skenderpašina 4; tel. (33) 220462; fax (33) 651789; e-mail bhdani@bih.net.ba; internet www.bhdani.com; independent; political and cultural; Editor-in-Chief EMIR IMAMOVIĆ; circ. 25,500 (2001).

Hrvatska Riječ (Croat Voice): 71000 Sarajevo, Titova 9A/4; tel. and fax (33) 444621; e-mail h_rijec@bih.net.ba; internet www .hrvatska-rijec.com; Croat weekly; Editor-in-Chief ALENKO ZORNIJA.

Ljiljan: 71000 Sarajevo, Sime Milutinovica Sarajlije 12; tel. (33) 664895; fax (33) 664697; e-mail ljiljan@bih.net.ba; internet www .nipplijljan.com; official newspaper of the PDA; Editor-in-Chief DŽEMALUDIN LATIĆ; circ. 8,000 (2001).

Slobodna Bosna (Free Bosnia): 71000 Sarajevo, Čekaluša Čikma 6; tel. (33) 444041; fax (33) 444895; e-mail info@slobodna-bosna.ba; independent; national and international politics; Editor SENAD AVDIĆ; circ. 28,000 (2001).

Start: 71000 Sarajevo, La Benevolencije 6; tel. and fax (33) 260210; e-mail redakcija@startbih.info; internet www.startbih.info; independent; Editor NIK DENAMEDA.

PERIODICALS

Buka: 88000 Banja Luka; tel. and fax (51) 319130; e-mail info@6yka .com; internet www.6yka.com; internet magazine published by the Banja Luka Centre for Informational Decontamination of the Young (Centar za informativnu dekontaminaciju mladih iz Banjaluke); Editor-in-Chief ALEKSANDAR TRIFUNOVIĆ.

Feniks (Phoenix): 88000 Mostar, Camp Ortijes; tel. and fax (36) 352064; e-mail feniks_magazine@yahoo.com; internet www.feniks .co.ba; current affairs, culture, science and technology; supports closer integration of Bosnia and Herzegovina with the European Union; Editor-in-Chief Lt-Col HOLGER FLÖGE.

Naša Ognjišta—Hrvatski katolički mjesečnik (Our Hearth—Croat Catholic Monthly): 80240 Tomislavgrad, trg fra Mije Čuića 1; tel. (34) 352295; fax (34) 352808; e-mail nasa.ognjista@tel.net.ba; monthly; Editor-in-Chief GABRIJEL MIOČ.

Reporter: 78000 Banja Luka, Grčka 20; tel. (51) 221220; fax (51) 221228; e-mail rep@inecco.net; f. 1996; independent; Editor PERICA VUCINIĆ.

Svjetlo Riječi (Light of the Word): 71000 Sarajevo, Zagrebačka 18; tel. (33) 726200; fax (33) 661364; e-mail svjetlo@svjetlorijeci.ba; internet www.svjetlorijeci.ba; f. 1983; Franciscan; monthly; Dir PETAR MATANOVIĆ; Editor-in-Chief ZDRAVKO KUJUNDŽIJA.

NEWS AGENCIES

Federal News Agency (FENA): Sarajevo, Cemalusa 1; tel. (33) 445247; e-mail direktor@fena.ba; internet www.fena.ba; f. 2000 by Federation Govt; Dir ZEHRUDIN ISAKOVIĆ; Editor-in-Chief ZORAN ILIĆ.

ONASA (Oslobođenje News Agency): 71000 Sarajevo, Zmaja od Bosna 4; tel. (33) 276580; fax (33) 276899; e-mail onasa@onasa.com .ba; internet www.onasa.com.ba; f. 1994; Gen. Man. MEHMED HUSIĆ.

SNRA—Srpska Novinska Agentsija (News Agency of Republika Srpska): 75320 Bijeljina, Sofke Nikolić 66; tel. (55) 201819; fax (55) 201810; e-mail : redakcija@srna.co.yu; internet www.srna.co.yu; f. 1992; bureaux in Banja Luka and East Sarajevo (Republika Srpska); Man. Dir DRAGAN DAVIDOVIĆ.

Publishers

Novi Glas (New Voice): 78000 Banja Luka, Borisa Kidriča 1; tel. (51) 12766; fax (51) 12758; general literature; Dir MIODRAG ŽIVANOVIĆ.

JP NIO Službeni List BiH Sarajevo (Co for Newspaper Publication Organization, Official Gazette of Bosnia and Herzegovina, Sarajevo): 71000 Sarajevo, Magribija 3; tel. (33) 663470; e-mail slist@bih.net.ba; internet www.sllist.ba; publishes legislation and other official publications; Dir MEHMEDALIJA HUREMOVIĆ.

Svjetlost (Light): 71000 Sarajevo, Petra Preradovića 3; tel. (33) 212144; fax (33) 272352; internet www.svjetlost.ba; f. 1945; text-books and literature, religion; Dir SAVO ZIROJEVIĆ.

TKD Šahinpašić: 71000 Sarajevo, Soukbunar 12; tel. (33) 220111; fax (33) 668856; e-mail info@btcsahinpasic.com; internet www .btcsahinpasic.com; f. 1989; publishers, importers exporters and retailers of books; Dir-Gen. TAJIB ŠAHINPAŠIĆ.

Veselin Masleša: 71000 Sarajevo, Obala Kulina Bana 4; tel. (33) 521476; fax (33) 272369; f. 1950; school and university textbooks, general literature; Dir RADOSLAV MIJATOVIĆ.

Zoro (Sarajevo): 71000 Sarajevo, Šenoina 14; tel. and fax (33) 214454; e-mail zorosa@bih.net.ba; internet www.zoro.hr; f. 1994 in Zagreb (Croatia); Dir SAMIR FAZLIĆ.

PUBLISHERS' ASSOCIATION

Asscn of Publishers and Booksellers of Bosnia and Herzegovina: 71000 Sarajevo, Zmaja od Bosne 8B; tel. (33) 213435; fax (33) 266630; e-mail bedita@nub.ba; Pres. IBRAHIM SPAHIĆ; Gen. Sec. B. ISLAMOVIĆ.

Broadcasting and Communications

TELECOMMUNICATIONS

Three principal service providers of telecommunications operate in Bosnia and Herzegovina: BH Telecom, which operates chiefly in Sarajevo and in Bosniak-majority cantons of the Federation; HT Mostar in Croat-majority cantons of the Federation; and Telekom Sprkse in Republika Srpska.

BH Telecom: 71000 Sarajevo, Zmaja od Bosna 8; tel. (33) 444123; fax (33) 656500; internet www.telecom.ba; Dir Jasminko Aksamija.

BH Mobile (GSMBIH): 71000 Sarajevo, Zmaja od Bosna 8; tel. (33) 444555; fax (33) 447960; e-mail gsm.podrska@telecom.ba; internet www.bhtelecom.ba/bhmobile.html; f. 1996; mobile cellular communications.

Hrvatske telekomunikacije Mostar (HT Mostar): 88000 Mostar, Kneza Branimira; tel. and fax (36) 395555; e-mail info@ht .ba; internet www.ht.ba; Dir Stipe Prlić.

Eronet: 88000 Mostar, Tvrtka Miloša bb; tel. (39) 663311; fax (39) 663391; e-mail info@eronet.ba; tel. www.eronet.ba; internet www .eronet.ba; f. 1996; 51% owned by Hrvatske Telekomunikacije Mostar, 49% owned by Hrvatski Telecom (Croatia); mobile cellular telecommunications; provides coverage in Western, Southern, Central and Northern regions of Bosnia and Herzegovina.

Telekom Srpske: Banja Luka, Kralja Petra I Karađorđevića 61A; tel. (51) 240100; fax (51) 211150; e-mail ts.office@telekom-rs.com; internet www.telekomsrpske.com; CEO Slavisha Krunić.

Mobi's: 78000 Banja Luka, Mladena Stojanovića 4; tel. ; fax ; e-mail s.markovic@telekomsrpske.com; internet www.065mobis .com; mobile cellular communications; provides coverage in a majority of regions of Bosnia and Herzegovina; f. 1999; Dir Nebojša Milovčević (acting); 506,500 subscribers (2003).

BROADCASTING

In 2002 there were 183 licensed broadcasters in Bosnia and Herzegovina (42 television stations and 141 radio stations), in addition to three nationwide public broadcasters comprising: the Public Broadcasting Service of BiH (PBS BiH); Radio and Television of the Federation of Bosnia and Herzegovina (RTV FBiH); and Radio and Television of Republika Srpska. In total, there were 78 public and 105 private broadcasting media outlets in the country, of which there were 16 public and 26 private television stations, and 62 public and 79 private radio stations.

Regulatory Authority

At the decision of the High Representative for Bosnia and Herzegovina, the Communication Regulatory Authority was established in 2001 through the merger of the former Independent Media Commission, which had regulated the broadcasting sector, and the Telecommunication Regulatory Agency, responsible for telecommunications. The new regulatory body was to have jurisdiction over both broadcasting and telecommunications as an independent state agency.

Communication Regulatory Agency (CRA) (Regulatorna agencija za komunikacije—RAK): Sarajevo, Vilsonovo setaliste 10; tel. (33) 250600; fax (33) 713080; e-mail info@rak.ba; internet www.rak .ba; f. 2001; Dir-Gen. Kemal Huseinović.

Radio

Public Broadcasting Service of Bosnia and Herzegovina (Javni RTV Servis Bosne i Hercegovina): 71000 Sarajevo, Bulevar Meše Selimovića 12; tel. (33) 461101; fax (33) 461569; e-mail drago .maric@pbsbih.ba; internet www.pbsbih.ba; f. 1969; 2 TV programmes; incorporated news channel (BHTV 1) in 2002; Dir-Gen. Drago Marić; Dir of TV Milan Trivić; Dir of Radio Sabina Bačvić.

Radio of the Federation of Bosnia and Herzegovina (Radio Federacije Bosne i Hercegovine): 71000 Sarajevo, Mesa Selimovica 12; tel. (33) 455102; fax (33) 455103; e-mail esadc@rtvbih.ba; internet www.rtvbih.ba?Program/radio%20FBiH; Dir Cerović Esad.

Radio-Televizija Republike Srpske (RTRS) (Radio and Television of Republika Srpska): 78000 Banja Luka, Kralja Petra I Karađorđevića 129; tel. (51) 317661; internet www.rtrs.tv; Dir-Gen. Aleksandar Tijanić.

Bosnian Radio Network (Bosanska Radio Mreža—BORAM): 71000 Sarajevo, Cumurija 2; tel. (33)202099; fax (33) 261231; e-mail web@bih.net.ba; internet www.web1.bih.net.ba; network of 20 local stations; nationwide broadcasts from 2002.

Radio Kameleon: 75000 Tuzla, Milana Jovanovića 6; tel. and fax (35) 250055; e-mail kameleon@kameleon.ba; internet www .kameleon.ba; f. 1992; independent radio station; Gen. Dir Zlatko Berbić.

Radio Q: 71300 Visoko, ul. Hazima Dedića 13; tel. and fax (32) 735280; fax (32) 735280; e-mail radioq@radioq.co.ba; internet www .radioq.co.ba.

Radio Slon (Radio Elephant): 75000 Tuzla, ul. S. Karamehmedović 39; tel. (35) 205530; fax (35) 250053; e-mail redakcija@radioslon.ba; internet www.radioslon.ba; f. 1995; Dir Šaban Pirić.

Radio ZID: 71000 Sarajevo, Husrefa Redzica 8; commenced broadcasts March 1993; independent radio station; cultural and educative programmes; broadcasts to Sarajevo and to neighbouring areas in Federation of Bosnia and Herzegovina and in Republika Srpska; Chair. Zdravko Grebo; Editor-in-Chief Vlado Azinović.

Studio 99: Sarajevo; e-mail redakcija@ntv99.ba; internet www .ntv99.ba; f. 1995; independent radio and tv station; political and current affairs; Editor-in-Chief Adil Kulenović; Editor of Programmes Erina Gakić.

Television

Public Broadcasting Service of Bosnia and Herzegovina (Javni RTV Servis Bosne i Hercegovina): 71000 Sarajevo, Bulevar Meše Selimovića 12; tel. (33) 461101; fax (33) 461569; e-mail drago .maric@pbsbih.ba; internet www.pbsbih.ba; f. 1969; 2 TV programmes; incorporated news channel (BHTV 1) in 2002; Dir-Gen. Drago Marić; Dir of TV Milan Trivić; Dir of Radio Sabina Bačvić.

Federation of Bosnia and Herzegovina Television (Federalna Televizija BiH—FTV): Mese Selimovica 12, Sarajevo; tel. (33) 462511; fax (33) 455148; e-mail tvdesk02@rtvfbih.ba.

Radio-Televizija Republike Srpske (RTRS) (Radio and Television of Republika Srpska): 78000 Banja Luka, Kralja Petra I Karađorđevića 129; tel. (51) 317661; internet www.rtrs.tv; Dir-Gen. Aleksandar Tijanić.

Alternativna Televizija Informisanje: 78000 Banja Luka, Kralja Petra I Karađorđeva 2; tel. and fax (51) 320770; e-mail info@atvbl .com; internet www.atvbl.com; f. 1996; Dir Nataša Tešanović.

NTV Hayat: 71000 Sarajevo, Avdage Sahinagica 14; tel. (33) 271110; fax (33) 271111; e-mail ntvhayat@ntvhayat.com; internet www.ntvhayat.com; f. 1991; broadcasts 18 hours daily; Dir-Gen. Elvir Švrakić.

Zetel: Stara čaršija bb, 72000 Zenica; tel. (32) 403900; fax (32) 284076; e-mail zetel@bih.net.ba; f. 1992; independent; transmits 13 hours per day to Zenica and surrounding area; cultural, political, educational and sports programmes; Dir Željko Lincner.

Finance

(cap. = capital; res = reserves; dep. = deposits; m. = million; amounts in konvertibilna marka (KM or convertible marks); brs = branches)

BANKING

At the end of 2004 33 banks were operating in Bosnia and Herzegovina (compared with 76 in 1997), with the largest 10 banks holding about 85% of the system's deposits.

Central Bank

Central Bank of Bosnia and Herzegovina: 71000 Sarajevo, 25 Maršala Tita; tel. (33) 278100; fax (33) 278299; e-mail contact@cbbh .gov.ba; internet www.cbbh.gov.ba; replaced the National Bank of the Federation of Bosnia and Herzegovina, and the National Bank of Republika Srpska, which ceased monetary operations in Aug. 1997; cap. and res 213.7m., total assets 2,742.0m. (Nov. 2003); Gov. Kemal Kozarić.

Selected Banks

ABS Banka d.d. Sarajevo: 71000 Sarajevo, Trampina 12/6; tel. (33) 277060; fax (33) 667674; e-mail abs@absbanka.com; internet www.absbanka.ba; f. 1991; cap. 16.6m., res 1.2m., dep. 87.1m. (2003); Gen. Man. Adnan Zukić.

Balkan Investment Bank a.d.: 78000 Banja Luka, Krajških Brigada 2; tel. (51) 216285; fax (51) 211445; e-mail contact@ balkaninvestment.com; internet www.balkaninvestment.com; f. 2000; cap. 18.0m., res 0.3m., dep. 23.1m. (Dec. 2003); Chair. Liu-Tauras Varanavičius.

Bobar Banka a.d.: 76300 Bijeljina, Njegoseva 1; tel. (55) 211153; fax (55) 401863; e-mail office@bobarbanka.com; internet www.bobar .com; f. 1998; cap. 15.1m., res 0.1m., dep. 15.1m. (Dec. 2003); Gen. Man. Dragan Radumilo.

Bosna Bank International d.d. Sarajevo: 71000 Sarajevo, trg Djece Sarajeva b.b.; tel. (33) 275131; fax (33) 472159; e-mail info@bbi .ba; internet www.bbi.ba; Islamic bank; f. 2000; cap. 45.3m., dep. 20.3m. (2003); Dr Abdul Rahman Ahmed Yusuf Abdulmalek.

Central Profit Banka d.d. Sarajevo: Sarajeva, Zelenih Beretki 24; tel. (33) 663307; fax (33) 238340; e-mail international@cpb.ba; internet www.cpb.ba; f. 1919; cap. 10.7m., res 4.1m., dep. 261.6m. (2001); Gen. Man. FEHIM F. KAPIDŽIĆ; 13 brs.

Hypo Alpe-Adria-Bank a.d. Banja Luka: 78000 Banja Luka, 1 F. Jukica 9; tel. (51) 241800; fax (51) 212878; e-mail bank.bl.bih@hypo-alpe-adria.com; internet www.hypo-alpe-adria.com; f. 2002; cap. 44.0m., res 6.8m., dep. 143.4m. (2002); Chair. KURT MAKULA.

Hypo Alpe-Adria Bank d.d.: 88000 Mostar, Kneza Branimira 2B; tel. and fax (36) 444235; fax (36) 444235; e-mail bank.bih@hypo-alpe-adria.com; internet www.hypo-alpe-adria.ba; f. 1999 as Auro banka d.d. Vitez; name changed in 2000; cap. 70.0m., res 0.1m., dep. 694.7m. (2003); Pres. GÜNTER STRIEDINGER.

Investiciono-Komercijalna Banka d.d., Zenica: 72000 Zenica, POB 62, trg Samoupravljača 1; tel. (32) 401804; fax (32) 417022; e-mail ikbsejo@ikbze.com.ba; internet www.ikbze.com.ba; f. 1990; cap. 10.7m., res 7.0m., dep. 76.4m. (Dec. 2000); Gen. Man. UZEIR FETIĆ.

LHB Banka a.d. Banja Luka: 78000 Banja Luka, Milana Tepica 4; tel. (51) 221610; fax (51) 221623; e-mail info@vbbanka.com; internet www.vbbanka.com; f. 1998 as VB Banka a.d. Banja Luka; name changed as above 2004; cap. 16.8m., res 1.0m., dep. 63.4m. (2003); Gen. Man. RADOVAN BAJIĆ.

Nova Banka a.d., Bijeljina: 76300 Bijeljina, ul. Svetog Save br. 46; tel. (55) 201409; fax (55) 201410; e-mail office@novabanka.com; internet www.novabanka.com; f. 1992 as Export Banka a.d. Bijeljina; name changed 1999; cap. 17.0m., res 2.0m., dep. 104.0m. (2003); Pres. MIHAJLO VIDIĆ; Chair. ZIVOJIN KRAJISNIK.

Privredna Banka Sarajevo d.d., Sarajevo: 71000 Sarajevo, Alipašina 6; tel. (33) 277700; fax (33) 210360; e-mail pbscba22@bih.net.ba; f. 1971; cap. 10.3m., res 1.1m., dep. 58.1m. (Dec. 2002); Gen. Man. MEVSUDIN DREKOVIĆ; 14 brs.

ProCredit Bank d.d.: 71000 Sarajevo, Sime Mlutinovica Sarajlije 4; tel. (33) 250950; fax (33) 250971; e-mail procreditbank@procreditbank.ba; internet www.procreditbank.ba; f. 1997 as Micro Enterprise Bank d.d. Sarajevo; name changed as above 2003; cap. 15.7m., res 2.5m., dep. 20.7m. (2003); Dir BOB ASSENBERG.

Raiffeisen Bank HPB d.d. Bosna i Hercegovina: 71000 Sarajevo, Danijela Ozme 3; tel. (33) 287100; fax (33) 213851; e-mail info.rbbh@rbb-sarajevo.raiffeisen.at; internet www.raiffeisenbank.ba; f. 1992 as Market Banka d.d.; name changed in 2000; cap. 49.3m., res 42.4m., dep. 1,247.3m. (2003); Pres. Dr HEBERT STEPIĆ.

Razvojna Banka Jugoistočne Evrope a.d. Banja Luka: 78000 Banja Luka, Kralja Petra I Karađorđevica 85A; tel. (51) 242100; fax (51) 242192; e-mail rb@razvojnabanka.com; internet www.razvojnabanka.com; f. 1997; present namesince 2002; cap. 19.9m., res 0.4m., dep. 180.9m. (2003); Pres. MIROSLAV DJORDJEVIĆ.

Turkish Ziraat Bank Bosnia d.d.: 71000 Sarajevo, Ferhadija 29/5; tel. (33) 252230; fax (33) 252245; e-mail ziraat@bih.net.ba; internet www.ziraatbosnia.com; f. 1996; cap. 25.0m., res 8.5m., dep. 21.0m. (Dec. 2003); Chair. MEHMET ZEKI SAYIN.

Tuzlanska Banka d.d. Tuzla: 75000 Tuzla, Maršala Tita 34; tel. (35) 259259; fax (35) 250596; e-mail tuzbank@bih.net.ba; internet www.tuzbank.ba; f. 1990; cap. 17.7m., res 8.4m., dep. 210.3m. (2003); Chair. IBRAHIM MORANKIĆ; 16 brs.

UniCredit Zagrebačka Banka d.d.: 88000 Mostar, Kardinala Štepinca b.b.; tel. (36) 312112; fax (36) 312129; e-mail zababh@zaba.hr; internet www.zaba.ba; f. 1992 as Hrvatska Banka d.d. Mostar; name changed to Zagrebačka Banka BH d.d. 2000; merged with Universal Banka d.d. Sarajevo and name changed as above July 2004; cap. 45.6m., res 18.8m., dep. 599.0m. (Dec. 2003); Chair. ZVONIMIR JURJEVIĆ.

Union Banka d.d. Sarajevo: 71000 Sarajevo, Dubrovačka 6; tel. (33) 664470; fax (33) 219201; e-mail unionban@bih.net.ba; f. 1955; cap. 34.1m., res 17.1m., dep. 59.4m. (2003); Pres. ESAD BEKTEŠEVIĆ.

Volksbank BH d.d.: 71000 Sarajevo, Fra Andjela Zvizdovića 1; tel. (33) 483265; fax (33) 263832; e-mail info@volksbank.ba; internet www.volksbank.ba; cap. 20.0m., dep. 133.1m. (2001); Gen. Man. Dr PETER SETZER.

Banking Agencies

Banking Agency of the Federation of Bosnia and Herzegovina (Agencija za Bankarstvo Federacije Bosne i Hercegovine): 71000 Sarajevo, Koševo 3; tel. (33) 721400; fax (33) 668811; e-mail public@fba.ba; internet www.fba.ba; f. 1996; Chair. ELDAR ARNAUTOVIĆ; Dir ZLATKO BARS.

Banking Agency of Republika Srpska (Agencija za Bankarstvo Republike Srpske): 78000 Banja Luka, Vase Pelagića 11A; tel. (51) 218111; fax (51) 216665; e-mail office@abrs.ba; internet www.abrs.ba; f. 1998; Chair. of Bd NOVO PLAKALOVIĆ; Dir DUSHANKA NOVAKOVIĆ.

STOCK EXCHANGE

Sarajevo Stock Exchange: 71000 Sarajevo, Zvizdovića 1; tel. (33) 251462; fax (33) 251478; e-mail uprava@sase.ba; internet www.sase.ba; f. 2002; Dir-Gen. ALMIR BEGIĆ.

Trade and Industry

GOVERNMENT AGENCIES

Foreign Investment Promotion Agency of Bosnia and Herzegovina: 71000 Sarajevo, Branilaca Sarajeva 21; tel. (33) 278000; fax (33) 278081; e-mail fipa@fipa.gov.ba; internet www.fipa.gov.ba; f. 1999; Gen. Dir MIRZA HAJRIĆ.

Federation of Bosnia and Herzegovina

Privatization Agency of the Federation of Bosnia and Herzegovina: Sarajevo, Alipašina 41; tel. (33) 212884; fax (33) 212883; e-mail apfbih@bih.net.ba; internet www.apf.com.ba; Dir ADNAN MUJAGIĆ.

Securities Commission of the Federation of Bosnia and Herzegovina (Komisija za vrijednosne papire Federacije Bosne i Hercegovine): 71000 Sarajevo, Ćemaluša 9; tel. (33) 665897; fax (33) 211655; e-mail komvp@komvp.gov.ba; internet www.komvp.gov.ba; f. 1999; Pres. HASAN ČELAM.

Republika Srpska

Republika Srpksa Directorate for Privatization: 78000 Banja Luka, Mladena Stoganovića 4; tel. (51) 308311; fax (51) 311245; e-mail dip@inecco.net; internet www.rsprivatizacija.com; Dir BORISLAV OBRADOVIĆ.

Republika Srpska Securities Commission (Komisija za khartije od vrijednosti Republike Srpske): 78000 Banja Luka, Vuka Karadžića 6; tel. (51) 218361; fax (51) 218362; e-mail kontakt@khov-rs.org; internet www.khov-rs.org/Index.htm; Pres. BRANKA BODROŽA.

DEVELOPMENT ORGANIZATIONS

Central Bosnia Local Economic Development Agency (Centralno Bosanska Agencija za Ekonomski Razvoj—CeBEDA): 72000 Travnik, Zenjak 21B; tel. (32) 511877; fax (32) 818945; e-mail lebeda@bih.net.ba; internet www.ilsleda.com; f. 1998; Dir MIROSLAV RADOŠ.

Directorate for the Reconstruction and Development of Sarajevo Canton (Zavod za planiranje i razvoja Kantona Sarajeva): 71000 Sarajevo, Branilaca Sarajeva 26; tel. (33) 664347; fax (33) 209543; e-mail webmaster@zavodzpr-sa.ba; internet www.zavodzpr-sa.ba; involved in assisting reconstruction projects in both Sarajevo Canton and Sarajevo City (Federation of Bosnia and Herzegovina); Dir SAID JAMAKOVIĆ.

Federation of Bosnia and Herzegovina Federal Development Planning Institution (Federacija BiH Federalni zavod za programiranje razvoja): Sarajevo, Alipašina 41; tel. (33) 667272; fax (33) 212625; e-mail info@fzzpr.gov.ba; internet www.fzzpr.gov.ba; Dir Prof. NEŠET MUMINAGIĆ.

CHAMBERS OF COMMERCE

Chamber of Commerce of Bosnia and Herzegovina (Privredna Komora BiH): 71000 Sarajevo, Branislava Đurđeva 10; tel. (33) 663631; fax (33) 663632; e-mail cis@komorabih.com; internet www.komorabih.com; Pres. MILAN LOVRIĆ.

Chamber of Commerce of the Federation of Bosnia and Herzegovina—Sarajevo (Privredna Komora FBiH—Sarajevo): 71000 Sarajevo, Branislava Đurđeva 10; tel. (33) 217782; fax (33) 217783; e-mail info@kfbih.com; internet www.kfbih.com; Pres. JASO LASIĆ.

Chamber of Commerce of the Federation of Bosnia and Herzegovina—Mostar (Privredna Komora FBiH—Mostar): 88000 Mostar, Zagrebačka 10; tel. (36) 332963; fax (36) 332966; e-mail gkfbih@tel.net.ba; internet www.kfbih.com; Sec. ŽELJANA BEVANDA.

Chamber of Commerce of Republika Srpska (Privredna komora RS): 78000 Banja Luka, Đure Daničića 1; tel. (51) 215744; fax (51) 215565; internet www.pkrs.inecco.net; Pres. MLADEN MIČIĆ.

Sarajevo Canton Chamber of Commerce (Privredna Komora Kantona Sarajevo): 71000 Sarajevo, La Benevolencije 8; tel. (33) 250100; fax (33) 250137; e-mail webmaster@pksa.com.ba; internet www.pksa.com.ba; Pres. KEMAL GREBO.

UTILITIES

Electricity

Elektroprivreda BiH: 71000 Sarajevo, Vilsonovo Šetalište 15; tel. and fax (33) 751000; fax (33) 751008; e-mail e.kreso@elektroprivreda .ba; internet www.elektroprivreda.ba; generation, transmission and distribution of electric energy; Dir-Gen. ENVER KRESO.

Gas

BH-Gas: 71000 Sarajevo, Hamdije Cemerlića 2; tel. (33) 279000; fax (33) 661621; e-mail management@bh-gas.ba; internet www.bh-gas .ba; f. 1997; Man. Dir ALMIR BEČAREVIĆ.

Water

Vodno Područje Slivova Rijeke Save: 71000 Sarajevo, ul. Grbavička 4/3; tel. (33) 209827; fax (33) 209903; e-mail info@voda.ba; internet www.voda.ba.

TRADE UNIONS

Confederation of Independent Trade Unions of Bosnia and Herzegovina (Savez samostalnih sindikata Bosne i Hercegovine — SSSBiH): 71000 Sarajevo, Obala Kulina Bana 1; tel. (33) 202029; fax (33) 664872.

Confederation of Trade Unions of Republika Srpska (Savez sindikata Republike Srpske—SSRS): 78000 Banja Luka, Srpska 32; tel. (51) 310711; fax (51) 304241; Chair. ČEDO BOLAŠ.

Transport

RAILWAYS

At the beginning of the 1990s the railway system consisted of some 1,030 km of track, of which 75% was electrified. Much of the system was damaged or destroyed during the civil war, but in July 1996 the Sarajevo–Mostar service was restored and in 1997 the Tuzla–Doboj service reopened. The Tuzla–Brčko service resumed in 2002. Following the outbreak of hostilities in 1992, the state railway company was divided into three regional state-owned companies: the Bosnia and Herzegovina Railway (ŽBH); the Herzeg-Bosnia Railway(ŽHB); and the Republika Srpska Railway (ZhRS), based in Doboj. In 1998 ŽBH and ŽHB were merged to form Railways of the Federation of Bosnia and Herzegovina(ŽFBH). In March 2000 the Presidents of Bosnia and Herzegovina and Croatia signed an agreement to recommence railway traffic between the two countries. By the end of that year post-war reconstruction assistance had resulted in the restoration of about 85% of track; however, by 2004 only limited passenger services were operating.

Željeznice Federacije Bosne i Hercegovine (ŽFBH) (Railways of the Federation of Bosnia and Herzegovina): 71000 Sarajevo, Musala 2; tel. (33) 663719; fax (33) 650075; e-mail zbh@bih.net.ba.

Zheleznice Republike Srpske (ZhRS) (Railways of Republika Srpska): 74000 Doboj, Svetog Save 71; tel. and fax (53) 224050.

ROADS

The transport infrastructure in Bosnia and Herzegovina was badly damaged during the conflict of 1992–95. Some 35% of the country's roads and 40% of its bridges were affected by the conflict. A new Transportation Corporation was established (with its headquarters in Sarajevo), under the terms of the Dayton accords, in order to organize and operate roads, ports and railways on the territory of the two entities. The agreement also provided for the construction of a new road linking the Goražde enclave, east of Sarajevo, with the rest of the Federation. There were 21,846 km of roads in Bosnia and Herzegovina in 2001, of which 14,020 km were paved. In 1997 an internationally-funded project to rehabilitate and rebuild the road network in Republika Srpska commenced. In June 2000 the Governments of Bosnia and Herzegovina and Croatia signed an accord on the construction of the Ploče–Budapest corridor.

Federation Ministry of Transport and Communications: 71000 Sarajevo, Alipašina 41; tel. (33) 668907; fax (33) 667866; internet www.fmpik.gov.ba.

Republika Srpska Directorate for Roads: 78000 Banja Luka, Vase Pelagića 10; tel. (51) 309061; fax (51) 308316; Dir NEMANJA VASIĆ.

Centrotrans-Eurolines BiH: 71000 Sarajevo, Mula Mustafa Bašeskije 5; tel. (33) 464045; fax (33) 464040; e-mail info@centrotrans .com; internet www.centrotrans.com; f. 1963; principal provider of inter-city passenger coach services; Dir M. SACIRAGIĆ.

CIVIL AVIATION

The country has an international airport at Sarajevo, and three smaller civil airports, at Tuzla, Banja Luka and Mostar. Civil aviation was severely disrupted by the 1992–95 civil war. Commercial flights resumed to Sarajevo in August 1996, to Banja Luka in November 1997 and to Mostar in July 1998. There are regular flights to and from Sarajevo from various cities in Northern, Central and Eastern Europe.

Department of Civil Aviation of Bosnia and Herzegovina: 33000 Sarajevo, Envera Sehovića 2; tel. (33) 653016; fax (33) 653008; e-mail bhdca@bhdca.gov.ba; internet www.bhdca.gov.ba.

Sarajevo International Airport: 71210 Sarajevo, Kurta Schorka 36; tel. (33) 289202; fax (33) 289201; e-mail opc@sarajevo-airport.ba; internet www.sarajevo-airport.ba.

Tourism

Tourism was adversely affected as a result of the war of 1992–95 and subsequent instability, as well as by the destruction or damage of many historic monuments, and by the prevalence of landmines in many regions. Although the tourist infrastructure remained underdeveloped in the mid-2000s, Bosnia and Herzegovina has many sites of potential interest to tourists, including mountain scenery, ski resorts and spas, rivers and waterfalls, the historic cities of Sarajevo, Mostar, Travnik, Trebinje and Jajce, and one resort on the Adriatic Sea, at Neum. A film festival has been held annually in Sarajevo since 1995. Tourist arrivals increased from 139,000 in 2001 to an estimated 160,000 in 2002. Receipts from tourism totalled an estimated US $112m. in 2002.

Tourism Asscn of the Federation of Bosnia and Herzegovina: 71000 Sarajevo, Ćumurija 5; tel. (33) 200582; fax (33) 532281; e-mail tour.off@bih.net.ba; internet www.tourism.ba.

Ministry of Trade and Tourism of Republika Srpska: 78000 Banja Luka, Vuka Karadžica 4; tel. (51) 331523; fax (51) 331499; e-mail mtt@mtt.vladars.net.

BOTSWANA

Introductory Survey

Location, Climate, Language, Religion, Flag, Capital

The Republic of Botswana is a land-locked country in southern Africa, with South Africa to the south and east, Zimbabwe to the north-east and Namibia to the west and north. A short section of the northern frontier adjoins Zambia. The climate is generally sub-tropical, with hot summers. Annual rainfall averages about 457 mm (18 ins), varying from 635 mm (25 ins) in the north to 228 mm (9 ins) or less in the western Kalahari desert. The country is largely near-desert, and most of its inhabitants live along the eastern border, close to the main railway line. English is the official language, and Setswana the national language. Most of the population follow traditional animist beliefs, but several Christian churches are also represented. The national flag (proportions 2 by 3) consists of a central horizontal stripe of black, edged with white, between two blue stripes. The capital is Gaborone.

Recent History

Botswana was formerly Bechuanaland, which became a British protectorate, at the request of the local rulers, in 1885. It was administered as one of the High Commission Territories in southern Africa, the others being the colony of Basutoland (now Lesotho) and the protectorate of Swaziland. The British Act of Parliament that established the Union of South Africa in 1910 also allowed for the inclusion in South Africa of the three High Commission Territories, on condition that the local inhabitants were consulted. Until 1960 successive South African Governments asked for the transfer of the three territories, but the native chiefs always objected to such a scheme.

Within Bechuanaland, gradual progress was made towards self-government, mainly through nominated advisory bodies. A new Constitution was introduced in December 1960, and a Legislative Council (partly elected, partly appointed) first met in June 1961. Bechuanaland was made independent of High Commission rule in September 1963, and the office of High Commissioner was abolished in August 1964. On 1 March 1965 internal self-government was achieved, and the territory's first direct election, for a Legislative Assembly, was held on the basis of universal adult suffrage. Of the Assembly's 31 seats, 28 were won by the Bechuanaland Democratic Party (BDP or Domkrag), founded in 1962. The leader of the BDP, Seretse Khama, was sworn in as the territory's first Prime Minister. Bechuanaland became the independent Republic of Botswana, within the Commonwealth, on 30 September 1966, with Sir Seretse Khama (as he had become) taking office as the country's first President, while the Legislative Assembly was renamed the National Assembly. The BDP, restyled the Botswana Democratic Party at independence, won elections to the National Assembly, with little opposition, in 1969, 1974 and 1979.

Upon Khama's death in July 1980, Dr Quett Masire (later Sir Ketumile Masire), hitherto Vice-President and Minister of Finance, was appointed to the presidency. Following elections to the National Assembly in September 1984, at which the BDP again achieved a decisive victory, Masire was re-elected President by the legislature. However, the BDP fared badly in local government elections, which were held simultaneously with the parliamentary elections, apparently reflecting discontent at the country's high level of unemployment. An unprecedented outbreak of rioting, in March 1987, was similarly attributed by observers to popular dissatisfaction with the Government as a result of increasing unemployment. At a referendum in September a large majority endorsed amendments to the electoral system, as defined by the Constitution, although the principal opposition party, the Botswana National Front (BNF), boycotted the vote.

Despite widespread labour unrest during 1989, in October the BDP received 65% of the votes cast at a general election to the National Assembly, winning 27 of the 30 elective seats (the remaining three seats were won by the BNF), and the new legislature re-elected Masire for a third term as President. In November 1991 the Government dismissed some 12,000 members of public-service trade unions who had been campaigning for wage increases.

In March 1992 the Vice-President and Chairman of the BDP, Peter Mmusi, resigned as Vice-President and Minister of Local Government and Lands, while the party's Secretary-General, Daniel Kwelagobe, resigned as Minister of Agriculture, having been accused of corruption involving the illegal transfer of land. Festus Mogae, the Minister of Finance and Development Planning, was appointed as the new Vice-President. In June Mmusi and Kwelagobe were suspended from the Central Committee of the BDP; both were, however, re-elected to their former positions within the party in July 1993. In July 1995 the Minister of Presidential Affairs and Public Administration, Ponatshego Kedikilwe, was elected Chairman of the BDP—a post that had remained vacant since the death of Mmusi in October 1994.

At the general election held in October 1994 the BDP, which received 53.1% of the votes cast, won 26 of the 40 available seats, while the BNF, which obtained 37.7% of the votes, increased its representation to 13 seats. More than 70% of registered voters participated in the election. The BDP remained dominant in rural areas, while the BNF received strong support in urban constituencies. The National Assembly subsequently re-elected Masire to the presidency.

In August 1997 the National Assembly formally adopted a constitutional amendment restricting the presidential mandate to two terms of office and providing for the automatic succession to the presidency of the Vice-President, in the event of the death or resignation of the President. In September a national referendum endorsed further revisions, lowering the age of eligibility to vote from 21 to 18 years and providing for the establishment of an independent electoral commission. In November Masire announced his intention to retire from politics in March 1998. In accordance with the amended Constitution, Vice-President Mogae was inaugurated as President on 1 April 1998, pending elections to be held in 1999, and subsequently appointed a new Cabinet, in which the only new minister was Lt-Gen. Seretse Ian Khama, son of Botswana's first President (the late Sir Seretse Khama) and hitherto Commander of the Botswana Defence Force (BDF). Khama received the portfolio of presidential affairs and public administration, and was later designated as Mogae's Vice-President, subject to his election to the National Assembly. Kedikilwe, who had been favoured for the vice-presidency by certain prominent members of the BDP leadership, was appointed Minister of Finance and Development Planning. Khama was elected to the National Assembly in July, and was sworn in as Vice-President in the same month.

Meanwhile, hostility between Kenneth Koma, the leader of the BNF, and his deputy, Michael Dingake, had led to a split in the party. At the BNF's annual congress in April 1998 relations deteriorated over the issue of dissident members who had been expelled from the party. Koma, supported by the dissidents, ordered the expulsion from the party of central committee members. His actions were upheld by the party's constitution, and ultimately on appeal by the High Court. In June members of the dissolved central committee formed the Botswana Congress Party (BCP), under the leadership of Dingake. The BCP was declared the official opposition in July, after 11 of the BNF's 13 deputies joined the new party.

In September 1999 Mogae declared a state of emergency in order to allow the Independent Electoral Commission (IEC) to complete its work and prevent the disenfranchisement of around 60,000 Batswana in the forthcoming general election. The general election was held, as scheduled, in mid-October, despite opposition demands that it be postponed owing to the Government's apparent disregard for correct electoral procedure. The BDP, which received 57.2% of the votes, increased its representation in the National Assembly from 26 to 33 seats, while the number of seats held by the BNF (with 26.0% of the votes) fell significantly to only six seats, and the BCP (having received 11.9%) obtained just one seat. The IEC declared that the election had been conducted in a free and fair manner, with 77.3% of the electorate participating in the polls. Mogae was re-elected to the presidency by the National Assembly on 20 October and formed a new Cabinet the following day.

In December 1999 Mogae provoked outrage among the opposition parties, and tension within the ruling party, when he granted Vice-President Khama an unprecedented one-year sabbatical leave, effective from 1 January 2000. In July 2000 Kedikilwe resigned as Minister of Education, a position he had held since October 1999. Khama resumed his duties as Vice-President in September 2000, and a minor cabinet reshuffle was effected.

The Government's attempts to relocate Basarwa (San/Bushmen) people from their homeland within the Central Kalahari Game Reserve to a new settlement outside the Reserve provoked international concern in 1996–2002. It was claimed that officials had forced many Bushmen to move by disconnecting water supplies and threatening military intervention; 2,160 Bushmen had been resettled by mid-2001, according to reports. At the end of January 2002 the Government withdrew services to the remaining Bushmen living in the Reserve (estimated to number 500–700), in accordance with a decision announced in August 2001. A legal appeal brought to a halt the process of relocation but the return of hunting rights to the Bushmen was rejected on a technicality in April 2002. In August a delegation from the European Union accused the Government of providing false information about the number of Bushmen remaining in the Reserve, and of failing to fulfil their human rights requirements, including the supply of fresh water. In October the Government awarded some P2m. in compensation to more than 3,000 Basarwa who had been removed from the Reserve. In late 2002 Survival International, a lobby group for the rights of indigenous peoples, alleged that the Government had relocated the Basarwa in order to allow mining companies to explore for diamonds in the Reserve; the Government vehemently rejected these claims, maintaining that it was acting in the socio-economic interests of the Bushmen. Some 240 Basarwa were reported to be taking legal action against the Government in late 2003 in order to be permitted to live in the Reserve; the case was ongoing in early 2005.

Meanwhile, in November 2001 a number of changes to the structure and conditions of service of the judiciary were approved in a national referendum, although less than 5% of the electorate were reported to have participated in the vote. Ethnic tensions arose over a clause providing for an increase in the retirement age for judges. Pitso Ya Batswana, a Tswana nationalist group, claimed that this proposal was evidence of the over-representation in the judiciary and other professions of the Kalanga people, who constituted approximately 10% of the population, and that the referendum represented an attempt by the Kalanga community to advance its own interests. However, the Kalanga, together with numerous other ethnic groups, were not recognized in the Constitution as one of the eight tribes with the right to be represented in the House of Chiefs, Botswana's second legislative house. The Government had established a constitutional commission in July 2000 to investigate allegations of discrimination against minority groups, including the Kalanga, Wayeyi and Basarwa. On the basis of the recommendations of this commission, in December 2001 the Government presented a number of draft constitutional amendments. Under the proposals, the House of Chiefs would be renamed the Ntlo ya Dikgosi and its membership increased from 15 to 35, comprising 30 members elected by senior tribal authorities and five members appointed by the President. Elections to the Ntlo ya Dikgosi would be held every five years. In April 2002 the draft amendments were revised to allow the eight paramount chiefs to retain their *ex-officio* status in the chamber. The proposed amendments were submitted to the legislature in late 2003, although they had yet to be approved by early 2005.

In June 2002 the National Assembly approved legislation providing for an expansion in its directly elected membership from 40 to 57, with effect from the next general election (due in 2004), and a gradual increase in both the number of ministries, from 12 to 16, and in the number of assistant ministers, from four to eight. In September these reforms were partly implemented in a cabinet reshuffle, with the creation of two new ministries, the Ministry of Communications, Science and Technology, and the Ministry of Conservation, Wildlife and Tourism, and the appointment of two additional assistant ministers.

In early 2003 dissidents from the BNF, led by Koma, who had been expelled from the party in 2002, formed a new party, the New Democratic Front. In July 2003, at the BDP congress, Vice-President Khama defeated Kedikilwe to become Chairman of the party. Later that month Lesego Motsumi replaced Joy Phumaphi as Minister of Health. In September the BNF, the

Botswana Alliance Movement and the Botswana People's Party announced the formation of an electoral alliance to contest the general election the following year.

At the election to the newly enlarged legislature, held on 30 October 2004, the BDP secured 44 seats, although it obtained a smaller share of the vote (51.7%) than at the previous general election. The BNF received 26.1% of the votes cast and increased its representation to 12 seats, while the BCP (with 16.6%) retained its solitary parliamentary seat. The rate of voter participation was recorded at 74.6%. President Mogae was sworn in for a second term of office on 2 November.

Although, as one of the 'front-line' states, Botswana did not have diplomatic links with the apartheid regime in South Africa, it was (and remains) heavily dependent on its neighbour for trade and communications. Botswana is a member of the Southern African Development Community (SADC, see p. 345), which superseded the Southern African Development Co-ordination Conference (SADCC), in 1992. SADC, of which South Africa became a member in 1994, has its headquarters in Gaborone.

From independence, it was the Botswana Government's stated policy not to permit any guerrilla groups to operate from its territory. Relations with South Africa deteriorated in May 1984, when President Masire accused the South African Government of exerting pressure on Botswana to sign a non-aggression pact, aimed at preventing the alleged use of Botswana's territory by guerrilla forces of the (then outlawed) African National Congress of South Africa (ANC). In the second half of the 1980s South African forces launched a number of raids on alleged ANC bases in Botswana, causing several deaths. Owing to Botswana's vulnerable position, however, the Government did not commit itself to the imposition of economic sanctions against South Africa when this was recommended by SADCC in August 1986. In 1988–89 Botswana took action against the extension onto its territory of hostilities between South African government and anti-apartheid forces. Two South African commandos, who had allegedly opened fire on Botswana security forces while engaged in a raid, were sentenced to 10 years' imprisonment, nine South Africans were expelled for 'security reasons', and five ANC members were convicted on firearms charges. It was reported in August 1989 that the South African army had erected an electrified fence along a 24-km section of the South Africa–Botswana border, in order to halt the reputed threat of guerrilla infiltration into South Africa via Botswana.

With the dismantling of apartheid in the first half of the 1990s, Botswana's relations with South Africa improved markedly, and full diplomatic relations were established in June 1994. In August it was announced that the 'front-line' states were to form a political and security wing within SADC. In April 1999 Botswana and South Africa signed a bilateral agreement on the administrative merger of their adjacent national parks. The Kgalagadi Transfrontier Park was formally opened in May 2000 by President Mogae and President Thabo Mbeki of South Africa. In November the inaugural meeting of the Botswana-South Africa joint permanent commission on defence and security was held in Gaborone.

In August 1998 Botswana participated in attempts made by SADC to resolve a political crisis in Lesotho, where opposition parties were demanding the annulment of elections held in May of that year. Following an increase in civil and military unrest and reports of an imminent coup attempt, on 22 September 200–300 members of the BDF and 600 South African troops entered Lesotho, in response to requests from the Prime Minister, Pakalitha Mosisili. The SADC-sponsored military intervention encountered strong resistance from dissident members of the Lesotho armed forces and civilians, but after three days of heavy fighting and looting, in which more than 70 people died, relative calm was restored to the devastated capital, Maseru. In early 1999 the role of the BDF troops in Lesotho was the subject of debate in Botswana itself, and in May all the remaining SADC forces were withdrawn. A group of instructors from Botswana and South Africa remained in Lesotho, in an advisory and training capacity, until May 2000.

In 1983, following allegations that armed dissidents from Zimbabwe were being harboured among Zimbabwean refugees encamped in Botswana, the Botswana Government agreed to impose stricter restrictions on the refugees. In May Botswana and Zimbabwe established full diplomatic relations. The first meeting of the Botswana-Zimbabwe joint commission for co-operation was held in October 1984. A new influx of refugees, following the Zimbabwe general election in July 1985, threatened to strain relations between the two countries. In April 1989 about 600 Zimbabwean refugees remained in Botswana, prompting the Botswana Government to announce that refugee status for Zimbabwean nationals was to be revoked; by September almost all former Zimbabwean refugees had reportedly left Botswana. In the mid-1990s, however, the Government expressed concern at the growing number of illegal immigrants in the country, the majority of whom were from Zimbabwe; of more than 40,000 illegal immigrants repatriated during 1995, more than 14,000 were Zimbabwean. Relations between the two countries were again strained in 2000, when Zimbabwe's construction of a railway line from Bulawayo (its second largest city) to Beitbridge (on the border with South Africa) severely reduced transit freight traffic on Botswana Railways. In late 2001 and early 2002 Mogae participated in SADC efforts to encourage the Zimbabwean President, Robert Mugabe, to conduct his Government's land reform programme within the rule of law. Following the controversial re-election of Mugabe to the Zimbabwean presidency in March 2002, the Botswana Government became more critical of government policy in Zimbabwe, as the economic crisis in that country prompted an influx of immigrants into Botswana, with many entering illegally. In late 2003 the Botswana Government began erecting a 3m-high electrified fence along the border with Zimbabwe, ostensibly to prevent the spread of foot-and-mouth disease, although it was widely regarded as a measure to prevent the entry of further illegal immigrants, with those already in Botswana estimated to number more than 100,000 in early 2004; by the end of that year the number was estimated at more than 200,000. Some 2,500 people—mainly Zimbabweans—were being deported every month, and the Government sought to amend the Immigration Act of 2003 to impose higher fines and stricter sentences on those deemed to have entered the country illegally.

Following Namibian independence, in July 1990 it was announced that a commission for bilateral co-operation was to be established by Botswana and Namibia. In 1992, however, a border dispute developed between the two countries regarding their rival territorial claims over a small island (Sedudu-Kasikili) in the Chobe river. In early 1995 the two states agreed to present the issue of the demarcation of their joint border for arbitration at the International Court of Justice (ICJ, in The Hague, Netherlands), and in February 1996 the two countries signed an agreement committing themselves in advance to the Court's eventual judgment. Meanwhile, Namibia appealed to Botswana to remove its troops—stated by the Botswana authorities to be anti-poaching patrols—and national flag from the island. In early 1997 it was reported that Namibia had been angered by Botswana's erection of a fence along Namibia's Caprivi Strip, which separates the two countries to the north; Botswana insisted, however, that the fence was simply a measure to control the spread of livestock diseases. In January 1998 an emergency meeting of the Botswana-Namibia joint commission on defence and security was held to discuss ownership of another island (Situngu) in the Chobe river, following allegations by Namibia that the BDF had occupied the island and was stealing crops planted by Namibian farmers resident there. In December 1999 the ICJ granted Botswana control over Sedudu-Kasikili. A joint technical commission was subsequently established to consider other demarcation disputes between Botswana and Namibia, and in March 2003 its report was accepted by the Presidents of both countries.

Meanwhile, in late 1998 relations between the two countries were further strained by the arrival in Botswana of more than 300 refugees (a number of whom were reportedly leading political dissidents) from the Caprivi Strip in Namibia. President Mogae rejected Namibian demands for the extradition of the refugees, whose number had increased to more than 2,000 by early 1999. In May, however, a formal agreement was signed by the two Governments, according to which prominent dissidents among the refugees would be allowed to leave Botswana for another country and an amnesty would be extended to other refugees returning to Namibia. In response to a request from the Namibian Government, in September 2001 the Gaborone Magistrates' Court ruled in favour of the extradition of a group of 13 suspected Caprivi separatists who were wanted to stand trial for alleged high treason; however, this decision was reversed by Botswana's High Court in December 2002. Meanwhile, in April 2002 officials from Botswana and Namibia concluded a tripartite agreement with the office of the UN High Commissioner for Refugees (UNHCR) on the voluntary repatriation of Namibian refugees in Botswana. Between August and October around 800 refugees were repatriated to Namibia (although

UNHCR reported that none of them originated from the Caprivi Strip), leaving some 1,200 in Botswana, who remained reluctant to return. In December 2003 UNHCR and human rights group criticized the deportation from Botswana to Namibia of a further eight Caprivians, seven of whom were subsequently charged with high treason over alleged separatist activities; the authorities in Botswana claimed that the eight had lost their refugee status by visiting Namibia after being granted asylum in Botswana.

Government

Legislative power is vested in Parliament, consisting of the President and the National Assembly. The National Assembly is elected for a term of five years and comprises 57 members directly elected by universal adult suffrage, together with four members who are elected by the National Assembly from a list of candidates submitted by the President; the President and the Attorney-General are also *ex-officio* members of the Assembly. The President is restricted to two terms of office. He appoints and leads a Cabinet, which is responsible to the Assembly. The President has powers to delay implementation of legislation for six months, and certain matters also have to be referred to the 15-member House of Chiefs for approval, although this advisory body has no power of veto. In early 2004 a number of draft constitutional amendments relating to the House of Chiefs remained under consideration. Under the proposals, the House of Chiefs would be renamed the Ntlo ya Dikgosi and its membership increased from 15 to 35, comprising 30 members elected by senior tribal authorities and five members appointed by the President; elections to the Ntlo ya Dikgosi would be held every five years. Local government is effected through nine district councils and four town councils.

Defence

Military service is voluntary. In August 2004 the total strength of the Botswana Defence Force was some 9,000, comprising an army of 8,500 and an air force of 500. In addition, there was a paramilitary police force of 1,500. There are plans to enlarge the strength of the army to 10,000 men. Projected budgetary expenditure on defence for 2004 was P1,600m.

Economic Affairs

In 2003, according to estimates by the World Bank, Botswana's gross national income (GNI), measured at average 2001–03 prices, was US $7,038m., equivalent to $3,430 per head (or $7,960 on an international purchasing-power parity basis). During 1990–2003, it was estimated, the population increased by an average of 2.3% per year, while gross domestic product (GDP) per head also increased, in real terms, by an average of 2.3% per year. Overall GDP increased, in real terms, at an average annual rate of 4.7% in 1990–2003; growth in 2003 was 4.7%.

Agriculture (including hunting, forestry and fishing) contributed 2.5% of GDP in 2002/03, according to provisional figures, and engaged 43.9% of the total labour force in 2003. The principal agricultural activity is cattle-raising (principally beef production), which supports about one-half of the population and contributes more than 80% of agricultural GDP. As a member of the African, Caribbean and Pacific (ACP) group of states and a signatory to successive Lomé Conventions, Botswana has traditionally enjoyed preferential trade relations with the European Union (EU), including a quota to supply 18,916 metric tons of beef per year. However, Botswana has never met this quota: in 2003 some 8,500 tons of beef was exported to the EU. Under the Cotonou Agreement, which was concluded in mid-2000, the quota was to be phased out by 2007, when Botswana and the other ACP states were to establish reciprocal trade arrangements with the EU in order to achieve compatibility with the rules of the World Trade Organization. The main subsistence crops are roots and tubers, pulses and vegetables although Botswana is not self-sufficient in basic foods. Agricultural GDP decreased at an average annual rate of 0.5% in 1990–2003; however, growth of 3.7% was recorded in 2003.

Industry (including mining, manufacturing, construction and power) engaged 25.5% of the employed labour force in 2001 and, according to provisional figures, provided 49.2% of GDP in 2002/03. Industrial GDP increased at an average annual rate of 4.1% in 1990–2003; growth in 2003 was 3.7%.

Mining contributed 36.4% of GDP in 2002/03, according to provisional figures, although the sector engaged only 2.9% of the employed labour force in 2001. In terms of value, Botswana is the world's largest producer of diamonds (which accounted for

87.1% of export earnings in 2002, according to provisional figures, and some two-thirds of foreign exchange); copper-nickel matte and soda ash are also exported. In addition, coal, gold, cobalt and salt are mined, and there are known reserves of plutonium, asbestos, chromite, fluorspar, iron, manganese, potash, silver, talc and uranium. In 1998 a new minerals code included measures to encourage non-diamond mining projects. According to provisional official figures, the GDP of the mining sector increased, in real terms, at an average annual rate of 5.0% in 1993/94–2002/03; mining GDP declined by 3.0% in 2001/02, but increased by 10.3% in 2002/03.

Manufacturing engaged 8.7% of the employed labour force in 2001 and provided 4.5% of GDP in 2002/03, according to provisional figures. The GDP of the manufacturing sector increased at an average annual rate of 3.6% in 1990–2003; growth in 2003 was 3.7%.

Energy is derived principally from fuel wood and coal; the use of solar power is currently being promoted as an alternative source of energy. According to provisional figures, imports of fuels accounted for 7.0% of the value of total imports in 2002.

The services sector contributed 48.3% of GDP in 2002/03, according to provisional figures, and engaged 61.5% of the employed labour force in 2001. Within the sector, tourism is of considerable importance, being the third largest source of total foreign exchange. The GDP of the services sector increased at an average annual rate of 6.6% in 1990–2003; growth in 2003 was 3.7%.

In 2002 Botswana recorded a visible trade surplus of US $676.3m., and there was a surplus of $170.2m. on the current account of the balance of payments. In 2002 countries of the Southern African Customs Union (SACU—see below) provided 77.0% of imports, while European countries provided 13.8%. European countries (principally the United Kingdom) took 89.0% of exports in 2001; other important purchasers were the countries of SACU (6.5%). The principal exports in 2002 were diamonds and copper-nickel matte. The principal imports were machinery and electrical equipment, food, beverages and tobacco, vehicles and transport equipment, chemicals and rubber products, wood and paper products, metals and metal products and fuels.

In the financial year to 31 March 2004 the central Government recorded a budgetary deficit of P24.4m,, originally forecast at some P2,200m. but greatly reduced through emergency measures. Botswana's external debt totalled US $479.9m. at the end of 2002, of which $463.9m. was long-term public debt. In 2001 the cost of debt-servicing was equivalent to 1.7% of the value of exports of goods and services. The average annual rate of inflation was 5.9% in 2000–03; consumer prices increased by an annual average of 9.3% in 2003. Some 19.6% of the labour force were unemployed in 2001.

Botswana is a member of the Southern African Development Community (SADC, see p. 345) and (with Lesotho, Namibia, South Africa and Swaziland) of SACU. In September 2000 SADC commenced the implementation phase of its Protocol on Trade, which provided for the establishment of a regional free-trade area; all trade tariffs between member countries were to be eliminated gradually over a 12-year period.

Since the 1970s Botswana's development from one of the poorest countries in the world to a stable middle-income country has been based predominantly on the successful exploitation of diamonds and other minerals. Revenues from diamonds declined in the early 2000s and a fall in demand was also recorded, particularly following the slowdown in global economic growth in 2001. However, in late 2003 a large kimberlite deposit was discovered in the north-west of the country, while in late 2004 a new gold mine at Mupane in north-eastern Botswana commenced production, with projected output of 100,000 troy oz per year. In September 2004 the De Beers diamond company introduced the first of two client diamond-polishing companies meaning that for the first time rough diamonds—both mined locally and imported—would be cut and polished in Botswana. Despite these advances, the need to reduce the country's dependence on the mining industry has been recognized in recent years, and the Government's ninth National Development Plan (2003/04–2008/09) aimed to effect economic diversification by embracing recent technological developments. Other government priorities included the creation of new employment opportunities and the maintenance of macroeconomic stability and financial discipline. In 2000, as part of efforts to diversify the economic base and create sustainable employment, the Government established an International Financial Services Centre (IFSC). Botswana's proximity to South Africa, substantial tax incentives and the stability of a well-established democratic system of government were all expected to attract international financial companies to the country; by July 2004 some 20 companies had projects approved for operation under the IFSC. In 2003 the Government issued bonds for the first time in order to raise additional revenue and encourage the development of the financial services sector. Meanwhile, the HIV/AIDS pandemic represented a significant threat to continued economic growth, diminishing the work-force and depleting government resources through expenditure on projects to counter the disease. The 2004/05 budget allocated resources totalling P415m. to measures targeted at combating HIV/AIDS, however, uptake of antiretroviral drugs remained poor; with more than one-third of the population estimated to be infected with HIV, estimated average life expectancy had declined from around 60 years in the early 1990s to 40 years by 2002, and was expected to fall to about 36 years by 2005. Reduced GDP growth of 3.7% was forecast in 2005 and the suspension of the scheduled privatization of Air Botswana highlighted the difficulties the Government was confronted with regarding its plans successfully to divest a number of state-owned enterprises.

Education

Although education is not compulsory in Botswana, enrolment ratios are high. Primary education, which is provided free of charge, begins at seven years of age and lasts for up to seven years. Secondary education, beginning at the age of 13, lasts for a further five years, comprising a first cycle of three years and a second of two years. Enrolment at primary schools in 2000/01 included 84% of children in the relevant age-group (boys 82%; girls 86%), while, according to UNESCO estimates, the comparable ratio for secondary enrolment was 59% (boys 55%; girls 63%). Botswana has the highest teacher-pupil ratio in Africa, but continues to rely heavily on expatriate secondary school teachers. In 2001 tertiary education was provided by 49 technical and vocational training centres (including health institutes), four teacher-training colleges, two further education colleges, an agricultural college and a university (which was attended by 15,414 students in 2004). Expenditure on education by the central Government in 2004/05 was forecast at P4,681.9m. (representing 25.8% of total government spending).

Public Holidays

2005: 1–2 January (New Year), 25–28 March (Easter), 1 May (Labour Day), 5 May (Ascension Day), 1 July (Sir Seretse Khama Day), 18–19 July (for President's Day), 30 September (Botswana Day), 25–26 December (Christmas).

2006: 1–2 January (New Year), 14–17 April (Easter), 1 May (Labour Day), 25 May (Ascension Day), 1 July (Sir Seretse Khama Day), 17–18 July (for President's Day), 30 September (Botswana Day), 25–26 December (Christmas).

Weights and Measures

The metric system is in use.

Statistical Survey

Source (unless otherwise stated): Central Statistics Office, Private Bag 0024, Gaborone; tel. 352200; fax 352201; e-mail csobots@gov.bw; internet www.cso .gov.bw/cso.

Area and Population

AREA, POPULATION AND DENSITY

Area (sq km)	581,730*
Population (census results)	
21 August 1991	1,326,796
17 August 2001	1,678,891
Males	813,488
Females	867,375
Total	1,680,863
Population (UN estimates at mid-year)† . . .	
2002	1,770,000
2003	1,785,000
Density (per sq km) at mid-2003	3.1

* 224,607 sq miles.
† Source: UN, *World Population Prospects: The 2002 Revision.*

ADMINISTRATIVE DISTRICTS
(population at census of August 2001)

Barolong . . .	47,477	Kweneng	230,535
Central	501,381	Lobatse	29,689
Central Kalahari			
Game Reserve .	689	Ngamiland . . .	122,024
Chobe	18,258	Ngwaketse West .	10,471
Delta	2,688	North-East . . .	49,399
Francistown . . .	83,023	Orapa	9,151
Gaborone	186,007	Selebi-Phikwe . .	49,849
Ghanzi	32,481	South-East . . .	60,623
Jwaneng	15,179	Southern	113,704
Kgalagadi . .	42,049	Sowa	2,879
Kgatleng	73,507		

PRINCIPAL TOWNS
(population at August 2001 census)

Gaborone (capital) .	186,007	Serowe	42,444
Francistown . . .	83,023	Kanye	40,628
Molepolole . . .	54,561	Mahalapye . . .	39,719
Selebi-Phikwe . .	49,849	Mochudi	36,692
Maun	43,776	Lobatse	29,689

Mid-2003 (UN estimate, incl. suburbs): Gaborone 198,822 (Source: UN, *World Urbanization Prospects: The 2003 Revision*).

BIRTHS AND DEATHS
(UN estimates, annual averages)

	1985–90	1990–95	1995–2000
Birth rate (per 1,000)	37.9	34.1	32.4
Death rate (per 1,000)	6.3	6.2	10.2

Source: UN, *World Population Prospects: The 2002 Revision.*

Expectation of life (WHO estimates, years at birth): 40.4 (males 40.2; females 40.6) in 2002 (Source: WHO, *World Health Report*).

ECONOMICALLY ACTIVE POPULATION*
('000 persons aged 12 years and over, 2001)

	Males	Females	Total
Agriculture, hunting, forestry and fishing	44.5	10.8	55.3
Mining and quarrying	11.9	1.2	13.1
Manufacturing	17.9	21.1	39.0
Electricity, gas and water supply .	3.2	0.6	3.8
Construction	49.5	9.1	58.6
Wholesale and retail trade; repair of motor vehicles, motorcycles and personal and household goods	26.1	35.0	61.1
Hotels and restaurants	4.1	8.7	12.7
Transport, storage and communications	11.6	3.7	15.2
Financial intermediation . . .	2.2	3.4	5.6
Real estate, renting and business services	16.1	8.4	24.5
Public administration and defence; compulsory social security . .	48.8	21.2	70.0
Education	14.3	23.6	37.9
Health and social work	4.8	9.2	14.0
Other community, social and personal service activities . .	6.5	5.8	12.3
Private households with employed persons	1.9	20.2	22.2
Extra-territorial organizations and bodies	0.4	0.3	0.7
Activities not adequately defined .	1.7	1.6	3.2
Total employed	265.2	183.8	449.0
Unemployed	51.9	57.6	109.5
Total labour force	317.2	241.4	558.6

* Excluding members of the armed forces and those not actively seeking work. Totals may not be equivalent to sums of component parts, owing to statistical discrepancy and rounding.

Source: ILO.

Mid-2003 (estimates, '000 persons): Agriculture, etc. 353; Total labour force 805 (Source: FAO).

Health and Welfare

KEY INDICATORS

Total fertility rate (children per woman, 2002) . . .	3.7
Under-5 mortality rate (per 1,000 live births, 2003) . .	112
HIV/AIDS (% of persons aged 15–49, 2003)	37.3
Physicians (per 1,000 head, 1994)	0.24
Hospital beds (per 1,000 head, 1990)	1.58
Health expenditure (2001): US $ per head (PPP) . . .	381
Health expenditure (2001): % of GDP	6.6
Health expenditure (2001): public (% of total) . . .	66.2
Access to water (% of persons, 2002)	95
Access to sanitation (% of persons, 2002)	41
Human Development Index (2002): ranking	128
Human Development Index (2002): value	0.589

For sources and definitions, see explanatory note on p. vi.

Agriculture

PRINCIPAL CROPS
('000 metric tons)

	2001	2002	2003
Maize*	10	10	10
Sorghum	15†	15†	32
Roots and tubers*	92	93	93
Pulses*	18	18	18
Vegetables*	17	17	16
Fruit*	11	11	11

* FAO estimates.
† Unofficial figure.

Source: FAO.

LIVESTOCK
(FAO estimates, '000 head, year ending September)

	2001	2002	2003
Cattle	1,600	1,700	1,700
Horses	33	33	33
Asses	330	330	330
Sheep	370	430	400
Goats	2,250	2,250	2,250
Pigs	8	8	8
Poultry	4,000	4,000	4,000

Source: FAO.

LIVESTOCK PRODUCTS
('000 metric tons)

	2001	2002	2003
Beef and veal	32*	31*	27
Goat meat*	6	6	6
Poultry meat*	9	8	9
Other meat*	14	15	15
Cows' milk*	102	102	102
Goats' milk*	4	4	4
Cheese*	4	5	2
Butter*	1	1	1
Hen eggs*	3*	3*	3†
Cattle hides*	4	4	4

* FAO estimate(s).
† Unofficial figure.

Source: FAO.

Forestry

ROUNDWOOD REMOVALS
(FAO estimates, '000 cubic metres, excl. bark)

	2001	2002	2003
Industrial wood	105	105	105
Fuel wood	640	645	650
Total	745	750	755

Source: FAO.

Fishing

(FAO estimates, metric tons, live weight)

	2000	2001	2002
Tilapias	92	88	101
Other freshwater fishes . . .	74	30	38
Total catch	166	118	139

Note: Figures exclude aquatic mammals, recorded by number rather than weight. The number of Nile crocodiles caught was: 11 in 2000; 152 in 2001; 0 in 2002.

Source: FAO.

Mining

(metric tons, unless otherwise indicated)

	2000	2001	2002
Hard coal	946,900	930,374	953,081
Copper ore*	22,218	20,355	21,182
Nickel ore*	20,286	18,585	20,005
Cobalt†	308	325	269
Salt	184,753	178,646	315,259
Diamonds ('000 carats)	24,635	26,416	28,397
Soda ash (natural)	191,043	251,231	283,197
Crushed stone (cu metres) . . .	1,070,700	2,140,523	3,602,257

* Figures refer to the metal content of ores.
† Figures refer to the cobalt content of copper-nickel matte exported for refining.

Source: US Geological Survey.

Industry

SELECTED PRODUCTS

	1998	1999	2000
Beer ('000 hectolitres)	1,019	1,591	1,976
Soft drinks ('000 hectolitres) . .	411	410	356
Electric energy (million kWh) . .	1,000	955	1,058

2001: Soft drinks ('000 hectolitres) 431.

Source: UN, *Industrial Commodity Statistics Yearbook*.

Finance

CURRENCY AND EXCHANGE RATES
Monetary Units
100 thebe = 1 pula (P).

Sterling, Dollar and Euro Equivalents (31 December 2004)
£1 sterling = 8.268 pula;
US $1 = 4.281 pula;
€1 = 5.831 pula;
100 pula = £12.09 = $23.36 = €17.15.

Average Exchange Rate (pula per US $)
2002   6.3278
2003   4.9499
2004   4.6929

BUDGET
(million pula, year ending 31 March)

Revenue*	2002/03†	2003/04‡	2004/05§
Taxation	12,259.4	13,043.8	16,097.1
Mineral revenues	7,502.7	6,721.0	8,070.4
Customs pool revenues . . .	1,568.9	2,262.5	3,293.8
Non-mineral income tax . . .	1,839.5	2,234.3	2,553.9
General sales tax	1,254.6	1,725.1	2,070.0
Other current revenue	1,967.2	2,938.4	1,911.9
Interest	226.8	170.2	58.5
Other property income . . .	1,063.9	1,136.1	469.6
Fees, charges, etc.	597.8	959.0	1,051.0
Sales of fixed assets and land .	78.7	673.1	332.7
Total	14,226.6	15,982.3	18,008.9

* Excluding grants received (million pula): 84.4 in 2002/03; 200.0 in 2003/04; 200.0 in 2004/05.
† Revised figures.
‡ Revised estimates.
§ Projected estimates.

Expenditure*	2002/03†	2003/04‡	2004/05§
General services (incl. defence)	4,263.1	4,994.5	4,897.1
Education	3,548.8	4,336.5	4,681.9
Health	1,104.2	1,439.8	1,819.9
Housing, urban and regional development	1,144.4	414.7	1,033.6
Food and social welfare programme	400.9	162.0	97.0
Other community and social services	548.7	540.1	582.5
Economic services	3,053.2	2,425.2	2,986.0
Agriculture, forestry and fishing	646.7	609.2	561.9
Mining	88.7	102.0	133.5
Electricity and water supply	905.4	647.7	835.9
Roads	615.4	583.0	503.8
Others	797.0	483.3	950.8
Deficit grants to local authorities	1,555.8	1,674.5	1,689.0
Interest on public debt	81.1	219.4	353.2
Other grants	10.0		
Total	**15,710.1**	**16,206.7**	**18,140.1**

* Including net lending (million pula): −81.2 in 2002/03; −1,051.3 in 2003/04; −40.4 in 2004/05.
† Revised figures.
‡ Revised estimates.
§ Projected estimates.

Source: Bank of Botswana, Gaborone.

INTERNATIONAL RESERVES
(US $ million at 31 December)

	2001	2002	2003
IMF special drawing rights	39.62	44.36	49.81
Reserve position in IMF	28.00	32.36	45.05
Foreign exchange	5,829.63	5,397.20	5,244.92
Total	**5,897.25**	**5,473.92**	**5,339.78**

Source: IMF, *International Financial Statistics.*

MONEY SUPPLY
(million pula at 31 December)

	2001	2002	2003
Currency outside banks	481	470	533
Demand deposits at commercial banks	1,869	2,054	2,290
Total money	**2,350**	**2,524**	**2,823**

Source: IMF, *International Financial Statistics.*

COST OF LIVING
(Consumer Price Index; base: 2000 = 100)

	2001	2002	2003
Food (incl. beverages)	102.6	112.2	125.0
Clothing (incl. footwear)	103.8	107.8	112.4
All items (incl. others)	**106.6**	**115.1**	**125.8**

Source: ILO.

NATIONAL ACCOUNTS
(million pula at current prices, year ending 30 June)

National Income and Product

	1997/98	1998/99	1999/2000
Compensation of employees	5,654.2	6,833.0	7,452.9
Operating surplus	10,458.8	10,127.9	12,350.0
Mixed income	126.8	137.7	157.0
Domestic primary incomes	16,239.8	17,098.6	19,959.9
Consumption of fixed capital	2,421.3	2,647.4	2,976.2
Gross domestic product (GDP) at factor cost	18,661.1	19,746.0	22,936.1
Taxes on production and imports	1,597.5	1,887.8	2,558.5
Less Subsidies	96.0	110.0	100.0
GDP in market prices	20,162.6	21,523.8	25,362.7
Primary incomes received from abroad / *Less* Primary incomes paid abroad	−11.7	−353.8	−1,326.2
Gross national income (GNI)	20,150.9	21,170.0	24,036.5
Less Consumption of fixed capital	2,421.3	2,647.4	2,976.2
Net national income	17,729.6	18,522.6	21,060.3
Current transfers from abroad / *Less* Current transfers paid abroad	−90.0	−30.1	−33.3
Net national disposable income	17,639.6	18,492.5	21,027

Source: UN, *National Accounts Statistics.*

Expenditure on the Gross Domestic Product
(provisional figures)

	2000/01	2001/02	2002/03
Government final consumption expenditure	8,741.8	10,552.7	12,167.5
Private final consumption expenditure	8,438.6	9,307.8	10,336.0
Increase in stocks	−1,291.2	607.6	2,002.2
Gross fixed capital formation	6,898.2	7,743.2	8,735.7
Total domestic expenditure	**22,787.3**	**28,211.0**	**33,241.4**
Exports of goods and services	17,555.0	15,564.3	16,132.4
Less Imports of goods and services	10,805.9	11,737.9	12,690.3
Net errors and omissions	−900.0	−115.0	−345.0
GDP in purchasers' values	**28,636.5**	**31,922.4**	**36,338.5**
GDP at constant 1993/94 prices	**16,535.3**	**16,905.8**	**18,038.5**

Source: Bank of Botswana, Gaborone.

Gross Domestic Product by Economic Activity
(provisional figures)

	2000/01	2001/02	2002/03
Agriculture, hunting, forestry and fishing	755.2	791.7	870.7
Mining and quarrying	10,085.6	11,238.4	12,635.5
Manufacturing	1,344.1	1,404.0	1,549.7
Water and electricity	689.0	749.9	926.8
Construction	1,562.7	1,738.0	1,976.2
Trade, restaurants and hotels	3,193.3	3,650.7	4,177.9
Transport	1,057.7	1,150.7	1,287.8
Finance, insurance and business services	3,201.9	3,644.0	4,096.5
Government services	4,567.6	5,264.1	5,818.0
Social and personal services	1,106.7	1,249.3	1,394.3
Sub-total	**27,563.8**	**30,880.7**	**34,733.4**
Less Imputed bank service charge	996.2	1,172.8	1,438.7
GDP at basic prices	**26,567.6**	**29,708.0**	**33,294.7**
Import duties	1,582.1	1,657.1	1,618.6
Taxes on products	606.8	735.7	1,583.4
Less Subsidies on products	120.0	178.5	159.3
GDP in purchasers' values	**28,636.5**	**31,922.1**	**36,337.5**

Source: Bank of Botswana, Gaborone.

BALANCE OF PAYMENTS
(US $ million)

	2000	2001	2002
Exports of goods f.o.b.	2,675.4	2,314.5	2,318.6
Imports of goods f.o.b.	−1,773.2	−1,604.1	−1,642.3
Trade balance	902.1	710.4	676.3
Exports of services	324.8	340.3	489.6
Imports of services	−547.5	−513.3	−509.7
Balance on goods and services	679.4	537.3	656.2
Other income received . . .	378.1	358.4	268.4
Other income paid	−729.5	−495.4	−966.6
Balance on goods, services and income	328.1	400.2	−42.1
Current transfers received . . .	426.1	383.0	400.4
Current transfers paid	−209.0	−185.5	−188.1
Current balance	545.2	597.7	170.2
Capital account (net)	38.1	5.8	15.7
Direct investment abroad . . .	−2.3	−370.9	−42.9
Direct investment from abroad .	57.2	22.1	403.4
Portfolio investment assets . .	−34.1	−68.4	−420.2
Portfolio investment liabilities .	−5.9	6.0	7.1
Financial derivatives liabilities .	−3.0	—	—
Other investment assets . . .	−263.6	−152.7	−221.1
Other investment liabilities . .	37.7	54.4	56.3
Net errors and omissions . . .	−1.9	75.8	92.0
Overall balance	367.4	170.0	60.6

Source: IMF, *International Financial Statistics*.

External Trade

PRINCIPAL COMMODITIES
(million pula)

Imports c.i.f.	1999	2000*	2001*
Food, beverages and tobacco . .	1,411.7	1,494.2	1,475.7
Fuels	494.9	523.2	711.7
Chemicals and rubber products .	940.6	1,033.4	1,090.3
Wood and paper products . . .	819.4	817.1	928.2
Textiles and footwear	596.1	616.5	494.1
Metals and metal products . . .	877.2	769.0	813.8
Machinery and electrical equipment	2,142.3	2,356.4	2,078.4
Vehicles and transport equipment	1,373.7	1,314.8	1,285.0
Total (incl. others)	10,164.4	10,613.1	10,556.9

* Provisional figures.

Exports f.o.b.	1999	2000*	2001*
Meat and meat products . . .	223.4	263.5	365.9
Diamonds	9,706.4	11,383.6	12,085.9
Copper-nickel matte	557.9	830.3	597.4
Textiles	248.5	243.7	193.0
Vehicles and parts	666.8	270.4	298.7
Total (incl. others)	12,227.8	13,834.7	14,306.5

* Provisional figures.

PRINCIPAL TRADING PARTNERS
(million pula)

Imports c.i.f.	1999	2000*	2001*
SACU†	7,783.6	7,846.1	8,193.4
Zimbabwe	396.6	366.6	335.2
United Kingdom	272.5	442.3	467.8
Other Europe	664.3	1,306.7	832.7
Korea, Repub.	264.0	21.5	22.2
USA	188.0	174.1	190.0
Total (incl. others)	10,164.4	10,613.1	10,556.9

Exports f.o.b.	1999	2000*	2001*
SACU†	1,270.9	927.1	924.1
Zimbabwe	291.0	540.6	373.8
Other Africa	137.2	125.8	107.7
United Kingdom	8,130.1	9,644.3	12,283.3
Other Europe	2,220.9	2,417.1	452.0
USA	86.5	81.6	35.3
Total (incl. others)	12,227.8	13,834.7	14,306.5

* Provisional figures.
† Southern African Customs Union, of which Botswana is a member; also including Lesotho, Namibia, South Africa and Swaziland.

Transport

RAILWAYS
(traffic)

	1998/99	1999/2000	2000/01
Number of passengers ('000) . .	360	310	637
Passenger-km (million) . . .	89	75	106
Freight ('000 metric tons) . . .	2,812	2,448	1,956
Freight net ton-km (million) . .	1,282	1,037	747

Source: Botswana Railways.

ROAD TRAFFIC
(registered vehicles)

	2000	2001	2002
Passenger cars	48,223	53,733	59,791
Lorries and vans	71,205	75,985	75,985
Buses	5,989	6,458	6,903
Tractors	2,688	3,165	3,133
Others	11,217	11,233	12,145
Total	139,322	150,574	162,807

Source: Department of National Transport and Road Safety.

CIVIL AVIATION
(traffic on scheduled services)

	1999	2000	2001
Kilometres flown (million) . . .	2	2	2
Passengers carried ('000) . . .	108	121	123
Passenger-km (million)	50	53	55
Total ton-km (million)	5	5	5

Source: UN, *Statistical Yearbook*.

Tourism

FOREIGN TOURIST ARRIVALS

Country of origin	1997	1998	1999
Namibia	17,433	35,508	39,952
South Africa	258,120	359,292	393,528
United Kingdom	15,329	14,426	15,519
Zambia	22,057	26,971	28,888
Zimbabwe	207,244	195,789	245,630
Total (incl. others)	606,790	749,535	843,314

2002 (provisional): Total arrivals 1,037,000.

Receipts from tourism (US $ million): 184 in 1997; 175 in 1998; 234 in 1999; 313 in 2000; 300 in 2001; 309 in 2002.

Source: World Tourism Organization.

Communications Media

	2000	2001	2002
Television receivers ('000 in use) .	40	n.a.	n.a.
Telephones ('000 main lines in use)	150.3	142.6	142.5
Mobile cellular telephones ('000 subscribers)	200	278	435
Personal computers ('000 in use) .	60	65	70
Internet users ('000)	15	50	60

Source: International Telecommunication Union.

Radio receivers ('000 in use): 237 in 1997 (Source: UNESCO, *Statistical Yearbook*).

Facsimile machines: 3,529 in use in 1997/98 (Source: UNESCO, *Statistical Yearbook*).

Book production (first editions only): 158 titles in 1991, including 61 pamphlets (Source: UNESCO, *Statistical Yearbook*).

Daily newspapers: 1 in 2000 (average circulation 50,000 copies) (Source: UNESCO, *Statistical Yearbook*).

Non-daily newspapers: 3 in 1996 (average circulation 51,000 copies) (Source: UNESCO, *Statistical Yearbook*).

Other periodicals: 14 titles in 1992 (average circulation 177,000 copies) (Source: UNESCO, *Statistical Yearbook*).

Education

(2001)

	Institutions	Teachers	Students
Primary	750	12,370	329,451
Secondary	265	9,261	151,847
Vocational and technical Education	49	1,126	11,507
Teacher training	4	191	1,404
Colleges of education	2	170*	1,495

* 1998 figure.

Source: Ministry of Education, Gaborone.

Agricultural college (2004): Teachers 120; Students 850 (Source: Botswana College of Agriculture).

University (2004): Teachers 788; Students 15,414 (Source: University of Botswana).

Adult literacy rate (UNESCO estimates): 78.9% (males 76.1%; females 81.5%) in 2002 (Source: UN Development Programme, *Human Development Report*).

Directory

The Constitution

The Constitution of the Republic of Botswana took effect at independence on 30 September 1966; it was amended in August and September 1997. Its main provisions, with subsequent amendments, are summarized below:

EXECUTIVE

President

Executive power lies with the President of Botswana, who is also Commander-in-Chief of the armed forces. Election for the office of President is linked with the election of members of the National Assembly. The President is restricted to two terms of office. Presidential candidates must be over 30 years of age and receive at least 1,000 nominations. If there is more than one candidate for the Presidency, each candidate for office in the Assembly must declare support for a presidential candidate. The candidate for President who commands the votes of more than one-half of the elected members of the Assembly will be declared President. In the event of the death or resignation of the President, the Vice-President will automatically assume the Presidency. The President, who is an *ex-officio* member of the National Assembly, holds office for the duration of Parliament. The President chooses four members of the National Assembly.

Cabinet

There is also a Vice-President, whose office is ministerial. The Vice-President is appointed by the President and deputizes in the absence of the President. The Cabinet consists of the President, the Vice-President and other Ministers, including Assistant Ministers, appointed by the President. The Cabinet is responsible to the National Assembly.

LEGISLATURE

Legislative power is vested in Parliament, consisting of the President and the National Assembly, acting after consultation in certain cases with the House of Chiefs. The President may withhold assent to a Bill passed by the National Assembly. If the same Bill is again presented after six months, the President is required to assent to it or to dissolve Parliament within 21 days.

House of Chiefs

The House of Chiefs comprises the Chiefs of the eight principal tribes of Botswana as *ex-officio* members, four members elected by sub-chiefs from their own number, and three members elected by the other 12 members of the House. Bills and motions relating to chieftaincy matters and alterations of the Constitution must be referred to the House, which may also deliberate and make representations on any matter. Proposals to rename the House of Chiefs as the Ntlo ya Dikgosi and to increase its membership from 15 to 35 were under consideration.

National Assembly

The National Assembly consists of 40 members directly elected by universal adult suffrage, together with four members who are elected by the National Assembly from a list of candidates submitted by the President; the President, the Speaker and the Attorney-General are also *ex-officio* members of the Assembly. The life of the Assembly is five years. In June 2002 the National Assembly voted to increase its membership from 40 directly elected members to 57, with effect from the following general election.

The Constitution contains a code of human rights, enforceable by the High Court.

The Government

HEAD OF STATE

President: Festus G. Mogae (took office 1 April 1998; sworn in 20 October 1999 and, for a second term, 2 November 2004).

Vice-President: Lt-Gen. Seretse Ian Khama.

CABINET
(March 2005)

President: Festus G. Mogae.

Vice-President: Lt-Gen. Seretse Khama Ian Khama.

Minister of Presidential Affairs and Public Administration: Phandu Skelemani.

Minister of Health: Prof. Sheila Tlou.

Minister of Agriculture: Johnnie K. Swartz.

Minister of Foreign Affairs: Lt-Gen. Mompati S. Merafhe.

Minister of Minerals, Energy and Water Affairs: Charles Tibone.

Minister of Trade and Industry: D. Neo Moroka.

Minister of Local Government: Dr Margaret N. Nasha.

Minister of Works and Transport: Lesego Motsumi.

Minister of Communications, Science and Technology: Pelonomi Venson.

Minister of Environment, Wildlife and Tourism: Capt. Kitso Mokaila.

Minister of Finance and Development Planning: Baledzi Gaolathe.

Minister of Education: Jacob Nkate.

Minister of Labour and Home Affairs: Maj.-Gen. Moeng Pheto.

Minister of Lands and Housing: Brig. Ramadeluka Seretse.

Attorney-General: Ian S. Kirby.

In addition, there are five Assistant Ministers.

MINISTRIES

Office of the President: Private Bag 001, Gaborone; tel. 3950825; fax 3950858; e-mail op.registry@gov.bw; internet www.gov.bw/government/ministry_of_state_president.html#office_of_the_president.

Ministry of Agriculture: Private Bag 003, Gaborone; tel. 3950602; fax 3975805; internet www.gov.bw/government/ministry_of_agriculture.html.

Ministry of Communications, Science and Technology: Gaborone; internet www.gov.bw/government/ministry_of_communications_science_and_technology.html.

Ministry of Education: Chief Education Officer, 2nd Floor, Block 6 Bldg, Government Enclave, Gaborone; Private Bag 005, Gaborone; tel. 3655400; fax 3655458; e-mail moe.webmaster@gov.bw; internet www.moe.gov.bw/moe/index.html.

Ministry of Environment, Wildlife and Tourism: Private Bag 0047, Standard House, 2nd Floor, Main Mall, Gaborone; tel. 3953024; fax 3908675.

Ministry of Finance and Development Planning: Private Bag 008, Gaborone; tel. 3950201; fax 3956086; e-mail gsethebe@gov.bw; internet www.finance.gov.bw.

Ministry of Foreign Affairs: Private Bag 00368, Gaborone; tel. 3600700; fax 3913366; e-mail empofu@gov.bw; internet www.gov.bw/government/ministry_of_foreign_affairs.html.

Ministry of Health: Private Bag 0038, Gaborone; tel. 3974104; fax 3902584; e-mail mgmodise@gov.bw; internet www.gov.bw/government/ministry_of_health.html.

Ministry of Labour and Home Affairs: Private Bag 002, Gaborone; tel. 3611100; fax 3913584; e-mail msetimela@gov.bw ; internet www.gov.bw/government/ministry_of_labour_and_home_affairs.html.

Ministry of Lands and Housing: Private Bag 00434, Gaborone; tel. 3904223; fax 3911591; f. 1999.

Ministry of Minerals, Energy and Water Affairs: Khama Crescent, Private Bag 0018, Gaborone; tel. 3656600; fax 3972738; internet www.gov.bw/government/ministry_of_minerals_energy_and_water_affairs.html.

Ministry of State President: Private Bag 001, Gaborone; tel. 3950815; e-mail bsentle@gov.bw; internet www.gov.bw/government/ministry_of_state_president.html.

Ministry of Trade and Industry: Private Bag 0014, Gaborone; tel. 3957406; fax 3972910; e-mail dia.hq@gov.bw; internet www.mti.gov.bw.

Ministry of Works and Transport: Private Bag 007, Gaborone; tel. 3958500; fax 3913303; internet www.gov.bw/government/ministry_of_works_and_transport.html.

Legislature

HOUSE OF CHIEFS

The House has a total of 15 members. Proposals to rename the House of Chiefs as the Ntlo ya Dikgosi and to increase its membership from 15 to 33 were under consideration.

Chairperson: Chief Mosadi Seboko.

NATIONAL ASSEMBLY

Speaker: Patrick Balopi.

General Election, 30 October 2004

Party	Votes	%	Seats
Botswana Democratic Party	213,308	51.7	44
Botswana National Front	107,451	26.1	12
Botswana Congress Party	68,556	16.6	1
Botswana Alliance Movement	11,716	2.8	—
Botswana People's Party	7,886	1.9	—
Others*	3,482	0.8	—
Total	**412,399**	**100.0**	**57†**

* Including independents and candidates representing the New Democratic Front and MELS Movement of Botswana.
† The President and the Attorney-General are also *ex-officio* members of the National Assembly.

Political Organizations

Botswana Alliance Movement (BAM): Private Bag BO 210, Gaborone; tel. 3913476; fax 3914634; f. 1998 as an alliance of three opposition parties to contest the 1999 general election; Botswana People's Party withdrew in July 2000; Pres. Lepetu Setshwaelo; Chair. Motsamai K. Mpho; Sec.-Gen. Matlhomola Modise.

  Independence Freedom Party (IFP): POB 3, Maun; f. by merger of Botswana Freedom Party and Botswana Independence Party; Pres. Motsamai K. Mpho.

  United Action Party (UAP): Private Bag BO 210, Gaborone; f. 1998; Leader Lepetu Setshwaelo.

Botswana Congress Party (BCP): POB 2918, Gaborone; tel. and fax 3181805; f. 1998 following a split in the Botswana National Front; Pres. Otlaadisa Koosaletse; Chair. Peba Sethantsho; Sec.-Gen. Mokgweetsi Kgosipula.

Botswana Democratic Party (BDP) (Domkrag): POB 28, Tsholetsa House, Gaborone; tel. 3952564; fax 3913911; e-mail domkrag@info.bw; f. 1962 as the Bechuanaland Democratic Party ; Pres. Festus G. Mogae; Chair. Ian Khama; Sec.-Gen. Daniel K. Kwelagobe.

Botswana Labour Party: POB 140, Mahalapye; f. 1989; Pres. Lenyeletse Koma.

Botswana National Front (BNF): POB 1720, Gaborone; tel. 3951789; fax 3184970; f. 1966; Pres. Otsweletse Moupo; Chair. Klaas Motshidisi.

Botswana People's Party (BPP): POB 484, Francistown; f. 1960; Leader Bernard Balikane.

Botswana Progressive Union (BPU): POB 328, Nkange; f. 1982; Leader G. Kaelo.

Botswana Workers' Front (BWF): POB 597, Jwaneng; tel. 5880420; f. 1993; Leader M. M. Akanyang.

MELS Movement of Botswana: POB 501818, Gaborone; tel. and fax 3906005; f. 1993; Leader Themba Joina.

New Democratic Front (NDF): Gaborone; f. 2003 following split in the BNF; Leader Dr Kenneth Koma.

Social Democratic Party (SDP): POB 201818, Gaborone; tel. 3956516; f. 1994; Leader O. Marumo.

United Socialist Party (USP): POB 233, Lobatse; f. 1994; Leader N. Modubule.

Diplomatic Representation

EMBASSIES AND HIGH COMMISSIONS IN BOTSWANA

Angola: 5131 Kopanyo House, Nelson Mandela Dr., Private Bag BR 111, Gaborone; tel. 3900204; fax 3975089; Ambassador Jose Agostinho Neto.

China, People's Republic: 3096 North Ring Rd, POB 1031, Gaborone; tel. 352209; fax 300156; e-mail china_embbw@mfa.gov.cn; Ambassador Lin Difu.

Cuba: Plot 5198, Village, POB 40261, Gaborone; tel. 3951750; fax 3911485; e-mail cubanembassy@botsnet.bw; Ambassador Ana Vilma Vallejera Rodríguez.

France: 761 Robinson Rd, POB 1424, Gaborone; tel. 3973863; fax 3971733; Ambassador Pierre Coulont.

Germany: Professional House, 3rd Floor, Segoditshane Way, Broadhurst, POB 315, Gaborone; tel. 3953143; fax 3953038; e-mail zreg@gabo.diplo.de; Ambassador Dr Hans-Dietrich von Bothmer.

India: Plot 5375, President's Dr., Private Bag 249, Gaborone; tel. 3972676; fax 3974636; e-mail hicomind@info.bw; internet www .highcommissionofindia.com; High Commissioner LAL THLA MUANA.

Kenya: Plot 5373, President's Dr., Private Bag 297, Gaborone; tel. 3951408; fax 3951409; e-mail kenya@info.bw; High Commissioner JAMES BINSAI CHEPSONGOL.

Libya: POB 180, Plot 8851 (Government Enclave), Gaborone; tel. 3952481.

Namibia: POB 987, Plot 186, Morara Close, Gaborone; tel. 3902181; fax 3902248; e-mail nhc.gabs@info.bw; High Commissioner THERESIA SAMARIA.

Nigeria: Plot 1086/92, Queens Rd, The Mall, POB 274, Gaborone; tel. 3913561; fax 3913738; High Commissioner FATIMA ABUBAKAR.

Russia: Plot 4711, Tawana Close, POB 81, Gaborone; tel. 3953389; fax 3952930; e-mail embrus@info.bw; Ambassador IGOR S. LIAKIN.

South Africa: Plot 29, Queens Rd, Private Bag 00402, Gaborone; tel. 3904800; fax 3905501; e-mail sahcgabs@botsnet.bw; High Commissioner E. V. G. KOMANE.

Sweden: NDB Bldg, 4th Floor, The Mall, Private Bag 0017, Gaborone; tel. 3953912; fax 3953942; e-mail ambassaden.gaborone@foreign.ministry.se; Ambassador ANNIKA JAGANDER.

United Kingdom: Plot 1079-1084, Main Mall, off Queens Road, Private Bag 0023, Gaborone; tel. 3952841; fax 3956105; e-mail bhc@botsnet.bw; internet www.britishhighcommission.gov.uk/botswana; High Commissioner DAVID BYRON MERRY.

USA: POB 90, Gaborone; tel. 3953982; fax 3956947; e-mail ircgaborone@state.gov; internet botswana.usembassy.gov; Ambassador JOSEPH HUGGINS.

Zambia: POB 362, Gaborone; tel. 3951951; fax 3953952; High Commissioner CECIL HOLMES.

Zimbabwe: Plot 8850, POB 1232, Gaborone; tel. 3914495; fax 3905863; Ambassador PHELEKEZELA MPHOKO.

Judicial System

There is a High Court at Lobatse and a branch at Francistown, and Magistrates' Courts in each district. Appeals lie to the Court of Appeal of Botswana. The Chief Justice and the President of the Court of Appeal are appointed by the President.

Chief Justice: JULIAN NGANUNU.

High Court
Private Bag 1, Lobatse; tel. 5330396; fax 5332317.

Judges of the High Court: ISAAC K. B. LESETEDI, MARUPING DIBOTELO, UNITY DOW, MOATLHODI MARUMO, STANLEY SAPIRE.

President of the Court of Appeal: PATRICK TEBBUTT.

Justices of Appeal: STANLEY MOORE, JULIAN NGANUNU, HEIN GROSSKOPF, NEVILLE ZIETSMAN, NICHOLAS JOHN MCNALLY, RODGER KORSAH, CHRIS PLEWMAN.

Registrar and Master: GODFREY NTHOMIWA.

Office of the Attorney-General
Private Bag 009, Gaborone; tel. 3954700; fax 3957089.

Attorney-General: IAN STUART KIRBY.

Religion

The majority of the population hold animist beliefs; an estimated 30% are thought to be Christians. There are Islamic mosques in Gaborone and Lobatse. The Bahá'í Faith is also represented.

CHRISTIANITY

Botswana Council of Churches (Lekgotla la Dikereke mo Botswana): POB 355, Gaborone; tel. and fax 3951981; e-mail bots.christ .c@info.bw; f. 1966; Pres. Rev. ODIRILE E. MERE; Gen. Sec. DAVID J. MODIEGA; 24 mem churches and orgs.

The Anglican Communion

Anglicans are adherents of the Church of the Province of Central Africa, comprising 12 dioceses and covering Botswana, Malawi, Zambia and Zimbabwe. The Province was established in 1955, and the diocese of Botswana was formed in 1972. There were some 10,500 adherents at mid-2000.

Archbishop of the Province of Central Africa and Bishop of Botswana: Most Rev. TREVOR MWAMBA, POB 769, Gaborone; fax 3913015; e-mail acenter@info.bw.

Protestant Churches
There were an estimated 178,000 adherents in the country at mid-2000.

African Methodist Episcopal Church: POB 141, Lobatse; tel. 5407520; e-mail mobeat@bpc.bw; Presiding Elder Rev. MOSES P. LEKHORI.

Evangelical Lutheran Church in Botswana (Kereke ya Luthere ya Efangele mo Botswana): POB 1976, Gaborone; tel. 3952227; fax 3913966; e-mail elcb@info.bw; f. 1979; Bishop Rev. PHILIP J. ROBINSON; 43 congregations; c. 25,000 mems (2004).

Evangelical Lutheran Church in Southern Africa (Botswana Diocese): POB 400, Gaborone; tel. 3953976; Bishop Rev. M. NTUPING.

Methodist Church of Southern Africa (Gaborone Circuit): POB 260, Gaborone; tel. 3167627; e-mail methodist@botsnet.bw; Circuit Supt Rev. O. E. MERE.

United Congregational Church of Southern Africa (Synod of Botswana): POB 1263, Gaborone; tel. 3952491; synod status since 1980; Chair. Rev. D. T. MAPITSE; Sec. Rev. M. P. P. DIBEELA; c. 24,000 mems.

Other denominations active in Botswana include the Church of God in Christ, the Dutch Reformed Church, the United Methodist Church and the Seventh-day Adventists.

The Roman Catholic Church
Botswana comprises one diocese and an apostolic vicariate. The metropolitan see is Bloemfontein, South Africa. The church was established in Botswana in 1928, and had an estimated 80,393 adherents (some 4.6% of the total population) in the country at 31 December 2002. The Bishop participates in the Southern African Catholic Bishops' Conference, currently based in Pretoria, South Africa.

Bishop of Gaborone: Rt Rev. BONIFACE TSHOSA SETLALEKGOSI, POB 218, Bishop's House, Gaborone; tel. 3912958; fax 3956970; e-mail gabs.diocese@botsnet.bw.

Vicar Apostolic of Francistown: Rt Rev. FRANKLYN NUBUASAH.

The Press

DAILY NEWSPAPERS

Dikgang tsa Gompieno (Daily News): Private Bag 0060, Gaborone; tel. 3952541; e-mail dailynews@gov.bw; internet www .gov.bw/news; f. 1964; publ. by Dept of Information and Broadcasting; Setswana and English; Mon.–Fri.; Editor ME GOLEKANYE MOLAPISI; circ. 60,000.

Mmegi/The Reporter: Private Bag BR 50, Gaborone; tel. 3974784; fax 3905508; e-mail dikgang@mmegi.bw; internet www.mmegi.bw; f. 1984; daily; Setswana and English; publ. by Dikgang Publishing Co; Man. Editor TITUS MBUYA; circ. 20,000.

PERIODICALS

Agrinews: Private Bag 003, Gaborone; f. 1971; publ. by the Ministry of Agriculture; monthly; agriculture and rural development; circ. 6,000.

Botswana Advertiser: POB 130, 5647 Nakedi Rd, Broadhurst, Gaborone; tel. 3912844; weekly.

Botswana Business Month Magazine: POB 1605, Gaborone; fax 3912774; bimonthly; Editor CLARA OLSEN; circ. 500.

Botswana Business News: Private Bag 00367, Gaborone; fax 3905375; monthly; publ. by Ministry of Trade and Industry; Editors MUKRAM SHEIKH, MONTY LETSHWITI; circ. 3,000.

The Botswana Gazette: 125 Sedimosa House, Millennium Park, Kgale View, POB 1605, Gaborone; tel. 3912833; fax 3972283; e-mail editor@gazette.bw; internet www.gazette.bw; f. 1985; weekly; Man. Editor CLARA OLSEN; circ. 19,000.

Botswana Guardian: POB 1641, Gaborone; tel. 3908432; fax 3908457; e-mail guardsun@info.bw; f. 1952; weekly; Editor OUTSA MOKONE; circ. 21,505.

Botswana Journal of Technology: University of Botswana, Private Bag 0061, Gaborone; tel. 3554210; fax 3952309; e-mail ngowiab@mopipi.ub.bw; 2 a year; science and technology; Reviews Editor Prof. A. B. NGOWI.

Business and Financial Times: Unit 9, Plot 64, Gaborone International Commerce Park, POB 402396, Gaborone; tel. 3939911; fax 3939910; e-mail businesstimes@botsnet.bw ; Editor JIMMY SWIRA.

Government Gazette: Private Bag 0081, Gaborone; tel. 353202; fax 312001; weekly.

Kutlwano: Private Bag BR 139, Gaborone; tel. 3653500; fax 3653630; e-mail kutlwano@gov.bw; monthly; Setswana and English; publ. by Dept of Information Services; Editor RUSS MOLOSIWA; circ. 45,000.

The Midweek Sun: POB 00153, Gaborone; tel. 3908432; fax 3908457; e-mail guardsun@info.bw; internet www.midweeksun.co .bw; f. 1989; weekly; Editor MIKE MOTHIBI; circ. 17,971.

Motswana Woman: 686 Botswana Rd, Gaborone; tel. 3975362; fax 3975378; monthly; women's interests; circ. 4,000.

Northern Advertiser: Village Mall, POB 1108, Francistown; tel. 212265; fax 213769; e-mail rsfish@global.bw; f. 1985; weekly; advertisements, local interest, sport; Editor GRACE FISH; circ. 6,000.

The Zebra's Voice: National Museum, 331 Independence Ave, Private Bag 00114, Gaborone; tel. 3974616; fax 3902797; e-mail bemotswakhumo@gov.bw; internet www.botswana-museum.gov .bw; f. 1980; quarterly; cultural affairs; Editor BERLINAH MOTSWAKHUMO; circ. 5,000.

NEWS AGENCIES

Department of Information Services, Botswana Press Agency (BOPA): Private Bag BR 139, Gaborone; tel. 3653525; fax 3653626; e-mail bopa@gov.bw; f. 1981; News Editor MABEL KEBOTSAMANG.

Foreign Bureaux

Deutsche Presse-Agentur (Germany) and **Reuters** (UK) are represented in Botswana.

Publishers

A. C. Braby (Botswana) (Pty) Ltd: Unit 3/A/2, Western Industrial Estate, 22100 Phase 4, Gaborone West, POB 1549, Gaborone; tel. 3971444; fax 3973462; e-mail phonebook@yellowpages.bw; internet www.yellowpages.bw; business directories.

The Botswana Society: POB 71, Gaborone; tel. 3919673; fax 3919745; e-mail info@botsoc.org.bw; internet www.botsoc.org.bw; f. 1968; archaeology, arts, history, law, sciences.

Heinemann Educational Botswana (Pty) Ltd: POB 10103, Village Post Office, Gaborone; tel. 3972305; fax 3971832; e-mail hein@ info.bw; internet www.heinemann.co.za; Man. Dir LESEDI SEITEI.

Longman Botswana (Pty) Ltd: POB 1083, Lobatse Rd, Gaborone; tel. 3922969; fax 3922682; e-mail lb@longman.info.bw; f. 1981; educational; Man. Dir J. K. CHALASHIKA.

Macmillan Botswana Publishing Co (Pty) Ltd: POB 1155, Plot 56305, Block 10, Airport Road; tel. 311770; fax 311987; e-mail uiterwykw@macmillan.bw; Gen. Man. W. UITERWYK.

Morula Press: Business School of Botswana, Ext 2, 222 Independence Ave, Selemelo, POB 402492, Gaborone; tel. 3906134; fax 3904809; f. 1994; business, law.

Printing and Publishing Co (Botswana) (Pty) Ltd (PPCB): POB 130, 5647 Nakedi Rd, Broadhurst, Gaborone; tel. 3912844; e-mail ppcb@info.bw; education; Man. Dir Y. MUSSA; Gen. Man. GAVIN BLAMIRE.

GOVERNMENT PUBLISHING HOUSE

Department of Government Printing and Publishing Service: Private Bag 0081, Gaborone; tel. 353202; fax 312001; Dir ANDREW SESINYI.

Broadcasting and Communications

TELECOMMUNICATIONS

In early 1998 two companies were granted licences to operate mobile cellular telephone networks.

Botswana Telecommunications Authority (BTA): Private Bag 00495, 206–207 Independence Ave, Gaborone; tel. 3957755; fax 3957976; e-mail info@bta.org.bw; internet www.bta.org.bw; f. 1996; Chair. C. M. LEKAUKAU.

Botswana Telecommunications Corporation: POB 700, Gaborone; tel. 3958411; fax 3952777; internet www.btc.bw; f. 1980; state-owned; Chair. WILFRED MANDLEBE; CEO NOEL HERRITY.

BROADCASTING

Department of Information and Broadcasting: Private Bag 0060, Gaborone; tel. 3952541; fax 3957138; e-mail asesinyi@btv.gov .bw; Dir O. ANDREW SESINYI.

Radio

Radio Botswana: Private Bag 0060, Gaborone; tel. 3952541; fax 3957138; e-mail rbeng@info.bw; broadcasts in Setswana and English; govt-owned; f. 1965; Dir ANDREW SESINYI; Chief Eng. HABUJI SOSOME.

Radio Botswana II: Private Bag 0060, Gaborone; tel. 3952541; fax 3971588; f. 1992; commercial service.

Yarona FM: POB 1607, Gaborone; tel. 3912305; fax 3901063; e-mail info@yaronafm.co.bw; f. 1999; independent; Station Man. DUMI LOPANG.

Television

Botswana Television: Dept of Information & Broadcasting, Private Bag 0060, Gaborone; tel. 3658000; fax 3900051; internet www .btv.gov.bw; e-mail mhillman@btv.gov.bw; govt-funded national TV service; broadcasts commenced in July 2000; Gen. Man. (vacant).

TV Association of Botswana: Gaborone; relays SABC-TV and BOP-TV programmes from South Africa.

Finance

(cap. = capital; res = reserves; dep. = deposits; m. = million; brs = branches; amounts in pula)

BANKING

Central Bank

Bank of Botswana: POB 712, Private Bag 154,17938 Khama Crescent, Gaborone; tel. 3606000; fax 3601100; e-mail rakhudue@ bob.bw; internet www.bankofbotswana.bw; f. 1975; bank of issue; cap. 25m., res 2,705.0m., dep. 10,339.1m. (Dec. 2003); Gov. LINAH MOHOHLO.

Commercial Banks

Bank of Baroda (Botswana) Ltd: POB 21559, Plot 50370, Ground Floor, Acumen Park, Gaborone; tel. 588878; fax 588879; e-mail md .botswana@bankofbaroda.com; internet www.bankofbaroda.com; f. 2001; subsidiary of the Bank of Baroda (India); Man. Dir M. M GADIGI.

Barclays Bank of Botswana Ltd: POB 478, Barclays House, 6th Floor, Plot 8842, Khama Crescent, Gaborone; tel. 3953411; fax 3913672; e-mail howard.sparke@barclaysmail.com; internet www .barclays.com; f. 1975; 74.9% owned by Barclays Bank PLC (UK); cap. 8.5m., res 369.3m., dep. 3,526.6m. (Dec. 2001); Chair. M. C. TIBONE; Man. Dir DUNCAN D. MLAZIE; 48 brs.

First National Bank of Botswana Ltd: POB 1552, Finance House, 5th Floor, Plot 8843, Khama Crescent, Gaborone; tel. 3911669; fax 3906130; e-mail pbellos@fnbbotswana.co.bw; internet www.fnbbotswana.co.bw; f. 1991; 69.5% owned by First National Bank Holdings Botswana Ltd; cap. and res 292.7m., total assets 3,198.7m. (June 2004); Chair. HENRY C. L. HERMANS; Man. Dir ALEXANDER W. PARK; 12 brs.

Kingdom Bank Africa Limited: Plot 133, Extension 3, Independence Ave, Gaborone; POB 45078, Riverwalk, Gaborone; tel. 3906863; fax 3906874; f. 2003; Chair. NIGEL CHANKIRA; Man. Dir IRENE CHAMNEY; Exec. Dir TAPIWA SHAMU.

Stanbic Bank Botswana Ltd: Private Bag 00168, Stanbic House, Plot 50672, Fairground (off Machel Dr.), Gaborone; tel. 301600; fax 300171; e-mail botswanainfo@stanbic.com; internet www.stanbic .com; f. 1992 by merger; subsidiary of Standard Bank Investment Corpn Africa Holdings Ltd; cap. and res 90.3m., total assets 1,138.4m. (Dec. 2001); Chair. O. M. GABORONE; Man. Dirs D. W. KENNEDY; W. L. V. PRICE; Exec. Dir G. D. MARAIS; 6 brs.

Standard Chartered Bank Botswana Ltd: POB 496, Standard House, 5th Floor, The Mall, Gaborone; tel. 3953111; fax 3972933; internet www.standardcharteredbank.com; f. 1975; 75% owned by Standard Chartered Holdings (Africa) BV, Amsterdam; cap. and res 196.5m., total assets 2,393.0m. (Dec. 2000); Chair. P. L. STEENKAMP; Chief Executive D. N. T. KUWANA; CEO NIGEL JONES; 14 brs; 4 agencies.

Other Banks

Botswana Savings Bank: Tshomarelo House, POB 1150, Gaborone; tel. 3971236; fax 3952608; e-mail bsb@info.bw; internet www.bsb.bw; f. 1992; cap. and res 48.4m., dep. 101.5m. (March 2000); Chair. F. MODISE; Man. Dir MICHAEL LESOLLE.

National Development Bank: POB 225, Development House, Queens Rd, Gaborone; tel. 3952801; fax 3974446; f. 1964; cap. 77.7m., res 17.2m., total assets 247.6m. (March 1999); priority given to agricultural credit for Botswana farmers, and co-operative credit and loans for local business ventures; Chair. F. Modise; Gen. Man. O. M. Ramasedi; 5 brs.

STOCK EXCHANGE

Botswana Stock Exchange: Private Bag 00417, Finance House, 4th Floor, Unit 11, Millennium Office Park, Kgale Mews, Gaborone; tel. 3180201; fax 3180175; e-mail enquiries@bse.co.bw; internet www.bse.co.bw; f. 1989; commenced formal functions of a stock exchange in 1995; Chair. Louis G. Nchindo; CEO Dr T. T. K. Matome.

INSURANCE

Botswana Co-operative Insurance Co Ltd: POB 199, Gaborone; tel. and fax 313654.

Botswana Eagle Insurance Co Ltd: POB 1221, 501 Botsalano House, Gaborone; tel. 3919910; fax 3919911; e-mail john.main@saeagle.co.za; subsidiary of SA Eagle; Gen. Man. John Main.

Botswana Insurance Holdings (BIHL): BIC House, The Mall, POB 336, Gaborone; tel. 3600500; fax 373457; 56% owned by African Life Assurance Co Ltd; Man. Dir John A. Burbidge; Gen. Man. Limited Quite (acting).

Botswana Life: Private Bag 00296, Gaborone; tel. 3951791; fax 3905884; e-mail blil@lifeinsurance.bw; CEO Regina Vaka.

Mutual and Federal Insurance Co of Botswana Ltd: Private Bag 00347, Gaborone; tel. 3903333; fax 3903400; e-mail tfitt@mf.co.za; Man. Dir Bryan Kelly.

Sedgwick James Insurance Brokers (Pty) Ltd: POB 103, Plot 730, The Mall, Botswana Rd, Gaborone; tel. 3953899; fax 3973120.

Trade and Industry

GOVERNMENT AGENCIES

Botswana Housing Corporation (BHC): POB 412, Gaborone; tel. 3605100; fax 3952070; e-mail info@bhc.bw; internet www.bhc.bw; f. 1971; provides housing for central govt and local authority needs and assists with private-sector housing schemes; Chair. Maclean C. Letshwiti; CEO Milidzani A. Majingo (acting).

Department of Food Resources: POB 96, Gaborone; tel. 3954124; f. 1982; procurement, storage and distribution of food commodities under the Drought Relief Programme; Admin. Officer M. S. Sehlulane.

Department of Town and Regional Planning: Private Bag 0042, Gaborone; tel. 3951935; e-mail infoterra@info.bw; f. 1972; responsible for physical planning matters throughout the country, including formulation of national physical planning policy; prepares devt plans for settlements and regions and provides physical planning advice to govt and local authorities as well as private bodies.

DEVELOPMENT ORGANIZATIONS

Botswana Development Corporation Ltd: Private Bag 160, Moedi, Plot 50380, Gaborone International Showgrounds, off Machel Dr., Gaborone; tel. 3651300; fax 3904193; e-mail enquiries@bdc.bw; internet www.bdc.bw; f. 1970; Chair. S. S. G. Tumelo; Man. Dir Kenneth O. Matambo.

Botswana Enterprise Development Unit (BEDU): POB 0014, Plot 1269, Lobatse Rd, Gaborone; f. 1974; promotes industrialization and rural devt; Dir J. Lindfors.

Botswana Export Development and Investment Authority (BEDIA): POB 3122, Plot 28, Matsitama Rd, The Main Mall, Gaborone; tel. 3181931; fax 3181941; e-mail bedia@bedia.bw; internet www.bedia.co.bw; f. 1998; promotes and facilitates local and foreign investment; Chair. Uttum Corea; CEO Mmasekegoa Masire-Mwamba.

Department of Trade and Investment Promotion (TIPA) Ministry of Trade and Industry: Private Bag 00367, Gaborone; tel. 3951790; fax 3905375; e-mail tipa@info.bw; internet www.tipa.bw; promotes industrial and commercial investment, diversification and expansion; offers consultancy, liaison and information services; participates in overseas trade fairs and trade and investment missions; Dir D. Tsheko.

Financial Services Co of Botswana (Pty) Ltd: POB 1129, Finance House, Khama Cres., Gaborone; tel. 3951363; fax 3957815; f. 1974; hire purchase, mortgages, industrial leasing and debt factoring; Chair. M. E. Hopkins; Man. Dir R. A. Pawson.

Integrated Field Services: Private Bag 004, Ministry of Trade and Industry, Gaborone; tel. 3953024; fax 3971539; promotes industrialization and rural development; Dir B. T. Tibone.

International Financial Services Centre: Private Bag 160, Plot 50380, Moedi, Fairgrounds Office Park, Gaborone; tel. 3651300; fax 3913075; e-mail ifsc@ifsc.co.bw; internet www.ifsc.co.bw; f. 2000; Chair. H. C. L. Hermans; CEO A. P. Boshwaen.

CHAMBER OF COMMERCE

Botswana National Chamber of Commerce and Industry: POB 20344, Gaborone; tel. 3952677.

INDUSTRIAL AND TRADE ASSOCIATIONS

Botswana Agricultural Marketing Board (BAMB): Private Bag 0053, 1227 Haile Selassie Rd, Gaborone; tel. 3951341; fax 3952926; Chair. Mmapula Modise; Gen. Man. S. B. Taukobong.

Botswana Meat Commission (BMC): Private Bag 4, Lobatse; tel. 5331000; fax 5332228; e-mail mmannathoko@bmc.bw; f. 1966; slaughter of livestock, export of hides and skins, carcasses, frozen and chilled boneless beef; operates tannery and beef products cannery; Exec. Chair. Dr M. V. Raborokgwe.

EMPLOYERS' ORGANIZATIONS

Botswana Confederation of Commerce, Industry and Manpower (BOCCIM): POB 432, BOCCIM House, Gaborone; e-mail boccim@info.bw; f. 1971; Pres. Mogolori Modisi; Dir Elias Dewah.

Botswana Federation for Secondary School Teachers (BOFESTE): Unit 5, Commerce Park, POB 404341, Broadhurst, Gaborone; tel. 3937472; fax 3170845; Pres. Baboloki Tlale.

Botswana Teachers' Union (BTU): BTU Centre, P/Bag 0019, Mogoditshane; tel. 3906774; fax 3909838; e-mail btu@it.bw; internet www.btu.co.bw; f. 1937 as the Bechuanaland Protectorate African Teachers' Association; present name adopted 1966; Pres. Japhta Radibe; Sec. Gen. Caiphus Dema; 13,000 mems.

UTILITIES

Electricity

Botswana Power Corporation: POB 48, Motlakase House, Macheng Way, Gaborone; tel. 3603203; fax 3973563; f. 1971; operates power stations at Selebi-Phikwe (capacity 65 MW) and Moropule (132 MW); Chair. C. M. Lekaukau; CEO Ketane Sithole.

Water

Department of Water Affairs: Khama Cres., Private Bag 0018, Gaborone; tel. 3656600; fax 3972738; provides public water supplies for rural areas.

Water Utilities Corporation: Private Bag 00276, Gaborone; tel. 3604400; fax 3973852; e-mail metsi@wuc.bw; internet www.wuc.bw; f. 1970; 100% state-owned; supplies water to main urban centres and major villages; Chair. Nozipho Mabe; Chief Exec. F. Maunge.

CO-OPERATIVES

Department of Co-operative Development: POB 003, Gaborone; tel. 3950730; fax 3951657; f. 1964; promotes marketing and supply, consumer, dairy, horticultural and fisheries co-operatives, thrift and loan societies, credit societies, a co-operative union and a co-operative bank; Commissioner W. Moatshe (acting).

TRADE UNIONS

Botswana Federation of Trade Unions: POB 440, Gaborone; tel. and fax 3952534; e-mail bot.ftu@info.bw; f. 1977; Pres. Ronald Dust Baipidi; 25,000 mems (2001).

Affiliated Unions

Botswana Bank Employees' Union (BOBEU): Ext 4, South Ring Rd, Dilalelo, POB 111, Gaborone; tel. 3905893; Gen. Sec. Alfred Seleke.

Botswana Construction Workers' Union: POB 1508, Gaborone; Gen. Sec. Joshua Kesiilwe.

Botswana Diamond Sorters-Valuators' Union (BDSVU): POB 1186, Gaborone; Gen. Sec. Edward Keloneilwe.

Botswana Mining Workers' Union: POB 86, Orapa; tel. 2970331; fax 2970067; Chair. Chimbidzani Chimidza.

Botswana Postal Services Workers' Union: POB 87, Gaborone; Chair. Aaron Lefu.

Botswana Power Corporation Workers' Union: Private Bag 0053, Gaborone; Gen. Sec. Molefe Modise.

Botswana Railways Amalgamated Workers' Union (BRAWU): POB 181, Gaborone; Chair. Letlampona Mokgalajwe.

Botswana Telecommunications Employees' Union (BOTEU): Gaborone; Pres. LESETSWE KOFA.

Principal Non-affiliated Unions

Botswana Commercial and General Workers' Union: POB 62, Gaborone; tel. 3911874; fax 3959360; split from the BFTU in 1988; Gen. Sec. KEDIRETSE MPETANG.

Botswana Local Authorities Workers' Union: Private Bag 40, Francistown; tel. 2413312; fax 2413312; e-mail info@bulgsa.org.bw ; internet www.bulgsa.org.bw; f. 1974 as the Botswana Unified Local Government Service Association; present name adopted 2005; Pres. PELOTSHWEU BAENG.

National Amalgamated Local and Central Government, Parastatal, Statutory Body and Manual Workers' Union: Ext. 15, Plot No. 4946/7, Jawara Rd, POB 374, Gaborone; tel. 352790; fax 357790; e-mail nalcgpwu@info.bwu; Chair. DAVID TSALAILE; Gen. Sec. SIMON KGAOGANANG.

Transport

RAILWAYS

The 960-km railway line from Mafikeng, South Africa, to Bulawayo, Zimbabwe, passes through Botswana and has been operated by Botswana Railways (BR) since 1987. In 1997 there were 888 km of 1,067-mm-gauge track within Botswana, including three branches serving the Selebi-Phikwe mining complex (56 km), the Morupule colliery (16 km) and the Sua Pan soda-ash deposits (175 km). BR derives 85%–90% of its earnings from freight traffic, although passenger services do operate between Gaborone and Francistown, and Lobatse and Bulawayo. Through its links with Spoornet, which operates the South African railways system and the National Railways of Zimbabwe, BR provides connections with Namibia and Swaziland to the south, and an uninterrupted rail link to Zambia, the Democratic Republic of the Congo, Angola, Mozambique, Tanzania and Malawi to the north. However, freight traffic on BR was severely reduced following Zimbabwe's construction, in 1999, of a rail link from Bulawayo to Beitbridge, on its border with South Africa.

Botswana Railways (BR): Private Bag 52, Mahalapye; tel. 4711375; fax 4711377; f. 1987; Chair. IQBAL EBRAHIM; Gen. Man. KGOTLA RAMAPHANE (acting).

ROADS

In 1999 there were 10,217 km of roads, including 3,360 km of main roads, and 2,210 km of secondary roads; some 55.0% of the road network was paved (including a main road from Gaborone, via Francistown, to Kazungula, where the borders of Botswana, Namibia, Zambia and Zimbabwe meet). The construction of a 340-km road between Nata and Maun was completed in the late 1990s. Construction of the 600-km Trans-Kalahari Highway, from Jwaneng to the port of Walvis Bay on the Namibian coast, commenced in 1990 and was completed in 1998. A car-ferry service operates from Kazungula across the Zambezi river into Zambia.

Department of Road Transport and Safety: Private Bag 0026, Gaborone; tel. 3905442; responsible for national road network; responsible to the Ministry of Works and Transport; Dir MOSES K. SEBOLAI.

CIVIL AVIATION

The main international airport is at Gaborone. Four other major airports are located at Kasane, Maun, Francistown and Ghanzi. In 2000 there were also 108 airfields throughout the country. Scheduled services of Air Botswana are supplemented by an active charter and business sector.

Air Botswana: POB 92, Sir Seretse Khama Airport, Gaborone; tel. 3952812; fax 3974802; e-mail commercial@airbotswana.co.bw; internet www.airbotswana.co.bw; f. 1972; 45% govt-owned; transfer to private sector suspended in April 2004; domestic services and regional services to countries in eastern and southern Africa; Chair. G. N. THIPE; Gen. Man. R. WILLIE MOKGATLHE; 150,000 passengers per year.

Tourism

There are five game reserves and three national parks, including Chobe, near Victoria Falls, on the Zambia–Zimbabwe border. Efforts to expand the tourism industry include plans for the construction of new hotels and the rehabilitation of existing hotel facilities. In 2002 foreign tourist arrivals were estimated at 1,037,000; receipts from tourism amounted to an estimated US $309m. in that year.

Department of Tourism: Ministry of Environment, Wildlife and Tourism, Private Bag 0047, Standard House, 2nd Floor, Main Mall, Gaborone; tel. 3953024; fax 3908675; e-mail botswanatourism@gov .bw; internet www.botswanatourism.org; f. 1994; Dir TLHABOLOGO NDZINGE.

Department of Wildlife and National Parks: POB 131, Gaborone; tel. 3971405; fax 3912354; e-mail dwnp@gov.bw; Dir J. MATLHARE.

Hospitality and Tourism Association of Botswana (HATAB): Private Bag 00423, Gaborone; tel. 3957144; fax 3903201; e-mail morera@hatab.bw; fmrly Hotel and Tourism Association of Botswana; CEO ODIRILE MEAFHE.

BRAZIL

Introductory Survey

Location, Climate, Language, Religion, Flag, Capital

The Federative Republic of Brazil, the fifth largest country in the world, lies in central and north-eastern South America. To the north are Venezuela, Colombia, Guyana, Suriname and French Guiana, to the west Peru and Bolivia, and to the south Paraguay, Argentina and Uruguay. Brazil has a very long coastline on the Atlantic Ocean. Climatic conditions vary from hot and wet in the tropical rainforest of the Amazon basin to temperate in the savannah grasslands of the central and southern uplands, which have warm summers and mild winters. In Rio de Janeiro temperatures are generally between 17°C (63°F) and 29°C (85°F). The official language is Portuguese. Almost all of the inhabitants profess Christianity, and about 90% are adherents of the Roman Catholic Church. The national flag (proportions 7 by 10) is green, bearing, at the centre, a yellow diamond containing a blue celestial globe with 26 white five-pointed stars (one for each of Brazil's states), arranged in the pattern of the southern firmament, below an equatorial scroll with the motto 'Ordem e Progresso' ('Order and Progress'), and a single star above the scroll. The capital is Brasília.

Recent History

Formerly a Portuguese possession, Brazil became an independent monarchy in 1822, and a republic in 1889. A federal constitution for the United States of Brazil was adopted in 1891. Following social unrest in the 1920s, the economic crisis of 1930 resulted in a major revolt, led by Dr Getúlio Vargas, who was installed as President. He governed the country as a benevolent dictator until forced to resign by the armed forces in December 1945. During Vargas's populist rule, Brazil enjoyed internal stability and steady economic progress. He established a strongly authoritarian corporate state, similar to fascist regimes in Europe, but in 1942 Brazil entered the Second World War on the side of the Allies.

A succession of ineffectual presidential terms (including another by Vargas, who was re-elected in 1950) failed to establish stable government in the late 1940s and early 1950s. President Jânio Quadros, elected in 1960, resigned after only seven months in office, and in September 1961 the Vice-President, João Goulart, was sworn in as President. Military leaders suspected Goulart, the leader of the Partido Trabalhista Brasileiro (PTB), of communist sympathies, and they were reluctant to let him succeed to the presidency. As a compromise, the Constitution was amended to restrict the powers of the President and to provide for a Prime Minister. However, following the appointment of three successive premiers during a 16-month period of mounting political crisis, the system was rejected when a referendum, conducted in January 1963, approved a return to the presidential system of government, whereupon President Goulart formed his own Cabinet.

Following a period of economic crisis, exacerbated by allegations of official corruption, the left-wing regime of President Goulart was overthrown in April 1964 by a bloodless right-wing military coup led by Gen. (later Marshal) Humberto Castelo Branco, the Army Chief of Staff, who was promptly elected President by the National Congress (Congresso Nacional). In October 1965 President Castelo Branco assumed dictatorial powers, and all 13 existing political parties were banned. In December, however, two artificially-created parties, the pro-Government Aliança Renovadora Nacional (ARENA) and the opposition Movimento Democrático Brasileiro (MDB), were granted official recognition. President Castelo Branco nominated as his successor the Minister of War, Marshal Artur da Costa e Silva, who was elected in October 1966 and took office in March 1967 as President of the redesignated Federative Republic of Brazil (a new Constitution was introduced simultaneously). The ailing President da Costa e Silva was forced to resign in September 1969 and was replaced by a triumvirate of military leaders.

The military regime granted the President wide-ranging powers to rule by decree. In October 1969 the ruling junta introduced a revised Constitution, vesting executive authority in an indirectly-elected President. The Congresso Nacional,

suspended since December 1968, was recalled and elected Gen. Emílio Garrastazú Médici as President. Médici was succeeded as President by Gen. Ernesto Geisel and Gen. João Baptista de Figueiredo, respectively. Despite the attempts of both Presidents to pursue a policy of *abertura*, or opening to democratization, opposition to military rule intensified throughout the 1970s and early 1980s. In November 1982 the government-sponsored Partido Democrático Social (PDS) suffered significant losses at elections to the Câmara dos Deputados (Chamber of Deputies), state governorships and municipal councils. However, the PDS secured a majority of seats in the Senado Federal (Federal Senate) and, owing to pre-election legislation, seemed set to enjoy a guaranteed majority in the electoral college, scheduled to choose a successor to Gen. Figueiredo in 1985.

However, in July 1984 Vice-President Antônio Chaves de Mendonça and the influential Marco de Oliveira Maciel, a former Governor of Pernambuco, formed an alliance of liberal PDS members with members of the Partido do Movimento Democrático Brasileiro (PMDB), which, in December, became an official political party, the Partido Frente Liberal (PFL). This offered the opposition a genuine opportunity to defeat the PDS in the electoral college and at the presidential election, conducted in January 1985, the PFL candidate, Tancredo Neves (Prime Minister in 1961–62) was elected as Brazil's first civilian President for 21 years. However, Neves died before he could be inaugurated and, as a result, the PFL vice-presidential candidate, José Sarney, took office as President in April. President Sarney affirmed his commitment to fulfilling the objectives of the late President-designate. In May the Congresso Nacional approved a constitutional amendment restoring direct elections by universal suffrage.

The introduction in February 1986 of an anti-inflation programme, the Cruzado Plan, proved, initially, to be successful. Support for the Government was demonstrated in November at elections to the Congresso Nacional, which was to operate as a Constitutional Assembly (Assembléia Constitucional). The constitutional debate was dominated by the issue of the length of the presidential mandate. In June 1988 the Assembly approved a presidential mandate of five years. The first round of voting for the presidential election was provisionally set for 15 November 1989, thereby enabling Sarney to remain in office until March 1990. This *de facto* victory for the President precipitated a series of resignations by some of the leading members of the PMDB, who subsequently formed a new centre-left party, the Partido da Social Democracia Brasileira (PSDB). The Constitution was approved by the Congresso Nacional on 22 September 1988 and was promulgated in early October. Among its 245 articles were provisions transferring many hitherto presidential powers to the legislature. In addition, censorship was abolished, as was the National Security Law, whereby many political dissidents had been detained; the minimum voting age was lowered to 16 years; and the principle of habeas corpus was recognized. However, the Constitution offered no guarantees of land reform, and was thought by many to be nationalistic and protectionist.

Brazil's first presidential election by direct voting since 1960 took place on 15 November 1989. The main contenders were the conservative Fernando Collor de Mello, of the newly-formed Partido de Reconstrução Nacional (PRN), Luiz Inácio (Lula) da Silva of the left-wing Partido dos Trabalhadores (PT) and Leonel Brizola of the centre-left Partido Democrático Trabalhista (PDT). A second round on 17 December, contested by the two leading candidates, Collor de Mello and da Silva, was won by Collor de Mello, with 53% of the votes cast. Following his inauguration on 15 March 1990, the new President announced an ambitious programme of economic reform, entitled 'New Brazil' (known as the 'Collor Plan'), with the principal aim of reducing inflation, which had reached a monthly rate of more than 80%. A new currency, the cruzeiro (to replace, at par, the novo cruzado) was also introduced. The PRN's poor performance in the congressional and state gubernatorial elections of October and November was largely attributed to the severity and apparent failure of its economic austerity programme. A second economic plan, presented as an intensification of the Collor

Plan, was implemented in February 1991. In March Collor de Mello announced a new Plan for National Reconstruction, which envisaged further deregulation and rationalization of many state-controlled areas, including the ports, and the communications and fuel sectors.

Collor de Mello's position became increasingly precarious towards the end of 1991, after allegations of mismanagement of federal funds were made against his wife and several associates in the President's home state of Alagoas. During informal multi-party negotiations in September 1991, the President attempted to achieve greater congressional consensus and to reinforce his own mandate. In the same month, Collor de Mello presented a comprehensive series of proposals for constitutional amendment before the Congresso. Nevertheless, allegations of high-level corruption persisted into 1992 and the President failed to dispel suspicions sufficiently to attract the wider political participation in government necessary to facilitate the passage of legislation through an increasingly ineffectual Congresso Nacional. In May the President became the focus of further allegations following a series of disclosures made by his younger brother which appeared to implicate the President in a number of corrupt practices orchestrated by Paulo César Farias, Collor de Mello's 1989 election campaign treasurer. As a result, the Congresso Nacional established a special commission of inquiry to investigate the affair and in early September, after the commission had delivered its report, and bolstered by massive popular support, a 49-member congressional committee authorized the initiation of impeachment proceedings against the President. On 29 September the Câmara dos Deputados voted to proceed with the impeachment of the President for abuses of authority and position, prompting the immediate resignation of the Cabinet. On 2 October Collor de Mello surrendered authority to Vice-President Itamar Franco for a six-month period, pending the final pronouncement regarding his future in office, to be decided by the Senado.

In December 1992 the Senado voted overwhelmingly to proceed with Collor de Mello's impeachment and to indict the President for 'crimes of responsibility'. Within minutes of the opening of the impeachment trial on 29 December, however, Collor de Mello announced his resignation from the presidency. Itamar Franco was immediately sworn in to serve the remainder of Collor de Mello's term. On the following day the Senado, which had agreed to continue with proceedings against Collor de Mello, announced that the former President's political rights (including immunity from prosecution) were to be removed. In January 1993 the Supreme Court announced that Collor de Mello was to stand trial as an ordinary citizen on charges of 'passive corruption and criminal association', and in December the Court endorsed the Senado's eight-year ban on his holding public office. In December 1994, however, the Tribunal voted to acquit Collor de Mello of the charges, owing to insufficient evidence. In January 1998 the former President was cleared of charges of illegal enrichment.

Following several unsuccessful attempts in late 1992 and early 1993 to address the problems of burgeoning inflation and massive budget deficit, in June 1993 the new Minister of the Economy, Fernando Henrique Cardoso, announced the terms of the Government's latest economic programme, the *plano de verdade* (real plan). A new currency, the cruzeiro real, was introduced in August. A programme for economic stability, announced in December, sought to regulate the flow of federal resources to states and municipalities. Congressional approval for the establishment of a Social Emergency Fund prompted the activation of a transitional index, the Unidade Real de Valor (URV), linked to the US dollar, on 1 March 1994. On 1 July the new currency, the real, was introduced, at par with the dollar.

In April 1993 the PDT announced its withdrawal from the ruling coalition, following Franco's decision to proceed with the privatization of the prestigious national steel company, the Companhia Siderúrgica Nacional (CSN). In August the Partido Socialista Brasileiro (PSB) also withdrew from the coalition, and in the following month the PMDB national council narrowly defeated a motion to end its association with the Government. The fragility of the Government was exacerbated by a new corruption scandal in October, in which numerous senior politicians were implicated in a fraudulent scheme in which political influence was allegedly exercised in order to secure state projects for individual construction companies, in exchange for bribes. A congressional committee of inquiry was established, and, as a result of the investigation, in April 1994 the Câmara dos Deputados voted to expel three deputies and to continue

investigations into four deputies who had recently resigned. In the same month the Congresso Nacional concluded a review of the Constitution, having adopted just six amendments, including a reduction in the length of the presidential term from five to four years.

Allegations of corruption and misconduct preceding the elections in October 1994 forced the replacement of the vice-presidential running mates of both Cardoso and da Silva and the withdrawal from the contest of the PL's presidential candidate. Cardoso, whose candidacy was supported by the PFL, the PTB, the Partido Liberal (PL) and the business community, won the presidential contest in the first round, with an overall majority of 54.3% of the votes, following a campaign that had focused largely on the success of his economic initiatives.

Cardoso was inaugurated as President on 1 January 1995 and a new Cabinet was installed on the following day. The multi-party composition of the Cabinet (with portfolios allocated not only to those parties that had supported his candidacy, but also to the PT and the PMDB) demonstrated the new President's need to maintain a broad base of congressional support in order to secure prompt endorsement for proposed constitutional reform of the taxation and social security systems. However, opposition to the ongoing programme of economic stabilization and to renewed efforts by the Government to introduce constitutional amendments, including those that would end state monopolies in the telecommunications and petroleum sectors, resulted, in May 1995, in a general strike. The President's decision to order military intervention in a number of crucial petroleum refineries was widely interpreted as evidence of the Government's intent to undermine the concerted action of the political opposition and the trade unions. However, a number of amendments, including to the petroleum sector and telecommunications, were subsequently approved by the Senado.

By December 1995, however, Cardoso's integrity had been seriously compromised by the alleged involvement of a number of his political associates in irregular financial transactions, and by an influence-peddling scandal arising from the award to a US company of the contract for development of an Amazon Regional Surveillance System (Sivam), which resulted in the resignation of the Minister of the Air Force. Meanwhile, investigation of the so-called 'pink folder' of politicians continued during 1996, as the banking sector was plunged into further crisis. In March it was revealed that the Government had withheld details of a US $5,000m.-fraud perpetrated at the Banco Nacional a decade earlier. Moreover, it emerged that the Government had extended a recent credit facility of US $5,800m. to the bank in order to facilitate its merger with UNIBANCO in November 1995.

The results of municipal elections conducted in October 1996 revealed a reduction in support for the PSDB and disappointed many veteran parties. None the less, Cardoso's own popularity benefited from the success of the Government's attempts to control inflation, although the unions remained dissatisfied with the Government's failure to halt rising levels of unemployment. In June the Government announced details of the next phase of its massive divestment programme. Several companies in the power sector, 31 ports and the prestigious mining company, Companhia Vale do Rio Doce (CVRD) were among those state concerns to be offered for sale. In July the Government announced that the state telecommunications company, Telebrás, together with large sections of the rail and power networks, would be privatized by the end of 1998. Further reductions in public spending were announced in August and October.

In March 1997 legislation was approved ending the long-standing monopoly of Petróleo Brasileiro (PETROBRAS) over the petroleum industry. In June the Senado's rejection of legislation to reform the civil service, nevertheless, was a major setback to the Government's programme of economic reform; however, following a series of compromises, in November the lower house gave its final approval to the legislation.

In mid-1997 a constitutional amendment to permit the President to stand for re-election in 1998 was approved by the Senado, and was swiftly ratified by Cardoso. As the 1998 presidential election approached, various potential candidates announced changes in their party affiliation. In August 1997 Ciro Gomes, a former Minister of Finance, defected from the PSDB to the smaller Partido Popular Socialista (PPS), thereby exacerbating the internal crisis within the PSDB. In July 1997 an investigation by the Senado into a financial scandal arising from fraudulent bond issues concluded that 20 prominent politicians and senior officials (including three state governors, the mayor of São Paulo, Celso Pitta, and his predecessor, Paulo Maluf) had been involved in a criminal operation. A total of 161 financial institutions, including Banco Bradesco, Brazil's largest private bank, were implicated in the scandal. In January 1998 Celso Pitta was found guilty of fraud,and finally stood down in 2000, after being impeached. In October 2004 Maluf was found guilty of sending R $5,000m. of public funds abroad. He also faced other charges of corruption.

Despite his declared commitment to further economic austerity measures, in October 1998 Cardoso, again the PSDB's candidate, became the first President to be re-elected for a second consecutive term, securing 53% of the valid votes cast. Da Silva won 32% of the votes, while Ciro Gomes of the PPS received 11%. At the concurrent legislative elections, the PSDB also performed well, securing 99 of the 513 seats in the lower chamber, while its electoral allies—the PFL, PMDB, Partido Progressista Brasileiro and PTB—won a total of 278 seats, bringing the coalition's total representation to 377.

In January 1999 Itamar Franco, the newly elected Governor of Minas Gerais, declared that the state was defaulting on its debt to the federal Government, indirectly precipitating the devaluation of the Brazilian currency. In the same month, however, both chambers of the Congreso Nacional endorsed long-proposed reforms to the country's munificent pension system, considerably enhancing the prospects of President Cardoso's programme of fiscal austerity. However, the Government suffered a set-back in March following the withdrawal of the PTB from the ruling coalition, as a result of the unexpected dismissal of the Minister of the Budget and Administration. The administration came under further pressure in May when the PFL announced its intention to present its own candidate at the next presidential election. In August demonstrations against the Government's economic and social policies culminated in the arrival in Brasília of as many as 100,000 marchers, comprising political opponents led by the PT, trade unionists and landless individuals.

In October 1999 a congressional commission of inquiry into allegations of organized crime exposed a nation-wide criminal network that allegedly encompassed politicians, government officials, judges, police officers, business executives and banking officials. Embarrassed by the scale of the revelations (which extended to reports of drugs-trafficking within the parliament building), President Cardoso announced the establishment of a new anti-corruption force to combat organized crime. In an effort to improve accountability and to strengthen congressional powers of investigation, the Senado approved a constitutional amendment to restrict presidential use of provisional measures, to which successive Governments had frequently resorted as a means to circumvent the cumbersome legislative process.

At municipal elections in October 2000 the PT made significant gains, obtaining 14.1% of votes cast; the PSDB received 15.9% of votes and the PMDB 15.7%.

Investigations into government corruption and organized crime continued during 2001 and 2002. In July 2001 Jader Barbalho, the President of the Senado, temporarily relinquished his position after it emerged that he had been involved in corrupt activities while Governor of the state of Pará in the 1980s. In October he resigned from the Senado in an attempt to prevent his own impeachment, were he to be found guilty of corruption. Meanwhile, in April the credibility of the ruling coalition was further undermined by the unauthorized release of telephone transcripts secretly recorded by police during investigations into the disappearance of some US $830m. from the Amazonian development agency, Superintendência do Desenvolvimento da Amazônia (SUDAM), with which Barbalho was personally connected. In the following month two senators and one cabinet minister resigned after allegations of corruption. In July 2002 Miguel Reale resigned as Minister of Justice after only three months in office, apparently in protest at President Cardoso's involvement in the reversal of a decision by the Attorney-General to request a federal judiciary investigation into organized crime in Espírito Santo, whose capital, Vitória, had the highest murder rate in Latin America.

The months preceding the presidential elections of October 2002 were dominated by infighting over party candidacies. The ruling PSDB-PFL-PMDB coalition suffered a set-back in August 2001 when the PFL proposed its own presidential candidate, Roseanna Sarney, the Governor of Maranhão. It had been widely predicted that the former President and current Governor of the state of Minas Gerais, Itamar Franco, would secure the PMDB's presidential nomination; however, following a dis-

pute between Franco and Cardoso, the President made clear his support for the nomination of José Serra, as the PMDB candidate. However, in early March 2002 the offices of one of Sarney's businesses were raided by the federal police as part of an investigation into the misappropriation of funds from SUDAM. Sarney claimed that the raid had been engineered by her political rivals, including the PMDB, and the PFL withdrew from the governing coalition in protest. Nevertheless, the accusations damaged her reputation enough to force her to withdraw from the presidential race in April. The campaign manifesto of Lula da Silva, once again the PT's candidate, pledged economic reform, GDP growth of 5%, the implementation of a 'Zero Hunger' poverty-alleviation programme and the creation of 10m. new jobs. Such pledges won him popular approval but aroused corresponding concern among international investors, who feared that the election of a left-wing President, who promised large increases in government expenditure, would result in Brazil defaulting on its foreign debt (see Economic Affairs).

In the presidential election of 6 October 2002 da Silva secured 46.4% of the votes cast in the first round ballot. Serra, the government-backed candidate, was second-placed with 23.2% of the ballot, followed by PSB nominee Anthony Garotinho with 17.9% and Ciro Gomes, the candidate of the centre-left PPS, who secured 12.0% of the ballot. As no candidate had achieved the required 50%, a second ballot between the two leading candidates was held, on 27 October. Aided by the support of Garotinho, Gomes and Sarney, da Silva secured 61.3% of the votes cast in this round (the largest ever proportion of the vote since the system's introduction in 1945), while Serra attracted 38.7%. In congressional elections, also held on 6 October, da Silva's party took 91 of the 513 seats in the Câmara dos Deputados and increased its representation in the Senado to 14 seats (two-thirds of the Senado's 81 seats were contested). The PFL secured 84 lower-house seats, followed by the PMDB with 74 seats and the PSDB with 71 seats. The PFL's representation in the Senado remained unchanged, at 19 seats; however, the number of PMDB senators decreased, from 27 seats to 19, as did the PSDB's upper-house representation, from 16 to 11 seats. PT candidates performed less well in the provincial elections, winning only three state governorships, despite contesting eight, and the party also lost control of the socialist heartland of Rio Grande do Sul to Germano Rogotto of the PMDB. The PSDB won seven governorships, including those of São Paulo and Minas Gerais, and the PMDB secured five.

Owing to the fractured nature of the new Congreso Nacional, da Silva had to confirm support from the centrist parties in order to form a Government. The PT entered a coalition agreement with the PFL and the PMDB, who led the Câmara dos Deputados. This, in combination with the severity of the economic situation during 2002, resulted in a more cautious approach from the President-elect and his advisers; a left-wing alliance with the political centre ensured greater support for new legislation and greater confidence from international investors. President da Silva took office on 2 January 2003. His new Cabinet was dominated by members of the PT, although it also included representatives from the PPS, PDT, PSB and the PL. Antônio Palocci of the PT was appointed Minister of Finance, while Guido Mantega, da Silva's economic adviser, became Minister of Planning, Budget and Administration. Several key posts were given to members of the business community, such as Roberto Rodrigues, head of the country's agribusiness federation, who was given the agriculture portfolio. Furthermore, some PT traditionalists were disturbed by the President's choice of the industrialist and friend of former President Cardoso, Luis Fernando Furlán, as Minister for Development, Industry and Commerce. José Sarney, a member of the PMDB and ally of da Silva, was elected President of the Senado. Another da Silva ally, João Paulo Cunha, became President of the lower house. In May da Silva appointed three new judges to the Supreme Federal Tribunal, including the first Afro-Brazilian. (A fourth judge was appointed in April 2004.)

Upon assuming the presidency, da Silva affirmed his intention to proceed with the poverty-alleviation programme, to effect pension reform, and to modernize Brazil's tax system. In addition to the postponement of a large defence project, the new President announced immediate spending cuts in all areas of government, in order to fund the anti-hunger campaign. The public-sector social security system, whereby civil servants could retire on much greater pensions than were paid to private-sector workers, was widely seen as a symptom of the inequality within Brazilian society. The Government's proposed reform of the sector would make provision for the taxing of pensions and raise the retirement age. Unsurprisingly, the proposals provoked discontent among government workers and the PT's traditional allies in the trade union movement. In early July 2003 a one-day strike was held in protest, in which, it was claimed, over one-half of government employees participated. Nevertheless, in early August the Câmara dos Deputados approved the reforms, although the Government was forced to make several alterations to the legislation. It received senate approval on 11 December, despite some opposition from members of da Silva's own party. It was estimated that the reforms would reduce the social security deficit by R \$50,000m. over 20 years. Three days after the pension reforms were passed three deputies and one senator were expelled from the PT for having voted against the legislation. On 18 August 2004 the Supreme Court upheld the Goverment's right to impose an 11% tax on the pensions of public servants.

President da Silva also promised major reform of the tax system. The proposed changes, announced in mid-April 2003, were intended to rationalize the existing system, reduce levies on industry and export sectors, and improve collection. They included standardizing the rate of value-added tax (which varied between states), making permanent the temporary financial tax introduced by the Cardoso Government, and, in an attempt to ensure the support of regional Governors, replacing the federal property tax with a state levy. In September the Câmara dos Deputados approved the reforms. In mid-December the Senado followed suit, but not before the Government was again forced to make concessions to legislators and state Governors. In January 2004 the first of three stages of tax reform came into effect.

In 2003 the new administration was criticized for focusing on economic, rather than social, issues. In October Oded Grajew, the President's special adviser on the 'Zero Hunger' campaign, resigned, after claiming that corruption was rife within the scheme. In the same month the Government announced that it had met its annual target of including 1m. families in the programme. In November President da Silva announced a new project, which aimed to connect every family to the electricity grid by 2008. At the beginning of December a wide-reaching plan aimed at improving child health care was also launched. It was estimated that the three-year plan would cost almost R \$56,000m. During 2003 the Government reached five agreements with international pharmaceutical companies to buy anti-retroviral drugs at discounted prices, as part of its continuing plan to distribute the drugs free of charge. It was estimated that the number of AIDS-related deaths in Brazil has been reduced by 50% since 1996.

In January 2004 President da Silva effected his first major ministerial reshuffle. He significantly changed his social policy team and broadened the governing coalition to include two ministers from the centrist PMDB. The appointments were interpreted as a reward for the PMDB's support of President da Silva's pension and tax reforms. In the following month evidence emerged that the former deputy of Cabinet Chief José Dirceu, Waldomiro Diniz, had offered government contracts in exchange for 2002 presidential campaign contributions from the head of an illegal gambling operation in the state of Rio de Janeiro. Diniz was dismissed from his post and a criminal investigation begun, but the opposition failed in its attempt to instigate a federal parliamentary investigation into the affair, partly owing to a lack of support from the PMDB, which had recently declared itself an ally of the PT. The revelations prompted President da Silva to issue a decree outlawing bingo halls, although the ruling was overturned by the Senado in early May. The Government was also criticized for obstructing the federal inquiry. In April the President had suffered an earlier set-back after the PL's senators left the governing bloc, reducing the coalition's majority in the upper house to just three.

In June 2004 following a difficult passage through the Câmara dos Deputados, the Government's proposal to increase the minimum wage by R \$20 per week was rejected by the Senado, which instead proposed an increase of R \$35. (Da Silva had pledged to double the minimum wage by 2007, but claimed that the Government could not raise the extra revenue needed to pay minimum wage-linked pensions.) In July the Central Unica dos Trabalhadores (CUT) trade-union confederation organized marches across the country in protest at the Government's economic performance. Furthermore, from August the passing of legislation in the Câmara came to a standstill after deputies

refused to vote on a number of presidential decrees (which took precedence over other legislation). The deputies were protesting at a controversial decree earlier in the month granting cabinet status to the Governor of the Central Bank, Henrique Meirelles. This gave him a level of legal immunity in relation to a senate investigation into alleged tax evasion. The congressional deadlock, which threatened the passage of crucial government legislation (see below), was only ended in November after the da Silva administration agreed to pledge R \$600m. to projects sponsored by members of the Congresso Nacional. On 17 November most of the the Government's ambitious judicial reforms were approved by the Senado. The proposals included the creation of a supervisory council for the judiciary, and gave the Supreme Court power to set binding precedents for lower courts. In the following month a law allowing for joint public-private investment in infrastructure projects was approved by both legislative chambers in the same day. The approval of the legislation was an integral part of the Government's plan to increase foreign investment in the country.

In the municipal elections held on 3 October 2004 (with run-offs on 30 October) the PT performed relatively well overall, considering the fall in the Government's popularity throughout the year. However, the party lost the key mayoral election in São Paulo, where the incumbent PT mayor, Marta Suplicy, was defeated by the PMDB's José Serra. The PT also lost Porto Alegre to the PPS.

On 4 November 2004 the Minister of Defence, José Viegas, resigned in protest at what was seen by many as an attempt by the military to justify the torture that took place during the period of military rule in Brazil. The Vice-President, José Alencar Gomes da Silva, assumed responsibility for the defence portfolio. In late 2004 divisions within the governing coalition emerged: on 11 December the Minister of National Integration, Ciro Gomes, resigned after his party, the PPS, announced its departure from the coalition, accusing the Government of being too 'conservative'. Then, one day later, members of the PMDB, which was the biggest party in the Senado and the second largest in the Câmara, also voted to leave the coalition Government, citing da Silva's failure to pursue an active social policy. The vote, however, which was instigated by right-wing members of the party, exposed fissures within the PMDB when its two cabinet members and several of its senators and deputies refused to abide by the decision (the vote was ruled invalid by the high court in December). It was thought that both parties were planning to field their own candidates in the 2006 presidential election.

In September 2004 further allegations of corruption within the government ranks emerged: it was announced that more than 500 deputies and government officials were being investigated as part of an inquiry into money-laundering at the Banco do Estado do Paraná (Banestado) during the 1990s. In December a congressional investigation recommended that 91 of these be indicted. Gustavo Franco, a former governor of the Central Bank, and Celso Pitta, the former mayor of São Paulo, were among those named.

In mid-February 2005 Severino Cavalcanti of the right-wing Partido Progressista was elected President of the Câmara dos Deputados, defeating the President's favoured candidate, Luiz Greenhalgh. The election of Cavalcanti was widely seen as an assertion of the legislature's independence from the executive. In late March President da Silva finally carried out a long-anticipated reallocation of cabinet portfolios, which was, however, composed of only low-profile changes.

From the mid-1990s the Government suffered from repeated criticism of its failure to address the demands of the Landless Peasant Movement, the Movimento dos Trabalhadores Rurais Sem-Terra (MST), which organized a number of illegal occupations of disputed land during 1995 in support of demands for an acceleration of the Government's programme of expropriation of uncultivated land for distribution to landless rural families. Rapidly deteriorating relations between the authorities and the MST were exacerbated in April 1996 by the violent intervention of the local military police in a demonstration at Eldorado de Carajás in the State of Pará, which resulted in the deaths of 19 demonstrators. Widespread public outrage prompted President Cardoso to request immediate congressional priority for legislation relating to land expropriation, and in April 1997 the Government announced new measures to accelerate the process of land reform.

In early 1998 the MST intensified its campaign for land reform and in March thousands of activists occupied government premises, a campaign that led to the suspension of São Paulo's land-expropriation proceedings when the state's agrarian reform institute was occupied by 500 MST members in September. In May 2000 in one of the largest demonstrations in history by the movement, over 30,000 members of the MST occupied a number of public buildings, including the Ministry of Finance and the Ministry of Agrarian Reform, to demand land reform. The occupations prompted the Government to introduce legislation preventing further land invasions. Following inconclusive negotiations with the Government, the MST scaled down its protest and ministers agreed to resume talks, although these too proved inconclusive. A constitutional crisis ensued, provoked by the request by the Governor of Minas Gerais, Itamar Franco, that federal troops, sent to protect the President's estate, withdraw. However, following the temporary retreat of MST activists, the Government agreed to resume negotiations with the movement, and in October it was announced that loans were to be made available for those already settled on their own land. In October 2001 hundreds of MST activists occupied the Senado building in an attempt to oblige the Minister of Agrarian Reform to meet with them.

Following the election of Lula da Silva to the presidency in October 2002, the MST, traditional supporters of the PT, agreed to a temporary suspension of illegal land occupations. However, in March 2003 the MST declared its autonomy from the Government, amid concerns that its policies were more conservative than expected, and resumed its policy of land invasions. By July the Government had resettled only 5% of the target number of landless families for 2003 and the MST intensified its campaign of land seizures, invading a total of 220 estates in that year. In November more than 1,000 MST activists marched on Brasília where they were addressed by the President. He pledged to accelerate land reform, doubling the funds set aside for the government programme, which aimed to settle 1m. landless families in the next four years. Nevertheless, the budget that was approved in January 2004 allocated only one-half of the finances necessary for the Government to achieve its 2004 target. Throughout that year MST land occupations continued, with concerted campaigns in April, July and November. By that latest month 270 estates had been occupied. An MST report, published in January 2005, claimed that only 30,000 families had been settled in 2004, from a Government target of 115,000. However, the Government asserted that 81,000 families had been given land.

The murder, in December 1988, of Francisco (Chico) Mendes, the leader of the rubber-tappers' union and a pioneering ecologist brought Brazil's environmental problems to international attention. Widespread concern was expressed that large-scale development projects, together with the 'slash-and-burn' farming techniques of cattle ranchers, peasant smallholders and loggers, and the release of large amounts of mercury into the environment by an estimated 60,000 gold prospectors (or *garimpeiros*) in the Amazon region, presented a serious threat to the survival of both the indigenous Indians and the rainforest. International criticism of the Government's poor response to the threat to the environment persisted into the 2000s. Of particular concern to many international observers was the plight of the Yanomami Indian tribe in Roraima. It was estimated that, since the arrival of the *garimpeiros* in the region, some 10%–15% of the Yanomami's total population had been exterminated as a result of pollution and disease, introduced to the area by the gold prospectors. The Fundação Nacional do Indio (FUNAI—National Indian Foundation) was heavily criticized for its role in the affair and was accused of failing to provide effective protection and support for Brazil's Indian population. In August 1993 international attention was again focused on the region, following the slaughter of 73 members of the Yanomami tribe by *garimpeiros*, in the context of the ongoing territorial dispute prompted by the miners' attempts to exploit the rich mineral deposits of the Yanomami land. In March 1996 a US $5,700m.-rainforest protection programme (to be funded by the Brazilian Government, the European Union (EU) and the G-7 group of industrialized countries over a five-year period) was concluded between President Cardoso and the UN Secretary-General. In the following year the G-7 group pledged an additional US $68m. Legislation to provide greater protection for Brazil's natural resources, through the establishment of criminal penalties for illegal activities, was approved by the President in February 1998. In August 2002 Cardoso's Government created the world's biggest national park in the Tumucumaque Mountains, with funding promised by the World Bank and the UN's

Global Environmental Facility. In September 2003 President da Silva was criticized by environmentalists following the announcement of a four-year government infrastructure plan, which aimed to increase electricity output and improve transport links in the Amazon region. It was claimed that the plan would accelerate rainforest destruction. In January 2004 the Government announced that, despite protests by farmers, it would continue its plans to create an Indian reservation of 1.75m. ha in Roraima.

In 1990 a series of bilateral trade agreements was signed with Argentina, representing the first stage in a process which led to the establishment of a Southern Cone Common Market (Mercado Comum do Sul—Mercosul, see p. 349), also to include Paraguay and Uruguay. Mercosul came into effect on 1 January 1995, following the signing, by the Presidents of the four member nations, of the Ouro Prêto Protocol. While a complete common external tariff was not expected until 2006, customs barriers on 80%–85% of mutually exchanged goods were removed immediately. In 1999, however, Brazil's commercial relations with Argentina, in particular, were severely strained by the devaluation of the real, which prompted the latter country to impose curbs on certain Brazilian exports. Argentina's currency devaluation, in January 2002, led to a further decrease in the trade between the two countries.

At the fifth Ministerial Conference of the World Trade Organization (WTO), held in Cancún, Mexico, in September 2003 Brazil led a group of countries opposed to the US-EU policy of subsidizing agricultural products. This group of developing nations (which came to be known as the G-20 group) demanded an end to subsidies in industrialized countries, in return for opening up their markets. In October 2003 President da Silva and his Argentine counterpart, Néstor Kirchner, signed the so-called 'Buenos Aires Consensus' on regional co-operation, which committed both countries to a common stance in negotiations towards the proposed Free Trade Area of the Americas (FTAA). Throughout 2003 and 2004 talks between Brazil and the USA on the FTAA remained at an impasse; however in early 2005 it seemed likely that negotiations would resume. In January 2004 Brazil commenced a two-year term as a member of the UN's Security Council and began to campaign for a permanent seat on the Security Council. During the first two years of the da Silva administration trade links were expanded with Asia, particularly the People's Republic of China. In June 2004 Brazil sent 1,200 troops to Haiti to cope with the deteriorating security situation there, and took command of the UN peace-keeping troops stationed in the country. In January 2005 Porto Alegre hosted the fifth World Social Forum, a broad-based conference on issues affecting developing countries, which was attended by President da Silva.

In May 1994 Brazil declared its full adherence to the 1967 Tlatelolco Treaty for the non-proliferation of nuclear weapons in Latin America and the Caribbean. The Treaty was promulgated by presidential decree in September 1994. Brazil signed the international Treaty on the Non-Proliferation of Nuclear Weapons (see p. 94) in June 1997. President Cardoso ratified this and also the Comprehensive Test Ban Treaty (see p. 94) in July 1998.

Government

Under the 1988 Constitution, the country is a federal republic comprising 26 States and a Federal District (Brasília). Legislative power is exercised by the bicameral Congresso Nacional (National Congress), comprising the Senado Federal (Federal Senate—members elected by the majority principle in rotation for eight years) and the Câmara dos Deputados (Chamber of Deputies—members elected by a system of proportional representation for four years). The number of deputies is based on the size of the population. Election is by universal adult suffrage. Executive power is exercised by the President, elected by direct ballot for four years. The President appoints and leads the Cabinet. Each State has a directly elected Governor and an elected legislature. For the purposes of local government, the States are divided into municipalities.

Defence

Military service, lasting 12 months, is compulsory for men between 18 and 45 years of age. In August 2004 the armed forces totalled 302,909 (including 45,707 conscripts): army 189,000 (40,000 conscripts), navy 48,600 (including 3,200 conscripts) and air force 65,309 (including 2,507 conscripts). Public security forces number about 385,600. Defence expenditure for 2004 was budgeted at R $27,900m.

Economic Affairs

In 2003, according to estimates by the World Bank, Brazil's gross national income (GNI), measured at average 2001–03 prices, was US $474,414.7m., equivalent to US $2,710 per head (or $7,480 per head on an international purchasing-power parity basis). During 1990–2003, it was estimated, the population increased at an average annual rate of 1.4%, while gross domestic product (GDP) per head increased, in real terms, by an average of 0.9% per year. Overall GDP increased, in real terms, at an average annual rate of 2.3% in 1990–2003; real GDP grew by 0.5% in 2003.

Agriculture (including hunting, forestry and fishing) engaged 18.7% of the economically active population, according to census figures, in 2000, and, according to the FAO, 15.0% in 2003. According to official figures, it contributed 9.4% of GDP in 2003. The principal cash crops are soya beans, coffee, tobacco, sugar cane and cocoa beans. Subsistence crops include wheat, maize, rice, potatoes, beans, cassava and sorghum. Beef and poultry production are also important, as is fishing (particularly tuna, crab and shrimp). In September 2003 and October 2004 temporary decrees permitted the planting of transgenic soy for the following year's harvest; it was anticipated that permanent legislation would follow. In June 2004 the World Trade Organization (WTO) ruled that US cotton subsidies were in violation of trade rules, thereby increasing export potential for Brazilian cotton. During 1990–2002, according to the World Bank, agricultural GDP increased at an average annual rate of 3.5%. Agricultural GDP increased by 5.7% in 2001 and by 5.8% in 2002.

Industry (including mining, manufacturing, construction and power) employed 21.4% of the working population in 2000 and provided 36.8% of GDP in 2003. During 1990–2002, according to the World Bank, industrial GDP increased at an average annual rate of 1.9%. Industrial GDP declined by 0.7% in 2001, but grew by 1.5% in 2002.

Mining contributed 3.7% of GDP in 2003. Mining GDP grew by 3.9% in 2001 and by 10.4% in 2002. The major mineral exports are iron ore (haematite—in terms of iron content, Brazil is the largest producer in the world), manganese, tin and aluminium. Gold, phosphates, platinum, uranium, copper and coal are also mined. Brazil was the world's largest producer of niobium (contributing some 94% of global output in 2001). Brazil's reserves of petroleum were estimated at 11.6m. 42-gallon barrels in 2003.

Manufacturing contributed 22.9% of GDP in 2003. In 2000 the sector engaged 13.5% of the total employed population. There is considerable state involvement in a broad range of manufacturing activity. While traditionally-dominant areas, including textiles and clothing, footwear and food- and beverage-processing, continue to contribute a large share to the sector, more recent developments in the sector have resulted in the emergence of machinery and transport equipment (including road vehicles and components, passenger jet aircraft and specialist machinery for the petroleum industry), construction materials (especially iron and steel), wood and sugar cane derivatives, and chemicals and petrochemicals as significant new manufacturing activities. According to the World Bank, manufacturing GDP increased at an average rate of 1.1% per year in 1990–2003; the sector's GDP grew by 1.4% in 2002 and by 2.7% in 2003.

In 2001 81.7% of total electricity production was provided by hydroelectric power. Other energy sources, including petroleum, coal and nuclear power, accounted for the remaining 18.3%. Attempts to exploit further the country's vast hydroelectric potential (estimated at 144,000 MW) were encouraged by the completion of ambitious dam projects at Itaipú, on the border with Paraguay (expected to produce as much as 35% of Brazil's total electricity requirements when fully operational), and at Tucuruí, on the Tocantins river. In late 2000 it was announced that plans were under way further to expand the hydroelectric power-station at Itaipú, increasing its generating capacity to 14,000 MW. Following energy shortages caused by a drought in 2001, there were plans for the construction of thermal power-stations; however, by 2005 the new plants had yet to be built and the country was still vulnerable to shortages. The Angra I nuclear power plant, inaugurated in 1985, has subsequently operated only intermittently, while financial constraints hindered the completion of the Angra II plant, which became operational in mid-2000, preventing further development of the country's nuclear programme. There were further plans to construct Angra III. In late 2004 it was announced that Brazil would begin to produce enriched uranium in 2005. In the same

month the Government made public its plan to construct a natural gas pipeline connecting the Urucu natural gas reserve in Amazonia to neighbouring cities. The pipeline was expected to carry 2.2m. cu m per day on becoming operational in 2006. Brazil is a major producer of ethanol from sugar cane, and in late 2004 plans were announced to increase production by 40%. Fuel imports comprised 15.3% of the value of total merchandise imports in 2002.

The services sector contributed an estimated 53.8% of GDP in 2003 and engaged 59.9% of the employed labour force in 2000. According to the World Bank, the GDP of the services sector increased at an average rate of 2.6% per year in 1990–2002. The GDP of the services sector was estimated to have increased by 2.1% in 2002.

In 2003 Brazil recorded a trade surplus of US $24,801m. There was a surplus of US $4,016m. on the current account of the balance of payments. In 2002 the principal source of imports (20.1%) was the USA, which was also the principal market for exports (23.1%). Other major trading partners were Germany, Argentina, Japan, the Netherlands, Mexico and the People's Republic of China. The principal exports in 2003 were machinery and transport equipment, food and live animals and basic manufactures. The principal imports in the same year were machinery and transport equipment, chemical products and mineral fuels (notably petroleum).

The 2003 federal budget recorded expenditure of R $318,383m. and revenue of R $357,891m. Brazil's external debt was R $227,932m. in 2002, of which US $183,710m. was long-term debt. In that year the cost of debt-servicing was equivalent to 68.9% of the value of exports of goods and services. The annual rate of inflation averaged 13.7% in 1994–2003. Consumer prices increased by an average of 8.4% in 2002 and by 14.8% in 2003. Official figures indicated an average unemployment rate of 7.1% of the labour force in 2003.

Brazil is a member of the Latin American Integration Association (ALADI, see p. 289), Mercosul/Mercosur (see p. 349), the Association of Tin Producing Countries (ATPC) and the Cairns Group (see p. 423). Brazil also joined the Comunidade dos Países de Língua Portuguesa (CPLP, see p. 383), founded in 1996. In December 2004 Brazil was one of 12 countries that were signatories to the agreement, signed in Cusco, Peru, creating the South American Community of Nations (Comunidade Sul-Americana de Nações), intended to promote greater regional economic integration and due to become operational by 2007.

Moves towards a proposed Free Trade Area of the Americas (FTAA), first broached at the First Summit of the Americas held in Miami, USA, in 1994 and to be concluded by 2005, faltered in 2003 and 2004 with Brazil's resistance to opening its markets further without receiving greater access to US markets in return; specifically targeted were agricultural products such as orange juice, sugar, cotton and soya, which enjoyed protection in the USA. The protected US steel industry was another source of contention. Following the failure of the fifth WTO Ministerial Conference, in Cancún, Mexico, in September 2003, in November the two countries reached an accord whereby countries would be able to opt out of individual clauses. Negotiations proceeded in 2004 and resumed in February 2005. In June 2004 a complaint against US cotton subsidies brought by Brazil was upheld by the WTO. Throughout 2004 Brazil sought to develop trade links with Russia and the People's Republic of China. It was hoped that by 2010 trade with China would be worth US $35,000m.

The predicted success of the left-wing candidate da Silva in the months preceding the presidential elections of October 2002 resulted in anxiety in international financial circles about the possibility of increased government expenditure should he come to power. This, coupled with a first-quarter decrease in GDP, led President Cardoso in June to draw US $10,000m. of a previously-negotiated IMF loan, in order to replenish reserves and buy back foreign debt. In mid-July the Central Bank unexpectedly cut interest rates, in an attempt to stimulate growth before the elections, while the Government further reduced budgetary expenditure. Nevertheless, the economy continued to flounder, and in August the IMF announced a rescue package of US $30,400m., the largest ever disbursed by the Fund. The deal was dependent on the agreement of all presidential candidates to maintain current fiscal policy and commit to a primary budget surplus of 3.75% of GDP in 2003. Although the IMF loan settled financial markets temporarily, the real continued to depreciate.

In its first two years in office, the Government of President da Silva adhered to a prudent fiscal policy, maintaining high interest rates and keeping to strict inflation targets in an attempt to stabilize Brazil's economy. Many of the new President's traditional supporters were dismayed at his decision to make economic, not social, policy a priority, but the international community and the IMF were impressed by the new Government's economic orthodoxy. The base interest rate reached 26.5% during 2003, although by the beginning of 2004 the rate had fallen to 16.5%. Foreign investment decreased in the first six months of 2003, but recovered in the second half of the year. In 2003 a new loan, worth US $14,800m., was negotiated with the IMF. In return, Brazil agreed to maintain a primary budget surplus equivalent to 4.25% of GDP. In December 2004 a further US $1,400m. was made available by the Fund. Throughout 2004 interest rates remained high, and in January 2005 the base interest rate was raised to 18.25%, despite criticism from industry representatives and the Minister of Development, Industry and Trade, Luiz Furlán; however, the rise contributed to a fall in the annual rate of inflation, to 7.6%, in 2004. Foreign investment also increased in 2004, to an estimated US $14,000m. (from $10,110m, in 2003). Overall growth was put at 5.1% for that year. In December 2004 the Congresso Nacional approved a balanced budget for 2005 of R $681,300m. The Central Bank predicted that GDP growth would be 3.7% in 2005, and that the annual rate of inflation would fall further, to 5.7%. However, in 2005 the Government would come under increasing pressure to relax its economic policies as the 2006 elections approached.

Education

Education is free in official pre-primary and primary schools and is compulsory between the ages of seven and 14 years. Primary education begins at seven years of age and lasts for eight years.

Secondary education, beginning at 15 years of age, lasts for three years and is also free in official schools. According to UNESCO, enrolment at primary schools in 2000/2001 included 97% of children in the relevant age group (boys 100%; girls 93%), while in secondary schools, the enrolment was 71% (boys 69%; girls 74%). The Federal Government is responsible for higher education, and in 1997 there were 150 universities, of which 77 were state-administered. Numerous private institutions exist at all levels of education. Expenditure on education by the central Government was forecast at R $5,100m. for 2000.

Public Holidays

2005: 1 January (New Year's Day—Universal Confraternization Day), 5–8 February (Carnival), 25 March (Good Friday), 21 April (Tiradentes Day—Discovery of Brazil), 2 May (for Labour Day), 5 May (Ascension Day), 26 May (Corpus Christi), 7 September (Independence Day), 12 October (Our Lady Aparecida, Patron Saint of Brazil), 2 November (All Souls' Day), 15 November (Proclamation of the Republic), 25 December (Christmas Day).

2006: 1 January (New Year's Day—Universal Confraternization Day), 25–28 February (Carnival), 14 April (Good Friday), 21 April (Tiradentes Day—Discovery of Brazil), 1 May (Labour Day), 25 May (Ascension Day), 15 June (Corpus Christi), 7 September (Independence Day), 12 October (Our Lady Aparecida, Patron Saint of Brazil), 2 November (All Souls' Day), 15 November (Proclamation of the Republic), 25 December (Christmas Day).

Other local holidays include 20 January (Foundation of Rio de Janeiro) and 25 January (Foundation of São Paulo).

Weights and Measures

The metric system is in force.

Statistical Survey

Sources (unless otherwise stated): Economic Research Department, Banco Central do Brasil, SBS, Q 03, Bloco B, Brasília, DF; tel. (61) 414-1074; fax (61) 414-2036; e-mail coace.depec.@bcb.gov.br; internet www.bcb.gov.br; Instituto Brasileiro de Geografia e Estatística (IBGE), Centro de Documentação e Disseminação de Informações (CDDI), Rua Gen. Canabarro 706, 2°, 20271-201 Maracanã, Rio de Janeiro, RJ; tel. (21) 2142-4781; fax (21) 2142-4933; e-mail webmaster@ibge.bov.br; internet www.ibge.gov.br.

Area and Population

AREA, POPULATION AND DENSITY

Area (sq km)	8,547,404*
Population (census results)†	
1 August 1996	157,070,163
1 August 2000	
Males	83,576,015
Females	86,223,155
Total	169,799,170
Population (official estimates at mid-year)	
2002	176,391,015
2003	178,985,306
2004	181,586,030
Density (per sq km) at mid-2004	21.2

* 3,300,170.9 sq miles.
† Excluding Indian jungle population (numbering 45,429 in 1950).

ADMINISTRATIVE DIVISIONS
(population at census of 1 August 2000)

State	Population	Capital
Acre (AC)	557,526	Rio Branco
Alagoas (AL)	2,822,621	Maceió
Amapá (AP)	477,032	Macapá
Amazonas (AM)	2,812,557	Manaus
Bahia (BA)	13,070,250	Salvador
Ceará (CE)	7,430,661	Fortaleza
Espírito Santo (ES)	3,097,232	Vitória
Goiás (GO)	5,033,228	Goiânia
Maranhão (MA)	5,651,475	São Luís
Mato Grosso (MT)	2,504,353	Cuiabá
Mato Grosso do Sul (MS) . .	2,078,001	Campo Grande
Minas Gerais (MG)	17,891,494	Belo Horizonte
Pará (PA)	6,192,307	Belém
Paraíba (PB)	3,443,825	João Pessoa
Paraná (PR)	9,563,458	Curitiba
Pernambuco (PE)	7,918,344	Recife
Piauí (PI)	2,843,278	Teresina
Rio de Janeiro (RJ)	14,391,282	Rio de Janeiro
Rio Grande do Norte (RN) . .	2,776,782	Natal
Rio Grande do Sul (RS) . .	10,187,798	Porto Alegre
Rondônia (RO)	1,379,787	Porto Velho
Roraima (RR)	324,397	Boa Vista
Santa Catarina (SC)	5,356,360	Florianópolis
São Paulo (SP)	37,032,403	São Paulo
Sergipe (SE)	1,784,475	Aracaju
Tocantins (TO)	1,157,098	Palmas
Distrito Federal (DF)	2,051,146	Brasília
Total	169,799,170	—

PRINCIPAL TOWNS
(population at census of 1 August 2000)*

São Paulo	10,434,252	Santo André	649,331
Rio de Janeiro	5,857,904	João Pessoa	597,934
Salvador	2,443,107	Jaboatão	581,556
Belo Horizonte	2,238,526	São José dos Campos	539,313
Fortaleza	2,141,402	Contagem	538,017
Brasília (capital)	2,051,146	Ribeirão Preto	504,923
Curitiba	1,587,315	Uberlândia	501,214
Recife	1,422,905	Sorocaba	493,468
Manaus	1,405,835	Cuiabá	483,346
Porto Alegre	1,360,590	Feira de Santana	480,949
Belém	1,280,614	Aracaju	461,534
Goiânia	1,093,607	Niterói	459,451
Guarulhos	1,072,717	Juíz de Fora	456,796
Campinas	969,396	São João de Meriti	449,476
Nova Iguaçu	920,599	Londrina	447,065
São Gonçalo	891,119	Joinville	429,604
São Luís	870,028	Santos	417,983
Maceió	797,759	Campos dos	
		Goytacazes	406,989
Duque de Caxias	775,456	Ananindeua	393,392
Teresina	715,360	Olinda	367,902
Natal	712,317	Mauá	363,392
São Bernardo do			
Campo	703,177	São José do Rio Preto	358,523
Campo Grande	663,621	Diadema	356,389
Osasco	652,593		

* Figures refer to *municípios*, which may contain rural districts.

Brasília (Distrito Federal) (official population estimates at mid-year): 2,180,279 in 2002; 2,231,101 in 2003; 2,282,049 in 2004.

BIRTHS, MARRIAGES AND DEATHS
(official estimates based on annual registrations)

	Birth rate (per 1,000)	Death rate (per 1,000)
1997	21.9	5.7
1998	25.5	5.8
1999	25.1	5.8
2000	24.1	5.6
2001	21.7	5.5
2002	22.1	5.7

Registered births (incl. births registered but not occurring during that year): 3,576,890 in 1997 (1,231,816 not occurring in that year); 4,218,204 in 1998 (1,758,929 not occurring in that year); 4,209,768 in 1999 (1,552,155 not occurring in that year); 4,107,757 in 2000 (1,496,335 not occurring in that year); 3,743,651 in 2001 (1,234,297 not occurring in that year); 3,853,869 in 2002 (1,272,814 not occurring in that year).

Registered marriages: 724,738 in 1997; 698,614 in 1998; 788,744 in 1999; 732,721 in 2000; 710,121 in 2001; 715,166 in 2002.

Registered deaths (incl. deaths registered but not occurring during that year): 932,358 in 1997 (23,541 not occurring in that year); 960,328 in 1998 (20,880 not occurring in that year); 966,010 in 1999 (22,486 not occurring in that year); 945,492 in 2000 (20,792 not occurring in that year); 953,519 in 2001 (25,174 not occurring in that year): 987,966 in 2002 (29,491 not occurring in that year).

Expectation of life (WHO estimates, years at birth): 68.9 (males 65.7; females 72.3) in 2002 (Source: WHO, *World Health Report*).

ECONOMICALLY ACTIVE POPULATION
(persons aged 10 years and over, census of 1 August 2000)

	Males	Females	Total
Agriculture, hunting and forestry	9,176,490	2,594,521	11,771,011
Fishing	319,400	28,979	348,378
Mining and quarrying	218,003	16,866	234,869
Manufacturing	6,001,199	2,755,840	8,757,040
Electricity, gas and water	275,081	53,837	328,918
Construction	4,397,397	170,998	4,568,396
Commerce, repair of automotive vehicles and household goods	7,256,900	3,642,097	10,898,997
Accommodation and food	1,627,910	1,443,904	3,071,814
Transport, storage and communications	2,918,456	400,358	3,318,814
Financial services	458,501	365,207	823,708
Real estate, rental and business services	2,546,652	1,217,150	3,763,802
Public administration, defence and social security	2,204,241	1,138,626	3,522,868
Education	845,937	2,976,451	3,822,388
Health and social services	598,538	1,533,368	2,151,906
Other community, social and personal services	1,104,286	1,287,766	2,392,052
Domestic services	376,268	4,640,001	5,016,269
International organizations and external institutions	1,387	1,452	2,839
Activities not adequately defined	533,449	302,374	835,823
Total employed	40,860,097	24,769,796	65,629,892
Unemployed	5,596,322	6,151,258	11,837,581
Total labour force	46,546,419	30,921,054	77,467,473

Mid–2003 (estimates in '000): Agriculture, etc. 12,404; Total (incl. others) 82,506 (Source: FAO).

Health and Welfare

KEY INDICATORS

Total fertility rate (children per woman, 2002)	2.2
Under-5 mortality rate (per 1,000 live births, 2003)	35
HIV/AIDS (% of persons aged 15–49, 2003)	0.7
Physicians (per 1,000 head, 1996)	1.27
Hospital beds (per 1,000 head, 1996)	3.11
Health expenditure (2001): US $ per head (PPP)	573
Health expenditure (2001): % of GDP	7.6
Health expenditure (2001): public (% of total)	41.6
Access to water (% of persons, 2002)	89
Access to sanitation (% of persons, 2002)	75
Human Development Index (2002): ranking	72
Human Development Index (2002): value	0.775

For sources and definitions, see explanatory note on p. vi.

Agriculture

PRINCIPAL CROPS
('000 metric tons)

	2001	2002	2003
Wheat	3,365	3,106	6,029
Rice (paddy)	10,184	10,457	10,319
Barley	298	245	336
Maize	41,955	35,933	47,988
Oats	342	299	415
Sorghum	914	787	1,755
Buckwheat*	50	48	48
Potatoes	2,849	3,126	3,047
Sweet potatoes	485	498	495*
Cassava (Manioc)	22,577	23,066	22,147
Yams*	235	230	230
Sugar cane	345,942	363,721	389,849
Dry beans	2,453	3,064	3,310
Brazil nuts	28	27	28*
Cashew nuts	124	164	178
Soybeans (Soya beans)	37,881	42,125	51,482
Groundnuts (in shell)	202	195	177
Coconuts	2,131	2,892	2,851
Oil palm fruit*	460	450	516
Castor beans	100	171	78
Sunflower seed†	158	150	168
Cottonseed†	1,665	1,363	1,402
Tomatoes	3,103	3,653	3,694
Onions (dry)	1,050	1,222	1,194
Garlic	102	114	122
Other fresh vegetables*	2,200	2,250	2,250
Watermelons*	600	620	620
Cantaloupes and other melons*	150	155	155
Bananas	6,177	6,423	6,775
Oranges	16,983	18,531	16,903
Tangerines, mandarins, clementines and satsumas	1,125	1,263	1,263*
Lemons and limes	965	984	950*
Grapefruit and pomelos*	66	67	67
Apples	716	857	835
Peaches and nectarines	223	218	215*
Grapes	1,058	1,149	1,065
Mangoes	782	842	845*
Avocados	154	174	173*
Pineapples	1,430	1,433	1,406
Persimmons*	65	65	66
Cashew-apple*	1,550	1,600	1,603
Papayas	1,489	1,598	1,600*
Coffee beans (green)‡	1,820	2,650	1,997
Cocoa beans	186	175	170
Mate	646	513	550*
Sisal	181	171	184
Cotton (lint)†	872	713	737
Other fibre crops	97	97	97*
Tobacco (leaves)	568	670	656
Natural rubber	88†	96†	96*

* FAO estimate(s).
† Unofficial figure(s).
‡ Official figures, reported in terms of dry cherries, have been converted into green coffee beans at 50%.

Source: FAO.

LIVESTOCK
('000 head, year ending September)

	2001	2002	2003
Cattle	176,389	185,347	189,513*
Buffaloes	1,119	1,115	1,200*
Horses	5,801	5,900*	5,900*
Asses	1,239	1,250*	1,250*
Mules	1,346	1,350*	1,350*
Pigs	32,605	32,013	32,605
Sheep	14,639	14,287	14,182†
Goats	9,537	9,429	9,087†
Chickens	883	908	1,050*
Ducks*	3,400	3,500	3,550
Turkeys*	12,600	13,000	13,500

* FAO estimate(s).
† Unofficial figure.
Source: FAO.

LIVESTOCK PRODUCTS
('000 metric tons)

	2001	2002	2003
Beef and veal	6,823	7,139	7,230
Mutton and lamb*	71	69	68
Goat meat*	39	40	40
Pig meat	2,637	2,798	3,059
Horse meat*	21	21	21
Poultry meat	6,380	7,239	7,967
Cows' milk	21,146	22,315	23,315†
Goats' milk*	138	138	138
Butter and ghee†	75	77	79
Cheese*	38	39	39
Hen eggs	1,539†	1,547†	1,550*
Other poultry eggs*	65	59	59
Honey	22	24	24*
Wool: greasy	12	11	11*
Wool: scoured*	7	8	8
Cattle hides (fresh)*	670	715	715
Goatskins (fresh)*	5	5	5
Sheepskins (fresh)*	15	16	16

* FAO estimate(s).
† Unofficial figures.
Source: FAO.

Forestry

ROUNDWOOD REMOVALS
(FAO estimates, '000 cubic metres, excl. bark)

	2001	2002	2003
Sawlogs, veneer logs and logs for sleepers	49,290	49,290	49,290
Pulpwood	45,861	45,861	45,861
Other industrial wood	7,843	7,843	7,843
Fuel wood	133,428	134,473	135,542
Total	236,422	237,467	238,536

Source: FAO.

SAWNWOOD PRODUCTION
(FAO estimates, '000 cubic metres, incl. railway sleepers)

	2000	2001	2002
Coniferous (softwood)	7,800	6,050	6,400
Broadleaved (hardwood)	15,300	14,800	14,800*
Total	23,100	20,850	21,200

* FAO estimate.
2003: Figures assumed to be unchanged from 2002 (FAO estimates).
Source: FAO.

Fishing
('000 metric tons, live weight)

	2000	2001	2002
Capture	766.8	806.7	822.2
Characins	67.1	22.8	22.0
Freshwater siluroids	58.5	58.7	59.6
Weakfishes	43.5	2.6	1.8
Whitemouth croaker	28.8	39.3	42.3
Brazilian sardinella	17.0	39.0	27.9
Skipjack tuna	25.2	24.1	18.3
Aquaculture	176.5	207.5	246.2
Common carp	54.6	55.5	54.5
Tilapias	32.5	35.8	42.0
Total catch	943.4	1,014.2	1,068.3

* FAO estimate.
Note: Figures exclude aquatic mammals, recorded by number rather than by weight. The number of toothed whales caught was: 1,057 in 2000; 23 in 2001; 131 in 2002. Also excluded are crocodiles. The number of spectacled caimans caught was: 8,286 in 2000; 1,253 in 2001; 6,048 in 2002. The number of Nile crocodiles caught was: 1,477 in 2000; 50 in 2001.
Source: FAO.

Mining

('000 metric tons, unless otherwise indicated)

	1999	2000	2001
Hard coal[1]	5,618	6,461	6,600[2]
Crude petroleum ('000 barrels)	413,121	464,280	487,640[2]
Natural gas (million cu m)	11,898	13,291	14,000[2]
Iron ore:			
gross weight	194,000	208,800	208,700[2]
metal content	128,040	138,600	140,000[2]
Copper (metric tons)[3]	193,014	184,564	212,243
Nickel ore (metric tons)[3,4]	32,268	31,991	32,624
Bauxite	13,839	13,846	13,850[2]
Lead concentrates (metric tons)[4]	10,281	8,832	8,800[2]
Zinc (metric tons)[3]	187,010	191,777	197,037
Tin concentrates (metric tons)[3,4]	12,787	13,823	12,109
Manganese ore	7,968	5,723	n.a.
Chromium ore (metric tons)[5]	207,123	276,105	190,000[2]
Tungsten concentrates (metric tons)[4]	13	14	14[2]
Niobium concentrates (metric tons)[4]	31,352	31,190	31,200[2]
Ilmenite (metric tons)	96,000	123,000	123,000[2]
Rutile (metric tons)	4,300	3,162	3,200[2]
Zirconium concentrates (metric tons)[6]	27,160	29,805	30,000[2]
Silver (kilograms)[7]	42,000	41,000	41,000[2]
Gold (kilograms)[8]	52,634	50,393	50,500[2]
Bentonite (beneficiated)	274.6	274.0	274.0[2]
Kaolin (beneficiated)	1,516.7	1,734.8	1,735.0[2]
Magnesite (beneficiated)	259.8	279.9	280.0[2]
Phosphate rock[9]	4,344	4,725	4,700[2]
Potash salts[10]	348.2	351.7	357.0[2]
Fluorspar (Fluorite) (metric tons)[2,11]	44,926	42,962	43,000[2]
Barite (Barytes) (beneficiated) (metric tons)	44,906	53,741	54,000[2]
Quartz (natural crystals) (metric tons)	1,470	3,651	3,700[2]
Salt (unrefined):			
marine	4,528	4,626	4,600[2]
rock	1,430	1,448	1,400[2]
Gypsum and anhydrite (crude)	1,456	1,541	1,540[2]
Graphite (natural) (metric tons)[2]	53,503	71,208	71,000[2]
Asbestos (fibre) (metric tons)[2]	188,386	209,332	209,300[2]
Mica (metric tons)	3,000	4,000	4,000[2]
Vermiculite (beneficiated) (metric tons)	23,400	23,400	23,400[2]
Talc and pyrophyllite (crude)	454	450	450[2]
Diamonds ('000 carats):[1]			
gem	900	1,000	1,000[2]
industrial	600	600	600[2]

[1] Figures refer to marketable products.
[2] Estimated production.
[3] Figures from the Ministério de Minas e Energia.
[4] Figures refer to the metal content of ores and concentrates.
[5] Figures refer to the chromic oxide (Cr_2O_3) content.
[6] Including production of baddeleyite-caldasite.
[7] Figures refer to primary production only. The production of secondary silver (in kilograms) was: 50,000 per year in 1999–2001.
[8] Including official production by independent miners (garimpeiros): 9,055 kg in 1999; 10,395 kg in 2000; 5,866 kg in 2001.
[9] Figures refer to the gross weight of concentrates. The phosphoric acid (P_2O_5) content (in '000 metric tons) was: 1,560 in 1998; 1,528 in 1999.
[10] Figures refer to the potassium oxide (K_2O) content.
[11] Acid-grade and metallurgical-grade concentrates.
Source: US Geological Survey.

2002 ('000 metric tons): Copper 184,814; Nickel ore (metal content) 29,950; Zinc 249,434; Tin concentrates (metal content) 12,031; Silicon 133,390 (Source: Ministério de Minas e Energia).

2003 ('000 metric tons): Copper 173,378; Nickel ore (metal content) 30,514; Zinc 262,998; Tin concentrates (metal content) 10,761; Silicon 180,937 (Source: Ministério de Minas e Energia).

Industry

SELECTED PRODUCTS
('000 metric tons, unless otherwise indicated)

	1999	2000	2001
Beer ('000 hl)	62,491	66,954	67,905
Soft drinks ('000 hl)	54,783	59,651	62,261
Wood pulp (sulphate and soda)	6,499	6,668	6,789
Newsprint	242	266	230
Caustic soda	1,352	1,353	1,174
Phosphate fertilizers	1,358	1,496	n.a.
Electric energy (million kWh)	334,716	348,909	n.a.
Pig-iron	24,549	27,723	27,391
Crude steel	24,975	27,843	26,691
Cement*	40,248	39,559	38,735
Passenger cars (units)	221,000	260,000	296,000
Buses and Coaches (units)	14,934	22,672	23,373
Lorries (units)	55,277	71,686	77,342
Motorcycles (units)	468,000	621,000	741,000

* Portland cement only.

Source: UN, *Industrial Commodity Statistics Yearbook*.

2002 ('000 metric tons unless otherwise indicated): Fertilizers 8,071; Paper 7,774; Crude steel 29,604; Cement 38,026; Motor vehicles ('000 units) 1,791.

2003 ('000 metric tons unless otherwise indicated): Fertilizers 9,070; Paper 7,811; Crude steel 31,147; Cement 34,011; Motor vehicles ('000 units) 1,827.

Source: Ministério de Desenvolvimento, Indústria e Comércio Exterior, Brasília.

Finance

CURRENCY AND EXCHANGE RATES
Monetary Units
100 centavos = 1 real (plural: reais).

Sterling, Dollar and Euro Equivalents (31 December 2004)
£1 sterling = 5.1252 reais;
US $1 = 2.6536
€1 = 3.6145 reais;
100 reais = £19.51 = $37.68 = €27.67.

Average Exchange Rates (reais per US $)
2002   2.9208
2003   3.0771
2004   2.9251

Note: In March 1986 the cruzeiro (CR $) was replaced by a new currency unit, the cruzado (CZ $), equivalent to 1,000 cruzeiros. In January 1989 the cruzado was, in turn, replaced by the new cruzado (NCZ $), equivalent to CZ $1,000 and initially at par with the US dollar (US $). In March 1990 the new cruzado was replaced by the cruzeiro (CR $), at an exchange rate of one new cruzado for one cruzeiro. In August 1993 the cruzeiro was replaced by the cruzeiro real, equivalent to CR $1,000. On 1 March 1994, in preparation for the introduction of a new currency, a transitional accounting unit, the Unidade Real de Valor (at par with the US $), came into operation, alongside the cruzeiro real. On 1 July 1994 the cruzeiro real was replaced by the real (R $), also at par with the US $ and thus equivalent to 2,750 cruzeiros reais.

BUDGET
(R $ million)*

Revenue	2001	2002	2003
Tax revenue	196,712	243,006	273,358
Income tax	64,909	85,803	93,016
Tax on profits of legal entities .	9,367	13,364	16,750
Value-added tax on industrial			
products	19,456	19,799	19,674
Tax on financial operations and			
export duty	3,584	4,022	4,450
Import duty	9,090	7,972	8,143
Other taxes and duties . . .	15,349	26,538	31,377
Social security contributions .	46,364	52,267	59,565
Contributions to Social			
Integration Programme and			
Financial Reserve Fund for			
Public Employees	11,396	12,872	17,337
Provisional contribution on			
financial transactions . . .	17,197	20,369	23,046
Social welfare contributions . .	62,491	71,027	80,732
Other income	12,724	7,809	3,801
Total	271,927	321,842	357,891

Expenditure	2001	2002	2003
Transfers to state and local			
governments†	46,024	56,138	60,226
Personnel	64,381	73,306	78,066
Social service and welfare			
transfers	75,329	88,029	107,135
Other expenditures	63,766	71,910	72,956
Total	249,500	289,383	318,383

* Figures refer to cash operations of the National Treasury, including the collection and transfer of earmarked revenues for social expenditure purposes. The data exclude the transactions of other funds and accounts controlled by the Federal Government.
† Constitutionally mandated participation funds.

CENTRAL BANK RESERVES
(US $ million at 31 December)

	2001	2002	2003
Gold*	127	153	186
IMF special drawing rights . .	11	275	2
Foreign exchange	35,729	37,409	49,108
Total	35,867	37,836	49,297

* Valued at market-related prices.

Source: IMF, *International Financial Statistics*.

MONEY SUPPLY
(R $ million at 31 December)

	2001	2002	2003
Currency outside banks . . .	32,625	42,351	43,064
Demand deposits at deposit money			
banks	50,880	64,680	65,879
Total money (incl. others) . .	83,550	107,208	111,541

Source: IMF, *International Financial Statistics*.

COST OF LIVING
(Consumer Price Index; base: 1995 = 100)

	2001	2002	2003
All items	153.2	166.1	190.6

Source: IMF, *International Financial Statistics*.

NATIONAL ACCOUNTS
(R $ million at current prices)

National Income and Product

	2001	2002	2003
Compensation of employees . .	444,067	486,457	554,149
Net operating surplus	490,327	564,323	668,926
Net mixed income	60,469	61,618	69,757
Gross domestic product			
(GDP) at factor cost . . .	994,863	1,112,397	1,292,832
Taxes on production and imports	208,578	237,061 ⎫	263,350
Less Subsidies	4,704	3,430 ⎬	
GDP in market prices			
(purchasers' values) . .	1,198,736	1,346,028	1,556,182
Primary incomes received from			
abroad	8,185	10,434	10,902
Less Primary incomes paid			
abroad	53,689	62,706	66,384
Statistical discrepancy . . .	220	328	332
Gross national income (GNI).	1,153,452	1,294,084	1,501,032
Current transfers from abroad .	4,936	8,341	9,694
Less Current transfers paid			
abroad	1,069	1,074	941
Net national disposable			
income	1,157,318	1,301,351	1,509,785

Expenditure on the Gross Domestic Product

	2001	2002	2003
Final consumption expenditure .	956,501	1,052,139	1,192,613
Households . . . . . ⎫			
Non-profit institutions serving ⎬	725,760	781,174	882,983
households . . . . . ⎭			
General government . . .	230,741	270,965	309,631
Gross capital formation . . .	254,137	265,953	307,491
Gross fixed capital formation .	233,384	246,606	276,741
Changes in inventories . . ⎫			
Acquisitions, less disposals, of ⎬	20,753	19,348	30,750
valuables . . . . . ⎭			
Total domestic expenditure .	1,210,638	1,318,092	1,500,104
Exports of goods and services .	158,501	208,489	254,832
Less Imports of goods and			
services	170,403	180,554	198,754
GDP in purchasers' values			
(market prices)	1,198,736	1,346,028	1,556,182
GDP at constant 2003 prices	1,518,489	1,547,748	1,556,182

Gross Domestic Product by Economic Activity

	2001	2002	2003
Agriculture, hunting, forestry and			
fishing	89,287	104,908	138,191
Mining and quarrying	30,538	40,725	54,888
Manufacturing	240,834	279,907	337,457
Electricity, gas and water . . .	38,796	43,206	47,594
Construction	91,006	95,469	100,951
Trade, restaurants and hotels .	79,431	92,190	107,501
Transport	28,696	30,912	34,186
Communications	28,780	32,570	44,151
Finance, insurance, real estate and			
business services	70,126	92,190	97,459
Government services	173,302	195,933	220,458
Rents	127,546	135,629	142,544
Other community, social and			
personal services	120,080	130,839	144,884
Sub-total	1,118,422	1,274,478	1,470,264
Less Financial intermediation			
services indirectly measured .	54,653	75,332	74,661
Gross value added in basic			
prices	1,063,769	1,199,146	1,395,604
Taxes, less subsidies, on products .	134,967	146,883	160,578
GDP in market prices . . .	1,198,736	1,346,028	1,556,182

BALANCE OF PAYMENTS
(US $ million)

	2001	2002	2003
Exports of goods f.o.b.	58,223	60,362	73,084
Imports of goods f.o.b.	−55,572	−47,240	−48,283
Trade balance	2,650	13,121	24,801
Exports of services	9,322	9,551	10,468
Imports of services	−17,081	−14,509	−15,568
Balance on goods and services	−5,109	8,164	19,701
Other income received . . .	3,280	3,295	3,339
Other income paid	−23,023	−21,486	−21,891
Balance on goods, services and income	−24,852	−10,026	1,149
Current transfers received . .	1,934	2,627	3,132
Current transfers paid . . .	−296	−237	−265
Current balance	−23,215	−7,636	4,016
Capital account (net) . . .	−36	433	498
Direct investment abroad . .	2,258	−2,482	−249
Direct investment from abroad .	22,457	16,590	10,144
Portfolio investment assets . .	−795	−321	179
Portfolio investment liabilities .	872	−4,797	5,129
Financial derivatives assets . .	567	933	683
Financial derivatives liabilities .	−1,038	−1,289	−834
Other investment assets . . .	−6,586	−3,211	−9,483
Other investment liabilities . .	2,596	−9,331	−5,731
Net errors and omissions . . .	−498	−154	−764
Overall balance	−3,418	−11,266	3,586

Source: IMF, *International Financial Statistics*.

External Trade

PRINCIPAL COMMODITIES
(distribution by SITC, US $ million)

Imports f.o.b.	1999	2000	2001
Food and live animals . . .	3,560.3	3,443.1	2,938.6
Cereals and cereal preparations . .	1,611.0	1,662.0	1,524.1
Crude materials (inedible) except fuels	1,680.9	1,978.6	1,532.3
Mineral fuels, lubricants, etc.	5,887.4	8,912.4	8,454.1
Petroleum, petroleum products, etc.	4,634.8	7,121.1	6,714.3
Crude petroleum and bituminous oils	2,277.9	3,304.9	3,320.9
Refined petroleum products . .	2,245.7	3,671.3	3,202.1
Gasoline and other light oils .	1,203.9	1,963.2	1,431.0
Chemicals and related products	9,512.4	10,363.4	10,561.6
Organic chemicals	3,041.7	3,159.8	3,269.9
Medicinal and pharmaceutical products	1,950.5	1,804.3	1,910.2
Artificial resins and plastic materials	1,295.0	1,656.2	1,593.0
Basic manufactures	5,161.6	6,016.7	5,919.3
Machinery and transport equipment	22,197.2	24,211.7	25,136.2
Power-generating machinery and equipment	2,335.1	2,165.8	3,129.0
Machinery specialized for particular industries . . .	2,383.6	2,196.4	2,205.7
General industrial machinery equipment and parts . . .	2,888.7	2,944.7	3,323.4
Office machines and automatic data-processing machines . .	1,614.5	2,054.9	1,905.3
Telecommunications and sound equipment	2,673.0	3,206.4	3,156.3
Other electrical machinery apparatus, etc.	4,604.8	6,041.1	5,888.7
Thermionic, microcircuits, transistors and valves, etc. .	1,634.8	2,638.6	2,118.9

Imports f.o.b.— *continued*	1999	2000	2001
Road vehicles and parts* . . .	3,583.0	3,861.6	3,894.7
Other transport equipment* . .	1,581.7	1,741.2	1,644.9
Miscellaneous manufactured articles	3,295.3	3,533.3	3,594.4
Total (incl. others)	51,747.4	58,931.2	58,509.9

* Excluding tyres, engines and electrical parts.

Exports f.o.b.	1999	2000	2001
Food and live animals . . .	10,384.8	9,230.9	11,647.3
Meat and meat preparations . .	1,929.1	1,927.2	2,883.0
Vegetables and fruit	1,690.9	1,525.0	1,288.3
Sugar, sugar preparations and honey	2,010.1	1,295.2	2,403.8
Sugar and honey	1,925.1	1,203.9	2,289.2
Coffee, tea, cocoa and spices . .	2,760.7	2,066.8	1,718.6
Coffee and coffee substitutes .	2,463.9	1,784.6	1,417.1
Unroasted coffee, coffee husks and skins	2,330.8	1,559.6	1,207.7
Feeding-stuff for animals (excl. unmilled cereals)	1,587.1	1,716.0	2,166.8
Oilcake and other residues of soya beans	1,503.6	1,652.6	2,067.4
Beverages and tobacco . . .	1,017.8	911.6	1,001.4
Tobacco and tobacco manufactures	961.2	841.5	944.3
Crude materials (inedible) except fuels	7,153.2	8,650.9	8,797.8
Oil seeds and oleaginous fruit .	1,595.1	2,189.9	2,731.3
Soya beans	1,593.3	2,187.9	2,725.5
Pulp and waste paper	1,243.6	1,602.4	1,247.6
Metalliferous ores and metal scrap	3,168.2	3,536.1	3,389.7
Iron ore and concentrates . .	2,746.0	3,048.2	2,931.5
Iron ore and concentrates, not agglomerated	1,726.0	1,852.9	1,916.9
Chemicals and related products	2,980.4	3,502.5	3,149.6
Basic manufactures	9,879.8	11,219.3	10,351.1
Iron and steel	3,139.3	3,685.0	3,191.2
Iron and steel in primary form .	1,295.0	1,635.0	1,221.9
Non-ferrous metals	1,499.3	1,772.0	1,352.6
Machinery and transport equipment	11,366.2	15,485.1	15,542.4
Power-generating machinery and equipment	1,384.3	1,514.5	1,695.5
General industrial machinery equipment and parts . . .	1,442.0	1,598.0	1,468.0
Telecommunications and sound equipment	724.7	1,648.5	1,793.2
Road vehicles and parts* . . .	3,499.6	4,367.8	4,325.6
Passenger motor cars (excl. buses)	1,138.5	1,768.5	1,951.4
Other transport equipment* . .	1,937.7	3,618.7	3,637.8
Miscellaneous manufactured articles	2,851.5	3,443.2	3,490.0
Total (incl. others)	48,011.4	55,282.5	58,222.6

* Excluding tyres, engines and electrical parts.
Source: UN, *International Trade Statistics Yearbook*.

Imports (US $ million, 2002): Crude petroleum 3,247.3; Motors, generators and electrical equipment 1,685.8; Motor vehicle parts 1,357.7; Medications for human and veterinary medicine 1,352.5; Electronic equipment 1,250.2; Fuel oils 1,097.6; Total (incl. others) 47,240.5.

Exports (US $ million, 2002): Metalliferous ores and concentrates 3,048.9; Soya 3,032.0; Aeroplanes 2,335.5; Oil-cake and other residues from soya beans 2,198.9; Passenger cars 2,005.2; Radio transmitters and receivers and parts thereof 1,782.3; Total (incl. others) 60,361.8.

Imports (US $ million, 2003): Crude petroleum 3,777.0; Motor vehicle parts 1,500.7; Electronic equipment 1,470.5; Medications for human and veterinary medicine 1,397.3; Motors, generators and electrical equipment 1,144.4; Wheat grain 1,009.7; Total (incl. others) 48,259.6.

Exports (US $ million, 2003): Soya 4,290.4; Metalliferous ores and concentrates 3,455.9; Passenger cars 2,655.7; Oil-cake and other residues from soya beans 2,602.4; Petroleum derivatives 2,121.9; Aeroplanes 1,938.6; Total (incl. others) 73,084.1.

Source: Ministério do Desenvolvimento, Indústria e Comércio Exterior, Brasília.

PRINCIPAL TRADING PARTNERS
(US $ million)*

Imports f.o.b.	2001	2002	2003
Algeria	1,096	1,098	n.a.
Argentina	6,207	4,743	4,673
Belgium-Luxembourg	585	546	515
Canada	927	740	749
Chile	862	649	798
China, People's Republic	1,328	1,554	2,148
France	2,083	1,777	1,768
Germany	4,812	4,419	4,205
Italy	2,185	1,762	1,757
Japan	3,064	2,348	2,521
Korea, Republic	1,574	1,067	1,079
Mexico	695	580	533
Netherlands	532	535	509
Paraguay	n.a.	383	475
Spain	1,226	975	974
United Kingdom	1,235	1,345	1,202
USA	12,894	10,438	9,725
Uruguay	503	485	538
Total (incl. others)	55,581	47,240	48,260

Exports f.o.b.	2001	2002	2003
Argentina	5,002	2,342	4,561
Belgium-Luxembourg	1,812	1,892	1,795
Canada	555	732	978
Chile	1,352	1,461	1,880
China, People's Republic	1,902	2,520	4,533
France	1,648	1,525	1,715
Germany	2,502	2,537	3,136
Italy	1,809	1,817	2,208
Japan	1,986	2,098	2,311
Korea, Republic	736	852	1,223
Mexico	1,868	2,342	2,741
Netherlands	2,863	3,182	4,246
Paraguay	720	558	707
Spain	1,042	1,120	1,552
United Kingdom	1,705	1,769	1,899
USA	14,190	15,355	16,900
Uruguay	641	410	404
Total (incl. others)	58,270	60,362	73,084

* Imports by country of purchase; exports by country of last consignment.

Source: Ministério do Desenvolvimento, Indústria e Comércio Exterior, Brasília, DF.

Transport

RAILWAYS*

	1998	1999	2000
Passengers ('000)	2,449	1,587	1,614
Passenger-km ('000)	430,637	437,500	601,908
Freight ('000 metric tons)	263,140	261,920	292,500
Freight ton-km (million)	143,170	140,600	155,590

* Including suburban and metro services.

Source: Secretaria de Transportes Terrestres, Ministério dos Transportes, Brasília.

Freight transport: 162,235m. ton-km in 2001; 320,992 metric tons and 170,177m. ton-km in 2002; 344,996 metric tons and 182,648m. ton-km in 2003.

Source: Agência Nacional de Transportes Terrestres, Ministério dos Transportes, Brasília.

ROAD TRAFFIC
(motor vehicles in use at 31 December)

	1998	1999	2000
Passenger cars	21,313,351	22,347,423	23,241,966
Buses and coaches	430,062	400,048	427,213
Light goods vehicles	3,313,774	3,193,058	3,469,927
Heavy goods vehicles	1,755,877	1,778,084	1,836,203
Motorcycles and mopeds	3,854,646	4,222,705	4,732,331

Source: Empresa Brasileira de Planejamento de Transportes (GEIPOT).

SHIPPING

Merchant Fleet
(registered at 31 December)

	2001	2002	2003
Number of vessels	475	476	482
Total displacement ('000 grt)	3,687	3,449	3,258

Source: Lloyd's Register-Fairplay, *World Fleet Statistics*.

International Sea-borne Freight Traffic
('000 metric tons)

	2000	2001	2002
Goods loaded	288,202	315,135	342,675
Goods unloaded	191,072	191,072	186,330

Source: Ministério dos Transportes.

CIVIL AVIATION
(embarked passengers, mail and cargo)

	2001	2002	2003
Number of passengers ('000)	36,001	35,923	33,420
Passenger-km (million)	50,789	50,526	n.a.
Freight ton-km ('000)*	6,930,295	6,976,683	6,801,204

* Including mail.

Source: Departamento de Aviação Civil (DAC), Comando da Aeronáutica, Ministério da Defesa, Brasília.

Tourism

FOREIGN TOURIST ARRIVALS

Country of origin	2001	2002	2003
Argentina	1,374,584	699,177	792,753
Bolivia	107,673	67,673	60,487
Canada	55,629	67,531	68,585
Chile	154,093	112,451	114,562
France	185,033	206,262	225,235
Germany	320,602	296,157	315,532
Italy	216,517	183,469	214,141
Netherlands	44,057	55,088	77,693
Paraguay	285,752	218,653	186,457
Portugal	165,908	168,329	228,153
Spain	126,973	110,177	120,234
Switzerland	71,562	56,175	62,829
United Kingdom	143,823	146,513	155,877
USA	594,309	636,063	670,863
Uruguay	305,084	222,410	239,885
Total (incl. others)	4,772,575	3,783,400	4,090,590

Receipts from tourism (US $ million): 3,700.9 in 2001; 3,120.1 in 2002; 3,386.0 in 2003.

Source: Instituto Brasileiro de Turismo—EMBRATUR, Brasília.

Communications Media

	2000	2001	2002
Personal computers ('000 in use) .	7,500	10,800	13,000
Internet users ('000)	5,000	8,000	14,300
Telephones in use ('000 main lines)	30,926	37,431	38,810
Mobile cellular telephones ('000 subscribers)	23,188	28,746	34,881

2003: 46,373,000 mobile cellular telephone subscribers.

Source: International Telecommunication Union (ITU).

Radio receivers ('000 in use): 71,000 in 1997 (Source: UNESCO, *Statistical Yearbook*).

Television receivers ('000 in use): 58,283 in 2000 (Source: International Telecommunication Union (ITU)).

Book production ('000 titles): 21,574 in 1994 (Source:: UN, *Statistical Yearbook*).

Daily newspapers: 372 (average circulation, '000 copies: 7,163) in 1998 (Source: UN, *Statistical Yearbook*).

Non-daily newspapers: 1,251 in 1998 (Source: UN, *Statistical Yearbook*).

Facsimile machines: 500,000 in 1997 (Source: UN, *Statistical Yearbook*).

Education

(2003, unless otherwise indicated)

	Institutions	Teachers	Students
Pre-primary	94,741	270,575	5,155,676
Literacy classes (Classe de Alfabetização) . .	27,670	37,508	598,589
Primary	169,075	1,603,851	34,438,749
Secondary	23,118	488,376	9,072,942
Higher	1,637*	219,947†	3,479,913*

* 2002 figure.
† 2001 figure.

Adult literacy rate: 87.6% in 2001.

Source: Ministério da Educação, Brasília.

Directory

The Constitution

A new Constitution was promulgated on 5 October 1988. The following is a summary of the main provisions:

The Federative Republic of Brazil, formed by the indissoluble union of the States, the Municipalities and the Federal District, is constituted as a democratic state. All power emanates from the people. The Federative Republic of Brazil seeks the economic, political, social and cultural integration of the peoples of Latin America.

All are equal before the law. The inviolability of the right to life, freedom, equality, security and property is guaranteed. No one shall be subjected to torture. Freedom of thought, conscience, religious belief and expression are guaranteed, as is privacy. The principles of habeas corpus and 'habeas data' (the latter giving citizens access to personal information held in government data banks) are granted. There is freedom of association, and the right to strike is guaranteed.

There is universal suffrage by direct secret ballot. Voting is compulsory for literate persons between 18 and 69 years of age, and optional for those who are illiterate, those over 70 years of age and those aged 16 and 17.

Brasília is the federal capital. The Union's competence includes maintaining relations with foreign states, and taking part in international organizations; declaring war and making peace; guaranteeing national defence; decreeing a state of siege; issuing currency; supervising credits, etc.; formulating and implementing plans for economic and social development; maintaining national services, including communications, energy, the judiciary and the police; legislating on civil, commercial, penal, procedural, electoral, agrarian, maritime, aeronautical, spatial and labour law, etc. The Union, States, Federal District and Municipalities must protect the Constitution, laws and democratic institutions, and preserve national heritage.

The States are responsible for electing their Governors by universal suffrage and direct secret ballot for a four-year term. The organization of the Municipalities, the Federal District and the Territories is regulated by law.

The Union may intervene in the States and in the Federal District only in certain circumstances, such as a threat to national security or public order, and then only after reference to the National Congress.

LEGISLATIVE POWER

The legislative power is exercised by the Congresso Nacional (National Congress), which is composed of the Câmara dos Deputados (Chamber of Deputies) and the Senado Federal (Federal Senate). Elections for deputies and senators take place simultaneously throughout the country; candidates for the Congresso must be Brazilian by birth and have full exercise of their political rights. They must be at least 21 years of age in the case of deputies and at least 35 years of age in the case of senators. The Congresso meets twice a year in ordinary sessions, and extraordinary sessions may be convened by the President of the Republic, the Presidents of the

Câmara and the Senado, or at the request of the majority of the members of either house.

The Câmara is made up of representatives of the people, elected by a system of proportional representation in each State, Territory and the Federal District for a period of four years. The total number of deputies representing the States and the Federal District will be established in proportion to the population; each Territory will elect four deputies.

The Senado is composed of representatives of the States and the Federal District, elected according to the principle of majority. Each State and the Federal District will elect three senators with a mandate of eight years, with elections after four years for one-third of the members and after another four years for the remaining two-thirds. Each Senator is elected with two substitutes. The Senado approves, by secret ballot, the choice of Magistrates, when required by the Constitution; of the Attorney-General of the Republic, of the Ministers of the Accounts Tribunal, of the Territorial Governors, of the president and directors of the central bank and of the permanent heads of diplomatic missions.

The Congresso is responsible for deciding on all matters within the competence of the Union, especially fiscal and budgetary arrangements, national, regional and local plans and programmes, the strength of the armed forces and territorial limits. It is also responsible for making definitive resolutions on international treaties, and for authorizing the President to declare war.

The powers of the Câmara include authorizing the instigation of legal proceedings against the President and Vice-President of the Republic and Ministers of State. The Senado may indict and impose sentence on the President and Vice-President of the Republic and Ministers of State.

Constitutional amendments may be proposed by at least one-third of the members of either house, by the President or by more than one-half of the legislative assemblies of the units of the Federation. Amendments must be ratified by three-fifths of the members of each house. The Constitution may not be amended during times of national emergency, such as a state of siege.

EXECUTIVE POWER

Executive power is exercised by the President of the Republic, aided by the Ministers of State. Candidates for the Presidency and Vice-Presidency must be Brazilian-born, be in full exercise of their political rights and be over 35 years of age. The candidate who obtains an absolute majority of votes will be elected President. If no candidate attains an absolute majority, the two candidates who have received the most votes proceed to a second round of voting, at which the candidate obtaining the majority of valid votes will be elected President. The President holds office for a term of four years and (under an amendment adopted in 1997) is eligible for re-election.

The Ministers of State are chosen by the President and their duties include countersigning acts and decrees signed by the President, expediting instructions for the enactment of laws, decrees and regulations, and presentation to the President of an annual report of their activities.

The Council of the Republic is the higher consultative organ of the President of the Republic. It comprises the Vice-President of the Republic, the Presidents of the Câmara and Senado, the leaders of the majority and of the minority in each house, the Minister of Justice, two members appointed by the President of the Republic, two elected by the Senado and two elected by the Câmara, the latter six having a mandate of three years.

The National Defence Council advises the President on matters relating to national sovereignty and defence. It comprises the Vice-President of the Republic, the Presidents of the Câmara and Senado, the Minister of Justice, military Ministers and the Ministers of Foreign Affairs and of Planning.

JUDICIAL POWER

Judicial power in the Union is exercised by the Supreme Federal Tribunal; the Higher Tribunal of Justice; the Regional Federal Tribunals and federal judges; Labour Tribunals and judges; Electoral Tribunals and judges; Military Tribunals and judges; and the States' Tribunals and judges. Judges are appointed for life; they may not undertake any other employment. The Tribunals elect their own controlling organs and organize their own internal structure.

The Supreme Federal Tribunal, situated in the Union capital, has jurisdiction over the whole national territory and is composed of 11 ministers. The ministers are nominated by the President after approval by the Senado, from Brazilian-born citizens, between the ages of 35 and 65 years, of proved judicial knowledge and experience.

The Government

HEAD OF STATE

President: Luiz Inácio (Lula) da Silva (PT) (took office 2 January 2003).

Vice-President: José Alencar Gomes da Silva (PL).

THE CABINET
(April 2005)

The Cabinet is composed of members of the Partido dos Trabalhadores (PT), the Partido Comunista do Brasil (PC do B), the Partido Liberal (PL), the Partido Socialista Brasileiro (PSB), the Partido do Movimento Democrático Brasileiro (PMDB), the Partido Progressista (PP) and Independents.

Minister of Foreign Affairs: Celso Amorim (Ind.).

Minister of Justice: Márcio Thomaz Bastos (PT).

Minister of Finance: Antônio Palocci, Filho (PT).

Minister of Defence: José Alencar Gomes da Silva (PL).

Minister of Agriculture, Fisheries and Food Supply: Roberto Rodrigues (Ind.).

Minister of Agrarian Development: Miguel Soldatelli Rossetto (PT).

Minister of Labour and Employment: Ricardo Berzoini (PT).

Minister of Transport: Alfredo Pereira do Nascimento (PL).

Minister of Cities: Olivio Dutra (PT).

Minister of Planning, Budget and Administration: Paulo Bernardo (PT).

Minister of Mines and Energy: Dilma Vana Rousseff (Ind.).

Minister of Culture: Gilberto Gil (Ind.).

Minister of the Environment: Maria Osmarina Marina da Silva Vaz de Lima (PT).

Minister of Development, Industry and Trade: Luiz Fernando Furlán (Ind.).

Minister of Education: Tarso Genro (PT).

Minister of Health: Humberto Sergio Costa Lima (PT).

Minister of National Integration: Ciro Ferreira Gomes (Ind.).

Minister of Social Security: Romero Jucá (PMDB).

Minister of Social Development and the Fight against Hunger: Patrus Ananías (PT).

Minister of Communications: Eunício Lopes de Oliveira (PMDB).

Minister of Science and Technology: Eduardo Campos (PSB).

Minister of Sport: Agnelo Santos Queiroz, Filho (PC do B).

Minister of Tourism: Walfrido do Mares Guia (Ind.).

Comptroller-General: Waldir Pires (PT).

Cabinet Chief and Joint Minister of Policy Development and Implementation: José Dirceu de Oliveira e Silva (PT).

There are also eight Secretaries of State

MINISTRIES

Office of the President: Palácio do Planalto, Praça dos 3 Poderes, 70150-900 Brasília, DF; tel. (61) 411-1573; fax (61) 323-1461; e-mail protocolo@planalto.gov.br; internet www.presidencia.gov.br.

Office of the Civilian Cabinet: Palácio do Planalto, 4° andar, Praça dos Três Poderes, 70150-900 Brasília, DF; tel. (61) 211-1034; fax (61) 321-5804; e-mail casacivil@planalto.gov.br; internet www.presidencia.gov.br/casacivil.

Ministry of Agrarian Development: Esplanada dos Ministérios, Bloco A, 8° andar, Brasília DF; tel. (61) 223-8002; fax (61) 322-0492; e-mail miguel.rossetto@mda.gov.br; internet www.mda.gov.br.

Ministry of Agriculture, Fisheries and Food Supply: Esplanada dos Ministérios, Bloco D, 8° andar, 70043-900 Brasília, DF; tel. (61) 226-5161; fax (61) 321-8360; e-mail cenagri@agricultura.gov.br; internet www.agricultura.gov.br.

Ministry of Cities: Esplanada dos Ministérios, Bloco A, Anexo 2, 70050-901 Brasília, DF; tel. (61) 2108-1770; fax (61) 226-2719; e-mail cidades@cidades.gov.br; internet www.cidades.gov.br.

Ministry of Communications: Esplanada dos Ministérios, Bloco R, 8° andar, 70044-900 Brasília, DF; tel. (61) 311-6000; e-mail webmaster@mc.gov.br; internet www.mc.gov.br.

Ministry of Culture: Esplanada dos Ministérios, Bloco B, 3° andar, 70068-900 Brasília, DF; tel. (61) 316-2170; fax (61) 225-9162; e-mail info@minc.gov.br; internet www.cultura.gov.br.

Ministry of Defence: Esplanada dos Ministérios, Bloco Q, 70049-900 Brasília, DF; tel. (61) 312-4000; fax (61) 321-2477; e-mail faleconosco@defesa.gov.br; internet www.defesa.gov.br.

Ministry of Development, Industry and Trade: Esplanada dos Ministérios, Bloco J, 7° andar, Sala 700, 70053-900 Brasília, DF; tel. (61) 325-2056; fax (61) 325-2063; e-mail ascom@desenvolvimento.gov.br; internet www.desenvolvimento.gov.br.

Ministry of Education: Esplanada dos Ministérios, Bloco L, Edif. Sede e Anexos, 70047-900 Brasília, DF; tel. (61) 2104-8744; fax (61) 2104-9172; e-mail acordabr@acb.mec.gov.br; internet www.mec.gov.br.

Ministry of the Environment: Esplanada dos Ministérios, Bloco B, 5–9° andar, 70068-900 Brasília, DF; tel. (61) 4009-1000; fax (61) 4009-1756; e-mail marina.silva@mma.gov.br; internet www.mma.gov.br.

Ministry of Finance: Esplanada dos Ministérios, Bloco P, 5° andar, 70048-900 Brasília, DF; tel. (61) 412-2000; fax (61) 226-9084; e-mail acs.df.gmf@fazenda.gov.br; internet www.fazenda.gov.br.

Ministry of Foreign Affairs: Palácio do Itamaraty, Esplanada dos Ministérios, Bloco H, 70170-900 Brasília, DF; tel. (61) 411-6161; fax (61) 225-1272; internet www.mre.gov.br.

Ministry of Health: Esplanada dos Ministérios, Bloco G, 70058-900 Brasília, DF; tel. (61) 315-2425; fax (61) 224-8747; internet www.saude.gov.br.

Ministry of Justice: Esplanada dos Ministérios, Bloco T, Edif. Sede, 70064-900 Brasília, DF; tel. (61) 429-3000; fax (61) 322-6817; e-mail acs@mj.gov.br; internet www.mj.gov.br.

Ministry of Labour and Employment: Esplanada dos Ministérios, Bloco F, 5° andar, 70059-900 Brasília, DF; tel. (61) 317-6000; fax (61) 226-3577; e-mail internacional@mtb.gov.br; internet www.mtb.gov.br.

Ministry of Mines and Energy: Esplanada dos Ministérios, Bloco U, 70065-900 Brasília, DF; tel. (61) 319-5555; fax (61) 225-5407; internet www.mme.gov.br.

Ministry of National Integration: Esplanada dos Ministérios, Bloco E, 70067-901 Brasília, DF; tel. (61) 414-5801; fax (61) 414-5483; e-mail impresa@integracao.gov.br; internet www.integracao.gov.br.

Ministry of Planning, Budget and Administration: Esplanada dos Ministérios, Bloco K, 70040-906 Brasília, DF; tel. (61) 429-4343; fax (61) 321-5292; e-mail info@planejamento.gov.br; internet www.planejamento.gov.br.

Ministry of Science and Technology: Esplanada dos Ministérios, Bloco E, 4° andar, 70067-900 Brasília, DF; tel. (61) 317-7600; fax (61) 225-1441; e-mail webgab@mct.gov.br; internet www.mct.gov.br.

Ministry of Social Development and the Fight against Hunger: Esplanada dos Ministérios, Bloco C, 5° andar, 70046-900 Brasília, DF; tel. (61) 313-1822; internet www.desenvolvimentosocial.gov.br.

Ministry of Social Security: Esplanada dos Ministérios, Bloco F, 70059-900 Brasília, DF; tel. (61) 317-5100; fax (61) 322-7463; internet www.mps.gov.br.

Ministry of Sport: Esplanada dos Ministérios, Bloco A, 70054-906 Brasília, DF; tel. (61) 217-1800; fax (61) 217-1707; internet www .esporte.gov.br.

Ministry of Tourism: Esplanada dos Ministérios, Bloco U, 3°–4° andares, 70065-900 Brasília, DF; tel. (61) 310-9491; e-mail sidney .acosta@turismo.gov.br; internet www.turismo.gov.br.

Ministry of Transport: Esplanada dos Ministérios, Bloco R, 70044-900 Brasília, DF; tel. (61) 311-7001; fax (61) 311-7876; e-mail alfredo.nascimento@transportes.gov.br; internet www.transportes .gov.br.

President and Legislature

PRESIDENT

Election, First Round, 6 October 2002

Candidate	Valid votes cast	% valid votes cast
Luiz Inácio (Lula) da Silva (PT) . . .	39,443,876	46.4
José Serra (PSDB)	19,700,470	23.2
Antônio Garotinho (PSB)	15,175,776	17.9
Ciro Gomes (PPS)	10,167,650	12.0
Others	440,646	0.5
Total	**84,928,418**	**100.0**

Election, Second Round, 27 October 2002

Candidate	Valid votes cast	% valid votes cast
Luiz Inácio (Lula) da Silva (PT) . . .	52,793,364	61.3
José Serra (PSDB)	33,370,739	38.7
Total	**86,164,103**	**100.0**

CONGRESSO NACIONAL

Câmara dos Deputados

Chamber of Deputies: Palácio do Congresso Nacional, Edif. Principal, Praça dos Três Poderes, 70160-900 Brasília, DF; tel. (61) 216-0000; internet www.camara.gov.br.

President: SEVERINO CAVALCANTI (PP).

The Chamber has 513 members who hold office for a four-year term.

General Election, 6 October 2002

Party	Seats at election	Seats at April 2005
Partido dos Trabalhadores (PT) . . .	91	91
Partido da Frente Liberal (PFL) . . .	84	62
Partido do Movimento Democrático Brasileiro (PMDB)	75	86
Partido da Social Democracia Brasileira (PSDB)	70	52
Partido Progressista Brasileiro (PPB)* .	49	51
Partido Liberal (PL)†	26	51‡
Partido Trabalhista Brasileiro (PTB) .	26	48
Partido Socialista Brasileiro (PSB) .	22	16
Partido Democrático Trabalhista (PDT)	21	14
Partido Popular Socialista (PPS) . . .	15	17
Partido Comunista do Brasil (PC do B)	12	9
Partido de Reedificação da Ordem Nacional (PRONA)	6	2
Partido Verde (PV)	5	6
Partido Social Cristão (PSC)	1	2
Partido Social Liberal (PSL)†	1	—
Independents	9	6
Total	**513**	**513**

* Known as the Partido Progressista (PP) from 2003.
† The PL and the PSL subsequently formed a coalition.
‡ Including seats belonging to the PSL.

Senado Federal

Federal Senate: Palácio do Congresso Nacional, 70165-900 Brasília, DF; tel. (61) 311-4141; fax (61) 311-3190; e-mail webmaster .secs@senado.gov.br; internet www.senado.gov.br.

President: RENAN CALHEIROS (PMDB).

The 81 members of the Senate are elected by the 26 States and the Federal District (three Senators for each) according to the principle of majority. The Senate's term of office is eight years, with elections after four years for one-third of the members and after another four years for the remaining two-thirds.

In the elections of 6 October 2002 54 seats were contested. In April 2005 the PMDB was represented by 23 senators, the PFL by 16, the PT and the PSDB by 13 each, and the PDT and the PL by four each. The PTB, the PSB, the P-SOL and the PPS were also represented.

Governors

STATES

Acre: JORGE NEY VIANA (PT).

Alagoas: RONALDO AUGUSTO LESSA (PSB).

Amapá: ANTONIO WALDEZ GÓES (PDT).

Amazonas: EDUARDO BRAGA (PPS).

Bahia: PAULO SOUTO (PFL).

Ceará: LÚCIO ALCÂNTARA (PSDB).

Espírito Santo: PAULO HARTUNG (PSB).

Goiás: MARCONI FERREIRA PERILLO (PSDB).

Maranhão: JOSÉ REINALDO (PFL).

Mato Grosso: BLAIRO MAGGI (PPS).

Mato Grosso do Sul: JOSÉ ORCÍRIO ZECA (PT).

Minas Gerais: AÉCIO NEVES (PSDB).

Pará: SIMÃO ROBISON OLIVEIRA JATENE (PSDB).

Paraíba: CASSIO CUNHA LIMA (PSDB).

Paraná: ROBERTO REQUIÃO (PMDB).

Pernambuco: JARBAS DE ANDRADE VASCONCELOS (PMDB).

Piauí: WELLINGTON DIAS (PT).

Rio de Janeiro: ROSINHA MATHEUS GAROTINHO (PSB).

Rio Grande do Norte: VILMA DE FARIA (PSB).

Rio Grande do Sul: GERMANO RIGOTTO (PMDB).

Rondônia: IVO CASSOL (PSDB).

Roraima: FLAMARION POTELA (PSL).

Santa Catarina: LUIZ ENRIQUE DA SILVEIRA (PMDB).

São Paulo: GERALDO ALCKMIN (PSDB).

Sergipe: JOÃO ALVES (PFL).

Tocantins: MARCELO MIRANDA (PFL).

FEDERAL DISTRICT

Brasília: JOAQUIM DOMINGOS RORIZ (PMDB).

Political Organizations

Partido Comunista do Brasil (PC do B): Av. Sarutaiá 185, Jardim Paulista, 01403-010 São Paulo, SP; tel. (11) 3054-1800; fax (11) 3051-7738; e-mail secretariageral@pcdob.org.br; internet www .vermelho.org.br/pcdob; f. 1922; Pres. RENATO REBELO; 185,000 mems.

Partido Democrático Trabalhista (PDT): Rua Marechal Câmara 160, 4°, 20050 Rio de Janeiro, RJ; fax (21) 2262-8834; e-mail fio@pdt.org.br; internet www.pdt.org.br; f. 1980; formerly the PTB (Partido Trabalhista Brasileiro), renamed 1980 when that name was awarded to a dissident group following controversial judicial proceedings; mem. of Socialist International; Pres. (vacant); Gen. Sec. MANOEL DIAS.

Partido da Frente Liberal (PFL): Senado Federal, Anexo 1, 26° andar, 70165-900 Brasília, DF; tel. (61) 311-4305; fax (61) 224-1912; e-mail pfl25@pfl.org.br; internet www.pfl.org.br; f. 1984 by moderate members of the PDS and PMDB; Pres. JORGE BORNHAUSEN; Gen. Sec. JOSÉ CARLOS ALELUIA.

Partido Liberal (PL): Câmara dos Deputados, Anexo 1, 26° andar, 70160-900 Brasília, DF; tel. (61) 318-5899; e-mail pl@pl.org.br; internet www.pl.org.br; Pres. VALDEMAR COSTA NETO; Sec.-Gen. GUILHERME FARHAT FERRAZ.

Partido do Movimento Democrático Brasileiro (PMDB): Câmara dos Deputados, Edif. Principal, 70160-900 Brasília, DF; tel. (61) 318-5120; e-mail presidente@pmdb.org.br; internet www.pmdb .org.br; f. 1980; moderate elements of former MDB; merged with Partido Popular in February 1982; Pres. MICHEL TEMER; Sec.-Gen.

SARIVA FELIPE; factions include the **Históricos** and the **Movimento da Unidade Progressiva (MUP)**.

Partido Popular Socialista (PPS): SCS Quadra 7, Bloco A, Edif. Executive Tower, SL 826/828, Pátio Brasil Shopping, Setor Comerical Sul, 70307-000 Brasília, DF; tel. (61) 223-0623; fax (61) 323-3623; e-mail pps23@pps.org.br; internet www.pps.org.br; f. 1922; Pres. ROBERTO FREIRE; Sec.-Gen. RUBENS BUENO.

Partido Progressista (PP): Senado Federal, Anexo 1, 17° andar, 70165-900 Brasília, DF; tel. (61) 311-3041; fax (61) 226-8192; internet www.pp.org.br; f. 1995 as Partido Progressista Brasileiro (PPB) by merger of Partido Progressista Reformador (PPR), Partido Progressista (PP) and the Partido Republicano Progressista (PRP); changed name as above in 2003; right-wing; Pres. PEDRO CORRÊA; Sec.-Gen. LEODEGAR TISCOSKI.

Partido Social Cristão (PSC): tel. (21) 2220-2185; e-mail psc@psc.org.br; internet www.psc.org.br; f. 1970 as Partido Democrático Republicano; Pres. VITOR JORGE ADBALA NÓSSEIS.

Partido da Social Democracia Brasileira (PSDB): Av. L2 Sul, Quadra 607, Edif. Metrópolis, , 70200-400 Brasília, DF; tel. (61) 424-0500; fax (61) 424-0519; e-mail tucano@psdb.org.br; internet www.psdb.org.br; f. 1988; centre-left; formed by dissident members of the PMDB (incl. Históricos), PFL, PDS, PDT, PSB and PTB; Pres. EDUARDO AZEREDO; Sec.-Gen. BISMARCK MAIA.

Partido Social Liberal (PSL): Rua Olinda Ellis 365, Campo Grande, RJ; tel. and fax (21) 3384-0102; e-mail psl@psl.org.br; internet www.psl.org.br; f. 1994; Pres. TACIANO VARRO.

Partido Socialismo e Liberdade (P-SOL): Edif. Venâncio V, Loja 28, 70300-000 Brasília, DF; internet www.psol.org.b; f. 2004 by fmr PT mems; Pres. HELOISA HELENA.

Partido Socialista Brasileiro (PSB): Câmara dos Deputados, Anexo II, Brasília, DF; tel. (61) 215-9650; fax (61) 215-9663; e-mail lid.psb@camara.gov.br; internet www.psb.org.br; f. 1947; Pres. MIGUEL ARRAES; Sec.-Gen. RENATO SOARES.

Partido dos Trabalhadores (PT): Congresso Nacional, 70160, Brasília, DF; tel. (61) 224-1699; internet www.pt.org.br; f. 1980; first independent labour party; associated with the *autêntico* branch of the trade union movement; 350,000 mems; Pres. JOSÉ GENOINO; Nat. Sec.-Gen. SILVIO PEREIRA.

Partido Trabalhista Brasileiro (PTB): SCLN 303, Bloco C, Sala 105, Asa Norte, 70735-530 Brasília, DF; tel. (61) 226-0477; fax (61) 225-4757; e-mail ptb@ptb.org.br; internet www.ptb.org.br; f. 1980; Pres. ROBERTO JEFFERSON MONTEIRO FRANCISCO; Sec.-Gen. LUIS ANTÔNIO FLEURY, Filho.

Other political parties represented in the Congresso Nacional include the Partido de Reedificação da Ordem Nacional (PRONA), the Partido Verde (PV; internet www.pv.org.br), the Partido Social-Democrático (PSD), the Partido Social Trabalhista (PST), the Partido da Mobilização Nacional (PMN; internet www.pmn.org.br) and the Partido Social Democrata Cristão (PSDC; internet www.psdc.org.br).

OTHER ORGANIZATION

Movimento dos Trabalhadores Rurais Sem Terra (MST): Alameda Barão de Limeira, 1232 Campos Elíseos, 01202-002 São Paulo, SP; tel. (11) 3361-3866; e-mail jst@mst.org.br; internet www.mst.org.br; landless peasant movt; Pres. JOÃO PERO STÉDILE; Nat. Co-ordinator GILMAR MAURO.

Diplomatic Representation

EMBASSIES IN BRAZIL

Algeria: SHIS, QI 09, Conj. 13, Casa 01, Lago Sul, 70472-900 Brasília, DF; tel. (61) 248-4039; fax (61) 248-4691; e-mail sanag277@bsb.terra.com.br; Ambassador LAHCÈNE MOUSSAOUI.

Angola: SHIS, QI 07, Conj. 11, Casa 09, 71615-310 Brasília, DF; tel. (61) 248-4489; fax (61) 248-1567; e-mail emb.angola@tecnolink.com.br; internet www.angola.org.br; Ambassador ALBERTO CORREIA NETO.

Argentina: SHIS, QL 02, Conj. 01, Casa 19, Lago Sul, 70442-900 Brasília, DF; tel. (61) 364-7600; fax (61) 364-7666; e-mail embarg@embarg.org.br; internet www.embarg.org.br; Ambassador JUAN PABLO LOHLÉ.

Australia: SES, Av. Das Nações, Quadra 801, Conj. K, Lote 7, 70200-010 Brasília, DF; tel. (61) 226-3111; fax (61) 226-1112; e-mail australemb@terra.com.br; internet www.brasil.embassy.gov.br; Ambassador JOHN WILLIAM SULLIVAN.

Austria: SES, Av. das Nações, Quadra 811, Lote 40, 70426-900 Brasília, DF; tel. (61) 443-3111; fax (61) 443-5233; e-mail brasilia.ob@bmaa.gv.at; Ambassador WERNER BRANDSTETTER.

Belgium: SES, Av. das Nações, Quadra 809, Lote 32, 70422-900 Brasília, DF; tel. (61) 443-1133; fax (61) 443-1219; e-mail brasilia@diplobel.org; internet www.belgica.org.br; Ambassador GODELIEVE VAN DEN BERGH.

Bolivia: SHIS, QI 19, Conj. 13, Casa 19, 71655-130 Brasília, DF; tel. (61) 366-3432; fax (61) 366-3136; e-mail embolivia-brasilia@embolivia-brasil.org.br; internet www.embolivia-brasil.org.br; Ambassador EDGAR CAMACHO OMISTE.

Bulgaria: SEN, Av. das Nações, Quadra 801, Lote 08, 70432-900 Brasília, DF; tel. (61) 223-6193; fax (61) 323-3285; e-mail bulagria@abordo.com.br; Ambassador VENTZISLAV ANGUELOV IVANOV.

Cameroon: SHIS, QI 09, Conj. 07, Casa 01, 71625-070 Brasília, DF; tel. (61) 248-5403; fax (61) 248-0443; e-mail embcameroun@embcameroun.org.br; internet www.embcameroon.org.br; Ambassador MARTIN MBARGA NGUELE.

Canada: SES, Av. das Nações, Quadra 803, Lote 16, 70410-900 Brasília, DF; tel. (61) 424-5400; fax (61) 424-5490; e-mail brsla@international.gc.ca; internet www.dfait-maeci.gc.ca/brazil; Ambassador SUZANNE LAPORTE.

Cape Verde: SHIS, QL 08, Conj. 08, Casa 07, 71620-285 Brasília, DF; tel. (61) 248-0543; fax (61) 364-4059; e-mail embcaboverde@rudah.com.br; Ambassador LUÍS ANTÓNIO VALADARES DUPRET.

Chile: SES, Av. das Nações, Quadra 803, Lote 11, 70409-700 Brasília, DF; tel. (61) 2103-5151; fax (61) 322-2966; e-mail embchile@embchile.org.br; internet www.embchile.org.br; Ambassador OSVALDO PUCCIO HUIDOBRO.

China, People's Republic: SES, Av. das Nações, Quadra 813, Lote 51, 70443-900 Brasília, DF; tel. (61) 346-4436; fax (61) 346-3299; internet www.embchina.org.br; Ambassador JIANG YUANDE.

Colombia: SES, Av. das Nações, Quadra 803, Lote 10, 70444-900 Brasília, DF; tel. (61) 226-8997; fax (61) 224-4732; e-mail embjcol@embcol.org.br; Ambassador CLAUDIA RODRÍGUEZ CASTELLANOS.

Congo, Democratic Republic: SHIS, QI 06, Conj. 04, Casa 15, Lago Sul, CP 71620-045, Brasília, DF; tel. (61) 365-4822; fax (61) 365-4823; e-mail ambaredeco@ig.com.br; Chargé d'affaires a.i. DANIEL MUANDA LENDO.

Costa Rica: SRTV/N 701, Conj. C, Ala A, Salas 308/310, Edif. Centro Empresarial Norte, 70710-200 Brasília, DF; tel. (61) 328-2219; fax (61) 328-2243; e-mail embrica@solar.com.br; Ambassador SARA FAIGENZICHT DE GLOOBE.

Côte d'Ivoire: Sen. Av. das Nações, Lote 09, 70473-900, Brasília, DF; tel. (61) 321-7320; fax (61) 321-1306; e-mail cotedivoire@cotedivoire.org.br; internet www.cotedivoire.org.br; Ambassador COLETTE GALLIE LAMBIN.

Croatia: SHIS, QI 09, Conj. 11, Casa 03, 71625-110 Brasília, DF; tel. and fax (61) 248-0610; e-mail embaixada.croacia@zaz.com.br; Ambassador (vacant).

Cuba: SHIS, QI 05, Conj. 18, Casa 01, 71615-180 Brasília, DF; tel. (61) 248-4710; fax (61) 248-6778; e-mail embacuba@uol.com.br; internet www.embaixadacuba.org.br; Ambassador PEDRO JUAN NUÑEZ MOSQUERA.

Czech Republic: Via L-3, Quadra 805, Lote 21, 70414-900, CP 170 Brasília, DF; tel. (61) 242-7785; fax (61) 242-7833; e-mail brasilia@embassy.mzv.cz; internet www.mzv.cz/brasilia; Ambassador VÁCLAV HUBINGER.

Denmark: SES, Av. das Nações, Quadra 807, Lote 26, 70416-900 Brasília, DF; tel. (61) 443-8188; fax (61) 443-5232; e-mail bsbamb@um.dk; internet www.denmark.org.br; Ambassador CHRISTIAN KONIGSFELDT.

Dominican Republic: SHIS, QL 14, Conj. 05, Casa 08/10, 71640-055 Brasília, DF; tel. (61) 248-1405; fax (61) 364-3214; e-mail embajadombrasil@nutecnet.com.br; Ambassador IVÁN BÁEZ BRUGAL.

Ecuador: SHIS, QI 11, Conj. 09, Casa 24, 71625-290 Brasília, DF; tel. (61) 248-5560; fax (61) 248-1290; e-mail embeq@solar.com.br; Ambassador DIEGO RIBADENEIRA ESPINOSA.

Egypt: SEN, Av. das Nações, Lote 12, 70435-900 Brasília, DF; tel. (61) 323-8800; fax (61) 323-1039; e-mail embegito@opengate.com.br; internet www.opengate.com.br/embegito; Ambassador MOHAMED ABDEL FATTAH ABDALLAH.

El Salvador: SHIS, QI 10, Conj. 01, Casa 15, 71630-100 Brasília, DF; tel. (61) 364-4141; fax (61) 364-2459; e-mail brasemb@es.com.sv; internet www.elsalvador.hpg.com.br; Ambassador (vacant).

Finland: SES, Av. das Nações, Quadra 807, Lote 27, 70417-900 Brasília, DF; tel. (61) 443-7151; fax (61) 443-3315; e-mail brasilia@finlandia.org.br; internet www.finlandia.org.br; Ambassador HANNU UUSI-VIDENOJA.

France: SES, Av. das Nações, Quadra 801, Lote 04, 70404-900 Brasília, DF; tel. (61) 312-9100; fax (61) 312-9108; e-mail france@

ambafrance.org.br; internet www.ambafrance.org.br; Ambassador JEAN DE GLINIASTY.

Gabon: SHIS, QI 09, Conj. 11, Casa 24, 71615-300 Brasília, DF; tel. (61) 248-3536; fax (61) 248-2241; e-mail mgabao@terra.com.br; Ambassador MARCEL ODONGUI-BONNARD.

Germany: SES, Av. das Nações, Quadra 807, Lote 25, 70415-900 Brasília, DF; tel. (61) 442-7000; fax (61) 443-7508; e-mail info .brasilia@alemanha.org.br; internet www.alemanha.org.br; Ambassador FRIEDRICH PROT VON KUNOW.

Ghana: SHIS, QL 10, Conj. 08, Casa 02, 70466-900 Brasília, DF; tel. (61) 248-6047; fax (61) 248-7913; e-mail ghaembra@zaz.com.br; Ambassador DANIEL YAW ADJEI.

Greece: SES, Av. das Nações, Quadra 805, Lote 22, 70480-900 Brasília, DF; tel. (61) 443-6573; fax (61) 443-6902; e-mail info@ emb-grecia.org.br; internet www.emb-grecia.org.br; Ambassador ANDONIOS NICOLAIDIS.

Guatemala: SHIS, QI 03, Conj. 10, Casa 01, Lago-Sul, 71605-300 Brasília, DF; tel. (61) 365-1908; fax (61) 365-1906; e-mail embaguate-brasil@minex.gob.gt; Ambassador MANUEL ESTUARDO ROLDÁN BARILLAS.

Guyana: SHIS, QI 05, Conj. 19, Casa 24, 71615-190 Brasília, DF; tel. (61) 248-0874; fax (61) 248-0886; e-mail embguyana@apis.com .br; Ambassador MARILYN CHERYL MILES.

Haiti: SHIS, QL 10, Conj. 06, Casa 16, Lago Sul, 71630-065 Brasília, DF; tel. (61) 248-6860; fax (61) 248-7472; e-mail embhaiti@zaz.com .br; Ambassador JEAN SOREL WENDEL CLAUDE.

Holy See: SES, Av. das Nações, Quadra 801, Lote 01, 70401-900 Brasília, DF; tel. (61) 223-0794; fax (61) 224-9365; e-mail nunapost@ solar.com.br; Apostolic Nuncio Most Rev. LORENZO BALDISSERI (Titular Archbishop of Diocleziana).

Honduras: SHIS, QI 19, Conj. 07, Casa 34, Lago Sul, 71655-070 Brasília, DF; tel. (61) 366-4082; fax (61) 366-4618; Ambassador VICTOR MANUEL LOZANO URBINA.

Hungary: SES, Av. das Nações, Quadra 805, Lote 19, 70413-900 Brasília, DF; tel. (61) 443-0836; fax (61) 443-3434; e-mail huembbrz@terra.com.br; internet www.hungria.org.br; Ambassador Dr JÓZSEF NÉMETH.

India: SHIS, QL 08, Conj. 08, Casa 01, 71620-285 Brasília, DF; tel. (61) 248-4006; fax (61) 248-7849; e-mail indemb@indianembassy.org .br; Ambassador AMITAVA TRIPATHI.

Indonesia: SES, Av. das Nações, Quadra 805, Lote 20, 70479-900 Brasília, DF; tel. (61) 443-8800; fax (61) 443-6732; e-mail kbribrasilia@persocom.com.br; Ambassador PIETER TARUYU VAU.

Iran: SES, Av. das Nações, Quadra 809, Lote 31, 70421-900 Brasília, DF; tel. (61) 242-5733; fax (61) 224-9640; e-mail webiran@webiran .org.br; internet www.webiran.org.br; Ambassador SEYED JAFAR HASHEMI.

Iraq: SES, Av. das Nações, Quadra 815, Lote 64, 70430-900 Brasília, DF; tel. (61) 346-2822; fax (61) 346-7034; Chargé d'affaires ALA ALDDIN ABBAS HILMI.

Ireland: SHIS QL 12, Conj. 05, Casa 09, Lago Sul, Brasilia, DF; tel. (61) 248-8800; fax (61) 248-8816; e-mail irishembassybrasilia@ eircom.net; Ambassador MARTIN GREENE.

Israel: SES, Av. das Nações, Quadra 809, Lote 38, 70424-900 Brasília, DF; tel. (61) 2105-0500; fax (61) 2105-0555; e-mail info@ brasilia.mfa.gov.il; internet www.brasilia.mfa.gov.il; Ambassador TZIPORA RIMON.

Italy: SES, Av. das Nações, Lote 30, 70420-900 Brasília, DF; tel. (61) 442-9900; fax (61) 443-1231; e-mail embitalia@embitalia.org.br; internet www.embitalia.org.br; Ambassador MICHELE VALENSISE.

Japan: SES, Av. das Nações, Quadra 811, Lote 39, 70425-900 Brasília, DF; tel. (61) 442-4200; fax (61) 242-0738; e-mail culturaljapao1@yawl.com.br; internet www.japao.org.br; Ambassador TAKAHIKO HORIMURA.

Jordan: SHIS, QI 09, Conj. 18, Casa 14, 70408-900 Brasília, DF; tel. (61) 248-5407; fax (61) 248-1698; e-mail jordania@apis.com.br; Ambassador FARIS SHAWKAT MUFTI.

Korea, Democratic People's Republic: SHIS, QI 25, Conj. 10, Casa 11, Brasília, DF; tel. and fax (61) 244-6544; e-mail embcorea@ hotmail.com; Ambassador (vacant).

Korea, Republic: SEN, Av. das Nações, Lote 14, 70436-900 Brasília, DF; tel. (61) 321-2500; fax (61) 321-2508; e-mail ebcoreia@terra .com.br; Ambassador KIM KWANG-DONG.

Kuwait: SHIS, QI 05, Chácara 30, 71600-580 Brasília, DF; tel. (61) 248-2323; fax (61) 248-0969; e-mail kuwait@opendf.com.br; Ambassador HAMOOD Y. M. AL-ROUDHAN.

Lebanon: SES, Av. das Nações, Quadra 805, Lote 17, 70411-900 Brasília, DF; tel. (61) 443-5552; fax (61) 443-8574; e-mail

embaixada@libano.org.br; internet www.libano.org.br; Ambassador FOUAD EL-KHOURY GHANEM.

Libya: SHIS, QI 15, Chácara 26, 71600-750 Brasília, DF; tel. (61) 248-6710; fax (61) 248-0598; e-mail emblibia@terra.com.br; Ambassador MOHAMED HEIMEDA SAAD MATRI.

Malaysia: SHIS, QI 05, Chácara 62, 70477-900 Brasília, DF; tel. (61) 248-5008; fax (61) 248-6307; e-mail mwbrasilia@persocom.com .br; Ambassador TAI KAT MENG.

Mexico: SES, Av. das Nações, Quadra 805, Lote 18, 70412-900 Brasília, DF; tel. (61) 244-1011; fax (61) 244-1755; e-mail embamexbra@cabonet.com.br; internet www.mexico.org.br; Ambassador CECILIA SOTO GONZÁLEZ.

Morocco: SEN, Av. das Nações, Quadra 801, Lote 02, 70432-900 Brasília, DF; tel. (61) 321-4487; fax (61) 321-0745; e-mail sifamarbr@ onix.com.br; Ambassador ALI ACHOUR.

Mozambique: SHIS, QL 12, Conj. 07, Casa 09, 71630-275 Brasília, DF; tel. (61) 248-4222; fax (61) 248-3917; e-mail embamoc-bsb@uol .com; Ambassador (vacant).

Myanmar: SHIS, QI 07, Conj. 14, Casa 05, 71615-340 Brasília, DF; tel. (61) 248-3747; fax (61) 364-2747; e-mail mebrsl@brnet.com.br; Ambassador HLA MYINT.

Namibia: SHIS QI 09, Conj. 08, Casa 11, Lago Sul, 71625–080 Brasília, DF; tel. (61) 248-6274; fax (61) 248-7135; e-mail namibianembassy-brazil@ibest.com.br; Ambassador PATRICK NANDAGO.

Netherlands: SES, Av. das Nações, Quadra 801, Lote 05, 70405-900 Brasília, DF; tel. (61) 321-4769; fax (61) 321-1518; e-mail bra@ minbuza.nl; internet www.embaixada-holanda.org.br; Ambassador (vacant).

New Zealand: SHIS, QI 09, Conj. 16, Casa 01, 71625-160 Brasília, DF; tel. (61) 248-9900; fax (61) 248-9916; e-mail zelandia@nwi.com .br; Ambassador DENISE JOAN ALMÃO.

Nicaragua: SHIS, QI 16, Conj. 04, Casa 15, 71640-245 Brasília, DF; tel. (61) 248-1115; fax (61) 248-1120; e-mail embanibra@zaz.com.br; Chargé d'affaires a.i. LIZA TUCKER.

Nigeria: SEN, Av. das Nações, Lote 05, 70459-900 Brasília, DF; tel. (61) 226-1717; fax (61) 226-5192; e-mail nigeria@persocom.com.br; internet www.nigerianembassy-brasilia.org.br; Ambassador JOSEF SOOKORE EGBUSON.

Norway: SES, Av. das Nações, Quadra 807, Lote 28, 70418-900 Brasília, DF; tel. (61) 443-8720; fax (61) 443-2942; e-mail embno@ terra.com.br; internet www.noruega.org.br; Ambassador JAN GERHARD LASSEN.

Pakistan: SHIS, QL 12, Conj. 02, Casa 19, 71615-140 Brasília, DF; tel. (61) 364-1632; fax (61) 248-0246; e-mail parepbra@bruturbo .com; Ambassador KHALID KHATTAK.

Panama: SHIS, QI 07, Conj. 09, Casa 08, 71615-290 Brasília, DF; tel. (61) 248-7309; fax (61) 248-2834; e-mail empanama@nettur.com .br; Ambassador (vacant).

Paraguay: SES, Av. das Nações, Quadra 811, Lote 42, 70427-900 Brasília, DF; tel. (61) 242-3732; fax (61) 242-4605; e-mail embapar@ yawl.com.br; Ambassador LUIS GONZÁLEZ ARIAS.

Peru: SES, Av. das Nações, Quadra 811, Lote 43, 70428-900 Brasília, DF; tel. (61) 242-9933; fax (61) 244-9344; e-mail embperu@ embperu.org.br; internet www.embperu.org.br; Ambassador HERNÁN COUTURIER MARIÁTEGUI.

Philippines: SEN, Av. das Nações, Lote 01, 70431-900 Brasília, DF; tel. (61) 223-5143; fax (61) 226-7411; e-mail ambaphilbr@persocom .com.br; Ambassador OSCAR GARCIA VALENZUELA.

Poland: SES, Av. das Nações, Lote 33, 70423-900 Brasília, DF; tel. (61) 443-3438; fax (61) 242-8543; e-mail embpolon@terra.com.br; Ambassador KRZYSZTOF JACEK HINZ.

Portugal: SES, Av. das Nações, Quadra 801, Lote 02, 70402-900 Brasília, DF; tel. (61) 3032-9600; fax (61) 3032-9642; e-mail embaixadaportugal@embaixadaportugal.org.br; Ambassador FRANCISCO MANUEL SEIXAS DE COSTA.

Romania: SEN, Av. das Nações, Lote 06, 70456-900 Brasília, DF; tel. (61) 226-0746; fax (61) 226-6629; e-mail romenia@solar.com.br; Ambassador MONICA-MARIANA GRIGORESCU.

Russia: SES, Av. das Nações, Quadra 801, Lote A, 70476-900 Brasília, DF; tel. (61) 223-3094; fax (61) 226-7319; e-mail emb@ embrus.brte.com.br; internet www.brazil.mid.ru; Ambassador VLADIMIR LVOVITCH TYURDENEV.

Saudi Arabia: SHIS, QL 10, Conj. 09, Casa 20, 70471-900 Brasília, DF; tel. (61) 248-3523; fax (61) 284-2905; e-mail embsaud@tba.com .br; Ambassador (vacant).

Senegal: SEN, Av. das Nações, Lote 18, QL 12, Conj. 04, Casa 13, Lago Sul, 70800-400 Brasília, DF; tel. (61) 223-6110; fax (61) 322-

7822; e-mail senebrasilia@bol.com.br; Ambassador MOUHAMADOU DOUDOU LO.

Serbia and Montenegro: SES, Av. das Nações, Quadra 803, Lote 15, 70409-900 Brasília, DF; tel. (61) 223-7272; fax (61) 223-8462; e-mail embiugos@nutecnet.com.br; Ambassador RADIVOJE LAZAREVIĆ.

Slovakia: Av. das Nações, Quadra 805, Lote 21, 70414-900 Brasília, DF; tel. (61) 443-1263; fax (61) 443-1267; e-mail eslovaca@brasil. mfa.sk; Chargé d'affaires a.i. TERÉZIA SAJGALIKOVÁ.

South Africa: SES, Av. das Nações, Quadra 801, Lote 06, 70406–900 Brasília, DF; tel. (61) 312-9502; fax (61) 312-9509; e-mail saemb@solar.com.br; internet www.africadosul-consp.org.br; Ambassador LINDIWE DAPHNE ZULU.

Spain: SES, Av. das Nações, Quadra 811, Lote 44, 70429-900 Brasília, DF; tel. (61) 244-2776; fax (61) 242-1781; e-mail embespbr@ correo.mae.es; Ambassador JOSÉ CODERCH PLANAS.

Sri Lanka: SHIS, QI 09, Conj. 09, Casa 07, Lago Sul, 71625-090 Brasília DF; tel. (61) 248-2701; fax (61) 364-5430; e-mail lankaemb@ yawl.com.br; Ambassador Gen. ROHAN DE SILVA DALUWATTE.

Sudan: SHIS, QI 11, Conj. 5, Casa 13, Lago Sul, Brasília, DF; tel. (61) 248-4835; fax (61) 248-4833; e-mail sdbrasilia@sudanbrasilia .org; internet www.sudanbrasilia.org; Ambassador RAHAMTALLA MOHAMED OSMAN.

Suriname: SHIS, QI 09, Conj. 08, Casa 24, 71625-080 Brasília, DF; tel. (61) 248-6705; fax (61) 248-3791; e-mail surinameemb@terra .com.br; Ambassador RADJENDRAKUMAR NIHALCHAND SONNY HIRA.

Sweden: SES, Av. das Nações, Quadra 807, Lote 29, 70419-900 Brasília, DF; tel. (61) 443-1444; fax (61) 443-1187; e-mail swebra@ opengate.com.br; Ambassador MARGARETA WINBERG.

Switzerland: SES, Av. das Nações, Lote 41, 70448-900 Brasília, DF; tel. (61) 443-5500; fax (61) 443-5711; e-mail vertretung@bra.rep .admin.ch; internet www.dfae.admin.ch/brasilia; Ambassador RUDOLF BAERFUSS.

Syria: SEN, Av. das Nações, Lote 11, 70434-900 Brasília, DF; tel. (61) 226-0970; fax (61) 223-2595; e-mail embsiria@uol.com.br; Ambassador ALI DIAB.

Thailand: SEN, Av. das Nações, Lote 10, 70433-900 Brasília, DF; tel. (61) 224-6943; fax (61) 223-7502; e-mail thaiemb@linkexpress .com.br; Ambassador SUPHAT CHITRANUKROH.

Trinidad and Tobago: SHIS, QL 02, Conj. 02, Casa 01, 71665-028 Brasília, DF; tel. (61) 365-1132; fax (61) 365-1733; e-mail trinbago@ terra.com.br; Ambassador WINSTON CLYDE MOORE.

Tunisia: SHIS, QI 09, Conj. 16, Casa 20, 71625-160 Brasília, DF; tel. (61) 248-7177; fax (61) 248-7355; e-mail at.brasilia@terra.com .br; Ambassador HASSINE BOUZID.

Turkey: SES, Av. das Nações, Quadra 805, Lote 23, 70452-900 Brasília, DF; tel. (61) 242-1850; fax (61) 242-1448; e-mail turquia@ conectanet.com.br; Ambassador AHMET GÜRKAN.

Ukraine: SHIS QI 05, Conj. 04, Casa 02, 71615-040 Brasília, DF; tel. (61) 365-3889; fax (61) 365-2127; e-mail brucremb@zaz.com.br; Ambassador YURII BOHAIEVSKYI.

United Arab Emirates: SHIS, QI 05, Chácara 54, 71600-580 Brasília, DF; tel. (61) 248-0717; fax (61) 248-7543; e-mail uae@uae .org.br; internet www.uae.org.br; Ambassador YOUSEF ALI AL-USAIMI.

United Kingdom: SES, Quadra 801, Conj. K, Lote 08, 70408-900 Brasília, DF; tel. (61) 329-2300; fax (61) 329-2369; e-mail contato@ reinounido.org.br; internet www.reinounido.org.br; Ambassador PETER SALMON COLLECOTT.

USA: SES, Av. das Nações, Quadra 801, Lote 03, 70403-900 Brasília, DF; tel. (61) 321-7000; fax (61) 321-7241; internet www .embaixada-americana.org.br; Ambassador JOHN J. DANILOVICH.

Uruguay: SES, Av. das Nações, Lote 14, 70450-900 Brasília, DF; tel. (61) 322-1200; fax (61) 322-6534; e-mail urubras@emburuguai .org.br; internet www.emburuguai.org.br; Ambassador JUAN JOSÉ REAL.

Venezuela: SES, Av. das Nações, Quadra 803, Lote 13, 70451-900 Brasília, DF; tel. (61) 322-1011; fax (61) 226-5633; e-mail embven1@ rudah.com.br; Ambassador JULIO JOSÉ GARCÍA MONTOYA.

Viet Nam: SHIS, QI 05, Conj. 14, Casa 21, 71615-140 Brasília, DF; tel. (61) 364-5876; fax (61) 364-5836; e-mail embavina@uol.com.br; Ambassador NGUYEN VAN HUYNH.

Zimbabwe: SHIS, QI 01, Conj. 04, Casa 25, Brasília, DF; tel. (61) 365-4801; fax (61) 365-4803; Ambassador THOMAS SUKUTAI BVUMA.

Judicial System

The judiciary powers of the State are held by the following: the Supreme Federal Tribunal, the Higher Tribunal of Justice, the five Regional Federal Tribunals and Federal Judges, the Higher Labour Tribunal, the 24 Regional Labour Tribunals, the Conciliation and Judgment Councils and Labour Judges, the Higher Electoral Tribunal, the 27 Regional Electoral Tribunals, the Electoral Judges and Electoral Councils, the Higher Military Tribunal, the Military Tribunals and Military Judges, the Tribunals of the States and Judges of the States, the Tribunal of the Federal District and of the Territories and Judges of the Federal District and of the Territories.

The Supreme Federal Tribunal comprises 11 ministers, nominated by the President and approved by the Senate. Its most important role is to rule on the final interpretation of the Constitution. The Supreme Federal Tribunal has the power to declare an act of Congress void if it is unconstitutional. It judges offences committed by persons such as the President, the Vice-President, members of the Congresso Nacional, Ministers of State, its own members, the Attorney General, judges of other higher courts, and heads of permanent diplomatic missions. It also judges cases of litigation between the Union and the States, between the States, or between foreign nations and the Union or the States; disputes as to jurisdiction between higher Tribunals, or between the latter and any other court, in cases involving the extradition of criminals, and others related to the writs of habeas corpus and habeas data, and in other cases.

The Higher Tribunal of Justice comprises at least 33 members, appointed by the President and approved by the Senado. Its jurisdiction includes the judgment of offences committed by State Governors. The Regional Federal Tribunals comprise at least seven judges, recruited when possible in the respective region and appointed by the President of the Republic. The Higher Labour Tribunal comprises 27 members, appointed by the President and approved by the Senado. The judges of the Regional Labour Tribunals are also appointed by the President. The Regional Electoral Tribunals are also composed of seven members. The Higher Military Tribunal comprises 15 life members, appointed by the President and approved by the Senate; three from the navy, four from the army, three from the air force and five civilian members. The States are responsible for the administration of their own justice, according to the principles established by the Constitution.

SUPREME FEDERAL TRIBUNAL

Supremo Tribunal Federal: Praça dos Três Poderes, 70175-900 Brasília, DF; tel. (61) 217-3000; fax (61) 316-5483; e-mail webmaster@stf.gov.br; internet www.stf.gov.br.

President: NELSON DE ACEVEDO JOBIM, Filho.

Vice-President: ELLEN GRACIE.

Justices: JOSÉ PAULO SEPÚLVEDA PERTENCE, JOSÉ CELSO DE MELLO, CARLOS VELLOSO, MARCO AURÉLIO, GILMAR MENDES, CEZAR PELUSO, CARLOS BRITTO, JOAQUIM BARBOSA, EROS GRAU.

Attorney-General: CLÁUDIO LEMOS FONTELES.

Director-General (Secretariat): MIGUEL AUGUSTO FONSECA DE CAMPOS.

Religion

According to the census of 2000, there were around 125m. Roman Catholics, 26m. Evangelical Christians, 1m. Jehovah's Witnesses, and 2m. Spiritualists. Other faiths include Islam (27,239), Buddhism (214,873) and Judaism (86,825). There are also followers of African and indigenous religions.

CHRISTIANITY

Conselho Nacional de Igrejas Cristãs do Brasil (CONIC) (National Council of Christian Churches in Brazil): SCS, Quadra 01, Bloco E, Edif. Ceará, Sala 713, 70303-900 Brasília, DF; tel. and fax (61) 321-8341; e-mail conic.brasil@terra.com.br; internet www.conic .org.br; f. 1982; seven mem. churches; Pres. Bishop ADRIEL DE SOUZA MAIA; Exec. Sec. P. ERVINO SCHMIDT.

The Roman Catholic Church

Brazil comprises 41 archdioceses, 212 dioceses (including one each for Catholics of the Maronite, Melkite and Ukrainian Rites), 13 territorial prelatures and one territorial abbacy. The Archbishop of São Sebastião do Rio de Janeiro is also the Ordinary for Catholics of other Oriental Rites in Brazil (estimated at 10,000 in 1994). The great majority of Brazil's population are adherents of the Roman Catholic Church. Adherents at 1 December 2002 represented an estimated 80.0% of the population.

Bishops' Conference: Conferência Nacional dos Bispos do Brasil, SE/Sul Quadra 801, Conj. B, CP 02067, 70259-970 Brasília, DF; tel. (61) 313-8300; fax (61) 313-8303; e-mail cnbb@cnbb.org.br; internet www.cnbb.org.br; f. 1980; statutes approved 2002; Pres. Cardinal

GERALDO MAJELLA AGNELO (Archbishop of São Salvador, BA); Sec.-Gen. ODILO PEDRO SCHERER.

Latin Rite

Archbishop of São Salvador da Bahia, BA: Cardinal GERALDO MAJELLA AGNELO, Primate of Brazil, Cúria Metropolitana, Rua Martin Afonso de Souza 270, 40100-050 Salvador, BA; tel. and fax (71) 328-6699; fax (71) 328-0068; e-mail gma@atarde.com.br.

Archbishop of Aparecida, SP: RAYMUNDO DAMASCENO ASSIS.

Archbishop of Aracaju, SE: JOSÉ PALMEIRA LESSA.

Archbishop of Belém do Pará, PA: ORANI JOÃO TEMPESTA.

Archbishop of Belo Horizonte, MG: WALMOR OLIVEIRA DE AZEVEDO.

Archbishop of Botucatu, SP: ALOYSIO JOSÉ LEAL PENNA.

Archbishop of Brasília, DF: JOÃO BRAZ DE AVIZ.

Archbishop of Campinas, SP: BRUNO GAMBERINI.

Archbishop of Campo Grande, MS: VITÓRIO PAVANELLO.

Archbishop of Cascavel, PR: LÚCIO IGNÁCIO BAUMGAERTNER.

Archbishop of Cuiabá, MT: MILTON ANTÔNIO DOS SANTOS.

Archbishop of Curitiba, PR: MOACYR JOSÉ VITTI.

Archbishop of Diamantina, MG: PAULO LOPES DE FARIA.

Archbishop of Feira de Santana, BA: ITAMAR VIAN.

Archbishop of Florianópolis, SC: MURILO SEBASTIÃO RAMOS KRIEGER.

Archbishop of Fortaleza, CE: JOSÉ ANTÔNIO APARECIDO TOSI MARQUES.

Archbishop of Goiânia, GO: WASHINGTON CRUZ.

Archbishop of Juiz de Fora, MG: EURICO DOS SANTOS VELOSO.

Archbishop of Londrina, PR: ALBANO BORTOLETTO CAVALLIN.

Archbishop of Maceió, AL: JOSÉ CARLOS MELO.

Archbishop of Manaus, AM: LUIZ SOARES VIEIRA.

Archbishop of Mariana, MG: LUCIANO PEDRO MENDES DE ALMEIDA.

Archbishop of Maringá, PR: ANUAR BATTISTI.

Archbishop of Montes Claros, MG: GERALDO MAJELA DE CASTRO.

Archbishop of Natal, RN: MATIAS PATRÍCIO DE MACÊDO.

Archbishop of Niterói, RJ: ALANO MARIA PENA.

Archbishop of Olinda e Recife, PE: JOSÉ CARDOSO SOBRINHO.

Archbishop of Palmas, PR: ALBERTO TAVEIRA CORRÊA.

Archbishop of Paraíba, PB: ALDO DE CILLO PAGOTTO.

Archbishop of Porto Alegre, RS: DADEUS GRINGS.

Archbishop of Porto Velho, RO: MOACYR GRECHI.

Archbishop of Pouso Alegre, MG: RICARDO PEDRO CHAVES PINTO, Filho.

Archbishop of Ribeirão Preto, SP: ARNALDO RIBEIRO.

Archbishop of São Luís do Maranhão, MA: PAULO EDUARDO DE ANDRADE PONTE.

Archbishop of São Paulo, SP: Cardinal CLÁUDIO HUMMES.

Archbishop of São Salvador da Bahia, BA: Cardinal GERALDO MAJELLA AGNELO.

Archbishop of São Sebastião do Rio de Janeiro, RJ: Cardinal EUSÉBIO OSCAR SCHEID.

Archbishop of Sorocaba, SP: JOSÉ LAMBERT.

Archbishop of Teresina, PI: CELSO JOSÉ PINTO DA SILVA.

Archbishop of Uberaba, MG: ALOÍSIO ROQUE OPPERMANN.

Archbishop of Vitória, ES: LUIZ MANCILHA VILELA.

Archbishop of Vitória da Conquista, BA: GERALDO LYRIO ROCHA.

Maronite Rite

Bishop of Nossa Senhora do Líbano em São Paulo, SP: JOSEPH MAHFOUZ.

Melkite Rite

Bishop of Nossa Senhora do Paraíso em São Paulo, SP: FARES MAAKAROUN.

Ukrainian Rite

Bishop of São João Batista em Curitiba, PR: EFRAIM BASÍLIO KREVEY.

The Anglican Communion

Anglicans form the Episcopal Anglican Church of Brazil (Igreja Episcopal Anglicana do Brasil), comprising seven dioceses.

Igreja Episcopal Anglicana do Brasil: Av. Ludolfo Boehl 256, Teresópolis, 91720-150 Porto Alegre, RS; tel. and fax (51) 3318-6200; e-mail ieabl@ieab.org.br; internet www.ieab.org.br; f. 1890; 103,021 mems (1997); Primate Right Rev. ORLANDO SANTO DE OLIVEIRA; Gen. Sec. CHRISTINA TAKATSU WINNISCHOFER; e-mail cwinnischofer@ieab.org.br.

Protestant Churches

Igreja Cristã Reformada do Brasil: Rua Domingos Rodrigues, 306/Lapa, 05075-000 São Paulo, SP; tel. (11) 260-7514; f. 1932; Pres. Rev. ANTÔNIO BONZOI.

Igreja Evangélica de Confissão Luterana no Brasil (IECLB): Rua Senhor dos Passos 202, 4° andar, CP 2876, 90020-180 Porto Alegre, RS; tel. (51) 3221-3433; fax (51) 3225-7244; e-mail secretariageral@ieclb.org.br; internet www.ieclb.org.br; f. 1949; 715,000 mems; Pres. Pastor WALTER ALTMANN; Sec.-Gen. Dr NESTOR PAULO FRIEDRICH.

Igreja Evangélica Congregacional do Brasil: CP 414, 98700 Ijuí, RS; tel. (55) 332-4656; f. 1942; 148,836 mems (2000); Pres. Rev. H. HARTMUT W. HACHTMANN.

Igreja Evangélica Luterana do Brasil: Rua Cel. Lucas de Oliveira 894, 90440-010 Porto Alegre, RS; tel. (51) 3332-2111; fax (51) 3332-8145; e-mail ielb@ielb.org.br; internet www.ielb.org.br; f. 1904; 223,588 mems; Pres. Rev. CARLOS WALTER WINTERLE; Sec. Rev. RONY RICARDO MARQUARDT.

Igreja Maná do Brasil: Rua Marie Satzke, 47, Jardim Marajoara, 04664-150, São Paulo, SP; tel. (11) 4033-5091; e-mail adm_brasil@igrejamana.com; internet www.igrejamana.com.

Igreja Metodista do Brasil: Av. Piassanguaba 3031, Planalto Paulista, 04060-004 São Paulo, SP; tel. (11) 5585-0032 ; fax (11) 5594-3328; e-mail isede.nacional@metodista.org.br; internet www.metodista.org.br; 340,963 mems (2000); Exec. Sec. Bishop JOÃO ALVES DE OLIVEIRA.

Igreja Presbiteriana Unida do Brasil (IPU): Av. Princesa Isabel 629, 1210/1, Edif. Vitória Center, 29010-360 Vitória, ES; tel. and fax (27) 3222-8024; e-mail ipu@terra.com.br; internet www.ipu.org.br; f. 1978; Moderator Rev. GERSON ANTÔNIO URBAN.

BAHÁ'Í FAITH

Bahá'í Community of Brazil: SHIS, QL 08, Conj. 02, CP 7035, 71620-285 Brasília, DF; tel. (61) 364-3594; fax (61) 364-3470; e-mail info@bahai.org.br; internet www.bahai.org.br; f. 1965; Sec. CARLOS ALBERTO SILVA.

BUDDHISM

Sociedade Budista do Brasil (Rio Buddhist Vihara): Dom Joaquim Mamede 45, Lagoinha, Santa Tereza, 20241-390 Rio de Janeiro, RJ; tel. (21) 2526-1411; e-mail sbbrj@yahoo.com; internet www.geocities.com/sbbrj; f. 1972; Principal Dr PUHULWELLE VIPASSI.

Sociedade Taoísta do Brasil: Rua Cosme Velho 355, Cosme Velho, 22241-090 Rio de Janeiro, RJ; tel. (21) 2225-2887; e-mail info@taoismo.com.br; internet www.taoismo.com.br; f. 1991.

The Press

The most striking feature of the Brazilian press is the relatively small circulation of newspapers in comparison with the size of the population. The newspapers with the largest circulations are *O Dia* (250,000), *O Globo* (350,000), *Fôlha de São Paulo* (560,000), and *O Estado de São Paulo* (242,000). The low circulation is mainly owing to high costs resulting from distribution difficulties. In consequence there are no national newspapers. In 1998 a total of 372 daily newspaper titles were published in Brazil.

DAILY NEWSPAPERS

Belém, PA

O Liberal: Rua Gaspar Viana 253, 66020 Belém, PA; tel. (91) 222-3000; fax (91) 224-1906; e-mail redacao@orm.com.br; internet www.oliberal.com.br; f. 1946; Pres. LUCIDEA MAIORANA; circ. 20,000.

Belo Horizonte, MG

Diário da Tarde: Av. Getúlio Vargas 291, 30112-020 Belo Horizonte, MG; tel. (31) 3263-5229; internet www.estaminas.com.br/dt; f. 1931; evening; Editor FÁBIO PROENÇA DOYLE; total circ. 150,000.

Diário do Comércio: Av. Américo Vespúcio 1660, Nova Esperança, 31230-250 Belo Horizonte, MG; tel. (31) 3469-1011; fax (31) 3469-1080; e-mail redacaodc@diariodocomercio.com.br; internet www.diariodocomercio.com.br; f. 1932; Pres. LUIZ CARLOS MOTTA COSTA.

Estado de Minas: Av. Getúlio Vargas 291, 30112-020 Belo Horizonte, MG; tel. (31) 3263-5000; fax (31) 3263-5070; internet www.uai .com.br/em.html; f. 1928; morning; independent; Pres. BRITALDO SILVEIRA SOARES; circ. 65,000.

Hoje em Dia: Rua Padre Rolim 652, Santa Efigênia, 30130-090 Belo Horizonte, MG; tel. (31) 3236-8000; fax (31) 3236-8046; e-mail comercial@hojeemdia.com.br; internet www.hojeemdia.com.br; Man. Dir REINALDO GILLI.

Blumenau, SC

Jornal de Santa Catarina: Rua São Paulo 1120, 89010-000 Blumenau, SC; tel. (2147) 340-1400; e-mail redacao@santa.com.br; f. 1971; Dir ALVARO IAHNIG; circ. 25,000.

Brasília, DF

Correio Brasiliense: SIG, Quadra 02, Lotes 340, 70610-901 Brasília, DF; tel. (61) 214-1100; fax (61) 214-1157; e-mail geral@ correioweb.com.br ; internet www.correioweb.com.br; f. 1960; Pres. ÁLVARO TEIXEIRA DA COSTA; circ. 30,000.

Jornal de Brasília: SIG, Trecho 1, Lotes 585/645, 70610-400 Brasília, DF; tel. (61) 225-2515; internet www.jornaldebrasilia.com.br; f. 1972; Dir-Gen. FERNANDO CÔMA; circ. 25,000.

Campinas, SP

Correio Popular: Rua 7 de Setembro 189, Vila Industrial, 13035-350 Campinas, SP; tel. (19) 3736-3050; fax (19) 3234-8984; e-mail sygon@rac.com.br; internet www.cpopular.com.br; f. 1927; Editorial Dir NELSON HOMEM DE MELLO; circ. 40,000.

Curitiba, PR

O Estado do Paraná: Rua João Tschannerl 800, Vista Alegre, 80820-010 Curitiba, PR; tel. (41) 335-5000; fax (41) 335-2838; internet www.parana-online.com.br; f. 1951; Pres. PAULO CRUZ PIMENTEL; circ. 15,000.

Gazeta do Povo: Rua Pedro Ivo 459, Centro, 80010-020, Curitiba, PR; tel. (41) 224-0522; fax (41) 225-6848; e-mail atendimento@ tudoparana.com; internet tudoparana.globo.com/gazetadepovo; f. 1919; Pres. FRANCISCO CUNHA PEREIRA, Filho; circ. 40,000.

Jornal Tribuna do Paraná: Rua João Tschannerl 800, 80820-010 Curitiba PR; tel. (41) 331-5000; fax (41) 335-2838; internet www .parana-online.com.br; f. 1956; Pres. PAULO CRUZ PIMENTEL; circ. 15,000.

Florianópolis, SC

O Estado: Rodovia SC-401, Km 3, 88030 Florianópolis, SC; tel. (482) 388-8888; fax (482) 380-0711; f. 1915; Pres. JOSÉ MATUSALÉM COMELLI; circ. 20,000.

Fortaleza, CE

Jornal O Povo: Av. Aguanambi 282, 60055 Fortaleza, CE; tel. (85) 3211-9666; fax (85) 3231-5792; internet www.noolhar.com/opovo; f. 1928; evening; Pres. DEMÓCRITO ROCHA DUMMAR; Editor-in-Chief FÁTIMA SUDÁRIO; circ. 20,000.

Tribuna do Ceará: Av. Desembarque Moreira 2900, 60170 Fortaleza, CE; tel. (85) 3247-3066; fax (85) 3272-2799; f. 1957; Dir JOSÉ A. SANCHO; circ. 12,000.

Goiânia, GO

Diário da Manhã: Av. Anhanguera 2833, Setor Leste Universitário, 74000 Goiânia, GO; tel. (62) 261-7371; internet www.dm.com .br; f. 1980; Editor BATISTA CUSTÓDIO; circ. 16,000.

Jornal O Popular: Rua Thómas Edson Q7, Setor Serrinha, 74835-130 Goiânia, GO; tel. (62) 250-1000; fax (62) 241-1018; f. 1938; Pres. JAIME CÁMARA JÚNIOR; circ. 65,000.

João Pessoa, PB

Correio da Paraíba: Av. Pedro II, Centro, João Pessoa, PB; tel. (83) 216-5000; fax (83) 216-5009; e-mail jcorreio@zaz.com.br; internet www.correiodaparaiba.com.br.

Londrina, PR

Fôlha de Londrina: Rua Piauí 241, 86010-909 Londrina, PR; tel. (43) 3374-2000; fax (43) 3321-1051; e-mail caf@folhadelondrina.com .br; internet www.bonde.com.br/folha; f. 1948; Pres. JOÃO MILANEZ; circ. 40,000.

Manaus, AM

A Crítica: Av. André Araújo, Km 3, 69060 Manaus, AM; tel. (92) 643-1233; fax (92) 643-1234; internet www.acritica.com.br; f. 1949; Dir RITA ARAÚJO CADERARO; circ. 19,000.

Natal, RN

Diario de Natal: Av. Deodoro 245, Petropólis, 59012-600, Natal, RN; tel. (84) 220-0166; internet www.diariodenatal.com.br; Dir ALBIMAR FURTADO.

Niterói, RJ

O Fluminense: Rua da Conceição 188, Lj 118, Niterói Shopping, Niterói, RJ; tel. (21) 2620-3311; internet www.ofluminense.com.br; f. 1878; Dirs NINA RITA TORRES, ALEXANDRE TORRES; circ. 80,000.

A Tribuna: Rua Barão do Amazonas 31, 24030111 Niterói, RJ; tel. (13) 2102-7000; fax (13) 3219-4466; e-mail icarai@urbi.com.br; f. 1936; daily; Dir-Supt GUSTAVO SANTANO AMÓRO; circ. 10,000.

Palmas, TO

O Girassol: 104 N (ACNE 2), Conj. 03, Lote 22, Pousada Araguaia, Palmas, TO; tel. and fax (63) 225-5456; e-mail ogirassol@ogirassol .com; internet www.ogirassol.com.br; Pres. WILBERGSON ESTRELA GOMES.

Porto Alegre, RS

Zero Hora: Av. Ipiranga 1075, Azenha, 90169-900 Porto Alegre, RS; tel. (51) 3218-4900; fax (51) 3218-4700; internet zh.clicrbs.com.br; f. 1964; Pres. NELSON SIROTSKY; circ. 165,000 Monday, 170,000 weekdays, 240,000 Sunday.

Recife, PE

Diário de Pernambuco: Rua do Veiga 600, Santo Amaro, 50040-110 Recife, PE; tel. (81) 2122-7666; fax (81) 2122-7603; e-mail faleconosco@pernambuco.com; internet www.pernambuco.com/ diario; f. 1825; morning; independent; Pres. JOEZEIL BARROS; circ. 31,000.

Ribeirão Preto, SP

Jornal Tribuna da Ribeirão Preto: Rua São Sebastião 1380, Centro, 14015-040 Ribeirão Preto, SP; tel. and fax (16) 3632-2200; e-mail tribuna@tribunariberao.com.br; internet www .tribunariberao.com.br; Dir FRANCISCO JORGE ROSA, Filho.

Rio de Janeiro, RJ

O Dia: Rua Riachuelo 359, 20235-900 Rio de Janeiro, RJ; fax (21) 2507-1228; internet odia.ig.com.br; f. 1951; morning; centrist labour; Pres. GIGI CARVALHO; circ. 250,000 weekdays, 500,000 Sundays.

O Globo: Rua Irineu Marinho 35, CP 1090, 20233-900 Rio de Janeiro, RJ; tel. (21) 2534-5000; fax (21) 2534-5510; internet oglobo .globo.com; f. 1925; morning; Editor-in-Chief JOYCE JANE; circ. 350,000 weekdays, 600,000 Sundays.

Jornal do Brasil: Rua São José 90, Centro, 20010-020 Rio de Janeiro, RJ; tel. (21) 2323-1000; e-mail jb@jbonline.com.br; internet www.jb.com.br; f. 1891; morning; Catholic, liberal; Vice-Pres. RICARDO CARVALHO; circ. 200,000 weekdays, 325,000 Sundays.

Jornal do Commercio: Rua do Livramento 189, 20221-191 Rio de Janeiro, RJ; tel. and fax (21) 2223-8500; e-mail jornaldocommercio@ jcom.com.br; internet www.jornaldocommercio.com.br; f. 1827; morning; Pres. MAURICIO DINEPI; circ. 31,000 weekdays.

Jornal dos Sports: Rua Pereira de Almeida 88, Praça de Bandeira, 20260-100 Rio de Janeiro, RJ; tel. (21) 2563-0363; e-mail falatorcedor@jsports.com.br; internet www.jsports.com.br; f. 1931; morning; sporting daily; Man. Dir ARMANDO G. COELHO; circ. 39,000.

Salvador, BA

Correio da Bahia: Rua Aristides Novis 123, Fereração, 40210-630 Salvador, BA; tel. (71) 32721-2850; fax (71) 203-1811; e-mail comercial.correio@redebahia.com.br; internet www.correiodabahia .com.br; f. 1979; Pres. ARMANDO GONÇALVES.

A Tarde: Av. Tancredo Neves 1092, Caminho das Árvores, 41822-900 Salvador, BA; tel. (71) 340-8500; fax (71) 231-1064; e-mail presidencia@atarde.com.br; internet www.atarde.com.br; f. 1912; evening; Pres. REGINA SIMÕES DE MELLO LEITÃO; circ. 54,000.

Santarém, PA

O Impacto—O Jornal da Amazônia: Av. Presidente Vargas, 3728, Caranaza, 68040-060 Santarém, PA; tel. (93) 523-3330; fax (93) 523-9131; e-mail oimpacto@oimpacto.com.br; internet www .oimpacto.com.br; Pres. ADMILTON ALMEIDA.

Santo André, SP

Diário do Grande ABC: Rua Catequese 562, Bairro Jardim, 09090-900 Santo André, SP; tel. (11) 4435-8100; fax (11) 4434-8307; e-mail online@dgabc.com.br; internet www.dgabc.com.br; f. 1958; Pres. MAURY DE CAMPOS DOTTO; circ. 78,500.

Santos, SP

A Tribuna: Rua General Câmara 90/94, 11010-903 Santos, SP; tel. (13) 3211-7000; fax (13) 3219-6783; e-mail digital@atribuna.com.br; internet www.atribuna.com.br; f. 1984; Dir ROBERTO M. SANTINI; circ. 40,000.

São Luís, MA

O Imparcial: Empresa Pacotilha Ltda, Rua Assis Chateaubriand s/n, Renascença 2, 65075-670 São Luís, MA; tel. (98) 3212-2010; e-mail redacao@pacotilha.com.br; internet www.oimparcial.com.br; f. 1926; Dir-Gen. PEDRO BATISTA FREIRE.

São Paulo, SP

Diário Comércio,Indústria e Serviços: Rua Bacaetava 191, 1°, 04705-010 São Paulo, SP; tel. (11) 5095-5200; e-mail redacao@dci .com.br; internet www.dci.com.br; f. 1933; morning; Man. Dir ORESTES QUÉRCIA; circ. 50,000.

Diário de São Paulo: Rua Major Quedinho 90, Centro, São Paulo, SP; tel. (11) 3658-8000; internet www.diariosp.com.br; f. 1884; fmrly Diário Popular; evening; owned by O Globo; Exec. Dir RICARDO GANDOUR; circ. 90,000.

O Estado de São Paulo: Av. Celestino Bourroul 68, 1°, 02710-000 São Paulo, SP; tel. (11) 3856-2122; fax (11) 3266-2206; e-mail falecom@estado.com.br; internet www.estado.com.br; f. 1875; morning; independent; Exec. Editor LUIZ OCTAVIO LIMA; circ. 242,000 weekdays, 460,000 Sundays.

Fôlha de São Paulo: Alameda Barão de Limeira 425, 6° andar, Campos Elíseos, 01202-900 São Paulo, SP; tel. (11) 3224-3678; fax (11) 3224-7550; e-mail falecomagente@folha.com.br; internet www .folha.com.br; f. 1921; morning; Exec. Dir ANA LUCIA BUSCH; circ. 557,650 weekdays, 1,401,178 Sundays.

Gazeta Mercantil: Vila Olimpia, Rua Ramos Batista 444, 11° andar, CP 04552-020 São Paulo, SP; tel. (11) 4501-1112; e-mail red@ gazetamercantil.com.br; internet www.gazeta.com.br; f. 1920; business paper; Pres. LUIZ FERREIRA LEVY; circ. 80,000.

Jornal da Tarde: Av. Eng. Caetano Álvares 55, Limão, 02598-000 São Paulo, SP; tel. (11) 3856-2122; fax (11) 3856-2257; internet www .jt.com.br; f. 1966; evening; independent; Dir FERNÃO LARA MESQUITA; circ. 120,000, 180,000 Mondays.

Vitória, ES

A Gazeta: Rua Charic Murad 902, 29050 Vitória, ES; tel. (27) 3321-8333; fax (27) 3321-8720; e-mail aleite@redegazeta.com.br; internet gazetaonline.globo.com; f. 1928; Editorial Dir ANTÓNIO CARLOS LEITE; circ. 19,000.

PERIODICALS

Rio de Janeiro, RJ

Amiga: Rua do Russel 766/804, 22214 Rio de Janeiro, RJ; tel. (21) 2285-0033; fax (21) 2205-9998; weekly; women's interest; Pres. ADOLPHO BLOCH; circ. 83,000.

Antenna-Eletrônica Popular: Av. Marechal Floriano 151, 20080-005 Rio de Janeiro, RJ; tel. (21) 2223-2442; fax (21) 2263-8840; e-mail antenna@anep.com.br; internet www.anep.com.br; f. 1926; monthly; telecommunications and electronics, radio, TV, hi-fi, amateur and CB radio; Dir MARIA BEATRIZ AFFONSO PENNA; circ. 15,000.

Carinho: Rua do Russel 766/804, 22214 Rio de Janeiro, RJ; tel. (21) 2285-0033; fax (21) 2205-9998; monthly; women's interest; Pres. ADOLPHO BLOCH; circ. 65,000.

Conjuntura Econômica: Praia de Botafogo 190, Sala 923, 22253-900 Rio de Janeiro, RJ; tel. (21) 2559-6040; fax (21) 2559-6039; e-mail conjunturaeconomica@fgv.br; internet www.fgv.br/ conjuntura.htm; f. 1947; monthly; economics and finance; published by Fundação Getúlio Vargas; Editor-in-Chief ROBERTO FENDT; circ. 25,000.

Desfile: Rua do Russel 766/804, 22214 Rio de Janeiro, RJ; tel. (21) 2285-0033; fax (21) 2205-9998; f. 1969; monthly; women's interest; Dir ADOLPHO BLOCH; circ. 120,000.

ECO21: Av. Copacabana 2, No 301, 28010-122 Rio de Janeiro, RJ; tel. (21) 2275-1490; internet www.eco21.com.br; ecological issues; Dirs LÚCIA CHAYB, RENÉ CAPRILES.

Ele Ela: Rua do Russel 766/804, 22214 Rio de Janeiro, RJ; tel. (21) 2285-0033; fax (21) 2205-9998; f. 1969; monthly; men's interest; Dir ADOLPHO BLOCH; circ. 150,000.

Manchete: Rua do Russel 766/804, 20214 Rio de Janeiro, RJ; tel. (21) 285-0033; fax (21) 205-9998; f. 1952; weekly; general; Dir ADOLPHO BLOCH; circ. 110,000.

São Paulo, SP

Caros Amigos: Rua Fidalga 162, Vila Madalena, São Paulo, SP; tel. (11) 3819-0130; internet www.carosamigos.com.br; f. 1997; monthly; political; Editor SÉRGIO DE SOUZA; circ. 50,000.

Casa e Jardim: Av. Jaguaré 1485, Jaguaré 05346-902 São Paulo, SP; tel. (11) 3797-7986; fax (11) 3797-7936; e-mail casaejardim@ edglobo.com,br; internet revistacasaejardim.globo.com; f. 1953; monthly; homes and gardens, illustrated; Dir JUAN OCERIN; circ. 120,000.

Claudia: Editora Abril, Avda das Nações Unidas 7221, Pinheiros 05425-902, São Paulo, SP; tel. (11) 3037-2000; internet www.claudia .abril.uol.com.br; f. 1962; monthly; women's magazine; Dir ROBERTO CIVITA; circ. 460,000.

Criativa: Av. Jaguaré 1485, 05346-902 São Paulo, SP; tel. (11) 3767-7812; fax (11) 3767-7771; e-mail criativa@edglobo.com.br; internet revistacriativa.globo.com; monthly; women's interest; Dir JUAN OCERIN; circ. 121,000.

Digesto Econômico: Associação Comercial de São Paulo, Rua Boa Vista 51, 01014-911 São Paulo, SP; tel. (11) 3244-3092; fax (11) 3244-3355; e-mail admdiario@acsp.com.br; every 2 months; Pres. ELVIO ALIPRANDI; Chief Editor JOÃO DE SCANTIMBURGO.

Disney Especial: Av. das Nações Unidas 7221, 05477-000 São Paulo, SP; tel. (11) 3037-2000; fax (11) 3037-4124; every 2 months; children's magazine; Dir ROBERTO CIVITA; circ. 211,600.

Elle: Av. das Nações Unidas 7221, 05425-902 São Paulo, SP; tel. (11) 3037-5197; fax (11) 3037-5451; internet www.uol.com.br/elle; f. 1988; monthly; women's magazine; Editor CARLOS COSTA; circ. 100,000.

Exame: Av. CP 11079, 05422-970 São Paulo, SP; fax (11) 3037-2027; e-mail portalexame@abril.com.br; internet portalexame.abril.com .br; f. 1967; 2 a week; business; Editorial Dir CLAYTON NETZ; circ. 168,300.

Máquinas e Metais: Alameda Olga 315, 01155-900, São Paulo, SP; tel. (11) 3824-5300; fax (11) 3662-0103; e-mail info@arandanet.com .br; internet www.arandanet.com.br; f. 1964; monthly; machine and metal industries; Editor JOSÉ ROBERTO GONÇALVES; circ. 15,000.

Marie Claire: Av. Jaguaré 1485, 05346-902 São Paulo, SP; tel. (11) 3767-7000; internet revistamarieclaire.globo.com; monthly; women's magazine; Editorial Dir MÔNICA DE ALBUQUERQUE LINS SERINO; circ. 273,000.

Mickey: Av. das Nações Unidas 7221, 05477-000 São Paulo, SP; tel. (11) 3037-2000; fax (11) 3037-4124; monthly; children's magazine; Dir ROBERTO CIVITA; circ. 76,000.

Micromundo-Computerworld do Brasil: Rua Caçapava 79, 01408 São Paulo, SP; tel. (11) 3289-1767; monthly; computers; Gen. Dir ERIC HIPPEAU; circ. 38,000.

Pato Donald: Av. das Nações Unidas 7221, 05477-000 São Paulo, SP; tel. (11) 3037-2000; fax (11) 3037-4124; every 2 weeks; children's magazine; Dir ROBERTO CIVITA; circ. 120,000.

Placar: Av. das Nações Unidas 7221, 14° andar, 05477-000 São Paulo, SP; tel. (11) 3037-5816; fax (11) 3037-5597; e-mail placar .leitor@email.abril.com.br; f. 1970; monthly; soccer magazine; Dir MARCELO DURATE; circ. 127,000.

Quatro Rodas: Av. das Nações Unidas 7221, 14°, 05425-902 São Paulo, SP; fax (11) 3037-5039; internet quatrorodas.abril.com.br; f. 1960; monthly; motoring; Dir PAULO NOGUEIRA; circ. 250,000.

Revista O Carreteiro: Rua Palacete das Aguias 395, 04635-021 São Paulo, SP; tel. (11) 5031-8646; fax (11) 5031-8647; e-mail redacao@ocarreteiro.com.br; internet www.ocarreteiro.com.br; f. 1970; monthly; transport; Dirs JOÃO ALBERTO ANTUNES DE FIGUEIREDO, EDSON PEREIRA COELHO; circ. 100,000.

Saúde: Av. das Nações Unidas 7221, 05477-000 São Paulo, SP; tel. (11) 3031-7675; fax (11) 3813-9115; internet saude.abril.com.br; monthly; health; Dir ANGELO ROSSI; circ. 180,000.

Veja: Av. das Nações Unidas 7221, CP 11079, 05422-970 São Paulo, SP; fax (11) 3037-5638; e-mail veja@abril.com.br; internet www.veja .com.br; f. 1968; news weekly; Dirs JOSÉ ROBERTO GUZZO, TALES ALVARENGA, EURIPEDES ALCÂNTARA; circ. 1,200,000.

NEWS AGENCIES

Editora Abril, SA: Av. Otaviano Alves de Lima 4400, CP 2372, 02909-970 São Paulo, SP; tel. (11) 3977-1322; fax (11) 3977-1640; f. 1950; Pres. ROBERTO CIVITA.

Agência ANDA: Edif. Correio Brasiliense, Setor das Indústrias Gráficas 300/350, Brasília, DF; Dir EDILSON VARELA.

Agência o Estado de São Paulo: Av. Eng. Caetano Alvares 55, 02588-900 São Paulo, SP; tel. (11) 3856-2122; Rep. SAMUEL DIRCEU F. BUENO.

Agência Fôlha de São Paulo: Alameda Barão de Limeira 425, 4°
andar, 01290-900 São Paulo, SP; tel. (11) 224-3790; fax (11) 221-
0675; Dir MARION STRECKER.

Agência Globo: Rua Irineu Marinho 35, 2° andar, Centro, 20233-
900 Rio de Janeiro, RJ; tel. (21) 2292-2000; fax (21) 2292-2000; Dir
CARLOS LEMOS.

Agência Jornal do Brasil: Av. Brasil 500, 6° andar, São Cristóvão,
20949-900 Rio de Janeiro, RJ; tel. (21) 2585-4453; fax (21) 2580-
9944; f. 1966; Exec. Dir. EDGAR LISBOA.

Foreign Bureaux

Agence France-Presse (AFP) (France): Av. Almirante Barroso 52,
1002, 20031-000 Rio de Janeiro, RJ; tel. (21) 2215-0222; fax (21)
2262-2399; e-mail afpriored@afp/com; Bureau Chief (Brazil) ALAIN
BOEBION.

Agencia EFE (Spain): Praia de Botafogo 228, Bloco B, Gr. 907,
22359-900 Rio de Janeiro, RJ; tel. (21) 2553-6355; fax (21) 2553-
8823; e-mail efe@efebrasil.com.br; internet www.efebrasil.com.br;
Bureau Chief FRANCISCO R. FIGUÉROA.

Agência Lusa de Informação (Portugal): São Paulo, SP; Bureau
Chief GONÇALO CÉSAR DE SÁ.

Agenzia Nazionale Stampa Associata (ANSA) (Italy): Av. São
Luís 258, 20° andar, Conj. 2004, 01046-000 São Paulo, SP; tel. (11)
3258-7022; fax (11) 3129-5543; e-mail ansasp@uol.com.br; internet
www.eurosul.com; Dir OLIVIERO PLUVIANO.

Associated Press (AP) (USA): Praia de Botofogo 228, Sala 1105,
Botafogo, 22250-906 Rio de Janeiro, RJ; tel. (21) 3288-5000; fax (21)
3288-5049; Correspondents MICHAEL ASTOR, JOSÉ HAROLD OLMOS.

Deutsche Presse-Agentur (dpa) (Germany): Av. das Américas,
700, Bloco 2, Sala 3, Barra da Tijuca, 22640-102 Rio de Janeiro, RJ;
tel. (21) 3803-7723; fax (21) 3803-7721; Bureau Chief ESTEBAN ENGEL.

**Informatsionnoye Telegrafnoye Agentstvo Rossii—
Telegrafnoye Agentstvo Suverennykh Stran (ITAR—TASS)**
(Russia): Av. Gastão Senges 55, 2003, 22631-280 Rio de Janeiro, RJ;
e-mail itartass@skydome.net.

Inter Press Service (IPS) (Italy): Av. Augusto Severo 156, 1106,
20021-040 Rio de Janeiro, RJ; tel. (21) 2509-4842; fax (21) 2509-
4842; Correspondent RICARDO BITTENCOURT.

Jiji Tsushin-Sha (Jiji Press) (Japan): Av. Paulista 854, 13° andar,
Conj. 133, Bela Vista, 01310-913 São Paulo, SP; tel. (11) 3285-0025;
fax (11) 3285-3816; e-mail jijisp@nethall.com.br; f. 1958; Chief Correspondent MUTSUHIRO TAKABAYASHI.

Kyodo Tsushin (Japan): Av. Oswaldo Cruz 149, 1206, Flamengo,
22250-060 Rio de Janeiro, RJ; tel. (21) 2533-5561; fax (21) 2553-
0276; e-mail kyodonews@uol.com.br; Bureau Chief TAKAYOSHI
MAKITA.

Prensa Latina (Cuba): Marechal Mascarenhas de Moraís 121, Apto
602, Copacabana, 22030-040 Rio de Janeiro, RJ; tel. and fax (21)
2237-1766; Correspondent FRANCISCO FORTEZA.

Reuters (United Kingdom): Av. das Nações Unidas 17891, 8° andar,
04795-100 São Paulo, SP; tel. (11) 5644-7720; fax (11) 5644-7878;
e-mail saopaolo.newsroom@reuters.com; internet www.reuters.com
.br; Bureau Chief (News and Television) ADRIAN DICKSON; also represented in Rio de Janeiro and Brasília.

**Rossiskoye Informatsionnoye Agentstvo—Novosti (RIA—
Novosti)** (Russia): Rua Sambaíba 176, 701, 22450-140 Rio de
Janeiro, RJ; tel. and fax (21) 2512-4729; e-mail novosti@uol.com.br;
Correspondent VLADIMIR STEPANOV.

Xinhua (New China) News Agency (People's Republic of China):
Rua do México 21, 701–02, 20031-144 Rio de Janeiro, RJ; tel. (21)
2275-6173; fax (21) 2524-6111; e-mail xinhuabr@hotmail.com; Chief
Correspondent WANG ZHIGEN.

Central News Agency (Taiwan) is also represented in Brazil.

PRESS ASSOCIATIONS

Associação Brasileira de Imprensa: Rua Araújo Porto Alegre 71,
Centro, 20030-010 Rio de Janeiro, RJ; f. 1908; 4,000 mems; Pres.
MAURÍCIO AZÊDO; Sec. FICHEL DAVIT CHARGEL.

Associação Nacional de Editores de Revistas (ANER): Rua
Deputado Lacerda Franco 300, 15°, Conj. 55, 05418-000 São Paulo,
SP; tel. (11) 3030-9392; fax (11) 3030-9393; e-mail mceliafurtado@
aner.org.br; Pres. ANGELO ROSSI; Exec. Dir MARIA CÉLIA FURTADO.

Federação Nacional dos Jornalistas (FENAJ): Higs 707, Bloco
R, Casa 54, 70351-718 Brasília, DF; tel. (61) 244-0650; fax (61) 242-
6616; e-mail fenaj@fenaj.org.br; internet www.fenaj.org.br; f. 1946;
represents 30 regional unions; Pres. ELISABETH VILLELA DA COSTA.

Publishers

RIO DE JANEIRO, RJ

Ao Livro Técnico Indústria e Comércio Ltda: Rua Sá Freire
36/40, São Cristóvão, 20930-430 Rio de Janeiro, RJ; tel. (21) 2580-
6230; fax (21) 2580-9955; internet www.editoraaolivrotécnico.com
.br; f. 1933; textbooks, children's and teenagers' fiction and non-
fiction, art books, dictionaries; Man. Dir REYNALDO MAX PAUL BLUHM.

Ediouro Publicações, SA: Rua Nova Jerusalém 345, CP 1880,
Bonsucesso, 21042-230 Rio de Janeiro, RJ; tel. (21) 3882-8200;
e-mail editoriallivros@ediouro.com.br; internet www.ediouro.com
.br; f. 1939; general; Pres. JORGE CARNEIRO.

Editora Campus: Rua Sete de Setembro 111, 16° andar, 20050-002
Rio de Janeiro, RJ; tel. (21) 3970-9300; fax (21) 2507-1991; e-mail c
.rothmuller@campus.com.br; internet www.campus.com.br; f. 1976;
business, computing, non-fiction; Man. Dir CLAUDIO ROTHMULLER.

Editora Delta, SA: Av. Nilo Peçanha 50, 2817, 20020-100 Rio de
Janeiro, RJ; tel. (21) 2262-5243; internet www.delta.com.br; f. 1930;
reference books; Pres. ANDRÉ KOOGAN BREITMAN.

Editora Expressão e Cultura—Exped Ltda: Estrada dos Bandeirantes 1700, Bloco H, 22710-113, Rio de Janeiro, RJ; tel. (21)
2444-0649; fax (21) 2444-0651; e-mail exped@ggh.com.br; internet
www.exped.com.br; f. 1966; textbooks, literature, reference; Gen.
Man. RICARDO AUGUSTO PAMPLONA VAZ.

Editora e Gráfica Miguel Couto, SA: Rua da Passagem 78, Loja
A, Botafogo, 22290-030 Rio de Janeiro, RJ; tel. (21) 541-5145; f. 1969;
engineering; Dir PAULO KOBLER PINTO LOPES SAMPAIO.

Editora Nova Fronteira, SA: Rua Bambina 25, Botafogo, 22251-
050 Rio de Janeiro, RJ; tel. (21) 2131-1111; fax (21) 2286-6755;
e-mail sac@novafronteira.com.br; internet www.novafronteira.com
.br; f. 1965; fiction, psychology, history, politics, science fiction,
poetry, leisure, reference; Pres. CARLOS AUGUSTO LACERDA.

Editora Record, SA: Rua Argentina 171, São Cristóvão, CP 884,
20001-970 Rio de Janeiro, RJ; tel. (21) 2585-2000; fax (21) 2585-
2085; e-mail record@record.com.br; internet www.record.com.br; f.
1941; general fiction and non-fiction, education, textbooks, fine arts;
Pres. SÉRGIO MACHADO.

Editora Vozes, Ltda: Rua Frei Luís 100, CP 90023, 25689-900
Petrópolis, RJ; tel. (24) 2233-9000; fax (24) 2231-4676; e-mail
editorial@vozes.com.br; internet www.vozes.com.br; f. 1901; Catholic publishers; management, theology, philosophy, history, linguistics, science, psychology, fiction, education, etc.; Dir ANTONIO MOSER.

Livraria Francisco Alves Editora, SA: Rua Uruguaiana, 94, 13°
andar, centro, Rio de Janeiro, RJ 20050-091; tel. (21) 2221-3198; fax
(21) 2242-3438; f. 1854; textbooks, fiction, non-fiction; Pres. CARLOS
LEAL.

Livraria José Olympio Editora, SA: Rua da Glória 344, 4° andar,
Glória, 20241-180 Rio de Janeiro, RJ; tel. (21) 2509-6939; fax (21)
2242-0802; f. 1931; juvenile, science, history, philosophy, psychology, sociology, fiction; Dir MANOEL ROBERTO DOMINGUES.

Pallas Editora: Rua Frederico de Albuquerque 56, Higienópolis,
21050-840 Rio de Janeiro, RJ; tel. and fax (21) 2270-0186; e-mail
pallas@alternex.com.br; internet www.pallaseditora.com.br; f. 1980;
Afro-Brazilian culture.

SÃO PAULO, SP

Atual Editora, Ltda: São Paulo, SP; tel. (11) 5071-2288; fax (11)
5071-3099; e-mail atendprof@atualeditora.com.br; internet www
.atualeditora.com.br; f. 1973; school and children's books, literature;
Dirs GELSON IEZZI, OSVALDO DOLCE.

Barsa Planeta Internacional: Rua Rego Freitas 192, Vila
Buarque, CP 299, 01059-970 São Paulo, SP; tel. (11) 3225-1900; fax
(11) 3225-1960; e-mail atendimento@barsaplaneta.com.br; internet
www.barsa.com; f. 1951; reference books.

Ebid-Editora Páginas Amarelas Ltda: Av. Liberdade 956, 5°
andar, 01502-001 São Paulo, SP; tel. (11) 3208-6622; fax (11) 3209-
8723; f. 1947; commercial directories.

Editora Abril, SA: Av. das Nações Unidas 7221, 10°, 05425-902 São
Paulo, SP; tel. (11) 3037-2000; fax (11) 3037-2100; e-mail fmendia@
abril.com.br; internet www.abril.com.br; f. 1950; magazines; Pres.
and Editor ROBERTO CIVITA.

Editora Atica, SA: Rua Barão de Iguape 110, 01507-900 São Paulo,
SP; tel. (11) 3346-3000; fax (11) 3277-4146; e-mail editora@atica.com
.br; internet www.atica.com.br; f. 1965; textbooks, Brazilian and
African literature; Pres. VICENTE PAZ FERNANDEZ.

Editora Atlas, SA: Rua Conselheiro Nébias 1384, Campos Elíseos,
01203-904 São Paulo, SP; tel. (11) 3357-9144; e-mail diretoria@
editora-atlas.com.br; internet www.editoraatlas.com.br; f. 1944;

business administration, data-processing, economics, accounting, law, education, social sciences; Pres. LUIZ HERRMANN.

Editora Brasiliense, SA: Rua Airi 22, Tatuapé, 03310-010 São Paulo, SP; tel. and fax (11) 6198-1488; e-mail brasilienseedit@uol .com.br; internet www.editorabrasiliense.com.br; f. 1943; education, racism, gender studies, human rights, ecology, history, literature, social sciences; Man. YOLANDA C. DA SILVA PRADO; Vice-Pres. MARIA TERESA B. DE LIMA.

Editora do Brasil, SA: Rua Conselheiro Nébias 887, Campos Elíseos, CP 4986, 01203-001 São Paulo, SP; tel. (11) 3226-0211; fax (11) 3226-9655; e-mail editora@editoradobrasil.com.br; internet www.editoradobrasil.com.br; f. 1943; education; Pres. Dr CARLOS COSTA.

Editora FTD, SA: Rua Rui Barbosa 156, Bairro Bela Vista, 01326-010 São Paulo, SP; tel. (11) 3253-5011; fax (11) 288-0132; internet www.ftd.com.br; f. 1902; textbooks; Pres. JOÃO TISSI.

Editora Globo, SA: Av. Jaguare 1485/1487, 05346-902 São Paulo, SP; tel. (11) 3767-7400; fax (11) 3767-7870; e-mail globolivros@ edglobo.com.br; internet globolivros.globo.com; f. 1957; fiction, engineering, agriculture, cookery, environmental studies; Gen. Man. JUAN OCERIN.

Editora Melhoramentos Ltda: Rua Tito 479, 05051-000 São Paulo, SP; tel. (11) 3874-0854; fax (11) 3874-0855; e-mail blerner@ melhoramentos.com.br; internet www.melhoramentos.com.br; f. 1890; general non-fiction; children's books, dictionaries; Dir BRENO LERNER.

Editora Michalany Ltda: Rua Laura dos Anjos Ramos 420, Jardim Santa Cruz—Interlagos, 04455-350 São Paulo, SP; tel. (11) 5611-3414; fax (11) 5614-1592; e-mail editora@editoramichalany .com.br; internet www.editoramichalany.com.br; f. 1965; biographies, economics, textbooks, geography, history, religion, maps; Dir DOUGLAS MICHALANY.

Editora Moderna, Ltda: Rua Padre Adelino 758, Belenzinho, 03303-904, São Paulo, SP; tel. (11) 6090-1316; fax (11) 6090-1369; e-mail moderna@moderna.com.br; internet www.moderna.com.br; Pres. RICARDO ARISSA FELTRE.

Editora Revista dos Tribunais Ltda: Rua do Bosque 820, 01136-000 São Paulo, SP; tel. (11) 3613-8400; fax (11) 3613-8474; e-mail gmarketing@rt.com.br; internet www.rt.com.br; f. 1912; law and jurisprudence books and periodicals; Dir CARLOS HENRIQUE DE CARVALHO, Filho.

Editora Rideel Ltda: Alameda Afonso Schmidt 879, Santa Terezinha, 02450-001 São Paulo, SP; tel. (11) 6977-8344; fax (11) 6976-7415; e-mail sac@rideel.com.br; internet www.rideel.com.br; f. 1971; general; Dir ITALO AMADIO.

Editora Saraiva: Av. Marquês de São Vicente 1697, CP 2362, 01139-904 São Paulo, SP; tel. (11) 3933-3366; fax (11) 861-3308; e-mail diretoria.editora@editorasaraiva.com.br; internet www .editorasaraiva.com.br; f. 1914; education, textbooks, law, economics; Pres. JORGE EDUARDO SARAIVA.

Editora Scipione Ltda: Praça Carlos Gomes 46, 01501-040 São Paulo, SP; tel. (11) 3241-2255; e-mail scipione@scipione.com.br; internet www.scipione.com.br; f. 1983; owned by Editora Abril, SA; school-books, literature, reference; Dir LUIZ ESTEVES SALLUM.

Instituto Brasileiro de Edições Pedagógicas, Ltda (Editoras IBEP Nacional): Avda Alexandre Mackenzie 619, Jaguaré, 05322-000 São Paulo, SP; tel. (11) 6099-7799; fax (11) 6694-5338; e-mail editoras@ibep-nacional.com.br; internet www.ibep-nacional.com.br; f. 1965; textbooks, foreign languages and reference books; Dirs JORGE YUNES, PAULO C. MARTI.

Lex Editora, SA: Frei Eusébio Soledade 94, Vila Mariana, 04106-030 São Paulo, SP; tel. (11) 5549-0122; fax (11) 5575-9138; e-mail adm@lexli.com.br; internet www.lexli.com.br; f. 1937; legislation and jurisprudence; Dir MILTON NICOLAU VITALE PATARA.

Thomson Pioneira: Rua Traipu 114, Perdizes, 01235-000 São Paulo, SP; tel. (11) 3665-9900; fax (11) 3665-9901; internet www .thomsonlearning.com.br; f. 1960 as Editora Pioneira; acquired by Thomson Learning in 2000; architecture, computers, political and social sciences, business studies, languages, children's books; Dirs ROBERTO GUAZZELLI, LILIANA GUAZZELLI.

BELO HORIZONTE, MG

Editora Lê, SA: Av. D. Pedro II 4550, Jardim Montanhês, CP 2585, 30730 Belo Horizonte, MG; internet www.le.com.br; tel. (31) 3413-1720; f. 1967; textbooks.

Editora Lemi, SA: Av. Nossa Senhora de Fátima 1945, CP 1890, 30000 Belo Horizonte, MG; tel. (31) 3201-8044; f. 1967; administration, accounting, law, ecology, economics, textbooks, children's books and reference books.

Editora Vigília, Ltda: Belo Horizonte, MG; e-mail lerg@ planetarium.com.br; tel. (31) 3337-2744; fax (31) 3337-2834; f. 1960; general.

CURITIBA, PR

Editora Educacional Brasileira, SA: Rua XV de Novembro 178, Salas 101/04, CP 7498, 80000 Curitiba, PR; tel. (41) 223-5012; f. 1963; biology, textbooks and reference books.

PUBLISHERS' ASSOCIATIONS

Associação Brasileira de Editores de Livros (Abrelivros): Rua Turiassu 143, 101/102, 05005-001 São Paulo, SP; tel. and fax (11) 3826-9071; e-mail abrelivros@abrelivros.org.br; internet www .abrelivros.org.br; Pres. Prof. WANDER SOARES.

Associação Brasileira do Livro (ABL): Av. 13 de Maio 23, 16°, Sala 1619/1620, 20031-000 Rio de Janeiro, RJ; tel. and fax (21) 2240-9115; e-mail abralivro@uol.com.br; Pres. ADENILSON JARBAS CABRAL.

Câmara Brasileira do Livro: Cristiano Viana 91, 05411-000 São Paulo, SP; tel. (11) 3069-1300; e-mail marketing@cbl.org.br; internet www.cbl.org.br; f. 1946; Pres. OSWALDO SICILIANO.

Sindicato Nacional dos Editores de Livros (SNEL): Av. Rio Branco 37, 1503/6 and 1510/12, 20090-003 Rio de Janeiro, RJ; tel. (21) 2233-6481; fax (21) 2253-8502; e-mail snel@snel.org.br; internet www.snel.org.br; 200 mems; Pres. PAULO ROBERTO ROCCO; Man. ANTÔNIO LASKOS.

There are also regional publishers' associations.

Broadcasting and Communications

TELECOMMUNICATIONS

BCP Telecomunicações: São Paulo, SP; internet www.bcp.com.br; tel. (11) 5509-6955; f. 1997; mobile services in São Paulo area; Pres. ROBERTO PEÓN.

Brasil Telecom: SIA Sul, Área dos Servicos Públicos, Lote D, Bloco B, 71.215-000 Brasília, DF; tel. (61) 415-1128; fax (61) 415-1133; internet www.brasiltelecom.com.br; fixed line services in 10 states; Chair. MODESTO SOUZA BARROS CARVALHOSO; Pres. HENRIQUE SUTTON DE SOUSA NEVES.

Empresa Brasileira de Telecomunicações, SA (EMBRATEL): Av. Pres. Vargas 1012, CP 2586, 20179-900 Rio de Janeiro, RJ; tel. (21) 2519-8182; e-mail cmsocial@embratel.net.br; internet www .embratel.com.br; f. 1965; operates national and international telecommunications system; controlled by Telmex, Mexico; Chair. DANIEL CRAWFORD.

Telecomunicações de São Paulo, SA (Telesp): Rua Martiniano de Carvalho 851, Bela Vista, 01321-000 São Paulo, SP; tel. (11) 3549-7200; fax (11) 3549-7202; e-mail webmaster@telesp.com.br; internet www.telesp.com.br; services operated by Telefónica, SA, of Spain; Pres. FERNANDO XAVIER FERREIRA; Chief Exec. SAMPAIO DORIA.

Telemar: Rua Lauro Muller 116, 22° andar, Botafogo, Rio de Janeiro, RJ; tel. (21) 2815-2921; fax (21) 2571-3050; internet www .telemar.com.br; fixed line services in 16 states; f. 1998 as Tele Norte Leste; Chair. CARLOS JEREISSATI; Pres. MANOEL DE SILVA.

VIVO: Av. Chucri Zaidan 2460, 5°, 04583-110 São Paulo, SP; tel. (11) 5105-1001; internet www.vivo.com.br; owned by Telefónica Móviles, SA of Spain (50%) and Portugal Telecom; mobile telephones; 24.6m. customers.

Regulatory Authority

Agência Nacional de Telecomunicações (ANATEL): SAUS Quadra 06, Bloco H, 3° andar, 70313-900 Brasília, DF; tel. (61) 312-2336; fax (61) 312-2211; e-mail biblioteca@anatel.gov.br; internet www.anatel.gov.br; f. 1998; regional office in each state; Pres. PEDRO JAIME ZILLER.

BROADCASTING

Radio

In April 1992 there were 2,917 radio stations in Brazil, including 20 in Brasília, 38 in Rio de Janeiro, 32 in São Paulo, 24 in Curitiba, 24 in Porto Alegre and 23 in Belo Horizonte.

The main broadcasting stations in Rio de Janeiro are: Rádio Nacional, Rádio Globo, Rádio Eldorado, Rádio Jornal do Brasil, Rádio Tupi and Rádio Mundial. In São Paulo the main stations are Rádio Bandeirantes, Rádio Mulher, Rádio Eldorado, Rádio Gazeta and Rádio Excelsior; and in Brasília: Rádio Nacional, Rádio Alvorada, Rádio Planalto and Rádio Capital.

Rádio Nacional do Brásil (RADIOBRÁS): CP 070747, 70359-970 Brasília, DF; tel. 321-3949; fax 321-7602; e-mail maurilio@radiobras .gov.br; internet www.radiobras.gov.br; Pres. Eugenio Bucci.

Television
The main television networks are:

RBS TV-TV Gaúcha, SA: Rua Rádio y TV Gaúcha 189, 90850-080 Porto Alegre, RS; tel. (51) 3218-5119; fax (51) 3218-5144; e-mail info@rbstv.com.br; internet www.rbs.com.br; Vice-Pres Walmor Bergesch.

TV Bandeirantes: Rádio e Televisão Bandeirantes Ltda, Rua Radiantes 13, Morumbi, 05699-900 São Paulo, SP; tel. (11) 3742-3011; fax (11) 3745-7622; e-mail cat@band.com.br; internet www.band.com .br; 65 TV stations and repeaters throughout Brazil; Pres. João Jorge Saad.

TV Record—Rede Record de Televisão—Radio Record, SA: Rua de Várzea 240, Barra Funda, 01140-080 São Paulo, SP; tel. (11) 3660-4761; fax (11) 3660-4756; e-mail tvrecord@rederecord.com.br; internet www.tvrecord.com.br; Pres. João Batista R. Silva; Exec. Vice-Pres. H. Gonçalves.

TV Rede Globo: Rua Lopes Quintas 303, Jardim Botânico, 22460-010 Rio de Janeiro, RJ; tel. (21) 2540-2000; fax (21) 2294-2092; e-mail webmaster@redeglobo.com.br; internet www.redeglobo.com .br; f. 1965; 8 stations; national network; Dir Adilson Pontes Malta.

TV SBT—Sistema Brasileira de Televisão—Canal 4 de São Paulo, SA: Av. Das Comunicações 4, Vila Jaraguá, 06278-905 São Paulo, SP; tel. (11) 7087-3000; fax (11) 7087-3509; internet www.sbt .com.br; Vice-Pres. Guilherme Stoliar.

Broadcasting Associations
Associação Brasileira de Emissoras de Rádio e Televisão (ABERT): Centro Empresarial Varig, SCN Quadra 04, Bloco B, Conj. 501, Pétala A, 70710-500 Brasília, DF; tel. (61) 327-4600; fax (61) 327-3660; e-mail abert@abert.org.br; internet www.abert.org .br; f. 1962; mems: 32 shortwave, 1,275 FM, 1,574 medium-wave and 80 tropical-wave radio stations and 258 television stations (1997); Pres. Paulo Machado de Carvalho Neto; Exec. Dir Oscar Piconez.

There are regional associations for Bahia, Ceará, Goiás, Minas Gerais, Rio Grande do Sul, Santa Catarina, São Paulo, Amazonas, Distrito Federal, Mato Grosso and Mato Grosso do Sul (combined) and Sergipe.

Finance
(cap. = capital; dep. = deposits; res = reserves; m. = million; brs = branches; amounts in reais, unless otherwise stated)

BANKING
Conselho Monetário Nacional: SBS, Q.03, Bloco B, Edif. Sede do Banco do Brasil, 21° andar, 70074-900 Brasília, DF; tel. (61) 414-1945; fax (61) 414-2528; e-mail cmn@bcb.gov.br; f. 1964 to formulate monetary policy and to supervise the banking system; Pres. Antônio Palocci, Filho (Minister of Finance).

Central Bank
Banco Central do Brasil: Setor Bancário Sul, Quadra 03, Mezanino 01, Bloco B, 70074-900 Brasília, DF; tel. (61) 414-1955; fax (61) 223-1033; e-mail secre.surel@bcb.gov.br; internet www.bcb.gov.br; f. 1965 to execute the decisions of the Conselho Monetário Nacional; bank of issue; cap. 2,576.4m., res 4,467.7m., dep. 317,639.4m. (Dec. 2003); Gov. Henrique de Campos Meirelles; 10 brs.

State Commercial Banks
Banco do Brasil, SA: Setor Bancário Sul, Quadra 01, Bloco C, Lote 32, Edif. Sede III, 70073-901 Brasília, DF; tel. (61) 310-4500; fax (61) 310-2444; internet www.bb.com.br; f. 1808; cap. 8,366.2m., res 3,805.6m., dep. 151,713.6m. (Dec. 2003); Pres. Cássio Casseb Lima; 3,241 brs.

Banco do Estado do Ceará (BEC): Rua Pedro Pereira 481, 3° andar, 60035-000 Fortaleza, CE; tel. (85) 3255-1818; fax (85) 3255-1933; e-mail bec@bec.com.br; internet www.bec.com.br; f. 1964; cap. 242.3m., res 37.7m., dep. 803.8m. (June 2003); Pres. João Batista Santos; 4 brs.

Banco do Estado do Rio Grande do Sul, SA (Banrisul): Rua Caldas Junior 108, 7° andar, 90018-900 Porto Alegre RS; tel. (51) 3215-2501; fax (51) 3215-1715; e-mail cambio_dg@banrisul.com.br; internet www.banrisul.com.br; f. 1928; cap. 600.0m., res 200.8m., dep. 9,515.7m. (Dec. 2003); Pres. Ario Zimmermann; 352 brs.

Banco do Estado de Santa Catarina SA: Rodovia SC 401, Km 5, 4600, Bairro Saco Grande II, 88032-000 Florianpólis, SC; tel. (48) 239-9000; fax (48) 239-9052; e-mail decam/dinte@besc.com.br; internet www.besc.com.br; f. 1962; cap. 1,319.0m., res -1,201.3m., dep. 1,690.8m. (Dec. 2003); Pres. Vitor Fontana.

Banco do Estado de São Paulo, SA (Banespa): Rua Antonio Prado 6, Centro, 01010-010 São Paulo, SP; tel. (11) 5538-7450; fax (11) 5538-6680; e-mail relacoesmercado@santander.combr; internet www.banespa.com.br; f. 1909; owned by Banco Santander (Spain); cap. 2,536.8m., res 2,219.9m., dep. 15,408.8m. (Dec. 2003); Pres. Gabriel Jaramillo Sanint; 1,404 brs.

Banco do Nordeste do Brasil, SA: Av. Paranjana 5700, Passaré, 60740-000 Fortaleza, CE; tel. (85) 3299-3333; fax (85) 3299-3878; e-mail info@banconordeste.gov.br; internet www.banconordeste.gov .br; f. 1952; cap. 1,162.0m., res 153.2m., dep. 2,946.6m. (Dec. 2003); Pres. and CEO Byron Costa de Queiroz; 186 brs.

Banco Nossa Caixa, SA: São Paulo, SP; tel. (11) 3856-7770; fax (11) 3856-7771; internet www.nossacaixa.com.br; f. 1917 as Caixa Econômica do Estado de São Paulo; cap. 1,27.4m., res 171.2m., dep. 16,793.3m. (June 2002); Pres. Valdery Frota de Albuqerque; 498 brs.

Other state commercial banks are the Banco do Estado do Pará and Banestes—the Banco do Estado do Espirito Santo.

Private Banks
Banco ABC Brasil SA: Av. Paulista 37, 01311-902 São Paulo, SP; tel. (11) 3170-2000; fax (11) 3170-2001; e-mail abcbrasil@abcbrasil .com.br; internet www.abcbrasil.com.br; f. 1989 as Banco ABC—Roma SA; cap. 222.1m., res 157.0m., dep. 998.2m. (Dec. 2003); Pres. and Gen. Man. Tito Enrique da Silva Neto; 2 brs.

Banco ABN AMRO SA: Av. Paulista 1374, 3°, 01310-916 São Paulo, SP; tel. (11) 3174-9615; fax (11) 3174-7052; internet www .bancoreal.com.br; cap. 7,458.2m., res 646.4m., dep. 25,822.3m. (Dec. 2003); 847 brs.

Banco Alfa de Investimento SA: Almadena Santos 466, 4° andar, 01418-000 Paraíso, SP; tel. (11) 3175-5074; fax (11) 3171-2438; internet www.bancoalfa.com.br; f. 1998; cap. 226.0m., res 357.9m., dep. 3,293.6m. (Dec. 2003); Pres. Paulo Guiherme Monteiro Lobato Ribeiro; 9 brs.

Banco da Amazônia, SA: Av. Presidente Vargas 800, 66017-000 Belém, PA; tel. (91) 4008-3252; fax (91) 223-5403; e-mail cambio@ bancoamazionia.com.br; internet www.bancoamazonia.com.br; f. 1942; cap. 1,205.2m., res 221.4m., dep. 1,588.3m. (Dec. 2003); Pres. Mâncio Lima Cordeiro; 88 brs.

Banco Banestado (BANESTADO): Rua Monsenhor Celso 151, 11° andar, 81110-150 Curitiba, PR; tel. (11) 5019-8101; fax (11) 5019-8103; e-mail helphb@email.banestado.com.br; internet www .banestado.com.br; f. 1928; Pres. Roberto Egydio Setubal; 374 brs.

Banco BBM SA: Rua Miguel Calmon 57, 2° andar, Comercis, 40015-010 Salvador, BA; tel. (71) 243-7675; fax (71) 243-2987; internet www.bancobbm.com.br; f. 1858 as Banco de Bahia; cap. 162.1m., res 150.5m., dep. 2,910.6m. (Dec. 2003); Pres. Pedro Henrique Mariani; 4 brs.

Banco BCN SA: Av. das Nações Unidas 12901, CENU—Torre Oeste, 15° andar, 04578-000 São Paulo, SP; tel. (11) 5509-2444; fax (11) 5509-2804; internet www.bcn.com.br; f. 1929 as Casa Bancaria Conde & Cia; cap. 2,270.1m., res 957.9m., dep. 14,797.6m. (Dec. 2003); Pres. José Luiz Acar Pedro; 222 brs.

Banco BMC, SA: Av. das Nações Unidas 12.995, 24° andar, 04578-000 São Paulo, SP; tel. (11) 5503-7500; fax (11) 5503-7676; e-mail bancobmc@bmc.com.br; internet www.bmc.com.br; f. 1939; adopted current name in 1990; cap. 164.8m., res 53.6m., dep. 1,562.1m. (Dec. 2003); Chair. and CEO Francisco Jaime Nogueira Pinheiro; 9 brs.

Banco BMG, SA: Av. Alvares Cabral 1707, Santo Agostinho, 30170-001 Belo Horizonte, MG; tel. (31) 3290-3700; fax (31) 3290-3168; e-mail bancobmg@bancobmg.com.br; internet www.bancobmg.com .br; f. 1930; cap. 201.8m., res 130.2m., dep. 1,498.4 (Dec. 2003); Pres. Flávio Pentagna Guimarães; 10 brs.

Banco Bemge, SA: Rua Albita 131, 30310-160 Belo Horizonte, MG; tel. (31) 5019-8101; fax (31) 5019-8103; f. 1967; fmrly Banco do Estado de Minas Gerais SA; acquired by Banco Itaú, SA, in Sept. 1998; cap. 250.8m., res –157.6m., dep. 2,450.3m. (Dec. 1997); Pres. and CEO José Afonso Beltrão da Silva.

Banco Boavista Interatlântico, SA: Praça Pio X 118-11, 20091-040 Rio de Janeiro, RJ; tel. (21) 3849-5535; e-mail boavista@ibm.net; internet www.boavista.com.br; f. 1997; acquired by Banco Bradesco in 2000; cap. 4,401.9m., res 278.7m., dep. 4,241.4m. (Dec. 2002); Pres. José Luiz Acar Pedro.

Banco Bradesco, SA: Cidade de Deus, Vila Yara, 06029–900 Osasco, SP; tel. (11) 3681-4011; fax (11) 3684-4630; internet www .bradesco.com.br; f. 1943; fmrly Banco Brasileiro de Descontos; cap. 7,000.0m., res 6,546.9m., dep. 97,663.5m. (Dec. 2003); Chair. Lázaro de Mello Brandão; Vice-Chair. Antônio Bornia; 3,054 brs.

Banco Brascan SA: Av. Almirante Barroso 52, 30° andar, Centro, 20031-000 Rio de Janeiro, RJ; tel. (21) 3231-3000; fax (21) 3231-3231; internet www.bancobrascan.com.br; cap. 167.9m., res 77.9m., dep. 621.7m. (Dec. 2003); Pres. ANTONIO PAULO DE AZEVEDO SODRE.

Banco Dibens, SA: Rua Boa Vista 162, 6° andar, Centro, 01014-902 São Paulo, SP; tel. (11) 3243-7533; fax (11) 3243-7534; internet www .dibens.com.br; f. 1989; jt owned by Unibanco and Grupo Verdi; cap. 110.7m., res 31.7m., dep. 1,993.3m. (Dec. 2001); Pres. MAURO SADDI; 23 brs.

Banco Fibra: Av. Brigadeiro Faria Lima 3064, Itaim Bibi, 01451-000 São Paulo, SP; tel. (11) 3847-6700; fax (11) 3847-6969; e-mail bancofibra@bancofibra.com.br; internet www.bancofibra.com.br; f. 1989; cap. 170.0m., res 244.7m., dep. 5,393.7m. (Dec. 2003); Pres. BENJAMIN STEINBRUCH; CEO JOÃO AYRES RABELLO, Filho.

Banco Industrial do Brasil: Av. Juscelino Kubitschek 1703, Itaim Bibi, 04543-000 São Paulo, SP; tel. (11) 3049-9700; fax (11) 3049-9810; internet www.bancoindustrial.com.br; cap. 103.0m., res 22.6m., dep. 562.8m. (Dec. 2003); Pres. CARLOS ALBERTO MANSUR.

Banco Industrial e Comercial, SA (Bicbanco): Av. Paulista 1048, Bela Vista, 01310-100 São Paulo, SP; tel. (11) 3179-9000; fax (11) 3179-9277; e-mail internationa@bicbanco.com.br; internet www .bicbanco.com.br; f. 1938; cap. 300.0m., res 61.1m., dep. 2,833.4m. (Dec. 2003); Pres. JOSÉ BEZERRA DE MENEZES; 36 brs.

Banco Itaú, SA: Praça Alfredo Egydio de Souza Aranha 100, Torre Itaúsa, 04344-902 São Paulo, SP; tel. (11) 5019-1549; fax (11) 5019-1133; e-mail investor.relations@itau.com.br; internet www.itau.com .br; f. 1944; cap. 5,525.0m., res 1,531.7m., dep. 55,326.2m. (Dec. 2003); Chair. OLAVO EGYDIO SETÚBAL; Pres. and CEO ROBERTO EGYDIO SETÚBAL; 1,677 brs.

Banco Itau BBA, SA: Av. Brigadeiro Faria Lima 3400, 4°, 04538-132 São Paulo, SP; tel. (11) 3708-8000; fax (11) 3708-8172; e-mail bancoitaubba@itaubba.com.br; internet www.itaubba.com.br; f. 1988; acquired by Banco Itaú in 2002; cap. 2,430.0m., res 685.6m., dep. 9,311.6m. (Dec. 2003); Pres. FERNÃO CARLOS BOTELHO BRACHER; 6 brs.

Banco Mercantil do Brasil, SA: Rua Rio de Janerio 654, 10°, Centro, 30160–912 Belo Horizante, MG; tel. (31) 3239-6314; fax (31) 3239-6975; e-mail sac@mercantil.com.br; internet www.mercantil .com.br; cap. 173.2m., res 215.1m., dep. 3,324.4m. (Dec. 2003); Chair., Pres. and CEO MILTON DE ARAÚJO; 204 brs.

Banco Mercantil de São Paulo: CP 4077, Av. Paulista 1450, 01310-917 São Paulo, SP; tel. (11) 3145–2121; fax (11) 3145-3180; e-mail finasa@finasa.com.br; internet www.finasa.com.br; f. 1938; owned by Banco Bradesco; cap. 817.4m., res 189.6m., dep. 3,832.6m. (Dec. 1999); Pres. Dr GASTÃO EDUARDO DE BUENO VIDIGAL.

Banco Pactual: Av. República do Chile 230, 28° e 29° andares, 20031-170 Rio de Janeiro, RJ; tel. (21) 2514-9600; fax 2514-8600; e-mail webmaster@pactual.com.br; internet www.pactual.com.br; f. 1983; cap. 208.1., res 296.5m., dep. 1,261.6m. (Dec. 2002); Pres. EDUARDO PLASS; 4 brs.

Banco de Pernambuco SA (Bandepe): Edif. Bandepe 5°, Cais do Apolo 222, Bairro do Recife, 50030-230 Recife, PE; tel. (11) 3425-6385; fax (11) 0812-2097; internet www.bandepe.com.br; f. 1938 as Banco do Estado de Pernambuco; cap. 2,412.4m., res –684.2m., dep. 868.1m. (Dec. 2002); Pres. FLORIS GUSTAAF HENDKIK DECKERS; 52 brs.

Banco Pine SA: Alameda Santos 1940, 12-13°, Cerqueira Cesar, 01418-200 São Paulo, SP; tel. (11) 3372-5200; fax (11) 3372-5403; e-mail bancopine@uol.com.br; internet www.bancopine.com.br; f. 1997; cap. 113.3m., res 38.6m., dep. 631.1m. (Dec. 2003); Man. Dirs Dr NELSON NOGUEIRA PINHEIRO, NORBERTO NOGUEIRA PINHEIRO.

Banco Rural SA: Av. Presidente Wilson 927, 6°, 20065-900 Rio de Janeiro, RJ; tel. (21) 3210-1310; fax (21) 3220-0198; internet www .rural.com.br; f. 1964; cap. 177.7m., res 432.0m., dep. 3,478.8m. (Dec. 2003); Pres. SABINO CORRÊA RABELLO; 78 brs.

Banco Safra, SA: Av. Paulista 2100, 9° andar, 01310-930 São Paulo, SP; tel. (11) 3175-7575; fax (11) 3175-7211; e-mail safrapact@ uol.com.br; internet www.safra.com.br; f. 1940; cap. 1,411.9m., res 1,646.0m., dep. 16,285.8m. (Dec. 2003); Pres. CARLOS ALBERTO VIEIRA; 77 brs.

Banco Santander Brasil, SA: Rua Amador Bueno 474, 04752-005 São Paulo, SP; tel. (11) 5538-6555; fax (11) 5538-7750; internet www .santander.com.br; f. 1942; fmrly Banco Geral do Comercio; cap. 1,248.2m., res 341.0m., dep. 15,839.0m. (Dec. 2003); Pres. GABRIEL JARAMILLO SANINT; 41 brs.

Banco Santander Meridional, SA: Rua Siqueira Campos 1125, Centro, 90010-001 Porto Alegre, RS; tel. (51) 3287-5700; fax (51) 3287-5672; internet www.meridional.com.br; f. 1973; fmrly Banco Sulbrasileiro, SA; taken over by the Govt in Aug. 1985; acquired by Banco Bozano, Simonsen in 1997; name changed in 2000 following acquisition by Banco Santander Brasil, SA; cap. 815.2m., res

149.7m., dep. 1,717.7m. (Dec. 2003); Pres. GABRIEL JARAMILLO SANINT; 227 brs.

Banco Société Générale Brasil SA: Av. Paulista 2300, 9° andar, Cerqueira Cesar, 01310-300 São Paulo, SP; tel. (11) 3217-8000; fax (11) 3217-8090; internet www.sgbrasil.com.br; f. 1981 as Banco Sogeral; cap. 125.1m., res –49.5m., dep. 206.6m. (Dec. 2003); Pres. FRANÇOIS DOSSA.

Banco Sudameris Brasil, SA: Av. Paulista 1000, 01310-912 São Paulo, SP; tel. (11) 3170-9899; fax (11) 3289-1239; internet www .sudameris.com.br; f. 1910; cap. 1,138.7m., res 200.8m., dep. 7,944.6m. (Dec. 2003); Exec. Dir. YVES L. J. LEJEUNE; 270 brs.

Banco Votorantim, SA: Av. Roque Petroni, Jr 999, 16° andar, 04707-910 São Paulo, SP; tel. (11) 5185-1700; fax (11) 5185-1900; internet www.bancovotorantim.com.br; cap. 1,500.2m., res 358.2m., dep. 12,610.1m. (June 2004); 4 brs.

UNIBANCO (União de Bancos Brasileiros, SA): Av. Eusébio Matoso 891, 05423-901 São Paulo, SP; tel. (11) 3097-1313; fax (11) 3813-6182; e-mail investor.relations@unibanco.com.br; internet www .unibanco.com.br; f. 1924; cap. 3,690.6m., res 3,465.3m., dep. 36,005.8m. (Dec. 2003); Chair. PEDRO MOREIRA SALLES; 809 brs.

Development Banks

Banco de Desenvolvimento de Minas Gerais, SA (BDMG): Rua da Bahia 1600, CP 1026, 30160-907 Belo Horizonte, MG; tel. (31) 3219-8000; fax 3226-3292; e-mail contastos@bdmg.mg.gov.br; internet www.bdmg.mg.gov.br; f. 1962; long-term credit operations; cap. 464.1m., res –178.8m. (Dec. 2002); Pres. ROMEU SCARIOLI.

Banco Nacional do Desenvolvimento Econômico e Social (BNDES): Av. República do Chile 100, Centro, 20031-917 Rio de Janeiro, RJ; tel. (21) 2277-7447; fax (21) 3088-7447; internet www .bndes.gov.br; f. 1952 to act as main instrument for financing of development schemes sponsored by the Government and to support programmes for the development of the national economy; charged with supervision of privatization programme of the 1990s; cap. 12,500.1m., res 576.4m., dep. 8,617.0m. (June 2002); Pres. GIUDO MANTEGA; 1 br.

Banco Regional de Desenvolvimento do Extremo Sul (BRDE): Rua Uruguai 155, 4°, CP 139, 90010-140 Porto Alegre, RS; tel. (51) 3215-5000; fax (51) 3215-5050; e-mail brde@brde.com.br; internet www.brde.com.br; f. 1961; development bank for the states of Paraná, Rio Grande do Sul and Santa Catarina; finances small and medium-sized enterprises; cap. 15m. (Dec. 1993); Pres. CASILDO JOÃO MALDANER; 3 brs.

Investment Banks

Banco de Investimentos Credit Suisse First Boston: Av. Brigadeiro Faria Lima 3064, 13° andar, Itaim Bibi, 01451-000 São Paulo, SP; tel. (11) 3842-9700; fax (11) 3842-9747; e-mail csam@ csam.br; internet www.csfb.com.br; f. 1971; fmrly Banco de Investimentos Garantia; subsidiary of Credit Suisse, Switzerland; cap. 956.6m., res 107.2m., dep. 1,794.7m. (Dec. 1996); Dir MAURO BERGSTEIN; 1 br.

Other investment banks include Banco Finasa de Investimento SA, Banco Fininvest SA.

State-owned Savings Bank

Caixa Econômica Federal: Brasília, DF; tel. (61) 321-9209; fax (61) 225-0215; internet www.caixa.gov.br; f. 1860; cap. 4,301.1m., res 564.4m., dep. 73,611.2m. (June 2002); Pres. EMÍLIO CARRAZAI; 2,026 brs.

Foreign Banks

American Express Bank Brasil (USA): Av. Bridadeiro Faria Lima 1355, 16° andar, 01452-022 São Paulo, SP; tel. (11) 3030-3000; fax (11) 3030-3030; e-mail biamex@biamex.com.br; internet www .biamex.com.br; f. 1988 as Mantrust SRL; present name adopted Dec. 2003; owned by American Express Bank; cap. 102.3m., res 1.6m., dep. 389.2m. (Dec. 2003); Pres. MARK W. GROSS.

Banco Barclays SA: Praça Prof. José Lannes 40, 5°, 04157-100 São Paulo, SP; tel. (11) 5509-3200; fax (11) 5509-3340; e-mail barclays@ uol.com.br; internet www.barclays.com; f. 1967 as Banco de Investimento; cap. 488.6m., res –320.2m., dep. 313.0m. (Dec. 2002); Pres. PETER ANDERSON.

Banco de la Nación Argentina: Av. Paulista 2319, Sobreloja, 01310 São Paulo, SP; tel. (11) 3083-1555; fax (11) 3081-4630; e-mail bnaspbb@dialdata.com.br; f. 1891; Dir-Gen. GERARDO LUIS PONCE; 2 brs.

Banco JP Morgan SA: Av. Brigadeiro Faria Lima 3729, 04538-905 São Paulo, SP; tel. (11) 3048-3700; fax (11) 3048-3500; internet www .jpmorgan.com; f. 1969; Pres. CHARLES WORTMAN.

Banco Sumitomo Mitsui Brasileiro SA: Av. Paulista 37, 12°, Paraiso, 01311-902 São Paulo, SP; tel. (11) 3178-8000; fax (11) 3289-1668; f. 1958; cap. 309.4m., res 12.8m., dep. 132.5m. (Dec. 2003); Pres. Takeaki Misumi; 1 br.

Banco de Tokyo-Mitsubishi SA: Av. Paulista 1274, Bela Vista, 01310-925 São Paulo, SP; tel. (11) 3268-0211; fax (11) 3268-0453; internet www.btm.com.br; f. 1972 as Banco de Tokyo; cap. 186.9m., res 150.3m., dep. 446.8m. (Dec. 2003); Pres. Yoshio Nozaki; 2 brs.

BankBoston SA: Av. Doutor Chucri Zaidan 246, Villa Cordeiro, Morumbi, 04583-110 São Paulo, SP; tel. (11) 3249-5622; fax (11) 3249-5529; internet www.bankboston.com.br; cap. 1,610.0m., res 304.6m., dep. 8,427.9m. (Dec. 2003); Pres. Geraldo José Carbone; 59 brs.

Deutsche Bank SA Banco Alemao: Rua Alexandre Dumas 2200, 04717-910 São Paulo, SP; tel. (11) 5189-5000; fax (11) 5189-5100; internet www.deutschebank.com.br; f. 1911; cap. 138.9m., res 118.3m., dep. 2,506.6m. (Dec. 2003); Pres. Roger I. Karam.

HSBC Bank Brasil SA-Banco Multiplo: Travessa Oliveira Belo 34, 4° andar, Centro, 80020-030 Curitiba, PR; tel. (41) 321-6161; fax (41) 340-2660; internet www.hsbc.com.br; f. 1997; cap. 1,340.6m., res 296.8m., dep. 16,934.2m. (Dec. 2003); Pres. Youssef Assaad Nasr; 966 brs.

ING Bank NV (Netherlands): Av. Brigadeiro Faria Lima 3064, 10°, 01451-000 São Paulo, SP; tel. (11) 3847-6274; fax (11) 3847-8274; e-mail deiwes.rubira@ing-barings.com.

Banking Associations

Associação Nacional dos Bancos de Investimentos—ANBID: Av. Brigadeiro Faria Lima 2179, 2° andar, 01451-001 São Paulo, SP; tel. (11) 3471-4200; fax (11) 3471-4230; e-mail anbid@anbid.com.br; internet www.anbid.com.br; investment banks; Pres. Alfredo Egydio Setúbal; Supt Luiz Kaufman.

Federação Brasileira dos Bancos: Rua Líbero Badaró 425, 17°, 01009-905 São Paulo, SP; tel. (11) 3244-9800; fax (11) 3107-8486; internet www.febraban.org.br; f. 1966; Dir-Gen. Wilson Roberto Levorato.

Sindicato dos Bancos dos Estados do Rio de Janeiro e Espírito Santo: Av. Rio Branco 81, 19° andar, Rio de Janeiro, RJ; Pres. Theóphilo de Azeredo Santos; Vice-Pres. Dr Nelson Mufarrej.

Sindicato dos Bancos dos Estados de São Paulo, Paraná, Mato Grosso e Mato Grosso do Sul: Rua Líbero Badaró 293, 13° andar, 01905 São Paulo, SP; f. 1924; Pres. Paulo de Queiroz.

There are other banking associations in Maceió, Salvador, Fortaleza, Belo Horizonte, João Pessoa, Recife and Porto Alegre.

STOCK EXCHANGES

Comissão de Valores Mobiliários (CVM): Rua Sete de Setembro 111, 13°, 26° e 34°, Centro, 20159-900 Rio de Janeiro, RJ; tel. (21) 3233-0200; fax (21) 2221-6769; e-mail soi@cvm.gov.br; internet www.cvm.gov.br; f. 1977 to supervise the operations of the stock exchanges and develop the Brazilian securities market; regional offices in Brasília and São Paulo; Chair. José Luiz Osorio de Almeida, Filho.

Bolsa de Mercadorias e Futuros—BM&F: Praça Antonio Prado 48, 01010-901 São Paulo, SP; tel. (11) 3199-2000; fax (11) 3242-7565; e-mail webmaster@bmf.com.br; internet www.bmf.com.br; f. 1985; mercantile and futures exchange; offices in Rio de Janeiro, Campo Grande, Santos and New York (USA); CEO Edemir Pinto.

Bolsa de Valores do Rio de Janeiro: Praça XV de Novembro 20, 20010-010 Rio de Janeiro, RJ; tel. (21) 2514-1069; fax (21) 2514-11107; e-mail info@bvrj.com.br; internet www.bvrj.com.br; f. 1845; focuses on the trading of fixed income government bonds and foreign exchange; Chair. Edson Figueiredo Menezes; Supt-Gen. Sergio Póvoa.

Bolsa de Valores de São Paulo (BOVESPA): Rua XV de Novembro 275, CP 3456, 01013-001 São Paulo, SP; tel. (11) 3233-2000; fax (11) 3233-3550; e-mail bovespa@bovespa.com.br; internet www.bovespa.com.br; f. 1890; offices in Rio de Janeiro and Porto Alegre; 550 companies listed in 1997; Pres. Raymundo Magliano, Filho; CEO Gilberto Mifano.

There are commodity exchanges at Paraná, Porto Alegre, Vitória, Recife, Santos and São Paulo.

INSURANCE

Supervisory Authorities

Superintendência de Seguros Privados (SUSEP): Rua Buenos Aires 256, 4°, 20061-000 Rio de Janeiro, RJ; tel. (21) 3086-9800; e-mail gabin@susep.gov.br; internet www.susep.gov.br; f. 1966; within Ministry of Finance; offices in Brasília, São Paulo and Porto

Alegre; Pres. Antônio Palocci, Filho (Minister of Finance); Supt René de Oliveira Garcia Júnior.

Conselho de Recursos do Sistema Nacional de Seguros Privados, de Previdência Abierta e de Capitalização (CRSNSP): Rua Buenos Aires 256, 20061-000 Rio de Janeiro, RJ; tel. (21) 3806-9815; f. 1966 as Conselho Nacional de Seguros Privados (CNSP); changed name in 1998; Sec. Theresa Christina Cunha Martins.

Federação Nacional dos Corretores de Seguros Privados, de Capitalização, de Previdência Privada e das Empresas Corretoras de Seguros (FENACOR): Av. Rio Branco 147, 6°, 20040-006 Rio de Janeiro, RJ; tel. (21) 2507-0033; fax (21) 2507-0037; e-mail leoncio@fenacor.com.br; internet www.fenacor.com.br; Pres. Armando Vergílio dos Santos Junior.

Federação Nacional das Empresas de Seguros Privados e de Capitalização (FENASEG): Rua Senador Dantas 74, Centro, 20031-200 Rio de Janeiro, RJ; tel. (21) 2510-7777; e-mail fenaseg@fenaseg.org.br; internet www.fenaseg.org.br; f. 1951; Pres. João Elisio Ferraz de Campos.

IRB-Brasil Resseguros: Av. Marechal Câmara 171, Castelo, 20020-900 Rio de Janeiro, RJ; tel. (21) 2272-0200; fax (21) 2240-8775; e-mail info@irb-brasilre.com.br; internet www.irb-brasilre.com.br; f. 1939; fmrly Instituto de Resseguros do Brasil; offices in Brasília, São Paulo and Porto Alegre; reinsurance; Pres. Lídio Duarte.

Principal Companies

The following is a list of the principal national insurance companies, selected on the basis of assets. The total assets of insurance companies operating in Brazil were US$ 21,465.7m. in December 2003.

AGF Vida e Previdência, SA: São Paulo, SP; separated from AGF Brasil Seguros and sold to Itau in 2003; total assets US $218.2m. (Dec. 2003).

Bradesco Saúde, SA: Rua Barão de Itapagipe 225, Rio Comprido, Rio de Janeiro, RJ 20261-901; tel. (21) 2503-1101; fax (21) 2293-9489; internet www.bradescosaude.com.br; health insurance; Pres. Luiz Carlos Trabuco Cappi.

Bradesco Seguros e Previdência, SA: Rua Barão de Itapagipe 225, 20269-900 Rio de Janeiro, RJ; tel. (21) 2503-1101; fax (21) 2293-9489; internet www.bradescoseguros.com.br; f. 1934; general; total assets US $354.7m. (Dec. 2003); Pres. Luiz Carlos Trabuco Cappi.

Bradesco Vida e Previdência, SA: Cidade de Deus s/n, Vila Yara, São Paulo, SP; tel. (11) 3684-2122; fax (11) 3684-5068; internet www.bradescoprevidencia.com.br; f. 2001; life insurance; total assets US $8,530.2m. (Dec. 2003); Pres. Marco Antonio Rossi.

Brasilprev Seguros e Prevedência, SA: Rua Verbo Divino 1711, Chácara Santo Antônio, 04719-002 São Paulo, SP; tel. (11) 5185-4240; e-mail atendimento@brasilprev.com.br; internet www.brasilprev.com.br; f. 1993; all classes; 50% owned by Banco do Brasil; total assets US $1,933.5m. (Dec. 2003); Pres. Fuad Noman.

Caixa Seguros: SCN Quadra 01, Bloco A, 15°–17° andares, Asa Norte, 70711-900 Brasília, DF; tel. (61) 429-2400; fax (61) 328-0600; internet www.caixaseguros.com.br; f. 1967; fmrly Sasse, Cia Nacional de Seguros; changed name to Sasse Caixa Seguros in 1998 and as above in 2000; general; total assets US $425.0m. (Dec. 2003); Pres. Thierry Marc Claude Claudon.

Caixa Vida e Previdência, SA: SCN Quadra 1, Bloco A, 15°, Asa Norte, 70711-900 Brasília, DF; tel. (61) 429-2400; fax (61) 328-0600; internet www.caixaprevidencia.com.br; part of Caixa Seguros group; total assets US $451.6m. (Dec. 2003).

Cia de Seguros Aliança do Brasil, SA: Rua Manuel da Nóbrega 1280, 9°, 04001-004 São Paulo, SP; tel. (11) 4689-5638; internet www.aliancadobrasil.com.br; f. 1996; total assets US $324.4m. (Dec. 2003); Pres. Khalid Mohammed Raouf.

HSBC Vida e Previdência(Brasil), SA: Rua Ten. Francisco Ferreira de Souza 805, Bloco 1, Ala 4, Vila Hauer, 81570-340 Curitiba, PR; tel. (41) 217-4555; fax (41) 321-8800; e-mail spariz@hsbc.com.vr; internet www.hsbc.com.br; f. 1938; all classes; total assets US $499.3m. (Dec. 2004); Supt Dir Vilson Andrade; Pension Funds Dir Sidney Pariz.

Icatu Hartford Seguros, SA: Av. Presidente Wilson 231, 10° andar, 20030-021 Rio de Janeiro, RJ; tel. 0800-285-3000; e-mail online@icatu.com.br; internet www.icatu-hartford.com.br; total assets US $329.2m. (Dec. 2003).

Itaú Seguros, SA: Praça Alfredo Egydio de Souza Aranha 100, Bloco A, 04344-920 São Paulo, SP; tel. (11) 5019-3322; fax (11) 5019-3530; e-mail itauseguros@itauseguros.com.br; internet www.itauseguros.com.br; f. 1921; all classes; total assets US $325.4m. (Dec. 2003); Pres. Luiz de Campos Salles.

Itaú Vida e Previdência, SA: internet www.itau.com.br; part of the Itaú group; total assets US $1,808.4m. (Dec. 2003).

Liberty Paulista Seguros, SA: Rua Dr Geraldo Campos Moreira 110, 04571-020 São Paulo, SP; tel. (11) 5503-4000; fax (11) 5505-2122; internet www.libertypaulista.com.br; f. 1906; general; total assets US $156.7m. (Dec. 2003); Pres. LUIS MAURETTE.

Marítima Seguros, SA: Rua Col. Xavier de Toledo 114, 10°, São Paulo, SP; tel. (11) 3156-1000; fax (11) 3156-1712; internet www.maritimaseguros.com.br; f. 1943; Pres. FRANCISCO CAIUBY VIDIGAL; Dir-Gen. MILTON BELLIZIA BELLIZIA, Filho.

Porto Seguro Cia de Seguros Gerais: Rua Guaianazes 1238, 12°, 01204-001 São Paulo, SP; tel. (11) 3366-5199; fax (11) 3366-5140; internet www.portoseguro.com.br; f. 1945; life, automotive and risk; total assets US $518.6m. (Dec. 2003); Pres. ROSA GARFINKEL.

Real Seguros, SA: Rua Samapiao Viana 44, 04004-902 Paraíso, SP; tel. (11) 3054-7000; internet www.realseguros.com.br; f. 1969; in 1999 became part of ABM AMRO; general; total assets US $165.8m. (Dec. 2003).

Real Vida e Previdência, SA: Rua Sampaio Viana 44, 04004-902 Paraíso, SP; tel. (11) 3054-7000; internet www.bancoreal.com.br; f. 1969; became part of the ABM AMRO group in 1999; total assets US $495.1m. (Dec. 2003).

Santander Seguros, SA: internet www.santander.com.br; part of the Banco Santander; total assets US $467.3m. (Dec. 2003).

Sul América, Cia Nacional de Seguros: Rua da Quitanda 86, 20091-000 Rio de Janeiro, RJ; tel. (21) 2506-8585; fax (21) 2506-8807; internet www.sulamerica.com.br; f. 1895; life and risk; total assets US $221.9m. (Dec. 2003); Pres. RONY CASTRO DE OLIVEIRA LYRIO.

Sul América Seguros de Vida e Previdência, SA: Rua Pedro Avacine 73, Morumbi, 05679-160 São Paulo, SP; tel. (11) 3779-7000; fax (11) 3758-8972; internet www.sulamerica.com.br; total assets US $348.3m. (Dec. 2003).

Unibanco AIG Previdência, SA: Av. Eusébio Matoso 1375, 0523-180 São Paulo, SP; tel. (11) 3039-4082; fax (11) 3039-4074; internet www.unibancoseguros.com.br; f. 2001 by merger of Unibanco Seguros and AIG Brasil; part of the Unibanco AIG group; Pres. JOSÉ CASTRO ARAÚJO RUDGE.

Unibanco AIG Seguros: Av. Eusébio Matoso 1375, 05423-180 São Paulo, SP; tel. (11) 3039-4082; fax (11) 3039-4074; internet www.unibancoseguros.com.br; f. 2001 by merger of Unibanco Seguros and AIG Brasil; part of the Unibanco AIG group; life; Pres. JOSÉ CASTRO ARAÚJO RUDGE.

Trade and Industry

GOVERNMENT AGENCIES

Agência Nacional de Petróleo (ANP): SGAM, Quadra 603, Módulo I, 3°, 70830-902 Brasília, DF; tel. (61) 226-0444; fax (61) 226-0699; internet www.anp.gov.br; f. 1998; regulatory body of the petroleum industry; Dir-Gen. VITOR MARTINS.

Agência de Promoção de Exportações do Brasil: SBN Quadra 1, Bloco B, 10° andar, Edif. CNC, 70041-902 Brasília, DF; tel. (61) 426-0202; fax (61) 426-0222; e-mail apex@apexbrasil.com.br; internet www.apexbrasil.com.br; promotes Brazilian exports; Pres. JUAN MANUEL QUIRÓS.

Comissão de Fusão e Incorporação de Empresa (COFIE): Ministério da Fazenda, Edif. Sede, Ala B, 1° andar, Esplanada dos Ministérios, Brasília, DF; tel. (61) 225-3405; mergers commission; Pres. SEBASTIÃO MARCOS VITAL; Exec. Sec. EDGAR BEZERRA LEITE, Filho.

Conselho de Desenvolvimento Comercial (CDC): Bloco R, Esplanada dos Ministérios, 70044 Brasília, DF; tel. (61) 223-0308; commercial development council; Exec. Sec. Dr RUY COUTINHO DO NASCIMENTO.

Conselho de Desenvolvimento Econômico (CDE): Bloco K, 7° andar, Esplanada dos Ministérios, 70063 Brasília, DF; tel. (61) 215-4100; f. 1974; economic development council; Gen. Sec. JOÃO BATISTA DE ABREU.

Conselho de Desenvolvimento Social (CDS): Bloco K, 3° andar, 382, Esplanada dos Ministérios, 70063 Brasília, DF; tel. (61) 215-4477; social development council; Exec. Sec. JOÃO A. TELES.

Conselho Nacional do Comércio Exterior (CONCEX): Fazenda, 5° andar, Gabinete do Ministro, Bloco 6, Esplanada dos Ministérios, 70048 Brasília, DF; tel. (61) 223-4856; f. 1966; responsible for foreign exchange and trade policies and for the control of export activities; Exec. Sec. NAMIR SALEK.

Conselho Nacional de Desenvolvimento Científico e Tecnológico (CNPq): SEPN 507, 3° andar, Brasília, DF; tel. (61) 348-9401; fax (61) 348-3941; e-mail presidencia@cnpq.br; internet www.cnpq.br; f. 1951; scientific and technological development council; Pres. ERNEY FELÍCIO PLESSMANN DE CAMARGO.

Conselho Nacional de Desenvolvimento Rural Sustentável (CNDRS): SCN, Quadra 01, Edif. Brasília Trade Centre, Sala 501, 70711-902 Brasília, DF; tel. (61) 328-5218; fax (61) 328-5175; internet www.cndrs.org.br; f. 2000 to promote sustainable rural development.

Conselho de Não-Ferrosos e de Siderurgia (CONSIDER): Ministério da Indústria e Comércio, Esplanada dos Ministérios, Bloco 7, 7° andar, 70056-900 Brasília, DF; tel. (61) 224-6039; f. 1973; exercises a supervisory role over development policy in the non-ferrous and iron and steel industries; Exec. Sec. WILLIAM ROCHA CANTAL.

Instituto Brasileiro de Geografia e Estatística (IBGE): Centro de Documentação e Disseminação de Informações (CDDI), Rua Gen. Canabarro 706, 2° andar, Maracanã, 20271-201 Rio de Janeiro, RJ; tel. (21) 2142-4781; fax (21) 2142-4933; e-mail webmaster@ibge.gov.br; internet www.ibge.gov.br; f. 1936; produces and analyses statistical, geographical, cartographic, geodetic, demographic and socioeconomic information; Pres. (IBGE) EDUARDO PEREIRA NUNES; Supt (CDDI) DAVID WU TAI.

Instituto Nacional de Colonização e Reforma Agraria (INCRA): Edif. Palácio do Desenvolvimento. 70057-900 Brasília, DF; e-mail incra@incra.gov.br; internet www.incra.gov.br; f. 1970; land reform agency; Pres. RALF HACKBART.

Instituto Nacional de Metrologia, Normalização e Qualidade Industrial (INMETRO): Rua Santa Alexandrina 416, 5°, Rio Comprido, 20261-232 Rio de Janeiro, RJ; tel. (21) 2502–1009; fax (21) 2563-2970; e-mail gabin@inmetro.gov.br; internet www.inmetro.gov.br; f. 1973; in 1981 INMETRO absorbed the Instituto Nacional de Pesos e Medidas (INPM), the weights and measures institute; Pres. ARMANDO MARIANTE CARVALHO.

Instituto de Pesquisa Econômica Aplicada (IPEA): Av. Presidente António Carlos 51, 13° andar, CP 2672, 20020-010 Rio de Janeiro, RS; tel. (21) 3804-8000; fax (21) 2240-1920; e-mail editrj@ipea.gov.br; internet www.ipea.gov.br; also has an office in Brasília; f. 1970; economics and planning institute; Pres. GLAUCO ARBIX.

Secretária de Desenvolvimento da Produção: Esplanada dos Ministérios, Bloco J, 5° andar, Brasília, DF; tel. (61) 2109-7182; internet www.desenvolvimento.gov.br; developing commercial, industrial and service production; Sec. CARLOS GASTALDONI.

REGIONAL DEVELOPMENT ORGANIZATIONS

Agência de Desenvolvimento da Amazônia (ADA): Av. Almirante Barroso 426, Marco, 66090-900 Belém, PA; tel. (91) 210-5440; fax (91) 266-0366; e-mail gabinete@ada.gov.br; internet www.ada.gov.br; f. 2001 to co-ordinate the development of resources in Amazonia; Dir-Gen. DJALMA BEZERRA MELLO.

Agência de Desenvolvimento do Nordeste (ADENE): Praça Ministro João Gonçalves de Souza s/n, Edif. Sudene, 50670-900 Recife, PE; tel. (81) 3416-2108; e-mail webmaster@adene.gov.br; internet www.adene.gov.br; f. 2001 to replace the defunct Superintendência de Desenvolvimiento do Nordeste (SUDENE); Dir-Gen. MANOEL BRANDÃO.

Companhia de Desenvolvimento dos Vales do São Francisco e do Parnaíba (CODEVASF): SGAN, Q 601, Lote 1, Edif. Manoel Novaes, 70830-901 Brasília, DF; tel. (61) 312-4747; fax (61) 311-7814; e-mail divulgacao@codevasf.gov.br; internet www.codevasf.gov.br; f. 1974; promotes integrated development of resources of São Francisco and Parnaíba Valley; Pres. LUIZ CARLOS EVERTON DE FARIAS.

Superintendência da Zona Franca de Manaus (SUFRAMA): Rua Ministro João Gonçalves de Souza s/n, Distrito Industrial, 69075-783 Manaus, AM; tel. (92) 237-1691; fax (92) 237-6549; e-mail gabin@suframa.gov.br; internet www.suframa.gov.br; to assist in the development of the Manaus Free Zone; Supt FLÁVIA SKROBOT BARBOSA GROSSO.

AGRICULTURAL, INDUSTRIAL AND TRADE ORGANIZATIONS

Associação Brasileira de Celulose e Papel—Bracelpa: Rua Afonso de Freitas 409, Bairro Paraíso, 04006-900 São Paulo, SP; tel. (11) 3885-1845; fax (11) 3885-3689; e-mail faleconosco@bracelpa.org.br; internet www.bracelpa.org.br; f. 1932; pulp and paper association; Pres. OSMAR ELIAS ZOGBI.

Associação Brasileira dos Produtores de Algodão—Abrapa: Sector Bancário Norte, Quadra 1, Bloco F, Sala 401, Edif. Palácio da Agricultura, 70040-908 Brasília, DF; tel. and fax (61) 425-2762; e-mail abrapa@abrapa.com.br; internet www.abrapa.com.br; f. 1999; cotton producers' association; Pres. JOÃO LUIZ RIBAS PESSA.

Associação de Comércio Exterior do Brasil (AEB): Av. General Justo 335, 4° andar, 20021-130 Rio de Janeiro, RJ; tel. (21) 2544-0048; fax (21) 2544-0577; e-mail aebbras@aeb.org.br; internet www.aeb.org.br; exporters' association.

Associação Comercial do Rio de Janeiro: Rua da Calendária 9, 11°–12° andares, Centro, 20091-020 Rio de Janeiro, RJ; tel. (21) 2291-1229; fax (21) 2253-6236; e-mail acrj@acrj.org.br; internet www.acrj.org.br; f. 1820; Pres. MARCÍLIO MARQUES MOREIRA.

Centro das Indústrias do Estado de São Paulo (CIESP): Rua Cel. Santos Cardos 537, Jardim Santista, CE, 08730-110 Mogi das Cruzes, SP; tel. 4735-3447; fax 4722-7251; e-mail ciesp@ciesp.com .br; internet www.ciesp.com.br; f. 1928; asscn of small and medium-sized businesses; Pres. CLÁUDIO VAZ.

Companhia de Pesquisa de Recursos Minerais (CPRM): Serviço Geológico do Brasil, Av. Pasteur 404, Urca, 22290-240 Rio de Janeiro, RJ; tel. (21) 2295-5337; fax (21) 2542-3647; e-mail cprm@ cprm.gov.br; internet www.cprm.gov.br; mining research, attached to the Ministry of Mines and Energy; Pres. UMBERTO RAIMUNDO COSTA.

Confederação da Agricultura e Pecuária do Brasil (CNA): SBN, Quadra 01, Bloco F, 3°-5°, Edif. Palácio da Agricultura, 70048-908 Brasília, DF; tel. (61) 424-1400; fax (61) 424-1490; e-mail cna@ cna.org.br; internet www.cna.org.br; f. 1964; national agricultural confederation; Pres. ALYSSON PAULINELLI.

Confederação Nacional do Comércio (CNC): SCS, Edif. Presidente Dutra, 4° andar, Quadra 11, 70327 Brasília, DF; tel. (61) 223-0578; national confederation comprising 35 affiliated federations of commerce; Pres. ANTÔNIO JOSÉ DOMINGUES DE OLIVEIRA SANTOS.

Confederação Nacional da Indústria (CNI): Rua Mariz e Barros 678, 2°, Maracaña, 20270-002 Rio de Janeiro, RJ; tel. (21) 2204-9513; fax (21) 2204-9522; e-mail sac@cni.org.br; internet www.cni.org.br; f. 1938; national confederation of industry comprising 27 state industrial federations; Pres. ARMANDO DE QUEIROZ MONTEIRO METO; First Vice-Pres. CARLOS EDUARDO MOREIRA FERREIRA.

Conselho dos Exportadores de Café Verde do Brasil (CECAFE): Av. Nove de Julho 4865, Torre A, Conj. 63, Chácara Itaim, 01407-200 São Paulo, SP; tel. (11) 3079-3755; fax (11) 3167-4060; internet www.cecafe.com; f. 1999, through merger of Federação Brasileira dos Exportadores de Café and Associação Brasileira dos Exportadores de Café; council of green coffee exporters.

Departamento Nacional da Produção Mineral (DNPM): SAN, Quadra 1, Bloco B, 3° andar, 70040-200 Brasília, DF; tel. (61) 224-7097; fax (61) 225-8274; e-mail webmaster@dnpm.gov.br; internet www.dnpm.gov.br; f. 1934; responsible for geological studies and control of exploration of mineral resources; Dir-Gen. JOÃO R. PIMENTEL.

Empresa Brasileira de Pesquisa Agropecuária (EMBRAPA): SAIN, Parque Rural, W/3 Norte, CP 040315, 70770-901 Brasília, DF; tel. (61) 348-4433; fax (61) 347-1041; f. 1973; attached to the Ministry of Agriculture, Fisheries and Food Supply; agricultural research; Pres. ALBERTO DUQUE PORTUGAL.

Federação das Indústrias do Estado do Rio de Janeiro (FIRJAN): Centro Empresarial FIRJAN, Avda Graça Aranha 1, Rio de Janeiro, RJ; tel. (21) 2563-4389; e-mail centrodeatendimento@ firjan.org.br; internet www.firjan.org; regional manufacturers' association; 102 affiliated sindicates.

Federação das Indústrias do Estado de São Paulo (FIESP): Av. Paulista 1313, 01311-923 São Paulo, SP; tel. (11) 3549-4499; internet www.fiesp.org.br; regional manufacturers' association; Pres. PAULO SKAF.

Instituto Brasileiro do Meio Ambiente e Recursos Naturais Renováveis (IBAMA): Edif. Sede IBAMA, Av. SAIN, L4 Norte, Bloco C, Subsolo, 70800-200 Brasília, DF; tel. (61) 316-1205; fax (61) 226-5094; e-mail cnia@sede.ibama.gov.br; internet www.ibama.gov .br; f. 1967; responsible for the annual formulation of national environmental plans; merged with SEMA (National Environmental Agency) in 1988 and replaced the IBDF in 1989; Pres. EDUARDO MAILIUS.

Instituto Brasileiro do Mineração (IBRAM): SCS, Quadra 2, Bloco D, Edif. Oscar Niemeyer, 11° andar, 70316-900 Brasília, DF; tel. (61) 226-9367; fax (61) 226-9580; e-mail ibram@ibram.org.br; internet ibram.org.br; f. 1976 to foster the development the mining industry; Pres. JOÃO SÉRGIO MARINHO NUNES.

Instituto Nacional da Propriedade Industrial (INPI): Praça Mauá 7, 18° andar, 20081-240 Rio de Janeiro, RJ; tel. (21) 2206-3000; fax (21) 2263-2539; e-mail inpipres@inpi.gov.br; internet www .inpi.gov.br; f. 1970; intellectual property, etc.; Pres. LUIZ OTÁVIO BEAKLINI.

Instituto Nacional de Tecnologia (INT): Av. Venezuela 82, 8° andar, 20081-310 Rio de Janeiro, RJ; tel. (21) 2123-1238; fax (21) 2123-1136; e-mail int@int.gov.br; internet www.int.gov.br; f. 1921; co-operates in national industrial development; Dir JOÃO LUIZ HANRIOT SELASCO.

União Democrática Ruralista (UDR): Brasília, DF; landowners' organization; Pres. LUIZ ANTÔNIO NABHAN GARCIA.

UTILITIES

Electricity

The auctioning of electricity supply contracts began in December 2004.

Centrais Elétricas Brasileiras, SA (ELETROBRÁS): Edif. Petrobrás, Rua Dois, Setor de Autarquias Norte, 70040-903 Brasília, DF; tel. (61) 223-5050; fax (61) 225-5502; e-mail maryann@ eletrobras.gov.br; internet www.eletrobras.gov.br; f. 1962; government holding company responsible for planning, financing and managing Brazil's electrical energy programme; scheduled for division into eight generating cos and privatization; Pres. FIRMINO FERREIRA SAMPAIO NETO.

Centrais Elétricas do Norte do Brasil, SA (ELETRONORTE): SCN, Quadra 6, Conj. A, Blocos B/C, Sala 602, Super Center Venâncio 3000, 70718-500 Brasília, DF; tel. (61) 429-5151; fax (61) 328-1566; e-mail elnweb@eln.gov.br; internet www.eln .gov.br; f. 1973; Pres. BENEDITO APARECIDO CARRARO.

Centrais Elétricas do Sul do Brasil, SA (ELETROSUL): Rua Deputado Antônio Edu Vieira 999, Pantanal, 88040-901 Florianópolis, SC; tel. (48) 231-7000; fax (48) 234-3434; Gerasul responsible for generating capacity; f. 1968; Pres. FIRMINO FERREIRA SAMPAIO NETO.

Companhia de Geração Térmica de Energia Elétrica (CGTEE): Rua Sete de Setembro 539, 90010-190 Porto Alegre, RS; tel. (51) 3287-1500; fax (51) 3287-1566; internet www.cgtee .gov.br; f. 1997; became part of Eletrobrás in 2000; Chair. CALTER LUIZ CARDEAL DE SOUZA; Pres. JÚLIO CESAR RIEMENSCHNEIDER DE QUADROS.

Companhia Hidro Elétrica do São Francisco (CHESF): 333 Edif. André Falcão, Bloco A, Sala 313 Bongi, Rua Delmiro Golveia, 50761-901 Recife, PE; tel. (81) 229-2000; fax (81) 229-2390; e-mail chesf@chesf.com.br; internet www.chesf.com.br; f. 1948; Pres. MOZART DE SIQUEIRA CAMPOS ARAÚJO.

Eletrobrás Termonuclear, SA (Eletronuclear): Rua da Candelária 65, Centro, 20091-020 Rio de Janeiro, RJ; tel. (21) 2588-7000; fax (21) 2588-7200; internet www.eletronuclear.gov.br; f. 1997 by fusion of the nuclear branch of Furnas with Nuclebrás Engenharia (NUCLEN); oprates two nuclear facilities, Angra 1 and 2; Angra 3 under construction; Chair. JOSÉ DRUMMOND SARAIVA; Pres. ZIELI DUTRA THOMÉ, Filho.

Furnas Centrais Elétricas, SA: Rua Real Grandeza 219, Bloco A, 16° andar, Botafogo, 22281-031 Rio de Janeiro, RJ; tel. (21) 2528-3970; fax (21) 2528-4480; e-mail presiden@furnas.com.br; internet www.furnas.com.br; f. 1957; Pres. JOSÉ PEDRO RODRIQUES DE OLIVEIRA.

Espírito Santo Centrais Elétricas, SA (ESCELSA): Rua Sete de Setembro 362, Centro, CP 01-0452, 29015-000 Vitória, ES; tel. (27) 3321-9000; fax (27) 3322-0378; internet www.escelsa.com.br; f. 1968; Pres. JOSÉ GUSTAVO DE SOUZA.

Centrais Elétricas de Santa Catarina, SA (CELESC): Rodovia SC 404, Km 3, Itacorubi, 88034-900 Florianópolis, SC; tel. (48) 231-5000; fax (48) 231-6530; e-mail celesc@celesc.com.br; internet www .celesc.com.br; production and distribution of electricity throughout state of Santa Catarina; Pres. FRANCISCO DE ASSIS KÜSTER.

Comissão Nacional de Energia Nuclear (CNEN): Rua General Severiano 90, Botafogo, 22290-901 Rio de Janeiro, RJ; tel. (21) 2295-9596; fax (21) 2295-86962; e-mail corin@cnen.gov.br; internet www .cnen.gov.br; f. 1956; state organization responsible for management of nuclear power programme; Pres. ODAIR DIAS GONCALVES.

Companhia de Eletricidade do Estado da Bahia (COELBA): Av. Edgard Santos 300, Cabula IV, 41186-900 Salvador, BA; tel. (71) 370-5130; fax (71) 370-5132; Pres. EDUARDO LÓPEZ ARANGUREN MARCOS.

Companhia de Eletricidade do Estado do Rio de Janeiro (CERJ): Rua Visconde do Rio Branco 429, Centro, 24020-003 Niterói, RJ; tel. (21) 2613-7120; fax (21) 2613-7196; e-mail cerj@cerj .com.br; internet www.cerj.com.br; f. 1907; privatized in 1996; Pres. ALEJANDRO DANÚS CHIRIGHIN.

Companhia Energética de Alagoas (CEAL): Av. Fernandes Lima 3496, Gruta de Lourdes, 57057-900 Maceió, AL; tel. (82) 218-9300; internet www.ceal.com.br; f. 1961; Man. Dir JOAQUIM BRITO.

Companhia Energética de Brasília (CEB): SCRS, Quadro 503, Bloco B, Lotes 13/14, Brasília, DF; tel. 0800 610196; e-mail info@ceb .com.br; internet www.ceb.com.br; services in DF; also operates gas distribution co CEBGAS.

Companhia Energética do Ceará (COELCE): Av. Barão de Studart 2917, 60120-002 Fortaleza, CE; tel. (85) 3247-1444; fax (85) 3272-4711; internet www.coelce.com.br; f. 1971; Pres. CARLOS EDUARDO CARVALHO ALVES.

Companhia Energética do Maranhão (CEMAR): Av. Colares Moreira 477, Renascença II, São Luis, MA ; internet www.cemar-ma .com.br; f. 1958 as Centrais Elétricas do Maranhão; changed name as above in 1984; owned by PPL Global, Inc, USA; Tech. Dir MARCELINO MACHADO DA CUNHA NETO.

Companhia Energética de Minas Gerais (CEMIG): Av. Barbacena 1200, 30190-131 Belo Horizonte, MG; tel. (31) 3299-4900; fax (31) 3299-3700; e-mail atendimento@cemig.com.br; internet www .cemig.com.br; fmrly state-owned, sold to a Brazilian-US consortium in May 1997; Pres. DJALMA BASTOS DE MORAIS.

Companhia Energética de Pernambuco (CELPE): Av. João de Barros 111, Sala 301, 50050-902 Recife, PE; tel. (81) 3217-5168; e-mail celpe@celpe.com.br; internet www.celpe.com.br; state distributor of electricity; CEO JOÃO BOSCO DE ALMEIDA.

Companhia Energética de São Paulo (CESP): Av. Nossa Senora do Sabará 5312, Bairro Pedreira, 04447-011 São Paulo, SP; tel. (11) 5613-2100; fax (11) 3262-5545; e-mail inform@cesp.com.br; internet www.cesp.com.br; f. 1966; Pres. MAURO GUILHERME JARDIM ARCE.

Companhia Força e Luz Cataguazes-Leopoldina: Praça Rui Barbosa 80, 36770-000 Cataguases, MG; tel. (32) 3429-6000; fax (32) 3421-4240; internet www.cataguazes.com.br; f. 1905; Pres. MANOEL OTONI NEIVA.

Companhia Paranaense de Energia (COPEL): Rua Coronel Dulcídio 800, 80420-170 Curitiba, PR; tel. (41) 322-3535; fax (41) 331-4145; e-mail copel@mail.copel.com.br; internet www.copel.com .br; f. 1954; state distributor of electricity and gas; Pres. NEY AMINTHAS DE BARROS BRAGA.

Companhia Paulista de Força e Luz: Rodovia Campinas Mogi-Mirim Km 2.5, 10388-900 Campinas, SP; tel. (19) 3253-8704; fax (19) 3252-7644; internet www.cpfl.com.br; provides electricity through govt concessions; Pres. WILSON PINTO FERREIRA JÚNIOR.

Eletricidade de São Paulo, SA (ELETROPAULO): Av. Alfredo Egidio de Souza Aranha 100, 04791-900 São Paulo, SP; tel. (11) 5546-1467; fax (11) 3241-1387; e-mail administracao@eletropaulo .com.br; internet www.eletropaulo.com.br; f. 1899; acquired by AES in 2001; Pres. MARC ANDRÉ PERREIRA.

Indústrias Nucleares do Brasil, SA (INB): Rua Mena Barreto 161, Botofogo, 22271-100 Rio de Janeiro, RJ; tel. (21) 2536-1600; fax (21) 2537-9391; e-mail inbrio@inb.gov.br; internet www.inb.gov.br; Pres. ROBERTO NOGUEIRA DA FRANCA.

Itaipú Binacional: Av. Tancredo Neves 6731, 85856-970 Foz de Iguaçu, PR; tel. (45) 520-5252; e-mail itaipu@ìtaipu.gov.br; internet www.itaipu.gov.br; f. 1974; 1,490 employees (Itaipú Brasil–1998); Dir-Gen. (Brazil) EUCLIDES SCALCO.

LIGHT—Serviços de Eletricidade, SA: Av. Marechal Floriano 168, CP 0571, 20080-002 Rio de Janeiro, RJ; tel. (21) 2211-7171; fax (21) 2233-1249; e-mail light@lightrio.com.br; internet www.lightrio .com.br; f. 1905; electricity generation and distribution in Rio de Janeiro; formerly state-owned, sold to a Brazilian-French-US consortium in 1996; Pres. LUIZ DAVID TRAVESSO.

Regulatory Agency

Agência Nacional de Energia Elétrica (ANEEL): SGAN 603, Módulo J, 70830-030 Brasília, DF; e-mail aneel@aneel.gov.br; internet www.aneel.gov.br; Pres. JERSON KELMAN; Dir EDUARDO HENRIQUE ELLERY, Filho.

Gas

Companhia Distribuidora de Gás do Rio de Janeiro (CEG): Av. Pedro II 68, São Cristovão, 20941-070 Rio de Janeiro, RJ; tel. (21) 2585-7575; fax (21) 2585-7070; internet www.ceg.com.br; f. 1969; gas distribution in the Rio de Janeiro region; privatized in July 1997.

Companhia de Gás de Alagoas, SA (ALGÁS): Rua Comendador Palmeria 129, Farol, 57051-150 Maceió, AL; tel. (82) 216-3600; fax (82) 216-3628; e-mail algas@algas.com.br; internet www.algas.com .br; 51% state-owned; Dir and Pres. Dr GERSON DA FONSECA.

Companhia de Gás de Bahia (BAHIAGÁS): Avda Tancredo Neves 450, Sala 1801, Edif. Suarez Trade, 41820-020 Salvador, BA; tel. (71) 340-9000; fax (71) 341-9001; e-mail bahiagas@bahiagas.com .br; internet www.bahiagas.com.br; 51% state-owned; Pres. Dr LUIZ FERNANDO MUELLER KOSER.

Companhia de Gás do Ceará (CEGÁS): Av. Santos Dumont 7700, 5°-6° andares, 20941-070 Fortaleza, CE; tel. (85) 3265-1144; fax (85) 3265-2026; e-mail cegas@secrel.com.br; internet www.cegas.com.br; 51% owned by the state of Amazonas; Pres. Dr JOSÉ REGO, Filho.

Companhia de Gás de Minas Gerais (GASMIG): Av. Álvares Cabral 1740, 7° andar, 30170-001 Belo Horizonte, MG; tel. (31) 3291-2001; e-mail gasmig@gasmig.com.br; internet www.gasmig.com.br; Pres. DJALMA BASTOS DE MORAIS.

Companhia de Gás de Pernambuco (COPERGÁS): Av. Eng. Domingo Ferreira 4060, 15° andar, 51021-040 Recife, PE; tel. (81) 3463-2000; e-mail copergas@copergas.com.br; internet www .copergas.com.br; 51% state-owned; Pres. Dr ROMERO DE OLIVEIRA E SILVA.

Companhia de Gás do Rio Grande do Sul (SULGÁS): Travessa Francisco Leonardo Truda 40, 90010-050 Porto Alegre, RS; tel. (51) 3227-4111; internet www.sulgas.rs.gov.br; 51% state-owned; Pres. Dr GILES CARRECONDE AZEVEDO.

Companhia de Gás de Santa Catarina (SCGÁS): Rua Antônia Luz 255, Centro Empresarial Hoepcke, 88010-410 Florianápolis, SC; tel. (48) 229-1200; fax (48) 229-1230; e-mail scgasonline.com.br; internet www.scgas.com.br; 51% state-owned; Pres. Dr LUIZ GOMES.

Companhia de Gás de São Paulo (COMGÁS): Rua Augusta 1600, 9° andar, 01304-901 São Paulo, SP; tel. (11) 3177-5000; fax (11) 3177-5359; e-mail comgas@comgas.com.br; internet www .comgas.com.br; f. 1978; distribution in São Paulo of gas; sold in April 1999 to consortium including British Gas PLC and Royal Dutch/Shell Group; Pres. LUIS DOMENECH.

Companhia Paraibana de Gás (PBGÁS): Av. Epitácio Pessoa 4840, Sala 210, 1° andar, Tambaú, 58030-001 João Pessoa, PB; tel. (83) 247-2244; e-mail cicero@pbgas.com.br; internet www.pbgas.com .br; 51% state-owned; Pres. Dr CÍCERO ERNESTO LEITE DE SOUZA.

Companhia Paranaense de Gás (COMPAGÁS): Rua Pasteur 463, 7° andar, Batel, 80250-080 Curitiba, PR; tel. (41) 312-1900; fax (41) 222-6633; e-mail compagas@mail.copel.br; internet www .compagas.com.br; Pres. Dr ANTÔNIO FERNANDO KREMPEL.

Companhia Potiguar de Gás (POTIGÁS): Rua Dão Silveira 3672, Candelária, 59066-180 Natal, RN; tel. (84) 217-3322; fax (84) 217-3309; e-mail ismael@potigas.com.br; internet www.potigas.com .br; 17% state-owned; Pres. Dr ISMAEL WANDERLEY GOMES, Filho.

Companhia Rondoniense de Gás, SA (RONGÁS): Av. Carlos Gomes 1223, Sala 403, Centro, 78903-000 Porto Velho, RO; tel. and fax (69) 229-0333; e-mail rongas@enter-net.com.br; internet www .rongas.com.br; f. 1998; 17% state-owned; Pres. GERSON ACURSI.

Empresa Sergipana de Gás, SA (EMSERGÁS): Rua Dom Bosco 1223 B, Suíça, 49050-220 Aracaju, SE; tel. and fax (79) 211-5213; e-mail emsergas@infonet.com.br; internet www.emsergas.com.br; Pres. Dr LUIZ MACHADO MENDONÇA.

Water

Agua e Esgotos do Piauí (AGESPISA): Av. Mal Castelo Branco 101, Cabral, 64000 Teresina, PI; tel. (86) 2239-300; f. 1962; state-owned; water and waste management; Pres. OLIVÃO GOMES DA SOUSA.

Companhia de Agua e Esgosto de Ceará (CAGECE): Rua Lauro Vieira Chaves 1030, Fortaleza, CE; tel. (85) 3247-2422; internet www.cagece.com.br; state-owned; water and sewerage services; Gen. Man. JOSÉ DE RIBAMAR DA SILVA.

Companhia Algoas Industrial (CINAL): Rodovia Divaldo Suruagy, Km 12, 57160-000 Marechal Deodoro, AL; tel. (82) 269-1100; fax (82) 269-1199; internet www.cinal.com.br; f. 1982; management of steam and treated water; Dir PAULO ALBERQUERQUE MARANHÃO.

Companhia Espírito Santense de Saneamento (CESAN): Av. Governador Bley, 186, Edif. BEMGE, 29010-150 Vitória ES; tel. (27) 3322-8399; fax (27) 3322-4551; internet www.cesan.com.br; f. 1968; state-owned; construction, maintenance and operation of water supply and sewerage systems; Pres. CLÁUDIO DE MORAES MACHADO.

Companhia Estadual de Aguas e Esgotos (CEDAE): Rua Sacadura Cabral 103, 9° andar, 20081-260 Rio de Janeiro, RJ; tel. (21) 2296-0025; fax (21) 2296-0416; internet www.cedae.rj.gov.br; state-owned; water supply and sewerage treatment; Pres. ALBERTO JOSÉ MENDES GOMES.

Companhia Pernambucana Saneamento (COMPESA): Av. Cruz Cabugá 1387, Bairro Santo Amaro, 50040-905 Recife, PE; tel. (81) 421-1711; fax (81) 421-2712; state-owned; management and operation of regional water supply in the state of Pernambuco; Pres. GUSTAVO DE MATTO PONTUAL SAMPAIO.

Companhia Riograndense de Saneamento (CORSAN): Rua Caldas Júnior 120, 18° andar, 90010-260 Porto Alegre, RS; tel. (51) 3215-5691; e-mail ascom@corsan.com.br; internet www.corsan.com .br; f. 1965; state-owned; management and operation of regional water supply and sanitation programmes; Dir DIETER WARTCHOW.

Companhia de Saneamento Básico do Estado de São Paulo (SABESP): Rua Costa Carvalho 300, 05429-000 São Paulo, SP; tel. (11) 3030-4000; internet www.sabesp.com.br; f. 1973; state-owned; supplies basic sanitation services for the state of São Paulo, including water treatment and supply; Pres. ARIOVALDO CARMIGNANI.

TRADE UNIONS

Central Unica dos Trabalhadores (CUT): Rua Caetano Pinto 575, Brás, 03041-000 São Paulo, SP; tel. (11) 3272-9411; e-mail duvaier@cut.org.br; internet www.cut.org.br; f. 1983; central union confederation; left-wing; Pres. Luiz Marinho; Gen. Sec. Gilmar Carneiro.

Confederação Geral dos Trabalhadores (CGT): Rua Tomaz Gonzaga 50, 2° andar, Liberdade, 01506-020 São Paulo, SP; tel. (11) 3209–6577; e-mail cgt@cgt.org.br; internet www.cgt.org.br; f. 1986; fmrly Coordenação Nacional das Classes Trabalhadoras; represents 1,012 labour organizations linked to PMDB, containing 6.3m workers; Pres. Antônio Carlos dos Reis Medeiros; Sec.-Gen. Francisco Canínde Pegado do Nascimento.

Confederação Nacional dos Metalúrgicos (Metal Workers): e-mail imprensa@cnmcut.org.br; internet www.cnmcut.org.br; f. 1985; Pres. Heiguiberto Guiba della Bella navarro; Gen. Sec. Fernando Augusto Moreira Lopes.

Confederação Nacional das Profissões Liberais (CNPL) (Liberal Professions): SAU/SUL, Edif. Belvedere Gr. 202, 70070-000 Brasília, DF; tel. (61) 223-1683; fax (61) 223-1944; e-mail cnpl@cnpl.org.br; internet www.cnpl.org.br; f. 1953; Pres. Luís Eduardo Gautério Gallo; Exec. Sec. José Antônio Brito Andrade.

Confederação Nacional dos Trabalhadores na Indústria (CNTI) (Industrial Workers): Av. W/3 Norte, Quadra 505, Lote 01, 70730-517 Brasília, DF; tel. (61) 274-4150; fax (61) 274-7001; f. 1946; Pres. José Calixto Ramos.

Confederação Nacional dos Trabalhadores no Comércio (CNTC) (Commercial Workers): Av. W/5 Sul, SGAS Quadra 902, Bloco C, 70390-020 Brasília, DF; tel. (61) 217-7100; fax (61) 217-7122; e-mail secretaria@cntc.org.br; internet www.cntc.org.br; f. 1946; Pres. Antônio de Oliveira Santos.

Confederação Nacional dos Trabalhadores em Transportes Marítimos, Fluviais e Aéreos (CONTTMAF) (Maritime, River and Air Transport Workers): Av. Pres. Vargas 446, gr. 2205, 20071 Rio de Janeiro, RJ; tel. (21) 2233-8329; f. 1957; Pres. Maurício Monteiro Sant'Anna.

Confederação Nacional dos Trabalhadores em Comunicações e Publicidade (CONTCOP) (Communications and Advertising Workers): SCS, Edif. Serra Dourada, 7° andar, No 705/709, Q 11, 70315 Brasília, DF; tel. (61) 224-7926; fax (61) 224-5686; f. 1964; 350,000 mems; Pres. Antônio Maria Thaumaturgo Cortizo.

Confederação Nacional dos Trabalhadores nas Empresas de Crédito (CONTEC) (Workers in Credit Institutions): SEP-SUL, Av. W4, EQ 707/907 Lote E, 70351 Brasília, DF; tel. (61) 244-5833; e-mail contec@yawl.com.br; internet www.contec.org.br; f. 1958; 814,532 mems (1988); Pres. Lourenço Ferreira do Prado.

Confederação Nacional dos Trabalhadores em Estabelecimentos de Educação e Cultura (CNTEEC) (Workers in Education and Culture): SAS, Quadra 4, Bloco B, 70070-908 Brasília, DF; tel. (61) 321-4140; fax (61) 321-2704; internet www.cnteec.org.br; f. 1966; Pres. Miguel Abrão Neto.

Confederação Nacional dos Trabalhadores na Agricultura (CONTAG) (Agricultural Workers): SDS, Edif. Venâncio VI, 1° andar, 70393-900 Brasília, DF; tel. (61) 321-2288; fax (61) 321-3229; internet www.contag.org.br; f. 1964; represents 25 state federations and 3,630 syndicates; Pres. Manoel José dos Santos.

Força Sindical (FS): Rua Galvão Bueno 782, Liberdade, São Paulo, SP; tel. (11) 3277-5877; e-mail secgeral@fsindical.org.br; internet www.fsindical.org.br; f. 1991; 6m. mems (1991); Pres. Paulo Pereira da Silva.

Transport

Ministério dos Transportes: see section on the Government (Ministries).

RAILWAYS

In 2003 there were 29,000 km of railway lines. There are also railways owned by state governments and several privately owned railways.

Companhia Brasileira de Trens Urbanos (CBTU): Estrada Velha da Tijuca 77, Usina, 20531-080 Rio de Janeiro, RJ; tel. (21) 2575-3399; fax (21) 2571-6149; internet www.cbtu.gov.br; f. 1984; fmrly responsible for surburban networks and metro systems throughout Brazil; 252 km in 1998; the transfer of each city network to its respective local government was under way; Pres. Luiz Otavio Mota Valadares.

Gerência de Trens Urbanos de João Pessoa (GTU/JP): Praça Napoleão Laureano 1, 58010-040 João Pessoa, PB; tel. (83) 241-4240; fax (83) 241-6388; 30 km.

Gerência de Trens Urbanos de Maceió (GTU/MAC): Rua Barão de Anadiva 121, 57020-630 Maceió, AL; tel. (82) 221-1839; fax (82) 223-4024; 32 km.

Gerência de Trens Urbanos de Natal: Praça Augusto Severo 302, 59012-380 Natal, RN; tel. (84) 221-3355; fax (84) 221-0181; 56 km.

Superintendência de Trens Urbanos de Belo Horizonte (STU/BH-Demetrô): Av. Afonso Pena 1500, 11°, 30130-005 Belo Horizonte, MG; tel. (31) 3250-4021; fax (31) 3250-4053; e-mail metrobh@gold.horizontes.com.br; f. 1986; 21.3 km open in 2002; Gen. Man. M. L. L. Siqueira.

Superintendência de Trens Urbanos de Recife (STU/REC): Rua José Natário 478, Areias, 50900-000 Recife, PE; tel. (81) 3455-4655; fax (81) 3455-4422; f. 1985; 53 km open in 2002; Supt Fernando Antônio C. Dueire.

Superintendência de Trens Urbanos de Salvador (STU/SAL): Praça Onze de Decembro, s/n, Bairro Calçada, 40410-360 Salvador, BA; tel. (71) 313-9512; fax (71) 313-8760; 14 km.

América Latina Logistica do Brasil, SA: Av. Setembro 2645, 80230-010 Curitiba, PR; tel. (41) 321-7459; e-mail call@all-logistica.com; internet www.all-logistica.com; f. 1997; 6,586 km in 2003; Pres. Alexandre Behring Costa.

Companhia Cearense de Transportes Metropolitanos, SA (Metrofor): Rua 24 de Maio 60, 60020-001 Fortaleza, CE; tel. (85) 3455-7000; fax (85) 3212-4848; e-mail metrofor@metrofor.ce.gov.br; internet www.metrofor.ce.gov.br; f. 1997; 46 km.

Companhia Ferroviária do Nordeste: Av. Francisco de Sá 4829, Bairro Carlito Pamplona, 60310-002 Fortaleza, CE; tel. (85) 3286-2525; fax (85) 3286-6156; e-mail kerley@cfn.com.br; internet www.cfn.com.br; 4,534 km in 2003; Dir Martiniano Dias.

Companhia do Metropolitano de São Paulo: Rua Augusta 1626, 01304-902 São Paulo, SP; tel. (11) 3371-7411; fax (11) 3283-5228; internet www.metro.sp.gov.br; f. 1974; 4-line metro system, 57.6 km open in 2002; Pres. Luiz Carlos Frayze David.

Companhia Paulista de Trens Metropolitanos (CPTM): Av. Paulista 402, 5° andar, 01310-000 São Paulo, SP; tel. (11) 3371-1530; fax (11) 3285-0323; e-mail ctpm@ctpm.sp.gov.br; internet www.ctpm.sp.gov.br; f. 1992 to incorporate suburban lines fmrly operated by the CBTU and FEPASA; 286 km; Dir and Pres. Mário Manuel Seabra Rodrigues Bandeira.

Departamento Metropolitano de Transportes Urbanos: SES, Quadra 4, Lote 6, Brasília, DF; tel. (61) 317-4090; fax (61) 226-9546; internet www.dmtu.df.gov.br; the first section of the Brasília metro, linking the capital with the western suburb of Samambaia, was inaugurated in 1994; 38.5 km open in 1997; Dir Leonardo de Faria e Silva.

Empresa de Trens Urbanos de Porto Alegre, SA: Av. Ernesto Neugebauer 1985, 90250-140 Porto Alegre, RS; tel. (51) 3371-5000; fax (51) 3371-1219; e-mail secos@trensurb.com.br; internet www.trensurb.gov.br; f. 1985; 31 km open in 1998; Pres. Marco Maia.

Estrada de Ferro do Amapá (EFA): Av. Santana 429, Porto de Santana, 68925-000 Santana, AP; tel. (96) 231-1719; fax (96) 281-1175; f. 1957; operated by Indústria e Comércio de Minérios, SA; 194 km open in 1998; Dir Supt José Luiz Ortiz Vergulino.

Estrada de Ferro Campos do Jordão: Rua Martin Cabral 87, CP 11, 12400-000 Pindamonhangaba, SP; tel. (22) 3644-7408; fax (22) 3643-2951; internet www.efcj.com.br; f. 1914; operated by the Tourism Secretariat of the State of São Paulo; 47 km open in 1998; Dir Arthur Ferreira dos Santos.

Estrada de Ferro Carajás: Av. dos Portugueses s/n, 65085-580 São Luís, MA; tel. (98) 3218-4000; fax (98) 3218-4530; f. 1985 for movement of minerals from the Serra do Carajás to the port at Ponta da Madeira; operated by the Companhia Vale do Rio Doce; 892 km open in 2002; Supt Juares Salibra.

Estrada de Ferro do Jari: Vila Mongouba s/n, Monte Dourado, 68230-000 Pará, PA; tel. (91) 3736-6526; fax (91) 3736-6490; transportation of timber and bauxite; 68 km open; Dir Armindo Luiz Baretta.

Estrada de Ferro Mineração Rio do Norte, SA: Praia do Flamengo 200, 5° e 6° andares, 22210-030 Rio de Janeiro, RJ; tel. (21) 2205-9112; fax (21) 2545-5717; 35 km open in 1998; Pres. Antônio João Torres.

Estrada de Ferro Paraná-Oeste, SA (Ferroeste): Av. Iguaçu 420-7°, 80230-902 Curitiba, PR; tel. (41) 322-1811; fax (41) 233-2147; internet www.pr.gov.br/ferroeste; f. 1988 to serve the grain-producing regions in Paraná and Mato Grosso do Sul; 249 km in 2003;

privatized in late 1996, Brazilian company, Ferropar, appointed as administrator; Pres. JOSÉ HERALDO CARNEIRO LOBO.

Estrada de Ferros Trombetas: Porto de Trombetas, 68275-000 Oriximiná, PA; tel. (91) 549-7010; fax (91) 549-1482; e-mail jcarlos@mrn.com.br; 30 km; bauxite transport to Trombetas port; operated by Mineração Rio do Norte; Pres. JOSÉ CARLOS SOARES.

Estrada de Ferro Vitória-Minas: Av. Carandaí 1115, 13°, Funcionários, 30130-915 Belo Horizonte, MG; tel. (31) 3279-4545; fax (31) 3279-4676; f. 1942; operated by Companhia Vale do Rio Doce; transport of iron ore, general cargo and passengers; 905 km open in 2003; Dir JOSÉ FRANCISCO MARTINS VIVEIROS.

Ferrovia Bandeirante, SA (Ferroban): Rua Dr Sales de Oliveira 1380, Vila Industrial, 13035-270 Campinas, SP; tel. (19) 3735-3100; fax (19) 3735-3196; e-mail ferroban@ferroban.com.br; internet www.ferroban.com.br; f. 1971 by merger of five railways operated by São Paulo State; transferred to private ownership in Nov. 1998; fmrly Ferrovia Paulista; 4,236 km open in 2003; Dir JOÃO GOUVEIA FERRÃO NETO.

Ferrovia Centro Atlântica, SA: Rua Sapucaí 383, Floresta 30150-904, Belo Horizonte, MG; tel. (31) 3279-5520; fax (31) 3279-5709; e-mail thiers@centro-atlantica.com.br; internet www.fcasa.com.br; f. 1996 following the privatization of Rede Ferroviária Federal, SA; industrial freight; 7,080 km; Man. Dir THIERS MANZANO BARSOTTI.

Ferrovia Norte-Sul: Avda Marechal Floriano 45, Centro, 20080-003 Rio de Janeiro, RJ; tel. (21) 2253-9659; fax (21) 2263-9119; e-mail valecascom@ferrovianortesul.com.br; internet www.ferrovianortesul.com.br; 2,066 km from Belém to Goiânia; Man. Dir LUIZ RAIMUNDO CARNEIRO DE AZEVEDO.

Ferrovia Novoeste, SA: Rua do Rócio 351, 3°, 04552-905 São Paulo, SP; tel. (11) 3845-4966; fax (11) 3841-9252; e-mail silviam@uol.com.br; 1,622 km in 2003; Man. Dir NÉLSON DE SAMPAIO BASTOS.

Ferrovia Tereza Cristina, SA: Rua dos Ferroviários 100, Oficinas, 88702-230 Tubarão, SC; tel. (48) 621-7700; fax (48) 621-7747; e-mail ftc@ftc.com.br; internet www.ftc.com.br; 164 km in 2003; Man. Dir BENONY SCHMIDT, Filho.

Ferrovias Norte do Brasil, SA (FERRONORTE): Rua do Rócio 351, 3° andar, Vila Olímpia, 04552-905 São Paulo, SP; tel. (11) 3845-4966; fax (11) 3841-9252; e-mail jhomero@novoeste.com.br; internet www.ferronorte.com.br; f. 1988; 403 km in 2003; affiliated with Ferrovia Novoeste and Ferroban; Man. Dir NELSON DE SAMPAIO BASTOS.

Metrô Rio: Av. Presidente Vargas 2000, Col. Centro, 20210-031 Rio de Janeiro, RJ; tel. (21) 3211-6300; e-mail sac@metrorio.com.br; internet www.metrorio.com.br; 2-line metro system, 42 km open in 1997; operated by Opportans Concessão Metroviária, SA; Pres. ALVARO J. M. SANTOS.

MRS Logística, SA: Praia de Botafogo 228, Sala 1201E, Ala B, Botafogo, 22359-900, Rio de Janeiro, RJ; tel. (21) 2559-4610; internet www.mrs.com.br; f. 1996; 1,974 km in 2003; CEO JULIO FONTANA NETO.

ROADS

In 2003 there were an estimated 1.7m. km of roads in Brazil, of which less than 10% were paved. Brasília has been a focal point for inter-regional development, and paved roads link the capital with every region of Brazil. The building of completely new roads has taken place predominantly in the north. Roads are the principal mode of transport, accounting for 63% of freight and 96% of passenger traffic, including long-distance bus services, in 1998. Major projects include the 5,000-km Transamazonian Highway, running from Recife and Cabedelo to the Peruvian border, the 4,138-km Cuibá–Santarém highway, which will run in a north–south direction, and the 3,555-km Trans-Brasiliana project, which will link Marabá, on the Trans-Amazonian highway, with Aceguá, on the Uruguayan frontier. A 20-year plan to construct a highway linking São Paulo with the Argentine and Chilean capitals was endorsed in 1992 within the context of the development of the Southern Cone Common Market (Mercosul). In 2004 an agreement was reached to construct a highway linking the Brazilian state of Acre with the coast of Peru.

Departamento Nacional de Estradas de Rodagem (DNER) (National Roads Development): SAN, Quadra 3, Blocos N/O, 4° andar, Edif. Núcleo dos Transportes, 70040-902 Brasília, DF; tel. (61) 315-4100; fax (61) 315-4050; e-mail diretoria.geral@dner.gov.br; internet www.dner.gov.br; f. 1945 to plan and execute federal road policy and to supervise state and municipal roads in order to integrate them into the national network; Exec. Dir ROGÉRIO GONZALES ALVES.

INLAND WATERWAYS

River transport plays only a minor part in the movement of goods. There are three major river systems, the Amazon, Paraná and the São Francisco. The Amazon is navigable for 3,680 km, as far as Iquitos in Peru, and ocean-going ships can reach Manaus, 1,600 km upstream. Plans have been drawn up to improve the inland waterway system and one plan is to link the Amazon and Upper Paraná to provide a navigable waterway across the centre of the country. In 1993 the member governments of Mercosul, together with Bolivia, reaffirmed their commitment to a 10-year development programme (initiated in 1992) for the extension of the Tietê Paraná river network along the Paraguay and Paraná rivers as far as Buenos Aires, improving access to Atlantic ports and creating a 3,442 km waterway system, navigable throughout the year.

Agência Nacional de Transportes Aquaviários: Ministério dos Transportes, SAN, Quadra 3, Blocos N/O, 70040-902 Brasília, DF; tel. (61) 315-8102; Sec. WILDJAN DA FONSECA MAGNO.

Administração da Hidrovia do Nordeste (AHINOR): Rua da Paz 561, 65020-450 São Luiz, MA.

Administração da Hidrovia do Paraguai (AHIPAR): Rua Treze de Junho 960, Corumbá, MS; tel. (67) 231-2841; fax (67) 231-2661; internet www.ahiper.gov.br; Supt PAULO CÉSAR C. GOMES DA SILVA.

Administração da Hidrovia do Paraná (AHRANA): Av. Brigadeiro Faria Lima 1884, 6°, 01451-000 São Paulo, SP; tel. (11) 3034-0270; fax (11) 3815-5435; e-mail ahrana@ahrana.gov.br; internet www.ahrana.gov.br; Supt LUIZ EDUARDO GARCIA.

Administração da Hidrovia do São Francisco (AHSFRA): Praça do Porto 70, Distrito Industrial, 39270-000 Pirapora, MG; tel. (38) 3741-2555; fax (38) 3741-2510; internet www.ahsfra.gov.br; Supt JOSÉ H. BORATO JABUR JÚNIOR.

Administração das Hidrovias da Amazônia Oriental (AHIMOR): Rua Joaquim Nabuco 8, Nazaré, 66055-300 Belém, PA; tel. (91) 241-3995; fax (91) 241-4589; e-mail ahimor@ahimor.gov.br; internet www.ahimor.gov.br.

Administração das Hidrovias do Sul (AHSUL): Praça Oswaldo Cruz 15, 3° andar, 90030-160 Porto Alegre, RS; tel. (51) 3228-3677; fax (51) 3226-9068; Supt JOSÉ LUIZ F. DE AZAMBUJA.

Administração das Hidrovias do Tocantins e Araguaia (AHITAR): Rua 85 971, Setor Sul, 74080-010 Goiânia, GO; tel. (62) 225-1744; e-mail ahitar@terra.com.br; internet www.ahitar.com.br.

Empresa de Navegação da Amazônia, SA (ENASA): Belém, PA; tel. (91) 223-3878; fax (91) 224-0528; f. 1967; cargo and passenger services on the Amazon river and its principal tributaries, connecting the port of Belém with all major river ports; Pres. ANTÓNIO DE SOUZA MENDONÇA; 48 vessels.

SHIPPING

There are more than 40 deep-water ports in Brazil, all but one of which (Imbituba) are directly or indirectly administered by the Government. The majority of ports are operated by state-owned concerns (Cia Docas do Pará, Estado de Ceará, Estado do Rio Grande do Norte, Bahia, Paraíba, Espírito Santo, Rio de Janeiro and Estado de São Paulo), while a smaller number (including Suape, Cabedelo, São Sebastião, Paranaguá, Antonina, São Francisco do Sul, Porto Alegre, Itajaí, Pelotas and Rio Grande) are administered by state governments.

The ports of Santos, Rio de Janeiro and Rio Grande have specialized container terminals handling more than 1,200,000 TEUs (20-ft equivalent units of containerized cargo) per year. Santos is the major container port in Brazil, accounting for 800,000 TEUs annually. The ports of Paranaguá, Itajaí, São Francisco do Sul, Salvador, Vitória and Imbituba cater for containerized cargo to a lesser extent.

Total cargo handled by Brazilian ports in 2002 amounted to 529m. tons, compared with 506m. tons in 2001. Some 43,000 vessels used Brazil's ports in 1998.

Brazil's merchant fleet comprised 482 vessels totalling 3,258,000 grt in December 2003.

Departamento de Marinha Mercante: Coordenação Geral de Transporte Maritimo, Av. Rio Branco 103, 6° e 8° andar, 20040-004 Rio de Janeiro, RJ; tel. (21) 2221-4014; fax (21) 2221-5929; Dir PAULO OCTÁVIO DE PAIVA ALMEIDA.

Port Authorities

Departamento de Portos: SAN, Quadra 3, Blocos N/O, CEP 70040-902 Brasília, DF; Dir PAULO ROBERTO K. TANNENBAUM.

Administração do Porto de Manaus (SNPH): Rua Governador Vitório 121, Centro, 69000 Manaus, AM; tel. (92) 621-4300; fax (92) 635-9464; internet faleconosco@portodemanaus.com.br; internet www.portodemanaus.com.br; private; operates the port of Manaus.

Administração do Porto de São Francisco do Sul (APSFS): Av. Eng. Leite Ribeiro 782, CP 71, 89240-000 São Francisco do Sul, SC; tel. (47) 471-1200; fax (47) 471-1211; e-mail porto@apsfs.sc.gov.br; internet www.apsfs.sc.gov.br; Dir-Gen. ARNALDO S. THIAGO.

Administração dos Portos de Paranaguá e Antonina (APPA): Rua Antonio Pereira 161, 83221-030 Paranaguá, PR; tel. (41) 420-1100; fax (41) 423-4252; internet www.pr.gov.br/portos; Port Admin. Eng. OSIRIS STENGHEL GUIMARÃES.

Companhia Docas do Espírito Santo (CODESA): Av. Getúlio Vargas 556, Centro, 29020-030 Vitória, ES; tel. (27) 3132-7360; fax (27) 3132-7311; e-mail assecs@codesa.com.br; internet www.codesa .com.br; f. 1983; Dir JOÃO LUIZ ZAGANELLI.

Companhia das Docas do Estado de Bahia: Av. da França 1551, 40010-000 Salvador, BA; tel. (71) 243-5066; fax (71) 241-6712; internet www.codeba.com.br; administers the ports of Aracaju, Salvador, Aratu, Ilhéus and Pirapora, and the São Francisco waterway (AHSFRA); Pres. JORGE FRANCISCO MEDAUAR.

Companhia Docas do Estado de Ceará (CDC): Praça Amigos da Marinha s/n, 60182-640 Fortaleza, CE; tel. (85) 3263-1551; fax (85) 3263-2433; internet www.docasdoceara.com.br; administers the port of Fortaleza; Dir MARCELO MOTA TEIXEIRA.

Companhia Docas do Estado de São Paulo (CODESP): Av. Conselheiro Rodrigues Alves s/n, Macuco, 11015-900 Santos, SP; tel. (13) 3233-6565; fax (13) 3222-3068; e-mail codesp@carrier.com.br; internet www.portodesantos.com; administers the ports of Santos, Charqueadas, Estrela, Cáceres, Corumbá/Ladário, and the waterways of Paraná (AHRANA), Paraguai (AHIPAR) and the South (AHSUL); Pres. JOSÉ CARLOS MELLO REGO.

Companhia Docas de Imbituba (CDI): Porto de Imbituba, Av. Presidente Vargas 100, 88780-000 Imbituba, SC; tel. (48) 255-0080; fax (48) 255-0701; e-mail docas@cdiport.com.br; internet www .cdiport.com.br; private-sector concession to administer the port of Imbituba; Man. Dir NILTON GARCIA DE ARAUJO.

Companhia Docas do Pará (CDP): Av. Pres. Vargas 41, 2° andar, 66010-000 Belém, PA; tel. (91) 216-2011; fax (91) 241-1741; internet www.cdp.com.br; f. 1967; administers the ports of Belém, Macapá, Santarém and Vila do Conde, and the waterways of the Eastern Amazon (AHIMOR) and Tocantins and Araguaia (AHITAR); Dir-Pres. CARLOS ACATAUSSÚ NUNES.

Companhia Docas da Paraíba (DOCAS-PB): Rua Presidente João Pessoa, s/n, 58310-000 Cabedelo, PB; internet www.pbnet.com .br/zaitek/porto-pb/index.htm; administers the port of Cabedelo.

Companhia Docas do Rio de Janeiro (CDRJ): Rua do Acre 21, 20081-000 Rio de Janeiro, RJ; tel. (21) 2219-8544; fax (21) 2253-0528; e-mail cdrj@portosrio.gov.br; internet www.portosrio.gov.br; administers the ports of Rio de Janeiro, Niterói, Sepetiba and Angra dos Reis; Pres. ANTÔNIO CARLOS SOARES LIMA.

Companhia Docas do Rio Grande do Norte (CODERN): Av. Hildebrando de Góis 220, Ribeira, 59010-700 Natal, RN; tel. (84) 211-5311; fax (84) 221-6072; administers the ports of Areia Branca, Natal, Recife and Maceió; Dir JOSÉ WALTER DE CARVALHO.

Empresa Maranhense de Administração Portuária (EMAP): Porto do Itaquí, s/n, 65085-370 São Luís, MA; tel. (98) 216-6000; fax (98) 216-6060; internet www.portodoitaqui.com.br; f. 2001 to administer ports of Itaquí as concession from the state of Maranhão; Pres. FERNANDO ANTONIO BRITO, Filho.

Sociedade de Portos e Hidrovias do Estado de Rondônia (SOPH): Terminal dos Milagres 400, Caiari; tel. (69) 229-2134; fax (69) 229-3943; operates the port of Porto Velho; Dir OBEDES OLIVEIRA DE QUEIROZ.

SUAPE—Complexo Industrial Portuário Governador Eraldo Gueiros: Rodovia PE-060, Km 10, Engenho Massangana, 55590-972 Município de Ipojuca, PE; tel. (81) 3527-5000; fax (81) 3527-5064; e-mail presidênciasuape.pe.gov.br; administers the port of Suape.

Superintendência do Porto de Itajaí: Rua Blumenau 5, Col. Centro, 88305-101 Itajaí, SC; tel. (47) 341-8000; e-mail atendimento@portoitajai.com.br; internet www.portoitajai.com.br.

Superintendência do Porto de Rio Grande (SUPRG): Av. Honório Bicalho, s/n, CP 198, 96201-020 Rio Grande do Sul, RS; tel. (53) 231-1366; fax (53) 231-1857; internet www.portoriogrande.com.br; f. 1996; Port Dir LUIZ FRANCISCO SPOTORNO.

Superintendência do Porto de Tubarão: Porto de Tubarão, 29072-970 Vitória, ES; tel. (27) 3228-1053; fax (27) 3228-1682; operated by the Companhia Vale do Rio Doce mining co; Port Dir CANDIDO COTTA PACHECO.

Superintendência de Portos e Hidrovias do Estado do Rio Grande do Sul (SPH): Av. Mauá 1050, 4°, 90010-110 Porto Alegre, RS; tel. (51) 3211-4849; fax (51) 3225-8954; e-mail executiva@sph.rs .gov.br; internet www.sph.rs.gov.br; administers the ports of Porto Alegre, Pelotas and Cachoeira do Sul, the São Gonçalo canal and other waterways.

State-owned Company

Companhia de Navegação do Estado de Rio de Janeiro: Praça 15 de Novembro 21, 20010-010 Rio de Janeiro, RJ; tel. (21) 2533-6661; fax (21) 2252-0524; Pres. MARCOS TEIXEIRA.

Private Companies

Aliança Navegação e Logística Ltda: Av. Pasteur 110, 5°-6°, Botafogo, 22290-240 Rio de Janeiro, RJ; tel. (21) 3873-3500; fax (21) 3873-3569; e-mail contact@rio.alianca.com.br; internet www.alianca .com.br; f. 1950; cargo services to Argentina, Uruguay, Europe, Baltic, Atlantic and North Sea ports; Pres. ARSÉNIO CARLOS NÓBREGA.

Companhia de Navegação do Norte (CONAN): Av. Rio Branco 23, 25° andar, 20090-003 Rio de Janeiro, RJ; tel. (21) 2223-4155; fax (21) 2253-7128; f. 1965; services to Brazil, Argentina, Uruguay and inland waterways; Chair. J. R. RIBEIRO SALOMÃO.

Companhia de Navegação do São Francisco: Av. São Francisco 1517, 39270-000 Pirapora, MG; tel. (38) 3741-1444; fax (38) 3741-1164; Pres. JOSÉ HUMBERTO BARATA JABUR.

Companhia Interamericana de Navegação e Comercio—CINCO: Av. 14 de Março 1700, 79370-000 Ladário, MS; tel. (67) 226-1010; fax (67) 226-1718; e-mail luiz.assy@cinconav.com.br; internet www.cinconav.com.br; f. 1989; Paraguay and Parana Rivers water transportation; Dirs LUIZ ALBERTO DO AMARAL ASSY, MICHEL CHAIM.

Companhia Libra de Navegação: Rua São Bento 8, 8°, Centro, 20090-010, Rio de Janeiro, RJ; tel. (21) 2203-5000; fax (21) 2283-3001; internet www.libra.com.br.

Frota Oceânica e Amazonica, SA (FOASA): Av. Venezuela 110, CP 21-020, 20081-310 Rio de Janeiro, RJ; tel. (21) 2203-3838; fax (21) 2253-6363; e-mail foasa@pamar.com.br; f. 1947; Pres. JOSÉ CARLOS FRAGOSO PIRES; Vice-Pres. LUIZ J. C. ALHANATI.

Petrobrás Transporte, SA (TRANSPETRO): Edif. Visconde de Itaboraí, Av. Presidente Vargas 328, Rio de Janeiro, RJ; internet www.transpetro.com.br; f. 1998; absorbed the Frota Nacional de Petroleiros (FRONAPE) in 1999; transport of petroleum and related products; 55 vessels; Pres. MAURO OROFINO CAMPOS.

Vale do Rio Doce Navegação, SA (DOCENAVE): Av. Graça Aranha 26, 8°–9° andar, 20005-900 Rio de Janerio, RJ; fax (21) 3814-4971; internet www.docenave.com.br; bulk carrier to Japan, Arabian Gulf, Europe, North America and Argentina; Pres. ALVARO DE OLIVEIRA, Filho.

Wilson Sons Agência Marítima: Rua Jardim Botânico 518, 3° andar, 22461-000 Rio de Janeiro, RJ; tel. (21) 2126-4222; fax (21) 2126-4190; e-mail box@wilsonsons.com.br; internet www .wilsonsons.com.br; f. 1837; shipping agency, port operations, towage, small shipyard.

CIVIL AVIATION

There are about 2,014 airports and airstrips and 417 helipads. Of the 67 principal airports 22 are international, although most international traffic is handled by the two airports at Rio de Janeiro and two at São Paulo. There were 16,454 aircraft registered in Brazil in 2003.

Departamento de Aviação Civil: Rua Santa Luiza 651, Castelo, 20030-040 Rio de Janeiro, RJ; tel. (21) 3814-6700; internet www.dac .gov.br; studies, plans and coordinates develops activities of public and private civil aviation; Dir-Gen. Maj.-Brig. CARLOS DE CAMPOS MACHADO.

Empresa Brasileira de Infra-Estrutura Aeroportuária (INFRAERO): SCS, Quadra 04, NR 58, Edif. Infraero, 6° andar, 70304-902 Brasília, DF; tel. (61) 312-3170; fax (61) 312-3105; e-mail fernandalima@infraero.gov.br; internet www.infraero.gov.br; Pres. EDUARDO BOGALHO PETTENGILL.

Principal Airlines

GOL Transportes Aéreos Ltda: Rua Tamios 246, Jardim Aeropuerto, 04630-000 São Paulo, SP; tel. (11) 5033-4200; internet www .voegol.com.br; Man. Dir CONSTANTINO OLIVEIRA JÚNIOR.

Líder Táxi Aéreo, SA: Av. Santa Rosa 123, 30535-630 Belo Horizonte, MG; tel. (31) 3490-4500; fax (31) 3490-4600; internet www .lideraviacao.com.br; helicopters and small jets; f. 1958; Pres. JOSÉ AFONSO ASSUMPÇÃO.

Oceanair Linhas Aéreas Ltda: Av. Marechal Câmara 160, Sala 1532, Centro, 20020-080 Rio de Janeiro, RJ; tel. (21) 2544-2181; fax (21) 2215-7181; internet www.oceanair.com.br; f. 1998; domestic services; Pres. GERMAN EFROMOVICH.

Pantanal Linhas Aéreas Sul-Matogrossenses, SA: Av. das Nações Unidas 10989, 8° andar, São Paulo, SP; tel. (11) 3040-3900; fax (11) 3846-3424; e-mail pantanal@uninet.com.br; internet www .pantanal-airlines.com.br; f. 1993; regional services; Pres. MARCOS FERREIRA SAMPAIO.

TAM Linhas Aéreas, SA (Transportes Aéreos Regionais—TAM): Av. Jurandir 856, Lote 4, 1°, Jardim Ceci, 04072-000 São Paulo, SP; tel. (11) 5582-8811; fax (11) 578-5946; e-mail tamimprensa@tam.com.br; internet www.tam.com.br; f. 1976; scheduled passenger and cargo services from São Paulo to destinations throughout Brazil; Pres. Daniel Mandelli Martin.

VARIG, SA (Viação Aérea Rio-Grandense): Av. Almirante Silvio de Noronha 365, Bloco C, 4°, 20021-010 Rio de Janeiro, RJ; tel. (21) 3814-5869; fax (21) 3814-5703; internet www.varig.com.br; f. 1927; international services throughout North, Central and South America, Africa, Western Europe and Asia; domestic services to major Brazilian cities; cargo services; also operates the domestic regional subsidiary airlines Nordeste and Rio-Sul; Man. Dir Manoel Guedes.

VASP, SA (Viação Aérea São Paulo): Praça Comte-Lineu Gomes s/n, Aeroporto Congonhas, 04626-910 São Paulo, SP; tel. (11) 5532-3000; fax (11) 5542-0880; internet www.vasp.com.br; f. 1933; privatized in Sept. 1990; domestic services throughout Brazil; international services to Argentina, Belgium, the Caribbean, South Korea and the USA; Pres. Wagner Canhedo Azevedo.

Tourism

In 2003 some 4.1m. tourists visited Brazil. In that year receipts from tourism totalled US $3,386m. Rio de Janeiro, with its famous beaches, is the centre of the tourist trade. Like Salvador, Recife and other towns, it has excellent examples of Portuguese colonial and modern architecture. The modern capital, Brasília, incorporates a new concept of city planning and is the nation's show-piece. Other attractions are the Iguaçu Falls, the seventh largest (by volume) in the world, the tropical forests of the Amazon basin and the wildlife of the Pantanal.

Instituto Brasileiro de Turismo (EMBRATUR): SCN, Q 02, Bloco G, 3° andar, 70710-500 Brasília, DF; tel. (61) 224-9100; fax (61) 223-9889; internet www.embratur.gov.br; f. 1966; Pres. Caio Luiz de Carvalho.

Seção de Feiras e Turismo/Departamento de Promoção Comercial: Ministério das Relações Exteriores, Esplanada dos Ministérios, 5° andar, Sala 523, 70170-900 Brasília, DF; tel. (61) 411-6394; fax (61) 322-0833; e-mail docstt@mre.gov.br; internet www.braziltradenet.gov.br; f. 1977; organizes Brazil's participation in trade fairs and commercial exhibitions abroad; Principal Officer Antônio J. M. de Souza e Silva.

Associação Brasileira da Indústria de Hotéis (ABIH): Avda Nilo Peçanha 12, Grups 1005, 20020-100 Rio de Janeiro, RJ; tel. (21) 2533-5768; fax (21) 2533-7632; e-mail abihnacional@abih.com.br; internet www.abih.com.br; f. 1936; hoteliers' association; Pres. Luiz Carlos Nunes; Sec. Marluce Margalhães.

BRUNEI
Introductory Survey

Location, Climate, Language, Religion, Flag, Capital

The Sultanate of Brunei (Negara Brunei Darussalam) lies in South-East Asia, on the north-west coast of the island of Borneo (most of which is comprised of the Indonesian territory of Kalimantan). It is surrounded and bisected on the landward side by Sarawak, one of the two eastern states of Malaysia. The country has a tropical climate, characterized by consistent temperature and humidity. Annual rainfall averages about 2,540 mm (100 ins) in coastal areas and about 3,300 mm (130 ins) in the interior. Temperatures are high, with average daily temperatures ranging from 24°C (75°F) to 32°C (90°F). The principal language is Malay, although Chinese is also spoken and English is widely used. The Malay population (an estimated 66.6% of the total in 2003) are mainly Sunni Muslims. Most of the Chinese in Brunei (11.0% of the population) are Buddhists, and some are adherents of Confucianism and Daoism. Europeans and Eurasians are predominantly Christians, and the majority of indigenous tribespeople (Iban, Dayak and Kelabit— 3.6% of the population) adhere to various animist beliefs. The flag (proportions 1 by 2) is yellow, with two diagonal stripes, of white and black, running from the upper hoist to the lower fly; superimposed in the centre is the state emblem (in red, with yellow Arabic inscriptions). The capital is Bandar Seri Begawan (formerly called Brunei Town).

Recent History

Brunei, a traditional Islamic monarchy, formerly included most of the coastal regions of North Borneo (now Sabah) and Sarawak, which later became states of Malaysia. During the 19th century the rulers of Brunei ceded large parts of their territory to the United Kingdom, reducing the sultanate to its present size. In 1888, when North Borneo became a British Protectorate, Brunei became a British Protected State. In accordance with an agreement made in 1906, a British Resident was appointed to the court of the ruling Sultan as an adviser on administration. Under this arrangement, a form of government that included an advisory body, the State Council, emerged.

Brunei was invaded by Japanese forces in December 1941, but reverted to its former status in 1945, when the Second World War ended. The British-appointed Governor of Sarawak was High Commissioner for Brunei from 1948 until the territory's first written Constitution was promulgated in September 1959, when a further agreement was made between the Sultan and the British Government. The United Kingdom continued to be responsible for Brunei's defence and external affairs until the Sultanate's declaration of independence in 1984.

In December 1962 a large-scale revolt broke out in Brunei and in parts of Sarawak and North Borneo. The rebellion was undertaken by the 'North Borneo Liberation Army', an organization linked with the Parti Rakyat Brunei (PRB—Brunei People's Party), led by Sheikh Ahmad Azahari, which was strongly opposed to the planned entry of Brunei into the Federation of Malaysia. The rebels proclaimed the 'revolutionary State of North Kalimantan', but the revolt was suppressed, after 10 days' fighting, with the aid of British forces from Singapore. A state of emergency was declared, the PRB was banned, and Azahari was given asylum in Malaya. In the event, the Sultan of Brunei, Sir Omar Ali Saifuddin III, decided in 1963 against joining the Federation. From 1962 he ruled by decree, and the state of emergency remained in force. In October 1967 Saifuddin, who had been Sultan since 1950, abdicated in favour of his son, Hassanal Bolkiah, who was then 21 years of age. Under an agreement signed in November 1971, Brunei was granted full internal self-government.

In December 1975 the UN General Assembly adopted a resolution advocating British withdrawal from Brunei, the return of political exiles and the holding of a general election. Negotiations in 1978, following assurances by Malaysia and Indonesia that they would respect Brunei's sovereignty, resulted in an agreement (signed in January 1979) that Brunei would become fully independent within five years. Independence was duly proclaimed on 1 January 1984, and the Sultan took office as Prime Minister and Minister of Finance and of Home Affairs,

presiding over a Cabinet of six other ministers (including two of the Sultan's brothers and his father, the former Sultan).

The future of the Chinese population, which controlled much of Brunei's private commercial sector but had become stateless since independence, appeared threatened in 1985, when the Sultan indicated that Brunei would become an Islamic state in which the indigenous, mainly Malay, inhabitants, known as *bumiputras* ('sons of the soil'), would receive preferential treatment. Several Hong Kong and Taiwan Chinese, who were not permanent Brunei residents, were repatriated.

In May 1985 a new political party, the Parti Kebangsaan Demokratik Brunei (PKDB—Brunei National Democratic Party), was formed. The new party, which comprised business executives loyal to the Sultan, based its policies on Islam and a form of liberal nationalism. However, the Sultan forbade employees of the Government (about 40% of the country's working population) from joining the party. Persons belonging to the Chinese community were also excluded from membership. Divisions within the new party led to the formation of a second group, the Parti Perpaduan Kebangsaan Brunei (PPKB— Brunei National Solidarity Party), in February 1986. This party, which also received the Sultan's official approval, placed greater emphasis on co-operation with the Government, and was open to both Muslim and non-Muslim ethnic groups.

Although the Sultan was not expected to allow any relaxation of restrictions on radical political activities, it became clear during 1985 and 1986 that a more progressive style of government was being adopted. The death of Sir Omar Ali Saifuddin, the Sultan's father, in September 1986 was expected to accelerate modernization. In October the Cabinet was enlarged to 11 members, and commoners and aristocrats were assigned portfolios that had previously been given to members of the royal family. In February 1988, however, the PKDB was dissolved by the authorities after it had demanded the resignation of the Sultan as Head of Government (although not as Head of State), an end to the 26-year state of emergency and the holding of democratic elections. The official reason for the dissolution of the party was its connections with a foreign organization, the Pacific Democratic Union. The leaders of the PKDB, Abdul Latif Hamid and Abdul Latif Chuchu, were arrested, under the provisions of the Internal Security Act, and detained until March 1990. Abdul Latif Hamid died in May of that year. In January 1990 the Government ordered the release of six political prisoners, who had been detained soon after the revolt in 1962.

In 1990 the Government encouraged the population to embrace *Melayu Islam Beraja* (Malay Islamic Monarchy) as the state ideology. This affirmation of traditional Bruneian values for Malay Muslims was widely believed to be a response to an increase in social problems, including the abuse of alcohol and mild narcotics. Muslims were encouraged to adhere more closely to the tenets of Islam, greater emphasis was laid on Islamic holiday celebrations, and the distribution of alcohol was discouraged.

Extremely moderate progress towards reform was apparent in subsequent years. In 1994 a constitutional committee, appointed by the Government and chaired by the Minister of Foreign Affairs, Prince Mohamad Bolkiah, submitted a recommendation that the Constitution be amended to provide for an elected legislature. In February 1995 the PPKB was given permission to convene a general assembly, at which Abdul Latif Chuchu, the former Secretary-General of the PKDB, was elected President. Latif Chuchu was, however, compelled to resign shortly afterwards, owing to a condition of his release from detention in 1990. In May 1998 the PKDB was permitted to hold a further annual general meeting, at which Hatta Zainal Abidin, the son of a former opposition leader, was elected party President.

In February 1997 the Sultan replaced his brother, Prince Jefri Bolkiah, as Minister of Finance. It was rumoured that the Sultan's assumption of the finance portfolio was due to alleged financial disagreements rather than Prince Jefri's frequently criticized extravagant lifestyle. In March the Sultan and Prince Jefri denied accusations of misconduct made by a former winner of a US beauty contest, Shannon Marketic. A US court granted the Sultan immunity from legal action in August, owing to his status as a foreign head of state; this immunity was extended to Prince Jefri in March 1998. Similar allegations against Prince Jefri, submitted to a court in Hawaii, resulted in an undisclosed financial settlement, following the judge's rejection of Prince Jefri's claims to immunity. Marketic subsequently appealed against the granting of exemption from prosecution in her case. Further allegations concerning the extravagant lifestyle of Prince Jefri emerged in a court case in the United Kingdom in February, in which Jefri was being sued for £80m. by two former business associates, Watche (Bob) and Rafi Manoukian. The Manoukian brothers claimed that Prince Jefri had reneged on two property agreements; Prince Jefri was counter-suing them for £100m., alleging that they had exploited their relationship with him to amass considerable wealth. The case, which was unreported in Brunei, was also settled out of court for an undisclosed sum.

Following the dismissal in March 1998, after 14 years in office, of Dato' Dr Haji Johar bin Dato' Haji Noordin, reportedly owing to the inadequacy of his response to the haze over Brunei caused by forest fires in Indonesia and Malaysia, Abdul Aziz assumed responsibility for the health portfolio. The resignations of the Attorney-General, Pengiran Haji Bahrin bin Pengiran Haji Abbas (who was granted leave from his position as Minister of Law), and of the Solicitor-General were accepted by the Sultan in June. An acting Attorney-General and Solicitor-General were appointed, while the Sultan assumed temporary responsibility for the law portfolio. On 10 August the Sultan's son, Prince Al-Muhtadee Billah Bolkiah, was installed as the heir to the throne.

Prince Jefri, who had left Brunei in April 1998, was removed as Chairman of the Brunei Investment Agency (BIA), which controls the country's overseas investments, at the end of July, following the collapse earlier in the month of his business conglomerate, the Amedeo Development Corporation. (The Amedeo Development Corporation was formally liquidated by the High Court of Brunei in July 1999, with reported debts of at least US $3,500m.) Prince Jefri was also removed from the boards of seven communications companies. He claimed that he was the victim of a conspiracy of conservative Islamists, led by his estranged brother, Prince Mohamad Bolkiah (the Minister of Foreign Affairs), and the Minister of Education, Pehin Dato' Haji Abdul Aziz bin Pehin Haji Umar. Prince Jefri's removal from positions of authority took place amid a more rigorous enforcement of the ban on alcohol and the confiscation from retailers of non-Islamic religious artefacts. Abdul Aziz, who replaced Prince Jefri as Chairman of the BIA, also headed an investigation (which was initiated in June) into the finances of the BIA. In September Abdul Aziz announced that large amounts of government funds had been misappropriated during Prince Jefri's tenure as Chairman. In January 2000, following a long period during which the Government made no significant comment about the misappropriation of BIA funds or about the role of the Sultan's younger brother in the affair, Prince Jefri returned to Brunei after many months of self-imposed exile. Private negotiations ensued between Prince Jefri and the parties involved in the investigation. These negotiations failed, however, and in February the Government and the BIA began civil proceedings against Prince Jefri, alleging his improper withdrawal and use of substantial BIA funds during the period in which he had served as Minister of Finance and Chairman of the BIA; 71 other people were named in the action, including Prince Jefri's eldest son, Prince Muda Abdul Hakeem, and his private secretary. In May an out-of-court settlement was reached between Prince Jefri and the prosecuting parties, in accordance with which all of Prince Jefri's assets, both in Brunei and overseas, that had been acquired with funds derived from the BIA were to be returned to the State. These assets were sold for £5.5m. at a public auction in August 2001.

In October 2000 Haji Awang Kassim, Prince Jefri's former confidential secretary, who was also former deputy managing director of the BIA and a prominent figure in Amedeo management, was arrested, following his extradition from the Philippines. Civil proceedings were also instigated against another six of Prince Jefri's former colleagues. In the mean time, legal wrangling over responsibility for Amedeo's huge losses continued. In October 2001 the Sultan, dissatisfied with the unsuccessful and expensive attempts by leading international accountancy and law companies, requested his newly created local company, Global Evergreen, to resolve the long-standing dis-

pute with more than 300 creditors who were owed an estimated B $1,000m. Negotiations proceeded swiftly, and creditors were strongly recommended to accept a new, highly favourable offer whereby they would be repaid on a 'sliding scale' according to the magnitude of their claim. Larger claims would be dealt with on an individual basis. The settlement brought to an end much of the legal contention arising from the Government's closure of the company two years previously.

In May 2002 it was reported that 13 foreign Global Evergreen employees (of whom three were citizens of Australia, four of the United Kingdom, five of New Zealand and one of Malaysia), who had been investigating the whereabouts of the state funds that had disappeared as a result of the Amedeo scandal, had been refused permission to leave the country, ostensibly owing to visa irregularities. It was thought that, during the course of their investigation, they had angered both the chairman of the company, Minister of Education Pehin Dato' Haji Abdul Aziz bin Pehin Haji Umar, and the Minister of Home Affairs, Pehin Dato' Haji Isa bin Pehin Haji Ibrahim. They were granted permission to leave Brunei shortly afterwards. In August the Sultan formally swore in Dato' Seri Paduka Dr Haji Ahmad bin Haji Jumat as the Minister of Development and Pehin Dato' Haji Abu Bakar bin Haji Apong as the Minister of Health. Meanwhile, following the introduction in October 2001 of a Local Newspapers (Amendment) Order establishing more stringent controls over Brunei's newspapers, the English-language *News Express* was forced to shut down its operations in September 2002; it had been unable to comply with new financial requirements.

In March 2004 it was reported that a businessman and two retired senior army and police intelligence officers had been imprisoned without trial under the Internal Security Act for allegedly 'leaking' government secrets. The police-officer, Nordin bin Haji Mohamad Noor, was also accused of treason, having allegedly provided classified documents to a foreign country.

In July 2004 the Sultan announced that Brunei's Legislative Council, suspended since 1984, would be reconvened later in the year in order to debate several proposed amendments to the Constitution. However, it was reported that the state of emergency that had been in place in the country since 1962 would not be lifted and that the council would be appointed, rather than elected. In September the 21-member Council was duly convened and later in that month it approved a series of amendments to the Constitution. These envisaged, amongst other changes, the direct election of 15 members of an expanded 45-member Legislative Council, although the remaining 30 members would be appointed by the Sultan. No schedule was established for the holding of the elections, and it was debatable how far the changes represented genuine progress towards democracy in Brunei.

In February 2000 the Brunei Darussalam Economic Council (BDEC), which had been established in September 1998 to explore ways of improving the Sultanate's economy, released a report in which it warned that Brunei's economy was becoming increasingly unsustainable. The report was endorsed by the Sultan, who appointed Prince Mohamad to oversee the implementation of the economic recovery plan recommended by the BDEC. In his address to mark Brunei's 16th National Day, also in February, the Sultan focused on the issue of the economy and the importance of the development of alternative sources of revenue, in an unprecedented acknowledgement of the country's fundamental economic problems. In November 2000 the Sultan launched the Islamic Development Bank of Brunei, as part of his efforts to create an international Islamic banking centre and transform Brunei into one of the region's most important financial centres. In September 2004 the IMF published a report stating that Brunei's principal challenge over the next 20 years would be to preserve its high standard of living in the face of the continued depletion of its petroleum reserves.

Relations with the United Kingdom, meanwhile, had become strained during 1983, following the Brunei Government's decision, in August, to transfer the management of its investment portfolio from the British Crown Agents to the newly created BIA. However, normal relations were restored in September, when the British Government agreed that a battalion of Gurkha troops, stationed in Brunei since 1971, should remain in Brunei after independence, at the Sultanate's expense, specifically to guard the oil and gas fields.

Brunei has developed close relations with the members of the Association of South East Asian Nations (ASEAN, see p. 162), in particular Singapore, and became a full member of the organization immediately after independence. Brunei also joined the UN, the Commonwealth (see p. 181) and the Organization of the Islamic Conference (see p. 327) in 1984. In September 1992 Brunei was formally admitted to the Non-aligned Movement (see p. 384). In late 1991 Brunei established diplomatic relations with the People's Republic of China at ambassadorial level. As a member of ASEAN, Brunei's relations with Viet Nam improved during 1991 (following Viet Nam's withdrawal from Cambodia in September 1989). In February 1992 diplomatic relations were formally established with Viet Nam during a visit to Brunei by the Vietnamese Prime Minister. In October 1993 the Brunei Government announced the establishment of diplomatic relations at ambassadorial level with Myanmar.

In July 1990, in response to the uncertainty over the future of US bases in the Philippines (see the chapter on the Philippines), Brunei joined Singapore in offering the USA the option of operating its forces from Brunei. A bilateral memorandum of understanding was subsequently signed, providing for up to three visits a year to Brunei by US warships. Under the memorandum, Brunei forces were to train with US personnel.

Conflicting claims (from Brunei, Viet Nam, the People's Republic of China, the Philippines, Malaysia and Taiwan) to all, or some, of the uninhabited Spratly Islands, situated in the South China Sea, remained a source of tension in the region. Brunei is the only claimant not to have stationed troops on the islands, which are both strategically important and possess potentially large reserves of petroleum. During the 1990s attempts to resolve the dispute through a negotiated settlement resulted in little progress, and military activity in the area increased. Talks at the annual summit meeting of ASEAN ministers of foreign affairs held in Hanoi, Viet Nam, in July 2001 failed to make any further advances in ending the impasse. However, during the annual ASEAN summit meeting held in Phnom-Penh, Cambodia, in November 2002, the members of the grouping signed an agreement with China approving a 'code of conduct' for the islands, which was aimed at resolving the conflict.

In February 2000 Brunei hosted its first Asia-Pacific Economic Co-operation (APEC, see p. 155) Senior Officials' Meeting, attended by 3,000 delegates from 21 countries. In April an ASEAN Regional Forum (ARF) meeting to discuss security issues was held in Brunei. In November Brunei hosted the annual summit meeting of APEC leaders; attended by some 6,000 delegates, this was the largest international event ever held in the country.

In an attempt to promote tourism and enhance the nation's international standing, in January 2001 the Sultan launched 'Visit Brunei Year' and 'Visit ASEAN Year 2002', in association with the regional Asian Tourism Forum. In August 2001 Brunei was the venue for the first International Islamic Exposition, attended by representatives from 25 other countries. In November Brunei hosted the seventh summit meeting of ASEAN leaders, which was also attended by representatives from the People's Republic of China, Japan and South Korea. At the end of the meeting Brunei pledged its support for a programme proposed by Philippine President Gloria Macapagal Arroyo, which focused on encouraging close regional co-operation in countering international terrorism in the aftermath of the September suicide attacks on the USA. In late July and early August 2002 the 35th ASEAN Ministerial Meeting, the ninth ARF and the Post-Ministerial Meeting were held in Brunei; ASEAN leaders subsequently signed a Declaration on Counter-Terrorism with the USA. In September 2002 the 34th ASEAN Economic Ministers' Meeting was also convened in the country.

Government

The 1959 Constitution confers supreme executive authority on the Sultan. He is assisted and advised by four Constitutional Councils: the Religious Council, the Privy Council, the Council of Cabinet Ministers and the Council of Succession. Following the rebellion of 1962, certain provisions of the Constitution (including those pertaining to elections and to a fifth Council, the Legislative Council) were suspended, and the Sultan has since ruled by decree. However, in September 2004 the Legislative Council was convened for the first time since the country became independent in 1984 and approved several constitutional amendments, including one providing for the direct election of 15 members of an expanded 45-member Legislative Council. The remaining members were to be appointed by the Sultan. No timetable was established for the holding of the elections.

Defence

At 1 August 2004 the Royal Brunei Malay Regiment numbered 7,000 (including 700 women): army 4,900; navy 1,000; air force 1,100. Military service is voluntary, but only Malays are eligible for service. Paramilitary forces comprised an estimated 3,750, including 1,750 Royal Brunei Police and a Gurkha Reserve Unit numbering some 2,000. Defence expenditure in 2004 was budgeted at an estimated B \$475m. One Gurkha battalion of the British army, comprising about 1,120 men, has been stationed in Brunei since 1971. There are also about 500 troops from Singapore operating a training school in Brunei.

Economic Affairs

In 1998, according to estimates by the World Bank, Brunei's gross national income (GNI), measured at average 1996–98 prices, was US \$7,754m., equivalent to US \$24,100 per head (or US \$24,910 on an international purchasing-power parity basis). In 1990–2003, it was estimated, the population increased by an annual average of 2.5%, while gross domestic product (GDP) per head decreased, in real terms, by an average of 0.7% per year during 1990–98. Brunei's overall GDP increased at an estimated average annual rate of 1.5% during 1990–2000. Real GDP grew by 3.1% in 2001, by 2.8% in 2002 and by 3.1% in 2003.

Agriculture (including forestry and fishing) employed less than an estimated 0.6% of the working population and provided an estimated 3.5% of GDP in 2003. In 2000 an estimated 1.3% of the total land area was cultivated; the principal crops include rice, cassava, bananas and pineapples. In the 1990s Brunei imported about 80% of its total food requirements. During 1990–98 agricultural GDP increased, in real terms, at an average annual rate of 2.7%. Agricultural GDP increased by an estimated 1.8% in 2000 and by an estimated 2.3% in 2001.

Industry (comprising mining, manufacturing, construction and utilities) employed 24.1% of the working population in 1991 and contributed an estimated 44.7% of GDP in 2003. Total industrial GDP increased at an average annual rate of 1.2% in 1990–98. Industrial GDP, including oil and gas services, increased by an average of 6.6% per year in 1993–97. Industrial GDP increased by an estimated 2.1% in 1997, but declined by 1.0% in 1998.

Brunei's economy depends almost entirely on its petroleum and natural gas resources. Mining and quarrying employed only 5.0% of the working population in 1991, but the petroleum sector provided an estimated 36.3% of GDP in 2001. Proven reserves of petroleum at the end of 2003 amounted to 1,100m. barrels, sufficient to sustain production at that year's levels (averaging 214,000 barrels per day) for approximately 14 years. Output of natural gas in 2003 totalled 12,400m. cu m, from proven reserves at the end of that year of some 350,000m. cu m (sustainable for less than 29 years). Crude petroleum, natural gas and petroleum products together accounted for an estimated 89.7% of total export earnings in 2000. The GDP of the petroleum and gas sector declined by an annual average of 0.3% in 1990–97 and by an estimated 1.6% in 1998. However, in 2002 sectoral GDP increased by 3.2% and in 2003 it increased by 3.6%.

Manufacturing is dominated by petroleum refining. The sector employed 3.8% of the working population in 1991 (increasing to 5.4% in 1995) and, together with mining and quarrying, contributed an estimated 40.1% of GDP in 2003. Since the mid-1980s Brunei has attempted to expand its manufacturing base. In the mid-1990s the textile industry provided the largest non-oil and -gas revenue; other industries included cement, mineral water, canned food, dairy products, silica sands products, footwear and leather products, the design and manufacture of printed circuits, publishing and printing. Manufacturing GDP (including mining and quarrying) increased by an estimated 3.5% in 2000 and by an estimated 1.0% in 2001.

Services employed 73.7% of the working population in 1991 and provided an estimated 51.8% of GDP in 2003. In that year the sector comprising wholesale and retail trade, restaurants and hotels contributed 9.5% of GDP, and the finance sector 8.5%. Plans were under way to develop Brunei as a regional centre for finance and banking. The GDP of the banking and finance sector increased by an annual average of 7.7% in 1993–97 and by an estimated 3.8% in 1998. The tourism sector was also being actively promoted as an important part of Brunei's policy of diversification away from its reliance on petroleum and natural gas. In 2000 1.3m. people visited Brunei, and in 1998 receipts from tourism totalled US \$37m. During 1990–98 the combined GDP of the service sectors increased, in real terms, at an average rate of 3.5% per year. GDP of the services sector increased by an estimated 7.1% in 1997 and by 3.9% in 1998.

In 2003 Brunei recorded a visible trade surplus of B \$5,513.0m. and, as a result of high investment income from abroad, in the same year there was a surplus of B \$7,499.8m. on the current account of the balance of payments. In 2003 the principal source of imports (20.2%) was Malaysia; other major suppliers were Singapore, the USA, Japan and the People's Republic of China. The principal market for exports in that year was Japan, which accounted for 41.0% of total exports (mainly natural gas on a long-term contract); other significant purchasers were the Republic of Korea (also a purchaser of natural gas), Thailand and the USA. Principal imports comprised machinery and transport equipment, basic manufactures, food and live animals and miscellaneous manufactured articles; principal exports were mineral fuels and lubricants.

In 2002 there was a budgetary deficit of B \$378.5m. Brunei has no external public debt. International reserves were unofficially estimated at US \$38,000m. in 1997 but were estimated to have declined to US \$20,000m. in late 1998. Annual inflation averaged 1.5% in 1992–2002; consumer prices decreased by 2.3% in 2002, but increased by 0.3% in 2003. Foreign workers, principally from Malaysia and the Philippines, have helped to ease the labour shortage resulting from the small size of the population, and comprised about 41% of the labour force in 2000, compared with 30% in 1998 (owing to an exodus of foreign workers in that year). However, the rate of unemployment was estimated at 3.5% in 2002, reflecting a shortage of non-manual jobs for the well-educated Bruneians.

Brunei is a member of the Association of South East Asian Nations (ASEAN, see p. 162). In October 1991 the member states formally announced the establishment of the ASEAN Free Trade Area (AFTA), which was to be implemented over 15 years (later reduced to 10), and, as a member of ASEAN, Brunei endorsed Malaysia's plan for an East Asia Economic Caucus. AFTA was formally established in 2002. Brunei was a founder member of the Asia-Pacific Economic Co-operation (APEC, see p. 155) forum, initiated in November 1989, and is also a member of the UN Economic and Social Commission for Asia and the Pacific (ESCAP, see p. 31), which aims to accelerate economic progress in the region. In 1994 the East ASEAN Growth Area (EAGA) was established, encompassing Mindanao, in the Philippines, Sarawak and Sabah, in Malaysia, Kalimantan and Sulawesi, in Indonesia, and Brunei.

The eighth (2001–05) National Development Plan continued the emphasis of the sixth (1991–95) and seventh (1996–2000) Plans on diversification of the economy to reduce the country's dependence on income from petroleum and natural gas. In 1996 the Government announced proposals to develop Brunei as a Service Hub for Trade and Tourism (SHuTT) by 2003, following earlier plans for the development of the private sector and the conversion of Brunei into a regional centre for banking and finance. Various measures were taken to accelerate the broadening of Brunei's economic base, which had been impeded by high labour costs, a limited internal market and a lack of a domestic entrepreneurial culture. However, the regional financial crisis, which began in 1997, resulted in an economic downturn in Brunei. The situation was compounded by a significant decline in the international price of petroleum from mid-1997, by the huge financial losses arising from alleged mismanagement of the Brunei Investment Agency (BIA), and by the collapse of the Amedeo Development Corporation, which was responsible for many building projects in Brunei (see Recent History). Concerns over the future of the Sultanate's economy continued to increase; a report released by the Brunei Darussalam Economic Council (BDEC) in February 2000 warned of its unsustainable nature. In December 2000, however, the discovery of significant new oil and gas reserves by Brunei Shell Petroleum provided a stimulus for renewed activity in the petroleum sector. While the disputes arising from the collapse of the Amedeo Corporation were largely resolved by the Sultan's formation of Global Evergreen in 2001, foreign investors continued to be deterred by the repercussions of the scandal. In early 2003 the Brunei Economic Development Board announced plans to attract foreign investment in the country through the solicitation of proposals for the development of a gas pipeline, power plant and jetty at Sungai Liang, as well as the develop-

ment of an additional port facility at Pulau Muara Besar; it was hoped that the projects would create an estimated 6,000 jobs and attract US \$4,500m. of investment over the next five years. Meanwhile, a report issued by the Asia-Pacific Economic forum focused on the need for Brunei's Government to improve levels of co-ordination among government agencies and thus overcome the challenges to increasing foreign investment posed by the slow bureaucratic procedures and a lack of transparency. In September 2004 the IMF released a report stating that Brunei's main challenge in the coming years would be to preserve its high living standards in the face of the ongoing depletion of its natural resources. Wide-ranging structural reforms would be necessary if the Government was to be successful in diversifying the country's economy and reducing its reliance on the oil and gas sector as the engine of economic growth. In particular, if the Government was to focus on developing the country as a regional financial centre, improved regulatory and supervisory measures would need to be implemented in order to prevent money laundering and encourage investment. The IMF predicted that GDP growth in 2004 would be approximately 1%.

Education

Education is free and is compulsory for 12 years from the age of five years. Islamic studies form an integral part of the school curriculum. Pupils who are Brunei citizens and reside more than 8 km (5 miles) from their schools are entitled to free accommodation in hostels, free transport or a subsistence allowance. Schools are classified according to the language of instruction, i.e. Malay, English or Chinese (Mandarin). In 1996 enrolment at pre-primary level was equivalent to 53% of children in the relevant age-group (males 53%; females 53%). Primary education lasts for six years from the age of six years. Secondary education, usually beginning at 12 years of age, lasts for seven years, comprising a first cycle of three years (lower secondary), a second of two years (upper secondary) and a third of two years (pre-tertiary). In 1996 enrolment at primary level was equivalent to 106% of children in the relevant age-group (males 109%; females 104%), while the comparable enrolment ratio at secondary level was 77% (males 72%; females 82%). In 2003 there were seven vocational colleges, one teacher-training college and two institutes of higher education, including one university. The University of Brunei Darussalam was formally established in 1985, but many students continue to attend universities abroad, at government expense. In 1994 enrolment at tertiary level was equivalent to 6.6% of the relevant age-group (males 5.3%; females 8.0%). Of total ordinary expenditure by the Government in 1997, 13.5% (B \$347m.) was for the Ministry of Education.

Public Holidays

2005: 1 January (New Year's Day), 21 January† (Hari Raya Aidiladha, Feast of the Sacrifice), 9 February* (Chinese New Year), 10 February† (Hijrah, Islamic New Year), 23 February (National Day), 21 April† (Hari Mouloud, Birth of the Prophet), 31 May (Royal Brunei Armed Forces Day), 15 July (Sultan's Birthday), 2 September† (Israk Mikraj, Ascension of the Prophet Muhammad), 5 October† (Beginning of Ramadan), 20 October† (Memperingati Nuzul Al-Quran, Anniversary of the Revelation of the Koran), 4 November† (Hari Raya Aidilfitri, end of Ramadan).

2006: 1 January (New Year's Day), 11 January† (Hari Raya Aidiladha, Feast of the Sacrifice), 29 January* (Chinese New Year), 31 January† (Hijrah, Islamic New Year), 23 February (National Day), 11 April† (Hari Mouloud, Birth of the Prophet), 31 May (Royal Brunei Armed Forces Day), 15 July (Sultan's Birthday), 22 August† (Israk Mikraj, Ascension of the Prophet Muhammad), 24 September† (Beginning of Ramadan), 9 October† (Memperingati Nuzul Al-Quran, Anniversary of the Revelation of the Koran), 24 October† (Hari Raya Aidilfitri, end of Ramadan).

*The first day of the first moon of the lunar calendar.

† These holidays are dependent on the Islamic lunar calendar and may vary by one or two days from the dates given.

Weights and Measures

The imperial system is in operation but local measures of weight and capacity are used. These include the gantang (1 gallon), the tahil (11/3 oz) and the kati (11/3 lb).

Statistical Survey

Source (unless otherwise stated): Department of Economic Planning and Development, Prime Minister's Office, Block 2A, Jalan Ong Sum Ping, Bandar Seri Begawan BA 1311; tel. 2244433; fax 2230236; e-mail info@jpke.gov.bn; internet www.depd.gov.bn.

AREA AND POPULATION

Area: 5,765 sq km (2,226 sq miles); *By District:* Brunei/Muara 570 sq km (220 sq miles), Seria/Belait 2,725 sq km (1,052 sq miles), Tutong 1,165 sq km (450 sq miles), Temburong 1,305 sq km (504 sq miles).

Population (excluding transients afloat): 260,482 at census of 7 August 1991; 332,844 (males 168,925, females 163,919) at census of 21 August 2001; 348,800 (males 176,300, females 172,500) in 2003 (official estimate). *By District* (official estimates, 2003): Brunei/Muara 242,600; Seria/Belait 58,000; Tutong 39,600; Temburong 8,600.

Density (2003): 60.5 per sq km.

Ethnic Groups (2003, official estimates): Malay 232,200, Chinese 38,200, Other indigenous 12,500, Others 65,900, Total 348,800.

Principal Towns: Bandar Seri Begawan (capital): population 27,285 at 2001 census, 45,900 at 1991 census; Kuala Belait: population 21,200 at 1991 census; Seria: population 21,100 at 1991 census; Tutong: population 13,000 at 1991 census. *Mid-2003* (UN estimate, incl. suburbs): Bandar Seri Begawan 60,874 (Source: UN, *World Urbanization Prospects: The 2003 Revision*).

Births, Marriages and Deaths (registrations, 2002): Live births 7,464 (birth rate 21.9 per 1,000); Deaths 1,041 (death rate 3.1 per 1,000); Marriages 2,288 (marriage rate 6.3 per 1,000 in 1999).

Expectation of Life (WHO estimates, years at birth): 76.1 (males 74.8; females 77.4) in 2002. Source: WHO, *World Health Report*.

Economically Active Population (persons aged 15 years and over, 2001 census, provisional): Agriculture, hunting, forestry and fishing 1,994; Mining and quarrying 3,954; Manufacturing 12,455; Electricity, gas and water 2,639; Construction 12,301; Trade, restaurants and hotels 20,038; Transport, storage and communications 4,803; Financing, insurance, real estate and business services 8,190; Community, social and personal services 79,880; *Total employed* 146,254 (males 85,820, females 60,434); Unemployed 11,340 (males 6,734, females 4,606); *Total labour force* 157,594 (males 92,554, females 65,040). *Mid-2003* (estimates): Agriculture, etc. 1,000; Total labour force 170,000 (Source: FAO).

HEALTH AND WELFARE

Key Indicators

Total Fertility Rate (children per woman, 2002): 2.5.

Under-5 Mortality Rate (per 1,000 live births, 2003): 6.

HIV/AIDS (% of persons aged 15–49, 2003): <0.1.

Physicians (per 1,000 head, 2002): 0.87.

Health Expenditure (2001): US $ per head (PPP): 638.

Health Expenditure (2001): % of GDP: 3.1.

Health Expenditure (2001): public (% of total): 79.4.

Human Development Index (2002): ranking: 33.

Human Development Index (2002): value: 0.867.

For sources and definitions, see explanatory note on p. vi.

AGRICULTURE, ETC.

Principal Crops ('000 metric tons, 2003): Rice (paddy) 0.6, Vegetables 10.4, Fruit 4.7.

Livestock ('000 head, 2003): Cattle 1.4, Buffaloes 5.9, Goats 3.1, Poultry 12,093.

Livestock Products (FAO estimates, '000 metric tons, 2002): Beef and veal 3.3, Poultry meat 12.8, Poultry eggs 5.9, Cattle hides (fresh) 0.6. Source: FAO.

Forestry ('000 cubic metres, 2003): Round timber 101.1; Sawn timber 50.9; Firewood 0.1; Bakau poles 89.9; Charcoal ('000 kg) 28.4; Poles ('000 pieces) 3.1.

Fishing (metric tons, live weight, 2003): Capture 14,546.4; Aquaculture 583.3; *Total catch* 15,129.7.

MINING

Production (2003): Crude petroleum ('000 barrels, incl. condensate) 75,642; Natural gas (million cu m, gross) 12,702. Source: US Geological Survey.

INDUSTRY

Production ('000 barrels, unless otherwise indicated, 2003): Motor spirit (petrol) 1,717; Distillate fuel oils 1,195; Residual fuel oil 511; Cement ('000 metric tons) 235; Electric energy (million kWh, 2000, estimate) 2,579. Source: mainly US Geological Survey.

FINANCE

Currency and Exchange Rates: 100 sen (cents) = 1 Brunei dollar (B $). *Sterling, US Dollar and Euro Equivalents* (31 December 2004): £1 sterling = B $3.1555; US $1 = B $1.6338; €1 = B $2.2254; B $100 = £31.69 = US $61.21 = €44.94. *Average Exchange Rate* (Brunei dollars per US $): 1.7906 in 2002; 1.7422 in 2003; 1.6902 in 2004. Note: The Brunei dollar is at par with the Singapore dollar.

Budget (B $ million, 2002): *Revenue:* Tax revenue 2,331.7 (Import duty 111.2; Corporate income tax 2,204.1); Non-tax revenue 1,936.1 (Commercial receipts 301.9; Property income 1,631.0); Total 4,267.8. *Expenditure:* Personal emoluments 1,337.4; Other annual recurrent charges 1,204.3; Other special expenditure charges 497.6; Development expenditure 419.8; Charged expenditure 1,137.2; Investment in public sector 50.1; Total 4,646.3.

Money Supply (B $ million, 2002): Currency outside banks 654.8; Demand deposits at banks 1,617.8; Total money 2,272.6.

Cost of Living (Consumer Price Index; base: 2002 = 100): *2003:* All items 100.3 (Food and non-alcoholic beverages 99.2; Clothing and footwear 97.1; Housing, water, electricity and maintenance 99.2; Transport goods, services and operations 98.5; Communications 95.5; Education 99.6; Medical and health 98.1; Recreation and entertainment 101.3; Miscellaneous goods and services 100.6).

Gross Domestic Product by Economic Activity (B $ million in current prices, 2003, provisional): Agriculture, hunting, forestry and fishing 294.5; Mining, quarrying and manufacturing 3,402.3; Electricity, gas and water 62.1; Construction 334.0; Trade, restaurants and hotels 803.7; Transport, storage and communications 431.9; Finance, insurance, real estate and business services 722.2; Community, social and personal services 2,441.1; *Sub-total* 8,491.8; *Less* Imputed bank service charge 254.8; *GDP in purchasers' values* 8,236.9.

Balance of Payments (B $ million, 2003): Exports of goods 7,704.3; Imports of goods –2,191.3; *Trade balance* 5,513.0; Exports of services 760.5; Imports of services –1,797.4; *Balance on goods and services* 4,476.1; Other income received 3,917.0; Other income paid –651.4; *Balance on goods, services and income* 7,741.7; Current transfers received 0; Current transfers paid –241.9; *Current balance* 7,499.8; Capital balance –16.6; Financial balance –4,613.5; *Overall balance* 2,869.7.

EXTERNAL TRADE

Principal Commodities (B $ million, 2003): *Imports c.i.f.:* Food and live animals 348.02; Chemicals 175.87; Basic manufactures 597.47; Machinery and transport equipment 815.20; Miscellaneous manufactured articles 264.03; Total (incl. others) 2,311.82. *Exports f.o.b.:* Mineral fuels, lubricants, etc. 6,754.15; Machinery and transport equipment 411.63; Miscellaneous manufactured articles 418.78; Total (incl. others) 7,704.33.

Principal Trading Partners (B $ million, 2003): *Imports:* Australia 68.9; People's Republic of China 112.5; France 38.6; Germany 74.6; Hong Kong 151.8; Indonesia 61.7; Italy 16.1; Japan 231.2; Republic of Korea 54.4; Malaysia 468.1; Netherlands 10.9; Singapore 465.2; United Kingdom 85.0; USA 266.0; Total (incl. others) 2,311.8. *Exports:* Japan 3,155.9; Republic of Korea 862.1; Malaysia 284.0; Singapore 344.4; Thailand 726.2; USA 597.1; Total (incl. others) 7,704.3.

TRANSPORT

Road Traffic (registered vehicles, 2001): Private cars 188,720; Goods vehicles 17,828; Motorcycles and scooters 7,162; Buses and taxis 2,267; Others 4,470.

Merchant Fleet (displacement, '000 grt at 31 December): 362.7 in 2001; 482.6 in 2002; 480.0 in 2003. Source: Lloyd's Register-Fairplay, *World Fleet Statistics*.

International Sea-borne Shipping (freight traffic, freight tons, 2003): Goods loaded 127,547; Goods unloaded 1,260,507. Note: One freight ton equals 40 cubic feet (1.133 cubic metres) of cargo.

Civil Aviation (2003): Passenger arrivals 487,768, passenger departures 487,701; freight loaded 16,038 metric tons, freight unloaded 11,265 metric tons; mail loaded 440 metric tons, mail unloaded 124 metric tons.

TOURISM

Visitor Arrivals by Nationality (incl. excursionists, 2000): Indonesia 68,527; Malaysia 974,132; Philippines 65,842; Singapore 27,995; United Kingdom 43,865; Total (incl. others) 1,306,764.

Tourism Receipts (US $ million): 38 in 1996; 39 in 1997; 37 in 1998. Source: World Bank.

COMMUNICATIONS MEDIA

Radio Receivers (2000, estimate): 362,712 in use.

Television Receivers (2000, estimate): 216,223 in use.

Telephones (2003): 81,900 direct exchange lines in use.

Facsimile Machines (1996, estimate): 2,000 in use. Source: UN, *Statistical Yearbook*.

Mobile Cellular Telephones (2003): 177,372 subscribers.

Personal Computers ('000 in use, 2001 estimate): 25. Source: International Telecommunication Union.

Internet Users ('000, 2001): 35.0. Source: International Telecommunication Union.

Book Production (1992): 25 titles; 56,000 copies. Source: UNESCO, *Statistical Yearbook*.

Newspapers (2002): Daily 4; Non-daily 3 (English 2, with circulation of 22,000 copies; Malay 3, with circulation of 39,500 copies; Malay and English 1, with circulation of 10,000 copies).

Other Periodicals (1998): 15 (estimated combined circulation 132,000 copies per issue).

EDUCATION

Pre-primary and Primary: 207 schools; 4,828 teachers; 58,837 pupils in 2003.

General Secondary: 33 schools; 2,913 teachers; 37,743 pupils in 2003.

Teacher Training: 1 college; 37 teachers; 244 students in 2003.

Vocational: 7 colleges; 501 teachers; 2,780 students in 2003.

Higher Education: 2 institutes (incl. 1 university); 392 teachers; 3,805 students in 2003.

Adult Literacy Rate (UNESCO estimates): 93.9% (males 96.3%; females 91.4%) in 2002. Source: UN Development Programme, *Human Development Report*.

Directory

The Constitution

Note: Certain sections of the Constitution relating to elections and the Legislative Council were in abeyance between 1962 and 2004.

A new Constitution was promulgated on 29 September 1959 (and amended significantly in 1971 and 1984). Under its provisions, sovereign authority is vested in the Sultan and Yang Di-Pertuan, who is assisted and advised by five Councils: the Religious Council, the Privy Council, the Council of Cabinet Ministers, the (inactive) Legislative Council and the Council of Succession. Power of appointment to the Councils is exercised by the Sultan.

The 1959 Constitution established the Chief Minister as the most senior official, with the British High Commissioner as adviser to the Government on all matters except those relating to Muslim and Malay customs.

In 1971 amendments were introduced reducing the power of the British Government, which retained responsibility for foreign affairs, while defence became the joint responsibility of both countries.

In 1984 further amendments were adopted as Brunei acceded to full independence and assumed responsibility for defence and foreign affairs.

THE RELIGIOUS COUNCIL

In his capacity as head of the Islamic faith in Brunei, the Sultan and Yang Di-Pertuan is advised on all Islamic matters by the Religious Council, whose members are appointed by the Sultan and Yang Di-Pertuan.

THE PRIVY COUNCIL

This Council, presided over by the Sultan and Yang Di-Pertuan, is to advise the Sultan on matters concerning the Royal prerogative of mercy, the amendment of the Constitution and the conferment of ranks, titles and honours.

THE COUNCIL OF CABINET MINISTERS

Presided over by the Sultan and Yang Di-Pertuan, the Council of Cabinet Ministers considers all executive matters.

THE LEGISLATIVE COUNCIL

The role of the Legislative Council is to scrutinize legislation. However, following political unrest in 1962, provisions of the Constitution relating, *inter alia*, to the Legislative Council were amended, and the Legislative Council has not met since 1984. In the absence of the Legislative Council, legislation is enacted by royal proclamation.

In July 2004 the Sultan announced that the Legislative Council would be reinstated by the end of that year. Its members were to be appointed by a governmental committee. However, the state of emergency that had been declared in 1962 would remain in force and the Sultan would continue to rule by decree.

THE COUNCIL OF SUCCESSION

Subject to the Constitution, this Council is to determine the succession to the throne, should the need arise.

The State is divided into four administrative districts, in each of which is a District Officer responsible to the Prime Minister and Minister of Home Affairs.

The Government

HEAD OF STATE

Sultan and Yang Di-Pertuan: HM Sultan Haji Hassanal Bolkiah (succeeded 4 October 1967; crowned 1 August 1968).

COUNCIL OF CABINET MINISTERS
(April 2005)

Prime Minister, Minister of Defence and of Finance: HM Sultan Haji Hassanal Bolkiah.

Minister of Foreign Affairs: HRH Prince Mohamed Bolkiah.

Minister of Home Affairs and Special Adviser to the Prime Minister: Pehin Dato' Haji Isa bin Pehin Haji Ibrahim.

Minister of Education: Pehin Dato' Haji Abdul Aziz bin Pehin Haji Umar.

Minister of Industry and Primary Resources: Dato' Haji Abdul Rahman Taib.

Minister of Religious Affairs: Pehin Dato' Dr Haji Mohamad Zain bin Haji Serudin.

Minister of Development: Dato' Seri Paduka Dr Haji Ahmad bin Haji Jumat.

Minister of Health: Pehin Dato' Haji Abu Bakar bin Haji Apong.

Minister of Culture, Youth and Sports: Pehin Dato' Haji Hussein bin Pehin Haji Mohamad Yosof.

Minister of Communications: Pehin Dato' Haji Zakaria bin Haji Suleiman.

There are, in addition, eight deputy ministers.

MINISTRIES

Office of the Prime Minister (Jabatan Perdana Menteri): Istana Nurul Iman, Bandar Seri Begawan BA 1000; tel. 2229988; fax 2241717; e-mail PRO@jpm.gov.bn; internet www.pmo.gov.bn.

Ministry of Communications (Kementerian Perhubungan): Jalan Menteri Besar, Bandar Seri Begawan BB 3910; tel. 2383838; fax 2380127; e-mail info@mincom.gov.bn; internet www.mincom.gov .bn.

Ministry of Culture, Youth and Sports (Kementerian Kebudayaan, Belia dan Sukan): Simpang 336, Jalan Kebangsaan, Bandar Seri Begawan BC 4415; tel. 2380911; fax 2380653; e-mail info@kkbs .gov.bn; internet www.kkbs.gov.bn.

Ministry of Defence (Kementerian Pertahanan): Bolkiah Garrison, Bandar Seri Begawan BB 3510; tel. 2386371; fax 2331615; e-mail info@mindef.gov.bn; internet www.mindef.gov.bn.

Ministry of Development (Kementerian Pembangunan): Old Airport, Jalan Berakas, Bandar Seri Begawan BB 3510; tel. 2241911; e-mail info@mod.gov.bn; internet www.mod.gov.bn.

Ministry of Education (Kementerian Pendidikan): Old Airport, Jalan Berakas, Bandar Seri Begawan BB 3510; tel. 2382233; fax 2380050; e-mail sutmoe@brunet.bn; internet www.moe.gov.bn.

Ministry of Finance (Kementerian Kewangan): Tingkat 5, Bangunan Kementerian Kewangan, Commonwealth Dr., Jalan Kebangsaan, Bandar Seri Begawan BB 3910; tel. 2241991; fax 2226132; e-mail info@finance.gov.bn; internet www.finance.gov.bn.

Ministry of Foreign Affairs (Kementerian Hal Ehwal Luar Negeri): Jalan Subok, Bandar Seri Begawan BD 2710; tel. 2261177; fax 2262904; e-mail info@mfa.gov.bn; internet www.mfa.gov.bn.

Ministry of Health (Kementerian Kesihatan): Jalan Menteri Besar, Bandar Seri Begawan BB 3910; tel. 2226640; fax 2240980; e-mail moh2@brunet.bn; internet www.moh.gov.bn.

Ministry of Home Affairs (Kementerian Hal Ehwal Dalam Negeri): Jalan Menteri Besar, Bandar Seri Begawan BB 3910; tel. 2223225; e-mail info@home-affairs.gov.bn; internet www .home-affairs.gov.bn.

Ministry of Industry and Primary Resources (Kementerian Perindustrian dan Sumber-sumber Utama): Jalan Menteri Besar, Bandar Seri Begawan BB 3910; tel. 2382822; fax 2382807; e-mail MIPRS2@brunet.bn; internet www.industry.gov.bn.

Ministry of Religious Affairs (Kementerian Hal Ehwal Ugama): Jalan Menteri Besar, Jalan Berakas, Bandar Seri Begawan BB 3910; tel. 2382525; fax 2382330; e-mail info@religious-affairs.gov .bn; internet www.religious-affairs.gov.bn.

Political Organizations

Parti Perpaduan Kebangsaan Brunei (PPKB) (Brunei National Solidarity Party—BNSP): Bandar Seri Begawan; f. 1986 after split in PKDB (see below); ceased political activity in 1988, but re-emerged in 1995; Pres. HATTA ZAINAL ABIDIN.

Former political organizations included: **Parti Rakyat Brunei—PRB** (Brunei People's Party), banned in 1962, leaders are all in exile; **Barisan Kemerdeka'an Rakyat—BAKER** (People's Independence Front), f. 1966 but no longer active; **Parti Perpaduan Kebangsaan Rakyat Brunei—PERKARA** (Brunei People's National United Party), f. 1968 but no longer active; and **Parti Kebangsaan Demokratik Brunei—PKDB** (Brunei National Democratic Party—BNDP), f. 1985 and dissolved by government order in 1988.

Diplomatic Representation

EMBASSIES AND HIGH COMMISSIONS IN BRUNEI

Australia: Teck Guan Plaza, 4th Floor, Jalan Sultan, Bandar Seri Begawan BS 8811; tel. 2229435; fax 2221652; e-mail austhicom .brunei@dfat.gov.au; internet www.australia.org.bn; High Commissioner CHRISTIAN BENNETT.

Bangladesh: 125 Kampong Kiulap, Bandar Seri Begawan BE 1518; tel. 2238420; fax 2238421; e-mail bdoot@brunet.bn; High Commissioner M. A. HAKIM.

Cambodia: 8 Simpang 845, Kampong Tasek, Meradun, Jalan Tutong, Bandar Seri Begawan BF 1520; tel. 2654046; fax 2650646; Ambassador ITH DETTOLA.

Canada: 5th Floor, Jalan McArthur Bldg, 1 Jalan McArthur, Bandar Seri Begawan BS 8711; tel. 2220043; fax 2220040; e-mail hicomcda@brunet.bn; internet www.dfait-maeci.gc.ca/Brunei; High Commissioner PAUL S. H. LAU.

China, People's Republic: 1, 3 & 5 Simpang 462, Kampong Sungai Hanching, Jalan Muara, Bandar Seri Begawan BC 2115; tel. 2334163; fax 2335710; e-mail embproc@brunet.bn; Ambassador YANG YANYI.

France: Kompleks Jalan Sultan, Units 301–306, 3rd Floor, 51–55 Jalan Sultan, Bandar Seri Begawan BS 8811; tel. 2220960; fax 2243373; e-mail france@brunet.bn; internet www.france.org.bn; Ambassador THIERRY BORJA DE MOZOTA.

Germany: Kompleks Bangunan Yayasan Sultan Haji Hassanal Bolkiah, Unit 2.01, Block A, 2nd Floor, Jalan Pretty, Bandar Seri Begawan BS 8711; tel. 2225547; fax 2225583; e-mail prgerman@ brunet.bn; Ambassador CONRAD KARL CAPPELL.

India: 'Baitussyifaa', Simpang 40–22, Jalan Sungai Akar, Bandar Seri Begawan BC 3915; tel. 2339947; fax 2339783; e-mail hicomind@ brunet.bn; internet www.brunet.bn/gov/emb/india; High Commissioner BUTSHIKAN SINGH.

Indonesia: Simpang 528, Lot 4498, Kampong Sungai Hanching Baru, Jalan Muara, Bandar Seri Begawan BC 2115; tel. 2330180; fax 2330646; e-mail kbribsb@brunet.bn; internet www.indonesia.org .bn; Ambassador YUSBAR DJAMIL.

Iran: 19 Simpang 477, Kampong Sungai Hanching, Jalan Muara, Bandar Seri Begawan BC 2115; tel. 2330021; fax 2331744; Ambassador ABBAS TALEBIFAR.

Japan: 1 & 3 Jalan Jawatan Dalam, 33 Simpang 122, Kampong Kiulap, Bandar Seri Begawan BE 1518; tel. 2229265; fax 2229481; e-mail embassy@japan.com.bn; internet www.bn.emb-japan.go.jp; Ambassador YOSHINOBU NISAKA.

Korea, Republic: POB 2169, Bandar Seri Begawan BS 8674; tel. 2426038; fax 2426041; e-mail koreaemb@brunet.bn; Ambassador KIM WOONG-NAM.

Laos: Lot 19824, 11 Simpang 480, Jalan Kebangsaan Lama, off Jalan Muara, Bandar Seri Begawan BC 4115; tel. 2345666; fax 2345888; e-mail LAOSEMBA@brunet.bn; Ambassador BOUNTHONG VONGSALY.

Malaysia: 61 Simpang 336, Jalan Kebangsaan, Kampong Sungai Akar, Bandar Seri Begawan BC 4115; tel. 2381095; fax 2381278; e-mail mwbrunei@brunet.bn; High Commissioner SAIFUL AZAM ABDULLAH (acting).

Myanmar: 14 Lot 2185/46292, Simpang 212, Jalan Kampong Rimba, Gadong, Bandar Seri Begawan BE 3119; tel. 2450506; fax 2451008; e-mail myanmar@brunet.bn; Ambassador U THET WIN.

Oman: 35 Simpang 100, Kampong Pengkalan, Jalan Tungku Link, Gadong, Bandar Seri Begawan BE 3719; tel. 2446953; fax 2449646; e-mail omnembsb@brunet.bn; Ambassador Haji MOHAMMAD BIN OMAR AHMAD AIDID.

Pakistan: 10A Simpang 350, Kampong Sungai Akar, Jalan Subok, Bandar Seri Begawan; tel. 2261355; fax 2261353; e-mail hcpak@ brunet.bn; internet www.brunet.bn/gov/emb/Pakistan; High Commissioner BADR-UD-DEEN.

Philippines: 17 Simpang 126, Km 2, Jalan Tutong, Bandar Seri Begawan BA 2111; tel. 2241465; fax 2237707; e-mail bruneipe@ brunet.bn; Ambassador VIRGINIA H. BENDAVIDEZ.

Saudi Arabia: 1 Simpang 570, Kampong Salar, Jalan Muara, Bandar Seri Begawan BT 2528; tel. 2792821; fax 2792826; e-mail bnemb@mofa.gov.sa; Ambassador ESAM BIN AHMED BIN JAMAL ABID AL-THAGAFI.

Singapore: 8 Simpang 74, Jalan Subok, Bandar Seri Begawan; tel. 2262741; fax 2262743; e-mail singa@brunet.bn; internet www.mfa .gov.sg/brunei; High Commissioner V. P. HIRUBALAN.

Thailand: 2 Simpang 682, Jalan Tutong, Kampong Bunut, Bandar Seri Begawan BF 1320; tel. 2653108; fax 2653032; e-mail thaiemb@ brunet.bn; Ambassador SORNSILP POLTEJA.

United Kingdom: POB 2197, Bandar Seri Begawan BS 8674; tel. 2222231; fax 2234315; e-mail brithc@brunet.bn; internet www .britishhighcommission.gov.uk/brunei; High Commissioner ANDREW CAIE.

USA: Teck Guan Plaza, 3rd Floor, Jalan Sultan, Bandar Seri Begawan BS 8811; tel. 2220384; fax 2225293; e-mail ConsularBrunei@state.gov; internet bandar.usembassy.gov; Ambassador GENE B. CHRISTY.

Viet Nam: 7 Simpang 5383719, Jalan (Duong) Kebangsaan Lama, Bandar Seri Begawan BC 2115; tel. 2343167; fax 2343169; e-mail vnembassy@hotmail.com; Ambassador HA HONG HAI.

Judicial System

SUPREME COURT

The Supreme Court consists of the Court of Appeal and the High Court. Syariah (*Shari'a*) courts coexist with the Supreme Court and deal with Islamic laws.

Office of the Supreme Court

Km 11/2, Jalan Tutong, Bandar Seri Begawan BA 1910; tel. 2225853; fax 2241984; e-mail judiciarybn@hotmail.com; internet www.judicial.gov.bn/supr_court.htm.

Chief Registrar: Haji HAIROLARNI ABD MAJID.

The Court of Appeal

Composed of the President and two Commissioners appointed by the Sultan. The Court of Appeal considers criminal and civil appeals against the decisions of the High Court and the Intermediate Court. The Court of Appeal is the highest appellate court for criminal cases. In civil cases an appeal may be referred to the Judicial Committee of Her Majesty's Privy Council in London if all parties agree to do so before the hearing of the appeal in the Brunei Court of Appeal.

President: Sir DEREK CONS.

The High Court

Composed of the Chief Justice and judges sworn in by the Sultan as Commissioners of the Supreme Court. In its appellate jurisdiction, the High Court considers appeals in criminal and civil matters against the decisions of the Subordinate Courts. The High Court has unlimited original jurisdiction in criminal and civil matters.

Chief Justice: Dato' Seri Paduka MOHAMMED SAIED.

OTHER COURTS

Intermediate Courts: have jurisdiction to try all offences other than those punishable by the death sentence and civil jurisdiction to try all actions and suits of a civil nature where the amount in dispute or value of the subject/matter does not exceed B $100,000.

The Subordinate Courts

Presided over by the Chief Magistrate and magistrates, with limited original jurisdiction in civil and criminal matters and civil jurisdiction to try all actions and suits of a civil nature where the amount in dispute does not exceed B $50,000 (for Chief Magistrate) and B $30,000 (for magistrates).

Chief Magistrate: ROSTAINA BINTI Pengiran Haji DURAMAN.

The Courts of Kathis

Deal solely with questions concerning Islamic religion, marriage and divorce. Appeals lie from these courts to the Sultan in the Religious Council.

Chief Kathi: Dato' Seri SETIA Haji SALIM BIN Haji BESAR.

Attorney-General: Dato' Paduka Haji KIFRAWI BIN Dato' Paduka Haji KIFLI, Attorney-General's Chambers, The Law Bldg, Km 1, Jalan Tutong, Bandar Seri Begawan BA 1910; tel. 2244872; fax 2223100; e-mail info@agc.gov.bn; internet www.agc.gov.bn.

Solicitor-General: Datin Paduka MAGDALENE CHONG.

Religion

The official religion of Brunei is Islam, and the Sultan is head of the Islamic community. The majority of the Malay population are Muslims of the Shafi'is school of the Sunni sect; at the 1991 census Muslims accounted for 67.2% of the total population. The Chinese population is either Buddhist (accounting for 12.8% of the total population at the 1991 census), Confucianist, Daoist or Christian. Large numbers of the indigenous ethnic groups practise traditional animist forms of religion. The remainder of the population are mostly Christians, generally Roman Catholics, Anglicans or members of the American Methodist Church of Southern Asia. At the 1991 census Christians accounted for 10.0% of the total population.

ISLAM

Supreme Head of Islam: HM Sultan Haji HASSANAL BOLKIAH (Sultan and Yang Di-Pertuan).

CHRISTIANITY

The Anglican Communion

Within the Church of the Province of South East Asia, Brunei forms part of the diocese of Kuching (Malaysia).

The Roman Catholic Church

Brunei comprises a single apostolic prefecture. At December 2002 an estimated 6.3% of the population were adherents.

Prefect Apostolic: Rev. CORNELIUS SIM, Church of Our Lady of the Assumption, POB 527, Bandar Seri Begawan BS 8670; tel. 2222261; fax 2238938; e-mail frcsim@brunet.bn; internet www.catholicbrunei.org.

The Press

NEWSPAPERS

Borneo Bulletin: Locked Bag No. 2, MPC (Old Airport, Berakas), Bandar Seri Begawan BB 3510; tel. 2451468; fax 2451461; e-mail borneobulletin2@brunet.bn; internet www.brunet.bn/news/bb; f. 1953; daily; English; independent; owned by QAF Group; Editor CHARLES REX DE SILVA; circ. 25,000.

Brunei Darussalam Newsletter: Dept of Information, Prime Minister's Office, Istana Nurul Iman, Bandar Seri Begawan BA 1000; tel. 2229988; fortnightly; English; govt newspaper; distributed free; circ. 14,000.

Daily News Digest: Dept of Information, Prime Minister's Office, Istana Nurul Iman, Bandar Seri Begawan BA 1000; internet www.brunet.bn/news/dndbd/digest.htm; English; govt newspaper.

Media Permata: Locked Bag No. 2, MPC (Old Airport, Berakas), Bandar Seri Begawan BB 3510; tel. 2451468; fax 2451461; e-mail mediapermata@brunet.bn; internet www.brunei-online.com/mp; f. 1995; daily (not Sun.); Malay; owned by QAF Group; Editor ABDUL LATIF; circ. 10,000.

Pelita Brunei: Dept of Information, Prime Minister's Office, Old Airport, Berakas BB 3510; tel. 2383941; fax 2381004; e-mail pelita@brunet.bn; internet www.brunet.bn/news/pelita/pelita1.htm; f. 1956; weekly (Wed.); Malay; govt newspaper; distributed free; Editor TIMBANG BIN BAKAR; circ. 27,500.

Salam: c/o Brunei Shell Petroleum Co Sdn Bhd, Seria 7082; tel. 34184; fax 34189; internet www.shell.com.bn/salam; f. 1953; monthly; Malay and English; distributed free to employees of the Brunei Shell Petroleum Co Sdn Bhd; Editor SAIFUL MAHADHIR NORDIN; circ. 46,000.

Publishers

Borneo Printers & Trading Sdn Bhd: POB 2211, Bandar Seri Begawan BS 8674; tel. 2651387; fax 2654342; e-mail bptl@brunet.bn.

Brunei Press Sdn Bhd: Lots 8 & 11, Perindustrian Beribi II, Jalan Gadong, Bandar Seri Begawan BE 1118; tel. 2451468; fax 2451462; e-mail brupress@brunet.bn; internet www.bruneipress.com.bn; f. 1953; Gen. Man. REGGIE SEE.

Capital Trading & Printing Pte Ltd: POB 1089, Bandar Seri Begawan; tel. 2244541.

Leong Bros: 52 Jalan Bunga Kuning, POB 164, Seria; tel. 322381.

Offset Printing House: POB 1111, Bandar Seri Begawan; tel. 2224477.

The Star Press: Bandar Seri Begawan; f. 1963; Man. F. W. ZIMMERMAN.

GOVERNMENT PUBLISHING HOUSE

Government Printer: Government Printing Department, Office of the Prime Minister, Bandar Seri Begawan BB 3510; tel. 2382541; fax 2381141; e-mail jpkkuu@brunet.bn; internet www.printing.gov.bn; Dir MOHIDIN BIN Haji DAUD.

Broadcasting and Communications

TELECOMMUNICATIONS

Authority for the Information Communication Technology Industry (AiTi): Block B14, Simpang 32-5, Kampong Anggrek Desa, Jalan Berakas, Bandar Seri Begawan BB 3713; tel. 2323232; fax 2382445; e-mail info@aiti.gov.bn; internet www.aiti.gov.bn; f. 2003; regulatory body for telecommunications industry; responsible for development of information communication technology industry; Chair. Dato' Paduka Awang Haji ABDULLAH BIN Haji BAKAR.

DST Communications Sdn Bhd: Block D, Yayasan Sultan Haji Hassanal Bolkiah Kompleks, Bandar Seri Begawan; tel. 2232323; e-mail dst-group@simpur.net.bn; internet www.dst-group.com; mobile service provider; signed agreement with Alcatel in 2003 to improve provision of mobile services in Brunei; Man. Dir Pengiran Haji MOHAMED ZIN BIN Pengiran DAMIT.

Jabatan Telecom Brunei (Department of Telecommunications of Brunei): Ministry of Communications, Jalan Berakas, Bandar Seri Begawan BB 3510; tel. 2382382; fax 2382445; e-mail info@telecom.gov.bn; internet www.telecom.gov.bn; telecommunications services provider; originally scheduled to become Telekom Brunei Bhd (govt-owned company) in 2003; corporatization later postponed indefinitely; Dir of Telecommunications Awang BUNTAR BIN OSMAN.

BROADCASTING

Radio

Radio Televisyen Brunei (RTB): Prime Minister's Office, Jalan Elizabeth II, Bandar Seri Begawan BS 8610; tel. 2243111; fax 2241882; e-mail rtbpits@brunet.bn; internet www.rtb.gov.bn; f. 1957; five radio networks: four broadcasting in Malay, the other in English, Chinese (Mandarin) and Gurkhali; also broadcasts on the internet; Dir Pengiran Dato' Paduka ISMAIL MOHAMED.

The British Forces Broadcasting Service (Military) broadcasts a 24-hour radio service to a limited area.

Television

Kristal Astro Sdn Bhd: Unit 1-345, 1st Floor, Gadong Properties Centre, Gadong, Bandar Seri Begawan BE 4119; tel. 2456828; fax 2420682; f. 2000; jt venture between Kristal Sdn Bhd and Malaysian Measat Broadcast Network Systems Sdn Bhd; provides more than 30 digital satellite subscription channels.

Kristal TV: DST Network Sdn Bhd, Unit 1-345, 1st Floor, Gadong Properties Centre, Gadong, Bandar Seri Begawan BE 4119; tel. 2456828; fax 2420682; f. 1999; 14 television channels.

Radio Televisyen Brunei (RTB): Prime Minister's Office, Jalan Elizabeth II, Bandar Seri Begawan BS 8610; tel. 2243111; fax 2241882; e-mail rtbpits@brunet.bn; internet www.rtb.gov.bn; f. 1957; three television channels with one satellite channel; Dir Pengiran Dato' Paduka ISMAIL MOHAMED.

Finance

(cap. = capital; res = reserves; dep. = deposits; brs = branches; amounts in Brunei dollars unless otherwise stated)

BANKING

The Department of Financial Services (Treasury), the Brunei Currency Board and the Brunei Investment Agency (see Government Agencies below), under the Ministry of Finance, perform most of the functions of a central bank.

Commercial Banks

Baiduri Bank Bhd: Block A, Units 1–4, Kiarong Complex, Lebuhraya Sultan Hassanal Bolkiah, Bandar Seri Begawan BE 1318; tel. 2455111; fax 2455599; e-mail bank@baiduri.com; internet www.baiduri.com; f. 1994; cap. 30m., res 32.0m., dep. 1,329.7m. (Dec. 2003); Chair. Pengiran ANAK ISTERI Pengiran ANAK HAJJAH ZARIAH; Gen. Man. PIERRE IMHOF; 10 brs.

Islamic Bank of Brunei Bhd: Lot 159, Bangunan IBB, Jalan Pemancha, POB 2725, Bandar Seri Begawan BS 8711; tel. 2235687; fax 2235722; e-mail ibb@brunet.bn; internet www.ibb.com.bn; f. 1981 as Island Development Bank; name changed from International Bank of Brunei Bhd to present name in Jan. 1993; practises Islamic banking principles; Chair. Haji ABDUL RAHMAN BIN Haji ABDUL KARIM; Man. Dir Haji ZAINASALLEHEN BIN Haji MOHAMED TAHIR; 13 brs.

Islamic Development Bank of Brunei Bhd: Ground–4th Floors, Kompleks Setia Kenangan, Kampong Kiulap, Jalan Gadong, Bandar Seri Begawan BE 1518; tel. 2232547; fax 2233540; e-mail dbbcom@brunet.bn; internet www.idbb-bank.com.bn; f. 1995 as Development Bank of Brunei Bhd; name changed to present in July 2000; practises Islamic banking principles; Man. Dir Pengiran Datin Paduka Hajah URAI Pengiran ALI; 3 brs.

Foreign Banks

Citibank NA (USA): Darussalam Complex, 12–15 Jalan Sultan, Bandar Seri Begawan BS 8811; tel. 2243983; fax 2237344; e-mail glen.rase@citicorp.com; Country Head GLEN RASE; 2 brs.

The Hongkong and Shanghai Banking Corpn Ltd (Hong Kong): Jalan Sultan, cnr Jalan Pemancha, Bandar Seri Begawan BS 8811; tel. 2252252; fax 2241316; e-mail hsbc@hsbc.com.bn; internet www.hsbc.com.bn; f. 1947; acquired assets of National Bank of Brunei in 1986; CEO MARCUS HURRY; 10 brs.

Maybank (Malaysia): 1 Jalan McArthur, Bandar Seri Begawan BS 8711; tel. 2226462; fax 2226404; e-mail maybank@brunet.bn; f. 1960; Country Man. AZIZUL ABDUL RASHID; 3 brs.

RHB Bank Bhd (Malaysia): Unit G. 02, Block D, Kompleks Bangunan Yayasan Sultan Haji Hassanal Bolkiah, Ground Floor, Jalan Pretty, Bandar Seri Begawan BS 8711; tel. 2222526; fax 2237487; e-mail rhbbsb@brunet.bn; fmrly Sime Bank Bhd; Country Man. APANDI BIN KLOMPOT; 1 br.

Standard Chartered Bank (United Kingdom): 1st Floor, 51–55 Jalan Sultan, POB 186, Bandar Seri Begawan BS 8811; tel. 2242386; fax 2220103; e-mail scb.brunei@bn.standardchartered.com; internet www.standardchartered.com/bn; f. 1958; CEO HANS THEILKUHL; 8 brs.

United Overseas Bank Ltd (Singapore): Unit G5, RBA Plaza, Jalan Sultan, Bandar Seri Begawan BS 8811; tel. 2225477; fax 2240792; f. 1973; Gen. Man. SIA KEE HENG; 2 brs.

'Offshore' Banks

The Brunei International Financial Centre (BIFC), under the Ministry of Finance, supervises the activities of the offshore banking sector in Brunei.

Royal Bank of Canada: 1 Jalan McArthur, 4A, 4th Floor, Bandar Seri Begawan BS 8711; tel. 2224366; fax 2224368; Gen. Man. MATTHEW YONG.

Sun Hung Kai International Bank (Brunei) Ltd (Hong Kong): Bandar Seri Begawan; f. 2004; Dir P. H. MARK.

STOCK EXCHANGE

In May 2002 the International Brunei Exchange Ltd (IBX) was granted an exclusive licence to establish an international securities exchange in Brunei.

International Brunei Exchange Ltd (IBX): The Empire, Muara-Tutong Highway, Jerudong BG 3122; tel. 2611222; fax 2611020; e-mail info@ibx.com.bn; internet www.ibx.com.bn; f. 2001; CEO B. C. YONG.

INSURANCE

In 1998 there were 18 general, three life and two composite (takaful) insurance companies operating in Brunei.

General Companies

The Asia Insurance Co Ltd: Unit A1 & A2, 1st Floor, Block A, Bangunan Hau Man Yong, Simpang 88, Kampong Kiulap, Bandar Seri Begawan BE 1518; tel. 2236100; fax 2236102; e-mail asiains_d.wong@brunet.bn; Man. DAVID WONG KOK MIN.

Aviva Insurance Bhd: Unit 311, 3rd Floor, Kompleks Mohd Yussof, Mile 1½, Jalan Tutong, Bandar Seri Begawan BA 1714; tel. 2223632; fax 2220965; e-mail aviva@brunet.bn; fmrly CGU Insurance Bhd; Man. LIANG VOON CHIANG.

AXA Insurance (B) Sdn Bhd: Unit 608, 6th Floor, Jalan Sultan Complex, 51–55 Jalan Sultan, Bandar Seri Begawan BS 8811; tel. 2226138; fax 2243474; fmrly GRE Insurance (B) Sdn Bhd; Man. MOK HAI TONG.

BALGI Insurance (B) Sdn Bhd: Unit 7, Simpang 88, Bangunan Haji Ahmad bin Hassan and Anak-Anak, Kampong Kiulap, Bandar Seri Begawan BE 1518; tel. 2234020; fax 2233981; Man. Dir PATRICK SIM SONG JUAY.

Borneo Insurance Sdn Bhd: Unit 103, Bangunan Kambang Pasang, Km 2, Jalan Gadong, Bandar Seri Begawan BE 4119; tel. 2420550; fax 2428550; Man. LIM TECK LEE.

Cosmic Insurance Corpn Sdn Bhd: Block J, Unit 11, Abdul Razak Complex, 1st Floor, Jalan Gadong, Bandar Seri Begawan BE 3919; tel. 2427112; fax 2427114; Man. RONNIE WONG.

ING General Insurance International NV: Shop Lot 86, 2nd Floor, Jalan Bunga Raya, Kuala Belait KA 1131; tel. 3335338; fax 3335338; Man. SHERRY SOON PECK ENG.

Liberty Citystate Insurance Pte Ltd: 1st Floor, Unit 25, Block C, Bangunan Hau Man Yong Complex, Simpang 88, Kampong Kiulap, Bandar Seri Begawan BE 1518; tel. 2238282; fax 2236848; e-mail libertyintl@brunet.bn; Man. ROBERT LAI CHIN YIN.

Malaysia National Insurance Bhd: 9 Bangunan Haji Mohd Salleh Simpang 103, 1st Floor, Jalan Gadong, Bandar Seri Begawan BE 4119; tel. 2443393; fax 2427451; e-mail tsang.py@brunet.bn; Man. ANDREW AK NYAGORN.

MBA Insurance Sdn Bhd: 7 Bangunan Hasbullah I, 1st Floor, Km 4, Jalan Gadong, Bandar Seri Begawan BE 3519; tel. 2441535; fax 2441534; e-mail cheahmbabrunei@brunet.bn; Man. CHEAH LYE CHONG.

Motor and General Insurance Sdn Bhd: 6 Bangunan Hasbullah II, Km 4, Jalan Gadong, Bandar Seri Begawan BE 3919; tel. 2440797; fax 2445342; Man. Dir Haji ABDUL AZIZ BIN ABDUL LATIF.

National Insurance Co Bhd: Scouts' Headquarters Bldg, Jalan Gadong, Bandar Seri Begawan BE 1118; tel. 2426888; fax 2429888; e-mail insurance@brunet.bn; internet www.national.com.bn; Gen. Man. CHAN LEK WEI.

Royal and Sun Alliance Insurance (Global) Ltd: Unit 7, 1st Floor, Block B, Kiarong Complex, Lebuhraya Sultan Hassanal Bolkiah, Bandar Seri Begawan BE 1318; tel. 2423233; fax 2423325; Gen. Man. Tommy Leong Tong Kaw.

South East Asia Insurance (B) Sdn Bhd: Unit 2, Block A, Abdul Razak Complex, 1st Floor, Jalan Gadong, Bandar Seri Begawan BE 3919; tel. 2443842; fax 2420860; Gen. Man. Shim Wei Hsiung.

Standard Insurance (B) Sdn Bhd: 2 Bangunan Hasbullah I, Ground Floor, Bandar Seri Begawan BE 3919; tel. 2450077; fax 2450076; e-mail feedback@standard-ins.com; internet www .standard-ins.com; Man. Paul Kong.

Winterthur Insurance (Far East) Pte Ltd: c/o Borneo Co (B) Sdn Bhd, Lot 9771, Km 3½, Jalan Gadong, Bandar Seri Begawan BE 4119; tel. 2422561; fax 2424352; Gen. Man. Anna Chong.

Life Companies

American International Assurance Co Ltd: Unit 509A, Wisma Jaya Building, 5th Floor, 85–94 Jalan Pemancha, Bandar Seri Begawan BS 8811; tel. 2239112; fax 2221667; e-mail Kenneth-WC .Ling@AIG.com; Man. Philip Tan.

The Asia Life Assurance Society Ltd: Unit 2, 1st Floor, Block D, Abdul Razak Complex, Jalan Gadong, Bandar Seri Begawan BE 4119; tel. 2423755; fax 2423754; e-mail asialife@simpur.net.bn; Br. Man. Joseph Wong Siong Lion.

The Great Eastern Life Assurance Co Ltd: Suite 1, Badi'ah Complex, 2nd Floor, Jalan Tutong, Bandar Seri Begawan BA 2111; tel. 2243792; fax 2225754; e-mail gelife@brunet.bn; Man. Helen Yeo.

Takaful (Composite Insurance) Companies

Syarikat Insurans Islam TAIB Sdn Bhd: Bangunan Pusat Komersil dan Perdagangan Bumiputera, Ground Floor, Jalan Cator, Bandar Seri Begawan BS 8811; tel. 2237724; fax 2237729; e-mail insuranstaib@brunet.bn; internet www.insuranstaib.com.bn; f. 1993; provides Islamic insurance products and services; Man. Dir Haji Mohamed Roselan bin Haji Mohamed Daud.

Takaful Bank Pembangunan Islam Sdn Bhd (TBPISB): Bangunan Seri Kiulap, Kampong Kiulap, Gadong, Bandar Seri Begawan; internet www.tbpisb.com; f. 2001; fmrly Takaful IDBB Sdn Bhd; name changed as above in 2003; Islamic life and non-life insurance products; Chair. Pehin Dato' Paduka Seri Laila Jasa Haji Awang Ahmad Wally Skinner; Man. Dir Haji Aishatul Akmar Sidek.

Takaful IBB Bhd: Unit 5, Block A, Kiarong Complex, Lebuhraya Sultan Hassanal Bolkiah, Bandar Seri Begawan BE 1318; tel. 2451804; fax 2451808; e-mail takaful@brunet.bn; internet www .takaful-ibb.com; f. 1993; Chair. Pehin Dato' Haji Abu Bakar bin Haji Apong Daud.

Insurance Association

General Insurance Association of Negara Brunei Darussalam (GIAB): Unit C2-2, Block C, Shakirin Complex, Kampong Kiulap, Bandar Seri Begawan BE 1318; tel. 2237898; fax 2237858; e-mail giab@brunet.bn; internet www.giab.com.bn; f. 1986; Chair. Dorothy Newn.

Trade and Industry

GOVERNMENT AGENCIES

Brunei Currency and Monetary Board (BCMB): Tingkat 5, Bangunan Kementerian Kewangan, Commonwealth Dr., Jalan Kebangsaan, Bandar Seri Begawan BB 3910; tel. 2383999; fax 2382232; e-mail bcb@brunet.bn; internet www.finance.gov.bn/bcb/ bcb_index.htm; f. 1967; maintains control of currency circulation; name changed as above Feb. 2004; Sec. Haji Mahadi Haji Ibrahim; Chair. HM Sultan Haji Hassanal Bolkiah (Minister of Finance).

Brunei Darussalam Economic Council (BDEC): Bandar Seri Begawan; internet www.brudirect.com/BruneiInfo/info/ BD_EconomicCouncil.htm; f. 1998; convened to examine the economic situation in Brunei and to recommend short- and long-term measures designed to revitalize the economy; Chair. HRH Prince Mohamed Bolkiah.

Brunei International Financial Centre (BIFC): Tingkat 14, Ministry of Finance, Commonwealth Dr., Jalan Kebangsaan, Bandar Seri Begawan BB 3910; tel. 2383750; fax 2383787; e-mail bifc@finance.gov.bn; internet www.bifc.finance.gov.bn; f. 2000; regulates international financial sector and encourages development of Brunei as investment destination; CEO Robert Miller.

Brunei Investment Agency: Tingkat 5, Bangunan Kementerian Kewangan, Commonwealth Dr., Jalan Kebangsaan, Bandar Seri Begawan BB 3910; f. 1973; Man. Dir Awang Haji Ali bin Haji Apong (acting).

DEVELOPMENT ORGANIZATIONS

Brunei Economic Development Board (BEDB): Block 2K, Jalan Ong Sum Ping, Bandar Seri Begawan BA 1311; tel. 2230111; fax 2230053; e-mail info@bedb.com.bn; internet www.bedb.com.bn; f. 2001; promotes Brunei as an investment destination; facilitates and assists industrial development; Chair. Pehin Dato' Haji Mohammad bin Haji Daud; CEO John A. Perry.

Brunei Industrial Development Authority (BINA): Ministry of Industry and Primary Resources, Km 8, Jalan Gadong, Bandar Seri Begawan BE 1118; tel. 2444100; fax 2423300; e-mail bruneibina@ brunet.bn; internet www.bina.gov.bn; f. 1996; Dir Haji Mohd Zain bin Haji Gaffar.

Brunei Islamic Trust Fund (Tabung Amanah Islam Brunei): Block A, Unit 2, Ground Floor, Kiarong Complex, Lebuhraya Sultan Hj Hassanal Bolkiah, Bandar Seri Begawan BE 1318; tel. 2452666; fax 2450877; f. 1991; promotes trade and industry; Chair. Haji Awang Yahya bin Haji Ibrahim.

Brunei Trade and Enterprise Development Council: Bandar Seri Begawan; facilitates the industrialization of Brunei; Chair. Dato' Haji Abdul Rahman Taib (Minister of Industry and Primary Resources).

Semaun Holdings Sdn Bhd: Unit 2.02, Block D, 2nd Floor, Yayasan Sultan Haji Hassanal Bolkiah Complex, Jalan Pretty, Bandar Seri Begawan BS 8711; tel. 2232950; e-mail semaun@brunet .bn; internet www.semaun.gov.bn; promotes industrial and commercial development through direct investment in key industrial sectors; 100% govt-owned; the board of directors is composed of ministers and senior govt officials; Chair. Dato' Haji Abdul Rahman Taib (Minister of Industry and Primary Resources); Man. Dir Pengiran Haji Mariana P. D. N. Pengiran Haji Abdul Momin.

CHAMBERS OF COMMERCE

Brunei Darussalam International Chamber of Commerce and Industry: Unit 402–403A, 4th Floor, Wisma Jaya, Jalan Pemancha, Bandar Seri Begawan BS 8811; tel. 2228382; fax 2228389; Chair. Sulaiman Haji Ahai; Sec. Haji Shazali bin Dato' Haji Sulaiman; 108 mems.

Brunei Malay Chamber of Commerce and Industry: POB 1099, Bandar Seri Begawan BS 8672; tel. 2422752; fax 2422753; f. 1964; Pres. Dato' A. A. Hapidz; 160 mems.

Chinese Chamber of Commerce: Chinese Chamber of Commerce Bldg, 72 Jalan Robert, 2nd–4th Floors, Bandar Seri Begawan BS 8811; tel. 2235494; fax 2235492; e-mail ccc@brunet.bn; internet www.bruneichinesechamber.com; Pres. Robert Koh Hoe Kiat.

Indian Chamber of Commerce: Lot 20021, Taman Aman Complex, Jalan Gadong-Tutong, Kampong Beribi, Bandar Seri Begawan BE 3188; tel. 2650793; fax 2650793.

National Chamber of Commerce and Industry of Brunei Darussalam: 2nd Floor, 144 Jalan Pemancha, Bandar Seri Begawan BS 8711; tel. 2243321; fax 2228737; e-mail abas@nccibd.com; internet www.bruneichamber.com; Pres. Sheikh Abas Sheikh Mohamad.

STATE HYDROCARBON COMPANIES

Brunei Gas Carriers Sdn Bhd (BGC): 7th Floor, Setia Kenangan Mall, Kampong Kiulap, Bandar Seri Begawan; internet www .syarikatbgc.com; f. 1998; LNG shipping co; owned jtly by Brunei Govt, Shell International Gas and Diamond Gas Carriers.

Brunei LNG Sdn Bhd: Lumut KC 2935, Seria; tel. 3236901; fax 3236749; e-mail GP-External-Affairs@BruneiLNG.com; internet www.blng.com.bn; f. 1969; natural gas liquefaction; owned jtly by the Brunei Govt, Shell and Mitsubishi Corpn; operates LNG plant at Lumut, which has a capacity of 7.2m. tons per year; Man. Dir Dato' Hamdillah H. A. Wahab.

Brunei National Petroleum Co Sdn Bhd (PetroleumBrunei): 5th Floor, Bangunan Bahirah, Jalan Menteri Besar, Bandar Seri Begawan BB 3910; tel. 2383022; fax 2383004; e-mail bnpc@brunet .bn; f. 2001; wholly govt-owned; CEO Alias Haji Mohd Yusof (acting).

Brunei Shell Marketing Co Bhd: Maya Puri Bldg, 36/37 Jalan Sultan, POB 385, Bandar Seri Begawan; tel. 2229304; fax 2240470; internet www.bsm.com.bn; f. 1978 (from the Shell Marketing Co of Brunei Ltd), when the Govt became equal partner with Shell; markets petroleum and chemical products throughout Brunei; Man. Dir Mat Suny Haji Mohd Hussein.

Brunei Shell Petroleum Co Sdn Bhd (BSP): Jalan Utara, Panagia, Seria KB 3534; tel. 3373999; fax 3372040; internet www.shell .com.bn; f. 1957; the largest industrial concern in the country; 50% state holding; Man. Dir Mark Carne; Dep. Man. Dir Haji Zainal Abidin Haji Mohamed Ali.

Jasra International Petroleum Sdn Bhd: RBA Plaza, 2nd Floor, Jalan Sultan, Bandar Seri Begawan; tel. 2228968; fax 2228929; petroleum exploration and production; Man. Dir ROBERT A. HARRISON.

TRADE UNIONS

Trade unions are legal in Brunei, but must be registered with the Government. In 2003 there were three officially registered trade unions, all in the petroleum sector, with a total membership constituting less than 5% of that sector's work-force. These included:

Brunei Oilfield Workers' Union: XDR/11, BSP Co Sdn Bhd, Seria KB 3534; f. 1964; 470 mems; Pres. SUHAINI Haji OTHMAN; Sec.-Gen. ABU TALIB BIN Haji MOHAMAD.

Transport

RAILWAYS

There are no public railways in Brunei. The Brunei Shell Petroleum Co Sdn Bhd maintains a 19.3-km section of light railway between Seria and Badas.

ROADS

In 1999 there were 1,150 km of roads in Brunei, of which almost 400 km were paved. The main highway connects Bandar Seri Begawan, Tutong and Kuala Belait. A 59-km coastal road links Muara and Tutong. The Eighth National Development Plan (2001–05) prioritized the development of Brunei's roads and, in particular, the construction of a network of main roads that would connect Brunei Muara, Tutong, Kuala Belait and Temburong. In September 2002 construction of the 15-km Jalan Lumut Bypass was completed.

Land Transport Department: 451979 Km 6, Jalan Gadong, Beribi, Bandar Seri Begawan BE 1110; tel. 2451979; fax 2424775; e-mail latis@brunet.bn; internet www.land-transport.gov.bn; Dir Awang Haji OTHMAN BIN Haji MOMIN.

SHIPPING

Most sea traffic is handled by a deep-water port at Muara, 28 km from the capital, which has a 611-m wharf and a draught of 8 m. The port has a container terminal, warehousing, freezer facilities and cement silos. In October 2000 a plan to deepen the port to enable its accommodation of larger vessels was announced. The original, smaller port at Bandar Seri Begawan itself is mainly used for local river-going vessels, for vessels to Malaysian ports in Sabah and Sarawak and for vessels under 30 m in length. There is a port at Kuala Belait, which takes shallow-draught vessels and serves mainly the Shell petroleum field and Seria. Owing to the shallow waters at Seria, tankers are unable to come up to the shore to load, and crude petroleum from the oil terminal is pumped through an underwater loading line to a single buoy mooring, to which the tankers are moored. At Lumut there is a 4.5-km jetty for liquefied natural gas (LNG) carriers.

Four main rivers, with numerous tributaries, are an important means of communication in the interior, and boats or water taxis are the main form of transport for most residents of the water villages. Larger water taxis operate daily to the Temburong district.

Bee Seng Shipping Co: 7 Block D, Sufri Complex, Km 2, Jalan Tutong, POB 1777, Bandar Seri Begawan; tel. 2220033; fax 2224495; e-mail beeseng@brunet.bn.

Belait Shipping Co (B) Sdn Bhd: B1, 2nd Floor, 94 Jalan McKerron, Kuala Belait 6081; POB 632, Kuala Belait; tel. 3335418; fax 3330239; f. 1977; Man. Dir Haji FATIMAH BINTE Haji ABDUL AZIZ.

Brunei Shell Tankers Sdn Bhd: Seria KB 3534; tel. 3373999; f. 1986; owned jtly by Brunei Govt (50%), a co in the Royal Dutch/Shell Group of Cos (25%) and Mitsubishi Corpn of Japan (25%); seven vessels operated by Shell International Trading and Shipping Co Ltd; delivers LNG to overseas markets; Man. Dir CHRIS FINLAYSON.

Harper Wira Sdn Bhd: B2 Bangunan Haji Mohd Yussof, Jalan Gadong, Bandar Seri Begawan 3188; tel. 2448529; fax 2448529.

Inchcape Borneo: Bangunan Inchcape Borneo, Km 4, Jalan Gadong, Bandar Seri Begawan; tel. 2422561; fax 2424352; f. 1856; Gen. Man. LO FAN KEE.

New Island Shipping: POB 850, Bandar Seri Begawan 1908; tel. 2451800; fax 2451480; f. 1975; Chair. TAN KOK VOON; Man. JIMMY VOON.

Pansar Co Sdn Bhd: First Floor, 27 Kompleks Mubibbah 3, Jalan Gadong, Bandar Seri Begawan 3180; tel. 2445246; fax 2445247.

Seatrade Shipping Co: POB 476, Bandar Seri Begawan 1904; tel. 2421457; fax 2421453.

Silver Line (B) Sdn Bhd: Muara Port; tel. 2445069; fax 2430276.

Wei Tat Shipping and Trading Co: Mile 41, Jalan Tutong, POB 103, Bandar Seri Begawan; tel. 265215.

CIVIL AVIATION

There is an international airport near Bandar Seri Begawan, which can handle up to 1.5m. passengers and 50,000 metric tons of cargo per year. The Brunei Shell Petroleum Co Sdn Bhd operates a private airfield at Anduki for helicopter services.

Department of Civil Aviation: Brunei International Airport, Bandar Seri Begawan BB 2513; tel. 2330142; fax 2331706; e-mail dea@brunet.bn; internet www.civil-aviation.gov.bn; Dir Haji KASIM BIN Haji LATIP.

Royal Brunei Airlines Ltd: RBA Plaza, Jalan Sultan, POB 737, Bandar Seri Begawan BS 8671; tel. 2240500; fax 2244737; e-mail feedback@rba.com.bn; internet www.bruneiair.com; f. 1974; operates services within the Far East and to the Middle East, Australia and Europe; Chair. Dato' Haji HAZAIR ABDULLAH; CEO PETER WILLIAM FOSTER.

Tourism

Tourist attractions in Brunei include the flora and fauna of the rain forest and the national parks, as well as mosques and water villages. There were 964,080 foreign visitor arrivals (including same-day visitors) in 1998. Foreign visitor arrivals increased to 1,306,764 in 2000. In 1998 international tourist receipts totalled US $37m. The year 2001 was designated 'Visit Brunei Year'.

Brunei Tourism: c/o Ministry of Industry and Primary Resources, Jalan Menteri Besar, Bandar Seri Begawan BB 3910; tel. 2382825; fax 2382824; e-mail info@tourismbrunei.com; internet www.tourismbrunei.com; Dir-Gen. Sheikh JAMALUDDIN BIN Sheikh MOHAMED.

BULGARIA

Introductory Survey

Location, Climate, Language, Religion, Flag, Capital

The Republic of Bulgaria lies in the eastern Balkans, in south-eastern Europe. It is bounded by Romania to the north, by Turkey and Greece to the south, by Serbia and Montenegro (Serbia) to the west and by the former Yugoslav republic of Macedonia to the south-west. The country has an eastern coastline on the Black Sea. The climate is one of fairly sharp contrasts between winter and summer. Temperatures in Sofia are generally between −5°C (23°F) and 28°C (82°F). The official language is Bulgarian, a Southern Slavonic language, written in the Cyrillic alphabet. Minority languages include Turkish and Macedonian. The majority of the population are Christian, most of whom adhere to the Bulgarian Orthodox Church, although there is a substantial minority of Muslims. The national flag (proportions 2 by 3) has three equal horizontal stripes, of white, green and red. The capital is Sofia.

Recent History

After almost 500 years of Ottoman rule, Bulgaria declared itself an independent kingdom in 1908. In both the First and Second World Wars Bulgaria allied itself with Germany, and in 1941 joined in the occupation of Yugoslavia. Soviet troops occupied Bulgaria in 1944. In September the Fatherland Front, a left-wing alliance formed in 1942, seized power, with help from the USSR, and installed a Government, led by Kimon Georgiev. In September 1946 the monarchy was abolished, following a popular referendum, and a republic was proclaimed. The first post-war election was held in October, when the Fatherland Front received 70.8% of the votes cast and won 364 seats in the 465-member Narodno Sobraniye (National Assembly), of which 277 were held by the Bulgarian Communist Party (BCP). In November Georgi Dimitrov, the First Secretary of the BCP and a veteran international revolutionary, became Chairman of the Council of Ministers (Prime Minister) in a Government that comprised members of the Fatherland Front. All opposition parties were abolished and a new Constitution, based on the Soviet model, was adopted in December 1947, when Bulgaria was designated a People's Republic. Dimitrov was replaced as Prime Minister by Vasil Kolarov in March 1949, but remained leader of the BCP until his death in July. His successor as party leader, Vulko Chervenkov, became Prime Minister in February 1950.

Todor Zhivkov succeeded Chervenkov as leader of the BCP in March 1954, although the latter remained Prime Minister until April 1956, when he was replaced by Anton Yugov. Following an ideological struggle within the BCP, Zhivkov was Prime Minister from November 1962 until July 1971, when, after the adoption of a new Constitution in May, Zhivkov became the first President of the newly formed State Council. He was re-elected in 1976, 1981 and 1986. At a BCP Congress held in March and April 1981 the party's leader was restyled General Secretary. In June, following elections to the Narodno Sobraniye, a new Government was formed; Grisha Filipov, a member of the BCP's Political Bureau, succeeded Stanko Todorov, who had been Prime Minister since 1971. In March 1986 Filipov was replaced by Georgi Atanasov, a former Vice-President of the State Council.

In local elections in March 1988, the nomination of candidates other than those endorsed by the BCP was permitted for the first time. Candidates presented by independent public organizations and workers' collectives obtained about one-quarter of the total votes cast. At a plenum of the BCP, held in July, several prominent proponents of reform were dismissed.

On 10 November 1989 Zhivkov was unexpectedly removed from his post of General Secretary of the BCP and from the Political Bureau. He was replaced as General Secretary by Petur Mladenov, Minister of Foreign Affairs since 1971, who also became President of the State Council. In mid-November 1989 the Narodno Sobraniye voted to abolish part of the penal code prohibiting 'anti-State propaganda' and to grant an amnesty to those convicted under its provisions. Zhivkov was subsequently denounced by the BCP and divested of his party membership, and an investigation into corruption during his tenure of power

was initiated. In 1990 Zhivkov was arrested on charges of embezzlement of state funds. (In January 1994 Zhivkov was sentenced to seven years' imprisonment on these charges, but in February 1996 the Supreme Court upheld his appeal against the sentence.)

In early December 1989 Angel Dimitrov became leader of the Bulgarian Agrarian People's Union (BAPU, the sole legal political party apart from the BCP, with which it was originally allied); the BAPU was subsequently reconstituted as an independent opposition party. In mid-December the BCP proposed amendments to the Constitution and the adoption of a new electoral law to permit free and democratic elections to be held in 1990. In January 1990 the Narodno Sobraniye voted to remove from the Constitution the article guaranteeing the BCP's dominant role in society and approved legislation permitting citizens to form independent groups and to stage demonstrations. Discussions regarding political and economic reforms commenced in early January 1990 between the BCP, the BAPU and the Union of Democratic Forces (UDF), a co-ordinating organization that comprised several dissident and independent groups. In early February the BCP adopted a new manifesto, pledging its commitment to extensive political and economic reforms, the separation of party and state, and the introduction of a multi-party system, while retaining its Marxist orientation. The party's organizational structures were substantially reformed, and Aleksandur Lilov, a former head of the BCP's ideology department, who had been expelled from the party in 1983 for criticism of Zhivkov, became Chairman of the Presidium of the Supreme Council. The President of the State Council, Mladenov, proposed the formation of an interim coalition government, pending elections to the Narodno Sobraniye. The UDF and the BAPU, however, rejected Mladenov's invitation to participate in such a coalition. Accordingly, the new Council of Ministers, appointed on 8 February 1990, was composed solely of BCP members, chaired by Andrei Lukanov, the former Minister of Foreign Economic Relations, who was regarded as an advocate of reform.

There was unrest in mid-February 1990, when an estimated 200,000 supporters of the UDF gathered in Sofia to demand the end of BCP rule. Following discussions in late March, with the participation of the BAPU and other political and public organizations, it was finally agreed that Mladenov was to be re-elected as President, pending elections to a Velikoto Narodno Sobraniye (Grand National Assembly), which would be empowered to approve a new constitution, in June. It was also decided to dissolve the State Council. In early April the Narodno Sobraniye adopted an electoral law, together with legislation that provided for political pluralism and guaranteed the right to form political parties. Also in early April the BCP voted to rename itself the Bulgarian Socialist Party (BSP).

Following an electoral campaign marred by acts of intimidation and violence, elections to a 400-member Velikoto Narodno Sobraniye were held in two rounds, on 10 and 17 June 1990. The BSP won 211 seats, but failed to obtain the two-thirds' majority of seats necessary to secure support for the approval of constitutional and economic reforms. The UDF, which won the majority of votes in urban areas, obtained 144 seats. The Movement for Rights and Freedoms (MRF), which had been established earlier in 1990 to represent the country's Muslim minority (principally ethnic Turks), secured 23 seats. The BAPU won 16 seats. The UDF, after initial protests against alleged electoral fraud, accepted the validity of the results, although it again rejected the BSP's invitation to join a coalition government. In July Mladenov announced his resignation as President, following a campaign of protests and strikes, led by students. Zhelyu Zhelev, the Chairman of the UDF, was elected to replace him in early August. Zhelev was succeeded as Chairman of the UDF first by Petur Beron, hitherto the party's Secretary, and, from December, by Filip Dimitrov, a lawyer and the Vice-President of the Green Party.

The severe deterioration in the economy in 1990 resulted in widespread shortages of food and fuel. Increasing division between conservative and reformist elements within the BSP became manifest in early November 1990, when 16 BSP delegates to the Velikoto Narodno Sobraniye announced their decision to form a separate group, as a result of which the party no longer held an absolute majority in the body. Following a four-day general strike organized by Podkrepa, Lukanov's Government resigned at the end of the month. Subsequent discussions between representatives of all the political forces in the Velikoto Narodno Sobraniye resulted in the formation of a new 'government of national consensus' in mid-December, comprising members of the BSP, the UDF, the BAPU and four independents. Dimitar Popov, a lawyer with no party affiliation, had been elected in early December to chair the new Council of Ministers.

In mid-November 1990 the Velikoto Narodno Sobraniye voted to rename the country the Republic of Bulgaria and to remove from the national flag the state emblem, which included communist symbols. The Velikoto Narodno Sobraniye adopted a new Constitution in mid-July 1991; it subsequently voted to dissolve itself, although it continued sessions in an interim capacity, pending legislative elections. (The new Constitution provided for elections to be held, on an *ad hoc* basis, to a Velikoto Narodno Sobraniye, the sole body empowered to adopt a new constitution, sanction territorial changes to the Republic, or certain constitutional amendments, although the permanent legislative body was to be the Narodno Sobraniye.) The Constitution stipulated, a five-year residency qualification for presidential candidates, effectively disqualifying the candidacy of Simeon Sakskoburg-gotski (Saxe-Coburg Gotha—'Simeon II'), the pretender to the Bulgarian throne, who had lived in exile since 1946. At the elections to the new, 240-seat Narodno Sobraniye, held on 13 October 1991, the UDF obtained the largest share of the votes cast (34.4%), narrowly defeating an alliance led by the BSP. The UDF won a total of 110 seats in the legislature, while the BSP obtained 106. The MRF became the third-strongest political force, securing 24 seats. The new Council of Ministers, composed of UDF members and six independents, was announced in early November. Dimitrov, the leader of the UDF, was elected Chairman of the new Government. A direct presidential election was held in January 1992. Following an inconclusive first round, a second ballot, involving the two leading candidates (the incumbent President, Zhelev, and Velko Valkanov, an independent supported by the BSP), took place. Zhelev was re-elected for a five-year term, receiving 53% of the votes cast.

In early April 1992, despite BSP opposition, the Government adopted legislation restoring ownership of land and property that had been transferred to the state during 1947–62; legislation approving the privatization of state-owned companies followed. In May Dimitrov threatened to resign as Prime Minister, unless the Minister of Defence, Dimitur Ludzhev, relinquished his post. Ludzhev resigned later that month, and Dimitrov implemented an extensive reorganization of the Council of Ministers. In July the former Prime Minister, Lukanov (by that time a BSP deputy), was arrested, prompting the remaining BSP deputies to withdraw from a meeting of the Narodno Sobraniye in protest. Legal proceedings were initiated against Lukanov and a further 60 former senior officials (including two other former Prime Ministers) on charges of misappropriating state funds. In mid-July 1992 there were strikes, supported by Podkrepa, by miners and other public-sector employees. In early August the Chairman of Podkrepa, Konstantin Trenchev, was arrested with 37 others and charged with incitement to destroy public property in 1990.

Meanwhile, relations between President Zhelev and the UDF became increasingly strained. At the end of October 1992 MRF and BSP deputies in the Narodno Sobraniye defeated the Government in a motion of confidence proposed by Dimitrov; the Government subsequently resigned. In November Zhelev invited Dimitrov (as the nominee of the party with the largest representation in the Narodno Sobraniye) to form a new government. The MRF, however, declined to form a coalition with the UDF, and Dimitrov's nomination was thus defeated in the Narodno Sobraniye. President Zhelev then rejected the candidacy of a BSP nominee, reportedly on the grounds that the candidate held dual nationality (although the Constitution did not place restrictions on such citizens). Following the failure of the UDF and the MRF to reach agreement for a coalition, in December the MRF nominated an academic, Prof. Lyuben Berov, hitherto an economic adviser to Zhelev, to the office of Prime Minister. The UDF accused Berov of collaborating with the former communist regime and organized a large rally to protest against his candidacy, while threatening to expel members who voted in his favour in the Narodno Sobraniye. In the

event, the majority of UDF deputies abstained, but Berov was approved as Prime Minister on 30 December by 124 votes to 25. Berov's proposed Council of Ministers, principally composed of non-partisan 'technocrats', was also accepted by the Narodno Sobraniye. On the same day, the BSP and the MRF voted in the Narodno Sobraniye to discharge Lukanov from custody.

In March 1993 internal divisions within the UDF became more apparent when a breakaway faction of the party formed a new, pro-Berov organization, the New Union for Democracy (NUD); in response, the UDF intensified its campaign of opposition. Large-scale demonstrations were staged by the UDF in Sofia and several other cities in June, to accuse Zhelev of attempting to restore communism, and to demand immediate elections. On 29 June the Vice-President, Blaga Dimitrova, resigned. The crisis finally subsided when three votes expressing 'no confidence' in Berov's Government, which were proposed by the UDF in the Narodno Sobraniye, proved unsuccessful; political unrest continued, however.

By May 1994 the Berov Government had survived its seventh motion of 'no confidence', after the controversial introduction of value-added tax (VAT), unpopular increases in fuel prices and the dramatic decline in value of the national currency, the lev, prompted thousands of demonstrators to protest in Sofia against government policies. In early September Berov's Government submitted its resignation, owing to criticism of the poor organization of the delayed privatization programme that had commenced in June. Both the BSP and the UDF refused presidential mandates to form a new Government. In October President Zhelev dissolved the Narodno Sobraniye and announced that a general election would take place in December. Later in October Zhelev appointed an interim, neutral Government, headed by Reneta Indzhova.

At the general election, which was held as scheduled on 18 December 1994, the BSP (in alliance, as the Democratic Left, with two small parties) obtained an outright majority in the Narodno Sobraniye, with 125 seats (43.5% of the total votes cast); the UDF won 69 seats (24.2%). Other groups that obtained more than the 4% of votes required for representation in the legislature were: the People's Union (an alliance of the BAPU and the Democratic Party), the MRF and the Bulgarian Business Bloc (BBB). A new Government, headed by the Chairman of the BSP, Zhan Videnov, was appointed at the end of January 1995.

In February 1995 the Narodno Sobraniye amended the 1992 property restitution law (see above), extending for a further three years the deadline by which certain properties had to be restored to their rightful owners. In March the Government drafted a programme for mass privatization, which envisaged payment through a combination of cash, debt bonds and investment vouchers (made available from January 1996). Demonstrations took place throughout March 1995, however, reflecting widespread dissatisfaction with government amendments to the Agricultural Land Tenure Act, which they feared would restrict landowners' rights to dispose of their property and would encourage the restoration of communist-style collective farms. In late April President Zhelev exercised his right of veto against the amendments. In late September the Government survived a motion of 'no confidence', which was introduced in protest at its failure to control the rapid increase in levels of crime. At municipal elections in late October and early November, the ruling coalition won 195 of a total of 255 mayoralties, although the UDF secured the mayoralties in the country's three main cities. In January 1996 a further motion of 'no confidence' in the Videnov administration, proposed in protest at a severe shortage of grain, was defeated, although the situation prompted the resignations of the Deputy Prime Minister and an additional two ministers. Meanwhile, a sharp devaluation of the lev resulted in further economic hardship. In June the UDF proposed a motion expressing 'no confidence' in the Government's management of the economy, which was, however, defeated by a large majority.

In primary elections for a UDF presidential candidate, which were conducted in early June 1996, Petar Stoyanov, a lawyer and senior member of the opposition alliance, secured 66% of the votes cast, defeating Zhelev. In July the Constitutional Court ruled that the candidacy of the Minister of Foreign Affairs, Georgi Pirinski, nominated on behalf of the BSP (and widely considered to be the most popular nominee), was ineligible, on the grounds that he was not a Bulgarian citizen by birth. In September the BSP selected the Minister of Culture, Ivan Marazov, as its presidential candidate; Marazov was to represent a newly formed electoral alliance, known as Together for Bulgaria. In early October the former Prime Minister, Andrei Lukanov (who had remained an influential member of the BSP), was assassinated. Ensuing speculation regarding the motive for the killing focused, in particular, on Lukanov's critical stance towards the Videnov administration's slow implementation of economic reforms. (In early March 2003 Ilya Pavlov, a prominent business executive, was shot and killed, one day after testifying in the trial of five people accused of the murder of Lukanov. In November of that year all five defendants were sentenced to life imprisonment for Lukanov's murder.)

In the first round of the presidential election, held on 27 October 1996, Stoyanov secured 44.1% of the votes cast; Marazov received only 27.0% of the votes, while the candidate of the BBB, Georgi Ganchev, won 21.9%. Only 61% of the electorate voted in the second round, which took place on 3 November, reflecting increasing public disaffection with the Government's economic management. Stoyanov was elected to the presidency, with 59.7% of the votes cast. He subsequently announced plans to establish a Council of National Salvation, which would devise measures to improve financial stability. In December the UDF staged a series of demonstrations to demand early legislative elections and the resignation of the Government. On 21 December Videnov tendered his resignation from the office of Prime Minister and the post of BSP party leader. Georgi Parvanov, who was a supporter of Videnov, subsequently replaced him as Chairman of the BSP. At the end of December the Narodno Sobraniye voted by a large majority to accept the resignation of Videnov's Government. The UDF, however, intensified its campaign of demonstrations; in early January an attempt by protesters to seize the parliamentary building was suppressed by security forces.

On 19 January 1997 Stoyanov was inaugurated as President, and at the end of January the BSP accepted a proposal by Stoyanov that the party form a new government, pending legislative elections. In early February the BSP announced the appointment of a new Council of Ministers under Nikolai Dobrev (the Minister of the Interior in the previous administration). However, following continued protests and strikes by supporters of the UDF, Dobrev agreed to relinquish the BSP's mandate to form a new government, owing to increasing concern that the disorder might escalate into civil conflict. The Consultative National Security Council adopted recommendations (which were approved by the Narodno Sobraniye) that, in the absence of agreement between the political parties represented in the legislature on the formation of a government, the President should appoint an interim council of ministers, dissolve the Narodno Sobraniye and schedule legislative elections. Stoyanov subsequently nominated the mayor of Sofia, Stefan Sofiyanski, to the office of Prime Minister, pending the elections, which were scheduled to be held in mid-April; the Narodno Sobraniye was dissolved on 19 February. In March the interim Government announced that Videnov was to be charged with criminal negligence as a result of government policies that had caused the severe shortage of grain in 1995–96; the Minister of Agriculture in the Videnov administration and three of his deputies were also prosecuted.

At the elections to the Narodno Sobraniye, which took place, as scheduled, on 19 April 1997, the UDF secured 137 seats, while the BSP (which again contested the elections in the Democratic Left alliance) obtained only 58 seats; the Alliance for National Salvation (a coalition comprising the MRF and other monarchist and centrist groups) won 19 seats, a newly established left-wing organization, known as Euro-Left, obtained 14 seats and the BBB 12 seats. Later in April the UDF formally nominated the party Chairman, Ivan Kostov, to the office of Prime Minister (subject to the approval of the Narodno Sobraniye). At the first session of the new legislature, which was convened in early May, deputies adopted a seven-point declaration of national consensus, which had been proposed by the UDF; the stated policies included the implementation of economic reforms that had been agreed with the IMF, the acceleration of measures to restore agricultural land to rightful ownership and support for Bulgaria's accession to the European Union (EU, see p. 217) and the North Atlantic Treaty Organization (NATO, see p. 301). Later in May the Narodno Sobraniye elected Kostov to the office of Prime Minister; only deputies belonging to the Democratic Left alliance opposed his nomination. The new Council of Ministers included five members of the outgoing interim administration.

At the end of July the Narodno Sobraniye voted in favour of declassifying security files on politicians and public officials, and adopted legislation to expedite the restoration of land to rightful ownership. In early September two parliamentary representatives of the BBB were expelled from the party after criticizing the leadership of Ganchev, who, they claimed, intended to establish links with the BSP; another deputy resigned in protest at their removal. The BBB was consequently obliged to dissolve its parliamentary group, which had been reduced to below the required minimum of 10 representatives. In October a government commission announced that 23 prominent public officials, including 14 members of the Narodno Sobraniye, had been members of the security services of the former communist regime. In January 1998 the Narodno Sobraniye rejected a motion expressing 'no confidence' in the Government, which had been proposed by Democratic Left deputies.

In April 1999 the Government, accused of nepotism and corruption, survived a second vote of 'no confidence' in the Narodno Sobraniye. Local government elections took place on 16 and 23 October: the UDF won 31.3% of the votes cast and the BSP secured 29.4%. In December Kostov reorganized the Council of Ministers. In May 2000 Kostov's administration survived a third vote of 'no confidence', and in February 2001 the Narodno Sobraniye rejected a further 'no confidence' motion, proposed in response to the worsening crime situation. Meanwhile, in January, in advance of presidential and legislative elections, the BSP attempted to consolidate support by forming an alliance, known as the Coalition for Bulgaria, with 14 other, smaller leftist and nationalist groups. Several parliamentary deputies subsequently defected from the UDF in order to form a new party, the Conservative Union. In April the former monarch, Simeon Sakskoburggotski, who returned to Bulgaria at the beginning of the month, failed to be permitted legally to register his new National Movement as a party. None the less, in May the Movement was permitted to form an alliance with two smaller, registered parties, the Party of Bulgarian Women and the Oborishte Party for National Revival, as the National Movement Simeon II (NMSII), under a nominal leader, Vesela Draganova, in order to participate in the legislative elections. Sakskoburggotski asserted that he had no desire to restore the monarchy, and pledged to combat official corruption and reform the economy, in order to fulfil the criteria for EU membership.

In the general election, held on 17 June 2001, the NMSII received 42.7% of the votes cast, obtaining 120 seats, while the incumbent UDF secured only 18.2% of the votes (51 seats). Other groups to win seats in parliament were the Coalition for Bulgaria, which obtained 17.1% of the votes (48 seats), and the MRF, with 7.5% of the votes (21 seats). The NMSII held just one seat fewer than the 121 required to secure an absolute majority in the Narodno Sobraniye; however, it had declared its intention to form a coalition government throughout its election campaign, and it approached the MRF and the UDF as potential partners. The MRF agreed to be represented in government, but the UDF refused to participate in a government that comprised members of the MRF; the BSP subsequently became an informal coalition partner. Sakskoburggotski was sworn in as Prime Minister on 24 July. The Council of Ministers, in which two ministerial portfolios were allocated to both the MRF and the BSP, was approved by the Narodno Sobraniye on the same day, although members of the UDF voted against the new cabinet, in protest at the presence of the BSP. Kostov subsequently resigned his leadership of the UDF.

In the first round of voting in the presidential election, held on 11 November 2001, at which the rate of participation by the electorate was just 39.2% (less than the 50% demanded by the Constitution), Parvanov, contesting the election for the Coalition for Bulgaria, won 36.4% of the votes cast, and the incumbent, Stoyanov, who stood as an independent candidate, secured 34.9% of the votes. Parvanov confirmed his victory in a second round of voting on 18 November, in which he obtained 54.1% of the votes cast, compared with the 45.9% of the votes received by Stoyanov; the rate of voter participation was some 54.6%. The result of the election, which was largely unanticipated, given the rejection of the BSP-led Coalition in the legislative elections and the support of both Sakskoburggotski and the UDF for the incumbent, was widely interpreted as an expression of protest by a frustrated electorate. Parvanov was sworn in as President on 19 January 2002 and took office three days later.

In December 2001 the Government released a report, which accused the Kostov Government of unscrupulous actions with regard to the privatization process, and announced the establishment of an investigative commission. In February 2002 the Government survived a vote of 'no confidence', which had been proposed by the UDF, by 134 votes to 50 (a number of BSP deputies abstained from voting). In March five members of the Narodno Sobraniye left the NMSII, in protest at Sakskoburggotski's perceived failure to fulfil electoral pledges. In April the NMSII was finally legally registered as a political party, and Sakskoburggotski was elected as its Chairman. The new post of Minister of European Affairs was created in late May, and Meglena Kuneva was appointed to it.

In early October 2002 the Narodno Sobraniye voted in favour of closing the third and fourth reactors of the Kozloduy nuclear power plant (in compliance with EU demands) following Bulgaria's accession to the Union, which was not anticipated before 2007. However, in mid-November 2002 the Government signed an agreement with the EU, according to which it undertook to decommission the reactors by 2006. Later in November 2002 the Government defeated votes of 'no confidence' brought by the UDF and the Coalition for Bulgaria, which, respectively, regarded the agreement as a violation of the Constitution and accused the Government of failing to act in the country's interests. In early January 2003, following a legal challenge by the BSP, the Supreme Administrative Court ruled the government agreement to be invalid, announcing that only the Narodno Sobraniye could decide on the closure of the two reactors. Meanwhile, in December 2002 the Government approved controversial draft legislation, which required all religious organizations, with the exception of the Bulgarian Orthodox Church, to be registered officially; the legislation was opposed by the NMSII's junior coalition partner, the MRF.

Following efforts by the Supreme Administrative Court to suspend the sales of both the state tobacco company, Bulgartabac, and the Bulgarian Telecommunications Company in late 2002 (see Economic Affairs), in January 2003 the Narodno Sobraniye approved controversial legislation removing the Court's power to block the privatization of principle state enterprises; divestments were, instead, to be decided by the Government, with the approval of the Narodno Sobraniye. In late February Parvanov exercised his right of veto, on the grounds that the legislation contravened the Constitution; later that month, however, the ruling majority in the Narodno Sobraniye voted to override the presidential veto. A petition was subsequently lodged with the Constitutional Court by Parvanov, the UDF and the BSP, and in mid-April the Court ruled that the amendments to the privatization bill had been unconstitutional. Meanwhile, in mid-February five members of parliament had left the NMSII, alleging widespread corruption within the Government, and thereby reducing the governing coalition's legislative majority to just 10 seats.

In May 2003 the Government survived a further vote of 'no confidence', proposed by the UDF. In July the Prime Minister implemented a reshuffle of the Council of Ministers; however, the MRF and the BSP remained dissatisfied, as the restructuring failed to ascribe them any greater influence, and opposition parties claimed that it had not been sufficiently far-reaching. Notably, a new deputy prime ministerial post, with special responsibility for EU integration, was created. In July the Narodno Sobraniye approved draft electoral legislation that introduced a mixed system of voting, whereby one-half of the Narodno Sobraniye's 240 members were to be elected by majority vote in their constituencies, and the remainder by proportional representation from a national list of candidates. In early August the Minister of Finance, Milen Velchev, tendered his resignation, citing a lack of support from within the Government; however, he subsequently withdrew his decision, following consultations with Sakskoburggotski. In late September the Narodno Sobraniye passed a number of amendments to the Constitution, as part of wider efforts to reform the judiciary and combat the increasingly prevalent problem of organized crime. The failure to address the strength of criminal structures had been widely regarded as a principal weakness of Sakskoburggotski's Government. Meanwhile, also in September the Prime Minister's nomination of a former head of the communist-era National Intelligence Service, Gen. Brigo Asparuhov, as an adviser on security issues led to concerns by opposition parties and western diplomats that relations with NATO (to which Bulgaria was to accede in 2004) could be adversely affected. Two members of parliament left the NMSII over the issue, although Asparuhov declined the nomination in the following month.

In municipal elections, which took place on 26 October and 2 November 2003, the BSP and the UDF secured the majority of seats, with many incumbents retaining their posts. The results, which were widely interpreted as a rejection of the NMSII in the first test of public support since its election to the Government in 2001, led to renewed pressure for a more extensive cabinet reshuffle. In mid-January 2004 Ekaterina Mihailova resigned her position as deputy leader of the UDF, in protest at the leadership of Nadezhda Mihailova. The latter was re-elected to the party leadership in February, prompting 26 UDF members, including the party's former Chairman, Ivan Kostov, to leave the party. Kostov subsequently founded a new party: Democrats for a Strong Bulgaria. In mid-March the Government survived its fifth vote of 'no confidence', which had been proposed by the BSP in the Narodno Sobraniye.

In May 2004 Stefan Sofianski, who was briefly Prime Minister on an interim basis in 1997, was suspended from his position as Mayor of Sofia for a short period while an investigation was pursued into his conduct of official affairs. The allegations of corruption made against Sofianski remained unresolved in early 2005 and were likely to damage his credibility as a potential leader of the fragmented political right wing before the parliamentary elections, which were due to held later that year. In December 2004 the Government, under pressure from New Time, a grouping that had left NMSII earlier in the year, announced an increase in expenditure on the education sector, in order to secure sufficient parliamentary support for the 2005 draft budget. In February 2005 the Narodno Sobraniye voted to dismiss Ognyan Gerdzhikov as its Chairman by a narrow majority. Gerdzhikov had been accused of systematic violation of the Narodno Sobraniye's rules of procedure after he refused to allow parliament to discuss the failed sale of Bulgartabac to British-American Tobacco (of the United Kingdom and the USA). The issue inspired a sixth vote of 'no confidence' in Sakskoburggotski's Government, which the ruling coalition narrowly survived, having received the support of New Time. Later in the same month, in an attempt to strengthen the ruling coalition before the elections, the Prime Minister effected a reorganization of the Council of Ministers. The parliamentary leader of New Time, Miroslav Sevlievski, was appointed as Minister of Energy and Energy Resources, while Sevlievski's predecessor in that post, Milko Kovachev, replaced Lidiya Shouleva as Deputy Prime Minister and Minister of the Economy; Shouleva was given responsibility for NMSII's electoral campaign and also for developing the party's national economic plan for 2005–10. Other ministerial changes included the establishment of a new Ministry of Culture and Tourism, headed by Nina Chilova, and the appointment of a new Minister of Agriculture and Forestry. On 23 February 2005 Borislav Velikov, of NMSII, was elected as the new Chairman of the Narodno Sobraniye.

Bulgaria's establishment of formal relations with the former Yugoslav republic of Macedonia (FYRM) in January 1992 prompted harsh criticism from the Greek Government, although relations with Greece appeared to improve thereafter. In November 1993 the FYRM expressed its desire to establish full diplomatic relations with Bulgaria, and in the following month Bulgaria announced that it was to open an embassy in the FYRM and relax border procedures between the two states. In February 1999 Prime Minister Kostov and the Prime Minister of the FYRM, Ljubčo Georgievski, signed a declaration pledging that neither country had a territorial claim on the other. In March the Ministers of Defence of Bulgaria and the FYRM signed a joint declaration providing for increased military co-operation, including joint exercises and the supply of military equipment to the FYRM, in connection with the aim of both countries to join NATO. Public opposition in Bulgaria to the aerial bombardment of Yugoslavia (now Serbia and Montenegro) by NATO forces in March–June 1999, increased, after a misdirected NATO missile damaged a private residence in the outskirts of Sofia in April. Nevertheless, the Bulgarian Narodno Sobraniye approved a decision made by the Council of Ministers to allow NATO use of the country's airspace.

In June 2000, after eight years of discussions, relations with Romania were significantly improved by the signature of an agreement on the construction of a second bridge over the River Danube, from Vidin to Calafat, in Romania; the link was to improve road connections between the Balkans and western Europe. Ties with Romania were strengthened from 2000, owing to that country's concurrent negotiations for accession to the EU, and in August 2001 Bulgaria and Romania agreed to campaign jointly for membership of both the EU and NATO.

Relations between Bulgaria and Russia improved in 1992, following the signature of co-operation agreements, and the visit of the Russian President, Boris Yeltsin, to Sofia in August. In April 1998 the Bulgarian Government signed an agreement with the Russian national gas company, Gazprom, providing for the supply and transit of Russian gas. In December 2000 Russia expressed its disappointment at Bulgaria's decision to terminate, in accordance with conditions for accession to the EU, a 1978 bilateral agreement on visa-free travel, with effect from June 2001. However, in March 2003 Russian President Vladimir Putin visited Bulgaria, resulting in strongly enhanced economic relations (already a significant trading partner, Russia sought to increase its influence with regard to Balkan power supplies), despite failing to persuade Bulgaria to withdraw its support for US-led military action in Iraq (see below).

Relations with neighbouring Turkey were intermittently strained from the mid-1980s, when the Zhivkov regime began a campaign of forced assimilation of Bulgaria's ethnic Turkish minority (which constitutes an estimated 10% of the total population). The ethnic Turks were forced to adopt Slavic names prior to the December 1985 census, and were banned from practising Islamic religious rites. In May 1989 Bulgarian militia units violently suppressed demonstrations by an estimated 30,000 ethnic Turks in eastern Bulgaria against the assimilation campaign. In June more than 80,000 ethnic Turks were expelled from Bulgaria, although the Bulgarian authorities claimed that the Turks had chosen to settle in Turkey, following a relaxation in passport regulations. By mid-August an estimated 310,000 Bulgarian Turks had crossed into Turkey, and in late August the Turkish Government, alarmed by the continued influx of refugees, closed the border. In the following month a substantial number of the Bulgarian Turks, disillusioned with conditions in Turkey, began to return to Bulgaria. The Turkish Government repeatedly proposed that discussions with the Bulgarian Government be held, under the auspices of the UN High Commissioner for Refugees, to establish the rights of the Bulgarian Turks and to formulate a clear immigration policy. Finally, Bulgaria agreed to negotiations and friendly relations between Bulgaria and Turkey had apparently been restored by late 1991.

Meanwhile, in December 1989 some 6,000 Pomaks (ethnic Bulgarian Muslims) held demonstrations to demand religious and cultural freedoms, as well as an official inquiry into alleged atrocities against Pomaks during Zhivkov's tenure of office. In January 1990 anti-Turkish demonstrations were held in the Kurdzhali district of southern Bulgaria, in protest at the Government's declared intention to restore civil and religious rights to the ethnic Turkish minority. Despite continuing demonstrations by Bulgarian nationalist protesters, in March the Narodno Sobraniye approved legislation that permitted ethnic Turks and Pomaks to use their original, non-Slavic, names. This development was welcomed by the Turkish Government. Nevertheless, inter-ethnic disturbances continued, particularly in the Kurdzhali region, during 1990. In May 1992 Prime Minister Dimitrov visited Turkey, and the two countries signed a treaty of friendship and co-operation. By 1993 ethnic tensions had generally been contained in Bulgaria, although there were reports of disturbances between ethnic Turks and ethnic Bulgarian Muslims in the south of the country. In July 1995 a visit by President Süleyman Demirel of Turkey to Bulgaria indicated a significant improvement in Bulgarian-Turkish relations. In June 1998 the Narodno Sobraniye ratified an agreement demarcating the border between Bulgaria and Turkey (which had been signed during an official visit to Sofia by the Turkish Prime Minister, Mesut Yılmaz, in December 1997). In February 2001 Bulgaria and Turkey signed a joint protocol on combating terrorism and organized crime.

Bulgaria's relations with the USA strengthened during 2002, and in February 2003 the Narodno Sobraniye voted to allow US forces to make use of Bulgarian airspace, as well as the air base at Sarafovo, on the Black Sea, for military operations during the impending US-led campaign to remove the regime of Saddam Hussein in Iraq (see the chapter on Iraq); Bulgaria had previously offered its support to the USA during its military campaign in Afghanistan from late 2001 (see the chapter on the USA). The conflict in Iraq (which commenced in March 2003) was strongly opposed by a number of European countries, notably France, and in February French President Jacques Chirac had condemned both Bulgaria and Romania as 'irresponsible' in offering the USA their support. In late December five members of the Bulgarian military contingent in Iraq were killed and 25 were wounded as the result of a suicide attack. Also in December the Narodno Sobraniye voted to allow the establishment of US bases on Bulgarian territory. In early 2004 the Iraqi media reported that in 1998 the BSP and a number of Bulgarian companies had received payments from the regime of Saddam Hussein; the Bulgarian Government established a parliamentary commission to investigate the claims. In 2004 two Bulgarian civilians were executed by militant groups in Iraq; however, Bulgaria pledged to maintain its 470-strong military presence in Iraq.

In mid-1992 Bulgaria became a member of the Council of Europe (see p. 199), and in May 1994 Bulgaria was granted associate partnership status by Western European Union (WEU, see p. 352). In 1996 Bulgaria submitted an official application for membership of the EU. In October of that year Bulgaria joined the World Trade Organization (see p. 357). Negotiations on Bulgaria's accession to the EU, which was conditional on the Government's fulfilment of certain criteria (see Economic Affairs), began in March 2000, and Bulgaria was expected to be admitted as a full member in 2007. In March 2004 the European Parliament praised Bulgaria's reform efforts and endorsed the planned date of 2007 for Bulgaria's accession, and in June Bulgaria (along with Romania) officially concluded the negotiation process with the EU (although the EU reserved the right, for the first time, to postpone the accession date if necessary). Meanwhile, in November 2002, at a NATO summit meeting held in Prague, Czech Republic, seven countries, including Bulgaria, were formally invited to become full members in 2004. Bulgaria duly joined the Alliance on 29 March 2004.

Government

Legislative power is held by the unicameral Narodno Sobraniye, comprising 240 members, who are elected for four years by universal adult suffrage. The President of the Republic (Head of State) is directly elected for a period of five years, and is also Supreme Commander-in-Chief of the Armed Forces. The Council of Ministers, the highest organ of state administration, is elected by the Narodno Sobraniye. For local administration purposes, Bulgaria comprises 28 regions (divided into a total of 259 municipalities).

Defence

Military service is compulsory and lasts for nine months. The total strength of the armed forces in August 2004 was estimated at 51,000 (including some 49,000 conscripts), comprising an army of 25,000, an air force of 13,100, a navy of an estimated 4,370, and 8,530 centrally controlled and Ministry of Defence staff. Paramilitary forces include an estimated 12,000 border guards, 18,000 railway and construction troops and 4,000 security police. The budget for 2004 allocated some 876m. new leva to defence. Bulgaria joined the North Atlantic Treaty Organization's (NATO) 'Partnership for Peace' (see p. 303) programme of military co-operation in 1994 and became a full member of the alliance on 29 March 2004.

Economic Affairs

In 2003, according to estimates by the World Bank, Bulgaria's gross national income (GNI), measured at average 2001–03 prices, was US $19,364.2m., equivalent to $2,130 per head (or $7,610 per head on an international purchasing-power parity basis). During 1990–2003, it was estimated, the population decreased at an average rate of 0.8% per year, while gross domestic product (GDP) per head increased, in real terms, at an average annual rate of 0.5%. According to the World Bank, Bulgaria's overall GDP declined, in real terms, by an average of 0.4% annually during 1990–2003. However, real GDP increased by 4.9% in 2002 and by 4.3% in 2003.

Agriculture contributed some 12.1% of GDP in 2003, and the sector (including hunting, forestry and fishing) engaged 25.6% of the employed labour force in 2002. In 1990 private farming was legalized, and farmland was to be restituted, in its former physical boundaries, to former owners and their heirs; by the end of 1999 96% of land restitution had been completed. In 1996 privately owned farms supplied 75.4% of total agricultural production. The principal crops are wheat, maize, barley, sunflower seeds, potatoes, tomatoes and melons. Bulgaria is also a major exporter of wine, and there is a large exportable surplus of processed agricultural products. During 1990–2003, according to the World Bank, the average annual GDP of the agricultural sector increased, in real terms, by 1.5%. Real agricultural GDP increased by 5.1% in 2002 and by 2.5% in 2003.

Industry provided some 27.3% of GDP in 2003 and the sector (including mining, manufacturing, construction and utilities) engaged 27.9% of the employed labour force in 2002. According to the World Bank, industrial GDP declined, in real terms, at an average annual rate of 2.8% in 1990–2003. However, real industrial GDP increased by 3.5% in 2002 and by 5.0% in 2003.

In 2002 mining accounted for some 1.4% of GDP and mining and quarrying engaged 1.2% of the employed labour force. Coal, iron ore, copper, manganese, lead and zinc are mined, and petroleum is extracted on the Black Sea coast.

The manufacturing sector accounted for 16.5% of GDP in 2003 and it engaged 20.5% of the employed labour force in 2002. Based on the value of output, in 1999 the main branches of manufacturing were food products, beverages and tobacco products, machinery, refined petroleum products, basic metals, chemicals and chemical products, and clothing. The GDP of the manufacturing sector increased by 6.5% in 1998, but declined by 5.9% in 1999.

Bulgaria's production of primary energy in 2001 was equivalent to 54.0% of gross consumption. Coal and nuclear power, produced by the country's sole nuclear power station, at Kozloduy, are the main domestic sources of energy. (A second nuclear power plant, at Belene, was scheduled to be completed by 2010.) In 2001 nuclear power provided 50.2% of electric energy, while coal accounted for 42.8% of electricity production. Bulgaria has established itself as a major regional electricity exporter and in 2004 supplied Greece with extra electricity for the Olympic Games. Imports of mineral fuels and electricity comprised 17.6% of the value of merchandise imports in 2003.

The services sector contributed some 60.6% of GDP in 2003 and engaged 46.4% of the employed labour force in 2002. Tourism revenues increased significantly in 2002–03. The World Bank estimated that the real GDP of the services sector decreased at an average rate of 1.9% per year in 1990–2003. However, the real GDP of the sector increased by 5.1% in 2002 and by 7.5% in 2003.

In 2003 Bulgaria recorded a visible trade deficit of US $2,437.7m., and there was a deficit of $1,648.0m. on the current account of the balance of payments. In that year the principal sources of imports were Germany, which provided 14.3% of the total and Russia, which provided 12.6%. Italy (10.2%), Greece (6.6%) and Turkey (6.1%) were also major suppliers. The main market for exports in 2003 was Italy (taking 14.0% of the total); Germany (10.8%), Greece (10.4%), Turkey (9.2%) and Belgium (6.1%) were also significant purchasers. The principal exports in 2003 were clothing and footwear, iron and steel, other metals and petroleum products. The principal imports in that year were mineral fuels (crude petroleum and natural gas), textiles, machines and equipment, vehicles and plastics and rubber.

In 2002 Bulgaria recorded a budgetary deficit of an estimated 876m. new leva (equivalent to 2.7% of GDP). Bulgaria's total external debt at the end of 2002 was US $10,462m., of which $8,585m. was long-term public debt. In that year the cost of debt-servicing was equivalent to 15.9% of revenue from exports of goods and services. The annual rate of inflation averaged 7.7% in 1997–2003. Consumer prices increased by 1,058.4% in 1997, but by only 18.7% in 1998 and by 2.5% in 1999, before increasing by 10.4% in 2000, by 7.4% in 2001, by 5.8% in 2002 and by 2.1% in 2003. Some 12.2% of the labour force were registered as unemployed at December 2004.

In 1990 Bulgaria became a member of the IMF and the World Bank, and it was a founding member of the European Bank for Reconstruction and Development (EBRD, see p. 212), established in the same year. Bulgaria is a member of the Organization of the Black Sea Economic Co-operation (see p. 325). The country's negotiations for accession to the European Union (EU, see p. 217) were successfully concluded in June 2004, and membership was expected to take effect from 2007.

At the beginning of the 1990s, in an effort to prevent economic collapse, the Government introduced an extensive programme of privatization and restructuring of the banking system, and adopted austerity measures in 1991. In May 1996 there was a dramatic reduction in the value of the lev, and in September the IMF suspended the disbursement of funds. Following the resumption of negotiations between a new, interim administration

(see Recent History) and the IMF, agreement was reached in March 1997 on the adoption of structural reforms. The Government established a currency control board in July, which fixed the exchange rate of the lev to that of the German Deutsche Mark. Bulgaria officially concluded accession talks with the EU in June 2004 and was scheduled to accede to the organization in 2007. In order to comply with conditions for EU membership, two of the Kozloduy nuclear power installation's six reactors were closed at the end of 2002; an agreement had been reached with the EU in November on the closure of two additional reactors by 2006, but in early 2003 the Supreme Administrative Court ruled the Government's decision on the early closure of the third and fourth reactors to be illegal. Although investor confidence had been undermined in late 2002, when long-delayed progress towards the privatization of the state tobacco company, Bulgartabac, and the Bulgarian Telecommunications Company (BTC) was halted owing to claims that legislation on privatization had been violated, a 65% stake in BTC was eventually divested in February 2004. The proposed sale of Bulgartabac to British-American Tobacco failed in January 2005, and the Narodno Sobraniye voted to reopen the privatization process in February. Meanwhile, plans for the partial privatization of seven electricity distribution companies were approved by the Government in November 2004. The budget for 2005 envisaged continued growth, of between 5.0% and 5.5%, and a lower annual rate of inflation of 3.6%, while further improvement of the transport infrastructure, the reduction of taxes and the stimulation of employment remained priorities for the Government. The draft budget set the projected budgetary deficit at just 0.5% of GDP; however, the plan was adjusted in order to gain parliamentary approval and, to the displeasure of the IMF, which was due to review a precautionary stand-by agreement of US $146m. with Bulgaria in March, extra expenditure of 100m. leva was allocated to education.

Education

Education is free and compulsory between the ages of seven and 16 years. Children between the ages of three and six years may attend kindergartens (in 2003/04 75% of pre-school age children attended). A 12-year system of schooling was introduced in 1998. Primary education, beginning at seven years of age, lasts for four years. Secondary education, from 11 years of age, lasts for up to eight years, comprising two cycles of four years each. Secondary education is undertaken at general schools, which provide a general academic course, or vocational and technical schools, and art schools, which offer specialized training. In 2003/04 primary enrolment included 100% of children in the relevant age-group, while enrolment at lower secondary and upper secondary schools included 84% and 77%, respectively, of those in the relevant age-group. In the mid-1990s the system of higher education was reorganized extensively. In 1997 enrolment in universities and equivalent higher colleges was equivalent to 24% of those in the relevant age-group. In 2003/04 there were a total of 42 higher educational institutions, with a total enrolment of 207,340 students, and an additional nine colleges. Tuition fees for university students were introduced in mid-1999. According to preliminary figures, the 2002 state budget allocated 568m. new leva to education (representing 4.9% of total expenditure by the central Government).

Public Holidays

2005: 1 January (New Year), 3 March (National Day), 29 April–2 May (Easter), 1 May (Labour Day), 6 May (St George's Day), 24 May (Education Day), 6 September (Union of Eastern Rumelia and the Bulgarian Principality), 22 September (Independence Day), 1 November (Commemoration of the Leaders of the Bulgarian National Revival), 24–26 December (Christmas).

2006: 1 January (New Year), 3 March (National Day), 21–24 April (Easter), 1 May (Labour Day), 6 May (St George's Day), 24 May (Education Day), 6 September (Union of Eastern Rumelia and the Bulgarian Principality), 22 September (Independence Day), 1 November (Commemoration of the Leaders of the Bulgarian National Revival), 24–26 December (Christmas).

Weights and Measures

The metric system is in force.

Statistical Survey

Sources (unless otherwise indicated): National Statistical Institute, 1038 Sofia, ul. P. Volov 2; tel. (2) 985-77-00; fax (2) 985-76-40; e-mail info@nsi.bg; internet www.nsi.bg; Bulgarian National Bank, 1000 Sofia, bul. A. Battenberg 1; tel. (2) 914-51-203; fax (2) 980-24-25; e-mail press_office@bnbank.org; internet www.bnb.bg; Center for Economic Development, 1408 Sofia, ul. J. K. Ivan Vazov 1/9; tel. (2) 953-42-04; e-mail stat@ced.bg; internet www.stat.bg.

Area and Population

AREA, POPULATION AND DENSITY

Area (sq km)*	110,994†
Population (census results)	
4 December 1992	8,487,317
1 March 2001	
Males	3,862,465
Females	4,066,436
Total	7,928,901
Population (official estimates at 31 December)	
2001	7,891,095
2002	7,845,499
2003	7,801,273
Density (per sq km) at 31 December 2003	70.3

* Including territorial waters of frontier rivers (261.4 sq km).
† 42,855 sq miles.

ETHNIC GROUPS
(2001 census)

	Number	%
Bulgarian	6,655,210	83.94
Turkish	746,664	9.42
Roma	370,908	4.68
Others*	156,119	1.97
Total	7,928,901	100.00

* Including 62,108 (0.78% of the total) who chose not to be defined by ethnic group, and 24,807 (0.31%) who did not respond to the question on ethnicity.

ADMINISTRATIVE REGIONS
(provisional results, 2001 census)

	Population
City Oblast	
Sofia City	1,173,988
Oblasts	
Blagoevgrad	341,245
Burgas	423,608
Dobrich	215,232
Gabrovo	144,150
Kardzhali	164,019
Khaskovo	277,483
Kyustendil	162,622
Lovech	169,951
Montana	182,267
Pazardzhik	310,741
Pernik	149,856
Pleven	312,018
Plovdiv	715,904
Razgrad	152,417
Ruse	266,213
Shumen	204,395
Silistra	142,003
Sliven	218,474
Smolyan	140,067
Sofia (Oblast)	273,252
Stara Zagora	370,665
Targovishche	137,689
Varna	462,218
Veliko Tarnovo	293,294
Vidin	130,094
Vratsa	243,039
Yambol	156,080
Total	7,932,984

Each oblast is named after its capital city.

PRINCIPAL TOWNS
(population at 2001 census)

Sofia (capital) . .	1,173,988	Sliven	136,148
Plovdiv	338,302	Pazardzhik	127,918
Varna	320,668	Pernik	104,626
Burgas (Bourgas) .	209,479	Shumen	104,473
Ruse (Roussé) . .	178,435	Dobrich*	100,000
Stara Zagora . .	167,708	Khaskovo	99,181
Pleven	149,174	Veliko Tarnovo	90,504

* Known as Tolbukhin in 1949–90.

Mid-2003: Sofia 1,075,791 (Source: UN, *World Urbanization Prospects: The 2003 Revision*).

BIRTHS, MARRIAGES AND DEATHS

	Registered live births		Registered marriages*		Registered deaths	
	Number	Rate (per 1,000)	Number	Rate (per 1,000)	Number	Rate (per 1,000)
1995 . .	71,967	8.6	36,795	4.4	114,670	13.6
1996 . .	72,188	8.6	n.a.	4.3	117,056	14.0
1997 . .	64,125	7.7	34,772	4.2	121,861	14.7
1998 . .	65,361	7.9	35,591	4.3	118,190	14.3
1999 . .	72,291	8.8	35,540	4.3	111,786	13.6
2000 . .	73,679	9.0	n.a.	4.3	115,087	14.1
2001 . .	68,180	8.6	n.a.	4.0	112,368	14.2
2002 . .	67,262	8.5	n.a.	3.7	112,858	14.3

* Including marriages of Bulgarian nationals outside the country, but excluding those of aliens in Bulgaria.

Source: partly UN, *Population and Vital Statistics* and *Monthly Bulletin of Statistics*.

Expectation of life (WHO estimates, years at birth): 71.9 (males 68.7; females 75.3) in 2002 (Source: WHO, *World Health Report*).

EMPLOYMENT
(annual averages, excluding armed forces)

	2000	2001	2002
Agriculture, hunting, forestry and fishing	781,566	766,796	767,134
Mining and quarrying	40,684	37,284	34,553
Manufacturing	615,691	609,460	614,289
Electricity, gas and water supply	59,710	59,648	58,462
Construction	127,554	125,361	128,558
Wholesale and retail trade; repair of motor vehicles, motorcycles and personal and household goods	352,383	360,027	380,367
Hotels and restaurants	85,059	86,007	89,838
Transport and communications	219,453	223,623	221,870
Financial intermediation . . .	32,791	35,926	33,008
Real estate, renting and business activities	121,035	132,752	135,614
Public administration; compulsory social security	91,700	98,124	98,939
Education	218,302	204,932	201,539
Health and social work	148,250	144,762	144,348
Other community, social and personal service activities . .	85,930	83,367	83,721
Total employees	2,980,108	2,968,069	2,992,240

Unemployment (persons registered at 31 December): 682,792 in 2000; 662,260 in 2001; 602,524 in 2002.

Health and Welfare

KEY INDICATORS

Total fertility rate (children per woman, 2002)	1.1
Under-5 mortality rate (per 1,000 live births, 2003) . . .	15
HIV/AIDS (% of persons aged 15–49, 2003)	<0.10
Physicians (per 1,000 head, 2001)	3.4
Hospital beds (per 1,000 head, 2001)	7.2
Health expenditure (2001): US $ per head (PPP) . . .	303
Health expenditure (2001): % of GDP	4.8
Health expenditure (2001): public (% of total)	82.1
Access to water (% of persons, 2002)	100
Access to sanitation (% of persons, 2002)	100
Human Development Index (2002): ranking	56
Human Development Index (2002): value	0.796

For sources and definitions, see explanatory note on p. vi.

Agriculture

PRINCIPAL CROPS
('000 metric tons)

	2001	2002	2003
Wheat	4,077.5	4,122.8	2,003.9
Rice (paddy)	18.7	18.0	23.7
Barley	930.9	1,211.4	525.0
Maize	872.6	1,288.1	1,161.1
Rye	39.0	18.3	11.9
Oats	98.8	62.4	51.5
Triticale (wheat-rye hybrid) . .	10.0	23.4	18.3
Other cereals*	28.4	29.0	23.2
Potatoes	600.4	627.3	630.0*
Sugar beet	18.9	51.3	9.1
Dry beans	10.8	8.1	9.0*
Sunflower seed	405.1	645.4	788.8
Cabbages	138.5	109.4	110.0*
Asparagus*	12.0	12.0	12.0
Tomatoes	393.5	390.0*	390.0*
Pumpkins, squash and gourds*	30.0	31.0	35.0
Cucumbers and gherkins . .	125.0†	125.0*	130.0*
Aubergines (Eggplants) . . .	30.7†	25.0*	25.0*
Chillies and green peppers . .	144.0	166.6	170.0*
Dry onions	71.9†	80.0*	75.0*
Garlic*	28.0	30.0	30.0
Green beans*	18.0	20.0	20.0
Carrots*	17.0*	20.0	20.0
Other vegetables*	109.9	118.5*	112.3†
Watermelons	203.5†	200.0*	210.0*
Apples	42.7	26.4	30.0*
Cherries	28.5	15.7	15.0*
Peaches and nectarines . . .	13.1	10.1	10.0*
Plums	73.2	48.9	60.0*
Strawberries	15.6	15.6	10.0*
Grapes	433.5	408.9	400.0*
Other fruit	34.2*	47.4*	45.4†
Tobacco (leaves)	57.8	62.3	60.0*

* FAO estimate(s).
† Unofficial figure.

Source: FAO.

LIVESTOCK
('000 head at 1 January each year)

	2001	2002	2003
Horses	140.3	150.7	151.0†
Asses	196.2	196.7	200.0†
Cattle	639.8	634.5	691.2
Pigs	1,143.6	788.5	966.5
Sheep	2,286.4	1,571.4	1,728.4
Goats	970.3	675.4	754.5
Poultry	14,991.0*	19,146.0†	19,140.0†
Rabbits	418.0	400.0†	500.0†

* FAO estimate.
† Unofficial figure.

Source: FAO.

LIVESTOCK PRODUCTS
('000 metric tons)

	2001	2002	2003
Beef and veal†	68.5	47.6	52.6
Mutton and lamb†	44.4	46.5	38.7
Goat meat†	7.4	7.5	7.3
Pig meat	237.0	248.0*	250.0*
Poultry meat	110.0	120.0	110.0†
Rabbit meat*	5	5	5
Cows' milk	1,224.1	1,305.9	1,188.8
Buffaloes' milk	5.3	4.4	4.6
Sheeps' milk	72.1	93.5	91.0
Goats' milk	173.2	104.8	105.3
Cheese	44.6	44.7	37.8*
Butter	1.1	1.1	1.0
Hen eggs†	82.3	90.6	88.5
Other poultry eggs†	1.6	2.3	2.1
Honey	4.9	4.9	4.9*
Wool: greasy	6.6	6.5	6.6*
Wool: scoured	3.9	3.9	3.9*
Sheepskins*	15	15	15
Goatskins*	2.3	2.1	2.3
Cattle and buffalo hides* . . .	8.5	8.3	8.4

* FAO estimate(s).
† Unofficial figure(s).

Source: FAO.

Forestry

ROUNDWOOD REMOVALS
('000 cubic metres, excl. bark)

	2003	2001	2002
Sawlogs, veneer logs and logs for sleepers	1,626	1,292	1,581
Pulpwood*	957	971	971
Other industrial wood*	94	94	94
Fuel wood	2,107	1,635	2,187
Total	**4,784**	**3,992**	**4,833**

* FAO estimates.
2003: Figures assumed to be unchanged from 2002 (FAO estimates).
Source: FAO.

SAWNWOOD PRODUCTION
('000 cubic metres, incl. sleepers)

	1999	2000	2001
Coniferous (softwood) . . .	290	258	253
Broadleaved (hardwood) . . .	35	54	79
Total	**325**	**312**	**332**

2002–03: Figures assumed to be unchanged from 2001 (FAO estimates).
Source: FAO.

Fishing

('000 metric tons, live weight)

	2000	2001	2002
Capture	7.0	6.4	15.0
Common carp	0.1	0.9	0.5
European sprat	1.7	0.7	11.6
Sea snails	3.8	3.4	0.7
Aquaculture	3.6	2.9	2.3
Common carp	1.3	0.5	0.5
Grass carp	0.7	0.0	0.0
Other cyprinids	0.9	1.5	1.5
Rainbow trout	0.4	0.8	0.0
Total catch	**10.6**	**9.4**	**17.3**

Source: FAO.

Mining

('000 metric tons, unless otherwise indicated)

	1999	2000	2001*
Anthracite	17	18	14
Other hard coal	106	100	101
Lignite	22,696	23,765	23,856
Other brown coal	3,074	3,211	3,151
Crude petroleum	39	41	32
Natural gas (million cu metres)	27	15	22
Iron ore: gross weight	699	559	325
Iron ore: metal content	223	178	92
Copper concentrate†	96	92	88
Lead concentrate*† . . .	17.0*	10.5	18.5
Zinc concentrate* †	10.2	9.4	12.1
Manganese ore*†	—	—	0.4
Silver (metric tons)† . . .	59	55	57
Gold (kilograms)‡	2,743	2,347	2,540
Bentonite	232	296	308
Kaolin (washed)	140*	150	150
Barite (Barytes)	1,124	875	825
Salt (unrefined)	1,300	1,700	1,931
Gypsum and anhydrite (crude) .	149	170	167

* Estimated production.
† Figures relate to the metal content of ores and concentrates.
‡ Figures relate to metal production.

Source: US Geological Survey.

Industry

SELECTED PRODUCTS
('000 metric tons, unless otherwise indicated)

	2000	2001	2002
Flour	590	639	479
Refined sugar	216	181	153
Wine ('000 hectolitres) . . .	1,833	1,208	836
Beer ('000 hectolitres) . . .	4,048	4,093	3,950
Cigarettes and cigars (metric tons)*	26,700	26,700	23,700
Cotton yarn (metric tons)[1] . .	19,100	20,700	17,600
Woven cotton fabrics ('000 metres)[2]	49,800	68,700†	45,300†
Wool yarn (metric tons)[1] .	3,900	3,700	3,500
Woven woollen fabrics ('000 metres)[2]	4,700	8,000†	8,400†
Woven fabrics of man-made fibres ('000 metres)[3] . . .	13,400	14,500	n.a.
Leather footwear ('000 pairs) .	5,700*	5,100*	2,500
Rubber footwear ('000 pairs) .			n.a.
Chemical wood pulp . . .	77.2	72.6	82.6
Paper and paperboard . . .	136.0	96.5	75.3
Sulphuric acid (100%) . . .	641	620	751
Nitrogenous fertilizers[4] . .	395	318	598
Phosphate fertilizers[4] . .	83	89	
Clay building bricks (million) .	166	144	158
Cement	2,209	2,088	2,134
Rolled iron (metric tons) . .	1,455	1,598	1,490
Aluminium (metric tons) . .	3,190	1,568	1,460
Refined copper—unwrought (metric tons)	33,900	41,900	40,700
Refined lead—unwrought (metric tons)	157,200	168,500	151,600
Zinc—unwrought (metric tons)	76,600	86,700	n.a.
Metal-working lathes (number)	1,563	1,916	1,587
Fork-lift trucks (number)*[5] .	1,200	1,100	1,100
Refrigerators—household (number)	17,900	n.a.	n.a.

— *continued*	2000	2001	2002
Construction: dwellings completed (number)[6] . . .	8,795	5,937	6,153
Electric energy (million kWh) .	40,925	43,968	42,555

[1] Pure and mixed yarn. Figures for wool include yarn of man-made staple.
[2] Pure and mixed fabrics, after undergoing finishing processes.
[3] Finished fabrics, including fabrics of natural silk.
[4] Figures for nitrogenous fertilizers are in terms of nitrogen, and for phosphate fertilizers in terms of phosphoric acid. Data for nitrogenous fertilizers include urea.
[5] Both electric and motor fork-lift trucks. Including hoisting gears.
[6] Including restorations and conversions.
* Figures are rounded.
† Million square metres.

Finance

CURRENCY AND EXCHANGE RATES

Monetary Units
100 stotinki (singular: stotinka) = 1 new lev (plural: leva).

Sterling, Dollar and Euro Equivalents (31 December 2004)
£1 sterling = 2.7733 new leva;
US $1 = 1.4359 new leva;
€1 = 1.9558 new leva;
100 new leva = £36.06= $69.64 = €51.13.

Average Exchange Rate (new leva per US$)
2002   2.0770
2003   1.7327
2004   1.5751

Note: On 5 July 1999 a new lev, equivalent to 1,000 old leva, was introduced. In January 1999 the value of the old lev had been linked to the German currency, the Deutsche Mark (DM), when an official exchange rate of DM1 = 1,000 old leva was established. The new lev was thus at par with the DM. From the establishment of the euro, on 1 January 1999, the German currency had a fixed exchange rate of €1 = 1.95583.

STATE BUDGET
(million new leva)*

Revenue†	2000	2001	2002‖
Taxation	7,140.7	7,495.5	7,991
Taxes on income, profits, etc. .	1,044.6	1,277.0	1,088
Social security contributions .	2,241.8	2,310.3	2,553
From employers	1,427.7	1,439.5	1,604
Domestic taxes on goods and services	3,529.8	3,603.7	4,026
Sales, turnover or value-added taxes	2,359.0	2,454.4	2,688
Excises	1,131.3	1,106.7	1,314
Taxes on international trade and transactions	220.7	195.4	188
Import duties	220.6	195.4	188
Other current revenue	1,872.2	2,310.3	2,162
Entrepreneurial and property income	480.1	973.0	n.a.
Administrative fees and charges, non-industrial and incidental sales	730.6	836.7	n.a.
Fines and forfeits	353.1	271.4	n.a.
Contributions to government employee pension and welfare funds	227.1	187.6	n.a.
Capital revenue	111.6	68.5	67
Total revenue	9,124.5	9,874.3	10,220

Expenditure‡	2000	2001	2002‖
General public services	731.8	673.0	686
Defence	644.3	622.2	565
Public order and safety	509.2	553.9	660
Education	425.7	456.1	568
Health	524.1	984.9	1,228
Social security and welfare . . .	3,461.4	3,622.1	3,898
Housing and community amenities	134.0	192.8	105
Recreational, cultural and religious affairs and services	153.5	143.3	151
Economic affairs and services . .	914.8	1,157.3	1,272
Fuel and energy	103.6	95.7	55
Agriculture, forestry, fishing and hunting	165.3	202.3	322
Transport and communications	515.9	489.9	515
Other purposes	1,945.9	1,806.9	2,557
Total expenditure	9,444.8	10,212.6	11,688
Current§	8,436.9	9,136.4	10,722
Capital	1,007.9	1,076.2	966

* Figures refer to the consolidated accounts of the central Government (including social security funds and other extrabudgetary units).
† Excluding grants received (million new leva): 215.4 in 2000; 394.0 in 2001; 419 in 2002.
‡ Excluding lending minus repayments (million new leva): −259.6 in 2000; −500.2 in 2001; −173 in 2002.
§ Including interest payments (million new leva): 1,067.0 in 2000; 1,095.6 in 2001; 702 in 2002.
‖ Preliminary figures.

Sources: IMF, *Government Finance Statistics Yearbook* and Ministry of Finance.

INTERNATIONAL RESERVES
(US $ million at 31 December)

	2001	2002	2003
Gold*	289.6	340.0	413.8
IMF special drawing rights . .	2.3	0.7	67.7
Reserve position in IMF . . .	41.2	44.6	48.7
Foreign exchange	3,247.3	4,361.8	6,174.6
Total	3,580.4	4,747.1	6,704.8

* Valued at market-related prices.

Source: IMF, *International Financial Statistics.*

MONEY SUPPLY
(million new leva at 31 December)

	2001	2002	2003
Currency outside banks . . .	3,081.0	3,334.9	3,874.1
Demand deposits at deposit money banks	1,654.8	2,086.1	2,807.2
Total money (incl. others) . .	4,883.2	5,542.3	6,801.0

Source: IMF, *International Financial Statistics.*

COST OF LIVING
(Consumer Price Index; base: 1995=100)

	2000	2001	2002
Food	3,003.5	3,199.1	3,198.1
Fuel and light	6,411.8	6,700.9	7,544.7
Clothing	2,492.5	2,500.2	2,494.7
Rent	6,795.8	7,584.6	8,277.0
All items (incl. others)	3,447.1	3,700.9	3,915.9

Source: ILO.

Consumer prices (Retail Price Index, base: 2000 = 100): 107.4 in 2001; 113.6 in 2002; 116.0 in 2003. Source: IMF, *International Financial Statistics.*

NATIONAL ACCOUNTS
(million new leva at current prices)

Expenditure on the Gross Domestic Product

	2001	2002	2003
Final consumption expenditure .	25,819	28,070	30,304
Government final consumption expenditure	5,177	5,832	6,532
Private final consumption expenditure	20,642	22,238	23,772
Gross capital formation	6,141	6,406	7,476
Gross fixed capital formation .	5,415	5,909	6,733
Changes in inventories . . .	726	497	743
Total domestic expenditure .	31,959	34,476	37,780
Exports of goods and services . .	16,510	17,180	18,314
Less Imports of goods and services	18,760	19,321	21,670
Statistical discrepancy	—	—	−13
GDP in market prices . . .	29,709	32,335	34,410

Source: IMF, *International Financial Statistics.*

Gross Domestic Product by Economic Activity

	2000	2001	2002
Agriculture	3,289	3,520	3,543
Forestry	12	13	14
Mining	386	403	403
Manufacturing	4,213	4,607	4,879
Electricity, gas and water . . .	1,216	1,349	1,381
Construction	1,087	1,203	1,264
Trade	1,952	2,179	2,332
Transport	1,656	1,953	2,126
Communications	1,061	1,433	1,795
Financial services	706	831	923
Other services	8,119	8,865	9,834
Gross value added in basic prices	23,697	26,356	28,494
Less Financial intermediation services indirectly measured .	−476	−539	−516
Taxes on products	3,311	3,697	4,158
Import duties	221	195	188
GDP in market prices . . .	26,753	29,709	32,324

BALANCE OF PAYMENTS
(US $ million)

	2001	2002	2003
Exports of goods f.o.b.	5,113.0	5,692.1	7,438.5
Imports of goods f.o.b.	−6,693.3	−7,286.6	−9,912.3
Trade balance	−1,580.3	−1,594.4	−2,473.7
Exports of services	2,425.9	2,594.0	3,108.2
Imports of services	−1,881.7	−2,000.3	−2,533.7
Balance on goods and services	−1,036.1	−1,000.8	−1,899.2
Other income received	351.8	319.7	327.9
Other income paid	−656.3	−550.0	−766.4
Balances on goods, services and income	−1,340.6	−1,231.0	−2,337.7
Current transfers received . . .	598.5	655.6	860.0
Current transfers paid	−100.1	−106.2	−170.3
Current balance	−842.2	−681.6	−1,648.0
Capital account (net)	−0.1	−0.1	−0.2
Direct investment abroad . . .	−9.8	−28.3	−20.1
Direct investment from abroad .	812.9	873.7	1,360.7
Portfolio investment assets . .	−40.4	218.3	−72.0
Portfolio investment liabilities .	105.1	−302.1	−134.6
Financial derivatives assets . .	17.5	6.8	−1.1
Other investment assets . . .	363.0	283.0	151.5
Other investment liabilities . .	−122.3	641.0	685.8
Net errors and omissions . . .	89.6	−295.5	410.0
Overall balance	373.3	715.2	732.0

Source: IMF, *International Financial Statistics.*

External Trade

PRINCIPAL COMMODITIES
(€ million)

Imports c.i.f.	2001	2002	2003
Furniture and household appliances	206.1	250.6	320.5
Medicines and cosmetics . . .	285.6	294.6	315.3
Ores	278.3	208.7	312.7
Textiles	1,060.1	1,162.6	1,321.0
Plastics and rubber	319.5	362.6	439.3
Machines and equipment	705.0	809.8	937.3
Electrical machines	356.6	282.0	316.8
Vehicles	453.1	438.0	541.6
Spare parts and equipment . .	273.4	309.9	360.3
Crude petroleum and natural gas .	1,389.6	1,362.1	1,302.3
Total (incl. others)	8,127.8	8,411.2	9,610.5

Exports f.o.b.	2001	2002	2003
Food	219.2	247.4	299.5
Clothing and footwear . . .	1,140.4	1,258.4	1,457.6
Medicines and cosmetics . . .	179.5	168.5	163.2
Furniture and household appliances	147.3	210.7	245.7
Iron and steel	395.6	393.2	541.4
Other metals	474.7	470.0	534.7
Chemicals	225.7	216.0	229.4
Textiles	205.6	239.7	278.2
Raw materials for the food industry	172.2	320.9	218.4
Machines and equipment . . .	263.1	297.6	310.4
Petroleum products	506.6	357.6	385.0
Other mineral fuels and electricity	260.9	233.4	171.6
Total (incl. others)	5,714.2	6,062.9	6,668.2

PRINCIPAL TRADING PARTNERS
(€ million)

Imports c.i.f.	2001	2002	2003
Austria	161.9	176.3	210.7
Belgium	119.9	118.3	130.6
Brazil	92.4	73.9	105.4
China	97.6	145.8	248.6
Czech Republic	130.1	130.8	156.0
France	489.5	475.4	541.7
Germany	1,241.9	1,199.5	1,370.4
Greece	460.6	507.9	637.6
Hungary	89.9	107.2	119.2
Italy	780.3	953.7	982.3
Japan	85.7	93.8	121.4
Netherlands	148.3	170.6	170.7
Poland	119.3	105.7	135.2
Romania	192.9	172.4	231.1
Russia	1,627.2	1,233.2	1,208.2
Spain	134.8	163.8	214.0
Sweden	100.9	89.1	110.9
Switzerland	94.7	106.3	108.2
Turkey	305.7	414.8	588.6
Ukraine	263.2	261.5	305.8
United Kingdom	202.3	219.9	239.5
USA	213.0	182.4	245.6
Total (incl. others)	8,127.8	8,411.2	9,610.5

Exports f.o.b.	2001	2002	2003
Austria	95.2	101.4	134.7
Belgium	279.5	291.1	404.7
France	320.5	324.3	338.2
Georgia	59.4	52.4	39.6
Germany	545.1	578.7	718.2
Greece	501.2	557.9	691.4
Italy	855.1	934.5	935.2
Macedonia, former Yugoslav republic	125.4	134.5	136.7
Netherlands	89.3	108.0	102.7
Romania	144.1	168.7	203.4
Russia	133.6	97.5	93.2
Spain	188.5	204.4	181.1
Switzerland	65.2	101.3	46.3
Turkey	461.1	565.1	610.2
Ukraine	69.2	56.3	52.5
United Kingdom	151.0	176.4	168.7
USA	319.1	285.3	297.9
Yugoslavia, Federal Republic* . .	235.2	183.6	220.2
Total (incl. others)	5,714.2	6,062.9	6,668.2

* Serbia and Montenegro from February 2003.

Transport

RAILWAYS
(traffic)

	2000	2001	2002
Passengers carried ('000) . . .	50,029	41,817	33,719
Passenger-kilometres (million) .	3,472	2,990	2,598
Freight carried ('000 metric tons) .	21,082	19,285	18,500
Freight net ton-kilometres (million)	5,538	4,904	4,628
Length of track, incl. sidings (km)	6,518	6,402	6,384

ROAD TRAFFIC
(motor vehicles in use at 31 December)

	2000	2001	2002
Passenger cars	1,908,392	2,085,730	2,254,222
Buses and coaches	41,971	42,870	44,255
Lorries and vans	271,463	245,962	262,641
Motorcycles and mopeds . . .	519,212	526,046	520,296

Source: International Road Federation, *World Road Statistics*.

INLAND WATERWAYS
(traffic)

	2000	2001	2002
Passengers carried ('000) . . .	76	67	60
Passenger-kilometres (million) .	1	—	—
Freight carried ('000 metric tons) .	1,846	1,300	1,621
Freight ton-kilometres (million) .	397	365	571

SHIPPING

Merchant Fleet
(registered at 31 December)

	2001	2002	2003
Number of vessels	172	165	151
Total displacement ('000 grt) . .	955.3	889.3	747.9

Source: Lloyd's Register-Fairplay, *World Fleet Statistics*.

Sea-borne Traffic
(international and coastal)

	2000	2001	2002
Freight ('000 metric tons) . . .	18,619	16,737	15,557
Freight ton-kilometres (million) .	74,391	67,551	60,814

CIVIL AVIATION
(traffic)

	1999	2000	2001
Passengers carried ('000) . . .	1,354	1,261	861
Passenger-kilometres (million) .	2,680	2,257	1,795
Freight carried ('000 metric tons) .	30	22	4
Freight ton-kilometres (million) .	63	46	2

Tourism

ARRIVALS OF FOREIGN VISITORS

Country of origin	2001	2002	2003
Austria	27,253	24,358	23,215
Belgium	24,946	29,076	32,176
Czech Republic	36,986	48,485	78,392
Denmark	19,372	31,628	42,708
Finland	29,178	38,108	48,833
France	27,305	30,983	35,766
Germany	374,323	480,460	534,582
Greece	344,677	391,386	547,700
Israel	50,368	64,064	69,055
Macedonia, former Yugoslav republic*	643,106	621,875	672,385
Poland	31,492	48,738	61,819
Romania*	227,286	92,826	76,645
Russia	130,886	99,389	121,332
Slovakia	30,999	42,452	63,912
Sweden	48,070	54,898	70,461
Turkey	44,243	29,645*	33,007
Ukraine	70,168	39,426	42,385
United Kingdom	69,202	110,902	159,341
USA	25,560	25,417	31,126
Yugoslavia, Federal Republic*†	359,467	534,816	591,781
Total (incl. others)	2,775,717	2,992,590	3,531,567

* Includes 'shuttle traders'.

† Serbia and Montenegro from February 2003.

Receipts from tourism (US $ million): 1,074 in 2000; 1,201 in 2001; 1,344 in 2002 (Source: World Bank).

Communications Media

	2001	2002	2003
Telephones ('000 main lines in use)	2,914	2,868	n.a.
Mobile cellular telephones ('000 subscribers)	1,550	2,598	n.a.
Personal computers ('000 in use)	380	405	n.a.
Internet users ('000)	605	630	1,545
Book production:*			
titles	4,984	6,018	5,511
copies ('000)	6,567	5,616	4,484
Newspapers:			
titles	465	401	386
total circulation ('000 copies) .	375,244	358,424	297,688
Magazines:†			
titles	678	673	661
total circulation ('000 copies) .	19,999	15,184	17,034

* Including pamphlets.
† Including bulletins.

Facsimile machines (number in use): 15,000 in 1995 (estimate).

Television receivers (number in use): 3,692,000 in 2000.

Sources: partly UN, *Statistical Yearbook*, UNESCO, *Statistical Yearbook*, and International Telecommunication Union.

Education

(2002/03)

	Institutions	Teachers	Students
Kindergartens	3,127	18,276	201,000
General schools	2,720	61,354	825,668
Special	132	2,229	15,252
Vocational technical	4	95	2,747
Secondary vocational	105	2,872	47,033
Technical colleges and schools of arts	377	15,608	149,567
Post-secondary vocational technical	18	234	3,165
Colleges	9	2,294	14,801*
Higher educational	42	18,710	215,712†

* Qualification degree 'specialist'.

† Including 4,440 post-graduates studying for 'specialist' degrees.

Adult literacy rate (UNESCO estimates): 98.6% (males 99.1%; females 98.1%) in 2002 (Source: UN Development Programme, *Human Development Report*).

Directory

The Constitution

The Constitution of the Republic of Bulgaria, summarized below, took effect upon its promulgation, on 13 July 1991, following its enactment on the previous day.

FUNDAMENTAL PRINCIPLES

Chapter One declares that the Republic of Bulgaria is to have a parliamentary form of government, with all state power derived from the people. The rule of law and the life, dignity and freedom of the individual are guaranteed. The Constitution is the supreme law; the power of the State is shared between the legislature, the executive and the judiciary. The Constitution upholds principles such as political and religious freedom (although no party may be formed on separatist, ethnic or religious lines), free economic initiative and respect for international law.

FUNDAMENTAL RIGHTS AND OBLIGATIONS OF CITIZENS

Chapter Two establishes the basic provisions for Bulgarian citizenship and fundamental human rights, such as the rights of privacy and movement, the freedoms of expression, assembly and association, and the enfranchisement of Bulgarian citizens aged over 18 years. The Constitution commits the State to the provision of basic social welfare and education and to the encouragement of culture,

science and the health of the population. The study and use of the Bulgarian language is required. Other obligations of the citizenry include military service and the payment of taxes.

THE NARODNO SOBRANIYE

The Narodno Sobraniye (National Assembly) is the legislature of Bulgaria and exercises parliamentary control over the country. It consists of 240 members, elected for a four-year term. Only Bulgarian citizens aged over 21 years (who do not hold a state post or another citizenship and are not under judicial interdiction or in prison) are eligible for election to parliament. A member of the Narodno Sobraniye ceases to serve as a deputy while holding ministerial office. The Narodno Sobraniye is a permanently acting body, which is free to determine its own recesses and elects its own Chairman and Deputy Chairmen. The Chairman represents and convenes the Narodno Sobraniye, organizes its proceedings, attests its enactments and promulgates its resolutions.

The Narodno Sobraniye may function when more than one-half of its members are present, and may pass legislation and other acts by a majority of more than one-half of the members present, except where a qualified majority is required by the Constitution. Ministers are free to, and can be obliged to, attend parliamentary sessions. The most important functions of the legislature are: the enactment of laws; the approval of the state budget; the scheduling of presidential elections; the election and dismissal of the Chairman of the Council of Ministers (Prime Minister) and of other members of the Council of

Ministers; the declaration of war or conclusion of peace; the foreign deployment of troops; and the ratification of any fundamental international instruments to which the Republic of Bulgaria has agreed. The laws and resolutions of the Narodno Sobraniye are binding on all state bodies and citizens. All enactments must be promulgated in the official gazette, *Durzhaven Vestnik*, within 15 days of their passage through the legislature.

THE PRESIDENT OF THE REPUBLIC

Chapter Four concerns the Head of State, the President of the Republic of Bulgaria, who is assisted by a Vice-President. The President and Vice-President are elected jointly, directly by the voters, for a period of five years. A candidate must be eligible for election to the Narodno Sobraniye, but also aged over 40 years and a resident of the country for the five years previous to the election. To be elected, a candidate must receive more than one-half of the valid votes cast, in an election in which more than one-half of the eligible electorate participate. If necessary, a second ballot must then be conducted, contested by the two candidates who received the most votes. The one who receives more votes becomes President. The President and Vice-President may hold the same office for only two terms and, during this time, may not engage in any unsuitable or potentially compromising activities. If the President resigns, is incapacitated, impeached or dies, the Vice-President carries out the presidential duties. If neither official can perform their duties, the Chairman of the Narodno Sobraniye assumes the prerogatives of the Presidency, until new elections take place.

The President's main responsibilities include the scheduling of elections and referendums, the conclusion of international treaties and the promulgation of laws. The President is responsible for appointing a Prime Minister-designate (priority must be given to the leaders of the two largest parties represented in the Narodno Sobraniye), who must then attempt to form a government.

The President is Supreme Commander-in-Chief of the Armed Forces of the Republic of Bulgaria and presides over the Consultative National Security Council. The President has certain emergency powers, usually subject to the later approval of the Narodno Sobraniye. Many of the President's actions must be approved by the Chairman of the Council of Ministers. The President may return legislation to the Narodno Sobraniye for further consideration, but can be overruled.

THE COUNCIL OF MINISTERS

The principal organ of executive government is the Council of Ministers, which supervises the implementation of state policy and the state budget, the administration of the country and the Armed Forces, and the maintenance of law and order. The Council of Ministers is headed and co-ordinated by the Chairman (Prime Minister), who is responsible for the overall policy of government. The Council of Ministers, which also includes Deputy Chairmen and Ministers, must resign upon the death of the Chairman or if the Narodno Sobraniye votes in favour of a motion of no confidence in the Council or in the Chairman.

JUDICIAL POWER

The judicial branch of government is independent. All judicial power is exercised in the name of the people. Individuals and legal entities are guaranteed basic rights, such as the right to contest administrative acts and the right to legal counsel. One of the principal organs is the Supreme Court of Cassation, which exercises supreme judicial responsibility for the precise and equal application of the law by all courts. The Supreme Administrative Court rules on all challenges to the legality of acts of any organ of government. The Chief Prosecutor supervises all other prosecutors and ensures that the law is observed, by initiating court actions and ensuring the enforcement of penalties, etc.

The Supreme Judicial Council is responsible for appointments within the ranks of the justices, prosecutors and investigating magistrates, and recommends to the President of the Republic the appointment or dismissal of the Chairmen of the two Supreme Courts and of the Chief Prosecutor (they are each appointed for a single, seven-year term). These last three officials are, *ex officio*, members of the Supreme Judicial Council, together with 22 others, who must be practising lawyers of high integrity and at least 15 years of professional experience. These members are elected for a term of five years, 11 of them by the Narodno Sobraniye and 11 by bodies of the judiciary. The Supreme Judicial Council is chaired by the Minister of Justice, who is not entitled to vote.

LOCAL SELF-GOVERNMENT

Chapter Seven provides for the division of Bulgaria into regions and municipalities. Municipalities are the basic administrative territorial unit at which local self-government is practised; their principal organ is the municipal council, which is elected directly by the population for a term of four years. The council elects the mayor, who is the principal organ of executive power. Bulgaria is also divided into regions. Regional government, which is entrusted to regional governors (appointed by the Council of Ministers) and administrations, is responsible for regional policy, the implementation of state policy at a local level and the harmonization of local and national interests.

THE CONSTITUTIONAL COURT

The Constitutional Court consists of 12 justices, four of whom are elected by the Narodno Sobraniye, four appointed by the President of the Republic and four elected by the justices of the two Supreme Courts. Candidates must have the same eligibility as for membership of the Supreme Judicial Council. They serve a single term of nine years, but a part of the membership changes every three years. A chairman is elected by a secret ballot of the members.

The Constitutional Court provides binding interpretations of the Constitution. It rules on the constitutionality of: laws and decrees; competence suits between organs of government; international agreements; national and presidential elections; and impeachments. A ruling of the Court requires a majority of more than one-half of the votes of all the justices.

CONSTITUTIONAL AMENDMENTS AND THE ADOPTION OF A NEW CONSTITUTION

Chapter Nine provides for constitutional changes. Except for those provisions reserved to the competence of a Velikoto Narodno Sobraniye (see below), the Narodno Sobraniye is empowered to amend the Constitution with a majority of three-quarters of all its Members, in three ballots on three different days. Amendments must be proposed by one-quarter of the parliamentary membership or by the President. In some cases, a majority of two-thirds of all the Members of the Narodno Sobraniye will suffice.

Velikoto Narodno Sobraniye

A Velikoto Narodno Sobraniye (Grand National Assembly) consists of 400 members, elected by the generally established procedure. It alone is empowered to adopt a new constitution, to sanction territorial changes to the Republic of Bulgaria, to resolve on any changes in the form of state structure or form of government, and to enact amendments to certain parts of the existing Constitution (concerning the direct application of the Constitution, the domestic application of international agreements, the irrevocable nature of fundamental civil rights and of certain basic individual rights even in times of emergency or war, and amendments to Chapter Nine itself).

Any bill requiring the convening of a Velikoto Narodno Sobraniye must be introduced by the President of the Republic or by one-third of the members of the Narodno Sobraniye. A decision to hold elections for a Grand National Assembly must be supported by two-thirds of the members of the Narodno Sobraniye. Enactments of the Velikoto Narodno Sobraniye require a majority of two-thirds of the votes of all the members, in three ballots on three different days. A Velikoto Narodno Sobraniye may resolve only on the proposals for which it was elected, whereupon its prerogatives normally expire.

The Government

HEAD OF STATE

President: GEORGI PARVANOV (elected 18 November 2001; inaugurated 19 January 2002; took office 22 January 2002).

COUNCIL OF MINISTERS
(April 2005)

A coalition of the National Movement Simeon II (NMSII), the Movement for Rights and Freedoms (MRF), the Bulgarian Socialist Party (BSP) and New Time.

Prime Minister: SIMEON SAKSKOBURGGOTSKI (NMSII).

Deputy Prime Minister: PLAMEN PANAYOTOV (NMSII).

Deputy Prime Minister and Minister of the Economy: MILKO KOVACHEV (NMSII).

Deputy Prime Minister and Minister of Transport and Communications: NIKOLAI VASSILEV (NMSII).

Minister of Defence: NIKOLAI AVRAMOV SVINAROV (NMSII).

Minister of Foreign Affairs: SOLOMON ISAK PASI (NMSII).

Minister of Finance: MILEN EMILOV VELCHEV (NMSII).

Minister of the Interior: GEORGI PETROV PETKANOV (BSP).

Minister of Justice: ANTON ILIEV STANKOV (NMSII).

Minister of Education and Science: IGOR DAMYANOV (NMSII).

Minister of European Affairs: MEGLENA KUNEVA (NMSII).

Minister of Agriculture and Forestry: NIHAT KABIL (MRF).

Minister of Regional Development and Public Works: VALENTIN IVANOV TSEROVSKI (NMSII).

Minister of Labour and Social Policy: HRISTINA HRISTOVA (NMSII).

Minister of Health: SLAVCHO BOGOEV (NMSII).

Minister of Culture and Tourism: BOZHIDAR NINA CHILOVA (NMSII).

Minister of the Environment and Water: DOLORES BORISOVA ARSENOVA (NMSII).

Minister of Energy and Energy Resources: MIROSLAV SEVLIEVSKI (New Time).

Minister of State Administration: DIMITAR GEORGIEV KALCHEV (BSP).

Minister of Youth and Sport: VASSIL MINCHEV IVANOV (NMSII).

Minister without Portfolio: FILIZ HYUSMENOVA (MRF).

MINISTRIES

Office of the President: 1123 Sofia, bul. Dondukov 2; tel. (2) 923-93-33; e-mail press@president.bg; internet www.president.bg.

Council of Ministers: 1000 Sofia, bul. Dondukov 1; tel. (2) 940-27-70; fax (2) 980-20-56; e-mail iprd@government.bg; internet www.government.bg.

Ministry of Agriculture and Forestry: 1040 Sofia, bul. Botev 55; tel. (2) 980-99-27; fax (2) 980-62-56; e-mail press@mzgar.government.bg; internet www.mzgar.government.bg.

Ministry of Culture and Tourism: 1040 Sofia, bul. A. Stamboliyski 17; tel. (2) 940-09-00; fax (2) 981-81-45; e-mail press.culture@bta.bg; internet www.culture.government.bg.

Ministry of Defence: 1000 Sofia, ul. Dyakon Ignatiy 3; tel. (2) 922-09-22; fax (2) 987-32-28; e-mail presscntr@mod.bg; internet www.md.government.bg.

Ministry of the Economy: 1000 Sofia, ul. Slavyanska 8; tel. (2) 940-73-03; fax (2) 988-55-32; e-mail public@mi.government.bg; internet www.mi.government.bg.

Ministry of Education and Science: 1540 Sofia, bul. A. Stamboliyski 18; tel. (2) 984-87-44; fax (2) 988-26-93; e-mail press_mon@minedu.government.bg; internet www.minedu.government.bg.

Ministry of Energy and Energy Resources: 1040 Sofia, ul. Triaditsa 8; tel. (2) 926-36-36; fax (2) 980-76-30; e-mail pressall@doe.bg; internet www.doe.bg.

Ministry of the Environment and Water: 1000 Sofia, ul. U. Gladston 67; tel. (2) 940-62-31; fax (2) 988-59-13; e-mail slavv@moew.government.bg; internet www.moew.government.bg.

Ministry of European Affairs: 1040 Sofia, ul. Al. Zhendov 1; tel. (2) 971-32-12; fax (2) 971-29-06; e-mail mkuneva@mfa.government.bg; internet www.evroportal.bg.

Ministry of Finance: 1000 Sofia, ul. G. S. Rakovski 102; tel. (2) 985-920-20; fax (2) 985-920-24; e-mail feedback@minfin.bg; internet www.minfin.government.bg.

Ministry of Foreign Affairs: 1504 Sofia, bul. E. Georgiyev 117; tel. (2) 946-30-79; fax (2) 870-30-41; e-mail iprd@mfa.government.bg; internet www.mfa.government.bg.

Ministry of Health: 1000 Sofia, pl. Sv. Nedelya 5; tel. (2) 930-011-01; fax (2) 981-26-39; e-mail press@mh.government.bg; internet www.mh.government.bg.

Ministry of the Interior: 1000 Sofia, ul. 6-ti Septemvri 29; tel. (2) 982-20-14; fax (2) 982-20-47; e-mail spvo@mvr.bg; internet www.mvr.bg.

Ministry of Justice: 1040 Sofia, ul. Slavyanska 1; tel. (2) 988-48-23; fax (2) 981-91-57; e-mail pr@justice.government.bg; internet www.mjeli.government.bg.

Ministry of Labour and Social Policy: 1051 Sofia, ul. Triaditsa 2; tel. (2) 811-94-43; fax (2) 988-44-05; e-mail mlsp@mlsp.government.bg; internet www.mlsp.government.bg.

Ministry of Regional Development and Public Works: 1000 Sofia, ul. Kiril i Metodiy 17–19; tel. (2) 988-29-54; fax (2) 987-58-56; e-mail press@mrrb.government.bg; internet www.mrrb.government.bg.

Ministry of State Administration: 1594 Sofia, bul. Dondukov 1; tel. (2) 940-27-17; fax (2) 940-21-70; e-mail k.zdravskovska@government.bg.

Ministry of Transport and Communications: 1000 Sofia, ul. Dyakon Ignatiy 9; tel. (2) 940-95-00; fax (2) 987-18-05; e-mail press@mtc.government.bg; internet www.mtc.government.bg.

Ministry of Youth and Sport: 1000 Sofia, ul. V. Levski 75; tel. (2) 930-05-55; e-mail info@mms.government.bg; internet www.youthsport.bg.

President and Legislature

PRESIDENT

Presidential Election, First Ballot, 11 November 2001

Candidates	% of votes
Georgi Parvanov (Coalition for Bulgaria)	36.4
Petar Stoyanov (Independent)	34.9
Bogomil Bonev (Civic Party for Bulgaria)	19.3
Reneta Indzhova (Democratic Alliance)	4.9
Others	4.5
Total	**100.0**

Second Ballot, 18 November 2001

Candidates	% of votes
Georgi Parvanov	54.1
Petar Stoyanov	45.9
Total	**100.0**

LEGISLATURE

Narodno Sobraniye
(National Assembly)

1169 Sofia, pl. Narodno Sobraniye 3; tel. (2) 980-85-01; fax (2) 981-01-81; e-mail infocenter@nt52.parliament.bg; internet www.parliament.bg.

Chairman: BORISLAV VELIKOV.

General Election, 17 June 2001

Parties	% of votes	Seats
National Movement Simeon II*.	42.73	120
United Democratic Forces	18.17	51
Coalition for Bulgaria†	17.14	48
Movement for Rights and Freedoms	7.45	21
Gergyovden (St Georges's Day) Movement-IMRO—Bulgarian National Movement coalition	3.63	—
Others	10.88	—
Total	**100.00**	**240**

* In coalition with the Party of Bulgarian Women and the Oborishte Party for National Revival.
† A coalition of 15 parties, led by the Bulgarian Socialist Party.

Political Organizations

Bulgarian Agrarian National Union—People's Union (Bulgarski Zemedelski Naroden Sayuz—BZNS—NS): 1000 Sofia, pl. Slaveikov 4A; tel. (2) 987-05-77; fax (2) 962-64-21; contested 2001 legislative elections as part of the United Democratic Forces coalition; Leader ANASTASIA MOSER.

Bulgarian Communist Party (Bulgarska Komunisticheska Partiya): 1404 Sofia, bul. P. J. Todorov 5B; tel. and fax (2) 959-16-73; e-mail spasov@internet-bg.net; internet www.bcp.hit.bg; re-formed in 1990; First Sec. of the Central Cttee VLADIMIR SPASOV.

Bulgarian Social Democrats (Balgarski Sotsialdemokrati): 1504 Sofia, ul.E. Yosif 37; tel. (2) 980-15-84; fax (2) 973-24-76; e-mail president@bsdp.net; internet www.bsdp.net; fmrly Bulgarian Social Democratic Party (United); contested 2001 legislative elections as part of the United Democratic Forces coalition; Pres. GEORGI ANASTASOV.

Bulgarian Socialist Party (BSP) (Bulgarska Sotsialisticheska Partiya): 1000 Sofia, ul. Positano 20; tel. (2) 981-57-08; fax (2) 981-17-88; e-mail bsp@bsp.bg; internet www.bsp.bg; f. 1891 as the Bulgarian Social Democratic Party (BSDP); renamed the Bulgarian Communist Party (BCP) in 1919; renamed as above in 1990; contested legislative elections in 2001 as part of the Coalition for Bulgaria in association with 14 other parties; Chair. SERGEY STANISHEV.

Civic Party for Bulgaria: Sofia; f. 2000; centre-right; Chair. BOGOMIL BONEV.

Democratic Party (Demokraticheskata Partiya): 1303 Sofia, bul. Botev 61; tel. (2) 930-80-30; fax (2) 930-80-31; re-formed 1990; contested the 2001 as part of the United Democratic Forces coalition; agreed coalition with Union of Democratic Forces (q.v.) in advance of 2005 legislative elections; Chair. ALEKSANDAR PRAMATARSKI.

Democratic Party of Justice: Sofia; f. 1994; ethnic Turkish group; fmrly part of the Movement for Rights and Freedoms; Chair. NEDIM GENDZHEV.

Democrats for a Strong Bulgaria (DSB) (Demokrati za silna Balgariya): 1000 Sofia, ul. G. Ignatiyev 10A; tel. (2) 980-53-34; fax (2) 987-17-51; e-mail mediacentre@dsb.bg; internet www.dsb.bg; f. 2004; right-wing; Chair. IVAN KOSTOV.

Fatherland Party of Labour: Sofia; nationalist; Chair. RUMEN POPOV.

Gergyovden (St George's Day) Movement: Sofia, bul. G. M. Dimitrov 16; tel. (2) 965-16-74; fax (2) 965-16-79; contested the legislative election of June 2001 in alliance with IMRO—Bulgarian National Movement; Pres. ORLIN CHOCHOV.

Green Party (Zelena Partiya v Balgariya): 1000 Sofia, ul. Lavele 30; tel. (2) 987-69-24; fax (2) 987-85-38; e-mail green@mail.bol.bg; internet www.greenparty.bg; f. 1989; Chair. ALEKSANDER KARAKACHANOV.

IMRO—Bulgarian National Movement (VMRO—Balgarsko natsionalno dvizheniye—VMRO—BND): 1301 Sofia, ul. Pirotska 5; tel. (2) 980-25-82; fax (2) 980-25-83; e-mail vmro@vmro.org; internet www.vmro.org; fmrly Inner Macedonian Revolutionary Organization—Bulgarian National Movement; contested the legislative election of June 2001 in alliance with the Gergyovden (St George's Day) Movement; Chair. KRASSIMIR KARAKACHANOV.

Liberal Democratic Alternative: 1000 Sofia, ul. Triaditsa 4; tel. and fax (2) 986-37-14; e-mail lda@bulgarianspace.com; f. 1997; Leader ZHELYU ZHELEV.

Movement for Rights and Freedoms (MRF) (Dvizhenie za Prava i Svobodi—DPS): 1301 Sofia, bul. Al. Stamboliyski 45A; tel. (2) 986-33-77; fax (2) 988-15-81; e-mail press@dps.bg; internet www.dps.bg; f. 1990 to represent interests of Muslim minority in Bulgaria; supports integration of Bulgaria into the EU and NATO; Pres. AKHMED DOGAN.

National Movement for Rights and Freedoms (Nationalno dvizheniye za prava i svobodi—NDPS): 1000 Sofia; f. 1999 as breakaway faction of the MRF (q.v.); formed an electoral coalition, the Bulgarian Republican Bloc, with the United Labour Bloc and the Bulgarian Agrarian National Association (led by Yano Yanev) in 2004; Leader GYUNER TAHIR.

National Movement Simeon II (NMSII) (Nationalno dvizheniye Simeon Vtori): 1000 Sofia, ul. Vrabcha 23; tel. (2) 980-38-09; fax (2) 980-38-07; e-mail ndsv@ndsv.bg; internet www.ndsv.bg; f. 2001 by supporters of the former monarch; contested the 2001 legislative elections as the National Movement, in coalition with the Party of Bulgarian Women and the Oborishte Party for National Revival; registered as a political party in 2002; Chair. SIMEON SAKSKOBURGGOTSKI.

New Time (Novoto vreme): c/o Narodno Sobraniye, 1169 Sofia, pl. Narodno Sobraniye 2; tel. (2) 939-31-79; fax (2) 981-47-40; e-mail pgnv@nt14.parliament.bg; internet www.novotovreme.bg; f. 2003 by fmr mems of the National Movement Simeon II; Leader EMIL KOSHLUKOV.

Union of Democratic Forces (UDF) (Sayuz na Demokratichnite Sili—SDS): 1000 Sofia, bul. Rakovski 134; tel. (2) 930-61-02; fax (2) 981-05-22; e-mail iac@sds.bg; internet www.sds.bg; f. 1989; fmrly principal member of the United Democratic Forces; supports the integration of Bulgaria into the European Union; pro-market; agreed coalition with Democratic Party in advance of 2005 legislative elections; Chair. NADEZHDA MIHAILOVA.

Union of Free Democrats (SSD) (Soyuz na svobodnite demokrati): 1000 Sofia, bul. Levski 91; tel. (2) 989-59-99; fax (2) 989-69-99; e-mail press@ssd.bg; internet www.ssd.bg; f. 2001 as a breakaway faction of the Union of Democratic Forces; support greater integration of Bulgaria into the EU and NATO; Leader STEFAN SOFIANSKI.

United Labour Bloc (Obedinen blok na truda—OBT): Sofia; f. 1997; formed an electoral coalition, the Bulgarian Republican Bloc, with the National Movement for Rights and Freedoms and the Bulgarian Agrarian National Association (led by Yano Yanev) in 2004; Chair. KRASTYU PETKOV.

Diplomatic Representation

EMBASSIES IN BULGARIA

Afghanistan: 1618 Sofia, Ovcha Kupel, ul. Boryana 61/216A/15; tel. (2) 955-61-96; fax (2) 955-99-76; e-mail ariana@sofianet.net; Ambassador MUHAMMAD FAZEL SAIFI.

Albania: 1000 Sofia, ul. Krakra 10; tel. (2) 946-12-22; fax (2) 943-30-69; Ambassador FATMIR KUMBARO.

Algeria: 1000 Sofia, ul. Slavyanska 16; tel. (2) 980-22-50; Ambassador ZINE EL-ABIDINE HACHICHI.

Argentina: 1000 Sofia, ul. D. Tsankov 36, POB 635; tel. (2) 971-25-39; fax (2) 71-61-30-28; Ambassador GERÓNIMO CORTÉS-FUNES.

Armenia: 1606 Sofia, ul. 20-ti April 11; tel. and fax (2) 952-60-46; e-mail armembsof@sof.omega.bg; Ambassador SERGEI MANASERIAN.

Austria: 1000 Sofia, ul. Shipka 4; tel. (2) 932-90-32; fax (2) 981-05-67; e-mail sofia-ob@bmaa.gov.at; Ambassador Dr KARL DIEM.

Belarus: 1113 Sofia, ul. Kokiche 20; tel. (2) 965-28-43; e-mail embassyblr@omega.bg; Ambassador ALYAKSANDR PETROV.

Belgium: 1164 Sofia, ul. V. Zavera 1; tel. (2) 988-72-90; fax (2) 963-36-38; e-mail ambabel@einet.bg; Ambassador EDMOND DE WILDE.

Brazil: 1113 Sofia, ul. F. Zh. Kyuri 19/1/6; tel. (2) 972-35-27; fax (2) 971-28-18; e-mail sofbrem@main.infotel.bg; Ambassador CARLOS ALBERTO PESSÔA PARDELLAS.

Cambodia: 1000 Sofia, bul. A. Sakharov 3; tel. (2) 975-71-35; fax (2) 975-40-09; Ambassador BO RASSI.

China, People's Republic: 1113 Sofia, ul. A. von Khumbolt 7; tel. (2) 973-39-10; fax (2) 971-10-81; internet www.chinaembassy.bg; Ambassador XIE HANGSHENG.

Croatia: 1087 Sofia, ul. Krakra 18; tel. (2) 943-32-55; fax (2) 946-13-55; e-mail dkp_rh@infotel.bg; Ambassador TONCI STANIČIĆ.

Cuba: 1113 Sofia, ul. K. Sharkelov 1; tel. (2) 970-46-22; fax (2) 972-04-60; e-mail consulcuba@mbox.digsys.bg; Ambassador LUIS FELIPE VÁZQUEZ.

Cyprus: 1087 Sofia, ul. Yu. Gagarin 22/154A/2; tel. (2) 972-09-96; fax (2) 972-04-60; e-mail embacu@mbox.digsys.bg; Chargé d'affaires a.i. JOSÉ DE LA C. ROSADO .

Czech Republic: 1504 Sofia, ul. Ya. Sakazov 9; tel. (2) 946-11-11; fax (2) 946-18-00; e-mail sofia@embassy.mzv.cz; internet www.czechembassy.org/wwwo/?zu=sofia; Ambassador PETR DOKLÁDAL.

Denmark: 1000 Sofia, bul. Dondukov 54, POB 1393; tel. (2) 917-01-00; fax (2) 980-99-01; e-mail sofamb@um.dk; internet www.ambsofia.um.dk; Ambassador CHRISTIAN FABER-ROD.

Egypt: 1087 Sofia, ul. 6-ti Septemvri 5; tel. (2) 987-02-15; fax (2) 980-12-63; e-mail egembsof@spnet.net; Ambassador OSAMA MUHAMMAD TAWFIK.

Finland: 1504 Sofia, ul. Krakra 16/4; tel. (2) 942-49-10; fax (2) 942-49-11; e-mail finembassy@online.bg; Ambassador TAISTO TOLVANEN.

France: 1054 Sofia, ul. Oborishte 27–29; tel. (2) 965-11-00; fax (2) 965-11-20; internet www.ambafrance-bg.org; Ambassador YVES SAINT-GEOURS.

Georgia: Sofia; Ambassador TEIMURAZ SHARASHENIDZE.

Germany: 1113 Sofia, ul. F. Zh. Kyuri 25, POB 869; tel. (2) 963-45-18; fax (2) 963-16-58; e-mail gemb@vilmat.com; internet www.german-embassy.bg; Ambassador Dr HARALD KINDERMANN.

Greece: 1504 Sofia, ul. San Stefano 23; tel. (2) 946-10-27; fax (2) 946-12-49; e-mail sofia@greekembassy.bg; internet www.greekembassy.bg; Ambassador PROKOPIOUS MANDZURANIS.

Holy See: 1000 Sofia, 11-ti Avgust 6, POB 9; tel. (2) 981-17-43; fax (2) 981-61-95; e-mail nuntius@mbox.digsys.bg; Apostolic Nuncio GIUSEPPE LEANZA.

Hungary: 1000 Sofia, ul. 6-ti Septemvri 57; tel. (2) 963-04-60; fax (2) 963-21-10; e-mail huemszof@netbg.com; Ambassador Dr BÉLA KOLOZSI.

India: Sofia, bul. Patriarkh Evtimii 31; tel. (2) 981-17-02; fax (2) 981-41-24; e-mail india@inet.bg; Ambassador DINKAR KHULLAR.

Indonesia: 1087 Sofia, bul. Simeonovsko shose 53/4; tel. (2) 962-52-40; fax (2) 962-58-42; e-mail indosof@geobiz.net; Ambassador R. BROTO UTOMO.

Iran: 1087 Sofia, ul. V. Levski 77; tel. (2) 987-61-73; Ambassador FEREIDUN HAKBIN.

Iraq: 1113 Sofia, ul. A. P. Chekhov 21; tel. (2) 973-33-48; fax (2) 971-11-97; e-mail sofemb@iraqmofa.net.

Israel: 1463 Sofia, pl. Balgaria 1, NDK Administration Bldg; tel. (2) 951-50-44; fax (2) 952-11-01; e-mail info@sofia.mfa.gov.il; Ambassador AVRAHAM SHARON.

Italy: 1087 Sofia, ul. Shipka 2; tel. (2) 980-45-07; fax (2) 980-37-17; e-mail italdiplsofia@online.bg; Ambassador GIOVAN BATTISTA CAMPAGNOLA.

Japan: 1087 Sofia, ul. Lyulyakova gradina 14; tel. (2) 971-27-08; fax (2) 971-10-95; internet www.bg.emb-japan.go.jp; Ambassador YASUYOSHI ICHIHASHI.

Korea, Democratic People's Republic: 1087 Sofia, bul. A. Sakharov 4; tel. (2) 977-53-48; Ambassador JO SUNG-JU.

Korea, Republic: 1414 Sofia, pl. Balgaria 1, NDK Administration BldgNDK Ad; tel. (2) 965-01-62; Ambassador PILL-JOO SUNG.

Kuwait: 1700 Sofia, bul. Simeonovsko shose 15; tel. (2) 962-51-30; e-mail kuwaitembassy-bulgaria@spnet.net; Ambassador MUHAMMAD A. AL-AWADHI.

Lebanon: 1113 Sofia, ul. F. Zh. Kyuri 19; tel. (2) 971-31-69; fax (2) 973-32-56; e-mail amliban@bgnet.bg; Ambassador HUSSEIN MOUSSAWI.

Libya: 1784 Sofia, bul. A. Sakharov 1; tel. (2) 974-35-56; fax (2) 974-32-73; Sec. of People's Bureau FARAG GIBRIL.

Macedonia, former Yugoslav republic: 1113 Sofia, ul. F. Zh. Kyuri 17/2/1; tel. and fax (2) 971-37-08; Ambassador LJUBISA GEORGIEVSKI.

Moldova: 1000 Sofia, bul. Patriarkh Evtimiy 17; tel. (2) 981-73-70; fax (2) 981-85-53; e-mail moldova@www1.infotel.bg; Ambassador VASILE STURZA.

Mongolia: 1113 Sofia, ul. F. Zh. Kyuri 52; tel. (2) 965-84-03; fax (2) 963-07-45; e-mail mongemb@mbox.infotel.bg.

Morocco: 1087 Sofia, bul. E. Georgiev 129; tel. (2) 944-27-94; fax (2) 946-10-43; e-mail sifmasof@bulnet.bg; Ambassador ABDESSELAM ALEM.

Netherlands: 1504 Sofia, ul. Oborishte 15; tel. (2) 816-03-00; fax (2) 816-03-01; e-mail info@netherlandsembassy.bg; internet www.netherlandsembassy.bg; Ambassador H. J. C. M. VAN LYNDEN.

Peru: 1113 Sofia, ul. F. Zh. Kyuri 17/2/2; tel. (2) 971-37-08; fax (2) 973-33-46; e-mail peru@mail.bol.bg; Chargé d'affaires JULIO VEGA ERAUSQUÍN.

Poland: 1504 Sofia, ul. E. Georgiev 125; tel. (2) 987-26-10; fax (2) 987-29-39; e-mail polamba@internet-bg.net; Ambassador JAROSŁAW LINDENBERG.

Portugal: 1087 Sofia, ul. Ivatz voyvoda 6; tel. (2) 943-36-67; fax (2) 943-30-89; e-mail embport@online.bg; Ambassador PAULO TIAGO GERÓNIMO DA SILVA.

Romania: 1087 Sofia, bul. Sitnyakovo 4; tel. (2) 971-28-58; fax (2) 973-34-12; e-mail ambsofro@exco.net; Ambassador CONSTANTIN GRIGORIE.

Russia: 1087 Sofia, ul. N. Mirchev 28; tel. (2) 963-44-58; fax (2) 963-41-03; e-mail consulate@datacom.bg; Ambassador ANATOLII POTAPOV.

Serbia and Montenegro: 1087 Sofia, ul. Veliko Tarnovo 3; tel. (2) 946-16-33; fax (2) 946-10-59; e-mail ambasada-scg-sofija@infotel.bg; Ambassador CEDOMIR RADOJKOVIĆ.

Slovakia: 1504 Sofia, bul. Ya. Sakazov 9; tel. (2) 942-92-10; fax (2) 942-92-35; e-mail embassy@sofia.mfa.sk; Ambassador MICHAL KOTTMAN.

Spain: 1087 Sofia, ul. Sheynovo 27; tel. (2) 943-30-32; fax (2) 946-12-01; e-mail embespbg@mail.mae.es; Ambassador JOSÉ ANGEL LÓPEZ JORRÍN.

Sweden: 1087 Sofia, ul. A. Nobel 4; tel. (2) 971-24-31; fax (2) 973-37-95; e-mail sweembg@einet.bg; Ambassador STEN ASK.

Switzerland: 1504 Sofia, ul. Shipka 33; tel. (2) 942-01-00; fax (2) 946-11-86; e-mail vertretung@sof.rep.admin.ch; Ambassador RUDOLF KNOBLAUCH.

Syria: 1087 Sofia, bul. Simeonovsko shose; tel. (2) 944-15-85; Chargé d'affaires SADDIK SADDIKNI.

Turkey: 1087 Sofia, bul. V. Levski 80; tel. (2) 987-14-64; fax (2) 981-93-58; e-mail turkel@techno-link.com; Ambassador HAYDAR BERK.

Ukraine: 1618 Sofia, Ovcha Kupel, ul. Boryana 29; tel. (2) 955-94-78; e-mail puvrb@mail.bol.bg; internet www.ukramb.bol.bg; Ambassador VYACHESLAV POKHVALSKYI.

United Kingdom: 1087 Sofia, ul. Moskovska 9; tel. (2) 933-92-22; fax (2) 933-92-19; e-mail britembsof@mbox.cit.bg; internet www.british-embassy.bg; Ambassador JEREMY HILL.

USA: 1087 Sofia, ul. Saborna 1; tel. (2) 980-52-41; fax (2) 981-89-77; e-mail irc@usembassy.bg; internet www.usembassy.bg; Ambassador JAMES W. PARDEW.

Venezuela: 1087 Sofia, ul. Tulovo 1; tel. (2) 943-30-61; fax (2) 943-30-10; e-mail embavenez@mbox.digsys.bg; Ambassador BOANERGES SALAZAR.

Viet Nam: 1113 Sofia, ul. Zhetvarka 1; tel. (2) 963-26-09; fax (2) 963-36-58; e-mail dsqvietnam@sf.icn.bg; Ambassador NGUYEN VAN DAC.

Judicial System

The 1991 Constitution provided for justice to be administered by the Supreme Court of Cassation, the Supreme Administrative Court, courts of appeal, courts of assizes, military courts and district courts. The main legal officials are the justices, or judges, of the higher courts, the prosecutors and investigating magistrates. The judicial system is independent, most appointments being made or recommended by the Supreme Judicial Council. The Ministry of Justice co-ordinates the administration of the judicial system and the prisons. There is also the Constitutional Court, which is the final arbiter of constitutional issues. Under transitional arrangements attached to the 1991 Constitution, the existing Supreme Court of Bulgaria was to exercise the prerogatives of the two new Supreme Courts until the new judicial system was enacted and established.

Supreme Court of Cassation: 1000 Sofia, bul. Vitosha 2; tel. (2) 987-76-98; fax (2) 988-39-85; Pres. IVAN GRIGOROV.

Supreme Administrative Court: 1000 Sofia, bul. A. Stamboliyski 18; tel. (2) 981-30-42; fax (2) 981-87-51; internet www.sac.government.bg; Chair. KONSTANTIN PENCHEV.

Constitutional Court: 1594 Sofia, bul. Dondukov 1; tel. (2) 987-50-08; fax (2) 987-19-86; e-mail s.petrova@constcourt.government.bg; internet www.constcourt.bg; Chair. NEDELCHO B. BERONOV; Sec.-Gen. KIRIL A. MANOV.

Supreme Judicial Council (Vissh Sadeben Savet): 1000 Sofia, ul. Saborna 9; tel. (2) 981-79-74; fax (2) 980-76-32; e-mail vss_adm@inet.bg; internet www.vss.justice.bg; Head, Minister of Justice.

Office of the Prosecutor-General: 1040 Sofia, bul. Vitosha 2; tel. and fax (2) 988-52-13; Prosecutor-General NIKOLA FILTCHEV.

Religion

Most of the population profess Christianity, the main denomination being the Bulgarian Orthodox Church, with a membership of more than 80% of the population. The 1991 Constitution guarantees freedom of religion, although Eastern Orthodox Christianity is declared to be the 'traditional religion in Bulgaria'. In accordance with the 1949 Bulgarian Law on Religious Faith, all new religious denominations must be registered by a governmental board before being allowed to operate freely. There is a significant Muslim minority (some 9% of the population), most of whom are ethnic Turks, although there are some ethnic Bulgarian Muslims, known as Pomaks. There is a small Jewish community.

Directorate of Religious Affairs: 1000 Sofia, bul. Dondukov 1; tel. and fax (2) 988-04-88; a dept of the Council of Ministers; conducts relations between govt and religious organizations; Chair. Dr IVAN ZHELEV DIMITROV.

CHRISTIANITY

In 1992 a schism occurred in the Bulgarian Orthodox Church.

Bulgarian Orthodox Church: 1090 Sofia, ul. Oborishte 4, Synod Palace; tel. (2) 987-56-11; fax (2) 989-76-00; f. 865; autocephalous Exarchate 1870 (recognized 1945); administered by the Bulgarian Patriarchy; 11 dioceses in Bulgaria and two dioceses abroad (Diocese of North and South America and Australia, and Diocese of West Europe), each under a Metropolitan; Chair. of the Bulgarian Patriarchy His Holiness Patriarch MAKSIM.

Armenian Apostolic Orthodox Church: Sofia 1080, ul. Nishka 31; tel. (2) 988-02-08; 20,000 adherents (1996); administered by Bishop DIRAYR MARDIKIYAN, resident in Bucharest, Romania; Chair. of the Diocesan Council in Bulgaria OWANES KIRAZIAN.

The Roman Catholic Church

The Latin (Western) Rite, which is organized in two dioceses, had 65,000 adherents at 31 December 2002. The Byzantine-Slav (Eastern) Rite is organized in one diocese, which had 15,000 adherents at 31 December 2002. All three dioceses are directly responsible to the Holy See.

Bishops' Conference: 1606 Sofia, ul. Lulin Planina 5; tel. (2) 953-04-06; fax (2) 952-61-86; e-mail cproykov@technolink.bg; Pres. CHRISTO NIKOLOV PROYKOV (Titular Bishop of Briula).

Western Rite

Bishop of Nicopolis: PETKO JORDANOV CHRISTOV, 7000 Ruse, ul. I. Vazov 26A; tel. (82) 22-52-45; fax (82) 82-28-81; e-mail dio_nicop@ elits.rousse.bg.

Diocese of Sofia and Plovdiv: GEORGI IVANOV JOVČEV (Apostolic Administrator), 4000 Plovdiv, bul. Maria Luisa 3; tel. (32) 62-20-42; fax (32) 62-15-22; e-mail lubovenkov@hotmail.com.

Eastern Rite

Apostolic Exarch of Sofia: CHRISTO NIKOLOV PROYKOV (Titular Bishop of Briula), 1606 Sofia, ul. Lulin Planina 5; tel. (2) 953-04-06; fax (2) 952-61-86; e-mail cproykov@technolink.bg.

Reformed Churches

Bulgarian Church of God: Sofia 1408, ul. P. Karavelov 1; tel. (2) 965-75-52; fax (2) 951-91-31; Head Pastor PAVEL IGNATOV.

Union of the Churches of the Seventh-day Adventists: 1000 Sofia, ul. Solunska 10; tel. (2) 988-12-18; fax (2) 980-17-09; e-mail sda.bg@sbline.net; 6,700 adherents (1997); Head Pastor AGOP TACH-MISSJAN.

Union of Evangelical Baptist Churches: 1303 Sofia, ul. Osogovo 63; tel. and fax (2) 931-06-82; 4,000 adherents (1999); Pres. Dr THEODOR ANGELOV.

Union of Evangelical Congregational Churches: 1000 Sofia, ul. Solunska 49; tel. (2) 980-56-85; fax (2) 980-69-02; e-mail sescbg@ yahoo.com; 4,000 adherents (1998); Head Pastor Rev. Dr CHRISTO KULICHEV.

Union of Evangelical Pentecostal Churches: 1557 Sofia, ul. Bacho Kiro 21; tel. (2) 983-51-69; f. 1928; Head Pastor VIKTOR VIRCHEV.

ISLAM

Supreme Muslim Theological Council: 1000 Sofia, ul. Bratya Miladinovi 27; tel. (2) 987-73-20; fax (2) 939-00-23; adherents estimated at 9% of the actively religious population, with an estimated 708 regional imams; Chair. RIDVAN KADIOV; Chief Mufti of the Muslims in Bulgaria FIKRI SALI.

JUDAISM

Central Jewish Theological Council: 1000 Sofia, Ekzarkh Yosif St 16; tel. (2) 983-12-73; fax (2) 983-50-85; e-mail sofia_synagogue@ mail.orbitel.bg; 5,000 adherents (1992); Head ROBERT DJERASSI.

The Press

PRINCIPAL DAILIES

24 Chasa (24 Hours): 1504 Sofia, bul. Tzarigradsko 47; tel. (2) 44-19-45; fax (2) 433-93-39; f. 1991; wholly owned by Westdeutsche Allgemeine Zeitung (Germany); Editor-in-Chief VALERI NAIDENOV; circ. 330,000.

Bulgarska Armiya (Bulgarian Army): 1080 Sofia, ul. I. Vasov St; tel. (2) 987-47-93; fax (2) 987-91-26; f. 1944 as *Narodna Armiya* (People's Army), name changed 1991; organ of the Ministry of Defence; Editor-in-Chief Col VLADI VLADKOV; circ. 30,000.

Chernomorsky Far (Black Sea Lighthouse): 8000 Burgas, ul. Milin Kamak 9; tel. (56) 84-22-48; fax (56) 84-01-78; f. 1958; independent regional newspaper; Editorial Dir GEORGI INGILISOV; circ. 37,000.

Dneven Trud (Daily Labour): 1000 Sofia, bul. Dondukov 52; tel. (2) 980-12-69; fax (2) 980-26-26; f. 1998; owned by Westdeutsche Allgemeine Zeitung (Germany); Editor TOSHO TOSHEV.

Dnevnik (Daily): 1000 Sofia, ul. I. Vazov 16; tel. (2) 937-63-00; fax (2) 937-62-35; internet www.dnevnik.bg; f. 2001; Editor-in-Chief GALYA PROKOPIEVA.

Duma (Word): 1000 Sofia, ul. Positano 20, POB 382; ; tel. (2) 980-12-91; fax (2) 980-52-91; e-mail bsp@mail.bol.bg; internet www.duma .bg; f. 1990 as an organ of the Bulgarian Socialist Party; resumed publication in Oct. 2001; Editor-in-Chief VYACHESLAV TUNEV.

Kontinent: 1202 Sofia, ul. Industrialna 11; tel. (2) 943-44-46; e-mail kont@bgnet.bg; f. 1992; independent; Editor-in-Chief BOIKO PAN-GELOV.

Maritza: 4000 Plovdiv, bul Kh. Botev 27A; tel. (32) 60-34-50; fax (32) 60-34-22; e-mail mpolit@maritsa.com; internet www.digsys.bg/ bgnews/maritsa; f. 1991; Editor-in-Chief ANTON BAYEV; circ. 30,000.

Monitor: 1504 Sofia, bul. D. Tsankov 37; tel. (2) 960-22-07; fax (2) 960-22-13; e-mail info@zone168.com; internet www.monitor.bg; Editor-in-Chief PETYO BLSKOV.

Narodno Delo (People's Cause): 9000 Varna, bul. Kh. Botev 3; tel. (52) 23-10-71; fax (52) 23-90-67; f. 1944; 6 a week; regional independent; business, politics and sport; Editor-in-Chief DIMITUR KRASI-MIROV; circ. 56,000.

Noshten Trud (Night Labour): 1000 Sofia, bul. Dondukov 52; tel. and fax (2) 987-70-63; f. 1992; 5 a week; Editor-in-Chief PLAMEN KAMENOV.

Nov Glas (New Voice): 5500 Lovech, ul. G. Dimitrov 24; tel. (68) 222-42; f. 1988; regional independent; Editor-in-Chief VENETSII GEORGIEV.

Novinar: 1505 Sofia, ul. Oborishte 44; tel. (2) 943-55-22; fax (2) 943-45-32; e-mail novinar@novinar.net; internet www.novinar.org; f. 1992; Editor-in-Chief Dr STOYKO TONEV; circ. 45,000 (1997).

Pari (Money): 1202 Sofia, ul. Industrialna 11; tel. (2) 917-87-02; fax (2) 917-87-03; e-mail office@pari.bg; internet www.pari.bg; f. 1991; 5 a week; financial and economic news online; Bulgarian and English; Editor-in-Chief STEFAN NEDELCHEV; circ. 10,000.

Podkrepa (Support): 1000 Sofia, ul. Ekzarkh Yosif 37; tel. (2) 983-12-27; fax (2) 946-73-74; f. 1991; organ of the Podkrepa (Support) Trade Union Confederation; Editor-in-Chief (vacant).

Sega: 1164 Sofia, bul. Dzh. Bauchar 23; tel. (2) 969-43-00; e-mail prepress@segbg.com; internet www.segabg.com; f. 1998; Editor-in-Chief DIMITRANA ALEKSANDROVA.

Shipka: Khaskovo; tel. (38) 12-52-52; fax (38) 3-76-28; f. 1988; independent regional newspaper; Editor-in-Chief DIMITUR DOBREV; circ. 25,000.

Sport: 1000 Sofia, Vassil Levski Stadium, Sektor V, POB 88; tel. (2) 88-03-43; fax (2) 88-36-28; f. 1927; Editor-in-Chief IVAN NANKOV; circ. 80,000.

Standart News Daily: 1504 Sofia, bul. Tzarigradsko 47; tel. (2) 960-43-43; fax (2) 960-43-12; e-mail root@standartnews.com; internet www.standartnews.com; f. 1992; Editor-in-Chief YULY MOSKOV; circ. 110,000.

Trud (Labour): 1000 Sofia, bul. Dondukov 52; tel. (2) 987-98-05; fax (2) 980-11-40; f. 1923; organ of the Confederation of Independent Trade Unions in Bulgaria; Editor-in-Chief TOSHO TOSHEV; circ. 200,000.

Zemedelsko Zname (Agrarian Banner): Sofia; tel. (2) 87-38-51; f. 1902; organ of the Aleksandur Stamboliyski Bulgarian Agrarian People's Union; Editor ILIYA DANOV.

Zemya (Earth): 1000 ofia, ul. 11-ti Avgust 18; tel. (2) 88-50-33; fax (2) 83-52-77; f. 1951 as *Kooperativno Selo* (Co-operative Village); renamed 1990; fmrly an organ of the Ministry of Agriculture; Editor-in-Chief KOSTA ANDREEV; circ. 53,000.

PRINCIPAL PERIODICALS

166 Politzeiski Vesti (166 Police News): 1680 Sofia, ul. Solun 25–26, J. K. Belite Brezi; tel. (2) 82-30-30; fax (2) 82-30-28; f. 1945; fmrly *Naroden Strazh*; weekly; criminology and public security; Editor-in-Chief PETAR VITANOV; circ. 22,000.

168 Chasa (168 Hours): 1504 Sofia, bul. Tzarigradsko 47; tel. (2) 433-92-88; fax (2) 433-93-15; f. 1990; weekly; business, politics, entertainment; owned by Westdeutsche Allgemeine Zeitung (Germany); Editor-in-Chief VASELKA VALILEVA; circ. 93,000.

Avto-moto Svyat (Automobile World): 1000 Sofia, ul. Sv. Sofia 6, POB 1348; tel. and fax (2) 88-08-08; f. 1957; monthly; illustrated publication on cars and motor sports; Editor-in-Chief ILJA SELIKTAR; circ. 33,600.

Az Buki (Alphabet): 1113 Sofia, bul. Tzarigradsko 125; tel. (2) 71-65-73; f. 1991; weekly; for schools; sponsored by the Ministry of Education and Science; Editor-in-Chief MILENA STRAKOVA; circ. 11,800.

Bulgarski Fermer (Bulgarian Farmer): 1202 Sofia, ul. Industrialna 11; f. 1990; weekly; Editor-in-Chief VASSIL ASPARUHOV; circ. 20,000.

Computer: 1504 Sofia, ul. Panayot Volov 11; tel. and fax (2) 943-41-28; e-mail office@newteck.bg; internet www.newteck.bg; f. 1991; monthly; information technology; Editor-in-Chief PETAR PETROV; circ. 7,000.

Computer World: 1421 Sofia, bul. Hr. Smirnenski 1B/1111; tel. (2) 963-20-17; fax (2) 963-28-41; f. 1991; weekly; US-Bulgarian jt-venture; information technology; Editor-in-Chief TATIANA HINOVA; circ. 7,000.

Darzhaven Vestnik (State Gazette): 1169 Sofia, bul. A. Battenberg 1; tel. (2) 986-10-76; e-mail dv@nt52.parliament.bg; f. 1879; 2 a week; official organ of the National Assembly; 2 bulletins of parliamentary proceedings and the publication in which all legislation is promulgated; Editor-in-Chief IVAN GAJDARSKI; circ. 42,000.

Ekho (Echo): 1000 Sofia, ul. V. Levski 75; tel. (2) 87-54-41; f. 1957; weekly; organ of the Bulgarian Tourist Union; tourism publication; Editor-in-Chief LUBOMIR GLIGOROV; circ. 7,000.

Film: Sofia; e-mail film@online.bg; f. 1993; monthly; Editor DIMA DIMOVA; circ. 11,000.

Futbol (Football): Sofia; f. 1988; weekly; independent soccer publication; Editor-in-Chief IVAN CHOMAKOV; circ. 132,500.

Ikonomichesky Zhivot (Economic Life): 1000 Sofia, Blvd Dondukov 11; tel. (2) 987-95-06; fax (2) 987-65-60; e-mail ikonzhiv@dir.bg; f. 1966; weekly; independent; marketing and finance; Editor-in-Chief VASIL ALEKSIEV; circ. 10,000.

Kapital: 1000 Sofia, ul. I. Vazov 20; tel. (2) 981-58-16; fax (2) 987-69-07; internet www.capital.bg; f. 1993; weekly; Man. Editor FILIP HARMANDJIEV; circ. 30,000 (1999).

Krile (Wings): 1784 Sofia, POB 11; tel. (2) 974-51-26; fax (2) 974-51-25; e-mail kaloian_1999@yahoo.com; f. 1911; fmrly *Kam Nebeto*, renamed 1991; monthly; official organ; civil and military aviation; Pres. and Editor-in-Chief ROSSEN KALUDOV PANTCHELIEV; circ. 20,000.

Kultura (Culture): 1040 Sofia, ul. A. Battenberg 4; tel. (2) 988-33-22; fax (2) 980-04-95; e-mail kultura@online.bg; internet www.online.bg/kultura; f. 1957; weekly; issue of the Culture Space Foundation; arts, publicity and cultural affairs; Editor-in-Chief KOPRINKA CHERVENKOVA; circ. 5,000.

Kurier 5 (Courier 5): 1000 Sofia, bul. Tzarigradsko 47; tel. (2) 46-30-26; f. 1991; weekdays; advertising newspaper; Editor-in-Chief STEPAN ERAMIAN; circ. 30,000.

LIK: 1000 Sofia, bul. Tzarigradsko 49; weekly; publication of the Bulgarian Telegraph Agency; literature, art and culture; Editor-in-Chief SIRMA VELEVA; circ. 19,000.

Literaturen Forum (Literary Forum): 1000 Sofia, ul. Rakovski 136; tel. (2) 88-10-69; fax (2) 88-10-69; e-mail litforum@slovoto.org; internet www.slovo.bg/litforum; f. 1990; weekly; independent; Dir MARIN GEORGIEV; circ. 5,300.

Makedonia (Macedonia): 1301 Sofia, ul. Pirotska 5; tel. (2) 80-05-32; fax 87-46-64; e-mail mpress@virbus.bg; f. 1990; weekly; organ of the IMRO (Bulgarian National Movement)-Union of Macedonian Societies; Editor-in-Chief DINKO DRAGANOV; circ. 22,000.

Missul (Thought): 1000 Sofia, ul. Pozitano 20, POB 382; tel. (2) 85-141; f. 1990; weekly; organ of the Marxist Alternative Movement; politics, culture; Editor-in-Chief GEORGI SVEZHIN; circ. 15,000.

Napravi Sam (Do It Yourself): 1504 Sofia, ul. Panayot Volov 11; tel. and fax (2) 943-41-28; e-mail newteck@einet.bg; internet www.newteck.bg; f. 1981; monthly; Editor-in-Chief GEORGI BALANSKI; circ. 8,000.

Nie Zhenite (We the Women): Sofia; f. 1990; weekly; organ of the Democratic Union of Women; Editor-in-Chief EVGINIA KIRANOVA.

Nov Den (New Day): 1000 Sofia, ul. Lege 5; tel. (2) 77-39-82; e-mail ivan_kalchev@yahoo.com; f. 1991; weekly; organ of the Union of Free Democrats; Editor-in-Chief IVAN KALCHEV; circ. 25,000.

Novo Vreme (New Time): 1000 Sofia, ul. Positano 20; tel. (2) 981-62-58; fax (2) 980-52-91; e-mail novovreme@novovreme.com; internet www.novovreme.com; six a year; organ of the Bulgarian Socialist Party; Editor-in-Chief I. BORISSOV.

Paraleli: 1040 Sofia, bul. Tzarigradsko 49; tel. (2) 87-40-35; f. 1964; weekly; illustrated publication of the Bulgarian Telegraph Agency; Editor-in-Chief KRASSIMIR DRUMEV; circ. 50,000.

Pardon: 1504 Sofia, bul. Tzarigradsko 47; tel. (2) 43-431; f. 1991; weekly; satirical publication; Editor-in-Chief CHAVDAR SHINOV; circ. 8,560.

Pogled (Review): Sofia; tel. (2) 87-70-97; fax (2) 65-80-23; f. 1930; weekly; organ of the Union of Bulgarian Journalists; Editor-in-Chief DAMYAN OBRECHKOV; circ. 47,300.

Prava i Svobodi (Rights and Freedoms): 1000 Sofia, bul. A. Stamboliyski 45; f. 1990; weekly; organ of the Movement for Rights and Freedoms; politics, culture; Editor-in-Chief (vacant); circ. 7,500.

Pro i Anti: 1000 Sofia, POB 1078; tel. (2) 66-18-75; fax (2) 963-42-36; e-mail anti_bg@yahoo.co.uk; internet www.pro-anti.net; f. 1991; weekly; Editor-in-Chief VASIL STANILOV; circ. 7,000.

Starshel (Hornet): 1000 Sofia, ul. S. Karadja 26; tel. and fax (2) 988-08-16; e-mail starshel@bulmail.net; internet www.starshel.bg; f. 1946; weekly; satirical; Editor-in-Chief MIAKHAIL VESHIM; circ. 45,200.

Televiziya i Radio (Television and Radio): 1756 Sofia, bul. Tzarigradsko 111; tel. (2) 970-01-88; fax (2) 974-36-93; e-mail petmar@mail.techno-link.com; f. 1964; weekly; broadcast listings; Editor-in-Chief LUBOMIR YANKOV; circ. 30,000 (1999).

Tsarkoven Vestnik (Church Newspaper): 1000 Sofia, ul. Oborishte 4; tel. (2) 87-56-11; f. 1900; weekly; organ of the Bulgarian Orthodox Church; Editor-in-Chief DIMITAR KIROV; circ. 4,000.

Uchitelsko Delo (Teachers' Cause): Sofia; tel. and fax (2) 981-35-28; internet www.sbubg.info/udelo; f. 1905; weekly; organ of the Union of Bulgarian Teachers; Editor-in-Chief MARGARITA CHOLAKOVA; circ. 12,000.

Zdrave (Health): Sofia; tel. (2) 44-30-26; f. 1955; monthly; published by Bulgarian Red Cross; Editor-in-Chief YAKOV YANAKIEV; circ. 55,000.

Zhenata Dnes (Women Today): 1000 Sofia, bul. Narodno Sobraniye 12; tel. (2) 89-16-00; f. 1946; monthly; Editor-in-Chief BOTIO ANGELOV; circ. 50,000.

NEWS AGENCIES

Bulgarska Telegrafna Agentsia (BTA) (Bulgarian Telegraph Agency): 1024 Sofia, bul. Tzarigradsko 49; tel. (2) 92-62-42; fax (2) 986-22-89; e-mail bta@bta.bg; internet www.bta.bg; f. 1898; official news agency; domestic, Balkan and international news in Bulgarian and English; also economic and sports news; publishes weekly surveys of science and technology, international affairs, literature and art; Gen. Dir MAKSIM MINCHEV.

Sofia-Press Agency: 1040 Sofia, ul. Slavyanska 29; tel. (2) 88-58-31; fax (2) 88-34-55; f. 1967; publishes socio-political and scientific literature, fiction, children's and tourist literature, publications on the arts, a newspaper, magazines and bulletins in foreign languages.

Foreign Bureaux

Agence France-Presse (AFP) (France): 1504 Sofia, bul. Ya. Sakazov 19; tel. (2) 944-10-78; fax (2) 46-34-63; e-mail afpsofia@afp.com.

Agencia EFE (Spain): 1000 Sofia, ul. Strandya 40; tel. (2) 87-03-54; Correspondent SAMUEL FRANCÉS.

Anadolu Ajansı (Turkey): 1000 Sofia, Graf Ignatiev St 44/A/2; tel. (2) 981-67-88; fax (2) 981-59-83; e-mail sofya@anadoluajansi.com.tr.

Ceska kancelar (CTK) (Czech Republic): Sofia; tel. (2) 70-91-36; Correspondent VĔRA IVANOVIČOVÁ.

Deutsche Presse-Agentur (dpa) (Germany): 1000 Sofia, ul. Geo Milev 40G; tel. (2) 70-86-44; Correspondent ELENA LALOVA.

ITAR-TASS (Information Telegraph Agency of Russia-Telegraphic Agency of the Sovereign Countries) (Russia): 1000 Sofia, ul. A. Gendov1/29; tel. (2) 87-38-03; Correspondent ALEKSANDR STEPANENKO.

Magyar Távirati Iroda (MTI) (Hungary): Sofia; Correspondent TIVADAR KELLER.

Polska Agencja Prasowa (PAP) (Poland): Sofia, Slatina Distr., Bl. 18v, apt 54; tel. (2) 944-14-39; Correspondent EVGENIA MANOŁOWA.

Reuters (United Kingdom): 1000 Sofia, Ivan Vazov St 16; tel. (2) 911-88; fax (2) 980-91-31; e-mail sofia.newsroom@reuters.com; Correspondent THALIA GRIFFITHS.

RIA—Novosti (Russian Information Agency—News (Russia): Sofia; Bureau Man. YEVGENII VOROBYOV.

Tanjug Novinska Agencija (Serbia and Montenegro): 1000 Sofia, ul. L. Koshut 33; tel. (2) 71-90-57; Correspondent PERO RAKOSEVIĆ.

Xinhua (New China) News Agency (People's Republic of China): 1000 Sofia, ul. Baba Ilitsa 80B; tel. (2) 54-81-88; Correspondent U. SIZIUN.

PRESS ASSOCIATION

Union of Bulgarian Journalists: 1000 Sofia, ul. Ekzarkh Yosif 37; tel. (2) 83-19-95; fax (2) 83-54-84; f. 1944; Pres. CHAVDAR TONCHEV; 5,500 mems.

Publishers

Bulgarski Houdozhnik (Bulgarian Artist) Publishing House: 1504 Sofia, ul. Shipka 6; tel. (2) 946-72-85; fax (2) 946-02-12; e-mail filchev@vip.bg; f. 1952; art books, children's books; Dir BOUYAN FILCHEV.

Bulgarski Pisatel (Bulgarian Writer) Publishing House: 1000 Sofia, ul. 6-ti Septemvri 35; tel. (2) 87-58-73; fax (2) 87-24-95; publishing house of the Union of Bulgarian Writers; Bulgarian fiction and poetry, criticism; Dir GERTCHO ATANASOV.

Christo G. Danov State Publishing House (Darzhavno Izdatelstvo 'Christo G. Danov'): 4005 Plovdiv, ul. S. Chalakov 1; tel. (32) 23-12-01; fax (32) 26-05-60; f. 1855; fiction, poetry, literary criticism; Dir NACHO CHRISTOSKOV.

Marin Drinov Academic Publishing House (Bulgarian Academy of Sciences) (Izdatelstvo na Bulgarskata Akademiya na Naukite 'Marin Drinov'): 1113 Sofia, ul. Acad. Georgi Bonchev 6; tel. (2) 72-09-22; fax (2) 870-40-54; e-mail baspress@abv.bg; f. 1869; scientific works and periodicals of the Bulgarian Academy of Sciences; Dir YATCHKO IVANOV.

Medizina i Fizkultura (Medicine and Physical Culture) Publishing House (Izdatelstvo 'Medizina i Fizkultura'): 1080 Sofia, pl. Slaveikov 11; tel. (2) 987-99-75; fax (2) 987-13-08; e-mail medpubl@abv.bg; f. 1948; medicine; Dir EMILIA NIKOLOVA.

Military Publishing House (Voenno Izdatelstvo): 1000 Sofia, ul. I. Vazov 12; tel. (2) 980-27-66; fax (2) 980-27-99; e-mail evtimov@vi-books.com; internet www.vi-books.com; Dir RONMEN EVTIMOV.

Naouka i Izkoustvo (Sciences and Arts) Publishing House: 1000 Sofia, pl. Slaveikov 11; tel. (2) 987-47-90; fax (2) 987-24-96; e-mail nauk_izk@sigma-bg.com; f. 1948; Man. LORETA PUSHKAROVA.

Narodna Kultura (National Culture) Publishing House: 1000 Sofia, ul. A. Kanchev 1, POB 421; tel. (2) 987-80-63; e-mail nauk-izk@sigma-bg.com; f. 1944; general; Dir PETAR MANOLOV.

Prosveta (Enlightenment) Publishing House: 1618 Sofia, ul. Zemedelska; tel. (2) 818-20-20; fax (2) 818-20-19; e-mail prosveta@intech.bg; internet www.prosveta.net; f. 1945; educational publishing house; Chair. JOANA TOMOVA; Dir YONKO YONCHEV.

Reporter Publishing House: 1184 Sofia, bul. Tzarigradsko 113; tel. (2) 975-23-82; fax (2) 975-23-84; e-mail reporter@techno-link.com; internet www.reporter-bg.com; f. 1990; private publishers of fiction and documentary literature; Man. KRUM BLAGOV.

Sinodalno (Synodal) Publishing House: 1000 Sofia, ul. Oborishte 4; tel. (2) 87-56-11; religious publishing house; Dir ANGEL VELITEHKOV.

Technica Publishing House': 1000 Sofia, pl. Slaveikov 1; tel. (2) 987-12-83; fax (2) 987-49-06; e-mail upravitel@technica-bg.com; internet www.technica-bg.com; f. 1958; textbooks for professional, higher and university education, technical literature, dictionaries and handbooks; Exec. Man. MARIA DAMIANOVA PARASKOVA.

Zemizdat Publishing House: 1504 Sofia, bul. Tzarigradsko 47; tel. (2) 44-18-29; f. 1949; specializes in works on agriculture, shooting, fishing, forestry, livestock-breeding, environmental studies and popular scientific literature and textbooks; Dir PETAR ANGELOV.

PUBLISHERS' ASSOCIATION

Bulgarian Book Association: 1000 Sofia, pl. Slaveikov 11, POB 1046; tel. (2) 986-79-70; fax (2) 986-79-93; e-mail bba@otel.net; internet www.bba-bg.org; f. 1994; Sec.-Gen. MADLENA ROMANOVA; Chair. RAYMOND WAGENSTEIN.

Broadcasting and Communications

TELECOMMUNICATIONS

In 2002 there were 2.9m. main telephone lines in use and there were 2.6m. subscribers to mobile cellular telephone services.

Communications Regulation Commission (CRC): 1000 Sofia, ul. Gurko 6; tel. (2) 981-29-49; fax (2) 971-27-29; e-mail info@crc.bg; internet www.crc.bg; f. 2002; Pres. GERGANA PETROVA SARBOVA-BOZHILOVA.

Association of Bulgarian Broadcasters (ABBRO): 1504 Sofia, bul. Evlogi Georgiev 44; tel. (2) 946-16-20; fax (2) 944-29-79; e-mail office@abbro-bg.org; internet www.abbro-bg.org; f. 1997; independent non-profit organization; represents 60 private media companies, including 160 radio and television stations; Exec. Dir ANTOANETA ARSOVA.

Bulgarian Telecommunications Co (Balgarska Telekomunikatsionna Kompaniya—BTC): 1606 Sofia, bul. Totleben 8; tel. (2) 949-46-24; fax (2) 952-10-98; e-mail pc@btc.bg; internet www.btc.bg; 65% owned by Viva Ventures (Austria), a subsidiary of Advent International (USA); Chair. JOANNA JAMES; 23,000 employees.

Mobikom (Radiotelecommunication Company Mobikom): 1000 Sofia, POB 101; tel. (2) 974-40-27; fax (2) 960-56-13; internet www.mobikom.com; f. 1992; 49% owned by Cable and Wireless (USA), 39% owned by Bulgarian Telecommunications Co; Man. Dir JOHN MUNNERY.

MobilTel EAD: 1309 Sofia, ul. Kukush 1/8; tel. (88) 850-00-31; fax (88) 850-00-32; e-mail pr@mobiltel.bg; internet www.mobiltel.bg; f. 1994; provides mobile telecommunications services.

BROADCASTING

National Radio and Television Council: 1504 Sofia, ul. San Stefano 29; Dir IVAN BORISLAVOV.

Radio

In 2003 there were 89 licensed radio stations in Bulgaria.

Bulgarian National Radio (Balgarsko Natsionalno Radio): 1040 Sofia, bul. D. Tsankov 4; tel. (2) 963-43-30; fax (2) 963-44-64; e-mail bgintrel@nationalradio.bg; internet www.nationalradio.bg; f. 1929; two Home Service programmes; local stations at Blagoevgrad, Plovdiv, Shumen, Stara Zagora and Varna. The Foreign Service broadcasts in Bulgarian, Albanian, Arabic, English, French, German, Greek, Russian, Serbian, Spanish and Turkish; Dir-Gen. POLYA STANCHEVA.

BG Radio: 1000 Sofia, POB 48; tel. (2) 951-62-24; fax (2) 952-38-45; e-mail bgradio@bgradio.net; internet www.bgradio.net; f. 2001; commercial music station; wholly owned by Metromedia International Telecommunications Inc (USA); Chief Exec. NIKOLAY YANCHOVICHIN.

Television

In 2003 there were 98 licensed television stations in Bulgaria.

bTV: 1463 Sofia, pl. Balgaria 1, NDK Administration Bldg; tel. (2) 917-68-00; fax (2) 952-14-83; internet www.btv.bg; f. 2000; daily news transmission of commercial news, family entertainment and locally-produced programmes, on bTV channel; owned by Balkan News Corpn Plc, a subsidiary of News Corpn Ltd (Australia); Chief Exec. MARTY POMPADUR.

Bulgarian National Television (Bulgarska Natsionalna Televiziya): 1504 Sofia, ul. San Stefano 29; tel. (2) 944-63-29; fax (2) 946-12-10; internet www.bnt.bg; f. 1959; daily transmission of programmes on Channel 1 and Efir 2 and on the satellite channel—TV Bulgaria; Dir-Gen. ULYANA PRUMOVA; 3,000 employees.

New Television (Novo Televiziya): 1000 Sofia, bul. N. Valtsarov 55; tel. (2) 933-18-40; fax (2) 933-18-20; e-mail pr@ntv.bg; internet www.ntv.bg; f. 1994; privately owned; news and entertainment.

Finance

(cap. = capital; dep. = deposits; res = reserves; m. = million; amounts in new leva)

BANKING

A currency board was established in July 1997. By early 2005 35 commercial banks were in operation in Bulgaria (of which six were branches of foreign banks). The country's remaining state-owned bank, DSK Bank, was privatized in 2003.

Central Bank

Bulgarian National Bank (Bulgarska Narodna Banka): 1000 Sofia, bul. A. Battenberg 1; tel. (2) 914-51-203; fax (2) 980-24-25; e-mail press_office@bnbank.org; internet www.bnb.bg; f. 1879; bank of issue; cap. 20m., res 1,664.8m., dep. 1,002.1m. (Dec. 2003); Gov. IVAN ISKROV; 3 brs.

Commercial Banks

Allianz Bulgaria Commercial Bank (Targovska Banka Aliantz Balgaria): 1202 Sofia, bul. Mariya Luiza 79; tel. (2) 921-54-07; fax (2) 981-93-07; e-mail admin@bank.allianz.bg; internet bank.allianz.bg; f. 1997 as Yambol Commercial Bank; 79.3% owned by Allianz Bulgaria Holding AD; cap. 23.9m., res 3.7m., dep. 268.2m. (Dec. 2003); Chair. of Supervisory Bd OLEG NEDYALKOV; Chair. of Management Bd DIMITAR ZHELEV; 30 brs.

BNP Paribas (Bulgaria): 1000 Sofia, bul. Tsar Osvoboditel 2, POB 11; tel. (2) 921-86-40; fax (2) 921-86-95; e-mail bulgaria_bnpparibas@bnpparibas.com; internet bulgaria.bnpparibas.com; f. 1994; present name adopted 2001; wholly owned by BNP Paribas (France); cap. 36.0m., res 12.8m., dep. 240.8m. (Dec. 2002); Chief Exec. ULLRICH-GÜNTER SCHUBERT.

Bulbank: 1000 Sofia, bul. Sv. Nedelya 7; tel. (2) 923-21-11; fax (2) 988-46-36; e-mail info@sof.bulbank.bg; internet www.bulbank.bg; f. 1964 as the Bulgarian Foreign Trade Bank; present name adopted 1994; 85.2% owned by UniCredito Italiano (Italy); cap. 166.4m., res 59.8m., dep. 2,194.3m. (Dec. 2003); Chair. and Chief Exec. LEVON HAMPARTZOUMIAN; 91 brs.

Bulgarian-American Credit Bank: 1504 Sofia, ul. Shipka 3; tel. (2) 965-83-45; fax (2) 944-50-10; e-mail bacb@baefinvest.com; f. 1996; cap. €6.7m., res €0.9m., dep. €23.5m. (Dec. 2003); Chief Exec. FRANK BAUER.

Central Co-operative Bank (Tsentralna Kooperativna Banka): 1086 Sofia, ul. G. S. Rakovski 103; tel. (2) 926-62-66; fax (2) 926-62-

02; e-mail office@ccbank.bg; internet www.ccbank.bg; f. 1991; cap. 32.3m., res 58.0m., dep. 20.4m. (Dec. 2004); Chair. ALEXANDER VODENICHAROV; 38 brs.

Corporate Commercial Bank (Korporativna Targovska Banka): 1000 Sofia, ul. Graf Ignatiev 10, POB 632; tel. (2) 980-93-62; fax (2) 980-89-48; e-mail corpbank@corpbank.bg; internet www.corpbank .bg; f. 1989 as BSFK Bulgarsovinvest; cap. 14.0m., res 4.3m., dep. 276.6m. (Dec. 2003); Chair. of Supervisory Bd TZVETAN VASSILEV; 10 brs.

D Commerce Bank (D Bank): 1000 Sofia, ul. Tsar Osvoboditel 8; tel. (2) 935-71-71; fax (2) 989-48-48; e-mail info@dbank.bg; internet www.dbank.bg; f. 1999 as Demirbank (Bulgaria); present name adopted 2005; cap. 20.0m., res −2.1m., dep. 32.4m. (Dec. 2003); Chief Exec. MUAMMER AKSIT OZKURAL.

DSK Bank (Banka DSK): 1040 Sofia, ul. Moskovska 19; tel. (2) 985-57-220; fax (2) 980-64-77; e-mail office@dskbank.bg; internet www .dskbank.bg; f. 1951 as State Savings Bank; present name adopted 1998; provides general retail banking services throughout the country; wholly owned by National Savings and Commercial Bank—OTP Bank (Hungary); cap. 94.0m., res 208.3m., dep. 2,050.8m. (Dec. 2003); Chair. and Chief Exec. Dr KRASSIMIR ANGARSKI; 323 brs and offices.

DZI Bank: 1000 Sofia, bul. Dondukov 4–6; tel. (2) 930-71-36; fax (2) 980-26-23; e-mail info@dzibank.bg; internet www.dzibank.bg; f. 1994; cap. 40.0m., res 1.2m., dep. 538.1m. (Dec. 2003); Chair. DIANA MLADENOVA; Chief Exec. Dir VLADIMIR VLADIMIROV.

EIBank—Economic and Investment Bank (SIBank—Stopanka i investitsionna banka): 1000 Sofia, ul. Slavyanska 2; tel. (2) 939-92-40; fax (2) 981-25-26; e-mail info@hq.eibank.bg; internet www .eibank.bg; f. 1994 as Bulgarian-Russian Investment Bank; present name adopted 2000; cap. 20.0m., res 9.7m., dep. 466.6m. (Dec. 2004); Exec. Dir VASSIL SIMOV; 16 brs.

Eurobank (Evrobank): 1407 Sofia, bul. Cherni Vrakh 43; tel. (2) 969-07-50; fax (2) 969-06-99; e-mail eurobank@eurobank.bg; internet www.eurobank.bg; f. 1993; cap. 15.0m., res 5.1m., dep. 250.1m. (Dec. 2002); Chair. and Exec. Dir EMIL ANGELOV; 30 brs.

First Investment Bank (Parva Investitsionna Banka): 1000 Sofia, ul. S. Karadzha 10; tel. (2) 910-01-00; fax (2) 980-50-33; e-mail fib@ fibank.bg; internet www.fibank.bg; f. 1993; 39% owned by European Privatization and Investment Corpn (Austria), 20% owned by the European Bank for Reconstruction and Development; cap. 64.7m., res 13.0m., dep. 913.0m. (Dec. 2003); Chief Exec. JONATHAN HARFIELD; Chair. of Supervisory Bd GEORGI DIMITROV MUTAFCHIEV; 22 brs.

Hebrosbank (Khebros Bank): 4018 Plovdiv, Blvd Tsar Boris III Obedinitel 37; tel. (32) 90-25-13; fax (32) 62-39-64; e-mail head .office@hebros.bg; internet www.hebros.bg; f. 1993; commercial, investment, corporate and retail banking; cap. 41.1m., res 28.1m., dep. 429.2m. (Dec. 2003); Chair. and Chief Exec. GAUTAM VIR; 47 brs.

HVB Bank Biochim: 1026 Sofia, ul. I. Vazov 1; tel. (2) 926-92-10; fax (2) 926-94-40; e-mail info@biochim.com; internet www.biochim .com; f. 1987; present name adopted 2004; 99.7% owned by Bank Austria Creditanstalt AG (Austria); name changed from Commercial Bank Biochim plc in 2004; cap. 36.8m., res 83.3m., dep. 902.6m. (Dec. 2003); Chair. of Man. Bd and Exec. Dir PETER HAROLD; 40 brs.

Investbank: 1000 Sofia, ul. Rakovski 155; tel. (2) 981-69-38; fax (2) 980-77-22; e-mail office@ibank.bg; internet www.ibank.bg; f. 1994; present name adopted 2002; cap. 16.0m., res 0.6m., dep. 82.2m. (Dec. 2003); Chair. of Supervisory Bd PETYA BARAKOVA-SLAVOVA; nine brs.

Municipal Bank (Obshchinska Banka): 1000 Sofia, ul. Vrabcha 6; tel. (2) 930-01-11; fax (2) 981-51-47; e-mail contacts@municipalbank .bg; internet www.municipalbank.bg; f. 1996; cap. 25.0m., res 10.4m., dep. 286.1m. (Dec. 2003); Chief Exec. VANYA VASSILEVA; 16 brs.

Postbank—Balgarska Poshchenska Banka: 1414 Sofia, pl. Balgaria 1; tel. (2) 963-20-96; fax (2) 963-04-82; e-mail intldiv@postbank .bg; internet www.postbank.bg; f. 1991; privatized in 1999; cap. 51.3m., res 34.8m., dep. 771.9m. (Dec. 2003); Chief Exec. PANAIOTIS VARELAS; 112 brs and offices.

Raiffeisenbank (Bulgaria) AD: 1504 Sofia, ul. Gogol 18–20; tel. (2) 919-85-101; fax (2) 943-45-28; e-mail ibgamts@rbb-sofia .raiffeisen.at; internet www.rbb.bg; f. 1994; wholly owned by Raiffeisen International Beteiligungs (Austria); cap. 26.5m., res 31.3m., dep. 696.6m. (Dec. 2003); Chair. and Exec. Gen. Man. MOMCHIL ANDREEV.

SG Expressbank: 9000 Varna, bul. Vl. Varnenchik 92; tel. (52) 66-04-80; fax (52) 60-13-24; e-mail office@sgexpressbank.bg; internet www.sgexpressbank.bg; f. 1993; 97.95% owned by Société Générale (France); cap. 28.5m., res 11.7m., dep. 547.8m. (Dec. 2003); Chief Exec. SANDY GILLIO; 20 brs.

Teximbank (Teksimbank): 1202 Sofia, bul. Mariya Luiza 107; tel. (2) 935-90-00; fax (2) 931-12-07; e-mail texim@omega.bg; internet www.teximbank.bg; f. 1992; private entrepreneurial bank; Pres. MARIA VIDOLOVA; nine brs.

International Asset Bank: 1303 Sofia, bul. T. Aleksandrov 81–83, POB 256; tel. (2) 812-01-11; fax (2) 920-42-01; e-mail office@feibbank .com; internet www.feibbank.com; f. 1989; fmrly First East International Bank; present name adopted 2004; cap. 20.1m., res 3.7m., dep. 105.1m. (Dec. 2003); Pres. and Chair. ANNA SABEVA; 28 brs.

Unionbank Commercial Bank (Yunionbank Targovska Banka): 1606 Sofia, ul. D. Gruev 10–12; tel. (2) 915-33-33; fax (2) 980-20-04; e-mail mainmail@unionbank.bg; internet www.unionbank.bg; f. 1992; cap. 15.4m., res 2.9m., dep. 181.3m. (Dec. 2003); Chair. of Bd EMANUIL MANOLOV; 10 brs.

United Bulgarian Bank (Obedinena Balgarska Banka): 1040 Sofia, ul. Sv. Sofia 5; tel. (2) 98-54-00; fax (2) 988-08-22; e-mail info@ sof.ubb.bg; internet www.ubb.bg; f. 1993; universal commercial bank; 89.9% owned by National Bank of Greece SA; cap. 76.0m., res 15.4m., dep. 1,489.5m. (Dec. 2003); Chief Exec. STILIAN P. VATEV; 114 brs.

STOCK EXCHANGE

Bulgarian Stock Exchange: 1040 Sofia, pl. Makedonia 1; tel. (2) 986-58-63; fax (2) 987-55-66; e-mail bse@bse-sofia.bg; internet www .bse-sofia.bg; Chair. BISTRA ILKOVA; Chief Exec. GEORGI DRAICHEV.

INSURANCE

In 1947 all insurance firms were nationalized, and reorganized into a single state insurance company. In 1989 private insurance companies began to reappear.

Bulstrad: 1000 Sofia, pl. Pozitano 5; tel. (2) 985-66-100; fax (2) 985-66-103; internet www.bulstrad.bg; f. 1961; 31% owned by TBIH Group (Netherlands); all classes of insurance and reinsurance; Chair. of Bd and Chief Exec. RUMEN YANCHEV; 13 brs.

DZI Insurance: 1000 Sofia, Georgi Benkovski St 3; tel. (2) 981-57-99; fax (2) 987-45-33; e-mail general.ins@dzi.bg; internet www.dzi .bg; f. 1946; privatization approved in 2002; all areas of insurance; Chair. DANCHO DANCHEV; 27 agencies, 101 brs.

Trade and Industry

GOVERNMENT AGENCY

Privatization Agency (Agentsia za Privatizatsiya): 1000 Sofia, ul. Aksakov 29; tel. (2) 897-75-79; fax (2) 981-62-01; e-mail bgpriv@priv .government.bg; internet www.priv.government.bg; f. 1992; organizes the privatization of state-owned enterprises; Exec. Dir ATANAS BANGACHEV.

INTERNATIONAL FREE-TRADE ZONES

Burgas Free-Trade Zone: 8000 Burgas, ul. Trapezitsa 5, POB 154; tel. (56) 84-20-47; fax (56) 84-15-62; e-mail freezone@bse.bg; internet www.freezonebourgas.com; f. 1989; Exec. Dirs ANGELIN POPOV, KRASIMIR GRUDOV.

Dragoman Free-Trade Zone: 2210 Dragoman, ul. G. Dimitrov 33; tel. and fax (2) 954-93-39.

Plovdiv Free-Trade Zone: 4003 Plovdiv, ul. V. Tarnovo 25,; tel. (32) 65-02-86; fax (32) 65-08-33; e-mail frzone@plovdiv.techno-link .com; internet www.freezone-plovdiv.com; f. 1990; Exec. Dir ALEKSANDAR NIKOLOV.

Ruse (Rousse) Free-Trade Zone: 7000 Ruse, ul. Knyazhevska 5, POB 108; tel. (82) 27-22-47; fax (82) 27-00-84; e-mail trade@ freezone-rousse.bg; internet www.freezone-rousse.bg; f. 1988; Gen. Man. YORDAN KAZAKOV.

Svilengrad Free-Trade Zone: 6500 Svilengrad; tel. (359) 379-74-45; fax (359) 379-75-41; e-mail sbz@svilengrad.com; internet www .svilengrad.com/sbz; f. 1990; Exec. Dir DIMO HARAKCHIEV.

Vidin Free-Trade Zone: 3700 Vidin; tel. (94) 60-20-40; fax (94) 60-20-46; internet www.vidin.net/ftz; f. 1988; Gen. Man. K. MARINOV.

CHAMBER OF COMMERCE

Bulgarian Chamber of Commerce and Industry (BCCI): 1058 Sofia, ul. Parchevich 42; tel. (2) 987-26-31; fax (2) 987-32-09; e-mail bcci@bcci.bg; internet www.bcci.bg; f. 1895; promotes economic relations and business contacts between Bulgarian and foreign cos and orgs; organizes participation in international fairs and exhibitions; publishes economic publs in Bulgarian and foreign languages; organizes foreign trade advertising and publicity; provides legal and economic consultations, etc.; registers all Bulgarian cos trading internationally (more than 40,000 at the end of 2000); Pres. BOZHIDAR BOZHINOV; 28 regional chambers.

EMPLOYERS' ASSOCIATIONS

Bulgarian Industrial Association (BIA) (Balgarska Stopanska Kamara—BSK): 1000 Sofia, ul. Alabin 16–20; tel. (2) 932-09-11; fax (2) 987-26-04; e-mail office@bia-bg.com; internet www.bia-bg.com; f. 1980; assists Bulgarian economic enterprises with promotion and foreign contacts; economic analysis; legal and arbitration services; intellectual property protection; training and qualification; Chair. and Exec. Pres. BOZHIDAR DANEV.

Employers Association of Bulgaria (EABG) (Sayuz na Rabotodatelite v Balgariya): 1202 Sofia, ul. Industrialna 11; tel. (2) 917-88-68; fax (2) 917-88-61; e-mail headoffice@eabg.org; internet www.eabg.org; f. 2000; Chair. VASIL VASILEV.

Union for Private Economic Enterprise in Bulgaria (UPEE) (Sayuz za Stopansko Initsiativa—SSI): 1407 Sofia, ul. T. Notchev 30; tel. (2) 962-47-84; fax (2) 962-48-36; e-mail office@ssi-bg.org; internet www.ssi-bg.org; f. 1989; voluntary assocn of private enterprises; Chair. of Bd Dr BORISLAV BORISOV; 140 brs.

Vazrazhdane (Renaissance) Union of Bulgarian Private Entrepreneurs (UPBE) (Vazrazhdane sayuz na chastnite predpremachi): 1504 Sofia, bul. Dondukov 68; tel. (2) 926-24-17; fax (2) 926-74-12; e-mail vuzrazdane@union-vuzrazdane.com; internet www.union-vuzrazdane.com; f. 1989; Chair. DOBROOMIR GUSHCHEROV.

UTILITIES

Electricity

National Electricity Company (Natsionalna Elektricheska Kompania—NEK): 1000 Sofia, ul. Veslets 5 ; tel. (2) 986-18-19; fax (2) 980-12-43; e-mail nek@nek.bg; internet www.nek.bg; f. 1991; wholly state-owned; responsible for hydroelectric power generation; national transmission of electricity; centralized purchase and sale of electrical energy; supervision of national power system; Chair. of Bd ANGEL MINEV; Exec. Dir VASIL ANASTASOV.

Nuclear Regulatory Agency (Agentsiya za yadreno regulirane): 1574 Sofia, bul. Shipchenski prokhod 69; tel. (2) 940-68-00; fax (2) 940-69-19; e-mail mail@bnsa.bas.bg; internet www.bnsa.bas.bg; f. 1957; Chair. SERGEY TSOCHEV.

Gas

Bulgargaz: 1336 Sofia, bul. P. Vladigerov 66, POB 3; tel. (2) 939-64-22; fax (2) 925-04-01; e-mail hq@bulgargaz.com; internet www.bulgargaz.com; f. 1973; renamed 1990; state-owned; import, transmission, distribution, storage and transit of natural gas; Chair. GATI AL-JEBOURI; Chief Exec. KIRIL GEORGIEV GEGOV.

Overgaz: 1407 Sofia, ul. F. Kutev St 5; tel. (2) 960-32-20; fax (2) 962-17-24; internet www.overgas.bg; f. 1992; owned by Gazprom (Russia); holds a majority share in 26 local gas distribution companies, including Sofiagas EAD and Varnagas AD; Exec. Dir SASHA DONTCHEV.

CO-OPERATIVE

Central Union of Workers' Productive Co-operatives: 1000 Sofia, bul. Dondukov 11 POB 55; tel. (2) 80-39-38; fax (2) 87-03-20; f. 1988; overarching organization of 164 workers' productive co-operatives; Pres. STILIAN BALASSOPOULOV; 60,000 mems.

TRADE UNIONS

Confederation of Independent Trade Unions in Bulgaria (CITUB) (Konfederatsia na Nezavisitimite Sindikati v Bulgaria—KNSB): 1040 Sofia, bul. Makedonia 1; tel. (2) 917-04-79; fax (2) 988-59-69; internet knsb-bg.org; f. 1904; name changed from Bulgarian Professional Union and independence declared from all parties and state structures in 1990; in 1998 remained the main trade-union organization; approx. 75 mem. federations and four associate mems (principal mems listed below); Chair. ZHELYAZKO KHRISTOV; Sec. MILADIN STOYNOV; some 3m. mems.

Podkrepa (Support) Trade Union Confederation: 1000 Sofia, ul. A. Kanchev 2; tel. (2) 981-45-51; fax (2) 981-29-28; e-mail press_center@podkrepa.org; internet www.podkrepa.org; f. 1989; 36 regional and 30 branch union orgs; Chair. KONSTANTIN TRENCHEV; Gen. Sec. PETAR GANCHEV; 150,000 mems (2003).

Principal CITUB Trade Unions

Federation of Independent Agricultural Trade Unions: 1606 Sofia, ul. D. Hadzhidimov 29; tel. (2) 952-15-40; Pres. LYUBEN KHARALAMPIEV; 44,600 mems.

Federation of Independent Trade Unions of Construction Workers: Sofia; tel. (2) 801-60-03; Chair. NIKOLAI RASHKOV; 220,000 mems.

Federation of the Independent Trade Unions of Employees of the State and Social Organizations: 1000 Sofia; tel. (2) 987-98-52; Chair. PETAR SUCHKOV; 144,900 mems.

Federation of Independent Mining Trade Unions: 1233 Sofia, 32 ul. Veania; tel. (2) 931-07-00; fax (2) 931-00-50; f. 1992; Pres. PENCHO TOKMAKCHIEV; 20,000 mems.

Federation of Light-Industry Trade Unions: 1040 Sofia, bul. Makedonia 1; tel. (2) 988-15-70; fax (2) 988-15-20; Chair. YORDAN IVANOV.

Federation of Trade Unions in the Chemical Industry: 1040 Sofia, bul. Makedonia 1; tel. (2) 987-39-07; Pres. LYUBEN MAKOV.

Federation of Trade Union Organizations in the Forestry and Woodworking Industries: 1606 Sofia, ul. Vladayska 29; tel. (2) 952-31-21; fax (2) 951-73-97; Pres. PETAR ABRACHEV.

Federation of Trade Unions of Health Services: 1202 Sofia, bul. Mariya Luiza 45; tel. (2) 988-20-97; fax (2) 983-18-14; e-mail fsz_citub@mail.orbitel.bg; f. 1990; Pres. Dr IVAN KOKALOV; 17,955 mems (2004).

Independent Trade Union Federation of the Co-operatives: 1000 Sofia, ul. Rakovski 99; tel. (2) 987-36-74; Chair. NIKOLAI NIKOLOV; 96,000 mems.

Independent Trade Union Federation for Trade Co-operatives, Services and Tourism: 1000 Sofia, ul. 6-ti Septemvri 4; tel. (2) 988-02-51; Chair. PETAR TSEKOV; 212,221 mems.

Independent Trade Union of Food-Industry Workers: 1606 Sofia, ul. D. Hadzhidimov 29; tel. (2) 952-30-72; fax (2) 952-16-70; Pres. SLAVKHO PETROV.

National Federation of Energy Workers: 1040 Sofia, bul. Makedonia 1; tel. (2) 988-48-22; f. 1927; Pres. BOZHIL PETROV; 15,000 mems.

National Trade Union Federation 'Metal-elektro': 1040 Sofia, bul. Makedonia 1, POB 543; tel. (2) 987-48-06; fax (2) 987-75-38; e-mail nsf-me@netbg.com; Pres. ASSEN ASSENOV.

Trade Union of Bulgarian Teachers: 1000 Sofia, ul. Gen. Parensov 11; tel. (2) 987-78-18; fax (2) 988-17-94; e-mail seb@internet-bg.net; internet sbu.internet-bg.net; f. 1905; Pres. YANKA TANEVA; 186,153 mems.

Trade Union of Metal workers (Metalicy): 1000 Sofia, bul. Macedonia 1; tel. (2) 988-48-21; fax (2) 988-27-10; e-mail metalicy@netbg.com; f. 1992; Pres. VASSIL YANACHKOV; 13,000 mems.

Union of Transport Workers: 1233 Sofia, bul. Mariya Luiza 106; tel. (2) 931-51-24; fax (2) 831-71-24; e-mail stsb@einet.bg; f. 1911; Pres. YORDANKA RADEVA; 16,018 mems (Dec. 2003).

Other Principal Trade Unions

Podkrepa Construction, Industry and Water Supply Federation: 1000 Sofia, ul. Uzundjovska 12; tel. (2) 987-96-70; fax (2) 998-87-38; e-mail fciw@mail.techno-link.com; Pres. YOANIS PARTENIOTIS; 15,000 mems.

Podkrepa National Union of Petrochemical Workers: 8000 Burgas, Neftohim EAD; tel. (56) 80-09-01; fax (56) 80-12-89.

Podkrepa Professional Trade Union for Chemistry, Geology and Metallurgy Workers: 1000 Sofia, ul. A. Kanchev 2; 15,000 mems.

Podkrepa Professional Trade Union for Doctors and Medical Personnel: 1000 Sofia, ul. A. Kanchev 2; Chair. Dr K. KRASTEV; 20,000 mems.

Podkrepa Union of Journalists: 1000 Sofia, ul. A. Kanchev 2; tel. (2) 987-21-98.

Union of Architects in Bulgaria: 1504 Sofia, ul. Krakra 11; tel. (2) 943-83-21; fax (2) 943-83-49; e-mail sab@bgnet.bg; internet www.bularch.org; f. 1893; Pres. IVAN STANISHEV.

Transport

RAILWAYS

In 2002 there were 6,384 km of track (including sidings) in Bulgaria. The international and domestic rail networks are centred on Sofia. Construction of a 52-km underground railway system for Sofia commenced in 1979; the first section, comprising 6.1 km, was opened in January 1998.

Bulgarian State Railways (Balgarski Darzhavni Zheleznitsi—BDZh): 1080 Sofia, ul. I. Vazov 3; tel. (2) 981-11-10; fax (2) 987-71-51; e-mail bdz@bdz.bg; internet www.bdz.bg; f. 1888; operates passenger and freight railway services; Pres. ANELIA KROUSHKOVA; Chief Exec. NASKO TSANEV; 18,131 employees (2004).

National Railway Infrastructure Company (Natsionalna Kompania 'Zhelezoputna Infrastruktura'): 1080 Sofia, ul. I. Vazov 3; e-mail intrel_1@rail.infra.bg; internet www.rail-infra.bg; f. 2002 to assume infrastructure responsibilities of Bulgarian State Railways into two entities; Gen. Dir DIMITAR GAIDAROV.

Railway Transport Executive Agency (Zhelezoputna Administratsiya): 1080 Sofia, ul. I. Vazov 3; tel. (2) 940-94-27; fax (2) 987-67-69; e-mail aburov@mtc.government.bg; internet www.railbg.com; f. 2001; regulatory and control functions; Exec. Dir GEORGI NIKOLOV.

ROADS

There were 37,077 km of roads in Bulgaria in 2002, of which 2,911 km were principal roads; 92% of the network was paved. Two important international motorways traverse the country and a major motorway runs from Sofia to the coast.

Road Executive Agency: 1606 Sofia, Blvd Makedonia 3; tel. (2) 952-17-68; fax (2) 951-54-22; e-mail pdikovsky@rea.bg; f. 1952; develops, manages and maintains the national road network; provides conditions for the realization of state road policy; Dir-Gen. PAVEL DIKOVSKY.

SHIPPING AND INLAND WATERWAYS

The Danube (Dunav) River is the main waterway, with Ruse (Rousse) and Lom the two main ports. There are external services from Black Sea ports (the largest being Varna and Burgas) to the former USSR, the Mediterranean and Western Europe.

Bulgarian Ports National Co (BPA) (Natsionalna Kompania 'Pristanishta'): 1000 Sofia, ul. Gen. Gurko 5; tel. (2) 940-97-73; fax (2) 987-94-80; e-mail bpa@port.bg; internet www.port.bg; f. 2000; Gen. Dir Capt. PEYCHO MANOLOV.

Bulgarian River Shipping Co (Parakhodstvo Balgarsko Rechno Plavane): 7000 Ruse, pl. Otets Paisiy 2; tel. (82) 82-20-81; fax (82) 82-21-30; e-mail main@brp.bg; internet www.brp.bg; f. 1935; shipment of cargo and passengers on the Danube; storage, handling and forwarding of cargo; scheduled for privatization; Chair. STEFAN ZAGOROV; Gen. Dir VRANGEL NIKIFOROV.

Bulgarski Morski Flot Co: 9000 Varna, ul. Panaguirishte 17; tel. (52) 22-63-16; fax (52) 22-53-94; carriage of goods and passengers on waterways; Dir-Gen. ATANAS YONKOV.

Burgas (Bourgas) Port Authority: 8000 Burgas, ul. A. Battenberg 1; tel. (56) 84-04-93; fax (56) 84-01-56; e-mail ivanov@port-burgas.com; internet www.port-burgas.com; Chief Exec. GEORGE DERELIEV.

Lom Port Authority: 3600 Lom, ul. Pristanishtna 21; tel. (971) 422-08; fax (971) 269-31.

Navigation maritime bulgare: 9000 Varna, Primorski bul. 1; tel. (52) 63-31-00; fax (52) 63-30-33; e-mail office@navbul.com; internet www.navbul.com; f. 1892; scheduled for privatization; sea transport and ship repair; owns 93 tankers, bulk carriers and container, ferry, cargo and passenger vessels with a capacity of 1.8m. dwt (2002);

owns Varna shipyard; Dir-Gen. Capt. IVAN BORISSOV; 5,000 employees.

Varna Port Authority: 9000 Varna, pl. Slaveykov 1; tel. (52) 60-21-91; fax (52) 63-29-53; e-mail headoffice@port-varna.bg; internet port-varna.bg; Exec. Dir DANAIL PAPAZOV.

CIVIL AVIATION

There are three international airports in Bulgaria; at Sofia, Varna and Burgas, and seven other airports for domestic services.

Civil Aviation Administration (Grazhdanska Vazdukhoplavatelna Administratsiya): 1000 Sofia, ul. Dyakon Ignatii 9; tel. (2) 987-07-84; fax (2) 980-53-37; e-mail caa@caa.bg; internet www.caa.bg; Dir Gen. KALIN BARZOV.

Air Sofia: 1000 Sofia, Blvd Patriiarkh Evtimii 64; tel. (2) 981-09-25; fax (2) 980-29-07; e-mail airsofia@airsofia.com; internet www.airsofia.com; f. 1992; international charter flights; Pres. LILIAN TODOROV; Man. Dir GEORGI IVANOV.

Air Via: 1000 Sofia, bul. Dimitros 54; tel. (2) 971-28-69; fax (2) 973-34-54; e-mail headoffice@air-via.com; internet www.air-via.com; f. 1990; began services in 1997; private charter airline, internal charter services to Burgas, Plovdiv and Varna; Man. Dir MIKHAIL DONSKY.

Bulgaria Air: 1540 Sofia, Sofia Airport; tel. (2) 937-32-43; fax (2) 937-32-54; e-mail office@air.bg; internet www.air.bg; f. 2002 as successor to Balkan Bulgarian Airlines (Balkanair); scheduled for privatization; international passenger and cargo services; Chair. of Bd ANDREY BRESHKOV; Chief Exec. KONSTANTIN TASKOV, FILIPP ALEKSIEV.

Hemus Air (Khemus Er): 100 Sofia, ul. U. Gladston 32; tel. (2) 981-54-57; e-mail office@hemusair.bg; internet www.hemusair.bg; f. 1991; 66% state-owned; domestic and international passenger and cargo services; Man. Dir DIMITAR PAVLOV.

Tourism

Bulgaria's tourist attractions include the resorts on the Black Sea coast, mountain scenery and ski resorts and historic centres. In 1997 the tourism authorities promoted the creation of a national system of tourist offices, to be managed by local governments. In 2003 there were 3,531,567 foreign visitor arrivals. Tourism receipts totalled US $1,344m. in 2002, compared with $496m. in 1997.

Bulgarian Tourist Chamber: 1000 Sofia, ul. Sv. Sofia 8; tel. (2) 987-40-59; fax (2) 986-51-33; e-mail btch@yahoo.com; internet www.btch.org; f. 1991; assists tourism enterprises, provides training, and co-ordinates non-governmental organizations; Chair. TSVETAN TONCHEV.

Balkantourist: 1301 Sofia, ul. Sv. Sofia 2; tel. (2) 987-51-92; fax (2) 981-01-14; e-mail sofia.agency@balkantourist.bg; internet www.balkantourist.bg; f. 1948; privately owned; leading tour operator and travel agent; Exec. Dir NELLY SANDALSKA.

BURKINA FASO

Introductory Survey

Location, Climate, Language, Religion, Flag, Capital

Burkina Faso (formerly the Republic of Upper Volta) is a land-locked state in West Africa, bordered by Mali to the west and north, by Niger to the east, and by Benin, Togo, Ghana and Côte d'Ivoire to the south. The climate is hot and mainly dry, with an average temperature of 27°C (81°F) in the dry season (December–May). A rainy season occurs between June and October. Levels of rainfall are generally higher in the south than in the north; average annual rainfall in Ouagadougou is 718 mm (28 ins). The official language is French, and there are numerous indigenous languages (principally Mossi), with many dialects. The majority of the population follow animist beliefs; about 30% are Muslims and some 10% Christians, mainly Roman Catholics. The national flag (proportions 2 by 3) has two equal horizontal stripes, of red and green, with a five-pointed gold star in the centre. The capital is Ouagadougou.

Recent History

Burkina Faso (Upper Volta until August 1984) became a self-governing republic within the French Community in December 1958 and achieved full independence on 5 August 1960, with Maurice Yaméogo as President. In January 1966 Yaméogo was deposed in a *coup d'état*, led by Lt-Col (later Gen.) Sangoulé Lamizana, the army Chief of Staff, who took office as President and Prime Minister. The new regime dissolved the legislature, suspended the Constitution and established a Conseil suprême des forces armées. Political activities were suspended between September 1966 and November 1969. A new Constitution, approved by referendum in June 1970, provided for a return to civilian rule after a four-year transitional period. The Union démocratique voltaïque (UDV) won 37 of the 57 seats in elections for an Assemblée nationale, held in December. In early 1971 Lamizana appointed the UDV leader, Gérard Ouédraogo, as Prime Minister at the head of a mixed civilian and military Council of Ministers.

Following a series of conflicts between the Government and the legislature, in February 1974 Lamizana announced that the army had again assumed power. The Assemblée nationale was replaced in July by a Conseil national consultatif pour le renouveau, with 65 members nominated by the President. Political parties were allowed to resume their activities in October 1977, and in the following month a referendum approved a draft Constitution providing for a return to civilian rule. The UDV won 28 of the 57 seats at elections to a new Assemblée nationale, held in April 1978, while the Union nationale pour la défense de la démocratie (UNDD), led by Hermann Yaméogo (the son of the former President), secured 13 seats. In May Lamizana was elected President, and in July the Assemblée elected Lamizana's nominee, Dr Joseph Conombo, as Prime Minister.

In November 1980 Lamizana was overthrown in a bloodless coup, led by Col Saye Zerbo, and a new Government, comprising both army officers and civilians, was formed. The Constitution was suspended, the legislature was dissolved, and political parties were banned. Opposition to the Zerbo regime soon emerged, and in November 1982 Zerbo was deposed by a group of non-commissioned army officers. Maj. Jean-Baptiste Ouédraogo emerged as leader of the new regime, and a predominantly civilian Government was formed. A power struggle within the Government became apparent with the arrest, in May 1983, of radical left-wing elements, including the recently appointed Prime Minister, Capt. Thomas Sankara. Sankara and his supporters were released following a rebellion by pro-Sankara commandos at Pô, near the border with Ghana, under the leadership of Capt. Blaise Compaoré.

In August 1983 Sankara seized power in a violent coup. A Conseil national révolutionnaire (CNR) was established, and Jean-Baptiste Ouédraogo and other perceived opponents of the new administration were placed under house arrest. Compaoré, as Minister of State at the Presidency, became the regime's second-in-command. Administrative, judicial and military reforms were announced, and citizens were urged to join Comités pour la défense de la révolution, which played an important role in consolidating Sankara's position.

In June 1984 seven army officers were executed, convicted of plotting to overthrow the Government. Sankara accused the outlawed Front progressiste voltaïque of complicity in the plot, alleging that it had been supported by France and other foreign powers; the French Government vigorously denied any involvement, and relations between the two countries were strained. In August the country was renamed Burkina Faso ('Land of the Incorruptible Men').

In December 1985 a long-standing border dispute with Mali erupted into a six-day war that left some 50 people dead. The conflict centred on a reputedly mineral-rich area known as the Agacher strip. Following a cease-fire, arranged by the regional defence grouping, Accord de non-agression et d'assistance en matière de défense, and as a result of an interim decision on the dispute delivered by the International Court of Justice (ICJ) in January 1986, troops were withdrawn from the Agacher area; both countries accepted the ICJ's ruling, made in December, that the territory be divided equally between the two.

On 15 October 1987 a self-styled Front populaire (FP), led by Compaoré, overthrew the CNR in a coup, in which Sankara and 13 of his entourage were killed. A predominantly civilian Council of Ministers included seven members of the previous administration. Compaoré became Head of State, with the title of Chairman of the FP. In April 1989 a new political grouping, the Organisation pour la démocratie populaire/Mouvement du travail (ODP/MT), was established, under the leadership of Clément Oumarou Ouédraogo. The swift dismissal of government members who had declined to join the new party was an indication that the ODP/MT was to assume a prominent role in Compaoré's regime.

In August 1989 an amnesty was proclaimed for all political prisoners. In the following month it was announced that the Commander-in-Chief of the Armed Forces and Minister of Popular Defence and Security, Maj. Jean-Baptiste Boukary Lingani, and the Minister of Economic Promotion, Capt. Henri Zongo (both of whom had been prominent at the time of the 1983 and 1987 coups), had been executed, together with two others, following the discovery of a plot to overthrow Compaoré. It was widely believed that Lingani and Zongo had been opposed to aspects of economic reform, notably the principle of co-operation with the IMF and the World Bank (funding negotiations with which had begun in 1988). Compaoré subsequently assumed personal responsibility for defence. In December 1989 it was announced that a further attempt to overthrow the Government had been thwarted.

The first congress of the FP, in March 1990, sanctioned the establishment of a commission to draft a new constitution that would define a process of 'democratization'. Hermann Yaméogo was appointed to the Executive Committee of the FP. (In June, however, Yaméogo and his supporters were expelled from the organization.) Meanwhile, in April Clément Oumarou Ouédraogo was dismissed from the Council of Ministers and replaced as Secretary for Political Affairs of the FP and as Secretary-General of the ODP/MT by Roch Marc-Christian Kaboré, hitherto Minister of Transport and Communications and, unlike Ouédraogo, a known supporter of Compaoré's ideals. In September Kaboré was appointed as a Minister of State.

The final draft of the constitution, which was completed in late 1990, delineated the division of power between the executive, legislature and judiciary, in a 'revolutionary, democratic, unitary and secular state'. Multi-party elections, by universal suffrage, would take place for a President and legislative Assemblée des députés du peuple (ADP), while provision was made for the establishment of a second, appointed and consultative chamber of the legislature, the Chambre des représentants, to be composed of the 'active forces of the nation'.

In March 1991, at its first congress, the ODP/MT adopted Compaoré as the party's presidential candidate and renounced its Marxist-Leninist ideology. In May 1991 a congress was convened to restructure the FP and to provide for the separation, upon the adoption of the draft constitution, of the functions of the FP and the organs of state. Compaoré, redesignated Secretary-General of the FP, was confirmed as Head of State pending the presidential election. Delegates also approved the rehabilitation of Maurice Yaméogo, and an appeal was made to all political exiles to return to Burkina. In June plans were announced for the construction of a memorial honouring Sankara.

About 49% of the registered electorate voted in the constitutional referendum, which took place on 2 June 1991: of these, 93% were reported to have endorsed the Constitution of what was to be designated the Fourth Republic. The new document took effect on 11 June. A transitional Government was subsequently appointed, its most senior member being Kaboré (as Minister of State, responsible for the Co-ordination of Government Action). The dominant role of the ODP/MT was widely criticized, and several nominated government members declined their posts. In July Hermann Yaméogo, now leader of the Alliance pour la démocratie et la fédération (ADF), and several other representatives of parties outside the FP were appointed to the Government. In August, however, Yaméogo (who had announced his intention to contest the presidency) was one of three government members who resigned in protest against proposed electoral procedures. Seven further opposition members resigned from the transitional administration in September, when Compaoré rejected demands for a national conference. Grouped in a Coordination des forces démocratiques (CFD), the opposition organized rallies and demonstrations in support of the campaign for a national conference. Attempts to achieve a compromise failed, and in October five CFD candidates withdrew from the presidential contest.

The presidential election proceeded on 1 December 1991, when Compaoré (who had resigned from the army to contest the presidency as a civilian) was elected, unopposed, with the support of 90.4% of those who voted. The CFD claimed that an abstention rate of 74.7% reflected the success of its appeal for a boycott of the poll. Compaoré emphasized the need for national reconciliation, but shortly after the election Clément Oumarou Ouédraogo was assassinated; attacks on other opposition members were also reported. Although the Government condemned the violence, the CFD denounced Compaoré as personally responsible for the incidents, and further disturbances followed Ouédraogo's funeral. Apparently in response, the Government announced the indefinite postponement of the legislative elections, which had been scheduled for January 1992. The CFD had been advocating a boycott of the elections, and few political parties had registered their intention to contest the poll.

Compaoré was inaugurated as President on 24 December 1991, and in January 1992 it was announced that some 4,000 people who had been convicted in connection with political or trade-union activities since the time of Sankara's accession to power were to be rehabilitated. Four opposition members were appointed to the Government in February, including Hermann Yaméogo as Minister of State.

A total of 27 political parties contested the legislative elections, which were finally held on 24 May 1992. The ODP/MT won 78 of the ADP's 107 seats, and nine other parties secured representation. The rate of participation by voters was reported to have been around 35%. In June Compaoré appointed Youssouf Ouédraogo, hitherto President of the Economic and Social Council, as Prime Minister. Although his Council of Ministers included representatives of seven political parties, the ODP/MT was allocated most strategic posts.

In March 1994 Ouédraogo resigned, apparently prompted by the failure of the Government to negotiate a settlement for salary increases acceptable to workers' representatives, following the 50% devaluation of the CFA franc in January. Kaboré, hitherto Minister of State, responsible for Relations with the Organs of State, was appointed as the new premier. In February 1996 Kadré Désiré Ouédraogo, hitherto Deputy Governor of the Banque centrale des états de l'Afrique de l'ouest, replaced Kaboré as Prime Minister. At this time a new, social-democratic party, the Congrès pour la démocratie et le progrès (CDP), was formed, uniting the ODP/MT and 10 other parties. The CDP was dominated by close allies of Compaoré, and the new premier subsequently joined the party.

Constitutional amendments and a new electoral code were approved by the ADP in January 1997. Notably, restrictions were removed on the renewal of the Head of State's mandate (hitherto renewable only once), the number of parliamentary seats was to be increased to 111 with effect from the forthcoming elections, and the ADP was renamed the Assemblée nationale.

Elections to the Assemblée nationale took place in May 1997, contested by some 569 candidates from 13 parties. The CDP won

a resounding victory, securing 101 seats; three other parties obtained representation in the legislature.

In April 1998, following consultations with pro-Government and opposition parties, the Council of Ministers adopted legislation providing for the establishment of an independent electoral commission: the 26-member Commission électorale nationale indépendante (CENI) was to be composed of six representatives of the parliamentary majority and an equal number of opposition delegates, together with civic representatives. However, when the CENI was inaugurated, in July, several opposition parties, including the principal opposition party in the legislature, the Parti pour la démocratie et le progrès (PDP), refused to take up their seats and indicated their intention to boycott the forthcoming presidential election. The Groupe du 14 février (G-14f) coalition, which had become a prominent focus of opposition to the Compaoré administration, protested about a lack of transparency in the electoral process, disputing the impartiality of the CENI and alleging unfair provisions for campaign funding.

Several prominent opposition figures, among them Hermann Yaméogo, whose party had absorbed a faction of the Rassemblement démocratique africain (RDA) to form the Alliance pour la démocratie et la fédération—Rassemblement démocratique africain (ADF—RDA), and Joseph Ki-Zerbo, the leader of the PDP, declined to participate in the presidential election, which took place, as scheduled, on 15 November 1998. Compaoré was challenged by two minor candidates: an ecologist, Ram Ouédraogo, and a representative of the faction of the RDA that remained outside Yaméogo's party, Frédéric Guirma. The provisional results, issued by the CENI on 18 November, confirmed a decisive victory for Compaoré, with 87.53% of the valid votes cast. Despite the appeal by the G-14f for a boycott, the rate of voter participation, at 56.08%, was considerably higher than in 1991. A new Government, again headed by Kadré Désiré Ouédraogo, was appointed in January 1999.

The political climate deteriorated rapidly after Norbert Zongo, the managing editor of the newspaper *L'Indépendant*, was found dead, together with three colleagues, in December 1998. Zongo, a frequent critic of the Compaoré regime, had been investigating allegations that David Ouédraogo, a driver employed by François Compaoré, younger brother and special adviser of the President, had been tortured and killed by members of the presidential guard. Opposition parties and human rights organizations, grouped in a Collectif d'organisations démocratiques de masse et de partis politiques, demanded a full investigation of the case. Opposition groups refused to participate in an independent commission of inquiry into Zongo's apparent murder, established by presidential decree in January 1999, stating that a similar commission had failed to bring to justice those responsible for the assassination of Clément Oumarou Ouédraogo in 1991. Shortly afterwards a three-day general strike was widely observed in the capital. In its final report, submitted in May 1999, the commission of inquiry stated that it had been unable to prove the identity of the culprits, but indicated the likelihood that the members of the presidential guard implicated in the death of David Ouédraogo were also responsible for the murders of the journalists. In mid-May three prominent members of the opposition, including Halidou Ouédraogo, the Chairman of the Collectif, and Hermann Yaméogo, were arrested by the security forces, accused of denouncing the presidential guard and of having plotted a *coup d'état*. Two were released after a brief detention, but Yaméogo remained in custody for three days. Shortly afterwards Compaoré stated that the examining magistrate responsible for the Zongo case would be given his full support. He further announced a reorganization of the presidential guard, an amnesty for all those arrested in recent protests, the reopening of educational establishments closed during the unrest, and compensation for the relatives of the victims of the murders that had provoked the political crisis.

In June 1999 Compaoré established a Collège des sages, composed of Burkinabè state elders, and religious and ethnic leaders. The 16-member Collège was to promote national reconciliation and, most notably, to investigate unpunished political crimes since independence. In mid-June the Collège ordered the arrest of the three members of the presidential guard accused of the murder of David Ouédraogo. The main recommendations of the Collège's report, published in August, were that a government of national unity should be formed, as well as a 'commission of truth and justice' to oversee the transition to a truly plural political system and to investigate unresolved political murders, including that of Sankara. The Collège also suggested that an amnesty should be granted to those implicated during the investigations of the commission, and that compensation should be paid to the families of victims. The Collège further recommended the creation of a commission to examine certain clauses of the Constitution and to formulate rules governing political parties, the organization of fresh elections to the Assemblée nationale and that Compaoré should not seek re-election. Although Compaoré praised the work of the Collège, opposition organizations rejected the proposed amnesty and criticized the need for the President to assent to any proposed reforms.

In September 1999 the Prime Minister, Kadré Désiré Ouédraogo, began consultations with the leaders of the main political parties in order to identify the principal objectives of any government of national unity. Most opposition parties stipulated that participation in such a government would be conditional on the expedition of legal action in the cases of David Ouédraogo and Norbert Zongo. Thus, the reshuffled Council of Ministers, announced in October, included just two, relatively uninfluential, representatives of the opposition. In November, in accordance with the recommendations of the Collège des sages, the two advisory commissions were inaugurated: one to consider possible changes to the Constitution, and another to promote national reconciliation. Despite official assurances that the commissions' findings would be binding, the G-14f refused to participate.

In January 2000 the ruling CDP organized a public demonstration in favour of the proposals of the advisory commission on political reform, which had recommended the modification of the electoral code and the reform of the judiciary and the Constitution. Most notably, the commission proposed that a restriction of the presidential mandate to no more than two successive terms be reintroduced. The Assemblée nationale subsequently voted to revise the electoral code, to accord greater powers to the CENI, and to postpone the municipal elections scheduled for February in order to allow the implementation of the revisions. The opposition, however, criticized what they perceived to be the limited nature of the reforms and expressed their determination to boycott any elections until the Ouédraogo and Zongo cases had been fully resolved. The advisory commission on national reconciliation published its report in February, urging the prosecution of those suspected of involvement in the embezzlement of public funds and in so-called political killings. The report also recommended that victims of political violence or their relations receive an official apology, compensation and a guarantee regarding their future security. The commission also called for greater freedom of speech, of the press, and of assembly, the resolution of legal proceedings in the Ouédraogo and Zongo cases, the enactment of an amnesty law, and the construction of a monument to former President Sankara.

The Assemblée nationale approved revisions to the electoral code in April 2000; under the new regulations, which introduced a system of proportional representation, 90 deputies would be elected from regional lists, while 21 would be elected from a national list. The new legislation also reduced the presidential mandate from seven to five years, renewable only once. However, as the new limits were not to take effect until the next election, Compaoré would be permitted to contest the presidential elections due in 2005 and 2010. In addition, the Assemblée approved significant judicial reforms, which provided for the eventual abolition of the Supreme Court and the replacement of its four permanent chambers with four new state institutions: a Constitutional Council, a Council of State, a Court of Appeal and a National Audit Court. In the same month Hermann Yaméogo was expelled from the G-14f for having criticized the group's refusal to co-operate with the Government.

In early May 2000 the Government announced that the postponed municipal elections would be held on 30 July. However, several opposition parties reiterated their demand for the Ouédraogo and Zongo cases to be resolved prior to the elections. In July the elections were postponed until 24 September, although the Collectif and the G-14f continued to call for a further delay. However, by mid-August several constituent parties of the Collectif and the G-14f had chosen to nominate candidates for the elections. As a result, three parties, including the ADF—RDA, were expelled from the Collectif and the G-14f. The increasingly fragmented nature of the opposition was also evident in the formation of several breakaway groups by former ADF—RDA members. The CDP held outright control of 40 of the 49 municipalities following the elections, which were contested by 25 parties, although the G-14f and the PDP boycotted the poll.

In November 2000, amid ongoing social unrest, Kadré Désiré Ouédraogo resigned as Prime Minister and was replaced by Paramanga Ernest Yonli, hitherto the Minister of the Civil Service and Institutional Development. President Compaoré subsequently formed a 36-member Council of Ministers, including 12 members of the opposition. The new appointments resulted from an agreement reached by Yonli and representatives from seven political parties, including the ruling CDP and the ADF—RDA, but not the principal opposition party, the PDP, which refused to participate. The agreement specified the parties' conditions for joining the Government, notably the prompt and thorough completion of pending legal cases. The leaders of the participating parties were to meet with the Prime Minister every three months to evaluate the implementation of the accord.

Meanwhile, the trial of the soldiers accused of murdering David Ouédraogo began in August 2000. Two of the defendants were acquitted by the military tribunal, but two members of Compaoré's presidential guard, including Marcel Kafando, head of the guard at the time of Ouédraogo's death, were sentenced to 20 years' imprisonment, with a third member sentenced to 10 years'. In early February 2001 Kafando was charged with arson and the murder of Norbert Zongo and three others. In late March, at a rally attended by some 30,000 people, President Compaoré apologized for some 176 unpunished crimes allegedly committed by state representatives since independence in 1960. This act constituted the most significant element of a 'day of forgiveness' that had been proposed by the Collège des sages, but which was boycotted by protesters, including relations of Sankara and Zongo. However, dissatisfaction at the Government's failure to resolve the Zongo case continued, and in June 2001 several thousand people participated in a demonstration in Ouagadougou calling for those whom they believed to have ordered the killing of Zongo, including François Compaoré, to be brought to justice. None the less, in August, following the appointment of two of their members to the CENI, the constituent parties of the G-14f announced their intention to contest the forthcoming legislative elections. Michel Tapsoba, a human rights activist, was elected as Chairman of the CENI in the following month. In November it was announced that the judicial investigation into Kafando's alleged involvement in Zongo's death had been hampered by the poor health of the defendant.

In February 2002 the Assemblée nationale adopted a constitutional amendment, providing for the abolition of the Chambre des représentants, following the failure to appoint replacement representatives for those whose terms had expired in December 2001. The Government announced proposals for the eventual replacement of the Chambre by a Conférence générale de la nation, the membership and responsibilities of which were to be determined in due course.

On 5 May 2002 some 30 parties contested elections to the Assemblée nationale, the first to be conducted with the use of a single ballot paper, in accordance with the demands of opposition parties. The CDP remained the largest party, securing 57 of the 111 seats, with 49.52% of the votes cast, although its representation was much reduced. The ADF—RDA won 17 seats, with 12.61% of the votes cast, becoming the largest opposition party, followed by the PDP—PS (as the PDP had become, following its merger with the Parti socialiste burkinabè in mid-2001), with 10 seats. Ten other parties secured legislative representation. Kaboré was elected as President of the Assemblée nationale in early June, prior to the reappointment of Yonli as Prime Minister. Despite the slim majority held by the CDP in the Assemblée nationale and the precedent set by the inclusion of ministers from opposition parties in the outgoing administration, the new 31-member Government, appointed in mid-June, did not contain any representatives of the opposition.

In June 2002 the Council of Ministers announced the appointment of First Presidents to head the new judicial institutions that were to replace the Supreme Court. In October the membership of the Constitutional Council was approved by the Council of Ministers, and the other three new judicial institutions were formally inaugurated in early December.

In early October 2003 the Government announced that the authorities had prevented a planned *coup d'état*. By early January 2004 15 members of the armed forces, including several members of the presidential guard, and two civilians, notably Norbert Tiendrébéogo, the Chairman of the Front des forces sociales, had been arrested on suspicion of involvement in the alleged plot. (International arrest warrants remained outstanding for a further two civilians.) It was announced that the detainees were to face charges of plotting and threatening the security of the State. The reputed leader of the group, Capt. Luther Ouali, was additionally to be charged with treason and complicity with a foreign power. In mid-January President Compaoré effected a minor government reshuffle. Notably, the Minister of Defence, Gen. Kouamé Lougué, was dismissed and replaced by Yéro Boly, hitherto head of the presidential administration. It was subsequently reported that Lougué had been questioned by the state prosecutor in connection with the alleged coup plot. Two other ministers were replaced, and a new minister-delegate position, responsible for technical education, was created. In mid-April Ouali was sentenced to 10 years' imprisonment; six other defendants received lesser sentences, and a further six were acquitted.

In late April 2004 the Assemblée nationale approved an amendment to the electoral code, changing the electoral unit from the region, which number 15, to the province, of which there are 45. The vote was boycotted by most opposition parties, which claimed that they would be disadvantaged by the revised electoral code as they would be unable to field candidates in all 45 electoral units. The amendment represented a return to the system in place prior to the reforms adopted in 2000: these were regarded as having contributed to the opposition's success in increasing significantly its legislative representation in the 2002 elections.

Compaoré has, in recent years, gained wide recognition for his efforts as a regional mediator and as a proponent of inter-African conflict-resolution initiatives. In the early 1990s, however, relations with some members of the Economic Community of West African States (ECOWAS, see p. 205) suffered a reverse, owing to the Compaoré Government's support for Charles Taylor's rebel National Patriotic Front of Liberia (NPFL) and Burkina's refusal to participate in the military intervention by the ECOWAS cease-fire monitoring group (ECOMOG, see p. 208) in Liberia. In September 1991 Compaoré admitted that Burkinabè troops had been dispatched to Liberia to assist the NPFL in the overthrow of Samuel Doe's regime in mid-1990, but asserted that the country's involvement in Liberia had ended. In November 1992 the US Government recalled its ambassador to Burkina, and announced that the recently appointed Burkinabè ambassador to the USA would not be welcome in Washington, DC, owing to Burkina's alleged role in transporting arms from Libya to the NPFL. Allegations of Burkinabè support for the NPFL persisted, but in September 1995 the Compaoré administration, stating that it regarded the peace agreement that had been signed in Abuja, Nigeria, in the previous month as more 'credible' than earlier peace settlements for Liberia, announced that Burkina would contribute peace-keeping troops to ECOMOG. In February 1997 the Burkinabè legislature approved legislation authorizing the participation of Burkinabè military personnel in the cease-fire monitoring group, and members of the Burkinabè military subsequently remained in Liberia to assist in the training of new armed forces.

In early 1999 President Ahmed Tejan Kabbah of Sierra Leone and the Nigerian Government alleged that Burkina Faso and Liberia were co-operating to provide support and supply arms to the rebel fighters of the Revolutionary United Front (RUF) in Sierra Leone. (Sierra Leonean refugees, entering Guinea in early 1998, had made similar accusations.) The Burkinabè Government denied any involvement, although in early 2000 a report to the UN Security Council accused Burkina of having supplied weapons to the RUF in exchange for diamonds on several occasions. It was also alleged that Burkina had supplied weapons to Liberia and to Angolan rebel groups, despite international embargoes on the supply of weapons to those countries. The report, which further accused Compaoré of having conducted personal negotiations with the Angolan rebel leader Jonas Savimbi, was strenuously denied by the Burkinabè Government. Two missions from the UN Security Council visited Burkina Faso in mid-2000, at the invitation of the Burkinabè Government, to investigate the claims regarding the breaching of arms embargoes against Angola and Sierra Leone. In December it was reported that Burkina Faso was to introduce measures aimed at controlling its weapons imports in an attempt to allay international concern. Although Compaoré, in May 2001, criticized a decision by the UN to impose travel restrictions on Liberian officials, relations with the Taylor Government subsequently became more distant. In July 2002 the Burkinabè Government hosted a conference intended to promote a peaceful resolution of the political crisis in Liberia, at

which Taylor's Government was not represented. Moreover, Compaoré stated that he regarded Taylor's resignation as President of Liberia in August 2003 as a positive development, which would encourage the stabilization of the region.

The Assemblée nationale authorized the dispatch of a Burkinabè military contingent to the surveillance mission for the Central African Republic (CAR) in February 1997, and a Burkinabè force remained in the CAR as part of the UN peace-keeping operation that succeeded the regional mission between April 1998 and February 2000. Burkina Faso has maintained close ties with Libya, and was a founder member of the Libyan-sponsored Community of Sahel-Saharan States (see p. 373) in 1997.

In early November 1999 a dispute over land rights between Burkinabè settlers in the south-west of Côte d'Ivoire and the indigenous minority Krou population led to the violent and systematic expulsion from the region of several hundred Burkinabè plantation workers. Several deaths were reported, and it was estimated that up to 20,000 expatriates subsequently returned to Burkina. Following the *coup d'état* in Côte d'Ivoire in December, the military authorities assured the Government of Burkina that the expulsions would cease and that measures would be taken in order to allow workers to return. None the less, tensions between the two countries intensified as the former Prime Minister of Côte d'Ivoire and leader of the Rassemblement des républicains, Alassane Ouattara, was excluded from participation in the Ivorian presidential election of October 2000 because of his Burkinabè origins. Following a coup attempt in Abidjan in early January 2001, which the Ivorian Government attributed to the influence of unnamed, neighbouring states, attacks on Burkinabè expatriates in Côte d'Ivoire reportedly increased; by late January it was reported that up to 10,000 Burkinabè were returning to Burkina each week. In June, following allegations that hundreds of Burkinabè children were working illegally on coffee and cocoa plantations in Côte d'Ivoire, the two countries announced that they would commence joint patrols of their common border. In early July a meeting between Compaoré and the Ivorian President, Laurent Gbagbo, in Sirte, Libya, was reported to have defused tensions somewhat between the two countries.

Following the outbreak of unrest in northern Côte d'Ivoire in mid-September 2002, Gbagbo again alleged that an unnamed, neighbouring country was implicated in the rebellion; these allegations were widely believed to refer to Burkina, although the Burkinabè Government denied any involvement in the uprising. However, in late November, following an attack on the residence of the Burkinabè President in Abidjan, the Ivorian Minister of Agriculture and Rural Development met Compaoré to express the Ivorian Government's regret for the attack. A statement by Compaoré in an interview with the French newspaper *Le Parisien*, in late January, to the effect that the restoration of peace in Côte d'Ivoire would necessitate the resignation of Gbagbo as President of that country, led to a further deterioration in relations between the two countries. As a result of the upsurge in violence in Côte d'Ivoire, at least 350,000 Burkinabè citizens were reported to have fled Côte d'Ivoire for Burkina by mid-2003. The Burkinabè authorities closed the common border of the two countries in September 2002, reopening it in September 2003. Relations between the two countries subsequently became more cordial, and in late 2003 Compaoré hosted meetings with several prominent Ivorian leaders, including Gbagbo, Prime Minister Seydou Diarra and former rebel leader Guillaume Soro, emphasizing the need to develop bilateral co-operation. In late March 2004, however, the Burkinabè Government announced that four of its citizens were among hundreds of people reportedly killed by the Ivorian security forces during protests in Abidjan, and in July Burkina accused Côte d'Ivoire of violating its airspace. Following the renewed outbreak of violence in Cote d'Ivoire in November, Compaoré again commented, this time in the French daily *Le Figaro*, that it would be impossible to resolve the Ivorian conflict under the present regime in that country.

During 2003–04 the Mauritanian President Col Maaouiya Sid'Ahmed Ould Taya and his administration repeatedly accused the Government of Burkina Faso of supporting a series of attempted *coups d'état* in Mauritania. The Burkinabé authorities denied claims that, in collaboration with Libya, they had provided refuge, funding, arms and training facilities to the rebels, particularly Maj. Saleh Ould Hanenna and Capt. Abderahmane Ould Mini, who admitted attempting to overthrow President Taya's regime during the trial of 181 suspects which commenced in Mauritania in late 2004. Also among the accused, tried *in absentia*, was Sidi Mohamed Mustapha Ould Limam Chavi, a Mauritanian-born adviser to President Campaoré. In protest at the alleged conduct of the Burkinabè Government, President Taya did not attend the 10th Summit of La Francophonie, held in Ouagadougou in November 2004. Meanwhile, in late 2004 the Burkinabè Government alleged Hermann Yaméogo had supplied the Mauritanian Government with false information regarding the existence of training camps in Burkina Faso and was colluding with the Governments of Côte d'Ivoire, Guinea and Mauritania in plans to destabilize Burkina.

Government

Under the terms of the Constitution of June 1991, as subsequently revised, executive power is vested in the President and in the Government, and is counterbalanced by a legislative Assemblée nationale, and by an independent judiciary. Presidential and legislative elections are conducted by universal adult suffrage, in the context of a multi-party political system. The President is elected for a seven-year term, and delegates to the Assemblée nationale are elected for a five-year term. In April 2000 the Assemblée nationale adopted legislation, effective from the next elections, which reduced the presidential mandate from seven to five years, renewable only once, and introduced a system of proportional representation for elections to the Assemblée nationale, according to which 90 deputies would be elected from a regional list, while 21 would be elected from a national list. The President is empowered to appoint a Prime Minister; however, the Assemblée nationale has the right to veto any such appointment.

Burkina is divided into 45 provinces, each of which is administered by a civilian governor.

Defence

National service is voluntary, and lasts for two years on a part-time basis. In August 2004 the active armed forces numbered 10,800 (army 6,400, air force 200, gendarmerie 4,200). Other units include a 'security company' of 250 and a part-time people's militia of 45,000. The defence budget for 2004 was estimated at 33,000m. francs CFA.

Economic Affairs

In 2003, according to estimates by the World Bank, Burkina Faso's gross national income (GNI), measured at average 2001–03 prices, was US $4,178m., equivalent to $300 per head (or $1,180 on an international purchasing-power parity basis). During 1990–2003, it was estimated, the population increased at an average annual rate of 2.4%, while gross domestic product (GDP) per head increased, in real terms, by an average of 1.9% per year. Overall GDP increased, in real terms, at an average annual rate of 4.4% in 1990–2003; growth in 2003 was 6.5%.

Agriculture (including forestry and fishing) contributed 31.0% of GDP in 2003, according to the World Bank. About 92.2% of the labour force were employed in agriculture in 2003. The principal cash crop is cotton (exports of which accounted for an estimated 54.1% of the value of total exports in 2002). Smaller amounts of other crops, including karité nuts (sheanuts) and sesame seed, are also exported. The main subsistence crops are millet, sorghum, maize and rice. Burkina is almost self-sufficient in basic foodstuffs in non-drought years. Livestock-rearing is of considerable significance, contributing 9.7% of GDP and 21.0% of export revenue in 2002, according to IMF estimates. During 1990–2003 agricultural GDP increased at an average annual rate of 4.3%. Agricultural GDP increased by 8.3% in 2002, but remained constant in 2003. In 2004 millet production and pasture lands in some northern regions of Burkina Faso were badly affected by low rainfall and locust swarms which spread across the Sahel region, raising fears of food shortages.

Industry (including mining, manufacturing, construction and power) contributed 18.9% of GDP in 2003, according to the World Bank, but engaged only 2.0% of the employed labour force in 1996. During 1990–2003 industrial GDP increased at an average annual rate of 2.5%; growth in 2003 was 0.7%, but industrial GDP neither increased or decreased in 2003.

Although Burkina has considerable mineral resources, extractive activities accounted for 0.4% of GDP in 2002, and engaged only 0.1% of the employed labour force in 1996. However, the development of reserves of gold (exports of which contributed an estimated 2.4% of the value of total exports in 2002) has since brought about an increase in the sector's economic importance, while there is considerable potential, subject to the development

of an adequate infrastructure, for the exploitation of manganese, zinc and limestone. The country's other known mineral reserves include phosphates, silver, lead and nickel.

The manufacturing sector engaged only 1.4% of the employed labour force in 1996, and contributed 12.9% of GDP in 2003, according to the World Bank. The sector is dominated by the processing of primary products: major activities are cotton-ginning, the production of textiles, food-processing (including milling and sugar-refining), brewing and the processing of tobacco and of hides and skins. Motorcycles and bicycles are also assembled. According to the World Bank, manufacturing GDP increased at an average annual rate of 1.4% in 1990–2003; no growth was recorded in 2003.

Two hydroelectric stations supplied about one-third of Burkina's electricity output in 1998; the remainder was derived from thermal power stations (using imported fuel). The country's hydropower capacity is being expanded, and in 2000 the interconnection of the south of Burkina Faso with the electricity network of Côte d'Ivoire was finalized; a link with Ghana's electricity grid is also planned. Imports of petroleum products comprised an estimated 18.6% of the value of total imports in 2002.

The services sector contributed 50.1% of GDP in 2003, and engaged 7.8% of the employed labour force in 1996. The GDP of the services sector increased at an average annual rate of 5.1% in 1990–2003; growth was 12.1% in 2003.

According to the Banque centrale des états de l'Afrique de l'ouest, in 2003 Burkina recorded an estimated visible trade deficit of 208,800m. francs CFA, while there was a deficit of an estimated 173,700m. francs CFA on the current account of the balance of payments. In 2002 the principal sources of imports were France (which provided 19.6% of the total) and Côte d'Ivoire (18.8%); Japan and Germany were also major suppliers. The principal markets for exports in that year were France (45.3%), Côte d'Ivoire and Singapore. The principal exports in 2002 were cotton, and livestock and livestock products (including hides and skins). In the same year the principal imports were capital equipment, petroleum products, food products and raw materials.

In 2003 Burkina recorded an overall budget deficit of an estimated 200,000m. francs CFA, equivalent to an estimated 8.1% of GDP. Burkina's total external debt was US $1,580m. at the end of 2002, of which $1,399m. was long-term public debt. In that year the cost of debt-servicing was equivalent to 16.0% of the value of exports of goods and services. The annual rate of inflation, which was negligible prior to the 50% devaluation of the CFA franc in January 1994, increased to 25.1% in 1994, but slowed thereafter, to 7.4% in 1995. In 1990–2003 the average annual rate of inflation was 4.1%. Consumer prices increased by 1.8% in 2003. Some 71,280 people were unemployed in 1996, according to the national census, equivalent to only 1.4% of the total labour force.

Burkina is a member of numerous regional organizations, including the Economic Community of West African States (ECOWAS, see p. 205), the West African organs of the Franc Zone (see p. 267), the Conseil de l'Entente (see p. 373), the Liptako–Gourma Integrated Development Authority (see p. 374), and the Permanent Inter-State Committee on Drought Control in the Sahel (CILSS, see p. 375).

Burkina Faso has experienced strong growth since the devaluation of the CFA franc in 1994, as the competitiveness of its principal exports has been enhanced. In September 1999 the IMF approved funding under an Enhanced Structural Adjustment Facility (later replaced by the Poverty Reduction and Growth Facility—PRGF), equivalent to some US $49m., in support of the Government's economic programme for 1999–2002. During this period considerable success was achieved in reducing inflation, from more than 5.0% in 1998 to 2.3% in 2002, and in lowering the external current-account deficit. However, the fiscal deficit increased during this period, as efforts to improve the collection of taxes met with only limited success. In July 2000 the IMF and the World Bank announced that Burkina Faso was to receive some $400m. in debt-service relief under their original initiative for heavily indebted poor countries and a further $300m. under an enhanced framework. However, unrest in Côte d'Ivoire (a significant trade route to and from Burkina) from late 2002 had a detrimental impact on the Burkinabè economy, leading to predictions of reduced growth for 2003. In June 2003 the IMF approved a PRGF, equivalent to some $34m., in support of the Government's economic programme for 2003–06, which aimed to contain inflation at less than 3% and achieve real GDP growth of 5.2% by 2005. In the event, heavy rainfall in 2003 facilitated a record cotton crop of some 500,000 metric tons, which, together with high international cotton prices, contributed to GDP growth of 6.5% for that year. The Government also pledged to advance its programme of structural reform, although the proposed privatizations of the telecommunications company, the Office National des Télécommunications, and of the electricity company, the Société Nationale Burkinabè d'Electricité, were delayed. In early 2004 a consortium of European banks agreed a loan of €62m. ($78m.) to the Société Burkinabè des Fibres Textiles, Burkina's parastatal cotton processing company, to aid the further growth of the cotton sector. In late 2004 Burkina Faso was granted an International Development Association credit of $84m. by the World Bank to assist in countering the damage caused by locust swarms in the north of the country that year and to fund programmes to reduce the region's future vulnerability to such infestations. Nevertheless, the economy of Burkina Faso remained dependent on a narrow resource base, particularly on cotton, and therefore vulnerable to external exigencies, while poverty remained widespread, particularly in rural areas.

Education

Education is provided free of charge, and is officially compulsory for six years between the ages of seven and 14. Primary education begins at seven years of age and lasts for six years. Secondary education, beginning at the age of 13, lasts for a further seven years, comprising a first cycle of four years and a second of three years. Enrolment levels are among the lowest in the region. In 2002/03 primary enrolment included 47.5% of children in the relevant age-group (males 53.8%; females 41.0%). By 2003/04, however, the rate of enrolment in the first year of primary education had increased by 29.7%, and overall primary enrolment reached 52.3%, according to official figures.

According to UNESCO estimates, secondary enrolment in 2000/01 included only 8% of children in the appropriate age-group (males 10%; females 6%). In 2001/02 there were approximately 46 pupils to every teacher in secondary education. There is a university in Ouagadougou, a polytechnic university at Bobo-Dioulasso and an école normale supérieure at Koudougou. The number of students enrolled at tertiary-level institutions in 2001/02 was 15,535. A radio service has been established to further general and technical education in rural areas. In 2000 spending on education represented 11.0% of total budgetary expenditure.

Public Holidays

2005: 1 January (New Year's Day), 21 January* (Aïd el Kebir—Tabaski, Feast of the Sacrifice), 8 March (International Women's Day), 28 March (Easter Monday), 21 April* (Mouloud, Birth of the Prophet), 1 May (Labour Day), 5 May (Ascension Day), 5 August (Independence Day), 15 August (Assumption), 1 November (All Saints' Day), 4 November* (Aïd es Segheir, end of Ramadan), 11 December (Proclamation of the Republic), 25 December (Christmas).

2006: 1 January (New Year's Day), 11 January* (Aïd el Kebir—Tabaski, Feast of the Sacrifice), 8 March (International Women's Day), 11 April* (Mouloud, Birth of the Prophet), 17 April (Easter Monday), 1 May (Labour Day), 25 May (Ascension Day), 5 August (Independence Day), 15 August (Assumption), 24 October* (Aïd es Segheir, end of Ramadan), 1 November (All Saints' Day), 11 December (Proclamation of the Republic), 25 December (Christmas).

*These holidays are dependent on the Islamic lunar calendar and may vary by one or two days from the dates given.

Weights and Measures

The metric system is in force.

Statistical Survey

Source (except where otherwise stated): Institut National de la Statistique et de la Démographie, 555 blvd de la Révolution, 01 BP 374, Ouagadougou 01; tel. 32-49-76; fax 31-07-60.

Area and Population

AREA, POPULATION AND DENSITY

Area (sq km)	274,200*
Population (census results)	
10–20 December 1985	7,964,705
10 December 1996	
Males	4,970,882
Females	5,341,727
Total	10,312,609
Population (UN estimates at mid-year)†	
2001	12,259,000
2002	12,624,000
2003	13,002,000
Density (per sq km) at mid-2003	47.4

* 105,870 sq miles.
† Source: UN, *World Population Prospects: The 2002 Revision.*

ETHNIC GROUPS

1995 (percentages): Mossi 47.9; Peul 10.3; Bobo 6.9; Lobi 6.9; Mandé 6.7; Sénoufo 5.3; Gourounsi 5.0; Gourmantché 4.8; Tuareg 3.1; others 3.1 (Source: La Francophonie).

PROVINCES

(population at 1996 census)

Province	Population	Capital	Population of capital
Balé	168,170	Boromo	n.a.
Bam	211,551	Kongoussi . . .	17,893
Banwa	215,297	Solenzo	n.a.
Bazèga . . .	213,824	Kombissiri . .	16,821
Bougouriba . .	76,498	Diébougou . .	11,637
Boulgou . . .	415,583	Tenkodogo . .	31,466
Boulkiemdé . .	421,302	Koudougou . .	72,490
Comoé	241,376	Banfora . . .	49,724
Ganzourgou . .	256,921	Zorgo	17,466

Province— continued	Population	Capital	Population of capital
Gnagna . . .	307,372	Bogandé . . .	8,960
Gourma . . .	220,116	Fada N'Gourma .	29,254
Houet	672,114	Bobo-Dioulasso .	309,771
Ioba	161,484	Dano	n.a.
Kadiogo . . .	941,894	Ouagadougou . .	709,736
Kénédougou . .	198,541	Orodara . . .	16,581
Komandjari . .	50,484	Gayéri	n.a.
Kompienga . .	40,766	Pama	n.a.
Kossi . . .	230,693	Nouna	19,105
Koulpélogo . .	187,399	Ouargaye . . .	n.a.
Kouritenga . .	250,117	Koupéla . . .	17,619
Kourwéogo . .	117,996	Boussé	n.a.
Léraba	92,927	Sindou	n.a.
Lorom . . .	111,339	Titao	n.a.
Mouhoun . . .	235,391	Dédougou . . .	33,815
Nahouri . . .	119,739	Pô	17,146
Namentenga . .	252,738	Boulsa	12,280
Nayala . . .	136,393	Toma	n.a.
Noumbiel . . .	51,431	Batié	n.a.
Oubritenga . .	197,237	Ziniaré . . .	11,153
Oudalan . . .	137,160	Gorom-Gorom .	5,669
Passoré . . .	271,864	Yako	18,472
Poni	195,900	Gaoua	6,424
Sanguié . . .	249,583	Réo	22,534
Sanmatenga . .	464,032	Kaya	33,958
Séno	201,760	Dori	23,768
Sissili . . .	153,434	Léo	18,988
Soum	252,993	Djibo	20,080
Sourou . . .	188,512	Tougan . . .	15,218
Tapoa . . .	234,968	Diapaga . . .	5,017
Tuy	160,722	Houndé . . .	21,830
Yagha . . .	116,419	Sebba	n.a.
Yatenga . . .	444,563	Ouahigouya . .	52,193
Ziro	119,219	Sapouy . . .	n.a.
Zondoma . . .	127,654	Gourcy	n.a.
Zoundwéogo . .	197,133	Manga	14,035
Total	10,312,609		

PRINCIPAL TOWNS
(population at 1996 census)

Ouagadougou				
(capital) . .	709,736	Ouahigouya . . .	52,193
Bobo-Dioulasso . .	309,771	Banfora . . .	49,724
Koudougou . . .	72,490	Kaya	33,958

Mid-2003 (UN estimate, incl. suburbs): Ouagadougou 821,474 (Source: UN, *World Urbanization Prospects: The 2003 Revision*).

BIRTHS AND DEATHS
(UN estimates, annual averages)

	1985–90	1990–95	1995–2000
Birth rate (per 1,000)	49.9	49.0	49.1
Death rate (per 1,000)	18.2	17.6	17.9

Source: UN, *World Population Prospects: The 2002 Revision*.

Expectation of life (WHO estimates, years at birth, 2001): 41.7 (males 40.6; females 42.6 (Source: WHO, *World Health Report*).

ECONOMICALLY ACTIVE POPULATION
(1996 census, persons aged 10 years and over)

	Males	Females	Total
Agriculture, hunting, forestry and fishing	2,284,744	2,229,124	4,513,868
Mining and quarrying	2,946	1,033	3,979
Manufacturing	46,404	25,161	71,565
Electricity, gas and water . . .	2,279	534	2,813
Construction	20,678	398	21,076
Trade, restaurants and hotels . .	98,295	126,286	224,581
Transport, storage and communications	20,024	556	20,580
Finance, insurance, real estate and business services	10,466	2,665	13,131
Community, social and personal services	76,690	27,236	103,926
Activities not adequately defined .	15,104	13,712	28,816
Total employed	2,577,630	2,426,705	5,004,335
Unemployed	51,523	19,757	71,280
Total labour force	2,629,153	2,446,462	5,075,615

Mid-2003 (estimates in '000): Agriculture, etc. 5,609; Total labour force 6,084 (Source: FAO).

Health and Welfare

KEY INDICATORS

Total fertility rate (children per woman, 2002)	6.7
Under-5 mortality rate (per 1,000 live births, 2003) . . .	207
HIV/AIDS (% of persons aged 15–49, 2003)	4.20
Physicians (per 1,000 head, 1997)	0.04
Hospital beds (per 1,000 head, 1996)	1.42
Health expenditure (2001): US $ per head (PPP) . . .	27
Health expenditure (2001): % of GDP	3
Health expenditure (2001): public (% of total)	60.1
Access to water (% of persons, 2002)	52
Access to sanitation (% of persons, 2002)	12
Human Development Index (2002): ranking	175
Human Development Index (2002): value	0.302

For sources and definitions, see explanatory note on p. vi.

Agriculture

PRINCIPAL CROPS
('000 metric tons)

	2001	2002	2003
Rice (paddy)	109.9	89.1	97.1
Maize	606.3	653.1	738.3
Millet	1,009.0	994.7	1,214.4
Sorghum	1,371.6	1,373.3	1,519.2
Sweet Potatoes	41.6	37.0	37.0*
Yams	70.7	25.2	25.0*
Sugar cane*	420	450	420
Cow peas (dry)	376.2	330.2	330.0*
Bambara beans	37.7	36.2	36.0*
Other pulses*	25	25	25
Groundnuts (in shell)	301.1	323.6	321.0†
Karité nuts (Sheanuts)* . . .	70	70	70
Cottonseed*	215	240†	250*
Okra*	26	26	26
Other vegetables*	206	206	206
Fruit*	74.1	74.1	74.1
Cotton (lint)†	114	160	163

* FAO estimate(s).
† Unofficial figure(s).

LIVESTOCK
('000 head, year ending September)

	2001	2002	2003
Cattle	4,894.2	4,992.1	5,091.9
Sheep*	6,800	6,800	6,900
Goats*	8,700	8,700	8,800
Pigs	634.9	647.6	660.6
Poultry*	23,000	23,000	24,000
Horses*	26.5	26.5	27.0
Asses*	511	521	531
Camels*	15.0	15.3	15.6

* FAO estimates.

Source: FAO.

LIVESTOCK PRODUCTS
(FAO estimates, '000 metric tons)

	2001	2002	2003
Beef and veal	48.8	54.6	56.5
Mutton and lamb	13.6	14.1	14.2
Goat meat	23.5	23.5	24.1
Pig meat	9.1	9.3	9.5
Poultry meat	27.0	27.0	28.2
Other meat	8.3	8.4	8.4
Cows' milk	176.2	179.8	183.3
Goats' milk	54.0	54.0	54.0
Ghee	1.3	1.4	1.4
Hen eggs	17.5	17.5	18.2
Cattle hides	8.0	8.9	9.3
Sheepskins	3.3	3.5	3.5
Goatskins	6.1	6.1	6.3

Source: FAO.

Forestry

ROUNDWOOD REMOVALS
('000 cubic metres, excluding bark)

	2001*	2002	2003
Sawlogs, veneer logs and logs for sleepers*	85	85	85
Other industrial wood	509	1,098	1,098
Fuel wood	7,402	6,009	6,152
Total	7,996	7,192	7,335

* FAO estimates.
Source: FAO.

SAWNWOOD PRODUCTION
('000 cubic metres)

	2001	2002	2003
Total (all broadleaved)	1.3	1.8	1.5

Source: FAO.

Fishing

(metric tons, live weight)

	2000	2001*	2002*
Capture	8,500	8,500	8,500
Freshwater fishes	8,500	8,500	8,500
Aquaculture	5	5	5
Total catch	8,505	8,505	8,505

* FAO estimates.

Source: FAO.

Mining

	2000	2001	2002
Industrial gold-mining production (kg)	553	209	390
Artisanal gold washing . . .	515	209	390
Industrial and semi-industrial production	38	—	—

Source: IMF, *Burkina Faso: Statistical Annex* (June 2003).

Industry

SELECTED PRODUCTS
(metric tons, unless otherwise indicated)

	2000	2001	2002*
Edible oils	17,888	19,452	19,626
Shea (karité) butter	186	101	21
Flour	12,289	13,686	10,005
Pasta	211	—	n.a.
Sugar	43,412	46,662	47,743
Beer ('000 hl)	494	500	546
Soft drinks ('000 hl)	221	222	250
Cigarettes (million packets) . .	85	78	78
Printed fabric ('000 sq metres) .	275	—	—
Soap	12,079	9,240	9,923
Matches (cartons)	9,358	4,956	3,009
Bicycles (units)	22,215	17,718	20,849
Mopeds (units)	16,531	19,333	19,702
Tyres ('000)	397	599	670
Inner tubes ('000)	2,655	3,217	2,751
Electric energy ('000 kWh) . .	390,322	364,902	361,000

* Estimates.

Source: IMF, *Burkina Faso: Statistical Annex* (June 2003).

Finance

CURRENCY AND EXCHANGE RATES

Monetary Units
100 centimes = 1 franc de la Communauté financière africaine (CFA).

Sterling, Dollar and Euro Equivalents (31 December 2004)
£1 sterling = 930.12 francs CFA;
US $1 = 481.58 francs CFA;
€1 = 655.96 francs CFA;
10,000 francs CFA = £10.75 = $20.77 = €15.24.

Average Exchange Rate (francs CFA per US $)
2002   696.99
2003   581.20
2004   528.29

Note: An exchange rate of 1 French franc = 50 francs CFA, established in 1948, remained in force until January 1994, when the CFA franc was devalued by 50%, with the exchange rate adjusted to 1 French franc = 100 francs CFA. This relationship to French currency remained in effect with the introduction of the euro on 1 January 1999. From that date, accordingly, a fixed exchange rate of €1 = 655.957 francs CFA has been in operation.

BUDGET
('000 million francs CFA)

Revenue*	2001	2002†	2003†
Tax revenue	213.2	240.9	270.1
Income taxes	56.1	61.7	67.2
Corporate	26.1	29.0	n.a.
Personal	23.7	26.9	n.a.
Goods and services . . .	111.8	130.2	147.2
Value-added tax	84.8	89.5	n.a.
Imports	37.1	32.1	n.a.
Domestic	47.7	54.8	n.a.
Single tax on petroleum products	6.2	17.5	n.a.
International trade	39.2	42.4	43.8
Import duties	30.7	34.2	n.a.
Non-tax revenue	14.7	18.5	30.8
Total	228.0	259.4	300.9

Expenditure‡	2001	2002†	2003†
Current expenditure	218.8	258.9	268.9
Wages and salaries . . .	98.2	103.0	112.1
Goods and services . . .	40.5	62.5	61.5
Interest payments . . .	17.5	16.8	16.3
Current transfers	60.1	70.1	70.7
Investment expenditure . . .	240.5	230.3	232.0
Domestically financed . . .	63.5	86.7	97.6
Externally financed . . .	177.1	143.5	134.4
Total	459.4	489.1	500.9

* Excluding grants received ('000 million francs CFA): 148.3 in 2001; 118.6 in 2002; 133.3 in 2003.
† Estimates.
‡ Excluding net lending ('000 million francs CFA): –1.9 in 2001; –2.7 in 2002; 23.5 in 2003.

Source: IMF, *Burkina Faso: Statistical Annex* (June 2003) and *Burkina Faso: First Review Under the Three-Year Arrangement Under the Poverty Reduction and Growth Facility, and Request for Waiver of Performance Criterion—Staff Report; Staff Supplement; Press Release on the Executive Board Discussion; and Statement by the Executive Director for Burkina Faso* (April 2004).

INTERNATIONAL RESERVES
(excluding gold, US $ million at 31 December)

	2001	2002	2003
IMF special drawing rights . .	0.5	0.4	0.3
Reserve position in IMF . . .	9.1	9.9	10.8
Foreign exchange	250.9	303.1	423.6
Total	260.5	313.4	434.7

Source: IMF, *International Financial Statistics*.

MONEY SUPPLY

('000 million francs CFA at 31 December)

	2001	2002	2003
Currency outside banks . . .	120.9	83.2	91.0
Demand deposits at deposit money banks*	135.7	152.9	183.3
Checking deposits at post office .	1.9	2.5	3.1
Total money (incl. others) . .	262.3	243.7	287.2

* Excluding the deposits of public establishments of an administrative or social nature.

Source: IMF, *International Financial Statistics*.

COST OF LIVING

(Consumer Price Index; base: 1996 = 100)

	2000	2001	2002
Food and beverages and tobacco .	101.1	110.0	113.4
Clothing	106.9	107.1	107.8
Housing, water, electricity and gas	104.3	103.4	109.5
All items (incl. others)	106.5	111.7	114.3

Source: Banque centrale des états de l'Afrique de l'ouest.

All items (Consumer Price Index; base 2000=100): 105.0 in 2001; 107.3 in 2002; 109.5 in 2003 (Source: IMF, *International Financial Statistics*).

NATIONAL ACCOUNTS

('000 million francs CFA at current prices)

Expenditure on the Gross Domestic Product

	2001	2002	2003
Final consumption expenditure .	1,958.7	2,140.9	2,290.6
Households, incl. non-profit institutions serving households	1,491.5	1,639.7	1,774.3
General government . . .	467.2	501.2	516.3
Gross capital formation . .	417.7	425.7	479.4
Gross fixed capital formation .	448.0	449.9	459.1
Changes in inventories . .			
Acquisitions, less disposals, of valuables	−30.3	−24.2	20.3
Total domestic expenditure .	2,376.4	2,566.6	2,770.0
Exports of goods and services .	190.1	202.1	221.5
Less Imports of goods and services	476.1	488.9	518.2
GDP in market prices . . .	2,090.4	2,279.9	2,473.3
GDP at constant 1985 prices .	1,477.3	1,545.1	1,645.0

Gross Domestic Product by Economic Activity

	2000	2001	2002
Agriculture, livestock, forestry and fishing	530.7	655.3	667.6
Mining	10.7	4.9	6.9
Manufacturing			
Electricity, gas and water . .	204.6	257.0	292.7
Construction and public works .	48.5	58.3	69.3
Trade	272.7	268.1	320.5
Transport and communications .	77.3	76.0	90.9
Non-marketable services . . .	205.6	212.6	225.6
Other services	172.4	199.0	237.8
Sub-total	1,522.5	1,731.2	1,911.3
Import taxes and duties . . .	38.2	84.5	92.5
GDP in purchasers' values .	1,560.6	1,815.7	2,003.8

Source: Banque centrale des états de l'Afrique de l'ouest.

BALANCE OF PAYMENTS

('000 million francs CFA)

	2001	2002	2003*
Exports of goods f.o.b.	163.8	170.8	189.5
Imports of goods f.o.b.	−373.3	−381.7	−398.3
Trade balance	−209.5	−210.9	−208.8
Services (net)	−76.7	−72.5	−80.1
Balance on goods and services	−286.2	−283.4	−288.9
Income (net)	−17.9	−14.7	−11.9
Balance on goods, services and income	−304.1	−298.1	−300.8
Private unrequited transfers (net)	25.8	29.8	22.0
Official unrequited transfers (net)	65.0	60.3	105.1
Current balance	−213.3	−208.0	−173.7
Capital account (net)	121.1	112.6	90.1
Direct investments (net) . . .	6.0	9.3	10.5
Portfolio investments (net) . . .	2.5	0.9	2.0
Other investments (net) . . .	85.7	99.1	82.1
Net errors and omissions . . .	2.4	−3.1	1.1
Overall balance	4.4	10.8	12.1

* Estimates.

Source: Banque centrale des états de l'Afrique de l'ouest.

External Trade

PRINCIPAL COMMODITIES

('000 million francs CFA)

Imports f.o.b.	2000	2001	2002*
Food products	45.0	53.6	48.5
Petroleum products	65.0	67.9	71.0
Capital equipment	122.8	115.5	124.5
Raw materials	33.3	36.5	38.7
Total (incl. others)	368.6	373.3	381.7

Exports f.o.b.	2000	2001	2002*
Livestock and livestock products .	32.1	31.0	34.4
Live animals	16.5	16.5	14.4
Hides and skins	13.8	11.4	18.0
Cotton	72.2	96.0	88.8
Gold	6.2	2.2	3.9
Total (incl. others)	146.4	163.8	164.2

* Estimates.

Source: IMF, *Burkina Faso: Statistical Annex* (June 2003).

PRINCIPAL TRADING PARTNERS

('000 million francs CFA)*

Imports c.i.f.	2000	2001	2002†
Belgium-Luxembourg . . .	10.5	7.9	12.3
China, People's Repub.	15.0	18.9	12.4
Côte d'Ivoire	83.8	89.5	83.1
France	82.7	84.8	86.9
Germany	13.3	13.5	26.7
Ghana	4.8	5.1	3.0
India	2.2	5.0	7.5
Italy	11.5	10.8	8.4
Japan	20.8	21.3	41.1
Netherlands	7.8	7.7	10.4
Nigeria	6.5	5.1	3.8
Pakistan	0.9	4.7	1.0
Senegal	5.7	3.3	2.3
Thailand	2.6	3.2	2.5
Togo	9.8	13.5	12.5
United Kingdom	9.7	8.6	7.2
USA	10.1	16.0	14.5
Total (incl. others)	368.9	404.0	443.2

Exports f.o.b.	2000	2001	2002†
Belgium-Luxembourg	10.5	5.1	1.6
Benin	0.2	1.1	0.5
Côte d'Ivoire	14.0	9.4	10.9
France	27.0	28.7	53.7
Ghana	1.9	3.0	2.6
Italy	5.0	6.0	2.3
Japan	1.7	1.9	3.5
Mali	6.3	5.1	4.8
Niger	4.3	6.5	2.6
Nigeria	0.1	0.1	1.2
Singapore	7.0	8.1	6.0
Togo	2.0	1.6	0.5
United Kingdom	1.9	4.0	1.7
Total (incl. others)	125.0	136.4	118.6

* Figures refer to recorded trade only.
† Estimates.

Source: IMF, *Burkina Faso: Statistical Annex* (June 2003).

Transport

RAILWAYS
(international freight traffic, '000 metric tons)

	1999	2000	2001
To Côte d'Ivoire	43.2	59.2	34.0
From Côte d'Ivoire	377.7	356.0	279.2

Source: IMF, *Burkina Faso: Selected Issues and Statistical Annex* (April 2002).

Passenger-km (million, 1993): 403 (Source: UN Economic Commission for Africa, *African Statistical Yearbook*).

ROAD TRAFFIC
('000 motor vehicles in use)

	1999	2000	2001
Passenger cars	26.3	26.5	26.5
Commercial vehicles . . .	19.6	22.6	22.6

Source: UN, *Statistical Yearbook*.

CIVIL AVIATION
(traffic on scheduled services)*

	1999	2000	2001
Kilometres flown (million) . .	4	4	2
Passengers carried ('000) . .	147	144	100
Passenger-km (million) . . .	269	253	158
Total ton-km (million) . . .	39	35	22

* Including an apportionment of the traffic of Air Afrique.

Source: UN, *Statistical Yearbook*.

Tourism

FOREIGN VISITORS BY COUNTRY OF ORIGIN*

	2000	2001	2002
Côte d'Ivoire	7,567	7,920	6,840
France	38,103	43,063	45,868
Germany	3,131	2,118	3,612
Mali	5,297	5,799	4,388
Niger	4,728	5,365	7,172
Senegal	4,171	4,607	5,456
Togo	3,938	4,016	4,780
USA	3,906	4,541	5,940
Total (incl. others)	125,699	128,449	148,904

* Arrivals at hotels and similar establishments.

Tourism receipts (US $ million): 34 in 2001.

Source: World Tourism Organization.

Communications Media

	2001	2002	2003
Telephones ('000 main lines in use)	57.6	61.9	65.4
Mobile cellular telephones ('000 subscribers)	75	113.0	227.0
Personal computers ('000 in use) .	17	19	26
Internet users ('000)	21	25	48

Source: International Telecommunication Union.

Television receivers ('000 in use, 2000): 140 (Source: UNESCO, *Statistical Yearbook*).

Radio receivers ('000 in use, 1997): 370 (Source: UNESCO, *Statistical Yearbook*).

Daily newspapers (1996): 4 (average circulation 14,000 copies) (Source: UNESCO, *Statistical Yearbook*).

Non-daily newspapers (1995): 9 (average circulation 42,000 copies) (Source: UNESCO, *Statistical Yearbook*).

Book production (first editions, 1996): 12 titles (14,000 copies) (Source: UNESCO, *Statistical Yearbook*).

Education

(2001/02*)

	Institu-tions	Teachers	Students Males	Females	Total
Secondary (general) . . .	428	3,999	122,248	77,778	200,026
Secondary (technical) . .	68	707	8,237	8,913	17,150
Higher	21	807	11,589	3,946	15,535

* Public and private institutions.

Pre-primary (1997/98): Institutions 147; Teachers 441; Students 18,045 (males 8,921, females 9,124).

Primary (2002/03): Students 1,012,150 (males 585,573, females 426,577).

Sources: Ministère de l'enseignement de base et de l'alphabétisation, Ouagadougou; Ministère des enseignements secondaire et supérieur et de la recherche scientifique, Ouagadougou; UNESCO, *Statistical Yearbook*.

Adult literacy rate (UNESCO estimates): 12.8% (males 18.5%; females 8.1%) in 2002 (Source: UN Development Programme, *Human Development Report*).

Directory

The Constitution

The present Constitution was approved in a national referendum on 2 June 1991, and was formally adopted on 11 June. The following are the main provisions of the Constitution, as amended in January 1997, April 2000 and February 2002:

The Constitution of the 'revolutionary, democratic, unitary and secular' Fourth Republic of Burkina Faso guarantees the collective and individual political and social rights of Burkinabè citizens, and delineates the powers of the executive, legislature and judiciary.

Executive power is vested in the President, who is Head of State, and in the Government, which is appointed by the President upon the recommendation of the Prime Minister. With effect from the election due in 2005, the President was to be elected, by universal suffrage, for a five-year term, renewable only once (previously a seven-year term had been served).

Legislative power is exercised by the multi-party Assemblée nationale. Deputies are elected, by universal suffrage, for a five-year term. The number of deputies and the mode of election is determined by law. The President appoints a Prime Minister and, at the suggestion of the Prime Minister, appoints the other ministers. The President may, having consulted the Prime Minister and the President of the Assemblée nationale, dissolve the Assemblée nationale. Both the Government and the Assemblée nationale may initiate legislation.

The judiciary is independent and, in accordance with constitutional amendments approved in April 2000 (see Judicial System), consists of a Court of Cassation, a Constitutional Council, a Council of State, a National Audit Court, a High Court of Justice, and other courts and tribunals instituted by law. Judges are accountable to a Higher Council, under the chairmanship of the Head of State, who is responsible for guaranteeing the independence of the judiciary.

The Constitution also makes provision for an Economic and Social Council, for a Higher Council of Information, and for a national ombudsman.

The Constitution denies legitimacy to any regime that might take power as the result of a *coup d'état*.

The Government

HEAD OF STATE

President: BLAISE COMPAORÉ (assumed power as Chairman of the Front populaire 15 October 1987; elected President 1 December 1991; re-elected 15 November 1998).

COUNCIL OF MINISTERS
(March 2005)

President: BLAISE COMPAORÉ.

Prime Minister: PARAMANGA ERNEST YONLI.

Minister of State, Minister of Foreign Affairs and Regional Co-operation: YOUSSOUF OUÉDRAOGO.

Minister of State, Minister of Agriculture, Water Resources and Fisheries: SALIF DIALLO.

Minister of Health: BÉDOUMA ALAIN YODA.

Minister of Justice, Keeper of the Seals: BOUREIMA BADINI.

Minister of Defence: YÉRO BOLY.

Minister of Territorial Administration and Decentralization: MOUMOUNI FABRÉ.

Minister of Security: DJIBRILL YIPÉNÉ BASSOLET.

Minister of Finance and the Budget: JEAN-BAPTISTE MARIE PASCAL COMPAORÉ.

Minister of the Economy and Development: SEYDOU BOUDA.

Minister of Employment, Labour and Youth: ALAIN LUDOVIC TOU.

Minister of Mines, Quarries and Energy: ABDUL KADER CISSÉ.

Minister of Trade, the Promotion of Business and Crafts: BENOÎT OUATTARA.

Minister of Infrastructure, Transport and Housing: HIPPOLYTE LINGANI.

Minister of Secondary and Higher Education and Scientific Research: LAYA SAWADOGO.

Minister of Basic Education and Literacy: MATHIEU R. OUÉDRAOGO.

Minister of the Civil Service and the Reform of the State: LASSANÉ SAWADOGO.

Minister of Culture, Arts and Tourism: MAHAMOUDOU OUÉDRAOGO.

Minister of Posts and Telecommunications: JUSTIN TIÈBA THIOMBIANO.

Minister of Animal Resources: ALPHONSE BONOU.

Minister of Social Action and National Solidarity: MARIAM LAMIZANA.

Minister of Information: JOSEPH KAHOUN.

Minister for the Promotion of Women: MARIE GISÈLE GUIGMA.

Minister of Relations with Parliament, Spokesperson for the Government: ADAMA FOFANA.

Minister for the Promotion of Human Rights: MONIQUE ILBOUDO.

Minister of the Environment and Quality of Life: LAURENT SÉDOGO.

Minister of Sport and Leisure: TIOUNDOUN SESSOUMA.

Minister-delegate attached to the Minister of Foreign Affairs and Regional Co-operation, responsible for Regional Co-operation: JEAN DE DIEU SOMDA.

Minister-delegate attached to the Minister of Infrastructure, Transport and Housing, responsible for Transport: PATRICE NIKIEMA.

Minister-delegate attached to the Minister of Secondary and Higher Education and Scientific Research, responsible for Technical and Professional Education: YOUMA ZERBO.

Minister-delegate attached to the Minister of Basic Education and Literacy, responsible for Literacy and Informal Education: ARSÈNE ARMAND HIEN.

Minister-delegate attached to the Minister of Employment, labour and Youth, responsible for Youth: DANIEL OUEDRAOGO.

General Secretary of the Government and the Council of Ministers: MARIE ODILE BONKOUNGOU BALIMA.

MINISTRIES

Office of the President: 03 BP 7030, Ouagadougou 03; tel. 30-66-30; fax 31-49-26; internet www.presidence.bf.

Office of the Prime Minister: 03 BP 7027, Ouagadougou 03; tel. 32-48-89; fax 31-47-61; internet www.primature.gov.bf.

Ministry of Agriculture, Water Resources and Fisheries: 03 BP 7005, Ouagadougou 03; tel. 32-41-14; fax 31-08-70; e-mail ministere-agriculture@cenatrin.bf; internet www.agriculture.gov.bf.

Ministry of Animal Resources: 03 BP 7026, Ouagadougou 03; tel. 32-61-07; fax 31-84-75; internet www.mra.gov.bf.

Ministry of Basic Education and Literacy: 03 BP 7032, Ouagadougou 03; tel. 30-66-00; fax 31-42-76; internet www.meba.gov.bf.

Ministry of the Civil Service and the Reform of the State: Immeuble de la Modernisation, 922 ave Kwamé N'Krumah, 03 BP 7006, Ouagadougou 03; tel. 30-19-52; fax 30-19-55; internet www.fonction-publique.gov.bf.

Ministry of Culture, Arts and Tourism: 03 BP 7007, Ouagadougou 03; tel. 33-09-63; fax 33-09-64; e-mail webmaster-mcat@mcc.gov.bf; internet www.culture.gov.bf.

Ministry of Defence: 01 BP 496, Ouagadougou 01; tel. 30-72-14; fax 31-36-10; internet www.defense.gov.bf.

Ministry of the Economy and Development: 03 BP 7050, Ouagadougou 03; tel. 32-43-18; fax 30-55-08; internet www.medev.gov.bf.

Ministry of the Environment and Quality of Life: 565 rue Neto, Koulouba, 03 BP 7044, Ouagadougou 03; tel. 32-40-74; fax 30-70-39; e-mail messp@liptinfor.bf; internet www.environnement.gov.bf.

Ministry of Finance and the Budget: 03 BP 7050, Ouagadougou 03; tel. 30-69-95; fax 31-27-15; e-mail finances@cenatrin.bf; internet www.finances.gov.bf.

Ministry of Foreign Affairs and Regional Co-operation: rue 988, blvd du Faso, 03 BP 7038, Ouagadougou 03; tel. 32-47-34; fax 30-87-92; e-mail webmaster.mae@mae.gov.bf; internet www.mae.gov.bf.

Ministry of Health: 03 BP 7009, Ouagadougou 03; tel. 32-41-71; fax 32-41-85; e-mail dgep@cenatrin.bf; internet www.sante.gov.bf.

Ministry of Information: 03 BP 7045, Ouagadougou 03; tel. 32-42-78; fax 31-56-71; internet www.information.gov.bf.

Ministry of Infrastructure, Transport and Housing: 03 BP 7011, Ouagadougou 03; tel. 30-73-33; fax 31-84-08; e-mail mith@cenatrin.bf; internet www.mith.gov.bf.

Ministry of Justice: 01 BP 526, Ouagadougou 01; tel. 32-48-33; fax 31-71-37; e-mail webmestre@justice.bf; internet www.justice.gov.bf.

Ministry of Labour, Employment and Youth: 03 BP 7016, Ouagadougou 03; tel. 30-09-60; fax 31-88-01; e-mail emploi@metss.gov.bf; internet www.emploi.gov.bf.

Ministry of Mines, Quarries and Energy: 01 BP 644, Ouagadougou 01; tel. 31-84-29; fax 31-84-30; internet www.mines.gov.bf.

Ministry of Posts and Telecommunications: 387 ave Georges Conseiga, 01 BP 5175, Ouagadougou 01; tel. 33-73-85; fax 33-73-87; e-mail mpt.secretariat@onatel.bf; internet www.mpt.bf.

Ministry for the Promotion of Human Rights: 01 BP 526, Ouagadougou 01; tel. 32-48-33; fax 33-50-95; internet www.mpdh.gov.bf.

Ministry for the Promotion of Women: BP 303, Ouagadougou; tel. 30-01-04; fax 30-01-02; e-mail sarah_tanou@hotmail.com; internet www.mpf.gov.bf.

Ministry of Relations with Parliament: 01 BP 2079, Ouagadougou 01; tel. 32-40-70; fax 30-78-94; e-mail cab_mrp@yahoo.fr; internet www.mrp.gov.bf.

Ministry of Secondary and Higher Education and Scientific Research: 03 BP 7047, Ouagadougou 03; tel. 32-45-67; fax 32-61-16; e-mail laya.saw@messrs.gov.bf; internet www.messrs.gov.bf.

Ministry of Security: 01 BP 6466, Ouagadougou 01; tel. 31-68-91; fax 31-58-87; internet www.securite.gov.bf.

Ministry of Social Action and National Solidarity: 01 BP 515, Ouagadougou 01; tel. 30-68-75; fax 31-67-37; e-mail massn@fasonet.bf; internet www.action-sociale.gov.bf.

Ministry of Sport and Leisure: 03 BP 7035, Ouagadougou 03; tel. 32-47-86; fax 33-08-18; internet www.sports.gov.bf.

Ministry of Territorial Administration and Decentralization: 01 BP 526, Ouagadougou 01; tel. 32-48-33; fax 31-72-00; internet www.matd.gov.bf.

Ministry of Trade, the Promotion of Business and Crafts: 01 BP 365, Ouagadougou 01; tel. 32-47-86; fax 31-84-97; internet www.commerce.gov.bf.

President and Legislature

PRESIDENT

Presidential Election, 15 November 1998

Candidate	Votes	% of votes
Blaise Compaoré	1,996,151	87.53
Ram Ouédraogo	150,793	6.61
Frédéric Guirma	133,552	5.86
Total	2,280,496*	100.00

*There were, in addition, 89,458 blank votes.

ASSEMBLÉE NATIONALE

Assemblée nationale: BP 6482, Ouagadougou 01; tel. 31-46-84; fax 31-45-90.

President: Roch Marc Christian Kaboré.

General Election, 5 May 2002

Parties	% of total votes*	National list seats	Total seats†
CDP	49.52	11	57
ADF—RDA	12.61	3	17
PDP—PS	7.01	2	10
CFD‡	4.38	1	5
PAI	3.62	1	5
PAREN	2.73	1	4
CPS	2.63	1	3
UNIR—MS	2.45	1	3
PDS	2.41	—	2
CNDP	2.02	—	2
UDPI	1.04	—	1
FPC	0.97	—	1
APL	0.67	—	1
Total (incl. others)	100.00	21	111

*Including votes from regional and national party lists.
†Including seats filled by voting from regional lists, totalling 90.
‡The Coalition des forces démocratiques, an electoral alliance of six parties.

Advisory Council

Economic and Social Council: 01 BP 6162, Ouagadougou 01; tel. 32-40-91; fax 31-06-54; e-mail ces@ces.gov.bf; internet www.ces.gov.bf; f. 1985; present name adopted in 1992; 90 mems; Pres. Thomas Sanon.

Political Organizations

Some 30 political parties contested the legislative elections held in May 2002. In early 2005 the most important political parties included the following:

Alliance pour la démocratie et la fédération—Rassemblement démocratique africain (ADF—RDA): 01 BP 1991, Ouagadougou 01; tel. 30-52-00; f. 1990 as Alliance pour la démocratie et la fédération, absorbed faction of Rassemblement démocratique africain in 1998; several factions broke away in 2000 and in mid-2003; Pres. Gilbert Noël Ouédraogo.

Alliance pour le progrès et la liberté (APL): 03 BP 7126, Ouagadougou 03; tel. 31-16-01; Sec.-Gen. Joséphine Tamboura-Sama.

Congrès pour la démocratie et le progrès (CDP): 1146 ave Dr Kwamé N'Krumah, 01 BP 1605, Ouagadougou 01; tel. 31-50-18; fax 31-43-93; e-mail contact@cdp-burkina.org; internet www.cdp-burkina.org; f. 1996 by merger, to succeed the Organisation pour la démocratie populaire/Mouvement du travail as the principal political org. supporting Pres. Compaoré; social democratic; Pres. Roch Marc Christian Kaboré.

Convention nationale des démocrates progressistes (CNDP): Ouagadougou; tel. 36-39-73; f. 2000; Leader Alfred Kaboré.

Convention panafricaine sankariste (CPS): BP 44, Bokin; tel. 45-72-93; f. 1999 by merger of four parties, expanded in 2000 to include two other parties; promotes the policies of fmr Pres. Sankara; Pres. Nongma Ernest Ouédraogo.

Convention pour la démocratie et la fédération (CDF): Ouagadougou; tel. 36-23-63; f. 1998; Pres. Amadou Dicko Diemdioda.

Convergence pour la démocratie sociale (CDS): Ouagadougou; f. 2002; socialist, opposed to Govt of Pres. Compaoré; Chair. Valérie Dieudonné Somé; Exec. Sec.-Gen. Sessouma Sanou.

Front des forces sociales (FFS): BP 255, Ouagadougou; tel. 32-32-32; e-mail tino8@caramail.com; internet membres.lycos.fr/FFS; f. 1996; Sankarist; member of the Groupe du 14 février and opposition Collectif d'organisations démocratiques de masse et de partis politiques; Chair. Norbert Michel Tiendrébéogo.

Front patriotique pour le changement (FPC): BP 8539, Ouagadougou; tel. 25-32-45; Pres. Tahirou Ibrahim Zon.

Mouvement du peuple pour le socialisme—Parti fédéral (MPS—PF): BP 3448, Ouagadougou; tel. 36-50-72; f. 2002 by split from PDP—PS; Leader Dr Pargui Emile Paré.

Mouvement pour la tolérance et le progrès/Moog Teeb Panpaasgo (MTP): BP 2364, Ouagadougou; tel. 36-45-35; f. 2000; Sankarist; contested 2002 legislative elections as part of the Coalition des forces démocratiques (CFD); Pres. Congo Emmanuel Nayabtigungu Kaboré.

Parti africain de l'indépendance (PAI): Ouagadougou; tel. 33-46-66; f. 1999; Sec.-Gen. SOUMANE TOURÉ.

Parti pour la démocratie et le progrès—Parti socialiste (PDP—PS): BP 606, Ouagadougou; tel. 33-44-80; f. 2001 by merger of the Parti pour la démocratie et le progrès and the Parti socialiste burkinabè; Nat. Pres. JOSEPH KI-ZERBO.

Parti pour la démocratie et le socialisme (PDS): Ouagadougou; tel. 34-34-04; Pres. FÉLIX SOUBÉIGA.

Parti de la renaissance nationale (PAREN): Ouagadougou; tel. 43-12-26; f. 2000; social-democratic; Pres. KILACHIA LAURENT BADO.

Parti socialiste unifié: Ouagadougou; f. 2001 by mems of fmr Parti socialiste burkinabè; Leader BENOÏT LOMPO.

Union des démocrates et progressistes indépendants (UDPI): BP 536, Ouagadougou; tel. 38-27-99; expelled from Groupe du 14 février in mid-2000; Leader LONGO DONGO.

Union nationale pour la démocratie et le développement (UNDD): 03 BP 7114, Ouagadougou 03; tel. 31-15-15; e-mail info@undd.bf; internet www.undd.org; f. 2003 by fmr mems of the ADF—RDA (q.v.); liberal; Pres. Me HERMANN YAMÉOGO.

Union pour la renaissance—Mouvement sankariste (UNIR—MS): Ouagadougou; tel. 36-30-45; f. 2000; Pres. BÉNÉWENDÉ STANISLAS SANKARA.

Diplomatic Representation

EMBASSIES IN BURKINA FASO

Algeria: place des Nations Unies, 01 BP 3893, Ouagadougou 01; tel. 30-64-01; fax 30-37-46; e-mail ambalg@cenatrin.bf; Ambassador MOHAMED EL AMINE BEN CHERIF.

Belgium: Immeuble Me Benoit SAWADOGO 994 rue Agostino, NETO, Koulouba, 01 BP 1264, Ouagadougou 01; tel. 31-21-64; fax 31-06-60; e-mail ouagadougou@diplobel.org; internet www.diplomatie.be/ouagadougou; Ambassador PAUL JANSEN.

Canada: rue Agostino Neto, 01 BP 548, Ouagadougou 01; tel. 31-18-94; fax 31-19-00; e-mail ouaga@dfait-maeci.gc.ca; internet www.dfait-maeci.gc.ca/burkina_faso; Ambassador DENIS BRIAND.

China (Taiwan): 994 rue Agostino Neto, 01 BP 5563, Ouagadougou 01; tel. 31-61-95; fax 31-61-97; e-mail ambachine@fasonet.bf; Ambassador TAO WEN-LUNG.

Côte d'Ivoire: place des Nations Unies, 01 BP 20, Ouagadougou 01; tel. 31-82-28; fax 31-82-30; e-mail ambci@cenatrin.bf; Ambassador RICHARD KODJO.

Cuba: rue 4/64, La Rotonde, Secteur 4, Ouagadougou; tel. 30-64-91; fax 31-73-24; e-mail embacuba.bf@fasonet.bf; Ambassador FERNANDO PRATS MARI.

Denmark: rue Agostino Neto, 01 BP 1760, Ouagadougou 01; tel. 31-31-92; fax 31-31-89; e-mail ouaamb@um.dk; internet www.danburkina.com; Ambasssador MARGIT THOMSEN.

Egypt: Zone du Conseil de L'Entente, blvd du Faso, BP 7042, Ouagadougou; tel. 30-66-39; fax 31-38-36; e-mail egyptianembassy@liptinfor.bf; Ambassador ABD EL-KADER ES-SAYED TANTAWI.

France: 33 rue Yalgado Ouédraogo, 01 BP 504, Ouagadougou 01; tel. 30-67-74; fax 31-41-66; e-mail ambassade@ambafrance-bf.org; internet www.ambafrance-bf.org; Ambassador FRANCIS BLONDET.

Germany: 01 399 ave Joseph Badoua, BP 600, Ouagadougou 01; tel. 30-67-31; fax 31-39-91; e-mail amb.allemagne@fasonet.bf; Ambassador MARC-ULRICH VON SCHWEINITZ.

Ghana: 22 ave d'Oubritenga, 01 BP 212, Ouagadougou 01; tel. 30-76-35; Ambassador GEORGES MINYILA.

Libya: 01 BP 1601, Ouagadougou 01; tel. 30-67-53; fax 31-34-70; Ambassador ABD AN-NASSER SALEH MUHAMMAD YOUNES.

Mali: 2569 ave Bassawarga, 01 BP 1911, Ouagadougou 01; tel. 38-19-22; Ambassador TOUMANY SISSOKO.

Mauritania: Ouagadougou; Ambassador MOHAMED OULD SID AHMED LEKHAL.

Morocco: Ouagadougou; Ambassador ABDELMAJID BOUAB.

Netherlands: 415 ave Dr Kwamé N'Krumah, 01 BP 1302, Ouagadougou 01; tel. 30-61-34; fax 30-76-95; e-mail oua@minbuza.nl; internet www.ambassadepays-bas.bf; Ambassador HENRICUS MAURITUS STEPHANUS SCHAAPVELD.

Nigeria: rue de l'Hôpital Yalgado, 01 BP 132, Ouagadougou 01; tel. 36-30-15; Ambassador AHMED KASHIM.

Saudi Arabia: Ouagadougou; Ambassador AID BIN MUHAMMAD ATH-THAKFI.

Senegal: ave de la Résistance du 17 Mai, 01 BP 3226, Ouagadougou 01; tel. 31-14-18; fax 31-14-01; e-mail ambasenebf@cenatrin.bf; Ambassador CHEIKH SYLLA.

USA: 602 ave Raoul Follereau, Koulouba, 01 BP 35, Ouagadougou 01; tel. 30-67-23; fax 31-23-68; e-mail amembouaga@state.gov; internet ouagadougou.usembassy.gov; Ambassador JOSEPH ANTHONY HOLMES.

Judicial System

In accordance with constitutional amendments approved by the Assemblée nationale in April 2000, the Supreme Court was abolished; its four permanent chambers were replaced by a Constitutional Council, a Council of State, a Court of Cassation and a National Audit Court, all of which commenced operations in December 2002. Judges are accountable to a Higher Council, under the chairmanship of the President of the Republic, in which capacity he is officially responsible for ensuring the independence of the judiciary. A High Court of Justice is competent to try the President and members of the Government in cases of treason, embezzlement of public funds, and other crimes and offences.

Constitutional Council: Ouagadougou; f. 2002 to replace Constitutional Chamber of fmr Supreme Court; Pres. IDRISSA TRAORÉ; Sec.-Gen. HONIBIPÈ MARIAM MARGUERITE OUÉDRAOGO.

Council of State: 03 BP 7024, Ouagadougou 03; tel. 33-52-11; e-mail webmasterconseil@justice.gov.bf; internet www.conseil-etat.gov.bf; f. 2002 to replace Administrative Chamber of fmr Supreme Court; First Pres. HARIDIATA DAKOURÉ.

Court of Cassation: 01 BP 586, Ouagadougou; tel. 30-64-15; fax 31-02-71; e-mail cdouedraogo@ahjudaf.org; f. 2002 to replace Judicial Chamber of fmr Supreme Court; First Pres. DIMKINSEDO CHEICK OUÉDRAOGO.

High Court of Justice: Ouagadougou; f. 1998; comprises six deputies of the Assemblée nationale and three magistrates appointed by the President of the Court of Cassation; Pres. YARGA LARBA; Vice-Pres. DÉ ALBERT MILLOGO.

National Audit Court: rue Guillaume Ouédraogo, Ouagadougou; internet www.cour-comptes.gov.bf; f. 2002 to replace Audit Chamber of fmr Supreme Court; First Pres. BOUREIMA PIERRE NEBIE.

Religion

The Constitution provides for freedom of religion, and the Government respects this right in practice. The country is a secular state. Islam, Christianity and traditional religions operate freely without government interference. More than 50% of the population follow animist beliefs.

ISLAM

An estimated 30% of the population are Muslims.

Association Islamique Tidjania du Burkina Faso: Ouagadougou; Pres. CHEICK ABOUBACAR MAÏGA II.

CHRISTIANITY

The Roman Catholic Church

Burkina Faso comprises three archdioceses and nine dioceses. At 31 December 2002 there were an estimated 1.5m. Roman Catholics in Burkina, comprising 12.1% of the total population.

Bishops' Conference

Conférence des Evêques de Burkina Faso et du Niger, 01 BP 1195, Ouagadougou 01; tel. 30-60-26; fax 31-64-81; e-mail ccbn@fasonet.bf. f. 1966; legally recognized 1978; Pres. Rt Rev. PHILIPPE OUÉDRAOGO (Bishop of Ouahigouya).

Archbishop of Bobo-Dioulasso: Most Rev. ANSELME TITIANMA SANON, Archevêché, Lafiaso, 01 BP 312, Bobo-Dioulasso; tel. 97-04-35; fax 97-04-38; e-mail ddec.bobo@fasonet.bf.

Archbishop of Koupéla: Most Rev. SÉRAPHIN F. ROUAMBA, Archevêché, BP 51, Koupéla; tel. 70-00-30; fax 70-02-65; e-mail archevkou@fasonet.bf.

Archbishop of Ouagadougou: Most Rev. JEAN-MARIE UNTAANI COMPAORÉ, Archevêché, 01 BP 1472, Ouagadougou 01; tel. 30-67-04; fax 30-72-75; e-mail archidiocese.ouaga@liptinfor.bf.

Protestant Churches

Assemblées de Dieu du Burkina Faso: 01 BP 458, Ouagadougou; tel. 30-54-60; e-mail ad@adburkina.org; internet www.adburkina.org; f. 1921; Pres. Pastor JEAN PAWENTAORÉ OUÉDRAOGO.

Fédération des Eglises et Missions Evangéliques (FEME): BP 108, Ouagadougou; tel. 36-14-26; e-mail feme@fasonet.bf; f. 1961; 10 churches and missions, 82,309 adherents; Pres. Pastor FREEMAN KOMPAORÉ.

BAHÁ'Í FAITH

Assemblée spirituelle nationale: 01 BP 977, Ouagadougou 01; tel. 34-29-95; e-mail gnampa@fasonet.bf; Nat. Sec. JEAN-PIERRE SWEDY.

The Press

Direction de la presse écrite: Ouagadougou; govt body responsible for press direction.

DAILIES

24 Heures: 01 BP 3654, Ouagadougou 01; tel. 31-41-08; fax 30-57-39; f. 2000; privately-owned; Dir BOUBAKAR DIALLO.

Bulletin de l'Agence d'Information du Burkina: 01 BP 1332, Ouagadougou; tel. 32-46-39; fax 32-46-40; e-mail aib.redaction@mcc.gov.bf; internet www.aib.bf; f. 1964 as L'Agence Voltaïque de Presse; current name adopted in 1984; Dir JAMES DABIRE.

L'Express du Faso: 01 BP 1, Bobo-Dioulasso 01; tel. 97-93-26; fax 33-50-27; e-mail kami.express@caramail.com; f. 1998; privately-owned; Dir of Publication KAMI MOUNTAMOU.

L'Observateur Paalga (New Observer): 01 BP 584, Ouagadougou 01; tel. 33-27-05; fax 31-45-79; e-mail lobservateur@zcp.bf; internet www.lobservateur.bf; f. 1973; relaunched in 1991; privately-owned; also a Sunday edn, *L'Observateur Dimanche*; Dir EDOUARD OUÉDRAOGO; circ. 7,000.

Le Pays: Cité 1200 logements, 01 BP 4577, Ouagadougou 01; tel. 36—20-46; fax 36-03-78; e-mail ed.lepays@cenatrin.bf; internet www.lepays.bf; f. 1991; independent; Dir-Gen. BOUREIMA JÉRÉMIE SIGUE; Editor-in-Chief MAHOROU KANAZOE; circ. 5,000.

Sidwaya Quotidien (Daily Truth): 5 rue du Marché, 01 BP 507, Ouagadougou 01; tel. 30-63-06; fax 31-03-62; e-mail sidwayas@mcc.gov.bf; internet www.sidwaya.bf; f. 1984; state-owned; Dir ISSAKA SOURWEMA; circ. 3,000.

PERIODICALS

L'Aurore: 01 BP 5104, Ouagadougou 01; tel. 25-22-81; e-mail enitiema@yahoo.fr; Dir of Publication ELIE NITIÈMA.

Bendré (Drum): 16.38 ave du Yatenga, 01 BP 6020, Ouagadougou 01; tel. 33-27-11; fax 31-28-53; e-mail bendrekan@hotmail.com; internet www.bendre.africa-web.org; f. 1990; weekly; current affairs; Dir SY MOUMINA CHERIFF; circ. 7,000 (2002).

Les Echos: Ouagadougou; f. 2002; weekly; Editor DAVID SANHOUIDI.

Evasion: Cité 1200 logements, 01 BP 4577, Ouagadougou 01; tel. 36-17-30; fax 36-03-78; e-mail ed.lepays@cenatrin.bf; internet www.lepays.bf; f. 1996; publ. by Editions le Pays; weekly; current affairs; Dir-Gen. BOUREIMA JÉRÉMIE SIGUE; Editor in Chief ABDOULAYE TAO.

L'Evènement: 01 BP 1860, Ouagadougou 01; tel. and fax 31-69-34; e-mail bangreib@yahoo.fr; internet www.cnpress-zongo.net/evenementbf; f. 2001; bimonthly; Editor-in-Chief NEWTON AHMED BARRY.

L'Hebdomadaire: Ouagadougou; tel. 31-47-62; e-mail hebdcom@fasonet.bf; internet www.hebdo.bf; f. 1999; Fridays; Dir ZÉPHIRIN KPODA; Editor-in-Chief DJIBRIL TOURÉ.

L'Indépendant: 01 BP 5663, Ouagadougou 01; tel. 33-37-75; e-mail sebgo@fasonet.bf; internet www.independant.bf; f. 1993 by Norbert Zongo; weekly, Tuesdays; Dir LIERMÉ DIEUDONNÉ SOMÉ; Editor-in-Chief TALATO SIID SAYA.

Le Journal du Jeudi (JJ): 01 BP 3654, Ouagadougou 01; tel. 31-41-08; fax 30-01-62; e-mail info@journaldujeudi.com; internet www.journaldujeudi.com; f. 1991; weekly; satirical; Dir BOUBAKAR DIALLO; Editor-in-Chief DAMIEN GLEZ; circ. 10,000.

Laabaali: Association Tin-Tua, BP 167, Fada N'Gourma; tel. 77-01-26; fax 77-02-08; e-mail info@tintua.org; f. 1988; monthly; promotes literacy, agricultual information, cultural affairs, Gourmanché; Dir of Publishing BENOÎT B. OUOBA; Editor-in-Chief SUZANNE OUOBA; circ. 4,000.

Label Magazine: Seydoni Production, 01 BP 4912, Ouagadougou 01; tel. 35-80-11; fax 36-21-34; e-mail cdt.burkina@fasonet.bf; f. 2001; music, arts, youth activities.

Le Marabout: 01 BP 3564, Ouagadougou 01; tel. 31-41-08; e-mail info@marabout.net; internet www.marabout.net; f. 2001; monthly; publ. by the Réseau africain pour la liberté d'informer; pan-African politics; satirical; Dir BOUBAKAR DIALLO; Editor-in-Chief DAMIEN GLEZ.

L'Opinion: 01 BP 6459, Ouagadougou 01; tel. 30-89-48; fax 30-89-47; e-mail zedcom@fasonet.bf; internet www.zedcom.bf; weekly; Editor ISSAKA LINGANI.

Regard: 01 BP 4707, Ouagadougou 01; tel. 31-16-70; fax 31-57-47; weekly; Dir CHRIS VALÉA; Editor PATRICK ILBOUDO; circ. 4,000.

San Finna: Immeuble Photo Luxe, 01 BP 2061, Ouagadougou 01; tel. and fax 33-09-09; e-mail maclau.y@fasonet.bf; internet www.sanfinna.com; f. 1999; Mondays; independent; current affairs, international politics; Editor-in-Chief MATHIEU N'DO.

Sidwaya Hebdo (Weekly Truth): 5 rue du Marché, 01 BP 507, Ouagadougou 01; tel. 31-36-05; fax 31-03-62; e-mail sidwayas@mcc.gov.bf; internet www.sidwaya.bf; f. 1997; state-owned; weekly; Dir ISSAKA SOURWEMA.

Sidwaya Magazine (Truth): 5 rue du Marché, 01 BP 507, Ouagadougou 01; tel. 30-63-07; fax 31-03-62; e-mail sidwayas@mcc.gov.bf; internet www.sidwaya.bf; f. 1989; state-owned; monthly; Editor-in-Chief BONIFACE COULIBALY; circ. 2,500.

La Voix du Sahel: 01 BP 5505, Ouagadougou; tel. 33-20-75; e-mail voixdusahel@yahoo.fr; privately-owned; Dir of Publication PROMOTHÉE KASSOUM BAKO.

Votre Santé: Cité 1200 logements, 01 BP 4577, Ouagadougou 01; tel. 36-20-46; fax 36-03-78; internet www.lepays.bf/mensuel/laune.asp; f. 1996; publ. by Editions le Pays; monthly; Dir-Gen. BOUREIMA JÉRÉMIE SIGUE; Editor-in-Chief SÉNI DABO.

NEWS AGENCY

Agence d'Information du Burkina (AIB): 01 BP 1332, Ouagadougou 01; tel. 32-46-39; fax 32-46-40; e-mail aib.redaction@delgi.gov.bf; internet www.aib.bf; f. 1964; fmrly Agence Voltaïque de Presse; state-controlled; Dir JAMES DABIRÉ.

PRESS ASSOCIATIONS

Association Rayimkudemdé—Association Nationale des Animateurs et Journalistes en Langues Nationales du Burkina Faso (ARK): Sigh-Noghin, Ouagadougou; f. 2001; Pres. RIGOBERT ILBOUDO; Sec.-Gen. PIERRE OUÉDRAOGO.

Centre National de Presse—Norbert Zongo (CNP—NZ): 04 BP 8524, Ouagadougou 04; tel. and fax 34-37-45; e-mail cnpress@fasonet.bf; internet www.cnpress-zongo.net; f. 1998 as Centre National de Presse; centre of information and documentation; provides journalistic training; incorporates Association des Journalistes du Burkina (f. 1988); Dir ABDOULAYE DIALLO.

Publishers

Editions Contact: 04 BP 8462, Ouagadougou 04; tel. 61-28-72; e-mail contact.evang@cenatrin.bf; f. 1992; evangelical Christian and other books in French.

Editions Découvertes du Burkina (ADDB): 06 BP 9237, Ouagadougou 06; tel. 36-22-38; e-mail jacques@liptinfor.bf; human and social sciences, poetry; Dir JACQUES GUÉGANÉ.

Editions Firmament: 01 BP 3392, Ouagadougou 01; tel. 38-44-25; e-mail roger.kabore@uemoa.int; literary fiction; Dir ROGER KABORÉ.

Editions Flamme: 01 BP 458, Ouagadougou 01; tel. 21-10-28; e-mail ad-lagengo-bf@cenatrin.bf; internet www.adburkina.org/imprimerie/flamme.html; owned by the Assembleés de Dieu du Burkina Faso; literature of Christian interest in French and in Mooré; Dir Pastor ZACHARIE DELMA.

Editions Gambidi: 01 BP 5743, Ouagadougou 01; tel. 36-59-42; e-mail jp.guigane@liptinfor.bf; politics, philosophy; Dir JEAN-PIERRE GUINGANÉ.

Graphic Technic International & Biomedical (GTI): 01 BP 3230, Ouagadougou 01; tel. and fax 31-67-69; e-mail hien.ignace@fasonet.bf; internet www.afrilivres.com/index.asp?navig=annuaire; medicine, literary, popular and children's fiction, poetry; Dir ANSOMWIN IGNACE HIEN.

Editions Hamaria: 01 BP 6788, Ouagadougou 01; tel. 34-38-04; e-mail edition.hamaria@fasonet.bf; sciences, fiction.

Presses Africaines SA: 01 BP 1471, Ouagadougou 01; tel. 30-71-75; fax 30-72-75; general fiction, religion, primary and secondary textbooks; Man. Dir A. WININGA.

Editions Sankofa et Gurli: 01 BP 3811, Ouagadougou 01; tel. 36–43–44; e-mail sankogur@hotmail.com; literary fiction, social sciences; in French and in national languages; Dir Jean-Claude Naba.

Editions Sidwaya: BP 810, Ouagadougou; f. 1998 to replace Société Nationale d'Editions et de Presse; state-owned; transfer to private ownership proposed; general, periodicals; Pres. Pierre Waongo.

Broadcasting and Communications

TELECOMMUNICATIONS

Regulatory Authority

Autorité nationale de Régulation des Télécommunications du Burkina Faso (ARTEL): ave Dimdolobsom, Porte 43, Rue 3.48, 01 BP 6437, Ouagadougou; tel. 33-41-98; fax 33-50-39; e-mail secretariat@artel.bf; internet www.artel.bf; f. 2000 prior to the proposed liberalization of the telecommunications sector; Pres. of the Administrative Council Zouli Bonkoungou.

Service Providers

Office National des Télécommunications (ONATEL): ave de la Nation, 01 BP 10000, Ouagadougou 01; tel. 49-44-02; fax 31-03-31; e-mail dcrp@onatel.bf; internet www.onatel.bf; 34% transfer to private ownership scheduled for 2004; Dir-Gen. Moussa Sanfo.

TELMOB: tel. 49-42-41; fax 49-42-78; e-mail wema.d@onatel.bf ; internet www.onatel.bf/telmob/index.htm; f. 2002; mobile cellular telephone operator in 19 cities; Dir Dieudonné Wema; 85,000 subscribers (Dec. 2003).

Celtel Burkina Faso: ave de la Résistance du 17 Mai, 01 BP 6622, Ouagadougou; tel. 33-14-00; fax 33-14-06; e-mail service_clientele@bf.celtel.com; internet www.bf.celtel.com; f. 2001; mobile cellular telephone operator in Ouagadougou, Bobo-Dioulasso and 19 other towns; subsidiary of MSI Cellular Investments Holding (Netherlands); Dir-Gen. Raymond Laforce; 55,000 subscribers (2003).

Telecel-Faso: ave de la Nation, 08 BP 11059, Ouagadougou 08; tel. 33-35-56; fax 33-35-58; e-mail infos@telecelfaso.bf; internet www.telecelfaso.bf; f. 2000; mobile cellular telephone operator in Ouagadougou, Bobo-Dioulasso and 19 other towns; 80% owned by Orascom Telecom (Egypt); Dir-Gen. Ahmed Cissé; 80,000 subscribers (Dec. 2003).

BROADCASTING

Regulatory Authority

Higher Council of Information: 290 ave Ho Chi Minh, 01 BP 6618, Ouagadougou 01; tel. 30-11-24; fax 30-11-33; e-mail csi@fasonet.bf; internet www.primature.gov.bf/republic/acc_csi.htm; f. 1995; Pres. Luc Adolphe Tiao.

Radio

In November 1999 there were 53 officially registered radio stations in Burkina Faso: four international stations, 17 commercial and two state-owned stations chiefly broadcasting music, six community stations, 10 other independent stations and 14 religious stations. There were 47 licensed FM radio stations in Burkina Faso in December 2001.

Radiodiffusion–Télévision du Burkina (RTB): 01 BP 2530, Ouagadougou 01; tel. 31-83-53; fax 32-48-09; f. 2001; Dir-Gen. Marcel Toe.

Radio Nationale du Burkina (La RNB): 03 BP 7029, Ouagadougou 03; tel. 32-43-02; fax 31-04-41; e-mail mafarmas@hotmail.com; f. 1959; state radio service; comprises national broadcaster of informative and discussion programmes, music stations *Canal Arc-En-Ciel* and *Canal Arc-en-Ciel Plus*, and two regional stations, broadcasting in local languages, in Bobo-Dialasso and Gaoua; Dir Mafarma Sanogo.

Radio Evangile Développement (RED): 04 BP 8050, Ouagadougou 04; tel. 43-51-56; e-mail regd.burkina@cenatrin.bf; f. 1993; broadcasts from Ouagadougou, Bobo-Dioulasso, Ouahigouya, Léo, Houndé, Koudougou and Yako; evangelical Christian; Dir-Gen. Joanna Ilboudo.

Horizon FM: 01 BP 2714, Ouagadougou 01; tel. 33-23-23; fax 35-60-54; e-mail horizonfm@fasonet.bf; f. 1990; private commercial station; broadcasts in French, English and eight vernacular languages; operates 10 stations nationally; Dir Moustapha Laabli Thiombiano.

Radio Locale-Radio Rurale: 03 BP 7029, Ouagadougou 03; tel. 31-27-81; fax 79-10-22; f. 1969; community broadcaster; local stations at Diapaga, Djibasso Gasson, Kongoussi, Orodara and Poura; Dir-Gen. Bélibié Soumaïla Bassole.

Radio Maria: Archevêché, 01 BP 90, Ouagadougou 01; tel. 31-70-70; fax 30-72-75; e-mail mcsburkina@yahoo.com; f. 1993; Roman Catholic; Dir Fr Dominique Yanogo.

Radio Salankoloto-Association Galian: 01 BP 1095, Ouagadougou 01; tel. 31-64-93; fax 31-64-71; e-mail radiosalankoloto@cenatrin.bf; f. 1996; community broadcaster; Dir Roger Nikiéma.

Radio Vive le Paysan: 05 BP 6274, Ouagadougou 05; tel. 31-16-36; fax 38-52-90; e-mail aeugene@fasonet.bf.

Radio la Voix du Paysan: BP 100, Ouahigouya; tel. 55-04-11; fax 55-01-62; community broadcaster; f. 1996; Pres. Bernard Lédéa Ouédraogo.

Television

Radio Télévision du Burkina: (see Radio); Dir of Television Inoussa Kinda.

Télévision Canal Viim Koéga—Fréquence Lumière: BP 108, Ouagadougou; tel. 30-76-40; e-mail cvktv@cvktv.org; internet www.cvktv.org; f. 1996; operated by the Fédération des Eglises et Missions Evangéliques.

Finance

(cap. = capital; res = reserves; dep. = deposits; m. = million; brs = branches; amounts in francs CFA)

BANKING

Central Bank

Banque Centrale des Etats de l'Afrique de l'Ouest (BCEAO): ave Gamal-Abdel-Nasser, BP 543, Ouagadougou; tel. 30-60-15; fax 30-63-76; e-mail akangni@bceao.int; internet www.bceao.int; HQ in Dakar, Senegal; f. 1962; bank of issue for the mem. states of the Union économique et monétaire ouest-africaine (UEMOA, comprising Benin, Burkina Faso, Côte d'Ivoire, Guinea-Bissau, Mali, Niger, Senegal and Togo); cap. and res 859,313m., total assets 5,671,675m. (Dec. 2002); Resident Representative Jérome Bro Grebe; br. in Bobo-Dioulasso.

Other Banks

Bank of Africa—Burkina Faso (BOA—B): 770 ave de la Résistance du 17 mai, 01 BP 1319, Ouagadougou 01; tel. 30-88-70; fax 30-88-74; e-mail boadg@fasonet.bf; internet www.bkofafrica.net/burkina.htm; f. 1998; cap. 1,500m., res 235m., dep. 53,817m. (Dec. 2003); Chair. Lassiné Diawara; Gen.-Man. Philippe Nadaud; 2 brs.

Banque Agricole et Commerciale du Burkina (BAC-B): 2 ave Gamal Abdel Nasser, Secteur 3, 01 BP 1644, Ouagadougou 01; tel. 33-33-33; fax 31-43-52; e-mail bacb@bacb.bf; f. 1980; fmrly Caisse Nationale de Crédit Agricole du Burkina (CNCA-B); present name adopted 2002; 25% state-owned; cap. 3,500m., res 1,126m., dep. 48,155m. (Dec. 2002); Pres. Tibila Kabore; Chair. & Gen.-Man. Léonce Kone; 4 brs.

Banque Commerciale du Burkina (BCB): 653 ave Dr Kwamé N'Krumah, 01 BP 1336, Ouagadougou 01; tel. 30-78-78; fax 31-06-28; e-mail bcb@bcb.bf; internet www.bcb.bf; f. 1988; 50% owned by Libyan Arab Foreign Bank, 25% state-owned, 25% owned by Caisse Nationale de Sécurité Sociale; res. 1,360m., dep. 42,336m., total assets 57,994m. (Feb. 2005); Pres. Jacques Zida; Gen.-Man. Mahmud Hammuda; 4 brs.

Banque Internationale du Burkina (BIB): 1340 ave Dimdolobsom, 01 BP 362, Ouagadougou 01; tel. 30-00-00; fax 31-00-94; e-mail bibouaga@fasonet.bf; f. 1974; 25% owned by Fonds Burkina de Développement Economique et Social., 24.2% owned by Compagnie de Financement et de Participation (Rep. of the Congo), 22.8% state-owned; cap. 4,800m., res 2,159.7m., dep. 108,716.5m. (Dec. 2002); Chair. Gaspard-Jean Ouédraogo; 21 brs.

Banque Internationale pour le Commerce, l'Industrie et l'Agriculture du Burkina (BICIA—B): 479 ave Dr Kwamé N'Krumah, 01 BP 08, Ouagadougou 01; tel. 31-31-31; fax 31-19-55; e-mail biciabdg@fasonet.bf; internet www.biciabnet.net; f. 1973; affiliated to BNP Paribas (France); 25% state-owned; cap. 5,000m., res 4,777m., dep. 188,842m. (Dec. 2002); Chair. Michel Kompaoré; Dir-Gen. Jean-Pierre Bajon-Arnal; 11 brs.

Ecobank Burkina: Immeuble espace Fadima, 633 rue Maurice Bishop, 01 BP 145, Ouagadougou 01; tel. 31-89-80; fax 31-89-81; e-mail ecobank@ecobank.com; internet www.ecobank.com; f. 1996; 59% owned by Ecobank Transnational Inc., 14.4% by private Burkinabé enterprises, 12% by Ecobank Benin, 12% by Ecobank Togo; cap.

1,500.0m., res 3,315.5m., dep. 61,337.0m.(Dec. 2004); Chair. ANDREA BAYALA; Dir-Gen. ASSIONGBON EKUÉ.

Société Générale de Banques au Burkina (SGBB): 4 rue du Marché, 01 BP 585, Ouagadougou 01; tel. 30-60-34; fax 31-05-61; e-mail bhfm.mail@socgen.com; internet www.sgbb.bf; f. 1998; 31% owned by Société Générale (France), 15% state-owned; cap. and res 1,600m., total assets 50,787m. (Dec. 2001); Pres. and Dir-Gen. EMILE PARÉ.

Credit Institutions

Burkina Bail, SA: 1043 ave du Dr Kwame Nkrumah, Immeuble SODIFA, 01 BP 1913, Ouagadougou 01; tel. 30-69-85; fax 30-70-02; e-mail asory@burkinabail.bf; internet www.burkinabail.bf; 51.9% owned by BIB; cap. 1,000., total assets 6,369m. (Dec. 2004); Dir-Gen. ABDOULAYE K. SORY.

Réseau des Caisses Populaires du Burkina (RCPB): Ouagadougou; tel. 30-48-41; Dir-Gen. DAOUDA SAWADOGA; 276,966 mems (June 2002), 104 co-operatives.

Société Burkinabè de Financement (SOBFI): Immeuble Nassa, 1242 ave Dr Kwamé N'Krumah, 10 BP 13876, Ouagadougou 10; tel. 31-80-04; fax 33-71-62; e-mail sobfi@fasonet.bf; f. 1997; cap. 500.0m., total assets 2,578.6m. (Dec. 2001); Pres. DIAWAR DIACK.

Bankers' Association

Association Professionnelle des Banques et Etablissements Financiers (APBEF-B): Ouagadougou; tel. 31-20-65; fax 31-20-66; e-mail apbef-b@cenatrin.bf; Pres. JOSÉ ESPEILLAC.

STOCK EXCHANGE

Bourse Régionale des Valeurs Mobilières (BRVM): s/c Chambre de Commerce, d'Industrie et d'Artisanat du Burkina, 01 BP 502, Ouagadougou 01; tel. 30-87-73; fax 30-87-19; e-mail louedraogo@brvm.org; internet www.brvm.org; f. 1998; national branch of BRVM (regional stock exchange based in Abidjan, Côte d'Ivoire, serving the member states of UEMOA); Man. LÉOPOLD OUÉDRAOGO.

INSURANCE

FONCIAS—TIARD: 99 ave Léo Frobénius, 01 BP 398, Ouagadougou 01; tel. 30-62-04; fax 31-01-53; e-mail groupe-foncias@foncias.bf; f. 1978; 51% owned by AGF (France), 20% state-owned; non-life insurance and reinsurance; cap. 400m.; Dir-Gen. BERNARD GIRARDIN; also **Foncias-Vie**, life insurance; Dir-Gen. JOSEPH BARO.

Gras Savoye Burkina Faso: avenue de la Résistance du 17 mai, 01 BP 1304, Ouagadougou 01; tel. 30-51-69; fax 30-51-73; e-mail grassavoye@fasonet.bf; internet www.grassavoye.com; affiliated to Gras Savoye (France); Dir-Gen. LAURENT SAWADOGO.

Société Nationale d'Assurances et de Réassurances (SONAR): 284 ave de Loudun, 01 BP 406, Ouagadougou 01; tel. 30-62-43; fax 30-89-75; e-mail sonar@cenatrin.bf; f. 1974; 42% owned by Burkinabè interests, 33% by French, Ivorian and US cos, 22% state-owned; life and non-life; cap. 720m. (SONAR-IARD, non-life), 500m. (SONAR-Vie, life); Dir-Gen. ANDRÉ BAYALA; 5 brs.

Union des Assurances du Burkina (UAB): 08 BP 11041, Ouagadougou 08; tel. 31-26-15; fax 31-26-20; e-mail uab@fasonet.bf; f. 1991; 42% owned by AXA Assurances Côte d'Ivoire; cap. 500m.; Pres. APPOLINAIRE COMPAORÉ; Dir-Gen. (non-life insurance) SI SALIFOU TRAORÉ; Dir-Gen. (life insurance) SOUMAÏLA SORGHO.

Trade and Industry

GOVERNMENT AGENCIES

Bureau des Mines et de la Géologie du Burkina (BUMIGEB): 4186 route de Fada–N'Gourma, 01 BP 601, Ouagadougou 01; tel. 36-48-02; fax 36-48-88; e-mail bumigeb@cenatrin.bf; internet www.bumigeb.bf; f. 1978; restructured 1997; research into geological and mineral resources; Pres. S. KY; Dir-Gen. PASCALE DIENDÉRÉ.

Commission de Privatisation: 01 BP 6451, Ouagadougou 01; tel. 33-58-93; fax 30-77-41; e-mail privatisation@fasonet.bf.

Comptoir Burkinabè des Métaux Précieux (CBMP): Ouagadougou; tel. 30-75-48; fax 31-56-34; promotes gold sector, liaises with artisanal producers; transfer to private management pending in 2004; Dir-Gen. YACOUBA BARRY.

Office National d'Aménagement des Terroirs (ONAT): 01 BP 3007, Ouagadougou 01; tel. 30-61-10; fax 30-61-12; f. 1974; fmrly Autorité des Aménagements des Vallées des Voltas; integrated rural development, including economic and social planning; Man. Dir ZACHARIE OUÉDRAOGO.

Office National des Barrages et des Aménagements Hydro-agricoles (ONBAH): 03 BP 7056, Ouagadougou 03; tel. 30-89-82; fax 31-04-26; e-mail onbah@cenatrin.bf; f. 1976; control and development of water for agricultural use, construction of dams, water and soil conservation; state-owned; Dir-Gen. AÏZO TINDANO.

Office National du Commerce Extérieur (ONAC): 30 ave Léo Frobénius, 01 BP 389, Ouagadougou 01; tel. 31-13-00; fax 31-14-69; e-mail info@tradepoint.bf; internet www.tradepoint.bf; f. 1974; promotes and supervises external trade; Man. Dir SÉRIBA OUATTARA (acting); br. at Bobo-Dioulasso.

DEVELOPMENT ORGANIZATIONS

Agence Française de Développement (AFD): 52 ave Nelson Mandela, 01 BP 529, Ouagadougou 01; tel. 30-60-92; fax 31-19-66; e-mail afdburkina@liptinfor.bf; internet www.afd.fr; fmrly Caisse Française de Développement; Dir YVES JORLIN.

Association Française des Volontaires du Progrès (AFVP): 01 BP 947, Ouagadougou 01; tel. 30-70-43; fax 31-44-91; e-mail afvp.bf@liptinfor.bf; internet www.afvp.org; f. 1973; supports small business; Nat. Delegate FRANÇOIS LECARPENTIER.

Bureau d'Appui aux Micro Entreprises (BAME): BP 610, Bobo-Dioulasso; tel. 97-16-28; fax 97-21-76; e-mail bame@fasonet.bf; f. 1991; supports small business; Dir FÉLIX SANON.

Cellule d'Appui à la Petite et Moyenne Entreprise d'Ouagadougou (CAPEO): 01 BP 6443, Ouagadougou 01; tel. 31-37-62; fax 31-37-64; e-mail capeod@fasonet.bf; internet www.spid.com/capeo; f. 1991; supports small and medium-sized enterprises.

Fondation pour la Promotion de l'Entreprise et de l'Emploi (FEE): Ouagadougou; tel. 31-27-90; promotes private enterprise.

Promotion du Développement Industriel, Artisanal et Agricole (PRODIA): Secteur 8, Gounghin, 01 BP 2344, Ouagadougou 01; tel. 34-31-11; fax 34-71-47; e-mail prodia@cenatrin.bf; internet www.afraca.org/frprodia.html; f. 1981; supports small business; issued 1,266 loans amounting to 391.7m. francs CFA in 1998; Dir MAMADOU OUÉDRAOGO.

CHAMBER OF COMMERCE

Chambre de Commerce, d'Industrie et d'Artisanat du Burkina: 180/220 rue 3-119, 01 BP 502, Ouagadougou 01; tel. 30-61-14; fax 30-61-16; e-mail webmaster.ccia@ccia.bf; internet www.ccia.bf; f. 1948; Pres. El Hadj OUMAROU KANAZOÉ; Dir-Gen. BENOÎT OUATTARA; brs in Bobo-Dioulasso, Koupéla and Ouahigouya.

EMPLOYERS' ORGANIZATIONS

Association Femmes Solidaritées (AFS): 01 BP 1749, Ouagadougou 01; tel. 30-01-50; association of female employers.

Club des Hommes d'Affaires Franco-Burkinabé: Ambassade de France au Burkina Faso, 01 BP 4382, Ouagadougou; tel. 31-32-73; fax 31-32-81; e-mail chafb@liptinfor.bf; internet www.chafb.bf; f. 1990; represents 65 major enterprises and seeks to develop trading relations between Burkina Faso and France; Pres. OUMAR YUGO.

Conseil National du Patronat Burkinabè (CNPB): 01 BP 660, Ouagadougou 02; tel. 33-29-24; fax 30-25-21; e-mail belco@fasonet.bf; f. 1998; comprises 27 professional groupings; Pres. El Hadj OUMAROU KANAZOE; Exec. Sec. EMILE KABORÉ.

Groupement Professionnel des Industriels: 01 BP 5381, Ouagadougou 01; tel. and fax 30-11-59; e-mail gpi@fasonet.bf; f. 1974; Pres. MARTIAL OUÉDRAOGO.

Fédération Nationale des Exportateurs du Burkina (FENEB): Ouagadougou; Permanent Sec. SEYDOU FOFANA.

Jeune Chambre du Burkina Faso: tel. 31-36-14; fax ; e-mail eras@fasonet.bf; internet www.jceburkina.bf; f. 1976; org. of entrepreneurs aged 18–40; affiliated to Junior Chambers International, Inc; Exec. Pres. ERNEST ROBERT TOE.

Syndicat des Commerçants Importateurs et Exportateurs du Burkina (SCIMPEX): 01 BP 552, Ouagadougou 01; tel. 31-18-70; fax 31-30-36; e-mail scimpex@cenatrin.bf; Pres. LASSINÉ DIAWARA.

UTILITIES

Electricity

Société Générale de Travaux et de Constructions Electriques (SOGETEL): Zone Industrielle, Gounghin, 01 BP 429, Ouagadougou 01; tel. 34-29-80; fax 34-25-70; e-mail sogetel@cenatrin.bf; internet www.cenatrin.bf/sogetel; transport and distribution of electricity.

Société Nationale Burkinabè d'Electricité (SONABEL): ave Nelson Mandela, 01 BP 54, Ouagadougou 01; tel. 30-61-00; fax 31-03-40; f. 1954; state-owned; partial privatization proposed for 2004;

production and distribution of electricity; Dir-Gen. SALIF LAMOUSSA KABORÉ.

Water

Office National de l'Eau et de l'Assainissement (ONEA): 01 BP 170, Ouagadougou 01; tel. 43-19-00; fax 43-19-11; e-mail onea@ fasonet.bf; f. 1977; storage, purification and distribution of water; transferred to private management (by Veolia Water Burkina Faso) in 2001; Dir-Gen. MAMADOU LAMINE KOUATE.

Veolia Water Burkina Faso: 06 BP 9525, Ouagadougou 06; tel. and fax 34-03-00; manages operation of water distribution and sewerage services; subsidiary of Veolia Environnement (France).

CO-OPERATIVES

Union des Coopératives Agricoles et Maraîchères du Burkina (UCOBAM): 01 BP 277, Ouagadougou 01; tel. 30-65-27; fax 30-65-28; e-mail ucobam@zcp.bf; f. 1968; comprises 8 regional co-operative unions (6,500 mems, representing 35,000 producers); production and marketing of fruit, vegetables, jams and conserves; Dir-Gen. MAHAMOUD SOBGO.

TRADE UNIONS

In 2001 there were more than 20 autonomous trade unions. The five trade-union syndicates were:

Confédération Générale du Travail Burkinabè (CGTB): 01 BP 547, Ouagadougou 01; tel. 31-36-71; f. 1988; confed. of several autonomous trade unions; Sec.-Gen. TOLÉ SAGNON.

Confédération Nationale des Travailleurs Burkinabè (CNTB): BP 445, Ouagadougou; tel. 31-23-95; f. 1972; Sec.-Gen. LAURENT OUÉDRAOGO; 10,000 mems.

Confédération Syndicale Burkinabè (CSB): 01 BP 1921 Ouagadougou 01; tel. and fax 31-83-98; e-mail cosybu2000@yahoo.fr; f. 1974; mainly public service unions; Sec.-Gen. JEAN MATHIAS LILIOU.

Organisation Nationale des Syndicats Libres (ONSL): 01 BP 99, Ouagadougou 01; tel. 30-72-77; f. 1960; 6,000 mems.

Union Syndicale des Travailleurs Burkinabè (USTB): BP 381, Ouagadougou; f. 1958; Sec.-Gen. BONIFACE SOMDAH; 35,000 mems in 45 affiliated orgs.

Transport

RAILWAY

At the end of 1991 there were some 622 km of track in Burkina Faso. A 105-km extension from Donsin to Ouagadougou was inaugurated in December of that year. Plans exist for the construction of an extension to the manganese deposits at Tambao.

SITARAIL—Transport Ferroviaire de Personnes et de Marchandises: rue Dioncolo, 01 BP 5699, Ouagadougou 01; tel. 31-07-35; fax 30-85-21; 67% owned by Groupe Bolloré, 15% state-owned, 15% owned by Govt of Côte d'Ivoire; national branch of SITARAIL (based in Abidjan, Côte d'Ivoire); responsible for operations on the railway line between Kaya, Ouagadougou and Abidjan (Côte d'Ivoire); Rep. in Burkina SOULEYMANE YAMÉOGO.

Société de Gestion du Patrimoine Ferroviaire du Burkina (SOPAFER—B): 01 BP 192, Ouagadougou 01; tel. 30-25-48; fax 31-35-94; railway network services; Dir-Gen. NÈBAMA KERE.

ROADS

In 1999 there were an estimated 58,461 km of roads, including 10,469 km of classified roads; only around 3% of the total network, or 19% of the length of classified roads, was paved at that time. A major aim of current road projects is to improve transport links with other countries of the region. In 1999 a US $37m. project was begun to upgrade the road linking Ouagadougou with the Ghanaian border via the more isolated southern provinces.

Interafricaine de Transport et de Transit (IATT): 04 BP 8242, Ouagadougou 04; tel. 30-25-12; fax 30-37-04.

Société Africaine de Transit (SAT): 01 BP 4249, Ouagadougou 01; tel. 31-09-16.

Société Africaine de Transports Routiers (SATR): 01 BP 5298, Ouagadougou 01; tel. 34-08-62.

Société Nationale du Transit du Burkina (SNTB): 474 ave Bishop, 01 BP 1192, Ouagadougou 01; tel. 30-60-54; fax 30-85-21; f. 1977; 31% owned by Groupe SAGA (France); 12% state-owned; road haulage and warehousing; Dir-Gen. SEYDOU DIAKITÉ.

CIVIL AVIATION

There are international airports at Ouagadougou and Bobo-Dioulasso, 49 small airfields and 13 private airstrips. Ouagadougou airport handled an estimated 275,400 passengers and 5,880 metric tons of freight in 1999.

Air Burkina: ave Loudun, 01 BP 1459, Ouagadougou 01; tel. 30-76-76; fax 31-48-80; f. 1967 as Air Volta; 56% owned by Aga Khan Group; 14% state-owned; operates domestic and regional services; Dir MOHAMED GHELALA.

Tourism

Burkina Faso, which possesses some 2.8m. ha of nature reserves, is considered to provide some of the best opportunities to observe wild animals in West Africa. Some big game hunting is also permitted. Several important cultural events are also held in Burkina Faso: the biennial pan-African film festival, FESPACO, is held in Ouagadougou, as is the biennial international exhibition of handicrafts, while Bobo-Dioulasso hosts the biennial week of national culture. In 2002 there were approximately 149,000 foreign visitors. Receipts from tourism were estimated at US $34m. in 2001.

Office National du Tourisme Burkinabè (ONTB): ave Frobénius, BP 1318, Ouagadougou; tel. 31-19-59; fax 31-44-34; e-mail ontb@ontb.bf; internet www.ontb.bf; Dir-Gen. ISIDORE NABALOUM.

BURUNDI

Introductory Survey

Location, Climate, Language, Religion, Flag, Capital

The Republic of Burundi is a land-locked country lying on the eastern shore of Lake Tanganyika, in central Africa, a little south of the Equator. It is bordered by Rwanda to the north, by Tanzania to the south and east, and by the Democratic Republic of the Congo (formerly Zaire) to the west. The climate is tropical (hot and humid) in the lowlands, and cool in the highlands, with an irregular rainfall. The population is composed of three ethnic groups: the Hutu (85%), the Tutsi (14%) and the Twa (1%). The official languages are French and Kirundi, while Swahili is used, in addition to French, in commercial circles. More than 65% of the inhabitants profess Christianity, with the great majority of the Christians being Roman Catholics. A large minority still adhere to traditional animist beliefs. The national flag (proportions 3 by 5) consists of a white diagonal cross on a background of red (above and below) and green (hoist and fly), with a white circle, containing three green-edged red stars, in the centre. The capital is Bujumbura.

Recent History

Burundi (formerly Urundi) became part of German East Africa in 1899. In 1916 the territory was occupied by Belgian forces from the Congo (now the Democratic Republic of the Congo, DRC). Subsequently, as part of Ruanda-Urundi, it was administered by Belgium under a League of Nations mandate and later as a UN Trust Territory. Elections in September 1961, conducted under UN supervision, were won by the Union pour le progrès national (UPRONA). Internal self-government was granted in January 1962 and full independence on 1 July, when the two parts of the Trust Territory became separate states, as Burundi and Rwanda. Tensions between Burundi's two main ethnic groups, the Tutsi (traditionally the dominant tribe, despite representing a minority of the overall population) and the Hutu, escalated during 1965. Following an unsuccessful attempt by the Hutu to overthrow the Tutsi-dominated Government in October, nearly all the Hutu political élite were executed, eliminating any significant participation by the Hutu in Burundi's political life until the late 1980s (see below). In July 1966 the Mwami (King), Mwambutsa IV, was deposed, after a reign of more than 50 years, by his son Charles, and the Constitution was suspended. In November Charles, now Mwami Ntare V, was himself deposed by his Prime Minister, Capt. (later Lt-Gen.) Michel Micombero, who declared Burundi a republic.

Several alleged plots against the Government in 1969 and 1971 were followed by an abortive coup in 1972, during which Ntare V was killed. Hutu activists were held responsible for the attempted coup, and this served as a pretext for the Tutsi to conduct a series of large-scale massacres of the rival tribe, in which, it was estimated, about 100,000 were killed; large numbers of the Hutu fled to neighbouring countries.

In 1972 Micombero began a prolonged restructuring of the executive, which resulted, in 1973, in the appointment of a seven-member Presidential Bureau, headed by himself. In July 1974 the Government introduced a new republican Constitution, which vested sovereignty in UPRONA, the sole legal political party. Micombero was elected Secretary-General of the party and re-elected for a seven-year presidential term.

In 1976 an army coup deposed Micombero, who died in exile in July 1983. The leader of the coup, Lt-Col (later Col) Jean-Baptiste Bagaza, was appointed President by the Supreme Revolutionary Council (composed of army officers), and a new Council of Ministers was formed. In October 1978 Bagaza abolished the post of Prime Minister. The first national congress of UPRONA was held in December 1979, and a party Central Committee, headed by Bagaza, was elected to take over the functions of the Supreme Revolutionary Council in January 1980. A new Constitution, adopted by national referendum in November 1981, provided for the establishment of a unicameral legislature, the Assemblée nationale, to be elected by universal adult suffrage. The first legislative elections were held in October 1982. Having been re-elected President of UPRONA in July 1984, Bagaza, the sole candidate, was elected President of Burundi by direct suffrage in August, winning 99.6% of the votes cast.

In September 1987 Bagaza was deposed in a military coup, led by Maj. Pierre Buyoya, who accused Bagaza of corruption. Buyoya immediately formed a Military Committee for National Salvation (CMSN) to administer the country, pending the appointment of a new President. The Constitution was suspended, and the Assemblée nationale was dissolved. On 2 October Buyoya was inaugurated as President of the Third Republic.

In August 1988 tribal tensions erupted into violence in the north of the country when groups of Hutus, claiming Tutsi provocation, slaughtered hundreds of Tutsis in the towns of Ntega and Marangara. The Tutsi-dominated army was immediately dispatched to the region to restore order, and large-scale tribal massacres occurred. In October Buyoya announced changes to the Council of Ministers, including the appointment of a Hutu, Adrien Sibomana, to the newly restored post of Prime Minister. For the first time the Council included a majority of Hutu representatives. Buyoya subsequently established a Committee for National Unity (comprising an equal number of Tutsis and Hutus) to investigate the massacres and make recommendations for national reconciliation. Following the publication of the Committee's report, Buyoya announced plans to introduce new regulations to combat all forms of discrimination against Hutus. Nevertheless, political tension remained at a high level in 1989.

In May 1990, in response to a new draft charter on national unity, Buyoya announced plans to replace military rule with a 'democratic constitution under a one-party government'. A charter designed to reconcile the Tutsi and the Hutu was to be the subject of a referendum. In December, at an extraordinary national congress of UPRONA, the CMSN was abolished and its functions transferred to an 80-member Central Committee, with Buyoya as Chairman and with a Hutu, Nicolas Mayugi, as Secretary-General. At a referendum in February 1991 the draft charter on national unity was overwhelmingly approved, despite criticism from opposition groups. Later in the month a ministerial reorganization, whereby Hutus were appointed to 12 of the 23 government portfolios, was viewed with scepticism by political opponents. In March a commission was established to prepare a report on the democratization of political structures, in preparation for the drafting of a new constitution. The commission's report, presented in September, recommended the establishment of a multi-party parliamentary system, which was to operate in conjunction with a renewable five-year presidential mandate. The proposals received the support of more than 90% of the voters in a referendum held on 9 March 1992, and the new Constitution was promulgated on 13 March.

In an extensive government reorganization in April 1992, Hutus were appointed to 15 of the 25 ministries, while Buyoya relinquished the defence portfolio. In the same month Buyoya approved legislation relating to the creation of new political parties in accordance with the new Constitution. New political parties were to be obliged to demonstrate impartiality with regard to ethnic or regional origin, gender and religion, and were to refrain from militarization. In October Buyoya announced the creation of the 33-member National Electoral Preparatory Commission (NEPC), comprising representatives of the eight recognized political parties, together with administrative, judicial, religious and military officials.

A presidential election, which took place on 1 June 1993, was won, with 64.8% of the votes cast, by Melchior Ndadaye, the candidate of the Front pour la démocratie au Burundi (FRODEBU), with the support of the Rassemblement du peuple burundien (RPB), the Parti du peuple and the Parti libéral; Buyoya received 32.4% of the vote as the UPRONA candidate, with support from the Rassemblement pour la démocratie et le développement économique et social (RADDES) and the Parti social démocrate. Elections for 81 seats in the Assemblée nationale were conducted on 29 June. FRODEBU again emerged as the most successful party, with 71% of the votes and 65 of the seats in the new legislature. UPRONA, with 21.4% of the votes, secured the remaining 16 seats. Ndadaye, Burundi's first Hutu

Head of State, assumed the presidency on 10 July. A Tutsi, Sylvie Kinigi, became Prime Minister, while the new Council of Ministers included a further six Tutsi representatives.

On 21 October 1993 more than 100 army paratroopers swiftly overwhelmed supporters of the Government and occupied the presidential palace and the headquarters of the national broadcasting company. Ndadaye and several other prominent Hutu politicians and officials were detained and subsequently killed by the insurgents, who later proclaimed François Ngeze, one of the few Hutu members of UPRONA and a minister in the Government of former President Buyoya, as head of a National Committee for Public Salvation (CPSN). While members of the Government sought refuge abroad and in the offices of foreign diplomatic missions in Bujumbura, the armed forces declared a state of emergency, closing national borders and the capital's airport. However, international condemnation of the coup, together with the scale and ferocity of renewed tribal violence (fuelled by reports of Tutsi-dominated army units seeking out and eliminating Hutu intellectuals), undermined support for the insurgents from within the armed forces, and precipitated the collapse of the CPSN, which was disbanded on 25 October. Kinigi ended the curfew, but remained in hiding and urged the deployment of an international force in Burundi to protect the civilian Government. On 28 October the UN confirmed that the Government had resumed control of the country. Ngeze and 10 coup leaders were arrested, while some 40 other insurgents were believed to have fled to Zaire (now the DRC).

Meanwhile, in early November 1993 several members of the Government, including the Prime Minister, had left the French embassy with a small escort of French troops, and on 8 November Kinigi met with 15 of the 17 surviving ministers, in an attempt to address the humanitarian crisis arising from the massacre and displacement of hundreds of thousands of Burundians following the failed coup. On the same day the Constitutional Court officially recognized the presidential vacancy resulting from the murder of both Ndadaye and his constitutional successor, Giles Bimazubute, the Speaker of the Assemblée nationale, and stated that presidential power should be exercised by the Council of Ministers, pending a presidential election, which was to be conducted within three months. However, the Minister of External Relations and Co-operation, Sylvestre Ntibantunganya (who succeeded Ndadaye as leader of FRODEBU), suggested that no electoral timetable should be considered before the resolution of internal security difficulties and the initiation of a comprehensive programme for the repatriation of refugees. In December Ntibantunganya was elected Speaker of the Assemblée nationale. The foreign affairs portfolio was assumed by Jean-Marie Ngendahayo, previously Minister of Communications and Government Spokesman.

Meanwhile, in November 1993, following repeated requests by the Government for an international contribution to the protection of government ministers in Burundi, the Organization of African Unity (OAU)—now the African Union (AU, see p. 144)—agreed to the deployment of a protection force (MIPROBU), to comprise some 180 civilian and military personnel, for a period of six months. In December opposition parties, including UPRONA and the RADDES, organized demonstrations in protest at the deployment of the contingent, scheduled for January 1994, claiming that it infringed Burundi's sovereignty. As a compromise, in March the Government secured a significant reduction in the size of MIPROBU, to comprise a military contingent of 47 and 20 civilian observers; its mandate was subsequently extended at three-monthly intervals.

In early January 1994 FRODEBU deputies in the Assemblée nationale approved a draft amendment to the Constitution, allowing a President of the Republic to be elected by the Assemblée nationale, in the event of the Constitutional Court's recognition of a presidential vacancy. UPRONA deputies, who had boycotted the vote, expressed concern that such a procedure represented election by indirect suffrage, in direct contravention of the terms of the Constitution. The continued boycott of the Assemblée nationale by UPRONA deputies forced the postponement, on 10 January, of an attempt by FRODEBU deputies to elect their presidential candidate, the Minister of Agriculture and Livestock, Cyprien Ntaryamira. Three days later, none the less, following the successful negotiation of a political truce with opposition parties, Ntaryamira was elected President by the Assemblée nationale. A Tutsi Prime Minister, Anatole Kanyenkiko, was appointed in early February, and the composition of a new multi-party Council of Ministers was subsequently agreed. During that month ethnic tension was renewed, as armed Hutu

and Tutsi extremist factions attempted to establish territorial strongholds.

On 6 April 1994, returning from a regional summit meeting in Dar es Salaam, Tanzania, Ntaryamira and three government ministers were killed when the aircraft of the Rwandan President, Juvénal Habyarimana, in which they were travelling, was the target of a rocket attack above Kigali airport, Rwanda, and exploded on landing. Habyarimana, who was also killed, was widely acknowledged to have been the intended victim of the attack. In contrast to the violent political and tribal chaos that erupted in Rwanda (q.v.) in the aftermath of the death of Habyarimana, Burundians responded positively to appeals for calm issued by Ntibantunganya, the Speaker of the Assemblée nationale, who, on 8 April, was confirmed (in accordance with the Constitution) as interim President for a three-month period. However, violent exchanges between Hutu extremist rebels and factions of the armed forces continued in April. The failure of the warring militias to respond to an ultimatum, issued by Ntibantunganya in late April, to surrender all illegal arms by 1 May, resulted in the military bombardment of several rebel strongholds, forcing the withdrawal and surrender of a number of insurgents.

Having discounted the possibility of organizing a general election, owing to security considerations, in June 1994 all major political parties joined lengthy negotiations to establish a procedure for the restoration of the presidency. The mandate of the interim President was extended for three months by the Constitutional Court in July, and by the end of August it had been decided that a new President would be elected by a broadly representative commission. A new power-sharing agreement, the Convention of Government, was announced on 10 September. Detailing the terms of government for a four-year transitional period (including the allocation of 45% of cabinet posts to opposition parties), it was incorporated into the Constitution on 22 September. The Convention also provided for the creation of a National Security Council (Conseil de sécurité nationale—CSN), which was formally inaugurated on 10 October. On 30 September the Convention elected Ntibantunganya to the presidency from a list of six candidates, including Charles Mukasi, the UPRONA leader. Ntibantunganya's appointment was endorsed by the Assemblée nationale, and he was formally inaugurated on 1 October. Anatole Kanyenkiko was reappointed as Prime Minister, and a coalition Government was announced in accordance with the terms of the Convention. In December, however, UPRONA announced its intention to withdraw from the Government and from the legislature, following the election earlier that month of Jean Minani (a prominent FRODEBU member) to the post of Speaker of the Assemblée nationale. UPRONA members accused Minani of having incited Hutu attacks against Tutsis in the aftermath of the October 1993 attempted coup. In January 1995 the political crisis was averted by agreement on a compromise FRODEBU candidate, Léonce Ngendakumana. Minani subsequently assumed the FRODEBU party leadership. Later that month Kanyenkiko resisted attempts by the UPRONA leadership to expel him from the party, for having failed to comply with party demands for the withdrawal from the Government of all party members over the Minani affair. Two UPRONA ministers were subsequently dismissed from the Government, in apparent retaliation, prompting Mukasi in mid-February to demand the resignation of the Prime Minister and to declare an indefinite general strike in support of this demand. In response to increased political opposition, Kanyenkiko acknowledged that he no longer commanded the necessary mandate to continue in office, and on 22 February Antoine Nduwayo, a UPRONA candidate selected in consultation with other opposition parties, was appointed Prime Minister by presidential decree. A new coalition Council of Ministers was announced on 1 March, but political stability was undermined immediately by the murder of the Hutu Minister of Energy and Mines, Ernest Kabushemeye.

Ethnic tension persisted in the second half of 1994, exacerbated by the scale and proximity of the violence in Rwanda and by the presence in Burundi of an estimated 200,000 Rwandan Hutu refugees. Frequent ethnically motivated killings, including those of several prominent politicians and government officials, resulted in the imposition of a partial curfew in the capital in December. Fears that the security crisis in Burundi would develop into civil war were exacerbated in late 1994 by reports that the 30,000-strong Force pour la défense de la démocratie (FDD), the armed wing of Nyangoma's extremist

Conseil national pour la défense de la démocratie (CNDD), was preparing for an armed struggle against the armed forces.

An escalation in the scale and frequency of incidents of politically and ethnically motivated violence during 1995 prompted renewed concern that the security crisis would precipitate a large-scale campaign of ethnic massacres similar to that in Rwanda during 1994. Government-sponsored military initiatives were concentrated in Hutu-dominated suburbs of Bujumbura and in the north-east, where an aggressive campaign was waged against the alleged insurgent activities of the Parti de libération du peuple hutu (PALIPEHUTU—a small, proscribed, Hutu opposition group based in Tanzania), resulting in the deaths of hundreds of Hutu civilians. The Government accused Hutu extremist militias of conducting an intimidating and violent programme of recruitment in the region. It was reported that as many as 130 civilians were killed in the ensuing hostilities. Also in June 1995 a report published by the human rights organization Amnesty International claimed that national security forces in Burundi had collaborated with extremist Tutsi factions in the murder of thousands of Hutus since 1993. Increased security measures announced by Ntibantunganya in the same month included restrictions on a number of civil liberties. None the less, in late June 1995 the Minister of State in charge of External Relations and Co-operation, Jean-Marie Ngendahayo, resigned, expressing dissatisfaction at the Government's inability to guarantee the safety and basic rights of the population.

By early 1996 reports of atrocities perpetrated against both Hutu and Tutsi civilians by rogue elements of the Tutsi-led armed forces (including militia known as the *Sans Echecs*) and by extremist Hutu rebel groups had become almost commonplace in rural areas. It was believed that the capital had been effectively 'cleansed' of any significant Hutu presence by the end of 1995. In late December the UN Secretary-General petitioned the Security Council to sanction some form of international military intervention in Burundi to address the crisis. However, the Burundian Government remained vehemently opposed to a foreign military presence.

In early April 1996 representatives of the US Agency for International Development and the Humanitarian Office of the European Union (EU, see p. 217) visited Burundi. Their findings, which were severely critical of the administration's failure to reconcile the country's various ethnic and political interests within government, prompted the USA and the EU immediately to suspend aid to Burundi. Despite pledges by Ntibantunganya in late April to undertake comprehensive reforms of the security forces and the judiciary, violence continued to escalate, prompting the suspension of French military co-operation with Burundi at the end of May.

Representatives of some 13 political parties (including FRODEBU and UPRONA) participated in discussions conducted in Mwanza, Tanzania, in April 1996, with mediation from the former President of Tanzania, Julius Nyerere. Talks resumed in Mwanza in early June; Mukasi, the UPRONA leader, with support from an informal coalition of seven smaller, predominantly Tutsi parties (the Rassemblement unitaire), accused FRODEBU deputies of seeking to abrogate the Convention of Government, a charge that was strenuously denied by FRODEBU following the talks. At a conference of regional powers in Arusha, Tanzania, in late June, it was reported that Ntibantunganya and Nduwayo had requested foreign intervention to protect government installations. By early July a regional technical commission to examine the request for 'security assistance' (comprising regional defence ministers, but not representatives of the Burundian armed forces) had convened in Arusha and had reached preliminary agreement, with UN support, for an intervention force. Meanwhile, significant differences with regard to the mandate of such a force had emerged between Ntibantunganya and Nduwayo (who suggested that the President was attempting to neutralize the country's military capability). At a mass rally in Bujumbura of Tutsi-dominated opposition parties, the Prime Minister joined Mukasi and other anti-Government figures in rejecting foreign military intervention. Some days later, however, full endorsement of the Arusha proposal for intervention was recorded by member nations of the OAU at a summit meeting convened in Yaoundé, Cameroon.

Political and ethnic enmities intensified still further when reports of a massacre of more than 300 Tutsi civilians at Bugendana, allegedly committed by Hutu extremists, including heavily armed Rwandan Hutu refugees, emerged shortly after the UN accused the Burundian authorities of collaborating with the Rwandan administration in a new initiative of (largely enforced) repatriation of Rwandan refugees in Burundi. While FRODEBU members made an urgent appeal for foreign intervention to contain the increasingly violent civil and military reaction to these events, students (with the support of the political opposition) began a second week of protests against regional military intervention, and demonstrated in support of demands for the removal of the country's leadership.

In late July 1996 the armed forces were extensively deployed in the capital in a military coup. A statement made by the Minister of National Defence, Lt-Col Firmin Sinzoyiheba, criticized the failure of the administration to safeguard national security, and announced the suspension of the Assemblée nationale and all political activity, the imposition of a nationwide curfew and the closure of national borders and the airport at Bujumbura. Former President Buyoya was declared interim President of a transitional republic, and immediately sought to reassure former ministers and government officials that their safety would be guaranteed by the new regime. Ntibantunganya conveyed his refusal to relinquish office, but Nduwayo resigned, attributing his failure to effect national reconciliation principally to Ntibantunganya's ineffective leadership. In response to widespread external condemnation of the coup, Buyoya announced that a largely civilian government of national unity would be promptly installed, and that future negotiations with all Hutu groups would be considered. The forced repatriation of Rwandan Hutu refugees was halted with immediate effect.

Despite the appointment at the end of July 1996 of Pascal-Firmin Ndimira, a Hutu member of UPRONA, as Prime Minister, and an urgent attempt by Buyoya to obtain regional support, the leaders of Ethiopia, Kenya, Rwanda, Tanzania, Uganda and Zaire, meeting in Arusha, under OAU auspices, declared their intention to impose stringent economic sanctions against the new regime unless constitutional government was restored immediately. In early August the composition of a new 23-member, multi-ethnic Cabinet was announced. In mid-August Buyoya announced that an expanded transitional Assemblée nationale, incorporating existing elected deputies, would be inaugurated during September for a three-year period. Buyoya was formally inaugurated as President on 27 September.

The regional sanctions that were imposed in early August 1996 resulted in the suspension of all significant trade and in Burundi's virtual economic isolation. However, the threat of a humanitarian crisis prompted the sanctions co-ordinating committee, meeting in Arusha in September, to authorize a relaxation of the embargo to facilitate the distribution of food and medical aid. An attempt by Buyoya later that month to secure the repeal of all sanctions by announcing an end to the ban on political parties and the restoration of the Assemblée nationale was received with scepticism by opponents, in view of the continued suspension of the Constitution and Buyoya's refusal to address preconditions to the ending of sanctions that required the organization of unconditional peace negotiations. In October Buyoya agreed to enter into negotiations with the CNDD, but a subsequent meeting of regional leaders in Arusha decided that sanctions should be maintained until evidence emerged of constructive progress in the negotiations. This prompted the Burundian Government to withdraw the offer of unconditional dialogue with the CNDD as long as sanctions remained in place. Meanwhile, in early October some 37 deputies had attended the formal reopening of the Assemblée nationale, which was boycotted by the majority of FRODEBU deputies.

Reports emerged that the armed forces were targeting Hutus (thousands were estimated to have been killed since the coup), in an attempt to safeguard rural and border regions for Tutsi communities, to which the CNDD and other Hutu militia retaliated with attacks against military installations near Bujumbura, as well as against Tutsi civilians. A UN report on the causes of the 1993 coup, published in August, implicated two of Buyoya's military leaders, who were subsequently dismissed. By late 1996 the military action in eastern Zaire had led to the repatriation of 30,000 Burundians and had severely weakened FDD fighting capacity, although some activists continued the fight from Tanzania. In December Amnesty International denounced what it termed a 'policy of systematic extermination of a section of population' on the part of the armed forces, alleging that the army had massacred as many as 500 Hutu civilians in Butaganza, in the north-west, earlier in the month. Such reports were denied by the Burundian Government. In January 1997 the office of the UN High Commissioner for Refugees (UNHCR) reported that the army had massed more than 100,000 (mainly Hutu) civilians in camps, as part of a 'regroupment' scheme, which the authorities claimed to be an initiative to protect villagers in areas of rebel activity. By mid-1997, according to government figures, some 200,000 civilians had been 'regrouped' in about 50 camps, while non-governmental organizations variously estimated the number of civilians affected at 350,000–500,000.

The trial began in May 1997 of some 79 military officers accused of involvement in the October 1993 coup attempt. (In May 1999 five of those accused were sentenced to death and a number of others received prison terms; however, all of the senior officers, including Bikomagu, were acquitted.) At the end of July 1997 it was reported that six people convicted of involvement in acts of genocide perpetrated in 1993 had been executed. During July–August the Burundian courts issued 30 death sentences in relation to such crimes; 10 defendants were sentenced to life imprisonment, and 19 to 20 years' custody.

Six ministers were replaced in a reorganization of Ndimira's Government in May 1997, and in August Ambroise Niyonsaba was allocated the new post of Minister of the Peace Process. Civil unrest continued later that year, and on 1 January 1998 an attack on Bujumbura airport by more than 1,000 Hutu rebels resulted in at least 250 deaths. Similar attacks, although on a smaller scale, continued during early 1998. On 18 February the second stage of the inter-Burundian peace talks was held. The discussions, which had been delayed following the death of the Minister of Defence in a helicopter crash, were attended by representatives of the Government, the political parties and the Assemblée nationale, and prominent civilians. The CNDD, however, suspended its participation in protest at human rights violations on the part of the Government. Following the announcement in late February that a regional summit, held in Kampala, Uganda, had voted to maintain the sanctions on Burundi, President Buyoya announced the impending repeal of travel restrictions that had been applied to former Presidents Bagaza and Ntibantunganya, and to the Speaker of the Assemblée nationale, Ngendakumana. In mid-March the courts dismissed a case against Ngendakumana, on charges of genocide.

Following negotiations between the Government and the Assemblée nationale concerning the expiry of FRODEBU's electoral mandate in June 1998, Buyoya and Ngendakumana publicly signed a political accord, and a new transitional Constitution was promulgated on 6 June. The new charter provided for institutional reforms, including the creation of two vice-presidencies to replace the office of Prime Minister, the enlargement of the Assemblée nationale from 81 to 121 seats, and the creation of a seven-member Constitutional Court, which was installed on 24 June. In accordance with the transitional Constitution, Buyoya was inaugurated as President on 11 June. On the following day the two Vice-Presidents were appointed: Frédérique Bavuginyumvira, a senior member of FRODEBU, who was allocated responsibility for political and administrative affairs, and Mathias Sinamenye (a Tutsi and hitherto the Governor of the Central Bank), with responsibility for economic and social issues. A new 22-member Council of Ministers included 13 Hutus and eight Tutsis. The newly enlarged Assemblée nationale, which was inaugurated in mid-July, incorporated nine representatives from smaller political parties (with four further seats remaining provisionally vacant), together with 27 civilian representatives and 21 new representatives of FRODEBU to replace those who had been killed or had fled into exile. On 22 July the inter-Burundian peace talks were adjourned at the request of the Government, as the parties were unable to reach agreement on the structure of the negotiations.

Meanwhile, little substantive progress was made in regional efforts to bring about direct peace talks between the Buyoya Government and its opponents. Consultations in Arusha in December 1996 were attended by representatives of the Buyoya administration, FRODEBU, the CNDD, PALIPEHUTU and other organizations. However, the Government's stipulation that fighting must be brought to a formal halt prior to any negotiations effectively precluded direct contacts. The first of a series of national discussions on the peace process began in January 1997, attended by academics, religious leaders, politicians and representatives of civil society. However, prominent political organizations, notably FRODEBU, refused to attend the talks. Buyoya attended the fourth Arusha summit meeting on the Burundi conflict in April. The leaders of the Great Lakes countries agreed to ease economic sanctions in the interest of alleviating conditions for the civilian population. The full revocation of sanctions was made dependent on the opening of direct,

unconditional peace talks between the Burundian Government and opposition.

Initial optimism that inter-party discussions, commencing in Arusha in August 1997, would achieve progress in ending the political crisis diminished as the Buyoya Government became increasingly hostile to the mediation of Nyerere, claiming him to be biased in favour of the opposition. After it became evident that the sanctions would not be revoked immediately upon the opening of negotiations, the Buyoya Government announced that it would not be attending the Arusha talks, stating that it required more time to prepare, and the session was subsequently abandoned. Nyerere openly condemned the stance of the Buyoya regime, appealing for wider international assistance in resolving the crisis. A meeting of regional leaders, convened (in Buyoya's absence) in the Tanzanian capital in early September, reaffirmed its support for Nyerere's mediation, criticized the Burundian Government for its intransigence, and resolved to maintain all existing sanctions.

In May 1998 dissension between the political and military wings of the CNDD resulted in a division of the organization, into a faction headed by Nyangoma (which retained the name CNDD) and a larger faction comprising most of its armed forces, led by the FDD Chief of Staff, Jean-Bosco Ndayikengurukiye (which became known as the CNDD—FDD). In that month Nyerere conducted discussions with Burundian political leaders, in preparation for the peace negotiations, which commenced in mid-June in Arusha. At the talks, which were attended by 17 groupings involved in the conflict, it was agreed that the next round of discussions would take place on 20 July, and that all factions would suspend hostilities on that date. The Government, however, expressed reservations concerning the cease-fire, citing the need to maintain state security. The CNDD—FDD also refused to accept the cease-fire. It was agreed that the negotiations were to continue for three months, and that commissions would be established to negotiate each of the main issues of contention. At the July discussions, however, little progress was made. Prior to the third round of negotiations, division emerged in UPRONA between those who supported Mukasi's opposition to the Arusha talks and those who were prepared to negotiate with the Hutu opposition. In October some moderate members of the UPRONA central committee elected a rival Chairman, Dr Luc Rukingama, the Minister of Information and a supporter of Buyoya. Mukasi was arrested in August, following outspoken criticism of the Government. The commissions were duly established during further discussions in October and January 1999.

At a regional summit meeting, which took place in Arusha in January 1999, following an appeal from the UN Security Council earlier in the month, regional Heads of State voted to suspend the economic sanctions, in recognition of the progress made in the peace negotiations, although they emphasized that the eventual lifting of the sanctions would be dependent on the progress made at the peace talks. In May Buyoya announced his proposals for reconciliation; these included a 10-year transitional period during which he would occupy the presidency for the first five years and a Hutu representative would assume the post for the second five years. The plan also envisaged the extension of the Assemblée nationale to include Hutu rebel factions, the creation of an upper legislative chamber, the establishment of communal police forces, to resolve the issue of Tutsi-dominated defence and security forces, and the establishment of a national truth commission. Buyoya's opponents dismissed the proposals, citing his failure to honour his commitment to return the country swiftly to civilian rule in 1996 and the absence of any reference to elections in his plan. A round of discussions took place in Arusha in July; Nyerere criticized the lack of progress achieved at the negotiations, and the failure of the commissions to reach agreement. The absence from the negotiations of the two most significant rebel movements, the CNDD—FDD and an armed wing of PALIPEHUTU, known as Forces nationales de libération (FNL), was also viewed as a major impediment to agreement on a peace plan. (The CNDD had rejoined the discussions.) Further talks at Arusha in September were impeded by the escalation of violence throughout the country, particularly around Bujumbura. Subsequent discussions were postponed, owing to the death of Nyerere in mid-October. All the participating parties expressed their commitment to the process, and nine organizations, including FRODEBU and UPRONA, created a movement for peace and solidarity, the Convergence nationale pour la paix et réconciliation (CNPR), which proposed that negotiations continue on neutral territory, owing to the alleged role of Tanzania in sheltering Hutu rebels. In December regional Heads of State, meeting in Arusha, nominated the former President of South Africa, Nelson Mandela, as the new mediator of the peace negotiations.

Unrest continued throughout 1999 and increased in the second half of the year. The escalation of Hutu-led attacks around the capital led to the alleged rearming of Tutsi militias by the Tutsi-dominated security forces, and the enforced relocation of more than 320,000 Hutus into 'regroupment' camps. While the authorities claimed that the camps provided protection for the civilian population, the UN, the USA and the EU all expressed concern at the Government's policy of enforced 'regroupment' of Hutus. In mid-October, following an ambush in which two UN aid workers were killed attempting to inspect a 'regroupment' camp, the UN announced that it was to restrict its operations and confine its staff to Bujumbura.

In June 1999 a new penal code was adopted by the Assemblée nationale; the code, which entered into effect on 1 January 2000, protected civil rights and liberties, and introduced controls to prohibit torture and reduce the length of detention. In January 2000 a major cabinet reorganization was effected. Peace negotiations (the first to be attended by Mandela) resumed in Arusha in late February. Mandela criticized Tutsi domination of public office and urged equal representation of Hutu and Tutsi in the armed forces, while also denouncing Hutu rebel attacks on civilians. At a further round of discussions, which commenced in Arusha in late March, agreement was reached on draft proposals for a new ethnically balanced armed force. (Nevertheless, government forces continued attacks against Hutu rebel positions, prompting fierce fighting south of Bujumbura.) In April Mandela visited Burundi for the first time, meeting government and militia leaders. Following a further meeting with Buyoya in Johannesburg, South Africa, in June, Mandela announced that the Burundian President had agreed to ensure equal representation of Hutu and Tutsi in the armed forces and the closure of 'regroupment' camps by the end of July.

In July 2000 Ndayikengurukiye, as leader of the CNDD—FDD, for the first time accepted an invitation by Mandela to participate in the peace negotiations. In the same month the drafting of a peace accord was finalized; the agreement stipulated the terms for the establishment of a transitional government for a period of three years, the integration of former Hutu rebels into the armed forces, and the creation of an electoral system that would ensure power-sharing between the Tutsi and the Hutu. At a summit meeting, which was attended by several regional Heads of State in Arusha, negotiating groups were presented with the draft peace agreement, which included compromise proposals on unresolved issues. However, the CNDD—FDD demanded the release by the authorities of political prisoners, the fulfilment of the pledge to dismantle the 'regroupment' camps, and bilateral negotiations with the armed forces, as a precondition to the cessation of hostilities. (The FNL had again failed to attend the discussions.) On 28 August the peace agreement was formally endorsed by representatives of the Government, the Assemblée nationale, seven Hutu political associations and seven Tutsi parties. The remaining three Tutsi groups that had attended the previous negotiations subsequently signed the accord at cease-fire discussions, which took place in Nairobi, Kenya, in late September, following assurances by Mandela that measures would be taken to ensure that the Hutu rebels cease hostilities. At the same time an Implementation and Monitoring Committee, comprising representatives of the negotiating parties, and international and civil society representatives, was established. Following the conclusion of these discussions, a statement was issued, demanding that the CNDD—FDD and FNL suspend rebel activity and sign the peace agreement.

In late 2000 negotiations on the establishment of power-sharing structures continued. In January 2001 14 of the 19 signatories of the peace accord agreed on the composition of a new Assemblée nationale, which would allocate Hutu parties 60% and Tutsi 40% representation in the legislature. Six candidates for the transitional presidency had emerged; however, the negotiating groups had failed to agree to return Buyoya to the office. Hostilities between government troops and Hutu rebels continued, and at the end of February the FNL launched an offensive on the northern outskirts of Bujumbura, which resulted in some 50,000 civilians fleeing to the centre of the capital. Government forces had regained control of Bujumbura by early March, but heavy fighting continued in regions outlying the capital. Later that month CNDD—FDD forces launched a

major attack against the principal town of Gitega, 100 km east of Bujumbura, which was repelled by government troops. On 18 April, while Buyoya was attending peace negotiations with the CNDD—FDD leadership in Gabon, Tutsi army officers seized control of the state radio station in Bujumbura and announced that the Government had been overthrown. Troops loyal to Buyoya rapidly suppressed the coup attempt, and about 40 members of the armed forces were subsequently arrested in connection with the uprising.

In June 2001 Mandela announced that a regional summit meeting was to be convened in Arusha on 23 July, in an effort to resolve the impasse in the peace process. On 22 July disaffected members of the armed forces staged an abortive coup attempt, kidnapping a senior military officer and endeavouring to seize the central prison in Bujumbura (where the instigators of the failed coup in April were in detention). Troops loyal to Buyoya counter-attacked the rebels, killing three and arresting many others. Nevertheless, the peace summit of regional Heads of State, chaired by Mandela, proceeded as scheduled, and the signatory groups to the Arusha accord finally reached agreement on the nature of the transitional leadership. A new multi-party transitional government, according the Hutu and Tutsi ethnic groups balanced representation, was to be installed on 1 November. The Secretary-General of FRODEBU, Domitien Ndayizeye, was nominated to the vice-presidency of the transitional administration. Buyoya was to continue in the office of President for 18 months (from 1 November), after which time he was to transfer the office to Ndayizeye. However, the CNDD—FDD and the FNL persisted in rejecting the peace accord and announced that they would continue hostilities against the transitional authorities, while one of the principal Tutsi opposition parties, the Parti pour le redressement national (PARENA), refused to join the proposed new government.

Following further negotiations in Arusha and in Pretoria, South Africa, in early October 2001, agreement was reached on the composition of the new 26-member transitional Government. FRODEBU and UPRONA were the most dominant parties in the new power-sharing administration, while portfolios were allocated to a further 13 parties that had signed the Arusha agreement. (In total, Hutus received 14 of the 26 ministerial posts.) On 29 October a transitional Constitution, which was drafted by a technical law commission and included principles incorporated in the previous Constitution of 1992 and the Arusha peace accord, was formally adopted by the Assemblée nationale. The new transitional Constitution provided for the establishment of an upper legislative chamber, the Sénat, and four new commissions to assist in the peace and reconciliation process. Former combatants belonging to political movements were to be integrated into the armed and security forces during the transitional period. Also at the end of October the South African Government dispatched troops to Burundi as part of a proposed 700-member contingent, in an effort, initiated by Mandela, to enforce national security and support the transitional authorities. In a reversal to the peace efforts, however, the CNDD—FDD had divided, with the emergence of a new faction, led by Jean-Pierre Nkurunziza, which commanded the support of most of the movement's combatants.

On 1 November 2001 the newly established transitional Government was officially installed, as scheduled. However, the FNL continued to launch attacks on the outskirts of Bujumbura, despite the deployment of the South African troops. In January 2002 the nomination to the transitional Assemblée nationale of a number of deputies, representing civil society and 14 of the political parties that had signed the peace agreement, was endorsed by the Constitutional Court. (FRODEBU and UPRONA retained their seats in the chamber.) Jean Minani, the Chairman of FRODEBU, was subsequently elected Speaker of the Assemblée nationale. At the end of that month the Constitutional Court approved the establishment of a 51-member Sénat.

Efforts to bring about a cease-fire in the civil conflict continued, with a series of meetings in Pretoria in February 2002, which were attended by representatives of the Government and armed forces, and both factions of the CNDD—FDD (but not by the FNL). In March a further regional summit meeting was convened in Dar es Salaam, which the FNL and Nkurunziza's CNDD—FDD faction again boycotted. In response to the continued lack of progress in peace efforts, FRODEBU issued a statement in April condemning the Government's failure to suppress the rebel militia. The South African Deputy Prime Minister, Jacob Zuma (who had replaced Mandela as the principal mediator), hosted a new series of consultations between the militia groups and the Burundi Government in Pretoria later that month. However, both the FNL and Nkurunziza's faction failed to participate, and Nkurunziza subsequently announced his opposition to Zuma's involvement in the cease-fire process. Further discussions between government and rebel delegations regarding the implementation of a cease-fire were scheduled to take place in Dar es Salaam in August. Early that month, following an attempt to remove the FNL 'hardline' leader, Agathon Rwasa, from his post, the movement divided: a new faction, led by Alain Mugabarabona, emerged, while Rwasa remained in control of most of the combatants. The peace negotiations, which commenced on 12 August, were attended for the first time by Mugabarabona's FNL faction and both CNDD—FDD factions. At the end of that month, however, renewed fighting between FNL supporters and government troops was reported on the outskirts of Bujumbura.

A summit meeting on Burundi (attended by regional Presidents), which was convened in Dar es Salaam on 7 October 2002, resulted in a cease-fire agreement between the Government, and Ndayikengurukiye's CNDD—FDD and Mugabarabona's FNL faction. Negotiations with the main CNDD—FDD continued, amid hostilities between government and rebel forces in central and northern Burundi. The authorities placed Bagaza (now the leader of PARENA) under house arrest, on suspicion of involvement with several attacks in Bujumbura. Also in November Maj.-Gen. Vincent Niyungeko, hitherto Chief of Staff of the armed forces, became the new Minister of Defence.

On 3 December 2002, following mediation from Uganda and South Africa, the Government finally reached a cease-fire agreement with the CNDD—FDD, which was scheduled to enter into effect at the end of that month. Under the Arusha agreement, the rebel factions were to be reconstituted as political parties, while Buyoya was to relinquish the presidency to Ndayizeye at the end of April 2003. However, the cease-fire agreement was not imposed at the end of December 2002, owing to delays in the arrival of observers from the AU. Hostilities between government and CNDD—FDD forces continued, particularly in Gitega, and Nkurunziza, attributing responsibility for the failure to implement the accord to the Government, suspended further discussions. In February 2003 the AU Cease-fire Observer Mission, comprising 35 monitors (from Burkina Faso, Mali, Togo and Tunisia), arrived in Bujumbura, with a mandate to monitor the peace agreement. In late April the first 100 members of an AU Mission in Burundi (AMIB) arrived in the country; the contingent (which was to comprise troops from South Africa, Ethiopia and Mozambique) was to assist in the enforcement of the cease-fire between the Government and the rebel factions. Despite the reported reluctance of Buyoya to relinquish the presidency, Ndayizeye was officially inaugurated as President for the scheduled period of 18 months on 30 April, thereby improving the prospects for sustained peace. On the same day Alphonse-Marie Kadege (who in December 2002 had replaced Rukingama as Chairman of the more moderate UPRONA faction) was appointed Vice-President. On 5 May Ndayizeye appointed a representative of Mugabarabona's FNL faction and Ndayikengurukiye's CNDD—FDD faction to the transitional Council of Ministers, as part of a government reorganization. In early May the Government announced that it had ended the ban on PARENA activities, imposed in November 2002.

On 7 July 2003 hostilities escalated into a major offensive by FNL forces against Bujumbura; by the time government troops had restored some control in the capital, four days later, some 170 people had been killed, and 6,000–7,000 civilians displaced, according to preliminary UN estimates. In mid-July the UN announced its decision to withdraw non-essential personnel from the capital, in response to the increasingly poor security situation. On 21 July, at further peace discussions in Dar es Salaam, the Government and Nkurunziza's CNDD—FDD faction reiterated their commitment to implementing the December 2002 cease-fire agreement. In late August the Assemblée nationale adopted legislation granting temporary immunity from prosecution (with regard to political crimes committed from July 1962) to political leaders returning from exile to participate in transitional organs of government. A regional summit meeting, convened in Dar es Salaam in mid-September, ended in failure, without agreement being reached between the Government and Nkurunziza's CNDD—FDD on political power-sharing. Further clashes occurred between FNL and government forces north of Bujumbura later that month, and it was reported that some 47,500 civilians had been displaced from the region during September.

On 8 October 2003, after four days of peace discussions in Pretoria, South Africa, under the mediation of Zuma and the South African President, Thabo Mbeki, Ndayizeye signed an agreement with Nkurunziza on political, military and security power-sharing. The CNDD—FDD faction was to be allocated four ministerial portfolios, 40% of army officers' posts, the vice-presidency of the Assemblée nationale, three provincial governorships, and two ambassadorial posts, while former CNDD—FDD combatants were to be demobilized. Mugabarabona and Ndayikengurukiye issued a statement condemning the accord, which was finally approved by the legislature on 22 October. Also in October AMIB reached its maximum strength of 3,128, following the deployment of the final peace-keeping forces from Ethiopia and Mozambique (which had been delayed, owing to lack of funding). On 16 November the Government and Nkurunziza's CNDD—FDD signed a final comprehensive peace agreement, endorsing the accords of December 2002, and of October and November 2003. On the same day regional Heads of State issued an ultimatum to Rwasa (as leader of the only rebel faction to remain in conflict with the Government) to join the peace process. On 23 November Ndayizeye reorganized the Government of national unity to include four representatives of Nkurunziza's CNDD—FDD faction, including Nkurunziza himself, who was appointed to the third most senior post, Minister of State with responsibility for Good Governance and State Inspection. In early December Nkurunziza arrived in Bujumbura for the first time since 1993, and it was reported that some 6,000 of his former combatants had been assembled for disarmament.

At the end of December 2003 the Holy See's apostolic nuncio to Burundi, Michael Courtney, died after being shot in a road ambush at Minago, 50 km south of Bujumbura. Rwasa's FNL faction denied accusations by the Government that it was responsible for the incident, and subsequently agreed to enter into peace discussions. On 7 January 2004 Ndayizeye established a 33-member Joint Military High Command, comprising 20 members of the existing armed forces and 13 of the former CNDD—FDD. In mid-January further fighting between government troops and FNL combatants in Bujumbura Rural Province resulted in the displacement of some 10,000 civilians. Later that month negotiations between Ndayizeye and an FNL delegation, convened in Oisterwijk, Netherlands, ended without agreement on a cease-fire being reached. The FNL continued to refuse to recognize the transitional authorities, and clashes between government and rebel forces continued in early February. In late March the AU renewed the mandate of AMIB (which was due to expire at the beginning of April) for a further month, and urged the UN Security Council to authorize the deployment of UN peace-keeping troops in Burundi. In April Nkurunziza announced the suspension of CNDD—FDD participation in the transitional institutions, on the grounds that the Government had failed to implement the November 2003 power-sharing accord. On 21 May the UN Security Council approved the replacement of the AMIB mission with a UN contingent, the Opération des Nations Unies au Burundi (ONUB). ONUB, which had a maximum strength of 5,650 military personnel, officially commenced deployment on 1 June.

In July 2004 the International Monitoring Committee charged with overseeing the implementation of the power-sharing arrangements urged political parties to reach consensus in efforts to adopt a new constitution (necessary to allow elections to proceed). A draft power-sharing accord (which provided for a Government and Assemblée nationale of 60% Hutu and 40% Tutsi composition) was reached in Pretoria later that month, but was rejected by predominantly Tutsi parties. (Also in July the CNDD—FDD announced the resumption of its participation in the Government of national unity.) On 6 August the accord, which would allow elections to proceed on 31 October, was signed in Pretoria by 20 of the 30 delegations, with Tutsi parties, notably UPRONA, refusing to accept the proposed power-sharing arrangements. Despite continuing speculation that the elections would be postponed, a five-member Commission électorale nationale indépendante (CENI) was established at the end of August. In early September initial regional peace discussions were conducted in Bujumbura. Following the massacre of refugees at the Gatumba camp in August (see below), however, government forces launched attacks against FNL troop positions during that month.

In September 2004 the International Criminal Court (ICC, see p. 275) announced that Burundi had ratified the signatory treaty, allowing prosecutions for civilian massacres to proceed.

Meanwhile, the main political groupings continued to fail to reach agreement on a proposed new Constitution, with 11 Tutsi parties, including UPRONA, objecting to the parliamentary ethnic representation vested in the draft. In mid-October the CENI announced that legislative elections, scheduled to take place at the end of that month, were to be postponed until 22 April 2005. On 20 October 2004 a new interim 'post-transitional' Constitution was officially adopted by Ndayizeye, after its approval by both chambers of the legislature. The new Constitution, which was to extend the mandate of the transitional organs of government from 1 November until the elections in April 2005, was scheduled to be endorsed at a national referendum in late November. Although five Tutsi political parties had withdrawn opposition to the Constitution, six continued to protest that it favoured the Hutu. In mid-November Ndayizeye dismissed Kadege from the office of Vice-President, owing to his public opposition to the Constitution, replacing him with Frederic Ngenzebuhoro, also of UPRONA. Later that month the CENI announced the postponement of the constitutional referendum until 22 December, citing lack of technical resources. (However, organization of the referendum was again delayed.) At the end of December the Government announced the creation of a new National Defence Force and of a new police force, comprising equal numbers of the existing Tutsi-dominated armed forces and Hutu former rebel combatants (mainly CNDD—FDD); a Tutsi was appointed head of the new army, while the post of deputy commander was allocated to a Hutu. In January 2005 both Hutu- and Tutsi-dominated political parties warned Ndayizeye against proposing amendments to the draft Constitution in order to seek re-election. Later in January the CENI again rescheduled the referendum, for 28 February.

The new Constitution, which enshrined the power-sharing principles of a Government and Assemblée nationale of 60% Hutu and 40% Tutsi composition, was endorsed at a referendum on 28 February 2005 by some 92% of votes cast (with an estimated 88% of the electorate participating in the ballot). Adoption of the Constitution was expected to allow legislative elections to proceed on 22 April, to be followed by the election of a President by the new Assemblée nationale. In late April, however, the Government announced that Ndayizeye's mandate was to be extended to allow elections to be rescheduled for 19 August, with the inauguration of a new President to take place on 26 August. In the same month the CNDD—FDD suspended participation in the Government, after Ndayizeye opposed the party's nomination to replace the Minister of the Interior (who had died in March).

The cross-border movement of vast numbers of refugees, provoked by regional ethnic and political violence, has dominated recent relations with Rwanda, Tanzania and the DRC (formerly Zaire), and has long been a matter of considerable concern to the international aid community. The uprising by Laurent-Désiré Kabila's Alliance des forces démocratiques pour la libération du Congo-Zaïre (AFDL) in eastern Zaire in January 1997 resulted in the return of large numbers of refugees to Burundi, reportedly undermining the operations from Zaire of FDD combatants. Moreover, the seizure of power by the AFDL in May was welcomed by the Buyoya regime, which moved to forge close relations with Kabila's DRC. Burundi initially denied any involvement in the civil war that commenced in the DRC in August, but by May 1999 some 3,000 Burundian troops were reported to be stationed in the east of the country, with the aim of destroying CNDD—FDD camps. (The CNDD—FDD supported the DRC Government in the civil war and used the conflict as an opportunity to regroup and rearm.) In June the DRC instituted proceedings against Burundi, together with Rwanda and Uganda, at the International Court of Justice (in The Hague, Netherlands), accusing them of acts of armed aggression in contravention of the terms of both the UN Charter and the Charter of the OAU. In early February 2001, however, the DRC abandoned proceedings against Burundi and Rwanda. In January 2002 the Burundian Government made a formal commitment to withdraw all troops (reported to number about 1,000) from the DRC, while the DRC authorities pledged to end their alliance with the CNDD—FDD. In mid-2004 intensified hostilities in eastern DRC resulted in the flight of a further 30,000 refugees to Burundi. In August some 160 Banyamulenge (Congolese Tutsi), numbering among those who had fled from Bukavu in June to take refuge in Burundi, were massacred at a refugee camp at Gatumba, near the border between the two countries. Although the FNL admitted responsibility for the atrocity (which prompted the further exodus of both Burundian

Tutsis and Banyamulenge refugees to Rwanda), the Governments of Burundi and Rwanda maintained that Hutu militia operating within the DRC were involved and threatened to resume military engagement in the country.

Meanwhile, the continued presence of large numbers of Burundian refugees in Tanzania, and increasingly strong accusations on the part of the Buyoya Government that Tanzania was supporting the Hutu rebellion, prompted tension between the two countries in mid-1997. In late August Tanzania announced that it had placed its armed forces on alert, stating that Burundian forces were mobilizing near the border in preparation for an invasion of the refugee camps. Meanwhile, the Buyoya Government's assertions that Nyerere was unduly biased in his role as mediator in the Burundian conflict further strained bilateral ties. In late 1997 Burundian allegations that the Tanzanian Government was involved in cross-border raids by Hutu militias, based in Tanzania, adversely affected relations, and in November there were reports of clashes between troops on the Tanzanian–Burundian border. In the same month Burundi's ambassador-designate to Tanzania was ordered to assume control of the Burundian embassy in Dar es Salaam, which was occupied by members of the CNDD and FRODEBU, but was arrested by the Tanzanian authorities and expelled. In 1998 bilateral relations improved slightly, and in July Tanzania agreed to the reopening of the Burundian embassy. Relations appeared to improve further in early 1999 and, following a meeting of the Burundian and Tanzanian ministers of foreign affairs, it was announced that a tripartite commission was to be established (with representatives from Burundi, Tanzania and UNHCR) to investigate allegations that armed militia groups had used Tanzania as a base from which to launch attacks on Burundi. Exchanges of fire between members of the Tanzanian armed forces and Burundian rebels on the border between the two countries were reported in September 2000. In late 2001 Tanzania denied further accusations by the Government of Burundi that Burundian rebels were operating from Tanzanian territory. At mid-2004, according to UNHCR estimates, some 757,000 Burundian refugees remained in Tanzania, with a further 20,000 in the DRC and 350 in Rwanda.

Government

Following the coup of 25 July 1996, the Constitution of March 1992 was suspended. A peace agreement, which was signed by representatives of the incumbent Government, the Assemblée nationale and 17 political groupings on 28 August 2000, provided for the installation of a transitional administration, in which power-sharing between the Hutu and Tutsi ethnic groups was guaranteed (see Recent History). A transitional Constitution, which was drafted by a technical law commission and included principles incorporated in the 1992 Constitution and the peace accord, was formally adopted on 29 October 2001. In accordance with the new Constitution, a transitional multi-party Government was installed on 1 November. Executive power was vested in the President, who was empowered to appoint the Council of Ministers. The incumbent Tutsi President remained in office for the first 18 months of a three-year transitional period; under the peace agreement, he then transferred the office to the Hutu Vice-President on 30 April 2003. The transitional Constitution vested legislative power in the 121-member Assemblée nationale (which included representatives of civil society and most of the political parties that had signed the peace agreement) and an upper chamber, the 51-member Sénat. In October 2004 a new interim 'post-transitional' Constitution was officially adopted by the President, after its approval by both chambers of the legislature. The new Constitution, which allowed the extension of the mandate of the transitional organs of government from 1 November until elections, was endorsed at a national referendum on 28 February 2005. Legislative elections were scheduled for 22 April, and were to be followed by the election of a President by the new Assemblée nationale. In April, however, the Government announced that the presidential mandate was to be extended to allow the elections to be rescheduled for 19 August, with the inauguration to take place on 26 August.

For the purposes of local government, Burundi comprises 15 provinces (administered by civilian governors), each of which is divided into districts and further subdivided into communes.

Defence

The total strength of the armed forces in August 2004 was 50,500, comprising an army of an estimated 45,000 and a paramilitary force of an estimated 5,500 gendarmes (including a

50-strong marine police force). The power-sharing agreement of August 2000 provided for the establishment of a new army, comprising equal proportions of existing government forces and former rebel combatants. At the end of 2004 the Government announced the creation of the new 30,000-member National Defence Force, which would incorporate 7,000 former rebel combatants, and of a new 20,000-member police force. Total military expenditure was estimated at 56,800m. Burundian francs (9.7% of GDP) in 2002. In April 2003 the deployment of the first members of an AU Mission in Burundi (AMIB) commenced; the contingent (which comprised mainly South African troops, with reinforcements from Ethiopia and Mozambique) was mandated to assist in the enforcement of the cease-fire between the Government and rebel factions. In May 2004 the UN Security Council approved the deployment of a Opération des Nations Unies au Burundi (ONUB), to replace AMIB. ONUB (which had a maximum authorized strength of 5,650 military personnel), totalled 5,454 uniformed personnel, supported by 506 civilian staff, at the end of 2004. Defence expenditure for 2004 was budgeted at an estimated 47,000m. Burundian francs.

Economic Affairs

In 2003, according to estimates by the World Bank, Burundi's gross national income (GNI), measured at average 2001–03 prices, was US $664m., equivalent to $100 per head (or $620 per head on an international purchasing-power parity basis). During 1990–2003, it was estimated, the population increased at an average annual rate of 2.2%, while gross domestic product (GDP) per head declined, in real terms, by an average of 3.0% per year. Overall GDP declined, in real terms, at an average annual rate of 0.9% in 1990–2003; growth in 2002 was 3.6%, but a decrease of 1.0% was recorded in 2003.

Agriculture (including forestry and fishing) contributed an estimated 49.0% of GDP in 2003. An estimated 89.9% of the labour force were employed in the sector in mid-2003. The principal cash crops are coffee (which accounted for 50.0% of export earnings in 2001) and tea. The main subsistence crops are cassava and sweet potatoes. Although Burundi is traditionally self-sufficient in food crops, population displacement as a result of the political crisis resulted in considerable disruption in the sector. The livestock-rearing sector was also severely affected by the civil war. During 1990–2003, according to the World Bank, agricultural GDP declined at an average annual rate of 0.1%, and it declined by 0.8% in 2003.

Industry (comprising mining, manufacturing, construction and utilities) engaged 21.8% of the employed labour force in 1991 and contributed an estimated 19.0% of GDP in 2003. Industrial GDP increased at an average annual rate of 0.3% in 1990–2002; growth of 25.4% was recorded in 2002.

Mining and power engaged 0.1% of the employed labour force in 1990 and, according to the IMF, contributed an estimated 1.1% of GDP in 2002. Gold (alluvial), tin, tungsten and columbo-tantalite are mined in small quantities, although much activity has hitherto been outside the formal sector. Burundi has important deposits of nickel (estimated at 5% of world reserves), vanadium and uranium. In addition, petroleum deposits have been discovered. The GDP of the mining sector increased at an average annual rate of 3.4% in 1997–2001, according to IMF estimates; growth in 2001 was an estimated 14.3%.

Manufacturing engaged 1.2% of the employed labour force in 1990 and, according to the IMF, contributed an estimated 8.4% of GDP in 2002. The sector consists largely of the processing of foodstuffs and agricultural products (coffee, cotton, tea and the extraction of vegetable oils), and of textiles and leather products. Manufacturing GDP increased at an average annual rate of 2.5% in 1997–2001, according to IMF estimates. Manufacturing GDP increased by 3.2% in 2000 and remained constant in 2001.

Energy is derived principally from hydroelectric power (an estimated 38.6% of electricity consumed in 2001 was imported). Peat is also exploited as an additional source of energy. Imports of refined petroleum products comprised 12.4% of the value of imports in 2001.

The services sector contributed an estimated 32.0% of GDP in 2003, but engaged only 4.4% of the employed labour force in 1990. According to the World Bank, the GDP of the services sector declined at an average annual rate of 0.2% in 1990–2002, but increased by 3.5% in 2002.

In 2003 Burundi recorded an estimated trade deficit of US $92.5m., and there was a deficit of $37.3m. on the current account of the balance of payments. In 2001 the principal source of imports (15.5%) was Belgium; other important suppliers in that year were Saudi Arabia, France and Kenya. The principal

market for exports in 2001 (31.0%) was the United Kingdom; other important markets were Belgium, Germany, Kenya and Rwanda. The main imports in 2001 were refined petroleum products, road vehicles and parts, medicinal and pharmaceutical products, and cereals and cereal preparations. The principal exports in that year were coffee, tea and gold.

In 2003 the budget deficit was 32,871.2m. Burundian francs, equivalent to some 5.0% of GDP. Burundi's external debt at the end of 2002 was US $1,204m., of which $1,095m. was long-term public debt. In that year the cost of debt-servicing was equivalent to 59.0% of revenue from the export of goods and services. The annual rate of inflation averaged 14.2% in 1992–2003. Consumer prices increased by 16.0% in 2003.

Burundi, with its neighbours Rwanda and the Democratic Republic of the Congo, is a member of the Economic Community of the Great Lakes Countries (CEPGL, see p. 374). Burundi is also a member of the Common Market for Eastern and Southern Africa (COMESA, see p. 179), and of the International Coffee Organization (see p. 370).

Burundi's acute economic decline after 1993, owing to the severe political upheaval and accompanying population displacement, was further exacerbated by the regional economic sanctions imposed following the coup of July 1996. In addition, the decline in the international price of coffee (the principal export crop) resulted in substantial losses in the sector from 1997. By early 1999, when sanctions were revoked, official reserves had become severely depleted, and the Government was obliged to borrow heavily in order to meet its financing requirements. As a result, domestic and foreign debts had accumulated at an unsustainable level, and Burundi was defaulting on its debt-servicing obligations, while smuggling and tax evasion were largely unchecked. In May 2000 the IMF and the World Bank announced the resumption of international credit to Burundi. Following the signing of a peace agreement in August of that year (see Recent History), a transitional power-sharing Government was installed in November 2001. Although hostilities continued in part of the country, further agreements improved prospects for reaching a permanent peace settlement. In January 2004 the IMF commended the Government's economic programme for 2002–03, which continued a strong recovery in 2001–02, and approved a three-year Poverty Reduction and Growth Facility (PRGF). Reduction of the unsustainably high external debt-servicing burden was a priority for the Government, and the country was expected to qualify for debt relief under the enhanced initiative of the IMF and World Bank for heavily indebted poor countries. Considerable funds pledged at an international donor conference, convened in Belgium earlier in January 2004, under the auspices of the UN Development Programme and the Belgian Government, were to support a number of reconstruction programmes, including the resettlement of refugees and internally displaced persons. The Government's main short-term objective under the PRGF-supported programme was to increase productivity in the agricultural sector, and, in particular, implement reforms of the coffee sector. In September 2004 the legislature approved a revised budget, which projected significantly increased expenditure, allocated to the establishment of a new expanded armed force (officially announced at the end of that year), demobilization of former rebel combatants and preparations for elections. In January 2005 the IMF, completing the first review of Burundi's progress under the PRGF-supported programme, granted the Government's request for waivers of non-observance of performance criteria and approved a further financial disbursement. Despite higher than expected growth in 2004, fiscal slippages, which reflected higher petroleum prices and spending associated with the peace process, together with the effects of revenue losses from the coffee sector, were reported. Also in January 2005 the Government introduced a temporary tax to combat drought-related famine in the north-east of the country.

Education

Education is provided free of charge. Kirundi is the language of instruction in primary schools, while French is used in secondary schools. Primary education, which is officially compulsory, begins at seven years of age and lasts for six years. Secondary education begins at the age of 13 and lasts for up to seven years, comprising a first cycle of four years and a second of three years. In 2000/01, according to UNESCO estimates, 54% of children in the relevant age-group (males 59%; females 49%) were enrolled at primary schools. Enrolment at secondary schools in that year was equivalent to only an estimated 10% of the population in the appropriate age-group (males 12%; females 9%). There is one university, in Bujumbura; in 1998 5,037 students were enrolled. Expenditure on education by the central Government in 2002 was estimated at 23,000m. Burundian francs (equivalent to 15.2% of total government expenditure).

Public Holidays

2005: 1 January (New Year's Day), 5 February (Unity Day), 28 March (Easter Monday), 1 May (Labour Day), 5 May (Ascension Day), 1 July (Independence Day), 15 August (Assumption), 18 September (Victory of UPRONA Party), 13 October (Rwagasore Day), 21 October (Ndadaye Day), 1 November (All Saints' Day), 25 December (Christmas).

2006: 1 January (New Year's Day), 5 February (Unity Day), 17 April (Easter Monday), 1 May (Labour Day), 25 May (Ascension Day), 1 July (Independence Day), 15 August (Assumption), 18 September (Victory of UPRONA Party), 13 October (Rwagasore Day), 21 October (Ndadaye Day), 1 November (All Saints' Day), 25 December (Christmas).

Weights and Measures

The metric system is in force.

Statistical Survey

Area and Population

AREA, POPULATION AND DENSITY

Area (sq km)	27,834*
Population (census results)†	
15–16 August 1979	4,028,420
16–30 August 1990	
Males	2,473,599
Females	2,665,474
Total	5,139,073
Population (UN estimates at mid-year)‡	
2001	6,412,000
2002	6,602,000
2003	6,825,000
Density (per sq km) at mid-2003	245.2

* 10,747 sq miles.
† Excluding adjustment for underenumeration.
‡ Source: UN, *World Population Prospects: The 2002 Revision.*

PRINCIPAL TOWNS: Bujumbura (capital), population 235,440 (census result, August 1990). *1978:* Gitega 15,943 (Source: Banque de la République du Burundi). *Mid-2003* (urban population, incl. suburbs): Bujumbura 378,397 (Source: UN, *World Urbanization Prospects: The 2003 Revision*).

BIRTHS AND DEATHS
(UN estimates, annual averages)

	1985–90	1990–95	1995–2000
Birth rate (per 1,000)	47.8	45.8	43.1
Death rate (per 1,000)	19.5	23.0	22.2

Source: UN, *World Population Prospects: The 2002 Revision.*

Expectation of life (WHO estimates, years at birth): 40.8 (males 38.7; females 43.0) in 2002 (Source: WHO, *World Health Report*).

ECONOMICALLY ACTIVE POPULATION*
(persons aged 10 years and over, 1990 census)

	Males	Females	Total
Agriculture, hunting, forestry and fishing	1,153,890	1,420,553	2,574,443
Mining and quarrying	1,146	39	1,185
Manufacturing	24,120	9,747	33,867
Electricity, gas and water	1,847	74	1,921
Construction	19,447	290	19,737
Trade, restaurants and hotels	19,667	6,155	25,822
Transport, storage and communications	8,193	311	8,504
Financing, insurance, real estate and business services	1,387	618	2,005
Community, social and personal services	68,905	16,286	85,191
Activities not adequately defined	8,653	4,617	13,270
Total labour force	1,307,255	1,458,690	2,765,945

* Figures exclude persons seeking work for the first time, totalling 13,832 (males 9,608, females 4,224), but include other unemployed persons.

Source: UN, *Demographic Yearbook*.

Mid-2003 (estimates in '000): Agriculture, etc. 3,234; Total 3,598 (Source: FAO).

Health and Welfare

KEY INDICATORS

Total fertility rate (children per woman, 2002)	6.8
Under-5 mortality rate (per 1,000 live births, 2003)	190
HIV/AIDS (% of persons aged 15–49, 2003)	6.0
Physicians (per 1,000 head, 1993)	0.06
Hospital beds (per 1,000 head, 1991)	0.66
Health expenditure (2001): US $ per head (PPP)	19
Health expenditure (2001): % of GDP	3.6
Health expenditure (2001): public (% of total)	59.0
Access to water (% of persons, 2002)	79
Access to sanitation (% of persons, 2002)	36
Human Development Index (2002): ranking	173
Human Development Index (2002): value	0.339

For sources and definitions, see explanatory note on p. vi.

Agriculture

PRINCIPAL CROPS
('000 metric tons)

	2001	2002	2003*
Wheat	8.7	8.7	8.7
Rice (paddy)	60.9	62.6	63.0
Maize	124.4	126.8	127.0
Millet	10.0†	10.7	10.7
Sorghum	69.1	73.2	73.5
Potatoes	27.3	28.0	28.0
Sweet potatoes	780.9	833.5	835.0
Cassava (Manioc)	712.7	749.9	750.0
Taro (Coco yam)	84.7	85.7	85.7
Yams	9.9	9.9	10.0
Sugar cane	200*	176	200
Dry beans	248.9	245.3	245.0
Dry peas	33.2*	33.3	33.5
Groundnuts (in shell)*	8.8	8.8	8.8
Oil palm fruit	9.5†	11.0†	13.0
Vegetables (incl. melons)*	250	250	250
Bananas and plantains	1,548.9	1,603.0	1,600
Other fruits*	85	85	85
Coffee (green)	15.8	36.0	20.1†
Tea (made)	9.0	6.6	6.6

* FAO estimate(s).
† Unofficial figure.

Source: FAO.

LIVESTOCK
('000 head, year ending September)

	2001	2002	2003*
Cattle	315*	324	325
Pigs*	70	70	70
Sheep	230*	230	230
Goats*	750	750	750
Poultry*	4,300	4,300	4,300

* FAO estimate(s).

Source: FAO.

LIVESTOCK PRODUCTS
(FAO estimates, '000 metric tons)

	2001	2002	2003
Beef and veal	9.1	9.1	9.1
Mutton and lamb	1.1	1.0	1.0
Goat meat	2.9	2.9	2.9
Pig meat	4.2	4.2	4.2
Poultry meat	6.1	6.1	6.1
Cows' milk	19.3	19.3	19.3
Sheep's milk	0.6	0.6	0.7
Goats' milk	8.4	8.4	8.4
Poultry eggs	3.0	3.0	3.0
Cattle hides (fresh)	1.8	1.8	1.8

Source: FAO.

Forestry

ROUNDWOOD REMOVALS
(FAO estimates, '000 cubic metres, excl. bark)

	2001	2002	2003
Sawlogs, veneer logs and logs for sleepers	266	266	266
Other industrial wood	67	67	67
Fuel wood	7,952	8,095	8,241
Total	8,285	8,428	8,574

Source: FAO.

SAWNWOOD PRODUCTION
(FAO estimates, '000 cubic metres, incl. railway sleepers)

	1998	1999	2000
Coniferous (softwood)	7	17	18
Broadleaved (hardwood)	26	63	65
Total	33	80	83

Figures for 2001–03 assumed to be unchanged from 2000 (FAO estimates).
Source: FAO.

Fishing

(metric tons, live weight)

	2000	2001	2002*
Capture	17,315	8,964	9,000
Freshwater perches	3,070	1,657	1,660
Dagaas	10,839	6,138	6,160
Aquaculture	100	100*	100
Total catch (incl. others)	17,415	9,064*	9,100

* FAO estimate(s).
Source: FAO.

Mining

(metric tons)

	2000	2001	2002
Tin ore*	7	4	—
Tantalum and niobium (columbium) concentrates†	31.2	122.5	72.4
Gold (kilograms)*	—	415	483
Kaolin	1,500	—	—
Peat‡	4,088	6,816	6,977

* Figures refer to the metal content of ores.
† The estimated tantalum content (in metric tons) was: 10.0 in 2000; 39.4 in 2001; 17.7 in 2002.
‡ Reported on basis of fiscal year beginning 1 May.

Source: US Geological Survey.

Industry

SELECTED PRODUCTS
('000 metric tons, unless otherwise indicated)

	1999	2000	2001*
Beer ('000 hectolitres)	984.1	891.6	702.2
Soft drinks ('000 hectolitres)	127.0	119.9	94.4
Cottonseed oil ('000 litres)	111.5	104.4	86.8
Sugar	20.6	18.3	18.2
Paint	0.4	0.4	0.5
Insecticides	1.2	0.2	—
Soap	2.9	3.2	3.2
Bottles	3.0	—	—
Blankets ('000)	136.0	141.9	121.6
Fibro-cement products	0.8	1.6	2.5
Batteries ('000 cartons)†	4.6	3.5	3.0
Electric energy (million kWh)	99.1	99.2	107.8

* Preliminary figures.
† Cartons of 240 batteries.
Source: IMF, *Burundi: Statistical Annex* (November 2002).

Finance

CURRENCY AND EXCHANGE RATES

Monetary Units
100 centimes = 1 Burundian franc.

Sterling, Dollar and Euro Equivalents (31 December 2004)
£1 sterling = 2,142.908 francs;
US $1 = 1,109.510 francs;
€1 = 1,511.265 francs;
10,000 Burundian francs = £4.67 = $9.01 = €6.62.

Average Exchange Rate (Burundian francs per US dollar)
2002   930.749
2003   1,082.620
2004   1,100.910

BUDGET
(million Burundian francs)*

Revenue†	1997	1998	1999
Tax revenue	42,880	61,554	66,627
Taxes on income and profits	10,322	13,139	15,122
Social security contributions	3,731	4,281	5,357
Domestic taxes on goods and services	20,744	25,305	31,640
Transaction tax	7,281	11,435	12,643
Excise tax	13,155	13,870	18,997
Taxes on international trade	7,229	18,829	14,508
Import duties	6,527	10,726	11,022
Export tax	702	4,562	28
Entrepreneurial and property income	1,920	3,106	3,071
Other current revenue	1,345	1,610	2,238
Capital revenue	108	64	111
Total	46,253	66,334	72,047

Expenditure‡	1997	1998	1999
General public services	18,154	20,513	25,122
Defence	21,100	23,325	24,564
Public order and safety	1,344	2,153	2,502
Education	11,204	14,080	15,990
Health	2,085	2,421	2,271
Social security and welfare . .	4,718	6,510	2,401
Recreational, cultural and religious affairs and services	334	286	345
Economic affairs and services . .	n.a.	3,062	3,721
Fuel and energy	n.a.	232	543
Agriculture, forestry, fishing and hunting	n.a.	1,499	1,941
Mining, manufacturing and construction	n.a.	995	1,068
Transport and communications .	n.a.	336	169
Other purposes	n.a.	25,711	28,265
Interest payments	6,071	6,844	9,507
Total	80,800	98,061	105,181
Current	58,207	74,082	80,966
Capital	12,322	23,979	24,215
Adjustment to total expenditure .	10,271	—	—

* Figures refer to the consolidated operations of the central Government, comprising the general budget, social security funds and extrabudgetary accounts (covering transactions undertaken through foreign borrowing arrangements and grants not recorded in treasury accounts). The data exclude the operations of other central government units with individual budgets.

† Excluding grants received.

‡ Excluding lending minus repayments.

Source: IMF, *Government Finance Statistics Yearbook*.

2000 ('000 million Burundian francs): *Revenue:* Tax revenue 93.7 (Income tax 20.0, Taxes on goods and services 46.8, Taxes on international trade 22.8); Non-tax revenue 4.7; Total 98.3, excl. grants received (15.9). *Expenditure:* Current 96.0 (Salaries 33.9, Goods and services 37.9, Transfers and subsidies 9.9, Interest payments 14.3); Capital 31.1 (Domestic resources 8.8, External resources 22.3); Total 127.2, excl. net lending (-3.6).

2001 ('000 million Burundian francs, estimates): *Revenue:* Tax revenue 103.1 (Income tax 28.5, Taxes on goods and services 48.7, Taxes on international trade 21.7); Non-tax revenue 7.0; Total 110.2, excl. grants received, (5.9). *Expenditure:* Current 118.6 (Salaries 40.1, Goods and services 44.2, Transfers and subsidies 15.9, Interest payments 18.5); Capital 35.1 (Domestic resources 18.5, External resources 16.6); Total 153.7, excl. net lending (-3.9).

2002 ('000 million Burundian francs, estimates): *Revenue:* Tax revenue 104.8 (Income tax 29.4, Taxes on goods and services 51.9, Taxes on international trade 23.2); Non-tax revenue 13.6; Total 118.4, excl. grants received, (13.1). *Expenditure:* Current 119.7 (Salaries 45.9, Goods and services 38.6, Transfers and subsidies 16.4, Interest payments 18.7); Capital 33.4 (Domestic resources 6.4, External resources 27.0); Total 153.0, excl. net lending (-1.4).

Sources: IMF, *Burundi: Use of Fund Resources—Request for Post-Conflict Emergency Assistance—Staff Report; and Press Release on the Executive Board Discussion* (May 2003), and *Burundi: Selected Issues and Statistical Appendix* (February 2004).

INTERNATIONAL RESERVES
(US $ million at 31 December)

	2001	2002	2003
Gold*	0.27	0.34	0.40
IMF special drawing rights . .	0.06	0.16	0.14
Reserve position in IMF . .	0.45	0.49	0.54
Foreign exchange	17.20	58.13	66.29
Total	17.98	59.12	67.37

* Valued at market-related prices.

Source: IMF, *International Financial Statistics*.

MONEY SUPPLY
(million Burundian francs at 31 December)

	2001	2002	2003
Currency outside banks . . .	34,058	42,752	44,515
Deposits at central bank . . .	347	449	1,158
Demand deposits at commercial banks	44,244	55,838	72,107
Demand deposits at other monetary institutions . . .	1,431	1,487	1,857
Total money	80,080	100,527	119,637

Source: IMF, *International Financial Statistics*.

COST OF LIVING
(Consumer Price Index for Bujumbura; base: January 1991 = 100)

	1999	2000	2001
Food	305.9	395.6	398.0
Clothing	403.7	469.8	407.9
Housing, heating and light . . .	282.3	327.5	433.7
Transport	210.2	344.8	367.2
All items (incl. others)	295.0	366.6	400.6

Source: IMF, *Burundi: Statistical Annex* (November 2002).

NATIONAL ACCOUNTS

Composition of the Gross National Product
(million Burundian francs at current prices)

	2001	2002	2003
Gross domestic product (GDP) in purchasers' values . . .	549,981	584,605	651,590
Net factor income from abroad . .	−11,545	−10,906	−18,778
Gross national product (GNP) .	538,436	573,699	632,812

Source: IMF, *International Financial Statistics*.

Expenditure on the Gross Domestic Product
(million Burundian francs at current prices)

	2001	2002	2003
Government final consumption expenditure	80,479	99,051	124,851
Private final consumption expenditure	512,657	505,882	580,060
Increase in stocks	—	25,674	—
Gross fixed capital formation . .	40,073	55,787	69,130
Total domestic expenditure .	633,209	686,394	774,041
Exports of goods and services . .	38,235	36,035	48,700
Less Imports of goods and services	121,464	137,849	171,120
Statistical discrepancy		25	−31
GDP in purchasers' values . .	549,981	584,605	651,590

Source: IMF, *International Financial Statistics*.

Gross Domestic Product by Economic Activity
('000 million Burundian francs at current prices)

	2000	2001	2002
Agriculture, hunting, forestry and fishing	184.0	195.9	213.2
Mining and quarrying . . . }	5.1	5.6	6.0
Electricity, gas and water . . }			
Manufacturing†	59.8	65.6	67.5
Construction	20.6	23.1	24.3
Trade, restaurants and hotels .	36.8	26.3	27.6
Transport, storage and communications	38.7	27.7	29.0
Other services	110.4	151.4	158.4
GDP at factor cost	455.5	495.6	526.0
Indirect taxes, *less* subsidies .	55.6	54.3	58.6
GDP in purchasers' values .	511.1	550.0	584.6

* Estimates.

† Including handicrafts ('000 million Burundian francs): 20.3 in 2000; 22.1 in 2001; 23.3 in 2002.

Source: IMF, *Burundi: Selected Issues and Statistical Annex* (February 2004).

BALANCE OF PAYMENTS
(US $ million)

	2001	2002	2003
Exports of goods f.o.b.	39.2	31.0	37.5
Imports of goods f.o.b.	−108.3	−104.8	−130.0
Trade balance	−69.1	−73.8	−92.5
Exports of services	5.2	6.3	5.6
Imports of services	−37.9	−43.2	−45.0
Balance on goods and services	−101.8	−110.7	−131.9
Other income received	1.9	0.9	1.3
Other income paid	−15.8	−12.6	−18.6
Balance on goods, services and income	−115.7	−122.4	−149.3
Current transfers received . . .	79.6	115.5	115.5
Current transfers paid . . .	−2.9	−3.3	−3.5
Current balance	−39.0	−10.2	−37.3
Capital account (net)	—	−0.5	−0.9
Other investment assets . . .	24.0	−4.3	−19.9
Other investment liabilities . .	−28.0	−36.2	−30.1
Net errors and omissions . . .	−31.2	3.9	−12.6
Overall balance	−74.3	−47.2	−100.9

Source: IMF, *International Financial Statistics.*

External Trade

PRINCIPAL COMMODITIES
(distribution by SITC, US $ million)

Imports c.i.f.	1999	2000	2001
Food and live animals . . .	12.9	20.4	16.4
Cereals and cereal preparations .	9.6	14.4	10.7
Malt (incl. malt flour) . . .	5.0	5.5	2.8
Crude materials (inedible) except fuels	5.6	5.6	5.7
Mineral fuels, lubricants, etc. .	19.1	17.9	17.4
Refined petroleum products . .	18.9	17.5	17.2
Motor spirit (gasoline) and other light oils	9.0	8.2	17.1
Motor spirit (incl. aviation spirit)	8.5	7.6	—
Gas oils	8.5	7.5	—
Animal and vegetable oils, fats and waxes	0.4	13.4	1.5
Chemicals and related products	20.9	19.6	25.2
Medicinal and pharmaceutical products	8.5	10.1	12.2
Basic manufactures	24.3	28.6	28.7
Non-metallic mineral manufactures	6.1	7.1	7.8
Lime, cement, etc.	5.3	6.1	6.8
Cement	5.3	6.0	6.7
Machinery and transport equipment	40.0	34.4	32.4
Telecommunications and sound equipment	2.1	13.1	3.4
Road vehicles and parts (excl. tyres, engines and electrical parts) .	22.1	8.8	12.8
Miscellaneous manufactured articles	6.9	8.7	10.6
Total (incl. others)	132.0	150.2	138.8

Exports f.o.b.	1999	2000	2001
Food and live animals . . .	43.6	36.7	29.4
Coffee, tea, cocoa and spices . .	42.7	34.4	28.0
Coffee (incl. husks and skins) .	41.5	31.4	21.1
Tea	1.2	3.0	6.8
Gold, non-monetary, unwrought or semi-manufactured	17.7	2.4	6.3
Total (incl. others)	62.4	42.8	42.2

Source: UN, *International Trade Statistics Yearbook.*

PRINCIPAL TRADING PARTNERS

Imports c.i.f. (US $ '000)	1997	1998	1999
Belgium	22,358	30,254	19,851
China, People's Repub.	2,812	6,403	3,961
France	11,645	14,217	5,980
Germany	8,042	9,585	5,901
Italy	4,220	4,811	3,423
Japan	7,567	5,989	3,677
Kenya	5,305	8,784	6,199
Netherlands	5,234	4,656	2,246
Tanzania	3,057	3,113	5,118
United Arab Emirates	5,445	5,224	3,909
United Kingdom	2,041	2,314	2,511
USA	2,281	2,339	2,557
Zambia	6,761	12,530	6,734
Zimbabwe	2,806	1,562	2,208
Total (incl. others)	122,745	156,944	117,658

Source: Banque de la République du Burundi.

2000 (US $ million): Belgium 18.3; China, People's Repub. 5.6; France 19.6; Kenya 7.7; Saudi Arabia 15.9; Tanzania 23.0; United Arab Emirates 4.8; Total (incl. others) 150.2 (Source: UN, *International Trade Statistics Yearbook*).

Exports (million Burundian francs)	1997	1998	1999
Belgium-Luxembourg	4,929.3	2,624.8	995.5
France	37.3	17.8	358.1
Germany	6,579.5	2,968.8	1,520.9
United Kingdom	8,305.7	8,125.9	10,278.9
Total (incl. others)	30,767.2	28,634.8	30,970.8

Source: Banque de la République du Burundi.

2000 (US $ million): Belgium 5.4; Switzerland and Liechtenstein 11.1; United Kingdom 5.4; Total (incl. others) 42.8 (Source: UN, *International Trade Statistics Yearbook*).

Transport

ROAD TRAFFIC
(estimates, '000 motor vehicles in use)

	1999	2000	2001
Passenger cars	6.9	7.0	7.0
Commercial vehicles	9.3	9.3	9.3

Source: UN, *Statistical Yearbook.*

LAKE TRAFFIC
(Bujumbura, '000 metric tons)

	1997	1998	1999
Goods:			
arrivals	70.9	123.1	142.5
departures	28.1	28.1	28.2

Source: Banque de la République du Burundi.

CIVIL AVIATION
(traffic on scheduled services)

	1996	1997	1998
Passengers carried ('000) . . .	9	12	12
Passenger-km (million)	2	8	8

Source: UN, *Statistical Yearbook.*

Tourism

TOURIST ARRIVALS BY REGION*

	1996	1997	1998
Africa	13,004	5,011	7,394
Americas	1,660	639	1,092
Asia	2,213	852	1,218
Europe	10,514	4,051	5,700
Total	27,391	10,553	15,404

* Including Burundian nationals residing abroad.

Tourist arrivals ('000): 26 in 1999; 29 in 2000; 36 in 2001.

Tourism receipts (US $ million): 1 in 2000; 1 in 2001; 1 in 2002 (estimate).

Source: World Tourism Organization.

Communications Media

	2001	2002	2003
Television receivers ('000 in use) .	200	n.a.	n.a.
Telephones ('000 main lines in use)	20.5	22.1	23.9
Mobile cellular telephones ('000 subscribers)	30.7	52.0	64.0
Personal computers ('000 in use) .	5	5	26
Internet users ('000)	7	8	14

Radio receivers ('000 in use): 440 in 1997.

Facsimile machines (number in use): 4,000 in 1996.

Daily newspapers: 1 in 1998.

Non-daily newspapers: 5 in 1998 (circulation 8,000 copies).

Sources: International Telecommunication Union; UNESCO, *Statistical Yearbook*.

Education

(1998, unless otherwise indicated)

	Institu-tions	Teachers	Students Males	Females	Total
Pre-primary . . .	n.a.	49*	2,455	2,438	4,938
Primary†	1,512	12,107	307,079	250,265	557,344
Secondary†:					
general	}		30,604	26,268	56,872
technical and vocational . .	} 400	3,546			
			n.a.	n.a.	4,610
Higher	n.a.	379	3,549	1,488	5,037

* Figure refers to 1988/89.
† Figures refer to public education only.

Source: UNESCO Institute for Statistics.

Adult literacy rate (UNESCO estimates): 50.4% (males 57.7%; females 43.6%) in 2002 (Source: UN Development Programme, *Human Development Report*).

Directory

The Constitution*

On 20 October 2004 an interim 'post-transitional' Constitution was officially adopted by the President, after its approval by both chambers of the legislature. The new Constitution, which extended the mandate of the transitional organs of government from 1 November until elections, scheduled for 22 April 2005, was endorsed at a national referendum on 28 February 2005 (replacing the Constitution of 28 October 2001). The main provisions are summarized below:

PREAMBLE

The transitional Constitution upholds the rights of the individual, and provides for a multi-party political system. The Government is based on the will of the people, and must be composed in order to represent all citizens. The function of the political system is to unite and reconcile all citizens and to ensure that the established Government serves the people. The Government must recognize the separation of powers, the primacy of the law and the principles of good governance and transparency in public affairs. All citizens have equal rights and are assured equal protection by the law. The civic obligations of the individual are emphasized.

POLITICAL PARTY SYSTEM

Political parties may be established freely, subject to conformity with the law. Their organization and activities must correspond to democratic principles and membership must be open to all civilians. They are not permitted to promote violence, discrimination or hate on any basis, including ethnical, regional or religious or tribal affilation. Members of defence and security bodies, and acting magistrates are prohibited from joining political parties. A five-member Commission électorale nationale indépendante guarantees the freedom, impartiality and independence of the electoral process.

EXECUTIVE POWER

Executive power is vested in the President, who is the Head of State. The President is elected by universal direct suffrage for a term of five years, which is renewable once. (The first post-transitional President is to be elected by a majority of two-thirds of members of both legislative chambers.) The President is assisted in the exercise of his powers by two Vice-Presidents, whom he appoints, and presides over the Government.

GOVERNMENT

The President appoints the Government in consultation with the Vice-Presidents. The Government is required to comprise a 60% proportion of Hutu ministers and deputy ministers and 40% of Tutsi ministers and deputy ministers, and to include a minimum 30% of women. Political parties that secured more than 5% of votes cast in legislative elections are entitled to nominate a proportionate number of representatives to the Government. The President is obliged to replace a minister in consultation with the political party that the minister represents.

LEGISLATURE

Legislative power is vested in the bicameral legislature, comprising a lower chamber, the Assemblée nationale, and an upper chamber, the Sénat. The Assemblée nationale has a minimum of 100 deputies, with a proportion of 60% Hutu and 40% Tutsi representives, and including a minimum 30% of women. Deputies are elected by direct universal suffrage for a term of five years, while the Twa ethnic group nominates three representatives. If the election results fail to conform to the stipulated ethnic composition, the inbalance will be redressed according to the electoral code. The Sénat comprises two deputies elected by ethnically balanced colleges from each of the country's provinces, and three Twa representatives, and includes a minimum 30% of women. Both chambers have a President and Vice-Presidents.

JUDICIARY

The President guarantees the independence of the judiciary, with the assistance of the Conseil Supérieur de la Magistrature. The highest judicial power is vested in the Cour Suprême. All appointments to these organs are made by the President, on the proposal of the Minister of Justice and in consultation with the Conseil Supérieur de la Magistrature, and are endorsed by the Sénat. The Cour Constitutionnelle interprets the provisions of the Constitution and ensures the conformity of new legislation. The Cour Constitution-nelle comprises seven members, who are appointed by the President, subject to the approval of the Sénat, for a six-year renewable term.

DEFENCE AND SECURITY FORCES

The establishment and operations of defence and security forces must conform to the law. Members of defence and security forces are prohibited from belonging to, participating in the activities of, or demonstrating prejudice towards, any political parties. All citizens are eligible to join the defence and security forces. During a period to be determined by the Sénat, defence and security forces are not permitted to comprise more than 50% of one single ethnic group, in order to ensure an ethnic balance and guard against acts of genocide and military coups.

* In April 2005 the Government announced that the presidential mandate was to be extended to allow elections to be rescheduled for 19 August, with the inauguration to take place on 26 August.

The Government

HEAD OF STATE

President: Maj. Domitien Ndayizeye (inaugurated 30 April 2003).

Vice-President: Frederic Ngenzebuhoro.

COUNCIL OF MINISTERS
(April 2005)

A transitional Government, comprising representatives of the Front pour la démocratie au Burundi (FRODEBU), the Union pour le progrès national (UPRONA), the Conseil national pour la défense de la démocratie—Force pour la défense de la démocratie (CNDD—FDD), the Alliance burundaise-africaine pour le salut (ABASA), the Alliance nationale pour les droits et le développement économique (ANADDE), the AV—Intware (Alliance of the Brave), the Conseil national pour la défense de la démocratie (CNDD), the faction of the Forces nationales de libération (FNL) led by Alain Mugabarabona, the Inkinzo y'Ijambo Ry'abarundi (Inkinzo), the Parti de libération du peuple hutu (PALIPEHUTU), the Parti du peuple (PP), the Parti pour la réconciliation du peuple (PRP), the Parti social démocrate (PSD), the Rassemblement pour la démocratie et le développement économique et social (RADDES) and the Rassemblement pour le peuple du Burundi (RPB).

Minister of State, with responsibility for Good Governance and State Inspection: Jean-Pierre Nkurunziza (CNDD—FDD).

Minister of External Relations and Co-operation: Térence Sinunguruza (UPRONA).

Minister of the Interior: (vacant).

Minister of Public Security: Col Donatien Sidnakira (FRODEBU).

Minister of Justice and Keeper of the Seals: Didace Kiganahe (FRODEBU).

Minister of National Defence: Maj.-Gen. Vincent Niyungeko (UPRONA).

Minister of Development, Planning and Reconstruction: Séraphine Wakana (UPRONA).

Minister of Communal Development and Handicrafts: Cyrille Hicintuka (FNL).

Minister of Relocation and Resettlement of Displaced and Repatriated Persons: Françoise Ngendahayo (Inkinzo).

Minister of Mobilization for Peace and National Reconciliation: Antoine Butoyi (ANADDE).

Minister of Territorial Development, the Environment and Tourism: Albert Mbonerane (CNDD).

Minister of Agriculture and Livestock: Pierre Ndikumagenge (UPRONA).

Minister of Handicrafts, Vocational Training and Adult Literacy: Godefroy Hakizimana (PSD).

Minister of Labour and Social Security: Dismas Nditabiriye (RADDES).

Minister of the Civil Service: Gaspard Kobako (CNDD—FDD).

Minister of Finance: Athanase Gahungu (ABASA).

Minister of Commerce and Industry: Thomas Minani (FRODEBU).

Minister of National Education: Salvator Ntihabade (FRODEBU).

Minister of Social Action and Women's Affairs: Marie-Goretti Nduwimana.

Minister of Culture, Youth and Sport: Barnabé Muteragiranwa (RPB).

Minister of Public Health: Jean Kamana (FRODEBU).

Minister of Communication and Government Spokesman: Onésime Nduwimana (CNDD—FDD).

Minister of Public Works and Equipment: Salvator Ntahome-nyereye (CNDD—FDD).

Minister of Transport, Posts and Telecommunications: Séverin Ndikumugongo (PP).

Minister of Energy and Mines: André Nkundikije (AV—Intware).

Minister of Human Rights, Institutional Reforms and Relations with the Assemblée nationale: Déogratias Rusengwamihigo (PRP).

Minister in the Office of the President, in charge of AIDS Control: Charles Nditije (UPRONA).

MINISTRIES

All ministries are based in Bujumbura

Office of the President: Bujumbura; tel. 226063.

Ministry of Agriculture and Livestock: Bujumbura; tel. 222087.

Ministry of Commerce and Industry: BP 492, Bujumbura; tel. 225330; fax 225595.

Ministry of Communication: BP 2870, Bujumbura.

Ministry of Culture, Youth and Sport: Bujumbura; tel. 226822.

Ministry of Development, Planning and Reconstruction: BP 1830, Bujumbura; tel. 223988.

Ministry of Energy and Mines: BP 745, Bujumbura; tel. 225909; fax 223337; e-mail dgee@cbinf.com.

Ministry of External Relations and Co-operation: Bujumbura; tel. 222150.

Ministry of Finance: BP 1830, Bujumbura; tel. 225142; fax 223128.

Ministry of Justice: Bujumbura; tel. 222148.

Ministry of Labour and Social Security: BP 1480, Bujumbura; tel. 225645; fax 228715; e-mail mtpe@cbinf.com; internet www .burundi.gov.bi/appofre.htm.

Ministry of Public Works and Equipment: BP 1860, Bujumbura; tel. 226841; fax 226840; e-mail mtpe@cbinf.com; internet www .burundi.gov.bi/appoffre.htm.

Ministry of Social Action and Women's Affairs: Bujumbura; tel. 225039.

Ministry of Transport, Posts and Telecommunications: BP 2000, Bujumbura; tel. 222923; fax 226900.

President and Legislature

PRESIDENT

In July 1996 the President elected by the Assemblée nationale, Cyprien Ntibantunganya, was deposed in a military coup and replaced by Maj. Pierre Buyoya. Under a power-sharing agreement, which was reached in August 2000, in Arusha, Tanzania, Buyoya remained in the office of the President for the first 18 months of a three-year transitional period (commencing on 1 November 2001). On 30 April 2003 he was replaced by the incumbent Vice-President, a Hutu leader, Maj. Domitien Ndayizeye, who was to serve for the following 18 months. Following the extension of the transitional process, the election of a President by a newly established Assemblée nationale (following legislative elections) was provisionally rescheduled for 26 August 2005.

SÉNAT

The transitional Constitution, adopted on 29 October 2001, provided for the creation of an upper chamber, the Sénat. In January 2002 the Constitutional Court approved the nomination of 51 deputies (48 representing the country's provinces) to a transitional ethnically balanced Sénat.

President: Libère Bararunyeretse (UPRONA).

ASSEMBLÉE NATIONALE*

President: Jean Minani (FRODEBU).

Vice-President: Frédéric Ngenzebuhoro (UPRONA).

Elections, 29 June 1993

Party	Votes	% of votes	Seats
FRODEBU	1,532,107	71.04	65
UPRONA	462,324	21.44	16
RPB	35,932	1.67	—
PRP	29,966	1.39	—
RADDES	26,631	1.23	—
PP	24,372	1.13	—
Independents	853	0.04	—
Invalid votes	44,474	2.06	—
Total	2,156,659	100.00	81

*The Assemblée nationale was suspended following the July 1996 coup, but was reconvened in October. Under transitional constitutional arrangements promulgated in June 1998, the membership of the Assemblée nationale was enlarged from 81 to 121 members in order to incorporate representatives of smaller parties and the civilian population. In January 2002 54 deputies representing 14 of the political parties signatory to the Arusha agreement of August 2000 were appointed to the expanded chamber.

Political Organizations

Political parties are required to demonstrate firm commitment to national unity, and impartiality with regard to ethnic or regional origin, gender and religion, in order to receive legal recognition. By early 2005 the number of registered political parties had increased to 34; these included former rebel organizations, with only Forces nationales de libération remaining in conflict with government forces.

Alliance burundaise-africaine pour le salut (ABASA): Bujumbura; f. 1993; Tutsi; Leader NSANZE TERENCE.

Alliance libérale pour le développement (Imboneza): f. Aug. 2002; Leader JOSEPH NTIDENDEREZA.

Alliance nationale pour les droits et le développement économique (ANADDE): Bujumbura; f. 1992; Tutsi; Leader PATRICE NSABABAGANWA.

Alliance nouvelle pour la démocratie et le développement au Burundi: f. Aug. 2002; Leader JEAN-PAUL BURAFUTA.

AV—Intware (Alliance of the Brave): Bujumbura; f. 1993; Tutsi; Leader ANDRÉ NKUNDIKIJE.

Conseil national pour la défense de la démocratie (CNDD): Bujumbura; e-mail cndd_bur@usa.net; internet www.club.euronet .be/pascal.karolero.cndd.burundi; f. 1994; Hutu; Leader LÉONARD NYANGOMA.

Conseil national pour la défense de la démocratie—Force pour la défense de la démocratie (CNDD—FDD): fmr armed wing of the Hutu CNDD; split into two factions in Oct. 2001, one led by JEAN-BOSCO NDAYIKENGURUKIYE and the other by JEAN-PIERRE NKURUNZIZA; Nkurunziza's faction incl. in Govt Nov. 2003, following peace agreement; registered as political org. Jan. 2005; Leader JEAN-PIERRE NKURUNZIZA; Sec.-Gen. HUSSEIN RADJABU.

Convergence nationale pour la paix et la réconciliation (CNPR): Bujumbura; f. Oct. 1999; alliance comprising Union pour le progrès national, a faction of Front pour la démocratie au Burundi and several Tutsi parties; Pres. AUGUSTIN NZOJIBWAMI.

Forces nationales de libération (FNL): fmr armed wing of Hutu Parti de libération du peuple hutu (PALIPEHUTU); split in Aug. 2002 ; in conflict with Govt in early 2005; Leader AGATHON RWASA.

Forum démocratique (FODE): Bujumbura; f. Nov. 1999; Leader DEOGRATIAS BABURIFATO.

Front national de libération Icanzo (FNL Icanzo): reconstituted Dec. 2002 from fmr faction of Forces nationales de libération; Leader Dr ALAIN MUGABARABONA.

Front pour la démocratie au Burundi (FRODEBU): Bujumbura; f. 1992; split in June 1999; Hutu; Chair. JEAN MINANI; Sec.-Gen. WELEONCE NGENDAKUMANA.

Inkinzo y'Ijambo Ry'abarundi (Inkinzo) (Guarantor of Freedom of Speech in Burundi): Bujumbura; f. 1993; Tutsi; Pres. Dr ALPHONSE RUGAMBARARA.

KAZE—Force pour la défense de la démocratie (KAZE—FDD): f. May 2004; reconstituted as a political party from a faction of the armed CNDD—FDD (see above); Leader JEAN-BOSCO NDAYIKENGURUKIYE.

Mouvement de la résistance pour la réhabilitation du citoyen (MRC—Rurenzangemero): Bujumbura; f. June 2001; regd Nov. 2002; Leader Lt-Col EPITACE BAYAGANAKANDI.

Parti de la consensus nationale (PACONA): f. Feb. 2004; Leader JEAN-BOSCO NDAYIZAMBAYE.

Parti indépendant des travailleurs (PIT): Bujumbura; f. 1993; Tutsi; Chair. NICEPHORE NDIMURUKU.

Parti libéral (PL): BP 2167, Bujumbura; tel. 214848; fax 225981; e-mail liberalburundi@yahoo.fr; f. 1992; Hutu; Leader JOSEPH NTIDENDEREZA.

Parti de libération du peuple hutu (PALIPEHUTU): Bujumbura; f. 1980 in Tanzania, with the aim of advancing the interests of the Hutu ethnic group; Chair. ETIENNE KARATASI.

Parti du peuple (PP): Bujumbura; f. 1992; Hutu; Leader SHADRAIK NIYONKURU.

Parti pour le démocratie et la réconciliation: f. May 2002; Leader AUGUSTIN NZOJLBWAMI.

Parti pour le développement et la solidarité des travailleurs (PML-Abanyamwete): Bujumbura; f. Oct. 2004; Leader PATRICIA NDAYIZEYE.

Parti pour la paix, la démocratie, la réconciliation et la reconstruction (PPDR): f. Dec. 2002 by fmr mems of FRODEBU (see above); registered March 2004; Leader JEAN-LEOPOLD NZOBONIMPA.

Parti pour la réconciliation du peuple (PRP): Bujumbura; f. 1992; Tutsi; Leader MATHIAS HITIMANA.

Parti pour le redressement intégral du Burundi (PARIBU): Bujumbura; f. Sept. 2004; Leader BENOIT NDORIMANA.

Parti pour le redressement national (PARENA): Bujumbura; f. 1994; Leader JEAN-BAPTISTE BAGAZA.

Parti pour la restitution de la monarchie et du dialogue (PRMD) (Abuhuza): Bujumbura; f. 2004; Leader GODEFROID KAMATARI.

Parti social démocrate (PSD): Bujumbura; f. 1993; Tutsi; Leader GODEFROID HAKIZIMANA.

Rassemblement pour la démocratie et le développement économique et social (RADDES): Bujumbura; f. 1992; Tutsi; Chair. JOSEPH NZEYZIMANA.

Rassemblement pour le peuple du Burundi (RPB): Bujumbura; f. 1992; Hutu; Leader BALTHAZAR BIGIRIMANA.

Solidarité pour la défense des minorités (SOJEDEM): Bujumbura.

Sonovi-Ruremesha (Party for a Non-Violent Society): f. Aug. 2002; Tutsi; Chair. DEOGRATIAS NDAYISHIMIYE.

Union pour la paix et le développement (Zigamibanga): f. Aug. 2002; Leader FREDDY FERUVI.

Union pour le progrès national (UPRONA): BP 1810, Bujumbura; tel. 225028; f. 1958; following the 1961 elections, the numerous small parties which had been defeated merged with UPRONA, which became the sole legal political party in 1966; party activities were suspended following the coup of Sept. 1987, but resumed in 1989; Chair. JOHN BAPTISTE MANWANGARI.

Diplomatic Representation

EMBASSIES IN BURUNDI

Belgium: 9 blvd de la Liberté, BP 1920, Bujumbura; tel. 223676; fax 223171; e-mail bujumbura@diplobel.org; Ambassador JAN F. MUTTON.

China, People's Republic: 675 sur la Parcelle, BP 2550, Bujumbura; tel. 224307; fax 213735; Ambassador SHI TONGNING.

Egypt: 31 ave de la Liberté, BP 1520, Bujumbura; tel. 223161; Ambassador MUHAMMAD MOUSA.

France: 60 blvd de l'Uprona, BP 1740, Bujumbura; tel. 226767; fax 221793; Ambassador ALAIN GIRMA.

Germany: 22 rue 18 septembre, BP 480, Bujumbura; tel. 226412; Ambassador Dr BERND MORAST.

Holy See: 46 chaussée Prince Louis-Rwagasore, BP 1068, Bujumbura; tel. 225415; fax 223176; e-mail nonciat@cbinf.com; Apostolic Nuncio Most Rev. PAUL RICHARD GALLAGHER (Titular Archbishop of Hodelm).

Korea, Democratic People's Republic: BP 1620, Bujumbura; tel. 222881; Ambassador PAE SOK JUN.

Russia: 78 blvd de l'UPRONA, BP 1034, Bujumbura; tel. 226098; fax 222984; Ambassador IGOR S. LIAKIN-FROLOV.

Rwanda: 24 ave du Zaïre, BP 400, Bujumbura; tel. 223140; Ambassador SYLVESTRE UWIBAJIJE.

Tanzania: BP 1653, Bujumbura; Ambassador Francis Mndolwa.

USA: ave des Etats-Unis, BP 1720, Bujumbura; tel. 223454; fax 222926; e-mail jyellin@bujumbura.us-state.gov; Ambassador James Yellin.

Judicial System

Constitutional Court: Bujumbura; comprises a minimum of seven judges, who are nominated by the President for a six-year term.

Supreme Court: BP 1460, Bujumbura; tel. and fax 213544; Court of final instance; three divisions: ordinary, cassation and administrative.

Courts of Appeal: Bujumbura, Gitega and Ngozi.

Tribunals of First Instance: There are 17 provincial tribunals and 123 smaller resident tribunals in other areas.

Tribunal of Trade: Bujumbura.

Tribunals of Labour: Bujumbura and Gitega.

Administrative Courts: Bujumbura and Gitega.

Religion

More than 65% of the population are Christians, the majority of whom are Roman Catholics. Anglicans number about 60,000. There are about 200,000 other Protestant adherents, of whom about 160,000 are Pentecostalists. Fewer than 40% of the population adhere to traditional beliefs, which include the worship of the god Imana. About 1% of the population are Muslims. The Bahá'í Faith is also active in Burundi.

CHRISTIANITY

Conseil National des Eglises Protestantes du Burundi (CNEB): BP 17, Bujumbura; tel. 224216; fax 227941; e-mail cneb@cbninf.com; f. 1935; 10 mem. churches; Pres. Rt Rev. Jean Nduwayo (Anglican Bishop of Gitega); Gen. Sec. Rev. Osias Habingabwa.

The Anglican Communion

The Church of the Province of Burundi, established in 1992, comprises five dioceses.

Archbishop of Burundi and Bishop of Buye: Most Rev. Samuel Ndayisenga, BP 94, Ngozi; fax 302317.

Provincial Secretary: Rev. Pascal Bigirimana, BP 2098, Bujumbura; tel. 224389; fax 229129; e-mail eebprov@cbinf.com.

The Roman Catholic Church

Burundi comprises one archdiocese and six dioceses. At 31 December 2002 there were an estimated 4,434,588 adherents, equivalent to 65.9% of the total population.

Bishops' Conference

Conférence des Evêques Catholiques du Burundi, 5 blvd de l'UPRONA, BP 1390, Bujumbura; tel. 223263; fax 223270; e-mail cecab@cbinf.com.

f. 1980; Pres. Most Rev. Simon Ntamwana (Archbishop of Gitega).

Archbishop of Gitega: Most Rev. Simon Ntamwana, Archevêché, BP 118, Gitega; tel. 402160; fax 402620; e-mail archigi@bujumbura.ocicnet.net.

Other Christian Churches

Union of Baptist Churches of Burundi: Rubura, DS 117, Bujumbura 1; Pres. Paul Baruhenamwo.

Other denominations active in the country include the Evangelical Christian Brotherhood of Burundi, the Free Methodist Church of Burundi and the United Methodist Church of Burundi.

BAHÁ'Í FAITH

National Spiritual Assembly: BP 1578, Bujumbura; tel. 955840; e-mail bahaiburundi@yahoo.fr; Sec. Christian Nsavye.

The Press

National Communications Council (Conseil national de la communication—CNC): Bujumbura; f. 2001 under the terms of the transitional Constitution; responsible for ensuring press freedom; Pres. Jean-Pierre Manda.

NEWSPAPERS

L'Aube de la Démocratie: Bujumbura; organ of Hutu Front pour la démocratie au Burundi.

Le Renouveau du Burundi: Ministry of Information, BP 2573, Bujumbura; tel. 226232; f. 1978; publ. by UPRONA; 3 a week; French; circ. 20,000; Dir Jean Nzeyimana.

La Tribune du Burundi: Bujumbura; f. 2004; Dir Justin Tagouh.

PERIODICALS

Au Coeur de l'Afrique: Association des conférences des ordinaires du Rwanda et Burundi, BP 1390, Bujumbura; fax 223027; e-mail cnid@cbinf.com; bimonthly; education; circ. 1,000.

Bulletin Économique et Financier: BP 482, Bujumbura; bimonthly.

Bulletin Mensuel: Banque de la République du Burundi, Service des études, BP 705, Bujumbura; tel. 225142; monthly.

In-Burundi: c/o Cyber Média, Bujumbura, BP 5270, ave du 18 septembre; tel. 244464; internet www.in-burundi.net; current affairs internet publication; Editor-in-Chief Edgar C. Mbanza.

Ndongozi Y'uburundi: Catholic Mission, BP 690, Bujumbura; tel. 222762; fax 228907; fortnightly; Kirundi.

Revue Administration et Juridique: Association d'études administratives et juridiques du Burundi, BP 1613, Bujumbura; quarterly; French.

PRESS ASSOCIATION

Burundian Association of Journalists (BAJ): Bujumbura; Pres. François Sendazirasa.

NEWS AGENCIES

Agence Burundaise de Presse (ABP): ave Nicolas Mayugi, BP 2870, Bujumbura; tel. 213083; fax (2) 22282; e-mail abp@cbinf.com; internet www.abp.info.bi; f. 1975; publ. daily bulletin.

Agence d'Information Net Press: Bujumbura; internet www.cbinf.com/netpress.bi; independent agency; operations suspended Jan. 2002; Dir Jean-Claude Kavumbagu.

Publishers

BURSTA: BP 1908, Bujumbura; tel. 231796; fax 232842; f. 1986; Dir Richard Kashirahamwe.

Editions Intore: 19 ave Matana, BP 2524, Bujumbura; tel. 223499; e-mail anbirabuza@yahoo.fr; f. 1992; philosophy, history, journalism, literature, social sciences; Dir Dr André Birabuza.

IMPARUDI: ave du 18 septembre 3, BP 3010, Bujumbura; tel. 223125; fax 222572; f. 1950; Dir-Gen. Théoneste Mutambuka.

Imprimerie la Licorne: 29 ave de la Mission, BP 2942, Bujumbura; tel. 223503; fax 227225; f. 1991.

Les Presses Lavigerie: 5 ave de l'UPRONA, BP 1640, Bujumbura; tel. 222368; fax 220318.

Régie de Productions Pédagogiques: BP 3118, Bujumbura II; tel. 226111; fax 222631; e-mail rpp@cbinf.com; f. 1984; school textbooks; Dir Abraham Mbonerane.

GOVERNMENT PUBLISHING HOUSE

Imprimerie Nationale du Burundi (INABU): BP 991, Bujumbura; tel. 224046; fax 225399; f. 1978; Dir Nicolas Nijimbere.

Broadcasting and Communications

TELECOMMUNICATIONS

Direction Générale des Transports, Postes et Télécommunications: BP 2390, Bujumbura; tel. 225422; fax 226900; govt telecommunications authority; Dir-Gen. Apollinaire Ndayizeye.

Office National des Télécommunications (ONATEL): BP 60, Bujumbura; tel. 223196; fax 226917; e-mail onatel@cbinf.com; f. 1979; service provider; privatization pending; Dir-Gen. Augustin Ndabihore.

Téléphonie Cellulaire du Burundi (TELECEL): Bujumbura; 40% govt-owned; mobile telephone service provider.

BROADCASTING

Radio

Radio Isanganiro: Bujumbura; internet www.ijambo.net; f. Nov. 2002; controlled by Association Ijambo, f. by Studio Ijambo (see below); broadcasts on 89.7 FM frequency, in Kirundi, French and Swahili; services cover Bujumbura area, and were to be extended to all Great Lakes region.

Radio Umwizero/Radio Hope: BP 5314, Bujumbura; tel. 217068; e-mail umwizero@cbinf.com; f. 1996; EU-funded, private station promoting national reconciliation, peace and development projects; broadcasts nine hours daily in Kirundi, Swahili and French; Dir HUBERT VIEILLE.

Studio Ijambo (Wise Words): Bujumbura; e-mail burundi@sfcg .org; internet www.studioijambo.org; f. 1995 by Search for Common Ground; promotes peace and reconciliation.

Voix de la Révolution/La Radiodiffusion et Télévision Nationale du Burundi (RTNB): BP 1900, Bujumbura; tel. 223742; fax 226547; e-mail rtnb@cbinf.com; internet www.burundi-quotidien .com; f. 1960; govt-controlled; daily radio broadcasts in Kirundi, Swahili, French and English; Dir-Gen. INNOCENT MUHOZI; Dir (Radio) EMMANUEL NZEYIMANA.

Television

Voix de la Révolution/La Radiodiffusion et Télévision Nationale du Burundi (RTNB): BP 1900, Bujumbura; tel. 223742; fax 226547; e-mail rtnb@cbinf.com; internet www.burundi-quotidien .com; f. 1960; govt-controlled; television service in Kirundi, Swahili, French and English; Dir (Television) DAVID HICUBURUMAI.

Finance

(cap. = capital; res = reserves; dep. = deposits; m. = million; brs = branches; amounts in Burundian francs)

BANKING

Central Bank

Banque de la République du Burundi (BRB): BP 705, Bujumbura; tel. 225142; fax 223128; e-mail brb@brb.bi; f. 1964 as Banque du Royaume du Burundi; state-owned; bank of issue; cap. and res 12,478.0m., dep. 11,233.4m. (Dec. 1999); Gov. SALVATOR TOYI; Vice-Gov. CYPRIEN SINZOBAHAMVYA; 2 brs.

Commercial Banks

Banque Burundaise pour le Commerce et l'Investissement SARL (BBCI): blvd du Peuple Murundi, BP 2320, Bujumbura; tel. 223328; fax 223339; f. 1988; cap. and res 846.4m., total assets 4,936.8m. (Dec. 2001); Pres. ABBÉ GABRIEL BAZIRUWISABIYE; Dir-Gen. CHARLES NIHANGAZA.

Banque Commerciale du Burundi SARL (BANCOBU): 84 chaussée Prince Louis-Rwagasore, BP 990, Bujumbura; tel. 222317; fax 221018; e-mail bancobu@cbinf.com; f. 1988 by merger; cap. 330.0m., res 1,610.6m., dep. 24,386.7m. (Dec. 2002); Pres. P. U. GAHUNGU; Man. Dir GASPARD SINDAYIGAYA; 6 brs.

Banque de Commerce et de Développement (BCD): ave de Grèce, BP 2020, Bujumbura; tel. 210950; fax 210952; e-mail bcd@ cbinf.com; f. 1999; cap. and res 1,238.2m., total assets 12,626.5m. (June 2001); Pres. FRANÇOIS BUTOKE; Man. Dir ANTOINE NDUWAYO.

Banque de Crédit de Bujumbura SM: ave Patrice Emery Lumumba, BP 300, Bujumbura; tel. 222091; fax 223007; e-mail direction@bcb.bi; internet www.bcb.bi; f. 1964; cap. 1,000.0m., res 3,825.2m., dep. 57,851.3m. (Dec. 2003); Pres. RÉNILDE BAZAHICA; 7 brs.

Banque de Gestion et de Financement: 1 blvd de la Liberté, BP 1035, Bujumbura; tel. 221352; fax 221351; e-mail bgf@usan.bu.net; f. 1996; cap. and res 1,517.4m., dep. 9,642.1m. (Dec. 2002); Pres. EVARISTE GATOGATO; Dir-Gen. MATHIAS NDIKUMANA.

Banque Populaire du Burundi (BPB): 10 ave du 18 septembre, BP 1780, Bujumbura; tel. 221257; fax 221256; e-mail bpb@cbinf .com; internet www.cbinf.com; f. 1992; cap. and res 1,474.0m., dep. 12,918.5m. (Dec. 2001); Pres. LÉONCE NDIHOKUBWAYO; Dir-Gen. DÉO BUKOBERO.

Interbank Burundi SARL: 15 ave de l'Industrie, BP 2970, Bujumbura; tel. 220629; fax 220461; e-mail interb@cbinf.com; internet www.interbankbdi.com; cap. and res 3,994.7m., total assets 38,560.7m. (Dec. 2001); Pres. GEORGES COUCOULIS.

Development Bank

Banque Nationale pour le Développement Economique SARL (BNDE): 3 ave du Marché, BP 1620, Bujumbura; tel. 222888; fax 223775; e-mail bnde@cbinf.com; f. 1966; cap. 740.0m., res 2,400.6m., dep. 16,198.5m. (Dec. 2002); Pres. and Dir-Gen. MATHIAS SINAMENYE.

Co-operative Bank

Banque Coopérative d'Epargne et de Crédit Mutuel (BCM): BP 1340, Bujumbura; operating licence granted in April 1995; Vice-Pres. JULIEN MUSARAGANY.

Financial Institutions

Société Burundaise de Financement S.M.: 6 rue de la Science, BP 270, Bujumbura; tel. 222126; fax 225437; e-mail sbf@cbinf.com; cap. and res 2,113.7m., total assets 8,837.5m. (Dec. 2001); Pres. DARIUS NAHAYO.

Société de Financement et de Leasing: 27 ave de l'Amitié, BP 2998, Bujumbura; tel. 243206; fax 243207; e-mail finalease@ spccdnets.com; cap. and res 675.3m., total assets 3,728.9m. (Dec. 2001); Pres. NICOLAS WATSON.

INSURANCE

Société d'Assurances du Burundi (SOCABU): 14–18 rue de l'Amitié, BP 2440, Bujumbura; tel. 226520; fax 226803; e-mail socabu@cbinf.com; f. 1977; cap. 540m.; Man. Dir ASTÈRE GIRUKWIGOMBA.

Société Générale d'Assurances et de Réassurance (SOGEAR): BP 2432, Bujumbura; tel. 222345; fax 229338; f. 1991; Pres. BENOÎT NDORIMANA; Dir-Gen. L. SAUSSEZ.

Union Commerciale d'Assurances et de Réassurance (UCAR): BP 3012, Bujumbura; tel. 223638; fax 223695; f. 1986; cap. 150m.; Chair. Lt-Col EDOUARD NZAMBIMANA; Man. Dir HENRY TARMO.

Trade and Industry

GOVERNMENT AGENCIES

Agences de Promotion des Echanges Extérieurs (APEE): Bujumbura; promotes and supervises foreign exchanges.

Office du Café du Burundi (OCBU): BP 450, Bujumbura; tel. 224017; fax 225532; e-mail dgo@usan-bu.net; f. 1964; supervises coffee plantations and coffee exports; Dir-Gen. BARTHÉLÉMY NIYIKIZA.

Office du Thé du Burundi (OTB): 52 blvd de l'UPRONA, Bujumbura; tel. 224228; fax 224657; e-mail otb@cbinf.com; f. 1979; supervises production and marketing of tea; Man. Dir SALVATORE NIMUBONA.

Office National du Commerce (ONC): Bujumbura; f. 1973; supervises international commercial operations between the Govt of Burundi and other states or private orgs; also organizes the import of essential materials; subsidiary offices in each province.

Office National du Logement (ONL): BP 2480, Bujumbura; tel. 226074; f. 1974 to supervise housing construction.

DEVELOPMENT ORGANIZATIONS

Compagnie Financière pour le Développement SA: Bldg INSS, 1 Route Nationale, BP 139, Ngozi; tel. 302279; fax 302296; Pres. ABBÉ EPHREM GIRUKWISHAKA.

Fonds de Développement Communal SP: BP 2799, Bujumbura; tel. 221963; fax 243268; e-mail fdc@cbinf.com; Pres. BÉATRICE BUKWARE.

Fonds de Promotion de l'Habitat Urbain: 6 ave de la Liberté, BP 1996, Bujumbura; tel. 227676; fax 223225; e-mail fphu@cbinf.com; cap. 818m. Burundian francs; Pres. DIDACE BIRABISHA.

Institut des Sciences Agronomiques du Burundi (ISABU): BP 795, Bujumbura; tel. 227349; fax 225798; e-mail isabu@usan-bu.net; f. 1962 for the scientific development of agriculture and livestock.

Office National de la Tourbe (ONATOUR): BP 2360, Bujumbura; tel. 226480; fax 226709; f. 1977 to promote the exploitation of peat deposits.

Société d'Economie pour l'Exploitation du Quinquina au Burundi (SOKINABU): 16 blvd Mwezi Gisabo, BP 1783, Bujumbura; tel. 223469; fax 218160; e-mail chiastos@yahoo.fr; f. 1975 to develop and exploit cinchona trees, the source of quinine; Dir CHRISTIAN REMEZO.

Société Régionale de Développement de l'IMBO (SRDI): Bujumbura; promotes development of IMBO region.

Société Régionale de Développement de Kayanza (SRD KAYANZA): Kayanza; promotes development of Kayanza region.

Société Régionale de Développement de Kirimiro (SRD KIRIMIRO): Bujumbura; promotes development of Kirimiro region.

Société Régionale de Développement de Kirundo (SRD KIRUNDO): Bujumbura; promotes development of Kirundo region.

Société Régionale de Développement de Mumirwa (SRD MUMIRWA): Bujumbura; promotes development of Mumirwa region.

Société Régionale de Développement de Rumonge (SRD RUMONGE): Bujumbura; promotes development of Rumonge region.

CHAMBER OF COMMERCE

Chambre de Commerce, d'Industrie, d'Agriculture et d'Artisanat du Burundi: BP 313, Bujumbura; tel. 222280; fax 227895; f. 1923; Pres. DIDACE NZOHABONAYO; Sec.-Gen. CYRILLE SINGEJEJE; 130 mems.

UTILITY

Régie de Distribution d'Eau et d'Electricité (REGIDESCO): Bujumbura; state-owned distributor of water and electricity services.

TRADE UNIONS

Confédération des Syndicats du Burundi (COSIBU): Bujumbura; Chair. Dr PIERRE-CLAVIER HAJAYANDI.

Union des Travailleurs du Burundi (UTB): BP 1340, Bujumbura; tel. 223884; f. 1967 by merger of all existing unions; closely allied with UPRONA; sole authorized trade union prior to 1994, with 18 affiliated nat. professional feds; Sec.-Gen. MARIUS RURAHENYE.

Transport

RAILWAYS

There are no railways in Burundi. Plans have been under consideration since 1987 for the construction of a line passing through Uganda, Rwanda and Burundi, to connect with the Kigoma–Dar es Salaam line in Tanzania. This rail link would relieve Burundi's isolated trade position.

ROADS

In 1996 Burundi had a total of 14,480 km of roads, of which 1,950 km were national highways and 2,530 km secondary roads. A new crossing of the Ruzizi River, the Bridge of Concord (Burundi's longest bridge), was opened in early 1992.

Office des Transports en Commun (OTRACO): BP 1486, Bujumbura; tel. 231313; fax 232051; 100% govt-owned; operates public transport.

INLAND WATERWAYS

Bujumbura is the principal port for both passenger and freight traffic on Lake Tanganyika, and the greater part of Burundi's external trade is dependent on the shipping services between Bujumbura and lake ports in Tanzania, Zambia and the Democratic Republic of the Congo.

Exploitation du Port de Bujumbura (EPB): Bujumbura; tel. 226036; f. 1967; 43% state-owned; controls Bujumbura port; Dir-Gen. MÉTHODE SHIRAMBERE.

CIVIL AVIATION

The international airport at Bujumbura is equipped to take large jet-engined aircraft.

Air Burundi: 40 ave du Commerce, BP 2460, Bujumbura; tel. 224609; fax 223452; e-mail airbdi@cbinf.com; f. 1971 as Société de Transports Aériens du Burundi; state-owned; operates charter and scheduled passenger services to destinations throughout central Africa; CEO Col ANTOINE GATOTO; Dir C. KAGARI.

Tourism

Tourism is relatively undeveloped. The annual total of tourist arrivals declined from 125,000 in 1991 to only 10,553 in 1997. Total arrivals increased gradually, from 15,404 in 1998 to an estimated 36,000 in 2001. Tourism receipts amounted to an estimated US $1m. in 2002. However, continued failure to resolve conflict between the Government and rebel groups effectively prevented any significant revival of tourism.

Office National du Tourisme (ONT): 2 ave des Euphorbes, BP 902, Bujumbura; tel. 224208; fax 229390; f. 1972; responsible for the promotion and supervision of tourism; Dir HERMENEGILDE NIMBONA (acting).

CAMBODIA

Introductory Survey

Location, Climate, Language, Religion, Flag, Capital

The Kingdom of Cambodia occupies part of the Indo-Chinese peninsula in South-East Asia. It is bordered by Thailand and Laos to the north, by Viet Nam to the east and by the Gulf of Thailand to the south. The climate is tropical and humid. There is a rainy season from June to November, with the heaviest rainfall in September. The temperature is generally between 20°C and 36°C (68°F to 97°F), with March and April usually the hottest months; the annual average temperature in Phnom-Penh is 27°C (81°F). The official language is Khmer, which is spoken by everybody except the Vietnamese and Chinese minorities. The state religion is Theravada Buddhism. The national flag (proportions 2 by 3) consists of three horizontal stripes, of dark blue, red (half the depth) and dark blue, with a stylized representation (in white) of the temple of Angkor Wat, showing three of its five towers, in the centre. The capital is Phnom-Penh.

Recent History

The Kingdom of Cambodia became a French protectorate in the 19th century and was incorporated into French Indo-China. In April 1941 Norodom Sihanouk, then aged 18, succeeded his grandfather as King. In May 1947 he promulgated a Constitution which provided for a bicameral Parliament, including an elected National Assembly. Cambodia became an Associate State of the French Union in November 1949 and attained independence on 9 November 1953. In order to become a political leader, King Sihanouk abdicated in March 1955 in favour of his father, Norodom Suramarit, and became known as Prince Sihanouk. He founded a mass movement, the Sangkum Reastr Niyum (Popular Socialist Community), which won all the seats in elections to the National Assembly in 1955, 1958, 1962 and 1966. King Suramarit died in April 1960, and in June Parliament elected Prince Sihanouk as Head of State. Prince Sihanouk's Government developed good relations with the People's Republic of China and with North Viet Nam, but it was highly critical of the USA's role in Asia. From 1964, however, the Government was confronted by an underground Marxist insurgency movement, the Khmers Rouges, while it also became increasingly difficult to isolate Cambodia from the war in Viet Nam.

In March 1970 Prince Sihanouk was deposed by a right-wing coup, led by the Prime Minister, Lt-Gen. (later Marshal) Lon Nol. The new Government pledged itself to the removal of foreign communist forces and appealed to the USA for military aid. Sihanouk went into exile and formed the Royal Government of National Union of Cambodia (GRUNC), supported by the Khmers Rouges. Sihanoukists and the Khmers Rouges formed the National United Front of Cambodia (FUNC). Their combined forces, aided by South Viet Nam's National Liberation Front and North Vietnamese troops, posed a serious threat to the new regime, but in October 1970 Marshal Lon Nol proclaimed the Khmer Republic. In June 1972 he was elected the first President. During 1973 several foreign states recognized GRUNC as the rightful government of Cambodia. In 1974 the republican regime's control was limited to a few urban enclaves, besieged by GRUNC forces, mainly Khmers Rouges, who gained control of Phnom-Penh on 17 April 1975. Prince Sihanouk became Head of State again but did not return from exile until September. The country was subjected to a pre-arranged programme of radical social deconstruction immediately after the Khmers Rouges' assumption of power; towns were largely evacuated, and their inhabitants forced to work in rural areas. During the following three years an estimated 1.7m. people died as a result of ill-treatment, hunger, disease and executions.

A new Constitution, promulgated in January 1976, renamed the country Democratic Kampuchea, and established a republican form of government; elections for a 250-member People's Representative Assembly were held in March 1976. In April Prince Sihanouk resigned as Head of State, and GRUNC was dissolved. The Assembly elected Khieu Samphan, formerly Deputy Prime Minister, to be President of the State Presidium (Head of State). The little-known Pol Pot (formerly Saloth Sar) became Prime Minister. In September 1977 it was officially disclosed that the ruling organization was the Communist Party of Kampuchea (CPK), with Pol Pot as the Secretary of its Central Committee.

After 1975 close links with the People's Republic of China developed, while relations with Viet Nam deteriorated. In 1978, following a two-year campaign of raids across the Vietnamese border by the Khmers Rouges, the Vietnamese army launched a series of offensives into Kampuchean territory. In December the establishment of the Kampuchean National United Front for National Salvation (KNUFNS, renamed Kampuchean United Front for National Construction and Defence—KUFNCD—in December 1981, and United Front for the Construction and Defence of the Kampuchean Fatherland—UFCDKF—in 1989), a communist-led movement opposed to Pol Pot and supported by Viet Nam, was announced. Later in the month Viet Nam invaded Kampuchea, supported by the KNUFNS.

On 7 January 1979 Phnom-Penh was captured by Vietnamese forces, and three days later the People's Republic of Kampuchea was proclaimed. A People's Revolutionary Council was established, with Heng Samrin, leader of the KNUFNS, as President. It pledged to restore freedom of movement, freedom of association and of religion, and to restore the family unit. The CPK was replaced as the governing party by the Kampuchean People's Revolutionary Party (KPRP). The Khmer Rouge forces, however, remained active in the western provinces, near the border with Thailand, and conducted sporadic guerrilla activities elsewhere in the country. Several groups opposing both the Khmers Rouges and the Heng Samrin regime were established, including the Khmer People's National Liberation Front (KPNLF), headed by a former Prime Minister, Son Sann. In July, claiming that Pol Pot's regime had been responsible for 3m. deaths, the KPRP administration sentenced Pol Pot and his former Minister of Foreign Affairs, Ieng Sary, to death *in absentia*. In January 1980 Khieu Samphan assumed the premiership of the deposed Khmer Rouge regime, while Pol Pot became Commander-in-Chief of the armed forces. In 1981 the CPK was reportedly dissolved and was replaced by the Party of Democratic Kampuchea (PDK).

During the first few years of the KPRP regime Viet Nam launched regular offensives on the Thai-Kampuchean border against the united armed forces of Democratic Kampuchea, the coalition Government-in-exile of anti-Vietnamese resistance groups formed in June 1982. As a result of the fighting, and the prevalence of starvation and disease, thousands of Kampuchean refugees crossed the border into Thailand; in turn, a large number of Vietnamese citizens subsequently settled on Kampuchean territory. The coalition Government-in-exile, of which Prince Sihanouk became President, Khieu Samphan (PDK) Vice-President and Son Sann (KPLNF) Prime Minister, received the support of the People's Republic of China and of member states of the Association of South East Asian Nations (ASEAN, see p. 162), whilst retaining the Kampuchean seat in the UN General Assembly.

In the mid-1980s an increasingly conciliatory attitude between the USSR and the People's Republic of China led to a number of diplomatic exchanges, aimed at reconciling the coalition Government-in-exile with the Government in Phnom-Penh, led by the General Secretary of the KPRP, Heng Samrin. Largely, however, because of mistrust of the PDK (due to Pol Pot's continuing influence), the Heng Samrin Government rejected peace proposals from ASEAN and the coalition Government-in-exile in 1985 and 1986. In September 1987 the Government of the People's Republic of China stated that it would accept a Kampuchean 'government of national reconciliation' under Prince Sihanouk, but that the presence of Vietnamese troops in Kampuchea remained a major obstacle. In the same month the USSR also declared that it was 'prepared to facilitate a political settlement' in Kampuchea. In October, having announced its readiness to conduct negotiations with some PDK leaders (but not Pol Pot), the Heng Samrin Government offered Prince Sihanouk a government post and issued a set of peace proposals which included the complete withdrawal of Vietnamese troops, internationally observed elections and the formation of a coalition government. In December 1987 Prince Sihanouk and Hun Sen, the Chairman of the Council of Ministers in the Heng Samrin Government, met in France for private discussions for the first time since the invasion by Viet Nam. The meeting ended in a joint communiqué, stating that the conflict was to be settled politically by negotiations among all the Kampuchean parties, and that any resulting agreement should be guaranteed by an international conference.

Under increasing pressure from the USSR and the People's Republic of China, the four Kampuchean factions participated in a series of 'informal meetings', held in Indonesia, which were also attended by representatives of Viet Nam, Laos and the six ASEAN members. At the first of these meetings, in July 1988, Viet Nam advanced its deadline for a complete withdrawal of its troops from Kampuchea to late 1989. In April 1989 the National Assembly in Phnom-Penh ratified several constitutional amendments, whereby the name of the country was changed to the State of Cambodia, a new national flag, emblem and anthem were introduced, Buddhism was reinstated as the state religion, and the death penalty was abolished. In July 1989 the Paris International Conference on Cambodia (PICC) met for the first time. The PICC agreed to send a UN reconnaissance party to Cambodia to study the prospects for a cease-fire and the installation of a peace-keeping force.

The withdrawal of Vietnamese forces, completed on schedule in September 1989, was followed by renewed offensives into Cambodia by the resistance forces, particularly the PDK. In November, following substantial military gains by the PDK, the UN General Assembly adopted a resolution supporting the formation of an interim government in Cambodia which would include members of the PDK, but which retained a clause, introduced in 1988, relating to past atrocities committed by the organization. The resolution also cast doubt on the Vietnamese withdrawal (since it had not been monitored by the UN) and, in reference to the alleged presence of 1m. Vietnamese settlers in Cambodia, condemned 'demographic changes' imposed in the country. An Australian peace initiative was unanimously approved by the five permanent members of the UN Security Council in January 1990. In February Prince Sihanouk declared that the coalition Government-in-exile would henceforth be known as the National Government of Cambodia.

In July 1990 the USA withdrew its support for the National Government of Cambodia's occupation of Cambodia's seat at the UN. In August the UN Security Council endorsed the framework for a comprehensive settlement in Cambodia. The agreement provided for UN supervision of an interim government, military arrangements for the transitional period, free elections and guarantees for the future neutrality of Cambodia. A special representative of the Secretary-General of the UN was to control the proposed UN Transitional Authority in Cambodia (UNTAC). The UN would also assume control of the Ministries of Foreign Affairs, National Defence, Finance, the Interior and Information, Press and Culture. China and the USSR pledged to cease supplies of military equipment to their respective allies, the PDK and the Phnom-Penh Government.

At a fourth 'informal meeting' in Jakarta in September 1990 the four Cambodian factions accepted the UN proposals. They also agreed to the formation of the Supreme National Council (SNC), with six representatives from the Phnom-Penh Government and six from the National Government of Cambodia. SNC decisions were to be taken by consensus, effectively allowing each faction the power of veto, and the SNC was to occupy the Cambodian seat at the UN General Assembly. Prince Sihanouk was subsequently elected to the chairmanship of the SNC (a position in which he would have final arbitration if a consensus could not be reached), and resigned as leader of the resistance coalition and as President of the National Government of Cambodia (positions to which Son Sann was appointed). Agreement was also reached on the four factions reducing their armed forces by 70% and the remaining 30% being placed in cantonments under UN supervision; the introduction of a system of multi-party democracy; the Phnom-Penh Government abandoning its demand for references to genocide to be included in a draft plan; and the holding of elections to a constituent assembly, which would subsequently become a legislative assembly comprising 120 seats.

Following the release of political prisoners by the Phnom-Penh Government in October 1991, including former 'reformist' associates of Hun Sen (who had been arrested in 1990 and replaced by supporters of the more conservative chairman of the National Assembly, Chea Sim), a congress of the KPRP was convened at which the party changed its name to the Cambodian People's Party (CPP). The communist insignia was removed from its emblem, Heng Samrin was replaced as Chairman of the Central Committee (formerly the Politburo) by Chea Sim and Hun Sen was elected as Vice-Chairman.

On 23 October 1991 the four factions signed the UN peace accord in Paris, under the auspices of the PICC. UNTAC was expected to be in place by August 1992. The mainly military UN Advance Mission in Cambodia (UNAMIC), comprising 300 men, was in place by the end of 1991. The peace-keeping operation was expected to be completed in 1993. The agreement also provided for the repatriation, under the supervision of the UN High Commissioner for Refugees, of the estimated 340,000 Cambodian refugees living in camps in Thailand. There were continuing fears that the PDK would, in an attempt to ensure electoral support, endeavour forcibly to repatriate refugees to areas of western Cambodia under their control.

In November 1991 Prince Sihanouk returned to Phnom-Penh, accompanied by Hun Sen. The CPP and the United National Front for an Independent, Neutral, Peaceful and Co-operative Cambodia (FUNCINPEC), led by Prince Sihanouk, subsequently formed an alliance and announced their intention to establish a coalition government. (The alliance was abandoned in December, in response to objections from the KPNLF and the PDK.) On 23 November the four factions endorsed the reinstatement of Prince Sihanouk as the Head of State of Cambodia, pending a presidential election in 1993. Political protest increased towards the end of 1991. An attack by demonstrators on Khieu Samphan on his return to Phnom-Penh in late November led senior PDK officials to flee to Bangkok where the SNC met and agreed that, henceforth, officials of the party would occupy the SNC headquarters in Phnom-Penh with members of UNAMIC. Further demonstrations took place in December and in January 1992. However, following an agreement with representatives of the UN Security Council, the Phnom-Penh Government released all remaining political prisoners between January and March 1992. The UN Security Council expanded UNAMIC's mandate to include mine-clearing operations, and in February authorized the dispatch of a 22,000-member peace-keeping force to Cambodia to establish UNTAC. In mid-March UNAMIC transferred responsibility for the implementation of the peace agreement to UNTAC.

The refugee repatriation programme, which began in March 1992, was threatened by continued cease-fire violations, which were concentrated in the central province of Kampong Thum. In June the continued obduracy of the PDK disrupted the implementation of the second phase of the peace-keeping operation, which comprised the cantonment and disarmament of the four factions' forces. Although by mid-July about 12,000 troops from three of the factions had reported to the designated areas, the PDK intensified its violations of the cease-fire agreement, continued to deny the UN access to its zones, and failed to attend meetings on the implementation of the peace agreement. At the Ministerial Conference on the Rehabilitation and Reconstruction of Cambodia, which was convened in Tokyo in late June, the application of economic sanctions against the PDK was considered. The PDK reiterated demands that power be transferred from the Phnom-Penh Government to the SNC and that both the SNC and UNTAC should co-operate in ensuring that all Vietnamese forces had withdrawn from Cambodia. During August Yasushi Akashi (who had been appointed UN Special Representative to Cambodia in charge of UNTAC in January 1992) affirmed that the elections would proceed without the participation of the PDK if it continued to refuse to co-operate. The UN set a deadline for compliance of 15 November. By the end of November, however, no consensus had been reached, and the Security Council adopted a resolution condemning PDK obduracy. The Security Council approved an embargo on the supplies of petroleum products to the PDK and endorsed a ban on the export of timber (a principal source of income for the party) from 31 December. On the day the sanctions were adopted, however, the PDK announced the formation of a subsidiary party to contest the forthcoming elections, the Cambodian National Unity Party, led by Khieu Samphan and Son Sen.

In December 1992 the seizure of six members of the UN peace-keeping forces in PDK-controlled areas reflected a growing distrust of UNTAC by the PDK, which had previously alleged UN bias in favour of the Phnom-Penh Government. The slow progress of the peace initiative, coupled with the poor conduct of UN troops, resulted in widespread disaffection with UNTAC, and in the latter part of 1992 resentment towards ethnic Vietnamese intensified, largely as a result of PDK and, subsequently, KPLNF propaganda.

By the final deadline at the end of January 1993 20 parties, excluding the PDK, had registered to contest the elections. The Phnom-Penh Government subsequently launched an offensive against the PDK in northern and western Cambodia, recovering much of the territory gained by the PDK since the signing of the peace agreement in October 1991. In early February 1993 Prince Sihanouk returned to Phnom-Penh from Beijing amidst intensifying politically motivated violence. There were also continuing attacks by the PDK on ethnic Vietnamese, and, following several rural massacres, thousands of Vietnamese took refuge in Viet Nam. Despite the violence, UNTAC's voter registration campaign, which ended in February, had been extremely successful; 4.7m. Cambodians were registered, constituting about 97% of the estimated eligible electorate. The repatriation programme for refugees on the Thai border was also successfully concluded; 360,000 refugees had been returned to Cambodia on schedule by the end of April.

On 23–28 May 1993 about 90% of the electorate participated in the elections to the Constituent Assembly. The PDK offered support to the FUNCINPEC Party, in the hope of securing a role in government following the elections but, owing to the massive voter participation in the election, Prince Sihanouk abandoned his proposals for the inclusion of the PDK in a future Government. Early results from the election, indicating a FUNCINPEC victory, prompted CPP allegations of electoral irregularities. UNTAC, however, rejected CPP requests for fresh elections in at least four provinces. In early June, without prior consultation with the UN and disregarding the incomplete election results, Prince Sihanouk announced the formation of a new Government, with himself as Prime Minister and Prince Ranariddh and Hun Sen as joint Deputy Prime Ministers. The coalition was created and renounced within hours, owing to objections from Prince Ranariddh, who had not been consulted, and to suggestions by UN officials that it was tantamount to a coup. Two days later the official results of the election were released: the FUNCINPEC Party secured 58 seats with 46% of the votes cast, the CPP 51 seats with 38% of the votes, the Buddhist Liberal Democratic Party (BLDP, founded by the KPNLF) 10 seats (3%) and a breakaway faction from the FUNCINPEC Party, MOLINAKA (National Liberation Movement of Cambodia), one seat. Despite the UN's endorsement of the election as fair, the CPP refused to dissolve the State of Cambodia Government in Phnom-Penh and announced that certain eastern provinces were threatening to secede unless demands for an independent examination of the results were met. Prince Norodom Chakrapong (a son of Prince Sihanouk who had been appointed to the Council of Ministers of the Phnom-Penh Government in December 1991) subsequently led a secessionist movement in seven provinces in the east and north-east of the country, which was reportedly sanctioned by the CPP leadership in an attempt to secure a power-sharing agreement with the FUNCINPEC Party.

On 14 June 1993, at the inaugural session of the Constituent Assembly, Prince Sihanouk was proclaimed Head of State, and 'full and special' powers were conferred on him. The Assembly adopted a resolution declaring null and void the overthrow of Prince Sihanouk 23 years previously and recognizing him retroactively as Head of State of Cambodia during that period. The secessionist movement in the eastern provinces collapsed, and on the following day an agreement was reached on the formation of an interim government, with Hun Sen and Prince Ranariddh as Co-Chairmen of the Provisional National Government of Cambodia, pending the drawing up of a new constitution. Prince Chakrapong returned to Phnom-Penh, where he was reconciled with Prince Sihanouk. A few days later the CPP officially recognized the results of the election.

The PDK had immediately accepted the results of the election and supported the formation of a coalition government, but continued to engage in military action to support its demands for inclusion in a future government. In July 1993 the PDK offered to incorporate its forces into the newly formed Cambodian National Armed Forces (later restyled the Royal Cambodian Armed Forces), which had been created through the merger of the forces of the other three factions in June. PDK offensives escalated, however, after the party was denied a role in government, largely owing to US threats to withhold economic aid from Cambodia if the PDK were included prior to a renunciation of violence. In late August Cambodia's united armed forces initiated a successful offensive against PDK positions in north-

western Cambodia. The Government rejected an appeal for urgent discussions by the PDK after government forces had captured PDK bases, insisting that the party surrender unconditionally the estimated 20% of Cambodian territory under its control. The PDK suffered from defections as disillusioned troops were offered the same rank in the Cambodian National Armed Forces under a government amnesty, which ended in January 1995.

On 21 September 1993 the Constituent Assembly adopted a new Constitution, which provided for an hereditary monarchy. On 24 September Prince Sihanouk promulgated the Constitution, thus terminating the mandate of UNTAC (whose personnel left the country by mid-November). The Constituent Assembly became the National Assembly, and Prince Sihanouk acceded to the throne of the new Kingdom of Cambodia. Chea Sim was re-elected Chairman of the National Assembly. Government ministers were to be chosen from parties represented in the National Assembly, thus precluding the involvement of the PDK. In October talks scheduled between the Cambodian Government and the PDK were postponed indefinitely, owing to the ill health of King Sihanouk. At the end of October the National Assembly approved the new Royal Government of Cambodia (previously endorsed by King Sihanouk), in which Prince Ranariddh was named First Prime Minister and Hun Sen Second Prime Minister. Between November 1993 and January 1994 initiatives to incorporate the PDK into the new Government failed, owing to objections from various parties. In May 1994 King Sihanouk threatened to stop negotiating with the PDK and the Government to end the fighting in the north-west of the country, which had reached a severity not witnessed since 1989, and forced the postponement of proposed peace talks in Pyongyang, the Democratic People's Republic of Korea. Following the failure of peace talks held in May and June 1994, the Government ordered the PDK to leave Phnom-Penh and closed the party's mission in the capital.

In July 1994 the Government claimed to have suppressed a coup attempt led by Prince Chakrapong and Gen. Sin Song, a former Minister of National Security under the State of Cambodia. Following a personal appeal from King Sihanouk, Prince Chakrapong, who protested his innocence, was exiled from Cambodia, while Gen. Sin Song was placed under arrest. (Gen. Sin Song escaped from prison in September and was captured by Thai authorities in November.) Hun Sen also suspected his rival, Sar Kheng, a Deputy Prime Minister and Minister of the Interior, of involvement in the alleged revolt. Sar Kheng was, however, protected by his powerful brother-in-law, Chea Sim. The coup attempt was also used by the increasingly divided Government as a pretext to suppress criticism of the regime. Newspapers were closed, editors fined and imprisoned and in September an editor renowned as an outspoken critic of the Government was killed by unidentified assailants.

Despite King Sihanouk's continued advocacy of national reconciliation, in July 1994 legislation providing for the outlawing of the PDK was adopted by the National Assembly (whilst allowing for an immediate six-month amnesty for the lower ranks of the party). In response, the PDK announced the formation of a Provisional Government of National Unity and National Salvation of Cambodia (PGNUNSC), under the premiership of Khieu Samphan, which was to co-ordinate opposition to the Government in Phnom-Penh from its headquarters in Preah Vihear in the north of the country. In October Sam Rainsy, who was highly regarded by independent foreign observers, was dismissed as Minister of Finance, apparently owing to his efforts to combat high-level corruption. Prince Sirivudh subsequently resigned as Minister of Foreign Affairs in protest at Rainsy's removal, which also demonstrated the decline in King Sihanouk's political influence—Prince Ranariddh and Hun Sen had jointly proposed Rainsy's dismissal in March, but King Sihanouk had withheld his consent. Prince Sirivudh also criticized the FUNCINPEC Party, of which he was Secretary-General, for submitting too readily to CPP demands, as it became increasingly apparent that real power lay with the former communists.

In May 1995 Rainsy was expelled from the FUNCINPEC Party and in April he was expelled from the National Assembly. This caused international disquiet and provoked criticism from human rights groups. Rainsy formed a new party, the Khmer Nation Party (KNP), which was officially launched in November. The Government declared the KNP illegal but refrained from action to disband it. Rainsy's expulsion from the National Assembly coincided with the adoption of the revised draft of a draconian press law, which imposed substantial fines and prison sentences for reporting issues affecting 'national security' or 'political stability'.

Politically motivated violence, organized crime and drugs-trafficking all developed as serious problems in Cambodia. The situation was exacerbated by the inadequacies of law enforcement, the lack of any specific legislation to deter 'money laundering' and endemic corruption among senior government officials and the armed forces. In October Prince Sirivudh was expelled from the National Assembly (and thus deprived of diplomatic immunity) and charged with conspiring to assassinate Hun Sen. Human rights groups declared that Prince Sirivudh, who protested his innocence, was a political prisoner. Under an agreement reached with King Sihanouk's intervention, Prince Sirivudh was allowed to go into exile in France in December on condition that he refrain from political activity. In January 1996 Prince Sirivudh was convicted and sentenced to 10 years' imprisonment *in absentia* on charges of criminal conspiracy and possession of unlicensed firearms. Also in January the Government began to adopt repressive measures against the KNP. In March Rainsy nominally merged the KNP with a defunct but still legally registered party, in an attempt to gain legal status. However, in April the Government ordered all parties without parliamentary representation to close their offices. Several KNP officials were assassinated during the year.

In August 1996 the prominent PDK leader, Ieng Sary, together with two military divisions that controlled the significant PDK strongholds of Pailin and Malai, defected from the movement and negotiated a peace agreement with the Government. Ieng Sary subsequently denied responsibility for the atrocities committed during Pol Pot's regime, and was granted a royal amnesty in September, at the request of both Hun Sen and Prince Ranariddh. Following his defection, Ieng Sary formed a new political organization, the Democratic National United Movement (DNUM), while his supporters retained control of Pailin and Malai, despite efforts by troops loyal to the PDK leadership to recapture the region (where lucrative mineral and timber resources were situated). Former PDK troops (numbering about 4,000) were integrated into the national army in November. An estimated 2,500 PDK troops transferred allegiance to the Government in October.

Throughout 1996 political instability increased. In September the partial dissolution of the PDK increased tensions within the ruling coalition, as both the CPP and the FUNCINPEC Party attempted to attract former PDK troops. However, as the FUNCINPEC Party appeared more successful than the CPP at recruiting former PDK commanders and cadres, Hun Sen became concerned that the alliance between the royalists and the PDK as former resistance forces would be re-established. In February 1997 Prince Ranariddh sent a helicopter mission to Anlong Veng to negotiate with the central PDK faction. However, PDK members opposed to peace talks ambushed the helicopter, killing the majority of the Prince's emissaries. Meanwhile, the two Prime Ministers were stockpiling weapons, violations of human and civil rights were becoming increasingly prevalent, corruption was rampant, and labour unrest was widespread. King Sihanouk announced his concern and raised the possibility of his abdication. The potential involvement of the popular monarch in the forthcoming polls provoked a threat from Hun Sen to cancel both the local and national elections and to amend the Constitution to prohibit all members of the royal family from participating in politics, to guarantee the neutrality of the constitutional monarchy. In March 1997 Rainsy, who had increased his attacks against Hun Sen and the CPP-controlled judicial system and police force, led a demonstration outside the National Assembly. The meeting was attacked by assailants who threw four grenades, killing 19 and injuring more than 100 protesters in a presumed attempt to assassinate Rainsy. Rainsy accused Hun Sen of orchestrating the attack and expressed no confidence in the commission established to investigate the incident.

In April 1997 Ung Phan, a former CPP member who had joined the FUNCINPEC Party in the early 1990s, led a rebellion against the party leadership of Prince Ranariddh, with the support of Hun Sen. The National Assembly, which was due to adopt legislation pertaining to local and national elections scheduled for 1998, was unable to convene, as the FUNCINPEC Party refused to attend until its dissident members were expelled from the Assembly, whereas the CPP insisted on their retention. In June the dissident FUNCINPEC members organized a party congress and formed a rival FUNCINPEC Party,

with Toan Chhay, the Governor of Siem Reap, as its chairman. Also in June Prince Sirivudh was prevented from returning to Cambodia, as he was refused permission to board flights to Cambodia in Hong Kong, owing to threats by Hun Sen, who had earlier refused to support a royal pardon for the Prince.

In May 1997 Khieu Samphan announced the creation of a new political party, the National Solidarity Party, which would support the National United Front (an alliance founded in February by Prince Ranariddh) at the next election. Prince Ranariddh declared that, if the notorious former leadership of the PDK were excluded, he would welcome such an alliance. Hun Sen, however, deemed the potential alliance to be a threat to the CPP and, following the seizure of a shipment of weapons destined for Prince Ranariddh, accused the Prince of illegally importing weapons to arm PDK soldiers. The PDK was divided over the issue of peace negotiations. Pol Pot began a violent purge, ordering the death of Son Sen and also that of Ta Mok. Following the execution of Son Sen and his family, many PDK commanders rallied behind Ta Mok, and fighting erupted between the two factions. Pol Pot and his supporters fled into the jungle, with Khieu Samphan as a hostage, but were captured by Ta Mok's forces and returned to the PDK base at Anlong Veng, near the Thai border. In late July a US journalist, Nate Thayer, was invited by the PDK to Anlong Veng to witness the trial of Pol Pot. He was condemned by a 'people's court' for 'destroying national unity' and for the killing of Son Sen and his family. In October Thayer was permitted to interview the former leader, who denied that atrocities had occurred under his regime.

In June 1997 Prince Ranariddh claimed that Pol Pot was under arrest and that Khieu Samphan would surrender. Hun Sen, meanwhile, demanded that Ranariddh choose between himself and Khieu as a partner in government. Tensions between Prince Ranariddh and Hun Sen increased, as FUNCINPEC military forces were strengthened. Hun Sen continued to warn that PDK defectors were massing in Phnom-Penh. On 3 July, following several attempts by CPP troops to detect the presence of PDK soldiers in FUNCINPEC units, CPP forces disarmed a unit of Prince Ranariddh's bodyguards, on the grounds that they were allegedly PDK troops. On the following day Prince Ranariddh left the country. On 5 July serious fighting erupted in Phnom-Penh, and on 6 July, the day on which Khieu Samphan had been scheduled to broadcast the PDK's agreement with the FUNCINPEC Party to end its resistance and rejoin the political system, Hun Sen appeared on television to demand Prince Ranariddh's arrest (on charges of negotiating with the PDK, introducing proscribed PDK troops into Phnom-Penh and secretly importing weapons to arm those forces) and to urge FUNCINPEC officials to select another leader. More than 24 hours of pillage then ensued. The UN subsequently claimed that it had documentary evidence showing that at least 43 people, principally from the royalist army structure, had been murdered by forces loyal to Hun Sen after the events of 5–6 July. Many more FUNCINPEC and KNP officials, as well as many FUNCINPEC members of the legislature, fled the country.

King Sihanouk's appeals for both sides to travel to the People's Republic of China to negotiate a settlement were rejected by Hun Sen. Prince Ranariddh announced from Paris that a resistance movement was being organized in western Cambodia. Meanwhile, Hun Sen began negotiations with certain prominent members of the FUNCINPEC Party who remained in Phnom-Penh in an effort to attain the two-thirds' majority of the National Assembly necessary for the investiture of a new government. By the end of July 1997 the National Assembly had reconvened, with 98 of the 120 deputies present, including 40 of the 58 FUNCINPEC deputies. Hun Sen protested to the international community that his actions did not constitute a *coup d'état*, as he had not abolished the Constitution or the monarchy and had not dissolved the Government or the National Assembly. He also declared that he was in favour of free elections in 1998. Despite these assurances, aid was temporarily suspended by the USA, Japan, Germany and later Australia. However, the UN refused to condemn Hun Sen by name, although it expressed a 'grave preoccupation' with the situation in Cambodia. King Sihanouk, who had been in the People's Republic of China since February, also insisted on remaining neutral and accepted that Chea Sim should continue to sign royal decrees in his absence. In August the National Assembly voted to remove Ranariddh's legal immunity (a warrant subsequently being issued for his arrest) and elected Ung Huot, the FUNCINPEC Minister of Foreign Affairs, to the post of First

Prime Minister. The USA opposed his election as undemocratic, but Japan resumed its aid programme, and China also accepted Prince Ranariddh's replacement.

In July 1997 troops loyal to Prince Ranariddh, led by Gen. Nhiek Bunchhay (the former military Deputy Chief of Staff and a principal negotiator with the PDK), were swiftly forced into the north-west of the country by CPP troops. They regrouped near the Thai border in an effective alliance with PDK troops under Ta Mok. Prolonged fighting took place for control of the town of O'Smach, about 70 km west of Anlong Veng, which was the last base for the resistance coalition led by Prince Ranariddh, the Union of Cambodian Democrats. At the end of August the King arrived in Siem Reap. Hun Sen rejected another proposal from the King to act as a mediator in peace talks, insisting that Ranariddh had to be tried for his alleged crimes.

In September 1997 Hun Sen announced a cabinet reorganization that effectively removed remaining supporters of Prince Ranariddh from the Government. However, in a secret ballot the National Assembly failed by 13 votes to approve the changes by the required two-thirds' majority. Hun Sen continued his efforts to encourage the return of all opposition representatives who had fled the country in July, except Ranariddh and Gen. Nhiek Bunchhay. In November Rainsy returned to Cambodia, whereupon he organized a peace march through Phnom-Penh, which was attended by several thousand supporters. In a conciliatory gesture in December, Hun Sen and Rainsy held a cordial meeting, at which they agreed to co-operate in the national interest.

In mid-December 1997 the National Assembly voted, for technical reasons, to postpone local and legislative elections from May until July 1998 and to increase the number of seats from 120 to 122, owing to Ieng Sary's decision in October 1997 to transfer nominal control of Pailin and Malai to the Government. At the beginning of February 1998 Rainsy withdrew the KNP from the electoral process in protest at the unlawful methods allegedly employed by Hun Sen, including the registration of a breakaway faction of the KNP bearing an identical title and logo and the fatal shooting in January of a KNP official and his daughter. Rainsy subsequently restyled the KNP the Sam Rainsy Party.

Hun Sen and Ranariddh agreed to the terms of a Japanese peace proposal in February 1998, which provided for the severance of Ranariddh's links with the PDK, the implementation of a cease-fire in the north-west (which came into effect on 27 February), a royal pardon for Ranariddh if he were convicted *in absentia* of the charges against him and his guaranteed safe return to participate in the general election. Ranariddh was convicted in March of illegally importing weapons and of conspiring with the proscribed PDK, and sentenced to 30 years' imprisonment and a fine of US $54m. for damage caused on 5–6 July 1997. At the formal request of Hun Sen, Sihanouk granted Ranariddh a royal pardon, but no amnesty was accorded to Nhiek Bunchhay or Serei Kosal, the commanders of Ranariddh's troops in the north-west, who were found guilty on the same day. Ranariddh returned to Phnom-Penh at the end of March 1998, but the FUNCINPEC Party had been severely weakened by the killing of many of its senior personnel, the closure of its offices across the country and the defection of some principal officials, including Loy Simchheang and You Hockry.

In March 1998 two divisions of PDK troops mutinied against their leader, Ta Mok; further divisions rebelled in the following week, surrendering control of the PDK headquarters, Anlong Veng, to government troops. During the ensuing clashes thousands of civilians were evacuated to Thailand. Pol Pot died on 15 April, shortly after his comrades had offered to surrender him for trial by an international tribunal. It was later reported that he had committed suicide. Ta Mok announced that he was prepared to reach agreement with the Government but demanded autonomy for Anlong Veng. Sporadic clashes between the remnants of the PDK and government forces continued in late 1998. The grouping was practically defunct, however, by the end of the year, following further significant defections in October and December. In late December Nuon Chea (Pol Pot's former deputy) and Khieu Samphan defected to the Government, seeking sanctuary in Pailin, an area effectively controlled by Ieng Sary. In February 1999 a final 4,332 PDK troops surrendered to the Co-Ministers of National Defence in Anlong Veng. Ta Mok, however, remained in the border area.

The election campaign period was characterized by intimidation and violence. All demonstrations were banned, as was the dissemination of political information by private news media. Ranariddh and, more particularly, Rainsy (who did finally contest the election) sought to exploit traditional Cambodian hatred of the Vietnamese. Hun Sen refused to campaign, but the ruling CPP dominated the National Election Committee, the Constitutional Council, the armed forces and the judiciary, as well as central and local government. However, the general election, which took place on 26 July 1998, was characterized by the UN-co-ordinated Joint International Observer Group as free and fair. Voting took place relatively peacefully, except for an attack on a polling station by PDK remnants, in which 10 people were killed; 90% of the 5,395,024 registered voters (representing 98% of the population of voting age) participated in the election, which was contested by 39 parties. Under a newly introduced modified system of proportional representation that favoured larger parties, the CPP secured 64 seats (with 41.4% of the popular vote), the FUNCINPEC Party 43 seats (31.7%) and the Sam Rainsy Party 15 seats (14.3%). At an audience with the King at the end of July Hun Sen proposed a three-party coalition, but this was rejected by Ranariddh and Rainsy, who demanded a national recount, on the grounds of electoral fraud, and threatened to boycott the new National Assembly.

In August 1998 Rainsy was detained for questioning, following a grenade explosion at the Ministry of the Interior. Several thousand Cambodians took part in a demonstration in Phnom-Penh, organized by Sam Rainsy, to denounce electoral fraud and to demand the removal of Hun Sen. Despite a ruling by the Constitutional Court upholding the National Election Committee's decision to reject allegations of electoral fraud, the peaceful demonstration outside the National Assembly lasted for more than two weeks. Talks between the three principal parties failed to produce a resolution. In September, however, following a grenade attack on a disused residence of Hun Sen, the protesters were violently dispersed by security forces, and Hun Sen ordered the arrest of Rainsy on charges of murder. The opposition accused Hun Sen of staging the incident in order to justify his suppression of the peaceful protest. Rainsy took refuge under the protection of the UN, and both Rainsy and Ranariddh abandoned claims for a recount. Sporadic violence continued, and Hun Sen announced that the FUNCINPEC Party and the Sam Rainsy Party would be expelled from the National Assembly if they failed to attend its inauguration on 24 September. Prior to the inauguration Hun Sen, Rainsy and Ranariddh met, under the chairmanship of Sihanouk, in Siem Reap Province, but failed to resolve the crisis. Tension was further heightened by a rocket-propelled grenade attack on a convoy of vehicles en route to the convening ceremony of the National Assembly. Hun Sen, who claimed to be the intended victim of the attack, issued retaliatory threats prompting Ranariddh and Rainsy to flee to Thailand. Following the failure of further negotiations in early October, a declaration was issued, stating that the present Government, which was due to leave office, would continue to administer the country until a new government was formed. The situation continued to deteriorate in October 1998 with the arrest, torture and execution of many opposition supporters.

Ranariddh agreed to return to Cambodia to attend a meeting with Hun Sen, under the auspices of King Sihanouk, from which Rainsy was excluded. In November 1998 agreement was reached on the formation of a coalition Government, which would be supported by 107 of the 122 deputies, with Hun Sen as Prime Minister and Ranariddh as the Chairman of the National Assembly. The accord also provided for the creation of a Senate (to be presided over by Chea Sim), the reintegration of resistance soldiers into the armed forces, royal pardons for Gen. Nhiek Bunchhay and Serei Kosal, as well as Prince Sirivudh and Prince Chakrapong, and restitution for property damaged during fighting in July 1997. On 25 November the National Assembly convened, and Ranariddh was duly elected Chairman of the Assembly, with two CPP deputies. The new Royal Government was approved on 30 November and included Co-Ministers for the influential Ministries of Defence and of the Interior, while the CPP controlled the foreign affairs and finance portfolios and the FUNCINPEC Party assumed responsibility for information and health. Rainsy became the official leader of the opposition. The Senate, which was empowered to scrutinize and amend bills passed by the National Assembly, held its inaugural session on 25 March 1999. Representation in the 61-member upper chamber was proportionate to elected strength in the National Assembly; the CPP was allocated 31 seats, the FUNCINPEC Party 21 and the Sam Rainsy Party seven, whilst a further two members were appointed by the King. Chea Sim was duly elected as Chairman, and Nhiek Bunchhay became one of the three Deputy Chairmen.

Reform of the Royal Cambodian Armed Forces began in January 1999 with Hun Sen's resignation as Commander-in-Chief, to demonstrate the neutrality of the armed forces. He was replaced by the former Chief of the General Staff, Gen. Ke Kimyan. By the end of September 15,551 'ghost' troops (soldiers who had been killed or had deserted, but whose pay continued to be collected by senior officers) had been removed from the army payroll. Plans announced in November 1999 provided for the demobilization of 11,500 troops in 2000, followed by a further 10,000 in both 2001 and 2002. The coalition Government also expressed its commitment to administrative and environmental reforms.

In March 1999 Ta Mok was captured near the Thai border and placed in detention. In May Kang Kek Ieu, known as Duch, the director of the Tuol Sleng detention centre where 16,000 detainees had been tortured and executed during the Democratic Kampuchean regime, was arrested and charged with belonging to a proscribed organization. These detentions intensified domestic and international pressure for the establishment of a tribunal to try former Khmer Rouge leaders for atrocities committed during 1975–79. Three jurists, commissioned by the UN to assess the evidence against the leaders of the PDK, recommended that 20–30 Khmer Rouge leaders be brought to trial and reparations be made to their victims. The Cambodian Government, however, in the interests of national reconciliation, was reluctant to indict former Khmer Rouge leaders who had surrendered to the Government, for fear that former PDK members might revert to armed insurrection. The Cambodian Government and the UN also differed as to the composition and structure of a tribunal. The UN doubted Cambodia's ability to conduct a trial in accordance with international standards and thus favoured an international tribunal, whereas Hun Sen claimed that this would constitute an infringement of Cambodian sovereignty and insisted that any trials take place within the existing Cambodian court structure. In April, however, Hun Sen conceded that UN-appointed foreign judges could take part in a trial in Cambodia, although he still favoured the nomination of a Cambodian prosecutor. Cambodia submitted draft legislation recommending a majority of Cambodian judges to the UN for approval in December. Hun Sen announced in January 2000 that the trials would begin on 17 April, the 25th anniversary of Pol Pot seizing control of Phnom-Penh, with or without UN support. The Government approved draft legislation establishing a court in January, but the UN finally issued its rejection of the draft in February, stating that the legislation did not conform to international standards. In December 1999 the office of the UN Secretary-General's special envoy to Cambodia was closed at the request of the Cambodian Government, despite UN pleas that it remain open for a further year. The Cambodian Government had, however, agreed in August to extend the mandate of the representative of the UN High Commissioner for Human Rights based in Cambodia, Thomas Hammarberg. Following the delays in establishing a tribunal, in August 1999 the National Assembly approved legislation extending pre-trial detention for those accused of genocide and crimes against humanity from six months to three years, effectively postponing the trials of Ta Mok and Duch. In September both Ta Mok and Duch were formally charged with genocide under a 1979 decree of the People's Republic of Kampuchea, and in the first half of 2002 both were also charged with having committed crimes against humanity; the pair remained in government custody, awaiting trial, in early 2005.

In June 1999, following pressure from Australia and the United Kingdom, Gen. Nuon Paet, a senior Khmer Rouge commander, was convicted in connection with the abduction and murder of three foreign tourists (Australian, British and French nationals) in July 1994 and sentenced to life imprisonment. Gen. Nuon Paet's sentence was upheld by the appeals court in September 2000 and again in September 2002. In July Col Chhouk Rin, one of a number of other Khmer Rouge leaders charged in connection with the murder of the three tourists, was freed after it was announced that he was covered by the amnesty granted to Khmer Rouge cadres who surrendered to the Cambodian Government. However, in September 2002, following formal protests from the Australian, British and French Governments, his acquittal was reversed by the appeals court and Col Chhouk Rin was sentenced to life imprisonment; he refused to recognize the verdict, despite the fact that it was upheld by another court in November 2003, and appealed to the Supreme Court against his conviction. He remained free pending the outcome of his appeal. In February 2005 the verdict was upheld, and the court ordered that Chhouk Rin be arrested and imprisoned immediately. Meanwhile, in May 2002 Gen. Sam Bith was arrested and charged in connection with the murder of the three tourists. In December, following a trial during which former Khmer Rouge leader Nuon Chea testified on his behalf, Bith was convicted of the charges against him and also received a life sentence; he subsequently appealed against his conviction. In April 2003 Judge Sok Sethamony, who had been responsible for sentencing Bith, was assassinated in Phnom-Penh.

In April 2000 US Senator John Kerry announced that, following extensive negotiations between the Cambodian Government and the UN, an agreement had been reached on a formula for the establishment of a tribunal to try former Khmer Rouge leaders for atrocities committed under the regime. The details of a draft accord on the establishment of the tribunal were finalized in July, whereupon the requisite legislation was submitted to the Cambodian National Assembly. In early August the Sam Rainsy Party presented a petition expressing unreserved support for the Government's agreement with the UN. Despite the opposition's support for the legislation, however, significant delays ensued; the National Assembly finally approved the draft legislation in January 2001. However, it specified that only those individuals deemed 'most responsible' for the atrocities would face the tribunal, thereby implicitly exempting significant numbers of middle- and lower-ranking former Khmer Rouge officials from prosecution. The legislation was approved by the Senate later the same month.

In July 2001 the final version of legislation providing for the trial of Khmer Rouge leaders was passed by the National Assembly, and, in the following month, after receiving the approval of the Constitutional Council, it was signed into law by King Sihanouk. The UN was left to determine whether or not the trial framework would ensure the adequate implementation of international standards of justice. In June, following the departure of the UN Secretary-General's Special Representative for Human Rights in Cambodia, Peter Leuprecht, who had voiced doubts as to the efficacy of the proposed legislation, Prime Minister Hun Sen accused the UN of interfering with Cambodian sovereignty. His views were reiterated by Prince Ranariddh.

In February 2002 the UN unexpectedly announced that it had decided to abandon negotiations with the Cambodian Government over a UN role in the establishment of a joint tribunal to try former Khmer Rouge leaders. It claimed that the legal framework created by the Government did not conform to international standards of justice and that it would not ensure either the independence or impartiality of proceedings. In response, the Government stated that it intended to proceed with the trials and that it would make no further concessions to the UN in order to facilitate the establishment of a tribunal. In June Peter Leuprecht visited the country again and intimated that attempts were under way to facilitate the restarting of talks, with the possibility that the trials could be conducted in a Cambodian court but with the inclusion of foreign judges. In the following month Prime Minister Hun Sen announced that Cambodia was prepared to compromise with the UN by amending the laws that would govern the establishment of any tribunal. In November the UN voted in favour of a draft resolution submitted by Japan and France requesting that it resume negotiations with the Cambodian Government without further delay. Hun Sen affirmed his Government's intention to co-operate with the UN in the renewal of efforts to establish a satisfactory judicial framework for the tribunal. Following a week of exploratory talks in January 2003, negotiations subsequently recommenced in March, resulting in the signing of a draft agreement concerning the tribunal. In June the two sides concluded a formal agreement providing for the establishment of a bicameral tribunal, composed of a Trial Chamber and a Supreme Court Chamber. Under the legislation approved in 2001, only those senior officials of the Khmers Rouges deemed to bear most responsibility for the atrocities of 1975–78 were to face trial. After a significant delay, owing to the prolonged political dispute that had arisen following the 2003 elections (see below), the legislation establishing the tribunal was finally ratified by the Cambodian legislature in October 2004 and promulgated by the King in the same month. In December 2004 a UN delegation arrived in the country to discuss funding. By March 2005 UN members had pledged a total of US $38.0m. (of which $21.6m.

had been allocated by the Japanese Government), thus permitting the establishment of the tribunal.

In November 2000, meanwhile, dozens of armed men launched an attack on official buildings in Phnom-Penh. At least seven of the gunmen were killed in the raid, which government officials initially attributed to unspecified 'terrorists'; however, some of those involved alleged that they had been brought to Phnom-Penh under false pretences and forced to carry weapons. The leader of the US-based Cambodian Freedom Fighters organization, Chhun Yasith (a citizen of the USA), subsequently issued a statement claiming responsibility for the attack on behalf of his organization and alleging that its principal intention had been to disrupt the forthcoming visit of the President of Viet Nam, Tran Duc Luong (which had originally been scheduled for late November, but which was then postponed indefinitely). Forty-seven people, including two members of the Sam Rainsy Party, were subsequently reported to have been charged with terrorism in connection with the attack.

In late June and July 2001 the trial of 32 of those who had participated in the attempted coup took place, amid accusations that the Government had played a part in fomenting the violence in order to facilitate the intimidation of political opponents by local leaders. Three US citizens, among those arrested, were sentenced to life imprisonment *in absentia*; 27 Cambodians were also given sentences ranging in length from three years to life. In November a further 26 nationals were imprisoned for terms of up to 15 years, following a second mass trial which had begun in October. Two people were released owing to lack of evidence. In February 2002 a further 20 people were tried in connection with the attempted coup and sentenced to prison terms; those convicted included one US citizen.

In 2001 the Prime Minister continued to prevaricate on questions of democratic reform. The stagnation of democracy in the country was reflected by the violence that surrounded the registration period for Cambodia's first multi-party local elections (scheduled for February 2002), which ended in August 2001. At least 20 of the candidates planning to mount a challenge to Hun Sen and the ruling CPP were shot dead during the election campaign. Furthermore, during the campaign period the opposition was denied access to the state-controlled media, effectively preventing it from communicating with potential voters.

In February 2002 polling for the 1,621 *khum* (communes) resulted in an overwhelming victory for the CPP, which secured control of 1,598 *khum*. The Sam Rainsy Party won control of 13 and the FUNCINPEC Party 10. Despite numerous allegations of intimidation and electoral irregularities, the opposition parties accepted the results; according to election monitors, however, the elections could be deemed neither free nor fair.

In 2002, following its disappointing performance in the local elections, a rift developed within the FUNCINPEC Party. As an indirect result, in May 2002 Prince Norodom Chakrapong, one of the sons of King Norodom Sihanouk, founded a new political party, the Prince Norodom Chakrapong Khmer Soul party. Meanwhile, in June the party was weakened further by the defection of one of its founding members, Hang Dara, who announced the formation of the Hang Dara Movement Democratic Party to contest the next general election.

On 27 July 2003 23 political parties contested elections to the 123-member National Assembly. The CPP secured 73 seats, the FUNCINPEC Party 26 and the Sam Rainsy Party 24. However, the failure of the CPP to secure the two-thirds' majority necessary to form a single-party government raised the prospect of a further period of political instability in Cambodia. The FUNCINPEC Party and the Sam Rainsy Party both refused to enter into a multi-party government and, instead, formed the 'Alliance of Democrats' to oppose the CPP. Initially, the Alliance insisted that it would agree to form a tripartite government only if Hun Sen tendered his resignation as Prime Minister. The stalemate continued, angering King Norodom Sihanouk, who indicated his displeasure by failing to attend the inauguration of the newly elected National Assembly, an event also boycotted by both opposition parties. King Sihanouk subsequently attempted to secure a resolution to the dispute by convening a series of talks between leading figures in the CPP and the opposition. These resulted in the conclusion of a provisional agreement by the three parties in early November regarding the formation of a joint administration, although disagreement continued as to the details of the proposed arrangement. In December the three parties finally began negotiations on the formation of a new government, and the first session of the incoming National Assembly took place later that month. However, the CPP continued to reject opposition demands concerning the composition of a new administration, insisting that Hun Sen would continue as Prime Minister. In early 2004 King Sihanouk announced that he had approved a request by the Chairman of the Senate, Chea Sim, to extend the Senate's mandate by one year in order to avert a constitutional crisis; elections to the Senate had been scheduled to take place in March of that year. In January 2004 the FUNCINPEC Party and the Sam Rainsy Party announced that they intended to merge in March, thereby forming the Alliance of Democrats Party. Meanwhile, a series of shootings of prominent opposition supporters in the aftermath of the elections to the National Assembly was believed to have been orchestrated by the CPP. In January the leader of the Free Trade Union of Workers of the Kingdom of Cambodia (FTUWKC), Chea Vichea, a prominent opponent of Hun Sen, was murdered in Phnom-Penh. His killing was believed to have been politically motivated.

At the end of June 2004 the political deadlock that had resulted from the 2003 national elections ended when the CPP and the FUNCINPEC Party signed a power-sharing agreement, whereby the two parties could establish a coalition Government. The formation of a new, 207-member Government (in which the CPP held 136 posts and the FUNCINPEC Party 71) was ratified by the National Assembly in the following month, and Hun Sen was once again confirmed as Prime Minister by royal decree. Prince Norodom Ranariddh of the FUNCINPEC Party was appointed President of the National Assembly. Some controversy was generated by Parliament's approval of legislation permitting the appointments of new government officials to be confirmed together rather than approved separately, as had been the case previously. Chea Sim, President of the Senate and acting Head of State during King Norodom Sihanouk's absence from the country on medical grounds, refused to sign the new legislation and left the country, purportedly also for medical reasons. The Vice-President of the Senate, and a Deputy Prime Minister in the incoming Government, Nhiek Bunchhay, subsequently approved the bill. The role of the Sam Rainsy Party remained unclear, and the party boycotted the National Assembly in protest at its exclusion from the new Government.

In October 2004 King Norodom Sihanouk unexpectedly announced his intention to abdicate, owing to ill health. As required by the Constitution, the Royal Council of the Throne was convened to appoint a successor. The Council subsequently announced that it had appointed one of Sihanouk's sons, Prince Norodom Sihamoni, to the throne. Sihamoni's coronation took place later in that month.

International relations were severely affected by the events of 5–6 July 1997. The USA, Germany and Japan suspended all but humanitarian assistance, and in October 1998 the US House of Representatives adopted a resolution accusing Hun Sen of genocide. One of the most serious international consequences of the events of July 1997 was the decision by ASEAN to postpone indefinitely Cambodia's admission to the grouping. Cambodia had attended an ASEAN meeting in July 1995 with official observer status, had had its application for membership accepted in July 1996 and had been due to join in late July 1997. Hun Sen was angered by ASEAN's decision and initially rejected the grouping's attempts to negotiate a diplomatic solution to the Cambodian crisis. However, at the end of July Hun Sen invited ASEAN to mediate in the dispute and held talks with the grouping in early August. At the end of August the Prime Minister of Singapore announced that Cambodia would not be considered for admission to ASEAN until after elections had been held. Prior to the ASEAN summit meeting in Hanoi in December 1998, despite the formation of a Cambodian coalition Government in November, Singapore, Thailand and the Philippines remained opposed to Cambodia's immediate accession to the organization. However, in the event, the host country, Viet Nam, announced that Cambodia had been accepted as the 10th member of ASEAN, although the formal admission was to take place at a later unspecified date. Cambodia duly acceded to ASEAN on 30 April 1999. A further significant consequence of the events of 5–6 July 1997 was the decision of the UN Accreditation Committee to leave Cambodia's seat at the UN vacant. However, following the formation of a coalition Government in November 1998, Cambodia regained its seat at the UN in December.

In August 2002, following a meeting of ASEAN in Brunei, Cambodia became a signatory to an anti-terrorism pact originally drawn up by Malaysia, Indonesia and the Philippines in May of that year; the pact was intended to increase regional co-operation on security issues. In November the country hosted the annual ASEAN summit meeting, which was also attended by the Republic of Korea, Japan and China, as well as India, which was present for the first time. During the meeting a framework agreement was signed to establish an ASEAN-China free trade area by 2010.

Relations between Cambodia and the People's Republic of China (which had formerly supported the PDK) had already improved during the mid-1990s. However, following the events of 5–6 July 1997, Hun Sen deliberately aligned himself with China, possibly as a reaction to the disapproval of ASEAN, which considered itself to be a counterbalance to the influence of China in the region. China continued to provide political and limited financial support, and in November 2000 President Jiang Zemin paid a two-day official visit to Cambodia, the first by a Chinese Head of State in more than 35 years. On the first day of Jiang's visit, China defended its support of the Khmers Rouges during the 1970s, claiming that its limited assistance had been intended to help maintain Cambodia's independence from foreign powers. Subsequent visits from other senior Chinese officials further consolidated cordial relations between the two countries.

In January 1994 Chuan Leekpai undertook the first-ever official visit to Cambodia by a Thai Prime Minister. Relations between Cambodia and Thailand had been strained by the Thai armed forces' unauthorized links with the PDK (which controlled illicit trade in gems and timber along the Thai border) and by Cambodian allegations of Thai involvement in the July 1994 coup attempt, but improved in September 1995 when the two countries signed an agreement to establish a joint border commission. Thailand remained neutral following the events of 5–6 July 1997, but extended humanitarian assistance to the estimated 35,000 refugees who crossed into Thailand to avoid the fighting in the north-west of Cambodia. In June 2001 the Thai Prime Minister, Thaksin Shinawatra, visited Cambodia, emphasizing the improved state of relations between the two countries and, in October, King Sihanouk presented Thaksin Shinawatra with an honorary medal for his efforts to promote bilateral ties. However, in January 2003 relations became extremely strained when demonstrators attacked the Thai embassy and several Thai-owned businesses in Phnom-Penh, having been provoked by comments, wrongly attributed to a Thai actress, that implied that the temples at Angkor Wat had been stolen from Thailand. The violence escalated, prompting the Thai Government to withdraw its ambassador, together with more than 500 Thai nationals resident in Cambodia, and to downgrade diplomatic relations. In the aftermath of the riots Prime Minister Hun Sen issued a formal apology to the Thai Government and promised compensation; bilateral relations subsequently began to improve and the joint border was re-opened. In April the Thai ambassador returned to Phnom-Penh and, in mid-2003, the Cambodian and Thai Cabinets held an unprecedented joint meeting. In September almost all of those Cambodians who had been imprisoned for their involvement in the riots were released and, in October 2004, the Thai embassy in Phnom-Penh finally reopened, following the completion of repairs to the building.

In April 1995 Cambodia, Thailand, Viet Nam and Laos signed an agreement providing for the establishment of the Mekong River Commission (see p. 375), which was to co-ordinate the sustainable development of the resources of the Lower Mekong River Basin. In October 1999 the leaders of Cambodia, Laos and Viet Nam convened in the Laotian capital for their first 'unofficial' Indo-Chinese summit meeting. The opening of Cambodia's first bridge over the Mekong River in December 2001 was intended to promote the country's trade links with Viet Nam and Laos. The bridge connected East and West Cambodia by road for the first time.

Government

The Kingdom of Cambodia is a constitutional monarchy. The monarch is the Head of State and is selected by the Throne Council from among descendants of three royal lines. Legislative power is vested in the 123-member National Assembly, the lower chamber, which is elected for a term of five years by universal adult suffrage, and the 61-member Senate, the upper chamber, whose members are appointed by political parties in proportion to their representation in the National Assembly. Executive power is held by the Cabinet (the Royal Government of Cambodia), headed by the Prime Minister, who is appointed by the King at the recommendation of the Chairman of the

National Assembly from among the representatives of the winning party.

For local administration the Kingdom of Cambodia is divided into provinces, municipalities, districts, *khan*, *khum* and *sangkat*.

Defence

In August 2004 the total strength of the Royal Cambodian Armed Forces was estimated to be 124,300, comprising an army of 75,000, a navy of 2,800, an air force of 1,500 and provincial forces of about 45,000. A system of conscription was officially in force, for those aged between 18 and 35, for five years; however, conscription has not been implemented since 1993. In 2004 government expenditure on defence was budgeted at an estimated 294,000m. riels.

Economic Affairs

In 2003, according to the World Bank, Cambodia's gross national income (GNI), measured at average 2001–03 prices, was US $4,055m., equivalent to $310 per head (or $2,060 per head on an international purchasing-power parity basis). During 1990–2003, it was estimated, the population increased at an average annual rate of 3.0%. while gross domestic product (GDP) per head increased, in real terms, by an average of 3.8% per year during 1993–2003. Cambodia's overall GDP increased, in real terms, at an average annual rate of 6.8% during 1993–2003. According to the Asian Development Bank (ADB), GDP increased by 5.5% in 2002 and by 5.2% in 2003.

Agriculture (including hunting, forestry and fishing) contributed an estimated 37.2% of GDP in 2003. In the previous year the sector engaged 70.2% of the economically active population, but remained extremely vulnerable to adverse weather conditions, this problem being compounded by inadequate rural infrastructure and a lack of farm inputs such as fertilizers. In October 1999 Cambodia announced its intention to export rice for the first time since 1970, owing to an estimated rice surplus of 140,000 metric tons. In 2003 rice production was estimated at 3.7m. tons. In 2004 dry-season paddy production was estimated at 873,000 tons, a 3.7% decline compared with 2003, which was attributable to drought in the first half of the year. Other principal crops include cassava, maize, sugar cane and bananas. Timber and rubber are the two principal export commodities. The forestry sector accounted for only an estimated 2.3% of GDP in 2002, as reserves continued to be depleted and reafforestation remained inadequate. The fishing sector was also adversely affected by deforestation, which caused reductions in freshwater fishing catches, owing to the silting up of lakes and rivers. According to official estimates, however, the GDP of the fishing sector increased at an average annual rate of 3.8% in 1995–2002, following a period of decline in the early 1990s, and contributed an estimated 12.2% of GDP in 2002. According to the ADB, agricultural GDP increased, in real terms, at an average annual rate of 3.0% during 1995–2003. The GDP of the agricultural sector contracted by 3.2% in 2002 but expanded by 9.6% in 2003, before declining by 2.4% in 2004.

Industry (including mining, manufacturing, construction and utilities) contributed an estimated 26.8% of GDP in 2003, and employed 10.5% of the labour force in the previous year. According to the ADB, in real terms, industrial GDP increased at an average annual rate of 14.9% during 1995–2003. Growth in industrial GDP was 17.7% in 2002, 6.6% in 2003 and 16.9% in 2004.

In 2003 mining and quarrying contributed only an estimated 0.5% of GDP. Cambodia has limited mineral resources, including phosphates, gem stones, iron ore, bauxite, silicon and manganese ore, of which only phosphates and gem stones are, at present, being exploited. In the 1990s several agreements on petroleum exploration were signed with foreign enterprises. Cambodia's resources of natural gas were unofficially estimated to be 1,500,000m.–3,500,000m. cu m in 1992, and petroleum reserves were estimated to be between 50m. and 100m. barrels. According to the ADB, the GDP of the mining sector increased, in real terms, at an average annual rate of 7.2% during 1995–2002; growth in mining GDP was 13.4% in 2001 and 18.9% in 2002.

The manufacturing sector contributed an estimated 19.3% of GDP in 2003 and employed 8.7% of the labour force in 2002. The sector is dominated by rice milling and the production of ready-made garments, household goods, textiles, tyres and pharmaceutical products. The manufacture of garments, mostly for export, grew rapidly during the 1990s, and by the end of 2000 160,000 workers were engaged in garment manufacture. This had risen to approximately 230,000 workers by 2003. Exports of clothing rose in value by 13.2% in 2001, compared with the previous year, to reach US $1,147m. In 2003 garment exports accounted for approximately 80% of Cambodia's total exports. However, the abandonment by the USA of the Multi-Fibre Arrangement—under which Cambodia was granted quotas to export textiles to the USA and Europe—at the end of 2004 would, it was feared, have a serious impact upon the performance of the Cambodian garment sector; many textile factories based in Cambodia were expected to relocate to China in order to take advantage of that country's lower labour costs and more secure business environment. The Government was also attempting to promote the establishment of agro-industrial enterprises (sugar and vegetable oil refineries and factories producing paper pulp) and to encourage the production of fertilizers, petroleum and heavy construction and mechanical equipment. According to the ADB, the GDP of the manufacturing sector increased, in real terms, at an average annual rate of 17.2% during 1995–2002. Growth in manufacturing GDP was 14.2% in 2001 and 15.1% in 2002.

Energy is derived principally from timber. All commercial energy used in Cambodia is imported. In the late 1990s the country had an installed capacity of 28.7 MW, of which 15 MW was accounted for by an oil-fired thermal power plant and the rest by diesel generating units. Owing to a lack of spare parts and a shortage of fuel, only a small percentage of the generating capacity can be utilized. Cambodia has considerable hydropower potential, and two hydropower plants were under construction in the late 1990s. In late 2002 Cambodia signed an agreement with China, Thailand, Laos, Myanmar and Viet Nam to form a regional power distribution system, enabling hydropower development in the Mekong River area.

The services sector contributed an estimated 36.0% of GDP in 2003 and engaged 19.5% of the economically active population in the previous year. The tourism sector has become increasingly significant. From 2000 greater political stability led to an increase in tourist arrivals. In 2001, despite the effects of the terrorist attacks on the USA in September, arrivals increased to 604,919 and receipts to US $380m. It was feared that the bombing in Bali, Indonesia, in October 2002 would affect the growth of Cambodia's tourism sector by deterring visitors to the region. In that year, however, 786,546 tourists visited Cambodia and receipts totalled an estimated $454m., but in 2003, designated 'Visit Cambodia Year' by the Government, tourist arrivals declined to 701,014. In real terms, according to the ADB, the GDP of the services sector increased at an average annual rate of 5.7% during 1995–2003. Growth in the sector was 4.3% in 2002, 2.1% in 2003 and 7.3% in 2004.

In 2002 Cambodia recorded a visible trade deficit of US $563.5m., while there was a deficit of $64.0m. on the current account of the balance of payments. In 2003 the principal sources of imports were Thailand (27.0%) and Hong Kong (14.7%); other major sources were Singapore, the People's Republic of China and the Republic of Korea. In the same year the principal market for exports was the USA (59.8%); other important purchasers were Germany, the United Kingdom and Singapore. The principal exports in 2003 were garments (accounting for an estimated 79.2% of the total), rubber, rice, fish and logs and sawn timber. The principal imports were petroleum products (accounting for 6.4% of the total), cigarettes, clothing, cement, vehicles and motorcycles. Re-exports (which were a result of the differences in tariffs on goods imported by Cambodia and its neighbours) declined in importance, from 53% of total exports in 1993 to an estimated 5.6% in 2003.

Cambodia's overall budget deficit in 2003 was 1,083,000m. riels. Cambodia's external debt at the end of 2002 totalled US $2,907m., of which $2,594m. was long-term public debt. In that year the cost of debt-servicing was equivalent to 0.8% of revenue from exports of goods and services. The annual rate of inflation averaged 4.6% during 1995–2003; consumer prices increased by 1.2% in 2003 and by an estimated 3.9% in 2004. The unemployment rate was estimated at 3.1% in 2004.

Cambodia is a member of the UN Economic and Social Commission for Asia and the Pacific (ESCAP, see p. 31), of the Asian Development Bank (see p. 159), of the Mekong River Commission (see p. 375) and of the Colombo Plan (see p. 373). Cambodia was formally admitted to the Association of South East Asian Nations (ASEAN, see p. 162) in April 1999. Following the implementation of the ASEAN Free Trade Area (AFTA, see p. 163) in January 2002, Cambodia was granted until 2007 to comply with the 0%–5% tariff agreement.

Cambodia has continued to be dependent on foreign aid to reduce poverty and promote economic growth in the country. At the annual meeting of bilateral and multilateral donors in Paris in May 2000, US $548m. of fresh aid was pledged to Cambodia in response to the Government's appeals. At the next annual meeting, held in Tokyo in June 2001, the country received a further $615m. and, in June 2002, at a meeting held in Phnom-Penh, it was awarded a further $635m. In December 2004, at the seventh donor meeting, held in Phnom-Penh, $504m. in aid was pledged for 2005. The Government had requested a total of $1,800m., to be disbursed over three years, but donors refused to commit funds for more than one year, making the extent of further aid dependent upon the outcome of an assessment of the progress that the Government had made in addressing the problem of widespread corruption in the country. Meanwhile, in 2001 the Government initiated its second Socioeconomic Development Plan, to be implemented in 2001–05, as part of its ongoing effort to combat poverty. The Plan aimed to expand opportunities for the poor through the promotion of stable and sustained economic growth. In November 2002 the Chinese Government announced that it had cancelled Cambodia's foreign debt, significantly improving the country's situation. However, it was widely recognized that the Government needed to continue to implement key reforms, particularly in the public sector, if Cambodia was eventually to be able to compete with its regional neighbours. The political uncertainty that ensued in the aftermath of the July 2003 general election acted as a deterrent to foreign investment and resulted in a significant delay in approval of the 2004 budget. However, following the eventual formation of a new Government in July 2004, the Prime Minister announced the so-called 'Rectangular Strategy', a policy intended to promote good governance that focused on promoting economic growth in the country through: the development of agriculture; the expansion of the private sector; the repair and construction of physical infrastructure; and the development of human resources. It was expected that the legislature's ratification of the country's membership of the World Trade Organization (WTO) in August 2004, following the organization's approval of Cambodia's membership application in September 2003, would significantly improve the country's economic prospects. In November 2004 the Government announced a new initiative intended to attract foreign investment into the country through the reform of existing procedures and a commitment to reducing the corruption endemic in Cambodia. In the following month international donors meeting in Phnom-Penh criticized the Government for the slow pace of reforms in the country and for its failure to take more decisive action to reduce corruption. The ADB estimated that the economy expanded by 6.0% in 2004. However, in 2005 it predicted that growth would reach only 2.3%, mainly as a result of the expiry of the Multi-Fibre Arrangement with the USA.

Education

Education is compulsory for six years between the ages of six and 12. Primary education begins at six and lasts for six years. In 1997 enrolment at primary level was equivalent to 113% of children in the relevant age-group (males 123%; females 104%). Secondary education comprises two cycles, each lasting three years. In 1997 enrolment at secondary level was equivalent to 24% of the relevant age-group (males 31%; females 17%). In the same year enrolment at tertiary level was equivalent to 1.0% of the relevant age-group (males 2.0%; females 0.5%). In 2003 the Ministry of Education, Youth and Sport was allocated 300,000m. riels (10.3% of total expenditure).

Public Holidays

2005: 1 January (International New Year's Day), 7 January (Remembrance Day), 13–15 April (Cambodian New Year), 1 May (Labour Day), 20 May (Day of Remembrance), 24 September (Constitution Day), 23 October (Anniversary of Paris Peace Agreement on Cambodia), 9 November (Independence Day).

2006: 1 January (International New Year's Day), 7 January (Remembrance Day), 13–15 April (Cambodian New Year), 1 May (Labour Day), 20 May (Day of Remembrance), 24 September (Constitution Day), 23 October (Anniversary of Paris Peace Agreement on Cambodia), 9 November (Independence Day).

Weights and Measures

The metric system is in force.

Statistical Survey

Source (unless otherwise stated): National Institute of Statistics, Ministry of Planning, Sangkat Boeung Keng Kong 2, blvd Monivong, Phnom-Penh; tel. (23) 216538; fax (23) 213650; e-mail census@camnet.com.kh; internet www.nis.gov.kh.

Note: Some of the statistics below represent only sectors of the economy controlled by the Government of the former Khmer Republic. During the years 1970–75 no figures were available for areas controlled by the Khmers Rouges.

Area and Population

AREA, POPULATION AND DENSITY

Area (sq km)	181,035*
Population (census results)†	
17 April 1962	5,728,771
Prior to elections of 1 May 1981	6,682,000
3 March 1998	
Males	5,511,408
Females	5,926,248
Total	11,437,656
Population (official estimates at mid-year)	
2001	13,148,363
2002	13,473,352
2003	13,798,237
Density (per sq km) at mid-2003	76.2

* 69,898 sq miles.
† Excluding adjustments for underenumeration.

PROVINCES
(1998 census)

	Area (sq km)*	Population	Density (per sq km)
Banteay Mean Chey	6,679	577,772	86.5
Bat Dambang	11,702	793,129	67.8
Kampong Cham	9,799	1,608,914	164.2
Kampong Chhnang	5,521	417,693	75.7
Kampong Spueu	7,017	598,882	85.3
Kampong Thum	13,814	569,060	41.2
Kampot	4,873	528,405	108.4
Kandal	3,568	1,075,125	301.3
Kaoh Kong	11,160	132,106	11.8
Kracheh	11,094	263,175	23.7
Mondol Kiri	14,288	32,407	2.3
Phnom Penh	290	999,804	3,447.6
Preah Vihear	13,788	119,261	8.6
Prey Veaeng	4,883	946,042	193.7
Pousat	12,692	360,445	28.4
Rotanak Kiri	10,782	94,243	8.7
Siem Reab	10,299	696,164	67.6
Krong Preah Sihanouk	868	155,690	179.4
Stueng Traeng	11,092	81,074	7.3
Svay Rieng	2,966	478,252	161.2
Takaev	3,563	790,168	221.8
Otdar Mean Chey	6,158	68,279	11.1
Krong Kaeb	336	28,660	85.3
Krong Pailin	803	22,906	28.5
Total	178,035	11,437,656	64.2

* Excluding Tonlé Sap lake (3,000 sq km).

PRINCIPAL TOWNS
(population at 1998 census)

Phnom-Penh (capital) . .	999,804	Bat Dambang (Battambang) . .	139,964
Preah Sihanouk (Sihanoukville)* .	155,690	Siem Reab (Siem Reap)	119,528

* Also known as Kampong Saom (Kompong Som).

Mid-2003 (UN estimate, incl. suburbs): Phnom-Penh 1,157,066 (Source: UN, *World Urbanization Prospects: The 2003 Revision*).

BIRTHS AND DEATHS
(annual averages)

	1985–90	1990–95	1995–2000*
Birth rate (per 1,000)	44.2	38.2	36.8
Death rate (per 1,000)	16.5	14.1	10.4

* UN estimates (Source: UN, *World Population Prospects: The 2002 Revision*).

Source (unless otherwise indicated): Ministry of Economy and Finance, Phnom-Penh.

1997: Death rate (per 1,000) 12.0 (Source: WHO).

1998: Birth rate (per 1,000) 38.0 (Source: WHO).

Expectation of life (WHO estimates, years at birth): 54.6 (males 51.9; females 57.1) in 2002 (Source: WHO, *World Health Report*).

EMPLOYMENT

	2000	2001	2002
Agriculture, forestry and fishing .	3,889,048	4,384,250	4,479,773
Mining and quarrying	3,328	13,525	10,751
Manufacturing	367,286	544,832	556,388
Electricity, gas and water . . .	3,799	3,795	4,704
Construction	69,773	94,077	100,123
Wholesale and retail trade . . .	436,308	644,307	628,960
Restaurants and hotels . . .	18,794	10,412	32,446
Transport and communications .	119,596	169,307	174,711
Financial intermediation, real estate and renting	16,636	11,854	16,224
Public administration	146,986	149,382	143,513
Education	87,385	88,446	102,331
Health and social work	30,235	24,810	36,190
Other social services	40,098	35,153	44,926
Other services	45,905	69,179	68,637
Total employed	5,275,177	6,243,329	6,399,677

Health and Welfare

KEY INDICATORS

Total fertility rate (children per woman, 2002)	4.8
Under-5 mortality rate (per 1,000 live births, 2003) . . .	140
HIV/AIDS (% of persons aged 15–49, 2003)	2.60
Physicians (per 1,000 head, 1998)	0.30
Hospital beds (per 1,000 head, 1990)	2.07
Health expenditure (2001): US $ per head (PPP)	184
Health expenditure (2001): % of GDP	11.8
Health expenditure (2001): public (% of total)	14.9
Access to water (% of persons, 2002)	34
Access to sanitation (% of persons, 2002)	16
Human Development Index (2002): ranking	130
Human Development Index (2002): value	0.568

For sources and definitions, see explanatory note on p. vi.

Agriculture

PRINCIPAL CROPS
('000 metric tons)

	2001	2002	2003
Rice (paddy)	4,099.0	3,822.5	4,300.0†
Maize	185.6	148.9	190.0†
Sweet potatoes	26.3	31.5	32.6*
Cassava (Manioc)	142.3	122.0	139.0*
Other roots and tubers*	26.0	27.0	27.0
Dry beans	17.2	23.9	24.0*
Soybeans (Soya beans)	24.7	38.8	39.0*
Groundnuts (in shell)	8.9	9.7	10.0*
Sesame seed	9.0	10.2	10.5*
Coconuts	58.0*	70.0†	71.0*
Sugar cane	169.3	208.8	220.0*
Tobacco (leaves)	4.7	4.7	4.7*
Natural rubber	38.7	32.4	47.0*
Vegetables*	473.0	475.0	475.0
Oranges	63.0	63.0	63.0*
Mangoes	35.0	35.0*	35.0*
Pineapples	16.0	16.0*	16.0*
Bananas	146.0	146.0	146.0*
Other fruits and berries*	62.2	62.2	62.7

* FAO estimate(s).
† Unofficial figure.
Source: FAO.

LIVESTOCK
('000 head, year ending September)

	2001	2002	2003*
Horses*	27	27	28
Cattle	2,869	2,924	2,950
Buffaloes	626	626	620
Pigs	2,115	2,105	2,150
Chickens	15,248	16,678	17,000
Ducks*	6,000	6,300	7,000

* FAO estimates.
Source: FAO.

LIVESTOCK PRODUCTS
('000 metric tons)

	2001	2002	2003
Beef and veal*	58.2	53.4	53.5
Buffalo meat*	8.8	8.8	12.8
Pig meat*	107.8	102.5	105.0
Poultry meat*	27.2	26.5	28.3
Cows' milk*	20.4	20.4	20.4
Hen eggs	11.7	13.2*	13.0*
Other poultry eggs*	3.3	3.5	3.5
Cattle hides (fresh)*	14.6	13.4	13.4
Buffalo hides (fresh)*	1.8	1.8	2.6

* FAO estimate(s).
Source: FAO.

Forestry

ROUNDWOOD REMOVALS
('000 cubic metres, excl. bark)

	2001	2002	2003*
Sawlogs, veneer logs and logs for sleepers	100	100*	100
Other industrial wood	23	25	25
Fuel wood*	9,924	9,737	9,558
Total	10,047	9,862	9,683

* FAO estimate(s).
Source: FAO.

SAWNWOOD PRODUCTION
('000 cubic metres, incl. railway sleepers)

	2001	2002	2003
Total (all broadleaved)	5	5*	5*

* FAO estimate.
Source: FAO.

Fishing

('000 metric tons, live weight)

	2000	2001	2002
Capture	284.4	428.2	406.2
Freshwater fishes	245.3	384.5	359.8
Marine fishes	26.6	31.0	33.8
Aquaculture*	14.4	14.0	14.6
Total catch *	298.8	442.2	420.8

* FAO estimates.
Note: Figures exclude crocodiles, recorded by number rather than by weight. The total number of estuarine crocodiles caught was: 26,300 in 2000; 35,970 in 2001; 50,850 in 2002.
Source: FAO.

Mining

('000 metric tons)

	2001	2002	2003
Salt (unrefined)	11.0	72.5	50.0*

* Estimate.
Source: US Geological Survey.

Industry

SELECTED PRODUCTS
('000 metric tons, unless otherwise indicated)

	1971	1972	1973
Distilled alcoholic beverages ('000 hectolitres)	45	55	36
Beer ('000 hectolitres)	26	23	18
Soft drinks ('000 hectolitres)	25	25*	25*
Cigarettes (million)	3,413	2,510	2,622
Cotton yarn—pure and mixed (metric tons)	1,068	1,094	415
Bicycle tyres and tubes ('000)	208	200*	200*
Rubber footwear ('000 pairs)	1,292	1,000*	1,000*
Soap (metric tons)	469	400*	400*
Motor spirit (petrol)	2	—	—
Distillate fuel oils	11	—	—
Residual fuel oils	14	—	—
Cement	44	53	78
Electric energy (million kWh)†	148	166	150

* Estimate.
† Production by public utilities only.

Cigarettes (million): 4,175 in 1987; 4,200 annually in 1988–92 (estimates by US Department of Agriculture).

Cement ('000 metric tons): 50 in 2001 (estimate by the US Geological Survey).

Electric energy (estimates, million kWh): 194 in 1995; 201 in 1996; 208 in 1997; 215 in 1998; 222 in 1999; 229 in 2000.

Plywood ('000 cu m): 15 in 1999; 18 in 2000; 14 in 2001; 14 in 2002 (FAO estimate); 14 in 2003 (FAO estimate) (Source: FAO).

Source: partly UN, *Industrial Commodity Statistics Yearbook*.

Finance

CURRENCY AND EXCHANGE RATES

Monetary Units
100 sen = 1 riel.

Sterling, Dollar and Euro Equivalents (31 December 2004)
£1 sterling = 7,777.749 riels;
US $1 = 4,027.000 riels;
€1 = 5,485.180 riels;
10,000 riels = £1.29 = $2.48 = €1.82.

Average Exchange Rate (riels per US $)
2002   3,912.080
2003   3,973.330
2004   4,016.250

BUDGET
('000 million riels)

Revenue*	2001	2002	2003
Tax revenue	1,087.1	1,209.8	1,178.6
Direct taxes	140.2	131.6	149.7
Profit tax	113.0	87.9	117.8
Indirect taxes	571.2	654.4	633.7
Turnover tax	9.9	7.9	10.9
Value-added tax . . .	402.8	429.3	385.4
Excise duties	154.8	210.3	208.0
Taxes on international trade	375.7	423.8	395.2
Import duties	364.1	407.8	374.9
Other current revenue . . .	423.8	500.5	525.1
Forestry	29.1	14.6	6.6
Receipts from public enterprises	74.5	62.8	52.6
Posts and telecommunications	122.3	122.6	119.8
Public services	119.6	146.5	186.9
Capital revenue	9.1	16.3	2.6
Total	**1,520.0**	**1,726.6**	**1,706.3**

Expenditure†	2001	2002	2003
Council of Ministers	101	82	95
Ministry of Defence	277	265	270
Ministry of the Interior . . .	140	174	171
Ministry of Economy and Finance	19	40	111
Ministry of Public Works and Transport	21	16	14
Ministry of Agriculture, Forestry, Hunting and Fisheries . . .	30	40	39
Ministry of Education, Youth and Sport	209	290	300
Ministry of Health	130	164	173
Ministry of Posts and Telecommunications . . .	41	36	35
Ministry of Social Affairs, Labour, Professional Training and Youth Rehabilitation	28	33	33
Total (incl. others)	**2,367**	**2,806**	**2,914**
Current expenditure	1,392	1,579	1,843
Capital expenditure	975	1,241	1,244
Cash adjustments	—	−15	−173

* Excluding grants received.
† Figures for individual ministries exclude externally financed capital expenditure ('000 million riels): 692 in 2001; 903 in 2002; 910 in 2003.

Source: IMF, *Cambodia: Statistical Appendix* (October 2004).

INTERNATIONAL RESERVES
(US $ million at 31 December)

	2001	2002	2003
IMF special drawing rights . .	0.51	0.55	0.20
Foreign exchange	586.30	775.60	815.33
Total	**586.81**	**776.15**	**815.53**

Source: IMF, *International Financial Statistics.*

MONEY SUPPLY
(million riels at 31 December)

	2001	2002	2003
Currency outside banks . . .	577,780	765,980	906,390
Demand deposits at deposit money banks	31,940	47,300	29,470
Total money	**609,720**	**813,280**	**935,860**

Source: IMF, *International Financial Statistics.*

COST OF LIVING
(Consumer Price Index for Phnom-Penh; base: December 2000 = 100)

	2001	2002	2003
Food, beverages and tobacco . .	97.86	99.58	101.06
Clothing and footwear . . .	95.22	89.18	87.35
Housing and utilities . . .	103.35	110.80	111.64
Household furnishings and operations	98.78	95.85	95.71
Medical care and health expenses	103.24	105.01	103.12
Transport and communication . .	95.59	95.88	100.62
Recreation and education . . .	107.49	109.55	108.77
Personal care and effects . . .	101.36	103.09	103.24
All items	**100.34**	**103.65**	**104.84**

NATIONAL ACCOUNTS
('000 million riels at current prices)

Expenditure on the Gross Domestic Product

	2001	2002	2003*
Government final consumption expenditure	827.9	913.2	1,012.0
Private final consumption expenditure	12,337.7	12,860.3	13,891.9
Increase in stocks	299.0	−68.8	32.0
Gross fixed capital formation . .	2,786.7	3,549.9	3,692.0
Statistical discrepancy	−247.3	−304.9	−880.0
Total domestic expenditure	**16,004.0**	**16,949.7**	**17,747.9**
Exports of goods and services . .	7,914.7	9,275.3	9,854.1
Less Imports of goods and services	9,374.9	10,557.8	10,952.0
GDP in purchasers' values .	**14,543.9**	**15,667.2**	**16,650.0**
GDP at constant 2000 prices .	**14,952.6**	**15,392.4**	**16,177.4**

* Preliminary figures.

Source: Asian Development Bank, *Key Indicators of Developing Asian and Pacific Countries.*

Gross Domestic Product by Economic Activity

	2001	2002	2003*
Agriculture, hunting, forestry and fishing	5,161.7	5,231.8	5,859.6
Mining and quarrying	39.6	46.6	85.0
Manufacturing	2,556.4	2,969.5	3,044.0
Electricity, gas and water . . .	56.8	75.8	84.6
Construction	867.1	1,023.1	1,014.4
Trade, restaurants and hotels . .	2,021.3	2,140.2	2,247.0
Transport, storage and communications	947.2	960.0	1,046.0
Financing, real estate and business services	980.8	964.8	950.0
Public administration	359.2	390.5	448.0
Other services	751.2	902.9	992.2
Sub-total	**13,741.2**	**14,705.0**	**15,770.8**
Less Imputed bank service charge	118.1	78.3	69.8
GDP at factor cost	**13,623.1**	**14,626.7**	**15,701.0**
Indirect taxes, *less* subsidies . .	920.7	1,040.4	879.8
Statistical discrepancy	—	—	69.2
GDP in purchasers' values .	**14,543.9**	**15,667.2**	**16,650.0**

* Preliminary figures.

Source: Asian Development Bank, *Key Indicators of Developing Asian and Pacific Countries.*

BALANCE OF PAYMENTS
(US $ million)

	2000	2001	2002
Exports of goods f.o.b.	1,401.1	1,571.2	1,750.1
Imports of goods f.o.b.	−1,939.3	−2,094.0	−2,313.5
Trade balance	−538.2	−522.8	−563.5
Exports of services	428.4	524.6	600.2
Imports of services	−327.9	−347.3	−379.6
Balance on goods and services	−437.7	−345.5	−342.8
Other income received	67.1	57.5	50.7
Other income paid	−189.6	−193.4	−219.2
Balance on goods, services and income	−560.2	−481.4	−511.2
Current transfers received	432.0	403.8	456.5
Current transfers paid	−7.3	−8.3	−9.3
Current balance	−135.4	−85.8	−64.0
Capital account (net)	79.8	102.8	76.7
Direct investment from abroad	148.5	148.1	53.8
Other investment assets	−183.7	−118.2	−11.9
Other investment liabilities	224.2	118.4	238.1
Net errors and omissions	16.6	−24.2	−50.2
Overall balance	92.0	68.1	165.7

Source: IMF, *International Financial Statistics*.

External Trade

PRINCIPAL COMMODITIES
(US $ million)

Imports c.i.f.	2001	2002	2003*
Cigarettes	70	68	69
Petroleum products	175	150	180
Motorcycles	21	28	30
Total (incl. others)	2,270	2,503	2,829

Exports f.o.b.	2001	2002	2003*
Crude rubber†	52	63	98
Logs and sawn timber†	68	38	25
Clothing	1,188	1,386	1,645
Fish	42	60	37
Rice	57	24	90
Total (incl. others)‡	1,571	1,749	2,076

* Estimates.
† Including estimates for unrecorded exports.
‡ Including re-exports (US $ million): 109 in 2001; 111 in 2002; 117 (estimate) in 2003.

Source: IMF, *Cambodia: Statistical Appendix* (October 2004).

PRINCIPAL TRADING PARTNERS
(US $ million)

Imports c.i.f.	2001	2002	2003
China, People's Republic	86.9	276.8	324.1
France	12.6	63.1	53.6
Hong Kong	116.9	372.8	411.2
Indonesia	9.9	75.7	84.5
Japan	19.7	76.8	67.3
Korea, Republic	49.6	126.8	144.6
Malaysia	19.3	60.4	68.9
Singapore	399.5	387.7	338.2
Thailand	503.9	567.0	756.5
Viet Nam	109.5	118.9	135.5
Total (incl. others)	1,600.3	2,311.0	2,469.0

Exports f.o.b.	2001	2002	2003
China, People's Republic	16.7	22.3	23.6
France	35.0	39.4	40.5
Germany	98.7	159.8	211.3
Netherlands	25.7	29.2	25.6
Singapore	28.0	76.8	67.8
Thailand	7.6	10.2	11.3
United Kingdom	126.3	122.1	150.3
USA	832.2	1,041.7	1,214.3
Viet Nam	24.5	26.6	30.3
Total (incl. others)	1,374.4	1,766.0	1,917.0

Source: Asian Development Bank, *Key Indicators of Developing Asian and Pacific Countries*.

Transport

RAILWAYS
(traffic)

	1997	1998	1999
Freight carried ('000 metric tons)	16	294	259
Freight ton-km ('000)	36,514	75,721	76,171
Passengers ('000)	553	438	431
Passenger-km ('000)	50,992	43,847	49,894

Source: Ministry of Economy and Finance, Phnom-Penh.

2000: Passenger-km ('000) 15; Freight ton-km ('000) 91 (Source: UN, *Statistical Yearbook*).

ROAD TRAFFIC
(estimated number of motor vehicles in use)

	2000	2001	2002
Passenger cars	193,851	200,561	209,128
Buses and coaches	2,918	2,996	3,196
Trucks	27,819	28,533	29,968
Other vehicles	371	396	421
Motorcycles and mopeds	513,503	565,931	586,278

Sources: Ministry of Public Works and Transport, Phnom-Penh, and Phnom-Penh Municipal Traffic Police.

SHIPPING

Merchant Fleet
(registered at 31 December)

	2001	2002	2003
Number of vessels	564	727	663
Displacement ('000 grt)	1,996.7	2,425.8	2,048.3

Source: Lloyd's Register-Fairplay, *World Fleet Statistics*.

International Sea-borne Freight Traffic
(estimates, '000 metric tons)

	1988	1989	1990
Goods loaded	10	10	11
Goods unloaded	100	100	95

Source: UN, *Monthly Bulletin of Statistics*.

CIVIL AVIATION
(traffic on scheduled services)

	1975	1976	1977
Passenger-kilometres (million)	42	42	42
Freight ton-kilometres ('000)	400	400	400

Source: Statistisches Bundesamt, Wiesbaden, Germany.

Tourism

FOREIGN TOURIST ARRIVALS
(by air)*

Country of residence	2001	2002	2003
Australia and New Zealand . .	15,266	19,467	16,809
Canada	6,191	8,221	5,915
China, People's Repub.	32,002	31,391	35,166
France	23,328	35,385	22,457
Germany	6,861	8,340	6,480
Japan	17,952	19,946	15,385
Korea, Republic	9,579	10,549	10,358
Malaysia	15,994	14,383	15,376
Singapore	10,982	9,263	6,499
Taiwan	23,098	30,035	31,584
Thailand	17,496	17,109	13,895
United Kingdom	17,686	15,425	15,510
USA	37,033	55,368	32,534
Viet Nam	7,828	7,671	2,102
Total (incl. others†)	408,377	522,978	455,972

* Figures for individual countries refer to arrivals at Pochentong (Phnom-Penh) airport only.

† Including arrivals at Siem Reap airport (133,688 in 2001; 202,791 in 2002; 186,298 in 2003).

Total arrivals (incl. arrivals by land and sea): 604,919 in 2001; 786,524 in 2002; 701,014 in 2003.

Tourism receipts (US $ million): 304 in 2000; 380 in 2001; 454 in 2002.

Source: Ministry of Tourism, Phnom-Penh.

Communications Media

	1999	2000	2001
Television receivers ('000 in use)	98	99	n.a.
Telephones ('000 main lines in use)	27.7	30.9	33.5
Mobile cellular telephones ('000 subscribers)	89.1	130.5	223.5
Personal computers ('000 in use)	13	15	20
Internet users ('000)	4.0	6.0	10.0

Facsimile machines (number in use): 884 in 1995; 1,470 in 1996; 2,995 in 1997.

Internet users ('000): 30.0 in 2002.

Source: International Telecommunication Union.

Radio receivers ('000 in use): 1,120 in 1995; 1,300 in 1996; 1,340 in 1997 (Source: UNESCO, *Statistical Yearbook*).

Education

(2002/03*)

	Institutions	Teachers	Students
Primary	5,915	48,433	2,747,411
Secondary	594	22,830	543,885
Junior high school	411	17,423	415,703
Senior high school	183	5,407	128,182

* Excluding technical and vocational education and higher education.

Source: IMF, *Cambodia: Statistical Appendix* (October 2004).

Adult literacy rate (UNESCO estimates): 69.4% (males 80.8%; females 59.3%) in 2002 (Source: UN Development Programme, *Human Development Report*).

Directory

The Constitution

The Constitution was promulgated on 21 September 1993; a number of amendments were passed on 4 March 1999. The main provisions are summarized below:

GENERAL PROVISIONS

The Kingdom of Cambodia is a unitary state in which the King abides by the Constitution and multi-party liberal democracy. Cambodian citizens have full right of freedom of belief; Buddhism is the state religion. The Kingdom of Cambodia has a market economy system.

THE KING

The King is Head of State and the Supreme Commander of the Khmer Royal Armed Forces. The monarchist regime is based on a system of selection: within seven days of the King's death the Royal Council of the Throne (comprising the Chairman of the Senate, the Chairman of the National Assembly, the Prime Minister, the Supreme Patriarchs of the Mohanikay and Thoammayutikanikay sects, the First and Second Vice-Chairmen of the Senate and the First and Second Vice-Chairmen of the National Assembly) must select a King. The King must be at least 30 years of age and be a descendant of King Ang Duong, King Norodom or King Sisowath. The King appoints the Prime Minister and the Cabinet. In the absence of the King, the Chairman of the Senate assumes the duty of acting Head of State.

THE LEGISLATURE

Legislative power is vested in the National Assembly (the lower chamber) and the Senate (the upper chamber). The National Assembly has 123 members who are elected by universal adult suffrage. A member of the National Assembly must be a Cambodian citizen by birth over the age of 25 years and has a term of office of five years, the term of the National Assembly. The National Assembly may not be dissolved except in the case where the Royal Government (Cabinet) has been dismissed twice in 12 months. The National Assembly may dismiss cabinet members or remove the Royal Government from office by passing a censure motion through a two-thirds' majority vote of all the representatives in the National Assembly. The Senate comprises nominated members, the number of which does not exceed one-half of all of the members of the National Assembly; two are nominated by the King, two are elected by the National Assembly and the remainder are elected by universal adult suffrage. A member of the Senate has a term of office of six years. The Senate reviews legislation passed by the National Assembly and acts as a co-ordinator between the National Assembly and the Royal Government. In special cases, the National Assembly and the Senate can assemble as the Congress to resolve issues of national importance.

THE CABINET

The Cabinet is the Royal Government of the Kingdom of Cambodia, which is led by a Prime Minister, assisted by Deputy Prime Ministers, with state ministers, ministers and state secretaries as members. The Prime Minister is designated by the King at the recommendation of the Chairman of the National Assembly from among the representatives of the winning party. The Prime Minister appoints the members of the Cabinet, who must be representatives in the National Assembly or members of parties represented in the National Assembly.

THE CONSTITUTIONAL COUNCIL

The Constitutional Council's competence is to interpret the Constitution and laws passed by the National Assembly and reviewed completely by the Senate. It has the right to examine and settle disputes relating to the election of members of the National Assembly and the Senate. The Constitutional Council consists of nine members with a nine-year mandate. One-third of the members are replaced every three years. Three members are appointed by the King, three elected by the National Assembly and three appointed by the Supreme Council of the Magistracy.

The Government

HEAD OF STATE

King: HM King Norodom Sihamoni (appointed by the Royal Council of the Throne on 14 October 2004).

ROYAL GOVERNMENT OF CAMBODIA
(April 2005)

A coalition of the Cambodian People's Party (CPP) and the FUNCINPEC Party.

Prime Minister: Hun Sen (CPP).

Deputy Prime Ministers and Co-Ministers of the Interior: Sar Kheng (CPP), Prince Norodom Sirivudh (FUNCINPEC).

Deputy Prime Ministers and Co-Ministers of National Defence: Tea Banh (CPP), Nhiek Bunchhay (FUNCINPEC).

Deputy Prime Minister and Minister of Foreign Affairs and International Co-operation: Hor Nam Hong (CPP).

Deputy Prime Minister and Minister of Rural Development: Lu Lay Sreng (FUNCINPEC).

Deputy Prime Minister and Minister in Charge of the Council of Ministers: Sok An (CPP).

Senior Ministers: Cham Prasidh (CPP), Chhay Thon (CPP), Keat Chhon (CPP), Im Chhun Lim (CPP), Men Sam On (CPP), Dr Mok Mareth (CPP), Nhim Vannda (CPP), Tav Senghuo (CPP), Hong Sun Huot (FUNCINPEC), Khun Haing (FUNCINPEC), Khy Taing Lim (FUNCINPEC), Kol Pheng (FUNCINPEC), Sirey Kosal (FUNCINPEC), Veng Sereivuth (FUNCINPEC), You Hockry (FUNCINPEC).

Minister of Agriculture, Forestry, Hunting and Fisheries: Chan Sarun (CPP).

Minister of Commerce: Cham Prasidh (CPP).

Minister of Cults and Religions: Khun Haing (FUNCINPEC).

Minister of Culture and Fine Arts: Sisovat Panara Sirivudh (FUNCINPEC).

Minister of Economy and Finance: Keat Chhon (CPP).

Minister of Education, Youth and Sport: Kol Pheng (FUNCINPEC).

Minister of Environment: Dr Mok Mareth (CPP).

Minister of Health: Nuth Sokhom (FUNCINPEC).

Minister of Industry, Mines and Energy: Suy Sem (CPP).

Minister of Information: Khieu Kanharith (CPP).

Minister of Justice: Ang Vong Vattana (CPP).

Minister of Parliamentary Affairs and Inspection: Men Sam On (CPP).

Minister of Planning: Chhay Thon (CPP).

Minister of Posts and Telecommunications: So Khun (CPP).

Minister of Public Works and Transport: Sun Chan Thol (FUNCINPEC).

Minister of Rural Development: Ly Thuch (FUNCINPEC).

Minister of Social Affairs and Youth Rehabilitation: Ith Sam Heng (CPP).

Minister of Territorial Organization, Urbanization and Construction: Im Chhun Lim (CPP).

Minister of Tourism: Lay Prohors (FUNCINPEC).

Minister of Vocational Training and Labour: Nhem Bun Chin (FUNCINPEC).

Minister of Water Resources and Meteorology: Lim Kean Hor (CPP).

Minister of Women's Affairs and Veterans: Ung Kantha Phavy (FUNCINPEC).

Secretary of State for Public Functions: Pich Bun Thin (CPP).

Secretary of State for Civil Aviation: Mao Hasvannal (FUNCINPEC).

There are also 133 further Secretaries of State.

MINISTRIES

Ministry of Agriculture, Forestry, Hunting and Fisheries: 200 blvd Norodom, Phnom-Penh; tel. (23) 211351; fax (23) 217320; e-mail info@maff.gov.kh; internet www.maff.gov.kh.

Ministry of Commerce: 20A–B blvd Norodom, Phnom-Penh; tel. (23) 427358; fax (23) 426396; e-mail kunkoet@moc.gov.kh; internet www.moc.gov.kh.

Ministry of Cults and Religions: Preah Sisowath Quay, cnr rue 240, Phnom-Penh; tel. (23) 725099; fax (23) 725699; e-mail morac@cambodia.gov.kh; internet www.morac.gov.kh.

Ministry of Culture and Fine Arts: 227 blvd Monivong, cnr rue Red Cross, Phnom-Penh; tel. (23) 217645; fax (23) 725749; e-mail mcfa@cambodia.gov.kh; internet www.mcfa.gov.kh.

Ministry of National Defence: blvd Confederation de la Russie, cnr rue 175, Phnom-Penh; tel. (23) 883184; fax (23) 366169; e-mail info@mond.gov.kh; internet www.mond.gov.kh.

Ministry of Economy and Finance: 60 rue 92, Phnom-Penh; tel. (23) 722863; fax (23) 427798; e-mail mefcg@hotmail.com; internet www.mef.gov.kh.

Ministry of Education, Youth and Sport: 80 blvd Norodom, Phnom-Penh; tel. (23) 210705; fax (23) 215096; e-mail crsmeys@camnet.com.kh; internet www.moeys.gov.kh.

Ministry of Environment: 48 blvd Sihanouk Tonle Bassac, Khan Chamkarmon, Phnom-Penh; tel. (23) 427894; fax (23) 427844; e-mail moe-cabinet@camnet.com.kh; internet www.moe.gov.kh.

Ministry of Foreign Affairs and International Co-operation: 161 Preah Sisowath Quay, cnr rue 240, Phnom-Penh; tel. (23) 216141; fax (23) 216144; e-mail mfaicasean@bigpond.com.kh; internet www.mfaic.gov.kh.

Ministry of Health: 151–153 blvd Kampuchea Krom, Phnom-Penh; tel. (23) 722873; fax (23) 426841; e-mail procure.pcu@bigpond.com.kh; internet www.moh.gov.kh.

Ministry of Industry, Mines and Energy: 45 blvd Preah Norodom, Phnom-Penh; tel. (23) 723077; fax (23) 428263; e-mail mine@cambodia.gov.kh; internet www.mine.gov.kh.

Ministry of Information: 62 blvd Monivong, Phnom-Penh; tel. (23) 724159; fax (23) 427475; e-mail information@cambodia.gov.kh; internet www.information.gov.kh.

Ministry of the Interior: 275 blvd Norodom, Khan Chamkarmon, Phnom-Penh; tel. (23) 726148; fax (23) 212708; e-mail moi@interior.gov.kh; internet www.interior.gov.kh.

Ministry of Justice: 14 blvd Sothearos, Phnom-Penh; tel. (23) 360327; fax (23) 364119; e-mail moj@cambodia.gov.kh; internet www.moj.gov.kh.

Ministry of Parliamentary Affairs and Inspection: rue Jawaharlal Nehru, Phnom-Penh; tel. (23) 884261; fax (23) 884264; e-mail mnasrl@cambodia.gov.kh; internet www.mnasrl.gov.kh.

Ministry of Planning: 386 blvd Monivong, Sangkat Boeung Keng Kong 2, Phnom-Penh; tel. (23) 212049; fax (23) 210698; e-mail mop@cambodia.gov.kh; internet www.mop.gov.kh.

Ministry of Posts and Telecommunications: cnr rue Preah Ang Eng and rue Ang Non, Phnom-Penh; tel. (23) 426510; fax (23) 426011; e-mail mptc@cambodia.gov.kh; internet www.mptc.gov.kh.

Ministry of Public Works and Transport: 106 blvd Norodom, Phnom-Penh; tel. (23) 427845; fax (23) 427852; e-mail mpwt@mpwt.gov.kh; internet www.mpwt.gov.kh.

Ministry of Rural Development: Jok Dimitrov, cnr rue 169, Phnom-Penh; tel. (23) 426850; fax (23) 366790; e-mail mrd@cambodia.gov.kh; internet www.mrd.gov.kh.

Ministry of Social Affairs, Labour, Vocational Training and Youth Rehabilitation: 788B blvd Monivong, Phnom-Penh; tel. (23) 218437; fax (23) 726086; e-mail mosalvy-gdlv@camnet.com.kh; internet www.mosalvy.gov.kh.

Ministry of Territorial Organization, Urbanization and Construction: 771–773 blvd Monivong, Phnom-Penh; tel. (23) 215660; fax (23) 217035; e-mail gdlmup-mlmupc@camnet.com.kh; internet www.mlmupc.gov.kh.

Ministry of Tourism: 3 blvd Monivong, Phnom-Penh 12258; tel. (23) 212837; fax (23) 426877; e-mail info@mot.gov.kh; internet www.mot.gov.kh.

Ministry of Water Resources and Meteorology: 47 blvd Norodom, Phnom-Penh; tel. (23) 724289; fax (23) 426345; e-mail mowram@cambodia.gov.kh; internet www.mowram.gov.kh.

Ministry of Women's Affairs and Veterans: 3 blvd Norodom, Phnom-Penh; tel. and fax (23) 428965; e-mail mwva.cabinet@bigpond.com.kh; internet www.mwva.gov.kh.

Legislature

PARLIAMENT

National Assembly

National Assembly, blvd Samdech Sothearos, cnr rue 240, Phnom-Penh; tel. (23) 214136; fax (23) 217769; e-mail kimhenglong@cambodian-parliament.org; internet www.cambodian-parliament.org.

Chairman: NORODOM RANARIDDH (FUNCINPEC).

Election, 27 July 2003

	% of Votes	Seats
Cambodian People's Party	47.35	73
FUNCINPEC Party	20.75	26
Sam Rainsy Party	21.87	24
Others	10.03	—
Total	100.00	123

Senate

Senate, Chamkarmon Palace, blvd Norodom, Phnom-Penh; tel. (23) 211446; fax (23) 211441; e-mail oum_sarith@camnet.com.kh; internet www.khmersenate.org.

Chairman: CHEA SIM (CPP).

First Vice-Chairman: CHIVAN MONIRAK (FUNCINPEC).

Second Vice-Chairman: NHIEK BUNCHHAY (FUNCINPEC).

Inauguration, 25 March 1999

	Seats
Cambodian People's Party	31
FUNCINPEC Party	21
Sam Rainsy Party	7
King's appointees	2
Total	61

Political Organizations

Alliance of Democrats (AD): Phnom-Penh; f. 2003; alliance of FUNCINPEC Party and Sam Rainsy Party; Pres. Prince NORODOM RANARIDDH; Vice-Pres. SAM RAINSY.

Buddhist Liberal Party (Kanakpak Serei Niyum Preah Put Sasna): Phnom-Penh; internet www.blp.org; f. 1998; Chair. IENG MULI; Gen. Sec. SIENG LAPRESSE.

Cambodia National Sustaining Party: 56 rue 598, Krom 25, Mondul 3, Sangkat Bang Kork II, Khan Toul Kork, Phnom-Penh; tel. (12) 655442; e-mail cnsp_cambodia@hotmail.com; internet www.pensovann.com; f. 1997 by Pen Sovann, fmr Sec.-Gen. of the Cen. Cttee of the CPP, to contest the 1998 legislative elections; boycotted 2003 legislative elections; Pres. PEN SOVANN.

Cambodian Freedom Fighters: 2728 E 10th Street, Long Beach, CA 90804, USA; tel. (562) 433-9930; fax (562) 433-7490; internet www.cffighters.org; f. 1998 in opposition to Hun Sen's leadership; Leader CHHUN YASITH; Sec.-Gen. RICHARD KIRI KIM.

Cambodian People's Party (CPP) (Kanakpak Pracheachon Kampuchea): 203 blvd Norodom, Sangkat Tonle Bassac, Khan Chamkarmon, Phnom-Penh; tel. and fax (23) 2158801; e-mail cpp@thecpp.org; internet www.thecpp.org; known as the Kampuchean People's Revolutionary Party 1979–91; 21-mem. Standing Cttee of the Cen. Cttee; Cen. Cttee of 153 full mems; Hon. Chair. of Cen. Cttee HENG SAMRIN; Chair. of Cen. Cttee CHEA SIM; Vice-Chair. HUN SEN; Chair. of Permanent Cttee SAY CHHUM.

Cambodian Women's Party: 22 rue 384, Sangkat Toul Svay Prey 1, Khan Chamkarmon, Phnom-Penh; tel. (23) 993297; f. 1998; Pres. NUON BUNNA.

Democratic National United Movement (DNUM): Pailin; f. 1996 by Ieng Sary, following his defection from the PDK; not a national political party, did not contest 1998 election; DNUM members are also free to join other political parties.

Farmers' Party: 21 rue 528, Sangkat Boeung Kak 1, Khan Chamkarmon, Phnom-Penh; tel. (16) 333200; Pres. PON PISITH.

FUNCINPEC Party (United National Front for an Independent, Neutral, Peaceful and Co-operative Cambodia Party): 11 blvd Monivong (93), Sangkat Sras Chak, Khan Daun Penh, Phnom Penh; tel. (23) 428864; fax (23) 426521; e-mail funcinpec@funcinpec.org; internet www.funcinpec.org; FUNCINPEC altered its title to the FUNCINPEC Party when it adopted political status in 1992; the party's military wing was the National Army of Independent Cambodia (fmrly the Armée Nationale Sihanoukiste—ANS); merged with the Son Sann Party in Jan. 1999; Pres. Prince NORODOM RANARIDDH; Sec.-Gen. Prince NORODOM SIRIVUDH.

Hang Dara Movement Democratic Party: 16 rue 430, Sangkat Phsardoeum Thkov, Khan Chamkarmon, Phnom-Penh; tel. (12) 672007; f. 2002 to contest 2003 general election; breakaway faction of the FUNCINPEC Party; Pres. HANG DARA.

Indra Buddra City Party: Commune, Chbarmon District, Kampong Spueu; tel. (12) 710331; Pres. NOREAK RATANAVATHANO.

Khmer Angkor Party: 27C rue 390, Sangkat Boeung Keng Kang 3, Khan Chamkarmon, Phnom-Penh; tel. (12) 865269; f. 1998; breakaway faction of Sam Rainsy Party; Pres. KUNG MUNI.

Khmer Citizens' Party (Kanakpak Pulroat Khmer): 94B rue 146, Sangkat Phsar Depo 2, Khan Toul Kork, Phnom-Penh; tel. (12) 827071; f. 1996; breakaway faction of Khmer Nation Party (now Sam Rainsy Party); Pres. KHIEU SENGKIM.

Khmer Democratic Party (Kanakpak Pracheathippatei Khmer): 79A rue 186, Sangkat Touek Laak 3, Khan Toul Kork, Phnom-Penh; tel. (12) 842947; Pres. OUK PHURIK.

Khmer Front Party (Ronakse Chuncheat Khmer): 40 St 566, Sangkat Boeungkok 1, Khan Tuolkok, Phnom-Penh; tel. (12) 762207; e-mail khmerfront@hotmail.com; internet www.khmerfrontparty.org; f. 2002 to contest 2003 general election; Pres. SUTH DINA; Vice-Pres. SUN SOKUNMEALEA.

Khmer Help Khmer Party (Khmer Chuoy Khmer): 21 rue 281, Sangkat Boeung Kak 1, Khan Toul Kork, Phnom-Penh; tel. (23) 885017; f. 1998 as Khmer New Life Party; name changed as above in 2003; Pres. KING SOVANN; Gen. Sec. TIT SARUN.

Khmer Neutral Party (Kanakpak Kampuchea Appyeakroet): 14A rue Keo Chea, Phnom-Penh; tel. (23) 62365; fax (23) 27340; e-mail Masavang@datagraphic.fr; Pres. BUO HEL.

Khmer Soul Party: 7 blvd Makara, Sangkat No. 4, Khan Mitta Pheap, Sihanoukville; tel. (12) 573345; Pres. MOEUNG MLOB.

Khmer Unity Party: 54 blvd Russia, Sangkat Phsar Depo 3, Khan Toul Kork, Phnom-Penh; tel. (12) 829092; e-mail kup@free.fr; internet kup.free.fr; Pres. BOU SARIN.

Liberal Democratic Party: 21 rue 614, Sangkat Boeung Kak 2, Khan Toul Kork, Phnom-Penh; tel. (12) 866576; f. 1993; receives support from members of the armed forces; pro-Government; Chair. Gen. CHHIM OM YON.

MOLINAKA (National Liberation Movement of Cambodia): 8 rue 292, Sangkat Boeung Keng Kang 2, Khan Chamkarmon, Phnom-Penh; tel. (12) 941029; f. 1992; a breakaway faction of FUNCINPEC; Pres. KHLOK PRITHY.

National Union Party (Kanakpak Ruop Ruom Cheat): Phnom-Penh; established by rebel mems of FUNCINPEC Party; Chair. (vacant); Sec.-Gen. UNG PHAN.

Norodom Chakrapong Khmer Soul Party (NCPPK): 61 rue 294, Sangkat Boeung Keng Kang 1, Khan Chamkarmon, Phnom-Penh; tel. (23) 212597; e-mail ncppk@bigpond.com.kh; internet www.ncppk.org; f. 2002 by Prince Norodom Chakrapong; breakaway faction of FUNCINPEC Party; Pres. Prince NORODOM CHAKRAPONG.

Reastr Niyum (Nationalist Party): blvd Norodom, Phnom-Penh; tel. (23) 215659; fax (23) 215279; f. 1998; breakaway faction of the FUNCINPEC Party; Pres. UNG HUOT; Sec.-Gen. PU SOTHIRAK.

Rice Party (Svor): 69 blvd Sotheoaros, Sangkat Tonle Bassac, Khan Chamkarmon, Phnom-Penh 12301; tel. (11) 860060; e-mail riceparty@asia.com; internet www.riceparty.itgo.com; f. 1992; Pres. NHOUNG SEAP.

Sam Rainsy Party (SRP): 71 blvd Sotheoaros, Sangkat Tonle Bassac, Khan Chamkarmon, Phnom-Penh; tel. and fax (23) 217452; e-mail samrainsy@samrainsyparty.org; internet www.samrainsyparty.org; f. 1995 as the Khmer Nation Party; name changed as above in 1998; 444,544 mems (Aug. 2001); Pres. SAM RAINSY; Sec.-Gen. MENG RITA (acting).

Union of National Solidarity Party (UNS): 75 rue 598, Sangkat Phnom Penh Thmei, Khan Roeusey Keo, Phnom-Penh; tel. (12) 829003; Pres. SIM SOKHOM.

United Front for the Construction and Defence of the Kampuchean Fatherland (UFCDKF): Phnom-Penh; f. 1978 as the Kampuchean National United Front for National Salvation (KNUFNS), renamed Kampuchean United Front for National Construction and Defence (KUFNCD) in 1981, present name adopted in 1989; mass organization supporting policies of the CPP; an 89-mem. Nat. Council and a seven-mem. hon. Presidium; Chair. of Nat. Council CHEA SIM; Sec.-Gen. ROS CHHUN.

Diplomatic Representation

EMBASSIES IN CAMBODIA

Australia: Villa 11, R. V. Senei Vinnavaut Oum (rue 254), Sangkat Chaktomouk, Khan Daun Penh, Phnom-Penh; tel. (23) 213470; fax (23) 213413; e-mail australian.embassy.cambodia@dfat.gov.au; internet www.embassy.gov.au/kh.html; Ambassador LISA KIM FILI-PETTO.

Brunei: 237 rue Pasteur 51, Sangkat Boeung Keng Kang 1, Khan Chamkarmon, Phnom-Penh; tel. (23) 211457; fax (23) 211455; e-mail brunei@bigpond.com.kh; Ambassador Awang Haji EMRAN B. BAHAR.

Bulgaria: 227/229 blvd Norodom, Phnom-Penh; tel. (23) 217504; fax (23) 212792; e-mail bulgembpnp@camnet.com.kh; Chargé d'affaires a.i. ROUMEN DONTCHEV.

Canada: Villa 9, R. V. Senei Vinnavaut Oum, Sangkat Chakto-mouk, Khan Daun Penh, Phnom-Penh; tel. (23) 213470; fax (23) 211389; e-mail pnmpn@dfait-maeci.gc.ca; internet www.dfait-maeci.gc.ca/cambodia; Ambassador DONICA POTTIE.

China, People's Republic: 156 blvd Mao Tse Toung, Phnom-Penh; tel. (23) 720920; fax (23) 364738; e-mail chinaemb_kh@mfa.gov.cn; Ambassador HU QIANWEN.

Cuba: 96/98 rue 214, Sangkat Veal Vong, Khan 7 Makara, Phnom-Penh; tel. (23) 213212; fax (23) 217428; e-mail embacuba@camnet.com.kh; Ambassador NIRSIA CASTRO GUEVARA.

France: 1 blvd Monivong, Phnom-Penh; tel. (23) 430020; fax (23) 430041; e-mail ambafrance@online.com.kh; internet www.ambafrance.gov.kh; Ambassador YVON ROÉ D'ALBERT.

Germany: 76–78 rue Yougoslavie, BP 60, Phnom-Penh; tel. (23) 216381; fax (23) 427746; e-mail germanembassy@everyday.com.kh; internet www.phnompenh.diplo.de; Ambassador PIUS FISCHER.

India: 777 blvd Monivong, Phnom-Penh; tel. (23) 210912; fax (23) 213640; e-mail hocembindia@online.com.kh; Ambassador ALOKE SEN.

Indonesia: 90 blvd Norodom, Phnom-Penh; tel. (23) 216148; fax (23) 216571; e-mail kukppenh@bigpond.com.kh; internet www.indonesia-phnompenh.org; Ambassador NURRACHMAN OERIP.

Japan: 194 blvd Norodom, Sangkat Tonle Bassac, Khan Cham-karmon, Phnom-Penh; tel. (23) 217161; fax (23) 216162; e-mail eojc@bigpond.com.kh; internet www.kh.emb-japan.go.jp; Ambassador FUMIAKI TAKAHASHI.

Korea, Democratic People's Republic: 39 rue 268, Phnom-Penh; tel. (15) 912567; fax (23) 426230; Ambassador CHOE HAN-CHUN.

Korea, Republic: 50 rue 214, Sangkar Beung Rain, Khan Daun Penh, Phnom-Penh; tel. (23) 211900; fax (23) 219200; e-mail cambodia@mofat.go.kr; internet www.koreanembcam.go.kr; Ambassador LEE HAN-GON.

Laos: 15–17 blvd Mao Tse Toung, POB 19, Phnom-Penh; tel. (23) 982632; fax (23) 720907; e-mail laoembpp@camintel.com; Ambassador THOUANE VORASARN.

Malaysia: 5 rue 242, Sangkat Chaktomouk, Khan Daun Penh, Phnom-Penh; tel. (23) 216176; fax (23) 216004; e-mail mwppenh@online.com.kh; Ambassador Datin Paduka MELANIE LEONG SOOK LEI.

Myanmar: 181 blvd Norodom, Phnom-Penh; tel. (23) 213664; fax (23) 213665; e-mail M.E.PHNOMPENH@bigpond.com.kh; Ambassador Dr AUNG NAING.

Philippines: 33 rue 294, Khan Chamkarmon, Sangkat Tonle Bassac, Phnom-Penh; tel. (23) 215145; fax (23) 215143; e-mail phnompenhpe@online.com.kh; Ambassador (vacant).

Poland: 767 blvd Monivong, BP 58, Phnom-Penh; tel. (23) 217782; fax (23) 217781; e-mail emb.pol.pp@online.com.kh; internet www.polishembassy-cambodia.org; Ambassador KAZIMIERZ A. DUCHOWSKI.

Russia: 213 blvd Sothearos, Phnom-Penh; tel. (23) 210931; fax (23) 216776; e-mail russemba@online.com.kh; internet www.embrusscambodia.mid.ru; Ambassador VALERII TERESHCHENKO.

Singapore: 92 blvd Norodom, Phnom-Penh; tel. (23) 360855; fax (23) 210862; e-mail singemb@bigpond.com.kh; internet www.mfa.gov.sg/phnompenh; Ambassador LAWRENCE ANDERSON.

Thailand: 196 Preah Norodom Blvd, Sangkat Tonle Bassac, Khan Chamkarmon, Phnom-Penh; tel. (23) 726306; fax (23) 726309; e-mail thaipnp@mfa.go.th; Ambassador PIYAWAT NIYOMRERKS.

United Kingdom: 27–29 rue 75, Sangkat Sras Chak, Khan Daun Penh, Phnom-Penh; tel. (23) 427124; fax (23) 427125; e-mail britemb@online.com.kh; internet www.britishembassy.gov.uk/cambodia; Ambassador DAVID GEORGE READER.

USA: 16 rue 228, Phnom-Penh; tel. (23) 216436; fax (23) 216437; internet phnompenh.usembassy.gov; Ambassador CHARLES AARON RAY.

Viet Nam: 436 blvd Monivong, Phnom-Penh; tel. (23) 362741; fax (23) 427385; e-mail embbvnpp@camnet.com.kh; Ambassador NGUYEN DU HONG.

Judicial System

An independent judiciary was established under the 1993 Constitution.

Supreme Court: rue 134, cnr rue 63, Phnom-Penh; tel. (17) 816663; Chair. DID MONTY.

Religion

BUDDHISM

The principal religion of Cambodia is Theravada Buddhism (Buddhism of the 'Tradition of the Elders'), the sacred language of which is Pali. A ban was imposed on all religious activity in 1975. By a constitutional amendment, which was adopted in April 1989, Buddhism was reinstated as the national religion and was retained as such under the 1993 Constitution. By 1992 2,800 monasteries (of a total of 3,369) had been restored and there were 21,800 Buddhist monks. In 1992 about 90% of the population were Buddhists.

Supreme Patriarchs: Ven. Patriarch TEP VONG, Ven. Patriarch BOU KRI.

Patriotic Kampuchean Buddhists' Association: Phnom-Penh; mem. of UFCDKF; Pres. LONG SIM.

CHRISTIANITY

The Roman Catholic Church

Cambodia comprises the Apostolic Vicariate of Phnom-Penh and the Apostolic Prefectures of Battambang and Kompong-Cham. At 31 December 2002 there were an estimated 15,301 adherents in the country, equivalent to about 0.1% of the population. An Episcopal Conference of Laos and Kampuchea was established in 1971. In 1975 the Government of Democratic Kampuchea banned all religious practice in Cambodia, and the right of Christians to meet to worship was not restored until 1990.

Vicar Apostolic of Phnom-Penh: Rt Rev. EMILE DESTOMBES (Titular Bishop of Altava), 787 blvd Monivong (rue 93), BP 123, Phnom-Penh; tel. and fax (23) 212462; e-mail evecam@camnet.com.kh.

ISLAM

Islam is practised by a minority in Cambodia. Islamic worship was also banned in 1975, but it was legalized in 1979, following the defeat of the Democratic Kampuchean regime.

The Press

According to Cambodia's Press Law, newspapers, magazines and foreign press agencies are required to register with the Department of Media at the Ministry of Information. In October 2002 160 Khmer language newspapers, 36 foreign language newspapers, 42 magazines, 19 bulletins and 12 foreign news agencies were registered.

NEWSPAPERS AND MAGAZINES

Newspapers are not widely available outside Phnom-Penh. In June 2004 Cambodia's first regional newspaper, *Somne Thmey*, was launched. It was to circulate in the country's four main provinces.

Areyathor (Civilization): 52 rue Lyuk Lay, Sangkat Chey, Chummneah, Phnom-Penh; tel. (23) 913662; Editor CHIN CHAN MONTY.

Bayon Pearnik: 3 rue 174, BP 2279, Phnom-Penh; tel. (12) 803968; fax (23) 211921; e-mail bp@forum.org.kh; internet www.bayonpearnik.com; f. 1995; English; monthly; Publr and Editor ADAM PARKER; circ. 10,000.

Cambodia Daily: 50B rue 240, Phnom-Penh; tel. (23) 426602; fax (23) 426573; e-mail aafc@forum.org.kh; internet www.cambodiadaily.com; f. 1993; in English and Khmer; Mon.–Sat.; Editor CHRIS DECHERD; Publr BERNARD KRISHER; circ. 3,500.

Cambodia New Vision: BP 158, Phnom-Penh; tel. (23) 219898; fax (23) 360666; e-mail cabinet1b@camnet.com.kh; internet www.cnv.org.kh; f. 1998; official newsletter of the Cambodian Govt.

Chakraval: 3 rue 181, Sangkat Tumnop Teuk, Khan Chamkarmon, Phnom-Penh; tel. (23) 211878; fax (23) 720141; e-mail chakraval@hotmail.com; Khmer; daily; Publr KEO SOPHORN; Editor SO SOVAN RITH.

Commercial News: 394 blvd Preah Sihanouk, Phnom-Penh; tel. (23) 721665; fax (23) 721709; e-mail tcnews@online.com.kh; internet www.thecommercialnews.com; f. 1993; Chinese; Chief Editor Liu Xiao Guang; circ. 6,000.

Construction (Kasang): 126 rue 336, Sangkat Phsar Deum Kor, Khan Tuol Kok, Phnom-Penh; tel. (18) 818292; Khmer; Editor Chhea Vary.

Equality Voice: 470 rue 163, Sangkat Boeung Keng Kang, Khan Chamkarmon, Phnom-Penh; tel. (12) 842471; Khmer; Publr Huon Mara.

Indradevi: 256 blvd Mao Tse Toung, Phnom-Penh; tel. (23) 215808; e-mail indradevi@camnet.com.kh; internet www.indradevi.com.kh; f. 1998; general interest magazine.

Kampuchea: 158 blvd Norodom, Phnom-Penh; tel. (23) 725559; f. 1979; weekly; Chief Editor Keo Prasat; circ. 55,000.

Kampuchea Thmey (New Cambodia): 805 rue Kampuchea Krom, Phnom-Penh; tel. (23) 882535; fax (23) 882656; e-mail kampucheathmey@camnet.com.kh; internet www.kampucheathmey.com; daily.

Khmer Wisdom: 1588 Khan Russei Keo, Phnom-Penh; tel. (12) 841377; Khmer; Publr Chea Chan Thon.

Khmer Youth Voice: 240 rue 374, Sangkat Toul Prey 2, Khan Chamkarmon, Phnom-Penh; tel. (23) 211336; fax (23) 210137; e-mail sovann@camnet.com.kh; Khmer; twice weekly; Editor Uo Sovann.

Koh Santepheap (Island of Peace): 41 rue 338, Sangkat Toul Svay Prey 1, Khan Chamkarmon, Phnom-Penh; tel. (23) 211818; fax (23) 220155; e-mail kohsantepheap@online.com.kh; internet www.kohsantepheapdaily.com.kh; Khmer; daily; Dir Thong Uy Pang.

Moneaksekar Khmer: 27 rue 318, Sangkat Toul Svay Prey 1, Khan Chamkarmon, Phnom-Penh; tel. (23) 990777; Editor Dam Sithik.

Neak Chea: 1 rue 158, Khan Daun Penh, Phnom-Penh; tel. (23) 428653; fax (23) 427229; e-mail adhoc@forum.org.kh; bulletin released by the Cambodia Human Rights and Development Association; Khmer; twice a month.

Phnom Penh Daily: 5 rue 84, Corner 61, Sangkat Srah Chak, Khan Daun Penh, Phnom-Penh; tel. (15) 917682; e-mail ppenhdaily@camnet.com.kn; internet www.phnompenhdaily.com.kh; Khmer; available online in English; Editor Va Dane.

Phnom Penh Post: 10A rue 264, Phnom-Penh; tel. (23) 210309; fax (23) 426568; e-mail michael.pppost@online.com.kh; internet www.phnompenhpost.com; f. 1992; English; fortnightly; Editor-in-Chief and Publr Michael Hayes.

Pracheachon (The People): 101 blvd Norodom, Phnom-Penh; tel. (23) 723665; f. 1985; 2 a week; organ of the CPP; Editor-in-Chief Som Kimsuor; circ. 50,000.

Rasmei Kampuchea: 476 blvd Monivong, Phnom-Penh; tel. (23) 362881; fax (23) 362472; e-mail rasmei_kampuchea@yahoo.com; daily; f. 1993; local newspaper in northern Cambodia; Editor Pen Samithy.

Samleng Thmei (New Voice): 91 rue 139, Sangkat Veal Vong, Khan 7, Phnom-Penh; tel. (15) 920589; Khmer; Editor Khun Ngor.

Somne Thmey (New Writing): 164B blvd Preah Norodom, Phnom-Penh; tel. (23) 224303; e-mail mcd.cambodia@online.com.kh; f. 2004; Khmer; weekly; publ. in Siem Reab, Preah Sihanouk, Kampong Cham and Bat Dambang; Editor-in-Chief Pen Bona.

NEWS AGENCIES

Agence Kampuchea Presse (AKP): 62 blvd Monivong, Phnom-Penh; tel. (23) 430564; e-mail akp@camnet.com.kh; internet www.camnet.com.kh/akp; f. 1978; Dir-Gen. Kit-Kim Huon.

Foreign Bureaux

Agence France-Presse (AFP) (France): 8 rue 214, BP 822, Phnom-Penh; tel. (23) 426227; fax (23) 426226; Bureau Chief Luke Hunt.

Associated Press (AP) (USA): 18c rue 19, BP 870, Phnom-Penh; tel. (23) 426607; e-mail ap@bigpond.com.kh; Correspondent Chris Fontaine.

Deutsche Presse-Agentur (dpa): 5E rue 178, Phnom-Penh; tel. (23) 427846; fax (23) 427846; Correspondent Joe Cochrane.

Reuters (UK): 201, 2nd Floor, Hong Kong Centre, 108–112 blvd Sothearos, Phnom-Penh; tel. (23) 216977; fax (23) 216970; Bureau Chief Robert Birsel.

Xinhua (New China) News Agency (People's Republic of China): 19 rue 294, Phnom-Penh; tel. (23) 211608; fax (23) 426613; Correspondent Lei Bosong.

ASSOCIATIONS

Cambodian Association for the Protection of Journalists (CAPJ): BP 816, 58 rue 336, Sangkat Psadoeum Khor, Khan Tuol Kok, Phnom-Penh; tel. (15) 997004; fax (23) 215834; e-mail umsarin@hotmail.com; Pres. Um Sarin.

Cambodian Club of Journalists: Phnom-Penh; Pres. Pen Samithy; Sec.-Gen. Prach Sim.

Khmer Journalists' Association: 101 blvd Preah Norodom, Phnom-Penh; tel. (23) 725459; f. 1979; mem. of UFCDKF; Pres. Pin Samkhon.

League of Cambodian Journalists (LCJ): 74 rue 205, Sangkat Toulsvayprey, Khan Chamkarmon, Phnom-Penh; tel. and fax (23) 360612; Pres. Om Chandara.

Broadcasting and Communications

TELECOMMUNICATIONS

Cambodia Samart Communication (CASACOM): 56 blvd Norodom, Sangkat Chey Chumneah, Khan Daun Penh, Phnom-Penh; tel. (16) 810001; fax (16) 810004; e-mail somchai.an@hello016-gsm.com; internet www.hello016-gsm.com; f. 1992; operates a national mobile telephone network; CEO Somchai (An) Lertwisettheerakul.

CamGSM Co Ltd: 33 blvd Preah Sihanouk, Phnom-Penh; tel. (12) 800800; fax (12) 801801; e-mail helpline@mobitel.com.kh; internet www.mobitel.com.kh; f. 1996; operates national GSM 900 mobile telephone network under trade name MobiTel; CEO David Spriggs.

Camintel: 1 cnr Terak Vithei Sisowath and Vithei Phsar Dek, Phnom-Penh; tel. (23) 986789; fax (23) 986277; e-mail victor@camintel.com; internet www.camintel.com; jt venture between the Ministry of Posts and Telecommunications and the Indonesian co, Indosat; operates domestic telephone network; Chair. Nhek Korsol Vythyea.

Camshin Corporation: Suite 6B–7B, Regency Sq., 294 blvd Mao Tse Toung, Phnom-Penh; tel. (23) 367801; fax (23) 367805; e-mail sales@camshin.com; internet www.camshin.com; a jt venture between the Ministry of Posts and Telecommunications and the Thai co, Shinawatra International Co Ltd; telephone communications co.

BROADCASTING

Radio

Apsara: 69 rue 360, 57, Sangkat Boeung Keng Kang 1, Khan Chamkarmon, Phnom-Penh; tel. (12) 949414; fax (23) 214302; e-mail tv11@camnet.com.kh; internet www.apsaratv.com.kh; f. 1996; Head of Admin. Keo Sopheap; News Editor Sin So Cheat.

Bayon: c/o Bayon Media Group, 954 rue 2, Takhmau, Kandal Province; tel. (23) 363695; fax (23) 363795; e-mail bayontv@camnet.com.kh; internet www.bayontv.com.kh; Dir-Gen. Kem Kunnavath.

Bee Hive Radio: 949 rue 360, Boeung Keng Kang, Khan Chamkarmon, Phnom-Penh; tel. (23) 992939; fax 240439; e-mail sok@online.com.kh; Dir-Gen. Mam Sonando.

FM 90 MHZ: 65 rue 178, Phnom-Penh; tel. (23) 363699; fax (23) 368623; Dir-Gen. Nhim Bun Thon; Dep. Dir-Gen. Tum Vann Det.

FM 99 MHZ: 41 rue 360, Phnom-Penh; tel. (23) 426794; Gen. Man. Som Chhaya.

FM 107 MHZ: 18 rue 562, Phnom-Penh; tel. (23) 880874; fax (23) 368212; e-mail tv9@camnet.com.kh; internet www.tv9.com.kh; Dir-Gen. Khun Hang.

Krusa FM: Phnom-Penh; e-mail febcam@bigpond.com.kh; f. 2002; controlled by Far East Broadcasting; religious programmes; Dir Samoeun Intal.

Phnom-Penh Municipality Radio: 131–132 blvd Pochentong, Phnom-Penh; tel. (23) 725205; fax (23) 360800; Gen. Man. Khampun Keomony.

Radio WMC: 30 rue 488, Sangkat Phsar Dem Thkov, Khan Chamkarmon, Phnom-Penh; tel. and fax (12) 847854; e-mail wmc@forum.org.kh; independent; radio station of Women's Media Centre of Cambodia; Dir Chea Sudaneth.

RCAF Radio: c/o Borei Keila, rue 169, Phnom-Penh; tel. (23) 366061; fax (23) 366063; f. 1994; Royal Cambodian Armed Forces radio station; Dir Tha Tana; News Editor Seng Kateka.

Ta Prohm Radio: 27B rue 472, Phnom-Penh; tel. (23) 213054; e-mail taprohm@yahoo.com; f. 2003; launched by FUNCINPEC Party as opposition radio station; broadcasts news programmes in Khmer to Phnom-Penh and surrounding area.

Vithyu Cheat Kampuchea (National Radio of Cambodia): rue Preah Kossamak, Phnom-Penh; tel. (12) 852741; fax (11) 745074; e-mail chaosang2002@yahoo.com; f. 1978; fmrly Vithyu Samleng Pracheachon Kampuchea (Voice of the Cambodian People); controlled by the Ministry of Information; home service in Khmer; daily external services in English, French, Lao, Vietnamese and Thai; Dir-Gen. VANN SENG LY; Dep. Dir-Gen. TAN YAN.

Voice of Cambodia: Phnom-Penh; e-mail vocri@vocri.org; internet www.vocri.org; Cambodia's first international internet radio station. There are also several private local radio stations.

Television

Apsara Television (TV11): 69 rue 360, 57, Sangkat Boeung Keng Kang 1, Khan Chamkarmon, Phnom-Penh; tel. (23) 303002; fax (23) 214302; e-mail tv11@camnet.com.kh; internet www.apsaratv.com.kh; Dir-Gen. SOK EISAN.

Bayon Television (TV27): 954 rue 2, Takhmau, Kandal Province; tel. (23) 363695; fax (23) 363795; e-mail bayontv@camnet.com.kh; internet www.bayontv.com.kh; Dir-Gen. KEM KUNNAVATH.

National Television of Cambodia (TVK): 62 blvd Preah Monivong, Phnom-Penh; tel. (23) 722983; fax (23) 426407; e-mail tvk@camnet.gov.kh; internet www.tvk.gov.kh; f. 1983; broadcasts for 10 hours per day in Khmer; Dir-Gen. (Head of Television) MAO AYUTH.

Phnom-Penh Television (TV3): 2 blvd Russia, Phnom-Penh; tel. (12) 814323; fax (23) 360800; e-mail tv3@camnet.com.kh; internet www.tv3.com.kh; Dir-Gen. KHAMPHUN KEOMONY.

RCAF Television (TV5): 165 rue 169, Borei Keila, Phnom-Penh; tel. (23) 366061; fax (23) 366063; e-mail mica.t.v.5@bigpond.com.kh; Editor-in-Chief PRUM KIM.

TV Khmer (TV9): 18 rue 562, Phnom-Penh; tel. (23) 880874; fax (23) 368212; e-mail tv9@camnet.com.kh; internet www.tv9.com.kh; f. 1992; Dir-Gen. KHOUN ELYNA; News Editor PHAN TITH.

Finance

(cap. = capital; res = reserves; dep. = deposits; brs = branches)

BANKING

The National Bank of Cambodia, which was established as the sole authorized bank in 1980 (following the abolition of the monetary system by the Government of Democratic Kampuchea in 1975), is the central bank, and assumed its present name in February 1992. The adoption of a market economy led to the licensing of privately owned and joint-venture banks from July 1991. Following the implementation of the 1999 Financial Institutions Law, 29 of the banks operative in Cambodia were considered for re-licensing. Between November 1999 and November 2002 17 banks were closed, many having failed to meet new capital requirements. At the end of July 2004 there were 17 banks (excluding the central bank) operating in Cambodia, comprising: one state-owned bank; three specialized banks; 10 locally-incorporated private banks; and three branches of foreign banks.

Central Bank

National Bank of Cambodia: 22–24 blvd Preah Norodom, BP 25, Phnom-Penh; tel. (23) 722563; fax (23) 426117; e-mail nbc@bigpond.com.kh; f. 1980; cap. 100,000m. riels, res 939,154m. riels, dep. 1,777,673m. riels (Dec. 2003); Gov. CHEA CHANTO; Dep. Gov. ENG THAYSAN.

State Bank

Foreign Trade Bank: 3 rue Kramoun Sar, Khan Daun Penh, Phnom-Penh; tel. (23) 724466; fax (23) 426108; e-mail info@ftbbank.com; internet www.ftbbank.com; f. 1979; removed from direct management of National Bank of Cambodia in 2000; scheduled for privatization; Man. TIM BO PHOL.

Specialized Banks

Cambodia Agriculture Industrial Specialized Bank: 87 blvd Preah Norodom, Sangkat Phsar Thmey III, Khan Daun Penh, Phnom-Penh; tel. (23) 218667; fax (23) 217751; e-mail kien@bigpond.com.kh; Man. CHHOR SANG.

Peng Heng SME Bank: 72 blvd Norodom, Phnom-Penh; tel. (23) 219243; fax (23) 219185; e-mail pengheng@camnet.com.kh; f. 2001.

Rural Development Bank: 9–13 rue 7, Sangkat Chaktomouk, Khan Daun Penh, Phnom-Penh; tel. (23) 220810; fax (23) 722388; e-mail rdb@online.com.kh; internet www.rdb.com.kh; f. 1998; provides credit to rural enterprises; Chair. and CEO SON KOUN THOR.

Private Banks

ACLEDA Bank PLC: 28 blvd Mao Tse Toung, Sangkat Beung Trabek, Khan Chamkarmon, Phnom-Penh; tel. (23) 364619; fax (23) 364914; e-mail acledabank@acledabank.com.kh; internet www.acledabank.com.kh; f. 1993; became specialized bank in Oct. 2000 and was awarded commercial banking licence in Dec. 2003; provides financial services to all sectors; Chair. CHEA SOK; Gen. Man. IN CHANNY; 115 brs and offices.

Advanced Bank of Asia Ltd: 97–99 blvd Preah Norodom, Sangkat Boeung Raing, Khan Daun Penh, Phnom-Penh; tel. (23) 720434; fax (23) 720435; e-mail aba@ababank.com.kh; Dir CHAE WAN CHO.

Cambodia Asia Bank Ltd: 252 blvd Preah Monivong, Sangkat Phsar Thmey II, Khan Daun Penh, Phnom-Penh; tel. (23) 722105; fax (23) 426628; e-mail cab@camnet.com.kh; Man. WONG TOW FOCK.

Cambodia Mekong Bank: 6 blvd Monivong, Khan Daun Penh, Phnom-Penh; tel. (23) 430980; fax (23) 430431; e-mail ho.mailbox@mekongbank.com; cap. US $13m., dep. US $5.9m. (Dec. 2003); Chair. MICHAEL C. STEPHEN; Pres. and CEO KHOV BOUN CHHAY.

Cambodian Commercial Bank Ltd: 26 blvd Preah Monivong, Sangkat Phsar Thmey II, Khan Daun Penh, Phnom-Penh; tel. (23) 426145; fax (23) 426116; e-mail ccbpp@online.com.kh; internet www.cbb-cambodia.com; f. 1991; cap. US $13m., dep. US $83.7m. (Dec. 2003); Chair. MALEERATNA PLUMCHITCHOM; Dir and Gen. Man. SAHASIN YUTTARAT; 4 brs.

Cambodian Public Bank (Campu Bank): Villa 23, rue Kramoun Sar, Sangkat Phsar Thmey II, Khan Daun Penh, Phnom-Penh; tel. (23) 214111; fax (23) 217655; e-mail campu@campubank.com.kh; f. 1992; cap. 79.5m. riels, dep. 395.0m. riels (Dec. 2003); Pres. Tan Sri Dato' Dr HONG PIOW TEH; Gen. Man. PHAN YING TONG.

Canadia Bank Ltd: 265–269 rue Preah Ang Duong, Sangkat Wat Phnom, Khan Daun Penh, Phnom-Penh; tel. (23) 215286; fax (23) 427064; e-mail canadia@camnet.com.kh; internet www.canadiabank.com; f. 1991; cap. 50.6m. riels, res 32.3m. riels, dep. 411.6m. riels (2001); Man. PUNG KHEAV SE; 10 brs.

Singapore Banking Corporation Ltd: 68 rue Samdech Pan, Sangkat Boeung Reang, Khan Daun Penh, Phnom-Penh; tel. (23) 211211; fax (23) 212121; e-mail info@sbc-bank.com; internet www.sbc-bank.com; f. 1993; cap. US $13m. (2003), dep. US $6.8m. (Dec. 2000); Pres. ANDY KUN SWEE TIONG; Chair. KUN KAY HONG.

Union Commercial Bank Ltd: UCB Bldg, 61 rue 130, Sangkat Phsar Chas, Khan Daun Penh, Phnom-Penh; tel. (23) 427995; fax (23) 427997; e-mail ucb@bigpond.com.kh; internet www.ucb.com.kh; f. 1994; cap. US $13m., dep. US $46m. (Dec. 2002), res US $4m. (Dec. 2001); CEO YUM SUI SANG; Chair. and Pres. YIU KAI KWONG; 3 brs.

Vattanac Bank: 89 blvd Preah Norodom, Sangkat Boeung Raing, Khan Daun Penh, Phnom-Penh; tel. (23) 212727; fax (23) 216687; e-mail service@vattanacbank.com; internet www.vattanacbank.com; f. 2002; cap. US $13m. (2004).

Foreign Banks

First Commercial Bank (Taiwan): 263 rue Preah Ang Duong, Sangkat Wat Phnom, Khan Daun Penh, Phnom-Penh; tel. (23) 210027; fax (23) 210029; e-mail fcbpp@bigpond.com.kh.

Krung Thai Bank PLC (Thailand): 149 rue Jawaharlal Nehru, Depot Market 1, Khan Tuolkok Division, Phnom-Penh; tel. (23) 366005; fax (23) 428737; e-mail ktbpmp@bigpond.com.kh; Man. NAKROB U-SETTHASAKDI.

Maybank Bhd (Malaysia): 4 rue Kramoun Sar, Sangkat Boeung Raing, Khan Daun Penh, Phnom-Penh; tel. (23) 210123; fax (23) 210099; e-mail mbb@camnet.com.kh; internet www.maybank2u.com.my; Man. ABDUL MALEK MOHD KHAIR.

INSURANCE

Asia Insurance (Cambodia) Ltd: 91 blvd Preah Norodom, Sangkat Boeung Raing, Khan Daun Penh, Phnom-Penh; tel. (23) 427981; fax (23) 216969; e-mail email@asiainsurance.com.kh; internet www.asiainsurance.com.kh; f. 1996; Gen. Man. PASCAL BRANDT-GAGNON.

Cambodia National Insurance Company (CAMINCO): cnr rue 106 and rue 19, Phnom-Penh; tel. (23) 772043; fax (23) 427810; e-mail caminco@caminco.com.kh; state-owned insurance co.

Commercial Union: 28 rue 47, Phnom-Penh; tel. (23) 426694; fax (23) 427171; general insurance; Gen. Man. PAUL CABLE.

Forte Insurance (Cambodia) Ltd: 325 blvd Mao Tse Toung, BP 565, Phnom-Penh; tel. (23) 885077; fax (23) 982907; e-mail forte@forte.com.kh; internet www.forteinsurance.com; f. 1996; Man. Dir CARLO CHEO.

Indochine Insurance Ltd: 55 rue 178, BP 808, Phnom-Penh; tel. (23) 210701; fax (23) 210501; e-mail info@indochine.com.kh; internet www.indochine.net; f. 1994; Man. Dir PHILIPPE LENAIN.

Trade and Industry

DEVELOPMENT ORGANIZATIONS

Council for the Development of Cambodia (CDC): Government Palace, quai Sisowath, Wat Phnom, BP 1225, Phnom-Penh; tel. (23) 981154; fax (23) 428426; e-mail cdc.cib@online.com.kh; internet www.cambodiainvestment.gov.kh; f. 1994; Chair. HUN SEN; Chair. HRH NORODOM RANARIDDH; Sec.-Gen. SOK CHENDA.

Cambodian Investment Board (CIB): Government Palace, quai Sisowath, Wat Phnom, Phnom-Penh; tel. (23) 981156; fax (23) 428426; e-mail CDC.CIB@bigpond.com.kh; internet www.cambodiainvestment.gov.kh; f. 1993; part of CDC; sole body responsible for approving foreign investment in Cambodia, also grants exemptions from customs duties and other taxes, and provides other facilities for investors; Chair. HUN SEN; Sec.-Gen. SOK CHENDA.

National Information Communications Technology Development Authority (NiDA): 3rd Floor, Satellite Bldg, Office of the Council of Ministers, blvd Confederation de la Russie, Phnom-Penh; tel. (23) 880635; fax (23) 880637; e-mail info@nida.gov.kh; internet www.nida.gov.kh; f. 2000; promotes information technology and formulates policy for its development; Chair. HUN SEN; Sec.-Gen. PHU LEEWOOD.

CHAMBER OF COMMERCE

Cambodia Chamber of Commerce: Office Vila 7B, cnr rue 81 and rue 109, Sangkat Boeung Reang, Khan Daun Penh, Phnom-Penh; tel. (23) 212265; fax (23) 212270; e-mail ppcc@camnet.com.kh; internet www.ppcc.org.kh; f. 1995; Pres. SOK KONG; Dir-Gen. Dr NANG SOTHY.

INDUSTRIAL AND TRADE ASSOCIATIONS

Export Promotion Department: Ministry of Commerce, 65–67–69 rue 136, Sangkat Phsar Kandal II, Khan Daun Penh, Phnom-Penh; tel. (23) 216948; fax (23) 217353; e-mail praknork@everyday.com.kh; internet www.moc.gov.kh; f. 1997; Dir PRAK NORK.

Garment Manufacturers' Association in Cambodia (GMAC): rue Jawaharlal Nehru, Phnom-Penh; tel. (23) 723796; fax (23) 369398; e-mail GMAC@bigpond.com.kh; Pres. VAN SOU IENG; Sec.-Gen. KEN LOO.

UTILITIES

Electricity

Electricité du Cambodge: EDC Bldg, rue 19, Wat Phnom, Khan Daun Penh, Phnom-Penh; tel. (23) 724771; fax (23) 426938; e-mail yim_nolson@bigpond.com.kh; f. 1996; state-owned; Man. Gen. TAN KIM VIN.

Electricity Authority of Cambodia (EAC): 2 rue 282, Boeng Keng Kang 1, Phnom-Penh; tel. (23) 217654; fax (23) 214144; e-mail admin@eac.gov.kh; internet www.eac.gov.kh; f. 2001; regulatory authority; Chair. Dr TY NORIN.

Water

Phnom-Penh Water Supply Authority: rue 108, 12201 Phnom-Penh; tel. (23) 724046; fax (23) 428969; e-mail eksonnchan@ppwsa.com.kh; f. 1996 as an autonomous public enterprise; Dir-Gen. EK SONN CHAN.

TRADE UNIONS

Association of Independent Cambodian Teachers: 33 rue 432, Sangkat Boeng Trabaek, Khan Chamkarmon, Phnom Penh; Pres. RUNG CHHUN; Gen.-Sec. CHEA MUNI.

Cambodia Federation of Independent Trade Unions (CFITU): 45 rue 63, Boeng Keng Kang 1, Khan Chamkarmon, Phnom-Penh; tel. (23) 213356; e-mail CFITU@bigpond.com.kh; f. 1979 as Cambodia Federation of Trade Unions; changed name as above in 1999; Chair. ROS SOK; Vice-Chair. TEP KIM VANNARY, KIENG THISOTHA.

Cambodia Labour Union Federation (CLUF): 78 rue 474, Sangkat Boeung Trabek, Khan Chamkarmon, Phnom-Penh; tel. (23) 866682; f. 1999; Pres. SOM AUN.

Cambodian Union Federation (CUF): 18 rue 112, Sangkat Phsar Depo III, Khan Toul Kok, Phnom-Penh; tel. (23) 882453; fax (23) 427632; e-mail CUF@bigpond.com.kh; f. 1997 with the support of the

CPP in response to the formation of the FTUWKC; Pres. CHUON MOM THOL.

Cambodian Union Federation of Building and Wood Workers: 18A rue 112, Sangkat Phsar Depo III, Khan Tuol Kok, Phnom-Penh; tel. (23) 842382; fax (23) 882453; f. 2001; Pres. SAY SAM ON.

Coalition of Cambodia Apparel Workers' Democratic Union: 6C rue 476, Sangkat Tuol Tum Pong I, Khan Chamkarmon, Phnom-Penh; tel. (23) 210481; f. 2001; Pres. CHHORN SOKHA.

Free Trade Union of Workers of the Kingdom of Cambodia (FTUWKC): 222B Sangkat Boeung Reang, Khan Daun Penh, Phnom-Penh; tel. and fax (23) 216870; e-mail ftuwkc@cambodiaworkers.org; internet www.cambodiaworkers.org; fmrly Free Trade Union of Khmer Workers; f. 1996 by Mary Ou with the assistance of Sam Rainsy; Pres. CHEA MUNNY; Gen. Sec. SUM SAMNEANG.

National Independent Federation Textile Union of Cambodia (NIFTUC): 29B rue 432, Sangkat Toul Tompoung II, Khan Chamkarmon, Phnom-Penh; tel. and fax (23) 219239; e-mail niftuc@forum.org.kh; f. 1999; Pres. MORM NHIM.

Transport

RAILWAYS

Royal Railway of Cambodia: Central Railway Station, Railway Sq., Sangkat Srach Chak, Khan Daun Penh, Phnom-Penh; tel. (12) 994168; fax (23) 430815; e-mail RRCcambodia@bigpond.com.kh; comprises two 1,000 mm-gauge single-track main lines with a total length of 650 km: the old 385-km Phnom-Penh to Poipet line (of which the 48-km Sisophon to Poipet link is awaiting restoration), the new 264-km Phnom-Penh to Sihanoukville line and branch lines and special purpose sidings 100 km; the condition of the tracks and bridges on both lines is very poor, with many temporary repairs, owing to mine damage, and the service also suffers from other operational difficulties, such as a shortage of rolling stock; there are 14 'Gares' (main stations), 19 stations and 38 halts; Pres. and Dir-Gen. SOKHOM PHEAKAVANMONY.

ROADS

In 1997 the total road network was 35,769 km in length, of which 4,165 km were highways and 3,604 km were secondary roads. In the same year about 7.5% of the road network was paved, but this figure rose to an estimated 11.6% in 1999. West and East Cambodia were linked by road for the first time in December 2001, with the opening of a bridge across the Mekong River.

INLAND WATERWAYS

The major routes are along the Mekong river, and up the Tonlé Sap river into the Tonlé Sap (Great Lake), covering, in all, about 2,400 km. The inland ports of Neak Luong, Kompong Cham and Prek Kdam have been supplied with motor ferries, and the ferry crossings have been improved.

SHIPPING

The main port is Sihanoukville, on the Gulf of Thailand, which has 11 berths and can accommodate vessels of 10,000–15,000 tons. Phnom-Penh port lies some distance inland. Steamers of up to 4,000 tons can be accommodated.

CIVIL AVIATION

There is an international airport at Pochentong, near Phnom-Penh. A further international airport, at Siem Reap, was inaugurated in December 2002. In mid-2003 construction of a new terminal at Pochentong International Airport was completed.

State Secretariat of Civil Aviation (SSCA): 62 blvd Norodom, Phnom-Penh; tel. (23) 360617; fax (23) 426169; e-mail civilaviation@cambodia.gov.kh; internet www.civilaviation.gov.kh; Dir-Gen. KEO SAPHAL.

Mekong Airlines: Hong Kong Centre, blvd Sotheoros, Phnom-Penh; tel. (23) 217299; fax (23) 217277; e-mail bookm8@everyday.com.kh; internet www.marveltour.com/mekong; f. 2002; jt venture between Hun Kim Leng Investment (51%) and Australian co Via Aviation (49%); domestic and international flights to eight destinations.

President Airlines: 298 blvd Mao Tse Toung, Phnom-Penh; tel. (23) 993088; fax (23) 212992; e-mail pnhrr@presidentairlines.com; internet www.presidentairlines.com; f. 1998; domestic and, from Aug. 2002, international passenger services.

Royal Khmer Airlines: 19 Unit 12, rue Preah Kossomak, Phnom-Penh; tel. (23) 216899; fax (23) 428279; f. 2000; domestic and international services.

Royal Phnom-Penh Airways: 209 rue 19, Sangkat Chey Chumneah, Khan Daun Penh, Phnom-Penh; tel. (23) 216487; fax (23) 217420; e-mail pnhairways@rlppairways.com; internet www .rlppairways.com; f. 1999; scheduled and charter passenger flights to domestic and regional destinations; Chair. Prince NORODOM CHAKRAPONG.

Siem Reap Airways International: 65 rue 214, Sangkat Beoung Rang, Khan Daun Penh, Phnom-Penh; tel. (23) 720022; fax (23) 720522; e-mail reservation@siemreapairways.com; internet www .siemreapairways.com; f. 2000; scheduled international and domestic passenger services; CEO PRASERT PRASARTTONG-OSOTH.

Tourism

Tourist arrivals increased to an estimated 466,365 in 2000, owing to the improvement in the security situation; in that year tourist receipts reached US $304m. Despite the repercussions of the terrorist attacks on the USA in September 2001, 604,919 tourists visited in that year, an increase of 29.7% compared with 2000. In 2002 tourist arrivals totalled 786,524 and receipts an estimated $454m. In an attempt to encourage the development of the tourism sector, 2003 was designated 'Visit Cambodia Year'. However, in that year tourist arrivals decreased by 10.9%, to 701,014.

Directorate-General of Tourism: 3 blvd Monivong, Phnom-Penh; tel. (23) 427130; fax (23) 426107; e-mail tourism@camnet.com.kh; f. 1988; Dir SO MARA.

CAMEROON

Introductory Survey

Location, Climate, Language, Religion, Flag, Capital

The Republic of Cameroon lies on the west coast of Africa, with Nigeria to the west, Chad and the Central African Republic to the east, and the Republic of the Congo, Equatorial Guinea and Gabon to the south. The climate is hot and humid in the south and west, with average temperatures of 26°C (80°F). Annual rainfall in Yaoundé averages 4,030 mm (159 ins). The north is drier, with more extreme temperatures. The official languages are French and English; many local languages are also spoken, including Fang, Bamileke and Duala. Approximately 53% of Cameroonians profess Christianity, 25% adhere to traditional religious beliefs, and about 22%, mostly in the north, are Muslims. The national flag (proportions 2 by 3) has three equal vertical stripes, of green, red and yellow, with a five-pointed gold star in the centre of the red stripe. The capital is Yaoundé.

Recent History

In 1884 a German protectorate was established in Cameroon (Kamerun). In 1916, during the First World War, the German administration was overthrown by British and French forces. Under an agreement reached between the occupying powers in 1919, Cameroon was divided into two zones: a French-ruled area in the east and south, and a smaller British-administered area in the west. In 1922 both zones became subject to mandates of the League of Nations, with France and the United Kingdom as the administering powers. In 1946 the zones were transformed into UN Trust Territories, with British and French rule continuing in their respective areas.

French Cameroons became an autonomous state within the French Community in 1957. Under the leadership of Ahmadou Ahidjo, a northerner who became Prime Minister in 1958, the territory became independent, as the Republic of Cameroon, on 1 January 1960. The first election for the country's National Assembly, held in April 1960, was won by Ahidjo's party, the Union camerounaise. In May the new National Assembly elected Ahidjo to be the country's first President.

British Cameroons, comprising a northern and a southern region, was attached to neighbouring Nigeria, for administrative purposes, prior to Nigeria's independence in October 1960. Plebiscites were held, under UN auspices, in the two regions of British Cameroons in February 1961. The northern area voted to merge with Nigeria (becoming the province of Sardauna), while the south voted for union with the Republic of Cameroon, which took place on 1 October 1961.

The enlarged country was named the Federal Republic of Cameroon, with French and English as joint official languages. It comprised two states: the former French zone became East Cameroon, while the former British portion became West Cameroon. John Ngu Foncha, the Prime Minister of West Cameroon and leader of the Kamerun National Democratic Party, became Vice-President of the Federal Republic. Under the continuing leadership of Ahidjo, who (as the sole candidate) was re-elected President in May 1965, the two states became increasingly integrated. In September 1966 the two governing parties and several opposition groups combined to form a single party, the Union nationale camerounaise (UNC). The only significant opposition party, the extreme left-wing Union des populations camerounaises (UPC), was suppressed in 1971 (although it was allowed to operate again in the early 1990s, following a return to multi-party politics). Meanwhile, Ahidjo was re-elected as President in March 1970, and Solomon Muna (who had replaced Foncha as Prime Minister of West Cameroon in 1968) became Vice-President.

In June 1972, following the approval by referendum of a new Constitution, the federal system was ended, and the country was officially renamed the United Republic of Cameroon. A centralized political and administrative system was rapidly introduced, and in May 1973 a new National Assembly was elected for a five-year term. After the re-election of Ahidjo as President in April 1975, the Constitution was revised, and a Prime Minister, Paul Biya (a bilingual Christian southerner), was appointed in June. In April 1980 Ahidjo was unanimously re-elected to the presidency for a fifth five-year term of office.

Ahidjo resigned as President in November 1982, and nominated Biya as his successor. In August 1983 Biya announced the discovery of a conspiracy to overthrow his Government, and simultaneously dismissed the Prime Minister and the Minister of the Armed Forces, both northern Muslims. Later in August Ahidjo resigned as President of the UNC, strongly criticizing Biya's regime. In September Biya was elected President of the ruling party, and in January 1984 he was re-elected as President of the Republic. The post of Prime Minister was subsequently abolished, and it was announced that the country's name was to revert to the Republic of Cameroon.

In February 1984 Ahidjo and two of his close military advisers were tried (Ahidjo *in absentia*) for their alleged complicity in the coup plot of August 1983, and received death sentences, which were, however, commuted to life imprisonment. On 6 April 1984 rebel elements in the presidential guard attempted to overthrow the Biya Government. After three days of intense fighting, in which hundreds of people were reported to have been killed, the rebellion was suppressed by forces loyal to the President; a total of 51 defendants subsequently received death sentences. Following extensive changes within the military hierarchy, the UNC Central Committee and the leadership of state-controlled companies, Biya reorganized his Government in July and introduced more stringent press censorship. In March 1985 the UNC was renamed the Rassemblement démocratique du peuple camerounais (RDPC).

Presidential and legislative elections were held in April 1988. Biya was re-elected unopposed to the presidency, securing 98.75% of the votes cast. In the elections to the National Assembly voters were presented with a choice of RDPC-approved candidates; 153 of the 180 deputies elected were new members.

In February 1990 11 people, including the former President of the Cameroonian Bar Association, Yondo Black, were arrested in connection with their alleged involvement in an unofficial opposition organization, the Social Democratic Front (SDF). In April Black was sentenced to three years' imprisonment on charges of 'subversion'. Later that month Biya announced that all the prisoners who had been detained in connection with the 1984 coup attempt were to be released. In May 1990 a demonstration organized by the SDF was violently suppressed by security forces, and six deaths were subsequently reported. In June the Vice-President of the RDPC, John Ngu Foncha, resigned, alleging corruption and human rights violations on the part of the Government, while the Congress of the RDPC re-elected Biya as President of the party. In response to continued civil unrest, Biya stated that he envisaged the future adoption of a multi-party system and announced a series of reforms, including the abolition of laws governing subversion, the revision of the law on political associations, and the reinforcement of press freedom. In December the National Assembly adopted legislation whereby Cameroon officially became a multi-party state.

In January 1991 anti-Government demonstrators protested at Biya's failure to grant an amnesty to prisoners implicated in the 1984 coup attempt. Meanwhile, opposition leaders reiterated demands for Biya's resignation and the convening of a national conference to formulate a timetable for multi-party elections. In April 1991 the principal anti-Government groups created an informal alliance, the National Co-ordination Committee of Opposition Parties (NCCOP), which organized a widely observed general strike. Later in April, in response to increasing pressure for political reform, the National Assembly approved legislation granting a general amnesty for political prisoners and reintroducing the post of Prime Minister. Biya subsequently appointed Sadou Hayatou, hitherto Secretary-General at the Presidency, to the position. Hayatou named a transitional Government, principally composed of members of the former Cabinet. The Government's refusal to comply with the NCCOP's demands for an unconditional amnesty for all political prisoners (the existing provisions for an amnesty excluded an estimated 400 political prisoners jailed for allegedly non-political crimes) and for the convening of a national conference prompted the alliance to organize a campaign of civil disobedience, culminating in a general strike in June. The Government placed seven of Cameroon's 10 provinces under military rule, prohibited opposition gatherings, and later in June, following continued civil disturbances, banned the NCCOP and several opposition parties, alleging that the opposition alliance was responsible for terrorist activities. Although opposition leaders announced that the campaign of civil disobedience would continue, the effect of the general strike declined in subsequent months.

In October 1991 Biya announced that legislative elections were to be held in February 1992, and that a Prime Minister would be appointed from the party that secured a majority in the National Assembly. Following tripartite negotiations between the Government, opposition parties and independent officials, in mid-November 1991 the Government and about 40 of the 47 registered opposition parties (including some parties belonging to the NCCOP) signed an agreement providing for the establishment of a committee to draft constitutional reforms. The opposition undertook to suspend the campaign of civil disobedience, while the Government agreed to end the ban on opposition meetings and to release all prisoners who had been arrested during anti-Government demonstrations. However, several principal opposition parties belonging to the NCCOP, including the SDF, subsequently declared the agreement to be invalid, and stated that the campaign of civil disobedience would continue. The Government revoked the ban on opposition gatherings later in November, and in December ended the military rule that had been imposed in seven provinces.

In January 1992 the Government postponed the legislative elections until March, in order to allow parties sufficient time for preparation. However, several opposition movements, including two of the principal parties, the SDF and the Union démocratique du Cameroun (UDC), refused to contest the elections, on the grounds that the scheduled date was still too early and benefited the RDPC. In February those opposition parties that had not accepted the tripartite agreement in November 1991 formed the Alliance pour le redressement du Cameroun (ARC), and announced that they were to boycott the elections.

The legislative elections, which took place on 1 March 1992, were contested by 32 political parties; the RDPC won 88 of the National Assembly's 180 seats, while the Union nationale pour la démocratie et le progrès (UNDP) obtained 68, the UPC 18 and the Mouvement pour la défense de la République (MDR) six seats. The RDPC subsequently formed an alliance with the MDR, thereby securing an absolute majority in the National Assembly. In April Biya formed a 25-member Cabinet, principally comprising members of the previous Government and including five MDR members; Simon Achidi Achu, an anglophone member of the RDPC, was appointed Prime Minister.

In August 1992 Biya announced that the forthcoming presidential election, scheduled for May 1993, was to be brought forward to 11 October 1992. In September Biya promulgated legislation regulating the election of the President that prohibited the formation of electoral alliances. Shortly before the election two of the seven opposition candidates withdrew in favour of the Chairman of the SDF, John Fru Ndi, who received the support of the ARC. The presidential election, which took place as scheduled, immediately provoked opposition allegations of malpractice on the part of the Government. In mid-October Fru Ndi proclaimed himself President, following unconfirmed reports that he had won the election. Later that month, however, the Government announced that Biya had been re-elected by 39.9% of the votes cast, while Fru Ndi had secured 35.9%, prompting violent demonstrations by opposition supporters in many areas. The Supreme Court rejected a subsequent appeal by Fru Ndi that the results of the election be declared invalid. At the end of October, in response to the continued unrest, the Government placed Fru Ndi and several of his supporters under house arrest. Biya was inaugurated as President on 3 November and pledged to implement further constitutional reforms. Later that month international condemnation of the Government increased, following the death by torture of a detained opposition member; the USA and Germany suspended economic aid to Cameroon in protest at the continued enforcement of the state of emergency. At the end of November Biya appointed a new 30-member Cabinet, which, in addition to three members of the MDR, included representatives of the UPC, the UNDP and the Parti national du progrès.

In March 1993 an informal alliance of opposition parties (led by the SDF), the Union pour le changement, organized a series of demonstrations and a boycott of French consumer goods (in protest at the French Government's involvement with Biya) in support of demands for a new presidential election. The Government accused the alliance of incitement to civil disorder and continued efforts to suppress opposition activity. In response to international pressure, however, the Government announced its intention to conduct a national debate on constitutional reform. In April a gathering organized by the Cameroon Anglophone Movement (CAM) in Buéa, in South-West Province, demanded the restoration of a federal system of government, in response to the traditional dominance of the French-speaking section of the population. In the following month the Government promulgated draft constitutional amendments that provided for the installation of a democratic political system, with the establishment of new organs of government, including an upper legislative chamber, to be known as the Senate, and restricted the power vested in the President (who was to serve a maximum of two five-year terms of office). The draft legislation retained a unitary state, but, in recognition of demands by supporters of federalism, envisaged a more decentralized system of local government.

During the second half of 1993 the opposition organized a series of anti-Government strikes and demonstrations, which led to the detention of many activists. In December public-sector workers initiated a general strike, with the support of the opposition, after the Government announced substantial salary reductions. In early 1994, however, strike action in protest at the devaluation of the CFA franc subsided, following the imposition of sanctions against striking civil servants. Meanwhile, in September 1993 a peace agreement was signed between the Kokoto and Arab Choa ethnic groups in Kousseri, although further clashes were reported later in the year. In February 1994 security forces killed some 50 members of the Arab Choa ethnic group at the village of Karena in northern Cameroon, apparently in retaliation for acts of armed banditry in the region, which were, however, widely attributed to former Chadian rebels.

In September 1994 an informal alliance of 16 opposition movements, the Front des alliés pour le changement (FAC), was established, effectively replacing the Union pour le changement; the FAC denounced alleged human rights violations on the part of the authorities, together with the indefinite postponement of municipal elections and the transfer of state-owned enterprises to the private sector. The UNDP and the UDC refused to join the alliance, however, on the grounds that it was dominated by the SDF. In November Biya announced that discussions on the revision of the Constitution were to resume, following the establishment of a Consultative Constitutional Review Committee, and that municipal elections were to take place in 1995. Constitutional discussions commenced in December 1994, but were boycotted by the opposition, which cited limitations in the agenda of the debate. In early 1995, however, the Consultative Constitutional Review Committee submitted revised constitutional amendments to Biya for consideration.

In July 1995 members of a new anglophone organization, the Southern Cameroons National Council (SCNC, which demanded that the former portion of the British Cameroons that had amalgamated with the Republic of Cameroon in 1961 be granted autonomy), staged a demonstration in Bamenda. In August representatives of anglophone movements, including the SCNC and the CAM, officially presented their demands for the establishment of an independent, English-speaking republic of Southern Cameroons at the UN; the organizations claimed that the plebiscite of 1961, whereby the former southern portion of British Cameroons had voted to merge with the Republic of Cameroon on terms of equal status, had been rendered invalid by subsequent francophone domination.

In October 1995 a special congress of the RDPC re-elected Biya as leader of the party for a further term of five years. Meanwhile, Cameroon's pending application for membership of the Commonwealth (which had been accepted, in principle, in 1993, subject to the Government's fulfilment of certain democratic conditions) prompted further controversy; opposition movements urged the Commonwealth to refuse admission to Cameroon on the grounds that no progress had been achieved with regard to human rights and the democratic process, while the SCNC submitted a rival application for membership on behalf of the proposed independent republic of Southern Cameroons. In November, however, Cameroon was formally admitted to the Commonwealth. In December 1995 the National Assembly adopted the revised constitutional amendments, submitted by Biya earlier that month, which increased the presidential mandate from five to seven years (while restricting the maximum tenure of office to two terms) and provided for the establishment of a Senate. In March 1996 the SDF and the UNDP urged a campaign of civil disobedience in protest at the Government's appointment by decree of representatives to replace the elected mayors in principal towns (following the municipal elections, the opposition had gained control of 13 towns). In April the Government imposed a total ban on all media reports of the SDF/UNDP campaign of civil disobedience. In May–June the two parties organized general strikes, which were principally observed in western and northern regions. In September Simon Achidi Achu was replaced as Prime Minister by Peter Mafany Musonge, the General Manager of the Cameroon Development Corporation, and a new Cabinet was appointed.

In January 1997 the Government postponed the legislative elections (which had been scheduled to take place in March) owing to organizational difficulties. In April the Government announced that the elections were to take place on 17 May. Pre-election violence, in which some five people were killed, prompted the imposition of increased security measures, including the closure of the country's borders. The elections, which were contested by 46 political parties, were monitored by a Commonwealth observer mission. The announcement of provisional results (which attributed a large majority of seats to the RDPC) prompted opposition claims of widespread electoral malpractice; the observer group also expressed general dissatisfaction with the election process. The Supreme Court, however, rejected opposition appeals against RDPC victories and in early June the official election results were announced: the RDPC had secured 109 of the 180 seats in the legislature, while the SDF had obtained 43, the UNDP 13 and the UDC five seats; the Mouvement pour la jeunesse du Cameroun, the UPC and the MDR obtained one seat each. The Cabinet remained virtually unchanged from the previous administration. In August further polls were conducted in seven constituencies where the results had been annulled, owing to alleged irregularities; the RDPC won all of the seats, thus increasing its representation in the National Assembly to 116 seats.

It was announced in September 1997 that the presidential election would be held on 12 October. Shortly afterwards the SDF, the UNDP and the UDC declared a boycott of all elections, in protest at the absence of an independent electoral commission. In mid-September Biya was officially elected as the RDPC presidential candidate. At the election, which was contested by seven candidates, Biya was re-elected, winning 92.6% of the votes cast. The level of voter participation in the election was much disputed, with official sources asserting that a record 81.4% of the electorate took part, while opposition leaders claimed that the abstention rate was higher than 80%. Biya was formally inaugurated on 3 November, beginning, in accordance with the revised Constitution, a seven-year term in office. Following talks with various opposition groups, the RDPC reached an agreement with the UNDP on the creation of a coalition government; the SDF, however, refused to co-operate with the ruling party. In December, having reappointed Musonge as Prime Minister, Biya effected a major cabinet reshuffle. The new Government included representatives from four of the country's many political groups, although the RDPC retained 45 of the 50 ministerial posts.

In July 1998 10 of the 43 SDF deputies resigned from the party, in protest at the perceived tribalism and authoritarianism of its leadership. In October the SDF expelled its First National Vice-President, Soulaimane Mahamad, following the latter's criticism of Fru Ndi as authoritarian. In January 1999 Fru Ndi announced that he was prepared to initiate direct dialogue with President Biya. It was, however, alleged that the leader of the SDF had announced this radical change of policy in the hope of securing a favourable verdict in his imminent court appearance on charges of defamation. In April Fru Ndi, none the less, found guilty and was fined and given a three-year suspended sentence. At the SDF party conference in the same month Fru Ndi was re-elected Chairman of the party by an overwhelming majority of delegates. The conference voted not to enter into dialogue with the Government until an independent electoral commission had been established.

Meanwhile, in September 1998 it was reported that some 60 English-speaking Cameroonians, who were alleged to be secessionists campaigning for the independence of Southern Cameroons, were being detained and tortured in Yaoundé, following attacks on police premises. There were counter-accusations

made by the opposition, however, that the raids had been staged by government agents as a pretext for further suppression of demands for increased decentralization. In January 1999 the opposition condemned the Government for the alleged marginalization of the anglophone minority in Cameroon, noting that only three of the 2,000 soldiers recently recruited by the armed forces were English-speaking. In June the trial of the alleged anglophone secessionists (the majority of whom had been arrested in 1997) began in Yaoundé. In July several of the defendants claimed that confessions that they were members of the separatist SCNC had been extracted under torture and threats of summary execution. In August the accused formally denied all charges against them, although several individuals admitted to being members of a cultural association linked to the SCNC. In October three of the defendants were sentenced to life imprisonment, others received lengthy prison sentences, while 29 were acquitted. The human rights organization Amnesty International criticized the verdicts, alluding to the alleged bias of the military court and the reported torture of detainees, and in November the UN Human Rights Committee criticized Cameroon for its alleged failure to protect and to respect fundamental human rights.

In September 1999 Mounchipou Seydou was dismissed as Minister of Posts and Telecommunications and was subsequently arrested. (In December 2003, after lengthy legal proceedings, Seydou was sentenced to 20 years' imprisonment for his involvement in the embezzlement of an estimated 2,400m. francs CFA in public funds.) In October 1999 a report by a German non-governmental organization, Transparency International (see p. 385), rated Cameroon as the most corrupt country in the world. Although the Government strenuously denied the claim, a meeting was held in November of the National Commission on Corruption, which had met infrequently since its creation in 1997, at which senior government officials outlined strategies to curb corruption in their areas of responsibility. None the less, in December 2004 Transparency International again rated Cameroon as the most corrupt country, reporting that some 10% of households had committed acts of bribery in the previous year.

There was a cabinet reshuffle in March 2000, which was widely interpreted as a response to an escalation in urban crime (several foreign diplomats, including the ambassadors of the USA and the Netherlands, had been attacked). All ministers linked to security matters were involved in the reshuffle. Furthermore, some 70% of senior police-officers were reportedly replaced. In November deputies staged a sit-in outside the National Assembly after the security forces prevented a protest march, from the legislative building to the presidential palace, from proceeding. The march had been organized by the SDF in support of demands for the creation of an independent electoral commission. In the following month the National Assembly adopted legislation on the establishment of a National Elections Observatory and on the regulation of state funding for political parties and electoral campaigns. However, five opposition parties boycotted the vote on the elections observatory, claiming that it would be unconstitutional, as it would perform the same functions as the Constitutional Council, and criticizing the President's role in appointing its 11 members. President Biya subsequently postponed municipal elections, due on 21 January 2001, until January 2002, ostensibly on the grounds that the new electoral legislation had yet to become fully operational, and that the 21st Franco-African summit was to convene in Yaoundé a few days prior to the original date.

A reorganization of the cabinet was effected in April 2001, following accusations of corruption against several ministers. At the beginning of October at least three people died in clashes with the security forces during a demonstration organized by the SCNC in Kumbo, in North-West Province, on the 40th anniversary of the reunification of Cameroon. Later that month the National Elections Observatory was inaugurated, amid opposition criticism that the 11 appointees were all supporters of the ruling RDPC. In December the municipal elections were postponed for a further six months.

Legislative and municipal elections were held concurrently on 30 June 2002, despite initial technical problems. Voting had been delayed by one week, owing to insufficient voting materials, leading to the dismissal of the Minister of Territorial Administration, Ferdinand Koungou Edima. Some 47 parties contested the elections to the National Assembly, at which the RDPC's majority increased to 133 seats, while its closest rival, the SDF, secured 21 seats, the UDC five, the UPC three and the

UNDP only one seat. Electoral turn-out was reported to be less than 50%, and the elections were boycotted by the SCNC. Voting for the remaining 17 seats was cancelled by the Supreme Court, in response to complaints of various irregularities in the nine constituencies concerned. At the municipal elections, the RDPC also performed strongly, winning 286 of the 336 council seats contested. Opposition parties alleged widespread electoral fraud, however, and demanded that the elections be declared void. The SDF initially refused to participate in the newly elected legislature and municipal councils, although in mid-July Fru Ndi announced the end of the boycott, provoking internal conflict within his party. Several SDF senior officials subsequently resigned from the party and formed the Alliance des forces progressistes, claiming that Fru Ndi's unilateral decision to end the boycott had been inspired by covert plans to join the Government. In August there was an extensive cabinet reshuffle, in which 18 new members of government were appointed. On 15 September voting took place for the 17 legislative seats that had remained vacant since June; the RDPC secured a further 16 seats, increasing its majority to 149 of the 180 seats in the National Assembly, while the SDF won the remaining seat.

In mid-2003 the activities of several independent media outlets, including the newspaper *Mutations*, a radio station and two privately owned television stations, were suspended. In December a further 12 independent radio stations, many of which were based in English-speaking regions of Cameroon, were ordered to cease transmission. International press freedom organizations claimed that the Government had taken this action in order to suppress speculation relating to the forthcoming presidential election, which was due in October 2004. Also in December 2003 the legislature approved a series of reforms to the National Elections Observatory, including the extension of appointees' terms from one year to three years and provisions for public consultations (carried out in early 2004) on appointments to the organization. Meanwhile, in November the SDF, the UDC and three other opposition parties announced the formation of an electoral coalition, with the intention of nominating a single candidate to contest the presidential election. However, owing to internal divisions the coalition collapsed in September 2004 and a total of 16 candidates were put forward by opposition parties (including the SDF and the UDC) to contest the presidential election of 11 October. Despite a constitutional limit of two terms in office, Biya was again re-elected to the presidency, securing some 75% of the vote. John Fru Ndi (SDF) and Adamou Ndam Njoya (UDC) were attributed just 17.1% and 4.7% of the vote, respectively. Although opposition groups strongly contested the validity of the result, accusing Biya and his allies of large-scale electoral fraud, a delegation of electoral observers composed of former members of the US Congress declared the elections to have been fairly conducted.

In December 2004 President Biya appointed a new cabinet and, notably, an English-speaking Prime Minister, Ephraim Inoni, hitherto Assistant Secretary-General of the Presidency. Despite the appointment of Inoni, representatives of Cameroon's Anglophone community demanded increased representation in government to counterbalance what they perceived as a disproportionate number of Francophone ministers. The new administration was again comprised largely of members of the RDPC, however, a number of portfolios, including posts and telecommunications and transport, were allocated to representatives of other parties.

In 1991 the Nigerian Government claimed that Cameroon had annexed nine Nigerian fishing settlements, following a long-standing border dispute, based on a 1913 agreement between Germany and the United Kingdom that ceded the Bakassi peninsula in the Gulf of Guinea (a region of strategic and economic significance) to Cameroon. Subsequent attempts by the Governments of Nigeria and Cameroon to resolve the dispute achieved little. In December 1993 some 500 Nigerian troops were dispatched to the region, in response to a number of incidents in which Nigerian nationals had been killed by Cameroonian security forces. Later that month the two nations agreed to establish a joint patrol in the disputed area, and to investigate the incidents. In February 1994, however, Cameroon announced that it was to submit the dispute for adjudication by the UN, the Organization of African Unity (OAU, now the African Union, see p. 144) and the International Court of Justice (see p. 19) (ICJ), based in The Hague, Netherlands. Subsequent reports of clashes between Cameroonian and Nigerian forces in the region prompted fears of a full-scale conflict. In March Cameroon

agreed to enter into negotiations with Nigeria (without the involvement of international mediators) to resolve the issue. In the same month the OAU issued a resolution urging the withdrawal of troops from the disputed region. In May negotiations between the two nations, with mediation by the Togolese Government, resumed in Yaoundé. In September the Cameroonian Government submitted additional claims to territory in north-eastern Nigeria to the ICJ.

In February 1996 renewed hostilities between Nigerian and Cameroonian forces in the Bakassi region resulted in several casualties. Later that month, however, Cameroon and Nigeria agreed to refrain from further military action, and delegations from the two countries resumed discussions, again with Togolese mediation. In March the ICJ ordered both nations to cease military operations in the region, to withdraw troops to former positions, and to co-operate with a UN investigative mission, which was to be dispatched to the area. In April, however, clashes continued, with each Government accusing the other of initiating the attacks. Claims by Nigeria that the Cameroonian forces were supported by troops from France were denied by the French Government. Diplomatic efforts to avoid further conflict increased. Nevertheless, both nations continued to reinforce their contingents in the region. In September both countries assured the UN investigative mission of their commitment to a peaceful settlement of the dispute. In December and again in May 1997, however, the Nigerian authorities claimed that Cameroonian troops had resumed attacks in the region. Further clashes were reported in late 1997 and early 1998.

In October 1998 further contention arose when Nigeria alleged that Cameroon had awarded a Canadian company a concession to prospect for petroleum in the disputed area. Cameroon insisted that no such concession had been granted. From late that year relations between Cameroon and Nigeria began to improve, and in November the International Committee of the Red Cross organized an exchange of prisoners between the two sides. In April 1999 the President-elect of Nigeria, Gen. Olusegun Obasanjo, visited Cameroon, the first such visit since the beginning of the border conflict in 1994. The two countries reportedly agreed to resolve the dispute 'in a fraternal way'. It was, however, announced that ICJ proceedings would be continued, and in late May 1999 Nigeria filed its defence. Following the submission to the ICJ of various written counter-claims by Cameroon and Nigeria in 2000–01, both countries presented their evidence at public hearings in The Hague in February and March 2002.

In October 2002 the ICJ issued its final verdict on the demarcation of the land and maritime boundary between Cameroon and Nigeria, notably ruling in favour of Cameroon's sovereignty over the Bakassi peninsula, citing the 1913 Anglo-German partition agreement, while upholding Nigeria's offshore boundary claims. Despite having no option to appeal, Nigeria refused to accept the Court's decision, and troop deployments began to increase on both sides of the border. In mid-November, however, at a meeting in Geneva, Switzerland, mediated by the Secretary-General of the UN, Kofi Annan, the Presidents of Cameroon and Nigeria signed a joint communiqué announcing the creation of a bilateral commission, to be headed by a UN Special Representative, with a mandate to achieve a peaceful solution to the Bakassi peninsula dispute. At its inaugural meeting in Yaoundé in December, the commission agreed on a 15-point peace agenda and decided to establish a sub-committee to undertake the demarcation of the boundary. In August 2003 Nigeria and Cameroon adopted a framework agreement for the implementation of the ICJ's judgment, providing for the withdrawal of all military and administrative personnel from the Bakassi region; the process of demarcation of boundaries between the two countries was expected to take up to three years to complete. The bilateral commission requested that the international community support the cost of the exercise, which was estimated at some US $12m. In December the Nigerian Government ceded control of 32 villages on its north-eastern border to Cameroon, but sovereignty over the disputed territory with petroleum resources remained under discussion. In January 2004 Presidents Biya and Obasanjo, meeting in Geneva, Switzerland, with UN mediation, agreed to exchange consular envoys, and to establish joint security patrols in the disputed region; the signing of a 'non-aggression' treaty was envisaged. Following a meeting in Yaoundé in late July between Biya and Obasanjo, it was confirmed that Nigerian troops would withdraw from Bakassi by 15 September. However, the Nigerian Government subsequently reneged on this agreement following legal appeals by Bakassi residents regarding the constitutional legality of ceding land held by Nigerians. The Nigerian Federal High Court rejected this appeal in October but by the end of December the Nigerian Government had still failed to withdraw troops from the disputed peninsula, citing difficulties over demarcating maritime boundaries.

Government

Under the amended 1972 Constitution, the Republic of Cameroon is a multi-party state. Executive power is vested in the President, as Head of State, who is elected by universal adult suffrage for a term of seven years, and may serve a maximum of two terms. Legislative power is held by the National Assembly, which comprises 180 members and is elected for a term of five years. In December 1995 constitutional amendments provided for the establishment of an upper legislative chamber (to be known as the Senate). The Cabinet is appointed by the President. Local administration is based on 10 provinces, each with a governor who is appointed by the President.

Defence

In August 2004 Cameroon's armed forces were estimated to total 23,100 men, including 9,000 in paramilitary forces. The army numbered 12,500, the navy about 1,300 and the air force 300. Cameroon has a bilateral defence agreement with France. The defence budget for 2004 was estimated at 105,000m. francs CFA.

Economic Affairs

In 2003, according to estimates by the World Bank, Cameroon's gross national income (GNI), measured at average 2001–03 prices, was US $11,933m., equivalent to $640 per head (or $1,980 per head on an international purchasing-power parity basis). During 1990–2003, it was estimated, the population increased at an average annual rate of 2.5%, while gross domestic product (GDP) per head declined, in real terms, by an average of 0.5% per year. Overall GDP increased, in real terms, at an average annual rate of 2.1% in 1990–2003; growth in 2003 was 4.2%.

Agriculture (including hunting, forestry and fishing) contributed 44.5% of GDP in 2003. An estimated 57.1% of the labour force were employed in agriculture in 2002. The principal cash crops are cocoa beans (which accounted for 6.5% of export earnings in 2001), cotton and coffee. The principal subsistence crops are roots and tubers (mainly cassava), maize and sorghum; Cameroon is not, however, self-sufficient in cereals. In 1995 an estimated 42% of the country's land area was covered by forest, but an inadequate transport infrastructure has impeded the development of the forestry sector. None the less, illegal logging and poaching in the country's forests remains a significant problem. Livestock-rearing makes an important contribution to the food supply. During 1990–2003, according to the World Bank, the real GDP of the agricultural sector increased at an average annual rate of 5.1%; growth in 2003 was 6.8%.

Industry (including mining, manufacturing, construction and power) employed 8.9% of the labour force in 1990, and contributed 18.9% of GDP in 2003. During 1990–2003, according to the World Bank, industrial GDP increased at an average annual rate of 0.7%; growth of 7.0% was recorded in 2003.

Mining contributed 4.0% of GDP in 2000/01, but employed only 0.1% of Cameroon's working population in 1985. Receipts from the exploitation of the country's petroleum reserves constitute a principal source of government revenue. Deposits of limestone are also quarried. Significant reserves of natural gas, bauxite, iron ore, uranium and tin remain largely undeveloped. According to the IMF, the GDP of the mining sector increased by an average of 2.5% per year in 1995/96–2000/01; growth in 2000/01 was 0.6%.

Manufacturing contributed an estimated 10.9% of GDP in 2003, and employed an estimated 7% of the working population in 1995. The sector is based on the processing of both indigenous primary products (petroleum-refining, agro-industrial activities) and of imported raw materials (an aluminium smelter uses alumina imported from Guinea). According to the World Bank, manufacturing GDP increased at an average annual rate of 3.3% in 1990–2003; growth in 2003 was 8.7%.

In 2001 hydroelectric power installations supplied 98.1% of Cameroon's energy. In 2001 imports of mineral fuels accounted for 18.4% of the value of total imports.

Services contributed 36.5% of GDP in 2003. During 1990–2003, according to the World Bank, the GDP of the services sector increased at an average annual rate of 0.4%; growth in 2002 was 1.8%.

In 2004 Cameroon recorded a visible trade surplus of an estimated 3,000m. francs CFA, but there was an estimated deficit of 206,000m. francs CFA on the current account of the balance of payments. In 2001 the principal source of imports (24.1%) was France; other major suppliers were Nigeria, the USA and Germany. The principal market for exports in that year (27.1%) was Italy; other significant purchasers were Spain, France, the Netherlands and the People's Republic of China. The principal exports in 2001 were crude petroleum and oils, timber and timber products, coffee, cocoa beans, raw cotton and aluminium. The principal imports in that year were machinery and transport equipment, semi-finished materials, mineral fuels and lubricants, and food and live animals.

In 2003 there was a budget deficit of 310,000m. francs CFA (equivalent to some 3.2% of GDP). Cameroon's total external debt at the end of 2002 was US $8,502m., of which $7,240m. was long-term public debt. The annual rate of inflation averaged 2.4% in 1990–2003; consumer prices increased by 0.6% in 2003. An estimated 5.8% of the labour force were unemployed in mid-1985.

Cameroon is a member of the Central African organs of the Franc Zone, see p. 267), of the Communauté économique des états de l'Afrique centrale (CEEAC, see p. 373), of the International Cocoa Organization (see p. 370) and of the International Coffee Organization (see p. 370).

In 1997 the IMF approved a three-year loan for Cameroon, equivalent to about US $221m., under the Enhanced Structural Adjustment Facility. In October 2000 the IMF and the World Bank's International Development Association agreed to support a debt-reduction package for Cameroon, worth an estimated $2,000m., under the enhanced initiative for heavily indebted poor countries, thus substantially reducing Cameroon's debt-service obligations and allowing increased expenditure on social and welfare services. In December the IMF approved another three-year loan, equivalent to about $144m., under the Poverty Reduction and Growth Facility (PRGF), in support of efforts to improve social services, reduce poverty and maintain a stable macroeconomic environment. In December 2003 the IMF approved the Government's request for a one-year extension of the programme, in view of unexpectedly slow progress on structural reforms to the economy and Cameroon's continued failure to repay its commercial creditors. In December of the following year, despite stating that Cameroon's public finances had significantly deteriorated in 2003–04, the IMF announced that, contingent on the Government's successful implementation of approved economic policies in 2005, it would consider offering Cameroon a new and favourable arrangement under the PRGF. Meanwhile, a 1,070-km pipeline to transport crude petroleum from Chad to the southern Cameroonian port of Kribi was inaugurated in October 2003. It was hoped that revenue from the pipeline, projected to reach some $500m. over a 25-year production period, would partially offset the decline in direct revenue from petroleum, daily production of which decreased from a peak of 164,000 barrels in the mid-1980s to some 85,000 barrels in 2002. However, in late 2004 non-governmental organizations and opposition groups expressed concerns that earnings from the pipeline were not properly accounted for and were subject to embezzlement. Real GDP growth was estimated at 4.2% in 2003, as a result of the expanding non-petroleum sector. None the less, by the end of 2004 the planned privatization of various public utilities was behind schedule, owing to a lack of interest from the private sector, and fraud and corruption remained a hindrance to economic development, as did the country's generally poor physical infrastructure.

Education

Since independence, Cameroon has achieved one of the highest rates of school attendance in Africa, but provision of educational facilities varies according to region. Education, which is bilingual, is provided by the Government, missionary societies and private concerns. Education in state schools is available free of charge, and the Government provides financial assistance for other schools. Primary education begins at six years of age. It lasts for six years in Eastern Cameroon (where it is officially compulsory), and for seven years in Western Cameroon. Secondary education, beginning at the age of 12 or 13, lasts for a further seven years, comprising two cycles of four years and three years in Eastern Cameroon and five years and two years in Western Cameroon. In 1999/2000 primary enrolment was equivalent to 91% of children in the appropriate age-group (males 98%; females 84%), while, according to UNESCO estimates, in 1998/99 enrolment at secondary schools was equivalent to only 20% (males 22%; females 17%). Expenditure on education by the central Government in 2004 was estimated at 213,143m. francs CFA (26.3% of total spending).

Public Holidays

2005: 1 January (New Year), 21 January* (Festival of Sheep), 11 February (Youth Day), 25 March (Good Friday), 28 March (Easter Monday), 1 May (Labour Day), 5 May (Ascension Day), 20 May (National Day), 15 August (Assumption), 4 November* (Djoulde Soumae, end of Ramadan), 25 December (Christmas).

2006: 1 January (New Year), 11 January* (Festival of Sheep), 11 February (Youth Day), 14 April (Good Friday), 17 April (Easter Monday), 1 May (Labour Day), 20 May (National Day), 25 May (Ascension Day), 15 August (Assumption), 24 September* (Djoulde Soumae, end of Ramadan), 25 December (Christmas).

* These holidays are dependent on the Islamic lunar calendar and may vary by one or two days from the dates given.

Weights and Measures

The metric system is in force.

Statistical Survey

Source (unless otherwise stated): Direction de la Prévision, Ministère de l'Economie et des Finances, BP 18, Yaoundé; tel. 223-4040; fax 223-2150.

Area and Population

AREA, POPULATION AND DENSITY

Area (sq km)	475,442*
Population (census results)	
9 April 1976†	7,663,246
9 April 1987	
Males	5,162,878
Females	5,330,777
Total	10,493,655
Population (UN estimates at mid-year)‡	
2001	15,429,000
2002	15,729,000
2003	16,018,000
Density (per sq km) at mid-2003	33.7

* 183,569 sq miles.
† Including an adjustment for underenumeration, estimated at 7.4%. The enumerated total was 7,090,115.
‡ Source: UN, *World Population Prospects: The 2002 Revision.*

PROVINCES
(population at 1987 census)

	Urban	Rural	Total
Centre	877,481	774,119	1,651,600
Littoral	1,093,323	259,510	1,352,833
West	431,337	908,454	1,339,791
South-West	258,940	579,102	838,042
North-West	271,114	966,234	1,237,348
North	234,572	597,593	832,165
East	152,787	364,411	517,198
South	104,023	269,775	373,798
Adamaoua	178,644	316,541	495,185
Far North	366,698	1,488,997	1,855,695
Total	3,968,919	6,524,736	10,493,655

PRINCIPAL TOWNS
(population at 1987 census)

Douala	810,000	Bamenda	110,000
Yaoundé (capital) .	649,000	Nkongsamba . . .	85,420
Garoua	142,000	Kumba	70,112
Maroua	123,000	Limbé	44,561
Bafoussam . . .	113,000		

Mid-2003 (estimated population, '000): Douala 1,858 (Source: UN, *World Urbanization Prospects: The 2003 Revision*).

BIRTHS AND DEATHS
(official estimates, annual averages)

	1987–92	1993–97	1998–2000
Birth rate (per 1,000)	41.7	39.7	38.2
Death rate (per 1,000)	12.8	11.4	10.1

Expectation of life (WHO estimates, years at birth): 48.1 (males 47.2; females 49.0) in 2002 (Source: WHO, *World Health Report*).

ECONOMICALLY ACTIVE POPULATION
(official estimates, persons aged six years and over, mid-1985)

	Males	Females	Total
Agriculture, hunting, forestry and fishing	1,574,946	1,325,925	2,900,871
Mining and quarrying	1,693	100	1,793
Manufacturing	137,671	36,827	174,498
Electricity, gas and water . . .	3,373	149	3,522
Construction	65,666	1,018	66,684
Trade, restaurants and hotels . .	115,269	38,745	154,014
Transport, storage and communications	50,664	1,024	51,688
Financing, insurance, real estate and business services . . .	7,447	562	8,009
Community, social and personal services	255,076	37,846	292,922
Activities not adequately defined .	18,515	17,444	35,959
Total in employment	2,230,320	1,459,640	3,689,960
Unemployed	180,016	47,659	227,675
Total labour force	2,410,336	1,507,299	3,917,635

Source: ILO, *Yearbook of Labour Statistics.*

Mid-2003 (estimates in '000): Agriculture, etc. 3,729; Total labour force 6,662 (Source: FAO).

Health and Welfare

KEY INDICATORS

Total fertility rate (children per woman, 2002)	4.7
Under-5 mortality rate (per 1,000 live births, 2003) . . .	166
HIV/AIDS (% of persons aged 15–49, 2003)	6.9
Physicians (per 1,000 head, 1996)	0.07
Hospital beds (per 1,000 head, 1990)	2.55
Health expenditure (2001): US $ per head (PPP)	20
Health expenditure (2001): % of GDP	3.3
Health expenditure (2001): public (% of total)	37.1
Access to water (% of persons, 2002)	63
Access to sanitation (% of persons, 2002)	48
Human Development Index (2002): ranking	141
Human Development Index (2002): value	0.501

For sources and definitions, see explanatory note on p. vi.

Agriculture

PRINCIPAL CROPS
('000 metric tons)

	2001	2002	2003
Rice (paddy)	62	62*	62*
Maize	739	750*	750*
Millet*	50	50	50
Sorghum*	505	525	550
Potatoes	134	134*	135*
Sweet potatoes	175	175*	175*
Cassava (Manioc)	1,947	1,950*	1,950*
Yams	264	265*	265*
Other roots and tubers* . . .	1,062	1,015	1,015
Sugar cane*	1,350	1,400	1,400
Dry beans	173	170*	170*
Groundnuts (in shell)	198	200*	200*
Pistachios*	120	120	120
Oil palm fruit*	1,150	1,150	1,200
Melonseed*	57	57	57
Cottonseed*	105	95	102
Tomatoes	370	370*	370*
Pumpkins, squash and gourds* .	122	122	122
Dry onions	67	67*	67*
Bananas	632	630*	630*
Plantains	1,187	1,200*	1,200*
Avocados*	50	52	52
Pineapples	44	45*	45*
Coffee (green)	71	41†	48†
Cocoa beans	122	125†	140†
Cotton (lint)	97	94	93
Natural rubber	53	52	46

* FAO estimate(s).
† Unofficial figure.
Source: FAO.

LIVESTOCK
(FAO estimates, '000 head, year ending September)

	2001	2002	2003
Horses	17	17	17
Asses	38	39	39
Cattle	5,900	5,900	5,950
Pigs	1,350	1,350	1,350
Sheep	3,800	3,800	3,800
Goats	4,400	4,400	4,400
Chickens	31,000	31,000	31,000

Source: FAO.

LIVESTOCK PRODUCTS
('000 metric tons)

	2001	2002	2003
Beef and veal	94.8*	94.8†	95.0†
Mutton and lamb†	16.4	16.4	16.4
Goat meat†	15.4	15.4	15.4
Pig meat†	16.2	16.2	16.2
Poultry meat†	29.2	29.2	29.2
Other meat	46.4	46.4	46.4
Cows' milk†	125.0	125.0	125.0
Sheep's milk†	17.0	17.0	17.0
Goats' milk†	42.0	42.0	42.0
Poultry eggs†	13.2	13.2	13.2
Honey†	3.0	3.0	3.0
Cattle hides (fresh)† . . .	13.0	13.0	13.0
Sheepskins (fresh)† . . .	2.7	2.7	2.7
Goatskins (fresh)†	1.5	1.5	1.5

* Unofficial figure.
† FAO estimate(s).
Source: FAO.

Forestry

ROUNDWOOD REMOVALS
('000 cubic metres, excl. bark)

	2001	2002	2003
Sawlogs, veneer logs and logs for sleepers	1,190	1,250	1,400
Other industrial wood	80	50	150
Fuel wood*	9,183	9,256	9,330
Total	10,453	10,556	10,880

* FAO estimates.
Source: FAO.

SAWNWOOD PRODUCTION
('000 cubic metres, incl. railway sleepers)

	2001	2002	2003
Total (all broadleaved)	800	652	658

Source: FAO.

Fishing

(FAO estimates, '000 metric tons, live weight)

	2000	2001	2002
Capture	112.1	111.0	120.1
Freshwater fishes	55.0	52.5	65.0
Cassava croaker	2.0	2.7	2.1
Bobo croaker	3.4	3.2	1.9
Other croakers and drums . .	3.3	2.4	1.9
Sardinellas	21.6	21.6	22.5
Bonga shad	21.6	21.6	21.8
Aquaculture	0.1	0.1	0.3
Total catch	112.2	111.1	120.5

Source: FAO.

Mining*

	2000	2001	2002
Crude petroleum (million barrels)	32.1	29.2	28.0
Gold (kilograms)†	1,000	1,000	1,000
Pozzolan ('000 metric tons) . . .	605	600	620
Limestone ('000 metric tons) . .	259	260	260

* Estimated production.
† Data refer to the metal content of ores.

Source: US Geological Survey.

Industry

SELECTED PRODUCTS
('000 metric tons, unless otherwise indicated)

	1998	1999	2000
Palm oil	136	132	136
Raw sugar*	52	62	82
Veneer sheets ('000 cu metres) .	59	53	70
Plywood ('000 cu metres) . . .	89	92	37
Aviation gasoline	17	18	18
Jet fuels†	10	11	57
Motor spirit (petrol)†	304	312	323
Kerosene†	248	251	250
Gas-diesel (distillate fuel) oil† . .	295	365	459
Residual fuel oils	490	342	397
Lubricating oils	22	19	17
Petroleum bitumen (asphalt)† . .	12	10	5
Liquefied petroleum gas . . .	28	33	26
Cement‡	400	850	890
Aluminium (unwrought)‡ . . .	82	90	86
Electric energy (million kWh) . .	3,214	3,435	3,441

* FAO estimates.
† Estimates.
‡ Data from the US Geological Survey.

2001 ('000 metric tons): Palm oil 138 (FAO estimate); Raw sugar 99 (unofficial figure); Veneer sheets ('000 cu metres) 55; Aluminium (unwrought) 81 (US Geological Survey figure).

2002 ('000 metric tons): Palm oil 144 (unofficial figure); Raw sugar 113 (unofficial figure); Veneer sheets ('000 cu metres) 50; Aluminium (unwrought) 80 (US Geological Survey figure).

Sources: UN, *Industrial Commodity Statistics Yearbook*; FAO.

Finance

CURRENCY AND EXCHANGE RATES

Monetary Units
100 centimes = 1 franc de la Coopération financière en Afrique central (CFA).

Sterling, Dollar and Euro Equivalents (31 December 2004)
£1 sterling = 930.1188 francs CFA;
US $1 = 481.5774 francs CFA;
€1 = 655.9570 francs CFA;
10,000 francs CFA = £10.75 = $20.77 = €15.24.

Average Exchange Rate (francs CFA per US $)
2002   696.99
2003   581.20
2004   528.29

Note: An exchange rate of 1 French franc = 50 francs CFA, established in 1948, remained in force until January 1994, when the CFA franc was devalued by 50%, with the exchange rate adjusted to 1 French franc = 100 francs CFA. This relationship to French currency remained in effect with the introduction of the euro on 1 January 1999. From that date, accordingly, a fixed exchange rate of €1 = 655.957 francs CFA has been in operation.

BUDGET
('000 million francs CFA, revised projections)

Revenue*	2002	2003	2004
Oil revenue	310	310	256
Non-oil revenue	976	1,052	1,191
Direct taxes	267	257	295
Special tax on petroleum products	62	80	88
Taxes on international trade .	172	161	182
Other taxes on goods and services	411	462	547
Value-added tax	344	358	426
Non-tax revenue	63	68	79
Other tax revenue	—	24	—
Total	**1,286**	**1,362**	**1,447**

Expenditure	2002	2003	2004
Current expenditure	1,039	1,045	1,058
Wages and salaries	410	421	455
Other goods and services . .	319	321	316
Subsidies and transfers . . .	119	128	129
Interest due	191	175	158
External	177	154	137
Domestic	15	21	21
Capital expenditure	298	198	270
Externally financed investment	97	54	70
Domestically financed investment	181	129	180
Restructuring	20	15	20
Total	**1,337**	**1,243**	**1,328**

* Excluding grants received ('000 million francs CFA): 36 in 2002; 66 in 2003; 50 in 2004.

Source: IMF, *Cameroon: Fourth Review Under the Three-Year Arrangement Under the Poverty Reduction and Growth Facility, and Requests for Extension of Arrangement, Waiver of Performance Criterion, and Extension of Interim Assistance Under the Enhanced Initiative for Heavily Indebted Poor Countries—Staff Report; Staff Supplement; Press Release on the Executive Board Discussion; and Statement by the Executive Director for Cameroon* (December 2003).

INTERNATIONAL RESERVES*
(US $ million at 31 December)

	2001	2002	2003
IMF special drawing rights . .	0.02	1.18	1.47
Reserve position in IMF . .	0.68	0.79	0.96
Foreign exchange	331.14	627.70	637.21
Total	**331.83**	**629.66**	**639.64**

* Excluding reserves of gold (30,000 troy ounces each year). At 31 December 2002 the national valuation of these reserves (based on market-related prices) was US $12.52 million.

Source: IMF, *International Financial Statistics*.

MONEY SUPPLY
('000 million francs CFA at 31 December)

	2001	2002	2003
Currency outside banks . . .	296.14	333.74	298.02
Demand deposits at deposit money banks	410.94	473.35	462.88
Total money (incl. others) . .	**711.98**	**813.63**	**771.21**

Source: IMF, *International Financial Statistics*.

COST OF LIVING
(Consumer Price Index; base: 1990 = 100)

	2001	2002	2003
All items	131.9	135.7	136.5

Source: UN, *Monthly Bulletin of Statistics*.

NATIONAL ACCOUNTS
('000 million francs CFA at current prices, year ending 30 June)

Expenditure on the Gross Domestic Product

	1998/99	1999/2000	2000/01
Government final consumption expenditure	542	593	706
Private final consumption expenditure	3,869	4,048	4,322
Gross capital formation	1,010	959	1,125
Total domestic expenditure .	**5,422**	**5,600**	**6,153**
Exports of goods and services . .	1,319	1,791	2,010
Less Imports of goods and services	1,334	1,564	1,843
GDP in purchasers' values . .	**5,406**	**5,827**	**6,320**
GDP at constant 1989/90 prices	**3,693**	**3,846**	**4,050**

Source: IMF, *Cameroon: Statistical Appendix* (August 2002).

Gross Domestic Product by Economic Activity

	1998/99	1999/2000	2000/01
Agriculture, hunting, forestry and fishing . . .	2,288	2,482	2,699
Mining and quarrying	211	227	246
Manufacturing	572	617	669
Electricity, gas and water . . .	81	87	95
Construction	200	215	229
Services	1,903	2,033	2,205
GDP at factor cost	5,255	5,661	6,143
Indirect taxes, *less* subsidies . .	152	164	177
GDP in purchasers' values . .	5,406	5,827	6,320

Source: IMF, *Cameroon: Statistical Appendix* (August 2002).

GDP in purchasers' values ('000 million francs CFA, year ending 30 June, revised figures): 6,010.6 in 1999; 6,613.6 in 2000; 7,043.8 in 2001 (Source: IMF, *International Financial Statistics*).

BALANCE OF PAYMENTS
('000 million francs CFA)

	2002*	2003†	2004†
Exports of goods f.o.b.	1,381	1,306	1,261
Imports of goods f.o.b.	−1,326	−1,233	−1,258
Trade balance	55	73	3
Services and other income (net) .	−628	−431	−326
Balance on goods, services and income	−573	−358	−323
Transfers (net)	92	133	117
Current balance	−480	−225	−206
Official capital (net)	−290	−229	−176
Private capital (net)	572	191	190
Overall balance	−198	−262	−193

* Estimates.
† Revised projections.

Source: IMF, *Cameroon: Fourth Review Under the Three-Year Arrangement Under the Poverty Reduction and Growth Facility, and Requests for Extension of Arrangement, Waiver of Performance Criterion, and Extension of Interim Assistance Under the Enhanced Initiative for Heavily Indebted Poor Countries—Staff Report; Staff Supplement; Press Release on the Executive Board Discussion; and Statement by the Executive Director for Cameroon* (December 2003).

External Trade

PRINCIPAL COMMODITIES
(US $ million)

Imports c.i.f.	1999	2000	2001
Food and live animals . . .	233.3	247.5	270.9
Cereals and cereal preparations .	122.7	125.5	153.2
Mineral fuels, lubricants, etc. .	207.8	345.5	340.7
Petroleum, petroleum products and related materials	206.6	342.1	339.1
Crude petroleum and oils . .	178.5	305.9	294.3
Chemicals and related products	168.1	174.7	201.1
Manufactured goods	193.6	221.4	383.0
Iron and steel	26.8	32.1	155.1
Tubes, pipes and fittings . . .	6.9	8.9	124.3
Machinery and transport equipment	345.5	341.1	481.5
Road vehicles	111.8	127.6	170.7
Total (incl. others)	1,315.8	1,488.8	1,852.3

Exports f.o.b.	1999	2000	2001
Food and live animals . . .	353.2	263.7	283.3
Coffee, tea, cocoa, spices, etc. . .	284.4	199.5	218.9
Cocoa and cocoa products . .	162.5	103.6	143.9
Cocoa beans (raw, roasted) .	126.4	72.9	113.1
Coffee (green, roasted) . . .	121.0	94.6	73.8
Crude materials, inedible, except fuels	446.5	386.4	372.4
Textile fibres and wastes . . .	80.4	68.5	98.2
Raw cotton (not carded or combed)	80.4	68.5	98.1
Mineral fuels, lubricants, etc. .	555.0	992.4	908.0
Petroleum, petroleum products and related materials	555.0	990.2	907.9
Crude petroleum and oils . .	552.1	880.1	809.5
Petroleum products (refined) .	2.8	109.8	98.2
Manufactured goods	136.7	161.5	155.6
Aluminium	94.5	101.9	93.5
Total (incl. others)	1,600.6	1,832.6	1,749.4

Source: UN, *International Trade Statistics Yearbook*.

PRINCIPAL TRADING PARTNERS
(estimates, US $ million)

Imports c.i.f.	1999	2000	2001
Canada	25	25	20
China, People's Repub.	37	44	50
Côte d'Ivoire	18	23	20
France (incl. Monaco) . . .	350	358	446
Germany	78	60	138
Guinea	44	57	75
Italy	52	47	57
Japan	71	73	84
Netherlands	39	36	34
Nigeria	168	286	259
Pakistan	13	7	11
Senegal	21	10	10
South Africa	—	18	32
Spain	18	18	29
Turkey	17	12	10
United Kingdom	34	31	44
USA	63	71	146
Total (incl. others)	1,316	1,489	1,852

Exports f.o.b.	1999	2000	2001
Angola	0	21	15
Belgium	39	39	40
Central African Republic . . .	16	—	—
Chad	21	10	12
China, People's Repub.	43	114	103
Congo, Democratic Repub. . . .	3	24	27
Congo, Repub.	17	18	19
France (incl. Monaco) . . .	281	240	190
Gabon	32	15	16
Germany	29	—	—
Italy	345	531	474
Korea, Repub.	33	1	1
Netherlands	149	134	157
Spain	199	141	264
Thailand	17	14	15
United Kingdom	28	29	29
USA	40	28	36
Total (incl. others)	1,601	1,833	1,750

Source: UN, *International Trade Statistics Yearbook*.

Transport

RAILWAYS
(traffic, year ending 30 June)

	1998/99	1999/00	2000/01
Freight ton-km (million) . . .	916	1,063	1,159
Passenger-km (million)	311	711	303

Source: UN, *Statistical Yearbook*.

ROAD TRAFFIC
(estimates, '000 motor vehicles in use)

	1998	1999	2000
Passenger cars	105.8	110.7	115.9
Commercial vehicles	43.2	45.3	47.4

Source: UN, *Statistical Yearbook*.

SHIPPING

Merchant Fleet
(registered at 31 December)

	2001	2002	2003
Number of vessels	58	59	61
Total displacement ('000 grt)	13.6	16.7	186.8

Source: Lloyd's Register-Fairplay, *World Fleet Statistics*.

International Sea-borne Freight Traffic
(freight traffic at Douala, '000 metric tons)

	1995	1996	1997
Goods loaded	1,841	1,967	2,385
Goods unloaded	2,317	2,211	2,497

Source: Banque des états de l'Afrique centrale, *Etudes et Statistiques*.

CIVIL AVIATION
(traffic on scheduled services)

	1999	2000	2001
Kilometres flown (million)	6	6	5
Passengers carried ('000)	293	312	247
Passenger-km (million)	597	646	489
Total ton-km (million)	106	115	91

Source: UN, *Statistical Yearbook*.

Tourism

FOREIGN VISITORS BY COUNTRY OF ORIGIN*

	1999	2000	2001
Belgium	40,033	41,050	4,374
Canada	10,107	10,662	2,568
France	37,310	38,771	53,950
Germany	15,518	16,616	7,268
Italy	6,523	5,537	4,575
Netherlands	9,332	9,970	3,046
Switzerland	11,553	11,077	9,609
United Kingdom	13,867	13,847	5,888
USA	11,842	12,462	10,043
Total (incl. others)	261,923	277,070	220,578

* Arrivals at hotels and similar establishments.

Receipts from tourism (US $ million): 39 in 2000.

Source: World Tourism Organization.

Communications Media

	2000	2001	2002
Television receivers ('000 in use)	520	n.a.	n.a.
Telephones ('000 main lines in use)	n.a.	106.3	110.9
Mobile cellular telephones ('000 subscribers)	148	310	702
Personal computers ('000 in use)	50	60	90
Internet users ('000)	40	45	60

Radio receivers ('000 in use): 2,270 in 1997.

Daily newspapers: 2 in 1996 (average circ. 91,000).

Non-daily newspapers: 7 in 1996 (average circ. 152,000).

2003 ('000 subscribers): Mobile cellular telephones 1,077.0.

Sources: mainly UNESCO, *Statistical Yearbook*; International Telecommunication Union.

Education
(1998, unless otherwise indicated)

	Institutions	Teachers	Students
Pre-primary	1,371	4,438	103,908
Primary	9,459	41,142	2,133,707
Secondary:			
General	700*	19,515	341,439
Vocational	324*	7,245*	122,122
Universities	6†	2,645	66,902

* 1995/96 figure.
† 1996/97 figure.

Sources: UNESCO Institute for Statistics; *Annuaire statistique du Cameroun*.

Adult literacy rate (UNESCO estimates): 67.9% (males 77.0%; females 59.8%) in 2002 (Source: UN Development Programme, *Human Development Report*).

Directory

The Constitution

In December 1995 the National Assembly formally adopted amendments to the 1972 Constiution that provided for a democratic system of government, with the establishment of an upper legislative chamber (to be known as the Senate), a Council of Supreme Judiciary Affairs, a Council of State, and a Civil Service High Authority, and restricted the power vested in the President, who was to serve a maximum of two seven-year terms. The restoration of decentralized local government areas was also envisaged. The main provisions of the 1972 Constitution, as amended, are summarized below:

The Constitution declares that the human being, without distinction as to race, religion, sex or belief, possesses inalienable and sacred rights. It affirms its attachment to the fundamental freedoms embodied in the Universal Declaration of Human Rights and the UN Charter. The State guarantees to all citizens of either sex the rights and freedoms set out in the preamble of the Constitution.

SOVEREIGNTY

1. The Republic of Cameroon shall be one and indivisible, democratic, secular and dedicated to social service. It shall ensure the equality before the law of all its citizens. Provisions that the official languages be French and English, for the motto, flag, national anthem and seal, that the capital be Yaoundé.

2–3. Sovereignty shall be vested in the people who shall exercise it either through the President of the Republic and the members returned by it to the National Assembly or by means of referendum. Elections are by universal suffrage, direct or indirect, by every citizen aged 21 or over in a secret ballot. Political parties or groups may take part in elections subject to the law and the principles of democracy and of national sovereignty and unity.

4. State authority shall be exercised by the President of the Republic and the National Assembly.

THE PRESIDENT OF THE REPUBLIC

5. The President of the Republic, as Head of State and Head of the Government, shall be responsible for the conduct of the affairs of the Republic. He shall define national policy and may charge the members of the Government with the implementation of this policy in certain spheres.

6–7. Candidates for the office of President must hold civic and political rights, be at least 35 years old and have resided in Cameroon for a minimum of 12 consecutive months, and may not hold any other elective office or professional activity. The President is elected for seven years, by a majority of votes cast by the people, and may serve a maximum of two terms. Provisions are made for the continuity of office in the case of the President's resignation.

8–9. The Ministers and Vice-Ministers are appointed by the President to whom they are responsible, and they may hold no other appointment. The President is also head of the armed forces, he negotiates and ratifies treaties, may exercise clemency after consultation with the Higher Judicial Council, promulgates and is responsible for the enforcement of laws, is responsible for internal and external security, makes civil and military appointments, provides for necessary administrative services.

10. The President, by reference to the Supreme Court, ensures that all laws passed are constitutional.

11. Provisions whereby the President may declare a state of emergency or state of siege.

THE NATIONAL ASSEMBLY

12. The National Assembly shall be renewed every five years, though it may at the instance of the President of the Republic legislate to extend or shorten its term of office. It shall be composed of 180 members elected by universal suffrage.

13–14. Laws shall normally be passed by a simple majority of those present, but if a bill is read a second time at the request of the President of the Republic a majority of the National Assembly as a whole is required.

15–16. The National Assembly shall meet twice a year, each session to last not more than 30 days; in one session it shall approve the budget. It may be recalled to an extraordinary session of not more than 15 days.

17–18. Elections and suitability of candidates and sitting members shall be governed by law.

RELATIONS BETWEEN THE EXECUTIVE AND THE LEGISLATURE

19. Bills may be introduced either by the President of the Republic or by any member of the National Assembly.

20. Reserved to the legislature are the fundamental rights and duties of the citizen; the law of persons and property; the political, administrative and judicial system in respect of elections to the National Assembly, general regulation of national defence, authorization of penalties and civil procedure etc., and the organization of the local authorities; currency, the budget, dues and taxes, legislation on public property; economic and social policy; the education system.

21. The National Assembly may empower the President of the Republic to legislate by way of ordinance for a limited period and for given purposes.

22–26. Other matters of procedure, including the right of the President of the Republic to address the Assembly and of the Ministers and Vice-Ministers to take part in debates.

27–29. The composition and conduct of the Assembly's programme of business. Provisions whereby the Assembly may inquire into governmental activity. The obligation of the President of the Republic to promulgate laws, which shall be published in both languages of the Republic.

30. Provisions whereby the President of the Republic, after consultation with the National Assembly, may submit to referendum certain reform bills liable to have profound repercussions on the future of the nation and national institutions.

THE JUDICIARY

31. Justice is administered in the name of the people. The President of the Republic shall ensure the independence of the judiciary and shall make appointments with the assistance of the Higher Judicial Council.

THE SUPREME COURT

32–33. The Supreme Court has powers to uphold the Constitution in such cases as the death or incapacity of the President and the admissibility of laws, to give final judgments on appeals on the Judgment of the Court of Appeal and to decide complaints against administrative acts. It may be assisted by experts appointed by the President of the Republic.

IMPEACHMENT

34. There shall be a Court of Impeachment with jurisdiction to try the President of the Republic for high treason and the Ministers and Vice-Ministers for conspiracy against the security of the State.

THE ECONOMIC AND SOCIAL COUNCIL

35. There shall be an Economic and Social Council, regulated by the law.

AMENDMENT OF THE CONSTITUTION

36–37. Bills to amend the Constitution may be introduced either by the President of the Republic or the National Assembly. The President may decide to submit any amendment to the people by way of a referendum. No procedure to amend the Constitution may be accepted if it tends to impair the republican character, unity or territorial integrity of the State, or the democratic principles by which the Republic is governed.

The Government

HEAD OF STATE

President: PAUL BIYA (took office 6 November 1982; elected 14 January 1984; re-elected 24 April 1988, 11 October 1992, 12 October 1997 and 11 October 2004).

CABINET
(April 2005)

A coalition of the Rassemblement démocratique du peuple camerounais (RDPC), the Union nationale pour la démocratie et le progrès (UNDP), the Union des populations camerounaises (UPC), the Mouvement pour la défense de la République (MDR) and the Alliance nationale pour la démocratie et le progrès (ANDP).

Prime Minister: EPHRAIM INONI (RDPC).

Deputy Prime Minister: AMADOU ALI (RDPC).

Ministers of State

Minister of State and Secretary-General of the Presidency: JEAN-MARIE ATANGANA MEBARA (RDPC).

Minister of State in charge of Territorial Administration and Decentralization: MARAFA HAMIDOU YAYA (RDPC).

Minister of State in charge of External Relations: LAURENT ESSO (RDPC).

Minister of State in charge of Commercial Development: LUC MAGOIRE MBARGA ATANGA (UNDP).

Minister of State in charge of Planning, Programme Execution, Development and Territorial Administration: AUGUSTIN FRÉDÉRIC KODOCK (UPC).

Minister of State in charge of Culture: FERDINAND LÉOPOLD OYONO.

Minister of State in charge of Agriculture and Rural Development: CLOBAIRE TCHATAT (RDPC).

Ministers

Minister of the Economy and Finance: POLYCARPE ABAH ABAH.

Minister of Scientific Research and Innovation: MADELEINE TCHUENTÉ (RDPC).

Minister of Small and Medium Businesses, Local Economy and Crafts: BERNARD MESSENGUE AVOM (RDPC).

Minister of Employment and Professional Training: ZACHARIE PÉRÉVET (RDPC).

Minister of Secondary Education: LOUIS BAPES BAPES.

Minister of Forests and Wildlife: HILMAN EGBÉ ACHU (RDPC).

Minister of Urban Development and Housing: ETIENNE CHARLES LÉKÉNÉ DONFACK (RDPC).

Minister of Higher Education: JACQUES FAME NDONGO (RDPC).

Minister of Social Affairs: CATHERINE BAKANG MBOCK (RDPC).

Minister of Public Works: MARTIN ARISTIDE OKOUDA (RDPC).

Minister of Energy and Water: ALPHONSE SIYAM SIWÉ (RDPC).

Minister of Estates and Land Affairs: LOIUS MARIE ABOGO NKONO (RDPC).

Minister of Transport: Dakolé Daïssala (MDR).

Minister of Labour and Social Welfare: Robert Nkili (RDPC).

Minister of Industry, Mines and Technological Development: Charles Salé (RDPC).

Minister of the Environment and the Protection of Nature: Pierre Hélé (RDPC).

Minister of Trade: Luc Magloire Mbanga Atangana.

Minister of Public Service and Administrative Reform: Benjamin Amama Amama.

Minister of Communication: Pierre Moukoko Mbonjo (RDPC).

Minister of Women's Affairs and the Family: Suzanne Bombak (RDPC).

Minister of National Education: Haman Adama (RDPC).

Minister of Livestock, Fisheries and Animal Industries: Dr Aboubakari Sarki (RDPC).

Minister of Public Service and Administrative Reform: Benjamin Amama Amama (RDPC).

Minister of Youth: Adoum Garoua.

Minister of Sports and Physical Education: Philippe Mbarg Mboa.

Minister of Posts and Telecommunications: Bello Bouba Maigari (UNDP).

Minister of Public Health: Urbain Olanguena Awono (RDPC).

Minister of Tourism: Baba Hamadou (RDPC).

Ministers-delegate

Minister-delegate at the Ministry of Finance and the Budget, in charge of the Budget: Henri Engoulou (RDPC).

Minister-delegate at the Ministry of Planning, Programme Execution, Development and Territorial Administration: Seini Kachala (RDPC).

Minister-delegate at the Presidency, in charge of Defence: Rémy Ze Meka (RDPC).

Minister-delegate at the Ministry of External Relations, in charge of Relations with the Commonwealth: Joseph Dion Nguté (RDPC).

Minister-delegate at the Ministry of External Relations, in charge of Relations with the Islamic World: Adoum Gargoum (RDPC).

Minister-delegate at the Ministry of Territorial Administration and Decentralization: Emmanuel Edou (RDPC).

Minister-delegate at the Ministry of the Environment and the Protection of Nature: Nana Aboubakar Djalloh (UNDP).

Minister-delegate at the Ministry of Communication: Gervais Mendo Zé (RDPC).

Minister-delegate at the Ministry of Justice: Maurice Kamto (RDPC).

Minister-delegate at the Presidency, in charge of Defence: Rémy Zé Meka (RDPC).

Minister-delegate at the Presidency, in charge of Relations with the National Assembly: Grégoire Owona (RDPC).

Minister-delegate at the Presidency, in charge of the Supreme State Audit: David Siegfried Etamé Massoma (RDPC).

Ministers-delegate at the Presidency without Portfolio: Justin Ndioro (RDPC), Hamadou Moustapha (ANDP), Elvis Ngole Ngole (RDPC).

Secretaries of State

Secretary of State for Estates and Land Affairs: Jean Claude Etogo (RDPC).

Secretary of State for the Economy and Finances: Denis Omarou (RDPC).

First Secretary of State for National Education: Emmanuel Ngafeeson (RDPC).

Second Secretary of State for National Education: Haman Adama (RDPC).

Secretary of State for Industrial and Commercial Development: Edmond Mouampéa Mbio (RDPC).

Secretary of State for Public Health: Alim Hayatou (RDPC).

Secretary of State for Youth and Sports, in charge of Youth: Denis Oumarou (RDPC).

Secretary of State for Public Works: Emmanuel Bonde (RDPC).

Secretary of State for Agriculture and Rural Development: Aboubakar Abdoulaye (RDPC).

Secretary of State for Housing and Urban Affairs, in charge of Lands: André Tsala Messi (RDPC).

Secretary of State for Transport: Edmond Monpéa Mbio (RDPC).

Secretary of State for Defence, in charge of the National Gendarmerie: Jean Marie Aléokol (RDPC).

Other Officials with the Rank of Minister

Assistant Secretary-General of the Presidency: René Owona (RDPC).

Director of the Cabinet of the President of the Republic: Ngo'o Mebe (RDPC).

MINISTRIES

Correspondence to ministries not holding post boxes should generally be addressed c/o the Central Post Office, Yaoundé.

Office of the President: Palais de l'Unité, Yaoundé; tel. 223-4025; internet www.camnet.cm/celcom/homepr.htm.

Office of the Prime Minister: Yaoundé; tel. 223-8005; fax 223-5735; e-mail spm@spm.gov.cm; internet www.spm.gov.cm.

Ministry of Agriculture and Rural Development: Quartier Administratif, Yaoundé; tel. 222-0553; fax 222-5091.

Ministry of Communication: Quartier Hippodrome, Yaoundé; tel. 223-3467; fax 223-3022; e-mail mincom@mincom.gov.cm; internet www.mincom.gov.cm.

Ministry of Culture: Quartier Hippodrome, Yaoundé; tel. 222-6579; fax 223-6579.

Ministry of Defence: Quartier Général, Yaoundé; tel. 223-4055.

Ministry of Economy and Finance: BP 13750, Quartier Administratif, Yaoundé; tel. and fax 723-2099; internet www.camnet.cm/investir/minfi/.

Ministry of Employment and Professional Training: Yaoundé; tel. 222-0186; fax 223-1820.

Ministry of Energy and Water: Quartier Administratif, BP 955, Yaoundé; tel. 223-3404; fax 223-3400; e-mail minmee@camnet.cm; internet www.camnet.cm/investir/minmee.

Ministry of the Environment and the Protection of Nature: Yaoundé.

Ministry of Estates and Land Affairs: Yaoundé.

Ministry of External Relations: Yaoundé; tel. 220-3850; fax 220-1133; internet www.diplocam.gov.cm.

Ministry of Forests and Wildlife: BP 1341, Yaoundé; tel. 220-4258; fax 222-9487; e-mail onadef@camnet.cm; internet www.camnet.cm/investir/envforet/index.htm.

Ministry of Higher Education: 2 ave du 20 Mai, BP 1457, Yaoundé; tel. 222-1770; fax 222-9724; e-mail aowono@uycdc.uninet.cm; internet www.mineup.gov.cm.

Ministry of Industry, Mines and Technological Development: Quartier Administratif, BP 955, Yaoundé; tel. 223-3404; fax 223-3400; e-mail minmee@camnet.cm; internet www.camnet.cm/investir/minmee.

Ministry of Justice: Quartier Administratif, Yaoundé; tel. 222-0189; fax 223-0005.

Ministry of Livestock, Fisheries and Animal Industries: Yaoundé; tel. 222-3311.

Ministry of National Education: Quartier Administratif, Yaoundé; tel. 223-4050; fax 223-1262.

Ministry of Posts and Telecommunications: Quartier Administratif, Yaoundé; tel. 223-0615; fax 223-3159; internet www.minpostel.gov.cm.

Ministry of Public Health: Quartier Administratif, Yaoundé; tel. 222-2901; fax 222-0233; internet www.camnet.cm/investir/hgy/index.htm.

Ministry of the Public Service and Administrative Reform: Yaoundé; tel. 222-0356; fax 223-0800.

Ministry of Public Works: Quartier Administratif, Yaoundé; tel. 222-1916; fax 222-0156.

Ministry of Scientific Research and Innovation: Yaoundé; tel. 222-1331; fax 222-1333; internet www.minrest.gov.cm.

Ministry of Secondary Education: Yaoundé.

Ministry of Small and Medium Businesses, Local Economy and Crafts: Yaoundé.

Ministry of Social Affairs: Quartier Administratif, Yaoundé; tel. 222-5867; fax 222-1121.

Ministry of Technical and Professional Training: Yaoundé.

Ministry of Territorial Administration and Decentralization: Quartier Administratif, Yaoundé; tel. 223-4090; fax 222-3735.

Ministry of Tourism: BP 266, Yaoundé; tel. 222-4411; fax 222-1295; e-mail mintour@camnet.cm; internet www.mintour.gov.cm.

Ministry of Transport: Quartier Administratif, Yaoundé; tel. 222-8709; fax 223-2238; e-mail mintrans@camnet.cm; internet www.camnet.cm/investir/transport.

Ministry of Urban Development and Housing: Yaoundé; tel. 223-2282.

Ministry of Women's Affairs and the Family: Quartier Administratif, Yaoundé; fax 223-3965.

Ministry of Youth: Quartier Administratif, Yaoundé; tel. 223-3257; e-mail minjes@minjes.gov.cm; internet www.minjes.gov.cm.

President and Legislature

PRESIDENT

Election, 11 October 2004

Candidate	% of votes
Paul Biya (RDPC)	75.24
John Fru Ndi (SDF)	17.13
Adamou Ndam Njoya (UDC)	4.71
Garga Haman Adji (ADD)	1.50
Others*	1.42
Total	100.00

* There were 12 other candidates.

NATIONAL ASSEMBLY

President: Cavaye Yéguié Djibril.

General Election, 30 June 2002*

Party	Seats
Rassemblement démocratique du peuple camerounais (RDPC)	149
Social Democratic Front (SDF)	22
Union démocratique du Cameroun (UDC)	5
Union des populations camerounaises (UPC)	3
Union nationale pour la démocratie et le progrès (UNDP)	1
Total	180

* Includes the results of voting in nine constituencies (for 17 seats) where the elections were postponed until 15 September 2002, owing to irregularities.

Political Organizations

At the time of the June 2002 legislative elections there were 159 legal political parties, of which the most important are listed below:

Action for Meritocracy and Equal Opportunity Party (AMEC): Leader Joachim Tabi Owono.

Alliance des forces progressistes (AFP): f. 2002; Leader Maidadi Saidou Yaya.

Alliance pour la démocratie et le développement (ADD): Sec.-Gen. Garga Haman Adji.

Alliance démocratique pour le progrès du Cameroun (ADPC): Garoua; f. 1991.

Alliance nationale pour la démocratie et le progrès: Yaoundé; Pres. Hamadou Moustapha.

Alliance pour le progrès et l'émancipation des dépossédés (APED): Yaoundé; f. 1991; Leader Bohin Bohin.

Alliance pour le redressement du Cameroun (ARC): f. 1992 by a number of opposition movements.

Association sociale-démocrate du Cameroun (ASDC): Maroua; f. 1991.

Cameroon Anglophone Movement (CAM): advocates a federal system of govt.

Congrès panafricain du Cameroun (CPC): BP 1248, Douala; f. 1991.

Convention libérale (CL): f. 1991; Leader Pierre-Flambeau Ngayap.

Démocratie intégrale au Cameroun (DIC): Douala; f. 1991; Leader Gustave Essaka.

Front des alliés pour le changement (FAC): Douala; f. 1994; alliance of 16 opposition movements; Leader Samuel Eboua.

Front démocratique et patriotique (FDP): f. 1994; alliance of six opposition parties.

Liberal Democratic Alliance (LDA): Buéa; Pres. Henri Fossung.

Mouvement africain pour la nouvelle indépendance et la démocratie (MANIDEM): fmrly a faction of the UPC; Leader Anicet Ekane.

Mouvement pour la défense de la République (MDR): f. 1991; Leader Dakole Daissala.

Mouvement pour la démocratie et le progrès (MDP): f. 1992; Leader Samuel Eboua.

Mouvement pour la jeunesse du Cameroun (MLJC): Leader Dieudonné Tina.

Mouvement pour la libération et le développement du Cameroun (MLDC): by a breakaway faction of the MLJC; Leader Marcel Yondo.

Mouvement social pour la nouvelle démocratie (MSND): Leader Yondo Black.

Nouvelle convention (NC): Yaoundé.

Parti des démocrates camerounais (PDC): BP 6909, Yaoundé; tel. 222-2842; f. 1991; Leader Louis-Tobie Mbida.

Parti libéral-démocrate (PLD): f. 1991; Leader Njoh Litumbe.

Parti populaire pour le développement (PPD): f. 1997.

Parti républicain du peuple camerounais (PRPC): Bertoua; f. 1991; Leader Ateba Ngoua.

Parti socialiste camerounais (PSC): Leader Jean-Pierre Dembele.

Parti socialiste démocratique (PSD): BP 141, Douala; tel. 342-1995; f. 1991; Leader Nsame Mbongo Joseph.

Parti socialiste démocratique du Cameroun (PSDC): Leader Jean Michel Tekam.

Rassemblement démocratique du peuple camerounais (RDPC): BP 867, Yaoundé; tel. 23-27-40; f. 1966 as Union nationale camerounaise by merger of the Union camerounaise; the Kamerun National Democratic Party and four opposition parties; adopted present name in 1985; sole legal party 1972–90; Pres. Paul Biya; Sec.-Gen. Joseph-Charles Doumba.

Rassemblement démocratique du peuple sans frontières (RDPF): f. 1997.

Social Democratic Front (SDF): BP 490, Bamenda; tel. 336-3949; fax 336-2991; e-mail webmaster@sdfparty.org; internet www.sdfparty.org; f. 1990; Chair. John Fru Ndi; Sec.-Gen. Prof. Tazoacha Asonganyi.

Social Democratic Movement (SDM): f. 1995; breakaway faction of the Social Democratic Front; Leader Siga Asanga.

Southern Cameroons National Council (SCNC): f. 1995; supports the establishment of an independent republic in anglophone Cameroon; Chair. Sam Ekontang Elad; Leader Chief Ette Otun Ayamba.

Union démocratique du Cameroun (UDC): BP 1638, Yaoundé; f. 1991; Leader Adamou Ndam Njoya.

Union des forces démocratiques du Cameroun (UFDC): Yaoundé; f. 1991; Leader Victorin Hameni Bieleu.

Union nationale pour la démocratie et le progrès (UNDP): BP 656, Douala; tel. 220-6394; f. 1991; split in 1995; Chair. Bello Bouba Maigari.

Union des populations camerounaises (UPC): Douala; f. 1948; split into two main factions in 1996: UPC (N), led by Ndeh Ntumazah and UPC (K), led by Augustin Frédéric Kodock.

Diplomatic Representation

EMBASSIES AND HIGH COMMISSIONS IN CAMEROON

Algeria: 433 rue 1828, Quartier Bastos, BP 1619, Yaoundé; tel. 221-5351; fax 231-5354; Ambassador (vacant).

Belgium: rue 1792, Quartier Bastos, BP 816, Yaoundé; tel. 220-0519; fax 220-0521; e-mail yaounde@diplobel.org; internet www.diplomatie.be/yaounde/; Ambassador Jan de Bruyne.

Brazil: BP 348, Yaoundé; tel. 221-4567; fax 221-1957; Chargé d'affaires a.i. SERGIO COURI ELIAS.

Canada: Immeuble Stamatiades, place de l'Hôtel de Ville, BP 572, Yaoundé; tel. 223-2311; fax 222-1090; e-mail yunde@dfait-maeci.gc.ca; internet www.infoexport.gc.ca/cm; High Commissioner MICHEL PERRAULT.

Central African Republic: 41 rue 1863, Quartier Bastos, Montée du Carrefour de la Vallée Nlongkak, BP 396, Yaoundé; tel. and fax 220-5155; Ambassador (vacant).

Chad: Quartier Bastos, BP 506, Yaoundé; tel. 221-0624; fax 220-8570; Ambassador (vacant).

China, People's Republic: Nouveau Bastos, BP 1307, Yaoundé; tel. 221-0083; fax 221-4395; e-mail chinaemb_cm@mfa.gov.cn; Ambassador WANG SIFA.

Congo, Democratic Republic: BP 632, Yaoundé; tel. 220-5103; Ambassador ZÉPHIRIN KIBIDI NGOVUKA.

Congo, Republic: rue Restaurant la Riviera, après Afrique Hôtel, BP 1422, Yaoundé; tel. 221-2458; Ambassador ALPHONSE NZIÉFFÉ.

Côte d'Ivoire: BP 11354, Yaoundé; tel. 221-3291; fax 221-3295; Ambassador PAUL AYOMAN AMBOHALÉ.

Egypt: 718 rue 1828, Quartier Bastos, BP 809, Yaoundé; tel. 220-3922; fax 220-2647; Ambassador ABD EL-HAMID SOLIMAN.

Equatorial Guinea: 82 rue 1851, Quartier Bastos, BP 277, Yaoundé; tel. and fax 221-0804; Ambassador PURIFICACIÓN ANGUE ONDO.

France: Plateau Atémengué, BP 1631, Yaoundé; tel. 222-7900; fax 222-7909; e-mail chancellerie.yaounde-amba@diplomatie.gouv.fr; internet www.ambafrance-cm.org; Ambassador JEAN-FRANÇOIS VALETTE.

Gabon: Quartier Bastos, Ekoudou, BP 4130, Yaoundé; tel. 220-2966; fax 221-0224; Ambassador FERDINAND MASSALA MALONGA.

Germany: Nouvelle Bastos, Bastos-Usine, Yaoundé; tel. 221-0566; fax 221-6211; e-mail info@jaun.diplo.de; Ambassador VOLKER SEITZ.

Greece: Quartier Mont Fébé, BP 82, Yaoundé; tel. and fax 221-0595; Ambassador IONNIS A. GEORGIADIS.

Holy See: rue du Vatican, BP 210, Yaoundé (Apostolic Nunciature); tel. 220-0475; fax 220-7513; Apostolic Pro-Nuncio Most Rev. ELISEO ANTONIO ARIOTTI (Titular Archbishop of Vibiana).

Israel: rue du Club Olympique à Bastos 154, Longkak, BP 5934, Yaoundé; tel. 221-1291; fax 221-0823; e-mail info@yaounde.mfa.gov.il; Ambassador BENNY OMER.

Italy: Plateau Bastos, BP 827, Yaoundé; tel. 220-3376; fax 221-5250; e-mail ambyaounde@iccnet.cm; internet www.ambitaliacamerun.org; Ambassador FAUSTINO BONAVENTURA TRONI.

Japan: 1513 rue 1828, Quartier Bastos, Ekoudou, BP 6868, Yaoundé; tel. 220-6202; fax 221-5179; Ambassador MASAKI KUNIEDA.

Korea, Democratic People's Republic: Ambassador KIM RYONG YONG.

Korea, Republic: BP 301, Yaoundé; tel. 221-3223; fax 220-1725; Ambassador DAE-TAEK LIM.

Liberia: Quartier Bastos, Ekoudou, BP 1185, Yaoundé; tel. 221-1296; fax 220-9781; Ambassador CARLTON ALEXWYN KARPEH.

Libya: Quartier Nylon Nlongkak, Quartier Bastos, BP 1980, Yaoundé; tel. 220-4138; fax 221-4298; Chargé d'affaires a.i. IBRAHIM O. AMAMI.

Morocco: Quartier Bastos, BP 1629, Yaoundé; tel. 220-5092; fax 221-7450; e-mail sifamayaoun@camnet.cm; Ambassador OMAR ENNAJI.

Nigeria: Quartier Bastos, BP 448, Yaoundé; tel. 223-5551; High Commissioner EMMANUEL CHAME QUILTOMI NJWAH.

Romania: Immeuble Dyna Immobilier, rue de Joseph Mballa Elounden, BP 6212, Yaoundé; tel. and fax 221-3986; Chargé d'affaires a.i. MIRCEA BONCU.

Russia: Quartier Bastos, BP 488, Yaoundé; tel. 220-1714; fax 220-7891; e-mail consrusse@camnet.cm; Ambassador POULATE KH. ABDOULAYEV.

Saudi Arabia: rue 1951, Quartier Bastos, BP 1602, Yaoundé; tel. 221-2675; fax 220-6689; Ambassador AHMED HUSSEIN ALBEDEWI.

Spain: blvd. de l'URSS, Quartier Bastos, BP 877, Yaoundé; tel. 220-3543; fax 220-6491; e-mail embespcm@mail.mae.es; Ambassador JOSÉ JAVIER SOLANO GADEA.

Tunisia: rue de Rotary, Quartier Bastos, BP 6074, Yaoundé; tel. 220-3368; fax 221-0507; Chargé d'affaires a.i. MOHAMED NACER KORT.

United Kingdom: ave Winston Churchill, BP 547, Yaoundé; tel. 222-0545; fax 222-0148; e-mail BHC@yaounde.mail.fco.gov.uk; internet www.britcam.org; High Commissioner RICHARD WILDASH.

USA: rue Nachtigal, BP 817, Yaoundé; tel. 223-4014; fax 223-0753; internet usembassy.state.gov/yaounde; Ambassador NIELS MARQUARDT.

Judicial System

Supreme Court

Yaoundé; tel. 222-0164; fax 222-0576.

Consists of a president, nine titular and substitute judges, a procureur général, an avocat général, deputies to the procureur général, a registrar and clerks.

President: ALEXANDRE DIPANDA MOUELLE.

High Court of Justice

Yaoundé.

Consists of nine titular judges and six substitute judges, all elected by the National Assembly.

Attorney-General: RISSOUCK A. MOULONG MARTIN.

Religion

It is estimated that 53% of the population are Christians (an estimated 25.4% of those are Roman Catholics), 25% adhere to traditional religious beliefs, and 22% are Muslims.

CHRISTIANITY

Protestant Churches

There are about 1m. Protestants in Cameroon, with about 3,000 church and mission workers, and four theological schools.

Fédération des Eglises et missions évangéliques du Cameroun (FEMEC): BP 491, Yaoundé; tel. and fax 223-8117; e-mail femec_org@yahoo.fr; internet www.wagne.net/femec; f. 1968; 10 mem. churches; Pres. Rev. Dr JEAN KOTTO (Evangelical Church of Cameroon); Admin. Sec. Rev. Dr GRÉGOIRE AMBADIANG DE MENDENG (Presbyterian Church of Cameroon).

Eglise évangélique du Cameroun (Evangelical Church of Cameroon): BP 89, Douala; tel. 342-3611; fax 342-4011; f. 1957; 500,000 mems (1992); Pres. Rev. CHARLES E. NJIKE; Sec. Rev. HANS EDJENGUELE.

Eglise presbytérienne camerounaise (Presbyterian Church of Cameroon): BP 519, Yaoundé; tel. 332-4236; independent since 1957; comprises four synods and 16 presbyteries; 220,000 mems (1985); Gen. Sec. Rev. GRÉGOIRE AMBADIANG DE MENDENG.

Eglise protestante africaine (African Protestant Church): BP 26, Lolodorf; f. 1934; 8,400 mems (1985); Dir-Gen. Rev. MARNIA WOUNGLY-MASSAGA.

Presbyterian Church in Cameroon: BP 19, Buéa; tel. 332-2336; 300,000 mems (1996); 302 ministers; Moderator Rev. NYANSAKO-NI-NKU.

Union des Eglises baptistes au Cameroun (Union of Baptist Churches of Cameroon): New Bell, BP 6007, Douala; tel. 342-4106; autonomous since 1957; 37,000 mems (1985); Gen. Sec. Rev. EMMANUEL MBENDA.

Other Protestant churches active in Cameroon include the Cameroon Baptist Church, the Cameroon Baptist Convention, the Church of the Lutheran Brethren of Cameroon, the Evangelical Lutheran Church of Cameroon, the Presbyterian Church in West Cameroon and the Union of Evangelical Churches of North Cameroon.

The Roman Catholic Church

Cameroon comprises five archdioceses and 18 dioceses. At 31 December 2001 adherents represented some 25.7% of the total population. There are several active missionary orders, and four major seminaries for African priests.

Bishops' Conference

Conférence Episcopale Nationale du Cameroun, BP 1963, Yaoundé; tel. 231-1592; fax 771-3542; e-mail ngoyambjulienne@yahoo.fr. f. 1989; Pres. Most Rev. SIMON-VICTOR TONYÉ BAKOT (Archbishop of Yaoundé).

Archbishop of Bamenda: Most Rev. PAUL VERDZEKOV, Archbishop's House, BP 82, Bamenda; tel. 336-1241; fax 336-3487; e-mail archbishop@refinedct.net.

Archbishop of Bertoua: Most Rev. ROGER PIRENNE, Archevêché, BP 40, Bertoua; tel. 224-1748; fax 224-2585.

Archbishop of Douala: Cardinal CHRISTIAN WIYGHAN TUMI, Archevêché, BP 179, Douala; tel. 342-3714; fax 342-1837.

Archbishop of Garoua: Most Rev. Antoine Ntalou, Archevêché, BP 272, Garoua; tel. 227-1353; fax 227-2942.

Archbishop of Yaoundé: Most Rev. Simon-Victor Tonyé Bakot, Archevêché, BP 207, Yaoundé; tel. 220-2461; fax 221-9735; e-mail procure.yde@rctmail.net.

BAHÁ'Í FAITH

National Spiritual Assembly: BP 145, Limbe; tel. 333-2146; mems in 1,744 localities.

The Press

DAILIES

Cameroon Tribune: route de l'Aéroport, BP 1218, Yaoundé; tel. 230-3689; fax 230-4362; e-mail cameroon-tribune@cameroon-tribune.cm; internet www.cameroon-tribune.cm; f. 1974; govt-controlled; French and English; Pub. Marie Claire Nnana; Man. Editor Patrice Etoundi Mballa; circ. 20,000.

Mutations: 183 rue 1055, Place Repiquet, BP 12348, Yaoundé; tel. and fax 222-5104; e-mail contact@quotidienmutations.net; internet www.quotidienmutations.net; daily; French; independent; Man. Editor Haman Mana.

Politiks Matinal: Yaoundé; f. 1999; independent; French; circ. 10,000.

Le Quotidien: BP 13088, Douala; tel. 339-1189; fax 339-1819; French; circ 29,000.

PERIODICALS

Affaires Légales: BP 3681, Douala; tel. 342-5838; fax 343-2259; monthly; legal periodical.

Afrique en Dossiers: Yaoundé; f. 1970; French and English; Dir Ebongue Soelle.

Cameroon Outlook: BP 124, Limbe; f. 1969; 3 a week; independent; English; Editor Jerome F. Gwellem; circ. 20,000.

Cameroon Panorama: BP 46, Buéa; tel. 332-2240; e-mail cainsbuea@yahoo.com; f. 1962; monthly; English; Roman Catholic; Editor Rev. Fr Moses Tazoh; circ. 4,500.

Cameroon Post: Yaoundé; weekly; independent; English; Publr Paddy Mbawa; Editor Julius Wamey; circ. 50,000.

Cameroon Review: BP 408, Limbe; monthly; Editor-in-Chief Jerome F. Gwellem; circ. 70,000.

Cameroon Times: BP 408, Limbe; f. 1960; weekly; English; Editor-in-Chief Jerome F. Gwellem; circ. 12,000.

Challenge Hebdo: BP 1388, Douala; weekly; Editor Benjamin Zebaze.

Le Combattant: Yaoundé; weekly; independent; Editor Benyimbe Joseph; circ. 21,000.

Courrier Sportif du Bénin: BP 17, Douala; weekly; Dir Henri Jong.

Dikalo: BP 4320, Douala; tel. 337-2122; fax 337-1906; f. 1991; independent; 2 a week; French; Publications Dir Tetteh M. Armah; Editor Henri Epee Ndoumbe.

Ecovox: BP 1256, Bafoussam; tel. 344-6267; fax 344-6669; internet www.wagne.net/ecovox; 2 a year; French; ecological news.

L'Effort Camerounais: BP 15231, Douala; tel. 343-2726; fax 343-1837; internet www.effortcamerounais.info.net; bi-monthly; Catholic; Editor-in-chief Antoine de Padou Chonang.

La Gazette: BP 5485, Douala; 2 a week; Editor Abodel Karimou; circ. 35,000.

The Herald: BP 1218, Yaoundé; tel. 231-5522; fax 231-8497; 3 a week; English; Dir Dr Boniface Forbin; circ. 1,568.

Al Houda: BP 1638, Yaoundé; quarterly; Islamic cultural review.

L'Indépendant Hebdo: Yaoundé; Chief Editor Evariste Menounga.

Le Jeune Observateur: Yaoundé; f. 1991; Editor Jules Koum (imprisoned for libel in January 2005).

J'informe: Yaoundé; tel. 993-6605; fax 220-5336; f. 2002; weekly; French; Editor Delor Magellan Kamgaing.

Journal Officiel de la République du Cameroun: BP 1603, Yaoundé; tel. and fax 221-5218; weekly; official govt notices; Man. Editor Joseph Marcel; circ. 4,000.

Le Messager: Rue des écoles, BP 5925, Douala; tel. 342-0214; fax 342-0439; internet www.lemessager.net; f. 1979; 3 a week; independent; Man. Editor Pius N. Njawe; circ. 20,000.

The Messenger: BP 15043, Douala; English-language edn of *Le Messager*; Editor Hilary Fokum.

Nleb Ensemble: Imprimerie Saint-Paul, BP 763, Yaoundé; tel. 223-9773; fax 223-5058; f. 1935; fortnightly; Ewondo; Dir Most Rev. Jean Zoa; Editor Joseph Befe Ateba; circ. 6,000.

La Nouvelle Expression: BP 15333, Douala; tel. 343-2227; fax 343-2669; independent; 3 a week; French; Man. Editor Séverin Tchounkeu.

La Nouvelle Presse: BP 2625, Messa, Yaoundé; tel. 996-6768; f. 2001; weekly; Publications Dir Jacques Blaise Mvie.

Ouest Echos: BP 767, Bafoussam; tel. and fax 344-1091; internet www.wagne.net/ouestechos/; weekly; regional; Dir Michel Eclador Pékoua.

Presbyterian Newsletter: BP 19, Buéa; quarterly.

Que Savoir: Douala; monthly; industry, commerce and tourism.

Recherches et Études Camerounaises: BP 193, Yaoundé; monthly; publ. by Office National de Recherches Scientifiques du Cameroun.

La Révélation: Yaoundé; Dir Bosco Tchoubet.

La Sentinelle: BP 24079, Douala; tel. and fax 339-1627; weekly; lifestyle; circ. 3,200.

Le Serment: Yaoundé; newspaper; Editor-in-Chief Anselme Mballa.

Le Serviteur: BP 1405, Yaoundé; monthly; Protestant; Dir Pastor Daniel Ako'o; circ. 3,000.

Le Travailleur/The Worker: BP 1610, Yaoundé; tel. 222-3315; f. 1972; monthly; French and English; journal of Organisation Syndicale des Travailleurs du Cameroun/Cameroon Trade Union Congress; Sec.-Gen. Louis Sombes; circ. 10,000.

Le Triomphe: BP 1862, Douala; tel. 342-8774; f. 2002; weekly; Publications Dir Sipowa Conscience Parfait.

L'Unité: BP 867, Yaoundé; weekly; French and English.

Weekly Post: Obili, Yaoundé; Publr Chief Bisong Etahoben.

NEWS AGENCIES

CamNews: c/o SOPECAM, BP 1218, Yaoundé; tel. 230-3830; fax 230-4362; Dir Jean Ngandjeu.

Foreign Bureaux

Xinhua (New China) News Agency (People's Republic of China): ave Joseph Omgba, BP 1583, Yaoundé; tel. 220-2572; Chief Correspondent Sun Xingwen.

Agence France-Presse (France), Reuters (United Kingdom) and ITAR—TASS (Russia) are also represented.

PRESS ASSOCIATIONS

Association des Journalistes Indépendants du Cameroun (AJIC): BP 2996, Yaoundé; tel. 222-3572; independent journalists' asscn; Pres. Célestin Lingo.

Conseil Camerounais des Médias (CCM): Yaoundé; f. 2005; created by the UJC to strengthen the quality and independence of journalism in Cameroon; 9 mems.

Union des Journalistes du Cameroun (UJC): Yaoundé; Pres. Célestin Lingo.

Publishers

AES Presses Universitaires d'Afrique: BP 8106, Yaoundé; tel. 222-0030; fax 222-2325; e-mail aes@iccnet.cm; f. 1986; literature, social sciences and law; Dir-Gen. Serge Dontchueng Kouam.

Editions Buma Kor: BP 727, Yaoundé; tel. 723-0768; fax 223-2903; f. 1977; general, children's, educational and Christian; English and French; Man. Dir B. D. Buma Kor.

Editions Clé: BP 1501, ave Maréchal Foch, Yaoundé; tel. 722-3554; fax 723-2709; e-mail edition@iccnet.cm; f. 1963; African and Christian literature and studies; school textbooks; medicine and science; general non-fiction; Dir Comlan Prosper.

Editions Le Flambeau: BP 113, Yaoundé; tel. 222-3672; f. 1977; general; Man. Dir Joseph Ndzie.

Editions Semences Africaines: BP 5329, Yaoundé-Nlongkak; tel. 222-4058; f. 1974; fiction, history, religion, textbooks; Man. Dir Philippe-Louis Ombede.

New Times Publishing House: Presbook Compound, BP 408, Limbe; tel. 333-3217; f. 1983; publishing and book-trade reference; Dir and Editor-in-Chief J. F. Gwellem.

GOVERNMENT PUBLISHING HOUSES

Centre d'Edition et de Production pour l'Enseignement et la Recherche (CEPER): BP 808, Yaoundé; tel. 723-1293; f. 1967; transfer pending to private ownership; general non-fiction, science and technology, tertiary, secondary and primary textbooks; Man. Dir JEAN CLAUDE FOUTH.

Imprimerie Nationale: BP 1603, Yaoundé; tel. 223-1277; scheduled for transfer to private ownership; Dir AMADOU VAMOULKE.

Société de Presse et d'Editions du Cameroun (SOPECAM): route de l'Aéroport, BP 1218, Yaoundé; tel. 230-4147; fax 230-4362; f. 1977; under the supervision of the Ministry of Communication; Pres. PAUL TESSA; Man. Editor MARIE CLAIRE NNANA.

Broadcasting and Communications

TELECOMMUNICATIONS

A Telecommunications Regulation Agency was established in early 1999.

Cameroon Telecommunications (CAMTEL): BP 1571, Yaoundé; tel. 223-4065; fax 223-0303; e-mail camtel@camnet.cm; internet www.camnet.cm; f. 1999 by merger of INTELCAM and the Dept of Telecommunications; 51% privatization pending; Pres. NFON VICTOR MUKETE; Dir-Gen. EMMANUEL NGUIAMBA NLOUTSIRI.

Mobile Telephone Networks Cameroon (MTNC): Douala; f. 1999 as CAMTEL Mobile; mobile cellular telephone operator; 70% owned by MTN South Africa.

Société Camerounaise de Mobiles: Yaoundé; internet www.fcr .fr/fr/identite/pays/cameroun.htm; f. 1999; mobile cellular telephone operator; operates in Yaoundé, Douala and Bafoussam; 100% owned by France Câbles et Radio; Dir-Gen. JEAN-PAUL GANDET.

BROADCASTING

Radio

Office de Radiodiffusion-Télévision Camerounaise (CRTV): BP 1634, Yaoundé; tel. 221-4077; fax 220-4340; internet www.crtv .cm; f. 1987 by merger; broadcasts in French and English; satellite broadcasts commenced in Jan. 2001, reaching some 80% of the national territory; Pres. of Council of Administration PIERRE MOUKOKO MBONJO (Minister of Communication); Dir-Gen. (vacant).

Radio Bertoua: BP 260, Bertoua; tel. 224-1445; fax 224-2275; Head of Station BAIVE NYONG PHILIP.

Radio Buéa: BP 86, Buéa; tel. 332-2615; programmes in English, French and 15 vernacular languages; Man. PETERSON CHIA YUH; Head of Station GIDEON MULU TAKA.

Radio Douala: BP 986, Douala; tel. 342-6060; programmes in French, English, Douala, Bassa, Ewondo, Bakoko and Bamiléké; Dir BRUNO DJEM; Head of Station LINUS ONANA MVONDO.

Radio Garoua: BP 103, Garoua; tel. 227-1167; programmes in French, Hausa, English, Foulfouldé, Arabic and Choa; Dir BELLO MALGANA; Head of Station MOUSSA EPOPA.

Radio Ngaoundéré: BP 135, Ngaoundéré; tel. 225-2148.

Radio Tam Tam: Yaoundé.

Radio Yaoundé FM 94: BP 1634, Yaoundé; tel. 220-2502; Head of Station LOUISE POM.

There are also provincial radio stations at Abong Mbang, Bafoussam, Bamenda, Ebolowa and Maroua.

Television

Television programmes from France were broadcast by the Office de Radiodiffusion-Télévision Camerounaise from early 1990.

Office de Radiodiffusion-Télévision Camerounaise (CRTV): see Radio.

Finance

(cap. = capital; res = reserves; dep. = deposits; m. = million; brs = branches; amounts in francs CFA)

BANKING

Central Bank

Banque des Etats de l'Afrique Centrale (BEAC): Ave Monseigneur Vogt 736, BP 1917, Yaoundé; tel. 223-4030; fax 223-3329; e-mail beac@beac.int; internet www.beac.int; f. 1973; bank of issue for mem. states of the Communauté économique et monétaire de l'Afrique centrale (CEMAC, fmrly Union douanière et économique de l'Afrique centrale) Cameroon, the Central African Repub., Chad, the Repub. of the Congo, Equatorial Guinea and Gabon); cap. 45,000m., res 176,661m., total assets 2,144,626m. (Nov. 2003); Gov. JEAN-FÉLIX MAMALEPOT; Dir in Cameroon SADOU HAYATOU; 5 brs in Cameroon.

Commercial Banks

Amity Bank Cameroon SA: BP 2705, Douala; tel. 343-2055; fax 343-2046; e-mail amibac@camnet.cm; f. 1990; cap. and res −2,671m., total assets 24,717m. (June 2002); Pres. VICTOR ANOMAH NGU; Dir-Gen. OUMAROU SANDA; 4 brs.

Banque Internationale du Cameroun pour l'Epargne et le Crédit (BICEC): ave du Général de Gaulle, BP 1925, Douala; tel. 342-8576; fax 342-6047; e-mail bicec@bicec.com; internet www.bicec .com; f. 1962 as Banque Internationale pour le Commerce et l'Industrie du Cameroun; name changed as above in 1997, following restructuring; 52.5% owned by Groupe Banques Populaires (France); cap. 3,000m., res 12,667m., dep. 250,043m., total assets 277,327m. (June 2002); Pres. JEAN-BAPTISTE BOKAM; Gen. Man. JEAN-PIERRE SCHIANO; 26 brs.

Citibank N.A. Cameroon: 96 rue Flatters, Bonanjo, BP 4571, Douala; tel. 342-4272; fax 342-4074; f. 1997; Dir-Gen. LOUIS ADANDE; Asst Dir-Gen. OSMAN EL TOUM.

Commercial Bank of Cameroon (CBC): BP 4004, Douala; tel. 442-0202; fax 443-3800; e-mail cbcbank@camnet.cm; f. 1997; cap. and res. 5,478m., total assets 89,027m. (June 2001); Pres. VICTOR FOTSO; Dir-Gen. JEAN-LOUIS CHAPUIS.

Crédit Lyonnais Cameroun SA: 530 rue du Roi George, BP 300, Douala; tel. 343-5400; fax 342-5413; f. 1989 as Société Commerciale de Banque—Crédit Lyonnais Cameroun; name changed as above in 2002; 35% state-owned; cap. and res 14,887m., total assets 258,316m. (Dec. 2004); Pres. MARTIN ARISTIDE OKOUDA; Gen. Man. FRANCIS DUBUS; Sec.-Gen. PIERRE SAM-NDOUMBE; 15 brs.

Ecobank Cameroun SA (Togo): blvd de la Liberté, BP 582, Douala; tel. 343-8250; fax 343-8487; e-mail ecobankcm@ecobank.com; internet www.ecobank.com; f. 2001; cap. 2,500m., res 89m., dep. 34,917m, total assets 56,070m. (Dec. 2004); Pres. ANDRÉ FOTSO; Dir-Gen. LOUIS VIEILLEDENT.

Highland Corporation Bank SA: Immeuble Hôtel Hilton, blvd du 20 mai, BP 10039, Yaoundé; tel. 223-9287; fax 232-9291; e-mail atnjp@camnet.cm; internet pcnet.ifrance.com/pcnet/hcb/; f. 1995; 100% privately owned; cap. 600m. (Dec. 1996); Exec. Pres. PAUL ATANGA NJI; Asst Dir-Gen. JOHANES MBATI.

Société Générale de Banques au Cameroun (SGBC): 78 rue Joss, BP 4042, Douala; tel. 342-7010; fax 343-0353; e-mail sgbcdla@ camnet.cm; f. 1963; 25.6% state-owned; cap. and res 17,213m., total assets 301,391m. (June 2001); Chair. AMADOU NJIFENJOU MOULIOM; Dir-Gen. ALAIN BELLISSARD; 15 brs.

Standard Chartered Bank Cameroon SA: blvd de la Liberté, BP 1784, Douala; tel. 343-5200; fax 342-8927; internet www .standardchartered.com/cm/index.html; f. 1980 as Boston Bank Cameroon; name changed 1986; 100% owned by Standard Chartered Bank (United Kingdom); cap. 7,000m., total assets 143,619m. (June 2002); Pres. EPHRAIM INONI; Gen. Man. ANDREW McGREGOR FLETCHER; 3 brs.

Development Banks

Banque de Développement des Etats de l'Afrique Centrale: see Franc Zone.

Crédit Foncier du Cameroun (CFC): 484 blvd du 20 mai 1972, BP 1531, Yaoundé; tel. 223-5215; fax 223-5221; f. 1977; 75% state-owned; cap. and res 8,355m., total assets 82,512m. (Dec. 2002); provides assistance for low-cost housing; Pres. ANDRÉ BOOTO A. NGON; Dir-Gen. JOSEPH EDOU; 10 brs.

Société Nationale d'Investissement du Cameroun (SNI): place du 20 mai, BP 423, Yaoundé; tel. 222-4422; fax 223-1332; e-mail sni@ sni.cm; internet www.sni.cm; f. 1964; state-owned investment and credit agency; cap. 19,000m., res 20,980m., total assets 33,426m. (June 2000); Dir-Gen. ESTHER BELIBI DANG.

Financial Institutions

Caisse Autonome d'Amortissement du Cameroun: BP 7167, Yaoundé; tel. 222-0187; fax 222-0129; e-mail camtis@camnet.cm; f. 1985; cap. 5,000m. (1998); Dir-Gen. DANIEL LAMERE NJANKOUO.

Caisse Camerounaise d'Epargne et de Crédit: Yaoundé; tel. 237-4532; fax 237-5026; e-mail cce@iccnet.cm; internet www.iccnet .cm/ccec.

Caisse Commune d'Epargne et d'Investissement (CCEI): place de l'Indépendance, BP 11834, Yaoundé; tel. 223-3068; fax 222-1785;

e-mail kengnea@hotmail.com; total assets 88,551m. (June 2000); Pres. Dr PAUL KANMOGNE FOKAM; Dir-Gen. DANIEL POTOUONJOU TAPONZIÉ.

Fonds d'Aide et de Garantie des Crédits aux Petites et Moyennes Entreprises (FOGAPE): BP 1591, Yaoundé; tel. 223-3859; fax 222-3274; f. 1984; cap. 1,000m. (Oct. 1997); Pres. JOSEPH HENGA; Vice-Pres. ARMAND FIRMIN MVONDO.

Société Camerounaise de Crédit Automobile (SOCCA): rue du Roi Albert, BP 554, Douala; tel. 342-7478; fax 342-1219; e-mail soccabail@camnet.cm; internet www.giefca.com/english/cameroun .htm; cap. 1,200m., res 2,705m., total assets 11,932m. (June 1999); Pres. VALENTIN MOUYOMBON; Dir-Gen. JOHANN BAUDOT.

Société Camerounaise de Crédit-Bail (SOCABAIL): rue du Roi Albert, BP 554, Douala; tel. 342-7478; fax 342-1219; e-mail soccabail@camnet.cm; cap. 500m., res 1,343m., total assets 5,880m. (June 1999); Pres. ALAIN GUYON.

STOCK EXCHANGE

Bourse des Valeurs de Douala (Douala Stock Exchange): 1450 blvd de la Liberté, BP 442, Douala; tel. 343-8582; fax 353-8584; e-mail dsx@dsx.cm; f. 2003; 23% state-owned; Chair. BÉNÉDICT BELIBI; Gen. Man. MATHURIN DOUMBE EPÉE.

INSURANCE

Activa Assurances: BP 12970, Douala; tel. 343-4503; fax 343-4572; e-mail activa.assur@camnet.cm; f. 1999; all branches except life insurance; cap. 400m.; 66% owned by Cameroonian investors, 33% by Ivorian investors; Chair. JEAN DIAGOU; Gen. Man. RICHARD LOWE.

AGF Cameroun Assurances: rue Manga Bell, BP 105, Douala; tel. 342-9203; fax 343-0324; e-mail agf.cameroun@agf-cm.com; f. 1974; all classes of insurance; cap. 700m.; Dir-Gen. BERNARD LIBOUREL.

Assurances Mutuelles Agricoles du Cameroun (AMACAM): BP 962, Yaoundé; tel. 222-4966; f. 1965; cap. 100m.; state-owned; privatization pending; Pres. SAMUEL NGBWA NGUELE; Dir-Gen. LUC CLAUDE NANFA.

Compagnie Camerounaise d'Assurances et de Réassurances (CCAR): 11 rue Franqueville, BP 4068, Douala; tel. 342-3159; fax 342-6453; f. 1974; cap. 499.5m.; Pres. YVETTE CHASSAGNE; Dir-Gen. CHRISTIAN LE GOFF.

Compagnie Nationale d'Assurances (CNA): BP 12125, Douala; tel. 342-4446; fax 342-4727; f. 1986; all classes of insurance; cap. 600m.; Chair. THÉODORE EBOBO; Man. Dir PROTAIS AYANGMA AMANG.

General and Equitable Assurance Cameroon Ltd (GEACAM): 56 blvd de la Liberté, BP 426, Douala; tel. 342-5985; fax 342-7103; cap. 300m.; Pres. V. A. NGU; Man. Dir J. CHEBAUT.

Société Camerounaise d'Assurances et de Réassurances (SOCAR): 1450 blvd de la Liberté, BP 280, Douala; tel. 342-5584; fax 342-1335; f. 1973; cap. 800m.; Chair. J. YONTA; Man. Dir R. BIOUELE.

Trade and Industry

GOVERNMENT AGENCY

Economic and Social Council: BP 1058, Yaoundé; tel. 223-2474; advises the Govt on economic and social problems; comprises 150 mems, which serve a five-year term, and a perm. secr.; Pres. LUC AYANG; Sec.-Gen. FRANÇOIS EYOK.

DEVELOPMENT ORGANIZATIONS

Agence Française de Développement (AFD): Plateau Atémengué, BP 46, Yaoundé; tel. 222-0015; fax 223-5707; e-mail afd .ynde@camnet.cm; internet www.afd.fr/; fmrly Caisse Française de Développement; Dir GUY LECAMUS.

Cameroon Development Corporation (CAMDEV): Bota Area, Limbe; tel. 333-2251; fax 343-2654; e-mail cdcbota@iccnet2000.com; f. 1947; reorg. 1982; cap. 15,626m. francs CFA; statutory corpn established to acquire and develop plantations of tropical crops for local and export markets; operates two oil mills, 11 banana-packing stations and seven rubber factories; Chair. Chief OKIAH NAMATA ELANGWE; Gen. Man. HENRY NJALLA QUAN.

Direction Générale des Grands Travaux du Cameroon (DGTC): BP 6604, Yaoundé; tel. 222-1803; fax 222-1300; f. 1988; commissioning, implementation and supervision of public works contracts; Chair. JEAN FOUMAN AKAME; Man. Dir MICHEL KOWALZICK.

Hévéa-Cameroun (HEVECAM): BP 1298, Douala and BP 174, Kribi; tel. 346-1919; f. 1975; state-owned; development of 15,000 ha rubber plantation; 4,500 employees; transferred to private owner-

ship in 1997; Pres. ELIE C. NYOKWEDI MALONGA; Man. Dir JEAN-MARC SEYMAN.

Mission d'Aménagement et d'Equipement des Terrains Urbains et Ruraux (MAETUR): BP 1248, Yaoundé; tel. 222-3113; fax 223-3190; e-mail maetur@gcnet.cm; internet www.maetur.gcnet .cm; f. 1977; Pres. PIERRE HÉLÉ; Dir-Gen. ANDRÉ MAMA FOUDA.

Mission de Développement de la Province du Nord-Ouest (MIDENO): BP 442, Bamenda; Dir ANDREW WAINDIM NDONYI.

Mission Française de Coopération et d'Action Culturelle: BP 1616, Yaoundé; tel. 223-0412; fax 222-5065; e-mail mission.coop@ camnet.cm; administers bilateral aid from France; Dir LUC HALLADE.

Office Céréalier dans la Province du Nord: BP 298, Garoua; tel. 227-1438; f. 1975 to combat effects of drought in northern Cameroon and stabilize cereal prices; Pres. Alhadji MAHAMAT; Dir-Gen. GILBERT GOURLEMOND.

Société de Développement du Cacao (SODECAO): BP 1651, Yaoundé; tel. 230-4544; fax 230-3395; e-mail sodecao@cameroun; f. 1974; reorg. 1980; cap. 425m. francs CFA; development of cocoa, coffee and food crop production in the Littoral, Centre, East and South provinces; Pres. JOSEPH-CHARLES DOUMBA; Dir-Gen. JOSEPH INGWAT II.

Société de Développement de l'Elevage (SODEVA): BP 50, Kousseri; cap. 50m. francs CFA; Dir Alhadji OUMAROU BAKARY.

Société de Développement et d'Exploitation des Productions Animales (SODEPA): BP 1410, Yaoundé; tel. 222-2428; f. 1974; cap. 375m. francs CFA; development of livestock and livestock products; Man. Dir ETIENNE ENGUELEGUELE.

Société de Développement de la Haute-Vallée du Noun (UNVDA): BP 25, N'Dop, North-West Province; f. 1970; cap. 1,380m. francs CFA; rice, maize and soya bean cultivation; Dir-Gen. SAMUEL BAWE CHI WANKI.

Société d'Expansion et de Modernisation de la Riziculture de Yagoua (SEMRY): BP 46, Yagoua; tel. 229-6213; f. 1971; cap. 4,580m. francs CFA; commercialization of rice products and expansion of rice-growing in areas where irrigation is possible; Pres. ALBERT EKONO; Dir-Gen. LIMANGANA TORI.

Société Immobilière du Cameroun (SIC): BP 387, Yaoundé; tel. 223-3411; fax 222-5119; f. 1952; cap. 1,000m. francs CFA; housing construction and development; Pres. ENOCH KWAYEB; Dir-Gen. GILLES-ROGER BELINGA.

CHAMBERS OF COMMERCE

Chambre d'Agriculture, d'Elevage et des Forêts du Cameroun: Parc Repiquet, BP 287, Yaoundé; tel. 223-1496; f. 1955; 120 mems; Pres. PHILÉMON ADJIBOLO; Sec.-Gen. SOLOMON NFOR GWEI; other chambers at Yaoundé, Ebolowa, Bertoua, Douala, Ngaoundéré, Garoua, Maroua, Buéa, Bumenda and Bafoussam.

Chambre de Commerce, d'Industrie et des Mines du Cameroun (CCIM): rue de Chambre de Commerce, BP 4011, Douala; also at BP 36, Yaoundé; BP 211, Limbe; BP 59, Garoua; BP 944, Bafoussam; BP 551, Bamenda; tel. 342-6855; fax 342-5596; e-mail cride-g77@camnet.cm; internet www.g77tin.org/ccimhp .html; f. 1921; 138 mems; Pres. PIERRE TCHANQUE; Sec.-Gen. SAÏDOU ABDOULAYE BOBBOY.

EMPLOYERS' ORGANIZATIONS

Association Professionnelle des Établissements de Crédit (APECCAM): BP 133, Yaoundé; tel. 223-5401; fax 223-5402; Pres. JEAN LOUIS CHAPUIS.

Groupement des Femmes d'Affaires du Cameroun (GFAC): BP 1940, Douala; tel. 342-464; Pres. FRANÇOISE FONING.

Groupement Interpatronal du Cameroun (GICAM): ave Konrad Adenauer, BP 1134, Yaoundé; also at BP 829, Douala; tel. 220-2722; fax 220-9694; e-mail gicam-yde@camnet.cm; tel. and fax 342-3141; f. 1957; Pres. ANDRÉ SIAKA; Sec.-Gen. FRANCIS SANZOUANGO.

Syndicat des Commerçants Importateurs-Exportateurs du Cameroun (SCIEC): 16 rue Quillien, BP 562, Douala; tel. 342-0304; Sec.-Gen. G. TOSCANO.

Syndicat des Industriels du Cameroun (SYNDUSTRICAM): 17 blvd de Liberté, BP 673, Douala; tel. 342-3058; fax 342-5616; f. 1953; Pres. CHARLES METOUCK.

Syndicat des Producteurs et Exportateurs de Bois du Cameroun: BP 570, Yaoundé; tel. 220-2722; fax 220-9694; Pres. CARLO ORIANI.

Syndicat Professionnel des Entreprises du Bâtiment, des Travaux Publics et des Activités Annexes: BP 1134, Yaoundé; also at BP 660, Douala; tel. and fax 220-2722; Pres. (vacant).

Syndicats Professionnels Forestiers et Activités connexes du Cameroun: BP 100, Douala.

Union des Syndicats Professionnels du Cameroun (USPC): BP 829, Douala; Pres. Moukoko Kingue.

West Cameroon Employers' Association (WCEA): BP 97, Tiko.

Utilities

Electricity

Société Nationale d'Electricité du Cameroun (SONEL): BP 4077, 63 ave de Gaulle, Douala; tel. 342-5444; fax 342-2209; e-mail sonel@camnet.cm; internet www.camnet.cm/investir/minmee/sonelind.htm; f. 1974; 44% state-owned; 56% stake acquired by AES Sirocco in 2001; CEO Jean Fouman Akame; Dir-Gen. Helen Tarnoy.

Water

Société Nationale des Eaux du Cameroun (SNEC): BP 157, Douala; tel. 342-8711; fax 342-2945; e-mail snec@camnet.cm; internet www.camnet.cm/investir/minmee/snec.htm; f. 1967; 73% state-owned; privatization suspended Dec. 2003; Pres. Amadou Ali; Dir-Gen. Basile Atangana Kouna.

PRINCIPAL CO-OPERATIVE ORGANIZATIONS

Centre National de Développement des Entreprises Coopératives (CENADEC): Yaoundé; f. 1970; promotes and organizes the co-operative movement; bureaux at BP 43, Kumba and BP 26, Bamenda; Dir Jacques Sangue.

Union Centrale des Coopératives Agricoles de l'Ouest (UCCAO): ave Samuel Wonko, BP 1002, Bafoussam; tel. 344-4296; fax 344-1845; e-mail mefinja@yahoo.fr; f. 1958; marketing of cocoa and coffee; 120,000 mems; Pres. Jacques Fotso Kankeu; Gen. Man. François Mefinja Foka.

West Cameroon Co-operative Association Ltd: BP 135, Kumba; founded as cen. financing body of the co-operative movement; provides short-term credits and agricultural services to mem. socs; policy-making body for the co-operative movement in West Cameroon; 142 mem. unions and socs representing c. 45,000 mems; Pres. Chief T. E. Njea.

TRADE UNION FEDERATION

Confederation of Cameroon Trade Unions (CCTU): BP 1610, Yaoundé; tel. 222-3315; f. 1985; fmrly the Union Nationale des Travailleurs du Cameroun (UNTC); Pres. Emmanuel Bakod; Sec.-Gen. Louis Sombes.

Transport

RAILWAYS

There are some 1,008 km of track—the West Line running from Douala to Nkongsamba (166 km), with a branch line leading southwest from Mbanga to Kumba (29 km), and the Transcameroon railway, which runs from Douala to Ngaoundéré (885 km), with a branch line from Ngoumou to Mbalmayo (30 km). In July 2002 the World Bank disbursed a loan of 15,600m. francs CFA to Cameroon to help rehabilitate the main line. In November the French Government approved a loan of US $12.5m. to Cameroon primarily to improve rolling stock.

Cameroon Railways (CAMRAIL): Gare Centrale de Bessengué, blvd de la Réunification, BP 766, Douala; tel. 340-6045; fax 340-8252; e-mail camrail.dg@iccnet2000.cm; f. 1999; Pres. Etienne Giros; Dir-Gen. Patrick Claes.

Office du Chemin de Fer Transcamerounais: BP 625, Yaoundé; tel. 222-4433; supervises the laying of new railway lines and improvements to existing lines, and undertakes relevant research; Dir-Gen. Luc Towa Fotso.

ROADS

In 1999 there were an estimated 349,300 km of roads, of which about 4,300 km were paved.

SHIPPING

There are seaports at Kribi and Limbé-Tiko, a river port at Garoua, and an estuary port at Douala-Bonabéri, the principal port and main outlet, which has 2,510 m of quays and a minimum depth of 5.8 m in the channels and 8.5 m at the quays. In 1997 the port handled 4,882,000 metric tons of cargo. Total handling capacity is 7m. metric tons annually. Plans are under way to increase the annual capacity of the container terminal. There are also plans to modernize Limbé-Tiko and to promote it internationally.

Office National des Ports/National Ports Authority: 81 rue de la Chambre de Commerce, BP 4023, Douala; tel. 342-0133; fax 342-6797; e-mail onpc@camnet.cm; internet www.camnet.cm/investir/transport/onpc; f. 1971; Chair. Daholé Daïssala (Minister of Transport); Dir-Gen. Alphonse Siyam Sive.

Cameroon Shipping Lines SA (CAMSHIP): Centre des Affaires Maritimes, BP 4054, Douala; tel. 342-0999; fax 342-7676; e-mail camship@camnet.cm; f. 1975; scheduled for transfer to private-sector ownership; 6 vessels trading with Western Europe, USA, Far East and Africa; Chair. François Sengat Kuo; Man. Dir René Mbayen.

    Camafrica Liner Ltd: Centre des Affaires Maritimes, BP 4054, Douala; non-vessel owner container carrier co. trading between West Africa and Europe.

Camtainer: Para-maratime Area, Douala Port, BP 4993, Douala; tel. 3342-7704; fax 342-7173; internet www.camnet.cm/investir/transpor/camtenair/sommaire.htm.

Compagnie Maritime Camerounaise SA (CMC): BP 3235, Douala; tel. 342-8540; fax 342-5842.

Conseil National des Chargeurs du Cameroun (CNCC): BP 1588, Douala; tel. 342-3206; fax 342-8901; f. 1986; promotion of the maritime sector; Gen. Man. Emmanuel Edou.

Delmas Cameroun: rue Kitchener, BP 263, Douala; tel. 342-4750; fax 342-8851; f. 1977; Pres. Jean-Guy Le Floch; Dir-Gen. Dany Chutaux.

MAERSK CAMEROUN SA—Douala: BP 12414, Douala; tel. 342-1185; fax 342-1186; e-mail dlasal@maersk.com.

Société Africaine de Transit et d'Affrètement (SATA): Douala; tel. 342-8209; f. 1950; Man. Dir Raymond Parizot.

Société Agence Maritime de l'Ouest Africain Cameroun (SAMOA): 5 blvd de la Liberté, BP 1127, Douala; tel. 342-1680; f. 1953; shipping agents; Dir Jean Perrier.

Société Camerounaise de Manutention et d'Acconage (SOCAMAC): BP 284, Douala; tel. 342-4051; e-mail socamac@camnet.cm; internet www.camnet.cm/investir/transpor/socamac/socamac.htm; f. 1976; freight handling; Pres. Mohamadou Talba; Dir-Gen. Harry J. Ghoos.

Société Camerounaise de Transport et d'Affrètement (SCTA): BP 974, Douala; tel. 342-1724; f. 1951; Pres. Jacques Viault; Dir-Gen. Gontran Frauciel.

Société Camerounaise de Transport Maritime: BP 12351, Douala; tel. 342-4550; fax 342-4946.

Société Ouest-Africaine d'Entreprises Maritimes—Cameroun (SOAEM—Cameroun): 5 blvd de la Liberté, BP 4057, Douala; tel. 342-5269; fax 342-0518; f. 1959; Pres. Jacques Colombani; Man. Dir Jean-Louis Greciet.

SOCOPAO Cameroun: BP 215, Douala; tel. 342-6464; f. 1951; shipping agents; Pres. Vincent Bollore; Man. Dir E. Dupuy.

Transcap Cameroun: BP 4059, Douala; tel. 342-7214; f. 1960; Pres. René Dupraz; Man. Dir Michel Bardou.

CIVIL AVIATION

There are international airports at Douala, Garoua and Yaoundé; there are, in addition, 11 domestic airports, as well as a number of secondary airfields.

Aéroports du Cameroun (ADC): Aéroport de Douala; tel. 342-3577; fax 342-3758; f. 1999; manages major airports; 35% owned by Aéroports de Paris, 29% state-owned.

Air Affaires Afrique: BP 1225, Douala; tel. 342-2977; fax 342-9903; f. 1978; regional and domestic charter passenger services; CEO Byron Byron-Exarcos.

Cameroon Airlines (CAMAIR): 151 rue de l'Hôtel de Ville, BP 4092, Douala; tel. 342-2525; fax 342-3459; e-mail camair@camnet.cm; internet www.camnet.cm/investir/transpor/index.htm; f. 1971; domestic flights and services to Africa and Europe; privatization pending; flights suspended since November 2003 ; 3 aeroplanes; Dir-Gen. Paul Ngamo Hamani (interim); Inspector-Gen. of Administration and Finance Esther Gouett.

Tourism

Tourists are attracted by Cameroon's cultural diversity and by its national parks, game reserves and sandy beaches. In 2001 408,377 tourists visited Cameroon. In 2000 receipts from tourism totalled US $39m.

Ministère du Tourisme: BP 266, Yaoundé; tel. 222-4411; fax 222-1295; e-mail mintour@camnet.cm; internet www.camnet.cm/mintour/tourisme/index.htm.

CANADA

Introductory Survey

Location, Climate, Language, Religion, Flag, Capital

Canada occupies the northern part of North America (excluding Alaska and Greenland) and is the second largest country in the world, after Russia. It extends from the Atlantic Ocean to the Pacific. Except for the boundary with Alaska in the north-west, Canada's frontier with the USA follows the upper St Lawrence Seaway and the Great Lakes, continuing west along latitude 49°N. The climate is an extreme one, particularly inland. Winter temperatures drop well below freezing but summers are generally hot. Rainfall varies from moderate to light and there are heavy falls of snow. The two official languages are English and French, the mother tongues of 59.7% and 23.2%, respectively, at the general census in 2001. Immigration during the 1990s made a profound impact on languages spoken in Canadian homes; at the 2001 census Chinese was the language most commonly spoken at home, after English and French. About 36% of the population are Roman Catholics. The main Protestant churches are the United Church of Canada and the Anglican Church of Canada. Numerous other religious denominations are represented. The national flag (proportions 1 by 2) consists of a red maple leaf on a white field, flanked by red panels. The capital is Ottawa.

Recent History

The Liberals, led by Pierre Trudeau, were returned to office at general elections in 1968, 1972, 1974, and again in 1980 after a short-lived minority Progressive Conservative Party (PC) administration. Popular support for the Liberals, however, was undermined by an economic recession, and the PC, led by Brian Mulroney, obtained a substantial legislative majority at general elections held in September 1984.

During 1986 the persistence of high rates of unemployment, together with the resignations in discordant circumstances of five cabinet ministers, led to a fall in the PC Government's popularity. Popular support for the Government further declined, in response to criticism by the Liberals and the New Democratic Party (NDP) of the Government's negotiation of a new US-Canadian trade treaty, which the Liberals and the NDP viewed as overly advantageous to US business interests and potentially damaging to Canada's national identity, and which was approved by the House of Commons in August 1988. Nevertheless, in general elections in November the PC was re-elected, although with a reduced majority, and full legislative ratification of the trade agreement followed in December. In February 1990 the federal Government opened negotiations with Mexico, to achieve a lowering of trade barriers. The US Government joined these discussions, and in December 1992 Canada, the USA and Mexico finalized terms for a tripartite North American Free Trade Agreement (NAFTA, see p. 299), with the aim of creating a free trade zone encompassing the whole of North America.

In the province of Québec, where four-fifths of the population speak French as a first language and which maintains its own cultural identity, the question of political self-determination has long been a sensitive issue. At provincial elections in 1976 the separatist Parti Québécois (PQ) came to power, and in 1977 made French the official language of education, business and government in Québec. In December 1985 the PQ was replaced by the Liberals as the province's governing party. The Liberals retained power at the next provincial elections, held in September 1989. However, political support for separatist aspirations was extended to the federal Parliament in May 1990, when seven PC members representing Québec constituencies, led by Lucien Bouchard (a former member of Mulroney's Cabinet), broke away from the party and formed the independent Bloc Québécois (BQ), with the object of acting in the interests of a 'sovereign Québec'. The BQ later expanded, with disaffected Liberal support, to nine members.

In 1982 the British Parliament transferred to Canada authority over all matters contained in British statutes relating to Canada, opening the way for institutional reform and the redistribution of legislative powers between Parliament and the provincial legislatures. All the provinces except Québec eventually accepted constitutional provisions that included a charter of rights and a formula for constitutional amendments, whereby such amendments would require the support of at least seven provinces representing more than 50% of the population. Québec, however, maintained that its legislature could exercise the right to veto constitutional provisions.

Following the return to office in 1985 of the Liberals in Québec, the federal Government adopted new initiatives to include Québec in the constitutional arrangements. In April 1987 Mulroney and the provincial premiers met at Meech Lake, Québec, to negotiate a constitutional accommodation for Québec. The resultant agreement, the Meech Lake Accord, recognized Québec as a 'distinct society' within the Canadian federation, and granted each of the provinces substantial new powers in the areas of federal parliamentary reform, judicial appointments and the creation of new provinces. The Accord was subject to ratification, not later than June 1990, by the federal Parliament and all provincial legislatures. By early 1990 the federal Parliament and each of the 10 provincial legislatures, except for New Brunswick and Manitoba, had approved the Accord.

Opposition to the Meech Lake arrangements, on the grounds that they afforded too much influence to Québec and failed to provide Inuit and Indian minorities with the same measure of protection as francophone groups, began to emerge in March 1990, when the Newfoundland legislature rescinded its earlier endorsement of the Accord. Following a meeting in June between Mulroney and the provincial premiers (at which a number of compromise amendments were adopted), the New Brunswick legislature agreed to accept the Accord, but the provinces of Manitoba and Newfoundland upheld their opposition. The Meech Lake Accord duly lapsed in late June, and the Québec Government, which had opposed any changes to the earlier terms of the Accord, responded by refusing to participate in future provincial conferences, and by appointing a commission to examine the province's political choices. In September 1991 the federal Government announced a new series of constitutional reform proposals, which, unlike the Meech Lake Accord, would require the assent of only seven provinces representing 50% of the total population. Under the new plan, Québec was to be recognized as a distinct society in terms of its language, culture and legal system, while each province would have full control of its cultural affairs. Native peoples were to receive full self-government within 10 years, inter-provincial trade barriers were to be abolished, and the federal Senate was to become an elected body with limited powers of legislative veto, except in matters involving natural resources, in which it would have full powers of veto. The reform proposals also included the creation of a Council of Federation to resolve disputes between the provinces and federal Government. A National Unity Committee, comprising an inter-party group of 30 federal legislators, was formed to ascertain public reaction to the plan, about which the Québec provincial government expressed initial reservations on economic grounds.

In March 1992 an all-party committee of the federal Parliament recommended new constitutional proposals providing for a system of 'co-operative federalism', which would grant Québec powers of veto over future constitutional changes, together with exclusive jurisdiction over the main areas of its provincial affairs. This plan was rejected by the Québec Government.

Further, inconclusive, discussions among the provincial premiers (in which Québec refused to participate) took place in mid-1992. Mulroney's proposal to revive the Meech Lake proposals was opposed by the western provinces, which sought increased representation in a reformed Senate and were unwilling to concede a constitutional veto to Québec until after these changes were carried out. In late August 1992, following resumed consultations between Mulroney and the provincial premiers, a new programme of constitutional reforms, known as the Charlottetown Agreement, was finalized for submission to a national referendum. The proposals, which were endorsed by all of the provincial premiers as well as the leaders of the three main political parties, provided for an equal and elected Senate, a guarantee in perpetuity to Québec of one-quarter of the seats in the federal House of Commons (regardless of future movements in population), as well as three of the nine seats on the Supreme Court of Canada. There was also to be recognition of provincial jurisdiction in cultural affairs, and increased provincial powers over certain economic affairs and immigration. The inherent right to self-government of the Indian and Inuit population was also to be recognized.

Despite the apparent political consensus, considerable opposition to the Charlottetown Agreement became evident prior to the referendum, which took place in October 1992. Disagreements emerged on a regional basis, as well as among NDP and Liberal supporters, and aspects of the proposed constitution were opposed by the PQ and the BQ, and by the Reform Party (RP), a conservative-populist movement which led opposition in the western provinces. Nationally, the proposals were defeated by a margin of 54.4% to 44.6%; only four of the provinces (Ontario, New Brunswick, Newfoundland and Prince Edward Island) and the Northwest Territories endorsed the Agreement.

The defeat of the Charlottetown Agreement, together with the persistence of adverse economic conditions, led to a rapid erosion in the prestige of the Government, and in Mulroney's personal popularity. A reorganization of Cabinet posts in January 1993 failed to restore public confidence, and in the following month Mulroney announced that he was to relinquish office in June. He was succeeded by the former Minister of Defence and Veterans' Affairs, Kim Campbell, who became Canada's first female Prime Minister.

The Campbell Government proved unable to restore the PC's political standing, and, faced with the expiry in November 1993 of its five-year parliamentary mandate, general elections were scheduled for October. The outcome of the elections, which were contested primarily on domestic economic issues, resulted in a decisive victory for the Liberals, led by Jean Chrétien. A significant realignment of political forces was reflected in the new Parliament, in which PC representation was reduced to only two seats. The the BQ, with 54 seats, became the official opposition party, and declared that it would pursue the achievement of full sovereignty for Québec. Kim Campbell, who lost her seat in the federal Parliament, resigned as PC leader and was succeeded by Jean Charest.

The new Liberal Government set out to implement an economic recovery programme. Substantial reductions in defence expenditure were announced, as well as a C $6,000m. job-creation scheme, and in December 1993, following the renegotiation of certain treaty protocols with the US Government, NAFTA, which had received Canadian legislative ratification in June, was formally promulgated, to take effect from January 1994. The Liberals were re-elected at general elections held in June 1997, although with a reduced majority in the House of Commons. The RP replaced the BQ as the main opposition party.

The issue of separatism in Québec was reopened by provincial elections held in September 1994, in which the PQ, led by Jacques Parizeau, defeated the incumbent Liberal administration by a margin of 44.7% to 44.3%. Parizeau, whose campaign had included an undertaking that a new referendum on independence would be held during 1995, was supported at federal level by the BQ, although the federal Government asserted that considerable uncertainty was felt within Québec over the possible economic consequences of secession. In June 1995 the PQ and the BQ, together with a smaller provincial nationalist group, the Action Démocratique du Québec, agreed a framework for the province's proposed independence and in mid-September the referendum received provincial legislative approval.

In the referendum, held on 30 October 1995, the sovereignty proposals were defeated by a margin of only 50,000 votes; in a turn-out of 93% of eligible voters, 49.4% were in favour of the sovereignty plan, and 50.6% opposed. Parizeau announced his intention to resign. In February 1996 Lucien Bouchard, having resigned from the federal House of Commons and relinquished the leadership of the BQ, succeeded Parizeau as Premier of Québec and leader of the PQ. Bouchard indicated that his administration viewed the sovereignty issue as less urgent than the resolution of Québec's immediate economic problems. In September 1997 Bouchard refused to attend a conference of provincial premiers and territorial commissioners, at which a seven-point framework on Canadian unity was agreed. The conference, held in Calgary, recognized the 'unique character' of Québec, but asserted that any future change in the constitutional powers of one province should be applicable to all prov-

inces. By June 1998 the resultant 'Calgary Declaration' had been endorsed by the legislatures of all provinces except Québec.

The Supreme Court, which had been requested in February 1998 to rule on the legality of a unilateral secession by Québec, declared in August that no province had the right, in constitutional or international law, to leave the federation without prior negotiations with the federal and provincial governments, and that secession would require the approval of the federal legislature, together with that of seven of the 10 provinces. It was further stated that an obligation would exist for negotiation with Québec if a clear majority of its voters expressed a wish to leave the federation.

In March 1998 Jean Charest resigned as leader of the PC, to accept the leadership of the Liberal Party of Québec, which had been perceived as losing popular support for its anti-separatist policy. At a provincial legislative election in November, however, an unexpected rise in support for the Liberals awarded them 43.7% of the popular vote, against 42.7% for the PQ, which, none the less, obtained 76 seats in the 125-seat legislature, compared with 48 seats for the Liberals. Following the election, Bouchard conceded that the PQ had failed to attract sufficient support to merit an early referendum.

In March 2000 members of the RP voted to form the Canadian Alliance (CA), an organization conceived at a convention held in September 1998 with the aim of uniting the major right-wing parties. The PC declined to join the CA, although a number of that party's prominent members chose to do so. Deborah Grey, formerly of the RP, became the temporary Leader of the Opposition, pending a formal contest for the leadership of the CA. In July Stockwell Day, a former PC member, was elected leader of the CA, defeating Preston Manning, the last leader of the RP. Day was elected to the House of Commons at a by-election in September.

In October 2000 Chrétien announced that a general election would be held on 27 November, despite his Government's mandate being valid until June 2002. At the election, Chrétien's Liberals received 41% of the votes cast and won 172 of the 301 seats in the House of Commons. The CA secured 26% of the votes cast and 66 parliamentary seats, while the BQ obtained 38 seats, the NDP 13 seats and the PC 12. The results demonstrated an increasing political polarization between the country's east and centre and its west—the CA won 50 of the 60 seats available in the two westernmost provinces, British Columbia and Alberta, but only two in Ontario (the Liberals being elected in 100 of the 103 constituencies in that province).

In January 2001 Bouchard announced his resignation as Premier of Québec, once a successor had been elected. He also resigned as a member of the provincial legislature and as leader of the PQ, stating that he had failed in his intention to achieve independence for the province and that he lacked both popular and party support. The BQ had lost several seats in Québec to the Liberals at the November 2000 federal general election and opinion polls continued to show a decline in support for the PQ's policy on independence. Also in January 2001 Lorne Calvert was elected Premier of Saskatchewan following the resignation of Roy Romanow. In early February Roger Grimes succeeded Brian Tobin as Premier of Newfoundland, following Tobin's appointment to the federal Government. (In December Newfoundland was officially renamed Newfoundland and Labrador.) In early March Bernard Landry of the PQ, hitherto Minister of Finance in the province, was elected the new Premier of Québec.

In May 2001, at provincial elections in British Columbia, the NDP, which had been in government since 1991, retained just two seats in the 79-seat Legislative Assembly. The Liberal Party secured the remaining 77 seats. The provincial Liberal leader, Gordon Campbell, became Premier.

In mid-July 2001, following several months of internal dissent in the party owing to its poor performance in the 2000 legislative elections, 13 CA members resigned from the party in protest at Day's refusal to resign the leadership. Day had offered to step down temporarily if he could appoint his successor, an offer that had been rejected by CA members. The dissident MPs formed a new parliamentary party, the Democratic Representative Caucus, which, in September, formed a coalition in the House of Representatives with the PC. Day eventually resigned in December, and stood for re-election in March 2002, but was defeated by Stephen Harper. In the same month Ernie Eves succeeded Mike Harris as Premier of Ontario.

Throughout 2002 the Government was subject to accusations of corruption. In May Chrétien dismissed the Minister of Defence, Art Eggleton, after it was revealed that Eggleton had awarded a C $36,000 contract in his ministry to a former girl-friend. At the same time, Don Boudria, who had been appointed Minister of Public Works and Services in January, was moved back to his former post as Leader of the Government in the House of Commons, a move widely regarded as a demotion, after he stayed in the holiday home of the head of a company that had been awarded lucrative government contracts. In June the Minister of Finance, Paul Martin, widely considered as a poten-tial successor to Chrétien, was dismissed and replaced by Deputy Prime Minister John Manley. It was widely believed that Martin, a longtime rival of Chrétien, had been planning to launch a leadership challenge. In August Chrétien announced that he would stand down as Prime Minister in February 2004, and pass the premiership to another member of the Liberal Party. In October the Government faced further criticism when the Solicitor-General, Lawrence MacAulay, resigned following accusations that he had been involved in the awarding of federal grants to a community college headed by his brother. He was replaced by Wayne Easter.

Legislative elections were held in 10 of the 13 provinces and territories in late 2002 and throughout 2003. Following elections in the Yukon Territory in November 2002, Dennis Fentie of the Yukon Party replaced Pat Duncan of the Liberal Party as Premier. In April 2003 Charest became Premier of Québec when the Liberal Party secured 76 seats in the 125-member legis-lature in provincial elections, compared with 45 seats for the PQ. The NDP increased its majority in Manitoba at elections in June and Gary Doer retained the premiership. In the same month the PC was re-elected in New Brunswick, although with a reduced majority. In August the PC retained office in Nova Scotia, although Premier John Hamm presided over a minority Govern-ment. In September the PC won a third successive term in office in Prince Edward Island and Patrick Binns retained the pre-miership. In October the Liberals assumed control of Ontario from the PC, taking 72 seats, compared with 24 for the PC; Dalton McGuinty was appointed provincial Premier. Later in the same month the PC assumed power from the Liberals in elections in Newfoundland and Labrador; Danny Williams became Premier. Elections were also held in Saskatchewan in early November, in which the NDP retained a narrow majority in the provincial legislature. Elections were held later that month in the Northwest Territories; Stephen Kakfwi, the incumbent Premier and Chairman of the territory's Executive Council, did not stand for re-election, and Joseph Handley was sworn in as his successor in the following month.

In April 2003 the World Health Organization (WHO) declared that travel to Toronto was inadvisable as a result of an outbreak of Severe Acute Respiratory Syndrome (SARS), a previously unknown atypical pneumonia that had originated in eastern Asia. Although WHO rescinded its travel advice at the end of that month, the city remained on WHO's list of areas affected by the disease until early July. A total of 41 people had died of SARS in the Toronto area by mid-July.

In June 2003 Ontario's Court of Appeal ruled that a definition of marriage which excluded same-sex couples was discrim-inatory and unconstitutional; one week later Prime Minister Chrétien announced that the federal Government would pre-pare draft legislation to define marriage as 'a heterosexual or homosexual union'. He also referred the issue to the federal Supreme Court, which ruled in favour of the Ontario ruling in December 2004, thus clearing the way for the Government to prepare draft legislation on the issue. (In May 2003 British Columbia's Court of Appeal also had approved same-sex mar-riages.)

In September 2003 the Liberal Party nominated Paul Martin as the successor to party leader Chrétien, who was due to retire in early 2004. However, Chrétien stood down as premier early, and on 12 December Paul Martin succeeded him as Prime Minister and as party leader. Martin subsequently carried out a wide-ranging reallocation of government portfolios; notable appointments included Anne McLennan as Deputy Prime Min-ister and Ralph Goodale to the Ministry of Finance, while Bill Graham remained Minister of Foreign Affairs. Also in December the PC and CA announced that they had merged to form a new party, the Conservative Party of Canada; in March 2004 Ste-phen Harper was elected party leader.

In February 2004 a report by the office of the Auditor-General concluded that the Government had misappropriated funds during a state campaign intended to promote national unity in Québec in 1997–2001. It was alleged that contracts worth some C $100m. had been awarded to advertising companies in Québec

with links to the Liberal Party, and that some of these contracts were false. Prime Minister Martin denied any involvement in the affair, which coincided with his time as Minister of Finance in the Chrétien Government, and ordered a public inquiry into the scandal. Nevertheless, the affair was widely believed to have affected support for the Liberal Party in the general election that was held on 28 June. The incumbent party won 43.8% of the votes cast, obtaining 135 seats in the newly enlarged 308-seat House of Commons, compared with the 172 seats it had secured in the previous election. As a result, the Liberals failed to obtain a parliamentary majority, and Prime Minister Martin was forced to form a minority Government. The Conservatives won 32.1% of the votes cast and a total of 99 parliamentary seats, while the BQ increased its legislative representation to 54 seats (from 33 seats). The NDP secured 19 seats and the one remaining seat was won by an independent candidate. Voter turn-out was the lowest ever, at 60.9% of the electorate.

On 22 November 2004 a provincial election was held in Alberta, in which the Conservatives maintained their majority, albeit a reduced one, winning 62 seats in the 83-member legis-lature. The Liberals took 16 seats and the NDP four, while the Alberta Alliance Party won its first seat. Ralph Klein was returned to office as provincial premier.

In mid-January 2005 Prime Minister Martin carried out his first reallocation of cabinet portfolios after the Minister of Citizenship and Immigration, Judy Sgro, was forced to resign over allegations that she had abused her ministerial position. An investigation was begun by the federal ethics commissioner. Guiseppe (Joseph) Volpe, hitherto Minister of Human Resources and Skills Development, succeeded her, while Lucienne Robil-lard, the Minister of Intergovernmental Affairs, took on Volpe's former portfolio.

The question of land treaty claims by Canada's indigenous peoples came to prominence in the latter part of the 20th century, when disputes over land rights arose in Ontario, Man-itoba and, most notably, Québec, where armed confrontations took place in 1990 between the civil authorities and militant indigenous groups. In September 1988, following 13 years of negotiations, the federal Government formally transferred to indigenous ownership an area covering 673,000 sq km in the Northwest Territories. In the Yukon Territory, an area of 41,000 sq km (representing 8.6% of the Territory's land) was trans-ferred to indigenous control. At the same time, debate had begun to intensify in the formulation of a new constitutional status for the Northwest Territories, in which a population of only 58,000 (of which Inuit and other indigenous peoples comprised about one-half) occupied an area comprising one-third of Canada's land mass. In December 1991 specific terms for the creation of a semi-autonomous Nunavut Territory, covering an area of 2.2m. sq km, to the east of a boundary running northwards from the Saskatchewan–Manitoba border, were agreed by Inuit repre-sentatives and the federal Government, and in May 1992 a plebiscite on a proposal to divide the Northwest Territories into two self-governing units was approved by the territories' resi-dents.

A formal agreement to settle all outstanding land treaty claims was finalized by the federal Government in May 1993, providing for Nunavut to come into official existence on 1 April 1999. Elections to a new, 17-seat Legislature for Nunavut, to be located at Iqaluit, were held in February 1999, and the new Territorial Government took office in April. In November 1996 an official inquiry into the social and economic condition of Canada's indigenous peoples recommended the creation of a new chamber of the federal Parliament to function as a permanent commission to review issues affecting the indigenous groups, and that these communities receive increased powers of self-government. In December 1997 the Supreme Court awarded legal title to 57,000 sq km of ancestral land to two native groups in British Columbia, and in the following month the federal Government offered a formal apology to all native groups for past mistreatment and injustices. The principle of 'aboriginal title', established by the Supreme Court ruling, was again exercised in April 1999 in British Columbia under the Nisga'a Agreement. The Agreement transferred some 2,000 sq km of land, together with substantial powers of self-government and C $196m., to 5,500 Nisga'a people; in return they ceded their wider aboriginal title. In August 2003 Chrétien signed an agree-ment that would transfer powers of self-government and 39,000 sq km of land to some 3,000 Tlicho people in the Northwest Territories; the agreement was due to be ratified by the federal Parliament and by the territorial legislature in 2005. An agreement worth C $350m., transferring powers of self-government to 5,300 Inuit people in north-west Labrador, was due to be signed at the end of January 2005.

Recent administrations have sought to emphasize Canada's independence from the USA in matters of foreign policy, while continuing the increased co-operation in areas such as trade and environmental protection. In the last two decades of the 20th century a number of bilateral environmental agreements were signed, including accords on gaseous emissions, both domestically and in the USA (which move northwards into Canada to produce environmentally destructive 'acid rain') and the elimination of industrial pollution from the Great Lakes, in conjunction with the implementation of a number of domestic environmental-improvement programmes. In 1997, at the third Conference of the Parties to the Framework Convention on Climate Change (see World Meteorological Organization, see p. 136), held in Kyoto, Japan, Canada undertook to implement reductions of its emissions of 'greenhouse gases' to 6% below 1990 levels by the year 2012. In July 2001, at the International Summit on Climate Change in Bonn, Germany, the Canadian Government pledged to ratify the Kyoto Protocol, although it had refused to do so the previous November at a summit in The Hague, Netherlands. The then Minister of Natural Resources, Ralph Goodale, criticized the USA for refusing to commit to reductions. In December 2002 the Canadian Government ratified the Protocol, despite opposition from the gas and petroleum industries and the province of Alberta, which threatened to challenge the legality of ratification in the Supreme Court. Canada assumed a leading role in the establishment, with seven other circumpolar countries, of the Arctic Council (see p. 372), which commenced operation in September 1996. The aims of the Council include the protection of the environment of the polar region, the formation of co-ordinated policies governing its future, and the safeguarding of the interests of its indigenous population groups.

There have been recurrent disagreements between Canada and France concerning the boundary of disputed waters near the French-controlled islands of Saint Pierre and Miquelon, off the southern coast of Newfoundland and Labrador. In June 1992 an international arbitration tribunal presented its report, generally regarded as favourable to Canada, and in December 1994 the two countries agreed a 10-year accord on the allocation of fishing rights around the islands. In September 2001 France and Canada held talks on energy exploration in the waters off Saint Pierre and Miquelon; geologists believed there were large petroleum and natural gas deposits between the islands and Newfoundland and Labrador and Nova Scotia.

In December 1992 Canada and the EC (European Community, now European Union—EU) announced the resolution of a seven-year disagreement over the allocation of fishing rights to European commercial fleets in the north-west Atlantic Ocean. In 1994, however, the EU unilaterally awarded itself almost 70% of the internationally agreed quota of Greenland halibut (also known as turbot) caught in the north-west Atlantic fishing grounds. This action was not recognized by other members of the Northwest Atlantic Fishing Organization (NAFO), and was vigorously contested by the Canadian Government, which declared that it would act to prevent EU fishing trawlers (principally from Spain and Portugal) from overfishing the already seriously depleted stocks of Greenland halibut. It was also announced that Canada was extending its maritime jurisdiction beyond its Exclusive Economic Zone (EEZ), already extending 200 nautical miles (370 km) from the coastline. This action was rejected by the EU as contrary to international law. (In November 2003 Canada ratified the UN Convention on the Law of the Sea which establishes the limit of the EEZ as being 200 nautical miles from the coastline.)

In February 1995 the Canadian Government warned the EU that force would be used if necessary to ensure that total catches by EU vessels did not exceed 3,400 tons of the NAFO-agreed world Greenland halibut quota of 27,000 tons. On 6 March the Canadian Government declared a 60-day moratorium on all trawling for this fish in the north-west Atlantic, and three days later its enforcement vessels fired on and impounded a Spanish trawler fishing in international waters. The EU responded by suspending all official political contacts with Canada, pending the release of the trawler. The impasse was eased by the release of the trawler on 15 March, when it was agreed to initiate quota allocation negotiations. Divisions began to emerge within the EU when the British Government refused to endorse an EU protest against these interceptions, and declared its support of

Canada's desire to conserve north-west Atlantic fishing stocks. A resolution was eventually reached in mid-April, under which Canada and EU countries each agreed to accept 41% of the 1996 Greenland halibut quota. It was agreed that independent observers would monitor the activities of trawlers in the north-west Atlantic fishing zone. However, during the negotiation of an accord in June 1996 governing bilateral relations between Canada and the EU, the Canadian Government rejected a Spanish request that it suspend the enforcement of its fishing regulations outside Canadian territorial waters. In early 2002 the Canadian Government imposed a ban on all vessels from Estonia and the Faeroe Islands from entering Canadian ports, accusing those fleets of violating NAFO-agreed shrimp quotas off the eastern coast of the country. In September the Government extended the ban to any foreign vessel which violated NAFO-agreed quotas. In December the ban on the Estonian fleet was lifted. In January–October 2004 Canadian officials boarded more than 100 foreign vessels and issued six summonses for illegal fishing.

Canada, which maintains significant economic and commercial links with Cuba and operates a policy of 'constructive engagement' in its relations with that country, adopted a prominent role in international opposition to efforts, initiated by the US Government in March 1996, to penalize investors whose business in any way involves property in Cuba that was confiscated from US citizens following the 1959 revolution. The imposition of these measures, known as the Helms-Burton Act, led in July 1996 to the exclusion from the USA of nine Canadian businessmen involved in nickel-mining operations in Cuba. The Canadian Government responded by introducing legislation prohibiting Canadian companies from compliance with the Helms-Burton Act, and refused to recognize foreign court rulings arising from the Act. With Mexico, which also conducts significant trade with Cuba, Canada co-ordinated a joint challenge to the US Government through NAFTA dispute procedures. In November 1996 Canada actively promoted a resolution by the UN General Assembly condemning the US trade sanctions against Cuba, and in the same month joined the EU in a complaint against the embargo to the World Trade Organization (WTO, see p. 357). In April 1998, following an official visit to Cuba by Chrétien, the Canadian Government signed a series of co-operation agreements with Cuba. However, relations between the two countries subsequently experienced a sharp decline, owing to increasing official and public concern in Canada at the Cuban Government's human rights record, particularly in relation to the treatment of political prisoners. In July 1999 the Canadian Government stated that it would implement no further assistance programmes to Cuba that did not clearly further the protection of human rights, and it was indicated that Canada would not support, or encourage other countries to support, the admission of Cuba to the Organization of American States (see p. 319).

Relations with the USA improved in June 1999 following the resolution of a long-standing disagreement over the demarcation of salmon-fishing rights off the Pacific coast. However, in September 2000 a dispute arose over the USA's threat to impose export tariffs on Canadian timber which, the USA claimed, was subsidized by the Canadian Government, and which undercut the price of US timber. Canada requested a WTO investigation into US anti-subsidy policies, after the USA imposed duties of 32% on softwood lumber imports from Canada in response. In August 2001 Canada won a preliminary victory at the WTO, which adopted a report agreeing that the Government was not subsidizing exports. Canada hoped to remove US duties and replace an earlier quota agreement, which expired in March 2001, with a system based on free trade; however, the USA imposed tariffs of 27% on softwood lumber imports from Canada in May 2002 in order to protect its own timber industry. Negotiations to resolve the issue failed, and in January 2004 the Canadian Government rejected a US proposal to remove the duties in exchange for quotas limiting Canadian exports to the US market. The USA continued to refuse to remove the duties and in August the WTO ruled that Canada could retaliate with trade sanctions. In December Canada was in discussion with eight other WTO members, including the EU and Japan, over co-ordinating trade sanctions against the USA.

Following the terrorist attacks on the USA on 11 September 2001, Canada and the USA increased co-operation on intelligence and security matters: under the 'Smart Border Declaration' signed by the two countries in December, 400 US National Guards were to be deployed at 43 crossings along both sides of the 6,400-km (4,000-mile) Canadian–US border. In the same month extensive anti-terrorist legislation was also introduced. Some 750 Canadian troops were deployed in Afghanistan in February 2002 as part of the US-led international forces present in that country. The Canadian contingent assisted in the continuing military campaign against the militant Islamist al-Qa'ida (Base) organization, suspected of orchestrating the attacks on the USA, although all Canadian forces had returned home by November 2002. However, in August 2003 around 1,900 Canadian troops were sent to Afghanistan as part of a NATO-led mission to protect the interim Government there and suppress militant resistance. The federal Government promised some C $300m. for the reconstruction of Iraq following the US-led invasion and occupation of that country and the fall of the Iraqi President, Saddam Hussain, in 2003. In January 2004 US President George W. Bush announced that Canadian companies would be allowed to tender bids for reconstruction projects in Iraq, worth an estimated US $18,600m.; the US Administration had previously declared that Canada, among other traditional allies, would not be invited to participate in such projects, following its opposition to the invasion of Iraq.

In the mid-1990s Canada actively sought to obtain an international ban on the manufacture and use of landmines. At a conference held in Ottawa in December 1997, Canada became the first signatory of the Ottawa Convention, a treaty agreed by 121 countries, undertaking to discontinue the use of these armaments and providing for the destruction of existing stockpiles. However, by early 2005 the USA, the Russian Federation and the People's Republic of China had not become parties to the agreement. Humanitarian concerns remained at the forefront of Canadian foreign policy: in 1999–2005 the Government contributed forces to humanitarian and peace-keeping operations in Kosovo, East Timor, Sierra Leone, the former Yugoslav republic of Macedonia and the Democratic Republic of Congo. In September 2000 the Canadian Government strongly urged governments of creditor nations to accelerate programmes of debt relief for heavily indebted poor countries—in December the Government announced a moratorium on debt repayments due from 11 such countries, with effect from January 2001. In June 2002 Canada hosted the G-8 summit of industrialized countries, in Kananaskis, British Columbia. Canada imposed a range of economic sanctions against Zimbabwe in May 2003 following the harassment of its citizens in that country, including its High Commissioner.

Government

Canada is a federal parliamentary state. Under the Constitution Act 1982, executive power is vested in the British monarch, as Head of State, and exercisable by her representative, the Governor-General, whom she appoints on the advice of the Canadian Prime Minister. The federal Parliament comprises the Head of State, a nominated Senate (a maximum of 112 members, appointed on a regional basis) and a House of Commons (308 members, elected by universal adult suffrage for single-member constituencies). A Parliament may last no longer than five years. The Governor-General appoints the Prime Minister and, on the latter's recommendation, other ministers to form the Cabinet. The Prime Minister should have the confidence of the House of Commons, to which the Cabinet is responsible. Canada comprises 10 provinces (each with a Lieutenant-Governor and a legislature, which may last no longer than five years, from which a Premier is chosen), and three territories constituted by Act of Parliament.

Defence

Canada co-operates with the USA in the defence of North America and is a member of NATO. Military service is voluntary. In August 2004 the armed forces numbered 52,300: army 19,300, navy 9,000, air force 13,500, and 10,500 not identified by service. There were 36,900 reserve troops. The federal Government's defence budget for 2004 was C $13,300m.

Economic Affairs

In 2003, according to estimates by the World Bank, Canada's gross national income (GNI), measured at average 2001–03 prices, was US $814,602m., equivalent to US $23,930 per head (or $29,740 on an international purchasing-power parity basis). The country's population increased at an average annual rate of 1.0% in 1990–2003, while gross domestic product (GDP) per head increased, in real terms, by an average of 1.7% per year. Overall GDP increased, in real terms, at an average rate of 2.7% per year in 1990–2003; GDP increased by 2.0% in 2003.

Agriculture (including forestry and fishing) contributed 2.2% of GDP (in constant 1997 prices) in 2003 and the sector (excluding forestry and fishing) engaged 2.1% of the economically active population in 2004. The principal crops are wheat, barley and other cereals, which, together with livestock production (chiefly cattle and pigs) and timber, provide an important source of export earnings. In 2003 the cattle industry was affected by the discovery of bovine spongiform encephalopathy (BSE—commonly known as 'mad cow disease') in Alberta; the USA, Japan and Australia subsequently suspended the import of Canadian beef. Canada is a leading world exporter of forest products and of fish and seafood. The production of furs is also important. In April–May 2004 the Government approved a cull of 350,000 harp seals. In real terms, the GDP of the agricultural sector decreased at an average annual rate of 0.1% in 1990–2001. Agricultural GDP decreased by 3.2% in 2002, but increased by 9.0% in 2003.

Industry (including mining, manufacturing, construction and power) provided 28.9% of GDP (in constant 1997 prices) in 2003, and the sector (including forestry and fishing) employed 23.1% of the economically active population in 2004. Industrial GDP increased, in real terms, at an average annual rate of 2.2% in 1990–2001. Industrial GDP increased by 1.8% in 2002 and by 1.5% in 2003.

Mining provided 3.7% of GDP (in constant 1997 prices) in 2003, but employed only 1.9% of the economically active population in 2004 (together with forestry, fishing, petroleum and gas). Canada is a major world producer of zinc, asbestos, nickel, potash and uranium. Gold, silver, iron, copper, cobalt and lead are also exploited. There are considerable reserves of petroleum and natural gas in Alberta, off the Atlantic coast and in the Canadian Arctic islands. The GDP of the mining sector increased, in real terms, at an average rate of 0.1% in 1997–2002. Mining GDP decreased by 1.3% in 2002, but increased by 6.5% in 2003.

Manufacturing contributed 17.1% of GDP (in constant 1997 prices) in 2003, and employed 14.2% of the economically active population, in 2004. The principal branches of manufacturing in 2003, measured by the value of shipments, were transport equipment (accounting for 22.2% of the total), food products (11.6%), chemical products (7.5%), paper and allied products (6.1%), primary metal industries (6.2%) and wood industries (5.7%). The GDP of the sector increased, in real terms, at an average rate of 2.8% per year in 1990–2001. Manufacturing GDP increased by 1.9% in 2002 and by 0.1% in 2003.

Energy is derived principally from hydroelectric power (which provided 56.7% of the electricity supply in 2001) and from geothermal and nuclear power-stations. In 2002 Canada's total energy production (including nuclear energy) totalled an estimated 562,935 kWh. In 2003 energy products accounted for 15.1% of Canada's exports and 5.7% of imports.

Services provided 68.9% of GDP (in constant 1997 prices) in 2003, and engaged 74.8% of the economically active population, in 2004. The combined GDP of the service sectors increased, in real terms, at an average rate of 3.0% per year in 1990–2001. Services GDP increased by 4.1% in 2002 and by 2.5% in 2003.

In 2002 Canada recorded a visible trade surplus of US $41,513m., and there was a surplus of US $17,628m. on the current account of the balance of payments. In 2003 the USA accounted for 82.6% of Canada's total exports and 70.2% of total imports; the countries of the European Union (EU, see p. 217) and Japan were also important trading partners. The principal exports in that year were machinery and equipment, motor vehicles and parts and industrial goods. The principal imports were machinery and equipment, motor vehicles and parts and industrial goods. In January 1989 a free trade agreement with the USA entered into force, whereby virtually all remaining trade tariffs imposed between the two countries were to be eliminated over a 10-year period. Negotiations with the USA and Mexico, aimed at the eventual creation of a full North American free trade area, concluded in December 1992 with the signing of an agreement. The North American Free Trade Agreement (NAFTA, see p. 299) entered into operation on 1 January 1994. Since the implementation of NAFTA, however, disagreements have persisted between Canada and the USA over alleged violations of the Agreement by the US Government in relation to bilateral trade in softwood lumber, wheat and other commodities. At a third Summit of the Americas, held in Québec in April 2001, a timetable for a proposed Free Trade Area of the Americas, to take effect by 2005, was agreed upon. Negotiations commenced in late 2002, and continued in 2005.

Since the mid-1990s the Canadian Government has implemented measures aimed at expanding trade in the Far East, notably with the People's Republic of China, the Republic of Korea, Indonesia and Viet Nam. In November 1996 Canada finalized a trade agreement with Chile, which, from June 1997, phased out most customs duties by 2002. In October 1998 negotiations began with the members of the European Free Trade Association (EFTA, see p. 214) for the creation of a free trade area, while Canada has also pursued efforts to develop similar arrangements with the EU. Bilateral agreements on trade, communications and the prevention of financial crime were signed with Mexico in 2003.

For the financial year 2003/04, there was a consolidated budget surplus of C $9,100m. The annual rate of inflation averaged 2.1% in 1990–2004. Consumer prices increased by an average of2.8% in 2003 and by 1.9% in 2004. The rate of unemployment averaged 7.6% in 2003 and 7.2% in 2004.

Many sectors of Canadian industry rely heavily on foreign investment. Following the international recession of the mid-1970s, Canada's average annual rate of inflation remained above 4% throughout the 1980s. A series of budgetary deficits, attributable largely to high interest rates, prevented a sustained economic recovery until the mid-1990s, when an emphasis on fiscal stringency led, in part, in August 1996, to the country's first current-account surplus in the balance of payments since 1984. The recovery was further aided by low rates of domestic inflation and by the beneficial effects of NAFTA on Canadian export sales to the USA, and continued strongly into the early 2000s. In 2001 Canada and Mexico agreed to eliminate tariffs on goods worth an annual US $1,950m. Proposals for the 2003/04 budget included provisions for increased expenditure on health care—some C $74,300m. over the following 10 years—and for reductions in corporate and personal rates of taxation—a five-year plan worth C $100,000m., implemented in 2004/05. At the same time, a budgetary surplus was achieved for the seventh successive year. In late 2001 the rate of inflation fell below 1%; although by the end of 2003 it had risen to 2.8%, it fell again, to 1.9%, by the end of 2004. GDP growth in 2003 was 2.0%. Growth was estimated at 3.0% in 2004 and was forecast to increase by 3.2% in 2005. The Government projected a combined budgetary surplus of C $29,500m. for the period 2004–10. Eleven of the 13 provinces and territories reported a budgetary deficit in 2003/04. The predominance of trade with the USA (in which Canada, assisted by currency fluctuations favourable to its exports, maintained a substantial surplus in the early 2000s) compensated for deficits with other major trading partners, including the EU and Japan, and allowed Canada to record substantial trade surpluses in the early 2000s. However, in spite of its strong recovery, the Canadian economy remains vulnerable to adverse movements in world prices for its major exports of raw materials. In 2003 the strength of the Canadian dollar also had a negative effect on exports. The Canadian airline industry was particularly badly affected by the terrorist attacks on the USA in September 2001; in November of that year Canada 3000, the country's second largest airline, ceased operations, and the national carrier Air Canada reported heavy losses and made 9,000 staff redundant. The ban on the import of Canadian beef in several countries in 2003 following the discovery of one cow infected with BSE in Alberta also had an adverse affect on the cattle industry. In late January 2005 a further case of BSE was identified in Alberta.

Education

Education policy is a provincial responsibility, and the period of compulsory school attendance varies. French-speaking students are entitled by law, in some provinces, to instruction in French. Primary education is from the age of five or six years to 13–14, followed by three to five years at secondary or high school. In 1999/2000 some 5,397,000 pupils attended primary and secondary schools. In 2002 there were 58 universities in the country. Total government budgetary expenditure on education totalled C $68,579m. (14.0% of total spending) in 2003/04.

Public Holidays*

2005: 1 January (New Year's Day), 25 March (Good Friday), 28 March (Easter Monday), 23 May (Victoria Day), 1 July (Canada Day), 5 September (Labour Day), 10 October (Thanksgiving Day), 11 November (Remembrance Day), 25 December (Christmas Day), 26 December (Boxing Day).

2006: 1 January (New Year's Day), 14 April (Good Friday), 17 April (Easter Monday), 22 May (Victoria Day), 1 July (Canada Day), 4 September (Labour Day), 9 October (Thanksgiving Day), 11 November (Remembrance Day), 25 December (Christmas Day), 26 December (Boxing Day).

*Standard public holidays comprise the listed days, together with any other day so proclaimed by individual provinces.

Weights and Measures

The metric system is in force.

Statistical Survey

Source (unless otherwise stated): Statistics Canada, Ottawa, ON K1A 0T6; tel. (613) 951-8116; fax (613) 951-0581; internet www.statcan.ca.

Area and Population

AREA, POPULATION AND DENSITY

Area (sq km)	
Land	9,093,507
Inland water	891,163
Total	9,984,670*
Population (census results)†	
14 May 1996	28,846,761
15 May 2001	
Males‡	14,706,850
Females‡	15,300,245
Total	30,007,094
Population (official postcensal estimates at 1 July)	
2002	31,414,000
2003	31,629,700
2004	31,946,300
Density (per sq km) at 1 July 2004	3.5§

* 3,855,101 sq miles.
† Excluding census data for one or more incompletely enumerated Indian reserves or Indian settlements and excluding adjustment for under-enumeration.
‡ Figures are rounded to nearest 5.
§ Land area only.

PROVINCES AND TERRITORIES

(census results, 15 May 2001)

	Land area (sq km)*	Population†	Capital
Provinces:			
Alberta	642,317	2,974,807	Edmonton
British Columbia .	925,186	3,907,738	Victoria
Manitoba . .	553,556	1,119,583	Winnipeg
New Brunswick .	71,450	729,498	Fredericton
Newfoundland‡ .	373,872	512,930	St John's
Nova Scotia . .	53,338	908,007	Halifax
Ontario	917,741	11,410,046	Toronto
Prince Edward			
Island	5,660	135,294	Charlottetown
Québec	1,365,128	7,237,479	Québec
Saskatchewan . .	591,670	978,933	Regina
Territories:			
Northwest			
Territories . .	1,183,085	37,360	Yellowknife
Nunavut Territory§	1,936,113	26,745	Iqaluit
Yukon Territory .	474,391	28,674	Whitehorse
Total	9,093,507	30,007,094	—

* Official estimates at 1 July 2003; the total land area recorded by the preliminary results of the 2001 census was 9,012,112 sq km.
† Excluding census data for one or more incompletely enumerated Indian reserves or Indian settlements.
‡ Newfoundland and Labrador from December 2001.
§ Formerly part of Northwest Territories. Constituted as a separate Territory with effect from 1 April 1999.

PRINCIPAL METROPOLITAN AREAS

(census results, 15 May 2001)

Toronto	4,682,897	London	432,451
Montréal* . . .	3,426,350	Kitchener . . .	414,284
Vancouver . . .	1,986,965	St Catharines–	
		Niagara . . .	377,009
Ottawa–Hull			
(capital) . .	1,063,664	Halifax	359,183
Edmonton . . .	951,395	Victoria	311,902
Calgary	937,845	Windsor	307,877
Québec	682,757	Oshawa	296,298
Winnipeg . . .	671,274	Saskatoon . . .	225,927
Hamilton	662,401		

* Excluding census data for one or more incompletely enumerated Indian reserves or Indian settlements.

BIRTHS, MARRIAGES AND DEATHS

	Registered live births*		Registered marriages†		Registered deaths*	
	Number	Rate (per 1,000)	Number	Rate (per 1,000)	Number	Rate (per 1,000)
1998/99 .	338,295	11.2	152,581	5.1	217,632	7.2
1999/2000 .	336,912	11.0	155,742	5.1	217,229	7.1
2000/01 .	327,107	10.6	157,395	5.1	219,114	7.1
2001/02 .	328,155	10.5	146,618	4.7	220,494	7.1
2002/03 .	329,307	10.4	147,634‡	n.a.	224,702	7.1
2003/04 .	330,803	10.4	148,752‡	n.a.	233,807	7.3

* Including Canadian residents temporarily in the USA but excluding US residents temporarily in Canada.
† Figures refer to the first of the two years, from January to December.
‡ Preliminary figures.

Expectation of life (WHO estimates, years at birth): 79.8 (males 77.2; females 82.3) in 2002 (Source: WHO, *World Health Report*).

IMMIGRATION

Origin	2000	2001	2002
Africa	20,033	23,451	22,145
Asia	140,138	155,580	141,095
India	26,114	27,870	28,906
Philippines	10,126	12,927	11,030
Europe	42,950	43,226	38,796
France	4,348	4,416	3,963
United Kingdom . . .	4,823	5,566	4,937
North and Central America . .	16,047	17,598	15,945
USA	5,831	5,915	5,304
Caribbean (West Indies) .	7,156	8,546	7,589
South America	6,780	8,499	8,829
Total (incl. others)	227,363	250,415	228,830

ECONOMICALLY ACTIVE POPULATION*

(annual averages, '000 persons aged 15 years and over)

	2002	2003	2004
Agriculture	330.0	339.5	334.3
Forestry, fishing, mining, petroleum and gas	272.0	289.7	297.8
Utilities	131.5	131.5	131.4
Construction	882.8	931.4	983.7
Manufacturing	2,326.2	2,294.0	2,282.4
Trade	2,430.0	2,460.7	2,501.8
Transportation and warehousing .	756.2	766.8	800.5
Finance, insurance, real estate and leasing	895.6	936.2	983.8
Professional, scientific and technical services	993.3	999.5	1,022.6
Management, administrative and other support	591.4	612.2	628.1
Educational services	1,015.9	1,050.3	1,055.0
Health care and social assistance .	1,607.0	1,684.3	1,750.0
Information, culture and recreation	704.8	704.5	720.9
Accommodation and food services .	1,003.9	1,022.3	1,011.7
Public administration	778.0	815.2	820.6
Other services	693.2	707.9	695.9
Total employed	15,411.8	15,746.0	16,020.5
Unemployed	1,277.6	1,300.9	1,248.8
Total labour force	16,689.4	17,046.8	17,269.2
Males	8,989.8	9,135.9	9,224.1
Females	7,699.6	7,910.9	8,045.2

* Figures exclude military personnel, inmates of institutions, residents of the Yukon, Northwest and Nunavut Territories, and Indian Reserves.

Health and Welfare

KEY INDICATORS

Total fertility rate (children per woman, 2002)	1.5
Under-5 mortality rate (per 1,000 live births, 2003) . . .	6
HIV/AIDS (% of persons aged 15–49, 2001)	0.3
Physicians (per 1,000 head, 2000)	2.1
Hospital beds (per 1,000 head, 1999)	3.9
Health expenditure (2001): US $ per head (PPP)	2,792
Health expenditure (2001): % of GDP	9.5
Health expenditure (2001): public (% of total)	70.8
Access to water (% of persons, 2002)	100
Access to sanitation (% of persons, 2002)	100
Human Development Index (2002): ranking	4
Human Development Index (2002): value	0.943

For sources and definitions, see explanatory note on p. vi.

Agriculture

PRINCIPAL CROPS
('000 metric tons)

	2002	2003	2004
Wheat	16,197.5	23,552.0	25,860.4
Barley	7,489.4	12,327.6	13,186.4
Corn for grain	8,998.8	9,587.3	8,835.7
Rye	133.8	327.1	417.9
Oats	2,910.7	3,691.0	3,683.1
Peas (dry)	1,365.5	2,124.4	3,338.2
Soybeans	2,335.7	2,268.3	3,048.0
Sunflower seed	157.4	150.3	54.4
Rapeseed (Canola)	4,407.1	6,771.2	7,728.1
Canary seed	175.7	226.4	300.5
Lentils	353.8	519.9	962.0
Linseed	679.4	754.4	516.9
Mustard seed	154.3	226.1	305.5
Tame hay	18,140.9	22,360.4	25,614.5

2000 ('000 metric tons): Potatoes 4,568.5.

2001 ('000 metric tons): Fodder corn 6,091.7.

LIVESTOCK
('000 head at 1 July)

	2001	2002	2003
Milch cows	1,073	1,072	1,055
Beef cattle	4,799	4,822	4,916
Sheep	1,248	1,253	n.a.
Pigs	14,105	14,672	14,608

2004 ('000 head at 1 July): Sheep 1,238; Pigs 14,838.

LIVESTOCK PRODUCTS

	2001	2002	2003
Beef and veal ('000 lbs)	2,781,370	2,852,088	2,624,048
Mutton and lamb ('000 lbs) . .	31,408	32,519	35,991
Pig meat ('000 lbs)	3,816,849	4,096,964	4,150,078
Poultry meat (metric tons) . .	1,102,433	1,102,492	1,100,968
Milk (kilolitres)	7,556,398	7,375,749	7,548,197
Creamery butter (metric tons) . .	83,970	75,831	84,180
Cheddar cheese (metric tons) . .	126,683	123,037	132,611
Ice-cream mix (kilolitres) . .	147,451	158,470	150,806
Eggs ('000 dozen)	566,659	575,791	576,533

Forestry

ROUNDWOOD REMOVALS
(2002, '000 cubic metres)

	Softwoods	Hardwoods	Total
Alberta*	15,207	9,487	24,694
British Columbia†	70,956	2,682	73,637
Manitoba	1,392	714	2,106
New Brunswick†	6,991	3,193	10,184
Newfoundland†‡	2,466	92	2,559
Northwest Territories†	22	0	22
Nova Scotia	5,179	887	6,066
Nunavut Territory	n.a.	n.a.	n.a.
Ontario†	19,486	6,841	26,327
Prince Edward Island†	463	162	626
Québec	31,564	9,961†	41,525†
Saskatchewan	2,025	2,283	4,309
Yukon Territory	42	n.a.	42
Total †	155,794	36,302	192,096

* Preliminary.
† Estimates.
‡ Newfoundland and Labrador from December 2001.
Sources: National Forestry Database Program.

SAWNWOOD PRODUCTION
('000 cubic metres, incl. railway sleepers)

	2001	2002	2003
Coniferous (softwood)*	52,613.6	56,750.3	55,891.7
Broadleaved (hardwood) . . .	1,094.0	1,731.0	1,654.0
Total	53,707.6	58,481.3	57,545.7

* Unofficial figures.

Source: FAO.

Fur Industry

NUMBER OF PELTS PRODUCED

	2000	2001	2002
Alberta	n.a.	133,800	148,100
British Columbia	266,700	n.a.	n.a.
Manitoba	137,700	146,100	115,500
Northwest Territories	13,100	18,400	31,800
Nova Scotia	447,700	506,600	487,200
Nunavut Territory	9,900	11,600	11,000
Ontario	469,100	568,200	526,200
Prince Edward Island	29,800	34,800	48,600
Québec	270,300	315,700	242,400
Saskatchewan	87,800	98,400	85,700
Yukon Territory	6,400	3,300	8,300
Total (incl. others)†	1,968,000	2,206,000	2,035,200

* Newfoundland and Labrador from December 2001.
† Includes undisclosed provincial and territorial data.

Fishing

('000 metric tons, live weight)

	2000	2001	2002
Capture	1,012.1	1,052.5	1,014.0
Atlantic cod	46.0	40.3	35.3
Atlantic herring	203.3	199.3	191.1
Atlantic mackerel	17.6	24.5	43.1
Marine fishes	27.0	69.6	—
Queen crab	93.5	95.3	106.8
American lobster	45.3	51.4	45.1
Northern prawn	100.1	94.3	102.1
American sea scallop . . .	83.9	89.2	94.0
Aquaculture	127.6	153.2	172.3
Atlantic salmon	72.5	95.6	114.9
Total catch	1,139.7	1,205.8	1,186.3

Note: Figures exclude aquatic plants ('000 metric tons, capture only): 34.5 in 2000; 14.9 in 2001; 16.8 in 2002. Also excluded are aquatic mammals, recorded by number rather than weight. The number of whales caught was: 1 in 2000; 934 in 2001; 1 in 2002. The number of seals caught was: 88,923 in 2000; 195,867 in 2001; 287,936 in 2002.

Sources: FAO.

Mining

('000 metric tons, unless otherwise indicated)

	2001	2002*	2003†
Metallic:			
Bismuth (metric tons) . . .	258	203	145
Cadmium (metric tons) . . .	979	899	710
Cobalt (metric tons) . . .	2,112	2,065	1,743
Copper (metric tons) . . .	614,312	584,195	534,287
Gold (kilograms)	158,875	151,904	140,529
Iron ore	27,119	30,902	32,957
Lead (metric tons)	150,389	101,330	77,140
Molybdenum (metric tons) . .	8,556	7,953	9,304
Nickel (metric tons)	184,300	179,800	155,007
Platinum group (kilograms) . .	20,694	24,372	18,514
Selenium (metric tons) . . .	238	175	253
Silver (metric tons)	1,265	1,352	1,255
Uranium (metric tons) . . .	12,991	12,855	10,294
Zinc (metric tons)	1,012,048	923,931	744,037
Non-metallic:			
Asbestos	277	242	n.a.
Gypsum	7,821	8,809	8,330
Nepheline syenite	710	717	697
Potash (K₂O)	8,237	8,361	9,145
Salt	13,725	12,736	13,390
Sulphur, in smelter gas . . .	762	703	589
Sulphur, elemental	8,154	7,671	7,920
Fuels:			
coal	70,355	66,608	62,163
natural gas (million cubic metres)	171,388	n.a.	n.a.
natural gas by-products ('000 cubic metres)	29,321	n.a.	n.a.
petroleum, crude ('000 cubic metres)	129,810	n.a.	n.a.
Structural materials:			
cement	12,986	13,710	14,063
stone	124,758	124,746	119,356

* Revised figures.
† Provisional figures.

Source: Natural Resources Canada.

Industry

VALUE OF SHIPMENTS
(C $ million)

	2001	2002	2003
Food industries	61,432.6	62,366.3	63,435.7
Beverage and tobacco products industries	11,699.1	11,657.3	12,031.6
Textile mills	4,050.7	3,843.4	3,421.1
Textile product mills . . .	2,664.3	2,562.5	2,297.4
Clothing industries	7,740.1	7,551.0	7,074.7
Leather and allied products industries	985.3	860.8	743.0
Wood product industries . . .	30,112.8	32,333.2	31,247.8
Paper industries	35,933.6	34,455.8	33,203.9
Printing, publishing and allied industries	11,625.0	11,674.5	11,590.5
Refined petroleum and coal products industries . . .	33,954.1	34,275.4	37,355.3
Chemical and chemical products industries	38,604.1	39,767.9	41,186.8
Plastics and rubber products industries	22,436.4	24,485.5	24,722.0
Non-metallic mineral products industries	10,367.8	11,390.0	11,993.8
Primary metal industries . . .	34,115.3	36,769.8	37,605.6
Fabricated metal products industries	30,136.6	30,914.0	31,025.6
Machinery industries (excl. electrical machinery)	25,714.3	26,344.5	25,575.7
Computer and electronic products industries	26,885.2	21,630.6	18,790.1
Electrical equipment, appliance and component industries . .	11,595.4	10,585.3	9,984.4
Transportation equipment industries	122,395.7	125,802.6	120,949.5
Furniture and fixture industries .	13,110.4	13,863.6	14,035.5
Other manufacturing industries .	6,758.2	7,241.4	7,495.1
Total	542,317.1	550,375.5	545,765.2

Electric energy (net production, million kWh): 590,134 in 2000; 588,077 in 2001 (Source: UN, *Industrial Commodity Statistics Yearbook*).

Finance

CURRENCY AND EXCHANGE RATES

Monetary Units
100 cents = 1 Canadian dollar (C $).

Sterling, US Dollar and Euro Equivalents (31 December 2004)
£1 sterling = C $2.3246;
US $1 = C $1.2036;
€1 = C $1.6394;
C $100 = £43.02 = US $83.08 = €61.00.

Average Exchange Rate (C $ per US $)
2002   1.5693
2003   1.4011
2004   1.3010

BUDGET
(C $ million, year ending 31 March)*

Revenue	2001/02	2002/03	2003/04
Income taxes	188,091	178,857	188,126
Property and related taxes . .	41,734	42,527	43,794
Consumption taxes	88,988	96,367	98,583
Health insurance premiums . .	2,282	2,996	3,018
Contributions to social security plans	59,927	63,450	66,757
Other taxes	14,901	15,920	16,355
Sales of goods and services . . .	34,371	35,500	36,381
Investment income	31,908	33,987	36,142
Other revenue from own sources .	4,901	6,504	6,942
Total own source revenue . .	467,102	476,108	496,099

Expenditure	2001/02	2002/03	2003/04
General government services . .	15,632	16,112	15,952
Protection of persons and property	35,393	37,004	37,275
Transport and communications .	18,829	19,476	20,081
Health	76,998	83,849	89,643
Social services	141,799	145,161	150,716
Education	66,218	65,959	68,579
Resource conservation and industrial development . . .	16,404	18,651	19,152
Environment	9,933	10,168	11,220
Recreation and culture	11,345	11,748	12,048
Labour, employment and immigration	3,006	3,374	3,237
Housing	3,303	4,008	4,323
Foreign affairs and international assistance	4,552	5,158	4,793
Regional planning and development	2,123	2,097	2,070
Research establishments . . .	1,740	1,861	2,242
Debt charges	52,034	49,192	47,430
Other expenditures	2,211	958	1,824
Total expenditure	461,521	474,775	490,585

* Figures refer to the consolidated accounts of federal, provincial and territorial governments.

INTERNATIONAL RESERVES
(US $ million at 31 December)

	2001	2002	2003
Gold*	291	205	45
IMF special drawing rights . .	614	719	838
Reserve position in IMF . . .	2,863	3,580	3,847
Foreign exchange	30,484	32,685	31,537
Total	34,253	37,189	36,267

* National valuation.

Source: IMF, *International Financial Statistics*.

MONEY SUPPLY
(C $ million at 31 December*)

	2001	2002	2003
Currency outside banks . . .	38,660	41,130	42,350
Demand deposits at deposit money banks	214,890	227,040	241,670
Total money (incl. others) . .	253,750	268,500	284,390

* Rounded to the nearest $10m.

Source: IMF, *International Financial Statistics*.

COST OF LIVING
(Consumer Price Index; base: 1992 = 100)

	2000	2001	2002
Food	112.2	117.2	120.3
Housing	108.8	112.8	113.8
Household expenses and furnishings	110.0	112.2	113.8
Clothing	105.5	106.0	105.2
Transport	130.7	130.8	134.4
Health and personal care . . .	112.0	114.2	115.5
Recreation, education and reading.	122.5	124.3	126.3
Tobacco and alcohol	97.6	105.1	123.6
All items	113.5	116.4	119.0

NATIONAL ACCOUNTS
National Income and Product
(C $ million at current prices)

	2001	2002	2003
Compensation of employees . .	570,008	592,692	613,718
Operating surplus	260,067	271,876	292,437
Domestic factor incomes . .	830,075	864,568	906,155
Consumption of fixed capital . .	147,608	156,146	164,403
Change in stocks	240	–2,959	4,876
Gross domestic product at factor cost	977,923	1,017,755	1,075,434
Indirect taxes, *less* subsidies . .	129,552	139,259	142,653
Statistical discrepancy	725	954	685
GDP at market prices . . .	1,108,200	1,157,968	1,218,772

Gross national income (C $ '000 million, quarterly data seasonally adjusted at annual rates): 1,077.85 in 2001; 1,127.56 in 2002; 1,189.54 in 2003 (Source: IMF, *International Financial Statistics*).

Gross national disposable income (C $ '000 million, quarterly data seasonally adjusted at annual rates): 1,079.53 in 2001; 1,128.92 in 2002; 1,190.09 in 2003 (Source: IMF, *International Financial Statistics*).

Expenditure on the Gross Domestic Product
(C $ million at current prices)

	2001	2002	2003
Government final consumption expenditure	211,115	223,677	237,711
Private final consumption expenditure	622,903	657,302	688,707
Increase in stocks	–6,270	–568	7,662
Gross fixed capital formation . .	217,631	227,400	237,391
Total domestic expenditure .	1,045,379	1,107,811	1,171,471
Exports of goods and services . .	483,053	479,358	461,596
Less Imports of goods and services	419,508	428,248	413,611
Statistical discrepancy	–724	–953	–684
GDP at market prices . . .	1,108,200	1,157,968	1,218,772
GDP at constant 1997 prices	1,038,844	1,074,620	1,096,359

Gross Domestic Product by Economic Activity
(C $ million at constant 1997 prices)

	2001	2002	2003
Agriculture, hunting, forestry and fishing	20,846	20,169	21,988
Mining, petroleum and gas extraction	35,650	35,204	37,493
Manufacturing	170,729	174,049	174,208
Electricity, gas and water . . .	25,678	26,338	25,780
Construction	52,182	53,797	56,193
Wholesale trade	54,910	58,757	62,163
Retail trade	53,219	56,088	57,716
Transportation and warehousing .	46,803	47,503	47,694
Finance, insurance, real estate and leasing	190,055	198,827	203,152
Professional, scientific and technical services	42,287	44,252	45,683
Administration and support, waste management and remediation services	19,814	20,779	21,589
Education	44,250	44,731	44,956
Health care and social assistance .	56,927	59,078	61,363
Information and cultural industries	39,540	41,817	42,496
Arts, entertainment and recreation	9,030	9,651	10,050
Accommodation and food services .	22,931	23,055	22,726
Public administration	53,575	54,895	56,547
Other services	23,056	23,734	24,172
GDP at basic prices	961,482	992,724	1,015,969

CANADA

BALANCE OF PAYMENTS
(US $ million)

	2001	2002	2003
Exports of goods f.o.b.	271,803	263,754	285,794
Imports of goods f.o.b.	−226,528	−227,318	−244,281
Trade balance	45,275	36,436	41,513
Exports of services	39,225	40,748	42,934
Imports of services	−43,880	−45,129	−50,661
Balance on goods and services	40,620	32,055	33,786
Other income received	16,742	19,881	23,500
Other income paid	−42,181	−38,133	−40,238
Balance on goods, services and income	15,181	13,803	17,047
Current transfers received	4,501	4,429	4,796
Current transfers paid	−3,473	−3,785	−4,575
Current balance	16,209	14,447	17,628
Capital account (net)	3,741	3,177	2,836
Direct investment abroad	−36,229	−26,461	−22,240
Direct investment from abroad	27,529	20,940	6,273
Portfolio investment assets	−24,374	−15,928	−9,139
Portfolio investment liabilities	24,631	13,365	13,160
Other investment assets	−10,544	−8,531	−20,555
Other investment liabilities	7,506	5,009	10,910
Net errors and omissions	−6,295	−6,204	−1,767
Overall balance	2,172	−185	−3,255

Source: IMF, *International Financial Statistics*.

External Trade

PRINCIPAL COMMODITIES
(C $ million)

Imports f.o.b.	2001	2002	2003
Agricultural and fishing products	20,373.1	21,780.0	21,517.5
Energy products	17,747.0	16,447.5	19,624.7
Crude petroleum	12,814.3	11,722.3	13,301.0
Industrial goods and materials	68,430.6	68,905.9	65,183.8
Metals and metal ores	15,245.3	16,470.6	14,945.0
Chemicals and plastics	25,164.3	25,747.1	25,051.7
Machinery and equipment (excl. automotive products)	112,524.8	105,847.8	98,236.4
Industrial and agricultural machinery	28,256.1	27,577.0	26,723.5
Aircraft and other transportation equipment	16,317.4	14,626.2	11,978.1
Office machines and equipment	17,730.2	15,700.3	14,521.5
Automotive products	72,577.9	81,466.5	76,359.5
Passenger automobiles and chassis	22,200.4	26,226.9	24,489.7
Trucks and other motor vehicles	9,624.6	11,776.2	13,057.2
Motor vehicle parts	40,752.9	43,463.4	38,812.6
Other consumer goods	42,923.1	46,444.4	46,259.2
Total (incl. others)	350,682.5	356,580.9	341,832.7

Exports f.o.b.	2001	2002	2003
Agricultural and fishing products	31,078.0	30,885.3	29,256.1
Energy products	55,751.9	49,308.9	60,498.1
Crude petroleum	15,370.2	18,550.8	20,644.3
Natural gas	25,595.1	18,372.0	26,083.4
Forestry products	40,287.5	37,252.1	34,453.7
Lumber and sawmill products	18,035.1	17,765.3	16,503.3
Newsprint and other paper and paperboard products	15,370.3	12,938.5	11,638.8
Industrial goods and materials	67,796.1	70,158.8	66,536.3
Chemicals, plastics and fertilizers	23,812.9	24,230.8	23,396.7
Metals and alloys	20,339.5	22,191.8	20,239.5
Machinery and equipment (excl. automotive products)	102,554.5	97,091.5	88,606.5
Industrial and agricultural machinery	19,995.4	20,299.9	18,909.4
Aircraft and other transportation equipment	24,483.6	22,432.8	20,589.2
Automotive products	92,526.6	96,676.1	87,373.8
Passenger automobiles and chassis	48,529.2	49,815.3	43,381.2
Trucks and other motor vehicles	17,342.9	17,856.4	16,106.9
Motor vehicle parts	26,654.5	29,004.4	27,885.7
Other consumer goods	16,305.8	17,678.1	17,183.0
Total (incl. others)	420,657.1	413,795.3	400,010.0

PRINCIPAL TRADING PARTNERS
(C $ million, balance of payments basis)

Imports	2001	2002	2003
Japan	10,572.0	11,732.9	10,644.9
United Kingdom	11,952.9	10,178.8	8,826.8
USA	254,949.4	255,093.2	239,870.7
Other European Union countries	23,197.0	25,860.8	25,982.7
Other OECD countries	18,645.5	19,680.7	19,676.5
Other countries	31,365.6	34,034.5	36,831.1
Total	350,682.5	356,580.9	341,832.7

Exports	2001	2002	2003
Japan	10,124.8	10,152.5	9,785.7
United Kingdom	6,912.9	6,184.8	7,697.8
USA	352,083.1	347,068.9	330,375.3
Other European Union countries	16,712.0	16,372.0	16,420.5
Other OECD countries	12,129.2	12,174.1	12,668.6
Other countries	22,695.0	21,843.0	23,062.1
Total	420,657.1	413,795.3	400,010.0

Transport

RAILWAYS
(revenue traffic)*

	2001	2002	2003
Passengers carried ('000)	4,112	4,223	4,024
Passenger train-km ('000)	11,809	11,919	11,671
Freight carried ('000 tons)	321,127	317,432	327,126
Freight train-km ('000)	113,784	116,185	117,278

* Intercity trains only.

Source: Railway Association of Canada, *Railway Trends*.

ROAD TRAFFIC
('000 vehicles registered at 31 December)

	1999	2000	2001
Total vehicle registrations . . .	23,637.1	23,627.4	23,427.2
Total road motor vehicle			
registrations	17,534.3	17,882.2	18,101.7
Passenger cars and light trucks	16,538	16,832.2	17,054.8
Heavy trucks	649	661.4	654.5
Buses	73	77.3	74.1
Motorcycles and mopeds . . .	274	311.3	318.3
Trailers	4,145.3	3,988.9	4,023.2
Other (off-road, construction, farm			
vehicles, etc.)	1,957.5	1,756.3	1,302.3

2003 ('000 vehicles registered at 31 December): Total vehicle registrations 24,665.4; Total road motor vehicle registrations 18,868.8.

INLAND WATER TRAFFIC
(St Lawrence Seaway, '000 metric tons)

	2002	2003	2004
Montréal–Lake Ontario	30,002	28,900	30,494
Welland Canal	32,108	31,870	33,945

Source: St Lawrence Seaway Management Corpn.

SHIPPING
Merchant Fleet
(registered at 31 December)

	2000	2001	2002
Number of vessels	861	875	902
Total displacement ('000 grt) . .	2,657.6	2,727.0	2,797.6

Source: Lloyd's Register of Shipping, *World Fleet Statistics*.

International Sea-borne Freight Traffic

	2000	2001	2002
Goods ('000 metric tons):			
loaded	187,834.4	174,723.6	174,270.2
unloaded	105,919.0	112,135.3	108,464.2
Vessels (number):			
arrived	26,233	24,142	24,466
departed	26,233	24,321	24,547

Source: Statistics Canada, Transportation Division and *Shipping in Canada*.

CIVIL AVIATION
(major Canadian airlines, '000)

	1999	2000	2001
Passengers	24,578	25,049	23,495
Passenger-km	65,699,586	68,215,299	64,117,271
Goods ton-km	2,013,821	1,930,970	1,631,127

Tourism

	1999	2000	2001
Travellers from the USA:			
number ('000)	15,180	15,189	15,570
expenditure (C $ million) . .	7,149	7,448	7,910
Travellers from other countries:			
number ('000)	4,231	4,438	4,109
expenditure (C $ million) . .	4,892	5,188	n.a.

Travellers from the USA ('000): 16,168 in 2002; 14,232 in 2003.

Travellers from the USA (expenditure, C $ million): 8,412 in 2002; 7,288 in 2003.

Communications Media

	2000	2001	2002
Total households ('000)	11,699	11,897	12,021
Homes with television ('000) . .	11,575	11,796	11,924
Telephones ('000 main lines in			
use)*	20,347.0	20,335.9	20,205.4
Mobile cellular telephones ('000			
subscribers)*	8,726.6	10,861.6	11,860.8
Personal computers ('000 in use)*	12,000	n.a.	15,300
Internet users ('000)*	12,700	13,500	15,200

Facsimile machines: 5,320,000 in 1998*.

Newspapers (titles, 2001): Daily 101; Non-daily 1,100.

Book production (titles): 17,931 in 1995; 19,900 in 1996 (Source: UNESCO, *Statistical Yearbook*).

* Source: International Telecommunication Union.

Education

(1999/2000)

	Institutions	Teachers*	Pupils*
Elementary–secondary . . .	15,595	302,977	5,397,000
Post-secondary colleges . . .	199†	27,832‡	407,000†
Universities	75†	33,801	591,000†

* Full-time only.
† Estimate.
‡ Preliminary figure.

Directory

The Constitution

Under the Constitution Act 1982, which was enacted as Schedule B to the Canada Act (UK) 1982, and which entered into force on 17 April 1982, executive authority is vested in the Sovereign, and exercised in her name by a Governor-General and Privy Council. Legislative power is exercised by a Parliament of two Houses, the Senate and the House of Commons. The Constitution includes a Charter of Rights and Freedoms, and provisions which recognize the nation's multicultural heritage, affirm the existing rights of native peoples, confirm the principle of equalization of benefits among the provinces and strengthen provincial ownership of natural resources.

THE GOVERNMENT

The national government operates through three main agencies: Parliament (consisting of the Sovereign as represented by the Gov-

ernor-General, the Senate and the House of Commons), which makes the laws; the Executive (the Cabinet or Ministry), which applies the laws; and the Judiciary, which interprets the laws.

The Prime Minister is appointed by the Governor-General and is habitually the leader of the political party commanding the confidence of the House of Commons. He chooses the members of his Cabinet from members of his party in Parliament, principally from those in the House of Commons. Each Minister or member of the Cabinet is usually responsible for the administration of a department, although there may be Ministers without portfolio whose experience and counsel are drawn upon to strengthen the Cabinet, but who are not at the head of departments. Each Minister of a department is responsible to Parliament for that department, and the Cabinet is collectively responsible before Parliament for government policy and administration generally.

Meetings of the Cabinet are presided over by the Prime Minister. From the Cabinet, signed orders and recommendations go to the Governor-General for his or her approval, and the Crown acts only on the advice of its responsible Ministers. The Cabinet takes the responsibility for its advice being in accordance with the support of Parliament and is held strictly accountable.

THE FEDERAL PARLIAMENT

Parliament must meet at least once a year, so that 12 months do not elapse between the last meeting in one session and the first meeting in the next. The duration of Parliament may not be longer than five years from the date of election of a House of Commons. Senators (normally a maximum of 104 in number) are appointed until age 75 by the Governor-General in Council. They must be at least 30 years of age, residents of the province they represent and in possession of C $4,000 of real property over and above their liabilities. Members of the House of Commons are elected by universal adult suffrage for the duration of a Parliament.

Under the Constitution, the federal Parliament has exclusive legislative authority in all matters relating to public debt and property; regulation of trade and commerce; raising of money by any mode of taxation; borrowing of money on the public credit; postal service, census and statistics; militia, military and naval service and defence; fixing and providing for salaries and allowances of the officers of the Government; beacons, buoys and lighthouses; navigation and shipping; quarantine and the establishment and maintenance of marine hospitals; sea-coast and inland fisheries; ferries on an international or interprovincial frontier; currency and coinage; banking, incorporation of banks, and issue of paper money; savings banks; weights and measures; bills of exchange and promissory notes; interest; legal tender; bankruptcy and insolvency; patents of invention and discovery; copyrights; Indians and lands reserved for Indians; naturalization and aliens; marriage and divorce; the criminal law, except the constitution of courts of criminal jurisdiction but including the procedure in criminal matters; the establishment, maintenance and management of penitentiaries; such classes of subjects as are expressly excepted in the enumeration of the classes of subjects exclusively assigned to the Legislatures of the provinces by the Act. Judicial interpretation and later amendment have, in certain cases, modified or clearly defined the respective powers of the federal Government and provincial governments.

Both the Parliament of Canada and the legislatures of the provinces may legislate with respect to agriculture and immigration, but provincial legislation shall have effect in and for the provinces as long and as far only as it is not repugnant to any Act of Parliament. Both Parliament and the provincial legislatures may legislate with respect to old age pensions and supplementary benefits, but no federal law shall affect the operation of any present or future law of a province in relation to these matters.

PROVINCIAL AND MUNICIPAL GOVERNMENT

In each of the 10 provinces the Sovereign is represented by a Lieutenant-Governor, appointed by the Governor-General in Council, and acting on the advice of the Ministry or Executive Council, which is responsible to the Legislature and resigns office when it ceases to enjoy the confidence of that body. The Legislatures are unicameral, consisting of an elected Legislative Assembly and the Lieutenant-Governor. The duration of a Legislature may not exceed five years from the date of the election of its members.

The Legislature in each province may exclusively make laws in relation to: amendment of the constitution of the province, except as regards the Lieutenant-Governor; direct taxation within the province; borrowing of money on the credit of the province; establishment and tenure of provincial offices and appointment and payment of provincial officers; the management and sale of public lands belonging to the province and of the timber and wood thereon; the establishment, maintenance and management of public and reformatory prisons in and for the province; the establishment, maintenance and management of hospitals, asylums, charities and charitable institutions in and for the province other than marine hospitals; municipal institutions in the province; shop, saloon, tavern, auctioneer and other licences issued for the raising of provincial or municipal revenue; local works and undertakings other than interprovincial or international lines of ships, railways, canals, telegraphs, etc., or works which, though wholly situated within the province are declared by the federal Parliament to be for the general advantage either of Canada or two or more provinces; the incorporation of companies with provincial objects; the solemnization of marriage in the province; property and civil rights in the province; the administration of justice in the province, including the constitution, maintenance and organization of provincial courts both in civil and criminal jurisdiction, and including procedure in civil matters in these courts; the imposition of punishment by fine, penalty or imprisonment for enforcing any law of the province relating to any of the aforesaid subjects; generally all matters of a merely local or private nature in the province. Further, provincial

Legislatures may exclusively make laws in relation to education, subject to the protection of religious minorities; and to non-renewable natural resources, forestry resources and electrical energy, including their export from one province to another, and to the right to impose any mode or system of taxation thereon, subject in both cases to such laws not being discriminatory.

Under the Constitution Act, the municipalities are the creations of the provincial governments. Their bases of organization and the extent of their authority vary in different provinces, but almost everywhere they have very considerable powers of local self-government.

The Government

Head of State: HM Queen ELIZABETH II (succeeded to the throne 6 February 1952).

Governor-General: ADRIENNE CLARKSON (took office 7 October 1999).

FEDERAL MINISTRY
(April 2005)

Prime Minister: PAUL MARTIN.

Leader of the Government in the Senate: JACOB AUSTIN.

Minister of Transport: JEAN-CLAUDE LAPIERRE.

Minister of Finance: RALPH E. GOODALE.

Deputy Prime Minister and Minister of Public Safety and Emergency Preparedness: ANNE McLELLAN.

President of the Queen's Privy Council for Canada and Minister of Intergovernmental Affairs and of Human Resources and Skills Development: LUCIENNE ROBILLARD.

Minister of the Environment: STÉPHANE DION.

Minister of Foreign Affairs: PIERRE STEWART PETTIGREW.

Minister of Indian Affairs and Northern Development and Federal Interlocutor for Métis and Non-Status Indians: ANDY SCOTT.

Minister of International Trade: JAMES SCOTT PETERSON.

Minister of Agriculture and Agri-Food: ANDREW MITCHELL.

Minister of National Defence: BILL GRAHAM.

Minister of Veterans' Affairs: ALBINA GUARNIERI.

President of the Treasury Board and Minister responsible for the Canadian Wheat Board: REGINALD B. ALCOCK.

Minister of Fisheries and Oceans: GEOFF REGAN.

Leader of the Government in the House of Commons: TONI VALERI.

Minister of International Co-operation: M. AILEEN CARROLL.

Minister of Justice and Attorney-General: IRWIN COTLER.

Minister of Natural Resources: RUBEN JOHN EFFORD.

Minister of Canadian Heritage and Minister responsible for the Status of Women: LIZA FRULLA.

Minister of Citizenship and Immigration: GIUSEPPE (JOSEPH) VOLPE.

Minister of Labour and Housing: JOSEPH FRANK FONTANA.

Minister of Public Works and Government Services: SCOTT BRISON.

Minister of Health: UJJAL DOSANJH.

Minister of Social Development: KEN DRYDEN.

Minister of Industry: DAVID EMERSON.

Minister of State (Northern Development): ETHEL BLONDIN-ANDREW.

Minister of State (Multiculturalism): RAYMOND CHAN.

Minister of State (Human Resources Development): CLAUDETTE BRADSHAW.

Minister of National Revenue: JOHN McCALLUM.

Minister of Western Economic Diversification and Minister of State (Sport): STEPHEN OWEN.

Minister of Atlantic Canada Opportunities Agency: JOSEPH McGUIRE.

Minister of State (Federal Economic Development Initiative for Northern Ontario): JOSEPH ROBERT COMUZZI.

Deputy Leader of the Government in the House of Commons, Minister responsible for Official Languages and for Demo-

cratic Reform, and Associate Minister of National Defence: Mauril Bélanger.

Minister of State (Public Health): Carolyn Bennett.

Minister of the Economic Development Agency of Canada for the Regions of Québec and Minister responsible for the Francophonie: Jacques Saada.

Minister of State (Infrastructure and Communities): John Ferguson Godfrey.

Minister of State (Families and Caregivers): Tony Ianno.

MINISTRIES

Office of the Prime Minister: Langevin Block, 80 Wellington St, Ottawa, ON K1A 0A3; tel. (613) 941-6888; fax (613) 941-6900; e-mail pm@pm.gc.ca; internet www.pm.gc.ca.

Agriculture and Agri-Food Canada: Sir John Carling Bldg, 930 Carling Ave, Ottawa, ON K1A 0C7; tel. (613) 759-1000; fax (613) 759-7977; e-mail info@agr.gc.ca; internet www.agr.gc.ca.

Atlantic Canada Opportunities Agency: 644 Main St, 3rd Floor, POB 6051, Moncton, NB E1C 9J8; tel. (506) 851-2271; fax (506) 851-7403; internet www.acoa-apeca.gc.ca.

Canada Economic Development for the Regions of Québec: Tour de la Bourse 800, pl. Victoria, Suite 3800, CP 247, Montréal, QC H4Z 1E8; tel. (514) 283-6412; fax (514) 283-3302; internet www.dec-ced.gc.ca.

Canada Revenue Agency: 871 Heron Rd, Ottawa, ON K1A 0L8; tel. (613) 952-0384; internet www.cra-arc.gc.ca.

Canadian Heritage: Les Terrasses de la Chaudière, 14 étage, bureau 1497, 25 rue Eddy, Gatineau, QC K1A 0M5; tel. (819) 997-0055; fax (819) 953-5382; internet www.pch.gc.ca.

Citizenship and Immigration Canada: Jean Edmonds Towers, 21st Floor, 365 Laurier Ave West, Ottawa, ON K1A 1L1; tel. (613) 954-1064; fax (613) 957-2688; e-mail minister@cic.gc.ca; internet www.cic.gc.ca.

Department of Justice Canada: East Memorial Bldg, 284 Wellington St, Ottawa, ON K1A 0H8; tel. (613) 957-4222; fax (613) 954-0811; e-mail webadmin@justice.gc.ca; internet www.canada.justice.gc.ca.

Department of National Defence: National Defence Headquarters, Maj.-Gen. George R. Pearkes Bldg, 101 Colonel By Dr., Ottawa, ON K1A 0K2; tel. (613) 992-4581; fax (613) 992-4241; internet www.forces.gc.ca.

Environment Canada: 70 rue Crémazie, Gatineau, QC K1A 0H3; tel. (819) 997-2800; fax (819) 953-2225; e-mail enviroinfo@ec.gc.ca; internet www.ec.gc.ca.

Finance Canada: East Tower, 19th Floor, 140 O'Connor St, Ottawa, ON K1A 0G5; tel. (613) 992-1573; fax (613) 996-2690; e-mail consltcomm@fin.gc.ca; internet www.fin.gc.ca.

Fisheries and Oceans Canada: 200 Kent St, 13th Floor, Station 13228, Ottawa, ON K1A 0E6; tel. (613) 993-0999; fax (613) 990-1866; e-mail info@dfo-mpo.gc.ca; internet www.dfo-mpo.gc.ca.

Foreign Affairs Canada: Lester B. Pearson Bldg, 125 Sussex Dr., Ottawa, ON K1A 0G2; tel. (613) 944-4000; fax (613) 996-9709; e-mail infotech@international.gc.ca; internet www.dfait-maeci.gc.ca.

Health Canada: Brooke Claxton Bldg, Tunney's Pasture, Ottawa, ON K1A 0K9; tel. (613) 957-2991; fax (613) 941-5366; e-mail info@hc-sc.gc.ca; internet www.hc-sc.gc.ca.

Human Resources and Skills Development Canada: 140 promenade du Portage, Gatineau, QC K1A 0J9; tel. (819) 994-6313; fax (819) 953-7260; internet www.hrsdc.gc.ca.

Indian and Northern Affairs Canada: Les Terrasses de la Chaudière, Pièce 1415, 10 rue Wellington, Gatineau, QC K1A 0H4; tel. (819) 997-0380; fax (819) 953-3017; e-mail infopubs@ainc-inac.gc.ca; internet www.ainc-inac.gc.ca.

Industry Canada: C. D. Howe Bldg, 235 Queen St, Ottawa, ON K1A 0H5; tel. (613) 947-7466; fax (613) 954-6436; internet www.ic.gc.ca.

International Trade Canada: Lester B. Pearson Bldg, 125 Sussex Dr., Ottawa, ON K1A 0G2; tel. (613) 944-4000; fax (613) 996-9709; e-mail enqserv@dfait-maeci.gc.ca; internet www.itcan-cican.gc.ca.

Natural Resources Canada: 580 Booth St, Ottawa, ON K1A 0E4; tel. (613) 995-0947; fax (613) 996-9094; internet www.nrcan-rncan.gc.ca.

Public Safety and Emergency Preparedness Canada: 340 Laurier Ave, Ottawa, ON K1G 4G4; tel. (613) 991-3283; fax (613) 990-9077; e-mail communications@ocipep-bpiepc.gc.ca; internet www.csis-scrs.gc.ca.

Public Works and Government Services Canada: pl. du Portage, rue Laurier, Gatineau, QC K1A 0S5; tel. (819) 956-3115; e-mail questions@pwgsc.gc.ca; internet www.pwgsc.gc.ca.

Social Development Canada: 140 promenade du Portage, Hull, QC K1A 0J9; tel. (819) 994-6313; fax (819) 953-7260; internet www.sdc.gc.ca.

Transport Canada: Tower C, 29th Floor, pl. de Ville, 330 Sparks St, Ottawa, ON K1A 0N5; tel. (613) 990-0700; fax (613) 995-0327; e-mail mintc@tc.gc.ca; internet www.tc.gc.ca.

Treasury Board: West Tower, 10th Floor, l'Esplanade Laurier, 300 Laurier Ave West, Ottawa, ON K1A 0R5; tel. (613) 957-2400; fax (613) 996-0518; e-mail tbs-sct@tbs-sct.gc.ca; internet www.tbs-sct.gc.ca.

Veterans Affairs Canada: 161 Grafton St, POB 7700, Charlottetown, PE C1A 8M9; tel. (902) 566-8888; fax (902) 566-8508; e-mail information@vac-acc.gc.ca; internet www.vac-acc.gc.ca.

Western Economic Diversification Canada: Canada Pl., Suite 1500, 9700 Jasper Ave, Edmonton, AB T5J 4H7; tel. (780) 495-4164; fax (403) 495-4557; internet www.wd.gc.ca.

Federal Legislature

THE SENATE

Speaker: Daniel Hays.

Seats at March 2005

Liberal	64
Conservative Party	23
Progressive Conservative	5
New Democratic Party of Canada	1
Independent	5
Vacant	7
Total	105

HOUSE OF COMMONS

Speaker: Peter Milliken.

General Election, 28 June 2004

	% of votes at election	Seats at election	Seats at March 2005
Liberal	36.7	135	132
Conservative	29.6	99	99
Bloc Québécois	12.4	54	54
New Democratic Party	15.7	19	19
Independent	5.6	1	3
Vacant	—	—	1
Total	100.0	308	308

Provincial Legislatures

ALBERTA

Lieutenant-Governor: Norman L. Kwong.

Premier: Ralph Klein.

Election, November 2004

	Seats at election
Progressive Conservative	62
Liberal	16
New Democratic Party	4
Alberta Alliance	1
Total	83

BRITISH COLUMBIA

Lieutenant-Governor: Iona Campagnolo.

Premier: Gordon Campbell.

Election, May 2001

	Seats at election	Seats at March 2005
Liberal	76	72
New Democratic Party	—	3
Democratic Reform of British Columbia	—	1
Independent	—	1
Vacant	—	2
Total	79	79

MANITOBA

Lieutenant-Governor: PETER M. LIBA.

Premier: GARY ALBERT DOER.

Election, June 2003

	Seats
New Democratic Party	35
Progressive Conservative	20
Liberal	2
Total	57

NEW BRUNSWICK

Lieutenant-Governor: HERMÉNÉGILDE CHIASSON.

Premier: BERNARD LORD.

Election, June 2003

	Seats at election	Seats at March 2005
Progressive Conservative	28	27
Liberal	26	26
New Democratic Party	1	1
Vacant	—	1
Total	55	55

NEWFOUNDLAND AND LABRADOR

Lieutenant-Governor: EDWARD MOXON ROBERTS.

Premier: DANNY WILLIAMS.

Election, October 2003

	Seats
Progressive Conservative	34
Liberal	12
New Democratic Party	2
Total	48

NOVA SCOTIA

Lieutenant-Governor: MYRA A. FREEMAN.

Premier: JOHN F. HAMM.

Election, August 2003

	Seats at election	Seats at March 2005
Progressive Conservative	25	24
New Democratic Party	15	15
Liberal	12	11
Independent	—	1
Vacant	—	1
Total	52	52

ONTARIO

Lieutenant-Governor: JAMES K. BARTLEMAN.

Premier: DALTON MCGUINTY.

Election, October 2003

	Seats at election	Seats at March 2005
Liberal	72	71
Progressive Conservative	24	24
New Democratic Party	7	8
Total	103	103

PRINCE EDWARD ISLAND

Lieutenant-Governor: J. LÉONCE BERNARD.

Premier: PATRICK G. BINNS.

Election, September 2003

	Seats
Progressive Conservative	23
Liberal	4
Total	27

QUÉBEC

Lieutenant-Governor: LISE THIBAULT.

Premier: JEAN CHAREST.

Election, April 2003

	Seats at election	Seats at March 2005
Liberal	76	73
Parti Québécois	45	46
Action Démocratique du Québec	4	5
Independent	—	1
Total	125	125

SASKATCHEWAN

Lieutenant-Governor: LYNDA HAVERSTOCK.

Premier: LORNE CALVERT.

Election, November 2003

	Seats
New Democratic Party	30
Saskatchewan Party	28
Total	58

Territorial Legislatures

NORTHWEST TERRITORIES

Commissioner: GLENNA F. HANSEN.

Premier and Minister of the Executive Department: JOSEPH HANDLEY.

The Legislative Assembly, elected in November 2003, consists of 19 independent members without formal party affiliation.

NUNAVUT TERRITORY

Commissioner: PETER IRNIQ.

Premier: PAUL OKALIK.

The Legislative Assembly, elected in February 2004, consists of 19 independent members without formal party affiliation.

YUKON TERRITORY

Commissioner: JACK CABLE.

Government Leader and Minister of the Executive Council Office: DENNIS FENTIE.

Election, November 2002

	Seats at election	Seats at March 2005
Yukon Party	12	11
New Democratic Party	5	5
Liberal	1	1
Independent	—	—
Total	**18**	**18**

Political Organizations

Action Démocratique du Québec: 740 rue Sainte-Maurice, bureau 108, Montréal, QC H3C 1L5; tel. (514) 270-4413; fax (514) 270-4469; e-mail adq@adq.qc.ca; internet www.adq.qc.ca; f. 1994; provincial nationalist; Leader MARIO DUMONT; Pres. GUY LAFOREST.

Bloc Québécois: 3750 Cremazie Est, bureau 307, Montréal, QC H2A 1B6; tel. (514) 526-3000; fax (514) 526-2868; e-mail infobloc@ bloc.org; internet www.blocquebecois.org; f. 1990 by group of seven Progressive Conservative MPs representing Québec constituencies in fed. parl.; seeks negotiated sovereignty for Québec; Leader GILLES DUCEPPE; Dir-Gen. GILBERT GARDENER.

Canadian Action Party: 99 Atlantic Ave, Suite 302, Toronto, ON M6K 3J8; tel. (416) 535-4144; fax (416) 535-6325; e-mail info@ canadianactionparty.ca; internet www.canadianactionparty.ca; f. 1997; Leader CONNIE FOGAL.

Christian Heritage Party of Canada: POB 4958, Station E, Ottawa, ON K1S 5J1; tel. (819) 568-6686; fax (819) 281-7174; e-mail edchp@qc.aira.com; internet www.chp.ca; f. 1986; Pres. THOMAS KROESBERGEN; Leader RONALD O. GRAY.

Communist Party of Canada: 290A Danforth Ave, Toronto, ON M4K 1N6; tel. (416) 469-2446; fax (416) 469-4063; e-mail info@ cpc-pcc.ca; internet www.communist-party.ca; f. 1921; Leader MIGUEL FIGUEROA.

Communist Party of Canada (Marxist-Leninist): 396 Cooper St, Suite 405, Ottawa, ON K2P 2H7; tel. (613) 565-6446; fax (613) 565-8787; e-mail office@cpcml.ca; internet www.cpcml.ca; f. 1970; Nat. Leader SANDRA SMITH.

Conservative Party of Canada: 130 Albert St, Suite 1720, Ottawa, ON K1P 5G4; tel. (613) 755-2000; fax (613) 755-2001; e-mail info@conservative.ca; internet www.conservative.ca; f. 2003 by merger of Canadian Alliance and Progressive Conservative Party of Canada; Leader STEPHEN HARPER.

Green Party of Canada: POB 997, Station B, Ottawa, ON K1P 5RI; tel. (866) 868-3447; e-mail info@greenparty.ca; internet www .greenparty.ca; f. 1983; environmentalist; Leader JIM HARRIS.

Liberal Party of Canada: 81 Metcalfe St, Suite 400, Ottawa, ON K1P 6M8; tel. (613) 237-0740; fax (613) 235-7208; e-mail info@liberal .ca; internet www.liberal.ca; supports comprehensive social security, economic growth and a balanced economy; Leader PAUL MARTIN; Pres. MIKE EIZENGA; Nat. Dir STEVE MACKINNON.

Libertarian Party of Canada: 2052 Ste Marie, Embrun, ON K0A 1W0; tel. (613) 443-5423; e-mail info@libertarian.ca; internet www .libertarian.ca; f. 1974; supports the extension of individual freedoms; Leader JEAN-SERGE BRISSON; Pres. GEORGE J. DANCE.

Marijuana Party: 74 Rachel St East, Suite 100, Montréal, QC H2W 1C6; tel. (514) 842-4900; internet www.marijuanaparty.com; f. 2000; campaigns for the legalization of marijuana; Leader MARC-BORIS ST-MAURICE.

New Democratic Party of Canada: 300-279 Laurier Ave West, Ottawa, ON K1P 5J9; tel. (613) 236-3613; fax (613) 230-9950; e-mail ndpadmin@fed.ndp.ca; internet www.ndp.ca; f. 1961; social democratic; Leader JACK LAYTON; Pres. ADAM GIAMBRONE; Federal Sec. CHRIS WATSON; 90,000 mems (2003).

Ontario Provincial Confederation of Regions Party: Toronto, ON; e-mail cor@mountaincable.net; f. 1990; Pres. TILTON BEAUMONT.

Parti Québécois: 1200 ave Papineau, Bureau 150, Montréal, QC H2K 4R5; tel. (514) 526-0020; fax (514) 526-0272; e-mail info@pq .org; internet www.pq.org; f. 1968; social democratic; seeks political sovereignty for Québec; governing party of Québec in 1976–85 and 1994–2003; Pres. BERNARD LANDRY; 200,000 mems (2001).

Saskatchewan Party: 1637 Victoria Ave, POB 546, Regina, SK S4P 3A2; tel. (306) 359-1638; fax (306) 359-9832; e-mail info@ saskparty.com; internet www.saskparty.com; f. 1997; Leader BRAD WALL.

Socialist Party of Canada: POB 4280, Victoria, BC V8X 3X8; tel. (250) 478-5670; e-mail spc@iname.com; internet www .worldsocialism.org/canada; f. 1905; Gen. Sec. JOHN AYERS.

Yukon Party: POB 31113, Whitehorse, YT Y1A 5P7; tel. (867) 668-6505; fax (867) 667-7660; e-mail info@yukonparty.com; internet www.yukonparty.com; Leader DENNIS FENTIE; Pres. MARIE COX.

Diplomatic Representation

EMBASSIES AND HIGH COMMISSIONS IN CANADA

Afghanistan: 246 Queen St, Suite 400, Ottawa, ON K1P 5E4; tel. (613) 563-4223; fax (613) 563-4962; e-mail afghanembott@ afghanistanembassy.ca; internet www.afghanistanembassy.ca; Ambassador OMAR SAMAD.

Albania: 130 Albert St, Suite 302, Ottawa, ON K1P 5G4 ; tel. (613) 236-4114; fax (613) 236-0804; e-mail embassyrepublicofalbania@on .aivn.com; Ambassador ADHURIM RESULI.

Algeria: 500 Wilbrod St, Ottawa, ON K1N 6N2; tel. (613) 789-8505; fax (613) 789-1406; e-mail ambalgcan@rogers.com; internet www .embassyalgeria.ca; Ambassador YOUCEF YOUSFI.

Angola: 189 Laurier Ave East, Ottawa, ON K1N 6P1; tel. (613) 234-1152; fax (613) 234-1179; e-mail info@ambangola-can.org; internet www.embangola-can.org; Ambassador MIGUEL MARIA N'ZAU PUNA.

Antigua and Barbuda, Dominica, Grenada, Montserrat, Saint Christopher and Nevis, Saint Lucia and Saint Vincent and the Grenadines: 130 Albert St, Suite 700, Ottawa, ON K1P 5G4; tel. (613) 236-8952; fax (613) 236-3042; e-mail echcc@travel-net.com; High Commissioner LORRAINE BERNADINE WILLIAMS.

Argentina: 90 Sparks St, Suite 910, Ottawa, ON K1P 5B4; tel. (613) 236-2351; fax (613) 235-2659; e-mail embargentina@ argentina-canada.net; internet www.argentina-canada.net; Ambassador ARTURO G. BOTHAMLEY.

Armenia: 7 Delaware Ave, Ottawa, ON K2P 0Z2; tel. (613) 234-3710; fax (613) 234-3444; e-mail erac@ican.net; internet www .armembassycanada.ca; Ambassador ARA PAPIAN.

Australia: 50 O'Connor St, Suite 710, Ottawa, ON K1P 6L2; tel. (613) 236-0841; fax (613) 236-4376; internet www.ahc-ottawa.org; High Commissioner ANTHONY JOHN HELY.

Austria: 445 Wilbrod St, Ottawa, ON K1N 6M7; tel. (613) 789-1444; fax (613) 789-3431; e-mail embassy-ob@bmaa.gv.at; internet www .austro.org; Ambassador OTTO DITZ.

Azerbaijan: 275 Slater St, Suite 904, Ottawa, ON K1P 5H9; tel. (613) 288-0497; fax (613) 230-8089; e-mail azerbaijan@azembassy .ca; internet www.azembassy.ca; Ambassador FAKHRADDIN GURBANOV.

Bahamas: 360 Albert St, Suite 1020, Ottawa, ON K1R 7X7; tel. (613) 232-1724; fax (613) 232-0097; e-mail ottawa-mission@bahighco .com; High Commissioner PHILIP PATRIC SMITH.

Bangladesh: 275 Bank St, Suite 302, Ottawa, ON K2P 2L6; tel. (613) 236-0138; fax (613) 567-3213; e-mail bang@bellnet.ca; internet www.iosphere.net/~bhc; High Commissioner RAFIQ AHMED KHAN.

Barbados: 130 Albert St, Suite 1204, Ottawa, ON K1P 5G4; tel. (613) 236-9517; fax (613) 230-4362; e-mail ottawa@foreign.gov.bb; High Commissioner GLYNE SAMUEL MURRAY.

Belarus: 130 Albert St, Suite 600, Ottawa, K1P 5G4; tel. (613) 233-9994; fax (613) 233-8500; e-mail belamb@igs.net; Ambassador NINA NIKOLAEVNA MAZAI.

Belgium: 360 Albert St, 8th Floor, Suite 820, Ottawa, ON K1R 7X7; tel. (613) 236-7267; fax (613) 236-7882; e-mail ottawa@diplobel.org; internet www.diplobel.org/canada; Ambassador DANIEL P. M. N. R. LEROY.

Benin: 58 Glebe Ave, Ottawa, ON K1S 2C3; tel. (613) 233-4429; fax (613) 233-8952; e-mail ambaben@benin.ca; internet www.benin.ca; Ambassador FRANCIS LOKO.

Bolivia: 130 Albert St, Suite 416, Ottawa, ON K1P 5G4; tel. (613) 236-5730; fax (613) 236-8237; e-mail embolivia-ottawa@rree.gov.bo; internet www.boliviaembassy.ca; Ambassador CARLOS ANTONIO CARRASCO FERNÁNDEZ.

Bosnia and Herzegovina: 130 Albert St, Suite 805, Ottawa, ON K1P 5G4; tel. (613) 236-0028; fax (613) 236-1139; e-mail embassyofbih@bellnet.ca; internet www.bhembassy.ca; Ambassador VJEKOSLAV DOMLJAN.

Brazil: 450 Wilbrod St, Ottawa, ON K1N 6M8; tel. (613) 237-1090; fax (613) 237-6144; e-mail mailbox@brasembottawa.org; internet www.brasembottawa.org; Ambassador VALDEMAR CARNEIRO LEÃO.

Brunei: 395 Laurier Ave East, Suite 400, Ottawa, ON K1N 6R4; tel. (603) 234-5656; fax (603) 234-4397; e-mail bhco@bellnet.ca; High Commissioner Hajah SITI RELAWATI HAJI MD IDRIS (acting).

Bulgaria: 325 Stewart St, Ottawa, ON K1N 6K5; tel. (613) 789-3215; fax (613) 789-3524; e-mail mailmn@storm.ca; Chargé d'affaires a.i. DIMITER DIMITROV.

Burkina Faso: 48 Range Rd, Ottawa, ON K1N 8J4; tel. (613) 238-4796; fax (613) 238-3812; e-mail burkina.faso@sympatico.ca; internet www.amba.burkina-canada.org; Ambassador JULIETTE BONKOUNGOU-YAMEOGO.

Burundi: 325 Dalhousie St, Suite 815, Ottawa, ON K1N 8J4; tel. (613) 789-0414; fax (613) 789-9537; Ambassador EPIPHANIE KABUSHEMEYE NTAMWANA.

Cameroon: 170 Clemow Ave, Ottawa, ON K1S 2B4; tel. (613) 236-1522; fax (613) 238-3885; High Commissioner PHILÉMON YUNJI YANG.

Chile: 50 O'Connor St, Suite 1413, Ottawa, ON K1N 6L2; tel. (613) 235-4402; fax (613) 235-1176; e-mail echile@chile.ca; internet www.chile.ca; Ambassador JOSÉ MIGUEL CRUZ SÁNCHEZ.

China, People's Republic: 515 St Patrick St, Ottawa, ON K1N 5H3; tel. (613) 789-3434; fax (613) 789-1911; e-mail cooffice@buildlink.com; internet www.chinaembassycanada.org; Ambassador SHUMIN LU.

Colombia: 360 Albert St, Suite 1002, Ottawa, ON K1R 7X7; tel. (613) 230-3760; fax (613) 230-4416; e-mail embajada@embajadacolombia.ca; internet www.embajadacolombia.ca; Ambassador JORGE ANIBAL VISBAL MARTELO.

Congo, Democratic Republic: 18 Range Rd, Ottawa, ON K1N 8J3; tel. (613)230-6391; fax (613) 230-1945; internet www.ambassadesrdcongo.org/ambass_canada.htm; Chargé d'affaires a.i. LOUISE NZANGA RAMAZANI.

Costa Rica: 325 Dalhousie St, Suite 407, Ottawa, ON K1N 7G2; tel. (613) 562-2855; fax (613) 562-2582; e-mail embcrica@travel-net.com; Ambassador CARLOS MIRANDA ARRINDA.

Côte d'Ivoire: 9 Marlborough Ave, Ottawa, ON K1N 8E6; tel. (613) 236-9919; fax (613) 563-8287; e-mail acica@ambaci-ottawa.org; internet www.ambaci-ottawa.org; Ambassador DIÉNÉBOU KABA.

Croatia: 229 Chapel St, Ottawa, ON K1N 7Y6; tel. (613) 562-7820; fax (613) 562-7821; e-mail croatia.emb@bellnet.ca; internet www.croatiaemb.net; Chargé d'affaires a.i. ANTE BARBIR.

Cuba: 388 Main St, Ottawa, ON K1S 1E3; tel. (613) 563-0141; fax (613) 563-0068; e-mail cuba@embacuba.ca; internet www.embacuba.ca; Ambassador ERNESTO ANTONIO SENTI DARIAS.

Czech Republic: 251 Cooper St, Ottawa, ON K2P 0G2; tel. (613) 562-3875; fax (613) 562-3878; e-mail ottawa@embassy.mzv.cz; internet www.czechembassy.org; Ambassador PAVEL VOŠALÍK.

Denmark: 47 Clarence St, Suite 450, Ottawa, ON K1N 9K1; tel. (613) 562-1811; fax (613) 562-1812; e-mail danemb@cyberus.ca; internet www.danish-embassy-canada.com; Ambassador POUL ERIK DAM KRISTENSEN.

Dominica: (see entry for Antigua and Barbuda).

Dominican Republic: 130 Albert St, Suite 418, Ottawa, ON K1P 5G4; tel. (613) 569-9893; fax (613) 569-8673; e-mail info@drembassy.org; internet www.drembassy.org; Ambassador EDUARDO J. TEJERA CURBELO.

Ecuador: 50 O'Connor St, Suite 316, Ottawa, ON K1P 6L2; tel. (613) 563-8206; fax (613) 235-5776; e-mail mecucan@sprint.ca; internet www.ncf.carleton.ca/ecuador; Ambassador MARIANO ALEJANDRO SUÁREZ PASCUAL.

Egypt: 454 Laurier Ave East, Ottawa, ON K1N 6R3; tel. (613) 234-4931; fax (613) 234-9347; internet www.egyptembassy.ca; e-mail egyptemb@sympatico.ca; Ambassador MAHMOUD F. EL-SAEED.

El Salvador: 209 Kent St, Ottawa, ON K2P 1Z8; tel. (613) 238-2939; fax (613) 238-6940; e-mail embajada@elsalvador-ca.org; Ambassador MAURICIO ROSALES RIVERA.

Estonia: 260 Dalhousie St, Suite 210, Ottawa, ON K1N 7E4; tel. (613) 789-4222; fax (613) 789-9555; e-mail estonianembassy@rogers.com; internet www.estemb.ca; Chargé d'affaires a.i. ARGO KÜÜNEMÄE.

Ethiopia: 151 Slater St, Suite 210, Ottawa, ON K1P 5H3; tel. (613) 235-6637; fax (613) 235-4638; e-mail cainfoethi@magi.com; internet www.ethiopia.ottawa.on.ca; Ambassador Dr BERHANU DIBABA KUMA.

Finland: 55 Metcalfe St, Suite 850, Ottawa, ON K1P 6L5; tel. (613) 288-2233; fax (613) 288-2244; e-mail embassy@finland.ca; internet www.finland.ca; Ambassador PASI MIKAEL PATOKALLIO.

France: 42 Sussex Dr., Ottawa, ON K1M 2C9; tel. (613) 789-1795; fax (613) 562-3735; e-mail politique@ambafrance-ca.org; internet www.ambafrance-ca.org; Ambassador DANIEL JOUANNEAU.

Gabon: 4 Range Rd, Ottawa, ON K1N 8J5; tel. (613) 232-5301; fax (613) 232-6916; e-mail ambgabon@sprint.ca; Ambassador JOSEPH OBIANG NDOUTOUME.

Germany: 1 Waverley St, Ottawa, ON K2P 0T8; tel. (613) 232-1101; fax (613) 594-9330; e-mail germanembassyottawa@on.aibn.com; internet www.ottawa.diplo.de; Ambassador CHRISTIAN FRIEDEMANN PAULS.

Ghana: 1 Clemow Ave, Ottawa, ON K1S 2A9; tel. (613) 236-0871; fax (613) 236-0874; e-mail ghanacom@ghanahighcommission-canada.com; internet www.ghanahighcommission-canada.com; High Commissioner SAMUEL ARTHUR ODOI-SYKES.

Greece: 76–80 MacLaren St, Ottawa, ON K2P 0K6; tel. (613) 238-6271; fax (613) 238-5676; e-mail embassy@greekembassy.ca; internet www.greekembassy.ca; Ambassador YIANNIS MOURIKIS.

Grenada: (see entry for Antigua and Barbuda).

Guatemala: 130 Albert St, Suite 1010, Ottawa, ON K1P 5G4; tel. (613) 233-7237; fax (613) 233-0135; e-mail embassy1@embaguate-canada.com; internet www.embaguate-canada.com; Ambassador CARLOS HUMBERTO JIMÉNEZ LICONA.

Guinea: 483 Wilbrod St, Ottawa, ON K1N 6N1; tel. (613) 789-8444; fax (613) 789-7560; e-mail ambguineaott@sympatico.ca; Ambassador ALY DIANE.

Guyana: Burnside Bldg, 151 Slater St, Suite 309, Ottawa, ON K1P 5H3; tel. (613) 235-7249; fax (613) 235-1447; e-mail guyanahcott@rogers.com; internet www.guyanamissionott.org; High Commissioner RAJNARINE SINGH.

Haiti: 130 Albert St, Suite 1409, Ottawa, ON K1P 5G4; tel. (613) 238-1628; fax (613) 238-2986; e-mail bohio@sympatico.ca; Chargé d'affaires CAROL JOSEPH.

Holy See: Apostolic Nunciature, 724 Manor Ave, Rockcliffe Park, Ottawa, ON K1M 0E3; tel. (613) 746-4914; fax (613) 746-4786; e-mail nuntius@bellnet.ca; Nuncio Most Rev. LUIGI VENTURA (Titular Archbishop of Equilio).

Honduras: 151 Slater St, Suite 805, Ottawa, ON K1P 5H3; tel. (613) 233-8900; fax (613) 232-0193; e-mail embhonca@magma.ca; Ambassador ANA CAROLINA GALEANO BURGOS.

Hungary: 299 Waverley St, Ottawa, ON K2P 0V9; tel. (613) 230-2717; fax (613) 230-7560; e-mail sysadmin@huembott.org; internet www.docuweb.ca/hungary; Ambassador DÉNES TOMAJ.

Iceland: 360 Albert St, Suite 710, Ottawa, ON K1R 7X7; tel. (613) 482-1944; fax (613) 482-1945; e-mail icemb.ottawa@utn.stjr.is; internet www.iceland.org/ca; Ambassador GUDMUNDUR EIRÍKSSON.

India: 10 Springfield Rd, Ottawa, ON K1M 1C9; tel. (613) 744-3751; fax (613) 744-0913; e-mail hicomind@hciottawa.ca; internet www.hciottawa.ca; High Commissioner SHYAMALA BALASUBRAMANIAN COWSIK.

Indonesia: 55 Parkdale Ave, Ottawa, ON K1Y 1E5; tel. (613) 724-1100; fax (613) 724-1105; e-mail info@prica.org; internet www.indonesia-ottawa.org; Chargé d'affaires a.i. SADEWO JOEDO.

Iran: 245 Metcalfe St, Ottawa, ON K2P 2K2; tel. (613) 235-4726; fax (613) 232-5712; e-mail iranemb@salamiran.org; internet www.salamiran.org; Ambassador SEYED MOUHAMMAD ALI MOOSAVI.

Iraq: 215 McLeod St, Ottawa, ON K2P 0Z8; tel. (613) 236-9177; fax (613) 567-1101; Ambassador HOWAR M. ZIAD.

Ireland: 130 Albert St, Suite 1105, Ottawa, ON K1P 5G4; tel. (613) 233-6281; fax (613) 233-5835; e-mail embassyofireland@rogers.com; Ambassador MARTIN BURKE.

Israel: 50 O'Connor St, Suite 1005, Ottawa, ON K1P 6L2; tel. (613) 567-6450; fax (613) 567-9878; e-mail info@ottawa.mfa.gov.il; internet www.embassyofisrael.ca; Ambassador ALAN BAKER.

Italy: 275 Slater St, 21st Floor, Ottawa, ON K1P 5H9; tel. (613) 232-2401; fax (613) 233-1484; e-mail ambital@italyincanada.com; internet www.italyincanada.com; Ambassador MARCO COLOMBO.

Jamaica: 275 Slater St, Suite 800, Ottawa, ON K1P 5H9; tel. (613) 233-9311; fax (613) 233-0611; e-mail hc@jhcottawa.ca; High Commissioner CARL O' NEAL MARSHALL.

Japan: 255 Sussex Dr., Ottawa, ON K1N 9E6; tel. (613) 241-8541; fax (613) 241-2232; e-mail infocul@embjapan.ca; internet www.ca.emb-japan.go.jp; Ambassador SADAAKI NUMATA.

Jordan: 100 Bronson Ave, Suite 701, Ottawa, ON K1R 6G8; tel. (613) 238-8090; fax (613) 232-3341; e-mail jordan@on.aibn.com; Ambassador FOUAD AYOUB.

Kenya: 415 Laurier Ave East, Ottawa, ON K1N 6R4; tel. (613) 563-1773; fax (613) 233-6599; e-mail kenyahighcommission@rogers.com; internet www.kenyahighcommission.ca; Ambassador PETER NICHOLAS RATENG O. OGEGO.

Korea, Republic: 150 Boteler St, Ottawa, ON K1N 5A6; tel. (613) 244-5010; fax (613) 244-5043; internet www.emb-korea.ottawa.on.ca; Ambassador YIM SUNG-JOON.

Kuwait: 333 Sussex Dr., Ottawa, ON K1N 1J9; tel. (613) 780-9999; fax (613) 780-9905; e-mail canada@embassyofkuwait.com; internet www.embassyofkuwait.com; Ambassador MUSAED RASHED A. AL-HAROUN (designate).

Latvia: 280 Albert St, Suite 300, Ottawa, ON K1P 5G8; tel. (613) 238-6014; fax (613) 238-7044; e-mail embassy.canada@mfa.gov.lv; internet www.ottawa.am.gov.lv; Ambassador ATIS SJANĪTS.

Lebanon: 640 Lyon St, Ottawa, ON K1S 3Z5; tel. (613) 236-5825; fax (613) 232-1609; e-mail info@lebanonembassy.ca; internet www.lebanonembassy.ca; Ambassador RAYMOND BAAKLINI.

Libya: 81 Metcalfe St, Suite 1000, Ottawa, ON K1P 6K7; tel. (613) 230-0919; fax (613) 230-0683; Chargé d'affaires a.i. AHMED ALI JARRUD.

Lithuania: 130 Albert St, Suite 204, Ottawa, ON K1P 5G4; tel. (613) 567-5458; fax (613) 567-5315; e-mail litemb@storm.ca; internet www.lithuanianembassy.ca; Ambassador SIGUTĖ JAKŠTONYTĖ.

Macedonia, former Yugoslav republic: 130 Albert St, Suite 1006, Ottawa, ON K1P 5G4; tel. (613) 234-3882; fax (613) 233-1852; e-mail emb.macedonia.ottawa@sympatico.ca; Ambassador SASKO NASEV.

Madagascar: 200 Catherine St, Suite 510, Ottawa, ON K2P 2K9; tel. (613) 567-0505; fax (613) 567-2882; e-mail ambamadcanada@yahoo.ca; internet www.madagascar-embassy.ca; Ambassador RAKOTOARISOA FLORENT.

Malawi: 7 Clemow Ave, Ottawa, ON K1S 2A9; tel. (613) 236-8931; fax (613) 236-1054; e-mail malawi.highcommission@bellnet.ca; High Commissioner KENNEDY AMOS MALISTA.

Malaysia: 60 Boteler St, Ottawa, ON K1N 8Y7; tel. (613) 241-5182; fax (613) 241-5214; e-mail malottawa@kln.gov.my; internet home.istar.ca/~mwottawa; High Commissioner Dato' DENNIS J. IGNATIUS.

Mali: 50 Goulburn Ave, Ottawa, ON K1N 8C8; tel. (613) 232-1501; fax (613) 232-7429; e-mail mbassadedumali@rogers.com; internet www.ambamalicanada.org; Ambassador MAMADOU BANDIOUGOU DIAWARA.

Mauritania: 121 Sherwood Dr., Ottawa, ON K1Y 3V1; tel. (613) 237-3283; fax (613) 237-3287; e-mail info@mauritania-canada.ca; internet www.mauritania-canada.ca; Ambassador MAHFOUDH BEN DEDDACH.

Mexico: 45 O'Connor St, Suite 1500, Ottawa, ON K1P 1A4; tel. (613) 233-8988; fax (613) 235-9123; e-mail info@embamexcan.com; internet www.embamexcan.com; Ambassador MARÍA TERESA GARCÍA SEGOVIA.

Mongolia: 151 Slater St, Suite 503, Ottawa, ON K1P 5H3; tel. (613) 569-3830; fax (613) 569–3916; internet mail@mongolembassy.org; e-mail ; internet www.mongolembassy.org; Ambassador GALSAN BATSUKH.

Montserrat: (see entry for Antigua and Barbuda).

Morocco: 38 Range Rd, Ottawa, ON K1N 8J4; tel. (613) 236-7391; fax (613) 236-6164; e-mail sifamaot@bellnet.ca; internet www.ambamaroc.ca; Ambassador MOHAMED TANGI.

Myanmar: 85 Range Rd, Suite 902/903, Ottawa, ON K1N 8J6; tel. (613) 232-6434; fax (613) 232-6435; e-mail meott@magma.ca; Chargé d'affaires a.i. U KYAW TIN.

Netherlands: 350 Albert St, Suite 2020, Ottawa, ON K1R 1A4; tel. (613) 237-5030; fax (613) 237-6471; e-mail nlgovott@netcom.ca; internet www.netherlandsembassy.ca; Ambassador JACQUES G. S. T. M. VAN HELLENBURG HUBAR.

New Zealand: Clarica Centre, 99 Bank St, Suite 727, Ottawa, ON K1P 6G3; tel. (613) 238-5991; fax (613) 238-5707; e-mail info@nzhcottawa.org; internet www.nzembassy.com/canada; High Commissioner GRAHAM DESMOND KELLY.

Niger: 38 Blackburn Ave, Ottawa, ON K1N 8A3; tel. (613) 232-4291; fax (613) 230-9808; Ambassador NANA AÏCHA MOUCTARI FOUMAKOYE.

Nigeria: 295 Metcalfe St, Ottawa, ON K2P 1R9; tel. (613) 236-0522; fax (613) 236-0529; e-mail hc@nigeriahighcommottawa.com; internet www.nigeriahighcommottawa; High Commissioner OLUFEMI OYEWALE GEORGE.

Norway: 90 Sparks St, Suite 532, Ottawa, ON K1P 5B4; tel. (613) 238-6571; fax (613) 238-2765; e-mail emb.ottawa@mfa.no; internet www.emb-norway.ca; Ambassador INGVARD MARTIN ARNE HAVNEN.

Pakistan: Burnside Bldg, 151 Slater St, Suite 608, Ottawa, ON K1P 5H3; tel. (613) 238-7881; fax (613) 238-7296; e-mail parepottawa@sprint.ca; internet www.pakmission.ca; High Commissioner SHAHID MALIK.

Panama: 130 Albert St, Suite 300, Ottawa, ON K1P 5G4; tel. (613) 236-7177; fax (613) 236-5775; e-mail pancanem@rapidweb.ca; Ambassador ROMY VÁSQUEZ DE GONZÁLEZ.

Papua New Guinea: 130 Albert St, Suite 300, Ottawa, ON K1A 5G4; fax (613) 236-5775; High Commissioner NAGORA Y. BOGAN.

Paraguay: 151 Slater St, Suite 501, Ottawa, ON K1P 5H3; tel. (613) 567-1283; fax (613) 567-1679; e-mail embapar@magmacom.com; internet www.embassyofparaguay.ca; Ambassador JUAN ESTEBAN O. AGUIRRE MARTÍNEZ.

Peru: 130 Albert St, Suite 1901, Ottawa, ON K1P 5G4; tel. (613) 238-1777; fax (613) 232-3062; e-mail emperuca@bellnet.ca; internet www.embassyofperu.ca; Ambassador JOSÉ E. ROMERO.

Philippines: 130 Albert St, Suite 606, Ottawa, ON K1P 5G4; tel. (613) 233-1121; fax (613) 233-4165; e-mail embassyofphilippines@rogers.com; internet members.rogers.com/embassyofphilippines; Ambassador FRANCISCO L. BENEDICTO.

Poland: 443 Daly Ave, Ottawa, ON K1N 6H3; tel. (613) 789-0468; fax (613) 789-1218; e-mail ottawa@polishembassy.ca; internet www.polishembassy.ca; Ambassador PIOTR OGRODZINSKI.

Portugal: 645 Island Park Dr., Ottawa, ON K1Y 0B8; tel. (613) 729-0883; fax (613) 729-4236; e-mail embportugal@embportugal-ottawa.org; internet www.embportugal-ottawa.org; Ambassador JOÃO PEDRO DA SILVEIRA CARVALHO.

Romania: 655 Rideau St, Ottawa, ON K1N 6A3; tel. (613) 789-3709; fax (613) 789-4365; e-mail romania@cyberus.ca; internet www.cyberus.ca/~romania; Ambassador LIVIU MAIOR.

Russia: 285 Charlotte St, Ottawa, ON K1N 8L5; tel. (613) 235-4341; fax (613) 236-6342; e-mail rusemb@intranet.ca; internet www.rusembcanada.mid.ru; Ambassador GEORGII MAMEDOV.

Rwanda: 123 Mackay St, Ottawa, ON K1M 2B4; Ambassador EUGENE MUNYAKAYANZA.

Saint Christopher and Nevis: (see entry for Antigua and Barbuda).

Saint Lucia: (see entry for Antigua and Barbuda).

Saint Vincent and the Grenadines: (see entry for Antigua and Barbuda).

Saudi Arabia: 99 Bank St, Suite 901, Ottawa, ON K1P 6B9; tel. (613) 237-4100; fax (613) 237-0567; e-mail caemb@mofa.gov.sa; Ambassador Dr MOHAMMED R. AL-HUSANI AL-SHARIF.

Senegal: 57 Marlborough Ave, Ottawa, ON K1N 8E8; tel. (613) 238-6392; fax (613) 238-2695; e-mail amadou@rogers.com; internet www.ambassenecanada.org; Ambassador AMADOU DIALLO.

Serbia and Montenegro: 17 Blackburn Ave, Ottawa, ON K1N 8A2; tel. (613) 233-6289; fax (613) 233-7850; e-mail diplomat@yuemb.ca; internet www.embscg.ca; Ambassador PERKO VUKOTIC.

Slovakia: 50 Rideau Terrace, Ottawa, ON K1M 2A1; tel. (613) 749-4442; fax (613) 749-4989; e-mail ottawa@slovakembassy.ca; internet www.ottawa.mfa.sk; Chargé d'affaires a.i. ŠTEFAN ROZKOPÁL.

Slovenia: 150 Metcalfe St, Suite 2101, Ottawa, ON K2P 1P1; tel. (613) 565-5781; fax (613) 565-5783; e-mail vot@mzz-dkp.gov.si; Ambassador VERONIKA STABEJ.

South Africa: 15 Sussex Dr., Ottawa, ON K1M 1M8; tel. (613) 744-0330; fax (613) 741-1639; e-mail rsafrica@southafrica-canada.ca; internet www.southafrica-canada.ca; High Commissioner THERESA MAY SOLOMON.

Spain: 74 Stanley Ave, Ottawa, ON K1M 1P4; tel. (613) 747-2252; fax (613) 744-1224; e-mail embespca@mail.mae.es; internet www.embaspain.ca; Ambassador JOSÉ IGNACIO CARBAJAL GÁRATE.

Sri Lanka: 333 Laurier Ave West, Suite 1204, Ottawa, ON K1P 1C1; tel. (613) 233-8449; fax (613) 238-8448; e-mail lankacom@magi.com; internet www.srilankahcottawa.org; High Commissioner M. N. GEETHANGANI DE SILVA.

Sudan: 354 Stewart St, Ottawa, ON K1N 6K8; tel. (613) 235-4000; fax (613) 235-6880; e-mail sudanembassy-canada@rogers.com; Ambassador Dr FAIZA HASSAN TAHA ARMOUSA.

Sweden: Mercury Court, 377 Dalhousie St, Ottawa, ON K1N 9N8; tel. (613) 241-8553; fax (613) 241-2277; e-mail sweden@cyberus.ca; internet www.swedishembassy.ca; Ambassador LENNART ALVIN.

Switzerland: 5 Marlborough Ave, Ottawa, ON K1N 8E6; tel. (613) 235-1837; fax (613) 563-1394; e-mail vertretung@ott.rep.admin.ch; internet www.eda.admin.ch/canada_all; Ambassador ANTON THALMANN.

Syria: 151 Slater St, Suite 1000, Ottawa, ON K1P 5H3; tel. (613) 569-5556; fax (613) 569-3800; e-mail syrianembassy@on.aibn.ca; internet www.syrianembassy.com; Chargé d'affaires a.i. IMAD ALAHMAR.

Tanzania: 50 Range Rd, Ottawa, ON K1N 8J4; tel. (613) 232-1500; fax (613) 232-5184; e-mail tzottawa@synapse.net; High Commissioner Dr BEN G. MOSES.

Thailand: 180 Island Park Dr., Ottawa, ON K1Y 0A2; tel. (613) 722-4444; fax (613) 722-6624; e-mail thaiott@magma.ca; internet www.magma.ca/~thaiott/mainpage.htm; Ambassador SNANCHART DEVAHASTIN.

Togo: 12 Range Rd, Ottawa, ON K1N 8J3; tel. (613) 238-5916; fax (613) 235-6425; e-mail ambatogoca@hotmail.com; Ambassador BAWOUMONDOM AMELETE.

Trinidad and Tobago: 200 First Ave, Ottawa, ON K1S 2G6; tel. (613) 232-2418; fax (613) 232-4349; e-mail ottawa@ttmissions.com; internet www.ttmissions.com; High Commissioner ARNOLD ALVIN PIGGOTT.

Tunisia: 515 O'Connor St, Ottawa, ON K1S 3P8; tel. (613) 237-0330; fax (613) 237-7939; Ambassador MUHAMMAD SAAD.

Turkey: 197 Wurtemburg St, Ottawa, ON K1N 8L9; tel. (613) 789-4044; fax (613) 789-3442; e-mail turkishottawa@mfa.gov.tr; internet www.turkishembassy.com; Ambassador AYDEMIR ERMAN.

Uganda: 231 Cobourg St, Ottawa, ON K1N 8J2; tel. (613) 789-7797; fax (613) 789-8909; e-mail ugandahighcomm@bellnet.ca; internet www.ugandahighcommission.ca; High Commissioner CISSY HELEN TALIWAKU.

Ukraine: 310 Somerset St West, Ottawa, ON K2P 0J9; tel. (613) 230-2961; fax (613) 230-2400; e-mail emb_ca@ukremb.ca; internet www.ukremb.ca; Ambassador MYKOLA MAIMESKUL.

United Arab Emirates: World Exchange Plaza, 45 O'Connor St, Suite 1800, Ottawa, ON K1P 1A4; tel. (613) 565-7272; fax (613) 565-8007; e-mail safara@uae-embassy.com; internet www.uae-embassy.com; Ambassador HASSAN MOHAMMED OBAID AL-SUWAIDI.

United Kingdom: 80 Elgin St, Ottawa, ON K1P 5K7; tel. (613) 237-1530; fax (613) 237-7980; e-mail generalenquiries@britanincanada.org; internet www.britanincanada.org; High Commissioner DAVID NORMAN REDDAWAY.

USA: 490 Sussex Dr., POB 866, Station B, Ottawa, ON K1P 5T1; tel. (613) 238-5335; fax (613) 688-3080; internet www.usembassycanada.gov; Ambassador (vacant).

Uruguay: 130 Albert St, Suite 1905, Ottawa, ON K1P 5G4; tel. (613) 234-2727; fax (613) 233-4670; e-mail urott@iosphere.net; internet www.iosphere.net/~uruott; Ambassador ALVARO MARCELO MOERZINGER PAGANI.

Venezuela: 32 Range Rd, Ottawa, ON K1N 8J4; tel. (613) 235-5151; fax (613) 235-3205; e-mail info.canada@misionvenezuela.org; internet www.misionvenezuela.org; Chargé d'affaires a.i. MARGARITA AYELLO.

Viet Nam: 470 Wilbrod St, Ottawa, ON K1M 6M8; tel. (613) 236-0772; fax (613) 236-2704; e-mail vietem@istar.ca; internet www.vietnamembassy-canada.ca; Ambassador NGUYEN THI HOI TRINH.

Yemen: 788 Island Park Dr., Ottawa, ON K1Y 0C2; tel. (613) 729-6627; fax (613) 729-8915; e-mail assistant@yemenincanada.ca; internet www.yemenincanada.ca; Ambassador Dr ABDULLA ABDULWALI NASHER.

Zimbabwe: 332 Somerset St West, Ottawa, ON K2P 0J9; tel. (613) 237-4388; fax (613) 563-8269; e-mail zim.highcomm@sympatico.ca; internet www.docuweb.ca/zimbabwe; Ambassador GABRIEL MHARADZE MACHINGA.

Judicial System

FEDERAL COURTS

The Supreme Court of Canada: Supreme Court Bldg, 301 Wellington St, Ottawa, ON K1A 0J1; tel. (613) 995-4330; fax (613) 996-9138; e-mail reception@scc-csc.gc.ca; internet www.scc-csc.gc.ca; ultimate court of appeal in both civil and criminal cases throughout Canada. The Supreme Court is also required to advise on questions referred to it by the Governor-General in Council. Important questions concerning the interpretation of the Constitution Act, the constitutionality or interpretation of any federal or provincial law, the powers of Parliament or of the provincial legislatures, among other matters, may be referred by the Government to the Supreme Court for consideration.

In most cases, appeals are heard by the Court only if leave to appeal is given from any final judgment of the highest court of last resort in a province or territory, or of the Federal Court of Appeal. Such leave, or permission, will be given by the Court when a case involves a question of public importance. There are cases, however, where leave is not required. In criminal cases, there is an automatic right of appeal where an acquittal has been set aside in the provincial court of appeal or where one judge in the provincial court of appeal dissents on a question of law.

Chief Justice of Canada: BEVERLEY MCLACHLIN.

Puisne Judges: FRANK IACOBUCCI, JOHN C. MAJOR, MICHEL BASTARACHE, W. IAN BINNIE, LOUISE ARBOUR, LOUIS LEBEL, MARIE DESCHAMPS, MORRIS J. FISH.

The Federal Court: Supreme Court Bldg, Kent and Wellington Sts, Ottawa, ON K1A 0H9; tel. (613) 996-6795; fax (613) 952-7226; e-mail reception@cas-satj.gc.ca; internet www.fca-caf.gc.ca; has jurisdiction in claims against the Crown, claims by the Crown, miscellaneous cases involving the Crown, claims against or concerning crown officers and servants, relief against Federal Boards, Commissions, and other tribunals, interprovincial and federal-provincial disputes, industrial or industrial property matters, admiralty, income tax and estate tax appeals, citizenship appeals, aeronautics, interprovincial works and undertakings, residuary jurisdiction for relief if there is no other Canadian court that has such jurisdiction, jurisdiction in specific matters conferred by federal statutes

Chief Justice: ALLAN LUTFY.

The Federal Court of Appeal

Supreme Court Bldg, Kent and Wellington Sts, Ottawa, ON K1A 0H9; tel. (613) 996-6795; fax (613) 952-7226; e-mail reception@cas-satj.gc.ca; internet www.fca-caf.gc.ca.

Has jurisdiction on appeals from the Trial Division, appeals from Federal Tribunals, review of decisions of Federal Boards and Commissions, appeals from Tribunals and Reviews under Section 28 of the Federal Court Act, and references by Federal Boards and Commissions. The Court has one central registry and consists of the principal office in Ottawa and local offices in major centres throughout Canada.

Chief Justice: JOHN D. RICHARD.

Trial Division Judges: YVON PINARD, FREDERICK E. GIBSON, SANDRA J. SIMPSON, DANIÈLE TREMBLAY-LAMER, DOUGLAS R. CAMPBELL, PIERRE BLAIS, FRANÇOIS LEMIEUX, JOHN A. O'KEEFE, ELIZABETH HENEGHAN, DOLORES HANSEN, ELEANOR R. DAWSON, EDMOND P. BLANCHARD, MICHAEL A. KELEN, MICHAEL BEAUDRY, LUC MARTINEAU, CAROLYN LAYDEN-STEVENSON, SIMON NOËL, JUDITH A. SNIDER, JAMES RUSSELL, JOHANNE GAUTHIER, JAMES O'REILLY, KONRAD W. VON FINCKENSTEIN, SEAN J. HARRINGTON, RICHARD MOSLEY, MICHEL M. J. SHORE, MICHAEL L. PHELAN, ANNE L. MACTAVISH, YVES DE MONTIGNY.

Court of Appeal Judges: ALICE DESJARDINS, ROBERT DÉCARY, ALLEN M. LINDEN, GILLES LÉTOURNEAU, MARSHALL E. ROTHSTEIN, MARC NOËL, MARC NADON, J. EDGAR SEXTON, JOHN MAXWELL EVANS, KAREN SHARLOW, J. D. DENIS PELLETIER, J. BRIAN MALONE.

PROVINCIAL AND TERRITORIAL COURTS

Alberta

Court of Appeal

Chief Justice of Alberta: CATHERINE A. FRASER (Edmonton).

Court of Queen's Bench

Chief Justice: ALLAN H. J. WACHOWICH (Edmonton).
Associate Chief Justice: A. B. SULATYCKY (Calgary).

British Columbia

Court of Appeal

Chief Justice of British Columbia: LANCE SIDNEY GEORGE FINCH.

Supreme Court

Chief Justice: DONALD IAN BRENNER.
Associate Chief Justice: PATRICK DONALD DOHM.

Manitoba

Court of Appeal

Chief Justice of Manitoba: R. J. SCOTT.

Court of Queen's Bench

Chief Justice: MARC M. MONNIN.
Associate Chief Justice: JEFFREY J. OLIPHANT.
Associate Chief Justice (Family Division): GERALD W. MERCIER.

New Brunswick

Court of Appeal

Chief Justice of New Brunswick: ERNEST DRAPEAU.

Court of Queen's Bench

Chief Justice: DAVID D. SMITH (Moncton).

Newfoundland and Labrador

Supreme Court—Court of Appeal

Chief Justice: CLYDE K. WELLS.

Trial Division

Chief Justice: J. D. GREEN.

Northwest Territories

Court of Appeal

Chief Justice: CATHERINE A. FRASER (Alberta).

Supreme Court

Judges of the Supreme Court: J. EDWARD RICHARD, JOHN Z. VERTES, VIRGINIA A. SCHULER.

Nova Scotia

Court of Appeal

Chief Justice of Nova Scotia: CONSTANCE R. GLUBE.

Supreme Court

Chief Justice: JOSEPH P. KENNEDY.
Associate Chief Justice: MICHAEL MACDONALD.

Supreme Court (Family Division)

Associate Chief Justice: R. F. FERGUSON.

Nunavut Territory

Court of Appeal

Chief Justice: CATHERINE A. FRASER (Alberta).

Court of Justice

Judges of the Court of Justice: B. A. BROWNE, R. G. KILPATRICK, E. D. JOHNSON.

Ontario

Court of Appeal

Chief Justice of Ontario: ROY R. MCMURTRY.
Associate Chief Justice of Ontario: DENNIS R. O'CONNOR.

Court of Justice

Chief Justice: HEATHER F. SMITH.
Associate Chief Justice: J. DOUGLAS CUNNINGHAM.

Prince Edward Island

Supreme Court—Appeal Division

Chief Justice: GERARD E. MITCHELL.

Supreme Court—Trial Division

Chief Justice: J. ARMAND DESROCHES.

Québec

Court of Appeal

Chief Justice of Québec: J. J. MICHEL ROBERT.

Superior Court

Chief Justice: FRANÇOIS ROLLAND.
Associate Chief Justice: ROBERT PIDGEON.

Saskatchewan

Court of Appeal

Chief Justice of Saskatchewan: E. D. BAYDA.

Court of Queen's Bench

Chief Justice: W. F. GEREIN (Regina).

Yukon Territory

Court of Appeal

Chief Justice: LANCE S. G. FINCH (British Columbia).

Supreme Court

Judges of the Supreme Court: L. F. GOWER HUDSON, R. S. VEALE (both of Whitehorse).

Religion

CHRISTIANITY

About 75% of the population belong to the three main Christian churches: Roman Catholic, United and Anglican. Numerous other religious denominations are active in Canada.

Canadian Council of Churches/Conseil canadien des Eglises: 159 Roxborough Dr., Toronto, ON M4W; tel. (416) 972-9494; fax (416) 927-0405; e-mail avedikia@ccc-cce.ca; internet www.ccc-cce.ca; f. 1944; 19 mem. churches, one assoc. mem; Pres. Prof. RICHARD SCHNEIDER (Orthodox Church in America); Gen. Sec. Rev. Dr KAREN HAMILTON.

The Anglican Communion

The Anglican Church of Canada (L'Eglise anglicane du Canada) comprises 30 dioceses in four ecclesiastical provinces (each with a Metropolitan archbishop). The Church had about 680,000 members in 1,800 parishes in 2004.

General Synod of the Anglican Church of Canada: 80 Hayden St, Toronto, ON M4Y 3G2; tel. (416) 924-9192; fax (416) 968-7983; e-mail info@national.anglican.ca; internet www.anglican.ca; Gen. Sec. Archdeacon JAMES BOYLES.

Primate of the Anglican Church of Canada: Most Rev. ANDREW HUTCHINSON.

Province of British Columbia and Yukon: Metropolitan Most Rev. DAVID P. CRAWLEY (Archbishop of Kootenay).

Province of Canada: Metropolitan Most Rev. BRUCE STAVERT (Archbishop of Québec).

Province of Ontario: Metropolitan Most Rev. CALEB LAWRENCE (Archbishop of Moosonee).

Province of Rupert's Land: Metropolitan Rt Rev. JOHN CLARKE (Bishop of Athabasca).

The Orthodox Churches

There were an estimated 580,000 adherents to Orthodox patriarchates at mid-2000.

Greek Orthodox Metropolis of Toronto (Canada): 1 Patriarch Bartholomew Way, East York, ON M4H 1C6; tel. (416) 429-5757; fax (416) 429-4588; e-mail greekomt@on.aibn.com; internet www.gocanada.org; 350,000 mems (1997); Metropolitan Archbishop SOTIRIOS ATHANASSOULAS.

Ukrainian Orthodox Church of Canada: 9 St John's Ave, Winnipeg, MB R2W 1G8; tel. (204) 586-3093; fax (204) 582-5241; e-mail chancery@archeparchy.ca; internet www.uocc.ca; f. 1918; 281 parishes; 30,000 mems (2001); Metropolitan of Winnipeg and of all Canada His Beatitude WASYLY (Fedak); Chair. Very Rev. Fr WILLIAM MAKARENKO.

The Russian, Belarusian, Polish, Romanian, Serbian, Coptic, Antiochian and Armenian Churches are also represented in Canada.

The Roman Catholic Church

For Catholics of the Latin rite, Canada comprises 18 archdioceses (including one directly responsible to the Holy See), 46 dioceses and one territorial abbacy. There are also one archdiocese and four dioceses of the Ukrainian rite. In addition, the Maronite, Melkite and Slovak rites are each represented by one diocese (all directly responsible to the Holy See). In December 2001 the Roman Catholic Church had about 11.3m. adherents in Canada.

Canadian Conference of Catholic Bishops/Conférence des évêques catholiques du Canada: 2500 Don Reid Dr., Ottawa, ON K1H 2J2; tel. (613) 241-9461; fax (613) 241-9048; e-mail cecc@cccb.ca; internet www.cccb.ca; Pres. Most Rev. BRENDAN M. O'BRIEN (Archbishop of St John's, NL); Vice-Pres. Most Rev. ANDRÉ GAUMOND (Archbishop of Sherbrooke, QC).

Latin Rite

Archbishop of Edmonton: Most Rev. THOMAS COLLINS.
Archbishop of Gatineau-Hull: Most Rev. ROGER ÉBACHER.
Archbishop of Grouard-McLennan: Most Rev. ARTHÉ GUIMOND.
Archbishop of Halifax: Most Rev. TERRENCE T. PRENDERGAST.
Archbishop of Keewatin-Le Pas: Most Rev. PETER ALFRED SUTTON.
Archbishop of Kingston: Most Rev. ANTHONY G. MEAGHER.
Archbishop of Moncton: Most Rev. ANDRÉ RICHARD.
Archbishop of Montréal: Most Rev. Cardinal JEAN-CLAUDE TURCOTTE.
Archbishop of Ottawa: Most Rev. MARCEL ANDRÉ J. GERVAIS.
Archbishop of Québec: Cardinal MARC OUELLET.
Archbishop of Regina: Most Rev. PETER J. MALLON.

Archbishop of Rimouski: Most Rev. Bertrand Blanchet.

Archbishop of St Boniface: Most Rev. Emilius Goulet.

Archbishop of St John's, NL: Most Rev. Brendan M. O'Brien.

Archbishop of Sherbrooke: Most Rev. André Gaumond.

Archbishop of Toronto: Cardinal Aloysius M. Ambrozic.

Archbishop of Vancouver: Most Rev. Raymond Roussin.

Archbishop of Winnipeg: Most Rev. Vernon J. Weisgerber.

Ukrainian Rite

Ukrainian Catholic Archeparchy of Winnipeg (Metropolitan See of Canada): 233 Scotia St, Winnipeg, MB R2V 1V7; tel. (204) 338-7801; fax (204) 339-4006; e-mail archepar@escape.ca; internet www.archeparchy.ca; 126,200 mems (2001); Archeparch-Metropolitan of Winnipeg Most Rev. Michael Bzdel.

The United Church of Canada

The United Church of Canada (L'Eglise unie du Canada) was founded in 1925 with the union of Methodist, Congregational and Presbyterian churches in Canada. The Evangelical United Brethren of Canada joined in 1968. In 2001 there were 3,677 congregations and 637,941 mems.

Moderator: Rev. Dr Peter Short.

General Secretary: Rev. Dr Jim Sinclair, 3250 Bloor St West, Suite 300, Toronto, ON M8X 2Y4; tel. (416) 231-5931; fax (416) 231-3103; e-mail info@uccan.org; internet www.uccan.org.

Other Christian Churches

Canadian Baptist Ministries: 7185 Millcreek Dr., Mississauga, ON L5N 5R4; tel. (905) 821-3533; fax (905) 826-3441; e-mail communications@cbmin.org; internet www.cbmin.org; 1,133 churches; 129,000 mems (1996); Gen. Sec. Rev. Dr Gary Nelson.

Christian Reformed Church in North America (Canadian Council): 3475 Mainway, POB 5070, Burlington, ON L7R 3Y8; tel. (905) 336-2920; fax (905) 336-8344; e-mail crcna@crcna.ca; internet www.crcna.org; f. 1857; 241 congregations; 81,250 mems (2003); Dir in Canada Rev. William Veenstra.

Church of Jesus Christ of Latter-day Saints (Mormon): 1185 Eglinton Ave East, POB 116, Toronto, ON M3C 3C6; tel. (416) 424-2485; fax (416) 424-3326; internet ldscanada.byondf1.com; f. 1832; 481 congregations; 166,505 mems in Canada (2004).

Evangelical Lutheran Church in Canada: 393 Portage Ave, Suite 302, Winnipeg, MB R3B 3H6; tel. (204) 984-9150; fax (204) 984-9185; e-mail pnjohnson@elcic.ca; internet www.elcic.ca; f. 1986; 623 congregations; 182,077 mems (2003); Bishop Rev. Raymond L. Schultz.

Lutheran Church–Canada: 3074 Portage Ave, Winnipeg, MB R3K 0Y2; tel. (204) 895-3433; fax (204) 832-3018; e-mail info@lutheranchurch.ca; internet www.lutheranchurch.ca; f. 1988; 321 congregations; 76,900 mems (2004); Pres. Rev. Ralph Mayan.

Pentecostal Assemblies of Canada: 2450 Milltower Court, Mississauga, ON L5N 5Z6; tel. (905) 542-7400; fax (905) 542-7313; e-mail info@paoc.org; internet www.paoc.org; f. 1919; 1,111 congregations; 236,579 mems (2005); Gen. Supt Dr William D. Morrow.

Presbyterian Church in Canada: 50 Wynford Dr., Toronto, ON M3C 1J7; tel. (416) 441-1111; fax (416) 441-2825; e-mail pccweb@presbycan.ca; internet www.presbyterian.ca; f. 1875; 997 congregations; 125,509 mems (2003); Moderator Rev. Dr Richard Fee; Prin. Clerk Rev. Stephen Kendall.

Religious Society of Friends: 91A Fourth Ave, Ottawa, ON K1S 2L1; tel. (613) 235-8553; fax (613) 235-1753; e-mail signy@canadiangeographic.ca; internet www.quaker.ca; Clerk of Canadian Yearly Meeting Rick McCutcheon-Ham (2004).

Seventh-day Adventists: 1148 King St East, Oshawa, ON L1H 1H8; tel. (905) 433-0011; fax (905) 433-0982; e-mail namorim@sdacc.org; internet www.sdacc.org; 328 congregations; 53,343 mems (2004); Pres. Daniel Jackson; Sec. Nilton Amorim.

BAHÁ'Í FAITH

Bahá'í Community of Canada: 7200 Leslie St, Thornhill, ON L3T 6L8; tel. (905) 889-8168; fax (905) 889-8184; e-mail info@ca.bahai.org; internet www.ca.bahai.org; f. 1902; 30,000 mems (2004); Sec. Judy Filson.

BUDDHISM

Buddhist Churches of Canada: 11786 Fentiman Place, Richmond, BC V7E 6M6; tel. (604) 272-3330; fax (604) 272-6865; e-mail bcc@bcc.ca; internet www.bcc.ca; f. 1905; Jodo Shinshu Hongwanji-ha of Mahayana Buddhism; Bishop Orai Fujikawa.

ISLAM

There are an estimated 260,000 Muslims in Canada.

Ahmadiyya Movement in Islam (Canada): 10610 Jane St, Maple, ON L6A 3A2; tel. (905) 832-2669; fax (905) 832-3220; e-mail info@ahmadiyya.ca; internet www.ahmadiyya.ca; f. 1965; Pres. and Missionary-in-Charge Naseem Mahdi; Gen. Sec. Dr Aslam Daud.

Canadian Islamic Congress: 420 Erb St West, Suite 424, Waterloo, ON N2L 6K6; tel. (519) 746-1242; fax (519) 746-2929; e-mail cic@canadianislamiccongress.com; internet www.canadianislamiccongress.com; Pres. Mohamed Elmasry.

Council of Muslim Communities of Canada: 1 Balmoral Ave, Suite 714, Toronto, ON M4V 3B9; f. 1971; co-ordinating agency; Pres. Hanny Hassan.

Organization of North American Shi'a Itha-Asheri Muslim Communities (NASIMCO): 300 John St, POB 87629, Thornhill, ON L3T 7R3; tel. (905) 763-7512; fax (905) 763-7509; e-mail info@nasimco.org; internet www.nasimco.org; Pres. Hussein Walji; Sec. Habib Dhalla.

JUDAISM

The are an estimated 350,000 Jews in Canada.

Canadian Council for Conservative Judaism: 1000 Finch Ave West, Suite 508, Toronto, ON M3J 2V5; tel. (416) 667-1717; fax (416) 667-1818; e-mail canadian@uscj.org; Pres. Paul Kochberg; Dir Loretta Tanenbaum.

Canadian Council for Reform Judaism: 36 Atkinson Ave, Thornhill, ON L4J 8C9; tel. (905) 709-2275; fax (905) 709-1895; e-mail ccrj@uahc.org; Pres. Charles Rothschild.

Canadian Jewish Congress: 100 Sparks St, Suite 650, Ottawa, ON K1P 5B7; tel. (613) 233-8703; fax (613) 233-8748; e-mail canadianjewishcongress@cjc.ca; internet www.cjc.ca; f. 1919; 10 regional offices; Exec. Vice-Pres. Jack Silverstone.

SIKHISM

There are an estimated 278,400 Sikhs in Canada.

World Sikh Organization of Canada (WSO Canada): 1183 Cecil Ave, Ottawa, ON K1H 7Z6; tel. (613) 521-1984; fax (613) 521-7454; e-mail info@worldsikh.org; internet www.worldsikh.org; Pres. Ajit Singh Sahota; Exec. Dir Anne Lowthian.

The Press

The daily press in Canada is essentially local and regional in coverage, influence and distribution. Chain ownership has traditionally been predominant: at the beginning of 2000 63.4% of daily newspaper circulation was represented by two major groups: Hollinger Inc (42.0% of daily newspaper circulation) and Quebecor Inc (21.4%). However, in 2000 both Hollinger and the Thomson Corpn (10.5%) divested themselves of significant proportions of their newspaper interests—Thomson retaining only the Toronto *Globe and Mail*, control of which was subsequently transferred to Bell Globemedia, Inc, a joint venture between companies including Thomson and the telecommunications operator, BCE, Inc. In November 2000 CanWest Global Communications Corpn acquired 14 daily metropolitan newspapers, a number of community newspapers and a 50% interest in the National Post (Canada's first national daily newspaper, launched by Hollinger's Southam Inc division in October 1998). Torstar (which owns the *Toronto Star*) accounted for 13.8% of total circulation in 2000.

In 2002 there were 102 daily newspapers with a combined circulation of almost 5.1m., and, in 2000, about 1,100 weekly and twice-weekly community newspapers serving mainly the more remote areas of the country. A significant feature of the Canadian press is the number of newspapers catering for immigrant groups: there are over 80 of these daily and weekly publications appearing in over 20 languages.

There are numerous periodicals for business, trade, professional, recreational and special interest readership, although periodical publishing, particularly, encounters substantial competition from publications originating in the USA.

The following are among the principal newspaper publishing groups:

CanWest Global Communications Corpn: 3100 TD Center, 201 Portage Ave, Winnipeg, MB R3B 3L7; tel. (204) 956-2025; fax (204) 947-9841; e-mail gelliot@canwest.com; internet www.canwestglobal.com; acquired Southam Publications in 2000; owns 11 English-language major metropolitan daily newspapers in Canada; Chair. Frank McKenna; Pres. and CEO Leonard J. Asper.

Quebecor Inc: 612 rue St-Jacques, Montréal, QC H3C 1C8; tel. (514) 877-9777; fax (514) 877-9790; e-mail qi_info@quebecor.com; internet www.quebecor.com; f. 1965; publishes eight major metropolitan daily newspapers, eight community daily newspapers and some 180 local weekly newspapers; Pres. and CEO PIERRE KARL PELADIEU.

Torstar Corpn: 1 Yonge St, Toronto, ON M5E 1P9; tel. (416) 869-4010; fax (416) 869-4183; e-mail torstar@torstar.com; internet www .torstar.com; incorporates the Citymedia Group and Metroland newspaper-publishing cos; Chair. JOHN R. EVANS; Pres. and CEO J. ROBERT PRITCHARD.

PRINCIPAL DAILY NEWSPAPERS

Alberta

Calgary Herald: 215 16th St, SE, POB 2400, Station M, Calgary, AB T2P 0W8; tel. (403) 235-7100; fax (403) 235-7379; e-mail llovestone@theherald.canwest.com; internet www.canada.com/calgary; f. 1883; Publr PETER MENZIES; Editor-in-Chief MALCOLM KIRK; circ. Mon. to Sat. 121,147, Sun. 114,020.

Calgary Sun: 2615 12th St, NE, Calgary, AB T2E 7W9; tel. (403) 250-4200; fax (403) 250-4180; e-mail cal-promotions@calgarysun .com; internet www.calgarysun.com; f. 1980; Publr GUY HUNTINGFORD; Editor-in-Chief CHRIS NELSON; circ. Mon. to Sat. 65,988, Sun. 98,941.

Daily Herald–Tribune: 10604 100th St, Postal Bag 3000, Grande Prairie, AB T8V 6V4; tel. (403) 532-1110; fax (403) 532-2120; e-mail frinne@bowesnet.com; internet www.dailyheraldtribune.com; f. 1913; evening; Publr KENT KEEBAUGH; Man. Editor FRED RINNE; circ. 9,047.

Edmonton Journal: POB 2421, Edmonton, AB T5J 2S6; tel. (780) 429-5100; fax (780) 429-5536; e-mail letters@thejournal.canwest .com; internet www.canada.com/edmonton; f. 1903; Pres. and Publr LINDA HUGHES; Editor-in-Chief ALLAN MAYER; circ. Mon. to Sat. 135,458, Sun. 130,572.

Edmonton Sun: 4990 92nd Ave, Suite 250, Edmonton, AB T6B 3A1; tel. (780) 468-0100; fax (780) 468-0128; e-mail letters@edm .sunpub.com; internet www.fyiedmonton.com/htdocs/edmsun.shtml; f. 1978; Publr and CEO CRAIG MARTIN; Publr CRAIG MARTIN; Editor GRAHAM DALZIEL; circ. Mon. to Sat. 70,984, Sun. 99,301.

Fort McMurray Today: 8550 Franklin Ave, Fort McMurray, AB T9H 3G1; tel. (403) 743-8186; fax (403) 790-1006; e-mail today@ ccinet.ab.ca; evening; Publr TIM O'ROURKE; Man. Editor MICHAEL HALL; circ. Mon. to Thurs. 4,163, Fri. 5,976.

Lethbridge Herald: 504 Seventh St South, POB 670, Lethbridge, AB T1J 3Z7; tel. (403) 328-4411; fax (403) 328-4536; e-mail dawn .sugimoto@lethbridgeherald.com; internet www.mysouthernalberta .com/leth/index.php; f. 1907; evening and Sun.; Publr MICHAEL J. HERTZ; Man. Editor DOYLE MACKINNON; circ. Mon. to Sat. 20,210, Sun. 18,179.

Medicine Hat News: 3257 Dunmore Rd, SE, POB 10, Medicine Hat, AB T1A 7E6; tel. (403) 527-1101; fax (403) 527-1244; e-mail apoirier@medicinehatnews.com; internet www.medicinehatnews .com; f. 1887; evening; Publr MICHAEL J. HERTZ; Man. Editor ALAN POIRIER; circ. 14,000.

Red Deer Advocate: 2950 Bremner Ave, Bag 5200, Red Deer, AB T4N 5G3; tel. (403) 314-4328; fax (403) 341-4772; e-mail editorial@ reddeeradvocate.com; internet www.reddeeradvocate.com; f. 1894; Publr FRED GORMAN; Man. Editor JOE MCLAUGHLIN; circ. Mon. to Sat. 19,000.

British Columbia

Alaska Highway News: 9916 89th St, Fort St John, BC V1J 3T8; tel. (250) 785-5631; fax (250) 785-3522; e-mail ahnews@awink.com; internet www.canada.com/fortstjohn; evening; Publr BRUCE LANTZ; Editor JOE PAVLIN; Man. Editor MIKE HEINTZMAN; circ. 4,000.

Alberini Valley Times: 4918 Napier St, POB 400, Port Alberini, BC V9Y 7N1; tel. (250) 723-8171; fax (250) 723-0586; e-mail avtimes@shaw.ca; Publr NIGEL E. HANNAFORD; Man. Editor KAREN BODEN; circ. Mon. to Sat. 6,000.

Daily Bulletin: 335 Spokane St, Kimberley, BC V1A 1Y9; tel. (250) 427-5333; fax (250) 427-5336; e-mail bulletin@cyberlink.bc.ca; f. 1932; evening; Publr STEEN JORGENSEN; Editor CHRIS DOUAN; circ. 2,000.

Daily Courier: 550 Doyle Ave, Kelowna, BC V1Y 7V1; tel. (250) 762-4445; fax (250) 763-0194; e-mail alison.yesilcimen@ok.bc.ca; internet www.theokangan.bc.ca; f. 1904; Mon. to Sat. evening, Sun. morning; Publr ALISON YESILCIMEN; Man. Editor JOHN HARDING; circ. Mon. to Sat. 16,128, Sun. 15,534.

Daily News: 2575 McCullough Rd, Nanaimo, BC V9S 5W5; tel. (250) 7529-4200; fax (250) 729-4288; e-mail pgodfrey@ nanaimodailynews.com; internet www.canada.com/nanaimo; f. 1874; evening; Publr CURT DUDDY; Man. Editor PETER GODFREY; circ. 9,000.

Daily Townsman: 822 Cranbrook St North, Cranbrook, BC V1C 3R9; tel. (250) 426-5201; fax (250) 426-5003; e-mail townsman@ cyberlink.bc.ca; evening; Publr STEEN JORGENSEN; Editor DAVID SANDS; circ. 4,000.

Kamloops Daily News: 393 Seymour St, Kamloops, BC V2C 6P6; tel. (250) 372-2331; fax (250) 374-3884; e-mail kamloopsnews@telus .net; internet www.kamloopsnews.ca; f. 1930; evening; Publr DALE BRIN; Editor SUSAN DUNCAN; circ. 15,000.

Nelson Daily News: 266 Baker St, Nelson, BC V1L 4H3; tel. (250) 352-3552; fax (250) 352-2418; e-mail news@nelsondailynews.com; internet www.nelsondailynews.com/home.html; f. 1902; evening; Publr PETER HOWIE; Editor DREW EDWARDS; circ. 3,000.

Peace River Block News: 901 100th Ave, Dawson Creek, BC V1G 1W2; tel. (250) 782-4888; fax (250) 782-6770; e-mail news@prbn.ca; internet www.canada.com/dawsoncreek; f. 1930; evening and Sun.; Publr SUSAN RAND; Editor JAMIE DIROM; circ. Mon. to Sat. 2,000, Sun. 10,000.

Penticton Herald: 186 Nanaimo Ave West, Suite 101, Penticton, BC V2A 1N4; tel. (250) 492-4002; fax (250) 492-2403; e-mail editor@ pentictonherald.ca; internet www.pentictonherald.ca; evening; Publr ALISON YESILCIMEN; Man. Editor S. PAUL VARGA; Gen. Man. ANDRÉ MARTIN; circ. 8,000.

Prince George Citizen: 150 Brunswick St, POB 5700, Prince George, BC V2L 5K9; tel. (250) 562-2441; fax (250) 562-7453; e-mail news@princegeorgecitizen.com; internet www.princegeorgecitizen .com; f. 1957; evening; Publr DEL LAVERDURE; Man. Editor DAVE PAULSON; circ. 16,000.

The Province: 200 Granville St, Suite 1, Vancouver, BC V6C 3N3; tel. (604) 605-2000; fax (604) 605-2720; internet www.canada.com/ vancouver/theprovince; f. 1898; Publr DENNIS SKULSKY; Editor-in-Chief WAYNE MORIARTY; circ. Mon. to Sat. 160,000, Sun. 196,000.

Sing Tao Daily News (Eastern Canada Edition): 8874 Hudson St, Vancouver, BC V6A 2V1; tel. (604) 261-5066; fax (604) 261-7093; e-mail editor@singtao.ca; internet singtao.ca; Chinese; Editor PAUL TSANG; circ. Mon. to Sat. 15,000.

Times Colonist: 2621 Douglas St, Victoria, BC V8T 4M2; tel. (250) 380-5211; fax (250) 380-5353; e-mail lchodan@tc.canwest.com; internet www.canada.com/victoria/timescolonist; f. 1980 by merger; Publr BOB MCKENZIE; Editor-in-Chief LUCINDA CHODAN; circ. Mon. to Sat. 73,087–85,728, Sun. 73,000.

Trail Daily Times: 1163 Cedar Ave, Trail, BC V1R 4B8; tel. (250) 368-8551; fax (250) 368-8550; e-mail editor@trailtimes.ca; internet www.trailtimes.ca; evening; Publr BARB BLATCHFORD; Editor TRACY GILCHRIST; circ. 5,000.

The Vancouver Sun: 200 Granville St, Suite 1, Vancouver, BC V6C 3N3; tel. (604) 605-2000; fax (604) 605-2720; e-mail info@png .canwest.com; internet www.canada.com/vancouver/vancouversun; f. 1886; Pres. and Publr DENNIS SKULSKY; Editor-in-Chief PATRICIA GRAHAM; circ. Mon. to Fri. 190,000, Sat. 238,000.

World Journal (Vancouver): 2288 Clark Dr., Vancouver, BC V5N 3G8; tel. (604) 876-1338; fax (604) 876-9191; internet www .worldjournal.com; Chinese; Publr WILSON CHIEN; circ. 10,000.

Manitoba

Brandon Sun: 501 Rosser Ave, Brandon, MB R7A 0K4; tel. (204) 727-2451; fax (204) 725-0976; e-mail bchester@brandonsun.com; internet www.brandonsun.com; f. 1882; evening and Sun.; Publr EWAN POW; Editor JAMES O'CONNOR; circ. Mon. to Sat. 16,000, Sun. 14,000.

Daily Graphic: 1941 Saskatchewan Ave West, POB 130, Portage La Prairie, MB R1N 3B4; tel. (204) 857-3427; fax (204) 239-1270; e-mail editor.dailygraphic@shawcable.com; internet www .portagedailygraphic.com; evening; Publr W. J. HAMILTON; Man. Editor MARK TORJUSEN; circ. 3,000.

Flin Flon Reminder: 10 North Ave, Flin Flon, MB R8A 0T2; tel. (204) 687-3454; fax (204) 687-4473; e-mail reminder@mb.sympatico .ca; f. 1946; evening; Publr RANDY DANELIUK; Editor RICH BILLY; circ. 4,000.

Winnipeg Free Press: 1355 Mountain Ave, Winnipeg, MB R2X 3B6; tel. (204) 697-7000; fax (204) 697-7375; e-mail nick.hurst@ freepress.mb.ca; internet www.winnipegfreepress.com; f. 1874; Mon. to Fri. evening, Sat., Sun. morning; Publr MURDOCH DAVIS; Editor NICHOLAS HIRST; circ. Mon. to Fri. 119,000, Sat. 170,000, Sun. 117,000.

Winnipeg Sun: 1700 Church Ave, Winnipeg, MB R2X 3A2; tel. (204) 694-2022; fax (204) 632-8709; e-mail bbrennan@wpgsun.com; internet www.winnipegsun.com; f. 1980; Publr and CEO ED HUCULAK; Man. Editor BILL DAVIDSON; circ. Mon. to Sat. 46,000, Sun. 58,000.

New Brunswick

L'Acadie Nouvelle: 476 blvd St-Pierre ouest, CP 5536, Caraquet, NB E1W 1B7; tel. (506) 727-4444; fax (506) 727-7620; e-mail infos@ acadienouvelle.com; internet www.acadienouvelle.com; f. 1984; Publr GILLES GAGNÉ; Editor BRUNO GODIN; circ. 18,000.

Daily Gleaner: POB 3370, Fredericton, NB E3B 5A2; tel. (506) 452-6671; fax (506) 452-7405; e-mail dgnews@nbnet.nb.ca; internet www .canadaeast.com; f. 1880; evening; Publr ERIC LAWSON; Editor-in-Chief KATHY JENKINS; circ. 25,000.

New Brunswick Telegraph–Journal: 210 Crown St, POB 2350, Saint John, NB E2L 3V8; tel. (506) 632-8888; fax (506) 648-2654; e-mail newsroom@nbpub.com; internet www.telegraphjournal.com; Publr JONATHAN FRANKLIN; Man. Editor PETER HAGGERT; circ. Mon. to Fri. 40,549, Sat. 45,000.

St John Times–Globe: 210 Crown St, POB 2350, Saint John, NB E2L 3V8; tel. (506) 632-8888; fax (506) 648-2654; e-mail tjetg@nbnet .nb.ca; internet www.nbnews.com; evening; Publr VICTOR MLODECKI; circ. 23,000.

The Times and Transcript: 939 Main St, POB 1001, Moncton, NB E1C 8P3; tel. (506) 859-4900; fax (506) 859-4899; e-mail news@ timestranscript.com; internet www.timestranscript.com; f. 1983; Mon. to Sat. evening, Sat. morning; Publr GREG LUTES; Man. Editor AL HOGAN; circ. Mon. to Fri. 38,000, Sat. 43,000.

Newfoundland and Labrador

Telegram: Columbus Dr., POB 5970, St John's, NL A1C 5X7; tel. (709) 364-6300; fax (709) 364-9333; e-mail rwanger@thetelegram .com; internet www.thetelegram.com; f. 1879; Mon. to Sat. morning; Publr MILLER H. AYRE; Editor RUSSELL WANGERSKY; circ. Mon. to Fri. 30,336, Sat. 53,000.

Western Star: 106 West St, POB 460, Corner Brook, NL A2H 6E7; tel. (709) 634-4668; fax (709) 634-9824; e-mail rwilliams@ thewesternstar.com; internet www.thewesternstar.com; f. 1900; Publr SHAWN WOODFORD; Man. Editor RICHARD WILLIAMS; circ. Mon. to Sat. 8,000.

Nova Scotia

Amherst Daily News: 147 South Albion St Town Sq., POB 280, Amherst, NS B4H 3Z2; tel. (902) 667-5102; fax (902) 667-0419; e-mail dcole@amherstdaily.com; internet www.amherstdaily.com; f. 1893; Publr EARL J. GOUCHIE; Man. Editor DARRELL COLE; circ. Mon. to Sat. 4,000.

Cape Breton Post: 255 George St, POB 1500, Sydney, NS B1P 6K6; tel. (902) 564-5451; fax (902) 562-7077; e-mail fjackson@cbpost.com; internet www.capebretonpost.com; f. 1901; Publr ANITA DELAZZER; Man. Editor FRED JACKSON; circ. Mon. to Sat. 25,100.

Chronicle–Herald: 1650 Argyle St, POB 610, Halifax, NS B3J 2T2; tel. (902) 426-2811; fax (902) 426-0449; e-mail newsroom@herald.ns .ca; internet www.herald.ns.ca; f. 1875; Publr GRAHAM W. DENNIS; Man. Editor TERRY O'NEIL; circ. Mon. to Sat. 93,000, Sun. 63,000.

Daily News: 1601 Lower Walker St, POB 8330, Station A, Halifax, NS B3K 5M1; tel. (902) 468-1222; fax (902) 468-3609; e-mail webeditor@hfxnews.ca; internet www.hfxnews.southam.ca; f. 1979; Publr JAMIE THOMSON; Man. Editor SHERRI AIKENHEAD; circ. Mon. to Sat. 24,000, Sun. 30,000.

The Evening News: 352 East River Rd, POB 159, New Glasgow, NS B2H 5E2; tel. (902) 752-3000; fax (902) 752-1945; e-mail news@ ngnews.ca; internet www.newglasgownews.com; f. 1910; evening; Publr RICHARD RUSSELL; Man. Editor DAVE GLENEN; circ. 8,000.

Mail–Star: 1650 Argyle St, POB 610, Halifax, NS B3J 2T2; tel. (902) 426-2811; fax (902) 426-3014; e-mail ombud@herald.ns.ca; internet www.herald.ns.ca; evening; Publr GRAHAM W. DENNIS; Man. Editor TERRY O'NEIL; circ. 21,000.

Truro Daily News: 6 Louise St, POB 220, Truro, NS B2N 5C3; tel. (902) 893-9405; fax (902) 893-0518; e-mail news@trurodaily.com; internet www.trurodaily.com; f. 1891; evening; Publr RICHARD RUSSELL; Man. Editor MIKE TURNER; circ. 7,000.

Ontario

Barrie Examiner: 571 Bayfield St North, Barrie, ON L4M 4Z9; tel. (705) 726-6537; fax (705) 726-5414; e-mail news@thebarrieexaminer .com; internet www.thebarrieexaminer.com; f. 1864; evening; Publr RON LAURIN; Man. Editor MIKE BEAUDIN; circ. 10,925.

Beacon–Herald: 16 Packham Rd, POB 430, Stratford, ON N5A 6T6; tel. (519) 271-2220; fax (519) 271-1026; e-mail jkastner@ bowesnet.com; f. 1854; evening; Publr AMBER OGILVIE; Man. Editor JOHN KASTNER; circ. 10,764.

Brockville Recorder and Times: 23 King St West, POB 10, Brockville, ON K6V 5T8; tel. (613) 342-4441; fax (613) 342-4456;

e-mail wb.raison@recorder.ca; internet www.recorder.ca; f. 1821; evening; Publr BOB PEARCE; Editor BARRY RAISON; circ. 12,389.

Cambridge Reporter: 26 Ainslie St South, POB 1510, Cambridge, ON N1R 5T2; tel. (519) 621-3810; fax (519) 621-8239; e-mail news@ cambridge-reporter.com; internet www.cambridge-reporter.com; f. 1846; evening; Publr L. R. (VERNE) SHAULL; Editor CLYDE WARRINGTON; circ. 7,000.

Chatham Daily News: 45 Fourth St, POB 2007, Chatham, ON N7M 5M6; tel. (519) 354-2000; fax (519) 354-9489; e-mail news@ chathamdailynews.ca; internet www.chathamdailynews.ca; f. 1862; evening; Publr JIM BLAKE; Man. Editor BRUCE CORCORAN; circ. 13,617.

Chronicle–Journal: 75 Cumberland St South, Thunder Bay, ON P7B 1A3; tel. (807) 343-6200; fax (807) 345-5991; e-mail cj-editorial@ cwconnect.ca; internet www.chroniclejournal.com; Publr COLIN BRUCE; Man. Editor BRIAN DRYDEN; circ. Mon. to Sat. 37,926, Sun. 28,565.

Cobourg Daily Star: 99 King St West, POB 400, Cobourg, ON K9A 4L1; tel. (905) 372-0131; fax (905) 372-4966; e-mail cdsletters@ northumberlandtoday.com; internet www.northumberlandtoday .com; evening; Publr MIKE WALSH; Man. Editor MANDY MARTIN; circ. 4,470.

Daily Observer: 186 Alexander St, Pembroke, ON K8A 4L9; tel. (613) 732-3691; fax (613) 732-2226; e-mail editor@thedailyobserver .ca; internet www.thedailyobserver.ca; f. 1855; evening; Publr STEVE GLOSTER; Man. Editor PETER LAPINSKIE; circ. 6,000.

Daily Press: 187 Cedar St South, POB 560, Timmins, ON P4N 2G9; tel. (705) 268-5050; fax (705) 268-7373; e-mail tdp@nt.net; internet www.timminspress.com; f. 1933; Publr and Gen. Man. BRUCE COWAN; Man. Editor TED RATH; circ. Mon. to Sat. 9,700.

Le Droit: 47 rue Clarence, bureau 222, CP 8860, succursale Terminus, Ottawa, ON K1G 3J9; tel. (613) 562-0111; fax (613) 562-6280; e-mail ledroit@ledroit.com; internet www.ledroit.com; f. 1913; Publr CLAUDE GAGNON; Man. Editor MICHEL GAUTHIER; circ. Mon. to Fri. 35,985, Sat. 40,494.

The Expositor: 53 Dalhousie St, POB 965, Brantford, ON N3T 5S8; tel. (519) 756-2020; fax (519) 756-9470; e-mail expnews@ theexpositor.com; internet www.brantfordexpositor.ca; f. 1852; Publr MICHAEL PEARCE; Editor DAVE JUDD; circ. 22,249.

Financial Post: 300 1450 Don Mills Rd, Don Mills, ON M3B 3R5; tel. (416) 3583-2300; fax (416) 383-2443; e-mail letters@finpost.com; internet www.financialpost.com; f. 1907; Publr ROBERT ATTALA; Editor-in-Chief TERENCE CORCORAN; circ. 91,000.

The Globe and Mail: 444 Front St West, Toronto, ON M5V 2S9; tel. (416) 585-5000; fax (416) 585-5085; e-mail newsroom@globeandmail .ca; internet www.globeandmail.com; f. 1844; Publr PHILLIP CRAWLEY; Editor EDWARD GREENSPON; circ. Mon. to Fri. 316,438, Sat. 394,260.

Guelph Mercury: 8–14 Macdonnell St, POB 3604, Guelph, ON N1H 6P7; tel. (519) 822-4310; fax (519) 767-1681; e-mail pyoung@ therecord.com; internet www.guelphmercury.com; f. 1854; evening; Group Publr FRED KUNTZ; Editor PATRICIA YOUNG; circ. 14,100.

Hamilton Spectator: 44 Frid St, Hamilton, ON L8N 3G3; tel. (905) 526-3333; fax (905) 526-1139; e-mail drobbins@thespec.com; internet www.thespec.com; f. 1846; Publr JAGODA PIKE; Editor-in-Chief DANA ROBBINS; circ. Mon. to Fri. 105,765, Sat. 122,621.

Intelligencer: 450 Bridge St East, POB 5600, Belleville, ON K8N 5C7; tel. (613) 962-9171; fax (613) 962-9652; e-mail newsroom@ intelligencer.ca; internet www.intelligencer.ca; f. 1870; evening; Publr MICHAEL A. POWER; Man. Editor NICK PALMER; circ. 15,756.

Kingston Whig–Standard: 6 Cataraqui St, POB 2300, Kingston, ON K7L 1Z7; tel. (613) 544-5000; fax (613) 530-4119; e-mail kinwhig@thewhig.com; internet www.kingstonwhigstandard.com; f. 1834; Publr FRED LAFLAMME; Man. Editor NOREEN RASBACH; circ. 27,695.

Lindsay Daily Post: 15 William St North, Lindsay, ON K9V 3Z8; tel. (705) 324-2114; fax (705) 324-0174; e-mail lineditorial@thepost .ca; internet www.thepost.ca; evening; Publr ANDY WHEELER; Editor CINDY WOODS; circ. 4,766.

London Free Press: 369 York St, POB 2280, London, ON N6A 4G1; tel. (519) 679-6666; fax (519) 667-4503; e-mail letters@lfpress .com; internet www.lfpress.com; f. 1849; Publr SUSAN MUSZAK; Editor-in-Chief PAUL BERTON; circ. 95,792.

Ming Pao Daily News: 1355 Huntingwood Dr., Scarborough, ON M1S 3J1; tel. (416) 321-0093; fax (416) 321-3499; e-mail newsdesk@ mingpaoca.com; Chinese; Editor-in-Chief RICHARD KWOK-KAI NG; circ. Mon. to Sat. 33,000, Sun. 51,000.

National Post: 1450 Don Mills Rd, Suite 300, Don Mills, ON M3B 2X7; tel. (416) 383-2300; fax (416) 442-2209; e-mail queries@ nationalpost.com; internet www.nationalpost.com; f. 1998; national newspaper with printing centres in nine cities; owned by CanWest

Global Communications Corpn; Publr ROBERT ATTALA; Editor-in-Chief MATTHEW FRASER; circ. Mon. to Fri. 246,504, Sat. 270,129.

Niagara Falls Review: 4801 Valley Way, POB 270, Niagara Falls, ON L2E 6T6; tel. (905) 358-5711; fax (905) 356-0785; e-mail reporter@nfreview.com; internet www.niagarafallsreview.ca; f. 1879; evening; Publr DAVID A. BEATTIE; Man. Editor JOE WALLACE; circ. 18,476.

North Bay Nugget: 259 Worthington St, POB 570, North Bay, ON P1B 3B5; tel. (705) 472-3200; fax (705) 472-1438; e-mail news@nugget.ca; internet www.nugget.ca; f. 1909; evening; Publr PAUL MCCUAIG; Man. Editor JOHN SIZE; circ. 17,539.

Northern Daily News: 8 Duncan Ave, POB 1030, Kirkland Lake, ON P2N 3L4; tel. (705) 567-5321; fax (705) 567-6162; f. 1922; evening; Publr TIM CRESWELL; Editor TOM PERRY; circ. 3,379.

Orillia Packet and Times: 31 Colborne St East, Orillia, ON L3V 1T4; tel. (705) 325-1355; fax (705) 325-4033; e-mail news@packetandtimes.com; internet www.orilliapacket.com; f. 1926 by merger; evening; Publr DAVE MARTINEAU; Man. Editor MARK BISSET; circ. 8,289.

Ottawa Citizen: 1101 Baxter Rd, POB 5020, Ottawa, ON K2C 3M4; tel. (613) 829-9100; fax (613) 596-3755; e-mail sanderson@thecitizen.canwest.com; internet www.canada.com/ottawa/ottawacitizen; f. 1845; Publr and Gen. Man. JAMES ORBAN; Editor-in-Chief SCOTT ANDERSON; circ. 137,474.

Ottawa Sun: 380 Hunt Club Rd, Station T, Ottawa, ON K1G 5H7; tel. (613) 739-7000; fax (613) 739-9383; e-mail rgibbons@ott.sunpub.com; Publr RICK GIBBONS; circ. Mon.-Fri. 50,000, Sat. 45,000, Sun. 54,000; Editor-in-Chief MIKE THERIEN.

Peterborough Examiner: 730 Kingsway, Peterborough, ON K9J 8L4; tel. (705) 745-4641; fax (705) 743-4581; e-mail news1@peterboroughexaminer.com; internet www.thepeterboroughexaminer.com; f. 1884; evening; Publr JIM AMBROSE; Man. Editor ED N. ARNOLD; circ. 22,501.

The Record: 225 Fairway Rd, Kitchener, ON N2G 4E5; tel. (519) 894-1500; fax (519) 894-1241; e-mail business@therecord.com; internet www.therecord.com; f. 1878; evening; Publr FRED KUNTZ; Editor LYNN HADDRALL; circ. 65,879.

St Catharines Standard: 17 Queen St, St Catharines, ON L2R 5G5; tel. (905) 684-7251; fax (905) 684-6032; e-mail standard@stcatharinesstandard.ca; internet www.stcatharinesstandard.ca; f. 1891; evening; Publr JULIA KAMULA; Man. Editor ANDREA KRILUCK; circ. Mon. to Fri. 30,925, Sat. 38,864.

St Thomas Times–Journal: 16 Hincks St, St Thomas, ON N5R 5Z2; tel. (519) 631-2790; fax (519) 631-5653; e-mail news@stthomastimesjournal.com; internet www.stthomastimesjournal.com; f. 1882; evening; Publr BEV PONTON; Man. Editor ROSS PORTER; circ. 7,939.

Sarnia Observer: 140 Front St South, POB 3009, Sarnia, ON N7T 7M8; tel. (519) 344-3641; fax (519) 332-2951; e-mail editorial@theobserver.ca; f. 1854; evening; Publr DARYL C. SMITH; Man. Editor TERRY SHAW; circ. 21,000.

Sault Star: 145 Old Garden River Rd, POB 460, Sault Ste Marie, ON P6A 5M5; tel. (705) 759-3035; fax (705) 759-0102; e-mail ssmstar@ssmsoutham.ca; internet www.saultstar.com; f. 1912; evening; Publr LOU A. MAULUCCI; Man. Editor JOHN HALUCHA; circ. 19,658.

Sentinel–Review: 16–18 Brock St, POB 1000, Woodstock, ON N4S 8A5; tel. (519) 537-2341; fax (519) 537-3049; fax (519) 537-8542; e-mail sentinelreview@bowesnet.com; internet www.woodstocksentinelreview.com; f. 1886; evening; Publr PAT LOGAN; Man. Editor BILL SCRIVEN; circ. 8,500.

Simcoe Reformer: 105 Donly Dr. South, POB 370, Simcoe, ON N3Y 4L2; tel. (519) 426-5710; fax (519) 426-9255; e-mail refedit@bowesnet.com; internet www.simcoereformer.ca; f. 1858; evening; Group Publr CAM MCKNIGHT; Man. Editor KIM NOVAK; circ. 8,433.

Sing Tao Daily News: 417 Dundas St West, Toronto, ON M5T 1G6; tel. (416) 596-8140; fax (416) 861-8169; internet www.singtao.ca; Chinese; Editor-in-Chief ROBERT LEUNG; circ. Mon. to Sun. 160,693.

Standard–Freeholder: 44 Pitt St, Cornwall, ON K6J 3P3; tel. (613) 933-3160; fax (613) 933-7168; e-mail maned@standard-freeholder.com; internet www.standard-freeholder.com; Publr MILTON S. ELLIS; Editor ALF LAFAVE; circ 14,865.

Sudbury Star: 33 MacKenzie St, Sudbury, ON P3C 4Y1; tel. (705) 674-5276; fax (705) 674-6834; e-mail editorial@thesudburystar.com; internet www.thesudburystar.com; f. 1909; evening; Publr KEN D. SEGUIN; Man. Editor ROGER CAZABON; circ. 18,437.

Sun Times: 290 Ninth St East, POB 200, Owen Sound, ON N4K 1N7; tel. (519) 376-2250; fax (519) 376-7190; e-mail cmcmenemy@owensoundsuntimes.com; internet www.owensoundsuntimes.com; f.

1853; evening; Publr CHERYL A. MCMENEMY; Man. Editor FRANK RUPNIK; circ. 15,830.

Toronto Star: 1 Yonge St, Toronto, ON M5E 1E6; tel. (416) 367-2000; fax (416) 869-4328; e-mail lettertoed@thestar.ca; internet www.thestar.com; f. 1892; Publr MICHAEL GOLDBLOOM; Man. Editor MARY DEANNE SHEARS; circ. 470,433.

Toronto Sun: 333 King St East, Toronto, ON M5A 3X5; tel. (416) 947-2222; fax (416) 947-3228; e-mail editor@tor.sunpub.com; internet www.torontosun.com; f. 1971; Publr and CEO NEIL FOWLER; Editor JIM JENNINGS; circ. Mon. to Sat. 226,956.

Welland-Port Colborne Tribune: 228 East Main St, POB 278, Welland, ON L3B 5P5; tel. (905) 732-2411; fax (905) 732-3660; e-mail tribune@wellandtribune.ca; internet www.wellandtribune.ca; f. 1863; Publr MIKE WALSH; Man. Editor GEORGE DUMA; circ. 14,905.

Windsor Star: 167 Ferry St, Windsor, ON N9A 4M5; tel. (519) 256-5533; fax (519) 255-5515; e-mail letters@win.southam.ca; internet www.southam.com/windsorstar; f. 1918; Publr JIM MCCORMACK; Editor MARY BENETEAU; circ. 76,395.

World Journal (Toronto): 415 Eastern Ave, Toronto, ON M4M 1B7; tel. (416) 778-0888; fax (416) 778-1037; internet www.worldjournal.com; Chinese; Pres. DAVID TING; Editor-in-Chief PAUL CHANG; circ. 38,000.

Prince Edward Island

Guardian: 165 Prince St, POB 760, Charlottetown, PE C1A 4R7; tel. (902) 629-6000; fax (902) 566-3808; e-mail letters@theguardian.pe.ca; internet www.theguardian.pe.ca; f. 1887; Publr DON BRANDER; Editor GARY MACDOUGALL; circ. Mon. to Sat. 20,777.

Journal–Pioneer: 4 Queen St, POB 2480, Summerside, PE C1N 4K5; tel. (902) 436-2121; fax (902) 436-0784; e-mail info@journalpioneer.com; internet www.journalpioneer.com; f. 1865; evening; Publr SANDY RUNDLE; Editor DARLENE SHEA; circ. 9,610.

Québec

Le Devoir: 2050 rue de Bleury, 9e étage, Montréal, QC H3A 3M9; tel. (514) 985-3333; fax (514) 985-3360; e-mail redaction@ledevoir.com; internet www.ledevoir.com; Publr BERNARD DESCÔTEAUX; Editor-in-Chief JEAN ROBERT SANSFAÇON; circ. Mon. to Fri. 25,903, Sat. 41,517.

The Gazette: 1010 rue Ste-Catherine ouest, Suite 200, Montréal, QC H3B 5L1; tel. (514) 987-2222; fax (514) 987-2270; e-mail letters@thegazette.canwest.com; internet www.canada.com/montreal/montrealgazette; f. 1778; English; Publr ALAN ALLNUTT; Editor-in-Chief ANDREW PHILLIPS; circ. Mon. to Fri. 142,552, Sat. 168,878, Sun. 137,685 (2003).

Le Journal de Montréal: 4545 rue Frontenac, Montréal, QC H2H 2R7; tel. (514) 521-4545; fax (514) 525-542; e-mail transmission@journalmtl.com; internet www.journalmtl.com; f. 1964; Editor-in-Chief DANY DOUCET; circ. Mon. to Fri. 267,194, Sat. 324,924, Sun. 268,950.

Le Journal de Québec: 450 ave Béchard, Vanier, QC G1M 2E9; tel. (418) 683-1573; fax (418) 683-1027; e-mail commentaires@journaldequebec.com; internet www.journaldequebec.com; f. 1967; Publr JEAN-CLAUDE L'ABBÉE; Chief Editor SERGE CÔTÉ; circ. Mon. to Fri. 98,606, Sat. 126,000, Sun. 101,000.

Le Nouvelliste: 1920 rue Bellefeuille, CP 668, Trois Rivières, QC G9A 5J6; tel. (819) 376-2501; fax (819) 376-0946; e-mail information@lenouvelliste.qc.ca; internet www.cyberpresse.ca/nouvelliste; f. 1920; Pres. and Publr RAYMOND TARDIF; Editor-in-Chief ANDRÉ POITRAS; circ. 43,000.

La Presse: 7 rue St-Jacques, Montréal, QC H2Y 1K9; tel. (514) 285-6880; fax (514) 285-6930; e-mail nouvelles@lapresse.ca; internet www.cyberpresse.ca/reseau; f. 1884; Pres. and Editor GUY CREVIER; circ. Mon. to Fri. 188,693, Sat. 277,777, Sun. 204,825.

Le Quotidien du Saguenay-Lac-St-Jean: 1051 blvd Talbot, Chicoutimi, QC G7H 5C1; tel. (418) 545-4474; fax (418) 690-8824; internet www.cyberpresse.ca/quotidien; f. 1973; Editor-in-Chief MICHEL SIMARD; circ. Mon. to Sat. 29,000.

The Record: 1195 Galt St East, CP 1200, Sherbrooke, QC J1H 5L6; tel. (819) 569-9511; fax (819) 569-3945; e-mail newsroom@sherbrookerecord.com; internet www.sherbrookerecord.com; f. 1897; Publr RANDY KINNEAR; Editor SHARON MCCULLY; circ. 5,100.

Le Soleil: 410 blvd Charest est, CP 1547, succursale Terminus, Québec, QC G1K 7J6; tel. (418) 686-3394; fax (418) 686-3374; e-mail redaction@lesoleil.com; internet www.cyberpresse.ca/soleil; f. 1896; Publr ANDRÉ PROVENCHER; Editor YVES BELLEFLEUR; circ. Mon. to Fri. 81,000, Sat. 117,723, Sun. 86,310.

La Tribune: 1950 rue Roy, Sherbrooke, QC J1K 2X8; tel. (819) 564-5454; fax (819) 564-8098; e-mail redaction@latribune.qc.ca; internet www.cyberpresse.ca/tribune; f. 1910; Pres. and Publr LOUISE BOIS-VERT; Editor-in-Chief MAURICE CLOUTIER; circ. Mon. to Fri. 32,043, Sat. 39,000.

La Voix de L'Est: 76 rue Dufferin, Granby, QC J2G 9L4; tel. (450) 375-4555; fax (450) 777-4865; e-mail redaction@lavoixdelest.qc.ca; internet www.cyberpresse.ca/vde; f. 1945; Pres. and Publr JACQUES PRONOVOST; circ. Mon. to Fri. 16,000, Sat. 19,176.

Saskatchewan

Daily Herald: 30 10th St East, Prince Albert, SK S6V 0Y5; tel. (306) 763-7202; fax (306) 763-3331; e-mail editorial@paherald.sk.ca; internet www.paherald.sk.ca; f. 1894; Publr IAN JENSEN; Man. Editor HEATHER PERSSON; circ. Mon. to Sat. 7,600.

Leader–Post: 1964 Park St, POB 2020, Regina, SK S4P 3G4; tel. (306) 565-8211; fax (306) 565-2588; e-mail feedback@leaderpost .canwest.com; internet www.canada.com/regina/leaderpost; f. 1883; Publr GREG MCLEAN; Editor JANICE DOCKHAM; circ. Mon to Fri. 49,781, Sat. 56,965.

StarPhoenix: 204 Fifth Ave North, Saskatoon, SK S7K 2P1; tel. (306) 657-6231; fax (306) 657-6437; e-mail spnews@sp.canwest.com; internet www.canada.com/saskatoon/starphoenix; f. 1902; Publr LYLE SINKEWICZ; Editor STEVE GIBB; circ. Mon. to Fri. 56,269, Sat 61,643.

Times–Herald: 44 Fairford St West, POB 3000, Moose Jaw, SK S6H 1V1; tel. (306) 692-6441; fax (306) 692-2101; e-mail editorial@ mjtimes.sk.ca; internet www.mjtimes.sk.ca; f. 1889; evening; Publr ROB CLARK; Editor LESLEY SHEPPARD; circ. 9,000.

Yukon Territory

Whitehorse Star: 2149 Second Ave, Whitehorse, Yukon, YT Y1A 1C5; tel. (867) 667-4481; fax (867) 668-7130; e-mail star@ whitehorsestar.com; internet www.whitehorsestar.com; f. 1900; evening; Publr JACKIE PIERCE; Editor JIM BUTLER; circ. 2,421.

SELECTED PERIODICALS

Alberta

Canadian Public Policy/Analyse de Politiques: Dept of Economics, University of Calgary, 2500 University Dr. NW, Calgary, AB T2N 1N4; tel. (403) 210-9490; fax (403) 282-5262; e-mail cpp@ ucalgary.ca; internet economics.ca/cpp; quarterly; Editor KENNETH J. MCKENZIE; circ. 1,100.

Oilweek: 133 Eighth St, SW, Suite 800, Calgary, AB T2R IM6; tel. (403) 266-8700; fax (403) 266-6634; e-mail oilweek@oilweek.com; internet www.oilweek.com; weekly letter and monthly magazine; f. 1948; Publr BILL WHITELAW; Man. Editor DARRELL STONEHOUSE; circ. 7,500.

Ukrainski Visti (Ukrainian News): 12227 107th Ave, Suite 1, Edmonton, AB T5M 1Y9; tel. (780) 488-3693; fax (780) 488-3859; e-mail ukrnews@compusmart.ab.ca; f. 1929; fortnightly; Ukrainian and English; Editor MARCO LEVYTSKY; circ. 4,000.

British Columbia

BC Outdoors—Sport, Fishing and Outdoor Adventure: OP Publishing Ltd, 1080 Howe St, Suite 900, Vancouver, BC V6Z 2T1; tel. (604) 606-4644; fax (604) 687-1925; e-mail bcoutdoors@ oppublishing.com; internet www.bcosportfishing.com; f. 1945; 6 a year; Co-ordinating Editor TRACEY ELLIS; circ. 24,000.

Pacific Yachting: OP Publishing Ltd, 1080 Howe St, Suite 900, Vancouver, BC V6Z 2T1; tel. (604) 606-4644; fax (604) 687-1925; e-mail editorial@pacificyachting.com; internet www.pacificyachting .com; f. 1968; monthly; Editor PETER A. ROBSON; circ. 15,700.

Vancouver Magazine: 2608 Granville St, Vancouver, BC V6H 3V3; tel. (604) 877-7732; fax (604) 877-4823; e-mail mail@ vancouvermagazine.com; internet www.vancouvermagazine.com; f. 1957; 10 a year; Publr LANCE NEALE; Editor MATTHEW MALLON; circ. 60,000.

Western Living: 2608 Granville St, Suite 560, Vancouver, BC V6H 3V3; tel. (604) 877-7732; fax (604) 877-4849; e-mail wlmail@ westernlivingmagazine.com; internet www.westernlivingmagazine .com; f. 1971; monthly; Publr LANCE NEAL; Editor JIM SUTHERLAND; circ. 218,000.

Westworld BC: 4180 Lougheed Highway, 4th Floor, Burnaby, BC V5C 6A7; tel. (604) 299-7311; fax (604) 299-9188; e-mail cwm@ canadawide.com; internet www.canadawide.com/westworldbc_ad .htm; f. 1974; quarterly; Editor ANNE ROSE; circ. 517,000.

Manitoba

The Beaver—Canada's History Magazine: 167 Lombard Ave, Suite 478, Winnipeg, MB R3B 0T6; tel. (204) 988-9300; fax (204) 988-9309; e-mail editors@historysociety.ca; internet www

.beavermagazine.ca; f. 1920; 6 a year; Canadian history; Editor ANNALEE GREENBERG; circ. 50,000.

Cattlemen: 220 Portage Ave, 8th Floor, Winnipeg, MB R3C 0A5; tel. (204) 944-5753; fax (204) 944-5416; e-mail gren@fbcpublishing .com; internet www.agcanada.com; f. 1938; monthly; animal husbandry; Editor GREN WINSLOW; circ. 30,000.

Country Guide: 220 Portage Ave, 8th Floor, Winnipeg, MB R3C 3K7; tel. (204) 944-5754; fax (204) 944-5416; e-mail davew@ fbcpublishing.com; internet www.agcanada.com; f. 1882; 10 a year; agriculture; Editor DAVID WREFORD; circ. 55,000.

Grainews: 220 Portage Ave, 8th Floor, Winnipeg, MB R3C 3K7; tel. (204) 944-5587; fax (204) 944-5416; e-mail andy@fbcpublishing.com; internet www.agcanada.com; f. 1975; 17 a year; grain and cattle farming; Editor ANDY SIRSKI; circ. 47,000.

Kanada Kurier: 955 Alexander Ave, POB 1054, Winnipeg, MB R3C 2X8; tel. (204) 774-1883; fax (204) 783-5740; e-mail kanadakurier@ mb.simpatico.ca; f. 1889; weekly; German; Editor RENATE ACHENBACH; circ. 25,000.

The Manitoba Co-operator: 220 Portage Ave, 8th Floor, POB 9800, Main Station, Winnipeg, MB R3C 3K7; tel. (204) 944-2222; fax (204) 942-8463; e-mail jay@fbcpublishing.com; f. 1925; weekly; farming; Editor JAY WHETTER; circ. 21,000.

New Brunswick

Brunswick Business Journal: 55 McKnight St, Suite 115, Fredericton, NB E3A 5W8599 Maint St, Suite 203, Moncton, NB E1E 1C8; tel. (506) 472-4783; fax (506) 459-4189; f. 1984; monthly; Editor SUZANNE MCDONALD-BOYCE.

Newfoundland and Labrador

Atlantic Business Magazine: 197 Water St, POB 2356, St John's, NL A1C 6E7; tel. (709) 726-9300; fax (709) 726-3013; e-mail dchafe@ atlanticbusinessmagazine.com; internet www .atlanticbusinessmagazine.com; 6 a year; business; Man. Editor EDWINA HUTTON; Editor DAWN CHAFE; circ. 29,060.

Northwest Territories

L'Aquilon: POB 1325, Yellowknife, NT X1A 2N9; tel. (867) 873-6603; fax (867) 873-2158; e-mail aquilon@internorth.com; internet www.aquilon.nt.ca; f. 1985; weekly; Editor ALAIN BESSETTE; circ. 1,000.

Hay River Hub: 8–4 Courtoreille St, Hay River, NT X0E 1G2; tel. (867) 874-6577; fax (867) 874-2679; e-mail thehub@ssimicro.com; f. 1973; weekly; Publr CHRIS BRODEUR; Man. Editor SEAN PERCY; circ. 3,000.

Northern News Service: 5108 50th St, Yellowknife, NT X1A 2R1; tel. (867) 873-4031; fax (867) 873-8507; e-mail nnsl@nnsl.com; internet www.nnsl.com; f. 1945 as *News/North*; weekly; Publr JACK SIGVALDASON; Man. Editor BRUCE VALPY; circ. 11,000.

Slave River Journal: 207 McDougal Rd, POB 990, Fort Smith, NT X0E 0P0; tel. (867) 872-2734; fax (867) 872-2754; e-mail srj@ auroranet.nt.ca; internet www.srji.com; f. 1978; weekly; Publr DON JAQUE; Man. Editor SANDRA JAQUE; circ. 2,193.

Yellowknifer: 5108 50th St, Yellowknife, NT X1A 2R1; tel. (867) 873-4031; fax (867) 873-8507; e-mail yellowknifer@nnsl.com; weekly; Editor BRUCE VALPY; circ. 6,200.

Nova Scotia

Atlantic Progress Magazine: 1660 Hollis St, Penthouse Suite 603, Halifax, NS B3J 1V7; tel. (902) 494-0999; fax (902) 494-0997; e-mail news@progresscorp.com; internet www.progresscorp.com; f. 1993; 11 a year; regional business; Editor DAVID HOLT; circ. 22,000.

Canadian Forum: 5502 Atlantic St, Halifax, NS B3H 1G4; tel. (902) 421-7022; fax (902) 425-0166; f. 1920; 10 a year; political, literary and economic; Editor ROBERT CLUDOS; circ. 9,000.

Nunavut Territory

Kivalliq News: Rankin Inlet, NU; tel. (867) 645-3223; fax (867) 645-3225; e-mail editor@arctic.ca; f. 1994; owned by Northern News Services; English and Inuktitut; Publr JACK SIGVALDASON; Editor DARRELL GREER; circ. 1,400.

Nunatsiaq News: POB 8, Iqaluit, NU X0A 0H0; tel. (867) 979-5357; fax (867) 979-4763; e-mail nunat@nunanet.com; internet www .nunatsiaq.com; f. 1973; weekly; English and Inuktitut; Publr STEVEN ROBERTS; Editor JIM BELL; circ. 8,000.

Ontario

Anglican Journal: 80 Hayden St, Toronto, ON M4Y 3G2; tel. (416) 924-9199; fax (416) 921-4452; e-mail editor@national.anglican.ca; internet www.anglicanjournal.com; f. 1871; 10 a year; official publ.

of the Anglican Church of Canada; Editor LEANNE LARMONDIN; circ. 215,000.

Better Farming: RR2, Vanleek Hill, ON K0B 1R0; tel. (613) 687-2232; fax (613) 678-5993; e-mail admin@betterfarming.com; internet www.betterfarming.com; f. 1999; monthly; Man. Editor ROBERT C. IRWIN.

CAmagazine: The Canadian Institute of Chartered Accountants, 277 Wellington St West, Toronto, ON M5V 3H2; tel. (416) 977-3222; fax (416) 204-3409; e-mail christian.bellavance@cica.ca; internet www.camagazine.com; f. 1911; monthly; Editor-in-Chief CHRISTIAN BELLAVANCE; circ. 75,000 (60,000 in English; 15,000 in French).

Campus Canada: 5397 Eglington Ave West, Suite 101, Toronto, ON M9C 5K6; tel. (416) 928-2909; fax (416) 928-1357; e-mail chris@campus.ca; internet www.campus.ca; f. 1983; quarterly; 30 campus edns; Man. Editor CHRISTIAN PEARCE; circ. 145,000.

Canada Gazette: Canada Gazette Directorate, Public Works and Govt Services Canada, 350 Albert St, Ottawa, ON K1A 0S5; tel. (613) 996-1268; fax (613) 991-3540; e-mail ncr.gazette@communication.gc.ca; internet canadagazette.gc.ca; f. 1867; weekly; official newspaper of the Govt of Canada; English and French; Dir CAROL KENNEDY.

Canadian Architect: 12 Concorde Pl., Suite 800, Toronto, ON M3B 2X7; tel. (416) 442-3390; fax (416) 442-2214; e-mail ichodikoff@canadianarchitect.com; internet www.canadianarchitect.com; f. 1955; monthly; Editorial Dir IAN CHODIKOFF; circ. 11,000.

Canadian Art: 51 Front St East, Suite 210, Toronto, ON M5E 1B3; tel. (416) 368-8854; fax (416) 368-6135; e-mail info@canadianart.ca; internet www.canadianart.ca; quarterly; Publr MELONY WARD; Man. Editor BRYNE MCLAUGHLIN; circ. 24,000.

Canadian Bar Review/Revue du Barreau canadien: Canadian Bar Foundation, 500–865 Carling Ave, Ottawa, ON K1S 5S8; tel. (613) 237-2925; fax (613) 237-0185; e-mail eveitch@cba.org; internet www.cba.org; f. 1923; quarterly; Editor Prof. EDWARD VEITCH; circ. 36,000.

Canadian Business: 1 Mount Pleasant Rd, 11th Floor, Toronto, ON M4Y 2Y5; tel. (416) 764-1200; fax (416) 764-1255; e-mail letters@canadianbusiness.rogers.com; internet www.canadianbusiness.com; f. 1927; 21 a year; Publr DEBORAH ROSSER; Editor-in-Chief JOE CHIDLEY; circ. 81,000.

Canadian Chemical News: 130 Slater St, Suite 550, Ottawa, ON K1P 6E2; tel. (613) 232-6252; fax (613) 232-5862; e-mail info@accn.ca; internet www.accn.ca; f. 1949; 10 a year; Editor MICHELLE PIQUETTE; circ. 5,800.

Canadian Defence Quarterly: 310 Dupont St, Toronto, ON M5R 1V9; tel. (416) 968-7252; fax (416) 968-2377; e-mail cdq@baxter.net; internet www.baxter.net/cdq; f. 1970; quarterly; Publr W. H. BAXTER; Editor MICHAEL POITEVIN; circ. 6,000.

Canadian Dental Association Journal: 1815 Alta Vista Dr., Ottawa, ON K1G 3Y6; tel. (613) 523-1770; fax (613) 523-7736; e-mail jokeefe@cda-adc.ca; internet www.cda-adc.ca; f. 1935; 11 a year; Editor Dr JOHN P. O'KEEFE.

Canadian Electronics: CLB Media Inc, 240 Edward St, Aurora, ON L4G 3S9; tel. (905) 727-0077; fax (905) 727-0017; e-mail tgouldson@clbmedia.ca; internet www.actioncom.com/cehomepage.htm; f. 1986; 7 a year; Editor TIM GOULDSON; circ. 22,000.

Canadian Geographic: 39 McArthur Ave, Ottawa, ON K1L 8L7; tel. (613) 745-4629; fax (613) 744-0947; e-mail editorial@canadiangeographic.ca; internet www.canadiangeographic.ca; f. 1930; 6 a year; publ. of the Royal Canadian Geographical Soc.; Editor RICK BOYCHUK; circ. 227,000.

Canadian Home Workshop: 340 Ferrier St, Suite 210, Markham, ON L3R 2Z5; tel. (905) 475-8440; fax (905) 475-9246; e-mail editorial@canadianhomeworkshop.com; internet www.canadianhomeworkshop.com; f. 1977; monthly; do-it-yourself; Editorial Dir DOUGLAS THOMPSON; circ. 104,000.

Canadian House & Home: 511 King St West, Suite 120, Toronto, ON M5V 2Z4; tel. (416) 593-0204; fax (416) 591-1630; e-mail chheditorial@canhomepub.com; internet www.canadianhouseandhome.com; f. 1982; 12 a year; Editor COBI LADNER; circ. 252,000.

Canadian Jewish News: 1500 Don Mills Rd, Suite 205, North York, ON M3B 3KY; tel. (416) 391-1836; fax (416) 391-0829; e-mail mbd@cjnews.com; internet www.cjnews.com; f. 1971; 50 a year; Editor MORDECHAI BEN-DAT; circ. 50,000.

Canadian Living: 25 Sheppard Ave West, Suite 100, North York, ON M2N 6S7; tel. (416) 733-7600; fax (416) 733-3398; e-mail letters@canadianliving.com; internet www.canadianliving.com; f. 1975; monthly; Editor CHARLOTTE EMPEY; circ. 563,000.

Canadian Medical Association Journal: 1867 Alta Vista Dr., Ottawa, ON K1G 3Y6; tel. (613) 731-8610; fax (613) 565-5471; e-mail pubs@cma.ca; internet www.cmaj.ca; f. 1911; 25 a year; Editor Dr JOHN HOEY; circ. 64,000.

Canadian Musician: 23 Hannover Dr., Suite 7, St Catharines, ON L2W 1A3; tel. (905) 641-3471; fax (905) 641-1648; e-mail info@nor.com; internet www.canadianmusician.com; f. 1979; 6 a year; Man. Editor JEFF MACKAY; circ. 27,000.

Canadian Nurse/L'infirmière canadienne: 50 Driveway, Ottawa, ON K2P 1E2; tel. (613) 237-2133; fax (613) 237-3520; e-mail cnj@cna-nurses.ca; f. 1905; 10 a year; journal of the Canadian Nurses' Asscn; English and French; Editor-in-Chief JUDITH HAINES; Editor (L'infirmière canadienne) DIANE ST-PIERRE; circ. 111,000.

Canadian Pharmaceutical Journal: 1785 Alta Vista Dr., Suite 105, Ottawa, ON K1G 3Y6; tel. (613) 523-7877; fax (613) 523-0445; e-mail cpj@pharmacists.ca; internet www.pharmacists.ca/content/hcp/resource_centre/cpj/cpj_contacts.cfm; f. 1868; 10 a year; Publr LEESA BRUCE; Editor POLLY THOMSON; circ. 17,000.

Canadian Travel Press Weekly: 310 Dupont St, Toronto, ON M5R 1V9; tel. (416) 968-7252; fax (416) 968-2377; e-mail ctp@baxter.net; internet www.travelpress.com; 46 a year; Editor-in-Chief EDITH BAXTER; circ. 13,000.

Chatelaine: 1 Mount Pleasant Rd, 8th Floor, Toronto, ON M4Y 2Y5; tel. (416) 764-1888; fax (416) 764-2413; e-mail chatcour@maclean.hunter-quebec.qc.ca; internet www.chatelaine.com; f. 1928; monthly; women's journal; Editor KIM PITTAWAY; circ. 803,000.

ComputerWorld Canada: 55 Town Centre Ct, Suite 302, Scarborough, ON M1P 4X4; tel. (416) 290-0240; fax (416) 290-0238; internet www.itworldcanada.com; f. 1984; 25 a year; Editor-in-Chief NORMAN TOLLINSKY; circ. 42,000.

Elm Street The Look Magazine: 111 Queen St East, Suite 320, Toronto, ON M5C 1S2; tel. (416) 364-3333; fax (416) 595-7217; e-mail elmstreet@elmstreet.ca; internet www.elmstreet.ca; f. 1996; 8 a year; women's interest; Editor-in-Chief LORI SEYMOUR; circ. 600,000.

Flare: 1 Mount Pleasant Rd, 8th Floor, Toronto, ON M4Y 2YS; tel. (416) 764-1829; fax (416) 764-2866; e-mail sarah.casselman@flare.rogers.com; internet www.flare.com; f. 1970; monthly; fashion, beauty and health; Editor-in-Chief SUZANNE BOYD; circ. 1.7m.

Hockey News: 777 Bay St, Suite 2700, Toronto, ON M5G 2N1; tel. (416) 340-8000; fax (416) 340-2786; internet www.thn.com; f. 1947; 42 a year; Editor-in-Chief STEVE DRYDEN; circ. 205,000.

Holstein Journal: 30 East Beaver Creek Rd, Suite 210, Richmond Hill, ON L4B 1J2; tel. (905) 886-4222; fax (905) 886-0037; e-mail subs@holsteinjournal.com; internet www.holsteinjournal.com; f. 1938; monthly; news and information pertaining to the Holstein dairy breed; Editor BONNIE E. COOPER; circ. 5,000.

Kanadai Magyarsag (Hungarian-Canadians): 74 Advance Rd, Etobicoke, ON M8Z 2T7; tel. (416) 233-3131; fax (416) 233-5984; e-mail magyarsag@wellerpublishing.com; weekly; circ. 10,000.

Legion Magazine: 359 Kent St, Suite 407, Ottawa, ON K2P 0R6; tel. (613) 235-8741; fax (613) 233-7159; e-mail editor@legionmagazine.com; internet www.legionmagazine.com; f. 1926; 6 a year; publ. of the Royal Canadian Legion; Editor MAC JOHNSTON; circ. 332,638.

Maclean's: 1 Mount Pleasant Rd, 11th Floor, Toronto, ON M4Y 2Y5; tel. (416) 764-1339; fax (416) 764-1332; e-mail letters@macleans.ca; internet www.macleans.ca; f. 1905 as *The Business Magazine*; present name adopted in 1911; weekly; Publr PAUL JONES; Editor ANTHONY WILSON-SMITH; circ. 500,000.

Northern Miner: 12 Concorde Pl., Suite 800, Toronto, ON M3C 4J2; tel. (416) 442-2122; fax (416) 442-2191; e-mail northernminer2@northernminer.com; internet www.northernminer.com; f. 1915; weekly; Editor JAMES B. WHYTE; circ. 23,000.

Now: 189 Church St, Toronto, ON M4K 1N1; tel. (416) 364-1300; fax (416) 364-1166; e-mail web@nowtoronto.com; internet www.nowtoronto.com; f. 1981; weekly; young adult; Publr and Editor MICHAEL HOLLETT; circ. 106,308.

Ontario Medical Review: 525 University Ave, Suite 300, Toronto, ON M5G 2K7; tel. (416) 599-2580; fax (416) 340-2232; e-mail jeff_henry@oma.org; internet www.oma.org; f. 1922; monthly; publ. of the Ontario Medical Asscn; Editor JEFF HENRY; circ. 26,600.

Oral Health: 12 Concorde Pl., Suite 800, Toronto, ON M3C 4J2; tel. (416) 510-6781; fax (416) 510-6785; e-mail cwilson@oralhealthjournal.com; internet www.oralhealthjournal.com; f. 1911; monthly; dentistry; Man. Editor CATHERINE WILSON; circ. 17,000.

Photo Life: 1 Dundas St West, Suite 2500, POB 84, Toronto, ON M5G 1G3; tel. (800) 905-7468; fax (800) 664-2739; e-mail editor@photolife.com; internet www.photolife.com; f. 1976; 6 a year; Editor-in-Chief ANITA DAMMER; circ. 55,000.

Quill & Quire: 111 Queen St East, 3rd Floor, Toronto, ON M5C 1S2; tel. (416) 364-3333; fax (416) 595-5415; e-mail info@ quillandquire.com; internet www.quillandquire.com; f. 1935; monthly; book-publishing industry; Editor DEREK WEILER; circ. 5,000.

Style: 555 Richmond St West, Suite 701, Toronto, ON M5V 3B1; tel. (416) 203-6737; fax (416) 203-1057; e-mail style@style.ca; internet www.style.ca; f. 1888; monthly; fashion and clothing trade publication; Editor MARILISA RACCO; circ. 12,000.

Style at Home: 25 Sheppard Ave West, Suite 100, Toronto, ON M2N 6S7; tel. (416) 733-7600; fax (416) 218-3632; e-mail letters@ styleathome.com; f. 1997; 8 a year; Editor GAIL JOHNSTON HABS; circ. 204,000.

Sympatico Netlife: 25 Sheppard Ave West, Suite 100, North York, ON M2N 6S7; tel. (416) 733-7600; fax (416) 733-8272; e-mail giffen@ sympatico.ca; internet www1.sympatico.ca/mags/netlife; 6 a year; computer technology; Editor PETER GIFFEN; circ. 450,000.

Toronto Life Magazine: Urban Group, St Joseph Media Corpn, Queen Richmond Centre, Toronto, ON M5C 1S2; tel. (416) 364-3333; fax (416) 861-1169; e-mail editorial@torontolife.com; internet www .torontolife.com; f. 1966; monthly; Publr MARINA GLOGOVAC; Editor JOHN MACFARLANE; circ. 97,000.

Tribute Magazine: 71 Barber Greene Rd, Don Mills, Toronto, ON M3C 2A2; tel. (416) 445-0544; fax (416) 445-2894; e-mail sstewart@ tribute.ca; internet www.tribute.ca; f. 1984; 9 a year; entertainment; Editor-in-Chief SANDRA I. STEWART; circ. 500,000.

TV Guide: 25 Sheppard Ave West, Suite 100, North York, ON M2N 6S7; tel. (416) 733-7600; fax (416) 733-3632; e-mail tvguide@indas .on.ca; internet www.tvguide.ca; f. 1976; weekly; Editor CHRISTOPHER LOUDON; circ. 838,000.

TV Times: 44 Frid St, Hamilton, ON L8N 3G3; tel. (905) 526-3501; fax (905) 526-3513; e-mail tvtimes@canada.com; internet www .canada.com/entertainment/television/tvtimes.html; f. 1969; weekly; 14 regional edns; Editor ERIC KOHANIK; circ. 1,941,000.

Québec

L'Actualité: 200 ave McGill College, bureau 800, Montréal, QC H3B 4G7; tel. (514) 845-2543; fax (514) 845-7503; e-mail redaction@ lactualite.com; internet www.lactualite.com; f. 1976; monthly; current affairs; Pres. and Editor MARC BLONDEAU; Editor-in-Chief CAROLE BEAULIEU; circ. 188,455.

Affaires Plus: 1100 blvd René-Lévesque ouest, 24e étage, Montréal, QC H3B 4X9; tel. (514) 392-9000; fax (514) 392-1586; e-mail aide .lesaffaires.com@transcontinental.ca; internet www.affairesplus .com; f. 1978; monthly; Editor-in-Chief MARIE-AGNÈS THELLIER; circ. 96,000.

Le Bulletin des Agriculteurs: 1001 blvd de Maisonneuve ouest, Montréal, QC H3A 3E1; tel. (514) 845-5141; fax (514) 845-6261; e-mail info@lebulletin.com; internet www.lebulletin.com; f. 1918; monthly; Editor-in-Chief SYLVIE BOUCHARD; circ. 24,000.

Châtelaine: 1001 blvd de Maisonneuve ouest, bureau 1100, Montréal, QC H3A 3E1; tel. (514) 843-2504; fax (514) 845-4302; e-mail lettres@chatelaine-quebec.com; internet www.chatelaine-quebec .com; f. 1960; monthly; Editor CATHERINE ELIE; circ. 207,000.

CIM Bulletin: 3400 blvd de Maisonneuve ouest, Bureau 1210, Montréal, QC H3Z 3B8; tel. (514) 939-2710; fax (514) 939-2714; e-mail cim@cim.org; internet www.cim.org; monthly; publ. by the Canadian Inst. of Mining, Metallurgy and Petroleum; Editor H. EDNIE; circ. 10,000.

Il Cittadino Canadese: 5960 Jean-Talon est, Bureau 209, Montréal, QC H1S 1M2; tel. (514) 253-2332; fax (514) 253-6574; e-mail journal@cittdinocanadese.com; internet www.cittdinocanadese .com; f. 1941; weekly; Italian; Editor BASILIO GIORDANO; circ. 36,000.

Harrowsmith Country Life: 3650 Pitfield Blvd, Montreal (Pierrefonds), QC H8Y 3L4; tel. (514) 327-4464; fax (514) 327-0514; e-mail info@harrowsmithcountrylife.ca; internet www .harrowsmithcountrylife.ca; f. 1976; 6 a year; Editor TOM CRUICKSHANK; circ. 190,000.

Le Lundi: 7 chemin Bates, Outremont, QC H2V 1A6; tel. (514) 270-1100; fax (514) 270-5395; f. 1976; weekly; Editor MICHAEL CHOINIÈRE; circ. 62,000.

Le Producteur de Lait Québécois: 555 blvd Roland-Thérrien, Longueuil, QC J4H 3Y9; tel. (514) 679-8483; fax (514) 670-4788; e-mail rloiseau@laterre.ca; internet www.lait.org/zone3/producteur/ index.asp; f. 1980; monthly; dairy farming; publ. by Fédération des producteurs de lait du Québec; Editor-in-Chief JEAN VIGNEAULT; circ. 12,000.

Progrès-Dimanche: 1051 blvd Talbot, Chicoutimi, QC G7H 5C1; tel. (418) 545-4474; fax (418) 690-8685; e-mail msimard@lequotidien .com; internet www.cyberpresse.ca/quotidien/progresdimanche; f. 1964; weekly; Editor-in-Chief MICHEL SIMARD; circ. 45,000.

Québec Science: 4388 rue St-Denis, bureau 300, Montréal, QC H2J 2L1; tel. (514) 843-6888; fax (514) 843-4897; e-mail courrier@ quebecscience.qc.ca; internet www.quebecscience.qc.ca; internet www.cybersciences.com; f. 1969; 10 a year; Editor-in-Chief RAYMOND LEMIEUX; circ. 32,000.

Reader's Digest/Sélection: 1100 René Lévesque Blvd West, Montréal, QC H3B 5H5; tel. (514) 934-0751; fax (514) 940-3637; internet www.readersdigest.ca; f. 1947; monthly; French and English edns; Editor-in-Chief PETER STORLAND (French edn); circ. 1.2m.

Rénovation Bricolage: 7 chemin Bates, Outremont, QC H2V 4V7; tel. (514) 848-7164; fax (514) 848-0309; e-mail renobrico@ tva-publications.com; f. 1976; 9 a year; Publr and Editor CLAUDE LECLERC; Editor-in-Chief VINCENT ROY; circ. 48,500.

Revue Commerce: 1100 blvd René-Lévesque ouest, 24e étage, Montréal, QC H3B 4X9; tel. (514) 392-9000; fax (514) 3921586; e-mail lesaffaires@postelinc.com; internet www.revuecommerce .com; f. 1898; monthly; Editor-in-Chief DIANE BÉRARD.

Sélection du Reader's Digest: 1100 blvd Réne-Lévesque ouest, Montréal, QC H3B 5H5; tel. (514) 940-0751; fax (514) 940-7340; e-mail manon.sylvain@readersdigest.com; internet www.selectionrd .ca; f. 1947; monthly; Editor ROBERT GOYETTE; circ. 321,000.

La Terre de Chez Nous: 555 blvd Roland-Thérrien, Longueuil, QC J4H 3Y9; tel. (450) 679-8483; fax (450) 679-4788; e-mail tcn@laterre .qc.ca; internet www.laterre.ca; f. 1929; weekly; agriculture and forestry; Editor-in-Chief LOÏC HAMON; Publr DANIEL BOULANGER; circ. 41,500.

TV Hebdo: 7 chemin Bates, Outremont, QCH2V 4V7; tel. (514) 848-7000; fax (514) 848-7070; e-mail tv@tvhebdo.com; internet www .tvhebdo.com; f. 1960; weekly; Editor-in-Chief JEAN-LOUIS PODLESAK; circ. 223,000.

Saskatchewan

Farm Light & Power: 2230 15th Ave, Regina, SK S4P 1A2; tel. (306) 525-3305; fax (306) 757-1810; f. 1959; monthly; Editor TOM BRADLEY; circ. 71,000.

Western Producer: 2310 Millar Ave, POB 2500, Saskatoon, SK S7K 2C4; tel. (306) 665-3544; fax (306) 934-2401; e-mail newsroom@ producer.com; internet www.producer.com; f. 1923; weekly; agriculture; Man. Editor BARB GLEN; circ. 74,000.

Yukon Territory

Yukon News: 211 Wood St, Whitehorse, YT Y1A 2E4; tel. (867) 667-6285; fax (867) 668-3755; e-mail plesniak@yukon-news.com; internet www.yukonweb.com/community/yukon-news; f. 1960; 3 a week; Editor PETER LESNIAK; circ. 8,000.

NEWS AGENCIES

The Canadian Press: 36 King St East, Toronto, ON M5C 2L9; tel. (416) 364-0321; fax (416) 364-0207; internet www.cp.org; f. 1917; national news co-operative; 99 newspaper mems; Editor-in-Chief SCOTT WHITE.

Foreign Bureaux

Agence France-Presse (AFP): 180 blvd Réné-Lévesque Est, Suite 200, Montréal, QC H2X 1N6; tel. (514) 288-2777; fax (514) 288-3506; e-mail afpcanada@afp.com; internet www.afp.com; Bureau Chief HERVÉ GUILBAUD; also office in Toronto.

Agencia EFE (Spain): 76 St Clarens Ave, Toronto, ON M6K 2S5; tel. (416) 535-2396; fax (416) 516-6909; e-mail durruti@interlog.com.

Agenzia Nazionale Stampa Associata (ANSA) (Italy): 150 Wellington St, Press Gallery, Rm 703, Ottawa, ON K1P 5A4; tel. (613) 235-4248; fax (613) 235-4248; Rep. ELIO COPPOLA.

Associated Press (USA): 36 King St East, Toronto, ON M5C 2L9; tel. (416) 368-1388; fax (416) 368-7552.

Deutsche Presse-Agentur (dpa) (Germany): 702 National Press Bldg, 150 Wellington St, Ottawa, ON K1P 5A4; tel. (613) 234-6024; Correspondent BARBARA HALSIG.

Informatsionnoye Telegrafnoye Agentstvo Rossii—Telegrafnoye Agentstvo Suverennykh Stran (ITAR—TASS) (Russia): 200 Rideau Terrace, Suite 1305, Ottawa, ON K1M OZ3; tel. (613) 745-4310; fax (613) 745-5581; e-mail tasscnd@simpatico.ca; Correspondent BORIS GROUSHIN.

Reuters (United Kingdom): 2020 rue Université, bureau 1020, Montréal, QC H3A 2A5; tel. (514) 282-0744; fax (514) 844-2327; also office in Vancouver.

Agencia EFE (Spain), Jiji Tsushin (Japan), Prensa Latina (Cuba), United Press International (USA) and Xinhua (New China) News Agency (People's Republic of China) are also represented.

PRESS ASSOCIATIONS

Canadian Business Press: 40 Shields Court, Suite 201, Markham, ON L3R 0M5; tel. (905) 946-8889; fax (905) 479-1711; e-mail jjcbp@ passport.ca; Chair. TERRY MALDEN; Pres. JUDY JOHNSON; 125 mems.

Canadian Community Newspapers Association: 90 Eglinton Ave East, Suite 206, Toronto, ON M4P 2Y3; tel. (416) 482-1090; fax (416) 482-1908; e-mail info@ccna.ca; internet www.ccna.ca; f. 1919; Exec. Dir SERGE LAVOIE; 692 mems.

Canadian Newspaper Association: 890 Yonge St, Suite 200, Toronto, ON M4W 3P4; tel. (416) 923-3567; fax (416) 923-7206; e-mail bcantley@cna-acj.ca; internet www.cna-acj.ca; f. 1996; Chair. RUSS MILLS; 102 mems.

Canadian Magazine Publishers Association: 130 Spadina Ave, Suite 202, Toronto, ON M5V 2L4; tel. (416) 504-0274; fax (416) 504-0437; e-mail cminfo@cmpa.ca; internet www.cmpa.ca; f. 1973; Chair. MICHAEL REA.

Magazines Canada: 425 Adelaide St West, Suite 700, Toronto, ON M5V 3C1; tel. (416) 596-5382; fax (416) 504-0437; e-mail info@ magazinescanada.com; internet www.magazinescanada.com; Pres. GARY GARLAND.

Publishers

Editions d'Acadie: 236 rue St-Georges, Moncton, NB E1C 8N8; tel. (506) 857-8490; fax (506) 855-3130; e-mail edacadie@nbnet.nb.ca; f. 1972; Gen. Dir MARCEL OUELLETTE.

Thomas Allen and Son Ltd: 390 Steelcase Rd East, Markham, ON L3R 1G2; tel. (416) 475-9126; fax (416) 475-6747; internet www .thomas-allen.com; f. 1916; Pres. T. J. ALLEN.

Annick Press Ltd: 15 Patricia Ave, Willowdale, ON M2M 1H9; tel. (416) 221-4802; fax (416) 221-8400; e-mail annickpress@annickpress .com; internet www.annickpress.com; f. 1976; children's; Dir RICK WILKS.

Arsenal Pulp Press Book Publishers Ltd: 1014 Homer St, Suite 103, Vancouver, BC V6B 2W9; tel. (604) 687-4233; fax (604) 669-8250; e-mail contact@arsenalpulp.com; internet www.arsenalpulp .com; f. 1982; literary, native, cultural studies; Publr BRIAN LAM.

Editions Bellarmin: 165 rue Deslauriers, Ville St-Laurent, QC H4N 2S4; tel. (514) 745-4290; fax (514) 745-4299; e-mail editions@ fides.qc.ca; internet www.fides.qc.ca; f. 1891; religious, educational, politics, sociology, ethnography, history, sport, leisure; Dir-Gen. ANTOINE DEL BUSSO.

Black Rose Books: CP 1258, succursale place du Parc, Montréal, QC H2W 1Y5; tel. (514) 844-4076; fax (514) 849-1956; e-mail blackrose@web.net; internet www.web.net/blackrosebooks; f. 1969; social studies, humanities; Pres. JACQUES ROUX.

Borealis Press Ltd: 110 Bloomindale St, Ottawa, ON K2C 4A4; tel. (613) 798-9299; fax (613) 798-9747; e-mail borealis@istar.ca; internet www.borealispress.com; f. 1972; Canadian fiction and non-fiction, drama, juvenile, poetry; Pres. FRANK TIERNEY; Vice-Pres. W. GLENN CLEVER.

Breakwater Books/Softwares Ltd: 100 Water St, POB 2188, St John's, NL A1C 6E6; tel. (709) 722-6680; fax (709) 753-0708; e-mail info@breakwater.nf.net; internet www.breakwater.nf.net; f. 1973; fiction, non-fiction, children's, educational, folklore; Pres. CLYDE ROSE.

Broadview Press: 280 Perry St, Unit 5, POB 1243, Peterborough, ON K9J 7H5; tel. (705) 743-8990; fax (705) 743-8353; e-mail customerservice@broadviewpress.com; internet www .broadviewpress.com; f. 1985; Pres. DON LePAN.

Canada Law Book Inc: 240 Edward St, Aurora, ON L4G 3S9; tel. (905) 841-6472; fax (905) 841-5085; internet www.canadalawbook .ca; f. 1855; law reports, law journals, legal textbooks, etc.; Pres. STUART MORRISON.

Carswell-Thomson Professional Publishing Canada: 2075 Kennedy Rd, Toronto, ON M1T 3V4; tel. (416) 609-8000; fax (416) 298-5094; internet www.carswell.com/carswell.home; f. 1864; Pres. and CEO DON VAN MEER.

Les Editions CEC Inc: 8101 blvd Métropolitain est, Anjou, Montréal, QC H1J 1J9; tel. (514) 351-6010; fax (514) 351-3534; e-mail infoped@cecditions.com; f. 1956; textbooks; Pres. and Dir-Gen. JACQUES ROCHEFORT.

Chenelière/McGraw-Hill: 7001 blvd St-Laurent, Montréal, QC H2S 3E3; tel. (514) 273-1066; fax (514) 276-0324; e-mail chene@ dlcmcgrawhill.ca; textbooks; Pres. MICHEL DE LA CHENELIÈRE.

Coach House Books: 401 Huron St, Toronto, ON M5S 2G5; tel. (416) 979-2217; fax (416) 977-1158; internet www.chbooks.com; f. 1965; fiction, poetry, drama; Publr STAN BEVINGTON.

Crabtree Publishing Co Ltd: 612 Welland Ave, St Catharines, ON L2M 5V6; tel. (905) 682-5221; fax (905) 682-7166; e-mail letters@ crabtreebooks.com; internet www.crabtreebooks.com; f. 1978; children's; Pres. PETER A. CRABTREE.

Douglas & McIntyre Ltd: 2323 Québec St, Suite 201, Vancouver, BC V5T 4S7; tel. (604) 254-7191; fax (604) 254-9099; e-mail dm@ douglas-mcintyre.com; internet www.douglas-mcintyre.com; f. 1964; fiction, general non-fiction; Pres. SCOTT McINTYRE.

The Dundurn Group: 8 Market St, Suite 200, Toronto, ON M5E 1M6; tel. (416) 214-5544; fax (416) 214-5556; e-mail info@dundurn .com; internet www.dundurn.com; f. 1972; drama and performing arts, history, reference, fiction and non-fiction; Pres. KIRK HOWARD.

Fenn Publishing Co Ltd: 34 Nixon Rd, Bolton, ON L7E 1W2; internet www.hbfenn.com; fiction and non-fiction; Pres. HAROLD FENN; Publr C. JORDAN FENN.

Editions Fides: 165 rue Deslauriers, Ville St-Laurent, PQ H4N 2S4; tel. (514) 745-4290; fax (514) 745-4299; e-mail editions@fides.qc .ca; internet www.editionsfides.com; f. 1937; juvenile, history, theology, textbooks and literature; Dir-Gen. ANTOINE DEL BUSSO.

Fifth House Publishers Ltd: 6125 11th St, SE, No. 9, Calgary, AB T2H 2L6; tel. (403) 571-5230; fax (403) 571-5235; e-mail godwit@ fitzhenry.ca; internet www.fitzhenry.ca/fifthhouse.htm; f. 1982; native, literary and non-fiction.

Fitzhenry & Whiteside Ltd: 195 Allstate Parkway, Markham, ON L3R 4T8; tel. (416) 477-9700; fax (416) 477-9179; e-mail godwit@ fitzhenry.ca; internet www.fitzhenry.ca; f. 1966; textbooks, trade, educational; Pres. SHARON FITZHENRY.

General Publishing Co Ltd: 895 Don Mills Rd, Toronto, ON M3C 1W3; tel. (416) 445-3333; fax (416) 445-5967; f. 1934; fiction, history, biography, children's, general, textbooks.

Grolier Ltd: 12 Banigan Dr., Toronto, ON M4H 1A6; tel. (416) 425-1924; fax (416) 425-4015; internet www.scholasticlibrary.com; f. 1912; division of Scholastic Library Publishing; reference, children's; Gen. Man. ROB FURLONGER.

Harcourt Canada: 55 Horner Ave, Toronto, ON M8Z 4X6; tel. (416) 255-4491; fax (416) 255-5608; internet www.harcourtcanada.com; f. 1922; medical, educational, scholarly; Pres. WENDY COCHRAN.

Harlequin Enterprises Ltd: 225 Duncan Mill Rd, Don Mills, ON M3B 3K9; tel. (416) 445-5860; fax (416) 445-8655; e-mail customer_ecare@harlequin.ca; internet www.eharlequin.com; f. 1949; fiction, paperbacks; Chair. and CEO DONNA M. HAYES.

HarperCollins Canada Ltd: 2 Bloor St East, Toronto, ON M4W 1A8; tel. (416) 975-9334; fax (416) 975-5223; e-mail hccanada@ harpercollins.com; internet www.harpercanada.com; f. 1932; trade, bibles, dictionaries, juvenile, paperbacks; Pres. and CEO DAVID KENT.

Editions de l'Hexagone: 1010 rue de la Gauchetière est, Montréal, QC H2L 2N5; tel. (514) 523-1182; fax (514) 282-7530; internet www .edhexagone.com; f. 1953; literature; Editorial Dir PIERRE GRAVELINE.

Hyperion Press Ltd: 300 Wales Ave, Winnipeg, MB R2M 2S9; tel. (204) 256-9204; fax (204) 255-7845; e-mail tamos@escape.ca; internet www.escape.ca/~tamos; children's illustrated, crafts; Pres. MARVIS TUTIAH.

Institut de Recherches psychologiques, inc/Institute of Psychological Research, Inc: 34 rue Fleury ouest, Montréal, QC H3L 1S9; tel. (514) 382-3000; fax (514) 382-3007; e-mail info@i-r-p.ca; internet www.i-r-p.ca; f. 1964; educational and psychological tests; Adviser ROBERT CHEVRIER.

Jesperson Publishing: 100 Water St, 3rd Floor, POB 2188, St John's, NL A1C 6E6; tel. (709) 757-2216; fax (709) 753-0708; e-mail info@jespersonpublishing.nf.net; internet www.jespersonpublishing .nf.net; f. 1974; educational and trade; Pres. DEBBIE HANLON.

Key Porter Books: 70 The Esplanade, 3rd Floor, Toronto, ON M5E 1R2; tel. (416) 862-7777; fax (416) 862-2304; e-mail iromain@ keyporter.com; internet www.keyporter.com; f. 1980; general trade; Pres. and CEO ANNA PORTER.

Leméac Editeur: 4609 d'Iberville, 3e étage, Montréal, QC H2H 2L9; tel. (514) 525-5558; fax (514) 524-3145; e-mail lemeac@lemeac .com; f. 1957; literary, academic, general; Gen. Dir LISE P. BERGEVIN.

Lidec Inc: 4350 ave de l'Hôtel-de-Ville, Montréal, QC H2W 2H5; tel. (514) 843-5991; fax (514) 843-5252; e-mail lidec@lidec.qc.ca; internet www.lidec.qc.ca; f. 1965; educational, textbooks; Pres. MARC-AIME GUÉRIN.

James Lorimer & Co Ltd: 35 Britain St, Toronto, ON M5A 1R7; tel. (416) 362-4762; fax (416) 362-3939; e-mail jlc@sympatico.ca; f. 1971; urban and labour studies, children's, general non-fiction; Pres. JAMES LORIMER.

McClelland and Stewart Ltd: 481 University Ave, Suite 900, Toronto, ON M5G 2E9; tel. (416) 598-1114; fax (416) 598-7764;

internet www.mcclelland.com; f. 1906; trade and illustrated; Pres. and Publr Douglas M. Gibson.

McGill-Queen's University Press: 3430 rue McTavish, Montréal, QC H3A 1X9; tel. (514) 398-3750; fax (514) 398-4333; e-mail philip .cercone@mcgill.ca; internet www.mqup.ca; f. 1960; scholarly and general interest; Exec. Dir Philip J. Cercone.

McGraw-Hill Educational Publishing: 300 Water St, Whitby, ON L1N 9B6; tel. (416) 430-5000; fax (416) 430-5191; internet www .mcgrawhill.ca; f. 1944; educational and general; three divisions: educational publishing, higher education and professional publishing; imprints include McGraw-Hill Lifetime Learning, Xebec/McGraw-Hill, McGraw-Hill Reyerson, McGraw-Hill Latin America/Spain, McGraw-Hill Europe, Middle East, Africa and McGraw-Hill Asia/Pacific; Pres. and CEO John Dill.

Editions du Noroît: 156 succursale de Lorimier, Montréal, QC H2H 2N6; tel. (514) 727-0005; fax (514) 723-6660; e-mail lenoroit@ lenoroit.com; internet www.lenoroit.com; f. 1971; poetry; Dir Paul Bélanger.

Oberon Press: 350 Sparks St, Suite 400, Ottawa, ON K1R 7S8; tel. and fax (613) 238-3275; e-mail oberon@sympatico.ca; internet www3 .sympatico.ca/oberon; f. 1966; poetry, children's, fiction and general non-fiction; Pres. Michael Macklem.

Oxford University Press Canada: 70 Wynford Dr., Don Mills, ON M3C 1J9; tel. (416) 441-2941; fax (416) 444-0427; e-mail custserv@ oupcan.com; internet www.oupcan.com; f. 1904; general, education, scholarly, Canadiana; Pres. Joanna Gertler.

Pearson Education Canada Inc: 26 Prince Andrew Pl., Toronto, ON M3C 2T8; tel. (416) 447-5101; fax (416) 443-0948; internet www .pearsoned.ca; educational; Pres. and CEO Tony Vander Woude.

Penguin Books Canada Ltd: 10 Alcorn Ave, Suite 300, Toronto, ON M4V 3B2; tel. (416) 925-2249; fax (416) 925-0068; e-mail oper@ penguin.ca; internet www.penguin.ca; f. 1974; division of Pearson; Pres. Ed Carson; Publr David Davidar.

Pippin Publishing Corpn: 85 Ellesmere Rd, Suite 232, Toronto, ON M1R 4B9; tel. (416) 510-2918; fax (416) 510-3359; e-mail jld@ pippinpub.com; internet www.pippinpub.com; f. 1995; educational and trade; Pres. Jonathan Lovat Dickson.

Pontifical Institute of Mediaeval Studies: 59 Queen's Park Cres. East, Toronto, ON M5S 2C4; tel. (416) 926-7144; fax (416) 926-7258; e-mail pontifex@chass.utoronto.ca; internet www.pims.ca; f. 1939; scholarly publs concerning the Middle Ages; Dir of Publs Dr Ron B. Thomson.

Prentice Hall Canada Inc: 1870 Birchmount Rd, Scarborough, ON M1P 2J7; tel. (416) 293-3621; fax (416) 299-2529; e-mail pub_canada@prenhall; internet www.prenhall.com; f. 1960; trade, textbooks; Pres. Brian Heer.

Les Presses de l'Université Laval: Pavillon Maurice-Pollack, bureau 3103, Cité Universitaire, Ste-Foy, QC G1K 7P4; tel. (418) 656-2803; fax (418) 656-3305; e-mail presses@pul.ulaval.ca; internet www.ulaval.ca/pul; f. 1950; scholarly; Publr Benoit Bernier.

Les Presses de l'Université de Montréal: 3535 chemin Queen-Mary, bureau 206, Montréal, QC H3V 1H8; tel. (514) 343-6933; fax (514) 343-2232; e-mail pum@umontreal.ca; internet www.pum .umontreal.ca; f. 1962; scholarly and general; Gen. Man. Antoine Del Busso.

Les Presses de l'Université du Québec: Edif. le Delta I, 2875 blvd Laurier, Suite 450, Ste-Foy, QC G1V 2M2; tel. (418) 657-4399; fax (418) 657-2096; e-mail puq@puq.uquebec.ca; internet www.puq .uquebec.ca; f. 1969; scholarly and general; Dir-Gen. Angèle Tremblay.

Random House of Canada Ltd: 1 Toronto St, Unit 300, Toronto, ON L4W M5C 2V6; tel. (416) 364-4449; fax (416) 364-6863; internet www.randomhouse.ca; f. 1944; merged with Doubleday Canada Ltd in 1999; Chair. and CEO John Neale.

Editions du Renouveau Pédagogique Inc: 5757 rue Cyphiot, St-Laurent, QC H4S 1R3; tel. (514) 334-2690; fax (514) 334-4720; e-mail info@erpi.com; internet www.erpi.com; f. 1965; textbooks; Pres. Normand Cléroux.

Scholastic Canada Ltd: 175 Hillmount Rd, Markham, ON L6C 1Z7; tel. (905) 887-7323; fax (905) 887-1131; internet www.scholastic .ca; f. 1957; Pres. F. C. Larry Muller.

Sélection du Reader's Digest (Canada) Ltée/The Reader's Digest Association (Canada) Ltd: 1125 Stanley St, Montréal, QC H3B 5H5; tel. (514) 940-0751; fax (514) 940-3637; e-mail customer .service@readersdigest.com; internet www.rd.ca; Pres. and CEO Andrea Martin.

Editions du Septentrion: 1300 ave Maguire, Sillery, QC G1T 1Z3; tel. (418) 688-3556; fax (418) 527-4978; e-mail sept@septentrion.qc .ca; internet www.septentrion.qc.ca; f. 1988; history, essays, general; Man. Denis Vaugeois.

Simon & Schuster Canada: 625 Cochrane Dr., Suite 600, Markham, ON L3R 9R9; tel. (905) 943-9942; fax (905) 943-9026; e-mail info@simonandschuster.ca; internet www.simonsays.com.

Thistledown Press Ltd: 633 Main St, Saskatoon, SK S7H 0J8; tel. (306) 244-1722; fax (306) 244-1762; e-mail thistle@sk.sympatico.ca; internet www.thistledown.sk.ca; f. 1975; Canadian fiction, non-fiction and poetry; Publrs Patrick O'Rourke, Allan Forrie.

Thomson Nelson: 1120 Birchmount Rd, Scarborough, ON M1K 5G4; tel. (416) 752-9448; fax (416) 752-8101; e-mail inquire@nelson .com; internet www.nelson.com; f. 1914; retailing, consumer affairs, textbooks; Pres. George W. Bergquist.

Thompson Educational Publishing Inc: 6 Ripley Ave, Suite 200, Toronto, ON M6S 3N9; tel. (416) 766-2763; fax (416) 766-0398; e-mail publisher@thompsonbooks.com; internet www .thompsonbooks.com; f. 1989; textbooks; Pres. Keith Thompson.

Turnstone Press Ltd: 100 Arthur St, Suite 607, Winnipeg, MB R3B 1H3; tel. (204) 947-1555; fax (204) 942-1555; e-mail editor@ turnstonepress.mb.ca; internet www.turnstonepress.com; f. 1976; literary, regional; Man. Editor Todd Besant.

University of Alberta Press: Ring House 2, Edmonton, AB T6G 2E1; tel. (780) 492-3662; fax (780) 492-0719; e-mail uap@ualberta.ca; internet www.uap.ualberta.ca; f. 1969; scholarly, general non-fiction; Dir Linda D. Cameron.

University of British Columbia Press (UBC Press): 2029 West Mall, Vancouver, BC V6T 1Z2; tel. (604) 822-5959; fax (604) 822-6083; e-mail info@ubcpress.ubc.ca; internet www.ubcpress.ubc.ca; f. 1971; humanities, forestry, social science; Dir R. Peter Milroy.

University of Calgary Press: 2500 University Dr., NW, Calgary, AB T2N 1N4; tel. (403) 220-7578; fax (403) 282-0085; e-mail whildebr@ucalgary.ca; internet www.uofcpress.com; f. 1981; Dir Walter Hildebrandt.

University of Manitoba Press: 423 University Cres., Winnipeg, MB R3T 2N2; tel. (204) 474-9495; fax (204) 474-7566; internet www .umanitoba.ca/uofmpress; f. 1967; regional history, Native, Icelandic and women's studies; Dir David Carr.

University of Ottawa Press/Presses de l'Université d'Ottawa: 542 ave King Edward, Ottawa, ON K1N 6N5; tel. (613) 562-5246; fax (613) 562-5247; e-mail press@uottawa.ca; internet www.uopress .uottawa.ca; f. 1936; university texts, scholarly works in English and French, Canadian literature; Dir Ruth Bradley-St-Cyr.

University of Toronto Press Inc: 10 St Mary St, Suite 700, Toronto, ON M4Y 2W8; tel. (416) 978-2239; fax (416) 978-4738; e-mail publishing@utpress.utoronto.ca; internet www.utpress .utoronto.ca; f. 1901; scholarly books and journals; Pres., Publr and CEO John Yates.

John Wiley and Sons Canada Ltd: 6045 Freemont Blvd, Mississauga, ON L5R 4J3; tel. (416) 236-4433; fax (416) 236-8743; e-mail canada@wiley.com; internet www.wiley.com; f. 1968; COO William Zerter.

Wilfrid Laurier University Press: Wilfrid Laurier University, 75 University Ave West, Waterloo, ON N2L 3C5; tel. (519) 884-0710; fax (519) 725-1399; e-mail brian@@press.wlu.ca; internet www .wlupress.wlu.ca; f. 1974; academic and scholarly; Dir Brian Henderson.

GOVERNMENT PUBLISHING HOUSE

Government of Canada Publications: Canadian Government Publishing, Public Works and Government Services Canada, Ottawa, ON K1A 0S5; tel. (613) 941-5995; fax (613) 954-5779; e-mail publications@pwgsc.gc.ca; internet publications.gc.ca; f. 1876; books and periodicals on numerous subjects, incl. agriculture, economics, environment, geology, history and sociology; Dir Christine Leduc.

ORGANIZATIONS AND ASSOCIATIONS

Association of Canadian Publishers: 110 Eglinton Ave West, Suite 401, Toronto, ON M4R 1A3; tel. (416) 487-6116; fax (416) 487-8815; e-mail admin@canbook.org; internet www.canbook.org; f. 1976; trade asscn of Canadian-owned English-language book publrs; represents Canadian publishing internationally; 145 mems; Exec. Dir John Pelletier.

Association of Canadian University Presses: c/o University of Toronto Press, 10 Saint Mary St, Suite 700, Toronto, ON M4Y 2W8; tel. (416) 978-2239; Exec. Dir Brian Henderson.

Canadian Copyright Institute: 192 Spadina Ave, Suite 107, Toronto, ON M5T 2C2; tel. (416) 975-1756; fax (416) 975-1839; e-mail bkper@interlog.com; internet www.zvaios.com/cci; 83 mems; Admin. Anne McClelland.

Canadian Publishers' Council: 250 Merton St, Suite 203, Toronto, ON M4S 1B1; tel. (416) 322-7011; fax (416) 322-6999; e-mail pubadmin@pubcouncil.ca; internet www.pubcouncil.ca; f. 1910; trade asscn of Canadian-owned publrs and Canadian-incorp. subsidiaries of British and US publrs; 24 mems; Pres. DEB WOODS.

Broadcasting and Communications

The 1968 Broadcasting Act established the Canadian Broadcasting Corporation (CBC) as the national, publicly owned, broadcasting service and created the Canadian Radio-Television and Telecommunications Commission (CRTC) as the agency regulating radio, television and cable television. The CRTC's telecommunications authority is currently derived from the 1985 Canadian Radio-Television and Telecommunications Act. Subsequent Broadcasting Acts, introduced in 1991 and 1993, reconfirmed the CRTC's regulatory powers.

Many privately owned television and radio stations have affiliation agreements with the CBC and help to distribute the national services. A number of the major private television networks (see below) also have affiliates.

Canadian Broadcasting Corporation/Société Radio Canada (CBC/SRC): 250 Lanark Ave, POB 3220, Station C, Ottawa, ON K1Y 1E4; tel. (613) 724-1200; fax (613) 724-5707; e-mail commho@cbc.ca; internet cbc.radio-canada.ca; f. 1936; financed mainly by public funds, with supplementary revenue from commercial advertising on CBC television; 8 nation-wide radio and television networks, numerous regional stations and affiliates, a digital television channel (Country Canada) and music network (Galaxie); services in French, English, and 8 native Canadian languages, incl. Dene and Inuktitut; Pres. and CEO ROBERT RABINOVITCH; Chair. CAROLE TAYLOR.

Canadian Radio-Television and Telecommunications Commission (CRTC): Ottawa, ON K1A 0N2; tel. (819) 997-0313 (Information); fax (819) 994-0218; e-mail info@crtc.gc.ca; internet www.crtc.gc.ca; f. 1968; offices in Halifax, Winnipeg and Vancouver; Chair. CHARLES DALFEN; Vice-Chair. ANDRÉE P. WYLIE (Broadcasting), RICHARD FRENCH (Telecommunications).

TELECOMMUNICATIONS

Principal Telecommunications Networks

Aliant Inc: Station Central RPO, POB 880, Halifax, NS B3J 2W3; tel. (877) 225-4268; internet www.aliant.ca; f. 1999 by merger of telecommunications providers in New Brunswick, Nova Scotia, Prince Edward Island and Newfoundland and Labrador; world-wide communications and information technology solutions; 39.2% owned by Bell Canada, 14.0% owned by BCE Inc; Pres. and CEO STEPHEN WETMORE.

   Island Tel: 69 Belevedere Ave, Charlottetown, PE C1A 7M1; tel. (902) 566-0131; fax (902) 566-4665; internet www.islandtel.pe.ca.

   Island Tel Mobility: 69 Belvedere Ave, POB 820, Charlottetown, PE C1A 7M1.

   Maritime Telegraph and Telephone Co Ltd (MTT): 1505 Barrington St, POB 880, Halifax, NS B3J 2W3; tel. (902) 487-4080; fax (902) 487-4161; internet www.mtt.ca; telecommunications for Nova Scotia.

   MTT Mobility: Network Services, Park Place Centre, Tower 1, 238 Brownlow Ave, Suite 200, Dartmouth, NS B3B 1Y2.

New Brunswick Telephone Co Ltd (NBTel): 1 Brunswick Sq., POB 1430, Saint John, NB E2L 4K2; tel. (506) 658-7917; fax (506) 694-2722; internet www.nbtel.nb.ca; telecommunications for New Brunswick.

   NBTel Mobility: 1 Brunswick Sq., POB 1430, Saint John, NB E2L 4K2.

Newfoundland Telephone Co Ltd (NewTel): Fort William Bldg, POB 2110, St John's, NL A1C 5H6; tel. (709) 739-2276; fax (709) 754-2500; internet www.newtel.com; telecommunications for Newfoundland and Labrador.

   NewTel Mobility: POB 2110, St John's, NL A1C 5H6.

Bell Canada Enterprises Inc (BCE Inc): 1000 de la Gauchetière St West, Suite 3700, Montréal, QC H3B 4Y7; tel. (514) 870-8777; fax (514) 870-4385; e-mail bcecomms.bce.ca; internet www.bce.ca; f. 1880; provides fixed-line and mobile telecommunications, satellite and internet services; Chair. RICHARD J. CURRIE; Pres. and CEO MICHAEL SABIA.

   Bell Canada: 1050 Beaver Hall Hill, POB 8787, Station A, Montréal, QC H3C 4R5; internet www.bell.ca; Canada's largest regional telephone operating co; holds a monopoly in most of Québec and Ontario; 80% owned by BCE Inc; Pres. EUGENE ROMAN.

   Bell Mobility: 105 rue Hotel de Ville, 5e étage, Hull, QC J8X 4H7; internet www.bellmobility.ca; mobile telecommunications.

Bell West: 111 Fifth Ave, SW, Calgary, AB T2P 3Y6; tel. (403) 410-8600; e-mail customercare@bell.ca; internet www.bell.ca; 100% owned by Bell Canada; Pres. (Western Region) PAUL HEALEY.

Manitoba Telecom Services (MTS): 333 Main St, POB 6666, Winnipeg, MB R3C 3V6; tel. (204) 225-5687; internet www.mts.ca; full-service telecommunications co for Manitoba, broadband services in Alberta and British Columbia; partly owned by BCE; CEO WILLIAM C. FRASER; Pres. CHERYL BARKER.

Northwestel Inc: 301 Lambert St, POB 2727, Whitehorse, YT Y1A 4Y4; tel. (867) 668-5300; fax (867) 668-7079; internet www.nwtel.ca; f. 1979, bought by BCE Inc in 1988; provides fixed line and mobile telecommunications services to 110,000 customers in Yukon Territory, Northwest Territories, Nunavut Territory and British Columbia; Chair. TERRY MOSEY; Pres. and CEO PAUL FLAHERTY.

Télébec Mobilité Inc: 555 ave Centrale, Val-d'Or, QC J9P 1P6; e-mail customerservice@nwtel.ca; internet www.telebecmobilite.ca; mobile telecommunications.

Téléglobe Inc: 1000 rue de la Gauchetière ouest, Montréal, QC H3B 4X5; tel. (514) 868-7272; fax (514) 868-7234; internet www.teleglobe.ca; f. 1949; operates international telecommunications services; CEO LIAM STRONG.

Telesat Canada: 1601 Telesat Court, Gloucester, ON K1B 5P4; tel. (613) 748-0123; fax (613) 748-8712; e-mail info@telesat.ca; internet www.telesat.ca; f. 1969 by act of parliament; owns and operates Canada's commercial and domestic satellite system; Chair. R. J. CURRIE.

Call-Net Enterprises Inc: 2235 Sheppard Ave East, Suite 600, North York, ON M2J 5B5; tel. (416) 718-6400; fax (416) 718-6477; internet www.callnet.ca; Chair. LAWRENCE G. TAPP; Pres. and CEO BILL LINTON.

Glentel: 8501 Commerce Court, Burnaby, BC V5A 4N3; tel. (604) 415-6500; fax (604) 415-6565; e-mail customer_service@glentel.com; internet www.glentel.com; f. 1963; wireless communications.

Globalstar Canada Co: 75 Watline Ave, Suite 140, Mississauga, ON L4Z 3E5; tel. (905) 890-1377; fax (905) 890-2175; e-mail info@globalstar.ca; internet www.globalstar.ca; mobile telecommunications.

Microcell Telecom: 1250 blvd René-Lévesque ouest, Suite 400, Montréal, QC H3B 4W8; tel. (514) 937-2121; fax (514) 937-2554; e-mail info.communications@microcell.ca; internet www.microcell.ca; Pres. and CEO ANDRÉ TREMBLAY.

Primus Telecommunications Canada Inc: 5343 Dundas St, West, Suite 400, Etobicoke, ON M9B 6K5; tel. (416) 236-3636; fax (416) 236-4749; e-mail info@primustel.ca; internet www.primustel.ca; long-distance, international and internet services; Pres. EDMUND CHISLETT.

Rogers Communications Inc: 333 Bloor St East, 9th Floor, Toronto, ON M4W 1G9; tel. (416) 935-8200; internet www.rogers.com; provides mobile, digital, cable and internet services; Chair. H. GARFIELD EMERSON; Pres. and CEO EDWARD S. ROGERS.

Saskatchewan Telecommunications (SaskTel) International: 2121 Saskatchewan Dr., 12th Floor, Regina, SK S4P 3Y2; tel. (306) 777-4509; fax (306) 359-7475; internet www.sasktel.com; f. 1986; provides mobile, satellite and internet services for Saskatchewan; Chair. REGINALD BIRD; Pres. and CEO DONALD R. CHING.

   SaskTel Mobility: 2550 Sandra Schmirler Way, Regina, SK S4P 3Y2; internet www.sasktelmobility.com.

Sierra Wireless, Inc: 13811 Wireless Way, Richmond, BC V6V 3A4; tel. (604) 231-1100; fax (604) 231-1109; e-mail kgallagher@sierrawireless.com; internet www.sierrawireless.com; Chair. and CEO DAVID B. SUTCLIFFE.

SR Telecom Inc: 8150 Trans-Canada Hwy, Montréal, QC H4S 1M5; tel. (514) 335-1210; fax (514) 334-7783; e-mail info@srtelecom.com; internet www.srtelecom.com; Chair. PAUL A. DICKIE; Pres. and CEO PIERRE ST-ARNAUD.

TELUS: 4595 Canada Way, Burnaby, BC V5G 1J9; tel. (604) 482-2800; fax (604) 482-2700; internet www.telus.com; f. 2001 following merger of TELUS Communications and BC Telecom; Chair. BRIAN A. CANFIELD; Pres. and CEO DARREN ENTWISTLE.

   TELUS Mobility: 200 Consilium Pl., Suite 1600, Scarborough, ON M1H 3J3; internet www.telusmobility.com; mobile telecommunications; incorporates Clearnet, QuébecTel and TELUS Mobility West; Pres. and CEO GEORGE COPE.

   TELUS Québec: 6 rue Jules-A. Brillant, Rimouski, QC G5L 7E4; tel. (418) 723-2271; fax (418) 722-2059; e-mail sacqt@telus.com; internet www.telusquebec.com; telecommunications for Québec; Pres. and CEO HUGUES ST-PIERRE.

RADIO

The CBC operates two AM and two FM networks, one each in English and French. The CBC's Northern Service provides both national network programming in English and French, and special local and short-wave programmes, some of which are broadcast in the eight principal languages of the Indian and Inuit peoples. In March 2004 there were 425 outlets for AM radio and 1,573 outlets for FM radio (including private affiliates and rebroadcasters). There were also 76 outlets for Digital Transitional Radio. The CBC radio service, which is virtually free of commercial advertising, is within reach of 99.5% of the population. Radio Canada International, the CBC's overseas short-wave service, broadcasts daily in nine languages and distributes recorded programmes for use world-wide.

TELEVISION

The CBC operates two television networks, one in English and one in French. CBC's Northern Service provides both radio and television service to 98% of the 90,000 inhabitants of northern Québec, the Northwest Territories, Nunavut and the Yukon. Almost 41% of these inhabitants are native Canadians, and programming is provided in Dene and Inuktitut languages as well as English and French. As of March 2004, CBC television was carried on 1,387 outlets. CBC television is available to approximately 99% of the English- and French-speaking population.

Canadian Satellite Communication Inc (Cancom) of Toronto has been licensed since 1981 by the CRTC to conduct a multi-channel television and radio broadcasting operation via satellite for the distribution of CTV programme output, Réseau de Télévision (TVA) and independent television and radio programmes to remote and under-served communities. Cancom also distributes by satellite the programme output of five US television networks. A second satellite broadcaster, Star Choice, was licensed by the CRTC in June 1998. A further satellite broadcaster, Anik F2, was launched in July 2004.

In March 2004 there were 663 licensed cable operators. There are five educational services: TV-Ontario in Ontario and Radio-Québec in Québec operate their own television stations and networks; the Learning and Skills Television of Alberta provides educational programming in that province; the Saskatchewan Communications Network Corporation distributes educational programming in Saskatchewan; and the Open Learning Agency (OLA) provides child and adult education by television in British Columbia. Programmes obtainable by pay television services have been in operation since 1983.

Aboriginal People's Television Network (APTN): 339 Portage Ave, 2nd Floor, Winnipeg, MB R3B 2C3; tel. (204) 947-9331; fax (204) 947-9307; e-mail info@aptn.ca; internet www.aptn.ca; f. 1999; fmrly Television Northern Canada—TVNC; broadcasts in English, French and a number of native Canadian languages; CEO JEAN LAROSE.

Canadian Satellite Communications Inc (Cancom): 50 Burnhamthorpe Rd West, Suite 1000, Mississauga, ON L5B 3C2; tel. (905) 272-4960; fax (905) 272-3399; e-mail pdumas@cancom.ca; internet www.cancom.ca; a division of Shaw Communications Inc; Chair. HAROLD ROOZEN; Pres. and CEO PETER CLASSON.

CTV Television Network: 9 Channel Nine Court, POB 9, Station O, Toronto, ON M4A 2M9; tel. (416) 299-2000; fax (416) 299-2643; internet www.ctv.ca; 25 privately-owned affiliated stations from coast to coast, with 247 rebroadcasters; covers 99% of Canadian TV households; Pres. and CEO TRINA McQUEEN.

Global Television Network: 81 Barber Greene Rd, Don Mills, ON M3C 2A2; tel. (416) 446-5311; fax (416) 446-5447; internet www.canada.com/globaltv; 11 stations in eight provinces; a subsidiary of CanWest Global Communications Corpn; Pres. GERRY NOBLE.

Réseau de Télévision (TVA): 1600 blvd de Maisonneuve est, CP 368, succursale C, Montréal, QC H2L 4P2; tel. (514) 526-0476; fax (514) 526-4285; internet www.tva.canoe.com; f. 1971; French-language network, with 10 stations in Québec and 19 rebroadcasters serving 98% of the province, together with francophone communities in Ontario and New Brunswick; Pres. and CEO JEAN GOUEPY.

Telesat Canada: 1601 Telesat Court, Gloucester, ON K1B 5P4; tel. (613) 748-0123; fax (613) 748-8712; e-mail info@telesat.ca; internet www.telesat.ca; a subsidiary of BCE Inc; f. 1969; Pres. LAURIER (LARRY) J. BOISVERT.

TQS Inc: 612 rue St-Jacques, Bureau 100, Montréal, QC H3C 5R1; tel. (514) 390-6035; fax (514) 390-6067; e-mail tvpublic@tqs.qc.ca; internet www.tqs.qc.ca; f. 1986; French-language; 2 stations, 6 rebroadcasters and 2 retransmitters serving 95% of the province of Québec; Pres. LOUIS V. AUDET.

ASSOCIATIONS

Canadian Association of Broadcasters/L'Association canadienne des radiodiffuseurs: 350 Sparks St, Suite 306, Ottawa, ON K1R 7S2; tel. (613) 233-4035; fax (613) 233-6961; e-mail cab@ cab-acr.ca; internet www.cab-acr.ca; f. 1926; 600 mem. broadcasting stations; Pres. and CEO GLENN O'FARRELL; Chair. (Radio) ROB BRAIDE; Chair. (Television) JOHN BURGIS.

Canadian Cable Television Association/Assocation canadienne de télévision par câble (CCTA/ACTC): 360 Albert St, Suite 1010, Ottawa, ON K1R 7X7; tel. (613) 232-2631; fax (613) 232-2137; e-mail ccta@ccta.com; internet www.ccta.ca; 559 mem. cos serving 5,739,446 subscribers in Canada; Chair. DEAN MACDONALD; Pres. MICHAEL HENNESSY.

Radio Advisory Board of Canada/Conseil consultatif canadien de la radio: 811-116 Albert St, Ottawa, ON K1P 5G3; tel. (613) 230-3261; fax (613) 728-3278; e-mail r.a.b.c@on.aibn.com; internet www.rabc.ottawa.on.ca; 21 mem. asscns; Gen. Man. E. R. (TED) CAMPBELL.

Television Bureau of Canada, Inc: 160 Bloor St East, Suite 1005, Toronto, ON M4W 1B9; tel. (416) 923-8813; fax (416) 923-8739; e-mail tvb@tvb.ca; internet www.tvb.ca; f. 1962; 150 mems; Pres. JIM PATTERSON.

Finance

(cap. = capital; auth. = authorized; res = reserves; dep. = deposits; m. = million; brs = branches; amounts in Canadian dollars)

BANKING

Since Confederation in 1867, the federal Government has exercised jurisdiction over banking operations throughout Canada. The Bank Act of 1980 created two categories of banking institution: Schedule I banks, in which no one interest is allowed to own more than 10% of the shares; and Schedule II banks, which are either subsidiaries of foreign financial institutions, or are banks controlled by Canadian non-bank financial institutions. In 2002 there were 10 Schedule I banks and 50 Schedule II banks. In that year there were more than 8,000 bank branches in Canada.

Major revisions to the Bank Act, the federal Trust and Loans Companies Act, the federal Insurance Companies Act and the Co-operative Credit Associations Act came into force in June 1992. This legislation permits federal financial institutions, with some restrictions, to diversify into each other's markets through subsidiaries. By 1 January 1995, following ratification of the North American Free Trade Agreement (NAFTA) and the enactment of the World Trade Organization Implementation Act, the domestic asset limitations on foreign-owned Schedule II banks in the Canadian market were removed.

In the past, the Bank Act was generally reviewed once every 10 years. As a result of extensive revisions to the federal financial institutions legislation in 1992, a further review of the Bank Act was carried out in 1997. In addition, a Task Force on the Future of the Canadian Financial Services Sector was appointed by the federal Government in 1996 to review the legislative framework of the financial services sector. The report of the Task Force, published in September 1998, recommended the abolition of existing barriers preventing financial institutions from providing unified services in banking, insurance and motor vehicle leasing. It was also proposed that commercial banks and trust companies (see below) be permitted to market all classes of insurance through their branch networks by 2002. The Task Force expressed support for the entry of foreign banks into the commercial loans market, and for the adoption of new regulations for consumer protection. In 1999 the Government adopted legislation permitting foreign banks to establish operations in Canada without their being obliged to establish Canadian-incorporated subsidiaries. Foreign bank branches (known as Schedule III banks) are prohibited from accepting deposits of less than C \$150,000. The Bank Act Reform, a series of extensive changes to federal financial institutions, finally entered into effect in October 2001. This provided for much greater flexibility of the financial services system, as recommended by the Task Force, and also included an increase in the maximum level of single ownership in large banks from 10% to 20%, while any one interest was henceforth permitted to control as much as 65% of a medium-sized bank; the minimum amount of capital required to apply for a bank licence was halved to C \$5m. In October 2004, according to the Office of the Superintendent of Financial Institutions, the banking industry included 19 domestic banks, 27 foreign bank subsidiaries (of which three were in the process of liquidation) and 18 full service foreign bank branches. At mid-2002 banks accounted for more than 70% of the total assets of the financial services sector, with the six largest domestic banks accounting for 90% of the assets of the banking industry.

Trust and loan companies, which were originally formed to provide mortgage finance and private customer loans, now occupy an important place in the financial system, offering current account facilities and providing access to money transfer services. In 2003 41 trust companies and 23 loan companies, which were regulated under the federal Trust and Loan Companies Act, were operating in Canada.

Central Bank

Bank of Canada: 234 Wellington St, Ottawa, ON K1A 0G9; tel. (613) 782-8111; fax (613) 782-8655; e-mail paffairs@bankofcanada.ca; internet www.bankofcanada.ca; f. 1934; bank of issue; cap. and res 30m., dep. 2,370.5m. (Dec. 2003); Gov. DAVID A. DODGE.

Commercial Banks

Schedule I Banks

Bank of Montréal: 129 rue St-Jacques, Montréal, QC H2Y 1L6; tel. (514) 877-7110; fax (514) 877-6922; e-mail info@bmo.com; internet www.bmo.com; f. 1817; cap. 5,108m., dep. 171,551m. (Oct. 2003); Chair. and CEO ANTHONY F. COMPER; 963 brs in Canada, 168 foreign brs.

Bank of Nova Scotia (Scotiabank): Scotia Plaza, 44 King St West, Toronto, ON M5H 1H1; tel. (416) 866-6161; fax (416) 866-3750; e-mail email@scotiabank.ca; internet www.scotiabank.ca; f. 1832; cap. 3,941m., dep. 192,672m. (Oct. 2003); Chair. ARTHUR R. A. SCACE; Pres. and CEO RICHARD E. WAUGH; 1,272 brs in Canada, 90 foreign brs.

Canadian Imperial Bank of Commerce: Commerce Court, Toronto, ON M5L 1A2; tel. (416) 980-2211; fax (416) 368-8843; internet www.cibc.com; f. 1961 through merger of Canadian Bank of Commerce (f. 1867) and Imperial Bank of Canada (f. 1875); cap. 6,307m., res 50m., dep. 188,130m. (Oct. 2003); Chair. and CEO JOHN S. HUNKIN; 1,453 brs in Canada.

Canadian Western Bank: 10303 Jasper Ave, Suite 2300, Edmonton, AB T5J 3X6; tel. (780) 423-8888; fax (780) 423-8897; e-mail comments@cwb.com; internet www.cwbank.com; f. 1988 by merger of the Bank of Alberta and the Western and Pacific Bank of Canada; cap. 150.7m., dep. 3,819.7m. (Oct. 2003); Chair. JACK C. DONALD; Pres. and CEO LARRY M. POLLOCK; 27 brs.

Laurentian Bank of Canada/Banque Laurentienne du Canada: Laurentian Bank Tower, 1981 ave Collège McGill, Montréal, QC H3A 3K3; tel. (514) 284-4500; fax (514) 284-3396; e-mail laurentianbank@com; internet www.laurentianbank.com; f. 1846 as Montreal City and District Savings Bank; name changed as above 1987; cap. 446.8m., dep. 13,292.9m. (Oct. 2003); Chair. DENIS DESAUTELS; Pres. and CEO RAYMOND MCMANUS.

National Bank of Canada/Banque Nationale du Canada: 600 rue de la Gauchetière ouest, Montréal, QC H3B 4L2; tel. (514) 394-5000; fax (514) 394-8434; internet www.nbc.ca; f. 1859; cap. 1,958m., dep. 51,463m. (Oct. 2003); Chair. ANDRÉ BÉRARD; Pres. and CEO RÉAL RAYMOND; 549 brs.

Royal Bank of Canada: 1 pl. Ville Marie, Montréal, QC H3C 3A9; tel. (514) 874-2110; fax (514) 974-4472; e-mail banks@rbc.com; internet www.rbc.com; f. 1869; cap. 7,812m., dep. 260,518m. (Oct. 2003); Chair GUY SAINT PIERRE; CEO GORDON M. NIXON; 1,311 brs in Canada, 807 foreign brs.

Toronto-Dominion Bank: Toronto-Dominion Centre, 55 King St West and Bay St, Toronto, ON M5K 1A2; tel. (416) 982-8222; fax (416) 982-5671; e-mail customer.service@td.com; internet www.tdbank.ca; f. 1955 by merger of the Bank of Toronto (f. 1855) and the Dominion Bank (f. 1869); cap. 4,714m., dep. 182,880m. (Oct. 2003); Chair. JOHN M. THOMPSON; Pres. and CEO W. EDMUND CLARKE; 953 brs.

Principal Schedule II Banks

Bank of Tokyo-Mitsubishi (Canada): Royal Bank Plaza, South Tower, Suite 2100, POB 42, Toronto, ON M5J 2J1; tel. (416) 865-0220; fax (416) 865-9511; f. 1996 by merger of Bank of Tokyo Canada (f. 1981) and Mitsubishi Bank of Canada (f. 1982); subsidiary of Bank of Tokyo-Mitsubishi (Japan); cap. 182.6m., dep. 1,947.1m. (Oct. 2003); Pres. and CEO JUN TAYA; 3 brs.

Citibank Canada: Citibank Pl., 123 Front St West, Suite 1000, Toronto, ON M5J 2M3; tel. (416) 947-5500; fax (416) 947-5628; internet www.citibank.com/canada; f. 1981; subsidiary of Citibank NA (USA); cap. 500m., dep. 5,105.0m. (Dec. 2003); Chair. and CEO KENNETH QUINN; 1 br.

HSBC Bank Canada: 300-885 West Georgia St, Vancouver, BC V6C 3E9; tel. (604) 685-1000; fax (604) 641-1849; e-mail info@hsbc.ca; internet www.hsbc.ca; f. 1981; subsidiary of HSBC Holdings plc (United Kingdom); cap. 1,075m., res 165m., dep 28,372m. (Dec. 2002); Chair. MARTIN GLYNN; Pres. and CEO LINDSAY GORDON; c. 170 brs.

Société Générale (Canada): 1501 ave Collège McGill, bureau 1800, Montréal, QC H3A 3M8; tel. (514) 841-6000; fax (514) 841-6250; internet www.socgen.com; f. 1981; subsidiary of Société Gén-érale SA (France); cap. 250.8m., dep. 173.4m. (Dec. 2003); Chair. JACQUES BOUHET; Pres. and CEO DIDIER COLIN; 3 brs.

Development Bank

Business Development Bank of Canada: 5 pl. Ville Marie, 4th Floor, Montréal, QC H3B 5E7; tel. (514) 283-5904; fax (514) 283-2872; e-mail info-bdc@bdc.ca; internet www.bdc.ca; f. 1944; fed. govt corpn; auth. shareholders' equity 923m. (March 2001); Chair. CEDRIC E. RITCHIE; Acting Pres. CEO and Exec. Vice-Pres. ANDRÉ BOURDEAU; 80 brs.

Principal Trust and Loan Companies

Bank of Nova Scotia Trust Co: Scotia Plaza, 44 King St West, Toronto, ON M5H 1H1; tel. (416) 933-3000; fax (416) 933-3009; internet www.scotiabank.com; assets 878m. (Dec. 1999); Pres. J. RORY MACDONALD.

Canada Trustco Mortgage Co: Canada Trust Tower, 275 Dundas St, London, ON N6A 4S4; tel. (519) 663-1500; fax (519) 663-5114; f. 1855; total assets 46,000m. (1997); Pres. and CEO W. EDMUND CLARK; 421 brs.

Canadian Western Trust Corporation: 2200 Park Pl., 666 Burrard St, Vancouver, BC V6C 2X8; tel. (604) 685-1208; fax (604) 685-9997; e-mail information@cwt.ca; internet www.cwt.ca; assets 285.0m. (Oct. 1999); COO ADRIAN BAKER.

National Trust Co Ltd: 1 Adelaide St East, Toronto, ON M5C 2W8; tel. (416) 361-3611; fax (416) 361-4037; f. 1898; subsidiary of Scotiabank; cap. and res 253.7m., dep. 13,849.1m. (Oct. 1996); Chair. and CEO PAUL CANTOR.

Royal Trust Corporation of Canada: Royal Trust Tower, POB 7500, Station A, Toronto, ON M5W 1P9; tel. (416) 974-1400; fax (416) 861-9658; f. 1899; total assets 11,500m. (July 1997); Pres. HELEN AZEVEDO.

TD Mortgage Corporation: Toronto-Dominion Centre, 55 King St West, POB 191, Toronto, ON M5K 1H6; tel. (416) 982-6744; fax (416) 944-5853; Pres. BRUCE SHIREFF.

Savings Institutions with Provincial Charters

Alberta Treasury Branches: ATB Pl., 9888 Jasper Ave, Edmonton, AB T5J 1P1; tel. (780) 408-7309; fax (780) 422-4178; internet www.atb.com; f. 1938; assets 15,300m. (December 2004); Pres. and CEO ROBERT NORMAND; 149 brs.

Province of Ontario Savings Office: 40 King St West, 6th Floor, Oshawa, ON L1H 1A4; tel. (905) 433-5788; fax (905) 433-6519; e-mail poso@ofina.ca; internet www.ofina.on.ca/poso; f. 1921; acquired by Desjardins Credit Union in Jan. 2003; dep. 2,300m. (Jan. 2003); Chair. SUSAN GUINN; 28 brs.

Bankers' Organizations

Canadian Bankers Association: Commerce Court West, Suite 3000, Box 348, Toronto, ON M5L 1G2; tel. (416) 362-6092; fax (416) 362-7705; e-mail inform@cba.ca; internet www.cba.ca; f. 1891; 5 regional brs, 48 mems; Chair. WARREN LAW; Pres. RAYMOND J. PROTTI.

Institute of Canadian Bankers: Tour Scotia, 1002 Sherbrooke St West, Suite 1000, Montréal, QC H3A 3M5; tel. (514) 282-9480; e-mail info@icb.org; internet www.icb.org; f. 1967; provides financial training.

STOCK EXCHANGES

Bourse de Montréal/Montreal Exchange: Tour de la Bourse, CP 61, 800 sq. Victoria, Montréal, QC H4Z 1A9; tel. (514) 871-2424; fax (514) 871-3568; e-mail info@m-x.ca; internet www.m-x.ca; f. 1874; 75 approved participants; Chair. JEAN TURMEL; Pres. and CEO LUC BERTRAND.

Toronto Venture Exchange: 609 Granville St, POB 10333, Vancouver, BC V7Y 1H1; tel. (604) 689-3334; fax (604) 688-6051; e-mail information@tsxventure.com; internet www.tsx.ca; f. 1999 by merger of Alberta and Vancouver Stock Exchanges; incorporated Winnipeg Stock Exchange in 2000; acquired by Toronto Stock Exchange (TSX) in 2001; fmrly the Canadian Venture Exchange; 68 mems; Pres. LINDA HOHOL.

TSX Group (Toronto Stock Exchange): The Exchange Tower, 130 King St West, Toronto, ON M5X 1J2; tel. (416) 947-4700; fax (416) 947-4662; e-mail info@tsx.com; internet www.tsx.com; f. 1852; volume of trade 61,277m. shares (valued at some C \$833,907m.) in 2004; 121 mems; Chair. WAYNE C. FOX; CEO RICHARD NESBITT.

INSURANCE

Principal Companies

Allianz Canada: 10 York Mills Rd, Suite 700, Toronto, ON M2P 2G5; tel. (416) 227-7800; fax (416) 227-9837; e-mail info@allianz.ca; internet www.allianz.ca; f. 1928; Pres. CHRISTIAN CASSEBAUM.

Blue Cross Life Insurance Co of Canada: 644 Main St, POB 220, Moncton, NB E1C 8L3; tel. (506) 853-1811; fax (506) 853-4646; e-mail cabcpwebmaster@pac.bluecross.ca; internet www.bluecross .ca; Pres. and CEO JIM GILLIGAN.

Canada Life Assurance Co: 330 University Ave, Toronto, ON M5G 1R8; tel. (416) 597-1456; fax (416) 597-1940; e-mail info@ canadalife.com; internet www.canadalife.com; f. 1847; Pres. DAVID A. NIELD.

Canadian General Insurance Co: 2206 Eglinton Ave East, Suite 500, Scarborough, ON M1L 4S8; tel. (416) 288-1800; fax (416) 288-9756; f. 1907; Pres. and CEO R. LEWIS DUNN.

Clarica: 227 King St South, Waterloo, ON N2J 4C5; tel. (519) 888-2290; fax (519) 888-2990; e-mail service@clarica.com; internet www .clarica.com; f. 1999 following demutualization of The Mutual Group (f. 1870); Pres. and CEO ROBERT ASTLEY.

Desjardins Financial Security Life Assurance Company: 200 ave des Commandeurs, Lévis, QC G6V 6R2; e-mail info@ desjardinsfinancialsecurity.com; internet www .desjardinsfinancialsecurity.com; f. 2001; following merger of Assurance vie Desjardins–Laurentienne with Imperial Life Assurance Co of Canada; Pres. and CEO FRANÇOIS JOLY.

Dominion of Canada General Insurance Co: 165 University Ave, Toronto, ON M5H 3B9; tel. (416) 362-7231; fax (416) 362-9918; f. 1887; Pres. and CEO GEORGE L. COOKE.

Federation Insurance Co of Canada: 1000 rue de la Gauchetière ouest, Bureau 500, Montréal, QC H3B 4W5; tel. (514) 875-5790; fax (514) 875-9769; f. 1947; Pres. NOEL WALPOLE.

GCAN Insurance Co: 480 University Ave, Toronto, ON M5G 1V6; tel. (416) 598-4651; fax (416) 598-5478; internet www.gcan.ca; f. 1955; Pres. ANDREAS H. HENKE.

General Accident Group of Canada: 2206 Eglinton Ave East, Toronto, ON M1L 4S8; tel. (416) 288-1800; fax (416) 288-9756; internet www.genacc.ca; f. 1906; Pres. R. LEWIS DUNN.

Gore Mutual Insurance Co: 262 Dundas St, Cambridge, ON N1R 5T3; tel. (519) 623-1910; fax (519) 623-8348; e-mail vision@ goremutual.ca; internet www.goremutual.ca; f. 1839; Pres. and CEO KEVIN W. MCNEIL.

Guardian Insurance Co of Canada: 181 University Ave, Toronto, ON M5W 3M7; tel. (416) 941-5050; fax (416) 941-9791; f. 1911; Pres. and CEO HENRY J. CURTIS.

Halifax Insurance Co: 75 Eglinton Ave East, Toronto, ON M4P 3A4; tel. (416) 440-1000; fax (416) 440-0799; internet www .halifaxinsurance.com; f. 1809; Pres. and CEO DONALD K. LOUGH.

Industrial Alliance Pacific Life Insurance Co: 2165 Broadway West, POB 5900, Vancouver, BC V6B 5H6; tel. (604) 734-1667; fax (604) 734-8221; e-mail intouch@iaplife.com; internet www.iaplife .com; f. 2000 by merger; Pres. JOHN B. GILL.

ING Canada: 181 University Ave, ING Tower, 7th Floor, Toronto, ON M5H 3M7; tel. (416) 941-5151; fax (416) 941-0014; e-mail info@ INGcanada.com; internet www.ingdirect.ca; Pres. and CEO YVES BROUILLETTE.

Kings Mutual Insurance Co: POB 10, Berwick, NS B0P 1E0; tel. (902) 538-3187; fax (902) 538-7271; e-mail kings.mutual@ns .sympatico.com; f. 1904; Pres. J. J. UEFFING.

Manufacturers Life Insurance Co (Manulife Financial): 200 Bloor St East, Toronto, ON M4W 1E5; tel. (416) 926-6624; fax (416) 926-3520; e-mail dominic_d'alessandro@manulife.com; internet www.manulife.com; f. 1887; acquired Commercial Union Life Assurance Co of Canada in 2001; merger with John Hancock Financial Services, Inc. announced Sept. 2003, scheduled for completion mid-2004; Pres. and CEO DOMINIC D'ALESSANDRO.

Metropolitan Life Insurance Co of Canada: Constitution Sq., 360 Albert St, Suite 1750, Ottawa, ON K1R 7X7; tel. (613) 237-7171; fax (613) 237-7585; internet www.metlife.ca; Pres. and CEO ROBERT M. ASTLEY.

The National Life Assurance Co of Canada: 522 University Ave, Toronto, ON M5G 1Y7; tel. (416) 598-2122; fax (416) 598-4948; internet www.nationallife.ca; f. 1897; Pres. VINCENT P. TONNA.

Portage La Prairie Mutual Insurance Co: 749 Saskatchewan Ave East, Portage La Prairie, MB R1N 3B8; tel. (204) 857-3415; fax (204) 239-6655; e-mail info@portagemutual.com; internet www .portagemutual.com; f. 1884; Pres. T. W. MCCARTNEY.

Royal & Sun Alliance Insurance Co of Canada: 10 Wellington St East, Toronto, ON M5E 1L5; tel. (416) 366-7511; fax (416) 367-9869; internet www.royalsunalliance.ca; f. 1851; Pres. and CEO MARCEL BUNDOCK.

Société Nationale d'Assurance Inc: 425 blvd de Maisonneuve ouest, Bureau 1500, Montréal, QC H3A 3G5; tel. (514) 288-8711; fax (514) 288-8269; f. 1940; Pres. ANDRÉ NADON.

Sun Life Financial Canada: POB 4150, Station A, Toronto, ON M5W 2C9; tel. (416) 979-9966; fax (416) 585-9546; e-mail service@ sunlife.com; internet www.sunlife.ca/canada; f. 1871; Chair. WILLIAM W. STINSON; Pres. ROBERT M. ASTLEY; CEO DONALD A. STEWART.

Toronto Mutual Life Insurance Co: 112 St Clair Ave West, Toronto, ON M4V 2Y3; tel. (416) 960-3463; fax (416) 960-0531; internet www.torontomutual.com; Pres. and CEO VAN M. CAMPBELL.

Wawanesa Mutual Insurance Co: 191 Broadway, Winnipeg, MB R3C 3P1; tel. (204) 985-3923; fax (204) 942-7724; internet www .wawanesa.com; f. 1896; Pres. and CEO G. J. HANSON.

Western Assurance Co: POB 3000, Stn Main, Ajax, ON L15 7L9; tel. (905) 686-8326; fax (416) 367-9869; f. 1851; Pres. and CEO LARRY SIMMONS.

Zurich Canada: 400 University Ave, Toronto, ON M5G 1S7; tel. (416) 586-3000; fax (416) 586-2990; internet www.zurichcanada .com; CEO PAUL VAN DE GEIJIN.

Insurance Organizations

Advocis (Financial Advisors' Association of Canada) (CAIFA): 350 Bloor St East, 2nd Floor, Toronto, ON M4W 3W8; tel. (416) 444-5251; fax (416) 444-8031; e-mail info@advocis.ca; internet www.advocis.ca; f. 1906; Chair. BRIAN MALLARD; CEO STEVE HOWARD; 18,000 mems.

Canadian Association of Mutual Insurance Companies: 311 McArthur Ave, Suite 205, Ottawa, ON K1L 6P1; tel. (613) 789-6851; fax (613) 789-6854; e-mail nflafreniere@camic.ca; internet www .camic.ca; Pres. NORMAN LAFRENIÈRE; 103 mems.

Canadian Life and Health Insurance Association Inc: 1 Queen St East, Suite 1700, Toronto, ON M5C 2X9; tel. (416) 777-2221; fax (416) 777-1895; e-mail info@clhia.ca; internet www.clhia.ca; f. 1894; Pres. G. R. TRAVERSY; Man. KOLETTE TABER; 74 mems.

Insurance Brokers Association of Canada: 155 University Ave, Suite 1920, Toronto, ON M5H 3B7; tel. (416) 367-1831; fax (416) 367-3687; e-mail info@ibac.ca; internet www.ibac.ca; f. 1921; Pres. DAN DANYLUK; 11 mem. asscns.

Insurance Bureau of Canada: 151 Yonge St, Suite 1900, Toronto, ON M5C 2W7; tel. (416) 362-2031; fax (416) 361-5952; internet www .ibc.ca; f. 1964; Pres. and CEO STANLEY I. GRIFFIN.

Insurance Institute of Canada: 18 King St East, 6th Floor, Toronto, ON M5C 1C4; tel. (416) 362-8586; fax (416) 362-4239; e-mail genmail@iic-iac.org; internet www.iic-iac.org; f. 1952; Pres. PETER HOHMAN; 31,000 mems.

Life Insurance Institute of Canada: 1155 North Service Road West, Suite 11, Oakville, ON L6M 3E3; tel. (905) 847-8966; fax (905) 847-8897; e-mail liic@loma.org; internet www.liic.ca; f. 1935; Exec. Dir DEBBIE COLE-GAUER; 57 mem. asscns.

Trade and Industry

CHAMBER OF COMMERCE

The Canadian Chamber of Commerce: 350 Sparks St, Suite 501, Ottawa, ON K1R 7S8; tel. (613) 238-4000; fax (613) 238-7643; e-mail info@chamber.ca; internet www.chamber.ca; f. 1925; mems: 500 community chambers of commerce and boards of trade, 80 nat. trade asscns and 2,500 business corpns; Nat. Pres. NANCY HUGHES ANTHONY.

INDUSTRIAL AND TRADE ASSOCIATIONS

Alliance of Manufacturers and Exporters Canada: 75 International Blvd, 4th Floor, Toronto, ON M9W 6L9; tel. (416) 798-8000; fax (416) 798-8050; e-mail national@the-alliance.com; internet www .palantir.ca/the-alliance; f. 1871; the nat. org. of mfrs and exporters of Canada; Pres. STEPHEN VAN HOUTEN; 3,500 mems.

Agriculture and Horticulture

Canada Beef Export Federation (Canada Beef): 235 6715-Eighth St, NE, Calgary, AB T2E 7H7; tel. (403) 274-0005; fax (403) 274-7275; e-mail canada@cbef.com; internet www.cbef.com; f. 1989; Chair. BEN THORKALSON; Dir GENE ROWE.

Canada Grains Council: 220 Portage Ave, Winnipeg, MB R3C 0A5; tel. (204) 925-2130; fax (204) 925-2132; e-mail office@

canadagrainscouncil.ca; internet www.canadagrainscouncil.ca; f. 1969; Chair. JIM WILSON; 33 mems.

Canadian Federation of Agriculture/Fédération Canadienne de l'agriculture (CFA/FCA): 75 Albert St, Suite 1101, Ottawa, ON K1P 5E7; tel. (613) 236-3633; fax (613) 236-5749; e-mail info@cfafca.ca; internet www.cfa-fca.ca; f. 1935; Exec. Dir BRIGID RIVOIRE; 21 mems.

Canadian Horticultural Council: 9 Corvus Court, Ottawa, ON K2E 724; tel. (613) 226-4880; fax (613) 226-4497; internet www.hortcouncil.ca; f. 1922; Exec. Vice-Pres. ANNE FOWLIE.

Canadian Nursery Landscape Association (Association Canadienne des Pépiniéristes et des Paysagistes): 7856 Fifth Line South, RR 4, Stn Main, Milton, ON L9T 2X8; tel. (905) 875-1399; fax (905) 875-1840; e-mail cnla@canadanursery.com; internet www.canadanursery.com; f. 1922 as the Eastern Canada Nurserymen's Asscn; present name adopted in 1999; Pres. HAROLD DEENEN; Exec. Dir CHRIS D. ANDREWS; 3,200 mems.

Canadian Seed Growers' Association: 202–240 Catherine St, Ottawa, ON K2P 2G8; tel. (613) 236-0497; fax (613) 563-7855; e-mail seeds@seedgrowers.ca; internet www.seedgrowers.ca; f. 1904; Pres. BARRY REISNER; Exec. Dir DALE ADOLPHE; 4,700 mems.

National Dairy Council of Canada: 221 Laurier Ave East, Ottawa, ON K1N 6P1; tel. (613) 238-4116; fax (613) 238-6247; e-mail info@ndcc.ca; f. 1918; Pres. KEMPTON MATTE; 69 mem asscns, 250 individual mems.

National Farmers Union (NFU): 2717 Wentz Ave, Saskatoon, SK S7K 4B6; tel. (306) 652-9465; fax (306) 664-6226; e-mail nfu@nfu.ca; internet www.nfu.ca; f. 1969; Pres. STEWART WELLS; Exec. Sec. TERRY PUGH; 10,000 mems.

Union des producteurs agricoles: 555 blvd Roland-Therrien, bureau 100, Longueuil, QC J4H 3Y9; tel. (450) 679-0530; fax (450) 679-5436; e-mail upa@upa.qc.ca; internet www.upa.qc.ca; f. 1924; Pres. LAURENT PELLERIN; 44,000 mems.

Building and Construction

Canadian Construction Association: 75 Albert St, Suite 400, Ottawa, ON K1P 5E7; tel. (613) 236-9455; fax (613) 236-9526; e-mail cca@cca-acc.com; internet www.cca-acc.com; f. 1918; Pres. MICHAEL ATKINSON; over 20,000 mems.

Canadian Institute of Steel Construction: 201 Consumers Rd, Suite 300, Willowdale, ON M2J 4G8; tel. (416) 491-4552; fax (416) 491-6461; e-mail info@cisc-icca.ca; internet www.cisc-icca.ca; f. 1930; Pres. MIKE GILMOR; 245 mems.

Canadian Paint and Coatings Association: 9900 blvd Cavendish, Bureau 103, St-Laurent, QC H4M 2V2; tel. (514) 745-2611; fax (514) 745-2031; e-mail cpca@cdnpaint.org; internet www.cdnpaint.org; f. 1913; Pres. RICHARD MURRY; 70 mems.

Canadian Precast/Prestressed Concrete Institute: 196 Bronson Ave, Suite 100, Ottawa, ON K1R 6H4; tel. (613) 232-2619; fax (613) 232-5139; e-mail info@cpci.ca; internet www.cpci.ca; Pres. JOHN R. FOWLER; 300 mems.

Ontario Painting Contractors Association: 211 Consumers Rd, Suite 305, Willowdale, ON M2J 4G8; tel. (416) 498-1897; fax (416) 498-6757; e-mail mmarquardt@attglobal.net; internet www.ontpca.org; f. 1967; Exec. Dir MAUREEN MARQUARDT; 100 mems.

Clothing and Textiles

Canadian Apparel Federation: 124 O'Connor St, Suite 504, Ottawa, ON K1P 5M9; tel. (613) 231-3220; fax (613) 231-2305; e-mail info@apparel.ca; internet www.apparel.ca; f. 1977; Exec. Dir BOB KIRKE.

Canadian Textiles Institute: 22 Somerset St West, Suite 500, Ottawa, ON K2P 2G3; tel. (613) 232-7195; fax (613) 232-8722; e-mail cti@textiles.ca; f. 1935; Pres. ELIZABETH SIWICKI; 60 mems.

Men's Clothing Manufacturers Association: 555 rue Chabanel ouest, bureau 801, Montréal, QC H2N 2H8; tel. (514) 383-1689; fax (514) 382-3846; e-mail mcma@macten.net; f. 1961; Exec. Dir DAVID BALINSKY; 67 mems.

Textile Federation of Canada: c/o Groupe CTT Group, 3000 rue Boullé, St-Hyacinthe, QC J2S 1H9; tel. (450) 778-1870; fax (450) 778-9016; e-mail rleclerc@ctt.ca; Exec. Sec. ROGER LECLERC; 1,950 mems.

Electrical and Electronics

Canadian Electrical Contractors Assocation: 23 Lesmill Rd, Suite 207, North York, ON M3B 3P6; tel. (416) 391-3226; fax (416) 391-3926; Exec. Sec. ERYL M. ROBERTS.

Canadian Electricity Association: see Utilities—Electricity.

Electrical and Electronic Manufacturers Association of Canada: 10 Carlson Court, Suite 500, Rexdale, ON M9W 6L2; tel. (905) 674-7410; fax (905) 674-7412; f. 1976; Pres. NORMAN ASPIN; 175 mems.

Fisheries

Canadian Association of Fish Exporters: 1770 Woodward Dr., Suite 212, Ottawa, ON K2C 0P8; tel. (613) 228-9220; fax (613) 228-9223; e-mail jbarnett@seafood.ca; internet www.seafood.ca/index.htm; f. 1978; Pres. Dr JANE BARNETT.

Fisheries Council of Canada: 38 Antares Dr., Suite 110, Ottawa, ON K2E 7V2; tel. (613) 727-7450; fax (613) 727-7453; e-mail info@fisheriescouncil.org; internet www.fisheriescouncil.ca; f. 1915; Pres. PATRICK MCGUINNESS; f. 1915; seven mem. asscns; over 135 mem. cos.

Food and Beverages

Association of Sales and Marketing Companies International: 58 Meadowbrook Ave, Suite 100, Unionville, ON L3R 2N9; tel. (905) 477-4644; fax (905) 477-9580; e-mail asmc-i@rogers.com; internet www.asmc.org; f. 1942; Pres. KEITH BRAY; 70 mems, 60 assoc. mems in 20 countries.

Baking Association of Canada: 7895 Tranmere Dr., Mississauga, ON L5S 1V9; tel. (905) 405-0288; fax (905) 405-0993; e-mail info@baking.ca; internet www.baking.ca; f. 1947; Pres. and CEO PAUL HETHERINGTON; 1,400 institutional mems, 200 assoc. mems.

Brewers Association of Canada: 155 Queen St, Suite 1200, Ottawa, ON K1P 6L1; tel. (613) 232-9601; fax (613) 232-2283; e-mail office@brewers.ca; internet www.brewers.ca; f. 1943; Pres. and CEO R. A. MORRISON; 29 mems.

Canadian Council of Grocery Distributors: CP 1082, succursale place-du-Parc, Montréal, QC H2W 2P4; tel. (514) 982-0267; fax (514) 849-3021; f. 1919; Pres. and CEO JOHN F. GECI; 69 institutional mems, 115 assoc. mems.

Canadian Food Brokers Association: 58 Meadowbrook Lane, Suite 100, Unionville, ON L3R 2N9; tel. (905) 477-4644; fax (905) 477-9580; e-mail cfba@rogers.com; f. 1942; Pres. KEITH BRAY; 70 mems, 60 assoc. mems.

Canadian Meat Council/Conseil des viandes du canada (CMC/CVC): 955 Green Valley Cres., Suite 305, Ottawa, ON K2C 3V4; tel. (613) 729-3911; fax (613) 729-4997; e-mail info@cmc-cvc.com; internet www.cmc-cvc.com; f. 1919; Pres. WILLIE VAN SOLKEMA; 19 mems.

Canadian National Millers' Association: 408 Queen St, Ottawa, ON K1R 5A7; tel. (613) 238-2293; fax (613) 235-5866; f. 1920; Pres. GORDON HARRISON; 15 mems.

Canadian Pork Council/Conseil canadien du porc (CPC/CCP): 75 Albert St, Suite 1101, Ottawa, ON K1P 5E7; tel. (613) 236-9239; fax (613) 236-6658; e-mail info@cpc-ccp.com; internet www.cpc-ccp.com; Pres. CLARE SCHLEGEL; Exec. Dir MARTIN RICE; 9 mems.

Confectionery Manufacturers Association of Canada: 885 Don Mills Rd, Suite 301, Don Mills, ON M3C 1V9; tel. (416) 510-8034; fax (416) 510-8044; e-mail carolh@fcpmc.com; f. 1919; Pres. CAROL L. HOCHU; 81 corporate mems.

Food and Consumer Products Manufacturers of Canada: 885 Don Mills Rd, Suite 301, Don Mills, ON M3C 1V9; tel. (416) 510-8024; fax (416) 510-8043; e-mail info@cpmc.com; internet www.fcpmc.com; Pres. GEORGE FLEISCHMANN; 180 corporate mems.

Food Institute of Canada: 1600 Scott St, Suite 415, Ottawa, ON K1Y 4N7; tel. (613) 722-1000; fax (613) 722-1404; e-mail fic@foodnet.fic.ca; internet www.fic.ca; f. 1989; Pres. JEAN GATTUSO; 200 mems.

Forestry, Lumber and Allied Industries

Canadian Lumbermen's Association/Association canadienne de l'industrie du bois (CLA/ACIB): 27 Goulburn Ave, Ottawa, ON K1N 8C7; tel. (613) 233-6205; fax (613) 233-1929; e-mail info@cla-ca.ca; internet www.cla-ca.ca; f. 1907; Pres. and Exec. Dir JEAN-FRANÇOIS HOUDE (acting); Chair. MARTIN MICHAUD; 217 mems.

Canadian Wood Council (CWC/CCB): 99 Bank St, Suite 400, Ottawa, ON K1P 6B9; tel. (613) 747-5544; fax (613) 747-6264; e-mail webmaster@cwc.ca; internet www.cwc.ca; f. 1959; Pres. PAULINE ROCHEFORT; Chair. YVES LAFLAMME; 14 mem. asscns.

Council of Forest Industries (COFI): I Business Bldg, Suite 1501, 700 West Pender St, Pender Pl., Vancouver, BC V6C 1G87; tel. (604) 684-0211; fax (604) 687-4930; e-mail info@cofi.org; internet www.cofi.org; f. 1960; Pres. and CEO JOHN ALLAN; 64 mems.

Forest Products Association of Canada/Association des produits forestiers du Canada (FPAC/APFC): 99 Bank St, Suite 410, Ottawa, ON KIP 6B9; tel. (613) 563-1441; fax (613) 563-4720; e-mail ottawa@fpac.ca; internet www.fpac.ca; f. 1913; fmrly the

Canadian Pulp and Paper Asscn; Pres.and CEO Avrim Lazar; 27 mems.

Ontario Forest Industries Association: 20 Toronto St West, Suite 820, Toronto, ON M5C 2B8; tel. (416) 368-6188; fax (416) 368-5445; e-mail info@ofia.com; internet www.ofia.com; f. 1943; Pres. and CEO Tim J. Millard; 17 mem. cos and 11 affiliate mems.

Hotels and Catering

Canadian Restaurant and Foodservices Association: 316 Bloor St West, Toronto, ON M5S 1W5; tel. (416) 923-8416; fax (416) 923-1450; e-mail info@crfa.ca; internet www.crfa.ca; f. 1944; Pres. Douglas Needham; 14,000 mems.

Hotel Association of Canada Inc: 130 Albert St, Suite 1206, Ottawa, ON K1P 5G4; tel. (613) 237-7149; fax (613) 237-8928; e-mail hac@hotels.ca; internet www.hotels.ca; f. 1929; Pres. Anthony Pollard.

Hotel and Restaurant Suppliers' Association Inc: 2435 rue Guénette, St-Laurent, QC H4R 2E9; tel. (514) 334-5161; fax (514) 334-1279; e-mail info@afhr.com; internet www.afhr.com; f. 1936; Pres. Denis Lamothe; Gen. Man. Gilbert Crevier.

Mining

Canadian Association of Petroleum Producers: 350 Seventh Ave, SW, Suite 2100, Calgary, AB T2P 3N9; tel. (403) 267-1100; fax (403) 261-4622; e-mail communication@capp.ca; internet www.capp.ca; f. 1952; Pres. Pierre Alvarez; 150 institutional mems, 140 assoc. mems.

Canadian Gas Association: See Utilities—Gas.

Canadian Mining Contractors Association: 1088 Staghorn Court, Mississauga, ON L5C 3R2; tel. (905) 279-0104; fax (905) 279-1646; e-mail bcampbell@istar.ca; Pres. Bruce Campbell.

Mining Association of Canada: 350 Sparks St, Suite 1105, Ottawa, ON K1R 7S8; tel. (613) 233-9391; fax (613) 233-8897; e-mail gpeeling@mining.ca; internet www.mining.ca; f. 1935; Pres. Gordon R. Pelling; 60 mems.

Northwest Territories & Nunavut Chamber of Mines: POB 2818, Yellowknife, NT X1A 2R1; tel. (867) 873-5281; fax (867) 920-2145; e-mail nwtmines@ssimicro.com; internet www.miningnorth.com; f. 1967; Gen. Man. Mike Vaydik; 380 mems.

Ontario Mining Association: 110 Yonge St, 15th Floor, Toronto, ON M5C 1T4; tel. (416) 364-9301; fax (416) 364-5986; f. 1920; Pres. Patrick Reid; 47 mems.

Petroleum Services Association of Canada: 800 Sixth Ave SW, Suite 1150, Calgary, AB T2P 3G3; tel. (403) 264-4195; fax (403) 263-7174; e-mail infor@psac.ca; internet www.psac.ca; Pres. Roger Soucy.

Yukon Chamber of Mines: 3151B Third Ave, Whitehorse, YT Y1A 1G1; tel. (867) 667-2090; fax (867) 668-7127; e-mail info@ycmines.ca; internet www.ycmines.ca; f. 1947; Pres. Scott Casselman; 350 mems.

Pharmaceutical

Canada's Research-Based Pharmaceuticals (Rx & D): 1111 Prince of Wales Dr., Suite 302, Ottawa, ON K2C 3T2; tel. (613) 727-1380; fax (613) 727-1407; e-mail info@canadapharma.org; internet www.canadapharma.org; f. 1914 as Pharmaceutical Mfrs Asscn of Canada; Pres. Murray J. Elston; 65 mems.

Canadian Drug Manufacturers Association: 4120 Yonge St, Suite 409, Toronto, ON M2P 2B8; tel. (416) 223-2333; fax (416) 223-2425; e-mail info@cdma-acfpp.org; internet www.cdma-acfpp.org; Pres. Jim Keon; 18 mems.

Retailing

Retail Council of Canada: 121 Bloor St, Suite 1210, Toronto, ON M4W 3M5; tel. (416) 922-6678; fax (416) 922-8011; internet www.retailcouncil.org; f. 1963; Pres. and CEO Diane J. Brisebois; 8,500 mems.

Retail Merchants' Association of Canada Inc: 1780 Birchmount Rd, Scarborough, ON M1P 2H8; tel. (416) 291-7903; fax (416) 291-5635; f. 1896; Pres. Sean McMahon; 3,000 mems.

Transport

Air Transport Association of Canada: see Transport—Civil Aviation.

Canadian Institute of Traffic and Transportation: 10 King St East, 4th Floor, Toronto, ON M5C 1C3; tel. (416) 363-5696; fax (416) 363-5698; e-mail citt@citt.ca; internet www.citt.ca; f. 1958; Chair. Susan Collins; 2,000 mems.

Canadian Shippers' Council: see Transport—Shipping.

Canadian Trucking Alliance: National Bldg, 130 Slater St, Suite 1025, Ottawa, ON K1P 6E2; tel. (613) 236-9426; fax (613) 563-2701; e-mail dugas@cantruck.com; internet www.cantruck.com; f. 1937; CEO David Bradley.

Canadian Vehicle Manufacturers' Association: 170 Attwell Dr., Suite 400, Toronto, ON M9W 5Z5; tel. (416) 364-9333; fax (416) 367-3221; e-mail cvma@cvma.ca; internet www.cvma.ca; f. 1926; Pres. Mark A. Nantais; 5 mems.

Railway Association of Canada: see Transport—Railways.

Shipping Federation of Canada: see Transport—Shipping.

Miscellaneous

Canadian Association of Importers and Exporters, Inc: 438 University Ave, Suite 1618, Box 60, Toronto, ON M5G 2K8; tel. (416) 595-5333; fax (416) 595-8226; internet www.importers.ca; f. 1932; Pres. Bob Armstrong; 550 mems.

Canadian Printing Industries Association: 75 Albert St, Suite 906, Ottawa, ON K1P 5E7; tel. (613) 236-7208; fax (613) 236-8169; e-mail pboucher@cpia-aci.ca; internet www.cpia-aci.ca; Pres. Pierre Boucher; 789 mems.

Canadian Tobacco Manufacturers' Council: Ottawa, ON; tel. (613) 238-2799; fax (613) 238-4463; f. 1963; Pres. Robert Parker.

Shipbuilding Association of Canada: 222 Queen St, Suite 1502, Ottawa, ON K1P 5V9; tel. (613) 232-7127; fax (613) 238-5519; e-mail pcairns@cfncon.com; internet www.shipbuilding.ca; f. 1995; Pres. Peter Cairns; 20 mems.

UTILITIES

Regulatory Authorities

Alberta Energy and Utilities Board: 640 Fifth Ave, SW, Calgary, AB T2P 3G4; tel. (403) 297-8311; fax (403) 297-8398; e-mail eub.info_services@eub.gov.ab.ca; internet www.eub.gov.ab.ca.

British Columbia Utilities Commission: 900 Howe St, 6th Floor, Box 250, Vancouver, BC V6Z 2N3; tel. (604) 660-4700; fax (604) 660-1102; e-mail commission.secretary@bcuc.com; internet www.bcuc.com; Chair. Peter Ostergaard.

Manitoba Public Utilities Board: 280 Smith St, 2nd Floor, Winnipeg, MB R3C 1K2; tel. (204) 945-2638; fax (204) 945-2643; Exec. Dir G. O. Barron.

National Energy Board: 444 Seventh Ave, SW, Calgary, AB T2P 0X8; tel. (403) 292-4800; fax (403) 292-5503; internet www.neb.gc.ca; fed. regulatory agency; Chair. Kenneth W. Vollman.

New Brunswick Board of Commissioners of Public Utilities: 110 Charlotte St, POB 5001, Saint John, NB E2L 4Y9; tel. (506) 658-2504; fax (506) 633-0163; e-mail dnichols@nbnet.nb.ca; Chair. David C. Nicholson.

Newfoundland and Labrador Board of Commissioners of Public Utilities: POB 21040, St John's, NL A1A 5B2; tel. (709) 726-8600; fax (709) 726-9604; e-mail cheryl@pub.nf.ca; internet www.pub.nf.ca; Chair. and CEO Robert Noseworthy.

Nova Scotia Utility and Review Board: POB 1692, Postal Unit M, Halifax, NS B3J 3S3; tel. (902) 424-4448; fax (902) 424-3919; e-mail uarb.board@gov.ns.ca; internet www.nsuarb.ca; Chair. P. W. Gurnham.

Ontario Energy Board: 2300 Yonge St, 26th Floor, Box 2319, Toronto, ON M4P 1E4; tel. (416) 481-1967; fax (416) 440-7656; e-mail boardsec@oeb.gov.on.ca; internet www.oeb.gov.on.ca; Chair. Floyd Laughren.

Prince Edward Island Regulatory and Appeals Commission: 134 Kent St, Suite 501, POB 577, Charlottetown PE C1A 7L1; tel. (902) 892-3501; fax (902) 566-4076; e-mail irac@irac.pe.ca; internet www.irac.pe.ca; Chair. and CEO Maurice Rodgerson.

Québec Electricity and Gas Board: 800 pl. Victoria, CP 001, succursale de la Bourse, Montréal, QC H4Z 1A2; tel. (514) 873-2070.

Saskatchewan Municipal Board: 2151 Scarth St, 4th Floor, Regina, SK S4P 3V7; tel. (306) 787-6221; fax (306) 787-1610; internet www.smb.gov.sk.ca; Chair. B. G. McNamee.

Electricity

ATCO Electric: 10035 105th St, POB 2426, Edmonton, AB T5J 2V6; internet www.atcoelectric.com; formerly Alberta Power Ltd; generates and distributes electricity in Alberta.

BC Hydro: 6911 Southpoint Dr., Burnaby, BC V3N 4X8; tel. (604) 528-1600; fax (604) 623-3901; e-mail customer.service@bchydro.com; internet www.bchydro.com; generation, transmission and distribution of energy in British Columbia; Chair. and CEO Larry I. Bell.

Canadian Electricity Association: 1155 rue Metcalfe, bureau 1120, Montréal, QC H3Z 2P9; tel. (514) 866-6121; fax (514) 866-1880; e-mail info@canelect.ca; internet www.intertower.com/cea .html; mems include 36 corporate utility enterprises accounting for c. 95% of Canada's installed generating capacity; Pres. and CEO HANS R. KONOW.

Hydro-Québec: 75 blvd René-Lévesque ouest, Montréal, QC H2Z 1A4; tel. (514) 289-2211; fax (514) 843-3163; internet www.hydro.mb .ca; Pres. ANDRÉ CAILLÉ.

Manitoba Hydro: 820 Taylor Ave, POB 815, Winnipeg, MB R3C 2P4; tel. (204) 474-3311; fax (204) 475-9044; e-mail publicaffairs@ hydro.mb.ca; internet www.hydro.mb.ca; Pres. and CEO ROBERT B. BRENNAN.

Newfoundland and Labrador Hydro: POB 12400, St John's, NL A1B 4K7; tel. (709) 737-1400; fax (709) 737-1231; internet www.nlh .nf.ca; Pres. and CEO WILLIAM E. WELLS.

Northwest Territories Power Corporation: 4 Capital Dr., Hay River, NT X0E 1G2; tel. (867) 874-5200; fax (867) 874-5251; e-mail info@ntpc.com; internet www.ntpc.com; f. 1988; Chair. RICHARD NER-YSOO; Pres. and CEO LEON COURNEYA.

Nova Scotia Power Inc: POB 910, Halifax, NS B3J 2W5; tel. (902) 428-6230; fax (902) 428-6110; internet www.nspower.ca; fmrly Crown Corporation of Nova Scotia; privatized 1992; distributes power to over 400,000 customers; CEO DAVID D. McCANN.

Ontario Power Generation: 700 University Ave, Toronto, ON M5G 1X6; tel. (416) 592-5111; fax (416) 971-3691; internet www .ontariopowergeneration.com; f. 1907 as Ontario Hydro, renamed as above in 1999; Canada's largest public utility corpn; also the main producer of nuclear power; Chair. WILLIAM FARLINGER; Pres. and CEO RONALD OSBORNE.

Prince Edward Island Energy Corporation: Jones Bldg, 11 Kent St, 4th Floor, POB 2000, Charlottetown, PE C1A 7N8; tel. (902) 894-0288; fax (902) 894-0290; e-mail dwmacquarrie@gov.pe.ca; internet www.gov.pe.ca; CEO WAYNE MACQUARRIE.

SaskPower: 2025 Victoria Ave, Regina, SK S4P 0S1; tel. (306) 566-2121; fax (306) 566-2330; e-mail enquiries@saskpower.com; internet www.saskpower.com; f. 1930; f. 1930; Pres. and CEO JOHN WRIGHT.

Gas

Canadian Gas Association: 20 Eglinton Ave West, Suite 1305, POB 1305, Toronto, ON M4R 1K8; tel. (416) 481-1828; fax (416) 481-2625; e-mail info@cga.ca; internet www.cga.ca; f. 1907; Pres. and CEO MARIE C. ROUNDING; 220 corporate mems.

Ontario Natural Gas Association: 77 Bloor St, Suite 1104, Toronto, ON M5S 1M2; tel. (416) 961-2339; fax (416) 961-1173; e-mail onga@sympatico.ca; Chair. BERNARD JONES.

TransCanada Pipelines Ltd: 111 Fifth Ave, SW, POB 1000, Station M, Calgary, AB T2P 4K5; tel. (403) 267-6100; fax (403) 267-6444; internet www.transcanada.com; production, storage, transmission and sale of natural gas through six subsidiary cos; Pres. and CEO DOUGLAS D. BALDWIN.

Westcoast Energy Inc: 666 Burrard St, Suite 3400, Park Place, Vancouver, BC V6C 3M8; tel. (604) 488-8000; fax (604) 488-8500; internet www.westcoastenergy.com; production, storage, transmission and sale of natural gas through four operating cos in British Columbia, Alberta and Manitoba; Chair. and CEO MICHAEL E. J. PHELPS.

Water

Northwest Territories Water Board: POB 1500, Yellowknife, NT X1A 2R3; tel. (867) 669-2772; fax (867) 669-2719; internet infosource .gc.ca/info_1/NTW-XI-e.html.

Nunavut Water Board: Gjoa Haven, NU X0E 1J0; e-mail rbecker@ polarnet.ca.

Resource Management and Environmental Protection Branch, Nova Scotia Department of Environment and Labour: 5151 Terminal Rd, 5th Floor, POB 2107, Halifax, NS B3J 3B7; tel. (902) 424-2554; fax (902) 424-0503; internet www.gov.ns.ca/ enla/rmep.

SaskWater: Victoria Place, 111 Fairford St East, Moose Jaw, SK 6SH 7X9; tel. (306) 694-3900; fax (306) 694-3944; e-mail comm@ saskwater.com; internet www.saskwater.com; Pres. CLARE KIRKLAND.

Water Management Branch, British Columbia Ministry of Environment, Lands and Parks: 2975 Jutland Rd, POB 9340, Victoria, BC V8W 9M1; tel. (250) 952-6806; internet www.elp.gov.bc .ca/wat; Dir JAMES S. MATTISON.

Water Resources Branch, Manitoba Natural Resources: 200 Saulteaux Cres., POB 80, Winnipeg, MB R3J 3W3; tel. (204) 945-7488; fax (204) 945-7419; Dir STEVEN TOPPING.

Water Resources Branch, Ontario, Ministry of Environment and Energy: 135 St Clair Ave West, 2nd Floor, Toronto, ON M4V 1P5; tel. (416) 323-4917; fax (416) 965-9807; Dir JIM ASHMAN.

Water Resources Division, Newfoundland and Labrador Department of Environment and Conservation: Confederation Bldg, POB 8700, St John's, NL A1B 4J6; tel. (709) 729-2563; fax (709) 729-0320; internet www.gov.nf.ca/env/env/water_resources .asp; Dir MARTIN GOEBEL.

Water Resources Division, Prince Edward Island Department of the Environment: Jones Bldg, 11 Kent St, POB 2000, Charlottetown, PE C1A 7N8; tel. (902) 368-5000; fax (902) 368-5830; e-mail jjyoung@gov.pe.ca; Dir JIM YOUNG.

Water Resources Planning Branch, New Brunswick Department of the Environment: Argyle Pl., POB 6000, Fredericton, NB E3B 5H1; tel. (506) 457-4846; fax (506) 453-2390; Man. WILLIAM C. AYER.

TRADE UNIONS

At the beginning of 2000 there were 4,057,000 union members in Canada, representing 25.8% of the civilian labour force. Of these, 29.5% belonged to unions with headquarters in the USA.

In 2000 unions affiliated to the Canadian Labour Congress represented 69.4% of total union membership.

Canadian Labour Congress: 2841 Riverside Dr., Ottawa, ON K1V 8X7; tel. (613) 521-3400; fax (613) 521-4655; internet www .clc-ctc.ca; f. 1956; Pres. KEN GEORGETTI; Sec.-Treas. NANCY RICHE; 2,500,000 mems (2001).

Affiliated unions with more than 15,000 members:

Amalgamated Transit Union: 1450 Meyerside Dr., Suite 701, Mississauga, ON L5T 2N5; tel. (905) 670-4710; fax (905) 670-3659; e-mail atucc@on.aibn.com; internet www.atuccanada.com; Canadian Dir KEN FOSTER; 24,000 mems (2000).

American Federation of Musicians of the United States and Canada: 75 The Donway West, Suite 1010, Don Mills, ON M3C 2E9; tel. (416) 391-5161; fax (416) 391-5165; e-mail afmcan@afm .org; internet www.afm.org; Vice-Pres. in Canada DAVID J. JANDRISCH; 18,000 mems (2001).

British Columbia Nurses' Union: 4060 Regent St, Burnaby, BC V5C 6P5; tel. (604) 433-2268; fax (604) 433-7945; internet www .bcnu.org; Pres. CATHY FERGUSON; 25,000 mems (2000).

Canadian Union of Postal Workers: 337 Bank St, Ottawa, ON K2P 1Y3; tel. (613) 236-7238; fax (613) 563-7861; internet www .cupw.ca; f. 1965; Nat. Pres. DEBORAH BOURQUE; 54,000 mems (2000).

Canadian Union of Public Employees: 21 Florence St, Ottawa, ON K2P 0W6; tel. (613) 237-1590; fax (613) 237-5508; internet www.cupe.ca; Nat. Pres. PAUL MOIST; 540,000 mems (2001).

Communications, Energy and Paperworkers Union of Canada: 350 Albert St, 19th Floor, Ottawa, ON K1R 1A4; tel. (613) 230-5200; fax (613) 230-5801; internet www.cep.ca; Pres. BRIAN PAYNE; 140,000 mems (2000).

Hotel Employees and Restaurant Employees International Union: 1140 blvd de Maisonneuve ouest, bureau 1150, Montréal, QC H3A 1M8; tel. (514) 844-4167; fax (514) 844-1536; e-mail jamesstamos@herecanadianoffice.com; Canadian Dir JAMES STAMOS; 31,000 mems (2001).

International Association of Fire Fighters: 350 Sparks St, Suite 403, Ottawa, ON K1R 7S8; tel. (613) 567-8988; fax (613) 567-8986; Asst to the Gen. Pres. JIM LEE; 18,400 mems (2000).

International Association of Machinists and Aerospace Workers: 100 Metcalfe St, Suite 300, Ottawa, ON K1P 5M1; tel. (613) 236-9761; fax (613) 563-7830; Gen. Vice-Pres. in Canada DAVE L. RITCHIE; 45,000 mems (2000).

International Brotherhood of Electrical Workers: 1450 Meyerside Dr., Suite 300, Mississauga, ON L5T 2N5; tel. (905) 564-5441; fax (905) 564-8114; e-mail ivpd_oi@ibew.org; Int. Vice-Pres. PHIL FLEMMING; 59,000 mems (1999).

International Union of Operating Engineers: 28 Aberdeen St, Kentville, NS B4N 3X9; tel. (902) 678-9950; fax (902) 678-1838; e-mail iuoe@glinx.com; Canadian Dir EDGAR DOULL; 40,000 mems (2000).

IWA Canada (Industrial Wood and Allied Workers of Canada): 1285 Pender St, Suite 500, Vancouver, BC V6E 4B2; tel. (604) 683-1117; fax (604) 688-6416; internet www.iwa.ca; f. 1937; Pres. D. C. HAGGARD; 44,000 mems (2001).

Labourers' International Union of North America: 44 Hughson St South, Hamilton, ON L8N 2A7; tel. (905) 522-7177;

fax (905) 522-9310; internet www.liuna.org; Canadian Dir and Vice-Pres. ENRICO H. MANCINELLI; 60,000 mems (2000).

National Automobile, Aerospace Transportation and General Workers Union of Canada (CAW–Canada): 205 Placer Court, North York, Willowdale, ON M2H 3H9; tel. (416) 497-4110; fax (416) 495-6552; e-mail caw@caw.ca; internet www.caw.ca; f. 1985; Nat. Pres. BUZZ HARGROVE; 270,000 mems (2004).

National Union of Public and General Employees: 15 Auriga Dr., Nepean, ON K2E 1B7; tel. (613) 228-9800; fax (613) 228-9801; e-mail national@nupge.ca; internet www.nupge.ca; Nat. Pres. JAMES CLANCY; 337,000 mems (2003).

Office and Professional Employees' International Union: 1200 ave Papineau, bureau 250, Montréal, QC H2K 4S6; tel. (514) 522-6511; fax (514) 522-9000; Canadian Dir JERRI NEW; 33,000 mems (2000).

Ontario English Catholic Teachers' Association: 65 St Clair Ave East, Suite 400, Toronto, ON M4T 2Y8; tel. (416) 925-2493; fax (416) 925-7764; internet www.oecta.on.ca; Pres. JIM SMITH; 30,000 mems (2000).

Ontario Secondary School Teachers' Federation: 60 Mobile Dr., Toronto, ON M4A 2P3; tel. (416) 751-8300; fax (416) 751-3394; e-mail brennan@osstf.on.ca; internet www.osstf.on.ca; Pres. EARL MANNERS; 50,000 mems (2002).

Public Service Alliance of Canada: 233 Gilmour St, Ottawa, ON K2P 0P1; tel. (613) 560-4200; fax (613) 567-0385; internet www.psac-afpc.com; f. 1966; Nat. Pres. NYCOLE TURMEL; 150,000 mems (2000).

Service Employees International Union: 75 The Donway West, Suite 810, North York, ON M3C 2E9; tel. (416) 447-2311; fax (416) 447-2428; e-mail stewarts@seiu.ca; internet www.seiu.ca; Vice-Pres. in Canada SHARLEEN STEWART; 90,000 mems (2000).

Teamsters Canada: 2540 Daniel-Johnson, bureau 804, Laval, QC H7T 2S3; tel. (450) 682-5521; fax (450) 681-1244; internet www.teamsters-canada.org; Canadian Pres. ROBERT BOUVIER; 115,000 mems (2003).

Union of Needletrades, Industrial and Textile Employees-Canada: 15 Gervais Dr., Suite 700, Toronto, ON M3C 1Y8; tel. (416) 441-1806; fax (416) 441-9680; internet www.unite-svti.org; Canadian Dir JOHN ALLERUZZO; 25,000 mems (2000).

United Association of Journeymen and Apprentices of the Plumbing and Pipe Fitting Industry of the United States and Canada: 1959 152nd St, Suite 316, Surrey, BC V4A 9E3; tel. (604) 531-0516; fax (604) 531-0547; e-mail uacanada@direct.ca; internet www.ua.org; Vice-Pres. and Canadian Dir GEORGE MESERVIER; 37,000 mems (2000).

United Brotherhood of Carpenters and Joiners of America: 5799 Young St, Suite 807, Willowdale, ON M2M 3V3; tel. (416) 225-8885; fax (416) 225-5390; internet www.carpenters.org; Gen. Exec. Bd Mem. JAMES E. SMITH; 56,000 mems (2000).

United Food and Commercial Workers Canada: 61 International Blvd, Suite 300, Rexdale, ON M9W 6K4; tel. (416) 675-1104; fax (416) 675-6919; e-mail ufcw@ufcw.ca; internet www.ufcw.ca; f. 1979; Canadian Dir MICHAEL J. FRASER; 220,000 mems (2000).

United Steelworkers of America: 234 Eglinton Ave East, 7th Floor, Toronto, ON M4P 1K7; tel. (416) 487-1571; fax (416) 482-5548; internet www.uswa.org; Nat. Dir in Canada LAWRENCE MCBREARTY; 190,000 mems (2000).

Other Central Congresses

Centrale des syndicats du Québec: 9405 rue Sherbrooke est, Montréal, QC H1L 6P3; tel. (514) 356-8888; fax (514) 356-9999; internet www.csq.qc.net; f. 1974; name changed as above 2000; Pres. RÉJEAN PARENT; 13 affiliated federations, 250 affiliated unions.

Affiliated union with over 15,000 members:

Fédération des syndicats de l'enseignment: 320 rue St-Joseph est, bureau 100, Québec, QC G1K 9E7; tel. (418) 649-8888; fax (418) 649-1914; internet www.fse.qc.net; Pres. JOHANNE FORTIER; 80,000 mems (2000).

Centrale des syndicats démocratiques: 801 4e rue, bureau 300, Québec, QC G1J 2T7; tel. (418) 529-2956; fax (418) 529-6323; f. 1972; Pres. FRANÇOIS VAUDREUIL; 2 federated and 382 affiliated unions (2000).

Confederation of Canadian Unions: 155 Skinner St, Suite 206, Nanaimo, BC V9R 5E8; tel. (250) 753-1060; fax (250) 753-1062; e-mail ccu@island.net; f. 1969; Pres. JOE ELWORTHY; 9 affiliated unions (1999).

Confédération des syndicats nationaux: 1601 ave de Lorimier, Montréal, QC H2K 4M5; tel. (514) 598-2121; fax (514) 598-2052;

e-mail intcsn@total.net; internet www.csn.qc.ca; f. 1921; Pres. MARC LAVIOLETTE; 9 federated unions.

Federated unions with over 15,000 members:

Fédération des employées et employés de services publics inc: 1601 ave de Lorimier, Montréal, QC H2K 4M5; tel. (514) 598-2231; fax (514) 598-2398; Pres. GINETTE GUÉRIN; 36,000 mems (2000).

Fédération du commerce inc: 1601 ave de Lorimier, Montréal, QC H2K 4M5; tel. (514) 598-2181; fax (514) 598-2304; Pres. JEAN LORTIE; 34,000 mems (2000).

Fédération de la métallurgie: 2100 blvd de Maisonneuve est, bureau 204, Montréal, QC H2K 4S1; tel. (514) 529-4937; fax (514) 529-4935; Pres. ALAIN LAMPRON; 20,000 mems (1998).

Fédération de la santé et des services sociaux: 1601 ave de Lorimier, Montréal, QC H2K 4M5; tel. (514) 598-2210; fax (514) 598-2223; Pres. PIERRE LAMY; 107,000 mems (2003).

Fédération nationale des enseignantes et des enseignants du Québec (FNEEQ): 1601 ave de Lorimier, Montréal, QC H2K 4M5; tel. (514) 598-2241; fax (514) 598-2190; e-mail fneeq@videotron.net; internet www.fneeq.qc.ca; f. 1969; Pres. PIERRE PATRY; 20,000 mems (2000).

The American Federation of Labor and Congress of Industrial Organizations (AFL–CIO), with headquarters in Washington, DC, USA, represented 0.4% of the total union membership in Canada, at the beginning of 1997.

Affiliated union with over 15,000 members:

International Association of Bridge, Structural and Ornamental Iron Workers: 1350 L'Heritage Dr., Sarnia, ON N7S 6H8; tel. (519) 542-1413; fax (519) 542-3790; Gen. Vice-Pres. JAMES PHAIR; 15,000 mems (2000).

Principal Unaffiliated Unions

Alberta Teachers' Association: 11010 142nd St, Edmonton, AB T5N 2R1; tel. (780) 447-9400; fax (780) 455-6481; e-mail postmaster@teachers.ab.ca; internet www.teachers.ab.ca; Pres. LARRY BOOI; 34,000 mems (2001).

British Columbia Teachers' Federation: 550 West Sixth Ave, Suite 100, Vancouver, BC V5Z 4P2; tel. (604) 871-2283; fax (604) 871-2294; internet www.bctf.bc.ca; Pres. DAVID CHUDNOVSKY; 44,000 mems (2000).

Canadian Telephone Employees' Association: pl. du Canada, bureau 360, Montréal, QC H3B 2N2; tel. (514) 861-9963; Pres. JUDITH KING; 16,000 mems (2000).

Christian Labour Association of Canada: 5920 Atlantic Dr., Mississauga, ON L4W 1N6; tel. (905) 670-7383; fax (905) 670-8416; e-mail headoffice@clac.ca; internet www.clac.ca; Pres. STAN BAKER; 22,000 mems (2000).

Elementary Teachers' Federation of Ontario: 480 University Ave, Suite 1000, Toronto, ON M5G 1V2; tel. (416) 962-3836; fax (416) 642-2424; internet www.etfo.on.ca; f. 1998; Pres. PHYLLIS BENEDICT; 52,000 mems (2000).

Fédération des infirmières et d'infirmiers du Québec: 2050 rue de Bleury, 4e étage, Montréal, QC H3A 2J5; tel. (514) 987-1141; fax (514) 987-7273; internet www.fiiq.qc.ca/default.htm; Pres. JENNIE SKENE; 48,000 mems (1998).

Ontario Nurses' Association: 85 Grenville St, Suite 400, Toronto, ON M5S 3A2; tel. (416) 964-8833; fax (416) 964-8864; e-mail onamail@mail.ona.on; internet www.ona.org; Pres. BARB WAHL; 45,000 mems (2001).

Professional Institute of the Public Service of Canada: 53 Auriga Dr., Nepean, ON K2E 8C3; tel. (613) 228-6310; fax (613) 228-9048; internet www.pipsc.ca; Pres. STEVE HINDLE; 45,000 mems (2002).

Syndicat de la fonction publique Québec: 5100 blvd des Gradins, Québec, QC G2J 1N4; tel. (418) 623-2424; fax (418) 623-6109; Gen. Pres. SERGE ROY; 39,000 mems (2000).

United Nurses of Alberta: Park Plaza, 9th Floor, 10611 98th Ave, Edmonton, AB T5K 2P7; tel. (403) 425-1025; fax (403) 426-2093; Pres. HEATHER SMITH; 17,000 mems (2000).

Transport

Owing to the size of the country, Canada's economy is particularly dependent upon its transport infrastructure. The St Lawrence Seaway allows ocean-going ships to reach the Great Lakes. In addition to an extensive railway network, the country's transport facilities are being increasingly augmented by new roads, air services and petroleum pipelines. The Trans-Canada Highway forms a main feature of a network of more than 900,000 km of roads and highways.

Canadian Transportation Agency (CTA): Ottawa, ON K1A 0N9; tel. (819) 997-0344; fax (819) 953-8353; internet www.cta-otc.gc.ca; f. 1996 to oversee the economic regulation of transport; Chair. MARIAN L. ROBSON.

RAILWAYS

BC Rail: POB 8770, Vancouver, BC V6B 4X6; tel. (604) 986-2012; fax (604) 984-5004; internet www.bcrail.com; f. 1912; publicly-owned; 2,314 km of track; Chair. J. GOLDSMITH; Pres. and CEO P. J. McELLIGOTT.

CN Rail: 935 rue de la Gauchetière ouest, CP 8100, succursale A, Montréal, QC H3C 3N4; tel. (514) 399-4937; fax (514) 399-6910; internet www.cn.ca; f. 1919; investor-owned; 32,500 km of track; Chair. DAVID G. A. SMITH; Pres. and CEO PAUL TELLIER.

CP Rail System (Canadian Pacific Railway): 401 Ninth Ave, SW, Calgary, AB T2P 4Z4; tel. (403) 319-7000; internet www.cpr.ca; f. 1881; 24,649 km of track; Pres. and CEO ROBERT RITCHIE.

Ontario Northland Transportation Commission: 555 Oak St East, North Bay, ON P1B 8L3; tel. (705) 472-4500; fax (705) 476-5598; internet www.ontc.on.ca; an agency of the Govt of Ontario; operates rail services over 1,211 km of track; Commissioner and Chair. TED HARGREAVES; Pres. and CEO STEVE CARMICHAEL.

VIA Rail Canada Inc: 3 pl. Ville-Marie, CP 8116, succursale A, Montréal, QC H3C 3N3; tel. (514) 871-6000; fax (514) 871-6463; internet www.viarail.ca; f. 1978; fed. govt corpn; proposed transfer to private sector pending; operates passenger services over rail routes covering 13,822 km of track throughout Canada; Chair. (vacant); Pres. and CEO PAUL CÔTÉ.

Association

Railway Association of Canada: 99 Bank St, Suite 1401, Ottawa, ON K1P 6B9; tel. (613) 567-8591; fax (613) 567-6726; e-mail rac@railcan.ca; internet www.railcan.ca; f. 1917; Pres. WILLIAM ROWAT; 60 mems.

ROADS

Provincial governments are responsible for roads within their boundaries. The federal Government is responsible for major roads in the Yukon, the Northwest Territories and Nunavut and in National Parks. In 2001 there were an estimated 1,427,000 km of roads (including 12,800 km of freeways and 192,700 km of highways). The Trans-Canada Highway extends from St John's, NL, to Victoria, BC.

INLAND WATERWAYS

The St Lawrence River and the Great Lakes provide Canada and the USA with a system of inland waterways extending from the Atlantic Ocean to the western end of Lake Superior, a distance of 3,769 km (2,342 miles). There is a 10.7-m (35-foot) navigation channel from Montréal to the sea and an 8.25-m (27-foot) channel from Montréal to Lake Erie. The St Lawrence Seaway (see below), which was opened in 1959, was initiated partly to provide a deep waterway and partly to satisfy the increasing demand for electric power. Power development has been undertaken by the provinces of Québec and Ontario, and by New York State. The navigation facilities and conditions are within the jurisdiction of the federal governments of the USA and Canada.

St Lawrence River and Great Lakes Shipping

St Lawrence Seaway Management Corporation: 202 Pitt St, Cornwall, ON K6J 3P7; tel. (613) 932-5170; fax (613) 932-7286; e-mail marketing@seaways.ca; internet www.greatlakes-seaway.com; f. 1998; responsible for management and operation of marine traffic through Canadian section of St Lawrence Seaway, which is operated jtly with the USA; Chair. ROBERT J. SWENOR; Pres. and CEO RICHARD CORTE.

Algoma Central Corpn: 62 Church St, Suite 600, St Catharines, ON L2R 3C4; tel. (905) 687-7888; fax (905) 687-7882; e-mail miatello@algonet.com; internet www.algonet.com; f. 1899; Pres. and CEO T. S. DOOL; 24 bulk cargo vessels.

Canada Steamship Lines Inc (CSL Group): 759 square Victoria, Montréal, QC H2Y 2K3; tel. (514) 982-3800; fax (514) 982-3802; e-mail ships@csltml.com; internet www.csl.ca; f. 1913; Pres. GERALD CARTER; 14 vessels.

Paterson, N. M., and Sons Ltd: 1918 Yonge St, Thunder Bay, ON P7C 4W6; tel. (807) 577-8421; fax (807) 475-3493; internet www.marmus.ca/marmus/PATSRN; f. 1908; bulk carriers; Pres. and CEO ROBERT J. PATERSON; 7 vessels; 95,536 grt.

SHIPPING

At 31 December 2003 the Canadian merchant fleet comprised 916 vessels, with a total displacement of 2,723,001 grt.

British Columbia Ferry Services Inc.: 1112 Fort St, Victoria, BC V8V 4V2; tel. (250) 381-1401; fax (250) 381-5452; internet www.bcferries.com; passenger and vehicle ferries; Pres.and CEO DAVID HAHN; 40 vessels.

Fednav Ltd: 1000 rue de la Gauchetière ouest, bureau 3500, Montréal, QC H3B 4W5; tel. (514) 878-6500; fax (514) 878-6642; e-mail info@fednav.com; internet www.fednav.com; f. 1944; shipowners, operators, contractors, terminal operators; Pres. L. G. PATHY; owned and chartered fleet of 68 vessels.

Groupe Desagnés Inc: 21 rue du Marché-Champlain, Bureau 100, Québec, QC G1K 8Z8; tel. (418) 692-1000; fax (418) 692-6044; Chair. and CEO LOUIS-MARIE BEAULIEU; 10 vessels.

Marine Atlantic Inc: 355 Purves St, North Sydney, NS B2A 3V2; tel. (800) 341-7891; fax (902) 564-7480; internet www.marine-atlantic.ca; vehicle and passenger ferries serving Atlantic coast of Canada; Chair. SID HYNES.

Associations

Canadian Shipowners Association: 350 Sparks St, Suite 705, Ottawa, ON K1R 7S8; tel. (613) 232-3539; fax (613) 232-6211; e-mail csa@shipowners.ca; internet www.shipowners.ca; f. 1953; Pres. DONALD MORRISON; 7 mems.

Shipping Federation of Canada: 300 rue St-Sacrement, bureau 326, Montréal, QC H2Y 1X4; tel. (514) 849-2325; fax (514) 849-6992; f. 1903; Pres. GILLES J. BÉLANGER; 75 mems.

CIVIL AVIATION

Principal Company

Air Canada: CP 14000, succursale St-Laurent, Montréal, QC H4Y 1H4; tel. (514) 422-5000; fax (514) 422-5909; internet www.aircanada.ca; f. 1937; investor-owned; acquired Canadian Airlines International in Jan. 2000; Pres. and CEO ROBERT MILTON; operates scheduled and charter services throughout Canada and to the USA; also serves Europe, the Middle East and the Caribbean.

Association

Air Transport Association of Canada: 255 Albert St, Suite 1100, Ottawa, ON K1P 6A9; tel. (613) 233-7727; fax (613) 230-8648; e-mail atac@atac.ca; internet www.atac.ca; f. 1934; Pres. J. CLIFFORD MACKAY; 300 mems.

Tourism

Most tourist visitors are from the USA (estimated at 15.6m. of a total 19.7m. in 2001). Expenditure by tourists in that year was estimated to total US $10,774m.

Canadian Tourism Commission: 235 Queen St, 8th Floor West, Ottawa, ON K1A 0H6; tel. (613) 946-1000; fax (613) 954-3964; e-mail ctc_feedback@businteractive.com; internet www.canadatourism.com; fed. govt org.; Chair. J. BUDD BUCHANAN; Pres. MICHELE MCKENZIE.

Tourism Industry Association of Canada: 130 Albert St, Suite 1608, Ottawa, ON K1P 5G4; tel. (613) 238-3883; fax (613) 238-3878; e-mail info@tiac-aitc.ca; internet www.tiac-aitc.ca; f. 1931; private-sector asscn; encourages travel to and within Canada; promotes devt of travel facilities and services; Pres. RANDY WILLIAMS.

CAPE VERDE

Introductory Survey

Location, Climate, Language, Religion, Flag, Capital

The Republic of Cape Verde is an archipelago of 10 islands and five islets in the North Atlantic Ocean, about 500 km (300 miles) west of Dakar, Senegal. The country lies in a semi-arid belt, with little rain and an average annual temperature of 24°C (76°F). The official language is Portuguese, of which the locally spoken form is Creole (Crioulo). There were plans to make Crioulo an official language in 2005. Virtually all of the inhabitants profess Christianity, and more than 95% are Roman Catholics. The national flag, adopted in 1992 (proportions 3 by 5), comprises five horizontal stripes: blue (half the depth) at the top, white, red, white (each one-twelfth) and blue. Superimposed, to the left of centre, is a circle of 10 five-pointed gold stars (four on the white stripes and three each on the blue stripes above and below). The capital is Cidade de Praia.

Recent History

The Cape Verde Islands were colonized by the Portuguese in the 15th century. From the 1950s liberation movements in Portugal's African colonies campaigned for independence, and, in this context, the archipelago was linked with the mainland territory of Portuguese Guinea (now Guinea-Bissau) under one nationalist movement, the Partido Africano da Independência do Guiné e Cabo Verde (PAIGC). The independence of Guinea-Bissau was recognized by Portugal in September 1974, but the PAIGC leadership in the Cape Verde Islands decided to pursue its independence claims separately, rather than enter into an immediate federation with Guinea-Bissau. In December 1974 a transitional Government, comprising representatives of the Portuguese Government and the PAIGC, was formed; members of other political parties were excluded. On 30 June 1975 elections for a legislative body, the Assembléia Nacional Popular (ANP—National People's Assembly) were held, in which only PAIGC candidates were allowed to participate. Independence was granted to the Republic of Cape Verde on 5 July 1975, with Aristides Pereira, Secretary-General of the PAIGC, becoming the country's first President. Cape Verde's first Constitution was approved in September 1980.

Although Cape Verde and Guinea-Bissau remained constitutionally separate, the PAIGC supervised the activities of both states. Progress towards the ultimate goal of unification was halted by the November 1980 coup in Guinea-Bissau. The Government of Cape Verde condemned the coup, and in January 1981 the Cape Verdean wing of the PAIGC was renamed the Partido Africano da Independência de Cabo Verde (PAICV). In February Pereira was re-elected as President by the ANP, and all articles concerning an eventual union with Guinea-Bissau were removed from the Constitution. Discussions concerning reconciliation were held in June 1982, however, and diplomatic relations between the two countries were subsequently normalized.

Meanwhile, elections to the ANP took place in December 1985. The candidates on the PAICV-approved list, not all of whom were members of the PAICV, obtained 94.5% of the votes cast. In January 1986 Pereira was re-elected for a further five-year term as President by the ANP. In 1989 two political commissions were established, to regulate legislative elections and to consider proposals for constitutional changes, and it was subsequently announced that, although elections to the ANP were to be held in 1990, local elections were to be deferred until 1991. In April 1990 a newly formed political organization, the Movimento para a Democracia (MPD), issued a manifesto in Paris, France, which advocated the immediate introduction of a multi-party system. Pereira subsequently announced that the next presidential election would be held, for the first time, on the basis of universal suffrage.

In July 1990, in an apparent response to increasing pressure from church and academic circles, a special congress of the PAICV reviewed proposals for new party statutes and the abolition of Article 4 of the Constitution, which guaranteed the supremacy of the PAICV. Pereira also resigned as Secretary-General of the PAICV, and was later replaced by the Prime Minister, Gen. Pedro Verona Rodrigues Pires, hitherto Deputy

Secretary-General of the party. In September the ANP approved a constitutional amendment abolishing the PAICV's monopoly of power and permitting a multi-party system. The MPD subsequently received official recognition as a political party. In November 1990 the MPD announced its support for an independent candidate, António Mascarenhas Monteiro, in the forthcoming presidential election. On 13 January 1991 the first multi-party elections to take place in lusophone Africa resulted in a decisive victory for the MPD, which secured 56 of the 79 seats in the ANP. Later that month Dr Carlos Alberto Wahnon de Carvalho Veiga, the leader of the MPD, was sworn in as Prime Minister at the head of an interim Government, mostly comprising members of the MPD. The presidential election, held in mid-February, resulted in victory for Mascarenhas, who secured 73.5% of the votes cast. The first multi-party local elections, held in December, resulted in another decisive victory for the MPD, which secured control of 10 of the 14 local councils.

On 25 September 1992 a new Constitution of the Republic of Cape Verde (also referred to as the 'Second Republic') came into force, enshrining the principles of multi-party democracy. In August 1993 the opposition PAICV elected Aristides Lima to the post of Secretary-General of the party, replacing Pires, who was appointed party Chairman. In December the Minister of Justice and Labour, Dr Eurico Correia Monteiro, was dismissed, following his announcement that he would be contesting the leadership of the MPD at an extraordinary national convention of the party, to take place in February 1994. At the convention Carlos Veiga was re-elected Chairman of the MPD. However, increasing conflict within the party resulted in some 30 party delegates, led by Monteiro, boycotting the convention. That month Monteiro announced the establishment of a new political party, the Partido da Convergência Democrática (PCD).

At legislative elections conducted in December 1995 the MPD secured an outright majority, taking 50 of the 72 seats in the Assembléia Nacional (AN, as the ANP had become in 1992). The PAICV won 21 seats, while the remaining seat was obtained by the PCD. At a presidential election conducted in February 1996 Mascarenhas, the sole candidate, was re-elected. However, the turn-out was only 45%. Veiga, meanwhile, expressed his intention to continue the policies of liberal economic and social reform that had been pursued in his previous term in office.

In May 1998 Veiga created several new ministries and appointed the Minister of Economic Co-ordination, António Gualberto do Rosário, to the newly created post of Deputy Prime Minister. In March 1999 Veiga stated that he would not seek re-election as the Chairman of the MPD at the next party convention. Do Rosário and the Mayor of Praia, Jacinto Santos, subsequently announced their candidacies for the chairmanship of the MPD, and thus the premiership. In municipal elections held in February 2000 the MPD sustained substantial losses, retaining only eight of 17 local councils and losing the capital to the PAICV, which re-emerged as a credible political force. Following the resignation of Pedro Pires, who announced his candidacy for the presidential election, the PAICV elected José Maria Neves as its new President in June. In the following month do Rosário was elected Chairman of the MPD, and Santos subsequently formed a new political party, the Partido da Renovação Democrática (PRD).

In late July 2000 Veiga announced his resignation as Prime Minister and confirmed his candidacy for the presidential election scheduled to take place in early 2001; he was replaced by do Rosário. In October 2000 it was announced that the PCD, the União Caboverdiana Independente e Democrática and the Partido de Trabalho e Solidariedade were to form a coalition (the Aliança Democrática para a Mudança—ADM) to participate in the forthcoming legislative elections.

At the legislative elections, held on 14 January 2001, the opposition PAICV secured 49.5% of the vote and 40 seats in the AN, compared with 40.5% (30 seats) for the MPD and 6.1% (two seats) for the ADM. A new Government, headed by Neves, was announced at the end of January; Prime Minister Neves indicated that his Government's priorities would include reducing unemployment levels and the rehabilitation of public finances.

At the presidential election, conducted on 11 February, no candidate received an overall majority, necessitating a second round, held on 25 February, at which Pires narrowly defeated Veiga, receiving 50.01% of valid votes cast. Appeals against the result by Veiga, who cited voting irregularities, were later rejected by the Supreme Court, which confirmed Pires as the new President. Aristides Raimundo Lima was elected Speaker of the AN in February. In December Agostinho Lopes was elected unopposed as the new Chairman of the MPD.

In June 2002, with famine threatening 30,000 inhabitants, the Government made its first appeal for emergency food aid in more than 20 years. The UN World Food Programme responded with an appeal to international donors for US $1.2m. in emergency aid. In October 2003 Carlos Burgo resigned as Minister of Finance, Planning and Regional Development. There was speculation that his resignation had been prompted by differences over the budget for 2004, which was to be debated by the AN later that month, although this was denied by the PAICV.

At local elections in March 2004, the MPD secured control of nine of the 17 municipalities, while the ruling PAICV won in only six. A government reshuffle was effected in April, with a new cabinet structure comprising 13 ministers and four secretaries of state. João Pinto Serra became Minister of Finance and Planning, while João Pereira Silva and Júlio Lopes Correia were appointed to the newly created portfolios of Economy, Growth and Competitiveness and Internal Affairs, respectively. In September this structure was amended to 14 ministers and three secretaries of state, with the creation of the Ministry of Social Communication. In December 2004 Agostinho Lopes was re-elected President of the MPD.

Cape Verde has traditionally professed a non-aligned stance in foreign affairs and maintains relations with virtually all the power blocs. On taking office in 1991, the MPD Government successfully sought to extend Cape Verde's range of international contacts, with special emphasis on potential new sources of development aid; substantial assistance has been received from both Israel and the Gulf states. The MPD Government enlarged the scope of Cape Verde's diplomatic contacts, establishing embassies in South Africa and Sweden, as well as diplomatic presences in Hong Kong, Macao, Singapore, Spain, the United Kingdom and the USA. In July 2001 the new PAICV administration established diplomatic relations at ambassadorial level with the People's Republic of China. In April 2002 the Government announced its intention to seek a 'special status' for Cape Verde with the European Union, thereby increasing trade and investment, and in November 2003 Prime Minister Neves visited a number of European countries in an attempt to gain support for this aim. In 2004 the Governments of Cape Verde and Portugal announced the creation of a commission designed to help Cape Verdean immigrants living in Portugal. The country has continued to maintain particularly close relations with Portugal and Brazil, and with other lusophone African former colonies—Angola, Guinea-Bissau, Mozambique and São Tomé and Príncipe, known collectively, with Cape Verde, as the Países Africanos da Língua Oficial Portuguesa (PALOP). In July 1996 a 'lusophone commonwealth', known as the Comunidade dos Países de Língua Portuguesa (CPLP), comprising the five PALOP countries together with Portugal and Brazil, was formed with the intention of benefiting each member state through joint co-operation on technical, cultural and social matters. In December 1996 Cape Verde became a full member of the Sommet francophone, a commonwealth comprising all the French-speaking nations of the world, and benefits in turn from membership of this body's Agence de coopération culturelle et technique.

Government

Under the 1992 Constitution, Cape Verde is a multi-party state, although the formation of parties on a religious or geographical basis is prohibited. Legislative power is vested in the Assembléia Nacional (AN—National Assembly), which comprises 72 deputies, elected by universal adult suffrage for a five-year term. The Head of State is the President of the Republic, who is elected by universal suffrage for a five-year term. Executive power is vested in the Prime Minister, who is nominated by the deputies of the AN, appointed by the President and governs with the assistance of a Council of Ministers.

Defence

The armed forces, initially formed from ex-combatants in the liberation wars, totalled about 1,200 (army 1,000, air force less than 100, coastguard 100) in August 2004. There is also a police force, the Police for Public Order, which is organized by the local municipal councils. National service is by selective conscription. In October 2002 the Government announced a programme of reform, involving the coastguard, the military police and special forces dealing with drugs-trafficking and terrorism offences. Government defence expenditure in 2004 was budgeted at an estimated 500m. escudos.

Economic Affairs

In 2003, according to estimates from the World Bank, Cape Verde's gross national income (GNI), measured at average 2001–03 prices, was US $815m., equivalent to $1,490 per head (or $5,440 per head on an international purchasing-power parity basis). During 1990–2003, it was estimated, the population increased at an average annual rate of 2.5%, while gross domestic product (GDP) per head increased, in real terms, by an average of 3.0% per year. Overall GDP increased, in real terms, at an average annual rate of 5.6% in 1990–2003; growth in 2003 was 5.0%.

Agriculture (including forestry and fishing) contributed 6.6% of GDP in 2003, and employed an estimated 21.7% of the economically active population in 2002. The staple crop is maize; sugar cane, coconuts, bananas, mangoes, sweet potatoes, potatoes, cassava, and vegetables are also cultivated. Drought and an invasion of locusts from mainland Africa severely reduced the harvest in 2004. Export earnings from fish and crustaceans declined from 262.0m. escudos (20.2% of the total value of exports, excluding fuel) in 1997 to 37.7m. escudos (1.9%) in 2001. Lobster and tuna are among the most important exports. Moreover, the total fish catch declined from 14,730 metric tons in 1981 to 6,573 tons in 1992. In 1994 a five-year project was announced for the redevelopment of the fishing industry, with investment of US $28m. By 2000 the annual catch had recovered somewhat to 10,821 tons, although it had declined to an estimated 8,000 tons by 2002. During 1990–2003 the GDP of the agricultural sector increased, in real terms, at an average annual rate of 3.5%; growth in 2003 was 1.6%.

Industry (including construction and power) contributed 18.9% of GDP in 2003, and employed 30.6% of the labour force in 1990. During 1990–2003 industrial GDP increased, in real terms, at an average annual rate of 5.2%; growth in 2003 was 4.5%.

Mining employed 0.4% of the labour force in 1990 and contributed less than 1% of GDP in 1998. Salt and pozzolana, a volcanic ash used in cement manufacture, are the main non-fuel minerals produced.

Manufacturing contributed 7.6% of GDP in 2003 and employed about 6% of the labour force in 1995. The most important branches, other than fish-processing, are clothing, footwear, rum distilling and bottling. Legislation enacted in 1999 provided for the transformation of industrial parks at Mindelo and Praia into free-trade zones, and for the establishment of a further free-trade zone on Sal island. During 1990–2003 the GDP of the manufacturing sector increased, in real terms, at an average annual rate of 4.0%; an increase of 4.8% was recorded in 2003.

Energy is derived principally from hydroelectric power and gas. Imports of mineral fuels comprised 5.6% of the value of total estimated imports in 2001.

Services accounted for 74.5% of GDP in 2003. Tourism has been identified as the area with the most potential for economic development. A new international airport on Santiago, due to open in March 2005, was expected to give considerable impetus to the development of the tourism sector. The airport on São Vicente island was upgraded to international capacity in 2000. Plans were also under way for the construction of two further international airports, on São Vicente and Boa Vista. The Government planned to spend €635m. upgrading the road network in 2005. Tourist arrivals increased from 52,000 in 1998 to 134,169 in 2001. During 1990–2003 the combined GDP of the service sectors increased, in real terms, at an average annual rate of 6.0%; growth in 2003 was 5.7%.

In 2003 Cape Verde recorded a trade deficit of US $291.1m., and there was a deficit of $77.3m. on the current account of the balance of payments. In 2003 the principal source of imports was Portugal (48.4%); other major suppliers were the Netherlands (14.7%) and Belgium (5.7%). Portugal was also the principal market for exports (70.1%) in that year; the other major purchaser was the USA (2.5%). The principal exports in 2001 were clothing (49.0%) and footwear (39.8%). The principal imports in that year were cereals and cereal preparations, refined petroleum and passenger vehicles.

In 2004 projected budget figures showed a deficit of 3,730m. escudos. Cape Verde's total external debt at the end of 2002 was US $413.5m., of which $385.2m. was long-term public debt. In that year the cost of debt-servicing was equivalent to 7.6% of the value of exports of goods and services. The annual rate of inflation averaged 4.3% in 1990–2003. Consumer prices increased by an average of 1.2% in 2003. In 2003 unemployment affected some 21% of the labour force, according to official figures.

Cape Verde is a member of the Economic Community of West African States (ECOWAS, see p. 205), which promotes trade and co-operation in West Africa, and is a signatory to the Lomé Convention and subsequent Cotonou Agreement (see p. 262).

Cape Verde's agricultural economy is highly vulnerable to severe periodic drought, making self-sufficiency in food production impossible; approximately 85% of the country's total food requirements are imported and in 2002 it was estimated that 36% of the country's population were living in poverty. The country benefits from considerable external assistance (which totalled 3,632m. escudos in 2000) and substantial remittances from emigrants. There are about 700,000 Cape Verdeans living outside the country, principally in the USA, the Netherlands, Portugal, Italy and Angola. In 2003, according to the central bank, private remittances from emigrants provided an estimated 7,928.5m. escudos. In 2002 the figure was 9,701.9m., equivalent to 13.2% of GDP. The Government has attempted to attract emigrants' capital into the light-industry and fishing sectors by offering favourable tax conditions to investors. In March 1998 Cape Verde and Portugal signed an agreement providing for their respective currencies to become linked through a fixed exchange rate, thus transforming the Cape Verde escudo into a convertible currency. In 2001 two financial co-operation agreements were signed by Portugal and Cape Verde, in an attempt to strengthen the Cape Verdean economy. In April 2002 the IMF approved a Poverty Reduction and Growth Facility worth some US $12.7m. in support of Cape Verde's economic programme for 2002–05 (as outlined in a new National Development Plan). By mid-2004 some $9m. of this had been accessed and, following a review, the IMF announced that a further $2m. would be made available. However, an IMF mission to Cape Verde in November found that the country had not met several of its economic and financial targets. In September 2003 the African Development Bank granted Cape Verde a $3.3m. loan to finance further economic reforms, and the Government and the UN signed an assistance framework plan, valid until 2005, aimed at aiding Cape Verde's development and reducing poverty. The Government implemented a number of fiscal reforms in early 2004, including the introduction of value-added tax. In July the UN announced plans to reclassify Cape Verde as a medium-developed country. This provoked fears, however, that levels of international aid would decline. In late 2004 the Prime Minister, José Maria Neves, announced that Cape Verde was considering adopting the euro as the country's currency. The Banco de Cabo Verde estimated that GDP would increase by 5% in the following year, while inflation would be between 1% and 2%.

Education

Primary education, beginning at six or seven years of age and lasting for six years, is compulsory. Secondary education, beginning at 13 years of age, is divided into two cycles, the first comprising a three-year general course, the second a two-year pre-university course. There are three teacher-training units and two industrial and commercial schools of further education. A private university, the Universidade Jean Piaget de Cabo Verde, opened in Praia in 2002. Primary enrolment in 2000/01 included 100% of children in the relevant age-group, while UNESCO estimated that secondary enrolment was equivalent to 76% of children in the relevant age-group (males 75%; females 77%). In 1996/97 there were 1,660 Cape Verdean students studying at overseas universities. In 2003 expenditure on education was budgeted at 4.8m. escudos, equivalent to 26% of the central Government's total public expenditure.

Public Holidays

2005: 1 January (New Year), 20 January (National Heroes' Day), 1 May (Labour Day), 5 July (Independence Day), 15 August (Assumption), 1 November (All Saints' Day), 25 December (Christmas Day).

2006: 1 January (New Year), 20 January (National Heroes' Day), 1 May (Labour Day), 5 July (Independence Day), 15 August (Assumption), 1 November (All Saints' Day), 25 December (Christmas Day).

Weights and Measures

The metric system is in force.

Statistical Survey

Sources (unless otherwise stated): Instituto Nacional de Estatística, Avda Amílcar Cabral, CP 116, Praia, Santiago; tel. 613960; e-mail inecv@mail.cvtelecom.cv; internet www.ine.cv; Statistical Service, Banco de Cabo Verde, 117 Avda Amílcar Cabral, CP 101, Praia, Santiago; tel. 2607060; fax 2611914; e-mail apericles@bcv.cv; internet www.bcv.cv.

AREA AND POPULATION

Area: 4,036 sq km (1,558 sq miles).

Population: 341,491 (males 161,494, females 179,997) at census of 23 June 1990; 434,625 at census of 16 June 2000. *2003:* 458,748 (official estimate). *By Island* (2000 census): Boa Vista 4,209; Brava 6,804; Fogo 37,421; Maio 6,754; Sal 14,816; Santo Antão 47,170; São Nicolau 13,661; Santiago 236,627; São Vicente 67,163. *2002* (official estimates): Boa Vista 4,661; Brava 6,678; Fogo 37,607; Maio 7,042; Sal 15,889; Santo Antão 47,312; São Nicolau 13,535; Santiago 247,947; São Vicente 69,837.

Density (2003): 113.7 per sq km.

Principal Towns (population at 2000 census): Praia (capital) 94,757; Mindelo 62,970. *Mid-2003* (UN estimate, incl. suburbs): Praia 107,045 (Source: UN, *World Urbanization Prospects: The 2003 Revision*).

Births, Marriages and Deaths (annual averages, 1995–2000, unless otherwise indicated): Birth rate 29.6 per 1,000 (2001); Registered marriages (1994) 1,200 (marriage rate 3.2 per 1,000); Death rate 5.8 per 1,000 (UN estimate). Sources: African Development Bank; and UN, *Demographic Yearbook* and *World Population Prospects: The 2002 Revision*.

Expectation of Life (WHO estimates, years at birth): 70.1 (males 66.6; females 72.9) in 2002. Source: WHO, *World Health Report*.

Economically Active Population (persons aged 10 years and over, 1990 census): Agriculture, hunting, forestry and fishing 29,876; Mining and quarrying 410; Manufacturing 5,520; Electricity, gas and water 883; Construction 22,722; Trade, restaurants and hotels 12,747; Transport, storage and communications 6,138; Financial, insurance, real estate and business services 821; Community, social and personal services 17,358; Activities not adequately defined 24,090; *Total labour force* 120,565 (males 75,786, females 44,779), including 31,049 unemployed persons (males 19,712, females 11,337) (Source: ILO). *2000 Census* (persons aged 10 years and over): Total employed 144,310; Unemployed 30,334; Total labour force 174,644. *Mid-2003* (FAO estimates): Agriculture, etc. 40,000; Total (incl. others) 190,000 (Source: FAO).

HEALTH AND WELFARE

Key Indicators

Total Fertility Rate (children per woman, 2002): 3.4.

Under-5 Mortality Rate (per 1,000 live births, 2003): 35.

Physicians (per 1,000 head, 2000): 0.38.

Hospital Beds (per 1,000 head, 2000): 1.60.

Health Expenditure (2001): US $ per head (PPP): 134.

Health Expenditure (2001): % of GDP: 3.7.

Health Expenditure (2001): public (% of total): 74.2.

Access to Water (% of persons, 2002): 80.

Access to Sanitation (% of persons, 2002): 42.

Human Development Index (2002): ranking: 105.

Human Development Index (2002): 0.717.
For sources and definitions, see explanatory note on p. vi.

AGRICULTURE, ETC.

Principal Crops (FAO estimates unless otherwise indicated, '000 metric tons, 2003): Maize 10,000 (unofficial figure); Potatoes 3.5; Sweet potatoes 4.0; Cassava 3.0; Sugar cane 14.0; Pulses 5.0; Coconuts 6.0; Cabbages 4.0; Tomatoes 4.5; Dry onions 1.6; Green beans 2.0; Cucumbers and gherkins 1.0; Bananas 6.0; Mangoes 4.5; Other fruits 4.5; Pimento and allspice 1.0. Source: FAO.

Livestock ('000 head, 2003): Cattle 21.8; Pigs 200.0 (FAO estimate); Sheep 9.2; Goats 112.3; Horses 0.5 (FAO estimate); Asses 14.0 (FAO estimate); Mules 1.8 (FAO estimate); Chickens 417. Source: FAO.

Livestock Products ('000 metric tons, 2003): Pig meat 7.0; Other meat 1.4; Cows' milk 4.8; Goats' milk 5.5; Hen eggs 1.6. Source: FAO.

Fishing (metric tons, live weight, 2002): Total catch 8,000 (FAO estimate) (Wahoo 552; Little tunny 108; Skipjack tuna 284; Yellowfin tuna 287). Source: FAO.

MINING

Production (estimates, metric tons, 2002): Salt (unrefined) 1,600. Clay, gypsum, limestone and volcanic rock were also produced, at unreported levels. Source: US Geological Survey.

INDUSTRY

Production (metric tons, 2001, unless otherwise indicated): Biscuits 348 (1990 figure); Bread 5,628 (1995 figure); Canned fish 200; Frozen fish 900; Flour 15,901 (1999 figure); Beer 4,104,546 litres (1999 figure); Soft drinks 922,714 litres (1996 figure); Cigarettes and tobacco 77 kg (1999 figure); Paint 628,243 kg (1997 figure); Footwear 670,676 pairs (1996 figure); Soap 1,371,045 kg (1999 figure); Electric energy 164.3m. kWh. Sources: mainly UN, *Industrial Commodity Statistics Yearbook*, and IMF, *Cape Verde: Statistical Appendix* (October 2001).

FINANCE

Currency and Exchange Rates: 100 centavos = 1 Cape Verde escudo; 1,000 escudos are known as a conto. *Sterling, Dollar and Euro Equivalents* (31 December 2004): £1 sterling = 156.36 escudos; US \$1 = 80.96 escudos; €1 = 110.27 escudos; 1,000 Cape Verde escudos = £6.39 = \$12.352 = €9.069. *Average Exchange Rate* (escudos per US dollar): 117.168 in 2002; 97.703 in 2003; 88.808 in 2004.

Budget ('000 million escudos, 2004, revised projections): *Revenue*: Taxation 17.18 (Taxes on income and profits 6.34, Taxes on international trade 3.88, Taxes on goods and services 1.67, Value-added tax 4.32, Other tax revenue 0.97); Non-tax revenue 2.19; Total 24,520 (incl. net lending 0.26, and external grants 4.88). *Expenditure*: Recurrent 18.52 (Wages and salaries 10.77, Acquisition of goods and services 1.66, Transfers and other subsidies 3.21, Other expenditures, Interest payments 2.07); Capital 9,730; Total 28.25. Source: IMF, *Cape Verde: Fourth Review Under the Three-Year Arrangement Under the Poverty Reduction and Growth Facility* (September 2004).

International Reserves (US \$ million at 31 December 2003): IMF special drawing rights 0.01; Foreign exchange 93.60; Total 93.61. Source: IMF, *International Financial Statistics*.

Money Supply (million escudos at 31 December 2003): Currency outside banks 6,515.6; Demand deposits at commercial banks 16,574.9; Total money (incl. others) 23,090.9. Source: IMF, *International Financial Statistics*.

Cost of Living (Consumer Price Index; base: 1989 = 100): 182.8 in 2001; 186.3 in 2002; 188.5 in 2003.

Expenditure on the Gross Domestic Product (million escudos at current prices, 2002): Government final consumption expenditure 19,698; Private final consumption expenditure 54,783; Gross fixed capital formation (incl. increase in stocks) 25,297; *Total domestic expenditure* 99,778; Exports of goods and services 22,883; *Less* Imports of goods and services 49,344; *GDP in purchasers' values* 73,317.

Gross Domestic Product by Economic Activity (million escudos at current prices, 2001): Agriculture, forestry and livestock 6,295; Fishing 594; Industry and energy 6,098; Construction 5,196; Commerce 10,088; Hotels 2,317; Transport and communications 12,198; Banks and insurance 3,624; Housing 4,062; Public service 9,312; Other services 1,968; *Sub-total* 61,751; Import taxes 7,041; *Less* Imputed bank service charges 2,097; *GDP at market prices* 66,695. Source: IMF, *Cape Verde: Statistical Appendix* (June 2003).

Balance of Payments (estimates, US \$ million, 2003): Exports of goods f.o.b. 52.83; Imports of goods f.o.b. -343.95; *Trade balance* -291.11; Exports of services 224.08; Imports of services -203.25; *Balance on goods and services* -270.29; Other income (net) -16.65; *Balance on goods, services and income* -286.93; Current transfers (net) 209.69; *Current balance* -77.25; Capital account (net) 21.07; Direct investment from abroad 14.78; Other capital (net) -9.24; Net errors and omissions -5.35; *Overall balance* -55.98. Source: IMF, *International Finance Statistics*.

EXTERNAL TRADE

Principal Commodities (distribution by SITC, US \$ million, 2001): *Imports c.i.f.*: Food and live animals 63.4 (Milk and cream 12.0, Cereals and cereal preparations 16.5, Vegetables and fruit 9.1, Sugar, sugar preparations and honey 7.8); Beverages and tobacco 15.4 (Alcoholic beverages 8.9); Mineral fuels, lubricants, etc. 13.9 (Refined petroleum 13.4); Basic manufactures 40.5 (Cement 8.6, Manufactures of metals 9.4); Machinery and transport equipment 68.7 (Power generating machinery 9.7, General industrial machinery and parts 8.4, Electric machinery and apparatus 10.8, Passenger vehicles 12.8); Miscellaneous manufactured articles 21.3; Total (incl. others) 247.5. *Exports f.o.b.*: Footwear 3.9; Miscellaneous manufactured articles 5.2 (Articles of apparel and clothing accessories 4.8); Total (incl. others) 9.8. Source: UN, *International Trade Statistics Yearbook*.

Principal Trading Partners (million escudos, 2003): *Imports c.i.f.*: Belgium 1,943.2; Brazil 922.0; Côte d'Ivoire 907.0; France 1,069.2; Italy 740.6; Netherlands 5,018.4; Portugal 16,576.6; Spain 906.0; USA 1,181.0; Total (incl. others) 34,235.2. *Exports f.o.b.*: Portugal 875.5; USA 278.6; Germany 13.4; Angola 10.0; Netherlands 4.8; Total (incl. others) 1,236.1.

TRANSPORT

Road Traffic (motor vehicles in use, 31 December 2001): Light vehicles 18,556; Heavy vehicles 3,924; Motorcycles 1,597.

Shipping: *Merchant Fleet* (registered at 31 December 2003): Number of vessels 41, total displacement ('000 grt) 20.9 (Source: Lloyd's Register-Fairplay, *World Fleet Statistics*). *International Seaborne Freight Traffic* (estimates, '000 metric tons, 1993): Goods loaded 144, goods unloaded 299 (Source: UN Economic Commission for Africa, *African Statistical Yearbook*).

Civil Aviation (traffic on scheduled services, 2001): Passengers carried 973,161; Cargo carried (tons) 5,372.

TOURISM

Tourist Arrivals by Country of Residence (2002): France 11,813; Germany 13,796; Italy 35,080; Portugal 34,292; South Africa 10,003; Spain 4,722; USA 1,665; Total (incl. others) 125,852.

Tourism Receipts (million escudos): 4,686.4 in 2000; 6,539.1 in 2001; 7,509.4 in 2002.

COMMUNICATIONS MEDIA

Radio Receivers* (1997): 73,000 in use.

Television Receivers† (2000): 2,000 in use.

Telephones† (2003): 71,700 main lines in use.

Mobile Cellular Telephones† (2003): 53,300 subscribers.

Facsimile Machines‡ (1996): 1,000 in use.

Internet Users† (2003): 20,400.

Non-daily Newspapers* (1996): 4 titles (average circulation 20,000 copies).

Book Production* (1989): 10 titles.
* Source: UNESCO, *Statistical Yearbook*.
† Source: International Telecommunication Union.
‡ Source: UN, *Statistical Yearbook*.

EDUCATION

Pre-primary (1986/87): 58 schools (1986/87); 136 teachers (1986/87); 19,879 pupils (2000/01).

Primary (2000/01): 370 schools (1990/91); 3,219 teachers (1997/98); 90,640 pupils.

Total Secondary (2002/03): 2,035 teachers; 49,131 pupils.

Higher (2000/01): 628 pupils.

Teacher Training: 25 teachers (1987/88); 889 pupils (1993/94).

Vocational Schools (1993/94): 94 teachers; 1,400 pupils. Source: mainly UNESCO, *Statistical Yearbook*.

Adult Literacy Rate (UNESCO estimates): 75.7% (males 85.4%; females 68.0) in 2002 (Source: UN Development Programme, *Human Development Report*).

Source: mainly Ministry of Education and Human Resources.

Directory

The Constitution

A new Constitution of the Republic of Cape Verde ('the Second Republic') came into force on 25 September 1992. The Constitution defines Cape Verde as a sovereign, unitary and democratic republic, guaranteeing respect for human dignity and recognizing the inviolable and inalienable rights of man as a fundament of humanity, peace and justice. It recognizes the equality of all citizens before the law, without distinction of social origin, social condition, economic status, race, sex, religion, political convictions or ideologies and promises transparency for all citizens in the practising of fundamental liberties. The Constitution gives assent to popular will, and has a fundamental objective in the realization of economic, political, social and cultural democracy and the construction of a society that is free, just and in solidarity.

The Head of State is the President of the Republic, who is elected by universal adult suffrage and must obtain two-thirds of the votes cast to win in the first round of the election. If no candidate secures the requisite majority, a new election is held within 21 days and contested by the two candidates who received the highest number of votes in the first round. Voting is conducted by secret ballot. Legislative power is vested in the Assembléia Nacional, which is also elected by universal adult suffrage. The Prime Minister is nominated by the Assembléia, to which he is responsible. On the recommendation of the Prime Minister, the President appoints the Council of Ministers, whose members must be elected deputies of the Assembléia. There are 17 local government councils, elected by universal suffrage for a period of five years.

A constitutional revision, adopted in July 1999, gave the President the right to dissolve the Assembléia Nacional, created a new advisory chamber (Conselho Económico e Social), and gave the State the right to adopt Crioulo as the country's second official language.

The Government

HEAD OF STATE

President: PEDRO DE VERONA RODRIGUES PIRES (elected 25 February 2001).

COUNCIL OF MINISTERS
(April 2005)

Prime Minister and Minister of Youth and Sports: JOSÉ MARIA PEREIRA NEVES.

Minister of State and of Infrastructure and Transport: MANUEL INOCÊNCIO SOUSA.

Minister of State and of Health: BASÍLIO MOSSO RAMOS.

Minister of Foreign Affairs, Co-operation and Communities: VÍCTOR MANUEL BARBOSA BORGES.

Minister of Justice: MARIA CRISTINA LOPES ALMEIDA FONTES LIMA.

Minister of Internal Administration: JÚLIO LOPES CORREIA.

Minister of Finance and Planning: JOÃO ANTÓNIO PINTO COELHO SERRA.

Minister of Defence and Parliamentary Affairs: ARMINDO CIPRIANO MAURÍCIO.

Minster of Culture: MANUEL MONTEIRO DA VEIGA.

Minister of the Environment, Agriculture and Fisheries: MARIA MADALENA DE BRITO NEVES.

Minister of Education and Human Resources: FILOMENA DE FÁTIMA RIBEIRO VIEIRA MARTINS.

Minister of Labour and Solidarity: SIDÓNIO FONTES LIMA MONTEIRO.

Minister of the Economy, Growth and Competitiveness: JOÃO PEREIRA SILVA.

Minister of State Reform and Public Administration: ILÍDIO ALEXANDRE DA CRUZ.

Minister of Social Communication and the Presidency of the Council of Ministers: JOÃO BAPTISTA PEREIRA.

Secretary of State for Youth and Sports: AMÉRICO SABINO SOARES NASCIMENTO.

Secretary of State for Decentralization and Regional Development: RAMIRO ANDRADE ALVES AZEVEDO.

Secretary of State for Foreign Affairs: DOMINGOS DIAS PEREIRA MASCARENHAS.

MINISTRIES

Office of the President: Presidência da República, CP 100, Plateau, Praia, Santiago; tel. 2616555; fax 2614356; internet www.presidenciarepublica.cv.

Office of the Prime Minister: Gabinete do Primeiro Ministro, Palácio do Governo, Várzea, CP 16, Praia, Santiago; tel. 2610513; fax 2613099; e-mail gab.imprensa@gpm.gov.cv; internet www.governo.cv.

Ministry of Culture: Praia, Santiago; tel. 2610567.

Ministry of Defence and Parliamentary Affairs: Palácio do Governo, Várzea, Praia, Santiago; tel. 2610344; fax 2612081; e-mail armindo.mauricio@palgov.cv.

Ministry of the Economy, Growth and Competitiveness: Praia, Santiago.

Ministry of Education and Human Resources: Palácio do Governo, Várzea, CP 111, Praia, Santiago; tel. 2610509; fax 2612764; internet www.minedu.cv.

Ministry of the Environment, Agriculture and Fisheries: Ponta Belém, Praia, Santiago; tel. 2615713; fax 2614054.

Ministry of Finance and Planning: 107 Avda Amílcar Cabral, CP 30, Praia, Santiago; tel. 2607400; internet ww.mf.cv.

Ministry of Foreign Affairs, Co-operation and Communities: Palácio das Comunidades, Achada de Santo António, Praia, Santiago; tel. 2615727; fax 2616262; e-mail mne@gov.cv.

Ministry of Health: Palácio do Governo, Várzea, Praia, Santiago; tel. 2610501.

Ministry of Infrastructure and Transport: Ponta Belém, Praia, Santiago; tel. 2615709; fax 2614141; e-mail margarida.lobo@mih.gov.cv.

Ministry of Internal Administration: Praia, Santiago.

Ministry of Justice: Rua Serpa Pinto, CP 205, Praia, Santiago; tel. 2623257; fax 2623261.

Ministry of Labour and Solidarity: Praia, Santiago.

Ministry of Social Communication and the Presidency of the Council of Ministers: Praia, Santiago.

Ministry of State Reform and Public Administration: Achada de Santo Antonio, Praia, Santiago; tel. 2622802; internet www.sereap.cv.

President and Legislature

PRESIDENT

Presidential Election, First ballot, 11 February 2001

Candidate	Votes	% of votes
Pedro Verona Rodrigues Pires (PAICV) .	61,389	46.51
Carlos Alberto de Carvalho Veiga (MPD) .	60,472	45.82
Jorge Carlos de Almeida Fonseca (PCD) .	5,182	3.93
David Hopffer de Cordeiro Almada (Ind.) .	4,936	3.74
Total	131,979	100.00

Second ballot, 25 February 2001

Candidate		Votes	% of votes
Pedro Verona Rodrigues Pires (PAICV)	.	75,828	50.01
Carlos Alberto de Carvalho Veiga (MPD)	.	75,811	49.99
Total		151,639	100.00

ASSEMBLÉIA NACIONAL

Assembléia Nacional: Achada de Santo António, CP 20 A, Praia, Santiago; tel. 2608000; fax 2622660; e-mail an-cv@cvtelecom.cv; internet www.parlamento.cv.

Speaker: ARISTIDES RAIMUNDO LIMA.

Legislative Elections, 14 January 2001

Party	Votes	% of votes	Seats
Partido Africano da Independência de Cabo Verde (PAICV)	67,862	49.5	40
Movimento para a Democracia (MPD)	55,581	40.5	30
Aliança Democrática para a Mudança (ADM)*	8,382	6.1	2
Partido da Renovação Democrática (PRD) . . .	4,644	3.4	—
Partido Socialista Democrático (PSD)	622	0.5	—
Total	137,091	100.0	72

*An alliance of the Partido da Convergência Democrática (PCD), the Partido de Trabalho e Solidariedade (PTS) and the União Caboverdiana Independente e Democrática—Partido Democrata Cristão (UCID—PDC), which disbanded following the elections.

Political Organizations

Movimento para a Democracia (MPD): Achada Santo António, CP 90A, Praia, Santiago; tel. 2614082; fax 2614122; e-mail webmaster@mpd.cv; internet www.mpd.cv; f. 1990; advocates administrative decentralization; governing party since Jan. 1991; Chair. AGOSTINHO LOPES.

Partido Africano da Independência de Cabo Verde (PAICV): Avda Amílcar Cabral, CP 22, Praia, Santiago; tel. 2612720; fax 2611410; internet www.paicv.org; f. 1956 as the Partido Africano da Independência do Guiné e Cabo Verde (PAIGC); name changed in 1981, following the 1980 coup in Guinea-Bissau; sole authorized political party 1975–90; Pres. JOSÉ MARIA NEVES; Sec.-Gen. ARISTIDES LIMA.

Partido da Convergência Democrática (PCD): Praia, Santiago; f. 1994 by fmr mems of the MPD; Pres. (vacant).

Partido da Renovação Democrática (PRD): Praia, Santiago; f. 2000 by fmr mems of the MPD; Pres. SIMÃO MONTEIRO.

Partido Socialista Democrático (PSD): Praia, Santiago; f. 1992; Sec.-Gen. JOÃO ALÉM.

Partido de Trabalho e Solidariedade (PTS): Praia, Santiago; f. 1998; Interim Leader ISAÍAS RODRIGUES.

União Caboverdiana Independente e Democrática—Partido Democrata Cristão (UCID—PDC): Praia, Santiago; f. 1974 by emigrants opposed to the PAICV; obtained legal recognition in 1991; name changed from UCID in 2001; Pres. MANUEL RODRIGUES.

Diplomatic Representation

EMBASSIES IN CAPE VERDE

Angola: Achada de Santo António, Praia, Santiago; tel. 2621296; fax 2623234; Ambassador JOSÉ AUGUSTO CÉSAR 'KILUANGE'.

Brazil: Chã de Areia 2, CP 93, Praia, Santiago; tel. 2615607; fax 2615609; e-mail emb.brasil@cvtelecom.cv; Ambassador VITOR CANDIDO PAIM GUBATO.

China, People's Republic: Achada de Santo António, CP 8, Praia, Santiago; tel. 2623029; fax 2623047; e-mail chinaemb_cv@mfa.gov.cn; Ambassador SUN RONGMAO.

Cuba: Achada de Santo António, Praia, Santiago; tel. 2615597; fax 2623720; e-mail ecubacpv@cvtelecom.cv; Ambassador PABLO REIS DOMINGUES.

France: Achada de Santo António, CP 192, Praia, Santiago; tel. 2615591; fax 2615590; e-mail fransula@cvtelecom.cv; internet www.ambafrance-cv.org; Ambassador JACQUES BUGUET.

Portugal: Avda OUA, Achada de Santo António, CP 160, Praia, Santiago; tel. 2626097; fax 2613222; e-mail emb.port@cvtelecom.cv; Ambassador FRANCISCO RIBEIRO TELLES.

Russia: Achada de Santo António, CP 31, Praia, Santiago; tel. 2622739; fax 2622738; e-mail embrus@cvtelecom.cv; Ambassador VLADIMIR E. PETUKHOV.

Senegal: Rua Abílio Macedo, Plateau, Praia, Santiago; tel. 2615221; e-mail silcarneyni@hotmail.com; Ambassador SILCARNEYNI GUEYE.

USA: Rua Abílio Macedo 81, Praia, Santiago; tel. 2615616; fax 2611355; internet www.praia.usembassy.gov; Ambassador DONALD C. JOHNSON.

Judicial System

Supremo Tribunal de Justiça

Gabinete do Juiz Presidente, Rua Cesário de Lacerda, (Edifício dos Correios), CP 117, Praia, Santiago; tel. 2615810; fax 2611751; e-mail stj@supremo.gov.cv; internet www.stj.cv.

f. 1975; the highest court; Pres. BENFEITO MOSSO RAMOS.

Attorney-General: FRANQUILIM AFONSO FURTADO.

There were plans to create a Constitutional Court in 2005.

Religion

CHRISTIANITY

At 31 December 2002 there were an estimated 550,193 adherents of the Roman Catholic Church, representing 93.1% of the total population. Protestant churches, among which the Church of the Nazarene is the most prominent, represent about 1% of the population.

The Roman Catholic Church

Cape Verde comprises two dioceses, directly responsible to the Holy See. The Bishops participate in the Episcopal Conference of Senegal, Mauritania, Cape Verde and Guinea-Bissau, currently based in Senegal.

Bishop of Mindelo: Rt Rev. ARLINDO GOMES FURTADO.

Bishop of Santiago de Cabo Verde: Rt Rev. PAULINO DO LIVRAMENTO ÉVORA, Avda Amílcar Cabral, Largo 5 de Outubro, CP 7600, Praia, Santiago; tel. 2611119; fax 2612126.

The Anglican Communion

Cape Verde forms part of the diocese of The Gambia, within the Church of the Province of West Africa. The Bishop is resident in Banjul, The Gambia.

Other Christian Churches

Church of the Nazarene: District Office, Avda Amílcar Cabral, Plateau, Praia, Santiago; tel. 2613611.

Other churches represented in Cape Verde include the Church of Assembly of God, the Church of Jesus Christ of Latter-day Saints, the Evangelical Baptist Church, the Maná Church, the New Apostolic Church, the Seventh-day Adventist Church and the Universal Church of the Kingdom of God.

BAHÁ'Í FAITH

National Spiritual Assembly: Rua Madragoa, Plateau, Praia, Santiago; tel. 2617739.

The Press

Agaviva: Mindelo, São Vicente; tel. 2312121; f. 1991; monthly; Editor GERMANO ALMEIDA; circ. 4,000.

Boletim Oficial da República de Cabo Verde: Imprensa Nacional, CP 113, Praia, Santiago; tel. 2614150; e-mail incv@cvtelecom.cv; weekly; official announcements.

O Cidadão: Praça Dr António Aurélio Gonçalves 2, CP 669, Mindelo, São Vicente; tel. 2325024; fax 2325022; e-mail cidadao@caboverde.zzn.com; internet www.hostultra.com/~caboverde/cidadao/; Editor JOSÉ MÁRIO CORREIA.

Contacto: CP 89C, Praia, Santiago; tel. 2615752; fax 2611442; f. 1993; quarterly; economic bulletin publ. by Centro de Promoção

Turística, de Investimento Externo e das Exportações (PROMEX); Co-ordinator MANUELA GARCIA; circ. 1,500.

Expresso das Ilhas: Santiago; internet www.expressodasilhas.cv; f. 2001 by the MPD; weekly; Dir FERNANDO MONTEIRO.

Horizonte: Achada de Santo António, CP 40, Praia, Santiago; tel. 2622447; fax 2623330; e-mail infopress@cvtelecom.cv; f. 1999; daily; pro-Government; Editor FERNANDO MONTEIRO; circ. 5,000.

Raízes: CP 98, Praia, Santiago; f. 1977; quarterly; cultural review; Editor ARNALDO FRANÇA; circ. 1,500.

A Semana: Rotunda do Palmarejo, CP 36-C, Praia, Santiago; tel. 2629860; fax 2628661; e-mail jornalsemana@mail.cvtelecom.cv; internet www.asemana.cv; weekly; independent; Editor FILOMENA SILVA; circ. 5,000.

Terra Nova: Rua Guiné-Bissau 1, CP 166, Mindelo, São Vicente; tel. 2322442; fax 2321475; e-mail terranova@cabonet.cv; f. 1975; monthly; Roman Catholic; Editor P. ANTÓNIO FIDALGO BARROS; circ. 3,000.

There is also an online newspaper, Visão News (www.visaonews.com), based in the USA.

NEWS AGENCIES

CaboPress: Achado Santo António, CP 40/A, Praia, Santiago; tel. 2615557; fax 2615555; f. 1991.

Inforpress: Achada de Santo António, CP 40/A, Praia, Santiago; tel. 2623025; fax 2623023; internet www.inforpress.cv; f. 1988 as Cabopress; Pres. JOSÉ MARIA ALMEIDA.

Foreign Bureaux

Agence France Presse: CP 26/118, Praia, Santiago; tel. 2613890.

Agência Lusa de Informação (Portugal): Prainha, Praia, Santiago; tel. 2613519; Bureau Chief FRANCISCO FONTES.

Inter Press Service (IPS) (Italy): CP 14, Mindelo, São Vicente; tel. 2314550; Rep. JUAN A. COLOMA.

Publishers

Instituto Caboverdeano do Livro e do Disco (ICL): Centro Cultural, CP 158, Praia, Santiago; tel. 2612346; books, journals, music.

GOVERNMENT PUBLISHING HOUSE

Imprensa Nacional: CP 113, Praia, Santiago; tel. 2614209; Admin. JOÃO DE PINA.

Broadcasting and Communications

TELECOMMUNICATIONS

Cabo Verde Telecom: Rua Cabo Verde Telecom, CP 220, Várzea, Praia, Santiago; tel. 2609200; fax 2613725; e-mail cvtelecom@cvtelecom.cv; internet www.cvtelecom.cv; f. 1995; Chief Exec. ANTÓNIO PIRES CORREIA.

Cabo Verde Telecom was the sole telephone, cable and internet provider, however, in 2004 the Government announced plans to open the telecommunications market by 2010. It was expected that a licence for a second provider would be granted in 2005.

BROADCASTING

Rádio Televisão de Cabo Verde (RTC): Rua 13 de Janeiro, CP 01A, Achada de Santo António, Praia, Santiago; tel. 2623051; fax 2623206; e-mail rtc@mail.cvtelecom.cv; govt-controlled; 18 radio transmitters and five solar relay radio transmitters; FM transmission only; radio broadcasts in Portuguese and Creole for 24 hours daily; one television transmitter and seven relay television transmitters; television broadcasts in Portuguese and Creole for eight hours daily with co-operation of RTPI (Portugal); Pres. MARCOS OLIVEIRA.

Televisão de Cabo Verde: Praia, Santiago; sole television broadcaster; part of Radio Televisão de Cabo Verde; Dir ORLANDO RODRIGUES.

Praia FM: Rua Visconde de S. Januario 19, 4° andar, CP 276-C, Praia, Santiago; tel. 2616356; fax 2616357; e-mail praiafm@cvtelecom.cv; internet www.praiafm.biz; Dir GIORDANO CUSTÓDIO.

Rádio Comercial: Achada Santo António, Prédio Gomes Irmãos 3° esq., CP 507, Praia, Santiago; tel. 2623156; fax 2622413; e-mail

multimedia.rc@cvtelecom.cv; internet www.radiocomercial.net; f. 1997; Admin. HENRIQUE PIRES; Dir CARLOS FILIPE GONÇALVES.

Rádio Educativa de Cabo Verde: Achada de Santo António, Praia, Santiago; tel. 2611161.

Rádio Morabeza: Rua da Guiné Bissau 3A, CP 456, Mindelo, São Vicente; tel. 2324431; fax 2300069; e-mail radiomorabeza@cvtelecom.cv.

Rádio Nacional de Cabo Verde (RNCV): CP 26, Praia, Santiago; tel. 2613729.

Rádio Nova—Emissora Cristã de Cabo Verde: CP 166, Mindelo, São Vicente; tel. 2322082; fax 2321475; internet www.radionovaonline.com; f. 2002; Roman Catholic station; Dir ANTÓNIO FIDALGO BARROS.

Voz de São Vicente: CP 29, Mindelo, São Vicente; fax 2311006; f. 1974; govt-controlled; Dir JOSÉ FONSECA SOARES.

Radiotelevisão Portuguesa International and Canal Plus International began broadcasting in 1995.

Finance

(cap. = capital; res = reserves; dep. = deposits; m. = million; brs = branches; amounts in Cape Verde escudos)

BANKING

Central Bank

Banco de Cabo Verde (BCV): 117 Avda Amílcar Cabral, CP 101, Praia, Santiago; tel. 2607080; fax 2617095; e-mail mcostabcv.cv; internet www.bcv.cv; f. 1976; bank of issue; cap. 200.0m., res 1,505.2m., dep. 11,610.9m. (Dec. 2003); Gov. OLAVO AVELINO GARCIA CORREIA.

Other Banks

Banco Caboverdiano de Negócios (BCN): Rua Justino Lopes 1, CP 593, Praia, Santiago; tel. 2611662; fax 2614006; e-mail btacv@cvtelecom.cv; f. 1996 as Banco Totta e Açores (Cabo Verde); renamed as above in 2004; owned by a Cape Verdian consortium; cap. €2.7m. (Oct. 2004); 3 brs.

Banco Comercial do Atlântico (BCA): Avda Amílcar Cabral, CP 474, Praia, Santiago; tel. 2615535; fax 2613235; e-mail bcdan@cvtelecom.cv; internet www.bca.cv; f. 1993; privatized in 2000; main commercial bank; cap. 1,000m., res 398.0m., dep. 35,092.0m. (Dec. 2003); Pres. MIGUEL AFONSO; Chair. JOÃO HENRIQUE REAL PEREIRA; 23 brs.

Banco Interatlântico: Avda Cidade de Lisboa, CP 131A, Praia, Santiago; tel. 2614008; fax 2614712; e-mail cdgcv@cvtelecom.cv; f. 1999; Pres. JOÃO HENRIQUE REAL PEREIRA.

Caixa Económica de Cabo Verde (CECV): Avda Cidade de Lisboa, CP 199, Praia, Santiago; tel. 2615561; fax 2615560; e-mail cecv@caixaeconomica.cv; internet www.caixaeconomica.cv; f. 1928; privatized in 1999; commercial bank; cap. 348.0m., res 814.7m., dep. 12,890.8m. (Dec. 2003); Pres. FRANCISCO JOSÉ GONÇALVES SIMÕES; 11 brs.

STOCK EXCHANGE

Bolsa de Valores de Cabo Verde: Achada de Santo António, CP 115A, Praia, Santiago; tel. 2603030; fax 2603035; e-mail bcv@mail.cvtelecom.cv; f. 1998; not operating, however, there were plans to reopen in 2005.

INSURANCE

Companhia Caboverdiana de Seguros (IMPAR): Avda Amílcar Cabral, CP 469, Praia, Santiago; tel. and fax 2613765; e-mail impar@cvtelecom.cv; f. 1991; Pres. Dr CORSINO ANTÓNIO FORTES.

Garantia Companhia de Seguros: Rua Guerra Mendes, CP 138, Praia, Santiago; tel. 2615661; fax 2612555; e-mail garantia@cvtelecom.cv; f. 1991; privatized in 2000; Pres. JOÃO HENRIQUE REAL PEREIRA.

Trade and Industry

GOVERNMENT AGENCIES

Agencia Caboverdiana de Investimentos e Exportações (ACIE): Praia, Santiago; f. 2004 to replace the Centro de Promoção Turística, de Investimento Externo e das Exportações (PROMEX);

promotes public-private investment partnerships in infrastructure and tourism.

Comissão de Investimento Externo e Empresa Franca (CIEF): Praia, Santiago; foreign investment commission.

Gabinete de Apoio à Reestruturação do Sector Empresarial do Estado (GARSEE; Cabo Verde Privatization): Praia, Santiago; tel. 2614748; fax 2612334; e-mail cvprivatization@mail.cvtelecom.cv; bureau in charge of planning and supervising restructuring and divestment of public enterprises; Project Dir Dr SÉRGIO CENTEIO.

DEVELOPMENT ORGANIZATION

Instituto Nacional de Investigação e Desenvolvimento Agrário (INIDA): CP 84, Praia, Santiago; tel. 2711147; fax 2711133; e-mail inida@inida.gov.cv; f. 1979; research and training on agricultural issues.

TRADE ASSOCIATION

Associação para Promoção de Pequenos Empresários (APME): Fazenda, Praia, Santiago; tel. 2606056.

CHAMBERS OF COMMERCE

Câmara de Comércio, Indústria e Serviços de Barlavento (CCISB): Rua da Luz 33, CP 728, Mindelo, São Vicente; tel. 2328495; fax 2328496; e-mail camara.com@cvtelecom.cv; f. 1996; Pres. MANUEL J. MONTEIRO.

Câmara de Comércio, Indústria e Serviços de Sotavento (CCISS): Avda Andrade Corvo, Edificio Shopping Moeda 2° andar, Praia, Santiago; tel. 2615352; fax 2617235; e-mail cciss@cvtelecom.cv.

STATE INDUSTRIAL ENTERPRISES

Empresa Nacional de Avicultura, SARL (ENAVI): Tira Chapéu Zona Industrial, CP 135, Praia; tel. 2627268; fax 2628441; e-mail enavi@cvtelecom.cv; poultry farming.

Empresa Nacional de Combustíveis, SARL (ENACOL): Largo John Miller's, CP 1, Mindelo, São Vicente; tel. 2323290; fax 2323425; e-mail enacolsv@mail.cvtelecom.cv; internet www.enacol.cv; f. 1979; sales 1,592m. escudos (1994); supervises import and distribution of petroleum; Dir Dr MÁRIO A. RODRIGUES.

Empresa Nacional de Produtos Farmacêuticos, SARL (EMPROFAC): Tira Chapéu Zona Industrial, CP 59, Praia, Santiago; tel. 2627895; fax 2627899; e-mail emprofac@cvtelecom.cv; f. 1979; state monopoly of pharmaceuticals and medical imports.

UTILITIES

Electricity and Water

Empresa de Electricidade e Água, SA (Electra): Avda Baltazar Lopes Silva 10-1, CP 137, Mindelo, São Vicente; tel. 2303030; fax 2324446; e-mail electra@electra.cv; internet www.electra.cv; f. 1982; privatized in 1999; Pres. RUI OLIVEIRA SANTOS.

CO-OPERATIVES

Instituto Nacional das Cooperativas: Fazenda, CP 218, Praia, Santiago; tel. 2614112; fax 2613959; central co-operative org.

TRADE UNIONS

Confederação Caboverdiana dos Sindicatos Livres (CCSL): Rua Dr Júlio Abreu, CP 155, Praia, Santiago; tel. and fax 2616319; e-mail ccsl@cvtelecom.cv; Sec.-Gen. JOSÉ MANUEL VAZ.

Sindicato dos Transportes, Comunicações e Turismo (STCT): Praia, Santiago; tel. 2616338.

União Nacional dos Trabalhadores de Cabo Verde—Central Sindical (UNTC—CS): Avda Cidade de Praia, CP 123, Praia, Santiago; tel. 2614305; fax 2613629; e-mail untc@mail.cvtelecom.cv; internet www.untc-cs.org; f. 1978; Chair. JÚLIO ASCENÇÃO SILVA.

Transport

ROADS

In 2004 there were an estimated 2,250 km of roads, of which 1,750 km were paved. In 2005 the Government planned to allocate €635m. to upgrade the road network, including building a ring road around Praia.

SHIPPING

Cargo-passenger ships call regularly at Porto Grande, Mindelo, on São Vicente, and Praia, on Santiago. In 2005 there were plans to upgrade the ports at Praia, Sal, São Vicente and Porto Novo (Santo Antão). There are small ports on the other inhabited islands. Cape Verde's registered merchant fleet at 31 December 2003 consisted of 41 vessels, totalling 20,900 grt.

Comissão de Gestão dos Transportes Marítimos de Cabo Verde: CP 153, São Vicente; tel. 2314979; fax 2312055.

Empresa Nacional de Administração dos Portos, SA (ENAPOR, SA): Avda Marginal, CP 82, Mindelo, São Vicente; tel. 2324414; fax 2324337; e-mail enapor@mail.cvtelecom.cv; internet www.enapor.cv; f. 1982; Chair. and Man. Dir FRANKLIM DO ROSÁRIO SPENCER.

Cape Verde National Shipping Line, SARL (Cs Line): Avda Cidade de Lisboa, CP 000, Praia, Santiago; tel. 2611206; fax 2611175; e-mail jose.lopes@cslinecv.com; internet www.cslinecv.com.

Companhia Caboverdiana de Navegação: Rua Cristiano Sena Barcelos 3–5, Mindelo, São Vicente; tel. 2322852.

Companhia de Navegação Estrela Negra: Avda 5 de Julho 17, CP 91, Mindelo, São Vicente; tel. 2325423; fax 2315382.

Linhas Marítimas Caboverdianas (LINMAC): CP 357, Praia, Santiago; tel. 2614352; fax 2613715; Dir ESTHER SPENCER.

Seage Agência de Navegação de Cabo Verde: Avda Cidade de Lisboa, CP 232, Praia, Santiago; tel. 2615758; fax 2612524; e-mail seage@cvtelecom.cv; f. 1986; Chair. CÉSAR MANUEL SEMEDO LOPES.

CIVIL AVIATION

The Amílcar Cabral international airport, at Espargos, on Sal island, can accommodate aircraft of up to 50 tons and 1m. passengers per year. The airport's facilities were expanded during the 1990s. A second international airport, under construction on Santiago, capable of accommodating long-range aircraft, was due to open in March 2005. There is also a small airport on each of the other inhabited islands. The airport on São Vicente was upgraded to international capacity in 2000. Plans were also under way for the construction of two further international airports, on Boa Vista and São Vicente.

Empresa Nacional de Aeroportos e Segurança AEREA, EP (ASA): Aeroporto Amílcar Cabral, CP 58, Ilha do Sal; tel. 2412626; fax 2411570; e-mail pca@asa.cv; internet www.asa.cv; airports and aircraft security; Pres. MÁRIO LOPES.

Transportes Aéreos de Cabo Verde (TACV): Avda Amílcar Cabral, CP 1, Praia, Santiago; tel. 2615813; fax 2613585; e-mail cv.airline@milton.cvtelecom.cv; internet www.tacv.cv; f. 1958; internal services connecting the nine inhabited islands; also operates regional services to Senegal, The Gambia and Guinea-Bissau, and long-distance services to Europe and the USA; privatization scheduled for 2005; Dir ALFREDO CARVALHO.

A private company, Inter Island Airlines, offers flights between the islands of Cape Verde.

Tourism

The islands of Santiago, Santo Antão, Fogo and Brava offer attractive mountain scenery. There are extensive beaches on the islands of Santiago, Sal, Boa Vista and Maio. In 2000 there were 88 hotels in Cape Verde. In 2002 there were some 2,305 rooms in Cape Verde (65% of these in hotels, the remainder in pensions and hostels), with 4,241 beds. Some 134,169 tourists visited Cape Verde during 2001 and tourism receipts totalled 6,539.1m. escudos in that year, increasing to 7,509.4m. escudos in 2002. The sector is undergoing rapid expansion, under the aegis of the Agencia Caboverdiana de Investimentos e Exportações (ACIE), with development in a number of Zonas de Desenvolvimento Turístico Integral, established in 1994. In late 2003 the Government began steps to have Fogo, which contains the only live volcano on Cape Verde, designated a UNESCO world heritage site. Plans were unveiled in March 2004 to promote the island of Santa Luzia as an eco-tourism destination. Construction of a large tourist resort on Santiago, expected to cost €550m., commenced in early 2005. Tourist arrivals are projected to increase to about 400,000 annually by 2008. It was hoped that the planned expansion of Cape Verde's airports would lead to an increase in tourist numbers.

THE CENTRAL AFRICAN REPUBLIC

Introductory Survey

Location, Climate, Language, Religion, Flag, Capital

The Central African Republic is a land-locked country in the heart of equatorial Africa. It is bordered by Chad to the north, by Sudan to the east, by the Democratic Republic of the Congo (formerly Zaire) and the Republic of the Congo to the south and by Cameroon to the west. The climate is tropical, with an average annual temperature of 26°C (79°F) and heavy rainfall in the south-western forest areas. The national language is Sango, but French is the official language and another 68 languages and dialects have been identified. It is estimated that about one-half of the population are Christian; another 15% are Muslims, while animist beliefs are held by an estimated 24%. The national flag (proportions 3 by 5) has four equal horizontal stripes, of blue, white, green and yellow, divided vertically by a central red stripe, with a five-pointed yellow star in the hoist corner of the blue stripe. The capital is Bangui.

Recent History

The former territory of Ubangi-Shari (Oubangui-Chari), within French Equatorial Africa, became the Central African Republic (CAR) on achieving self-government in December 1958. David Dacko led the country to full independence became the first President, on 13 August 1960. In 1962 a one-party state was established, with the ruling Mouvement d'évolution sociale de l'Afrique noire (MESAN) as the sole authorized party. President Dacko was overthrown on 31 December 1965 by a military coup, which brought to power his cousin, Col (later Marshal) Jean-Bédel Bokassa, Commander-in-Chief of the armed forces.

In January 1966 Bokassa formed a new Government, rescinded the Constitution and dissolved the legislature, the Assemblée nationale. Bokassa, who became Life President in March 1972 and Marshal of the Republic in May 1974, forestalled several alleged coup attempts and employed increasingly repressive measures against dissidents. From January 1975 to April 1976 Elisabeth Domitien, the Vice-President of MESAN, was Prime Minister; she was the first woman to hold this position in any African country.

In September 1976 the Council of Ministers was replaced by the Council for the Central African Revolution, and former President Dacko was appointed personal adviser to the President. In December the Republic was renamed the Central African Empire (CAE), and a new Constitution was instituted. Bokassa was proclaimed the first Emperor, and Dacko became his Personal Counsellor. The Imperial Constitution provided for the establishment of an Assemblée nationale, but no elections were held. In May 1978 Bokassa reorganized the army leadership and strengthened its powers, however, on 20 September 1979, while Bokassa was in Libya, Dacko deposed him in a bloodless coup, which received considerable support from France. The country was again designated a republic, with Dacko as its President and Henri Maidou as Vice-President.

President Dacko's principal concern was to establish order and economic stability, but his Government encountered opposition, particularly from students who objected to the continuation in office of CAE ministers. In August 1980 Dacko accepted demands for the dismissal of both Maidou and the Prime Minister, Bernard Christian Ayandho. Bokassa, at that time in exile in Côte d'Ivoire (and subsequently in Paris), was sentenced to death *in absentia* in December. In February 1981 a new Constitution, providing for a multi-party system, was approved by referendum and promulgated by Dacko. He won a presidential election in March, amid allegations of electoral malpractice, and was sworn in for a six-year term in April. Political tension intensified in subsequent months, and on 1 September the Chief of Staff of the Armed Forces, Gen. André Kolingba, deposed Dacko in a bloodless coup. Kolingba was declared President, and a ruling Comité militaire pour le redressement national (CMRN) and an all-military Government were formed. All political activity was suspended.

In March 1982 the exiled leader of the banned Mouvement pour la libération du peuple centrafricain (MLPC), Ange-Félix Patassé, returned to Bangui and was implicated in an unsuccessful coup attempt. Patassé, who had been Prime Minister

under Bokassa in 1976–78 and who had contested the 1981 presidential election, sought asylum in the French embassy in Bangui, from where he was transported to exile in Togo. A visit by President Mitterrand of France to the CAR in October 1982 normalized bilateral relations, which had been strained by French support for Patassé. Domestic opposition to Kolingba's regime continued, and in August 1983 elements of the three main opposition parties formed a united front.

In September 1985 the CMRN was dissolved and, for the first time since Kolingba's assumption of power, civilians were appointed to the Council of Ministers. In early 1986 a specially convened commission drafted a new Constitution, which provided for the creation of a sole legal political party, the Rassemblement démocratique centrafricain (RDC), and conferred extensive executive powers on the President, while defining a predominantly advisory role for the legislature. At a referendum in November some 91.17% of voters approved the draft Constitution and granted Kolingba a mandate to serve a further six-year term as President. The Council of Ministers was reorganized in December to include a majority of civilians. The RDC was officially established in February 1987, with Kolingba as founding President, and elections to the new Assemblée nationale took place in July, at which 142 candidates, all nominated by the RDC, contested the 52 seats.

In October 1986 Bokassa returned unexpectedly to the CAR and was immediately arrested. His new trial opened in November and continued until June 1987, when the former Emperor was sentenced to death, having been convicted on charges of murder, conspiracy to murder, the illegal detention of prisoners and embezzlement. In February 1988 Kolingba commuted the sentence to one of life imprisonment with hard labour.

The appointment during 1988 of former associates of Bokassa, Dacko and Patassé to prominent public offices appeared to represent an attempt by Kolingba to consolidate national unity. In August 1989, however, 12 opponents of his regime, including members of the Front patriotique oubanguien-Parti du travail and the leader of the Rassemblement populaire pour la reconstruction de la Centrafrique, Brig.-Gen. (later Gen.) François Bozizé, were arrested in Benin, where they had been living in exile, and extradited to the CAR. Bozizé was subsequently found guilty of complicity in the 1982 coup attempt.

In 1990 opposition movements exerted pressure on the Government to introduce a plural political system. In December the Executive Council of the RDC recommended a review of the Constitution and the re-establishment of the premiership. Accordingly, in March 1991 Edouard Franck, a former Minister of State at the Presidency, was appointed Prime Minister, and in July the Assemblée nationale approved a constitutional amendment providing for the establishment of a multi-party political system. Kolingba resigned from the presidency of the RDC in the following month, in order to remain 'above parties'. In December Kolingba pardoned Bozizé.

Kolingba convened a Grand National Debate in August 1992, but it was boycotted by the influential Concertation des forces démocratiques (CFD), an alliance of opposition groupings, which announced that it would only participate in a multi-party national conference with sovereign powers. At the end of August the Assemblée nationale approved legislation in accordance with decisions taken by the Grand National Debate: constitutional amendments provided for the strict separation of executive, legislative and judicial powers, and Kolingba was granted temporary powers to rule by decree until the election of a new multi-party legislature. Concurrent legislative and presidential elections commenced in October, but were suspended by presidential decree and subsequently annulled by the Supreme Court, owing to alleged sabotage of the electoral process. In December Franck resigned as Prime Minister and was replaced by Gen. Timothée Malendoma, the leader of the Forum civique.

In February 1993 Malendoma, who had accused Kolingba of curtailing his powers, was dismissed from the premiership and replaced by Enoch Derant Lakoué, the leader of the Parti social-démocrate. In response to mounting pressure from both the opposition and the French Government, two rounds of concurrent legislative and presidential elections were held in late August and mid-September. The MLPC won 34 of the 85 seats in the Assemblée nationale, while the RDC, in second place, secured 13 seats. Patassé, the MLPC leader and former Prime Minister, was elected President, winning 52.47% of the votes cast at a second round of voting. The seven other presidential candidates included Kolingba, Prof. Abel Goumba (the leader of the CFD) and former President Dacko. In late August Kolingba attempted to delay the publication of the election results by issuing two decrees that modified the electoral code and altered the composition of the Supreme Court; however, the decrees were revoked, after the French Government threatened to suspend all co-operation with the CAR in protest.

In September 1993 Bokassa was released from prison under a general amnesty for convicts; however, the former Emperor was banned for life from participating in elections and demoted from the military rank of marshal. He died in November 1996.

In October 1993 Patassé was inaugurated as President. Soon afterwards he appointed Jean-Luc Mandaba, the Vice-President of the MLPC, as Prime Minister; Mandaba formed a coalition Government, which had a working majority of 53 seats in the Assemblée nationale.

In December 1994 a draft Constitution was approved by 82% of voters in a national referendum. The new Constitution, which was adopted in January 1995, included provisions empowering the President to nominate senior military, civil service and judicial officials, and requiring the Prime Minister to implement policies decided by the President. In addition, provision was made for the creation of directly elected regional assemblies and for the establishment of an advisory State Council, which was to deliberate on administrative issues. Several groups in the governing coalition (notably the Mouvement pour la démocratie et le développement—MDD, led by Dacko) expressed concern at the powers afforded to the President.

In April 1995 Mandaba resigned as Prime Minister, pre-empting a threatened vote of 'no confidence' in his administration (initiated by his own party), following accusations of corruption and incompetence. Patassé appointed Gabriel Koyambounou, formerly a civil servant, as the new Prime Minister. Koyambounou subsequently nominated a new Council of Ministers, with an enlarged membership. In December several opposition movements (including the MDD, but not the RDC) united to form the Conseil démocratique des partis politiques de l'opposition (CODEPO), which aimed to campaign against alleged corruption and mismanagement by the Patassé regime.

In the mid-1990s the Government repeatedly failed to pay the salaries of public-sector employees and members of the security forces, prompting frequent strikes and mounting political unrest. In mid-April 1996 CODEPO staged an anti-Government rally in Bangui. Shortly afterwards part of the national army mutinied in the capital and demanded the immediate settlement of all salary arrears. Patassé promised that part of the overdue salaries would be paid and that the mutineers would not be subject to prosecution. The presence of French troops (the Eléments français d'assistance opérationelle—EFAO) in Bangui, with a mandate to secure the safety of foreign nationals and (in accordance with a bilateral military accord) to protect the presidential palace and other key installations, contributed to the swift collapse of the rebellion. In late April Patassé appointed a new Chief of Staff of the Armed Forces, Col Maurice Regonessa, and banned all public demonstrations. In May, however, discontent resurfaced, and CODEPO organized another rally in Bangui, at which it demanded the resignation of the Government. Soon afterwards, in an attempt to tighten his hold on power, the President ordered that control of the national armoury should be transferred from the regular army to the presidential guard. However, adverse reaction to this move within the ranks of the armed forces rapidly escalated into a second, more determined insurrection. Once again EFAO troops were deployed to protect the Patassé administration; some 500 reinforcements were brought in from Chad and Gabon to consolidate the resident French military presence (numbering 1,400). Five hostages were taken by the mutineers, including Col Regonessa, a government minister and the President of the Assemblée nationale. After five days of fierce fighting between dissident and loyalist troops, the French forces intervened to suppress the rebellion. France's military action (which allegedly resulted in civilian deaths) prompted intense scrutiny of the role of the former colonial power, and precipitated large pro- and anti-French demonstrations in Bangui. In total, 11 soldiers and

32 civilians were reported to have been killed in the second army mutiny. Following extended negotiations, the mutineers and government representatives eventually signed an accord, providing for an amnesty for the rebels (who were to return to barracks under EFAO guard), the immediate release of hostages, and the installation of a new government of national unity.

In June 1996 the Government and the opposition signed a protocol providing for the establishment of a government of national unity, led by a civilian Prime Minister with no official party ties. Following the publication of the protocol, Koyambounou's Government resigned. Jean-Paul Ngoupandé, hitherto ambassador to France and with no official political affiliation (although he had been Secretary-General of the RDC in the late 1980s), was appointed as the new Prime Minister and immediately nominated a new Council of Ministers. National co-operation, however, remained elusive, as CODEPO, dissatisfied with the level of its ministerial representation, immediately withdrew from the Government of National Unity. Moreover, a growing animosity was reported between Patassé and Ngoupandé, with the former refusing to transfer any effective power to the latter.

At a conference on national defence held in August–September 1996, several resolutions were adopted regarding restructuring and improving conditions within the army. In October, however, it was reported that troops who had been involved in the insurrections of April and May were refusing to be transferred from their barracks in the capital to a more remote location; Patassé insisted that their departure would take place none the less. However, in mid-November a further mutiny erupted among these troops. A substantial part of Bangui was occupied by the rebels, and a number of hostages were taken. The latest uprising appeared to have a strong tribal and political motivation: the mutineers, who demanded the resignation of Patassé, belonged to the Yakoma ethnic group of Kolingba. EFAO troops were deployed once again, ostensibly to maintain order and protect foreign residents; however, by guarding key installations and government buildings, they also effectively prevented the overthrow of the Patassé administration. More than 100 people were killed in the unrest during late November and early December.

In December 1996 the Presidents of Burkina Faso, Chad, Gabon and Mali negotiated a 15-day truce, which was supervised by the former transitional President of Mali, Gen. Amadou Toumani Touré; a one-month extension to the cease-fire was subsequently agreed. In January 1997, following the killing of two French soldiers in Bangui (reportedly by mutineers), EFAO troops retaliated by killing at least 10 members of the rebel forces; French military involvement in the CAR was condemned by the opposition, which also sought (without success) to initiate impeachment proceedings against Patassé. Subsequent to the renewal of violence, Touré again came to Bangui as mediator and helped to create a cross-party Committee of Consultation and Dialogue. The 'Bangui Accords', drawn up by this committee, were signed towards the end of January; these, as well as offering an amnesty to the mutineers, provided for the formation of a new government of national unity and for the replacement of the EFAO troops by peace-keeping forces from African nations. The opposition at first threatened to boycott the new Government, largely owing to the appointment of Michel Gbezera-Bria (a close associate of Patassé and hitherto the Minister of Foreign Affairs) as Prime Minister. However, with the creation of new ministerial posts for opposition politicians, a 'Government of Action' (which did not include Ngoupandé) was formed on 18 February; soon afterwards Gen. Bozizé replaced Gen. Regonessa as Chief of Staff of the Armed Forces.

In February 1997 responsibility for peace-keeping operations was transferred from the EFAO to forces of the newly formed Mission interafricaine de surveillance des accords de Bangui (MISAB), comprising some 700 soldiers from Burkina Faso, Chad, Gabon, Mali, Senegal and Togo (with logistical support from 50 French military personnel). MISAB soldiers were also to assist in disarming the former mutineers; however, when in late March they attempted to do so, fighting broke out in which some 20 MISAB soldiers were killed. A spokesman for the rebels, Capt. Anicet Saulet, claimed that the lack of representation of the former mutineers in the new Government constituted a breach of the Bangui Accords. Following a meeting between Saulet and Patassé in early April, the Council of Ministers was expanded to include two military officers as representatives of the rebels. Later that month several hundred former mutineers attended a ceremony marking their reintegration into the regular armed forces.

In May 1997, following the deaths in police custody of three former rebels suspected of criminal activities, nine ministers representing the G11 (a grouping of 11 opposition parties, including the MDD—which had left CODEPO in November 1996—and the RDC), as well as the two representatives of the former mutineers, suspended participation in the Government. In June violent clashes erupted once again between MISAB forces and former mutineers. In response to several attacks on the French embassy by the rebels, several hundred EFAO troops were redeployed on the streets of Bangui, and MISAB forces launched a major offensive in the capital, capturing most of the rebel-controlled districts. This assault led to the arrest of more than 80 former mutineers, but also to some 100 deaths, both of soldiers and of civilians. Soon afterwards some 500 demonstrators gathered outside the French embassy to protest against alleged abuses of human rights by MISAB troops; MISAB officials claimed that criminals were impersonating their soldiers in order to perpetrate atrocities. On the same day Touré returned to Bangui in his capacity as Chairman of MISAB, and negotiated a four-day truce, which took effect at the end of June, followed by a 10-day cease-fire agreement, signed at the beginning of July; all of the former mutineers were to be reintegrated into the regular armed forces, and their safety and that of the people living in the districts under their control was guaranteed; the rebels, for their part, were to relinquish their weaponry. Towards the end of July many of the people who had been held in custody in relation to the previous month's violence were released by the authorities, and the curfew in Bangui was eased, while it was reported that almost all of the former mutineers had rejoined the regular armed forces. In September the nine representatives of opposition parties in the Council of Ministers resumed their vacant posts.

In July 1997, in accordance with a decision to disengage forces from its former African colonies, France announced its intention to withdraw its troops from the CAR by April 1998; the first troops left the country in October 1997. France campaigned vigorously for the formation of a UN force, but encountered initial resistance from the USA. A National Reconciliation Conference, held in Bangui, in February 1998 led to the signing on 5 March of a National Reconciliation Pact by President Patassé and 40 representatives of all the country's political and social groups. The accord was countersigned by Gen. Touré and witnessed by many other African Heads of State. The Pact restated the main provisions of the Bangui Accords and of the political protocol of June 1996. It provided for military and political restructuring, to be implemented by a civilian Prime Minister, supported by all of the country's social and political groups. The powers and position of the President were, however, guaranteed, and a presidential election was scheduled for late 1999.

The signature of the Pact facilitated the authorization, later in March 1998, by the UN Security Council of the establishment of a peace-keeping mission, the UN Mission in the Central African Republic (MINURCA), to replace MISAB. MINURCA comprised 1,345 troops from Benin, Burkina Faso, Canada, Chad, Côte d'Ivoire, Egypt, France, Gabon, Mali, Portugal, Senegal and Togo, and was granted a mandate to remain in the country for an initial period of three months. The mission was subsequently extended until the end of February 1999.

There was substantial support for the new political solution. However, preparations for the legislative elections were marked by disagreement between the Government and the G11 over electoral procedure. When the authorities announced in August that the elections were to be postponed, owing to the difficulties of registering rural voters, the opposition claimed that there was little political will for the elections in government circles.

Elections to the newly reorganized Assemblée nationale, which were contested by 29 parties, finally took place on 22 November and 13 December 1998. The MPLC won 47 of the 109 seats in the legislature, but secured the co-operation of seven independent members. The opposition won 55 seats; however, the defection, amid allegations of bribery, of a newly elected deputy belonging to the Parti social-démocrate (PSD) gave the ruling MPLC a majority in the Assemblée. The opposition called for the defector to give up his seat, and the opening of the Assemblée nationale was delayed. Most of the opposition representatives boycotted the opening of the legislature, which was eventually held on 4 January 1999, and MINURCA troops were deployed to protect deputies from anti-Government protesters gathered outside. Patassé's decision to call on a close associate,

the nominally independent erstwhile Minister of Finance, Anicet Georges Dologuélé, to form a new Government provoked public demonstrations and caused the opposition formally to withdraw from the legislature (the boycott lasted until March). Dologuélé announced the composition of a new coalition Council of Ministers in early January, but 10 opposition ministers immediately resigned in protest at the MPLC's alleged disregard for the results of the election. In mid-January Dologuélé announced the formation of another Council of Ministers, which included four members of the MDD, despite an earlier agreement made by the opposition not to accept posts in the new Government. The MDD leadership subsequently ordered its members to resign from their government positions; three of the four ministers did so, but Armand Sama, the nominated Minister of Town Planning, Housing and Public Buildings, defied his party's directives and retained his portfolio. In March two PSD deputies resigned from the party, announcing their intention to retain their seats in the Assemblée nationale as independents.

In February 1999 the UN Security Council extended MINURCA's mandate until mid-November in order that it might assist in preparations for, and the conduct of, the presidential election, which was scheduled to be held on 29 August. France was reported to have opposed an extension of the mandate, and in February the French contingent withdrew from MINURCA (as did the troops from Côte d'Ivoire in April). The UN Secretary-General, Kofi Annan, called on all factions in the CAR to co-operate in preparations for the presidential election. In particular, Annan criticized delays in the appointment of the independent electoral commission, the Commission électorale mixte indépendante (CEMI), the 27 members of which were finally approved in May. In July the Constitutional Court authorized 10 candidates to stand in the election. President Patassé was to seek re-election, while other candidates included two former Presidents, Kolingba and Dacko, two former Prime Ministers, Ngoupandé and Lakoué, as well as Goumba, the opposition candidate in the 1993 presidential election. In August, at the request of bilateral creditors and the UN, a 45-member body was established to supervise the activities of the CEMI, which comprised members of both opposition and pro-Patassé parties. In the event, the election was not held until 19 September, owing to organizational problems. International observers reported that, despite some attempts at fraud by a number of individuals, no widespread irregularities had been discovered. On 2 October the Constitutional Court announced that Patassé had been re-elected President, with 51.6% of the total votes cast. Patassé's nearest rivals were Kolingba, who won 19.4% of the votes, Dacko (11.2%), and Goumba (6.1%).On 22 October Patassé was sworn in as President for a further six-year term. In early November recently reappointed Prime Minister Dologuélé announced the formation of a new Council of Ministers, which included members of parties loyal to Patassé, as well as independents, three opposition representatives and two members of the armed forces. The Government stated that its main priorities were to improve human development in the CAR and to combat poverty; particular emphasis was also laid on the restructuring of the public sector and of the armed forces.

In October 1999 Kofi Annan requested that the UN Security Council authorize the gradual withdrawal of MINURCA from the CAR over a three-month period following the end of its mandate on 15 November. In December the UN announced proposals to establish a Bureau de soutien à la consolidation de la paix en Centrafrique (BONUCA), in Bangui, the role of which would be to monitor developments in the CAR in the areas of politics, socio-economics, human rights and security issues, as well as to facilitate dialogue between political figures. BONUCA began its operation on the same day as the final withdrawal of MINURCA, 15 February 2000, with a mandate for a one-year period. In September 2000 BONUCA's mandate was extended until the end of 2001, and in September 2001, following continued unrest, it was extended for a further one-year period.

In April 2000 the Dologuélé Government survived a vote of 'no confidence', which was proposed by the opposition, in the Assemblée nationale. The Government was subject to further pressure in November, when thousands of civil servants staged a strike in support of their demands for the payment of at least 12 of the 30 months' salary arrears owed to them. The paralysis of public services exacerbated social tensions, and youths joined the protest movement, erecting barricades. Later that month 15 opposition parties united to demand the resignation of Patassé and to announce, in December, the formation of a co-ordination committee with the aim of organizing a peaceful transfer of

power. In April 2001 Patassé dismissed the Dologuélé administration. Martin Ziguélé was appointed as Prime Minister, and
a new Government was formed.

On 28 May 2001 rebellious soldiers, thought to be supporters
of Kolingba, attacked Patassé's official residence in an
attempted coup. However, the insurgency was suppressed by
troops loyal to Patassé, and at least 59 people were killed. Libya
sent troops and helicopters, while a contingent of rebels from the
Democratic Republic of the Congo (DRC) arrived to support the
Patassé regime. Violence ensued throughout the country, with
heavy fighting in Bangui resulting in some 300 deaths. Of an
estimated 60,000–70,000 civilians who were reported to have
fled the capital following the coup attempt, some 10,000 had
returned by July, according to aid agencies. In August 2002
Kolingba and 21 associates were sentenced to death *in absentia*
for their alleged involvement in the coup; a further 500 defendants were reported to have received prison terms of 10–20 years.

In August 2001 the Council of Ministers was reshuffled; most
notably, the Minister of National Defence, Jean-Jacques Déma-
fouth, was replaced, following allegations regarding his involvement in the attempted coup in May (he was, however, acquitted
of all charges at his trial in October 2002). In October 2001 Gen.
Bozizé was dismissed from the post of Chief of Staff of the Armed
Forces because of similar allegations. However, in early
November violence erupted in Bangui between supporters of
Bozizé and the presidential guard (supported by forces from
Libya) after attempts were made to arrest Bozizé, at the request
of a judicial commission of inquiry into the failed coup attempt.
International and regional efforts to mediate between Bozizé
and the CAR administration were unsuccessful, and later that
month Bozizé fled to the southern town of Sarh in Chad, where
he was granted refuge, with about 300 of his armed supporters.
Tension reportedly increased between the CAR and Chad, as
security forces pursued those loyal to Bozizé along the border
between the two countries. At a meeting of the Communauté
économique et monétaire de l'Afrique centrale (CEMAC) in
Libreville, Gabon, on 6 December, a commission was created,
chaired by President Omar Bongo of Gabon, and also comprising
Presidents Idriss Deby and Denis Sassou-Nguesso of Chad and
the Republic of the Congo, respectively, to find a lasting solution
to the crisis in the CAR. In late December the CAR judiciary
abandoned legal proceedings against Bozizé, and in January
2002, during a meeting held in Chad, a government delegation
invited Bozizé and his supporters to return to the CAR.

In April 2002, in consultation with political parties and development organizations, the Government announced a series of
measures to reform public services and promote good governance. In July the Minister of State in charge of Finance and the
Budget, Eric Sorongopé, was arrested on suspicion of embezzling government funds reportedly in excess of US $3m. More
than 20 government officials were also detained on charges
relating to the scandal. The subsequent withdrawal of IMF and
World Bank representatives from Bangui also threatened to
aggravate the ongoing budget crisis, and protests continued at
the Government's failure to pay public-sector wages. In September BONUCA's mandate was extended until December
2003.

On 25 October 2002 the northern suburbs of Bangui were
invaded by forces loyal to Bozizé (who had been granted asylum
in France earlier in the month, in accordance with an agreement
reached at a CEMAC summit aimed at defusing tension between
the CAR and Chad—see below). After five days of heavy
fighting, pro-Government forces, supported by Libyan troops
and some 1,000 fighters from a DRC rebel grouping, the Mouvement pour la libération du Congo (MLC), succeeded in repelling
Bozizé's insurgents. Initial reports indicated that some 28
people had been killed during the fighting. None the less, by
December the Patassé Government had failed fully to suppress
the forces allied to Bozizé, and the CAR was effectively divided
between loyalist areas in the south and east and rebel-held
northern regions between the Chadian border and Bangui.
Concerns were raised by the UN for the welfare of the approximately 150,000 refugees and displaced civilians positioned
between Bozizé's forces and pursuing.

In December 2002 the first contingent of a CEMAC peace-
keeping force (eventually to number 350) arrived in Bangui, and
in January 2003 Libyan forces were withdrawn. Clashes were
frequently claimed to have occurred between the regular CAR
army and its allies, culminating in reports (denied by the CAR
Government) of a massacre of MLC soldiers in December. In
February 2003, however, MLC fighters began to withdraw from

the CAR, in response to international pressure on the Patassé
Government, which claimed that all 'misunderstandings'
between fighters from the DRC and its own troops had been
resolved. In late February 2003 Patassé announced the establishment of a new commission to rehabilitate officials returning
from exile, and in March the RDC and other opposition parties
resumed their participation in the Assemblée nationale. A ministerial reshuffle was effected in January 2003.

On 15 March 2003 armed supporters of Bozizé entered
Bangui, encountering little resistance from government troops.
President Patassé, who had been attending a regional summit in
Niger, was forced to withdraw to the Cameroonian capital,
Yaoundé, after shots were fired at his aeroplane as it attempted
to land at Bangui. Reports suggested that casualties during the
coup had numbered no more than 15 people; in response to an
outbreak of looting throughout Bangui, a curfew was imposed on
16 March. Following the surrender of the largely demoralized
security forces in the capital, Bozizé declared himself Head of
State, dissolved the Assemblée nationale and suspended the
Constitution. Although the coup was condemned by the African
Union, the UN, CEMAC, France and the USA, Bozizé insisted
that his actions constituted only a 'temporary suspension of
democracy' and that a new consensus government would be
formed in consultation with the former opposition, human rights
groups and development agencies. Following this announcement, Bozizé secured the approval of the Governments of Gabon
and the Republic of the Congo at a meeting with the foreign
ministers of those countries. France deployed some 300 troops in
Bangui in order to assist foreign nationals intending to leave the
CAR. Bozizé also gained the support of opposition parties, which
pledged to oppose any attempt by Patassé to return to power. In
late March Abel Goumba, the leader of the Front patriotique
pour le progrès, was appointed as Prime Minister, and a new,
broad-based transitional Government was subsequently formed.
Despite only receiving two positions in the new Council of
Ministers, in mid-April the MLPC declared that it would adhere
to the transitional arrangements decreed by Bozizé. Meanwhile,
some 100,000 people were reported to have demonstrated in
support of Bozizé in Bangui in late March. In April public
support for the new regime increased further, following the
payment of public-sector salaries for the first time in more than
two years, and an amnesty for those convicted of involvement in
the coup attempt of May 2001 was proclaimed.

On 30 May 2003 Bozizé inaugurated a 98-member, advisory
Conseil national de transition (CNT), which included representatives of political parties, trade unions, religious organizations and human rights groups, in order to assist him in
exercising legislative power during the transitional period,
which was to last 18–30 months. The CNT maintained its
opposition to any involvement by former President Patassé in
the political process, and elected Nicolas Tiangaye, a prominent
human rights activist, as its Speaker. Meanwhile, Bozizé confirmed his intention to return the country to civilian rule in
January 2005, and a timetable for the resumption of democracy
was announced.

In June 2003 the Government announced plans for the demobilization of 5,700 former fighters: 1,200 loyal to Bozizé, 3,500
loyal to Patassé and 1,000 returning from exile. Two military
training centres were subsequently established for former combatants who were to be integrated into the CAR army. In July
UN agencies announced the resumption of food aid to the CAR,
following its suspension in March. The CNT resolved that the
long-delayed national dialogue, towards which the previous
administration had made tentative efforts, would take place in
mid-September. Several prominent political figures were
invited to participate, including former Presidents Dacko (who
died in November) and Kolingba, but Patassé was excluded.
Meanwhile, the Government continued its investigations into
widely acknowledged corruption within the country's economic
institutions and civil service. In June the executive boards of the
state electricity and telecommunications companies were dismissed after the reported discovery of widespread accounting
irregularities, and in July 866 non-existent workers were
removed from the public-sector payroll. Moreover, in the same
month the judicial authorities began an investigation into the
whereabouts of some 4,800m. francs CFA donated by the Japanese Government for the Patassé administration's reconciliation
plans, and ordered the suspension of mineral and timber interests controlled by the former President, while the Government
issued guidelines obliging government officials and politicians
to declare their personal assets. In August the state prosecutor

issued an international arrest warrant for Patassé, now in exile in Togo, on charges including murder and embezzlement. In September BONUCA's mandate was extended until December 2004.

Some 350 delegates, representing government, political organizations, trade unions, civil society and ethnic groups, participated in the national dialogue, which ended in late October 2003, and a 21-member panel was created to oversee the implementation of the delegates' recommendations, which included the eventual establishment of a Truth and Reconciliation Commission. The curfew imposed in March was definitively lifted at the end of October. In December Prime Minister Goumba was appointed Vice-President, and his previous post was allocated to Célestin-Leroy Gaombalet, a former financier. Gaombalet subsequently effected a government reshuffle, in which 14 ministers retained their porfolios; the changes mainly reflected popular dissatisfaction with deteriorating public security in Bangui, and new appointees also included several political figures linked to previous administrations. In late December the chief of presidential security, Col Danzoumi Yalo, and his brother, Sani Yalo (a businessman who had been implicated in a major financial scandal in 1999), were arrested on suspicion of plotting a coup, amid reports of continuing insecurity in the country. In the same month a new mining code was promulgated, following the recommendations of a conference held in August. The legislation appeared to limit the President's discretion over awarding contracts for mineral exploitation, and strengthened the role of the security forces in monitoring illegal mining.

An eight-member interministerial committee, headed by Prime Minister Gaombalet, was established in January 2004 to oversee the forthcoming electoral process. According to a revised schedule, a referendum on a new constitution, which was to be drafted by the CNT, would be held in November, with municipal, presidential and legislative elections to follow between December and January 2005. Bozizé had earlier stated that he would not contest the presidential election but in mid-June 2004 he declared his candidature possible. In early December the newly-appointed Transitional Constitutional Court (TCC) oversaw the planned referendum on a new Constitution, which was approved by 87.2% of those who voted. The new Constitution provided for a presidential term of five years, renewable only once, and increased powers for the Prime Minister. Following the referendum Bozizé announced that presidential and legislative elections were to be rescheduled for mid-February 2005 and that he would stand as an independent candidate for the presidency. In late December 2004 the TCC disqualified nine presidential candidates including, notably, former President Patassé and former Prime Minister Ngoupandé. However, the TCC's decision provoked popular unrest and in early January 2005 Bozizé annulled the disqualification of Ngoupandé and two other candidates.

Following administrative delays, presidential and legislative elections were held concurrently on 13 March 2005. In the presidential election Bozizé secured 43.0% of the votes cast, while the former Prime Minister Ziguélé obtained 23.5% and Kolingba 16.0%. As no candidate had won an absolute majority, the two leading candidates, Bozizé and Ziguélé, proceeded to a second round of voting, scheduled to be held on 8 May. More than 900 candidates contested the 105 seats in the new legislature. According to official announcements, 17 seats were secured, however, the remaining parliamentarians would not be appointed until after a second round of voting—also scheduled to be held on 8 May—had taken place.

In May 1997 the CAR recognized the administration of President Laurent Kabila in the DRC (formerly Zaire). In the same month the CAR and the DRC signed a mutual assistance pact, which provided for permanent consultation on internal security and defence. The pact also sought to guarantee border security; however, during mid-1997 armed troops of what had been the Zairean army were reported to be fleeing troops loyal to Kabila and crossing the Oubangui river into the CAR. In January 1999 there was a further influx of DRC civilians to the CAR. The refugees crossed the Oubangui river to escape the fighting between government and rebel soldiers, who were occupying the northern part of the DRC. In August the regional office of the UN High Commissioner for Refugees (UNHCR) estimated that the CAR was sheltering about 54,000 refugees from the DRC, Chad and Sudan. However, in December 2001 UNHCR announced plans to establish a new camp in the DRC for refugees who had fled the CAR. Following the attempted coup in

the CAR in May 2001, UNHCR estimated that 23,000 people had escaped to the DRC; further movements were reported in the aftermath of the attempted coup of October 2002. In June 2003 Gen. Bozizé and President Joseph Kabila of the DRC agreed to re-establish existing bilateral security arrangements. In August 2004 officials from both countries met to discuss reopening the common border and, subsequently, an agreement was signed under the auspices of the UNHCR allowing some 10,000 Congolese refugees in the CAR to be repatriated. The process of repatriation was reported to have begun in October.

In late 1994 the CAR and Chad agreed to establish a bilateral security structure to ensure mutual border security. In 1994 the CAR also became the fifth member of the Lake Chad Basin Commission (see p. 374). In December 1999 it was reported that some 1,500 Chadian refugees were preparing to leave the CAR, allegedly owing to fears for their security following the imminent departure of MINURCA forces. Relations between the CAR and Chad deteriorated when armed men, led by a Chadian rebel, raided southern Chad from the CAR on 29 and 31 December 2001; four people were killed during the raids. A further outbreak of violence in the border area was reported in April 2002, which resulted in at least one fatality. Despite pledges by both countries to increase co-operation, further clashes in August resulted in the deaths of 20 CAR soldiers. An emergency CEMAC summit took place later that month, chaired by the Gabonese President, Omar Bongo, and an observer mission was dispatched to examine the security situation along the common border. At the end of August the mission reported that, although tension remained high in the region, there was no concentration of troops on the border. The CAR's decision to appoint Col Martin Khoumtan-Madji (believed by the Chadian authorities to be an alias of Abdoulaye Miskine, a former senior Chadian rebel leader, who had been based in the CAR since 1998) as the head of a special unit in the CAR military, charged with securing the common border, further strained relations, as did Chad's reputed sponsorship of forces loyal to Bozizé. In early October a CEMAC summit in Libreville, Gabon, sought to defuse tensions between the two countries; in accordance with an accord reached at the summit, Bozizé and Khoumtan-Madji were subsequently granted asylum in France and Togo, respectively, and in December the first contingent of a CEMAC force was deployed in Bangui, initially to protect Patassé and later to monitor joint patrols of the border by Chadian and CAR troops. Relations between the two countries subsequently began to improve somewhat, and in January 2003 the Governments of the CAR, Chad and Sudan announced their intention to establish a tripartite committee to oversee the security and stability of their joint borders. Following Bozizé's assumption of power in the CAR in mid-March 2003, the Chadian Government dispatched some 400 troops to Bangui; 120 Chadian troops were subsequently integrated into CEMAC's operations in the CAR, which were scheduled to end in January 2005, with the remainder withdrawn. In November 2004 the issue of border security was again raised after a massacre in the northern town of Birao, perpetrated, according to some local witnesses, by a raiding Chadian militia. The defence ministers of Sudan, Chad and the CAR subsequently met to finalize plans for joint patrols and information sharing in order to strengthen security along their common borders.

The CAR maintains amicable relations with Nigeria, and in June 1999 the two countries signed a bilateral trade agreement. The CAR is also a close ally of Libya, and in April 1999 joined the Libyan-sponsored Community of Sahel-Saharan States (see p. 373). Diplomatic relations with Libya (which had been closely allied with the Patassé Government) were resumed in July 2003, following discussions between President Bozizé and the Libyan leader, Col Muammar al-Qaddafi.

Government

Following the overthrow of President Ange-Félix Patassé in mid-March 2003, the Constitution of January 1995 was suspended, and the Assemblée nationale dissolved. The self-proclaimed Head of State, Gen. François Bozizé, appointed a 63-member Conseil national de transition, to assist him in exercising legislative power, and a transitional Government. The transitional period was to last 18–30 months. A new constitution was approved by referendum on 5 December 2004. Legislative, presidential and municipal elections were held on 13 March 2005. A second round of elections was scheduled to take place on 8 May.

For administrative purposes, the country is divided into 14 prefectures, two economic prefectures (Gribingui and Sangha), and one commune (Bangui). It is further divided into 67 sub-prefectures and two postes de contrôle administratif. At community level there are 65 communes urbaines, 102 communes rurales and seven communes d'élevage.

Defence

In August 2004 the armed forces numbered about 2,550 men (army 1,400, air force 150 and gendarmerie 1,000). Military service is selective and lasts for two years. The full withdrawal of the 1,345 troops of the United Nations Mission in the Central African Republic (MINURCA) was completed in mid-February 2000. In December 2002 the first contingent of a peace-keeping force from the Communauté économique et monétaire de l'Afrique centrale (CEMAC) arrived in Bangui. At early 2004 380 CEMAC troops were deployed in the CAR. Some 300 French troops also remained in the country, and were engaged in training CAR soldiers. Government expenditure on defence in 2004 was estimated at 20,000m. francs CFA.

Economic Affairs

In 2003, according to estimates by the World Bank, the CAR's gross national income (GNI), measured at average 2001–03 prices, was US $1,194.1m., equivalent to $260 per head (or $1,080 per head on an international purchasing-power parity basis). During 1990–2003, it was estimated, the population increased at an average annual rate of 2.2%, while gross domestic product (GDP) per head declined, in real terms, by an average of 1.4% per year. Overall GDP increased, in real terms, at an average annual rate of 0.7% in 1990–2003; in 2003, GDP contracted by 7.3%, according to the World Bank.

Agriculture (including hunting, forestry and fishing) contributed an estimated 56.9% of GDP in 2003. About 71.8% of the economically active population were employed in the sector in 2002. The principal cash crops have traditionally been cotton (which accounted for an estimated 6.5% of export earnings in 2002) and coffee (only an estimated 1.0% of total exports in 2002, compared with 9.4% in 1999). In mid-2003 FAO warned that, although improved security would allow the 2003 cotton harvest to be sent to ginning complexes in Chad, there remained a severe shortage of seeds for the April–May 2004 planting season. In June 2004 the IMF reported that cotton production had largely ceased. However, it was subsequently reported that the French company Développement des Agro-industries du Sud (DAGRIS) would make substantial investments from March 2005 towards reconstructing the cotton industry. Livestock and tobacco are also exported. The major subsistence crops are cassava (manioc) and yams. The Government is encouraging the cultivation of horticultural produce for export. The exploitation of the country's large forest resources represents a significant source of export revenue (exports of wood accounted for an estimated 50.1% of the total in 2002, increasing from 31.0% in 1999). Rare butterflies are also exported. Agricultural GDP increased at an average annual rate of 3.8% during 1990–2003; growth in 2003 was 4.0%.

Industry (including mining, manufacturing, construction and power) engaged 3.5% of the employed labour force in 1990 and provided an estimated 14.8% of GDP in 2003. Industrial GDP increased at an average annual rate of 1.7% in 1990–2003; growth in 2003 was 4.0%.

Mining and quarrying engaged a labour force estimated at between 40,000 and 80,000 in the late 1990s, and contributed an estimated 6.9% of GDP in 2003. The principal activity is the extraction of predominantly gem diamonds (exports of diamonds totalled an estimated 415,000 carats and provided some 36.6% of total export revenue in 2002, rising to an estimated 40% in 2004). The introduction of gem-cutting facilities and the eradication of widespread 'black market' smuggling operations would substantially increase revenue from diamond mining. However, in the CAR diamonds are predominantly found in widely scattered 'alluvial' deposits (mainly in the south-west and west of the country), rather than Kimberlite deposits, which are concentrated and, thus, more easily exploited and policed. The reopening in 1997 of the Bangui diamond bourse, which had been established in 1996, was intended to increase revenue by levying a 10% sales tax on transactions. In July 2003 the CAR became a participant in the Kimberley Process, an international certification scheme aimed at excluding diamonds from the world market that have been traded for arms by rebel movements in conflict zones. Deposits of gold are also exploited. The development of uranium resources may proceed, and reserves of iron ore, copper, tin and zinc have also been located, although the country's insecurity and poor infrastructure have generally

deterred mining companies from attempting commercial exploitation of these reserves. Mining activity was largely suspended following Gen. François Bozizé's seizure of power in March 2003, pending an audit of companies involved in the sector. It was hoped that the adoption of a new mining code in December would revive the sector and increase transparency in licensing procedures. According to IMF estimates, the GDP of the mining sector increased by an average of 7.0% per year during 1992–94, but declined by an average of 4.6% per year in 1994–97, before increasing by 0.8% in 1998 and by 3.5% in 1999.

The manufacturing sector engaged 1.6% of the employed labour force in 1988. Manufacturing, which contributed an estimated 2.4% of GDP in 2003, is based on the processing of primary products. In real terms, the GDP of the manufacturing sector increased at an average annual rate of 1.0% in 1990–2003; growth in 2003 was 4.0%.

In 1999, according to preliminary figures, 97.7% of electrical energy generated within the CAR was derived from the country's two hydroelectric power installations. Imports of petroleum products comprised an estimated 9.7% of the cost of merchandise imports in 2002.

Services engaged 15.5% of the employed labour force in 1988 and provided an estimated 28.3% of GDP in 2003. In real terms, the GDP of the services sector decreased at an average rate of 6.7% per year during 1990–2003; it declined by 14.9% in 2002 and by 40.5% in 2003.

In 2003 the CAR recorded a visible trade surplus of an estimated 5,000m. francs CFA, but there was a deficit of an estimated 33,400m. francs CFA on the current account of the balance of payments. In 1996 the principal source of imports was France (providing 39.5% of the total), while the principal markets for exports were Belgium-Luxembourg (accounting for 60.1% of the total) and France (30.9%). Other major trading partners in that year were Cameroon, Japan and the United Kingdom. The principal exports in 2002 were wood products, diamonds and cotton. The principal imports in 1996 were road vehicles, machinery, basic manufactures, cotton, mineral fuels and lubricants, chemical products and food.

In 2003 there was an estimated budget surplus of 16,900m. francs CFA (equivalent to an estimated 2.4% of GDP). At the end of 2002 the CAR's external debt was US $1,066m., of which $980m. was long-term public debt. In 2001 the cost of debt-servicing was equivalent to 11.9% of revenue from exports of goods and services. Consumer prices rose by 24.5% in 1994, following the devaluation of the currency, and by 19.2% in 1995. The annual rate of inflation averaged 3.8% in 1990–2003; consumer prices increased by an average of 5.4% in 2003. In 1995 7.6% of the labour force were unemployed.

The CAR is a member of the Central African organs of the Franc Zone (see p. 267) and of the Communauté economique des états de l'Afrique centrale (CEEAC, see p. 373).

The CAR's land-locked position, the inadequacy of the transport infrastructure and the country's vulnerability to adverse climatic conditions and to fluctuations in international prices for its main agricultural exports have impeded sustained economic growth. Periodic political instability has also severely disrupted economic activity and unrest, following the attempted coups in May 2001 and October 2002, coupled with the consequent disruption to road links with Cameroon, destabilized the domestic economy and adversely affected international trade. The corruption scandal of July 2002 (see above) also undermined creditor confidence in the CAR. The Government was unable to complete its IMF-approved programme of structural and fiscal reforms, and the IMF and the World Bank suspended operations in the CAR. However, in June 2004 the IMF approved a loan of some US $8.2m. in Emergency Post-Conflict Assistance and in August it initiated, in conjunction with the World Bank, programmes aimed at stimulating foreign investment and financing in the CAR. Between October 2002 and March 2003 economic activity was disrupted by civil conflict and, as a consequence of the military coup, the US Government suspended all financial aid to the CAR except in the areas of humanitarian aid and the promotion of democracy. Following his assumption of power in March, Bozizé and his new transitional Government began diplomatic efforts to secure financial assistance from international donors. In May the UN appealed for $9.5m. in emergency aid for the CAR, estimating that some 2.2m. people were 'in a situation of humanitarian distress'. One of the first actions of the new administration was to commence payment of salary arrears owed to public servants, as industrial action over non-payment had paralysed many sectors of the economy, but by the end of 2004 public-sector salaries were still some five months in arrears. Anti-corruption measures were implemented, and in mid-2003 the new regime suspended mining and timber licences awarded under the previous administration, pending a review of the sectors. It was estimated that 50% of potential revenue from taxes on diamond exports were lost to smuggling and corruption under the Patassé administration. Meanwhile, insecurity persisted in much of the country, particularly in rural areas, adversely affecting agricultural production. In 2004 the fall in world prices for coffee and cotton adversely affected these key agricultural sectors while real GDP contracted by some 7% in 2003. Some two-thirds of the population continued to live in acute deprivation, subsisting on less than $1 per day, according to a UN report in December 2004. However, it was hoped that the new Constitution approved at a referendum in that month (see above) would facilitate the return to stability and civilian rule, which, in turn, would precipitate improvements in social provision and infrastructure to reduce poverty and increase the attraction of the CAR to international investors and donors.

Education

Education is officially compulsory for eight years between six and 14 years of age. Primary education begins at the age of six and lasts for six years. Secondary education begins at the age of 12 and lasts for up to seven years, comprising a first cycle of four years and a second of three years. In 2000/01 enrolment at primary schools included 55% of children in the relevant age-group (64% of boys; 45% of girls), according to UNESCO estimates, while in 1991 secondary enrolment was equivalent to only 10% (boys 15%; girls 6%). Current expenditure by the Ministry of Education in 1995 totalled 8,820m. francs CFA, equivalent to 1.6% of gross national income. The provision of state-funded education was severely disrupted during the 1990s and early 2000s, owing to the inadequacy of the Government's resources.

Public Holidays

2005: 1 January (New Year), 28 March (Easter Monday), 29 March (Anniversary of death of Barthélemy Boganda), 1 May (May Day), 5 May (Ascension Day), 16 May (Whit Monday), 30 June (National Day of Prayer), 13 August (Independence Day), 15 August (Assumption), 1 November (All Saints' Day), 1 December (National Day), 25 December (Christmas).

2006: 1 January (New Year), 29 March (Anniversary of death of Barthélemy Boganda), 17 April (Easter Monday), 1 May (May Day), 25 May (Ascension Day), 5 June (Whit Monday), 30 June (National Day of Prayer), 13 August (Independence Day), 15 August (Assumption), 1 November (All Saints' Day), 1 December (National Day), 25 December (Christmas).

Weights and Measures

The metric system is officially in force.

Statistical Survey

Source (unless otherwise stated): Division des Statistiques et des Etudes Economiques, Ministère de l'Economie, du Plan et de la Coopération Internationale, Bangui.

Area and Population

AREA, POPULATION AND DENSITY

Area (sq km)	622,984*
Population (census results)	
8 December 1975	2,054,610
8 December 1988	
Males	1,210,734
Females	1,252,882
Total	2,463,616
Population (UN estimates at mid-year)†	
2001	3,770,000
2002	3,819,000
2003	3,865,000
Density (per sq km) at mid-2003	6.2

* 240,535 sq miles.

† Source: UN, *World Population Prospects: The 2002 Revision.*

PRINCIPAL TOWNS

(estimated population at mid-1994)

Bangui (capital) . .	524,000	Carnot	41,000
Berbérati	47,000	Bambari	41,000
Bouar	43,000	Bossangoa . . .	33,000

Mid-2003 (incl. suburbs): Bangui 697,690 (Source: UN, *World Urbanization Prospects: The 2003 Revision*).

BIRTHS AND DEATHS

(UN estimates, annual averages)

	1985–90	1990–95	1995–2000
Birth rate (per 1,000)	42.6	41.8	40.0
Death rate (per 1,000)	18.0	18.1	20.3

Source: UN, *World Population Prospects: The 2002 Revision.*

1994: Registered live births 124,707 (birth rate 41.6 per 1,000); Registered deaths 50,063 (death rate 16.7 per 1,000) (Source: UN, *Population and Vital Statistics Report*).

Expectation of life (WHO estimates, years at birth): 42.9 (males 42.1; females 43.7) in 2002 (Source: WHO, *World Health Report*).

ECONOMICALLY ACTIVE POPULATION

(persons aged 6 years and over, 1988 census)

	Males	Females	Total
Agriculture, hunting, forestry and fishing	417,630	463,007	880,637
Mining and quarrying	11,823	586	12,409
Manufacturing	16,096	1,250	17,346
Electricity, gas and water . . .	751	58	809
Construction	5,583	49	5,632
Trade, restaurants and hotels . .	37,435	54,563	91,998
Transport, storage and communications	6,601	150	6,751
Financing, insurance, real estate and business services . . .	505	147	652
Community, social and personal services	61,764	8,537	70,301
Activities not adequately defined .	7,042	4,627	11,669
Total employed	565,230	532,974	1,098,204
Unemployed	66,624	22,144	88,768
Total labour force	631,854	555,118	1,186,972

Source: ILO.

Mid-2003 (estimates in '000): Agriculture, etc. 1,267; Total labour force 1,809 (Source: FAO).

Health and Welfare

KEY INDICATORS

Total fertility rate (children per woman, 2002)	5.0
Under-5 mortality rate (per 1,000 live births, 2003) . . .	180
HIV/AIDS (% of persons aged 15–49, 2003)	13.50
Physicians (per 1,000 head, 1995)	0.04
Hospital beds (per 1,000 head, 1991)	0.87
Health expenditure (2001): US $ per head (PPP)	58
Health expenditure (2001): % of GDP	4.5
Health expenditure (2001): public (% of total)	51.2
Access to water (% of persons, 2002)	75
Access to sanitation (% of persons, 2002)	27
Human Development Index (2002): ranking	169
Human Development Index (2002): value	0.361

For sources and definitions, see explanatory note on p. vi.

Agriculture

PRINCIPAL CROPS
('000 metric tons)

	2001	2002	2003
Rice (paddy)	25.3	27.4	29.7
Maize	107.0	113.0	119.0
Millet*	10.1	10.6	10.6
Sorghum*	40.2	42.3	42.5
Cassava (Manioc)	561.7	563.0	563.0†
Taro (Coco yam)†	105.0	100.0	100.0
Yams†	380.0	350.0	350.0
Sugar cane†	90.0	90.0	90.0
Pulses†	31.0	30.0	30.0
Groundnuts (in shell) . . .	121.9	127.8	133.6
Oil palm fruit†	30.0	30.0	30.0
Sesame seed	39.4	41.1	42.8
Melonseed	25.5	26.8	27.9
Pumpkins, squash and gourds† .	5.9	5.9	5.9
Other vegetables†	58.0	58.0	58.0
Bananas†	118.0	115.0	110.0
Plantains†	83.0	82.0	80.0
Oranges†	24.0	22.0	20.0
Pineapples†	14.1	14.0	13.8
Coffee (green)	12.3*	13.0	7.5*
Cottonseed	14.2	14.0*	14.0*
Cotton (lint)	10.3	10.0†	10.0*

* Unofficial figure(s).
† FAO estimate(s).
Source: FAO.

LIVESTOCK
('000 head, year ending September)

	2001	2002	2003
Cattle	3,200	3,273	3,347
Goats	2,763	2,921	3,087
Sheep	234	246	259
Pigs	707	738	771
Chickens	4,389	4,575	4,769

Source: FAO.

LIVESTOCK PRODUCTS
('000 metric tons)

	2001	2002	2003
Beef and veal	67.0	69.0	71.0*
Mutton and lamb*	1.3	1.4	1.4
Goat meat	10.2*	11.0	11.0*
Pig meat	12.5*	12.5	12.9
Poultry meat	3.5*	4.1	4.3*
Other meat*	8.8	8.8	8.8
Cows' milk*	63.0	65.0	65.0
Cattle hides (fresh)* . . .	9.2	9.2	9.5
Goatskins (fresh)*	1.1	1.2	1.2
Hen eggs*	1.5	1.5	1.5
Honey*	13.0	13.0	13.0

* FAO estimate(s).
Source: FAO.

Forestry

ROUNDWOOD REMOVALS
('000 cubic metres, excluding bark)

	1999	2000	2001
Sawlogs, veneer logs and logs for sleepers	553	703	750
Other industrial wood*	308	308	308
Fuel wood	2,000	2,000	2,000*
Total	2,861	3,011	3,058

* FAO estimate(s).
2002–03: Figures assumed to be unchanged from 2001 (FAO estimates).
Source: FAO.

SAWNWOOD PRODUCTION
('000 cubic metres, including railway sleepers)

	1999	2000	2001
Total (all broadleaved)	79	102	150

2002–03: Figures assumed to be unchanged from 2001 (FAO estimates).
Source: FAO.

Fishing

('000 metric tons, live weight)

	2000	2001	2002
Capture*	15.0	15.0	15.0
Aquaculture	0.1	0.1	0.0
Total catch (freshwater fishes) .	15.1	15.1	15.0

* FAO estimates.
Source: FAO.

Mining

	2000	2001	2002
Gold (kg, metal content of ore) .	12	20*	20
Diamonds ('000 carats)	461	449	415†

* Estimate.
† Reported figure.
Source: US Geological Survey.

Industry

SELECTED PRODUCTS
('000 metric tons, unless otherwise indicated)

	2001	2002	2003
Beer ('000 hectolitres)	159.5	132.2	121.7
Sugar (raw, centrifugal)* . . .	13	12	12
Soft drinks and syrups ('000 hectolitres)	46.7	42.4	38.4
Cigarettes (million packets) . .	16.1	16.6	16.1
Palm oil	2.0	2.7	n.a.
Groundnut oil	1.8	1.3	n.a.
Plywood ('000 cubic metres) . .	1.8	2.0	1.9

* FAO estimates.

Sources: mostly IMF, *Central African Republic: Selected Issues and Statistical Appendix* (August 2004).

Electric energy (million kWh, estimates): 104 in 1998; 107 in 1999; 107 in 2000 (Source: UN, *Industrial Commodity Statistics Yearbook*).

Finance

CURRENCY AND EXCHANGE RATES

Monetary Units
100 centimes = 1 franc de la Coopération financière en Afrique centrale (CFA).

Sterling, Dollar and Euro Equivalents (31 December 2004)
£1 sterling = 930.119 francs CFA;
US $1 = 481.577 francs CFA;
€1 = 655.957 francs CFA;
10,000 francs CFA = £10.75 = $20.77 = €15.24.

Average Exchange Rate (francs CFA per US $)
2002   696.988
2003   581.200
2004   528.285

Note: The exchange rate of 1 French franc = 50 francs CFA, established in 1948, remained in force until January 1994, when the CFA franc was devalued by 50%, with the exchange rate adjusted to 1 French franc = 100 francs CFA. This relationship to French currency remained in effect with the introduction of the euro on 1 January 1999. From that date, accordingly, a fixed exchange rate of €1 = 655.957 francs CFA has been in operation.

BUDGET
('000 million francs CFA)

Revenue*	2001	2002	2003†
Tax revenue	51.8	61.4	45.3
Taxes on income and profits .	15.2	17.2	14.0
Domestic taxes on goods and services	24.8	33.3	20.5
Taxes on international trade .	11.8	10.9	10.7
Import duties and taxes . .	7.0	7.6	7.7
Other receipts	11.4	17.0	8.4
Total	63.2	78.4	53.7

Expenditure‡	2001	2002	2003†
Current expenditure . . .	60.9	68.6	66.0
Wages and salaries . . .	29.2	33.1	34.5
Other goods and services . .	14.6	17.1	16.3
Transfers and subsidies . .	7.2	7.1	7.3
Interest payments . . .	9.8	11.3	7.9
Public investment programme . .	32.8	46.0	19.5
Domestically financed . .	1.3	3.9	2.9
Externally financed . . .	8.5	7.3	5.0
Total	93.6	114.6	85.5

* Excluding grants received ('000 million francs CFA): 24.3 in 2001; 27.5 in 2002; 10.1 in 2003.
† Estimates.
‡ Excluding adjustment for payment arrears ('000 million francs CFA): 7.3 in 2001; −21.3 in 2002; −28.4 in 2003.

Source: IMF, *Central African Republic: Selected Issues and Statistical Annex* (August 2004).

INTERNATIONAL RESERVES
(US $ million at 31 December)

	2001	2002	2003
Gold*	3.09	3.81	4.65
IMF special drawing rights . .	0.01	0.01	0.01
Reserve position in IMF . .	0.14	0.16	0.24
Foreign exchange	118.60	123.06	132.17
Total	121.84	127.04	137.07

* National valuation of reserves based on market-related prices.

Source: IMF, *International Financial Statistics*.

MONEY SUPPLY
(million francs CFA at 31 December)

	2001	2002	2003
Currency outside banks . .	82,566	77,431	70,370
Demand deposits at commercial and development banks . .	16,584	17,306	15,060
Total money (incl. others) . .	99,151	94,739	85,440

Source: IMF, *International Financial Statistics*.

COST OF LIVING
(Consumer Price Index for Bangui; base: 1990 = 100)

	1998	1999	2000
Food	144.2	139.8	145.2
Fuel and light	120.9	119.8	125.5
Clothing	148.1	155.3	150.3
All items (incl. others)* . . .	145.0	141.6	145.9

* Excluding rent.

All items (excl. rent) (Consumer Price Index for Bangui; base 2000=100)): 103.7 in 2001; 105.2 in 2002; 110.9 in 2003.

Source: ILO.

NATIONAL ACCOUNTS
('000 million francs CFA at current prices)

Expenditure on the Gross Domestic Product

	2001	2002	2003*
Government final consumption expenditure	84.4	93.7	72.7
Private final consumption expenditure	597.4	598.8	620.2
Increase in stocks . . . . } Gross fixed capital formation . }	59.3	65.1	41.9
Total domestic expenditure .	741.1	757.6	734.8
Exports of goods and services .	117.2	112.9	77.5
Less Imports of goods and services	149.0	144.2	115.9
GDP in purchasers' values .	709.3	726.3	696.4

* Estimates.

Source: IMF, *Central African Republic: Selected Issues and Statistical Appendix* (August 2004).

Gross Domestic Product by Economic Activity

	2001	2002	2003*
Agriculture, hunting, forestry and fishing	365.2	370.4	378.8
Mining and quarrying . . .	46.0	47.7	46.1
Manufacturing	24.6	21.5	16.1
Electricity, gas and water . . .	5.4	5.2	5.4
Construction	29.0	29.7	30.9
Transport and communications .	26.8	27.9	26.6
Commerce	75.2	75.7	72.3
Other merchant services . .	38.7	39.0	37.6
Government services	39.8	45.1	47.0
Technical assistance	21.8	19.9	4.5
GDP at factor cost	672.6	682.1	665.2
Indirect taxes	29.6	36.5	23.6
Customs duties	7.0	7.6	7.7
GDP in purchasers' values . .	709.2	726.2	696.4

* Estimates.

Source: IMF, *Central African Republic: Selected Issues and Statistical Appendix* (August 2004).

BALANCE OF PAYMENTS
('000 million francs CFA)

	2001	2002	2003*
Exports of goods	104.1	101.3	67.9
Imports of goods	−78.5	−81.7	−62.9
Trade balance	25.6	19.6	5.0
Services (net)	−57.4	−50.9	−43.4
Balance on goods and services	−31.8	−31.3	−38.4
Income (net)	−7.5	−5.1	−2.2
Balance on goods, services, and income	−39.3	−36.4	−40.6
Current transfers (net)	21.3	19.0	7.2
Current balance	−18.0	−17.4	−33.4
Capital account (net)	13.1	13.6	6.9
Public sector financing (net) . .	−4.2	−13.1	−11.4
Private sector financing (net) . .	−3.8	−17.1	−1.9
Net errors and omissions . . .	−14.9	−2.3	8.2
Overall balance	−27.7	−36.3	−31.5

* Estimates.

Source: IMF, *Central African Republic: Selected Issues and Statistical Appendix* (August 2004).

External Trade

PRINCIPAL COMMODITIES
(distribution by SITC, US $'000)

Imports c.i.f.	1994	1995	1996
Food and live animals . . .	24,635	27,587	12,585
Cereals and cereal preparations .	17,183	15,010	5,915
Flour of wheat or meslin . . .	13,990	7,999	3,442
Beverages and tobacco . . .	14,238	12,128	8,977
Tobacco and tobacco manufactures	12,216	9,244	6,709
Unmanufactured tobacco and tobacco refuse	4,417	8,510	3,632
Cigarettes	7,799	734	3,077
Crude materials (inedible) except fuels	10,353	27,184	25,177
Cork and wood	97	2,466	4,365
Coniferous sawlogs and veneer logs	90	1,921	3,901
Textile fibres (excl. wool tops) and waste	9,361	22,443	19,132
Cotton	7,951	20,547	17,501
Mineral fuels, lubricants, etc. .	11,606	23,063	14,594
Petroleum, petroleum products, etc.	11,374	22,755	14,550
Refined petroleum products . .	11,223	22,715	14,447
Motor spirit (gasoline) and other light oils	3,223	8,364	4,756
Chemicals and related products	25,037	20,721	14,056
Medicinal and pharmaceutical products	16,759	9,522	6,416
Medicaments	15,912	8,300	5,960
Basic manufactures	21,404	29,201	19,118
Non-ferrous metals	4,685	3,548	1,812
Machinery and transport equipment	36,668	112,122	67,289
Machinery specialized for particular industries . . .	2,809	26,240	7,912
Civil engineering and contractors' plant and equipment . .	876	23,753	4,939
Construction and mining machinery	460	20,437	3,685
Self propelled bulldozers, angledozers and levellers	366	14,872	472
General industrial machinery, equipment and parts . . .	5,969	9,441	5,042
Telecommunications and sound equipment	3,131	12,119	4,777
Television and radio transmitters, etc. . . .	983	6,170	2,496

Imports c.i.f.— *continued*	1994	1995	1996
Road vehicles and parts* . . .	16,456	49,770	33,043
Passenger motor cars (excl. buses)	2,948	8,935	5,473
Motor vehicles for goods transport and special purposes	4,847	17,160	13,314
Goods vehicles (lorries and trucks)	4,500	11,006	11,387
Parts and accessories for cars, buses, lorries, etc.* . . .	4,204	9,836	7,056
Other transport equipment* . .	557	1,963	5,771
Aircraft, associated equipment and parts*	548	1,791	5,771
Miscellaneous manufactured articles	7,040	12,019	10,386
Armoured fighting vehicles, arms of war and ammunition	17	6	7,152
Tanks and other armoured fighting vehicles, motorized, and parts .	—	—	6,830
Total (incl. others)	154,162	265,499	179,942

* Excluding tyres, engines and electrical parts.

Exports f.o.b.	1994	1995	1996
Food and live animals . . .	2,605	4,142	1,295
Crude materials (inedible) except fuels	42,858	59,829	57,334
Cork and wood	1,299	2,790	4,756
Coniferous sawlogs and veneer logs	142	1,736	3,883
Textile fibres (excl. wool tops) and waste	7,531	20,351	22,379
Cotton	7,528	20,309	22,379
Crude fertilizers and crude minerals (excl. coal, petroleum and precious stones)	33,545	35,998	29,437
Industrial diamonds (sorted) .	33,545	35,998	29,435
Basic manufactures	31,114	41,776	40,107
Non-metallic mineral manufactures	30,839	39,887	39,725
Diamonds (excl. sorted industrial diamonds), unmounted . .	30,836	39,880	39,715
Sorted non-industrial diamonds, rough or simply worked	29,877	39,812	39,663
Machinery and transport equipment	2,239	10,543	8,663
Road vehicles and parts* . . .	2,008	9,259	7,119
Parts and accessories for cars, buses, lorries, etc.*	1,237	3,351	4,141
Armoured fighting vehicles, arms of war and ammunition	692	—	6,992
Tanks and other armoured fighting vehicles, motorized, and parts .	—	—	6,829
Total (incl. others)	81,451	119,522	115,128

* Excluding tyres, engines and electrical parts.

Source: UN, *International Trade Statistics Yearbook*.

PRINCIPAL TRADING PARTNERS
(US $'000)*

Imports c.i.f.	1994	1995	1996
Belgium-Luxembourg	2,675	6,589	2,805
Cameroon	8,448	12,880	7,103
Congo, Dem. Repub.	1,386	1,841	1,938
Congo, Repub.	18,047	4,738	3,371
France (incl. Monaco)	59,149	90,739	71,137
Germany	3,213	7,626	2,792
Italy	1,332	2,921	1,674
Japan	8,586	52,303	15,676
Netherlands	1,085	2,815	1,845
United Kingdom	1,437	1,563	3,148
USA	2,447	4,871	2,971
Total (incl. others) . . .	154,162	265,499	179,942

Exports f.o.b.	1994	1995	1996
Belgium-Luxembourg	64,906	75,487	69,192
Cameroon	226	1,825	1,184
Congo, Dem. Repub.	437	1,917	1,904
Congo, Repub.	1,012	1,374	850
France (incl. Monaco)	9,862	30,207	35,556
Spain	1,154	4	—
United Kingdom	270	2,069	3,996
Total (incl. others)	81,451	119,522	115,128

* Imports by country of production; exports by country of consumption.

Source: UN, *International Trade Statistics Yearbook*.

Transport

ROAD TRAFFIC
(motor vehicles in use)

	1999	2000	2001
Passenger cars	4,900	5,300	5,300
Commercial vehicles	5,800	6,300	6,300

Source: UN, *Statistical Yearbook*.

INLAND WATERWAYS TRAFFIC—INTERNATIONAL SHIPPING
(metric tons)

	1996	1997	1998
Freight unloaded at Bangui . .	60,311	56,206	57,513
Freight loaded at Bangui . . .	5,348	5,907	12,524
Total	65,659	62,113	70,037

Source: Banque des états de l'Afrique centrale, *Etudes et Statistiques*.

CIVIL AVIATION
(traffic on scheduled services)*

	1999	2000	2001
Kilometres flown (million) . . .	3	3	1
Passengers carried ('000) . . .	84	77	46
Passenger-km (million)	235	216	130
Total ton-km (million)	36	32	19

* Including an apportionment of the traffic of Air Afrique.

Source: UN, *Statistical Yearbook*.

Tourism

	1997	1998	1999
Tourist arrivals ('000)	26	7	10
Tourism receipts (US $ million) .	5	6	n.a.

Source: World Tourism Organization.

Communications Media

	2000	2001	2002
Television receivers ('000 in use) .	21	n.a.	n.a.
Telephones ('000 main lines in use)	9.5	8.9	9.0
Mobile cellular telephones ('000 subscribers)	5.0	11.0	12.6
Personal computers ('000 in use) .	6	7	8
Internet users ('000)	1.5	3.0	5.0

Source: International Telecommunication Union.

Radio receivers: 283,000 in use in 1997 (Source: UNESCO, *Statistical Yearbook*).

Mobile cellular telephones ('000 subscribers): 13.0 in 2003.

Daily newspapers: 3 in 1996 (average circulation 6,000) (Source: UNESCO, *Statistical Yearbook*).

Non-daily newspapers: 1 in 1995 (average circulation 2,000) (Source: UNESCO, *Statistical Yearbook*).

Education

(1990/91, unless otherwise indicated)

	Schools	Teachers	Pupils
Pre-primary	162	572*	15,734
Primary	930	4,004	308,409
Secondary:			
general	46† }	1,005 {	46,989
vocational	n.a.		1,862
Higher	n.a.	136	2,823

* 1987/88 figure.

† State-funded general secondary schools.

1991/92: Primary pupils 277,961; General secondary pupils 42,263; Vocational secondary pupils 1,477; University teachers 139; University students 2,923.

1998: Primary teachers 3,125; Primary pupils 284,398; University teachers 300; University students 6,229 (Sources: UNESCO, *Statistical Yearbook*; UNESCO Institute for Statistics).

Adult literacy rate (UNESCO estimates): 48.6% (males 64.7%; females 33.5%) in 2002 (Source: UN Development Programme, *Human Development Report*).

Directory

The Constitution

Following the overthrow of President Ange-Félix Patassé in mid-March 2003, the Constitution of January 1995 was suspended. In December 2004 a new constitution was approved at a referendum by 87.2% of the electorate. The new Constitution provides for a presidential term of five years, renewable only once.

The Government

HEAD OF STATE

President of the Republic and Minister of National Defence, the Restructuring of the Armed Forces and Disarmament: Gen. François Bozizé (assumed power 16 March 2003).

COUNCIL OF MINISTERS
(March 2005)

Following the *coup d'état* of March 2003, a broadly-based transitional Government was formed.

Prime Minister and Head of Government: Célestin-Leroy Gaombalet (CPC).

Minister of State, responsible for National Education, Literacy, Higher Education and Scientific Research: Abdou Karim Méckassoua (CPC).

Minister of Agriculture and Animal Husbandry: Lt-Col Parfait-Anicet M'baye.

Minister of Planning, the Economy, Finance, the Budget and International Co-operation: Daniel N'ditiféï Boysémbé (MDI-PS).

Minister of Foreign and Francophone Affairs, and Regional Integration: Charles-Hervé Wénézoui (Ind.).

Minister of the Interior, responsible for Territorial Administration: Lt-Col MICHEL SALLÉ.

Minister of Justice, Keeper of Seals: (vacant).

Minister of Equipment and Transport: M'POKOMANDJI SOLINY (FPP).

Minister of Mines and Energy: Maj. SYLVAIN N'DOUTINGAÏ.

Minister of Communication, National Reconciliation and Democratic and Civic Culture: JOSEPH KITIKI KOUAMBA (FPP).

Minister of Water Resources, Forests, Hunting and Fishing: DENIS KOSSI-BELLA (MLPC).

Minister in charge of the Secretariat-General of the Government and Relations with the National Transitional Council: Me ZARAMBAUD ASSINGAMBI (Ind.).

Minister of Public Health and Population: Prof. NESTOR MAMADOU NALI (Ind.).

Minister of the Reconstruction of Public Buildings, Urban Planning and Housing: ABRAHAM NGOTTO BOULOUM (FODEM).

Minister of Posts and Telecommunications, responsible for New Technologies: IDRISS SALAO (RDC).

Minister of the Civil Service, Labour and Social Security: JACQUES BOTI (USTC).

Minister of Youth, Sports, Culture and the Arts: DÉSIRÉ KOLINGBA (PSD).

Minister of Tourism Development and Artisanal Industries: BRUNO DACKO (MDD).

Minister of Family, Social Affairs, and National Solidarity: SOLANGE PAGONÉNDJI N'DACKALA (Ind.).

Minister of Trade, Industry and the Promotion of the Public Sector: DIDIER WANGUÉ (Ind.).

Minister-delegate responsible for Public Security: Col JULES-BERNARD OUANDÉ.

Minister-delegate responsible for Planning, International Co-operation, Finance and the Budget: Col MOHAMED MAHADI MARBOUA.

Minister-delegate responsible for Primary and Secondary Education: ETIENNE NATALO.

Minister-Delegate responsible for Foreign Affairs, Regional Integration and Francophone Affairs: GUY MOSKIT.

MINISTRIES

All ministries are based in Bangui.

Office of the President: Palais de la Renaissance, Bangui; tel. 61-46-63.

Ministry of the Civil Service, Labour and Social Security: Bangui; tel. 61-01-44.

Ministry of Communication, National Reconciliation and Democratic and Civic Culture: BP 940, Bangui; tel. 61-27-66; fax 61-59-85.

Ministry of Equipment and Transport: BP 941, Bangui.

Ministry of Foreign and Francophone Affairs, and Regional Integration: Bangui; tel. 61-35-55; fax 61-20-76.

Ministry of Justice, Human Rights and Good Governance: Bangui; tel. 61-16-44.

Ministry of Mines and Energy: Bangui; tel. 61-20-54; fax 61-60-76.

Ministry of National Defence, the Restructuring of the Armed Forces and Disarmament: Bangui; tel. 61-46-11.

Ministry of National Education, Literacy, Higher Education and Research: BP 791, Bangui.

Ministry of Planning, the Economy, Finance, the Budget and International Co-operation: BP 912, Bangui; tel. 61-70-55; fax 61-63-98.

Ministry of Public Health and Population: Bangui; tel. 61-29-01.

President and Legislature

Following the overthrow of President Ange-Félix Patassé in mid-March 2003, Gen. François Bozizé assumed power and dissolved the Assemblée nationale. A 98-member Conseil national de transition was to prepare for new presidential and legislative elections, which were held concurrently on 13 March 2005. At the presidential election Bozizé secured 43.0% of the votes cast, while the former Prime Minister, Martin Ziguélé, obtained 23.5% and the former President, Gen. André Kolingba, 16.0%. Bozizé and Ziguélé proceeded to a second round of voting, which was scheduled to take place on 8 May. A second round of voting in legislative elections was also to take place on that day: in the first round 17 of the 105 seats in the new legislature had been secured.

Conseil national de transition: Speaker NICOLAS TIANGAYE.

Political Organizations

Alliance pour la démocratie et le progrès (ADP): Bangui; f. 1991; progressive; Leader JOSPEH THÉOPHILE DOUACLÉ.

Collectif des Centrafricains en France (CCF): Paris (France); f. 1984; umbrella org. for political representatives resident in France; Gen. Sec. ANDRÉ DOUNGOUMA-FOKY.

Concertation des Partis Politiques d'Opposition (CPPO): Bangui; umbrella org. of 12 parties opposed to former President Patassé.

Conseil démocratique des partis politiques de l'opposition (CODEPO): Bangui; f. 1995; political alliance led by AUGUSTE BOU-KANGA; comprises the following parties.

> **Mouvement démocratique pour la renaissance et l'évolution de la République Centrafricaine (MDRERC):** Bangui; Chair. JOSEPH BENDOUNGA; Sec.-Gen. LÉON SEBOU.

> **Parti républicain centrafricain (PRC):** Bangui.

Convention nationale (CN): Bangui; f. 1991; Leader DAVID GALIAMBO.

Coordination des Patriotes Centrafricains (CPC): Paris (France) and Bangui; f. 2003; Umbrella org. for groups opposed to former President Patassé and affiliated to the uprising of March 2003; Sec.-Gen. ABDOU KARIM MÉCKASSOUA.

Forum civique (FC): Bangui; Leader Gen. TIMOTHÉE MALENDOMA.

Forum démocratique pour la modernité (FODEM): Bangui; tel. 61-29-54; e-mail eric.neris@wanadoo.fr; internet membres.lycos.fr/fodem/; f. 1998; Pres. CHARLES MASSI.

Front patriotique pour le progrès (FPP): BP 259, Bangui; tel. 61-52-23; fax 61-10-93; f. 1972; aims to promote political education and debate; Leader Prof. ABEL GOUMBA.

G11: Bangui; f. 1997; alliance of 11 opposition parties led by Prof. ABEL GOUMBA; principal mems: ADP, FPP, MDD and RDC.

Mouvement d'évolution sociale de l'Afrique noire (MESAN): Bangui; f. 1949; comprises two factions, MESAN and MESAN-BOGANDA, led respectively by FIDÈLE OGBAMI and JOSEPH NGBANGA-DIBO.

Mouvement National pour le Renouveau: Bangui; Leader PAUL BELLET.

Mouvement pour la démocratie et le développement (MDD): Bangui; f. 1993; aims to safeguard national unity and the equitable distribution of national wealth; Leader LOUIS PAPENIAH.

Mouvement pour la démocratie, l'indépendance et le progrès social (MDI-PS): BP 1404, Bangui; tel. 61-18-21; e-mail mdicentrafrique@chez.com; internet www.chez.com/mdicentrafrique; Sec.-Gen. DANIEL NDITIFEI BOYSEMBE.

Mouvement pour la libération du peuple centrafricain (MLPC): Bangui; internet www.patasse.com/; f. 1979; leading party in govt Oct. 1993–March 2003; Pres. ANGE-FÉLIX PATASSÉ (in exile in Togo); Interim Pres. LUC-APOLLINAIRE DONDON-KONAMBAYÉ.

Parti africain de développement (PAD): Bangui.

Parti libéral-démocrate (PLD): Bangui; Leader NESTOR KOMBO-NAGUEMON.

Parti social-démocrate (PSD): BP 543, Bangui; tel. 61-59-02; fax 61-58-44; Leader ENOCH DERANT LAKOUÉ.

Parti de l'unité nationale (PUN): Bangui; Leader JEAN-PAUL NGOUPANDÉ.

Rassemblement démocratique centrafricain (RDC): BP 503, Bangui; tel. 61-53-75; f. 1987; sole legal political party 1987–91; Leader Gen. ANDRÉ KOLINGBA.

Rassemblement populaire pour la reconstruction de la Centrafrique (RPRC): Bangui; Leader Gen. FRANÇOIS BOZIZÉ.

Union des démocrates pour le renouveau panafricain (UDRP): Bangui; Leader BENOÎT LIKITI.

Union des forces acquises à la paix (UFAP): Bangui; f. 1998; opposition alliance, including political parties, trade unions and human rights orgs; weakened by withdrawals in Nov. 1999; Pres. PAUL BELLET.

Union nationale démocratique du peuple centrafricain (UNDPC): Bangui; f. 1998; Islamic fundamentalist; based in southeast CAR; Leader MAHAMAT SALEH.

Union pour le Progrès en Centrafrique (UPCA): Bangui; Leader FAUSTIN YERIMA.

Union pour la république (UPR): Bangui; leader PIERRE SAMMY MAKFOY.

Diplomatic Representation

EMBASSIES IN THE CENTRAL AFRICAN REPUBLIC

Cameroon: rue du Languedoc, BP 935, Bangui; tel. 61-18-57; fax 61-16-87; Chargé d'affaires a.i. GILBERT NOULA.

Chad: ave Valéry Giscard d'Estaing, BP 461, Bangui; tel. 61-46-77; Ambassador MAINTINE DJOUMBE.

China, People's Republic: ave des Martyrs, BP 1430, Bangui; tel. 61-27-60; fax 61-31-83; e-mail chinaemb_cf@mfa.gov.cn; Ambassador HE SIJI.

Congo, Democratic Republic: Ambassador EMBE ISEA MBAMBE.

Congo, Republic: BP 1414, Bangui; tel. 61-18-77; fax 61-03-09; Ambassador ERIC EPÉNY OBONDZO.

Egypt: angle ave Léopold Sédar Senghor et rue Emile Gentil, BP 1422, Bangui; tel. 61-46-88; fax 61-35-45; Ambassador AZMY HASSAN KHALIFAH.

France: blvd du Général de Gaulle, BP 884, Bangui; tel. 61-30-05; fax 61-74-04; e-mail chancellerie.bangui-amba@diplomatie.gouv.fr; internet www.ambafrance-cf.org; Ambassador JEAN-PIERRE DESTOUESSE.

Holy See: ave Boganda, BP 1447, Bangui; tel. 61-26-54; fax 61-03-71; e-mail nonrca@intnet.cf; Apostolic Nuncio Most Rev. JOSEPH CHENNOTH (Titular Archbishop of Milevum).

Japan: Temporarily closed; affairs handled through the Embassy of Japan, Yaoundé, Cameroon, since October 2003.

Libya: Bangui; tel. 61-46-62; fax 61-12-79; Ambassador (vacant).

Nigeria: ave des Martyrs, BP 1010, Bangui; tel. 61-40-97; fax 61-12-79; Ambassador A. A. ILEMIA.

Russia: ave du Président Gamal Abdel Nasser, BP 1405, Bangui; tel. 61-03-11; fax 61-56-45; e-mail ruscons@intent.cf; e-mail rusconsrca@yandex.ru; Ambassador IGOR P. LABUZOV.

Sudan: ave de France, BP 1351, Bangui; tel. 61-38-21; Ambassador Dr SULEIMA MOHAMED MUSTAPHA.

Judicial System

Supreme Court: BP 926, Bangui; tel. 61-41-33; highest judicial organ; acts as a Court of Cassation in civil and penal cases and as Court of Appeal in administrative cases; comprises four chambers: constitutional, judicial, administrative and financial; Pres. EDOUARD FRANCK.

There is also a Court of Appeal, a Criminal Court, 16 tribunaux de grande instance, 37 tribunaux d'instance, six labour tribunals and a permanent military tribunal. A High Court of Justice was established under the 1986 Constitution, with jurisdiction in all cases of crimes against state security, including high treason by the President of the Republic. The 1995 Constitution (which was suspended by Gen. François Bozizé in mid-March 2003) established a Constitutional Court, the judges of which were to be appointed by the President. In December 2004 Bozizé appointed a Transitional Constitutional Court that oversaw the referendum on a new constitution held in the same month.

Religion

It is estimated that 24% of the population hold animist beliefs, 50% are Christians (25% Roman Catholic, 25% Protestant) and 15% are Muslims. There is no official state religion.

CHRISTIANITY

The Roman Catholic Church

The Central African Republic comprises one archdiocese and seven dioceses. There were an estimated 752,402 adherents at 31 December 2003.

Bishops' Conference

Conférence Episcopale Centrafricaine, BP 1518, Bangui; tel. 61-70-72; fax 61-46-92; e-mail ceca_rca@yahoo.fr.

f. 1982; Pres. Rt Rev. FRANÇOIS XAVIER YOMBANDJÉ (Bishop of Bossangoa).

Archbishop of Bangui: Most Rev. PAULIN POMODIMO, Archevêché, BP 1518, Bangui; tel. 61-31-48; fax 61-46-92; e-mail cent-afr@intnet.cf.

Protestant Church

Eglise Protestante du Christ Roi: BP 608, Bangui; tel. 61-14-35.

The Press

The independent press is highly regulated. Independent publications must hold a trading licence and prove their status as a commercial enterprise. They must also have proof that they fulfil taxation requirements. There is little press activity outside Bangui.

DAILIES

E le Songo: Bangui; f. 1986.

Le Citoyen: BP 974, Bangui; tel. 61-89-16; independent; Publr MAKA GBOSSOKOTTO; circ. 3,000.

Le Novateur: BP 913, Bangui; tel. 61-48-84; fax 61-87-03; e-mail ccea_ln@intnet.cf; independent; Publr MARCEL MOKWAPI; circ. 750.

PERIODICALS

Bangui Match: Bangui; monthly.

Centrafrique-Presse: BP 1058, Bangui; tel. and fax 61-39-57; e-mail redaction@centrafrique-presse.com; internet www.centrafrique-presse.com; weekly; Publr PROSPER N'DOUBA.

Le Courrier Rural: BP 850, Bangui; publ. by Chambre d'Agriculture.

Le Délit d'Opinion: Bangui; independent.

Demain le Monde: BP 650, Bangui; tel. 61-23-15; f. 1985; fortnightly; independent; Editor-in-Chief NGANAM NÖEL.

Journal Officiel de la République Centrafricaine: BP 739, Bangui; f. 1974; fortnightly; economic data; Dir-Gen. GABRIEL AGBA.

Nations Nouvelles: BP 965, Bangui; publ. by Organisation Commune Africaine et Mauricienne; politics and current affairs.

Le Peuple: BP 569, Bangui; tel. 61-76-34; f. 1995; weekly; Editor-in-Chief VERMOND TCHENDO.

Le Progrès: BP 154, Bangui; tel. 61-70-26; f. 1991; monthly; Editor-in-Chief BELIBANGA CLÉMENT; circ. 2,000.

Le Rassemblement: Bangui; organ of the RDC; Editor-in-Chief MATHIAS GONEVO REAPOGO.

La Tortue Déchaînée: Bangui; independent; satirical; Publr MAKA GBOSSOKOTTO.

PRESS ASSOCIATION

Groupement des Editeurs de la Presse privée indépendante de Centrafrique (GEPAIC): Bangui; Pres. MAKA GBOSSOKOTO.

NEWS AGENCIES

Agence Centrafricaine de Presse (ACAP): BP 40, Bangui; tel. 61-10-88; f. 1974; Gen. Man. VICTOR DETO TETEYA.

Informatsionnoye Telegrafnoye Agentstvo Rossii—Telegrafnoye Agentstvo Suverennykh Stran (ITAR—TASS) (Russia) and Agence France-Presse are represented in the CAR.

Publisher

GOVERNMENT PUBLISHING HOUSE

Imprimerie Centrafricaine: BP 329, Bangui; tel. 61-72-24; f. 1974; Dir-Gen. PIERRE SALAMATE-KOILET.

Broadcasting and Communications

TELECOMMUNICATIONS

Société Centrafricaine de Télécommunications (SOCATEL): BP 939, Bangui; tel. 61-42-68; fax 61-44-72; e-mail dg-socatel@

socatel.cf; internet www.socatel.intnet.cf; f. 1990; 60% state-owned; 40% owned by France Câbles et Radio (France Télécoms); further privatization suspended March 2003; Dir-Gen. VALENTIN NZAPAOKO.

CARATEL Entreprises: BP 2439, Bangui; tel. 61-44-10; fax 61-44-49; e-mail telecomp@intnet.cf; internet www.socatel.intnet.cf; mobile cellular telephone operator.

Telecel: BP 939, Bangui; tel. 61-19-30; fax 61-16-99; mobile cellular telephone operator.

BROADCASTING

Radiodiffusion-Télévision Centrafricaine: BP 940, Bangui; tel. 61-25-88; f. 1958 as Radiodiffusion Nationale Centrafricaine; govt-controlled; broadcasts in French and Sango; Sec.-Gen. DELPHINE ZOUTA.

Radio Rurale: community stations operating in Bouar, Nola, Berbérati and Bambari.

Radio Ndeke Luka: community station operated by UN.

Radio Nostalgie: commercial radio station in Bangui.

Radio Notre-Dame: radio station operated by Roman Catholic Church.

Finance

(cap. = capital; res = reserves; dep. = deposits; m. = million; amounts in francs CFA)

BANKING

Central Bank

Banque des Etats de l'Afrique Centrale (BEAC): BP 851, Bangui; tel. 61-40-00; fax 61-19-95; e-mail beacbgf@beac.int; HQ in Yaoundé, Cameroon; f. 1973; bank of issue for mem. states of the Communauté économique et monétaire de l'Afrique centrale (CEMAC, fmrly Union douanière et économique de l'Afrique centrale), comprising Cameroon, the Central African Repub., Chad, the Repub. of the Congo, Equatorial Guinea and Gabon; cap. 45,000m., res 176,661m., total assets 2,144,626m. (Nov. 2003); Gov. JEAN-FÉLIX MAMALEPOT; Dir in CAR ENOCH DERANT-LAKOUE.

Commercial Banks

Banque Internationale pour le Centrafrique (BICA): place de la République, BP 910, Bangui; tel. 61-00-42; fax 61-61-36; e-mail bica@intnet.cf; internet www.socatel.intnet.cf/bica.html; f. 1946; present name adopted 1996; 35% owned by Banque Belgolaise SA, Brussels, 15% by group of African investors (COFIPA), 40% by private citizens, 10% by Govt; cap. and res 1,117m., total assets 19,616m. (Dec. 2001); Pres. MARTIN BABA; Dir-Gen. JEAN-CLAUDE PORCHER; 2 brs.

Banque Populaire Maroco-Centrafricaine (BPMC): rue Guérillot, BP 844, Bangui; tel. 61-31-90; fax 61-62-30; e-mail bpmc@intnet.cf; f. 1991; 62.5% owned by Groupe Banque Populaire (Morocco), and 37.5% state-owned; cap. and res 2,776m., total assets 11,551m. (Dec. 2001); Dir-Gen. MOHAMMED NAITSSI.

Commercial Bank Centrafrique (CBCA): rue de Brazza, BP 59, Bangui; tel. 61-29-90; fax 61-34-54; e-mail cbca@intnet.cf; internet www.socatel.intnet.cf/ubac.htm; f. 1962; 51% owned by Groupe Fotso; 39% owned by CAR private shareholders; 10% state-owned; cap. and res 1,851m., total assets 19,520m. (Dec. 2001); Pres. SERGE PSIMHIS; Dir-Gen. THÉODORE DABANGA; 1 br.

Development Bank

Banque de Développement des Etats de l'Afrique Centrale: see Franc Zone.

Financial Institutions

Caisse Autonome d'Amortissement de la République Centrafricaine: Bangui; tel. 61-53-60; fax 61-21-82; management of state funds; Dir-Gen. JOSEPH PINGAMA.

Caisse Nationale d'Epargne (CNE): Office national des postes et de l'épargne, Bangui; tel. 61-22-96; fax 61-78-80; Pres. SIMONE BODEMO-MODOYANGBA; Dir-Gen. AMBROISE DAOUDA; Man. ANTOINE BEKOUANEBANDI.

Bankers' Association

Association Professionnelle des Banques: Bangui.

Development Agencies

Agence Française de Développement: rue de la Moyenne corniche, BP 817, Bangui; tel. 61-03-06; fax 61-22-40; e-mail afd@intnet.cf; e-mail dorbeaud@afd.fr; internet www.afd.fr; administers economic aid and finances specific development projects; Man. DELPHINE DORBEAU.

Mission Française de Coopération et d'Action Culturelle: BP 934, Bangui; tel. 61-63-34; fax 61-28-24; administers bilateral aid from France; Dir HERVÉ CRONEL.

INSURANCE

Agence Centrafricaine d'Assurances (ACA): BP 512, Bangui; tel. 61-06-23; f. 1956; Dir R. CERBELLAUD.

Assureurs Conseils Centrafricains (ACCAF): ave Barthélemy Boganda, BP 743, Bangui; tel. 61-19-33; fax 61-44-70; e-mail accaf@ascoma.com; internet www.ascoma.com; f. 1968; owned by Ascoma (Monaco); Chair. JEAN-CLAUDE ROY; Dir-Gen. SYLVAIN COUSIN.

Entreprise d'Etat d'Assurances et de Réassurances (SIRIRI): Bangui; tel. 61-36-55; f. 1972; Pres. EMMANUEL DOKOUNA; Dir-Gen. MARTIN ZIGUÉLÉ.

Legendre, A. & Cie: rue de la Victoire, BP 896, Bangui; Pres. and Dir-Gen. ANDRÉ LEGENDRE.

Union Centrafricaine d'Assurances et de Réassurances: rue du Général de Gaulle, BP 343, Bangui; tel. 61-36-66; fax 61-33-40; e-mail ucardg@intnet.cf; Dir-Gen. ALAIN BLANCHARD.

Trade and Industry

DEVELOPMENT ORGANIZATION

Société Centrafricaine de Développement Agricole (SOCADA): ave David Dacko, BP 997, Bangui; tel. 61-30-33; f. 1964; reorg. 1980; 75% state-owned, 25% Cie Française pour le Développement des Fibres Textiles (France); purchasing, transport and marketing of cotton, cotton-ginning, production of cottonseed oil and groundnut oil; Pres. MAURICE METHOT.

INDUSTRIAL AND TRADE ASSOCIATIONS

Agence de Développement de la Zone Caféière (ADECAF): BP 1935, Bangui; tel. 61-47-30; coffee producers' asscn; assists coffee marketing co-operatives; Dir-Gen. J. J. NIMIZIAMBI.

Agence Nationale pour le Développement de l'Elevage (ANDE): BP 1509, Bangui; tel. 61-69-60; fax 61-50-83; assists with development of livestock.

Bourse Internationale de Diamant de Bangui: BP 26, Bangui; tel. 61-58-63; fax 61-60-76; diamond exchange; supervised by the Ministry of Mines and Energy.

Caisse de Stabilisation et de Péréquation des Produits Agricoles (CAISTAB): BP 76, Bangui; tel. 61-08-00; supervises marketing and pricing of agricultural produce; Dir-Gen. M. BOUNANDELE-KOUMBA.

Fédération Nationale des Eleveurs Centrafricains (FNEC): ave des Martyrs, BP 588, Bangui; tel. 61-23-97; fax 61-47-24.

Groupement des industries centrafricaines (GICA): Bangui; umbrella group representing 12 principal companies of various industries.

Office National des Forêts (ONF): BP 915, Bangui; tel. 61-38-27; f. 1969; reafforestation, development of forest resources; Dir-Gen. C. D. SONGUET.

CHAMBERS OF COMMERCE

Chambre d'Agriculture, d'Elevage, des Eaux, Forêts, Chasses, Pêches et Tourisme: BP 850, Bangui; tel. 61-76-76; f. 1964; Sec.-Gen. MOÏSE DENISSIO.

Chambre de Commerce, d'Industrie, des Mines et de l'Artisanat (CCIMA): Boulevard Charles de Gaulle, BP 823, Bangui.; tel. 61-16-68; fax 61-35-70; e-mail ccici@africaonline.co.ci; internet www.admin.cf/ccima; Pres. RIGOBERT YOMBO; Sec. GERTRUDE ZOUTA-YAMANDJA.

EMPLOYERS' ORGANIZATION

Union Nationale du Patronat Centrafricain (UNPC): Rue Durand Ferté, BP 2180, Bangui; tel. and fax 61-42-10; e-mail unpc-rca@intnet.cf; Pres. FAUSTIN ZAGUI.

UTILITIES

Electricity

Société Energie de Centrafrique (ENERCA): ave de l'Indépendance, BP 880, Bangui; tel. 61-20-22; fax 61-54-43; e-mail enerca@intnet.cf; f. 1967; state-owned; production and distribution of electric energy; 119,1 GWh produced for the Bangui grid in 2003; Dir-Gen. SAMUEL TOZOUI.

Water

Société de Distribution d'Eau en Centrafrique (SODECA): BP 1838, Bangui; tel. 61-59-66; fax 61-25-49; f. 1975 as the Société Nationale des Eaux; state-owned co responsible for supply, treatment and distribution of water; Dir-Gen. FRANÇOIS FARRA-FROND.

TRADE UNIONS

There are five officially recognized trade-union federations, including:

Organization of Free Public-Sector Unions: Bangui.

Union Syndicale des Travailleurs de la Centrafrique (USTC): BP 1390, Bangui; tel. 61-71-64; fax 61-62-62; affiliated with the International Confed. of Free Trade Unions; Sec.-Gen. THÉOPHILE SONNY KOLLE.

Transport

RAILWAYS

There are no railways at present. There are long-term plans to connect Bangui to the Transcameroon railway. A line linking Sudan's Darfur region with the CAR's Vakaga province has also been proposed.

ROADS

In 1999 there were an estimated 23,810 km of roads. Only about 3% of the total network is paved. Eight main routes serve Bangui, and those that are surfaced are toll roads. Both the total road length and the condition of the roads are inadequate for current requirements. In 1997 the European Union provided 32,500m. francs CFA to improve infrastructure in the CAR. In September a vast road-improvement scheme was launched, concentrating initially on roads to the south and north-west of Bangui. The CAR is linked with Cameroon by the Transafrican Lagos–Mombasa highway. Roads are frequently impassable in the rainy season (July–October).

Bureau d'Affrètement Routier Centrafricain (BARC): Gare routière, BP 523, Bangui; tel. 61-20-55; fax 61-37-44; Dir-Gen. J. M. LAGUEREMA-YADINGUIN.

Compagnie Nationale des Transports Routiers (CNTR): Bangui; tel. 61-46-44; state-owned; Dir-Gen. GEORGES YABADA.

Fonds Routier: BP 962, Bangui; tel. 61-62-95; fax 61-68-63.

Projet Sectoriel de Transports (PST): BP 941, Bangui; tel. 61-62-94; fax 61-65-79.

TBC Cameroun SARL: BP 637, Bangui; tel. 61-20-16; fax 61-13-19; e-mail info@tbclogistics.com; internet www.tbclogistics.com; f. 1963.

INLAND WATERWAYS

There are some 2,800 km of navigable waterways along two main water courses. The first, formed by the Congo river and its tributary the Oubangui, can accommodate convoys of barges (of up to 800 metric tons load) between Bangui and Brazzaville and Pointe-Noire in the Republic of the Congo, except during the dry season, when the route is impassable. The second is the river Sangha, also a tributary of the Congo, on which traffic is again seasonal. There are two ports, at Bangui and Salo, on the rivers Oubangui and Sangha respectively. Bangui port has a handling capacity of 350,000 tons, with 350 m of wharfs and 24,000 sq m of warehousing. Efforts are being made to develop the Sangha upstream from Salo to increase the transportation of timber from this area, and to develop Nola as a timber port.

Agence Centrafricaine des Communications Fluviales (ACCF): BP 822, Bangui; tel. 61-09-67; fax 61-02-11; f. 1969; state-owned; supervises development of inland waterways transport system; Chair. GUY MAMADOU MARABENA.

Société Centrafricaine de Transports Fluviaux (SOCA-TRAF): Rue Parent, BP 1445, Bangui; tel. and fax 61-43-15; e-mail socatraf@intnet.cf; f. 1980; 51% owned by ACCF; Man. Dir FRANÇOIS TOUSSAINT.

CIVIL AVIATION

The international airport is at Bangui-M'Poko. There are also 37 small airports for internal services.

Agence pour la sécurité de la navigation aérienne en Afrique et Madagascar (ASECNA): 32-38, Avenue Jean Jaurès, BP 828, Bangui; tel. 61-33-80; fax 61-49-18; e-mail contact@asecna.aero; internet www.asecna.com; Dir-Gen. OUSMANE ISSOUFOU OUBANDAWAKI.

Centrafrican Airlines (CAL): Aéroport Bangui-M'Poko; f. 1999; privately-owned; internal flights.

Mondial Air Fret (MAF): BP 1883, Bangui; tel. 61-14-58; fax 61-62-62; f. 1998; Dir THÉOPHILE SONNY COLE.

Tourism

Although tourism remains relatively undeveloped, the Central African Republic possesses considerable scenic attractions in its waterfalls, forests and wildlife. Tourist arrivals were estimated at 10,000 in 1999, compared with only 1,599 in 1990. In 1998 receipts from tourism were estimated at US $6m.

Office National Centrafricain du Tourisme (OCATOUR): rue Roger Guérillot, BP 645, Bangui; tel. 61-45-66.

CHAD

Introductory Survey

Location, Climate, Language, Religion, Flag, Capital

The Republic of Chad is a land-locked country in north central Africa, bordered to the north by Libya, to the south by the Central African Republic, to the west by Niger, Nigeria and Cameroon, and to the east by Sudan. The climate is hot and arid in the northern desert regions of the Sahara but very wet, with annual rainfall of 5,000 mm (197 ins) in the south. The official languages are French and Arabic, and various African languages are also widely spoken. Almost one-half of the population are Muslims, living in the north. About 30% of the population are Christians. Most of the remainder follow animist beliefs. The national flag (proportions 2 by 3) has three equal vertical stripes, of dark blue, yellow and red. The capital is N'Djamena.

Recent History

Formerly a province of French Equatorial Africa, Chad achieved full independence on 11 August 1960. However, the sparsely populated northern territory of Borkou-Ennedi-Tibesti, accounting for some 47% of the area of Chad, remained under French military control until 1965. The first President of the independent republic was François (later Ngarta) Tombalbaye, a southerner and leader of the Parti progressiste tchadien (PPT). In 1962 the PPT was declared the sole political party. In 1965 a full-scale insurgency began, concentrated mainly in the north. The Muslims of northern Chad have historically been in conflict with their black southern compatriots, who are mainly Christians or animists. The banned Front de libération nationale du Tchad (FROLINAT, founded in Sudan in 1966) assumed leadership of the revolt. The rebellion was partially quelled in 1968, following French military intervention.

In 1973 several prominent figures in the regime, including Gen. Félix Malloum, the Army Chief of Staff, were imprisoned on charges of conspiracy. Also in that year Libyan troops occupied the so-called 'Aozou strip', an apparently mineral-rich region of some 114,000 sq km (44,000 sq miles) in northern Chad, over which Libya claimed sovereignty.

In April 1975 Tombalbaye was killed in a military coup. Malloum was released and appointed President, leading a military regime; the Mouvement national pour la révolution culturelle et sociale, which had succeeded the PPT in 1973, was dissolved. In early 1978 FROLINAT, which received clandestine military assistance from Libya, seized control of a large area of the north before its advance was halted by French military intervention. In August, after negotiations with Malloum, Hissène Habré, a former leader of FROLINAT, was appointed Prime Minister. However, disagreements developed between Habré (a Muslim from the north) and Malloum over the status of Muslims in Chad.

In February 1979 armed conflict broke out between Habré's Forces armées du nord (FAN) and the government armed forces, the Forces armées tchadiennes (FAT). The FAN gained control of the capital, N'Djamena, and in March Malloum resigned and fled the country. In April a provisional Government was formed, comprising representatives of several groups, including FROLINAT, the FAN and the FAT, but sporadic fighting continued. In August 11 factions formed a Gouvernement d'union nationale de transition (GUNT), with Goukouni Oueddei, the leader of FROLINAT, as President and Lt-Col (later Gen.) Wadal Abdelkader Kamougué as Vice-President.

Goukouni's authority was undermined by continual disagreements with Habré, and in March 1980 fighting resumed. In October Libyan forces intervened directly in the hostilities, in support of Goukouni. By December Habré had been defeated, and a Libyan force of some 15,000 men was established in the country. In November 1981 Libyan troops were withdrawn, and a peace-keeping force was installed under the auspices of the Organization of African Unity (OAU—now the African Union, see p. 144). The conflict intensified, however, and in June 1982 Habré's forces captured N'Djamena. Habré was formally inaugurated as President in October, and Goukouni formed a rival administration in Bardaï.

In January 1983 some members of the FAT joined Habré's FAN to form the Forces armées nationales tchadiennes (FANT).

In August Goukouni's rebel forces, with Libyan support, captured the northern administrative centre of Faya-Largeau. France dispatched a further 3,000 troops to Chad and imposed an 'interdiction line' to separate the warring factions. In September it was announced that fighting had ceased. In June 1984, in an attempt to consolidate his political support in the south, Habré replaced the FROLINAT-FAN movement with a new organization, the Union nationale pour l'indépendance et la révolution (UNIR). In September Libya and France agreed to withdraw their troops from Chad. By mid-November all French troops had left the country; however, it was reported that some 3,000 Libyan troops remained in Chad. By the end of 1985 hostilities in southern Chad had ceased. In February 1986, however, GUNT forces, with support from Libya, attacked government positions south of the 'interdiction line'. Habré appealed for French military assistance, and France agreed to establish a defensive air-strike force (designated Opération Epervier) in N'Djamena. The GUNT, meanwhile, began to disintegrate. Kamougué resigned as Goukouni's Vice-President in June, and in February 1987 declared his support for Habré. In August 1986, meanwhile, Acheikh Ibn Oumar's Conseil démocratique révolutionnaire (CDR) also withdrew support from Goukouni. In October, following armed clashes between the Libyan-supported CDR and his own Forces armées populaires (FAP), Goukouni declared himself willing to seek a reconciliation with Habré.

In December 1986 clashes began in the Tibesti region between Libyan forces and the (now pro-Habré) FAP. FANT troops moved into northern Chad and, with increased logistical support from France and the USA, forced Libya to withdraw from Faya-Largeau. In May 1987 Libyan troops retreated to the 'Aozou strip'. In August FANT troops attacked and occupied the town of Aozou, which was, however, recaptured by Libyan forces three weeks later. In September the FANT made an incursion into southern Libya. An OAU-brokered cease-fire took effect, but sporadic fighting continued, and the Chadian Government claimed that Libyan aircraft were repeatedly violating Chadian airspace.

Following negotiations between the Ministers of Foreign Affairs of Chad and Libya in Gabon in July 1988, agreement was reached, in principle, to restore diplomatic relations. However, the issues of the sovereignty of the Aozou region, the fate of Libyan prisoners of war in Chad, and the security of common borders remained unresolved. In October 1988 diplomatic relations were resumed, and the September 1987 cease-fire agreement was reaffirmed, although Chad continued to accuse Libya of violating the conditions of the agreement.

The cohesion of the GUNT was undermined in 1988 by a dispute between Goukouni and Acheikh Ibn Oumar. Several former opposition groups transferred their support to Habré, and in November, following negotiations with UNIR, Acheikh Ibn Oumar and his supporters returned to Chad. He was appointed Minister of Foreign Affairs in March 1989. In April Mahamat Itno, the Minister of the Interior and Territorial Administration, was arrested following the discovery of an alleged plot to overthrow Habré. Idriss Deby, a former Commander-in-Chief of the Armed Forces, who was also implicated in the attempted coup, fled to Sudan, where he established a new opposition group.

In June 1989 the Government accused Libya of planning a military offensive against Chad, with the complicity of Sudan. In July the Libyan leader, Col Muammar al-Qaddafi, and Habré met for the first time, in Mali, but their negotiations were inconclusive. On 31 August, however, Acheikh Ibn Oumar met his Libyan counterpart in Algiers, where they signed an outline peace accord. Under its terms, if a negotiated settlement to the dispute over sovereignty of the 'Aozou strip' was not achieved within one year, the issue was to be submitted to the International Court of Justice (ICJ) for adjudication. Provision was made for the withdrawal of all armed forces from the Aozou region and the release of all prisoners of war. No agreement was reached at discussions between Habré and Qaddafi in Morocco in August 1990, and the territorial dispute was referred for adjudication by the ICJ.

In December 1989 a new Constitution was reportedly approved by 99.94% of voters in a national referendum. In endorsing the document, the electorate also approved Habré in the office of President for a further seven-year term. The new Constitution confirmed UNIR as the sole legal party, and provided for the establishment of an elected legislature. Elections to this 123-seat Assemblée nationale followed in July 1990.

In November 1990 the Mouvement patriotique du salut (MPS—previously styled the Forces patriotiques du salut) invaded Chad from Sudan. Although a previous attack, in March, had been successfully countered by government forces, on this occasion the MPS forces were able to advance rapidly towards N'Djamena. France reiterated its policy of non-interference in Chad's internal affairs, and on 30 November Habré and his associates fled Chad. Deby arrived in N'Djamena two days later. The Assemblée nationale was dissolved, and the Constitution suspended, pending the proposed introduction of a multi-party political system. Deby became interim Head of State. Several members of the former Habré regime, including Acheikh Ibn Oumar, were included in the new Government.

Following Deby's accession to power, many political organizations that had opposed Habré announced their support for the MPS. Deby announced that a smaller national army, to be known as the Armée nationale tchadienne (ANT), was to replace the FANT. The French Government responded favourably to the new administration, and the Libyan and Sudanese Governments declared their support for the MPS, undertaking not to allow forces hostile to Deby to operate on their territory. Deby, however, reiterated Chad's claim to the Aozou region, which remained under consideration by the ICJ. In March 1991 the Government promulgated a National Charter to operate for a 30-month transitional period, confirming Deby's appointment as President, Head of State and Chairman of the MPS, and creating a Council of Ministers (headed by Jean Bawoyeu Alingué) and a 31-member legislative Conseil de la République. In May Deby announced that a national conference would be convened in May 1992 to prepare a new Constitution. Interim arrangements permitting the registration of political parties would enter into force in January 1992.

In September 1991 forces loyal to Habré apparently entered Chad from Niger and attacked military garrisons in the north of the country. In the following month disaffected ANT troops attacked an arsenal at N'Djamena airport in an attempt to seize power; some 40 people were killed in the ensuing fighting. Several officials, including the Minister of the Interior, were arrested on charges connected with the incident, which some analysts believed had been provoked by discontent within the Hadjerai ethnic group at its perceived under-representation in government. France reaffirmed its support for the MPS and announced that an additional 300 troops would be dispatched to Chad. Following the coup attempt, Chad abrogated a recent co-operation agreement with Libya, on the grounds that the sovereignty of the Aozou region remained in dispute. In December some 3,000 pro-Habré rebels of the Libya-based Mouvement pour la démocratie et le développement (MDD) attacked towns in the Lake Chad region. Following expressions of concern by France (which had dispatched reinforcements for the Epervier contingent) at reported abuses of human rights, including the summary execution of a number of rebels, the Deby administration reiterated its commitment to the democratic process, and declared a general amnesty for political prisoners. In February 1992 a further *coup d'état* was attempted by members of the armed forces.

In April 1992 the MDD claimed that more than 40 of its activists, including its leader, Goukouni Guët, had been arrested in Nigeria, extradited to Chad, and subsequently imprisoned or executed. In May MDD rebels launched a new offensive in the Lake Chad region. In the same month a number of amendments to the National Charter were adopted, and Joseph Yodoyman, a member of the opposition Alliance nationale pour la démocratie et le développement (ANDD), was appointed Prime Minister. A new Council of Ministers included, for the first time, members of several opposition parties and human rights organizations. In June an agreement between the Government and the Comité de sursaut national pour la paix et la démocratie (CSNPD), the dissident faction of the armed forces responsible for the abortive coup attempt in February, provided for the release of detained members of the CSNPD and their reintegration into the ANT. In June an agreement was signed in

Libreville, Gabon, providing for a cessation of hostilities between government forces and the MDD. In July Yodoyman was expelled from the ANDD, and another member of the ANDD subsequently left the Government. A reorganization of the Council of Ministers took place in August, after three representatives of human rights organizations resigned from the Government.

In September 1992 an agreement was reached by the Government and an opposition group based in Sudan, the Front national du Tchad (FNT), which granted the FNT the status of a political party. Later that month the Government signed further peace agreements with the MDD, which had resumed activities in the Lake Chad region, and with the CSNPD, which had engaged in clashes with government forces in Doba, in the south, in August. In October, however, the MDD was reported to have begun a renewed offensive against government forces at Bagassola, near Lake Chad, and at the end of that month the MDD declared the peace agreement to be invalid, alleging that the Government was preparing to resume hostilities.

The national conference was finally convened in January 1993. In April the conference, which had been accorded sovereign status, adopted a Transitional Charter, elected Dr Fidel Moungar, hitherto Minister of National and Higher Education, as Prime Minister, and established a 57-member interim legislature, the Conseil supérieur de la transition (CST). The leader of the Rassemblement pour la démocratie et le progrès (RDP), Lol Mahamat Choua—who had briefly served as President in 1979, was elected Chairman of the CST. Under the terms of the Transitional Charter, Deby was to remain Head of State and Commander-in-Chief of the Armed Forces for a period of one year (with provision for one extension), while a Transitional Government, under the supervision of the CST, was to implement economic, political and social programmes as drafted by the conference.

In mid-1993 the Government announced that the ANT and other security forces were to be reorganized, in response to widespread public concern at increasing violence involving the armed and security forces; in May the Government had confirmed the findings of a commission of inquiry that its forces had carried out massacres of civilians in southern Chad earlier that year. Moungar announced that members of the armed forces who were implicated in the violence had been arrested, that military units in the region were to be replaced, and that a judicial investigation was to be instituted. In August, none the less, armed men killed 82 civilians in the southern prefecture of Ouaddaï. Shortly afterwards it was reported that some 41 people had been killed when a demonstration in N'Djamena, organized in protest at the massacre, was suppressed by the Republican Guard.

In October 1993 the CST approved a motion expressing 'no confidence' in the Moungar administration, apparently initiated by supporters of Deby. Moungar resigned, and in November the CST elected Kassire Delwa Koumakoye, hitherto Minister of Justice, Keeper of the Seals, as Prime Minister. In December teachers and other government employees began strike action in protest at the Government's failure to pay salary arrears. The 50% devaluation of the CFA franc, in January 1994, precipitated further unrest.

Meanwhile, rebel activities by the so-called 'politico-military' movements continued. In January 1994 members of the FNT (who were to have been integrated into the ANT following the peace agreement with the Government) attacked a military garrison at Abéché, in the north-east. In February negotiations between the Chadian authorities and the CSNPD, with mediation by the Central African Republic (CAR), failed to secure a lasting peace, and further clashes were reported in southern Chad in late March.

In February 1994 the ICJ ruled in favour of Chad in the issue of the sovereignty of the Aozou region. In May 1994 the Governments of Chad and Libya issued a joint statement confirming that the withdrawal of Libyan troops from the region had been completed as scheduled. In June a co-operation agreement consolidated relations between the two countries.

In March 1994 an Institutional Committee submitted constitutional recommendations, which included provisions for the introduction of a five-year presidential term, the installation of a bicameral legislature and a Constitutional Court, and the establishment of a decentralized administrative structure. In April the CST extended the transitional period by one year. A new electoral timetable was adopted, whereby the Government was obliged to provide funds for the organization of the elections, to reach an agreement with the Union des syndicats du Tchad (UST) in order to end industrial unrest, and, by June, to adopt an electoral code, to establish a national reconciliation council (to negotiate a peace settlement with the rebel movements), and to appoint electoral and human rights commissions. Government efforts to negotiate a settlement with the UST were impeded by strike action by public-sector workers in mid-1994, when agreement was reached on limited salary increases and the payment of arrears. In May Deby effected a comprehensive reorganization of the Government.

In August 1994 the Chadian authorities and the CSNPD signed a cease-fire agreement, providing for the recognition of the CSNPD as a legal political organization and the integration of its forces into the ANT. Later that month government troops were reported to have killed 26 civilians in the south, in reprisal for attacks by members of another rebel faction, the Forces armées pour la République fédérale (FARF). In September it was reported that the Minister of Mines and Energy, Lt-Col Mahamat Garfa (who had recently been dismissed as Chief of Army Staff), had fled N'Djamena with substantial government funds, and, together with some 600 members of the ANT, had joined rebel forces of the Conseil national de redressement du Tchad in eastern Chad; Garfa subsequently established a co-ordination of eight rebel groups operative in eastern Chad from abroad, the Alliance nationale de la résistance (ANR), while remaining in exile himself. In October Choua was replaced as Chairman of the CST by a member of the MPS, Mahamat Bachar Ghadaia. Choua subsequently accused the Government of human rights violations, including the assassination of two prominent members of the RDP.

Deby officially announced in November 1994 that the process of democratic transition would conclude on 9 April 1995, following presidential and legislative elections. In December 1994 Deby declared a general amnesty for political prisoners and opposition members in exile, notably excluding Habré. In the same month an independent national electoral commission was established. In January 1995 the CST adopted a new electoral code and subsequently approved the draft Constitution, which had been amended in accordance with recommendations made by a national conference in August 1994. In March 1995 the CST extended the transitional period for a further year and amended the National Charter to debar the incumbent Prime Minister from contesting the forthcoming presidential election or from belonging to a political party. In April the Court of Appeal annulled the results of an electoral census conducted in February, citing procedural irregularities. In the same month the CST, which had criticized the Government's lack of progress in organizing democratic elections, voted to remove Koumakoye from the premiership and subsequently elected Djimasta Koibla, a prominent member of the Union pour la démocratie et la République (UDR), as Prime Minister.

In August 1995 the Chairman and other members of the Executive Bureau of the CST resigned, following accusations of the misappropriation of funds. In late August security forces raided the home of Saleh Kebzabo, the leader of the opposition Union nationale pour le développement et le renouveau (UNDR). In protest, an informal alliance of opposition parties, to which the UNDR belonged, announced that it was to suspend participation in the CST and demanded the resignation of the head of the security forces.

In November 1995 the Government and the MDD agreed to a cease-fire, an exchange of prisoners and the integration of a number of MDD troops into the ANT. Reconciliation discussions between the Chadian Government and its opponents were convened in Franceville, Gabon, in January 1996. In March the Government and 13 opposition parties signed a cease-fire agreement. Although it appeared that the majority of the armed movements had rejected the agreement, the conclusion of the Franceville accord allowed the electoral programme to proceed. Although several opposition parties, particularly the southern-based organizations that favoured the adoption of a federal system of government, urged their supporters to reject the draft Constitution (which enshrined a unitary state), the new Constitution was endorsed by 63.5% of votes cast at a national referendum on 31 March 1996.

Deby was among 15 candidates authorized to contest the presidential election scheduled for mid-1996. In the first round of voting, held on 2 June, Deby secured 43.9% of the votes cast, followed by Kamougué, with 12.4%, and Kebzabo, with 8.5%. Deby and Kamougué proceeded to a second round of voting on 3 July. Although most of the unsuccessful first-round candidates

urged a boycott of the vote, Kebzabo announced his support for Deby, who won a decisive victory, receiving 69.1% of votes cast. The rate of participation by voters exceeded 75% of the registered electorate. Deby was inaugurated as President on 8 August, and subsequently reappointed Koibla as Prime Minister. Koibla named an interim Council of Ministers, which included several former opposition members, among them Kebzabo as Minister of Foreign Affairs. In September representatives of the Government and the MDD signed a peace agreement in Niger.

At legislative elections held on 5 January and 23 February 1997 the MPS secured an absolute majority in the 125-member Assemblée nationale, winning 65 seats, while Kamougué's Union pour le renouveau et la démocratie (URD) secured 29 seats, and Kebzabo's UNDR 15. The new Assemblée nationale was inaugurated on 4 April, and in May Kamougué was elected as its President, with the support of the MPS and the UNDR, as well as his own URD. Koibla's transitional Government resigned in the same month. Nassour Guélengdouksia Ouaïdou, hitherto Secretary-General at the Presidency, was named as the new Prime Minister. His Government retained Kebzabo, as Minister of State for Public Works, Transport, Housing and Town Planning, although most strategic portfolios remained under the control of the MPS.

In April 1997 the Government and the FARF signed a conclusive peace agreement, providing for the cessation of all hostilities, a general amnesty for FARF members, the integration of its civilian and armed members into the state apparatus, and the legalization of the movement as a political party, the Front patriotique pour la démocratie. In August the Government was reported to have negotiated a peace agreement with the FAP, the military wing of Goukouni's FROLINAT. Agreement was reached on a general amnesty for the FNT, the Front national du Tchad renové (FNTR—a breakaway group from the FNT) and the Mouvement pour la justice sociale et la démocratie at reconciliation talks with the Government in October. However, later that month fighting erupted in Logone Occidental prefecture between FARF rebels and government troops; according to official figures, 42 FARF fighters, 52 civilians and four members of the ANT were killed. The FARF accused the Government of reneging on its commitment to integrate FARF fighters into the regular armed forces. In an extensive government reshuffle in January 1998 Kebzabo was redesignated Minister of State, Minister of Mines, Energy and Petroleum, a new post. Meanwhile, insecurity persisted. Responsibility for the kidnap, in February 1998, of four French nationals in Moyen Chari prefecture was claimed by the Union des forces démocratiques (UFD). It was subsequently reported that 11 rebels had been killed, and 19 arrested, in an operation to liberate the hostages. French troops were mobilized in support of the Chadian security forces, although the military attaché at the French embassy in N'Djamena, said to be an associate of the UFD leader, Dr Mahamout Nahour, was declared *persona non grata* by the Chadian authorities after Nahour demanded only to negotiate with him. In May Kebzabo and two UNDR secretaries of state were removed from the Government. In the same month a presidential envoy and the FARF Chief of General Staff signed an agreement envisaging an immediate end to rebel activity; the Government undertook to withdraw élite elements of the National Nomadic Guard from the south, and there was to be a general amnesty for FARF militants. The terms of the April 1997 peace accord, whereby the FARF was to be legalized as a political party, were also to be renewed.

Reports emerged from late 1998 of a rebellion in the Tibesti region of northern Chad, led by the Mouvement pour la démocratie et la justice au Tchad (MDJT) of Youssouf Togoimi, who had been dismissed as Minister of the Armed Forces in 1997. The Government did not acknowledge the existence of any rebellion in Tibesti until March 1999; even then, the authorities asserted that Togoimi was leading a group of only some 30 Toubou rebels. It was confirmed that the Government had deployed military reinforcements, including a 3,000-strong élite force, and the authorities admitted that the ANT had suffered some losses in operations against the MDJT. However, claims by Togoimi that his movement was in control of much of the north of the country were categorically denied. In June FROLINAT announced that it was giving political and logistical support to the Tibesti rebellion. In November the MDJT announced that it had defeated ANT forces in Aozou, killing 80 and capturing 47 (a further 42 ANT troops were said to have defected to the rebellion).

Ouaïdou resigned as Prime Minister in December 1999. He was replaced by Nagoum Yamassoum, whose new Government included five UNDR members, among them Kebzabo as Minister of State, Minister of Agriculture. A minor government reshuffle was effected in March 2000. Meanwhile, in December 1999 it was announced that 13 'politico-military' groups, including FROLINAT and the FNTR, had formed a new anti-Government alliance led by Antoine Bangui, the Coordination des mouvements armés et partis politiques de l'opposition (CMAP). In the same month another four 'politico-military' groups, led by Acheikh Ibn Oumar of the CDR, formed the Comité politique d'action et de liaison (CPAL). In February 2000 it was reported that the former armed wing of the MDD had renamed itself the Mouvement pour l'unité et la République and allied itself with the MDJT and the CDR. No significant progress was achieved at talks held in Libya in April 2000 between Deby and Goukouni Oueddei, the leader of FROLINAT-Conseil provisoire de la révolution (FROLINAT-CPR), as the organization had been renamed.

In July 2000 the MDJT attacked a garrison in Bardaï and proclaimed its control of four towns in Tibesti. Official sources stated that 57 rebels and 13 government troops were killed during the fighting. The Prime Minister visited the region and invited MDJT negotiators to take part in peace discussions. In September it was reported that Moïse Ketté Nodji, the leader of the CSNPD, had been killed during clashes with ANT forces; it was subsequently reported that the CSNPD had been dissolved. In September Togoimi met with Deby for the first time, in Sirte, Libya. Togoimi's proposal for multilateral peace discussions, incorporating all opposition groups and Deby's administration, was followed later that month by a conference at which Deby met with representatives of some 30 organizations (including trade unions and civil society groups, in addition to political parties), styling themselves the Forces vives, who were reportedly united in their disapproval of a new electoral code (see below). However, renewed fighting broke out in October between members of the MDJT and government forces in the far north and subsequently intensified.

Meanwhile, in July 2000 the Assemblée nationale approved proposals for the creation of an independent electoral body, the Commission électorale nationale indépendante (CENI), which was to plan a reorganization of constituencies in advance of elections due to be held in 2001. An extensive reshuffle of the Government at the end of August 2000 followed the dismissal of ministers belonging to the URD, owing to their party's rejection of the new electoral code.

In February 2001 it was announced that a presidential election would take place on 20 May and that legislative elections, initially scheduled for April, would be postponed until March 2002 for financial reasons. Municipal and local elections, which would have elected the bodies that, in turn, were to elect the members of the proposed upper parliamentary chamber, the Sénat, were postponed indefinitely. In March 2001 opposition leaders and the CENI called for the presidential election to be postponed, alleging that large-scale fraud had been committed in the compilation of the electoral register, although a subsequent legal challenge to have the electoral census annulled failed. In April Deby dismissed all UNDR ministers from the Government, apparently in response to Kebzabo's announcement that he was to contest the presidential election. The Secretary-General of the Parti pour la liberté et le développement (PLD), Ibn Oumar Mahamat Saleh, who was also a presidential candidate, subsequently ordered his party's three ministers to withdraw from the Government. In early May the six opposition presidential candidates, including Kamougué, Yorongar and former Prime Minister Alingué, signed an electoral pact, pledging to unite behind a single candidate in the event of a second round of voting. Meanwhile, in addition to the MDS, 27 political organizations, including the RDP, rallied behind Deby.

The presidential election took place, as scheduled, on 20 May 2001. Although international and national observers pronounced themselves largely satisfied with its conduct, the six opposition candidates alleged widespread fraud and malpractice. In late May, prior to the announcement of the results, eight members of the CENI resigned, in response to apparent irregularities in the vote counting. Following the CENI's announcement of preliminary results crediting Deby with 67.35% of the votes cast, all six opposition candidates were briefly arrested at Kebzabo's home, reportedly for breaching a temporary ban on political meetings. The unsuccessful candidates were subsequently rearrested on charges of inciting violence and civil disobedience, as they attempted to organize a protest march to coincide with the funeral of a dead activist. Although the arrests were promptly rescinded, the Forces vives condemned the election result as fraudulent and called a general strike. Moreover, the opposition presented a petition to the Constitutional Council, requesting that the election be annulled. On 13 June the Constitutional Council issued the final results of the election, according to which Deby had won 63.17% of the valid votes cast, followed by Yorongar, with 16.35%. (Yorongar's supporters claimed that he had won more than one-half of the votes cast.) A turn-out of 61.4% was declared, compared with the 80.9% that had been announced initially. Following Deby's inauguration on 8 August, Yamassoum was reappointed as Prime Minister; the new 35-member Government comprised 20 representatives from the MPS, five from the RDP and 10 other allies of Deby. The CDR condemned the appointments, and, despite a promise by Deby to review the electoral register, opposition parties continued to urge a boycott of the legislative elections scheduled for early 2002.

Disagreements between the CMAP and the CPAL became apparent in late 2001, following a declaration by Deby in August that he was willing to engage in dialogue with the two groups. In September FROLINAT-CPR was expelled from the CMAP, which accused Goukouni's party of engaging in separate discussions with the Government. In late October, however, the CMAP expressed a willingness to enter into discussions with Deby and offered to send a delegation to N'Djamena if its security could be assured; the CPAL continued to oppose any negotiations. In December the CMAP presented the Government with proposals for a peace plan, and in the following month the Minister of Foreign Affairs, Mahamat Saleh Annadif, held discussions with CMAP members in France and with other exiled opposition members in Benin and Nigeria. Meanwhile, negotiations took place in N'Djamena between the Government and principal opposition leaders (with the notable exception of Yorongar); although some progress was reported, opposition parties continued to demand a full reorganization of the voter registration exercise. In late January 2002 Deby announced that the elections would be held on 21 April; according to the revised electoral code, the Assemblée nationale was to be enlarged to 155 members.

Meanwhile, reports emerged in December 2001 that the Libyan Government, which was mediating between MDJT rebels and the Chadian Government, had assured the rebels of its support. (The insurgency in northern Chad had intensified in the second half of 2001; reports, in mid-July, that MDJT forces had captured the town of Fada, killing 86 government troops, were denied by the authorities.) The involvement of Libya in the peace process was regarded as a major factor in the beneficial terms offered to the MDJT in a peace agreement, signed by the group's deputy leader, Adoum Togoi Abbo (a former Chadian ambassador to Libya), and the Chadian Government in early January 2002. According to the agreement, both sides would institute an immediate cease-fire and a general amnesty for prisoners. Moreover, the MDJT was to participate in the Chadian Government and other state institutions, while the rebel forces were to be regularized. Notably, the Libyan Government was to be responsible for monitoring the implementation of the agreement. However, Togoimi did not give his approval to the arrangements and, as a split in the rebel group became evident, in early April the MDJT issued a statement accusing the Government of inhibiting the peace process by its refusal to postpone legislative elections in order to allow the appointment of MDJT representatives to the Government. (It was, however, subsequently reported that Togoimi had demanded to be appointed as Prime Minister of Chad; some elements within the MDJT, moreover, stated that Togoi had been expelled from the organization.) In late April the CMAP also announced the suspension of peace negotiations with the Government.

Elections to the Assemblée nationale, which took place on 21 April 2002, were contested by 472 candidates, representing some 40 parties, although the UDR and PLD boycotted the polls. According to the final election results, the MPS won 110 seats in the Assemblée nationale, significantly increasing its representation. (It was reported that MPS candidates were unopposed in some 50 constituencies.) The RDP became the second largest party, with 12 seats, while the FAR became the largest opposition party, with nine seats. Koumakoye's VIVA—Rassemblement national pour la démocratie et le progrès and the UNDR each won five seats, and the URD's representation was significantly reduced, to only three seats. The Constitutional Council annulled the results of voting in two constituencies. In mid-June Ouaïdou was elected as President of the Assemblée nationale, and Deby appointed his special counsellor, Haroun Kabadi, a senior official in the MPS, as Prime Minister, to head a 28-member Council of Ministers, in which several important ministers retained their portfolios. Notably, a new Ministry of Petroleum was created, distinct from the Ministry of Mines and Energy.

Meanwhile, in mid-May 2002 it was reported that Togoi was being held in detention by forces loyal to Togoimi, who had confirmed his rejection of the peace agreement signed in January; MDJT commanders denied that Togoi had been killed. None the less, in early July some 200 former MDJT fighters were reported to have joined government forces. In early June the FNTR announced the cessation of its armed struggle. An attack, in mid-September, on the eastern village of Tissi was attributed by the Chadian Government to troops supported by the CAR, although the ANR, which been dormant for several years, claimed responsibility for the raid and, amid heightened tension with the CAR (see below), emphasized that the perpetrators of the attack were resident in Chad.

The death of Togoimi, in Libya, in late September 2002, while being treated for injuries sustained in a landmine explosion in northern Chad in August, raised hopes that peace talks between the Government and the MDJT would be reconvened, and Deby visited the north in order to encourage a resumption of negotiations. The leadership of the MDJT was assumed, in an acting capacity, by Adoum Maurice Hel-Bongo, although a split in the organization, between those loyal to Togoi and those loyal to Hel-Bongo became evident in subsequent months. In early October renewed fighting broke out in the north; following an attack by the MDJT on an airport at Faya N'Gourma, in which some 20 ANT soldiers reportedly died, further clashes were reported near Fada, in which, according to official figures, 50 MDJT rebels were killed. Later in the month the Government announced that the ANT had mounted an offensive against the MDJT near Ennedi, killing 123 MDJT fighters and capturing a futher 63, as well as releasing 20 Sudanese and four Libyan civilians held hostage by the rebels. (These figures were disputed by the MDJT.) In mid-November rebels of the Forces des organisations nationales pour l'alternance et les libertés au Tchad (FONALT), one of the constituent groups of the ANR, claimed to have killed 116 ANT soldiers in clashes near Adré, close to the borders with Sudan and the CAR, although the Chadian Government made no official confirmation or denial of these reports.

A minor ministerial reshuffle was effected in mid-November 2002; notably, the Secretary-General of the MPS, Mahamat Saleh Ahmat, hitherto Minster of State, responsible for Land Management, Town Planning and Housing, left the Government, while a new Minister of Mines and Energy, Mahamat Madadou Adji, was among those appointed.

In early January 2003, following negotiations in Libreville, Gabon, hosted by the Gabonese President, Omar Bongo, the Government and the ANR signed a peace memorandum, in which rebels of the organization were granted a general amnesty prior to their reintegration into the civilian sector. Moreover, Garfa, the leader of the ANR, returned to Chad for the first time since 1994. However, the FONALT rejected the terms of the accord. During the first half of 2003 reports emerged of the formation of a new 'umbrella' grouping of 'politico-military' organizations opposed to the Deby regime, the Front uni pour la démocratie et la paix (FUDP). The initiative to establish the FUDP had apparently come from among Chadian exiles in Benin, although, following pressure from the Beninois authorities, several influential members of the group left Benin for Togo. In April Hel-Bongo resigned as acting president of the MDJT. By mid-July, when Togoi was elected as President of the FUDP, at a congress reportedly held in Nigeria, several 'politico-military' organizations had announced their affiliation to the grouping, including the FNTR, the MDD and the faction of the MDJT loyal to Togoi. The FUDP stated as its objective the establishment of a new constitution and of a transitional government, prior to the holding of free and transparent elections. In late August the faction of the MDJT that had remained outside the FUDP elected Col Hassan Abdallah Mardigué as its leader. In early September more than 200 MDJT fighters were reported to have surrendered to government forces near Fada; following the signing of a peace accord between the Minister of National Defence, Veterans and Victims of War, Gen. Mahamat Nouri, and a local MDJT commander, Col Mahamat Abdramane

Darbai, these former rebels were to be integrated into the ANT. None the less, later in the month MDJT rebels in Tibesti claimed that the organization had captured Bardai airport, killing some 35 government troops; the Government denied these claims, stating that 10 MDJT fighters had been killed in an unsuccessful attack on the airport.

Meanwhile, in mid-May 2003 15 deputies were elected to serve at the High Court of Justice, one of the institutions that had been established by the 1996 Constitution, but had hitherto remained in abeyance. It was reported that the Minister of the Economy and Finance, Idriss Ahmed Idriss, intended to press charges at the court against the Minister of Public Security and Immigration, Mahamat Ali Abdallah, who was alleged to have redirected some 40,000m. francs CFA of public funds. (However, it was subsequently reported that the Assemblée nationale had voted to reject Idriss's proposal, pending the findings of an *ad hoc* parliamentary commission into the accusations.) In a minor government reorganization effected later in the month Abdallah became Minister of Trade, Industry and Crafts, but was not reappointed to a new Council of Ministers formed in June, which was headed by a close ally of Deby, Moussa Mahamat Faki, as Prime Minister, and included 11 new members; the dismissal of Kabadi as Prime Minister followed his removal, earlier in June, from the executive committee of the MPS. In late July it was reported that the Assemblée nationale had approved legislation delegating presidential prerogatives to Faki until October, while Deby received medical treatment in France, although the Chadian ambassador to France denied claims that the President was seriously ill.

The Minister of Justice, Keeper of the Seals, Djimnaye Koudji Gaou, died in early September 2003; his successor, Kalzeubé Pahimi, was appointed in early October, when a minor ministerial reshuffle was effected. In mid-November some 20 opposition parties, including the URD and the UNDR, as well as the RDP, which had increasingly distanced itself from the Deby administration, issued a document calling for a programme of electoral reform. Meanwhile, in response to speculation that Deby and his supporters were seeking to amend the Constitution to permit the President to contest a further term of office, the two RDP ministers announced their resignation from the Government in late November; they were replaced by two members of the MPS later in the month. Moreover, Choua, the leader of the RDP, subsequently announced that the party would no longer support the MPS in the Assemblée nationale. In mid-November a motion of 'no confidence' in Prime Minister Faki was overwhelmingly defeated in the Assemblée nationale. In late November Mahamat Hissène, a former communications adviser to Deby and a close ally of the President, was elected as Secretary-General of the MPS. In mid-December the Government signed a peace agreement with Togoi in Ouagadougou, Burkina Faso (where Togoi had been resident since 2000), providing for an immediate cease-fire, an amnesty for MDJT fighters and supporters, and for the eventual inclusion of an undisclosed number of MDJT ministers in the Chadian Government. However, 'hardline' factions of the MDJT rejected the terms of the agreement, claiming to have killed up to 30 government troops in renewed clashes in Tibesti shortly after the agreement had been signed.

In early February 2004 Deby reorganized the Council of Ministers, making changes to seven government positions. Idriss Ahmed Idriss left the Ministry of the Economy and Finance to become the National Director of the regional bank, the Banque des états de l'Afrique centrale; he was replaced by Ahmat Awat Sakine, hitherto Director-General of the Treasury. Gen. Nouri retired as Minister of National Defence, Veterans and Victims of War, reportedly on grounds of ill health, and was replaced by Gen. Allafouz Koni.

A number of new opposition coalitions were formed in 2004. In March six 'politico-military' organizations, including a faction of the MDJT, the MDD, the CDR and the MUR, formed the Union des forces pour le changement (UFC). Acheikh Ibn Oumar was named as Provisional National Co-ordinator of the new grouping, which declared itself committed to the development of national unity and the holding of fair and free elections. In April Ahmat Hassaballah Soubiane, a founder member of the MPS and the former Chadian ambassador to the USA and Canada (a post from which he was reportedly dismissed earlier in the year after criticizing Deby's plans to change the Constitution and seek a third term in office), announced in Washington, DC, the formation of the Coalition pour la défense de la démocratie et des droits constitutionnels (CDDC). In May 25 opposition parties, including the URD, the UNDR and the RDP, announced that they had formed the Coordination des partis politiques pour la défense de la Constitution (CPDC), which, like the CDDC, sought to resist Deby's proposed constitutional modifications.

In a national address in mid-May 2004 Deby confirmed reports that an attempted military coup had been quashed without bloodshed, and that the mutinous soldiers had been forced to surrender after two days of negotiations, claiming that the rebellion had been a response to recent army reforms. Eight constitutional amendments were approved by the Assemblée nationale later that month, the most notable of which removed the restriction limiting the President to serving two terms of office. The changes, which required endorsement in a national referendum, were vigorously criticized by opposition parties, which boycotted the vote, called a national strike (not widely observed) and urged people to demonstrate outside the legislative building. In June the Constitutional Council rejected an opposition appeal to annul the constitutional revisions. In late July Deby effected a major reorganization of the Council of Ministers, dismissing nine ministers—among them Gen. Koni, who was replaced as Minister of National Defence, Veterans and Victims of War by Emmanuel Nadingar, hitherto Assistant Secretary-General to the Government—and creating a new Ministry of State Control and Moralization. Representatives of a number of smaller parties that had supported Deby in the 2001 presidential election were allocated posts in the new Government, although the MPS retained control of the most important portfolios and Faki remained Prime Minister.

In January 2005 the Government launched a census to determine the composition of the electorate in anticipation of the referendum on constitutional amendment. Despite the CPDC's stated policy of boycotting the referendum, the UNDR leader, Saleh Kebzaboh, urged his party members to participate in the census and acquire voting cards, provoking speculation that he was preparing to withdraw from the coalition.

In early 1998 it was reported that Chad was to seek the extradition from Senegal of former President Habré, with a view to his prosecution in relation to human-rights abuses and in connection with the embezzlement of state funds. A committee of inquiry, established by the Deby administration, held Habré's 'political police' responsible for the deaths of some 40,000 people and the torture of 200,000 others. In February 2000, following a ruling by a Senegalese court that he could be tried in that country, Habré was charged with complicity in acts of torture committed in Chad under his leadership, and placed under house arrest. The charges were dismissed in July, however, on the grounds that Senegal lacked the appropriate penal procedure to process such a case. In March 2001 the Senegalese Court of Cassation upheld this ruling. Habré remained in Senegal in early 2004, although his alleged victims were seeking his extradition to stand trial in Belgium, under a law that (as amended in 2003) gave that country's courts universal jurisdiction in cases of human rights abuses and war crimes, if Belgian citizens or long-term residents were among the plaintiffs. (Several of the alleged victims of abuses committed under Habré's regime had been granted Belgian citizenship.)

Relations with France appeared uneasy in the late 1990s, particularly following the expulsion of a French military attaché in early 1998. Further tension arose in March 2000, when the Chadian Government demanded the recall of the French ambassador to Chad, Alain du Boispéan. However, relations subsequently improved, and in September 2002 President Jacques Chirac became the first French Head of State to visit Chad for more than 30 years. The French Minister of Defence, Michèle Alliot-Marie, met Deby on a visit to Chad in April 2003, when she expressed support for the actions of Chadian troops in the force deployed by the Communauté économique et monétaire de l'Afrique centrale (CEMAC) in the CAR (see below). Additionally, Deby undertook a state visit to France in September of that year .

In response to an attempted coup in the CAR in May 2001, Chad reportedly dispatched troops to defend the Government of President Ange-Félix Patassé. In early November heightened unrest broke out in the CAR, following an attempt to arrest the recently dismissed Chief of Staff of the Armed Forces, Gen. François Bozizé, in connection with the May coup attempt. Bozizé crossed into Chad, with an estimated 300 armed supporters, and was granted refuge in Sarh. Chad was subsequently involved in efforts by both the Libyan-sponsored Community of Sahel-Saharan States (see p. 373) and CEMAC to find a lasting solution to the crisis in the CAR. In late December the

CAR judiciary abandoned legal proceedings against Bozizé. Meanwhile, repeated clashes were reported at the Chad–CAR border and an additional source of tension was the appointment of Col Martin Khoumtan-Madji (believed by the Chadian authorities to be an alias of Abdoulaye Miskine, a former senior member of the CSNPD based in the CAR since 1998) as the head of a special unit in the CAR military, comprising some 300 soldiers, including many former Chadian rebels, and answerable directly to the presidency, charged with securing the common border of the two countries.

In early August 2002 the CAR Prime Minister, Martin Ziguélé, accused Chadian troops of launching cross-border attacks in the CAR, precipitating an emergency CEMAC summit later that month, chaired by President Bongo of Gabon. (Chadian sources stated that the troops that had launched the attacks in the CAR were loyal to Bozizé, and not affiliated to the ANT.) A report issued by a CEMAC observer mission, at the end of August, stated that, although tension remained high in the border region, there was no concentration of troops on the border, or of foreign troops in either country. An attack by the ANR in eastern Chad (see above), in early September, was attributed by the Chadian Government to troops supported by the CAR. In early October a CEMAC summit in Libreville, Gabon, sought to defuse tensions between the two countries; in accordance with an accord reached at the summit, Bozizé and Khoumtan-Madji were subsequently granted asylum in France and Togo, respectively; a CEMAC force was subsequently deployed to monitor joint patrols of the border by Chadian and CAR troops. Tensions subsequently abated somewhat, and in late January 2003 the Governments of Chad, the CAR and Sudan announced their intention to establish a tripartite committee to oversee the security and stability of their joint borders. In mid-February the Presidents of Chad and the CAR met in Bangui in an attempt to normalize relations between the two countries. Later that month some 20,000 refugees (many of whom were Chadian nationals who had been resident in the CAR for many years) entered southern Chad, fleeing renewed fighting in the CAR. Following Bozizé's assumption of power in mid-March, some 400 Chadian troops were reportedly dispatched to the CAR; around 120 Chadian troops were subsequently integrated into the CEMAC force that had been deployed in the CAR in late 2002. Relations improved between the two countries during 2003, and in December Deby was a guest of honour at celebrations for the National Day of the CAR in Bangui.

Following the outbreak of a violent rebellion in the Darfur region of western Sudan in February 2003 (see the chapter on Sudan), Deby played a major role in promoting diplomatic measures intended to restore peace to the region, meeting the Sudanese President, Lt-Gen. Omar Hassan Ahmad al-Bashir, in April, August and December. In early November Sudanese and Chadian officials agreed to establish a joint force to patrol the countries' common border, amid rising concerns about cross-border banditry associated with the rebellion. Peace talks between representatives of the Sudanese Government and the rebel Sudan Liberation Movement (SLM) were held in N'Djamena in December, but were inconclusive; the Chadian Government issued a statement blaming the SLM for the breakdown in negotiations. By March 2004 some 130,000 Sudanese citizens had sought refuge in eastern Chad, where many of the population belonged to the same tribe as the refugees from Darfur. At the end of that month indirect peace talks between the Government, the SLM and the Sudan Justice and Equality Movement (SJEM), attended by international observers, commenced in Chad, and on 8 April a 45-day humanitarian ceasefire was signed by representatives of the three parties. Further talks were held in Chad between the Government, the SLM and the SJEM later that month, but little progress was made. Although it was agreed that the cease-fire could be renewed for additional 45-day periods, it failed to hold. Furthermore, in late April and early May a series of clashes occurred between Chadian troops and Sudanese militiamen, known as the *Janjaweed*, pursuing Sudanese rebels across the border; the Chadian Government denounced the incursions and protested to the Sudanese Government. In mid-June the Chadian Government announced that its troops had killed 69 *Janjaweed* fighters who had attacked the Chadian village of Birak, some 6 km from the Sudanese border. By December an estimated 200,000 Sudanese had fled to Chad, according to the office of the UN High Commissioner for Refugees, placing considerable strain on food and water resources in the border region. In that month the Sudanese Government concluded a ceasefire in N'Djamena with a previously unidentified rebel group, the National Movement for Reform and Development (NMRD), which described itself as a breakaway faction of the SJEM. It was hoped that these negotiations would lead to the return of significant numbers of refugees to Sudan, although little progress had been observed by early 2005, and violent clashes in the border area continued.

Further concerns regarding regional security emerged in March 2004, when clashes at the Niger–Chad border between Islamist militants belonging to the Algerian-based Groupe salafiste pour la prédication et le combat (GSPC) and Chadian and Nigerien troops resulted in the deaths of some 43 GSPC fighters and three Chadian soldiers, according to the Chadian Government. It was announced that month that the Governments of Algeria, Chad, Mali and Niger were to reinforce security cooperation in the regions of their common borders. Meanwhile, the MDJT had reportedly captured a prominent GSPC leader, Amara Saïfi (also known as Abderrazak le Para). In July it was reported that the MDJT had released Saïfi, whose faction of the GSPC had apparently united with the Chadian rebel group to fight the Chadian army.

Government

A new Constitution was adopted by national referendum on 31 March 1996. Under the terms of the Constitution, the Republic of Chad is a unitary state with a multi-party political system. Executive power is vested in the President, who is the Head of State and Commander-in-Chief of the Armed Forces. The President is elected by direct universal suffrage for a maximum of two five-year terms of office. The President appoints the Prime Minister, who nominates the Council of Ministers. Legislative power is vested in a bicameral legislature, comprising the 155-member Assemblée nationale, which is elected by direct universal suffrage for a four-year term, and a Sénat, which has a six-year mandate (with one-third of the membership renewable every two years). However, by early 2004 the Sénat had still to be established, as the organs of local government that were to elect its members had not yet been inaugurated, while the constitutional amendments adopted by the Assemblée nationale in May 2004, if approved by the referendum scheduled to take place in 2005, would abolish the Sénat altogether. Chad is divided into 28 administrative departments.

Defence

In August 2004 the Armée nationale tchadienne (ANT) was estimated to number 30,350 (army approximately 25,000, air force 350, Republican Guard 5,000). In addition, there was a 4,500-strong gendarmerie. The army has been undergoing restructuring since 1996. Military service is by conscription. Under defence agreements with France, the army receives technical and other aid: in August 2004 the number of troops deployed in Chad by France numbered 950. Direct aid from France to the Chadian army in 1999 was an estimated 6,160m. francs CFA. Defence expenditure for 2004 was budgeted at an estimated 21,000m. francs CFA.

Economic Affairs

In 2003, according to estimates by the World Bank, Chad's gross national income (GNI), measured at average 2001–03 prices, was US $2,420m., equivalent to $250 per head (or $1,100 on an international purchasing-power parity basis). During 1990–2003, it was estimated, the population increased at an average annual rate of 3.0%, while gross domestic product (GDP) per head increased, in real terms, by an average of 0.6% per year. Overall GDP increased, in real terms, at an average annual rate of 3.8% in 1990–2003, according to the World Bank; growth in 2003 was 9.9%.

Agriculture contributed 37.7% of GDP in 2003, according to the World Bank; some 72.4% of the labour force were employed in the sector in 2003. The principal cash crop is cotton (exports of which contributed an estimated 15.8% of total export revenue in 2003, a decline from 41.1% in 2001). The principal subsistence crops are sorghum, groundnuts and millet. Livestock-rearing, which contributed an estimated 21.0% of exports in 2003, also makes an important contribution to the domestic food supply. During 1990–2003 agricultural GDP increased at an average annual rate of 5.2%; growth in 2002 was 4.6%.

Industry contributed 16.7% of GDP in 2003. About 4.2% of the population were employed in the sector in 1990. During 1990–2003 industrial GDP increased at an average annual rate of 5.9%; it increased by 25.4% in both 2002 and 2003, partly owing to the revenues from petroleum extraction (see below).

The mining sector (including fishing) contributed 3.2% of GDP in 2000, according to the IMF. For many years the only minerals exploited were natron (sodium carbonate), salt, alluvial gold and materials for the construction industry. However, long-delayed plans to develop sizeable petroleum reserves in the Doba Basin and at Sedigi, in the south of the country, were being pursued in the early 2000s, and production of petroleum at Doba commenced in mid-2003 (see below). There is believed to be considerable potential for the further exploitation of gold, bauxite and uranium. During 1994–2000 the GDP of the mining sector (including fishing) declined at an average annual rate of 0.2%, according to the IMF; growth of 0.8% was recorded in 2000.

The manufacturing sector, which contributed 14.7% of GDP in 2003, operates mainly in the south of the country, and is dominated by agro-industrial activities, notably the processing of the cotton crop by the state-controlled Société Cotonnière du Tchad (COTONTCHAD). During 1994–2000 manufacturing GDP increased at an average annual rate of 14.0%, according to the IMF; however, the GDP of the sector declined by 1.9% in 2000.

Chad is heavily dependent on imports of mineral fuels (principally from Cameroon and Nigeria) for the generation of electricity. Imports of mineral fuels comprised an estimated 65.1% of the total value of merchandise imports in 2003. The use of wood-based fuel products by most households has contributed to the severe depletion of Chad's forest resources. In November 2000 the Cameroonian Prime Minister announced the creation of a technical committee to instigate the export of electricity to Chad. None the less, by 2002 only 2% of households in Chad had access to electricity.

Services contributed 45.6% of GDP in 2003. The GDP of the sector increased at an average annual rate of 2.8% in 1990–2003; growth in 2003 was 7.6%.

In 2002 Chad recorded an estimated visible trade deficit of 198,800m. francs CFA, and there was a deficit of 563,700m. francs CFA on the current account of the balance of payments. In 1995 Chad's principal source of imports (41.3%) was France; other major suppliers were Cameroon, Nigeria and the USA. The principal markets for exports include Cameroon and France. The principal exports in 2003 were petroleum, livestock and cotton. The principal imports in 1995 were petroleum products, road vehicles and parts, sugar and cereals.

In 2002 Chad recorded an overall budgetary deficit of 65,600m. francs CFA (equivalent to 4.7% of GDP). Chad's external debt at the end of 2002 totalled US $1,281m., of which $1,148m. was long-term public debt. In 2001 the cost of debt-servicing was equivalent to 7.9% of earnings from exports of goods and services. Consumer prices increased by an annual average of 5.1% in 2000–03, but in 2003 they declined by 1.9%.

Chad is a member of the Central African organs of the Franc Zone (see p. 267) and of the Communauté économique des états de l'Afrique centrale (CEEAC, see p. 373); the Lake Chad Basin Commission (see p. 374) is based in N'Djamena.

Traditionally, economic growth in Chad has been inhibited by a number of factors: conflict has deterred investment in the development of considerable mineral wealth and other resources, leaving the economy over-dependent on cotton, while the country's land-locked position has been compounded by infrastructural deficiencies. However, in late 2000 a consortium led by the US ExxonMobil Corporation, and supported by Petronas of Malaysia and the US ChevronTexaco Corporation, began work to develop substantial petroleum resources in three fields in the Doba Basin, believed to contain reserves of approximately 900m. barrels. Operations commenced in July 2003, and a 1,070-km pipeline to transport petroleum from Doba to the port of Kribi in Cameroon was officially inaugurated in October. Initial output was estimated at 50,000 barrels per day (b/d), but had reached some 200,000 b/d, by mid-2004; production was expected to continue for 25–30 years. It was predicted that the commencement of petroleum exports would contribute to an increase in GDP of 39.5% in 2004, and forecasts indicated that per capita income in Chad, hitherto among the lowest in the world, would double in 2005. In 1998, the Assemblée nationale had adopted legislation whereby 72% of state revenue from the petroleum sector would be dedicated to the development of health, education, agriculture and infrastructure, while a further 10% would be held in trust for future generations. In 2000 work commenced on the construction of a pipeline from petroleum reserves at Sedigi to a new refinery in Farcha, near N'Djamena. The refinery would supply a new 16-MW power station in the capital, and provide fuel for local transportation requirements. In January 2005, in a visit to Taiwan, President Deby approved a $100m. investment agreement for Chad's petroleum sector with the state-owned Chinese Petroleum Corporation. Meanwhile, in January 2000 the IMF approved funding under its Poverty Reduction and Growth Facility (PRGF) in support of the Government's economic programme for 1999–2002. Furthermore, in May 2001 the Bretton Woods institutions declared Chad eligible for debt-service relief under their enhanced initiative for heavily indebted poor countries. The IMF increased Chad's PRGF by some US $6.8m. in January 2002, in order to alleviate the adverse effects of declining world prices for cotton, and in October the IMF agreed to a request by the Chadian authorities to extend the facility to December 2003. It was hoped that the increase in GDP provided by petroleum revenues would enable the Government to address effectively the large social and development needs of the country's population and to take measures to combat poverty. Nevertheless, the Government was warned against over-reliance on the petroleum sector for future economic growth and was urged to improve expenditure management and to further reform the cotton, domestic energy, and financial sectors.

Education

Education is officially compulsory for six years between six and 12 years of age. Primary education begins at the age of six and lasts for six years. Secondary education, from the age of 12, lasts for seven years, comprising a first cycle of four years and a second of three years. In 2000/01 primary enrolment included 58% of children in the relevant age-group (males 70%; females 47%), while in 1999/2000 secondary enrolment included only 8% of children in the appropriate age-group (males 12%; females 4%). The Université du Tchad was opened at N'Djamena in 1971. In addition, there are several technical colleges. Some 5,901 students were enrolled at higher education institutions in 1999/2000. Total expenditure on education by the central Government (including foreign-financed investment) in 1996 was 32,196m. francs CFA (21.2% of total government expenditure).

Public Holidays

2005: 1 January (New Year), 21 January* (Id al-Adha, Feast of the Sacrifice), 28 March (Easter Monday), 21 April* (Maloud, Birth of the Prophet), 1 May (Labour Day), 16 May (Whit Monday), 25 May ('Liberation of Africa', anniversary of the OAU's foundation), 11 August (Independence Day), 15 August (Assumption), 1 November (All Saints' Day), 4 November* (Id al-Fitr, end of Ramadan), 28 November (Proclamation of the Republic), 1 December (Liberation and Democracy Day, anniversary of the 1990 coup d'état), 25 December (Christmas).

2006: 1 January (New Year), 11 January* (Id al-Adha, Feast of the Sacrifice), 11 April* (Maloud, Birth of the Prophet), 17 April (Easter Monday), 1 May (Labour Day), 25 May ('Liberation of Africa', anniversary of the OAU's foundation), 5 June (Whit Monday), 11 August (Independence Day), 15 August (Assumption), 1 November (All Saints' Day), 24 October* (Id al-Fitr, end of Ramadan), 28 November (Proclamation of the Republic), 1 December (Liberation and Democracy Day, anniversary of the 1990 coup d'état), 25 December (Christmas).

*These holidays are dependent on the Islamic lunar calendar and may vary by one or two days from the dates given.

Weights and Measures

The metric system is officially in force.

Statistical Survey

Source (unless otherwise stated): Direction de la Statistique, des Etudes Economiques et Démographiques, BP 453, N'Djamena; tel. 52-31-64.

Area and Population

AREA, POPULATION AND DENSITY

Area (sq km)	
Land	1,259,200
Inland waters	24,800
Total	1,284,000*
Population (sample survey)	
December 1963–August 1964	3,254,000†
Population (census result)	
8 April 1993‡	
Males	2,950,415
Females	3,208,577
Total	6,158,992
Population (UN estimates at mid-year)§	
2001	8,103,000
2002	8,348,000
2003	8,598,000
Density (per sq km) at mid-2002	6.7

* 495,800 sq miles.
† Including areas not covered by the survey.
‡ Figures are provisional. The revised total, including an adjustment for underenumeration (estimated at 1.4%), is 6,279,931.
§ Source: UN, *World Population Prospects: The 2002 Revision.*

ETHNIC GROUPS

1995 (percentages): Sara, Bongo and Baguirmi 20.1; Chadic 17.7; Arab 14.3; M'Bourn 6.3; Masalit, Maba and Mimi 6.1; Tama 6.1; Adamawa 6.0; Sudanese 6.0; Mubi 4.1; Hausa 2.1; Kanori 2.1; Massa 2.1; Kotoko 2.0; Peul 0.5; Others 4.5 (Source: La Francophonie).

PREFECTURES
(1993 census)

	Area (sq km)	Population*	Density (per sq km)	Principal city
Batha	88,800	288,458	3.2	Ati
Biltine	46,850	184,807	3.9	Biltine
Borkou-Ennedi-Tibesti (BET)	600,350	73,185	0.1	Faya-Largeau
Chari-Baguirmi† . .	82,910	1,251,906	15.1	N'Djamena
Guéra	58,950	306,253	5.2	Mongo
Kanem	114,520	279,927	2.4	Mao
Lac	22,320	252,932	11.3	Bol
Logone Occidental . .	8,695	455,489	52.4	Moundou
Logone Oriental . .	28,035	441,064	15.7	Doba
Mayo-Kebbi	30,105	825,158	27.4	Bongor
Moyen Chari . . .	45,180	738,595	16.3	Sarh
Ouaddaï	76,240	543,900	7.1	Abéché
Salamat	63,000	184,403	2.9	Am-Timan
Tandjile	18,045	453,854	25.2	Lai
Total	1,284,000	6,279,931	4.9	

* Including adjustment for underenumeration.
† Including the capital district, N'Djamena (population 530,965).
Note: As a result of administrative reform, Chad's former prefectures have been replaced by the following departments: Assongha (principal city Adré), Baguirmi (Massenya), Bahr el Gazal (Moussoro), Bahr Kôh (Sarh), Batha Est (Oum-Hadjer), Batha Ouest (Ati), Biltine (Biltine), Borkou (Faya-Largeau), Dababa (Bokoro), Ennedi (Fada), Guera (Mongo), Hadjer Lamis (Massaguet), Kabia (Gounou Gaya), Kanem (Mao), Lac (Bol), Lac Iro (Kyabe), Logone Occidental (Moundou), Logone Oriental (Doba), Mandoul (Koumra), Mayo Boneye (Bongor), Mayo Dallah (Pala), Monts de Lam (Baïbokoum), Ouaddaï (Abéché), Salamat (Am-Timan), Sila (Goz-Beïda), Tandjile Est (Lai), Tandjile Ouest (Kelo), Tibesti (Bardaï). The capital city, N'Djamena, constitutes a separate administrative unit.

PRINCIPAL TOWNS
(population at 1993 census)

N'Djamena (capital)	530,965	Koumra	26,702
Moundou	99,530	Pala	26,115
Sarh	75,496	Am Timan	21,269
Abéché	54,628	Bongor	20,448
Kelo	31,319	Mongo	20,443

Mid-2003 (UN estimate, incl. suburbs): N'Djamena 796,853 (Source: UN, *World Urbanization Prospects: The 2003 Revision*).

BIRTHS AND DEATHS
(UN estimates, annual averages)

	1985–90	1990–95	1995–2000
Birth rate (per 1,000)	48.3	48.7	48.3
Death rate (per 1,000)	20.8	20.3	20.1

Source: UN, *World Population Prospects: The 2002 Revision*.

Expectation of life (WHO estimates, years at birth): 47.7 (males 46.1; females 49.3) in 2002 (Source: WHO, *World Health Report*).

ECONOMICALLY ACTIVE POPULATION
(ILO estimates, '000 persons at mid-1990)

	Males	Females	Total
Agriculture, hunting, forestry and fishing	1,179	1,102	2,281
Industry	105	9	115
Manufacturing	50	6	56
Services	245	100	344
Total labour force	1,529	1,211	2,740

Source: ILO.

1993 census (persons aged six years and over): Total labour force 2,719,443 (males 1,416,449; females 1,302,994) (Source: ILO, *Yearbook of Labour Statistics*).

Mid-2003 (estimates in '000): Agriculture, etc. 2,831; Total 3,912 (Source: FAO).

Health and Welfare

KEY INDICATORS

Total fertility rate (children per woman, 2002)	6.7
Under-5 mortality rate (per 1,000 live births, 2003)	200
HIV/AIDS (% of persons aged 15–49, 2003)	4.80
Physicians (per 1,000 head, 1994)	0.03
Hospital beds (per 1,000 head, 1996)	0.72
Health expenditure (2001): US $ per head (PPP)	17
Health expenditure (2001): % of GDP	2.6
Health expenditure (2001): public (% of total)	76.0
Access to water (% of persons, 2002)	34
Access to sanitation (% of persons, 2002)	8
Human Development Index (2002): ranking	167
Human Development Index (2002): value	0.379

For sources and definitions, see explanatory note on p. vi.

Agriculture

PRINCIPAL CROPS
('000 metric tons)

	2001	2002	2003
Wheat	2.8	4.0	3.7*
Rice (paddy)	112.2	134.9	139.0*
Maize	105.3	84.3	120.0*
Millet	397.6	357.4	430.0*
Sorghum	497.2	480.7	560.0*
Other cereals	206.2	151.1	170.0*
Potatoes†	33	33	33
Sweet potatoes†	64	64	64
Cassava (Manioc)	306.0	322.0†	325.0†
Taro (Coco yam)†	38	38	38
Yams†	230	230	230
Sugar cane†	350.0	355.0	355.0
Dry beans	83.3	78.0†	78.0†
Other pulses	42.5	43.0†	43.0†
Groundnuts (in shell)	448.1	450.0*	450.0*
Sesame seed	43.4	35.0*	35.0*
Melonseed†	20	20	20
Cottonseed*	110	113	77
Dry onions†	14	14	14
Other vegetables†	81	81	81
Dates†	18	18	18
Mangoes†	32	32	32
Other fruit†	63	63	63
Cotton (lint)*	70	71	49

* Unofficial figure(s).
† FAO estimate(s).

Source: FAO.

LIVESTOCK
('000 head, year ending September)

	2001	2002	2003
Cattle	5,992	6,128*	6,268*
Goats	5,304	5,463*	5,588*
Sheep	2,431	2,454*	2,511*
Pigs†	22	24	24
Horses*	225	261	267
Asses	364	372†	380†
Camels†	725	725	730
Poultry†	5,000	5,000	120

* Unofficial figure(s).
† FAO estimate(s).

Source: FAO.

LIVESTOCK PRODUCTS
(FAO estimates, '000 metric tons)

	2001	2002	2003
Beef and veal	77.0	76.3	78.3
Mutton and lamb	12.1	12.7	13.0
Goat meat	19.8	20.4	20.9
Poultry meat	4.7	4.7	4.7
Other meat	5.2	5.2	5.3
Cows' milk	161.7	165.5	169.3
Sheep's milk	9.0	9.2	9.4
Goats' milk	31.8	32.8	33.5
Poultry eggs	4.5	4.5	4.5
Cattle hides (fresh)	14.1	14.0	14.4
Sheepskins (fresh)	2.0	2.1	2.2
Goatskins (fresh)	4.0	4.1	4.2

Source: FAO.

Forestry

ROUNDWOOD REMOVALS
(FAO estimates, '000 cubic metres, excl. bark)

	2001	2002	2003
Sawlogs, veneer logs and logs for sleepers*	14	14	14
Other industrial wood	747	747	747
Fuel wood	6,001	6,119	6,239
Total	6,762	6,880	7,000

* Output assumed to be unchanged since 1993.

Source: FAO.

SAWNWOOD PRODUCTION
('000 cubic metres, incl. railway sleepers)

	1994	1995	1996
Total (all broadleaved)	2.4*	2.4	2.4

* FAO estimate.

1997–2003: Annual production as in 1996 (FAO estimates).

Source: FAO.

Fishing

('000 metric tons, live weight)

	1996	1997	1998
Total catch (freshwater fishes)	100.0	85.0	84.0

1999–2002: Figures assumed to be unchanged from 1998 (FAO estimates).

Source: FAO.

Industry

SELECTED PRODUCTS

	2000	2001	2002
Oil of groundnuts ('000 metric tons)*	33.1	36.6	36.6
Sugar (centrifugal, raw, '000 metric tons)	29.8	24.7	23.1
Beer of millet ('000 metric tons)*	9.5	13.5	12.5
Cigarettes (million packs)	29.5	29.6	36.0
Electric energy (million kWh)	82.3	90.9	106.6

* Estimates.

Sources: mostly FAO; IMF, *Chad: Statistical Appendix* (April 2004).

Finance

CURRENCY AND EXCHANGE RATES

Monetary Units
100 centimes = 1 franc de la Coopération financière en Afrique centrale (CFA).

Sterling, Dollar and Euro Equivalents (31 December 2004)
£1 sterling = 930.12 francs CFA;
US $1 = 481.58 francs CFA;
€1 = 655.96 francs CFA.
10,000 francs CFA = £10.75 = $20.77 = €15.24.

Average Exchange Rate (francs CFA per US $)
2002   696.99
2003   581.20
2004   528.29

Note: An exchange rate of 1 French franc = 50 francs CFA, established in 1948, remained in force until January 1994, when the CFA franc was devalued by 50%, with the exchange rate adjusted to 1 French franc = 100 francs CFA. This relationship to French currency remained in effect with the introduction of the euro on 1 January 1999. From that date, accordingly, a fixed exchange rate of €1 = 655.957 francs CFA has been in operation.

BUDGET
('000 million francs CFA)

Revenue*	2000	2001	2002
Tax revenue	68.3	78.6	98.4
Taxes on income and profits	22.7	28.2	43.0
Companies	11.3	12.5	19.0
Individuals	10.0	12.6	22.0
Employers' payroll tax	1.5	3.1	2.0
Property tax	1.6	1.8	2.6
Taxes on goods and services	18.8	19.7	19.5
Turnover tax	11.7	13.0	13.6
Tax on petroleum products	6.0	4.1	4.4
Taxes on international trade	21.8	27.2	31.9
Import taxes	18.5	23.5	28.3
Export taxes	2.2	2.3	1.6
Other tax revenues	3.4	1.6	1.6
Other revenue	11.9	13.1	11.6
Property income	1.9	2.4	1.6
Administrative fees	2.6	4.4	1.9
Non-industrial sales	1.7	1.9	2.3
Total	80.2	91.7	110.0

Expenditure†	2000	2001	2002
Current expenditure	99.9	109.8	137.9
Primary current expenditure	88.0	100.7	126.0
Wages and salaries	38.5	44.3	48.9
Materials and supplies	20.8	22.6	24.5
Health	4.2	5.2	4.9
Education	4.0	4.6	5.7
Transfers	11.3	6.9	18.9
Subsidies	7.1	3.5	6.9
Defence	15.2	19.2	23.9
Salaries	10.2	12.4	13.2
Materials and supplies	5.0	6.8	10.7
Famine relief	—	3.1	—
Elections	0.4	4.7	2.0
Peace accord implementation	—	—	5.2
Interest	10.3	9.1	12.0
External	8.9	8.6	10.6
Investment expenditure	103.3	110.5	140.3
Domestically-financed	10.7	11.4	16.9
Foreign-financed	92.6	99.1	123.5
Grants	48.0	48.2	74.4
Loans	44.6	50.8	49.0
Total	203.2	220.3	278.2

* Excluding grants received ('000 million francs CFA): 55.2 in 2000; 68.8 in 2001; 95.9 in 2002.
† Excluding adjustment for payments arrears ('000 million francs CFA): −2.6 in 2000; 9.3 in 2001; −6.7 in 2002.

Source: IMF, *Chad: Statistical Appendix* (April 2004).

INTERNATIONAL RESERVES
(US $ million at 31 December)

	2001	2002	2003
Gold*	3.09	3.81	4.65
IMF special drawing rights	0.00	0.01	0.00
Reserve position in IMF	0.35	0.38	0.42
Foreign exchange	122.02	218.31	186.68
Total	125.46	222.52	191.75

* Valued at market-related prices.

Source: IMF, *International Financial Statistics*.

MONEY SUPPLY
('000 million francs CFA at 31 December)

	2001	2002	2003
Currency outside banks	94.77	116.80	110.92
Demand deposits at commercial and development banks	43.43	59.79	60.23
Total money (incl. others)	138.69	176.59	171.17

Source: IMF, *International Financial Statistics*.

COST OF LIVING
(Consumer Price Index for African households in N'Djamena; base: 2000 = 100)

	2001	2002	2003
All items	112.4	118.3	116.0

Source: IMF, *International Financial Statistics*.

NATIONAL ACCOUNTS
('000 million francs CFA at current prices)

Expenditure on the Gross Domestic Product

	2001	2002	2003*
Government final consumption expenditure	90.8	110.2	108.6
Private final consumption expenditure	998.1	1,078.6	1,177.3
Gross fixed capital formation†	569.8	924.2	755.7
Total domestic expenditure	1,658.7	2,113.0	2,041.6
Exports of goods and services	183.9	171.4	310.1
Less Imports of goods and services	621.9	910.0	774.9
GDP in purchasers' values	1,220.6	1,374.3	1,576.8

* Estimates.
† Includes variation in stocks.

Source: Banque des états de l'Afrique centrale.

Gross Domestic Product by Economic Activity

	2000	2001	2002
Agriculture*	368.8	469.5	476.9
Mining and quarrying†	32.5	35.5	47.7
Electricity, gas and water	6.0	6.6	7.6
Manufacturing	85.0	100.7	119.5
Construction	14.9	16.3	20.0
Petroleum sector	2.1	24.3	51.9
Wholesale and retail trade, restaurants and hotels / Transport and communications	232.5	279.3	342.0
Public administration	118.3	134.3	149.9
Other services	93.1	109.3	125.7
GDP at factor cost	953.2	1,175.7	1,341.1
Indirect taxes, *less* subsidies	37.5	45.5	50.7
GDP in purchasers' values	990.7	1,221.1	1,391.8

* Excluding fishing.
† Including fishing.

Source: IMF, *Chad: Statistical Appendix* (April 2004).

BALANCE OF PAYMENTS
('000 million francs CFA)

	2001	2002	2003
Exports of goods f.o.b.	138.3	123.8	259.4
Cotton	56.9	38.9	41.0
Livestock	49.5	52.0	54.6
Petroleum	0.0	0.0	127.8
Imports of goods f.o.b.	−377.7	−590.1	−458.2
Trade balance	−239.4	−446.3	−198.8
Services (net)	−198.7	−272.3	−266.0
Balance on goods and services	−438.1	−738.6	−464.8
Other income (net)	−16.5	−41.3	−158.2
Balance on goods, services and income	−454.6	−779.9	−623.0
Private unrequited transfers (net)	25.7	22.2	22.9
Official unrequited transfers (net)	24.6	19.5	36.4
Current balance	−404.3	−738.2	−563.7
Public capital	48.2	74.4	47.4
Private capital	1.0	1.8	1.0
Direct investments	319.8	643.9	434.5
Other investments	43.6	47.7	44.3
Net errors and omissions	−16.4	12.3	9.3
Overall balance	−8.1	41.9	−27.2

Source: Banque des états de l'Afrique centrale.

External Trade

PRINCIPAL COMMODITIES

Imports c.i.f. (US $'000)	1995
Food and live animals	41,182
Cereals and cereal preparations	16,028
Wheat and meslin (unmilled)	8,945
Sugar, sugar preparations and honey	17,078
Refined sugars, etc.	16,825
Beverages and tobacco	7,175
Mineral fuels, lubricants, etc.	38,592
Refined petroleum products	38,551
Motor spirit (gasoline) and other light oils	6,490
Kerosene and other medium oils	8,456
Gas oils	23,318
Chemicals and related products	15,507
Medicinal and pharmaceutical products	7,789
Basic manufactures	26,190
Non-metallic mineral manufactures	7,654
Metal manufactures	8,804
Machinery and transport equipment	51,246
General industrial machinery, equipment and parts	8,175
Road vehicles (incl. air-cushion vehicles) and parts*	17,873
Parts and accessories for cars, lorries, buses, etc.*	8,253
Miscellaneous manufactured articles	27,335
Printed matter	13,565
Postage stamps, banknotes, etc.	11,622
Total (incl. others)	215,171

* Excluding tyres, engines and electrical parts.

Source: UN, *International Trade Statistics Yearbook*.

Exports ('000 million francs CFA)	2000	2001	2002*
Cotton	50.6	56.9	33.2
Livestock	48.8	49.5	52.0
Total (incl. others)	130.2	138.3	118.0

* Estimates.

Source: La Zone Franc, *Rapport Annuel 2002*.

Total imports c.i.f. (million francs CFA): 169,733 in 1996; 194,732 in 1997; 210,207 in 1998; 194,523 in 1999; 224,386 in 2000; 497,417 in 2001; 1,356,632 in 2002 (Source: IMF, *International Financial Statistics*).

PRINCIPAL TRADING PARTNERS

Imports c.i.f. (US $'000)	1995
Belgium-Luxembourg	4,771
Cameroon	33,911
Central African Repub.	3,010
China, People's Repub.	6,251
France	88,887
Germany	2,988
Italy	6,452
Japan	5,121
Malaysia	2,234
Netherlands	2,843
Nigeria	25,269
Spain	3,402
USA	13,966
Total (incl. others)	215,171

Source: UN, *International Trade Statistics Yearbook*.

Transport

ROAD TRAFFIC
(motor vehicles in use at 31 December)

	1994	1995*	1996*
Passenger cars	8,720	9,700	10,560
Buses and coaches	708	760	820
Lorries and vans	12,650	13,720	14,550
Tractors	1,413	1,500	1,580
Motorcycles and mopeds . . .	1,855	2,730	3,640

* Estimates.

Source: International Road Federation, *World Road Statistics*.

CIVIL AVIATION
(traffic on scheduled services*)

	1999	2000	2001
Kilometres flown (million) . . .	3	3	1
Passengers carried ('000) . . .	84	77	46
Passengers-km (million) . . .	235	216	130
Total ton-km (million)	36	32	19

* Including an apportionment of the traffic of Air Afrique.

Source: UN, *Statistical Yearbook*.

Tourism

FOREIGN VISITORS BY COUNTRY OF ORIGIN*

	2000	2001	2002
Canada	2,470	1,226	1,212
Central African countries . . .	6,621	4,896	3,773
France	13,707	22,274	10,835
Germany	1,361	1,003	469
Italy	1,254	1,109	328
USA	5,320	3,695	4,913
West Africa	4,137	2,156	2,424
Total (incl. others)	43,034	56,850	32,334

* Arrivals at hotels and similar establishments.

Tourism receipts (US $ million): 10 in 1996; 9 in 1997; 10 in 1998.

Source: World Tourism Organization.

Communications Media

	2001	2002
Telephones ('000 main lines in use)	11.0	11.8
Mobile cellular telephones ('000 subscribers) .	22.0	34.2
Personal computers ('000 in use)	12	13
Internet users ('000)	4.0	15.0

Television receivers ('000 in use): 10.9 in 2000.

Radio receivers ('000 in use): 1,670 in 1997.

Facsimile machines (number in use): 182 in 1999.

Daily newspapers: 1 in 1996 (average circulation 2,000 copies); 2 in 1997; 2 in 1998.

Non-daily newspapers: 2 in 1995 (average circulation 10,000 copies); n.a. in 1996; 14 in 1997; 10 in 1998.

Periodicals: 51 in 1997; 53 in 1998.

2003 ('000 subscribers): Mobile cellular telephones 65.0.

Sources: International Telecommunication Union; UNESCO, *Statistical Yearbook*; UN, *Statistical Yearbook*.

Education

(1996/97, unless otherwise indicated)

	Institu-tions	Teachers	Students Males	Students Females	Students Total
Pre-primary* . . .	24	67	938	735	1,673
Primary	2,660†	10,151	447,685	233,224	680,909
Secondary:					
general	153†	2,598	77,622	19,389	97,011
teacher training . .	6†	46	360	265	625
vocational . . .	12†	148	1,506	647	2,153
Tertiary‡	n.a.	n.a.	5,016	885	5,901

* 1994/95 figures; public education only.
† 1995/96 figure.
‡ 1999/2000 figures.

Source: mainly UNESCO, *Statistical Yearbook*.

1997/98: *Primary:* 786,537 students, *Secondary:* 112,268 students, *Higher:* 4,799 students.

1998/99: *Primary:* 839,932 students.

Adult literacy rate (UNESCO estimates): 45.8% (males 54.5%; females 37.5%) in 2002 (Source: UN Development Programme, *Human Development Report*).

Directory

The Constitution

The Constitution of the Republic of Chad, which was adopted by national referendum on 31 March 1996, enshrines a unitary state. The President is elected for a term of five years by direct universal adult suffrage, and is restricted to a maximum of two terms in office. The Prime Minister, who is appointed by the President, nominates the Council of Ministers. The bicameral legislature includes a 155-member Assemblée nationale, which is elected by direct universal adult suffrage for a term of four years. Provision is also made for an upper legislative chamber, the Sénat, with one-third of members renewed every two years. The Constitution provides for an independent judicial system, with a High Court of Justice, and the establishment of a Constitutional Court and a High Council for Communication.

Constitutional amendments approved by the Assemblée nationale in May 2004 provided for the abolition of the restriction on the number of terms that the President is permitted to serve, and for the abolition of the Sénat (which had not, however, been established). These amendments were to be presented for approval by referendum, prior to their eventual implementation.

The Government

HEAD OF STATE

President: Gen. IDRISS DEBY (assumed office 4 December 1990; elected President 3 July 1996; re-elected 20 May 2001).

COUNCIL OF MINISTERS
(March 2005)

Prime Minister: PASCAL YOADIMNADJI.

Minister of State, Minister of Foreign Affairs and African Integration: NAGOUM YAMASSOUM.

Minister of Agriculture: LAOKEIN KOURAYO MEDARD.

Minister of Planning, Development and Co-operation: MAHAMAT ALI HASSAN.

Minister of National Defence, Veterans and Victims of War: EMMANUEL NADINGAR.

Minister of Territorial Administration: MAHAMAT ZENE BADA.

Minister of Justice, Keeper of the Seals: KALZEUBÉ PAYIMI DABEUT.

Minister of Public Security and Immigration: ABDERAHMANE MOUSSA.

Minister of the Economy and Finance: NGUEYAM DJAIBE.

Minister of Public Works and Transport: ADOUM YOUNOUSMI.

Minister of Public Health: AZIZA BAROUD.

Minister of National Education: MAHAMAT MAOULOUD IZZADINE.

Minister of Trade, Industry and Crafts: ROUTOUANGE YOMA GOLOM.

Minister of the Environment and Water: ADOUM DIAR.

Minister of the Civil Service, Labour and Employment: MAHAMAT NOUR MALLAYE.

Minister of Social Welfare and the Family: FATIME KIMTO.

Minister of Livestock: MAHAMAT ABDOULAYE.

Minister of Communication, Government Spokesman: NATOINGAR BAILODJI BARTHELEMY.

Minister of Land Management, Town Planning and Housing: SANDJIMA DOUNIA.

Minister of Petroleum: YOUSSOUF ABASSALAH.

Minister of Mines and Energy: MAHAMAT NASSER HASSANE.

Minister of Posts and Telecommunications: Dr BRAHIM SEID.

Minister of Higher Education, Scientific Research and Professional Training: Prof. AVOCKSOUMA DJONA.

Minister of State Control and Moralization: Dr HAOUA OUTMAN DJAMÉ.

Minister of Culture, Youth and Sports: BARADINE HAROUNE.

Minister of the Development of Tourism: OUMAR KADJALLAMI BOUKAR.

Minister, Secretary-General of the Government responsible for Relations with Parliament: ABAKAR MALLAH MOURCHI.

Minister-delegate to the Prime Minister, responsible for Decentralization: OUMAR BOUKAR.

Secretary of State for the Economy and Finance: ABBAS MAHAMAT TOLLI.

Assistant Secretary-General to the Government: DJIVIDI BOUKAR DIBEING.

MINISTRIES

Office of the President: Palais rose, BP 74, N'Djamena; tel. 51-44-37; fax 52-45-01; e-mail presidence@tchad.td; internet rapidrecettes .com/sodt.

Office of the Prime Minister: N'Djamena; tel. 52-69-77; fax 52-20-89.

Office of the Minister, Secretary-General of the Government responsible for Relations with Parliament: BP 59, N'Djamena; tel. 52-52-82.

Ministry of Agriculture: BP 441, N'Djamena; tel. 52-69-79; fax 52-51-19.

Ministry of the Civil Service, Labour and Employment: BP 637, N'Djamena; tel. 52-21-98; fax 52-68-34.

Ministry of Communication: BP 892, N'Djamena; tel. 52-40-97; fax 52-65-60.

Ministry of Culture, Youth and Sports: BP 519, N'Djamena; tel. 52-26-58.

Ministry of the Development of Tourism: BP 86, N'Djamena; tel. 52-32-55.

Ministry of the Economy and Finance: BP 816, N'Djamena; tel. 52-33-98; fax 52-49-08.

Ministry of the Environment and Water: BP 905, N'Djamena; tel. 52-60-12; fax 52-38-39; e-mail facdrem@intnet.td.

Ministry of Foreign Affairs and African Integration: BP 746, N'Djamena; tel. 51-80-50; fax 51-45-85.

Ministry of Higher Education, Scientific Research and Professional Training: BP 743, N'Djamena; tel. 51-61-58; fax 51-92-31.

Ministry of Justice: BP 426, N'Djamena; tel. 52-21-72; fax 52-21-39; e-mail justice@intnet.td.

Ministry of Land Management, Town Planning and Housing: BP 436, N'Djamena; tel. 52-31-89; fax 52-39-35.

Ministry of Livestock: BP 750, N'Djamena; tel. 52-98-53.

Ministry of Mines and Energy: BP 816, N'Djamena; tel. 52-20-88; fax 52-25-65.

Ministry of National Defence, Veterans and Victims of War: BP 916, N'Djamena; tel. 52-35-13; fax 52-65-44.

Ministry of National Education: BP 743, N'Djamena; tel. 51-92-65; fax 51-45-12.

Ministry of Petroleum: BP 816, N'Djamena; tel. 52-50-87; fax 52-25-65.

Ministry of Planning, Development and Co-operation: BP 286, N'Djamena; tel. 51-89-81; fax 51-51-85.

Ministry of Posts and Telecommunications: BP 154, N'Djamena; tel. 52-15-79; fax 52-15-30; e-mail dabye@intnet.td.

Ministry of Public Health: BP 440, N'Djamena; tel. 51-51-14; fax 51-58-00.

Ministry of Public Security and Immigration: BP 916, N'Djamena; tel. 52-05-76.

Ministry of Public Works and Transport: BP 436, N'Djamena; tel. 52-06-60; fax 52-39-35.

Ministry of Social Welfare and the Family: BP 80, N'Djamena; tel. 52-25-32; fax 52-48-88.

Ministry of State Control and Moralization: N'Djamena.

Ministry of Territorial Administration: BP 742, N'Djamena; tel. 52-56-09; fax 52-59-06.

Ministry of Trade, Industry and Crafts: BP 424, N'Djamena; tel. 52-21-99; fax 52-27-33.

President and Legislature

PRESIDENT

Election, 20 May 2001

Candidate	Votes	% of vote
Idriss Deby (MPS*)	1,533,509	63.17
Ngarledjy Yorongar (FAR)	396,864	16.35
Saleh Kebzaboh (UNDR)	169,917	7.00
Gen. Wadal Abdelkader Kamougué (URD)	146,125	6.02
Ibn Oumar Mahamat Saleh (PLD)	70,248	2.89
Kassire Delwa Koumakoye (VIVA—RNDP)	57,382	2.36
Dr Jean Bawoyeu Alingué (UDR)	53,513	2.20
Total	**2,427,558**	**100.00**

*In coalition with 27 other parties.

ASSEMBLÉE NATIONALE

Assemblée nationale: Palais du 15 janvier, BP 01, N'Djamena; tel. 53-08-25; fax 31-45-90.

President: NASSOUR GUÉLENDOUKSIA OUAÏDOU.

General Election, 21 April 2002

Party	Seats
Mouvement patriotique du salut (MPS)	110
Rassemblement pour la démocratie et le progrès (RDP)	12
Fédération action pour la République (FAR)	9
VIVA—Rassemblement national pour la démocratie et le progrès (VIVA—RNDP)	5
Union nationale pour le développement et le renouveau (UNDR)	5
Union pour le renouveau et la démocratie (URD)	3
Others*	9
Vacant†	2
Total	**155**

*There were nine other parties.
† The Constitutional Council annulled the results of voting in two constituencies, in which by-elections were subsequently to be held.

Note: The 1996 Constitution also makes provision for an upper house of the legislature, the Sénat. This was not, however, subsequently established. Amendments to the Constitution that were adopted by the Assemblée nationale in May 2004 provided (subject to approval by national referendum) *inter alia* for the abolition of the upper house.

Political Organizations

Legislation permitting the operation of political associations, subject to official registration, took effect in October 1991. In early 2005 there were about 60 active political organizations, of which the following were among the most important:

Alliance nationale pour la démocratie et le développement (AND): BP 4066, N'Djamena; tel. 51-46-72; f. 1992; Leader SALIBOU GARBA.

Alliance tchadienne pour la démocratie et le développement (ATD): N'Djamena; e-mail info@atd-tchad.com; Leader ABDERAMAN DJASNABAILLE.

Action tchadienne pour l'unité et le socialisme (ACTUS): N'Djamena; e-mail actus@club-internet.fr; f. 1981; Marxist-Leninist; Sec.-Gen. Dr DJIMADOUM LEY-NGARDIGAL.

Coalition pour la defense de la démocratie et des droits constitutionnels (CDDC): f. 2004 to unite opposition groups in resisting President Deby's proposed revision of the Constitution; Co-ordinator AHMAT HASSABALLAH SOUBIANE.

Convention pour la démocratie et le fédéralisme: N'Djamena; f. 2002; socialist; supports the establishment of a federal state; Leader ALI GOLHOR.

Convention nationale démocratique et sociale (CNDS): N'Djamena; Leader ADOUM DAYE ZERE.

Coordination des partis politiques pour la défense de la Constitution (CPDC): f. 2004 to oppose President Deby's proposed constitutional modifications; mems include the RDP, the URD and the UNDR.

Fédération action pour la République (FAR): BP 4197, N'Djamena; tel. 51-91-12; fax 51-78-60; e-mail yorongar@intnet.td; internet www.yorongar.com; supports the establishment of a federal republic; Leader NGARLEDJY YORONGAR.

Mouvement patriotique du salut (MPS): Assemblée nationale, Palais du 15 janvier, BP 01, N'Djamena; e-mail administrateur@tchad-gpmps.org; internet www.tchad-gpmps.org; f. 1990 as a coalition of several opposition movements; other opposition groups joined during the Nov. 1990 offensive against the regime of Hissène Habré, and following the movement's accession to power in Dec. 1990; Pres.of group D'IDRISS NDELE MOUSSA.

Parti pour la liberté et le développement (PLD): N'Djamena; f. 1993; boycotted legislative elections in 2002; Sec.-Gen. IBN OUMAR MAHAMAT SALEH.

Rassemblement pour la démocratie et le progrès (RDP): N'Djamena; f. 1992; seeks to create a secure political environment by the establishment of a reformed national army; supported the re-election of Pres. Deby in 2001, but withdrew support from the Govt in Nov. 2003; Leader LOL MAHAMAT CHOUA.

Union pour la démocratie et la République (UDR): N'Djamena; f. 1992; supports liberal economic policies and a secular, decentralized republic; boycotted legislative elections in 2002; Leader Dr JEAN BAWOYEU ALINGUÉ.

Union nationale pour le développement et le renouveau (UNDR): N'Djamena; supports greater decentralization and increased limitations on the power of the state; Pres. SALEH KEBZABOH; Sec.-Gen. CÉLESTIN TOPONA.

Union pour le renouveau et la démocratie (URD): BP 92, N'Djamena; tel. 51-44-23; fax 51-41-87; f. 1992; Leader Gen. WADAL ABDELKADER KAMOUGUÉ.

VIVA—Rassemblement national pour la démocratie et le progrès (VIVA—RNDP): N'Djamena; f. 1992; supports a unitary, democratic republic; Pres. KASSIRE DELWA KOUMAKOYE.

A number of unregistered dissident groups (some based abroad) are also active. In early 2005 these organizations, largely 'politico-military', included the following:

Alliance nationale de la résistance (ANR): f. 1996 as alliance of five movements; in early 2003 comprised eight rebel groups based in eastern Chad; signed peace agreement with Govt in Jan. 2003, although FONALT rejected this accord; Leader Col MAHAMAT GARFA.

Armée nationale tchadienne en dissidence (ANTD): f. 1994; Leader Col MAHAMAT GARFA.

Forces des organisations nationales pour l'alternance et les libertés au Tchad (FONALT): rejected cease-fire signed by ANR with Govt in Jan. 2003; Leader Col ABDOULAYE ISSAKA SARWA.

Coordination des mouvements armés et partis politiques de l'opposition (CMAP): internet www.maxpages.com/tchad/cmap2; f. 1999 by 13 'politico-military' organizations; a number of groups subsequently left, several of which later joined the FUDP (q.v.); Leader ANTOINE BANGUI.

Front extérieur pour la rénovation: Leader ANTOINE BANGUI.

Front de libération nationale du Tchad-Conseil provisoire de la révolution (FROLINAT-CPR): f. 1968 in Sudan; based in Algeria; Leader GOUKOUNI OUEDDEI.

Front uni pour la démocratie et la paix (FUDP): f. 2003 in Benin; seeks by all possible means to establish a new constitution and a transitional govt in advance of free and transparent elections; faction of MDJT (q.v.) led by Adoum Togoi Abbo claims membership, but this is rejected by principal faction of MDJT; Pres. Brig.-Gen. ADOUM TOGOI ABBO.

Conseil national de résistance (CNR): leadership of group forced to leave Benin for Togo in mid-2003; Pres. HISSÈNE KOTY YACOUB.

Convention populaire de résistance (CPR): e-mail cpr60@voila.fr; f. 2001 by fmr mems of CNR (q.v.); Leader ABDEL-AZIZ ABDALLAH KODOK.

Front national du Tchad renové (FNTR): Dabo; e-mail yasaid2001@yahoo.fr; internet www.maxpages.com/tchad/fntr; f. 1996 in Sudan by fmr mems of FNT (q.v.); based in Dabo (France); announced abandonment of armed struggle in 2002; new leadership elected in early 2003; seeks establishment of semi-presidential and social-democratic system of govt; publishes monthly bulletin, *Al-Widha*, in French and Arabic; Hon. Pres. MAHAMAT MOUSSA; Sec-Gen. SALAHADINE MAHADI.

Mouvement pour la démocratie et le développement (MDD): tel. and fax 34-46-17; e-mail mdd@mdd-tchad.com; internet membres.lycos.fr/mddtchad; comprises two factions, led by ISSA FAKI MAHAMAT and BRAHIM MALLAH.

Mouvement des Renovateurs Tchadiens (MNRT): e-mail fpls@romandie.com; democratic opposition in exile; Sec.-Gen. ALI MUHAMMAD DIALLO.

Union des forces pour le changement (UFC): f. 2004; advocates suspension of the 1996 Constitution and the composition of a new Charter of the Republic to develop national unity, free, transparent elections and the rule of law; National Co-ordinator ACHEIKH IBN OUMAR.

Conseil démocratique révolutionnaire (CDR): Leader ACHEIKH IBN OUMAR.

Front démocratique populaire (FDP): Leader Dr MAHAMOUT NAHOR.

Front populaire pour la renaissance nationale.

Mouvement pour la démocratie et le développement (MDD): tel. and fax 34-46-17; e-mail mdd@mdd-tchad.com; internet membres.lycos.fr/mddtchad; comprises two factions, led by ISSA FAKI MAHAMAT and BRAHIM MALLAH.

Mouvement pour la démocratie et la justice au Tchad (MDJT): based in Tibesti, northern Chad; e-mail admin@mdjt.net; internet www.mdjt.net; fmr deputy leader, Brig.-Gen. ADOUM TOGOI ABBO, signed a peace agreement with Govt in Jan. 2002, although this was subsequently rejected by elements close to fmr leader, YOUSSOUF TOGOIMI (who died in Sept. 2002); split into two factions in 2003; the faction led by Togoi claimed membership of the FUDP (q.v.) and signed a peace agreement with the Govt in Dec. 2003, which was rejected by the faction led by Chair. Col HASSAN ABDALLAH MARDIGUÉ.

Mouvement pour l'unité et la République (MUR): f. 2000 by faction of the MDD (q.v.); Leader GAILETH GATOUL BOURKOUMANDAH.

Union des forces démocratiques (UFD): Leader Dr MAHAMAT NAHOUR.

Diplomatic Representation

EMBASSIES IN CHAD

Algeria: BP 178, N'Djamena; tel. 52-38-15; fax 52-37-92; Ambassador BOUBAKEUR OGAB.

Cameroon: rue des Poids Lourds, BP 58, N'Djamena; tel. 52-28-94.

Central African Republic: rue 1036, près du Rond-Point de la Garde, BP 115, N'Djamena; tel. 52-25-75; Ambassador DAVID NGUINDO.

China (Taiwan): BP 1150, N'Djamena; tel. 52-44-05; fax 52-44-02; e-mail ambchine@mail.intnet.td; Ambassador SHIN CHENG.

Congo, Democratic Republic: ave du 20 août, BP 910, N'Djamena; tel. 52-29-35; Ambassador (vacant).

Egypt: BP 1094, N'Djamena; tel. 51-09-72; fax 51-09-73; Ambassador AZIZ M. NOUR ED-DIN.

France: rue du Lt Franjoux, BP 431, N'Djamena; tel. 52-25-75; fax 52-28-55; e-mail amba.france@intnet.td; internet www .ambafrance-td.org; Ambassador JEAN-PIERRE BERÇOT.

Holy See: rue de Béguinage, BP 490, N'Djamena; tel. 52-31-15; fax 52-38-27; e-mail nonceapo@intnet.td; Apostolic Nuncio Most Rev. JOSEPH CHENNOTH (Titular Archbishop of Milevum).

Libya: BP 1096, N'Djamena; tel. 52-39-79; Ambassador GHAYTH SALIM.

Nigeria: 35 ave Charles de Gaulle, BP 752, N'Djamena; tel. 52-24-98; fax 52-30-92; Ambassador M. M. BAUCHI.

Russia: 2 rue Adjutant Collin, BP 891, N'Djamena; tel. 52-57-19; fax 51-31-72; e-mail amrus@intnet.td; Ambassador VLADIMIR NIKOLAE-VICH MARTYNOV.

Saudi Arabia: quartier Aéroport, rue Jander Miry, BP 974, N'Djamena; tel. 52-36-95; fax 52-33-28; e-mail tdemb@mofa.gov.sa.

Sudan: rue de la Gendarmerie, BP 45, N'Djamena; tel. 52-43-59; e-mail amb.soudan@intnet.td; Ambassador HASSAN BESHIR ABDEL-WAHAB.

USA: ave Félix Eboué, BP 413, N'Djamena; tel. 51-70-09; fax 51-56-54; e-mail YingraD@state.gov; internet usembassy.state.gov/ndjamena; Ambassador MARC M. WALL.

Judicial System

The highest judicial authority is the Supreme Court, which comprises a Judicial Chamber, an Administrative Chamber and an Audit Chamber. There is also a Constitutional Council, with final jurisdiction in matters of state. The legal structure also comprises the Court of Appeal, and magistrate and criminal courts. A High Court of Justice, which is competent to try the President or members of the Government in cases of treason, embezzlement of public funds, and certain other crimes and offences, was inaugurated in June 2003.

Supreme Court: rue 0221, Quartier Résidentiel, 1er arrondissement, N'Djamena; tel. 52-00-00; fax 53-00-00; e-mail ccsrp@intnet .td; internet www.coursupreme.td; Pres. ABDERAHIM BIREME HAMID; Pres. of the Judicial Chamber BELKOULAYE BEN COUMAREAUX; Pres. of the Administrative Chamber OUSMAME SALAH IDJEMI; Pres. of the Audit Chamber DOLOTAN NOUDJALBAYE; Prosecutor-Gen. EDOUARD NGARTA M'BAIOUROUM.

Constitutional Council: BP 5500, N'Djamena; tel. 52-03-41; e-mail conseil.sg@intnet.td; Pres. PASCAL YOADIMNADJI.

Court of Appeal: N'Djamena; tel. 51-24-26; Pres. MAKI ADAM ISSAKA.

High Court of Justice: N'Djamena; f. 2003; comprises 15 deputies of the Assemblée nationale, of whom 10 are titular judges and five supplementaries, who serve in the absence of a titular judge. All 15 are elected for the term of four years by their peers; competent to try the President and members of the Government in cases of treason, embezzlement of public funds, and certain other crimes and offences; Pres. ADOUM GOUDJA.

Religion

It is estimated that some 50% of the population are Muslims and about 30% Christians. Most of the remainder follow animist beliefs.

ISLAM

Conseil Suprême des Affaires Islamiques
POB 1101, N'Djamena; tel. 51-81-80; fax 52-58-84.

Head of the Islamic Community: Imam MOUSSA IBRAHIM.

CHRISTIANITY

The Roman Catholic Church
Chad comprises one archdiocese, six dioceses and one apostolic prefecture. At 31 December 2004 baptized Roman Catholics numbered approximately 855,000, most of whom resided in the south of the country and in N'Djamena.

Bishops' Conference
Conférence Episcopale du Tchad, BP 456, N'Djamena; tel. 52-37-79; fax 52-50-51; e-mail secreta.cet@intnet.td.
f. 1991; Pres. Most Rev. JEAN-CLAUDE BOUCHARD (Bishop of Pala).

Archbishop of N'Djamena: Most Rev. MATTHIAS N'GARTÉRI MAYADI, Archevêché, BP 456, N'Djamena; tel. 51-74-44; fax 52-50-51; e-mail diocndja@intnet.td.

Protestant Churches

Entente des Eglises et Missions Evangéliques au Tchad (EEMET): BP 2006, N'Djamena; tel. 51-53-93; fax 51-87-20; e-mail eemet@intnet.td; asscn of churches and missions working in Chad; includes Assemblées Chrétiennes au Tchad (ACT), Assemblées de Dieu au Tchad (ADT), Eglise Evangélique des Frères au Tchad (EEFT), Eglise Evangélique au Tchad (EET), Eglise Fraternelle Luthérienne au Tchad (EFLT), Eglise Evangélique en Afrique Centrale au Tchad (EEACT), Eglise Evangélique Missionnaire au Tchad (EEMT); also five assoc. mems: Union des Jeunes Chrétiens (UJC), Groupe Biblique des Hôpitaux au Tchad (GBHT), Mission Evangélique contre la Lèpre (MECL), Croix Bleue du Tchad (CBT).

BAHÁ'Í FAITH

National Spiritual Assembly: BP 181, N'Djamena; tel. 51-47-05; e-mail ntirandaz@aol.com.

The Press

Al-Watan: N'Djamena; tel. 51-57-96; weekly; Editor-in-Chief MOUSSA NDORKOÏ.

Audy Magazine: BP 780, N'Djamena; tel. 51-49-59; f. 2000; 2 a month; women's interest; Dir TONGRONGOU AGOUNA GRÂCE.

Bulletin Mensuel de Statistiques du Tchad: BP 453, N'Djamena; monthly.

Carrefour: Centre al-Mouna, BP 456, N'Djamena; tel. 51-42-54; e-mail almouna@intnet.td; f. 2000; every 2 months; Dir Sister NADIA KARAKI; circ. 1,000 (2001).

Chronique: Association pour la Promotion des Libertés Fondamentales Tchad (APLFT), BP 4037, N'Djamena; tel. 51-91-14; monthly; promotes civic information and popular understanding of civic law; Dir MAOUNDONODJI GILBERT.

Comnat: BP 731, N'Djamena; tel. 51-46-75; fax 51-46-71; quarterly; publ. by Commission Nationale Tchadienne for UNESCO.

Grenier: BP 1128, N'Djamena; tel. 53-30-14; e-mail cedesep@intnet .td; monthly; economics; finance; Dir KOHOM NGAR-ONE DAVID.

Info-Tchad: BP 670, N'Djamena; tel. 51-58-67; news bulletin issued by Agence-Info Tchad; daily; French.

Informations Economiques: BP 458, N'Djamena; publ. by the Chambre de Commerce, d'Agriculture et d'Industrie; weekly.

La Lettre: BP 2037, N'Djamena; tel. and fax 51-91-09; e-mail ltdh@ intnet.td; f. 1993; monthly; publ. by the Ligue Tchadienne des droits de l'Homme; Dir DOBIAN ASSINGAR.

N'Djamena Bi-Hebdo: BP 4498, N'Djamena; tel. 51-53-14; fax 52-14-98; e-mail ndjh@intnet.td; 2 a week; Arabic and French; f. 1989; Dir YALDET BÉGOTO OULATAR; Editor-in-Chief DIEUDONNÉ DJONABAYE; circ. 3,500 (2001).

Notre Temps: BP 4352, N'Djamena; tel. and fax 51-46-50; e-mail ntemps.presse@yahoo.fr; f. 2000; weekly; opposed to the Govt of Pres. Deby; Editorial Dir NADJIKIMO BENOUDJITA; circ. 3,000 (2001).

L'Observateur: BP 2031, N'Djamena; tel. and fax 51-80-05; e-mail observer.presse@intnet.td; f. 1997; weekly; Dir SY KOUMBO SINGA GALI; circ. 4,000 (2001).

Le Progrès: 1976 ave Charles de Gaulle, BP 3055, N'Djamena; tel. 51-55-86; fax 51-02-56; e-mail progres@intnet.td; f. 1993; daily; Dir MAHAMAT HISSÈNE; circ. 3,000 (2001).

Revue Juridique Tchadienne: BP 907, N'Djamena; internet www .cefod.org/Revuejuridique/Sommaire_rjt.htm; f. 1999; Dir MAHAMAT SALEH BEN BIANG.

Tchad et Culture: BP 907, N'Djamena; tel. 51-54-32; fax 51-91-50; e-mail cefod@intnet.td; internet www.cefod.org; f. 1961; monthly; Dir RONELNGUÉ TORIAÏRA; Editor-in-Chief NAYGOTIMTI BAMBÉ; circ. 4,500 (2002).

Le Temps: face Ecole Belle-vue, Moursal, BP 1333, N'Djamena; tel. 51-70-28; fax 51-99-24; e-mail temps.presse@intnet.td; f. 1995; weekly; Dir MICHAËL N. DIDAMA; circ. 6,000 (2001).

Victoire Al Nassr: BP 1331, N'Djamena; tel. 51-64-17; weekly; Dir ABOUBAKAR MAHAMAT BORGHO.

La Voix du Paysan: BP 1671, N'Djamena; tel. 51-82-66; monthly; Dir DJALDI TABDI GASSISSOU NASSER.

NEWS AGENCIES

Agence-Info Tchad: BP 670, N'Djamena; tel. 52-58-67; f. 1966; Dir ABAKAR HASSAN ACHEICK.

Foreign Bureau

Agence France-Presse (AFP): N'Djamena; tel. 51-54-71; Correspondent ALDOM NADJI TITO.

Publisher

Imprimerie du Tchad (IDT): BP 456, N'Djamena; tel. 52-44-40; fax 52-28-60; Gen.-Dir D. E. MAURIN.

Broadcasting and Communications

TELECOMMUNICATIONS

Société des Télécommunications du Tchad (SOTEL TCHAD): Siége sociale, BP 1132, N'Djamena; tel. 52-14-36; e-mail sotel@intnet.td; internet www.sotel.td; fax 52-14-42; f. 2000 by merger of telecommunications services of fmr Office National des Postes et des Télécommunications and the Société des Télécommunications Internationales du Tchad; privatization proposed; Dir-Gen. ALI MAHAMAT ZÈNE ALI FADEL.

Celtel-Tchad: N'Djamena; tel. 52-04-11; fax 52-02-33; internet www.mti-cellular.com; f. 2000; affiliated to MSI-Cellular (United Kingdom); provides mobile cellular telecommunications in N'Djamena and Moundou; Dir-Gen. RAYMOND LAFORCE.

Tchad Mobile-Libertis: ave Charles de Gaulle, BP 5742, N'Djamena; tel. 52-02-00; fax 52-01-39; e-mail mobichad@intnet.td; f. 2000; provides mobile cellular telecommunications in N'Djamena, Abéché, Doba, Moundou and Sarh; jointly owned by Orascom Telecom (Egypt) and SOTEL TCHAD; operations suspended in July 2004; Dir-Gen. SAMEH MANGOURY.

BROADCASTING

Regulatory Authority

High Council of Communication (HCC): N'Djamena; f. 1994; responsible for registration and regulation of radio and television stations, in addition to the printed press; funds independent radio stations; Pres. EMMANUEL TOUADÉ.

Radio

Private radio stations have been permitted to operate in Chad since 1994, although private broadcasts did not begin until 1997. By mid-2002 15 private and community stations had received licences, of which nine had commenced broadcasts. There was, additionally, a state-owned broadcaster, with four regional stations.

Radio Nationale Tchadienne (RNT): BP 4589, N'Djamena; tel. 53-32-00; f. 1955; state-controlled; programmes in French, Arabic and 11 vernacular languages; four regional stations; Dir N'GUÉRÉBAYE ADOUM SALEH.

Radio Abéché: BP 36, Abéché, Ouaddaï; tel. 69-81-49.

Radio Faya-Largeau: Faya-Largeau, Borkou.

Radio Moundou: BP 122, Moundou, Logone Occidental; tel. 69-13-22; programmes in French, Sara and Arabic; Dir DIMANANGAR DJAÏNTA.

Radio Sarh: BP 270, Sarh, Bahr Kôh; tel. 68-13-61; programmes in French, Sara and Arabic; Dir BIANA FOUDA NACTOUANDI.

Union des radios privées du Tchad (URPT): N'Djamena; f. 2002 as a federation of nine private and community radio stations, including the following.

DJA FM: BP 1312, N'Djamena; tel. 51-64-90; fax 52-14-52; e-mail myzara@intnet.td; f. 1999; music, cultural and informative programmes in French, Arabic and Sara; Dir ZARA YACOUB.

Radio Brakoss (Radio de l'Agriculture): Moïssala, Mandoul; f. 2000; community radio station; operations suspended by the Govt in Feb.2004; Dir TCHANGUIZ VATANKHAH.

Radio Duji Lohar: BP 155, Moundou, Logone Occidental; tel. 69-17-14; fax 69-12-11; e-mail cdave@intnet.td; f. 2001.

Radio FM Liberté: BP 892, N'Djamena; tel. 51-42-53; f. 2000; financed by nine civil-society organizations; broadcasts in French, Arabic and Sara; Dir DOBIAN ASSINGAR.

Radio Lotiko: Diocese de Sarh, BP 87, Sahr; tel. 68-12-46; fax 68-14-79; e-mail lotiko@intnet.td; internet www.lotiko.org; f. 2001; community radio station; Dir FABRIZIO COLOMBO.

La Voix du Paysan: BP 22, Doba, Logone Oriental; f. 1996; Roman Catholic; Dir DJALDI TABDI GASSISSOU NASSER.

Television

TVT Télévision tchadienne: BP 274, N'Djamena; tel. 52-26-79; fax 52-29-23; state-controlled; broadcasts c. 12 hours per week in French and Arabic; Dir OUROUMADJI MOUSSA.

Broadcasts from Canal France International, TV5, CNN and seven Arabic television stations are also received in Chad.

Finance

(cap. = capital; res = reserves; dep. = deposits; m. = million; br. = branch; amounts in francs CFA)

BANKING

Central Bank

Banque des Etats de l'Afrique Centrale (BEAC): ave Charles de Gaulle, BP 50, N'Djamena; tel. 52-21-65; fax 52-44-87; e-mail beacndj@beac.int; internet www.beac.int; HQ in Yaoundé, Cameroon; f. 1973; bank of issue for mem. states of the Communauté économique et monétaire de l'Afrique centrale (CEMAC, fmrly Union douanière et économique de l'Afrique centrale), comprising Cameroon, the Central African Repub., Chad, the Repub. of the Congo, Equatorial Guinea and Gabon; cap. 45,000m., res 176,661m., total assets 2,144,626m. (Nov. 2003); Gov. JEAN-FÉLIX MAMALEPOT; Dir in Chad IDRISS AHMED IDRISS; brs at Moundou and Sara.

Other Banks

Banque Agricole du Soudan au Tchad (BAST): ave el-Niméry, BP 1727, N'Djamena; tel. 51-90-41; fax 51-90-40; e-mail bast@intnet.td; cap. 1,200m. (2002), total assets 1,845m. (Dec. 1999); Pres. MOUHAMED OUSMAN AWAD; Dir-Gen. ABDELKADER OUSMAN HASSAN; 1 br.

Banque Commerciale du Chari (BCC): ave Charles de Gaulle, BP 757, N'Djamena; tel. 51-89-58; fax 51-62-49; e-mail bcc@intnet.td; 50% state-owned, 50% owned by Libya Arab Foreign Bank (Libya); cap. and res 3,567m., total assets 20,931m. (Dec. 2001); Pres. BIDJERE BINDJAKI; Dir-Gen. HAMED EL MISTIRI.

Banque Internationale pour l'Afrique au Tchad (BIAT): ave Charles de Gaulle, BP 87, N'Djamena; tel. 52-43-14; fax 52-23-45; e-mail biat@intnet.td; f. 1954; current name adopted 1981; 80.6% owned by Compagnie de Financement et de Participation (Bamako, Mali); cap. 3,000m. res 1,317m., dep. 24,876m. (Dec. 2003); Chair. BABER TOUNKARA; Dir-Gen. GUY MALLETT.

Commerical Bank Tchad (CBT): rue du Capitaine Ohrel, BP 19, N'Djamena; tel. 52-28-28; fax 52-33-18; e-mail expbdt@intnet.td; f. 1962; 50.7% owned by Groupe FOTSO (Cameroon), 17.5% state-owned; fmrly Banque de Développement du Tchad; cap. 4,019.8m., res 1,305.3m., dep. 22,255.9m. (March 2005); Pres. YOUSSOUF ABBASALAH; Dir-Gen. GEORGES DJADJO; 1 br.

Financial Bank Tchad (FBT): BP 804, N'Djamena; tel. 52-33-89; fax 52-29-05; e-mail fbt@intnet.td; f. 1992; 97.9% owned by Financial BC (Switzerland); cap. and res 956m., total assets 18,674m. (Dec. 2001); Pres. RÉMY BAYSSET; Dir-Gen. JEAN-LOUIS CASTEL.

Société Générale Tchadienne de Banque (SGTB): 2–6 rue Robert Lévy, BP 461, N'Djamena; tel. 52-28-01; fax 52-37-13; e-mail sgtb@intnet.td; internet www.sgtb.td; f. 1963; 30% owned by Société Générale (France), 15% by Sociéte Générale de Banque au Cameroun; cap. and res 3,603m., total assets 36,579m. (Dec. 2003); Pres. and Dir-Gen. CHEMI KOGRIMI; 3 brs.

Bankers' Organizations

Association Professionnelle des Banques au Tchad: 2–6 rue Robert Lévy, BP 461, N'Djamena; tel. 52-41-90; fax 52-17-13; Pres. CHEMI KOGRIMI.

Conseil National de Crédit: N'Djamena; f. 1965 to formulate a national credit policy and to organize the banking profession.

INSURANCE

Assureurs Conseils Tchadiens Cecar et Jutheau: rue du Havre, BP 139, N'Djamena; tel. 52-21-15; fax 52-35-39; e-mail biliou.alikeke@intnet.td; f. 1966; Dir BILIOU ALIKEKE.

Gras Savoye Tchad: rue du Général Thillo, BP 5620, N'Djamena; tel. 52-00-72; fax 52-00-71; e-mail gras.savoye@intnet.td; internet www.grassavoye.com; affiliated to Gras Savoye (France); Man. DOMKRÉO DJAMON.

Société Mutuelle d'Assurances des Cadres des Professions Libérales et des Indépendants (SMAC): BP 644, N'Djamena; tel. 51-70-19; fax 51-70-61.

Société de Représentation d'Assurances et de Réassurances Africaines (SORARAF): N'Djamena; Dir Mme FOURNIER.

Société Tchadienne d'Assurances et de Réassurances (La STAR Nationale): ave Charles de Gaulle, BP 914, N'Djamena; tel. 52-56-77; fax 52-51-89; e-mail star@intnet.td; internet www .lastarnationale.com; f. 1977; privatized in 1995; cap. 260,300m. francs CFA; Dir-Gen. RAKHIS MANNANY.

Trade and Industry

DEVELOPMENT ORGANIZATIONS

Agence Française de Développement (AFD): BP 478, route de Farcha, N'Djamena; tel. 52-70-71; fax 52-78-31; e-mail afdndjdi@ intnet.td; internet www.afd.fr; fmrly Caisse Française de Développement; Dir LOUIS L'AOT.

Association Française des Volontaires du Progrès (AFVP): BP 448, N'Djamena; tel. 52-20-53; fax 52-26-56; e-mail afvptchd@ intnet.td; internet www.afvp.org; f. 1965; Nat. Rep. CAROLE SAMBA.

Association Tchadienne pour le Développement: BP 470, Quartier Sabangali, N'Djamena; tel. 51-43-69; fax 51-89-23; e-mail darna.dnla@intnet.td; Dir DIGALI ZEUHINBA.

Mission Française de Coopération et d'Action Culturelle: BP 898, N'Djamena; tel. 52-42-87; fax 52-44-38; administers bilateral aid from France; Dir EDOUARD LAPORTE.

Office National de Développement Rural (ONDR): BP 896, N'Djamena; tel. 51-48-64; f. 1968; Dir MICKAEL DJIBRAEL.

Société pour le Développement du Lac (SODELAC): BP 782, N'Djamena; tel. 51-35-03; f. 1967 to develop the area of Lake Chad; cap. 180m. francs CFA; Pres. CHERIF ABDELWAHAB; Dir-Gen. MAHAMAT MOCTAR ALI.

CHAMBER OF COMMERCE

Chambre de Commerce, d'Industrie, d'Agriculture, des Mines et d'Artisanat: 13 rue du Col Moll, BP 458, N'Djamena; tel. 52-52-64; fax 52-14-52; f. 1935; brs at Sarh, Moundou, Bol and Abéché; Pres. Dr NICOLE FROUD; Dir-Gen. BEKOUTOU TAIGAM.

TRADE ASSOCIATIONS

Office National des Céréales (ONC): BP 21, N'Djamena; tel. 52-37-31; fax 52-20-18; e-mail onc1@intnet.td; f. 1978; production and marketing of cereals; Dir-Gen. MAHAMAT ALI HASSABALLAH; 11 regional offices.

Société Nationale de Commercialisation du Tchad (SONACOT): N'Djamena; f. 1965; cap. 150m. francs CFA; 76% state-owned; nat. marketing, distribution and import-export co; Man. Dir MARBROUCK NATROUD.

EMPLOYERS' ORANIZATIONS

Conseil National du Patronat Tchadien (CNPT): 17 ave Charles de Gaulle, BP 34, N'Djamena; tel. 52-25-71; fax 51-60-65; Pres. RAKHIS MANNANY; Sec.-Gen. MARC MADENGAR BEREMADJI; 67 mem. enterprises with total work-force of 8,000 (2002).

Union des Transporteurs Tchadiens: N'Djamena; tel. 51-45-27.

UTILITIES

Veolia Water—STEE (Société Tchadienne d'Eau et d'Electricité): 11 rue du Col Largeau, BP 44, N'Djamena; tel. 51-28-81; fax 51-21-34; f. 1968; state-owned; managed privately by subsidiary of Veolia Environnement (France—fmrly Vivendi) since 2000; production and distribution of electricity and water; Pres. GOMON MAWATA WAKAG; Dir-Gen. ISMAEL MAHAMAT ADOUM.

TRADE UNIONS

Confédération Libre des Travailleurs du Tchad (CLTT): ave Charles de Gaulle, BP 553, N'Djamena; tel. 51-76-11; fax 52-44-56; Sec.-Gen. BRAHIM BAKAS; 22,500 mems (2001).

Union des Syndicats du Tchad (UST): BP 1143, N'Djamena; tel. 51-42-75; fax 51-48-08; f. 1988; federation of trade unions; Pres. DOMBAL DJIMBAGUE; Sec.-Gen. DJIBRINE ASSALI HAMDALLAH.

Transport

RAILWAYS

There are no railways in Chad. In 1962 the Governments of Chad and Cameroon signed an agreement to extend the Transcameroon railway from Ngaoundéré to Sarh, a distance of 500 km. Although the Transcameroon reached Ngaoundéré in 1974, its proposed extension into Chad remains indefinitely postponed.

ROADS

The total length of the road network in 1999 was an estimated 40,000 km, of which 3,100 km were principal roads and 1,400 km were secondary roads; only 412 km of the network was paved. There are also some 20,000 km of tracks suitable for motor traffic during the October–July dry season. The European Union is contributing to the construction of a highway connecting N'Djamena with Sarh and Léré, on the Cameroon border, and of a 400-km highway linking Moundou and Ngaoundéré.

Coopérative des Transportateurs Tchadiens (CTT): BP 336, N'Djamena; tel. 51-43-55; road haulage; Pres. SALEH KHALIFA; brs at Sarh, Moundou, Bangui (CAR), Douala and Ngaoundéré (Cameroon).

Société Générale d'Entreprise Routière (SGER): BP 175, N'Djamena; tel. and fax 51-55-12; e-mail itralu@intnet.td; devt and maintenance of roads; 95% owned by Arcory International (Sudan); Pres. PATRICK MORIN.

Société Tchadienne d'Affrètement et de Transit (STAT): 21 ave Félix Eboué, BP 100, N'Djamena; tel. 51-88-72; fax 51-74-24; e-mail stat.tchad@intnet.td; affiliated to Groupe Saga (France); road haulage.

INLAND WATERWAYS

The Chari and Logone rivers, which converge to the south of N'Djamena, are navigable. These waterways connect Sarh with N'Djamena on the Chari and Bongor and Moundou with N'Djamena on the Logone.

CIVIL AVIATION

The international airport is at N'Djamena. There are also more than 40 smaller airfields.

Air Affaires Tchad: BP 256, N'Djamena; tel. 51-06-20; e-mail airaffaires@yahoo.st; passenger and freight internal and charter flights.

Air Tchad: BP 168, N'Djamena; tel. 52-45-64; fax 52-35-82; internal flights.

Minair Tchad: ave Charles de Gaulle, BP 1239, N'Djamena; tel. 51-31-51; fax 51-07-80; passenger and freight air transport.

Tourism

Chad's potential attractions for tourists include a variety of scenery from the dense forests of the south to the deserts of the north. Receipts from tourism in 1998 totalled an estimated US $10m. A total of 32,334 tourists visited Chad in 2002, compared with 56,850 in 2001.

Direction du Tourisme: BP 86, N'Djamena; tel. 52-23-03; fax 52-22-61.

CHILE

Introductory Survey

Location, Climate, Language, Religion, Flag, Capital

The Republic of Chile is a long, narrow country lying along the Pacific coast of South America, extending from Peru and Bolivia in the north to Cape Horn in the far south. Isla de Pascua (Rapa Nui or Easter Island), about 3,780 km (2,350 miles) off shore, and several other small islands form part of Chile. To the east, Chile is separated from Argentina by the high Andes mountains. Both the mountains and the cold Humboldt Current influence the climate; between Arica in the north and Punta Arenas in the extreme south, a distance of about 4,000 km (2,500 miles), the average maximum temperature varies by no more than 13°C. Rainfall varies widely between the arid desert in the north and the rainy south. The language is Spanish. There is no state religion but the great majority of the inhabitants profess Christianity, and some 72% are adherents of the Roman Catholic Church. The national flag (proportions 2 by 3) is divided horizontally: the lower half is red, while the upper half has a five-pointed white star on a blue square, at the hoist, with the remainder white. The capital is Santiago.

Recent History

Chile was ruled by Spain from the 16th century until its independence in 1818. For most of the 19th century it was governed by a small oligarchy of landowners. Chile won the War of the Pacific (1879–83) against Peru and Bolivia. The greater part of the 20th century was characterized by the struggle for power between right- and left-wing forces.

In September 1970 Dr Salvador Allende Gossens, the Marxist candidate of Unidad Popular (a coalition of five left-wing parties, including the Partido Comunista de Chile—PCCh), was elected to succeed Eduardo Frei Montalva, a Christian Democrat who was President between 1964 and 1970. Allende promised to transform Chilean society by constitutional means, and imposed an extensive programme of nationalization. The Government failed to obtain a congressional majority in the elections of March 1973 and encountered a deteriorating economic situation as well as an intensification of violent opposition to its policies. Accelerated inflation led to food shortages and there were repeated clashes between pro- and anti-Government activists. The armed forces finally intervened in September 1973. President Allende died during the coup. The Congreso (Congress) was subsequently dissolved, all political activity banned and strict censorship introduced. The military Junta dedicated itself to the eradication of Marxism and the 'reconstruction' of Chile, and its leader, Gen. Augusto Pinochet Ugarte, became Supreme Chief of State in June 1974 and President in December. The Junta was widely criticized abroad for its repressive policies and violations of human rights. Critics of the regime were tortured and imprisoned, and several thousand were abducted or 'disappeared'. Some of those who had been imprisoned were released, as a result of international pressure, and sent into exile.

In September 1976 three constitutional acts were promulgated with the aim of creating an 'authoritarian democracy'. All political parties were banned in March 1977, when the state of siege was extended. Following a UN General Assembly resolution, adopted in December 1977, which condemned the Government for violating human rights, President Pinochet organized a referendum in January 1978 to seek endorsement of the regime's policies. Since more than 75% of the voters supported the President in his defence of Chile 'in the face of international aggression', the state of siege (in force since 1973) was ended and was replaced by a state of emergency.

At a plebiscite held in September 1980, 67% of voters endorsed a new Constitution, drafted by the Government, although dubious electoral practices were allegedly employed. Although the new Constitution was described as providing a 'transition to democracy' and President Pinochet ceased to be head of the armed forces, additional clauses allowed him to maintain his firm hold on power until 1989. The new Constitution became effective from March 1981. Political parties, which were still officially outlawed, began to re-emerge, and in mid-1983 five moderate parties formed a coalition, the Alianza Democrática, which advocated a return to democratic rule within 18 months. A left-wing coalition was also created.

In February 1984 the Council of State, a government-appointed consultative body, began drafting a law to legalize political parties and to prepare for elections in 1989. Despite the Government's strenuous attempts to eradicate internal opposition through the introduction of anti-terrorist legislation and extensive security measures, a campaign of explosions and public protests continued throughout 1984 and 1985. A number of protesters were killed in violent clashes with security forces, and many opposition leaders and trade unionists were detained and sent into internal exile.

Throughout 1986 President Pinochet's regime came under increasing attack from the Roman Catholic Church, guerrilla organizations (principally the Frente Patriótico Manuel Rodríguez—FPMR) and international critics, including the US administration, which had previously refrained from condemning the regime's notorious record of violations of human rights. In September the FPMR made an unsuccessful attempt to assassinate Pinochet. The regime's immediate response was to impose a state of siege throughout Chile, under which leading members of the opposition were detained and strict censorship was introduced. One consequence of the state of siege was the reappearance of right-wing 'death squads', which were implicated in a series of murders following the assassination attempt.

President Pinochet clearly indicated his intention to remain in office beyond 1989 by securing, in mid-1987, the sole presidential candidacy, should it be approved by the same plebiscite that would decide the future electoral timetable. The referendum, to be held on 5 October 1988, asked if the sole candidate nominated by the Pinochet regime should be confirmed as President. If the Government lost the referendum, it would be obliged to hold open elections within one year. Several political parties and opposition groups established the Comando por el No campaign to co-ordinate the anti-Government vote. The official result recorded 55% of the votes cast for the anti-Pinochet campaign, and 43% for the President. Following the plebiscite, the opposition made repeated demands for changes to the Constitution, in order to accelerate the democratic process, and sought to initiate discussions with the armed forces. However, Pinochet rejected the opposition's proposals, and affirmed his intention to remain in office until March 1990. Elections were to be held in December 1989.

In mid-1989 Patricio Aylwin Azócar, a lawyer and former senator who had been a vociferous supporter of the 'no' vote in the 1988 plebiscite, emerged as the sole presidential candidate for the centre-left Concertación de los Partidos de la Democracia (CPD, formerly the Comando por el No), an alliance of 17 parties including the Partido Demócrata Cristiano (PDC), of which Aylwin had hitherto been President. Throughout 1989 the election campaign was dominated by demands from both the CPD and right-wing parties for constitutional reform. A document detailing 54 amendments (including the legalization of Marxist political parties) ratified by the Junta was finally accepted by the opposition, with some reservations, and the constitutional reforms were approved by 86% of voters in a national referendum in July 1989.

The electoral campaign was conducted amid intermittent outbursts of political violence and government intervention. Uncertainty regarding President Pinochet's own intentions concerning the forthcoming elections was finally dispelled in mid-1989, when he dismissed the possibility of his candidacy as unconstitutional, but reiterated his intention to continue as Commander-in-Chief of the Army for at least four years. Opposition leaders interpreted subsequent actions by the Government (including the implementation of a law providing for the autonomy of the Banco Central de Chile, the appointment of directors to state-owned companies with mandates of up to 10 years and curbs on the Government's power to remove state officials from their posts) as an attempt by the President to retain a degree of influence beyond his term of office.

The presidential and congressional elections were conducted on 14 December 1989. In the presidential ballot, Aylwin Azócar of the centre-left CPD won a clear victory over the government-supported candidate, former Minister of Finance Hernán Büchi Buc. The transfer of power took place on 11 March 1990. Two members of the outgoing Junta remained as commanders of the air force and police.

Having failed to obtain the support of the two-thirds' majority in the Congreso necessary to amend the 1981 Constitution significantly, Aylwin's new CPD administration was forced to reconcile attempts to fulfil campaign promises as quickly as possible with the need to adopt a conciliatory approach towards more right-wing parties in the Congreso. Agreement was reached almost immediately on a series of modifications to the tax laws, but attempts to amend existing legislation considered repressive by the new administration, including the death penalty and provisions for the censorship of the press, were less successful. (The death penalty was finally abolished in April 2001 and a press freedom law was approved in the following month.)

In April 1990 the Government created the National Commission for Truth and Reconciliation (Comisión Nacional de Verdad y Reconciliación—CNVR) to document and investigate alleged violations of human rights during the previous administration. Although Pinochet, before leaving office, had provided for the impunity of the former military Junta with regard to abuses of human rights, it was suggested by human rights organizations that such safeguards might be circumvented by indicting known perpetrators of atrocities on charges of 'crimes against humanity', a provision which gained considerable public support following the discovery, during 1990, of a number of mass graves containing the remains of political opponents of the 1973–90 military regime. The army High Command condemned the Commission for undermining the prestige of the armed forces and attempting to contravene the terms of a comprehensive amnesty declared in 1978. Although a new accord between military leaders and the Government-Elect had been negotiated in January 1990 (whereby the role of the armed forces was redefined as essentially subservient to the Ministry of Defence), relations between the new Government and the army High Command remained tense. Pinochet became the focus for widespread disaffection with the military élite, but resisted demands for his resignation, reiterating his intention to continue as Commander-in-Chief of the Army until 1997.

Escalating public and political antagonism towards the former military leadership was fuelled throughout 1990 and 1991 by further revelations of abuses of human rights and financial corruption, and erupted into widespread popular outrage and renewed political violence following the publication, in March 1991, of the findings of the CNVR. The report documented the deaths of 2,279 alleged political opponents of the former regime who were executed, died as a result of torture or disappeared (and were presumed to be dead) in 1973–90. In accordance with President Aylwin's recommendation that the report should foster national reconciliation and fulfil an expositionary rather than judicial function, those responsible for the deaths were identified only by the institutions to which they belonged. However, Aylwin pledged full government co-operation for families wishing to pursue private prosecutions. The report concluded that the military Government had embarked upon a 'systematic policy of extermination' of its opponents through the illegal activities of the covert military intelligence agency, Dirección de Inteligencia Nacional (Dina), and was also highly critical of the Chilean judiciary for failing to protect the rights of individuals by refusing thousands of petitions for habeas corpus submitted by human rights lawyers. Pinochet publicly denounced the document and declared his opposition to government plans to make material reparation to the families of the victims named in the report. Left-wing extremists meanwhile embarked on a series of attacks against right-wing opponents; however, fears of an escalation in extremist violence were partially dispelled by the announcement, in May 1991, of the FPMR's intention to renounce its armed struggle and join the political mainstream as the Movimiento Patriótico Manuel Rodríguez.

In November 1993, following a prolonged investigation and a controversial trial, former Dina officials Gen. Manuel Contreras and Col. Pedro Espinoza were convicted of the murder of Orlando Letelier, a former cabinet minister (and Chile's ambassador to the USA during the Government of Salvador Allende in the early 1970s), who was assassinated in 1976, together with a US associate, in Washington, DC. In April Contreras was sentenced to 15 years' imprisonment for the kidnapping of Miguel

Sandoval, a left-wing activist who had disappeared in 1975 (the sentence was reduced to six years in January 2004 and in late 2004 Contreras was released from prison).The judge in the case, Alejandro Solís, rejected the defendant's invocation of the amnesty law, ruling that it did not apply in cases of 'disappearance', on the grounds that such unresolved cases of abduction should be considered as ongoing. In November 2004 the Supreme Court upheld this decision on appeal (see below).

In November 1991, as part of the new Government's commitment to political decentralization, the Congreso approved constitutional amendments to local government statutes, which provided for the replacement of centrally-appointed local officials with directly-elected representatives. However, the considerable right-wing opposition in the Congreso continued to frustrate President Aylwin's attempts to enact legislation. Proposals to accelerate the prosecution of military personnel accused of human rights abuses, while safeguarding their anonymity, put forward by the President in August 1993, were rejected by the right as ill-considered and precipitate, while left-wing groups accused the Government of being concessionary. In September Aylwin was forced to withdraw the proposals from the Congreso, following a declaration of opposition to the legislation, made by two member parties of the ruling coalition, in response to the petitions of human rights organizations.

A presidential election, held on 11 December 1993, was won by the CPD candidate Eduardo Frei Ruiz-Tagle, a PDC senator, with 58% of the votes cast, ahead of Arturo Alessandri Besa, the candidate of the right-wing coalition, the Unión para el Progreso de Chile (UPC), who received 24% of the votes. However, the ruling coalition failed to make significant gains at concurrently conducted congressional elections. In February 1994 formal congressional endorsement was secured for constitutional reform, whereby henceforth the length of the non-renewable presidential term would be fixed at six years.

On assuming the presidency in March 1994 Frei identified the immediate aims of his Government as the alleviation of poverty, the elimination of corrupt government, and the fostering of significant economic growth. However, the President's affirmation of Pinochet's right to remain in office until 1997 appeared to compromise his pre-election demands for greater powers for the executive to nominate and remove the military High Command. In August Frei presented several constitutional reform proposals to the Congreso, including the abolition of the nine seats for appointed senators (installed by the former military regime) and the introduction of an electoral system based on proportional representation (to replace the unrepresentative binomial system). However, Frei encountered the same level of opposition to constitutional reform (particularly from the right and from the upper house), that had undermined most attempts at constitutional amendment made by the previous administration.

In November 1995 the Government secured the support of the opposition Partido Renovación Nacional (RN) for revised proposals for new legislation relating to human rights and constitutional reform. However, the compromised nature of the agreement provoked considerable disaffection within the RN, and within the opposition UPC alliance in general, which was effectively dissolved following the departure of the Partido Unión Demócrata Independiente (UDI) and the Unión de Centro-Centro (UCC) in protest at the actions of the RN. Concern was also expressed by members of the Partido Socialista (PS—within the ruling coalition) that the human rights legislation had been severely compromised.

During 1997 government efforts to abolish the designated seats in the Senado intensified in response to Pinochet's stated intention to assume one of the seats assigned to former Presidents on retirement as Commander-in-Chief of the Army in March 1998. In July 1997 the Senado rejected the Government's latest petition for reform to the system of appointments. In October it was announced that Maj.-Gen. Ricardo Izurieta, previously chief of defence staff, was to succeed Pinochet as Commander-in-Chief of the Army. The announcement was made amid a number of changes in the military High Command, which appeared to confirm earlier predictions that military influence would henceforth be concentrated in the Senado, where it would bolster the political right wing.

Legislative elections to renew all 120 seats in the Cámara de Diputados and 20 of the elective seats in the Senado were conducted on 11 December 1997. The governing Concertación secured 51% of the votes for deputies and retained (with 70 seats) a comfortable majority in the lower house. The elections revealed a shifting balance of power within the two major political groupings (support for the UDI, in particular, appeared to have superseded that for the RN within the Unión por Chile), and prompted renewed criticism of the country's binomial system of voting, the PCCh having failed to secure congressional representation despite attracting 8% and 7% of the votes to the upper and lower houses, respectively.

In December 1997 Pinochet reiterated his intention to assert his constitutional right, on retirement, to assume an *ex-officio* seat (for life) in the Senado (in addition to the nine designated senators). A number of centre-left politicians pledged to obstruct Pinochet's accession to the Senado in protest. Separate attempts were made in January 1998 by junior members of the Concertación (despite the declarations of senior members of the Government—anxious to ensure a peaceful exchange of offices in March—that such action was untimely and politically inconvenient) and by the leadership of the PCCh to begin judicial proceedings against Pinochet on charges related to gross abuses of human rights. Pinochet responded by announcing that he would not retire as Commander-in-Chief of the Army on 26 January, as previously suggested, but would continue in office until 10 March, thereby preserving the immunity from prosecution provided by the position for as long as possible.

On 6 March 1998 the military High Command announced that Pinochet had been named an honorary commander-in-chief—a position with no historical precedent. On 11 March Pinochet assumed his seat in the Senado. A largely symbolic, and unsuccessful, attempt by 11 Concertación deputies to instigate a formal impeachment action against Pinochet was initiated in the Cámara de Diputados in the same month. The motion's defeat prompted a crisis within the Concertación—the majority of PDC deputies having voted against it.

At the presidential poll, held on 12 December 1999, the candidate of the ruling Concertación, Ricardo Lagos Escobar of the PS, received 47.96% of the total votes cast, with Joaquín Lavín, representing the Alianza por Chile (formed by the RN and the UDI), obtaining 47.52%. Four minor candidates, among whom only Gladys Marín (representing the PCCh) received more than 3.0% of the poll, were eliminated. At the second round of voting, which took place on 16 January 2000, Lagos emerged victorious with 51.3% of the total votes, while Lavín received 48.7%. (Lavín was subsequently elected Mayor of Santiago in local elections held in October.) Lagos was sworn in as President on 11 March. He set out a reduction in unemployment and an increase in economic growth to be the main priorities for his new Government.

As the controversy surrounding the detention of former President Pinochet in the United Kingdom continued in 1999 (see below), domestic attention was once again focused on the actions of the security forces during the post-1973 military regime. In June the arrest of five retired army officers (former commanders of a notorious élite army unit popularly referred to as the 'caravan of death') was ordered by an appeal court judge following renewed investigation into the disappearance of 72 political prisoners in the immediate aftermath of the 1973 military coup. The decision to prosecute the five men on charges of aggravated kidnapping was considered a breakthrough in Chilean judicial practice, since the absence of physical or documented evidence of the deaths of the prisoners meant that the crimes were technically in continuance, and that the accused men were not protected by the 1978 amnesty which guaranteed the impunity of military personnel for crimes committed before that year. In July 1999 the legality of the arrests was confirmed by the Supreme Court, and the indictment (and extradition from the USA) of a sixth former army officer was sought in connection with the case in August. Attempts by the Government to stem the resurgence of popular resentment of the past actions of the armed forces included, in August, the first direct discussions of the fate of the 'disappeared' between representatives of the armed forces and human rights organizations. However, tensions were exacerbated by the US National Security Council's declassification, in June, of some 5,800 CIA documents which recorded abuses of human rights during 1973–78, and appeared to support claims that the Chilean armed forces had falsified evidence purporting to demonstrate the threat posed by the Allende administration in order to justify the 1973 coup. In September 1999 the Supreme Court had ruled in favour of criminal proceedings brought against two retired generals, Humberto Gordon Rubio and Roberto Schmied, earlier in the month for their alleged involvement in the murder of trade union leader Tucapel Jiménez in 1982. (In August 2002 12 former military officers, including four generals, were sentenced

to terms of imprisonment for their involvement in the murder of Jiménez.). In the following month an arrest warrant was issued against Gen. (retd) Hugo Salas Wendel, a former Director of Dina, on charges of complicity in the killings in 1987 of 12 alleged members of a left-wing guerrilla group. In June 2000 the Mesa de Diálogo, a round-table discussion between human rights lawyers and the military, agreed to guarantee the anonymity of any military person offering information on the whereabouts of any 'disappeared' person. The first official report as a result of the agreement in January 2001 disclosed information on the fate of 200 people—151 were allegedly thrown into the sea, 20 were buried in a mass grave and 29 were scattered in graves around central Chile.

Proposed reforms to the Constitution under discussion in 2001 included the abolition of seats for non-elected senators and a revision of the binominal electoral system, which reformers believed entrenched the interests of the former authoritarian regime against social change. However, the results of legislative elections, held on 16 December, threatened progress on constitutional issues, as the right-wing UDI, a member of the Alianza por Chile, made significant gains in the Senado and the Cámara de Diputados. In the Senado, where 18 of the 38 elective seats were contested, the CPD won 51.3% of the votes cast and an overall 20 seats, but lost its one-seat majority, while the Alianza por Chile won 44.0% and increased its representation to 16 seats (the UDI's total increased to nine seats). The remaining two seats were won by Independents. In the Cámara de Diputados the CPD won 47.9% of the votes and 62 seats, a substantially reduced majority, while the Alianza por Chile secured 44.3% of the ballot and 57 seats (the UDI's representation increased to 35 deputies, replacing the PDC as Chile's largest party).

On 16 October 1998 former President Pinochet was arrested during a visit to London, United Kingdom, in response to a preliminary request, made to the British authorities by a Spanish judge, Baltazar Garzón, that Pinochet should be extradited to Spain to answer charges of 'genocide and terrorism' committed against some 4,000 individuals, including Spanish nationals, by his administration during 1973–90. A second Spanish request for Pinochet's extradition, received later in the month, cited his alleged involvement in institutionalized torture, conspiracy and the taking of hostages. In early November a formal request for extradition was made, although the Spanish Government (like the British Government) was anxious to emphasize its neutrality in what it considered to be a purely judicial affair. In Chile the Frei Government protested that Pinochet's diplomatic immunity had been infringed, while the British Government denied Pinochet's status as an accredited diplomat. Meanwhile, supporters and opponents of Pinochet clashed during demonstrations in Santiago, and there were concerns that Pinochet's detention was threatening to undermine the country's delicate political and military balance.

The British House of Lords' hearing of the extradition appeal in late November 1998 overturned a high court ruling in October that Pinochet was entitled to 'sovereign immunity' as a former head of state. Despite the remonstrances of the Chilean Minister of Foreign Affairs, José Miguel Insulza, and pressure from the USA to allow Pinochet to return to Chile, on 9 December the British Government authorized the start of formal extradition proceedings. President Frei reacted angrily to the decision, recalling the Chilean ambassador in London for consultations. Meanwhile, however, it had emerged that one of the three law lords who had rejected Pinochet's immunity in the November ruling had failed to declare potentially compromising personal links to the international human rights campaign group Amnesty International. As a result, in December a new appeal panel unanimously suspended the November pronouncement and ordered the case to be re-submitted to a new appellate committee. Meanwhile, Pinochet remained under effective house arrest in the United Kingdom. In March 1999 the appellate committee ruled itself to be in support of the original pronouncement overturning Pinochet's claims to immunity. However, the committee also found that only charges relating to events subsequent to December 1988 (at which time the 1984 UN Convention against Torture and Other Cruel, Inhuman or Degrading Treatment or Punishment had entered into British law) should be considered relevant, thus reducing the number of draft charges brought by Spain from 33 to three. Formal extradition proceedings were initiated in September, and in October a court found that Pinochet could be lawfully extradited to Spain. Pinochet's lawyers made a formal appeal against the decision. However, in early March 2000, after an independent doctors' report had concluded that Pinochet was medically unfit to undergo further legal proceedings, the British Secretary of State for the Home Department, Jack Straw, announced that Pinochet was to be released, and on the following day the former President returned to Chile.

The return of Pinochet to Chile was interpreted as a triumph for the former dictator and included a public welcome by the heads of the armed forces but no representation from the civilian Government. Initially, expectations that Pinochet would ever stand trial in Chile were very low; however, these were raised in June 2000 following the Santiago Appeal Court's ruling to lift the former dictator's political immunity. In August, in an historical judgment, the Supreme Court confirmed the decision. The judgment was made possible by changes to Chile's judiciary, several members of which had retired and had been replaced by more independent-minded judges. Foremost among these was Juan Guzmán Tapia, who vigorously took up the legal case against Pinochet and others accused of human rights' infringements. Over 200 lawsuits were filed against Pinochet. The former President's lawyers, meanwhile, argued that it would be too undignified for their client to submit to a medical examination to determine whether he was mentally fit to stand trial (compulsory in Chile for all citizens over the age of 70). In October an Argentine judge requested the extradition of Pinochet to stand trial for the 1974 killing, in Buenos Aires, of former Chilean army chief Carlos Prats and his wife. In November the Supreme Court ruled that Pinochet must not leave the country and on 1 December Judge Guzmán indicted Pinochet on charges of aggravated kidnapping and murder in the 'caravan of death' case (see above) and placed him under house arrest. However, the Santiago Appeal Court overturned the house arrest order on the grounds that his case had been improperly handled (he was not questioned before being charged), a decision subsequently confirmed by the Supreme Court. The Supreme Court also ruled that Pinochet must face interrogation by Judge Guzmán within 20 days, though not before undergoing the medical tests required by law. In early January 2001, after failing to appear for previously scheduled tests, Pinochet finally consented to the medical examination and was subsequently questioned. On 31 January Judge Guzmán issued an order for the former General's arrest on charges of kidnap and murder. However, following an appeal by Pinochet, in March the Santiago Appeal Court ruled that the charges should be reduced to conspiracy to cover up the events, as opposed to responsibility for the 'caravan of death', and in July the Court ruled that the former dictator was mentally unfit to stand trial. In July 2002 the Supreme Court voted to close the case against Pinochet permanently, as he was suffering from 'incurable' and 'irreversible' dementia. Within days Pinochet relinquished his position as senator for life. In October 2003, despite Pinochet's lucid appearance in a recent television interview, the Supreme Court dismissed a further attempt to overturn the ruling. However, in May 2004 the Santiago Court of Appeal voted to remove Pinochet's immunity from prosecution for the crimes allegedly committed as part of 'Plan Condor', an intelligence operation to eliminate opponents of the Latin American military dictatorships in the 1970s; on 26 October the Supreme Court voted to uphold this ruling.

In mid-July 2004 a US senate report on the accounts of the Washington, DC-based Riggs Bank alleged that, between 1985 and 2002, Pinochet and his wife had deposited up to US $12m. into secret accounts there. The Chilean authorities immediately initiated an investigation into the origin of the funds and, in response to separate, ongoing investigations by Spanish judge Baltazar Garzón, on 9 November Attorney-General Mónica Maldonado Croquevielle recommended that Pinochet's assets be 'frozen' while investigations continued. Meanwhile, on 26 August the Supreme Court upheld a decision by the appeals court in May to strip Pinochet of his immunity from prosecution. The decision opened the way for Pinochet to be interrogated by Judge Guzmán over his role in 'Plan Condor'. In the following month the former dictator's legal representatives unsuccessfully petitioned the Supreme Court to disbar Guzmán from the case on the grounds that his supposed personal animosity towards the former President that would compromise his impartiality. On 25 September Pinochet was formally interrogated by Judge Guzmán and, despite Pinochet's lawyers claiming that he had recently suffered a significant deterioration in his mental condition, on 13 December Guzmán declared him to be of sufficiently sound mind to stand trial; the Supreme Court upheld this decision (by three votes to two) on 4 January 2005. The

following day Pinochet was placed under house arrest pending trial, although one week later he was released on bail.

In late 2002 the President encountered serious political difficulties when the Government became embroiled in a corruption scandal. A number of government officials were accused of accepting bribes from a consultancy company, Gate, during 1999–2000, and it was alleged that some of the money had been used to finance CPD election campaigns. Lagos was quick to announce plans to increase government accountability and improve the transparency of party funding, but allegations of corruption within the ruling CPD continued and two close associates of Lagos were subsequently arrested on bribery charges. In January 2003 the Supreme Court stripped five CPD congressmen of their parliamentary immunity in order that they too face corruption charges. As a result, the representation of Lagos's Concertación alliance was reduced to 58 seats in the Cámara de Diputados, compared with 57 for the opposition Alianza por Chile. In February there were reports of a further manipulation of public office, this time in connection with the alleged theft and transferral of some US $100m. of deposits belonging to CORFO (Corporación de Fomento de la Producción), a government development agency. In February, in an attempt to regain public confidence, President Lagos carried out a cabinet reshuffle. Most notably, Luis Bates Hidalgo—a former leading member of the anti-corruption campaign group Transparency International—was appointed Minister of Justice.

In August 2003 President Lagos announced a series of measures intended to resolve issues relating to human rights violations during the military dictatorship. These included increases in compensation paid to victims of political violence and their relatives, as well as measures to facilitate criminal prosecutions of former military personnel. However, he did not pledge to repeal the 1978 amnesty law, an omission that prompted criticism from relatives of the 'disappeared'. None the less, in November 2004 the Supreme Court, in reference to the prosecution, on charges of involvement in 'Plan Condor', of the former head of Dina, Manuel Contreras, and three other former secret policemen, ruled against the invocation of the amnesty law in cases of 'disappearance', on the grounds that, until the body of the kidnapped person was found, such unresolved cases of abduction should be considered as ongoing. The Supreme Court's ruling opened the way for many other cases of human rights abuses during 1973–90 to be brought. Also in November 2004, the testimonies of some 35,000 victims of abuses under the Pinochet regime were published in a report by the National Commission on Political Imprisonment and Torture. Although victims' and human rights groups welcomed the report, many criticized it for omitting the names of those accused of the abuses. Prior to the report's publication, the Commander-in-Chief of the Chilean Army, Gen. Juan Emilio Cheyre Espinosa, issued on behalf of the armed forces a public apology, in which for the first time institutional responsibility was accepted for the systematic abuse of opponents of the Pinochet regime. On 29 November President Lagos announced that some 28,000 of the victims who gave testimony in the report would be eligible for a pension, equivalent to nearly US $200 per month.

In September 2003 the Senado voted in favour of a proposed constitutional amendment legalizing divorce. Chile remained the only country in the Western hemisphere where divorce was banned. The Roman Catholic Church strongly opposed the move, and began a lobbying campaign to dilute the legislation. Nevertheless, in March 2004 the Cámara de Diputados approved a new civil matrimony law that allowed divorce after one year of marriage. The law was promulgated by President Lagos in May and came into effect in November.

In September 2004 President Lagos carried out a cabinet reshuffle, in which, notably, the Minister of National Defence, Michelle Bachelet Jeria, and the Minister of Foreign Affairs, María Soledad Alvear Valenzuela, lost their portfolios. Both women subsequently announced their intention to stand as candidates in the forthcoming presidential election, scheduled for 14 December 2005. In mid-January 2005 Alvear was chosen as her party's, the PDC, nominee; however, she faced intense competition in winning the presidential candidacy of the ruling Concertación as a whole from Bachelet of the PS. The successful Concertación candidate's main rival in the presidential ballot would once again be the Alianza por Chile's Joaquín Lavín.

In late October and early November 2004 the Senado finally approved a number of constitutional reforms. These included: the abolition of non-elected senators and of senators-for-life; the restoration of the President's power to dismiss the head of the armed forces and the police; and a reduction of the presidential term from six years to four. The constitutional reforms required subsequent approval by the Cámara de Diputados.

In 2000 and 2001 a series of mining, dam and forestry projects prompted violent protests by the Mapuche indigenous peoples who were campaigning for the restitution of land they claimed under ancestral right. In May 2000 a Historical Truth and New Deal Commission was created to consider the demands and needs of indigenous communities. However, in October the Cámara de Diputados rejected legislation that would have granted constitutional recognition to the Mapuche peoples. In November 2003 the Commission produced its final report, which recommended the extension of constitutional and property rights to indigenous peoples and confirmation of their entitlement to participate in national politics. In early 2004 it was alleged that forest fires in the Bíobío region had been started by groups of Mapuche activists opposed to the activities of the timber industry. In August five Mapuche activists were convicted under anti-terrorism legislation passed during the Pinochet regime of setting fire to property of the logging company Forestal Mininco. Human rights organizations condemned the use of the legislation as disproportionate. In early November seven Mapuche activists (and one non-Mapuche sympathizer) were acquitted on charges of conspiring to commit terrorist acts. Meanwhile, in August, after some eight years of legal dispute between the Spanish energy company Endesa, SA, and a coalition of ecological and indigenous groups of Pehuenche ethnicity, an agreement was finally reached that would allow construction of a hydroelectric plant in the River Bíobío basin. It was predicted that the plant, inaugurated in September, would supply 3,100 GWh annually, equivalent to some 9% of Chile's electricity requirements.

In August 1991 Argentina and Chile reached a settlement regarding disputed territory in the Antarctic region. Responsibility for the contentious Laguna del Desierto region, however, was to be decided by international arbitration. In October 1994 Argentina's claim to the territory was upheld by a five-member international arbitration panel. In July 1997 it was announced unexpectedly that the two countries were to conduct joint military exercises in 1998, and in September it was agreed to proceed with the creation of a conciliation commission, originally envisaged within the terms of a peace and friendship treaty concluded in 1984. Joint naval exercises began in August 1998. In December agreement on border demarcation of the still disputed 'continental glaciers' territory in the Antarctic region was reached by the Presidents of the two countries. In September 2000 both countries ratified the Mining and Co-operation Integration Treaty, signed in 1997, which allowed joint exploitation of mineral deposits along their shared border. Relations between the two countries were strained in mid-2004, however, following the decision of Argentine President Néstor Carlos Kirchner to reduce exports of gas to Chile by some 25% in order to meet a critical shortfall in stocks for domestic consumption. The Lagos administration claimed that this violated an agreement signed in 1995. Tensions between the two countries were exacerbated following the appointment of Ignacio Walker Prieto as the Chilean Minister of Foreign Affairs in September. In a newspaper editorial prior to his appointment Walker had criticized both President Kirchner for opportunism and Peronism in general for displaying 'authoritarian' and 'fascistic' traits.

Prospects for renewed diplomatic relations with Bolivia (which severed relations with Chile in 1978 over the issue of Bolivian access to the Pacific Ocean) were frustrated during the 1990s. The Bolivian Government made repeated requests in 1997 for the renewal of discussions on Bolivian access to the sea, and sought Peru's assistance in the dispute; however, subsequent ministerial discussions failed to produce an effective formula for the restoration of diplomatic relations. In late 2003 the new Bolivian Government reiterated its historic claims to sovereign access to the Pacific. In early 2004 President Lagos indicated his intention to seek consultations with Peru, although the Government continued to refuse any prospect of ceding territory to Bolivia. The Lagos administration's decision in October to privatize the port of Arica elicited vehement objections from the Bolivian Government, which feared this would adversely effect Bolivia's external trade, owing to significant increases in port tariffs (supposedly in contravention of the 1904 treaty that guaranteed duty-free passage of Bolivian goods through Arica). However, in the following month there were moves towards *rapprochement* at the Rio Group summit in

Brazil after the Bolivian delegation notably omitted mention of its demand for sovereign access to the Pacific.

A free trade agreement with Colombia, the Acuerdo de Complementación Económica (ACE), took effect from 1 January 1994. However, tensions arose between the two countries in September 2004 following Chile's imposition of restrictions on imports of Colombian sugar and Colombia's reciprocal imposition of tariffs on Chilean wine, fruit and vehicles. A free trade agreement with Ecuador came into effect on 1 January 1995. In December 1994 the signatory nations to the North American Free Trade Agreement (NAFTA) issued a formal invitation to Chile to join the group. However US President Bill Clinton failed to secure US congressional support for 'fast track' authorization for Chile's accession to the Agreement. In November 2000 President Clinton announced that the USA would negotiate a bilateral trade deal with Chile, as opposed to it formally becoming a full member of NAFTA. In the context of this delay, Chile intensified attempts to negotiate a bilateral free-trade agreement with Canada and a formal trade agreement with the Mercado Común del Sur (Mercosur, see p. 349). In November 1996 agreement was reached with Canada on the removal of tariffs on three-quarters of bilateral trade, with the gradual removal of remaining duties over a five-year period. The agreement came into effect in July 1997 and its terms were modified and expanded in early 1998. Meanwhile, in October 1996, Chile became an associate member of Mercosur, following negotiations which established the immediate reduction of tariffs on 90% of Chilean goods, and the subsequent elimination of tariffs on 'sensitive' goods including meat, sugar, edible oils and wheat, over an 18-year period. However, Chile's decision to negotiate a bilateral free trade accord with the USA in 2000 effectively stalled further negotiations on full membership.

In April 1998 Chile and Mexico signed a free trade agreement, expanding the terms of an ACE in force since 1992. In June 1998 Chile signed a similar agreement with Peru, abolishing customs duties on 2,500 products. The agreement also envisaged the free passage of 50% of all products by 2003 and the creation of a free-trade area within 18 years. With the exception of Bolivia, Chile has now negotiated free trade agreements throughout the South American continent. At a third 'Summit of the Americas', in Québec, Canada, in April 2001, attended by representatives of all nations in the region (with the exception of Cuba), a timetable on the establishment of a Free Trade Area of the Americas (FTAA) by 2005 was agreed upon. Negotiations were to conclude by January 2005, although by this time no agreement had been reached. In December 2002 Chile and the USA finally agreed on a free trade pact that would eliminate immediately all barriers on 85% of trade between the two countries, with the remaining trade restrictions being phased out within 12 years. The agreement came into effect in January 2004. In February 2003 an association agreement for political and economic co-operation between Chile and the European Union came into effect. In the same month a new free trade agreement was signed with the Republic of Korea; the accord was ratified by the South Korean legislature in February 2004. A free trade accord between Chile and the European Free Trade Association (EFTA, see p. 214) came into effect also in February 2004. In early December Chile successfully applied for observer status at the Andean Community of Nations (see p. 148). Later that month Chile was one of 12 countries that were signatories to the agreement, signed in Cusco, Peru, creating the South American Community of Nations (Comunidad Sudamericana de Naciones), intended to promote greater regional economic integration, due to become operational by 2007.

Government

Chile is a republic, divided into 12 regions and a metropolitan area. Easter Island enjoys 'special territory' status within Chile. Under the terms of the Constitution, executive power is vested in the President, who is directly elected for a six-year term. The President is assisted by a Cabinet. Legislative power is vested in the bicameral Congreso Nacional (National Congress), comprising the 49-member Senado (Senate) and the 120-member Cámara de Diputados (Chamber of Deputies).

Defence

Military service is for one year (army) or 22 months (navy and air force) and is compulsory for men at 19 years of age. In August 2004 the army had a strength of 47,700, the navy 19,000 and the air force 11,000. Paramilitary security forces numbered about 38,000 carabineros. Defence expenditure for 2004 was budgeted at 947,000m. pesos.

Economic Affairs

In 2003, according to estimates by the World Bank, Chile's gross national product (GNI), measured at average 2001–03 prices, was US $69,598m., equivalent to $4,390 per head (or $9,810 per head on an international purchasing-power parity basis). During 1990–2003, it was estimated, the population increased by an average of 1.4% per year, while gross domestic product (GDP) per head increased, in real terms, at an average annual rate of 4.1%. Overall GDP increased, in real terms, at an average annual rate of 5.6% in 1990–2003; real GDP increased by 3.3% in 2003.

According to preliminary estimates, agriculture (including forestry and fishing) contributed an estimated 6.1% of GDP, at constant prices, in 2003. An estimated 13.4% of the employed labour force were engaged in this sector in late 2004. Important subsistence crops include wheat, oats, barley, rice, beans, lentils, maize and chick-peas. Industrial crops include sugar beet, sunflower seed and rapeseed. Fruit and vegetables are also important export commodities (together contributing 11.1% of total export revenues in 2003), particularly, beans, asparagus, onions, garlic, grapes, citrus fruits, avocados, pears, peaches, plums and nuts. The production and export of wine has increased significantly in recent years. Forestry and fishing, and derivatives from both activities, also make important contributions to the sector. During 1990–2003 agricultural GDP increased, in real terms, by an average of 2.5% per year; agricultural GDP growth was estimated at 5.7% in 2002 and at 0.9% in 2003.

According to preliminary figures, industry (including mining, manufacturing, construction and power) contributed an estimated 37.2% of GDP, at constant prices, in 2003 and accounted for an estimated 23.6% of the employed labour force in late 2004. During 1990–2003 industrial GDP increased by an average of 5.2% per year. GDP growth in all industrial sectors was estimated at 0.9% in 2002 and at 3.5% in 2003.

Mining contributed an estimated 8.6% of GDP, at constant prices, in 2003 and engaged an estimated 1.3% of the employed labour force in late 2004. Chile, with some 22% of the world's known reserves, is the world's largest producer and exporter of copper. Copper accounted for 87.5% of Chile's total export earnings in 1970, but the proportion had decreased to about 25.7% by 2001. However, in 2004 the contribution of copper to total export earnings increased to an estimated 54% (some US $14,340m.). Gold, silver, iron ore, nitrates, molybdenum, manganese, lead and coal are also mined, and the whole sector contributed 40.1% of total export earnings in 2001. In real terms, the sector's GDP was estimated to have decreased by 3.9% in 2002, but the sector increased by an estimated 5.4% in 2003. Petroleum and natural gas deposits have been located in the south and, in 2004, offshore. In 2002 Chile was the world's largest producer of lithium carbonate, producing some 31,320 metric tons in the previous year.

According to preliminary estimates, manufacturing contributed 17.1% of GDP, at constant prices, in 2003, and engaged an estimated 13.7% of the employed labour force in late 2004. The most important branches of manufacturing are food and non-ferrous metals. Manufacturing GDP increased by an average of 3.9% per year in 1990–2003. Growth in sectoral GDP was put at 2.7% in 2002 and at 2.4% in 2003.

In 2001 electric energy was derived mainly from hydroelectric power (49.4%), coal (16.5%) and natural gas (28.7%). Chile produces some 40% of its national energy requirements. Plans are under consideration to exploit further Chile's vast hydro-electric potential (estimated at 18,700 MW—the largest in the world). Meanwhile, Chile imported fuel and energy products equivalent to some 16.2% of the value of total merchandise imports in 2003.

The services sector, according to preliminary estimates, contributed an estimated 56.5% of GDP, at constant prices, in 2003 and engaged an estimated 63.0% of the employed labour force in late 2004. The financial sector continued to expand in the early 21st century, fuelled, in part, by the success of private pension funds. During 1990–2003 services GDP increased by an average of 4.8% per year. The sector's GDP increased, in real terms, by an estimated 2.8% in 2002 and by a further estimated 3.0% in 2003.

In 2003 Chile recorded a visible trade surplus of US $3,015m., but there was a deficit of $594m. on the current account of the balance of payments. In 2001 Argentina was the principal source of imports (19.1%), while the USA was the principal market for exports (18.6%). Other major trading partners were

Japan, the United Kingdom, Brazil and the People's Republic of China. In 2001 the principal exports were copper and copper manufactures (25.7% of total export revenue), fish (8.7%), fruit (6.5%) and chemical products (6.2%). The principal imports in that year were machinery and transport equipment, and mineral and chemical products.

In 2002 there was a budgetary deficit of some 186,510m. pesos (equivalent to 4.0% of GDP). Chile's external debt totalled some US $43,396m. at the end of 2003, of which $4,551m. was long-term public debt. Debt-servicing costs in 2002 were equivalent to some 32.8% of the value of exports of goods and services. The annual rate of inflation averaged 7.4% in 1990–2004, and stood at 1.0% in 2004. An estimated 7.8% of the labour force were unemployed in late 2004.

Chile is a member of the Latin American Integration Association (ALADI, see p. 289) and was admitted to the Rio Group (see p. 385) in 1990 and to the Asia-Pacific Economic Co-operation group (APEC, see p. 155) in 1994. Chile is also among the founding members of the World Trade Organization (WTO, see p. 357).

Owing to the relaxation of import duties in the early 1980s, Chile's potential in the agricultural and manufacturing sectors was stifled by cheaper imported goods. Exports of fruit, seafoods and wines, however, expanded considerably, although in 2004 Chile remained heavily dependent on exports of copper and on the stability of the world copper market. Largely as a result of depressed world prices for copper, in 1999 Chile's economy contracted by 1.1%. In an attempt to stimulate exports, in September the Central Bank abandoned its strict regulation of the peso, allowing the currency to float against the US dollar. In an attempt to stimulate recovery, the new Government of President Lagos initiated a public works programme, designed to increase the incomes of skilled and semi-skilled workers, and introduced tax rebates of up to US $400 for about 1m. people. Other government initiatives included encouraging foreign investment in growth areas such as tourism and new technology and promoting investment in Chile's disparate regions. Tax and financial sector reforms were introduced to encourage inward investment and improve tax collection in 2001. In January 2005 the Government claimed that it had reduced tax evasion in the previous year by $760m. and that total tax revenue had increased by $806m. However, high unemployment and low investment levels continued to stifle consumer demand. Although high imported petroleum prices and declining prices for copper continued to stifle growth in 2001 and 2002 (when the economy grew by 3.4% and 2.2%, respectively), Chile's trade balance none the less remained stable, as market confidence increased. By 2004 unemployment remained high (at an estimated 7.8% in October–December). Nevertheless, in that year, as international prices for Chile's principal commodities improved, growth was estimated at 3.3%. A free trade agreement with the USA, traditionally Chile's largest trading partner, came into effect in January 2004; by November it was reported that trade between the two countries had increased by some 25%, compared with the same period in the previous year. None the less, in 2003 the People's Republic of China overtook the USA to become Chile's largest export market. In April 2004 the Governments of Chile and China began negotiations on a free trade agreement and plans were announced for increased Chinese investment in the Chilean copper industry. A free trade agreement with the Republic of Korea came into effect in February of that year, while in January 2005 a similar bilateral accord was signed with the Government of India. GDP was estimated to have grown by 5.8% in 2004 and similar growth was predicted for 2005.

Education

Pre-primary education is widely available for all children from five years of age. Primary education is officially compulsory, and is provided free of charge, for eight years, beginning at six or seven years of age. It is divided into two cycles: the first lasts for four years and provides a general education; the second cycle offers more specialized schooling. Secondary education, beginning at 13 or 14 years of age, is divided into the humanities-science programme (lasting for four years), with the emphasis on general education and possible entrance to university, and the technical-professional programme (lasting for between four and six years), designed to fulfil the requirements of specialist training. In 1996 the total enrolment at primary schools included an estimated 98.2% of children in the relevant age-group, while the comparable ratio for secondary enrolment was

85.9%. Higher education is provided by three kinds of institution: universities, professional institutes and centres of technical information. The provision for education in the 2002 central government budget was 1,958,540m. pesos (18.7% of total spending).

Public Holidays

2005: 1 January (New Year's Day), 25–26 March (Good Friday and Easter Saturday), 2 May (for Labour Day), 21 May (Battle of Iquique), 15 August (Assumption), 4 September (National Unity Day), 19 September (for Independence Day), 12 October (Day of the Race, anniversary of the discovery of America), 1

November (All Saints' Day), 8 December (Immaculate Conception), 25 December (Christmas Day).

2006: 1 January (New Year's Day), 14–15 April (Good Friday and Easter Saturday), 1 May (Labour Day), 21 May (Battle of Iquique), 15 August (Assumption), 4 September (National Unity Day), 18 September (Independence Day), 12 October (Day of the Race, anniversary of the discovery of America), 1 November (All Saints' Day), 8 December (Immaculate Conception), 25 December (Christmas Day).

Weights and Measures

The metric system is officially in force.

Statistical Survey

Sources (unless otherwise stated): Instituto Nacional de Estadísticas, Avda Bulnes 418, Casilla 498-3, Correo 3, Santiago; tel. (2) 366-7777; fax (2) 671-2169; e-mail inesdadm@reuna.cl; internet www.ine.cl ; Banco Central de Chile, Agustinas 1180, Santiago; tel. (2) 696-2281; fax (2) 698-4847; e-mail bcch@bcentral.cl; internet www.bcentral.cl.

Area and Population

AREA, POPULATION AND DENSITY*

Area (sq km)	756,096†
Population (census results)‡	
22 April 1992	13,348,401
24 April 2002	
Males	7,447,695
Females	7,668,740
Total	15,116,435
Population (official estimates at mid-year)	
2002	15,589,147
2003	15,773,504
2004	15,955,631
Density (per sq km) at mid-2004	21.1

* Excluding Chilean Antarctic Territory (approximately 1,250,000 sq km).
† 291,930 sq miles.
‡ Excluding adjustment for underenumeration.

REGIONS
(2002 census)

	Area (sq km)	Population ('000)	Density (per sq km)	Capital
I De Tarapacá . . .	59,099.1	428.6	7.3	Iquique
II De Antofagasta .	126,049.1	494.0	3.9	Antofagasta
III De Atacama . .	75,176.2	254.3	3.4	Copiapó
IV De Coquimbo . .	40,579.9	603.2	14.9	La Serena
V De Valparaíso .	16,396.1	1,539.9	93.9	Valparaíso
VI Del Libertador Gen. Bernardo O'Higgins	16,387.0	780.6	47.6	Rancagua
VII Del Maule	30,296.1	908.1	30.0	Talca
VIII Del Bíobío	37,062.6	1,861.6	50.2	Concepción
IX De la Araucanía .	31,842.3	869.5	27.3	Temuco
X De Los Lagos . . .	67,013.1	1,073.1	16.0	Puerto Montt
XI Aisén del Gen. Carlos Ibáñez del Campo .	108,494.4	91.5	0.8	Coihaique
XII De Magallanes y Antártica Chilena .	132,297.2	150.8	1.1	Punta Arenas
Metropolitan Region (Santiago) . .	15,403.2	6,061.2	393.5	—
Total	756,096.3	15,116.4	19.9	—

PRINCIPAL TOWNS
(2002 census)

Gran Santiago (capital)	4,668,473		Talca	201,797
Puente Alto . . .	492,915		Arica	185,268
Viña del Mar . .	286,931		Puerto Montt . .	175,938
Antofagasta . . .	296,905		Los Angeles . . .	166,556
Valparaíso . . .	275,982		Coquimbo . . .	163,036
Talcahuano . . .	250,348		Chillán	161,953
Temuco . . .	245,347		La Serena . . .	160,148
San Bernardo .	246,762		Osorno	145,475
Concepción . .	216,061		Valdivia . . .	140,559
Iquique . . .	216,419		Calama	138,402
Rancagua . . .	214,344			

BIRTHS, MARRIAGES AND DEATHS

	Registered live births*		Registered marriages		Registered deaths	
	Number	Rate (per 1,000)	Number	Rate (per 1,000)	Number	Rate (per 1,000)
1994 . .	288,175	20.6	91,555	6.5	75,445	5.4
1995 . .	279,928	19.7	87,205	6.1	78,531	5.5
1996 . .	278,729	19.3	83,547	5.8	79,123	5.5
1997 . .	273,641	18.7	78,077	5.3	78,472	5.4
1998 . .	270,637	18.3	73,456	5.0	80,257	5.4
1999 . .	263,867	17.6	69,765	4.6	81,984	5.5
2000 . .	261,993	17.2	66,607	4.4	78,814	5.2
2001 . .	259,069	16.8	64,088	4.2	81,873	5.3

* Adjusted for underenumeration.
Source: partly UN, *Demographic Yearbook*.

Expectation of life (WHO estimates, years at birth): 76.7 (males 73.4; females 80.0) in 2002 (Source: WHO, *World Health Report*).

ECONOMICALLY ACTIVE POPULATION*
('000 persons aged 15 years and over, October–December)

	2002	2003†	2004†
Agriculture, hunting, forestry and fishing	746.6	771.8	783.2
Mining and quarrying	69.8	71.9	73.8
Manufacturing	780.4	797.2	805.1
Electricity, gas and water	29.5	31.2	31.9
Construction	439.9	427.4	473.0
Trade, restaurants and hotels	1,073.1	1,066.8	1,127.5
Transport, storage and communications	444.8	483.3	461.2
Financing, insurance, real estate and business services	430.9	453.5	472.6
Community, social and personal services	1,516.2	1,572.1	1,634.7
Total employed	**5,531.3**	**5,675.1**	**5,862.9**
Unemployed	468.7	453.1	494.7
Total labour force	**5,999.9**	**6,128.2**	**6,357.6**

* Figures are based on sample surveys, covering 36,000 households, and exclude members of the armed forces. Estimates are made independently, therefore totals are not always the sum of the component parts.
† Preliminary figures.

Health and Welfare

KEY INDICATORS

Total fertility rate (children per woman, 2002)	2.4
Under-5 mortality rate (per 1,000 live births, 2003)	9
HIV/AIDS (% of persons aged 15–49, 2003)	0.3
Physicians (per 1,000 head, 1995)	1.08
Hospital beds (per 1,000 head, 1996)	2.67
Health expenditure (2001): US $ per head (PPP)	792
Health expenditure (2001): % of GDP	7.0
Health expenditure (2001): public (% of total)	44.0
Access to water (% of persons, 2002)	95
Access to sanitation (% of persons, 2002)	92
Human Development Index (2002): ranking	43
Human Development Index (2002): value	0.839

For sources and definitions, see explanatory note on p. vi.

Agriculture

PRINCIPAL CROPS
('000 metric tons)

	2001	2002	2003
Wheat	1,780	1,820	1,780*
Rice (paddy)	143	142	141
Barley	65	77	50*
Maize	778	924	1,190
Oats	345	416	420*
Potatoes	1,210	1,303	1,094
Sugar beet	3,232	3,555	2,100
Dry beans	60	45	48
Rapeseed	59	2	13*
Cabbages†	68	68	70
Lettuce†	85	86	87
Tomatoes	1,263*	1,287*	1,300†
Pumpkins, squash and gourds†	105	106	105
Green chillies and peppers†	60	62	63
Dry onions†	285	287	290
Carrots†	98	99	99
Green corn†	240	245	250
Other vegetables†	335	342	338
Watermelons†	80	83	83
Cantaloupes and other melons†	63	64	65
Oranges	101	114	118
Lemons and limes	132	140	150
Apples	1,135	1,050	1,100
Pears	205	202	205
Peaches and nectarines	290	274	275†

— continued	2001	2002	2003
Plums	211	230	240
Grapes	1,785*	1,720	1,750†
Avocados	110	130	135
Kiwi fruit	135†	128	125

* Unofficial figure.
† FAO estimate(s).
Source: FAO.

LIVESTOCK
('000 head, year ending September)

	2001	2002	2003
Horses*	650	660	670
Cattle†	3,980	3,927	3,932
Pigs*	2,750	3,100	3,200
Sheep*	4,090	4,050	4,100
Goats*	750	880	990
Chickens*	82,000	74,700	80,000
Turkeys*	24,900	23,100	18,500

* FAO estimates.
† Unofficial figures.
Source: FAO.

LIVESTOCK PRODUCTS
('000 metric tons)

	2001	2002	2003
Beef and veal	217.6	200.0	190.0
Mutton and lamb	10.9	9.9	10.8
Pig meat	303.0	350.7	385.8
Horse meat	10.8	11.1	11.2*
Poultry meat*	487.8	452.6	457.6
Cows' milk	2,190	2,170	2,170
Goats' milk*	10.4	10.5	10.5
Butter	11.8	11.6	11.6*
Cheese	57.2	59.7	59.7*
Hen eggs	115.6†	113.8†	116.5
Wool: greasy*	16.2	16.0	16.0
Cattle hides*	31.3	28.8	27.0

* FAO estimate(s).
† Unofficial figure.
Source: FAO.

Forestry

ROUNDWOOD REMOVALS
('000 cubic metres, excluding bark)

	2001	2002	2003
Sawlogs, veneer logs and logs for sleepers	13,107	13,962	13,279
Pulpwood	12,386	11,321	11,321
Other industrial wood	189	208	208
Fuel wood	12,108	12,326*	12,712*
Total	**37,790**	**37,817**	**37,520**

* FAO estimate.
Source: FAO.

SAWNWOOD PRODUCTION
('000 cubic metres, including railway sleepers)

	2001	2002	2003
Coniferous (softwood)	5,581	6,193	6,758
Broadleaved (hardwood)	291	246	246
Total	**5,872**	**6,439**	**7,004**

Source: FAO.

Fishing

('000 metric tons, live weight)

	2000	2001	2002
Capture	4,300.2	3,797.1	4,271.5
Patagonian grenadier . . .	91.3	162.1	133.4
Araucanian herring	722.5	324.6	347.4
Anchoveta (Peruvian anchovy) .	1,700.6	852.8	1,526.9
Chilean jack mackerel . . .	1,234.3	1,649.9	1,519.0
Chub mackerel	95.8	365.0	343.4
Aquaculture	391.6	566.1	545.7
Atlantic salmon	166.9	253.9	265.7
Coho (silver) salmon	93.4	136.9	102.5
Total catch	**4,691.7**	**4,363.2**	**4,817.1**

Note: Figures exclude aquatic plants ('000 metric tons): 280.8 (capture 247.4, aquaculture 33.5) in 2000; 299.8 (capture 234.3, aquaculture 65.5) in 2001; 315.7 in 2002 (capture 244.0, aquaculture 71.6).

Source: FAO.

Mining

('000 metric tons, unless otherwise indicated)

	2000	2001	2002
Copper (metal content)	4,602.0	4,739.0	4,580.6
Coal	503.4	568.1	451.6
Iron ore*	8,728.9	5,437.1	7,268.8
Calcium carbonate	5,395.2	5,563.2	5,887.7
Sodium sulphate (metric tons) . .	56,501	67,760	70,776
Zinc—metal content (metric tons) .	31,403	32,762	36,161
Molybdenum—metal content (metric tons)	33,639	33,492	29,467
Manganese (metric tons)† . . .	41,716	31,320	12,195
Gold (kilograms)	54,143	42,673	38,688
Silver (kilograms)	1,242.2	1,348.7	1,210.5
Petroleum ('000 cubic metres) . .	325.8	309.8	336.4

* Gross weight. The estimated iron content is 61%.
† Gross weight. The estimated metal content is 32%.

Sources: Servicio Nacional de Geología y Minería; CODELCO.

Industry

SELECTED PRODUCTS

('000 metric tons, unless otherwise indicated)

	1999	2000	2001
Refined sugar	434	432	476
Beer (million litres)	334	322	337
Wine*	480.7	667.4	565.2
Soft drinks (million litres) . . .	1,154	1,225	2,212
Cigarettes (million)	13,271	13,796	13,305
Non-rubber footwear ('000 pairs) .	6,237	5,735	5,251
Particle board ('000 cu metres) .	301	366	360
Mattresses ('000)	1,082	1,132	1,016
Sulphuric acid	2,436	2,363	2,736
Motor spirit (petrol)	2,129	2,170	n.a.
Kerosene and jet fuel	830	716	n.a.
Distillate fuel oils	3,436	3,716	n.a.
Residual fuel oils	1,425	1,592	n.a.
Cement	2,508	2,686	3,145
Tyres ('000)	2,551	3,084	3,246
Glass sheets ('000 sq metres) . .	21,523	23,180	20,714
Blister copper	2,835	n.a.	n.a.
Refined copper, unwrought . . .	2,666	2,668	2,882
Copper wire	5.8	5.9	5.7
Electric energy (million kWh) . .	38,389	41,268	n.a.

2002: Wine 575.2*.

* Source: FAO.

Source (unless otherwise indicated): UN, *Industrial Commodity Statistics Yearbook*.

Finance

CURRENCY AND EXCHANGE RATES

Monetary Units
100 centavos = 1 Chilean peso.

Sterling, Dollar and Euro Equivalents (31 December 2004)
£1 sterling = 1,081.26 pesos;
US $1 = 559.83 pesos;
€1 = 762.54 pesos;
10,000 Chilean pesos = £9.25 = $17.86 = €13.11.

Average Exchange Rate (pesos per US $)
2002   688.936
2003   691.433
2004   609.369

BUDGET

('000 million pesos)

Revenue	2002	2003*	2004*
Current revenue	9,917.23	10,845.52	11,307.07
Operating revenue . . .	665.12	696.99	699.63
Social security contributions .	678.90	718.96	817.48
Net tax revenues	7,709.00	8,336.28	8,899.21
Net copper revenue . . .	345.59	447.18	496.72
Transfers	85.72	90.25	38.93
Other revenue	432.89	528.46	326.64
Operating revenue of previous years	—	27.39	28.46
Capital revenue	211.30	201.12	177.48
Sale of assets	36.90	30.34	25.93
Repayment of loans . . .	174.40	170.78	151.55
Total revenue	**10,128.52**	**11,046.64**	**11,484.55**

* Projections.

Expenditure*	2000	2001	2002
Government	332.79	365.24	415.01
Defence	708.78	746.25	780.70
Public order and safety	508.12	569.80	627.57
Education	1,580.11	1,774.41	1,958.54
Health	1,099.11	1,232.84	1,326.35
Social security and welfare . .	2,599.64	2,830.24	2,916.89
Housing	355.54	382.01	409.62
Subsidies	246.96	256.32	272.50
Other social services	411.11	441.20	446.29
Economic services	1,035.62	1,107.09	1,204.51
Interest payments	180.34	202.76	135.09
Sub-total	**9,058.09**	**9,908.15**	**10,493.06**
Less Lending included in expenditure	204.76	174.35	178.03
Total expenditure	**8,853.33**	**9,733.81**	**10,315.03**
Current	7,555.88	8,269.76	8,713.39
Capital	1,297.45	1,464.05	1,601.64

* Excluding net lending.

2003 ('000 million pesos, excluding net lending, projections): Current expenditure 9,306.92; Capital expenditure 1,818.50; Total expenditure 11,125.42.

2004 ('000 million pesos, excluding net lending, projections): Current expenditure 9,872.33; Capital expenditure 1,847.97; Total expenditure 11,720.30.

Source: Dirección de Presupuestos, Santiago.

INTERNATIONAL RESERVES

(US $ million at 31 December)

	2001	2002	2003
Gold*	18.6	2.3	2.7
IMF special drawing rights . .	28.9	36.5	45.7
Reserve position in IMF . . .	308.7	490.7	582.9
Foreign exchange	14,041.3	14,813.9	15,211.0
Total	**14,397.5**	**15,343.4**	**15,842.3**

* National valuation.

Source: IMF, *International Financial Statistics*.

MONEY SUPPLY
('000 million pesos at 31 December)

	2001	2002	2003
Currency outside banks . . .	1,214.7	1,301.5	1,379.7
Demand deposits at commercial banks	2,847.6	3,129.3	3,551.0
Total money	4,062.3	4,430.8	4,930.7

Source: IMF, *International Financial Statistics*.

COST OF LIVING
(Consumer Price Index for Santiago; base: 2000 = 100)

	2001	2002	2003
Food (incl. beverages)	100.8	102.9	105.8
Rent, fuel and light	106.1	109.6	115.0
Clothing (incl. footwear) . . .	94.3	90.6	86.2
All items (incl. others)	103.6	106.1	109.1

Source: ILO.

NATIONAL ACCOUNTS
('000 million pesos at current prices)

Expenditure on the Gross Domestic Product

	2001	2002	2003
Government final consumption expenditure	5,480.8	5,942.1	6,288.0
Private final consumption expenditure	27,743.0	29,184.7	31,123.6
Increase in stocks	167.6	359.2	296.5
Gross fixed capital formation . .	9,382.3	9,846.9	10,543.9
Total domestic expenditure .	42,773.7	45,332.9	48,252.0
Exports of goods and services . .	14,501.0	15,749.8	18,141.1
Less Imports of goods and services	13,833.3	14,671.4	16,573.8
GDP in purchasers' values .	43,441.4	46,411.3	49,819.3
Net primary income from abroad .	−1,588.0	−2,012.3	−2,248.1
Gross national income (GNI) .	41,853.4	44,399.0	47,571.2
GDP at constant 1996 prices .	36,854.9	37,670.2	38,900.4

Source: IMF, *International Financial Statistics*.

Gross Domestic Product by Economic Activity

	2000	2001*	2002*
Agriculture and forestry . . .	1,755.8	1,643.1	1,902.3
Fishing	490.1	465.4	516.3
Mining and quarrying	2,844.0	2,933.1	3,270.7
Manufacturing	7,149.4	8,079.5	8,538.7
Electricity, gas and water . . .	1,242.9	1,342.0	1,489.4
Construction	2,869.6	3,074.9	3,305.0
Trade, restaurants and hotels . .	4,226.8	4,534.9	4,478.6
Transport, storage and communications	2,829.7	3,045.0	3,191.9
Financial services†	5,511.3	6,035.4	6,367.9
Sale of real estate	2,313.1	2,447.5	2,547.1
Personal services	5,099.2	5,577.3	6,075.3
Public administration	1,814.2	1,904.4	2,013.1
Sub-total	38,146.1	41,082.5	43,696.3
Value-added tax	3,128.3	3,353.5	3,716.6
Import duties	709.1	668.7	665.0
Less Imputed bank service charge	1,408.2	1,663.4	1,666.6
GDP in purchasers' values .	40,575.3	43,441.4	46,411.3

* Provisional figures.
† Including insurance, renting of property and business loans.

BALANCE OF PAYMENTS
(US $ million)

	2001	2002	2003
Exports of goods f.o.b.	18,272	18,177	21,046
Imports of goods f.o.b.	−16,428	−15,921	−18,031
Trade balance	1,844	2,256	3,015
Exports of services	4,138	4,332	4,805
Imports of services	−4,983	−4,988	−5,571
Balance on goods and services	999	1,600	2,249
Other income received . . .	1,458	1,046	1,114
Other income paid	−3,985	−3,960	−4,394
Balance on goods, services and income	−1,527	−1,315	−1,031
Current transfers received . . .	713	792	748
Current transfers paid	−286	−362	−310
Current balance	−1,100	−885	−594
Direct investment abroad . . .	−1,610	−294	−1,395
Direct investment from abroad .	4,200	1,888	2,982
Portfolio investment assets .	−1,386	−3,083	−5,327
Portfolio investment liabilities .	1,525	999	1,701
Financial derivatives liabilities	−86	−124	118
Other investment assets . . .	−1,326	1,624	−387
Other investment liabilities . .	44	1,087	1,678
Net errors and omissions . . .	−861	−1,027	866
Overall balance	−599	185	−357

Source: IMF, *International Financial Statistics*.

External Trade

PRINCIPAL COMMODITIES
(distribution by SITC, US $ million)

Imports c.i.f.	1999	2000	2001
Food and live animals . . .	999.8	1,080.7	1,053.8
Mineral fuels, lubricants, etc. .	1,869.3	3,022.8	2,738.9
Petroleum, petroleum products, etc.	1,387.4	2,428.8	2,111.9
Crude petroleum oils, etc. . .	1,099.9	1,982.6	1,726.6
Gas, natural and manufactured	299.5	418.3	486.1
Chemicals and related products	1,865.4	2,044.4	2,141.3
Basic manufactures	1,969.5	2,342.9	2,423.3
Iron and steel	284.2	384.0	406.1
Machinery and transport equipment	5,081.4	5,791.0	5,598.9
Machinery specialized for particular industries	550.4	681.4	733.9
General industrial machinery equipment and parts . . .	909.0	981.6	1,032.5
Office machines and automatic data-processing equipment . .	614.2	654.4	573.3
Automatic data-processing equipment	435.3	469.2	414.7
Telecommunications and sound equipment	891.3	960.4	817.6
Other electrical machinery apparatus, etc.	621.4	656.1	702.7
Road vehicles and parts* . .	982.6	1,529.1	1,343.0
Passenger motor cars (excl. buses)	415.2	629.4	535.0
Lorries and trucks	270.3	548.1	467.2
Miscellaneous manufactured articles	1,598.5	1,808.2	1,761.1
Total (incl. others)	13,891.5	16,619.7	16,136.2

* Data on parts exclude tyres, engines and electrical parts.

Exports f.o.b.	1999	2000	2001
Food and live animals . . .	3,684.0	3,788.2	4,197.0
Fish, crustaceans and molluscs and preparations thereof . . .	1,404.3	1,546.2	1,629.9
Fish, fresh (live or dead), chilled or frozen	1,060.4	1,190.1	1,259.3
Frozen fish	509.8	537.2	547.3
Vegetables and fruit	1,533.4	1,536.7	1,613.2
Fruit and nuts (excl. oil nuts) fresh or dried	1,109.8	1,191.7	1,221.0
Feeding-stuff for animals (excl. unmilled cereals)	303.6	255.0	328.3
Beverages and tobacco . . .	569.3	607.2	679.0
Beverages	556.3	593.8	661.5
Wine of fresh grapes . . .	523.7	576.8	645.0
Crude materials (inedible) except fuels	3,877.3	4,929.3	4,774.0
Cork and wood	649.4	643.4	780.3
Pulp and waste paper . . .	768.3	1,113.8	1,068.2
Chemical wood pulp . . .	766.7	1,110.4	1,066.2
Chemical wood pulp, bleached or semi-bleached	641.3	955.6	898.5
Metalliferous ores and metal scrap	2,164.9	2,877.7	2,622.9
Copper ores and concentrates (excl. matte)	1,735.1	2,393.7	2,162.8
Chemicals and related products	750.6	1,015.3	1,158.6
Basic manufactures	5,290.7	6,162.8	6,088.6
Non-ferrous metals	4,383.2	5,164.6	4,921.3
Copper	4,249.8	5,063.8	4,816.2
Copper and copper alloys refined or not, unwrought .	4,154.5	4,954.5	4,689.4
Refined copper (incl. copper alloys other than master alloys), unwrought . .	3,909.6	4,661.5	4,396.4
Machinery and transport equipment	495.0	494.6	522.6
Total (incl. others)	15,619.2	18,214.5	18,745.4

Source: UN, *International Trade Statistics Yearbook*.

2002 (US $ million): *Imports c.i.f.* (provisional): Consumer goods 2,836.2 (Durables 1,001.7; Semi-durables 1,044.3); Intermediate goods 9,634.2 (Mineral fuels and lubricants 2,462.7, *of which* Petroleum 1,615.1); Capital goods 3,470.2; Franc zone 986.6; Total 16,927.2 *Exports f.o.b.:* Food and live animals 4,545.3 (Fish, crustaceans and molluscs and preparations thereof 1,657.2; Vegetables and fruit 1,955.7); Beverages and tobacco 627.0; Crude materials (inedible) except fuels 4,063.4 (Cork and wood 749.2; Pulp and waste paper 813.3; Metalliferous ores and metal scrap 2,235.3); Chemicals and related products 1,123.8; Basic manufactures 5,758.6 (Non-ferrous metals 4,726.2); Total (incl. others) 17,051.4.

2003 (US $ million): *Imports c.i.f.* (provisional): Consumer goods 3,166.6 (Durables 1,186.1; Semi-durables 1,080.5); Intermediate goods 10,956.2 (Mineral fuels and lubricants 3,100.2, *of which* Petroleum 2,125.6); Capital goods 3,667.9; Franc zone 1,291.6; Total 19,082.4 *Exports f.o.b.:* Food and live animals 5,094.3 (Fish, crustaceans and molluscs and preparations thereof 1,799.2; Vegetables and fruit 2,201.9); Beverages and tobacco 701.6; Crude materials (inedible) except fuels 5,120.4 (Cork and wood 813.6; Pulp and waste paper 890.6; Metalliferous ores and metal scrap 3,094.8); Chemicals and related products 1,327.8; Basic manufactures 6,453.4 (Non-ferrous metals 5,275.2); Total (incl. others) 19,807.3.

PRINCIPAL TRADING PARTNERS
(US $ million)

Imports c.i.f.	1999	2000	2001
Argentina	2,014.7	2,866.4	3,074.1
Brazil	965.7	1,329.8	1,490.8
Canada	406.1	508.4	423.3
China, People's Republic . . .	658.4	949.5	1,013.1
Colombia	165.9	204.9	188.8
Ecuador	227.4	254.2	123.3
France	411.2	442.4	572.9
Germany	615.1	599.8	684.1
Italy	513.1	417.6	435.0
Japan	631.6	701.8	548.5
Korea, Republic	404.7	534.6	538.5
Mexico	578.4	615.1	532.1
Nigeria	131.4	313.0	122.6
Peru	168.4	255.4	285.3
Spain	408.7	426.3	464.1
Sweden	270.1	281.6	180.2
Switzerland	153.8	123.1	109.1
United Kingdom	181.2	176.3	193.4
USA	2,986.1	3,273.2	2,976.1
Venezuela	210.1	236.7	184.8
Total (incl. others)	13,891.5	16,619.7	16,136.2

Exports f.o.b.	1999	2000	2001
Argentina	726.3	639.0	618.7
Belgium	287.6	374.6	244.0
Bolivia	190.3	164.0	165.2
Brazil	701.3	969.4	909.6
Canada	175.5	244.1	285.4
China, People's Republic . . .	357.3	901.8	1,065.0
Colombia	205.8	236.3	286.5
Ecuador	109.6	158.7	260.9
France	492.1	631.7	621.1
Germany	532.7	458.7	547.0
Italy	638.9	822.5	830.2
Japan	2,279.7	2,546.6	2,311.9
Korea, Republic	693.5	809.1	596.0
Mexico	621.0	815.6	917.0
Netherlands	506.6	446.5	551.6
Peru	356.6	439.3	586.7
Spain	312.5	377.0	354.1
United Kingdom	1,063.1	1,064.6	1,243.2
USA	2,811.1	3,007.8	3,483.6
Venezuela	195.2	228.4	306.8
Total (incl. others)	15,619.2	18,214.5	18,745.4

Transport

PRINCIPAL RAILWAYS

	2000	2001	2003*
Passenger journeys ('000) . .	13,197	16,095	14,364
Passenger-kilometres ('000) . .	736,696	870,836	861,064
Freight ('000 metric tons) . . .	21,982	22,514	22,750
Freight ton-kilometres (million) .	3,135	3,318	3,581

* Provisional figures; data for 2002 not available.

ROAD TRAFFIC
(motor vehicles in use)

	2000	2001	2002
Passenger cars (excl. taxis) .	1,209,968	1,247,985	1,270,516
Buses and coaches (incl. taxis) .	166,429	160,586	161,125
Lorries and vans	645,461	656,209	675,518
Specialized vehicles (incl. tractors)	14,377	16,204	16,426
Motorcycles and mopeds . . .	27,284	26,318	24,761

SHIPPING

Merchant Fleet
(registered at 31 December)

	2001	2002	2003
Number of vessels	480	525	532
Total displacement ('000 grt) . .	880.3	879.6	964.0

Source: Lloyd's Register-Fairplay, *World Fleet Statistics*.

International Sea-borne Shipping
(freight traffic, '000 metric tons)

	1999	2000	2001
Goods loaded	31,287	34,074	37,113
Goods unloaded	19,456	19,888	15,257

CIVIL AVIATION
(traffic on scheduled services)

	1999	2000	2001
Kilometres flown (million) . . .	107	108	110
Passengers ('000)	5,188	5,175	5,316
Passenger-km (million) . . .	10,650	10,859	11,520
Freight (million ton-km) . . .	2,107	2,296	2,329

Source: UN, *Statistical Yearbook*.

Tourism

ARRIVALS BY NATIONALITY

	2002	2003	2004
Argentina	514,711	536,010	473,003
Bolivia	107,703	132,312	108,911
Brazil	79,198	100,341	99,324
France	38,241	42,644	37,253
Germany	41,598	54,402	42,095
Peru	154,842	163,718	153,215
Spain	34,655	42,841	36,668
United Kingdom	37,269	50,984	39,752
USA	130,568	147,321	129,252
Total (incl. others)	1,412,315	1,613,523	1,421,076

Tourism receipts (US $ million): 819 in 2000; 799 in 2001; 845 in 2002.

Sources: World Tourism Organization; Servicio Nacional de Turismo.

Communications Media

	2000	2001	2002
Television receivers ('000 in use)	4,300	4,400	n.a.
Telephones ('000 main lines in use)	3,365.0	3,703.3	3,467.2
Mobile cellular telephones ('000 subscribers)	3,401.5	5,271.6	6,445.7
Personal computers ('000 in use) .	1,260	1,300	1,796
Internet users ('000)	2,537	3,102	3,575

2003: Telephones ('000 main lines in use) 3,401; Mobile cellular telephones ('000 subscribers) 7,581; Internet users ('000) 4,000.

Radio receivers ('000 in use): 5,180 in 1997.

Facsimile machines: 40,000 in use in 1997.

Daily newspapers: 52 in 1996.

Sources: mainly UNESCO, *Statistical Yearbook*; UN, *Statistical Yearbook*; International Telecommunication Union.

Education

(2002)

	Institutions	Teachers	Students
Pre-primary		10,014	298,419
Special primary		4,878	64,806
Primary	n.a.*	71,062	2,276,713
Secondary		32,464	896,470
Adult		1,911	195,482
Higher (incl. universities) . .	226	n.a.	521,609

* Many schools offer more than one level of education. A detailed breakdown is given below.

Schools (2002): Pre-primary: 641; Special 509; Primary 3,768; Secondary 479; Adult 257; Pre-primary and special 4; Pre-primary and primary 3,261; Pre-primary and secondary 2; Special and primary 13; Special and secondary 1; Special and adult 4; Primary and secondary 283; Primary and adult 94; Secondary and adult 156; Pre-primary, special and primary 61; Pre-primary, special and adult 1; Pre-primary, primary and secondary 940; Pre-primary, primary and adult 241; Special, primary and secondary 1; Primary, secondary and adult 46; Pre-primary, special, primary and secondary 7; Pre-primary, special, primary and adult 11; Pre-primary, primary, secondary and adult 97; Pre-primary, special, primary, secondary and adult 2; Total 10,879.

Adult literacy rate (UNESCO estimates): 95.7% (males 95.8%; females 95.6%) in 2001 (Source: UN Development Programme, *Human Development Report*).

Directory

The Constitution

The 1981 Constitution, described as a 'transition to democracy', separated the presidency from the Junta and provided for presidential elections and for the re-establishment of the bicameral legislature, consisting of an upper chamber (Senado) of both elected and appointed senators, who are to serve an eight-year term, and a lower chamber (Cámara de Diputados) of 120 deputies elected for a four-year term. All former Presidents are to be senators for life. There is a National Security Council consisting of the President of the Republic, the heads of the armed forces and the police, and the Presidents of the Supreme Court and the Senado.

In July 1989 a national referendum approved 54 reforms to the Constitution, including 47 proposed by the Government and seven by the Military Junta. Among provisions made within the articles were an increase in the number of directly elected senators from 26 to 38, the abolition of the need for the approval of two successive Congresos for constitutional amendments (the support of two-thirds of the Cámara de Diputados and the Senado being sufficient), the reduction in term of office for the President to be elected in 1989 from eight to four years, with no immediate re-election possible, and the redrafting of the provision that outlawed Marxist groups so as to ensure 'true and responsible political pluralism'. The President's right to dismiss the Congreso and sentence to internal exile were eliminated.

In November 1991 the Congreso approved constitutional changes to local government. The amendments provided for the replacement of centrally appointed local officials with directly elected representatives.

In February 1994 an amendment to the Constitution was approved whereby the length of the presidential term was reduced from eight to six years.

The Government

HEAD OF STATE

President: Ricardo Lagos Escobar (took office 10 March 2000).

THE CABINET
(April 2005)

A coalition of parties represented in the Concertación de los Partidos de la Democracia (CPD) (including the Partido Demócrata Cristiano—PDC, the Partido Socialista de Chile—PS, the Partido por la Democracia—PPD, and the Partido Radical Socialdemócrata—PRSD) and five Independents (Ind.).

Minister of the Interior: José Miguel Angel Insulza Salinas (PS).

Minister of Foreign Affairs: IGNACIO WALKER PRIETO (PDC).

Minister of National Defence: JAIME RAVINET DE LA FUENTE (PDC).

Minister of Finance: NICOLÁS EYZAGUIRRE GUZMÁN (PPD).

Minister, Secretary-General of the Presidency: EDUARDO DOCKENDORFF VALLEJOS (PDC).

Minister, Secretary-General of the Government: FRANCISCO VIDAL SALINAS (PPD).

Minister of the Economy and Energy: JORGE RODRÍGUEZ GROSSI (PDC).

Minister of Mining: ALFONSO DULANTO RENCORET (Ind.).

Minister of Planning and Co-operation: YASNA PROVOSTE (Ind.).

Minister of Education: SERGIO BITAR CHACRA (PPD).

Minister of Justice: LUIS BATES HIDALGO (Ind.).

Minister of Labour and Social Security: RICARDO SOLARI SAAVEDRA (PS).

Minister of Public Works, Transport and Telecommunications: JAVIER ETCHEVERRY CELHAY (PPD).

Minister of Health: PEDRO GARCÍA ASPILLAGA (Ind.).

Minister of Housing and Urban Planning: SONIA TSCHORNE (PS).

Minister of Agriculture: JAIME CAMPOS QUIROGA (PRSD).

Minister of the National Women's Service (Sernam): CECILIA PÉREZ DÍAZ (Ind.).

MINISTRIES

Ministry of Agriculture: Teatinos 40, Santiago; tel. (2) 393-5000; fax (2) 393-5050; e-mail contacto@minagri.gob.cl; internet www.minagri.gob.cl.

Ministry of the Economy and Energy: Teatinos 120, 10°, Santiago; tel. (2) 672-5522; fax (2) 696-6305; e-mail economia@minecon.cl; internet www.economia.cl.

Ministry of Education: Alameda 1371, 7°, Santiago; tel. (2) 390-4000; fax (2) 380-0317; internet www.mineduc.cl.

Ministry of Finance: Teatinos 120, 12°, Santiago; tel. (2) 675-5800; fax (2) 671-8064; e-mail webmaster@minhda.cl; internet www.minhda.cl.

Ministry of Foreign Affairs: Catedral 1158, Santiago; tel. (2) 679-4200; fax (2) 699-4202; e-mail info@minrel.cl; internet www.minrel.cl.

Ministry of Health: Enrique MacIver 541, 3°, Santiago; tel. (2) 639-4001; fax (2) 633-5875; e-mail consulta@minsal.cl; internet www.minsal.cl.

Ministry of Housing and Urban Development: Alameda 924, Santiago; tel. (2) 638-0801; fax (2) 633-3892; e-mail contactenos@minvu.cl; internet www.minvu.cl.

Ministry of the Interior: Palacio de la Moneda, Santiago; tel. (2) 690-4000; fax (2) 699-2165; internet www.interior.cl.

Ministry of Justice: Morandé 107, Santiago; tel. (2) 674-3100; fax (2) 698-7098; internet www.minjusticia.cl.

Ministry of Labour and Social Security: Huérfanos 1273, 6°, Santiago; tel. (2) 695-5133; fax (2) 698-8473; e-mail mintrab@mintrab.gob.cl; internet www.mintrab.cl.

Ministry of Mining: Teatinos 120, Santiago; tel. (2) 671-4373; fax (2) 698-9262; internet www.minmineria.cl.

Ministry of National Defence: Villavicencio 364, 22°, Edif. Diego Portales, Santiago; tel. (2) 222-1202; fax (2) 633-0568; internet www.emdn.cl.

Ministry of the National Women's Service (Sernam): Teatinos 950, 5°, Santiago; tel. (2) 549-6100; fax (2) 549-6148; e-mail mlobos@sernam.gov.cl; internet www.sernam.gov.cl.

Ministry of Planning and Co-operation (MIDEPLAN): Ahumada 48, 7°, Santiago; tel. (2) 675-1400; fax (2) 672-1879; internet www.mideplan.cl.

Ministry of Public Works: Morandé 59, Of. 545, Santiago; tel. (2) 361-2641; fax (2) 361-2700; internet www.mop.cl.

Ministry of Transport: Amunátegui 139, 3°, Santiago; tel. (2) 421-3000; fax (2) 421-3552; e-mail mtt@mtt.cl; internet www.mtt.cl.

Office of the Minister, Secretary-General of the Government: Palacio de la Moneda, Santiago; tel. (2) 690-4160; fax (2) 697-1756; e-mail cmladini@segegob.cl; internet www.segegob.cl.

Office of the Minister, Secretary-General of the Presidency: Palacio de la Moneda, Santiago; tel. (2) 690-4218; fax (2) 690-4329.

President and Legislature

PRESIDENT

Election, 12 December 1999 and 16 January 2000

	% of votes cast, 12 Dec. 1999	% of votes cast, 16 Jan. 2000
Ricardo Lagos Escobar (CPD) . .	48.0	51.3
Joaquín Lavín Infante (Alianza por Chile)	47.5	48.7
Gladys Marín Millie (PCCh) . .	3.2	—
Tomás Hirsch Goldschmidt (PH) .	0.5	—
Sara Larraín Ruiz-Tagle . . .	0.4	—
Arturo Frei Bolívar (UCCP) . . .	0.4	—
Total	**100.0**	**100.0**

CONGRESO NACIONAL

Senado*
(Senate)

President: ANDRÉS ZALDÍVAR LARRAÍN (PDC).

General Election, 16 December 2001*

	% of valid votes	Seats
Concertación de Partidos por la Democracia (CPD)†	51.3	20
Alianza por Chile‡	44.0	16
Partido Comunista de Chile (PCCh) . . .	2.6	—
Independents	1.6	2
Partido Humanista (PH)	0.4	—
Partido Liberal (PL)	0.1	—
Total	**100.0**	**38**

1,716,942 valid votes were cast. In addition, there were 71,522 blank and 68,802 spoiled votes.

* Results of elections to renew 18 of the 38 elective seats in the Senado. In addition, there are nine designated senators, and a constitutional provision for former Presidents to assume a seat for life, in an ex-officio capacity. In July 2002 former President Pinochet resigned his senatorial seat, bringing the total number of senators to 48.

† Including the Partido Demócrata Cristiano (PDC), which won 12 seats, the Partido Socialista de Chile (PS), with five seats, and the Partido por la Democracia (PPD), with three seats.

‡ Including the Partido Unión Demócrata Independiente (UDI), which won nine seats, and the Partido Renovación Nacional (RN), which won seven seats.

Cámara de Diputados
(Chamber of Deputies)

President: ISABEL ALLENDE (PPD).

General Election, 16 December 2001

	Valid votes	% of valid votes	Seats
Concertación de Partidos por la Democracia (CPD)* . . .	2,925,800	47.9	62
Alianza por Chile†	2,703,701	44.3	57
Partido Comunista de Chile (PCCh)	318,638	5.2	—
Independents	86,283	1.4	1
Partido Humanista (PH) . .	69,265	1.1	—
Partido Liberal (PL)	3,453	0.1	—
Total	**6,107,140**	**100.0**	**120**

In addition, there were 236,132 blank and 648,232 spoiled votes.

* Including the Partido Demócrata Cristiano (PDC), which won 24 seats, the Partido por la Democracia (PPD), which won 21 seats, the Partido Socialista de Chile (PS), with 11 seats, and the Partido Radical Socialdemócrata (PRSD), with six seats.

† Including the Partido Unión Demócrata Independiente (UDI), which won 35 seats, and the Partido Renovación Nacional (RN), which won 22 seats.

Political Organizations

Alianza por Chile: Santiago; f. 1996 as the Unión por Chile; name changed to above in 1999; right-wing alliance; Leader JOAQUÍN LAVÍN INFANTE.

Partido Renovación Nacional (RN): Antonio Varas 454, Providencia, Santiago; tel. (2) 373-8740; fax (2) 373-8704; e-mail cmonckeberg@rn.cl; internet www.rn.cl; f. 1987; right-wing; Pres. SERGIO DIEZ URZÚA; Sec.-Gen. CRISTIAN MONCKEBERG BRUNETT.

Partido Unión Demócrata Independiente (UDI): Suecia 286, Providencia, Santiago; tel. (2) 241-4200; fax (2) 233-6189; e-mail udi@caudi.cl; internet www.udi.cl; f. 1989; right-wing; Pres. PABLO LONGUEIRA MONTES; Sec.-Gen. PATRICIO MELERO ABAROA.

Concertación de Partidos por la Democracia (CPD): Londres 57, Santiago; tel. and fax (2) 639-7170; fax (2) 639-7449; e-mail concert@ctcreuna.cl; f. 1988 as the Comando por el No, an opposition front to campaign against the military regime in the plebiscite of 5 October 1988; name changed to above following plebiscite; Leader RICARDO LAGOS ESCOBAR.

Partido Demócrata Cristiano (PDC): Alameda B. O'Higgins 1460, 2°, Santiago; tel. (2) 757-4400; fax (2) 757-4400; e-mail info@pdc.cl; internet www.pdc.cl; f. 1957; member of CPD; Pres. ADOLFO ZALDÍVAR; Sec.-Gen. JAIME MULET MARTÍNEZ.

Partido Liberal (PL): Eduardo de la Barra 1384, Of. 404, Providencia, Santiago; tel. (2) 335-5233 ; fax (2) 233-2750; e-mail info@partidoliberal.cl; internet www.partidoliberal.cl; liberal party; f. 1998 by dissident centrist politicians; Pres. JOSÉ DUCCI CLARO; Sec.-Gen. CELSO HORMAZÁBAL SUAZO.

Partido por la Democracia (PPD): Erasmo Escala 2154, Santiago; tel. (2) 735-2824; fax (2) 735-1692; internet www.ppd.cl; f. 1989; Pres. VÍCTOR BARRUETO; Sec.-Gen. ESTEBAN VALENZUELA VAN TREEK.

Partido Radical Socialdemócrata (PRSD): Miraflores 495, Santiago; tel. (2) 632-2161; fax (2) 632-2161; centre-left; allied to CPD; Sec.-Gen. ISIDRO SOLIS PALMA.

Partido Socialista de Chile (PS): Paris 873, Santiago; tel. (2) 630-6900; fax (2) 672-0507; e-mail pschile@pschile.cl; internet www.pschile.cl; f. 1933; left-wing; mem. of Socialist International; Pres. RICARDO NÚÑEZ; Sec.-Gen. ARTURO BARRIOS OTEÍZA.

Partido Comunista de Chile (PCCh): Avda Vicuña Mackenna 31, Santiago; tel. and fax (2) 695-4791; fax (2) 695-1150; e-mail www@pcchile.cl; internet www.pcchile.cl; f. 1912; achieved legal status in October 1990; Sec-Gen. GUILLERMO TELLIER.

Partido Humanista (PH): Quebec 564, Providencia, Santiago; tel. (2) 269-6116; internet www.partidohumanista.cl; e-mail secretario@partidohumanista.cl; Pres. EFREN OSORIO; Sec.-Gen. MARILEN CABRERA.

Partido Izquierda Cristiana (PIC): Compañia 2404, Santiago; tel. (2) 671-7681; fax (2) 671-7837; e-mail hmario@ctcinternet.cl; Pres. CARLOS DONOSO PACHECO; Sec.-Gen. PATRICIO VÉJAR MERCADO.

Diplomatic Representation

EMBASSIES IN CHILE

Argentina: Miraflores 285, Santiago; tel. ((2) 582-2500; fax (2) 639-3321; e-mail embajador@embargentina.cl; internet www.embargentina.cl; Ambassador CARLOS ENRIQUE ABIHAGGLE.

Australia: Isidora Goyenechea 3621, 12° y 13°, Casilla 33, Correo 10 Las Condes, Santiago; tel. (2) 550-3500; fax (2) 331-5960; e-mail consular.santiago@dfat.gov.au; internet www.chile.embassy.gov.au; Ambassador ELIZABETH SCHICK.

Austria: Isidora Goyenechea 2934, Of. 601, Las Condes, Santiago; tel. (2) 233-0557; fax (2) 233-6971; e-mail santiagodechile@bmaa.gv.at; Ambassador WALTER HOWADT.

Belgium: Edif. Forum, Providencia 2653, 11°, Of. 1103, Santiago; tel. (2) 232-1071; fax (2) 232-1073; e-mail santiago@diplobel.org; Ambassador JOHAN BALLEGEER.

Brazil: Alonso Ovalle 1665, Casilla 1497, Santiago; tel. (2)698-2486; fax (2) 671-5961; internet www.brasembsantiago.cl; e-mail embrasil@brasembsantiago.cl; Ambassador GELSON FONSECA JÚNIOR.

Bulgaria: Rodolfo Bentjerodt 4895, Vitacura, Santiago; tel. (2) 228-3110; fax (2) 208-0404; e-mail embajada.debul0001@chilnet.cl.

Canada: Nueva Tajamar 481, 12°, Santiago; tel. (2) 362-9663; fax (2) 362-9665; e-mail stago@dfait-maeci.gc.ca; internet www.dfait-maeci.gc.ca/santiago; Ambassador BERNARD GIROUX.

China, People's Republic: Pedro de Valdivia 550, Santiago; tel. (2) 233-9880; fax (2) 234-1129; e-mail em.na@ctcinternet.cl; Ambassador LI CHANGHUA.

Colombia: Presidente Errázuriz 3943, Las Condes, Santiago; tel. (2) 206-1314; fax (2) 208-0712; e-mail esantiag@minrelext.gov.co; Ambassador ALBERTO VELÁSQUEZ MARTÍNEZ.

Costa Rica: Calle Zurich 255, Dpto 85, Las Condes, Santiago; tel. (2) 334-9486; fax (2) 334-9490; e-mail embacostarica@adsl.tie.cr; Ambassador GUSTAVO CAMPOS FALLAS.

Croatia: Ezequias Alliende 2370, Providencia, Santiago; tel. (2) 269-6141; fax (2) 269-6092; e-mail embajada@croacia.cl; Ambassador BORIS MARUNA.

Cuba: Avda Los Leones 1346, Providencia, Santiago; tel. (2) 494-1485; fax (2) 494-1495; e-mail emcuchil@embacuba.cl; Ambassador ALFONSO FRAGA PÉREZ.

Czech Republic: Avda El Golf 254, Santiago; tel. (2) 232–1066; fax (2) 232-0707; e-mail santiago@embassy.mzv.cz; internet www.mfa.cz/santiago; Ambassador LUBOMÍR HLADÍK.

Denmark: Jacques Cazotte 5531, Casilla 13430, Vitacura, Santiago; tel. (2) 941-5100; fax (2) 218-1736; e-mail sclamb@um.dk; internet www.denmark.cl; Ambassador ANITA HUGAU.

Dominican Republic: Augusto Leguia Sur 79, Of. 1802, Las Condes, Santiago; tel. (2) 245-0667; fax (2) 245-1648; e-mail embajada@rd.tie.cl; Ambassador AMABLE PADILLA GUERRERO.

Ecuador: Avda Providencia 1979 y Pedro Valdivia, 5°, Santiago; tel. (2) 231-5073; fax (2) 232-5833; e-mail embajadaecuador@adsl.tie.cl; Ambassador GONZALO SALVADOR HOLGUÍN.

Egypt: Roberto del Río 1871, Providencia, Santiago; tel. (2) 274-8881; fax (2) 274-6334; e-mail egipto@ctcinternet.cl; Ambassador ABD-EL MOHSEN OMAR MAKHION.

El Salvador: Coronel 2330, 5°, Of. 51, Santiago; tel. (2) 233-8324; fax (2) 231-0960; e-mail embajada.deels001@chilnet.cl; Ambassador MARIO JOSÉ IGNACIO AVILA ROMERO.

Finland: Alcántara 200, Of. 201, Las Condes, Santiago; tel. (2) 263-4917; fax (2) 263-4701; e-mail sanomat.snt@formin.fi; Ambassador PEKKA J. KORVENHEIMO.

France: Condell 65, Casilla 38D , Providencia, Santiago; tel. (2) 470-8000; fax (2) 470-8050; e-mail ambafran@ia.cl; internet www.france.cl; Ambassador ALAIN LE GOURRIÉREC.

Germany: Las Hualtatas 5677, Vitacura, Santiago; tel. (2) 463-2500; fax (2) 463-2525; e-mail central@embajadadealemania.cl; internet www.caracas.diplo.de; Ambassador JOACHIM SCHMILLEN.

Greece: Jorge Sexto 306, Las Condes, Santiago; tel. (2) 212-7900; fax (2) 212-8048; e-mail embassygr@tie.cl; internet www.grecia.cl; Ambassador HARIS DIMITRIOU.

Guatemala: Las Urbinas, Of. 1-A, Providencia, Santiago; tel. (2) 334-8273; fax (2) 334-8276; e-mail echilegu@intelnet.net.gt; Ambassador ANTONIO R. CASTELLANOS.

Haiti: Zurich 255, Of. 21, Las Condes, Santiago; tel. (2) 650-8180; fax (2) 334-0384; e-mail embhai@terra.cl; Ambassador RONALD PIERRE.

Holy See: Calle Nuncio Sótero Sanz 200, Casilla 16.836, Correo 9, Santiago (Apostolic Nunciature); tel. (2) 231-2020; fax (2) 231-0868; e-mail nunciatu@entelchile.net; Nuncio Most Rev. ALDO CAVALLI (Titular Archbishop of Vibo Valentia).

Honduras: Zurich 255, Dpto 51, Las Condes, Santiago; tel. (2) 234-4069; fax (2) 334-7946; e-mail honduras@entelchile.net; Ambassador EDUARDO KAWAS GATTAS.

Hungary: Avda Los Leones 2279, Providencia, Santiago; tel. (2) 204-2210; fax (2) 234-1227; e-mail huembstg@entelchile-net; internet www.chilenet.net/huembstg; Ambassador GYULA BARCSI.

India: Triana 871, Casilla 10433, Santiago; tel. (2) 235-2005; fax (2) 235-9607; e-mail embindia@entelchile.net; Ambassador SUSMITA GONGULEE THOMAS.

Indonesia: Nueva Costanera 3318, Vitacura, Santiago; tel. (2) 207-6266; fax (2) 207-9901; e-mail kbristgo@mi-mail.cl; Ambassador SUWARNO ATMOPRAWIRO.

Israel: San Sebastián 2812, 5°, Casilla 1224, Santiago; tel. (2) 750-0500; fax (2) 750-0555; e-mail eisraelp@rdc.cl; Ambassador ORI NOY.

Italy: Clemente Fabres 1050, Providencia, Santiago; tel. (2) 470-8400; fax (2) 223-2467; e-mail info@embitalia.cl; internet www.embitalia.cl; Ambassador GIOVANNI FERRERO.

Japan: Avda Ricardo Lyon 520, Santiago; tel. (2) 232-1807; fax (2) 232-1812; internet www.cl.emb-japan.go.jp; e-mail embajada.dejap001@chilnet.cl; Ambassador HAJIME OGAWA.

Jordan: San Pascual 446, Las Condes, Casilla 00562, Santiago; tel. (2) 325-7748; fax (2) 325-7754; e-mail jordanemb@vtr.net; Ambassador ATEF HALASA.

Korea, Democratic People's Republic: Ambassador YU CHANG UN (resident in Peru).

Korea, Republic: Alcántara 74, Casilla 1301, Santiago; tel. (2) 228-4214; fax (2) 206-2355; e-mail corembad@tie.cl; Ambassador SHIN JANG-BUM.

Lebanon: Alianza 1728, Casilla 1950, Santiago; tel. (2) 219-9724; fax (2) 219-3502; e-mail libano@netline.cl; Ambassador MOURAD JAMMAL.

Malaysia: Tajamar 183, 10° y 11°, Of. 1002, Correo 35, Las Condes, Santiago; tel. (2) 233-6698; fax (2) 234-3853; e-mail mwstg@embdemalasia.cl; Ambassador A. GANAPATHY.

Mexico: Félix de Amesti 128, Las Condes, Santiago; tel. (2) 206-6133; fax (2) 206-6147; e-mail embamex@mi.cl; Ambassador RICARDO VILLANUEVA HALLAL.

Morocco: Avda Luis Pasteur 5850, Of. 203, Vitacura, Santiago; tel. (2) 218-0311; fax (2) 219-4280; e-mail ambmarch@terra.cl; internet www.marruecos.cl; Ambassador ABDELHADI BOUCETTA.

Netherlands: Las Violetas 2368, Casilla 56-D, Santiago; tel. (2) 756-9200; fax (2) 756-9226; e-mail stg@minbuza.nl; internet www.holanda-paisesbajos.cl; Ambassador HINKINUS NIJENHUIS.

New Zealand: El Golf 99, Of. 703, Las Condes, Santiago; tel. (2) 290-9800; fax (2) 458-0940; e-mail nzembassychile@adsl.tie.cl; Ambassador RICHARD MANN.

Nicaragua: Zurich 255, Of. 111, Las Condes, Santiago; tel. (2) 234-1808; fax (2) 234-5071; e-mail embanic@embajadadenicaragua.tie.cl; Ambassador EDGARD ESCOBAR FORNOS.

Norway: San Sebastián 2839, Of. 509, Casilla 2431, Santiago; tel. (2) 234-2888; fax (2) 234-2201; e-mail emb.santiago@mfa.no; Ambassador PÅL MOE.

Panama: La Reconquista 640, Las Condes, Santiago; tel. (2) 202-6318; fax (2) 202-5439; e-mail embajada@panamachile.tie.cl; Ambassador ALEJANDRO YOUNG DOWNEY.

Paraguay: Huérfanos 886, 5°, Ofs 514–515, Santiago; tel. (2) 639-4640; fax (2) 633-4426; e-mail epychemb@entelchile.net; Ambassador JUAN ANDRÉS CARDOZO DOMÍNGUEZ.

Peru: Avda Andrés Bello 1751, Casilla 16277, Providencia, Santiago; tel. (2) 235-2356; fax (2) 235-8139; e-mail embstgo@entelchile.net; Ambassador JORGE COLUNGE VILLACORTA.

Philippines: Félix de Amesti 367, Santiago; tel. (2) 208-1313; fax (2) 208-1400; e-mail embajada.defil001@chilnet.cl; Ambassador HERMENEGILDO C. CRUZ.

Poland: Mar del Plata 2055, Santiago; tel. (2) 204-1213; fax (2) 204-9332; internet www.polonia.cl; e-mail embchile@entelchile.net; Ambassador JAROSŁAW SPYRA.

Portugal: Nueva Tajamar 555, Torre Norte 16°, Las Condes, Santiago; tel. (2) 203-0542; fax (2) 203-0545; e-mail embaixada.portugal@entelchile.net; Ambassador ANTÓNIO MACHADO DE FARIA E MAYA.

Romania: Benjamín 2955, Las Condes, Santiago; tel. (2) 231-1893; fax (2) 232-3441; e-mail embajada@rumania.tie.cl; internet www.embajadaderumania.cl; Ambassador ION VÎLCU.

Russia: Cristobal Colón 4152, Las Condes, Santiago; tel. (2) 208-6254; fax (2) 206-8892; e-mail embajada@rusia.tie.cl; internet www.rucl.virtualave.net; Ambassador VLADIMIR V. CHKHIKVADZE.

South Africa: Avda 11 de Septiembre 2353, 16°, Torre San Ramón, Santiago; tel. (2) 231-2860; fax (2) 231-3185; e-mail embsachi@interaccess.cl; internet www.embajada-sudafrica.cl; Ambassador VICTOR ZAZERAJ.

Spain: Avda Andrés Bello 1895, Casilla 16456, Providencia, Santiago; tel. (2) 235-2755; fax (2) 235-1049; e-mail embespcl@correo.mae.es; Ambassador JUAN ALFONSO ORTIZ RAMOS.

Sweden: CP 16639, Santiago; tel. (2) 940-1700; fax (2) 940-1730; e-mail ambassaden.santiago-de-chile@foreign.ministry.se; internet www.embajadasuecia.cl; Ambassador ARNE RODIN.

Switzerland: Avda Américo Vespucio Sur 100, 14°, Las Condes, Santiago; tel. (2) 263-4211; fax (2) 263-4094; e-mail vertretung@san.rep.admin.ch; internet www.eda.admin.ch/santiago_emb/s/home.html; Chargé d'affaires a.i. DIETER CAVALLERI.

Syria: Carmencita 111, Casilla 12, Correo 10, Santiago; tel. (2) 232-7471; Ambassador HISHAM HALLAJ.

Thailand: Avda Américo Vespucio 100, 15°, Las Condes, Santiago; tel. (2) 263-0710; fax (2) 263-0803; e-mail thaichil@ctcreuna.cl; internet www.rte-chile.thaiembdc.org; Ambassador PITHAYA POOKAMAN.

Turkey: Edif. Montolin, Of. 71, Monseñor Sotero Sanz 55, Providencia, Santiago; tel. (2) 231-8952; fax (2) 231-7762; e-mail turquia@manquehue.net; Ambassador AYSENUR ALPASLAN.

United Kingdom: Avda el Bosque Norte 0125, Casilla 72 D, Santiago; tel. (2) 370-4100; fax (2) 370-4180; e-mail chancery.santiago@fco.gov.uk; internet www.britemb.cl; Ambassador RICHARD WILKINSON (until Sept. 2005); Ambassador HOWARD DRAKE (designate).

USA: Avda Andrés Bello 2800, Las Condes, Santiago; tel. (2) 232-2600; fax (2) 330-3710; internet www.usembassy.cl; Ambassador CRAIG KELLY.

Uruguay: Avda Pedro de Valdivia 711, Casilla 2636, Santiago; tel. (2) 204-7988; fax (2) 274-4066; e-mail urusgo@uruguay.cl; internet www.uruguay.cl/; Ambassador ALEJANDRO ANTONIO LORENZO Y LOSADA ALDUNATE.

Venezuela: Bustos 2021, Providencia, Santiago; tel. (2) 225-0021; fax (2) 223-1170; e-mail embajada@embavenez.cl; internet www.embavenez.cl; Ambassador VÍCTOR ELOY DELGADO MONSALVE.

Judicial System

The Supreme Courts consist of 21 members.

There are Courts of Appeal (in the cities or departments of Arica, Iquique, Antofagasta, Copiapó, La Serena, Valparaíso, Santiago, San Miguel, Rancagua, Talca, Chillán, Concepción, Temuco, Valdivia, Puerto Montt, Coyhaique and Punta Arenas) whose members are appointed from a list submitted to the President of the Republic by the Supreme Court. The number of members of each court varies. Judges of the lower courts are appointed in a similar manner from lists submitted by the Court of Appeal of the district in which the vacancy arises. Judges and Ministers of the Supreme Court do not continue in office beyond the age of 75 years.

In March 1998 a major reform of the judiciary was implemented, including an increase, from 17 to 21, in the number of Ministers of the Supreme Court.

Corte Suprema

Bandera 344, 2°, Santiago; tel. (2) 873-5258; fax (2) 873-5276; e-mail mgonzalezp@poderjudicial.cl; internet www.poderjudicial.cl.

President of the Supreme Court: MARCOS LIBEDINSKY TSCHORNE.

Ministers of the Supreme Court: HERNÁN ALVAREZ GARCÍA, ELEODORO ORTIZ SEPÚLVEDA, JOSÉ BENQUIS CAMHI, ENRIQUE TAPIA WITTING, RICARDO GÁLVEZ BLANCO, ALBERTO CHAIGNEAU DEL CAMPO, JORGE RODRÍGUEZ ARIZTÍA, ENRIQUE CURY URZÚA, JOSÉ LUIS PÉREZ ZAÑARTU, ORLANDO ALVAREZ HERNÁNDEZ, URBANO MARÍN VALLEJO, DOMINGO YURAC SOTO, HUMBERTO ESPEJO ZÚÑIGA, JORGE MEDINA CUEVAS, DOMINGO ALFONSO MOURGUES, MILTON IVAN ARANCIBIA, NIBALDO SEGURA PEÑA, MARIA MORALES VILLAGRAN, ADALIS OYARZUN MIRANDA, JAIME DEL CARMEN RODRÍGUEZ ESPOZ.

Attorney-General: MONICA MALDONADO CROQUEVIELLE.

Secretary of the Court: CARLOS A. MENESES PIZARRO.

Religion

CHRISTIANITY

The Roman Catholic Church

Some 72% of the population are Roman Catholics; there were an estimated 11.0m. adherents at 31 December 2002. Chile comprises five archdioceses, 18 dioceses, two territorial prelatures and one apostolic vicariate.

Bishops' Conference

Conferencia Episcopal de Chile, Echaurren 4, 6°, Casilla 517-V, Correo 21, Santiago; tel. (2) 671-7733; fax (2) 698-1416; e-mail secretariageneral@episcopado.cl; internet www.iglesia.cl.

f. 1955 (statutes approved 2000); Pres. Mgr ALEJANDRO GOIC KARMELIC O. Rancagua (Archbishop of Santiago de Chile).

Archbishop of Antofagasta: PABLO LIZAMA RIQUELME, San Martín 2628, Casilla E, Antofagasta; tel. (55) 26-8856; e-mail arzoanto@cechnet.cl.

Archbishop of Concepción: ANTONIO MORENO CASAMITJANA, Calle Barros Arana 544, Casilla 65-C, Concepción; e-mail amoreno@episcopado.cl; tel. (41) 22-8173; fax (41) 23-2844.

Archbishop of La Serena: MANUEL DONOSO DONOSO, Los Carrera 450, Casilla 613, La Serena; tel. (51) 21-2325; fax (51) 22-5886; e-mail laserena@episcopado.cl.

Archbishop of Puerto Montt: Cristián Caro Cordero, Calle Benavente 385, Casilla 17, Puerto Montt; tel. (65) 25-2215; fax (65) 27-1861; e-mail puertomontt@episcopado.cl.

Archbishop of Santiago de Chile: Cardinal Francisco Javier Errázuriz Ossa, Erasmo Escala 1884, Casilla 30-D, Santiago; tel. (2) 696-3275; fax (2) 671-2042; e-mail curiasantiago@arzobispado.tie.cl.

The Anglican Communion

Anglicans in Chile come within the Diocese of the Southern Cone of America, which forms part of the Anglican Church of the Southern Cone of America, covering Argentina, Bolivia, Chile, Paraguay, Peru and Uruguay.

Bishop of Chile: Rt Rev. H. F. Zavala M, Iglesia Anglicana, José Miguel de la Barra 480, Of. 205, Casilla 50675, Correo Central, Santiago, Santiago; tel. (2) 639-1509; fax (2) 639-4581; e-mail fzavala@evangel.cl; internet www.iglesiaanglicana.cl.

Other Christian Churches

Baptist Evangelical Convention: Casilla 41-22, Santiago; tel. (2) 222-4085; fax (2) 635-4104; f. 1908; Pres. Moisés Pinto; Gen. Sec. Víctor Olivares.

Evangelical Lutheran Church: Pedro de Valdivia 3420-H, Dpto 33, Ñuñoa, Casilla 15167, Santiago; tel. (2) 225-0091; fax (2) 205-2193; e-mail iglesia_evangelica_ielch@adsl.tie.cl; f. 1937 as German Evangelical Church in Chile; present name adopted in 1959; Pres. Gloria Rojas; 3,000 mems.

Jehovah's Witnesses: Avda Concha y Toro 3456, Puente Alto; tel. (2) 288-1264; fax (2) 288-1257; Dir Pedro J. Lovato Grosso.

Methodist Church: Sargento Aldea 1041, Casilla 67, Santiago; tel. (2) 556-6074; fax (2) 554-1763; autonomous since 1969; 7,317 mems; Bishop Neftalí Aravena Bravo.

Orthodox Church of the Patriarch of Antioch: Avda Perú 502, Recoleta, Santiago; tel. and fax (2) 737-4697; Archbishop Mgr. Sergio Abad.

Pentecostal Church: Calle Pena 1103, Casilla de Correo 2, Curicó; tel. (75) 1035; f. 1945; 90,000 mems; Bishop Enrique Chávez Campos.

Pentecostal Church Mission: Calle Passy 32, Santiago; tel. (2) 634-6785; fax (2) 634-6786; f. 1952; Sec. Rev. Daniel Godoy Fernández; Pres. Rev. Erasmo Farfán Figueroa; 12,000 mems.

JUDAISM

Comité Representativo de las Entidades Judías en Chile (CREJ): Avda Ricardo Lyon 812, Providencia, Santiago; tel. (2) 274-7101; fax (2) 269-7005; Pres. Elimat Y. Jason.

Comunidad Israelita Sefardi de Chile: Avda Ricardo Lyon 812, Providencia, Santiago; tel. (2) 209-8086; fax (2) 204-7382; Pres. Salomon Camhi Avayu, Rabbi Iosef Gabay.

ISLAM

Sociedad Unión Musulmana: Mezquita As-Salam, Campoamor 2975, esq. Chile-España, Ñuñoa, Santiago; tel. (2) 343-1376; fax (2) 343-11378; Pres. Ousama Abughazalé.

BAHÁ'Í FAITH

National Spiritual Assembly: Manuel de Salas 356, Casilla 3731, Ñuñoa, Santiago; tel. (2) 269-2005; fax (2) 225-8276; e-mail secretaria@bahai.cl; internet www.bahai.cl; Co-ordinator Reed Chandler Reed; Sec. Farbod Youssefi.

The Press

Most newspapers of nation-wide circulation in Chile are published in Santiago.

DAILIES

Circulation figures listed below are supplied mainly by the Asociación Nacional de la Prensa. Other sources give much lower figures.

Santiago

La Cuarta: Diagonal Vicuña Mackenna 1842, Casilla 2795, Santiago; tel. (2) 555-0034; fax (2) 556-1017; e-mail lacuarta@copesa.cl; internet www.lacuarta.cl; morning; Gen. Man. Juan Carlos Larraín Wormald.

El Diario Financiero: San Crescente 81, 3°, Las Condes, Santiago; tel. (2) 339-1000; fax (2) 231-3340; e-mail buzon@eldiario; internet www.eldiario.cl; f. 1988; morning; Dir Guillermo Turner Olea; Gen. Man. José Miguel Respaldiza Chicharro; circ. 20,000.

Diario Oficial de la República de Chile: Casilla 81-D, Agustinas 1269, Santiago; tel. (2) 698-3969; fax (2) 698-1059; internet www.diarioficial.cl; f. 1877; Dir Florencio Ceballos Bustos; circ. 10,000.

Estrategia: Luis Carrera 1298, Vitacura, Santiago; tel. (2) 655-6228; fax (2) 655-6256; e-mail estrategia@edgestion.cl; internet www.estrategia.cl; f. 1978; morning; Editor Mónica Haberland.

El Mercurio: Avda Santa María 5542, Casilla 13-D, Santiago; tel. (2) 330-1111; fax (2) 242-1131; e-mail jpillanes@mercurio.cl; internet www.elmercurio.cl; f. 1827; morning; conservative; Gen. Man. Fernando Cisternas Bravo; circ. 120,000 (weekdays), 280,000 (Sun.).

La Nación: Agustinas 1269, Casilla 81-D, Santiago; tel. (2) 787-0100; fax (2) 698-1059; internet www.lanacion.cl; f. 1917 to replace govt-subsidized *El Cronista*; morning; financial; Propr Soc. Periodística La Nación; Dir Juan Walker Edwards; Gen. Man. Francisco Feres Nazarala; circ. 45,000.

Santiago Times: tel. (2) 777-5376; e-mail info@santiagotimes.cl; internet www.santiagotimes.cl; daily; national news in English; Editor Stephen Anderson; 10,000 subscribers.

La Segunda: Avda Santa María 5542, Casilla 13-D, Santiago; tel. (2) 330-1111; fax (2) 228-9289; e-mail redaccion@lasegunda.cl; internet www.lasegunda.com; f. 1931; owned by proprs of *El Mercurio*; evening; Dir Cristián Zegers Ariztía; circ. 40,000.

La Tercera: Avda Vicuña Mackenna 1962, Ñuñoa, Santiago; tel. (2) 550-7000; fax (2) 550-7999; e-mail latercera@copesa.cl; internet www.latercera.cl; f. 1950; morning; Dir Cristián Bofill Rodríguez; circ. 200,000.

Las Ultimas Noticias: Bellavista 0112, Providencia, Santiago; tel. (2) 730-3000; fax (2) 730-3331; e-mail rodolfo.gambetti@lun.cl; internet www.lun.cl; f. 1902; morning; Dir Agustín Edwards del Río; Gen. Man. Juan Enrique Canales Besa; owned by the proprs of *El Mercurio*; circ. 150,000 (except Sat. and Sun.).

Antofagasta

La Estrella del Norte: Manuel Antonio Matta 2112, Antofagasta; tel. (55) 26-4835; f. 1966; evening; Dir Caupolicán Márquez Vergara; circ. 5,000.

El Mercurio: Manuel Antonio Matta 2112, Antofagasta; tel. (55) 45-3600; fax (55) 425-3612; e-mail cronicafta@mercurio.cl; internet www.mercurioantofagasta.cl; f. 1906; morning; conservative independent; proprs Soc. Chilena de Publicaciones; Dir Arturo Romá Herrera; circ. 9,000.

Arica

La Estrella de Arica: San Marcos 580, Arica; tel. (58) 22-5024; fax (58) 25-2890; f. 1976; Dir Reinaldo Neira Ruiz; circ. 10,000.

Atacama

Chañarcillo: Los Carrera 801, Chañaral, Atacama; tel. (52) 21-9044; f. 1992; morning; Dir Luis Cerpa Hidalgo.

Calama

El Mercurio: Abaroa 2051, Calama; tel. (55) 34-1604; fax (55) 36-4255; e-mail cronicacalama@mercurio.cl; internet www.mercuriocalama.cl; f. 1968; propr Soc. Chilena de Publicaciones; Dir Roberto Gaete; circ. 4,500 (weekdays), 7,000 (Sun.).

Chillán

La Discusión de Chillán, SA: Calle 18 de Septiembre 721, Casilla 479, Chillán; tel. (42) 21-2650; fax (42) 21-3578; f. 1870; morning; independent; Dir Tito Castillo Peralta; circ. 5,000.

Concepción

El Sur: Calle Freire 799, Casilla 8-C, Concepción; tel. (41) 23-5825; f. 1882; morning; independent; Dir Rafael Maira Lamas; circ. 28,000 (weekdays), 45,000 (Sun.).

Copiapó

Atacama: Manuel Rodríguez 740, Copiapó; tel. (52) 2255; morning; independent; Dir Samuel Salgado; circ. 6,500.

Coyhaique

El Diario de Aisén: 21 de Mayo 410, Coyhaique; tel. (67) 234-850; fax (67) 232-318; Dir Aldo Marchesse Compodónico.

Curicó

La Prensa: Merced 373, Curicó; tel. (75) 31-0453; fax (75) 31-1924; e-mail laprensa@entelchile.net; internet diariolaprensa.cl; f. 1898; morning; right-wing; Man. Dir Manuel Massa Mautino; Editor Carlos Pozo Carvacho; Pres. Carlos Lazcano Alfonso; circ. 6,000.

Iquique

La Estrella de Iquique: Luis Uribe 452, Iquique; tel. (57) 42-2805; fax (57) 42-7975; f. 1966; evening; Dir Sergio Montivera Bruna; circ. 10,000.

El Nortino: Baquedano 1470, Iquique; tel. (57) 41-6666; fax (57) 41-2997; f. 1992; morning; Dir-Gen. Reynaldo Berríos González.

La Serena

El Día: Brasil 431, La Serena; tel. (51) 22-2863; fax (51) 22-2844; f. 1944; morning; Dir Antonio Puga Rodríguez; circ. 10,800.

Los Angeles

La Tribuna: Calle Colo Colo 464, Casilla 15-D, Los Angeles; tel. (43) 31-3315; fax (43) 31-1040; independent; Dir Cirilo Guzmán de la Fuente; circ. 4,500.

Osorno

El Diario Austral: Yungay 499, Valdivia; tel. (64) 23-5191; fax (64) 23-5192; e-mail vpineda@australvaldivia.cl; internet www .australvaldivia.cl; f. 1982; Dir Verónica Moreno Aguilera; circ. 6,500 (weekdays), 7,300 (Sun.).

Ovalle

El Ovallino: Victoria 323-B, Ovalle; tel. and fax (53) 627-557; Dir Jorge Contador Araya.

Puerto Montt

El Llanquíhue: Antonio Varas 167, Puerto Montt; tel. (65) 25-5115; fax (65) 432-401; f. 1885; Dir Ernesto Montalba; circ. 4,800 (weekdays), 5,700 (Sun.).

Punta Arenas

La Prensa Austral: Waldo Seguel 636, Casilla 9-D, Punta Arenas; tel. (61) 20-4000; fax (61) 24-7406; e-mail direccion@laprensaaustral .cl; internet www.laprensaaustral.cl; f. 1941; morning; independent; Dir Manuel González Araya; circ. 10,000, Sunday (*El Magallanes*; f. 1894) 12,000.

Quillota

El Observador: La Concepción 277, Casilla 1-D, Quillota; tel. (33) 312-096; fax (33) 311-417; e-mail elobser@entelchile.net; internet www.diarioelobservador.cl; f. 1970; Tuesdays and Fridays; Man. Dir Roberto Silva Bijit.

Rancagua

El Rancagüino: O'Carroll 518, Casilla 50, Rancagua; tel. (72) 23-0358; fax (72) 22-1483; e-mail prensaelrancaguino@adsl.tie.cl; internet www.elrancaguino.cl; f. 1915; independent; Dir Alejandro González; Gen. Man. Fernando Reyes; circ. 10,000.

Talca

El Centro: Tres Oriente 798, Talca; tel. (71) 22-0946; fax (71) 22-0924; f. 1989; Gen. Man. Hugo Saavedra Oteiza.

Temuco

El Diario Austral: Antonio Varas 945, Casilla 1-D, Temuco; tel. (45) 21-2575; fax (45) 23-9189; f. 1916; morning; commercial, industrial and agricultural interests; Dir Marco Antonio Pinto Zepeda; propr Soc. Periodística Araucanía, SA; circ. 15,100 (weekdays), 23,500 (Sun.).

Tocopilla

La Prensa de Tocopilla: Bolívar 1244, Tocopilla; tel. (83) 81-3036; f. 1924; morning; independent; Gen. Man. Jorge Leiva Concha; circ. 3,000.

Valdivia

El Diario Austral: Yungay 499, Valdivia; tel. (63) 24-2200; fax (63) 24-2209; internet www.australvaldivia.cl; f. 1982; Dir Gustavo Serrano Cotapos; circ. 5,600.

Valparaíso

La Estrella: Esmeralda 1002, Casilla 57-V, Valparaíso; tel. (32) 26-4264; fax (32) 26-4241; internet www.mercurio.cl; e-mail purzua@mercurio.cl; f. 1921; evening; independent; Dir Alfonso Castagneto; owned by the proprs of *El Mercurio*; circ. 28,000 (weekdays), 35,000 (Sat.).

El Mercurio: Esmeralda 1002, Casilla 57-V, Valparaíso; tel. (32) 26-4264; fax (32) 26-4138; internet www.elmercuriovalpo.cl; f. 1827;

morning; Dir Marco Antonio Pinto Zepada; owned by the proprs of *El Mercurio* in Santiago; circ. 65,000.

PERIODICALS

Santiago

América Economía: Apoquindo 4499, 10°, Las Condes, Santiago; tel. (2) 290-9400; fax (2) 206-6005; e-mail icolodro@aeconomia.cl; internet www.americaeconomia.com; e-mail rferro@aeconomia.cl; f. 1986; monthly; business; CEO Elías Selman; Publisher Nils Strandberg; Editorial Dir Raúl Ferro Isakaz.

Apsi: Santiago; tel. (2) 77-5450; f. 1976; fortnightly; current affairs; Dir Marcelo Contreras Nieto; circ. 15,000.

La Bicicleta: José Fagnano 614, Santiago; tel. (2) 222-3969; satirical; Dir Antonio de la Fuente.

CA (Ciudad/Arquitectura) Revista Oficial del Colegio de Arquitectos de Chile AG: Manuel Montt 515, Santiago; tel. (2) 235-3368; fax (2) 235-8403; f. 1964; 4 a year; architects' magazine; Editor Arq. Jaime Márquez Rojas; circ. 3,500.

Caras: Reyes Lavalle 3194, Las Condes, Santiago; tel. (2) 399-6399; fax 399-6299; internet www.caras.cl; e-mail revista@caras.cl; women's interest; Dir Patricia Guzmán.

Carola: San Francisco 116, Casilla 1858, Santiago; tel. (2) 33-6433; fortnightly; women's magazine; published by Editorial Antártica, SA; Dir Isabel Margarita Aguirre de Maino.

Cauce: Huérfanos 713, Of. 604–60, Santiago; tel. (2) 38-2304; fortnightly; political, economic and cultural affairs; Dir Angel Flisfich; circ. 10,000.

Chile Agrícola: Teresa Vial 1170, Casilla 2, Correo 13, Santiago; tel. and fax (2) 522-2627; e-mail chileagricola@hotmail.com; f. 1975; 6 a year; organic farming; Dir Ing. Agr. Raúl González Valenzuela; circ. 7,000.

Chile Forestal: Avda Bulnes 285, Of. 601, Santiago; tel. (2) 390-0213; fax (2) 696-6724; e-mail mespejo@conaf.cl; internet www.conaf .cl; f. 1974; 10 a year; state-owned; technical information and features on forestry sector; Editor Ricardo San Martín; Dir Mariela Espejo Suazo; circ. 4,000.

Cinegrama: Avda Holanda 279, Providencia, Santiago; tel. (2) 422-8500; fax (2) 422-8570; internet www.cinegrama.cl; e-mail cinegrama@holanda.cl; monthly; cinema; Dir Jaime Godoy; Editor Leyla López.

The Clinic: Santo Domingo 550, Santiago; tel. (2) 633-9584; fax (2) 639-6584; fortnightly; political and social satire; Dir Patricio Fernández.

Conozca Más: Reyes Lavalle 3193, Las Condes, Santiago; tel. (2) 366-7100; fax (2) 246-2810; e-mail viamail@conozcamas.cl; internet www.conozcamas.cl; monthly; science; Dir Paula Aviles; circ. 90,000.

Cosas: Almirante Pastene 329, Providencia, Santiago; tel. (2) 364-5100; fax (2) 235-8331; f. 1976; fortnightly; entertainment and lifestyle; Dir Mónica Comandari Kaiser; circ. 40,000.

Creces: Luis Uribe 2610, Ñuñoa, Santiago; tel. and fax (2) 341-5829; internet www.creces.cl; e-mail creceswebmaster@entelchile.net; monthly; science and technology; Dir Sergio Prenafeta; circ. 12,000.

Deporte Total: Santiago; tel. (2) 251-6236; fax (2) 204-7420; f. 1981; weekly; sport, illustrated; Dir Juan Ignacio Oto Larios; circ. 25,000.

Ercilla: Avda Holanda 279, Providencia, Santiago; tel. (2) 422-8500; fax (2) 422-8570; e-mail ercilla@holanda.cl; internet www.ercilla.cl; f. 1936; weekly; general interest; conservative; Dir Eugenio González; circ. 28,000.

Gestión: Luis Carrera 1289, Vitacura, Santiago; tel. (2) 655-6100; fax (2) 655-6439; f. 1975; monthly; business matters; Dir Maira Jordan; circ. 38,000.

Internet: Avda Carlos Valdovinos 251; tel. (2) 552-5599; monthly; internet and new technology; Dir Florencio Uteras.

Mensaje: Almirante Barroso 24, Casilla 10445, Santiago; tel. (2) 696-0653; fax (2) 671-7030; e-mail rrpp@mensaje.cl; internet www .mensaje.cl; f. 1951; monthly; national, church and international affairs; Dir Antonio Delfau; circ. 6,000.

Mujer a Mujer: Vicuña McKenna 1870, Ñuñoa, Santiago; tel. (2) 550-7000; fax (2) 550-7379; internet www.mujeramujer.cl; e-mail mujer@latercera.cl; weekly; women's interest; Dir Jackeline Otey.

News Review: Casilla 151/9, Santiago; tel. (2) 236-9511; fax (2) 236-0887; f. 1991; weekly; English language news; Dir Graham A. Wigg.

Paula: Avda Santa María 0120, Providencia, Santiago; tel. (2) 200-0407; fax (2) 200-0490; e-mail paula@paulacom.cl; internet www .paula.cl; f. 1967; monthly; women's interest; Dir Paula Recart; circ. 85,000.

Punto Final: San Diego 31, Of. 606, Casilla 13954, Correo 21, Santiago; tel. and fax (2) 697-0615; e-mail punto@interaccess.cl; internet www.puntofinal.cl; f. 1965; fortnightly; politics; left-wing; Dir MANUEL CABIESES DONOSO; circ. 15,000.

¿Qué Pasa?: Vicuña Mackenna 1870, Ñuñoa, Santiago; tel. (2) 550-7523; fax (2) 550-7529; internet www.quepasa.cl; e-mail quepasa@copesa.cl; f. 1971; weekly; general interest; Dir BERNADITA DEL SOLAR VERA; circ. 30,000.

Semanario Datos Sur: Avda Urmeneta 231, Puerto Montt; tel. (65) 26-6934; e-mail datossur@telsur.cl; internet www.datossur.cl; weekly; regional, national and business news; Dir ALEX BERKHOFF ALCARRAZ.

Semanario El Siglo: Diagonal Paraguay 458, Of. 1, Casilla 13479, Correo 21, Santiago; tel. and fax (2) 633-0074; e-mail elsiglo@elsiglo.cl; internet www.elsiglo.cl; f. 1940; fortnightly; published by the Communist Party of Chile (PCCh); Dir CLAUDIO DE NEGRI QUINTANA; circ. 15,000.

Vea: Avda Holanda 279, Providencia, Santiago; tel. (2) 422-8500; fax (2) 422-8571; e-mail revistavea@holanda.cl; internet www.vea.cl; f. 1939; weekly; general interest, illustrated; Dir JAIME GODOY CARTES; circ. 150,000.

PRESS ASSOCIATION

Asociación Nacional de la Prensa: Carlos Antúnez 2048, Santiago; tel. 232-1004; fax 232-1006; e-mail info@anp.cl; internet www.anp.cl; f. 1951; Pres. JUAN LUIS SOMMERS COMANDARI; Sec. DANIELA ROJAS.

NEWS AGENCIES

Agencia Chile Noticias (ACN): Carlos Antúnez 1884, Of. 104, Providencia, Santiago; tel. and fax (2) 223 0205; e-mail jfranco@chilenoticias.cl; internet www.chilenoticias.cl; f. 1993; Dir JEANETE FRANCO N.

Agencia Orbe: Avda Phillips 56, Of. 66, Santiago; tel. (2) 639-4774; fax (2) 639-6826; Bureau Chief PATRICIA ESCALONA CÁCERES.

Agencia UPI: Avda Nataniel 47, 9°, Santiago; tel. (2) 696-0162; fax (2) 698-6605; Bureau Chief FRANCISCO JARA ARANCIBIA.

Business News Americas: Carmencita 106, Las Condes, Santiago; tel. (2) 232-0302; fax (2) 232-9376; e-mail info@bnamericas.com; internet www.bnamericas.com; internet-based business information; CEO GREGORY BARTON.

Chile Information Project (CHIP): Avda Santa María 227, Of. 12, Recoleta, Santiago; tel. (-2) 738-0150; fax (2) 735-2267; e-mail anderson@chip.mic.cl; internet www.santiagotimes.cl; English language; Dir STEPHEN J. ANDERSON.

Europa Press: Biarritz 1913, Providencia, Santiago; tel. and fax (2) 274-3552; e-mail europapress@rdc.cl; Dir JOSÉ RÍOS VIAL.

Foreign Bureaux

Agence France-Presse (France): Avda B. O'Higgins 1316, 9°, Apdo 92, Santiago; tel. (2) 696-0559; fax (2) 695-5036; Correspondent HUMBERTO ZUMARÁN ARAYA.

Agencia EFE (Spain): Coronel Santiago Bueras 188, Santiago; tel. (2) 638-0179; fax (2) 633-6130; e-mail direccion@agenciaefe.tie.cl; internet www.efe.es; f. 1966; Bureau Chief Man. MANUEL FUENTES GARCÍA.

Agenzia Nazionale Stampa Associata (ANSA) (Italy): Moneda 1040, Of. 702, Santiago; tel. (2) 698-5811; fax (2) 698-3447; e-mail ansacile@entelchile.net; f. 1945; Bureau Chief GIORGIO BAGONI BETTOLLINI.

Associated Press (AP) (USA): Tenderini 85, 10°, Of. 100, Casilla 2653, Santiago; tel. (2) 633-5015; fax 633-8368; Bureau Chief EDUARDO GALLARDO.

Bloomberg News (USA): Miraflores 222, Santiago; tel. (2) 638-6820; fax (2) 698-3447; Dir MIKE SMITH.

Deutsche Presse-Agentur (dpa) (Germany): San Antonio 427, Of. 306, Santiago; tel. (2) 639-3633; Correspondent CARLOS DORAT.

Inter Press Service (IPS) (Italy): Santiago; tel. (2) 39-7091; Dir and Correspondent GUSTAVO GONZÁLEZ RODRÍGUEZ.

Prensa Latina (Cuba): Bombero Ossa 1010, Of. 1104, Santiago; tel. (2) 671-8222; fax (2) 695-8605; Correspondent LIDIA SEÑARIS CEJAS.

Reuters (United Kingdom): Nueva York 33, 10°, Casilla 4248, Santiago; tel. (2) 672-8800; fax (2) 696-0161; Correspondent RAÚL CUEVAS.

Xinhua (New China) News Agency (People's Republic of China): Biarritz 1981, Providencia, Santiago; tel. (2) 25-5033; Correspondent SUN KUOGUOWEIN.

Association

Asociación de Corresponsales de la Prensa Extranjera en Chile: Coronel Santiago Bueras 188, Santiago; tel. (2) 688-0424; fax (2) 633-6130; Pres. OMAR RUZ.

Publishers

Arrayán Editores: Bernarda Morin 435, Providencia, Santiago; tel. (2) 431-4200; fax (2) 274-1041; internet www.arrayan.cl; f. 1982; general; Gen. Man. PABLO MARINKOVIC.

Distribuidora Molino, SA: Abtao 574, Quinta Normal, Santiago; tel. (2) 786-3000; fax (2) 776-6425; e-mail molino@molinoxxi.cl; Admin. Man. JORGE VARGAS ARAYA.

Ediciones y Comunicaciones Ltda: Luis Thayer Ojeda 0115, Of. 402, Providencia, Santiago; tel. (2) 232-1241; fax (2) 234-9467; e-mail edicom@chilnet.cl; internet www.chilnet.cl/edicom/; publs include *Anuario Farmacológico*; Gen. Man. MARIO SILVA MARTÍNEZ.

Ediciones San Pablo: Vicuña Mackenna 10777, Casilla 3746, Santiago; tel. (2) 288-2025; fax (2) 288-2026; e-mail dgraledi@cnet.net; Catholic texts; Dir-Gen. P. LUIS NEIRA RAMÍREZ.

Ediciones Técnicas Ltda: El Condor 844, Of. 203, Huechuraba, Santiago; tel. (2) 757-4200; fax (2) 757-4201; e-mail editec@editec.cl; internet www.editec.cl; Pres. RICARDO CORTES DONOSO; Gen. Man. ROLY SOLIS SEPÚLVEDA.

Ediciones Universitarias de Valparaíso: Universidad Católica de Valparaíso, 12 de Febrero 187, Casilla 1415, Valparaíso; tel. (32) 27-3087; fax (32) 27-3429; e-mail euvsa@ucv.cl; internet www.euv.cl; f. 1970; literature, social and general sciences, engineering, education, music, arts, textbooks; Gen. Man. ALEJANDRO DAMIÁN VILARREAL.

Ediciones Urano: Avda Francisco Bilbao 2809, Providencia, Santiago; tel. (2) 341-6731; fax (2) 225-3896; e-mail chile@edicionesurano.com; internet www.edicionesurano.com; f. 1983; self-help, mystical and scholarly.

Editorial Andrés Bello/Jurídica de Chile: Avda Ricardo Lyon 946, Casilla 4256, Providencia, Santiago; tel. (2) 461-9500; fax (2) 225-3600; e-mail julio_serrano@entelchile.net; internet www.editorialandresbello.com; f. 1947; history, arts, literature, politics, economics, textbooks, law and social science; Gen. Man. JULIO SERRANO LAMAS.

Editorial Antártica, SA: San Francisco 116, Santiago; tel. (2) 639-3476; fax (2) 633-3402; e-mail plaborde@antartica; internet www.antartica.cl; f. 1978; Gen. Man. PAUL LABORDE U.

Editorial Borlando: Avda Victoria 151, Santiago; tel. (2) 555-9566; fax (2) 555-9564; internet www.editorialborlando.cl; scholarly, juvenile, educational and reference; f. 1984.

Editorial Cuatro Vientos Ltda: Jaime Guzmán Errázuriz 3293, Ñuñoa, Santiago; tel. (2) 225-8381; fax (2) 341-3107; e-mail 4vientos@netline.cl; internet www.cuatrovientos.net; f. 1980; Man. Editor JUAN FRANCISCO HUNEEUS COX.

Editorial El Sembrador: Sargento Aldea 1041, Casilla 2037, Santiago; tel. (2) 556-9454; Dir ISAÍAS GUTIÉRREZ.

Editorial y Distribuidora Lenguaje y Pensamiento Ltda: Avda Apoquindo 6275, Of. 36, Las Condes, Santiago; tel. (2) 245-2909; fax (2) 202-8263; internet www.juegosdidacticos.cl.

Editorial Evolución, SA: General del Canto 105, Of. 707, Santiago; tel. (2) 236-4789; fax (2) 236-4796; e-mail jbravo@evolucion.cl; internet www.evolucion.cl; business and management.

Editorial Fondo de Cultura Económica Chile SA: Paseo Bulnes 152, Santiago; tel. (2) 699-0189; fax (2) 696-2329.

Editorial Renacimiento: Huérfanos 623, Santiago; tel. (2) 632-7334; fax (2) 633-9374; internet www.feriachiledellibro.cl; Gen. Man. MANUEL VILCHES.

Editorial Terra Chile: Pabellón 11, Santiago; tel. (2) 737-4455; fax (2) 738-0445; Gen. Man. ORLANDO MILESI.

Editorial Texido: Einstein 921, Recoleta, Santiago; tel. (2) 622-4652; fax (2) 622-4660; f. 1969; Gen. Man. ELSA ZLATER.

Editorial Tiempo Presente Ltda: Almirante Pastene 329, Casilla 303, Correo 22, Providencia, Santiago; tel. (2) 364-5100; fax (2) 235-8331; e-mail cosas@cosas.com; internet www.cosas.com; Gen. Man. JUAN LUIS SOMMERS.

Editorial Trineo, SA: Los Olmos 3685, Macul, Santiago; tel. (2) 750-1000; fax (2) 750-1001; e-mail trineo@trineo.cl; internet www.trineo.cl; Gen. Man. CARLOS JÉREZ HERNÁNDEZ.

Editorial Universitaria, SA: María Luisa Santander 0447, Casilla 10220, Providencia, Santiago; tel. (2) 487-0700; fax (2) 487-0702; e-mail comunicaciones@universitaria.cl; internet www

.universitaria.cl; f. 1947; general literature, social science, technical, textbooks; Man. Dir RODRIGO CASTRO.

Empresa Editora Zig-Zag SA: Los Conquistadores 1700, 17°, Of. B, Providencia, Santiago; tel. (2) 335-7477; fax (2) 335-7445; e-mail zigzag@zigzag.cl; internet www.zigzag.cl; f. 1934; general publishers of literary works, reference books and magazines; Pres. GONZALO VIAL C; Gen. Man. FRANCISCO PÉREZ FRUGONE.

Lexis-Nexis Chile: Miraflores 383, 11°, Santiago; tel. (2) 510-5000; fax (2) 510-5110; internet www.lexisnexis.cl; legal, business, government and academic; f. 1973.

McGraw-Hill/Interamericana de Chile Ltda: Pocuro 2151, Providencia, Casilla 150, Correo 29, Santiago; tel. (2) 373-3000; fax (2) 635-4467; e-mail gerardo_aguayo@mcgraw-hill.com.cl; internet www.mcgraw-hill.cl.

Norma de Chile, SA: Avda Providencia 1760, Of. 502, Providencia, Santiago; tel. (2) 236-3355; fax (2) 236-3362; e-mail ventasnorma@carvajal.cl; internet www.norma.com; f. 1960; part of Editorial Norma of Colombia; Gen. Man. ELSY SALAZAR CAMPO.

Pehuen Editores Ltda: Antonio Varas 2043, Santiago; tel. (2) 204-9399; fax (2) 204-9399; e-mail pehuen@cmet.net; f. 1983; literature and sociology; Gen. Man. ALICIA Z. CERDA.

Publicaciones Técnicas, SA (PUBLITECSA): Miraflores 383, 11°, Santiago; tel. (2) 510-5000; fax (2) 365-8010; e-mail acliente@publitecsa.cl; internet www.publitecsa.cl; official information; Commercial Man. CARLOS MUNIZAGA.

RIL Editores (fmrly Red Internacional del Libro Ltda): Alférez Real 1464, Providencia, CP 750-0960, Santiago; tel. (2) 223-8100; fax (2) 225-4269; e-mail ril@rileditores.com; internet www.rileditores.com; literature, poetry, scholarly and political; f. 1991; Dir ELEONORA FINKELSTEIN; Dir of Publications DANIEL CALABRESE.

PUBLISHERS' ASSOCIATION

Cámara Chilena del Libro AG: Avda B. O'Higgins 1370, Of. 501, Casilla 13526, Santiago; tel. (2) 698-9519; fax (2) 687-4088; e-mail camlibro@terra.cl; internet www.camlibro.cl; Pres. EDUARDO CASTILLO GARCÍA; Exec. Sec. RAQUEL TORNERO GÓMEZ.

Broadcasting and Communications

TELECOMMUNICATIONS

Regulatory Authority

Subsecretaría de Telecomunicaciones (Department of Telecommunications, Ministry of Public Works): Amunátegui 139, 5°, Casilla 120, Correo 21, Santiago; tel. (2) 421-3000; fax (2) 421-3553; e-mail subtel@subtel.cl; Under-Sec. CHRISTIAN NICOLAI ORELLANA.

Major Operators

Alcatel de Chile: Monseñor Sótero Sanz 55, 3°, Providencia, Santiago; tel. (2) 230-3000; fax (2) 231-1862; internet www.alcatel.com; Chair. and CEO SERGE TCHURUK; Pres. and COO PHILIPPE GERMOND.

AT&T Chile: Rinconada El Salto 202, Huechuraba, Santiago; tel. (2) 582 5000; fax (2) 585-5079; e-mail info@firstcom.cl; internet www.attla.cl; Pres. ALEJANDRO ROJAS; Dir-Gen. JAIME CHICO PARDO.

Chilesat: Rinconada El Salto 202, Huechuraba, Casilla 12, Santiago; tel. (2) 380-0171; fax (2) 382-5142; e-mail tlchile@chilesat.net; internet www.chilesat.net; Pres. JUAN EDUARDO IBÁÑEZ WALKER; Gen. Man. RAMÓN VALDIVIESO.

CMET Compañía de Telefónos: Avda Los Leones 1412, Providencia, Santiago; tel. (2) 251-3333; fax (2) 274-9573; Pres. RAFAEL BARRA CARMONA; Gen. Man. AGUSTÍN CASTELLÓN RAUCH.

Empresa Nacional de Telecomunicaciones, SA—ENTEL Chile, SA: Andrés Bello 2687, 14°, Casilla 4254, Las Condes, Santiago; tel. (2) 360-0123; fax (2) 360-3424; internet www.entel.cl; f. 1964; operates the Chilean land satellite stations of Longovilo, Punta Arenas and Coihaique, linked to INTELSAT system; 52% owned by Telecom Italia; Pres. CARLOS HURTADO.

Telefónica Chile: Providencia 111, Santiago; tel. (2) 691-2020; fax (2) 691-2018; internet www.ctc.cl; fmrly Compañía de Telecomunicaciones de Chile, SA; privatized in 1988; owned by Telefónica, SA (Spain); CEO CLAUDIO MUÑOZ.

Telefónica Móvil de Chile: Miraflores 130, Santiago; tel. (2) 661-6000; internet www.telefonicamovil.c; f. 1996; mobile telephone services.

TELEX-CHILE, SA: Rinconada El Salto 202, Huechuraba, Santiago; tel. (2) 382-5786; fax (2) 382-5142; e-mail tlchile@chilesat.net; internet www.telex.cl; Pres. JORGE AWAD MEHECH; Gen. Man. RAMÓN VALDIVIESO RÍOS.

VTR GlobalCom: Reyes Lavalle 3340, 9°, Las Condes, Santiago; tel. (2) 310-1000; fax (2) 310-1560; internet www.vtr.cl; Pres. BLAS TOMIC; Gen. Man. PEDRO GUTIÉRREZ SÁNCHEZ.

BROADCASTING

Regulatory Authority

Asociación de Radiodifusores de Chile (ARCHI): Pasaje Matte 956, Of. 801, Casilla 10476, Santiago; tel. (2) 639-8755; fax (2) 639-4205; e-mail archi@archiradios.cl; internet www.archiradios.cl; f. 1936; 455 broadcasting stations; Pres. CÉSAR MOLFINO MENDOZA.

Radio

In December 2000 there were 1,153 radio stations (981 FM and 172 AM) transmitting in Chile.

Agricultura (AM y FM): Avda Manuel Rodríguez 15, Santiago; tel. (2) 695-3088; fax (2) 672-2749; owned by Sociedad Nacional de Agricultura; Pres. MANUEL VALDÉS VALDÉS; Gen. Man. GUIDO ERRÁZURIZ MORENO.

Aurora FM: Eliodoro Yáñez 1783, Providencia, Santiago; tel. (2) 390-2112; fax (2) 632-5860; f. 1982; part of Ibero American media group; Pres. ERNESTO CORONA BOZZO; Gen. Man. JUAN CARRASCO HERNÁNDEZ.

Beethoven FM: Garibaldi 1620, Ñuñoa, Santiago; tel. (2) 225-0222; fax (2) 274-3323; e-mail director@redfm.cl; internet www.beethovenfm.cl; f. 1981; mainly classical music; affiliate stations in Viña del Mar and Temuco; Exec. Dir and legal rep. RICARDO GUTIÉRREZ GATICA.

Belén AM: Benavente 385, 3°, Casilla 17, Puerto Montt; tel. (65) 25-8048; fax (65) 25-8097; e-mail radiobel.en001@chilnet.cl; f. 1990; owned by Archbishopric of Puerto Montt; Dir NELSON GONZÁLEZ ANDRADE; Gen. Man. CARLOS WAGNER CATALÁN.

Bío Bío La Radio: Avda Libertador Bernardo O'Higgins 680, Concepción; tel. (41) 225-660; fax (41) 226-742; affiliate stations in Concepción, Los Angeles, Temuco, Ancud, Castro, Osorno, Puerto Montt and Valdivia.

Compañía Radio Chilena: Phillips 40, 2°, Casilla 10277, Santiago; tel. (2) 463-5000; fax (2) 463-5050; e-mail jsilva@radiochilena.cl; internet www.radiochilena.com; f. 1922; news; FM, AM and satellite; Exec. Dir JUAN LUIS SILVA DIBARRART.

Radio El Conquistador FM: El Conquistador del Monte 4644, Huechuraba, Santiago; tel. (2) 740-0000; fax (2) 740-0259; e-mail rconquis@entelchile.net; internet www.elconquistadorfm.cl; f. 1962; affiliate stations in Santiago, Iquique, Antofagasta, La Serena, Viña del Mar, Rancagua, Talca, Chillán, Concepción, Talcahuano, Pucón, Temuco, Villarrica, Lago Llanquihue, Osorno, Puerto Montt, Puerto Varas, Valdivia and Punta Arenas; Pres. JOAQUÍN MOLFINO.

Radio Cooperativa (AM y FM): Antonio Bellet 353, Casilla 16367, Correo 9, Santiago; tel. (2) 364-8000; fax (2) 236-0535; e-mail info@cooperativa.cl; internet www.cooperativa.cl; f. 1936; affiliate stations in Copiapó, Arica, Coquimbo, La Serena, Valparaíso, Concepción, Calama, Temuco and Castro; Pres. LUIS AJENJO ISASI; Gen. Man. SERGIO PARRA GODOY.

La Clave FM: Monjitas 454, Of. 406, Santiago; tel. (2) 633-1621; fax (2) 639-2914; f. 1980; Pres. MIGUEL NASUR ALLEL; Gen. Man. VÍCTOR IBARRA NEGRETE.

Duna FM: Eliodoro Yáñez 1804, Providencia, Santiago; tel. (2) 225-5494; fax (2) 225-6013; e-mail contacto@duna.cl; internet www.duna.cl; affiliate stations in Viña del Mar and Concepción; Pres. FELIPE LAMARCA CLARO; Dir A. HOLUIGUE.

Estrella del Mar AM: Eleuterio Ramírez 207, Ancud-Isla de Chiloé; tel. (65) 63-2900; fax (65) 63-2900; f. 1982; affiliate stations in Castro and Quellón; Dir MIGUEL ANGEL MILLAR SILVA.

Festival AM: Quinta 124 A, Viña del Mar; tel. (32) 68-9328; fax (32) 68-0266; e-mail servicios@festival.cl; internet www.festival.cl; f. 1976; Pres. LUIS MUÑOZ AHUMADA; Dir-Gen. SANTIAGO CHIESA HOWARD.

Finísima FM: Luis Thayer Ojeda 1145, Santiago; tel. (2) 233-5771; fax (2) 231-0611; affiliate stations in Santiago, Arica, Iquique, Calama, Copiapó, La Serena, Ovalle, Isla de Pascua, Quilpe, San Antonio, San Felipe, Villa Alemana, Viña del Mar, Rancagua, Talca, Chillán, Concepción, Los Angeles, Temuco, Puerto Montt, Coihayque, Puerto Aysen and Punto Arenas; Gen. Man. CRISTIÁN WAGNER MUÑOZ.

FM-Hit: Eliodoro Yáñez 1783, Providencia, Santiago; tel. (2) 274-6737; fax (2) 274-8928; internet www.concierto.cl; f. 1999; part of Ibero American media group; affiliate stations in Santiago, Iquique, Antofagasta, San Antonio, La Serena, Viña del Mar, Concepción, Temuco, Osorno and Puerto Montt; Gen. Man. JAIME VEGA DE KUYPER.

Horizonte: Avda Los Leones 1625, Providencia, Santiago; tel. (2) 274-6737; fax (2) 410-5400; internet www.horizonte.cl; f. 1985;

affiliate stations in Arica, Antofagasta, Iquique, La Serena, Viña del Mar, Concepción, San Antonio, Temuco, Villarrica, Puerto Montt, Punta Arenas and Osorno.

Infinita FM: Avda Los Leones 1285, Providencia, Santiago; tel. (2) 754-4400; fax (2) 341-6727; internet www.infinita.cl; f. 1977; affiliate stations in Santiago, Viña del Mar, Concepción and Valdivia; Gen. Man. CARLOS ALBERTO PEÑAFIEL GUARACHI.

Radio Nacional de Chile: Argomedo 369, Santiago; tel. (2) 638-1348; fax (2) 632-1065; affiliate stations in Arica and Punta Arenas; Gen. Man. SANTIAGO AGLIATI.

Para Ti FM: El Conquistador del Monte 4644, Huechuraba, Santiago; tel. (2) 740-9393; fax (2) 740-0405; internet www.fmparati.cl; 16 affiliate stations throughout Chile; Gen. Man. FELIPE MOLFINO BURKERT.

Radio Polar: Bories 871, 2°, Punta Arenas; tel. (61) 24-1909; fax (61) 22-8344; f. 1940; Pres. RENÉ VENEGAS OLMEDO.

Pudahuel FM: Eliodoro Yáñez 1783, Providencia, Santiago; tel. (2) 223-0704; fax (2) 223-7589; e-mail radio@pudahuel.cl; internet www .pudahuel.cl; f. 1966; part of Ibero American media group; affiliate stations in Arica, Iquique, Antofagasta, Calama, Copiapó, Coquimbo, La Serena, Ovalle, San Felipe, Valparaíso, Viña del Mar, Rancagua, Curico, Linares, Talca, Chillán, Concepción, Los Angeles, Talcahuano, Pucón, Temuco, Villarrica, Ancud-Castro, Osorno, Puerto Montt, Valdivia and Punta Arenas; Pres. SUSANA MUTINELLI ANCHUBIDART; Gen. Man. JOAQUÍN BLAYA BARRIOS.

Santa María de Guadalupe: Miguel Claro 161, Casilla 2626, Santiago; tel. (2) 235-7996; fax (2) 235-8527; e-mail radio@ santamariadeguadalupe.com; internet www .santamariadeguadalupe.com; religious broadcasting; affiliate stations in Arica, Iquique, Antofagasta, La Serena, Viña del Mar, Temuco, Puerto Varas, Coihayque and Punta Arenas; Dir ALFONSO CHADWICK.

Superandina FM: Santa Rosa 441, Of. 34, Casilla 401, Los Andes; tel. (34) 42-2515; fax (34) 90-4091; internet www.superandina.cl; f. 1987; Dir JOSÉ ANDRÉS GÁLVEZ.

Universo FM: Félix de Amesti 124, 8°, Las Condes, Santiago; tel. (2) 206-6065; fax (2) 206-6049; affiliate stations in 18 cities, including Iquique, Copiapó, La Serena, Ovalle, Concepción, Temuco, Puerto Montt, Coihayque and Punta Arenas; Pres. ÁLVARO LARRAÍN.

Television

Corporación de Televisión de la Universidad Católica de Chile—Canal 13: Inés Matte Urrejola 0848, Casilla 14600, Providencia, Santiago; tel. (2) 251-4000; fax (2) 630-2040; e-mail dasein@ reuna.cl; internet www.canal13.cl; f. 1959; non-commercial; Exec. Dir ELEODORO RODRÍGUEZ MATTE; Gen. Man. JAIME BELLOLIO RODRÍGUEZ.

La Red Televisión, S.A./TV Azteca Chile, S.A.: Manquehue Sur 1201, Las Condes, Santiago; tel. (2) 385-4000; fax (2) 385-4020; internet www.redtv.cl; e-mail administracion@lared.cl; f. 1991; Pres. JUAN CARLOS LATORRE; Gen. Man. MARCELO PAMDOLFO.

Megavisión, S.A.—Canal 9: Avda Vicuña Mackenna 1348, Ñuñoa, Santiago; tel. (2) 810-8000; fax (2) 551-8369; e-mail mega@mcl.cl; internet www.mega.cl; f. 1990; Pres. RICARDO CLARO VALDÉS; Gen. Man. CRISTÓBAL BULNES SERRANO.

Red de Televisión SA/Chilevisión—Canal 11: Inés Matte Urrejola 0825, Casilla 16547, Correo 9, Providencia, Santiago; tel. (2) 461-5100; fax (2) 461-5371; e-mail info@chilevision.cl; internet www .chilevision.cl; part of Ibero American media group; News Dir FELIPE POZO.

Televisión Nacional de Chile—Canal 7: Bellavista 0990, Casilla 16104, Providencia, Santiago; tel. (2) 707-7777; fax (2) 707-7766; e-mail rrpp@tvn.cl; internet www.tvn.cl; government network of 140 stations and an international satellite signal; Chair. LUIS ORTIZ QUIROGA; Exec. Dir PABLO PIÑEIRA ECHENIQUE.

Corporación de Televisión de la Universidad Católica de Valparaíso: Agua Santa Alta 2455, Casilla 247, Viña del Mar; tel. (32) 616-000; fax (32) 610-505; e-mail tv@ucv.cl; f. 1957; Dir JORGE A. BORNSCHEUER.

Finance

(cap. = capital; res = reserves; dep. = deposits; m. = million; brs = branches; amounts in pesos unless otherwise specified)

BANKING

Supervisory Authority

Superintendencia de Bancos e Instituciones Financieras: Moneda 1123, 6°, Casilla 15-D, Santiago; tel. (2) 442-6200; fax (2) 441-0914; e-mail superintendente@sbif.cl; internet www.sbif.cl; f. 1925; affiliated to Ministry of Finance; Supt ENRIQUE MARSHALL RIVERA.

Central Bank

Banco Central de Chile: Agustinas 1180, Santiago; tel. (2) 670-2000; fax (2) 670-2099; e-mail bcch@bcentral.cl; internet www .bcentral.cl; f. 1926; under Ministry of Finance until Dec. 1989, when autonomy was granted; bank of issue; cap. 257,604.6m., total assets 17,985,161.2m. (Dec. 2002); Pres. VITTORO CORBO; Gen. Man. CAMILO CARRASCO.

State Bank

Banco del Estado de Chile: Avda B. O'Higgins 1111, Santiago; tel. (2) 670-7000; fax (2) 670-5711; internet www.bancoestado.cl; f. 1953; state bank; cap. and res 328,551m., dep. 3,492,359m. (May 2002); Chair. JAIME ESTÉVEZ; Gen. Man. JOSÉ MANUEL MENA; 294 brs.

Commercial Banks

Banco de A. Edwards: Huérfanos 740, Santiago; tel. (2) 388-3000; fax (2) 388-4428; internet www.banedwards.cl; f. 1851; acquired by Banco de Chile in Jan. 2002.

Banco BICE: Teatinos 220, Santiago; tel. (2) 692-2000; fax (2) 696-5324; e-mail webmaster@bice.cl; internet www.bice.cl; f. 1979 as Banco Industrial y de Comercio Exterior; name changed as above in 1988; cap. and res 94,987m. (Dec. 2003); Pres. BERNARDO MATTE LARRAÍN; Gen. Man. RENÉ LÉHUEDÉ FUENZALIDA; 9 brs.

Banco de Chile: Ahumada 251, Casilla 151-D, Santiago; tel. (2) 637-1111; fax (2) 637-3434; internet www.bancochile.cl; f. 1894; 42% owned by SAOS, SA; cap. 482,504m., res 82,619m., dep. 7,265,620m. (Dec. 2003); Chair. SEGISMUNDO SCHULIN-ZEUTHEN SERRANO; CEO PABLO GRANIFO LAVÍN; 243 brs.

Banco Conosur: Avda B. O'Higgins 1980, 7°, Santiago; tel. (2) 697-1491; fax (2) 696-3133; internet www.bancoconosur.cl; Pres. LIONEL OLAVARRÍA LEYTON; Vice-Pres. ADOLFO GARCÍA-HUIDOBRO OCHAGAVÍA.

Banco de Crédito e Inversiones (Bci): Huérfanos 1134, Casilla 136-D, Santiago; tel. (2) 692-7000; fax (2) 695-3775; e-mail webmaster@bci.cl; internet www.bci.cl; f. 1937; cap. and res 287,854m., dep. 4,126,771m. (Dec. 2003); Pres. LUIS ENRIQUE YARUR REY; Gen. Man. LIONEL OLAVARRÍA; 112 brs.

Banco del Desarrollo: Avda B. O'Higgins 949, 3°, Casilla 320-V, Casilla 1, Santiago; tel. (2) 674-5000; fax (2) 671-5547; e-mail bdd@ bandes.cl; internet www.bdd.cl; f. 1983; cap. 117,417m., res 209.6m., dep. 1,190,039m. (Dec. 2003); Chair. VICENTE CARUZ MIDDLETON; Gen. Man. HUGO TRIVELLI; 83 brs.

Banco Internacional: Moneda 818, Casilla 135-D, Santiago; tel. (2) 369-7000; fax (2) 369-7367; e-mail banco@binter.cl; internet www .bancointernacional.cl; f. 1944; cap. and res 14,489m., dep. 153,025m. (Dec. 2002); Pres. and Chair. ALEJANDRO L. FURMAN SIHMAN; Gen. Man. ALVARO ACHONDO GONZÁLEZ; 11 brs.

Banco Santander Chile: Bandera 140, 13°, Casilla 57-D, Santiago; tel. (2) 320-2000; fax (2) 320-8877; e-mail webmaster@santander.cl; internet www.santandersantiago.cl; f. 1926; cap. and res 810,420m., dep. 8,750,867m. (Dec. 2003); subsidiary of Banco de Santander (Spain); incorporated Banco Osorno y La Unión in 1996; Chair. MAURICIO LARRAÍN GARCES; CEO FERNANDO CAÑAS BERKOWITZ; 72 brs.

Banco Security: AApoquindo 3100, Las Condes, Santiago; tel. (2) 584-4000; fax (2) 270-4001; e-mail bancosecurity@security.cl; internet www.security.cl; f. 1981; fmrly Banco Urquijo de Chile; cap. and res 80,606m., dep. 970,284m. (Dec. 2003); Pres. and Chair. FRANCISCO SILVA S.; Gen. Man. RAMÓN ELUCHANS O.; 11 brs.

BBVA Banco BHIF: Huérfanos 1234, Casilla 517, Santiago; tel. (2) 679-1000; fax (2) 698-5640; e-mail bhif@bhif.cl; internet www.bhif.cl; f. 1883; was merged with Banco Nacional in 1989; acquired Banesto Chile Bank in Feb. 1995; controlling interest acquired by Banco Bilbao Vizcaya (Spain) in Sept. 1998; name changed as above in 1999; cap. and res 228,163m., dep. 1,349,303m. (May 2002); Pres. JOSÉ SAID SAFFIE; CEO RAMÓN MONELL V.; 78 brs.

Corpbanca: Huérfanos 1072, Casilla 80-D, Santiago; tel. (2) 687-8000; fax (2) 696-5763; e-mail ggeneral@corpbanca.cl; internet www .corpbanca.cl; f. 1871 as Banco de Concepción, current name adopted in 1997; cap. 270,002m., res 18,895m., dep. 2,144,606m. (Dec. 2003); Chair. CARLOS ABUMOHOR TOUMA; CEO CHRISTIAN SAMSING S.; 64 brs.

Dresdner Bank Lateinamerika AG: Huérfanos 1219, Casilla 10492, Santiago; tel. (2) 731-4444; fax (2) 671-3307; e-mail info@dbla .com; internet www.dbla.cl; f. 1958 as Banco Continental; bought by Crédit Lyonnais in Sept. 1987, subsequently by Dresdner BNP; current name adopted in 2002; cap. 20,131m., res 6,139m., dep. 149,107m. (Dec. 2003); Pres. EWALD DOERNER; Gen. Man. ROLAND JACOB; 4 brs.

Scotiabank Sud Americano: Morandé 226, Casilla 90-D, Santiago; tel. (2) 692-6000; fax (2) 698-6008; e-mail scotiabank@scotiabank.cl; internet www.scotiabank.cl; f. 1944; cap. 65,366m., res 32,433m., dep. 1,407,886m. (Dec. 2002); Chair. PETER C. CARDINAL; CEO LUIS FERNANDO TOBÓN; 49 brs.

Finance Corporations

Financiera Atlas, SA: Nueva de Lyon 72, 7°, Santiago; tel. (2) 233-3151; fax (2) 233-3152; Gen. Man. NEIL A. DENTON FEILMANN.

Banking Association

Asociación de Bancos e Instituciones Financieras de Chile AG: Ahumada 179, 12°, Santiago; tel. (2) 636-7100; fax (2) 698-8945; e-mail general@abif.cl; internet www.abif.cl; f. 1945; Pres. HERNÁN SOMERVILLE SENN; Gen. Man. ALEJANDRO ALARCÓN PÉREZ.

Other Financial Supervisory Bodies

Superintendencia de Administradoras de Fondos de Pensiones (SAFP) (Superintendency of Pension Funds): Huérfanos 1273, 9°, Casilla 3955, Santiago; tel. (2) 753-0100; fax (2) 753-0122; internet www.safp.cl; f. 1981; Supt GUILLERMO LARRAÍN RÍOS.

Superintendencia de Seguridad Social (Superintendency of Social Security): Huérfanos 1376, 5°, Santiago; tel. (2) 620-4500; fax (2) 696-4672; e-mail secgral@suseso.cl; internet www.suseso.gov.cl; f. 1927; Supt XIMENA C. RINCÓN GONZÁLEZ.

STOCK EXCHANGES

Bolsa de Comercio de Santiago: La Bolsa 64, Casilla 123-D, Santiago; tel. (2) 399-3000; fax (2) 318-1961; e-mail chathaway@bolsadesantiago.com; internet www.bolsadesantiago.com; f. 1893; 34 mems; Pres. PABLO YRARRÁZAVAL VALDÉS; Gen. Man. JOSÉ ANTONIO MARTÍNEZ ZUGARRAMURDI.

Bolsa de Corredores—Valores de Valparaíso: Prat 798, Casilla 218-V, Valparaíso; tel. (32) 25-0677; fax (32) 21-2764; e-mail bolsadec.orred001@chilnet.cl; internet www.bovalpo.com; f. 1905; Pres. CARLOS F. MARÍN ORREGO; Man. ARIE JOEL GELFENSTEIN FREUNDLICH.

Bolsa Electrónica de Chile: Huérfanos 770, 14°, Santiago; tel. (2) 639-4699; fax (2) 633-4174; e-mail info@bolchile.cl; internet www.bolchile.cl; Gen. Man. JUAN CARLOS SPENCER OSSA.

INSURANCE

In 2002 there were 55 general, life and reinsurance companies operating in Chile.

Supervisory Authority

Superintendencia de Valores y Seguros: Avda Libertador Bernardo O'Higgins 1449, Santiago 834-0518; tel. (2) 473-4000; fax (2) 473-4101; internet www.svs.cl; f. 1931; under Ministry of Finance; Supt ALEJANDRO FERREIRO YAZIGI.

Principal Companies

Aetna Chile Seguros de Vida, SA: Suecia 211, 7°, Santiago; tel. (2) 364-2000; fax (2) 364-2010; e-mail jdupre@aetna.cl; internet www.aetna.cl; f. 1981; life; Pres. SERGIO BAEZA VALDÉS; Gen. Man. FERNANDO HASENBERG NATOLI.

Aseguradora Magallanes, SA: Agustinas 1022, Of. 722; tel. (2) 365-4848; fax (2) 365-4860; e-mail fvarela@magallanes.cl; internet www.magallanes.cl; f. 1957; general; Pres. SERGIO LARRAÍN PRIETO; Gen. Man. FERNANDO VARELA.

Axa Seguros Generales, SA: Huérfanos 1189, 2°, 3° y 4°, Casilla 429-V, Santiago; tel. (2) 679-9200; fax (2) 679-9300; internet www.axa.cl; f. 1936; general; Gen. Man. BERNARDO SERRANO LÓPEZ.

Chilena Consolidada, SA: Pedro de Valdivia 195, Casilla 16587, Correo 9, Providencia, Santiago; tel. (2) 200-7000; fax (2) 274-9933; internet www.chilena.cl; f. 1853; owned by Zurich group; general and life; Gen. Man. IGNACIO BARRIGA UGARTE.

Chubb de Chile, SA: Gertrudis Echeñique 30, 4°, Santiago; tel. (2) 206-2191; fax (2) 206-2735; internet www.chubb.com/chile; f. 1992; general; Gen. Man. CLAUDIO M. ROSSI.

Cía de Seguros de Crédito Continental, SA: Avda Isidora Goyenechea 3162, 6°, Edif. Parque 1 Golf, Santiago; tel. (2) 636-4000; fax (2) 636-4001; e-mail comer@continental.cl; f. 1990; general; Gen. Man. FRANCISCO ARTIGAS CELIS.

Cía de Seguros Generales Aetna Chile, SA: Suecia 211, Santiago; tel. (2) 364-2000; fax (2) 364-2060; internet www.aetna.cl; f. 1899; general; Pres. SERGIO BAEZA VALDÉS; Gen. Man. MÁXIMO ERRÁZURIZ DE SOLMINIHAC.

Cía de Seguros Generales Consorcio Nacional de Seguros, SA: El Bosque Sur 130, Santiago; tel. (2) 230-4000; fax (2) 250-2525; f. 1992; general; Gen. Man. MARCOS BÜCHI BUC.

Cía de Seguros Generales Cruz del Sur, SA: Avda El Golf 150, Santiago; tel. (2) 461-8000; fax (2) 461-8715; internet www.cruzdelsur.cl; f. 1974; general; Pres. JOSÉ TOMÁS GUZMÁN DUMAS; Gen. Man. MIKEL URIARTE PLAZAOLA.

Cía de Seguros Generales Euroamérica, SA: Agustinas 1127, 2°, Casilla 180-D, Santiago; tel. (2) 672-7242; fax (2) 696-4086; internet www.euroamerica.cl; f. 1986; general; Gen. Man. PATRICIA JAIME VÉLIZ.

Cía de Seguros de Vida Consorcio Nacional de Seguros, SA: Avda El Bosque Sur 180, 3°, Casilla 232, Correo 35, Providencia, Santiago; tel. (2) 230-4000; fax (2) 230-4050; f. 1916; life; Pres. JUAN BILBAO HORMAECHE; Gen. Man. MARCOS BÜCHI BUC.

Cía de Seguros de Vida La Construcción, SA: Avda Providencia 1806, 11°–18°, Providencia, Santiago; tel. (2) 340-3000; fax (2) 340-3024; internet www.laconstruccion.sa.cl; f. 1985; life; Pres. VÍCTOR MANUEL JARPA RIVEROS; Gen. Man. MANUEL ZEGERS IRARRÁZAVAL.

Cía de Seguros de Vida Cruz del Sur, SA: El Golf 150, Santiago; tel. (2) 461-8000; fax (2) 461-8715; internet www.cruzdelsur.cl; f. 1992; life; Pres. ROBERTO ANGELINI; Gen. Man. MIKEL URIARTE PLAZAOLA.

Cía de Seguros de Vida Euroamérica, SA: Agustinas 1127, 3°, Casilla 21-D, Santiago; tel. (2) 782-7000; fax (2) 699-0732; e-mail deptoservicio@eurovida.cl; internet www.eurovida.cl; f. 1962; life; Pres. BENJAMIN DAVIS CLARKE; Gen. Man. PATRICIA JAIME VÉLIZ.

Cía de Seguros de Vida Santander, SA: Bandera 150, Santiago; tel. (2) 640-1177; fax (2) 640-1377; e-mail servicio@santanderseg.cl; internet www.netra.santanderseg.cl/index; f. 1989; life; Pres. FRANCISCO MARTÍN LÓPEZ-QUESADA.

ING, Seguros de Vida, SA: Avda Suecia 211, Providencia, Casilla 13224, Santiago; tel. (2) 252-1464; fax (2) 364-2060; internet www.ing.cl; f. 1989; life; Gen. Man. ÁLVARO JIMÉNEZ URRUTIA.

La Interamericana Compañía de Seguros de Vida: Agustinas 640, 9°, Casilla 111, Correo Central, Santiago; tel. (2) 630-3000; fax (2) 639-5859; internet www.interamericana.cl; f. 1980; life; Pres. RICARDO PERALTA VALENZUELA; Gen. Man. RICARDO GARCÍA HOLTZ.

Le Mans—ISE Compañia Seguros Generales, SA: Encomenderos 113, Casilla 185-D, Centro 192, Las Condes, Santiago; tel. (2) 422-9000; fax (2) 232-0471; e-mail lemans@lemans.cl; internet www.lemansise.cl; f. 1888; general; Pres. IGNACIO WALKER CONCHA; Gen. Man. MARC GARÇON.

Mapfre Garantías y Crédito, SA: Teatinos 280, 5°, Santiago; tel. (2) 870-1500; fax (2) 870-1501; internet www.mapfregc.cl; f. 1991; general; Gen. Man. RODRIGO CAMPERO PETERS.

Renta Nacional Compañía de Seguros de Vida, SA: Amunátegui 178, 2°, Santiago; tel. (2) 670-0200; fax (2) 670-0045; f. 1982; life; Gen. Man. GENARO LAYMUNS HEILMAIER.

Seguros Vida Security Previsión, SA: Hendaya 60, 7°, Las Condes, Santiago; tel. (2) 750-2300; fax (2) 750-2440; internet www.vidasecurity.cl; f. 2002 through merger of Seguros Security and Seguros Previsión Vida; Gen. Man. ALEJANDRO ALZÉRRECA LUNA.

Reinsurance

Caja Reaseguradora de Chile, SA: Apoquindo 4449, 8°, Santiago; tel. (2) 338-1200; fax (2) 206-4063; f. 1934; life; Pres. ANDRÉS JIMÉNES.

Insurance Association

Asociación de Aseguradores de Chile, AG: La Concepción 322, Of. 501, Providencia, Santiago; tel. (2) 236-2596; fax (2) 235-1502; e-mail seguros@aach.cl; internet www.aach.cl; f. 1931; Pres. MIKEL URIARTE PLAZAOLA; Gen. Man. JORGE CLAUDE BOURDEL.

Trade and Industry

GOVERNMENT AGENCIES

Comisión Nacional del Medio Ambiente (CONAMA): Obispo Donoso 6, Providencia, Santiago; tel. (2) 240-5600; fax (2) 244-1262; e-mail informaciones@conama.cl; internet www.conama.cl; f. 1994; environmental regulatory body; Exec. Dir GIANNI LÓPEZ RAMIREZ.

Corporación de Fomento de la Producción (CORFO): Moneda 921, Casilla 3886, Santiago; tel. (2) 631-8200; e-mail info@corfo.cl; internet www.corfo.cl; f. 1939; holding group of principal state enterprises; grants loans and guarantees to private sector; responsible for sale of non-strategic state enterprises; promotes entrepreneurship; CEO and Exec. Vice-Pres. OSCAR LANDERRETCHE GACITÚA; Gen. Man. BERNARDO ESPINOZA; 13 brs.

PROCHILE (Dirección General de Relaciones Económicas Internacionales): Alameda 1315, 2°, Casilla 14087, Correo 21, Santiago; tel. (2) 565-9000; fax (2) 696-0639; e-mail info@prochile.cl; internet www.prochile.cl; f. 1974; bureau of international economic affairs; Dir HUGO LAVADES M.

Servicio Nacional de Capacitación y Empleo (National Training and Employment Service): Teatinos 333, 8°, Santiago; tel. (2) 870-6222; fax (2) 696-7103; internet www.sence.cl; attached to Ministry of Labour and Social Security; Dir JOSSIÉ ESCÁRATE.

STATE CORPORATIONS

Corporación Nacional del Cobre de Chile (CODELCO-Chile): Huérfanos 1270, Casilla 150-D, Santiago; tel. (2) 690-3000; fax (2) 690-3059; e-mail comunica@stgo.codelco.cl; internet www.codelcochile.com; f. 1976 as a state-owned enterprise with copper-producing operational divisions at Chuquicamata, Radomiro Tomić, Salvador, Andina, Salvador, Talleres Rancagua and El Teniente; attached to Ministry of Mining; Pres. JORGE RODRÍGUEZ GROSSI; Exec. Pres. JUAN VILLARZÚ RHODE; 18,496 employees.

Empresa Nacional de Petróleo (ENAP): Vitacura 2736, 10°, Las Condes, Santiago; tel. (2) 280-3000; fax (2) 280-3199; e-mail webenap@enap.cl; internet www.enap.cl; f. 1950; state-owned petroleum and gas exploration and production corporation; Pres. ALFONSO DULANTO RENCORET; Gen. Man. ENRIQUE DÁVILA ALVEAL; 3,286 employees.

DEVELOPMENT ORGANIZATIONS

Comisión Chilena de Energía Nuclear: Amunátegui 95, Casilla 188-D, Santiago; tel. (2) 699-0070; fax (2) 699-1618; e-mail lvillanu@CCHEN.cl; internet www.cchen.cl; f. 1965; government body to develop peaceful uses of atomic energy; concentrates, regulates and controls all matters related to nuclear energy; Pres. Dr ROBERTO HOJMAN G.; Exec. Dir LORETO VILLANUEVA Z.

Corporación Nacional de Desarrollo Indígena (Conadi): Aldunate 620, 8°, Temuco, Chile; tel. (45) 641-500; fax (45) 641-520; e-mail ctranamil@conadi.gov.cl; internet www.conadi.cl; promotes the economic and social development of indigenous communities.

Corporación Nacional Forestal (CONAF): Región Metropolitana, Valenzuela Castillo 1868, Santiago; tel. (2) 225-0428; fax (2) 225-00641; e-mail consulta@conaf.cl; internet www.conaf.cl; f. 1970 to promote forestry activities, to enforce forestry law, to promote afforestation, to administer subsidies for afforestation projects and to increase and preserve forest resources; manages 13.97m. ha designated as National Parks, Natural Monuments and National Reserves; under Ministry of Agriculture; Exec. Dir Ing. CARLOS WEBER BONTE.

Empresa Nacional de Minería (ENAMI): MacIver 459, 2°, Casilla 100-D, Santiago; tel. (2) 637-5278; fax (2) 637-5452; e-mail webmaster@enami.cl; internet www.enami.cl; promotes the development of small and medium-sized mines; attached to Ministry of Mining; partially privatized; Exec. Vice-Pres. JAIME PÉREZ DE ARCE ARAYA.

CHAMBERS OF COMMERCE

There are chambers of commerce in all major towns.

Cámara de Comercio de Santiago de Chile, AG: Edif. Del Comercio, Monjitas 392, Santiago; tel. (2) 360-7000; fax (2) 633-3595; e-mail cpn@ccs.cl; internet www.ccs.cl; f. 1919; 1,300 mems; Pres. ESTEBAN ALBANO; Man. CLAUDIO ORTIZ TELLO.

Cámara de la Producción y del Comercio de Concepción: Cauplicán 567, 2°, Concepción; tel. (41) 241-121; fax (41) 227-903; e-mail lmandiola@cpcc.cl; internet www.cpcc.cl; Pres. PEDRO SCHLACK HARNECKER; First Vice-Pres. GUSTAVO VALENZUELA G.; Gen. Man. LEONCIO TORO ARAYA.

Cámara Nacional de Comercio, Servicios y Turismo de Chile: Merced 230, Santiago; tel. (2) 365-4000; fax (2) 365-4001; internet www.cnc.cl; f. 1858; Pres. PEDRO CORONA BOZZO; Vice-Pres. HÉCTOR VALENCIA BRINGAS; 120 mems.

Cámara de Comercio de Antofagasta: Latorre 2580, Dpto 21, Antofagasta; tel. (55) 225-125; fax (55) 222-053; e-mail info@comercioantofagasta.cl; internet www.comercioantofagasta.cl; f. 1924; Man. JORGE MOZÓ GREZ.

Cámara de Comercio, Servicios y Turismo de Temuco, A.G.: Vicuña Mackenna 396, Temuco; tel. (45) 210-556; fax (45) 237-047; internet www.camaratemuco.cl; Pres. HANS KÜHN BEISSER; Vice-Pres. MAX HENZI IBARRA.

INDUSTRIAL AND TRADE ASSOCIATIONS

Servicio Agrícola y Ganadero (SAG): Avda Bulnes 140, Santiago; tel. (2) 345-1100; fax (2) 345-1102; e-mail dirnac@sag.gob.cl; internet www.sag.cl; under Ministry of Agriculture; responsible for the protection and development of safe practice in the sector; Nat. Dir DIONISIO FAULBAUM.

Servicio Nacional de Pesca (SERNAPESCA): Victoria 2832, Valparaíso; tel. (32) 81-9100; fax (32) 25-6311; e-mail informaciones@sernapesca.cl; internet www.sernapesca.cl; f. 1978; government regulator of the fishing industry.

Sociedad Agrícola y Servicios Isla de Pascua (SASIPA): Alfredo Lecannelier 1940, Providencia, Santiago; tel. (2) 232-7497; fax (2) 232-7497; administers agriculture and public services on Easter Island; Gen. Man. GERARDO VELASCO.

EMPLOYERS' ORGANIZATIONS

Confederación de la Producción y del Comercio: Monseñor Sótero Sanz 182, Providencia, Santiago; tel. (2) 231-9764; fax (2) 231-9808; e-mail procomer@entelchile.net; internet www.cpc.cl; f. 1936; Pres. HERNÁN GUILLERMO SOMERVILLE SENN.

Affiliated organizations:

Asociación de Bancos e Instituciones Financieras de Chile AG: see Finance (Banking Association).

Cámara Nacional de Comercio, Servicios y Turismo: see above.

Cámara Chilena de la Construcción: Marchant Pereira 10, 3°, Providencia, Código Postal 6640721, Santiago; tel. (2) 376-3300; fax (2) 371-3430; internet www.camaraconstruccion.cl; f. 1951; Pres. OTTO KUNZ SOMMER; Vice-Pres. JUAN MACKENNA IÑIGUEZ; 17,442 mems.

Sociedad de Fomento Fabril, FG (SOFOFA): Avda Andrés Bello 2777, 3°, Las Condes, Santiago; tel. (2) 391-3100; fax (2) 391-3200; internet www.sofofa.cl; f. 1883; largest employers' organization; Pres. JUAN CLARO; Sec.-Gen. ANDRÉS CONCHA; 2,500 mems.

Sociedad Nacional de Agricultura—Federación Gremial (SNA): Tenderini 187, 2°, CP 6500978, Santiago; tel. (2) 639-6710; fax (2) 633-7771; e-mail info@sna.cl; internet www.sna.cl; f. 1838; landowners' association; controls Radio Stations CB 57 and XQB8 (FM) in Santiago, CB-97 in Valparaíso, CD-120 in Los Angeles, CA-144 in La Serena, CD-127 in Temuco; Pres. ANDRÉS SANTA CRUZ; Dir JUAN MIGUEL OVALLE.

Sociedad Nacional de Minería (SONAMI): Avda Apoquindo 3000, 5°, Santiago; tel. (2) 335-9300; fax (2) 334-9700; e-mail monica.cavallini@sonami.cl; internet www.sonami.cl; f. 1883; Pres. ALFREDO OVALLE RODRÍGUEZ; Gen. Man. JAIME ALÉ YARAD; 48 mem. cos.

Confederación de Asociaciones Gremiales y Federaciones de Agricultores de Chile: Lautaro 218, Los Angeles; regd 1981; Pres. DOMINGO DURÁN NEUMANN; Gen. Sec. ADOLFO LARRAÍN V.

Confederación del Comercio Detallista y Turismo de Chile, AG: Merced 380, 8°, Of. 74, Santiago; tel. (2) 639-1264; fax (2) 638-0338; e-mail comerciodetallista@confedech.cl; internet www.comerciodetallista.cl; f. 1938; retail trade; Nat. Pres. RAFAEL CUMSILLE ZAPAPA; Sec.-Gen. ROBERTO ZUÑIGA BELAUZARÁN.

Confederación Gremial Nacional Unida de la Mediana y Pequeña Industria, Servicios y Artesanado (CONUPIA): General Parra 703, Providencia, Santiago; tel. (2) 235-8022; internet www.conupia.cl; e-mail gerencia@conupia.cl; small and medium-sized industries and crafts; Pres. GERMÁN DASTRES GONZÁLEZ; Vice-Pres. CHAQUIB SUFÁN AIDAR; Sec.-Gen. MARIO PONCE DÍAZ.

There are many federations of private industrialists, organized by industry and region.

UTILITIES

Comisión Nacional de Energía: Teatinos 120, 7°, Clasificador 14, Correo 21, Santiago; tel. (2) 460-6800; fax (2) 365-6800; e-mail energia@cne.cl; internet www.cne.cl; Minister-Pres. JORGE RODRÍGUEZ GROSSI; Exec. Sec. LUIS SÁNCHEZ CASTELLÓN.

Superintendencia de Electricidad y Combustibles (SEC): Amunátegui 58, Santiago; internet www.sec.cl; Supt SERGIO ESPEJO YAKSIC; Gen. Sec. MARTA CABEZA VARGAS.

General

Colbún, SA: Avda 11 de Septiembre 2355; tel. (2) 460-4000; fax (2) 460-4005; e-mail contacto@colbun.cl; internet www.colbun.cl; f. 1986; hydroelectricity producer; fmrly state-owned, acquired by Tracebel SA of Belgium; Pres. EMILIO PELLEGRINI RIPAMONTI; CEO FRANCISCO J. COURBIS GREZ; 226 employees.

Electricity

The four national power grids are SING (operated by CODELCO and EDELNOR), SIC, Aysén and Magallanes.

AES Gener, SA: Mariano Sánchez Fontecilla 310, 3°, Santiago; tel. (2) 686-8900; fax (2) 686-8991; e-mail gener@gener.cl; internet www.gener.cl; f. 1981 as Chilectra Generación, SA, following the restructuring of Compañía Chilena de Electricidad, SA; privatized in 1988 and Chilgener, SA, adopted in 1989; current name adopted in 1998; owned by AES Corpn (USA); responsible for operation of power plants Renca, Ventanas, Laguna Verde, El Indio, Altalfal, Maitenes, Queltehues and Volcán; total output 10,169.0 GWh (Dec. 2002); also operates subsidiaries in Argentina and Colombia; Pres. JOSEPH BRANDT; Gen. Man. FELIPE CERÓN; 1,121 employees (group).

Empresa Eléctrica Guacolda, SA: Miraflores 222, 16°, Santiago; tel. (2) 362-4000; fax (2) 360-1675; internet www.guacolda.cl; operates a thermoelectric power-station in Huasco; installed capacity of 304 MW; Gen. Man. JOSÉ FLORENCIO GUZMÁN.

Empresa Eléctrica Santiago: Jorge Hirmas 2964, Renca, Santiago; tel. (2) 680-4760; fax (2) 680-4743; operates the Nueva Renca thermoelectric plant in Santiago; installed capacity of 379 MW; Gen. Man. HÉCTOR ROJAS.

Energía Verde: O'Higgins 940, Of. 90, Concepción; tel. (43) 431-363; fax (43) 431-357; operates two co-generation power-stations at Constitución and Laja and a steam plant at Nacimiento; supplies the Cabrero industrial plant; CEO JAIME ZUAZAGOITÍA.

Norgener, SA: Jorge Hirmas 2964, Renca, Santiago; tel. (2) 680-4870; fax (2) 680-4895; northern subsidiary supplying the mining industry; operates power plants with installed capacity of 276 MW; Gen. Man. CARLOS AGUIRRE.

Arauco Generación: Vitacura 2771, 9°, Las Condes, Santiago; tel. (2) 560-6700; fax (2) 236-5090; e-mail gic@arauco.cl; f. 1994 to commercialize surplus power from pulp processing facility; Pres. CARLOS CROXATTO S.; Gen. Man. HERNÁN ARRIAGADA.

BMV Industrias Eléctricas: Avda Vicuña Mackenna 1540, Ñuñoa, Santiago; tel. (2) 555-8806; fax (2) 555-8807; e-mail bmv@bmv.cl; internet www.bmv.cl; Gen. Man. ANGÉLICA PADOVANI.

Chilquinta Energía, SA: General Cruz 222, Valparaíso; tel. (32) 502-000; fax (32) 231-171; e-mail contactoweb@chiquinta.cl; internet www.chilquinta.cl; f. 1995; owned by Sempra and PSEG of the USA; Pres. HÉCTOR MADARIAGA; Gen. Man. CRISTIÁN ARNOLDS.

Compañía Eléctrica del Litoral, SA: San Sebastián 2952, Of. 202, Las Condes, Santiago; tel. (2) 481-195; fax (2) 483-313; internet www.litoral.cl; e-mail fmartine@litoral.cl; f. 1949; Gen. Man. MARCELO LUENGO.

Compañía General de Electricidad, SA (CGE): Teatinos 280, Santiago; tel. (2) 624-3243; fax (2) 680-7104; e-mail cge@cge.cl; internet www.cge.cl; installed capacity of 662 MW; Pres. GABRIEL DEL REAL; Gen. Man. GUILLERMO MATTA FUENZALIDA.

Empresa Eléctrica Emec, SA: Los Talleres 1831, Barrio Industrial, Coquimbo; tel. (51) 20-1000; fax (51) 20-1188; internet www.emec.cl; e-mail info@emec.cl; f. 1980; Pres. JOSÉ HORNAUER LÓPEZ; Gen. Man. SERGI JORDANA DE BUEN.

Empresa Eléctrica de Aysén, SA: Francisco Bilbao 412, Casilla 280, Coyhaique; tel. (67) 23-3105; e-mail ggral@entelchile.net; f. 1983; Gen. Man. JORGE ILLANES SENN.

Empresa Eléctrica de Magallanes, SA (Edelmag, SA): Croacia 444, Punta Arenas; tel. (71) 40-00; fax (71) 40-77; e-mail edelmag@edelmag.cl; internet www.edelmag.cl; f. 1981; Pres. JORGE JORDAN FRANULIC; Gen. Man. CARLOS YÁÑEZ ANTONUCCI; 111 employees.

Empresa Eléctrica del Norte Grande (EDELNOR): Avda Apoquindo 3721, Santiago; tel. (2) 353-3200; fax (2) 206-2154; f. 1981; acquired by Codelco and Tractebel of Belgium in Dec. 2002; Gen. Man. JUAN CLAVERÍA A.; 365 employees.

Empresas Emel, SA: Avda Libertador Bernardo O'Higgins 886, Central Post Office, 5° y 6°, Santiago; tel. (2) 376-6500; fax (2) 633-3849; holding co for the Emel group of electricity cos, owned by PPL Corpn of the USA; output in 2000 totalled 18,6124 MWh; CEO ALFONSO G. TORO; Emel group comprises:

ELECDA (Empresa Eléctrica de Antofagasta, SA): José Miguel Carrera 1587, Antofagasta 1250; tel. (55) 649-100; Dir EDUARDO ARTURO APABLAZA DAU.

ELIQSA (Empresa Eléctrica de Iquique, SA): Zegeres 469, Iquique; tel. (57) 40-5400; fax (57) 42-7181; e-mail eliqsa@eliqsa.cl; CEO AQUILES IVAN MELÉNDEZ VARGAS.

EMELAT (Empresa Eléctrica Atacama, SA): Circunvalación Ignacio Carrera Pinto 51, Copiapó; tel. (52) 205-100; fax (52) 205-103; f. 1981; distribution company; Pres. MICHAEL FRIEDLANDER; Gen. Man. EDUARDO ARTURO APABLAZA DAU.

EMELARI (Empresa Eléctrica de Arica, SA): Baquedano 731, Arica; tel. (58) 201-100; fax (58) 23-1105; Dir JOHN FOGARTY.

ENERSIS, SA: Avda Kennedy 5454, Casilla 1557, Vitacura, Santiago; tel. (2) 353-4400; fax (2) 378-4768; e-mail comunicacion@e

.enersis.cl; internet www.enersis.com; f. 1981; holding co for Spanish group generating and distributing electricity through its subsidiaries throughout South America; 60.62% owned by Endesa S.A.; Gen. Man. MARIO VALCARCE; 10,957 employees.

Chilectra, SA: Santo Domingo 789, Casilla 1557, Santiago; tel. (2) 632-2000; fax (2) 639-3280; e-mail rrpp@chilectra.cl; internet www.chilectra.cl; f. 1921; transmission and distribution arm of ENERSIS (see above); supplies distribution cos, including the Empresa Eléctrica Municipal de Lo Barnechea, Empresa Municipal de Til-Til, and the Empresa Eléctrica de Colina, SA; holds overseas distribution concessions in Argentina, Peru and Brazil; acquired by ENERSIS of Spain in 1999; Pres. JORGE ROSENBLUT; Gen. Man. JULIO VALENZUELA.

Empresa Eléctrica Pehuenche, SA (EEP): Santa Rosa 76, 14°, Santiago; tel. (2) 630-9000; fax (2) 696-5568; f. 1986; part of ENERSIS group; Gen. Man. LUCIO CASTRO MÁRQUEZ.

Empresa Nacional de Electricidad, SA (ENDESA): Santa Rosa 76, Casilla 1392, Santiago; tel. (2) 630-9000; fax (2) 635-4720; e-mail comunicacion@endesa.cl; internet www.endesa.cl; f. 1943; installed capacity 4,035 MW (Feb. 2002); ENERSIS obtained majority control of ENDESA Chile in April 1999; Pres. LUIS RIVERA NOVO; Gen. Man. HECTOR LÓPEZ VILASECO.

SAESA (Sociedad Austral de Electricidad, SA): Manuel Bulnes 441, Osorno; tel. (64) 20-6200; fax (64) 20-6209; e-mail saesa@saesa.cl; internet www.saesa.cl; owned by PSEG Corpn of the USA; Gen. Man. JORGE BRAHM BARRIL.

Gas

Abastecedora de Combustible (Abastible, SA): Avda Vicuña Mackenna 55, Providencia, Santiago; tel. (2) 693-0000; fax (2) 693-9304; internet www.abastible.cl; owned by COPEC; Pres. FELIPE LAMARCA CLARO; Gen. Man. JOSÉ ODONE.

AGA Chile, SA: Juan Bautista Pistene 2344, Santiago; tel. (2) 907-6888; f. 1920; natural and industrial gases utility; owned by Linde Gas Corpn of Germany.

Compañía de Consumidores de Gas de Santiago (GASCO, SA): 1061 Santo Domingo, Casilla 8-D, Santiago; tel. (2) 694-4444; fax (2) 694-4370; e-mail info@gasco.cl; internet www.gasco.cl; natural gas utility; supplies Santiago and Punta Arenas regions; owned by CGE; Pres. MATÍAS PÉREZ CRUZ; Gen. Man. JOSÉ LUIS HORNAUER HERRMANN.

Electrogas: Evaristo Lillo 78, Of. 41, Las Condes, Santiago; tel. (2) 377-1458; fax (2) 233-4931; owned by ENDESA (q.v.); Gen. Man. CARLOS ANDREANI.

Gas Valpo: Camino Internacional 1420, Viña del Mar; tel. (32) 27-7000; fax (32) 21-3092; e-mail info@gasvalpo.cl; internet www.gasvalpo.cl; f. 1853; owned by AGL of Australia.

GasAndes: Avda. Isidora Goyenechea 3600, Las Condes, Santiago Santiago; tel. (2) 362-4200; distributes gas transported from the Argentine province of Mendoza via a 463-km pipeline.

GasAtacama: natural-gas producer and transporter; CEO RUDOLF ARANEDA.

Lipigas: Las Urbinas 53, 13°, Of.131, Providencia, Santiago; tel. (32) 656-500; fax (32) 656-595; e-mail info@lipigas.cl; internet www.lipigas.cl; Pres. JAIME SANTA CRUZ; Gen. Man. MARIO FERNÁNDEZ.

Agrogas: Lo Ovalle 1321, Santiago; tel. (2) 511-0904; owned by Empresas Lipigas, SA; supplier of liquid gas.

Industrias Codigas: Las Urbinas 53, 9°, Providencia, Santiago; tel. (2) 520-4700; fax (2) 520-4733; e-mail info@codigas.cl; internet www.codigas.cl; f. 1959; owned by Empresas Lipigas, SA; Pres. HUGO YACONI MERINO; Gen. Man. JOSÉ LUIS MEIER.

Metrogas: El Bosque Norte 0177, 11°, Las Condes, Santiago; tel. (2) 337-8000; fax (2) 337-8173; internet www.metrogas.cl; natural gas utility; owned by GASCO and COPEC; Pres. MATÍAS PÉREZ CRUZ; Gen. Man. EDUARDO MORANDÉ.

Water

Aguas Andinas, SA: Avda Presidente Balmaceda 1398, Santiago; tel. (2) 688-1000; fax (2) 698-5871; e-mail info@aguasandinas.cl; internet www.aguasandinas.cl; water supply and sanitation services to Santiago and the surrounding area; sold to a French-Spanish consortium in June 1999; Gen. Man. ANGEL SIMÓN GRIMALDOS.

Empresa de Obras Sanitarias de Valparaíso, SA (Esval): Cochrane 751, Valparaíso; tel. (32) 209-000; fax (32) 209-502; e-mail infoesval@entelchile.net; internet www.esval.cl; f. 1989; sanitation and irrigation co serving Valparaíso; Chair. EDMUNDO DUPRÉ ECHEVERRÍA; Gen. Man. GUSTAVO GONZÁLEZ DOORMAN; 377 employees.

Sigsig Ltda (Tecnagent): Presidente Errázuriz 3262, Casilla 7550295, Las Condes, Santiago; tel. (2) 335-2001; fax (2) 334-8466;

e-mail tecnagent@tecnagent.cl; internet www.tecnagent.cl; Pres. RAÚL SIGREN BINDHOFF; Gen. Man. RAÚL A. SIGREN ORFILA.

TRADE UNIONS

There are more than 50 national labour federations and unions.

Union Confederations

There are 37 union confederations, of which the following are among the most important:

Agrupación Nacional de Empleados Fiscales (ANEF): Edif. Tucapel Jiménez, Alameda 1603, Santiago; tel. (2) 696-2957; fax 699-3806; internet www.anef.cl; f. 1943; affiliated to CUT; public-service workers; Pres. RAÚL DE LA PUENTE PEÑA; Sec.-Gen. JEANETTE SOTO FUENTES.

Confederación Bancaria: Santiago; tel. (2) 699-5597; affiliated to CUT; Pres. DIEGO OLIVARES ARAVENA; Sec.-Gen. RAÚL REQUENA MARTÍNEZ.

Confederación de Empleados Particulares de Chile (CEPCH): Santiago; tel. (2) 72-2093; trade union for workers in private sector; affiliated to CUT; Pres. ANGÉLICA CARVALLO PRENAFETA; Sec.-Gen. ANDRÉS BUSTOS GONZÁLEZ.

Confederación General de Trabajadores del Transporte Terrestre (CGTT): Almirante Latorre 355, 2°, Of. 3, Santiago; tel. and fax (2) 695-9551; affiliated to CUT; road transport workers; Pres. ULISES MARTÍNEZ SEPÚLVEDA; Sec.-Gen. RODOLFO DOSSETTO UGALDE.

Confederación Nacional Campesina: Gorbea 1769, Santiago; tel. and fax (2) 695-2017; affiliated to CUT; Pres. EUGENIO LEÓN GAJARDO; Sec.-Gen. RENÉ ASTUDILLO R.

Confederación Nacional de Federaciones y Sindicatos de Empresas e Interempresas de Trabajadores del Transporte Terrestre y Afines (CONATRACH): Concha y Toro 2A, 2°, Santiago; tel. and fax (2) 698-0810; Pres. PEDRO MONSALVE FUENTES; Sec.-Gen. PEDRO JARA ESPINOZA.

Confederación Nacional de Federaciones y Sindicatos de Trabajadores Textiles y Ramos Similares (CONTEXTIL): Nataniel Cox 152 B, 1°, Santiago; tel. and fax (2) 696-8098; affiliated to CUT; Pres. PATRICIA C. CARRILLO; Sec.-Gen. MARÍA FELISA GARAY ASTUDILLO.

Confederación Nacional de Gente de Mar, Marítimos, Portuarios y Pesqueros (CONGEMAR): Tomás Ramos 158–172, Valparaíso; tel. (32) 255-430; fax (32) 257-580; affiliated to CUT; Pres. WALTER ASTORGA LOBOS; Sec.-Gen. JUAN GUZMÁN CARRASCO.

Confederación Nacional de Sindicatos Agrícolas—Unidad Obrero Campesina (UOC): Eleuterio Ramírez 1463, Santiago; tel. and fax (2) 696-6342; e-mail confe.uocchile@uocchile.cl; affiliated to CUT; Pres. SEGUNDO JUAN CORVALÁN HUERTA; Sec.-Gen. PEDRO REYES BAHAMONDEZ.

Confederación Nacional de Sindicatos de Trabajadores de la Construcción, Maderas, Materiales de Edificación y Actividades Conexas: Almirante Hurtado 2069, Santiago; tel. (2) 695-3908; fax (2) 696-4536; affiliated to CUT; Pres. MIGUEL ANGEL SOLÍS VIERA; Sec.-Gen. ADRIAN FUENTES HERMOSILLA.

Confederación Nacional de Sindicatos y Federaciones de Trabajadores Metalúrgicos (CONSTRAMET): Avda Francia 1317, Independencia, Santiago; tel. (2) 737-6875; fax (2) 443-0039; e-mail contrame@mailnet.rdc.cl; affiliated to CUT; Pres. MIGUEL SOTO ROA; Sec.-Gen. MIGUEL CHÁVEZ SOAZO.

Confederación Nacional de Suplementeros de Chile (CONASUCH): Tucapel Jiménez 26, Santiago; tel. (2) 695-7639; fax (2) 699-1646; f. 1942; Pres. IVAN ENCINA CARO; Sec. JOSÉ CANALES ORTIZ.

Confederación Nacional de Trabajadores de la Alimentación y Afines (CONTALCH): Liszt 3082, San Joaquín, Santiago; tel. and fax (2) 553-2193; affiliated to CUT; Pres. CIJIFREDO VERA VERA.

Confederación Nacional de Trabajadores de la Industria del Pan (CONAPAN): Tucapel Jiménez 32, 2°, Santiago; tel. and fax (2) 672-1622; affiliated to CUT; Pres. LUIS ALEGRÍA ALEGRÍA; Sec. LUIS PALACIOS CAMPOS.

Confederación Nacional de Trabajadores de la Industria Textil (CONTEVECH): Agustinas 2349, Santiago; tel. (2) 699-3442; fax (2) 687-3269; affiliated to CUT; Pres. MIGUEL VEGA FUENTES; Sec.-Gen. OSCAR CÁCERES YÁNEZ.

Confederación Nacional de Trabajadores del Comercio (CONATRADECO): Santiago; tel. and fax (2) 638-6718; Pres. EDMUNDO LILLO ARAVENA; Sec.-Gen. FEDERICO MUJICA CANALES.

Confederación Nacional de Trabajadores del Comercio (CONSFECOVE): Monjitas 454, Of. 606, Santiago; tel. (2) 632-2950; fax (2) 632-2884; affiliated to CUT; Pres. CLAUDIO ARAVENA ALVAREZ; Sec.-Gen. SUSANA ROSAS VALDEBENITO.

Confederación Nacional de Trabajadores del Cuero y Calzado (FONACC): Arturo Prat 1490, Santiago; tel. (2) 556-9602;

affiliated to CUT; Pres. MANUEL JIMÉNEZ TORRES; Sec.-Gen. VÍCTOR LABBÉ SILVA.

Confederación Nacional de Trabajadores Electrometalúrgicos, Mineros y Automotrices de Chile (CONSFETEMA): Vicuña Mackenna 3101, San Joaquín, Santiago; tel. (2) 238-1732; fax (2) 553-6494; e-mail consfetema@123mail.cl; Pres. LUIS SEPÚLVEDA DEL RÍO.

Confederación Nacional de Trabajadores Forestales (CTF): Rengo 884, Casilla 2717, Concepción; tel. and fax (41) 220-0407; Pres. JORGE GONZÁLEZ CASTILLO; Sec.-Gen. GUSTAVO CARRASO SALAZAR.

Confederación Nacional de Trabajadores Molineros: Bascuñan Guerrero 1739, Casilla 703, Correo 21, Santiago; tel. and fax (2) 683-8882; Pres. JOSÉ VÁSQUEZ ALIAGA.

Confederación Nacional Minera: Príncipe de Gales 88, Casilla 10361, Correo Central, Santiago; tel. and fax (2) 696-6945; Pres. MOISÉS LABRAÑA MENA; Sec.-Gen. JOSÉ CARRILLO BERMEDO.

Confederación Nacional Sindical Campesina y del Agro 'El Surco': Chacabuco 625, Santiago; tel. and fax (2) 681-1032; e-mail asurco@entelchile.net; affiliated to CUT; Pres. FERNANDO VALÁSQUEZ SERRANO; Sec.-Gen. SERGIO DÍAZ TAPIA.

There are also 45 union federations and over 100 individual unions.

Transport

RAILWAYS

State Railways

Empresa de los Ferrocarriles del Estado: Avda B. O'Higgins 3170, Santiago; tel. (2) 376-8500; fax (2) 776-2609; e-mail contacto@efe.cl; internet www.efe.cl; f. 1851; 3,977 km of track (2000); the State Railways are divided between the Ferrocarril Arica–La Paz, La Calera Puerto Montt, and Metro Regional de Valparaíso (passenger service only); several lines scheduled for privatization; Pres. LUIS AJENJO ISASI; Gen. Man. EDUARDO CASTILLO AGUIRRE.

Parastatal Railways

Ferrocarril del Pacífico, SA (FEPASA): Málaga 120, 5°, Las Condes, Santiago; tel. (2) 412-1000; fax (2) 412-1040; e-mail oguevara@fepasa.cl; internet www.fepasa.cl; f. 1993; privatized freight services; Pres. RAMÓN ABOITIZ MUSATADI; Vice-Pres. JUAN EDUARDO ERRÁZURIZ OSSA; Gen. Man. GAMALIEL VILLALOBOS ARANDA.

Metro de Santiago: Empresa de Transporte de Pasajeros Metro, SA, Avda B. O'Higgins 1414, Santiago; tel. (2) 250-3000; fax (2) 699-2475; internet www.metrosantiago.cl; started operations 1975; 40.2 km (2003); 3 lines; Pres. FERNANDO BUSTAMENTE HUENTA; Gen. Man. R. AZÓCAR HIDALGO.

Private Railways

Empresa de Transporte Ferroviario, SA (Ferronor): Huérfanos 587, Ofs 301 y 302, Santiago; tel. (2) 638-0430; e-mail ferronor@ferronor.cl; internet www.ferronor.cl; 2,300 km of track (2002); established as a public/private concern, following the transfer of the Ferrocarril Regional del Norte de Chile to the then Ministry of Production Development (CORFO) as a *Sociedad Anónima* in 1989; operates cargo services only; Commercial Man. PABLO ARRANZ; Pres. ROBERTO PIRAZZOLI.

Ferrocarril Codelco-Chile: Barquito, Region III, Atacama; tel. (52) 48-8521; fax (52) 48-8522; Gen. Man. B. BEHN THEUNE.

Diego de Almagro a Potrerillos: transport of forest products, minerals and manufactures; 99 km.

Ferrocarril Rancagua–Teniente: transport of forest products, livestock, minerals and manufactures; 68 km.

Ferrocarril de Antofagasta a Bolivia (FCAB): Bolívar 255, Casillas ST, Antofagasta; tel. (55) 20-6700; fax (55) 20-6220; e-mail webmaster@fcab.cl; internet www.fcab.cl; f. 1888; owned by Luksic conglomerate (Quiñenco); operates an international railway to Bolivia and Argentina; cargo forwarding services; total track length 934 km; Chair. ANDRÓNICO LUKSIC ABAROA; Gen. Man. M. V. SEPÚLVEDA.

Ferrocarril Tocopilla–Toco: Calle Arturo Prat 1060, Casilla 2098, Tocopilla; tel. (55) 81-2139; fax (55) 81-2650; owned by Sociedad Química y Minera de Chile, SA; 117 km (1995); Gen. Man. SEGISFREDO HURTADO GUERRERO.

Association

Asociación Chilena de Conservación de Patrimonio Ferroviario (ACCPF—Chilean Railway Society): Concha y Toro 10, Barrio Brasil, Santiago; tel. (2) 699-4607; fax (2) 280-0252; e-mail rsandoval@ucinf.cl; internet www.accpf.cl; Pres. CARLOS ROA VAL-ANZUELA; Vice-Pres. SERGIO GONZÁLEZ RODRÍGUEZ.

ROADS

The total length of roads in Chile in 2001 was an estimated 79,604 km, of which some 6,279 km were highways and some 16,409 km were secondary roads. The road system includes the entirely paved Pan-American Highway, extending 3,455 km from north to south. Toll gates exist on major motorways. The 1,200-km Carretera Austral (Southern Highway), linking Puerto Montt and Puerto Yungay, was completed in 1996, at an estimated total cost of US $200m.

SHIPPING

As a consequence of Chile's difficult topography, maritime transport is of particular importance. In 1997 90% of the country's foreign trade was carried by sea (51m. metric tons). The principal ports are Valparaíso, Talcahuano, Antofagasta, San Antonio, Arica, Iquique, Coquimbo, San Vicente, Puerto Montt and Punta Arenas. Most port operations were privatized in the late 1990s.

Chile's merchant fleet amounted to 963,966 grt (comprising 532 vessels) at December 2003.

Supervisory Authorities

Asociación Nacional de Armadores: Blanco 869, 3°, Valparaíso; tel. (32) 21-2057; fax (32) 21-2017; e-mail armadore@entelchile.net; f. 1931; shipowners' association; Pres. ERICH STRELOW CASTILLO; Gen. Man. ARTURO SIERRA MERINO.

Cámara Marítima y Portuaria de Chile, AG: Blanco 869, 3°, Valparaíso; tel. (32) 25-3443; fax (32) 25-0231; e-mail camport@entelchile.net; Pres. BELTRÁN SAÉZ M.; Vice-Pres. RODOLFO GARCÍA SÁNCHEZ.

Dirección General de Territorio Marítimo y Marina Mercante: Errázuriz 537, 4°, Valparaíso; tel. (32) 20-8000; fax (32) 25-2539; e-mail webmaster@directemar.cl; internet www.directemar.cl; maritime admin. of the coast and national waters, control of the merchant navy; ship registry; Dir Rear Adm. FERNANDO LAZCANO.

Cargo Handling Companies

Empresa Portuaria Antofagasta: Grecia s/n, Antofagasta; tel. (55) 25-1737; fax (55) 22-3171; e-mail epa@puertoantofagasta.cl; internet www.puertoantofagasta.cl; Pres. BLAS ENRIQUE ESPINOZA SEPÚLVEDA; Gen. Man. ALVARO FERNÁNDEZ SLATER.

Empresa Portuaria Arica: Máximo Lira 389, Arica; tel. (58) 25-5078; fax (58) 23-2284; e-mail puertoarica@puertoarica.cl; internet www.puertoarica.cl; Pres. CARLOS EDUARDO MENA KEYMER; Gen. Man. PATRICIO CAMPAÑA CUELLO.

Empresa Portuaria Austral: B. O'Higgins 1385, Punta Arenas; tel. (61) 24-1111; fax (61) 24-1111; e-mail portspuq@epa.co.cl; internet www.epa.co.cl; Pres. LAUTARO HERNÁN POBLETE KNUDTZON-TRAMPE; Dir FERNANDO ARTURO JOFRÉ WEISS.

Empresa Portuaria Chacabuco: B. O'Higgins s/n, Puerto Chacabuco; tel. (67) 35-1198; fax (67) 35-1174; e-mail ptochb@entelchile.net; Pres. LUIS MUSALEM MUSALEM; Dir RAIMUNDO CRISTI SAAVEDRA.

Empresa Portuaria Coquimbo: Melgareja 676, Coquimbo; tel. (51) 31-3606; fax (51) 32-6146; e-mail ptoqq@entelchile.net; Pres. ARMANDO ARANCIBIA CALDERÓN; Gen. Man. MIGUEL ZUVIC MUJICA.

Empresa Portuaria Iquique: Jorge Barrera 62, Iquique; tel. (57) 40-0100; fax (57) 41-3176; e-mail epi@epi.cl; internet www.port-iquique.cl; f. 1998; Pres. PATRICIO ARRAU PONS; Gen. Man. PEDRO DÁVILA PINO.

Empresa Portuaria Puerto Montt: Angelmó 1673, Puerto Montt; tel. (65) 25-2247; e-mail info@empormontt.cl; internet www.empormontt.cl; Pres. JOSÉ DANIEL BARRETA SÁEZ; Gen. Man. LUÍS RIVAS APABLAZA.

Empresa Portuaria San Antonio: Alan Macowan 0245, San Antonio; tel. (35) 58-6110; fax (35) 58-6010; e-mail correo@saiport.cl; internet www.saiport.cl; f. 1998; Pres. ERNESTO EDWARDS RISOPATRÓN; Gen. Man. RUBEN ALVARADO VIGAR.

Empresa Portuaria Talcahuano-San Vicente: Latorre 1590, Talcahuano; tel. (41) 54-1419; fax (41) 54-1807; e-mail eportuaria@ptotalsve.co.cl; Pres. JUAN ENRIQUE COEYMANS AVARIA; Gen. Man. PATRICIO CAMPAÑA CUELLO.

Empresa Portuaria Valparaíso: Errázuriz 25, 4°, Of. 1, Valparaíso; tel. (32) 44-8800; fax (32) 22-4190; e-mail gcomercial@portvalparaiso.cl; internet www.portvalparaiso.cl; Pres. GABRIEL ALDONEY V.; Gen. Man. HARALD JAEGER KARL.

Principal Shipping Companies

Santiago

Cía Chilena de Navegación Interoceánica, SA: Plaza de la Justicia 59, Valparaíso; tel. (32) 275-500; fax (32) 255-949; e-mail info@ccni.cl; internet www.ccni.cl; f. 1930; regular sailings to Japan, Republic of Korea, Taiwan, Hong Kong, USA, Mexico, South Pacific, South Africa and Europe; bulk and dry cargo services; owned by Empresas Navieras, SA; Chair. BELTRÁN F. URENDA SALAMANCA; Gen. Man. ALEJANDRO PATTILLO MOREIRA; 116 employees.

Naviera Magallanes, SA (NAVIMAG): Avda El Bosque, Norte 0440, 11°, Of. 1103/1104, Las Condes, Santiago; tel. (2) 442-3150; fax (2) 442-3156; f. 1979; Chair. PEDRO LECAROS MENÉNDEZ; Gen. Man. HÉCTOR HENRÍQUEZ NEGRÓN.

Nisa Navegación, SA: Avda El Bosque Norte 0440, 11°, Casilla 2829, Santiago; tel. (2) 203-5180; fax (2) 203-5190; Chair. PEDRO LECAROS MENÉNDEZ; Fleet Man. C. SALINAS.

Sociedad Anónima de Navegación Petrolera (SONAP): Moneda 970, 20°, Casilla 13D, Santiago; tel. (2) 630-1009; fax (2) 630-1041; e-mail valsonap@sonap.cl; f. 1954; tanker services; Chair. FELIPE VIAL C.; Gen. Man. JOSÉ THOMSEN Q.

Valparaíso

Agencias Universales, SA (AGUNSA): Avda Andrés Bello 2687, 15°, Las Condes, Santiago; tel. (2) 203-9000; fax (2) 203-9009; internet www.agunsa.com; f. 1960; maritime transportation and shipping, port and docking services; owned by Empresas Navieras, SA; Chair. JOSÉ URENDA SALAMANCA; Gen. Man. FRANCO MONTALBETTI.

A. J. Broom y Cía, SAC: Blanco 951, Casilla 910, Valparaíso and MacIver 225, 10°, Casilla 448, Santiago; tel. (32) 26-8200; fax (32) 21-3308; e-mail genmanager@ajbroom.cl; internet www.broomgroup.com; f. 1920; ship owners and brokers; Pres. GASTÓN ANRÍQUEZ; Man. Dir JAMES C. WELLS M.

Cía Sud-Americana de Vapores: Plaza Sotomayor 50, Casilla 49-V, Valparaíso; also Hendaya 60, 12°, Santiago; tel. (32) 20-3000; tel. (2) 330-7000; fax (32) 20-3333; e-mail info@csav.com; internet www.csav.com; f. 1872; regular service between South America and US/Canadian ports, US Gulf ports, North European, Mediterranean, Scandinavian and Far East ports; bulk carriers, tramp and reefer services; part of Cristalchile group; Pres. RICARDO CLARO VALDÉS; Gen. Man. FRANCISCO SILVA DONOSO.

Empresa Marítima, SA (Empremar Chile): Almirante Gómez Carreño 49, Casilla 105-V, Valparaíso; tel. (32) 25-8061; fax (32) 21-3904; f. 1953; international and coastal services; Chair. LORENZO CAGLEVIC; Gen. Man. E. ESPINOZA.

Naviera Chilena del Pacífico, SA (Nachipa): Almirante Señoret 70, 6°, Casilla 370, Valparaíso; also Serrano 14, Of. 502, Casilla 2290, Santiago; tel. (32) 25-1253; fax (32) 25-3869; e-mail valparaiso@nachipa.com; cargo; Pres. ARTURO FERNÁNDEZ ZEGERS; Gen. Man. PABLO SIMIAN ZAMORANO.

Sudamericana Agencias Aéreas y Marítimas, SA. (SAAM): Blanco 895, Valparaíso; tel. (32) 20-1000; fax (32) 20-1481; e-mail gerenciavap@saamsa.com; internet www.saamsa.com; f. 1961; cargo services; Pres. VÍCTOR PINO; Gen. Man. ALEJANDRO GARCÍA-HUIDOBRO.

Transmares Naviera Chilena Ltda: Moneda 970, 20°, Edif. Eurocentro, Casilla 193-D, Santiago; also Cochrane 813, 8°, Casilla 52-V, Valparaíso; tel. (32) 20-2000; fax (32) 25-6607; e-mail transmares@transmares.cl; f. 1969; dry cargo service Chile–Uruguay–Brazil; Chair. WOLF VON APPEN; Gen. Man. C. KUHLENTHAL.

Several foreign shipping companies operate services to Valparaíso.

Punta Arenas

Cía Marítima de Punta Arenas, SA: Avda Independencia 830, Casilla 337, Punta Arenas; also Casilla 2829, Santiago; tel. (61) 22-1871; tel. (2) 203-5180; fax (61) 22-7514; fax (2) 203-5191; f. 1949; shipping agents and owners operating in the Magellan Straits; Pres. PEDRO LECAROS MENÉNDEZ; Gen. Man. ARTURO STORAKER MOLINA.

Puerto Montt

Transporte Marítimo Chiloé-Aysén, SA: Angelmo 2187, Puerto Montt; tel. (65) 27-0419; Deputy Man. PEDRO HERNÁNDEZ LEHMAN.

San Antonio

Naviera Aysén Ltda: San Antonio; also Huérfanos 1147, Of. 542, Santiago; tel. (35) 32578; tel. (2) 698-8680; Man. RAÚL QUINTANA A.

CIVIL AVIATION

There are 325 airfields in the country, of which eight have long runways. Arturo Merino Benítez, 20 km north-east of Santiago, and Chacalluta, 14 km north-east of Arica, are the principal international airports.

Aero Continente: Marchant Pereira 381, Providencia, Santiago; tel. (2) 242-4242; fax (2) 205-2575; internet www.aerocontinente .com; operations suspended in 2002; owned by Nordic Air of Finland; Pres. LUPE ZEVALLOS.

Aerocardal: Aeropuerto CAMB, Pudahuel, Casilla 64, Santiago; tel. (2) 377-7400; fax (2) 377-7406; e-mail aerocard@aerocardal.cl; f. 1989; charter services; Chair. ALEX CASASEMPERE.

Aerovías DAP: Avda B. O'Higgins 891, Casilla 406, Punta Arenas; tel. (61) 22-3340; fax (61) 22-1693; e-mail ventas@aeroviasdap.cl; internet www.aeroviasdap.cl; f. 1980; domestic services; CEO ALEX PISCEVIC.

Línea Aérea Nacional de Chile (LAN-Chile): Américo Vespucio 901, Renca, Santiago; tel. (2) 565-2525; fax (2) 565-1729; internet www.lanchile.com; f. 1929; operates scheduled domestic passenger and cargo services, also Santiago–Easter Island; international services to French Polynesia, Spain, and throughout North and South America; under the Govt's privatization programme, 99% of LAN-Chile shares have been sold to private interests since 1989; Pres. JORGE AWAD MEHECH; CEO ENRIQUE CUETO.

Tourism

Chile has a wide variety of attractions for the tourist, including fine beaches, ski resorts in the Andes, lakes, rivers and desert scenery. There are many opportunities for hunting and fishing in the southern archipelago, where there are plans to make an integrated tourist area with Argentina, requiring investment of US $120m. Isla de Pascua (Easter Island) may also be visited by tourists. In 2004 there were an estimated 1.4m. tourist arrivals. In 2002 receipts from tourism totalled $845m.

Servicio Nacional de Turismo (SERNATUR): Avda Providencia 1550, 2°, Santiago; tel. (2) 731-8419; fax (2) 236-1417; e-mail pcasanova@sernatur.cl; internet www.sernatur.cl; f. 1975; Dir Dr OSCAR SANTELICES ALTAMIRANO.

Asociación Chilena de Empresas de Turismo (ACHET): Moneda 973, Of. 647, Santiago; tel. (2) 699-2140; fax (2) 699-4245; e-mail achet@achet.cl; internet www.achet.cl; f. 1945; 155 mems; Pres. GUILLERMO CORREA SANFUENTES; Dir GUIDO FERNÁNDEZ SALINAS.

THE PEOPLE'S REPUBLIC OF CHINA

Introductory Survey

Location, Climate, Language, Religion, Flag, Capital

The People's Republic of China covers a vast area of eastern Asia, with Mongolia and Russia to the north, Tajikistan, Kyrgyzstan and Kazakhstan to the north-west, Afghanistan and Pakistan to the west, and India, Nepal, Bhutan, Myanmar (formerly Burma), Laos and Viet Nam to the south. The country borders the Democratic People's Republic of Korea in the north-east, and has a long coastline on the Pacific Ocean. The climate ranges from subtropical in the far south to an annual average temperature of below 10°C (50°F) in the north, and from the monsoon climate of eastern China to the aridity of the north-west. The principal language is Northern Chinese (Mandarin); in the south and south-east local dialects are spoken. The Xizangzu (Tibetans), Wei Wuer (Uygurs), Menggus (Mongols) and other groups have their own languages. The traditional religions and philosophies of life are Confucianism, Buddhism and Daoism. There are also Muslim and Christian minorities. The national flag (proportions 2 by 3) is plain red, with one large five-pointed gold star and four similar but smaller stars, arranged in an arc, in the upper hoist. The capital is Beijing (Peking).

Recent History

The People's Republic of China was proclaimed on 1 October 1949, following the victory of Communist forces over the Kuomintang (KMT) Government, which fled to the island province of Taiwan. The new Communist regime received widespread international recognition, but it was not until 1971 that the People's Republic was admitted to the United Nations, in place of the KMT regime, as the representative of China. Most countries now recognize the People's Republic.

With the establishment of the People's Republic, the leading political figure was Mao Zedong, who was Chairman of the Chinese Communist Party (CCP) from 1935 until his death in 1976. Chairman Mao, as he was known, also became Head of State in October 1949, but he relinquished this post in December 1958. His successor was Liu Shaoqi, First Vice-Chairman of the CCP, who was elected Head of State in April 1959. Liu was dismissed in October 1968, during the Cultural Revolution (see below), and died in prison in 1969. The post of Head of State was left vacant, and was formally abolished in January 1975, when a new Constitution was adopted. The first Premier (Head of Government) of the People's Republic was Zhou Enlai, who held this office from October 1949 until his death in 1976. Zhou was also Minister of Foreign Affairs from 1949 to 1958.

The economic progress of the early years of Communist rule enabled China to withstand the effects of the industrialization programmes of the late 1950s (called the 'Great Leap Forward'), the drought of 1960–62 and the withdrawal of Soviet aid in 1960. To prevent the establishment of a ruling class, Chairman Mao launched the Great Proletarian Cultural Revolution in 1966. The ensuing excesses of the Red Guards caused the army to intervene; Liu Shaoqi and Deng Xiaoping, General Secretary of the CCP, were disgraced. In 1971 an attempted coup by the Defence Minister, Marshal Lin Biao, was unsuccessful, and by 1973 it was apparent that Chairman Mao and Premier Zhou Enlai had retained power. In 1975 Deng Xiaoping re-emerged as first Vice-Premier and Chief of the General Staff. Zhou Enlai died in January 1976. Hua Guofeng, hitherto Minister of Public Security, was appointed Premier, and Deng was dismissed. Mao died in September 1976. His widow, Jiang Qing, tried unsuccessfully to seize power, with the help of three radical members of the CCP's Politburo. The 'gang of four' and six associates of Lin Biao were tried in November 1980. All were found guilty and were given lengthy terms of imprisonment. (Jiang Qing committed suicide in May 1991.) The 10th anniversary of Mao's death was marked in September 1986 by an official reassessment of his life; while his accomplishments were praised, it was now acknowledged that he had made mistakes, although most of the criticism was directed at the 'gang of four'.

In October 1976 Hua Guofeng succeeded Mao as Chairman of the CCP and Commander-in-Chief of the People's Liberation Army (PLA). The 11th National Congress of the CCP, held in

August 1977, restored Deng Xiaoping to his former posts. In September 1980 Hua Guofeng resigned as Premier, but retained his chairmanship of the CCP. The appointment of Zhao Ziyang, a Vice-Premier since April 1980, to succeed Hua as Premier confirmed the dominance of the moderate faction of Deng Xiaoping. In June 1981 Hua Guofeng was replaced as Chairman of the CCP by Hu Yaobang, former Secretary-General of the Politburo, and as Chairman of the party's Central Military Commission by Deng Xiaoping. A sustained campaign by Deng to purge the Politburo of leftist elements led to Hua's demotion to a Vice-Chairman of the CCP and, in September 1982, to his exclusion from the Politburo.

In September 1982 the CCP was reorganized and the post of Party Chairman abolished. Hu Yaobang became, instead, General Secretary of the CCP. A year later a 'rectification' (purge) of the CCP was launched, aimed at expelling 'Maoists', who had risen to power during the Cultural Revolution, and those opposed to the pragmatic policies of Deng. China's new Constitution, adopted in December 1982, restored the office of Head of State, and in June 1983 Li Xiannian, a former Minister of Finance, became President of China. In September 1986 the sixth plenary session of the 12th CCP Central Committee adopted a detailed resolution on the 'guiding principles for building a socialist society', which redefined the general ideology of the CCP, to provide a theoretical basis for the programme of modernization and the 'open door' policy of economic reform.

In January 1986 a high-level 'anti-corruption' campaign was launched, to investigate reports that many officials had exploited the programme of economic reform for their own gain. The field of culture and the arts underwent significant liberalization in 1986, with a revival of the 'Hundred Flowers' movement of 1956–57, which had encouraged the development of intellectual debate. However, a series of student demonstrations in major cities in late 1986 was regarded by China's leaders as an indication of excessive 'bourgeois liberalization'. In January 1987 Hu Yaobang unexpectedly resigned as CCP General Secretary, being accused of 'mistakes on major issues of political principles'. Zhao Ziyang became acting General Secretary. At the 13th National Congress of the CCP, which opened in October, Deng Xiaoping retired from the Central Committee, but amendments to the Constitution of the CCP permitted him to retain the influential positions of Chairman of the State and of the CCP Central Military Commissions. A new Politburo was appointed by the Central Committee in November. The majority of its 18 members were relatively young officials, who supported Deng Xiaoping's policies. The membership of the new Politburo also indicated a decline in military influence in Chinese politics. The newly-appointed Standing Committee of the Politburo was regarded, on balance, as being 'pro-reform'. In late November Li Peng was appointed Acting Premier of the State Council, in place of Zhao Ziyang. At the first session of the Seventh National People's Congress (NPC), held in March–April 1988, Li Peng was confirmed as Premier, and Yang Shangkun (a member of the CCP Politburo) was elected President.

The death of Hu Yaobang in April 1989 led to the most serious student demonstrations ever seen in the People's Republic. The students criticized the alleged prevalence of corruption and nepotism within the Government, and sought a limited degree of Soviet-style *glasnost* in public life. When negotiations between government officials and the students' leaders had failed to satisfy the protesters' demands, workers from various professions joined the demonstrations in Tiananmen Square, Beijing, which had now become the focal point of the protests. At one stage more than 1m. people congregated in the Square, as demonstrations spread to more than 20 other Chinese cities. In mid-May some 3,000 students began a hunger strike in Tiananmen Square, while protesters demanded the resignation of both Deng Xiaoping and Li Peng, and invited President Gorbachev of the USSR, who was visiting Beijing, to address them. The students ended their hunger strike at the request of Zhao Ziyang, who was generally regarded as being sympathetic to the students' demands. On 20 May a state of martial law was declared in Beijing. Within days, some 300,000 troops had assembled. At the end of May the students erected a 30 m-high replica of the US Statue of Liberty in the Square.

On 3 June 1989 a further unsuccessful attempt was made to dislodge the demonstrators, but on the following day troops of the PLA attacked protesters on and around Tiananmen Square, killing an unspecified number of people. Television evidence and eye-witness accounts estimated the total dead at between 1,000 and 5,000. The Government immediately rejected these figures and claimed, furthermore, that the larger part of the casualties had been soldiers and that a counter-revolutionary rebellion had been taking place. Arrests and executions ensued, although some student leaders eluded capture and fled to Hong Kong. Zhao Ziyang was dismissed from all his party posts and replaced as General Secretary of the CCP by Jiang Zemin, hitherto the secretary of the Shanghai municipal party committee. Zhao was accused of participating in a conspiracy to overthrow the CCP and placed under house arrest. In November Deng resigned as Chairman of the CCP Central Military Commission, his sole remaining party position, and was succeeded by Jiang Zemin, who was hailed as the first of China's 'third generation' of communist leaders (Mao being representative of the first, and Deng of the second). In January 1990 martial law was lifted in Beijing, and it was announced that a total of 573 prisoners, detained following the pro-democracy demonstrations, had been freed. Further groups of detainees were released subsequently. In March Deng Xiaoping resigned from his last official post, that of Chairman of the State Central Military Commission, and was succeeded by Jiang Zemin. An extensive military reshuffle ensued. At the CCP's 14th National Congress, held in October 1992, a new 319-member Central Committee was elected. The Politburo was expanded and a new Secretariat was chosen by the incoming Central Committee. Many opponents of Deng Xiaoping's support for a 'socialist market economy' were replaced.

At the first session of the Eighth NPC, convened in March 1993, Jiang Zemin was elected as the country's President, remaining CCP General Secretary. Li Peng was reappointed as Premier, and an extensive reorganization of the State Council was announced. The Congress also approved amendments to the 1982 Constitution. Changes included confirmation of the State's practice of a 'socialist market economy'. During 1993, however, the Government became concerned at the growing disparity between urban and rural incomes (exacerbated by the heavy taxes imposed on farmers) and the resultant problem of rural migration, and at the decline in support for the CCP in the countryside. In June thousands of peasants took part in demonstrations in Sichuan Province to protest against excessive official levies. In response to the ensuing riots, the central Government banned the imposition of additional local taxes.

In March 1995, at the third session of the Eighth NPC, the appointment of Wu Bangguo and of Jiang Chunyun as Vice-Premiers of the State Council was approved. In an unprecedented display of opposition, however, neither nominee received the NPC's full endorsement. Nevertheless, the position of Jiang Zemin, now regarded by many as the eventual successor to the 'paramount' leadership of the ailing Deng Xiaoping, appeared to have been strengthened. Personnel changes in the military hierarchy later in the year were also viewed as favourable to Jiang Zemin. In April 1996 the Government initiated 'Strike Hard', a new campaign against crime, executing hundreds of people.

The death of Deng Xiaoping, on 19 February 1997, precipitated a period of uncertainty regarding China's future direction. President Jiang Zemin, however, declared that the economic reforms would continue, and this was reiterated in Premier Li Peng's address to the fifth session of the Eighth NPC in March 1997, which included a commitment to restructure state-owned enterprises (SOEs). Delegates at the Congress approved legislation reinforcing the CCP's control over the PLA, and revisions to the criminal code were also promulgated, whereby statutes concerning 'counter-revolutionary' acts (under which many of the pro-democracy demonstrators had been charged in 1989) were removed from the code, but were replaced by 11 crimes of 'endangering state security'. Financial offences, such as money-laundering, were also included for the first time.

At the 15th National Congress of the CCP, convened in September 1997, emphasis was placed on radical reform of the 370,000 SOEs. Delegates approved amendments to the party Constitution, enshrining the 'Deng Xiaoping Theory' of socialism with Chinese characteristics alongside 'Mao Zedong Thought' as the guiding ideology of the CCP. The Congress

elected a new 344-member Central Committee, which re-elected Jiang Zemin as General Secretary of the CCP, and appointed a 22-member Politburo. The composition of the new Politburo appeared to confirm Jiang Zemin's enhanced authority: Qiao Shi, a reformist and Jiang's most influential rival, who was ranked third in the party hierarchy, was excluded, reportedly because of his age, as was Gen. Liu Huaqing, China's most senior military figure. Zhu Rongji, a former mayor of Shanghai, replaced Qiao Shi, and was also widely regarded as the likely successor to Li Peng, on Li's retirement as Premier of the State Council in March 1998. Gen. Liu was replaced by a civilian, Wei Jinxiang, who was responsible for combating corruption within the CCP. The absence of the military from the Politburo, and the composition of the new Central Military Commission, confirmed Jiang's increased authority over the PLA.

At the first session of the Ninth NPC, which commenced in early March 1998, the number of ministry-level bodies was reduced from 40 to 29, mainly through mergers. On 16 March Jiang Zemin was re-elected President, and Hu Jintao was elected Vice-President. Li Peng resigned as Premier and was replaced by Zhu Rongji, who received overwhelming support from the NPC delegates. Li Peng replaced Qiao Shi as Chairman of the NPC, despite a lack of support from a number of delegates. Zhu's appointments to a new 39-member State Council included a number of associates of Jiang Zemin. Zhu also promoted a number of technocrats who were supportive of his own policies.

At the second session of the Ninth NPC, held in March 1999, a number of constitutional amendments were ratified, including the elevation in status of private-sector and other non-state enterprises to 'important components of the socialist market economy', a recommendation for adherence to the rule of law, and the incorporation of Deng Xiaoping's ideology into the Constitution alongside Marxism-Leninism and 'Mao Zedong thought'. In October Hu Jintao was appointed a Vice-Chairman of the Central Military Commission, and in December Zeng Qinghong became a full member of the Politburo.

Public disquiet over corruption within the CCP, the state bureaucracy and economic enterprises was acknowledged in August 1993, when the Party initiated an anti-corruption campaign. Hundreds of executions of officials were subsequently reported, and in April 1995, following allegations of corruption, Wang Baosen, a deputy mayor of Beijing, committed suicide. In the same month Chen Xitong, Secretary of the Beijing Municipality Committee, was arrested. An extensive inquiry concluded that Wang Baosen, a protégé of Chen Xitong, had been responsible for serious irregularities, including the embezzlement of the equivalent of millions of US dollars. In September, having been similarly disgraced, Chen Xitong was expelled from the Politburo and from the Central Committee of the CCP, later being expelled from the CCP itself. Owing to his implication in the scandal, the mayor of Beijing, Li Qiyan, finally resigned in October 1996. The campaign against corruption intensified in 1997 with the sentencing in August of Chen Xiaotong, son of Chen Xitong, to 12 years' imprisonment for the misappropriation of public funds. In August 1998 Chen Xitong was sentenced to 16 years' imprisonment for corruption and dereliction of duty. It was reported that between October 1992 and June 1997 121,000 people had been expelled from the CCP for corruption, while 37,500 others had faced criminal charges. In an attempt to eradicate illicit trade, in July 1998 President Jiang Zemin ordered the closure of all the business interests of the PLA, comprising some 15,000 companies across all sections of the economy. The divestment of all the PLA's enterprises to a state body, was completed in mid-December.

Corruption appeared to be rife throughout 2000 in many areas of government, including customs, finance, the military and the Three Gorges dam project. Among the most notable cases was that of a former Vice-Chairman of the Standing Committee of the NPC, Cheng Kejie, who was executed in September for accepting huge bribes. Also in September, Maj.-Gen. Ji Shengde, the former head of military intelligence of the PLA, was formally charged with taking massive bribes while in office. His trial formed part of the biggest corruption and smuggling case in the history of the People's Republic, with several senior officials in various Chinese cities facing prosecution. Fourteen were executed, while other defendants received sentences of life imprisonment. In October 2000, following a two-year investigation, government auditors reported the embezzlement or serious misuse of the equivalent of more than US $11,000m. of public funds by government officials. Further revelations of corruption emerged in January 2001 when the official media reported that Liu Yong, a municipal party official in Shenyang, had operated a criminal gang and used the proceeds to support his business activities. In June more than 100 officials from Shenyang, including the city's mayor, Mu Suixin, were detained in connection with their association to Liu.

In January 2002 Wang Xuebing, the president of China Construction Bank and an ally of Zhu Rongji, was placed under investigation for alleged financial mismanagement, and in November he was expelled from the CCP on bribe-taking charges. In February Huang Jin, an official at Minsheng Bank, was charged with illegally procuring and expropriating loans, and in March a 'money-laundering' and illegal loans scandal emerged at the Bank of China, the perpetrators having fled overseas. In August another banking official, Zhu Xiaohua, the former president of Everbright Bank, was expelled from the CCP and subsequently sentenced to 15 years' imprisonment on corruption charges. In September three officials from CITIC Industrial Bank were arrested on suspicion of massive fraud. In June, meanwhile, Yang Rong, one of China's richest men and a former chairman of China Brilliance Automotive Holdings, fled the country owing to corruption allegations. Also in June, the authorities reported that companies in Jiangsu Province had paid bribes to local officials. In August Zhao Keming, a former deputy mayor of Xiamen, was sentenced to death, with a two-year reprieve, for accepting bribes. In December the former customs chief in Shenzhen, Zhao Yucun, was sentenced to life imprisonment, also for receiving bribes. In an unrelated scandal, the former chairman of Shenzhen Urban Construction Group, Li Yuguo, received a suspended death sentence for similar offences.

In February 2003 one of the perpetrators involved in the Bank of China scandal, branch manager Yu Zhendong, was arrested in the USA. In May the Governor of Yunnan Province, Li Jiating, received a suspended death sentence for taking bribes totalling more than the equivalent of US$2,200m. Also in May, Zhou Zhengyi, chairman of a Shanghai property company, Nongkai Development Group, was placed under investigation amid allegations of fraudulent loan-taking. One of these loans, for US$270m., had been received from the Bank of China in 2002. Speculation over the Bank of China's involvement in the scandal intensified following the removal of the chief executive of the bank's Hong Kong branch, Liu Jinbao, in late May. Zhou Zhengyi was also known to have been an associate of former President Jiang Zemin. Zhou was formally arrested in September 2003 on charges of fabricating documents and manipulating his company's trading price on the stock market. Meanwhile, in July Yang Bin, who had been the proposed governor of the Sinuiju free trade area on China's border with North Korea (see below), was sentenced to 18 years' imprisonment for fraud and corruption. In another development in October, China's Minister of Land and Natural Resources, Tian Fengshan, was removed from office as a result of allegations related to corruption in the real-estate market (see below).

In February 2004 the CCP announced the introduction of new regulations for the supervision of its officials, intended to reduce corruption within the party. Also in February Liu Jinbao, former chief executive of the Bank of China in Hong Kong (see above), was arrested. In June businessman Zhou Zhengyi (see above) was sentenced to three years' imprisonment. A report issued by the Government in August stated that approximately 4,000 officials had left China after appropriating public funds since the mid-1980s, and that the total sum embezzled had amounted to around5,000m. yuan during that time.

In January 1991, meanwhile, the trials of many of those arrested during the pro-democracy protests of 1989 commenced. Most activists received relatively short prison sentences. In July 1992 Bao Tong, a senior aide of Zhao Ziyang, the former General Secretary of the CCP, was found guilty of involvement in the pro-democracy unrest of mid-1989. In February 1994 Asia Watch, an independent New York-based human rights organization, issued a highly critical report of the situation in China, detailing the cases of more than 1,700 detainees, imprisoned for their political, ethnic or religious views. In July the trial on charges of counter-revolutionary activity of 14 members of a dissident group, in detention since 1992, commenced. In December 1994 nine of the defendants received heavy prison sentences.

In February 1993 Wang Dan and Guo Haifeng, leading student activists in the 1989 demonstrations, were freed. In late 1994, however, complaining of police harassment, Wang Dan filed a lawsuit against the authorities. He was rearrested in May 1995. The imposition of an 11-year sentence on Wang Dan at the conclusion of his cursory trial on charges of conspiracy, in October 1996, received international condemnation. In April 1998 he was released on medical parole and sent into exile in the USA. In May 1993, having served 12 years of a 15-year sentence, Xu Wenli was released from prison. He was rearrested in April 1994, but released shortly afterwards. In August 1993 the arrest and expulsion from China of Han Dongfang, a trade union activist who had attempted to return to his homeland after a year in the USA, attracted much international attention.

In June 1995 Liu Gang, a leader of the 1989 uprising, was released from prison, and in May 1996 he was granted temporary asylum in the USA. Two further dissidents, Ren Wanding and Zhang Xianliang, were freed upon completion of their prison terms in June 1996. Having been released in the same month, Wang Xizhe escaped from Guangzhou and was permitted to enter the USA in October. His fellow activist, Liu Xiaobo, was arrested in Beijing, however, and ordered to serve three years in a labour camp. In November Chen Zeming, another alleged leader of the 1989 pro-democracy demonstrations, was released on medical parole.

In 1997 there was increasing pressure on the CCP to reconsider its assessment of the 1989 Tiananmen Square pro-democracy demonstrations as a 'counter-revolutionary rebellion'. In June 1997, in an unprecedented decision, a court in Liaoning Province overturned convictions of 'counter-revolution' against four dissidents imprisoned for their role in the 1989 pro-democracy movement. However, an appeal to the CCP National Congress by Zhao Ziyang (who remained under house arrest) to reassess the official verdict was dismissed. In mid-1997 Beijing refuted reports by the human rights organization Amnesty International that several pro-democracy activists remained among the numerous political prisoners in China, classifying as criminals the estimated 2,000 people imprisoned on charges of 'counter-revolution'.

China's treatment of political dissidents attracted international attention in November 1997, with the release on medical grounds into exile in the USA of Wei Jingsheng. Wei had been imprisoned in 1979, but was released on parole in September 1993. He was rearrested, however, in April 1994, and detained incommunicado until December 1995, when he was convicted of conspiring to overthrow the Government. His sentencing to 14 years' imprisonment provoked an international outcry, and he was released shortly after Jiang Zemin's visit to the USA in 1997(see below). Bao Ge, a prominent Shanghai dissident and campaigner for compensation for Chinese victims of Japanese war aggression, was released from three years' imprisonment without trial in June 1997. He left for the USA in November.

In September 1998 Amnesty International released a report stating that China had executed 1,876 people in 1997, more than the rest of the world combined. This figure, however, represented a considerable reduction compared with the 4,367 executions documented in 1996. Also in September 1998, the UN High Commissioner for Human Rights, Mary Robinson, made an unprecedented official visit to China, including Tibet, and Hong Kong. Following the visit, in October China signed the International Covenant on Civil and Political Rights in New York, guaranteeing freedom of expression, a fair trial and protection against arbitrary arrest. Although the Government's signing of the Covenant was hailed as a great advance in its attitude towards human rights, the treaty would only come into force once ratified by the NPC. No date was set for ratification.

In 1998 attempts by dissidents in Beijing and the provinces to create and register an opposition party, the Chinese Democratic Party (CDP), with the principal aim of democratic elections, were suppressed by the Government. In November the Government published a judicial interpretation of the crimes of political subversion (thereby expanding existing punishable offences), specifying that 'incitement to subvert state power' would result in imprisonment for between three years and life for any publisher, musician, author, artist or film-maker found guilty of the charge. In December at least 30 members of the CDP were detained, and three veteran activists, Xu Wenli, Qin Yongmin and Wang Youcai, were sentenced to 13, 12 and 11 years' imprisonment, respectively, provoking strong international condemnation. Human rights groups declared the release on medical parole and subsequent exile to the USA of the prominent dissident, Liu Nianchun, shortly before the conviction of the CDP activists, to be an attempt to deflect criticism of their trials. A speech by President Jiang Zemin in December appeared to confirm the end of a period of relative tolerance of political dissent. By November 1999 a further 18 CDP leaders had been convicted of subverting state power and sentenced to lengthy terms of imprisonment.

At the first Sino-US discussions on human rights for four years in Washington, DC, in January 1999 members of the US delegation urged their Chinese counterparts to halt the harsh treatment of dissidents. In February of that year two dissidents, Gao Yu (a journalist) and Sun Weibang, who had received substantial sentences, were released ahead of schedule, prompting speculation that Beijing was attempting to counter criticism before the imminent visit to the People's Republic by the US Secretary of State and the forthcoming meeting of the UN Commission on Human Rights in Geneva. None the less, China continued its suppression of dissent. In late April, however, a US-sponsored resolution at the aforementioned UN Commission meeting, condemning China's human rights record, was defeated. The resolution was again defeated in April 2000. A number of activists were detained in June 1999 in advance of the 10th anniversary of the killings in Tiananmen Square; despite official fears, the day passed without major incident in Beijing. (In Hong Kong, however, thousands attended a commemorative rally.) The Square had been closed for some time, ostensibly for repairs before the 50th anniversary of the founding of the People's Republic in October, and did not reopen until late June. In April 2000 it was reported that four academics had been dismissed from a Chinese academy, accused of being 'a branch of opposition within the Party', following the publication of an essay by one of them advocating political reform. In August 2000 a group of Chinese dissidents filed a lawsuit in the USA accusing Li Peng of crimes against humanity for sanctioning the events of June 1989 in Tiananmen Square. China made a request to the USA that the case be abandoned, describing it as 'political farce'.

Following a further visit by Mary Robinson to Beijing in March 2000 (during which China refuted her right to criticize its conduct of internal affairs), in November a human rights training agreement was signed which, it was hoped, would be a precursor to ratification of the International Covenant on Civil and Political Rights (see above). Attempts were made by the Government in February and in November 2000 to regulate the publication of material on the internet, with the issuing of new rules first granting the regime the right to 'reorganize' or close down offending websites, and then requiring government approval prior to the posting of news bulletins. In February 2001 the trial began of the first webmaster to have been prosecuted for publishing subversive material on the internet, and between April and November 2001 some 17,000 internet cafés were shut down in a nation-wide campaign against pornographic and subversive websites.

The killings in Tiananmen Square attracted renewed attention in early January 2001 following the 'leak' of papers and transcripts of government meetings at the time, which had been smuggled out of China by a reformist civil servant and subsequently published abroad as 'The Tiananmen Papers'. The papers, which were immediately denounced by the Government as forgeries, appeared to show a split in the leadership over how to deal with the protesters, with Zhao Ziyang having favoured a conciliatory approach, while Li Peng supported decisive action against the students, regarding them as part of a 'counter-revolutionary rebellion'. Deng Xiaoping had taken the decision to suppress the protesters, with the support of a group of semi-retired elders. The papers also indicated that Jiang Zemin had been appointed to his positions directly by Deng, thus circumventing the Party's rules of selection. In June 2002 the authorities reportedly detained at least 23 people in connection with the publication of 'The Tiananmen Papers' following a lengthy investigation into the matter.

In early 2002 a report by Amnesty International claimed that there had been a total of 2,468 executions in China during 2001. The victims of the suppression reportedly included ethnic separatists, 'underground' churches, unregistered internet cafés, tax-evading peasants and also Chinese scholars returning from overseas, five of whom were US citizens. The Government's campaign also resulted in the removal in June 2001 of two editors from *Southern Weekend* for criticizing the penal system. Other newspapers also faced punishment for their investigations into growing social dissatisfaction and injustices. In August 2002 the US-based group Human Rights Watch reported that growing numbers of political dissidents were being detained in mental institutions, estimating that at least 3,000 people had been subjected to psychiatric detention for political

activity in the preceding two decades. Those detained included members of Falun Gong (see below), independent labour organizers and other organized anti-Government activists.

Attempts by the authorities to maintain order prior to the Party Congress resulted in renewed measures to curb access to the internet during 2002. In June, at the beginning of a three-month offensive, three leading internet providers were punished for disseminating harmful content and were forced to suspend a number of services. This was accompanied by a campaign to close down illegal internet cafés, after a fire at one such facility killed 24 people. By August 2002 it had been announced that 14,000 'cybercafés' had been closed, 3,100 of which were permanent closures. The official reasons for the closures were to improve workplace safety practices. In early September the authorities temporarily blocked access to the US-based 'Google' internet search engine, in order to limit access to potentially subversive material, but subsequently imposed new selective mechanisms to limit what could be accessed via 'Google'. Despite this, by 2002 China was the world's third largest user of the internet, usage having risen by 72% in 2001–02 to reach 45m. users. At the same time, the authorities arrested 23 people in connection with the 'leak' and publication of official documents concerning the Tiananmen massacres (see above).

In late December 2002 the authorities acknowledged that they had again arrested the US-based activist, Wang Bingzhang. Wang had disappeared in mid-2002 in Viet Nam, where he had travelled with two other Chinese dissidents, Yue Wu and Zhang Qi, in order to hold meetings with other activists. Wang was charged with espionage on behalf of Taiwan, and with terrorism—charges condemned by the China Democratic Party—and he went on trial in late January 2003. In early February he was sentenced to life imprisonment, and at the end of that month he lost his appeal. Also in late December 2002 the authorities released, on the basis of 'medical parole', Xu Wenli, who immediately returned to the USA. Xu's release was widely seen as a goodwill gesture towards the USA, Xu himself describing his release as 'political'. In mid-January 2003 the authorities charged an internet dissident, Ouyang Yi, with trying to overthrow the Government. Later that month the authorities expelled another prominent dissident, Fang Jue, to exile in the USA. Fang had, a few years previously, called for direct elections at all levels of government and for press freedom. He had been released from prison in July 2002, but had subsequently been detained during the CCP Congress in November. In early March 2003 the authorities released Zhang Qi, who immediately returned to the USA, where she was based. Also in March, publication of the Guangzhou newspaper *21st Century Herald* was suspended after it published an interview criticizing the Government's refusal to submit to a democratic vote.

The outbreak of Severe Acute Respiratory Syndrome (SARS, see below) in early 2003 seemed to bring about a brief period of relative media openness, with the press refuting official claims that the spread of the disease had not been concealed by the authorities. There were also press reports criticizing the treatment of Jiang Yanyong, a military doctor who had called for information on SARS to be made public. However, press freedom appeared to be more restricted once again from June 2003, with lists of banned topics being issued to journalists, and in August an order was issued restraining public debate on political reform and on constitutional amendments, as well as on reassessment of historical events (the latter was believed to refer to the 1989 student protests). Despite increasing privatization of the media sector, with newspapers being required to become financially independent of the State, there were few signs that the Government was relinquishing its control over the reporting of sensitive issues. The Government also continued to exercise tight control over the internet throughout 2003, with a police force of between 30,000 and 40,000 being employed to monitor activities on the web. In May 2003 four internet activists were imprisoned after publishing demands for political reform on the web, and in September another internet dissident, Li Zhi, was arrested on similar charges. In December 2003 a well-known internet satirist, Liu Di, was released after having being held without charge for over a year.

A report published by Amnesty International in early 2003 stated that there had been more executions in China in 2002 than in any other country, the number exceeding two-thirds of the known world total of more than 1,500. According to Amnesty, during 2003 the number of people arrested in connection with anti-Government internet activities increased sharply, with 54 confirmed cases, and the real number of arrests was believed to be considerably higher.

In February 2004 it was announced that foreign investment in Chinese media companies was to be allowed; however, this would be permitted only on the condition that foreign investors agreed to adhere to government regulations on media content. In March pro-democracy activist Wang Youcai (see above) was released and permitted to travel to the USA on medical grounds. Also in March, several members of the staff of *Southern Metropolis Daily* were arrested, reportedly in connection with articles published by the newspaper on the SARS epidemic (editor-in-chief Cheng Yizhong was released in August). Again in March, the second session of the NPC approved an amendment to the Constitution that introduced an explicit reference to human rights. This was described by official sources as a significant step for human rights protection in China. Other observers, however, criticized the amendment as vague and ineffectual. In April a resolution condemning China's human rights record was rejected at a meeting of the UN Commission on Human Rights for the 11th time. In June public recognition of the 15th anniversary of the 1989 Tiananmen Square demonstration was not permitted. In the same month the Government's continuing fear of the potential of the internet to facilitate subversion was evident with the launch of an official website that encouraged internet users to report illegal information. During 2004 it was reported that a number of organizations based in the West were providing software that enabled Chinese internet users to circumvent censorship. In July a new campaign for censorship of text messages was announced, with telephone companies being required to use filtering technology to identify words and numbers that were considered suspicious. In October Zhao Yan, a Chinese national working as a researcher for the *New York Times*, was arrested and charged with providing state secrets to foreigners following the newspaper's publication of a report stating Jiang Zemin's intention to resign as head of China's military (see below) before this had been officially announced. In December three leading intellectuals, Yu Jie, Liu Xiaobo and Zhang Zhuhua, who were known to have expressed critical views, were detained for questioning.

In March 2004, meanwhile, Amnesty International issued a report requesting a moratorium on the death penalty in China, stating that dysfunction in the judicial system meant that fair trial could not be ensured. In late 2004 it was reported that China was revising its legislation on capital punishment to make the Supreme People's Court the highest body of appeal in death penalty cases. It was believed that such a reform would lead to a significant reduction in the number of executions. The exact number of executions in China remained a state secret, with some estimates suggesting that as many as 15,000 a year were being carried out.

The emergence of Falun Gong in the late 1990s posed new challenges to the supremacy of the CCP, which banned the popular religious cult in July 1999, on the grounds that it constituted a threat to society. The group, which was also known as Falun Dafa, had been established in 1992 by Li Hongzhi, who was based in the USA, and from 1999 it attracted increasing attention in China and abroad, claiming tens of millions of adherents, mainly in China. The ban imposed in 1999 was prompted by demonstrations, attended by tens of thousands of supporters in numerous towns and cities, in protest at the arrest of more than 100 adherents of the sect. The authorities embarked on a campaign of harsh persecution of those who refused to renounce their faith, and by the end of the month more than 6,000 arrests had been made. A peaceful protest in central Beijing was attended by some 10,000 practitioners in April. Four members of the sect were imprisoned in December, with sentences ranging from seven to 18 years, for their part in organizing the demonstration. This followed the conviction and imprisonment of four of Falun Gong's provincial leaders in November. The authorities were also concerned by the high level of Falun Gong membership among CCP and PLA officials. The CCP took the opportunity to demonstrate its continuing power on 1 October 1999, with lavish but strictly-controlled, celebrations of the 50th anniversary of the foundation of the People's Republic of China. In a highly symbolic gesture, a picture of Jiang Zemin was paraded alongside portraits of Mao Zedong and Deng Xiaoping: the first time that the current President had been publicly placed on a par with his predecessors. Despite condemnation and prosecution by the full force of the law, and the lack of public appearances by Li Hongzhi, Falun Gong members continued to make quiet protests on a regular basis

during 2000. The CCP's fear of losing its authority in the face of this increasing religious adherence became evident in October 2000, when Falun Gong was declared to be a political rival to the CCP and an enemy of the nation. The suppression of Falun Gong continued throughout 2001, with dispersals of rallies, arrests and detentions in 're-education camps'. In July an anti-cult exhibition was held, and in late August the authorities sentenced 45 'die-hard' members to long prison sentences for organizing resistance. The group claimed in September that some 278 members had died in custody since 1999, while the Government blamed the group for the deaths of 1,600 people, including suicides. In November 2001 and February 2002 the authorities expelled on both occasions 30–40 Western followers of Falun Gong who had demonstrated in Tiananmen Square.

In early 2002 Falun Gong showed renewed signs of activity by infiltrating Chinese television broadcasts in several different cities and transmitting messages from Li Hongzhi, as well as short programmes contradicting the official government position on the sect. These activities reached new heights in late June with the heavy 'jamming' of *Sinosat* transmitters, prompting an admission by the Government that such interference had taken place, and emphasizing the technological sophistication and resourcefulness of Falun Gong. In late September 15 Falun Gong members were sentenced to between four and 20 years' imprisonment for violating anti-cult laws and damaging broadcasting equipment. At the same time the Government stated that Falun Gong had used Taiwan as a base from which to 'hijack' Chinese satellite transmissions and, while refraining from blaming the Taiwanese Government, urged it to curb the activities of the sect. In March 2003 a US national, Charles Li, was sentenced to three years' imprisonment by a Chinese court on charges related to 'hijacking' by the Falun Gong of Chinese television broadcasts. In November 2003 four people, including British national Wayne Tan Cho-sang, were arrested in Shenzhen for their involvement with Falun Gong. In February 2004 five Falun Gong practitioners were sentenced in Chongqing.

In January 2000, meanwhile, five Catholic bishops were ordained in a display of strength by the state-controlled Chinese Catholic Church, impeding any improvement in relations with the Vatican, which opposed the ordination. In August 1999 Beijing had refused to grant permission for the Pope to visit Hong Kong, owing to the Vatican's links with Taiwan. According to a US-based Catholic organization, the arrest of an archbishop belonging to the clandestine Roman Catholic Church in February 2000 was part of an attempt by China to undermine allegiance to the Vatican. During the year there was substantial evidence of the CCP's intensification of repression of all non-official religious movements, many of which were classified as 'evil cults', with widespread arrests and church closures. In October the situation was exacerbated when, on China's National Day, the Pope canonized 120 missionary and Chinese Roman Catholic martyrs. Beijing responded with allegations of serious crimes perpetrated by several of the new saints. Despite a subsequent apology by the Pope for any errors committed by missionaries in China, relations between the two sides were severely damaged. By October 2001, however, there were signs that Beijing and the Vatican were moving towards a *rapprochement*, which would potentially allow the restoration of full diplomatic relations, thereby not only impelling the Vatican (and possibly several Catholic Latin American nations) to sever links with Taiwan but also diminishing the problems arising from the existence of an 'underground' Catholic church in China. In mid-October Catholic scholars from around the world gathered in Beijing to commemorate the 400th anniversary of the start of Italian Jesuit Matteo Ricci's mission to China in 1601. The event was downgraded somewhat, but Pope John Paul II expressed regret for past Vatican actions and appealed for the establishment of diplomatic relations. Meanwhile, it was estimated that 70% of Chinese bishops received mutual recognition from the Chinese Bishops' Conference and the Vatican.

In December 2001 a senior-level conference on religion was held in Beijing, attended by all seven members of the Politburo Standing Committee. The conference acknowledged the increasing importance of religion in China, in contrast to the anti-religious ideology of the past, and aimed to bring independent churches under state control, thereby obviating the need for clandestine churches. It was thought that Protestant churches were to be the main beneficiaries of the conference; Falun Gong remained illegal. Despite this conference, however, a Hong Kong businessman, Li Guangqiang, was arrested for delivering bibles to an evangelical group in south-eastern China, and in January 2002 he was sentenced to two years in prison, apparently receiving a light sentence in order to deflect criticism from the USA.

In February 2002 documents smuggled out of the country by Chinese Christians revealed that the authorities were working hard to suppress unauthorized religious faiths, such as Christian sects, as well as Falun Gong (see above). In May the authorities arrested more than 100 South Korean missionaries for assisting North Korean refugees fleeing to China. In mid-2002, however, the Government began co-operating with underground Christians in combating an extremist Christian fringe sect known as 'Eastern Lightning', which had kidnapped and attempted forcibly to convert 34 Christians in April. 'Eastern Lightning' had emerged in 1990 under Zhao Weishan, and its belief in the reincarnation of Jesus as a woman bore a resemblance to that of a group that had started an anti-Government rebellion in the 19th century. 'Eastern Lightning' had, like Falun Gong, been designated an 'evil cult' and an enemy of the State. Despite such co-operation, however, in late July the authorities sentenced three underground Roman Catholic priests to three years' labour for 'cult' activities, and in September they arrested the underground bishop of Qiqihar, Heilongjiang Province. In October 2002 the US State Department's annual report on religious freedom continued to designate China as a country engaged in widespread repression of religion.

By early 2003 China and the Vatican had held several rounds of informal discussions on improving bilateral relations. However, Beijing was in confrontation with Bishop Joseph Zen Zekiun, the head of the Catholic Church in the Hong Kong SAR, who had become increasingly critical of Beijing's administration in Hong Kong and its religious policies in China. Observers noted that the division between the officially-endorsed 'patriotic' Catholic Church and the unofficial church was gradually being reduced, with 'patriotic' bishops privately seeking the Vatican's endorsement and guidance. In October 2003 a senior member of the state-approved Catholic Patriotic Association announced plans to build four new Catholic churches in Beijing. Also in October, however, 12 priests and seminarians of the unofficial Catholic church were arrested in Hebei Province. In April 2004 Gu Xianggao, a member of an unofficial Christian group, died in police custody. China was one of the few countries not represented at the funeral of Pope John Paul II in April 2005.

In February 2000, in an attempt definitively to refute the growing belief that China must eventually abandon one-party rule, Jiang Zemin had launched a new political theory entitled 'The Three Represents', which declared that the CCP would 'always represent the development needs of China's advanced social productive forces, always represent the onward direction of China's advanced culture and always represent the fundamental interests of the largest number of Chinese people'. It appeared, however, that with the advent of significant social change the CCP was finding it increasingly difficult to maintain control over its members. In the following months there was harsh repression of provincial labour unrest. In April 2000 it was also reported that the number of labour disputes had totalled more than 120,000 in 1999. Workers had become increasingly restless since 1998, when SOE restructuring had begun to result in widespread redundancies.

The third session of the Ninth NPC, which convened in Beijing in March 2000, focused mainly on economic issues but also made a commitment to ending official corruption and smuggling. Earlier that month a former provincial deputy governor had been executed for bribery and possession of property acquired from unidentified sources. At its Plenary Session in October, the CCP announced a new five-year plan, under which China was to concentrate on rural development, the creation of employment, economic modernization and combating corruption.

During the fourth session of the Ninth NPC, held in March 2001, Premier Zhu Rongji outlined plans for economic restructuring in preparation for China's membership of the World Trade Organization (WTO), and also called for scientific and technological advancement, the improvement of living standards, the reduction of rural poverty, development of the western regions, opening to the outside world and strengthening of the military. A 17.7% increase in the defence budget was also announced in March. In the mean time, from April 2001 the authorities renewed their action against dissent, as part of the latest nation-wide 'Strike Hard' campaign, which was believed to reflect political manoeuvring in advance of the CCP Congress in 2002. The campaign was co-ordinated by Luo Gan, a protégé

of Li Peng, with the approval of Jiang Zemin. In April Jin Ruchao was sentenced to death for his alleged role in setting off a series of bombs in Hebei in March, which killed a total of 108 people.

In mid-May 2001 a prominent intellectual who also served as a deputy director of economic reform, Pan Yue, presented to President Jiang a plan to transform the CCP into a more broadly representative body; the plan was subsequently discussed by the Politburo Standing Committee and reportedly contained a right-wing nationalist leaning combined with strong, centralized rule. Pan's plan was believed to reflect the views of an increasing number of party cadres, as a means to prolong CCP rule without effecting democratization. In early June the CCP released the *China Investigation Report 2000–2001: Studies of Contradictions Within the People under New Conditions*, which publicly acknowledged that its rule might be undermined by social discontent arising from the country's free-market reforms. It warned that growing inequality and corruption were important sources of discontent, ranging from angry farmers to dismissed workers. The report was chaired by Zeng Qinghong, a senior aide of Jiang, who was vying for a senior position at the 2002 CCP Congress.

On 1 July 2001, in a speech to mark the 80th anniversary of the foundation of the CCP, President Jiang urged the modernization of the Party and for the first time stated that business people would be welcome as party members, a formal reversal of decades of hostility to the entrepreneurial class. Jiang also spoke of the need to eliminate corruption, and warned that the alternative to CCP rule was chaos and the disintegration of the country. Jiang's rightward shift was not universally welcomed, however, and in mid-August he shut down a leading left-wing magazine, *Zhenli de Zhuiqiu* (*Search for the Truth*), in a move that reflected increasing discord between the Party's leftist and rightist factions. The left-wing forces, which included orthodox Communists, supporters of moderate socialism, the agricultural lobby and liberals, all opposed the transformation of the CCP into a more business-orientated party. In mid-July, meanwhile, despite the growing campaign against dissent, the International Olympic Committee (IOC) awarded the 2008 Olympic Games to Beijing, resulting in mass celebrations across the country.

The end of 2001 and most of 2002 was dominated by preparations for the 16th CCP Congress. The 25th anniversary of the death of Mao Zedong passed without commemoration in early September 2001, a silence attributed to the debate within the CCP over future policy and to President Jiang's attempt to secure his own legacy—he was reportedly seeking to retain influence as an elder statesman by keeping the post of Chairman of the Central Military Commission. Other senior officials, including Premier Zhu Rongji and NPC Chairman Li Peng, were also expected to be replaced in March 2003, when the 10th NPC was scheduled to be convened. Jiang's designated successor was Vice-President Hu Jintao, who had slowly gained prominence and had made a tour of European countries in late 2001 to introduce himself to world leaders (see below). In November Jiang appointed the Deputy Party Secretary for Shanxi Province, Li Jingtian, to his personal staff, which also included policy aide Wang Huning, Jia Tingan and speechwriter Tang Wensheng. In December the mayor of Shanghai, Xu Kuangdi unexpectedly resigned to assume an academic post, reportedly owing to his differences with the Shanghai Party Secretary, Huang Ju.

Meanwhile, in March 2002 tens of thousands of workers who had been made redundant staged demonstrations in the north-eastern industrial cities of Daqing and Liaoyang, protesting against job losses and the lack of adequate social security measures. (Since 1998 some 25m. workers had been laid off from State enterprises, according to official sources.) The principal organizer, Yao Fuxin, was arrested, prompting further demonstrations for his release. The events emphasized the potentially destabilizing effects of economic restructuring following China's admission to the WTO (see below). In April hundreds staged similar protests in Lanzhou. Several more such disturbances occurred during subsequent months, albeit on a smaller scale. In response, the Ministry of Labour urged enterprises to re-employ some workers and ensure the timely payment of allowances and pensions. Additionally, bureaucrats and civil servants received pay rises in July, in an attempt to raise consumer spending and to reduce corruption. In an effort to maintain social stability, poorer urban dwellers were also allocated new allowances in July, under a new registration system that would allow the Government accurately to count the numbers within that group.

In July 2002 senior CCP officials gathered at the coastal resort of Beidaihe to determine the new positions to be allocated at the Congress, amid strong indications that Jiang Zemin would remain CCP General Secretary for another term. In late October Huang Ju and Jia Qinglin, the CCP secretaries in charge of Shanghai and Beijing respectively, and close allies of Jiang Zemin, were transferred to new central government posts.

The 16th CCP Congress was finally held in early November 2002, having been delayed from September, and resulted in the long-awaited transfer of power to the 'fourth generation' leadership headed by the new General Secretary, Hu Jintao. A new 356-member Central Committee was elected, as well as a 24-member Politburo, the Standing Committee (the highest decision-making body) of which was expanded from seven to nine members, of whom Hu was the only incumbent to be retained. The new members of the Standing Committee were Wu Bangguo, Wen Jiabao, Jia Qinglin, Zeng Qinghong, Huang Ju, Wu Guanzheng, Li Changchun and Luo Gan. Of these, Jia, Zeng, Huang, and Li were all known to be close allies of Jiang, who had successfully prevented rival Li Ruihuan from being re-elected to the Standing Committee. Luo Gan, however, was a protégé of NPC Chairman Li Peng. As expected, Jiang retained the chairmanship of the CCP Central Military Commission, which also contained three important military allies of his, Generals Cao Gangchuan, Guo Boxiong, and Xu Caihou, of whom Cao and Guo were also appointed to the Politburo. Another Jiang ally, Gen. Liang Guanglie, hitherto Commander of the Nanjing Military Region, was appointed Chief of the PLA's General Staff. Jiang thus retained full control of the powerful PLA.

The Congress stressed continuity in policy, but introduced some economic reforms. Although state ownership would retain a dominant role, private businesses would be able to compete on a more equal basis, and there would be a greater emphasis on private capital. Discriminatory regulations on investment, financing, taxation, land use and foreign trade would be revised, and private property would be granted greater legal protection. However, there were no major political reforms, and foreign policy was to remain unchanged. In early December 2002 Zhou Yongkang, hitherto the party secretary for Sichuan Province, was appointed Minister of Public Security, replacing Jia Chunwang. In mid-January 2003 two men, including Yao Fuxin, went on trial accused of organizing the massive labour unrest of early 2002.

The final stage of the transfer of power to the 'fourth generation' of Chinese leadership took place during the 10th NPC, in mid-March 2003. As expected, Hu Jintao was appointed President, succeeding Jiang Zemin, while Zeng Qinghong became Vice-President. Wen Jiabao succeeded Zhu Rongji as premier, and appointed Huang Ju, Wu Yi, Zeng Peiyan, and Hui Liangyu as Vice-Premiers. The new State Council also included Ma Kai as Minister of State Development and Reform Commission, Jin Renqing as Minister of Finance, and Lu Fuyuan as Minister of Commerce. Both Ma and Jin were known to have economics backgrounds. Li Zhaoxing, a former ambassador to the USA and the UN and hitherto a Vice-Minister of Foreign Affairs, was appointed Minister of Foreign Affairs, replacing Tang Jiaxuan, who became one of five state councillors. Gen. Cao Gangchuan was appointed Minister of National Defence. Hua Jianmin, an ally of Jiang, was appointed Secretary-General of the State Council. The new Chairman of the NPC was Wu Bangguo, replacing Li Peng. Despite the change of personnel, the new leadership was widely expected to maintain continuity with the policies of recent years.

The incoming leadership immediately faced a new challenge with the outbreak of SARS, a previously unknown illness, which by the end of April 2003 had affected almost 3,500 people and resulted in more than 150 deaths in the People's Republic alone. As the pneumonia-like virus spread across Asia and also to Canada, the Chinese authorities' initial lack of openness attracted much international criticism. Thousands of people were placed in quarantine in Beijing, and many public facilities and schools were closed. The Minister of Public Health, Zhang Wenkang, and the mayor of Beijing, Meng Xuenong, were accused of having concealed the extent of the disease and were relieved of their party and state positions. Wang Qishan, hitherto vice-mayor, was appointed mayor of Beijing. The SARS epidemic was officially declared to be over in mid-June 2003, and the World Health Organization (WHO) removed its ban on travel to Beijing. There was speculation that the Government's initial mishandling of the SARS crisis might prompt develop-

ments on political reform. A committee was established in April under NPC Standing Committee Chairman Wu Bangguo to discuss various issues of constitutional change, including workers' rights and direct election of officials above the village level.

The closing of sluice gates of the Three Gorges dam on the Changjiang (River Yangtze) in June 2003 represented the final stage of the world's largest hydroelectric project. The damming of the river provoked some criticism, following reports that cracks had appeared in the dam, and there was also renewed concern over the forced relocation of 1.3m. former residents of the area. Meanwhile, in May 2003 the principal organizer of labour protests in north-eastern industrial cities in 2002 (see above), Yao Fuxin, was sentenced to seven years' imprisonment.

In July 2003 President Hu Jintao and Premier Wen Jiabao took the unusual step of cancelling the leadership's annual retreat to the resort of Beidaihe, with the stated intention of saving government money by removing leaders' privileges. In August 2003 the Government introduced a further significant change with the announcement of new marriage regulations to take effect from October. Under the new regulations, couples would no longer be subject to pre-marital health checks and would not need to seek employers' permission for their marriage.

The rapid growth of China's property industry posed problems for the Government in 2003, following protests and suicide attempts by residents evicted from homes scheduled for demolition by private developers and local officials. In Beijing residential areas were bulldozed as part of a modernization programme in preparation for the 2008 Olympic Games (a marketing plan for Beijing's hosting of the Games was announced in September 2003). In October 2003 the Government detained five property developers who had allegedly carried out evictions by violent means. In the same month the Minister of Land and Natural Resources, Tian Fengshan, was removed from office, amid reports of corruption in connection with the property market.

Meanwhile, in August 2003, the period of relative openness in the aftermath of the SARS crisis seemed to come to an end with the issuing of government directives banning media discussion of political and constitutional reform. There were, none the less, some signs of reform in the second half of 2003. In district elections in Beijing in December two seats were secured by independent candidates, this being the first time that independent candidates had won seats in the District People's Congress for more than 20 years. Also in December, in an important development, a constitutional amendment to provide protection of private property was introduced by members of the NPC. This amendment, first proposed at the third plenary session of the 16th CCP Central Committee in October, represented the first legal protection of private property rights in China since 1949. The changes were endorsed at the second session of the 10th NPC in March 2004. Detailed amendments to the Constitution were subsequently made, stating in Article 13 that 'citizens' lawful private property is inviolable'. Another important constitutional change approved at the NPC session was a new reference to the 'Three Represents' theory (see above) as a guiding ideology. At the same session Premier Wen Jiabao also outlined plans for eliminating agricultural taxation and reducing economic inequalities.

In February 2004, meanwhile, Bo Xilai, hitherto Governor of Liaoning Province, replaced Lu Fuyuan as Minister of Commerce. In March it was reported in Western newspapers that Jiang Yanyong, the military doctor who had accused the Government of concealing the extent of the SARS outbreak in 2003 (see above), had written a letter to the NPC requesting a reappraisal of the 1989 pro-democracy protests. In April the mother of a student involved in SARS research became the first person to die of the disease since 2003. However, there was no large-scale outbreak of SARS in early 2004, and in June the Government closed its SARS prevention office, declaring that the disease had been brought under control. In the same month Jiang Yanyong and his wife were arrested prior to a planned visit to the USA. Jiang's wife was released later in the month, and Jiang himself was released in July, having reportedly been subject to political indoctrination. Also in July, the Government announced a scheme intended to increase the number of female births (including incentives such as tax exemptions and financial support for girls' education), in an attempt to address the serious problem of gender imbalance in the population, which was believed to have been exacerbated by the one-child policy and the traditional preference for boys. Later in the year there was speculation that China was considering a relaxation of its family-planning regulations, amid concerns over the consequences of an ageing population.

In August 2004 a former government official was sentenced to death for stealing hundreds of cultural relics in what was believed to be the largest such theft since 1949. Also in August, the 100th anniversary of the birth of the late Deng Xiaoping was celebrated. In the same month, former Premier Li Peng, who had been widely seen as bearing primary responsibility for the killing of student demonstrators in 1989, claimed that the violent suppression of the Tiananmen Square demonstration had been strongly supported by Deng.

An important development took place at the fourth plenary session of the 16th CCP Congress in September 2004, when former President Jiang Zemin relinquished his last official post, that of Chairman of the Central Military Commission, to Hu Jintao. Hu was thus seen as having consolidated his position. There was speculation that the departure of Jiang might lead to changes of government policy in some areas. It seemed clear, however, that Hu did not intend to use his stronger position to introduce major democratic reforms. In a speech prior to the Congress, Hu had emphasized his belief that 'indiscriminately copying Western political systems is a blind alley for China.'

In 2004 an increase in social unrest in China was reported. Official statistics released in June estimated that 3m. people had taken part in some form of public protest, including labour strikes and riots, over the past year, representing an increase of almost 15% in comparison with the previous 12 months. Widening financial disparities as a consequence of economic growth, as well as frequent instances of official corruption, were believed to be the main causes of this disaffection. In October there was an outbreak of violence between members of the Muslim Hui minority and the Han Chinese population in Henan Province, leading to the imposition of martial law in some parts of the province in November. The incident was not described as an ethnic conflict in the Chinese media.

In January 2005 the death of former Premier and CCP leader Zhao Ziyang, who had been removed from his post and placed under house arrest following the student protests of 1989, prompted speculation of a revival of pro-democracy protests, with security around Tiananmen Square being reinforced. Whilst the Government was concerned that Zhao's death might elicit a resurgence of pro-democracy sentiments, it was generally considered unlikely that an anti-Government movement would be initiated by a generation of students who were too young to remember the Tiananmen massacre and who were reaping the benefits of China's economic growth. Following Zhao's death, the Government reiterated its refusal to reassess the events of 1989, emphasizing that suppression of the democracy movement had been necessary to ensure the social stability upon which China's economic successes since 1989 had depended. Zhao was described by foreign media sources as 'the ghost at the feast'. His death received limited coverage in the Chinese media, and mourning for him took place under strict government surveillance.

From the late 1990s there was increasing concern about the spread of HIV/AIDS in China. During 2001 the authorities acknowledged the seriousness of the problem, and in January new legislation was introduced in Chengdu that forbade infected people from marrying; compulsory tests were to be carried out on high-risk groups such as prostitutes, drug addicts and those who had spent extended time abroad. In early June it was reported that as many as 500,000 people in Henan Province had been infected with HIV after selling their blood plasma to companies that had employed unhygienic practices; these donations of blood had been encouraged by the local health authorities. At the UNAIDS summit meeting in late June, the Minister of Public Health, Zhang Wenkang, stated that there were 600,000 people infected with HIV in China; however, UN estimates placed the number at 1.5m. In late August the Vice-Minister of Health formally acknowledged the gravity of the AIDS crisis. The authorities announced an increase in funds to US $12m. annually to counter the spread of the virus, and an allocation of $117m. in 2001–02 to improve the safety of blood banks. In November 2001 China held its first national HIV/AIDS conference. In April 2002 the authorities reported a 17% increase in HIV cases to 850,000, a figure still well below UN estimates, and in June a UN report warned that China was on the brink of an AIDS catastrophe, estimating that the total number of cases could rise to 10m. by 2010. The fear was that, if unrestrained, the virus would spread from rural areas (the worst-affected regions) to the general urban population. In late

August China's most prominent AIDS activist, Wan Yanhai, who had exposed the Henan epidemic, was detained by the Bureau of State Security. In September the authorities admitted that as many as 1m. might be infected with HIV, and initially announced that they would start mass-manufacturing anti-AIDS drugs, possibly in violation of international patents—although the latter was later denied. However, the authorities also for the first time requested international assistance in combating the virus, and released Wan Yanhai in late September. In late November it was reported that the health authorities in Guangdong Province were planning to issue, on a trial basis, sterile needles to drug users, in an attempt to limit the spread of HIV, and on 1 December—World AIDS Day—the Government announced a renewed effort to promote AIDS awareness. However, in early 2003 a draft UN report warned that China would be unlikely to meet its target of halting or reversing the increase in HIV/AIDS by 2010.

Following the SARS crisis in early 2003, there were signs that the Chinese Government was taking new steps to provide improved access to health information and to affordable health care. Measures included the supply of free drugs to HIV/AIDS sufferers who were on a low income and the provision of AIDS training to doctors at provincial level. In December 2003 Premier Wen Jiabao publicly associated himself with the campaign against HIV/AIDS by visiting AIDS patients in a Beijing hospital on World Aids Day. Nevertheless, according to a report published by Human Rights Watch in September 2003, official government figures continued to conceal the true extent of the spread of the virus, whilst HIV/AIDS sufferers experienced employment discrimination and were sometimes denied access to treatment. In April 2004 the Government announced that free AIDS tests would be available to the entire population, and that financial support would be given to AIDS patients who were unable to pay for their own treatment. According to the UN, by 2004 more than 200,000 people had died of AIDs in China, with a further 840,000 being infected with HIV.

In November and early December 2001, meanwhile, the authorities announced plans to accelerate the development of China's space programme, including the launching of more satellites, space probes and a manned space flight, to be followed by a manned mission to the moon. In March 2002 China successfully launched and returned to earth an unmanned space capsule, *Shenzhou III*, and in January 2003 achieved the same results with *Shenzhou IV*, both of which could be used to carry astronauts into orbit. Also in January 2003 China announced plans to launch its first manned space flight later in that year, thereby becoming the third nation after the former USSR and the USA, to launch such missions. The long-term goal was to develop a space station and moon base. In October 2003 a spacecraft carrying astronaut Yang Liwei was successfully launched into orbit. A second manned space flight was scheduled to take place in 2005.

Tibet (Xizang), a semi-independent region of western China, was occupied in October 1950 by Chinese Communist forces. In March 1959 there was an unsuccessful armed uprising by Tibetans opposed to Chinese rule. The Dalai Lama, the head of Tibet's Buddhist clergy and thus the region's spiritual leader, fled with some 100,000 supporters to Dharamsala, northern India, where a government-in-exile was established. The Chinese ended the former dominance of the lamas (Buddhist monks) and destroyed many monasteries. Tibet became an 'Autonomous Region' of China in September 1965, but the majority of Tibetans have continued to regard the Dalai Lama as their 'god-king', and to resent the Chinese presence. In October 1987 violent clashes occurred in Lhasa (the regional capital) between the Chinese authorities and Tibetans seeking independence. Further demonstrations during a religious festival in March 1988 resulted in a riot and several deaths, and a number of Tibetan separatists were arrested and detained without trial. The Dalai Lama, however, renounced demands for complete independence, and in 1988 proposed that Tibet become a self-governing Chinese territory, in all respects except foreign affairs. In December 1988 an offer from the Dalai Lama to meet Chinese representatives in Geneva was rejected, and later that month two more demonstrators were killed by security forces during a march to commemorate the 40th anniversary of the UN General Assembly's adoption of the Universal Declaration of Human Rights.

On 7 March 1989 martial law was imposed in Lhasa for the first time since 1959, after further violent clashes between separatists and the Chinese police, which resulted in the deaths of 16 protesters. In October the Chinese Government condemned as an interference in its internal affairs the award of the Nobel Peace Prize to the Dalai Lama. In November several Tibetan Buddhist nuns claimed to have been severely tortured for their part in the demonstrations in March 1989. In May 1990 martial law was lifted in Lhasa. Human rights groups claimed that during the last six months of the period of martial law as many as 2,000 persons had been executed. Furthermore, political and religious repression and torture were reported to be continuing throughout 1990. Renewed anti-Chinese protests were reported in October 1991 and in March 1992. In May a report issued by Amnesty International was critical of the Chinese authorities' violations of the human rights of the monks and nuns of Tibet. In May 1993 several thousand Tibetans were reported to have demonstrated in Lhasa against Chinese rule. A number of protesters were believed to have been killed by the security forces. In January 1994 two prominent Tibetan activists were released from detention. In July, however, five secessionists were found guilty of counter-revolutionary acts and received prison sentences of up to 15 years.

In April 1994 China condemned the Dalai Lama's meeting with President Clinton during the former's lecture tour of the USA. In September the Dalai Lama warned China that Tibet might resort to armed uprising if oppression continued to worsen. In late 1994 the construction of new monasteries and temples in Tibet was banned. In March 1995 regulations restricting the number of Buddhist monks were announced, and in the same month the Dalai Lama's proposal that a referendum be held on the future of Tibet was dismissed by China. In May the Dalai Lama's nomination of the 11th incarnation of the Panchen Lama (the second position in the spiritual hierarchy, the 10th incumbent having died in 1989) was condemned by the Chinese authorities, which banned the six-year old boy, Gedhun Choekyi Nyima, from travelling to Dharamsala. In September 1995, as the 30th anniversary of the imposition of Chinese rule approached, it was reported that independence activists had carried out two bombings in Lhasa.

In September 1995, during the UN World Conference on Women and the Non-Governmental Organizations' Forum held concurrently in China, a silent protest by a group of female Tibetan exiles attracted much attention. Following an informal meeting between the Dalai Lama and US President Clinton in Washington in mid-September, China lodged a strong protest. In November the Chinese Government announced Gyaltsen (Gyaincain) Norbu as its own nomination of a new Panchen Lama. The boy was enthroned at a ceremony in Lhasa in December, the whereabouts of the Dalai Lama's choice remaining unknown until mid-1996, when China's ambassador to the UN in Geneva admitted that the boy was in detention in Beijing. There were violent confrontations in Tibet in May 1996, following the banning of any public display of images of the Dalai Lama. During the latter part of 1996 visits by the Dalai Lama to the United Kingdom and Australia aroused further protests from the Chinese Government. A series of minor explosions during 1996 culminated in late December with the detonation of a powerful bomb outside a government office in Lhasa, which injured several people. The attack was denounced by the Dalai Lama. In an unprecedented admission, the Chinese Government acknowledged the existence of a terrorist problem in Tibet.

The Chinese leadership condemned the Dalai Lama's visit to Taiwan in March 1997, despite assurances that he was visiting in his capacity as a spiritual leader. In May it was reported that Chadrel Rinpoche, an official in the Tibetan administration and one of Tibet's most senior monks, had been sentenced to six years' imprisonment for allegedly revealing information to the Dalai Lama about Beijing's search for the new Panchen Lama. The USA's decision in mid-1997 to appoint a special co-ordinator for Tibet was criticized by the Chinese authorities. In October the Dalai Lama appealed to the Chinese Government to reopen negotiations over the status of Tibet, confirming that he did not seek full independence for the region. In December the Geneva-based International Commission of Jurists (see p. 389) published a report accusing China of suppressing nationalist dissent in Tibet and attempting to extinguish Tibetan culture, and appealed for a referendum, under the auspices of the UN, to decide the territory's future status.

In April 1998 China agreed to allow envoys of the European Union (EU) to make a one-week investigatory visit to Tibet. Later that month in New Delhi, India, Thupten Ngodup, one of six Tibetan exiles who had been engaged in a hunger strike for

49 days, died after setting himself alight as security forces attempted forcibly to transport the protesters to hospital to end their hunger strike. The hunger strikers had declared their intention of starving themselves to death unless the UN agreed to debate the issue of Tibet in the General Assembly, to appoint a special rapporteur to investigate human rights violations and to oversee a referendum on independence. The protest was arranged by the Tibetan Youth Congress (TYC), a movement advocating independence for Tibet. In May 1998 the EU adopted two resolutions relating to China, condemning the sale of organs of executed prisoners and calling for a UN committee to investigate the transactions and, furthermore, urging the UN to appoint a rapporteur for Tibet issues.

During his visit to China and Hong Kong in late June 1998 (see below), the US President, Bill Clinton, discussed Tibet with Chinese leaders, with the Dalai Lama's support. Beijing proclaimed its readiness to open negotiations if the Dalai Lama first declared both Tibet and Taiwan to be inalienable parts of China. This statement was repeated regularly during 1998. In October the Dalai Lama admitted that since the 1960s he had received US $1.7m. annually from the Central Intelligence Agency (CIA) to support the Tibetan separatist movement. Whilst visiting the USA in early November, the Dalai Lama had an unofficial meeting with Bill Clinton, thereby angering the Chinese authorities. In January 1999 a new US special co-ordinator for Tibetan affairs was appointed, amid opposition from China. Earlier in the month TYC activists had attempted to storm the Chinese embassy in New Delhi and had burnt Chinese flags outside the building to protest against China's occupation of Tibet. In May the Dalai Lama visited the United Kingdom and met the British Prime Minister, Tony Blair. In order to avoid criticism from Beijing, it was reported that Blair had received the religious leader in a spiritual capacity.

In January 2000 the Chinese Government was embarrassed by the flight of Tibet's second most important Lama, the Karmapa, from Tibet to Dharamsala. Frequent requests by him to be permitted to visit his guru in India had been ignored. The Karmapa, who had, unusually, been recognized both by the Dalai Lama and by Beijing, had previously been rewarded by the latter for his perceived loyalty to the Chinese regime. Reports that the Karmapa's parents had been detained by the Chinese authorities, following anti-China remarks by their son, were denied. The Karmapa's request for political asylum placed the Indian authorities in a difficult position; India maintained close contact with both the Dalai Lama and with Beijing, but by the end of 2000 no decision had been reached. Meanwhile, there was some discord between followers of the Karmapa and other Tibetans, the former proclaiming their leader to be the Dalai Lama's equal. Furthermore, three other people staked their claim to be the real Karmapa. In January 2000 in Lhasa, Soinam Puncog, a two-year-old boy selected by the Chinese authorities but rejected by followers of the Dalai Lama, was ordained as the new Reting Lama.

China continued to exert great influence over the Dalai Lama's movements in 2000. Following the UN's decision to exclude him from a summit meeting of world religious leaders in August, in October the Republic of Korea refused to grant a visa to the Dalai Lama, on the grounds that it would be 'inappropriate'. Reports confirmed that Beijing had expressed strong opposition to a trip planned by the Dalai Lama for the following month. In April, however, despite warnings from Beijing, Japan had granted the Dalai Lama a visa to lecture at a Buddhist college. He also made his first-ever visit to Northern Ireland, to promote peace, in October 2000. Also in October, the newly appointed Party Secretary for Tibet, Guo Jinlong, announced that he would continue to oppose separatism, but would open up the region's economy. In November the head of a visiting EU delegation urged Beijing to appoint the Dalai Lama as governor of Tibet, a suggestion that was immediately rebuffed. In December contact was resumed between the Dalai Lama and the Chinese authorities, following a visit to Beijing by the former's brother. Meanwhile, in October in Lhasa, a bomb explosion was attributed to the continuing campaign of resistance to Chinese rule.

In February 2001 Beijing announced plans for the first railway link between Tibet and the rest of China. The new railway, linking Lhasa with Golmud, Qinghai Province, was to be 1,118 km long. Construction began at the end of June. Scheduled for completion in 2007, the project was one of several planned for the region, including a massive expansion of Lhasa and five new airports, which were aimed not only at raising the level of development but also at discouraging separatist dissent. Also in February, the Australian Minister of Health visited Tibet while touring China, the first visit to the region by an Australian minister in 13 years. In early April the Dalai Lama paid a 10-day visit to Taiwan, which was largely religious in nature, but he none the less met President Chen Shui-bian and addressed the legislature, thus antagonizing Beijing, which opposed any co-operation between its two principal 'renegade provinces'. Later in the month, the Karmapa spoke for the first time about his escape from China in the previous year. In late May the CCP organized commemorative ceremonies in Tibet to mark the 50th anniversary of the 'peaceful liberation' (the signing of the 1951 treaty) of the region, with official media praising the 'great social progress' made since China's assumption of power. On the anniversary the Dalai Lama had a meeting with US President George W. Bush in Washington, DC, greatly angering Beijing.

In early July 2001 Beijing's chosen Panchen Lama visited Shanghai and Zhejiang Province at the invitation of Beijing, the trip being regarded as a move to promote him as an alternative Tibetan leader to the Dalai Lama. Later in the month, Beijing announced that it would build a monument to commemorate Chinese rule over Tibet in the grounds of the Potala Palace, the former winter residence of the Dalai Lama. The monument was completed in early 2002. In early August 2001 the Chinese Government declared that, upon the death of the current incumbent, it would appoint its own Dalai Lama, thus disregarding traditional Tibetan procedures for selecting the spiritual leader; the plan was condemned by the Tibetan government-in-exile. Later in August Chinese troops seized the largest Tibetan monastery, Serthar, and forced thousands of monks and nuns to denounce the Dalai Lama. Many of the buildings there were reportedly destroyed. At the same time, Beijing refused to free Chadrel Rinpoche, imprisoned since 1997 (see above). Also in late August, Chinese geologists announced the discovery of extensive new petroleum and gas deposits in a 100-km belt in Tibet's Qiangtang basin. Many Tibetans feared, however, that massive development schemes, and the considerable influx of Han Chinese from neighbouring provinces (who dominated the new economy), were irreversibly transforming the character and culture of the region.

In November 2001 the Chinese Government announced the creation of a new enterprise zone in Lhasa, and issued a document outlining its main achievements during its 50 years of rule in Tibet. The issue of the document coincided with a visit to China by the UN High Commissioner for Human Rights, Mary Robinson, who urged Chinese leaders not to use the USA's 'war on terrorism' as a pretext for suppressing ethnic minorities.

In January 2002 Beijing released Ngawang Choephel, a Tibetan music scholar serving an 18-year sentence on spying charges, and in April the authorities released, on medical grounds, Tanag Jigme Sangpo, who had first been imprisoned in 1965, and again since 1983, for campaigning against Chinese rule. He was believed to be the country's longest-serving political prisoner, having endured a total of 32 years in detention. Both releases constituted apparent goodwill gestures to the USA. Tanag Jigme Sangpo subsequently sought medical treatment in the USA in mid-July 2002. In February, meanwhile, Beijing reiterated its request to the Dalai Lama for him to return from exile. In June the Party Secretary for Tibet, Guo Jinlong, visited Australia and met the Minister of Foreign Affairs, Alexander Downer, amid criticism of the latter for his refusal to meet the Dalai Lama. Also in June, CCP officials in Tibet formally welcomed Gyaltsen Norbu as the new Panchen Lama. In July the Dalai Lama announced the privatization of the Government-in-exile's businesses in India and Nepal, owing to their poor performance. However, in August the Russian authorities refused him a visa to visit three traditionally Buddhist Republics of the Russian Federation—Buryatiya, Tyva, and Kalmykiya—as Moscow sought to avoid displeasing Beijing.

In September 2002 exiled Tibetan officials travelled to China (including Tibet—the first such visit there since 1985) in a 16-day tour arranged by the elder brother of the Dalai Lama, Gyalo Thondup, who had visited Beijing in August. During the tour, the Dalai Lama's envoy to the USA, Lodi Gyaltsen Gyari, and the envoy to Europe, Kelsang Gyaltsen, held the first meetings with government officials since 1993, amid hopes of a more conciliatory attitude by Beijing. After returning to India, Gyari spoke favourably of the exchange. In late October the authorities freed Ngawang Sangdrol, a Tibetan nun whose three-year sentence in 1992 had been extended until 2011. In early November

the Dalai Lama finally visited Mongolia, although the Chinese Government denounced the visit. Meanwhile, in the middle of that month, Beijing revealed that the Dalai Lama's chosen Panchen Lama, in detention since 1995, was 'very happy' and living with his family in Tibet. In December 2002, however, the authorities sentenced to death two Tibetans for their alleged role in a series of bombings in Sichuan Province during 1998–2002. The two men were from Ganzi, a region of Sichuan which had a Tibetan majority and had once been part of the territory. In late January 2003 10 more people were arrested in connection with the bombings, and one of the two men sentenced earlier was executed.

In early June 2003 discussions between Chinese officials and envoys of the Dalai Lama were held in Beijing. The Dalai Lama's representative in the USA, Lodi Gyaltsen Gyari, who led the delegation, said that the visit had been encouraging despite remaining disagreements. Also in June, Indian Prime Minister Atal Bihari Vajpayee acknowledged Tibet as part of China in writing for the first time. Again in June, 18 Tibetans were deported to China from Nepal, despite condemnation of this action by the UN. In September 2003 US President George W. Bush held talks with the Dalai Lama, which prompted protests from Beijing. Meanwhile, in November 2003, a Tibetan political prisoner, Nyima Drakpa, died aged 29. There were claims that he had been tortured by Chinese authorities. In February 2004 Phuntsog Nyidron, a Tibetan Buddhist nun believed to have received the longest sentence ever given to a female political prisoner in China, was released after 15 years in prison. In March the Dalai Lama made a statement to mark the 45th anniversary of his flight from Tibet, declaring that he hoped for an improvement in relations with China during the coming year. However, in May the Government issued a document entitled 'Regional Ethnic Autonomy in Tibet', requiring the Dalai Lama to abandon any attempts to control developments there, even though he had expressed willingness to accept limited autonomy rather than full Tibetan independence. In August Gyaltsen Norbu, the boy nominated by Beijing as the new Panchen Lama in 1995, made a visit to Tibet. In September a third round of talks between Chinese officials and envoys of the Dalai Lama were held in Beijing to discuss the terms of a possible return of the Dalai Lama from exile.

Anti-Chinese sentiment in the Xinjiang Uygur Autonomous Region intensified in the 1990s, resulting in the initiation of a new, often brutal, campaign by the authorities to repress the Islamist separatist movement, whose goal was to establish an independent 'East Turkestan'. The region had been conquered by the Chinese Manchus in the mid-18th century, and it had subsequently enjoyed brief periods of independence. However, Han Chinese had, for decades after 1949, been encouraged or forced to move to the region by Beijing, thereby reducing the proportion of the indigenous Uygur population and compounding resentment. The Han Chinese and the Uygur communities often had little contact with one another, with the Han occupying the higher-status jobs, and forming majorities in the cities. Separatist movements such as the Xinjiang Liberation Front and the Uygur Liberation Organization (ULO) often had support of the Uygur diaspora in Kyrgyzstan and Uzbekistan. Suppression of separatism increased in 1996, following a number of violent incidents. Hundreds of people were detained for their part in rioting and bomb attacks, and many were subsequently executed or imprisoned. Reports in late 1997 indicated that there had been a renewal of armed separatist activity, in which more than 300 people had been killed. In January 1998 13 people were executed in Xinjiang, allegedly for robbery and murder, although unofficial reports suggested that those executed were Muslim separatist demonstrators. Muslim separatists were believed to be responsible for an incendiary device on a bus in Wuhan in February, which killed 16 people. Two leading activists, Yibulayin Simayi and Abudureyimu Aisha, were executed in January 1999. Detentions continued during the year, and a further 10 separatists were reportedly executed at the end of May. Three Muslims were sentenced to death in September for participating in the separatist campaign, whilst six others received long prison sentences. In October 2000 Abduhelil Abdulmejit, a leading organizer of resistance to Chinese rule in Xinjiang who had been imprisoned three years previously, was reported to have died of pneumonia while in custody; international groups alleged that he had been tortured and murdered.

Meanwhile, the NATO attacks on Yugoslavia in March–June 1999 greatly alarmed military planners in Beijing, who feared that the USA might carry out a similar operation in Xinjiang, on the grounds of humanitarian intervention on behalf of the Uygur separatists. The region was strategically important to China owing to its petroleum and gas reserves and its proximity to the increasingly important Caspian Sea-Central Asian region. Stability in Xinjiang remained crucial to China's 'go west' programme of developing the country's remote inner regions. Construction work on a 4,200-km gas pipeline from Xinjiang to Shanghai commenced in 2002, and the pipeline became operational in 2004.

During 2001 the authorities continued the 'Strike Hard' campaign against separatists, with multiple executions reported. In early August the PLA conducted large-scale military exercises involving 50,000 troops in the region. China's fears of Islamist separatism were heightened after the terrorist attacks on New York and Washington, DC, USA, on 11 September 2001, and Beijing stated that as many as 1,000 Uygur Islamist fighters had been trained in terrorist camps in Afghanistan operated by the al-Qa'ida network of the Saudi-born dissident, Osama bin Laden. In late September Chinese troops began anti-guerrilla operations in the Afghan border region of Xinjiang, aimed at preventing Islamist infiltration. International human rights groups, however, feared that Beijing would use the pretext of fighting terrorism to increase repression, and in November the Minister of Foreign Affairs, Tang Jiaxuan, likened China's anti-separatist campaign to the USA's 'war on terror'. In December, following the collapse of Afghanistan's ruling Taliban regime, China urged the USA to surrender captured Uygur Islamist fighters; the USA refused to comply, stating that it did not view the separatists as terrorists. At the same time, Jiang warned that religion should not be used to challenge the CCP or to undermine China's unity. In January 2002 Beijing released a new report alleging links between the separatists and Osama bin Laden, in an apparent bid to win international approval for its anti-separatist activities.

In March 2002 Amnesty International reported that thousands of Muslim Uygurs had been detained since 11 September 2001, and that up to 8,000 had been given 'political education' courses. In June 2002 the authorities announced that from September Xinjiang University would no longer teach courses in the Uygur language (for 50 years students had had a choice of studying in Uygur or Mandarin). The authorities claimed that this would raise the standards of education for Uygurs, but the latter viewed the changes as an attack on their culture and identity. In late August the USA designated the East Turkestan Islamic Movement a terrorist group and 'froze' the organization's assets, in a conciliatory gesture towards Beijing. The UN also added the organization to its list of terrorist organizations in September. In 2003 China continued to portray its suppression of Uygur separatism in Xinjiang, previously considered an internal affair, as part of the war on global terrorism. In December Beijing issued a 'terrorist' list that named the Eastern Turkestan Liberation Organization, the World Uygur Youth Congress and the East Turkestan Information Centre, as well as the East Turkestan Islamic Movement, as 'terrorist' organizations. Of these, only the East Turkestan Islamic Movement was considered a terrorist movement by the USA.

In March 2004 it was reported that Rebiya Kadeer, an Uygur businesswoman and rights activist who had been imprisoned in 1999 for sending newspaper articles to her husband in the USA, would be released in 2006. In July 2004, during a visit by President Hu to Tashkent (see below), a statement was signed by China and Uzbekistan whereby Uzbekistan agreed to co-operate with China in suppressing separatist activities in Xinjiang as part of a wider effort to combat terrorist activities. During 2004 Erkin Alptekin, son of Isa Yusuf Alptekin who had been head of a brief Uygur government in the 1940s, reportedly emerged as leader of a Uygur exile movement committed to achieving independence for Xinjiang, or East Turkestan, by peaceful means. In September an East Turkestan government-in-exile was proclaimed by Anwar Yusuf Turani, head of the East Turkestan National Freedom Centre. Many Uygur groups, however, did not recognize the government-in-exile. Rebiya Kadeer was released in March 2005, prior to a visit to Beijing by US Secretary of State Condoleezza Rice

In September 1984, following protracted negotiations, China reached agreement with the British Government over the terms of the future administration of Hong Kong upon the territory's return to Chinese sovereignty, scheduled for 1 July 1997. In 1985 a Basic Law Drafting Committee (BLDC), including 25 representatives from Hong Kong, was established in Beijing to

prepare a new Basic Law (Constitution) for Hong Kong, which was duly approved by the NPC in April 1990. Relations between China and the United Kingdom were strained in 1992 by the announcement of ambitious plans for democratic reform in Hong Kong prior to 1997. In December 1993 China declared that it would regard as null and void any laws enacted by the territory's Legislative Council. In October 1995 Qian Qichen, the Chinese Vice-Premier and Minister of Foreign Affairs, visited London for discussions with the British Prime Minister and his Foreign Secretary. In January 1996 the 150-member Preparatory Committee of the Hong Kong Special Administrative Region (SAR) was formally established in Beijing, in succession to the Preliminary Working Committee (PWC), which had been formed in July 1993 to study issues relating to the transfer of sovereignty. The new body duly appointed a 400-member Selection Committee, responsible for the choice of Hong Kong's future Chief Executive. In December 1996 the Selection Committee chose Tung Chee-hwa as the SAR's first Chief Executive and elected the 60 members of the Provisional Legislative Council (PLC).

The transfer of Hong Kong from British to Chinese sovereignty was effected at midnight on 30 June 1997, whereupon some 4,000 PLA troops were deployed in the territory. In December 36 deputies from Hong Kong were directly elected to the Ninth NPC in Beijing. Elections for the SAR's new Legislative Council took place in May 1998. In March 2001 the Hong Kong Government introduced the Chief Executive Election Bill, which was passed in July. Tung was re-elected unopposed in March 2002, and in June appointed a cabinet-style expanded Executive Council, under new powers accorded to him. In July 2003 mass demonstrations took place in Hong Kong against proposed new anti-subversion laws, which critics feared would undermine the 'one country, two systems' model and give Beijing greater control over Hong Kong's affairs. In September the controversial anti-subversion bill was withdrawn as a consequence of public opposition, representing a serious challenge to Beijing's authority in Hong Kong. Economic co-operation between Hong Kong and the mainland continued to develop, none the less, with the signing of a free-trade agreement, the Closer Economic Partnership Arrangement (CEPA), in June. In November it was announced that Hong Kong banks would be able to conduct personal banking services in Chinese yuan from the beginning of 2004. In April 2004 a meeting of the Standing Committee of the NPC was held to consider the future procedures for selecting Hong Kong's Chief Executive and Legislative Council. The Committee subsequently ruled that there was no possibility of direct election of the Chief Executive in 2007 or of universal suffrage in legislative elections in 2008. The ruling prompted protests by democracy campaigners in Hong Kong. However, in the elections to the Legislative Council held in September 2004, support for the pro-democracy faction was less evident than had been widely expected. Tung Chee-hwa resigned in March 2005. (See the chapter on Hong Kong for further information.)

In June 1986 China and Portugal opened formal negotiations for the return of the Portuguese overseas territory of Macao to full Chinese sovereignty. In January 1987 it was agreed that this would take place in December 1999. The agreement was based upon the 'one country, two systems' principle, which had formed the basis of China's negotiated settlement regarding the return of Hong Kong. In March 1993 the final draft of the Basic Law for Macao was approved by the NPC. In May 1995 China proposed the swift establishment of a preparatory working committee to facilitate the transfer of sovereignty. Cordial relations were maintained, and the Portuguese Minister of Foreign Affairs visited Beijing in February 1996. The two sides agreed to accelerate the pace of work of the Sino-Portuguese Joint Liaison Group (JLG). In January 1997 the Chinese Vice-Premier and Minister of Foreign Affairs, Qian Qichen, travelled to Portugal for discussions. It was subsequently announced that China would station an 'appropriate' number of troops in the territory to help combat the increasing problem of organized crime and ensure public security upon its resumption of sovereignty in December 1999.

In April 1999 the 200-member Selection Committee, which was comprised entirely of residents of the territory and which was to be responsible for the appointment of members of Macao's post-1999 government, was established in Beijing. In the following month Edmund Ho, a banker and a member of the legislature since 1988, was elected the first Chief Executive of Macao. China resumed sovereignty of the territory at midnight on 19 December 1999, whereupon Ho was duly inaugurated and the PLA garrison was established. President Jiang Zemin visited Macao in December 2000 to mark the first anniversary of the territory's reversion to Chinese sovereignty, and praised the local administration. Ho visited Beijing in March 2001 to attend the fourth session of the Ninth NPC. During 2001 and 2002 Beijing, Hong Kong, and Macao increased co-operation in combating cross-border crime. In March 2002 a new representative office of the Macao SAR was opened in Beijing, and in July Beijing dispatched a new representative to the territory. Macao continued to develop economic relations with several provinces on the mainland. In October 2003 a free-trade agreement, a CEPA, was signed between Macao and the mainland. President Hu visited Macao in December 2004 to mark the fifth anniversary of the territory's return to Chinese rule. (See the chapter on Macao for further information.)

Taiwan has repeatedly rejected China's proposals for reunification, whereby the island would become a 'special administrative region' along the lines of Hong Kong and Macao, and has sought reunification under its own terms. China has never relinquished sovereignty over the island, however, and has repeatedly threatened to use military force against Taiwan should it formally declare itself independent of the mainland. During the early 1990s relations improved as both sides held meetings of their respective cross-Straits organizations, the mainland's Association for Relations Across the Taiwan Straits (ARATS, established in 1991) and Taiwan's Straits Exchange Foundation (SEF, established in 1990). However, in early 1996 China conducted massive military exercises near Taiwan, coinciding with the island's first-ever presidential elections. Taiwan refused to be intimidated, and tensions later eased. Beijing became increasingly angry, however, at Taiwan's insistence on state-to-state negotiations, and the island's possible inclusion in a US-led Theater Missile Defense (TMD) system. China responded by increasing its missile build-up in coastal regions facing Taiwan. In early 2000 China warned that it would invade Taiwan if it indefinitely postponed reunification talks, and reacted negatively to the election of Chen Shui-bian as President, amid fears that a new, Taiwanese identity was developing. By 2000 the island's politics had increasingly become polarized between 'native Taiwanese' (approximately 65% of the population) and mainlanders and their offspring (approximately 35% of the population). A PLA military document in late 2000 added two additional possible pretexts for invasion, namely a declaration of independence or occupation by a third country. Nevertheless, despite frequent political disputes, cross-Straits business ties flourished as Taiwanese investment continued to flow into the mainland. In late 2001 President Chen removed long-standing investment restrictions with the mainland, marking a new 'aggressive opening' policy. Beijing remained unenthusiastic on the issue of full direct transport links unless Taiwan recognized the 'One China' principle, but by 2002 was showing greater flexibility towards the island. Chen had, in August 2002, supported the notion of a referendum to determine the island's future. In January 2003 China permitted several Taiwanese airliners on charter flights to land in China for the first time in over 50 years. However, the operation of full cross-Straits transport links remained unlikely in the immediate future. In June 2003 President Hu Jintao assumed control over Beijing's relations with Taiwan, taking over from former President Jiang Zemin. In July a US military report claimed that China was increasing its short-range missile capacity in preparation for possible conflict with Taiwan. In November tensions between Taiwan and the mainland were exacerbated after Taiwan's legislature approved a bill allowing referendums to take place on the island. Although the legislation in its final version prohibited a vote on Taiwan's sovereignty except in the event of an external attack, China feared that the new law might lead to a vote on Taiwan's independence. The Beijing Government did not attempt directly to influence the presidential election when it was held in March 2004, resulting in a narrow victory for Chen. Concurrently with the election, President Chen held a referendum on the subject of Taiwan's response to the deployment of Chinese missiles, but this failed to produce a valid result. China conducted a further series of military exercises in the Straits in July, including a mock invasion of Taiwan. Also in July, a Chinese government official warned that there was a possibility that Beijing might attack Taiwan should President Chen proceed with plans for constitutional reform. In elections to Taiwan's Legislative Yuan held in December, the pan-green alliance led by President Chen's Democratic Progressive Party (DPP) secured fewer seats than the pan-blue alliance, which

incorporated the KMT. The Taiwanese Government was thus faced with an opposition majority in the legislature, which was expected to hinder Chen's reform programme. In December the Standing Committee of China's NPC approved a draft of anti-secession legislation aimed at preventing Taiwan from declaring independence. The draft was approved by the third plenum of the 10th NPC in March 2005. In early 2005 it was agreed that, for the first time ever, direct flights between Taipei and the Chinese mainland were to be permitted during the forthcoming Lunar New Year. In April–May, during an historic visit to the mainland by Lien Chan, leader of the opposition KMT, President Hu Jintao and the former Premier of Taiwan agreed to uphold their opposition to Taiwanese independence. (See the chapter on Taiwan for further information.)

In the early years of the People's Republic, China was dependent on the USSR for economic and military aid, and Chinese planning was based on the Soviet model, with highly centralized control. From 1955, however, Mao Zedong set out to develop a distinctively Chinese form of socialism. As a result, the USSR withdrew all technical aid to China in August 1960. Chinese hostility to the USSR increased, in what became known as the 'Sino-Soviet Split', and was aggravated by territorial disputes, and by the Soviet invasion of Afghanistan and the Soviet-supported Vietnamese invasion of Cambodia in the late 1970s. Sino-Soviet relations remained strained until 1987, when representatives of the two countries signed a partial agreement concerning the exact demarcation of the disputed common border at the Amur River. The withdrawal of Soviet troops from Afghanistan (completed in February 1989) and Viet Nam's assurance that it would end its military presence in Cambodia by September 1989 resulted in a further *rapprochement*. In May 1989 a full summit meeting was held in Beijing, at which normal state and party relations between China and the USSR were formally restored. During the next two years senior Chinese officials visited the USSR. In December 1991, upon the dissolution of the USSR, China recognized the newly independent states of the former union. The President of Russia, Boris Yeltsin, visited China in December 1992. In May 1994, in Beijing, Premier Li Peng and his Russian counterpart signed various co-operation agreements. In September President Jiang Zemin travelled to Moscow, the first visit to Russia by a Chinese Head of State since 1957. The two sides reached agreement on the formal demarcation of the western section of the border (the eastern section having been delimited in May 1991), and each pledged not to aim nuclear missiles at the other. In June 1995 the Chinese Premier paid an official visit to Russia, where several bilateral agreements were signed.

Sino-Russian relations continued to improve, and in April 1996 in Beijing Presidents Jiang and Yeltsin signed a series of agreements, envisaging the development of closer co-operation in areas such as energy, space research, environmental protection, and the combating of organized crime. Together with their counterparts from Kazakhstan, Kyrgyzstan and Tajikistan, the two Presidents also signed a treaty aimed at reducing tension along their respective borders. Progress on the Sino-Russian border question, and also on matters such as trade, was made during the Chinese Premier's visit to Moscow in December 1996. A further treaty on military co-operation and border demilitarization was signed by the Presidents of China, Russia, Kazakhstan, Kyrgyzstan and Tajikistan in April 1997, during a visit by President Jiang Zemin to Russia. Presidents Jiang and Yeltsin affirmed their commitment to building a strategic, co-operative partnership, and a Sino-Russian committee on friendship, peace and development was established. Progress on the Sino-Russian border issue culminated in the signing of an agreement, during President Yeltsin's visit to Beijing in November, which formally ended the territorial dispute.

In May 1998 a direct telephone link was established between Jiang Zemin and President Yeltsin of Russia. In November, in Moscow, representatives from Russia, China and the Democratic People's Republic of Korea signed an inter-governmental agreement on the delimitation of their borders along the Tumannaya River. Relations continued to improve between China and Russia in 1999. In February 11 agreements on bilateral economic and trade co-operation were signed during a visit to Russia by Zhu Rongji. In June, following a visit to China by the Russian Minister of Foreign Affairs, it was announced that a final accord on the demarcation of a common border between the two countries had been agreed after seven years of negotiations. During a summit meeting of China, Russia, Kazakhstan, Kyrgyzstan and Tajikistan (collectively known as the 'Shanghai

Five'—see below) in the Kyrgyz capital, Bishkek, agreements were signed on the China–Kazakhstan–Kyrgyzstan and the Chinese–Kyrgyz borders. In November it was announced that all Chinese–Kazakh border issues had been completely resolved.

Following the resignation of Boris Yeltsin as Russian President in December 1999, his successor, Vladimir Putin, confirmed his commitment to maintaining and improving links with China. A 'significant upgrading' in Sino-Russian relations occurred during Putin's visit to Beijing in July 2000, when the two countries issued a joint statement condemning US plans for the deployment of a missile defence system (see above). Presidents Jiang and Putin expressed fears of a new nuclear arms race, should installation of the system be implemented. NPC Chairman Li Peng visited Russia in September 2000, mainly to discuss economic co-operation, particularly in energy issues. In November the Russian Prime Minister, Mikhail Kasyanov, visited China and concluded the sale of five A-50 early warning aircraft and two advanced naval destroyers to the Chinese armed forces.

In July 2001 Presidents Jiang and Putin signed a new 20-year Sino-Russian 'Good-neighbourly Treaty of Friendship and Co-operation' in Moscow and reaffirmed their opposition to the USA's plans for a National Missile Defence (NMD) system. The new treaty was a 'strategic partnership' rather than a military alliance, however, and was not officially aimed at any third countries. The treaty also agreed to further cultural, economic and scientific co-operation, and stated that neither country had any territorial claims on the other; the latter had become an important issue in the 1990s as an increasing number of illegal Chinese labourers had settled in the Russian Far East, raising fears in Russia that China would seek to reclaim territories ceded to Russia in the 19th century. Following the summit meeting, it was announced that China would purchase as many as 38 advanced Su-30 fighter aircraft from Russia, valued at US $2,000m. Since the 1990s Russia had sold between 70 and 100 advanced fighter aircraft, many of which were jointly produced by the two countries in Shenyang. In August the Russian gas monopoly, Gazprom, indicated that it would help build new pipelines connecting Siberia with northern China. In September Prime Minister Zhu Rongji visited Russia and signed several trade agreements, and in late October Vice-President Hu Jintao visited Moscow, where he met Putin.

In January 2002 Russia announced that it would build two new advanced warships for the Chinese navy by 2006, and in April the Russian state arms export agency, Rosoboroneksport, agreed to sell China hundreds of millions of dollars' worth of air defence missiles and related equipment. In May China and Russia reached agreement on the former's purchase of eight submarines costing US $1,500m., and at the end of that month the Russian Minister of Defence, Sergei Ivanov, visited Beijing and reiterated Moscow's commitment to their strategic partnership, which China feared was being undermined by Russia's increasingly pro-US and pro-NATO posture after the terrorist attacks on the USA in the previous September. In June China and Russia submitted a joint proposal to the UN Conference on Disarmament for a new international treaty to ban space weapons—a move aimed at preventing the USA from militarizing outer space. Russian Prime Minister Mikhail Kasyanov visited Beijing in late August to discuss strategic issues, and Putin himself visited China at the beginning of December to meet Jiang Zemin and Hu Jintao. The two countries issued a joint declaration on a number of global strategic issues, particularly urging a peaceful resolution to the USA's diplomatic crisis with Iraq, and for the USA and North Korea to normalize relations, with the latter abandoning its nuclear weapons programme. The two countries also sought to increase bilateral trade and economic co-operation, although there were disagreements regarding plans for a pipeline that would export Russian oil to Daqing, in north-eastern China, the route length and costs being the inhibiting factors.

Hu Jintao visited Russia during his first overseas trip in his capacity as China's President in May 2003. During the visit President Hu and President Putin discussed the use of Siberian oil resources in China, as well as international relations in the context of the recent military action in Iraq. President Putin visited China in October 2004 for official talks, which were dominated by China's wish to reach an agreement on the Daqing oil pipeline. However, President Putin stated that the decision on the route for the pipeline would be based on Russian interests.

During the 1990s China steadily consolidated its relations with the former Soviet republics of Central Asia. China shared with these republics a fear of the spread of Islamist terrorism, along with a common interest in developing and transporting the petroleum and gas deposits of the Caspian Sea-Central Asia region. In the late 1990s China, along with Russia, Kazakhstan, Kyrgyzstan, and Tajikistan, established the 'Shanghai Five' group (renamed the Shanghai Co-operation Organization—SCO at their annual meeting in June 2001, when Uzbekistan became the sixth member). The grouping aimed to stabilize the region in order to promote development. Both China and Russia hoped that the SCO would help counter US influence in Central Asia, but at a meeting of SCO ministers of foreign affairs in January 2002, it had become clear that following the US attack on Afghanistan in late 2001, the organization lacked cohesiveness and influence. During 2000–01 China also gradually began improving relations with the Taliban regime in Afghanistan, signing several economic and technical agreements in the expectation that the Taliban would cease supporting Islamist Uygur fighters in Xinjiang. Following the collapse of the Taliban regime in late 2001, the new Afghan Prime Minister, Hamid Karzai, visited Beijing in January 2002 to discuss Chinese aid towards the reconstruction of his country. Meanwhile, China strengthened its relations with Kyrgyzstan during 2002. In May of that year Kyrgyzstan ratified a 1999 border treaty which ceded nearly 95,000 ha of disputed territory to China, and in October 2002 the two countries staged their first-ever joint military exercises, under the auspices of the SCO. In December 2002 the President of Kazakhstan, Nursultan Nazarbayev, visited Beijing, where he reached an agreement to construct a pipeline from Kazakhstan to western China. On his first state visit as China's President, Hu Jintao visited Kazakhstan in early June 2003. In June 2004 President Hu visited Uzbekistan to attend an SCO summit meeting, and signed an agreement with Uzbek President Islam Karimov to co-operate in combating 'terrorism, separatism and extremism' (see also above). In the same month 11 Chinese aid workers were murdered in Afghanistan, in what was described by the Chinese media as a terrorist attack.

During the 1970s there was an improvement in China's relations with the West and also with Japan. Almost all Western countries had recognized the Government of the People's Republic as the sole legitimate government of China, and had consequently withdrawn recognition from the 'Republic of China', which had been confined to Taiwan since 1949. For many years, however, the USA refused to recognize the People's Republic, regarding the Taiwan administration as the legitimate Chinese government. In February 1972 President Richard Nixon of the USA visited the People's Republic and acknowledged that 'Taiwan is a part of China'. In January 1979 the USA recognized the People's Republic and severed diplomatic relations with Taiwan.

China's relations with the USA improved steadily throughout the 1980s. Following the suppression of the pro-democracy movement in 1989, however, all high-level government exchanges were suspended, and the export of weapons to China was prohibited. In November 1990 President George Bush received the Chinese Minister of Foreign Affairs in Washington, thereby resuming contact at the most senior level. In August 1993 the USA imposed sanctions on China, in response to the latter's sales of technology for nuclear-capable missiles to Pakistan, in alleged violation of international non-proliferation guidelines. The sanctions remained in force until October 1994. In October 1995 Sino-US relations appeared to improve when, at a meeting in New York, Presidents Jiang Zemin and Bill Clinton agreed to resume dialogue on various issues, the USA reaffirming its commitment to the 'one China' policy. In November the two countries reached agreement on the resumption of bilateral military contacts. During 1996 there were several causes of renewed Sino-US tension, mainly related to various trade issues.

Another obstacle to good relations between China and the USA is the question of Taiwan and, in particular, the continued sale of US armaments to Taiwan. Sino-US relations deteriorated in September 1992, upon President Bush's announcement of the sale of fighter aircraft to Taiwan. China condemned the USA's decision, in September 1994, to expand its official links with Taiwan. In June 1995, following President Clinton's highly controversial decision to grant him a visa, President Lee of Taiwan embarked upon an unofficial visit to the USA, where he met members of the US Congress. The visit so outraged Beijing that the Chinese ambassador to Washington was withdrawn. In March 1996, as China began a new series of missile tests, the USA stationed two naval convoys east of Taiwan, its largest deployment in Asia since 1975. President Clinton's decision to sell anti-aircraft missiles and other defensive weapons to Taiwan was condemned by China.

In October 1999 the Taiwan Security Enhancement Act (TSEA), establishing direct military ties between the USA and Taiwan, was adopted, albeit in modified form, by the International Relations Committee of the US House of Representatives, despite opposition from the Clinton Administration. Reaction from the People's Republic was unfavourable, and its displeasure increased in February 2000 when the House of Representatives overwhelmingly approved the Act, the consideration of which was postponed by the US Senate in April 2000 at the behest of Taiwanese President-elect Chen Shui-bian (in order not to antagonize Beijing during the sensitive period preceding his inauguration). In the same month the US Government announced that it had decided to defer the sale of four naval destroyers to Taiwan, although it was prepared to supply long-range radar and medium-range air-to-air missiles.

Negotiations on the issue of human rights, the USA's growing trade deficit with China, and China's proposed entry into the WTO were the focus of Sino-US relations in 1997. President Jiang Zemin visited the USA in October, the first such visit by a Chinese Head of State since 1985. Measures to reduce the US trade deficit with China and to accelerate China's entry into the WTO were negotiated. In addition, the Chinese Government agreed to control the export of nuclear-related materials, in return for the removal of sanctions on the sale of nuclear-reactor technology to the People's Republic.

In April 1998 the US Secretary of State, Madeleine Albright, visited China to prepare for an official visit by President Clinton in late June and early July. Prior to his visit it was announced that China's most favoured nation (subsequently restyled normal trading relations) status would be renewed for a further year. Although Clinton continued to be criticized for his constructive engagement policy, the visit was a diplomatic success, being notable for an unprecedented live broadcast in which Clinton and Jiang debated such issues as human rights, freedom of speech and the 1989 events in Tiananmen Square. In response to China's pledge in March 1998 to sign the International Covenant on Civil and Political Rights, the USA announced that it would abandon its sponsorship of an annual resolution of the UN Commission on Human Rights condemning China for human rights abuses. The decision, which followed a similar commitment by the EU in February, was deplored by human rights organizations.

Sino-US relations deteriorated significantly during 1999, owing to continued differences over China's human rights record, Tibet, trade relations, espionage and US plans for a missile defence system for Asia. During an official visit by Albright to the People's Republic at the end of February, she reiterated US disapproval at the suppression of organized dissent in China and urged the release of a number of political prisoners (although emphasizing that the USA would continue its policy of separating human rights issues from trade relations). Further acrimonious exchanges took place concerning demands from the US Congress that the proposed US TMD system, which was principally designed to protect Japan and the Republic of Korea, be extended to include Taiwan. During a visit to the USA by Zhu Rongji in April, despite the Chinese Premier's offer of a number of economic concessions in return for a bilateral trade agreement to facilitate WTO entry, no agreement was reached. At a final press conference, however, the two sides affirmed their commitment to signing an agreement by the end of 1999. Although China suspended bilateral negotiations in May, following the NATO bombing of the Chinese embassy in Yugoslavia (see below), China's normal trade relations status was renewed in July. China agreed to resume talks in September, and in November (following 13 years of negotiations) a bilateral trade agreement was concluded, which would allow for China's eventual accession to the WTO. The agreement with the USA facilitated the conclusion of bilateral trade agreements with the EU and other WTO members during 2000.

It was widely believed that the failure to reach a trade agreement in April 1999 was, in part, due to popular US anti-Chinese sentiment, which had been exacerbated by US claims in March that a Chinese spy had stolen important nuclear data during the 1980s. A further disclosure of Chinese espionage (which had allegedly taken place in 1995), involving information

relevant to the construction of a 'neutron' bomb emerged during Zhu's visit to the USA. The findings of a select committee of the US House of Representatives, which were released in May, confirmed that Chinese spies had systematically stolen US nuclear technology from the late 1970s until the mid-1990s. China denounced the document as a plot to encourage anti-Chinese sentiment and to deflect attention from the bombing of the Chinese embassy in Yugoslavia, which had occurred earlier that month. China had vigorously opposed the NATO bombing of Yugoslavia, during which the Chinese embassy had been severely damaged, leading to the deaths of three people and injuring 20 others. In July the USA agreed to pay US $4.5m. in compensation to the families of those killed and injured by the bombing, leading to the lifting of a ban on US military access to Hong Kong. In December compensation of US $28m. was agreed for damage caused to the Chinese embassy building, and in April 2000 the CIA dismissed one intelligence officer and reprimanded six managers for errors that had led to the bombing.

In June 2000 the US Secretary of State, Madeleine Albright, visited China, the most senior US official to do so since the events of May 1999. She criticized the People's Republic's human rights record and urged Beijing to increase its efforts for peace with Taiwan. In retaliation, the Chinese Government insisted that US military aid to Taiwan be immediately suspended. In October the situation improved upon the signature of a law granting China the status of Permanent Normal Trading Relations. In the following month Bill Clinton announced the waiving of penalties against China for supplying missile parts to Iran and Pakistan.

There were initial fears that the election of George W. Bush to the presidency of the USA in late 2000 would lead to the termination of that country's policy of engagement of recent years. Bush, and his Republican Party in particular, had been critical of Clinton's policy on China. Jiang Zemin, however, pronounced himself optimistic that relations would continue to develop positively. In February 2001 the US State Department's annual report on human rights stated that China's situation had deteriorated for the third consecutive year, particularly owing to the campaign against Falun Gong practitioners. Beijing responded by releasing, for the second year, its own report on human rights abuses in the USA. The USA at the same time announced that it would sponsor a resolution condemning China's human rights record at a UN meeting in March. Vice-Premier Qian Qichen visited the USA in March 2001, when he met several senior officials to discuss bilateral ties and urged against the sale of advanced weapons to Taiwan. Relations quickly became strained following the revelation that Senior Colonel Xu Junping of the PLA had defected while visiting the USA in December 2000, becoming the highest-level defector in over a decade. A US-based Chinese scholar, Gao Zhan, was also detained in China along with her husband and son, the latter a US citizen. Gao was accused of spying, although her husband and son were released. Gao was one of several US residents or citizens of Chinese origin who had been detained in China in late 2000 and early 2001.

A major test for Sino-US relations came at the beginning of April 2001, when a US surveillance plane was forced to make an emergency landing at an airbase on Hainan Island, off the coast of southern China, following its collision with a Chinese fighter aircraft over the South China Sea. The Chinese pilot was killed in the incident, while the spy plane's crew of 24 was detained by the Chinese authorities. Intense negotiations followed, and the crew was released on 12 April, after a partial apology from the US ambassador. The aircraft remained on Hainan, however, while the Chinese military studied its technology, and was returned to the USA in components in early July. In the immediate aftermath of the incident, the USA announced that it would sell Taiwan a US $4,000m. armaments 'package', consisting of navy destroyers, anti-submarine aircraft, diesel submarines, amphibious assault vehicles, and surface-to-air missiles and torpedoes. Bush also announced that the USA would do whatever was necessary to defend Taiwan from China. However, the transaction stopped short of selling an advanced combat-radar system, which had been requested by Taiwan. In early May the USA resumed reconnaissance flights near the Chinese coast, and stated that military exchanges with China would be downgraded. At the same time, Beijing reiterated its warnings against the USA's planned NMD system, fearing that it would also protect Taiwan.

Relations between China and the USA were further strained by a meeting between President Bush and the Dalai Lama in

Washington, DC, in late May 2001, and by a stopover by Taiwanese President Chen Shui-bian in New York during the same week. However, in early June the USA and China reached new trade accords, facilitating China's entry into the WTO. The USA reacted negatively, however, to the conviction of two US-based Chinese academics, Gao Zhan, and Qin Guangguang, for espionage in late July. Gao, Qin and another academic, Li Shaomin, were freed prior to a visit by the US Secretary of State, Colin Powell, who sought to improve bilateral relations after recent tensions. In late August a US aircraft carrier made a visit to Hong Kong; however, two US Navy aircraft carrier battle groups staged a one-day exercise in the South China Sea, coinciding with Chinese military exercises in the Taiwan Straits.

In early September 2001 the USA sought to reduce China's fears over its NMD programme by promising to keep China informed of its development and by abandoning its objections to China's build-up of its nuclear forces, in return for China's acceptance of NMD. The USA also urged China not to transfer ballistic missile technology to countries it considered 'rogue states'. The terrorist attacks against the USA on 11 September 2001 were strongly condemned by China, which pledged co-operation in the US-led 'war on terror'. In late October Bush made his first official visit to China to attend the summit meeting of Asia-Pacific Economic Co-operation (APEC), which was dominated by the issue of terrorism. However, the USA did not share Beijing's view that Uygur and Tibetan separatists in Xinjiang and Tibet respectively were terrorists. Disagreements also remained over the USA's successful NMD interceptor test in December. At the end of 2001 President Bush signed proclamations granting China 'permanent normal trading relations' commencing 1 January 2002, and also ended the Jackson-Vanik regulation preventing communist states from having normal trading relations with the USA if they restricted emigration.

US President Bush visited Beijing in February 2002, and held discussions with Jiang. The talks were candid, but the two sides disagreed on the issues of human rights, China's close ties with Iran, Iraq and North Korea (countries the US President had described as forming an 'axis of evil'), the USA's planned missile defence system, China's export of nuclear technology to Pakistan and US support for Taiwan. Relations deteriorated somewhat during March, however, as Beijing released for the third consecutive year a report on human rights abuses in the USA, in response to the latter's annual report on the human rights situation in China. More significantly, the Taiwanese Minister of National Defense made the first non-transit visit to the USA since 1979 to attend a private security conference, and it was revealed that the USA maintained contingency plans for a nuclear attack on seven states, including China.

In late April 2002 Hu Jintao made his first official visit to the USA, where he held discussions with President Bush, and was introduced to senior governmental and business leaders in preparation for his accession to power as President Jiang's successor. Hu emphasized the importance of Taiwan as a major determinant of bilateral relations. Meanwhile, the former US President, Bill Clinton, made a private visit to China in May. In late June military officials from both countries began discussions to restore bilateral military relations, and in July the US Department of Defense sent a team to China to discover the remains of several US servicemen who had disappeared during Cold War espionage missions. Despite this progress, the release of two new reports in the USA in mid-July highlighted remaining concerns about China. The first report, issued by the US Department of Defense, warned that China was increasing its defence spending in order to intimidate Taiwan. The second, issued by the Congressional US-China Security Review Commission, warned that China had become a leading proliferator of missile technology to countries opposed to the USA, and that US corporations and their investments in China were assisting its emergence as a major economic power, to the detriment of the US trade balance. In late August China introduced the 'Regulations on Export Control of Missiles and Missile-related Items and Technologies' to curb the export of missiles and related technology, in an apparent goodwill gesture to the visiting US Deputy Secretary of State, Richard Armitage. In return, the USA designated the East Turkestan Islamic Movement a terrorist group (see above), in line with Beijing's view.

In late October 2002 Jiang Zemin visited the USA and was hosted by President George W. Bush at his ranch in Texas, a gesture of hospitality conferred on few other world leaders. The major issues discussed were the emerging diplomatic crises over

Iraq and North Korea; China opposed any US attack on Iraq without UN authorization, while the USA urged China to put pressure on North Korea to end its nuclear weapons programme. Also on the agenda were the fight against global terrorism and the issue of Taiwan. However, Jiang was keen to avoid confrontation with the USA, regarding the improvement in bilateral relations as a major accomplishment of his presidency. The two leaders also attended the APEC summit meeting in Mexico at the end of October. In late November a US warship arrived in Qingdao, the first such visit since the Hainan aircraft incident of April 2001. In early December 2002, in Washington, DC, China and the USA held their first formal senior-level military talks since Bush assumed office, and days later the commander of US forces in the Pacific, Adm. Thomas Fargo, visited Beijing.

In January 2003 two major US aerospace companies, Hughes Electronics and Boeing Satellite Systems, were charged with illegally providing China with technology that could be used for the purposes of intercontinental missiles. Both companies were fined millions of dollars. There was strong opposition in China to the US military intervention in Iraq in March 2003, with the Chinese Ministry of Foreign Affairs voicing concerns that the action represented a threat to world security. President Hu none the less stated that the Iraq conflict should not affect the continuing development of Sino-US relations, and public protests in China against the war were banned. In August 2003 China hosted talks attended by six countries, including the USA, on North Korea's nuclear programme. Chinese intelligence services had confirmed US claims that North Korea was developing nuclear weapons at an advanced level, and Chinese officials had played a central role in bringing about North Korean participation in the discussions. Tensions over trade issues affected the Sino-US relationship in late 2003. During a visit to Beijing in September US Secretary of the Treasury John Snow criticized China's refusal to revalue its currency, amid US concerns that undervaluation of the yuan was having an adverse effect on the US economy. China in turn expressed strong criticism of the USA's imposition of quotas on Chinese textile exports in November 2003. In December the issue of Taiwan dominated a visit by Chinese Premier Wen Jiabao to Washington, with Wen seeking assurance from Washington that the USA would not support moves towards Taiwanese independence following the introduction of a new referendum law in Taiwan (see above).

The US State Department's annual report on human rights for 2003, published in February 2004, contained especially strong criticism of human rights protection in China, accusing the Chinese Government of 'back-sliding' on a number of issues. In March 2004 dialogue between China and the USA was suspended following the latter's decision to sponsor a resolution condemning China's human rights record. The resolution was rejected at a UN meeting in April (see above). Also in April, US Vice-President Dick Cheney made an official visit to Beijing, and held discussions with the Chinese leadership on issues relating to Taiwan and North Korea, as well as on economic matters. In the same month Chinese Vice-Premier Wu Yi made an official visit to the USA in an attempt to resolve trade disputes. In May China rejected renewed criticism by the USA of its human rights record, and accused the US Government of failing to investigate alleged abuse of Iraqi prisoners by US soldiers in its annual human rights report. An official US report on China's military capability, published in June, claimed that there was evidence that Beijing was preparing for military conflict over Taiwan. There were also suggestions by the USA that China had sold nuclear technology to Iran in return for oil. In July, during a visit to Beijing by US National Security Adviser Condoleezza Rice, a US official expressed his country's intention to continue selling advanced military equipment to Taiwan, despite strong Chinese opposition. In August China expressed outrage following an incident in which a Chinese businesswoman was beaten and injured by a US border official. Immediately prior to the US presidential election in November, the former Chinese Vice-Premier and Minister of Foreign Affairs, Qian Qichen, launched a scathing attack on the foreign policy of US President Bush, claiming that the latter was attempting to 'rule the world'. The Chinese Government sought to distance itself from Qian's remarks.

China's relations with Japan began to deteriorate in 1982, after China complained that passages in Japanese school textbooks sought to justify the Japanese invasion of China in 1937. In June 1989 the Japanese Government criticized the Chinese Government's suppression of the pro-democracy movement and suspended (until late 1990) a five-year aid programme to China. In April 1992 Jiang Zemin travelled to Japan, the first visit by the General Secretary of the CCP for nine years. In October Emperor Akihito made the first ever imperial visit to the People's Republic. Japan was one of many countries to criticize China's resumption of underground nuclear testing, at Lop Nor in Xinjiang Province, in October 1993. Relations were seriously strained in May 1994, when the Japanese Minister of Justice referred to the 1937 Nanjing massacre (in which more than 300,000 Chinese citizens were killed by Japanese soldiers) as a 'fabrication', and again in August, when a second Japanese minister was obliged to resign, following further controversial remarks about his country's war record. In May 1995, during a visit to Beijing, the Japanese Prime Minister expressed his deep remorse for the wartime atrocities, but offered no formal apology.

China's continuation of its nuclear-testing programme, in defiance of international opinion, prompted Japan to announce a reduction in financial aid to China. In August 1995 Japan suspended most of its grant aid to China. Following China's conduct of its 'final' nuclear test in July 1996, and its declaration of a moratorium, Japan resumed grant aid in March 1997. (China signed the Comprehensive Nuclear Test Ban Treaty in September 1996.) In July 1996, however, Sino-Japanese relations were affected by a territorial dispute relating to the Diaoyu (or Senkaku) Islands, a group of uninhabited islets in the East China Sea, which China had claimed as its own since ancient times, and Japan since 1895, and to which Taiwan also laid claim. The construction of a lighthouse on one of the islands by a group of Japanese nationalists led to strong protests from the Governments of both the People's Republic and Taiwan. The Japanese Government sought to defuse the tension by withholding recognition of the lighthouse, but did not condemn the right-wing activists responsible.

At a meeting with President Jiang Zemin during the APEC conference in November 1996, the Japanese Prime Minister apologized for Japanese aggression during the Second World War, and emphasized his desire to resolve the dispute over the Diaoyu Islands. In May 1997, following the landing on one of the Islands by a member of the Japanese Diet, the Japanese Government distanced itself from the incident. The US-Japanese agreement on expanded military co-operation caused further tension in Sino-Japanese relations. Nevertheless, Japan's support for China's entry into the WTO remained firm, while China backed Japanese proposals for a permanent seat on the UN Security Council.

Following the normalization of ties between the Japanese Communist Party (JCP) and its Chinese equivalent after a period of more than 30 years, the Chairman of the JCP, Tetsuzo Fuwa, paid an official visit to China in July 1998. During a visit by Jiang Zemin to Japan in November, the first of its kind by a Chinese Head of State, relations were strained when Japan failed to issue an unequivocal apology for its invasion and occupation of China during 1937–45. The summit meeting between Jiang and the Japanese Prime Minister, Keizo Obuchi, was, nevertheless, deemed to have been successful. Keizo Obuchi paid a reciprocal visit to the People's Republic, intended to repair ties, in July 1999, during which he held summit talks with Zhu Rongji and Jiang Zemin. Tensions remained, but a number of co-operation agreements were reached, including a bilateral accord on terms for China's WTO entry. The People's Republic, however, opposed the new US-Japan defence co-operation guide-lines, as it suspected that they could be invoked to defend Taiwan. Obuchi refused to guarantee that Taiwan be excluded from the security arrangements.

In April 2001 NPC Chairman Li Peng cancelled a visit to Japan, apparently in response to Tokyo's decision to permit former Taiwanese President Lee Teng-hui to visit Japan, and the publication of a new history textbook that attenuated Japan's wartime atrocities in China and South-East Asia. By mid-2001 China and Japan had become embroiled in trade disputes involving tariffs on imported goods. China was further angered by the visit of the Japanese Prime Minister, Junichiro Koizumi, to a controversial war memorial in Tokyo that glorified Japan's war dead, including several prominent war criminals. China claimed that the visit demonstrated that Japan did not regret its conquest of large parts of China in the 1930s.

China reacted cautiously to Japan's announcement in October 2001 that it would send warships to the Indian Ocean in support of the USA's 'war on terror'. However, some Chinese leaders feared that the USA was seeking to increase Japan's military power in order to contain China. Prime Minister Koizumi made a brief visit to China in early October and issued an apology for Japan's wartime atrocities in China. In early November China, Japan and South Korea agreed to hold regular meetings of their economy, finance and foreign ministers to foster closer co-operation.

Li Peng finally visited Japan in early April 2002, when he met Koizumi and toured Japan's regions. At the same time, a Japanese opposition leader, Ichiro Ozawa, publicly stated that Japan could rapidly become a major nuclear power, if challenged by China, drawing a muted response from Beijing. Later that month, Koizumi visited China to attend the Boao Forum, where he met Zhu Rongji. Relations were strained in May, however, when Chinese security forces forcibly removed North Korean refugees seeking asylum at a number of foreign diplomatic missions, including the Japanese consulate in Shenyang, thus violating international protocol. A diplomatic impasse was resolved in June when Beijing agreed to release the asylum-seekers to a third country. In August, meanwhile, a Tokyo court finally admitted that Japan had conducted biological warfare in China during the Second World War, but rejected the demands by 180 Chinese plaintiffs for individual compensation. Despite China's bitterness over Japanese wartime occupation, economic relations between the two remained strong, with increasing bilateral trade, and rising Japanese investment in China. In January 2003, however, the Diaoyu/Senkaku Islands dispute re-emerged when Japan announced plans to lease the islands to a private owner, prompting protests from Beijing. Also in January, Prime Minister Koizumi made a further visit to a controversial war shrine (see above), which provoked renewed anger from Beijing. Two further incidents related to Japan's wartime atrocities caused tensions in the Sino-Japanese relationship in 2003. In August 29 people were poisoned by chemical weapons that had been left buried in north-eastern China after the Japanese invasion of the area during the war. In September an orgy involving the use of Chinese prostitutes by Japanese tourists also caused deep offence in China, especially as the event coincided with an anniversary of the Japanese occupation.

In January 2004 there was further conflict over the Diaoyu/Senkaku Islands when a Japanese ship fired a water cannon at a Chinese boat. In March there were protests in China following the arrest by Japanese police of seven Chinese activists who had landed on the islands. Strong anti-Japanese sentiment was evident in rioting by Chinese football supporters after Japan's football team defeated China in the Asia Cup final in August. Japanese officials made a complaint to the Chinese Government following an incident in which a Chinese submarine was found to have entered Japanese waters. China later apologized for the intrusion. In April 2005 violent demonstrations took place across China in protest at Japan's bid for a permanent seat on the UN Security Council, as well as at the publication of new Japanese school textbooks reportedly omitting mention of Japanese atrocities in China during the Second World War.

The long-standing border dispute with India, which gave rise to a short military conflict in 1962, remained unresolved. Discussions on the issue were held in 1988 and in 1991, and in September 1993 the two countries signed an agreement to reduce their troops along the frontier and to resolve the dispute by peaceful means. In December 1994 China and India agreed to hold joint military exercises in mid-1995. In August 1995 it was confirmed that the two countries were to disengage their troops from four border posts in Arunachal Pradesh. Further progress was made at the ninth round of Sino-Indian border discussions, held in October 1996, and during the visit of President Jiang Zemin to India (the first by a Chinese Head of State) in November. In May 1998, immediately prior to India's nuclear tests, the Indian Minister of Defence, George Fernandes, stated that China constituted India's main long-term security threat, citing its aid to Pakistan's nuclear programme and its military facilities in the Andaman Sea. However, the Indian Minister of External Affairs, Jaswant Singh, denied that India viewed China as a threat, when he visited Beijing in June 1999. The two countries subsequently improved relations following a series of bilateral meetings. Li Peng visited India in January 2001, and discussions were held with a view to the restoration of normal relations. Outstanding Indian concerns included the increasing levels of imports of cheap Chinese goods and the question of China's nuclear co-operation with Pakistan, while China resented India's decades-long hosting of Tibetan separatist organizations. However, in early January 2002 Prime Minister

Zhu Rongji led a business delegation to India, seeking greater commercial links and improved relations. In April officials from the two countries held discussions in New Delhi, aimed at establishing joint counter-terrorism measures.

In late April 2003 the Indian Minister of Defence, George Fernandes, began a week-long visit to Beijing, to discuss outstanding bilateral issues, including China's support for Pakistan and Chinese observation posts in the Bay of Bengal. In June Atal Bihari Vajpayee visited Beijing, the first visit by an Indian Prime Minister in over a decade. There appeared to be some significant developments as a result of this visit: the Indian Prime Minister officially recognized Tibet as part of China, and China agreed to trade with India's north-eastern state of Sikkim, thus implicitly recognizing India's control of that area. In November China and India held joint naval exercises, representing the first ever joint military exercises between the two countries. Further negotiations took place in 2004 in an attempt to move towards resolution of remaining border disputes, with Chinese Minister of National Defence Cao Gangchuan making an official visit to India in March (the first such visit by a Chinese defence minister), and a further round of talks taking place in July. During an historic visit to India in March 2005, the Chinese Premier signed an agreement aimed at resolving the border dispute.

In late December 2001 China hosted Pakistani President Pervez Musharraf, who arrived to mark the 50th anniversary of relations between the two countries. China and Pakistan had long been close allies, and co-operated in economic and military issues. In March 2001 Pakistan's Chasma Nuclear Power Plant in Punjab Province, which had been built in the 1990s with substantial assistance from the China National Nuclear Corporation, was opened. In early January 2002 it was reported that China had supplied several dozen fighter aircraft and air defence missiles to Pakistan. The two countries were also co-operating to develop a new fighter aircraft by 2005. Musharraf visited Beijing again in August 2002 and reaffirmed the close relations between the two countries. China had been increasingly concerned that Pakistan's closer relations with the USA since the terrorist attacks of 11 September 2001, would be at its own risk. In October 2003 the Chinese and Pakistani navies conducted joint military exercises. In November President Musharraf made another visit to Beijing during which various Sino-Pakistani agreements were concluded, including trade agreements and an extradition treaty. Despite expectations, plans for Chinese assistance to Pakistan in building a nuclear plant were not finalized. However, an agreement for the construction of a second nuclear plant was signed in May 2004. The value of the contract between the Pakistan Atomic Energy Commission and China National Nuclear Corporation was estimated at US $600m. Chinese Premier Wen Jiabao visited Pakistan in April 2005.

The question of the sovereignty of the Spratly (Nansha) Islands, situated in the South China Sea and claimed by six countries (Brunei, China, Malaysia, the Philippines, Taiwan and Viet Nam), remained unresolved in the early 21st century. The strategic importance of the sea was due to the major international shipping routes passing through the area, and China's claim to the islands and the sea raised concerns about its possible expansionist ambitions. By 1994 both China and Viet Nam had awarded petroleum exploration concessions to US companies, leading to increased tension among the claimants. In February 1995 it emerged that Chinese forces had occupied a reef to which the Philippines laid claim, resulting in a formal diplomatic protest from Manila. More than 60 Chinese fishermen and several vessels were subsequently detained by the Philippine authorities. Following consultations in August, China and the Philippines declared their intention to resolve peacefully their claims to the Spratly Islands. In January 1996 the Chinese Government denied any involvement in a naval skirmish in Philippine waters, during which a ship flying the Chinese flag and a Philippine patrol boat exchanged gunfire. In March China and the Philippines agreed to co-operate in combating piracy in the region. In November 1998 China angered the Philippine Government by building permanent structures on the disputed Mischief Reef. In late November 20 Chinese fishermen were arrested near Mischief Reef by the Philippine navy. Following Chinese protests, the men were released. In December China reiterated both its claim to sovereignty over the Spratly Islands and surrounding waters and its commitment to pursuing a peaceful solution through negotiation. Discussions between the two countries in April 1999 were unsuccessful, and

relations deteriorated further in May when a Chinese fishing vessel sank following a collision with a Philippine navy boat, which was claimed to be accidental by the Philippines but deliberate by the People's Republic. A further Chinese fishing vessel sank in a collision with a Philippine navy vessel in July. A similar territorial dispute relating to the Paracel (Xisha) Islands, which had been seized by China from South Vietnamese forces in 1974, also remained unresolved. In May 1996, despite having agreed to abide by the UN Convention on the Law of the Sea, China declared an extension of its maritime boundaries in the South China Sea. Other claimants to the Paracel Islands, in particular Indonesia, the Philippines and Viet Nam, expressed grave concern at China's apparent expansionism. In November 2002, in Phnom-Penh, Cambodia, Prime Minister Zhu Rongji signed a landmark 'declaration on the conduct of parties in the South China Sea' with members of the Association of South East Asian Nations (ASEAN, see p. 162), which aimed to avoid conflict in the area. Under this agreement, which was similar to one drafted in late 1999 but not implemented, claimants would practise self-restraint in the event of potentially hostile action (such as inhabiting the islands), effect confidence-building measures and give advance notice of military exercises in the region. However, the agreement did not include the Paracel Islands, and disagreements continued among the signatories on what the accord should encompass. Additionally, China introduced a provision requiring consensus to resolve outstanding issues, thereby allowing for future indecision among ASEAN members. In September 2003 China proposed a joint development and petroleum exploration strategy for the Spratly Islands. In November the Philippines Government complained that China had violated the 2002 accord by installing markers in parts of the Islands. There were a number of similar disputes in 2004, with China protesting at a move by Viet Nam to conduct tourist boat tours of the Islands.

In August and October 1990 diplomatic relations were established with Indonesia and Singapore respectively. In late 1991, following many years of mutual hostility resulting from a border dispute and from the Vietnamese intervention in Kampuchea (now Cambodia) in 1978, the restoration of normal relations between China and Viet Nam was announced. Bilateral relations continued to improve throughout the 1990s; in late February 2002 President Jiang Zemin began his second official visit to Viet Nam. In November 2000 meanwhile, President Jiang Zemin toured Laos, Cambodia and Brunei, the tour culminating in his attendance at the APEC conference in Brunei. His visit to Cambodia was the first by a Chinese Head of State for more than 30 years. Local security forces suppressed protests at China's support for the Khmer Rouge regime in the late 1970s. In December 2001 Jiang visited Myanmar, seeking to increase China's influence there vis-à-vis India and promising US $100m. in finance towards investment projects. China hoped to develop a new transport corridor from its land-locked southwestern provinces to Myanmar's Indian Ocean ports, allowing the easier export of goods. During 2000–01 China also increased links with a number of South Pacific island nations, providing aid and investment. Furthermore, China played a leading role in organizing the private Boao Forum of regional business and political leaders, held on China's Hainan Island in April 2002. In September 2002 China and Indonesia signed an agreement to export liquefied natural gas from the Indonesian province of Papua (formerly West Papua), valued at US $8,000m., as bilateral relations improved. At the ASEAN summit meeting in Phnom-Penh, Cambodia, in November 2002, China and 10 South-East Asian nations signed an agreement to establish the world's largest free-trade area by 2010. In January 2003 the head of Myanmar's ruling State Peace and Development Council, Gen. Than Shwe, visited Beijing, where he was promised US $200m. in development loans. In August, in defiance of US attempts to isolate Myanmar's leadership, 32 members of Myanmar's military junta visited Beijing to hold discussions with the Chinese authorities. In October China's links with ASEAN were strengthened when China signed ASEAN's Treaty of Amity and Co-operation, a pact for the promotion of regional stability, at an ASEAN summit meeting in Bali. China and ASEAN also agreed to work towards a free-trade agreement. In November 2004 a trade agreement was signed between China and ASEAN members committing countries to lower tariffs on goods trade by 2010. Also in November, Soe Win, Myanmar's new Prime Minister, made an official visit to China.

During 1992 China established diplomatic relations with the Republic of Korea (South Korea). China remained committed to the achievement of peace on the Korean peninsula, and in June 1996 it was reported that secret discussions between representatives of the Republic and of the Democratic People's Republic of Korea (North Korea) had been held in Beijing. In late 1997 China participated in quadripartite negotiations, together with the USA, the Democratic People's Republic of Korea and the Republic of Korea, to resolve the Korean issue. Further quadripartite negotiations took place throughout 1999. In May 2000 the North Korean leader, Kim Jong Il, visited China, on his first trip abroad for 17 years. China was pleased in the following month by the holding of the first ever-inter-Korean presidential summit meeting in the Democratic People's Republic of Korea. Regular inter-Korean meetings followed. Kim Jong Il visited China again in January 2001, and President Jiang visited North Korea in September. During 2001, however, China increased measures to counter the growing number of North Korean refugees entering the country. Premier Zhu Rongji made his first trip to the Republic of Korea in October 2000.

During 2002 China continued to play an important role on the Korean peninsula, its main interest being a reduction of tensions and the reconnection of the inter-Korean railway lines and their subsequent connection with China's own railway system. However, there were tensions with South Korea over the introduction of a bill that would grant special rights to ethnic Koreans in China and China's forcible removal of North Korean refugees from South Korean embassies in the People's Republic. In late June Beijing allowed 24 northern refugees who had been concealed in the embassy of South Korea to leave for that country. After the incident, Beijing began an operation against South Korean activists and missionaries who had been helping northerners to flee via China. In October North Korea appointed a Chinese businessman of Dutch citizenship, Yang Bin, as the new governor of its recently created Sinuiju Special Administrative Region; however, the Chinese authorities arrested him on charges of bribery and fraud, thereby preventing him from assuming the post. By early 2003 China was becoming increasingly concerned about the growing diplomatic crisis between North Korea and the USA over the former's decision formally to restart its nuclear programme. In January 2003 the vice-ministers of foreign affairs of China and South Korea met to discuss the crisis. In July South Korean President Roh Moo-Hyun visited Beijing for discussions with Hu Jintao on the subject of North Korea. Later in the month a Chinese envoy delivered a letter from Hu Jintao to North Korean leader Kim Jong Il. Chinese diplomatic efforts played a major role in ensuring North Korean participation in the six-party talks on the nuclear issue attended by North Korea, South Korea, China, the USA, Japan and Russia, which were held in Beijing in August 2003. Chinese Minister of Foreign Affairs Li Zhaoxing paid his first visit to Pyongyang in March 2004. Kim Jong Il made an unofficial visit to Beijing in April 2004, which became public following a major railway accident that coincided with Kim's return journey from China. During 2004 a number of North Korean officials visited China to study that country's development, reportedly as a model for economic reform in North Korea. Relations with South Korea were affected in 2004 by a dispute over the ancient kingdom of Koguryo, believed by Koreans to have been ruled by their own ancestors, but which China claimed had been ruled by one of its own ethnic groups. In August references to Koguryo were deleted from the Chinese Ministry of Foreign Affairs website.

After a fourth round of six-party talks on the North Korean nuclear issue, scheduled for September 2004, was delayed, the Chinese Government joined the USA in attempting to persuade Pyongyang to return to the negotiating table. In November 2004 an official at the Chinese Ministry of Foreign Affairs supported North Korea in refuting speculation on political instability in the country following reports that portraits of Kim Jong Il had been removed.

Following the reversion of Hong Kong to Chinese sovereignty, relations between China and the United Kingdom improved significantly in 1998. The British Secretary of State for Foreign and Commonwealth Affairs, Robin Cook, paid a visit to China and Hong Kong in January. The first China-EU summit meeting, which was scheduled to become an annual event, took place in London in April, prior to the Asia-Europe Meeting (ASEM). China and the EU committed themselves to greater mutual co-operation in the area of trade and economic relations. The Chinese Premier also had talks with his British counterpart, Tony Blair. Blair visited China and Hong Kong in October 1998. He declared his intention to broach the issue of human

rights through 'persuasion and dialogue' rather than 'confrontation and empty rhetoric'. Following the visit, the two sides pledged to increase co-operation in a number of areas, and in October 1999 Jiang Zemin became the first Chinese Head of State to visit the United Kingdom. This visit was part of a six-nation tour, which also included France, Portugal, Morocco, Algeria and Saudi Arabia. In the United Kingdom and France, however, Jiang's visit prompted protests by supporters of human rights, resulting in complaints from the Chinese authorities. In December, during a China-EU summit meeting in Beijing, the Chinese Government rejected criticism of its human rights record, reiterating its previous position that economic development would precede an improvement in human rightsIn October 2000 China concluded bilateral trade agreements with the EU necessary for WTO accession. In May 2001 Beijing hosted an EU delegation, seeking a new comprehensive partnership with China, particularly in the area of commerce. The fourth annual China-EU summit meeting took place in Brussels in early September, and discussed access by EU companies to China's insurance market, the last obstacle to China's admission to the WTO (which took place in December 2001). In late October–early November Vice-President Hu Jintao made his first official trip to the EU, visiting the United Kingdom, France, Germany and Spain. Jiang Zemin visited Germany in April 2002, the latter being the biggest European investor in China. In July 2003 Tony Blair made a diplomatic visit to China during which he sought to enhance trade links between China and the United Kingdom. In October there were developments towards greater economic co-operation between China and the EU at a China-EU summit meeting in Beijing. A new visa system was agreed to give Chinese tourists easier access to European countries. China also agreed to work with the EU on the Galileo satellite project, which once completed would represent a more advanced alternative to the US Global Positioning System. In January 2004 President Hu Jintao held talks in Paris with French President Jacques Chirac. In the course of President Hu's visit, President Chirac expressed his support for China's opposition to a proposed referendum in Taiwan (see above), stating that this proposition was a 'grave mistake'. President Chirac's support of China on this issue provoked anger in Taiwan. President Hu's visit to Paris also provoked protests by French government members and human rights activists.

In early 2004 in was reported that the EU was expected to become China's largest bilateral trading partner, overtaking the USA and Japan, following the forthcoming accession of 10 new member states to the EU. Premier Wen Jiabao made his first official visit to EU headquarters in Brussels shortly after the expansion of the Union in May 2004. In the same month Wen visited the United Kingdom and had discussions with Tony Blair on various issues, including human rights in the context of reported abuse of prisoners by British soldiers deployed in Iraq, as well as of political developments in Hong Kong and mainland China. In June Chinese and British fleets carried out the first ever joint navy exercises. During 2004 the EU continued to resist calls to lift a ban on weapons trade with China which had been in place since 1989, but some EU countries, including France and Germany, expressed opposition to the ban. In early 2005 it was reported that the embargo was expected to be removed later in the year. This was confirmed by the British Secretary of State for Foreign and Commonwealth Affairs, Jack Straw, during a visit to Beijing in January. There was renewed opposition to the removal of the ban within both the EU and the USA, however, following the approval of an anti-secession law by the Chinese NPC in March 2005.

China established diplomatic relations with Israel in 1992, and during the 1990s co-operated in several military technology projects, including China's indigenous fighter aircraft programme. However, the USA, fearing that this would strengthen China's position against Taiwan, exerted pressure on Israel to cancel a lucrative contract to supply airborne warning and control (AWACS) aircraft to China in early 2000. Initially, Israel refused to comply, particularly after Jiang Zemin had made the first official trip to the country by a Chinese Head of State, in April. In July, however, Israel was obliged to yield to pressure, as it could not risk losing the USA as a major ally. In January 2003 Israel ceased exports of weapons to China. In October 2000, meanwhile, China improved its relations with African nations when, during a Sino-African forum in Beijing, the People's Republic announced its decision to reduce or exempt outstanding debt totalling US \$1,200m. China also maintained friendly relations with a number of Middle Eastern nations, including Iran and Iraq, and in June 2000 hosted Iranian President Muhammad Khatami, who was seeking closer economic ties. President Hosni Mubarak of Egypt visited Beijing in January 2002. In April 2001 President Jiang visited several Latin American nations, including Argentina, Brazil, Chile, Cuba, Uruguay and Venezuela, attempting to foster economic links. In August the Minister of National Defence, Gen. Chi Haotian, also visited Venezuela, and discussed energy and security issues with President Hugo Chávez. The pattern of cultivating relations with countries in the developing world continued during 2002: in April Zhu Rongji visited Turkey and Egypt, and Jiang made a tour of Libya, Nigeria, Tunisia and Iran. The issues discussed included business and energy, defence co-operation, and the war against global terrorism. In late February 2003 China hosted the visiting Cuban President, Fidel Castro. China did not support the US-led military action against Iraq in March 2003, but the Chinese Government did provide humanitarian assistance to Iraqi refugees. China also expressed its interest in reconstruction projects in Iraq, such as petroleum exploration ventures. There were developments towards close economic co-operation with Brazil in 2004, when in May President Lula da Silva visited Beijing to discuss possibilities for increasing trade between the two countries, and President Hu visited Brazil in November for talks on trade deals. During 2004 there was also a strengthening of relations between China and Iran, China's second largest source of oil imports. In November China signed a deal for the development of Iran's Yadavaran oil field, the value of which was estimated at US $70,000m. During a visit to Tehran in November 2004 the Chinese Minister of Foreign Affairs indicated that he did not support US plans to exert pressure on Iran over the issue of its nuclear programme.

Government

China is a unitary state. Directly under the Central Government there are 22 provinces, five autonomous regions, including Xizang (Tibet), and four municipalities (Beijing, Chongqing, Shanghai and Tianjin). The highest organ of state power is the National People's Congress (NPC). In March 2003 the first session of the 10th NPC was attended by 2,916 deputies, indirectly elected for five years by the people's congresses of the provinces, autonomous regions, municipalities directly under the Central Government, and the People's Liberation Army. The NPC elects a Standing Committee to be its permanent organ. The current Constitution, adopted by the NPC in December 1982 and amended in 1993, was China's fourth since 1949. It restored the office of Head of State (President of the Republic). Executive power is exercised by the State Council (Cabinet), comprising the Premier, Vice-Premiers and other ministers heading ministries and commissions. The State Council is appointed by, and accountable to, the NPC.

Political power is held by the Chinese Communist Party (CCP). The CCP's highest authority is the Party Congress, convened every five years. In November 2002 the CCP's 16th National Congress elected a Central Committee of 198 full members and 158 alternate members. To direct policy, the Central Committee elected a 24-member Politburo. The incoming Standing Committee of the Politburo comprised nine members.

Provincial people's congresses are the local organs of state power. Local revolutionary committees, created during the Cultural Revolution, were abolished in January 1980 and replaced by provincial people's governments.

Defence

China is divided into seven major military units. All armed services are grouped in the People's Liberation Army (PLA). In August 2004, according to Western estimates, the regular forces totalled 2,255,000, of whom approximately 1,000,000 were believed to be conscripts, and of whom some 136,000 were women: the army numbered 1,600,000, the navy 255,000 (including a naval air force of 26,000), and the air force 400,000 (including 210,000 air defence personnel). Reserves numbered some 800,000, and the People's Armed Police comprised an estimated 1.5m. Military service is by selective conscription, and lasts for two years in all services. Defence expenditure for 2004 was budgeted at 207,000m. yuan. At the third plenary session of the 10th NPC in March 2005 plans were announced for an increase of 12% in military expenditure, with military spending thus expected to amount to approximately 247,700m. yuan.

Economic Affairs

In 2003, according to estimates by the World Bank, China's gross national income (GNI), measured at average 2001–03 prices, was US $1,409,768m., equivalent to some $1,100 per head (or $4,990 on an international purchasing-power parity basis). During 1990–2003, it was estimated, the population increased at an average annual rate of 1.0%, while gross domestic product (GDP) per head increased, in real terms, by an average annual rate of 8.6%, one of the highest growth rates in the world. Overall GDP increased, in real terms, at an average annual rate of 9.7% in 1990–2003; growth in 2002 was 8.0% and in 2003 reached 9.1%, compared with the previous year.

Agriculture (including forestry and fishing) contributed 14.6% of GDP in 2003, and employed 44.1% of the working population 2002. China's principal crops are rice (production of which accounted for almost 30% of the total world harvest in 2003), sweet potatoes, wheat, maize, soybeans, sugar cane, tobacco, cotton and jute. According to the World Bank, agricultural GDP increased at an average annual rate of 3.6%, in real terms, in 1990–2003. Growth in agricultural GDP was 2.4% in 2003, compared with the previous year.

Industry (including mining, manufacturing, construction and power) contributed 52.3% of GDP in 2003 and engaged 21.4% of the employed labour force in 2002. According to the World Bank, industrial GDP increased at an average annual rate of 12.6%, in real terms, in 1990–2003. Growth in industrial GDP was 10.2% in 2003, compared with the previous year.

The mining sector accounted for less than 0.8% of total employment in 2002. Output in the sector accounted for some 5.3% of total industrial production in 2002. China has enormous mineral reserves and is the world's largest producer of natural graphite, antimony, tungsten and zinc. Other important minerals include coal, iron ore, molybdenum, tin, lead, mercury, bauxite, phosphate rock, diamonds, gold, manganese, crude petroleum and natural gas.

The manufacturing sector contributed an estimated 43.6% of GDP in 2003, and the sector accounted for 11.3% of total employment in 2002. China is a leading world producer of chemical fertilizers, cement and steel. In the early 2000s industries such as information technology, electronics and motor vehicles expanded rapidly. The GDP of the manufacturing sector increased at an average annual rate of 11.9%, in real terms, during 1990–2003, according to the World Bank. Growth in the GDP of the manufacturing sector was 10.4% in 2003 compared with the previous year.

Energy is derived principally from coal (67.1% in 2003); other sources are petroleum (22.7%), hydroelectric power (7.4%) and natural gas (2.8%).China became a net importer of crude petroleum in 1993 and became the world's second largest importer in 2003, having overtaken Japan. By December 1999 the People's Republic's largest hydroelectric power station, at Ertan, was fully functioning. The 18,200-MW Three Gorges hydropower scheme on the Changjiang (River Yangtze), the world's largest civil engineering project, is scheduled for completion in 2009 and will have a potential annual output of 84,700m. kWh. China's national grid was also scheduled for completion in that year. The Three Gorges hydropower scheme began supplying power to eastern and central provinces in July 2003. Imports of mineral fuels comprised 6.6% of the cost of total imports in 2002.

Services contributed 33.2% of GDP in 2003 and engaged 28.6% of the employed labour force in 2002. Tourism, along with retail and wholesale trade, is expanding rapidly. Mainly as a result of the outbreak of Severe Acute Respiratory Syndrome (SARS) , however, the number of tourists declined from 97.9m. in 2002 to fewer than 91.7m. in 2003, while receipts from tourism decreased from US $20,385m. in 2002 to $17,406m. in 2003. The 2008 Olympic Games were to be held in Beijing. During 1990–2003, according to the World Bank, the GDP of the services sector increased at an average annual rate of 8.9%in real terms. Growth in the GDP of the services sector was 8.4% in 2003 compared with the previous year.

In 2003 China recorded a trade surplus of US $44,652m., and there was a surplus of $45,875m. on the current account of the balance of payments. In 2003 the principal source of imports was Japan (which provided 18.0% of total imports). Other important suppliers were Taiwan (12.0%), the Republic of Korea (10.4%) and the USA (8.2%). The principal markets for exports in 2002 were the USA (21.1% of total exports), Hong Kong (17.4%) and Japan (13.6%). Most of the goods exported to Hong Kong are subsequently re-exported. China became Japan's largest trading partner in 2004, replacing the USA. The principal imports in 2002 were machinery and transport equipment, chemicals and related products, and basic manufactures such as textiles. The principal exports in that year were machinery and transport equipment and textiles and clothing.

In 2003 China's overall budget deficit was 293,470m. yuan, equivalent to 2.5% of GDP. China's total external debt at the end of 2001 stood at US $168,255m., of which $88,531m. was long-term public debt. In 2002 the cost of debt-servicing was equivalent to 8.2% of the value of exports of goods and services. The annual rate of inflation averaged 6.0% in 1990–2002. Consumer prices declined by 0.8% in 2002 but increased by 1.2% in 2003. The rate of inflation was estimated by the Asian Development Bank (ADB) to be 3.9% in 2004. In 2003, according to official statistics, the total number of registered unemployed in urban areas was some 4.3% of the urban labour force. According to the ADB, however, official figures significantly underestimated the extent of urban unemployment, as they did not include workers who had been made redundant through reform of state-owned enterprises, or unemployed persons from rural areas who had migrated to urban areas in search of work. Meanwhile, in the early 2000s the number of rural unemployed was unofficially estimated at between 130m. and 150m.

China joined the Asian Development Bank (ADB, see p. 159) in 1986 and the Asia-Pacific Economic Co-operation forum (APEC, see p. 155) in 1991. In 1994 China became a member of the Association of Tin Producing Countries (ATPC). In July 1995 China was granted observer status at the World Trade Organization (WTO, see p. 357), which had succeeded the General Agreement on Tariffs and Trade (GATT) in January of that year. China was finally admitted as a full member in December 2001. China joined the Bank for International Settlements (BIS, see p. 170) in 1996. In the same year the secretariat of the Tumen River Economic Development Area (TREDA) was established in Beijing by the Governments of China, North and South Korea, Mongolia and Russia. China is also a member of the UN Economic and Social Commission for Asia and the Pacific (ESCAP, see p. 31).

In 1978 Deng Xiaoping introduced the 'open door' reform policy, which aimed to decentralize the economic system and to attract overseas investment to China. The state monopoly on foreign trade was gradually relinquished, commercial links with foreign countries were diversified and several Special Economic Zones were established. China subsequently experienced many years of rapid economic expansion, becoming one of the fastest-growing economies in the world. By the late 1990s, however, the revitalization of the loss-making state-owned enterprises (SOEs) and the reform of the weak banking sector had become increasingly urgent issues. The process of SOE reform was constrained by the necessity to minimize the number of workers being made redundant, amid concerns about possible social unrest. It was hoped that the restructuring of the SOEs would lead the enterprises away from traditional heavy industries in favour of more knowledge-based and consumer-orientated industries, with the assistance of private entrepreneurship. The objectives of the Tenth Five-Year Plan, for the period 2001–06, included a growth rate of 7% per annum, greater scientific and technological advancement, the intensification of infrastructure projects and improved environmental protection, as well as the completion of the transition to a socialist market economy. In August 2001, in preparation for WTO membership, the Government removed price controls on 128 items, but retained controls of prices of some strategic commodities, such as natural gas, electricity supplies and basic telecommunication services. China's accession to the WTO finally took place in December 2001, following which both external trade and foreign direct investment showed strong expansion. Foreign direct investment reached US $53,510m. in 2003, and increased to an estimated $59,700m. in 2004. After years of successive increases, the value of exports reportedly rose by more than 35% in 2004. In the same year the value of China's total foreign trade became the third largest in the world. As a result of WTO membership, China was required to make substantial changes to its legal system. A new foreign trade law, removing restrictions on foreign investment in the retail and distribution sectors, came into effect in mid-2004. Despite such reforms, the European Commission in 2004 continued to classify China as a transitional economy, rather than a market economy, citing remaining inadequacies in legislation on accounting, bankruptcy and property. In a report on China's WTO implementation published in September 2004, the US Chamber of Commerce highlighted intellectual property rights protection as an area in which China was failing to meet its WTO commitments. Fears that the repercussions of the 2003 outbreak of Severe Acute Respiratory Syndrome (SARS) would affect the economy were confirmed in July of that year when it was revealed that the rate of GDP growth had decreased to 6.7% in the second quarter of 2003, with growth in the services sector slowing to a mere 0.8%. However, from mid-2003 the economy made a rapid recovery. The official growth rate of 9.1% for 2003 as a whole represented the highest level of annual GDP growth since 1996, and concerns were raised that the Chinese economy might be 'overheating'. In the second half of 2004 efforts were made by the Government to curb the high rate of economic growth by limiting investment and raising interest rates. GDP growth was none the less reported to have reached 9.5% for 2004 as a whole. Despite this, China's economy faced several serious problems in the medium term. Much of the impressive economic growth of recent years had been state-generated, in the form of major public-works projects, and this had resulted in substantial budgetary deficits. The Government therefore needed to reduce public spending, at a time when social security provisions were coming under increasing pressure from the growing numbers of newly redundant workers. Whilst China's rapid development had clearly led to a marked improvement in average living standards and GDP per head had risen in real terms by more than 50% between 1997 and 2003 alone, much of this growth had taken place in the southern and eastern urban coastal regions. Despite the Government's initiatives to develop the western areas of the country, the resultant regional disparities had become increasingly evident. In 2004 an estimated 85m. people, mainly in rural areas, continued to live below the official 'poverty line' of an annual income of 637 yuan. Furthermore, energy shortages emerged as a growing problem in 2004, with some factories being forced to halt production owing to lack of power. Oil imports were reported to have increased by 40% in the first eight months of 2004. In the long term China's energy needs were expected to increase multifold; private car ownership, for example, was projected to increase from 10m. vehicles in 2004 to approximately 120m. in 2020. In the early 2000s there was also growing international pressure on China to liberalize its exchange-rate policy, amid concerns that the yuan was undervalued, at the fixed rate of 8.3 to the US dollar. In late 2004 there were suggestions from officials at the People's Bank of China that negotiations were taking place on liberalization of the exchange rate and that this might be realized in the near future. The ADB forecast a GDP growth rate of 8.5% in 2005. A major challenge for the Chinese Government in the early 21st century, meanwhile, remained the balancing of economic reform with political stability and with environmental concerns. In September 2004 an official at the State Environmental Protection Administration warned that China's environmental problems, such as air and water pollution, had reached crisis levels. Whilst the economic policies and rule of the CCP had been successful in bringing about massive economic growth since the early 1980s, controversy remained over the long-term effects of a non-democratic political system on China's economic development.

Education

The education system expanded rapidly after 1949. Fees are charged at all levels. Much importance is attached to kindergartens. Primary education begins for most children at seven years of age and lasts for five years. Secondary education usually begins at 12 years of age and lasts for a further five years, comprising a first cycle of three years and a second cycle of two years. Free higher education was abolished in 1985; instead, college students have to compete for scholarships, which are awarded according to academic ability. As a result of the student disturbances in 1989, college students were required to complete one year's political education, prior to entering college. Since 1979 education has been included as one of the main priorities for modernization. The whole educational system was being reformed in the late 1990s and early 2000s, with the aim of introducing nine-year compulsory education. According to official statistics, 90% of the population had been covered by the compulsory education scheme by 2002. The establishment of private schools has been permitted since the early 1980s. As a proportion of the total school-age population, enrolment at primary and secondary schools in 1997 was equivalent to 98% (boys 99%; girls 96%). In that year 100% of both boys and girls in the relevant age-group were enrolled at primary schools. Total enrolment at secondary schools in 1997 was equivalent to 70% of the total school-age population (males 74%; females 66%). In 1996 enrolment at tertiary level schools was equivalent to 5.7% of the relevant age-group (males 7.3%; females 3.9%). In 1999, according to UNESCO, the rate had reached to 16.5% (males 8.8%, females 24.5%). The 2003 budget allocated an estimated 349,140m. yuan to education. The numbers of Chinese students studying abroad were increasing in the early 21st century, with around 32,000 Chinese students reported to have been studying in British higher education institutions alone in 2002/03.

Public Holidays

2005: 1 January (Solar New Year), 9–12 February* (Lunar New Year), 8 March (International Women's Day, women only), 1

May (Labour Day), 1 August (Army Day), 9 September (Teachers' Day), 1–2 October (National Days).
2006: 1 January (Solar New Year), 29 January–1 February* (Lunar New Year), 8 March (International Women's Day, women only), 1 May (Labour Day), 1 August (Army Day), 9 September (Teachers' Day), 1–2 October (National Days).
*From the first to the fourth day of the first moon of the lunar calendar.

Weights and Measures

The metric system is officially in force, but some traditional Chinese units are still used.

Statistical Survey

Source (unless otherwise stated): National Bureau of Statistics of China, 38 Yuetan Nan Jie, Sanlihe, Beijing 100826; tel. (10) 68515074; fax (10) 68515078; e-mail service@stats.gov.cn; internet www.stats.gov.cn.

Note: Wherever possible, figures in this Survey exclude Taiwan. In the case of unofficial estimates for China, it is not always clear if Taiwan is included or excluded. Where a Taiwan component is known, either it has been deducted from the all-China figure or its inclusion is noted. Figures for the Hong Kong Special Administrative Region (SAR) and for the Macao SAR are listed separately. Transactions between the SARs and the rest of the People's Republic continue to be treated as external transactions.

Area and Population

AREA, POPULATION AND DENSITY

Area (sq km)	9,572,900*
Population (census results)	
1 July 1990	1,130,510,638
1 November 2000	
Males	640,275,969
Females	602,336,257
Total	1,242,612,226
Population (official estimates at 31 December)	
2001	1,276,270,000
2002	1,284,530,000
2003	1,292,270,000
Density (per sq km) at 31 December 2003	134.9

* 3,696,100 sq miles.

PRINCIPAL ETHNIC GROUPS
(at census of 1 November 2000)

	Number	%
Han (Chinese)	1,137,386,112	91.53
Zhuang	16,178,811	1.30
Manchu	10,682,262	0.86
Hui	9,816,805	0.79
Miao	8,940,116	0.72
Uygur (Uigur)	8,399,393	0.68
Tujia	8,028,133	0.65
Yi	7,762,272	0.63
Mongolian	5,813,947	0.47
Tibetan	5,416,021	0.44
Bouyei	2,971,460	0.24
Dong	2,960,293	0.24
Yao	2,637,421	0.21
Korean	1,923,842	0.16
Bai	1,858,063	0.09
Hani	1,439,673	0.12
Kazakh	1,250,458	0.10
Li	1,247,814	0.10
Dai	1,158,989	0.09
She	709,592	0.06
Lisu	634,912	0.05
Gelao	579,357	0.05
Dongxiang	513,805	0.04
Others	3,568,237	0.29
Unknown	734,438	0.06
Total	1,242,612,226	100.00

PRINCIPAL TOWNS
(Wade-Giles or other spellings in brackets)

Population at mid-2003
(UN estimates, incl. suburbs)

Shanghai (Shang-hai) .	12,759,367	Changsha (Chang-sha) .	1,935,042
Beijing (Pei-ching or Peking, the capital) .	10,847,827	Liuan	1,934,029
Tianjin (T'ien-chin or Tientsin) . . .	9,271,376	Hangzhou (Hang-chou or Hangchow)	1,882,986
Wuhan (Wu-han or Hankow) . . .	5,652,919	Wanxian	1,878,625
Shenyang (Shen-yang or Mukden) . . .	4,881,757	Tianmen	1,878,423
Chongqing (Ch'ung-ch'ing or Chungking) .	4,847,689	Jinxi	1,799,947
Guangzhou (Kuang-chou or Canton) . . .	3,886,934	Lanzhou (Lan-chou or Lanchow)	1,764,859
Chengdu (Ch'eng-tu) .	3,403,732	Heze	1,743,220
Xian (Hsi-an or Sian) .	3,203,019	Tangshan	1,731,705
Changchun (Ch'ang-ch'un) . . .	3,009,884	Kunming (K'un-ming) .	1,729,233
Harbin (Ha-erh-pin) .	2,911,071	Xiantao	1,698,901
Nanjing (Nan-ching or Nanking) . . .	2,780,117	Nanchang (Nan-ch'ang)	1,695,587
Zibo	2,734,961	Shijiazhuang (Shih-chia-chuang or Shihkiachwang) . .	1,679,955
Dalian (Ta-lien or Dairen)	2,676,733	Yantai	1,666,787
Jinan (Chi-nan or Tsinan)	2,619,328	Yulin	1,636,762
Taiyuan (T'ai-yüan) . .	2,475,566	Yancheng	1,630,761
Guiyang	2,401,839	Xuzhou	1,620,840
Qingdao (Ch'ing-tao or Tsingtao) . . .	2,384,606	Xinghua	1,575,009
Zhengzhou (Cheng-chou or Chengchow) . .	2,176,109	Pingxiang	1,538,343
Zaozhuang . . .	2,131,478	Luoyang	1,535,468
Liupanshui . . .	2,079,960	Taian	1,530,915
Handan	2,069,505	Wulumuqi (Urumqi) .	1,501,399
Linyi	1,993,391		

Source: UN, *World Urbanization Prospects: The 2003 Revision.*

ADMINISTRATIVE DIVISIONS
(previous or other spelling given in brackets)

	Area ('000 sq km)	Population at 1 November 2000		Capital of province or region	Estimated population ('000) at mid-2000*
		Total	Density (per sq km)		
Provinces					
Sichuan (Szechwan)	487.0	82,348,296	169	Chengdu (Chengtu)	3,294
Henan (Honan)	167.0	91,236,854	546	Zhengzhou (Chengchow)	2,070
Shandong (Shantung) . . .	153.3	89,971,789	587	Jinan (Tsinan)	2,568
Jiangsu (Kiangsu)	102.6	73,043,577	712	Nanjing (Nanking)	2,740
Guangdong (Kwangtung) . .	197.1	85,225,007	432	Guangzhou (Canton)	3,893
Hebei (Hopei)	202.7	66,684,419	329	Shijiazhuang (Shihkiachwang)	1,603
Hunan (Hunan)	210.5	63,274,173	301	Changsha (Changsha)	1,775
Anhui (Anhwei)	139.9	58,999,948	422	Hefei (Hofei)	1,242
Hubei (Hupeh)	187.5	59,508,870	317	Wuhan (Wuhan)	5,169
Zhejiang (Chekiang) . . .	101.8	45,930,651	451	Hangzhou (Hangchow)	1,780
Liaoning (Liaoning)	151.0	41,824,412	277	Shenyang (Shenyang)	4,828
Jiangxi (Kiangsi)	164.8	40,397,598	245	Nanchang (Nanchang)	1,722
Yunnan (Yunnan)	436.2	42,360,089	97	Kunming (Kunming)	1,701
Heilongjiang (Heilungkiang) .	463.6	36,237,576	78	Harbin (Harbin)	2,928
Guizhou (Kweichow)	174.0	35,247,695	203	Guiyang (Kweiyang)	2,533
Shaanxi (Shensi)	195.8	35,365,072	171	Xian (Sian)	3,123
Fujian (Fukien)	123.1	34,097,947†	277	Fuzhou (Foochow)	1,397
Shanxi (Shansi)	157.1	32,471,242	207	Taiyuan (Taiyuan)	2,415
Jilin (Kirin)	187.0	26,802,191	143	Changchun (Changchun)	3,093
Gansu (Kansu)	366.5	25,124,282	69	Lanzhou (Lanchow)	1,730
Hainan	34.3	7,559,035	220	Haikou	438‡
Qinghai (Tsinghai)	721.0	4,822,963	7	Xining (Hsining)	691‡
Autonomous regions					
Guangxi Zhuang (Kwangsi Chuang)	220.4	43,854,538	199	Nanning (Nanning)	1,311
Nei Mongol (Inner Mongolia) .	1,177.5	23,323,347	20	Hohhot (Huhehot)	978
Xinjiang Uygur (Sinkiang Uighur)	1,646.9	18,459,511	11	Urumqi (Urumchi)	1,415
Ningxia Hui (Ninghsia Hui) . .	66.4	5,486,393	83	Yinchuan (Yinchuen)	530‡
Tibet (Xizang)	1,221.6	2,616,329	2	Lhasa (Lhasa)	105§
Municipalities					
Shanghai	6.2	16,407,734	2,646	—	12,887
Beijing (Peking)	16.8	13,569,194	808	—	10,839
Tianjin (Tientsin)	11.3	9,848,731	872	—	9,156
Chongqing (Chungking) . . .	82.0	30,512,763	372	—	4,900
Total	9,572.9	1,242,612,226‖	130		

* UN estimates, excluding population in counties under cities' administration.

† Excluding islands administered by Taiwan, mainly Jinmen (Quemoy) and Mazu (Matsu), with 49,050 inhabitants according to figures released by the Taiwan authorities at the end of March 1990.

‡ December 1998 figure.

§ 1982 figure.

‖ Including 2,500,000 military personnel and 1,050,000 persons with unregistered households.

BIRTHS AND DEATHS
(sample surveys)

	2001	2002	2003
Birth rate (per 1,000)	13.38	12.86	12.41
Death rate (per 1,000)	6.43	6.41	6.40

Marriages (number registered): 7,971,100 in 2001; 7,788,000 in 2002; 8,035,000 in 2003.

Expectation of life (WHO estimates, years at birth): 71.1 (males 69.6; females 72.7) in 2002 (Source: WHO, *World Health Report*).

EMPLOYMENT*
(official estimates, '000 persons at 31 December)

	2000	2001	2002
Agriculture, forestry and fishing .	333,550	329,740	324,870
Mining	5,970	5,610	5,580
Manufacturing	80,430	80,830	83,070
Electricity, gas and water . . .	2,840	2,880	2,900
Construction	35,520	36,690	38,930
Geological prospecting and water conservancy	1,100	1,050	980
Transport, storage and communications	20,290	20,370	20,840

— *continued*	2000	2001	2002
Wholesale and retail trade and catering	46,860	47,370	49,690
Banking and insurance	3,270	3,360	3,400
Real estate	1,000	1,070	1,180
Social services	9,210	9,760	10,940
Health care, sports and social welfare	4,880	4,930	4,930
Education, culture, art, radio, film and television broadcasting . .	15,650	15,680	15,650
Scientific research and polytechnic services	1,740	1,650	1,630
Government agencies, etc. . . .	11,040	11,010	10,750
Others	56,430	58,520	62,450
Total	629,780	630,520	637,790

* In addition to employment statistics, sample surveys of the economically active population are conducted. On the basis of these surveys, the total labour force ('000 persons at 31 December) was: 744,320 in 2001; 753,600 in 2002; 760,750 in 2003. Of these totals, the number of employed persons ('000 at 31 December) was: 730,250 (agriculture, etc. 365,130, industry 162,840, services 202,280) in 2001; 737,400 (agriculture, etc. 368,700, industry 157,800, services 210,900) in 2002; 744,320 (agriculture, etc. 365,460, industry 160,770, services 218,090) in 2003.

Health and Welfare

KEY INDICATORS

Total fertility rate (children per woman, 2002)	1.8
Under-5 mortality rate (per 1,000 live births, 2003) . . .	37
HIV/AIDS (% of persons aged 15–49, 2003)	0.1
Physicians (per 1,000 head, 2002)	1.67
Hospital beds (per 1,000 head, 2000)	2.38
Health expenditure (2001): US $ per head (PPP)	224
Health expenditure (2001): % of GDP	5.5
Health expenditure (2001): public (% of total)	37.2
Access to water (% of persons, 2002)	77
Access to sanitation (% of persons, 2002)	44
Human Development Index (2002): ranking	94
Human Development Index (2002): value	0.745

For sources and definitions, see explanatory note on p. vi.

Agriculture

PRINCIPAL CROPS
('000 metric tons)

	2001	2002	2003
Wheat	93,873	90,290	86,100
Rice (paddy)	177,581	174,539	164,800
Barley*	2,893	3,324	3,115
Maize	114,088	121,310	114,000
Rye†	701	580	510
Oats†	790	490	465
Millet	1,966	2,176	1,950
Sorghum	2,696	3,329	2,845
Buckwheat†	1,245	968	800
Triticale (wheat-rye hybrid) . .	644	980	1,060
Potatoes	64,564	75,230	66,775
Sweet potatoes	113,591	108,075	100,000*
Cassava (Manioc)†	3,850	3,900	3,900
Taro (Coco yam)†	1,500	1,550	1,550
Sugar cane	75,663	90,107	90,510
Sugar beet	10,889	12,820	6,190
Dry beans*	1,800	2,150	1,900
Dry broad beans*	1,950	2,100	1,800
Dry peas*	1,120	1,500	1,230
Other pulses*	246	262	270
Soybeans (Soya beans)	15,407	16,507	16,500
Groundnuts (in shell)	14,416	14,818	13,370
Oil palm fruit	650	660	660
Castor beans	300*	370*	400†
Sunflower seed	1,478	1,946	2,000*
Rapeseed	11,331	10,552	11,410
Tung nuts	407	388	405†
Sesame seed	804	895	825†
Tallowtree seeds†	835	850	850
Linseed	253	420*	466
Cottonseed	10,647	9,832	10,400
Other oilseeds	845	875†	883†
Cabbages†	24,650	27,400	30,000
Asparagus†	4,200	5,000	5,500
Lettuce†	7,600	9,000	10,000
Spinach†	7,400	9,000	10,000
Tomatoes†	24,000	27,000	28,700
Cauliflower†	6,100	6,500	7,000
Pumpkins, squash and gourds† .	3,700	5,000	5,500
Cucumbers and gherkins† . . .	21,600	24,000	25,000
Aubergines (Eggplants)† . . .	14,000	15,400	16,000
Green chillies and peppers† . .	9,850	10,500	11,500
Green onions and shallots† . .	300	400	500
Dry onions†	15,000	16,500	17,500
Garlic†	7,800	9,000	10,000
Green beans†	1,800	2,000	2,250
Green peas†	1,530	1,700	2,000
Carrots†	6,000	7,000	8,000
Mushrooms†	960	1,050	1,300
Other vegetables†	128,126	137,150	n.a.
Watermelons	57,178	61,608†	66,000*
Cantaloupes and other melons .	11,670	12,618*	13,600
Grapes	3,680	4,479	3,850*
Apples	20,015	19,241	20,000*
Pears	8,796	9,309	9,300*
Peaches and nectarines	4,562	5,230	5,500*
Plums*	4,026	4,363	4,200

— continued	2001	2002	2003
Oranges	1,352	1,501	1,505*
Tangerines, mandarins, clementines and satsumas . .	8,749	8,824	8,850*
Lemons and limes*	376	505	580
Grapefruit and pomelos* . . .	233	261	260
Other citrus fruit*	896	920	900
Mangoes*	3,060	3,300	3,200
Pineapples	869	827	900*
Persimmons	1,585	1,741	1,700*
Bananas	5,272	5,557	5,600*
Other fruits and berries* . . .	3,089	3,462	3,366
Walnuts	252	343	360†
Other treenuts†	689	803	816
Tea (made)	702	745	780
Pimento and allspice†	215	220	230
Other spices†	347	365	375
Tobacco (leaves)	2,350	2,447	2,300*
Jute and jute-like fibres . . .	106*	159*	180†
Other fibre crops	575	809*	821†

* Unofficial figure(s).
† FAO estimate(s).

Source: mainly FAO.

LIVESTOCK
('000 head at 31 December)

	2001	2002	2003
Horses	8,766	8,260	8,088
Mules	4,530	4,362	4,194
Asses	9,227	8,815	8,499
Cattle	105,905	100,959	103,318
Buffaloes	22,758	22,684	22,724
Camels	326	279	264
Pigs	446,815	457,430	462,915
Sheep	133,160	135,893	143,793
Goats	157,159	161,292	172,759
Rabbits	190,000*	191,247	194,221
Chickens	3,650,000*	3,980,000†	3,860,000†
Ducks	625,000*	676,000†	650,000†
Geese	205,000*	232,506†	225,230†

* FAO estimate.
† Unofficial figure.

Source: FAO.

LIVESTOCK PRODUCTS
('000 metric tons)

	2001	2002	2003
Beef and veal*	5,110	5,460	6,200
Buffalo meat*	378	386	400
Mutton and lamb*	1,540	1,680	1,991
Goat meat*	1,387	1,487	1,600
Pig meat	41,845	43,266	45,000*
Horse meat†	156	156	156
Rabbit meat	406	423	440*
Poultry meat*	12,103	12,498	12,922
Other meat†	414	510	491
Cows' milk	10,255	12,998	14,000†
Buffaloes' milk†	2,680	2,700	2,700
Sheep's milk	974	1,006	1,025
Goats' milk†	225	220	225
Butter†	84	88	92
Cheese†	217	225	230
Hen eggs	19,862	20,933	22,000†
Other poultry eggs	3,506	3,694	3,800†
Honey	252	265	270†
Raw silk (incl. waste)	94*	100*	102†
Wool: greasy	298	308	315†
Wool: scoured	149	154	158†
Cattle hides (fresh)†	1,272	1,365	1,365
Buffalo hides (fresh)†	113	116	120
Sheepskins (fresh)†	300	321	321
Goatskins (fresh)†	297	319	319

* Unofficial figures.
† FAO estimates.

Source: FAO.

Forestry

ROUNDWOOD REMOVALS

(FAO estimates, '000 cubic metres, excl. bark)

	2001	2002	2003
Sawlogs, veneer logs and logs for sleepers	51,500	51,160	51,160
Pulpwood	5,500	5,400	5,400
Other industrial wood	35,000	34,700	34,700
Fuel wood	190,883	190,883	190,883
Total	282,883	282,143	282,143

Source: FAO.

Timber production (official figures, '000 cubic metres): 45,520 in 2001; 44,361 in 2002.

SAWNWOOD PRODUCTION

('000 cubic metres, incl. railway sleepers)

	2001	2002	2003*
Coniferous (softwood)	4,853	5,112	5,112
Broadleaved (hardwood)	2,785*	3,408	3,408
Total	7,638	8,520	8,520

* FAO estimate(s).
Source: FAO.

Fishing

('000 metric tons, live weight)

	2000	2001	2002
Capture	16,987.3	16,529.4	16,553.1
Freshwater fishes	1,223.0	1,033.3	924.2
Japanese anchovy	1,142.9	1,260.7	1,173.2
Largehead hairtail	1,285.5	1,282.7	1,287.8
Aquaculture	24,580.7	26,050.1	27,767.2
Common carp	2,119.8	2,193.2	2,235.6
Crucian carp	1,375.4	1,523.4	1,697.2
Bighead carp	1,614.0	1,637.9	1,701.0
Grass carp (White amur)	3,162.6	3,310.9	3,419.6
Silver carp	3,227.9	3,275.9	3,401.9
Pacific cupped oyster	3,291.9	3,491.0	3,625.5
Japanese carpet shell	1,616.4	2,014.4	2,300.9
Total catch	41,568.0	42,579.5	44,320.4

Note: Figures exclude aquatic plants ('000 metric tons, wet weight): 8,067.8 (capture 204.3, aquaculture 7,863.5) in 2000; 8,426.3 (capture 266.9, aquaculture 8,159.5) in 2001; 9,106.3 (capture 297.2, aquaculture 8,809.1) in 2002.

Source: FAO.

Aquatic products (official figures, '000 metric tons): 42,784.8 (marine 25,387.4, freshwater 17,397.5) in 2000; 43,813.4 (marine 25,717.0, freshwater 18,096.4) in 2001; 45,645 (marine 26,463, freshwater 19,182) in 2002; 47,046 (marine 26,858, freshwater 20,188) in 2003. The totals include artificially cultured products ('000 metric tons): 25,746.7 (marine 10,612.9, freshwater 15,133.8) in 2000; 27,261.3 (marine 11,310.8, freshwater 15,950.5) in 2001; 29,058 (marine 12,128, freshwater 16,930) in 2002; 30,253 (marine 12,533, freshwater 17,720) in 2003. Figures include aquatic plants on a dry-weight basis ('000 metric tons): 1,222.0 in 2000; 1,249 in 2001; 1,333 in 2002; 1,413 in 2003. Freshwater plants are not included.

Mining

(estimates, '000 metric tons, unless otherwise indicated)

	2000	2001	2002
Coal*	998,000	1,160,000	1,380,000
Crude petroleum*	163,000	163,959	167,000
Natural gas (million cu m)*	27,200	30,329	32,661
Iron ore: gross weight	223,000	220,000	231,000
Iron ore: metal content	67,200	n.a	n.a.
Copper ore†	593	587	568
Nickel ore (metric tons)†	50,300	51,500	54,000
Bauxite	9,000	9,800	11,000
Lead ore†	660	676	641
Zinc ore†	1,780	1,700	1,550
Tin concentrates (metric tons)†	99,400	95,000	62,000
Manganese ore: gross weight	3,500	4,300	4,500
Manganese ore: metal content	800	n.a.	n.a.
Tungsten concentrates (metric tons)†	37,000	38,500	49,500
Ilmenite	185	n.a.	n.a.
Molybdenum ore (metric tons)†	28,800	28,200	29,300
Vanadium (metric tons)†	30,000	30,000	33,000
Zirconium concentrates (metric tons)	15,000	n.a.	n.a.
Antimony ore (metric tons)†	110,000	140,000	100,000
Cobalt ore (metric tons)†	90	150	1,000
Mercury (metric tons)†	200	190	495
Silver (metric tons)†	1,600	1,910	2,950
Uranium (metric tons)†‡	500	655	730
Gold (metric tons)†	180	185	192
Magnesite	4,070	3,580	3,700
Phosphate rock and apatite§	19,400	n.a.	n.a.
Potash‖	380	385	450
Native sulphur	290	290	290
Fluorspar	2,450	2,450	2,450
Barite (Barytes)	3,500	3,600	3,100
Arsenic trioxide (metric tons)	16,000	n.a.	n.a.
Salt (unrefined)*	31,280	34,105	36,024
Gypsum (crude)	6,800	6,800	6,850
Graphite (natural)	430	450	450
Asbestos	315	310	270
Talc and related materials	3,500	3,500	3,600
Diamonds ('000 carats):			
gem	230	235	n.a.
industrial	920	950	n.a.

* Official figures. Figures for coal include brown coal and waste. Production of coal in 2003 was 1,667,000 ('000 metric tons). Figures for petroleum include oil from shale and coal. Production of petroleum in 2003 was 169,600 ('000 metric tons). Figures for natural gas refer to gross volume of output. Production of natural gas in 2003 was 35,051 (million cu m). Production of salt in 2003 was 34,377 ('000 metric tons).

† Figures refer to the metal content of ores, concentrates or (in the case of vanadium) slag.

‡ Data from the World Nuclear Association (London, United Kingdom). The amount of uranium mined in 2003 was 750 metric tons.

§ Figures refer to gross weight. The estimated phosphoric acid content was 30%.

‖ Potassium oxide (K_2O) content of potash salts mined.

Source: mainly US Geological Survey.

Industry

SELECTED PRODUCTS

Unofficial Figures
('000 metric tons, unless otherwise indicated)

	1999	2000	2001
Plywood ('000 cu m)*†	8,103	10,735	9,856
Mechanical wood pulp*† . . .	455	480	565
Chemical wood pulp*†	1,695	1,745	1,785
Other fibre pulp*†	13,646	14,276	14,321
Sulphur‡§‖(a)	1,630	1,900	2,000
Sulphur‡§‖(b)	3,860	3,370	3,090
Kerosene	7,438	8,723	n.a.
Residual fuel oil	19,594	20,537	n.a.
Lubricating oils	2,658	2,887	n.a.
Paraffin wax	1,276	1,386	n.a.
Petroleum coke	4,253	4,619	n.a.
Petroleum bitumen (asphalt) . .	3,545	3,849	n.a.
Liquefied petroleum gas . . .	8,166	9,166	n.a.
Aluminium (unwrought) . . .	2,808.9	2,989.2	3,575.8
Refined copper (unwrought) . .	1,170.0	1,370.0	1,440.0
Lead (unwrought)	945.1	1,113.4	1,195.4
Tin (unwrought)	90.5	101.3	105.1
Zinc (unwrought)	1,669.8	1,931.7	2,037.6

* Data from the FAO.
† Including Taiwan.
‡ Data from the US Geological Survey.
§ Figures refer to (a) sulphur recovered as a by-product in the purification of coal-gas, in petroleum refineries, gas plants and from copper, lead and zinc sulphide ores; and (b) the sulphur content of iron and copper pyrites, including pyrite concentrates obtained from copper, lead and zinc ores.
‖ Provisional or estimated figure(s).

Source: UN, *Industrial Commodity Statistics Yearbook*.

Official Figures
('000 metric tons, unless otherwise indicated)

	2001	2002	2003
Edible vegetable oils	13,831.7	15,312.2	15,842.9
Raw sugar	6,531	9,260.0	10,839.4
Beer	22,889.3	24,027.0	25,404.8
Cigarettes ('000 cases)	34,021	34,670.8	35,808.6
Cotton yarn (pure and mixed) . .	7,607	8,500	9,836
Woven cotton fabrics—pure and mixed (million metres) . .	29,000	32,239	35,352
Woollen fabrics ('000 metres) . .	343,033.9	326,912.1	442,945.8
Silk fabrics (metric tons) . . .	87,300	98,200	111,000
Chemical fibres	8,414	9,912	11,812
Paper and paperboard	37,770.7	46,669.9	48,493.3
Rubber tyres ('000)	135,730.0	163,065.9	193,119.6
Sulphuric acid	26,963.2	30,504.0	33,712.2
Caustic soda (Sodium hydroxide) .	7,879.6	8,779.7	9,452.7
Soda ash (Sodium carbonate) . .	9,143.7	10,331.5	11,335.6
Insecticides	787	929	767
Nitrogenous fertilizers (a)* . . .	25,273.7	28,084.8	28,145.2
Phosphate fertilizers (b)* . . .	7,525.6	8,010.3	9,780.8
Potash fertilizers (c)*	1,030.8	1,814.9	887.1
Synthetic rubber	1,219.8	1,362.1	1,348.3
Plastics	12,887.1	14,556.7	16,520.8
Motor spirit (gasoline)	41,546.6	43,207.6	47,908.6
Distillate fuel oil (diesel oil) . .	74,856.6	77,061.0	85,327.8
Coke	131,307.7	142,798.1	177,757.1
Cement	661,040	725,000	862,081
Pig-iron	155,542.5	170,846	213,667
Crude steel	151,634	182,366	222,336
Internal combustion engines ('000 horse-power)†	205,311.7	285,057.5	318,513.0
Tractors—over 20 horse-power (number)	38,200	45,400	48,800
Railway freight wagons (number) .	30,700	31,300	31,200
Road motor vehicles ('000) . . .	2,342	3,251	4,444
Bicycles ('000)	29,022.6	39,575.2	54,517.0
Electric fans ('000)	96,161.0	107,613.3	129,809.2
Mobile telephones ('000 units) . .	80,316.6	121,463.5	182,313.7
Floppy disks ('000)	488,000	718,000	671,000
Microcomputers ('000)	8,777	14,635	32,167
Large semiconductor integrated circuits ('000)	2,226,000	4,132,000	6,863,000
Colour television receivers ('000)	40,937	51,550	65,414

— continued	2001	2002	2003
Cameras ('000)	59,620.9	53,096.1	61,981.4
Electric energy (million kWh) . .	1,480,802	1,654,000	1,910,575

* Production in terms of (a) nitrogen; (b) phosphoric acid; or (c) potassium oxide.
† Sales.

Finance

CURRENCY AND EXCHANGE RATES

Monetary Units
100 fen (cents) = 10 jiao (chiao) = 1 renminbiao (People's Bank Dollar), usually called a yuan.

Sterling, Dollar and Euro Equivalents (31 December 2004)
£1 sterling = 15.985 yuan;
US $1 = 8.277 yuan;
€1 = 11.273 yuan;
1,000 yuan = £62.56 = $120.82 = €88.70.

Average Exchange Rate (yuan per US $)
2002   8.2770
2003   8.2770
2004   8.2770

Note: Since 1 January 1994 the official rate has been based on the prevailing rate in the interbank market for foreign exchange.

STATE BUDGET
(million yuan)*

Revenue	2001	2002	2003
Taxes	1,530,138	1,763,645	2,001,731
Company income tax . .	263,087	308,279	291,951
Tariffs	84,052	70,427	92,313
Agricultural and animal husbandry taxes . . .	48,170	71,785	87,177
Business tax	206,409	245,033	284,445
Consumption tax . . .	92,999	104,632	118,226
Value-added tax . . .	535,713	617,839	723,654
Other receipts	138,470	152,679	192,432
Sub-total	1,668,608	1,916,324	2,194,163
Less Subsidies for losses by enterprises	30,004	25,960	22,638
Total	1,638,604	1,890,364	2,171,525
Central Government . .	858,274	1,038,864	1,186,527
Local authorities . . .	780,330	851,500	984,998

Expenditure†	2001	2002	2003
Capital construction	251,064	314,298	342,930
Circulation of capital . . .	2,271	1,897	1,195
Agriculture, forestry and water conservancy	91,796	110,270	113,486
Culture, education, science and health care‡	336,102	397,908	450,551
National defence	144,204	170,778	190,787
Administration	219,752	297,942	343,768
Pensions and social welfare . .	26,668	37,297	49,882
Subsidies to compensate price increases	74,151	64,507	61,728
Promotion of innovation, science and technology	99,156	96,838	109,299
Operating expenses of industry, transport and commerce . . .	20,012	23,238	28,523
Geological prospecting . . .	9,901	10,289	10,694
Total (incl. others) . . .	1,890,258	2,205,315	2,464,995
Central Government . . .	576,802	677,170	742,010
Local authorities	1,313,456	1,528,145	1,722,985

* Figures represent a consolidation of the regular (current) and construction (capital) budgets of the central Government and local administrative organs. The data exclude extrabudgetary transactions, totalling (in million yuan): Revenue 382,643 (central 24,763, local 357,879) in 2000; 430,000 (central 34,700, local 395,300) in 2001; 447,900 (central 44,000, local 403,900) in 2002. Expenditure 352,901 (central 21,074, local 331,828) in 2000; 385,000 (central 25,813, local 359,187) in 2001; 383,100 (central 25,900, local 357,200) in 2002.
† Excluding payments of debt interest.
‡ Current expenditure only.

INTERNATIONAL RESERVES
(US $ million at 31 December)

	2001	2002	2003
Gold*	3,093	4,074	4,074
IMF special drawing rights	851	998	1,102
Reserve position in IMF	2,590	3,723	3,798
Foreign exchange†	212,165	286,407	403,251
Total†	218,698	295,202	412,225

* Valued at SDR 35 per troy ounce.
† Excluding the Bank of China's holdings of foreign exchange.

Source: IMF, *International Financial Statistics*.

MONEY SUPPLY
(million yuan at 31 December)*

	2001	2002	2003
Currency outside banking institutions	1,568,730	1,727,800	1,974,600
Demand deposits at banking institutions	4,414,010	5,356,210	6,431,420
Total money (incl. others)	6,168,850	7,266,540	8,644,890

* Figures are rounded to the nearest 10 million yuan.

Source: IMF, *International Financial Statistics*.

COST OF LIVING
(General Consumer Price Index; base: previous year = 100)

	2001	2002	2003
Food	100.0	99.4	103.4
Clothing	98.1	97.6	97.8
Housing*	101.2	99.9	102.1
All items (incl. others)	100.7	99.2	101.2

* Including water, electricity and fuels.

NATIONAL ACCOUNTS
(million yuan at current prices)

Expenditure on the Gross Domestic Product*

	2001	2002	2003
Government final consumption expenditure	1,302,930	1,391,690	1,476,400
Private final consumption expenditure	4,589,810	4,888,160	5,267,850
Increase in stocks	64,750	38,660	13,440
Gross fixed capital formation	3,681,330	4,191,830	5,124,830
Total domestic expenditure	9,638,820	10,510,340	11,882,520
Exports of goods and services *Less* Imports of goods and services	220,470	279,420	268,620
Sub-total	9,859,290	10,789,760	12,151,140
Statistical discrepancy†	−127,810	−272,530	−425,950
GDP in purchasers' values	9,731,480	10,517,230	11,725,190

* Figures are rounded to the nearest 10 million yuan.
† Referring to the difference between the sum of the expenditure components and official estimates of GDP, compiled from the production approach.

Gross Domestic Product by Economic Activity*

	2001	2002	2003
Agriculture, forestry and fishing	1,541,180	1,611,730	1,709,210
Industry†	4,237,460	4,597,520	5,309,290
Construction	637,540	700,500	818,130
Transport, storage and communications	596,830	642,030	671,560
Wholesale and retail trade and catering	791,980	847,670	923,810
Other services	1,926,590	2,117,780	2,293,200
Total	9,731,480	10,517,230	11,725,190

* Figures are rounded to the nearest 10 million yuan.
† Includes mining, manufacturing, electricity, gas and water.

BALANCE OF PAYMENTS
(US $ million)

	2001	2002	2003
Exports of goods f.o.b.	266,075	325,651	438,270
Imports of goods f.o.b.	−232,058	−281,484	−393,618
Trade balance	34,017	44,167	44,652
Exports of services	33,334	39,745	46,734
Imports of services	−39,267	−46,528	−55,306
Balance on goods and services	28,084	37,383	36,079
Other income received	9,338	8,344	16,095
Other income paid	−28,563	−23,289	−23,933
Balance on goods, services and income	8,909	22,438	28,241
Current transfers received	9,125	13,795	18,482
Current transfers paid	−633	−811	−848
Current balance	17,401	35,422	45,875
Capital account (net)	−54	−50	−48
Direct investment abroad	−6,884	−2,518	152
Direct investment from abroad	44,241	49,308	47,077
Portfolio investment assets	−20,654	−12,095	2,983
Portfolio investment liabilities	1,249	1,752	8,444
Other investment assets	20,813	−3,077	−17,922
Other investment liabilities	−3,933	−1,029	12,040
Net errors and omissions	−4,732	7,504	17,985
Overall balance	47,447	75,217	116,586

Source: IMF, *International Financial Statistics*.

External Trade

PRINCIPAL COMMODITIES
(distribution by SITC, US $ million)

Imports c.i.f.	2000	2001	2002
Food and live animals	4,742.3	4,967.3	5,224.1
Crude materials (inedible) except fuels	19,685.8	21,828.8	22,506.9
Metalliferous ores and metal scrap	5,801.6	7,326.6	7,265.0
Mineral fuels, lubricants, etc.	20,756.6	17,618.5	19,490.0
Petroleum, petroleum products, etc.	19,049.3	16,049.7	17,430.2
Crude petroleum oils, etc.	14,860.7	11,661.3	12,757.3
Chemicals and related products	29,768.7	31,603.0	38,370.9
Organic chemicals	8,301.5	8,867.8	10,979.1
Artificial resins, plastic materials, etc.	13,012.0	13,822.7	15,650.6
Products of polymerization, etc.	10,273.4	11,142.7	12,138.8
Basic manufactures	42,493.0	42,667.6	49,085.9
Textile yarn, fabrics, etc.	13,108.4	12,819.1	13,270.3
Iron and steel	9,795.2	10,870.8	13,680.5
Machinery and transport equipment	91,866.0	106,884.7	136,904.1
Machinery specialized for particular industries	10,556.8	12,397.4	15,252.2
General industrial machinery, equipment and parts	7,995.0	10,062.7	12,607.2
Office machines and automatic data-processing equipment	10,858.4	12,659.8	17,094.0
Telecommunications and sound equipment	12,412.8	13,293.2	14,149.9
Other electrical machinery, apparatus, etc.	35,641.7	39,903.5	55,488.8
Thermionic valves, tubes, etc.	21,155.6	23,611.9	35,167.4
Electronic microcircuits	13,300.0	16,591.4	25,644.1
Road vehicles and transport equipment *	6,348.3	9,988.0	11,482.6
Miscellaneous manufactured articles	12,699.8	15,119.3	20,000.3
Total (incl. others)	225,093.7	243,552.9	295,170.1

Exports f.o.b.	2000	2001	2002
Food and live animals . . .	12,270.8	12,764.8	14,601.7
Mineral fuels, lubricants, etc. .	7,862.3	8,415.2	8,449.3
Chemicals and related products	11,917.5	13,145.7	15,062.0
Basic manufactures . . .	43,305.0	44,604.6	53,744.4
Textile yarn, fabrics, etc. . . .	16,316.4	17,031.4	20,769.8
Machinery and transport equipment	82,443.7	94,774.4	126,853.2
Office machines and automatic data-processing equipment . .	18,637.9	23,572.4	36,227.8
Automatic data-processing machines and units . .	10,994.1	13,093.8	20,132.3
Telecommunications and sound equipment	19,508.3	23,758.7	32,016.8
Other electrical machinery, apparatus, etc.	24,655.4	25,986.2	32,845.6
Road vehicles and transport equipment*	8,918.1	9,026.3	10,137.3
Miscellaneous manufactured articles	85,582.8	86,682.1	100,760.8
Clothing and accessories (excl. footwear)	36,147.3	36,723.8	41,384.9
Footwear	9,466.6	9,676.4	10,680.6
Baby carriages, toys, games and sporting goods	10,112.4	9,886.2	12,561.2
Children's toys, indoor games, etc.	8,555.3	8,318.2	10,713.1
Total (incl. others)	249,202.6	266,098.2	325,596.0

* Data on parts exclude tyres, engines and electrical parts.

Source: UN, *International Trade Statistics Yearbook*.

PRINCIPAL TRADING PARTNERS
(US $ million)*

Imports c.i.f.	2001	2002	2003
Australia	5,425.9	5,850.6	7,300.1
Brazil	2,347.3	3,003.0	5,842.3
Canada	4,027.8	3,626.9	4,374.5
Finland	2,376.3	1,512.8	1,788.4
France	4,104.8	4,253.1	6,098.7
Germany	13,772.1	16,416.4	24,291.9
Hong Kong	9,423.0	10,726.2	11,118.7
Indonesia	3,887.9	4,508.4	5,747.0
Italy	3,784.3	4,319.5	5,080.6
Japan	42,787.3	53,466.0	74,148.1
Korea, Republic	23,377.0	28,568.0	43,128.1
Malaysia	6,204.0	9,296.3	13,986.4
Oman	1,609.6	1,446.5	1,985.8
Russia	7,958.8	8,406.7	9,728.1
Singapore	5,128.3	7,046.6	10,484.9
Sweden	2,167.4	1,791.0	2,715.9
Taiwan	27,338.8	38,061.4	49,360.4
Thailand	4,713.9	5,599.6	8,826.8
United Kingdom	3,527.0	3,336.0	3,570.3
USA	26,199.9	27,237.6	33,866.1
Total (incl. others)	243,557.2	295,170.1	412,759.8

Exports f.o.b.	2001	2002	2003
Australia	3,569.5	4,585.0	6,263.6
Canada	3,345.9	4,303.5	5,632.2
France	3,685.7	4,071.9	7,293.5
Germany	9,755.1	11,371.9	17,442.1
Hong Kong†	46,541.2	58,463.2	76,274.4
Indonesia	2,835.7	3,426.5	4,481.9
Italy	3,991.6	4,827.4	6,652.3
Japan	44,940.5	48,433.8	59,408.7
Korea, Republic	12,518.8	15,534.6	20,094.8
Malaysia	3,221.1	4,974.2	6,140.9
Netherlands	7,278.4	9,107.6	13,501.2
Russia	2,710.5	3,520.7	6,029.9
Singapore	5,790.7	6,984.2	8,863.8
Taiwan	4,999.6	6,585.7	9,004.1

Exports f.o.b.— *continued*	2001	2002	2003
United Kingdom	6,780.5	8,059.4	10,823.7
USA	54,279.5	69,945.8	92,466.8
Total (incl. others)	266,098.2	325,596.0	438,227.8

* Imports by country of origin; exports by country of consumption.
† The majority of China's exports to Hong Kong are re-exported.

Transport

	2001	2002	2003
Freight (million ton-km):			
railways	1,457,510	1,551,560	1,724,670
roads	633,040	678,250	709,950
waterways	2,598,890	2,751,060	2,871,580
air	4,372	5,155	5,790
Passenger-km (million):			
railways	476,680	496,940	478,860
roads	720,710	780,580	769,560
waterways	8,990	8,180	6,310
air	109,140	126,870	126,319

Road Traffic
('000 motor vehicles in use)*

	2001	2002	2003
Passenger cars and buses . . .	9,939.6	12,023.7	14,788.1
Goods vehicles	7,652.4	8,122.2	8,535.1
Total (incl. others)	18,020.4	20,531.7	23,829.3

* Excluding military vehicles.

Shipping

Merchant Fleet
(registered at 31 December)

	2001	2002	2003
Number of vessels	3,280	3,326	3,376
Total displacement ('000 grt) . .	16,646.1	17,315.5	18,428.0

Source: Lloyd's Register-Fairplay, *World Fleet Statistics*.

Sea-borne Shipping
(freight traffic, '000 metric tons)

	2001	2002	2003
Goods loaded and unloaded . .	1,426,340	1,666,280	2,011,260

Tourism

FOREIGN VISITORS
(arrivals, '000)

Country of origin	2001	2002	2003
Hong Kong and Macao . . .	74,344.5	80,808.2	77,527.3
Taiwan	3,442.0	3,660.6	2,731.9
Australia	255.1	291.3	245.4
Canada	253.9	291.3	230.3
France	199.5	222.1	156.1
Germany	253.4	281.8	222.0
Indonesia	224.2	274.7	231.8
Japan	2,385.7	2,925.6	2,254.8
Korea, Republic	1,678.8	2,124.3	1,945.5
Malaysia	468.6	592.4	430.1
Mongolia	387.1	453.1	418.3
Philippines	408.0	508.6	457.7
Russia	1,196.2	1,271.6	1,380.7
Singapore	415.0	497.1	378.1
Thailand	298.4	386.3	275.4
United Kingdom	302.5	343.0	288.3
USA	949.2	1,121.2	822.5
Total (incl. others)	89,012.9	97,908.3	91,662.1

Total tourism receipts (US $ million): 17,792 in 2001; 20,385 in 2002; 17,406 in 2003.

Communications Media

	2001	2002	2003
Telephones ('000 main lines in use)*	180,368	214,420	263,000
Mobile cellular telephones ('000 subscribers)*	144,820	206,620	269,000
Personal computers ('000 in use)*	25,000	35,500	n.a.
Internet users ('000)*	33,700	59,100	79,500
Book production:			
titles	154,526	170,962	190,391
copies (million)	6,310.0	6,870.0	6,670.0
Newspapers:			
number	2,111	2,137	2,119
average circulation ('000 copies)	181,300	187,210	190,720
Magazines:			
number	8,889	9,029	9,074
average circulation ('000 copies)	206,970	204,060	199,090

* Source: International Telecommunication Union.

1997 ('000 in use): Radio receivers 417,000; Facsimile machines 2,000 (Sources: UNESCO, *Statistical Yearbook*, and UN, *Statistical Yearbook*).

2000 ('000 in use): 380,000 television receivers (Source: International Telecommunication Union).

Education

(2003)

	Institutions	Full-time teachers ('000)	Students ('000)
Kindergartens	116,390	613	20,039
Primary schools	425,846	5,703	116,897
General secondary schools	79,490	4,537	85,832
Specialized secondary schools (technical and teacher training schools)	3,065	199	5,024
Agricultural and vocational schools	6,843	289	5,282
Special schools	1,551	30	365
Higher education	1,552	725	11,086

Adult literacy rate (based on census data): 90.9% (males 95.1%; females 86.5%) in 2002 (Source: UN Development Programme, *Human Development Report*).

Directory

The Constitution

A new Constitution was adopted on 4 December 1982 by the Fifth Session of the Fifth National People's Congress. Its principal provisions, including amendments made in 1993, 1999 and 2004, are detailed below. The Preamble, which is not included here, states that 'Taiwan is part of the sacred territory of the People's Republic of China'. The seventh paragraph of the Preamble was amended in 1993 and 1999 to state: 'The basic task of the nation is to concentrate its efforts on socialist modernization by following the road of building socialism with Chinese characteristics. Under the leadership of the Communist Party of China and the guidance of Marxism-Leninism, Mao Zedong Thought and Deng Xiaoping Theory, the Chinese people of all nationalities will continue to adhere to the people's democratic dictatorship-'. The paragraph was further amended in 2004 to refer to 'Chinese-style socialism' and to 'the important thought of the Three Represents'.

GENERAL PRINCIPLES

Article 1: The People's Republic of China is a socialist state under the people's democratic dictatorship led by the working class and based on the alliance of workers and peasants.

The socialist system is the basic system of the People's Republic of China. Sabotage of the socialist system by any organization or individual is prohibited.

Article 2: All power in the People's Republic of China belongs to the people.

The organs through which the people exercise state power are the National People's Congress and the local people's congresses at different levels.

The people administer state affairs and manage economic, cultural and social affairs through various channels and in various ways in accordance with the law.

Article 3: The state organs of the People's Republic of China apply the principle of democratic centralism.

The National People's Congress and the local people's congresses at different levels are instituted through democratic election. They are responsible to the people and subject to their supervision.

All administrative, judicial and procuratorial organs of the State are created by the people's congresses to which they are responsible and under whose supervision they operate.

The division of functions and powers between the central and local state organs is guided by the principle of giving full play to the initiative and enthusiasm of the local authorities under the unified leadership of the central authorities.

Article 4: All nationalities in the People's Republic of China are equal. The State protects the lawful rights and interests of the minority nationalities and upholds and develops the relationship of equality, unity and mutual assistance among all of China's nationalities. Discrimination against and oppression of any nationality are prohibited; any acts that undermine the unity of the nationalities or instigate their secession are prohibited.

The State helps the areas inhabited by minority nationalities speed up their economic and cultural development in accordance with the peculiarities and needs of the different minority nationalities.

Regional autonomy is practised in areas where people of minority nationalities live in compact communities; in these areas organs of self-government are established for the exercise of the right of autonomy. All the national autonomous areas are inalienable parts of the People's Republic of China.

The people of all nationalities have the freedom to use and develop their own spoken and written languages, and to preserve or reform their own ways and customs.

Article 5: The People's Republic of China shall be governed according to law and shall be built into a socialist country based on the rule of law.

The State upholds the uniformity and dignity of the socialist legal system.

No law or administrative or local rules and regulations shall contravene the Constitution.

All state organs, the armed forces, all political parties and public organizations and all enterprises and undertakings must abide by the Constitution and the law. All acts in violation of the Constitution and the law must be looked into.

No organization or individual may enjoy the privilege of being above the Constitution and the law.

Article 6: The basis of the socialist economic system of the People's Republic of China is socialist public ownership of the means of production, namely, ownership by the whole people and collective ownership by the working people.

The system of socialist public ownership supersedes the system of exploitation of man by man; it applies the principle of 'from each according to his ability, to each according to his work.'

In the initial stage of socialism, the country shall uphold the basic economic system in which the public ownership is dominant and diverse forms of ownership develop side by side, and it shall uphold the distribution system with distribution according to work remaining dominant and a variety of modes of distribution coexisting.

Article 7: The state-owned economy, namely the socialist economy under the ownership of the whole people, is the leading force in the national economy. The State ensures the consolidation and growth of the state-owned economy.

Article 8: The rural collective economic organizations shall implement a two-tier operations system that combines unified operations with independent operations on the basis of household contract operations and different co-operative economic forms in the rural areas—the producers', supply and marketing, credit, and consumers' co-operatives—are part of the socialist economy collectively owned by the working people. Working people who are all members of rural economic collectives have the right, within the limits prescribed by law, to farm plots of cropland and hilly land allotted for their private use, engage in household sideline production and raise privately-owned livestock.

The various forms of co-operative economy in the cities and towns, such as those in the handicraft, industrial, building, transport, commercial and service trades, all belong to the sector of socialist economy under collective ownership by the working people.

The State protects the lawful rights and interests of the urban and rural economic collectives and encourages, guides and helps the growth of the collective economy.

Article 9: Mineral resources, waters, forests, mountains, grassland, unreclaimed land, beaches and other natural resources are owned by the State, that is, by the whole people, with the exception of the forests, mountains, grassland, unreclaimed land and beaches that are owned by collectives in accordance with the law.

The State ensures the rational use of natural resources and protects rare animals and plants. The appropriation or damage of natural resources by any organization or individual by whatever means is prohibited.

Article 10: Land in the cities is owned by the State.

Land in the rural and suburban areas is owned by collectives except for those portions which belong to the State in accordance with the law; house sites and private plots of cropland and hilly land are also owned by collectives.

The State may, in the public interest and in accordance with the provisions of law, expropriate or requisition land for its use and shall make compensation for the land expropriated or requisitioned.

No organization or individual may appropriate, buy, sell or lease land, or unlawfully transfer land in other ways.

All organizations and individuals who use land must make rational use of the land.

Article 11: The non-public sector of the economy comprising the individual and private sectors, operating within the limits prescribed by law, is an important component of the socialist market economy.

The State protects the lawful rights and interests of the non-public sectors of the economy such as the individual and private sectors of the economy. The State encourages, supports and guides the development of the non-public sectors of the economy and, in accordance with the law, exercises supervision and control over the non-public sectors of the economy.

Article 12: Socialist public property is sacred and inviolable.

The State protects socialist public property. Appropriation or damage of state or collective property by any organization or individual by whatever means is prohibited.

Article 13: Citizens' lawful private property is inviolable.

The State, in accordance with the law, protects the rights of citizens to private property and to its inheritance.

The State may, in the public interest and in accordance with the law, expropriate or requisition private property for its use and shall make compensation for private property expropriated or requisitioned.

Article 14: The State continuously raises labour productivity, improves economic results and develops the productive forces by enhancing the enthusiasm of the working people, raising the level of their technical skill, disseminating advanced science and technology, improving the systems of economic administration and enterprise operation and management, instituting the socialist system of responsibility in various forms and improving organization of work.

The State practises strict economy and combats waste.

The State properly apportions accumulation and consumption, pays attention to the interests of the collective and the individual as well as of the State and, on the basis of expanded production, gradually improves the material and cultural life of the people.

The State establishes a sound social security system compatible with the level of economic development.

Article 15: The State practises a socialist market economy. The State strengthens economic legislation and perfects macro-control. The State prohibits, according to the law, disturbance of society's economic order by any organization or individual.

Article 16: State-owned enterprises have decision-making power in operations within the limits prescribed by law.

State-owned enterprises practise democratic management through congresses of workers and staff and in other ways in accordance with the law.

Article 17: Collective economic organizations have decision-making power in conducting economic activities on the condition that they abide by the relevant laws. Collective economic organizations practise democratic management, elect and remove managerial personnel, and decide on major issues in accordance with the law.

Article 18: The People's Republic of China permits foreign enterprises, other foreign economic organizations and individual foreigners to invest in China and to enter into various forms of economic co-operation with Chinese enterprises and other economic organizations in accordance with the law of the People's Republic of China.

All foreign enterprises and other foreign economic organizations in China, as well as joint ventures with Chinese and foreign investment located in China, shall abide by the law of the People's Republic of China. Their lawful rights and interests are protected by the law of the People's Republic of China.

Article 19: The State develops socialist educational undertakings and works to raise the scientific and cultural level of the whole nation.

The State runs schools of various types, makes primary education compulsory and universal, develops secondary, vocational and higher education and promotes pre-school education.

The State develops educational facilities of various types in order to wipe out illiteracy and provide political, cultural, scientific, technical and professional education for workers, peasants, state functionaries and other working people. It encourages people to become educated through self-study.

The State encourages the collective economic organizations, state enterprises and undertakings and other social forces to set up educational institutions of various types in accordance with the law.

The State promotes the nation-wide use of Putonghua (common speech based on Beijing pronunciation).

Article 20: The State promotes the development of the natural and social sciences, disseminates scientific and technical knowledge, and commends and rewards achievements in scientific research as well as technological discoveries and inventions.

Article 21: The State develops medical and health services, promotes modern medicine and traditional Chinese medicine, encourages and supports the setting up of various medical and health facilities by the rural economic collectives, state enterprises and undertakings and neighbourhood organizations, and promotes sanitation activities of a mass character, all to protect the people's health.

The State develops physical culture and promotes mass sports activities to build up the people's physique.

Article 22: The State promotes the development of literature and art, the press, broadcasting and television undertakings, publishing and distribution services, libraries, museums, cultural centres and other cultural undertakings, that serve the people and socialism, and sponsors mass cultural activities.

The State protects places of scenic and historical interest, valuable cultural monuments and relics and other important items of China's historical and cultural heritage.

Article 23: The State trains specialized personnel in all fields who serve socialism, increases the number of intellectuals and creates conditions to give full scope to their role in socialist modernization.

Article 24: The State strengthens the building of socialist spiritual civilization through spreading education in high ideals and morality, general education and education in discipline and the legal system, and through promoting the formulation and observance of rules of conduct and common pledges by different sections of the people in urban and rural areas.

The State advocates the civic virtues of love for the motherland, for the people, for labour, for science and for socialism; it educates the people in patriotism, collectivism, internationalism and communism and in dialectical and historical materialism; it combats capitalist, feudalist and other decadent ideas.

Article 25: The State promotes family planning so that population growth may fit the plans for economic and social development.

Article 26: The State protects and improves the living environment and the ecological environment, and prevents and remedies pollution and other public hazards.

The State organizes and encourages afforestation and the protection of forests.

Article 27: All state organs carry out the principle of simple and efficient administration, the system of responsibility for work and the system of training functionaries and appraising their work in order constantly to improve quality of work and efficiency and combat bureaucratism.

All state organs and functionaries must rely on the support of the people, keep in close touch with them, heed their opinions and suggestions, accept their supervision and work hard to serve them.

Article 28: The State maintains public order and suppresses treasonable and other criminal activities that endanger national security; it penalizes activities that endanger public security and disrupt the socialist economy as well as other criminal activities; and it punishes and reforms criminals.

Article 29: The armed forces of the People's Republic of China belong to the people. Their tasks are to strengthen national defence, resist aggression, defend the motherland, safeguard the people's peaceful labour, participate in national reconstruction, and work hard to serve the people.

The State strengthens the revolutionization, modernization and regularization of the armed forces in order to increase the national defence capability.

Article 30: The administrative division of the People's Republic of China is as follows:

(1) The country is divided into provinces, autonomous regions and municipalities directly under the central government;

(2) Provinces and autonomous regions are divided into autonomous prefectures, counties, autonomous counties and cities;

(3) Counties and autonomous counties are divided into townships, nationality townships and towns.

Municipalities directly under the central government and other large cities are divided into districts and counties. Autonomous prefectures are divided into counties, autonomous counties, and cities.

All autonomous regions, autonomous prefectures and autonomous counties are national autonomous areas.

Article 31: The State may establish special administrative regions when necessary. The systems to be instituted in special administrative regions shall be prescribed by law enacted by the National People's Congress in the light of the specific conditions.

Article 32: The People's Republic of China protects the lawful rights and interests of foreigners within Chinese territory, and while on Chinese territory foreigners must abide by the law of the People's Republic of China.

The People's Republic of China may grant asylum to foreigners who request it for political reasons.

FUNDAMENTAL RIGHTS AND DUTIES OF CITIZENS

Article 33: All persons holding the nationality of the People's Republic of China are citizens of the People's Republic of China.

All citizens of the People's Republic of China are equal before the law.

Every citizen enjoys the rights and at the same time must perform the duties prescribed by the Constitution and the law.

The State respects and preserves human rights.

Article 34: All citizens of the People's Republic of China who have reached the age of 18 have the right to vote and stand for election, regardless of nationality, race, sex, occupation, family background, religious belief, education, property status, or length of residence, except persons deprived of political rights according to law.

Article 35: Citizens of the People's Republic of China enjoy freedom of speech, of the press, of assembly, of association, of procession and of demonstration.

Article 36: Citizens of the People's Republic of China enjoy freedom of religious belief.

No state organ, public organization or individual may compel citizens to believe in, or not to believe in, any religion; nor may they discriminate against citizens who believe in, or do not believe in, any religion.

The State protects normal religious activities. No one may make use of religion to engage in activities that disrupt public order, impair the health of citizens or interfere with the educational system of the state.

Religious bodies and religious affairs are not subject to any foreign domination.

Article 37: The freedom of person of citizens of the People's Republic of China is inviolable.

No citizen may be arrested except with the approval or by decision of a people's procuratorate or by decision of a people's court, and arrests must be made by a public security organ.

Unlawful deprivation or restriction of citizens' freedom of person by detention or other means is prohibited; and unlawful search of the person of citizens is prohibited.

Article 38: The personal dignity of citizens of the People's Republic of China is inviolable. Insult, libel, false charge or frame-up directed against citizens by any means is prohibited.

Article 39: The home of citizens of the People's Republic of China is inviolable. Unlawful search of, or intrusion into, a citizen's home is prohibited.

Article 40: The freedom and privacy of correspondence of citizens of the People's Republic of China are protected by law. No organization or individual may, on any ground, infringe upon the freedom and privacy of citizens' correspondence except in cases where, to meet the needs of state security or of investigation into criminal offences, public security or procuratorial organs are permitted to censor correspondence in accordance with procedures prescribed by law.

Article 41: Citizens of the People's Republic of China have the right to criticize and make suggestions to any state organ or functionary. Citizens have the right to make to relevant state organs complaints and charges against, or exposures of, violation of the law or dereliction of duty by any state organ or functionary; but fabrication or distortion of facts with the intention of libel or frame-up is prohibited.

In case of complaints, charges or exposures made by citizens, the state organ concerned must deal with them in a responsible manner after ascertaining the facts. No one may suppress such complaints, charges and exposures, or retaliate against the citizen making them.

Citizens who have suffered losses through infringement of their civic rights by any state organ or functionary have the right to compensation in accordance with the law.

Article 42: Citizens of the People's Republic of China have the right as well as the duty to work.

Using various channels, the State creates conditions for employment, strengthens labour protection, improves working conditions and, on the basis of expanded production, increases remuneration for work and social benefits.

Work is the glorious duty of every able-bodied citizen. All working people in state-owned enterprises and in urban and rural economic collectives should perform their tasks with an attitude consonant with their status as masters of the country. The State promotes socialist labour emulation, and commends and rewards model and advanced workers. The State encourages citizens to take part in voluntary labour.

The State provides necessary vocational training to citizens before they are employed.

Article 43: Working people in the People's Republic of China have the right to rest.

The State expands facilities for rest and recuperation of working people, and prescribes working hours and vacations for workers and staff.

Article 44: The State prescribes by law the system of retirement for workers and staff in enterprises and undertakings and for functionaries of organs of state. The livelihood of retired personnel is ensured by the State and society.

Article 45: Citizens of the People's Republic of China have the right to material assistance from the State and society when they are old, ill or disabled. The State develops the social insurance, social relief and medical and health services that are required to enable citizens to enjoy this right.

The State and society ensure the livelihood of disabled members of the armed forces, provide pensions to the families of martyrs and give preferential treatment to the families of military personnel.

The State and society help make arrangements for the work, livelihood and education of the blind, deaf-mute and other handicapped citizens.

Article 46: Citizens of the People's Republic of China have the duty as well as the right to receive education.

The State promotes the all-round moral, intellectual and physical development of children and young people.

Article 47: Citizens of the People's Republic of China have the freedom to engage in scientific research, literary and artistic creation and other cultural pursuits. The State encourages and assists creative endeavours conducive to the interests of the people that are made by citizens engaged in education, science, technology, literature, art and other cultural work.

Article 48: Women in the People's Republic of China enjoy equal rights with men in all spheres of life, political, economic, cultural and social, including family life.

The State protects the rights and interests of women, applies the principle of equal pay for equal work for men and women alike and trains and selects cadres from among women.

Article 49: Marriage, the family and mother and child are protected by the State.

Both husband and wife have the duty to practise family planning.

Parents have the duty to rear and educate their minor children, and children who have come of age have the duty to support and assist their parents.

Violation of the freedom of marriage is prohibited. Maltreatment of old people, women and children is prohibited.

Article 50: The People's Republic of China protects the legitimate rights and interests of Chinese nationals residing abroad and protects the lawful rights and interests of returned overseas Chinese and of the family members of Chinese nationals residing abroad.

Article 51: The exercise by citizens of the People's Republic of China of their freedoms and rights may not infringe upon the interests of the State, of society and of the collective, or upon the lawful freedoms and rights of other citizens.

Article 52: It is the duty of citizens of the People's Republic of China to safeguard the unity of the country and the unity of all its nationalities.

Article 53: Citizens of the People's Republic of China must abide by the Constitution and the law, keep state secrets, protect public property and observe labour discipline and public order and respect social ethics.

Article 54: It is the duty of citizens of the People's Republic of China to safeguard the security, honour and interests of the motherland; they must not commit acts detrimental to the security, honour and interests of the motherland.

Article 55: It is the sacred obligation of every citizen of the People's Republic of China to defend the motherland and resist aggression.

It is the honourable duty of citizens of the People's Republic of China to perform military service and join the militia in accordance with the law.

Article 56: It is the duty of citizens of the People's Republic of China to pay taxes in accordance with the law.

STRUCTURE OF THE STATE

The National People's Congress

Article 57: The National People's Congress of the People's Republic of China is the highest organ of state power. Its permanent body is the Standing Committee of the National People's Congress.

Article 58: The National People's Congress and its Standing Committee exercise the legislative power of the State.

Article 59: The National People's Congress is composed of deputies elected from the provinces, autonomous regions, municipalities directly under the Central Government, and the special administrative regions, and of deputies elected from the armed forces. All the minority nationalities are entitled to appropriate representation.

Election of deputies to the National People's Congress is conducted by the Standing Committee of the National People's Congress.

The number of deputies to the National People's Congress and the manner of their election are prescribed by law.

Article 60: The National People's Congress is elected for a term of five years.

Two months before the expiration of the term of office of a National People's Congress, its Standing Committee must ensure that the election of deputies to the succeeding National People's Congress is completed. Should exceptional circumstances prevent such an election, it may be postponed by decision of a majority vote of more than two-thirds of all those on the Standing Committee of the incumbent National People's Congress, and the term of office of the incumbent National People's Congress may be extended. The election of deputies to the succeeding National People's Congress must be completed within one year after the termination of such exceptional circumstances.

Article 61: The National People's Congress meets in session once a year and is convened by its Standing Committee. A session of the National People's Congress may be convened at any time the Standing Committee deems this necessary, or when more than one-fifth of the deputies to the National People's Congress so propose.

When the National People's Congress meets, it elects a presidium to conduct its session.

Article 62: The National People's Congress exercises the following functions and powers:

(1) to amend the Constitution;

(2) to supervise the enforcement of the Constitution;

(3) to enact and amend basic statutes concerning criminal offences, civil affairs, the state organs and other matters;

(4) to elect the President and the Vice-President of the People's Republic of China;

(5) to decide on the choice of the Premier of the State Council upon nomination by the President of the People's Republic of China, and to decide on the choice of the Vice-Premiers, State Councillors, Ministers in charge of Ministries or Commissions and the Auditor-General and the Secretary-General of the State Council upon nomination by the Premier;

(6) to elect the Chairman of the Central Military Commission and, upon his nomination, to decide on the choice of all the others on the Central Military Commission;

(7) to elect the President of the Supreme People's Court;

(8) to elect the Procurator-General of the Supreme People's Procuratorate;

(9) to examine and approve the plan for national economic and social development and the reports on its implementation;

(10) to examine and approve the state budget and the report on its implementation;

(11) to alter or annul inappropriate decisions of the Standing Committee of the National People's Congress;

(12) to approve the establishment of provinces, autonomous regions, and municipalities directly under the Central Government;

(13) to decide on the establishment of special administrative regions and the systems to be instituted there;

(14) to decide on questions of war and peace; and

(15) to exercise such other functions and powers as the highest organ of state power should exercise.

Article 63: The National People's Congress has the power to recall or remove from office the following persons:

(1) the President and the Vice-President of the People's Republic of China;

(2) the Premier, Vice-Premiers, State Councillors, Ministers in charge of Ministries or Commissions and the Auditor-General and the Secretary-General of the State Council;

(3) the Chairman of the Central Military Commission and others on the Commission;

(4) the President of the Supreme People's Court; and

(5) the Procurator-General of the Supreme People's Procuratorate.

Article 64: Amendments to the Constitution are to be proposed by the Standing Committee of the National People's Congress or by more than one-fifth of the deputies to the National People's Congress and adopted by a majority vote of more than two-thirds of all the deputies to the Congress.

Statutes and resolutions are adopted by a majority vote of more than one-half of all the deputies to the National People's Congress.

Article 65: The Standing Committee of the National People's Congress is composed of the following:

the Chairman;

the Vice-Chairmen;

the Secretary-General; and

members.

Minority nationalities are entitled to appropriate representation on the Standing Committee of the National People's Congress.

The National People's Congress elects, and has the power to recall, all those on its Standing Committee.

No one on the Standing Committee of the National People's Congress shall hold any post in any of the administrative, judicial or procuratorial organs of the State.

Article 66: The Standing Committee of the National People's Congress is elected for the same term as the National People's Congress; it exercises its functions and powers until a new Standing Committee is elected by the succeeding National People's Congress.

The Chairman and Vice-Chairmen of the Standing Committee shall serve no more than two consecutive terms.

Article 67: The Standing Committee of the National People's Congress exercises the following functions and powers:

(1) to interpret the Constitution and supervise its enforcement;

(2) to enact and amend statutes with the exception of those which should be enacted by the National People's Congress;

(3) to enact, when the National People's Congress is not in session, partial supplements and amendments to statutes enacted by the National People's Congress provided that they do not contravene the basic principles of these statutes;

(4) to interpret statutes;

(5) to examine and approve, when the National People's Congress is not in session, partial adjustments to the plan for national economic and social development and to the state budget that prove necessary in the course of their implementation;

(6) to supervise the work of the State Council, the Central Military Commission, the Supreme People's Court and the Supreme People's Procuratorate;

(7) to annul those administrative rules and regulations, decisions or orders of the State Council that contravene the Constitution or the statutes;

(8) to annul those local regulations or decisions of the organs of state power of provinces, autonomous regions and municipalities directly under the Central Government that contravene the Constitution, the statutes or the administrative rules and regulations;

(9) to decide, when the National People's Congress is not in session, on the choice of Ministers in charge of Ministries or Commissions or the Auditor-General and the Secretary-General of the State Council upon nomination by the Premier of the State Council;

(10) to decide, upon nomination by the Chairman of the Central Military Commission, on the choice of others on the Commission, when the National People's Congress is not in session.

(11) to appoint and remove the Vice-Presidents and judges of the Supreme People's Court, members of its Judicial Committee and the President of the Military Court at the suggestion of the President of the Supreme People's Court;

(12) to appoint and remove the Deputy Procurators-General and Procurators of the Supreme People's Procuratorate, members of its Procuratorial Committee and the Chief Procurator of the Military Procuratorate at the request of the Procurator-General of the Supreme People's Procuratorate, and to approve the appointment and removal of the Chief Procurators of the People's Procuratorates of provinces, autonomous regions and municipalities directly under the Central Government;

(13) to decide on the appointment and recall of plenipotentiary representatives abroad;

(14) to decide on the ratification and abrogation of treaties and important agreements concluded with foreign states;

(15) to institute systems of titles and ranks for military and diplomatic personnel and of other specific titles and ranks;

(16) to institute state medals and titles of honour and decide on their conferment;

(17) to decide on the granting of special pardons;

(18) to decide, when the National People's Congress is not in session, on the proclamation of a state of war in the event of an armed attack on the country or in fulfilment of international treaty obligations concerning common defence against aggression;

(19) to decide on general mobilization or partial mobilization;

(20) to decide on entering the state of emergency throughout the country or in particular provinces, autonomous regions, or municipalities directly under the Central Government; and

(21) to exercise such other functions and powers as the National People's Congress may assign to it.

Article 68: The Chairman of the Standing Committee of the National People's Congress presides over the work of the Standing Committee and convenes its meetings. The Vice-Chairmen and the Secretary-General assist the Chairman in his work.

Chairmanship meetings with the participation of the Chairman, Vice-Chairmen and Secretary-General handle the important day-to-day work of the Standing Committee of the National People's Congress.

Article 69: The Standing Committee of the National People's Congress is responsible to the National People's Congress and reports on its work to the Congress.

Article 70: The National People's Congress establishes a Nationalities Committee, a Law Committee, a Finance and Economic Committee, an Education, Science, Culture and Public Health Committee, a Foreign Affairs Committee, an Overseas Chinese Committee and such other special committees as are necessary. These special committees work under the direction of the Standing Committee of the National People's Congress when the Congress is not in session.

The special committees examine, discuss and draw up relevant bills and draft resolutions under the direction of the National People's Congress and its Standing Committee.

Article 71: The National People's Congress and its Standing Committee may, when they deem it necessary, appoint committees of inquiry into specific questions and adopt relevant resolutions in the light of their reports.

All organs of State, public organizations and citizens concerned are obliged to supply the necessary information to those committees of inquiry when they conduct investigations.

Article 72: Deputies to the National People's Congress and all those on its Standing Committee have the right, in accordance with procedures prescribed by law, to submit bills and proposals within the scope of the respective functions and powers of the National People's Congress and its Standing Committee.

Article 73: Deputies to the National People's Congress during its sessions, and all those on its Standing Committee during its meetings, have the right to address questions, in accordance with procedures prescribed by law, to the State Council or the Ministries and Commissions under the State Council, which must answer the questions in a responsible manner.

Article 74: No deputy to the National People's Congress may be arrested or placed on criminal trial without the consent of the presidium of the current session of the National People's Congress or, when the National People's Congress is not in session, without the consent of its Standing Committee.

Article 75: Deputies to the National People's Congress may not be called to legal account for their speeches or votes at its meetings.

Article 76: Deputies to the National People's Congress must play an exemplary role in abiding by the Constitution and the law and keeping state secrets and, in production and other work and their public activities, assist in the enforcement of the Constitution and the law.

Deputies to the National People's Congress should maintain close contact with the units which elected them and with the people, listen to and convey the opinions and demands of the people and work hard to serve them.

Article 77: Deputies to the National People's Congress are subject to the supervision of the units which elected them. The electoral units have the power, through procedures prescribed by law, to recall the deputies whom they elected.

Article 78: The organization and working procedures of the National People's Congress and its Standing Committee are prescribed by law.

The President of the People's Republic of China

Article 79: The President and Vice-President of the People's Republic of China are elected by the National People's Congress.

Citizens of the People's Republic of China who have the right to vote and to stand for election and who have reached the age of 45 are eligible for election as President or Vice-President of the People's Republic of China.

The term of office of the President and Vice-President of the People's Republic of China is the same as that of the National People's Congress, and they shall serve no more than two consecutive terms.

Article 80: The President of the People's Republic of China, in pursuance of decisions of the National People's Congress and its Standing Committee, promulgates statutes; appoints and removes the Premier, Vice-Premiers, State Councillors, Ministers in charge of Ministries or Commissions, and the Auditor-General and the Secretary-General of the State Council; confers state medals and titles of honour; issues orders of special pardons; proclaims entering the state of emergency; proclaims a state of war; and issues mobilization orders.

Article 81: The President of the People's Republic of China, on behalf of the People's Republic of China, engages in activities involving State affairs and receives foreign diplomatic representatives and, in pursuance of decisions of the Standing Committee of the National People's Congress, appoints and recalls plenipotentiary representatives abroad, and ratifies and abrogates treaties and important agreements concluded with foreign states.

Article 82: The Vice-President of the People's Republic of China assists the President in his work.

The Vice-President of the People's Republic of China may exercise such parts of the functions and powers of the President as the President may entrust to him.

Article 83: The President and Vice-President of the People's Republic of China exercise their functions and powers until the new President and Vice-President elected by the succeeding National People's Congress assume office.

Article 84: In case the office of the President of the People's Republic of China falls vacant, the Vice-President succeeds to the office of President.

In case the office of the Vice-President of the People's Republic of China falls vacant, the National People's Congress shall elect a new Vice-President to fill the vacancy.

In the event that the offices of both the President and the Vice-President of the People's Republic of China fall vacant, the National People's Congress shall elect a new President and a new Vice-President. Prior to such election, the Chairman of the Standing Committee of the National People's Congress shall temporarily act as the President of the People's Republic of China.

The State Council

Article 85: The State Council, that is, the Central People's Government, of the People's Republic of China is the executive body of the highest organ of state power; it is the highest organ of state administration.

Article 86: The State Council is composed of the following: the Premier; the Vice-Premiers; the State Councillors; the Ministers in charge of ministries; the Ministers in charge of commissions; the Auditor-General; and the Secretary-General.

The Premier has overall responsibility for the State Council. The Ministers have overall responsibility for the respective ministries or commissions under their charge.

The organization of the State Council is prescribed by law.

Article 87: The term of office of the State Council is the same as that of the National People's Congress.

The Premier, Vice-Premiers and State Councillors shall serve no more than two consecutive terms.

Article 88: The Premier directs the work of the State Council. The Vice-Premiers and State Councillors assist the Premier in his work.

Executive meetings of the State Council are composed of the Premier, the Vice-Premiers, the State Councillors and the Secretary-General of the State Council.

The Premier convenes and presides over the executive meetings and plenary meetings of the State Council.

Article 89: The State Council exercises the following functions and powers:

(1) to adopt administrative measures, enact administrative rules and regulations and issue decisions and orders in accordance with the Constitution and the statutes;

(2) to submit proposals to the National People's Congress or its Standing Committee;

(3) to lay down the tasks and responsibilities of the ministries and commissions of the State Council, to exercise unified leadership over the work of the ministries and commissions and to direct all other administrative work of a national character that does not fall within the jurisdiction of the ministries and commissions;

(4) to exercise unified leadership over the work of local organs of state administration at different levels throughout the country, and to lay down the detailed division of functions and powers between the Central Government and the organs of state administration of provinces, autonomous regions and municipalities directly under the Central Government;

(5) to draw up and implement the plan for national economic and social development and the state budget;

(6) to direct and administer economic work and urban and rural development;

(7) to direct and administer the work concerning education, science, culture, public health, physical culture and family planning;

(8) to direct and administer the work concerning civil affairs, public security, judicial administration, supervision and other related matters;

(9) to conduct foreign affairs and conclude treaties and agreements with foreign states;

(10) to direct and administer the building of national defence;

(11) to direct and administer affairs concerning the nationalities, and to safeguard the equal rights of minority nationalities and the right of autonomy of the national autonomous areas;

(12) to protect the legitimate rights and interests of Chinese nationals residing abroad and protect the lawful rights and interests of returned overseas Chinese and of the family members of Chinese nationals residing abroad;

(13) to alter or annul inappropriate orders, directives and regulations issued by the ministries or commissions;

(14) to alter or annul inappropriate decisions and orders issued by local organs of state administration at different levels;

(15) to approve the geographic division of provinces, autonomous regions and municipalities directly under the Central Government, and to approve the establishment and geographic division of autonomous prefectures, counties, autonomous counties and cities;

(16) in accordance with the provisions of law, to decide on entering the state of emergency in parts of provinces, autonomous regions, and municipalities directly under the Central Government;

(17) to examine and decide on the size of administrative organs and, in accordance with the law, to appoint, remove and train administrative officers, appraise their work and reward or punish them; and

(18) to exercise such other functions and powers as the National People's Congress or its Standing Committee may assign it.

Article 90: The Ministers in charge of ministries or commissions of the State Council are responsible for the work of their respective departments and convene and preside over their ministerial meetings or commission meetings that discuss and decide on major issues in the work of their respective departments.

The ministries and commissions issue orders, directives and regulations within the jurisdiction of their respective departments and in accordance with the statutes and the administrative rules and regulations, decisions and orders issued by the State Council.

Article 91: The State Council establishes an auditing body to supervise through auditing the revenue and expenditure of all departments under the State Council and of the local government at different levels, and those of the state financial and monetary organizations and of enterprises and undertakings.

Under the direction of the Premier of the State Council, the auditing body independently exercises its power to supervise through auditing in accordance with the law, subject to no interference by any other administrative organ or any public organization or individual.

Article 92: The State Council is responsible, and reports on its work, to the National People's Congress or, when the National People's Congress is not in session, to its Standing Committee.

The Central Military Commission

Article 93: The Central Military Commission of the People's Republic of China directs the armed forces of the country.

The Central Military Commission is composed of the following: the Chairman; the Vice-Chairmen; and members.

The Chairman of the Central Military Commission has overall responsibility for the Commission.

The term of office of the Central Military Commission is the same as that of the National People's Congress.

Article 94: The Chairman of the Central Military Commission is responsible to the National People's Congress and its Standing Committee.

Two further sections, not included here, deal with the Local People's Congresses and Government and with the Organs of Self-Government of National Autonomous Areas, respectively.

The People's Courts and the People's Procuratorates

Article 123: The people's courts in the People's Republic of China are the judicial organs of the State.

Article 124: The People's Republic of China establishes the Supreme People's Court and the local people's courts at different levels, military courts and other special people's courts.

The term of office of the President of the Supreme People's Court is the same as that of the National People's Congress; he shall serve no more than two consecutive terms.

The organization of people's courts is prescribed by law.

Article 125: All cases handled by the people's courts, except for those involving special circumstances as specified by law, shall be heard in public. The accused has the right of defence.

Article 126: The people's courts shall, in accordance with the law, exercise judicial power independently and are not subject to interference by administrative organs, public organizations or individuals.

Article 127: The Supreme People's Court is the highest judicial organ.

The Supreme People's Court supervises the administration of justice by the local people's courts at different levels and by the special people's courts; people's courts at higher levels supervise the administration of justice by those at lower levels.

Article 128: The Supreme People's Court is responsible to the National People's Congress and its Standing Committee. Local people's courts at different levels are responsible to the organs of state power which created them.

Article 129: The people's procuratorates of the People's Republic of China are state organs for legal supervision.

Article 130: The People's Republic of China establishes the Supreme People's Procuratorate and the local people's procuratorates at different levels, military procuratorates and other special people's procuratorates.

The term of office of the Procurator-General of the Supreme People's Procuratorate is the same as that of the National People's Congress; he shall serve no more than two consecutive terms.

The organization of people's procuratorates is prescribed by law.

Article 131: People's procuratorates shall, in accordance with the law, exercise procuratorial power independently and are not subject to interference by administrative organs, public organizations or individuals.

Article 132: The Supreme People's Procuratorate is the highest procuratorial organ.

The Supreme People's Procuratorate directs the work of the local people's procuratorates at different levels and of the special people's procuratorates; people's procuratorates at higher levels direct the work of those at lower levels.

Article 133: The Supreme People's Procuratorate is responsible to the National People's Congress and its Standing Committee. Local people's procuratorates at different levels are responsible to the organs of state power at the corresponding levels which created them and to the people's procuratorates at the higher level.

Article 134: Citizens of all nationalities have the right to use the spoken and written languages of their own nationalities in court proceedings. The people's courts and people's procuratorates should provide translation for any party to the court proceedings who is not familiar with the spoken or written languages in common use in the locality.

In an area where people of a minority nationality live in a compact community or where a number of nationalities live together, hearings should be conducted in the language or languages in common use in the locality; indictments, judgments, notices and other documents should be written, according to actual needs, in the language or languages in common use in the locality.

Article 135: The people's courts, people's procuratorates and public security organs shall, in handling criminal cases, divide their functions, each taking responsibility for its own work, and they shall co-ordinate their efforts and check each other to ensure correct and effective enforcement of law.

THE NATIONAL FLAG, THE NATIONAL ANTHEM, THE NATIONAL EMBLEM AND THE CAPITAL

Article 136: The national flag of the People's Republic of China is a red flag with five stars.

The National Anthem of the People's Republic of China is the March of the Volunteers.

Article 137: The national emblem of the People's Republic of China is the Tiananmen (Gate of Heavenly Peace) in the centre, illuminated by five stars and encircled by ears of grain and a cogwheel.

Article 138: The capital of the People's Republic of China is Beijing (Peking).

The Government

HEAD OF STATE

President: Hu Jintao (elected by the 10th National People's Congress on 15 March 2003).

Vice-President: Zeng Qinghong.

STATE COUNCIL
(April 2005)

Premier: WEN JIABAO.

Vice-Premiers: HUANG JU, WU YI, ZENG PEIYAN, HUI LIANGYU.

State Councillors: ZHOU YONGKANG, Gen. CAO GANGCHUAN, TANG JIAXUAN, HUA JIANMIN, CHEN ZHILI.

Secretary-General: HUA JIANMIN.

Minister of Foreign Affairs: LI ZHAOXING.

Minister of National Defence: Gen. CAO GANGCHUAN.

Minister of State Development and Reform Commission: MA KAI.

Minister of Education: ZHOU JI.

Minister of Science and Technology: XU GUANHUA.

Minister of State Commission of Science, Technology and Industry for National Defence: ZHANG YUNCHUAN.

Minister of State Nationalities Affairs Commission: LI DEZHU.

Minister of Public Security: ZHOU YONGKANG.

Minister of State Security: XU YONGYUE.

Minister of Supervision: LI ZHILUN.

Minister of Civil Affairs: LI XUEJU.

Minister of Justice: ZHANG FUSEN.

Minister of Finance: JIN RENQING.

Minister of Personnel: ZHANG BAILIN.

Minister of Labour and Social Security: ZHENG SILIN.

Minister of Land and Natural Resources: SUN WENSHENG.

Minister of Construction: WANG GUANGTAO.

Minister of Railways: LIU ZHIJUN.

Minister of Communications: ZHANG CHUNXIAN.

Minister of Information Industry: WANG XUDONG.

Minister of Water Resources: WANG SHUCHENG.

Minister of Agriculture: DU QINGLIN.

Minister of Commerce: BO XILAI.

Minister of Culture: SUN JIAZHENG.

Minister of Public Health: WU YI.

Minister of Population and State Family Planning Commission: ZHANG WEIQING.

Governor of the People's Bank of China: ZHOU XIAOCHUAN.

Auditor-General of the National Audit Office: LI JINHUA.

MINISTRIES

Ministry of Agriculture: 11 Nongzhanguan Nanli, Chao Yang Qu, Beijing 100026; tel. (10) 64192293; fax (10) 64192468; e-mail webmaster@agri.gov.cn; internet www.agri.gov.cn.

Ministry of Civil Affairs: 147 Beiheyan Dajie, Dongcheng Qu, Beijing 100721; tel. (10) 65135333; fax (10) 65135332.

Ministry of Communications: 11 Jianguomennei Dajie, Dongcheng Qu. Beijing 100736; tel. (10) 65292114; fax (10) 65292345; internet www.moc.gov.cn.

Ministry of Construction: 9 Sanlihe Dajie, Xicheng Qu, Beijing 100835; tel. (10) 68394215; fax (10) 68393333; e-mail webmaster@mail.cin.gov.cn; internet www.cin.gov.cn.

Ministry of Culture: 10 Chaoyangmen Bei Jie, Dongcheng Qu, Beijing 100020; tel. (10) 65551432; fax (10) 65551433; e-mail webmaster@whb1.ccnt.com.cn; internet www.ccnt.com.cn.

Ministry of Education: 37 Damucang Hutong, Xicheng Qu, Beijing 100816; tel. (10) 66096114; fax (10) 66011049; e-mail webmaster@moe.edu.cn; internet www.moe.edu.cn.

Ministry of Finance: 3 Nansanxiang, Sanlihe, Xicheng Qu, Beijing 100820; tel. (10) 68551888; fax (10) 68533635; e-mail webmaster@mof.gov.cn; internet www.mof.gov.cn.

Ministry of Foreign Affairs: 225 Chaoyangmennei Dajie, Dongsi, Beijing 100701; tel. (10) 65961114; fax (10) 65962146; e-mail webmaster@fmprc.gov.cn; internet www.fmprc.gov.cn.

Ministry of Foreign Trade and Economic Co-operation: 2 Dongchangan Jie, Dongcheng Qu, Beijing 100731; tel. (10) 67081526; fax (10) 67081513; e-mail webmaster@moftec.gov.cn; internet www.moftec.gov.cn.

Ministry of Information Industry: 13 Xichangan Jie, Beijing 100804; tel. (10) 66014249; fax (10) 66034248; e-mail webmaster@mii.gov.cn; internet www.mii.gov.cn.

Ministry of Justice: 10 Chaoyangmennan Dajie, Chao Yang Qu, Beijing 100020; tel. (10) 65205114; fax (10) 65205316.

Ministry of Labour and Social Security: 12 Hepinglizhong Jie, Dongcheng Qu, Beijing 100716; tel. (10) 84201235; fax (10) 64218350.

Ministry of Land and Natural Resources: 3 Guanyingyuanxiqu, Xicheng Qu, Beijing 100035; tel. (10) 66127001; fax (10) 66175348; e-mail bzxx@mail.mlr.gov.cn; internet www.mlr.gov.cn.

Ministry of National Defence: 20 Jingshanqian Jie, Beijing 100009; tel. (10) 66730000; fax (10) 65962146.

Ministry of Personnel: 12 Hepinglizhong Jie, Dongcheng Qu, Beijing 100716; tel. (10) 84223240; fax (10) 64211417.

Ministry of Public Health: 1 Xizhinenwai Bei Lu, Xicheng Qu, Beijing 100044; tel. (10) 68792114; fax (10) 64012369; e-mail zhou@chsi.moh.gov.cn; internet www.moh.gov.cn.

Ministry of Public Security: 14 Dongchangan Jie, Dongcheng Qu, Beijing 100741; tel. (10) 65122831; fax (10) 65136577.

Ministry of Railways: 10 Fuxing Lu, Haidian Qu, Beijing 100844; tel. (10) 63244150; fax (10) 63242150; e-mail webmaster@ns.chinamor.cn.net; internet www.chinamor.cn.net.

Ministry of Science and Technology: 15B Fuxing Lu, Haidian Qu, Beijing 100862; tel. (10) 68515050; fax (10) 68515006; e-mail officemail@mail.most.gov.cn; internet www.most.gov.cn.

Ministry of State Security: 14 Dongchangan Jie, Dongcheng Qu, Beijing 100741; tel. (10) 65244702.

Ministry of Supervision: 4 Zaojunmiao, Haidian Qu, Beijing 100081; tel. (10) 62256677; fax (10) 62254181.

Ministry of Water Resources: 2 Baiguang Lu, Ertiao, Xuanwu Qu, Beijing 100053; tel. (10) 63203069; fax (10) 63202650; internet www.mwr.gov.cn.

STATE COMMISSIONS

State Commission of Science, Technology and Industry for National Defence: 2A Guang'anmennan Jie, Xuanwu Qu, Beijing 100053; tel. (10) 63571397; fax (10) 63571398; internet www.costind.gov.cn.

State Development and Reform Commission: 38 Yuetannan Jie, Xicheng Qu, Beijing 100824; tel. (10) 68504409; fax (10) 68512929; e-mail news@sdpc.gov.cn; internet www.sdpc.gov.cn.

State Economic and Trade Commission: 26 Xuanwumenxi Dajie, Xuanwumen Qu, Beijing 100053; tel. (10) 63192334; fax (10) 63192348; e-mail webmaster@setc.gov.cn; internet www.setc.gov.cn.

State Nationalities Affairs Commission: 252 Taipingqiao Dajie, Xicheng Qu, Beijing 100800; tel. and fax (10) 66017375.

State Population and Family Planning Commission: 14 Zhichun Lu, Haidian Qu, Beijing 100088; tel. (10) 62046622; fax (10) 62051865; e-mail sfpcdfa@public.bta.net.cn; internet www.sfpc.gov.cn.

Legislature

QUANGUO RENMIN DAIBIAO DAHUI
(National People's Congress)

The National People's Congress (NPC) is the highest organ of state power, and is indirectly elected for a five-year term. The first plenary session of the 10th NPC was convened in Beijing in March 2003, and was attended by 2,916 deputies. The first session of the 10th National Committee of the Chinese People's Political Consultative Conference (CPPCC, Chair. Jia Qinglin), a revolutionary united front organization led by the Communist Party, took place simultaneously. The CPPCC holds discussions and consultations on the important affairs in the nation's political life. Members of the CPPCC National Committee or of its Standing Committee may be invited to attend the NPC or its Standing Committee as observers.

Standing Committee

In March 2003 158 members were elected to the Standing Committee, in addition to the following:

Chairman: WU BANGGUO.

Vice-Chairmen: WANG ZHAOGUO, LI TIEYING, ISMAIL AMAT, HE LULI, DING SHISUN, CHENG SIWEI, XU JIALU, JIANG ZHENGHUA, GU XIULIAN, RAIDI, SHENG HUAREN, LU YONGXIANG, UYUNQIMG, HAN QIDE, FU TIESHAN.

Secretary-General: SHENG HUAREN.

Provincial People's Congresses

CHAIRMEN OF STANDING COMMITTEES OF PEOPLE'S CONGRESSES:

Provinces: Wang Taihua (Anhui), Song Defu (Fujian), (vacant) (Gansu), Lu Zhonghe (Guangdong), Qian Yunlu (Guizhou), Wang Xiaofeng (Hainan), Bai Keming (Hebei), Song Fatan (Heilongjiang), Li Keqiang (Henan), Yang Yongliang (Hubei), Yang Zhengwu (Hunan), Li Yuanchao (Jiangsu), Meng Jianzhu (Jiangxi), Wang Yunkun (Jilin), Wen Shizhen (Liaoning), Zhao Leji (Qinghai), Li Jianguo (Shaanxi), Zhang Gaoli (Shandong), Tian Chengping (Shanxi), Zhang Xuezhong (Sichuan), Bai Enpei (Yunnan), Xi Jinping (Zhejiang).

Special Municipalities: Yu Junbo (Beijing), Huang Zhendong (Chongqing), Gong Xueping (Shanghai), Fang Fengyou (Tianjin).

Autonomous Regions: Cao Bochun (Guangxi Zhuang), Chu Bo (Nei Monggol), Chen Jianguo (Ningxia Hui), Legqog (Tibet—Xizang), Abudureyimu Amiti (acting—Xinjiang Uygur).

People's Governments

PROVINCES

Governors: Wang Jinshan (Anhui), Lu Zhangong (Fujian), Lu Hao (Gansu), Huang Huahua (Guangdong), Shi Xiushi (Guizhou), Wei Liucheng (Hainan), Ji Yunshi (Hebei), Zhang Zuoji (Heilongjiang), Li Chengyu (Henan), Luo Qingquan (Hubei), Zhou Bohua (Hunan), Liang Baohua (Jiangsu), Huang Zhiquan (Jiangxi), Wang Min (Jilin), Zhang Wenyue (Liaoning), Yang Chuantang (Qinghai), Chen Deming (acting—Shaanxi), Han Yuqun (Shandong), Zhang Baoshun (Shanxi), Zhang Zhongwei (Sichuan), Xu Rongkai (Yunnan), Lu Zushan (Zhejiang).

SPECIAL MUNICIPALITIES

Mayors: Wang Qishan (Beijing), Wang Hongju (Chongqing), Han Zheng (Shanghai), Dai Xianglong (Tianjin).

AUTONOMOUS REGIONS

Chairmen: Lu Bing (Guangxi Zhuang), Yang Jing (Nei Monggol), Ma Qizhi (Ningxia Hui), Qiangba Puncog (Tibet—Xizang), Ismail Tiliwaldi (Xinjiang Uygur).

Political Organizations

COMMUNIST PARTY

Zhongguo Gongchan Dang (Chinese Communist Party—CCP): Beijing; f. 1921; 61m. mems in Dec. 1998; at the 16th Nat. Congress of the CCP in Nov. 2002, a new Cen. Cttee of 198 full mems and 158 alternate mems was elected; at its first plenary session the 16th Cen. Cttee appointed a new Politburo.

Sixteenth Central Committee

General Secretary: Hu Jintao.

Politburo

Members of the Standing Committee: Hu Jintao, Wu Bangguo, Wen Jiabao, Jia Qinglin, Zeng Qinghong, Huang Ju, Wu Guanzheng, Li Changchun, Luo Gan.

Other Full Members: Wang Lequan, Wang Zhaoguo, Hui Liangyu, Liu Qi, Liu Yunshan, Li Changchun, Wu Yi, Wu Bangguo, Wu Guanzheng, Zhang Lichang, Zhang Dejiang, Chen Liangyu, Luo Gan, Zhou Yongkang, Hu Jintao, Yu Zhengsheng, He Guoqiang, Jia Qinglin, Gen. Guo Boxiong, Huang Ju, Gen. Cao Gangchuan, Zeng Qinghong, Zeng Peiyan, Wen Jiabao.

Alternate Member: Wang Gang.

Secretariat: Zeng Qinghong, Liu Yunshan, Zhou Yongkang, He Guoqiang, Wang Gang, Gen. Xu Caihou, He Yong.

OTHER POLITICAL ORGANIZATIONS

China Association for Promoting Democracy: 98 Xinanli Guloufangzhuangchang, Beijing 100009; tel. (10) 64033452; f. 1945; mems drawn mainly from literary, cultural and educational circles; Chair. Xu Jialu; Sec.-Gen. Zhao Guanghua.

China Democratic League: 1 Beixing Dongchang Hutong, Beijing 100006; tel. (10) 65137983; fax (10) 65125090; f. 1941; formed from reorganization of League of Democratic Parties and Organizations of China; 131,300 mems, mainly intellectuals active in education, science and culture; Chair. Ding Shisun; Sec.-Gen. Zhang Baowen.

China National Democratic Construction Association: 208 Jixiangli, Chaowai Lu, Beijing 100020; tel. (10) 65523229; fax (10) 65523518; e-mail bgt@cndca.org.cn; internet www.cndca.org.cn; f. 1945; 99,260 mems, mainly industrialists and business executives; Chair. Cheng Siwei; Sec.-Gen. Zhang Jiao.

China Zhi Gong Dang (Party for Public Interests): Beijing; e-mail zhigong@public2.east.net.cn; f. 1925; reorg. 1947; mems are mainly returned overseas Chinese and scholars; Chair. Luo Haocai; Sec.-Gen. Qiu Guoyi.

Chinese Communist Youth League: 10 Qianmen Dongdajie, Beijing 100051; tel. (10) 67018132; fax (10) 67018131; e-mail guoji3acyt@yahoo.com; f. 1922; 68.5m. mems; First Sec. of Cen. Cttee Zhou Qiang.

Chinese Peasants' and Workers' Democratic Party: f. 1930 as the Provisional Action Cttee of the Kuomintang; took present name in 1947; more than 65,000 mems, active mainly in public health and medicine; Chair. Jiang Zhenghua; Sec.-Gen. Jiao Pingsheng (acting).

Jiu San (3 September) Society: f. 1946; fmrly Democratic and Science Soc.; 68,400 mems, mainly scientists and technologists; Chair. Han Qide; Sec.-Gen. Xu Guoquan.

Revolutionary Committee of the Chinese Kuomintang: tel. (10) 6550388; f. 1948; mainly fmr Kuomintang mems, and those in cultural, educational, health and financial fields; Chair. He Luli; Sec.-Gen. Liu Minfu.

Taiwan Democratic Self-Government League: f. 1947; recruits Taiwanese living on the mainland; Chair. Zhang Kehui; Sec.-Gen. Zhang Huajun.

During 1998 there were repeated failed attempts by pro-democracy activists to register an opposition party, the Chinese Democratic Party. The leaders of the party (Wang Youcai, Xu Wenli and Qin Yongmin) were sentenced to lengthy terms of imprisonment, and many other members of the party were detained.

Diplomatic Representation

EMBASSIES IN THE PEOPLE'S REPUBLIC OF CHINA

Afghanistan: 8 Dong Zhi Men Wai Dajie, Chao Yang Qu, Beijing 100600; tel. (10) 65321532; fax (10) 653226603; e-mail afgemb_beijing@yahoo.com; Ambassador Dr Qyamuddin Rahi Barlas.

Albania: 28 Guang Hua Lu, Jian Guo Men Wai, Beijing 100600; tel. (10) 65321120; fax (10) 65325451; Ambassador Kujtim Xhani.

Algeria: 2 Dong Zhi Men Wai Dajie, Chao Yang Qu, Beijing 100600; tel. (10) 65321231; fax (10) 65321648; Ambassador Madjid Bouguerra.

Angola: 1-13-1 Tayuan Diplomatic Office Bldg, Beijing 100600; tel. (10) 65326968; Ambassador João Manuel Bernardo.

Antigua and Barbuda: Guomen Bldg, Rm 1N, 1 Zuo Jia Zhuang, Chao Yang Qu, Beijing; tel. (10) 65326518; fax (10) 65326520; Ambassador James Thomas.

Argentina: Bldg 11, 5 Dong Wu Jie, San Li Tun, Beijing 100600; tel. (10) 65322090; fax (10) 65322319; e-mail echin@public.bta.net.cn; Ambassador Juan Carlos Morelli.

Armenia: 9-2-61 Tayuan Diplomatic Office Bldg, Beijing 100600; tel. (10) 65325677; fax (10) 65325654; e-mail armemb@public3.bta.net.cn; Ambassador Vasili Ghazaryan.

Australia: 21 Dong Zhi Men Wai Dajie, San Li Tun, Beijing 100600; tel. (10) 65322331; fax (10) 65326718; e-mail pubaff.beijing@dfat.gov.au; internet www.austemb.org.cn; Ambassador Dr Alan William Thomas.

Austria: 5 Xiu Shui Nan Jie, Jian Guo Men Wai, Beijing 100600; tel. (10) 65322726; fax (10) 65321505; e-mail oebpekin@public.bta.net.cn; Ambassador Hans Dietmar Schweisgut.

Azerbaijan: 3-2-31 San Li Tun Diplomatic Compound, Beijing 100600; tel. (10) 65324614; fax (10) 65324615; e-mail mailbox@azerbembassy.org.cn; internet www.azerbembassy.org.cn; Ambassador Yashar Tofigi Aliyev.

Bahrain: 2-9-1 Tayuan Diplomatic Office Bldg, Beijing 100600; tel. (10) 65325025; fax (10) 65325016; Ambassador Karim Ebrahim al-Shakar.

Bangladesh: 42 Guang Hua Lu, Beijing 100600; tel. (10) 65321819; fax (10) 65324346; e-mail bdemb@public3.bta.net.cn; internet www.bangladeshembassy.com.cn; Ambassador Ashfaqur Rahman.

Belarus: 2-10-1 Tayuan Diplomatic Office Bldg, Xin Dong Lu, Chao Yang Qu, Beijing 100600; tel. (10) 65326426; fax (10) 65326417; Ambassador ANATOL KHARLAP.

Belgium: 6 San Li Tun Lu, Beijing 100600; tel. (10) 65321736; fax (10) 65325097; e-mail Beijing@diplobel.org; Ambassador GASTON VAN DUYSE-ADAM.

Benin: 38 Guang Hua Lu, Jian Guo Men Wai, Beijing 100600; tel. (10) 65323054; fax (10) 65325103; Ambassador PIERRE AGO DOSSOU.

Bolivia: 2-3-2 Tayuan Diplomatic Office Bldg, Beijing 100600; tel. (10) 65323074; fax (10) 65324686; e-mail embolch@public3.bta.net.cn; Ambassador AUGUSTO ARGUEDAS DEL CARPIO.

Bosnia and Herzegovina: 1-5-1 Tayuan Diplomatic Office Bldg; tel. (10) 65326587; fax (10) 65326418; Ambassador BORISLAV MARIĆ.

Botswana: 1-8-1/2 Tayuan Diplomatic Office Bldg, Beijing 100600; tel. (10) 65325751; fax (10) 65325713; Ambassador KGOSI SEEPAPITSO IV.

Brazil: 27 Guang Hua Lu, Jian Guo Men Wai, Beijing 100600; tel. (10) 65322881; fax (10) 65322751; e-mail empequim@public.bta.net.cn; Ambassador LUIZ CASTRO NEVES.

Brunei: Villa No. 3, Qijiayuan Diplomatic Compound, Jian Guo Men Wai Dajie, Chao Yang Qu, Beijing 100600; tel. (10) 65324094; fax (10) 65324097; Ambassador Haji ABD. HAMID ABD. JALIL.

Bulgaria: 4 Xiu Shui Bei Jie, Jian Guo Men Wai, Beijing 100600; tel. (10) 65321946; fax (10) 65324502; e-mail bulemb@public.bta.net.cn; Ambassador ANGEL ORBETSOV.

Burundi: 25 Guang Hua Lu, Jian Guo Men Wai, Beijing 100600; tel. (10) 65321801; fax (10) 65322381; e-mail ambbubei@yahoo.fr; Ambassador ALFRED NKURUNZIZA.

Cambodia: 9 Dong Zhi Men Wai Dajie, Beijing 100600; tel. (10) 65321889; fax (10) 65323507; Ambassador KHEK LERANG.

Cameroon: 7 San Li Tun, Dong Wu Jie, Beijing 100600; tel. (10) 65321771; fax (10) 65321761; Ambassador ELEIH-ELLE ETIAN.

Canada: 19 Dong Zhi Men Wai Dajie, Chao Yang Qu, Beijing 100600; tel. (10) 65323536; fax (10) 65324311; internet www.beijing.gc.ca; Ambassador JOSEPH CARON.

Cape Verde: 6-2-121, Tayuan Diplomatic Office Bldg, Beijing; tel. (10) 65327547; fax (10) 65327546.

Central African Republic: 1-1-132, Ta Yuan Diplomatic Office Bldg, No. 1 Xin Dong Lu, Chaoyang Qu; tel. 65327353; fax 65327354; e-mail centra_chine@yahoo.fr; Ambassador CHRISTOPHE GAZAM-BETTE.

Chile: 1 Dong Si Jie, San Li Tun, Beijing 100600; tel. (10) 65321591; fax (10) 65323170; e-mail echilecn@public3.bta.net.cn; Ambassador PEDRO PABLO CABRERA.

Colombia: 34 Guang Hua Lu, Jian Guo Men Wai, Beijing 100600; tel. (10) 65321713; fax (10) 65321969; Ambassador GUILLERMO RICARDO VÉLEZ LONDOÑO.

Congo, Democratic Republic: 6 Dong Wu Jie, San Li Tun, Beijing 100600; tel. (10) 65321995; fax (10) 65321360; Ambassador JOHNSON BACLONGANDI WA BINANA.

Congo, Republic: 7 Dong Si Jie, San Li Tun, Beijing 100600; tel. (10) 65321658; Ambassador PIERRE PASSI.

Côte d'Ivoire: 9 San Li Tun, Bei Xiao Jie, Beijing 100600; tel. (10) 65321223; fax (10) 65322407; Ambassador KONAN KRAMO.

Croatia: 2-72 San Li Tun Diplomatic Office Bldg, Beijing 100600; tel. (10) 65326241; fax (10) 65326257; e-mail vrhpek@public.bta.net.cn; Ambassador BORIS VELIĆ.

Cuba: 1 Xiu Shui Nan Jie, Jian Guo Men Wai, Beijing 100600; tel. (10) 65321714; fax (10) 65322870; Ambassador ALBERTO RODRÍGUEZ ARUFE.

Cyprus: 2-13-2 Tayuan Diplomatic Office Bldg, Liang Ma He Nan Lu, Chao Yang Qu, Beijing 100600; tel. (10) 65325057; fax (10) 65324244; e-mail cyembpek@public3.bta.net.cn; Ambassador PETROS KESTORAS.

Czech Republic: Ri Tan Lu, Jian Guo Men Wai, Beijing 100600; tel. (10) 65326902; fax (10) 65325653; e-mail beijing@embassy.mzv.cz; internet www.mzv.cz/beijing; Ambassador Dr VITESLAV GREPL.

Denmark: 1 Dong Wu Jie, San Li Tun, Beijing 100600; tel. (10) 65322431; fax (10) 65322439; e-mail bjsamb@um.dk; internet www.dk-embassy-cn.org/; Ambassador LAURIDS MIKAELSEN.

Djibouti: 2-2-102 Tayuan Diplomatic Office Bldg, Beijing; tel. (10) 65327857; fax (10) 65327858; Ambassador MOUSSA BOUH ODOWA.

Dominica: Beijing; Ambassador DAVID KING HSIU.

Ecuador: 2-62, San Li Tun Office Bldg, Chaoyang Qu, Beijing 100600; tel. (10) 65323158; fax (10) 65324371; e-mail embecuat@public3bta.net.cn; Ambassador RODRIGO YEPES ENRIQUEZ HERRERA.

Egypt: 2 Ri Tan Dong Lu, Jian Guo Men Wai, Beijing 100600; tel. (10) 65321825; fax (10) 65325365; Ambassador ALI HOUSSAM EL DIN MAHMOUD ELHEFNY.

Equatorial Guinea: 2 Dong Si Jie, San Li Tun; tel. (10) 65323709; fax (10) 65323805; e-mail ntugabeso@hotmail.com; Ambassador NARCISO NTUGU ABESO OYANA.

Eritrea: Tayuan Diplomatic Office Bldg, Beijing; tel. (10) 56326534; fax (10) 65326532; Ambassador TSEGGAI TESFATSION SEREKE.

Ethiopia: 3 Xiu Shui Nan Jie, Jian Guo Men Wai, Beijing 100600; tel. (10) 65325258; fax (10) 65325591; e-mail ethembcn@public.bta.net.cn; Ambassador MAIT MARTINSON.

Fiji: 1-15-2 Tayuan Diplomatic Office Bldg, Beijing 100600; tel. (10) 65327305; fax (10) 6532 7253; e-mail lvratuvuki@hotmail.com; Ambassador JEREMAIA WAQANISAU.

Finland: Beijing Kerry Centre, 26/F South Tower, 1 Guanghua Lu, Beijing 100020; tel. (10) 85298541; fax (10) 85298547; e-mail sanomat.pek@formin.fi; internet www.finland-in-china.com; Ambassador BENJAMIN BASSIN.

France: 3 Dong San Jie, San Li Tun, Chao Yang Qu, Beijing 100600; tel. (10) 65321331; fax (10) 65324841; internet www.ambafrance-cn.org; Ambassador PHILIPPE GUELLUY.

Gabon: 36 Guang Hua Lu, Jian Guo Men Wai, Beijing 100600; tel. (10) 65322810; fax (10) 65322621; Ambassador EMMANUEL MBA-ALLO.

Georgia: Beijing; Chargé d'affaires a.i. ARCHIL SOKHADZE.

Germany: 17 Dong Zhi Men Wai Dajie, San Li Tun, Beijing 100600; tel. (10) 65322161; fax (10) 65325336; e-mail embassy@peki.diplo.de; internet www.beijing.diplo.de; Ambassador VOLKER STANZEL.

Ghana: 8 San Li Tun Lu, Beijing 100600; tel. (10) 65321319; fax (10) 65323602; Ambassador AFARE APEADU DONKOR.

Greece: 19 Guang Hua Lu, Jian Guo Men Wai, Beijing 100600; tel. (10) 65321588; fax (10) 65321277; Ambassador CHARALAMBOS ROCANAS.

Guinea: 2 Xi Liu Jie, San Li Tun, Beijing 100600; tel. (10) 65323649; fax (10) 65324957; Ambassador EL HADJI DJIGUI CAMARA.

Guinea-Bissau: Beijing; Ambassador NICOLAU DOS SANTOS.

Guyana: 1 Xiu Shui Dong Jie, Jian Guo Men Wai, Beijing 100600; tel. (10) 65321601; fax (10) 65325741; Ambassador RONALD MORTIMER AUSTIN.

Hungary: 10 Dong Zhi Men Wai Dajie, San Li Tun, Beijing 100600; tel. (10) 65321431; fax (10) 65325053; Ambassador MESZAROS SANDOR.

Iceland: Landmark Tower 1, 802, 8 North Dongsanhuan Lu, Beijing 100004; tel. (10) 65907795; fax (10) 65907801; e-mail icemb.beijing@utn.stjr.is; internet www.iceland.org/cn; Ambassador EIDUR GUDNASON.

India: 1 Ri Tan Dong Lu, Jian Guo Men Wai, Beijing 100600; tel. (10) 65321927; fax (10) 65324684; internet www.indianembassy.org.cn; Ambassador NALIN SURIE.

Indonesia: Diplomatic Office Bldg B, San Li Tun, Beijing 100600; tel. (10) 65325486; fax (10) 65325368; e-mail kombei@public3.bta.net.cn; Ambassador AA KUSTIA.

Iran: 13 Dong Liu Jie, San Li Tun, Beijing 100600; tel. (10) 65322040; fax (10) 65321403; Ambassador FEREYDOUN VERDINEJAD.

Iraq: 25 Xiu Shui Bei Jie, Jian Guo Men Wai, Beijing 100600; tel. (10) 65324355; fax (10) 65321599; e-mail iraqbeijing@yahoo.com; Ambassador MOHAMMAD SABIR ISMAIL.

Ireland: 3 Ri Tan Dong Lu, Jian Guo Men Wai, Beijing 100600; tel. (10) 65322691; fax (10) 65326857; Ambassador DECLAN KELLEHER.

Israel: Room 405, West Wing Office, 1 Jian Guo Men Wai Dajie, Beijing 100004; tel. (10) 65052970; fax (10) 65050328; e-mail israemb@public.bta.net.cn; Ambassador YEHOYADA HAIM.

Italy: 2 Dong Er Jie, San Li Tun, Beijing 100600; tel. (10) 65322131; fax (10) 65324676; e-mail ambpech@ambpech.org.cn; internet www.italianembassy.org.cn; Ambassador GABRIELE MENEGATTI.

Japan: 7 Ri Tan Lu, Jian Guo Men Wai, Beijing 100600; tel. (10) 65322361; fax (10) 65324625; Ambassador KORESHIGE ANAMI.

Jordan: 5 Dong Liu Jie, San Li Tun, Beijing 100600; tel. (10) 65323906; fax (10) 65323283; Ambassador ANMAR ABDULHALIM NAMIR HARMUD.

Kazakhstan: 9 Dong Liu Jie, San Li Tun, Beijing 100600; tel. (10) 65326182; fax (10) 65326183; e-mail kazconscan@on.aibn.com; Ambassador ZHANYBEK SALIMOVICH KARIBZHANOV.

Kenya: 4 Xi Liu Jie, San Li Tun, Beijing 100600; tel. (10) 65323381; fax (10) 65321770; Ambassador RUTH SERETI SOLITEI.

Korea, Democratic People's Republic: Ri Tan Bei Lu, Jian Guo Men Wai, Beijing 100600; tel. (10) 65321186; fax (10) 65326056; Ambassador CHOE JIN SU.

Korea, Republic: 3rd–4th Floors, China World Trade Centre, 1 Jian Guo Men Wai Dajie, Beijing 100600; tel. (10) 65053171; fax (10) 65053458; Ambassador KIM HA-JOONG.

Kuwait: 23 Guang Hua Lu, Jian Guo Men Wai, Beijing 100600; tel. (10) 65322216; fax (10) 65321607; Ambassador FAISAL RASHED AL-GHAIS.

Kyrgyzstan: 2-4-1 Tayuan Diplomatic Office Bldg, Beijing 100600; tel. (10) 65326458; fax (10) 65326459; e-mail kyrgyzch@public2.east .net.cn; Ambassador ERLAN ABDYLDAEV.

Laos: 11 Dong Si Jie, San Li Tun, Chao Yang Qu, Beijing 100600; tel. (10) 65321224; fax (10) 65326748; e-mail laoemcn@public.east.cn .net; Ambassador VICHIT XINDAVONG.

Latvia: Unit 71, Green Land Garden, No. 1A Green Land Road, Chao Yang Qu, Beijing 100016; tel. (10) 64333863; fax (10) 64333810; e-mail kinas@163bj.com; Ambassador JANIS LOVNIKS.

Lebanon: 10 Dong Liu Jie, San Li Tun, Beijing 100600; tel. (10) 65322197; fax (10) 65322770; Ambassador SLEIMAN RASSI.

Lesotho: 2-3-13 San Li Tun Diplomatic Apartment, Beijing 100600; tel. (10) 65326842; fax (10) 65326845; e-mail doemli@public.bta.net .cn; Ambassador LEBOHANG K. MOLEKO.

Libya: 3 Dong Liu Jie, San Li Tun, Beijing 100600; tel. (10) 65323666; fax (10) 65323391; Secretary of the People's Bureau MUFTAH OTMAN MADI.

Lithuania: B30 King's Garden, 18 Xiaoyun Lu, Chaoyang Qu, Beijing 100016; tel. (10) 84518520; fax (10) 84514442; e-mail emlituan@public3.bta.net.cn; Ambassador ARTURAS ZURAUSKAS.

Luxembourg: 21 Nei Wu Bu Jie, Beijing 100600; tel. (10) 65135937; fax (10) 65137268; e-mail pekin.amb@mae.etat.lu; Ambassador MARC UNGEHEUER.

Macedonia, former Yugoslav republic: 3-2-21 San Li Tun Diplomatic Office Bldg, 100600 Beijing; tel. (10) 65327846; fax (10) 65327847; e-mail macdebas@public3.bta.net.cn; Chargé d'affaires a.i. DANCO MARKOVSKI.

Madagascar: 3 Dong Jie, San Li Tun, Beijing 100600; tel. (10) 65321353; fax (10) 65322102; e-mail ambpek@public2.bta.net.cn; Ambassador VICTOR SIKONINA.

Malaysia: 2 Liang Ma Qiao Bei Jie, Chaoyang Qu, San Li Tun, 100600 Beijing; tel. (10) 65322531; fax (10) 65325032; e-mail mwbjing@kln.gov.my; Ambassador Dato' ABDUL MAJID.

Mali: 8 Dong Si Jie, San Li Tun, Beijing 100600; tel. (10) 65321704; fax (10) 65321618; Ambassador MODIBO TIEMOKO TRAORE.

Malta: 1-52 San Li Tun Diplomatic Compound, Beijing 100600; tel. (10) 65323114; fax (10) 65326125; e-mail maltaemb@public3.bta.net .cn; Ambassador Dr SAVIOUR GAUCI.

Mauritania: 9 Dong San Jie, San Li Tun, Beijing 100600; tel. (10) 65321346; fax (10) 65321685; Ambassador N'GAIDE LAMINE KAYOU.

Mauritius: 202 Dong Wai Diplomatic Office Bldg, 23 Dong Zhi Men Wai Dajie, Chao Yang Qu, Beijing; tel. (10) 65325695; fax (10) 65325706; Ambassador L. K. C. LAM PO TANG.

Mexico: 5 Dong Wu Jie, San Li Tun, Beijing 100600; tel. (10) 65321717; fax (10) 65323744; e-mail embmxchn@public.bta.net.cn; Ambassador SERGIO LEY-LÓPEZ.

Moldova: 3-1-152 Tayuan Diplomatic Office Bldg, Beijing 100600; tel. (10) 65325379; Ambassador VICTOR BORSEVICI.

Mongolia: 2 Xiu Shui Bei Jie, Jian Guo Men Wai, Beijing 100600; tel. (10) 65321203; fax (10) 65325045; e-mail monembbj@public3.bta .net.cn; Ambassador L. AMARSANAA.

Morocco: 16 San Li Tun Lu, Beijing 100600; tel. (10) 65321489; fax (10) 65321453; e-mail embmor@public.bta.net.cn; Ambassador MOHAMED CHERTI.

Mozambique: 1-7-2 Tayuan Diplomatic Office Bldg, Beijing 100600; tel. (10) 65323664; fax (10) 65325189; e-mail embamoc@ public.bta.net.cn; Ambassador ANTÓNIO INÁCIO JÚNIOR.

Myanmar: 6 Dong Zhi Men Wai Dajie, Chao Yang Qu, Beijing 100600; tel. (10) 65321584; fax (10) 65321344; Ambassador U THEIN LWIN.

Namibia: 2-9-2 Tayuan Diplomatic Office Bldg, Beijing 100600; tel. (10) 65324810; fax (10) 65324549; e-mail namemb@eastnet.com.cn; Ambassador H. U. IPINGE.

Nepal: 1 Xi Liu Jie, San Li Tun Lu, Beijing 100600; tel. (10) 65322739; fax (10) 65323251; Ambassador NARENDRA RAJ PANDAY.

Netherlands: 4 Liang Ma He Nan Lu, Beijing 100600; tel. (10) 65321131; fax (10) 65324689; Ambassador PHILIP DE HEER.

New Zealand: 1 Ri Tan, Dong Er Jie, Chao Yang Qu, Beijing 100600; tel. (10) 65322731; fax (10) 65324317; e-mail nzemb@ eastnet.com.cn; internet www.nzembassy.com/china; Ambassador TONY BROWNE.

Niger: 3-2-12 San Li Tun, Beijing 100600; tel. (10) 65324279; e-mail nigerbj@public.bta.net.cn; Ambassador BOZARI SEYDOU.

Nigeria: 2 Dong Wu Jie, San Li Tun, Beijing; tel. (10) 65323631; fax (10) 65321650; Ambassador JONATHAN OLUWOLE COKER.

Norway: 1 Dong Yi Jie, San Li Tun, Beijing 100600; tel. (10) 65322261; fax (10) 65322392; e-mail emb.beijing@mfa.no; internet www.norway.cn; Ambassador TOR CHR. HILDAN.

Oman: 6 Liang Ma He Nan Lu, San Li Tun, Beijing 100600; tel. (10) 65323956; fax (10) 65325030; Ambassador ABDULLAH HOSNY.

Pakistan: 1 Dong Zhi Men Wai Dajie, San Li Tun, Beijing 100600; tel. (10) 65322504; fax (10) 65322715; e-mail pak@public.bta.net.cn; Ambassador SALMAN BASHIR.

Papua New Guinea: 2-11-2 Tayuan Diplomatic Office Bldg, Beijing 100600; tel. (10) 65324312; fax (10) 65325483; Ambassador MAX RAI.

Peru: 1-91 San Li Tun, Bangonglou, Beijing 100600; tel. (10) 65323477; fax (10) 65322178; e-mail 1pekin@public.bta.net.cn; internet www.embperu.cn.net; Ambassador LUIS V. CHANG REYES.

Philippines: 23 Xiu Shui Bei Jie, Jian Guo Men Wai, Beijing 100600; tel. (10) 65321872; fax (10) 65323761; e-mail beijingpe@ cinet.com.cn; internet www.philembassy-china.org; Ambassador WILLY C. GAA.

Poland: 1 Ri Tan Lu, Jian Guo Men Wai, Chaoyang Qu, Beijing 100600; tel. (10) 65321235; fax (10) 65321745; e-mail polska@public2 .bta.net.cn; internet www.polandembassychina.net; Ambassador KSAWERY BURSKI.

Portugal: 8 San Li Tun Dong Wu Jie, Beijing 100600; tel. (10) 65323497; fax (10) 65324637; Ambassador ANTONIO NUNES DE CARVALHO SANTANA.

Qatar: 2-9-2 Tayuan Diplomatic Office Bldg, 14 Liang Ma He Nan Lu, Beijing 100600; tel. (10) 65322231; fax (10) 65325274; Ambassador SALEH ABDULLA AL-BOUANIN.

Romania: Ri Tan Lu, Dong Er Jie, Beijing 100600; tel. (10) 65323442; fax (10) 65325728; e-mail roamb@ht.rol.cn.net; Ambassador VIOREL ISTICIOAIA-BUDURA.

Russia: 4 Dong Zhi Men Nei, Bei Zhong Jie, Beijing 100600; tel. (10) 65322051; fax (10) 65324851; e-mail embassy@russia.org.cn; internet www.russia.org.cn; Ambassador ROGACHEV IGOR ALEXEYEVICH.

Rwanda: 30 Xiu Shui Bei Jie, Jian Guo Men Wai, Beijing 100600; tel. (10) 65322193; fax (10) 65322006; e-mail ambarwda@public3.bta .net.cn; internet www.embarwanda-china.com; Ambassador BEN MATHIAS RUGANGAZI.

Saudi Arabia: 1 Bei Xiao Jie, San Li Tun, Beijing 100600; tel. (10) 65324825; fax (10) 65325324; Ambassador MOHAMMED A. AL-BESHIR.

Serbia and Montenegro: 1 Dong Liu Jie, San Li Tun, Beijing 100600; tel. (10) 65323516; fax (10) 65321207; e-mail ambjug@ netchina.com.cn; internet www.emb-serbia-montenegro.org.cn; Ambassador DRAGAN MOMCILOVIĆ.

Sierra Leone: 7 Dong Zhi Men Wai Dajie, Beijing 100600; tel. (10) 65322174; fax (10) 65323752; e-mail sejohnny@163bj.com; Ambassador SAHR E. JOHNNY.

Singapore: 1 Xiu Shui Bei Jie, Jian Guo Men Wai, Beijing 100600; tel. (10) 65323926; fax (10) 65322215; Ambassador CHIN SIAT-YOON.

Slovakia: Ri Tan Lu, Jian Guo Men Wai, Beijing 100600; tel. (10) 65321531; fax (10) 65324814; Ambassador ZIGMUND BERTOK.

Slovenia: Block F, 57 Ya Qu Yuan, King's Garden Villas, 18 Xiao Yun Lu, Chao Yang Qu, Beijing 100016; tel. (10) 64681030; fax (10) 64681040; Ambassador VLADIMIR GASPARIĆ.

Somalia: 2 San Li Tun Lu, Beijing 100600; tel. (10) 65321752; Ambassador MOHAMED HASSAN SAID.

South Africa: 5 Dongzhimen Wai Dajie, Chao Yang Qu, Beijing 100600; tel. (10) 65320171; fax (10) 65327319; e-mail safrican@163bj .com; Ambassador THEMBA M. N. KUBHEKA.

Spain: 9 San Li Tun Lu, Beijing 100600; tel. (10) 65321986; fax (10) 65323401; Ambassador JOSÉ PEDRO SEBASTIÁN DE ERICE Y GÓMEZ-ACEBO.

Sri Lanka: 3 Jian Hua Lu, Jian Guo Men Wai, Beijing 100600; tel. (10) 65321861; fax (10) 65325426; e-mail lkembj@public.east.cn.net; Ambassador NIHAL RODRIGO.

Sudan: Bldg 27, San Li Tun, Beijing 100600; tel. (10) 65323715; fax (10) 65321280; e-mail mission.sudan@itu.cn; Ambassador MIRHGANI MOHAMED SALIH.

Suriname: 1-3-31 Diplomatic Compound, Jianguomenwai Beijing 100600; tel. (10) 65322938; fax (10) 65322941; Ambassador Roy Marinus Wong Lun Hing.

Sweden: 3 Dong Zhi Men Wai Dajie, San Li Tun, Beijing 100600; tel. (10) 65329790; fax (10) 65325008; e-mail ambassaden.peking@foreign.ministry.se; internet www.swedemb-cn.org.cn; Ambassador Borje Ljunggren.

Switzerland: 3 Dong Wu Jie, San Li Tun, Beijing 100600; tel. (10) 65322736; fax (10) 65324353; Ambassador Dante Martinelli.

Syria: 6 Dong Si Jie, San Li Tun, Beijing 100600; tel. (10) 65321563; fax (10) 65321575; Ambassador Mohammed Kheir al-Wadi.

Tajikistan: 5-1-41 Tayuan Diplomatic Office Bldg, Beijing 100600; tel. (10) 65322598; internet (10) 65323039; Ambassador Bokhadyr Najmidinovich Abdoullayev.

Tanzania: 8 Liang Ma He Nan Lu, San Li Tun, Beijing 100600; tel. (10) 65321408; fax (10) 65324985; Ambassador Charles Asilia Sanga.

Thailand: 40 Guang Hua Lu, Jian Guo Men Wai, Beijing 100600; tel. (10) 65321903; fax (10) 65321748; Ambassador Jullapong Nonsrichai.

Timor-Leste: Beijing.

Togo: 11 Dong Zhi Men Wai Dajie, Beijing 100600; tel. (10) 65322202; fax (10) 65325884; Ambassador Nolana Ta-Ama.

Tunisia: 1 Dong Jie, San Li Tun, Beijing 100600; tel. (10) 65322435; fax (10) 65325818; e-mail ambtun@public.netchina.com.cn; Ambassador Mohamed Sahbi Basli.

Turkey: 9 Dong Wu Jie, San Li Tun, Beijing 100600; tel. (10) 65322490; fax (10) 65325480; e-mail trkelcn@public.bta.net.cn; Ambassador Oktay Ozuye.

Turkmenistan: King's Garden, Villa D-26, 18 Xiao Yuan Rd, Beijing; tel. (10) 65326975; fax (10) 65326976; e-mail China@a-1.net.cn; Ambassador Gurbanmukhammet Kasymov.

Uganda: 5 Dong Jie, San Li Tun, Beijing 100600; tel. (10) 65322370; fax (10) 65322242; e-mail ugembssy@public.bta.net.cn; internet www.uganda.cn777.com.cn; Ambassador Philip Idro.

Ukraine: 11 Dong Liu Jie, San Li Tun, Beijing 100600; tel. (10) 65324013; fax (10) 65326359; e-mail ukrembcn@public3.bta.net.cn; internet www.ukrembcn.org; Ambassador Sergey Alekseevich Kamyshev.

United Arab Emirates: C801 Lufthansa Center, Office Building 50, Liangmaqiao Lu, Chao Yang Qu, Beijing 100016; tel. (10) 84514416; fax (10) 84514451; Ambassador Mohammed Rashid Ali Al-Boot.

United Kingdom: 11 Guang Hua Lu, Jian Guo Men Wai, Beijing 100600; tel. (10) 65321961; fax (10) 65321937; internet www.britishembassy.org.cn; Ambassador Sir Christopher Hum.

USA: 3 Xiu Shui Bei Jie, Beijing 100600; tel. (10) 65323831; fax (10) 65323178; internet www.usembassy-china.org.cn; Ambassador Clark T. Randt.

Uruguay: 1-11-2 Tayuan Diplomatic Office Bldg, Beijing 100600; tel. (10) 65324445; fax (10) 65327375; e-mail urubei@public.bta.net.cn; Ambassador Pelayo Joaquín Díaz Muguerza.

Uzbekistan: 11 Bei Xiao Jie, San Li Tun, Beijing 100600; tel. (10) 65326305; fax (10) 65326304; Ambassador Nosirzhon Yusupov.

Venezuela: 14 San Li Tun Lu, Beijing 100600; tel. (10) 65321295; fax (10) 65323817; e-mail embvenez@public.bta.net.cn; Ambassador Rocio Maneiro González.

Viet Nam: 32 Guang Hua Lu, Jian Guo Men Wai, Beijing 100600; tel. (10) 65321155; fax (10) 65325720; Ambassador Tran Van Luat.

Yemen: 5 Dong San Jie, San Li Tun, Beijing 100600; tel. (10) 65321558; fax (10) 65324305; Ambassador Marwan Abdullah Nu'man.

Zambia: 5 Dong Si Jie, San Li Tun, Beijing 100600; tel. (10) 65321554; fax (10) 65321891; Ambassador David Clifford Saviye.

Zimbabwe: 7 Dong San Jie, San Li Tun, Beijing 100600; tel. (10) 65323795; fax (10) 65325383; Ambassador Christopher Hatikuri Mutsvangwa.

Judicial System

The general principles of the Chinese judicial system are laid down in Articles 123–135 of the December 1982 Constitution (q.v.).

PEOPLE'S COURTS

Supreme People's Court: 27 Dongjiaomin Xiang, Beijing 100745; tel. (10) 65136195; f. 1949; the highest judicial organ of the State; handles first instance cases of national importance; handles cases of appeals and protests lodged against judgments and orders of higher people's courts and special people's courts, and cases of protests lodged by the Supreme People's Procuratorate in accordance with the procedures of judicial supervision; reviews death sentences meted out by local courts, supervises the administration of justice by local people's courts; interprets issues concerning specific applications of laws in judicial proceedings; its judgments and rulings are final; Pres. Xiao Yang (five-year term of office coincides with that of National People's Congress, by which the President is elected).

Local People's Courts: comprise higher courts, intermediate courts and basic courts.

Special People's Courts: include military courts, maritime courts and railway transport courts.

PEOPLE'S PROCURATORATES

Supreme People's Procuratorate: 147 Beiheyan Dajie, Beijing 100726; tel. (10) 65126655; acts for the National People's Congress in examining govt depts, civil servants and citizens, to ensure observance of the law; prosecutes in criminal cases; Procurator-Gen. Jia Chunwang (elected by the National People's Congress for five years).

Local People's Procuratorates: undertake the same duties at the local level. Ensure that the judicial activities of the people's courts, the execution of sentences in criminal cases and the activities of departments in charge of reform through labour conform to the law; institute, or intervene in, important civil cases that affect the interest of the State and the people.

Religion

During the 'Cultural Revolution' places of worship were closed. After 1977 the Government adopted a policy of religious tolerance, and the 1982 Constitution states that citizens enjoy freedom of religious belief and that legitimate religious activities are protected. Many temples, churches and mosques subsequently reopened. Since 1994 all religious organizations have been required to register with the Bureau of Religious Affairs. In the late 1990s a new religious sect, the Falun Gong (also known as Falun Dafa), emerged and quickly gained new adherents. However, the authorities banned the group, describing it as an 'evil cult'.

Bureau of Religious Affairs: Beijing; tel. (10) 652625; Dir Ye Xiaowen.

ANCESTOR WORSHIP

Ancestor worship is believed to have originated with the deification and worship of all important natural phenomena. The divine and human were not clearly defined; all the dead became gods and were worshipped by their descendants. The practice has no code or dogma and the ritual is limited to sacrifices made during festivals and on birth and death anniversaries.

BUDDHISM

Buddhism was introduced into China from India in AD 67, and flourished during the Sui and Tang dynasties (6th–8th century), when eight sects were established. The Chan and Pure Land sects are the most popular. According to official sources, in 1998 there were 9,500 Buddhist temples in China. There were 100m. believers in 1997.

Buddhist Association of China (BAC): f. 1953; Pres. Yi Cheng; Sec.-Gen. Xue Cheng.

Tibetan Institute of Lamaism
Pres. Bumi Jangbaluozhu; Vice-Pres. Cemolin Danzengchilie.

14th Dalai Lama: His Holiness the Dalai Lama Tenzin Gyatso, Thekchen Choeling, McLeod Ganj, Dharamsala 176 219, Himachal Pradesh, India; tel. (91) 1892-21343; fax (91) 1892-21813; e-mail ohhdl@cta.unv.ernet.ind.

Spiritual and temporal leader of Tibet; fled to India after failure of Tibetan national uprising in 1959.

CHRISTIANITY

During the 19th century and the first half of the 20th century large numbers of foreign Christian missionaries worked in China. According to official sources, there were 10m. Protestants and more than 4m. Catholics in China in 2000, although unofficial sources estimate that the Christian total could be as high as 90m. The Catholic Church in China operates independently of the Vatican. In addition, there is an increasing number of Christian sects in China.

Three-Self Patriotic Movement Committee of Protestant Churches of China: Pres.and acting Sec.-Gen. Ji Jianhong.

China Christian Council: 219 Jiujiang Lu, Shanghai 200002; tel. (21) 63210806; fax (21) 63232605; e-mail tspmccc@online.sh.cn; f.

1980; comprises provincial Christian councils; Pres. and acting Sec.-Gen. Rev. CAO SHENGJIE.

The Catholic Church: Catholic Mission, Si-She-Ku, Beijing; Bishop of Beijing MICHAEL FU TIESHAN (not recognized by the Vatican).

Chinese Patriotic Catholic Association: Pres. MICHAEL FU TIESHAN; Sec.-Gen. LIU BAINIAN; c. 3m. mems (1988).

CONFUCIANISM

Confucianism is a philosophy and a system of ethics, without ritual or priesthood. The respects that adherents accord to Confucius are not bestowed on a prophet or god, but on a great sage whose teachings promote peace and good order in society and whose philosophy encourages moral living.

DAOISM

Daoism was founded by Zhang Daoling during the Eastern Han dynasty (AD 125–144). Lao Zi, a philosopher of the Zhou dynasty (born 604 BC), is its principal inspiration, and is honoured as Lord the Most High by Daoists. According to official sources, there were 600 Daoist temples in China in 1998.

China Daoist Association: Temple of the White Cloud, Xi Bian Men, Beijing 100045; tel. (10) 6367179; f. 1957; Pres. (vacant); Sec.-Gen. YUAN BINGDONG.

ISLAM

According to Muslim history, Islam was introduced into China in AD 651. There were some 18m. adherents in China in 1997, chiefly among the Wei Wuer (Uygur) and Hui people, although unofficial sources estimate that the total is far higher, in the tens of millions.

Beijing Islamic Association: Dongsi Mosque, Beijing; f. 1979; Chair. Imam Al-Hadji CHEN GUANGYUAN.

China Islamic Association: Beijing 100053; tel. (10) 63546384; fax (10) 63529483; f. 1953; Chair. Imam Al-Hadji CHEN GUANGYUAN; Sec.-Gen. YU ZHENGUI.

The Press

In 2003 China had 2,119 newspaper titles (including those below provincial level) and 9,074 periodicals. Each province publishes its own daily. Only the major newspapers and periodicals are listed below. In late 1999 the Government announced its intention to merge or close down a number of newspapers, leaving a single publication in each province. Foreign investment in some areas of the print media was allowed for the first time in December 2002. In June 2003 the Government barred all newspapers and periodicals from taking subscriptions for 2004, in an attempt to prevent publications from coercing readers into buying subscriptions. In November 2003 the Government suspended 673 unprofitable state-run newspapers under new regulations requiring the large majority of newspapers to become financially independent from the central Government.

PRINCIPAL NEWSPAPERS

Anhui Ribao (Anhui Daily): 206 Jinzhai Lu, Hefei, Anhui 230061; tel. (551) 2827842; fax (551) 2847302; e-mail ahrb@ahrb.com.cn; internet www.ahrb.com.cn; Editor-in-Chief ZHANG YUXUAN.

Beijing Ribao (Beijing Daily): 34 Xi Biaobei Hutong, Dongdan, Beijing 100743; tel. (10) 65131071; fax (10) 65136522; f. 1952; organ of the Beijing municipal cttee of the CCP; Dir WAN YUNLAI; Editor-in-Chief LIU ZONGMING; circ. 700,000.

Beijing Wanbao (Beijing Evening News): 34 Xi Biaobei Hutong, Dongdan, Beijing 100743; tel. (10) 65132233; fax (10) 65126581; f. 1958; Editor-in-Chief REN HUANYING; circ. 800,000.

Beijing Youth Daily: Beijing; national and local news; promotes ethics and social service; circ. 3m.–4m.

Changsha Wanbao (Changsha Evening News): 161 Caie Zhong Lu, Changsha, Hunan 410005; tel. (731) 4424457; fax (731) 4445167.

Chengdu Wanbao (Chengdu Evening News): Qingyun Nan Jie, Chengdu 610017; tel. (28) 664501; fax (28) 666597; circ. 700,000.

China Business Times: Beijing; f. 1989; Editor HUANG WENFU; circ. 500,000.

Chongqing Ribao (Chongqing Daily): Chongqing; Dir and Editor-in-Chief LI HUANIAN.

Chungcheng Wanbao (Chungcheng Evening News): 51 Xinwen Lu, Kunming, Yunnan 650032; tel. (871) 4144642; fax (871) 4154192.

Dazhong Ribao (Dazhong Daily): 46 Jinshi Lu, Jinan, Shandong 250014; tel. (531) 2968989; fax (531) 2962450; internet www.dzdaily.com.cn; f. 1939; Dir XU XIYU; Editor-in-Chief LIU GUANGDONG; circ. 2,100,000.

Fujian Ribao (Fujian Daily): Hualin Lu, Fuzhou, Fujian; tel. (591) 57756; daily; Dir HUANG SHIYUN; Editor-in-Chief HUANG ZHONGSHENG.

Gongren Ribao (Workers' Daily): Liupukang, Andingmen Wai, Beijing 100718; tel. (10) 64211561; fax (10) 64214890; f. 1949; trade union activities and workers' lives; also major home and overseas news; Dir LIU YUMING; Editor-in-Chief SHENG MINGFU; circ. 2.5m.

Guangming Ribao (Guangming Daily): 106 Yongan Lu, Beijing 100050; tel. (10) 63017788; fax (10) 63039387; f. 1949; literature, art, science, education, history, economics, philosophy; Editor-in-Chief YUAN ZHIFA; circ. 920,000.

Guangxi Ribao (Guangxi Daily): Guangxi Region; Dir and Editor-in-Chief CHENG ZHENSHENG.

Guangzhou Ribao (Canton Daily): 10 Dongle Lu, Renmin Zhonglu, Guangzhou, Guangdong; tel. (20) 81887294; fax (20) 81862022; f. 1952; daily; social, economic and current affairs; Editor-in-Chief LI YUANJIANG; circ. 600,000.

Guizhou Ribao (Guizhou Daily): Guiyang, Guizhou; tel. (851) 627779; f. 1949; Dir GAO ZONGWEN; Editor-in-Chief GAN ZHENGSHU; circ. 300,000.

Hainan Ribao (Hainan Daily): 7 Xinhua Nan Lu, Haikou, Hainan 570001; tel. (898) 6222021; Dir ZHOU WENZHANG; Editor-in-Chief CHANG FUTANG.

Hebei Ribao (Hebei Daily): 210 Yuhuazhong Lu, Shijiazhuang, Hebei 050013; tel. (311) 6048901; fax (311) 6046969; f. 1949; Dir GUO ZENGPEI; Editor-in-Chief PAN GUILIANG; circ. 500,000.

Heilongjiang Ribao (Heilongjiang Daily): Heilongjiang Province; Dir JIA HONGTU; Editor-in-Chief AI HE.

Henan Ribao (Henan Daily): 1 Weiyi Lu, Zhengzhou, Henan; tel. (371) 5958319; fax (371) 5955636; f. 1949; Dir YANG YONGDE; Editor-in-Chief GUO ZHENGLING; circ. 390,000.

Huadong Xinwen (Eastern China News): f. 1995; published by Renmin Ribao.

Huanan Xinwen (South China News): Guangzhou; f. 1997; published by Renmin Ribao.

Hubei Ribao (Hubei Daily): 65 Huangli Lu, Wuhan, Hubei 430077; tel. (27) 6833522; fax (27) 6813989; f. 1949; Dir ZHOU NIANFENG; Editor-in-Chief SONG HANYAN; circ. 800,000.

Hunan Ribao (Hunan Daily): 18 Furong Zhong Lu, Changsha, Hunan 410071; tel. (731) 4312999; fax (731) 4314029; Dir JIANG XIANLI; Editor-in-Chief WAN MAOHUA.

Jiangxi Ribao (Jiangxi Daily): 175 Yangming Jie, Nanchang, Jiangxi; tel. (791) 6849888; fax (791) 6772590; f. 1949; Dir ZHOU JINGUANG; circ. 300,000.

Jiefang Ribao (Liberation Daily): 300 Han Kou Lu, Shanghai 200001; tel. (21) 63521111; fax (21) 63516517; f. 1949; Editor-in-Chief JIA SHUMEI; circ. 1m.

Jiefangjun Bao (Liberation Army Daily): Beijing; f. 1956; official organ of the Central Military Comm.; Dir Maj.-Gen. ZHANG SHIGANG; Editor-in-Chief WANG MENGYUN; circ. 800,000.

Jilin Ribao (Jilin Daily): Jilin Province; Dir and Editor-in-Chief YI HONGBIN.

Jingji Ribao (Economic Daily): 2 Bai Zhi Fang Dong Jie, Beijing 100054; tel. (10) 63559988; fax (10) 63539408; f. 1983; financial affairs, domestic and foreign trade; administered by the State Council; Editor-in-Chief FENG BING; circ. 1.2m.

Jinrong Shibao (Financial News): 44 Taipingqiao Fengtaiqu, Beijing 100073; tel. (10) 63269233; fax (10) 68424931.

Liaoning Ribao (Liaoning Daily): Liaoning Province; Dir XIE ZHENGQIAN.

Nanfang Ribao (Nanfang Daily): 289 Guangzhou Da Lu, Guangzhou, Guangdong 510601; tel. (20) 87373998; fax (20) 87375203; f. 1949; Nanfang Daily Group also publishes *Nanfang Dushi Bao* (Southern Metropolis Daily), *Ershiyi Shiji Jingji Baodao* (21st Century Economic Herald), and weekly edn *Nanfang Zhoumou* (Southern Weekend); Editor-in-Chief, *Nanfang Dushi Bao* CHENG YIZHONG; Gen. Man., *Nanfang Dushi Bao* (vacant); circ. 1m.

Nanjing Ribao (Nanjing Daily): 53 Jiefang Lu, Nanjing, Jiangsu 210016; tel. (25) 4496564; fax (25) 4496544.

Nongmin Ribao (Peasants' Daily): Shilipu Beili, Chao Yang Qu, Beijing 100025; tel. (10) 65005522; fax (10) 65071154; f. 1980; 6 a week; circulates in rural areas nation-wide; Dir ZHANG DEXIU; Editor-in-Chief ZHANG WENBAO; circ. 1m.

Renmin Ribao (People's Daily): 2 Jin Tai Xi Lu, Chao Yang Qu, Beijing 100733; tel. (10) 65368971; fax (10) 65368974; internet www .people.com.cn; f. 1948; organ of the CCP; also publishes overseas edn; Pres. WANG CHEN; Editor-in-Chief ZHANG YANNONG; circ. 2.15m.

Shaanxi Ribao (Shaanxi Daily): Shaanxi Province; Dir LI DONG-SHENG; Editor-in-Chief DU YAOFENG.

Shanxi Ribao (Shanxi Daily): 24 Shuangtasi Jie, Taiyuan, Shanxi; tel. (351) 446561; fax (351) 441771; Dir ZHAO WENBIN; Editor-in-Chief LI DONGXI; circ. 300,000.

Shenzhen Tequ Bao (Shenzhen Special Economic Zone Daily): 4 Shennan Zhonglu, Shenzhen 518009; tel. (755) 3902688; fax (755) 3906900; f. 1982; reports on special economic zones, as well as mainland, Hong Kong and Macao; Editor-in-Chief HUANG YANGLUE.

Sichuan Ribao (Sichuan Daily): Sichuan Daily Press Group, 70 Hongxing Zhong Lu, Erduan, Chengdu, Sichuan 610012; tel. and fax (28) 86968000; internet www.sconline.com.cn; f. 1952; Chair. of Bd LI ZHIXIA; Editor-in-Chief YU CHANGQIU; circ. 8m.

Tianjin Ribao (Tianjin Daily): 873 Dagu Nan Lu, Heri Qu, Tianjin 300211; tel. (22) 7301024; fax (22) 7305803; f. 1949; Dir and Editor-in-Chief ZHANG JIANXING; circ. 600,000.

Wenhui Bao (Wenhui Daily): 50 Huqiu Lu, Shanghai 200002; tel. (21) 63211410; fax (21) 63230198; f. 1938; Editor-in-Chief WU ZHEN-BIAO; circ. 500,000.

Xin Min Wan Bao (Xin Min Evening News): 839 Yan An Zhong Lu, Shanghai 200040; tel. (21) 62791234; fax (21) 62473220; f. 1929; specializes in public policy, education and social affairs; Editor-in-Chief HU JINGJUN; circ. 1.8m.

Xinhua Ribao (New China Daily): 55 Zhongshan Lu, Nanjing, Jiangsu 210005; tel. (21) 741757; fax (21) 741023; Editor-in-Chief ZHOU ZHENGRONG; circ. 900,000.

Xinjiang Ribao (Xinjiang Daily): Xinjiang Region; Editor-in-Chief HUANG YANCAI.

Xizang Ribao (Tibet Daily): Tibet; Editor-in-Chief LI ERLIANG.

Yangcheng Wanbao (Yangcheng Evening News): 733 Dongfeng Dong Lu, Guangzhou, Guangdong 510085; tel. (20) 87776211; fax (20) 87765103; e-mail ycwbic@ycwb.com.cn; internet www.ycwb.com .cn; f. 1957; Editor-in-Chief PAN WEIWEN; circ. 1.3m.

Yunnan Ribao (Yunnan Daily): Yunnan Province; Editor-in-Chief SUN GUANSHENG.

Zhejiang Ribao (Zhejiang Daily): Zhejiang Province; Dir CHEN MINER; Editor-in-Chief YANG DAJIN.

Zhongguo Qingnian Bao (China Youth News): 2 Haiyuncang, Dong Zhi Men Nei, Beijing 100702; tel. (10) 64032233; fax (10) 64033792; f. 1951; daily; aimed at 14–40 age-group; Dir XU ZHUQING; Editor-in-Chief LI XUEQIAN; circ. 1.0m.

Zhongguo Ribao (China Daily): 15 Huixin Dongjie, Chao Yang Qu, Beijing 100029; tel. (10) 64918633; fax (10) 64918377; internet www .chinadaily.com.cn; f. 1981; English; China's political, economic and cultural developments; world, financial and sports news; also publishes *Business Weekly* (f. 1985), *Beijing Weekend* (f. 1991), *Shanghai Star* (f. 1992), *Reports from China* (f. 1992), *21st Century* (f. 1993); Editor-in-Chief ZHU YINGHUANG; circ. 300,000.

Zhongguo Xinwen (China News): 12 Baiwanzhuang Nanjie, Beijing; tel. (10) 68315012; f. 1952; daily; Editor-in-Chief WANG XIJIN; current affairs.

SELECTED PERIODICALS

Ban Yue Tan (China Comment): Beijing; tel. (10) 6668521; f. 1980; in Chinese and Wei Wuer (Uygur); Editor-in-Chief DONG RUISHENG; circ. 6m.

Beijing Review: 24 Baiwanzhuang Lu, Beijing 100037; tel. (10) 68326085; fax (10) 68326628; e-mail bjreview@public3.bta.net.cn; internet www.bjreview.com.cn; f. 1958; weekly; edns in English, French, Spanish, Japanese and German; also **Chinafrica** (monthly in English and French); Publr WANG GANGYI; Editor-in-Chief LII HAIBO.

BJ TV Weekly: 2 Fu Xing Men Wai Zhenwumiao Jie, Beijing 100045; tel. (10) 6366036; fax (10) 63262388; circ. 1m.

Caijing: 10th Floor, Prime Tower 22 Chaoyangmenwai Lu, Beijing 100020; tel. (10) 65885047; fax (10) 65885046; internet www.caijing .com.cn/english/; f. 1998; business and finance, 2 a month; Editor HU SHULI.

China TV Weekly: 15 Huixin Dong Jie, Chao Yang Qu, Beijing 100013; tel. (10) 64214197; circ. 1.7m.

Chinese Literature Press: 24 Baiwanzhuang Lu, Beijing 100037; tel. (10) 68326010; fax (10) 68326678; e-mail chinalit@public.east.cn .net; f. 1951; monthly (bilingual in English); quarterly (bilingual in

French); contemporary and classical writing, poetry, literary criticism and arts; Exec. Editor LING YUAN.

Dianying Xinzuo (New Films): 796 Huaihai Zhong Lu, Shanghai; tel. (21) 64379710; f. 1979; bi-monthly; introduces new films.

Dianzi yu Diannao (Electronics and Computers): Beijing; f. 1985; popularized information on computers and microcomputers.

Dushu (Reading): Beijing; internet www.dushu.net; academic journal on social science and humanities; Editor WANG HUI.

Elle (China): 14 Lane 955, Yan'an Zhong Lu, Shanghai; tel. (21) 62790974; fax (21) 62479056; f. 1988; monthly; fashion; Pres. YANG XINCI; Chief Editor WU YING; circ. 300,000.

Family Magazine: 14 Siheng Lu, Xinhepu, Dongshan Qu, Guangzhou 510080; tel. (20) 7777718; fax (20) 7185670; monthly; circ. 2.5m.

Feitian (Fly Skywards): 50 Donggan Xilu, Lanzhou, Gansu; tel. (931) 25803; f. 1961; monthly.

Guoji Xin Jishu (New International Technology): Zhanwang Publishing House, Beijing; f. 1984; also publ. in Hong Kong; international technology, scientific and technical information.

Guowai Keji Dongtai (Recent Developments in Science and Technology Abroad): Institute of Scientific and Technical Information of China, 54 San Li He Lu, Beijing 100045; tel. (10) 68570713; fax (10) 68511839; e-mail kjdt@istic.ac.cn; internet www.wanfang.com.cn; f. 1962; monthly; scientific journal; Editor-in-Chief GUO YUEHUA; circ. 40,000.

Hai Xia (The Strait): 27 De Gui Xiang, Fuzhou, Fujian; tel. (10) 33656; f. 1981; quarterly; literary journal; CEOs YANG YU, JWO JONG LIN.

Huasheng Monthly (Voice for Overseas Chinese): 12 Bai Wan Zhuang Nan Jie, Beijing 100037; tel. (10) 68311578; fax (10) 68315039; f. 1995; monthly; intended mainly for overseas Chinese and Chinese nationals resident abroad; Editor-in-Chief FAN DONG-SHENG.

Jianzhu (Construction): Baiwanzhuang, Beijing; tel. (10) 68992849; f. 1956; monthly; Editor FANG YUEGUANG; circ. 500,000.

Jinri Zhongguo (China Today): 24 Baiwanzhuang Lu, Beijing 100037; tel. (10) 68326037; fax (10) 68328338; internet www .chinatoday.com.cn; f. 1952; fmrly *China Reconstructs*; monthly; edns in English, Spanish, French, Arabic, German, and Chinese; economic, social and cultural affairs; illustrated; Pres. and Editor-in-Chief HUANG ZU'AN.

Liaowang (Outlook): 57 Xuanwumen Xijie, Beijing; tel. (10) 63073049; f. 1981; weekly; current affairs; Gen. Man. ZHOU YICHANG; Editor-in-Chief JI BIN; circ. 500,000.

Luxingjia (Traveller): Beijing; tel. (10) 6552631; f. 1955; monthly; Chinese scenery, customs, culture.

Meishu Zhi You (Chinese Art Digest): 32 Beizongbu Hutong, East City Region, Beijing; tel. (10) 65591404; f. 1982; every 2 months; art review journal, also providing information on fine arts publs in China and abroad; Editors ZONGYUAN GAO, PEI CHENG.

Nianqingren (Young People): 169 Mayuanlin, Changsha, Hunan; tel. (731) 23610; f. 1981; monthly; general interest for young people.

Nongye Zhishi (Agricultural Knowledge): 21 Ming Zi Qian Lu, Jinan, Shandong 250100; tel. (531) 8932238; e-mail sdnyzs@ jn-public.sd.cninfo.net; internet www.sdny.com.cn; f. 1950; fortnightly; popular agricultural science; Dir YANG LIJIAN; circ. 410,000.

Qiushi (Seeking Truth): 2 Shatan Beijie, Beijing 100727; tel. (10) 64037005; fax (10) 64018174; f. 1988 to succeed *Hong Qi*(Red Flag); 2 a month; theoretical journal of the CCP; Editor-in-Chief LI BAOSHAN; circ. 1.83m.

Renmin Huabao (China Pictorial): Huayuancun, West Suburbs, Beijing 100044; tel. (10) 68411144; fax (10) 68413023; f. 1950; monthly; edns: two in Chinese, one in Tibetan and 12 in foreign languages; Dir and Editor-in-Chief ZHANG JIAHUA.

Shichang Zhoubao (Market Weekly): 2 Duan, Sanhao Jie, Heping Qu, Shenyang, Liaoning; tel. (24) 482983; f. 1979; weekly in Chinese; trade, commodities, and financial and economic affairs; circ. 1m.

Shufa (Calligraphy): 81 Qingzhou Nan Lu, Shanghai 200233; tel. (21) 64519008; fax (21) 64519015; f. 1977; every 2 months; journal on ancient and modern calligraphy; Chief Editor LU FUSHENG.

Tiyu Kexue (Sports Science): 8 Tiyuguan Lu, Beijing 100763; tel. (10) 67112233; f. 1981; sponsored by the China Sports Science Soc.; every 2 months; summary in English; Chief Officer YUAN WEIMIN; in Chinese; circ. 20,000.

Wenxue Qingnian (Youth Literature Journal): 27 Mu Tse Fang, Wenzhou, Zhejiang; tel. (577) 3578; f. 1981; monthly; Editor-in-Chief CHEN YUSHEN; circ. 80,000.

Women of China English Monthly: 15 Jian Guo Men Dajie, Beijing 100730; tel. (10) 65134616; fax (10) 65225380; e-mail geo@womenofchina.com.cn; internet www.womenofchina.com.cn; f. 1956; monthly; in English; administered by All-China Women's Federation; women's rights and status, views and lifestyle, education and arts, etc.; Editor-in-Chief YUN PENGJU.

Xian Dai Faxue (Modern Law Science): Southwest University of Political Science and Law, Chongqing, Sichuan 400031; tel. (23) 65382256; fax (23) 65382527; e-mail MLS@swupl.edu.cn; internet www.swupl.edu.cn; f. 1979; bi-monthly; with summaries in English; Editor-in-Chief SUN CHANGYONG.

Yinyue Aihaozhe (Music Lovers): 74 Shaoxing Lu, Shanghai 200020; tel. (21) 64372608; fax (21) 64332019; f. 1979; every two months; music knowledge; illustrated; Editor-in-Chief CHEN XUEYA; circ. 50,000.

Zhongguo Duiwai Maoyi Ming Lu (Directory of China's Foreign Trade): CCPIT Bldg, 1 Fuxingmen Wai Da Jie, Beijing 100860; tel. (10) 68022948; fax (10) 68510201; e-mail inform@press-media.com; f. 1974; monthly; edns in Chinese and English; information on Chinese imports and exports, foreign trade and economic policies; Editor-in-Chief YANG HAIQING.

Zhongguo Ertong (Chinese Children): 21 Xiang 12, Dongsi, Beijing; tel. (10) 6444761; f. 1980; monthly; illustrated journal for elementary school pupils.

Zhongguo Guangbo Dianshi (China Radio and Television): 12 Fucheng Lu, Beijing; tel. (10) 6896217; f. 1982; monthly; reports and comments.

Zhongguo Sheying (Chinese Photography): 61 Hongxing Hutong, Dongdan, Beijing 100005; tel. (10) 65252277; fax (10) 65257623; e-mail cphoto@public.bta.net.cn; internet www.cphoto.com.cn; f. 1957; monthly; photographs and comments; Editor WU CHANGYUN.

Zhongguo Zhenjiu (Chinese Acupuncture and Moxibustion): China Academy of Traditional Chinese Medicine, Dongzhimen Nei, Beijing 100700; tel. (10) 84014607; fax (10) 84046331; e-mail webmaster@cjacupuncture.com; internet www.cjacupuncture.com; f. 1981; monthly; publ. by Chinese Soc. of Acupuncture and Moxibustion; abstract in English; Editor-in-Chief Prof. DENG LIANGYUE.

Zijing (Bauhinia): Pres. and Editor-in-Chief CHEN HONG.

Other popular magazines include **Gongchandang Yuan** (Communists, circ. 1.63m.) and **Nongmin Wenzhai** (Peasants' Digest, circ. 3.54m.).

NEWS AGENCIES

Xinhua (New China) News Agency: 57 Xuanwumen Xidajie, Beijing 100803; tel. (10) 63071114; fax (10) 63071210; internet www.xinhuanet.com; f. 1931; offices in all Chinese provincial capitals, and about 100 overseas bureaux; news service in Chinese, English, French, Spanish, Portuguese, Arabic and Russian, feature and photographic services; Pres. TIAN CONGMING; Editor-in-Chief NAN ZHENZHONG.

Zhongguo Xinwen She (China News Agency): POB 1114, Beijing; f. 1952; office in Hong Kong; supplies news features, special articles and photographs for newspapers and magazines in Chinese printed overseas; services in Chinese; Dir WANG SHIGU.

Foreign Bureaux

Agence France-Presse (AFP) (France): 11-11 Jian Guo Men Wai, Diplomatic Apts, Beijing 100600; tel. (10) 65321409; fax (10) 65322371; e-mail afppek@afp.com; Bureau Chief ELIZABETH ZINGO.

Agencia EFE (Spain): 2-2-132 Jian Guo Men Wai, Beijing 100600; tel. (10) 65323449; fax (10) 65323688; Rep. CARLOS REDONDO.

Agenzia Nazionale Stampa Associata (ANSA) (Italy): 1-11 Ban Gong Lu, San Li Tun, Beijing 100600; tel. (10) 65323651; fax (10) 65321954; e-mail barbara@public3.bta.net.cn; Bureau Chief BARBARA ALIGHIERO.

Allgemeiner Deutscher Nachrichtendienst (ADN) (Germany): 7-2-61, Jian Guo Men Wai, Qi Jia Yuan Gong Yu, Beijing 100600; tel. and fax (10) 65321115; Correspondent Dr LUTZ POHLE.

Associated Press (AP) (USA): 6-2-22 Jian Guo Men Wai, Diplomatic Quarters, Beijing 100600; tel. (10) 65326650; fax (10) 65323419; Bureau Chief ELAINE KURTENBACH.

Deutsche Presse-Agentur (dpa) (Germany): Ban Gong Lou, Apt 1-31, San Li Tun, Beijing 100600; tel. (10) 65321473; fax (10) 65321615; e-mail dpa@public3.bta.net.cn; Bureau Chief ANDREAS LANDWEHR.

Informatsionnoye Telegrafnoye Agentstvo Rossii (ITAR—TASS) (Russia): 6-1-41 Tayuan Diplomatic Office Bldg, Beijing 100600; tel. (10) 65324821; fax (10) 65324820; e-mail tassbj@itar-tass.com; Bureau Chief ANDREY KIRILLOV.

Inter Press Service (TIPS) (Italy): 15 Fuxing Lu, POB 3811, Beijing 100038; tel. (10) 68514046; fax (10) 68518210; e-mail tipscn@istic.ac.cn; internet www.tips.org.cn; Dir WANG XIAOYING.

Jiji Tsushin (Japan): 9-1-13 Jian Guo Men Wai, Waijiao, Beijing; tel. (10) 65322924; fax (10) 65323413; Correspondents YOSHIHISA MURAYAMA, TETSUYA NISHIMURA.

Korean Central News Agency (Democratic People's Republic of Korea): Beijing; e-mail kcnab@xinhuanet.com; Bureau Chief RI YONG.

Kyodo News Service (Japan): 3-91 Jian Guo Men Wai, Beijing; tel. (10) 6532680; fax (10) 65322273; e-mail kyodob@ccnet.cn.net; Bureau Chief YASUHIRO MORI.

Magyar Távirati Iroda (MTI) (Hungary): 1-42 Ban Gong Lu, San Li Tun, Beijing 100600; tel. (10) 65321744; Correspondent GYÖRGY BARTA.

Prensa Latina (Cuba): 4-1-23 Jianguomenwai, Beijing 100600; tel. and fax (10) 65321914; e-mail prelatin@public.bta.net.cn; Correspondent ILSA RODRÍGUEZ SANTANA.

Press Trust of India: 5-131 Diplomatic Apts, Jian Guo Men Wai, Beijing 100600; tel. and fax (10) 65322221.

Reuters (UK): Hilton Beijing, 1 Dong Fang Lu/Bei Dong Sanhuan Lu, Chao Yang Qu, Beijing; tel. (10) 64662288; fax (10) 64653052; e-mail hilton@hiltonbeijing.com.cn; internet www.hilton.com; Bureau Man. RICHARD PASCOE.

Tanjug News Agency (Serbia and Montenegro): Qijayuan Diplomatic Apt, Beijing 100600; tel. (10) 65324821.

United Press International (UPI) (USA): 7-1-11 Qi Jia Yuan, Beijing; tel. (10) 65323271; Bureau Chief CHRISTIAAN VIRANT.

The following are also represented: Rompres (Romania) and VNA (Viet Nam).

PRESS ORGANIZATIONS

All China Journalists' Association: Xijiaominxiang, Beijing 100031; tel. (10) 66023981; fax (10) 66014658; Chair. SHAO HUAZE.

China Newspapers Association: Beijing; Chair. WANG CHEN.

The Press and Publication Administration of the People's Republic of China (State Copyright Bureau): 85 Dongsi Nan Dajie, East District, Beijing 100703; tel. (10) 65124433; fax (10) 65127875; Dir SHI ZONGYUAN.

Publishers

In 2003 there were 570 publishing houses in China. A total of 190,391 titles (and 6,670m. copies) were published in that year. In 2004 it was announced that foreign companies were to be allowed to enter the book distribution market. However, direct involvement by foreign companies in the publishing business remained restricted.

Beijing Chubanshe Chuban Jituan (Beijing Publishing House Group): 6 Bei Sanhuan Zhong Lu, Beijing 100011; tel. (10) 62016699; fax (10) 62012339; e-mail geo@bph.com.cn; internet www.bph.com.cn; f. 1956; politics, history, law, economics, geography, science, literature, art, etc.; Dir ZHU SHUXIN; Editor-in-Chief TAO XINCHENG.

Beijing Daxue Chubanshe (Beijing University Press): 205 Chengfu Lu, Zhongguancun, Haidian Qu, Beijing 100871; tel. (10) 62752024; fax (10) 62556201; f. 1979; academic and general.

China International Book Trading Corpn: POB 399, 35 Chegongzhuang Xilu, Beijing 100044; tel. (10) 68433113; fax (10) 68420340; e-mail bk@mail.cibtc.co.cn; internet www.cibtc.com.cn; f. 1949; foreign trade org. specializing in publs, including books, periodicals, art and crafts, microfilms, etc.; import and export distributors; Pres. QI PINGJIN.

China Publishing Group: Beijing; f. 2002; aims to restructure and consolidate publishing sector; comprises 12 major publishing houses; Pres. of the Bd YANG MUZHI.

CITIC Publishing House: Ta Yuan Diplomatic Office Bldg, 14 Liangmahe Lu, Chao Yang Qu, Beijing 100600; tel. (10) 85323366; fax (10) 85322505; e-mail liyinghong@citicpub.com; internet www.publish.citic.com; f. 1988; finance, investment, economics and business; Pres. WANG BIN.

Dianzi Gongye Chubanshe (Publishing House of the Electronics Industry—PHEI): POB 173, Wan Shou Lu, Beijing 100036; tel. (10) 68159028; fax (10) 68159025; f. 1982; electronic sciences and technology; Pres. LIANG XIANGFENG; Vice-Pres. WANG MINGJUN.

Dolphin Books: 24 Baiwanzhuang Lu, Beijing 100037; tel. (10) 68326332; fax (10) 68326642; f. 1986; children's books in Chinese and foreign languages; Dir WANG YANRONG.

Falü Chubanshe (Law Publishing House): Lianhuachi Xili, Fengtai Qu, Beijing 100073; tel. (10) 6815325; e-mail international@ lawpress.com.cn; internet www.lawpress.com.cn; f. 1980; current laws and decrees, legal textbooks, translations of important foreign legal works; Dir LAN MINGLIANG.

Foreign Languages Press: 19 Chegongzhuang Xi Lu, Fu Xing Men Wai, Beijing 100044; tel. (10) 68413344; fax (10) 68424931; e-mail info@flp.com.cn; internet www.flp.com.cn; f. 1952; books in 20 foreign languages reflecting political and economic developments in People's Republic of China and features of Chinese culture; Dir GUO JIEXIN; Editor-in-Chief XU MINGQIANG.

Gaodeng Jiaoyu Chubanshe (Higher Education Press): 55 Shatan Houjie, Beijing 100009; tel. (10) 64014043; fax (10) 64054602; e-mail linm@public.bta.net.cn; internet www.hep.edu.cn; f. 1954; academic, textbooks; Pres. LIU ZHIPENG; Editor-in-Chief ZHANG ZENGSHUN.

Gongren Chubanshe (Workers' Publishing House): Liupukeng, Andingmen Wai, Beijing; tel. (10) 64215278; f. 1949; labour movement, trade unions, science and technology related to industrial production.

Guangdong Keji Chubanshe (Guangdong Science and Technology Press): 11 Shuiyin Lu, Huanshidong Lu, Guangzhou, Guangdong 510075; tel. (20) 37607770; fax (20) 37607770; e-mail gdkjzbb@ 21cn.com; internet www.gdstp.com.cn; f. 1978; natural sciences, technology, agriculture, medicine, computing, English language teaching; Dir HUANG DAQUAN.

Heilongjiang Kexue Jishu Chubanshe (Heilongjiang Science and Technology Press): 41 Jianshe Jie, Nangang Qu, Harbin 150001, Heilongjiang; tel. and fax (451) 3642127; f. 1979; industrial and agricultural technology, natural sciences, economics and management, popular science, children's and general.

Huashan Wenyi Chubanshe (Huashan Literature and Art Publishing House): 45 Bei Malu, Shijiazhuang, Hebei; tel. 22501; f. 1982; novels, poetry, drama, etc.

Kexue Chubanshe (Science Press): 16 Donghuangchenggen Beijie, Beijing 100717; tel. (10) 64034313; fax (10) 64020094; e-mail icd@ cspg.net; f. 1954; books and journals on science and technology.

Lingnan Meishu Chubanshe (Lingnan Art Publishing House): 11 Shuiyin Lu, Guangzhou, Guangdong 510075; tel. (20) 87771044; fax (20) 87771049; f. 1981; works on classical and modern painting, picture albums, photographic, painting techniques; Pres. CAO LIXIANG.

Minzu Chubanshe (The Ethnic Publishing House): 14 Hepingli Beijie, Beijing 100013; tel. (10) 64211126; e-mail nova126@sina.com; f. 1953; books and periodicals in minority languages, e.g. Mongolian, Tibetan, Uygur, Korean, Kazakh, etc.; Editor-in-Chief HUANG ZHONGCAI.

Qunzhong Chubanshe (Masses Publishing House): Bldg 15, Part 3, Fangxingyuan, Fangzhuan Lu, Beijing 100078; tel. (10) 67633344; f. 1956; politics, law, judicial affairs, criminology, public security, etc.

Renmin Chubanshe (People's Publishing House): 8 Hepinglidongjie, Andingmenwai, Beijing; tel. (10) 4213713; managed by the Ministry of Communications; science and technology, textbooks, laws and specifications of communications; Dir and Editor-in-Chief XUE DEZHEN.

Renmin Jiaoyu Chubanshe (People's Education Press): 55 Sha Tan Hou Jie, Beijing 100009; tel. (10) 64035745; fax (10) 64010370; f. 1950; school textbooks, guidebooks, teaching materials, etc.

Renmin Meishu Chubanshe (People's Fine Arts Publishing House): Beijing; tel. (10) 65122371; fax (10) 65122370; f. 1951; works by Chinese and foreign painters, sculptors and other artists, picture albums, photographic, painting techniques; Dir GAO ZONGYUAN; Editor-in-Chief CHENG DALI.

Renmin Weisheng Chubanshe (People's Medical Publishing House): Beijing; tel. (10) 67617283; fax (10) 645143; f. 1953; medicine (Western and traditional Chinese), pharmacology, dentistry, public health; Pres. LIU YIQING.

Renmin Wenxue Chubanshe (People's Literature Publishing House): 166 Chaoyangmen Nei Dajie, Beijing 100705; tel. and fax (10) 65138394; e-mail rwzbs@sina.com; internet www.rw-cn.com; f. 1951; largest publisher of literary works and translations into Chinese; Dir and Editor-in-Chief NIE ZHENNING.

Shanghai Guji Chubanshe (Shanghai Classics Publishing House): 272 Ruijin Erlu, Shanghai 200020; tel. (21) 64370011; fax (21) 64339287; e-mail guji1@guji.com.cn; internet www.guji.com.cn; f. 1956; classical Chinese literature, history, art, philosophy, geography, linguistics, science and technology.

Shanghai Jiaoyu Chubanshe (Shanghai Educational Publishing House): 123 Yongfu Lu, Shanghai 200031; tel. (21) 64377165; fax (21) 64339995; f. 1958; academic; Dir and Editor-in-Chief CHEN HE.

Shanghai Yiwen Chubanshe (Shanghai Translation Publishing House): 193 Fujian Lu, Shanghai 200001; tel. (21) 53594508; fax (21) 63914291; e-mail info@yiwen.com.cn ; internet www.yiwen.com.cn; f. 1978; translations of foreign classic and modern literature; philosophy, social sciences, dictionaries, etc.

Shangwu Yinshuguan (The Commercial Press): 36 Wangfujing Dajie, Beijing 100710; tel. (10) 65252026; fax (10) 65134942; e-mail billyhu@sohu.com; internet www.cp.com.cn; f. 1897; dictionaries and reference books in Chinese and foreign languages, translations of foreign works on social sciences; Editor HU LONGBIAO; Pres. YANG DEYAN.

Shaonian Ertong Chubanshe (Juvenile and Children's Publishing House): 1538 Yan An Xi Lu, Shanghai 200052; tel. (21) 62823025; fax (21) 62821726; e-mail forwardz@public4.sta.net.cn; f. 1952; children's educational and literary works, teaching aids and periodicals; Gen. Man. ZHOU SHUNPEI.

Shijie Wenhua Chubanshe (World Culture Publishing House): Dir ZHU LIE.

Wenwu Chubanshe (Cultural Relics Publishing House): 29 Wusi Dajie, Beijing 100009; tel. (10) 64048057; fax (10) 64010698; e-mail web@wenwu.com; internet www.wenwu.com; f. 1956; books and catalogues of Chinese relics in museums and those recently discovered; Dir SU SHISHU.

Wuhan Daxue Chubanshe (Wuhan University Press): Luojia Hill, Wuhan, Hubei; tel. (27) 87218069; fax (27) 87218069; e-mail wdp3@ whu.edu.cn; internet www.wdp.whu.edu.cn; f. 1981; reference books, academic works, maps, audio-visual works etc.; Pres. and Editor-in-Chief Prof. JIANG JIANQIN.

Xiandai Chubanshe (Modern Press): 504 Anhua Li, Andingmenwai, Beijing 100011; tel. (10) 64263515; fax (10) 64214540; f. 1981; directories, reference books, etc.; Dir ZHOU HONGLI.

Xinhua Chubanshe (Xinhua Publishing House): 8 Jungyuan Lu, Shijingshan, Beijing 100000; tel. (10) 63074407; fax (10) 63073880; e-mail wjybox@xinhuanet.com; f. 1979; social sciences, economy, politics, history, geography, directories, dictionaries, etc.; Dir LUO HAIYUAN.

Xuelin Chubanshe (Scholar Books Publishing House): 120 Wenmiao Lu, Shanghai 200010; tel. and fax (21) 63768540; f. 1981; academic, including personal academic works at authors' own expense; Dir LEI QUNMING.

Zhongguo Caizheng Jingji Chubanshe (China Financial and Economic Publishing House): 8 Dafosi Dongjie, Dongcheng Qu, Beijing; tel. (10) 64011805; f. 1961; finance, economics, commerce and accounting.

Zhongguo Dabaike Quanshu Chubanshe (Encyclopaedia of China Publishing House): 17 Fu Cheng Men Bei Dajie, Beijing 100037; tel. (10) 68315610; fax (10) 68316510; e-mail ygh@bj.col.com .cn; f. 1978; specializes in encyclopaedias; Dir SHAN JIFU.

Zhongguo Ditu Chubanshe (SinoMaps Press): 3 Baizhifang Xijie, Beijing 100054; tel. (10) 63530808; fax (10) 63531961; e-mail wuqinjie@sinomaps.com; internet www.sinomaps.com; f. 1954; cartographic publr; Dir Dr BAI BO.

Zhongguo Funü Chubanshe (China Women Publishing House): 24A Shijia Hutong, 100010 Beijing; tel. (10) 65126986; f. 1981; women's movement, marriage and family, child-care, etc.; Dir LI ZHONGXIU.

Zhongguo Qingnian Chubanzongshe (China Youth Publishing Group): 21 Dongsi Shiertiao, Beijing 100708; tel. (10) 84015396; fax (10) 64031803; e-mail rightscenter@cyp.com.cn; internet www.cyp .com.cn; f. 1950; literature, social and natural sciences, youth work, autobiography; also periodicals; Pres. XI JIEYING; Editor-in-Chief WEN YUXIN.

Zhongguo Shehui Kexue Chubanshe (China Social Sciences Publishing House): 158A Gulou Xidajie, Beijing 100720; tel. (10) 64073837; fax (10) 64074509; f. 1978; Dir ZHENG WENLIN.

Zhongguo Xiju Chubanshe (China Theatrical Publishing House): 52 Dongsi Batiao Hutong, Beijing; tel. (10) 64015815; f. 1957; traditional and modern Chinese drama.

Zhongguo Youyi Chuban Gongsi (China Friendship Publishing Corpn): e-mail tmdoxu@public.east.cn.net; Dir YANG WEI.

Zhonghua Shuju (Zhonghua Book Co): 38 Taipingqiao Xili, Fenglai Qu, Beijing; tel. (10) 63458226; f. 1912; general; Pres. SONG YIFU.

PUBLISHERS' ASSOCIATION

Publishers' Association of China: Beijing; f. 1979; arranges academic exchanges with foreign publrs; Hon. Chair. SONG MUWEN; Chair. YU YOUXIAN.

Broadcasting and Communications

TELECOMMUNICATIONS

Ministry of Information Industry: see under Ministries.

China Mobile Communications Corpn (China Mobile): internet www.chinamobile.com; f. 2000; Pres. WANG JIANZHOU.

China Netcom Corpn: Beijing 100032; 9–15/F, Building A, 15/F, Bldg C, Corporate Sq., 35 Financial St, Xicheng Qu; tel. (10) 8809-3588; fax (10) 8809-1446; e-mail cnc@china-netcom.com; internet www.cnc.net.cn; f. 1999; internet telephone service provider; merged with China Telecom northern operations (10 provinces) in May 2002; Chair. YAN YIXUN; Pres. ZHANG CHUNJIANG.

China Satellite Communications Corpn (CHINA SATCOM): 42 Xueyuan Lu, Haidian Qu, Beijing 100083; internet www .chinasatcom.com; f. 2001 to provide internet, telephone and related services; Pres. ZHANG HAINAN.

China Telecom: 5th Floor, North Wing, Xibianmennei Jie, Xuanwu Qu, Beijing 100053; e-mail info@chinatelecom.com.cn; internet www .chinatelecom.com.cn; f. 1997 as a vehicle for foreign investment in telecommunications sector; operates 'Xiao Ling Tong' mobile phone services; restructured in May 2002 with responsibility for fixed-line network in 21 southern and western provinces; Pres. ZHOU DEQIANG.

China United Telecommunications Corpn (UNICOM): 1/F, Hongji Centre Office Bldg, 18 Jianguomenei Dajie, Beijing; tel. (10) 65181800; fax (10) 65183405; e-mail webmaster@chinaunicom.com .cn; internet www.chinaunicom.com.cn; f. 1994; cellular telecommunications; Chair. and Pres. WANG JIANZHOU.

Netease.com: Rm 1901, Tower E3, The Towers, Oriental Plaza No.1, East Chang An Jie, Dong Cheng Qu, Beijing 100738; tel. (10) 85180163; fax (10) 85183618; internet www.netease.com; Nasdaq-listed internet portal; CEO TED SUN.

Sina.com: Soho New Town, 16F Bldg C, 88 Jianguo Lu, Chaoyang Qu, Beijing 100022; tel. (10) 65665009; fax (10) 85801740; internet www.sina.com.cn; Nasdaq-listed internet portal; Pres. WANG YAN.

Sohu.com: 15th Floor, Tower 2, Bright China Chang An Bldg, 7 Jianguomen Nei Jie, Beijing 100005; tel. (10) 65102160; fax (10) 65101377; internet www.sohu.com; ; Nasdaq-listed internet portal; Chair. CHARLES ZHANG.

BROADCASTING

In 2003 there were 277 radio broadcasting stations, 742 radio transmitting and relay stations (covering 93.7% of the population), 317 television stations and 51,659 television transmitting and relay stations (covering 95.0% of the population).

Regulatory Authority

State Administration of Radio, Film and Television (SARFT): 2 Fu Xing Men Wai Dajie, POB 4501, Beijing 100866; tel. (10) 68513409; fax (10) 68512174; internet www.dns.incmrft.gov.cn; controls the Central People's Broadcasting Station, the Central TV Station, Radio Beijing, China Record Co, Beijing Broadcasting Institute, Broadcasting Research Institute, the China Broadcasting Art Troupe, etc.; Dir XU GUANGCHUN.

Radio

China National Radio (CNR): 2 Fu Xing Men Wai Dajie, Beijing 100866; tel. (10) 68045630; fax (10) 68045631; internet www.cnradio .com; f. 1945; domestic service in Chinese, Zang Wen (Tibetan), Min Nan Hua (Amoy), Ke Jia (Hakka), Hasaka (Kazakh), Wei Wuer (Uygur), Menggu Hua (Mongolian) and Chaoxian (Korean); Dir-Gen. YANG BO.

Zhongguo Guoji Guangbo Diantai (China Radio International): 16A Shijingshan Lu, Beijing 100039; tel. (10) 68891001; fax (10) 68891582; e-mail crieng@public.bta.net.cn; internet www.cri.com .cn; f. 1941; fmrly Radio Beijing; foreign service in 38 languages incl. Arabic, Burmese, Czech, English, Esperanto, French, German, Indonesian, Italian, Japanese, Lao, Polish, Portuguese, Russian, Spanish, Turkish and Vietnamese; Dir LI DAN.

Television

China Central Television (CCTV): 11 Fuxing Lu, Haidian, Beijing 100859; tel. (10) 8500000; fax (10) 8513025; internet www.wtdb .com/CCTV/about.htm; operates under Bureau of Broadcasting

Affairs of the State Council, Beijing; f. 1958; operates eight networks; 24-hour global satellite service commenced in 1996; Pres. ZHAO HUAYONG.

In October 1993 the Government approved new regulations, attempting to restrict access to foreign satellite broadcasts. In April 1994 foreign companies were prohibited from establishing or operating cable TV stations in China. By mid-1996 there were more than 3,000 cable television stations in operation, with networks covering 45m. households. The largest subscriber service is Beijing Cable TV (Dir Guo Junjin). Satellite services are available in some areas: millions of satellite receivers are in use. In September 2001 the Government signed a deal that would allow News Corpn and AOL Time Warner to become the first foreign broadcasters to have direct access to China's markets, although broadcasts would be restricted to Guangdong Province. In February 2004 it was announced that restrictions on foreign investment in TV and film production companies were to be removed. However, foreign media companies would be required to comply with government regulations on media content.

Finance

(cap. = capital; auth. = authorized; p.u. = paid up; res = reserves; dep. = deposits; m. = million; amounts in yuan unless otherwise stated)

BANKING

Radical economic reforms, introduced in 1994, included the strengthening of the role of the central bank and the establishment of new commercial banks. The Commercial Bank Law took effect in July 1995.

Regulatory Authority

China Banking Regulatory Commission: 33 Cheng Fang Lu, Xi Qu, Beijing; internet www.cbrc.gov.cn; f. 2003; Chair. LIU MINGKANG.

Central Bank

People's Bank of China: 32 Chengfang Jie, Xicheng Qu, Beijing 100800; tel. (10) 66194114; fax (10) 66015346; e-mail master@pbc .gov.cn; internet www.pbc.gov.cn; f. 1948; bank of issue; decides and implements China's monetary policies; Gov. ZHOU XIAOCHUAN; 2,204 brs.

Other Banks

Agricultural Bank of China: 23A Fuxing Lu, Haidian Qu, Beijing 100036; tel. (10) 68424388; fax (10) 68424437; e-mail webmaster@ intl.abocn.com; internet www.abchina.com; f. 1951; serves mainly China's rural financial operations, providing services for agriculture, industry, commerce, transport, etc. in rural areas; cap. 129,252m., res 3,183m., dep. 2,620,746m. (Dec. 2002); Pres. YANG MINGSHENG; 37,000 brs (domestic).

Agricultural Development Bank of China: 2A Yuetanbei Jie, Xicheng Qu, Beijing 100045; tel. (10) 68081557; fax (10) 68081773; f. 1994; cap. 20,000m.; Pres. HE LINXIANG.

Bank of China Ltd: 1 Fu Xing Men Nei Dajie, Beijing 100818; tel. (10) 66016688; fax (10) 66016869; e-mail webmaster@bank-of-china .com; internet www.bank-of-china.com; f. 1912; handles foreign exchange and international settlements; operates Orient AMC (asset management corporation) since 1999; fmrly Bank of China, became shareholding company in Aug. 2004, initial public offering expected in 2005; cap. 186,390m., res 19,000m., dep. 3,515,115m. (Dec. 2003); Chair. XIAO GANG; Pres. LI LIHUI; Dir ANTHONY NEOH; 121 brs.

Bank of Communications Ltd: 188 Yin Cheng Lu, Shanghai 200120; tel. (21) 58781234; fax (21) 58880559; e-mail webmaster@hq .bankcomm.com; internet www.bankcomm.com; f. 1908; commercial bank; cap. 17,108.2m., res 23,391.5m., dep. 643,741.9m. (Dec. 2003); a 19.9% stake was acquired by HSBC in Aug. 2004; Chair. JIANG CHAOLIANG; Pres. ZHANG JIANGGUO; 90 brs.

Bank of Shanghai Co Ltd: 585 Zhongshan Lu (E2), Shanghai 200010; tel. (21) 63370888; fax (21) 63370777; e-mail shenjie@ bankofshanghai.com.cn; internet www.bankofshanghai.com; f. 1995 as Shanghai City United Bank, assumed present name in 1998; cap. 2,600m., res 4,000.9m., dep 177,192.1m. (Dec. 2003); Chair. FU JIANHUA; Pres. XIN CHEN.

Beijing City Commercial Bank Corpn Ltd: 2nd Floor, Tower B, Beijing International Financial Bldg, 156 Fu Xing Men Nei Jie, Beijing 100031; tel. (10) 66426928; fax (10) 66426691; e-mail bccbibd@sina.com; internet www.bccb.com.cn; f. 1996 as Beijing City United Bank Corpn, assumed present name in 1998; cap 2,009.9m., res 1,448.4m., dep 89,773.6m. (Dec. 2001); Chair. YAN BINGZHU; Pres. YAN XIAOYAN.

BNP Paribas (China) Ltd: 13th Floor, North Tower, Shanghai Stock Exchange Bldg, 528 Pudong Nan Lu, Shanghai 200120; tel. (21) 58405500; fax (21) 58889232; f. 1992; fmrly International Bank of Paris and Shanghai; name changed as above 2004; 100% owned by BNP Paribas SA, Paris; cap. US $67.1m., res US $2.2m., dep. US $70.7m. (Dec. 2003); Chair. and Pres. DIDIER BALME.

Bohai Bank: Tianjin; f. 2004; 20% stake owned by Standard Chartered Bank.

Changsha City Commercial Bank: 1 Furong Zhong Lu, Changsha, Hunan; tel. (73) 14305570; fax (73) 14305560; internet www.hncccb.com.cn; f. 1997; cap. 312.0m., res 37.5m., dep. 16,785.4m. (Dec. 2002); Chair. YE ZHANG; Pres. XIANG LILI.

China Construction Bank (CCB): 25 Jinrong Jie, Beijing 100032; tel. (10) 67598628; fax (10) 67598544; e-mail ccb@bj.china.com; internet www.ccb.com.cn; f. 1954; fmrly People's Construction Bank of China; makes payments for capital construction projects in accordance with state plans and budgets; issues medium- and long-term loans to enterprises and short-term loans to construction enterprises and others; also handles foreign-exchange business; housing loans; operates Cinda AMC (asset management corporation) since 1998 and China Great Wall AMC since 1999; cap. 186,230m., res 36m., dep. 3,246,145m. (Dec. 2003); 49 brs; Chair. (vacant).

China Everbright Bank: Everbright Tower, 6 Fu Xing Men Wai Lu, Beijing 100045; tel. (10) 68565577; fax (10) 68561260; e-mail eb@cebbank.com; internet www.cebbank.com; f. 1992 as Everbright Bank of China; acquired China Investment Bank and assumed present name in 1999; cap. 8,216.9m., res 4,629.6m., dep. 375,869.3m. (Dec. 2003); Pres. WANG CHUAN; Chair. WANG MINGQUAN; 10 brs.

China International Capital Corporation (CICC): 28th Floor, China World Tower 2, 1 Jian Guo Men Wai Dajie, Beijing 100004; tel. (10) 65051166; fax (10) 65051156; e-mail info@cicc.com.cn; internet www.cicc.com.cn; f. 1995; international investment bank; 42.5% owned by China Construction Bank, 34.3% owned by Morgan Stanley; registered cap. US $100m.; CEO LEVIN ZHU.

China International Trust and Investment Corporation (CITIC): Capital Mansion, 6 Xianyuannan Lu, Chao Yang Qu, Beijing 100004; tel. (10) 64661105; fax (10) 64662137; e-mail g-office@citic.com.cn; internet www.citic.com.cn; f. 1979; economic and technological co-operation; finance, banking, investment and trade; registered cap. 3,000m.; sales US $3,462.7m. (1999/2000); Chair. WANG JUN; Pres. KONG DAN.

China Merchants Bank: China Merchants Bank Tower, 7088 Shennan Blvd, Shenzhen 518040; tel. (755) 83198888; fax (755) 83195061; e-mail 00430@oa.cmbchina.com; internet www.cmbchina .com; f. 1987; cap. 5,706.8m., res 10,231.6m., dep. 475,510.4m. (Dec. 2003); Pres. and CEO MA WEIHUA; 19 brs.

China Minsheng Banking Corporation: 8/F, 2 Fuxingmen Nei Dajie, Xicheng Qu, Beijing 100031; tel. (10) 58560623; fax (10) 58560742; e-mail service@cmbc.com.cn; internet www.cmbc.com.cn; first non-state national commercial bank, opened Jan. 1996; cap. 3,625.3m., res 4,530.9m., dep. 345,382.1m. (Dec. 2003); Chair. JING SHUPING; Pres. DONG WENBIAO; 5 brs.

Chinese Mercantile Bank: Ground and 23rd Floors, Dongfeng Bldg, 2 Yannan Lu, Futian Qu, Shenzhen 518031; tel. (755) 3257880; fax (755) 3257801; e-mail szcmbank@public.szptt.net.cn; f. 1993; owned by Hong Kong Chinese Bank 40%, CTS Hong Kong 30%, Industrial and Commercial Bank of China 30%; Pres. HUANG MIN-GXIANG.

CITIC Industrial Bank: Block C, Fuhua Bldg, 8 Chao Yang Men Bei Dajie, Dongcheng Qu, Beijing 100027; tel. (10) 65541658; fax (10) 65541671; e-mail webmaster@citicib.com.cn; internet www.citicib .com.cn; f. 1987; cap. 14,032.2m., res 1,332.9m., dep. 370,823.7m. (Dec. 2003); Chair. WANG JUN; Pres. DOU JIANZHONG; 26 brs.

Export and Import Bank of China (China Exim Bank): Jinyun Tower B, No. 43-A, Xizhimenbei Lu, Beijing 100044; tel. (10) 62231626; fax (10) 62231236; internet www.eximbank.gov.cn; f. 1994; provides trade credits for export of large machinery, electronics, ships, etc.; Chair. and Pres. YANG ZILIN.

Fujian Asia Bank Ltd: 2nd Floor, Yuan Hong Bldg, 32 Wuyi Lu, Fuzhou, Fujian 350005; tel. (591) 3330788; fax (591) 3330843; e-mail fablls@pub2.fz.fj.cn; f. 1993; cap. US $27.0m., res US $2.1m., dep. US $0.2m. (Dec. 2002); Chair. MA HONG; Gen. Man. SONG JIANXIN.

Fujian Industrial Bank: Zhong Shang Bldg, 154 Hudong Lu, Hualin, Fuzhou, Fujian 350003; tel. (591) 7839338; fax (591) 7841932; e-mail fjib@pub3.fz.fj.cn; internet www.fib.com.cn; f. 1982; cap. 3,000m., res 2,867.8m., dep. 117,935.2m. (Dec. 2001); Pres. GAO JIANPING; 19 brs.

Guangdong Development Bank: 83 Nonglinxia Lu, Dongshan Qu, Guangzhou, Guangdong 510080; tel. (20) 87310888; fax (20) 87310779; internet www.gdb.com.cn; f. 1988; cap. 3,585.7m., res 1,388.7m., dep. 166,079.3m. (Dec. 2001); Chair. LI RUOHONG; Pres. ZHANG GUANGHUA; 24 brs.

Hua Xia Bank: 22 Hua Xia Bank Mansions, Jianguomennei St, Dongcheng Qu, Beijing 100005; tel. (10) 85239607; fax (10) 85239601; e-mail zhgjb@hxb.cc; internet www.hxb.cc; f. 1992 as part of Shougang Corpn; cap. 3,500m., res 4,856.0m., dep. 231,132.2m. (Dec. 2003); Chair. LIU HAIYAN; Pres. WU JIAN.

Industrial and Commercial Bank of China: 55 Fuxingmennan Dajie, Xicheng Qu, Beijing 100031; tel. (10) 66106071; fax (10) 66106053; e-mail webmaster@icbc.com.cn; internet www.icbc.com .cn; f. 1984; handles industrial and commercial credits and international business; operates Huarong AMC (asset management corporation) since 1999; cap. 167,417m., res 15,908m., dep. 3,873,732m. (Dec. 2001); Chair. and Pres. JIANG JIANQING; Gen. Man. CHEN AIPING.

Nantong City Commercial Bank Co Ltd: 300 Nanda Lu, Nantong, Jiangsu 226006; tel. (513) 5123040; fax (513) 5123039; e-mail ntccb.id@pub.nt.jsinfo.net; internet www.ntccb.com; f. 1997 as Nantong City United Bank; assumed present name in 1998; cap. 215.7m., res 25.4m., dep. 7,444.1m. (Dec. 2003); Chair. and Pres. LIU CHANGJI.

Qingdao International Bank: Full Hope Mansion C, 12 Hong Kong Middle Rd, Qingdao, Shandong 266071; tel. (532) 5026230; fax (532) 5026222; e-mail qibankc@public.qd.sd.cn; internet www .qibank.net; f. 1996; joint venture between Industrial and Commercial Bank of China and Korea First Bank; cap. 165.5m., res 11.8m., dep. 167.3m. (Dec. 2003); Chair. KYO JOONG YOON; Pres. SUNG JAE CHUNG.

Shanghai Pudong Development Bank: 12 Zhongshan Dong Yi Lu, Shanghai 200002; tel. (21) 63296188; fax (21) 63232036; internet www.spdb.com.cn; f. 1993; cap. 3,915.0m., res 7,612.0m., dep. 350,744.3m. (Dec. 2003); Chair. ZHANG GUANGSHENG; Pres. JIN YUN.

Shenzhen Commercial Bank: Shenzhen Commercial Bank Bldg, 1099 Shennan Lu, Central, Shenzhen 518031; tel. (755) 25878092; fax (755) 25878212; e-mail ibd@bankofshenzhen.com; internet www .18ebank.com; cap. US $193m., res US $15m., dep. US $4,044m. (Dec. 2002); f. 1995; Chair. CHEN ZEMING; Pres. WANG JI; 45 brs.

Shenzhen Development Bank Co Ltd: 5047 Shennan Dong Lu, Shenzhen 518001; tel. (755) 2088888; fax (755) 2081018; e-mail shudi@sdb.com.cn; internet www.sdb.com.cn; f. 1987; cap. 1,945.8m., res 2,370.0m., dep. 158,946.2m. (Dec. 2002); Chair. CHEN ZHAOMIN; Pres. ZHOU LIN.

State Development Bank (SDB): 29 Fuchengmenwai Lu, Xicheng Qu, Beijing 100037; tel. (10) 68306557; fax (10) 68306541; f. 1994; merged with China Investment Bank 1998; handles low-interest loans for infrastructural projects and basic industries; Gov. CHEN YUAN.

Xiamen International Bank: 8–10 Jiang Lu, Xiamen, Fujian 361001; tel. (592) 2078888; fax (592) 2988788; e-mail xib@public.xm .fj.cn; internet www.xib.com.cn; f. 1985; cap. HK $800m., res HK $354.9m., dep. HK $9,891.6m. (Dec. 2003); Chair. CHEN GUI ZONG; Pres. LU YAO MING; 3 brs.

Zhejiang Commercial Bank Ltd: 88 Xi Zhongshan Lu, Ningbo 315010; tel. (574) 87252668; fax (574) 87245409; e-mail zcbho@mail .nbptt.zj.cn; internet www.zcbl.com; f. 1993; cap. US $49.2m. (1998); dep. US $54.8m. (Dec. 2002); Pres. and Chair. DUAN YONGKUAN.

Foreign Banks

Before mid-1995 foreign banks were permitted only to open representative offices in China. The first foreign bank established a full branch in Beijing in mid-1995, and by March 1998 there were 51 foreign banks in China. In March 1997 foreign banks were allowed for the first time to conduct business in yuan. However, they are only entitled to accept yuan deposits from joint-venture companies. Representative offices totalled 519 in December 1996. In March 1999 the Government announced that foreign banks, hitherto restricted to 23 cities and Hainan Province, were to be permitted to open branches in all major cities.

STOCK EXCHANGES

Several stock exchanges were in the process of development in the mid-1990s, and by early 1995 the number of sharcholders had reached 38m. By 1995 a total of 15 futures exchanges were in operation, dealing in various commodities, building materials and currencies. The number of companies listed on the Shanghai and Shenzhen Stock Exchanges rose from 323 in 1995 to 1,287 in 2003. In August 1997, in response to unruly conditions, the Government ordered the China Securities Regulatory Commission (see below) to assume direct control of the Shanghai and Shenzhen exchanges.

Stock Exchange Executive Council (SEEC): Beijing; tel. (10) 64935210; f. 1989 to oversee the development of financial markets in China; mems comprise leading non-bank financial institutions authorized to handle securities; Vice-Pres. WANG BOMING.

Securities Association of China (SAC): Olympic Hotel, 52 Baishiqiao Lu, Beijing 100081; tel. (10) 68316688; fax (10) 68318390; f. 1991; non-governmental organization comprising 122 mems (stock exchanges and securities cos) and 35 individual mems; Pres. ZHUANG XINYI.

Beijing Securities Exchange: 5 Anding Lu, Chao Yang Qu, Beijing 100029; tel. (10) 64939366; fax (10) 64936233.

Shanghai Stock Exchange: 528 Pudong Nan Lu, Shanghai 200120; tel. (21) 68808888; fax (21) 68807813; e-mail webmaster@ sse.com.cn; internet www.sse.com.cn; f. 1990; Chair. GENG LIANG; Pres. ZHU CONGJIU.

Shenzhen Stock Exchange: 5045 Shennan Dong Lu, Shenzhen, Guangdong 518010; tel. (755) 20833333; fax (755) 2083117; internet www.sse.org.cn; f. 1991; Chair. ZHENG KELIN; Pres. GUI MINJIE.

Regulatory Authorities

Operations are regulated by the State Council Securities Policy Committee and by the following:

China Securities Regulatory Commission (CSRC): Bldg 3, Area 3, Fangqunyuan, Fangzhuang, Beijing 100078; tel. (10) 67617343; fax (10) 67653117; e-mail csrcweb@publicf.bta.net.cn; internet www.csrc.gov.cn; f. 1993; Chair. SHANG FULIN.

INSURANCE

A new Insurance Law, formulated to standardize activities and to strengthen the supervision and administration of the industry, took effect in October 1995. Changes included the separation of life insurance and property insurance businesses. By the end of 2003 the number of insurance institutions operating in China totalled 62, of which 15 were joint-venture corporations and 21 were foreign-funded insurance branches. Total premiums rose from 44,000m. yuan in 1994 to some 388,000m. yuan in 2003. Of the latter figure, property insurance accounted for 86,900m. yuan and life insurance for 301,100m. yuan.

AXA-Minmetals Assurance Co: 12/F China Merchants Tower, 161 Jia Zui Dong Lu, Pudong, Shanghai 200120; tel. (21) 58792288; fax (21) 58792299; f. 1999; joint venture by Groupe AXA (France) and China Minmetals Group; CEO ALLAN LAM.

China Insurance (Holdings) Co Ltd: 28 Xuanwumen Xi Lu, Xuanwu Qu, Beijing; tel. (10) 63600601; fax (10) 63600605; internet www.chinainsurance.com; fmrly China Insurance Co, renamed Aug. 2002; f. 1931; cargo, hull, freight, fire, life, personal accident, industrial injury, motor insurance, reinsurance, etc.; Chair. YANG CHAO.

China Insurance Group: 410 Fu Cheng Men Nei Dajie, Beijing; tel. (10) 66016688; fax (10) 66011869; f. 1996; fmrly People's Insurance Co of China (PICC), f. 1949; hull, marine cargo, aviation, motor, life, fire, accident, liability and reinsurance, etc.; 300m. policyholders (1996); Chair. and Pres. MA YONGWEI.

China Life Insurance Co: 16 Chaowai Dajie, Chaoyang Qu, Beijing 10020; tel. (10) 85659999; internet www.chinalife.com.cn; f. 1999; formed from People's Insurance (Life) Co, division of fmr People's Insurance Co of China—PICC; restructured into a parent company and a shareholding company Aug. 2003; initial public offering Dec. 2003; Chair. and Pres. WANG XIANZHANG.

China Pacific Insurance Co Ltd (CPIC): 1226 Zhongshan Lu (Bei 1), Shanghai ; tel. (21) 65367846; internet www.cpic.com.cn; internet www.cpicbj.com.cn/en; f. 1991; joint-stock co; Chair. WANG GUOLIANG; Pres. HUO LIANHONG.

China Ping An Insurance Co: Ping An Bldg, Bagua San Lu, Bagualing, Shenzhen 518029; tel. (755) 82262888; fax (755) 82431019; internet www.pa18.com; f. 1988; Chair. and CEO MA MINGZHE.

Hua Tai Insurance Co of China Ltd: Corporate Square, 35 Jinrong Lu, Zicheng Qu, Beijing; tel. (10) 66218833; fax (10) 88091750; internet www.ehuatai.com; f. 1996 by 63 industrial cos; Pres. LIU XUE.

Pacific-Aetna Life Insurance Co: 30/F New Shanghai International Tower, Pudong Nan Lu, Shanghai 200120; tel. (21) 68863183; fax (21) 68862920; f. 1998 by CPIC and Aetna Life Insurance Co; China's first Sino-US insurance co.

Tai Ping Insurance Co Ltd: 410 Fu Cheng Men Nei Dajie, Beijing 100034; tel. (10) 66016688; fax (10) 66011869; marine freight, hull, cargo, fire, personal accident, industrial injury, motor insurance, reinsurance, etc.; Pres. SUN XIYUE.

Taikang Life Insurance Co Ltd: Zhongyi Bldg, 6 Xizhimenwai Lu, Xicheng Qu, Beijing 100044; tel. (10) 68330586; f. 1996; Chair. CHEN DONGSHENG.

Joint-stock companies include the Xinhua (New China) Life Insurance Co Ltd (Gen. Man. Sun Bing).

Regulatory Authority

China Insurance Regulatory Commission (CIRC): 410 Fu Cheng Men Nei Dajie, Beijing 100034; tel. (10) 66016688; fax (10) 66018871; internet www.circ.gov.cn; f. 1998; under direct authority of the State Council; Chair. WU DINGFU.

Trade and Industry

GOVERNMENT AGENCIES

Chinese General Association of Light Industry: 22B Fuwai Dajie, Beijing 100833; tel. (10) 68396329; e-mail webmaster@clii .com.cn; internet www.clii.com.cn; under supervision of State Council; Chair. CHEN SHINENG.

Chinese General Association of Textile Industry: 12 Dong Chang An Jie, Beijing 100742; tel. (10) 65129545; under supervision of State Council; Chair. SHI WANPENG.

Ministry of Foreign Trade and Economic Co-operation: see under Ministries.

State Administration for Industry and Commerce: 8 San Li He Dong Lu, Xicheng Qu, Beijing 100820; tel. (10) 68010463; fax (10) 68020848; responsible for market supervision and administrative execution of industrial and commercial laws; functions under the direct supervision of the State Council; Dir WANG ZHONGFU.

State-owned Assets Supervision and Administration Commission: Beijing; e-mail iecc@sasac.gov.cn ; internet www.sasac.gov .cn; f. 2003; supervision and administration of state-owned assets, regulation of ownership transfers of state-owned enterprises; Chair. LI RONGRONG.

Takeover Office for Military, Armed Police, Government and Judiciary Businesses: Beijing; f. 1998 to assume control of enterprises formerly operated by the People's Liberation Army.

CHAMBERS OF COMMERCE

All-China Federation of Industry and Commerce: 93 Beiheyan Dajie, Beijing 100006; tel. (10) 65136677; fax (10) 65122631; f. 1953; promotes overseas trade relations; Chair. HUANG MENGFU.

China Council for the Promotion of International Trade (CCPIT)—China Chamber of International Commerce (CCOIC): 1 Fuxingmenwai Lu, Beijing 100860; tel. (10) 68020229; fax (10) 68011370; e-mail info@ccpit.org; internet www.ccpit.org; Chair. WAN JIFEI.

TRADE AND INDUSTRIAL ORGANIZATIONS

Anshan Iron and Steel Co: Huangang Lu, Tiexi Qu, Anshan 114021; tel. and fax (412) 6723090; e-mail info@ansteel.com.cn; internet www.ansteel.com.cn; Pres. LIU JIE.

Baotou Iron and Steel Co: Gangtie Dajie, Kundulun Qu, Baotou 014010, Inner Mongolia; tel. (472) 2125619; fax (472) 2183708; Pres. and Chair. LIN DONGLU.

Beijing Urban Construction Group Co Ltd: 62 Xueyuannan Lu, Haidian, Beijing 100081; tel. (10) 62255511; fax (10) 62256027; e-mail cjp@mail.bucg.com; internet www.bucg.com; construction of civil and industrial buildings and infrastructure.

China Aviation Industry Corporation II: 67 Jiao Nan Street, Beijing 100712; tel. (10) 64094013; fax (10) 64032109; e-mail avic@ public3.bta.net.cn; Pres. ZHANG HONGBIAO.

China Aviation Supplies Corpn: 155 Xi Dongsi Jie, Beijing 100013; tel. (10) 64012233; fax (10) 64016392; f. 1980; Pres. LI HAI.

China Civil Engineering Construction Corpn (CCECC): 4 Beifeng Wo, Haidian Qu, Beijing 100038; tel. (10) 63263392; fax (10) 63263864; e-mail zongban@ccecc.com.cn; f. 1953; general contracting, provision of technical and labour services, consulting and design, etc.; Pres. DING YUANCHEN.

China Construction International Inc: 9 Sanlihe Lu, Haidian Qu, Beijing; tel. (10) 68394086; fax (10) 68394097; Pres. FU RENZHANG.

China Electronics Corpn: 27 Wanshou Lu, Haidian Qu, Beijing 100846; tel. (10) 68218529; fax (10) 68213745; e-mail cec@public.gb .com.cn; internet www.cec.com.cn; Pres. YANG XIAOTANG.

China Garment Industry Corpn: 9A Taiyanggong Beisanhuandong Lu, Chao Yang Qu, Beijing 100028; tel. (10) 64216660; fax (10) 64239134; Pres. DONG BINGGEN.

China General Technology (Group) Holding Ltd: f. 1998; through merger of China National Technical Import and Export

Corpn, China National Machinery Import and Export Corpn, China National Instruments Import and Export Corpn and China National Corpn for Overseas Economic Co-operation; total assets 16,000m. yuan; Chair. and Pres. CHEN WEIGEN.

China Gold Co: 1 Bei Jie, Qingnianhu, Andingmenwai, Beijing; tel. (10) 64214831; Pres. CHENG FUMIN.

China Great Wall Computer Group: 38A Xueyuan Lu, Haidian Qu, Beijing 100083; tel. (10) 68342714; fax (10) 62011240; internet www.gwssi.com.cn; f. 1988; Chair. CHEN ZHAOXIONG; Pres. LU MING.

China Great Wall Industry Corpn: Hangtian Changcheng Bldg, 30 Haidian Nanlu, Haidian Qu, Beijing 100080; tel. (10) 68748737; fax (10) 68748865; e-mail cgwic@cgwic.com; internet www.cgwic.com.cn; registered cap. 200m. yuan; Pres. ZHANG XINXIA.

China International Book Trading Corpn: see under Publishers.

China International Contractors Association: 28 Donghouxiang, Andingmenwai, Beijing 100710; tel. (10) 64211159; fax (10) 64213959; Chair. LI RONGMIN.

China International Futures Co Ltd (CIFCO): 20/F, 1050 Huaqiang Bei Rd, Shenzhen 518031; tel. (755) 83281693; fax (755) 83281807; e-mail lizongping@cifco.net.cn; internet www.szcifco.com; Chair. TIAN YUAN.

China International Telecommunications Construction Corpn (CITCC): 22 Yuyou Lane, Xicheng Qu, Beijing 100035; tel. (10) 66012244; fax (10) 66024103; Pres. QI FUSHENG.

China International Water and Electric Corpn: 3 Liupukang Yiqu Zhongjie, Xicheng Qu, Beijing 100011; tel. (10) 64015511; fax (10) 64014075; e-mail cwe@mx.cei.go.cn; f. 1956 as China Water and Electric International Corpn, name changed 1983; imports and exports equipment for projects in the field of water and electrical engineering; undertakes such projects; provides technical and labour services; Pres. WANG SHUOHAO.

China Iron and Steel Industry and Trade Group Corpn: 17B Xichangan Jie, Beijing 100031; tel. (10) 66067733; fax (10) 66078450; e-mail support@sinosteel.com.cn; internet www.sinosteel.com; f. 1999 by merger of China National Metallurgical Import and Export Corpn, China Metallurgical Raw Materials Corpn and China Metallurgical Steel Products Processing Corpn; Pres. BAI BAOHUA.

China National Aerotechnology Import and Export Corpn: 5 Liangguochang, Dongcheng Qu, Beijing 100010; tel. (10) 64017722; fax (10) 64015381; f. 1952; exports signal flares, electric detonators, tachometers, parachutes, general purpose aircraft, etc.; Pres. YANG CHUNSHU; Gen. Man. LIU GUOMIN.

China National Animal Breeding Stock Import and Export Corpn (CABS): 10 Yangyi Hutong Jia, Dongdan, Beijing 100005; tel. (10) 65131107; fax (10) 65128694; sole agency for import and export of stud animals including cattle, sheep, goats, swine, horses, donkeys, camels, rabbits, poultry, etc., as well as pasture and turf grass seeds, feed additives, medicines, etc.; Pres. YANG CHENGSHAN.

China National Arts and Crafts Import and Export Corpn: Arts and Crafts Bldg, 103 Jixiangli, Chao Yang Men Wai, Chao Yang Qu, Beijing 100020; tel. (10) 65931075; fax (10) 65931036; e-mail po@mbox.cnart.com.cn; internet www.cnart-group.com; deals in jewellery, ceramics, handicrafts, embroidery, pottery, wicker, bamboo, etc.; Pres. CHEN KUN.

China National Automotive Industry Corpn (CNAIC): 46 Fucheng Lu, Haidian Qu, Beijing 100036; tel. (10) 88123968; fax (10) 68125556; Pres. CHEN XULIN.

China National Automotive Industry Import and Export Corpn (CAIEC): 5 Beisihuan Xi Lu, Beijing 100083; tel. (10) 62310650; fax (10) 62310688; e-mail info@chinacaiec.com; internet www.chinacaiec.com; sales US $540m. (1995); Pres. ZHANG FUSHENG; 1,100 employees.

China National Cereals, Oils and Foodstuffs Import and Export Corpn (COFCO): 7th–13th Floors, Tower A, COFCO Plaza, Jian Guo Men Nei Dajie, Beijing 100005; tel. (10) 65268888; fax (10) 65278612; e-mail minnie@cofco.com.cn; internet www.cofco.com.cn; f. 1952; imports, exports and processes grains, oils, foodstuffs, etc.; also hotel management and property development; sales US $12,099.2m. (1999/2000); Chair. ZHOU MINGCHEN; Pres. LIU FUCHUN.

China National Chartering Corpn (SINOCHART): Rm 1601/1602, 1607/1608, Jiu Ling Bldg, 21 Xisanhuan Bei Lu, Beijing 100081; tel. (10) 68405601; fax (10) 68405628; e-mail sinochrt@public.intercom.co.cn; f. 1950; functions under Ministry of Foreign Trade and Economic Co-operation; subsidiary of SINOTRANS (see below); arranges chartering of ships, reservation of space, managing and operating chartered vessels; Pres. LIU SHUNLONG; Gen. Man. ZHANG JIANWEI.

China National Chemical Construction Corpn: Bldg No. 15, Songu, Anzhenxili, Chao Yang Qu, Beijing 100029; tel. (10) 64429966; fax (10) 64419698; e-mail cnccc@cnccc.com.cn; internet www.cnccc.com.cn; registered cap. 50m.; Pres. CHEN LIHUA.

China National Chemicals Import and Export Corporation (SINOCHEM): SINOCHEM Tower, A2 Fuxingmenwai Dajie, Beijing 100045; tel. (10) 68568888; fax (10) 68568890; internet www.sinochem.com; f. 1950; import and export, domestic trade and entrepôt trade of oil, fertilizer, rubber, plastics and chemicals; it has made notable development in other areas like industry, finance, insurance, transportation and warehousing; sales US $15,066.2m. (1999/2000); Pres. LIU DESHU.

China National Coal Industry Import and Export Corpn (CNCIEC): 88B Andingmenwai, Dongcheng Qu, Beijing 100011; tel. (10) 64287188; fax (10) 64287166; e-mail cnciec@chinacoal.com; internet www.chinacoal.com; f. 1982; sales US $800m. (1992); imports and exports coal and tech. equipment for coal industry, joint coal development and compensation trade; Chair. and Pres. WANG CHANGCHUN.

China National Coal Mine Corpn: 21 Bei Jie, Heipingli, Beijing 100013; tel. (10) 64217766; Pres. WANG SENHAO.

China National Complete Plant Import and Export Corpn (Group): 9 Xi Bin He Lu, An Ding Men, Beijing; tel. (10) 64253388; fax (10) 64211382; Chair. HU ZHAOQING; Pres. TANG JIANGUO.

China National Electronics Import and Export Corpn: 8th Floor, Electronics Bldg, 23A Fuxing Lu, Beijing 100036; tel. (10) 68219550; fax (10) 68212352; e-mail ceiec@ceiec.com.cn; internet www.ceiec.com.cn; imports and exports electronics equipment, light industrial products, ferrous and non-ferrous metals; advertising; consultancy; Chair. and Pres. QIAN BENYUAN.

China National Export Bases Development Corpn: Bldg 16–17, District 3, Fang Xing Yuan, Fang Zhuang Xiaoqu, Fengtai Qu, Beijing 100078; tel. (10) 67628899; fax (10) 67628803; Pres. XUE ZHAO.

China National Foreign Trade Transportation Corpn (Group) (SINOTRANS): Sinotrans Plaza, A43, Xizhimen Beidajie, Beijing 100044; tel. (10) 62295900; fax (10) 62295901; e-mail office@sinotrans.com; internet www.sinotrans.com; f. 1950; agents for Ministry's import and export corpns; arranges customs clearance, deliveries, forwarding and insurance for sea, land and air transportation; registered cap. 150m. yuan; Pres. ZHANG JIANWEI; Chair. MENG XIANGANG.

China National Import and Export Commodities Inspection Corpn: 15 Fanghuadi Xi Jie, Chao Yang Qu, Beijing 100020; tel. (10) 65013951; fax (10) 65004625; internet www.ccic.com; inspects, tests and surveys import and export commodities for overseas trade, transport, insurance and manufacturing firms; Pres. ZHOU WENHUI.

China National Instruments Import and Export Corpn (Instrimpex): Instrimpex Bldg, 6 Xizhimenwai Jie, Beijing 100044; tel. (10) 68330618; fax (10) 68330528; e-mail zcb@instrimpex.com.cn; internet www.instrimpex.com.cn; f. 1955; imports and exports; technical service, real estate, manufacturing, information service, etc.; Pres. ZHANG RUEN.

China National Light Industrial Products Import and Export Corpn: 910, 9th Section, Jin Song, Chao Yang Qu, Beijing 100021; tel. (10) 67766688; fax (10) 67747246; e-mail info@chinalight.com.cn; internet www.chinalight.com.cn; imports and exports household electrical appliances, audio equipment, photographic equipment, films, paper goods, building materials, bicycles, sewing machines, enamelware, glassware, stainless steel goods, footwear, leather goods, watches and clocks, cosmetics, stationery, sporting goods, etc.; Pres. XU LIEJUN.

China National Machine Tool Corpn: 19 Fang Jia Xiaoxiang, An Nei, Beijing 100007; tel. (10) 64033767; fax (10) 64015657; f. 1979; imports and exports machine tools and tool products, components and equipment; supplies apparatus for machine-building industry; Pres. QUAN YILU.

China National Machinery and Equipment Import and Export Corpn (Group): 6 Xisanhuannan Lu, Liuliqiao, Beijing 100073; tel. (10) 63271392; fax (10) 63261865; f. 1978; imports and exports machine tools, all kinds of machinery, automobiles, hoisting and transport equipment, electric motors, photographic equipment, etc.; Pres. LI SHUZHI.

China National Medicine and Health Products Import and Export Corpn: Meheco Plaza, 18 Guangming Zhong Jie, Chongwen Qu, Beijing 100061; tel. (10) 67116688; fax (10) 67021579; e-mail webmaster@meheco.com.cn; internet www.meheco.com.cn; Pres. LIU GUOSHENG.

China National Metals and Minerals Import and Export Corpn: Bldg 15, Block 4, Anhuili, Chao Yang Qu, Beijing 100101; tel. (10) 64916666; fax (10) 64916421; e-mail support@minmetals

.com.cn; internet www.minmetals.com.cn; f. 1950; principal imports and exports include steel, antimony, tungsten concentrates and ferrotungsten, zinc ingots, tin, mercury, pig-iron, cement, etc.; Pres. Miao Gengshu.

China National Native Produce and Animal By-Products Import and Export Corpn (TUHSU): Sanli Bldg, 208 Andingmenwai Jie, Beijing 100011; tel. (10) 64248899; fax (10) 64204099; e-mail info@china-tuhsu.com; internet www.china-tuhsu.com; f. 1949; imports and exports include tea, coffee, cocoa, fibres, etc.; 23 subsidiary enterprises; 9 tea brs; 23 overseas subsidiaries; Pres. Pan Deyuan.

China National Non-Ferrous Metals Import and Export Corpn (CNIEC): 12B Fuxing Lu, Beijing 100814; tel. (10) 63975588; fax (10) 63964424; Chair. Wu Jianchang; Pres. Xiao Junqing.

China National Nuclear Corpn: 1 Nansanxiang, Sanlihe, Beijing; tel. (10) 68512211; fax (10) 68533989; internet www.cnnc.com.cn; Pres. Kang Rixin.

China National Offshore Oil Corpn (CNOOC): PO Box 4705, No. 6 Dongzhimenwai, Xiaojie, Beijing 100027; tel. (10) 84521010; fax (10) 84521044; e-mail webmaster@cnooc.com.cn; internet www .cnooc.com.cn; f. 1982; operates offshore exploration and production of petroleum; sales US $1,341.5m. (1999/2000); Pres. Fu Chengyu.

China National Oil Development Corpn: Liupukang, Beijing 100006; tel. (10) 6444313; Pres. Cheng Shouli.

China National Packaging Import and Export Corpn: Xinfu Bldg B, 3 Dong San Huan Bei Lu, Chao Yang Qu, Beijing 100027; tel. (10) 64611166; fax (10) 64616437; e-mail info@chinapack.net; internet www.chinapack.net; handles import and export of packaging materials, containers, machines and tools; contracts for the processing and converting of packaging machines and materials supplied by foreign customers; registered cap. US $30m.; Pres. Zheng Chongxiang.

China National Petroleum Corpn (CNPC) (PetroChina): 6 Liupukang Jie, Xicheng Qu, Beijing 100724; tel. (10) 62094538; fax (10) 62094806; e-mail admin@hq.cnpc.com.cn; internet www.cnpc.com .cn; restructured mid-1998; responsible for petroleum extraction and refining in northern and western China, and for setting retail prices of petroleum products; Pres. Chen Geng.

China National Publications Import and Export Corpn: 16 Gongrentiyuguandong Lu, Chao Yang Qu, Beijing; tel. (10) 65066688; fax (10) 65063101; e-mail cnpiec@cnpiec.com.cn; internet www.cnpiec.com.cn; imports and exports books, newspapers and periodicals, records, CD-ROMs, etc.; Pres. Jiao Guoying.

China National Publishing Industry Trading Corpn: POB 782, 504 An Hua Li, Andingmenwai, Beijing 100011; tel. (10) 64215031; fax (10) 64214540; f. 1981; imports and exports publications, printing equipment technology; holds book fairs abroad; undertakes joint publication; Pres. Wu Jiangjiang.

China National Seed Group Corpn: 16A Xibahe, Chao Yang Qu, Beijing 100028; tel. (10) 64201817; fax (10) 64201820; imports and exports crop seeds, including cereals, cotton, oil-bearing crops, teas, flowers and vegetables; seed production for foreign seed companies etc.; Pres. He Zhonghua.

China National Silk Import and Export Corpn: 105 Bei He Yan Jie, Dongcheng Qu, Beijing 100006; tel. (10) 65123338; fax (10) 65125125; e-mail cnsiec@public.bta.net.cn; internet www.chinasilk .com; Pres. Chen Yiqing.

China National Star Petroleum Corpn: 1 Bei Si Huan Xi Lu, Beijing; e-mail jf@mail.cnspc.com.cn; internet www.cnspc.com.cn; f. 1997; petroleum and gas exploration, development and production; Pres. Zhu Jiazhen.

China National Technical Import and Export Corpn: Jiuling Bldg, 21 Xisanhuan Beilu, Beijing 100081; tel. (10) 68404000; fax (10) 68414877; e-mail info@cntic.com.cn; internet www.cntic.com.cn; f. 1952; imports all kinds of complete plant and equipment, acquires modern technology and expertise from abroad, undertakes co-production and jt ventures, and technical consultation and updating of existing enterprises; registered cap. 200m.; Pres. Wang Huiheng.

China National Textiles Import and Export Corpn: 82 Donganmen Jie, Beijing 100747; tel. (10) 65123844; fax (10) 65124711; e-mail webmaster@chinatex.com; internet www.chinatex-group .com; imports synthetic fibres, raw cotton, wool, garment accessories, etc.; exports cotton yarn, cotton fabric, knitwear, woven garments, etc.; Pres. Zhao Boya.

China National Tobacco Import and Export Corpn: 11 Hufang Lu, Xuanwu Qu, Beijing 100052; tel. (10) 63533399; fax (10) 63015331; Pres. Xun Xinghua.

China National United Oil Corpn: 57 Wangfujing Jie, Dongcheng Qu, Beijing 100006; tel. (10) 65223828; fax (10) 65223817; Chair. Zhang Jiaren; Pres. Zhu Yaobin.

China North Industries Group: 46 Sanlihe Lu, Beijing 100821; tel. (10) 68594210; fax (10) 68594232; internet www.corincogroup .com.cn; exports vehicles and mechanical products, light industrial products, chemical products, opto-electronic products, building materials, military products, etc.; Pres. Ma Zhigeng.

China Nuclear Energy Industry Corpn (CNEIC): 1A Yuetan Bei Jie, Xicheng Qu, Beijing 100037; tel. (10) 68013395; fax (10) 68512393; internet www.cnnc.com.cn; exports air filters, vacuum valves, dosimeters, radioactive detection elements and optical instruments; Pres. Zhang Zhifeng.

China Petroleum and Chemical Corporation (SINOPEC): No. A6 Huixin Dong Jie, Chao Yang Qu, Beijing 100029; tel. (10) 64225533; fax (10) 64212429; e-mail webmaster@sinopec.com.cn; internet www.sinopec.com.cn; f. 2000; exploration, development, production, refining, transport and marketing of petroleum and natural gas, production and sales of petrochemicals, chemical fibres, chemical fertilizers, and other chemicals, research and development and application of technology and information; sales US $29m. (1999/2000); Pres. Wang Jiming; Chair. of Bd Chen Tonghai.

> **SINOPEC Shanghai Petrochemical Co Ltd:** Wei Er Lu, Jinshanwei, Shanghai 200540; tel. (21) 57943143; fax (21) 57940050; e-mail spc@spc.com.cn; internet www.spc.com.cn; processing of crude petroleum into synthetic fibres, resins and plastics, and other petroleum products; cap. and res 12,294.8m. (1997), sales US $1,695.6m. (1999/2000); Chair. Lu Yiping.

> **SINOPEC Yizheng Chemical Fibre Co Ltd:** Zhenzhou, Yizheng, Jiangsu 211900; tel. (514) 3232235; fax (514) 3233880; internet www.sinopec.com.cn; f. 1993; chemical products; China's largest manufacturer of chemical fibre and world's fifth largest polyester maker (2001); revenue US $1,088.9m. (2000); Dir and Gen. Man. Xu Zhengning.

> **SINOPEC Zhenhai Refining and Chemical Co Ltd:** Zhenhai Qu, Ningbo, Zhejiang 315207; tel. (574) 6456425; fax (574) 6456155; internet www.zrcc.com.cn; f. 1974; petroleum refining and production of related chemicals; sales US $1,330.6m. (1999/2000); Chair. Sun Weijun.

China Road and Bridge Corpn: Zhonglu Bldg, 88C, An Ding Men Wai Dajie, Beijing 100011; tel. (10) 64285616; fax (10) 64285686; e-mail crbc@crbc.com; internet www.crbc.com; overseas and domestic building of highways, urban roads, bridges, tunnels, industrial and residential buildings, airport runways and parking areas; contracts to do surveying, designing, pipe-laying, water supply and sewerage, building, etc., and/or to provide technical or labour services; Chair. Ma Guodong; Pres. Zhou Jichang.

China Shipbuilding Trading Corpn Ltd: 56 Zhongguancun Nan Dajie, Beijing 100044; tel. (10) 88026037; fax (10) 88026000; e-mail webmaster@cstc.com.cn; internet www.chinaships.com; Pres. Li Zhushi.

China State Construction Engineering Corpn: Baiwanzhuang, Xicheng Qu, Beijing 100835; tel. (10) 68347766; fax (10) 68314326; e-mail cscec-us@worldnet.att.net; internet www.cscec.com; sales US $4,726.8m. (1999/2000); Pres. Sun Wenjie.

China State Shipbuilding Corpn: 5 Yuetan Beijie, Beijing; tel. (10) 68030208; fax (10) 68031579; Pres. Chen Xiaojin; Gen. Man. Xu Penghang.

China Tea Import and Export Corpn: Zhongtuchu Bldg, 208 Andingmenwai Jie, Beijing 100011; tel. (10) 64204127; fax (10) 64204101; e-mail info@teachina.com; internet www.chinatea.com .cn; Pres. Tong Jinhan.

China Xinshidai (New Era) Corpn: 40 Xie Zuo Hu Tong, Dongcheng Qu, Beijing 100007; tel. (10) 64017384; fax (10) 64032935; Pres. Qin Zhongxing.

Chinese General Co of Astronautics Industry (State Aerospace Bureau): 8 Fucheng Lu, Haidian Qu, Beijing 100712; tel. (10) 68586047; fax (10) 68370080; Pres. Liu Jiyuan.

Daqing Petroleum Administration Bureau: Sartu Qu, Daqing, Heilongjiang; tel. (459) 814649; fax (459) 322845; Gen. Man. Wang Zhiwu.

Handan Iron and Steel Co Ltd: Handan; e-mail hdgt@mail.hgjt .com.cn; internet www.hdgt.com.cn; f. 1958; Chair. Liu Rujun.

Ma'anshan Iron and Steel Co: 8 Hongqibei Lu, Maanshan 243003, Anhui; tel. (555) 2883492; fax (555) 2324350; Chair. Hang Yongyi; Pres. Li Zongbi.

Shanghai Baosteel Group Corpn: Baosteel Tower, 370 Pudian Lu, Pudong New District, Shanghai; tel. (21) 58358888; fax (21) 68404832; e-mail webman@baosteel.com; internet www.bstl.sh.cn; f. 1998; incorporating Baoshan Iron and Steel Corpn, and absorption of Shanghai Metallurgical Holding Group Corpn, and Shanghai Meishan Group Corpn Ltd; produces steel and steel products; sales US $14,548.0m. (2003); Pres. Ai Baojun; Chair. Xie Qihua.

Shanghai Foreign Trade Corpn: 27 Zhongshan Dong Yi Lu, Shanghai 200002; tel. (21) 63217350; fax (21) 63290044; f. 1988; handles import-export trade, foreign trade transportation, chartering, export commodity packaging, storage and advertising for Shanghai municipality; Gen. Man. WANG MEIJUN.

Shanghai International Trust Trading Corpn: 201 Zhaojiabang Lu, Shanghai 200032; tel. (21) 64033866; fax (21) 64034722; f. 1979; present name adopted 1988; handles import and export business, international mail orders, processing, assembling, compensation, trade, etc.

Shougang Group: Shijingshan, Beijing 100041; tel. (10) 88294166; fax (10) 88295578; e-mail sgjtglb01@shougang.com.cn; internet www.shougang.com.cn; f. 1919; produces iron and steel; sales US $4,396.8m. (1999/2000); Pres. ZHU JIMIN.

State Bureau of Non-Ferrous Metals Industry: 12B Fuxing Lu, Beijing 100814; tel. (10) 68514477; fax (10) 68515360; under supervision of State Economic and Trade Commission; Dir ZHANG WULE.

Wuhan Iron and Steel (Group) Co: Qingshan Qu, Wuhan, Hubei Province; tel. (27) 6892004; fax (27) 6862325; proposals for merger with two other steel producers in Hubei announced late 1997; Pres. LIU BENREN.

Xinxing Oil Co (XOC): Beijing; f. 1997; exploration, development and production of domestic and overseas petroleum and gas resources; Gen. Man. ZHU JIAZHEN.

Yuxi Cigarette Factory: Yujiang Lu, Yuxi, Yunnan Province; tel. and fax (877) 2052343; Gen. Man. CHU SHIJIAN.

Zhongjiang Group: Nanjing, Jiansu; f. 1998; multinational operation mainly in imports and exports, contract projects and real estate; group consists of 126 subsidiaries, incl. 25 foreign ventures.

UTILITIES

Regulatory Authority

State Electricity Regulatory Commission: 86 Xichangan Dajie, Beijing 100031; internet www.serc.gov.cn; f. 2003; Chair. CHAI SONG-YUE.

Electricity

Beijing Power Supply Co: Qianmen Xidajie, Beijing 100031; tel. (10) 63129201.

Central China Electric Power Group Co: 47 Xudong Lu, Wuchang, Wuhan 430077; tel. (27) 6813398.

Changsha Electric Power Bureau: 162 Jiefang Sicun, Changsha 410002; tel. (731) 5912121; fax (731) 5523240.

China Atomic Energy Authority: e-mail webmaster@caea.gov.cn; internet www.caea.gov.cn; Chair. ZHANG HUAZHU.

China Northwest Electric Power Group Co: 57 Shangde Lu, Xian 710004; tel. (29) 7275061; fax (29) 7212451; Chair. LIU HONG.

China Power Grid Development (CPG): f. to manage transmission and transformation lines for the Three Gorges hydroelectric scheme; Pres. ZHOU XIAOQIAN.

China Power Investment Corpn: e-mail engweb@cpicorp.com.cn; internet www.zdt.com.cn; f. 2002; from part of the constituent businesses of fmr State Power Corpn; parent company of China Power International; Pres. WANG BINGHUA.

China Southern Power Grid Co: f. 2002 from power grids in southern provinces of fmr State Power Corpn.

China Yangtze Electric Power Corpn: subsidiary of China Yangtze River Three Gorges Project Development Corpn; initial public offering on the Shanghai Stock Exchange Nov. 2003; Gen. Man. LI YONGAN.

China Yangtze Three Gorges Project Development Corpn: 1 Jianshe Dajie, Yichang, Hubei Province; tel. (717) 6762212; fax (717) 6731787; Pres. LI YONGAN.

Datang International Power Generation Co Ltd: 8/F, 482 Guanganmennei Dajie, Xuanwu Qu, Beijing 100053; internet www.dtpower.com; one of China's largest independent power producers; Chair. ZHAI RUOYU.

Dalian Power Supply Co: 102 Zhongshan Lu, Dalian 116001; tel. (411) 2637560; fax (411) 2634430; Chief Gen. Man. LIU ZONGXIANG.

Fujian Electric Industry Bureau: 4 Xingang Dao, Taijrang Qu, Fuzhou 350009; tel. and fax (591) 3268514; Dir WANG CHAOXU.

Gansu Bureau of Electric Power: 306 Xijin Dong Lu, Qilihe Qu, Lanzhou 730050; tel. (931) 2334311; fax (93) 2331042; Dir ZHANG MINGXI.

Guangdong Electric Power Bureau: 757 Dongfeng Dong Lu, Guangzhou 510600; tel. (20) 87767888; fax (20) 87770307.

Guangdong Shantou Electric Power Bureau: Jinsha Zhong Lu, Shantou 515041; tel. (754) 8257606.

Guangxi Electric Power Bureau: 6 Minzhu Lu, Nanning 530023; tel. (771) 2801123; fax (771) 2803414.

Guangzhou Electric Power Co: 9th Floor, Huale Bldg, 53 Huale Lu, Guangzhou 510060; tel. (20) 83821111; fax (20) 83808559.

Guodian Power Group: transfer of Jianbi power plant from fmr State Power Corpn completed Sept. 2003.

Hainan Electric Power Industry Bureau: 34 Haifu Dadao, Haikou 570203; tel. (898) 5334777; fax (898) 5333230.

Heilongjiang Electric Power Co: B12Fl High Tech Development Zone, Harbin 150001; tel. (451) 2308810; fax (451) 2525878; Chair. XUE YANG.

Huadian Power Intenational Corpn Ltd: 14 Jingsan Lu, Jinan, Shandong 250001; f. 1994; fmrly Shandong International Power Development, renamed as above 2003; Chair. HE GONG; Dir CHEN JIANHUA.

Huadong Electric Power Group Corpn: 201 Nanjing Dong Lu, Shanghai; tel. (21) 63290000; fax (21) 63290727; power supply.

Huaneng Power International: West Wing, Building C, Tianyin Mansion, 2C Fuxingmennan Lu, Xicheng, Beijing; tel. (10) 66491999; fax (10) 66491888; e-mail ir@hpi.com.cn; internet www.hpi.com.cn; f. 1998; transfer of generating assets from fmr State Power Corpn completed Sept. 2003; Chair. and Pres. LI XIAOPENG.

Huazhong Electric Power Group Corpn: Liyuan, Donghu, Wuhan, Hubei Province; tel. (27) 6813398; fax (27) 6813143; electrical engineering; Gen. Man. LIN KONGXING.

Inner Mongolia Electric Power Co: 28 Xilin Nan Lu, Huhehaose 010021; tel. (471) 6942222; fax (471) 6924863.

Jiangmen Electric Power Supply Bureau: 87 Gangkou Lu, Jiangmen 529030; tel. and fax (750) 3360133.

Jiangxi Electric Power Bureau: 13 Yongwai Zheng Jie, Nanchang 330006; tel. (791) 6224701; fax (791) 6224830.

National Grid Construction Co: established to oversee completion of the National Grid by 2009.

North China Grid Company Ltd: 482 Guanganmen Nei Dajie, Xuanwu Qu, Beijing 100053; tel. and fax (10) 63263377; Pres. ZHU GUOZHEN.

Northeast China Electric Power Group: 11 Shiyiwei Lu, Heping Qu, Shenyang 110003; tel. (24) 3114382; fax (24) 3872665.

Shandong Electric Power Group Corpn: 150 Jinger Lu, Jinan 250001; tel. (531) 6911919.

Shandong Rizhao Power Co Ltd: 1st Floor, Bldg 29, 30 Northern Section, Shunyu Xiaoqu, Jinan 250002; tel. (531) 2952462; fax (531) 2942561.

Shanghai Electric Power Co: 181 Nanjing Dong Lu, Huangpu Qu, Shanghai 200002; tel. (21) 63291010; fax (21) 63291440; e-mail smepc@smepc.com; internet www.smepc.com; total assets 61,946m. yuan, sales 28,183m. yuan (2003); Dir SHUAI JUNQING; 18,531 employees.

Shenzhen Power Supply Co: 2 Yanhe Xi Lu, Luohu Qu, Shenzhen 518000; tel. (755) 5561920.

Sichuan Electric Power Co: Room 1, Waishi Bldg, Dongfeng Lu, Chengdu 610061; tel. (28) 444321; fax (28) 6661888.

State Power Grid Corpn: No. 1 Lane 2, Baiguang Lu, Beijing 100761; tel. (10) 63416475; fax (10) 63548152; e-mail webmaster@sp.com.cn; internet www.cep.gov.cn; f. 1997; from holdings of Ministry of Electric Power; fmrly State Power Corpn of China; became a grid company following division of State Power Corpn into 11 independent companies (five generating companies, four construction companies and two transmission companies) in Dec. 2002; generating assets to be transferred to Huaneng Group, Huadian Group, Guodian Group, China Power Investment Corpn and Datang Group; Gen. Man. ZHAO XICHENG.

Tianjin Electric Power Industry Bureau: 29 Jinbu Dao, Hebei Qu, Tianjin 300010; tel. (22) 24406326; fax (22) 22346327.

Wenergy Co Ltd: 81 Wuhu Lu, Hefei 230001; tel. (551) 2626906; fax (551) 2648061.

Wuhan Power Supply Bureau: 981 Jiefang Dadao, Hankou, Wuhan 430013; tel. (27) 2426455; fax (27) 2415605.

Wuxi Power Supply Bureau: 8 Houxixi, Wuxi 214001; tel. (510) 2717678; fax (510) 2719182.

Xiamen Power Transformation and Transmission Engineering Co: 67 Wenyuan Lu, Xiamen 361004; tel. (592) 2046763.

Xian Power Supply Bureau: Huancheng Dong Lu, Xian 710032; tel. (29) 7271483.

Gas

Beijing Gas Co: 30 Dongsanhuan Zhong Lu, Beijing 100020; tel. (10) 65024131; fax (10) 65023815; Dir LIU BINGIUN.

Beijing Natural Gas Co: Bldg 5, Dixingju, An Ding Men Wai, Beijing 100011; tel. (10) 64262244.

Changchun Gas Co: 30 Tongzhi Jie, Changchun 130021; tel. (431) 8926479.

Changsha Gas Co: 18 Shoshan Lu, Changsha 410011; tel. (731) 4427246.

Qingdao Gas Co: 399A Renmin Lu, Qingdao 266032; tel. (532) 4851461; fax (532) 4858653.

Shanghai Gas Supply Co: 656 Xizang Zhong Lu, Shanghai 200003; tel. (21) 63222333; fax (21) 63528600; Gen. Man. LI LONG-LING.

Wuhan Gas Co: Qingnian Lu, Hankou, Wuhan 430015; tel. (27) 5866223.

Xiamen Gas Corpn: Ming Gong Bldg, Douxi Lukou, Hubin Nan Lu, Xiamen 361004; tel. (592) 2025937; fax (592) 2033290.

Water

Beijing District Heating Co: 1 Xidawang Lu, Hongmiao, Chao Yang Qu, Beijing 100026; tel. (10) 65060066; fax (10) 65678891.

Beijing Municipal Water Works Co: 19 Yangrou Hutong, Xicheng Qu, Beijing 100034; tel. (10) 66167744; fax (10) 66168028.

Changchun Water Co: 53 Dajing Lu, Changchun 130000; tel. (431) 8968366.

Chengdu Water Co: 16 Shierqiao Jie, Shudu Dadao, Chengdu 610072; tel. (28) 77663122; fax (28) 7776876.

The China Water Company: internet www.chinawater.com.hk; f. to develop investment opportunities for water projects.

Guangzhou Water Supply Co: 5 Huanshi Xi Lu, Guangzhou 510010; tel. (20) 81816951.

Haikou Water Co: 31 Datong Lu, Haikou 570001; tel. (898) 6774412.

Harbin Water Co: 49 Xi Shidao Jie, Daoli Qu, Harbin 150010; tel. (451) 4610522; fax (451) 4611726.

Jiangmen Water Co: 44 Jianshe Lu, Jiangmen 529000; tel. (750) 3300138; fax (750) 3353704.

Qinhuangdao Pacific Water Co: Hebei; Sino-US water supply project; f. 1998.

Shanghai Municipal Waterworks Co: 484 Jiangxi Zhong Lu, Shanghai 200002; tel. (21) 63215577; fax (21) 63231346; service provider for municipality of Shanghai.

Shenzhen Water Supply Group Co: Water Bldg, 1019 Shennan Zhong Lu, Shenzhen 518031; tel. (755) 2137836; fax (755) 2137888; e-mail webmaster@waterchina.com; internet www.waterchina.com.

Tianjin Waterworks Group: 54 Jianshe Lu, Heping Qu, Tianjin 300040; tel. (22) 3393887; fax (22) 3306720.

Xian Water Co: Huancheng Xi Lu, Xian 710082; tel. (29) 4244881.

Zhanjiang Water Co: 20 Renmin Dadaonan, Zhanjiang 524001; tel. (759) 2286394.

Zhongshan Water Supply Co: 23 Yinzhu Jie, Zhuyuan Lu, Zhongshan 528403; tel. (760) 8312969; fax (760) 6326429.

Zhuhai Water Supply General Corpn: Yuehai Zhong Lu, Gongbei, Zhuhai 519020; tel. (756) 8881160; fax (756) 8884405.

TRADE UNIONS

All-China Federation of Trade Unions (ACFTU): 10 Fu Xing Men Wai Jie, Beijing 100865; tel. (10) 68592114; fax (10) 68562030; e-mail webmaster@acftu.org.cn; internet www.acftu.org.cn; f. 1925; organized on an industrial basis; 15 affiliated national industrial unions, 30 affiliated local trade union councils; membership is voluntary; trade unionists enjoy extensive benefits; 103,996,000 mems (1995); Chair. WANG ZHAOGUO; First Sec. ZHANG JUNJIU.

Principal affiliated unions:

All-China Federation of Railway Workers' Unions: Chair. HUANG SICHUAN.

Architectural Workers' Trade Union: Sec. SONG ANRU.

China Self-Employed Workers' Association: Pres. REN ZHONGLIN.

Educational Workers' Trade Union: Chair. JIANG WENLIANG.

Light Industrial Workers' Trade Union: Chair. LI SHUYING.

Machinery Metallurgical Workers' Union: Chair. ZHANG CUNEN.

National Defence Workers' Union: Chair. GUAN HENGCAI.

Postal and Telecommunications Workers' Trade Union of China: Chair. LUO SHUZHEN.

Seamen's Trade Union of China: Chair. ZHANG SHIHUI.

Water Resources and Electric Power Workers' Trade Union: Chair. DONG YUNQI.

Workers' Autonomous Federation (WAF): f. 1989; aims to create new trade union movement in China, independent of the All-China Federation of Trade Unions.

Transport

RAILWAYS

Ministry of Railways: see under Ministries; controls all railways through regional divisions. The railway network has been extended to all provinces and regions except Tibet (Xizang), where construction is in progress. Total length in operation in December 2003 was 73,002 km, of which about 18,100 km were electrified. The major routes include Beijing–Guangzhou, Tianjin–Shanghai, Manzhouli–Vladivostok, Jiaozuo–Zhicheng and Lanzhou–Badou. In addition, special railways serve factories and mines. A new 2,536-km line from Beijing to Kowloon (Hong Kong) was completed in late 1995. Plans for a 1,450-km high-speed link between Beijing and Shanghai were announced in 1994, and construction was scheduled to begin by 2005. A high-speed link between Beijing and Guangzhou was also planned. China's first high-speed service, linking Guangzhou and Shenzhen, commenced in December 1994. A direct service between Shanghai and Hong Kong commenced in 1997.

An extensive programme to develop the rail network was announced in early 1998, which aimed to increase the total network to 68,000 km by the year 2000, and to more than 75,000 km by 2005. Railways were to be constructed along the Changjiang valley, starting at Sichuan, and along China's east coast, originating at Harbin. In December 1999 plans were announced for a railway to Kazakhstan. In June 2001 construction began on a new 1,118-km railway linking Tibet with the rest of China, to be completed after 10 years. A new magnetic-levitation ('maglev') railway linking Shanghai to Pudong International airport was built in co-operation with a German consortium in 2002. The first journey on this railway line was made at the beginnning of 2003. The 'maglev' train was expected to carry 10m. passengers a year by 2005.

City Underground Railways

Beijing Metro Corpn: 2 Beiheyan Lu, Xicheng, Beijing 100044; tel. (10) 68024566; f. 1969; total length 54 km, with 98 km of further lines to be built by the year 2010; Gen. Man. FENG SHUANGSHENG.

Guangzhou Metro: 204 Huanshi Lu, Guangzhou 510010; tel. (20) 6665287; fax (20) 6678232; opened June 1997; total length of 18.5 km, with a further 133 km planned; Gen. Man. CHEN QINGQUAN.

Shanghai Metro Corpn: 12 Heng Shan Lu, Shanghai 200031; tel. (21) 64312460; fax (21) 64339598; f. 1995; 65.8 km open, with at least a further 181.5 km under construction or planned; Pres. SHI LIAN.

Tianjin Metro: 97 Jiefangbei Lu, Heping, Tianjin 300041; tel. (22) 23395410; fax (22) 23396194; f. 1984; total planned network 154 km; Gen. Man. WANG YUJI.

Underground systems were under construction in Chongqing, Nanjing, and Shenzhen, and planned for Chengdu and Qingdao.

ROADS

At the end of 2003 China had 1,809,828 km of highways. Four major highways link Lhasa (Tibet) with Sichuan, Xinjiang, Qinghai Hu and Kathmandu (Nepal). A programme of expressway construction began in the mid-1980s. By 2003 there were 29,745 km of expressways, routes including the following: Shenyang–Dalian, Beijing–Tanggu, Shanghai–Jiading, Guangzhou–Foshan and Xian–Lintong. Expressway construction was to continue, linking all main cities and totalling 55,000 km by 2020. A new 123-km highway linking Shenzhen (near the border with Hong Kong) to Guangzhou opened in 1994. A 58-km road between Guangzhou and Zhongshan connects with Zhuhai, near the border with Macao. Construction of a bridge, linking Zhuhai with Macao, began in June 1998 and was completed in late 1999. A bridge connecting the mainland with Hong Kong was to be built, with feasibility studies being conducted in 2004.

INLAND WATERWAYS

At the end of 2003 there were some 123,964 km of navigable inland waterways in China. The main navigable rivers are the Changjiang

(Yangtze River), the Zhujiang (Pearl River), the Heilongjiang, the Grand Canal and the Xiangjiang. The Changjiang is navigable by vessels of 10,000 tons as far as Wuhan, more than 1,000 km from the coast. Vessels of 1,000 tons can continue to Chongqing upstream.

There were 5,142 river ports at the end of 1996. In 1997 there were some 5,100 companies involved in inland waterway shipping.

SHIPPING

China has a network of more than 2,000 ports, of which more than 130 are open to foreign vessels. In May 2001 plans were announced for the biggest container port in the world to be built on the Yangshan Islands, off shore from Shanghai. The main ports include Dalian, Qinhuangdao, Tianjin, Yantai, Qingdao, Rizhao, Lianyungang, Shanghai, Ningbo, Guangzhou and Zhanjiang. In 2003 the main coastal ports handled 2,011.3m. metric tons of cargo. In December 2003 China's merchant fleet comprised 3,376 ships, totalling 18.4m. grt.

Bureau of Water Transportation: Beijing; controls rivers and coastal traffic.

China International Marine Containers Group Co Ltd: 5/F, Finance Centre, Shekou, Shenzhen 518067; tel. (755) 26691130; fax (755) 26692707; internet www.cimc.com; f. 1980; container-manufacturing, supply and storage; revenue US $1,081.6m. (2000); Chair. and Dir LI JIANHONG.

China National Chartering Corpn (SINOCHART): see Trade and Industrial Organizations.

China Ocean Shipping (Group) Co (COSCO): 11th and 12th Floors, Ocean Plaza, 158 Fu Xing Men Nei, Xi Cheng Qu Chao Yang Qu, Beijing 100031; tel. (10) 66493388; fax (10) 66492288; internet www.cosco.com.cn; reorg. 1993, re-established 1997; head office transferred to Tianjin late 1997; br. offices: Shanghai, Guangzhou, Tianjin, Qingdao, Dalian; 200 subsidiaries (incl. China Ocean Shipping Agency—PENAVIC) and joint ventures in China and abroad, engaged in ship-repair, container-manufacturing, warehousing, insurance, etc.; merchant fleet of 600 vessels; 47 routes; Pres. WEI JIAFU.

China Shipping (Group) Co: Shanghai; e-mail cscas@cnshipping .com; internet www.cnshipping.com; f. 1997; Pres. LI KELIN.

China Shipping Container Lines Co Ltd: 5th Floor, Shipping Tower, 700 Dong Da Ming Lu, Shanghai 200080; tel. (21) 65966978; fax (21) 65966498; Chair. LI SHAODE.

China Shipping Development Co Ltd Tanker Co: 168 Yuanshen Lu, Pudong New Area, Shanghai 200120; tel. (21) 68757170; fax (21) 68757929.

Fujian Shipping Co: 151 Zhong Ping Lu, Fuzhou 350009; tel. (591) 3259900; fax (591) 3259716; e-mail fusco@pub2.fz.fj.cn; internet www.fusco-cn.com; f. 1950; transport of bulk cargo, crude petroleum products, container and related services; Gen. Man. LIU QIMIN.

Guangzhou Maritime Transport (Group) Co: 22 Shamian Nan Jie, Guangzhou 510131; tel. (20) 81861255; fax (20) 84428954.

CIVIL AVIATION

Air travel is expanding very rapidly. In 2002 a total of 141 civil airports were in operation. Chinese airlines carried a total of 87.6m. passengers in 2003. In October 2002 the Government merged the nine largest airlines into three groups, based in Guangzhou, Shanghai and Beijing. Air China incorporated China National Aviation Corpn (which also controls Zhejiang Airlines and 43% of Hong Kong's Dragonair) and China Southwest Airlines; China Eastern Airlines incorporated China Northwest Airlines and Yunnan Airlines; and China Southern Airlines incorporated Air Xinjiang and China Northern Airlines.

General Administration of Civil Aviation of China (CAAC): POB 644, 155 Dongsixi Jie, Beijing 100710; tel. (10) 64014104; fax (10) 64016918; f. 1949 as Civil Aviation Administration of China; restructured in 1988 as a purely supervisory agency, its operational functions being transferred to new, semi-autonomous airlines (see below); also China United Airlines (division of the Air Force) and China Capital Helicopter Service; domestic flights throughout China; external services are mostly operated by **Air China, China Eastern** and **China Southern Airlines**; Dir YANG YUANYUAN.

Air China: Beijing International Airport, POB 644, Beijing 100621; tel. (10) 64599068; fax (10) 64599064; e-mail webmaster@mail .airchina.com.cn; internet www.airchina.com.cn; international and domestic scheduled passenger and cargo services; Pres. WANG KAIYUAN.

Changan Airlines: 16/F, Jierui Bldg, 5 South Er Huan Rd, Xian, Shaanxi 710068; tel. (29) 8707412; fax (29) 8707911; e-mail liulei@ hnair.com; internet www.changanair.com; f. 1992; local passenger and cargo services; Pres. SHE YINING.

China Eastern Airlines: 2550 Hongqiao Rd, Hongqiao Airport, Shanghai 200335; tel. (21) 62686268; fax (21) 62686116; e-mail webmaster@cea.online.sh.cn; internet www.cea.online.sh.cn; f. 1987; domestic services; overseas destinations include USA, Europe, Japan, Sydney, Singapore, Seoul and Bangkok; Pres. LIU SHAOYONG.

China General Aviation Corpn: Wusu Airport, Taiyuan, Shanxi 030031; tel. (351) 7040600; fax (351) 7040094; f. 1989; 34 domestic routes; Pres. ZHANG CHANGJING.

China National Aviation Corpn: 23 Qianmen Dong Dajie, Dongcheng Qu, Beijing 100006; tel. (10) 5133060; fax (10) 5133060; controls Zhejiang Airlines and 43% of Hong Kong's Dragonair; merged with Air China Oct. 2002.

China Northern Airlines: 3-1 Xiaoheyan Lu, Dadong Qu, Shenyang, Liaoning 110043; tel. (24) 88294432; fax (24) 88294037; e-mail northern_air@163.net; internet www.cna.com.cn; f. 1990; scheduled flights to the Republic of Korea, Russia, Hong Kong, Macao and Japan; merged with China Southern Airlines Oct. 2002; Pres. JIANG LIANYING.

China Northwest Airlines: Laodong Nan Lu, Xian, Shaanxi 710082; tel. (29) 7298000; fax (29) 8624068; e-mail cnwadzz@pub .xa-online.sn.cn; internet www.cnwa.com; f. 1992; domestic services and flights to Macao, Singapore and Japan; merged with China Eastern Airlines in Oct. 2002; Pres. GAO JUNQUI.

China Southern Airlines: Baiyuan International Airport, Guangzhou, Guangdong 510406; tel. (20) 86128473; fax (20) 86658989; e-mail webmaster@cs-air.com; internet www.cs-air.com; f. 1991; merged with Zhong Yuan Airlines, 2000; domestic services; overseas destinations include Bangkok, Fukuoka, Hanoi, Ho Chi Minh City, Kuala Lumpur, Penang, Singapore, Manila, Vientiane, Jakarta and Surabaya; Chair. LIANG HUANFU; Pres. WANG CHANGSHUN.

China Southwest Airlines: Shuangliu Airport, Chengdu, Sichuan 610202; tel. (28) 5814466; fax (28) 5582630; e-mail szmaster@cswa .com; internet www.cswa.com; f. 1987; 70 domestic routes; international services to Singapore, Bangkok, Japan, the Republic of Korea and Kathmandu (Nepal); merged with Air China Oct. 2002; Pres. ZHOU ZHENGQUAN.

China Xinhua Airlines: 1 Jinsong Nan Lu, Chao Yang Qu, Beijing 100021; tel. (10) 67740116; fax (10) 67740126; e-mail infocxh@ homeway.com.cn; internet www.chinaxinhuaair.com; f. 1992; Pres. ZHAO ZHONGYING.

China Xinjiang Airlines: Diwopu International Airport, Urumqi 830016; tel. (991) 3801703; fax (991) 3711084; f. 1985; 30 domestic routes; international services to Kazakhstan, Russia, Pakistan, and Uzbekistan; merged with China Southern Airlines Oct. 2002; Pres. ZHANG RUIFU.

Hainan Airlines: Haihang Devt Bldg, 29 Haixiu Lu, Haikou, Hainan 570206; tel. (898) 6711524; fax (898) 6798976; e-mail webmaster@hnair.com; internet www.hnair.com; f. 1989; undergoing major expansion in 2001–02; 300 domestic services; international services to Korea; 14.8% owned by financier George Soros; Chair. FENG CHEN.

Shandong Airlines: Jinan International Airport, Jinan, Shandong 250107; tel. (531) 8734625; fax (531) 8734616; e-mail webmaster@ shandongair.com.cn; internet www.shandongair.com; f. 1994; domestic services; Pres. SUN DEHAN.

Shanghai Air Lines: 212 Jiangming Lu, Shanghai 200040; tel. (21) 62558888; fax (21) 62558885; e-mail liw@shanghai-air.com; internet www.shanghai-air.com; f. 1985; domestic services; also serves Phnom-Penh (Cambodia); Pres. ZHOU CHI.

Shenzhen Airlines: Lingtian Tian, Lingxiao Garden, Shenzhen Airport, Shenzhen, Guangdong 518128; tel. (755) 7771999; fax (755) 7777242; internet www.shenzhenair.com; f. 1993; domestic services; Pres. DUAN DAYANG.

Sichuan Airlines: Chengdu Shuangliu International Airport, Chengdu, Sichuan 610202; tel. (28) 5393001; fax (28) 5393888; e-mail scaloi@public.cd.sc.cn; internet www.hpis.com/sichuan/ sichuan.htm; f. 1986; domestic services; Pres. LAN XINGGUO.

Wuhan Air Lines: 435 Jianshe Dajie, Wuhan 430030; tel. (87) 63603888; fax (87) 83625693; e-mail wuhanair@public.wh.hb.cn; f. 1986; domestic services; Pres. CHENG YAOKUN.

Xiamen Airlines: Gaoqi International Airport, Xiamen, Fujian 361009; tel. (592) 5739888; fax (592) 5739777; internet www .xiamenair.com.cn; f. 1992; domestic services; also serves Bangkok (Thailand); Pres. WU RONGNAN.

Yunnan Airlines: Wujaba Airport, Kunming 650200; tel. (871) 7112999; fax (871) 7151509; internet www.chinayunnanair.com; f. 1992; 49 domestic services; also serves Bangkok, Singapore, and Vientiane (Laos); merged with China Eastern Airlines Oct. 2002; Pres. XUE XIAOMING.

Zhejiang Airlines: Jian Qiao Airport, 78 Shiqiao Lu, Hangzhou, Zhejiang 310021; tel. (571) 8082490; fax (571) 5173015; e-mail zjair@public.hz.zj.cn; internet www.zjair.com; f. 1990; domestic services; owned by China National Aviation Corpn; Pres. LUO QIANG.

Tourism

China has enormous potential for tourism, and the sector is developing rapidly. Attractions include dramatic scenery and places of historical interest such as the Temple of Heaven and the Forbidden City in Beijing, the Great Wall, the Ming Tombs, and also the terracotta warriors at Xian. Tibet (Xizang), with its monasteries and temples, has also been opened to tourists. Tours of China are organized for groups of visitors, and Western-style hotels have been built as joint ventures in many areas. In 2003 9,751 tourist hotels were in operation. A total of 91.7m. tourists visited China in 2003. In that year receipts from tourism totalled US $17,406m. The 2008 Olympic Games were to be held in Beijing.

China International Travel Service (CITS): 103 Fu Xing Men Nei Dajie, Beijing 100800; tel. (10) 66011122; fax (10) 66039331; e-mail mktng@cits.com.cn; internet www.cits.net; f. 1954; makes travel arrangements for foreign tourists; subsidiary overseas companies in 10 countries and regions; Pres. GAI ZHIXIN.

China National Tourism Administration (CNTA): 9A Jian Guo Men Nei Dajie, Beijing 100740; tel. (10) 65138866; fax (10) 65122096; Dir HE GUANGWEI.

Chinese People's Association for Friendship with Foreign Countries: 1 Tai Ji Chang Dajie, Beijing 100740; tel. (10) 65122474; fax (10) 65128354; f. 1954; Pres. CHEN HAOSU; Sec.-Gen. LUO QIN.

State Bureau of Tourism: Jie 3, Jian Guo Men Nei Dajie, Beijing 100740; tel. (10) 65122847; fax (10) 65122095; Dir LIU YI.

CHINESE SPECIAL ADMINISTRATIVE REGIONS

HONG KONG

Introductory Survey

Location, Climate, Language, Religion, Flag, Capital

The Special Administrative Region (SAR) of Hong Kong, as the territory became on 1 July 1997, lies in eastern Asia, off the south coast of the People's Republic of China. The SAR consists of the island of Hong Kong, Stonecutters Island, the Kowloon Peninsula and the New Territories, which are partly on the mainland. The climate is sunny and dry in winter, and hot and humid in summer. The average annual rainfall is 2,214 mm (87 ins), of which about 80% falls between May and September. The official languages are Chinese and English. Cantonese is spoken by the majority of the Chinese community, while Putonghua (Mandarin) is widely understood and of increasing significance. The main religion is Buddhism. Confucianism, Islam, Hinduism and Daoism are also practised, and there is a large Christian community. The flag of the Hong Kong SAR (proportions 2 by 3), flown subordinate to the flag of the People's Republic of China, displays a bauhinia flower consisting of five white petals, each bearing a red line and a red five-pointed star, at the centre of a red field. The capital is Victoria.

Recent History

Hong Kong Island was ceded to the United Kingdom under the terms of the Treaty of Nanking (Nanjing) in 1842. The Kowloon Peninsula was acquired by the Convention of Peking (Beijing) in 1860. The New Territories were leased from China in 1898 for a period of 99 years. From the establishment of the People's Republic in 1949, the Chinese Government asserted that the 'unequal' treaties giving Britain control over Hong Kong were no longer valid.

Japanese forces invaded Hong Kong in December 1941, forcing the British administration to surrender. In August 1945, at the end of the Second World War, the territory was recaptured by British forces. Colonial rule was restored, with a British military administration until May 1946. Upon the restoration of civilian rule, the territory was again administered in accordance with the 1917 Constitution, which vested full powers in the British-appointed Governor. In 1946 the returning Governor promised a greater measure of self-government but, after the communist revolution in China in 1949, plans for constitutional reform were abandoned. Thus, unlike most other British colonies, Hong Kong did not proceed, through stages, to democratic rule. The essential features of the colonial regime remained unaltered until 1985, when, following the Sino-British Joint Declaration (see below), the first changes were introduced into the administrative system. Prior to 1985 the Executive and Legislative Councils consisted entirely of nominated members, including many civil servants in the colonial administration. There were, however, direct elections for one-half of the seats on the Urban Council, responsible for public health and other amenities, but participation was low.

Between 1949 and 1964 an estimated 1m. refugees crossed from the People's Republic to Hong Kong, imposing serious strains on Hong Kong's housing and other social services. More than 460,000 Chinese immigrants arrived, many of them illegally, between 1975 and 1980. Strict measures, introduced in October 1980, reduced the continuous flow of refugees from China, but the number of legal immigrants remained at a high level.

During the 1980s the influx of large numbers of refugees from Viet Nam, most of whom lived for substantial periods in detention camps, was problematic. The Hong Kong authorities, meanwhile, exerted pressure on the British Government to end its policy of granting first asylum to these refugees. In response, legislation was introduced in June 1988 to distinguish between political refugees and 'economic migrants'. The latter were to be denied refugee status, and in October the British and Viet-

namese Governments agreed terms for their voluntary repatriation. In March 1989 the first group of co-operative 'economic migrants' flew back to Viet Nam. The number of Vietnamese arrivals increased sharply in the late 1980s, despite the unpleasant conditions in the camps where they were confined on arrival, and the restricting of the definition of refugee status. The relative paucity of those who agreed to return to Viet Nam (totalling 1,225 by February 1990) prompted the British Government to attempt, unsuccessfully, to gain general international endorsement for a policy of compulsory repatriation (which, it was claimed, would discourage further large-scale immigration). The Vietnamese Government announced in December 1989 that an agreement had been concluded between the United Kingdom and Viet Nam on a programme of 'involuntary' repatriation, whereby 'economic migrants' could be returned to Viet Nam against their will, on condition that no physical force was used. Reports of forcible repatriation caused violent disturbances in many of the camps. The programme was subsequently halted. At a meeting in January 1990, the UN steering committee for the Comprehensive Plan of Action on Indo-Chinese refugees failed to agree upon a policy. By May 1990 no further cases of the involuntary repatriation of Vietnamese had been reported. At an international conference held in that month, Hong Kong and the member countries of the Association of South East Asian Nations (ASEAN) threatened to refuse asylum to Vietnamese refugees altogether, unless the USA and Viet Nam gave approval to the policy of involuntary repatriation. In September Hong Kong, Viet Nam and the United Kingdom reached an agreement, supported by the UN High Commissioner for Refugees (UNHCR), to allow the repatriation of a new category of refugees—those who were not volunteering to return but who had indicated that they would not actively resist repatriation. This policy had little success, and the number of refugees increased. In October 1991, following protracted negotiations, it was announced that Viet Nam had agreed to the mandatory repatriation of refugees from Hong Kong. The first forcible deportation (mainly of recent arrivals) under the agreement was carried out in November. Tension and violence in the camps continued. In May 1992 an agreement between the United Kingdom and Viet Nam provided for the forcible repatriation of all economic migrants. By the end of 1995 the detention camp population had been greatly reduced, with only 1,479 being classified as refugees. Unrest in the camps continued intermittently. The People's Republic of China, meanwhile, continued to insist that all camps be cleared prior to the transfer of sovereignty in mid-1997. The Whitehead Detention Centre was closed in January 1997, and the refugees were transferred to other camps. Despite an acceleration in the repatriation programme, some 1,200 Vietnamese migrants remained in Hong Kong in December 1997. In January 1998 the SAR administration (see below) announced that it was abolishing the 'port of asylum' policy which had been applied to Vietnamese refugees. Those arriving illegally would no longer be given time to apply for asylum. At the end of May 2000 the last Vietnamese refugee camp, at Pillar Point, was closed. Most of the refugees were granted residency in the SAR.

Meanwhile, following a visit to Hong Kong by the British Prime Minister in September 1982, discussions between the United Kingdom and China were held regarding the territory's future status. In 1984 the United Kingdom conceded that in mid-1997, upon the expiry of the lease on the New Territories, China would regain sovereignty over the whole of Hong Kong. In September 1984 British and Chinese representatives met in Beijing and initialled a legally binding agreement, the Sino-British Joint Declaration, containing detailed assurances on the future of Hong Kong. China guaranteed the continuation of the territory's capitalist economy and life-style for 50 years after 1997. The territory, as a Special Administrative Region of the People's Republic, would be designated 'Hong Kong, China', and would continue to enjoy a high degree of autonomy, except in matters of defence and foreign affairs. It was agreed that Hong Kong would retain its identity as a free port and separate customs territory, and its citizens would be guaranteed freedom of speech, of assembly, of association, of travel and of religious belief. In December 1984, after being approved by the National People's Congress (NPC—the Chinese legislature) and the British Parliament, the agreement was signed in Beijing by the British and Chinese Prime Ministers, and in May 1985 the two Governments exchanged documents ratifying the agreement. A Joint Liaison Group (JLG), comprising British and Chinese representatives, was established to monitor the provisions of the agreement, and this group held its first meeting in July 1985. A 58-member Basic Law Drafting Committee (BLDC), including 23 representatives from Hong Kong, was formed in Beijing in June, with the aim of drawing up a new Basic Law (Constitution) for Hong Kong, in accordance with Article 31 of the Chinese Constitution, which provides for special administrative regions within the People's Republic.

The majority of the population reportedly accepted the terms of the Joint Declaration, but the sensitive issue of the future nationality of Hong Kong residents proved controversial. The 1981 British Nationality Act had already caused alarm in the territory, where the reclassification of 2.3m. citizens was perceived as a downgrading of their status. As holders of Hong Kong residents' permits, they had no citizenship status under British laws. Following the approval of the Hong Kong agreement, the British Government announced a new form of nationality, to be effective from 1997, designated 'British National (Overseas)', which would not be transferable to descendants and would confer no right of abode in the United Kingdom.

In September 1985 indirect elections were held for 24 new members of an expanded Legislative Council (Legco), to replace the former appointees and government officials. The participation rate among the very small proportion of the population eligible to vote in the elections was low. In March 1986 municipal elections were held for the urban and regional councils, which were thus, for the first time, wholly directly elected. A new Governor, Sir David Wilson (who had played a prominent part in the Sino-British negotiations on the territory's future), formally assumed office in April 1987, following the death of his predecessor, Sir Edward Youde, in December 1986. In May 1987 the Hong Kong Government published proposals regarding the development of representative government during the final decade of British rule. Among the options that it proposed was the introduction, in 1988, of direct elections to the Legislative Council, based upon universal adult suffrage. In spite of the disapproval of the Chinese Government, in February 1988 the Hong Kong Government published, with the support of the majority of the population, a policy document on the development of representative government; the principal proposal was the introduction, in 1991, of 10 (subsequently increased) directly elected members of the Legislative Council.

In April 1988 the first draft of the Basic Law for Hong Kong was published, and a Basic Law Consultative Committee (BLCC) was established in Hong Kong, initially with 176 members, to collect public comments on its provisions, over a five-month period; the draft was to be debated by the Legislative Council and by the Parliament of the United Kingdom, but no referendum was to be held in Hong Kong, and final approval of the Basic Law rested with the NPC of China. The draft offered five options for the election of a chief executive and four regarding the composition of the future Legislative Council, none of which, however, proposed that the Council should be elected entirely by universal suffrage. Although the legislature would be empowered to impeach the chief executive for wrongdoing, the Chinese Government would have final responsibility for his removal.

In November 1988 the UN Commission on Human Rights criticized the British attitude to the transfer of Hong Kong, with particular reference to the lack of direct elections. A second draft of the Basic Law was approved by the Chinese NPC in February 1989, which ignored all five options previously proposed for the election of a chief executive. In May there were massive demonstrations in Hong Kong in support of the anti-Government protests taking place in China. In June, following the killing of thousands of protesters by the Chinese armed forces in Tiananmen Square in Beijing, further demonstrations and a general strike took place in Hong Kong, expressing the inhabitants' revulsion at the massacres and their doubts as to whether the Basic Law would, in practice, be honoured by the Chinese

Government after 1997. The British Government refused to consider renegotiating the Sino-British Joint Declaration but, in response to demands that the British nationality laws should be changed to allow Hong Kong residents the right to settle in the United Kingdom after 1997, it announced in December 1989 that the British Parliament would be asked to enact legislation enabling as many as 50,000 Hong Kong residents (chosen on a 'points system', which was expected to favour leading civil servants, business executives and professional workers), and an estimated 175,000 dependants, to be given the right of abode in the United Kingdom. The measure was intended to 'maintain confidence' in the colony during the transition to Chinese sovereignty, by curbing the emigration of skilled personnel. The Hong Kong authorities cautiously welcomed the announcement, but China warned prospective applicants that it would not recognize their British nationality after 1997. Widespread popular protests took place in Hong Kong itself over the unfairness of a scheme which was perceived as elitist. The bill containing the measures was approved in the United Kingdom's House of Commons in April 1990.

Among other recommendations made by the parliamentary select committee were the introduction of a Bill of Rights for Hong Kong and an increase in the number of seats subject to direct election in the Hong Kong Legislative Council, to one-half of the total in 1991, leading to full direct elections in 1995. A draft Bill of Rights, based on the UN International Covenant on Civil and Political Rights, was published by the Hong Kong Government in March 1990. The draft was criticized in principle because its provisions would have been subordinate, in the case of conflict, to the provisions of the Basic Law. Nevertheless, the Bill of Rights entered into law in June 1991.

China's NPC approved a final draft of the Basic Law for Hong Kong in April 1990. In this version, 24 of the 60 seats in the Legislative Council would be subject to direct election from 1999, and 30 seats from 2003; a referendum, to be held after 2007, would consult public opinion on the future composition of the Council, although the ultimate authority to make any changes would rest with the NPC. The British Government had agreed to co-operate with these measures by offering 18 seats for direct election in 1991 and 20 seats in 1995. Under the Basic Law, the Chief Executive of the Hong Kong Special Administrative Region (SAR), as the territory was to be designated in 1997, would initially be elected for a five-year term by a special 800-member election committee; a referendum was to be held during the third term of office in order to help to determine whether the post should be subject to a general election. However, no person with the right of residence in another country would be permitted to hold an important government post. Particular concern was expressed over a clause in the Law that would 'prohibit political organizations and groups in the Hong Kong SAR from establishing contacts with foreign political organizations or groups'.

In April 1990 liberal groups founded Hong Kong's first formal political party, the United Democrats of Hong Kong (UDHK), with Martin Lee as its Chairman. The party subsequently became the main opposition to the conservatives, and achieved considerable success in local elections in March and May 1991, and in the territory's first direct legislative elections in September. Of the 18 seats in the Legislative Council subject to election by universal suffrage, 17 were won by members of the UDHK and like-minded liberal and independent candidates. Only 39% of registered electors, however, reportedly voted. Despite the party's electoral success, the Governor nominated only one of the UDHK's 20 suggested candidates when selecting his direct appointees to the Legislative Council. Changes in the membership of the Executive Council were announced in October, liberal citizens again being excluded by the Governor.

In April 1992 Christopher Patten, hitherto Chairman of the Conservative Party in the United Kingdom, was appointed Governor to replace Sir David Wilson upon his retirement. Patten took office in July. Plans for democratic reform in the territory, announced by the Governor in October, included the separation of the Executive Council from the Legislative Council. The former was reorganized to include prominent lawyers and academics. At the 1995 elections to the latter, the number of directly elected members was to be increased to the maximum permissible of 20; the franchise for the existing 21 'functional constituencies', representing occupational and professional groups, was to be widened and nine additional constituencies were to be established, in order to encompass all categories of workers. Various social and economic reforms were also announced. In the same month Patten paid his first visit to China.

The proposed electoral changes were denounced by China as a contravention of the Basic Law and of the 1984 Joint Declaration. Although Patten's programme received the general support of the Legislative Council, many conservative business leaders were opposed to the proposals. In November 1992, following Hong Kong's announcement that it was to proceed with the next stage of preparations for the disputed construction of a new airport (without, as yet, the Chinese Government's agreement to the revised financing of the project), China threatened to cancel, in 1997, all commercial contracts, leases and agreements between the Hong Kong Government and the private sector that had been signed without its full approval. The dispute continued in early 1993, China's criticism of the territory's Governor becoming increasingly acrimonious. In February China announced plans to establish a 'second stove', or alternative administration for Hong Kong, if the Governor's proposed reforms were implemented. In April, however, the impasse was broken when the United Kingdom and China agreed to resume negotiations. In July the 57-member Preliminary Working Committee (PWC), established to study issues relating to the forthcoming transfer of sovereignty and chaired by the Chinese Minister of Foreign Affairs, held its inaugural meeting in Beijing. Negotiations between the United Kingdom and China continued intermittently throughout 1993. In December, however, no progress having been made, proposed electoral reforms were submitted to the Legislative Council. The Governor's decision to proceed unilaterally was denounced by China, which declared that it would regard as null and void any laws enacted in Hong Kong.

In February 1994 the Legislative Council approved the first stage of the reform programme, which included the lowering of the voting age from 21 to 18 years. China confirmed that all recently elected bodies would be disbanded in 1997. The second stage was presented to the Legislative Council in March. Relations with China deteriorated further in April, upon the publication of a British parliamentary report endorsing Patten's democratic reforms. In the same month the UDHK and Meeting Point, a smaller party, merged and formed the Democratic Party of Hong Kong. In April the trial in camera of a Beijing journalist (who worked for a respected Hong Kong newspaper) on imprecise charges of 'stealing state secrets' and his subsequent severe prison sentence aroused widespread concern in the territory over future press freedom. Hundreds of journalists took part in a protest march through the streets of Hong Kong.

In June 1994, in an unprecedented development that reflected growing unease with Patten's style of government, the Legislative Council passed a motion of censure formally rebuking the Governor for refusing to permit a debate on an amendment to the budget. Nevertheless, at the end of the month the Legislative Council approved further constitutional reforms, entailing an increase in the number of its directly elected members and an extension of the franchise. Despite China's strong opposition to these reforms, shortly afterwards the People's Republic and the United Kingdom concluded an agreement on the transfer of defence sites, some of which were to be retained for military purposes and upgraded prior to 1997, while others were to be released for redevelopment. At the end of August, following the issuing of a report by the PWC in the previous month, the Standing Committee of the NPC in Beijing approved a decision on the abolition, in 1997, of the current political structure of Hong Kong.

In September 1994, at elections to the 18 District Boards (the first to be held on a fully democratic basis), 75 of the 346 seats were won by the Democratic Party. The pro-Beijing Democratic Alliance for the Betterment of Hong Kong (DAB) won 37 seats, the progressive Association for Democracy and People's Livelihood (ADPL) 29 seats, and the pro-Beijing Liberal Party and Liberal Democratic Foundation 18 seats and 11 seats, respectively. Independent candidates secured 167 seats. The level of voter participation was a record 33.1%. In December 1994 the director of the State Council's Hong Kong and Macao Affairs Office and secretary-general of the PWC, Lu Ping, formally confirmed that the Legislative Council would be disbanded in 1997.

Elections for the 32 seats on the Urban Council and the 27 seats on the Regional Council took place in March 1995. The Democratic Party took 23 seats, the DAB eight seats and the ADPL also eight seats. Fewer than 26% of those eligible voted in the polls. In the same month Donald Tsang was nominated as

Financial Secretary; his predecessor, along with other expatriate senior officials, had been requested to take early retirement to allow for the appointment of a local civil servant. Tsang took office in September.

Following a redrafting of the legislation, in June 1995 the United Kingdom and China reached agreement on the establishment of the Court of Final Appeal. Contrary to the Governor's original wishes, this new body would not now be constituted until after the transfer of sovereignty in mid-1997. The agreement was approved by the Legislative Council in July 1995. In the same month an unprecedented motion of 'no confidence' in the Governor was defeated at a session of the Legislative Council. Also in July the territory's Chief Secretary, Anson Chan, confirmed that she had had clandestine meetings with senior Chinese officials during a three-day visit to Beijing.

At elections to the Legislative Council in September 1995, for the first time all 60 seats were determined by election. The Democratic Party won 19 seats in total, including 12 of the 20 seats open to direct election on the basis of geographical constituencies and two of the 10 chosen by an electoral committee. The Liberal Party took nine of the 60 seats, the pro-Beijing DAB six, and the ADPL four. Independent candidates won 17 seats.

The Governor aroused much controversy in September 1995, when he urged the United Kingdom to grant the right of abode to more than 3m. citizens of Hong Kong. The proposals were rebuffed by the British Home Secretary. In October, however, an improvement in Sino-British relations was confirmed by the visit of the Chinese Minister of Foreign Affairs to London. The two sides reached agreement on the establishment of a liaison office to improve bilateral contacts between civil servants. China's disclosure of a plan to establish a parallel administration six months prior to the transfer of sovereignty provoked outrage in Hong Kong.

In January 1996 the 150-member Preparatory Committee of the Hong Kong SAR was formally established in Beijing to succeed the PWC. The 94 Hong Kong delegates included representatives of the territory's business and academic communities. The Democratic Party was excluded from the new body, which was to appoint a 400-member Selection Committee responsible for the choice of the territory's future Chief Executive.

In March 1996, during a visit to the territory, the British Prime Minister announced that more than 2m. holders of the forthcoming Hong Kong SAR passports would be granted visa-free access to (but not residency in) the United Kingdom. The Preparatory Committee in Beijing approved a resolution to appoint a provisional body to replace the Legislative Council. Towards the end of March, as the final deadline approached, thousands of Hong Kong residents rushed to submit applications for British Dependent Territories Citizenship (BDTC) which, although conferring no right of abode in the United Kingdom, would provide an alternative travel document to the new SAR passports. In April Anson Chan travelled to Beijing for discussions with Lu Ping. A visit to Hong Kong by Lu Ping earlier in the month had been disrupted by pro-democracy demonstrators. In early July eight pro-democracy politicians from Hong Kong, including five members of the Legislative Council, were refused entry to China to deliver a petition of 60,000 signatures against the proposed establishment of a provisional legislative body for Hong Kong. In mid-August nominations opened for candidacy for the 400-member Selection Committee. In the same month a new pro-democracy movement, The Frontier, comprising teachers, students and trade unionists, was established. In October 1996 the Chinese Minister of Foreign Affairs declared that from mid-1997 the annual protests against the Tiananmen Square massacre of 1989 (and similar demonstrations) would not be tolerated in Hong Kong; furthermore, criticism of the Chinese leadership by the territory's press would not be permitted.

In December 1996 the second ballot for the selection of Hong Kong's Chief Executive (the first having been held in November) resulted in the choice of Tung Chee-hwa, a shipping magnate and former member of the territory's Executive Council, who obtained 320 of the 400 votes. Later in the month the Selection Committee chose the 60 members of the SAR's controversial Provisional Legislative Council (PLC). More than 30 of the new appointees were members of the existing Legislative Council, belonging mainly to the DAB and to the Liberal Party. Despite much criticism of the PLC's establishment, the new body held its inaugural meeting in Shenzhen in January 1997, and elected Rita Fan as its President.

In early 1997 the Chief Executive-designate announced the composition of the Executive Council, which was to comprise three ex-officio members (as previously) and initially 11 non-official members. Anson Chan was to remain as Chief Secretary, while Donald Tsang was to continue as Financial Secretary; Elsie Leung was to become Justice Secretary, replacing the incumbent Attorney General. China's approval of Tung Chee-hwa's recommendations that senior civil servants be retained did much to enhance confidence in the territory's future. In February, however, relations with the outgoing administration deteriorated when the Preparatory Committee voted over-whelmingly in favour of proposals to repeal or amend 25 laws, thereby reducing the territory's civil liberties.

Meanwhile, Lawrence Leung had abruptly resigned as Director of Immigration in July 1996 for 'personal reasons'. In January 1997 he cast doubt on the integrity of the Hong Kong Government when he appeared before a hearing of the Legis-lative Council and claimed that he had in fact been dismissed, thus denying the official version of his departure from office. The scandal deepened with the revelation that Leung had been found to possess undisclosed business interests. Newspaper reports alleged that Leung had been involved in espionage activities on behalf of China. The Government finally admitted that Leung had indeed been dismissed, but denied the reports of espionage.

In May 1997 the PLC approved its first legislation (a bill on public holidays), despite protests from the British Government and pro-democracy groups in Hong Kong that the PLC was not entitled to pass laws during the transition period. The PLC declared, however, that the legislation would come into effect only on 1 July. Following the circulation in April of a public consultation document on proposed legislation governing civil liberties and social order, a series of amendments, relating to the holding of public demonstrations and the funding of political organizations, was announced in May. Pro-democracy groups and the outgoing administration remained dissatisfied with the legislation.

Shortly after the transfer of Hong Kong from British to Chinese sovereignty at midnight on 30 June 1997, the inaugura-tion of the SAR Executive Council, the PLC and members of the judiciary was held. Some 4,000 dignitaries attended the cere-monies, although the British Prime Minister and Foreign Secre-tary, and the US Secretary of State, did not attend the inaugura-tion of the PLC, to register their disapproval at the undemo-cratic nature of its formation. Pro-democracy groups and mem-bers of the former legislature staged peaceful demonstrations in protest at the abolition of the Legislative Council. More than 4,000 Chinese troops of the People's Liberation Army entered Hong Kong shortly after the handover ceremony, joining the small number of Chinese military personnel that had been deployed in the territory in April, following protracted negotia-tions with the British Government; a further 500 had entered the territory on 30 June, immediately prior to the handover.

Details of the procedure for elections to a new Legislative Council, which would replace the PLC, were announced by the SAR Government in early July 1997. The elections were sched-uled to take place in May 1998 and were to be conducted under a new system of voting. Of the 60 seats in the legislature, 20 were to be directly elected by means of a revised system of proportional representation, 30 were to be elected by 'functional constituencies' (comprising professional and special interest groups) and 10 by an 800-member electoral college. Legislative amendments governing the electoral arrangements were approved by the PLC in late September 1997. The significant reduction of the franchise, by comparison with the 1995 legis-lative elections, was condemned by the Democratic Party. The appointment by indirect election of 36 Hong Kong delegates to the Chinese NPC, in December 1997, also attracted criticism from pro-democracy activists.

Following the transfer of sovereignty to China, concerns con-tinued about freedom of expression in the SAR. In March 1998 a prominent publisher and a member of the Chinese People's Political Consultative Conference (CPPCC), Xu Simin, chal-lenged the right of the public broadcaster, Radio Television Hong Kong, to criticize government policy, while Tung stated on the same day that government policies should be positively presented by the media. Following expressions of popular dis-content, Tung issued a denial that Xu's position reflected gov-ernment policy. In the same month the Secretary of Justice, Elsie Leung, was criticized following the Government's decision not to prosecute another prominent publisher, CPPCC member

and a friend of Tung's, Sally Aw Sian, for corruption, despite a ruling against her by the Independent Commission Against Corruption. Pro-democracy groups expressed fears regarding the independence of the Justice Department. This occurred two weeks after Leung had declined to prosecute the official Chinese news agency, Xinhua, for an alleged breach of privacy laws, after it took 10 months (despite a legal 40-day limit) to issue a denial that it possessed information pertaining to Emily Lau, the leader of The Frontier. (In March 1999 a motion of 'no con-fidence' in Elsie Leung, prompted by these controversial legal decisions, was defeated in the Legislative Council.) In May 1998 two pro-democracy activists were found guilty of defacing flags of China and the Hong Kong SAR at a rally in January, the first such conviction since Hong Kong's transfer to Chinese sover-eignty. In March 1999 the Court of Final Appeal ruled that the law prohibiting the defacing of the SAR flag was an unconstitu-tional restriction of freedom of expression. In December, how-ever, under pressure from Beijing, the Court rescinded its own decision, and the conviction was confirmed, provoking protests from civil rights organizations. In January 1998 a demonstra-tion was staged to coincide with the visit of the former Chinese President, Yang Shangkun, who was regarded as one of those responsible for the Tiananmen Square massacre in 1989. Sim-ilar protests were conducted during a visit by Qiao Shi, the Chairman of the Standing Committee of the Eighth Chinese NPC, in February 1998, and in June a commemoration of the 1989 massacre took place without incident. In the following year, the 10th anniversary of the massacre was marked by a peaceful demonstration, attended by 70,000 protesters. On the second anniversary of the resumption of Chinese sovereignty, on 1 July 1999, more than 2,000 pro-democracy demonstrators protested against Chinese control. Tung Chee-hwa's unpopular policies were the subject of similar demonstrations on 1 July 2000.

In October 1999 the SAR administration announced the sudden transfer of Cheung Man-yee, Director of Broadcasting of the government-owned Radio Television Hong Kong, to a post as senior economic and trade representative in Tokyo, Japan. It was suspected that Cheung's defence of the broadcaster's edito-rial independence had made her unpopular with the pro-China establishment, resulting in her removal for political reasons. Shortly afterwards Emily Lau announced that she would report the transfer to the UN Committee on Human Rights, citing it as an example of the erosion of freedom of expression in Hong Kong.

In April 2000 there were renewed fears for the freedom of the Hong Kong media after a warning by Beijing against the reporting of any remarks advocating Taiwanese independence. The statement was issued following the broadcast in Hong Kong of an interview with Taiwanese Vice-President-elect Annette Lu, during which she made 'separatist' remarks. China's inter-ference was widely condemned, prompting an assurance by Tung Chee-hwa that freedom of the press and freedom of speech continued to be guaranteed under the provisions of the Basic Law. In October, in Beijing, relations between the Hong Kong media and the People's Republic were further damaged when Hong Kong reporters were accused by Jiang Zemin of being 'naïve' for implying that Beijing's support for the Chief Execu-tive would lead to Tung Chee-hwa's reappointment without election. A number of unprecedented personal attacks on the Chinese President subsequently appeared in the Hong Kong media, and in the following month journalists from the SAR were banned from attending celebrations in China to mark the 20th anniversary of the establishment of the Shenzhen Special Economic Zone. Those who attempted to contravene the ban were detained until after the ceremony. In November Willy Wo-Lap Lam, a prominent journalist and critic of mainland policy, resigned from the *South China Morning Post*. His work had been subject to 'pre-screening' for any material likely to anger the People's Republic.

Also in November 2000, students held the latest in a series of protests against the Public Order Ordinance (POO), which stipulated that permission for demonstrations had to be obtained from the security forces at least seven days in advance. Earlier in the month the Government had postponed until December a debate on POO in the Legislative Council, after opposition politicians protested that the administration was trying to enact the law by forcible means.

Fears concerning the SAR's autonomy were exacerbated by the rapid adoption by the PLC in April 1998 of the Adaptation of Laws Bill. The Bill was ostensibly simply to replace references to the British crown in existing legislation but in practice it exempted Xinhua, the office of the Chinese Ministry of Foreign Affairs and the garrison of the People's Liberation Army from all laws unless otherwise stated. Concerns about the territory's legal autonomy were also raised by the conviction and execution, in November and December respectively, of five criminals from Hong Kong in the People's Republic.

At the elections to the first Legislative Council of the SAR on 24 May 1998, participation (53.3% of registered voters) was the highest since the introduction of direct elections in Hong Kong. The Democratic Party and other pro-democracy parties suffered a reduction in their overall political strength in the legislature, despite the fact that they won 14 of the 20 directly elective seats. A total of 19 seats were secured by pro-democracy candidates, including 13 by the Democratic Party (nine directly elected), led by Martin Lee, which became the largest party in the Legislative Council. Lee advocated direct elections by universal suffrage for all 60 seats in the next poll, to be held in 2000. Pro-Beijing supporters dominated the functional constituencies and the election committee ballot. The pro-business Liberal Party, led by Allen Lee, failed to win a single seat in the direct elections but obtained nine in the other constituencies. The DAB also won nine seats, five of which were directly elective.

The powers of the new legislature were curbed by the Basic Law. Legislative Councillors were not permitted to introduce bills related to political expenditure, the political structure or the operation of the government. The passage of private members' bills or motions also required a majority of votes of both groups of councillors—those elected directly and those returned through functional constituencies and the election committee. At its first session in July 1998 the Legislative Council elected Rita Fan as its President. The division between the Chief Executive, who rarely consulted the legislature, and the Legislative Council became more apparent after Tung Chee-hwa's second annual policy address in October. He announced the abolition of urban and regional councils, a move opposed by many members of the legislature, who also criticized the Executive Council for failing to stimulate the territory's ailing economy.

In March 1999 Anson Chan agreed to continue serving as Chief Secretary for two years beyond her normal retirement age, until 2002, when Tung Chee-hwa's term of office was to end. In April 1999 the administration decided to abolish the municipal and regional councils, while existing district boards were to be replaced by district councils. Although the public had been dissatisfied with the performance of the municipal councils, there was resentment at the restructuring of local democracy, which was perceived as a regressive step. In November the Democratic Party threatened legal action if the plan was not abandoned, as it contravened the Basic Law. The first district elections in the Hong Kong SAR took place on 28 November. The Democratic Party won the largest number of elected seats (86), but the pro-Beijing DAB substantially increased its representation, from 37 seats to 83.

Popular support for the SAR Government declined substantially throughout 2000, and public unrest increased. In February Tung Chee-hwa effected a reshuffle of senior officials following the retirement of three officials from the civil service. In May Elsie Leung was reappointed Secretary of Justice for an additional two years. The reappointment was contentious as Leung was regarded as unpopular, having been responsible for some controversial decisions (see above). In June Tung Chee-hwa's administration was embarrassed by the resignation of Rosanna Wong as Secretary for Housing. Three days later the Legislative Council passed a vote of 'no confidence' in Wong and one of her senior officials, holding them responsible for a series of scandals relating to sub-standard construction works. Wong, however, remained a member of the Executive Council. This affair appeared to justify the resignation in April of the prominent opposition politician, Christine Loh, from the Legislative Council. Loh had cited her frustration with the Government's reluctance to share power with the legislature. According to a public opinion poll conducted in July, only 20% of those surveyed were satisfied with the Government's performance. This was the lowest level of approval recorded in these surveys, which had been conducted regularly since the transfer of sovereignty to China. In September one of Tung Chee-hwa's aides and two officials of Hong Kong University resigned after an independent inquiry found them guilty of attempting to suppress the results of public opinion polls conducted by a university researcher.

The second elections to the Legislative Council took place on 10 September 2000. Twenty-four (increased from 20 in the previous legislature) of the seats were directly elective, with 30 seats elected by 'functional constituencies' and six (reduced from 10) by an 800-member electoral college. The level of voter participation was 43.6%. The Democratic Party won the highest number of seats, with 12 (of which nine were directly elected), just ahead of the DAB, which obtained 11 seats. The Democratic Party's share of the votes cast, however, was inferior to that obtained in the 1998 elections. Public apathy was attributed to dissatisfaction with the Government and to the main political parties' failure to publicize coherent manifestos. Nine days later the DAB legislator-elect, Gary Cheng, resigned from the Legislative Council following a scandal over his failure to declare business interests. (A by-election held in December was won by an independent candidate.) At the first session of the new Legislative Council, Rita Fan was re-elected President.

The Government suffered a reverse in January 2001, when Anson Chan unexpectedly announced that she was to resign, for 'personal reasons'. While visiting Beijing in September 2000, she had been publicly reprimanded by China for her perceived lack of support for the Chief Executive. Chan, who had been widely respected by the international community, was succeeded in April by Donald Tsang, and the latter was replaced as Financial Secretary by Antony Leung, a former banker and member of the Executive Council, who was known to be close to Tung Chee-hwa.

In March 2001 the Hong Kong Government presented the new Chief Executive Election Bill, proposing the recognition of the powers of the central Government in Beijing to remove the Chief Executive and providing details of the procedure for the next election for that post, scheduled for 24 March 2002 (but see below). The new incumbent was to serve a five-year term commencing on 30 June 2002. The Bill was approved by the Legislative Council by 36 votes to 18 in July 2001 after minor amendments, but critics of the Bill regarded it as a set-back for the democratic process.

In early 2001 the Chinese Government warned that it would not allow Hong Kong to become a centre for the activities of Falun Gong, a religious sect banned on the mainland since mid-1999, and in May 2001 the Hong Kong Government increased its efforts to prevent the movement's followers from congregating in the territory in advance of a business forum. The conference was to be attended by President Jiang Zemin, former US President Bill Clinton, Thai Prime Minister Thaksin Shinawatra and hundreds of business leaders. Prior to Jiang's visit, scores of Falun Gong followers were prevented from entering Hong Kong; however, a small demonstration by followers was permitted to take place some 300 m from the forum venue. At the conference itself, President Jiang promised to guarantee Hong Kong's autonomy, and praised Tung Chee-hwa's work. At the same time, however, more than 100 Hong Kong academics urged Beijing to release Chinese scholars detained on the mainland in previous months (some of whom were citizens or residents of the USA, or residents of Hong Kong), including Li Shaomin and Gao Zhan, who had both been convicted for espionage. The two were freed in late July, and Li was allowed to resume his academic duties. Li's case was an apparent triumph of the autonomy of Hong Kong; however, it was feared that his case would deter Hong Kong's academics from writing about 'sensitive' topics relating to democracy and making trips to the mainland, thereby stifling intellectual debate. By late July, meanwhile, a Falun Gong spokesman claimed that its membership in Hong Kong had fallen by 50% during the past two years to 500 people.

In October 2001 the Hong Kong Government proposed to Beijing draft legislation that would allow mainland citizens to invest legally in Hong Kong's stock market, as part of a plan to develop closer financial links with the mainland. The proposal threatened to increase the rivalry between Hong Kong and Shanghai for the position of China's foremost financial centre, however, with the Chinese Government thought to favour the latter. At the same time, Tung Chee-hwa delivered his fifth annual policy address to the Legislative Council, in which he announced major new infrastructure projects and warned of economic hardship ahead. However, his speech was criticized for lacking bold initiatives needed to improve the economy.

In November 2001 opposition groups and trade unions, led by Emily Lau, announced the formation of a coalition aimed at preventing the re-election of Tung Chee-hwa as Chief Executive. In early December Lau strongly criticized the procedures for the election of the Chief Executive as undemocratic, and accused

Tung of cronyism and of being an unsuitable leader, adding that greater checks and balances were needed. Despite his growing unpopularity, in mid-December Tung announced his intention to stand for a second five-year term as Chief Executive, and was quickly endorsed by President Jiang Zemin, thus making his re-election certain. Tung was also endorsed by the convenor of the Executive Council, Leung Chun-ying, Liberal Party leader James Tien and the director of the Beijing Liaison Office, Jiang Enzhu. Martin Lee and his Democratic Party, however, boycotted the reception at which Tung formally announced his re-election bid. In late December the Chief Executive visited Beijing where he discussed the establishment of a free-trade arrangement between Hong Kong and the mainland. On 28 February 2002 Tung was nominated for re-election by 714 members of the 800-member Election Committee, thereby securing him a second term in office without challenge. He was formally sworn in for a second term on 1 July.

In mid-March 2002, meanwhile, police charged 16 Falun Gong members (11 locals, one New Zealander and four Swiss nationals) with obstruction following demonstrations outside the Beijing Liaison Office—the first time that legal action had been taken against the group in the SAR. The 16 went on trial in mid-June and were convicted in mid-August. Their HK $4,000 fines, however, were paid by an anonymous benefactor. Members of the group also demonstrated on 13 May 2002 to mark the 10th anniversary of the creation of the sect, and the birthday of its founder, Li Hongzhi.

In mid-April 2002 Harry Wu Hongda, a prominent US-based human rights activist, was prevented from entering Hong Kong. His detention on arrival at Chek Lap Kok airport, and deportation the following day, prompted concerns that Hong Kong's freedoms were increasingly under threat, particularly since Wu did not require a visa to enter the SAR, and had visited unimpeded on numerous occasions. Wu was again denied permission to enter the SAR in late June. In late April, the dismissal of the China correspondent of the *South China Morning Post*, Jasper Becker, led to fears that critical coverage of mainland issues would be suppressed.

Plans for a major reorganization of government structures were announced in mid-April 2002. Under the new system, the Executive Council would be expanded into a cabinet-style body consisting of 14 ministers, all appointed by the Chief Executive, and which would administer the 184,000-member civil service. Critics of the proposals warned that the new system would strengthen Tung's (and therefore Beijing's) control over the territory and compromise the independence of the professional civil service. The Legislative Council none the less adopted the changes, and a new cabinet was appointed in late June. However, Beijing's influence was highlighted by the fact that Tung's appointments were delayed by a few days while Beijing subjected them to scrutiny. When finally announced on 24 June 2002, the new Executive Council notably included five appointees from the private sector. These were Henry Tang Ying-yen, the new Secretary for Commerce, Industry and Technology; Arthur Li, the Secretary for Education and Manpower; Patrick Ho, the Secretary for Home Affairs; Sarah Liao, the Secretary for Environment, Transport and Works; and Frederick Ma, the Secretary for Financial Services and the Treasury. The portfolios of several leading officials, such as Donald Tsang, the Chief Secretary for Administration, Antony Leung, the Financial Secretary, and Elsie Leung, the Secretary for Justice, remained unchanged.

Hong Kong marked the fifth anniversary of its reversion to the People's Republic on 1 July 2002, amid calls from Jiang Zemin for Hong Kong's citizens to identify more closely with the mainland. Jiang, who was visiting the SAR, also issued a rare note of criticism of the territory's Government, urging it to improve its performance. At the same time, Vice-Premier Qian Qichen seemingly ruled out democratic reforms in 2007, as promised by the Basic Law, instead emphasizing the need for stability. Tung had described the priority of economic recovery as his greatest challenge during his second term. However, by July there were also increasing tensions between Tung and the civil service following new legislation that allowed the Government to reduce civil service pay by 4.42%, owing to the growing budget deficit. Some 30,000 public servants marched in protest at the cuts, in the largest demonstrations in Hong Kong since 1989. By late August, Tung's approval rating had fallen to 16%—its lowest level since he assumed office—amid increasing concerns about the economy, record levels of unemployment and the new governmental structures.

In late September 2002 the Government revealed proposals for new anti-subversion laws, which it was required to introduce under Article 23 of the Basic Law, but which had thus far remained unimplemented. Chinese Vice-Premier Qian Qichen had, in June, specifically urged the SAR Government to introduce these laws, giving the impression that Beijing was seeking to extend its laws into the SAR. Critics immediately feared that the new laws would undermine civil liberties and freedom of speech. Suspicions were increased by the fact that a draft of the laws was not made available to the public. The proposals specifically sought to criminalize treason, secession, sedition and subversion, and would also give police the powers to conduct emergency 'search and entry' acts without a warrant. 'Secession' referred to attempts to break away from China, while 'subversion' was defined as threatening or using force to intimidate or overthrow the Government. The Government would also be able to ban any groups affiliated with a mainland organization that had been proscribed in the mainland by the central authorities on national security grounds. Furthermore, the laws could also ban any 'seditious publications' that incited treason, secession or subversion, or disclosed state secrets. A maximum penalty of life imprisonment would be imposed on violators of the new laws. The Secretary for Security, Regina Ip, stated that the laws would not be used to target specific groups such as Falun Gong, or specific individuals, and that existing freedoms would not be affected. In November 10 human rights groups, including the local branches of Amnesty International and Human Rights Watch, urged the Government to abandon the proposed laws, and the US Government expressed its own concerns. Hong Kong's financial community also feared that the laws would hinder the free flow of information, which had long constituted a competitive advantage for the SAR. At the end of that month a Hong Kong court convicted three democracy activists of organizing an unauthorized protest, the first such convictions since the territory's return to Chinese rule. The three offenders were released on bail with a warning.

In September 2002 the head of the Catholic Church in Hong Kong, Cardinal John Baptist Wu, died after a long illness and was succeeded by his deputy, Bishop Joseph Zen Ze-kiun. The latter was a strong critic of the Chinese and Hong Kong Governments, and in 1998 had been banned from visiting the mainland. In early December he publicly criticized the proposed anti-subversion laws, stating that they jeopardized the Falun Gong sect.

On 1 December 2002 Martin Lee retired from the leadership of the Democratic Party, after completing four two-year terms (the maximum allowed), and was succeeded by a former party vice-chairman, Yeung Sum. Lee remained a member of the Legislative Council, however, and was expected to continue pressing for greater democratization of the SAR. In early December the Hong Kong Bar Association condemned the anti-subversion laws, describing them as unacceptable and harmful to the territory's freedoms. In mid-December between 20,000 and 60,000 people from a broad section of society demonstrated against the planned anti-subversion laws, and demonstrations in late December by those in favour of the laws attracted 10,000 people. By late January 2003 the Government indicated that, following the end of a three-month public consultation period, some aspects of the laws would be scaled down, namely provisions dealing with the possession of seditious publications, and a ban on access to state secrets.

The outbreak of Severe Acute Respiratory Syndrome (SARS, a hitherto-unknown pneumonia-like illness) in Hong Kong in early 2003, which killed almost 300 people in the territory before the disease was brought under control in June, led to further problems for the Government. There were demands for Tung Chee-hwa to resign, following accusations that the Chief Executive had mishandled the SARS crisis. Meanwhile, there was continuing public disquiet over the proposed security legislation, which was due to be introduced in early July. At the beginning of July, on the sixth anniversary of Hong Kong's reversion to Chinese sovereignty, 500,000 people took part in a demonstration against the proposed new laws. Following the protests, the Liberal Party chairman, James Tien, resigned from his position in the Government, stating that his party would not support the bill in the Legislative Council vote. Tung Chee-hwa subsequently delayed the introduction of the legislation. In late July two government ministers, Secretary for Security Regina Ip and Financial Secretary Antony Leung, resigned from their positions. Both officials had been a target of criticism in the protests at the beginning of the month, and both were known to have close ties with the Chinese Government in Beijing. In early September the controversial anti-subversion bill was withdrawn by Tung Chee-hwa owing to popular opposition; this represented an indirect challenge to the authority of the Chinese Government in Hong Kong. In November Chinese Vice-Premier Zeng Peiyan visited Hong Kong and expressed Beijing's continuing support for Tung Chee-hwa. At local government elections held in Hong Kong at the end of November the pro-Beijing DAB suffered heavy losses, prompting the resignation of the alliance's chairman, Tsang Yok-sing.

In early January 2004 there were further popular protests demanding the direct election of Hong Kong's Chief Executive and for all seats in the Legislative Council. In February a group of Hong Kong politicians led by Chief Secretary for Administration Donald Tsang visited Beijing to hold talks with the Chinese Government on the future political development of Hong Kong. Chinese officials stated that any decisions on changes to the procedures for election of the Chief Executive and the Legislative Council would by made by the mainland Chinese leadership. In April the Standing Committee of the NPC in Beijing ruled that the SAR's next Chief Executive would not be chosen by direct election in 2007. The introduction of direct elections for all members of the Legislative Council was similarly postponed. Chinese Premier Wen Jiabao stated later in the month that direct elections for the Chief Executive and the entire legislature in Hong Kong remained China's ultimate aim, but that this objective was not a possibility in the near future. The NPC ruling prompted protests by democracy campaigners in Hong Kong, who claimed that the decision contravened Hong Kong's Basic Law. At the end of April eight Chinese ships entered Hong Kong harbour, representing the strongest show of force by the Chinese navy since 1997. In May there were renewed concerns over the freedom of the media after two well-known radio broadcasters, Albert Cheng and Raymond Wong, left Hong Kong, citing attempts to limit their freedom of speech and threats of violence by pro-Beijing groups. The Chinese Government denied having had any part in threatening the broadcasters. Shortly after the departures of Cheng and Wong, a third broadcaster, Allen Lee, who had replaced Cheng as host of a popular radio talk show, resigned as well, claiming to have been subjected to similar instances of intimidation. Lee also resigned from his position as a Hong Kong delegate to China's NPC, claiming that he had not been able to express his opinions freely. In June Chief Executive Tung held talks with pro-democracy leaders and reiterated the promise that universal suffrage would eventually be realized in Hong Kong. Also in June it was reported that the offices of democracy campaigner Emily Lau had been vandalized and that she had received death threats. At the beginning of July, on the seventh anniversary of Hong Kong's return to Chinese sovereignty, as many as 500,000 people, according to one estimate, took part in a demonstration demanding universal suffrage. In the same month the Secretary for Health, Welfare and Food, Yeoh Eng-kiong, resigned following publication of a report on the 2003 SARS epidemic. In August a Chinese military parade, involving some 3,000 troops, took place in Hong Kong. Also in August there were reports of voter intimidation by pro-Beijing factions in advance of the forthcoming legislative elections. In the same month Democratic Party candidate Ho Wai-to was arrested in Guangdong on charges of hiring a prostitute. Ho and his family denied the allegations and claimed that the incident had been staged by the Chinese authorities.

At the elections to the Legislative Council held on 12 September 2004, in which 30 of the total of 60 members were directly elected, support for the pro-democracy faction was less evident than had been widely expected. Of the directly elective seats, 18 were won by democratic parties and 12 by pro-Beijing parties, despite pre-election polls having suggested that the democratic parties might secure as many as 21 of these seats. In the Legislative Council as a whole, pro-Beijing parties held 34 of 60 seats after the election, thus retaining their majority. Voter participation in the election was high, at 55.6%. There was speculation that following the election the mainland Chinese Government would attempt to expand its influence in the SAR.

In January 2005 a candle-lit vigil was held in Hong Kong to mourn the death of Chinese reformist leader Zhao Ziyang, who had remained under house arrest since the repression of the Tiananmen Square protests in 1989.

In March 2005 Tung Chee-hwa resigned from his post as Chief Executive, two years before his term in office was due to end. Chief Secretary for Administration Donald Tsang Yam-kuen

became acting Chief Executive, with a permanent appointment expected to be made within six months. Tung cited adverse health effects as the reason for his departure from the Chief Executive post. He was to become Vice-Chairman of the Chinese People's Political Consultative Conference, a body of the mainland Chinese Government. There was speculation that Tung had been removed from his post by the Beijing Government owing to his unpopularity in the SAR.

Legislation approved by the PLC in July 1997, meanwhile, included the introduction of measures to restrict the immigration into the territory of mainland-born children of Hong Kong residents. However, in January 1998 a judge ruled that this new legislation contravened the Basic Law. The Court of Final Appeal ruled against the SAR Government in January 1999, upholding the judgment that the legislation was unconstitutional, prompting condemnation of the Court by the People's Republic of China. Fearing that the ruling on the right of abode by the Court of Final Appeal would result in an influx of more than 1.6m. mainland Chinese, the SAR administration asked the Court in February to clarify its judgment, which apparently asserted the Court's right to overrule decisions relating to the Basic Law made by the NPC in Beijing. The Court of Final Appeal declared that it recognized the authority of the Standing Committee of the Chinese NPC. In May the Legislative Council voted to request the Standing Committee of the NPC to interpret the relevant articles of the Basic Law, to the dissatisfaction of lawyers and democrats, who protested that the SAR's autonomy was being undermined. The NPC published its interpretation, which was not retroactive, in June, stating that the Court of Final Appeal had failed to adhere to the Basic Law in not requesting an interpretation before delivering its judgment. The NPC stipulated that mainlanders were to be granted the right of abode in Hong Kong only if at least one parent had been permanently resident in the territory at the time of their birth and that mainland children of Hong Kong parents who wished to settle in the territory had to apply for mainland approval before entering the SAR. These changes to the interpretation of the Basic Law were estimated to reduce the number of successful applicants to 200,000. In December 17 immigrants with parents resident in Hong Kong were denied the right of abode by the Court of Final Appeal, which recognized China's unrestricted powers to interpret the Basic Law (three subsequently obtained permission to reside in the territory). Violent clashes between demonstrators and the security forces followed the ruling.

In August 2000 disaffected mainland Chinese immigrants seeking the right of abode in Hong Kong firebombed the Immigration Department building. Two people were killed, including one immigration officer; 22 people were subsequently arrested and charged with murder. In July 2001 Hong Kong's Court of Final Appeal ruled that a three-year-old boy born in Hong Kong while his mother was visiting the territory had the right to reside there, in a move praised as a triumph of rule of law. However, in early August the same court ordered the deportation of a 14-year-old girl to the mainland owing to the fact that she had been born there and subsequently adopted by Hong Kong parents. In June 2001 the Government planned to deport 5,000 migrants to the mainland, pending the outcome of a court case. The Court of Final Appeal in January 2002 announced that all except about 200 of these 5,000 people would be returned to the mainland by the end of March. Although some 400 people returned to the mainland before the 31 March deadline, approximately 4,300 refused to do so, and in April the authorities began forcibly deporting the remaining abode-seekers. The actions were particularly criticized because they resulted in children being separated from their parents and families being split up. Scores began legal proceedings against the deportations, amid strong protests by those concerned, and Bishop Joseph Zen personally intervened on behalf of several mentally ill or sick abode-seekers who were facing expulsion. It was reported in January 2003 that some 2,302 child abode-seekers had been deported to the mainland during 2002. In February 2003 plans were announced to ease immigration restrictions for skilled workers and business people from the Chinese mainland wishing to enter Hong Kong. This policy, the so-called Admission Scheme for Mainland Professionals, was introduced in July, and by December 1,545 applications for residence in Hong Kong had been received under the Scheme, of which 1,143 had been approved. In July 2003 further changes in immigration policy were introduced affecting dependants of permanent Hong Kong residents. Under these new regulations, persons holding a dependant visa were no longer entitled to take up employment in Hong Kong. Meanwhile, there were continuing efforts to prevent illegal immigration from mainland China, with 18,621 mainland Chinese being refused entry to Hong Kong in 2003.

In September 1998 the Sino-British JLG met in Hong Kong, for the first time since Hong Kong's transfer to China, to resolve outstanding issues. The most significant problem was that of the 1,100 Vietnamese refugees remaining in Hong Kong; China requested funds from the United Kingdom to facilitate their repatriation. At the final meeting of the JLG before its dissolution (on 1 January 2000), in December 1999 there was a disagreement over the treatment of a Hong Kong resident who had reportedly been arrested in Thailand and deported to the People's Republic of China without any formal extradition proceedings. The man, who had a British National Overseas passport, was entitled to British consular protection. The Chinese authorities, however, maintained that, as he was a Chinese national suspected of perpetrating crimes in the mainland, their jurisdiction applied.

Despite the tensions surrounding the transfer of sovereignty, many citizens of Hong Kong supported the Government of the People's Republic of China in its territorial dispute with Japan regarding the Diaoyu (or Senkaku) Islands. In September 1996 a Hong Kong activist, David Chan, was accidentally drowned during a protest against Japan's claim to the islands. As issues of patriotism assumed greater significance in Hong Kong, more than 10,000 people attended a demonstration to mourn the death of David Chan and to denounce Japan. In October protesters from Hong Kong joined a flotilla of small boats from Taiwan and Macao, which successfully evaded Japanese patrol vessels and raised the flags of China and Taiwan on the disputed islands.

The European Union (EU, see p. 217) agreed in December 2000 to grant residents of Hong Kong and Macao visa-free access to member states. This took effect from April 2001.

In July 2001 Tung Chee-hwa visited Washington, DC, and held a meeting with US President George W. Bush, at which Hong Kong's handling of Falun Gong and other issues of freedom were discussed. In August a US aircraft carrier made a visit to Hong Kong, in a sign of improving Sino-US ties. However, in March 2002 Beijing refused permission for a US warship to make a routine visit to Hong Kong, mainly in protest at the increasing links between the USA and Taiwan. In April, however, the ban was removed. In November, following an undercover operation by the US Federal Bureau of Investigation (FBI), three men were arrested for allegedly seeking to sells drugs in exchange for anti-aircraft missiles for the Islamist al-Qa'ida group. They agreed in January 2003 to be extradited to the USA. During a visit to Hong Kong in July 2003 British Prime Minister Tony Blair expressed his support for movement towards greater democracy in Hong Kong, following mass protests earlier in the month (see above), but also stated that it was important to maintain stability in the territory. In March 2004 a group of democracy activists, led by Martin Lee, visited the USA in order to discuss with representatives of the US Government their concerns over human rights in Hong Kong. Also in March, Chan Yu-lam, a resident of Hong Kong and a British citizen who had formerly been employed at the Hong Kong branch of the Xinhua state news agency of China, was accused of having spied on behalf of the United Kingdom and sentenced to life imprisonment by a court in Guangzhou. (Two other Hong Kong officials, Wei Pinguan and Cai Xiaohong, were imprisoned later in the year after also having been charged with spying for the United Kingdom.) Following the ruling of the Standing Committee of China's NPC in April, vetoing direct elections in Hong Kong (see above), the British Foreign and Commonwealth Office issued a statement claiming that the ruling had broken the promise of a high degree of autonomy for Hong Kong which been made by the Chinese Government in 1997. In May the head of the Catholic Church in Hong Kong, Bishop Joseph Zen Ze-kiun, an outspoken supporter of democracy in the territory who had been banned from visiting the mainland in 1998 (see above), was permitted to make a three-day visit to Shanghai.

Government

Since 1 July 1997 the Hong Kong SAR has been administered by a Chief Executive, who is accountable to the State Council of the People's Republic of China and serves a five-year term, there being a limit of two consecutive terms. The first incumbent was chosen by a 400-member Selection Committee in December 1996. Upon the expiry of his first term in 2002, the Chief Executive was chosen by an 800-member Election Committee.

In July 2002 a new government structure was introduced, which expanded the Executive Council into a cabinet-style body comprising 14 ex-officio members known as principal officials (each with an individual portfolio) and five non-official members, all accountable to the Chief Executive. Elections to the third four-year term of the 60-member Legislative Council took place in September 2004; 30 of the seats (compared with 24 in the previous legislature) were directly elective (under a system of proportional representation), with 30 seats being determined by 'functional constituencies' (comprising professional and special interest groups).

Defence

In December 1996 the Standing Committee of the National People's Congress in Beijing adopted the Hong Kong Garrison Law, which provided for the stationing in Hong Kong of troops of the People's Liberation Army (PLA). The Garrison Law defined the duties and obligations of the troops, jurisdiction over them and also the relationship between the troops and the Government of the Hong Kong SAR. The legislation took effect on 1 July 1997. The garrison can intervene in local matters only at the request of the Hong Kong Government, which remains responsible for internal security. In August 2004 a total of 7,000 Chinese troops were stationed in Hong Kong.

Economic Affairs

In 2003, according to estimates by the World Bank, Hong Kong's gross national income (GNI), measured at average 2001–03 prices, was US $163,020m., equivalent to US $25,430 per head (or US $28,810 on an international purchasing-power parity basis). During 1990–2003, it was estimated, the population increased by an average of 1.4% per year, while gross domestic product (GDP) per head increased, in real terms, at an average annual rate of 2.5% per year. Overall GDP increased, in real terms, at an average rate of 3.9% in 1990–2003; growth in 2003 was 3.3%, compared with the previous year.

Agriculture and fishing together employed only 0.2% of the working population in 2003, and contributed less than 0.1% of GDP in 2002. Crop production is largely restricted to flowers, vegetables and some fruit and nuts, while pigs and poultry are the principal livestock. An outbreak of avian influenza led to the slaughter of some 1.25m. poultry in May 2001. In early 2004 a new outbreak in neighbouring countries prompted the Government to implement stringent preventative measures. Hong Kong relies heavily on imports for its food supplies.

Industry (including mining, manufacturing, construction and power) provided an estimated 12.4% of GDP in 2002 and employed 17.2% of the working population in 2003.

Manufacturing employed 7.8% of the working population in 2003, and contributed an estimated 4.5% of GDP in 2002. Measured by the value of output, the principal branches of manufacturing are textiles and clothing, plastic products, metal products and electrical machinery (particularly radio and television sets).

The services sector plays the most important role in the economy, accounting for an estimated 87.5% of GDP in 2002 and employing 76.0% of the working population in 2003. The value of Hong Kong's invisible exports (financial services, tourism, shipping, etc.) was US $45,203m. in 2003. Revenue from tourism totalled an estimated US $10,117m. in 2002. The repercussions of the terrorist attacks on the USA in September 2001 adversely affected the tourism industry, as did the outbreak of Severe Acute Respiratory Syndrome (SARS) in April 2003 (see below). The number of visitors to the territory rose from 15.5m. in 2003 to a record 21.8m. (of whom 12.2m. were tourists from mainland China) in 2004. A new Disney theme park, the first phase of which was scheduled to open in September 2005, was expected further to increase the number of visitors to Hong Kong. The territory's banking and mercantile houses have branches throughout the region, and Hong Kong is regarded as a major financial centre, owing partly to the existence of an excellent international telecommunications network and to the absence of restrictions on capital inflows.

In 2003 Hong Kong recorded a visible trade deficit of US $5,779m. and there was a surplus of US $16,734m. on the current account of the balance of payments. Re-exports constituted 93.8% of total exports in 2004. The principal sources of Hong Kong's imports in 2004 were the People's Republic of China (43.5%) and Japan (12.1%); the principal markets for exports (including re-exports) were the People's Republic of China (44.0%) and the USA (16.9%). Other major trading partners included Taiwan, Germany and the United Kingdom. In

2002 the principal domestic exports were clothing, textiles, electrical machinery, data-processing equipment, and photographic apparatus. The principal imports in that year were foodstuffs, chemicals, textiles, machinery, transport equipment, and other manufactured articles.

In 2003/04 the budget deficit was an estimated HK $49,000m. (equivalent to 4.0% of GDP), the shortfall being considerably lower than the previous projection of HK $78,000m. A further improvement was anticipated for 2004/05, a deficit of HK $42,600m. (3.4% of GDP) being projected. The Government stated that it hoped to balance the budget by 2008/09, planning to reduce public spending by around 20%. The annual rate of inflation averaged 3.9% in 1990–2002. The consumer price index declined by 3.0% in 2002 and by 2.6 in 2003. Consumer prices continued to decrease in the first half of 2004, but Hong Kong returned to inflationary conditions for the first time in 68 months in July 2004, with a 0.9% increase in consumer prices being recorded in that month (compared with the corresponding month of the previous year). In 2004 as a whole, however, consumer prices decreased by 0.4%. As a result of the SARS crisis, the rate of unemployment increased dramatically in mid-2003, to reach a record 8.7% of the labour force, but declined during 2004 to stand at an estimated 6.5% in the final quarter of the year. The shortage of skilled labour continued.

Hong Kong is a member of the Asian Development Bank (ADB, see p. 159) and an associate member of the UN Economic and Social Commission for Asia and the Pacific (ESCAP, see p. 31). The territory became a member of Asia-Pacific Economic Co-operation (APEC, see p. 155) in 1991. Hong Kong joined the Bank for International Settlements (BIS, see p. 170) in 1996, and in early 1997 announced its participation in the IMF's New Arrangements to Borrow (NAB) scheme. After mid-1997 Hong Kong remained a separate customs territory, within the World Trade Organization (WTO, see p. 357).

Under the terms of the Basic Law, Hong Kong's financial system remained unchanged following the transfer to Chinese sovereignty in mid-1997. The territory continued as a free port, and the Hong Kong dollar was retained, remaining freely convertible and linked to the US currency. In 2001 the deceleration in the economy of the USA resulted in the weakening of one of Hong Kong's major export markets, which was compounded by the events of 11 September of that year. Despite Hong Kong's general recovery from the recessionary conditions of the late 1990s, consumer prices remained in decline until mid-2004 when prices began to rise modestly. In response to a decline in the property market, in September 2001 the Government declared a moratorium on the sale of subsidized public housing, which was removed in July 2002. In November 2002, however, the Government imposed a moratorium on property sales and land auctions until the end of 2003, in an attempt to halt the decline in property prices, which had decreased by 65% since 1997. The Hong Kong Monetary Authority stated in June 2002 that some 150,000 homeowners were experiencing negative equity. By late 2003, however, the property market appeared to be recovering, and compared with the same month of the previous year a 55% increase in property sales was reported for January 2004. It was estimated that the number of households with negative equity decreased by 30% in the second quarter of 2004, to 28,200. The Hong Kong stock market, as measured by the Hang Seng Index, remained subdued during 2002, but recovered during 2003 and increased by 13% in 2004, representing the first consecutive annual increase since 1996. Unemployment increased sharply from 2001, as companies downsized operations and new graduates entered the labour market, these developments being compounded by the effects of the SARS outbreak in 2003. There was some improvement in the labour market from late 2003, however, with unemployment continuing to decrease during 2004. Nevertheless, it was predicted at the beginning of 2005 that any further substantial decrease in unemployment was unlikely in the near future. The number of bankruptcy orders, meanwhile, rose from 9,151 in 2001 to 25,238 in 2002, declining slightly to 24,922 in 2003. As the budget deficit continued to place pressure on the economy, in early 2004 the Government declared its aim to raise HK $112,000m. over the next five years, in an effort to balance the budget. During 2004/05 government bonds up to the value of HK $20,000m. were to be issued, specifically to finance infrastructural projects. The introduction of a goods-and-services tax, as a means of expanding Hong Kong's narrow tax base, was also reported to be under consideration. By late 2002 there was increasing debate about delinking (and therefore devaluing) the

Hong Kong dollar from its US counterpart, in order to allow Hong Kong prices to adjust more easily to those of mainland China, and granting Hong Kong more flexibility in monetary policy. In the longer term, Hong Kong faced rising competition from Shanghai as China's leading financial centre. An increasing number of foreign investors were conducting business directly with the mainland and transferring regional offices there, where in the past Hong Kong had acted as an intermediary. Furthermore, Shanghai was expected to overtake Hong Kong as the world's largest container port by 2015. The opening of a large airport in Guangzhou in August 2004 was also believed to represent a potential threat to Hong Kong's status as a hub for international air traffic. In April 2003, meanwhile, following the outbreak of SARS, the World Health Organization (WHO) issued a warning against travel to Hong Kong, prompting the Government to announce a range of measures to assist those in the most vulnerable sectors of the economy, such as tourism, catering and retailing. Visitor arrivals in Hong Kong decreased by 67.9% in May 2003 compared with the corresponding month of the previous year. However, following the removal of the WHO travel warning in late May and the apparent end of the SARS epidemic in June, from mid-2003 the economy began to show signs of a quick recovery. It was believed that the SARS crisis had made little impact on Hong Kong's economy in the long term. The tourism sector benefited especially from a sharp increase in tourist arrivals from the Chinese mainland, following the implementation in July of a new policy to allow Guangdong residents to visit Hong Kong individually rather than as part of a tour group. The scheme was subsequently extended to encompass residents of Beijing, Shanghai and certain other areas of mainland China. Despite political tensions, economic relations with the Chinese mainland were expected to develop following the signing of the Closer Economic Partnership Agreement (CEPA) in June 2003. Under this agreement, various taxes levied by China on Hong Kong's products were to be removed or substantially reduced. From February 2004 Hong Kong banks were permitted to conduct personal banking services in Chinese yuan. Piracy remained a serious problem for Hong Kong's economy. It was estimated that in 2003 52% of software installed on computers in Hong Kong lacked official authorization. Environmental issues were also a continuing concern, with record levels of air pollution being reported in September 2004. In the same year there were protests by environmental groups against land reclamation projects planned by the Government. GDP growth for 2004 was initially projected at 6%, with the prediction being increased to 7.5% later in the year. For 2005 growth of around 4.5% was anticipated.

Education

In 2003/04 an estimated 136,000 children attended kindergarten. Full-time education is compulsory between the ages of six and 15. Primary education has been free in all government schools and in nearly all aided schools since 1971 and junior secondary education since 1978. There are three main types of secondary school: grammar, technical and pre-vocational. The four government-run teacher-training colleges merged to form the Hong Kong Institute of Education in 1994. The Hong Kong Institute of Vocational Education (IVE), which was founded in 1999, incorporates seven government-funded technical institutes and two colleges. In 1995 total enrolment at primary and secondary schools was equivalent to 82% of the school-age population (males 80%, females 84%). Primary enrolment in that year included 91% of children in the relevant age-group (males 90%, females 92%), while the comparable ratio for secondary enrolment was 71% (males 69%, females 73%). An education reform programme was in progress from 2000, including reform of curriculum and education management, and the establishment of Project Yi Jin, a life-long learning initiative. In 2003/04 the seven universities, (including Lingnan University, formerly Lingnan College, renamed in July 1999) and the Hong Kong Institute of Education had an estimated combined enrolment of 90,400 full-time and part-time students. The Open University of Hong Kong (founded in 1989 as the Open Learning Institute of Hong Kong), had 40,800 students in 2003/04. Budgetary expenditure (capital and recurrent) on education was an estimated HK $57,748m. for the financial year 2003/04.

Public Holidays

2005: 3 January (first weekday in January), 9–11 February (Chinese New Year), 5 April (Ching Ming), 25–28 March (Easter), 2 May (Labour Day), 16 May (the Buddha's birthday),

11 June (Tuen Ng, Dragon Boat Festival), 1 July (SAR Establishment Day), 19 September (Chinese Mid-Autumn Festival), 1 October (National Day), 11 October (Chung Yeung Festival), 25–26 December (Christmas).

2006: 2 January (first weekday in January), 29 –31 January (Chinese New Year), 5 April (Ching Ming), 14–17 April (Easter), 1 May (Labour Day), 5 May (the Buddha's birthday), 31 May (Tuen Ng, Dragon Boat Festival), 1 July (SAR Establishment Day), 1 October (National Day), 7 October (Chinese Mid-Autumn Festival), 30 October (Chung Yeung Festival), 25–26 December (Christmas).

Weights and Measures

The metric system is in force. Chinese units include: tsün (37.147 mm), chek or ch'ih (37.147 cm); kan or catty (604.8 grams), tam or picul (60.479 kg).

Statistical Survey

Source (unless otherwise stated): Census and Statistics Department, 19/F Wanchai Tower, 12 Harbour Rd, Hong Kong; tel. 25825073; fax 28271708; e-mail genenq@censtatd.gcn.gov.hk; internet www.info.gov.hk/censtatd/eng/hkstat/index2.html/.

Area and Population

AREA, POPULATION AND DENSITY

Land area (sq km)	1,103*
Population (census results)†	
15 March 1996	6,412,937
15 March 2001	
Males	3,285,344
Females	3,423,045
Total	6,708,389
Population (official estimates at mid-year)‡	
2001	6,724,900
2002	6,787,000
2003	6,803,100
Density (per sq km) at mid-2003	6,167.8

* 424 sq miles.
† All residents (including mobile residents) on the census date, including those who were temporarily absent from Hong Kong.
‡ Revised figures, referring to resident population, including mobile residents.

DISTRICTS
(2001 census)

	Area (sq km)	Population*	Density (per sq km)
Hong Kong Island . . .	80.28	1,335,469	16,635
Kowloon	46.85	2,023,979	43,201
New Territories . . .	970.91	3,343,046	3,443
Total	1,098.04†	6,702,494	6,104

* Excluding marine population (5,895).
† Total area was subsequently revised to 1,103 sq km.

PRINCIPAL TOWNS
(population at 1996 census)

Kowloon*	1,988,515	Tai Po	271,661
Victoria (capital) .	1,011,433	Tseun Wan . . .	268,659
Tuen Mun . . .	445,771	Sheung Shui . . .	192,321
Sha Tin	445,383	Tsing Yu . . .	185,495
Kwai Chung . . .	285,231	Aberdeen	164,439

* Including New Kowloon.

BIRTHS, MARRIAGES AND DEATHS*

	Known live births		Registered marriages		Known deaths	
	Number	Rate (per '000)	Number	Rate (per '000)	Number	Rate (per '000)
1996 . . .	64,559†	10.2	37,045	5.9	32,049†	5.1
1997‡ . .	60,379†	9.1	37,593	5.8	32,079†	4.9
1998‡ . .	53,356†	7.9	31,673	4.7	32,680†	4.8
1999‡ . .	50,513	7.5	31,287	4.6	33,387	4.8
2000‡ . .	53,720	8.1	30,879	4.6	33,993	5.1
2001‡ . .	49,144	7.2	32,825	4.9	33,305	5.0
2002‡ . .	48,200	7.1	32,070	4.7	34,300	5.0
2003‡ . .	46,200	6.8	35,400	5.2	36,500	5.4

* Excluding Vietnamese migrants.
† Figure calculated by year of registration.
‡ Provisional. Figures prior to 2000 have not been revised to take account of the results of the 2001 population census.

Expectation of life (years at birth, 2002, provisional): Males 78.7; Females 84.7.

ECONOMICALLY ACTIVE POPULATION
('000 persons aged 15 years and over, excl. armed forces)

	2001	2002	2003
Agriculture and fishing	7.2	9.9	7.5
Mining and quarrying	0.2	0.4	0.4
Manufacturing	326.4	289.5	272.4
Electricity, gas and water . . .	15.7	15.9	16.2
Construction	291.4	286.7	266.1
Wholesale, retail and import/export trades, restaurants and hotels .	981.1	983.7	993.2
Transport, storage and communications	353.4	346.0	346.4
Financing, insurance, real estate and business services . . .	478.1	474.7	470.2
Community, social and personal services	798.9	825.6	850.8
Total employed	3,252.3	3,232.3	3,223.3
Unemployed	174.8	255.5	277.6
Total labour force	3,427.1	3,487.8	3,500.9
Males	1,965.2	1,964.6	1,962.3
Females	1,461.9	1,523.2	1,538.5

Source: ILO.

Health and Welfare

KEY INDICATORS

Total fertility rate (children per woman, 1995–2000) . . .	1.2
Under-5 mortality rate (per 1,000 live births, provisional, 2001)	2.7
HIV/AIDS (% of persons aged 15–49, 2003)	0.1
Physicians (per 1,000 head, provisional, 2002)	1.6
Hospital beds (per 1,000 head, provisional, 2002)	5.2
Human Development Index (2002): ranking	23
Human Development Index (2002): value	0.903

For sources and definitions, see explanatory note on p. vi.

Agriculture

PRINCIPAL CROPS
(FAO estimates, '000 metric tons)

	2001	2002	2003
Lettuce	5	5	5
Spinach	11	11	11
Onions and shallots (green) . . .	4	4	4
Other vegetables	14	14	4
Fruit	4	4	4

Source: FAO.

LIVESTOCK
(FAO estimates, '000 head, year ending September)

	2001	2002	2003
Cattle (head)	1,500	1,500	1,500
Pigs	100	100	95
Chickens	1,000	1,000	1,000
Ducks	250	250	250

Source: FAO.

LIVESTOCK PRODUCTS
('000 metric tons)

	2001	2002	2003
Beef and veal*	15	14	13
Pig meat*	165	163	148
Poultry meat	62	61	60
Game meat†	6	6	6
Cattle hides (fresh)†	2	2	2

* Unofficial figures.
† FAO estimates.

Source: FAO.

Fishing

(FAO estimates, '000 metric tons, live weight)

	2000	2001	2002
Capture	157.0	174.0	169.8
Lizardfishes	5.8	6.4	6.3
Threadfin breams	17.0	18.8	18.3
Shrimps and prawns . . .	4.6	5.1	5.0
Squids	7.3	8.1	7.9
Aquaculture	5.0	5.6	4.3
Total catch	162.0	179.6	174.1

Source: FAO.

Industry

SELECTED PRODUCTS
('000 metric tons, unless otherwise indicated)

	1999	2000	2001
Crude groundnut oil	18	n.a.	n.a.
Uncooked macaroni and noodle products	127	83	62
Cotton yarn (pure and mixed) . .	n.a.	n.a.	90.9
Cotton woven fabrics (million sq m)	366	306	378
Knitted sweaters ('000) . . .	117,738	103,519	151,965
Men's and boys' jackets ('000) . .	6,414	2,027	1,838
Men's and boys' trousers ('000) .	32,937	20,457	14,139
Women's and girls' blouses ('000) .	63,596	93,323	187,209
Women's and girls' dresses ('000) .	5,668	1,375	2,242
Women's and girls' skirts, slacks and shorts ('000)	77,344	35,141	23,823
Men's and boys' shirts ('000) . .	41,040	149,824	105,254
Watches ('000)	31,926	28,729	16,774
Electric energy (million kWh) . .	29,496	31,329	n.a.

Source: UN, *Industrial Commodity Statistics Yearbook*.

Finance

CURRENCY AND EXCHANGE RATES

Monetary Units
100 cents = 1 Hong Kong dollar (HK $).

Sterling, US Dollar and Euro Equivalents (31 December 2004)
£1 sterling = HK $15.014;
US $1 = HK $7.774;
€1 = HK $10.588;
HK $1,000 = £66.61 = US $128.64 = €94.44.

Average Exchange Rate (HK $ per US $)
2002   7.7990
2003   7.7868
2004   7.7880

BUDGET
(HK $ million, year ending 31 March)

Revenue	2001/02	2002/03	2003/04*
Direct taxes:			
Earnings and profits tax . . .	77,749	73,028	78,080
Indirect taxes:			
Estate duty	1,928	1,403	1,500
Duties on petroleum products, beverages, tobacco and cosmetics	6,981	6,620	6,539
General rates (property tax) .	12,727	8,923	11,131
Motor vehicle taxes	2,676	2,510	2,712
Royalties and concessions . .	1,881	1,726	1,654
Others	21,077	19,464	22,595
Fines, forfeitures and penalties .	926	843	822
Receipts from properties and investments	8,621	8,015	7,708
Reimbursements and contributions	4,154	4,405	3,212
Operating revenue from utilities:			
Water	2,471	1,458	2,093
Others	895	610	757
Fees and charges	10,916	9,687	10,369
Interest receipts (operating revenue)	225	2,766	5,886
Land Fund (investment income) .	106	13,281	17,150
Capital Works Reserve Fund (land sales and interest)	10,683	12,190	6,025
Capital Investment Fund . . .	2,816	2,432	2,423
Loan funds	5,382	4,464	17,551
Other capital revenue	3,345	3,664	5,630
Total government revenue . .	175,559	177,489	203,837

Expenditure†	2001/02	2002/03	2003/04*
Economic affairs and services . .	13,714	13,748	15,561
Internal security	21,679	21,085	21,151
Immigration	2,301	2,531	2,805
Other security services	3,574	3,452	3,500
Social welfare	30,059	32,282	33,997
Health services	34,213	33,199	34,485
Education	52,232	54,785	57,748
Environmental services	11,207	11,443	11,213
Recreation, culture and amenities .	6,381	6,026	6,433
Other community and external affairs	1,844	2,051	2,093
Transport	6,399	7,732	9,920
Land and buildings	10,768	9,385	9,686
Water supply	7,711	7,473	6,757
Support	35,222	34,297	35,980
Housing	32,055	24,031	27,854
Total	269,359	263,520	279,183
Recurrent	210,445	211,728	214,460
Capital	58,914	51,792	64,723

* Revised estimates.
† Figures refer to consolidated expenditure by the public sector.

INTERNATIONAL RESERVES
(US $ million at 31 December)

	2001	2002	2003
Gold*	19	23	28
Foreign exchange†	111,155	111,898	118,360
Total	111,174	111,921	118,388

* National valuation.
† Including the foreign exchange reserves of the Hong Kong Special Administrative Region Government's Land Fund.

Source: IMF, *International Financial Statistics.*

MONEY SUPPLY
(HK $ '000 million at 31 December)

	2001	2002	2003
Currency outside banks . . .	101.4	113.0	127.6
Demand deposits at banking institutions	109.5	127.4	196.4
Total money	210.9	240.4	324.1

Source: IMF, *International Financial Statistics.*

COST OF LIVING
(Consumer price index; base: 2000 = 100)

	2001	2002	2003
Food	99.2	97.1	95.7
Housing	97.0	91.4	87.0
Electricity, gas and other fuels .	98.0	91.3	92.5
Clothing and footwear	95.4	96.1	93.6
All items (incl. others)	98.4	95.4	93.0

Source: ILO.

NATIONAL ACCOUNTS
(HK $ million at current prices)

Expenditure on the Gross Domestic Product

	2001	2002	2003
Government final consumption expenditure	128,846	131,279	130,067
Private final consumption expenditure	765,105	728,092	704,863
Change in stocks	−4,060	5,660	9,471
Gross domestic fixed capital formation	333,036	286,020	269,127
Total domestic expenditure .	1,222,927	1,151,051	1,113,528
Net exports of goods and services .	46,969	96,330	106,321
GDP in purchasers' values .	1,269,896	1,247,381	1,219,849
GDP at constant 2000 prices .	1,294,306	1,318,743	1,361,036

Gross Domestic Product by Economic Activity
(at factor price)

	2000	2001	2002
Agriculture and fishing	920	1,003	1,002
Mining and quarrying	241	174	136
Manufacturing	71,655	63,519	54,848
Electricity, gas and water . . .	38,853	40,126	41,540
Construction	64,026	58,971	53,089
Wholesale, retail and import/export trades, restaurants and hotels .	324,622	324,654	324,131
Transport, storage and communications	125,724	124,260	128,278
Financing, insurance, real estate and business services . . .	291,062	274,030	267,537
Community, social and personal services	252,435	265,081	267,659
Ownership of premises* . . .	59,358	63,537	67,258
Sub-total	1,228,897	1,215,354	1,205,479

— *continued*	2000	2001	2002
Taxes on production and imports .	57,908	53,917	43,325
Statistical discrepancy	1,533	625	−1,423
GDP in market prices . . .	1,288,338	1,269,896	1,247,381

* Including adjustments for financial intermediation services indirectly measured.

Source: Asian Development Bank, *Key Indicators of Developing Asian and Pacific Countries.*

BALANCE OF PAYMENTS
(US $ million)

	2001	2002	2003
Exports of goods f.o.b.	190,926	200,300	224,656
Imports of goods f.o.b.	−199,257	−205,353	−230,435
Trade balance	−8,331	−5,053	−5,779
Exports of services	39,449	43,008	45,203
Imports of services	−24,677	−25,603	−25,185
Balance on goods and services	6,441	12,352	14,239
Other income received	49,315	43,223	42,198
Other income paid	−44,036	−41,083	−37,813
Balance on goods, services and income	11,721	14,492	18,623
Current transfers received . . .	605	777	574
Current transfers paid . . .	−2,385	−2,673	−2,463
Current balance	9,941	12,596	16,734
Capital account (net)	−1,174	−2,011	−1,016
Direct investment abroad . .	−11,345	−17,463	−3,747
Direct investment from abroad	23,776	9,682	13,538
Portfolio investment assets .	−40,133	−37,702	−31,458
Portfolio investment liabilities .	−1,161	−1,084	991
Financial derivatives assets . .	17,971	20,035	25,435
Financial derivatives liabilities .	−12,888	−13,424	−15,224
Other investment assets . .	59,137	46,617	−22,181
Other investment liabilities .	−41,985	−26,412	15,193
Net errors and omissions . .	2,543	6,788	2,729
Overall balance	4,684	−2,377	994

Source: IMF, *International Financial Statistics.*

External Trade

PRINCIPAL COMMODITIES
(US $ million)

Imports c.i.f.	2000	2001	2002
Food and live animals . . .	7,328.5	6,949.3	6,869.9
Chemicals and related products	13,203.8	11,355.3	11,852.4
Basic manufactures . . .	36,684.6	32,925.6	33,589.9
Textile yarn, fabrics, made-up articles, etc.	13,726.0	12,183.7	12,072.2
Machinery and transport equipment	90,774.2	88,151.0	95,670.8
Office machines and automatic data-processing equipment .	18,341.5	18,938.5	20,100.9
Telecommunications and sound recording and reproducing apparatus and equipment . .	20,742.3	20,348.1	23,254.3
Electrical machinery, apparatus and appliances n.e.s., and electrical parts thereof . . .	37,407.0	33,980.2	38,101.1
Miscellaneous manufactured articles	55,304.6	53,127.0	51,060.7
Clothing (excl. footwear) . . .	16,028.4	16,121.1	15,718.4
Footwear	5,318.2	4,863.1	4,766.8
Photographic apparatus, equipment and supplies, optical goods, watches and clocks . .	7,166.3	6,998.3	6,955.2
Total (incl. others)	214,041.7	202,008.0	207,969.0

Exports f.o.b.	2000	2001	2002
Chemicals and related products	10,318.3	9,166.0	9,558.6
Basic manufactures	30,203.5	27,065.0	27,919.5
Textile yarn, fabrics, made-up articles, etc.	13,455.4	12,233.8	12,431.2
Machinery and transport equipment	77,699.1	75,981.0	87,605.2
Office machines and automatic data-processing equipment	16,402.5	17,746.5	20,398.7
Telecommunications and sound recording and reproducing apparatus and equipment	19,618.2	18,696.5	22,877.8
Electrical machinery, apparatus and appliances n.e.s., and electrical parts thereof	32,357.4	30,649.9	34,018.3
Miscellaneous manufactured articles	76,710.3	71,670.6	69,126.0
Clothing (excl. footwear)	24,239.6	23,472.3	22,453.6
Photographic apparatus, equipment and supplies, optical goods, watches and clocks	9,058.3	8,563.2	8,381.8
Total (incl. others)	202,683.2	191,066.2	201,927.8

Source: UN, *International Trade Statistics Yearbook*.

2003 (HK $ million): Total imports 1,805,800; Domestic exports 121,700; Re-exports 1,620,700; Total exports 1,742,400.

PRINCIPAL TRADING PARTNERS
(HK $ million, excl. gold)

Imports	2002	2003	2004
China, People's Repub.	717,074	785,625	918,275
Germany	32,997	41,222	39,999
Japan	182,569	213,995	256,141
Korea, Repub.	75,955	87,340	100,467
Malaysia	39,729	44,637	51,941
Singapore	75,740	90,570	110,986
Taiwan	115,906	125,203	153,812
Thailand	29,556	33,194	37,782
USA	91,478	98,730	111,994
Total (incl. others)	1,619,419	1,805,770	2,111,123

Domestic exports	2002	2003	2004
Canada	2,411	2,237	1,976
China, People's Repub.	41,374	36,757	37,898
Germany	4,273	4,853	4,985
Japan	2,969	2,848	2,812
Netherlands	3,470	2,473	2,616
Singapore	2,161	2,237	3,149
Taiwan	4,388	3,653	4,664
United Kingdom	7,588	7,762	8,190
USA	41,908	39,130	38,636
Total (incl. others)	130,926	121,687	125,982

Re-exports	2002	2003	2004
China, People's Repub.	571,870	705,787	850,645
France	19,243	20,676	24,964
Germany	44,567	51,369	57,915
Japan	80,743	91,154	104,733
Korea, Repub.	29,264	34,336	42,673
Netherlands	22,775	25,498	30,524
Singapore	29,424	33,468	40,428
Taiwan	30,193	38,616	44,447
United Kingdom	46,644	49,625	57,663
USA	291,043	285,084	302,964
Total (incl. others)	1,429,590	1,620,749	1,893,132

Transport

RAILWAYS
(traffic)

	2001	2002	2003
Passenger train journeys	3,001	n.a.	n.a.
Freight (metric tons):			
loaded	97,139	102,000	76,000
unloaded	273,051	283,000	253,000

ROAD TRAFFIC
(registered motor vehicles at 31 December)

	2001	2002*	2003*
Private cars	381,757	341,000	339,000
Buses (private and public)	13,297	13,000	13,000
Light buses (private and public)	6,448	6,000	6,000
Taxis	18,138	18,000	18,000
Goods vehicles	126,233	111,000	110,000
Motorcycles	36,191	28,000	30,000
Government vehicles (excl. military vehicles)	7,127	7,000	7,000
Total (incl. others)	589,808	526,000	524,000

* Preliminary figures, rounded.
Note: Figures do not include tramcars.

SHIPPING

Merchant Fleet
(registered at 31 December)

	2001	2002	2003
Number of vessels	646	766	901
Total displacement ('000 grt)	13,709.7	16,164.3	20,507.5

Source: Lloyd's Register-Fairplay, *World Fleet Statistics*.

Traffic
(2003)

	Ocean-going vessels	River vessels
Total capacity (million nrt)	591	181
Cargo landed ('000 metric tons)*	97,600	28,900
Cargo loaded ('000 metric tons)*	48,100	29,400

* Provisional figures.

Passenger traffic ('000, ocean-going vessels and river vessels, 2003): Passengers landed 8,879; Passengers embarked 9,765.

CIVIL AVIATION

	2001	2002	2003
Passengers:			
arrivals	11,533,000	11,841,000	9,486,000
departures	11,488,000	11,722,000	9,361,000
Freight (in metric tons):*			
landed	894,000	1,004,000	1,035,000
loaded	1,180,000	1,475,000	1,608,000

* Provisional figures.

Tourism

VISITOR ARRIVALS BY COUNTRY OF RESIDENCE

	2000	2001	2002
Australia	352,409	324,156	343,294
Canada	253,095	249,707	264,967
China, People's Repub.	3,785,845	4,448,583	6,825,199
Germany	193,837	173,359	172,654
Indonesia	236,275	212,260	223,590
Japan	1,382,417	1,336,538	1,395,020
Korea, Repub.	372,639	425,732	457,438
Macao	449,947	532,391	534,590
Malaysia	314,857	286,338	318,854
Philippines	278,460	293,105	329,604
Singapore	450,569	421,513	426,166
Taiwan	2,385,739	2,418,827	2,428,776
Thailand	228,774	241,480	259,336
United Kingdom	367,938	360,581	379,965
USA and Guam	966,008	935,717	1,000,844
Total (incl. others)	13,059,477	13,725,332	16,566,382

Source: Hong Kong Tourist Board.

Receipts from tourism (US $ million): 7,886 in 2000; 8,282 in 2001; 10,117 in 2002.

Communications Media

	2001	2002	2003
Telephones ('000 in use)	3,897.6	3,831.8	3,801.3
Facsimile machines (number in use)	411,000	546,000	n.a.
Mobile cellular telephones ('000 subscribers)	5,776.4	6,395.7	7,241.4
Personal computers ('000 in use)	2,600	2,864	n.a.
Internet users ('000)	2,601.3	2,918.8	3,212.8

1997 ('000 in use): Radio receivers 4,450.

2000 ('000 in use): Television receivers 3,105.

2002: Daily newspapers 52; Periodicals 754.

Sources: partly UNESCO, *Statistical Yearbook;* UN, *Statistical Yearbook;* International Telecommunication Union.

Education

(2003/04)

	Institutions	Full-time teachers*	Students†
Kindergartens	768	9,159	136,100
Primary schools	785	22,845	468,800
Secondary schools	537	25,093	470,500
Special schools	74	1,671	10,200
Institute of Vocational Education‡	1	1,033	59,400
Approved post-secondary college	2	117	4,000
Other post-secondary colleges	12	—	2,900
UGC-funded institutions§	8	5,620	90,400
Open University of Hong Kong	1	105	40,800
Adult education institutions	2,128	—	201,100

* As of 2000/01.

† Figures are rounded to the nearest 100.

‡ Formed by merger of two technical colleges and seven technical institutes in 1999.

§ Funded by the University Grants Committee.

Adult literacy rate (UNESCO estimates): 93.5% (males 96.9%; females 89.6%) in 2002 (Source: UN Development Programme, *Human Development Report*).

Directory

The Constitution

Under the terms of the Basic Law of the Hong Kong Special Administrative Region, the Government comprises the Chief Executive, the Executive Council and the Legislative Council. The Chief Executive must be a Chinese citizen of at least 40 years of age; he is appointed for a five-year term, with a limit of two consecutive terms; in 2002 he was chosen by an 800-member Election Committee; he is accountable to the State Council of the People's Republic of China, and has no military authority; he appoints the Executive Council, judges and the principal government officials; he makes laws with the advice and consent of the legislature; he has a veto over legislation, but can be overruled by a two-thirds' majority; he may dissolve the legislature once in a term, but must resign if the legislative impasse continues with the new body. The Legislative Council has 60 members; in September 2004 candidates for 30 seats were directly elected under a system of proportional representation and 30 seats were determined by elections within 'functional constituencies' (comprising professional and special interest groups). The Legislative Council is responsible for enacting, revising and abrogating laws, for approving the budget, taxation and public expenditure, for debating the policy address of the Chief Executive and for approving the appointment of the judges of the Court of Final Appeal and of the Chief Justice of the High Court.

The Government

Chief Executive: DONALD TSANG YAM-KUEN (acting, assumed office 10 March 2005).

EXECUTIVE COUNCIL
(April 2005)

Chairman: The Chief Executive.

Ex-Officio Members (Principal Officials)

Chief Secretary for Administration: DONALD TSANG YAM-KUEN.

Financial Secretary: HENRY TANG YING-YEN.

Secretary for Justice: ELSIE LEUNG OI-SIE.

Secretary for Commerce, Industry and Technology: JOHN TSANG CHUN-WAH.

Secretary for Housing, Planning and Lands: MICHAEL SUEN MING-YEUNG.

Secretary for Education and Manpower: ARTHUR LI KWOK-CHEUNG.

Secretary for Health, Welfare and Food: Dr YORK CHOW YAT-NGOK.

Secretary for the Civil Service: JOSEPH WONG WING-PING.

Secretary for Home Affairs: PATRICK HO CHI-PING.

Secretary for Security: AMBROSE LEE SIU-KWONG.

Secretary for Economic Development and Labour: STEPHEN IP SHU-KWAN.

Secretary for the Environment, Transport and Works: Dr SARAH LIAO SAU-TUNG.

Secretary for Financial Services and the Treasury: FREDERICK MA SI-HANG.

Secretary for Constitutional Affairs: STEPHEN LAM SUI-LUNG.

Non-Official Members

LEUNG CHUN-YING, SELINA CHOW LIANG SHUK-YEE, JASPER TSANG YOK-SING, CHENG YIU-TONG, ANDREW LIAO CHEUNG-SING, LAURA M. CHA, BERNARD C. CHAN.

GOVERNMENT OFFICES

Executive Council: Central Government Offices, Lower Albert Rd, Central; tel. 28102545; fax 28450176.

Office of the Chief Executive: 5/F Main Wing, Central Government Offices, Lower Albert Rd, Central; tel. 28783300; fax 25090577.

Government Secretariat: Central Government Offices, Lower Albert Rd, Central; tel. 28102900; fax 28457895.

Government Information Services: Murray Bldg, Garden Rd, Central; tel. 28428777; fax 28459078; internet www.info.gov.hk.

Legislature

LEGISLATIVE COUNCIL

The third Legislative Council to follow Hong Kong's transfer to Chinese sovereignty was elected on 12 September 2004. The Legislative Council comprises 60 members: 30 chosen by functional constituencies and 30 (increased from 24 in the previous legislature)

Hong Kong

by direct election in five geographical constituencies. The term of office of the Legislative Council was to last for four years.

President: RITA FAN HSU LAI-TAI.

Election, 12 September 2004

Party	Directly-elective seats	Functional Constituency seats	Total seats
Democratic Alliance for the Betterment of Hong Kong	9	3	12
Liberal Party	2	8	10
Democratic Party of Hong Kong	8	1	9
Article 45 Concern Group	3	1	4
Hong Kong Confederation of Trade Unions . . .	2	—	2
The Frontier	1	—	1
Association for Democracy and People's Livelihood	1	—	1
Neighbourhood and Worker's Service Centre	1	—	1
April Fifth Action . . .	1	—	1
Hong Kong Federation of Trade Unions . . .	—	1	1
Independents	2	16	18
Total	**30**	**30**	**60**

Political Organizations

April Fifth Action: internet act.to/45; socialist group, anti-Beijing; Spokesperson LEUNG KWOK-HUNG.

Article 45 Concern Group: internet www.article45.org; pro-democracy, supports election of Hong Kong's Chief Executive by universal suffrage.

Association for Democracy and People's Livelihood (ADPL): Sun Beam Commercial Bldg, Room 1104, 469–471 Nathan Rd, Kowloon; tel. 27822699; fax 27823137; e-mail info@adpl.org.hk; internet www.adpl.org.hk; advocates democracy; Chair. FREDERICK FUNG KIN-KEE; Gen. Sec. TAM KWOK-KIU.

Citizens' Party: GPOB 321, Central, Hong Kong; tel. 28930029; e-mail enquiry@citizensparty.org; internet www.citizensparty.org; f. 1997; urges mass participation in politics; established by Christine Loh, Chairwoman 1997–2000; Chair ALEX CHAN.

Democratic Alliance for the Betterment and Progress of Hong Kong (DAB): SUP Tower, 12/F, 83 King's Rd, North Point; tel. 25280136; fax 25284339; e-mail info@dab.org.hk; internet www.dab.org.hk; f. 2005; pro-Beijing; formed by merger of the Democratic Alliance for the Betterment of Hong Kong (f. 1992, supported return of Hong Kong to the motherland and implementation of the Basic Law) and the Hong Kong Progressive Alliance (f. 1994, supported by business and professional community); Chair. MA LIK; Sec.-Gen. KAN CHI-HO.

Democratic Party: Hanley House, 4/F, 776–778 Nathan Rd, Kowloon; tel. 23977033; fax 23978998; e-mail waiyin@dphk.ecoffiz.com; internet www.dphk.org; f. 1994 by merger of United Democrats of Hong Kong (UDHK—declared a formal political party in 1990) and Meeting Point; liberal grouping; advocates democracy; Chair. LEE WING TAT; Sec.-Gen. CHEUNG YIN-TUNG.

The Frontier: Flat B, 1/F, Kam Wah Bldg, 514-516 Nathan Rd, Yau Ma Tei, Kowloon; tel. 25249899; fax 25245310; e-mail frontier@frontier.org.hk; internet www.frontier.org.hk; f. 1996; pro-democracy movement, comprising teachers, students and trade unionists; Spokesperson EMILY LAU.

Hong Kong Democratic Foundation: Hong Kong House, Room 301, 17–19 Wellington St, Central; GPOB 12287; tel. 28696443; fax 28696318; advocates democracy; Chair. ALAN LUNG.

Hong Kong Voice of Democracy: 7/F, 57 Peking Rd, Tsimshatsui; tel. 92676489; fax 27915801; e-mail editor@democracy.org.hk; internet www.democracy.org.hk; pro-democracy movement; Dir LAU SAN-CHING.

Liberal Party: 4/F Henley Bldg, 5 Queen's Road, Central; tel. 28696833; fax 25334239; e-mail liberal@liberal.org.hk; internet www.liberal.org.hk; f. 1993 by mems of Co-operative Resources Centre (CRC); business-orientated; pro-Beijing; Leader ALLEN LEE PENG-FEI; Chair. JAMES TIEN.

Neighbourhood and Worker's Service Centre: e-mail nwsc@netvigator.com; internet www.nwsc.org.hk.

New Hong Kong Alliance: 4/F, 14–15 Wo On Lane, Central; fax 28691110; pro-China.

At the elections of September 2004, the Hong Kong Confederation of Trade Unions and the Hong Federation of Trade Unions also secured seats in the Legislative Council (see Trade and Industry section for details of these organizations).

The **Chinese Communist Party** (based in the People's Republic) and the **Kuomintang** (Nationalist Party of China, based in Taiwan) also maintain organizations.

Judicial System

The Court of Final Appeal was established on 1 July 1997 upon the commencement of the Hong Kong Court of Final Appeal Ordinance. It replaced the Privy Council in London as the highest appellate court in Hong Kong to safeguard the rule of law. The Court comprises five judges—the Chief Justice, three permanent judges and one non-permanent Hong Kong judge or one judge from another common-law jurisdiction.

The High Court consists of a Court of Appeal and a Court of First Instance. The Court of First Instance has unlimited jurisdiction in civil and criminal cases, while the District Court has limited jurisdiction. Appeals from these courts lie to the Court of Appeal, presided over by the Chief Judge or a Vice-President of the Court of Appeal with one or two Justices of Appeal. Appeals from Magistrates' Courts are heard by a Court of First Instance judge.

Court of Final Appeal

1 Battery Path, Central; tel. 21230123; fax 21210300; internet www.judiciary.gov.hk.

Chief Justice of the Court of Final Appeal: ANDREW K. N. LI.

Permanent Judges of the Court of Final Appeal: R. A. V. RIBEIRO, PATRICK S. O. CHAN, K. BOKHARY.

High Court

38 Queensway; tel. 28690869; fax 28690640; internet www.judiciary.gov.hk.

Chief Judge of the High Court: GEOFFREY T.L. MA.

Justices of Appeal: K. H. WOO, M. STUART-MOORE, F. STOCK, Mrs D. LE PICHON, P. C. Y. CHEUNG, A. G. ROGERS, M. C. K. N. YUEN, W. C. K. YEUNG, R. C. TANG.

Judges of the Court of First Instance: G. J. LUGAR-MAWSON, A. O. T. CHUNG, T. M. GALL, D. Y. K. YAM, W. S. Y. WAUNG, M. P. BURRELL, Ms C. F. L. CHU, Mrs V. S. BOKHARY, K. K. PANG, W. D. STONE, Ms C. M. BEESON, P. V. T. NGUYEN, M. J. HARTMANN, A. R. SUFFIAD, A. H. SAKHRANI, L. P. S. TONG, Miss S. S. H. KWAN, M. A. MCMAHON, J. M. H. LAM, A. K. N. CHEUNG, M. V. LUNN, A. T. BARMA, A. F. T. REYES.

OTHER COURTS

District Courts: There are 34 District Judges.

Magistrates' Courts: There are 59 Magistrates and 11 Special Magistrates, sitting in 9 magistracies.

Religion

The population is predominantly Buddhist. The number of active Buddhists is estimated at between 650,000 and 700,000, and there were more than 600 temples in 2003. Confucianism and Daoism are widely practised. The three religions are frequently found in the same temple. In 2003 there were some 540,000 Christians, approximately 70,000 Muslims, 15,000 Hindus, and 8,000 Sikhs. Judaism, the Bahá'í faith and Zoroastrianism are also represented.

BUDDHISM

Hong Kong Buddhist Association: 1/F, 338 Lockhart Rd; tel. 25749371; fax 28340789; internet www.hkbuddhist.org; Pres. Ven. KOK KWONG.

CHRISTIANITY

Hong Kong Christian Council: 9/F, 33 Granville Rd, Kowloon; tel. 23687123; fax 27242131; e-mail hkcc@hkcc.org.hk; internet www.hkcc.org.hk; f. 1954; 22 mem. orgs; Chair. Rev.Dr SOO YEE-PO THOMAS; Gen. Sec. Rev. SO SHING-YIT ERIC.

The Anglican Communion

Primate of Hong Kong Sheng Kung Hui and Bishop of Hong Kong Island and Macao: Most Rev. PETER K. K. KWONG, Bishop's House, 1 Lower Albert Rd, Central; tel. 25265355; fax 25212199; e-mail office1@hkskh.org.

Bishop of Eastern Kowloon: Rt Rev. LOUIS TSUI, Holy Trinity Bradbury Centre, 4/F, 139 Ma Tau Chung Rd, Kowloon; tel. 27139983; fax 27111609; e-mail ekoffice@ekhkskh.org.hk.

Bishop of Western Kowloon: Rt Rev. Thomas Soo, Ultra Grace Commercial Bldg, 15/F, 5 Jordan Rd, Kowloon; tel. 27830811; fax 27830799; e-mail hkskhdwk@netvigator.com.

The Lutheran Church

Evangelical Lutheran Church of Hong Kong: 50A Waterloo Rd, Kowloon; tel. 23885847; fax 23887539; e-mail info@elchk.org.hk; internet www.elchk.org.hk; 13,000 mems; Pres. Rev. Tso Shui-wan.

The Roman Catholic Church

For ecclesiastical purposes, Hong Kong forms a single diocese, nominally suffragan to the archdiocese of Canton (Guangzhou), China. According to Vatican sources, in December 2002 there were an estimated 367,402 adherents in the territory, representing more than 5% of the total population.

Bishop of Hong Kong: Joseph Zen Ze-kiun, Catholic Diocese Centre, 12/F, 16 Caine Rd; tel. 257652; fax 254707; e-mail bishopzen@catholic.org.uk.

The Press

Hong Kong has a thriving press. At the end of 2003, according to government figures, there were 52 daily newspapers, including 28 Chinese-language and 11 English-language dailies, and 864 periodicals.

PRINCIPAL DAILY NEWSPAPERS

English Language

Asian Wall Street Journal: GPOB 9825; tel. 25737121; fax 28345291; f. 1976; business; Editor Reginald Chua; circ. 85,000.

China Daily: Hong Kong edition of China's official English-language newspaper; launched 1997; Editor Liu Dizhong; circ. 11,000.

International Herald Tribune: 1201 K Wah Centre, 191 Java Rd, North Point; tel. 29221188; fax 29221190; internet www.iht.com; Correspondent Kevin Murphy.

South China Morning Post: Morning Post Centre, Dai Fat St, Tai Po Industrial Centre, Tai Po, New Territories; tel. 26808888; fax 26616984; internet www.scmp.com; f. 1903; CEO Owen Jonathan; Editor Robert Keatley; circ. 118,000.

The Standard: Sing Tao Bldg, 3/F, 1 Wang Kwong Rd, Kowloon Bay, Kowloon; tel. 27982798; fax 27953009; e-mail webmaster@thestandard.com.hk; internet www.thestandard.com.hk; f. 1949; Editor Karl Wilson; circ. 45,000.

Target Intelligent Report: Suite 2901, Bank of America Tower, 12 Harcourd Rd, Central; tel. 25730379; fax 28381597; e-mail info@targetnewspapers.com; internet www.targetnewspapers.com; f. 1972; financial news, commentary, politics, property, litigations, etc.

Chinese Language

Hong Kong Commercial Daily: 1/F, 499 King's Rd, North Point; tel. 25905322; fax 25658947.

Hong Kong Daily News: All Flats, Hong Kong Industrial Bldg, 17/F, 444–452 Des Voeux Rd West; tel. 28555111; fax 28198717; internet www.hkdailynews.net; f. 1958; morning; CEO Roddy Yu; Chief Editor K. K. Yeung; circ. 120,000.

Hong Kong Economic Journal: North Point Industrial Bldg, 22/F, 499 King's Rd; tel. 28567567; fax 28111070; e-mail info@hkej.com; Editor-in-Chief H. C. Chiu; circ. 70,000.

Hong Kong Economic Times: Kodak House, Block 2, 6/F, 321 Java Rd, North Point; tel. 28802888; fax 28111926; f. 1988; Publr Perry Mak; Chief Editor Eric Chan; circ. 64,565.

Hong Kong Sheung Po (Hong Kong Commercial Daily): 499 King's Rd, North Point; tel. 25640788; f. 1952; morning; Editor-in-Chief H. Cheung; circ. 110,000.

Hsin Wan Pao (New Evening Post): 342 Hennessy Rd, Wanchai; tel. 28911604; fax 28382307; f. 1950; Editor-in-Chief Chao Tse-lung; circ. 90,000.

Ming Pao Daily News: Block A, Ming Pao Industrial Centre, 15/F, 18 Ka Yip St, Chai Wan; tel. 25953111; fax 28982534; e-mail mingpao@mingpao.com; internet www.mingpao.com; f. 1959; morning; Chief Editor Paul Cheung; circ. 95,578.

Oriental Daily News: Oriental Press Centre, Wang Tai Rd, Kowloon Bay, Kowloon; tel. 27951111; fax 27955599; Chair. C. F. Ma; Editor-in-Chief Ma Kai Lun; circ. 650,000.

Ping Kuo Jih Pao (Apple Daily): Hong Kong; tel. 29908388; fax 27410830; e-mail adnews@appledaily.com; internet appledaily.atnext.com; f. 1995; published by Next Media; Propr Jimmy Lai; Publr Loh Chan; circ. 400,000.

Seng Weng Evening News: f. 1957; Editor Wong Long-chau; circ. 60,000.

Sing Pao Daily News: Sing Pao Bldg, 101 King's Rd, North Point; tel. 25702201; fax 28870348; f. 1939; morning; Chief Editor Hon Chung-suen; circ. 229,250.

Sing Tao Daily: Sing Tao Bldg, 3/F, 1 Wang Kwong Rd, Kowloon Bay, Kowloon; tel. 27982575; fax 27953022; f. 1938; morning; Editor-in-Chief Luk Kam Wing; circ. 60,000.

Ta Kung Pao: 342 Hennessy Rd, Wanchai; tel. 25757181; fax 28345104; e-mail tkp@takungpao.com; internet www.takungpao.com; f. 1902; morning; supports People's Republic of China; Editor T. S. Tsang; circ. 150,000.

Wen Wei Po: Hing Wai Centre, 2–4/F, 7 Tin Wan Praya Rd, Aberdeen; tel. 28738288; fax 28730657; internet www.wenweipo.com; f. 1948; morning; communist; Dir Zhang Guo-liang; First Editor-in-Chief Cheung Ching-wan; Editor-in-Chief Wong Bak Yao; circ. 200,000.

SELECTED PERIODICALS

English Language

Asian Business: c/o TPL Corporation (HK) Ltd, Block C, 10/F, Seaview Estate, 2–8 Watson Rd, North Point; tel. 25668381; fax 25080197; e-mail absales@asianbusiness.com.hk; internet www.asianbusinessnet.com; monthly; Publr and Executive Editor James Leung; circ. 75,000.

Asian Medical News: Pacific Plaza, 8/F, 410 Des Voeux Rd West; tel. 25595888; fax 25596910; e-mail amn@medimedia.com.hk; internet www.amn.com; f. 1979; monthly; Man. Editor Ross Garbett; circ. 28,300.

Asian Profile: Asian Research Service, GPOB 2232; tel. 25707227; fax 25128050; f. 1973; 6 a year; multi-disciplinary study of Asian affairs.

Business Traveller Asia/Pacific: 7/F Printing Hse, 6 Duddell St, Central; tel. 25119317; fax 25196846; e-mail enquiry@businesstravellerasia.com; f. 1982; consumer business travel; 10 a year; Publr Peggy Teo; circ. 25,647.

Far Eastern Economic Review: Central Plaza, 25/F, 18 Harbour Rd, Wanchai, GPOB 160; tel. 25737121; fax 25031530; e-mail review@feer.com; internet www.feer.com; f. 1946; 10 edns annually; Man. Dir Winnie Wong; Editor Hugh Restall; circ. 95,570.

Hong Kong Electronics: Office Tower, Convention Plaza, 38/F, 1 Harbour Rd; tel. 25844333; fax 28240249; e-mail hktdc@tdc.org.hk; internet www.tdctrade.com; f. 1985; bi-monthly; publ. by the Hong Kong Trade Development Council; Editor Geoff Picker; circ. 90,000.

Hong Kong Enterprise: Office Tower, Convention Plaza, 38/F, 1 Harbour Rd; tel. 25844333; fax 28240249; e-mail hktdc@tdc.org.hk; internet www.tdctrade.com; f. 1967; monthly; publ. by the Hong Kong Trade Development Council; Editor Geoff Picker; circ. 150,000.

Hong Kong Household: Office Tower, Convention Plaza, 38/F, 1 Harbour Rd, Wanchai; tel. 25844333; fax 28240249; e-mail hktdc@tdc.org.hk; internet www.tdctrade.com; f. 1983; publ. by the Hong Kong Trade Development Council; household and hardware products; 2 a year; Editor Geoff Picker; circ. 90,000.

Hong Kong Industrialist: Federation of Hong Kong Industries, Hankow Centre, 4/F, 5–15 Hankow Rd, Tsimshatsui, Kowloon; tel. 27323188; fax 27213494; e-mail fhki@fhki.org.hk; monthly; publ. by the Federation of Hong Kong Industries; Editor Lim Siong Hoon; circ. 6,000.

Hong Kong Special Administrative Region Government Gazette: Printing Division, Government Logistics Department, Cornwall House, Taikoo Place, 979 King's Rd, Quarry Bay; tel. 25649500; weekly.

Hong Kong Trader: Office Tower, Convention Plaza, 38/F, 1 Harbour Rd, Wanchai; tel. 25844333; fax 28243485; e-mail trader@tdc.org.hk; internet www.tdc.org.hk/hktrader; f. 1983; publ. by the Hong Kong Trade Development Council; trade, economics, financial and general business news; monthly; Man. Editor Sophy Fisher; circ. 70,000.

Official Hong Kong Guide: c/o HKTB, Citicorp Centre, 9–11/F, 18 Whitfield Rd, North Point; f. 1982; monthly; information on sightseeing, shopping, dining, etc. for overseas visitors; published by the Hong Kong Tourism Board.

Orientations: 17/F, 200 Lockhart Rd; tel. 25111368; fax 25074620; e-mail omag@netvigator.com; internet www.orientations.com.hk; f. 1970; 8 a year; arts of East Asia, the Indian subcontinent and South-East Asia; Publr and Editorial Dir Elizabeth Knight.

Reader's Digest (Asia Edn): Reader's Digest Association Far East Ltd, 19/F Cyber Centre, 3 Tung Wong Rd, Shau Kei Wan; tel.

96906381; fax 96906389; e-mail friends@rdasia.com.hk; f. 1963; general topics; monthly; Editor PETER DOCKRILL; circ. 332,000.

Spike: 2606 Westley Sq., 48 Hoi Yuen Rd, Kwun Tong, Kowloon; tel. 31058921; fax 31058927; e-mail editorial@spikehk.com; internet www.spikehk.com; f. 2003; weekly magazine; Publr STEPHEN VINES; Editor JON MARSH.

Sunday Examiner: Catholic Diocese Centre, 11/F, 16 Caine Rd; tel. 25220487; fax 25369939; e-mail sundayex@catholic.org.hk; internet sundayex.catholic.org.hk; f. 1946; religious; weekly; Deputy Editor-in-Chief Fr JIM MULRONEY; circ. 6,500.

Textile Asia: c/o Business Press Ltd, California Tower, 11/F, 30–32 D'Aguilar St, GPOB 185, Central; tel. 25233744; fax 28106966; e-mail texasia@netvigator.com; f. 1970; monthly; textile and clothing industry; Publr and Editor-in-Chief KAYSER W. SUNG; circ. 17,000.

Travel Business Analyst: GPO Box 12761; tel. 25072310; e-mail TBAoffice@aol.com; internet www.travelbusinessanalyst.com; f. 1982; travel trade; monthly; Editor MURRAY BAILEY.

Chinese Language

Affairs Weekly: Hong Kong; tel. 28950801; fax 25767842; f. 1980; general interest; Editor WONG WAI MAN; circ. 130,000.

Cheng Ming Monthly: Hennessy Rd, POB 20370; tel. 25740664; Chief Editor WAN FAI.

City Magazine: Hang Seng Bldg, 7/F, 200 Hennessy Rd, Wanchai; tel. 28931393; fax 28388761; f. 1976; monthly; fashion, wine, cars, society, etc.; Publr JOHN K. C. CHAN; Chief Editor PETER WONG; circ. 30,000.

Contemporary Monthly: Unit 705, Westlands Centre, 20 Westlands Rd, Quarry Bay; tel. 25638122; fax 25632984; f. 1989; monthly; current affairs; 'China-watch'; Editor-in-Chief CHING CHEONG; circ. 50,000.

Disc Jockey: Fuk Keung Ind. Bldg, B2, 14/F, 66–68 Tong Mei Rd, Taikoktsui, Kowloon; tel. 23905461; fax 27893869; e-mail vinpres@netvigator.com; f. 1990; monthly; music; Publr VINCENT LEUNG; Editor ALGE CHEUNG; circ. 32,000.

Elegance HK: Aik San Bldg, 14/F, 14 Westlands Rd, Quarry Bay; tel. 2963011; fax 25658217; f. 1977; monthly; for thinking women; Chief Editor WINNIE YUEN; circ. 75,000.

Kung Kao Po (Catholic Chinese Weekly): 16 Caine Rd; tel. 25220487; fax 25213095; e-mail kkp@catholic.org.hk; internet kkp .catholic.org.hk; f. 1928; religious; weekly; Editor-in-Chief Fr TERESA YUEN.

Metropolitan Weekly: f. 1983; weekly; entertainment, social news; Chief Editor CHARLES YOU; circ. 130,000.

Ming Pao Monthly: Ming Pao Industrial Centre, 15/F, Block A, 18 Ka Yip St, Chai Wan; tel. 25155107; fax 28982566; Chief Editor KOO SIU-SUN.

Next Magazine: 8 Chun Ying St, T. K. O. Industrial Estate West, Tseung Kwan O, Hong Kong; tel. 27442733; fax 29907210; internet www.nextmedia.com; f. 1989; weekly; news, business, lifestyle, entertainment; Editor-in-Chief CHEUNG KIM HUNG; circ. 172,708.

Open Magazine: Causeway Bay, POB 31429; tel. 28939197; fax 28915591; e-mail open@open.com.hk; internet www.open.com.hk; f. 1990; monthly; Chief Editor JIN CHONG; circ. 15,000.

Oriental Sunday: Oriental Press Centre, Wang Tai Rd, Kowloon Bay, Kowloon; tel. 27951111; fax 27952299; f. 1991; weekly; leisure magazine; Chair. C. F. MA; circ. 120,000.

Reader's Digest (Chinese Edn): Reader's Digest Association Far East Ltd, 19/F Cyber Centre, 3 Tung Wong Rd, Shau Kei Wan; tel. 28845678; fax 25671479; e-mail chrd@netvigator.com; f. 1965; monthly; Editor-in-Chief JOEL POON; circ. 200,000.

Today's Living: Prospect Mansion, Flat D, 1/F, 66–72 Paterson St, Causeway Bay; tel. 28822230; fax 28823949; e-mail magazine@todayliving.com; f. 1987; monthly; interior design; Publr and Editor-in-Chief KENNETH LI; circ. 35,000.

Yazhou Zhoukan: Block A, Ming Pao Industrial Centre, 15/F, 18 Ka Yip St, Chai Wan; tel. 25155358; fax 25059662; e-mail loppoon@mingpao.com; internet www.yzzk.com; f. 1987; international Chinese news weekly; Chief Editor YAU LOP-POON; circ. 110,000.

Yuk Long TV Weekly: Hong Kong; tel. 25657883; fax 25659958; f. 1977; entertainment, fashion, etc.; Publr TONY WONG; circ. 82,508.

NEWS AGENCIES

International News Service: 2E Cheong Shing Mansion, 33–39 Wing Hing St, Causeway Bay; tel. 25665668; Rep. AU KIT MING.

Xinhua (New China) News Agency, Hong Kong SAR Bureau: 387 Queen's Rd East, Wanchai; tel. 28314126; f. 2000; from fmr news dept of branch office of Xinhua (responsibility for other activities being assumed by Liaison Office of the Central People's Government in the Hong Kong SAR); Dir ZHANG GUOLIANG.

Foreign Bureaux

Agence France-Presse (AFP): Telecom House, Room 1840, 18/F, 3 Gloucester Rd, Wanchai, GPOB 5613; tel. 28020224; fax 28027292; Regional Dir YVAN CHEMLA.

Agencia EFE (Spain): 10A Benny View House, 63–65 Wong Nai Chung Rd, Happy Valley; tel. 28080199; fax 28823101; Correspondent MIREN GUTIERREZ.

Associated Press (AP) (USA): 1282 New Mercury House, Waterfront Rd; tel. 25274324; Bureau Chief ROBERT LIU.

Central News Agency (CNA) Inc (Taiwan): Hong Kong Bureau Chief CONRAD LU.

Jiji Tsushin-Sha (Japan): 3503 Far East Finance Centre, 16 Harcourt Rd; tel. 25237112; fax 28459013; e-mail webmaster@jiji.com; internet www.jiji.com; Bureau Man. KATSUHIKO KABASAWA.

Kyodo News Service (Japan): Unit 1303, 13/F, 9 Queen's Rd, Central; tel. 25249750; fax 28105591; e-mail tyoko@po.iijnet.or.jp; Correspondent TSUKASA YOKOYAMA.

Reuters Hong Kong Ltd: 10/F, Cityplaza 3, Taikoo Shing, Quarry Bay, Hong Kong; tel. 28450419; fax ; Technical Man. CYRIL CHUI.

United Press International (UPI) (USA): Unit C, 8/F Sincere Insurance Bldg, 4 Hennessy Rd; tel. 28037579; fax 28037579; Vice-Pres. (Asia) ARNOLD ZEITLIN; Editor (Asia) PAUL H. ANDERSON.

PRESS ASSOCIATIONS

Chinese Language Press Institute: Tower A, Sing Tao Bldg, 1 Wang Kwong Rd, Kowloon Bay, Kowloon; tel. 27982501; fax 27953017; Pres. TIONG HIEW KING.

Hong Kong Chinese Press Association: Rm 2208, 22/F, 33 Queen's Rd Central; tel. 28613622; fax 28661933; 13 mems; Chair. HUE PUE-YING.

Hong Kong Journalists Association: GPOB 11726, Henfa Commercial Bldg, Flat 15A, 348–350 Lockhart Rd, Waichai; tel. 25910692; fax 25727329; e-mail hkja@hk.super.net; internet www .hkja.org.hk; f. 1968; 413 mems; Chair. CHEUNG PING LING.

Newspaper Society of Hong Kong: Rm 904, 75–83 King's Rd, North Point; tel. 25713102; fax 25712676; f. 1954; Chair. LEE CHO-JAT.

Publishers

Art House of Collectors HK Ltd: 37 Lyndhurst Terrace, Ground Floor, Central; tel. 28818026; fax 28904304; Dir LI LAP FONG.

Asia 2000 Ltd: Rm A, 18/F, Hollywood Centre, 77–91 Queen's Rd West; tel. 25301409; fax 25261107; e-mail sales@asia2000.com.hk; internet www.asia2000.com.hk; Asian studies, politics, photography, fiction; Man. Dir MICHAEL MORROW.

Asian Research Service: GPOB 2232; tel. 25707227; fax 25128050; f. 1972; maps, atlases, monographs on Asian studies and journals; Dir NELSON LEUNG.

Chinese University Press: Chinese University of Hong Kong, Sha Tin, New Territories; tel. 26096508; fax 26036692; e-mail cup@cuhk .edu.hk; internet www.chineseupress.com; f. 1977; studies on China and Hong Kong and other academic works; Dir Dr STEVEN K. LUK.

Commercial Press (Hong Kong) Ltd: Eastern Central Plaza, 8/F, 3 Yiu Hing Rd, Shau Kei Wan; tel. 25651371; fax 25645277; e-mail webmaster@commercialpress.com.hk; internet www .commercialpress.com.hk; f. 1897; trade books, dictionaries, textbooks, Chinese classics, art, etc.; Chair. and Man. Dir CHAN MAN HUNG.

Excerpta Medica Asia Ltd: 1601, 16/F, Leighton Centre, 77 Leighton Rd, Causeway Bay; tel. 29651300; fax 29760778; e-mail emal@excerptahk.com; internet www.excerptahk.com; subsidiary of Elsevier; f. 1980; sponsored medical publications, abstracts, journals etc.

Hoi Fung Publisher Co: 125 Lockhart Rd, 2/F, Wanchai; tel. 25286246; fax 25286249; Dir. K. K. TSE.

Hong Kong University Press: Hing Wai Centre, 14/F, 7 Tin Wan Praya Rd, Aberdeen; tel. 25502703; fax 28750734; e-mail hkupress@hkucc.hku.hk; internet www.hkupress.org; f. 1956; Publr COLIN DAY.

Ismay Publications Ltd: C. C. Wu Bldg; tel. 25752270; Man. Dir MINNIE YEUNG.

Ling Kee Publishing Co Ltd: Zung Fu Industrial Bldg, 1067 King's Rd, Quarry Bay; tel. 25616151; fax 28111980; e-mail admin@

lingkee.com; internet www.lingkee.com; f. 1956; educational and reference; Chair. B. L. Au; Man. Dir K. W. Au.

Oxford University Press (China) Ltd: Warwick House East, 18/F, 979 King's Rd, Taikoo Place, Quarry Bay; tel. 25163222; fax 25658491; e-mail oupchina@oupchina.com.hk; internet www.oupchina.com.hk; f. 1961; school textbooks, reference, academic and general works relating to Hong Kong, Taiwan and China; Regional Dir Simon Li.

Taosheng Publishing House: Lutheran Bldg, 3/F, 50A Waterloo Rd, Yau Ma Tei, Kowloon; tel. 23887061; fax 27810413; e-mail taosheng@elchk.org.hk; Dir Chang Chun Wa.

Textile Asia/Business Press Ltd: California Tower, 11/F, 30–32 D'Aguilar St, GPOB 185, Central; tel. 25233744; fax 28106966; e-mail texasia@netvigator.com; internet www.textileasia-businesspress.com; f. 1970; textile magazine; Man. Dir Kayser W. Sung.

The Woods Publishing Co: Li Yuen Building, 2/F, 7 Li Yuen St West, Central; tel. 25233002; fax 28453296; e-mail tybook@netvigator.com; Production Man. Tong Sze Hong.

Times Publishing (Hong Kong) Ltd: Seaview Estate, Block C, 10/F, 2–8 Watson Rd, North Point; tel. 25668381; fax 25080255; e-mail abeditor@asianbusiness.com.hk; internet www.asianbusinessnet.com; trade magazines and directories; CEO Colin Yam; Executive Editor James Leung.

GOVERNMENT PUBLISHING HOUSE

Government Information Services: see Government Offices.

PUBLISHERS' ASSOCIATIONS

Hong Kong Publishers' and Distributors' Association: Flat C, 4/F, 240–246 Nathan Rd, Kowloon; tel. 23674412; 45 mems; Chair. Ho Kam-ling; Sec. Ho Nai-chi.

Society of Publishers in Asia: c/o Perfect Promotion Ltd, Room 1001, 10/F Tak Woo Hse, 17-19 D'Aguilar St, Central; tel. 28822555; fax 28824673; e-mail perfectp@netvigator.com.

Broadcasting and Communications

TELECOMMUNICATIONS

Asia Satellite Telecommunications Co Ltd (AsiaSat): East Exchange Tower, 23/F, 38–40 Leighton Rd; tel. 25000895; fax 25000888; e-mail wpang@asiasat.com; internet www.asiasat.com; CEO Peter Jackson.

Pacific Century CyberWorks (PCCW): 39/F PCCW Tower, Taikoo Place, 979 King's Rd, Quarry Bay; tel. 28882888; fax 28778877; e-mail general@pccw.com; internet www.pccw.com; fmrly Cable and Wireless HKT Ltd, acquired by PCCW August 2000; telecommunications/internet services provider; CEO Jack So.

Regulatory Authority

Telecommunications Authority: statutory regulator, responsible for implementation of the Govt's pro-competition and pro-consumer policies; Dir.Gen. Anthony S. K. Wong.

Hutchison Telecom, New T and T Hong Kong Ltd, and New World Telecom also operate local services. In 2000 six companies were licensed to provide mobile telecommunications services, serving over 5.2m. customers.

BROADCASTING

Regulatory Authority

Broadcasting Authority: 39/F Revenue Tower, 5 Gloucester Rd, Wanchai; tel. 25945721; fax 25072219; e-mail ba@tela.gov.hk; internet www.hkba.org.hk; regulatory body; administers and issues broadcasting licences; Chair. Daniel R. Fung.

Radio

Hong Kong Commercial Broadcasting Co Ltd: 3 Broadcast Drive, KCPOB 73000; tel. 23365111; fax 23380021; e-mail comradio@crhk.com.hk; internet www.crhk.com.hk; f. 1959; broadcasts in English and Chinese on three radio frequencies; Chair. G. J. Ho; Dir and CEO Winnie Yu.

Metro Broadcast Corpn Ltd (Metro Broadcast): Basement 2, Site 6, Whampoa Garden, Hunghom, Kowloon; tel. 21239877; fax 21239888; e-mail webmaster@metroradio.com.hk; internet www.metroradio.com.hk; f. 1991; broadcasts on three channels in English, Cantonese and Mandarin; Gen. Man. Craig B. Quick.

Radio Television Hong Kong: Broadcasting House, 30 Broadcast Drive, Kowloon; tel. 23396300; fax 23380279; e-mail admin@rthk

.org.hk; internet www.rthk.org.hk; f. 1928; govt-funded; 24-hour service in English and Chinese on seven radio channels; service in Putonghua inaugurated in 1997; Dir Chu Pui-hing.

Star Radio: Hutchison House, 12/F, 10 Harcourt Rd, Central; f. 1995; satellite broadcasts in Mandarin and English; Gen. Man. Mike Mackay.

Television

Asia Television Ltd (ATV): Television House, 81 Broadcast Drive, Kowloon; tel. 29928888; fax 23380438; e-mail atv@hkatv.com; internet www.hkatv.com; f. 1973; operates two commercial television services (English and Chinese) and produces television programmes; Dir and CEO Feng Xiao Ping.

STAR Group Ltd: One Harbourfront, 8/F, 18 Tak Fung St, Hunghom, Kowloon; tel. 26218888; fax 26213050; e-mail corp_aff@startv.com; internet www.startv.com; f. 1990; subsidiary of the News Corpn Ltd; broadcasts over 40 channels in English, Hindi, Tamil, Mandarin, Cantonese, Korean and Thai, including a range of sports programmes, music, movies, news, entertainment and documentaries. STAR reaches more than 300m. people in 53 countries across Asia, India and the Middle East, with a daily audience of about 100m. people. STAR also owns a contemporary Chinese film library with more than 600 titles. Additionally, STAR has interests in cable systems in India and Taiwan. Its services also extend to interactive cable TV, radio, wireless and digital media platforms; Chair. and CEO Michelle Guthrie; Pres. Steve Askew.

Radio Television Hong Kong: see Radio; produces drama, documentary and public affairs programmes; also operates an educational service for transmission by two local commercial stations; Dir Chu Pui-hing (acting).

Television Broadcasts Ltd (TVB): TVB City, 77 Chun Choi St, Tseung Kwan O Industrial Estate, Kowloon; tel. 23352288; fax 23581300; e-mail external.affairs@tvb.com.hk; internet www.tvb.com; f. 1967; operates Chinese and English language services; two colour networks; Exec. Chair. Sir Run Run Shaw; Man. Dir Louis Page.

Wharf Cable Ltd: Wharf Cable Tower, 4/F, 9 Hoi Shing Rd, Tsuen Wan; tel. 26115533; fax 24171511; f. 1993; 24-hour subscription service of news, sport and entertainment on 35 channels; carries BBC World Service Television; Chair. Peter Woo; Man. Dir Stephen Ng.

Finance

(cap. = capital; res = reserves; dep. = deposits; m. = million; brs = branches; amounts in Hong Kong dollars unless otherwise stated)

BANKING

In December 2003 there were 134 licensed banks operating in Hong Kong. There were also 42 restricted licence banks (formerly known as licensed deposit-taking companies), 39 deposit-taking companies, and 87 foreign banks' representative offices.

Hong Kong Monetary Authority (HKMA): 55/F, Two International Finance Centre, 8 Finance St, Central, Hong Kong; tel. 28788196; fax 28788197; e-mail hkma@hkma.gov.hk; internet www.hkma.gov.hk; f. 1993 by merger of Office of the Commissioner of Banking and Office of the Exchange Fund; carries out central banking functions; maintains Hong Kong dollar stability within the framework of the linked exchange rate system; supervises licensed banks, restricted licence banks and deposit-taking cos, their overseas brs and representative offices; manages foreign currency reserves; Chief Exec. Joseph Yam; Deputy Chief Execs Peter Pang, William Ryback, Norman Chan.

Banks of Issue

Bank of China (Hong Kong) Ltd (People's Repub. of China): Bank of China Tower, 1 Garden Rd, Central; tel. 28266888; fax 28105963; internet www.bochk.com; f. 1917; became third bank of issue in May 1994; merged in Oct. 2001 with the local branches of 11 mainland banks (incl. Kwangtung Provincial Bank, Sin Hua Bank Ltd, China and the South Sea Bank Ltd, Kincheng Banking Corpn, China State Bank, National Commercial Bank Ltd, Yien Yieh Commercial Bank Ltd, Hua Chiao Commercial Bank Ltd and Po Sang Bank Ltd, to form the Bank of China (Hong Kong)); cap. 43,043m., res 13,159m., dep. 676,065m. (Dec. 2003); CEO He Guangbei; 369 brs.

The Hongkong and Shanghai Banking Corporation Ltd: 1 Queen's Rd, Central; tel. 28221111; fax 28101112; internet www.asiapacific.hsbc.com; f. 1865; personal and commercial banking; cap. 51,603m., res 12,855m., dep. 1,823,109m. (Dec. 2003); Chair. David Eldon; CEO Michael R.P. Smith; more than 600 offices worldwide.

Standard Chartered Bank: Standard Chartered Bank Bldg, 4–4A Des Voeux Rd, Central; tel. 28203333; fax 28569129; internet www.standardchartered.com.hk; f. 1859; CEO PETER SULLIVAN.

Other Commercial Banks

Asia Commercial Bank Ltd: Asia Financial Centre, 120 Des Voeux Rd, Central; tel. 25419222; fax 25410009; e-mail contact@afh.com.hk; internet www.asia-commercial.com; f. 1934; fmrly Commercial Bank of Hong Kong; cap. 810.0m., res 455,979.0m., dep. 11,171.0m. (Dec. 2003); Chair. and CEO ROBIN Y. H. CHAN; Gen. Man. and Exec. Dir STEPHEN TAN; 13 domestic, 1 overseas br.

Bank of East Asia Ltd: Bank of East Asia Bldg, 16/F, 10 Des Voeux Rd, Central; tel. 28423200; fax 28459333; internet www.hkbea.com; inc in Hong Kong in 1918, absorbed United Chinese Bank Ltd in Aug. 2001, and First Pacific Bank (FPB) in Apr. 2002; cap. 3,668.6m., res 13,327.1m., dep. etc. 168,464.5m. (Dec. 2002); Chair. and Chief Exec. DAVID K. P. LI; 99 brs in Hong Kong and 18 overseas brs.

Chiyu Banking Corpn Ltd: 78 Des Voeux Rd, Central; tel. 28430111; fax 25267420; f. 1947; cap. 300m., res 2,970.5m., dep. 24,244.3m. (Dec. 2002); Chair. TAN KONG PIAT; 15 brs.

CITIC Ka Wah Bank Ltd: 232 Des Voeux Rd, Central; tel. 25457131; fax 25417029; e-mail info@citickawahbank.com; internet www.citickawahbank.com; f. 1922; cap. 2,393.3m., res 2,544.1m., dep. 66,612.1m. (Dec. 2003); acquired Hong Kong Chinese Bank Ltd Jan. 2002; Chair. DAN KONG; CEO KENNETH KONG SIU CHEE; Dir JU WEIMIN; 26 domestic brs, 2 overseas brs.

Dah Sing Bank Ltd: Dah Sing Financial Centre, 36/F, 108 Gloucester Rd, Central; tel. 25078866; fax 25985052; e-mail ops@dahsing.com.hk; internet www.dahsing.com; f. 1947; cap. 800.0m., res 1,057.7m., dep. 47,387.4m. (Dec. 2003); Chair. DAVID S. Y. WONG; Man. Dir DEREK H. H. WONG; 39 domestic brs.

DBS Bank (Hong Kong) Ltd: 11/F, The Center, 99 Queen's Rd, Central; tel. 22188822; fax 21678222; e-mail hkcs@dbs.com; internet www.dbs.com.hk; f. 1938; inc 1954 as Kwong On Bank, name changed 2000; subsidiary of the Development Bank of Singapore; cap. 5,200m., res 10,656.2m., dep. 130,540.8m. (Dec. 2003); acquired Dao Heng Bank and Overseas Trust Bank July 2003; Chair. FRANK WONG; CEO RANDOLPH GORDON SULLIVAN; 32 brs.

Hang Seng Bank Ltd: 83 Des Voeux Rd, Central; tel. 21981111; fax 28684047; e-mail ccd@hangseng.com; internet www.hangseng.com; f. 1933; The Hongkong and Shanghai Banking Corporation Ltd, 62.14%; cap. 9,559m., res 10,362m., dep. 441,115m. (Dec. 2003); Chair. DAVID ELDON; Vice-Chair. and CEO VINCENT CHENG; 155 domestic brs, 7 overseas brs.

Industrial and Commercial Bank of China (Asia): ICBC Tower, 122–126 Queen's Rd, Central; tel. 25343333; fax 28051166; internet www.icbcasia.com; f. 1964; fmrly Union Bank of Hong Kong; cap. 2,259.8m., res 2,636.0m., dep. 64,558.0m. (Dec. 2003); Chair. JIANG JIANQING; 20 brs.

International Bank of Asia Ltd: International Bank of Asia Bldg, 38 Des Voeux Rd, Central; tel. 28426222; fax 28401190; e-mail iba-info@iba.com.hk; internet www.iba.com.hk; f. 1982 as Sun Hung Kai Bank Ltd, name changed 1986; subsidiary of Arab Banking Corpn; cap. 1,172.2m., res 1,124.5m., dep. 33,501.1m. (Dec. 2003); Man. Dir and CEO MIKE M. MURAD; 26 brs.

Jian Sing Bank Ltd: F/41, Tower 1, Lippo Centre, 89 Queensway, Hong Kong; tel. 25410088; fax 25447145; e-mail admin@jsb.com.hk; internet www.jsb.com.hk; f. 1964 as Hongkong Industrial and Commercial Bank Ltd, acquired by Dah Sing Bank Ltd in 1987, 40% interest acquired by China Construction Bank in 1994, resulting in name change, China Construction Bank acquired 100% stake in 2002; subsidiary of China Construction Bank; cap. 300.0m., res 81,971.0m., dep. 2,645.7m. (Dec. 2003); Chair. LUO ZHEFU; CEO and Dir PATRICK P. T. HO.

Liu Chong Hing Bank Ltd: POB 2535, G/F New World Tower, 16-18 Queen's Rd, Central; tel. 28417417; fax 28459134; e-mail info@lchbank.com; internet www.lchbank.com; f. 1948; cap. 217.5m., res 5,726.9m., dep. 33,627.0m. (Dec. 2003); Chair. and Man. Dir LIU LIT-MAN; 34 domestic brs, 3 overseas brs.

Nanyang Commercial Bank Ltd: Nanyang Commercial Bank Bldg, 151 Des Voeux Rd, Central; tel. 28520888; fax 28153333; e-mail webmaster@ncb.com.hk; internet www.ncb.com.hk; f. 1949; cap. 600m., res 1,107.4m., dep. 75,720.1m. (Dec. 2003); Chair. HE GUANGBEI; 41 brs, 6 mainland brs, 1 overseas br.

Shanghai Commercial Bank Ltd: 12 Queen's Rd, Central; tel. 28415415; fax 28104623; e-mail contact@shacombank.com.hk; internet www.shacombank.com.hk; f. 1950; cap. 2,000m., res 7,222.5m., dep. 62,942.2m. (Dec. 2003); CEO, Man. Dir and Gen. Man. JOHN KAM-PAK YAN; 40 domestic brs, 4 overseas brs.

Standard Bank Asia Ltd: 36/F, Two Pacific Place, 88 Queensway; tel. 28227888; fax 28227999; e-mail ashbanking@standardbank.com.hk; internet www.standardbank.com; f. 1970 as Jardine Fleming & Company Ltd, renamed Jardine Fleming Bank Ltd in 1993, absorbed by Standard Bank Investment Corpn Ltd and name changed as present in July 2001; cap. 72m., res 90m., dep. 1,356.3m. (Dec. 2003); Chair. ROB A. G. LEITH.

Tai Yau Bank Ltd: 16/F Tak Shing House, 20 Des Voeux Rd, Central; tel. 25229002; fax 28685334; f. 1947; cap. 300.0m., res 129.2m., dep 1,495.2m. (Dec. 2003); Chair. KO FOOK KAU.

Wing Hang Bank Ltd: 161 Queen's Rd, Central; tel. 28525111; fax 25410036; e-mail whbpsd@whbhk.com; internet www.whbhk.com; f. 1937; cap. 293.8m., res 6,393.1m., dep. 77,477.0m. (Dec. 2003); acquired Chekiang First Bank Ltd, Aug. 2004; Chair. and Chief Exec. PATRICK Y. B. FUNG; 26 domestic brs, 12 overseas brs.

Wing Lung Bank Ltd: 45 Des Voeux Rd, Central; tel. 28268333; fax 28100592; e-mail wlb@winglungbank.com; internet www.winglungbank.com; f. 1933; cap. 1,161.0m., res 7,447.7m., dep. 55,200.6m. (Dec. 2003); Chair. MICHAEL PO-KO WU; Exec. Dir and Gen. Man. CHE-SHUM CHUNG; 33 domestic brs, 2 representative offices in China.

Principal Foreign Banks

ABN AMRO Bank NV (Netherlands): Edinburgh Tower, 3–4/F, Landmark, 15 Queen's Rd, Central; tel. 28429211; fax 28459049; CEO (China) SERGIO RIAL; 3 brs.

American Express Bank Ltd (USA): One Pacific Place, 36/F, 88 Queensway, Central; tel. 28440688; fax 28453637; Senior Country Exec. DOUGLAS H. SHORT III; 3 brs.

Australia and New Zealand Banking Group Ltd: 27/F, One Exchange Square, 8 Connaught Place, Central; tel. 28437111; fax 28680089; Gen. Man. PETER RICHARDSON.

Bangkok Bank Public Co Ltd (Thailand): Bangkok Bank Bldg, 28 Des Voeux Rd, Central; tel. 28016688; fax 28451805; Gen. Man. CHEN MAN YING; 2 brs.

Bank of America (Asia) Ltd: GPOB 799, 2/F, Bank of America Tower, 12 Harcourt Rd; tel. 28476666; fax 28100821; internet www.bankofamerica.com.hk; Chair. COLM MCCARTHY; Man. Dir and CEO FREDERICK CHIN.

Bank of Communications, Hong Kong Branch: 20 Pedder St, Central; tel. 28419611; fax 28106993; f. 1934; Gen. Man. FANG LIANKUI; 41 brs.

Bank of India: Ruttonjee House, 2/F, 11 Duddell St, Central; tel. 25240186; fax 28106149; e-mail boihk@netvigator.com; Chief Exec. O. P. GUPTA.

Bank of Scotland: Jardine House, 15/F, 1 Connaught Place, Central; tel. 25212155; fax 28459007; Regional Dir I. A. MCKINNEY; 1 br.

Barclays Capital Asia Ltd: Citibank Tower, 42/F, 3 Garden Rd, Central; tel. 29032000; fax 29032999; internet www.barclayscapital.com; f. 1972; Chair. and CEO ROBERT A. MORRICE.

BNP Paribas (France): Central Tower, 4–14/F, 28 Queen's Rd, Central; tel. 29098888; fax 25302707; e-mail didier.balme@bnpgroup.com; internet www.bnpparibas.com.hk; f. 1958; Man. DIDIER BALME; 2 brs.

Citibank, NA (USA): Citibank Tower, 39–40/F and 44–50/F, Citibank Plaza, 3 Garden Rd, Central; tel. 28688888; fax 23068111; 20 brs.

Commerzbank AG (Germany): Hong Kong Club Bldg, 21/F, 3A Chater Rd, Central; tel. 28429666; fax 28681414; 1 br.

Crédit Agricole Indosuez (France): One Exchange Square, 42–45/F, 8 Connaught Rd, Central; tel. 28489000; fax 28681406; Sr Country Officer CHARLES REYBET-DEGAT; 1 br.

Deutsche Bank AG (Germany): 51–56/F, Cheung Kong Center, 2 Queen's Rd, Central; tel. 22038888; fax 28459056; Gen. Mans Dr MICHAEL THOMAS, REINER RUSCH; 1 br.

Equitable PCI Bank (Philippines): 7/F, No. 1, Silver Fortune Plaza, Wellington St; tel. 28680323; fax 28100050; Vice-Pres. PAUL LANG; 1 br.

Fortis Bank (Belgium): Fortis Bank Tower, 26/F, 77–79 Gloucester Rd, Wanchai; tel. 28230456; fax 25276851; e-mail info@fortisbank.com.hk; internet www.fortisbank.com.hk; Gen. Man. DAVID YU; 28 brs.

Indian Overseas Bank: POB 182, Ruttonjee House, 3/F, 11 Duddell St, Central; tel. 25227249; fax 28450159; 2 brs.

JP Morgan Chase Bank (USA): 39/F, One Exchange Square, Connaught Place, Central; tel. 28431234; fax 28414396.

Malayan Banking Berhad (Malaysia): Entertainment Bldg, 18–19/F, 30 Queen's Rd, Central; tel. 25227141; fax 28106013; trades in Hong Kong as Maybank; Man. Hwan Woon Han; 2 brs.

Mevas Bank: 36/F, Dah Sing Financial Centre, 108 Gloucester Rd; tel. 31013286; fax 31013298; e-mail contactus@mevas.com; internet www.mevas.com; Chair. David S. Y. Wong.

Mizuho Corporate Asia (HK) Ltd (Japan): 17/F, 2 Pacific Place, 88 Queensway, Admiralty; tel. 21033040; fax 28101326; Man. Dir and CEO Noboru Akatsuka; 1 br.

National Bank of Pakistan: 18/F, ING Tower, 308–320 Des Voeux Rd, Central; tel. 25217321; fax 28451703; e-mail nbphkkm@netvigator.com; CEO Ghulam Hussain Azhar; 2 brs.

Oversea-Chinese Banking Corpn Ltd (Singapore): 9/F, 9 Queen's Rd, Central; tel. 28682086; fax 28453439; Gen. Man. Benjamin Yeung; 3 brs.

Philippine National Bank: 26/F, Worldwide Hse, 19 Des Voeux Rd, Central; tel. 25431066; fax 25416645; e-mail pnbhkgrp@pnbhk.com; Gen. Man. Danilo T. Flores; 1 br.

N. M. Rothschild and Sons (Hong Kong) Ltd: 16/F, Alexandra House, 16–20 Chater Rd, Central; tel. 25255333; fax 28681728; e-mail jackson.woo@rothschild.com.hk; internet www.rothschild.com.hk; Dir Jackson Woo.

Société Générale Asia Ltd (France): 42/F, Edinburgh Tower, The Landmark, 15 Queen's Rd; tel. 25838600; fax 28400738; internet www.sgcib.com; CEO Jackson Cheung.

Sumitomo Mitsui Banking Corpn (SMBC) (Japan): 7–8F/, One International Finance Centre, 1 Harbour View St, Central; tel. 22062000; fax 22062888; Gen. Man. Toshio Morikawa; 1 br.

Tokyo-Mitsubishi International (HK) Ltd (Japan): 14/F, Tower 1, Admiralty Centre, 18 Harcourt Rd; tel. 28627888; fax 25291550; Man. Dir and CEO Yoshiaki Watanabe.

UBAF (Hong Kong) Ltd (France): Far East Finance Centre, 18/F, 16 Harcourt Rd, Central; tel. 25201361; fax 25274256; e-mail info@ubafhk.com; internet www.ubafhk.com; Man. Dir G. Alejandro.

UFJ International Finance Asia Ltd (Japan): 6/F, Hong Kong Club Bldg, 3A Chater Rd, Central; tel. 25334300; fax 28453518; internet www.ufjifal.com; CEO and Man. Dir Akihiko Kobayashi.

United Overseas Bank Ltd (Singapore): United Overseas Bank Bldg, 54–58 Des Voeux Rd, Central; tel. 28425666; fax 28105773; Sr Vice-Pres. and CEO Robert Chan Tze Leung; 5 brs.

Banking Associations

The Chinese Banks' Association Ltd: South China Bldg, 5/F, 1–3 Wyndham St, Central; tel. 25224789; fax 28775102; 1,666 mems; chaired by Bank of East Asia.

The DTC Association (The Hong Kong Association of Restricted Licence Banks and Deposit-Taking Companies): Unit 2404, 24/F, Bonham Trade Centre, 50 Bonham Strand East, Sheung Wan; internet www.dtca.org.hk; tel. 25264079; fax 25230180.

The Hong Kong Association of Banks: Rm 525, Prince's Building, Central, Hong Kong; tel. 25211169; fax 28685035; e-mail info@hkab.org.hk; internet www.hkab.org.hk; f. 1981 to succeed The Exchange Banks' Asscn of Hong Kong; all licensed banks in Hong Kong are required by law to be mems of this statutory body, the function of which is to represent and further the interests of the banking sector; 133 mems; chaired by Bank of China (Hong Kong) Ltd; Sec. Rona Morgan.

STOCK EXCHANGE

Honk Kong Exchanges and Clearing Ltd: 1 International Finance Centre, 12/F, 1 Harbour View St, Central; tel. 25221122; fax 22953106; e-mail info@hkex.com.hk; internet www.hkex.com.hk; f. 2000 by unification of the Stock Exchange of Hong Kong, the Hong Kong Futures Exchange and the Hong Kong Securities Clearing Co; 572 mems; Chair. Lee Yeh Kwong; CEO Kwong Ki Chi.

In 1998 Exchange Fund Investment Ltd was established by the Government to manage its stock portfolio acquired during the intervention of August (Chair. Yang Ti-liang).

SUPERVISORY BODY

Securities and Futures Commission (SFC): 8/F, Chater House, 8 Connaught Rd, Central; tel. 28409222; fax 25217836; e-mail enquiry@hksfc.org.hk; internet www.hksfc.org.hk; f. 1989 to supervise the stock and futures markets; Chair. Andrew Sheng; Dir and COO Peter Au-yang.

INSURANCE

In December 2003 there were 188 authorized insurance companies, including 94 overseas companies. The following are among the principal companies:

Asia Insurance Co Ltd: World-Wide House, 16/F, 19 Des Voeux Rd, Central; tel. 28677988; fax 28100218; e-mail kclau@asiainsurance.com.hk; internet www.asiainsurance.com.hk; Chair. Sebastian Ki Chit Lau.

CGU International Insurance plc: Cityplaza One, 9/F, Taikoo Shing; tel. 28940555; fax 28905741; e-mail cguasia.com; Gen. Man. Andrew Lo.

Hong Kong Export Credit Insurance Corpn: South Seas Centre, Tower I, 2/F, 75 Mody Rd, Tsim Sha Tsui East, Kowloon; fax 27226277; Commr D. K. Dowding.

Ming An Insurance Co (HK) Ltd: Ming An Plaza, 19/F, 8 Sunning Rd, Causeway Bay; tel. 28151551; fax 25416567; e-mail mai@mingan.com.hk; internet www.mingan.com; Dir and Gen. Man. K. P. Cheng.

National Mutual Insurance Co (Bermuda) Ltd: 151 Gloucester Rd, Wanchai; tel. 25191111; fax 25987204; life and general insurance; Chair. Sir David Akers-Jones; CEO Terry Smith.

Prudential Assurance Co Ltd: Cityplaza 4, 10/F, 12 Taikoo Wan Rd, Taikoo Shing; tel. 29773888; fax 28776994; life and general; CEO James C. K. Wong.

Royal and Sun Alliance (Hong Kong) Ltd: Dorset House, 32/F, Taikoo Place, 979 King's Road, Quarry Bay; tel. 29683000; fax 29685111; Man. Dir Keith Land.

Summit Insurance (Asia) Ltd: 7/F Hsin Chong Center, 107-109 Wai Yip St, Kwun Tong, Kowloon; fax 25166992; e-mail agnesc@hcg.com.hk; internet www.hsinchong.com/summit; CEO Iu Po Sing.

Swiss Re Hong Kong Branch: 61/F Central Plaza, 18 Harbour Rd, Wanchai; tel. 25825608; acquired Mercantile and General Reinsurance in 1996; Gen. Man. Simon Lam.

Willis China (Hong Kong) Ltd: 3502, The Lee Gardens, 33 Hysan Ave, Causeway Bay; tel. 28270111; fax 28270966; internet www.willis.com; Man. Dir Kirk Austin.

Winterthur Life Hong Kong: 33rd Floor, Central Plaza, 18 Harbour Rd, Wanchai; tel. 21173000; fax 21173002; internet www.winterthur.com.hk; mem. of Crédit Suisse Group.

Insurance Associations

Hong Kong Federation of Insurers (HKFI): 29/F, Sunshine Plaza, 353 Lockhart Rd, Wanchai; tel. 25201868; fax 25201967; e-mail hkfi@hkfi.org.hk; internet www.hkfi.org.hk; f. 1988; 117 general insurance and 42 life insurance mems; Chair. Choy Chung Foo; Exec. Dir Louisa Fong.

Insurance Institute of Hong Kong: GPO Box 6747; tel. 25825601; fax 28276033; internet www.iihk.org.hk; f. 1967; Pres. Stephen Law.

Trade and Industry

Hong Kong Trade Development Council: Office Tower, 38/F, Convention Plaza, 1 Harbour Rd, Wanchai; tel. 1830668; fax 28240249; e-mail hktdc@tdc.org.hk; internet www.tdctrade.com; f. 1966; Chair. Peter Woo Kwong-ching; Exec. Dir Frederick Lam.

Trade and Industry Department: Trade and Industry Department Tower, 700 Nathan Rd, Kowloon; tel. 23985333; fax 27892491; e-mail enquiry@tid.gov.hk; internet www.tid.gov.hk; Dir-Gen. Kevin Ho.

DEVELOPMENT ORGANIZATIONS

Hong Kong Housing Authority: 33 Fat Kwong St, Homantin, Kowloon; tel. 27615002; fax 27621110; f. 1973; plans, builds and manages public housing; Chair. Dominic Wong; Dir of Housing J. A. Miller.

Hong Kong Productivity Council: HKPC Bldg, 78 Tat Chee Ave, Yau Yat Chuen, Kowloon Tong, Kowloon; tel. 27885678; fax 27885900; e-mail justina@hkpc.org; internet www.hkpc.org; f. 1967 to promote increased productivity of industry and to encourage optimum utilization of resources; council of 23 mems appointed by the Government, representing management, labour, academic and professional interests, and govt depts associated with productivity matters; Chair. Andrew Leung; Exec. Dir K. K. Yeung.

Kadoorie Agricultural Aid Loan Fund: c/o Director of Agriculture, Fisheries and Conservation, Cheung Sha Wan Govt Offices, 5/F, 303 Cheung Sha Wan Rd, Kowloon; tel. 21506666; fax 23113731; e-mail mailbox@afcd.gov.hk; f. 1954; provides low-interest loans to farmers; HK \$9.9m. was loaned in 2004/05.

J. E. Joseph Trust Fund: c/o Director of Agriculture, Fisheries and Conservation, Cheung Sha Wan Govt Offices, 5/F, 303 Cheung Sha Wan Rd, Kowloon; tel. 21506666; fax 23113731; e-mail mailbox@afcd .gov.hk; f. 1954; grants low-interest credit facilities to farmers and farmers' co-operative socs; HK $9.1m. was loaned in 2004/05.

CHAMBERS OF COMMERCE

Chinese Chamber of Commerce, Kowloon: 2/F, 8–10 Nga Tsin Long Rd, Kowloon; tel. 23822309; f. 1936; 234 mems; Chair. and Exec. Dir YEUNG CHOR-HANG.

The Chinese General Chamber of Commerce: 4/F, 24–25 Connaught Rd, Central; tel. 25256385; fax 28452610; e-mail cgcc@cgcc .org.hk; internet www.cgcc.org.hk; f. 1900; 6,200 mems; Chair. Dr TSANG HIN-CHI.

Hong Kong General Chamber of Commerce: United Centre, 22/F, 95 Queensway, POB 852; tel. 25299229; fax 25279843; e-mail chamber@chamber.org.hk; internet www.chamber.org.hk; f. 1861; 4,000 mems; Chair. ANTHONY NIGHTINGALE; CEO EDEN WOON.

Kowloon Chamber of Commerce: KCC Bldg, 3/F, 2 Liberty Ave, Homantin, Kowloon; tel. 27600393; fax 27610166; e-mail kcc02@ hkkcc.biz.com.hk; internet www.hkkcc.org.hk; f. 1938; 1,640 mems; Chair. TONG KWOK-WAH; Sec. of Gen. Affairs CHENG PO-WO.

FOREIGN TRADE ORGANIZATIONS

Hong Kong Chinese Importers' and Exporters' Association: Champion Bldg, 7–8/F, 287–291 Des Voeux Rd, Central; tel. 25448474; fax 25444677; e-mail info@hkciea.org.hk; internet www .hkciea.org.hk; f. 1954; 3,000 mems; Pres. WONG TING KWONG.

Hong Kong Exporters' Association: Room 825, Star House, 3 Salisbury Rd, Tsimshatsui, Kowloon; tel. 27309851; fax 27301869; e-mail exporter@exporters.org.hk; internet www.exporters.org.hk; f. 1955; 660 mems comprising leading merchants and manufacturing exporters; Pres. CLIFF K. SUN; Exec. Dir SHIRLEY SO.

INDUSTRIAL AND TRADE ASSOCIATIONS

Chinese Manufacturers' Association of Hong Kong: CMA Bldg, 64 Connaught Rd, Central; tel. 25456166; fax 25414541; e-mail info@cma.org.hk; internet www.cma.org.hk; f. 1934 to promote and protect industrial and trading interests; operates testing and certification laboratories; 3,700 mems; Pres. JOSE YU SUN-SAY; Sec.-Gen. FRANCIS T. M. LAU.

Federation of Hong Kong Garment Manufacturers: Cheung Lee Commercial Bldg, Room 401–3, 25 Kimberley Rd, Tsimshatsui, Kowloon; tel. 27211383; fax 23111062; e-mail fhkgmfrs@hkstar.com; internet www.garment.org.hk; f. 1964; 180 mems; Pres. NORMAN TAM; Sec.-Gen. MICHAEL LEUNG.

Federation of Hong Kong Industries (FKHI): Hankow Centre, 4/F, 5–15 Hankow Rd, Tsimshatsui, Kowloon; tel. 27323188; fax 27213494; e-mail fhki@fhki.org.hk; internet www.fhki.org.hk; f. 1960; 3,000 mems; Chair. ANDREW LEUNG.

Federation of Hong Kong Watch Trades and Industries Ltd: Peter Bldg, Room 604, 58–62 Queen's Rd, Central; tel. 25233232; fax 28684485; e-mail hkwatch@netvigator.com; internet www.hkwatch .org; f. 1947; 650 mems; Chair. LUTHER WONG.

Hong Kong Association for the Advancement of Science and Technology Ltd: 2A, Tak Lee Commercial Bldg, 113–17 Wanchai Rd, Wanchai; tel. 28913388; fax 28381823; e-mail info@hkaast.org .hk; internet www.hkaast.org.hk; Pres. Prof. LEE WING BUN.

Hong Kong Biotechnology Association Ltd: Rm 789, HITEC, 1 Trademart Drive, Kowloon Bay, Kowloon; tel. 26209955; fax 26201238; e-mail etang@hkbta.org.hk; internet www.hkbta.org.hk; Chair. LO YUK LAM.

Hong Kong Chinese Enterprises Association: Harbour Centre, Room 2104–6, 25 Harbour Rd, Wanchai; tel. 28272831; fax 28272606; e-mail info@hkcea.com; internet www.hkcea.com; f. 1991; 1,000 mems; CEO ZHOU JIE.

Hong Kong Chinese Textile Mills Association: 11/F, 38–40 Tai Po Rd, Sham Shiu Po, Kowloon; tel. 27778236; fax 27881836; f. 1931; 150 mems; Pres. LEE CHUNG-CHIU.

Hong Kong Construction Association Ltd: 3/F, 180–182 Hennessy Rd, Wanchai; tel. 25724414; fax 25727104; e-mail admin@ hkca.com.hk; internet www.hkca.com.hk; f. 1920; 372 mems; Pres. BILLY WONG; Sec.-Gen. PATRICK CHAN.

Hong Kong Electronic Industries Association Ltd: Rm 1201, 12/F, Harbour Crystal Centre, 100 Granville Rd, Tsimshatsui, Kowloon; tel. 27788328; fax 27882200; e-mail hkeia@hkeia.org; internet www.hkeia.org; 350 mems; Chair. Dr K. B. CHAN; Exec. Dir CHARLES CHAPMAN.

Hong Kong Garment Manufacturers Association: 401–3, Cheung Lee Commercial Bldg, 25 Kimberley Rd, Tsimshatsui, Kowloon; tel. 23052893; fax 23052493; e-mail mleung@textilecouncil .com; f. 1987; 40 mems; Chair. PETER WANG.

Hong Kong Information Technology Federation Ltd: The Center, 21/F, 99 Queen's Rd, Central; tel. 22878017; fax 22878038; e-mail info@hkitf.com; internet www.hkitf.org.hk; 316 mems; f. 1980; Pres. CHARLES MOK.

Hong Kong Jewellery and Jade Manufacturers Association: Flat A, 12/F, Kaiser Estate Phase 1, 41 Man Yue St, Hunghom, Kowloon; tel. 25430543; fax 28150164; e-mail hkjja@hkstar.com; internet www.jewellery-hk.org; f. 1965; 227 mems; Pres. CHARLES CHAN; Chair. KING LI; Gen. Man. CATHERINE CHAN.

Hong Kong Jewelry Manufacturers' Association: Unit G, 2/F, Kaiser Estate Phase 2, 51 Man Yue St, Hunghom, Kowloon; tel. 27663002; fax 23623647; e-mail hkjma@jewelry.org.hk; internet www.jewelry.org.hk; f. 1988; 260 mems; Chair. AARON SHUM.

Hong Kong Knitwear Exporters and Manufacturers Association: Cheung Lee Commercial Bldg, Rm 401–03, Tsimshatsui, Kowloon; tel. 27552621; fax 27565672; f. 1966; 80 mems; Chair. WILLY LIN; Exec. Sec. SHIRLEY LIU.

Hong Kong and Kowloon Footwear Manufacturers' Association: Kam Fung Bldg, 3/F, Flat D, 8 Cleverly St, Sheung Wan; tel. and fax 25414499; 88 mems; Pres. LOK WAI-TO; Sec. LEE SUM-HUNG.

Hong Kong Optical Manufacturers' Association Ltd: 2/F, 11 Fa Yuen St, Mongkok, Kowloon; tel. 23326505; fax 27705786; e-mail hkoma@netvigator.com; internet www.hkoptical.org.hk; f. 1982; 112 mems; Pres. HUI LEUNG-WAH.

Hong Kong Plastics Manufacturers Association Ltd: Fu Yuen Bldg, 1/F, Flat B, 39–49 Wanchai Rd; tel. 25742230; fax 25742843; f. 1957; 200 mems; Chair. JEFFREY LAM; Pres. DENNIS H. S. TING.

Hong Kong Printers Association: 1/F, 48–50 Johnston Rd, Wanchai; tel. 25275050; fax 28610463; e-mail printers@hkprinters.org; internet www.hkprinters.org; f. 1939; 437 mems; Chair. HO KA-HUN.

Hong Kong Rubber and Footwear Manufacturers' Association: Kar Tseuk Bldg, Block A, 2/F, 185 Prince Edward Rd, Kowloon; tel. 23812297; fax 23976927; e-mail hkrfma@netvigator.com; f. 1948; 180 mems; Chair. CHEUNG KAM; Pres. BENJAMIN KO.

Hong Kong Sze Yap Commercial and Industrial Association: Cosco Tower, Unit 1205–6, 183 Queen's Rd, Central; tel. 25438095; fax 25449495; f. 1909; 1,082 mems; Chair. LOUIE CHICK-NAN; Sec. WONG KA CHUN.

Hong Kong Toys Council: Hankow Centre, 4/F, 5–15 Hankow Rd, Tsimshatsui, Kowloon; tel. 27323188; fax 27213494; e-mail fhki@ fhki.org.hk; internet www.toyshk.org; f. 1986; 200 mems; Chair. SAMSON CHAN.

Hong Kong Watch Manufacturers' Association: Yu Wing Bldg, 3/F and 11/F, Unit A, 64–66 Wellington St, Central; tel. 25225238; fax 28106614; e-mail hkwma@netvigator.com; internet www .hkwma.org; 616 mems; Pres. KELVIN K. W. LAU; Sec.-Gen. RICKY W. K. LAW.

Information and Software Industry Association Ltd: Suite 2, 8/F, Tower 6, China Hong Kong City, 33 Canton Rd, Tsimshatsui; tel. 26222867; fax 26222731; e-mail info@isia.org.hk; internet www .isia.org.hk; Chair. SATTI WONG.

Internet and Telecom Association of Hong Kong: GPOB 13461; tel. 25042732; fax 25042752; e-mail info@itahk.org.hk; internet www.itahk.org.hk; 130 mems; Chair. TONY HAU.

New Territories Commercial and Industrial General Association Ltd: Cheong Hay Bldg, 2/F, 107 Hoi Pa St, Tsuen Wan; tel. 24145316; fax 24934130; f. 1973; 2,663 mems; Pres. LAU YUE SUN; Chair. HOK LIM WAN; Sec.-Gen. KAM CHUEN NGAN.

Real Estate Developers Association of Hong Kong: Worldwide House, Room 1403, 19 Des Voeux Rd, Central; tel. 28260111; fax 28452521; f. 1965; 779 mems; Pres. Dr STANLEY HO; Chair. KEITH KERR; Sec.-Gen. LOUIS LOONG.

Textile Council of Hong Kong Ltd: 401-3, Cheung Lee Commercial Bldg, 25 Kimberley Rd, Tsimshatsui , Kowloon; tel. 23052893; fax 23052493; e-mail mleung@textilecouncil.com; internet www .textilecouncil.com; f. 1989; 10 mems; Chair. ANDREW LEUNG; Exec. Dir MICHAEL LEUNG.

Toys Manufacturers' Association of Hong Kong Ltd: Room 1302, Metroplaza, Tower 2, 223 Hing Fong Rd, Kwai Chung, New Territories; tel. 24221209; fax 24221639; e-mail tm_hk@hotmail .com; internet www.tmhk.net; 250 mems; Pres. ARTHUR CHAN; Sec. Y. M. KO.

EMPLOYERS' ORGANIZATIONS

Employers' Federation of Hong Kong: Suite 2004, Sino Plaza, 255–257 Gloucester Rd, Causeway Bay; tel. 25280033; fax 28655285; e-mail efhk@efhk.org.hk; internet www.efhk.org.hk; f. 1947; 504 mems; Chair. VICTOR APPS; Exec. Dir JACKIE MA.

Hong Kong Factory Owners' Association Ltd: Wing Wong Bldg, 11/F, 557–559 Nathan Rd, Kowloon; tel. 23882372; fax 23857129; f. 1982; 1,179 mems; Pres. HWANG JEN; Sec. CHA KIT YEN.

UTILITIES

Electricity

CLP Power Ltd: 147 Argyle St, Kowloon; tel. 26788111; fax 27604448; internet www.clpgroup.com; f. 1918; fmrly China Light and Power Co Ltd; generation and supply of electricity to Kowloon and the New Territories; Chair. MICHAEL D. KADOORIE; Man. Dir ROSS SAYERS.

The Hongkong Electric Co Ltd: 44 Kennedy Rd; tel. 28433111; fax 28100506; e-mail mail@hec.com.hk; internet www.hec.com.hk; generation and supply of electricity to Hong Kong Island, and the islands of Ap Lei Chau and Lamma; Chair. GEORGE C. MAGNUS; Man. Dir K. S. TSO.

Gas

Gas Authority: all gas supply cos, gas installers and contractors are required to be registered with the Gas Authority. At the end of 2003 there were seven registered gas supply cos.

Hong Kong and China Gas Co Ltd: 23/F, 363 Java Rd, North Point; tel. 29633388; fax 25632233; internet www.towngas.com; production, distribution and marketing of town gas and gas appliances; operates two plants; Chair. LEE SHAU-KEE; Man. Dir ALFRED W. K. CHAN.

Water

Drainage Services Department: responsible for planning, designing, constructing, operating and maintaining the sewerage, sewage treatment and stormwater drainage infrastructures.

Water Supplies Department: tel. 28294709; fax 25881594; e-mail wsdinfo@wsd.gov.hk; internet www.info.gov.hk/wsd/; responsible for water supplies; approx. 2.4m. customers (2001).

TRADE UNIONS

In December 2003 there were 689 trade unions in Hong Kong, comprising 644 employees' unions, 23 employers' associations and 22 mixed organizations.

Hong Kong and Kowloon Trades Union Council (TUC): 12/F, Kam Shek Commercial Bldg, 17 Waterloo Rd, Mongkok, Kowloon; tel. 23845150; fax 27705396; f. 1949; 66 affiliated unions, mostly covering the catering and building trades; 28,200 mems; supports Taiwan; affiliated to ICFTU; Officer-in-Charge WONG YIU KAM.

Hong Kong Confederation of Trade Unions: Wing Wong Commercial Bldg, 19/F, 557–559 Nathan Rd, Kowloon; tel. 27708668; fax 27707388; e-mail hkctu@hkctu.org.hk; internet www.hkctu.org.hk; registered Feb. 1990; 63 affiliated independent unions and federations; 165,000 mems; Chair. CHENG CHING-FAT.

Hong Kong Federation of Trade Unions (FTU): 7/F, 50 Ma Tau Chung Rd, Tokwawan, Kowloon; tel. 27120231; fax 27608477; e-mail external@ftu.org.hk; internet www.ftu.org.hk; f. 1948; 176 member unions, mostly concentrated in shipyards, public transport, textile mills, construction, department stores, printing and public utilities; supports the People's Republic of China; 310,000 mems; Chair. WONG KWOK-KIN; Gen. Sec. LAM SHUK-YEE.

Also active are the **Federation of Hong Kong and Kowloon Labour Unions** (31 affiliated unions with 21,700 mems) and the **Federation of Civil Service Unions** (29 affiliated unions with 12,000 mems).

Transport

Transport Department: Immigration Tower, 41/F, 7 Gloucester Rd, Wanchai; tel. 28042600; fax 28240433; internet www.info.gov.hk/td.

RAILWAYS

Kowloon–Canton Railway Corpn: KCRC House, 9 Lok King St, Fo Tan, Sha Tin, New Territories; tel. 26881333; fax 26880983; internet www.kcrc.com; f. 1982; operated by the Kowloon–Canton Railway Corpn, a public statutory body; plans for merger with MTR Corpn announced in 2004; operates both heavy and light rail systems; the 34-km East Rail runs from the terminus at Hung Hom to the frontier at Lo Wu; through passenger services to Guangzhou

(Canton), suspended in 1949, were resumed in 1979; the electrification and double-tracking of the entire length and redevelopment of all stations has been completed, and full electric train service came into operation in 1983; in 1988 a light railway network serving the north-western New Territories was opened; passenger service extended to Foshan in 1993, Dongguan in 1994, Zhaoqing in 1995 and Shanghai in 1997; direct Kowloon–Beijing service commenced in May 1997; also freight services to several destinations in China; West Rail, a domestic passenger line, links Tuen Mun and Yuen Long with Kowloon; three East Rail extensions were due for completion in 2004–07; a Kowloon Southern Link connecting West Rail and East Rail was due for completion in 2008/09; a new 17-km railway linking Sha Tin and Central via a new cross-harbour tunnel was due to be completed in 2011, providing the first direct rail route from the Chinese border to Hong Kong Island; Chair. and CEO SAMUEL M. H. LAI.

MTR Corporation: MTR Tower, Telford Plaza, Kowloon Bay; tel. 29932111; fax 27988822; internet www.mtr.com.hk; f. 1975; privatized in 2000, shares commenced trading on Hong Kong Stock Exchange in Oct. 2000; plans for merger with Kowloon-Canton Railway Corpn announced in 2004; network of 87.7 km of railway lines and 50 stations; the first section of the underground mass transit railway (MTR) system opened in 1979; a 15.6-km line from Kwun Tong to Central opened in 1980; a 10.5-km Tsuen Wan extension opened in 1982; the 12.5-km Island Line opened in 1985–86; in 1989 a second harbour crossing between Cha Kwo Ling and Quarry Bay, known as the Eastern Harbour Crossing, commenced operation, adding 4.6 km to the railway system; 34-km link to new airport at Chek Lap Kok and to Tung Chung New Town opened in mid-1998; an additional line, the Tseung Kwan O Extension, was completed in August 2002; additional lines were also planned for 2006; CEO C. K. CHOW; Chair. Dr RAYMOND K. F. CH'IEN.

TRAMWAYS

Hong Kong Tramways Ltd: Whitty Street Tram Depot, Connaught Rd West, Western District; tel. 21186338; fax 21186038; f. 1904; operates six routes and 161 double-deck trams between Kennedy Town and Shaukeiwan; Dir and Gen. Man. FRANKIE YICK.

ROADS

At the end of 2003 there were 1,934 km of roads and 1,057 highway structures. Almost all of them are concrete or asphalt surfaced. Owing to the hilly terrain, and the density of building development, the scope for substantial increase in the road network is limited. A new 29-km steel bridge linking Hong Kong's Lantau Island with Macao and Zhuhai City, in the Chinese province of Guangdong, was being planned in in the early 21st century, with studies being carried out to determine the project's financial and technological feasibility.

Highways Department: Ho Man Tin Government Offices, 5/F, 88 Chung Hau St, Ho Man Tin, Kowloon; tel. 27623304; fax 27145216; e-mail hyd@hyd.gov.hk; internet www.hyd.gov.hk; f. 1986; planning, design, construction and maintenance of the public road system; co-ordination of major highway and railway projects; Dir MAK CHAI-KWONG.

FERRIES

Conventional ferries, hoverferries and catamarans operate between Hong Kong, China and Macao. There is also an extensive network of ferry services to outlying districts.

Hongkong and Yaumati Ferry Co Ltd: 98 Tam Kon Shan Rd, Ngau Kok Wan, North Tsing Yi, New Territories; tel. 23944294; fax 27869001; e-mail hkferry@hkf.com; internet www.hkf.com; licensed routes on ferry services, incl. excursion, vehicular and dangerous goods; Gen. Man. DAVID C. S. HO.

Hongkong Macao Hydrofoil Co Ltd: Turbojet Ferry Services (Guangzhou) Ltd, 83 Hing Wah St West, Lai Chi Kok, Kowloon; operates services to Macao, Fu Yong (Shenzhen airport) and East River Guangzhou.

'Star' Ferry Co Ltd: Kowloon Point Pier, Tsimshatsui, Kowloon; tel. 21186223; fax 21186028; e-mail sf@starferry.com.hk; f. 1898; operates 13 passenger ferries between the Kowloon Peninsula and Central, the main business district of Hong Kong; between Central and Hung Hom; between Tsimshatsui and Wanchai; between Tsimshatsui and Central; and between Wanchai and Hung Hom; Man. JOHNNY LEUNG.

SHIPPING

Hong Kong is one of the world's largest shipping centres and is a major container port. Hong Kong was a British port of registry until the inauguration of a new and independent shipping register in December 1990. Following Hong Kong's reunification with the People's Republic of China, Hong Kong maintains full autonomy in its maritime policy. At the end of 2003 the register comprised a fleet of

901 vessels, totalling 20.5m. grt. The eight container terminals at Kwai Chung, which are privately-owned and operated, comprised 19 berths in 2003. The construction of a ninth terminal (CT9) commenced in 1998. CT9 was expected to be fully operational by 2005. Lantau Island has been designated as the site for any future expansion.

Marine Department, Hong Kong Special Administrative Region Government: Harbour Bldg, 22/F, 38 Pier Rd, Central, GPOB 4155; tel. 28523001; fax 25449241; e-mail mdenquiry@ mardep.gov.hk; internet www.mardep.gov.hk; Dir of Marine S. Y. Tsui.

Shipping Companies

Anglo-Eastern Ship Management Ltd: Universal Trade Centre, 14/F, 3 Arbuthnot Rd, Central, POB 11400; tel. 28636111; fax 28612419; e-mail allhx470@gncomtext.com; internet www.webhk .com/angloeastern/; Chair. Peter Cremers; Man. Dir Marcel Liedts.

Chung Gai Ship Management Co Ltd: Admiralty Centre Tower 1, 31/F, 18 Harcourt Rd; tel. 25295541; fax 28656206; Chair. S. Koda; Man. Dir K. Ichihara.

COSCO (Hong Kong) Shipping Co Ltd (CHS): 50-51/F, Cosco Tower, 183 Queen's Rd, Central; tel. 28098688; fax 25461041; internet www.coscochs.com.hk; established by merger of former Ocean Tramping Co Ltd and Yick Fung Shipping and Enterprise Co; Chair. Wei Jiafu; Pres. and CEO Liu Guoyuan.

Fairmont Shipping (HK) Ltd: Fairmont House, 21/F, 8 Cotton Tree Drive; tel. 25218338; fax 28104560; Man. Charles Leung.

Far East Enterprising Co (HK) Ltd: 2/F Yuen Fat Admin Bldg, Yen Chow St West, West Kowloon Reclamation, Sahm Shui Po, Kowloon; tel. 28283668; fax 28275584; e-mail farensnp@farenco .com; f. 1949; shipping, chartering, brokering; Gen. Man. Lau Pak Shing.

Gulfeast Shipmanagement Ltd: Great Eagle Centre, 9/F, 23 Harbour Rd, Wanchai; tel. 28313344; Finance Dir A. T. Mirmohammadi.

Hong Kong Borneo Shipping Co Ltd: 815 International Bldg, 141 Des Voeux Rd, Central; tel. 25413797; fax 28153473; Pres. Datuk Lai Fook Kim.

Hong Kong Ming Wah Shipping Co: Unit 3701, China Merchants Tower, 37/F, Shun Tak Centre, 168–200 Connaught Rd, Central; tel. 25172128; fax 25473482.

Island Navigation Corpn International Ltd: Harbour Centre, 28–29/F, 25 Harbour Rd, Wanchai; tel. 28333222; fax 28270001; Man. Dir F. S. Shih.

Jardine Shipping Services: 18/F, Tower Two, Ever Gain Plaza, 88 Container Port Rd, Kwai Chung; tel. 25793388; fax 28569927; e-mail terence.sit@jsa.com.hk; internet www.jardine-shipping.com; Pres. Terence Sit.

Oak Maritime (HK) Inc Ltd: 2301 China Resources Bldg, 26 Harbour Rd, Wanchai; tel. 25063866; fax 25063563; Chair. Steve G. K. Hsu; Pres. Fred C. P. Tsai.

Orient Overseas Container Line Ltd: Harbour Centre, 31/F, 25 Harbour Rd, Wanchai; tel. 28333888; fax 25318122; internet www .oocl.com; member of the Grand Alliance of shipping cos (five partners); Chair. C. C. Tung.

Teh-Hu Cargocean Management Co Ltd: Unit B, Fortis Bank Tower, 15/F, 77–79 Gloucester Rd, Wanchai; tel. 25988688; fax 28249339; e-mail tehhuhk@on-nets.com; f. 1974; Man. Dir Kenneth K. W. Lo.

Wah Kwong Shipping Agency Co Ltd: Shanghai Industrial Investment Bldg, 26/F, 48–62 Hennessy Rd, POB 283; tel. 25279227; fax 28656544; e-mail wk@wahkwong.com.hk; Chair. George S. K. Chao.

Wah Tung Shipping Agency Co Ltd: China Resources Bldg, Rooms 2101–5, 21/F, 26 Harbour Rd, Wanchai; tel. 28272818; fax 28275361; e-mail mgr@watunship.com.hk; f. 1981; Dir and Gen. Man. B. L. Liu.

Wallem Shipmanagement Ltd: Hopewell Centre, 46/F, 183 Queen's Rd East; tel. 28768200; fax 28761234; e-mail rgb@wallem .com; Man. Dir R. G. Buchanan.

Worldwide Shipping Agency Ltd: 23/F, 9 Des Voeux Rd West; tel. 28423888; fax 28100617; e-mail wwsalkc@pacific.net.hk; f. 1958; Man. Stephen Pan.

Associations

Hong Kong Cargo-Vessel Traders' Association: 21–23 Man Wai Bldg, 2/F, Ferry Point, Kowloon; tel. 23847102; fax 27820342; 978 mems; Chair. Chow Yat-tak; Sec. Chan Bak.

Hong Kong Shipowners' Association: Queen's Centre, 12/F, 58–64 Queen's Rd East, Wanchai; tel. 25200206; fax 25298246; e-mail hksoa@hksoa.org.hk; internet www.hksoa.org.hk; 220 mems; Chair. Frank Tsao; Dir Arthur Bowring.

Hong Kong Shippers' Council: Rm 2407, Hopewell Centre, 183 Queen's Rd East; tel. 28340010; fax 28919787; e-mail shippers@ hkshippers.org.hk; internet www.hkshippers.org.hk; 63 mems; Chair. Willy Lin; Exec. Dir Sunny Ho.

CIVIL AVIATION

At the end of 2003 Hong Kong was served by 71 scheduled airlines. A new international airport, on the island of Chek Lap Kok, near Lantau Island, to replace that at Kai Tak, opened in July 1998, following delays in the construction of a connecting high-speed rail-link. The airport has two runways, with the capacity to handle 35m. passengers and 3m. metric tons of cargo per year. The second runway commenced operations in May 1999. A helicopter link with Macao was established in 1990.

Airport Authority of Hong Kong: Cheong Yip Rd, Hong Kong International Airport, Lantau; tel. 21887111; fax 28240717; scheduled for privatization; f. 1995; Chair. Dr Victor Fung Kwok-king; CEO Dr David J. Pang.

Civil Aviation Department: Queensway Government Offices, 46/F, 66 Queensway; tel. 28674203; fax 28690093; e-mail enquiry@ cad.gov.hk; internet www.info.gov.hk/cad/; Dir-Gen. Norman Lo Shung-man.

AHK Air Hong Kong Ltd: 4/F, South Tower, Cathay Pacific City, 8 Scenic Rd, Hong Kong International Airport; tel. 27618588; fax 27618586; e-mail ahk.hq@airhongkong.com.hk; f. 1986; international cargo carrier; Chief Operating Officer David Saechiu.

Cathay Pacific Airways Ltd: South Tower, 5/F, Cathay Pacific City, 8 Scenic Rd, Hong Kong International Airport, Lantau; tel. 27475000; fax 28106563; internet www.cathaypacific.com/hk; f. 1946; services to more than 40 major cities in the Far East, Middle East, North America, Europe, South Africa, Australia and New Zealand; Chair. and CEO David Turnbull.

Hong Kong Dragon Airlines Ltd (Dragonair): Dragonair House, 11 Tung Fai Rd, Hong Kong International Airport, Lantau; tel. 31933193; fax 31933194; internet www.dragonair.com; f. 1985; scheduled and charter flights to destinations throughout mainland China and to Bangladesh, Thailand, Cambodia, Brunei, Malaysia, Taiwan and Japan; 43% owned by China National Aviation Corpn; Dir and CEO Stanley Hui.

Tourism

Tourism is a major source of foreign exchange, tourist receipts reaching US $10,117m. in 2002. Some 15.5m. people visited Hong Kong in 2003, compared with 16.6m. in the previous year. In December 2002 there were some 98 hotels, and the number of rooms available totalled 38,949. In November 1999 it was agreed that a new Disneyland theme park would be constructed in Hong Kong, the first phase of which was scheduled to open in 2005. The Government expected the park to create a huge influx of tourists to the territory.

Hong Kong Tourism Board: Citicorp Centre, 9–11/F, 18 Whitfield Rd, North Point; tel. 28076543; fax 28076595; e-mail info@ discoverhongkong.com; internet www.DiscoverHongKong.com; f. 1957; reconstituted as Hong Kong Tourism Board 1 April 2001; co-ordinates and promotes the tourist industry; has govt support and financial assistance; up to 20 mems of the Board represent the Govt, the private sector and the tourism industry; Chair. Selina Chow; Exec. Dir Clara Chong.

MACAO

Introductory Survey

Location, Climate, Language, Religion, Flag, Capital

The Special Administrative Region (SAR) of Macao comprises the peninsula of Macao, an enclave on the mainland of southern China, and two nearby islands, Taipa, which is linked to the mainland by two bridges (with a third bridge being under construction in 2003), and Coloane. The latter island is connected to Taipa by a causeway and by an area of reclaimed land. The territory lies opposite Hong Kong on the western side of the mouth of the Xijiang (Sikiang) River. The climate is subtropical, with temperatures averaging 15°C in January and 29°C in July. There are two official languages, Chinese (Cantonese being the principal dialect) and Portuguese. English is also widely spoken. The predominant religions are Roman Catholicism, Chinese Buddhism, Daoism and Confucianism. The flag of the Macao SAR (proportions 2 by 3), introduced upon the territory's reversion to Chinese sovereignty in December 1999 and flown subordinate to the flag of the People's Republic of China, displays a stylized white flower below an arc of one large and four small yellow stars, above five white lines, on a green background. The capital, the city of Macao, is situated on the peninsula.

Recent History

Established by Portugal in 1557 as a permanent trading post with China, Macao became a Portuguese Overseas Province in 1951. After the military coup in Portugal in April 1974, Col José Garcia Leandro was appointed Governor of the province. A new statute, promulgated in February 1976, redefined Macao as a 'Special Territory' under Portuguese jurisdiction, but with a great measure of administrative and economic independence. Proposals to enlarge the Legislative Assembly from 17 to 21 members, thus giving the Chinese population an increased role in the administration of Macao, were abandoned when they did not receive the approval of the Government of the People's Republic of China in March 1980. China and Portugal established diplomatic relations in February 1979. In the same month Col Leandro was replaced as Governor by Gen. Nuno de Melo Egídio, deputy chief of staff of Portugal's armed forces. In June 1981 Gen. Egídio was, in turn, replaced by Cdre (later Rear-Adm.) Vasco Almeida e Costa, a Portuguese former minister and naval commander. Following a constitutional dispute in March 1984 over the Governor's plans for electoral reform (extending the franchise to the ethnic Chinese majority), the Legislative Assembly was dissolved. Elections for a new Assembly were held in August, at which the Chinese majority were allowed to vote for the first time, regardless of their length of residence in the territory. Following the elections, the Assembly was for the first time dominated by ethnic Chinese deputies.

In January 1986 Governor Almeida e Costa resigned. In May he was replaced by Joaquim Pinto Machado, whose appointment represented a break in the tradition of military governors for Macao. His political inexperience, however, placed him at a disadvantage. In May 1987 he resigned, citing 'reasons of institutional dignity' (apparently referring to the problem of corruption in the Macao administration). He was replaced in August by Carlos Melancia, a former Socialist deputy in the Portuguese legislature, who had held ministerial posts in several Portuguese governments.

The first round of negotiations between the Portuguese and Chinese Governments on the future of Macao took place in June 1986 in Beijing. Portugal's acceptance of China's sovereignty greatly simplified the issue. On 13 April 1987, following the conclusion of the fourth round of negotiations, a joint declaration was formally signed in Beijing by the Portuguese and Chinese Governments, during an official visit to China by the Prime Minister of Portugal. According to the agreement (which was formally ratified in January 1988), Macao was to become a 'special administrative region' (SAR) of the People's Republic (to be known as Macao, China) on 20 December 1999. Macao was thus to have the same status as that agreed (with effect from 1997) for Hong Kong, and was to enjoy autonomy in most matters except defence and foreign policy. A Sino-Portuguese Joint Liaison Group (JLG), established to oversee the transfer of

power, held its inaugural meeting in Lisbon in April 1988. In 1999 a Chief Executive for Macao was to be appointed by the Chinese Government, following 'elections or consultations to be held in Macao', and the territory's legislature was to contain 'a majority of elected members'. The inhabitants of Macao were to become citizens of the People's Republic of China. The Chinese Government refused to allow the possibility of dual Sino-Portuguese citizenship, although Macao residents in possession of Portuguese passports were apparently to be permitted to retain them for travel purposes. The agreement guaranteed a 50-year period during which Macao would be permitted to retain its free capitalist economy, and to be financially independent of China.

In August 1988 a Macao Basic Law Drafting Committee was formed. Comprising 30 Chinese members and 19 representatives from Macao, the Committee was to draft a law determining the territory's future constitutional status within the People's Republic of China. Elections to the Legislative Assembly were held in October 1988. Low participation (fewer than 30% of the electorate) was recorded, and a 'liberal' grouping secured three of the seats reserved for directly elected candidates, while a coalition of pro-Beijing and conservative Macanese (lusophone Eurasian) groups, won the other three.

In January 1989 it was announced that Portuguese passports were to be issued to about 100,000 ethnic Chinese inhabitants, born in Macao before October 1981, and it was anticipated that as many as a further 100,000 would be granted before 1999. Unlike their counterparts in the neighbouring British dependent territory of Hong Kong, therefore, these Macao residents (but not all) were to be granted the full rights of a citizen of the European Community (EC, now European Union—EU, see p. 217). In February 1989 President Mário Soares of Portugal visited Macao, in order to discuss the transfer of the territory's administration to China.

Following the violent suppression of the pro-democracy movement in China in June 1989, as many as 100,000 residents of Macao participated in demonstrations in the enclave to protest against the Chinese Government's action. The events in the People's Republic caused great concern in Macao. In August, however, China assured Portugal that it would honour the agreement to maintain the capitalist system of the territory after 1999.

In March 1990 the implementation of a programme to grant permanent registration to parents of 4,200 Chinese residents, the latter having already secured the right of abode in Macao, developed into chaos when other illegal immigrants demanded a similar concession. The authorities decided to declare a general amnesty, but were unprepared for the numbers of illegal residents, some 50,000 in total, who rushed to take advantage of the scheme, thereby revealing the true extent of previous immigration from China. Border security was subsequently increased, in an effort to prevent any further illegal immigration.

In late March 1990 the Legislative Assembly approved the final draft of the territory's revised Organic Law. The Law was approved by the Portuguese Assembly of the Republic in mid-April, and granted Macao greater administrative, economic, financial and legislative autonomy, in advance of 1999. The powers of the Governor and of the Legislative Assembly, where six additional seats were to be created, were therefore increased. The post of military commander of the security forces was abolished, responsibility for the territory's security being assumed by a civilian Under-Secretary.

Meanwhile, in February 1990, it was alleged that Carlos Melancia had accepted a substantial bribe from a foreign company in connection with a contract for the construction of the new airport in Macao. In September Melancia was served with a summons relating to the alleged bribery. Although he denied any involvement in the affair, the Governor resigned, and was replaced on an acting basis by the Under-Secretary for Economic Affairs, Dr Francisco Murteira Nabo. In September 1991 it was announced that Melancia and five others were to stand trial on charges of corruption. Melancia's trial opened in April 1993. In August the former Governor was acquitted on the grounds of insufficient evidence. In February 1994, however, it was announced that Melancia was to be retried, owing to irregularities in his defence case.

Meanwhile, many observers believed that the enclave was being adversely affected by the political situation in Lisbon, as differences between the socialist President and centre-right Prime Minister were being reflected in rivalries between officials in Macao. In an attempt to restore confidence, therefore, President Soares visited the territory in November 1990. In January 1991, upon his re-election as Head of State, the President appointed Gen. Vasco Rocha Vieira (who had previously served as the territory's Chief of Staff and as Under-Secretary for Public Works and Transport) Governor of Macao. In March 1991 the Legislative Assembly was expanded from 17 to 23 members. All seven Under-Secretaries were replaced in May.

Following his arrival in Macao, Gen. Rocha Vieira announced that China would be consulted on all future developments in the territory. The 10th meeting of the Sino-Portuguese JLG took place in Beijing in April 1991. Topics under regular discussion included the participation of Macao in international organizations, progress towards an increase in the number of local officials employed in the civil service (hitherto dominated by Portuguese and Macanese personnel) and the status of the Chinese language. The progress of the working group on the translation of local laws from Portuguese into Chinese was also examined, a particular problem being the lack of suitably qualified bilingual legal personnel. It was agreed that Portuguese was to remain an official language after 1999. The two sides also reached agreement on the exchange of identity cards for those Macao residents who would require them in 1999. Regular meetings of the JLG continued.

In July 1991 the Macao Draft Basic Law was published by the People's Republic of China. Confidence in the territory's future was enhanced by China's apparent flexibility on a number of issues. Unlike the Hong Kong Basic Law, that of Macao did not impose restrictions on holders of foreign passports assuming senior posts in the territory's administration after 1999, the only exception being the future Chief Executive. Furthermore, the draft contained no provision for the stationing of troops from China in Macao after the territory's return to Chinese administration.

In November 1991 the Governor of Macao visited the People's Republic of China, where it was confirmed that the 'one country, two systems' policy would operate in Macao from 1999. In March 1993 the final draft of the Basic Law of the Macao SAR was ratified by the National People's Congress (NPC) in Beijing, which also approved the design of the future SAR's flag. The adoption of the legislation was welcomed by the Governor of Macao, who reiterated his desire for a smooth transfer of power in 1999. The Chief Executive of the SAR was to be selected by local representatives. The SAR's first Legislative Council was to comprise 23 members, of whom eight would be directly elected. Its term of office would expire in October 2001, when it would be expanded to 27 members, of whom 10 would be directly elected.

Meanwhile, elections to the Legislative Assembly were held in September 1992. The level of participation was higher than on previous occasions, with 59% of the registered electorate (albeit only 13.5% of the population) attending the polls. Fifty candidates contested the eight directly elective seats, four of which were won by members of the main pro-Beijing parties, the União Promotora para o Progresso (UPP) and the União para o Desenvolvimento (UPD).

Relations between Portugal and China remained cordial. In June 1993 the two countries reached agreement on all outstanding issues regarding the construction of the territory's airport and the future use of Chinese air space. Furthermore, Macao was to be permitted to negotiate air traffic agreements with other countries. Later in the year visits by President Soares of Portugal to Macao and by the Chinese President, Jiang Zemin, to Lisbon took place. In February 1994 the Chinese Minister of Communications visited Macao to discuss with the Governor the progress of the airport project.

In April 1994, during a visit to China, the Portuguese Prime Minister received an assurance that Chinese nationality would not be imposed on Macanese people of Portuguese descent, who would be able to retain their Portuguese passports. Speaking in Macao itself, the Prime Minister expressed confidence in the territory's future. Regarding the issue as increasingly one of foreign policy, he stated his desire to transfer jurisdiction over Macao from the Presidency of the Republic to the Government, despite the necessity for a constitutional amendment.

In July 1994 a group of local journalists dispatched a letter, alleging intimidation and persecution in Macao, to President Soares, urging him to intervene to defend the territory's press

freedom. The journalists' appeal followed an incident involving the director of the daily *Gazeta Macaense*, who had been fined for reproducing an article from a Lisbon weekly newspaper, and now faced trial. The territory's press had been critical of the Macao Supreme Court's decision to extradite ethnic Chinese to the mainland (despite the absence of any extradition treaty) to face criminal charges and a possible death sentence.

The draft of the new penal code for Macao did not incorporate the death penalty. In January 1995, during a visit to Portugal, Vice-Premier Zhu Rongji of China confirmed that the People's Republic would not impose the death penalty in Macao after 1999, regarding the question as a matter for the authorities of the future SAR. The new penal code, prohibiting capital punishment, took effect in January 1996.

On another visit to the territory in April 1995, President Soares emphasized the need for Macao to assert its identity, and stressed the importance of three issues: the modification of the territory's legislation; the rights of the individual; and the preservation of the Portuguese language. Travelling on to Beijing, accompanied by Gen. Rocha Vieira, the Portuguese President had successful discussions with his Chinese counterpart on various matters relating to the transition.

In May 1995, during a four-day visit to the territory, Lu Ping, the director of the mainland Hong Kong and Macao Affairs Office, proposed the swift establishment of a preparatory working committee (PWC) to facilitate the transfer of sovereignty. He urged that faster progress be made on the issues of the localization of civil servants and of the law, and on the use of Chinese as the official language. Lu Ping also expressed his desire that the reorganized legislative and municipal bodies to be elected in 1996–97 conform with the Basic Law.

In December 1995, while attending the celebrations to mark the inauguration of the territory's new airport, President Soares had discussions with the Chinese Vice-President, Rong Yiren. During a four-day visit to Beijing in February 1996, the Portuguese Minister of Foreign Affairs, Jaime Gama (who urged that the rights and aspirations of the people of Macao be protected), met President Jiang Zemin and other senior officials, describing the discussions as positive. While acknowledging the sound progress of recent years, Gama and the Chinese Minister of Foreign Affairs agreed on an acceleration in the pace of work of the Sino-Portuguese JLG. In the same month Gen. Rocha Vieira was reappointed Governor of Macao by the newly elected President of Portugal, Jorge Sampaio. António Guterres, the new Portuguese Prime Minister, confirmed his desire for constitutional consensus regarding the transition of Macao.

At elections to the Legislative Assembly in September 1996 the pro-Beijing UPP received 15.2% of the votes and won two of the eight directly elective seats, while the UPD won 14.5% and retained one of its two seats. The business-orientated groups were more successful: the Associação Promotora para a Economia de Macau took 16.6% of the votes and secured two seats; the Convergência para o Desenvolvimento (CODEM) and the União Geral para o Desenvolvimento de Macau each won one seat. The pro-democracy Associação de Novo Macau Democrático (ANMD) also won one seat. The level of voter participation was 64%. The 23-member legislature was to remain in place beyond the transfer of sovereignty in 1999.

In October 1996 Portugal and China announced the establishment of a mechanism for regular consultation on matters pertaining to international relations. In the same month citizens of Macao joined a flotilla of small boats carrying activists from Taiwan and Hong Kong to protest against a right-wing Japanese group's construction of a lighthouse on the disputed Diaoyu (or Senkaku) Islands, situated in the East China Sea (see the chapter on the People's Republic of China). Having successfully evaded Japanese patrol vessels, the protesters raised the flags of China and Taiwan on the disputed islands. In November activists from around the world attended a three-day conference in Macao, in order to discuss their strategy for the protection of the islands.

Meanwhile, the rising level of violent criminal activity had become a cause of increasing concern. During 1996 there were numerous bomb attacks and brutal assaults, including several serious attacks on local casino staff. Violent incidents continued in 1997, giving rise to fears for the future of the territory's vital tourism industry. Many attributed the alarming increase in organized crime to the opening of the airport in Macao, which was believed to have facilitated the entry of rival gangsters from mainland China, Taiwan and Hong Kong. In May, following the murder of three men believed to have associations with one such group of gangsters, the Chinese Government expressed its concern at the deterioration of public order in Macao and urged Portugal to observe its responsibility, as undertaken in the Sino-Portuguese joint declaration of 1987, to maintain the enclave's social stability during the transitional period, whilst pledging the enhanced co-operation of the Chinese security forces in the effort to curb organized crime in Macao.

The freedom of Macao's press was jeopardized in June 1997, when several Chinese-language newspapers, along with a television station, received threats instructing them to cease reporting on the activities of the notorious 14K triad, a 10,000-member secret society to which much of the violence had been attributed. In July an explosive device was detonated in the grounds of the Governor's palace, although it caused no serious damage. In the following month China deployed 500 armed police-officers to reinforce the border with Macao in order to intensify its efforts to combat illegal immigration, contraband and the smuggling of arms into the enclave. Despite the approval in July of a law further to restrict activities such as extortion and 'protection rackets', organized crime continued unabated. In early October the police forces of Macao and China initiated a joint campaign against illegal immigration.

Meanwhile, the slow progress of the 'three localizations' (civil service, laws and the implementation of Chinese as an official language) continued to concern the Government of China. In mid-1996 almost 50% of senior government posts were still held by Portuguese expatriates. In January 1997 the Governor pledged to accelerate the process with regard to local legislation, the priority being the training of the requisite personnel. In February President Sampaio travelled to both Macao and China, where he urged respect for Macao's identity and for the Luso-Chinese declaration regarding the transfer of sovereignty. In December 1997 details of the establishment in Macao of the office of the Chinese Ministry of Foreign Affairs, which was to commence operations in December 1999, were announced. In January 1998 the Macao Government declared that the vast majority of senior civil service posts were now held by local officials.

In March 1998 the Chinese authorities reiterated their concern at the deteriorating situation in Macao. In April, by which month none of the 34 triad-related murders committed since January 1997 had been solved, the Portuguese and Chinese Governments agreed to co-operate in the exchange of information about organized criminal activities. Also in April 1998 the trial, on charges of breaching the gaming laws, of the head of the 14K triad, Wan Kuok-koi ('Broken Tooth'), was adjourned for two months, owing to the apparent reluctance of witnesses to appear in court. In early May Wan Kuok-koi was rearrested and charged with the attempted murder of Macao's chief of police, António Marques Baptista, in a car-bomb attack. The case was dismissed by a judge three days later on the grounds of insufficient evidence. Wan Kuok-koi remained in prison, charged with other serious offences. His renewed detention led to a spate of arson attacks. The Portuguese Government was reported to have dispatched intelligence officers to the enclave to reinforce the local security forces. In June Marques Baptista travelled to Beijing and Guangzhou for discussions on the problems of cross-border criminal activity and drugs-trafficking.

The Preparatory Committee for the Establishment of the Macao SAR, which was to oversee the territory's transfer to Chinese sovereignty and was to comprise representatives from both the People's Republic and Macao, was inaugurated in Beijing in May 1998. Four subordinate working groups (supervising administrative, legal, economic, and social and cultural affairs) were subsequently established. The second plenary session of the Preparatory Committee was convened in July 1998, discussions encompassing issues such as the 'localization' of civil servants, public security and the drafting of the territory's fiscal budget for 2000. In July 1998, during a meeting with the Chinese Premier, the Governor of Macao requested an increase in the mainland's investment in the territory prior to the 1999 transfer of sovereignty.

In July 1998, as abductions continued and as it was revealed, furthermore, that the victims had included two serving members of the Legislative Assembly, President Jiang Zemin of China urged the triads of Macao to cease their campaign of intimidation. The police forces of Macao, Hong Kong and Guangdong Province launched 'S Plan', an operation aiming to curb the activities of rival criminal gangs. In August, in an apparent attempt to intimidate the judiciary, the territory's Attorney-General and his wife were shot and slightly wounded. In the

following month five police-officers and 10 journalists who were investigating a bomb attack were injured when a second bomb exploded.

In August 1998 representatives of the JLG agreed to intensify Luso-Chinese consultations on matters relating to the transitional period. In September, in response to the increasing security problems, China unexpectedly announced that, upon the transfer of sovereignty, it was to station troops in the territory. This abandonment of a previous assurance to the contrary caused much disquiet in Portugal, where the proposed deployment was deemed unnecessary. Although the Basic Law made no specific provision for the stationing of a mainland garrison, China asserted that it was to be ultimately responsible for the enclave's defence. By October, furthermore, about 4,000 soldiers of the People's Liberation Army (PLA) were on duty at various Chinese border posts adjacent to Macao. During a one-week visit to Beijing, the territory's Under-Secretary for Public Security had discussions with senior officials, including the Chinese Minister of Public Security. In mid-October four alleged members of the 14K triad were detained without bail in connection with the May car-bombing and other incidents.

In November 1998 procedures for the election of the 200 members of the Selection Committee were established by the Preparatory Committee. Responsible for the appointment of the members of Macao's post-1999 Government, the delegates of the Selection Committee were required to be permanent residents of the territory: 60 members were to be drawn from the business and financial communities, 50 from cultural, educational and professional spheres, 50 from labour, social service and religious circles and the remaining 40 were to be former political personages.

In November 1998 raids on casinos believed to be engaged in illegal activities, conducted by the authorities, resulted in several arrests. Further violence took place in December. At the end of that month it was confirmed that Macao residents of wholly Chinese origin would be entitled to full mainland citizenship, while those of mixed Chinese and Portuguese descent would be obliged to decide between the two nationalities. In January 1999 several protesters were arrested during demonstrations to draw attention to the plight of numerous immigrant children, who had been brought illegally from China to Macao to join their legitimately resident parents. The problem had first emerged in 1996 when, owing to inadequate conditions, the authorities had closed down an unofficial school attended by 200 children, who because of their irregular status were not entitled to the territory's education, health and social services.

In January 1999 details of the composition of the future PLA garrison were disclosed. The troops were to comprise solely ground forces, totalling fewer than 1,000 soldiers and directly responsible to the Commander of the Guangzhou Military Unit. They would be permitted to intervene to maintain social order in the enclave only if the local police were unable to control major triad-related violence or if street demonstrations posed a threat of serious unrest. In March, during a trip to Macao (where he had discussions with the visiting Portuguese President), Qian Qichen, a Chinese Vice-Premier, indicated that an advance contingent of PLA soldiers would be deployed in Macao prior to the transfer of sovereignty. Other sources of contention between China and Portugal remained the unresolved question of the post-1999 status of those Macao residents who had been granted Portuguese nationality and also the issue of the court of final appeal.

In April 1999, at the first plenary meeting of the Selection Committee, candidates for the post of the SAR's Chief Executive were elected. Edmund Ho received 125 of the 200 votes, while Stanley Au garnered 65 votes. Three other candidates failed to secure the requisite minimum of 20 votes. Edmund Ho and Stanley Au, both bankers and regarded as moderate pro-business candidates, thus proceeded to the second round of voting by secret ballot, held in May. Edmund Ho received 163 of the 199 votes cast, and confirmed his intention to address the problems of law and order, security and the economy. The Chief Executive-designate also fully endorsed China's decision to deploy troops in Macao.

During 1999, in co-operation with the Macao authorities, the police forces of Guangdong Province, and of Zhuhai in particular, initiated a new offensive against the criminal activities of the triads, which had been in regular evidence with further murders throughout the year. China's desire to deploy an advance contingent of troops prior to December 1999, however, reportedly continued to be obstructed by Portugal. Furthermore, the announcement that, subject to certain conditions, the future garrison was to be granted law-enforcement powers raised various constitutional issues. Some observers feared the imposition of martial law, if organized crime were to continue unabated. Many Macao residents, however, appeared to welcome the mainland's decision to station troops in the enclave. In a further effort to address the deteriorating security situation, from December 1999 Macao's 5,800-member police force was to be restructured.

In July 1999 the penultimate meeting of the JLG took place in Lisbon. In August, in accordance with the nominations of the Chief Executive-designate, the composition of the Government of the future SAR was announced by the State Council in Beijing. Appointments included that of Florinda da Rosa Silva Chan as Secretary for Administration and Justice. Also in August an outspoken pro-Chinese member of the Legislative Assembly was attacked and injured by a group of unidentified assailants. This apparently random assault on a serving politician again focused attention on the decline in law and order in the enclave. In September the Governor urged improved co-operation with the authorities of Guangdong Province in order to combat organized crime, revealing that the majority of the inmates of Macao's prisons were not residents of the territory. In the same month it was reported that 90 former Gurkhas of the British army were being drafted in as prison warders, following the intimidation of local officers. In September the Chief Executive-designate announced the appointment of seven new members of the Legislative Council, which was to succeed the Legislative Assembly in December 1999. While the seven nominees of the Governor in the existing Legislative Assembly were thus to be replaced, 15 of the 16 elected members (one having resigned) were to remain in office as members of the successor Legislative Council. The composition of the 10-member Executive Council was also announced.

In October 1999 President Jiang Zemin paid a two-day visit to Portugal, following which it was declared that the outstanding question of the deployment of an advance contingent of Chinese troops in Macao had been resolved. The advance party was to be restricted to a technical mission, which entered the territory in early December. In November the 37th and last session of the JLG took place in Beijing, where in the same month the Governor of Macao held final discussions with President Jiang Zemin.

Meanwhile, in April 1999 Wan Kuok-koi had been acquitted of charges of coercing croupiers. In November his trial on other serious charges concluded: he was found guilty of criminal association and other illegal gambling-related activities and sentenced to 15 years' imprisonment. Eight co-defendants received lesser sentences. In a separate trial Artur Chiang Calderon, a former police officer alleged to be Wan Kuok-koi's military adviser, received a prison sentence of 10 years and six months for involvement in organized crime. While two other defendants were also imprisoned, 19 were released on the grounds of insufficient evidence. As the transfer of the territory's sovereignty approached, by mid-December almost 40 people had been murdered in triad-related violence in Macao since January 1999.

In late November 1999 representatives of the JLG reached agreement on details regarding the deployment of Chinese troops in Macao and on the retention of Portuguese as an official language. At midnight on 19 December 1999, therefore, in a ceremony attended by the Presidents and heads of government of Portugal and China, the sovereignty of Macao was duly transferred; 12 hours later (only after the departure from the newly inaugurated SAR of the Portuguese delegation), 500 soldiers of the 1,000-strong force of the PLA, in a convoy of armoured vehicles, crossed the border into Macao, where they were installed in a makeshift barracks. Prior to the ceremony, however, it was reported that the authorities of Guangdong Province had detained almost 3,000 persons, including 15 residents of Macao, suspected of association with criminal gangs. The celebrations in Macao were also marred by the authorities' handling of demonstrations by members of Falun Gong, a religious movement recently outlawed in China. The expulsion from Macao of several members of the sect in the days preceding the territory's transfer and the arrest of 30 adherents on the final day of Portuguese sovereignty prompted strong criticism from President Jorge Sampaio of Portugal. Nevertheless, in an effort to consolidate relations with the EU, in May 2000 the first official overseas visit of the SAR's Chief Executive was to Europe, his itinerary including Portugal. The EU agreed in principle in December 2000 to grant residents of Hong Kong and

Macao visa-free access to member states, subject to final approval by the European Parliament.

Meanwhile, a spate of arson attacks on vehicles in February 2000 was followed by the fatal shooting, in a residential district of Macao, of a Hong Kong citizen believed to have triad connections. In March, in an important change to the immigration rules, it was announced that children of Chinese nationality whose parents were permanent residents of Macao would shortly be allowed to apply for residency permits. A monthly quota of 420 successful applicants was established, while the youngest children were to receive priority.

In May 2000 hundreds of demonstrators participated in a march to protest against Macao's high level of unemployment. This shortage of jobs was attributed to the territory's use of immigrant workers, mainly from mainland China and South-East Asia, who were estimated to total 28,000. During the ensuing clashes several police officers and one demonstrator were reportedly injured. Trade unions continued to organize protests, and in July (for the first time since the unrest arising from the Chinese Cultural Revolution of 1966) tear gas and water cannon were used to disperse about 200 demonstrators who were demanding that the immigration of foreign workers be halted by the Government. In the same month it was announced that, in early 2001, an office of the Macao SAR was to be established in Beijing, in order to promote links between the two Governments. In Guangzhou in August 2000, as cross-border crime continued to increase, senior officials of Macao's criminal investigation unit met with their counterparts from China and Hong Kong for discussions on methods of improving co-operation. It was agreed that further meetings were henceforth to be held twice a year, alternately in Beijing and Macao.

Celebrations to mark the first anniversary of the reversion to Chinese sovereignty were attended by Jiang Zemin, who made a speech praising Macao's local administration, but warning strongly against those seeking to use either of the SARs as a base for subversion. A number of Falun Gong adherents from Hong Kong who had attempted to enter Macao for the celebrations were expelled. The same fate befell two Hong Kong human rights activists who had hoped to petition Jiang Zemin during his stay in Macao about the human rights situation in the People's Republic. A group of Falun Gong members in Macao, who held a protest the day before the Chinese President's arrival, were detained in custody and subsequently alleged that they had suffered police brutality.

In January 2001 China urged the USA to cease interfering in its internal affairs, following the signature by President Bill Clinton of the US Macao Policy Act, which related to the control of Macao's exports and the monitoring of its autonomy. In the same month voter registration began in Macao, in preparation for the expiry of the first Legislative Council's term of office in October and the election of a new assembly. In his Chinese Lunar New Year address on 23 January, Edmund Ho called for new efforts to revitalize the economy and achieve social progress.

The Governor of Guangdong Province, Lu Ruihua, made an official visit to Macao in early February 2001 to improve links between the two regions. At the same time, the Legislative Council announced plans to strengthen ties with legislative bodies in the mainland, and the President of the Legislative Council, Susana Chou, visited Beijing where she held discussions with Vice-Premier Qian Qichen. Also in February, a Macao resident was charged with publishing on-line articles about Falun Gong.

Edmund Ho visited Beijing in early March 2001 to attend the fourth session of the Ninth NPC, and held talks with President Jiang Zemin, who praised the former's achievements since the reversion of Macao to Chinese rule. On returning to Macao, Ho received the President of Estonia, Lennart Meri, who was touring the mainland and who thus became the first head of state to visit the SAR since its reversion to China. The two leaders discussed co-operation in the fields of tourism, trade, information technology and telecommunications, with Ho apparently seeking to learn from Estonia's experience in opening the telecommunications market. The EU announced in mid-March that SAR passport holders would, from May 2001, no longer require visas to enter EU countries. In the same month Jorge Neto Valente, a prominent lawyer and reputedly the wealthiest Portuguese person in Macao, was kidnapped by a gang, but freed in a dramatic police operation. The incident was the highest-profile kidnapping case in Macao since the return to Chinese rule.

The Macao, Hong Kong and mainland police forces established a working group in mid-March 2001 to combat cross-border crime, with a special emphasis on narcotics, and in late March the Macao, Hong Kong and Guangdong police forces conducted a joint anti-drugs operation, 'Spring Thunder', resulting in the arrest of 1,243 suspected traffickers and producers, and the seizure of large quantities of heroin, ecstasy, and marijuana. As part of the growing campaign against crime, a Shanghai court sentenced to death a Macao-based gangster, Zeng Jijun, on charges of running a debt-recovery group, members of which had committed murder. Three of Zeng's associates were given long prison sentences.

In May 2001 Macao and Portugal signed an agreement to strengthen co-operation in the fields of economy, culture, public security and justice during the visit of the Portuguese Minister of Foreign Affairs, Jaime Gama, the highest-ranking Portuguese official to visit Macao since its reversion to Chinese rule.

In early June 2001 Macao's Secretary for Security, Cheong Kuoc Va, visited Beijing and signed new crime-fighting accords aimed at reducing the trafficking of drugs, guns and people. In mid-June Chief Executive Edmund Ho made his first official visit to the headquarters of the EU in Brussels, where he sought to promote contacts and exchanges between the SAR and the EU.

China's most senior representative in Macao, Wang Qiren, died of cancer at the beginning of July 2001. Later in the month, another major campaign against illegal activities related to the triads was conducted by the Macao, Hong Kong and Guangdong police forces, and formed part of ongoing attempts to eradicate organized crime. At the end of the month, the Secretary for Security reported that cases of violent crime had declined by 37.3% year-on-year in the first half of 2001, and murders, robberies, arson, drug-trafficking and kidnapping had all decreased significantly over the same period. In a further sign of co-operation between Macao and the mainland against crime, the two sides signed an agreement on mutual judicial co-operation and assistance in late August, the first of its kind.

In September 2001 José Proença Branco and Choi Lai Hang were appointed police commander and customs chief respectively. Following the terrorist attacks in New York and Washington, DC, on 11 September, several Pakistanis were detained in Macao; however, it was quickly announced that the detentions were not connected to the world-wide terrorist searches that had been initiated. In the mean time, the Macao, Hong Kong and Guangdong police departments began examining measures and directing activities aimed at fighting terrorism.

Elections to the Legislative Assembly (Council) were held on 23 September 2001, the first since Macao's reversion to Chinese rule. The number of seats was increased from 23 to 27: seven members were appointed by the Chief Executive, 10 elected directly and 10 indirectly. Of the 10 directly elective seats, two seats each were won by the business-orientated CODEM, the pro-Beijing factions UPP and UPD and the pro-democracy ANMD. Two other factions won one seat each. Of the 10 indirectly elective seats, four were won by the OMKC (a group representing business interests), and two seats each were one by the DCAR (a group representing welfare, cultural, educational, and sports interests), the CCCAE (a group representing labour), and the OMCY (a group representing professionals).

In mid-October 2001 China appointed Bai Zhijian as director of its liaison office in Macao, and later in the month Cui Shiping was selected as Macao's representative in the NPC, replacing the late Wang Qiren. At the same time, Edmund Ho attended the summit meeting of Asia-Pacific Economic Co-operation (APEC) in Shanghai, and the EU-Macao Joint Committee held a meeting in the SAR, aimed at improving trade, tourism and legal co-operation between the two entities. During late 2001, meanwhile, Macao increased co-operation with Hong Kong and the mainland in fighting crime and combating terrorism, amid reports that Russian mafias were becoming increasingly active in the SARs, and in mid-November the three police departments held an anti-drugs forum in Hong Kong. Later in the month, Edmund Ho announced that personal income tax would be waived and industrial and commercial taxes reduced for 2002, in order to alleviate the impact of the economic downturn. Ho also pledged to create 6,000 new jobs and invest more in infrastructure, and urged employers to avoid staff reductions.

In December 2001 the Government moved finally to break the 40-year monopoly on casinos and gambling held by Stanley Ho and his long-established company, the Sociedade de Turismo e Diversões de Macau (SDTM). Under the new arrangements,

some 21 companies, none of which was Chinese-owned, were to be permitted to bid for three new operating licences for casinos in the SAR. The intention was to improve the image of the gambling industry, ridding the territory of its reputation for vice and making it more business- and family-orientated. Meanwhile, Stanley Ho's daughter Pansy was playing an increasingly prominent role in managing the family businesses (which included the shipping, property and hotel conglomerate, Shun Tak holdings); in December the group opened a new convention and entertainment centre.

Also in December 2001 Edmund Ho paid a visit to Beijing, where he and President Jiang Zemin discussed the situation in Macao. In early January 2002 Ho visited the mainland city of Chongqing, seeking to reinforce economic ties between the two places, and stating that Macao would play a more active role in developing the region. Also in January, the Government granted permission to the Taipei Trade and Cultural Office (TTCO) to issue visas for Taiwan-bound visitors from Macao and the mainland. In February Li Peng, Chairman of the Standing Committee of the NPC, paid an official visit to Macao, where he held discussions with the Chief Executive of the SAR. During Li's visit, a leading Macao political activist, along with several activists from the Hong Kong-based 'April 5th Action Group', were arrested for planning to stage protests against Li for his role in the Tiananmen Square suppression of 1989 and in favour of the release of mainland political dissidents. The Hong Kong activists were immediately deported. At the same time the Hong Kong media reported that a Hong Kong-based cameraman had been beaten and had his camera destroyed by a Macao policeman when he attempted to film the interception of the activists. Other journalists also claimed to have been treated aggressively, their allegations being disputed by the Macao police.

In early March 2002 a new representative office of the Macao SAR was established in Beijing, with the aim of enhancing ties between the SAR and the central Government and mainland. Wu Beiming was named as its director. At its inaugural ceremony, Edmund Ho and Chinese Vice-Premier Qian Qichen praised the 'one country, two systems' model, and the director of the central government liaison office in Macao, Bai Zhijian, suggested that Macao might become a model for Taiwan's eventual reunification with the mainland.

On 1 April 2002 Stanley Ho's STDM formally relinquished its 40-year monopoly on casinos. However, Ho retained influence in the gambling sector after his Macao Gaming Holding Company (SJM) won an 18-year licence to operate casinos (see Economy, below). Also in early April, Edmund Ho attended the first annual conference of the Boao Forum for Asia (BFA—a non-profit NGO), held on Hainan Island, China, where he met Hong Kong Chief Executive Tung Chee-hwa and Chinese Premier Zhu Rongji, as well as business leaders from both places.

The US Government in early April 2002 issued its second annual 'United States-Macao Policy Act Report'. This stated that the SAR continued to develop in a positive direction, citing its support for the USA's anti-terrorism campaign, the opening of the economy, the reorganization of its customs services, efforts to counter organized crime and the preservation of its own identity, including maintaining basic civil and human rights. As a result, Macao would continue to be accorded a special status distinct from mainland China under US law and policy. In the middle of the month the United Kingdom announced that it was granting visa-free access to holders of Macao SAR passports, and in late May the visiting Portuguese Minister of Foreign Affairs, António Martins da Cruz, also expressed confidence in Macao's future. In early June Macao hosted the Euro-China Business meeting, aimed at promoting small- and medium-sized enterprises in China to European investors. Also at this time, the Taiwanese Government eased restrictions on residents of Hong Kong and Macao applying for landing visas, essentially allowing those persons to obtain such visas on their first visit to Taiwan. However, in late July a Macao official criticized Taiwanese President Chen Shui-bian and accused him of seeking independence from the mainland.

In mid-June 2002 the Procurator-General, Ho Chio Meng, visited Portugal to promote judicial co-operation between the two territories, the first such visit by a Macao delegation since the territory's return to Chinese rule. Later in the month José Chu was appointed director of the Public Administration and Civil Services Bureau of the SAR.

Meanwhile, the Macao police force continued to maintain co-operation with Hong Kong and the mainland. In late June it was announced that almost 1,000 people had been arrested in Hong Kong during a one-month operation with the Macao police aimed at reducing cross-border and organized crime. At the end of July the Secretary for Security, Cheong Kuoc Va, stated that although overall crime had increased by 1.8% during the first half of the year, serious crimes had registered significant decreases.

In early July 2002 Beijing appointed Wan Yongxiang as the special commissioner of the Office of Special Commissioner of the Chinese Ministry of Foreign Affairs in the Macao SAR, succeeding Yuan Tao, who had held that post since 1999, when the office was established. At the end of July the Government announced the introduction of new identity cards, to be introduced in December 2002 over a period of four years. The cards were expected to function additionally as driving licences, border and medical access passes, and electronic payment methods.

The Russian Minister of Foreign Affairs, Igor Ivanov, visited Macao in late July 2002, mainly seeking to consolidate bilateral economic and trading relations, and to encourage Macao businesses to invest in Russia. In early August Edmund Ho visited the Chinese Autonomous Region of Nei Mongol (Inner Mongolia) to examine the possibility of developing links with the Sino-Russian border region, and later in the month he visited Guangzhou, in southern China, to discuss further economic co-operation and the joint development of Hengqin island (which is under the jurisdiction of Zhuhai City but located very close to Macao). In late September Ho visited Mozambique, where he and President Joaquim Alberto Chissano agreed to strengthen bilateral economic relations. At the same time, Secretary for Security Cheong Kuoc Va visited Portugal and signed security co-operation agreements aimed at combating transnational crime. In mid-October Edmund Ho visited the Republic of Korea (South Korea) and met President Kim Dae-Jung. While there, Ho sought increased investment and to promote tourism from South Korea. The two leaders also agreed to extend reciprocal visa-free visits from a maximum of 30 days to 90 days, effective from January 2003.

In early December 2002 Macao selected its 12 candidates for the 10th National People's Congress, to be held in Beijing in March 2003. At the same time, Edmund Ho paid a routine visit to Beijing, where he held discussions with Jiang Zemin and Vice-President Hu Jintao. The Macao SAR and the EU signed a four-year legal co-operation programme in early December, aimed at consolidating Macao's legal system. In early January 2003 the Chairman of the National Committee of the Chinese People's Political Consultative Conference (CPPCC), Li Ruihuan, visited Macao and praised the way in which the territory had been administered. Observers noted that Beijing was more satisfied with the governance of the Macao SAR than that of Hong Kong. In March 2003 deputies from Macao duly attended the first plenary session of the 10th NPC in Beijing. In the same month Edmund Ho held a meeting with the new Chinese Premier, Wen Jiabao, at which the future development of Macao under the policy of 'one country, two systems' was discussed.

Following the outbreak of a hitherto-unknown virus, Severe Acute Respiratory Syndrome (SARS), on the Chinese mainland and in neighbouring Hong Kong in early 2003, strict measures were introduced to prevent the disease from spreading to Macao, including travel restrictions and health checks on passengers entering the territory. The disease containment programme appeared to have been successful by June 2003, with Macao's only confirmed case of SARS having been discharged from hospital.

In October 2003 Chinese Vice-President Zeng Qinghong visited Macao to attend the signing ceremony of the Closer Economic Partnership Arrangement (CEPA—see below) between Macao and the Chinese mainland. Also in October, Chinese Vice-Premier Wu Yi attended a trade forum in Macao relating to China's trade relations with Portuguese-speaking countries (see below). Celebrations took place in December 2003 to mark the fourth anniversary of the establishment of the Macao SAR.

In a Policy Address in November 2003, Edmund Ho outlined plans for administrative reform of Macao's Government, alongside legal reform, to begin in 2004. Also in November, Xiao Yang, President of China's Supreme People's Court, delivered a speech emphasizing the importance of judicial co-operation between Macao and the mainland.

In June 2004 it was announced that the re-election of the Chief Executive would take place in late August. Edmund Ho began his election campaign in mid-August, and was duly re-

elected on 29 August, securing 296 of the 300 votes of the members of the Election Committee. In December 2004 Chinese President Hu Jintao visited Macao to mark the fifth anniversary of Macao's reunification with the People's Republic. During his visit Hu praised the successful implementation of 'one country, two systems' in Macao. In January 2005 President Sampaio of Portugal visited Macao, at the conclusion of an official visit to China.

Government

The Macao Special Administrative Region (SAR) is governed by a Chief Executive, who was first chosen by a 200-member Selection Committee in May 1999. The incumbent Chief Executive was re-elected in August 2004 by a Selection Committee of 300 members. The Chief Executive is accountable to the State Council of China, the term of office being five years, with a limit of two consecutive terms. Upon the territory's transfer to Chinese sovereignty in December 1999, a 10-member Executive Council, appointed by the Chief Executive to assist in policy-making, assumed office. It comprises five Secretaries, who hold individual portfolios, and five other members. In 2001 the Legislative Council (commonly referred to as the Legislative Assembly) was expanded from 23 to 27 members, of whom 10 were directly elected, 10 indirectly elected and seven appointed by the Chief Executive, all with a mandate of four years. In 2005 the membership of the Legislative Council was to be increased to 29, to incorporate two additional deputies to be chosen by direct election. For the purposes of local government, the islands of Taipa and Coloane are administered separately.

Defence

The 1998 budget allocated 1,200m. patacas to Macao's security. Upon the territory's transfer of sovereignty in December 1999, troops of the People's Liberation Army (PLA) were deployed in Macao. The force comprises around 1,000 troops: a maximum of 500 soldiers are stationed in Macao, the remainder being positioned in China, on the border with the SAR. The unit is directly responsible to the Commander of the Guangzhou Military Region and to the Central Military Commission. The Macao garrison is composed mainly of ground troops. Naval and air defence tasks are performed by the naval vessel unit of the PLA garrison in Hong Kong and by the airforce unit in Huizhou. Subject to certain conditions, the garrison was granted law-enforcement powers, to assist the maintenance of public security.

Economic Affairs

In 2001, according to estimates by the World Bank, Macao's gross national income (GNI), measured at average 1999–2001 prices, was US $6,207m., equivalent to $14,600 per head. In 2002 GNI was $21,920 per head on an international purchasing-power parity basis. During 1990–2003, it was estimated, the population increased at an average annual rate of 1.4%, while gross domestic product (GDP) per head increased, in real terms, at an average annual rate of 1.7% during 1990–2002. Overall GDP increased, in real terms, at an average annual rate of 3.1% in 1990–2002. In 2001 GDP growth decelerated to 2.2%, reflecting the global economic slowdown. GDP increased by 10.0% in 2002, and by an estimated 15.6% in 2003.

Agriculture is of minor importance. The main crops are rice and vegetables. Cattle, pigs and chickens are reared.

Industry (including mining, manufacturing, construction and public utilities) accounted for 12.0% of total GDP in 2002 and employed 27.0% of the economically active population in 2003. The mining sector is negligible.

The manufacturing sector contributed 6.9% of total GDP in 2002 and engaged 18.3% of the economically active population in 2003. The most important manufacturing industry is the production of textiles and garments, which accounted for 61.0% of the value of total output in 2000. Exports of textiles and garments increased from 15,616.8m. patacas in 2002 to 16,904.9m. patacas in 2003. Other industries include footwear and furniture.

Macao possesses few natural resources. Energy is derived principally from imported petroleum. Imports of petroleum and its products accounted for 5.9% of total import costs in 2003. The territory receives some electricity and water supplies from the People's Republic of China.

The services sector accounted for 88.0% of GDP in 2002 and employed 73.0% of the economically active population in 2003. Tourism and related gambling activities make a substantial contribution to the territory's economy. In 2000, according to official figures, the tourism and gambling industries contributed an estimated 38% of GDP, while the licensed casinos employed 6% of the labour force. Revenue from taxes on gambling was higher than expected in 2003, amounting to an estimated 9,100m. patacas in the first 11 months of the year alone. It was reported that the gross revenue of the casino business in 2004 reached 40,000m patacas, of which 14,000m. (35%) was payable in taxes to the Government. The number of tourist arrivals increased steadily from the 1990s, with visitors from the People's Republic of China rising particularly rapidly. Despite the outbreak of Severe Acute Respiratory Syndrome (SARS) in early 2003, the number of tourist arrivals increased from 11.53m. in 2002 to 11.88m. in 2003. In 2004 visitor arrivals rose by 40.3% to total 16.67m. The number of visitors from mainland China continued to increase rapidly, rising by 66% in 2004 to account for 57% of all arrivals, while those from Hong Kong accounted for 30% of total arrivals in 2004.

Legislation regulating 'offshore' banking was introduced in 1987. It was hoped that the territory would develop as an international financial centre. The Financial System Act, which took effect in September 1993, aimed to improve the reputation of Macao's banks by curbing the unauthorized acceptance of deposits. A law enacted in April 1995 aimed to attract overseas investment by offering the right of abode in Macao to entrepreneurs with substantial funds (at least US $250,000) at their disposal. From December 1999, upon the territory's reversion to Chinese sovereignty, Macao administered its own finances and was exempt from taxes imposed by central government. The pataca was retained, remaining freely convertible.

Macao's trade deficit rose from 1,397.1m. patacas in 2003 to 5,342.9m. patacas in 2004. The principal sources of imports in 2004 were the People's Republic of China (which supplied 44.4% of the total), followed by Hong Kong (10.6%) and Japan (9.6%). The principal market for exports was the USA (which purchased 48.7%), followed by the People's Republic of China (13.9%), Germany (8.3%) and Hong Kong (7.6%). The main exports were textiles and garments (which accounted for 80.1% of the total in 2004), machinery and apparatus, and footwear. The principal imports were raw materials for industry, notably textiles, fuels, foodstuffs and other consumer goods. In December 1999 Macao retained its status as a free port and remained a separate customs territory.

In 2003 a budgetary surplus of 2,657.6m. patacas was recorded. The average annual rate of inflation (excluding rents) between 1990 and 1998 was 5.9%. An average annual deflation rate (including rents) of 2.0% was registered in 1999–2003. Having decreased by 1.6% in 2003, consumer prices rose by nearly 1.0% in 2004. According to official figures, the level of unemployment decreased from a peak of 7.1% of the labour force in early 2000 to 6.3% in 2002, declining further to 6.0% in 2003 and to 4.1% in the final quarter of 2004. There is a shortage of skilled labour in Macao.

In 1991 Macao became a party to the General Agreement on Tariffs and Trade (GATT, subsequently superseded by the World Trade Organization—WTO, see p. 357) and an associate member of the UN Economic and Social Commission for Asia and the Pacific (ESCAP, see p. 31). In June 1992 Macao and the European Community (now the European Union) signed a five-year trade and economic co-operation agreement, granting mutual preferential treatment on tariffs and other commercial matters. The agreement was extended in December 1997. Macao remained a 'privileged partner' of the EU after December 1999. Macao also retained its membership of WTO after December 1999. The Multi-Fibre Arrangement (MFA), which for many years had governed Macao's exports of textiles and garments through a preferential system of quotas, ended in January 2005, when the integration of the relevant regulations into the WTO framework was completed.

After recording trade surpluses between 1998 and 2000, Macao's trade balance reverted to deficit in 2001. This deficit increased sharply in 2002, remaining at a similar level in 2003. Macao's trading position had been considerably weakened by the relative appreciation of the pataca against the currencies of its South-East Asian competitors. Attempts to diversify the economy in order to reduce dependence on tourism and the textile industry were made, although during the 1990s many non-textile operations were relocated to China and to South-East Asia, where labour costs were lower. Notably, Macao faced increasing competition from the nearby Zhuhai Special Economic Zone on the Chinese mainland. Nevertheless, foreign investment in Macao rose strongly during the first half of 2002,

totalling 1,000m. patacas, an increase of 20% year-on-year. The Closer Economic Partnership Arrangement (CEPA—see below) with mainland China, signed in 2003, was expected further to increase flows of foreign investment to Macao. In 1993, meanwhile, the Macao Government announced a major land-reclamation programme, the 470,000-sq m Nam Van Lakes project, which was planned to enlarge the territory's peninsular area by 20%. The development was to incorporate residential and business accommodation for 60,000 people and was reported to be approaching completion in 2004. This scheme was just one of several large projects being developed in the SAR and had led to the creation of many new jobs. In October 2002 construction work began on a third bridge linking Macao and Taipa Island. This bridge, the Sai Van Bridge, was inaugurated in December 2004. Gambling continued to be an important source of income for the SAR. In December 2001 STDM lost its long-standing monopoly of the gambling industry (see Recent History), and the Government awarded casino-operating licences to three companies (including Galaxy Casino Co Ltd and Las Vegas-backed Wynn Resorts (Macao) Ltd, as well as Macao Gaming Holding Co, a subsidiary of Ho's STDM). A 12th casino was opened by Stanley Ho in January 2004. In May 2004 Las Vegas Sands Inc, operating under a sub-concession granted by Galaxy Casino, opened a new casino, The Sands, representing the effective end of Stanley Ho's monopoly on the gambling industry. Las Vegas Sands planned to open a second casino, The Venetian Macau, by 2006. In early 2005 there were reportedly 16 casinos in operation in Macao, 14 of which were owned by Stanley Ho. In late 2004 Ho reached an agreement with Australian businessman Kerry Packer for the joint development of casino projects by 2007. Macao's tourist industry was adversely affected by the travel restrictions imposed following the outbreak of Severe Acute Respiratory Syndrome (SARS) on the Chinese mainland in early 2003. In mid-2003, therefore, the Macao Government initiated a tourism promotion scheme, costing 30m. patacas. By the end of 2003 Macao's tourism industry appeared to have recovered completely from the effect of SARS, with tourist arrivals for the year reaching 11,887,876m. The Chinese authorities planned greater integration of Macao within the Zhujiang (Pearl River) Delta region, particularly with regard to infrastructural development. The Macao SAR and the mainland Zhuhai Special Economic Zone planned jointly to develop a new industrial zone, which was officially inaugurated in December 2003. In January 2004 the Macao Government opened bidding for a land-reclamation project in connection with the cross-border industrial park. Meanwhile, in October 2003 the Closer Economic Partnership Arrangement (CEPA), a free-trade agreement, was signed between Macao and mainland China. In addition, Macao's importance to China's trade relations with Portuguese-speaking countries was emphasized at the first Forum for Economic and Trade Co-operation between China and Portuguese-Speaking Countries, which was held in Macao in October 2003. Following the economic contraction of 1996–99 and the recovery of 2000–01, Macao's GDP expanded strongly in 2002–03, the growth rate of 15.6% in 2003 being considerably higher than that registered in the previous year. This trend continued in 2004, with a GDP growth rate of 21.7% being recorded for the third quarter of that year.

Education

The education system in Macao comprises: pre-school education (lasting two years); primary preparatory year (one year); primary education (six years); secondary education (five–six years, divided into junior secondary of three years and senior secondary of two–three years). Schooling normally lasts from the ages of three to 17. In 2002/03 schools enrolled a total of 95,823 pupils (including kindergarten 12,737; primary 41,535; secondary 41,551). From 1995/96 free education was extended from government schools to private schools. Private schools provide education for more than 90% of children. The majority of these schools have joined the free education system, and together with the government schools they form the public school system, in which all pupils from primary preparatory year up to the junior secondary level (10 years) receive free tuition. Based on the four years of free education, compulsory education was implemented from 1999/2000. In 2001/02 the enrolment rate was as follows: pre-school education and primary preparatory year 86.9% (some families leave their children in China); primary education 104.2%; secondary education (including vocational and technical) 82.0%; and higher education (24.4%). In higher learning, there are 12 public and private universities, polytechnic institutes and research centres. Some 11,995 students attended courses offered by those institutions in the academic year 2002/03, ranging from the bacharelato (three-year courses) to doctorate programmes. The University of Macao was inaugurated, as the University of East Asia, in 1981 (passing from private to government control in 1988), and had 3,314 students, with 231 teachers, in 1999/2000. The languages of instruction are primarily English, Cantonese and Portuguese. The 2003 budget allocated 1,886.6m. patacas to education and training (including administration costs and equal to 16.23% of total government expenditure).

Public Holidays

2005: 1 January (New Year), 9–11 February (Chinese Lunar New Year), 4 April (Ching Ming), 25–26 March (Easter), 1 May (Labour Day), 15 May (Feast of Buddha), 11 June (Dragon Boat Festival), 19 September (day following Chinese Mid-Autumn Festival), 1–2 October (National Day of the People's Republic of China and day following), 11 October (Festival of Ancestors—Chung Yeung), 2 November (All Souls' Day), 8 December (Immaculate Conception), 20 December (SAR Establishment Day), 22 December (Winter Solstice), 24–25 December (Christmas).

2006 (provisional): 1 January (New Year), 29 January–31 January (Chinese Lunar New Year), 3 April (Ching Ming), 14–15 April (Easter), 1 May (Labour Day), 5 May (Feast of Buddha), 31 May (Dragon Boat Festival), 1–2 October (National Day of the People's Republic of China and day following), 7 October (Chinese Mid-Autumn Festival), 30 October (Festival of Ancestors—Chung Yeung), 2 November (All Souls' Day), 8 December (Immaculate Conception), 20 December (SAR Establishment Day), 22 December (Winter Solstice), 24–25 December (Christmas).

Weights and Measures

The metric system is in force.

Statistical Survey

Source (unless otherwise indicated): Direcção dos Serviços de Estatística e Censos, Alameda Dr Carlos d'Assumpção 411–417, Dynasty Plaza, 17° andar, Macao; tel. 3995311; fax 307825; e-mail info@dsec.gov.mo; internet www.dsec.gov.mo.

AREA AND POPULATION

Area (2003): 27.3 sq km (10.54 sq miles).

Population: 435,235 (males 208,865, females 226,370) at census of 23 August 2001 (414,200 inhabitants were of Chinese nationality and 8,793 inhabitants were of Portuguese nationality); 448,495 (official estimate) at 31 December 2003.

Density (31 December 2003): 16,428 per sq km.

Births, Marriages and Deaths (2003): Registered live births 3,212 (birth rate 7.2 per 1,000); Registered marriages 1,309 (marriage rate 2.9 per 1,000); Registered deaths 1,474 (death rate 3.3 per 1,000).

Expectation of Life (years at birth, 1998–2001): 78.9 (males 77.2; females 81.5).

Economically Active Population (2003): Manufacturing 37,077; Production and distribution of electricity, gas and water 1,333; Construction 16,283; Wholesale and retail trade; repair of motor vehicles, motorcycles and personal and household goods 32,824; Hotels, restaurants and similar activities 22,114; Transport, storage and communications 14,215; Financial activities 6,211; Real estate, renting and services to companies 11,883; Public administration, defence and compulsory social security 17,812; Education 9,617; Health and social work 4,643; Other community, social and personal service activities 23,469; Private households with employed persons 4,278; Others 829; *Total employed* 202,588.

HEALTH AND WELFARE

Key Indicators

Under-5 Mortality Rate (per 1,000 live births, 2003): 1.6.

HIV/AIDS (% persons aged 15–49, 2003): 0.001.

Physicians (per 1,000 head, 2003): 2.13.

Hospital Beds (per 1,000 head, 2003): 2.24.

Human Development Index (2001): value 0.898. For definitions, see explanatory note on p. vi.

AGRICULTURE, ETC.

Livestock ('000 head, 2003): Poultry 700 (FAO estimate). Source: FAO.

Livestock Products ('000 metric tons, 2003): Beef and veal 1.0*; Pig meat 9.5; Poultry meat 6.4*; Hen eggs 1.1*.
*FAO estimate.
Source: FAO.

Fishing (FAO estimates, metric tons, live weight, 2002): Marine fishes 1,020; Shrimps and prawns 230; Other marine crustaceans 210; Total catch (incl. others) 1,500. Source: FAO.

INDUSTRY

Production (2002, unless otherwise indicated): Wine 1,291,061 litres; Knitwear 39.46m. units; Footwear 10.47m. pairs; Clothing 223.27m. units; Furniture 4,431 units; Electric energy 1,719.2 million kWh (2003).

FINANCE

Currency and Exchange Rates: 100 avos = 1 pataca. *Sterling, Dollar and Euro Equivalents* (31 December 2004): £1 sterling = 15.470 patacas; US $1 = 8.010 patacas; €1 = 10.910 patacas; 1,000 patacas = £64.64 = $124.85= €91.66. *Average Exchange Rate* (patacas per US dollar): 8.033 in 2002; 8.021 in 2003; 8.022 in 2004. Note: The pataca has a fixed link with the value of the Hong Kong dollar (HK $1 = 1.030 patacas).

Budget (million patacas, 2003, provisional): *Total revenue*: 14,279.1 (direct taxes 11,342.8, indirect taxes 987.6, others 1,948.7). *Total expenditure*: 11,621.5.

International Reserves (US $ million at 31 December 2003): Foreign exchange 4,343.4; Total 4,343.4.

Money Supply (million patacas at 31 December 2003): Currency outside banks 2,361.7; Demand deposits at commercial banks 6,427.8; Total money 8,789.5. Source: IMF, *International Financial Statistics*.

Cost of Living (Consumer Price Index; base: Oct. 1999–Sept. 2000 = 100): All items 97.52 in 2001; 94.94 in 2002; 93.46 in 2003.

Gross Domestic Product (million patacas at current prices): 49,862 in 2001; 54,295 in 2002; 63,365 in 2003.

Expenditure on the Gross Domestic Product (provisional, million patacas at current prices, 2003): Government final consumption expenditure 6,600.2; Private consumption expenditure 21,900.2; Changes in inventories 262.0; Gross fixed capital formation 8,412.2; *Total domestic expenditure* 37,174.5; Exports of goods and services 62,469.8; *Less* Imports of goods and services 36,279.0; *GDP in purchasers' values* 63,365.4.

Gross Domestic Product by Economic Activity (provisional, million patacas at current prices, 2002): Mining and quarrying 7.1; Manufacturing 3,217.3; Electricity, gas and water supply 1,235.2; Construction 1,144.1; Trade, restaurants and hotels 5,398.0; Transport, storage and communications 3,003.5; Financial intermediation, real estate, renting and business activities 9,409.6; Public administration, other community, social and personal services (incl. gaming services) 23,310.4; *Sub-total* 46,725.2; *Less* Financial intermediation services indirectly measured 2,342.5; *GDP at basic prices* 44,382.6; Taxes on products (net) 9,453.0; *GDP in purchasers' values* 53,835.6.

Balance of Payments (US $ million, 2002): Exports of goods f.o.b. 2,357; Imports of goods f.o.b. –3,191; *Trade balance* –833; Exports of services 4,467; Imports of services –1,050; *Balance on goods and services* 2,584; Other income received 449; Other income paid –469; *Balance on goods, services and income* 2,564; Current transfers received 99; Current transfers paid –97; *Current balance* 2,565; Capital account (net) 128; Direct investment abroad –60; Direct investment from abroad 418; Portfolio investment assets –903; Portfolio investment liabilities 1; Financial derivatives assets 118; Other investment assets –866; Other investment liabilities 213; Net errors and omissions –1,320; *Overall balance* 293. Source: IMF, *International Financial Statistics*.

EXTERNAL TRADE

Principal Commodities (million patacas, 2003): *Imports c.i.f.*: (distribution by SITC): Food and live animals 1,422.2; Beverages and tobacco 1,414.4 (Beverages 930.9); Mineral fuels, lubricants, etc. 1,593.0 (Petroleum, petroleum products, etc. 1,299.8); Chemicals and related products 898.4; Basic manufactures 7,349.2 (Textile yarn, fabrics, etc. 6,175.0); Machinery and transport equipment 4,721.7 (Electrical machinery, apparatus, etc. 1,932.2; Transport equipment and parts 1,283.3); Miscellaneous manufactured articles 4,327.1 (Clothing and accessories 2,454.5); Total (incl.others) 22,097.2. *Exports f.o.b.*: Textile yarn and thread 733.4; Textile fabrics 1,531.5; Machinery and mechanical appliances 684.7; Clothing 14,640.0; Footwear 755.9; Total (incl. others) 20,700.1.

Principal Trading Partners (million patacas, 2003): *Imports c.i.f.*: Australia 307.9; China, People's Republic 9,489.9; France 751.4; Germany 603.3; Hong Kong 2,794.4; Italy 281.5; Japan 1,986.8; Korea, Republic 696.2; Singapore 777.1; Taiwan 1,282.0; United Kingdom 408.7; USA 871.9; Total (incl. others) 22,097.2. *Exports f.o.b.*: Canada 337.7; China, People's Republic 2,844.2; France 690.4; Germany 1,697.3; Hong Kong 1,361.7; Netherlands 433.4; United Kingdom 898.8; USA 10,320.2; Total (incl. others) 20,700.1.

TRANSPORT

Road Traffic (motor vehicles in use, December 2003): Light vehicles 59,556; Heavy vehicles 4,517; Motorcycles 66,399.

Shipping (international sea-borne freight traffic*, '000 metric tons, 2003): Goods loaded 159.2; Goods unloaded 74.5.
* Containerized cargo only.

Civil Aviation (2003): Passenger arrivals 780,522; Passenger departures 777,830; Goods landed (tons) 20,220; Goods loaded (tons) 68,449.

TOURISM

Visitor Arrivals by Country of Residence (2003): China, People's Republic 5,742,036; Hong Kong 4,623,162; Japan 85,613; Taiwan 1,022,830; Total (incl. others) 11,887,876.

Receipts from Tourism (US $ million): 3,205 in 2000; 3,745 in 2001; 4,415 in 2002.

COMMUNICATIONS MEDIA

Radio Receivers (1997): 160,000 in use.

Television Receivers (2000): 125,115 in use.

Daily Newspapers (2003): 11.

Telephones (Dec. 2003): 174,621 main lines in use.

Facsimile Machines (1999): 6,290 in use.

Mobile Cellular Telephones (2003): 364,031 subscribers.

Personal Computers (2001): 60,390 households.

Internet Users (2003): 59,401.
Sources: partly International Telecommunication Union and UNESCO, *Statistical Yearbook*.

EDUCATION

(2002/03)

Kindergarten: 62 schools; 465 teachers; 12,737 pupils.

Primary: 83 schools; 1,619 teachers; 41,535 pupils.

Secondary (incl. technical colleges): 56 schools; 1,995 teachers; 41,551 pupils.

Higher: 12 institutes; 1,112 teachers; 11,995 students.

Adult Literacy Rate: 91.3% at 2001 census.
Notes: Figures for schools and teachers refer to all those for which the category is applicable. Some schools and teachers provide education at more than one level. Institutions of higher education refer to those recognized by the Government of Macao Special Administrative Region.

Directory

The Constitution

Under the terms of the Basic Law of the Macao Special Administrative Region (SAR), which took effect on 20 December 1999, the Macao SAR is an inalienable part of the People's Republic of China. The Macao SAR, which comprises the Macao peninsula and the islands of Taipa and Coloane, exercises a high degree of autonomy and enjoys executive, legislative and independent judicial power,

including that of final adjudication. The executive authorities and legislature are composed of permanent residents of Macao. The socialist system and policies shall not be practised in the Macao SAR, and the existing capitalist system and way of life shall not be changed for 50 years. In addition to the Chinese language, the Portuguese language may also be used by the executive, legislative and judicial organs.

The central people's Government is responsible for foreign affairs and for defence. The Government of Macao is responsible for maintaining social order in the SAR. The central people's Government appoints and dismisses the Chief Executive, principal executive officials and Procurator-General.

The Chief Executive of the Macao SAR is accountable to the central people's Government. The Chief Executive shall be a Chinese national of no less than 40 years of age, who is a permanent resident of the region and who has resided in Macao for a continuous period of 20 years. He or she is elected locally by a broadly-representative Selection Committee and appointed by the central people's Government.

The Basic Law provides for a 300-member Election Committee, which serves a five-year term. The Election Committee shall be composed of 300 members from the following sectors; 100 members from industrial, commercial and financial sectors; 80 from cultural, educational, and professional sectors; 80 from labour, social welfare and religious sectors; and 40 from the Legislative Council, municipal organs, Macao deputies to the National People's Congress (NPC), and representatives of Macao members of the National Committee of the Chinese People's Political Consultative Conference (NCCPPCC). The term of office of the Chief Executive of the Macao SAR is five years; he or she may serve two consecutive terms. The Chief Executive's functions include the appointment of a portion of the legislative councillors and the appointment or removal of members of the Executive Council.

With the exception of the first term (which expired on 15 October 2001) the term of office of members of the Legislative Council (commonly known as the Legislative Assembly) shall be four years. The second Legislative Council shall be composed of 27 members, of whom 10 shall be returned by direct election, 10 by indirect election and seven by appointment. The third and subsequent Legislative Councils shall comprise 29 members, of whom 12 shall be returned by direct election, 10 by indirect election and seven by appointment.

The Macao SAR shall maintain independent finances. The central People's Government shall not levy taxes in the SAR, which shall practise an independent taxation system. The Macao pataca will remain the legal currency. The Macao SAR shall retain its status as a free port and as a separate customs territory.

The Government

Chief Executive: EDMUND HO HAU WAH (assumed office 20 December 1999; re-elected 29 August 2004).

EXECUTIVE COUNCIL
(April 2005)

Secretary for Administration and Justice: FLORINDA DA ROSA SILVA CHAN.

Secretary for Economy and Finance: FRANCIS TAM PAK YUEN.

Secretary for Security: CHEONG KUOC VA.

Secretary for Social and Cultural Affairs: FERNANDO CHUI SAI ON.

Secretary for Transport and Public Works: AO MAN LONG.

Other Members: TONG CHI KIN (Spokesman), LEONG HENG TENG, VICTOR NG, LIU CHAK WAN, MA IAO LAI.

GOVERNMENT OFFICES

Office of the Chief Executive: Headquarters of the Government of the Macao Special Administrative Region, Av. da Praia Grande; tel. 726886; fax 726665; internet www.gov.mo.

Office of the Secretary for Administration and Justice: Headquarters of the Government of the Macao Special Administrative Region, Av. da Praia Grande; tel. 9895-179; internet www.gov.mo.

Office of the Secretary for Economy and Finance: Headquarters of the Government of the Macao Special Administrative Region, Av. da Praia Grande; tel. 726886; fax 726665.

Office of the Secretary for Security: Calçada dos Quarteis, Quartel de S. Francisco; tel. 7997518; fax 580702.

Office of the Secretary for Social and Cultural Affairs: Headquarters of the Government of the Macao Special Administrative Region, Av. da Praia Grande; tel. 726886; fax 726168.

Office of the Secretary for Transport and Public Works: 1° andar, Edif. dos Secretários, Rua de S. Lourenço 28; tel. 726886; fax 727566.

Macao Government Information Bureau: Gabinete de Comunicação Social do Governo de Macau, Rua de S. Domingos 1, POB 706; tel. 332886; fax 355426; e-mail info@gcs.gov.mo; internet www.gcs .gov.mo; Dir VICTOR CHAN CHI PING.

Economic Services Bureau: Direcção dos Serviços de Economia, Rua Dr Pedro José Lobo 1–3, Edif. Luso Internacional, 25/F; tel. 386937; fax 590310; e-mail info@economia.gov.mo; internet www .economia.gov.mo.

Legislature

LEGISLATIVE COUNCIL (LEGISLATIVE ASSEMBLY)

Following the election of 23 September 2001, the Legislative Assembly comprised 27 members: seven appointed by the Chief Executive, 10 elected directly and 10 indirectly. Members serve for four years. The Assembly chooses its President from among its members, by secret vote. At the election of September 2001, the business-orientated Convergência para o Desenvolvimento de Macau (CODEM) won two of the 10 directly-elective seats. The Associação dos Empregados e Assalariados (AEA) and Associação Reforma Social-Economia de Macau (ARSEM) each won one of the 10 directly-elective seats. The pro-Beijing candidates of the União Promotora para o Progresso (UPP) and of the União para o Desenvolvimento (UPD) won two seats each. The pro-democracy Associação de Novo Macau Democrático (ANMD) also took two seats. Four of the 10 directly-elective seats were taken by the OMKC, a group representing business interests. Groups representing various other interests occupied the remaining six seats. The Legislative Assembly was superseded, under the terms of the Basic Law, by the Legislative Council. In practice, however, the legislature continues to be referred to as the Legislative Assembly.

Legislative Council (Legislative Assembly): Edif. da Assembléia Legislativa, Praça da Assembléia Legislativa, Aterros da Baía da Praia Grande; tel. 728377; fax 727857.

President: SUSANA CHOU.

Political Organizations

There are no formal political parties, but a number of registered civic associations exist and may participate in elections for the Legislative Assembly by presenting a list of candidates. These include the União Promotora para o Progresso (UNIPRO), Associação Promotora para a Economia de Macau (APPEM), União para o Desenvolvimento (UPD), Associação de Novo Macau Democrático (ANMD), Convergência para o Desenvolvimento (CODEM), União Geral para o Desenvolvimento de Macau (UDM), Associação de Amizade (AMI), Aliança para o Desenvolvimento da Economia (ADE), Associação dos Empregados e Assalariados (AEA) and Associação pela Democracia e Bem-Estar Social de Macau (ADBSM). Civic associations that are considerably active in civic, educational, and charity activities and services are: Associação Geral dos Operários de Macau (General Workers' Association of Macao), União Geral das Associações dos Moradores de Macau (Union of Neighbourhood Associations), Instituto do Novo Macau (New Macao Institute), Santa Casa Misericórdia (Charity Organization), Tong Sin Tong (Charity Organization), and Associação dos Trabalhadores da Função Pública de Macau (Macao Civil Servants Association).

Judicial System

Formal autonomy was granted to the territory's judiciary in 1993. A new penal code took effect in January 1996. Macao operates its own five major codes, namely the Penal Code, the Code of Criminal Procedure, the Civil Code, the Code of Civil Procedure and the Commercial Code. In March 1999 the authority of final appeal was granted to the supreme court of Macao, effective from June. The judicial system operates independently of the mainland Chinese system.

Court of Final Appeal

Praçeta 25 de Abril, Edif. dos Tribunais de Segunda Instância e Ultima Instância; tel. 3984117; fax 326744; e-mail ptui@court.gov .mo; internet www.court.gov.mo.

Pres. SAM HOU FAI.

Procurator-General: HO CHIO MENG.

Religion

The majority of residents profess Buddhism, and there are numerous places of worship, Daoism and Confucianism also being widely practised. The Protestant community numbers about 2,500. There are small Muslim and Hindu communities.

CHRISTIANITY

The Roman Catholic Church

Macao forms a single diocese, directly responsible to the Holy See. At 31 December 2002 there were 18,122 adherents in the territory.

Bishop of Macao: Rt Rev. JOSÉ LAI HUNG SENG, Paço Episcopal, Largo da Sé s/n, POB 324; tel. 309954; fax 309861; e-mail mdiocese@ macau.ctm.net.

The Anglican Communion

Macao forms part of the Anglican diocese of Hong Kong (q.v.).

The Press

A new Press Law, prescribing journalists' rights and obligations, was enacted in August 1990.

PORTUGUESE LANGUAGE

Boletim Oficial: Rua da Imprensa Nacional, POB 33; tel. 573822; fax 596802; e-mail info@imprensa.macau.gov.mo; internet www .imprensa.macau.gov.mo; f. 1838; weekly govt gazette; Dir Dr ANTÓNIO GOMES MARTINS.

O Clarim: Rua Central 26-A; tel. 573860; fax 307867; e-mail clarim@macau.ctm.net; f. 1948; weekly; Editor ALBINO BENTO PAIS; circ. 1,500.

Hoje Macau: Av. Dr Rodrigues 600E, Edif. Centro Comercial First National, 14° andar, Sala 1408; tel. 752401; fax 752405; e-mail hoje@ macau.ctm.net; internet www.hojemacau.com; daily; Dir CARLOS MORAIS JOSÉ; circ. 1,000.

Jornal Tribuna de Macau: Av. Almeida Ribeiro 99, Edif. Comercial Nam Wah, 6 andar, Salas 603–05; tel. 378057; fax 337305; internet www.jtm.com.mo; f. 1998; through merger of Jornal de Macau (f. 1982) and Tribuna de Macau (f. 1982); daily; Dir JOSÉ FIRMINO DA ROCHA DINIS; circ. 1,000.

Ponto Final: Rua Cidade do Porto, 315, Edif. Kam Yuen, Loja AL; tel. 339566; fax 339563; e-mail editor@pontofinalmacau.com ; internet www.pontofinalmacau.com; Dir RICARDO PINTO; circ. 1,500.

CHINESE LANGUAGE

Boletim Oficial: see above; Chinese edn.

Cheng Pou: Av. da Praia Grande, 63, Edif. Hang Cheong, E–F; tel. 965972; fax 965741; daily; Dir KUNG SU KAN; Editor-in-Chief LEONG CHI CHUN; circ. 5,000.

Jornal Informação: Rua de Francisco 22, 1° C, Edif. Mei Fun; tel. 561557; fax 566575; weekly; Dir CHAO CHONG PENG; circ. 8,000.

Jornal San Wa Ou: Av. Venseslau de Morais 221, Edif. Ind. Nam Fong, 2a Fase, 15°, Bloco E; tel. 717569; fax 717572; e-mail correiro@ macau.ctm.net; daily; Dir LAM CHONG; circ. 1,500.

Jornal 'Si-Si': Rua de Brás da Rosa 58, 2/F; tel. 974354; weekly; Dir and Editor-in-Chief CHEANG VENG PENG; circ. 3,000.

Jornal Va Kio: Rua da Alfândega 7–9; tel. 345888; fax 580638; f. 1937; daily; Dir CHIANG SAO MENG; Editor-in-Chief LEONG CHI SANG; circ. 21,000.

O Pulso de Macau: Rua Oito do Bairro Iao Hon S/N, Edif. Hong Tai, Apt F058 R/C; tel. 400194; fax 400284; e-mail pulsomo@yahoo.com .hk; internet www.pulso.com.mo; weekly; Dir HO SI VO.

Ou Mun Iat Pou (Macao Daily News): Rua Pedro Nolasco da Silva 37; tel. 371688; fax 331998; f. 1958; daily; Dir LEI SENG CHUN; Dir and Editor-in-Chief LEI PANG CHU; circ. 100,000.

Semanário Desportivo de Macau: Estrada D. Maria II, Edif. Kin Chit Garden, 2 G–H; tel. 718259; fax 718285; weekly; sport; Dir FONG NIM LAM; Editor-in-Chief FONG NIM SEONG; circ. 2,000.

Semenário Recreativo de Macau: Av. Sidónio Pais 31 D, 3/F A; tel. 553216; fax 516792; weekly; Dir IEONG CHEOK KONG; Editor-in-Chief TONG IOK WA.

Seng Pou (Star): Travessa da Caldeira 9; tel. 938387; fax 388192; f. 1963; daily; Dir and Editor-in-Chief KUOK KAM SENG; Deputy Editor-in-Chief TOU MAN KUM; circ. 6,000.

Si Man Pou (Jornal do Cidadão): Rua dos Pescadores, Edif. Ind. Ocean, Bl. 2, 2/F–B; tel. 722111; fax 722133; f. 1944; daily; Dir and Editor-in-Chief KUNG MAN; circ. 8,000.

Tai Chung Pou: Rua Dr Lourenço; P. Marques 7A, 2/F; tel. 939888; fax 934114; f. 1933; daily; Dir VONG U. KUONG; Editor-in-Chief CHAN TAI PAC; circ. 8,000.

Today Macau Journal: Pátio da Barca 20, R/C; tel. 215050; fax 210478; daily; Dir LAM VO I; Editor-in-Chief IU VENG ION; circ. 6,000.

NEWS AGENCIES

Associated Press (AP) (USA): POB 221; tel. 5994187; fax 519423; e-mail adamlee4@macau.ctm.net; Correspondent ADAM LEE.

China News Service: Av. Gov. Jaime Silveiro Marques, Edif. Zhu Kuan, 14/F, Y/Z; tel. 594585; fax 594585.

LUSA (Agência de Notícias de Portugal): Av. Conselheiro Ferreira de Almeida 95-A; tel. 967601; fax 967605; e-mail jcsantos@lusa.pt; internet www.lusa.pt; Dir JOSÉ COSTA SANTOS.

Reuters (United Kingdom): Rua de Penha, No. 22 Edif. Pearl Terrace, 7/F; tel. 345888; fax 930076; Correspondent HARALD BRUNING.

Xinhua (New China) News Agency Macao SAR Branch: Av. Gov. Jaime Silvério Marques, Edif. Zhu Kuan, 13 andar-V; tel. 727710; fax 700548; Dir PAN GUO JUN.

PRESS ASSOCIATIONS

Macao Chinese Media Workers Association: Travessa do Matadouro, Edif. 3, 3B; tel. 939486; e-mail mcju@macau.ctm.net; Pres. LEI PANG CHU.

Macao Journalists Association: Rua de Jorge Alvares, 7–7B, Viva Court, 17F, Flat A; tel. 569819; fax 569819; e-mail macauja@macau.ctm.net; internet home.macau.ctm.net/~macauja; f. 1999; Pres. CHEANG UT MENG.

Macao Journalists Club: Estrada do Repouso, Edif. Tak Fai 18B; tel. 921395; fax 921395; e-mail cjm@macau.ctm.net; Pres. DAVID CHAN CHI WA.

Macao Media Club: Rua de Santa Clara 5–7E, Edif. Ribeiro, 4B; tel. 330035; fax 330036; Pres. CHEONG CHI SENG.

Macao Sports Press Association: Av. Olímpica, Estádio de Macau 33; tel. 838206, ext. 151; fax 718285; e-mail macsport@macau.ctm.net; Pres. LAO LU KONG.

Publishers

Associação Beneficência Leitores Jornal Ou Mun: Nova-Guia 339; tel. 711631; fax 711630.

Fundação Macau: Av. República 6; tel. 966777; fax 968658; internet www.fmac.org.mo.

Instituto Cultural de Macau: see under Tourism; publishes literature, social sciences and history.

Livros do Oriente: Av. Amizade 876, Edif. Marina Gardens, 15 E; tel. 700320; fax 700423; e-mail lilau@macau.ctm.net; internet www.loriente.com; f. 1990; publishes in Portuguese, English and Chinese on regional history, culture, etc.; Gen. Man. ROGÉRIO BELTRÃO COELHO; Exec. Man. CECÍLIA JORGE.

Universidade de Macau—Centro de Publicações: Av. Padre Tomás Pereira, SJ, Taipa; tel. 3974504; fax 3974506; e-mail PUB_GRP@umac.mo; internet www.umac.mo/pc; f. 1993; art, economics, education, political science, history, literature, management, social sciences, etc.; Head Dr RAYMOND WONG.

GOVERNMENT PUBLISHER

Imprensa Oficial: Rua da Imprensa Nacional s/n; tel. 573822; fax 596802; e-mail info@imprensa.macau.gov.mo.

Broadcasting and Communications

TELECOMMUNICATIONS

The Government initiated a liberalization of the mobile telecommunications market in 2001.

Companhia de Telecomunicações de Macau, SARL (CTM): Rua de Lagos, Edif. Telecentro, Taipa; tel. 833833; fax 8913031; e-mail comm@macau.ctm.net; internet www.ctm.net; holds local telecommunications monopoly; shareholders include Cable and Wireless (51%) Portugal Telecom (28%), and CITIC Pacific (20%); Chair. JAMES CHEESEWRIGHT; CEO DAVID KAY; 900 employees.

Hutchison Telephone (Macau) Co Ltd: Macao; e-mail cs_web@htmac.com; internet www.hutchisonmacau.com; mobile telecommunications operator; subsidiary of Hutchison Whampoa Group (Hong Kong); local capital participation.

SmarTone Mobile (Macau) Ltd: Macao; e-mail enquiry@smartone.com.mo; internet www.smartone.com.mo; mobile telecommunications provider; subsidiary of SmarTone Mobile Communications Ltd (Hong Kong); local capital participation.

Regulatory Authority

Office for the Development of Telecommunications and Information Technology (GDTTI): Av. da Praia Grande 789, 3/F; tel. 3969161; fax 356328; e-mail ifx@gdtti.gov.mo; internet www.gdtti.gov.mo.

BROADCASTING

Radio

Rádio Vila Verde: Macao Jockey Club, Taipa; tel. 822163; private radio station; programmes in Chinese; Man. KOK HOI.

Television

Teledifusão de Macau, SARL (TDM): Rua Francisco Xavier Pereira 157-A, POB 446; tel. 335888 (Radio), 519188 (TV); fax 520208; privately owned; two radio channels: **Rádio Macau** (Av. Dr Rodrigo Rodrigues, Edif. Nam Kwong, 7/F; fax 343220) in Portuguese, broadcasting 24 hours per day in Portuguese on **TDM Canal 1** (incl. broadcasts from RTP International in Portugal) and 17 hours per day in Chinese on **TDM Channel 2**; Chair. STANLEY HO; Exec. Vice-Chair. Dr MANUEL GONÇALVES.

Macao Satellite Television: c/o Cosmos Televisão por Satélite, Av. Infante D. Henrique 29, Edif. Va Iong, 4/F A; commenced transmissions in 2000; operated by Cosmos Televisão por Satélite, SARL; domestic and international broadcasts in Chinese aimed at Chinese-speaking audiences world-wide.

Macao is within transmission range of the Hong Kong television stations.

Cosmos Televisão por Satélite, SARL: Av. Infante D. Henrique 29, Edif. Va Iong, 4/F A; tel. 785731; fax 788234; commenced trial satellite transmissions in 1999, initially for three hours per day; by the year 2003 the company planned to provide up to six channels; Chair. NG FOK.

Finance

(cap. = capital; res = reserves; dep. = deposits; m. = million; brs = branches; amounts in patacas unless otherwise indicated)

BANKING

Macao has no foreign-exchange controls, its external payments system being fully liberalized on current and capital transactions. The Financial System Act, aiming to improve the reputation of the territory's banks and to comply with international standards, took effect in September 1993.

Issuing Authority

Autoridade Monetária de Macau (AMCM) (Monetary Authority of Macao): Calçada do Gaio 24–26, POB 3017; tel. 568288; fax 325432; e-mail general@amcm.gov.mo; internet www.amcm.macau.gov.mo; f. 1989 as Autoridade Monetária e Cambial de Macau (AMCM), to replace the Instituto Emissor de Macau; govt-owned; Pres. ANSELMO L. S. TENG.

Banks of Issue

Banco Nacional Ultramarino (BNU), SA: Av. Almeida Ribeiro 22, POB 465; tel. 355111; fax 355653; e-mail markt@bnu.com.mo; internet www.bnu.com.mo; f. 1864; est. in Macao 1902; subsidiary of Caixa Geral de Depósitos since 2001; agent of Macao Government; agreement whereby the Bank remains an agent of the treasury signed with the administration of the Macao SAR in 2000; to remain a note-issuing bank until 2010; Gen. Man. Dr HERCULANO J. SOUSA; 11 brs.

Bank of China: Bank of China Bldg, Av. Dr Mário Soares; tel. 781828; fax 781833; e-mail bocmacau@macau.ctm.net; internet www.bocmacau.com; f. 1950 as Nan Tung Bank, name changed 1987; authorized to issue banknotes from Oct. 1995; Gen. Man. ZHANG HONGYI; 24 brs.

Other Commercial Banks

Banco da América (Macau), SA (Bank of America (Macau) Ltd): Av. Almeida Ribeiro 70–76, POB 165; tel. 568821; fax 570386; f. 1937; fmrly Banco Asiático Segurança Pacífico / Banco de Cantão; cap. 100m., res 55.7m., dep. 1,507.0m. (Dec. 2003); Chair. SAMUEL NG TSIEN; Man. Dr KIN HONG CHEONG.

Banco Comercial de Macau, SA: Av. da Praia Grande 572, POB 545; tel. 7910000; fax 595817; e-mail bcmbank@bcm.com.mo; f. 1995; total net assets US $855m. (Dec. 2003); Chair. JORGE JARDIM GONÇALVES; 17 brs.

Banco Delta Asia, SARL: Av. Conselheiro Ferreira de Almeida 79; tel. 559898; fax 570068; e-mail contact@bdam.com; internet www

.delta-asia.com; f. 1935; fmrly Banco Hang Sang; cap. 210.0m., res 173.2m., dep. 3,323.1m. (Dec. 2004); Chair. STANLEY AU; Exec. Dir PHILIP NG; 10 brs.

Banco Seng Heng, SARL: Av. da Amizade 555, Macau Landmark, Torre Banco Seng Heng; tel. 555222; fax 338064; e-mail sengheng@macau.ctm.net; internet www.senghengbank.com; f. 1972; cap. 150.0m., res 1,046.7m., dep. 16,030.8m. (Dec. 2003); Chair. STANLEY HO; Gen. Man. ALEX LI; 6 brs.

Banco Tai Fung, SARL: Tai Fung Bank Bldg, Av. Alameda Dr Carlos d'Assumpção 418; tel. 322323; fax 570737; e-mail tfbsecr@taifungbank.com; internet www.taifungbank.com; f. 1971; cap. 1,000m., dep. 22,139m. (Dec. 2003); Chair. FUNG KA YORK; Gen. Man. LONG RONGSHEN; 20 brs.

Banco Weng Hang, SA: Av. Almeida Ribeiro 241; tel. 335678; fax 576527; e-mail bwhhrd@whbmac.com; internet www.whbmac.com; f. 1973; subsidiary of Wing Hang Bank Ltd, Hong Kong; res 559m., dep. 9,516m. (Dec. 2004); Chair. PATRICK FUNG YUK-BUN; Gen. Man. and Dir LEE TAK LIM; 10 brs.

Guangdong Development Bank: Av. Dr Carlos d'Assumpção, 181–187, Centro Comercial do Grupo Brihantismo, 18° andar; tel. 750328; fax 750728; Gen. Man. GUO ZHI-HANG.

Luso International Banking Ltd: Av. Dr Mário Soares 47; tel. 378977; fax 711100; e-mail lusobank@lusobank.com.mo; internet www.lusobank.com.mo; f. 1974; cap. 300.0m., res 103.3m., dep. 7,113.3m. (Dec. 2003); Chair. LU YAO MING; Gen. Man. IP KAI MING; 10 brs.

Foreign Banks

Banco Comercial Português (Portugal): Av. da Praia Grande 594, BCM Bldg, 12/F; tel. 786769; fax 786772; Gen. Man. Dr ANTONIO MATOS.

Banco Espírito Santo do Oriente (Portugal): Av. Dr Mário Soares 323, Bank of China Bldg, 28/F, E–F; tel. 785222; fax 785228; e-mail besor@macau.ctm.net; f. 1996; subsidiary of Banco Espírito Santo, SA (Portugal); Exec. Dir JOÃO MANUEL AMBRÓSIO; Chair. and CEO JOSÉ MORGADO.

Bank of East Asia Ltd (Hong Kong): Av. da Praia Grande 697, Edif. Tai Wah R/C; tel. 335511; fax 337557; e-mail beamo@hkbea.com.mo; Gen. Man. LAI TZE HIM.

BNP Paribas (France): Av. Central Plaza, 10/F, Almeida Ribeiro 61; tel. 562777; fax 560626; f. 1979; Man. SANCO SZE.

Citibank NA (USA): Rua da Praia Grande 251–53; tel. 378188; fax 578451; Pres. DANIEL CHOW SHIU LUN.

DBS Bank (Hong Kong) Ltd: Rua de Santa Clara, 5-7E, Edif. Ribeiro, Lojas C&D; tel. 329338; fax 323711.

Hang Seng Bank: 20/F, Central Plaza, 61 Av. de Almeida Ribeiro; tel. 323321; fax 330612; internet main.hangseng.com/eng/abo/cu/macbro/index.html; Macao branch opened March 2004.

The Hongkong and Shanghai Banking Corporation Ltd (Hong Kong): Av. da Praia Grande 639; tel. 553669; fax 315421; e-mail hsbc@macau.ctm.net; f. 1972; CEO THOMAS YAM.

Industrial and Commercial Bank of China: Alameda Dr Carlos d'Assumpção 393–437, Edif. Dynasty Plaza, E, F, G e H; tel. 786338; fax 786328.

International Bank of Taipei (Taiwan): Av. Infante D. Henrique 52–58; tel. 715175; fax 715035; e-mail tppmonx@macau.ctm.net; f. 1996; fmrly Taipei Business Bank; Gen. Man. KEVIN CHIOU.

Liu Chong Hing Bank Ltd (Hong Kong): Av. da Praia Grande 693, Edif. Tai Wah, R/C; tel. 339982; fax 339990; Gen. Man. LAM MAN KING.

Macau Chinese Bank Ltd: Av. da Praia Grande 811; tel. 322678; fax 322680; fmrly Finibanco (Portugal).

Overseas Trust Bank Limited (Hong Kong): Rua de Santa Clara 5–7E, Edif. Ribeiro, Loja C e D; tel. 329338; fax 323711; e-mail otbmacau@macau.ctm.net; Senior Man. LAU CHI KEUNG.

Standard Chartered Bank (UK): 8/F Office Tower, Macao Landmark, Av. de Amizade; tel. 786111; fax 786222; f. 1982; Man. KIN YIP CHAN.

Banking Association

Associação de Bancos de Macau (ABM) (The Macau Association of Banks): Av. da Praia Grande 575, Edif. 'Finanças', 15/F; tel. 511921; fax 346049; e-mail abm@macau.ctm.net; Chair. ZHANG HONGYI.

INSURANCE

ACE Seguradora, SA: Rua Dr Pedro José Lobo 1–3, Luso Bank Bldg, 17/F, Apt 1701–02; tel. 557191; fax 570188; Rep. ANDY AU.

American Home Assurance Co: Av. Almeida Ribeiro 61, Central Plaza, 15/F, 'G'; non-life insurance.

American International Assurance Co (Bermuda) Ltd: Av. Almeida Ribeiro 61, Central Plaza, 13/F; tel. 9881888; fax 315900; life insurance; Rep. ALEXANDRA FOO CHEUK LING.

Asia Insurance Co Ltd: Rua do Dr Pedro José Lobo 1–3, Luso International Bank Bldg, 11/F, Units 1103–04; tel. 570439; fax 570438; non-life insurance; Rep. S. T. CHAN.

AXA China Region Insurance Company: Rua de Xangai 175, Edif. da Associação Comercial de Macau, 17/F; tel. 781188; fax 780022; life insurance; Rep. WRESTLY WONG.

CGU International Insurance plc: Av. da Praia Grande 693, Edif. Tai Wah A & B, 13/F; tel. 923329; fax 923349; non-life insurance; Man. VICTOR WU.

China Insurance Co Ltd: Av. Dr. Rodrigo Rodrigues, Edif. Seguros da China, 19/F; non-life insurance.

China Life Insurance Co Ltd: Av. Dr Rodrigo Rodrigues Quarteirão 11, Lote A, Zape, China Insurance Bldg, 15/F; tel. 558918; fax 787287; e-mail cic@macau.ctm.net; Rep. CHENG MINGJIN.

Companhia de Seguros Fidelidade: Av. Almeida Ribeiro 22–38 (BNU); tel. 374072; fax 511085; life and non-life insurance; Man. LEONEL ALBERTO RANGE RODRIGUES.

Companhia de Seguros Delta SA: Av. da Praia Grande 369–71, Edif. Keng Ou, 13/F, D; tel. 337036; fax 337037; Rep. JOHNNY CHENG.

Crown Life Insurance Co: Av. da Praia Grande 287, Nam Yuet Commercial Centre, Bl. B, 8/F; tel. 570828; fax 570844; Rep. STEVEN SIU.

Delta Asia Insurance Company Ltd: Av. da Praia Grande, 369–371, Edif. Keng Ou, 13/F.

HSBC Life Insurance (Asia) Ltd: Av. da Praia Grande 619, Edif. Comercial Si Toi, 1/F; tel. 212323; fax 217162; non-life insurance; Rep. NORA CHIO.

Ing Life Insurance Co (Macao) Ltd: Av. Almeida Ribeiro 61, 11/F, Unit C and D; tel. 9886060; fax 9886100; internet www.ing.com.mo; Man. STEVEN CHIK YIU KAI.

Insurance Co of North America: Av. Almeida Ribeiro 32, Tai Fung Bank Bldg, Rm 806–7; tel. 557191; fax 570188; Rep. JOSEPH LO.

Luen Fung Hang Insurance Co Ltd: Rua de Pequim 202A–246, Macao Finance Centre, 6/F–A; tel. 700033; fax 700088; e-mail lfhins@macau.ctm.net; internet www.lfhins.com; non-life insurance; Rep. SI CHI HOK.

Macao Life Insurance Co (Macao Insurance Company): Av. da Praia Grande 574, Edif. BCM, 10-11F; tel. 555078; fax 551074; life and non-life insurance (Macao Insurance Company); Rep. MANUEL BALCÃO REIS.

Manulife (International) Ltd: Av. da Praia Grande 517, Edif. Comercial Nam Tung, 8/F, Unit B & C; tel. 3980388; fax 323312; internet www.manulife.com.hk; Rep. DANIEL TANG.

MassMutual Asia Ltd: Av. da Praia Grande 517, Edif. Nam Tung 16, 6/F; life insurance.

Min Xin Insurance Co Ltd: Rua do Dr Pedro José Lobo 1–3, Luso International Bank Bldg, 27/F, Rm 2704; tel. 305684; fax 305600; non-life insurance; Rep. PETER CHAN.

Mitsui Sumitomo Insurance Co Ltd: Rua Dr Pedro José Lobo 1–3, Edif. Banco Luso, 11/F, Apartment 1202; tel. 385917; fax 596667; non-life insurance; Rep. TAKAO YASUKOCHI.

QBE Insurance (International) Ltd: Av. da Praia Grande 369–71, Edif. Keng On 'B', 9/F; tel. 323909; fax 323911; non-life insurance; Rep. SALLY SIU.

The Wing On Fire & Marine Insurance Co Ltd: Av. Almeida Ribeiro 61, Central Plaza, 7/F, Block E; tel. 356688; fax 333710; non-life insurance; Rep. CHIANG AO LAI LAI.

Winterthur Swiss Insurance (Macao) Ltd: Av. da Praia Grande 369-371, Edif. Keng Ou, 13/F, C; tel. 356618; fax 356800; non-life insurance; Man. ALLAN YU KIN NAM.

Insurers' Association

Federation of Macao Professional Insurance Intermediaries: Rua de Pequim 244–46, Macao Finance Centre, 6/F, G; tel. 703268; fax 703266; Rep. DAVID KONG.

Macao Insurance Agents and Brokers Association: Av. da Praia Grande 309, Nam Yuet Commercial Centre, 8/F, D; tel. 378901; fax 570848; Rep. JACK LI KWOK TAI.

Macao Insurers' Association: Av. da Praia Grande 575, Edif. 'Finanças', 15/F; tel. 511923; fax 337531; e-mail mia@macau.ctm.net; Pres. JIANG YIDAO.

Trade and Industry

CHAMBER OF COMMERCE

Associação Comercial de Macau (Macao Chamber of Commerce): Rua de Xangai 175, Edif. ACM, 5/F; tel. 576833; fax 594513; internet www.acm.org.mo; Pres. MA MAN KEI.

INDUSTRIAL AND TRADE ASSOCIATIONS

Associação dos Construtores Civis e Empresas de Fomento Predial de Macau (Macao Association of Building Contractors and Developers): Rua do Campo 9–11; tel. 323854; fax 345710; Pres. CHUI TAK KEI.

Associação dos Exportadores e Importadores de Macau (Macau Importers and Exporters Association): Av. Infante D. Henrique 60–62, Centro Comercial 'Central', 3/F; tel. 375859; fax 512174; e-mail aeim@macau.ctm.net; exporters' and importers' asscn; Chair. LIU CHAK WAN.

Associação dos Industriais de Tecelagem e Fiação de Lã de Macau (Macao Weaving and Spinning of Wool Manufacturers' Asscn): Av. da Amizade 271, Edif. Kam Wa Kok, 6/F–A; tel. 553378; fax 511105; Pres. WONG SHOO KEE.

Associação Industrial de Macau (Industrial Association of Macau): Rua Dr Pedro José Lobo 34–36, Edif. AIM, 17/F, POB 70; tel. 574125; fax 578305; e-mail aim@macau.ctm.net; internet www.madeinmacau.net; f. 1959; Pres. PETER PAN.

Centro de Produtividade e Transferência de Tecnologia de Macau (Macao Productivity and Technology Transfer Centre): Rua de Xangai 175, Edif. ACM, 6/F; tel. 781313; fax 788233; e-mail cpttm@cpttm.org.mo; internet www.cpttm.org.mo; vocational or professional training; Pres. Dr ERIC YEUNG; Dir-Gen. VICTOR KUAN.

Euro-Info Centre Macao: Av. da Amizade, 918, Edif. World Trade Center, 2° andar; tel. 713338; fax 713339; e-mail eic@macau.ctm.net; internet www.ieem.org.mo/eic/eicmacau.html; promotes trade with EU; Man. YVONNE SUN; Pres. JOSÉ LUÍS DE SALES MARQUES.

Instituto de Promoção do Comércio e do Investimento de Macau (IPIM) (Macao Trade and Investment Promotion Institute): Av. da Amizade 918, World Trade Center Bldg, 1°–4° andares; tel. 710300; fax 590309; e-mail ipim@ipim.gov.mo; internet www.ipim.gov.mo; Pres. LEE PENG HONG.

SDPIM (Macao Industrial Parks Development Co Ltd): Av. da Amizade 918, World Trade Center Bldg, 13/F A & B; tel. 786636; fax 785374; e-mail sdpim@macau.ctm.net; internet www.sdpim.com.mo; f. 1993; management and development of Macao Park of Zhuhai-Macao Cross Border Industrial Zone, Concordia Industrial Park, and other industrial parks in Macau; Pres. of the Bd PAULINA Y. ALVES DOS SANTOS.

World Trade Center Macao, SARL: Av. da Amizade 918, Edif. World Trade Center, 16/F–19/F; tel. 727666; fax 727633; e-mail wtcmc@macau.ctm.net; internet www.wtc-macau.com; f. 1995; trade information and business services, office rentals, exhibition and conference facilities; Man. Dir Dr ANTÓNIO LEÇA DA VEIGA PAZ.

UTILITIES

Electricity

Companhia de Electricidade de Macau, SARL (CEM): Estrada D. Maria II 32–36, Edif. CEM; tel. 339933; fax 719760; f. 1972; sole distributor; 6% owned by China Power International Holding Ltd; Pres. Eng. CUSTÓDIO MIGUENS.

Water

Sociedade de Abastecimento de Aguas de Macau, SARL (SAAM) (Macao Water): Av. do Conselheiro Borja 718; tel. 233332; fax 220150; e-mail mwater@macau.ctm.net; internet www.macaowater.com; f. 1985 as jt venture with Suez Lyonnaise des Eaux; Exec. Dir PHILIPPE WIND.

TRADE UNIONS

Macao Federation of Trade Unions: Rua Ribeira do Patane 2; tel. 576231; fax 553110; Pres. PUN IOK LAN.

Transport

RAILWAYS

There are no railways in Macao. A plan to connect Macao with Zhuhai and Guangzhou (People's Republic of China) is under consideration. Construction of the Zhuhai–Guangzhou section was under way in mainland China in the early 21st century.

ROADS

In 2000 the public road network extended to 341 km. The peninsula of Macao is linked to the islands of Taipa and Coloane by two bridges and by a 2.2-km causeway respectively. The first bridge (2.6 km) opened in 1974. In conjunction with the construction of an airport on Taipa (see below), a 4.4-km four-lane bridge to the Macao peninsula was opened in April 1994. A second connection to the mainland, the 1.5-km six-lane road bridge (the Lotus Bridge) linking Macao with Hengqin Island (in Zhuhai, Guangdong Province), opened to traffic in December 1999. A new 29-km steel bridge linking Macao with Hong Kong's Lantau Island and Zhuhai City, Guangdong Province, was being planned in 2003, with studies being carried out to determine the project's financial and technological feasibility. A third link between Macao and Taipa, a double-deck bridge, was inaugurated in late 2004.

SHIPPING

There are representatives of shipping agencies for international lines in Macao. There are passenger and cargo services to the People's Republic of China. Regular services between Macao and Hong Kong are run by the Hong Kong-based **New World First Ferry** and **Shun Tak–China Travel Ship Management Ltd** companies. A new terminal opened in late 1993. The new port of Kao-ho (on the island of Coloane), which handles cargo and operates container services, entered into service in 1991.

CTS Parkview Holdings Ltd: Av. Amizade, Porto Exterior, Terminal Marítimo de Macau, Sala 2006B; tel. 726789; fax 727112; purchased by STDM in 1998.

STDM Shipping Dept: Av. da Amizade Terminal Marítimo do Porto Exterior; tel. 726111; fax 726234; affiliated to Sociedade de Turismo e Diversões de Macau; Gen. Man. ALAN HO; Exec. Man. Capt. AUGUSTO LIZARDO.

Association

Associação de Agências de Navegação e Congêneres de Macau (Macau Shipping Association): Av. Horta e Costa 7D–E, POB 6133; tel. 528207; fax 302667; e-mail machpg@hotmail.com; Pres. VONG KOK SENG.

Port Authority

Capitania dos Portos de Macau: Rampa da Barra, Quartel dos Mouros, POB 47; tel. 559922; fax 511986; e-mail webmaster@marine.gov.mo; internet www.marine.gov.mo.

CIVIL AVIATION

In August 1987 plans were approved for the construction of an international airport, on reclaimed land near the island of Taipa, and work began in 1989. The final cost of the project was 8,900m. patacas. Macau International Airport was officially opened in December 1995. The terminal has the capacity to handle 6m. passengers a year. By 2002 a total of 9 airlines operated 436 scheduled flights weekly to 21 destinations, mostly in China, but also to the Democratic People's Republic of Korea, the Philippines, Singapore, Taiwan, and Thailand. Between January and December 2003 Macau International Airport handled a total of 2,905,811 passengers and 141,223 tons of cargo. A helicopter service between Hong Kong and Macao was put into operation in 1990 by East Asia Airlines, and a scheduled helicopter flight service between Macao and Shenzhen provided by the same company commenced in January 2003. East Asia Airlines transported a total of 99,985 helicopter passengers on its Macao–Hong Kong route and 2,691 helicopter passengers on their Macao–Shenzhen route in 2002. In late 2003 Air Macau launched direct flights between Macao and Chengdu, capital of Sichuan Province.

AACM (Civil Aviation Authority Macao): Rua Dr Pedro José Lobo 1–3, Luso International Bldg, 26/F; tel. 511213; fax 338089; e-mail aacm@macau.ctm.net; internet www.macau-airport.gov.mo; f. 1991; Pres. RUI ALFREDO BALACÓ MOREIRA.

Administração de Aeroportos, Lda (ADA): Av. de João IV, Centro Comercial Iat Teng Hou, 5/F; tel. 711808; fax 711803; e-mail adamkt@macau.ctm.net; internet www.ada.com.mo; Dir CARLOS SERUCA SALGADO.

CAM (Sociedade do Aeroporto Internacional de Macau, SARL): Av. Dr Mário Soares, Bank of China Bldg, 29/F; tel. 785448; fax 785465; e-mail cam@macau.ctm.net; internet www.macau-airport.gov.mo; f. 1989; airport owner, responsible for design, construction, development and international marketing of Macao International Airport; Chair. DENG JUN.

Air Macau: 398 Alameda Dr Carlos d'Assumpção, 12°-18° andar; tel. 3966888; fax 3966866; e-mail airmacau@airmacau.com.mo; internet www.airmacau.com.mo; f. 1994; controlled by China National Aviation Corporation (Group) Macao Co Ltd; services to several cities in the People's Republic of China, the Republic of Korea, the Philippines, Taiwan and Thailand; other destinations planned; Chair. GU TIEFEI; CEO DAVID H. J. FEI.

Tourism

Tourism is now a major industry, a substantial portion of the Government's revenue being derived from the territory's casinos. The other attractions are the cultural heritage and museums, dog-racing, horse-racing, and annual events such as Chinese New Year (January/February), the Macao Arts Festival (February/March), Dragon Boat Festival (May/June), the Macao International Fireworks Festival (September/October), the International Music Festival, (October) the Macao Grand Prix for racing cars and motorcycles (November) and the Macao International Marathon (December). At the end of 2002 there were 25 hotels of two-stars and above. A total of 9,168 hotel rooms were available in December 2004. Average per caput visitor spending in 2002 was 1,454 patacas. Total visitor arrivals rose from 11.88m. in 2003 to 16.67m. in 2004. Of the latter figure, 9.5m. were arrivals from the People's Republic of China and 5.1m. were arrivals from Hong Kong. Receipts from tourism were US $4,415m. in 2002.

Macao Government Tourist Office (MGTO): Alameda Dr Carlos d'Assumpção, 335-341, Edif. Hot Line, 12° andar; tel. 315566; fax 510104; e-mail mgto@macautourism.gov.mo; internet www.macautourism.gov.mo; Dir Eng. JOÃO MANUEL COSTA ANTUNES.

Instituto Cultural de Macau: Praçeta de Miramar 87U, Edif. San On; tel. 700391; fax 700405; e-mail postoffice@icm.gov.mo; internet www.icm.gov.mo; f. 1982; organizes performances, concerts, exhibitions, festivals, etc.; library facilities; Pres. HEIDI HO.

Macau Hotel Association: Rua Luís Gonzaga Gomes s/n, Bl. IV, r/c, Centro de Actividades Turísticas, Cabinet A; tel. 703416; fax 703415; e-mail nhacmo@macau.ctm.net; internet www.macauhotel.org.

Sociedade de Turismo e Diversões de Macau (STDM), SARL: Hotel Lisboa, 9F, Old Wing, POB 3036; tel. 566065; fax 371981; e-mail stdmmdof@macau.ctm.net; fmrly operated 10 casinos; since ending of STDM's monopoly franchise in 2002, operation of the casinos has been handled by STDM's subsidiary Macao Gaming Company Ltd; Man. Dir Dr STANLEY HO.

CHINA (TAIWAN)

Introductory Survey

Location, Climate, Language, Religion, Flag, Capital

The Republic of China has, since 1949, been confined mainly to the province of Taiwan (comprising one large island and several much smaller ones), which lies off the south-east coast of the Chinese mainland. The territory under the Republic's effective jurisdiction consists of the island of Taiwan (also known as Formosa) and nearby islands, including the P'enghu (Pescadores) group, together with a few other islands which lie just off the mainland and form part of the province of Fujian (Fukien), west of Taiwan. The largest of these is Kinmen (Jinmen), also known as Quemoy, which (with three smaller islands) is about 10 km from the port of Xiamen (Amoy), while five other islands under Taiwan's control, mainly Matsu (Mazu), lie further north, near Fuzhou. Taiwan itself is separated from the mainland by the Taiwan (Formosa) Strait, which is about 130 km (80 miles) wide at its narrowest point. The island's climate is one of rainy summers and mild winters. Average temperatures are about 15°C (59°F) in the winter and 26°C (79°F) in the summer. The average annual rainfall is 2,580 mm (102 in). The official language is Northern Chinese (Mandarin), but Taiwanese, a dialect based on the language of Fujian Province, is widely spoken. The predominant religions are Buddhism and Daoism (Taoism), but there are also adherents of I-kuan Tao, Christianity (mainly Roman Catholics and Protestants) and Islam. The philosophy of Confucianism has a large following. The national flag (proportions 2 by 3) is red, with a dark blue rectangular canton, containing a white sun, in the upper hoist. The capital is Taipei.

Recent History

China ceded Taiwan to Japan in 1895. The island remained under Japanese rule until the end of the Second World War in 1945, when it was returned to Chinese control, becoming a province of the Republic of China, then ruled by the Kuomintang (KMT, Nationalist Party). The leader of the KMT was Gen. Chiang Kai-shek, President of the Republic since 1928. The KMT Government's forces were defeated in 1949 by the Communist revolution in China. President Chiang and many of his supporters withdrew from the Chinese mainland to Taiwan, where they established a KMT regime in succession to their previous all-China administration. This regime continued to assert that it was the rightful Chinese Government, in opposition to the People's Republic of China, proclaimed by the victorious Communists in 1949. The Nationalists successfully resisted attacks by their Communist rivals, and declared that they intended to recover control of mainland China.

Although its effective control was limited to Taiwan, the KMT regime continued to be dominated by politicians who had formerly been in power on the mainland. Unable to replenish their mainland representation, the National Assembly (last elected fully in 1947) and other legislative organs extended their terms of office indefinitely, although fewer than half of the original members were alive on Taiwan by the 1980s. The political domination of the island by immigrants from the mainland caused some resentment among native Taiwanese, and led to demands for increased democratization and for the recognition of Taiwan as a state independent of China. The KMT, however, consistently rejected demands for independence, restating the party's long-standing policy of seeking political reunification, although under KMT terms, with the mainland.

The KMT regime continued to represent China at the United Nations (and as a permanent member of the UN Security Council) until October 1971, when it was replaced by the People's Republic. After 1971 a number of countries broke off diplomatic relations with Taiwan and recognized the People's Republic. In mid-2004 the Taiwan Government was recognized by some 26 countries, following the withdrawal of diplomatic recognition by Dominica in late March. After its removal from the UN in 1971, Nationalist China was subsequently expelled from several other international organizations. In November 1991, however, as 'Chinese Taipei', Taiwan joined the Asia-Pacific Economic Co-operation forum (APEC). In September 1992, under the name of the 'Separate Customs Territory of Taiwan, P'enghu, Kinmen and Matsu', Taiwan was granted observer status at the General Agreement on Tariffs and Trade (GATT) and was finally approved for membership of the successor body in September 2001, after 11 years of bidding: on 1 January 2002 Taiwan formally became a member of the World Trade Organization (WTO, see p. 357). In June 1995 Taiwan offered to make a donation of US $1,000m., to be used for the establishment of an international development fund, if the island were permitted to rejoin the UN. In February 2004 it was announced that Taiwan would become a member of the Commission for the Conservation and Management of Highly Migratory Fish Stocks in the Western and Central Pacific Ocean (responsible for implementing the 1995 UN Fish Stocks Agreement). Following its admission to the WTO, therefore, this represented the second recognition of Taiwan by an international organization. In September 2004, for the 12th consecutive year, the General Committee of the UN General Assembly rejected a proposal urging Taiwan's participation in the UN. However, Taiwan's leaders pledged to continue the island's campaign to gain re-entry. In April 1997 the Minister of Foreign Affairs announced that Taiwan had applied to be an observer of the World Health Organization (WHO) and would be seeking similar status in other UN agencies. Its application was unsuccessful, however, as was a second attempt to gain observer status in May 1998 and subsequent annual attempts.

In 1973 the Government of Taiwan rejected an offer from the People's Republic to hold secret discussions on the reunification of China. In October 1981 Taiwan rejected China's suggested terms for reunification, whereby Taiwan would become a 'special administrative region' and would have a substantial degree of autonomy, including the retention of its own armed forces. In 1983 China renewed its offer, including a guarantee to maintain the status quo in Taiwan for 100 years if the province agreed to reunification. In 1984, following the agreement between the People's Republic of China and the United Kingdom that China would regain sovereignty over the British colony of Hong Kong in 1997, mainland Chinese leaders urged Taiwan to accept similar proposals for reunification on the basis of 'one country—two systems'. The Taipei Government insisted that Taiwan would never negotiate with Beijing until the mainland regime renounced communism. In May 1986, however, the Government was forced to make direct contact with the Beijing Government for the first time, over the issue of a Taiwanese pilot who had defected to the mainland. In October 1987 the Government announced the repeal of the 38-year ban on visits to the mainland by Taiwanese citizens, with the exception of civil servants and military personnel. These regulations were relaxed in November 1998.

In April 1989 the Government announced that it was considering a 'One China, two governments' formula, whereby China would be a single country under two administrations, one in Beijing and one in Taipei. In May a delegation led by the Minister of Finance attended a meeting of the Asian Development Bank (ADB) in Beijing, as representatives of 'Taipei, China', demonstrating a considerable relaxation in Taiwan's stance. Reconciliation initiatives were abruptly halted, however, by the violent suppression of the pro-democracy movement in Beijing in June. In May 1990 a proposal by the President of Taiwan to open direct dialogue on a government-to-government basis with the People's Republic was rejected by Beijing, which continued to maintain that it would negotiate only on a party-to-party basis with the KMT. In December Taiwan announced that the state of war with the People's Republic would be formally ended by May 1991 (see below).

In February 1991 the recently formed National Unification Council, under the chairmanship of the President of Taiwan, put forward radical new proposals, whereby Taiwan and the People's Republic of China might recognize each other as separate political entities. In March a national unification programme, which incorporated the demand that Taiwan be acknowledged as an independent and equal entity, was approved by the Central Standing Committee of the KMT. The programme also included a proposal for direct postal, commercial and shipping links with the mainland.

In April 1991 a delegation from the Straits Exchange Foundation (SEF), established in late 1990 to deal with bilateral issues, travelled to Beijing for discussions, the first such delegation ever to visit the People's Republic. In August 1991 a Beijing magazine published an informal 10-point plan for the eventual reunification of China, whereby Taiwan would become a special administrative region and retain its own legislative, administrative and judicial authority. Two senior envoys of the mainland Chinese Red Cross were allowed to enter Taiwan in August on a humanitarian mission.

As the Beijing Government continued to warn against independence for Taiwan, in September 1991 the island's President asserted that conditions were not appropriate for reunification with the mainland and that Taiwan was a *de facto* sovereign and autonomous country. The President of the People's Republic indicated that force might be used to prevent the separation of Taiwan. In December the non-governmental Association for Relations across the Taiwan Straits (ARATS) was established in Beijing. In January 1992 the SEF protested to the People's Republic over the detention of a former pilot of the mainland air force who had defected to Taiwan in 1965 and, upon returning to his homeland for a family reunion in December 1991, had been arrested. He subsequently received a 15-year prison sentence. In May 1992 the National Unification Council's proposal for a non-aggression pact between Taiwan and the People's Republic was rejected.

In July 1992 the Taiwanese Government reiterated that it would not consider party-to-party talks with Beijing. In the same month President Lee urged the establishment of 'one country, one good system'. In mid-July statutes to permit the further expansion of economic and political links with the People's Republic were adopted by the Legislative Yuan. In August the vice-president of the mainland Red Cross travelled to the island, thus becoming the most senior representative of the People's Republic to visit Taiwan since 1949. Delegates from the SEF and ARATS met in Hong Kong in October 1992 for discussions. The Chairman of the Mainland Affairs Council, however, insisted upon the People's Republic's renunciation of the use of military force prior to any dialogue on the reunification question. Upon taking office in February 1993, the new Premier of Taiwan confirmed the continuation of the 'One China' policy.

In 1993 divisions between Taiwan's business sector and political groupings (the former advocating much closer links with the People's Republic, the latter urging greater caution) became evident. In January, and again later in the year, the Secretary-General of the SEF resigned, following disagreement with the Mainland Affairs Council. Historic talks between the Chairmen of the SEF and of the ARATS were held in Singapore in April. Engaging in the highest level of contact since 1949, Taiwan and the People's Republic agreed on the establishment of a formal structure for future negotiations on economic and social issues.

In August 1993 the People's Republic issued a document entitled *The Taiwan Question and the Reunification of China*, reiterating its claim to sovereignty over the island. Relations were further strained by a series of aircraft hijackings to Taiwan from the mainland. An SEF-ARATS meeting, held in Taiwan in December, attempted to address the issue of the repatriation of hijackers. Incidents of air piracy continued in 1994, substantial prison sentences being imposed on the hijackers by the Taiwanese authorities.

Further meetings between delegates of the SEF and ARATS were held in early 1994. In April, however, 24 Taiwanese tourists were among those robbed and killed on board a pleasure boat plying Qiandao Lake, in mainland China. Taiwan suspended all commercial and cultural exchanges with the People's Republic. In June three men were convicted of the murders and promptly executed. In February 1995 compensation totalling 1.2m. yuan was awarded to the victims' families by the People's Republic.

In July 1994 the Taiwanese Government released a White Paper on mainland affairs, urging that the division be acknowledged and the island accepted as a separate political entity. In August the SEF-ARATS talks were resumed when Tang Shubei, Vice-Chairman and Secretary-General of the ARATS, flew to Taipei for discussions with his Taiwanese counterpart, Chiao Jen-ho. Tang thus became the most senior Communist Chinese official ever to visit the island. Although the visit was marred by opposition protesters, the two sides reached tentative agreement on several issues, including the repatriation of hijackers and illegal immigrants from Taiwan to the mainland. Procedures for the settlement of cross-Straits fishing disputes were

also established. In mid-November relations were strained once again when, in an apparent accident during a training exercise, Taiwanese anti-aircraft shells landed on a mainland village, injuring several people. Nevertheless, in late November a further round of SEF-ARATS talks took place in Nanjing, at which agreement in principle on the procedure for the repatriation of hijackers and illegal immigrants was confirmed. Further progress was made at meetings in Beijing in January 1995, although no accord was signed. It was announced in March that the functions of the SEF were to be enhanced. To improve co-ordination, the SEF board of directors would henceforth include government officials, while meetings of the Mainland Affairs Council would be attended by officials of the SEF. In the same month the Mainland Affairs Council approved a resolution providing for the relaxation of restrictions on visits by mainland officials and civilians.

In 1995 President Jiang Zemin's Lunar New Year address, incorporating the mainland's 'eight-point' policy on Taiwan, was regarded as more conciliatory than hitherto. In April, in response, President Lee proposed a 'six-point' programme for cross-Straits relations: unification according to the reality of separate rules; increased exchanges on the basis of Chinese culture; increased economic and trade relations; admission to international organizations on an equal footing; the renunciation of the use of force against each other; and joint participation in Hong Kong and Macao affairs. In late April, however, the eighth round of working-level SEF-ARATS discussions was postponed, owing to disagreement over the agenda.

In May 1995 the SEF Chairman, Koo Chen-fu, and his mainland counterpart, Wang Daohan, formally agreed to meet in Beijing in July. In June, however, this proposed second session of senior-level negotiations was postponed by the ARATS, in protest at President Lee's recent visit to the USA. Tension between the two sides increased in July, when the People's Republic unexpectedly announced that it was about to conduct an eight-day programme of guided missile and artillery-firing tests off the northern coast of Taiwan. A second series of exercises took place in August, again arousing much anxiety on the island. In mid-August President Jiang Zemin confirmed that the People's Republic would not renounce the use of force against Taiwan. Nevertheless, at the end of that month President Lee reaffirmed the KMT's commitment to reunification. In October President Jiang Zemin's offer to visit Taiwan in person was cautiously received on the island. President Lee confirmed his Government's anti-independence stance in November.

In January 1996 the Taiwanese Premier again urged the early resumption of cross-Straits dialogue. In February there were unconfirmed reports of the extensive mobilization of mainland troops. In the same month, upon his appointment as Chairman of the Mainland Affairs Council, Chang King-yuh pledged to attempt to improve relations with the mainland. In March the People's Republic began a new series of missile tests, including the firing of surface-to-surface missiles into coastal areas around Taiwan. Live artillery exercises continued in the Taiwan Strait until after the island's presidential election, arousing international concern. The USA deployed two naval task forces in the area (see below).

In April 1996, as tension eased, the Mainland Affairs Council removed the ban on visits to Taiwan by officials of the People's Republic. The Ministry of Transportation and Communications announced that mainland container traffic was to be permitted direct entry to Taiwanese ports. At the end of April the SEF, which had lodged a strong protest with the ARATS during the missile tests of March, urged the resumption of bilateral discussions. In July President Lee reaffirmed his commitment to peaceful reunification.

In November 1996 the Mainland Affairs Council announced that the permanent stationing of mainland media representatives in Taiwan was to be permitted. President Lee's renewed offer to travel to the People's Republic was rejected and, despite repeated SEF requests, Tang Shubei of the ARATS continued to assert that Taiwan's pursuit of its 'two Chinas' policy (a reference to President Lee's attempts to raise the diplomatic profile of the island) prevented the resumption of cross-Straits discussions. In January 1997, however, as the reversion of the entrepôt of Hong Kong to Chinese sovereignty approached, shipping representatives of Taiwan and of the People's Republic reached a preliminary consensus on the establishment of direct sea links. Limited services resumed in April, thus ending a ban of 48 years. In March 1998 it was reported that Taiwan had agreed to allow a mainland Chinese shipping company to operate a direct shipping link between Shanghai and the northern Taiwanese port of Keelung.

In July 1997, upon the reversion to Chinese sovereignty of the British colony of Hong Kong, President Lee firmly rejected the concept of 'one country, two systems' and any parallel with Taiwan. In September the Taiwanese Minister of Finance and the Governor of the central bank were obliged to cancel a visit to Hong Kong, where they had planned to have informal discussions with delegates to the forthcoming IMF/World Bank meeting, owing to Hong Kong's failure to issue them with visas.

The declaration by an ARATS official in January 1998 that Taiwan did not need to recognize the Government of the People's Republic as the central Government as a precondition for dialogue was regarded as a significant concession on the part of the mainland authorities. However, Taiwan continued to insist that China abandon its demand that talks be conducted under its 'One China' principle. In February the ARATS sent a letter to the SEF requesting the resumption of political and economic dialogue between the two sides, and inviting a senior SEF official to visit the mainland. The SEF responded positively to the invitation in March, and proposed that a delegation be sent to the People's Republic to discuss procedural details, prior to a visit to the mainland by the SEF Chairman.

In April 1998 a delegation of the SEF visited the People's Republic. Following negotiations with the ARATS, it was announced that the Chairman of the SEF would visit the People's Republic later in 1998 formally to resume the dialogue, which had been suspended since 1995. The arrest on the mainland in May 1998 of four Taiwanese business executives on charges of espionage, and their subsequent conviction, and the visit to Malaysia by the Taiwanese Premier, in April, threatened to reverse the recent improvement in relations. However, in July the Chinese Minister of Science and Technology visited Taiwan, the first such visit by a mainland Minister since the civil war. This was followed later in the month by a formal visit to Taiwan by the Deputy Secretary-General of the ARATS. The kidnap and murder in August in the People's Republic of a Taiwanese local government official caused serious concern for the Taiwanese authorities. In October Koo Chen-fu, the SEF Chairman, duly travelled to the People's Republic, where he held several meetings with his ARATS counterpart, Wang Daohan, met with President Jiang Zemin (the highest level of bilateral contact since 1949) and had discussions with other senior officials. A four-point agreement was reached, allowing for increased communications between the two sides, but little was achieved in terms of a substantive breakthrough. However, the talks were considered to mark an important improvement in cross-Straits relations, and Wang Daohan accepted an invitation to visit Taiwan in March 1999.

In January 1999 the ARATS invited the SEF Deputy Secretary-General to visit the People's Republic for talks in order to prepare for Wang Daohan's visit. The SEF made a counter-proposal that ARATS officials visit Taiwan to discuss preparations. In March the Government announced that it was to establish a supra-ministerial task force to examine the suitability of trips by certain former government officials to the People's Republic of China, owing to security concerns. In the same month an ARATS delegation visited Taiwan. In April President Lee reaffirmed that Beijing should recognize Taiwan as being of equal status, that cross-Straits negotiations should concentrate on practical issues and that reunification could take place only if the mainland were to become a democracy. An SEF group went to Beijing in March, and preliminary agreement was reached that the ARATS Chairman would visit Taiwan in either mid-September or mid-October. In August, however, the ARATS suspended contacts with the SEF, following President Lee's insistence on the 'two-state theory' (see below), and it was confirmed in October that Wang Daohan would not visit Taiwan while the island continued to adhere to the theory.

Meanwhile, China was becoming increasingly demonstrative in its opposition to Taiwan's inclusion in the US-led Theater Missile Defence (TMD) anti-missile system. Ballistic missiles were deployed in mainland coastal regions facing Taiwan, and fears were heightened within the international community in July 1999 when the People's Republic announced that it had developed a neutron bomb, after declaring itself ready for war should Taiwan attempt to gain independence. This declaration was prompted by a radio interview given by President Lee, during which he asserted that relations with the People's Republic were 'state-to-state'. Chinese military exercises took place in the Taiwan Strait later that month, following which

Taiwan promised that it would not amend its Constitution to enshrine its claim to statehood in law. In August the USA reaffirmed its readiness to defend Taiwan against Chinese military action. Shortly afterwards the Taiwanese Government refused a request by Beijing that it retract the 'state-to-state' theory with regard to cross-Straits relations, and tension increased in late August when the KMT incorporated the 'two-state theory' into the party resolution, claiming that this would henceforth become the administrative guide-line and priority of the Taiwanese authorities. Later that month the Mainland Affairs Council announced that former Taiwan government officials involved in affairs related to national intelligence or secrets were not to be permitted to travel to China within three years of leaving their posts. In September, following a severe earthquake in Taiwan that killed or injured several thousand people, China was among the many countries to offer emergency assistance to the island. Taiwan, however, accused the People's Republic of contravening humanitarian principles by trying to force other countries to seek its approval before offering help. Relations became increasingly strained following the reversion of the Portuguese territory of Macao to Chinese sovereignty in December 1999. The People's Republic announced that reunification of the two sides of the Taiwan Strait would also be on the basis of 'one country, two systems'.

In February 2000 the People's Republic threatened to attack Taiwan if it indefinitely postponed reunification talks. The approval in the Legislative Yuan in March of a law providing for the first direct transport links between Taiwan's outlying islands and mainland China for 50 years did not substantially improve matters, and in April the Vice President-elect, Annette Lu, was denounced by the Chinese media after she made 'separatist' remarks, televised in Hong Kong, declaring that Taiwan was only a 'remote relative and close neighbour' of China. A Taiwanese opposition group subsequently endorsed a motion to dismiss Lu for putting the island at risk by provoking China. In an attempt to improve relations with the People's Republic, President Chen offered to compromise and to reopen negotiations on the basis that each side was free to interpret the 'One China' formula as it saw fit. Chinese Premier Zhu Rongji rejected the suggestion, and questioned Taiwan's motives, effectively dispelling all hopes of restarting negotiations in the near future. In July 2000 the Chinese authorities responded angrily when the United Kingdom issued a visa to former President Lee Teng-hui, who continued to be perceived as a dissident by the People's Republic. Despite the fact that Lee's visa was for the purpose of a private visit by an individual, and specified as a condition that no public statements would be made during the trip, China took action against British governmental and trade interests to register its displeasure.

In October 2000 Beijing published a policy document on its national defence, which confirmed that the People's Republic would use force to prevent Taiwanese secession, to stop occupation of the island, and also in the event of Taiwan indefinitely postponing reunification with the mainland. In November, however, there were signs of an improvement in relations when Wu Po-hsiung, the Vice-Chairman of the KMT, travelled to Beijing and met unofficially with Chinese Vice-Premier Qian Qichen. Wu was the most senior KMT official to visit mainland China for more than 50 years, and it was thought that Beijing was attempting to isolate Chen Shui-bian by consorting with his political rivals. During the meeting both sides agreed to hold important academic forums to discuss cross-Straits relations and to attempt to devise common positions. Qian stressed, however, the importance of Taiwan's recognition of the 'One China' principle before official negotiations could resume.

Also in November 2000, Taiwan announced that journalists from the People's Republic were to be granted permission to stay in Taiwan for periods of up to one month, during which time they would be invited to attend any press conferences called by the President's office and the Executive Yuan, in order to enhance cross-Straits exchanges and understanding. In the following month plans were announced for 'mini three links' with China, providing for direct trade, transport and postal links between Kinmen and Matsu islands and the mainland. The Taiwanese Government stressed, however, that any future direct links with Taiwan itself would be subject to rigorous security checks. In early January 2001 groups sailed from Kinmen and Matsu to Xiamen and Fuzhou, respectively, in the People's Republic. Beijing's response toward the initiative was guarded.

In March 2001, in Beijing, the press spokesman for the Fourth Session of the Ninth National People's Congress (NPC) reiterated that China did not favour the confederal system of reunification, but rather the 'one country, two systems' model. Also in that month, exiled pro-democracy activist Wei Jingsheng visited Taiwan and had discussions with Vice-President Lu. By April cross-Straits relations had become strained, following the visit of the Dalai Lama to Taiwan, and the forthcoming sale of weapons by the USA to Taiwan (see above).

In May 2001 President Chen announced that he aspired to become the first Taiwanese leader to visit the mainland since 1949 by attending the APEC forum to be held there in October; however, Beijing rejected Chen's proposal. Although official cross-Straits relations were often hostile, links continued to develop between Taiwan and the mainland, particularly in the business sphere. Many Taiwanese companies continued to invest in the mainland. President Chen in late August endorsed a plan by a special advisory committee to expand economic and commercial links with the People's Republic, a reversal of the previous Government's 'no haste, be patient' policy of limiting trade with the mainland for fear of becoming over-dependent on Taiwan. The new policy of 'aggressive opening' included the removal of a US $50m. limit on individual investments in the mainland. Beijing responded cautiously to Chen's initiative, declaring that direct full transport links between the mainland and Taiwan would have to wait until Chen respected the 'One China' reunification formula, but a senior Chinese trade official stated that China would not block further Taiwanese investment. At the same time, state-owned oil companies from Taiwan and China announced plans to resume co-operative exploration of the Taiwan Straits. Chen's critics warned that his new policy would make Taiwan too economically dependent on the mainland. In September 2001 the Taiwanese Government approved a proposal allowing Chinese investment in Taiwan's land and property market, as part of the new opening to the mainland. The limit on individual investments in the mainland was formally removed in November; restrictions on direct remits to and from the mainland via Taiwanese banks were also abolished.

In late October 2001, meanwhile, Taiwan boycotted the APEC summit meeting in Shanghai, following Beijing's refusal to allow Taiwan's chosen delegate, former Vice-President Li Yuan-tsu, to attend, on the grounds that he was not an 'economic' official. Despite this, the opposition Democratic Progressive Party (DPP—see below) deleted from its charter a vow to achieve the island's formal independence, since it was already a *de facto* separate entity. The change indicated a growing acceptance of the status quo by the DPP. It was hoped that the acceptance of China and Taiwan into the WTO in mid-November would improve cross-Straits relations, by enhancing communications in the field of trade.

The heavy defeat of the pro-mainland KMT by the pro-independence DPP at the legislative elections of December 2001 (see below) was initially seen as a reverse to cross-Straits relations; however, Beijing reacted with moderation to the event, in contrast to past bellicosity during elections, but insisted that Taiwan accept the 'One China' principle as a precondition for bilateral dialogue. Meanwhile, the Control Yuan reported that some 200 recently retired Taiwanese military and intelligence officials had visited Hong Kong and the mainland in violation of laws stipulating that they wait three years before doing so. There were fears that a number of these officials had divulged military secrets to mainland military officials, thereby jeopardizing the island's security.

In January 2002 the Government announced a new passport design incorporating the words 'issued in Taiwan' on the cover, ostensibly to differentiate clearly Taiwanese passports from mainland ones. The initiative was regarded disapprovingly by Beijing, as a sign of symbolic statehood. In mid-January the Government announced a list of more than 2,000 items that would thenceforth be legally importable from the mainland, mostly consumer but also agricultural goods, and at the same time facilitated direct transport links with the mainland. Later in the month, Chinese Vice-Premier Qian Qichen invited members of the DPP to visit the mainland, stating that most DPP members were not independence activists. President Chen welcomed Qian's remarks, and Premier Yu said he was planning to send a delegation to the mainland, but ruled out negotiations on the so-called '1992 consensus'.

In a sign of improving financial links, in early March 2002 Beijing announced that, for the first time, two Taiwanese banks would be allowed to open offices on the mainland. Taiwan would also allow mainland banks to establish offices on the island. At the end of the month, Taiwan eased restrictions on the island's

companies investing in computer-chip manufacturing on the mainland; however, restrictions would remain on the number of plants established and type of chips produced. Underlying these restrictions was a fear that Taiwan's valuable electronics industry might become dependent on the mainland, and that the mainland might gain access to advanced semiconductor technology used to guide missiles. It was thought that Taiwan's efforts to open up to the mainland were being hampered by former President Lee Teng-hui's new political party, upon which the DPP depended to maintain a majority in the legislature and which generally favoured a slower approach to improving bilateral commercial relations.

At the beginning of May 2002 an official Chinese newspaper published Beijing's strongest criticism to date of President Chen, describing him as a 'troublemaker' who sought to damage bilateral relations, and criticizing his efforts to promote a separate 'Taiwanese' identity. The comments were thought to be a response to the strengthening of relations between Taiwan and the USA (see below). None the less, Taiwan at the same time reluctantly allowed China to ship more than 2,300 tons of water to its outlying islands in order to help relieve the worst drought in many years, an arrangement that would have been unthinkable a few years previously. Meanwhile, Chen in early May announced that he planned to send a DPP delegation to the mainland later in the year, in response to Qian Qichen's conciliatory speech in January. At the end of May the Mainland Affairs Council planned to introduce changes that would allow non-governmental organizations a greater role in promoting cross-Straits dialogue. Two state-owned oil companies from both sides at this time agreed upon a joint venture to explore petroleum and gas deposits in the straits. Taiwan's arrest in mid-June of one of its own military officers for passing military secrets to China failed to damage these improving commercial links, but offered a reminder that the intelligence 'war' between the two sides was far from over. Earlier, in mid-April, Taiwan had dispatched several navy vessels to monitor a Chinese research vessel operating just outside Taiwanese waters, and had tested an indigenously developed air-defence missile in May. Despite mutual suspicions, several Taiwanese legislators and retired generals secretly travelled to Beijing in June and discussed defence issues with their mainland counterparts.

Bilateral relations again deteriorated in late July 2002, when the Pacific island nation of Nauru transferred its recognition from Taiwan to the People's Republic of China, thereby undermining Taipei diplomatically and prompting Chen to warn that Taiwan might have to chart its own future path. At the same time Taiwan's Ministry of National Defense warned in a biannual report that China's military spending was accelerating rapidly and that it would possess 600 short-range missiles targeting the island by 2005. Chen further incensed Beijing in early August by supporting demands for a referendum to determine the island's future, and referring to China and Taiwan as two countries. However, DPP officials stated that there had been no change in policy, and Chen subsequently softened his rhetoric. Taiwan then cancelled planned military exercises as a gesture of good faith, but Chen's comments delayed the introduction of direct transport links. At the end of July the Government announced that Chinese products could be advertised on the island and that Chinese employees of Taiwanese or foreign companies would be allowed to work in Taiwan. A Taiwanese semiconductor manufacturer, the world's largest, also announced plans to build a new factory on the Chinese mainland, in Shanghai.

The political atmosphere between Taiwan and the mainland remained volatile, however, and in early September 2002 Chen described China's threats against the island as a form of 'terrorism'. Later that month Beijing accused Taiwan of allowing the banned Falun Gong sect to use the island as a base for disrupting Chinese television and satellite broadcasts, although it did not accuse Taipei of directly supporting the group. A Chinese official stated that the source of the sect's propaganda transmissions had been traced to the island, but a Taiwanese investigation revealed nothing, and the unofficial leader of Falun Gong in Taiwan, Chang Ching-hsi, emphasized that the sect had no desire to exacerbate the tensions in cross-Straits relations. At the same time, a retired Taiwanese air force officer, his wife and their son were charged with spying for China in the late 1980s. In mid-October 2002 a Taiwanese army officer fled to China via Thailand with his wife and family.

Attempts to restore direct transport links between China and Taiwan gained momentum in October 2002 when Beijing abandoned the 'One China' principle as a condition for such links and agreed that these could be described as 'cross-Straits' rather than 'domestic'. However, two weeks later President Chen seemingly retreated from the proposal. A report by the Control Yuan in September 2002 had stated that only 2% of the money invested by Taiwanese firms in China was repatriated, and it was believed that Chen was reassessing the economic benefits of cross-Straits links. Elements in the DPP had long argued that these links with China were to Taiwan's economic disadvantage.

The 16th Congress of the Chinese Communist Party (CCP) held in Beijing in November 2002 stressed continuity in cross-Straits relations. However, the 'arms race' between China and Taiwan continued during the year, with the two sides acquiring advanced weaponry from Russia and the USA respectively. In mid-October two Chinese ships and a submarine sailed around the east coast of Taiwan en route to the South China Sea, where the Chinese navy was staging military exercises. The voyage served to warn Taiwan that Beijing could encircle the island if necessary, prompting the Minister of National Defense, Tang Yao-ming, to urge a strengthening of Taiwan's navy. Analysts noted, however, that Taiwan's defence spending had been reduced in recent years, owing to the economic downturn.

Tension between Taipei and Beijing intensified in January 2003, however, when President Chen stated that Taiwan was a sovereign state, and would never accept a Hong Kong-style solution nor federate with the mainland. At the same time, Vice-President Lu described China as being of a 'terrorist nature', referring to its missile build-up across the Taiwan Straits and to its coercive diplomacy. In late January 2003, none the less, following discussions earlier in that month, the first Taiwanese airliner in more than 50 years flew to mainland China, via Hong Kong, landing in Shanghai. The flight was one of 16 charter operations organized by the Taiwanese carrier, China Airlines (CAL), to transport Taiwanese visitors in China home for Chinese New Year celebrations. The instigation of direct cross-Straits flights on a regular basis, however, appeared unlikely to be realized in the near future.

In late February 2003 the Minister of National Defense stated that Taiwan would not reduce weapons purchases from the USA in return for the dismantling of Chinese missiles targeting the island. His remarks came in response to Chinese President Jiang Zemin's offer of such an arrangement, made to President Bush in October 2002.

Relations between the sides were antagonized following the outbreak on the mainland of a pneumonia-like virus, Severe Acute Respiratory Syndrome (SARS), which spread to Taiwan in early 2003. Taipei accused Beijing of concealing the seriousness of the outbreak, thereby endangering Taiwan and neighbouring countries. In May Taiwan formally rejected an aid programme offered by China to assist in countering the SARS epidemic on the island. Also in May, China continued to stress its opposition to Taiwan's membership of WHO at a meeting of the World Health Assembly in Geneva, Switzerland. However, Beijing did agree to Taiwan's participation in a global conference on SARS in June 2003.

Despite increased trade and educational connections between the two sides, cross-Straits relations continued to be dominated by political tensions. In early August 2003 the island's authorities arrested two Taiwanese citizens and a Taiwanese American on charges of spying for China. Also in August, a Chinese surveillance vessel was seen to the north of Taiwan, in advance of large-scale military exercises in that area. Military exercises simulating an attack on Taiwan by China were conducted in early September 2003. Also in September, in a move likely to anger Beijing further, Taiwan announced that it was to issue new passports for its citizens, which for the first time would have the word 'Taiwan' printed on the front. Cross-Straits tensions in September were again heightened by mass protests in Taipei at the beginning of the month demanding that the name 'Taiwan' be used officially by government agencies and private companies (see below). In October Taiwan's legislature passed the so-called Act Governing Relations between Peoples of the Taiwan Area and the Mainland Area, which was to provide a framework for the regulation of travel and business links between Taiwan and the mainland.

In November 2003 tensions between Taiwan and the mainland were further exacerbated after Taiwan's legislature approved a bill allowing referendums to take place on the island (see below). Although the legislation in its final version prohibited a vote on Taiwan's sovereignty except in the event of an external attack, Beijing feared that the new law might lead to

the holding of a vote on Taiwan's independence. An official at China's Taiwan Affairs Office warned that President Chen would be 'risking war' should he initiate any move towards Taiwanese independence. In December the issue of Taiwan dominated a visit by Chinese Premier Wen Jiabao to Washington, DC, with Wen seeking assurance from the USA that it would not support moves towards Taiwanese independence, following the introduction of the new referendum law. In the same month President Chen defended plans to hold a referendum in March 2004 on the subject of a proposed request to China that it remove hundreds of missiles aimed at the island. In January 2004 President Chen suggested that the referendum might be presented as an opportunity to reduce bilateral tensions. He stated that the referendum might include 'counter-proposals' such as direct transport links between Taiwan and China if the latter were to withdraw its missiles. In February, furthermore, President Chen suggested the establishment of a demilitarized zone between the mainland and Taiwan in order to facilitate joint discussions. Chen also stated that he would not declare Taiwanese independence, were he to win the presidential election in March 2004, although his attitude to relations with the Chinese mainland, for example in rejecting the 'one country, two systems' model advocated by Beijing, was regarded by some as tantamount to stating that independence already existed.

The Beijing Government did not attempt directly to influence the election when it was held in March 2004, resulting in a narrow victory for Chen. However, following widespread controversy and protests over the election result, the Chinese Government stated that it would not tolerate social instability in Taiwan. In the event, President Chen's referendum, held concurrently with the presidential election, did not produce a valid result (see below). The Beijing Government remained suspicious of Chen. At the end of July 2004 a senior Chinese official warned of an attack on Taiwan by 2008, if Chen were to proceed with constitutional reforms outlined in the Taiwanese President's inaugural speech in May, despite pledges from Chen that the amendments would not address the question of Taiwan's sovereignty. In August President Chen cancelled a military exercise scheduled for September after China removed 3,000 troops from the island of Dongshan owing to a typhoon threat. Chen's stated intention was to show goodwill towards the mainland. In September, however, following public opposition to a special budget for the purchase of weapons from the USA (see below), President Chen again drew attention to the mainland military threat, stating that the number of Chinese missiles aimed at Taiwan had increased to 610 from 496 at the end of 2003. In late December the Standing Committee of China's NPC approved a draft of anti-secession legislation aimed at preventing Taiwan from declaring independence. The legislation was approved by the third plenum of the 10th NPC in March 2005.

In January 2005 it was announced that for the first time direct flights between Taipei and the Chinese mainland would be permitted over the Lunar New Year period. The first direct commercial flights between Taipei and Beijing duly took place at the end of the month. In late April, in the first such visit since 1949, the Chairman of the (opposition) KMT, Lien Chan, embarked upon an official visit to the mainland, where he and Chinese President Hu Jintao agreed to remain opposed to Taiwanese independence. The initiative provoked mixed reactions among the citizens of Taiwan.

In domestic affairs, in December 1972 legislative elections were held, for the first time in 24 years, to fill 53 seats in the National Assembly. The new members, elected for a fixed term of six years, joined 1,376 surviving 'life-term' members of the Assembly. President Chiang Kai-shek remained in office until his death in April 1975. He was succeeded as leader of the ruling KMT by his son, Gen. Chiang Ching-kuo, who had hitherto been Premier. Dr Yen Chia-kan, Vice-President since 1966, became the new President. In 1978 President Yen retired and was succeeded by Gen. Chiang. At elections for 71 seats in the Legislative Yuan in December 1983, the KMT won an overwhelming victory, confirming its dominance over the independent 'Tangwai' (non-party) candidates. In March 1984 President Chiang was re-elected for a second six-year term, and Lee Teng-hui, a former Mayor of Taipei and a native Taiwanese, became Vice-President. President Chiang died in January 1988 and was succeeded by Lee Teng-hui.

In September 1986 135 leading opposition politicians formed the DPP, in defiance of the KMT's ban on the formation of new political parties. Partial elections to the National Assembly and the Legislative Yuan were held in December. The KMT achieved a decisive victory, but the DPP received about one-quarter of the total votes, and more than doubled the non-KMT representation. In February 1987 the KMT began to implement a programme of political reform. Martial law (in force since 1949) was replaced by the National Security Law in July and, under the terms of the new legislation, political parties other than the KMT were permitted, and civilians were removed from the jurisdiction of military courts. In April seven major posts in a reorganization of the Executive Yuan were allocated to reformist members of the KMT. In November 1987 the second annual Congress of the DPP approved a resolution declaring that Taiwanese citizens had the right to advocate independence. In January 1988, however, two opposition activists were imprisoned, on charges of sedition, for voicing such demands.

In February 1988 a plan to restructure the legislative bodies was approved by the Central Standing Committee of the KMT. Voluntary resignations were to be sought from 'life-term' members of the Legislative Yuan and National Assembly, and seats were no longer to be reserved for representatives of mainland constituencies. The 13th national Congress of the KMT was held in July. Following a decision to hold free elections for two-thirds of the members of the KMT's Central Committee, numerous new members were elected, and the proportion of native Taiwanese increased sharply. In January 1989 three legislative measures were enacted: a revision of regulations concerning the registration of political parties; a retirement plan for those members of the three legislative assemblies who had been elected by mainland constituencies in 1947; and a new law aiming to give greater autonomy to the Taiwan Provincial Government and its assembly, and in the following month the KMT became the first political party to register under the new legislation. Despite objections to the new laws, regarding the size of the retirement pensions being offered and the terms of the Civic Organizations Law (under which political parties were obliged to reject communism and any notion of official political independence for Taiwan), the DPP applied for official registration in April.

Partial elections to the Legislative Yuan and the Taiwan Provincial Assembly were held on 2 December 1989. A total of 101 seats in the Legislative Yuan were contested, with the KMT obtaining 72 seats and the DPP winning 21, thus securing the prerogative to propose legislation in the Legislative Yuan. In February 1990 the opening of the National Assembly's 35-day plenary session, convened every six years to elect the country's President, was disrupted by DPP members' violent action in a protest against the continuing domination of the Assembly by elderly KMT politicians, who had been elected on the Chinese mainland prior to 1949 and who had never been obliged to seek re-election. Many injuries resulted from clashes between riot police and demonstrators. In March 1990 DPP members were barred from the National Assembly for refusing to swear allegiance to 'The Republic of China', attempting instead to substitute 'Taiwan' upon taking the oath. Various amendments to the Temporary Provisions, which for more than 40 years had permitted the effective suspension of the Constitution, were approved by the National Assembly in mid-March. Revisions included measures to strengthen the position of the mainland-elected KMT members, who were granted new powers to initiate and veto legislation, and also an amendment to permit the National Assembly to meet annually. The revisions were opposed not only by the DPP but also by more moderate members of the KMT, and led to a large protest rally in Taipei, demanding the abolition of the National Assembly and the holding of direct presidential elections. Nevertheless, President Lee was duly re-elected, unopposed, by the National Assembly for a six-year term, two rival KMT candidates having withdrawn from the contest.

The National Affairs Conference (NAC) convened in June 1990 to discuss proposals for reform. A Constitutional Reform Planning Group was subsequently established. The NAC reached consensus on the issue of direct presidential elections, which would permit the citizens of Taiwan, rather than the members of the National Assembly, to select the Head of State. Meanwhile, the Council of Grand Justices had ruled that elderly members of the National Assembly and of the Legislative Yuan should step down by the end of 1991.

In October 1990 the National Unification Council, chaired by President Lee, was formed. In the same month the Mainland Affairs Council, comprising heads of government departments and led by the Vice-Premier of the Executive Yuan, was founded. In December President Lee announced that Taiwan would for-

mally end the state of war with the mainland; the declaration of emergency was to be rescinded by May 1991. Plans were announced for gradual constitutional reform, to be implemented in 1991–93. Meanwhile, in early December 1990 Huang Hwa, the leader of a faction of the DPP and independence activist, had received a 10-year prison sentence upon being found guilty of 'preparing to commit sedition'.

In April 1991 the National Assembly was convened, the session again being marred by violent clashes between KMT and DPP members. The DPP subsequently boycotted the session, arguing that a completely new constitution should be introduced and that elderly KMT delegates, who did not represent Taiwan constituencies, should not have the right to make amendments to the existing Constitution. Some 20,000 demonstrators attended a DPP-organized protest march. Nevertheless, the National Assembly duly approved the constitutional amendments, and at midnight on 30 April the 'period of mobilization for the suppression of the Communist rebellion' and the Temporary Provisions were formally terminated. The existence, but not the legitimacy, of the Government of the People's Republic was officially acknowledged by President Lee. Furthermore, Taiwan remained committed to its 'One China' policy. In May 1991 widespread protests following the arrest of four advocates of independence for Taiwan led to the abolition of the Statute of Punishment for Sedition. The law had been adopted in 1949 and had been frequently employed by the KMT to suppress political dissent.

A senior UN official visited the island in August 1991, the first trip by such a representative since Taiwan's withdrawal from the organization in 1971. Large-scale rallies calling for a referendum to be held on the issue of Taiwan's readmission to the UN as an independent state, resulting in clashes between demonstrators and the security forces, took place in September and October.

In August 1991 the opposition DPP officially announced its alternative draft constitution for 'Taiwan', rather than for 'the Republic of China', thus acknowledging the *de facto* position regarding sovereignty. In September, after being reinstated in the Legislative Yuan, Huang Hsin-chieh, the Chairman of the DPP, relinquished his seat in the legislature and urged other senior deputies to do likewise. Huang had been deprived of his seat and imprisoned in 1980, following his conviction on charges of sedition. At the party congress in October 1991, Huang was replaced as DPP Chairman by Hsu Hsin-liang. Risking prosecution by the authorities, the DPP congress adopted a resolution henceforth to advocate the establishment of 'the Republic of Taiwan', and urged the Government to declare the island's independence.

Elections to the new 405-member National Assembly, which was to be responsible for amending the Constitution, were held in December 1991. The 225 seats open to direct election were widely contested. The campaign was dominated by the issue of Taiwan's possible independence. The opposition's independence proposal was overwhelmingly rejected by the electorate, the DPP suffering a humiliating defeat. The KMT secured a total of 318 seats (179 of which were won by direct election), while the DPP won 75 seats (41 by direct election). All elderly mainland-elected delegates were obliged to relinquish their seats. In February 1992 20,000 demonstrators protested against the sedition laws and demanded a referendum on the issue of independence.

In March 1992, at a plenary session of the KMT Central Committee, it was agreed to reduce the President's term of office from six to four years. The principal question of arrangements for future presidential elections, however, remained unresolved. In April street demonstrations were organized by the DPP to support demands for direct presidential elections. In May the National Assembly adopted eight amendments to the Constitution, one of which empowered the President to appoint members of the Control Yuan.

Meanwhile, the radical dissident, (Stella) Chen Wan-chen, who had established the pro-independence Organization for Taiwan Nation-Building upon her return from the USA in 1991, was sentenced to 46 months' imprisonment in March 1992, having been found guilty of 'preparing to commit sedition'. In May, however, Taiwan's severe sedition law was amended, non-violent acts ceasing to be a criminal offence. Several independence activists were released from prison and other dissidents were able to return from overseas exile. Nevertheless, in June (George) Chang Tsang-hung, the chairman of the banned, US-based World United Formosans for Independence (WUFI), who had returned from exile in the USA in December 1991, received a prison sentence of five (commuted from 10) years upon conviction on charges of sedition and attempted murder, involving the dispatch of letter-bombs to government officials in 1976. Chang was released for medical treatment in October 1992. In March 1993 he was acquitted of the sedition charges, on the grounds of insufficient evidence.

Taiwan's first full elections since the establishment of Nationalist rule in 1949 were held in December 1992. The KMT retained 102 of the 161 seats in the Legislative Yuan. The DPP, however, garnered 31% of the votes and more than doubled its representation in the legislature, winning 50 seats. Following this set-back, the Premier and the KMT Secretary-General resigned. In February 1993 Lien Chan, hitherto Governor of Taiwan Province, became the island's first Premier of Taiwanese descent.

In May 1993 about 30 conservative rebels resigned from the KMT, and formed the New Alliance Nationalist Party. Furthermore, in June the Government was defeated in the Legislative Yuan, when a group of KMT deputies voted with the opposition to approve legislation on financial disclosure requirements for elected and appointed public officials. The unity of the KMT was further undermined in August, when six dissident legislators belonging to the New Kuomintang Alliance, which had registered as a political group in March, announced their decision to leave the ruling party in order to establish the New Party (NP). Nevertheless, in August 1993, at the 14th KMT Congress, Lee Teng-hui was re-elected Chairman of the party. A new 31-member Central Standing Committee and 210-member Central Committee, comprising mainly Lee's supporters, were selected. In a conciliatory gesture by the KMT Chairman, four vice-chairmanships were created, the new positions being filled by representatives of different factions of the party.

In September 1993, following a series of bribery scandals, the Executive Yuan approved measures to combat corruption. The administrative reform plan included stricter supervision of public officials and harsher penalties for those found guilty of misconduct. In the same month a KMT member of the Legislative Yuan was sentenced to 14 years' imprisonment for bribery of voters during the 1992 election campaign; similar convictions followed. At local government elections held in November 1993, although its share of the votes declined, the KMT secured 15 of the 23 posts at stake. The DPP, which accused the KMT of malpractice, won only six posts, despite receiving a substantial proportion of the votes; it retained control of Taipei County. Following allegations of extensive bribery at further local polls in early 1994 (at which the DPP and independent candidates made strong gains), the Ministry of Justice intensified its campaign against corruption. Proposals for constitutional amendments to permit the direct election in 1996 of the Taiwanese President by popular vote (rather than by electoral college) and to limit the powers of the Premier were approved by the National Assembly in July 1994.

At gubernatorial and mayoral elections in December 1994 the DPP took control of the Taipei mayoralty, in the first such direct polls for 30 years, while the KMT succeeded in retaining the provincial governorship of Taiwan, in the first ever popular election for the post, and the mayoralty of Kaohsiung. The NP established itself as a major political force, its candidate for the mayoralty of Taipei receiving more votes than the KMT incumbent.

In March 1995, following the President's formal apology at a ceremony of commemoration in February, the Legislative Yuan approved a law granting compensation to the relatives of the victims of a massacre by Nationalist troops in 1947 (the 'February 28 Incident'), in which an estimated 18,000 native Taiwanese had been killed.

Elections to the Legislative Yuan were held on 2 December 1995. A major campaign issue was that of corruption, allegations of malpractice and indictments having reached alarming levels. The KMT's strength declined to 84 of the 164 seats, the party faring particularly badly in Taipei. The DPP increased its representation to 53 seats. The NP, which favoured reconciliation with the mainland, secured 21 seats. The first direct presidential election was scheduled for March 1996, to coincide with the National Assembly polls. President Lee had declared his intention to stand for re-election in August 1995. There were a number of other candidates for the presidency. The campaign was dominated by the issue of reunification with the mainland. In mid-March a DPP demonstration on the streets of Taipei, in support of demands for Taiwan's independence, was attended by

50,000 protesters. At the presidential election, held on 23 March 1996, the incumbent President Lee received 54.0% of the votes cast, thus securing his re-election for a four-year term. At the concurrent elections for the National Assembly, the KMT took 183 of the 334 seats. The DPP won 99 seats and the NP 46 seats. The Chairman of the DPP, Shih Ming-teh, resigned and Hsu Hsin-liang, who had resigned in November 1993, subsequently returned to the post.

In June 1996 the President's announcement of the composition of the new Executive Yuan aroused much controversy. Although several members retained their previous portfolios, the President (apparently under pressure from within the KMT and disregarding public concern at the rising levels of corruption and organized crime) demoted the popular Ministers of Justice, and of Transportation and Communications, who had exposed malpractice and initiated campaigns against corruption. Other changes included the replacement of the Minister of Foreign Affairs by John Chang, the grandson of Chiang Kai-shek. The most controversial nomination, however, was the reappointment as Premier of Lien Chan, despite his recent election as the island's Vice-President. As fears of a constitutional crisis grew, opposition members of the Legislative Yuan, along with a number of KMT delegates, demanded that the President submit the membership of the Executive Yuan to the legislature for approval, and threatened to boycott the chamber.

In December 1996 the multi-party National Development Conference (NDC), established to review the island's political system, held its inaugural meeting. The convention approved KMT proposals to abolish the Legislative Yuan's right to confirm the President's choice of Premier, to permit the legislature to introduce motions of no confidence in the Premier and to empower the President to dismiss the legislature. The Provincial Governor, (James) Soong Chu-yu, subsequently tendered his resignation in protest at the NDC's recommendations that elections for the provincial governorship and assembly be abolished, as the first stage of the dissolution of the provincial apparatus. The Provincial Government was responsible for the entire island, with the exception of the cities of Taipei and Kaohsiung. In January 1997 President Lee refused to accept the Governor's resignation, but the affair drew attention to the uneasy relationship between the island's President and its Governor, and brought to the fore the question of reunification with the mainland. In July the National Assembly approved a series of constitutional reforms, implementing the NDC's recommendations.

In early May 1997 more than 50,000 demonstrators, protesting against the problem of increasing crime (particularly crimes of violence), demanded the resignation of President Lee. Three members of the Executive Yuan subsequently resigned. The appointment of Yeh Chin-feng as Minister of the Interior (the first woman to oversee Taiwan's police force) did little to appease the public, which remained highly suspicious of the alleged connections between senior politicians and the perpetrators of organized crime. In mid-May thousands of protesters, despairing of the rapid deterioration in social order, again took to the streets of Taipei, renewing their challenge to President Lee's leadership and demanding the immediate resignation of Premier Lien Chan. In late June a 'Say No to China' rally attracted as many as 70,000 supporters.

In August 1997 Vincent Siew, former Chairman of the Council for Economic Planning and Development and also of the Mainland Affairs Council, replaced Lien Chan as Premier (Lien Chan retained the post of Vice-President), and John Chang was appointed Vice-Premier. In the same month President Lee was re-elected unopposed as Chairman of the ruling KMT. The KMT experienced a serious set-back in elections at mayoral and magistrate levels, held in November 1997. The DPP, which had campaigned on a platform of more open government, won 12 of the 23 constituency posts contested, while the KMT achieved only eight posts. Consequently, more than 70% of Taiwan's population was to come under DPP administration. Following the KMT's poor performance in the ballot, the Secretary-General of the party resigned, and was replaced by John Chang. A major reorganization of the party followed.

At local elections held in January 1998, the KMT won an overwhelming majority of the seats contested, while the DPP, in a reversal of fortune, performed badly. In April the Minister of Justice tendered, and then subsequently withdrew, his resignation, claiming that lawmakers with connections to organized crime were exerting pressure on the Government to dismiss him. However, in July he was forced to resign, following his mishandling of an alleged scandal concerning the acting head of the Investigation Bureau.

In June 1998 the first-ever direct election for the leadership of the DPP was held. Lin Yi-hsiung won a convincing victory, assuming the chairmanship of the party in August. Meanwhile, in local elections in June, the KMT suffered a set-back, winning fewer than 50% of the seats contested. Independent candidates performed well. In August 17 new members were elected to the KMT Central Standing Committee, the 16 others being appointed by President Lee.

Elections to the newly expanded 225-member Legislative Yuan took place on 5 December 1998. The KMT won 46.4% of the votes cast, securing 125 seats, the DPP received 29.6% of the votes and won 72 seats, while the pro-unification NP secured only 7.1% of the votes and 11 seats. The New Nation Alliance, a breakaway group from the DPP (formed in September), won only one seat (with 1.6% of the votes cast). The KMT's victory was widely attributed to its management of the economy, in view of the Asian financial crisis, the developments in cross-Straits dialogue and a decline in factionalism within the party in 1998. In the election (held simultaneously) to select the mayor of Taipei, the KMT candidate, Ma Ying-jeou, a popular former Minister of Justice, defeated the DPP incumbent, Chen Shui-bian. However, Frank Hsieh, the DPP candidate, won the office of mayor of Kaohsiung. The KMT retained control of both city councils.

Chiou I-jen resigned as Secretary-General of the DPP in December 1998 and was replaced by Yu Shyi-kun. Later that month Chao Shu-po, a Minister without Portfolio, was appointed Governor of Taiwan Province, replacing the elected incumbent, James Soong, as part of the plans to dismantle the provincial government, agreed in 1997. In March 1999 an unprecedented vote of 'no confidence' in the leadership of Premier Vincent Siew was defeated in the Legislative Yuan. The motion was presented by the opposition following Siew's reversal of his earlier position and his decision to reduce the tax on share transactions, apparently as a result of pressure from President Lee. The National Assembly passed a controversial constitutional amendment on 4 September, which, *inter alia*, extended the terms of the deputies from May 2000 to June 2002. Election to the Assembly was henceforth to be on the basis of party proportional representation. Shortly afterwards, the KMT leadership expelled the Speaker of the National Assembly, Su Nan-cheng, from the party on the grounds that he had violated its policy on the tenure extension, thereby also removing him from his parliamentary seat and the post of Speaker. There was widespread dissatisfaction regarding the National Assembly's action, and in March 2000 the Council of Grand Justices of the Judicial Yuan ruled it to be unconstitutional. Later that month the DPP and the KMT reached an agreement on the abolition of the body and the cancellation of elections scheduled for early May. In April the National Assembly convened, and approved a series of constitutional amendments, which effectively deprived the body of most of its powers, and reduced it to an *ad hoc* institution. The powers to initiate constitutional amendments, to impeach the President or Vice-President and to approve the appointment of senior officials were transferred to the Legislative Yuan. The National Assembly was to retain the functions of ratifying constitutional amendments and impeachment proceedings, in which case 300 delegates, appointed by political parties according to a system of proportional representation, would convene for a session of a maximum duration of one month.

In November 1999 it was announced that a presidential election was to be held in March 2000. Five candidates registered: Lien Chan (with Vincent Siew as candidate for Vice-President) was the KMT nominee, while Chen Shui-bian, a former mayor of Taipei, was to stand for the DPP (with the feminist Annette Lu as vice-presidential candidate), and Li Ao was to represent the NP; the former DPP Chairman, Hsu Hsin-liang, qualified as an independent candidate, as did James Soong who, along with a number of his supporters, was consequently expelled from the KMT, his prospects being jeopardized by charges of embezzlement. In January 2000 Lien Chan, in an attempt to regain the support of disillusioned voters, proposed that the KMT's extensive business holdings be placed in trust and that the party terminate its direct role in the management of the numerous companies in which it owned shares. The KMT adopted the proposal shortly afterwards. In a reflection of the tense political situation between Taiwan and China, Chen Shui-bian of the DPP modified the party's stance

and pledged not to declare formal independence for the island unless Beijing attacked.

The presidential election, held on 18 March 2000, was won by Chen Shui-bian, who obtained 39.3% of the votes cast. James Soong, his closest rival, received 36.8% of the votes. (On the day after the election he founded the People First Party (PFP), in an attempt to take advantage of his popularity.) Lien Chan of the KMT secured only 23.1% of the votes. The remaining candidates obtained less than 1%. The poll attracted a high level of participation, 82.7% of the electorate taking part. (Upon his inauguration in May, Chen would thus become Taiwan's first non-KMT President since 1945.) Violence erupted as disappointed KMT supporters besieged the party's headquarters, attributing the KMT's defeat to the leadership's expulsion of James Soong and the resultant division of the party. Lee Teng-hui subsequently accepted responsibility for the defeat and resigned from the chairmanship of the party. Lien Chan assumed the leadership. As the KMT continued to dominate the Legislative Yuan, however, the party did not entirely relinquish its influence, and in early April gave permission for Tang Fei, a KMT member and hitherto Minister of National Defense, to serve as Premier, although he was to be suspended from party activities while in the post. Following protracted negotiations, the membership of the new Executive Yuan, which incorporated 11 DPP members and 13 KMT members, was approved in early May. The incoming Government largely lacked ministerial experience. Furthermore, the DPP's lack of a legislative majority impeded the passage of favourable legislation. The size of the budget deficit also made it difficult for the DPP to fulfil specific electoral pledges on health, housing and education. In July Frank Hsieh replaced Lin Yi-hsiung as Chairman of the DPP.

In July 2000 the Government was heavily criticized after a river accident in which four workers, stranded by a flash flood, drowned as a result of the authorities' failure to provide a rescue helicopter. While the various government departments deliberated over the allocation of responsibility, the victims' final hours were broadcast live on national television. The Vice-Premier and Chairman of the Consumer Protection Commission, Yu Shyi-kun, subsequently resigned, as did senior officials of the emergency services. The Premier's offer of resignation was refused by President Chen Shui-bian. In October, however, Tang Fei resigned as Premier, ostensibly owing to ill-health. It was suggested his departure from the post was due to the Government's failure to agree upon the fate of Taiwan's fourth nuclear power plant, the DPP being opposed to the project. Vice-Premier Chang Chun-hsiung was appointed Premier, and a minor cabinet reorganization was effected. Changes included the appointment of Yen Ching-chang as Minister of Finance, his predecessor having resigned following a sharp decline in the stock market.

Political disputes over the construction of Taiwan's fourth nuclear power plant intensified later in October 2000. The Minister of Economic Affairs, Lin Hsin-yi, was expelled from the KMT for 'seriously opposing KMT policies and impairing the people's interests' after he had demonstrated his support for the cancellation of the project. At the end of the month Chang Chun-hsiung announced that the Executive Yuan had decided to halt construction of the plant for financial and economic reasons. Although environmentalists were pleased, citing Taiwan's inability to process nuclear waste and to cope with accidents, the KMT reacted furiously, rejecting the Government's right to cancel a project approved by the legislature, and, together with the NP and the PFP, immediately began collecting legislators' signatures for the recall (dismissal) of Chen Shui-bian. The opposition was not mollified by a subsequent apology from Chen, and shortly afterwards the Legislative Yuan passed revised legislation on the process for presidential impeachment. Owing to the controversy, KMT member Vincent Siew refused to act as the President's representative to the annual APEC forum in Brunei in November and was replaced by Perng Fai-nan, the Governor of the Central Bank. The dispute became so serious that the business community issued an unprecedented public message that economic recovery should take priority over political differences, but in December some 10,000 protesters in Taipei demanded that Chen resign. In November the Government requested a constitutional interpretation on the issue from the Council of Grand Justices, which it agreed to be bound by. The Council ruled in mid-January 2001 that the Government should have sought the legislature's approval before halting construction of the plant, and in mid-February the Government decided immediately to resume construction of the plant. In

March a minor government reorganization was effected. The most notable change was the appointment of Hu Ching-piao, hitherto a Minister without Portfolio, as Chairman of the Atomic Energy Council, replacing Hsia Der-yu.

Meanwhile, in September 2000 four retired naval officers and one still serving were arrested in connection with the suspected murder in 1993 of a naval captain, Yin Ching-feng, to prevent him from revealing a scandal surrounding Taiwan's 1991 purchase of French-built frigates. It was alleged that bribery had influenced the award of the contract, which had been abruptly withdrawn from a South Korean firm. In October the Control Yuan impeached three former naval admirals, including the former Commander-in-Chief of the Navy, Adm. (retd) Yeh Chang-tung, for their involvement in the affair. In December the Taiwanese authorities appealed to the French Government for information to assist their investigations. The report of a two-year investigation by the Control Yuan, released in March 2002, strongly criticized the Ministry of National Defense and the navy command for failing to investigate fully Capt. Yin's murder, and recommended the court-martial of Adm. (retd) Yeh and former Prime Minister and Minister of National Defense Hau Pei-tsun.

By March 2001 President Chen had lost popularity within his DPP for softening his stance on two of its key policies—independence for Taiwan and commitment to a nuclear power-free island. Fears emerged that the DPP might lose seats in legislative elections due in December, although opinion polls showed that some 60% of the public supported construction of the nuclear plant. However, polls also showed Chen's popularity to be in decline, with much of the optimism that had greeted his inauguration being replaced with concerns about his inexperience and lack of authority, his handling of the economy and the political gridlock in domestic affairs, as well as the impasse in cross-Straits relations.

Concerns about the economy were heightened in May 2001 when 20,000 demonstrators from 18 trade unions marched in Taipei to protest against the Government's inability to reduce the unemployment rate, which at nearly 4% was at a 16-year high; furthermore, economic growth had declined to its lowest rate in 26 years. Later in the month Chen announced that he was planning to form the island's first coalition government after the December elections, in order to end the political infighting. In late June Chen received a major political boost when former President Lee Teng-hui offered his public support and suggested that he would back Chen in the December elections. Lee had disagreed with KMT leader Lien Chan, and his possible defection to Chen's support base threatened significantly to weaken the KMT. The emerging alliance between the two pro-independence leaders signalled a potential realignment in Taiwanese politics into pro-mainland and pro-independence forces.

Moves toward such a political environment gained momentum in early July 2001, when the KMT issued a policy paper arguing that Taiwan's best option in terms of its relations with China was to form a 'confederation' with the mainland—the furthest that any political party had moved in calling for a union with China. The architect of the new KMT policy, Su Chi, described this as being 'somewhere in the middle ground between independence and unification', although the party had adopted a noticeably more pro-reunification stance under Lien Chan. However, the KMT's Central Standing Committee in late July refrained from adopting the proposal, reflecting the party's uncertainty over mainland policy. In August 2001 a new political party, the Taiwan Solidarity Union (TSU), was formally launched with the support of former President Lee, and consisting of breakaway members of the KMT and DPP, led by the former Minister of the Interior, Huang Chu-wen. The party was formed in an attempt to secure for President Chen a majority in December's elections, an important goal given that the KMT had used its majority to block many of Chen's reforms during the previous one-year period. However, there were fears that the new party would drain support from Chen's DPP. Lee himself was expelled from the KMT in late September for supporting the TSU.

The last months of 2001 were dominated by campaigning for legislative elections The KMT and PFP drew their support from those who had fled the mainland in 1949 and their descendants (approximately 15% of the population), while native Taiwanese (who comprised 65% of the population) supported the DPP and the TSU. Despite the economic recession, Chen's popularity rose in the period prior to the elections, amid rumours that the DPP

would form a coalition to secure a majority. The DPP hoped that a coalition would enable reforms to the legislature, notably the abolition of the multi-member constituencies in favour of a single-seat, 'first-past-the-post' system, thereby ending the need for candidates from the same party to compete against each other.

At the elections held on 1 December 2001 the DPP emerged as the biggest single party in the new legislature, having won 36.6% of the votes cast and 87 seats, but failed to win a majority. The KMT won 31.3% of votes and 68 seats, thereby losing its dominance of the Legislative Yuan for the first time in its history. The PFP came third, winning 20.3% of the votes and 46 seats, while the newly formed TSU came fourth, with 8.5% of the votes and 13 seats. The NP won only 2.9% of the votes and one seat, while independents took nine seats. The level of voter participation was registered as 66.2%.

In the immediate aftermath of the elections, political manoeuvring to establish a coalition began, as the DPP and KMT sought to have their candidate elected as Vice-President of the Legislative Yuan. On 21 January 2002 President Chen reorganized the Executive Yuan, appointing his hitherto Secretary-General, Yu Shyi-kun, as Premier. The move was seen as a consolidation of the President's power, aimed at improving his prospects for re-election in 2004; the new Premier was also thought to be a more efficient administrator than his predecessor. Other notable appointments included Chen Shih-meng, hitherto deputy governor of the Central Bank, as the Secretary-General to the President, replacing Yu. Lin Hsin-i, hitherto Minister of Economic Affairs, was appointed Vice-Premier and Chairman of the Council for Economic Planning and Development, Eugene Chien, hitherto Deputy Secretary-General to the President, as Minister of Foreign Affairs, and Gen. Tang Yao-ming, hitherto Chief of the General Staff, as the new Minister of National Defense. Tang was the first native-born Taiwanese to hold the newly augmented defence post in a mainlander-dominated military, and he was to oversee military reforms in early 2002. Lee Yung-san, Chairman of the International Commercial Bank of China, was appointed Minister of Finance, while Lee Ying-yuan, hitherto deputy representative in Washington, DC, was appointed Secretary-General to the Executive Yuan; however, the ministers in charge of mainland and overseas Chinese affairs were retained, suggesting a desire for continuity in relations with China.

In late January 2002 elections were held for provincial city and township councillors. Although the KMT won the largest number of seats in these elections, it failed to expand its popularity on a national level, with the results reflecting the KMT's competent organizational mobilization methods. At the beginning of February an alliance of the KMT and PFP ('pan-blue camp') successfully blocked the DPP-TSU ('pan-green camp') candidate for the post of Vice-President of the Legislative Yuan, electing Chiang Ping-kun of the KMT to that position. At the same time, the incumbent President of the legislature, Wang Jin-pyng of the KMT, was re-elected to his post.

In February 2002 the KMT-PFP alliance immediately challenged the new Government by attempting to force it to accept revisions to legislation concerning local budget allocations, which had been approved by the outgoing Legislative Yuan in December 2001. However, in the decisive vote in the new Legislative Yuan, the KMT and PFP failed to secure the majority necessary to accomplish this, thereby giving the Government a minor victory. The narrowness of this victory, however, indicated that the KMT continued to pose a formidable obstacle to the new administration. An early set-back for the Government came in late March 2002 when the Minister of Economic Affairs, Christine Tsung, resigned, citing a hostile political environment, particularly in the Legislative Yuan. She was replaced by her deputy, Lin Yi-fu.

A major political scandal erupted in late March 2002 when one daily and one weekly newspaper reported that the Government of former President Lee Teng-hui had, in co-operation with the island's intelligence service (National Security Bureau—NSB), clandestinely established an unauthorized fund worth US $100m. to finance covert operations on the mainland and to further Taiwanese interests among influential lobby groups abroad, including the USA. Prosecutors immediately raided the offices of the two newspapers and seized the offending copies, accusing the editors of revealing state secrets. The scandal threatened to damage Lee's position, as well as jeopardize intelligence-gathering missions on the mainland and Taiwan's reputation for maintaining confidentiality; it was widely believed that the source of the 'leaks' was a former NSB colonel who had embezzled $5.5m. and then fled the island. Following the revelations, President Chen reiterated his commitment to press freedom and proposed new oversights for the NSB.

In early April 2002 the Executive Yuan approved plans to abolish the posts of Speaker and Deputy Speaker of the National Assembly, and replace them with that of a chairman of the session. In early May the Government revealed proposals to reform the electoral system, which would reduce the number of seats in the Legislative Yuan from 225 to 150 and extend the term of legislators from three to four years. Some 90 seats would be filled from single-seat constituencies (thereby eliminating the need for candidates from the same party to compete against each other, as in the existing multi-seat constituencies), with the remaining seats divided proportionally among parties that received more than 5% of the total vote. It was hoped that such reforms would make government more efficient and less dependent upon the availability of finance. A disadvantage of the system of multi-seat constituencies was that it required the participation of larger numbers of candidates and thus greater funding, thereby encouraging corruption.

Also in early May 2002, KMT Chairman Lien Chan announced that his party would form an official alliance with the PFP in order to strengthen opposition to the ruling DPP. However, plans for a joint candidacy in the 2004 presidential elections were hampered by regulations stipulating that the presidential and vice-presidential candidates should belong to the same party. Meanwhile, in mid-May thousands of people demonstrated in favour of changing Taiwan's official name from the 'Republic of China' to 'Taiwan'—an initiative that was supported by 70% of respondents in an opinion poll conducted by the Ministry of Foreign Affairs in 2001.

In mid-June 2002 Premier Yu Shyi-kun appointed Liu Shyh-fang as the first female Secretary-General of the Executive Yuan, replacing Lee Ying-yuan, who was standing as the DPP's candidate in elections for the mayoralty of Taipei, in December. In late July President Chen Shui-bian formally assumed the chairmanship of the DPP, in a move designed to bring party policy into line with the Government. However, critics suggested that the dual leadership style was reminiscent of the excessively strong executive characterized by the decades of KMT rule. In mid-September 2002 the Executive Yuan approved drafts of the new Political Party Law, which would ban political parties from operating or investing in profit-making enterprises, and allow the Government to investigate and confiscate assets unlawfully obtained by political parties. Although ostensibly aimed at creating greater political fairness and financial openness, the draft legislation was viewed as being directed at the KMT which, during the decades of its rule, had amassed a vast commercial fortune worth an estimated NT $53,750m. (US $1,600m.) in 2001. As a result, the KMT would be obliged to sell many of its assets.

A new political dispute emerged in late September 2002 over planned reforms of the debt-ridden agricultural and fishermen's credit co-operatives. The Government sought to reduce the activities of these local financial bodies, which had traditionally been used as a source of funds and influence for local KMT politicians. However, opposition to the reforms from farmers, KMT politicians and also Lee Teng-hui and the TSU was so intense that by late November President Chen was forced to suspend the plans. At the same time, more than 120,000 farmers and fishermen marched through Taipei to protest against the reforms, in what was the largest demonstration on the island since Chen took office. The protesters also demanded the establishment of a new agricultural development fund to alleviate the difficulties caused by Taiwan's entry into the WTO. Premier Yu Shyi-kun offered to resign, but was retained by Chen, who instead accepted the resignations of the Minister of Finance, Lee Yung-san, and the Chairman of the Council of Agriculture, Fan Chen-tsung. They were replaced by Lin Chuan and Lee Chin-lung, respectively. The departure of the respected Lee Yung-san, and the appointment of the third finance minister in as many years, raised concerns about political stability.

Meanwhile, Taiwan's political forces were also increasingly focused on elections for the mayoralties of Taipei and Kaohsiung, which took place in early December 2002, and were widely regarded as a preparation for the 2004 presidential elections. In Taipei the incumbent mayor, Ma Ying-jeou of the KMT, defeated his DPP rival, Lee Ying-yuan, winning 64.1% of the votes cast. Thus, he immediately emerged as a potential presidential candidate. His popularity complicated efforts by the KMT and PFP ('pan-blue camp') to select one of respective party chairmen Lien Chan and James Soong as their joint presidential candidate. In mid-December the two formally committed themselves to this goal. In Kaohsiung the incumbent mayor, Frank Hsieh of the DPP, narrowly defeated his KMT rival Huang Chun-ying, by 50.0% to 46.8% of the votes cast.

In late December 2002–early January 2003 a political scandal in the Kaohsiung City Council embarrassed both the DPP and KMT, when it was alleged that Chu An-hsiung, a businessman and politician, had bribed councillors from both parties in order to secure his election as speaker of the city council. This was the second scandal in Kaohsiung in recent months. In late 2002 it was alleged that a local businesswoman, Su Hui-chen, had bribed officials in the DPP and KMT in order to win favourable treatment for her property company, Zanadau Development. The incidents led to renewed demands for the reform of campaign finance laws, to limit the use of irregular funding in Taiwan's politics.

In January 2003 the release from 'death row' of three men accused of a double murder in 1991 prompted fresh calls for a substantial reform of the judicial system. The men were released on the grounds of insufficient evidence, and human rights activists and lawyers hoped that the case would set a precedent for establishing a clearer burden of proof in future capital cases. New legislation was to take effect from September 2003, which would give a greater role for defence counsels in courts. Also on the agenda were reforms aimed at divesting political parties of their media interests, namely in radio and television stations. During the decades of KMT rule, the party had amassed control or ownership of various media outlets, which the DPP now sought to dismantle.

In early February 2003 President Chen appointed Chiou I-jen, hitherto Secretary-General of the National Security Council, as Secretary-General to the President, while Kang Ning-hsiang, hitherto Vice-Minister of National Defense, succeeded Chiou in his former position. Later that month the leaders of the KMT and PFP again pledged to present a joint candidate for the presidency of Taiwan in 2004, with Lien Chan ostensibly the presidential candidate, and Soong as his running mate.

Following the outbreak of SARS in early 2003, in April the Executive Yuan issued a bill containing urgent measures to prevent the spread of the disease, including restrictions on travel between Taiwan and Hong Kong. In May the Taiwanese Minister of Health, Twu Shiing-jer, resigned over the SARS crisis, and the Legislative Yuan announced that US $3,100m. would be spent on combating the effects of the disease, which by June had killed more than 80 people on the island. The epidemic was under control by mid-2003.

The issue of Taiwan's very identity came to the fore once again in early September 2003, when as many as 150,000 independence activists, led by former President Lee Teng-hui, rallied in Taipei to demand that the island's name be formally changed from 'Republic of China' to 'Taiwan'. The continued use of the former had remained the source of much international confusion and diplomatic tensions, and it was believed that the adoption of 'Taiwan' would facilitate wider diplomatic recognition. On the following day a rival rally, attended mainly by descendants of Chiang Kai-shek and veterans of the civil war (who continued to favour eventual reunification with the mainland), attracted several thousand supporters. The two rallies highlighted divisions on the island over the issue of Taiwanese independence. Also in September, President Chen made proposals for the drafting of a new Taiwanese constitution to replace the operative constitution that had been introduced by Chiang Kai-shek and the KMT, declaring Taiwan to be a part of China. President Chen stated that he wanted a new constitution to be drafted by 2006, then approved by referendum and enacted by 2008. Furthermore, in October 2003 around 1,000 people, mostly ex-servicemen, gathered to commemorate Soong Mei-ling (the widow of Chiang Kai-shek), following her death in the US city of New York.

In November 2003 Taiwan's legislature passed a new law to allow referendums to be held on the island, prompting strong criticism from China (see above). The approval of the legislation came shortly after President Chen formally declared his intention to stand for re-election in the March 2004 presidential election. In December 2003 President Chen announced plans to hold a referendum on the issue of China's deployment of missiles against Taiwan (see above), to coincide with the forthcoming presidential poll. Also in December 2003, President Chen confirmed that Vice-President Annette Lu, a vocal supporter of

Taiwanese independence, would stand alongside him in the presidential election. Opposition presidential candidate Lien Chan and vice-presidential candidate James Soong, of the KMT and of the allied PFP respectively, as well as the popular mayor of Taipei, Ma Ying-jeou of the KMT, voiced strong opposition to the proposed referendum. In February 2004 popular demonstrations involving more than 70,000 people took place in southern Taiwan in support of the referendum, amid demands for China's removal of the missiles targeted at the island. At the end of February, in Taiwan's largest ever demonstration, an estimated 1.5m. people formed a 500-km 'human chain', linking hands across the island to protest against China's deployment of missiles. Meanwhile, the wording of the referendum question had been modified to ask voters whether, in the event of China's refusal to withdraw its missiles, they would favour a strengthening of Taiwan's defence system.

In a dramatic development on the day prior to the presidential election, scheduled for 20 March 2004, while campaigning in Tainan both President Chen and Vice-President Lu were wounded in a shooting incident. Neither was critically injured in the apparent assassination attempt, and the poll proceeded as planned. President Chen was re-elected by a narrow margin of 29,518 votes, equivalent to only 0.2% of valid votes, with 337,297 ballot papers being declared invalid. A turn-out of 80.28% of the electorate was recorded. In the concurrent referendum on the issue of Taiwan's response to the deployment of mainland missiles, however, the majority of citizens declined to vote on President Chen's proposals, thus indicating widespread division within Taiwan on the issue of the island's relationship with China. President Chen's re-election was immediately challenged by opposition candidate Lien Chan, who claimed that there had been irregularities in the electoral process, and demanded a recount of the votes. Supporters of Lien rioted in Taipei and other cities. There was also some speculation that the assassination attempt on President Chen had been deliberately staged in order to further his election prospects. Ballot papers were subsequently reported to have been seized by the judicial authorities. President Chen's re-election was none the less officially confirmed by Taiwan's Central Election Commission, amid further protests by supporters of Lien Chan.

In early April 2004 Minister of the Interior Yu Cheng-hsien resigned, citing the failure to prevent the shooting of Chen during the election campaign as the reason for his departure. In the same month, in a separate development, Minister of Foreign Affairs Eugene Y. H. Chien resigned in connection with the resignation of the head of the American Institute in Taiwan (see below). A recount of votes cast in the presidential election was completed on 19 May. It was estimated that 38,000 ballots were controversial, and that of these 23,000 were votes for Chen. This conclusion was not likely to reverse Chen's re-election, however; in addition to the controversial ballots, there remained unanswered questions surrounding the apparent attempt to assassinate Chen on the day before his re-election. In July US forensic expert Henry Lee, who had been investigating the shooting, stated that the truth about the incident might never be established, although the likelihood that the attack had been staged was reportedly believed to be minimal. Also in July remarks by Vice-President Annette Lu suggesting a resettlement of Taiwan's aboriginal communities to South America caused widespread offence among the island's indigenous population. Meanwhile, President Chen was inaugurated for his second term on 20 May, despite ongoing controversy over the election result, and on the same day he announced appointments to the new Executive Yuan. Yu Shyi-kun was retained as Premier. In June the Executive Yuan approved a special defence budget of NT $610,800m. for the purchase of weapons from the USA (first agreed in 2001). In July a new political party, the pro-independence Formosa Party, was inaugurated. In the same month it was announced that the remains of former President Chiang Kai-shek would be permanently buried in Taiwan, despite his wish to be buried on the mainland. In August the Legislative Yuan approved a bill on constitutional changes, which included plans for a reduction in the number of legislators and for reform of the electoral system. Also in August there was controversy surrounding the establishment of an independent committee to investigate the March shooting of President Chen, with the President of the Judicial Yuan claiming that the investigatory powers being given to this body were unconstitutional. In September protests took place in Taipei against the proposed special budget for the purchase of US weapons, which had been approved by the Executive Yuan in June. Protesters

feared that the purchase would exacerbate tensions with mainland China and also objected to the Government's plan to finance the weapons by privatizing state assets, claiming that the money should instead be spent on public welfare. In October observers speculated that continuing public opposition to the defence budget was likely to deter the Legislative Yuan from approving the weapons purchase plan.

In an election to the Legislative Yuan held in December 2004 the pan-green alliance, consisting of the DPP and the TSU, secured 101 seats, whereas the pan-blue alliance, comprising the KMT, the PFP and NP, secured 114 seats. The resulting opposition majority in the legislature was expected to hinder President Chen's proposals on constitutional changes and on relations with mainland China. President Chen resigned as DPP Chairman after the election, taking responsibility for the party's failure to gain a larger number of seats. Meanwhile, disputes over the legitimacy of President Chen's victory in March continued, with a High Court rejecting two opposition attempts, in November and December respectively, to nullify the presidential election result. The case was expected to be brought before the Supreme Court. There was a suggestion during 2004 of a merger between the KMT and the PFP, with plans for this being announced in advance of President Chen's inauguration in May; however, in December PFP Chairman James Soong stated that such a merger was no longer a possibility. Following the DPP's disappointing election performance in December, there was speculation that instead a coalition between the PFP and the DPP might be formed.

In January 2005 the Executive Yuan approved a draft amendment to the referendum law (see above), requiring any changes to Taiwan's boundaries to be approved by the population. This was seen by some as an attempt to counter the anti-secession law introduced by the Standing Committee of China's NPC in late 2004 (see above). Later in January Premier Yu Shyi-kun and all ministers of the Executive Yuan resigned prior to the first meeting of the new Legislative Yuan, according to tradition. President Chen subsequently appointed Frank Hsieh, Mayor of Kaohsiung and a leading member of the DPP, as Premier. New government appointments were made later in the month. Also in January Secretary-General Su Tseng-chang was appointed Chairman of the DPP, replacing Chen.

In foreign relations, meanwhile, in January 1979 Taiwan suffered a serious set-back when the USA established full diplomatic relations with the People's Republic of China and severed relations with Taiwan. The USA also terminated the 1954 mutual security treaty with Taiwan. Commercial links are still maintained, however, and Taiwan's purchase of armaments from the USA has remained a controversial issue. In August 1982 a joint Sino-US communiqué was published, in which the USA pledged to reduce gradually its sale of armaments to Taiwan. In September 1992 President George Bush announced the sale of up to 150 F-16 fighter aircraft to Taiwan. The announcement was condemned by the People's Republic. In December the US trade representative became the first senior US government official to visit the island since 1979. In September 1994 the USA announced a modification of its policy towards Taiwan, henceforth permitting senior-level bilateral meetings to be held in US government offices. In December the US Secretary of Transportation visited the Ministry of Foreign Affairs in Taipei, the first US official of cabinet rank to visit Taiwan for more than 15 years. In June 1995 President Lee was permitted to make a four-day unofficial visit to the USA, where he gave a speech at Cornell University, and met members of the US Congress. This visit provoked outrage in Beijing, and the Chinese ambassador to Washington was recalled. During 1996 the Taiwanese Vice-President was granted transit visas permitting him to disembark in the USA on a number of occasions.

In March 1996, as the mainland began a new series of missile tests off the Taiwanese coast (see above), the USA stationed two naval convoys in waters east of the island, representing the largest US deployment in Asia since 1975. The sale of defensive weapons to Taiwan was agreed. In September 1996 President Lee and the US Deputy Treasury Secretary met in Taipei for discussions, the most senior-level contact between the two sides since 1994. In late 1996, however, Taiwanese donors were implicated in reported irregularities in the financing of President Clinton's re-election campaign and in a large illicit contribution to the US Democratic Party. In early 1997 the first of the Patriot anti-missile air defence systems, purchased from the USA under an arrangement made in 1993, were reported to have been deployed on the island. The first of the F-16s were delivered to Taiwan in April 1997. The Taiwanese Government expressed satisfaction at the USA's continued commitment to Taiwan's security, confirmed following the visit to the USA of the President of the People's Republic, Jiang Zemin, in October and again in June 1998, during President Clinton's visit to the People's Republic. However, a statement by Clinton affirming that the USA would not support Taiwan's membership of the UN was sharply criticized in Taiwan. In late October 1998 the Taiwanese Chief of Staff, Gen. Tang Fei, made a secret two-week visit to the USA. This was regarded as an extremely sensitive matter, in view of the fact that the SEF Chairman had recently met with Jiang Zemin. In the following month the People's Republic complained to the USA following the US Energy Secretary's visit to Taiwan.

In January 1999 the People's Republic was angered by Taiwan's proposed inclusion in the US-led TMD system (see above). Tensions continued throughout the year, and in August the USA reaffirmed its commitment to defend Taiwan against Chinese military action. In the following month, however, the USA again refused to support Taiwan's application for UN membership. In October of that year the island welcomed the adoption, albeit in modified form, of the Taiwan Security Enhancement Act (TSEA), establishing direct military ties, by the International Relations Committee of the US House of Representatives, despite opposition from the Clinton Administration. Reaction from the People's Republic was unfavourable, and its displeasure increased in early February 2000 when the House of Representatives overwhelmingly approved the Act. In April of that year the US Senate postponed consideration of the Act at the behest of the Taiwanese President-elect, Chen Shui-bian, in order not to antagonize Beijing during the sensitive period preceding his inauguration. In the same month the US Government announced that it had decided to defer the sale of four naval destroyers to Taiwan, although it was prepared to supply long-range radar and medium-range air-to-air missiles. In September the USA granted a transit visa to Taiwanese Vice-President Annette Lu to stay in New York en route to Central America. Lu subsequently declared that the stopover had marked a breakthrough in talks between the USA and Taiwan. In October China was angered by a resolution passed by the US Congress supporting Taiwan's participation in the UN and other international organizations.

The election of George W. Bush to the US Presidency in late 2000 was widely expected to boost US-Taiwan relations at the expense of the USA's relations with the mainland, since Bush had used uncompromising rhetoric against the latter in his election campaign. This became more apparent after the crisis over the detention of a US reconnaissance plane and its crew following its collision with a Chinese fighter aircraft on 1 April 2001 (see the chapter on the People's Republic of China). Following that incident, in late April the USA agreed to sell Taiwan armaments worth a total of US $4,000m., consisting of navy destroyers, anti-submarine aircraft, diesel submarines, amphibious assault vehicles, and surface-to-air missiles and torpedoes, all of which would substantially bolster the island's defences. However, the USA stopped short of selling Taiwan an advanced combat-radar system, for fear of provoking Beijing. At the same time President Bush declared that the USA would do whatever was necessary to defend Taiwan, in the event of an invasion by mainland forces. Beijing was further angered by the visit of President Chen Shui-bian to the USA in late May 2001, when he met business leaders and members of the US Congress. Chen's visit was followed by that of his predecessor, Lee Teng-hui, in late June, as well as by a group of Taiwanese military and intelligence officials on an exchange programme, the first such exchange since 1979. Also in June, Taiwan successfully tested its US-made 'Patriot' air defence missiles for the first time.

In late August 2001 two US Navy aircraft carrier battle groups staged a one-day exercise in the South China Sea coinciding with Chinese military exercises in the Taiwan Straits, a further reminder that the USA was committed to protecting Taiwan. In October the Minister of National Defense, Wu Shih-wen, began finalizing the purchase of the naval destroyers offered earlier in the year, and the USA also offered Taiwan anti-tank missiles. In December the US House of Representatives approved the 2002 Defense Authorization Act, which included weapons sales to Taiwan and the promise of US help in acquiring submarines.

In January 2002 the Bush Administration rejected demands by a former US State Department official, Richard Holbrooke, that a fourth communiqué on US-Taiwan relations was needed,

stating that the existing 1982 communiqué was satisfactory. At the same time, a delegation from a US 'think tank', consisting of retired generals and officials, visited the mainland, and subsequently Taiwan, where they met President Chen and other senior officials and discussed the island's security. Also in January, Vice-President Annette Lu made a brief stopover in New York, en route to South America, and former President Lee Teng-hui announced that he planned to visit the USA in May to raise Taiwan's profile. During his visit to Beijing in late February 2002, President Bush pledged to adhere to the 1979 Taiwan Relations Act—the first time a US President had stated this in China itself.

There were indications that the USA's long-standing 'strategic ambiguity' regarding Taiwan was gradually coming to an end in early 2002. In mid-March the Minister of National Defense, Gen. (retd) Tang Yao-ming visited the USA to attend a private three-day defence and security conference in Florida, where he met the US Deputy Secretary of Defense, Paul Wolfowitz, and Assistant Secretary of State James Kelly. During the conference, Wolfowitz reportedly stated that the USA would assist in training Taiwan's military in areas of command and doctrine. Tang was the first incumbent to make a non-transit visit to the USA since 1979, and the event emphasized the increasingly important security links between the two sides. China condemned Tang's visit as interference in its affairs and responded by denying permission for a US warship to visit Hong Kong in April. Meanwhile, the scandal in late March concerning former President Lee Teng-hui's co-operation with the island's intelligence services in secretly establishing an unauthorized fund (see below) embarrassed Taiwan and several US lobbying groups, which had received sums of this money. Lee subsequently postponed his planned visit to the USA. In mid-April, however, the US Under-Secretary of Commerce for International Trade, Grant Aldonas, became the highest-ranking official of George W. Bush's Administration to visit Taiwan, where he met Chen Shui-bian. The latter proposed the establishment of a free-trade pact with the USA and Japan.

Reflecting the occasional political aspects of commercial relations with the USA, in September 2002 the Taiwanese Government urged the state-owned airline, CAL, to place a US $2,000m. order for 12 aircraft for its fleet with Boeing (of the USA) rather than the rival European-manufactured Airbus. However, in October CAL awarded the contract to Airbus, while also purchasing 10 Boeing aircraft for cargo and long-haul routes. Also in September 2002, the US Congress approved the Foreign Relations Authorization Act, Fiscal Year 2003, which for the first time allowed staff of the US State Department and other government agencies to work at the American Institute in Taiwan, the unofficial US mission to the island. Previously, US officials were required to embark upon sabbatical leave before serving at the institute. US military officers would also be allowed to work there, albeit not in uniform. The bill also recognized Taiwan as a major non-NATO ally of the USA, and served to strengthen US-Taiwanese relations.

President Chen in early January 2003 noted that only nine members of the US Congress had visited Taiwan during 2002, the lowest number in 20 years, and far fewer than the number visiting mainland China. Also in January 2003, the USA was considering participating in Taiwan's annual military exercises. In mid-February the Vice-Minister of National Defense, Chen Chao-min (who had succeeded Kang), attended a defence industry meeting in San Antonio, Texas, which was also attended by several US defence officials. In March a US delegation, led by Pentagon official Mary Tighe, visited Taipei to assess Taiwan's defence capability in the event of a Chinese missile attack. In mid-May the first round of Taiwan's 19th Hankuang military exercises took place. The US delegation sent to observe these exercises was reported to have been the largest ever, and included senior officials from the US Department of Defense.

In August 2003 plans for Taiwan's purchase of four new Kidd-class destroyers from the USA, first discussed in September 2002, were finalized. Taiwan also made an advance payment towards the acquisition of eight new diesel-submarines from the USA, which had been agreed in June 2002. Also in August, again reflecting the political influences on Taiwan's trade relations with the USA, CAL purchased 12 aircraft engines from US company General Electric, rejecting an alternative purchase from European company Rolls-Royce. At the end of August the USA expressed concern that China's increased military capability could pose a threat to Taiwan and reaffirmed US willingness to sell weapons to Taipei. At the same time, the Taiwanese Ministry of National Defense stated that its budget for 2005 would include special funds for the purchase of US-made Patriot PAC-3 anti-missile weaponry. Taiwan conducted further large-scale military exercises in early September.

In November 2003 President Chen made a visit to New York, in the course of which he was permitted to make a public speech. However, during a visit by Chinese Premier Wen Jiabao to Washington, DC, in December the Bush Administration appeared to support China's opposition to referendum plans in Taiwan, reaffirming its 'one China' policy and opposing any unilateral decision by either China or Taiwan to change the status quo. In January 2004 President Chen attempted to placate US concerns over his proposed referendum on Chinese missiles (see above) by suggesting that the referendum might be presented as an opportunity to reduce tensions between Taiwan and mainland China.

In April 2004 Therese Shaheen, head of the American Institute in Taiwan, resigned after reportedly having misrepresented US policy on Taiwanese independence. Her departure prompted the resignation of Taiwan's Minister of Foreign Affairs, Eugene Y. H. Chien. In June the Executive Yuan approved a special defence budget for the purchase of weapons from the USA, which had been agreed in April 2001 (see above). In October 2004 comments made in Beijing by US Secretary of State Colin Powell, suggesting that Taiwan was not an independent country and that it would eventually be reunified with China, caused concern on the island. Following public opposition in Taiwan to a special defence budget for purchase of US weapons (see above), the USA warned that there would be serious implications if the armaments purchase was not approved by the Legislative Yuan.

Taiwan severed diplomatic relations with Japan in 1972, following Tokyo's *rapprochement* with Beijing. Mainland displeasure was compounded in February 1993, however, when, for the first time in two decades, the Taiwanese Minister of Foreign Affairs paid a visit to Japan. In September 1994 pressure from Beijing resulted in the withdrawal of President Lee's invitation to attend the forthcoming Asian Games in Hiroshima. Instead, however, the Taiwanese Vice-Premier was permitted to visit Japan. Similarly, in July 1995 Japan announced that the Taiwanese Vice-Premier would not be permitted to attend a meeting of APEC members to be held in Osaka in November. Instead, President Lee was represented by Koo Chen-fu, the SEF Chairman. The latter also attended the APEC meeting in the Philippines in November 1996. At the Kuala Lumpur APEC summit in November 1998 President Lee was represented by a Minister without Portfolio, Chiang Ping-kun, who also attended the 1999 APEC conference, held in September in Auckland, New Zealand. Perng Fai-nan, the Governor of the Central Bank, represented President Chen Shui-bian at the APEC meeting in Brunei in November 2000.

In 1996 Taiwan's relations with Japan continued to be strained by the issue of adequate compensation for the thousands of Asian (mostly Korean) women used by Japanese troops for sexual purposes during the Second World War. In October Taiwan rejected a Japanese offer of nominal compensation for Taiwanese women. Relations deteriorated further during 1996 on account of a dispute relating to a group of uninhabited islets in the East China Sea: known as the Tiaoyutai (Diaoyu Dao) in Chinese, or Senkaku in Japanese, the islands were claimed by Taiwan, China and Japan. In July, following the construction of a lighthouse on one of the islands by a Japanese right-wing group, the Taiwanese Ministry of Foreign Affairs lodged a strong protest over Japan's decision to incorporate the islands within its 200-mile (370-km) exclusive economic zone. In early October further discussions with Japan on the question of Taiwanese fishing rights within the disputed waters ended without agreement. In the same month a flotilla of small boats, operated by activists from Taiwan, Hong Kong and Macao, succeeded in evading Japanese patrol vessels. Having reached the disputed islands, protesters raised the flags of Taiwan and of China. In May 1997 the Taiwanese Minister of Foreign Affairs expressed grave concern, following the landing and planting of their national flag on one of the disputed islands by a Japanese politician and three aides. A number of protesters and journalists from Taiwan and Hong Kong set sail from the port of Shenao, ostensibly to participate in an international fishing contest. They were intercepted by Japanese coastguard vessels and failed to gain access to the islands. Reports in October that Japanese patrol boats were forcibly intercepting Taiwanese fishing vessels were a further cause for concern for the Taiwa-

nese authorities. There was a significant development in relations between the two countries in November 1999, when the Governor of Tokyo paid an official visit to Taiwan, the most senior Japanese official to do so since the severing of diplomatic relations. The People's Republic condemned the visit, claiming that it undermined Sino-Japanese relations. The former President of Taiwan, Lee Teng-hui, made a private visit to Japan in late April 2001, ostensibly for medical treatment. In order to minimize tensions with Beijing, the Japanese authorities forbade Lee from making political statements while in Japan. In March 2002 it was revealed that Japanese politicians, including former Prime Minister Ryutaro Hashimoto, had received money from an unauthorized fund established by Lee in order to procure influence in Japan. However, the incident failed to damage bilateral relations, and in late 2001–early 2002 officials from both sides were investigating the possibility of establishing a free-trade agreement. In November 2002 the Japanese Government refused Lee a visa to visit Keio University, which subsequently withdrew its invitation for him to deliver a speech there. In January 2003 Taiwan, along with China, condemned Japan's moves to assert sovereignty over the Tiaoyutai islands in the East China Sea by renting them out to private companies. In May Japan's Minister of Foreign Affairs allegedly told a Chinese official that Japan supported Taiwan's bid to join WHO with observer status. Discussions on a free-trade agreement between Japan and Taiwan remained unresolved in 2003; this was thought to have been due partly to China's opposition to such an agreement. In September 2003 the second Taiwan-Japan Forum opened in Tokyo, at which issues of mutual concern were discussed.

In March 1989, meanwhile, President Lee paid a state visit to Singapore, the first official visit overseas by a President of Taiwan for 12 years. In a further attempt to end diplomatic isolation, Lee said that he would visit any foreign country, even if it maintained diplomatic relations with Beijing. In January 1993 official confirmation of Taiwan's purchase of 60 Mirage fighter aircraft from France provoked strong protest from Beijing. In January 1994 Taiwan suffered a reverse when (following pressure from the People's Republic) France recognized Taiwan as an integral part of Chinese territory and agreed not to sell weapons to the island. In February President Lee embarked upon an eight-day tour of South-East Asia. His itinerary incorporated the Philippines, Indonesia and Thailand, all three of which maintained diplomatic relations with the People's Republic of China. Although the tour was described as informal, President Lee had meetings with the three heads of state, leading to protests from Beijing. In May the Taiwanese President visited Nicaragua, Costa Rica, South Africa (the island's only remaining major diplomatic ally) and Swaziland. In March 1995 it was reported that Taiwan was to purchase shoulder-fired anti-aircraft missiles from a French company, despite France's previous assurances to the People's Republic that it would not sell weapons to Taiwan (the purchase was confirmed in 1996). In April President Lee travelled to the United Arab Emirates and to Jordan. Although accompanied by senior members of the Executive Yuan, the visits were described as private (Taiwan having no diplomatic relations with these countries). In June the Taiwanese Premier visited Austria, Hungary and the Czech Republic, where he had private meetings with his Czech counterpart and with President Václav Havel. Again, the visits provoked strong protest from China.

In August 1996, as Beijing continued to urge Pretoria to sever its diplomatic links with Taipei, Vice-Premier Hsu Li-teh led a delegation of government and business representatives to South Africa. In September, however, the Taiwanese Minister of Foreign Affairs was obliged to curtail an ostensibly private visit to Jakarta (where he was reported to have had discussions with his Indonesian counterpart), following protests from the People's Republic of China. Also in 1996, the first delivery of Mirage aircraft to Taiwan from France (first announced in 1993) took place. At the same time, it was confirmed that France would sell six Lafayette-class frigates to Taiwan (delivery of these was completed in March 1998). In January 1997 the Vice-President was received by the Pope during a visit to the Holy See, the only European state that continued to recognize Taiwan. In the same month the Minister of Foreign Affairs embarked upon a tour of seven African nations, in order to consolidate relations. His itinerary included South Africa, despite that country's recent announcement of its intention to sever diplomatic relations with Taiwan. In March 1997 a six-day visit to Taiwan by the Dalai Lama was strongly condemned by the People's Republic of

China, which denounced a meeting between President Lee and the exiled spiritual leader of Tibet as a 'collusion of splittists'. A second visit by the Dalai Lama, scheduled for July 1998, was postponed, following mainland China's criticism of the opening of a representative office of the Dalai Lama's religious foundation in Taiwan.

In July 1997, following the Bahamas' withdrawal of recognition from Taiwan and establishment of diplomatic relations with the People's Republic of China, the Taiwanese Minister of Foreign Affairs undertook an extensive tour of the countries of Central America and the Caribbean, in an effort to maintain their support. In September, during a tour of Central America (the six nations of the region having become the core of Taiwan's remaining diplomatic allies), President Lee attended an international conference on the development of the Panama Canal. The USA granted a transit visa to the Taiwanese President, enabling him to stop over in Hawaii en route to and from Central America. A visit to Europe in October by Vice-President Lien Chan was curtailed when pressure from Beijing forced the Spanish Government to withdraw an invitation. The Malaysian and Singaporean Prime Ministers met their Taiwanese counterpart in Taiwan in November, on their return from the APEC forum in Canada. The People's Republic expressed concern at the meetings.

In January 1998 the Taiwanese Premier, Vincent Siew, met senior officials during a visit to the Philippines and Singapore. It was believed that discussions had focused on the possibility of Taiwan extending economic assistance to those countries. Moreover, the Taiwanese Government expressed its intention to pursue the creation of a multilateral Asian fund, under the auspices of APEC, to support the ailing Asian economies. Relations with Taiwan's Asian neighbours were further strengthened in February, when a leading member of the KMT visited the Republic of Korea, again, it was understood, to discuss financial assistance in the wake of the Asian economic crisis. Negotiations between the Malaysian Deputy Prime Minister and Finance Minister and the Taiwanese Premier, held in Taiwan in February, also concentrated on economic and financial issues. Vincent Siew made a return visit to Malaysia in April. China was highly critical of these visits, accusing Taiwan of seeking to gain political advantage from the regional economic crisis.

In August 1999 the Taiwanese Government threatened to refuse entry to the island to Philippine labourers in retaliation for Manila's unilateral termination of its aviation agreement with Taipei. In October the Philippine authorities decided to close the country to Taiwanese aircraft. Access was, however, temporarily granted in November during talks on the renewal of the agreement. Negotiations faltered in December, but reached a successful conclusion in early 2000, thus permitting flights to the Philippines to resume. In March, however, the agreement collapsed, and flights were suspended again. In June the Taiwanese Government imposed a three-month ban on new work permits for Philippine nationals, citing interference by the Philippines' representative office in Taiwan concerning labour disputes. Any connection with the aviation dispute was denied. In September a new aviation agreement, enabling flights between Taipei and Manila to restart, was signed.

Following the withdrawal of diplomatic recognition by South Africa, in 1998 Taiwan made extensive efforts to maintain relations with the island's other allies. The Minister of Foreign Affairs visited eight African countries in February, and in April it was announced that Taiwan's overseas aid budget was to be substantially increased, in an attempt to retain diplomatic support. In May the Vice-President, Lien Chan, visited Taiwan's Central American and Caribbean allies. China expressed serious concern in November at New Zealand's decision to grant Taiwanese officials in Wellington privileges accorded to accredited diplomats. Following the loss of four allies during 1998, relations were established with the Marshall Islands in November of that year, and with the former Yugoslav republic of Macedonia in January 1999. The latter rapidly benefited from its contacts with Taiwan, receiving extensive aid following the Kosovo conflict. The Prime Minister of Papua New Guinea initiated diplomatic relations with Taiwan in early July 1999. Following his resignation later that month, recognition was withdrawn from Taiwan, allegedly because of a failure to adhere to correct procedures for the establishment of relations. Full diplomatic relations were established with Palau in December of that year, and Taiwan opened an embassy on the island in March 2000. In August 2000 the new Taiwanese President,

Chen Shui-bian, embarked upon a tour of diplomatic allies in Central America and West Africa. In October Taiwan was concerned that it might lose a diplomatic ally when the Minister of Foreign Affairs of Solomon Islands unexpectedly cancelled a visit to Taipei and travelled instead to Beijing. The Premier of Solomon Islands did not attend a regional forum, instead visiting Taipei to make amends and to reiterate his commitment to maintaining relations. There was speculation that this commitment arose from a need for substantial financial assistance from Taiwan.

In November 2000, after eight years' suspension, the 25th Joint Conference of Korea-Taiwan Business Councils took place in Seoul. It was agreed that henceforth conferences would be held annually alternately in Taipei and Seoul, and Taiwan ultimately hoped for a resumption of ministerial-level discussions on the establishment of bilateral air links. In the same month the European Parliament passed a resolution on strengthening relations with Taiwan, and in December Taiwan and Egypt agreed to exchange representative offices. Also in December, France refused to grant a visa to the Taiwanese Minister of Justice.

Throughout 2001 Taiwan continued to seek a higher diplomatic profile. President Chen in late May began a tour of five Latin American nations—El Salvador, Guatemala, Panama, Paraguay, and Honduras—as part of Taiwan's 'dollar diplomacy'—a practice of giving aid and bringing investment in return for diplomatic recognition. While in El Salvador, Chen met eight regional leaders, who pledged support for Taiwan. Both Taiwan and the People's Republic of China were increasingly bidding for support in this region to boost their overall global standing. Taiwan was also in competition with China for support from Pacific island nations, five of which (Marshall Islands, Nauru, Palau, Solomon Islands and Tuvalu) recognized Taiwan. Two of these nations, Solomon Islands and the Marshall Islands, were thought to be wavering in their support of Taiwan. The Dalai Lama visited Taiwan in March–April 2001 and held talks with President Chen, much to the anger of Beijing. In June the former Yugoslav republic of Macedonia announced that it would recognize the People's Republic of China, thus leading to a break in relations with Taiwan. In November Wu Shu-chen, wife of President Chen, travelled to Strasbourg, France, to accept the 'Prize for Freedom' awarded to her husband by Liberal International, a world grouping of liberal parties. Chen himself had been refused a visa by the European Union (EU).

In January 2002 it was reported that Taiwan had secretly been developing military and intelligence links with India, through mutual co-operation including bilateral visits of military personnel and the exchange of intelligence data. Also in January, Vice-President Lu visited Nicaragua and Paraguay, having visited The Gambia in December 2001. Vice-President Lu also visited Indonesia in mid-August 2002 and met several ministers, but not President Megawati Sukarnoputri, owing to pressure on the latter by Beijing. While in Indonesia, Lu discussed possible liquefied natural gas projects, investment and migrant labour. Taiwanese companies had in previous years invested US $17,000m. in Indonesia, the home of some 100,000 of Taiwan's migrant workers. President Chen completed a four-nation tour of Africa in early July 2002, having visited Senegal, São Tomé and Príncipe, Malawi and Swaziland. While en route to Swaziland, he was refused permission to land in South Africa, Pretoria being concerned not to offend Beijing. Diplomatic relations between Taiwan and Nauru were terminated in late July 2002 after the latter established relations with the People's Republic of China. In September 2002 Taiwan announced the opening of a trade and economic affairs representative office in Mongolia. In late 2002 Taiwan and the Democratic People's Republic of Korea (North Korea) were planning to open economic liaison offices in the respective capitals, the latter keen to attract new sources of investment. President Chen was forced to cancel a trip to Indonesia in December after the South-East Asian country came under heavy pressure from Beijing.

In March 2003 President Chen was again refused a visa by the EU, and was thus unable to address members of the European Parliament in Brussels. Also in March, the Taiwanese Government issued a warning that several Pakistani citizens with links to terrorist networks might be attempting to enter Taiwan. Taiwan expressed concern over the political situation in the West African state of São Tomé and Príncipe following a military coup there in July 2003. There were also concerns in mid-2003 that the violent conflict in Liberia might affect that nation's diplomatic relations with Taiwan, and in October Liberia transferred its recognition to the People's Republic of China, in the hope of obtaining reconstruction aid from Beijing. In August, meanwhile, Taiwan signed a free trade agreement with Panama, which was expected to take effect in January 2004. In November 2003 Kiribati granted diplomatic recognition to Taiwan, and a Taiwanese embassy opened on the Pacific island in January 2004. Also in January, there were tensions in Taiwan's relations with France after French President Jacques Chirac expressed his support for China's opposition to a proposed referendum in Taiwan (see above) during a visit by Chinese President Hu Jintao to Paris. President Chirac declared that the holding of a referendum in Taiwan on the issue of Chinese missiles would be a 'grave mistake'. Following President Chirac's remarks, two state visits by Taiwanese ministers to France were cancelled. Joint military exercises between the French and Chinese navies were held in March 2004 off Taiwan's northern coast. Also in March, Dominica withdrew its diplomatic recognition of Taiwan.

In September 2004 a disparaging remark by the Taiwanese Minister of Foreign Affairs, Chen Tan-sun, relating to the 'tiny country' of Singapore caused widespread offence. Minister Chen's remark was made in response to comments by the Singaporean Minister of Foreign Affairs indicating that pro-independence sentiments in Taiwan were a threat to regional stability. Chen refused to apologize for his remark, stating that the incident was indicative of the intimidation of Taiwan that China was able to provoke.

In November 2004 it was announced that Vanuatu had established diplomatic relations with Taiwan, but the validity of this agreement was disputed both by mainland China and by politicians within the Government of Vanuatu. The status of Vanuatu's diplomatic relations with Taiwan and China remained unresolved at the end of 2004, with some sources having suggested that this might represent an unprecedented dual recognition of both Taiwan and the People's Republic. In January 2005 Grenada re-established diplomatic relations with mainland China and severed its ties with Taiwan. Also in January, President Chen undertook an official visit to Palau, thus becoming the first Taiwanese President to visit the Pacific nation. He also travelled to Solomon Islands, where he strenuously denied accusations of 'money diplomacy', and to the US territory of Guam. A visit to Taipei by the President of the Marshall Islands in late 2004 was to be reciprocated in May 2005.

The question of the sovereignty of the Spratly Islands, situated in the South China Sea and believed to possess petroleum resources, to which five countries as well as Taiwan laid claim, remained unresolved. A contingent of Taiwanese marines is maintained on Taiping Island, the largest of the disputed islands, located some 1,574 km south-west of Taiwan. A satellite telecommunications link between Taiping and Kaohsiung was inaugurated in October 1995. In August 1993 Taiwan announced its intention to construct an airbase on Taiping Island, but in January 1996 the scheme was postponed. In late December 1998 the Legislative Yuan approved the first legal definition of Taiwan's sea borders. The Spratly Islands were claimed, as were the disputed Tiaoyutai Islands, within the 12- and 24-nautical mile zones. In November 2002, in Phnom-Penh, Cambodia, members of the Association of South East Asian Nations (ASEAN, see p. 162) signed a landmark 'declaration on the conduct of parties in the South China Sea', which aimed to avoid conflict in the area. Under this agreement, which was similar to one drafted in late 1999 but not implemented, claimants would practise self-restraint in the event of potentially hostile action (such as inhabiting the islands), effect confidence-building measures and give advance notice of military exercises in the region. However, the agreement did not include the Paracel Islands, and disagreements continued among the signatories on what the accord should encompass. Additionally, China introduced a provision requiring consensus to resolve outstanding issues, thereby allowing for future indecision among ASEAN members. It was unclear how the declaration affected Taiwan, since it was not a member of ASEAN. In August 2003 Minister of the Interior Yu Cheng-hsien visited Taiping Island and reaffirmed Taiwanese sovereignty.

Government

Under the provisions of the amended 1947 Constitution, the Head of State is the President, who is elected by popular vote for a four-year term. There are five Yuans (governing bodies), the highest legislative organ being the Legislative Yuan, to which

the Executive Yuan (the Council of Ministers) is responsible. Following elections in December 2001, the Legislative Yuan comprised 225 members; 168 chosen by direct election, most of the remainder being appointed from separate lists of candidates on the basis of proportional representation. The Legislative Yuan serves a three-year term. There are also Control, Judicial and Examination Yuans. Their respective functions are: to investigate the work of the executive; to interpret the Constitution and national laws; and to supervise examinations for entry into public offices. In April 2000 the role of the National Assembly was revised. The powers to initiate constitutional amendments, to impeach the President or Vice-President, and to approve the appointment of senior officials were transferred to the Legislative Yuan. The National Assembly retained the functions of ratifying constitutional amendments and responsibility for impeachment proceedings, in which case 300 delegates appointed by political parties according to a system of proportional representation were to convene for a session of a maximum duration of one month. The Taiwan Provincial Government handles the general administrative affairs of the island (excluding the cities of Taipei and Kaohsiung). Its policy-making body is the Taiwan Provincial Government Council. In July 1997 the National Assembly approved a series of constitutional amendments, including the suspension of elections at local government level, as the first stage of the dissolution of the provincial apparatus. Accordingly, the elected Governor of Taiwan was replaced by an appointed Governor in December 1998. The Taiwan Provincial Assembly exercises the province's legislative power. The Fukien (Fujian) Provincial Government is responsible for the administration of Quemoy and Matsu.

Defence

In August 2004 the armed forces totalled an estimated 290,000: army 200,000 (with deployments of 15,000–20,000 and 8,000–10,000, respectively, on the islands of Quemoy and Matsu), air force 45,000 and navy 45,000 (including 15,000 marines). Paramilitary forces numbered 26,650. Reserves totalled 1,657,500. The total number of military personnel was reduced during 2002. Military service lasts for 20 months. Projected budgetary defence expenditure for 2004 was estimated at NT $251,000m.

Economic Affairs

In 2003, according to official figures, Taiwan's gross national income (GNI), at current prices, totalled US $295,557m., equivalent to US $13,139 per head. During 1990–2003, it was estimated, the population increased at an average annual rate of 0.8%, while in terms of US dollars real gross domestic product (GDP) per head increased by an average of 3.7% per year. Overall GDP increased, in terms of New Taiwan dollars, at an average annual rate of 7.1% in 1990–1995. The average annual rate of increase in 1995–2003 was 4.1%. Having increased by 3.9% in 2002, GDP increased by 3.3% in 2003.

Agriculture (including hunting, forestry and fishing) contributed 1.7% of GDP in 2003, and employed 6.9% of the labour force. The principal crops are rice, sugar cane, maize, sweet potatoes and pineapples. Agricultural GDP decreased by 0.3%, in real terms, during 1995–2003. Compared with the previous year, agricultural GDP decreased by 0.2% in 2003.

Industry (comprising mining, manufacturing, construction and utilities) employed 33.1% of the labour force, and provided 28.8% of GDP in 2003. Industrial GDP increased, in real terms, at an average rate of 3.2% per year between 1995 and 2003. Compared with the previous year, industrial GDP increased by 4.5% in 2003.

Mining contributed 0.4% of GDP in 2003, and employed less than 0.1% of the labour force. Coal, marble and dolomite are the principal minerals extracted. Taiwan also has substantial reserves of natural gas. The GDP of the mining sector decreased at an average rate of 9.0% per year between 1995 and 2003. Mining GDP decreased by 19.0% in 2003.

Manufacturing contributed 24.2% of GDP in 2003, and employed 25.7% of the labour force. The most important branches, measured by gross value of output, are electronics (particularly personal computers), plastic goods, synthetic yarns and the motor vehicle industry. The sector's GDP grew at an average annual rate of 4.3%, in real terms, in 1995–2003. Manufacturing GDP increased by 5.7% in 2003, compared with the previous year.

In 2003 50.7% of Taiwan's energy supply was derived from imported petroleum. Imports of crude petroleum accounted for 7.5% of total import expenditure in 2003. In that year nuclear power supplied 8.0% of Taiwan's energy requirements.

The services sector contributed 69.4% of GDP in 2003, while engaging 48.1% of the labour force. In 1995–2003 the GDP of this sector increased at an average annual rate of 4.9%. In 2003 services GDP increased by 3.4%, compared with the previous year.

In 2003 Taiwan recorded a visible trade surplus of US $24,899m., and there was a surplus of US $29,202m. on the current account of the balance of payments. In 2003 the principal sources of imports were Japan (accounting for 25.6%) and the USA (13.2%). The principal markets for exports in that year were Hong Kong (19.7%) and the USA (18.0%). Trade with the People's Republic of China (mainly via Hong Kong) is of increasing significance. The value of exports to the People's Republic of China increased from US $9,945.0m. in 2002 to US $21,417.3 in 2003. Taiwan's principal imports in 2003 were electronic products, machinery, mineral products and chemical and related products. The principal exports in that year were electronic products, machinery and electrical and mechanical appliances, textiles, and base metals.

The 2003 budget included revenue of NT $1,319,995m. and expenditure of NT $1,618,913m., the deficit thus being NT $298,918m. In 2004 expenditure was estimated at NT $1,591,570m., while revenue was projected at NT $1,334,723m. At the end of March 2004 Taiwan's long-term external public debt was US $214m. The cost of debt-servicing remained equivalent to a negligible percentage of the value of exports of goods and services. The annual rate of inflation averaged 1.9% during the period 1990–2003. Consumer prices declined by 0.2% in 2002 and by 0.3% in 2003, before rising in 2004. Some 4.31% of the labour force were unemployed in October 2004 (compared with 5.21% a year earlier). There is a shortage of labour in certain sectors.

Taiwan became a member of the Asian Development Bank (ADB, see p. 159) in 1966, and of the Asia-Pacific Economic Co-operation forum (APEC, see p. 155) in late 1991. In September 1992 Taiwan was granted observer status at the General Agreement on Tariffs and Trade (GATT), and was finally granted membership of the successor World Trade Organization (WTO, see p. 357) in November 2001, effective from 1 January 2002.

Taiwan's economic growth since 1949 has been substantial, with its economy usually proving to be very resilient to world recession, owing to the versatility of its manufacturing base and its large reserves of foreign exchange (estimated at US $231,609m. in August 2004). In 2001, however, the economic deceleration in the USA (Taiwan's major export market) adversely affected the island's growth. Exports, normally accounting for approximately 50% of GDP, decreased sharply, with the electronics industry being particularly badly affected, and by late 2001 Taiwan was experiencing its worst recession in 40 years. The level of unemployment rose steadily, despite an extensive government-initiated employment-creation programme, but from late 2002, as economic growth resumed, the rate of unemployment began to decline. In May 2002 the Government announced a new six-year national development plan, Challenge 2008, consisting of US $75,000m. of spending on infrastructure and public construction projects, as well as US $1,440m. in low-interest loans for research and development, and enhanced English-language education to take into account the growth of 'e-commerce' and the internet. One of the largest infrastructure projects in recent years, a US $12,800m. high-speed railway linking Taipei and Kaohsiung, when completed in late 2005, was expected to integrate the island's western seaboard into a single commercial zone, as well as provide technology transfers from its Japanese developers. The national development plan also aimed to create 700,000 new jobs, with a view to keeping average unemployment below 4%, and maintaining GDP growth at above 5%. The Government also hoped that the plan would double the number of tourist visits. Despite such plans, compared with the previous year direct investment from abroad declined by 64.8% in 2002, partly owing to increasing competition from China. Foreign investment decreased again, by 68.7%, in 2003. Furthermore, the

Government feared that the increasing cross-Straits links it had been promoting were causing an excessive outflow of funds to China. Having decreased in 2002, Taiwan's direct investment abroad rose substantially in 2003. The island's privatization programme (first introduced in 1989) continued intermittently, having been delayed by opposition from labour unions and vested interest groups. The Taiwan Salt Company was fully privatized at the end of 2003. In mid-2004 companies scheduled for transfer to the private sector included Chinese Petroleum, China Shipbuilding, Chunghwa Telecom, Taiwan Sugar Corporation, Tang Eng Iron Works and Taiwan Power. From 2002 moves toward a consolidation of the banking and financial sector gathered momentum, as regulatory barriers separating banks, insurance companies and securities firms were removed, following the introduction of a new law in late 2001. In May 2002 the Government announced plans to privatize several state-owned banks by 2006, and sell all its stakes in commercial banks by 2010. Estimates for GDP growth were lowered following the outbreak of Severe Acute Respiratory Syndrome (SARS) in Taiwan in early 2003. From mid-2003, however, the Taiwanese economy recovered rapidly from the effects of SARS, with record growth in exports in the second half of the year. GDP thus expanded by 3.3% in 2003. Despite political tensions, economic links with the People's Republic of China were becoming increasingly significant, with the value of exports to the mainland rising from 7.6% of total exports in 2002 to 14.9% in 2003. In mid-2004 some sources estimated that exports to the mainland amounted to as much as 25% of Taiwan's exports. GDP growth for 2004 was initially projected at 4.7%; however, following strong economic performance in the first half of the year this estimate was later revised to 5.9%. The rate of growth was reported to be decelerating during the second half of 2004, and for 2005 a lower growth rate, of around 4.5%, was predicted.

Education

Education at primary schools and junior high schools is free and compulsory between the ages of six and 15 years. Secondary schools consist of junior and senior middle schools, normal schools for teacher-training and vocational schools. There are also a number of private schools. Higher education is provided in universities, colleges, junior colleges and graduate schools. Total projected budgetary expenditure on education, science and culture in 2004 was NT $306,446m. (equivalent to 19.3% of total projected expenditure). In 2003/04 there were over 1,912,791m. pupils enrolled in state primary schools. There were 1,676,970m. children in secondary schools. There were 158 universities and other institutes of higher education in 2003/04. The adult literacy rate in 2001 was 95.8%.

Public Holidays

2005: 1–2 January (Founding of the Republic/New Year), 9–12 February (Chinese New Year), 5 April (Ching Ming/Tomb-Sweeping Day and Death of President Chiang Kai-shek), 11 June (Dragon Boat Festival), 19 September (Mid-Autumn Moon Festival), 28 September (Teachers' Day/Birthday of Confucius), 10 October (Double Tenth Day, anniversary of 1911 revolution), 25 October (Retrocession Day, anniversary of end of Japanese occupation), 12 November (Birthday of Sun Yat-sen), 25 December (Constitution Day).

2006: 1–2 January (Founding of the Republic/New Year), 29 January–1 February (Chinese New Year), 5 April (Ching Ming/Death of President Chiang Kai-shek), 31 May (Dragon Boat Festival), 28 September (Teachers' Day/Birthday of Confucius), 7 October (Mid-Autumn Moon Festival and Teachers' Day/Birthday of Confucius), 10 October (Double Tenth Day, anniversary of 1911 revolution), 25 October (Retrocession Day, anniversary of end of Japanese occupation), 12 November (Birthday of Sun Yat-sen), 25 December (Constitution Day).

Weights and Measures

The metric system is officially in force, but some traditional Chinese units are still used.

Statistical Survey

Source (unless otherwise stated): Bureau of Statistics, Directorate-General of Budget, Accounting and Statistics (DGBAS), Executive Yuan, 2 Kwang Chow St, Taipei 10065; tel. (2) 23803542; fax (2) 23803547; e-mail sicbs@dgbas.gov.tw; internet www.dgbas.gov.tw.

Area and Population

AREA, POPULATION AND DENSITY

Area (sq km)	36,188*
Population (census results)	
16 December 1990	20,393,628
16 December 2000	
Males	11,386,084
Females	10,914,845
Total	22,300,929
Population (official figures at 31 December)	
2001	22,405,568
2002	22,520,776
2003	22,604,550
Density (per sq km) at 31 December 2003	624.6

* 13,972 sq miles.

PRINCIPAL TOWNS
(population at 31 December 2003)

Taipei (capital) . .	2,627,138	Hsinchu	382,897
Kaohsiung . . .	1,509,350	Taoyuan . . .	357,647
Taichung . . .	1,009,387	Jhongli . . .	339,586
Tainan . . .	749,628	Fongshan . . .	328,878
Banciao . . .	539,356	Sindian . . .	280,661
Jhunghe . . .	406,325	Chiayi . . .	269,594
Keelung . . .	392,242	Jhanghua . . .	233,435
Sanchong . . .	384,618	Yonghe . . .	231,816
Sinjhuang . . .	383,745	Pingdong . . .	216,338

BIRTHS, MARRIAGES AND DEATHS
(registered)

	Live births		Marriages		Deaths	
	Number	Rate (per 1,000)	Number	Rate (per 1,000)	Number	Rate (per 1,000)
1996 . .	325,545	15.18	169,424	7.90	122,489	5.71
1997 . .	326,002	15.07	166,216	7.68	121,000	5.59
1998 . .	271,450	12.43	145,976	6.69	123,180	5.64
1999 . .	283,661	12.89	173,209	7.87	126,113	5.73
2000 . .	305,312	13.76	181,642	8.19	125,958	5.68
2001 . .	260,354	11.65	170,515	7.63	127,647	5.71
2002 . .	247,530	11.02	172,655	7.69	128,636	5.73
2003 . .	227,070	10.06	171,483	7.60	130,801	5.80

Expectation of life (years at birth, 2003): Males 73.4; Females 79.1.

ECONOMICALLY ACTIVE POPULATION
(annual averages, '000 persons aged 15 years and over)*

	2001	2002	2003
Agriculture, forestry and fishing .	706	709	696
Mining and quarrying	10	9	8
Manufacturing	2,587	2,563	2,590
Construction	746	725	702
Electricity, gas and water . . .	35	35	35
Trade, hotels and restaurants . .	2,207	2,268	2,283
Transport, storage and communications	487	477	484
Finance, insurance and real estate	432	438	442
Professional and technical services	267	285	285
Social, personal and related community services	918	950	988
Public administration	327	329	369
Total employed (incl. others) .	9,383	9,454	9,573
Unemployed	450	515	503

— *continued*	2001	2002	2003
Total labour force	9,832	9,970	10,076
Males	5,855	5,896	5,904
Females	3,977	4,074	4,172

* Excluding members of the armed forces and persons in institutional households.

Health and Welfare

KEY INDICATORS

Total fertility rate (children per woman, 2003)	1.24
Under-5 mortality rate (per 1,000 live births, 2002) . . .	1.32
HIV/AIDS (% of persons aged 15–49, 2003)	0.03
Physicians (per 1,000 head, 2002)	1.58
Hospital beds (per 1,000 head, 2002)	5.92
Health expenditure (2000): US $ per head (PPP)	752
Health expenditure (2001): % of GDP	5.84
Health expenditure (2001): public (% of total)	64.9
Human Development Index (2002): value	0.891

For definitions, see explanatory note on p. vi.

Agriculture

PRINCIPAL CROPS
('000 metric tons)

	2001	2002	2003
Potatoes	32.1	38.3	44.3
Rice*	1,396.3	1,460.7	1,338.3
Sweet potatoes	188.7	191.4	199.8
Sorghum	21.7	17.9	17.5
Maize	166.0	188.9	167.9
Tea	19.8	20.3	20.7
Tobacco	9.2	7.6	5.2
Groundnuts	56.1	77.5	73.5
Sugar cane	2,180.3	1,973.1	1,695.7
Bananas	204.7	226.5	223.1
Pineapples	388.7	416.3	447.8
Citrus fruit	463.5	459.6	529.1
Vegetables	3,045.6	3,461.8	3,094.0

* Figures are in terms of brown rice. The equivalent in paddy rice (in '000 metric tons) was: 1,723.9 in 2001; 1,803.2 in 2002; 1,648.3 in 2003.

LIVESTOCK
('000 head at 31 December)

	2001	2002	2003
Cattle	146.0	144.1	144.0
Buffaloes	6.5	5.4	4.9
Pigs	7,164.6	6,793.9	6,778.8
Sheep and goats	184.7	161.9	241.0
Chickens	117,310	118,846	113,048
Ducks	10,104	10,124	10,112
Geese	2,613	2,542	2,757
Turkeys	235	191	186

LIVESTOCK PRODUCTS

	2001	2002	2003
Beef (metric tons)	5,057	5,303	5,523
Pig meat (metric tons)	1,165,998	1,125,721	1,082,224
Goat meat (metric tons)	7,219	6,789	6,591
Chickens ('000 head)*	376,196	377,522	371,420
Ducks ('000 head)*	32,142	31,012	31,040
Geese ('000 head)*	6,330	6,178	6,402
Turkeys ('000 head)*	458	387	364
Milk (metric tons)	346,079	357,804	354,421
Duck eggs ('000)	481,789	472,326	477,041
Hen eggs ('000)	7,325,125	7,069,644	7,018,647

* Figures refer to numbers slaughtered.

Forestry

ROUNDWOOD REMOVALS
('000 cubic metres)

	2001	2002	2003
Industrial wood	26.4	31.1	26.1
Fuel wood	6.0	4.0	15.0
Total	32.4	35.1	41.1

Fishing

('000 metric tons, live weight, incl. aquaculture)

	2001	2002	2003
Tilapias	82.9	85.1	85.4
Other freshwater fishes	19.2	18.8	16.3
Japanese eel	34.2	34.9	35.1
Milkfish	59.4	72.4	77.9
Pacific saury	39.8	51.3	91.5
Skipjack tuna	186.7	232.6	180.6
Albacore	64.1	62.8	54.1
Yellowfin tuna	109.6	97.2	96.8
Bigeye tuna	81.2	104.3	108.4
Chub mackerel	42.7	57.0	53.8
Sharks, rays, skates, etc.	44.2	45.3	67.5
Other fishes (incl. unspecified)	260.7	282.6	315.6
Total fish	1,024.7	1,144.3	1,183.0
Marine shrimps and prawns	29.0	25.2	42.0
Other crustaceans	9.8	9.9	17.4
Pacific cupped oyster	16.6	19.6	23.5
Common squids	13.7	14.1	17.2
Argentine shortfin squid	147.6	111.7	147.2
Flying squids	4.5	2.4	3.1
Other molluscs	0.4	0.5	0.8
Other aquatic animals	47.5	60.5	53.5
Total catch	1,301.2	1,388.2	1,487.7

Note: Figures exclude aquatic plants, totalling (in '000 metric tons): 31.8 in 2001; 43.6 in 2002; 40.9 in 2003.

Mining

(metric tons, unless otherwise indicated)

	2001	2002	2003
Crude petroleum ('000 litres)	44,380	51,106	45,760
Natural gas ('000 cu m)	849,158	886,828	830,893
Salt	66,150	56,720	191
Sulphur	223,659	212,343	225,006
Marble (raw material)	20,475,479	23,736,157	21,040,986
Dolomite	70,698	54,913	53,815

Industry

SELECTED PRODUCTS
('000 metric tons, unless otherwise indicated)

	2001	2002	2003
Wheat flour	784.3	781.2	798.1
Granulated sugar	201.8	176.3	210.6
Carbonated beverages ('000 litres)	442,241	434,998	447,417
Alcoholic beverages—excl. beer ('000 hectolitres)	2,482.4	562.2	482.4
Cigarettes (million)	22,226	19,383	20,493
Cotton yarn	313.6	306.4	286.7
Paper	803.6	801.0	781.9
Paperboard	2,590.5	3,235.3	3,403.8
Sulphuric acid	895.5	917.4	1,067.3
Spun yarn	360.3	316.0	308.8
Cement	18,127.6	19,362.9	18,474.2
Steel ingots	16,399.0	17,423.2	17,638.3
Sewing machines ('000 units)	194.2	235.6	243.2
Electric fans ('000 units)	15,644.3	14,844.4	13,375.5
Personal computers ('000 units)	14,130.1	14,462.2	10,511.7
Monitors ('000 units)	6,752.7	5,104.9	4,214.9
Radio cassette recorders ('000 units)	4,023.4	3,955.7	4,358.4
Radio receivers ('000 units)	1,390.1	426.2	371.9
Television receivers ('000 units)	927.6	1,014.8	1,248.0
Picture tubes ('000 units)	8,444	3,784	233
Integrated circuits (million units)	4,924.2	6,160.0	6,532.2
Electronic condensers (million units)	121,670.8	149,959.0	199,089.3
Telephone sets ('000 units)	1,911.0	215.2	352.5
Passenger motor cars (units)	266,237	326,270	388,002
Trucks and buses (units)	2,654	3,432	4,106
Bicycles ('000 units)	4,746.5	4,674.6	4,616.0
Ships ('000 dwt)*	1,014.3	833.7	n.a.
Electric energy (million kWh)	178,358	187,910	n.a.
Liquefied petroleum gas	1,278.5	1,366.1	n.a.

* Excluding motor yachts.

Finance

CURRENCY AND EXCHANGE RATES

Monetary Units
100 cents = 1 New Taiwan dollar (NT $).

Sterling, US Dollar and Euro Equivalents (31 December 2004)
£1 sterling = NT $61.6445;
US $1 = NT $31.9170;
€1 = NT $43.4742;
NT $1,000 = £16.22 = US $31.33 = €23.00.

Average Exchange Rate (NT $ per US $)
2002   34.575
2003   34.418
2004   33.422

BUDGET
(NT $ million, year ending 31 December)

Revenue	2002	2003	2004*
Taxes	820,051	828,551	903,088
Monopoly profits	346	—	—
Non-tax revenue from other sources	484,270	491,444	431,635
Total	1,304,667	1,319,995	1,334,723

* Forecasts.

Expenditure	2002	2003	2004*
General administration	162,255	167,738	168,258
National defence	225,243	227,742	250,949
Education, science and culture .	267,008	300,196	306,446
Economic development	291,166	295,569	244,883
Social welfare	262,241	284,680	281,919
Community development and			
environmental protection . .	23,433	28,680	25,139
Pensions and survivors' benefits .	124,288	125,414	123,757
Obligations	152,240	144,634	133,362
Subsidies to provincial and			
municipal governments . . .	37,909	39,957	42,695
Other expenditure	6,159	4,303	14,162
Total	1,551,943	1,618,913	1,591,570

* Forecasts.
Note: Figures refer to central government accounts, including Taiwan Province.

INTERNATIONAL RESERVES
(US $ million at 31 December)

	2001	2002	2003
Gold*	4,361	4,390	4,508
Foreign exchange	122,211	161,656	206,632
Total	126,572	166,046	211,140

* National valuation.

MONEY SUPPLY
(NT $ million at 31 December)

	2001	2002	2003
Currency outside banks . . .	525,659	527,278	608,205
Demand deposits at deposit money			
banks	4,500,201	4,964,311	5,944,627
Total money	5,025,860	5,491,589	6,552,832

COST OF LIVING
(Consumer Price Index; base: 2001 = 100)

	2000	2002	2003
Food	100.93	99.80	99.72
Clothing	101.70	100.58	101.96
Housing	100.34	98.88	97.81
Transport and communications .	98.95	97.78	98.38
Medicines and medical care . .	98.68	101.29	104.65
Education and entertainment . .	97.92	100.11	98.81
All items (incl. others)	100.01	99.80	99.52

NATIONAL ACCOUNTS
(NT $ million in current prices)

National Income and Product

	2000	2001	2002
Compensation of employees . .	4,939,685	4,809,210	4,765,265
Operating surplus	3,163,763	3,141,257	3,321,091
Domestic factor incomes . .	8,103,448	7,950,467	8,086,356
Consumption of fixed capital . .	878,482	932,853	997,948
Gross domestic product (GDP)			
at factor cost	8,981,930	8,883,320	9,084,304
Indirect taxes	727,193	683,302	715,190
Less Subsidies	45,735	59,998	50,683
GDP in purchasers' values . .	9,663,388	9,506,624	9,748,811
Factor income from abroad . .	286,688	314,956	357,203
Less Factor income paid abroad .	146,728	123,533	102,973
Gross national product (GNP) .	9,803,348	9,698,047	10,003,041
Less Consumption of fixed capital	878,482	932,853	997,948
National income in market			
prices	8,924,866	8,765,194	9,005,093

— *continued*	2000	2001	2002
Other current transfers from			
abroad	99,990	88,131	90,620
Less Other current transfers paid			
abroad	181,477	180,353	176,770
National disposable income .	8,843,379	8,672,972	8,918,943

Expenditure on the Gross Domestic Product

	2001	2002	2003
Government final consumption			
expenditure	1,240,437	1,232,676	1,261,414
Private final consumption			
expenditure	6,042,628	6,149,507	6,186,554
Increase in stocks	−99,598	−84,111	−34,617
Gross fixed capital formation . .	1,781,752	1,728,279	1,724,373
Total domestic expenditure .	8,965,219	9,026,351	9,137,724
Exports of goods and services . .	4,839,820	5,245,948	5,721,983
Less Imports of goods and services	4,298,415	4,523,488	5,012,152
GDP in purchasers' values . .	9,506,624	9,748,811	9,847,555
GDP at constant 1996 prices .	9,349,923	9,685,551	9,999,787

Gross Domestic Product by Economic Activity

	2001	2002	2003
Agriculture, hunting, forestry and			
fishing	185,182	181,000	179,657
Mining and quarrying	37,986	41,986	36,597
Manufacturing	2,431,213	2,519,581	2,515,260
Construction	277,651	249,632	219,924
Electricity, gas and water . . .	208,871	215,610	220,325
Transport, storage and			
communications	656,292	675,988	674,329
Trade, restaurants and hotels . .	1,833,533	1,895,476	1,954,911
Finance, insurance and real estate*	1,948,157	2,034,401	2,068,970
Business services	269,092	270,235	277,721
Community, social and personal			
services	962,939	1,009,031	1,040,492
Government services	1,011,122	1,024,869	1,064,656
Other services	114,981	121,283	119,692
Sub-total	9,937,019	10,239,092	10,372,534
Value-added tax	167,247	182,762	180,732
Import duties	119,100	126,370	128,710
Less Imputed bank service charge	716,742	799,413	834,421
GDP in purchasers' values . .	9,506,624	9,748,811	9,847,555

* Including imputed rents of owner-occupied dwellings.

BALANCE OF PAYMENTS
(US $ million)

	2001	2002	2003
Exports of goods f.o.b.	122,079	129,850	143,447
Imports of goods f.o.b.	−102,215	−105,657	−118,548
Trade balance	19,864	24,193	24,899
Exports of services	19,547	21,635	23,102
Imports of services	−24,465	−24,719	−25,635
Balance on goods and services	14,946	21,109	22,366
Other income received	9,327	10,334	12,991
Other income paid	−3,648	−3,321	−3,436
Balance on goods, services and			
income	20,625	28,122	31,921
Current transfers received . . .	2,607	2,621	2,673
Current transfers paid	−5,341	−5,113	−5,392
Current balance	17,891	25,630	29,202
Capital account (net)	−163	−139	−87
Direct investment abroad . .	−5,480	−4,886	−5,679
Direct investment from abroad .	4,109	1,445	453
Portfolio investment assets . .	−12,427	−15,711	−35,620
Portfolio investment liabilities .	11,136	6,644	29,693
Other investment assets . . .	−1,770	11,990	2,455
Other investment liabilities . .	4,048	9,268	15,438
Net errors and omissions . . .	9	−577	1,237
Overall balance	17,353	33,664	37,092

External Trade

PRINCIPAL COMMODITIES
(US $ million)

Imports c.i.f.	2001	2002	2003
Mineral products	12,763.6	12,617.8	16,332.1
Crude petroleum	6,808.6	6,752.5	9,564.4
Products of chemical or allied industries	10,231.9	11,340.2	13,494.7
Organic chemicals	3,901.2	4,368.1	n.a.
Base metals and articles thereof	7,783.6	9,187.0	11,292.0
Iron and steel products	3,788.2	4,852.0	6,259.1
Metal products (excl. iron and steel)	3,995.4	4,335.0	5,032.9
Machinery and mechanical appliances; electrical equipment; sound and television apparatus	47,549.3	50,115.4	52,933.2
Electronic products	21,026.8	23,105.2	25,391.9
Machineries	10,489.0	9,764.7	11,468.6
Electrical machinery products	4,282.4	4,615.7	4,942.7
Information and communication products	8,119.5	8,246.4	6,093.9
Vehicles, aircraft, vessels and associated transport equipment	4,237.9	3,469.5	3,886.8
Optical, photographic, cinematographic, measuring, precision and medical apparatus; clocks and watches; musical instruments	6,213.5	6,614.4	8,627.4
Total (incl. others)	107,237.4	112,530.1	127,248.5

Exports f.o.b.	2001	2002	2003
Chemicals	4,137.9	4,667.0	5,661.4
Plastics, rubber and articles thereof	7,992.8	8,798.6	9,975.4
Textiles and textile articles	12,630.1	12,149.7	11,877.5
Fibre and yarn	8,981.7	8,654.1	8,373.5
Base metals and articles thereof	11,330.9	12,542.7	14,330.3
Iron and steel	6,888.0	7,825.7	9,351.0
Metal products (excl. iron and steel)	4,442.8	4,716.8	4,979.3
Machinery and mechanical appliances; electrical equipment; sound and television apparatus	66,851.5	70,633.3	75,352.3
Electronic products	23,601.1	25,838.0	31,158.4
Machineries	8,348.1	9,258.4	9,864.9
Electrical machinery products	4,665.1	5,898.7	6,012.3
Information and communication products	15,668.1	16,039.0	14,056.7
Vehicles, aircraft, vessels and associated transport equipment	4,441.6	4,830.5	5,672.0
Total (incl. others)	122,866.3	130,596.8	144,179.5

PRINCIPAL TRADING PARTNERS
(US $ million)

Imports c.i.f.	2001	2002	2003
Australia	3,084.9	2,832.6	2,726.6
Canada	996.1	945.0	1,078.8
China, People's Republic	5,901.9	7,947.7	10,960.5
France	2,130.5	1,551.3	1,628.3
Germany	4,246.0	4,421.5	4,964.5
Hong Kong	1,848.9	1,738.6	1,725.2
Indonesia	2,523.4	2,588.1	2,921.5
Italy	1,084.1	1,089.7	1,131.6
Japan	25,848.4	27,277.3	32,635.4
Korea, Republic	6,705.1	7,711.1	8,687.9
Malaysia	4,213.7	4,151.9	4,749.0
Netherlands	1,524.2	1,438.0	1,295.0
Philippines	3,250.5	3,651.6	3,081.0
Russia	603.5	927.1	1,299.3
Saudi Arabia	2,745.4	2,406.3	4,275.5
Singapore	3,367.2	3,543.6	3,860.9
Switzerland	865.8	807.0	1,074.9
Thailand	2,181.0	2,170.8	2,364.9
United Kingdom	1,442.8	1,356.8	1,416.1
USA	18,229.2	18,094.3	16,820.1
Total (incl. others)	107,237.4	112,530.1	127,248.5

Exports f.o.b.	2001	2002	2003
Australia	1,362.7	1,586.6	1,884.4
Canada	1,564.3	1,533.6	1,470.4
China, People's Republic	4,745.4	9,945.0	21,417.3
France	1,166.0	1,122.8	1,251.0
Germany	4,480.4	3,836.0	4,207.5
Hong Kong*	26,961.4	30,845.3	28,353.6
Indonesia	1,474.6	1,462.9	1,514.0
Italy	1,254.5	1,254.0	1,460.2
Japan	12,759.0	11,983.8	11,912.5
Korea, Republic	3,275.6	3,866.5	4,573.6
Malaysia	3,061.4	3,132.6	3,046.2
Netherlands	4,229.2	3,772.0	4,126.2
Philippines	2,148.7	1,971.5	2,300.4
Singapore	4,051.5	4,377.8	4,982.7
Thailand	2,125.7	2,292.7	2,565.3
United Kingdom	3,329.3	2,908.8	2,884.3
USA	27,654.5	26,763.7	25,941.5
Viet Nam	1,726.9	2,287.2	2,664.3
Total (incl. others)	122,866.3	130,596.8	144,179.5

* The majority of Taiwan's exports to Hong Kong are re-exported.

Transport

RAILWAYS
(traffic)

	2001	2002	2003
Passengers ('000)	476,214	500,464	478,228
Passenger-km ('000)	12,268,691	12,147,500	11,177,092
Freight ('000 metric tons)	19,287	18,217	16,735
Freight ton-km ('000)	1,009,863	940,603	863,912

ROAD TRAFFIC
(motor vehicles in use at 31 December)

	2001	2002	2003
Passenger cars	4,825,581	4,989,336	5,169,733
Buses and coaches	24,053	25,079	25,628
Goods vehicles	830,673	856,783	885,780
Motorcycles and scooters	11,733,202	11,983,757	12,366,864

SHIPPING

Merchant Fleet
(at 31 December)

	2001	2002	2003
Number of vessels	656	649	637
Total displacement ('000 grt)	4,617.9	4,289.0	3,477.1

Source: Lloyd's Register-Fairplay, *World Fleet Statistics*.

Sea-borne freight traffic
('000 metric tons)

	2001	2002	2003
Goods loaded	221,154	243,914	254,640
Goods unloaded	331,719	362,796	380,937

CIVIL AVIATION
(traffic on scheduled services)

	2001	2002	2003
Passengers carried ('000)	46,084.4	44,185.6	37,879.4
Freight carried ('000 metric tons)	1,310.2	1,513.9	1,622.7

Tourism

TOURIST ARRIVALS BY COUNTRY OF ORIGIN

	2001	2002	2003
Hong Kong	80,752	76,690	56,076
Indonesia	89,476	87,728	38,078
Japan	971,190	998,497	657,053
Korea, Republic	82,684	83,624	92,893
Malaysia	56,834	66,304	67,014
Philippines	69,118	79,261	80,026
Singapore	96,777	111,024	78,739
Thailand	116,420	110,650	98,390
USA	339,390	377,470	272,858
Overseas Chinese*	325,266	623,675	436,083
Total (incl. others)	2,617,137	2,977,692	2,248,117

* i.e. those bearing Taiwan passports.

Tourism receipts (US $ million): 4,152 in 2001; 4,584 in 2002; 2,976 in 2003.

Communications Media

	2001	2002	2003
Book production (titles)	36,546	38,953	39,138
Newspapers	454	474	602
Magazines	7,236	8,140	n.a.
Telephone subscribers ('000)	12,858	13,099	13,355
Mobile telephones ('000 in use)	21,633	23,905	25,090
Personal computers ('000 in use)*	5,000	n.a.	n.a.
Internet users ('000)*	6,232	7,459	7,828

Television receivers (2002): Colour television receivers per 100 households: 99.56; Cable television receivers per 100 households: 74.81.

Radio receivers (1994): more than 16 million in use.

* Source: International Telecommunication Union.

Education

(2003/04)

	Schools	Full-time teachers	Students
Pre-school	3,306	21,251	240,926
Primary	2,638	103,793	1,912,791
Secondary (incl. vocational)	1,192	97,738	1,679,970
Higher	158	47,472	1,270,194
Special	24	1,687	5,921
Supplementary	934	2,896	278,124
Total (incl. others)	8,252	274,837	5,384,926

Directory

The Constitution

On 1 January 1947 a new Constitution was promulgated for the Republic of China. When the Chinese Communist Party established the People's Republic of China on the Chinese mainland in 1949, the Government of the Republic of China, led by the Kuomintang (KMT), relocated to Taiwan, where it maintained jurisdiction over Taiwan, Penghu, Kinmen, Matsu and numerous other islets. The two sides of the Taiwan Strait have since been governed as separate territories. The form of government that was incorporated in the Constitution is based on a five-power system and has the major features of both cabinet and presidential government. A process of constitutional reform, initiated in 1991, continued in the early 21st century. The following is a summary of the Constitution, as subsequently amended:

PRESIDENT

The President shall be directly elected by popular vote for a term of four years. Both the President and Vice-President are eligible for re-election to a second term. The President represents the country at all state functions, including foreign relations; commands land, sea and air forces, promulgates laws, issues mandates, concludes treaties, declares war, makes peace, declares martial law, grants amnesties, appoints and removes civil and military officers, and confers honours and decorations. The President convenes the National Assembly and, subject to certain limitations, may issue emergency orders to deal with national calamities and ensure national security; may dissolve the Legislative Yuan; also nominates the Premier (who may be appointed without the Legislative Yuan's confirmation), and the officials of the Judicial Yuan, the Examination Yuan and the Control Yuan.

EXECUTIVE YUAN

The Executive Yuan is the highest administrative organ of the nation and is responsible to the Legislative Yuan; has three categories of subordinate organization:

Executive Yuan Council (policy-making organization);

Ministries and Commissions (executive organization);

Subordinate organization (19 bodies, including the Secretariat, Government Information Office, Directorate-General of Budget, Accounting and Statistics, Council for Economic Planning and Development, and Environmental Protection Administration).

LEGISLATIVE YUAN

The Legislative Yuan is the highest legislative organ of the State, empowered to hear administrative reports of the Executive Yuan, and to change government policy. It may hold a binding vote of 'no confidence' in the Executive Yuan. It comprises 225 members: 168 are chosen by direct election from two special municipalities and other cities and counties, eight members are elected from and by aborigines, and eight from and by overseas Chinese. The remaining 41 members are elected from a nation-wide constituency on the basis of proportional representation. Members serve for three years and are eligible for re-election.

JUDICIAL YUAN

The Judicial Yuan is the highest judicial organ of state and has charge of civil, criminal and administrative cases, and of cases concerning disciplinary measures against public functionaries (see Judicial System).

EXAMINATION YUAN

The Examination Yuan supervises examinations for entry into public offices, and deals with personnel matters of the civil service, implements training and protection measures for public functionaries, and supervises the public service pension fund.

CONTROL YUAN

The Control Yuan is the highest control organ of the State, exercising powers of impeachment, censure and audit, comprising 29 members serving a six-year term. (According to the Additional Articles of the Constitution of the Republic of China in April 2000, the members of the Control Yuan shall be nominated by the President of the State, and with the consent of the Legislative Yuan). The Control Yuan may impeach or censure a public functionary at central or local level, who is deemed guilty of violation of law or dereliction of duty, and shall refer the matter to the law courts for action in cases involving a criminal offence; the Control Yuan may propose corrective measures to the Executive Yuan or to its subordinate organs.

The Government

HEAD OF STATE

President: CHEN SHUI-BIAN (inaugurated 20 May 2000; re-elected 20 March 2004).

Vice-President: HSU-LIEN ANNETTE LU.

Secretary-General: YU SHYI-KUN.

THE EXECUTIVE YUAN
(April 2005)

Premier: FRANK HSIEH CHANG-TING.

Vice-Premier and Minister of the Consumer Protection Commission: WU RONG-I.

Secretary-General: LEE YING-YUAN.

Ministers without Portfolio: CHO JUNG-TAI, HU SHENG-CHENG (Minister of the Council for Economic Planning and Development), CHEN CHI-MAI, FU LI-YEH, LIN SHENG-FENG, KUO YAO-CHI (Minister of the Public Construction Commission), LIN FERNG-CHING.

Minister of the Interior: SU JIA-CHYUAN.

Minister of Foreign Affairs: CHEN TAN-SUN.

Minister of National Defense: LEE JYE.

Minister of Finance: LIN CHUAN.

Minister of Education: TU CHENG-SHENG.

Minister of Justice: SHIH MAO-LIN.

Minister of Economic Affairs: HO MEI-YUEH.

Minister of Transportation and Communications: LIN LING-SAN.

Minister of the Mongolian and Tibetan Affairs Commission: HSU CHIH-HSIUNG.

Minister of the Overseas Chinese Affairs Commission: CHANG FU-MEI.

Minister of the Directorate-General of Budget, Accounting and Statistics: HSU JAN-YAU.

Minister of Central Personnel Administration: CHANG CHUN-YEN.

Minister of the Government Information Office: PASUYA WEN-CHIH YAO.

Minister of Health: HOU SHENG-MOU.

Minister of the Environmental Protection Administration: CHANG JUU-EN.

Minister of the Coast Guard Administration: SHI HWEI-YOW.

Minister of the Mainland Affairs Council: JAUSHIEH JOSEPH WU.

Minister of the Veterans' Affairs Commission: KAO HUA-CHU.

Minister of the National Youth Commission: CHENG LI-CHIUN.

Minister of the Atomic Energy Council: OUYANG MIN-SHEN.

Minister of the National Science Council: WU MAW-KUEN.

Minister of the Research, Development and Evaluation Commission: YEH JIUNN-RONG.

Minister of the Council of Agriculture: LEE CHING-LUNG.

Minister of the Council for Cultural Affairs: CHEN CHI-NAN.

Minister of the Council of Labor Affairs: CHEN CHU.

Minister of the Fair Trade Commission: HWANG TZONG-LEH.

Minister of the Council of Indigenous Peoples: WALIS PELIN.

Minister of the National Council on Physical Fitness and Sports: CHEN CHUAN-SHOW.

Minister of the Council for Hakka Affairs: LEE YUNG-TE.

Governor of the Central Bank of China: PERNG FAI-NAN.

Chairperson of the Central Election Commission: MASA J. S. CHANG.

Chairperson of the Co-ordination Council for North American Affairs: LIN FANG-MEI.

Director of the National Palace Museum: SHIH SHOU-CHIEN.

Minister of the Financial Supervisory Commission: KONG JAW-SHENG.

MINISTRIES, COMMISSIONS, ETC.

Office of the President: 122 Chungking South Rd, Sec. 1, Taipei; tel. (2) 23113731; fax (2) 23311604; e-mail public@mail.oop.gov.tw; internet www.president.gov.tw.

Ministry of Economic Affairs: 15 Foo Chou St, Taipei; tel. (2) 23212200; fax (2) 23919398; e-mail service@moea.gov.tw; internet www.moea.gov.tw.

Ministry of Education: 5 Chung Shan South Rd, Taipei 10040; tel. (2) 23566051; fax (2) 23976978; internet www.moe.gov.tw.

Ministry of Finance: 2 Ai Kuo West Rd, Taipei; tel. (2) 23228000; fax (2) 23965829; e-mail root@www.mof.gov.tw; internet www.mof.gov.tw.

Ministry of Foreign Affairs: 2 Chiehshou Rd, Taipei 10016; tel. (2) 23119292; fax (2) 23144972; internet www.mofa.gov.tw.

Ministry of the Interior: 5–9/F, 5 Hsu Chou Rd, Taipei; tel. (2) 23565005; fax (2) 23566201; e-mail gethics@mail.moi.gov.tw; internet www.moi.gov.tw.

Ministry of Justice: 130 Chungking South Rd, Sec. 1, Taipei 100 10036; tel. (2) 23146871; fax (2) 23896759; internet www.moj.gov.tw.

Ministry of National Defense: 2/F, 164 Po Ai Rd, Taipei; tel. (2) 23116117; fax (2) 23144221; internet www.ndmc.edu.tw.

Ministry of Transportation and Communications: 2 Chang Sha St, Sec. 1, Taipei; tel. (2) 23492900; fax (2) 23118587; e-mail motceyes@motc.gov.tw; internet www.motc.gov.tw.

Mongolian and Tibetan Affairs Commission: 4/F, 5 Hsu Chou Rd, Sec. 1, Taipei; tel. (2) 23566166; fax (2) 23566432; internet www.mtac.gov.tw.

Overseas Chinese Affairs Commission: 4/F, 5 Hsu Chou Rd, Taipei; tel. (2) 23566166; fax (2) 23566323; e-mail ocacinfo@mail.ocac.gov.tw; internet www.ocac.gov.tw.

Directorate-General of Budget, Accounting and Statistics: 5/F, 2 Kwang Chow St, Taipei 10065; tel. (2) 23803542; fax (2) 23803547; e-mail sicbs@dgbas.gov.tw; internet www.dgbas.gov.tw.

Government Information Office: 2 Tientsin St, Taipei; tel. (2) 33568888; fax (2) 23568733; e-mail service@mail.gio.gov.tw; internet www.gio.gov.tw.

Council of Indigenous Peoples: 16–17/F, 4 Chung Hsiao West Rd, Sec. 1, Taipei; tel. (2) 23882122; fax (2) 23891967.

Council of Agriculture: see under Trade and Industry—Government Agencies.

Atomic Energy Council (AEC): 80 Cheng Kung Rd, Sec. 1, Taipei 234; tel. (2) 82317919; fax (2) 82317864; internet www.aec.gov.tw.

Central Personnel Administration: 109 Huai Ning St, Taipei; tel. (2) 23111720; fax (2) 23715252; internet www.cpa.gov.tw.

Consumer Protection Commission: 1 Chung Hsiao East Rd, Sec. 1, Taipei; tel. (2) 23566600; fax (2) 23214538; e-mail tcpc@ms1.hinet.net; internet www.cpc.gov.tw.

Council for Cultural Affairs: 102 Ai Kuo East Rd, Taipei; tel. (2) 25225300; fax (2) 25519011; e-mail wwwadm@ccpdunx.ccpd.gov.tw; internet expo96.org.tw/cca/welcome_c.html.

Council for Economic Planning and Development: 9/F, 87 Nanking East Rd, Sec. 2, Taipei; tel. (2) 25225300; fax (2) 25519011; internet www.cepd.gov.tw.

Environmental Protection Administration: 41 Chung Hua Rd, Sec. 1, Taipei; tel. (2) 23117722; fax (2) 23116071; e-mail www@sun.epa.gov.tw; internet www.epa.gov.tw.

Fair Trade Commission: 12–14/F, 2-2 Chi Nan Rd, Sec. 2, Taipei; tel. (2) 23517588; fax (2) 23974997; e-mail ftcse@ftc.gov.tw; internet www.ftc.gov.tw.

Department of Health: 12/F, 100 Ai Kuo East Rd, Taipei; tel. (2) 23210151; fax (2) 2392-9723; internet www.doh.gov.tw.

Council of Labor Affairs: 5–15/F, 132 Min Sheng East Rd, Sec. 3, Taipei; tel. (2) 27182512; fax (2) 25149240; internet www.cla.gov.tw.

Mainland Affairs Council: 5–13/F, 2-2 Chi Nan Rd, Sec. 1, Taipei; tel. (2) 23975589; fax (2) 23975700; e-mail macst@mac.gov.tw; internet www.mac.gov.tw.

National Science Council: 17–22/F, 106 Ho Ping East Rd, Sec. 2, Taipei; tel. (2) 27377501; fax (2) 27377668; e-mail nsc@nsc.gov.tw; internet www.nsc.gov.tw.

National Youth Commission: 14/F, 5 Hsu Chou Rd, Taipei; tel. (2) 23566272; fax (2) 23566307; e-mail nycen@nyc.gov.tw ; internet www.nyc.gov.tw.

Research, Development and Evaluation Commission: 7/F, 2-2 Chi Nan Rd, Sec. 1, Taipei; tel. (2) 23419066; fax (2) 23928133; e-mail service@rdec.gov.tw; internet rdec.gov.tw.

Veterans' Affairs Commission: 222 Chung Hsiao East Rd, Sec. 5, Taipei; tel. (2) 27255700; fax (2) 27253578; e-mail hsc@www.vac.gov.tw; internet vac.gov.tw.

Co-ordination Council for North American Affairs: 133 Po-ai Rd, Taipei; tel. (2) 23119212; fax (2) 23822651; headquarters for

Taipei Economic and Cultural Representative Office (TECRO) in the USA.

Financial Supervisory Commission: 18/F, No.7, Sec. 2, Hsien Ming Blvd, Panchiao City, Taipei County 220; tel. (2) 89680899; e-mail fscey@fscey.gov.tw; internet www.fscey.gov.tw.

President and Legislature

PRESIDENT

Election, 20 March 2004 (provisional results)

Candidate*	Votes	% of votes
Chen Shui-bian (Democratic Progressive Party—DPP)	. 6,471,970	50.11
Lien Chan (Kuomintang—KMT) . . .	. 6,442,452	49.89
Total	.12,914,422†	100.00

* The vice-presidential candidates were respectively Annette Hsiu-lien Lu of the DPP and James C. Y. Soong of the People First Party (PFP).

† Not including invalid or spoiled ballot papers, which numbered 337,297. Results were subject to revision, following a recount conducted in May 2004 and subsequent judicial review, which remained in progress in early 2005.

LI-FA YUAN
(Legislative Yuan)

The Legislative Yuan is the highest legislative organ of the State. It comprises 225 seats. The 168 directly elected members come from two special municipalities and other cities and counties. Eight members are elected from and by aborigines. Eight members are overseas Chinese. Overseas Chinese members and the remaining 41 members are elected from a nation-wide constituency on the basis of proportional representation. Members serve for three years and are eligible for re-election.

President: WANG JIN-PYNG.

General Election, 11 December 2004

Party	% of votes	Seats
Democratic Progressive Party (DPP) . .	35.72	89
Kuomintang (KMT)	32.83	79
People First Party (PFP)	13.90	34
Taiwan Solidarity Union (TSU)	7.79	12
New Party (NP)	0.12	1
Independents and others	9.64	10
Total	100.0	225

Political Organizations

Legislation adopted in 1989 permitted political parties other than the KMT to function. By mid-2004 a total of 105 parties had registered with the Ministry of the Interior.

China Democratic Socialist Party (CDSP): 6/F, 7 Heping East Rd, Sec. 3, Taipei; tel. (2) 27072883; f. 1932 by merger of National Socialists and Democratic Constitutionalists; aims to promote democracy, to protect fundamental freedoms, and to improve public welfare and social security; Chair. I BUH-LUEN; Sec.-Gen. SUEN SHANN-HAUR.

China Young Party: 12/F, 2 Sinsheng South Rd, Sec. 3, Taipei; tel. (2) 23626715; f. 1923; aims to recover sovereignty over mainland China, to safeguard the Constitution and democracy, and to foster understanding between Taiwan and the non-communist world; Chair. JEAN JYI-YUAN.

Chinese Republican Party (CRP): 3/F, 26 Lane 90, Jongshun St, Sec. 2, Taipei; tel. (2) 29366572; f. 1988; advocates peaceful struggle for the salvation of China and the promotion of world peace; Chair. WANG YING-CHYUN.

Democratic Liberal Party (DLP): 4/F, 20 Lane 5, Cingtian, Taipei; tel. (2) 23121595; f. 1989; aims to promote political democracy and economic liberty for the people of Taiwan; Chair. HER WEI-KANG.

Democratic Progressive Party (DPP): 10/F, 30 Beiping East Rd, Taipei; tel. and fax (2) 23929989; e-mail foreign@dpp.org.tw; internet www.dpp.org.tw; f. 1986; advocates 'self-determination' for the people of Taiwan and UN membership; supports establishment

of independent Taiwan following plebiscite; 140,000 mems; Chair. SU TSENG-CHANG; Sec.-Gen. CHANG CHUN-HSIUNG.

Democratic Union of Taiwan (DUT): 16/F, 15-1 Hangjhou South Rd, Sec. 1, Taipei; tel. (2) 23211531; f. 1998; Chair. HSU CHERNG-KUEN.

Formosa Party: Taipei; f. 2004; pro-independence; Chair. WILLIAM HUANG; Sec.-Gen. CHEN DA-CHENG.

Green Party: 11/F-1, 273 Roosevelt Rd, Sec. 3, Taipei; tel. (2) 23621362; f. 1996 by breakaway faction of the DPP; Chair. CHEN GUANG-YEU.

Jiann Gwo Party (Taiwan Independence Party—TAIP): 9/F, 15–8 Nanjing East Rd, Sec. 5, Taipei; tel. (2) 22800879; internet www.taip .org/index.htm; f. 1996 by dissident mems of DPP; Chair. HUANG CHIEN-MING; Sec.-Gen. LI SHENG-HSIUNG.

Kungtang (KT) (Labour Party): 1 Lane 44, Jianguo South Rd, Sec. 1, Taipei; tel. (2) 27739044; fax (2) 27739050; f. 1987; aims to become the main political movement of Taiwan's industrial work-force; 10,000 mems; Chair. WU CHING-FU; Sec.-Gen. JENG JIN-YANG.

Kuomintang (KMT) (Nationalist Party of China): 11 Jongshan South Rd, Taipei 100; tel. (2) 23121472; fax (2) 23434561; internet www.kmt.org.tw; f. 1894; fmr ruling party; aims to supplant communist rule in mainland China; supports democratic, constitutional government, and advocates the unification of China under the 'Three Principles of the People'; aims to promote market economy and equitable distribution of wealth; plans for merger with PFP announced May 2004; 2,523,984 mems; Chair. LIEN CHAN; Sec.-Gen. LIN FONG-CHENG.

Nationwide Democratic Non-Partisan Union (NDNU): 13/F, 42-1 Huaining St, Taipei; Chair. YEH SHIANN-SHIOU.

New Nation Alliance: 14/F, 9 Songjiang Rd, Taipei; tel. (2) 23585643; f. 1998; promotes independence for Taiwan and the establishment of a 'new nation, new society and new culture'; Chair. PERNG BAE-SHEAN.

New Party (NP): 4/F, 65 Guangfu South Rd, Taipei; tel. (2) 27562222; fax (2) 27565750; e-mail webmaster@mail.np.org.tw; internet www.np.org.tw; f. 1993 by dissident KMT legislators (hith-erto mems of New Kuomintang Alliance faction); merged with China Social Democratic Party in late 1993; advocates co-operation with the KMT and DPP in negotiations with the People's Republic, the maintenance of security in the Taiwan Straits, the modernization of the island's defence systems, measures to combat government corruption, the support of small and medium businesses and the establishment of a universal social security system; 80,000 mems; Chair. YOK MU-MING.

Non-Partisan Solidarity Union: internet www.npsu.org.tw; f. 2004; Chair. CHANG PO-YA.

People First Party (PFP): 1/F, 63 Chang-an East Rd, Sec. 2, Taipei; tel. (2) 25068555; internet www.pfp.org.tw; f. 2000; plans for merger with KMT announced May 2004; Chair. JAMES C. Y. SOONG; Sec.-Gen. TSAI CHUNG-HSIUNG.

Taiwan Solidarity Union (TSU): 9/F, 65 Guancian Rd, Taipei; tel. (2) 23706686; fax (2) 23706616; internet www.tsu.org.tw; f. 2001 by a breakaway faction of the Kuomintang (KMT); Chair. SU CHIN-CHIANG; Sec.-Gen. CHEN CHIEN-MING.

Workers' Party: 2/F, 181 Fusing South Rd, Sec. 2, Taipei; tel. (2) 27555868; f. 1989 by breakaway faction of the Kungtang; radical; Leader LOU MEIWEN.

Various pro-independence groups (some based overseas and, until 1992, banned in Taiwan) are in operation. These include the **World United Formosans for Independence** (WUFI—4,000 mems world-wide; Chair. GEORGE CHANG) and the **Organization for Taiwan Nation-Building.**

Diplomatic Representation

EMBASSIES IN THE REPUBLIC OF CHINA

Belize: 11/F, 9 Lane 62, Tien Mou West Rd, Taipei 111; tel. (2) 28760894; fax (2) 28760896; e-mail embelroc@ms41.hinet.net; internet www.embassyofbelize.org.tw; Ambassador WILLIAM QUINTO.

Burkina Faso: 6/F, 9-1 Lane 62, Tien Mou West Rd, Taipei 111; tel. (2) 28733096; fax (2) 28733071; e-mail abftap94@ms17.hinet.net; Ambassador JACQUES Y. SAWADOGO.

Chad: 8/F, 9 Lane 62, Tien Mou West Rd, Taipei; tel. (2) 28742943; fax (2) 28742971; e-mail amchadtp@ms23.hinet.net; Ambassador HISSEIN BRAHIM TAHA.

Costa Rica: 5/F, 9-1 Lane 62, Tien Mou West Rd, Taipei 111; tel. (2) 28752964; fax (2) 28753151; e-mail oscaralv@ttn.net; Ambassador Dr OSCAR ALVAREZ.

Dominican Republic: 6/F, Lane 62, Tien Mou West Rd, Taipei 111; tel. (2) 28751357; fax (2) 28752661; e-mail embajada_dom_entaipei@hotmail.com; Ambassador Víctor Manuel Sánchez.

El Salvador: 2/F, 9 Lane 62, Tien Mou West Rd, Shih Lin, Taipei 111; tel. (2) 28763606; fax (2) 28763514; e-mail embasal.taipei@msa.hinet.net; Ambassador Francisco Ricardo Santana Berríos.

The Gambia: 9/F, 9-1 Lane 62, Tien Mou West Rd, Taipei 111; tel. (2) 28753911; fax (2) 28752775; e-mail gm.roc@msa.hinet.net; Ambassador John-Paul Bojang.

Guatemala: 3/F, 9-1 Lane 62, Tien Mou West Rd, Taipei 111; tel. (2) 28756952; fax (2) 28740699; e-mail embchina@minex.gob.gt; Ambassador Manuel Ernesto Galvez Coronado.

Haiti: 8/F, 9-1 Lane 62, Tien Mou West Rd, Taipei 111; tel. (2) 28766718; fax (2) 28766719; e-mail haiti@ms26.hinet.net; Chargé d'affaires Mario Chouloute.

Holy See: 87 Ai Kuo East Rd, Taipei 106 (Apostolic Nunciature); tel. (2) 23216847; fax (2) 23911926; Chargé d'affaires a.i. Mgr Ambrose Madtha.

Honduras: 9/F, 9 Lane 62, Tien Mou West Rd, Taipei 111; tel. (2) 28755507; fax (2) 28755726; e-mail honduras@ms9.hinet.net; Ambassador Marlene Villela de Talbott.

Malawi: 2/F, 9-1 Lane 62, Tien Mou West Rd, Taipei 111; tel. (2) 28762284; fax (2) 28763545; Ambassador Thengo Maloya.

Marshall Islands: 4/F, 9-1 Lane 62, Tien Mou West Rd, Taipei 111; tel. (2) 28734884; fax (2) 28734904; internet www.rmiembassy.org.tw; Ambassador Alex Carter Bing.

Nicaragua: 3/F, Jyi Shyan Rd, Lu Chow, Taipei; tel. (2) 82814512; fax (2) 82814515; e-mail icaza@ms13.hinet.net; Ambassador Salvador Stadthagen.

Palau: 5/F, 9 Lane B2, Tien Mou West Rd, Taipei 111; tel. (2) 28765415; fax (2) 28760436; Ambassador Johnson Toribiong.

Panama: 6/F, 111 Sung Kiang Rd, Taipei 104; tel. (2) 25099189; fax (2) 25099801; Ambassador Julio Mock.

Paraguay: 7/F, 9-1 Lane 62, Tien Mou West Rd, Taipei 111; tel. (2) 28736310; fax (2) 28736312; e-mail eptaipei@seed.net.tw; Ambassador Jorge Cravid (acting).

São Tomé and Príncipe: 3/F, 18 Chi-lin Rd, Taipei 104; tel. (2) 25114111; fax (2) 25116255; e-mail ladislaualmeida@yahoo.co.uk; Ambassador Ladislau d'Almeida.

Senegal: 10/F, 9-1 Lane 62, Tien Mou West Rd, Taipei 111; tel. (2) 28766519; fax (2) 28734909; e-mail sngol.taipei@msa.hinet.net; Ambassador Youssou Diagne.

Solomon Islands: 7/F, 9-1 Lane 62, Tien Mou West Rd, Taipei 111; tel. (2) 28731168; fax (2) 28735224; Ambassador Beraki Jino.

Swaziland: 10/F, 9 Lane 62, Tien Mou West Rd, Taipei 111; tel. (2) 28725934; fax (2) 28726511; e-mail swazitpi@ms41.hinet.net; Ambassador Njabuliso Gwebu.

Judicial System

Under Articles 78 and 79 of the Constitution and Article 5 of the Constitutional Amendments, 15 Justices of the Constitutional Court (including the President and Vice-President of the Judicial Yuan) have the authority to interpret the Constitution, and to render uniform interpretations of statutes and regulations whenever they are in conflict, and to declare the dissolution of any political party in violation of the Constitution. All of the Justices of the Constitutional Court are nominated and, with the consent of the Legislative Yuan (Congress), appointed by the President of the Republic of China. The Justices serve an eight-year term and may not be reappointed. However, the President and the Vice-President of the Judicial Yuan do not have the same term of protection. Due to a transition to a staggered system of appointment, of 15 Justices appointed in 2003, eight, including the President and Vice-President of the Judicial Yuan, serve a four-year term, while the others serve an eight-year term.

Judicial Yuan: 124 Chungking South Rd, Sec. 1, Taipei; tel. (2) 23618577; fax (2) 23898923; e-mail judicial@mail.judicial.gov.tw; internet www.judicial.gov.tw; Pres. Weng Yueh-sheng; Vice-Pres. Cheng Chung-mo; Sec.-Gen. Fan Kuang-chun; the highest judicial organ, and the interpreter of the constitution and national laws and ordinances; supervises the following:

> **Supreme Court:** 6 Chang Sha St, Sec. 1, Taipei; tel. (2) 23141160; fax (2) 23114246; e-mail tpsemail@mail.judicial.gov.tw; Court of third and final instance for civil and criminal cases; Pres. Wu Chii-pin.

> **High Courts:** Courts of second instance for appeals of civil and criminal cases.

> **District Courts:** Courts of first instance in civil, criminal and non-contentious cases.

> **Supreme Administrative Court:** 1 Lane 126, Chungking South Rd, Sec. 1, Taipei; tel. (2) 23113691; fax (2) 23111791; e-mail jessie@judicial.gov.tw; Court of final resort in cases brought against govt agencies; Pres. Chang Deng-ke.

> **High Administrative Courts:** Courts of first instance in cases brought against govt agencies.

> **Commission on Disciplinary Sanctions Against Functionaries:** 124 Chungking South Rd, 3/F, Sec. 1, Taipei 10036; tel. (2) 23111639; fax (2) 23826255; decides on disciplinary measures against public functionaries impeached by the Control Yuan; Chief Commissioner Lin Kuo-hsien.

Religion

According to the Ministry of the Interior, in 2002 24% of the population were adherents of Buddhism, 20% of Daoism (Taoism), 3.7% of I-kuan Tao and 2.6% of Christianity.

BUDDHISM

Buddhist Association of Taiwan: Mahayana and Theravada schools; 1,613 group mems and more than 9.61m. adherents; Leader Ven. Chin-hsin.

CHRISTIANITY

The Roman Catholic Church

Taiwan comprises one archdiocese, six dioceses and one apostolic administrative area. In December 2002, according to official figures, there were 298,451 adherents.

Bishops' Conference

Chinese Regional Bishops' Conference, 34 Lane 32, Kuangfu South Rd, Taipei 10552; tel. (2) 25782355; fax (2) 25773874; e-mail bishconf@ms1.hinet.net; internet www.catholic.org.tw.

f. 1967; Pres. Cardinal Paul Shan Kuo-hsi (Bishop of Kaohsiung).

Archbishop of Taipei: Most Rev. Joseph Cheng Tsai-fa, Archbishop's House, 94 Loli Rd, Taipei 10668; tel. (2) 27371311; fax (2) 27373710.

The Anglican Communion

Anglicans in Taiwan are adherents of the Protestant Episcopal Church. In 1999 the Church had 2,000 members.

Bishop of Taiwan: Rt Rev. Dr John Chien, 7 Lane 105, Hangchow South Rd, Sec. 1, Taipei 100; tel. (2) 23411265; fax (2) 23962014; e-mail skhtpe@ms12.hinet.net; internet www.dfms.org/taiwan.

Presbyterian Church

Tai-oan Ki-tok Tiu-Lo Kau-Hoe (Presbyterian Church in Taiwan): No. 3, Lane 269, Roosevelt Rd, Sec. 3, Taipei 106; tel. (2) 23625282; fax (2) 23628096; f. 1865; Gen. Sec. Rev. L. K. Lo; 224,679 mems (2000).

DAOISM (TAOISM)

In 2002 there were about 4.54m. adherents. Temples numbered 8,604, and clergy totalled 33,850.

I-KUAN TAO

Introduced to Taiwan in the 1950s, this 'Religion of One Unity' is a modern, syncretic religion, drawn mainly from Confucian, Buddhist and Daoist principles and incorporating ancestor worship. In 1998 there were 108 temples and 18,000 family shrines. Adherents totalled 845,000.

ISLAM

Leader Mohammed Ni Guo-an; 53,000 adherents in 2002.

The Press

In 1999 the number of registered newspapers stood at 367. The majority of newspapers are privately owned.

PRINCIPAL DAILIES

Taipei

Central Daily News: 260 Pa Teh Rd, Sec. 2, Taipei; tel. (2) 27765368; fax (2) 27775835; internet www.cdn.com.tw; f. 1928;

morning; Chinese; official Kuomintang organ; Publr and CEO SHAW YU-MING; circ. 600,000.

The China Post: 8 Fu Shun St, Taipei 104; tel. (2) 25969971; fax (2) 25957962; e-mail cpost@msl.hinet.net; internet www.chinapost.com.tw; f. 1952; morning; English; Publr and Editor JACK HUANG; readership 250,000.

China Times: 132 Da Li St, Taipei; tel. (2) 23087111; fax (2) 23063312; f. 1950; morning; Chinese; Chair. YU CHI-CHUNG; Publr YU ALBERT CHIEN-HSIN; circ. 1.2m.

China Times Express: 132 Da Li St, Taipei; tel. (2) 23087111; fax (2) 23081341; e-mail tang@mail.chinatimes.com.tw; f. 1988; evening; Chinese; Publr S. F. LIN; Editor H. T. YANG; circ. 400,000.

Commercial Times: 132 Da Li St, Taipei; tel. (2) 23087111; fax (2) 23069456; e-mail commercialtimes@mail.chinatimes.com.tw; f. 1978; morning; Chinese; Publr PENG CHWEI-MING; Editor-in-Chief SIMON CHENG; circ. 300,000.

Economic Daily News: 555 Chung Hsiao East Rd, Sec. 4, Taipei; tel. (2) 27681234; fax (2) 27600129; f. 1967; morning; Chinese; Publr WANG PI-CHEN.

The Great News: 216 Chen Teh Rd, Sec. 3, Taipei; tel. (2) 25973111; f. 1988; morning; also *The Great News Daily-Entertainment* (circ. 460,000).

Liberty Times: 11/F, 137 Nanking East Rd, Sec. 2, Taipei; tel. (2) 25042828; fax (2) 25042212; f. 1988; Publr WU A-MING; Editor-in-Chief ROGER CHEN.

Mandarin Daily News: 2 Foo Chou St, Taipei; tel. (2) 23921133; fax (2) 23410203; f. 1948; morning; Publr LIN LIANG.

Min Sheng Daily: 555 Chung Hsiao East Rd, Sec. 4, Taipei; tel. (2) 27681234; fax (2) 27560955; f. 1978; sport and leisure; Publr WANG SHAW-LAN.

Taiwan Hsin Sheng Pao: 260 Pa Teh Rd, Sec. 2, Taipei; tel. (2) 87723058; fax (2) 87723026; f. 1945; morning; Chinese; Publr LIU CHZ-SHIEN.

Taiwan News: 7/F, 88 Hsin Yi Rd, Sec. 2, Taipei 106; tel. (2) 23517666; fax (2) 23518389; e-mail editor@etaiwannews.com; internet www.etaiwannews.com; f. 1949; morning; English; Chair. T. C. KAO; Publr LUIS KO.

United Daily News: 555 Chung Hsiao East Rd, Sec. 4, Taipei; tel. (2) 27681234; fax (2) 27632303; e-mail secretariat@udngroup.com.tw; f. 1951; morning; Publr WANG SHAW-LAN; Editor-in-Chief HUANG SHU-CHUAN; circ. 1.2m.

Provincial

China Daily News (Southern Edn): 57 Hsi Hwa St, Tainan; tel. (6) 2202691; fax (6) 2201804; f. 1946; morning; Publr LIU CHZ-SHIEN; circ. 670,000.

The Commons Daily: 180 Min Chuan 2 Rd, Kaohsiung; tel. (7) 3363131; fax (7) 3363604; f. 1950; fmrly Min Chung Daily News; morning; Executive-in-Chief WANG CHIN-HSIUNG; circ. 148,000.

Keng Sheng Daily News: 36 Wuchuan St, Hualien; tel. (38) 340131; fax (38) 329664; f. 1947; morning; Publr HSIEH YING-YIN; circ. 50,000.

Taiwan Daily News: 361 Wen Shin Rd, Sec. 3, Taichung; tel. (4) 22958511; fax (4) 2958950; f. 1964; morning; Publr ANTONIO CHIANG; Editor-in-Chief LIU CHIH TSUNG; circ. 250,000.

Taiwan Hsin Wen Daily News: 3 Woo Fu I Rd, Kaohsiung; tel. (7) 2226666; f. 1949; morning; Publr CHANG REI-TE.

Taiwan Times: 32 Kaonan Rd, Jen Wu Shan, Kaohsiung; tel. (7) 3428666; fax (7) 3102828; f. 1978; Publr WANG YUH-FA.

SELECTED PERIODICALS

Artist Magazine: 6/F, 147 Chung Ching South Rd, Sec. 1, Taipei; tel. (2) 23886715; fax (2) 23317096; e-mail artvenue@seed.net.tw; f. 1975; monthly; Publr HO CHENG KUANG; circ. 28,000.

Better Life Monthly: 11 Lane 199, Hsin-yih Rd, Sec. 4, Taipei; tel. (2) 27549588; fax (2) 27016068; e-mail bettlife@ms14.hinet.net; f. 1987; Publr JACK S. LIN.

Brain: 9/F, 47 Nanking East Rd, Sec. 4, Taipei; tel. (2) 27132644; fax (2) 27137318; f. 1977; monthly; Publr JOHNSON WU.

Business Weekly: 12/F, No.141, Sec. 2, Minsheng East Rd, Jhongshan District, Taipei 104; tel. (2) 25056789; fax (2) 27364620; internet www.businessweekly.com.tw; f. 1987; Publr JIN WEI-TSUN.

Car Magazine: 1/F, 3 Lane 3, Tung-Shan St, Taipei; tel. (2) 23218128; fax (2) 23935614; e-mail carguide@ms13.hinet.net; f. 1982; monthly; Publr H. K. LIN; Editor-in-Chief TA-WEI LIN; circ. 85,000.

Central Monthly: 7/F, 11 Chung Shan South Rd, Taipei; tel. (2) 23433140; fax (2) 23435417; f. 1950; Publr HUANG HUI-TSEN.

China Times Weekly: 5/F, 25 Min Chuan East Rd, Sec. 6, Taipei; tel. (2) 27936000; fax (2) 27912238; f. 1978; weekly; Chinese; Publr CHANG KUO-LI.

Commonwealth Monthly: 11/F, No. 139, Sec. 2, Nanking East Rd, Taipei 104; tel. (2) 85078629; fax (2) 25079011; f. 1981; monthly; business; Pres. CHARLES H. C. KAO; Publr and Editor DIANE YING; circ. 83,000.

Cosmopolitan: 5/F, 8 Lane 181, Jiou-Tzung Rd, Nei Hu Area, Taipei; tel. (2) 287978900; fax (2) 287978990; e-mail hwaker@ms13.hinet.net; f. 1992; monthly; Publr MINCHUN CHANG.

Country Road: 14 Wenchow St, Taipei; tel. (2) 23628148; fax (2) 23636724; e-mail h3628148@ms15.hinet.net; internet www.harvest.org.tw; f. 1975; monthly; Editor YU SHU-LIEN; Publr SUN MING-HSIEN.

Crown Magazine: 50 Alley 120, Tun Hua North Rd, Sec. 4, Taipei; tel. (2) 27168888; fax (2) 25148285; f. 1954; monthly; literature and arts; Publr PING HSIN TAO; Editor CHEN LIH-HWA; circ. 76,000.

Defense Technology Monthly: 6/F, 6 Nanking East Rd, Sec. 5, Taipei; tel. (2) 27669628; fax (2) 27666092; f. 1894; Publr J. D. BIH.

Earth Geographic Monthly: 4/F, 16 Lane 130, Min Chuan Rd, Hsin-Tien, Taipei; tel. (2) 22182218; fax (2) 22185418; f. 1988; Publr HSU CHUNG-JUNG.

Elle Taiwan: 9/F, 5 Lane 30, Sec. 3, Min Sheng East Rd, Taipei; tel. (2) 87706168; fax (2) 87706178; e-mail newmedia@hft.com.tw; internet www.elle.com.tw; f. 1991; monthly; women's magazine; Publr JEAN DE WITT; Editors-in-Chief CINDY HU, DORIS LEE; circ. 50,000.

Evergreen Monthly: 11/F, 2 Pa Teh Rd, Sec. 3, Taipei; tel. (2) 25782321; fax (2) 25786838; f. 1983; health care knowledge; Publr LIANG GUANG-MING; circ. 50,000.

Excellence Magazine: 3/F, 15 Lane 2, Sec. 2, Chien Kuo North Rd, Taipei; tel. (2) 25093578; fax (2) 25173607; f. 1984; monthly; business; Man. LIN HSIN-JYH; Editor-in-Chief LIU JEN; circ. 70,000.

Families Monthly: 11/F, 2 Pa Teh Rd, Sec. 3, Taipei; tel. (2) 25785078; fax (2) 25786838; f. 1976; family life; Editor-in-Chief THELMA KU; circ. 155,000.

Foresight Investment Weekly: 7/F, 52 Nanking East Rd, Sec. 1, Taipei; tel. (2) 25512561; fax (2) 25119596; f. 1980; weekly; Dir and Publr SUN WUN HSIUNG; Editor-in-Chief WU WEN SHIN; circ. 55,000.

Global Views Monthly: 2/F, 1 Lane 93, Sungkiang Rd, Taipei; tel. (2) 25064617; fax (2) 25082941; f. 1986; Editor-in-Chief TIAO MING-FANG.

Gourmet World: 3/F, No. 53, Sec. 1, Jen-Ai Rd, Taipei; tel. (2) 23972215; fax (2) 23412184; f. 1992; Publr HSU TANG-JEN.

Harvest Farm Magazine: 14 Wenchow St, Taipei; tel. (2) 23628148; fax (2) 23636724; e-mail h3628148@ms15.hinet.net; internet www.harvest.org.tw; f. 1951; every 2 weeks; Publr YU SHU-LIEN; Editor SUN MING-HSIEN.

Information and Computer: 10/F, 116 Nang King East Rd, Taipei; tel. (2) 25422540; fax (2) 25310760; f. 1980; monthly; Chinese; Publr LIN FERNG-CHIN; Editor JENNIFER CHIU; circ. 28,000.

Issues and Studies: A Social Science Quarterly on China, Taiwan and East Asian Affairs: Institute of International Relations, National Chengchi University, 64 Wan Shou Rd, Wenshan, Taipei 116; tel. (2) 29386763; fax (2) 82377231; e-mail issues@nccu.edu.tw; internet http://iir.nccu.edu.tw/English/I&S.htm; f. 1965; quarterly; English; contemporary Chinese studies and East Asian affairs; Editor CHEN-SHEN J. YEN.

Jade Biweekly Magazine: 7/F, 222 Sung Chiang Rd, Taipei; tel. (2) 25811665; fax (2) 25210586; f. 1982; economics, social affairs, leisure; Publr HSU CHIA-CHUNG; circ. 98,000.

The Journalist: 16/F, 218 Tun Hua South Rd, Sec. 2, Taipei; tel. (2) 23779977; fax (2) 23775850; f. 1987; weekly; Publr WANG SHIN-CHING.

Ladies Magazine: 11/F, 3, 187 Shin Yi Rd, Sec. 4, Taipei; tel. (2) 27026908; fax (2) 27014090; f. 1978; monthly; Publr CHENG CHIN-SHAN; Editor-in-Chief THERESA LEE; circ. 60,000.

Living: 6/F, 100 Ai Kuo East Rd, Hsin Tien, Taipei; tel. (2) 23222266; fax (2) 33225050; f. 1997; monthly; Publr LISA WU.

Madame Figaro Taiwan: f. 2001; published by Stone Media.

Management Magazine: 5/F, 220 Ta Tung Rd, Sec. 3, Hsichih, Taipei; tel. (2) 86471828; fax (2) 86471466; e-mail frankhung@mail.chinamgt.com; internet www.harment.com; f. 1973; monthly; Chinese; Publr and Editor FRANK L. HUNG; Pres. KATHY T. KUO; circ. 65,000.

Money Monthly: 10/F, 289 Chung Hsiao East Rd, Taipei; tel. (2) 25149822; fax (2) 27154657; f. 1986; monthly; personal financial management; Publr PATRICK SUN; Man. Editor JENNIE SHUE; circ. 55,000.

Music and Audiophile: 2/F, 2 Kingshan South Rd, Sec. 1, Taipei; tel. (2) 25684607; fax (2) 23958654; f. 1973; Publr CHANG KUO-CHING; Editor-in-Chief CHARLES HUANG.

National Palace Museum Monthly of Chinese Art: No. 221, Sec. 2, Jishan Rd, Shrlin Chiu, Taipei 11102; tel. (2) 28821230; fax (2) 28821440; f. 1983; monthly in Chinese; Publr TU CHENG-SHENG; circ. 10,000.

National Geographic/The Earth: 4/F, 319, Sec. 4, Bade Rd, Taipei 105; tel. (2) 27485988; fax (2) 27480188.

Nong Nong Magazine: 11/F, 141, Sec. 2, Minsheng East Rd, Taipei 104; tel. (2) 25058989; fax (2) 25001986; e-mail group@nongnong .com.tw; f. 1984; monthly; women's interest; Publr ANTHONY TSAI; Editor VIVIAN LIN; circ. 70,000.

PC Home: 4/F, 141, Sec. 2, Minsheng East Rd, Taipei 104; tel. (2) 25000888; fax (2) 25006609; f. 1996; monthly; Publr HUNG-TZE JANG.

PC Office: 11/F, 8 Tun Hua North Rd, Taipei; tel. (2) 25007779; fax (2) 25007903; f. 1997; monthly; Publr HUNG-TZE JANG.

Reader's Digest (Chinese Edn): 2/F, 2 Ming Sheng East Rd, Sec. 5, Taipei; tel. (2) 27607262; fax (2) 27461588; monthly; Editor-in-Chief VICTOR FUNG.

Sinorama: 5/F, 54 Chunghsiao East Rd, Sec. 1, Taipei 100; tel. (2) 23922256; fax (2) 23970655; f. 1976; monthly; cultural; bilingual magazine with edns in Chinese with Japanese, Spanish and English; Publr SU TZA-PING; Editor-in-Chief ANNA Y. WANG; circ. 110,000.

Studio Classroom: 10 Lane 62, Ta-Chih St, Taipei; tel. (2) 25338082; fax (2) 25331009; internet www.studioclassroom.com; f. 1962; monthly; Publr DORIS BROUGHAM.

Taipei Journal: 2 Tientsin St, Taipei 10041; tel. (2) 23970180; fax (2) 23568233; e-mail tj@mail.gio.gov.tw; internet taipeijournal.nat .gov.tw; f. 1964; fmrly Free China Journal; weekly; English; news review; Publr ARTHUR IAP; Exec. Editor-in-Chief MICHAEL CHEN; circ. 30,000.

Taipei Times: 5/F, 137 Nanking East Rd, Sec. 2, Taipei; tel. (2) 25182728; fax (2) 25189154; internet www.taipeitimes.com; f. 1999; Publr ANTONIO CHIANG.

Taiwan Review: 2 Tientsin St, Taipei 100; tel. (2) 23516419; e-mail tr@mail.gio.gov.tw; f. 1951; fmrly *Taipei Review*, renamed as above March 2003; monthly; English; illustrated; Publr Dr LIN CHIA-LUNG; Editor-in-Chief ANDREW T. H. CHENG.

Time Express: 7/F, 2, 76 Tun Hua South Rd, Sec. 2, Taipei; tel. (2) 27084410; fax (2) 27084420; f. 1973; monthly; Publr RICHARD C. C. HUANG.

Unitas: 10/F, 180 Keelung Rd, Sec. 1, Taipei; tel. (2) 27666759; fax (2) 27567914; e-mail unitas@udngroup.com.tw; monthly; Chinese; literary journal; Publr CHANG PAO-CHING; Editor-in-Chief HSU HUI-CHIH.

Vi Vi Magazine: 7/F, 550 Chung Hsiao East Rd, Sec. 5, Taipei; tel. (2) 27275336; fax (2) 27592031; f. 1984; monthly; women's interest; Pres. TSENG CHING-TANG; circ. 60,000.

Vogue/GQ Conde Nast Interculture: 15/F, 51, Sec. 2, Keelung Rd, Sinyi District, Taipei 110; tel. (2) 27328899; fax (2) 27390504; f. 1996; monthly; Publr BENTHAM LIU.

Wealth Magazine: 7/F, 52 Nanking East Rd, Sec. 1, Taipei; tel. (2) 25816196; fax (2) 25119596; f. 1974; monthly; finance; Pres. TSHAI YEN-KUEN; Editor ANDY LIAN; circ. 75,000.

Win Win Weekly: 7/F, 52 Nanking East Rd, Taipei; tel. (2) 25816196; fax (2) 25119596; f. 1996; Publr GIN-HO HSHIE.

Youth Juvenile Monthly: 3/F, 66-1 Chung Cheng South Rd, Sec. 1, Taipei; tel. (2) 23112832; fax (2) 23612239; e-mail youth@ms2.hinet .net; internet www.youth.com.tw; f. 1965; Publr LEE CHUNG-GUAI.

NEWS AGENCIES

Central News Agency (CNA): 209 Sung Chiang Rd, Taipei 104; tel. (2) 25058379; fax (2) 25023805; e-mail cnamark@mail.cna.com .tw; internet www.cna.com.tw; f. 1924; news service in Chinese, English and Spanish; feature and photographic services; 12 domestic and 30 overseas bureaux; Pres. WAN LAI-LEE (acting).

Foreign Bureaux

Agence France-Presse (AFP): Rm 617, 6/F, 209 Sung Chiang Rd, Taipei; tel. (2) 25016395; fax (2) 25011881; e-mail AFPTPE@ms11 .hitnet.tw; Bureau Chief YANG HSIN-HSIN.

Associated Press (AP) (USA): Rm 630, 6/F, 209 Sung Chiang Rd, Taipei; tel. (2) 25036651; fax (2) 25007133; Bureau Chief WILLIAM FOREMAN.

Reuters (UK): 10/F, 196 Chien Kuo North Rd, Sec. 2, Taipei; tel. (2) 25033034; fax (2) 25092624; Bureau Chief TIFFANY WU.

Publishers

There are 7,810 publishing houses. In 2001 a total of 40,235 titles were published.

Art Book Co: 1/F, 18 Lane 283, Roosevelt Rd, Sec. 3, Taipei; tel. (2) 23620578; fax (2) 23623594; e-mail artbook@ms43.hinet.net; Publr HO KUNG SHANG.

Cheng Wen Publishing Co: 3/F, 277 Roosevelt Rd, Sec. 3, Taipei; tel. (2) 23628032; fax (2) 23660806; e-mail ccicncwp@ms17.hinet.net; Publr LARRY C. HUANG.

Children Publication Co Ltd: 1F-1, 314 Nei-Hu Rd, Taipei; tel. (2) 87972799; fax (2) 87972700; e-mail cplemail@ms11.hinet.net; internet www.012book.com.tw; f. 1994.

China Times Publishing Co: 2/F, 240 Hoping West Rd, Sec. 3, Taipei; tel. (2) 23686222; fax (2) 23049302; e-mail ctpc@mse.hinet .net; internet www.readingtimes.com.tw; f. 1975; Pres. MO CHAO-PING.

Chinese Culture University Press: 55 Hua Kang Rd, Yangming-shan, Taipei; tel. (2) 28611861; fax (2) 28617164; e-mail ccup@staff .pccu.edu.tw; Publr LEE FU-CHEN.

Cite Publishing Ltd: 2/F, 141 Mingsheng East Rd, Sec. 2, Taipei; tel. (2) 25000888; fax (2) 25001941; e-mail sales@cite.com.tw; internet www.cite.com.tw; f. 1996.

The Commercial Press Ltd: 37 Chungking South Rd, Sec. 1, Taipei; tel. (2) 23115538; fax (2) 23716274; e-mail cptw@ms12.hinet .net; f. 1897; Editor NANCY YI-YING CHIANG.

Commonwealth Publishing Co: 2/F, 1 Lane 93, Sung Chiang Rd, Taipei; tel. (2) 25076735; fax (2) 25082941; e-mail jeffchen@cwgv .com.tw; internet www.bookzone.com.tw; f. 1982.

Crown Publishing Group: 50 Lane 120, Tun Hua North Rd, Taipei; tel. (2) 27168888; fax (2) 27133422; e-mail edit3@crown.com .tw; internet www.crown.com.tw; f. 1954; Publr PHILIP PING; 90 employees.

The Eastern Publishing Co Ltd: 121 Chungking South Rd, Sec. 1, Taipei; tel. (2) 23114514; fax (2) 23814132; Publr CHENG LI-TSU.

Elite Publishing Co: 1/F, 33-1 Lane 113, Hsiamen St, Taipei 100; tel. (2) 23671021; fax (2) 23657047; e-mail elite113@ms12.hinet.net; f. 1975; Publr KO CHING-HWA.

Far East Book Co: 10/F, 66-1 Chungking South Rd, Sec. 1, Taipei; tel. (2) 23118740; fax (2) 23114184; e-mail service@mail.fareast.com .tw; internet www.fareast.com.tw; art, education, history, physics, mathematics, law, literature, dictionaries, textbooks, language tapes, Chinese-English dictionary; Publr GEORGE C. L. PU.

International Cultural Enterprises: Rm 612, 6/F, 25 Po Ai Rd, Taipei 100; tel. (2) 23318080; fax (2) 23318090; e-mail itsits@ms69 .hinet.net; internet www.itsits.com.tw; Publr LAKE HU.

Kwang Hwa Publishing Co: 5/F, 54 Chung Hsiao East Rd, Sec. 1, Taipei; tel. (2) 23922256; fax (2) 23970655; e-mail service@sinorama .com.tw; internet www.sinorama.com.tw; Publr ARTHUR IAP.

Li-Ming Cultural Enterprise Co: 2/F, 49 Chungking South Rd, Sec. 1, Taipei 100; tel. (2) 23310537; fax (2) 23821244; e-mail liming03@ms57.hinet.net; internet www.limingco.com.tw; f. 1971; Pres. SHEN FANG-SHIN.

Linking Publishing Co Ltd: 555, Sec. 4, Jhongsiao East Rd, Taipei; tel. (2) 27681234; fax (2) 27493734; e-mail linkingp@ms9 .hinet.net; internet www.udngroup.com.tw/linkingp; Publr LIU KUO-JUEI.

Locus Publishing Co: 11/F, 25 Nanking East Rd, Sec.4, Taipei; tel. (2) 87123898; fax (2) 87123897; e-mail locus@locuspublishing.com; internet www.locuspublishing.com; f. 1996.

San Min Book Co Ltd: 386 Fushing North Rd, Taipei; tel. (2) 25006600; fax (2) 25064000; e-mail editor@sanmin.com.tw; internet www.sanmin.com.tw; f. 1953; literature, history, philosophy, social sciences, dictionaries, art, politics, law; Publr LIU CHEN-CHIANG.

Sitak Publishing Group: 10/F, 15 Lane 174, Hsin Ming Rd, Neihu Dist., Taipei; tel. (2) 27911197; fax (2) 27918606; e-mail readers@ sitak.com.tw; internet www.sitak.com.tw; Publr CHU PAO-LOUNG; Dir KELLY CHU.

Taiwan Kaiming Book Co: 77 Chung Shan North Rd, Sec. 1, Taipei; tel. (2) 25510820; fax (2) 25212894; Publr LUCY CHOH LIU.

Tung Hua Book Co Ltd: 105 Emei St, Taipei; tel. (2) 23114027; fax (2) 23116615; e-mail service@bookcake.com.tw; internet www .bookcake.com.tw; f. 1965; Publr CHARLES CHOH.

The World Book Co: 6/F, 99 Chungking South Rd, Sec. 1, Taipei; tel. (2) 23113834; fax (2) 23317963; e-mail wbc.ltd@msa.hinet.com; internet www.worldbook.com.tw; f. 1921; literature, textbooks; Chair. YEN FENG-CHANG; Publr YEN ANGELA CHU.

Youth Cultural Enterprise Co Ltd: 3/F, 66-1 Chungking South Rd, Sec. 1, Taipei; tel. (2) 23112832; fax (2) 23113309; e-mail howei@ hotmail.com; internet www.youth.com.tw; f. 1958; Publr LEE CHUNG-KUEI.

Yuan Liou Publishing Co Ltd: 6/F, 81, Sec. 2, Nanchang Rd, Taipei; tel. (2) 23926899; fax (2) 33223707; e-mail ylib@ylib.com; internet www.ylib.com; f. 1975; fiction, non-fiction, children's; Publr WANG JUNG-WEN.

Broadcasting and Communications

TELECOMMUNICATIONS

Directorate-General of Telecommunications: Ministry of Transportation and Communications, 16 Chinan Rd, Sec. 2, Taipei; tel. (2) 23433969; internet www.dgt.gov.tw; regulatory authority.

Chunghwa Telecommunications Co Ltd: 21 Hsinyi Rd, Sec. 1, Taipei; tel. (2) 23445385; fax (2) 23919166; e-mail chtir@cht.com.tw; internet www.cht.com.tw; f. 1996; state-controlled company, privatization commenced 2000; Chair. HO-CHEN TAN.

Far EasTone Telecom: 334 Sze Chuan Rd, Sec. 1, Taipei; tel. (2) 29505478; internet www.fareastone.com.tw; mobile telephone services.

KG Telecom: 43 Kuan Chien Rd, Taipei; tel. (2) 23888800; e-mail kgtweb@kgt.com.tw; internet www.kgt.com.tw; mobile telephone services.

Taiwan Cellular Corpn: internet www.twngsm.com.tw; f. 1998 as Pacific Cellular Corpn; mobile telephone and internet services; Pres. JOSEPH FAN.

BROADCASTING

Broadcasting stations are mostly commercial. The Ministry of Transportation and Communications determines power and frequencies, and the Government Information Office supervises the operation of all stations, whether private or governmental.

Radio

In July 2004 there were 155 radio broadcasting corporations in operation.

Broadcasting Corpn of China (BCC): 10/F, 375 Sung Chiang Rd, Taipei 104; tel. (2) 25019688; fax (2) 25018545; internet www.bcc .com.tw; f. 1928; domestic (6 networks and 1 channel) services; 9 local stations, 131 transmitters; Pres. LEE CHING-PING; Chair. CHAO SHOU-PO.

Central Broadcasting System (CBS): 55 Pei An Rd, Tachih, Taipei 104; tel. (2) 28856168; fax (2) 28852315; e-mail rtm@cbs.org .tw; internet www.cbs.org.tw; domestic and international service; Dir LIN FONG-CHEN.

Cheng Sheng Broadcasting Corpn Ltd: 7/F, 66-1 Chungking South Rd, Sec. 1, Taipei; tel. (2) 23617231; fax (2) 23715665; internet www.csbc.com.tw; f. 1950; 6 stations, 3 relay stations; Chair. WENG YEN-CHING; Pres. PANG WEI-NANG.

International Community Radio Taipei (ICRT): 2/F, 373 Sung Chiang Rd, Taipei; tel. (2) 25184899; fax (2) 25183666; internet www .icrt.com.tw; predominantly English-language broadcaster; Gen. Man. DOC CASEY.

Kiss Radio: 34/F, 6 Min Chuan 2 Rd, Kaohsiung; tel. (7) 3365888; fax (7) 3364931; internet www.kiss.com.tw; Pres. HELENA YUAN.

M-radio Broadcasting Corpn: 810/F-1, 1-18 Taichung Kang Rd, Sec. 2, Taichung City; tel. (4) 23235656; fax (4) 23231199; e-mail jason@mradio.com.tw; internet www.mradio.com.tw; Pres. CHEN WEI-LIANG; Gen. Man. JASON C. LIN.

UFO Broadcasting Co Ltd: 25/F, 102 Roosevelt Rd, Sec. 2, Taipei; tel. (2) 23636600; fax (2) 23673083; internet www.ufo.net.tw; Pres. JAW SHAU-KONG.

Voice of Taipei Broadcasting Co Ltd: 10/F, B Rm, 15-1 Han Chou South Rd, Sec. 1, Taipei; tel. (2) 23957255; fax (2) 23947855; internet www.vot.com.tw; Pres. NITA ING.

Television

Legislation to place cable broadcasting on a legal basis was adopted in mid-1993, and by June 2004 63 cable television companies were in operation. A non-commercial station, Public Television (PTV), went on air in July 1998. Legislation to place satellite broadcasting on a legal basis was adopted in February 1999, and by May 2004 132 satellite broadcasting channels (provided by 60 domestic and 19 international companies) and 5 domestic and 3 international Digital Broadcasting System (DBS) channels were in operation.

China Television Co (CTV): 120 Chung Yang Rd, Nan Kang District, Taipei; tel. (2) 27838308; fax (2) 27826007; e-mail pubr@ mail.chinatv.com.tw; internet www.chinatv.com.tw; f. 1969; Pres. JIANG FENG-CHYI; Chair. CHENG SUMING.

Chinese Television System (CTS): 100 Kuang Fu South Rd, Taipei 10658; tel. (2) 27510321; fax (2) 27775414; e-mail public@mail .cts.com.tw; internet www.cts.com.tw; f. 1971; cultural and educational; Chair. JOU RUNG-SHENG; Pres. SHI LU.

Formosa Television Co (FTV): 14/F, 30 Pa Teh Rd, Sec. 3, Taipei; tel. (2) 25702570; fax (2) 25773170; internet www.ftv.com.tw; f. 1997; Chair. TSAI TUNG-RONG; Pres. CHEN KANG-HSING.

Public Television Service Foundation (PTS): 90 Lane 95, Sec. 9, Kang Ning Rd, Neihu, Taipei; tel. (2) 26329533; fax (2) 26338124; e-mail pts@mail.pts.org.tw; internet www.pts.org.tw; Chair. FRANK WU; Pres. YUNG-PE LEE.

Taiwan Television Enterprise (TTV): 10 Pa Teh Rd, Sec. 3, Taipei 10560; tel. (2) 25781515; fax (2) 25799626; internet www.ttv .com.tw; f. 1962; Chair. LAI KUO-CHOU; Pres. JENG IOU.

Finance

(cap. = capital; dep. = deposits; m. = million; brs = branches; amounts in New Taiwan dollars unless otherwise stated)

BANKING

In June 1991 the Ministry of Finance granted 15 new banking licences to private banks. A 16th bank was authorized in May 1992; further authorizations followed. Restrictions on the establishment of offshore banking units were relaxed in 1994. The banking sector was undergoing consolidation during 2002–03. At the end of May 2002 there were 52 banks in Taiwan. In September 2002 the Ministry of Finance announced plans to privatize government banks by 2006, and sell its stake in commercial banks by 2010. The Financial Supervisory Commission (see under Ministries) was established in 2004.

Central Bank

Central Bank of China: 2 Roosevelt Rd, Sec. 1, Taipei 100; tel. (2) 23936161; fax (2) 23571974; e-mail adminrol@mail.cbc.gov.tw; internet www.cbc.gov.tw; f. 1928; bank of issue; cap. 80,000m., dep. 6,090,191m. (Dec. 2003); Gov. PERNG FAI-NAN.

Domestic Banks

Bank of Taiwan: 120 Chungking South Rd, Sec. 1, Taipei 10036; tel. (2) 23493456; fax (2) 23315840; e-mail botservice@mail.bot.com .tw; internet www.bot.com.tw; f. 1899; cap. 48,000m., dep. 2,004,733m. (Dec. 2003); Chair. JOSEPH JYE-CHERNG LYU; Pres. SHENG-YANN LII; 134 brs, incl. 7 overseas.

Chiao Tung Bank: 91 Heng Yang Rd, Taipei 100; tel. (2) 23613000; fax (2) 23310398; e-mail dp092@ctnbank.com.tw; internet www .ctnbank.com.tw; f. 1907; fmrly Bank of Communications; cap. 26,848.9m., res 25,125.5m., dep. 418,109.7m. (Dec. 2003); Chair. SHEN-CHIH CHENG; Pres. KUO HSIUNG-CHUANG; 34 brs, incl. 2 overseas.

Export-Import Bank of the Republic of China (Eximbank): 8/F, 3 Nan Hai Rd, Taipei 100; tel. (2) 23210511; fax (2) 23940630; e-mail eximbank@eximbank.com.tw; internet www.eximbank.com .tw; f. 1979; cap. 12,000m., res 865.2m.(Dec. 2003); Chair. PAULINE FU; Pres. JOSEPH W. TSAI; 3 brs.

Farmers Bank of China: 85 Nanking East Rd, Sec. 2, Taipei 104; tel. (2) 21003456; fax (2) 25515425; internet www.farmerbank.com .tw; f. 1933; cap. 12,474m., res 1,538.9m., dep. 495,879.5m. (Dec. 2003); Chair. HENRY K.C. CHEN; Pres. PONG-LONG LIN; 76 brs.

International Commercial Bank of China (ICBC): 100 Chi Lin Rd, Taipei 10424; tel. (2) 25633156; fax (2) 25611216; e-mail service@icbc.com.tw; internet www.icbc.com.tw; f. 1912; cap. 37,261.0m., res 22,830.7m., dep. 924,673.5m. (Dec. 2003); Chair. TZONG-YEONG LIN; Pres. Y. T. (MCKINNEY) TSAI; 82 brs, incl. 18 overseas.

Land Bank of Taiwan: 46 Kuan Chien Rd, Taipei 10038; tel. (2) 23483456; fax (2) 23757023; e-mail lbot@imail.landbank.com.tw; internet www.landbank.com.tw; f. 1946; plans to merge with Bank of Taiwan and Central Trust of China in 2002 suspended; to be privatized by 2006; cap. 25,000m., res 50,404.3m., dep. 1,590,583.4m. (Dec. 2003); Chair. CHI-LIN WEA; 110 brs.

Taiwan Co-operative Bank: 77 Kuan Chien Rd, Taipei 10038; tel. (2) 23118811; fax (2) 23890704; e-mail tacbid01@14.hinet.net; internet www.tcb-bank.com.tw; f. 1946; acts as central bank for co-operatives, and as major agricultural credit institution; cap. 22,085.5m., res 35,762.1m., dep. 1,889,670.4m. (Dec. 2003); Chair. PATRICK C. J. LIANG; Pres. WILLIAM MING-CHUNG TSENG; 144 brs.

Commercial Banks

Bank of Kaohsiung: 168 Po Ai 2nd Rd, Kaohsiung 813; tel. (7) 5570535; fax (7) 5580529; e-mail service@mail.bok.com.tw; internet www.bok.com.tw; f. 1982; cap. 5,034.2m. (Aug. 2004); Chair. FLANDY SU; Pres. S. H. CHUANG; 36 brs.

Bank of Overseas Chinese: 8 Hsiang Yang Rd, Taipei 10014; tel. (2) 23715181; fax (2) 23814056; e-mail plan@mail.booc.com.tw; internet www.booc.com.tw; f. 1961; cap. 11,376.0m., res 202.7m., dep. 253,750.0m. (Dec. 2003); Chair. HERBERT S. S. CHUNG; Pres. WEN-LONG LIN; 56 brs.

Bank of Panhsin: 18 Cheng Tu St, Ban Chiau, 220, Taipei; tel. (2) 29629170; fax (2) 29572011; internet www.bop.com.tw; f. 1997; cap. 6,000m., res 2,459.1m., dep. 95,532.0m. (Dec. 2002); Chair. PING-HUI LIU; Pres. ROGER CHUANG; 28 brs.

Bank SinoPac: 9-1 Chien Kuo North Rd, Sec. 2, Taipei; tel. (2) 25082288; fax (2) 25083456; internet www.banksinopac.com.tw; f. 1992; cap. 19,444.0m., res 3,948.8m., dep. 364,758.9m. (Dec. 2003); Chair. PAUL C. Lo; Pres. ANGUS CHEN; 35 brs.

Bowa Bank: B1, 11, 2/F, 123, Sec. 2, Chung Hsiao East Rd, Taipei 100; tel. (2) 23279998; fax (2) 33931565; e-mail bowa605@bowabank .com; internet www.bowabank.com; f. 1992; fmrly Pan Asia Bank; cap. 14,700m. (Dec. 2003); Chair. WEI-CHI LIU; Pres. WEN-KE WU; 41 brs.

Cathay United Bank: 1/F, 7, Sung Jen Rd, Taipei, 110; tel. (2) 87226666; fax (2) 87898789; internet www.cathaybk.com.tw; cap. 43,182.4, res 22,638.1m., dep. 811,163.1 (Dec. 2003); merged with United World Chinese Commercial Bank in 2003.; Chair. GREGORY K.H. WANG; Pres. ROGER WU.

Central Trust of China: 49 Wu Chang St, Sec. 1, Taipei 10006; tel. (2) 23111511; fax (2) 23611544; e-mail ctc17001@ctc.com.tw; internet www.ctoc.com.tw; f. 1935; cap. 10,000m., res 4,886.4m., dep. 198,583.4m. (Dec. 2002); Chair. JIA-DONG SHEA; Pres. RUEY-SONG HUANG; 19 brs; plans to merge with Bank of Taiwan and Land Bank of Taiwan in 2002 suspended.

Chang Hwa Commercial Bank Ltd: 57, Sec. 2, Chungshan North Rd, Taipei; tel. (2) 25362951; fax (2) 25716871; e-mail customem@ ms1.chb.com.tw; internet www.chb.com.tw; f. 1905; cap. 49,594.8m., res 21,720.7m., dep. 1,212,158.7m. (Dec. 2003); Chair. PO-SHIN CHANG; Pres. MIKE S. E. CHANG; 153 brs, 7 overseas.

China Development Industrial Bank: F/3, 125 Nan King East Rd, Sec. 5, Taipei 105; tel. (2) 27638800; fax (2) 27660047; internet www.cdibank.com.tw; Chair. ANGELO J.Y. KOO; Pres. JEFFREY SUEN.

Chinatrust Commercial Bank: 3 Sung Shou Rd, Taipei 110; tel. (2) 27222002; fax (2) 27251499; internet www.chinatrust.com.tw; f. 1966; cap. 48,554.3m., dep. 765,189.4m. (Dec. 2002); Chinatrust Financial Holding Co; Chair. JEFFREY L. S. KOO; Pres. ERIC CHEN; 57 brs, 11 overseas.

The Chinese Bank: 6 Chung Hsiao West Rd, Sec. 1, Taipei 100; tel. (2) 55586666; fax (2) 55584556; e-mail tcb014@mail.chinesebank .com.tw; internet www.chinesebank.com.tw; f. 1992; cap. 15,171m., res 648.4m., dep. 195,831.8m. (Dec. 2003); Chair. FAN-HSIUNG KAO; 30 brs.

Chinfon Commercial Bank: 1 Nanyang St, Taipei 100; tel. (2) 23114881; fax (2) 23712395; e-mail ibd@chinfonbank.com.tw; internet www.chinfonbank.com.tw; f. 1971; cap 11,128m., res 78.2m., dep. 139,151.3m. (Dec. 2003); Chair. HUANG SHI-HUI; Pres GREGORY C. P. CHANG; 34 brs, 2 overseas.

Chung Shing Bank: 30, Su Wei 4th Rd, Kaohsiung 802; tel. (7) 3386033; internet www.csbank.com.tw; f. 1992; Chair. NAN-HWA WANG; Pres. CHIEN-CHING KUO; 25 brs.

Cosmos Bank: 5-10F., Tun Hua South Rd, Sec. 2, Taipei 106; tel. (2) 27011777; fax (2) 27849848; e-mail ibd@cosmosbank.com.tw; internet www.cosmosbank.com.tw; f. 1992; cap. 17,710m., res. 866.9m., dep. 219,108.3m. (Dec. 2003); Chair. HSUI SHENG-FA; Pres. C. C. HU; 35 brs.

Cota Commercial Bank: 59, Shih Fu Rd, Taichung 400; tel. (4) 22245161; fax (4) 22275237; internet www.cotabank.com.tw; f. 1995; cap. 3,184m., dep. 53,906m. (Dec. 2001); Chair. LIAO CHUN-TSE; Pres CHANG YING-CHE; 18 brs.

E. Sun Commercial Bank: 3/F, 115 Minsheng East Rd, Sec. 3, Taipei; tel. (2) 21751313; fax (2) 25475613; e-mail esbintl@email .esunbank.com.tw; internet www.esunbank.com.tw; f. 1992; cap. 18,175.0m., res 261.9m., dep. 289,142.8m. (Dec. 2003); acquired Kaohsiung Business Bank in 2004; Chair. HUANG YUNG-JEN; Pres. HOU YUNG-HSUNG; 114 brs.

Enterprise Bank of Hualien: 1-7 Kung Yuan Rd, Hualien, 970; tel. (38) 351101; fax (38) 359162; e-mail hebsecd@ms27.hinet.nt; internet www.banklotus.com.tw; Chair. JASON KAO; Pres. HO PING-TUNG.

Entie Commercial Bank: 158 Min Sheng East Rd, Sec. 3, Taipei; tel. (2) 27189999; fax (2) 27187843; internet www.entiebank.com.tw; f. 1993; cap. 14,093m., dep. 174,572m. (Dec. 2001); Chair. PAUL C.H. CHIU; Pres. ANDREW C.Y. TSAI; 39 brs.

Far Eastern International Bank: 207 Tun Hua South Rd, Sec. 2, Taipei; tel. (2) 23786868; fax (2) 23779000; e-mail 800@mail.feib.com .tw; internet www.feib.com.tw; f. 1992; cap. 15,248m., res 1,308.3m., dep. 188,040.7m. (Dec. 2002); Chair. DOUGLAS T. HSU; Pres. ELI HONG; 30 brs.

First Commercial Bank: 30, Sec. 1, Chung Ching South Rd, Taipei 100; tel. (2) 23481111; fax (2) 23892967; e-mail fcb@mail.firstbank .com.tw; internet www.firstbank.com.tw; f. 1899; cap. 46,216m., res 24,991.8m., dep. 1,374,734.9m. (Dec. 2003); Chair. STEVE S. F. SHIEH; Pres. LONG-I LIAO; 159 brs, 11 overseas.

Fuhwa Commercial Bank: 4, Sec. 1, Chung Hsiao West Rd, Taipei 100; tel. (2) 23801888; fax (2) 23801700; e-mail service@fuhwabank .com.tw; internet www.fuhwabank.com.tw; Chair. KANG-SHIEN KAO; Pres. CHUNG-HSING CHEN.

Hsinchu International Bank: 106 Chung Yang Rd, Hsinchu 300; tel. (3) 5245131; fax (35) 250977; internet www.hibank.com.tw; f. 1948; cap. 12,901.1m., res 651.2m., dep. 307,355.5m. (Dec. 2003); Chair. S. Y. CHAN; Pres C. W. WU; 73 brs.

Hua Nan Commercial Bank: 38 Chung Ching South Rd, Sec. 1, Taipei; tel. (2) 23713111; fax (2) 23316741; e-mail service@ms.hncb .com.tw; internet www.hncb.com.tw; f. 1919; cap. 37,091m., res 12,580.9m., dep. 1,353,331m. (Dec. 2003); Chair. LIN MING-CHEN; Pres. HSU TEH-NAN; 138 brs, 5 overseas.

Hwatai Commercial Bank: 246 Chang An E. Rd, Sec. 2, Taipei; tel. (2) 27525252; fax (2) 87725177; e-mail h0014@hwataibank.com .tw; internet www.hwataibank.com.tw; f. 1999; cap. 4,166m., res 2,049m., dep. 67,228m. (Sept. 2003); Chair. M. H. LIN; Pres. THOMAS C. W. LEE; 30 brs.

Industrial Bank of Taiwan: F/3, 97 Sung Jen Rd, Taipei 110; tel. (2) 23451101; fax (2) 87933568; internet www.ibt.com.tw; Chair. KENNETH C. M. LO; Pres. HENRY W. PANG.

International Bank of Taipei: 36 Nanking East Rd, Sec. 3, Taipei; tel. (2) 25063333; fax (2) 25063744; e-mail b630@ibtpe.com.tw; internet www.ibtpe.com.tw; f. 1948; cap. 21,159m., res 9,737.7m., dep. 331,292.6m. (Dec. 2003); Chair. S. C. HO; Pres. K. C. YU; 88 brs.

Jih Sun International Bank: 10 Chung King South Rd, Sec. 1, Taipei 100; tel. (2) 23119888; fax (2) 23613988; internet www .jihsunbank.com.tw; f. 1992 as Baodao Commercial Bank, assumed present name in December 2001; cap. 10,815m., dep. 148,405m. (May 2000); Chair. EDWARD K. H. CHEN; Pres. DOLLY YANG; 24 brs.

Kao Shin Commercial Bank: 75 Lih Wen Rd, Kaohsiung 813; tel. (7) 5580711; fax (7) 5592980; e-mail www.ksbank.com.tw; f. 1997; Chair. F. T. CHAO; Pres. CHARLES W. CHUNG; 27 brs.

Lucky Bank: 35 Chung Hua Rd, Sec. 1, Taichung 403; tel. (4) 22259111; fax (4) 22258624; e-mail iclkbank@ms23.hinet.net; internet www.luckybank.com.tw; f. 1997; Chair. C. C. CHANG; Pres. T. Y. SU; 27 brs.

Macoto Bank: 134 Hsi Chang St, Taipei 108; tel. (2) 23812160; fax (2) 23752538; e-mail master@macoto.com.tw; internet www .macotobank.com.tw; f. 1997; cap. 7,090m., res 3,446m., dep. 201,171.4m. (Dec. 2003); Chair. C. I. LIN; Pres. FRANK HUNG; 49 brs.

Shanghai Commercial and Savings Bank: 2 Min Chuan East Rd, Sec. 1, Taipei 104; tel. (2) 25817111; fax (2) 25318501; internet www.scsb.com.tw; f. 1915; cap. 14,340m., dep. 313,022m. (Dec. 2003); Chair. H. C. YUNG; Pres. Y. P. CHEN; 58 brs.

Sunny Bank: 88 Shih Pai Rd, Sec. 1, Taipei 112; tel. (2) 28208166; fax (2) 28233414; internet www.esunnybank.com.tw; f. 1997; cap. 6,161.7m., res 134.2m., dep. 126,305.1m. (Dec. 2002); Chair. S. H. CHEN; Pres. CHUEH-YANG HU; 22 brs.

Ta Chong Commercial Bank: 58 Chungcheng 2nd Rd, Kaohsiung; tel. (2) 8786988; fax (2) 2509883; e-mail service@tcbank.com.tw; internet www.tcbank.com.tw; f. 1992; Chair. TIAN-MAO CHEN; Pres. CHIN-TANG HUANG; 38 brs.

Taichung Commercial Bank: 87 Min Chuan Rd, Taichung 403; tel. (4) 22236021; fax (4) 22240748; e-mail webmaster@ms1.tcbbank .com.tw; internet www.tcbbank.com.tw; f. 1953; cap. 15,380m. (Dec. 2000), dep. 207,440m. (Dec. 2002); Chair. Y. F. TSAI; Pres. Y. C. TSAI; 80 brs.

Tainan Business Bank: 506 His Men Rd, Sec. 1, Tainan 700; tel. (6) 2139171; fax (6) 2136885; e-mail tnb@ms5.hinet.net; internet www.tnb.com.tw; Chair. CHEN PING-CHUN; Pres. CHEN FANG-LIEH.

Taipei Fubon Bank: internet www.taipeibank.com.tw; internet www.fubonbank.com.tw; f. 1969; fmrly City Bank of Taipei; acquired by Fubon Financial Holding in August 2002. Official merger of Taipei Bank and Fubon Commercial Bank in Jan. 2005, renamed as above; 124 brs, 3 overseas.

Taishin International Bank: 44 Chung Shan North Rd, Sec. 2, Taipei 104; tel. (2) 25683988; fax (2) 251177434551; e-mail pr@ taishinbank.com.tw; internet www.taishinbank.com.tw; f. 1992; absorbed Dah An Commercial Bank in Feb. 2002; cap. 28,467.8m., res 7,298.2m., dep. 510,332.3m. (Dec. 2003); Chair. THOMAS T. L. WU; Pres. CHARLES WANG; 39 brs.

Taitung Business Bank: 354 Chung Hwa Rd, Sec. 1, Taitung 950; tel. (89) 331191; fax (89) 331194; e-mail secretpb@ttbb.com.tw; internet www.ttbb.com.tw; f. 1955; Chair. TEIN-KON SHAW; Pres. K. T. CHEN.

Taiwan Business Bank: 30 Tacheng St, Taipei 103; tel. (2) 25597171; fax (2) 25507942; e-mail tbb3688@hotmail.com; internet www.tbb.com.tw; f. 1915; reassumed present name 1994; cap. 31,357.2m., res 7,642.8m., dep. 924,371.7m. (Dec. 2003); Chair. RONG-JOU WANG; Pres. JIN-FONG SOO.

Union Bank of Taiwan: 109 Ming Sheng East Rd, Sec. 3, Taipei 105; tel. (2) 27180001; fax (2) 27174093; e-mail 014_0199@email .ubot.com.tw; internet www.ubot.com.tw; f. 1992; cap. 14,889.3m., res 510.0m., dep. 182,851m. (Dec. 2003); Chair. C. C. HUANG; Pres. S. C. LEE; 40 brs.

United-Credit Commercial Bank: 126 Chung Hwa Rd, Sec. 1, Taichung 400; tel. (4) 22203176; fax (4) 22232912; e-mail ucbank@ mail.ucbank.com.tw; internet www.ucbank.com.tw; Chair. CHIU CHING-TE; Pres. LEE TSENG-CHANG.

There are also a number of Medium Business Banks throughout the country.

Community Financial System

The community financial institutions include both credit co-operatives and credit departments of farmers' and fishermen's associations. These local financial institutions focus upon providing savings and loan services for the community. At the end of 2003 there were 35 credit co-operatives, 253 credit departments of farmers' associations and 25 credit departments of fishermen's associations, with a combined total deposit balance of NT $1,932,900m., while outstanding loans amounted to NT $818,800m.

Foreign Banks

In December 2002 a total of 36 foreign banks were in operation in Taiwan.

STOCK EXCHANGE

In January 1991 the stock exchange was opened to direct investment by foreign institutions, and in March 1996 it was also opened to direct investment by foreign individuals. By the end of June 2003 702 foreign institutional investors had been approved to invest in the local securities market. Various liberalization measures have been introduced since 1994. In March 1999 the limits on both single and aggregate foreign investment in domestic shares were raised to 50% of the outstanding shares of a listed company. In November of that year the 'ceiling' of investment amount for each qualified foreign institutional investor in domestic securities markets was increased from US $600m. to US $1,200m. In July 2003 the Securities and Futures Commission relaxed relevant rules and regulations on foreign institutional investors.

Taiwan Stock Exchange Corpn: 13/F, 17 Po Ai Rd, Taipei 100; tel. (2) 23485678; fax (2) 23485324; f. 1962; Chair. C. Y. LEE.

Supervisory Body

Securities and Futures Bureau: 85 Hsin Sheng South Rd, Sec. 1, Da-an District, Taipei 106; tel. (2) 87735100; fax (2) 8734143; Dir-Gen. WU TANG-CHIEH.

INSURANCE

In 1993 the Ministry of Finance issued eight new insurance licences, the first for more than 30 years. Two more were issued in 1994.

Aegon Life Insurance (Taiwan) Inc: 8/F, 39 Chung Hua Rd, Sec. 1, Taipei; tel. (2) 23707270; fax (2) 23707280; internet www.aegon .com.tw; f. 2001; Chair. JAMES H. C. LIU.

Allianz President General Insurance Co Ltd: 11/F, 69 Ming Sheng East Rd, Sec. 3, Taipei; tel. (2) 25157177; fax (2) 25077506; e-mail azpl@ms2.seeder.net; internet www.allianz.com.tw; f. 1995; Chair. NAN-TEN CHUNG; Gen. Man. NICHOLAS CHANG.

Cathay Life Insurance Co Ltd: 296 Jen Ai Rd, Sec. 4, Taipei 10650; tel. (2) 27551399; fax (2) 27551322; e-mail master@cathlife .com.tw; internet www.cathlife.com.tw; f. 1962; Chair. TSAI HONG-TU; Pres. LIU CHIU-TE; Gen. Man. LIU QIU-DE.

Central Insurance Co Ltd: 6 Chung Hsiao West Rd, Sec. 1, Taipei; tel. (2) 23819910; fax (2) 23116901; e-mail mngnt@cins.com.tw; internet www.cins.com.tw; f. 1962; Chair. HSEIN KUANG SHE; Gen. Man. CHING CHIANG HUANG.

Central Reinsurance Corpn: 12th Floor, 53 Nanking East Rd, Sec. 2, Taipei 104; tel. (2) 25115211; fax (2) 25235350; e-mail centralre@centralre.com; internet www.centralre.com; f. 1968; Chair. CHENG-TUI YANG; Pres. SOLOMON C. F. CHIU; 124 employees (2003).

Central Trust of China, Life Insurance Dept: 3–8/F, 69 Tun Hua South Rd, Sec. 2, Taipei; tel. (2) 27849151; fax (2) 27052214; e-mail sectrl@ctclife.com.tw; internet www.ctclife.com.tw; f. 1941; life insurance; Pres. EDWARD LO; Gen. Man. MAN-HSIUNG TSAI.

China Life Insurance Co Ltd: 122 Tun Hua North Rd, Taipei; tel. (2) 27196678; fax (2) 27125966; e-mail services@mail.chinalife.com .tw; internet www.chinalife.com.tw; f. 1963; Chair. C. F. KOO; Gen. Man. CHESTER C. Y. KOO.

China Mariners' Assurance Corpn Ltd: 11/F, 2 Kuan Chien Rd, Taipei; tel. (2) 23757676; fax (2) 23756363; internet www.cmac.com .tw; f. 1948; Chair. VINCENT M. S. FAN; Pres. W. H. HUNG.

Chung Kuo Insurance Co Ltd: 10–12/F, ICBC Bldg, 100 Chilin Rd, Taipei 10424; tel. (2) 25513345; fax (2) 25414046; f. 1931; fmrly China Insurance Co Ltd; Chair. S. Y. LIU; Pres. C. Y. LIU.

Chung Shing Life Insurance Co Ltd: 18/F, 200 Keelung Rd, Sec. 1, Taipei 110; tel. (2) 27583099; fax (2) 23451635; f. 1993; Chair. T. S. CHAO; Gen. Man. DAH-WEI CHEN.

The First Insurance Co Ltd: 54 Chung Hsiao East Rd, Sec. 1, Taipei; tel. (2) 23913271; fax (2) 23930685; internet www.firsin.com .tw; f. 1962; Chair. CHENG HANG LEE; Pres. JAMES LAI.

Fubon Insurance Co Ltd: 237 Chien Kuo South Rd, Sec. 1, Taipei; tel. (2) 27067890; fax (2) 27042915; internet www.fubon-ins.com.tw; f. 1961; Chair. TSAI MING-CHUNG; Gen. Man. T. M. SHIH.

Fubon Life Assurance Co Ltd: 14/F, 108 Tun Hua South Rd, Sec. 1, Taipei; tel. (2) 87716699; fax (2) 87715919; f. 1993; Chair. RICHARD M. TSAI; Gen. Man. PEN-YUAN CHENG.

Global Life Insurance Co Ltd: 18 Chung Yang South Rd, Sec. 2, Peitou, Taipei 11235; tel. (2) 28967899; fax (2) 28958312; e-mail jimbolin@globallife.com.tw; internet www.globallife.com.tw; f. 1993; Chair. JOHN TSENG; Pres. GIN-CHUNG LIN.

Hontai Life Insurance Co Ltd: 7/F, 70 Cheng Teh Rd, Sec. 1, Taipei; tel. (2) 25595151; fax (2) 25562840; internet www.hontai.com .tw; f. 1994; fmrly Hung Fu Life Insurance Co; Chair. TONY SHE; Gen. Man. YU-CHIEH YANG.

Kuo Hua Insurance Co Ltd: 166 Chang An East Rd, Sec. 2, Taipei; tel. (2) 27514225; fax (2) 27819388; e-mail kh11601@kuohua.com.tw; internet www.kuohua.com.tw; f. 1962; Chair. and Gen. Man. J. B. WANG.

Kuo Hua Life Insurance Co Ltd: 42 Chung Shan North Rd, Sec. 2, Taipei; tel. (2) 25621101; fax (2) 25423832; internet www.khl.com .tw; f. 1963; Chair. DANIEL OUNG; Pres. C. T. KUO.

Mercuries Life Insurance Co Ltd: 6/F, 2 Lane 150, Hsin-Yi North Rd, Sec. 5, Taipei; tel. (2) 23455511; fax (2) 23456616; internet www .mli.com.tw; f. 1993; Chair. HARVEY TANG; Gen. Man. CHUNG-SHIN LU.

Mingtai Fire and Marine Insurance Co Ltd: 1 Jen Ai Rd, Sec. 4, Taipei; tel. (2) 27725678; fax (2) 27729932; internet www.mingtai .com.tw; f. 1961; Chair. LARRY P. C. LIN; Gen. Man. H. T. CHEN.

Nan Shan Life Insurance Co Ltd: 144 Min Chuan East Rd, Sec. 2, Taipei 104; tel. (2) 25013333; fax (2) 25012555; internet www .nanshanlife.com.tw; f. 1963; Chair. EDMUND TSE; Pres. SUNNY LIN.

Newa Insurance Co Ltd: 6/F, 458 Hsin Yi Rd, Sec. 4, Taipei; tel. (2) 27205522; fax (2) 87891190; internet www.newa.com.tw; f. 1999; Chair. KENNETH K. T. YEN; Gen. Man. CHUNG-KENG CHEN.

Prudential Life Assurance Co Ltd: 12/F, 550 Chung Hsiao East Rd, Sec. 4, Taipei; tel. (2) 27582727; fax (2) 27086758; internet www .prudential-uk.com.tw; f. 1999; Chair. DOMINIC LEUNG KA KUI; CEO DAN L. TING.

Shin Fu Life Insurance Co Ltd: 8/F, 6 Chung Hsiao West Rd, Sec. 1, Taipei; tel. (2) 23817172; fax (2) 23817162; f. 1993; Chair. and Gen. Man. SONG CHI CHIENG.

Shin Kong Insurance Co Ltd: 15 Chien Kuo North Rd, Sec. 2, Taipei; tel. (2) 25075335; fax (2) 25074580; internet www.shinkong .com.tw; f. 1963; Chair. ANTHONY T. S. WU; Pres. YIH HSIUNG LEE.

Shin Kong Life Insurance Co Ltd: 66 Chung Hsiao West Rd, Sec. 1, Taipei; tel. (2) 23895858; fax (2) 23758688; internet www.skl.com .tw; f. 1963; Chair. EUGENE T. C. WU; Gen. Man. HONG-CHI CHENG.

Sinon Life Insurance Co Ltd: 11-2/F, 155 Tsu Chih St, Taichung; tel. (4) 3721653; fax (4) 3722008; e-mail sinonlife@mail.sinonlife.com .tw; internet www.sinonlife.com.tw; f. 1993; Chair. PO-YEN HORNG; Gen. Man. P. T. LAI.

South China Insurance Co Ltd: 5/F, 560 Chung Hsiao East Rd, Sec. 4, Taipei; tel. and fax (2) 27298022; internet www.south-china .com.tw; f. 1963; Chair. C. F. LIAO; Pres. ALLAN I. R. HUANG.

Tai Ping Insurance Co Ltd: 3–5/F, 550 Chung Hsiao East Rd, Sec. 4, Taipei; tel. (2) 27582700; fax (2) 27295681; f. 1929; Chair. C. C. HUANG; Gen. Man. JAMES SUN.

Taian Insurance Co Ltd: 59 Kwantsien Rd, Taipei; tel. (2) 23819678; fax (2) 23315332; e-mail taian@mail.taian.com.tw; f. 1961; Chair. C. H. CHEN; Gen. Man. PATRICK S. LEE.

Taiwan Fire and Marine Insurance Co Ltd: 8–9/F, 49 Kuan Chien Rd, Jungjeng Chiu, Taipei; tel. (2) 23821666; fax (2) 23882555; e-mail tfmi@mail.tfmi.com.tw; internet www.tfmi.com.tw; f. 1948; Chair. W. Y. LEE; Gen. Man. JOSEPH N. S. CHANG.

Taiwan Life Insurance Co Ltd: 16–19/F, 17 Hsu Chang St, Taipei; tel. (2) 23116411; fax (2) 23759714; e-mail service1@twlife .com.tw; internet www.twlife.com.tw; f. 1947; Chair. PING-YU CHU; Pres. CHENG-TAO LIN.

Union Insurance Co Ltd: 12/F, 219 Chung Hsiao East Rd, Sec. 4, Taipei; tel. (2) 27765567; fax (2) 27737199; internet www.unionins .com.tw; f. 1963; Chair. S. H. CHIN; Gen. Man. FRANK S. WANG.

Zurich Insurance Taiwan Ltd: 56 Tun Hua North Rd, Taipei; tel. (2) 27752888; fax (2) 27416004; internet www.zurich.com.tw; f. 1961; Chair. DEAN T. CHIANG; Gen. Man. YUNG H. CHEN.

Trade and Industry

GOVERNMENT AGENCIES

Bureau of Foreign Trade (Ministry of Economic Affairs): 1 Houkow St, Taipei; tel. (2) 23510271; fax (2) 23513603; e-mail boft@ trade.gov.tw; internet www.trade.gov.tw; Dir-Gen. HUANG CHIH-PENG.

Council of Agriculture (COA): 37 Nan Hai Rd, Taipei 100; tel. (2) 23812991; fax (2) 23310341; e-mail webmaster@www.coa.gov.tw; f. 1984; govt agency directly under the Executive Yuan, with ministerial status; a policy-making body in charge of national agriculture, forestry, fisheries, the animal industry and food administration; promotes technology and provides external assistance; Chair. Dr LEE CHING-LUNG; Chief Sec. CHEN CHIH-CHING.

Industrial Development Bureau (Ministry of Economic Affairs): 41-3 Hsin Yi Rd, Sec. 3, Taipei; tel. (2) 27541255; fax (2) 27030160; e-mail service@moeaidb.gov.tw; internet www.moeaidb .gov.tw; Dir-Gen. CHEN CHAO-YIH.

Industrial Development and Investment Center (Ministry of Economic Affairs): 8/F, 71 Guancian Rd, Taipei 10047; tel. (2) 23892111; fax (2) 23820497; e-mail idic@mail.idic.gov.tw; internet www.idic.gov.tw; f. 1959 to assist investment and planning; Dir-Gen. ANGELA T. CHU.

CHAMBER OF COMMERCE

General Chamber of Commerce of the Republic of China: 6/F, 390 Fu Hsing South Rd, Sec. 1, Taipei; tel. (2) 27012671; fax (2) 27542107; f. 1946; 65 mems, incl. 40 nat. feds of trade asscns, 22 district export asscns and 3 district chambers of commerce; Chair. Dr GARY WANG; Sec.-Gen. CHIU JAW-SHIN.

INDUSTRIAL AND TRADE ASSOCIATIONS

China Productivity Center: 2/F, 79 Hsin Tai 5 Rd, Sec. 1, Hsichih, Taipei County; tel. (2) 26982989; fax (2) 26982976; internet www.cpc .org.tw; f. 1956; management, technology, training, etc.; Pres. CHEN MING-CHANG.

Chinese National Association of Industry and Commerce: 13/F, 390 Fu Hsing South Rd, Sec. 1, Taipei; tel. (2) 27070111; fax (2) 27017601; Chair. JEFFREY L. S. KOO.

Chinese National Federation of Industries (CNFI): 12/F, 390 Fu Hsing South Rd, Sec. 1, Taipei; tel. (2) 27033500; fax (2) 27033982; e-mail cnfi@mail.industry.net.tw; internet www.cnfi.org .tw; f. 1948; 142 mem. asscns; Chair. LIN KUNG-CHUNG; Sec.-Gen. Y. H. KUO.

Taiwan External Trade Development Council: 5–7/F, 333 Keelung Rd, Sec. 1, Taipei 11003; tel. (2) 27255200; fax (2) 27576653;

e-mail taitra@taitra.org.tw; internet www.taiwantrade.org.tw; trade promotion body; Pres. CHAO YUEN-CHUAN.

Taiwan Handicraft Promotion Centre: 1 Hsu Chou Rd, Taipei; tel. (2) 23217233; fax (2) 23937330; e-mail chm0811@ms7.hinet.net; internet www.handicraft.org.tw; f. 1957; Pres. J. H. LIN.

Trading Department of Central Trust of China: 49 Wuchang St, Sec. 1, Taipei 10006; tel. (2) 23111511; fax (2) 23821047; f. 1935; export and import agent for private and govt-owned enterprises.

UTILITIES

Electricity

Taiwan Power Co (Taipower): 242 Roosevelt Rd, Sec. 3, Taipei 10016; tel. (2) 23651234; fax (2) 23678593; e-mail service@taipower .com.tw; internet www.taipower.com.tw; f. 1946; electricity generation; in process of privatization from 2001; Pres. and Chair. LIN CHING-CHI.

Gas

The Great Taipei Gas Corpn: 5/F, 35 Kwang Fu North Rd, Taipei; tel. (2) 27684999; fax (2) 27630480; supply of gas and gas equipment.

Water

Taipei Water Dept: 131 Changxing St, Taipei; tel. (2) 7352141; fax (2) 7353185; f. 1907; responsible for water supply in Taipei and suburban areas; Commr LIN WEN-YUAN.

CO-OPERATIVES

In December 2003 there were 5,161 co-operatives, with a total membership of 5,138,145 and total capital of NT $23,524m. Of the specialized co-operatives the most important was the consumers' co-operative (4,023 co-ops).

The Co-operative League (f. 1940) is a national organization responsible for co-ordination, education and training and the movement's national and international interests (Chair. T. C. HWANG).

TRADE UNIONS

Chinese Federation of Labour: 7/F, 17 Jin Shan South Rd, Sec.1, Taipei 100; tel. (2) 33225111; fax (2) 33225121; e-mail cfllabor@ms10 .hinet.net; internet www.cfl.org.tw; f. 1954; mems: 43 federations of unions representing 1,000,000 workers; Pres. LIN HUI-KUAN.

National Federations

Chunghwa Postal Workers' Union: 9/F, 45 Chungking South Rd, Sec. 2, Taipei 100; tel. (2) 23921380; fax (2) 23414510; e-mail cpwu8331@ms18.hinet.net; internet www.cpwu.org.tw; f. 1930; fmrly Chinese Federation of Postal Workers; restructuring completed July 2003; 25,000 mems; Pres. TSAI LIANG-CHUAN.

National Chinese Seamen's Union: 8/F, 25 Nanking East Rd, Sec. 3, Taipei; tel. (2) 25150265; fax (2) 25078211; f. 1913; 21,705 mems; Pres. FANG FU-LIANG.

Taiwan Railway Labor Union: Rm 6044, 6/F, 3 Peiping West Rd, Taipei; tel. (2) 23896115; fax (2) 23896134; f. 1947; 15,579 mems; Pres. CHEN HAN-CHIN.

Regional Federations

Taiwan Federation of Textile and Dyeing Industry Workers' Unions (TFTDWU): 2 Lane 64, Chung Hsiao East Rd, Sec. 2, Taipei; tel. (2) 23415627; f. 1958; 11,906 mems; Chair. CHANG MING-KEN.

Taiwan Provincial Federation of Labour: 92 Sungann Rd, Sec.1, Taichung; tel. (4) 22309009; fax (2) 22309012; f. 1948; 81 mem. unions and 1,571,826 mems; Pres. CHEN JEA; Sec.-Gen. HUANG YAO-TUNG.

Transport

RAILWAYS

Taiwan Railway Administration (TRA): 3 Peiping West Rd, Taipei 10026; tel. (2) 23815226; fax (2) 23831367; f. 1891; a public utility under the Ministry of Communications and Transportation; operates both the west line and east line systems, with a route length of 1,097.2 km, of which 685.0 km are electrified; the west line is the main trunk line from Keelung, in the north, to Fangliao, in the south, with several branches; electrification of the main trunk line was completed in 1979; the east line runs along the east coast, linking Hualien with Taitung; the north link line, with a length of 79.2 km from Suao Sing to Hualien, was opened in 1980; the south link line, with a length of 98.2 km from Taitung Shin to Fangliao, opened in late 1991, completing the round-the-island system; Dir-Gen. T. W. Hsu.

Bureau of High Speed Rail (BOHSR): 9/F, 7 Sianmin Blvd, Sec. 2, Banchiao City, Taipei County; tel. (2) 80723333; high-speed rail link between Taipei and Kaohsiung under construction and scheduled for completion in 2005; Dir-Gen. N. H. Ho.

Taipei Rapid Transit Corporation (TRTC): 7 Lane 48, Zhong Shan North Rd, Sec. 2, Taipei; tel. (2) 21812345; fax (2) 25115003; internet www.trtc.com.tw; f. 1994; 66 km (incl. 10.5 km light rail) open, with further lines under construction; Chair. RICHARD C. L. CHEN; Pres. Dr HUEL-SHENG TSAY.

ROADS

There were 20,947 km of highways in 2002, most of them asphalt-paved. The Sun Yat-sen Freeway was completed in 1978. Construction of a 505-km Second Freeway, which was to extend to Pingtung, in southern Taiwan, began in July 1987 and was completed in late 2003. The Nantou branch, from the Wufeng system interchange of the Second Freeway to Puli in central Taiwan, with a length of 38 km, was scheduled for completion in 2008. Work on the Taipei–Ilan freeway began in 1991. The 31-km freeway and its 24.1-km extension, from Toucheng to Suao, were scheduled to be completed in 2005.

Taiwan Area National Expressway Engineering Bureau: 1 Lane 1, Hoping East Rd, Sec. 3, Taipei; tel. (2) 27078808; fax (2) 27017818; e-mail neebeyes@taneeb.gov.tw; internet www.taneeb.gov.tw; f. 1990; responsible for planning, design, construction and maintenance of provincial and county highways; Dir-Gen. BANE L. B. CHIOU.

Taiwan Area National Freeway Bureau: POB 75, Hsinchuang, Taipei 242; tel. (2) 29096141; fax (2) 29093218; e-mail tanfb1@freeway.gov.tw; internet www.freeway.gov.tw; f. 1970; Dir-Gen. LIANG YUEH.

Taiwan Motor Transport Co Ltd: 5/F, 17 Hsu Chang St, Taipei; tel. (2) 23715364; fax (2) 23820634; f. 1980; operates national bus service; Gen. Man. CHEN WU-SHIUNG.

SHIPPING

Taiwan has six international ports: Anping, Kaohsiung, Keelung, Taichung, Hualien and Suao. In 2003 the merchant fleet comprised 637 vessels, with a total displacement of almost 3.5m. grt.

Evergreen International Storage & Transport Corpn: 899, Ching Kuo Rd, Taoyuan; tel. (3) 3252060; fax (3) 3252059.

Evergreen Marine Corpn: 166 Ming Sheng East Rd, Sec. 2, Taipei 104; tel. (2) 25057766; fax (2) 25055256; e-mail prd@evergreen-marine.com; internet www.evergreen-marine.com; f. 1968; world-wide container liner services; Chair. KUO SHIUAN-YU; Pres. ARNOLD WONG.

Taiwan Navigation Co Ltd: 29 Chi Nan Rd, Sec. 2, Taipei 104; tel. (2) 23941769; fax (2) 23919316; e-mail tnctpe@taiwanline.com.tw; internet www.taiwanline.com.tw; Chair. HSIU-PING HSIEH; Pres. I. Y. CHANG.

U-Ming Marine Transport Corpn: 29/F, Taipei Metro Tower, 207 Tun Hua South Rd, Sec. 2, Taipei; tel. (2) 27338000; fax (2) 27359900; e-mail uming@metro.feg.com.tw; internet www.feg.hinet.net/u-ming.html; world-wide transportation services; Chair. DOUGLAS HSU; Pres. C. K. ONG.

Wan Hai Lines Ltd: 10/F, 136 Sung Chiang Rd, Taipei; tel. (2) 25677961; fax (2) 25216000; e-mail serv@wanhai.com.tw; internet www.wanhai.com.tw; f. 1965; regional container liner services; Chair. CHEN CHAO HON; Pres. CHEN PO TING.

Yang Ming Marine Transport Corpn (Yang Ming Line): 271 Ming De 1st Rd, Chidu, Keelung 206; tel. (2) 24550357; fax (2) 24550781; e-mail richardyu@yml.com.tw; internet www.yml.com.tw; f. 1972; world-wide container liner services, bulk carrier and supertanker services; Chair. FRANK LU; Pres. HUANG WANG-HSIU.

CIVIL AVIATION

There are two international airports, Chiang Kai-shek at Taoyuan, near Taipei, which opened in 1979 (a second passenger terminal and expansion of freight facilities being completed in 2000), and Hsiao-kang, in Kaohsiung (where an international terminal building was inaugurated in 1997). There are also 16 domestic airports. In March 2004 Air Macau opened a new passenger air route between Shenzhen Airport, on the mainland, with Taipei via Macao.

Civil Aeronautics Administration: 340 Tun Hua North Rd, Taipei; tel. (2) 23496000; fax (2) 23496277; e-mail gencaa@mail.caa.gov.tw; internet www.caa.gov.tw; Dir-Gen. BILLY K. C. CHANG.

China Airlines Ltd (CAL): 131 Nanking East Rd, Sec. 3, Taipei; tel. (2) 25062345; fax (2) 25145754; e-mail ju-reng_chen@email.china-airlines.com; internet www.china-airlines.com; f. 1959; international services to destinations in the Far East, Europe, the Middle East, the USA and Australia; Chair. Capt. Y. L. LEE; Pres. WEI HSING-HSIUNG.

EVA Airways (EVA): Eva Air Bldg, 376 Hsin-nan Rd, Sec. 1, Luchu, Taoyuan Hsien; tel. (3) 3515151; fax (3) 3510023; e-mail sammykao@evaair.com; internet www.evaair.com.tw; f. 1989; subsidiary of Evergreen Group; commenced flights in 1991; services to destinations in Asia (incl. Hong Kong and Macao), the Middle East, Europe, North America, Australia and New Zealand; Chair. CHANG KUO-CHENG; Pres. LIN BOU-SHIU.

Far Eastern Air Transport Corpn (FAT): 5 Alley 123, Lane 405, Tun Hua North Rd, Taipei 10592; tel. (2) 27121555; fax (2) 27122428; internet www.fat.com.tw; f. 1957; domestic services and regional international services; Chair. STEPHEN J. TSUEI; Pres. M. W. CHENG.

Mandarin Airlines (MDA): 13/F, 134 Ming Sheng East Rd, Sec. 3, Taipei; tel. (2) 27171188; fax (2) 27170716; e-mail mandarin@mandarin-airlines.com; internet www.mandarin-airlines.com; f. 1991; subsidiary of CAL; merged with Formosa Airlines 1999; domestic and regional international services; Chair. Y. L. LEE; Pres. MICHAEL LO.

TransAsia Airways (TNA): 9/F, 139 Chengchou Rd, Taipei; tel. (2) 25575767; fax (2) 25570643; internet www.tna.com.tw; f. 1951; fmrly Foshing Airlines; domestic flights and international services; Chair. FAN CHIEH-CHIANG; Pres. SUN HUANG-HSIANG.

UNI Airways Corpn (UIA): 7/F, 100 Chang An East Rd, Sec. 2, Taipei; tel. (2) 25135533; fax (2) 25133202; internet www.uniair.com.tw; f. 1989; fmrly Makung Airlines; merged with Great China Airlines and Taiwan Airlines 1998; domestic flights and international services (to Kota Kinabalu, Malaysia; Bali, Indonesia; Phuket, Thailand); Chair. JENG KUNG-YEUN; Pres. TONY SU.

Tourism

The principal tourist attractions are the cuisine, the cultural artefacts and the island scenery. In 2003 there were 2,248,117 visitor arrivals (including 436,083 overseas Chinese) in Taiwan. Receipts from tourism in 2003 totalled US $2,976m. To strengthen the development of the tourism industry, a 'Doubling Tourist Arrivals Plan', targeting 5m. arrivals in 2008, was inaugurated in September 2002. The plan also proclaimed 2004 as 'Visit Taiwan Year', in which travel incentives were to be offered to foreign visitors.

Tourism Bureau, Ministry of Transportation and Communications: 9/F, 290 Chung Hsiao East Rd, Sec. 4, Taipei 106; tel. (2) 23491635; fax (2) 27717036; e-mail tbroc@tbroc.gov.tw; internet taiwan.net.tw; f. 1972; Dir-Gen. SU CHERNG TYAN.

Taiwan Visitors Association: 5/F, 9 Min Chuan East Rd, Sec. 2, Taipei 104; tel. (2) 25943261; fax (2) 25943265; internet www.tva.org.tw; f. 1956; promotes domestic and international tourism; Chair. CHANG SHUO LAO.

COLOMBIA

Introductory Survey

Location, Climate, Language, Religion, Flag, Capital

The Republic of Colombia lies in the north-west of South America, with the Caribbean Sea to the north and the Pacific Ocean to the west. Its continental neighbours are Venezuela and Brazil to the east, and Peru and Ecuador to the south, while Panama connects it with Central America. The coastal areas have a tropical rain forest climate, the plateaux are temperate, and in the Andes mountains there are areas of permanent snow. The language is Spanish. Almost all of the inhabitants profess Christianity, and about 90% are Roman Catholics. There are small Protestant and Jewish minorities. The national flag (proportions 2 by 3) has three horizontal stripes, of yellow (one-half of the depth) over dark blue over red. The capital is Santafé de Bogotá (formerly Bogotá).

Recent History

Colombia was under Spanish rule from the 16th century until 1819, when it achieved independence as part of Gran Colombia, which included Ecuador, Panama and Venezuela. Ecuador and Venezuela seceded in 1830, when Colombia (then including Panama) became a separate republic. In 1903 the province of Panama successfully rebelled and became an independent country. For more than a century, ruling power in Colombia has been shared between two political parties, the Conservatives (Partido Conservador Colombiano, PCC) and the Liberals (Partido Liberal Colombiano, PL), whose rivalry has often led to violence. President Laureano Gómez of the PCC, who was elected 'unopposed' in November 1949, ruled as a dictator until his overthrow by Gen. Gustavo Rojas Pinilla in a coup in June 1953. President Rojas established a right-wing dictatorship but, following widespread rioting, he was deposed in May 1957, when a five-man military junta took power. According to official estimates, lawlessness during 1949–58, known as 'La Violencia', caused the deaths of about 280,000 people.

In an attempt to restore peace and stability, the PCC and the PL agreed to co-operate in a National Front. Under this arrangement, the presidency was to be held by the PCC and the PL in rotation, while cabinet portfolios would be divided equally between the two parties and both would have an equal number of seats in each house of the bicameral Congreso (Congress). In December 1957, in Colombia's first vote on the basis of universal adult suffrage, this agreement was overwhelmingly approved by a referendum and was subsequently incorporated in Colombia's Constitution, dating from 1886.

In May 1958 the first presidential election under the amended Constitution was won by the National Front candidate, Dr Alberto Lleras Camargo, a PL member who had been President in 1945–46. He took office in August 1958, when the ruling junta relinquished power. As provided by the 1957 agreement, he was succeeded by a member of the PCC, Dr Guillermo León Valencia, who was, in turn, succeeded by a PL candidate, Dr Carlos Lleras Restrepo, in 1966.

At the presidential election in April 1970, the National Front candidate, Dr Misael Pastrana Borrero (PCC) narrowly defeated Gen. Rojas, the former dictator, who campaigned as leader of the Alianza Nacional Popular (ANAPO), with policies that had considerable appeal for the poorer sections of the population. At elections to the Congreso, held simultaneously, the National Front lost its majority in each of the two houses, while ANAPO became the main opposition group in each. The result of the presidential election was challenged by supporters of ANAPO, and an armed wing of the party, the Movimiento 19 de Abril (M-19), began to organize guerrilla activity against the Government. It was joined by dissident members of a pro-Soviet guerrilla group, the Fuerzas Armadas Revolucionarias de Colombia—Ejército del Pueblo (FARC—EP), established in 1966.

The bipartisan form of government ended formally with the presidential and legislative elections of April 1974, although the 1974–78 Cabinet remained subject to the parity agreement. The PCC and the PL together won an overwhelming majority of seats in the Congreso, and support for ANAPO was greatly reduced. The presidential election was won by the PL candidate, Dr Alfonso López Michelsen.

At elections to the Congreso in February 1978, the PL won a clear majority in both houses, and in June the PL candidate, Dr Julio César Turbay Ayala, won the presidential election. President Turbay continued to observe the National Front agreement, and attempted to address the problems of urban terrorism and drugs-trafficking. In 1982 the guerrillas suffered heavy losses after successful counter-insurgency operations, combined with the activities of a new anti-guerrilla group associated with drugs-smuggling enterprises, the Muerte a Secuestradores (MAS, Death to Kidnappers), whose targets later became trade union leaders, academics and human rights activists.

At congressional elections in March 1982, the PL maintained its majority in both houses. In May the PCC candidate, Dr Belisario Betancur Cuartas, won the presidential election, benefiting from a division within the PL. President Betancur, who took office in August, declared a broad amnesty for guerrillas in November, reconvened the Peace Commission (first established in 1981) and ordered an investigation into the MAS. Despite the Peace Commission's successful negotiation of cease-fire agreements with the FARC—EP, the M-19 (now operating as a left-wing guerrilla movement) and the Ejército Popular de Liberación (EPL) during 1984, factions of all three groups which were opposed to the truce continued to conduct guerrilla warfare against the authorities. In May 1984 the Government's campaign for internal peace was severely hampered by the assassination of the Minister of Justice. His murder was regarded as a consequence of his energetic attempts to eradicate the flourishing drugs industry, and Colombia's leading drugs dealers were implicated in the killing. The Government declared a nation-wide state of siege and announced its intention to enforce its hitherto unobserved extradition treaty with the USA.

Relations between the M-19 and the armed forces deteriorated during 1985, and in June the M-19 formally withdrew from the cease-fire agreement. In November a dramatic siege by the M-19 at the Palace of Justice in the capital, during which more than 100 people were killed, resulted in severe public criticism of the Government and the armed forces for their handling of events. Negotiations with the M-19 were suspended indefinitely.

At congressional elections in March 1986, the traditional wing of the PL secured a clear victory over the PCC. The Unión Patriótica (UP), formed by the FARC—EP in 1985, won seats in both houses. At the presidential election in May, Dr Virgilio Barco Vargas of the PL was elected President. The large majority secured by the PL at both elections obliged the PCC to form the first formal opposition to a government for 30 years.

Attempts by the new administration to address the problems of political violence and the cultivation and trafficking of illicit drugs enjoyed little success during 1986–87. Hopes that an indefinite cease-fire agreement, concluded between the FARC—EP and the Government in March 1986, would facilitate the full participation of the UP in the political process were largely frustrated by the Government's failure to respond effectively to a campaign of assassinations of UP members, conducted by paramilitary 'death squads' during 1985–87, which resulted in an estimated 450 deaths. The crisis was compounded in October 1987 by the decision of six guerrilla groups, including the FARC—EP, the Ejército de Liberación Nacional (ELN) and the M-19, to form a joint front, the Coordinadora Guerrillera Simón Bolívar (CGSB). Although in 1987 the Government extended police powers against drugs dealers, its efforts were severely hampered by the Supreme Court's ruling that Colombia's extradition treaty with the USA was unconstitutional. A peace initiative in September 1988, committing the Government to entering into dialogue with those guerrilla groups that renounced violence, also had little success.

In January 1989 the Government and the M-19 concluded an agreement to initiate direct dialogue between the Government, all political parties in the Congreso and the CGSB. In March the M-19 and the Government signed a document providing for the reintegration of the guerrillas into society. In the same month, the ELN, the EPL and the FARC—EP publicly confirmed their willingness to participate in peace talks with the Government. In September the M-19 announced that it had reached agreement with the Government on a peace treaty, under which its members were to demobilize and disarm in exchange for a full pardon. In addition, the movement was to enter the political mainstream; in October the M-19 was formally constituted as a political party. By March 1990 all M-19 guerrilla forces had surrendered their weapons. In exchange for firm commitments from the Barco administration that a referendum would be held to decide the question of constitutional reform and that proposals for comprehensive changes to the electoral law would be introduced in the Congreso, members of the M-19 were guaranteed a general amnesty, reintegration into civilian life and full political participation in forthcoming elections.

The increasingly destabilizing influence of the drugs cartels, meanwhile, continued to undermine government initiatives. In August 1989 President Barco introduced emergency measures, including the reactivation of Colombia's extradition treaty with the USA. The US Administration requested the arrest by the Colombian authorities of 12 leading drugs-traffickers, popularly known as the 'Extraditables', who responded to the USA's request by issuing a declaration of 'total war' against the Government and all journalists, judges and trade unionists opposed to their activities.

A presidential election was scheduled to be held in May 1990. In March Bernardo Jaramillo, the presidential candidate of the UP was assassinated, and in April Carlos Pizarro of the M-19 became the third presidential candidate to be killed by hired assassins since August 1989. Pizarro was replaced by Antonio Navarro Wolff as M-19 presidential candidate, in conjunction with the recently established Convergencia Democrática (later Alianza Democrática—AD), an alliance of 13 (mainly left-wing) groups and factions. César Gaviria Trujillo of the PL was proclaimed the winner of the election, with 47% of the votes cast. Some 90% of voters indicated their approval of proposals for the creation of a National Constituent Assembly in a *de facto* referendum held simultaneously.

Gaviria's Cabinet was described as a cabinet of 'national unity' and comprised seven members of the PL, four of the PCC and, most surprisingly, Navarro Wolff, the AD—M-19 presidential nominee. President Gaviria confirmed his commitment to continuing the strenuous efforts to combat drugs-trafficking, having previously made comprehensive changes to police and military personnel in an apparent attempt to strengthen the Government's resistance to infiltration by the cartels. In October the Government proposed an initiative by which some articles of law would be relaxed and others not invoked (including the extradition treaty) for suspected drugs-traffickers who were prepared to surrender to the authorities.

In October 1990 the creation of the National Constituent Assembly was declared constitutionally acceptable by the Supreme Court. Candidates for the AD—M-19 secured 19 of the 70 contested Assembly seats, forcing the ruling PL and the Conservatives to seek support from them and seven elected independents for the successful enactment of reform proposals. In February 1991 the five-month session of the National Constituent Assembly was inaugurated. The composition of the Assembly had been expanded from 70 to 73 members in order to incorporate three invited members of former guerrilla groupings (two from the EPL and one from the Partido Revolucionario de Trabajadores—PRT) and was later expanded further to accommodate a representative of the Comando Quintín Lame. By June a political pact had been negotiated between President Gaviria and representatives of the PL, the AD—M-19 and the conservative Movimiento de Salvación Nacional (MSN), and an agreement was reached that, in order to facilitate the process of political and constitutional renovation, the Congreso should be dissolved prematurely. The Assembly subsequently voted to dismiss the Congreso, pending new congressional and gubernatorial elections, to be conducted in October (although congressional elections had not been scheduled to take place until 1994).

The new Constitution became effective on 6 July 1991. At the same time, the state of siege, imposed in 1984 in response to the escalation in political and drugs-related violence, was ended. The Constitution placed considerable emphasis upon provisions to encourage greater political participation and to restrict electoral corruption and misrepresentation. It also identified and sought to protect a comprehensive list of civil liberties, among which, controversially, was the prohibition of the extradition of Colombian nationals (see below). While the Constitution was welcomed enthusiastically by the majority of the population,

reservations were expressed that clauses relating to the armed forces remained largely unchanged and that provisions which recognized the democratic rights of indigenous groups did not extend to their territorial claims.

Relations with the Medellín cartel improved considerably following the release, in May 1991, of two remaining hostages, and in June, following the decision to prohibit constitutionally the practice of extradition, the Government's efforts were rewarded with the surrender of Pablo Escobar, the supposed head of the Medellín cartel. Charges later brought against Escobar included several of murder, kidnapping and terrorism. In July spokesmen for the Medellín drugs cartel announced that its military operations were to be suspended and that the 'Extraditables' were to be disbanded. Hopes that Escobar's surrender might precipitate a decline in drugs-related violence were frustrated by reports that Escobar was continuing to direct the operations of the Medellín cocaine cartels from his purpose-built prison at Envigado, and by the emergence of the powerful Cali drugs cartel, which was expected to compensate for any shortfall in the supply of illicit drugs resulting from the demise of the Medellín cartel.

The Liberals were most successful in the congressional elections of October 1991, with a clear majority of seats in both chambers. The traditional Conservative opposition suffered from a division in their support between the PCC, the MSN and the Nueva Fuerza Democrática, securing around one-quarter of the seats in both houses between them. The AD—M-19 received only 10% of the votes cast, equivalent to nine seats in the Senado and 15 seats in the Cámara de Representantes.

Meanwhile, in February 1990 the Government had established the National Council for Normalization, in an attempt to repeat the success of recent peace initiatives with the M-19 in negotiations with other revolutionary groups. The EPL announced the end of its armed struggle in August and joined the political mainstream (retaining the initials EPL as the Partido de Esperanza, Paz y Libertad), along with the Comando Quintín Lame and the PRT, in 1991. Attempts to negotiate with the FARC—EP and the ELN, however, proved fruitless, and violent clashes between the remaining guerrilla groups (now co-ordinating actions as the Coordinadora Nacional Guerrillera Simón Bolívar—CNGSB) and security forces persisted.

An escalation in guerrilla activity in 1992 prompted the Government to intensify anti-insurgency measures. In October the Congreso approved government proposals for an increased counter-insurgency budget and for the creation of new armed units to combat terrorism. The Government's rejection of any agenda for renewed negotiations provoked an intensification of the conflict, and this prompted Gaviria to declare a 90-day state of internal disturbance in November. As a result, the M-19 announced that it was to withdraw from the Government and resume an active opposition role.

As security situation continued to deteriorate, in February 1993 the Government announced a significant increase in its budget allocation for security, and in April, doubled the length of prison terms for terrorist acts. The state of internal disturbance was also extended twice. Attempts by the Government and the ELN to negotiate a truce were frustrated by a perceived lack of commitment to compromise on both sides, and the prospects for future successful discussions were undermined by the insistence of security forces that ELN members were responsible for the murder of the Vice-President of the Senado in November. In December negotiations with the Corriente de Renovación Socialista (CRS), a dissident faction of the ELN more disposed to political assimilation, produced a tentative agreement for the guerrillas' reincorporation into civilian life and transformation into a legitimate political force. In April 1994, under the supervision of international observers, the CRS duly surrendered its weapons, and was subsequently awarded two seats in the newly elected Cámara de Representantes (see below).

An intensification of drugs-related violence in the capital during early 1993 was attributed to an attempt by Pablo Escobar (who had escaped from prison in mid-1992) to force the Government to negotiate more favourable conditions for his surrender, and prompted the formation of a vigilante group, Pepe (Perseguidos por Pablo Escobar—those Persecuted by Pablo Escobar), which launched a campaign of retaliatory violence against Escobar's family, associates and property. Pepe was thought to number among its members several of Escobar's disgruntled rivals from the Medellín cartel. A simultaneous and sustained assault by Pepe and by the security forces against the remnants of the Medellín cartel resulted in the death or surrender of many notable cartel members, culminating in the death of Escobar himself, in December, during an exchange of fire with security forces attempting to effect his arrest.

The results of congressional and local elections conducted in March 1994 represented a serious reversal for the political left in Colombia, and re-established the traditional two-party dominance of the PL and the PCC. Following a second round of voting in the presidential election on 19 June between the two leading candidates, Ernesto Samper Pizano (PL) and Andrés Pastrana Arango (PCC), Samper was declared the winner. He was inaugurated on 7 August and a new Cabinet was installed.

Shortly after President Samper took office, allegations emerged that his election campaign had been partly funded by contributions from the Cali cartel. Tape recordings of conversations suggesting that contact had at least been made with the cartels were dismissed by the Prosecutor-General as insufficient proof of such contributions actually having been made. In July 1994 a similar recording, which appeared to implicate the Colombian Chief of National Police in the payment of a bribe by the Cali cartel, prompted the US Senate to vote to make the disbursement of future aid to Colombia dependent on an assessment of the level of its co-operation in anti-drugs programmes.

A CNGSB offensive during the weeks preceding the transfer of power from Gaviria to Samper in August resulted in numerous deaths on both sides and considerable damage inflicted on power installations and the transport infrastructure. Guerrilla activities further intensified after the new administration took office and included the murder of the UP's Manuel Cepeda Vargas (the only left-wing member of the Senado). However, in November President Samper complied with a guerrilla request that imprisoned rebel leaders should be moved from military installations to civilian prisons, and also declared the Government's willingness to enter into unconditional dialogue with the guerrillas.

In September 1994, under intense international pressure to formalize a greater commitment to respect for human rights, following a series of revelations in which the security forces were implicated in abuses of human rights, the Minister of the Interior, Horacio Serpa Uribe, announced an initiative to address the human rights crisis; these included the reform of the National Police and to disband all paramilitary units.

In February 1995, in the context of the US Government's persistence in attaching preconditions to the disbursement of financial aid to Colombia, President Samper reiterated his commitment to the eradication of all illegal drugs-related activities in the country. A number of initiatives to address the problem were launched in Cali, resulting in the capture of the head of the Cali drugs cartel, Gilberto Rodríguez Orejuela, and four other cartel leaders in mid-1995 (Orejuela was extradited to the USA to face charges of drugs-trafficking in December 2004). Meanwhile, in April 1995 nine prominent PL politicians were suspended from the party pending their investigation by the office of the Prosecutor-General, following allegations of their maintaining links with the Cali cartel. In the following months it was confirmed that the Comptroller-General and the Attorney-General were also to be the subject of investigation as a result of similar allegations, while Samper's former election campaign treasurer, Santiago Medina, was arrested on charges related to the processing of drugs cartel contributions through Samper's election fund. In August the Minister of National Defence, Fernando Botero Zea, resigned, having been implicated in the affair by evidence submitted to the authorities by Medina. Medina also insisted that Samper had been fully aware of the origin of the funds, an accusation denied by the President.

In May 1995 the Government extended an offer of participation in legislative and consultative processes to the FARC—EP, in the hope of securing their commitment to surrender arms. While the FARC—EP responded positively to the initial proposal, further progress was to be dependent on the Government's successful execution of its stated intention to demilitarize the sensitive north-eastern region of La Uribe. However, negotiations were hampered by renewed FARC—EP and ELN offensives in late May. An escalation in the number of acts of violence perpetrated by guerrilla forces and by paramilitary defence groups in the north-western Urabá region prompted Samper to declare a state of internal disturbance for a 90-day period. In October, however, the Constitutional Court rejected the terms of the state of emergency. Following the assassination in November of a prominent Conservative politician, the President declared a new 90-day state of internal disturbance.

In December 1995 the congressional accusations committee voted against the initiation of a full-scale inquiry into allegations of Samper's impropriety in the use of funds proceeding from drugs cartels, on the grounds of insufficient evidence at that time. The repercussions of the scandal, however, were considered to have severely undermined the political integrity of the Government. Relations between the US Government and the Samper administration deteriorated dramatically during 1995, culminating in allegations—made by official sources in Colombia—that the US Government was attempting to destabilize the administration through the covert actions of the US Drugs Enforcement Agency (DEA). In January 1996 Botero reiterated Medina's claim that Samper had been in full possession of the facts regarding the cartel's funding of his election campaign, prompting the PCC to announce an immediate suspension of co-operation with the Government and the resignation of two of the four incumbent PCC members of the Cabinet. Evidence collected by the Prosecutor-General was submitted to the accusations committee in February, together with four formal charges to be brought against the President, including that of illegal enrichment. Later in the month congressional commissions of both parliamentary chambers decided to launch a new and public investigation into the matter. In March Samper testified before the accusations committee and denied allegations that he had contrived the plan to solicit funding from the Cali cartel; however, he did concede that the cartel had part-financed the campaign, albeit without his knowledge. In June the Congreso voted to acquit Samper of charges of having been aware of the part-financing of his election campaign by drugs-traffickers. The US Administration condemned the result and threatened to impose trade sanctions against Colombia. Furthermore, in the following month, the US Government revoked Samper's visa to travel to the USA.

In April 1996 the Supreme Court took the unprecedented step of requesting that the Senado suspend the Attorney-General, Orlando Vásquez Velásquez, in order that he face charges of obstructing the course of justice (he had allegedly fabricated evidence to discredit the Prosecutor-General). In October Vásquez Velásquez was found guilty of the charges; he was dismissed as Attorney-General and banned from holding public office for a five-year period. Moreover, in December 1997 he was sentenced to eight years' imprisonment on drugs charges. During 1996 Botero, Medina and María Izquierdo, a former PL senator, were all sentenced to terms of imprisonment for their involvement in the Samper affair.

Civil unrest and guerrilla activity continued during 1996. The state of internal disturbance was extended for a further 90 days in January, and then again in April following a CNGSB-organized nation-wide 'armed industrial strike', which had resulted in as many as 40 deaths. In March a FARC—EP attack on a drugs-control police unit had renewed speculation of links between guerrilla groups and the drugs cartels. Moreover, a major offensive launched in August by FARC—EP and ELN rebels (resulting in as many as 100 fatalities) coincided with large-scale protests by coca growers demanding a review of the coca-eradication programme, particularly the use of aerial spraying. Although 26 members of the FARC—EP and some 250 dissident EPL rebels surrendered to the authorities during September and October, violent skirmishes continued unabated, and disaffected members of the ELN were reported to have regrouped as the Ejército Revolucionario del Pueblo.

In September 1996 Samper's credibility was undermined by the resignation of the Vice-President, Humberto de la Calle, who appealed to the President to renounce his office in order to prevent the country from descending into 'total chaos'. Later in the same month Samper was again humiliated by the discovery of 3.7 kg of heroin aboard the aircraft in which he had been scheduled to fly to the USA (using a diplomat visa) to attend a meeting of the UN General Assembly. (A subsequent investigation into the drugs seizure did not implicate the President in any way.) In December the Congreso approved controversial legislation to allow for the confiscation of drugs-traffickers' assets.

In early 1997 the Samper administration encountered increasing pressure from the USA to address the issues of drugs-trafficking and corruption. The USA again refused to 'certify' Colombia, claiming that there had been a substantial increase in the production of illicit drugs in that country during 1996. Legislation passed in November permitting the extradition of Colombian nationals sought for criminal offences abroad was strongly criticized by the US Administration as it would not have retroactive effect. (In March 2005 Samper was cleared of allegations by a US Federal Attorney that he had accepted US $5m. from the Cali Cartel to ensure that the legislation would not have retro-active effect).

In the months preceding the October 1997 local elections the activities of guerrilla and paramilitary groups in Colombia intensified. More than 40 candidates were killed, some 200 were kidnapped and as many as 1,900 withdrew after receiving death threats. In May the Government agreed to the temporary demilitarization of part of the Caquetá department in order to secure the release of 70 members of the armed forces captured by the FARC—EP. Voting was cancelled in numerous municipalities, while reports of secret preliminary peace negotiations between government representatives and the FARC—EP were undermined by a major military offensive in September, in which 652 FARC—EP guerrillas were killed and a further 1,600 were captured.

At congressional elections, conducted in March 1998, the PL retained a narrow overall majority in both chambers of the legislature. An estimated 54% of the electorate participated in the elections, which were preceded by a period of violent attacks on the security forces by guerrilla groups; in one incident 80 counter-insurgency troops were killed by the FARC—EP, and a further 43 were taken prisoner. In May tens of thousands of Colombians staged a demonstration to protest at the escalation of violence by guerrillas and paramilitary groups.

The first round of the presidential election was held in May 1998. The PL candidate, Horacio Serpa Uribe, secured 34.6% of the valid votes cast, followed by the PCC nominee Pastrana (34.3%), an independent candidate Noemí Sanín Posada (26.9%), and Gen. (retd) Bedoya (1.8%). Serpa's candidacy had been strongly opposed by the US Administration as he was alleged to have links with drugs-traffickers. A second ballot was held in June, at which Pastrana defeated Serpa, winning 50.4% of the valid votes cast. Pastrana was inaugurated as President on 7 August.

In July 1998 President-elect Pastrana announced that he had held secret talks with Manuel Marulanda Vélez (alias 'Tirofijo'), the FARC—EP leader, and that he had agreed to demilitarize five southern municipalities for a 90-day period (commencing in November) in order to facilitate negotiations with the guerrillas. Pastrana subsequently recognized the political status of the FARC—EP, thereby allowing the Government to negotiate with an outlawed group. Notwithstanding, FARC—EP attacks on the security forces continued. Shortly before the negotiations between the Government and the FARC—EP began in January 1999, it was revealed that in December the FARC—EP had held informal talks in Costa Rica with government officials from the USA and Colombia. (Relations between Colombia and the USA had improved notably under the Pastrana administration: in October Pastrana made an official visit to the USA—the first by a Colombian Head of State in 23 years—and in December the two countries agreed on measures to improve military co-operation in the fight against the drugs trade.) In mid-January 1999 the FARC—EP suspended talks with the Government until the authorities provided evidence that they were taking action against paramilitary groups, which claimed responsibility for the massacre of more than 130 civilians earlier in the month. In February Pastrana announced the extension of the period of demilitarization by three months, in order to facilitate negotiations.

The ELN, meanwhile, made tentative moves to negotiate a peace settlement during 1998. In February the group signed an accord with government peace negotiators in Madrid, Spain, on the holding of preliminary peace talks. In April the ELN disclosed that its leader, Gregorio Manuel Pérez Martínez, had died shortly afterwards; a collective leadership was appointed subsequently. In July, at a meeting in Mainz, Germany, between the ELN and representatives of Colombian 'civil society' (grouped in the National Peace Council—Consejo Nacional de Paz—CNP), the ELN made concessions on the 'humanization' of the war and agreed to facilitate talks between its members and the Government. The guerrillas subsequently postponed a meeting with the CNP in protest at its signing of an agreement with the Autodefensas Unidas de Colombia (AUC), an organization representing most of Colombia's paramilitary groups, to hold parallel peace talks. Nevertheless, in October representatives of the ELN, the CNP and the Government agreed on a timetable for preliminary peace talks, beginning in February 1999, which would culminate in the assembling of a national convention. The Government recognized the political status of

the ELN, but the group did not cease hostilities. The planned peace negotiations failed to begin in February 1999, not least because of the Government's refusal to agree to the ELN's request that four districts in the department of Bolívar be demilitarized. The ELN intensified its operations, in an apparent attempt to increase pressure on the Government to accede to its demands. The guerrillas hijacked an AVIANCA domestic flight in April, kidnapping all 46 people on board, and abducted some 140 members of the congregation of a church in Cali in May. In June Pastrana withdrew political recognition of the ELN and made the release of hostages a precondition for future peace talks. A civilian commission was subsequently appointed by the Government to negotiate towards this end. The ELN freed the last hostage in November 2000.

Little progress was achieved in negotiations with the FARC—EP until April 1999, as the guerrillas continued to insist that the Government demonstrate some success in its actions against paramilitary groups prior to a resumption of talks. The enforced resignation in that month of two senior army officers, alleged to have collaborated with paramilitary groups, appeared to appease the FARC—EP, however, and in early May talks between Marulanda and President Pastrana resulted in an agreement on a comprehensive agenda for future peace negotiations; the period of demilitarization was again extended. However, Pastrana's strategy was not entirely supported by his administration, and at the end of May Rodrigo Lloreda, the Minister of National Defence, resigned in protest at concessions granted to the FARC—EP. Pastrana's position was further undermined by the Congreso's rejection of legislation aimed at increasing the President's power concerning the peace process. Furthermore, the FARC—EP continued to pursue its military campaign. The postponement of talks in July, owing to a failure to agree on the role of international observers, was followed by a nation-wide guerrilla offensive that resulted in more than 200 deaths. The talks were subsequently postponed indefinitely, with the Government insisting that international monitors be allowed to investigate abuses allegedly committed by the FARC—EP in the demilitarized zone. As negotiations resumed in October in La Uribe, after Pastrana had apparently withdrawn his demand for international observers, demonstrations for peace were attended by some 10m. people throughout the country.

Relations between the US Government and the Colombian administration continued to improve under President Pastrana, notably regarding anti-drugs activities. In March 1999 the USA decided to 'certify' Colombia's efforts to combat drugs-trafficking and in September Pastrana announced the establishment of a new anti-narcotics battalion, to be trained and financed by the USA. Collaboration between the Colombian and US authorities led to the arrest of more than 60 suspected drugs-traffickers in two major operations conducted in October and December. However, the most important progress in Colombian-US relations came in 2000 with the development of Pastrana's so-called 'Plan Colombia'. This was an ambitious, US $7,500m. project intended to strengthen the Colombian state by increasing the efficiency of the security forces and the judicial system, eliminating drugs production through both eradication and crop substitution, and reducing unemployment. In July 2000 the US Congress approved a contribution to the Plan of $1,300m., which included a military component of $1,000m., but also significant sums for judicial reform and human rights education. Human rights organizations warned of an escalation of human rights abuses following the Plan's implementation, as the main aid component was allocated to strengthening the security forces, whose links to paramilitary groups were, allegedly, yet to be severed. At the same time, Colombia's Andean neighbours feared that an escalation in violence would force thousands of refugees on to their territory, and subsequently reinforced their borders.

At negotiations in September 2000 the FARC—EP threatened to halt the peace process if plans for the US military component of Plan Colombia, to be directed against coca-growing areas of Putumayo, were implemented. The FARC—EP effectively blockaded Putumayo from the end of that month to retain control of the province, and it succeeded in delaying the aerial spraying of coca plantations, which was scheduled to begin in November. (The military offensive against the plantations began in December, although in February 2001 the aerial spraying of crops was suspended in the Putumayo region after local authorities warned of the adverse effects the herbicides used could have on people and licit crops.) In October the Government dismissed 388 members of the armed forces in a move designed to improve military efficiency as well as to allay accusations of corruption and violations of human rights. However, the dismissals did not prevent the FARC—EP from withdrawing from peace talks in November in order to demand greater government action in combating the AUC. By the end of the year President Pastrana was under increasing pressure to take back by force control of the demilitarized zone; a report released in December estimated a 30% increase in FARC—EP military capacity since the zone was created. The murder in late December of Diego Turbay Cote, President of the congressional peace commission, allegedly by members of the FARC—EP, further heightened tensions. (The Vice-President of the peace commission was killed in September 2001.) However, following threats by the FARC—EP that failure to prolong the demilitarized zone would lead to 'total war', Pastrana extended the deadline until the end of January 2001. A further extension was granted in February, after which the FARC—EP leadership met the President in the demilitarized zone and signed a 13-point 'Pact of Los Pozos', including an agreement to revive the stalled negotiations, to expedite an exchange of sick prisoners, and to begin discussions on a cease-fire. In March diplomats representing governments from Latin America, Europe, Japan and Canada met with FARC—EP leaders to monitor the peace process. The new US Administration of George W. Bush refused an invitation to join the peace process, preferring instead to focus on drugs eradication policies. In July the US House of Representatives approved a US $670m. aid package, known as the Andean Regional Initiative, to support Plan Colombia and to promote stability in the rest of the Andean region.

Violence escalated during 2001. In the first four months of the year an estimated 760 people were killed, and in the first seven months 1,700 were kidnapped, a significant increase on the previous year. However, in June progress was made in peace negotiations when the FARC—EP signed a prisoner-exchange agreement with the Government; about 300 prisoners were released by the FARC—EP at the end of the month. Nevertheless, in August President Pastrana signed legislation giving new powers to the military to combat guerrilla forces. The legislation was controversial as it allowed for less scrutiny from government investigators, and was opposed by human rights organizations. In the same month three Irish nationals, suspected to have links to the Provisional Irish Republican Army (IRA), were arrested in the demilitarized zone on suspicion of collaborating with the FARC—EP on training methods. The arrests, together with the murder of former culture minister Consuelo Araújo in late September, threatened to derail the fragile peace process. (The men were acquitted in April 2004, although this acquittal was overturned in December. Following this ruling, the men absconded, and were believed to have fled the country.) None the less, in October the Government extended the existence of the demilitarized zone until January 2002, after the FARC—EP agreed to reduce the number of kidnappings and to begin cease-fire negotiations. However, the Government refused demands by the FARC—EP to remove military controls around the demilitarized zone. This impasse effectively prevented any progress on substantive issues such as cease-fire negotiations during the rest of the year. Finally, in a move that signalled the end of the peace process, on 9 January 2002 Pastrana announced that the FARC—EP had 48 hours to leave the demilitarized zone. Hours before the expiry of the deadline the FARC—EP rescinded demands for relaxed security around the demilitarized zone and agreed to recommence negotiations; as a result the guerrillas were able to continue their occupation of the zone. On 20 January, with the help of representatives from 10 facilitating countries and UN envoy James LeMoyne, agreement was reached on an extension, to early April, to the deadline for a cease-fire agreement. However, on 20 February, following the hijacking of an aeroplane and the kidnapping of a prominent senator, Pastrana terminated peace talks with the FARC—EP and ordered the armed forces to regain control of the demilitarized zone. In May the FARC—EP was held responsible for the deaths of at least 117 civilians sheltering in a church in Bojayá, in the department of Chocó. The church was hit by a FARC—EP mortar bomb during a battle to regain control of the town from the AUC.

In April 2000 an agreement was reached with the ELN on the establishment of a demilitarized zone, similar to that granted to the FARC—EP, in southern Bolívar. However, the Government faced much local opposition to the proposed zone, including roadblocks and demonstrations. In July informal discussions on a national convention, as demanded by the guerrilla movement

as a precursor to peace talks, were held with the ELN in Geneva, Switzerland, with envoys from Cuba, France, Norway, Spain and Switzerland present. These ended without agreement. In response, the ELN continued to sabotage Colombia's oil industry by attacking pipeline transport. Tentative moves towards peace recommenced in December after the ELN released 42 hostages. Negotiations in Havana, Cuba, at the end of the year resulted in a preliminary agreement on the terms and conditions of the demilitarized zone in Bolívar, though it was conditional on the acceptance by the ELN of the presence of an international verification committee in the region, as well as representatives from local and judicial institutions and one civilian police agency. The agreement was strongly opposed by the AUC and by residents of the proposed region, and in February 2001 more than 10,000 people in Bolívar participated in a demonstration against the establishment of the zone. The prospects for a demilitarized zone were reduced after the ELN suspended negotiations with the Government in March in protest at the aerial spraying of coca in the Bolívar region. At the same time, the AUC began an offensive in the area in order to prevent the establishment of the demilitarized zone. The ELN resumed peace negotiations in April but later that month members of the guerrilla organization allegedly kidnapped 92 workers from the US oil firm Occidental. They were subsequently released. Peace negotiations faltered again in August when President Pastrana suspended unofficial talks, which had been taking place in Venezuela, accusing the ELN of inflexibility. Bomb attacks in Medellín and other parts of the country later that month were widely assumed to be the response of the ELN to the suspension of the talks. Although contact between the two sides resumed in December in Cuba, and in January 2002, following a Christmas truce, negotiations on a permanent cease-fire were initiated, the ELN withdrew from talks with the Pastrana administration in May.

In legislative elections, held on 10 March 2002, the most significant gains were made by independents and parties allied to Alvaro Uribe Vélez, the former Governor of Antioquia and a candidate in the forthcoming presidential elections. The PL remained the largest single party in the Senado and the Cámara de Representantes, with 29 and 54 seats, respectively. However, its representation was substantially reduced, while the representation of the PCC diminished to 13 seats in the Senado and 21 lower-house seats. The rate of voter participation was 42.3%.

A presidential election was held on 26 May 2002, amid a climate of increased intimidation by both guerrilla and paramilitary groups. (Voter participation was estimated at only 46% of the electorate.) Uribe, a dissident member of the PL, was elected President with 54.0% of the votes cast, compared with 32.3% secured by his nearest rival, Horacio Serpa, the PL's official candidate. Luis Eduardo Garzón (the leader of the main trade-union federation, the Central Unitaria de Trabajadores) and Noemí Sanín (again standing as an independent) won 6.3% and 5.9% of the votes, respectively. The PCC had withdrawn its candidate following the party's disappointing results in the legislative elections; the PCC, the PL and a number of independents subsequently declared their support for the President-elect and his pledge to impose 'democratic security', thus giving him an overwhelming majority in both parliamentary chambers.

Upon taking office in August 2002, President Uribe resolved to strengthen the capacity of the Colombian Government to achieve a lasting victory over the rebel groups. To this end, the new President issued a decree establishing a 'state of internal disturbance' and introducing a war tax in September (intended to raise US $750m.). The decree also extended police powers to military units and designated two 'Rehabilitation and Consolidation Zones' in the north eastern departments of Sucre, Bolívar and Arauca, within which media access and civil liberties were to be drastically curtailed. Moreover, Uribe pledged to double the size of the army (to some 100,000 professional soldiers), recruit a further 100,000 police officers, create localized militias of 'peasant soldiers' and establish a network of 'informants' to ensure public security along the road network. As a result of the measures, the President's popularity soared. According to the US Department of State, between May 2002 and September 2004 the murder rate in the country decreased by 17.6%, while that of acts of terrorism fell by 18.4%, kidnappings by 35.1% and the massacre rate by 55.4%. In November the internal disturbance decree was renewed for a further 90-day period, despite a Constitutional Court ruling against it in July. In December the Congreso approved labour, pension and fiscal reforms which provided for an increase in military spending. Despite concerns over reports of human rights infringements by the security forces, throughout 2003 and 2004 the Government achieved apparent progress in its campaign against the rebel groups.

In December 2002 agreement was reached in the Congreso on some 15 proposed economic and political reforms, which were to be included in a national referendum. In July 2003 the Constitutional Court approved the terms of the so-called 'austerity referendum' (the first in Colombia's history), which was to be held on 25 October. The proposals included: a two-year 'freeze' on public-sector salaries, and reductions in civil service pensions; the transfer of responsibility for regional finances to the federal authorities; the reduction in the number of seats in the Congreso; and an increase in prison terms for those convicted of corruption. However, despite President Uribe's pledge that popular endorsement of the measures would improve governability and avert possible financial disaster, the necessary 25% of the electorate failed to vote. This was, in part, owing to the complexity of the referendum document, but also to widespread fears of violence and to the scheduling of the referendum one day before local elections. The failure of the proposals meant that the Uribe administration had to gain congressional approval for its reforms. The following day President Uribe suffered a further defeat when left-wing opposition groups performed well in the regional elections, at the expense of the pro-Government parties.

The Government's referendum defeat led to the resignations, in early November 2003, of several members of President Uribe's Cabinet, including the Minister of the Interior and Justice, Fernando Londoño Hoyos. In the following week Uribe dismissed both the head of the national police force, following corruption allegations, and the Chief of the Armed Forces, Jorge Mora Rangel. The President had become increasingly frustrated at the military's lack of progress in the civil war. In December President Uribe announced his intention to contest the result of the referendum: he asked the Consejo Nacional Electoral (CNE) to remove deceased voters from the electoral roll, in the hope of increasing the participation rate in the referendum to above 25%. Nevertheless, in the following month the CNE confirmed that the plebiscite had been inquorate. In late December the Government succeeded in gaining congressional approval for a series of tax reforms, although key aspects of the proposals, including an increase in value-added tax, were omitted from the legislation. Furthermore, in the same month the Congreso also approved a series of anti-terrorism measures proposed by the Government, granting extensive powers to the police and military. However, in late August 2004 the Constitutional Court ruled, by five votes to four, that the measures were unconstitutional, owing to irregularities in the congressional voting procedure. Earlier in the month the Court had also overturned parts of the Government's proposed reform to the pension system. Following these defeats, a controversial clause was added to a proposed amendment to the Constitution, to allow a President to serve two consecutive terms in office, under consideration by the legislature in 2004. The provision stated that the Constitutional Court was not empowered to overturn the legislation. The constitutional amendment was approved by the Congreso in December, and was due to be implemented before the presidential election that was scheduled for May 2006.

Following a declaration of cease-fire in December 2002, in mid-July 2003 the leaders of the AUC declared that their federation, which totalled some 13,000 fighters, would proceed with peace talks and disband by December 2005. Formal negotiations towards a settlement began in July 2004. In late October proposals by AUC adviser Carlos Alonso Lucio that AUC combatants be incorporated to the Colombian military were rejected following vociferous objections by human rights organizations and senior military officials. In late November AUC leader Salvatore Mancuso began the demobilization of AUC combatants under the Government-sponsored programme of reinsertion to civilian society. In that month the Supreme Court ruled that Mancuso (and FARC—EP leader Juvenal Ovidio Ricardo Palmera, known as 'Simón Trinidad') should be extradited to the USA to face charges of drugs-trafficking. Although Palmera was extradited in late December, it was widely understood that President Uribe would allow Mancuso to stay, conditional upon the continued demobilization of AUC combatants. Also in that month, the US Government pledged US $3m. towards the demobilization process. However, in early 2005 the process came under threat after the Congreso failed to reach agreement on the legal status of former paramilitaries.

Meanwhile, in 2003–04 the Colombian military continued to mount offensives against the FARC—EP (which announced an alliance with the ELN in August 2003, the month in which the aerial spraying of coca plantations was resumed in Putumayo). In April 2004 the Government announced the initiation of the so-called 'Plan Patriota', a largely US-funded military campaign in which some 17,000 troops were to be deployed in the traditional FARC—EP strongholds of Caquetá, Guaviare, Meta and Putumayo. However, the announcement met with some opposition: in May the UN Special Envoy to Colombia, Jan Egeland, expressed concerns that Plan Patriota could lead to increased numbers of internally displaced refugees and human rights abuses. (In January 2005 it was announced that Egeland's successor, James LeMoyne, was to be withdrawn, since a negotiated settlement between the Government and the FARC—EP had been deemed impossible.) Nevertheless, in mid-September the Government announced the capture of nearly 6,000 alleged insurgents and the death of some 1,500 more as a result of Plan Patriota. However, in February 2005 there were reports that the FARC—EP had launched a counter-offensive against the army in three provinces. In October 2004 the US Congress approved an increase in the number of US troops in Colombia from 400 to 800. The US budget for 2005 provided for some US $463m. of aid for Colombia, including at least $100m. for Plan Patriota, pending congressional approval. Total US expenditure under Plan Colombia in the period 2000–04 was estimated at some $3,000m.

In August 2004 the Minister of National Defence, Jorge Alberto Uribe Echavarría, proposed the creation of a regional armed force to combat drugs-trafficking. The proposal received, in general, an unenthusiastic response from the other countries in the region, who feared it could lead to Colombia's internal armed conflict spreading beyond its borders and, as an indirect consequence, an excessive increase in US influence in the region. In September the Uribe administration announced plans to introduce legislation that would allow the confiscation of some 150,000 ha of land used to cultivate illicit crops. It was also reported that under the Uribe presidency some 300,000 ha of coca had been fumigated (of which, the Government conceded, some 85% was subsequently replanted). Also in September, the assets, worth some US $200m., of former Cali cartel leaders Miguel and Gilberto Rodríguez Orejuela (see above) were confiscated by security forces. However, the authorities expressed concern at the discovery in December of extremely large, high-yielding and high-potency coca plants, thought to have been genetically modified.

Colombia has a long-standing border dispute with Venezuela. However, relations between the countries improved following the signing, in October 1989, of a border integration agreement, which included a provision on joint co-operation in the campaign to eradicate drugs-trafficking. In March 1990 the San Pedro Alejandrino agreement, signed by the two countries, sought to initiate the implementation of recommendations made by existing bilateral border commissions and to establish a number of new commissions, including one to examine the territorial claims of both sides. Colombia's efforts to improve relations with Venezuela were hampered by the activities of FARC—EP guerrillas in the border region, leading the two countries to sign an agreement to improve border co-operation in February 1997; however, in April Venezuela deployed 5,000 troops along its frontier with Colombia in an attempt to halt repeated incursions by Colombian guerrillas. Agreements were subsequently signed by the two countries to strengthen military co-operation and intelligence sharing. In 2000 relations deteriorated, owing to Venezuelan President Hugo Chávez's opposition to Plan Colombia and accusations by Colombia that Venezuela was covertly aiding the guerrilla forces. Relations deteriorated further in 2001, after Venezuela refused to allow the extradition to Colombia of a suspect in the April 1999 hijack of an AVIANCA flight (see above). Following the appointment of President Uribe, bilateral relations improved: in November 2002 Chávez and Uribe held a meeting at which they agreed on measures to promote bilateral trade and, notably, to establish a system to deal with problems on their common border. Despite repeated incursions into Venezuelan territory by Colombian combatants and drugs-traffickers in 2004 (including an incident in September that resulted in the death of five Venezuelan soldiers), in a public demonstration of amity, President Uribe and President Chávez met in Cartagena in early November to discuss border security and economic co-operation. However, relations were severely strained in mid-December following the arrest of

Rodrigo Granda Escobar, the supposed international spokes-person of the FARC—EP. It was subsequently alleged by the Venezuelan Government that Granda, although ultimately arrested in Cúcuta, Colombia, was first kidnapped in Caracas by Venezuelan and Colombian agents in the pay of the Colombian Government and with the collusion of US intelligence services. Although President Chávez repeatedly demanded an apology for this perceived violation of Venezuelan sovereignty, the Uribe Government denied all accusations of wrongdoing and the US Government denied all involvement. In consequence, in January 2005 President Chávez recalled the Venezuelan ambassador to Colombia and imposed restrictions on trade and passage between the two countries. Diplomatic interventions were made by Brazil and Peru to expedite a resolution to the dispute. Following an expression of regret by the Colombian Government in late January and a visit to the Venezuelan capital by President Uribe in mid-February, relations between the two countries were normalized. Also in that month, the Venezuelan authorities arrested a middle-ranking member of the FARC—EP, Gentil Galvis Patiño.

In 1980 Nicaragua laid claim to the Colombian-controlled islands of Providencia and San Andrés. Colombia has a territorial dispute with Honduras over cays in the San Andrés and Providencia archipelago. In October 1986 the Colombian Senado approved a delimitation treaty of marine and submarine waters in the Caribbean Sea, which had been signed by the Governments of Colombia and Honduras in August. In late 1999 the Honduran National Assembly finally ratified the treaty, strengthening Colombia's claim to the islands of Providencia and San Andrés, and thus angering Nicaragua, which filed a complaint with the International Court of Justice (ICJ). In July 2003 the Colombian Government disputed the jurisdiction of the ICJ in this affair, an objection dismissed by the Nicaraguan Government in January 2004.

On 1 January 1994 a 10-year trade liberalization programme came into effect between Colombia, Mexico and Venezuela. A free trade agreement with Chile, the Acuerdo de Complementación Económica (ACE), also took effect on the same day, and was expected to have eliminated tariffs on most goods by the time of its full implementation on 1 January 1999. Negotiations on a free trade agreement between the USA and Colombia, Ecuador and Peru were scheduled to conclude in late January 2005. By this time, however, the prospects for an agreement remained uncertain, owing to disagreements between the countries over matters including agriculture and intellectual property, together with protests by public-service workers and indigenous groups in late 2004 in the three Andean countries concerned.

Government

Executive power is exercised by the President (assisted by a Cabinet), who is elected for a four-year term by universal adult suffrage. Legislative power is vested in the bicameral Congress, consisting of the Senate (102 members elected for four years) and the House of Representatives (161 members elected for four years). The country is divided into 32 Departments and one Capital District.

Defence

At 18 years of age, every male (with the exception of students) must present himself as a candidate for military service of between one and two years. In August 2004 the strength of the army was an estimated 178,000 (including 63,800 conscripts), the navy 22,000 (including 14,000 marines) and the air force 7,000 (including 3,900 conscripts). The paramilitary police force numbers about 129,000 men. Some 7,400,000m. pesos were allocated to defence expenditure as part of the state budget for 2004.

Economic Affairs

In 2003, according to estimates by the World Bank, Colombia's gross national income (GNI), measured at average 2001–03 prices, was US $74,559m., equivalent to $1,810 per head (or $6,520 per head on an international purchasing-power parity basis). During 1990–2003, it was estimated, the population increased at an average annual rate of 1.9%, while gross domestic product (GDP) per head increased, in real terms, by an average of 0.6% per year. Colombia's overall GDP increased, in real terms, by an average of 2.4% per year in 1990–2003; GDP grew by 3.7% in 2003.

Agriculture (including hunting, forestry and fishing) contributed an estimated 14.0% of GDP and employed some 21.6% of the labour force in 2003. The principal cash crops are coffee

(which accounted for 6.2% of official export earnings in 2003), cocoa, sugar cane, bananas, tobacco, cotton and cut flowers. Rice, cassava, plantains and potatoes are the principal food crops. Timber and beef production are also important. During 1990–2003 agricultural GDP decreased at an average annual rate of 0.7%. Agricultural GDP increased by 0.7% in 2002 and by 3.1% in 2003.

Industry (including mining, manufacturing, construction and power) employed 19.1% of the labour force and contributed an estimated 30.6% of GDP in 2003. During 1990–2003 real industrial GDP increased at an average annual rate of 1.6%. Industrial GDP increased by 1.7% in 2002 and by 3.4% in 2003.

Mining employed 1.0% of the labour force in 2003 and, according to preliminary estimates, contributed 4.7% of GDP in 2002. Petroleum, natural gas, coal, nickel, emeralds and gold are the principal minerals exploited. Silver, platinum, iron, lead, zinc, copper, mercury, limestone and phosphates are also mined. Mining GDP decreased by 6.1% in 2001 and, according to provisional estimates, by 2.4% in 2002.

Manufacturing contributed an estimated 15.9% of GDP and employed 13.3% of the labour force in 2003. During 1990–2003 manufacturing GDP declined at an average annual rate of 0.6%. Manufacturing GDP increased by 1.1% in 2002 and by 4.4% in 2003. Based on the value of output, the most important branches of manufacturing were food products, beverages, chemical products, textiles and transport equipment.

Hydroelectricity provided 73.2% of Colombia's electricity requirements in 2001. In the early 1990s a rapid expansion programme of thermal power-stations was undertaken in order to increase electricity output in line with demand, which increased by 4.5% per year in the 1990s, and to reduce reliance on hydroelectric power. Natural gas provided some 18.0% of electricity requirements in 2001. The country is self-sufficient in petroleum and coal, and these minerals accounted for 36.7% of export revenues in 2003.

The services sector contributed an estimated 55.4% of GDP in 2003, and engaged 59.3% of the labour force in 2003. During 1990–2003 the combined GDP of the service sectors increased, in real terms, at an estimated average rate of 3.4% per year. The GDP of the services sector increased by 1.9% in 2002 and by 1.4% in 2003.

In 2003 Colombia recorded a visible trade surplus of US $435m. and there was a deficit of $1,345m. on the current account of the balance of payments. The country's principal trading partner in 2003 was the USA, which provided 29.4% of imports and took 44.3% of exports. Other important trading partners in that year were Brazil, Mexico, Venezuela and Ecuador. The principal exports in 2003 were minerals (particularly petroleum and its derivatives and coal), chemicals, vegetables and vegetable products, textiles and leather products, and foodstuffs, beverages and tobacco. The principal imports in 2003 were machinery and transport equipment, chemicals, foodstuffs, beverages and tobacco, textiles and leather products, and vegetables and vegetable products. A significant amount of foreign exchange is believed to be obtained from illegal trade in gold, emeralds and, particularly, the drug cocaine.

In 2003 there was an estimated general budgetary deficit of 9,398,800m. pesos, equivalent to 4.1% of GDP. Colombia's external debt amounted to US $33,853m. at the end of 2002, of which $30,052m. was long-term public debt. Debt-servicing was equivalent to 43.3% of the value of exports of goods and services. In 1992–2003 the average annual rate of inflation was 14.9%; consumer prices increased by an annual average of 7.3% in 2002 and by a further 7.3% in 2003. Some 14.8% of the labour force were unemployed in August 2003.

Colombia is a member of ALADI (see p. 289) and of the Andean Community (see p. 148). Both organizations attempt to increase trade and economic co-operation within the region. Colombia was one of 12 countries that were signatories to the agreement, signed in Cusco, Peru, creating the South American Community of Nations (Comunidad Sudamericana de Naciones), intended to promote greater regional economic integration, due to become operational by 2007.

A programme of structural reform was adopted in 1990–94, resulting in the liberalization of trade and the reorganization of the public sector. Strong economic growth was recorded during this period, not least because of the discovery of significant petroleum reserves. However, during 1994–98 GDP slowed, unemployment soared and the fiscal deficit widened. In the late 1990s economic problems in Colombia were compounded by a fall in the international price of the country's principal export commodities, petroleum and coffee, and by high interest rates, which had led to a rise in the cost of debt-servicing. The Government's economic programme for 1999–2002 emphasized further fiscal reform, the restructuring of the financial sector and a reduction in public spending, as well as the introduction of new social welfare programmes to alleviate the effects of austerity measures and a privatization programme. However, the sale of electrical companies was delayed as a result of guerrilla attacks on power installations and that of public banks because of low investor interest. Furthermore, Colombia was unable to take full advantage of the high price of petroleum in 2000 and 2001 because of guerrilla attacks on pipelines. One of the priorities of President Alvaro Uribe's Government on assuming office in August 2002 was the reform of the tax, pensions and labour sectors. In support of these proposed reforms, in January 2003 the IMF and the World Bank announced new loans to Colombia of US $2,200m. and $3,300m., respectively. Although the government proposals were defeated in a referendum in October 2003, and the Congreso approved only limited fiscal measures in December, in January 2004 the IMF nevertheless endorsed Colombia's economic performance, and made available a further $145m. in loans. Throughout 2004 growth remained strong and the Government's progress in its campaign against rebel groups, especially the demobilization of the AUC begun in November (see Recent History), improved investor confidence. In that year the European Union (see p. 217) donated €422m. in aid for social improvements and the USA donated an estimated $751.3m, mostly for military aid and anti-narcotics operations. The Uribe administration proposed a budget for 2005 of some 92,000m pesos, representing an annual increase in government expenditure of some 19%. The increase in expenditure was intended primarily to finance counter-insurgency and counter-narcotics operations and was to be met through a widening of the tax base, improved tax collection, increased government borrowing and privatization revenues. Growth was estimated at 4.0% in 2004 and was forecast at 3.5% in 2005.

Education

Primary education is free and compulsory for five years, to be undertaken by children between six and 12 years of age. No child may be admitted to secondary school unless these five years have been successfully completed. Secondary education, beginning at the age of 11, lasts for up to six years. Following completion of a first cycle of four years, pupils may pursue a further two years of vocational study, leading to the Bachiller examination. In 1996 the total enrolment at primary schools included 89% of pupils in the relevant age-group, while the comparable ratio for secondary education in 1995 was 50%. In 2001 there were 24 public universities in Colombia. Government expenditure on education in the 1999 budget was 5,789,000m. pesos, representing 19.7% of total spending.

Public Holidays

2005: 1 January (New Year's Day), 6 January (Epiphany), 19 March (St Joseph's Day), 24 March (Maundy Thursday), 25 March (Good Friday), 1 May (Labour Day), 5 May (Ascension Day), 26 May (Corpus Christi), 17 June (Sacred Heart of Jesus), 29 June (SS Peter and Paul), 20 July (Independence), 7 August (Battle of Boyacá), 15 August (Assumption), 12 October (Discovery of the Americas), 1 November (All Saints' Day), 11 November (Independence of Cartagena), 8 December (Immaculate Conception), 25 December (Christmas Day).

2006: 1 January (New Year's Day), 6 January (Epiphany), 19 March (St Joseph's Day), 13 April (Maundy Thursday), 14 April (Good Friday), 1 May (Labour Day), 25 May (Ascension Day), 15 June (Corpus Christi), 19 June (Sacred Heart of Jesus), 29 June (SS Peter and Paul), 20 July (Independence), 7 August (Battle of Boyacá), 15 August (Assumption), 12 October (Discovery of the Americas), 1 November (All Saints' Day), 11 November (Independence of Cartagena), 8 December (Immaculate Conception), 25 December (Christmas Day).

Weights and Measures

The metric system is in force.

Statistical Survey

Sources (unless otherwise stated): Departamento Administrativo Nacional de Estadística (DANE), Transversal 45 No 26-70, Interior I-CAN, Santafé de Bogotá, DC; tel. (1) 597-8300; fax (1) 597-8399; e-mail dane@dane.gov.co; internet www.dane.gov.co; Banco de la República, Carrera 7A, No 14-78, 5°, Apdo Aéreo 3531, Santafé de Bogotá, DC; tel. (1) 343-1111; fax (1) 286-1686; e-mail wbanco@banrep.gov.co; internet www.banrep.gov.co.

Area and Population

AREA, POPULATION AND DENSITY

Area (sq km)	1,141,748*
Population (census results)†	
15 October 1985	
Males	14,642,835
Females	14,838,160
Total	29,480,995
24 October 1993	37,664,711
Population (official estimates at mid-year)	
2002	43,834,117
2003	44,583,575
2004	45,325,260
Density (per sq km) at mid-2004	39.7

* 440,831 sq miles.
† Revised figures, including adjustment for underenumeration. The enumerated total was 27,853,436 (males 13,785,523, females 14,067,913) in 1985 and 33,109,840 (males 16,296,539, females 16,813,301) in 1993.

DEPARTMENTS
(census of 24 October 1993)*

Department	Area (sq km)	Population	Capital (with population)
Amazonas	109,665	56,399	Leticia (30,045)
Antioquia	63,612	4,919,619	Medellín (1,834,881)
Arauca	23,818	185,882	Arauca (59,805)
Atlántico	3,388	1,837,468	Barranquilla (1,090,618)
Bolívar	25,978	1,702,188	Cartagena (747,390)
Boyacá	23,189	1,315,579	Tunja (112,807)
Caldas	7,888	1,055,577	Manizales (345,539)
Caquetá	88,965	367,898	Florencia (107,620)
Casanare	44,640	211,329	Yopal (57,279)
Cauca	29,308	1,127,678	Popayán (207,700)
César	22,905	827,219	Valledupar (278,216)
Chocó	46,530	406,199	Quibdó (122,371)
Córdoba	25,020	1,275,623	Montería (308,506)
Cundinamarca . .	22,623	1,875,337	Santafé de Bogotá†
Guainía	72,238	28,478	Puerto Inírida (18,270)
La Guajira . . .	20,848	433,361	Riohacha (109,474)
Guaviare	42,327	97,602	San José del Guaviare (48,237)
Huila	19,890	843,798	Neiva (278,350)
Magdalena . . .	23,188	1,127,691	Santa Marta (313,072)
Meta	85,635	618,427	Villavicencio (272,118)
Nariño	33,268	1,443,671	Pasto (331,866)
Norte de Santander .	21,658	1,162,474	Cúcuta (538,126)
Putumayo	24,885	264,291	Mocoa (25,910)
Quindío	1,845	495,212	Armenia (258,990)
Risaralda	4,140	844,184	Pereira (401,909)
San Andrés y Providencia Islands	44	61,040	San Andrés (56,361)
Santander del Sur	30,537	1,811,740	Bucaramanga (472,461)
Sucre	10,917	701,105	Sincelejo (194,962)
Tolima	23,562	1,286,078	Ibagué (399,838)
Valle del Cauca . .	22,140	3,736,090	Cali (1,847,176)
Vaupés	65,268	24,671	Mitú (13,177)
Vichada	100,242	62,073	Puerto Carreño (11,452)
Capital District			
Santafé de Bogotá, DC	1,587	5,484,244	Bogotá†
Total	1,141,748	37,664,711	—

* Adjusted for underenumeration.
† The capital city, Santafé de Bogotá, exists as the capital of a department as well as the Capital District. The city's population is included only in Santafé de Bogotá, DC.

PRINCIPAL TOWNS
(estimated population at mid-1999)

Santafé de Bogotá, DC (capital)	6,260,862	Neiva	300,052
Cali	2,077,386	Soledad . . .	295,058
Medellín . . .	1,861,265	Armenia . . .	281,422
Barranquilla . .	1,223,260	Villavicencio . .	273,140
Cartagena . . .	805,757	Soacha . . .	272,058
Cúcuta . . .	606,932	Valledupar . . .	263,247
Bucaramanga . .	515,555	Montería . . .	248,245
Ibagué . . .	393,664	Itagüí	228,985
Pereira . . .	381,725	Palmira . . .	226,509
Santa Marta . .	359,147	Buenaventura . .	224,336
Manizales . .	337,580	Floridablanca . .	221,913
Bello	333,470	Sincelejo . . .	220,704
Pasto	332,396	Popayán	200,719

Mid-2003 (UN estimate, incl. suburbs): Santafé de Bogotá 7,289,646 (Source: UN, *World Urbanization Prospects: The 2003 Revision*).

BIRTHS, MARRIAGES AND DEATHS*

	Registered live births	Registered deaths
1996	n.a.	173,506
1997	n.a.	170,753
1998	720,984	175,363
1999	746,194	183,553
2000	752,834	187,432
2001	724,319	191,513
2002	700,455	192,262
2003†	697,029	189,073

* Data are tabulated by year of registration rather than by year of occurrence, although registration is incomplete. According to UN estimates, the average annual rates in 1985–90 were births 27.8 per 1,000; deaths 6.5 per 1,000; in 1990–95: births 27.0 per 1,000; deaths 6.4 per 1,000; and in 1995–2000: births 24.5 per 1,000; deaths 5.7 per 1,000 (Source: UN, *World Population Prospects: The 2002 Revision*).
† Preliminary figures.

Registered marriages: 102,448 in 1980; 95,845 in 1981; 70,350 in 1986.

Expectation of life (WHO estimates, years at birth): 71.8 (males 67.5; females 76.3) in 2002 (Source: WHO, *World Health Report*).

ECONOMICALLY ACTIVE POPULATION
(household survey, '000 persons, September)

	2001	2002	2003
Agriculture, hunting, forestry and fishing	3,661	3,492	3,769
Mining and quarrying	192	181	177
Manufacturing	2,119	2,200	2,328
Electricity, gas and water . . .	88	74	62
Construction	643	760	767
Trade, restaurants and hotels . .	4,235	4,193	4,375
Transport, storage and communications	1,069	1,069	1,133
Finance, insurance, real estate and business services . . .	843	888	935
Community, social and personal services	3,645	3,745	3,917
Activities not adequately described	5	18	5
Total labour force	16,498	16,619	17,467

Source: ILO.

Health and Welfare

KEY INDICATORS

Total fertility rate (children per woman, 2002)	2.6
Under-5 mortality rate (per 1,000 live births, 2003) . . .	21
HIV/AIDS (% of persons aged 15–49, 2003)	0.7
Physicians (per 1,000 head, 1997)	1.16
Hospital beds (per 1,000 head, 1996)	1.46
Health expenditure (2001): US $ per head (PPP)	356
Health expenditure (2001): % of GDP	5.5
Health expenditure (2001): public (% of total)	65.7
Access to water (% of persons, 2002)	92
Access to sanitation (% of persons, 2002)	86
Human Development Index (2002): ranking	73
Human Development Index (2002): value	0.773

For sources and definitions, see explanatory note on p. vi.

Agriculture

PRINCIPAL CROPS
('000 metric tons)

	2001	2002	2003
Rice (paddy)	2,314	2,348	2,543
Maize	1,197	1,174	1,289
Sorghum	212	223	260
Potatoes	2,874	2,835	2,872
Cassava (Manioc)	1,980	1,779	1,841
Yams	255	237	283
Other roots and tubers* . . .	73	64	75
Sugar cane*	33,400	35,800	37,000
Dry beans	124	120	136
Soybeans (Soya beans) . . .	56	57	58
Coconuts	99	96	105
Oil palm fruit*	2,600	2,600	2,633
Cottonseed*	70	60	88
Cabbages*	295	300	305
Tomatoes	398	423	369
Green chillies and peppers . . .	46	53	27
Dry onions	412	419	583
Carrots	190	152	180
Other vegetables*	200	201	205
Watermelons	64	70	66
Bananas	1,375	1,424	1,511
Plantains	2,928	2,921	2,911
Oranges	238	298	300*
Mangoes	134	141	167
Avocados	137	142	162
Pineapples	314	353	406
Papayas	111	86	88
Other fruit*	1,270	1,325	1,352
Coffee (green)	656	691	703

* FAO estimate(s).

Source: FAO.

LIVESTOCK
('000 head, year ending September)

	2001	2002	2003
Horses*	2,600	2,650	2,700
Mules*	605	610	615
Asses*	720	723	725
Cattle	24,510	24,765	25,000*
Pigs	2,198	2,234	2,300*
Sheep	2,256	2,045	2,100*
Goats	1,136	1,105	1,150*
Poultry*	110,000	115,000	118,000

* FAO estimate(s).

Source: FAO.

LIVESTOCK PRODUCTS
(FAO estimates, '000 metric tons)

	2001	2002	2003
Beef and veal	700	676	680
Mutton and lamb	6.9	6.2	6.5
Goat meat	6.4	6.3	6.5
Pig meat	98.4	110.0	110.0
Horse meat	5.5	5.6	5.7
Poultry meat	581	629	630
Cows' milk	5,877	6,021	5,920
Cheese	53	54.0	54.8
Butter and ghee	18.8	19.2	19.6
Hen eggs	354.9	314.4	325.0
Cattle hides	77.9	75.3	75.9

Source: FAO.

Forestry

ROUNDWOOD REMOVALS
('000 cu metres, excl. bark)

	2001	2002	2003
Sawlogs, veneer logs and logs for sleepers	1,190	1,161	1,148
Pulpwood	500	778	836
Other industrial wood	51	73	84
Fuel wood	10,760	9,598	7,891
Total	12,501	11,610	9,959

Source: FAO.

SAWNWOOD PRODUCTION
('000 cu metres, incl. railway sleepers)

	2001	2002	2003
Coniferous (softwood)	18	18	144
Broadleaved (hardwood) . . .	521	509	455
Total	539	527	599

Source: FAO.

Fishing

('000 metric tons, live weight)

	2000	2001	2002
Capture*	129.6	130.0	135.0
Characins*	6.6	6.6	6.6
Freshwater siluroids* . . .	10.5	10.6	10.6
Other freshwater fishes* . .	7.8	7.8	7.8
Pacific anchoveta	22.5*	25.1	25.0*
Skipjack tuna	5.9	1.9	2.3
Yellowfin tuna	17.4	25.6	30.8
Aquaculture	61.8	65.0*	65.0*
Tilapias	22.9	24.0*	24.0*
Cachama blanca	15.0	15.8*	15.8*
Rainbow trout	9.0	9.5*	9.5*
Whiteleg shrimp	11.4	12.0*	12.0*
Total catch*	191.4	195.0	200.0

* FAO estimate(s).

Note: Figures exclude crocodiles, recorded by number rather than by weight. The number of spectacled caimans caught was: 832,203 in 2000; 704,313 in 2001; 585,000 in 2002.

Source: FAO.

Mining

('000 metric tons, unless otherwise indicated)

	2000	2001	2002
Gold (kilograms)	37,018	21,813	20,799
Silver (kilograms)	7,970	7,242	6,986
Salt	461	395	527
Hard coal	38,142	43,910	39,500
Iron ore*	660	637	688
Crude petroleum ('000 barrels)	250,755	220,460	211,000

* Figures refer to the gross weight of ore. The estimated iron content is 46%.

Source: US Geological Survey.

Industry

SELECTED PRODUCTS

('000 metric tons, unless otherwise indicated)

	1996	1997	1998
Sugar	2,149.2	2,136.2	2,125.6
Cement	8,590.1	8,870.4	8,464.0
Steel ingots	298.4	344.9	264.5
Diesel oil ('000 barrels) . . .	24,552	24,266	23,210
Fuel oil ('000 barrels) . . .	19,453	19,700	18,758
Motor fuel ('000 barrels) . . .	41,160	34,445	38,354

Finance

CURRENCY AND EXCHANGE RATES

Monetary Units

100 centavos = 1 Colombian peso.

Sterling, Dollar and Euro Equivalents (31 December 2004)

£1 sterling = 4,658.73 pesos;

US $1 = 2,412.10 pesos;

€1 = 3,285.52 pesos;

10,000 Colombian pesos = £2.15 = $4.15 = €3.04.

Average Exchange Rate (pesos per US $)

2002   2,504.24

2003   2,877.65

2004   2,628.61

CENTRAL GOVERNMENT BUDGET

('000 million pesos)

Revenue	1996	1997	1998
Direct taxation	4,804.9	5,038.7	7,280.7
Indirect taxation	7,720.1	8,247.9	8,285.5
Rates and fines	102.7	399.7	104.6
Revenue under contracts . . .	290.8	30.3	—
Credit resources	5,380.2	8,721.9	10,527.9
Other	2,387.4	4,386.4	2,047.6
Total	20,686.1	26,824.9	28,246.3

Expenditure*	1996	1997	1998
Congress and comptrollership . .	186.4	238.9	281.0
General administration	879.7	856.0	742.0
Home office and foreign affairs .	123.2	127.7	147.8
Finance and public credit . .	3,184.6	3,509.1	3,263.7
Public works and transportation .	1,370.6	1,519.6	1,207.4
Defence	2,039.5	2,466.6	2,605.4
Police	973.0	1,237.4	1,471.4
Agriculture	811.8	622.3	425.0
Health	1,309.4	1,597.9	1,862.7
Education	2,950.3	3,656.9	4,706.9
Development, labour, mines and communications . . .	1,411.4	1,674.5	1,765.3
Justice and legal affairs . . .	947.7	1,118.2	1,234.8
Trade	31.1	26.2	21.2
Environment	139.0	167.5	138.7
Culture	—	12.4	64.3
Total	16,357.7	18,831.1	19,937.4

* Excluding public debt.

General budget ('000 million pesos): *Revenue:* 20,144.0 in 1999; 23,285.3 in 2000; 28,941.6 in 2001; 31,459.1 in 2002; 35,798.3 in 2003. *Expenditure:* 28,153.8 (excl. lending minus repayments 879.1) in 1999; 34,444.4 (excl. lending minus repayments 786.4) in 2000; 38,640.9 (excl. lending minus repayments 1,470.4) in 2001; 41,789.6 (excl. lending minus repayments 1,185.9) in 2002; 46,061.6 (excl. lending minus repayments 864.8) in 2003 (Source: IMF, *International Financial Statistics*).

INTERNATIONAL RESERVES

(US $ million at 31 December)

	2001	2002	2003
Gold*	91	112	136
IMF special drawing rights . .	135	154	171
Reserve position in IMF . . .	359	389	425
Foreign exchange	9,659	10,190	10,188
Total	10,244	10,844	10,920

* National valuation.

Source: IMF, *International Financial Statistics*.

MONEY SUPPLY

('000 million pesos at 31 December)

	2001	2002	2003
Currency outside banks . . .	8,653.6	10,188.5	12,196.6
Demand deposits at commercial banks	9,622.9	11,256.3	12,737.1
Total money (incl. others) . .	18,450.6	21,576.4	25,108.9

Source: IMF, *International Financial Statistics*.

COST OF LIVING

(Consumer price index for low-income families; base: 2000 = 100)

	2001	2002	2003
Food and beverages	108.7	118.4	127.2
Clothing and footwear . . .	103.8	105.8	107.2
Rent, fuel and light*	102.7	105.1	108.3
All items (incl. others)	108.6	116.5	125.0

* Including certain household equipment.

Source: ILO.

NATIONAL ACCOUNTS
('000 million pesos at current prices, rounded figures)

Composition of the Gross National Product

	1999	2000	2001*
Compensation of employees . .	56,482	62,118	66,289
Operating surplus . . . . .} Consumption of fixed capital .}	81,671	95,743	102,222
Gross domestic product (GDP) at factor cost . . .	138,153	157,861	168,512
Indirect taxes	14,242	18,048	20,590
Less Subsidies	831	1,013	1,166
GDP in purchasers' values .	151,565	174,896	187,936
Net factor income from abroad .	−2,663	−4,835	−5,963
Gross national product (GNP)	148,902	170,061	181,973

* Provisional figures.

Expenditure on the Gross Domestic Product

	2000	2001	2002
Government final consumption expenditure	37,057	37,910	42,070
Private final consumption expenditure	110,217	122,929	132,838
Increase in stocks	1,991	1,877	0
Gross fixed capital formation . .	21,952	26,593	30,758
Total domestic expenditure .	171,217	189,309	205,666
Exports of goods and services . .	37,606	39,153	39,779
Less Imports of goods and services	33,926	40,526	42,792
GDP in purchasers' values . .	174,896	187,936	202,653

Source: UN *Statistical Yearbook for Latin America and the Caribbean.*

2003 ('000 million pesos at current prices): *Total domestic expenditure* 233,333; Exports of goods and services 46,757; *Less* Imports of goods and services 52,356; *GDP in purchasers' values* 227,734 (Source: IMF, *International Financial Statistics*).

Gross Domestic Product by Economic Activity

	1999	2000	2001*
Agriculture, hunting and forestry	19,146	21,988	23,401
Fishing	559	640	750
Mining and quarrying	7,990	10,842	9,618
Manufacturing	21,034	25,622	26,916
Electricity, gas and water . . .	5,168	6,237	8,001
Construction	6,351	6,378	7,214
Wholesale and retail trade; repair of motor vehicles, motorcycles, and personal and household goods	13,232	14,843	16,077
Hotels and restaurants . . .	3,424	3,695	3,994
Transport, storage and communications	11,048	12,426	14,043
Financial intermediation . . .	7,609	7,753	8,608
Real estate, renting and business activities	17,592	18,457	19,034
Public administration and defence; compulsory social security	15,387	17,672	18,087
Education	9,798	10,648	11,971
Health and social work . . .	6,748	7,310	7,966
Other community, social and personal service activities . .	2,638	2,844	3,078
Private households with employed persons	726	768	818
Sub-total	148,449	168,124	179,576
Less Imputed bank service charge	7,305	6,778	7,465
GDP in basic prices	141,144	161,346	172,112
Taxes on products	10,695	13,819	16,033
Less Subsidies on products . .	274	269	209
GDP in purchasers' values .	151,565	174,896	187,936

* Provisional figures.

BALANCE OF PAYMENTS
(US $ million)

	2001	2002	2003
Exports of goods f.o.b.	12,848	12,316	13,693
Imports of goods f.o.b.	−12,269	−12,077	−13,258
Trade balance	579	239	435
Exports of services	2,190	1,866	1,879
Imports of services	−3,623	−3,332	−3,392
Balance on goods and services	−854	−1,227	−1,078
Other income received	914	711	548
Other income paid	−3,529	−3,559	−3,994
Balance on goods, services and income	−3,468	−4,075	−4,525
Current transfers received . . .	2,656	3,008	3,568
Current transfers paid	−302	−304	−234
Current balance	−1,114	−1,371	−1,191
Direct investment abroad . . .	−16	−857	−938
Direct investment from abroad .	2,525	2,115	1,793
Portfolio investment assets . .	−3,460	2,030	−1,741
Portfolio investment liabilities .	3,453	−933	130
Financial derivatives liabilities .	−113	−82	−45
Other investment assets . . .	231	282	1,652
Other investment liabilities . .	−136	−1,246	−39
Net errors and omissions . . .	−145	201	191
Overall balance	1,225	139	−188

Source: IMF, *International Financial Statistics.*

External Trade

PRINCIPAL COMMODITIES
(US $ million)

Imports c.i.f.	2001	2002	2003
Vegetables and vegetable products	724	836	855
Prepared foodstuffs, beverages and tobacco	852	788	799
Textiles and leather products . .	745	702	741
Paper and paper products . . .	435	436	454
Chemical products	2,725	2,770	3,757
Petroleum and its derivatives . .	219	239	292
Metals	574	562	678
Mechanical, electrical and transport equipment	5,558	5,441	6,157
Total (incl. others)	12,821	12,691	13,881

Exports f.o.b.	2001	2002	2003
Vegetables and vegetable products	1,108	1,193	1,188
Coffee	764	772	806
Coal	1,197	991	1,422
Petroleum and its derivatives . .	3,285	3,275	3,383
Prepared foodstuffs, beverages and tobacco	980	944	1,000
Textiles and leather products . .	1,015	880	1,017
Paper and publishing	399	373	398
Chemicals	1,522	1,509	1,371
Mechanical, electrical and transport equipment	1,093	931	665
Total (incl. others)	12,330	11,975	13,092

Source: Dirección de Impuestos y Aduanas Nacionales.

PRINCIPAL TRADING PARTNERS
(US $ million)

Imports c.i.f.	2001	2002	2003
Argentina	202.3	211.1	257.1
Bolivia	131.2	139.9	198.3
Brazil	582.1	642.8	619.4
Canada	344.2	313.5	274.1
Chile	262.5	299.9	280.8
China, People's Rep.	475.4	532.8	688.7
Ecuador	318.2	367.2	409.7
France	350.0	236.1	381.3
Germany	560.1	508.3	611.7
Italy	401.0	275.0	289.5
Japan	559.0	619.4	642.9
Korea, Rep.	266.3	311.5	337.8
Mexico	596.2	678.0	744.4
Peru	159.2	160.3	193.4
Spain	246.7	260.4	255.5
Switzerland	158.8	147.7	171.0
Taiwan	166.4	161.8	164.5
United Kingdom	179.6	161.8	164.3
USA	4,413.9	4,020.1	4,081.2
Venezuela	792.7	788.1	727.4
Total (incl. others)	12,820.6	12,690.4	13,880.6

Exports f.o.b.	2001	2002	2003
Belgium-Luxembourg	210.4	241.8	227.7
Canada	142.5	164.2	176.3
Chile	168.0	174.1	188.0
Costa Rica	149.8	192.5	153.9
Ecuador	699.9	814.0	778.6
France	134.0	138.3	145.2
Germany	416.9	332.3	264.1
Italy	196.1	222.4	279.9
Japan	164.7	193.8	198.7
Mexico	261.3	310.4	356.6
Netherlands	114.3	129.2	301.1
Panama	265.2	216.1	170.1
Peru	277.5	348.5	394.5
Puerto Rico	90.1	178.4	361.9
Spain	140.5	206.1	195.4
United Kingdom	287.3	159.3	182.7
USA	5,254.3	5,159.7	5,758.2
Venezuela	1,737.4	1,123.3	693.5
Total (incl. others)	12,301.5	11,938.9	13,010.1

Transport

RAILWAYS
(traffic)

	1996	1997	1998
Freight ('000 metric tons)	321	348	281
Freight ton-km ('000)	746,544	736,427	657,585

Source: Sociedad de Transporte Ferroviario, SA.

ROAD TRAFFIC
(motor vehicles in use)

	1997	1998	1999
Passenger cars	1,694,323	1,776,100	1,803,201
Buses	126,362	131,987	134,799
Goods vehicles	179,530	183,335	184,495
Motorcycles	385,378	450,283	479,073

Source: IRF, *World Road Statistics*.

SHIPPING
Merchant Fleet
(registered at 31 December)

	2001	2002	2003
Number of vessels	105	109	121
Total displacement ('000 grt)	65.6	67.8	71.1

Source: Lloyd's Register-Fairplay, *World Fleet Statistics*.

Domestic Sea-borne Freight Traffic
('000 metric tons)

	1987	1988	1989
Goods loaded and unloaded	772.1	944.8	464.6

International Sea-borne Freight Traffic
('000 metric tons)

	1999	2000	2001
Goods loaded	4,111	3,543	3,832
Goods unloaded	1,274	1,114	1,399

CIVIL AVIATION
(traffic)

	2001	2002	2003
Domestic			
Passengers carried ('000)	7,560	7,732	7,438
Freight carried (metric tons)	103,826	121,636	131,187
International			
Passengers ('000):			
arrivals	1,446	1,429	1,460
departures	1,605	1,455	1,484
Freight (metric tons):			
loaded	129,557	127,688	146,142
unloaded	242,780	257,293	299,463

Source: Departamento Administrativo de Aeronáutica Civil.

Tourism

TOURIST ARRIVALS
('000)

Country of origin	2000	2001	2002
Argentina	19.4	17.8	12.9
Brazil	14.3	14.6	13.1
Canada	21.6	20.6	15.6
Costa Rica	13.5	12.5	10.6
Ecuador	48.9	59.5	53.0
France	15.0	16.3	15.9
Germany	19.6	17.2	13.1
Mexico	24.0	24.5	23.9
Panama	13.3	16.9	17.0
Peru	22.0	23.9	22.3
Spain	26.4	29.0	28.3
United Kingdom	14.1	13.6	9.4
USA	137.1	156.7	149.5
Venezuela	62.2	58.3	63.4
Total (incl. others)	557.3	615.7	541.4

Source: World Tourism Organization, *Yearbook of Tourism Statistics*.

Tourism receipts (US $ million): 1,026 in 2000; 1,209 in 2001; 962 in 2002 (Source: World Tourism Organization).

Communications Media

	2001	2002	2003
Telephones ('000 main lines in use)	7,371.5	7,766.0	8,768.1
Mobile cellular telephones ('000 subscribers)	3,265.3	4,596.6	6,186.2
Personal computers ('000 in use) .	1,800	2,133	n.a.
Internet users ('000)	1,154.0	2,000.0	2,732.2

1996: 37 daily newspapers.

1997 ('000 in use): 21,000 radio receivers; 173 facsimile machines.

2000 ('000 in use): 11,936 television receivers.

Book production: 1,481 titles in 1991.

Sources: UN, *Statistical Yearbook*; UNESCO, *Statistical Yearbook*; International Telecommunication Union.

Education

(2002)

	Institutions	Teachers	Pupils
Nursery	32,432	50,713	1,080,555
Primary	55,869	193,606	5,205,489
Secondary	12,921	177,940	3,515,716
Higher (incl. universities) . . .	321	97,522	981,458

Source: partly Ministerio de Educación Nacional.

Adult literacy rate (UNESCO estimates): 92.1% (males 92.1%; females 92.2%) in 2002 (Source: UN Development Programme, *Human Development Report*).

Directory

The Constitution

A new, 380-article Constitution, drafted by a 74-member National Constituent Assembly, took effect from 6 July 1991. The new Constitution retained the institutional framework of a directly elected President with a non-renewable four-year term of office, together with a bicameral legislature composed of an upper house or Senate (with 102 directly elected members) and a lower house or House of Representatives (with 161 members, to include at least two representatives of each national department). On 14 December 2004 both chambers of the Congreso approved a constitutional amendment to allow re-election of the President. The reform was scheduled to be implemented before the presidential election that was due in May 2006. A Vice-President is elected at the same time as the President, and also holds office for a term of four years.

The new Constitution also contained comprehensive provisions for the recognition and protection of civil rights, and for the reform of the structures and procedures of political participation and of the judiciary.

The fundamental principles upon which the new Constitution is based are embodied in articles 1–10.

Article 1: Colombia is a lawful state, organized as a single Republic, decentralized, with autonomous territorial entities, democratic, participatory and pluralist, founded on respect for human dignity, on the labour and solidarity of its people and on the prevalence of the general interest.

Article 2: The essential aims of the State are: to serve the community, to promote general prosperity and to guarantee the effectiveness of the principles, rights and obligations embodied in the Constitution, to facilitate the participation of all in the decisions which affect them and in the economic, political, administrative and cultural life of the nation; to defend national independence, to maintain territorial integrity and to ensure peaceful coexistence and the validity of the law.

The authorities of the Republic are instituted to protect the residents of Colombia, in regard to their life, honour, goods, beliefs and other rights and liberties, and to ensure the fulfilment of the obligations of the State and of the individual.

Article 3: Sovereignty rests exclusively with the people, from whom public power emanates. The people exercise power directly or through their representatives in the manner established by the Constitution.

Article 4: The Constitution is the highest authority. In all cases of incompatability between the Constitution and the law or other juridical rules, constitutional dispositions will apply.

It is the duty of nationals and foreigners in Colombia to observe the Constitution and the law, and to respect and obey the authorities.

Article 5: The State recognizes, without discrimination, the primacy of the inalienable rights of the individual and protects the family as the basic institution of society.

Article 6: Individuals are solely responsible to the authorities for infringements of the Constitution and of the law. Public servants are equally accountable and are responsible to the authorities for failure to fulfil their function or abuse of their position.

Article 7: The State recognizes and protects the ethnic diversity of the Colombian nation.

Article 8: It is an obligation of the State and of the people to protect the cultural and natural riches of the nation.

Article 9: The foreign relations of the State are based on national sovereignty, with respect for self-determination of people and with recognition of the principles of international law accepted by Colombia.

Similarly, Colombia's external politics will be directed towards Caribbean and Latin American integration.

Article 10: Spanish (Castellano) is the official language of Colombia. The languages and dialects of ethnic groups are officially recognized within their territories. Education in communities with their own linguistic traditions will be bilingual.

The Government

HEAD OF STATE

President: Alvaro Uribe Vélez (took office 7 August 2002).

Vice-President: Francisco Santos Calderón (took office 7 August 2002).

CABINET
(April 2005)

A coalition of the Partido Conservador Colombiano, the Partido Liberal Colombiano and independents.

Minister of the Interior and Justice: Sabas Pretelt de la Vega.

Minister of Foreign Affairs: Carolina Barco.

Minister of Finance and Public Credit: Alberto Carrasquilla Barrera.

Minister of National Defence: Jorge Alberto Uribe Echavarría.

Minister of Agriculture and Rural Development: Carlos Gustavo Cano Sanz.

Minister of Labour, Social Security and Health: Diego Palacio Betancourt.

Minister of Mines and Energy: Luis Ernesto Mejía Castro.

Minister of Trade, Industry and Tourism: Jorge Humberto Botero.

Minister of National Education: Cecilia María Vélez White.

Minister of the Environment, Housing and Territorial Development: Sandra Suárez Pérez.

Minister of Communications: Martha Elena Pinto de Hart.

Minister of Transport: Andrés Uriel Gallego Henao.

Minister of Culture: María Consuelo Araújo Castro.

MINISTRIES

Office of the President: Palacio de Nariño, Carrera 8a, No 7-26, Santafé de Bogotá, DC; tel. (1) 562-9300; fax (1) 286-8063.

Ministry of Agriculture and Rural Development: Avda Jiménez, No 7-65, Santafé de Bogotá, DC; tel. (1) 334-1199; fax (1) 284-1775; e-mail minagric@colomsat.net.co; internet www.minagricultura.gov.co.

Ministry of Communications: Edif. Murillo Toro, Carrera 7 y 8, Calle 12 y 13, Apdo Aéreo 14515, Santafé de Bogotá, DC; tel. (1) 286-6911; fax (1) 344-3434; internet www.mincomunicaciones.gov.co.

Ministry of Culture: Calle 8, No 6-97, Santafé de Bogotá, DC; tel. (1) 342-4100; fax (1) 342-1721; e-mail fvasquez@mincultura.gov.co; internet www.mincultura.gov.co.

Ministry of the Environment, Housing and Territorial Development: Calle 37, No 8-40, Santafé de Bogotá, DC; tel. (1) 288-6877; fax (1) 288-9788; internet www.minambiente.gov.co.

Ministry of Finance and Public Credit: Carrera 8a, No 6-64, Of. 305, Santafé de Bogotá, DC; tel. (1) 381-1700; fax (1) 350-9344; internet www.minhacienda.gov.co.

Ministry of Foreign Affairs: Palacio de San Carlos, Calle 10A, No 5-51, Santafé de Bogotá, DC; tel. (1) 282-7811; fax (1) 341-6777; internet www.minrelext.gov.co.

Ministry of the Interior and Justice: Palacio Echeverry, Carrera 8A, No 8-09, Santafé de Bogotá, DC; tel. (1) 334-0630; fax (1) 341-9583; internet www.presidencia.gov.co/ministerios.

Ministry of Labour, Social Security and Health: Carrera 7A, No 34-50, Santafé de Bogotá, DC; tel. (1) 287-3434; fax (1) 285-7091; e-mail oaai@tutopia.com.

Ministry of Mines and Energy: Centro Administrativo Nacional (CAN), Avda El Dorado, Santafé de Bogotá, DC; tel. (1) 222-4555; fax (1) 222-3651; internet www.minminas.gov.co.

Ministry of National Defence: Centro Administrativo Nacional (CAN), 2°, Avda El Dorado, Santafé de Bogotá, DC; tel. (1) 220-4999; fax (1) 222-1874; internet www.mindefensa.gov.co.

Ministry of National Education: Centro Administrativo Nacional (CAN), Of. 501, Avda El Dorado, Santafé de Bogotá, DC; tel. (1) 222-2800; fax (1) 222-4578; e-mail dci@mineducacion.gov.co; internet www.mineducacion.gov.co.

Ministry of Trade, Industry and Tourism: Calle 28, No 13A-15, 18°, Edif. Centro de Comercio Internacional, Santafé de Bogotá, DC; tel. (1) 382-1307; fax (1) 352-2101; internet www.mincomercio.gov .co.

Ministry of Transport: Centro Administrativo Nacional (CAN), Of. 409, Avda El Dorado, Santafé de Bogotá, DC; tel. (1) 222-4411; fax (1) 222-1647; internet www.mintransporte.gov.co.

President and Legislature

PRESIDENT

Presidential Election, 26 May 2002

	Votes	% of votes cast
Alvaro Uribe Vélez	5,862,655	54.0
Horacio Serpa Uribe	3,514,779	32.3
Luis Eduardo Garzón	680,245	6.3
Noemí Sanín Posada	641,884	5.9
Others	155,966	1.5
Total*	10,855,529	100.0

*Excluding 196,116 blank ballots.

CONGRESO

Senado
(Senate)

President: GERMÁN VARGAS LLERAS.

General Election, 10 March 2002

	Seats	% of votes cast
Independent groups	52	51.5
Partido Liberal Colombiano (PL)	29	30.6
Partido Conservador Colombiano (PCC)	13	9.9
Coalitions	6	6.3
Indigenous groups*	2	1.7
Total	102	100.0

*Under the reforms of the Constitution in 1991, at least two Senate seats are reserved for indigenous groups.

Cámara de Representantes
(House of Representatives)

President: ALONSO ACOSTA OSIO.

General Election, 10 March 2002

	Seats	% of votes cast
Independent groups	69	52.6
Partido Liberal Colombiano (PL)	54	32.0
Partido Conservador Colombiano (PCC)	21	7.3
Coalitions	17	8.1
Total	161	100.0

Political Organizations

Alianza Democrática—M-19 (AD—M-19): Transversal 28, No 37-78, Santafé de Bogotá, DC; tel. (1) 368-9436; f. 1990; alliance of centre-left groups (including factions of Unión Patriótica, Colombia Unida, Frente Popular and Socialismo Democrático) which supported the M-19 campaign for elections to the National Constituent Assembly in December 1990; Leader DIEGO MONTAÑA CUÉLLAR.

Alianza Nacional Popular (ANAPO): Carrera 18, No 33-95, Santafé de Bogotá, DC; tel. (1) 287-7050; fax (1) 245-3138; f. 1971 by supporters of Gen. Gustavo Rojas Pinilla; populist party; Leader MARÍA EUGENIA ROJAS DE MORENO DÍAZ.

Democracia Cristiana: Avda 42, No 18-08, Apdo 25867, Santafé de Bogotá, DC; tel. (1) 285-6639; f. 1964; Christian Democrat party; 10,000 mems; Pres. JUAN A. POLO FIGUEROA; Sec.-Gen. DIEGO ARANGO OSORIO.

Frente Social y Político: f. 2001; left-wing; Presidential Candidate LUIS EDUARDO GARZÓN.

Frente por la Unidad del Pueblo (FUP): Santafé de Bogotá, DC; extreme left-wing front comprising socialists and Maoists.

Movimiento 19 de Abril (M-19): Calle 26, No 13B-09, Of. 1401, Santafé de Bogotá, DC; tel. (1) 282-7891; fax (1) 282-8129; f. 1970 by followers of Gen. Gustavo Rojas Pinilla and dissident factions from the FARC—EP (see below); left-wing urban guerrilla group, until formally constituted as a political party in Oct. 1989; mem. of the Coordinadora Nacional Guerrilla Simón Bolívar (CNGSB); Leader OTTY PATIÑO.

Movimiento Colombia Unida (CU): Santafé de Bogotá, DC; left-wing group allied to the UP; Leader ADALBERTO CARVAJAL.

Movimiento Nacional Conservador (MNC): Carrera 16, No 33-24, Santafé de Bogotá, DC; tel. (1) 245-4418; fax (1) 284-8529; Sec.-Gen. JUAN PABLO CEPERA MÁRQUEZ.

Movimiento Nacional Progresista (MNP): Carrera 10, No 19-45, Of. 708, Santafé de Bogotá, DC; tel. (1) 286-7517; fax (1) 341-9368; Sec.-Gen. EDUARDO AISAMAK LEÓN BELTRÁN.

Movimiento Obrero Independiente Revolucionario (MOIR): Avda Caracas 33–39, Santafé de Bogotá, DC; tel. (1) 287-0732; e-mail moir@moir.org.co; internet www.moir.org.co; left-wing workers' movement; Maoist; Leader HÉCTOR VALENGA.

Movimiento de Salvación Nacional (MSN): Carrera 7A, No 58-00, Santafé de Bogotá, DC; tel. (1) 249-0209; fax (1) 310-1991; f. 1990; split from the Partido Conservador Colombiano.

Mujeres para la Democracia: Santafé de Bogotá, DC; f. 1991; women's party; Leader ANGELA CUEVAS DE DOLMETSCH.

Organización Nacional Indígena de Colombia (ONIC): Calle 13, No 4–38, Santafé de Bogotá; tel. (1) 284-2168; fax (1) 284-3465; e-mail onic@onic.org.co; internet www.onic.org.co; f. 1982; asscn of indigenous political and development groups.

Partido Conservador Colombiano (PCC): Avda 22, No 37-09, Santafé de Bogotá, DC; tel. (1) 369-3923; fax (1) 369-0053; internet www.partidoconservador.com; f. 1849; 2.9m. mems; Sec.-Gen. ALVARO GUILLERMO RENDÓN LÓPEZ.

Partido de Esperanza, Paz y Libertad (EPL): f. 1969 as Maoist guerrilla movement Ejército Popular de Liberación; splinter group from Communist Party; abandoned armed struggle in March 1991; Leader FRANCISCO CARABALLO.

Partido Liberal Colombiano (PL): Avda Caracas, No 36-01, Santafé de Bogotá, DC; tel. (1) 288-1138; fax (1) 288-4200; e-mail medios@partidoliberal.org.co; internet www.partidoliberal.org.co; f. 1848; divided into two factions: the official group (HERNANDO DURÁN LUSSÁN, MIGUEL PINEDO) and the independent group, Nuevo Liberalismo (New Liberalism, led by Dr ALBERTO SANTOFIMIO BOTERO, ERNESTO SAMPER PIZANO, EDUARDO MESTRE); Dir ALPHER ROJAS CARVAJAL; Sec.-Gen. JUAN CARLOS POSADA GARCÍA-PEÑA.

Partido Nacional Cristiano (PNC): Calle 22C, No 31-01, Santafé de Bogotá, DC; tel. (1) 337-9211; fax (1) 269-3621; e-mail mision2@latino.net.co; Pres. LIÑO LEAL COLLAZOS.

Polo Democrático Independiente (PDI): Carrera 17A 37-27, Santafé de Bogotá; tel. (1) 288-6188; internet www.polodemocratico .net; f. 2002 as electoral alliance, constituted as a political party in July 2003; founded by fmr mems of the Movimiento 19 de Abril (q.v.); left-wing; Leader SAMUEL MORENO ROJAS.

Unidad Democrática de la Izquierda (Democratic Unity of the Left): Santafé de Bogotá, DC; f. 1982; left-wing coalition incorporating the following parties:

Firmes: Santafé de Bogotá, DC; democratic party.

Partido Comunista Colombiano (PC): Calle 18A, No 14-56, Apdo Aéreo 2523, Santafé de Bogotá, DC; tel. (1) 334-1947; fax (1) 281-8259; f. 1930; Marxist-Leninist party; Sec.-Gen. ALVARO VÁSQUEZ DEL REAL.

Partido Socialista de los Trabajadores (PST): Santafé de Bogotá, DC; workers' socialist party; Leader María SOCORRO RAMÍREZ.

Unión Patriótica (UP): Carrera 13A, No 38-32, Of. 204, Santafé de Bogota, DC; fax (1) 570-4400; f. 1985; Marxist party formed by the FARC—EP (see below); obtained legal status in 1986; Pres. ERNÁN PASTRANA; Exec. Sec. OVIDIO SALINAS.

The following guerrilla groups and illegal organizations were active:

Autodefensas Campesinas de Córdoba y Urabá (ACCU): right-wing paramilitary org.; Leaders CARLOS CASTAÑO, SALVATORE MANCUSO.

Autodefensas Unidas de Colombia (AUC): e-mail auc_inspeccion@yahoo.es; internet www.colombialibre.org; right-wing paramilitary org.; announced cease-fire in Dec. 2002; demobilization began in November 2004; c. 10,000 mems; Leader JULIÁN BOLÍVAR; Inspector-Gen. ADOLFO PAZ; Commdr-Gen. RAMÓN ISAZA; Political Dir ERNESTO BÁEZ.

Ejército de Liberación Nacional (ELN): internet www.eln-voces .com; Castroite guerrilla movement; f. 1964; 3,500 mems; political status recognized by the Govt in 1998; mem. of the Coordinadora Nacional Guerrilla Simón Bolívar (CNGSB); Leader NICOLÁS ROGRÍGUEZ BAUTISTA.

Frente Popular de Liberación Nacional (FPLN): f. 1994 by dissident mems of the ELN and the EPL.

Fuerzas Armadas Revolucionarias de Colombia—Ejercito del Pueblo (FARC—EP): internet www.farcep.org; fmrly military wing of the Communist Party; composed of 39 armed fronts and about 17,000 mems; political status recognized by the Govt in 1998; mem. of the Coordinadora Nacional Guerrilla Simón Bolívar (CNGSB); C-in-C PEDRO ANTONIO MARÍN (alias MANUEL MARULANDA VÉLEZ or 'TIROFIJO') (reported dead in mid-2004); Leader of the Bolivarian Movt GUILLERMO LEÓN SAENZ VARGAS (alias ALFONSO CANO).

Movimiento de Autodefensa Obrera (MAO): workers' self-defence movement; Trotskyite; Leader ADELAIDA ABADIA REY.

Movimiento de Restauración Nacional (MORENA): right-wing; Leader ARMANDO VALENZUELA RUIZ.

Muerte a Secuestradores (MAS) (Death to Kidnappers): right-wing paramilitary org.; funded by drugs-traffickers.

Nuevo Frente Revolucionario del Pueblo: f. 1986; faction of M-19; active in Cundinamarca region.

Patria Libre: f. 1985; left-wing guerrilla movement.

Diplomatic Representation

EMBASSIES IN COLOMBIA

Algeria: Carrera 11, No 93-53, Of. 302, Santafé de Bogotá, DC; tel. (1) 635-0520; fax (1) 635-0531; e-mail ambalgbg@cable.net.co; Ambassador OMAR BENCHEHIDA.

Argentina: Avda 40A, No 13-09, 16°, Apdo Aéreo 53013, Santafé de Bogotá, DC; tel. (1) 288-0900; fax (1) 288-8868; e-mail ecolo@mrecic .gov.ar; Ambassador MARTÍN ANTONIO BALZA.

Austria: Edif. Fiducafe, 4°, Carrera 9, No 73-44, Santafé de Bogotá, DC; tel. (1) 326-2680; fax (1) 317-7639; e-mail eaustria@cable.net.co; internet www.austria.cjb.net; Ambassador HANS PETER GLANZER.

Belgium: Calle 26, No 4A-45, 7°, Apdo Aéreo 3564, Santafé de Bogotá, DC; tel. (1) 380-0370; fax (1) 380-0340; e-mail bogota@ diplobel.org; internet www.diplobel.org/colombia; Ambassador JEAN-LUC BODSON.

Bolivia: Transversal 14A, No 118A-26, Apdo Aéreo 96219, Santa Barbara, Santafé de Bogotá, DC; tel. (1) 629-8237; fax (1) 619-4940; e-mail embolivia-bogota@rree.gov.bo; Ambassador JESÚS HERMAN ANTELO LAUGHLIN.

Brazil: Calle 93, No 14-20, 8°, Santafé de Bogotá, DC; tel. (1) 218-0800; fax (1) 218-8393; internet www.brasil.org.co; Ambassador MARÍA CELINA DE ACEVEDO RODRIGUES.

Canada: Carretera 7, No 115-33, 14°, Apdo Aéreo 110067, Santafé de Bogotá, DC; tel. (1) 657-9800; fax (1) 657-9912; e-mail bgota@ international.gc.ca; internet www.dfait-maeci.gc.ca/colombia; Ambassador JEAN-MARC DUVAL.

Chile: Calle 100, No 11B-44, Santafé de Bogotá, DC; tel. (1) 214-7990; fax (1) 619-3863; e-mail echileco@colomsat.net.co; internet www.embajadadechile.com.co; Ambassador AUGUSTO BERMUDEZ ARANCIBIA.

China, People's Republic: Carrera 16, No 98-30, Santafé de Bogotá, DC; tel. (1) 622-3215; fax (1) 622-3114; e-mail embchina@ andinet.com; Ambassador WU CHANGSHENG.

Costa Rica: Carrera 8, No 95-48, Santafé de Bogotá, DC; tel. (1) 623-0205; fax (1) 691-8558; e-mail embacosta@andinet.com; Ambassador MELVIN ALFREDO SAENZ BIOLLEY.

Cuba: Carrera 9, No 92-54, Santafé de Bogotá, DC; tel. (1) 621-7054; fax (1) 611-4382; e-mail embacuba@cable.net.co; Ambassador LUIS HERNÁNDEZ OJEDA.

Czech Republic: Carrera 7, No 115-33, Ofs 603 y 604, 6°, Santafé de Bogotá, DC; tel. (1) 640-0600; fax (1) 640-0599; e-mail bogota@ embassy.msv.cz; internet www.mzv.cz/bogota; Ambassador JOSEF RYCHTAR.

Dominican Republic: Carrera 7, No 115-33, Of. 403, Torre ABN AMRO, Santafé de Bogotá, DC; tel. (1) 640-0560; fax (1) 522-0102; e-mail embajado@cable.net.co; Ambassador RAÚL FERNANDO BARRIENTOS-LARA.

Ecuador: Calle 89, No 13-07, Santafé de Bogotá, DC; tel. (1) 635-0322; fax (1) 257-9799; e-mail mecucol@cable.net.co; internet www .embajadadaecuacol.net; Ambassador Gen. WILSON TORRES ZAPATA.

Egypt: Transversal 19A 101–10, Santafé de Bogotá, DC; tel. (1) 256-2940; fax (1) 256-9255; e-mail embegyptbta@unete.com; Ambassador ATEF ANWAR ALI HASSANEIN.

El Salvador: Carrera 9A, No 80-15, Of. 503, Edif. El Nogal, Santafé de Bogotá, DC; tel. (1) 349-6765; fax (1) 349-6670; e-mail elsalvadorcolombia@cable.net.co; Ambassador GUILLERMO RUBIO FUNES.

France: Carrera 11, No 93-12, Santafé de Bogotá, DC; tel. (1) 638-1400; fax (1) 638-1430; internet www.ambafrance-co.org; Ambassador CAMILLE ROHOU.

Germany: Edif. World Business Port, Carrera 69, No 43B-44, 7°, Santafé de Bogotá, DC; tel. (1) 423-2600; fax (1) 429-3145; e-mail embajalemana@andinet.com; internet www .embajada-alemana-bogota.de; Ambassador MATEI ION HOFFMANN.

Guatemala: Diagonal 145A, No 32-37, Santafé de Bogotá, DC; tel. (1) 636-1724; fax (1) 274-1196; e-mail embcolombia@minex.gob.gt; Ambassador FERNANDO SESENNA OLIVERO.

Holy See: Carrera 15, No 36-33, Apdo Aéreo 3740, Santafé de Bogotá, DC (Apostolic Nunciature); tel. (1) 320-0289; fax (1) 285-1817; e-mail nunciatura@cable.net.co; Apostolic Nuncio Most Rev. BENIAMINO STELLA (Titular Archbishop of Midila).

Honduras: Calle 121, No 13A-59, Santafé de Bogotá, DC; tel. (1) 215-4259; fax (1) 637-0686; e-mail emhoncol@andinet.com; Ambassador VICENTE MACHADO VALLE.

Hungary: Carrera 6A, No 77-46, Santafé de Bogotá, DC; tel. (1) 347-1467; fax (1) 347-1469; e-mail informacion@embajadahungria.org .co; internet www.embajadahungria.org.co; Ambassador BÉLA BARDÓCZ.

India: Edif. Bancafe, Torre B, Carrera 7, No 71-21, Of. 1001, Santafé de Bogotá, DC; tel. (1) 317-4865; fax (1) 317-4976; e-mail indembog@ cable.net.co; internet www.embajadaindia.org; Ambassador NILIMA MITRA.

Indonesia: Carrera 9, No 76-27, Santafé de Bogotá, DC; tel. (1) 217-6738; fax (1) 326-2165; e-mail info@indonesiabogota.org.co; internet www.indonesiabogota.org.co; Ambassador SETIJANTO POEDJOWARSITO.

Iran: Calle 96, No 11A-16/20, Santafé de Bogotá, DC; tel. (1) 218-6205; fax (1) 610-2556; e-mail embajadairan@andinet.com.co; Ambassador ABDULRAHIM SADATIFAR.

Israel: Calle 35, No 7-25, 14°, Santafé de Bogotá, DC; tel. (1) 288-4637; fax (1) 287-7783; e-mail embisrae@cable.net.co; Ambassador YAIR RECANATI.

Italy: Calle 93B, No 9-92, Apdo Aéreo 50901, Santafé de Bogotá, DC; tel. (1) 218-6604; fax (1) 610-5886; e-mail ambitbog@cable.net.co; internet www.ambitaliabogota.org; Ambassador FRANCESCO CAMILLO PEANO.

Jamaica: Avda 19, No 106A-83, Of. 304, Apdo Aéreo 102428, Santafé de Bogotá, DC; tel. (1) 612-3389; fax (1) 612-3479; e-mail emjacol@cable.net.com; Chargé d'affaires a.i. ELAINE TOWNSEND DE SÁNCHEZ.

Japan: Carrera 7A, No 71-21, 11°, Torre B, Santafé de Bogotá, DC; tel. (1) 317-5001; fax (1) 317-5007; e-mail embajapol@colomsat.net .co; Ambassador WATARU HAYASHI.

Korea, Democratic People's Republic: No 98-30, Carrera 16, Santafé de Bogotá; Ambassador WU CHANGSHENG.

Korea, Republic: Calle 94, No 9-39, Santafé de Bogotá, DC; tel. (1) 616-7200; fax (1) 610-0338; e-mail embcorea@mofat.go.kr; Ambassador PARK SANG-KYOON.

Lebanon: Calle 74, No 12-44, Santafé de Bogotá, DC; tel. (1) 212-8360; fax (1) 347-9106; e-mail emblibanco@hotmail.com; Ambassador MOUNIR KHREICH.

Mexico: Calle 114, No 9-01, Of. 204, Torre A, Santafé de Bogotá, DC; tel. (1) 629-4989; fax (1) 629-5121; e-mail emcolmex@007mundo .com; internet www.sre.gob.mx/colombia; Ambassador MARIO CHACÓN CARILLO.

Morocco: Carrera 10, No 93-16, Santafé de Bogotá, DC; tel. (1) 530-9300; fax (1) 530-8979; e-mail sifamabogot@aldato.com.co; internet www.embamarruecos.org.co; Ambassador MOHAMED MAOULAININE.

Netherlands: Carrera 13, No 93-40, 5°, Apdo Aéreo 43585, Santafé de Bogotá, DC; tel. (1) 638-4200; fax (1) 623-3020; e-mail nlgovbog@ etb.net.co; internet www.embajadadeholanda.org.co; Ambassador FRANS B.A.M. VAN HAREN.

Nicaragua: Calle 108A, No 25-42, Santafé de Bogotá, DC; tel. (1) 619-8934; fax (1) 612-6050; e-mail embnicaragua@007mundo.com; Ambassador DONALD CASTILLO RIVAS.

Norway: Carrera 9, No 73-44, 8°, Santafé de Bogotá, DC; tel. (1) 317-7851; fax (1) 317-7851; e-mail emb.bogota@mfa.no; Chargé d'affaires a.i. TOM TYRIHJELL.

Panama: Calle 92, No 7A-40, Santafé de Bogotá, DC; tel. (1) 257-5058; fax (1) 257-5067; e-mail embpacol@cable.net.co; Ambassador CARLOS OZORES TYPALDOS.

Paraguay: Carrera 7, No 72-28, Of. 302, Santafé de Bogotá, DC; tel. (1) 347-0322; e-mail embaparcolombia@yagua.com.py; Ambassador FELIPE ROBERTI.

Peru: Calle 80A, No 6-50, Santafé de Bogotá, DC; tel. (1) 257-0505; fax (1) 249-8581; e-mail lbogota@cable.net.co; Ambassador JOSÉ LUIS PÉREZ SÁNCHEZ-CERRO.

Poland: Calle 104A, No 23-48, Santafé de Bogotá, DC; tel. (1) 214-0400; fax (1) 214-0854; e-mail polemb@cable.net.co; Ambassador HENRIK KOBIEROWSKI.

Portugal: Carrera 12, No 93-37, Of. 302, Santafé de Bogotá, DC; tel. (1) 622-1334; fax (1) 622-1134; e-mail embporbo@andinet.com; Ambassador JOAQUIM JOSÉ FERREIRA DA FONSECA.

Romania: Carrera 7A, No 92-58, Santafé de Bogotá, DC; tel. (1) 256-6438; fax (1) 256-6158; e-mail emrubog@colomsat.net.co; Ambassador RADU URZICA.

Russia: Carrera 4, No 75-02, Apdo Aéreo 90600, Santafé de Bogotá, DC; tel. (1) 212-1881; fax (1) 210-4694; e-mail embajadarusia@cable .net.co; internet www.colombia.mid.ru; Ambassador VLADIMIR TRUJA-NOVSKI.

Spain: Calle 92, No 12-68, Santafé de Bogotá, DC; tel. (1) 622-0090; fax (1) 621-0809; e-mail embespco@correo.mae.es; Ambassador CARLOS GÓMEZ-MÚGICA SANZ.

Sweden: Calle 72-bis, No 5-83, 8°, Santafé de Bogotá, DC; tel. (1) 325-2165; fax (1) 325-2166; e-mail embsueca@cable.net.co; internet www.swedenabroad.com/bogota; Chargé d'affaires INGEMAR CEDER-BERG.

Switzerland: Carrera 9, No 74-08/1101, 11°, Santafé de Bogotá, DC; tel. (1) 349-7230; fax (1) 349-7195; e-mail vertretung@bog.rep .admin.ch; internet www.eda.admin.ch/bogota; Ambassador THOMAS KUPFER.

United Kingdom: Edif. ING Barings, Carrera 9, No 76-49, 9°, Santafé de Bogotá, DC; tel. (1) 317-6690; fax (1) 317-6265; e-mail britain@cable.net.co; internet www.britain.gov.co; Ambassador Sir THOMAS DUGGIN (until Sept. 2005); Ambassador HAYDON WARREN-GASH (designate).

USA: Calle 22D-bis, No 47-51, Apdo Aéreo 3831, Santafé de Bogotá, DC; tel. (1) 315-0811; fax (1) 315-2197; internet bogota.usembassy .gov; Ambassador WILLIAM BRAUCHER WOOD.

Uruguay: Carrera 9A, No 80-15, 11°, Apdo Aéreo 101466, Santafé de Bogotá, DC; tel. (1) 235-2748; fax (1) 248-3734; e-mail urucolom@ 007mundo.com; Ambassador EDUARDO CÉSAR AÑÓN NOCETI.

Venezuela: Carrera 11, No 87-51, 5°, Santafé de Bogotá, DC; tel. (1) 640-1213; fax (1) 640-1242; e-mail embajada@embaven.org.co; internet www.embaven.org.co; Ambassador CARLOS RODOLFO SANTIAGO RAMÍREZ.

Judicial System

The constitutional integrity of the State is ensured by the Constitutional Court. The Constitutional Court is composed of nine judges who are elected by the Senate for eight years. Judges of the Constitutional Court are not eligible for re-election.

President of the Constitutional Court: Dr CLARA INÉS VARGAS HERNÁNDEZ.

Judges of the Constitutional Court: JAIME ARAUJO RENTERÍA, ALFREDO BELTRÁN SIERRA, MANUEL JOSÉ CEPEDA ESPIÑOSA, JAIME CÓRDOBA TRIVIÑO, RODRIGO ESCOBAR GIL, MARCO GERARDO MONROY CABRA, EDUARDO MONTEALEGRE LYNETT, ALVARO TAFUR GAVIS.

The ordinary judicial integrity of the State is ensured by the Supreme Court of Justice. The Supreme Court of Justice is composed of the Courts of Civil and Agrarian, Penal and Laboral Cassation. Judges of the Supreme Court of Justice are selected from the nominees of the Higher Council of Justice and serve an eight-year term of office which is not renewable.

Prosecutor-General: LUIS CAMILO OSORIO.

Attorney-General: EDGARDO MAYA VILLAZÓN.

SUPREME COURT OF JUSTICE

Supreme Court of Justice
Carrera 7A, No 27-18, Santafé de Bogotá, DC; fax (1) 334-8745; internet www.ramajudicial.gov.co.

President: SILVIO FERNANDO TREJOS BUENO.

Court of Civil and Agrarian Cassation (seven judges): President JORGE ANTONIO CASTILLO RUGELES.

Court of Penal Cassation (nine judges): President YESID RAMIREZ BASTIDAS.

Court of Laboral Cassation (seven judges): President FERNANDO VÁSQUEZ BOTERO.

Religion

CHRISTIANITY

The Roman Catholic Church
At 31 December 2002 Roman Catholicism had 37.7m. adherents in Colombia, equivalent to 91.1% of the population. Colombia comprises 12 archdioceses, 49 dioceses and 10 apostolic vicariates.

Bishops' Conference
Conferencia Episcopal de Colombia, Carrera 47, No 84-85, Apdo Aéreo 7448, Santafé de Bogotá, DC; tel. (1) 311-4277; fax (1) 311-5575; e-mail colcec@cable.net.co.

f. 1978; statutes approved 1996; Pres. Cardinal PEDRO RUBIANO SÁENZ (Archbishop of Santafé de Bogotá).

Archbishop of Barranquilla: RUBÉN SALAZAR GÓMEZ, Carrera 45, No 53-122, Apdo Aéreo 1160, Barranquilla 4, Atlántico; tel. (5) 349-1145; fax (5) 349-1530; e-mail arquidio@arquidiocesibaq.org.co.

Archbishop of Bucaramanga: VÍCTOR MANUEL LÓPEZ FORERO, Calle 33, No 21-18, Bucaramanga, Santander; tel. (7) 642-4387; fax (7) 642-1361; e-mail informativo2002@operamail.com.

Archbishop of Cali: JUAN FRANCISCO SARASTI JARAMILLO, Carrera 4, No 7-17, Apdo Aéreo 8924, Cali, Valle del Cauca; tel. (2) 889-0562; fax (2) 83-7980.

Archbishop of Cartagena: CARLOS JOSÉ RUISECO VIEIRA, Apdo Aéreo 400, Cartagena; tel. (5) 664-5308; fax (5) 664-4974; e-mail arzoctg@ telecartagena.com.

Archbishop of Ibagué: FLAVIO CALLE ZAPATA, Calle 10, No 2-58, Ibagué, Tolima; tel. (82) 61-1680; fax (82) 63-2681.

Archbishop of Manizales: FABIO BETANCUR TIRADO, Carrera 23, No 19-22, Manizales, Caldas; tel. (68) 84-0114; fax (68) 82-1853.

Archbishop of Medellín: ALBERTO GIRALDO JARAMILLO, Calle 57, No 49-44, 3°, Medellín; tel. (4) 251-7700; fax (4) 251-9395; e-mail arquidiomed@epm.net.co.

Archbishop of Nueva Pamplona: GUSTAVO MARTÍNEZ FRÍAS, Carrera 5, No 4-87, Nueva Pamplona; tel. (75) 68-1329; fax (75) 68-4540; e-mail rtarazona@latinmail.com.

Archbishop of Popayán: IVÁN MARÍN-LÓPEZ, Calle 5, No 6-71, Apdo Aéreo 593, Popayán; tel. (928) 24-1710; fax (928) 24-0101; e-mail ivanarzo@emtel.net.co.

Archbishop of Santa Fe de Antioquia: Ignacio Gómez Aristizábal, Plazuela Martínez Pardo, No 12-11, Santa Fe de Antioquia; tel. (94) 853-1155; fax (94) 853-1596; e-mail arquistafe@edatel.net.co.

Archbishop of Santafé de Bogotá: Cardinal Pedro Rubiano Sáenz, Carrera 7A, No 10-20, Santafé de Bogotá, DC; tel. (1) 350-5511; fax (1) 350-7290; e-mail cancilleria@arquidiocesisbogota.org.co.

Archbishop of Tunja: Luis Augusto Castro Quiroga, Calle 17, No 9-85, Apdo Aéreo 1019, Tunja, Boyacá; tel. (987) 742-2094; fax (987) 743-3130; e-mail arquidio@telecom.com.co.

The Anglican Communion

Anglicans in Colombia are members of the Episcopal Church in the USA.

Bishop of Colombia: Rt Rev. Bernardo Merino Botero, Carrera 6, No 49-85, Apdo Aéreo 52964, Santafé de Bogotá, DC; tel. (1) 288-3167; fax (1) 288-3248; there are 3,500 baptized mems, 2,000 communicant mems, 29 parishes, missions and preaching stations; 5 schools and 1 orphanage; 8 clergy.

Protestant Churches

Baptist Convention: Medellín; tel. (4) 38-9623; Pres. Ramón Medina Ibáñez; Exec. Sec. Rev. Ramiro Pérez Hoyos.

Iglesia Evangélica Luterana de Colombia: Calle 75, No 20-54, Apdo Aéreo 51538, Santafé de Bogotá, DC; tel. (1) 212-5735; fax (1) 212-5714; e-mail ofcentral@ielco.org; 3,000 mems; Pres. Bishop Sigifrido Daniel Buitrago Pachón.

BAHÁ'Í FAITH

National Spiritual Assembly of the Bahá'ís of Colombia: Apdo Aéreo 51387, Santafé de Bogotá, DC; tel. (1) 268-1658; fax (1) 268-1665; e-mail bahaicol@colombianet.net; adherents in 1,013 localities.

JUDAISM

There is a community of about 25,000 with 66 synagogues.

The Press

DAILIES

Santafé de Bogotá, DC

El Espacio: Carrera 61, No 45-35, Apdo Aéreo 80111, Avda El Dorado, Santafé de Bogotá, DC; tel. (1) 425-1570; fax (1) 410-4595; internet www.elespacio.com.co; f. 1965; evening; Dir Jaime Ardila Casamitjana; circ. 159,000.

El Nuevo Siglo: Calle 45A, No 102-02, Apdo Aéreo 5452, Santafé de Bogotá, DC; tel. (1) 413-9200; fax (1) 413-8547; internet www .elnuevosiglo.com.co; f. 1925; Conservative; Dirs Juan Pablo Uribe, Juan Gabriel Uribe; circ. 68,000.

La República: Calle 46, No 103-59, Santafé de Bogotá, DC; tel. (1) 413-5077; fax (1) 413-3725; e-mail diario@larepublica.com.co; internet www.la-republica.com.co; f. 1953; morning; finance and economics; Dir Rodrigo Ospina Hernández; Editor Jorge Emilio Sierra M.; circ. 55,000.

El Tiempo: Avda El Dorado, No 59-70, Apdo Aéreo 3633, Santafé de Bogotá, DC; tel. (1) 294-0100; fax (1) 410-5088; internet www .eltiempo.com; f. 1911; morning; Liberal; Dir Enrique Santos Calderón; Editor Francisco Santos; circ. 265,118 (weekdays), 536,377 (Sundays).

Barranquilla, Atlántico

El Heraldo: Calle 53B, No 46-25, Barranquilla, Atlántico; tel. (5) 371-5000; fax (5) 371-5091; internet www.elheraldo.com.co; f. 1933; morning; Liberal; Gen. Editor Hugo Penton; circ. 70,000.

La Libertad: Carrera 53, No 55-166, Barranquilla, Atlántico; tel. (5) 349-1175; e-mail libertad@metrotel.net.co; internet www .lalibertad.com.co; Liberal; Dir Roberto Esper Rebaje; circ. 25,000.

El Tiempo Caribe: Carrera 50B, No 41-18, Barranquilla, Atlántico; tel. (5) 379-1510; fax (5) 341-7715; e-mail orlgam@eltiempo.com.co; internet www.eltiempo.com; f. 1956; daily; Liberal; Dir Orlanda Gamboa; circ. 45,000.

Bucaramanga, Santander del Sur

El Frente: Calle 35, No 12-22, Apdo Aéreo 665, Bucaramanga, Santander del Sur; tel. (7) 42-5369; fax (7) 33-4541; f. 1942; morning; Conservative; Dir Rafael Serrano Prada; circ. 10,000.

Vanguardia Liberal: Calle 34, No 13-42, Bucaramanga, Santander del Sur; tel. (7) 680-0700; fax (7) 630-2443; e-mail vanglibe@colomsat.net.co; internet www.vanguardia.com; f. 1919; morning; Liberal; Sunday illustrated literary supplement and women's supplement; Dir Eduardo Muñoz Serpa; Editor Marco Antonio Ibarra Penalosa; circ. 48,000.

Cali, Valle del Cauca

Occidente: Calle 12, No 5-22, Cali, Valle del Cauca; tel. (2) 895-9756; fax (2) 884-6572; e-mail occidente@cali.cercol.net.co; f. 1961; morning; Conservative; Dir Jorge Enrique Almario; circ. 25,000.

El País: Carrera 2A, No 24-46, Apdo Aéreo 4766, Cali, Valle del Cauca; tel. (2) 883-1183; fax (2) 883-5014; e-mail diario@elpais-cali .com; internet www.elpais-cali.com; f. 1950; Conservative; Dir Eduardo Fernández de Soto; Gen. Man. María Elvira Domínguez; circ. 60,000 (weekdays), 120,000 (Saturdays), 108,304 (Sundays).

El Pueblo: Avda 3A, Norte 35-N-10, Cali, Valle del Cauca; tel. (2) 68-8110; morning; Liberal; Dir Luis Fernando Londoño Capurro; circ. 50,000.

Cartagena, Bolívar

El Universal: Pie del Cerro Calle 30, No 17-36, Cartagena, Bolívar; tel. (5) 664-7310; fax (5) 666-1964; e-mail director@eluniversal.com .co; internet www.eluniversal.com.co; f. 1948; daily; Liberal; Editor Sonia Gedeon; Dir Pedro Luis Mogolón; circ. 167,000.

Cúcuta, Norte de Santander

La Opinión: Avda 4, No 16-12, Cúcuta, Norte de Santander; tel. (75) 71-9999; fax (75) 71-7869; e-mail gerencialaopinion@coll.telecom .com.co; f. 1960; morning; Liberal; Dir Dr José Eustorgio Colmenares Ossa; circ. 27,000.

Manizales, Caldas

La Patria: Carrera 20, No 21-51, Apdo Aéreo 70, Manizales, Caldas; tel. (68) 84-2460; fax (68) 84-7158; e-mail lapatria@lapatria.com; f. 1921; morning; Independent; Dir Dr Luis José Restrepo Restrepo; circ. 22,000.

Medellín, Antioquia

El Colombiano: Carrera 48, No 30 sur-119, Apdo Aéreo 80636, Medellín, Antioquia; tel. (4) 331-5252; fax (4) 331-4858; e-mail elcolombiano@elcolombiano.com.co; internet www.elcolombiano .com; f. 1912; morning; Conservative; Dir Ana Mercedes Gómez Martínez; circ. 90,000.

El Mundo: Calle 53, No 74-50, Apdo Aéreo 53874, Medellín, Antioquia; tel. (4) 264-2800; fax (4) 264-3729; e-mail elmundo@elmundo .com; internet www.elmundo.com; f. 1979; Dir Guillermo Gaviria Echeverri; Man. Carlos Alberto Gil Valencia; circ. 20,000.

Montería, Córdoba

El Meridiano de Córdoba: Avda Circunvalar, No 38-30, Montería, Córdoba; tel. (47) 82-6888; fax (47) 82-6996; e-mail publicidad@ elmeridianodecordoba.com; internet www.elmeridianodecordoba .com; f. 1995; morning; Dir William Enrique Salleg Taboada; circ. 18,000.

Neiva

Diario del Huila: Calle 8A, No 6-30, Neiva; tel. (8) 871-2542; fax (8) 871-2543; internet www.diariodelhuila.com; f. 1966; Gen. Editor Alfredo Rubio; circ. 12,000.

Pasto, Nariño

El Derecho: Calle 20, No 26-20, Pasto, Nariño; tel. (277) 2170; f. 1928; Conservative; Pres. Dr José Elías del Hierro; Dir Eduardo F. Mazuera; circ. 12,000.

Pereira, Risaralda

Diario del Otún: Carrera 8A, No 22-75, Apdo Aéreo 2533, Pereira, Risaralda; tel. (63) 51313; fax (63) 324-1900; e-mail eldiario@interco .net.co; internet www.eldiario.com.co; f. 1982; Financial Dir Javier Ignacio Ramírez Múnera; circ. 30,000.

El Imparcial: km 11 vía Pereira-Armenia, El Jordán, Pereira, Risaralda; tel. (63) 25-9935; fax (63) 25-9934; f. 1948; morning; Dir Zahur Klemath Zapata; circ. 15,000.

La Tarde: Carrera 9A, No 20-54, Pereira, Risaralda; tel. (63) 335-4666; fax (63) 335-4832; internet www.latarde.com; f. 1975; evening; Dir Sonia Díaz Mantilla; circ. 30,000.

Directory

Popayán, Cauca

El Liberal: Carrera 3, No 2-60, Apdo Aéreo 538, Popayán, Cauca; tel. (28) 24-2418; fax (28) 23-3888; f. 1938; Man. CARLOS ALBERTO CABAL JIMÉNEZ; circ. 6,500.

Santa Marta, Magdalena

El Informador: Calle 21, No 5-06, Santa Marta, Magdalena; f. 1921; Liberal; Dir JOSÉ B. VIVES; circ. 9,000.

Villavicencio, Meta

Clarín del Llano: Villavicencio, Meta; tel. (866) 23207; Conservative; Dir ELÍAS MATUS TORRES; circ. 5,000.

PERIODICALS

Santafé de Bogotá, DC

Antena: Santafé de Bogotá, DC; television, cinema and show business; circ. 10,000.

Arco: Carrera 6, No 35-39, Apdo Aéreo 8624, Santafé de Bogotá, DC; tel. (1) 285-1500; f. 1959; monthly; history, philosophy, literature and humanities; Dir ALVARO VALENCIA TOVAR; circ. 10,000.

ART NEXUS/Arte en Colombia: Carrera 5, No 67-19, Apdo Aéreo 90193, Santafé de Bogotá, DC; tel. (1) 312-9332; fax (1) 312-9252; e-mail artnexus@artnexus.com; f. 1976; quarterly; Latin American art, photography, visual arts; editions in English and Spanish; Dir CELIA SREDNI DE BIRBRAGHER; Exec. Editor IVONNE PINI; circ. 26,000.

El Campesino: Carrera 39A, No 15-11, Santafé de Bogotá, DC; f. 1958; weekly; cultural; Dir JOAQUÍN GUTIÉRREZ MACÍAS; circ. 70,000.

Consigna: Diagonal 34, No 5-11, Santafé de Bogotá, DC; tel. (1) 287-1157; fortnightly; Turbayista; Dir (vacant); circ. 10,000.

Coyuntura Económica: Calle 78, No 9-91, Apdo Aéreo 75074, Santafé de Bogotá, DC; tel. (1) 312-5300; fax (1) 212-6073; e-mail bibliote@fedesarrollo.org.co; f. 1970; quarterly; economics; published by Fundación para Educación Superior y el Desarrollo (FEDESARROLLO); Editor MARÍA ANGÉLICA ARBELAEZ; circ. 1,500.

Cromos Magazine: Calle 70A, No 7-81, Apdo Aéreo 59317, Santafé de Bogotá, DC; f. 1916; weekly; illustrated; general news; Dir ALBERTO ZALAMEA; circ. 102,000.

As Deportes: Calle 20, No 4-55, Santafé de Bogotá, DC; f. 1978; sports; circ. 25,000.

Economía Colombiana: Dirección Economía y Finanzas, San Agustín 6-45, Of. 126A, Santafé de Bogotá, DC; tel. (1) 282-4597; fax (1) 282-3737; f. 1984; published by Contraloría General de la República; 6 a year; economics.

El Espectador: Carrera 68, No 23-71, Apdo Aéreo 3441, Santafé de Bogotá, DC; tel. (1) 294-5555; fax (1) 260-2323; e-mail redactor@elespectador.com; internet www.elespectador.com; f. 1887 as a daily paper, published weekly from 2001; Editor FIDEL CANO; circ. 200,000.

Estrategia: Carrera 4A, 25A-12B, Santafé de Bogotá, DC; monthly; economics; Dir RODRIGO OTERO.

Guión: Carrera 16, No 36-89, Apdo Aéreo 19857; Santafé de Bogotá, DC; tel. (1) 232-2660; f. 1977; weekly; general; Conservative; Dir JUAN CARLOS PASTRANA; circ. 35,000.

Hit: Calle 20, No 4-55, Santafé de Bogotá, DC; cinema and show business; circ. 20,000.

Informe Financiero: Dirección Economía y Finanzas, San Agustín 6-45, Of. 126A, Santafé de Bogotá, DC; tel. (1) 282-4597; fax (1) 282-3737; published by Contraloría General de la República; monthly; economics.

Insurrección: internet www.eln-voces.com; f. 1998; fortnightly; fmrly Correo de Magdalena; organ of the Ejército de Liberación Nacional (ELN).

Menorah: Apdo Aéreo 9081, Santafé de Bogotá, DC; tel. (1) 611-2014; f. 1950; independent monthly review for the Jewish community; Dir ELIÉCER CELNIK; circ. 10,000.

Nueva Frontera: Carrera 7A, No 17-01, 5°, Santafé de Bogotá, DC; tel. (1) 334-3763; f. 1974; weekly; politics, society, arts and culture; Liberal; Dir CARLOS LLERAS RESTREPO; circ. 23,000.

Pluma: Apdo Aéreo 12190, Santafé de Bogotá, DC; monthly; art and literature; Dir (vacant); circ. 70,000.

Que Hubo: Santafé de Bogotá, DC; weekly; general; Editor CONSUELO MONTEJO; circ. 15,000.

Resistencia: e-mail elbarcinocolombia@yahoo.com; internet www.farcep.org/resistencia; f. 1993; quarterly; organ of the Fuerzas Armadas Revolucionarias de Colombia—Ejército del Pueblo (FARC—EP); Dir RAÚL REYES.

Revista Escala: Calle 30, No 17-752, Santafé de Bogotá, DC; tel. (1) 287-8200; fax (1) 285-9882; e-mail escala@col-online.com; f. 1962; fortnightly; architecture; Dir DAVID SERNA CÁRDENAS; circ. 18,000.

Revista Diners: Calle 85, No 18-32, 6°, Santafé de Bogotá, DC; tel. (1) 636-0508; fax (1) 623-1762; e-mail diners@cable.net.co; f. 1963; monthly; Dir GERMÁN SANTAMARÍA; circ. 110,000.

Semana: Calle 93B, No 13-47, Santafé de Bogotá, DC; tel. (1) 622-2277; fax (1) 621-0475; general; Pres. FELIPE LÓPEZ CABALLERO.

Síntesis Económica: Calle 70A, No 10-52, Santafé de Bogotá, DC; tel. (1) 212-5121; fax (1) 212-8365; f. 1975; weekly; economics; Dir FÉLIX LAFAURIE RIVERA; circ. 16,000.

Tribuna Médica: Calle 8B, No 68A-41, y Calle 123, No 8-20, Santafé de Bogotá, DC; tel. (1) 262-6085; fax (1) 262-4459; f. 1961; monthly; medical and scientific; Editor JACK ALBERTO GRIMBERG; circ. 50,000.

Tribuna Roja: Santafé de Bogotá, DC; tel. (1) 243-0371; e-mail tribojar@moir.org.co; internet www.moir.org.co/tribuna/tribuna.htm; f. 1971; quarterly; organ of the MOIR (pro-Maoist Communist party); Dir CARLOS NARANJO; circ. 300,000.

Vea: Calle 20, No 4-55, Santafé de Bogotá, DC; weekly; popular; circ. 90,000.

Voz La Verdad del Pueblo: Carrera 8, No 19-34, Ofs 310–311, Santafé de Bogotá, DC; tel. (1) 284-5209; fax (1) 342-5041; weekly; left-wing; Dir CARLOS A. LOZANO G; circ. 45,000.

NEWS AGENCIES

Ciep—El País: Carrera 16, No 36-35, Santafé de Bogotá, DC; tel. (1) 232-6816; fax (1) 288-0236; Dir JORGE TÉLLEZ.

Colprensa: Diagonal 34, No 5-63, Apdo Aéreo 20333, Santafé de Bogotá, DC; tel. (1) 287-2200; fax (1) 285-5915; e-mail colpre@elsitio.net.co; f. 1980; Dir ROBERTO VARGAS GALVIS.

Foreign Bureaux

Agence France-Presse (AFP): Carrera 5, No 16-14, Of. 807, Apdo Aéreo 4654, Santafé de Bogotá, DC; tel. (1) 281-8613; Dir MARIE SANZ.

Agencia EFE (Spain): Carrera 16, No 39A-69, Apdo Aéreo 16038, Santafé de Bogotá, DC; tel. (1) 285-1576; fax (1) 285-1598; e-mail efecol@efebogota.com.co; Bureau Chief ENRIQUE IBAÑEZ.

Agencia de Noticias Nueva Colombia (ANNCOL): Vattenledningsvägen 47, 126 34 Hägersten, Stockholm, Sweden; e-mail news@anncol.com; internet www.anncol.org; f. 1996; extreme left-wing news agency reporting on Colombian political and military affairs; founded in Sweden by expatriate dissident Colombians and sympathizers of the Fuerzas Armadas Revolucionarias de Colombia—Ejército del Pueblo (FARC—EP); Pres. of Editorial Bd LEIF LARSEN; Sr Editor ROBERTO GUTIÉRREZ.

Agenzia Nazionale Stampa Associata (ANSA) (Italy): Carrera 4, No 67-30, Apdo Aéreo 16077, Santafé de Bogotá, DC; tel. (1) 211-9617; fax (1) 212-5409; Bureau Chief ALBERTO ROJAS MORALES.

Associated Press (AP) (USA): Transversal 14, No 122-36, Apdo Aéreo 093643, Santafé de Bogotá, DC; tel. (1) 619-3487; fax (1) 213-8467; e-mail apbogota@bigfoot.com; Bureau Chief FRANK BAJAK.

Central News Agency Inc. (Taiwan): Carrera 13A, No 98-34, Santafé de Bogotá, DC; tel. (1) 25-6342; Correspondent CHRISTINA CHOW.

Deutsche Presse-Agentur (dpa) (Germany): Carrera 15, No 76-60, Of. 302, Santafé de Bogotá, DC; tel. (1) 618-3788; fax (1) 635-2516; e-mail presse@hbg.dpa.de; internet www.dpa.de; Correspondent RODRIGO RUIZ TOVAR.

Informatsionnoye Telegrafnoye Agentstvo Rossii—Telegrafnoye Agentstvo Suverennykh Stran (ITAR—TASS) (Russia): Calle 20, No 7-17, Of. 901, Santafé de Bogotá, DC; tel. (1) 243-6720; Correspondent GENNADII KOCHUK.

Inter Press Service (IPS) (Italy): Calle 19, No 3-50, Of. 602, Apdo Aéreo 7739, Santafé de Bogotá, DC; tel. (1) 341-8841; fax (1) 334-2249; Correspondent MARÍA ISABEL GARCÍA NAVARRETE.

Prensa Latina: Carrera 3, No 21-46, Apdo Aéreo 30372, Santafé de Bogotá, DC; tel. (1) 282-4527; fax (1) 281-7286; Bureau Chief FAUSTO TRIANA.

Reuters (United Kingdom): Calle 94A, No 13-34, 4°, Apdo Aéreo 29848, Santafé de Bogotá, DC; tel. (1) 634-4090; fax (1) 610-7733; e-mail bogota.newsroom@reuters.com; Bureau Chief JASON WEBB.

Xinhua (New China) News Agency (People's Republic of China): Calle 74, No 4-26, Apdo Aéreo 501, Santafé de Bogotá, DC; tel. (1) 211-5347; Dir HOU YAOQI.

PRESS ASSOCIATIONS

Asociación Colombiana de Periodistas: Avda Jiménez, No 8-74, Of. 510, Santafé de Bogotá, DC; tel. (1) 243-6056.

Asociación Nacional de Diarios Colombianos (ANDIARIOS): Calle 61, No 5-20, Apdo Aéreo 13663, Santafé de Bogotá, DC; tel. (1) 212-8694; fax (1) 212-7894; f. 1962; 30 affiliated newspapers; Pres. LUIS MIGUEL DE BEDOUT; Vice-Pres. LUIS FERNANDO BAENA.

Asociación de la Prensa Extranjera: Pedro Meléndez, No 87-93, Santafé de Bogotá, DC; tel. (1) 288-3011.

Círculo de Periodistas de Santafé de Bogotá, DC (CPB): Calle 26, No 13A-23, 23°, Santafé de Bogotá, DC; tel. (1) 282-4217; Pres. MARÍA TERESA HERRÁN.

Publishers

SANTAFÉ DE BOGOTÁ, DC

Comunicadores Técnicos Ltda: Carrera 18, No 46-58, Apdo Aéreo 28797, Santafé de Bogotá, DC; technical; Dir PEDRO P. MORCILLO.

Ediciones Aula XXI: Calle 19, No 44-10, Santafé de Bogotá, DC; tel. (1) 574-3990; fax (1) 244-6129; e-mail gerencia@edicionesaulaxxi .com; internet www.edicionesaulaxxi.com; general interest, reference, fiction and educational; Legal Rep. CARLOS MARIO ESCOBAR BRAVO.

Ediciones Cultural Colombiana Ltda: Calle 72, No 16-15 y 16-21, Apdo Aéreo 6307, Santafé de Bogotá, DC; tel. (1) 217-6529; fax (1) 217-6570; f. 1951; textbooks; Dir JOSÉ PORTO VÁSQUEZ.

Ediciones Gaviota: Transversal 43, No 99-13, Santafé de Bogotá, DC; tel. (1) 613-6650; fax (1) 613-9117; e-mail gaviotalibros@ edicionesgaviota. com.co.

Ediciones Lerner Ltda: Calle 8A, No 68A-41, Apdo Aéreo 8304, Santafé de Bogotá, DC; tel. (1) 420-0650; fax (1) 262-4459; f. 1959; general; Commercial Man. FABIO CAICEDO GÓMEZ.

Ediciones Modernas: Carrera 41A, No 22F, Santafé de Bogotá, DC; tel. (1) 269-0072; fax (1) 244-0706; e-mail edimodernas@ edimodernas.com.co; internet www.empresario.com.co/ edimodernas; f. 1991; juvenile.

Editora Cinco, SA: Calle 61, No 13-23, 7°, Apdo Aéreo 15188, Santafé de Bogotá, DC; tel. (1) 285-6200; recreation, culture, textbooks, general; Man. PEDRO VARGAS G.

Editorial Cypres Ltda: Carrera 15, No 80-36, Of. 302, Santafé de Bogotá, DC; tel. (1) 691-0578; fax (1) 636-3824; e-mail cypres@etb .net.co; general interest and educational.

Editorial El Globo, SA: Calle 16, No 4-96, Apdo Aéreo 6806, Santafé de Bogotá, DC.

Editorial Hispanoámerica: Carrera 56B, No 45-27, Santafé de Bogotá, DC; tel. (1) 221-3020; fax (1) 315-5587; e-mail info@ hispanoamerica.com.co; internet www.hispanoamerica.com.co; f. 1984; materials for primary education; Man. GABY TERESA CORTÉS; Editor ALVARO PINZÓN.

Editorial Paulinas: Calle 161A, No 31-50, Santafé de Bogotá, DC; tel. (1) 522-0828; fax (1) 671-0992; e-mail ventasp@paulinas.org.co; internet www.paulinas.org.co; Christian and self-help.

Editorial Presencia, Ltda: Calle 23, No 24-20, Apdo Aéreo 41500, Santafé de Bogotá, DC; tel. (1) 269-2188; fax (1) 269-6830; textbooks, tradebooks; Gen. Man. MARÍA UMAÑA DE TANCO.

Editorial San Pablo: Carrera 46, No 22A–90, Quintaparedes, Apdo Aéreo 080152, Santafé de Bogotá, DC; tel. (1) 368-2099; fax (1) 244-4383; e-mail editorial@sanpablo.com.co; internet www.sanpablo .com.co; f. 1914; religion (Catholic); Editorial Dir P. VICENTE MIOTTO.

Editorial Temis SA: Calle 17, No 68D, 46 PBX, Santafé de Bogotá, DC; tel. (1) 424-7855; fax (1) 292-5801; e-mail editorial@ editorialtemis.com; internet www.editorialtemis.com; f. 1951; law, sociology, politics; Man. Dir JORGE GUERRERO.

Editorial Voluntad, SA: Carrera 7A, No 24-89, 24°, Santafé de Bogotá, DC; tel. (1) 286-0666; fax (1) 286-5540; e-mail voluntad@ colomsat.net.co; f. 1930; school books; Pres. GASTÓN DE BEDOUT.

Fondo de Cultura Económica: Calle 16, No 80-18, Santafé de Bogotá, DC; tel. (1) 531-2288; fax (1) 531-1322; internet www.fce .com.co; f. 1934; academic; Dir CONSUELO SÁIZAR GUERRERO.

Fundación Centro de Investigación y Educación Popular (CINEP): Carrera 5A, No 33A-08, Apdo Aéreo 25916, Santafé de Bogotá, DC; tel. (1) 285-8977; fax (1) 287-9089; f. 1977; education and social sciences; Man. Dir FRANCISCO DE ROUX.

Instituto Caro y Cuervo: Carrera 11, No 64-37, PBX 3456004, Apdo Aéreo 51502, Santafé de Bogotá, DC; tel. (1) 255-8289; fax (1) 217-0243; e-mail direcciongeneral@caroycuervo.gov.co; internet www.caroycuervo.gov.co; f. 1942; philology, general linguistics and reference; Man. Dir IGNACIO CHAVES CUEVAS; Gen. Sec. CARLOS JULIO LUQUE CAGUA.

Inversiones Cromos SA: Calle 70A, No 7-81, Apdo Aéreo 59317, Santafé de Bogotá, DC; tel. (1) 217-1754; fax (1) 211-2642; f. 1916; Dir ALBERTO ZALAMEA; Gen. Man. JORGE EDUARDO CORREA ROBLEDO.

Legis, SA: Avda El Dorado, No 81-10, Apdo Aéreo 98888, Santafé de Bogotá, DC; tel. (1) 263-4100; fax (1) 295-2650; e-mail jcastrof@legis .com.co; internet www.legis.com.co; f. 1952; economics, law, general; Man. JUAN ALBERTO CASTRO.

McGraw Hill Interamericana, SA: Avda Américas, No 46-41, Apdo Aéreo 81078, Santafé de Bogotá, DC; tel. (1) 406-9000; fax (1) 245-4786; university textbooks; Dir-Gen. CARLOS G. MÁRQUEZ.

Publicar, SA: Avda 68, No 75A-50, 4°, Centro Comercial Metrópolis, Apdo Aéreo 8010, Santafé de Bogotá, DC; tel. (1) 225-5555; fax (1) 225-4015; e-mail m-navia@publicar.com; internet www.publicar .com; f. 1954; directories; CEO MARÍA SOL NAVIA.

Siglo del Hombre Editores Ltda: Carrera 32, No 25-46, Santafé de Bogotá, DC; tel. (1) 337-7700; fax (1) 337-7665; e-mail siglodelhombre@sky.net.co; f. 1992; arts, politics, anthropology, history, fiction, etc.; Gen. Man. EMILIA FRANCO DE ARCILA.

Tercer Mundo Editores SA: Transversal 2A, No 67-27, Apdo Aéreo 4817, Santafé de Bogotá, DC; tel. (1) 255-1539; fax (1) 212-5976; e-mail tmundoed@polcola.com.co; f. 1963; social sciences; Pres. SANTIAGO POMBO VEJARANO.

Thomson PLM: Calle 98, No 19A-21, Apdo Aéreo 52998, Santafé de Bogotá, DC; tel. (1) 257-4400; fax (1) 616-7620; internet www .plmlatina.com; medical; Commerical Dir DANILO SÁNCHEZ.

VillegasEditores: Avda 82, No 11-50, Interior 3, Santafé de Bogotá, DC; tel. (1) 616-1788; fax (1) 616-0020; internet www.villegaseditor .com; f. 1985; illustrated and scholarly.

ASSOCIATIONS

Cámara Colombiana del Libro: Carrera 17A, No 37-27, Apdo Aéreo 8998, Santafé de Bogotá, DC; tel. (1) 288-6188; fax (1) 287-3320; e-mail camlibro@camlibro.com.co; internet www.camlibro.com .co; f. 1951; Pres. ENRIQUE GONZÁLEZ VILLA; Exec. Dir JULIANA CÁLAD; 120 mems.

Colcultura: Biblioteca Nacional de Colombia, Calle 24, No 5-60, Apdo Aéreo 27600, Santafé de Bogotá, DC; tel. (1) 282-8656; fax (1) 341-4028; e-mail mgiraldo@mincultura.go.co; Dir ISADORA DE NORDEN.

Fundalectura: Avda 40, No 16-46, Santafé de Bogotá, DC; tel. (1) 320-1511; fax (1) 287-7071; e-mail contactenos@fundalectura.org.co; internet www.fundalectura.org.co; Exec. Dir CARMEN BARVO.

Broadcasting and Communications

Ministerio de Comunicaciones, Dirección de Telecomunicaciones: Edif. Murillo Toro, Carreras 7A y 8A, entre Calle 12A y 13, Apdo Aéreo 14515, Santafé de Bogotá, DC; tel. (1) 344-3460; fax (1) 286-1185; internet www.mincomunicaciones.gov.co; broadcasting authority; Dir MARTHA ELENA PINTO DE HART (Minister of Communications).

Instituto Nacional de Radio y Televisión (INRAVISION): Centro Administrativo Nacional (CAN), Avda El Dorado, Santafé de Bogotá, DC; tel. (1) 222-0700; fax (1) 222-0080; internet www .inravision.gov.co; f. 1954; govt-run TV and radio broadcasting network; educational and commercial broadcasting; Dir GILBERTO SAMPER RAMIREZ VALBUENA.

TELECOMMUNICATIONS

BellSouth Colombia, SA: Calle 100, No 7-33, Edif. Capital Tower, Santafé de Bogotá, DC; tel. (1) 650-0000; internet www.bellsouth .com.co; f. 1994; owned by Telefónica Móviles, SA (Spain); mobile telephone services.

Celumóvil SA: Calle 71A, No 6-30, 18°, Santafé de Bogotá, DC; tel. (1) 346-1666; fax (1) 211-2031; Sec.-Gen. CARLOS BERNARDO CARREÑO R.

Colombia Telecomunicaciones, SA (TELECOM): Calle 23, No 13-49, Santafé de Bogotá, DC; tel. (1) 286-0077; fax (1) 282-8768; internet www.telecom.com.co; f. June 2003 following dissolution of Empresa Nacional de Telecomunicaciones (f. 1947); national telecommunications enterprise; Pres. ALFONSO GÓMEZ PALACIO.

Empresa de Telecomunicaciones de Santafé de Bogotá (ETB): Carrera 7A, No 20-37, Santafé de Bogotá, DC; tel. (1) 341-4233; fax (1) 342-3550; e-mail sugeetb@axesnet.com; internet www .etb.com.co; Bogotá telephone co; partially privatized in May 2003; Pres. SERGIO REGUEROS.

BROADCASTING

Radio

The principal radio networks are as follows:

Cadena Melodía de Colombia: Calle 45, No 13-70, Santafé de Bogotá, DC; tel. (1) 323-1500; fax (1) 288-4020; Pres. EFRAÍN PÁEZ ESPITIA.

Cadena Radial Auténtica: Calle 32, No 16-12, Apdo Aéreo 18350, Santafé de Bogotá, DC; tel. (1) 285-3360; fax (1) 285-2505; f. 1983; stations include Radio Auténtica and Radio Mundial; Pres. JORGE ENRIQUE GÓMEZ MONTEALEGRE.

Cadena Radial La Libertad Ltda: Carrera 53, No 55-166, Apdo Aéreo 3143, Barranquilla; tel. (5) 31-1517; fax (5) 32-1279; news and music programmes for Barranquilla, Cartagena and Santa Marta; stations include Emisora Ondas del Caribe (youth programmes), Radio Libertad (classical music programmes) and Emisora Fuentes.

Cadena Super: Calle 16A, No 86A-78, Santafé de Bogotá, DC; tel. (1) 618-1371; fax (1) 618-1360; internet www.889.com.co; f. 1971; stations include Radio Super and Super Stereo FM; Pres. JAIME PAVA NAVARRO.

CARACOL, SA (Primera Cadena Radial Colombiana, SA): Carretera 39A, No 15-81, Apdo Aéreo 9291, Santafé de Bogotá, DC; tel. (1) 337-8866; fax (1) 337-7126; internet www.caracol.com.co; f. 1948; 107 stations; Pres. JOSÉ MANUEL RESTREPO FERNÁNDEZ DE SOTO.

Circuito Todelar de Colombia: Avda 13, No 84-42, Apdo Aéreo 27344, Santafé de Bogotá, DC; tel. (1) 616-1011; fax (1) 616-0056; f. 1953; 74 stations; Pres. BERNARDO TOBÓN DE LA ROCHE.

Colmundo Radio, SA ('La Cadena de la Paz'): Diagonal 58, 26A-29, Apdo Aéreo 36750, Santafé de Bogotá, DC; tel. (1) 217-8911; fax (1) 217-9358; f. 1989; Pres. Dr NÉSTOR CHAMORRO P.

Organización Radial Olímpica, SA (ORO, SA): Calle 72, No 48-37, 2°, Apdo Aéreo 51266, Barranquilla; tel. (5) 358-0500; fax (5) 345-9080; programmes for the Antioquia and Atlantic coast regions.

Radio Cadena Nacional, SA (RCN Radio): Carrera 13A, No 37-32, Santafé de Bogotá, DC; tel. (1) 314-7070; fax (1) 288-6130; e-mail rcn@impsat.net.co; internet www.rcn.com.co; 116 stations; official network; Pres. RICARDO LONDOÑO LONDOÑO.

Radiodifusora Nacional de Colombia: Centro Administrativo Nacional (CAN), Avda El Dorado, Santafé de Bogotá, DC; tel. (1) 222-0415; fax (1) 222-0409; e-mail radiodifusora@hotmail.com; f. 1940; national public radio; Dir ATHALA MORRIS.

Radiodifusores Unidos, SA (RAU): Carrera 13, No 85-51, Of. 705, Santafé de Bogotá, DC; tel. (1) 617-0584; commercial network of independent local and regional stations throughout the country.

Television

Television services began in 1954, and the NTSC colour television system was adopted in 1979. The government-run broadcasting network, INRAVISION, controls three national stations. Two national, privately-run stations began broadcasts in mid-1988. There are also two regional stations and one local, non-profit station. Broadcasting time is distributed among competing programmers through a public tender.

Cadena Uno: Centro Administrativo Nacional (CAN), Avda El Dorado, Santafé de Bogotá, DC; tel. (1) 342-3777; fax (1) 341-6198; e-mail cadena1@latino.net.co; internet www.cadena1.com.co; f. 1992; Dir FERNANDO BARRERO CHÁVEZ.

Canal 3: Centro Administrativo Nacional (CAN), Avda El Dorado, Santafé de Bogotá, DC; tel. (1) 222-1640; fax (1) 222-1514; f. 1970; Exec. Dir RODRIGO ANTONIO DURÁN BUSTOS.

Canal A: Calle 35, No 7-51, CENPRO, Santafé de Bogotá, DC; tel. (1) 232-3196; fax (1) 245-7526; f. 1966; Gen. Man. ROCÍO FERNÁNDEZ DEL CASTILLO.

Caracol Televisión, SA: Calle 76, No 11-35, Apdo Aéreo 26484, Santafé de Bogotá, DC; tel. (1) 319-0860; fax (1) 321-1720; internet www.canalcaracol.com; f. 1969; Pres. RICARDO ALARCÓN GAVIRIA.

Teleantioquia: Carrera 41, No 52-28, Edif. EDA, 3°, Apdo Aéreo 8183, Medellín, Antioquia; tel. (4) 262-0311; fax (4) 262-0832; e-mail info@teleantioquia.com.co; internet www.teleantioquia.com.co; f. 1985.

Telecafé: Carrera 19A, Calle 43, Sacatín contiguo Universidad Autónoma, Manizales, Caldas; tel. (68) 86-2949; fax (68) 86-3009; e-mail telecafe2004@epm.net.co; f. 1986; Gen. Man. ALBERTO LÓPEZ MARÍN.

Telecaribe: Carrera 54, No 72-142, 11°, Barranquilla, Atlántico; tel. (5) 358-2297; fax (5) 356-0924; e-mail ealviz@canal.telecaribe.com.co; internet www.telecaribe.com.co; f. 1986; Gen. Man. IVÁN OVALLE POVEDA.

Telepacífico: Calle 5A, No 38A-14, 3°, esq. Centro Comercial Imbanaco, Cali, Valle del Cauca; tel. (2) 589-933; fax (2) 588-281; e-mail telepacifico@emcali.net.co; Gen. Man. LUIS GUILLERMO RESTREPO.

TV Cúcuta: tel. (75) 74-7874; fax (75) 75-2922; f. 1992; Pres. JOSÉ A. ARMELLA.

ASSOCIATIONS

Asociación Nacional de Medios de Comunicación (ASOMEDIOS): Carrera 22, No 85-72, Santafé de Bogotá, DC; tel. (1) 611-1300; fax (1) 621-6292; e-mail asomedio@cable.net.co; internet www.asomedios.com; f. 1978; merged with ANRADIO (Asociación Nacional de Radio, Televisión y Cine de Colombia) in 1980; Pres. SERGIO ARBOLEDA CASAS.

Finance

(cap. = capital; res = reserves; dep. = deposits; m. = million; amounts in pesos, unless otherwise indicated)

Contraloría General de la República: Carrera 10, No 17-18, Torre Colseguros, 27°, Santafé de Bogotá, DC; tel. (1) 353-7700; fax (1) 353-7616; e-mail ahernandez@contraloriagen.gov.co; internet www.contraloriagen.gov.co; Controller-Gen. Dr ANTONIO HERNÁNDEZ GAMARRA.

BANKING

Supervisory Authority

Superintendencia Bancaria: Calle 7, No 4-49, 11°, Apdo Aéreo 3460, Santafé de Bogotá, DC; tel. (1) 594-0200; fax (1) 350-7999; e-mail super@superbancaria.gov.co; internet www.superbancaria.gov.co; Banking Supt JORGE PINZÓN SÁNCHEZ.

Central Bank

Banco de la República: Carrera 7A, No 14-78, 5°, Apdo Aéreo 3531, Santafé de Bogotá, DC; tel. (1) 343-1111; fax (1) 286-1686; e-mail wbanco@banrep.gov.co; internet www.banrep.gov.co; f. 1923; sole bank of issue; cap. 12.7m., res 20,900.0m., dep. 2,264.0m. (Dec. 2002); Man. Dir JOSÉ DARÍO URIBE; 28 brs.

Commercial Banks

Santafé de Bogotá, DC

ABN AMRO Bank (Colombia), SA (fmrly Banco Real de Colombia): KRA7, No 115-33, 17°, Santafé de Bogotá, DC; tel. (1) 521-9100; fax (1) 640-0675; f. 1975; Pres. CARLOS EDUARDO ARRUDA PENTEADO; 17 brs.

Bancafe: Calle 28, No 13A-15, 6°, Apdo Aéreo 240332, Santafé de Bogotá, DC; tel. (1) 606-7614; fax (1) 606-7727; e-mail c.gaona@bancafe.com.co; internet www.bancafe.com; f. 1953; fmrly Banco Cafetero, SA; 99% owned by Fondo de Garantías de Instituciones Financieras de Colombia; cap. 108,794.0m., res 75,750.2m., dep. 5,015,437.5m. (Dec. 2003); 283 brs; Pres. PEDRO NEL OSPINA SANTA MARÍA.

Banco Agrario de Colombia: Carrera 8, No 15-43, Santafé de Bogotá, DC; tel. (1) 212-3404; fax (1) 345-2279; internet www.bancoagrario.gov.co; f. 1999; state-owned; Pres. JORGE RESTREPO PALACIOS.

Banco America Colombia (fmrly Banco Colombo-Americano): Carrera 7, No 71-52, Torre B, 4°, Apdo Aéreo 12327, Santafé de Bogotá, DC; tel. (1) 312-2020; fax (1) 312-1645; cap. 3,268m., res 6,205m., dep. 14,475m. (Dec. 1993); wholly-owned subsidiary of Bank of America; Pres. EDUARDO ROMERO JARAMILLO; 1 br.

Banco de Bogotá: Calle 36, No 7-47, 15°, Apdo Aéreo 3436, Santafé de Bogotá, DC; tel. (1) 332-0032; fax (1) 338-3302; internet www.bancodebogota.com.co; f. 1870; acquired Banco del Comercio in 1992; cap. 2,253.8m., res 858,248.1m., dep. 4,697,327.6m. (Dec. 2002); Pres. Dr ALEJANDRO FIGUEROA JARAMILLO; 274 brs.

Banco Caja Social: Carrera 7, No 77-65, 11°, Santafé de Bogotá, DC; tel. (1) 313-8000; fax (1) 321-6912; e-mail ep_manrique@fundacion-social.com.co; internet www.bancocajasocial.com; f. 1911; savings bank; cap. 89,999m., res 74,527m., dep. 1,360,862m. (Dec. 2004); Pres. EULALIA ARBOLEDA DE MONTES; 135 brs.

Banco Colpatria, SA: Carrera 7A, No 24-89, 12°, Apdo Aéreo 30241, Santafé de Bogotá, DC; tel. (1) 286-8277; fax (1) 334-0867; internet www.colpatria.com.co; f. 1955; cap. 15,575m., dep. 197,390m. (Dec. 1994); Pres. CARLOS ESCOBAR BARCO; 26 brs.

Banco de Comercio Exterior de Colombia, SA (BANCOLDEX): Calle 28, No 13A-15, 38°, Apdo Aéreo 240092, Santafé de Bogotá, DC; tel. (1) 382-1515; fax (1) 282-5071; internet www.bancoldex.com; f. 1992; provides financing alternatives for Colombian exporters; affiliate trust company FIDUCOLDEX, SA, manages PROEXPORT (Export Promotion Trust); Pres. MIGUEL GÓMEZ MARTÍNEZ.

Banco de Crédito: Calle 27, No 6-48, Santafé de Bogotá, DC; tel. (1) 286-8400; fax (1) 251-8381; internet www.bancodecredito.com; f. 1963; cap. 36,952.8m., res 73,409.6m., dep. 944,129.3m. (Dec. 1999); Man. LUIS FERNANDO MESA PRIETO; 24 brs.

Banco Granahorrar: Carrera 6, No 15-32, 11°, Apdo Aéreo 3637, Santafé de Bogotá, DC; tel. (1) 382-2090; fax (1) 282-2802; www.granahorrar.com.co; f. 1932; fmrly Banco Central Hipotecario; assets 4,072,000m. (June 2003); Pres. Dr ALBERTO MONTOYA PUYANA; 132 brs.

Banco Mercantil de Colombia, SA (fmrly Banco de los Trabajadores): Avda 82, No 12-18, 8°, Santafé de Bogotá, DC; tel. (1) 635-0017; fax (1) 623-7770; e-mail amartinez@bancomercantil.com.co; internet www.bancomercantil.com; f. 1974; wholly-owned subsidiary of Banco Mercantil (Venezuela); Pres. GUSTAVO MARTURET; 10 brs.

Banco del Pacífico, SA: Calle 72, 10-07, 2°, Santafé de Bogotá, DC; tel. (1) 345-0111; fax (1) 217-9436; e-mail jcbernal@banpacifico.com.co; internet www.bp.fin.ec; f. 1994; wholly-owned by Banco del Pacífico, SA, Guayaquil (Ecuador); Exec. Pres. MARCEL LANIADO; 1 br.

Banco Popular, SA: Calle 17, No 7-43, 3°, Apdo Aéreo 6796, Santafé de Bogotá, DC; tel. (1) 339-5449; fax (1) 281-9448; e-mail vpinternacional@bancopopular.com.co; internet www.bancopopular.com.co; f. 1951; res 155.8m., dep. 3,140.2m. (June 2004); Int. Man. HERNANDO VIVAS V.; 158 brs.

Banco Standard Chartered: Calle 74, No 6-65, Santafé de Bogotá, DC; tel. (1) 217-7200; fax (1) 212-5786; f. 1982; cap. 10,312m., res 5,574m., dep. 84,200m. (Dec. 1996); Pres. HANS JUERGUEN HEILKUHL OCHOA; 11 brs.

Banco Sudameris Colombia (fmrly Banco Francés e Italiano): Carrera 11, No 94A-03, 5°, Apdo Aéreo 3440, Santafé de Bogotá, DC; tel. (1) 636-8785; fax (1) 636-7702; internet www.sudameris.com.co; affiliate of Banque Sudameris, SA (France); Pres. and Chair. JORGE RAMÍREZ OCAMPO; 6 brs.

Banco Tequendama, SA: Diagonal 27, No 6-70, 2°, Santafé de Bogotá, DC; tel. (1) 343-3900; fax (1) 346-7127; f. 1976; wholly-owned subsidiary of Banco Construcción (Venezuela); Pres. RUBÉN LOAIZA NEGREIROS; 11 brs.

Banco Unión Colombiano (fmrly Banco Royal Colombiano): Torre Banco Unión Colombiano, Carrera 7A, No 71-52, 2°, Apdo Aéreo 3438, Santafé de Bogotá, DC; tel. (1) 312-0411; fax (1) 312-0843; internet www.bancounion.com.co; f. 1925; cap. 33,708.1m. res 18,818.4m., dep. 354,047.1m. (Dec. 2001); Pres. JUAN FERNANDO POSADA CORPAS; 20 brs.

BBVA Colombia: Carrera 9A, No 72-21, 11°, Apdo Aéreo 53859, Santafé de Bogotá, DC; tel. (1) 312-4666; fax (1) 347-1600; internet www.bbvaganadero.com; f. 1956 as Banco Ganadero; name changed as above 2003; 73.7% owned by Banco Bilbao Vizcaya Argentaria, SA (Spain); cap. 879,467.8m., dep. 2,989,659.8m. (Dec. 1998); fmrly BBV-Banco Ganadero; Exec. Pres. LUIS B JUANGO FITERO; 279 brs.

Citibank Colombia, SA: Carrera 9A, No 99-02, 3°, Santafé de Bogotá, DC; tel. (1) 618-4455; fax (1) 621-0259; internet www.latam.citibank.com/colombia; wholly-owned subsidiary of Citibank (USA); Pres. ANTONIO URIBE; 23 brs.

Lloyds TSB Bank, SA (fmrly Banco Anglo Colombiano): Carrera 7, No 71-21, Torre B, 16°, Apdo Aéreo 3532, Santafé de Bogotá, DC; tel. (1) 286-3155; fax (1) 281-8646; e-mail contactenos@lloydstsbbank.com.co; internet www.grupolloyds.com.co; f. 1976; cap. 14,990.7m., res 24,983.8m., dep. 229,629.3m. (Dec. 1996); Pres. NIGEL LUSON; 52 brs.

Cali

Banco de Occidente: Carrera 4, No 7-61, 12°, Apdo Aéreo 7607, Cali, Valle del Cauca; tel. (2) 886-1111; fax (2) 886-1298; e-mail dinternacional@bancodeoccidente.com.co; internet www.bancodeoccidente.com.co; cap. 3,821.1m., res 467,898.1m., dep. 4,057,732.6m. (Dec. 2003); 78.2% owned by Grupo Aval Acciones y Valores; Pres. EFRAIN OTERO ÁLVAREZ; 122 brs.

Medellín

Bancolombia, SA (fmrly Banco Industrial de Colombia): Carrera 50, No 51-66, Medellín, Antioquia; tel. (4) 576-6060; fax (4) 513-4827; e-mail mfranco@bancolombia.com.co; internet www.bancolombia.com.co; f. 1945; renamed 1998; following merger with Banco de Colombia; cap. 288,348m., res 942,515m., dep. 7,771,159m. (Dec. 2003); Pres. JORGE LONDOÑO SALDARRIAGA; Chair. JUAN CAMILO OCHOA; 361 brs.

Banco Santander: Edif. Bavaria, 16°, Carrera 46, No 52-36, Medellín, Antioquia; tel. (1) 284-3100; fax (1) 281-0311; internet www.bancosantander.com.co; f. 1961; fmrly Banco Comercial Antioqueño, SA; subsidiary of Banco Santander (Spain); Pres. MONICA IÑES MARÍA APARICIO SMITH; 30 brs.

Banking Associations

Asociación Bancaria y de Entidades Financieras de Colombia: Carrera 9A, No 74-08, 9°, Santafé de Bogotá, DC; tel. (1) 249-6411; fax (1) 211-9915; e-mail info@asobancaria.com; internet www.asobancaria.com; f. 1936; 56 mem. banks; Pres. PATRICIA CÁRDENAS SANTA MARÍA.

Asociación Nacional de Instituciones Financieras (ANIF): Calle 70A, No 7-86, Santafé de Bogotá, DC; tel. (1) 310-1500; fax (1) 235-5947; internet www.anif.org; Pres. Dr FABIO VILLEGAS RAMÍREZ.

STOCK EXCHANGES

Superintendencia de Valores: Avda El Dorado, Calle 26, No 68-85, Torre Suramericana, 2° y 3°, Santafé de Bogotá, DC; tel. (1) 427-0222; fax (1) 427-0871; internet www.supervalores.gov.co; f. 1979 to regulate the securities market; Supt CLEMENTE DEL VALLE BORRÁEZ.

Bolsa de Bogotá: Carrera 8A, No 13-82, 4°–8°, Apdo Aéreo 3584, Santafé de Bogotá, DC; tel. (1) 243-6501; fax (1) 243-7327; internet www.bolsabogota.com.co; f. 1928; Pres. AUGUSTO ACOSTA TORRES; Sec.-Gen. MARÍA FERNANDA TORRES.

INSURANCE

Principal National Companies

ACE Seguros, SA: Calle 72, No 10-51, 6°, 7° y 8°, Apdo Aéreo 29782, Santafé de Bogotá, DC; tel. (1) 319-0300; fax (1) 319-0304; internet www.ace-ina.com; fmrly Cigna Seguros de Colombia, SA; Pres. ALVARO A. ROZO PALOU.

Aseguradora Colseguros, SA: Carrera 13A, No 29-24, Parque Central Bavaria, Apdo Aéreo 3537, Santafé de Bogotá, DC; tel. (1) 560-0600; fax (1) 561-6695; internet www.colseguros.com; f. 1874; Pres. MAX THIERMANN.

Aseguradora El Libertador, SA: Carrera 13, No 26-45, 9°, Apdo Aéreo 10285, Santafé de Bogotá, DC; tel. (1) 281-2427; fax (1) 286-0662; e-mail aselib@impsat.net.co; Pres. FERNANDO ROJAS CÁRDENAS.

Aseguradora Solidaria de Colombia: Carrera 12, No 93-30, Apdo Aéreo 252030, Santafé de Bogotá, DC; tel. (1) 621-4330; fax (1) 621-4321; e-mail eguzman@solidaria.com.co; Pres. CARLOS GUZMÁN.

Chubb de Colombia Cía de Seguros, SA: Carrera 7A, No 71-52, Torre B, 10°, Santafé de Bogotá, DC; tel. (1) 326-6200; fax (1) 326-6210; e-mail esaavedra@chubb.com.co; internet www.chubb.com.co; f. 1972; Pres. MANUEL OBREGÓN; 4 brs.

Cía Agrícola de Seguros, SA: Carrera 11, No 93-46, Apdo Aéreo 7212, Santafé de Bogotá, DC; tel. (1) 635-5827; fax (1) 635-5876; f. 1952; Pres. Dr JOSÉ F. JARAMILLO HOYOS.

Cía Aseguradora de Fianzas, SA (Confianza): Calle 82, No 11-37, 7°, Apdo Aéreo 056965, Santafé de Bogotá, DC; tel. (1) 617-0899; fax (1) 610-8866; e-mail ccorreos@confianza.com.co; internet www.confianza.com.co; Pres. RODRIGO JARAMILLO ARANGO.

Cía Central de Seguros, SA: Carrera 7A, No 76-07, 9°, Apdo Aéreo 5764, Santafé de Bogotá, DC; tel. (1) 319-0700; fax (1) 640-5553; e-mail recursos@centralseguros.com.co; internet www.centralseguros.com.co; f. 1956; Pres. SYLVIA LUZ RINCÓN LEMA.

Cía de Seguros Atlas, SA: Calle 21, No 23-22, 3°–11°, Apdo Aéreo 413, Manizales, Caldas; tel. (68) 84-1500; fax (68) 84-1447; e-mail satlas@andi.org.co; internet www.andi.org.co/seguros_atlas.htm; Pres. JORGE HOYOS MAYA.

Cía de Seguros Bolívar, SA: Carrera 10A, No 16-39, Apdo Aéreo 4421, Santafé de Bogotá, DC; tel. (1) 341-0077; fax (1) 281-8262; internet www.segurosbolivar.com.co; f. 1939; Pres. (vacant).

Cía de Seguros Colmena, SA: Calle 72, No 10-07, 7° y 8°, Apdo Aéreo 6774, Santafé de Bogotá, DC; tel. (1) 211-9111; fax (1) 211-4952; Pres. JUAN MANUEL DÍAZ-GRANADOS.

Cía de Seguros Generales Aurora, SA: Edif. Seguros Aurora, 1°, 2° y 3°, Carrera 7, No 74-21, Apdo Aéreo 8006, Santafé de Bogotá, DC; tel. (1) 212-2800; fax (1) 212-2138; Pres. GERMÁN ESPINOSA.

Cía Mundial de Seguros, SA: Calle 33, No 6-94, 2° y 3°, Santafé de Bogotá, DC; tel. (1) 285-5600; fax (1) 285-1220; Dir-Gen. CAMILO FERNÁNDEZ ESCOVAR.

Cía Suramericana de Seguros, SA: Centro Suramericana,Carrera 64B, No 49A-30, Apdo Aéreo 780, Medellín, Antioquia; tel. (4) 260-2100; fax (4) 260-3194; e-mail contactenos@suramericana.com.co; internet www.suramericana.com.co; f. 1944; Pres. Dr NICANOR RESTREPO SANTAMARÍA.

Condor, SA, Cía de Seguros Generales: Calle 119, No 16-59, Apdo Aéreo 57018, Santafé de Bogotá, DC; tel. (1) 612-0666; fax (1) 215-6121; Pres. Eudoro Carvajal Ibáñez.

Generali Colombia—Seguros Generales, SA: Carrera 7A, No 72-13, 1°, 7° y 8°, Apdo Aéreo 076478, Santafé de Bogotá, DC; tel. (1) 217-8411; fax (1) 255-1164; Pres. Marco Papini.

La Ganadera Cía de Seguros, SA: Carrera 7, No 71-52, Torre B, 11°, Apdo Aéreo 052347, Santafé de Bogotá, DC; tel. (1) 312-2630; fax (1) 312-2599; e-mail ganadera@impsat.net.co; internet www .laganadera.com.co; Pres. Carlos Vergara Gómez.

La Interamericana Cía de Seguros Generales, SA: Calle 78, No 9-57, 4° y 5°, Apdo Aéreo 92381, Santafé de Bogotá, DC; tel. (1) 210-2200; fax (1) 210-2021; Pres. Didier Serrano.

La Previsora, SA, Cía de Seguros: Calle 57, No 8-93, Apdo Aéreo 52946, Santafé de Bogotá, DC; tel. (1) 211-2880; fax (1) 211-8717; Pres. Alvaro Escallón Emiliani.

Liberty Seguros, SA: Calle 71A, No 6-30, 2°, 3°, 4° y 14°, Apdo Aéreo 100327, Santafé de Bogotá, DC; tel. (1) 212-4900; fax (1) 212-7706; e-mail lhernandez@impsat.net.co; f. 1954; fmrly Latinoamericana de Seguros, SA; Pres. Mauricio García Ortiz.

Mapfre Seguros Generales de Colombia, SA: Carrera 7A, No 74-36, 2°, Apdo Aéreo 28525, Santafé de Bogotá, DC; tel. (1) 346-8702; fax (1) 346-8793; Pres. José Manuel Inchausti.

Pan American de Colombia Cía de Seguros de Vida, SA: Carrera 7A, No 75-09, Apdo Aéreo 76000, Santafé de Bogotá, DC; tel. (1) 212-1300; fax (1) 217-8799; Pres. Alfonso Pontón.

Real Seguros, SA: Carrera 7A, No 115-33, 10°, Apdo Aéreo 7412, Santafé de Bogotá, DC; tel. (1) 523-1400; fax (1) 523-4010; Gen. Man. José Luiz Tomazini.

Royal and Sun Alliance Seguros (Colombia), SA: Carrera 7A, No 32-33, 6°, 7°, 11° y 12°, Santafé de Bogotá, DC; tel. (1) 561-0380; fax (1) 320-3726; internet www.royalsunalliance.com.co; fmrly Seguros Fénix, SA; Pres. Dinand Blom.

Segurexpo de Colombia, SA: Calle 72, No 6-44, 12°, Apdo Aéreo 75140, Santafé de Bogotá, DC; tel. (1) 217-0900; fax (1) 211-0218; Pres. Juan Pablo Luque Luque.

Seguros Alfa, SA: Carrera 13, No 27-47, 22° y 23°, Apdo Aéreo 27718, Santafé de Bogotá, DC; tel. (1) 344-4720; fax (1) 344-6770; Pres. Jesús Hernando Gómez.

Seguros Colpatria, SA: Carrera 7A, No 24-89, 9°, Apdo Aéreo 7762, Santafé de Bogotá, DC; tel. (1) 616-6655; fax (1) 281-5053; Pres. Dr Fernando Quintero.

Seguros La Equidad, OC: Calle 19, No 6-68, 10°, 11° y 12°, Apdo Aéreo 30261, Santafé de Bogotá, DC; tel. (1) 284-1910; fax (1) 286-5124; Pres. Dr Julio Enrique Medrano León.

Seguros del Estado, SA: Carrera 11, No 90-20, Apdo Aéreo 6810, Santafé de Bogotá, DC; tel. (1) 218-6977; fax (1) 218-0971; Pres. Dr Jorge Mora Sánchez.

Skandia Seguros de Vida, SA: Avda 19, No 113-30, Apdo Aéreo 100327, Santafé de Bogotá, DC; tel. (1) 214-1200; fax (1) 214-0038; Pres. Rafael Jaramillo Samper.

Insurance Association

Federación de Aseguradores Colombianos (FASECOLDA): Carrera 7A, No 26-20, 11° y 12°, Apdo Aéreo 5233, Santafé de Bogotá, DC; tel. (1) 210-8080; fax (1) 210-7090; e-mail fasecolda@fasecolda .com; internet www.fasecolda.com; f. 1976; 33 mems; Pres. Dr William R. Fadul Vergara.

Trade and Industry

GOVERNMENT AGENCIES

Agencia Nacional de Hidrocarburos (ANH): Edif. Guadalupe, Calle 37, 7-43, 5°, Santafé de Bogotá; tel. (1) 234-4519; fax (1) 234-4671; e-mail info@anh.gov.co; internet www.anh.gov.co; f. 2003; govt agency responsible for regulation of the petroleum industry.

Departamento Nacional de Planeación: Calle 26, No 13-19, 14°, Santafé de Bogotá, DC; tel. (1) 336-1600; fax (1) 281-3348; f. 1958; supervises and administers devt projects; approves foreign investments; Dir José Antonio Ocampo Gaviria.

Instituto Colombiano de la Reforma Agraria (INCORA): Centro Administrativo Nacional (CAN), Avda El Dorado, Apdo Aéreo 151046, Santafé de Bogotá, DC; tel. (1) 222-0963; fax (1) 222-1536; internet www.incora.gov.co; f. 1962; a public institution which, on behalf of the govt, administers public lands and those it acquires; reclaims land by irrigation and drainage facilities, roads, etc., to increase productivity in agriculture and stock-breeding; provides

technical assistance and loans; supervises the distribution of land throughout the country; Dir Jorge Cardoso.

Superintendencia de Industria y Comercio (SUPERINDUS-TRIA): Carrera 13, No 27-00, 5°, Santafé de Bogotá, DC; tel. (1) 523-1131; fax (1) 382-2696; e-mail info@sic.gov.co; internet www.sic.gov .co; supervises chambers of commerce; controls standards and prices; Supt Jairo Rubio Escobar.

Superintendencia de Sociedades (SUPERSOCIEDADES): Avda El Dorado, No 46-80, Apdo Aéreo 4188, Santafé de Bogotá, DC; tel. (1) 324-5777; fax (1) 324-5000; e-mail webmaster@ supersociedades.gov.co; internet www.supersociedades.gov.co; f. 1931; oversees activities of local and foreign corpns; Supt Rodolfo Daniés Lacouture.

DEVELOPMENT AGENCIES

Fondo Nacional de Proyectos de Desarrollo (FONADE): Calle 26, No 13-19, 19°–22°, Apdo Aéreo 24110, Santafé de Bogotá, DC; tel. (1) 594-0407; fax (1) 282-6018; e-mail fonade@colomsat.net.co; internet www.fonade.gov.co; f. 1968; responsible for channelling loans towards economic devt projects; administered by a cttee under the head of the Departamento Nacional de Planeación; FONADE works in close association with other official planning orgs; Gen. Man. Dr Elvira Forero Hernández.

Fundación para el Desarrollo Integral del Valle del Cauca (FDI): Calle 8, No 3-14, 17°, Apdo Aéreo 7482, Cali, Valle del Cauca; tel. (2) 80-6660; fax (2) 82-4627; f. 1969; industrial devt org.; Pres. Gunnar Lindahl Hellberg; Exec. Pres. Fabio Rodríguez González.

CHAMBERS OF COMMERCE

Confederación Colombiana de Cámaras de Comercio (CON-FECAMARAS): Carrera 13, No 27-47, Of. 502, Apdo Aéreo 29750, Santafé de Bogotá, DC; tel. (1) 346-7055; fax (1) 346-7026; e-mail confecamaras@inter.net.co; internet www.confecamaras.org.co; f. 1969; 56 mem. orgs; Exec. Pres. Eugenio Marulanda Gómez.

Cámara Colombo Venezolana: Carrera 20, No 82–40, Of. 301; tel. (1) 530-0626 ; fax (1) 530-0628; e-mail info@comvenezuela.com; internet www.comvenezuela.com; f. 1977; Colombian–Venezuelan trade asscn; 19 mem. cos; Pres. María Luisa Chiappe.

Cámara de Comercio de Bogotá: Carrera 9A, No 16-21, Santafé de Bogotá, DC; tel. (1) 381-0328; fax (1) 284-7735; internet www.ccb .org.co; f. 1878; 3,650 mem. orgs; Dir Ariel Jaramillo Jaramillo; Exec.-Pres. Dr María Fernanda Campo Saavedra.

There are also local Chambers of Commerce in the capital towns of all the Departments and in many of the other trading centres.

INDUSTRIAL AND TRADE ASSOCATIONS

Colombiana de Minería (COLMINAS): Santafé de Bogotá, DC; state mining concern; Man. Alfonso Rodríguez Kilber.

Corporación de la Industria Aeronáutica Colombiana, SA (CIAC SA): Aeropuerto Internacional El Dorado, Entrada 1 y 2, Apdo Aéreo 14446, Santafé de Bogotá, DC; tel. (1) 413-9735; fax (1) 413-8673; Gen. Man. Alberto Meléndez.

Empresa Colombia de Niquel (ECONIQUEL): Santafé de Bogotá, DC; tel. (1) 232-3839; administers state nickel resources; Dir Javier Restrepo Toro.

Empresa Colombiana de Uranio (COLURANIO): Centro Administrativo Nacional (CAN), 4°, Ministerio de Minas y Energía, Santafé de Bogotá, DC; tel. (1) 244-5440; f. 1977 to further the exploration, processing and marketing of radio-active minerals; initial cap. US $750,000; Dir Jaime García.

Empresa de Comercialización de Productos Perecederos (EMCOPER): Santafé de Bogotá, DC; tel. (1) 235-5507; attached to Ministry of Agriculture and Rural Development; Dir Luis Fernando Londoño Ruiz.

Industria Militar (INDUMIL): Diagonal 40, No 47-75, Apdo Aéreo 7272, Santafé de Bogotá, DC; tel. (1) 222-3001; fax (1) 222-4889; attached to Ministry of National Defence; Man. Adm. (retd) Manuel F. Avendaño.

Instituto Colombiano Agropecuario (ICA): Calle 37, No 8-43, 4° y 5°, Santafé de Bogotá, DC; tel. (1) 285-5520; fax (1) 232-4689; e-mail comunicaciones@ica.gov.co; internet www.ica.gov.co; f. 1962; institute for promotion, co-ordination and implementation of research into and teaching and devt of agriculture and animal husbandry; Dir Dr Alvaro Abisambra Abisambra.

Instituto de Fomento Industrial (IFI): Calle 16, No 6-66, Edif. Avianca, 7°–15°, Apdo Aéreo 4222, Santafé de Bogotá, DC; tel. (1) 336-0377; fax (1) 286-4166; f. 1940; state finance corpn for enterprise devt; cap. 469,808m. pesos, total assets 2,246,480m. pesos (Dec. 1998); Pres. Enrique Camacho Matamoros.

Instituto de Hidrología, Meteorología y Estudios Ambientales (IDEAM): Diagonal 97, No 17-60, 1°, 2°, 3° y 7°, Santafé de Bogotá, DC; tel. (1) 283-6927; fax (1) 635-6218; f. 1995; responsible for irrigation, flood control, drainage, hydrology and meteorology; Dir PABLO LEYVA.

Instituto de Investigación e Información Geocientífica, Mineroambiental y Nuclear (INGEOMINAS): Diagonal 53, No 34-53, Apdo Aéreo 4865, Santafé de Bogotá, DC; tel. (1) 222-1811; fax (1) 220-0582; e-mail aalarcon@ingeomin.gov.co; internet www.ingeominas.gov.co; f. 1968; responsible for mineral research, geological mapping and research including hydrogeology, remote sensing, geochemistry, geophysics and geological hazards; Dir Dr ADOLFO ALARCÓN GUZMÁN.

Instituto de Mercadeo Agropecuario (IDEMA): Carrera 10A, No 16-82, Of. 1006, Santafé de Bogotá, DC; tel. (1) 342-2596; fax (1) 283-1838; state enterprise for the marketing of agricultural products; Dir-Gen. ENRIQUE CARLOS RUIZ RAAD.

Instituto Nacional de Fomento Municipal (INSFOPAL): Centro Administrativo Nacional (CAN), Avda El Dorado, Santafé de Bogotá, DC; tel. (1) 222-3177; Gen. Man. JAIME MARIO SALAZAR VELÁSQUEZ.

Instituto Nacional de los Recursos Naturales Renovables y del Ambiente (INDERENA): Diagonal 34, No 5-18, 3°, Santafé de Bogotá, DC; tel. (1) 285-4417; f. 1968; govt agency regulating the devt of natural resources.

Minerales de Colombia, SA (MINERALCO): Calle 32, No 13-07, Apdo Aéreo 17878, Santafé de Bogotá, DC; tel. (1) 287-7136; fax (1) 87-4606; administers state resources of emerald, copper, gold, sulphur, gypsum, phosphate rock and other minerals except coal, petroleum and uranium; Gen. Man. ORLANDO ALVAREZ PÉREZ.

Sociedad Minera del Guainía (SMG): Santafé de Bogotá, DC; f. 1987; state enterprise for exploration, mining and marketing of gold; Pres. Dr JORGE BENDECK OLIVELLA.

There are several other agricultural and regional development organizations.

EMPLOYERS' AND PRODUCERS' ORGANIZATIONS

Asociación Colombiana Popular de Industriales (ACOPI): Carrera 23, No 41-94, Apdo Aéreo 16451, Santafé de Bogotá, DC; tel. (1) 244-2741; fax (1) 268-8965; f. 1951; asscn of small industrialists; Pres. JUAN A. PINTO SAAVEDRA; Man. MIGUEL CARRILLO M.

Asociación de Cultivadores de Caña de Azúcar de Colombia (ASOCAÑA): Calle 58N, No 3N-15, Apdo Aéreo 4448, Cali, Valle del Cauca; tel. (2) 64-7902; fax (2) 64-5888; f. 1959; sugar planters' asscn; Pres. Dr RICARDO VILLAVECES PARDO.

Asociación Nacional de Empresarios (ANDI) (National Asscn of Manufacturers): Calle 52, No 47-48, Apdo Aéreo 997, Medellín, Antioquia; tel. (4) 511-1177; fax (4) 511-7575; e-mail comercial@andi.com.co; internet www.andi.com.co; f. 1944; Pres. LUIS CARLOS VILLEGAS ECHEVERRI; 9 brs; 756 mems.

Asociación Nacional de Exportadores (ANALDEX): Carrera 10, No 27, Int. 137, Of. 902, Apdo Aéreo 29812, Santafé de Bogotá, DC; tel. (1) 342-0788; fax (1) 284-6911; exporters' asscn; Pres. JORGE RAMÍREZ OCAMPO.

Asociación Nacional de Exportadores de Café de Colombia: Calle 72, No 10-07, Of. 1101, Santafé de Bogotá, DC; tel. (1) 347-8419; fax (1) 347-9523; e-mail asoexport@asoexport.org; internet www.asoexport.org; f. 1938; private asscn of coffee exporters; Pres. JORGE E. LOZANO MANCERA.

Expocafé Ltda: Edif. Seguros Caribe, Carrera 7A, No 74-36, 3°, Apdo Aéreo 41244, Santafé de Bogotá, DC; tel. (1) 217-8900; fax (1) 217-3554; f. 1985; coffee exporting org.; Gen. Man. LUIS JOSÉ ALVAREZ L.

Federación Colombiana de Ganaderos (FEDEGAN): Carrera 14, No 36-65, Apdo Aéreo 9709, Santafé de Bogotá, DC; tel. (1) 245-3041; fax (1) 232-7153; e-mail fedegan@fedegan.org.co; internet www.fedegan.org.co; f. 1963; cattle raisers' asscn; about 350,000 affiliates; Pres. JORGE VISBAL MARTELO.

Federación Nacional de Cacaoteros: Carrera 17, No 30-39, Apdo Aéreo 17736, Santafé de Bogotá, DC; tel. (1) 288-7188; fax (1) 288-4424; e-mail f_cacaoteros@hotmail.com; fed. of cocoa growers; Gen. Man. Dr JOSÉ OMAR PINZÓN USECHE.

Federación Nacional de Cafeteros de Colombia (FEDERACAFE) (National Federation of Coffee Growers): Calle 73, No 8-13, Apdo Aéreo 57534, Santafé de Bogotá, DC; tel. (1) 217-0600; fax (1) 217-1021; internet www.cafedecolombia.com; f. 1927; totally responsible for fostering and regulating the coffee economy; Gen. Man. GABRIEL SILVA LUJÁN; 203,000 mems.

Federación Nacional de Comerciantes (FENALCO): Carrera 4, No 19-85, 7°, Santafé de Bogotá, DC; tel. (1) 350-0600; fax (1) 350-9424; e-mail fenalco@fenalco.com.co; internet www.fenalco.com.co; fed. of businessmen; Pres. GUILLERMO BOTERO NIETO.

Federación Nacional de Cultivadores de Cereales y Leguminosas (FENALCE): Carrera 14, No 97-62, Apdo Aéreo 8694, Santafé de Bogotá, DC; tel. (1) 218-2114; fax (1) 218-9463; e-mail fenalce@cable.net.co; f. 1960; fed. of grain growers; Gen. Man. JOSÉ ADEL CANCELADO PERRY; 30,000 mems.

Sociedad de Agricultores de Colombia (SAC) (Colombian Farmers' Society): Carrera 7A, No 24-89, 44°, Apdo Aéreo 3638, Santafé de Bogotá, DC; tel. (1) 281-0263; fax (1) 284-4572; e-mail socdeagr@impsat.net.co; f. 1871; Pres. JUAN MANUEL OSPINA RESTREPO; Sec.-Gen. Dr GABRIEL MARTÍNEZ TELÁEZ.

There are several other organizations, including those for rice growers, engineers and financiers.

UTILITIES

Electricity

Corporación Eléctrica de la Costa Atlántica (Corelca): Calle 55, No 72-109, 9°, Barranquilla, Atlántico; tel. (5) 356-0200; fax (5) 356-2370; responsible for supplying electricity to the Atlantic departments; generates more than 2,000m. kWh annually from thermal power-stations; Man. Dir HERNÁN CORREA NOGUERA.

Empresa de Energía Eléctrica de Bogotá, SA (EEB): Avda El Dorado, No 55-51, Santafé de Bogotá, DC; tel. (1) 221-1665; fax (1) 221-6858; internet www.eeb.com.co; provides electricity for Bogotá area by generating capacity of 680 MW, mainly hydroelectric; Man. Dir LUIS EDUARDO GARZÓN.

Instituto Colombiano de Energía Eléctrica (ICEL): Carrera 13, No 27-00, 3°, Apdo Aéreo 16243, Santafé de Bogotá, DC; tel. (1) 342-0181; fax (1) 286-2934; formulates policy for the devt of electrical energy; constructs systems for the generation, transmission and distribution of electrical energy; Man. DOUGLAS VELÁSQUEZ JACOME; Sec.-Gen. PATRICIA OLIVEROS LAVERDE.

Interconexión Eléctrica, SA (ISA): Calle 12 Sur, No 18-168, El Poblado, Apdo Aéreo 8915, Medellín, Antioquia; tel. (4) 325-2270; fax (4) 317-0848; e-mail isa@isa.com.co; internet www.isa.com.co; f. 1967; created by Colombia's principal electricity production and distribution cos to form a national network; installed capacity of 2,641m. kWh; operates major power-stations at Chivor and San Carlos; public co; Man. Dir JAVIER GUTIÉRREZ JACOME.

Isagen: Medellín, Antioquia; e-mail isagen@isagen.com.co; internet www.isagen.com.co; f. 1995 following division of ISA (q.v.); state-owned, scheduled for privatization; generates electricity from three hydraulic and two thermal power plants; Gen. Man. Ing. FERNANDO RICO PINZÓN.

Gas

Empresa Colombiana de Gas (Ecogás): Carrera 34, No 41-51, Bucaramanga, Santander; tel. (7) 632-0002; fax (7) 632-5525; e-mail jramirez@ecogas.com.co; internet www.ecogas.com.co; f. 1997; operation and maintenance of gas-distribution network; Pres. CARLOS ALBERTO GÓMEZ GÓMEZ; Sec.-Gen. DANIELA GALVIS VILLAREAL; Administrative Vice-Pres. Dr JOSÉ GREGORIO RAMÍREZ AMAYA.

Gas Natural ESP: Avda 40A, No 13-09, 9°, Santafé de Bogotá, DC; tel. (1) 338-1199; fax (1) 288-0807; f. 1987; private gas corpn; Pres. ANTONI PERIS MINGOT.

Gasoriente: distributes gas to eight municipalities in north-eastern Colombia.

TRADE UNIONS

According to official figures, an estimated 900 of Colombia's 2,000 trade unions are independent.

Central Unitaria de Trabajadores (CUT): Calle 35, No 7-25, 9°, Apdo Aéreo 221, Santafé de Bogotá, DC; tel. (1) 323-7550; fax (1) 323-7550; e-mail cut@cut.org.co; f. 1986; comprises 50 feds and 80% of all trade-union members; Pres. CARLOS RODRÍGUEZ DÍAZ; Sec.-Gen. BORIS MONTES DE OCA ANAYA.

Unión Sindical Obrera de la Indústria del Petróleo (USO): Avda del Ferrocarril, 28-43 Galán, Barrancabermeja, Santander; tel. (7) 622-7856; fax (7) 622-9150; e-mail usocol@1.telecom.com; internet www.nodo50.org/usocolombia; f. 1922; petroleum workers' union; affiliated to CUT; Sec.-Gen. (vacant); 3,200 mems.

Frente Sindical Democrática (FSD): f. 1984; centre-right trade-union alliance; comprises:

Confederación de Trabajadores de Colombia (CTC) (Colombian Confederation of Workers): Calle 39, No 26A-23, 5°, Apdo Aéreo 4780, Santafé de Bogotá, DC; tel. (1) 269-7119; f. 1934; mainly Liberal; 600 affiliates, including 6 national orgs and 20 regional feds; admitted to ICFTU; Pres. ALVIS FERNÁNDEZ; 400,000 mems.

Confederación de Trabajadores Democráticos de Colombia (CTDC): Carrera 13, No 59-52, Of. 303, Santafé de Bogotá, DC; tel. (1) 255-3146; fax (1) 484-581; f. 1988; comprises 23 industrial feds and 22 national unions; Pres. MARIO DE J. VALDERRAMA.

Confederación General de Trabajadores Democráticos (CGTD): Calle 39A, No 14-48, Apdo Aéreo 5415, Santafé de Bogotá, DC; tel. (1) 288-1560; fax (1) 573-4021; e-mail cgt@etb.net .co; internet www.cgtcolombia.org; Sec.-Gen. JULIO ROBERTO GÓMEZ ESGUERRA.

Transport

Land transport in Colombia is rendered difficult by high mountains, so the principal means of long-distance transport is by air. As a result of the development of the El Cerrejón coalfield, Colombia's first deep-water port was constructed at Bahía de Portete and a 150-km rail link between El Cerrejón and the port became operational in 1989.

Instituto Nacional del Transporte (INTRA): Edif. Minobras (CAN), 6°, Apdo Aéreo 24990, Santafé de Bogotá, DC; tel. (1) 222-4100; govt body; Dir Dr GUILLERMO ANZOLA LIZARAZO.

RAILWAYS

In 2000 there were 3,304 km of track.

Dirección General de Transporte Férreo y Masivo: Ministerio de Transporte, Centro Administrativo Nacional (CAN), Avda El Dorado, Santafé de Bogotá, DC; e-mail dgtuf@mintransporte.gov.co; internet www.mintransporte.gov.co/Ministerio/DGTFM/dgtferreo/html; part of the Ministry of Transport; formulates railway transport policies; Dir JUAN GONZALO JARAMILLO.

Empresa Colombiana de Vías Férreas (Ferrovías): Calle 16, No 96-64, 8°, Santafé de Bogotá, DC; tel. (1) 287-9888; fax (1) 287-2515; responsible for the maintenance and devt of the national rail network; Dir JUAN GONZALO JARAMILLO.

Ferroviario Atlántico, SA: Calle 72, No 13-23, 2°, Santafé de Bogotá, DC; tel. (1) 255-8684; fax (1) 255-8704; links port of Santa Marta with Santafé de Bogotá, DC; operated on a 30-year concession, awarded in 1998 to Asociación Futura Ferrocarriles de la Paz (Fepaz); 1,490 km (1993).

Fondo de Pasivo Social de Ferrocarriles Nacionales de Colombia: Santafé de Bogotá, DC; administers welfare services for existing and former employees of the FNC.

El Cerrejón Mine Railway: International Colombia Resources Corpn, Carrera 54, No 72-80, Apdo Aéreo 52499, Barranquilla, Atlántico; tel. (5) 350-5389; fax (5) 350-2249; f. 1989 to link the mine and the port at Bahía de Portete; 150 km (1996); Supt M. MENDOZA.

Metro de Medellín Ltda: Calle 44, No 46-001, Apdo Aéreo 9128, Medellín, Antioquia; tel. (4) 452-6000; fax (4) 452-4450; e-mail emetro@col3.telecom.com.co; two-line metro with 25 stations opened in stages in 1995–96; 29 km; Gen. Man. LUIS GUILLERMO GÓMEZ A.

Sociedad de Transporte Férreo de Occidente, SA: Avda Vásquez Cobo, Estación Ferrocarril, 2°, Cali; tel. (2) 660-3314; fax (2) 660-3320; runs freight services between Cali and the port of Buenaventura; Gen. Man. R. A. GUZMAN.

ROADS

In 2002 there were 110,000 km of roads, of which 26,000 km was paved. The country's main highways are the Caribbean Trunk Highway, the Eastern and Western Trunk Highways, the Central Trunk Highway and there are also roads into the interior. There are plans to construct a Jungle Edge highway to give access to the interior, a link road between Turbo, Bahía Solano and Medellín, a highway between Bogotá and Villavicencio and to complete the short section of the Pan-American Highway between Panama and Colombia.

There are a number of national bus companies and road haulage companies.

Dirección General de Carreteras: Ministerio de Transporte, Centro Administrativo Nacional (CAN), Of. 508, Avda El Dorado, Santafé de Bogotá, DC; tel. (1) 222-7308; fax (2) 428-6749; e-mail dcarreteras@mintransporte.gov.co; internet www.mintransporte .gov.co/Ministerio/DGTCarreteras/; part of the Ministry of Transport; formulates road transport policies; Dir MANUEL ARIAS MOLANO.

Instituto Nacional de Vías: Transversal 45, Entrada 2, Santafé de Bogotá, DC; tel. (1) 428-0400; fax (1) 315-6713; e-mail director@ latino.net.co; f. 1966; reorganized 1994; wholly state-owned; responsible to the Ministry of Transport; maintenance and construction of national road network; Gen. Man. LUIS E. TOBON CARDONA.

INLAND WATERWAYS

The Magdalena–Cauca river system is the centre of river traffic and is navigable for 1,500 km, while the Atrato is navigable for 687 km. The Orinoco system has more than five navigable rivers, which total more than 4,000 km of potential navigation (mainly through Venezuela); the Amazon system has four main rivers, which total 3,000 navigable km (mainly through Brazil). There are plans to connect the Arauca with the Meta, and the Putumayo with the Amazon, and also to construct an Atrato–Truandó inter-oceanic canal.

Dirección General de Transporte Fluvial: Ministerio de Transporte, Centro Administrativo Nacional (CAN), Avda El Dorado, Santafé de Bogotá, DC; tel. (1) 428-7332; fax (2) 428-6233; e-mail omedina@mintransporte.gov.co; internet www.mintransporte.gov .co/Ministerio/DGTFLUVIAL/dgtfluvial.html; part of the Ministry of Transport; formulates river transport policies; Dir LUIS ALEJANDRO ESPINOSA FIERRO.

Dirección de Navegación y Puertos: Edif. Minobras (CAN), Of. 562, Santafé de Bogotá, DC; tel. (1) 222-1248; responsible for river works and transport; the waterways system is divided into four sectors: Magdalena, Atrato, Orinoquia, and Amazonia; Dir ALBERTO RODRÍGUEZ ROJAS.

SHIPPING

The four most important ocean terminals are Buenaventura on the Pacific coast and Santa Marta, Barranquilla and Cartagena on the Atlantic coast. The port of Tumaco on the Pacific coast is gaining in importance and there are plans for construction of a deep-water port at Bahía Solano.

In 2003 Colombia's merchant fleet totalled 71,131 grt.

Dirección General de Transporte Marítimo y Puertos: Ministerio de Transporte, Centro Administrativo Nacional (CAN), Avda El Dorado, Santafé de Bogotá, DC; tel. (1) 428-7332; fax (2) 428-6233; e-mail omedina@mintransporte.gov.co; internet www .mintransporte.gov.co/Ministerio/DGTMARITIMO/dgtmar.html; part of the Ministry of Transport; formulates shipping policies; Dir OSCAR HUMBERTO MEDINA MORA.

Port Authorities

Port of Barranquilla: Sociedad Portuaria Regional de Barranquilla, Carrera 38, Calle 1A, Barranquilla, Atlántico; tel. (5) 379-9555; fax (5) 379-9557; e-mail sprbbaq@latino.net.co; internet www .sprb.com.co; privatized in 1993; Port Man. ANÍBAL DAU.

Port of Buenaventura: Empresa Puertos de Colombia, Edif. El Café, Of. 1, Buenaventura; tel. (224) 22543; fax (224) 34447; Port Man. VÍCTOR GONZÁLEZ.

Port of Cartagena: Sociedad Portuaria Regional de Cartagena, SA, Manga, Terminal Marítimo, Cartagena, Bolívar; tel. (5) 660-8071; fax (5) 650-2239; e-mail comercial@sprc.com.co; internet www.sprc .com.co; f. 1959; Port Man. ALFONSO SALAS TRUJILLO; Harbour Master Capt. GONZALO PARRA.

Port of Santa Marta: Empresa Puertos de Colombia, Calle 15, No 3-25, 11°, Santa Marta, Magdalena; tel. (54) 210739; fax (54) 210711; e-mail spsm@spsm.com.co; internet www.spsm.com.co; Port Man. JULIÁN PALACIOS.

Principal Shipping Companies

Colombiana Internacional de Vapores, Ltda (Colvapores): Avda Caracas, No 35-02, Apdo Aéreo 17227, Santafé de Bogotá, DC; cargo services mainly to the USA.

Flota Mercante Grancolombiana, SA: Edif. Grancolombiana, Carrera 13, No 27-75, Apdo Aéreo 4482, Santafé de Bogotá, DC; tel. (1) 286-0200; fax (1) 286-9028; f. 1946; owned by the Colombian Coffee Growers' Federation (80%) and Ecuador Development Bank (20%); f. 1946 one of Latin America's leading cargo carriers serving 45 countries world-wide; Pres. LUIS FERNANDO ALARCÓN MANTILLA.

Líneas Agromar, Ltda: Calle 73, Vía 40-350, Apdo Aéreo 3256, Barranquilla, Atlántico; tel. (5) 345-1874; fax (5) 345-9634; Pres. MANUEL DEL DAGO FERNÁNDEZ.

Petromar Ltda: Bosque, Diagonal 23, No 56-152, Apdo Aéreo 505, Cartagena, Bolívar; tel. (5) 662-7208; fax (5) 662-7592; Chair. SAVERIO MINERVINI S.

Transportadora Colombiana de Graneles, SA (NAVESCO, SA): Avda 19, No 118-95, Of. 214-301, Santafé de Bogotá, DC; tel. (1) 620-9035; fax (1) 620-8801; e-mail navesco@colomsat.net.co; Gen. Man. GUILLERMO SOLANO VARELA.

Several foreign shipping lines call at Colombian ports.

CIVIL AVIATION

Colombia has more than 100 airports, including 11 international airports: Santafé de Bogotá, DC (El Dorado International Airport),

Medellín, Cali, Barranquilla, Bucaramanga, Cartagena, Cúcuta, Leticia, Pereira, San Andrés and Santa Marta.

Dirección General de Transporte Aéreo: Ministerio de Transporte, Centro Administrativo Nacional (CAN), Of. 304, Avda El Dorado, Santafé de Bogotá, DC; tel. (1) 428-7397; fax (2) 428-7034; e-mail aereo@mintransporte.gov.co; internet www.mintransporte.gov.co/Ministerio/DGTAEREO/dgtaereo.html; part of the Ministry of Transport; formulates air transport policies; Dir JUAN CARLOS SALAZAR GÓMEZ.

Airports Authority

Unidad Administrativa Especial de Aeronáutica Civil: Aeropuerto Internacional El Dorado, 4°, Santafé de Bogotá, DC; tel. (1) 413-9500; fax (1) 413-9878; f. 1967 as Departamento Administrativo de Aeronáutica Civil, reorganized 1993; wholly state-owned; Dir ERNESTO HUERTAS ESACALLÓN.

National Airlines

Aerotaca, SA (Aerotransportes Casanare): Avda El Dorado, Entrada 1, Interior 20, Santafé de Bogotá, DC; tel. (1) 413-9884; fax (1) 413-5256; f. 1965; scheduled regional and domestic passenger services; Gen. Man. RAFAEL URDANETA.

AVIANCA (Aerovías Nacionales de Colombia, SA): Avda El Dorado, No 93-30, 5°, Santafé de Bogotá, DC; tel. (1) 413-9511; fax (1) 413-8716; internet www.avianca.com; f. 1919; operates domestic services to all cities in Colombia and international services to the USA, France, Spain and throughout Central and Southern America; merged with Aerolíneas Centrales de Colombia, SA (ACES) and Sociedad Aeronáutica de Medellín Consolidada, SA (SAM) in 2002; Chair. ANDRÉS OBREGÓN SANTO DOMINGO; Pres. JUAN EMILIO POSADA.

Intercontinental de Aviación: Avda El Dorado, Entrada 2, Interior 6, Santafé de Bogotá, DC; tel. (1) 413-9700; fax (1) 413-8458; internet www.insite-network.com/inter; f. 1965 as Aeropesca Colombia (Aerovías de Pesca y Colonización del Suroeste Colombiano); operates scheduled domestic, regional and international passenger and cargo services; Pres. Capt. LUIS HERNÁNDEZ ZIA.

Servicio de Aeronavegación a Territorios Nacionales (Satena): Avda El Dorado, Entrada 1, Interior 11, Apdo Aéreo 11163, Santafé de Bogotá, DC; tel. (1) 413-7100; fax (1) 413-8178; internet www.satena.com; f. 1962; commercial enterprise attached to the Ministry of National Defence; internal services; CEO and Gen. Man. Maj.-Gen. HECTOR CAMPO.

Tampa Cargo SA: Terminal de Carga, Aeropuerto Internacional José María Córdova, Apdo Aéreo 494, Ríonegro, Antioquia; tel. (574) 569–9200; fax (4) 569–9247; e-mail amartinez@tampacargo.com; internet www.tampacargo.com.co; f. 1973; operates international cargo services to destinations throughout the Americas; Pres. FREDERICK JACOBSEN; Head of Corp. Communications ISABEL MARTÍNEZ.

In addition, the following airlines operate international and domestic charter cargo services: Aerosucre Colombia, Aero Transcolombiana de Carga (ATC), Aires Colombia and Líneas Aéreas Suramericanas (LAS).

Tourism

The principal tourist attractions are the Caribbean coast (including the island of San Andrés), the 16th-century walled city of Cartagena, the Amazonian town of Leticia, the Andes mountains rising to 5,700m above sea-level, the extensive forests and jungles, pre-Columbian relics and monuments of colonial art. In 2002 there were 541,372 visitors (compared with 615,719 in 2001), most of whom came from the USA, Ecuador and Venezuela. In that year tourism receipts were US $962m.

Ministerio de Comercio, Industria y Turismo: Calle 28, No 13A-15, 18°, Edif. Centro de Comercio Internacional, Santafé de Bogotá, DC; tel. (1) 382-1307; fax (1) 352-2101; internet www.mincomercio.gov.co; Dir of Tourism ADOLFO TORO VELÁSQUEZ.

Asociación Colombiana de Agencias de Viajes y Turismo (ANATO): Carrera 21, No 83-63, Apdo Aereo 7088, Santafé de Bogotá, DC; tel. (1) 610-7099; fax (1) 236-2424; e-mail direccionejecutiva@anato.org; internet www.anato.com.co; f. 1949; Pres. Dr OSCAR RUEDA GARCÍA; Exec. Dir LUIS BETANCUR.

THE COMOROS*

Introductory Survey

Location, Climate, Language, Religion, Flag, Capital

The Union of the Comoros (formerly the Federal Islamic Republic of the Comoros) is an archipelago in the Mozambique Channel, between the island of Madagascar and the east coast of the African mainland. The group comprises four main islands (Ngazidja, Nzwani and Mwali, formerly Grande-Comore, Anjouan and Mohéli respectively, and Mayotte) and numerous islets and coral reefs. The climate is tropical, with average temperatures ranging from 23°C (73.4°F) to 28°C (82.4°F). Average annual rainfall is between 1,500 mm (59 ins) and 5,000 mm (197 ins). The official languages are Comorian (a blend of Swahili and Arabic), French and Arabic. Islam is the state religion. The flag (proportions 2 by 3) has four equal horizontal stripes, of yellow, white, red and blue, with a green triangle at the hoist depicting a white crescent moon and a vertical row of four five-pointed white stars. The capital, which is situated on Ngazidja, is Moroni.

Recent History

Formerly attached to Madagascar, the Comoros became a separate French Overseas Territory in 1947. The islands achieved internal self-government in December 1961, with a Chambre des députés and a Government Council responsible for local administration.

Elections in December 1972 resulted in a large majority for parties advocating independence. Ahmed Abdallah became President of the Government Council and in June 1973 was restyled President of the Government. At a referendum in December 1974 96% of the voters expressed support for independence, despite the opposition of the Mayotte Party, which sought the status of a French Department for the island of Mayotte. On 6 July 1975, the Chambre des députés voted for immediate independence, elected Abdallah to be first President of the Comoros and reconstituted itself as the Assemblée nationale. Although France made no attempt to intervene, it maintained control of Mayotte. Abdallah was deposed in August, and the Assemblée nationale was abolished. A National Executive Council was established, with Prince Saïd Mohammed Jaffar, leader of the opposition party, the Front national uni, as its head, and Ali Soilih, leader of the coup, among its members. In November the Comoros was admitted to the UN, as a unified state comprising the whole archipelago. In December France officially recognized the independence of Ngazidja, Nzwani and Mwali, but all relations between France and the Comoros were effectively suspended. In February 1976 Mayotte voted overwhelmingly to retain its links with France.

In January 1976 Ali Soilih was elected Head of State, and adopted extended powers under the terms of a new Constitution. In May 1978 Soilih was killed, following a coup by a group of European mercenaries, led by a Frenchman, Col Robert Denard, on behalf of the exiled former President, Ahmed Abdallah, and the Comoros was proclaimed a Federal Islamic Republic. Shortly afterwards diplomatic relations with France were restored.

In October 1978 a new Constitution was approved in a referendum, on the three islands excluding Mayotte, by 99.3% of the votes cast. Abdallah was elected President in the same month, and in December elections for a new legislature, the Assemblée fédérale, took place. In January 1979 the Assemblée fédérale approved the formation of a one-party state (unofficial opposition groups, however, continued to exist). Ali Mroudjae, hitherto Minister of Foreign Affairs and Co-operation, was appointed Prime Minister in February 1982, and legislative elections took place in March. Constitutional amendments adopted in October vested additional powers in the President. In September 1984 Abdallah was re-elected President. In January 1985, following further amendments to the Constitution, the position of Prime Minister was abolished, and Abdallah assumed the office of Head of Government.

In February 1987 Abdallah indicated that independent opposition candidates would be permitted to contest legislative elections scheduled for March. In the event, however, opposition candidates were only allowed to contest 20 seats on Ngazidja, where they received 35% of the total votes, and pro-Government candidates retained full control of the 42-seat Assemblée fédérale. There were allegations of widespread fraud and intimidation of opposition candidates.

In November 1989 a constitutional amendment permitting Abdallah to remain in office for a third six-year term was approved by 92.5% of votes cast in a popular referendum. The result of the referendum, however, was disputed by the President's opponents. Violent demonstrations followed, and opposition leaders were detained. On the night of 26–27 November Abdallah was assassinated by members of the presidential guard, under the command of Denard. The President of the Supreme Court, Saïd Mohamed Djohar, was appointed interim Head of State, however, Denard and his supporters defeated the regular army in a coup. The mercenaries' action provoked international condemnation, despite denials by Denard of complicity in Abdallah's death. (In May 1999 Denard stood trial in Paris, France, in connection with the assassination. Both Denard and his co-defendant, Dominique Malacrino, were acquitted of the murder charge.) In mid-December Denard agreed to relinquish power and, following the arrival of French paratroops in Moroni, was transported to South Africa, together with the remaining mercenaries. Djohar subsequently announced that the French troops were to remain in the Comoros for up to two years in order to train local security forces.

At the end of December 1989 the main political groups formed a provisional Government of National Unity. An amnesty for all political prisoners was proclaimed, and an inquiry into the death of Abdallah was instigated. It was announced that a multi-candidate presidential election, which was to end the system of single-party rule, was to take place in January 1990. Following delays caused by alleged widespread irregularities and an inconclusive first round held on 4 March, Djohar, the official candidate for the Union comorienne pour le progrès (Udzima), was elected President on 11 March, with 55.3% of the votes cast, defeating Mohamed Taki Abdulkarim, the leader of the Union nationale pour la démocratie aux Comores (UNDC). Djohar appointed a new Government, in which the eight political parties that had supported his presidential candidacy were represented.

In August 1991 the President of the Supreme Court, Ibrahim Ahmed Halidi, announced the dismissal of Djohar, on the grounds of negligence, and proclaimed himself interim President with the support of the Supreme Court. Opposition leaders declared the seizure of power to be legitimate under the terms of the Constitution. However, the Government condemned the coup attempt, and Halidi and several other members of the Supreme Court were arrested. A state of emergency was imposed, and remained in force until early September. A number of demonstrations in favour of Djohar took place in early August, although members of Udzima did not express support for the Government. Later that month the Government banned all public demonstrations.

In August 1991 Djohar established a new coalition Government, which included two members of the Front démocratique (FD) and, in an attempt to appease increasing discontent on Mwali, two members of the Mwalian opposition. However, the two leading political associations represented in the coalition Government, Udzima and the Parti comorien pour la démocratie et le progrès (PCDP), objected to the reshuffle, and shortly afterwards the ministers belonging to the two parties resigned. In November Udzima (which had been officially renamed Parti Udzima) withdrew its support for Djohar and joined the opposition. Opposition leaders demanded the dissolution of the Assemblée fédérale, which was declared to be invalid on the grounds that it had been elected under the former one-party system. Later in November agreement was reached between Djohar and

---

*Some of the information contained in this chapter refers to the whole Comoros archipelago, which the independent Comoran state claims as its national territory. However, the island of Mayotte (Mahoré) is, in fact, administered by France. Separate information on Mayotte may be found in the chapter on French Overseas Possessions.

the principal opposition leaders to initiate a process of national reconciliation, which would include the formation of a government of national unity and the convening of a constitutional conference. The accord also guaranteed the legitimacy of Djohar's election as President. In January 1992 a new transitional Government of National Unity was formed, under the leadership of Taki as its Co-ordinator, pending legislative elections.

In May 1992 opposition parties demanded the resignation of Djohar's son-in-law, Mohamed Saïd Abdallah M'Changama, as Minister of Finance, Commerce and Planning, following allegations of irregularities in the negotiation of government contracts. Djohar subsequently formed a new interim Council of Ministers, in which, however, M'Changama retained his portfolio. At a constitutional referendum, held on 7 June, reform proposals, which had been submitted in April, were approved by 74.3% of the votes cast, despite opposition from eight parties, notably Udzima and the FD. The new Constitution limited the presidential tenure to a maximum of two five-year terms of office and provided for a bicameral legislature, comprising an Assemblée fédérale, elected for a term of four years, and a 15-member Sénat, selected for a six-year term by the regional Councils. In early July Djohar dismissed Taki, following the latter's appointment of a former mercenary to a financial advisory post in the Government. Later that month Djohar formed a new Government, although the post of Co-ordinator remained vacant.

In mid-1992 social and economic conditions on the Comoros deteriorated, following strikes in a number of sectors. In September Djohar announced that legislative elections were to commence in the following month. Also in September an abortive coup attempt was staged by disaffected members of the armed forces. Six opposition leaders and six members of the armed forces, including two sons of the former President, Ahmed Abdallah, were subsequently charged with involvement in the attempted coup. In October some 100 rebel troops, led by a former member of Abdallah's presidential guard, attacked the military garrison of Kandani, in an attempt to release the detainees. Government forces attacked the rebels at Mbeni, to the north-east of Moroni; fighting was also reported on Nzwani. Later in October a demonstration was staged in protest at the French Government's support of Djohar. By the end of that month some 25 people had been killed in clashes between rebels and government forces in Moroni.

In October 1992 Djohar agreed to reschedule the legislative elections for late November, although opposition parties demanded a further postponement, and Udzima and the UNDC advocated a boycott. The first round of the legislative elections, which took place on 22 November, was contested by some 320 candidates representing 21 political parties. Numerous electoral irregularities and violent incidents were reported, however, and several opposition parties demanded that the results be declared invalid and joined the boycott. Election results in six constituencies were subsequently annulled, while the second round of voting on 29 November took place in only 34 of the 42 constituencies. Following partial elections on 13 and 30 December, reports indicated that candidates supporting Djohar—including seven members of the Union des démocrates pour la démocratie (UDD), a pro-Government organization based on Nzwani—had secured a narrow majority in the Assemblée fédérale. The leader of the UDD, Ibrahim Abdérémane Halidi, was appointed Prime Minister on 1 January 1993 and formed a new Council of Ministers. Later in January a Mwalian, Amir Attoumane, was elected as Speaker of the Assemblée fédérale, in response to demands by Mwalian deputies. Shortly after the new Government took office, however, disagreement between Djohar and Halidi was reported, while the presidential majority in the Assemblée fédérale fragmented into three dissenting factions.

In April 1993 nine people, including Abdallah's sons and two prominent members of Udzima, were convicted on charges of involvement in the coup attempt of September 1992 and sentenced to death. Following considerable domestic and international pressure, however, Djohar commuted the sentences to terms of imprisonment. In May 1993 eight supporters of M'Changama, allied with a number of opposition deputies, proposed a motion of 'no confidence' in the Government (apparently with the tacit support of Djohar), which was approved by 23 of the 42 deputies. Shortly afterwards, Djohar appointed an associate of M'Changama, Saïd Ali Mohamed, as Prime Minister, and a new Council of Ministers was formed. In June an alliance of pro-Halidi deputies proposed a motion of censure against the new Government, on the grounds that the Prime

Minister had not been appointed from a party that commanded a majority in the Assemblée fédérale. Djohar, however, declared the motion to be unconstitutional and, in view of the continued absence of a viable parliamentary majority, dissolved the Assemblée fédérale and announced legislative elections. He subsequently dismissed Mohamed and appointed a former presidential adviser, Ahmed Ben Cheikh Attoumane, as Prime Minister. Shortly afterwards an interim Council of Ministers was formed (although two of the newly appointed ministers immediately resigned).

Following the dissolution of the Assemblée fédérale, opposition parties declared Djohar unfit to hold office, in view of the increasing political confusion, and demanded that legislative elections take place within the period of 40 days stipulated in the Constitution. In July 1993, however, Djohar announced that the legislative elections (which were to take place concurrently with local elections) were to be postponed until October—they were later postponed until November. In response, opposition parties organized a one-day strike, in support of demands that Djohar bring forward the date of the legislative elections or resign. In September a number of opposition movements, notably Udzima and the UNDC, established an informal electoral alliance, known as the Union pour la République et le progrès, while the FD, the PCDP, CHUMA (Islands' Fraternity and Unity Party) and the Mouvement pour la démocratie et le progrès (MDP) agreed to present joint candidates. In October Djohar (who had failed to induce the political parties that supported him to form an electoral alliance, owing to their hostility towards M'Changama) established a political organization, the Rassemblement pour la démocratie et le renouveau (RDR), principally comprising supporters of M'Changama and several prominent members of the Government. In November the legislative elections were rescheduled for December, while the local elections were postponed indefinitely. Later in November Djohar reorganized the Council of Ministers and established a new National Electoral Commission (NEC), in response to opposition demands.

At the first round of the legislative elections, which took place on 12 December 1993, four opposition candidates secured seats in the Assemblée fédérale, apparently prompting concern in the Government. Following a second round of voting on 20 December, the NEC declared the results in several constituencies to be invalid. Opposition candidates refused to participate in further elections in these constituencies, on the grounds that voting was again to be conducted under the supervision of the authorities, rather than that of the NEC; RDR candidates consequently won all 10 contested seats, and 22 seats overall, thereby securing a narrow majority in the Assemblée fédérale. In January 1994 Djohar appointed the Secretary-General of the RDR, Mohamed Abdou Madi, as Prime Minister. The new Council of Ministers included several supporters of M'Changama, who was elected Speaker of the Assemblée fédérale. Later in January 12 principal opposition parties, which claimed that the RDR had assumed power illegally, formed a new alliance, the Forum pour le redressement national (FRN).

In May 1994 teachers (and later health workers) initiated strike action in support of demands for an increase in salaries and the reorganization of the public sector. In mid-June it was reported that five people had been killed on Mwali, after an opposition demonstration in support of the public-sector strike was violently suppressed by security forces. In September public-sector workers initiated further strike action; union officials refused to enter into negotiations with the authorities while Abdou Madi's Government remained in power. In October Djohar dismissed Abdou Madi from the office of Prime Minister and appointed Halifa Houmadi to the post.

In December 1994 Djohar failed to accede to a request by the Assemblée fédérale that political prisoners who had been implicated in the abortive coup attempt in September 1992 be granted amnesty. In January 1995 public-sector workers suspended strike action, after the Government agreed to a number of union demands. In the same month Djohar condemned a decision by the French Government to reimpose visa requirements for Comoran nationals entering Mayotte (which further undermined the Comoros' claim of sovereignty over the territory). A demonstration at the French embassy in Moroni, which was staged in protest at the measure, was suppressed by security forces, after degenerating into violence. Later in January division emerged within the RDR, after both the party's Chairman and its Secretary-General (Abdou Madi) criticized the Government's failure to contain subsequent hostility towards

French citizens. At a congress of the RDR in February the two officials were removed from the party, and Houmadi became Chairman. In the same month the Government announced that elections to the regional councils were to take place in April (later postponed until July) and were to be followed by the establishment of an upper legislative chamber, the Sénat, and a Constitutional Council. The opposition, however, accused Djohar of acting unconstitutionally in the preparation for elections and claimed that he planned to assume control of the electoral process.

In April 1995 reports emerged of a widening rift between Djohar and Houmadi, after the Prime Minister apparently claimed that Djohar and M'Changama had engaged in financial malpractice. At the end of that month Djohar dismissed Houmadi from the premiership and appointed a former Minister of Finance, Mohamed Caabi El Yachroutu, as his successor. A 13-member Council of Ministers, which included only five members of the previous administration, was established. In May three former Prime Ministers (Mohamed, Abdou Madi and Houmadi) conducted a series of political meetings urging public support for the removal of M'Changama (who, they claimed, exerted undue influence over Djohar) and demanded the dissolution of the Assemblée fédérale. In July further tension developed within the Government over an agreement whereby Air Comores was to be transferred to the joint management of an airline based in the United Arab Emirates; M'Changama and the Minister of Transport and Tourism, Ahmed Saïd Issilame, claimed that the agreement was technically invalid on the grounds that it had been signed by Djohar before legislation providing for the privatization of Air Comores had been approved in the Assemblée fédérale. Meanwhile, it was feared that the further postponement of elections to the regional councils would delay the presidential election. In an effort to facilitate the organization of the presidential election, the Government introduced minor constitutional amendments, including the relaxation of regulations governing the registration of political candidates and a provision empowering the Prime Minister to act as interim Head of State. At the end of July Djohar removed Issilame and a further three associates of M'Changama from the Council of Ministers.

In September 1995 about 30 European mercenaries, led by Denard, staged a military coup, seizing control of the garrison at Kandani and capturing Djohar. The mercenaries, who were joined by some 300 members of the Comoran armed forces, released a number of prisoners (including those detained for involvement in the failed coup attempt in September 1992) and installed a former associate of Denard, Capt. Ayouba Combo, as leader of a Transitional Military Committee. The French Government denounced the coup and suspended economic aid to the Comoros, but initially refused to take military action, despite requests for assistance from El Yachroutu, who had taken refuge in the French embassy. In October Combo announced that he had transferred authority to Mohamed Taki Abdulkarim and the leader of CHUMA, Saïd Ali Kemal, (who had both welcomed the coup) as joint civilian Presidents, apparently in an attempt to avert military repercussions by the French Government. The FRN, however, rejected the new leadership and entered into negotiations with El Yachroutu. Following a further appeal for intervention from El Yachroutu, who invoked a defence co-operation agreement that had been established between the two countries in 1978, some 900 French military personnel landed on the Comoros and surrounded the mercenaries at Kandani. Shortly afterwards Denard and his associates, together with the disaffected members of the Comoran armed forces, surrendered to the French troops. (In October 1996, following his release from imprisonment in France in July, Denard claimed that the coup attempt had been planned at the request of several Comoran officials, including Taki.)

Following the French military intervention, El Yachroutu declared himself interim President, in accordance with the Constitution, and formed a Government of National Unity, which included members of the constituent parties of the FRN. Djohar (who had been transported to Réunion by the French in order to receive medical treatment) rejected El Yachroutu's assumption of power and announced the reappointment of Saïd Ali Mohamed as Prime Minister. Later in October 1995 a National Reconciliation Conference decided that El Yachroutu would remain interim President, pending the forthcoming election, which was provisionally scheduled for early 1996. The incumbent administration opposed Djohar's stated intention to return to the Comoros and announced that measures would be taken to prevent him from entering the country. At the end of

October El Yachroutu granted an amnesty to all Comorans involved in the coup attempt and appointed representatives of the UNDC and Udzima (which had supported the coup) to the new Council of Ministers. In November Djohar announced the formation of a rival Government, headed by Mohamed. El Yachroutu, who was supported by the Comoran armed forces, refused to recognize the legitimacy of Djohar's appointments, while opposition parties equally opposed his return to power; only elements of the RDR continued to support Djohar's authority. It was reported that representatives of the Organization of African Unity (OAU, now the African Union—AU, see p. 144), who visited the Comoros and Réunion in November in an effort to resolve the situation, had unofficially concluded that only El Yachroutu's administration was capable of governing. There was also widespread speculation that the French Government had believed Djohar's authority to be untenable and had tacitly supported his removal from power. Later that month, however, supporters of Djohar, including M'Changama, organized a political gathering to demand the resignation of El Yachroutu's administration. Meanwhile, political leaders on Mwali rejected the authority of both rival Governments, urged a campaign of civil disobedience and established a 'citizens' committee' to govern the island; discontent with the central administration also emerged on Nzwani.

In January 1995 Djohar returned to the Comoros, after apparently signing an agreement stipulating that he would retain only symbolic presidential powers. A presidential election took place, in two rounds, on 6 and 16 March. At the first round, which was contested by some 15 candidates, Taki obtained the highest number of votes, with 21%, while the leader of the FRN, Abbas Djoussouf, secured about 15% of the votes. Taki was elected to the presidency on 16 March, obtaining 64% of the vote. International observers were satisfied with the electoral process; officials reported that 62% of the electorate had participated in the second round. The new Head of State was sworn in on 25 March. Taki appointed a new Council of Ministers, which included five of the presidential candidates who had supported him in the second round of the election.

In April 1996 Taki dissolved the Assemblée fédérale and announced that legislative elections would take place in October, despite the constitutional requirement that elections be held within a period of 40 days following the dissolution of the legislature. New Governors, all belonging to the UNDC, were appointed to each of the three islands. In August Taki issued a decree awarding himself absolute powers. This measure was widely criticized in the media and by opposition groups as being in violation of the Constitution.

In September 1996 Taki established a constitutional consultative committee, comprising 42 representatives of political parties and other organizations, which was to provide advice concerning the drafting of a new constitution; the FRN refused to participate in the committee. Also in that month the legislative elections were postponed until November. A national referendum to endorse a new draft Constitution was scheduled for 20 October. In order to comply with a constitutional proposal, which effectively restricted the number of political parties to a maximum of three, 24 pro-Taki political organizations merged to form one presidential party, the Rassemblement national pour le développement (RND). The opposition condemned the extensive powers that the draft Constitution vested in the President, and the rapidity with which it was to be installed, and urged a boycott of the referendum. The new Constitution, however, was approved by 85% of votes cast. The new Constitution vested legislative power in a unicameral parliament, the Assemblée fédérale, (thereby abolishing the Sénat) and extended the presidential term to six years, with an unrestricted number of consecutive mandates. Political parties were required to have two parliamentary deputies from each island (following legislative elections) to be considered legal; organizations that did not fulfil these stipulations were to be dissolved. Extensive executive powers were vested in the President, who was to appoint the Governors of the islands and gained the right to initiate constitutional amendments. The official result of the referendum was disputed by the opposition parties.

Following unsuccessful negotiations with the Government, which rejected demands for the creation of an independent electoral commission and the revision of electoral lists, the opposition parties (having formed a new alliance) refused to participate in the electoral process. Consequently, the legislative elections, which took place after a further delay, in two rounds, in December 1996, were only contested by the RND and the Front national pour la justice (FNJ), a fundamentalist Islamic organization, together with 23 independent candidates (in apparent contravention of a stipulation in the new Constitution that only legally created political parties were entitled to participate in national elections). The RND secured 36 of the 43 seats in the Assemblée fédérale, while the FNJ won three, with four seats taken by independent candidates. Taki nominated Ahmed Abdou, who had served in the administration of former President Ahmed Abdallah, as Prime Minister to head a new Council of Ministers.

In December 1996 industrial action in the public sector in support of demands by civil servants for the payment of salary arrears resulted in severe disruption in government services. Civil unrest, exacerbated by severe shortages of water and electricity, culminated in February in a one-day general strike. Meanwhile, discontent with the Government intensified on Nzwani; in March a general strike escalated into riots, when some 3,000 demonstrators (reported to be secessionists) clashed with the security forces in Mutsamudu, the main town. Taki replaced the Governor of Nzwani and other senior island officials and carried out a government reshuffle. However, sympathy for the separatist movements on both Nzwani and Mwali continued to increase, amid claims that the Government had consistently ignored their political and economic interests. Separatist leaders declared their intention to seek the restoration of French rule and established a 'political directorate' on Nzwani, chaired by Abdallah Ibrahim, the leader of the Mouvement populaire anjouanais, a grouping of separatist movements on Nzwani. (The relative prosperity of neighbouring Mayotte appeared to have prompted the demand for a return to French rule; it was reported that up to 200 illegal migrants a day attempted to enter Mayotte from Nzwani.) Military reinforcements were sent to Nzwani and the Governor of the island was replaced once again.

On 3 August 1997 the 'political directorate' unilaterally declared Nzwani's secession from the Comoros. The separatists subsequently elected Ibrahim as president of a 13-member 'politico-administrative co-ordination', which included Abdou Madi, a former Prime Minister during Djohar's presidency, as spokesperson. The declaration of independence was condemned by Djoussouf, who appealed for French mediation in the crisis. However, France, while denouncing the secession, declared itself in favour of the intervention of the OAU. The OAU responded by sending a special envoy, Pierre Yéré, to the Comoros. Meanwhile, separatist agitation intensified on Mwali, culminating on 11 August, when secessionists declared Mwali's independence from the Comoros, appointed a president and a prime minister to head a 12-member government, and called for reattachment to France.

As OAU mediation efforts continued, it was announced in mid-August 1997 that secessionist leaders on Mwali and Nzwani had agreed to negotiate with the authorities in Moroni, although those on Nzwani had insisted on the immediate withdrawal of the military reinforcements that had been sent to the island in July. By late August the Government had complied with this demand, and the OAU announced its intention to hold a reconciliation conference in September in Addis Ababa, Ethiopia, while maintaining that secession was unacceptable. Nzwani's Governor resigned and was not replaced. In early September, despite OAU and French opposition to military intervention, Taki despatched some 300 troops to Nzwani in an attempt forcibly to suppress the separatist insurrection. After two days of heavy fighting between secessionist and government forces, the OAU declared that the government troops had failed to quash the rebellion. The Government claimed that the separatists had been aided by foreign elements and expressed regret at France's refusal to support the military operation. As it emerged that some 40 Comoran soldiers and 16 Nzwani residents had been killed in the fighting, with many more injured, demonstrators demanding Taki's resignation clashed violently with the security forces in Moroni. The separatists on Nzwani reaffirmed their independence and empowered Ibrahim to rule by decree. Taki subsequently declared a state of emergency, assumed absolute power and dismissed the Government of Ahmed Abdou and his military and civilian advisers. (Abdou had reportedly resigned his position in late August, although this had not been announced publicly.) Shortly afterwards, Taki established a State Transition Commission, which included representatives from Nzwani and Mwali. The reconciliation conference was postponed indefinitely by the OAU. The League of Arab States (Arab League, see p. 290) agreed to a request from

Taki for assistance, and following talks with the OAU regarding the co-ordination of the mediation effort, all three islands hosted discussions in late September, which were convened by envoys from both organizations. The opposition continued to call for Taki's resignation, the decentralization of power through constitutional reform and the organization of new elections.

In September 1997, despite the misgivings of some members of the 'politico-administrative co-ordination', notably Abdou Madi, Ibrahim announced his decision to hold a referendum on self-determination for Nzwani on 26 October, prior to a reconciliation conference sponsored by both the OAU and the Arab League, which all parties had agreed to attend. Despite international opposition, the referendum was conducted as scheduled; according to separatist officials, 99.9% of the electorate voted in favour of independence for Nzwani. The following day Ibrahim dissolved the 'politico-administrative co-ordination' and appointed a temporary government, which was charged with preparing a constitution and organizing a presidential election, although it did not receive international recognition. Taki responded by severing Nzwani's telephone lines, suspending air and maritime links and establishing a commission to liaise with opposition leaders prior to the appointment of a government of national unity. However, the opposition refused to participate in such a government before the reconciliation conference had taken place. The conference had been postponed several times, largely owing to disagreements regarding the composition and strength of the delegations. In November the OAU announced plans to deploy a force of military observers in the Comoros, despite the separatists' insistence that the force would not be allowed to land on Nzwani; an initial eight-member contingent, which arrived that month, was subsequently to be increased to 25 and was to receive logistical support from France.

In early December 1997 Taki formed a new Council of Ministers, appointing Nourdine Bourhane as Prime Minister. The inter-Comoran reconciliation conference was held later that month; some agreement was reached on proposals for the establishment of an international commission of inquiry to investigate September's military intervention and on the holding of a Comoran inter-island conference to discuss institutional reform. In January 1998, following the first meeting in Fomboni, Mwali, of a committee charged with pursuing negotiations on the crisis, the OAU announced that both the Comoran Government and the Nzwani separatists had agreed to a number of conciliatory measures, including the restoration of air and maritime links and the release of federal soldiers still detained on Nzwani. However, Ibrahim subsequently rejected all the agreements that his delegation had signed in Fomboni, with the exception of the release of detainees.

In February 1998 tension increased further on Nzwani, where several rival separatist factions had emerged; fighting broke out between Ibrahim's supporters and followers of Abdou Madi with the apparent support of both Taki and the OAU, in an abortive attempt to mount resistance to the secessionists. Later in February a separatist constitution was approved by a reported 99.5% of voters in a referendum on Nzwani. Ibrahim subsequently appointed a new separatist government. OAU mediation efforts effectively broke down in March, following an unsuccessful visit to Nzwani by a ministerial delegation.

In Moroni public discontent intensified in May 1998, when at least three people were reported to have been killed in violent anti-Government protests. Later that month Taki, who appeared to be moderating his stance, acted to break the political deadlock, forming a committee to re-establish dialogue with the opposition, appointing a new Council of Ministers, and releasing a prominent separatist from detention in Moroni. Abdou Madi returned to federal government, and, seemingly as a conciliatory gesture to the secessionists, the premiership (a position traditionally held by a Nzwanian) was left vacant. In June Taki held discussions with a number of opposition leaders, although the FRN refused to participate.

In July 1998, as social unrest on Nzwani escalated, a dispute over the future aims of the secessionist movement led to the dismissal of the island's government, provoking violent clashes between islanders loyal to Ibrahim, who favoured independence within the framework of an association of the Comoran islands, and supporters of the outgoing prime minister of the island, Chamassi Saïd Omar, who continued to advocate reattachment to France.

Meanwhile, as social and economic conditions deteriorated further, with salaries still unpaid and strike action ongoing, Taki sought overseas assistance in resolving the crisis. In

August 1998 the Government provisionally suspended transport links with both Nzwani and Mayotte. France later refused the Government's request for a suspension of links between Mayotte and Nzwani, thus worsening the already fragile relations between the two countries. As industrial action continued into September, it was reported that the Government had banned news broadcasts by privately-owned radio and television stations. At meetings with Djoussouf and the leadership of his own party in October, Taki proposed the establishment of a government of public salvation, an idea opposed by many members of the RND and several government ministers.

On 6 November 1998 President Taki died unexpectedly, reportedly having suffered a heart attack, although several senior officials expressed serious doubts about the cause of death. Tadjidine Ben Saïd Massoundi, the President of the High Council of the Republic and a former Prime Minister, was designated acting President, in accordance with the Constitution, pending an election, which would be held after 30–90 days. Massoundi immediately revoked the ban on the movement of people and goods to Nzwani and, despite the continued opposition of several government ministers, proceeded with Taki's project for the formation of a government of public salvation. Djoussouf, the main opposition leader, was subsequently appointed Prime Minister, to head a Council of Ministers composed of members of the FRN and the RND. Divisions within the RND over its participation in the new Government led to a split in the party. In January 1999 Massoundi extended his presidential mandate, which was soon to expire, pending a resolution of the crisis dividing the islands.

Meanwhile, renewed tension within the separatist administration on Nzwani escalated in December 1998, provoking eight days of armed clashes between rival militias, which reportedly resulted in at least 60 deaths before a cease-fire agreement was signed. In January 1999 Ibrahim agreed to relinquish some of his powers to a five-member 'politico-administrative directorate', as meetings commenced between the rival separatist factions. No consensus was reached in the following months, however, and when Ibrahim replaced the directorate with a 'committee of national security' in March, the new administration was immediately rejected by rival leaders.

At an OAU-sponsored inter-island conference, held in Antananarivo, Madagascar, in April 1999, an agreement was reached that envisaged substantial autonomy for Nzwani and Mwali, the changing of the country's name to the Union of the Comoran Islands and the rotation of the presidency among the three islands. However, the delegates from Nzwani refused to sign the agreement, insisting on the need to consult the Nzwani population prior to a full endorsement. Several days of rioting followed in Moroni, as demonstrators protested against Nzwani's failure to ratify the accord. On 30 April the Chief of Staff of the Comoran armed forces, Col Assoumani Azali, seized power in a bloodless coup, deposing Massoundi and dissolving the Government, the Assemblée fédérale and all other constitutional institutions. Azali promulgated a new constitutional charter, in which he proclaimed himself head of state and of government and Commander-in-Chief of the armed forces, and sought to justify the coup by claiming that the authorities had not taken the political measures necessary to control the security situation in the Comoros. Full legislative functions were also vested in Azali, who announced his intention to stay in power for one year only, during which time he pledged to oversee the creation of the new institutions envisaged in the Antananarivo accord. The appointment of a State Committee (composed of six members from Ngazidja, four from Mwali and two from Nzwani) was followed by that of a State Council, which was to supervise the activities of the State Committee and comprised eight civilians and 11 army officers. The coup was condemned by the OAU; the UN, however, sent representatives to Azali's inauguration.

In June 1999 Azali created five technical commissions, which were charged with directing the implementation of the Antananarivo accord, including the drafting of new constitutions for the proposed union and its component parts. However, amid increasing discontent with the new administration, the main political parties boycotted a meeting at which they were to have nominated representatives to serve on the new commissions. Lt-Col Saïd Abeid Abdérémane, who had previously held the role of 'national mediator' on Nzwani, formed a government of national unity on the island and assumed the role of 'national co-ordinator'. In July delegates from the three islands, including Azali and Abeid, met on Mwali for talks aimed at resolving the

political crisis. The negotiations represented the most senior-level contact between the islands since the secessions of August 1997.

In August 1999 elections to establish an Assemblée nationale on Nzwani were held. No official results were released, but reports indicated that the most staunch separatists won the majority of seats. In August and October the OAU Secretary-General's newly appointed special envoy for the Comoros, Francisco Caetano José Madeira, visited the islands in unsuccessful attempts to persuade the separatists on Nzwani to sign the Antananarivo accord. In December the OAU adopted a tougher stance towards the Nzwani separatists by threatening the imposition of sanctions on the island should its leaders not have signed the peace accord by 1 February 2000. In response, Abeid announced that a referendum would be held on Nzwani in January 2000 regarding the signing of the Antananarivo accord. According to the separatist authorities of Nzwani, the results of the referendum revealed an overwhelming majority (94.47%) in favour of full independence for the island; the OAU, however, announced that it did not recognize the outcome of the ballot, following allegations of intimidation and repression of those in favour of reconciliation.

Meanwhile, following a series of meetings between Azali and a number of political parties from all three islands regarding the establishment of a more representative and decentralized government in Moroni, the State Committee underwent an extensive reorganization in December 1999, including the appointment of a Prime Minister, Bianrifi Tarmidi (from Mwali). Although Mwali was well represented in the new executive, only one Nzwanian minister was appointed.

In February 2000, as threatened, the OAU imposed economic sanctions on Nzwani; the overseas assets of the separatist leaders were 'frozen' and they themselves were confined to the island. Furthermore, as part of the OAU sanctions, the federal Government suspended sea and air transport links, as well as telephone communications with Nzwani.

In March 2000 army units, led by Capt. Abdérémane Ahmed Abdallah (the son of former President Ahmed Abdallah), reportedly attempted, unsuccessfully, to overthrow Azali; Abdallah was subsequently arrested. In the following month demonstrations were organized by a number of political parties in protest at Azali's failure to transfer the country to civilian rule by 14 April, as he had promised following the April 1999 coup (see above). Azali later claimed that the conditions set for the holding of elections, namely the signing of the Antananarivo accord by the Nzwanian separatists, had not been met.

In May 2000 the OAU announced that the lifting of sanctions against Nzwanian separatists was dependent on a return to constitutional order on the Comoros; it advocated the restoration of the October 1996 Constitution, the reinstatement of Tajidine Ben Saïd Massoundi as Head of State, as well as the appointment of an interim government and Prime Minister. The following month an OAU delegation, led by Madeira, arrived in Moroni in an attempt to revive peace talks. However, Abeid reiterated his rejection of the Antananarivo accord. The possibility of armed intervention on Nzwani was rejected at an OAU summit, held in July, although it was agreed to establish a total maritime blockade of Nzwani.

In August 2000 an agreement, known as the Fomboni Accord, was reached by Azali and Abeid following negotiations on Mwali. The agreement provided for the establishment of a new Comoran entity and granted the three islands considerable control over internal matters. A new constitution was to be drafted and approved, by referendum, within 12 months. Moreover, Abeid and Azali called for the sanctions imposed on Nzwani to be lifted. The declaration was rejected by the OAU, however, on the grounds that it contravened the Antananarivo accord and threatened the integrity of the Comoros. Demonstrations, organized by opposition members displeased with the new settlement, took place on Nzwani following the signing of the declaration. Nevertheless, a tripartite commission, comprising delegates from Ngazidja, Nzwani and Mwali, was established to define the terms of the new constitution. In November Bianrifi Tarmidi was replaced as Prime Minister by Hamada Madi 'Boléro', who subsequently formed a new Government. Despite attempts to include them in the new Government and the tripartite commission, opposition members refused to participate, instead presenting to international mediators their own proposals for a resolution to the crisis.

With the mediation of the OAU and the Organisation internationale de la francophonie (OIF), negotiations between opposition and government members continued throughout late 2000 and early 2001. In February the Framework Agreement for Reconciliation in the Comoros was signed in Fomboni by representatives of the Comoran Government, the Nzwani administration, opposition parties and civil society. The OAU, the OIF and the European Union (EU) were to be guarantors of the peace accord, which provided for the establishment of a new Comoran entity. Under the provisions of the agreement, an independent tripartite commission (comprising equal numbers of delegates from each of the islands, representing all the signatory groups) was to draft a new constitution, which would be subject to approval in a national referendum. The new constitution was to define the areas of jurisdiction of the new entity and the individual islands, although the central administration would retain control over religion, nationality, currency, foreign affairs and defence. An independent national electoral commission was also to be created. Following the constitutional referendum, a transitional government of national union was to be formed and charged with creating the new institutions by 31 December. However, in March, following disagreements over the composition of a follow-up committee intended to monitor the implementation of the Fomboni accord, the opposition withdrew from the reconciliation process. Nevertheless, the OAU suspended sanctions against Nzwani in May.

On 8–9 August 2001 a bloodless military coup on Nzwani resulted in the removal from power of Saïd Abeid Abdérémane. Abeid was replaced by a collective presidency, comprising Maj. Mohamed Bacar, Maj. Hassane Ali Toihili and Maj. Charif Halidi; a government of eight civilian commissioners (none of whom had been members of the previous government) was appointed. The new leadership stated its commitment to the Fomboni agreement. However, on 24 September a further bloodless military coup was instigated by the deputy head of the Comoran army and close ally of Col Azali, Maj. Ayouba Combo. Although Combo was initially declared leader of the army, and Ahmed Aboubakar Foundi was installed as leader of Nzwani, they were captured the following day, before subsequently escaping the island. In November Abeid attempted unsuccessfully to regain control of Nzwani in a military coup; he was defeated by forces loyal to Bacar and was obliged to flee the island; the attempted coup was strongly condemned by the Government, which reaffirmed its support for the island's authorities. Abeid, however, denied his involvement in the events, maintaining that the instigator had in fact been Allaoui Ahmed, who had reportedly allied himself with the Organisation pour l'indépendance d'Anjouan, a political alliance that opposed the proposed constitutional changes.

At the constitutional referendum, which took place on 23 December 2001, 76.4% of the electorate voted in favour of the proposed new constitution. The country, which was to change its name to the Union of the Comoros, was to be led by the President of the Union, at the head of a Council of the Union, and governed by a legislative assembly, the Assemblée de l'Union. The position of President was to rotate between the islands, while the Vice-Presidents, who were also members of the Council of the Union, were to be inhabitants of the two remaining islands; the first President was to come from Ngazidja. Each of the three islands was to become financially autonomous and was to be ruled by its own local government and institutions. The Union was to be responsible for matters of religion, nationality, currency, foreign affairs and external defence, while shared responsibilities between the Union and the islands were to be determined at a later date. A transitional government was to be installed to monitor the implementation of the new institutions.

In January 2002 Prime Minister Hamadi Madi 'Boléro' tendered his resignation. A transitional Government of National Unity was installed, with 'Boléro' reappointed as Prime Minister, and included members of the former Government, opposition representatives and two of Nzwani's separatist leaders. However, on the following day the Government collapsed, following the withdrawal of the opposition representatives, as a result of a disagreement over the allocation of ministerial portfolios. Meanwhile, Col Azali resigned as Head of State and announced his intention to stand as an independent candidate in the forthcoming presidential election; 'Boléro' was to serve as President *ad interim*. In February 2002 the Government of National Unity was re-established; notably, Soilihi Ali Mohammed, a member of the opposition, became Minister of Finance, the Budget and Privatization, replacing Assoumany Aboudou, who was appointed as Minister of the Interior and

Decentralization, the position that Mohammed had been allocated in January.

In March and April 2002 voters on Nzwani, Mwali and Ngazidja approved new local Constitutions. In a first round of voting in the federal presidential election on 17 March, contested by nine candidates, Col Azali secured 39.8% of the vote. Mahamoud Mradabi won 15.7% and Saïd Ali Kemal 10.7%; however, both Mradabi and Kemal boycotted the second round. Consequently, on 14 April Col Azali was elected unopposed as Federal President of the Union of the Comoros, reportedly securing more than 75% of the votes cast. However, the result was declared invalid by the NEC, on the grounds that the election had not been free and fair. Nevertheless, following the dissolution of the NEC, and the appointment of an independent electoral body, Col Azali was declared Federal President. Meanwhile, in late March and early April, Maj. Mohamed Bacar and Mohamed Saïd Fazul were elected as regional Presidents of Nzwani and Mwali, respectively; on 19 May Abdou Soule Elbak was elected regional President of Ngazidja. The regional Presidents subsequently formed local Governments. Col Azali appointed a new federal Government in early June.

However, the process of local devolution was complicated by uncertainty about the boundaries of jurisdiction on Ngazidja, as Moroni was to be the seat of government for both Azali and Elbak. According to a report issued by the World Bank, this confusion had hindered the ability of international organizations to implement aid programmes. In June 2002 disagreement over the new political structure prompted the occupation of a number of federal government buildings by troops. In response, the Government of Ngazidja boycotted the inauguration of the new head of the armed forces, Col Soilihi Ali Mohammed, and warned the OAU that it suspected a coup was being planned, to be led by Soilihi. President Elbak also dismissed a number of local government figures loyal to Azali.

In July 2002 Col Azali declared his intention to bring forward the process of national reconciliation, holding legislative elections in September. As a result of a meeting in August, Ngazidja was also granted its own internal security forces by Azali. Nevertheless, at the end of August street barricades were erected in Moroni, in protest at incomplete devolution on Ngazidja, which left Elbak with less authority than the other islands' Presidents. Later in the year Col Azali postponed the legislative elections until March–April 2003, despite assertions from international representatives that the absence of institutions for dialogue was a threat to the national reconciliation process. In September 2002 supporters of Azali formed a new political party, the Convention pour le renouveau des Comores (CRC). Later that month Elbak accused Azali of secretly monitoring his telephone conversations, while Mohamed Sasani, Elbak's cabinet director, circulated a letter to international bodies, including the EU, alleging an assassination plot by Azali against Elbak. The accusations were wholly rejected by the Azali administration.

In January 2003 the follow-up committee on the implementation of the reconciliation agreement proposed that elections to the islands' local assemblies be held in April and elections to the Assemblée de l'Union in May. In February two ministers in the local Government of Ngazidja and 12 police-officers were arrested for involvement in an apparent coup plot against Col Azali. Elbak denied any involvement, and one of the ministers and 10 of the police-officers were later released without charge. In early March Elbak and Bacar denounced Azali's failure to implement measures to resolve the institutional crisis and accused the federal President of repeated constitutional violations, requesting that the EU temporarily delay payment for fishing rights to the federal Government. In March the federal Government announced the indefinite postponement of the legislative elections.

In August 2003, at an AU-sponsored meeting in Pretoria, South Africa, aimed at resolving the ongoing political uncertainty, representatives of the federal and island governments signed a memorandum, according to which the federal Government would retain control of the army, but the administration of the police force would be devolved to the island Governments. Agreement was also reached that, during a transitional period leading to legislative elections, the customs services would be managed by a joint board, with taxes shared between the federal and island administrations. In November the army fired on an anti-Union demonstration led by President Elbak; it was reported that at least 15 people were injured. In December, following further mediation by the AU, the agreement reached in August was ratified by Azali and the three island Presidents at a ceremony in Moroni. A follow-up committee was appointed to monitor the implementation of the accord.

Elections to the three island assemblies were held on 14 and 21 March 2004. Pro-Azali candidates won an overall total of only 12 seats in the assemblies, while candidates allied to Elbak secured 14 of the 20 seats in the Ngazidja assembly, supporters of Bacar were reported to have won 19 of the 25 seats available on Nzwani, and nine allies of Fazul were elected to the 10-member assembly on Mwali. Elections to the Assemblée de l'Union took place on 18 and 25 April. According to final results, declared on 28 April, the CRC won only six of the 18 directly elected seats, while a loose coalition supporting the three island Presidents secured 11 seats, and CHUMA took one seat. The rate of participation by eligible voters at the second round was 68.5%. The remaining 15 seats in the 33-member federal assembly were taken by five nominees each from the island legislatures. The inauguration of the Assemblée, scheduled for 27 May, was postponed by President Azali and finally took place on 4 June. Saïd Dhuffur Bounnou was elected Speaker. In mid-July President Azali unveiled his new ministerial team, granting responsibility for co-ordinating Union affairs on their home islands to the two Vice-Presidents. The new cabinet comprised the two Vice-Presidents, seven ministers of state and two secretaries of state, and included a member of CHUMA, and representatives nominated by the island Presidents of Nzwani and Mwali. President Bacar declined to participate in the creation of the Government.

The Constitutional Court was inaugurated in September 2004, and Abdallah Ahmed Sourette was elected President in October. In the same month President Bacar effected a cabinet reshuffle on Nzwani. On 19 November, in a follow-up to the 2001 Framework Agreement for Reconciliation signed in Fomboni, long-awaited legislation on the division of power between the national and island authorities was passed by the Assemblée de l'Union. The bill, which was supported by President Azali, had provoked much controversy as it sought to clarify authority over security forces and public assets. Authority over the gendarmerie was granted to the island Presidents, precipitating a demonstration by the armed forces, led by the Minister of Defence, Msaidie Houmedi. The island Presidents also expressed their dissatisfaction with the bill, which, they claimed, had been amended by the Assemblée de l'Union without their consent. It was subsequently declared invalid by the Constitutional Court and returned to the Assemblée.

Diplomatic relations between the Comoros and France, suspended in December 1975, were restored in July 1978; in November of that year the two countries signed agreements on military and economic co-operation, apparently deferring any decision on the future of Mayotte. In subsequent years, however, member countries of the UN General Assembly repeatedly voted in favour of a resolution affirming the Comoros' sovereignty over Mayotte, with only France dissenting. Following Djohar's accession to power, diplomatic relations were established with the USA in June 1990. In September 1993 the Arab League accepted an application for membership from the Comoros. In mid-1999, following the military coup headed by Col Azali, France and the USA suspended all military co-operation with the Comoros; France resumed military co-operation in September 2002. In September 2004 the USA claimed that the Comoros was harbouring a militant Islamist group, Al Haramain. In mid-2004 a joint commission with Sudan was created, and there were plans for the reinstatement of the Franco-Comoran commission, after a hiatus of 10 years.

Government

Under the Constitution of 23 December 2001, each of the islands in the Union of the Comoros is headed by a local government and is partially autonomous. The Head of State of the Union of the Comoros is the President, who appoints the members of the Government and heads the Council of the Union, which also comprises the two Vice-Presidents. The members of the Council are elected for a four-year term, and the position of President rotates between the islands, while the Vice-Presidents are inhabitants of the two remaining islands. Federal legislative power is vested in the Assemblée de l'Union, which serves a five-year term and is composed of 33 deputies, 18 of whom are directly elected (nine on Ngazidja, seven on Nzwani and two on Mwali), with the remaining 15 seats divided equally among representatives of the three islands. Each island also elects its own legislative local assembly and president. A final transition to a federalized system was achieved in June 2004.

Defence

In mid-1997 the national army, the Force Comorienne de Défense (FCD), numbered about 1,500 men. Government expenditure on defence in 1994 was an estimated US $3m. In December 1996 an agreement was ratified with France, which provided for the permanent presence of a French military contingent in the Comoros, which was to be renewed by rotation. French military co-operation with the Comoros was suspended after the coup of April 1999, but resumed in September 2002.

Economic Affairs

In 2003, according to estimates from the World Bank, the gross national income (GNI) of the Comoros (excluding Mayotte), measured at average 2001–03 prices, was US $323m., equivalent to $450 per head (or $1,760 per head on an international purchasing-power parity basis). During 1990–2003, it was estimated, the population increased at an average annual rate of 2.6%, while gross domestic product (GDP) per head declined, in real terms, by an average of 1.3% per year. Overall GDP increased, in real terms, at an average annual rate of 1.2% in 1990–2003; growth in 2003 was 2.5%.

Agriculture (including hunting, forestry and fishing) contributed 40.9% of GDP in 2003. Approximately 72.3% of the labour force were employed in the agricultural sector in that year. In 2000 the sector accounted for some 88.4% of export earnings, however, in 2004 the output of cloves and vanilla was reported to have declined. The principal cash crops are vanilla, ylang ylang and cloves. The Comoros produces an estimated 80% of the ylang ylang consumed globally. Cassava, taro, rice, maize, pulses, coconuts and bananas are also cultivated. According to the World Bank, the real GDP of the agricultural sector increased at an average annual rate of 4.3% in 1990–2003; growth in 2003 was 5.7%.

Industry (including manufacturing, construction and power) contributed 11.9% of GDP in 2003. Some 9.4% of the labour force were employed in the industrial sector in 1990. According to the World Bank, the Comoros' industrial GDP increased at an average annual rate of 8.3% in 1990–2003; industrial GDP increased by 5.8% in 2003.

The manufacturing sector contributed 4.2% of GDP in 2003. The sector consists primarily of the processing of agricultural produce, particularly of vanilla and essential oils. According to the World Bank, manufacturing GDP increased at an average annual rate of 5.1% in 1990–2003; manufacturing GDP increased by 5.3% in 2003.

Electrical energy is derived from wood (some 80%), and from thermal installations. Imports of petroleum products comprised an estimated 19.6% of the total cost of imports in 2003 and some 33.5m. kW hours of electricity were produced in the Comoros in 2002.

The services sector contributed 47.2% of GDP in 2003. Strong growth in tourism from 1991 led to a significant expansion in trade, restaurant and hotel activities, although political instability inhibited subsequent growth. According to the World Bank, the GDP of the services sector decreased at an average rate of 5.1% per year in 1990–2003. It declined by 6.8% in 2003.

In 2002, according to the IMF, the Comoros recorded a visible trade deficit of 13,920m. Comoros francs and there was a deficit of 1,059m. Comoros francs on the current account of the balance of payments. In 2000 the principal source of imports was South Africa (accounting for some 54.2% of the total); other major sources were France, Pakistan and Kenya. France was the principal market for exports (43.5%); other important purchasers were Singapore, the USA and the United Kingdom. The leading exports in 2003 were vanilla (providing 78.1% of the total), cloves (13.4%) and ylang ylang (5.7%). The principal imports in that year were petroleum products (19.6%), vehicles and parts (12.5%), rice (9.5%), meat and fish (9.3%) and cement (5.2%).

The Comoran budget deficit, excluding grants received, was estimated at 8,800m. Comoros francs in 2003. The Comoros' external public debt at the end of 2002 totalled US $270.1m., of which $239.9m. was long-term public debt. In 2001 the cost of debt-servicing was equivalent to 3.7% of the value of exports of goods and services. According to the IMF, the annual rate of inflation averaged 3.7% during 1999–2002. In 2002 the rate was 3.3%. An estimated 19.7% of the labour force were unemployed in 2002.

In 1985 the Comoros joined the Indian Ocean Commission (IOC, see p. 374). The country is also a member of the Common

Market for Eastern and Southern Africa (COMESA, see p. 179) and of the Franc Zone (see p. 266).

The Comoros has a relatively undeveloped economy, with high unemployment, a limited transport system, a severe shortage of natural resources and heavy dependence on foreign aid, particularly from France. An intensification of political instability on the islands, following the seizure of power by the army in April 1999, had a particularly adverse effect on maritime trade and tourism. Following the conclusion of an agreement on national reconciliation in February 2001 (see above), in July a group of 'Friends of the Comoros', co-ordinated by the World Bank (and also including the European Union (EU), the Organisation internationale de la francophonie, France, Mauritius and Morocco), pledged some US $11.5m. in aid to assist with constitutional developments towards the establishment of a new Comoran entity, as well as to alleviate poverty and improve the economy. Furthermore, it was hoped that a number of agreements reached later that year, worth an estimated €5.9m., would encourage the further development of the production of vanilla, ylang ylang and cloves, and increase international demand for those crops. In November 2002 the federal Government and the EU signed a National Indicator Programme on co-operation during 2002–07; the Comoros was to receive €27.3m. under the Programme, mostly for education. During much of 2003 considerable economic disruption was caused, particularly on Ngazidja, by disputes over the distribution of political power and revenues following partial devolution. Meanwhile, the value of Comoran vanilla exports increased substantially, as international prices for the commodity escalated, owing to a severe decline in output in Madagascar, the world's principal producer. However, prices for cloves remained low throughout the year, and widespread poverty in the Comoros was exacerbated by steep rises in prices for essential foodstuffs. In early 2004 a transitional budget for the first half of the year was approved, however, an independent audit in September revealed serious irregularities in the national Government's accounts and in those of the island Governments of Nzwani and Mwali. In mid-2004 the IMF stated that political instability in the archipelago continued to have an adverse affect on economic development, although in November an IMF team visited the Comoros with the long-term aim of creating an IMF mission to the country. Conditions for the creation of a mission included reaching an agreement on power sharing between the national and island Governments, and complying with the 2005 budget. GDP growth in 2005 was forecast at 2%.

Education

Education is officially compulsory for 10 years between six and 16 years of age. Primary education begins at the age of six and lasts for six years. Secondary education, beginning at 12 years of age, lasts for seven years, comprising a first cycle of four years and a second of three years. Enrolment at primary schools in 2000/01 included 56% of children in the relevant age-group (males 60%; females 52%), according to UNESCO estimates. Children may also receive a basic education through traditional Koranic schools, which are staffed by Comoran teachers. Enrolment at secondary schools in 1999/2000 was equivalent to 21% of children in the relevant age-group (males 23%; females 18%), according to UNESCO estimates. The Comoros' first university opened in December 2003, with an enrolment of 1,200 students. Current expenditure by the Ministry of Education in 1995 was 3,381m. Comoros francs, representing 21.1% of total current government expenditure.

Public Holidays

2005: 1 January (New Year's Day), 21 January* (Id al-Adha, Feast of the Sacrifice), 10 February* (Muharram, Islamic New Year), 19 February* (Ashoura), 21 April* (Mouloud, Birth of the Prophet), 1 May (International Labour Day), 6 July (Independence Day), 2 September* (Leilat al-Meiraj, Ascension of the Prophet), 5 October* (Ramadan begins), 4 November* (Id al-Fitr, end of Ramadan), 27 November (Anniversary of President Abdallah's assassination).

2006: 1 January (New Year's Day), 11 January* (Id al-Adha, Feast of the Sacrifice), 31 January* (Muharram, Islamic New Year), 9 February* (Ashoura), 11 April* (Mouloud, Birth of the Prophet), 1 May (International Labour Day), 6 July (Independence Day), 22 August* (Leilat al-Meiraj, Ascension of the Prophet), 24 September* (Ramadan begins), 24 October* (Id al-Fitr, end of Ramadan), 27 November (Anniversary of President Abdallah's assassination).

*Religious holidays, which are dependent on the Islamic lunar calendar, may differ by one or two days from the dates given.

Weights and Measures

The metric system is in force.

Statistical Survey

Note: Unless otherwise indicated, figures in this Statistical Survey exclude data for Mayotte.

AREA AND POPULATION

Area: 1,862 sq km (719 sq miles). *By Island*: Ngazidja (Grande-Comore) 1,146 sq km, Nzwani (Anjouan) 424 sq km, Mwali (Mohéli) 290 sq km.

Population: 335,150 (males 167,089, females 168,061), excluding Mayotte (estimated population 50,740), at census of 15 September 1980; 446,817 (males 221,152, females 225,665), excluding Mayotte, at census of 15 September 1991; 527,900 in 1998. *Mid-2003* (UN estimate): 768,000 (males 386,000, females 382,000) (Source: UN, *World Population Prospects: The 2002 Revision*). *By Island* (1991 census): Ngazidja (Grande-Comore) 233,533, Nzwani (Anjouan) 188,953, Mwali (Mohéli) 24,331.

Density (per sq km, mid-2003): 412.5.

Principal Towns (population estimates, 2003): Moroni (capital) 53,420 (official estimate); Mutsamudu 30,900; Mitsamiouli 21,400; Domoni 19,100; Fomboni 13,300. Source: mostly Stefan Helders, *World Gazetteer* (internet www.world-gazetteer.com).

Births and Deaths (including figures for Mayotte, UN estimates, 1995–2000): Average annual birth rate 38.6 per 1,000; average annual death rate 9.4 per 1,000. Source: UN, *World Population Prospects: The 2002 Revision*.

Expectation of Life (WHO estimates, years at birth, including Mayotte): 63.3 (males 61.6; females 64.9) in 2002. Source: WHO, *World Health Report*.

Economically Active Population (ILO estimates, '000 persons at mid-1980, including figures for Mayotte): Agriculture, forestry and fishing 150; Industry 10; Services 20; Total 181 (males 104, females 77) (Source: ILO, *Economically Active Population Estimates and Projections, 1950–2025*). *1991 Census* (persons aged 12 years and over, excluding Mayotte): Total labour force 126,510 (males 88,034, females 38,476) (Source: UN, *Demographic Yearbook*). *Mid-2003* (estimates in '000): Agriculture, etc. 263; Total labour force 364 (Source: FAO).

HEALTH AND WELFARE

Key Indicators

Total Fertility Rate (children per woman, 2002): 4.9.

Under-5 Mortality Rate (per 1,000 live births, 2003): 73.

HIV/AIDS (% of persons aged 15–49, 1999): 0.12.

Physicians (per 1,000 head, 1997): 0.01.

Hospital Beds (per 1,000 head, 1990): 2.76.

Health Expenditure (2001): US $ per head (PPP): 29.

Health Expenditure (2001): % of GDP: 3.1.

Health Expenditure (2001): public (% of total): 60.0.

Access to Water (% of persons, 2002): 94.

Access to Sanitation (% of persons, 2002): 23.

Human Development Index (2002): ranking: 136.

Human Development Index (2002): value: 0.530.

For sources and definitions, see explanatory note on p. vi.

AGRICULTURE, ETC.

Principal Crops (FAO estimates, '000 metric tons, unless otherwise indicated, 2003): Rice (paddy) 17.0; Maize 4.0; Potatoes 0.5; Sweet potatoes 5.5; Cassava (Manioc) 55.0; Taro 9.0; Yams 3.8; Pulses 14.3; Groundnuts (in shell) 0.9; Coconuts 77.0; Oil crops 10.3; Tomatoes 0.5; Other vegetables 3.0; Bananas 60.0; Other fruits 3.5; Vanilla (dried, metric tons) 110; Cloves 3.0 (official figure); Ylang ylang 45. Source: FAO.

Livestock (FAO estimates, '000 head, year ending September 2003): Asses 5.0; Cattle 45.0; Sheep 21.0; Goats 115.0; Chickens 510. Source: FAO.

Livestock Products (FAO estimates, metric tons, 2003): Beef and veal 1,320; Sheep and goat meat 435; Chicken meat 560; Cow milk 4,550; Hen eggs 776. Source: FAO.

Fishing (FAO estimates, '000 metric tons, live weight, 2001): Total catch 12.2 (Carangids 0.5; Sardinellas 0.8; Anchovies, etc. 0.2; Skipjack tuna 2.0; Yellowfin tuna 5.2). *2002:* Figures assumed to be unchanged from 2001 (FAO estimates). Source: FAO.

INDUSTRY

Electric Energy (million kWh): 35.2 in 2000; 36.6 in 2001; 32.5 in 2002. Source: mainly Banque Centrale des Comores, *Rapport Annuel.*

FINANCE

Currency and Exchange Rates: 100 centimes = 1 Comoros franc. *Sterling, Dollar and Euro Equivalents* (31 December 2004): £1 sterling = 697.589 Comoros francs; US $1 = 361.183 Comoros francs; €1 = 491.968 Comoros francs; 1,000 Comoros francs = £1.434 = $2.769 = €2.033. *Average Exchange Rate* (Comoros francs per US $): 522.741 in 2002; 435.900 in 2003; 396.214 in 2004. Note: The Comoros franc was introduced in 1981, replacing (at par) the CFA franc. The fixed link to French currency was retained, with the exchange rate set at 1 French franc = 50 Comoros francs. This remained in effect until January 1994, when the Comoros franc was devalued by 33.3%, with the exchange rate adjusted to 1 French franc = 75 Comoros francs. This relationship to French currency remained in effect with the introduction of the euro on 1 January 1999. From that date, accordingly, a fixed exchange rate of €1 = 491.968 Comoros francs has been in operation.

Budget (estimates, million Comoros francs, 2003): *Revenue:* Tax revenue 19,622; Other revenue 2,713; Total 22,335, excluding grants received (3,147). *Expenditure:* Budgetary current expenditure 22,769 (Wages and salaries 11,493; Goods and services 5,297; Transfers 2,041; Interest payments 1,431; Current expenditure under technical assistance programmes 2,507); Budgetary capital expenditure 7,578; (Capital expenditure financed with external resources 4,793); Total (incl. others) 31,161. Source: La Zone Franc, *Rapport Annuel 2003.*

International Reserves (US $ million at 31 December 2003): Gold 0.24; IMF special drawing rights 0.01; Reserve position in IMF 0.81; Foreign exchange 93.48; Total 94.54. Source: IMF, *International Financial Statistics.*

Money Supply (million Comoros francs at 31 December 2003): Currency outside deposit money banks 11,505; Demand deposits at deposit money banks 11,075; Total money (incl. others) 24,793. Source: IMF, *International Financial Statistics.*

Cost of Living (Consumer Price Index; base: 1999= 100): All items 104.6 in 2000; 112.1 in 2001; 115.8 in 2002. Source: IMF, *Comoros: Selected Issues and Statistical Appendix* (August 2004).

Expenditure on the Gross Domestic Product (million Comoros francs at current prices, 2002): Government final consumption expenditure 20,538; Private final consumption expenditure 110,195; Gross fixed capital formation 13,300; Increase in stocks 2,500; *Total domestic expenditure* 146,533; Exports of goods and services 21,983; *Less* Imports of goods and services 39,536; *GDP in purchasers' values* 128,980. Source: IMF, *Comoros: Selected Issues and Statistical Appendix* (August 2004).

Gross Domestic Product by Economic Activity (million Comoros francs at current prices, 2002): Agriculture, hunting, forestry and fishing 53,000; Manufacturing 5,400; Electricity, gas and water 2,000; Construction and public works 7,837; Trade, restaurants and hotels 33,000; Transport and communications 6,652; Finance, insurance, real estate and business services 5,800; Government services 17,949; Other services 692; *Sub-total 132,330; Less* Imputed bank service charge 3,350; *GDP in purchasers' values* 128,980. Source: IMF, *Comoros: Selected Issues and Statistical Appendix* (August 2004).

Balance of Payments (million Comoros francs, 2002): Exports of goods f.o.b. 11,662; Imports of goods f.o.b. –25,582; *Trade balance* –13,920; Services (net) –3,646; *Balance on goods and services* – 17,566; Private transfers (net) 11,098; Current transfers (net) 5,408; *Current balance* –1,059; Net capital account (incl. errors and omissions) 4,335; *Overall balance* 3,276. Source: IMF, *Comoros: Selected Issues and Statistical Appendix* (August 2004).

EXTERNAL TRADE

Principal Commodities (provisional, million Comoros francs, 2003): *Imports c.i.f.:* Meat and fish 2,807; Rice 2,866; Petroleum products 5,949; Cement 1,563; Iron and steel 1,172; Vehicles and parts 3,790; Total (incl. others) 30,311. *Exports f.o.b.:* Vanilla 9,130; Cloves 1,563; Ylang ylang 664; Total (incl. others) 11,695. Source: La Zone Franc, *Rapport Annuel 2003.*

Principal Trading Partners (US $ million, 2000): *Imports:* Belgium 1.3; France-Monaco 14.0; Indonesia 1.5; Kenya 3.9; Pakistan 4.9; South Africa 39.0; United Arab Emirates 1.9; Total (incl. others) 71.9. *Exports:* Canada 0.3; France-Monaco 3.0; Germany 0.5; Israel 0.2; Singapore 1.1; United Kingdom 0.6; USA 1.1; Total (incl. others) 6.9. Source: UN, *International Trade Statistics Yearbook.*

TRANSPORT

Road Traffic (estimates, motor vehicles in use, 1996): Passenger cars 9,100; Lorries and vans 4,950. Source: International Road Federation, *World Road Statistics.*

Shipping: *Merchant Fleet* (registered at 31 December 2003): Number of vessels 105; Total displacement (grt) 416,739 (Source: Lloyd's Register-Fairplay, *World Fleet Statistics). International Seaborne Freight Traffic* (estimates, '000 metric tons, 1991): Goods loaded 12; Goods unloaded 107 (Source: UN Economic Commission for Africa, *African Statistical Yearbook).*

Civil Aviation (traffic on scheduled services, 1996): Passengers carried ('000) 27; Passenger-km (million) 3. Source: UN, *Statistical Yearbook.*

TOURISM

Tourist Arrivals (2002): France 9,076; Reunion 2,164; South Africa 1,247; Total (incl. others) 18,936. Source: World Tourism Organization, *Yearbook of Tourism Statistics* .

Receipts from Tourism (US $ million): 16 in 1998; 19 in 1999; 15 in 2000. Source: World Tourism Organization.

COMMUNICATIONS MEDIA

Radio Receivers (1997): 90,000 in use. Source: UNESCO, *Statistical Yearbook.*

Television Receivers (1997): 1,000 in use. Source: UNESCO, *Statistical Yearbook.*

Telephones (2003): 13,200 main lines in use. Source: International Telecommunication Union.

Mobile Cellular Telephones (2003): 2,000. Source: International Telecommunication Union.

Facsimile Machines (1998): 173 in use. Source: UN, *Statistical Yearbook.*

Personal Computers (2003): 5,000 in use. Source: International Telecommunication Union.

Internet Users (2003): 5,000. Source: International Telecommunication Union.

EDUCATION

Primary: 348 schools (1998); 2,381 teachers (1998); 94,405 pupils (2002). Sources: UNESCO Institute for Statistics and IMF, *Comoros: Selected Issues and Statistical Appendix* (August 2004).

Secondary: Teachers: general education 591 (1995/96, public education only); teacher training 11 (1991/92); vocational 31 (1986/87). Pupils: 35,193 (2002). Sources: UNESCO Institute for Statistics and IMF, *Comoros: Selected Issues and Statistical Appendix* (August 2004).

Vocational (1998/9): Pupils 232. Source: IMF, *Comoros: Selected Issues and Statistical Appendix* (August 2004).

Higher (1998/9): 67 teachers; 649 pupils. Sources: UNESCO Institute for Statistics and IMF, *Comoros: Selected Issues and Statistical Appendix* (August 2004).

Adult Literacy Rate: 56.2% (males 63.5%; females 49.1%) in 2002. Source: UN Development Programme, *Human Development Report.*

Directory

The Constitution

In accordance with an agreement on national reconciliation, signed on 17 February 2001 by representatives of the Government, the separatist administration on Nzwani, opposition parties and civil society, a new Constitution was presented in August and approved by referendum on 23 December. Under the terms of the new Constitution, the country was renamed the Union of the Comoros, and each of the three islands, Ngazidja, Nzwani and Mwali, were to be granted partial autonomy and were to be headed by a local government. The Union, governed by a central government, was to be headed by the President. The main provisions of the Constitution are summarized below.

PREAMBLE

The preamble affirms the will of the Comoran people to derive from the state religion, Islam, inspiration for the principles and laws that the State and its institutions govern; to guarantee the pursuit of a common future; to establish new institutions based on the rule of law, democracy and good governance, which guarantee an equal division of power between the Union and those islands that compose it; to adhere to the principles laid down by the Charters of the UN, the Organization of African Unity (now the African Union) and the Organization of the Islamic Conference and by the Treaty of the League of Arab States; and to guarantee the rights of all citizens, without discrimination, in accordance with the UN Declaration of Human Rights and the African Charter of Human Rights.

The preamble guarantees solidarity between the Union and the islands, as well as between the islands themselves; equality amongst the islands and their inhabitants, regardless of race, origin, or religion; the right to freedom of expression, education, health and justice; the freedom and security of individuals; the inviolability of an individual's home or property; and the right of children to be protected against abandonment, exploitation and violence.

THE UNION OF THE COMOROS

The Comoros archipelago constitutes a republic. Sovereignty belongs to the people, and is exercised through their elected representatives or by the process of referendum. There is universal secret suffrage, which can be direct or indirect, for all citizens who are over the age of 18 and in full possession of their civil and political rights. Political parties and groups operate freely, respecting national sovereignty, democracy and territorial integrity.

COMPETENCIES OF THE UNION AND THE ISLANDS

Each island freely administers its own affairs, while respecting the unity of the Union and its territorial integrity. Each island establishes its own fundamental laws, which must respect the Constitution. All Comorans within the Union have equal rights, freedoms and duties. All the islands are headed by an elected executive and assembly. The Union has ultimate authority over the individual islands and legislates on matters of religion, nationality, currency, foreign affairs, external defence and national identity. As regards those competencies shared by both the Union and the islands, the Union has ultimate jurisdiction only if the issue concerned affects more than one island, if the matter cannot be resolved by one island alone, or if the judicial, economic or social integrity of the Union may be compromised. The islands are responsible for those matters not covered by the Union, or by shared responsibility. The islands are financially autonomous.

THE UNION'S INSTITUTIONS

Executive Power

The President of the Union is the symbol of national unity. He is the guarantor of national independence, the unity of the Republic, the autonomy of the islands, territorial integrity and adherence to international agreements. He is the Head of State and is responsible for external defence and security, foreign affairs and negotiating and ratifying treaties.

The Council of the Union is composed of the President and two Vice-Presidents, selected from each island. The members of the Council are elected for a four-year term, and the position of President rotates between the islands, while the Vice-Presidents are inhabitants of the two remaining islands. The President appoints the members of the Government (ministers of the Union) and determines their respective portfolios. The composition of the Government must represent all of the islands equally.

Legislative Power

Legislative power is vested in the Assemblée de l'Union, which is composed of 33 deputies, elected for a period of five years. Fifteen of the deputies are selected by the islands' local assemblies (five deputies per island) and 18 are directly elected by universal suffrage. The Assemblée de l'Union sits for two sessions each year and, if necessary, for extraordinary sessions.

Judicial Power

Judicial power is independent of executive and legislative power. The President of the Union is the guarantor of the independence of the judicial system and is assisted by the Higher Council of the Magistracy (Conseil Supérieur de la Magistrature). The Supreme Court (Cour Suprême) is the highest ruling authority in judicial, administrative and fiscal matters, and its rulings are final and binding. A Constitutional Court (Cour Constitutionelle) was created in 2004.

THE HIGH COUNCIL

The High Council considers constitutional matters, oversees the results of elections and referendums and guarantees basic human rights and civil liberties. Moreover, the High Council is responsible for ruling on any conflicts regarding the separate competencies of the Union and the islands. The President of the Union, the Vice-Presidents, the President of the Assemblée de l'Union, and each President of the local island executives appoint one member to the High Council. Members are elected for a six-year mandate, renewable once; the President of the High Council is appointed by the members for a six-year term.

REVISION OF THE CONSTITUTION

The power to initiate constitutional revision is jointly vested in the President of the Union and the members of the Assemblée de l'Union. Constitutional revision must be approved by a majority of two-thirds of the deputies in the Assemblée de l'Union and by two-thirds of the members of the islands' local assemblies. However, the organizational structure of the Union cannot be revised, and any revision that may affect the unity and territorial boundaries of the Union is not permitted.

PROVISIONAL ARRANGEMENTS

The Union's institutions, as defined in the Constitution, are to be established in accordance with the terms laid out in the agreement on national reconciliation of 17 February 2001. Institutions on the island of Mayotte will be established within a maximum period of six months following the island's decision to rejoin the Union of the Comoros.

The Government

HEAD OF STATE

Federal President: Col Assoumani Azali (elected 14 April 2002).

REGIONAL PRESIDENTS

Mwali: Mohamed Saïd Fazul.
Ngazidja: Abdou Soule Elbak.
Nzwani: Maj. Mohamed Bacar.

GOVERNMENT OF THE UNION OF THE COMOROS
(March 2005)

The Government is a coalition of the CRC, CHUMA and representatives of the island Presidents. The President of Ngazidja, however, refused to participate in the coalition Government. Each island also has its own administration.

Vice-President, with responsibility for Solidarity, Health, the Population, Social Welfare and State Reform, and Co-ordinator of Union Administrative Services on Nzwani: Mohamed Caabi El Yachroutu (CRC).

Vice-President, with responsibility for Islamic Affairs, Human Rights, and Co-ordinator of Union Administrative Services on Mwali: Rachid Ben Massoundi (CRC).

Minister of State, Minister of Finance and the Budget: Abdoul Bastoi Ahamadi (Nzwani).

Minister of State, Minister of the Economy, Foreign Trade and Industrial Promotion: CHARIF MAOULANA (CRC).

Minister of State, Minister of External Defence, Territorial Security, Strategic Infrastructure and Communications, Relations with the Assemblies, and Government Spokesman: MSAIDIE HOUMEDI (CRC).

Minister of State, Minister of Foreign Affairs, Co-operation, with responsibility for Comorans Abroad: MOHAMED EL AMINE SOEUF (CRC).

Minister of State, Minister of Rural Development, Fisheries, Crafts, Privatization and the Environment: ABDOULHAMID MOHAMED (CHUMA).

Minister of State, Minister of Planning and Territorial Development: HAMZA SAÏD (Mwali).

Minister of State, Minister of National Education, Higher Education and Research: MOHAMED ELYAS YAHAYA (CRC).

Secretary of State for Co-operation: ABDOU MOUSTADRANE (CRC).

Secretary of State for Territorial Security and Communication: MARI ABDOU MARI (Mwali).

MINISTRIES

Office of the Head of State: BP 521, Moroni; tel. (74) 4808; fax (74) 4829; internet www.presidence-uniondescomores.com/v3/fr.

Ministry of the Economy, Foreign Trade and Industrial Promotion: Moroni; tel. (73) 0951; fax (73) 1981.

Ministry of External Defence, Territorial Security, Strategic Infrastructure and Communications and Relations with the Assemblies: Moroni; tel. (74) 4862.

Ministry of Finance and the Budget: BP 324, Moroni; tel. (74) 4161; fax (74) 4140.

Ministry of Foreign Affairs, Co-operation and Comorans abroad: BP 428, Moroni; tel. (74) 4100; fax (74) 4111.

Ministry of Human Rights and Islamic Affairs: Moroni; tel. (74) 4200.

Ministry of National Education, Higher Education and Research: Moroni.

Ministry of Planning and Territorial Development: Moroni.

Ministry of Rural Development, Fisheries, Crafts, Privatization and the Environment: Moroni.

Ministry of Solidarity, Health, the Population, Social Welfare and State Reform: Moroni.

President and Legislature

PRESIDENT

Presidential Election, First ballot, 17 March 2002

Candidate	% of votes
Col Assoumani Azali	39.8
Mahamoud Mradabi	15.7
Saïd Ali Kemal	10.7
Mtara Maécha	7.9
Abbas Djoussouf	7.8
Youssouf Saïd	6.1
Abdallah Halifa	4.5
Ali Mroudjaé	4.2
Moustoifa S. Cheick	3.4
Total	**100.0**

At the second ballot, held on 14 April 2002, Col ASSOUMANI AZALI was elected unopposed as Federal President of the Union of the Comoros after the withdrawal of his two qualifying opponents. Regional Presidents were elected on Mwali, Ngazidja and Nzwani in March–May 2002.

ASSEMBLÉE DE L'UNION

Assemblée de l'Union: BP 447, Moroni; tel. (74) 4000; fax (74) 4011.

President: SAID DHIUFFUR BOUNOU.

Elections, 18 and 25 April 2004

Party	Seats
Coalition supporting the three regional Presidents .	11
Convention pour le renouveau des Comores (CRC) .	6
CHUMA	1
Total	**33***

* The remaining 15 seats were filled by nominees from the islands' local assemblies, members of which had been elected on 14 and 21 March 2004.

Political Organizations

CHUMA (Islands' Fraternity and Unity Party): Moroni; e-mail chuma@pourlescomores.com; f. 1985; Leader SAÏD ALI KEMAL.

Convention pour le renouveau des Comores (CRC): presidential party; f. 2002; Leader Col ASSOUMANI AZALI; Sec.-Gen. ABDOU SOEFOU.

Djawabu: Leader YOUSSOUF SAÏD SOILIHI.

Forces pour l'action républicaine (FAR): Leader Col ABDOURAZAK ABDULHAMID.

Front de la action pour la democratie et le développment (FADD): Nzwani; main opposition party on Nzwani.

Front démocratique (FD): BP 758, Moroni; tel. (73) 3603; e-mail idriss@snpt.km; f. 1982; Chair. MOUSTOIFA SAÏD CHEIKH; Sec.-Gen. ABDALLAH HALIFA.

Front national pour la justice (FNJ): Islamic fundamentalist orientation; Leader AHMED RACHID.

Mouvement des citoyens pour la République (MCR): f. 1998; Leader MAHAMOUD MRADABI.

Mouvement populaire anjouanais (MPA): f. 1997 by merger of Organisation pour l'indépendance d'Anjouan and Mouvement séparatiste anjouanais; principal separatist movement on Nzwani (Anjouan).

Mouvement pour la démocratie et le progrès (MDP—NGDC): Moroni; founder-mem. of the FRN (see above), from which it withdrew in May 1999; Leader ABBAS DJOUSSOUF.

Mouvement pour le socialisme et la démocratie (MSD): Moroni; f. 2000 by splinter group of the FD; Leader ABDOU SOEFOU.

Parti comorien pour la démocratie et le progrès (PCDP): Route Djivani, BP 179, Moroni; tel. (73) 1733; fax (73) 0650; Leader ABDOU SOULE ELBAK.

Parti républicain des Comores (PRC): BP 665, Moroni; tel. (73) 3489; fax (73) 3329; e-mail prc@online.fr; internet www.chez.com/prc; f. 1998; Leader MOHAMED SAÏD ABDALLAH M'CHANGAMA.

Parti socialiste des Comores (Pasoco): tel. (73) 1328; Leader AHMED AFFANDI ALI.

Rassemblement pour une initiative de développement avec une jeunesse avertie (RIDJA): BP 1905, Moroni; tel. and fax (73) 3356; f. 1999; opposed to President Azali and the CRC in 2004 elections; Leader SAÏD LARIFOU; Sec.-Gen. AHAMED ACHIRAFI.

Rassemblement national pour le développement (RND): f. 1996; Chair. OMAR TAMOU; Sec. Gen. ABDOULHAMID AFFRAITANE.

Shawiri: Moroni; Leader Col MAHAMOUD MRADABI.

Shawiri—Unafasiya (SU): Moroni; f. 2003 following a split in Shawiri; Sec.-Gen. HADJI BEN SAÏD.

Union national pour la démocratie aux Comores (UNDC): Moroni; f. 1996; Pres. KAMAR EZZAMANE MOHAMED.

There are also a number of Islamist groups.

Diplomatic Representation

EMBASSIES IN THE COMOROS

China, People's Republic: Coulée de Lave, C109, BP 442, Moroni; tel. (73) 2521; fax (73) 2866; e-mail ambassadechine@snpt.km; Ambassador ZHAO CHUNSHENG.

France: blvd de Strasbourg, BP 465, Moroni; tel. (73) 0615; fax (73) 0922; e-mail pierre.lanners@snpt.km; Ambassador JEAN-PIERRE LAJAUNIE.

Libya: BP 1787, Moroni; tel. (73) 2819; Ambassador MUSSBAH AL-MOUNTASER KARIM FARFAR.

Judicial System

Under the terms of the Constitution, the President is the guarantor of the independence of the judicial system, and is assisted by the Higher Council of the Magistracy (Conseil Supérieur de la Magistrature). The highest ruling authority in judicial, administrative and fiscal matters is the Supreme Court (Cour Suprême). The High Council considers constitutional matters. A Constitutional Court (Cour Constitutionelle), comprising seven members, appointed by the President of the Union of the Comoros, the two Vice-Presidents and the three regional Presidents, was established in 2004. Abdallah Ahmed Sourette was elected President of the Constitutional Court in October of that year.

Constitutional Court: Moroni; Pres. ABDALLAH AHMED SOURETTE.

Religion

The majority of the population are Muslims, mostly Sunni. At 31 December 2002 there were an estimated 2,075 adherents of the Roman Catholic Church, equivalent to 0.3% of the total population.

CHRISTIANITY

The Roman Catholic Church

Office of Apostolic Administrator of the Comoros: Mission Catholique, BP 46, Moroni; tel. (73) 0570; fax (73) 0503; e-mail mcatholique@snpt.km; Apostolic Pro-Admin. JAN SZPILKA.

ISLAM

Organisation Islamique des Comores: BP 596, Coulée, Moroni; tel. (73) 2071.

The Press

Al Watwan: Nagoudjou, BP 984, Moroni-Coulée; tel. and fax (74) 4047; e-mail alwatwan@snpt.km; internet www.comores-online .com/al-watwan; f. 1985; weekly; state-owned; Dir-Gen. AMAD MDAHOMA; Editor-in-Chief AHMED ALIAMIR; circ. 1,500.

Comores Aujourd'hui: Moroni; pro-President Azali; Dir HAMADA MADI.

La Gazette des Comores: BP 2216, Moroni; tel. (73) 5234; e-mail la_gazette@snpt.km; internet site.voila.fr/la_gazette; weekly; Publication Dir ALLAOUI SAÏD OMAR.

Le Matin des Comores: BP 1040, Moroni; tel. (73) 2995; fax (73) 2939; e-mail contact@agendadescomores.com; internet www .lematindescomores.com; daily; Dir ALILOIAFA MOHAMED SAÏD.

There is also an online newspaper, *Conscience Comorienne* (www.conscience-comorienne.org)

NEWS AGENCY

Agence Comores Presse (ACP): Moroni.

Publisher

KomÉdit: BP 535, Moroni; general.

Broadcasting and Communications

TELECOMMUNICATIONS

Comtel: BP 5000, Moroni; tel. (74) 4300; fax (73) 1079; e-mail snpt@ snpt.km; internet www.snpt.km; formerly Société Nationale des Postes et des Télécommunications; post and telecommunications operations separated in 2004; undergoing privatization in 2005; there were further plans to divide the mobile telecommunications and fixed line branches of Comtel; Administrator DJAMALIDINE MOISSULI.

BROADCASTING

Transmissions to the Comoros from Radio France Internationale commenced in early 1994. A number of privately owned radio and TV stations also broadcast in the Comoros. In 2004 a Comoran TV station was being established with funds from the People's Republic of China.

Office de la radio télévision des Comores (ORTC): Moroni; Comoran state broadcasting company; CEO HAMADA MADI.

Radio

Radio-Comoro: BP 250, Moroni; tel. (73) 2531; fax (73) 0303; govt-controlled; domestic programmes in Comoran and French; international broadcasts in Swahili, Arabic and French; Dir-Gen. ISMAIL IBOUROI; Tech. Dir ABDULLAH RADJAB.

Radio Dzialandzé Mutsamudu (RDM): Mutsamudu, Nzwani; f. 1992; broadcasts on Nzwani; Co-ordinator SAÏD ALI DACAR MGAZI.

Radio KAZ: Mkazi, BP 1933; tel. (73) 5201.

Radio Ngazidja: Moroni; broadcasts on Ngazidja; Man. ABDOU DJIBABA.

Television

Djabal TV: Iconi, BP 675, Moroni; tel. (73) 6767.

Mtsangani Television (MTV): Mtsangani, BP 845, Moroni; tel. (73) 3316.

TV—SHA: Shashagnogo; tel. (73) 3636.

Finance

BANKING

(cap. = capital; res = reserves; dep. = deposits; m. = million; brs = branches; amounts in Comoros francs)

Central Bank

Banque Centrale des Comores: place de France, BP 405, Moroni; tel. (73) 1002; fax (73) 0349; e-mail bancecom@snpt.km; f. 1981; bank of issue; cap. 1,100m., res 7,260m., dep. 5,640m. (Dec. 1999); Gov. IBRAHIM BEN ALI; Pres. SALIM AHMED ADBALLAH.

Commercial Bank

Banque pour l'Industrie et le Commerce—Comores (BIC): place de France, BP 175, Moroni; tel. (73) 0243; fax (73) 1229; e-mail bic@snpt.km; f. 1990; 51% owned by BNP Paribas Participations (France); 34% state-owned; cap. 300m., res 1,737m., dep. 19,311m. (Dec. 2003); Pres. ABDOUL AZIZ MOHAMED YOUSSOUF; Dir-Gen. CHRISTIAN GOUT; 6 brs.

There are a number of offshore financial institutions based in the Comoros.

Development Bank

Banque de Développement des Comores: place de France, BP 298, Moroni; tel. (73) 0154; fax (73) 0397; e-mail bdc.moroni@snpt .km; f. 1982; provides loans, guarantees and equity participation for small- and medium-scale projects; 50% state-owned; cap. and res 1,242.0m., total assets 3,470.5m. (Dec. 2002); Pres. MZE CHEI OUBEIDI; Gen. Man. SAÏD ABDILLAHI.

Trade and Industry

GOVERNMENT AGENCIES

Office National du Commerce: Moroni; state-operated agency for the promotion and development of domestic and external trade.

Office National d'Importation et de Commercialisation du Riz (ONICOR): BP 748, Itsambouni, Moroni; tel. (73) 5566; fax (73) 0144; e-mail onicor_moroni@snpt.km.

Société de Développement de la Pêche Artisanale des Comores (SODEPAC): Moroni; state-operated agency overseeing fisheries development programme.

DEVELOPMENT ORGANIZATION

Centre Fédéral d'Appui au Développement Rural (CEFADER): Moroni; rural development org. with branches on each island.

CHAMBERS OF COMMERCE

Union des Chambres de Commerce des Comores: BP 763, Moroni; tel. (73) 0958; fax (73) 1983; privatized in 1995; Pres. MOINSALIMA MAHAMOUD SOIDIKI.

TRADE ASSOCIATION

Organisation Comorienne de la Vanille (OCOVA): BP 472, Moroni; tel. (73) 2709; fax (73) 2719.

EMPLOYERS' ORGANIZATIONS

Club d'Actions des Promoteurs Economiques: Moroni; f. 1999; Head SAÏD HASSANE DINI.

Organisation du Patronat Comorien (OPACO): Pres. SAÏD HASSANE NOURDINE.

UTILITIES

MA-MWE—Gestion de l'Eau et de l'Electricité aux Comores: BP 1762, Moroni; tel. (73) 3130; fax (73) 2359; e-mail cee@snpt.km; f. as Electricité et Eau des Comores; transferred to private management and renamed Comorienne de l'Eau et de l'Electricité in 1997; renationalized and renamed Service Public de l'Eau et de l'Electricité in 2001; reprivatized in Jan. 2002 and renamed as above; responsible for the production and distribution of electricity and water; Dir-Gen. ALLOUI SAÏD ABASSE.

Société d'Electricité d'Anjouan (EDA): Nzwani; Technical Dir YOUSSOUF ALI OICHEH.

STATE-OWNED ENTERPRISE

Comores Hydrocarbures : BP 3840, Moroni; tel. (73) 0490; fax (73) 1818; imports petroleum products; transfer to private management pending; Man. Dir ABDOU SOEFOU.

TRADE UNION

Union des Syndicats Autonomes des Travailleurs des Comores: BP 1199, Moroni; tel. and fax (73) 5143; f. 1996; Sec.-Gen. IBOUROI ALI TABIBOU.

Transport

ROADS

In 1999 there were an estimated 880 km of classified roads. About 76.5% of the network was paved in that year.

SHIPPING

The port of Mutsamudu, on Ngazidja, can accommodate vessels of up to 11 m draught. Goods from Europe are routed via Madagascar, and coastal vessels connect the Comoros with the east coast of Africa. The country's registered merchant fleet at 31 December 2003 numbered 105 vessels, totalling 416,739 grt. Mayotte suspended ferry services to the other islands in the archipelago in late 2004 due to safety issues.

Société Comorienne de Navigation: Moroni; services to Madagascar.

CIVIL AVIATION

The international airport is at Moroni-Hahaya on Nzwani. Work began on the upgrading of the airport in late 2004. Each of the other islands has a small airfield. At the end of 1995 it was announced that Air Comores, the national airline, was to be liquidated. In October 1999 Yemen Airways (Yemenia), following negotiations with the Comoran Government, was granted the status of the national airline of the Comoros and the use of the Comoran air traffic rights between Moroni and Paris, France. In 2004 Air Bourbon (Réunion) planned to launch a national carrier, Air Comores International, however, it was declared bankrupt in November of that year. At late 2004 international services were operated by Air Austral (Réunion), Air Mayotte, Air Tanzania, Sudan Airways, Precision Air (Tanzania) and Yemenia, while Ocean Airlines, based in Moroni, also offered regular international services in association with Emirates.

Comores Air Services: Moroni; tel. (73) 3366; internal services and international flights to Madagascar.

Comores Aviation: Moroni; tel. (73) 3400; f. 1999; twice-weekly charter flights between Moroni and Mayotte; Dir JEAN-MARC HEINTZ.

Ocean Airlines: route de la Cornice, BP 2556, Moroni; tel. (73) 1916; fax (73) 1917; e-mail infotz@fastair.org; internet www.fastair.org/ocean; f. 2002; internal flights and international services to Tanzania; Dir CHARLES NGARAMBE.

Tourism

The principal tourist attractions are the beaches, underwater fishing and mountain scenery. In 2000 hotel capacity amounted to an estimated 820 beds. Receipts from tourism totalled US $26m. in 1997, but decreased to $16m. in 1998, before recovering very slightly to $17m. in 1999. Tourist arrivals increased to 27,474 in 1998, but had decreased to 18,936 in 2002, mainly as a result of the unstable political situation. In late 2004 the ferry service to Mayotte was suspended, disrupting the tourism sector as many tourists travel via Mayotte.

Société Comorienne de Tourisme et d'Hôtellerie (COMOTEL): Itsandra Hotel, BP 1027, Moroni; tel. (73) 2365; national tourist agency; Dir-Gen. SITTI ATTOMANE.

THE DEMOCRATIC REPUBLIC OF THE CONGO

Introductory Survey

Location, Climate, Language, Religion, Flag, Capital

The Democratic Republic of the Congo (formerly Zaire) lies in central Africa, bordered by the Republic of the Congo to the north-west, by the Central African Republic and Sudan to the north, by Uganda, Rwanda, Burundi and Tanzania to the east and by Zambia and Angola to the south. There is a short coastline at the outlet of the River Congo. The climate is tropical, with an average temperature of 27°C (80°F) and an annual rainfall of 150 cm–200 cm (59 ins–97 ins). French is the official language. More than 400 Sudanese and Bantu dialects are spoken; Kiswahili, Kiluba, Kikongo and Lingala being the most widespread. An estimated 50% of the population is Roman Catholic, and there is a smaller Protestant community. Many inhabitants follow traditional (mostly animist) beliefs. The national flag (proportions 2 by 3) is blue, with a large central yellow star and six smaller yellow stars arranged vertically at the hoist. The capital is Kinshasa.

Recent History

The Democratic Republic of the Congo, formerly the Belgian Congo, became independent from Belgium as the Republic of the Congo on 30 June 1960. Five days later the armed forces mutinied, and the UN subsequently dispatched troops to the region to maintain order. In September the Head of State, Joseph Kasavubu, dismissed the Prime Minister, Patrice Lumumba. Later in that month control of government was assumed temporarily by Col (subsequently Marshal) Joseph-Désiré Mobutu. Mobutu returned power to President Kasavubu in February 1961. A few days later Lumumba was murdered. In August a new Government was formed, with Cyrille Adoula as Prime Minister. In July 1964 Kasavubu appointed Moïse Tshombe, the former leader of a group supporting the secession of the Katangan region, as interim Prime Minister, pending elections, and in August the country was renamed the Democratic Republic of the Congo. Following elections in March and April 1965, a power struggle developed between Tshombe and Kasavubu; in November Mobutu intervened, seizing power and proclaiming himself head of the 'Second Republic'. In late 1970 Mobutu, as sole candidate, was elected President. (From January 1972, as part of a national policy of 'authenticity', he became known as Mobutu Sese Seko.) In November 1970 elections to a new National Assembly (subsequently renamed the National Legislative Council, NLC) took place. In October 1971 the Democratic Republic of the Congo was renamed the Republic of Zaire, and one year later the Government of Zaire and the Executive Committee of the Mouvement populaire de la révolution (MPR), the sole legal political party, merged into the National Executive Council (NEC).

In March 1977, and again in May 1978, Katangan separatists invaded Zaire from Angola, taking much of Shaba (formerly Katanga) region; however, the separatists were repulsed on both occasions by the Zairean army, with armed support from a number of Western Governments. The invasion of 1977 prompted Mobutu to introduce a number of political reforms. Legislative elections took place in October, and, at a presidential election in December, Mobutu (again the sole candidate) was re-elected for a further seven-year term. In August 1980 he assumed the new post of Chairman of the MPR. In early 1982 opponents of Zaire's one-party system of government formed the Union pour la démocratie et le progrès social (UDPS). This was followed by the formation of the Front congolais pour le rétablissement de la démocratie (FCD), a coalition of opposition parties, led by Nguza Karl-I-Bond, the First State Commissioner (Prime Minister) from August 1980 until April 1981. Léon Kengo Wa Dondo was appointed First State Commissioner in a ministerial reshuffle in November 1982. Mobutu was re-elected President in July 1984. Elections to the NLC were held in September 1987. In November 1988 Mobutu replaced about one-third of the members of the NEC and reappointed Kengo Wa Dondo to the post of First State Commissioner, from which he had been removed in October 1986.

In April 1990 Mobutu announced that a plural political system, initially to comprise three parties, would be introduced after a transitional period of one year; the UDPS was immediately granted legal status. At the same time Mobutu declared the inauguration of the 'Third Republic' and relinquished the posts of Chairman of the MPR and State Commissioner for National Defence in the NEC, although remaining Head of State. N'Singa Udjuu Ongwakebi Untube, who had been First State Commissioner in 1981–82, was subsequently appointed the new Chairman of the MPR. The NEC was dissolved and Kengo Wa Dondo was replaced as First State Commissioner by Prof. Lunda Bululu, previously an adviser to Mobutu. In May 1990 a new, smaller, transitional NEC was formed, and Mobutu announced the imminent 'depoliticization' of the security forces and of the administration in general. In June Mobutu relinquished presidential control of the NEC and of foreign policy, and authorized the formation of independent trade unions. In October it was announced that a full multi-party political system would be established, and in November the necessary legislation was introduced. In the same month the USA announced that it was to suspend military and economic aid to Zaire, following renewed allegations of human rights abuses by the Mobutu regime (and continued speculation that Mobutu had personally misappropriated funds).

By February 1991 a large number of new parties had emerged. Prominent among them was the Union des fédéralistes et républicains indépendants (UFERI), led by Nguza Karl-I-Bond. An enlarged transitional Government, appointed in March and reshuffled in April, included members of minor opposition groups. None of the major opposition parties, including the UDPS and the UFERI, agreed to join the new Government. Prof. Mulumba Lukoji, an economist who had served in previous administrations, was appointed First State Commissioner.

In early April 1991 Mobutu announced that a National Conference of government and opposition representatives would be convened at the end of that month to draft a new constitution. However, the Conference was postponed, owing to widespread disturbances and anti-Government demonstrations in several parts of the country. In late April Mobutu resumed the chairmanship of the MPR. In July some 130 opposition movements formed a united front, the Union sacrée. Later in July Lukoji resigned as First State Commissioner. Etienne Tshisekedi Wa Mulumba, the leader of the UDPS, was nominated in his place, but refused the post following threats to his life, and Lukoji was subsequently reappointed. The National Conference was convened at the beginning of August, but was repeatedly suspended, initially owing to the dissatisfaction of the Union sacrée with the composition of its participants, and eventually by the Government, prompting renewed civil unrest and the dispatch of French and Belgian troops to Zaire to evacuate nationals of those countries. Although Tshisekedi finally accepted the post of First State Commissioner in September, he later refused to swear allegiance to the President and the Constitution; shortly afterwards he was replaced as First State Commissioner by Bernardin Mungul Diaka, also a member of the opposition. In November Mobutu dismissed Mungul and appointed Nguza Karl-I-Bond to the premiership. The Union sacrée denounced the appointment and expelled UFERI members from its ranks. Despite the expiry of his mandate as President in early December, Mobutu remained in office.

In April 1992 the National Conference reopened and declared its status to be sovereign and its decisions to be binding. Mobutu reacted with cautious opposition to the erosion of his powers. In mid-August the National Conference elected Tshisekedi as First State Commissioner, following the resignation of Nguza Karl-I-Bond. A 'transition act', adopted by the Conference in early August, afforded Tshisekedi a mandate to govern for 24 months, pending the promulgation of a new constitution that would curtail the powers of the President. Later that month Tshisekedi appointed a transitional 'Government of National Union', which included opponents of Mobutu.

The political interests of Tshisekedi and Mobutu clashed almost immediately when the President declared his intention to promote the adoption of a 'semi-presidential constitution', in opposition to the parliamentary system favoured by the Conference. In November 1992 the National Conference (without the participation of Mobutu's supporters) adopted a draft Constitution, providing for the establishment of a 'Federal Republic of the Congo', the introduction of a bicameral legislature and the election of a President (who would fulfil a largely ceremonial function) by universal suffrage. (Executive and military power was to be exercised by the Prime Minister.) The draft document was vigorously opposed by Mobutu, who unsuccessfully attempted in early December to remove the Tshisekedi Government. In early December the National Conference dissolved itself and was succeeded by a 453-member High Council of the Republic (HCR), headed by Archbishop Monsengwo, which, as the supreme interim executive and legislative authority, was empowered to amend and adopt the new Constitution and to organize legislative and presidential elections. At the same time Monsengwo declared that the report of a special commission, established by the Conference in order to examine allegations of corruption brought against Mobutu and his associates, would be considered by the HCR. Mobutu responded by ordering the suspension of the HCR and the Government. Attempts by the presidential guard to obstruct the convening of the HCR ended, following the organization of a public rally in Kinshasa by Monsengwo and other members of the HCR. With support from the USA, Belgium and France, Monsengwo reiterated the HCR's recognition of Tshisekedi as head of Zaire's Government.

In mid-January 1993 the HCR declared Mobutu to be guilty of treason, on account of his mismanagement of state affairs, and threatened impeachment proceedings unless he recognized the legitimacy of the 'Government of National Union'. In early March, in an attempt to reassert his political authority, Mobutu convened a special 'conclave' of political forces to debate the country's future. The HCR and the Union sacrée refused to attend. In mid-March the 'conclave' appointed Faustin Birindwa, a former UDPS member and adviser to Tshisekedi, as Prime Minister, charged with the formation of a 'Government of National Salvation'. The NLC was also revived to rival the HCR, and was reconvened to operate within the terms of reference of the old Mobutu-inspired Constitution. Birindwa's Cabinet, appointed in April, included Nguza Karl-I-Bond (as First Deputy Prime Minister in charge of Defence) and three members of the Union sacrée, who were immediately expelled from that organization. While the Birindwa administration was denied widespread official international recognition, Tshisekedi became increasingly frustrated at the impotence of his own Government (the armed forces recommenced blocking access to the HCR) and the deteriorating stability of the country. During April the army embarked upon a campaign of intimidation of opposition members, while tribal warfare re-emerged in Shaba and also erupted in the north-eastern region of Kivu. Tshisekedi urged the intervention of the UN to address these problems, and in July the Secretary-General of the UN appointed a Special Envoy to Zaire.

At the end of September 1993 an agreement was concluded between representatives of President Mobutu and of the principal opposition groups, providing for the adoption of a single constitutional text for the transitional period, which would be subject to approval by a national referendum. Under the provisions of the agreement, national transitional institutions would include the President of the Republic, a reorganized parliament, a government and national judiciary. During October, however, attempts to finalize the terms of the agreement were complicated by the insistence of Tshisekedi's supporters that he should continue in the office of Prime Minister, despite the objections of Mobutu's representatives that Tshisekedi's mandate had been superseded by the September agreement. The opposing positions of the principal political parties (largely polarized as the pro-Tshisekedi Union sacrée de l'opposition radicale—USOR—and the pro-Mobutu Forces politiques du conclave—FPC) became more firmly entrenched during November and December.

An ultimatum, issued to all political parties by President Mobutu in early January 1994, in an attempt to end the political impasse, resulted in the conclusion of an agreement to form a government of national reconciliation, signed by all major con-stituent parties of the FPC and the USOR (with the notable exception of Tshisekedi's own UDPS). Encouraged by the unexpected level of political support for the initiative, in mid-January Mobutu announced the dissolution of the HCR and the NLC, the dismissal of the Government of National Salvation, headed by Birindwa, and the candidacy for the premiership of two contestants, Tshisekedi and Lukoji, to be decided by the transitional legislature (to be known as the Haut Conseil de la République—Parlement de Transition, HCR—PT). Despite widespread condemnation of Mobutu's procedural circumvention of the HCR's authority, the HCR—PT was convened for the first time on 23 January. The HCR—PT promptly rejected Mobutu's procedure for the selection of a new Prime Minister. Subsequent attempts by the legislature to formulate a new procedure were frustrated by the increasingly divergent interests of the member parties of the USOR, and by Tshisekedi's insistence of his legitimate claim to the office.

On 8 April 1994 the HCR—PT endorsed a new Transitional Constitution Act, reiterating the provisions of previous accords for the organization of a constitutional referendum and presidential and legislative elections, and defining the functions of transitional institutions during a 15-month period. The Government, to be accountable to the HCR—PT, was to assume some former powers of the President, including the control of the Central Bank and the security forces. A new Prime Minister was to be appointed from opposition candidates, to be nominated within 10 days of the President's promulgation of the Act (on 9 April). Widening divisions within the USOR frustrated attempts to unite the opposition behind Tshisekedi as sole candidate, prompting the expulsion, in May, of 10 dissident parties from the USOR.

In June 1994 the HCR—PT ratified the candidature of seven opposition representatives for the premiership, rejecting that of Tshisekedi on a technicality. On 14 June it was reported that Léon Kengo Wa Dondo had been elected Prime Minister by 322 votes to 133 in the HCR—PT. However, Kengo Wa Dondo's election was immediately denounced as illegitimate, under the terms of the April Constitution Act, by the opposition and by the Speaker of the HCR—PT, Monsengwo Pasinya (who refused to endorse the actions of the legislature). A new transitional Government, announced on 6 July, was similarly rejected by the radical opposition. On 11 July, during a motion of confidence, the Government received overwhelming support from the HCR—PT. In October an expanded radical opposition grouping (the Union sacrée de l'opposition radicale et ses alliés, USORAL) resumed its participation in the HCR—PT, having boycotted proceedings since the election of Kengo Wa Dondo in June.

In late June 1995 political consensus between the FPC and the USORAL resulted in the HCR—PT's adoption of a constitutional amendment (approved by Mobutu) whereby the period of national transition (due to end on 9 July) was to be extended by two years, owing to a shortage of government resources. On 1 July deputies from both groups voted to remove Monsengwo Pasinya from the post of President of the transitional legislature. Meanwhile, opposition frustration at the Government's failure to publish an electoral timetable intensified. In late July an anti-Government demonstration in the capital, organized by the Parti lumumbiste unifié (a group supporting the aims of the murdered former Prime Minister, Patrice Lumumba), led to violent clashes that resulted in 10 fatalities. A subsequent anti-Government protest in Kinshasa, organized by USORAL in August, denounced international endorsement of Prime Minister Kengo Wa Dondo and urged his removal. In December opposition groups unanimously rejected a government offer to participate in a national coalition government and reiterated their demands for the prompt announcement of a timetable for multi-party elections. A National Electoral Commission, comprising 44 members (22 from both of the major political groupings) and headed by Bayona Bameya (a close political associate of President Mobutu), was formally installed in April 1996.

In mid-April 1996 it was announced that multi-party presidential and legislative elections would be conducted in May 1997, and would be preceded by a referendum on a new constitution in December 1996. President Mobutu announced that he was to contest the presidential poll. (However, neither the elections nor the referendum took place, as the security situation in the country worsened—see below.) A draft of the new Constitution, which provided for a federal state with a parliamentary system of government and a president with limited powers, was approved by the Government in late May.

In the mid-1990s existing ethnic tensions in eastern Zaire were heightened by the inflow of an estimated 1m. Hutu refugees from Rwanda (see below). The plight of the region's Zairean Tutsis (Banyamulenge) aroused international concern in late 1996, following reports of the organized persecution of Banyamulenge communities by elements of the Zairean security forces and by extremist Hutu refugees. In October the Sud-Kivu regional administration ordered all Banyamulenge to leave the area within one week or risk internment or forced expulsion. Although the order was subsequently rescinded, this threat provoked the mobilization of armed Banyamulenge rebels, who launched a violent counter-offensive, allegedly supported by the Tutsi-dominated authorities in Rwanda and Burundi. Support for the rebels from dissidents of diverse ethnic origin (including Shaba and Kasaï secessionists, and local Mai-Mai warriors) increased during the month, and later in October the rebels announced the formation of the Alliance des forces démocratiques pour la libération du Congo-Zaïre (AFDL), under the leadership of Laurent-Désiré Kabila (hitherto leader of the Parti de la révolution populaire, and a known opponent of the Mobutu regime since the 1960s). AFDL forces made rapid territorial gains, and the movement soon gathered momentum, emerging as a national rebellion aimed at overthrowing Mobutu. Counter-attacks by Zairean troops from January 1997 failed to recapture any significant area of territory. In March the AFDL entered the strategically important northern town of Kisangani (which had served as the centre of military operations for the Government), and in early April Mbuji-Mayi fell to the rebels. Nguza Karl-I-Bond, now leader of the pro-Mobutu FPC, urged his followers (for the most part Shaba secessionists) to support the AFDL. AFDL troops, entering Lubumbashi on 9 April, were welcomed as liberators, while government troops withdrew from the city. The Zairean Government continued to make allegations that the AFDL offensive was being supported by government troops from Rwanda, Uganda, Burundi and Angola, while the AFDL, in turn, claimed that the Zairean army was being augmented by white mercenary soldiers and by forces of the União Nacional para a Independência Total de Angola (UNITA).

Meanwhile, in August 1996 Mobutu had travelled to Switzerland to receive treatment for cancer. His absence, and uncertainties as to the state of his health, contributed to the poor co-ordination of the Zairean Government's response to the AFDL, which by the end of November was in control of most of Kivu. In that month the HCR—PT urged the expulsion of all Tutsis from Zairean territory; following attacks on Tutsis and their property, many Tutsi residents of Kinshasa fled to Brazzaville (Republic of the Congo). In the same month repeated public demonstrations demanded the resignation of Kengo Wa Dondo (himself part Tutsi in origin) for having failed to respond effectively to the insurrection. In December Mobutu returned to Zaire, appointed Gen. Mahele Bokungu as Chief of General Staff and reorganized the Government, retaining Kengo Wa Dondo as Prime Minister.

The continued exclusion of Tshisekedi from the Government prompted his supporters to mount a campaign of civil disobedience, and in January 1997 his faction of the UDPS announced its support for the AFDL. In March, following the capture of Kisangani, the HCR—PT voted to dismiss Kengo Wa Dondo, who tendered his resignation as Prime Minister later that month. He was replaced at the beginning of April by Tshisekedi, who, having offered government posts to members of the AFDL (which they refused), announced that he was dissolving the HCR—PT. Parliament, in turn, voted to dismiss Tshisekedi, whose supporters organized a demonstration of support in Kinshasa, only to come under attack from the security forces. On 8 April Mobutu declared a national state of emergency, dissolving the Government and ordering the deployment of security forces throughout Kinshasa. Gen. Likulia Bolongo was appointed Prime Minister at the head of a new 28-member 'Government of National Salvation', in which USORAL refused to participate. An arrest warrant was subsequently issued for Kengo Wa Dondo, who was alleged to have fled to Switzerland with funds from the national treasury.

After peace talks between Mobutu and Kabila, mediated by the South African President, Nelson Mandela, ended in failure in early May 1997, Kabila reiterated his intention to take the capital by force. On 16 May Mobutu left Kinshasa (travelling to Togo, and then to Morocco, where he died in September), while many of his supporters and family fled across the border to Brazzaville. On 17 May AFDL troops entered Kinshasa (encountering no resistance), and Kabila, speaking from Lubumbashi,

declared himself President of the Democratic Republic of the Congo (DRC, the name in use during 1964–71), which swiftly gained international recognition. He immediately announced plans to form a provisional government within 72 hours and a commission to draft a new constitution within 60 days; presidential and parliamentary elections were to be held in April 1999. On 20 May 1997 Kabila arrived in Kinshasa and on 23 May Kabila formed a transitional Government, which, while dominated by members of the AFDL, also included members of the UDPS and of the Front patriotique. No Prime Minister was appointed, and Tshisekedi was not offered a cabinet post; he refused to recognize the new Government and urged public protest against the administration, but failed to raise the mass support that he had previously enjoyed. On 26 May, following a number of protests, Kabila issued a decree indefinitely banning all political parties and public demonstrations. On 28 May Kabila issued a constitutional decree (which was to remain in force pending the adoption of a new constitution), investing the President with virtually absolute legislative and executive power, as well as control over the armed forces and the treasury. Of the previously existing state institutions, only the judiciary was not dissolved.

On 29 May 1997 Kabila was sworn in as President of the DRC, assuming full executive, legislative and military powers. Despite concern regarding the new administration's treatment of refugees, Kabila's assumption of power was well received internationally.

In August 1997 a military Court of Justice was established by decree, and at the end of October two statutory orders were signed by Kabila; one redesignated the administrative areas and local authorities of the DRC (the nine former regions were reorganized into 11 provinces), while the other created a paramilitary force (the Service national), which, under the control of the President, was to monitor and facilitate national reconstruction. In late October Kabila appointed a 42-member Constitutional Commission (originally due to be appointed in June), which was to draft a new constitution by March 1998. In the following month Kabila reaffirmed that the activities of political parties were suspended, pending presidential and legislative elections, scheduled to take place in 1999. At the end of November 1997 Kabila's Special Adviser for Security and the acting Army Chief of Staff, Gen. Masasu Nindanga, was arrested, and charged with maintaining a private militia and conspiring with state enemies; he was later sentenced to 20 years' imprisonment.

In early January 1998 Kabila reorganized the Cabinet, creating two new ministerial posts. Later that month Joseph Olenghankoy, the Chairman of the opposition Forces novatrices pour l'union et la solidarité (FONUS), was arrested for reasons believed to be related to a complaint he had made against two government ministers. He was subsequently sentenced by a military court to 15 years' imprisonment for violating the ban on political activity, although he was released from prison in June 1999. In February 1998 Tshisekedi was banished to his native village and placed under house arrest for his continued political activity on behalf of the UDPS. In March the new draft Constitution was presented to Kabila. In April UNESCO suspended co-operation with the DRC Government in protest at the detention of Arthur Z'ahidi Ngoma, a UNESCO official and political activist who had been arrested in November 1997. Z'ahidi Ngoma received a 12-month suspended sentence for breaking the ban on political activity in May 1998 and was released in June. In July Tshisekedi was returned to Kinshasa and announced that he was willing to co-operate with Kabila.

Following accusations of financial impropriety against several members of the Cabinet, in early June 1998 Kabila announced a cabinet reorganization, in which five ministers suspected of fraud or corruption were dismissed. Eight new posts were created, increasing the number of ministers from 29 to 37. In July a UN investigative team, which, despite continued obstruction by the Government, had conducted enquiries in the DRC between November 1997 and early 1998, published its report, concluding that the AFDL had massacred a large number of Rwandan Hutu refugees in 1996 and 1997; these findings were rejected by the Government on the grounds that they were based on an incomplete investigation.

In late July 1998 Kabila issued a decree expelling Rwandan troops from the country. He had earlier replaced the DRC Chief of Staff, James Kabereke, a Rwandan national, with Célestin Kifwa, a DRC citizen. In early August a rebellion was launched in Nord-Kivu province, in the east of the DRC, which was reported to have Rwandan and French support. The Minister of State for the Presidency, Deogratias Bugera, and the Minister of Foreign Affairs, Bizima Karaha, defected from the Government and joined the rebellion. Karaha was subsequently replaced by Jean-Charles Okoto, formerly deputy Governor of Kasaï Oriental province. Western Governments advised their citizens to leave the country, and several diplomatic missions were closed. The rebels advanced quickly in the east of the country and were soon reported to have captured Bukavu and Goma. Shortly afterwards a second front was opened from Kitona, in the west of the country, where further advances resulted in the rebels gaining control of Boma, Banana and Matadi. The Inga Dam, which supplies both electricity and water to Kinshasa and the Katanga mining region, was also captured, enabling the rebels to interrupt power supplies. At that time the rebel forces announced that they had formed a political organization, the Rassemblement congolais démocratique (RCD), with the aim of introducing political democracy in the DRC. The RCD leadership included Z'ahidi Ngoma, together with a former Prime Minister, Lunda Bululu, and Ernest Wamba dia Wamba. In mid-August Kabila was reported to have left Kinshasa for Lubumbashi, the former base of the AFDL insurgency. Kabila, who had installed his son, Joseph, as Chief of Staff, returned to Kinshasa at the end of the month.

Other countries in the region were, meanwhile, becoming involved in the conflict. While Rwanda had initially denied accusations that it was supporting the rebels, it quickly became evident that the anti-Kabila insurgents had the support of both Rwanda and Uganda, and that Kabila was receiving support from Angola, Namibia and Zimbabwe. Angolan troops, in particular, were instrumental in recapturing rebel-held towns in the western DRC, and in early September 1998 had expelled the rebels from that part of the country. Regional divisions were clearly evident at a meeting of Ministers of Defence of the Southern African Development Community (SADC, see p. 345), convened by President Mugabe of Zimbabwe on 18–19 August, to mobilize support for Kabila; only one-half of the participating delegates favoured intervention in the conflict. Regional efforts to reach a political solution to the civil conflict continued in September. The Government refused to negotiate with the RCD and a newly formed rebel grouping, the Mouvement pour la libération du Congo (MLC), however, on the grounds that their activities were supported by Rwanda and Uganda, respectively.

In September 1998 an Institutional Reform Commission (IRC), headed by the Minister of Justice, was established by Kabila to examine the draft Constitution. Kabila maintained that elections would be held in April 1999, and, as part of the electoral preparations, a census was to be conducted in October 1998. At the end of that month the IRC presented the revised draft Constitution to Kabila.

Although their advance had been halted in the west, the rebels continued to make progress in the east, capturing towns in Kasaï Oriental and Katanga. Despite their continued military successes, however, the rebels lacked popular support, and the movement was widely perceived as a Rwandan-backed Tutsi invasion. In mid-October the rebels shot down a passenger plane, which, they claimed, was transporting troops to the front; the Government denied this and stated that a number of civilians had been on board. In January 1999 the ongoing civil war led to the declaration of a state of siege in six of the 11 provinces of the DRC. On 29 January Kabila issued a decree ending the ban on political parties. However, the new system was widely criticized for continuing restrictions, which effectively prevented many existing parties from registering. Kabila also announced that the AFDL was to be transformed into People's Power Committees to encourage involvement in the political process at a local level. Following Kabila's dissolution of the Cabinet on 20 February, a new Government was formed in March and was subsequently enlarged to comprise 37 members.

In May 1999 the RCD announced changes to its executive committee; Wamba dia Wamba was replaced as President by Dr Emile Ilunga. (Z'ahidi Ngoma had resigned in February.) However, a number of the RCD's founding members opposed this move, and Wamba dia Wamba denounced it as a coup. Following clashes in Kisangani between supporters of Wamba dia Wamba and those of Ilunga, two factions emerged; one of these, led by Ilunga, was based in Goma, with the support of Rwanda, while the other, led by Wamba dia Wamba, was based in Kisangani and supported by Uganda. In June the DRC began proceedings at the International Court of Justice against Burundi, Rwanda and Uganda for acts of armed aggression, which it claimed to

have been in contravention of both the charters of the Organization of African Unity (OAU, now the African Union, see p. 144) and the UN. (In February 2001 the DRC abandoned the proceedings against Burundi and Rwanda.)

Despite a number of regional initiatives to end the civil war in late 1998 and early 1999, no lasting cease-fire agreement was negotiated, largely owing to Kabila's continued insistence that the rebels were supported by Rwanda and Uganda, and that they, therefore, be excluded from any talks. Although Col Muammar al-Qaddafi, the Libyan leader, hosted two rounds of regional talks in Sirte (Libya), it was in Lusaka, Zambia, under the mediation of Zambia's President Chiluba, that the rebels were first accorded a place at the negotiations, during a summit held in late June. Following this meeting, a cease-fire agreement was signed by the Heads of State of the DRC, Angola, Namibia, Zimbabwe, Rwanda and Uganda on 10 July (witnessed by the OAU, SADC, the UN and Zambia), by the leader of the MLC, Jean-Pierre Bemba, on 1 August and, following the resolution of a dispute (owing to the divisions within the RCD), by all 50 founding members of the RCD on 31 August. The agreement provided for an immediate cease-fire, the establishment of a Joint Military Commission (JMC), which was to investigate cease-fire violations, disarm militia groups and monitor the withdrawal of foreign troops, the deployment of a UN peace-keeping force and the organization of a national debate within the DRC. However, the UN stressed that authorization for a full peace-keeping force would have to be preceded by a 90-member military liaison mission and a subsequent 500-strong military observer mission. In July a general amnesty for rebels within the DRC was announced, and in that month the JMC was formed, comprising representatives of the rebel groups and the six Lusaka signatory states (the DRC, Angola, Namibia, Rwanda, Uganda and Zimbabwe). In mid-August the UN military liaison mission received official approval.

In August 1999 further fighting erupted in Kisangani between forces from Rwanda and Uganda and their respective factions of the RCD. A cease-fire was negotiated in late August, and at the end of the month the Ilunga faction of the RCD (known as RCD—Goma) announced a new executive committee. An investigation into the causes of the fighting recommended that all fighting forces be removed from Kisangani; as a result, the MLC transferred its headquarters to Gbadolite, while the Wamba dia Wamba faction of the RCD, known as the RCD—Mouvement de libération (RCD—ML), withdrew from Bunia. In early September the rebels raised objections to the composition of the cease-fire commission and voiced doubts over the neutrality of the mediators. At the end of the month, however, the rebels and the Government agreed that the national debate would be facilitated by the Italian Sant'Egidio Roman Catholic Community, although differences remained over the location for the conference and over OAU involvement.

Unrest became increasingly evident in late 1999. In November both factions of the RCD announced that they no longer respected the cease-fire (having previously denied violations), and the Ilunga faction of the movement accused the Government of openly breaching the agreement. In early November the UN Security Council voted to extend the mandate of the military liaison mission until mid-January 2000, owing to the difficulties experienced in obtaining security assurances and permission to deploy throughout the DRC. On 30 November 1999 the Council approved the establishment of a UN Mission in the Democratic Republic of the Congo (MONUC, see p. 75), to comprise some 5,000 troops, together with up to 500 military observers and liaison and technical assessment officers, with an initial mandate until March 2000. At a meeting of the UN Security Council concerning the conflict in the DRC, which took place in New York, USA, in January 2000, regional Heads of State expressed support for the rapid deployment of MONUC forces to support the Lusaka peace accord. In late February the UN Security Council authorized the expansion of MONUC to number 5,537 and the extension of its mandate to the end of August.

Also in late February 2000 the national debate was convened in Kinshasa, but was boycotted by opposition politicians, as well as by representatives of the rebel groups. Participants in the discussions subsequently submitted a final report, urging the establishment of a new national assembly and the revision of the Lusaka accord. The rebel groups rejected an offer by Kabila of a general amnesty in return for the cessation of hostilities, and fierce fighting between government and rebel forces continued in the east of the country, particularly in Kasaï Occidental. In early April participants at a meeting of the JMC signed a new cease-fire agreement, whereby all the forces involved in the conflict were to suspend hostilities and remain in position for a period of three months, pending the deployment of MONUC personnel to form a neutral zone between them. In early May, however, Ugandan and Rwandan forces again clashed in Kisangani, in violation of the cease-fire. After meeting a UN Security Council delegation, the Rwandan and Ugandan contingents agreed to the demilitarization of the town, and its transfer to the control of MONUC. Later that month RCD, Rwandan and Ugandan forces commenced withdrawal to a certain distance from the town. In June, however, it was reported that some 400 civilians had been killed in further hostilities between Rwandan and Ugandan troops in Kisangani. At the end of the month UN military personnel confirmed that Rwandan and Ugandan forces had withdrawn from the town, although some RCD members remained.

In June 2000 three ministers were arrested in connection with fraudulent activities and subsequently removed from office. In early July the Government withdrew the DRC ambassador in Belgium, in protest at an international arrest warrant issued by a Belgian magistrate against the Minister of State for Foreign Affairs and International Co-operation, Abdoulaye Yérodia Ndombasi, for crimes against humanity. (DRC refugees in Belgium had submitted a legal appeal accusing Ndombasi of inciting violence against the Tutsi ethnic group.) In the same month 240 deputies of a new 300-member transitional Parliament were elected by a commission under the supervision of the Ministry of Internal Affairs, while the remaining 60 were nominated by Kabila. A presidential decree, adopted in that month, provided for the decentralization of the Government, with the transferral of the legislature to Lubumbashi and the Supreme Court to Kisangani. On 22 August the new transitional Parliament was inaugurated in Lubumbashi, despite criticism from the international community, which accused Kabila of acting in contravention of the Lusaka accord.

In August 2000 the UN Security Council adopted a resolution extending the mandate of MONUC until mid-October to allow further time for the implementation of the cease-fire agreement. Kabila subsequently informed the UN that he authorized the immediate deployment of MONUC troops throughout the DRC. In early September the Cabinet was extensively reorganized, following the dismissal of the ministers in June. In October, in a reorganization of the RCD—Goma leadership, Ilunga was replaced by Adolphe Onusumba. In the same month an attempt to oust Wamba dia Wamba from the leadership of the RCD—ML was suppressed by Ugandan troops. The RCD—ML subsequently divided, following the establishment of a dissident breakaway faction, led by Roger Lumbala, which became known as RCD—National (RCD—N). In early December, following renewed fierce fighting, RCD—Goma, supported by Rwandan troops, succeeded in gaining control of the significant town of Pweto, in the south-eastern province of Katanga. The six countries and three rebel groups involved in the conflict subsequently signed an agreement in Harare, Zimbabwe, pledging to withdraw forces 15 km from positions of military engagement, prior to the deployment of MONUC troops (which was scheduled to take place within 45 days). Nevertheless, hostilities subsequently continued at Pweto, and in other eastern regions, while RCD—Goma refused to withdraw its forces in accordance with the agreement until the Government entered into bilateral discussions with the rebels and permitted the complete deployment of MONUC troops. In mid-December the UN Security Council adopted a resolution in favour of extending the mandate of MONUC to mid-June 2001.

On 16 January 2001 Kabila was fatally injured by one of his bodyguards at his private residence in Kinshasa. (The circumstances of his assassination remained unclear, and a committee of investigation was established in early February.) The transitional Parliament approved the nomination by the political leadership of his son, Joseph (hitherto Chief of Staff), as interim President. Following his inauguration on 26 January, Maj.-Gen. Joseph Kabila immediately engaged in international diplomatic efforts to resolve the conflict and urged rebel leaders to attend peace discussions with him. Following a meeting with Kabila in early February, the President of Rwanda, Maj.-Gen. Paul Kagame, announced that Rwandan troops would be withdrawn from Pweto on condition that control of the town was transferred to MONUC. However, the UN Security Council continued to demand that the DRC Government demonstrate its commitment to peace prior to the deployment of MONUC troops and

insisted that the implementation of the disengagement plan agreed in December was essential to this end. At a meeting of the UN Security Council in mid-February Kabila accepted the former Botswanan President, Sir Quett Ketumile Masire, as mediator to the conflict. (Laurent Kabila had previously opposed Masire's nomination to the post.) Following a further meeting of the UN Security Council later that month, attended by representatives of the six countries and three rebel factions involved in the conflict, it was agreed that the 15 km withdrawal of forces was to commence by mid-March.

The withdrawal from positions of military engagement duly commenced in mid-March 2001, in accordance with the UN-sponsored agreement, with the retreat from Pweto of the RCD—Goma and allied Rwandan troops. The first contingents of MONUC troops arrived in the DRC, and by the end of the month were stationed in the north-east of the country. At the beginning of April, however, the Ugandan-supported Forces pour la libération du Congo (FLC, which had been formed earlier that year by breakaway members of the MLC and the RCD—ML) refused to proceed with the withdrawal from military positions near Kisangani until MONUC guaranteed security in the region. The deployment of MONUC troops in the east of the country was delayed, after RCD forces initially prevented the peace-keeping forces from entering Kisangani. In mid-April Kabila appointed a new, enlarged Cabinet, which included only four members of the previous administration; it was reported that he had removed all ministers opposed to negotiating a settlement with the rebels.

In April 2001 a UN commission of experts issued a report, which accused Rwandan and Ugandan troops of systematic illegal exploitation of the DRC's mineral resources, and urged the Security Council to impose a trade embargo against the two countries. The Ugandan Government pledged to investigate the allegations of corruption (which implicated close members of the Ugandan President's family) and to complete the withdrawal of its forces from the DRC. In early May representatives of the DRC Government and the rebel factions, meeting in Lusaka, under the aegis of the OAU, SADC and the UN, signed a declaration establishing the principles for an 'Inter-Congolese National Dialogue' (a formal process of national consultation, with the aim of reaching a permanent peace settlement). It was decided that Masire (as organizer of the dialogue) would visit each province to gather public opinion for a proposed agenda, prior to further preparatory discussions, which were scheduled for mid-June. Later in May Kabila ended the remaining restrictions on political activity (thereby removing a major impediment to conducting the Inter-Congolese National Dialogue) and ordered the release of a number of detained human rights activists. (The preliminary discussions were rescheduled for mid-July, and subsequently for August.)

In late May 2001 a report by the state prosecutor claimed that forces opposing the Government (the RCD factions, and Rwandan and Ugandan troops) had conspired in the assassination of Laurent-Désiré Kabila, with the aim of seizing power. In June the UN Security Council approved a resolution extending the mandate of MONUC until mid-2002; the Council welcomed the progress towards negotiating a peace settlement, but reiterated demands that all foreign forces complete their withdrawal from the country. In early August, however, Kagame insisted that Kabila fulfil pledges to demobilize Rwandan Hutu militia, known as Interahamwe (who had become allied with DRC government forces, after participating in the genocide in Rwanda in 1994), as a precondition to withdrawing the Rwandan troops deployed in the country. Also in August Wamba dia Wamba was ousted as the RCD—ML leader by Mbusa Nyamwisi.

Preparatory discussions between Kabila and the leaders of the FLC and the RCD factions, mediated by Masire, which were for the first time attended by unarmed opposition groups and civic associations, were conducted in Gaborone, Botswana, in late August 2001. Agreement was reached on a number of significant issues for the organization of the Inter-Congolese National Dialogue, which was to commence in the Ethiopian capital, Addis Ababa, in mid-October and was expected to continue for 45 days. In early September the Namibian Government announced that it had withdrawn its troops (numbering some 1,850) from the DRC.

In mid-October 2001 the Inter-Congolese National Dialogue was convened in Addis Ababa; however, negotiations were suspended one week later, after the Government withdrew in protest at the absence of the allied Mai-Mai delegation. At the beginning of 2002, however, international donors pledged considerable development aid to support further efforts, in recognition of the progress achieved. In early January Ugandan troops were redeployed in the north-east of the country, near the town of Bunia, to prevent escalating fighting between the rebel factions from reaching the border with Uganda. Later that month RCD representatives, meeting with opposition parties and civil groups, reached consensus on a basis for the continuation of political dialogue, including the establishment of a new transitional government, conditions under which elections would be conducted, and the length of the period of transition.

The Inter-Congolese National Dialogue was reconvened in Sun City, South Africa, in February 2002, but was initially boycotted by Bemba. In April it was announced that the Government and the MLC had reached a compromise agreement, providing for the establishment of an administration of national unity: Kabila was to remain President and Bemba became Prime Minister for a transitional period, prior to general elections. The parties that signed the agreement commenced discussions in Matadi in May to draft a new constitution, while RCD—Goma and the UDPS announced their intention to form a political alliance to oppose the accord between Kabila and Bemba. (In late August it was announced that some progress had been achieved in negotiations, with agreement reached on an arrangement that would allow the Kabila Government and the MLC to share control of a national armed force.) At the end of July, after discussions mediated by Mbeki and Annan, a peace agreement was signed by Kabila and President Kagame of Rwanda in Pretoria, South Africa. Under the accord, Kabila pledged to arrest and disarm the Interahamwe militia in the DRC, while the Rwandan Government was to withdraw all troops from the country (thereby also providing for the integration of RCD—Goma into the peace process). President Robert Mugabe of Zimbabwe subsequently announced his intention of withdrawing the remaining Zimbabwean troops supporting the DRC Government. In August, however, following further fighting between Rwandan troops and armed groups in Sud-Kivu province, the DRC accused Rwanda of violating the cease-fire, while Rwanda, in turn, accused the Kabila Government of continuing to provide armaments to the Interahamwe militia. In early September the DRC and Uganda reached an accord in the Angolan capital, Luanda, providing for the normalization of relations between the two countries, and the full withdrawal of Ugandan troops in the DRC. The Ugandan and Zimbabwean Governments subsequently commenced the withdrawal of forces from the DRC (although the UN permitted some Ugandan troops provisionally to remain near the north-eastern town of Bunia to assist in the maintenance of security). At the end of September the withdrawal of Rwandan forces commenced, and it was announced that all 23,400 Rwandan troops had left the country by early October.

In mid-October 2002 Mai-Mai militia attacked RCD—Goma forces in the east of the country, following the departure of the Rwandan forces supporting the rebels. Later that month a five-member Panel of Experts on the illicit exploitation of the DRC's mineral resources submitted a report to the UN Security Council. Kabila subsequently suspended six ministers and a number of senior officials (including the head of the National Security Agency) who had been implicated in the report, and reorganized the Council of Ministers. (Several Zimbabwean ministers, and Ugandan and Rwandan military officers, were also cited in the report as being connected to illegal activities.) On 4 December the UN Security Council approved a resolution providing for the enlargement of MONUC to 8,700 personnel. Following the convening of a peace conference in early December, in Pretoria, the Government and rebels signed an extensive power-sharing agreement on 17 of that month. Under the terms of this accord, Kabila was to remain as President, while four vice-presidential posts were to be allocated, respectively, to the incumbent Government, opposition parties, RCD—Goma and the MLC. The new 36-member transitional administration, to remain in power for a two-year period, was to comprise representatives of the Government, all three RCD factions, the MLC, the opposition and civil society. At the end of December the MLC and the RCD factions signed a cease-fire agreement in Gbadolite, which was to allow the transportation of humanitarian assistance in the region. (However, all rebel factions subsequently failed to observe the cease-fire, and continued hostilities near the border with Uganda were reported.) In early January 2003 a military court in Kinshasa imposed death sentences on 26 defendants, and custodial terms on a

further 64, for their involvement in the assassination of President Laurent-Désiré Kabila. Later in January the UN Security Council adopted a resolution extending the mandate of the Panel of Experts on the exploitation of the DRC's resources for a further six months. In February the Minister of Finance tendered his resignation, after the Council of Ministers rejected the proposed budget for that year (which had incorporated stringent IMF-recommended reforms). In early March the power-sharing agreement was endangered, when clashes erupted near Bunia between an armed organization of the Lendu ethnic group, the Front de l'intégration pour la pacification de l'Ituri, which was supported by Ugandan troops, and a rival militia of the Hema ethnic group, known as Union des patriotes congolais (UPC). A further agreement to restore peace in the region was signed by the DRC and Ugandan Governments and the local rebel groups later that month. Meanwhile, further discussions on constitutional and security issues for the transitional period were conducted in Pretoria; agreement was reached on the adoption of a draft constitution and the deployment of a neutral international force in the country, pending the establishment of a new national army (which would include former rebel combatants). All measures agreed by the participating groups under the December 2002 settlement were to be ratified at a final session of the Inter-Congolese National Dialogue. However, the Rwandan Government renewed threats to resume military engagement in eastern DRC if the UN failed to secure the total withdrawal of Ugandan forces. On 20 March 2003, in response to continuing violence near Bunia, in contravention of the cease-fire agreement, the UN Security Council adopted a resolution urging an increase in the number of military and humanitarian observers stationed in the DRC under the MONUC mandate, and an immediate withdrawal of the Ugandan troops. At the final peace conference, which was convened at Sun City on 2 April, government and rebel representatives endorsed the establishment of the two-year transitional administration. The official adoption of the Constitution on 4 April was followed by Kabila's inauguration as interim Head of State on 7 April. The Ugandan Government subsequently pledged to withdraw forces from the DRC, in accordance with the peace agreement, and the departure of some 7,000 from the north-east commenced at the beginning of May. Despite the deployment of some 700 (mainly Uruguayan) MONUC troops at Bunia to compensate for the Ugandan withdrawal, UPC forces recaptured the town following intensive fighting, during which large numbers of civilians were massacred. On 30 May, in response to the developing humanitarian crisis, the UN Security Council authorized the establishment of a 1,500-member Interim Emergency Multinational Force, with a three-month mandate to restore order. Deployment of the contingent (which comprised troops from several European Union (see p. 217) nations, principally France) commenced in early June (despite protests from the various factions at French involvement in the conflict). Later that month it was announced that the UPC leadership was prepared to withdraw forces from Bunia.

In early May 2003 the nomination of the four Vice-Presidents to the new transitional Government was announced: these were Bemba; the new leader of RCD—Goma, Azarias Ruberwa; a former minister (representing the incumbent administration), Abdoulaye Yerodia Ndombasi; and the former UNESCO official detained in 1997–98, Z'ahidi Ngoma, as the representative of the political opposition. However, RCD—Goma protested at the nomination of Z'ahidi Ngoma, owing to his former leadership of the rebel faction, and temporarily withdrew from negotiations. As a result of protracted dissension, the transitional schedule, including the inauguration of the Vice-Presidents, which was originally scheduled for 29 May, was delayed. On 29 June all former combatant groups finally signed an agreement on power-sharing in the future integrated transitional armed forces. This final stage in the peace process allowed Kabila on the following day to nominate a transitional Government, in which portfolios were divided between representatives of the former rebel factions, the incumbent administration, political opposition and civil society organizations. While Kabila's Government, RCD—Goma, and the MLC were allocated the most significant portfolios, the new administration also included Nyamwisi (representing the RCD—ML), and Lumbala (representing RCD—N). The four Vice-Presidents were finally inaugurated on 17 July, after the arrival of the rebel representatives in Kinshasa. The inauguration of some ministers belonging to RCD—Goma was also delayed, owing to their reluctance to pledge allegiance to Kabila, but the new power-sharing Government was finally installed on 24 July. At the end of that month the UN Security Council approved a one-year extension of MONUC's mandate, and increased the contingent's military strength significantly; it was envisaged that these MONUC reinforcements would replace the Interim Emergency Multinational Force at the beginning of September. The new International Criminal Court, which had been established on 1 July 2002 at The Hague, Netherlands, announced that it was to initiate investigations into alleged atrocities committed in the Ituri region. On 20 August 2003 Kabila announced nominations to the military leadership of the new unified armed forces, which was to incorporate elements of all the former rebel groups and the Mai-Mai militia; former RCD—Goma and MLC commanders were appointed to senior posts, including those of services Chiefs of Staff. On 22 August the inaugural session of the new bicameral transitional Parliament was conducted; representation in the 500-member National Assembly and 120-member Senate was likewise divided between the former rebel groups, the Mai-Mai, the incumbent Government, political opposition and civil society. At the beginning of September the Interim Emergency Multinational Force officially transferred control of the Ituri region to MONUC reinforcements; the remaining French troops belonging to the contingent were finally withdrawn by the end of that month.

In November 2003, following a final report by the Panel of Experts, the UN Security Council issued a statement condemning the widespread illicit exploitation of the DRC's natural resources, which had financed the activities of former combatant groups, and urged the imposition of state authority throughout the country. Some 85 companies, including many large multinationals, were cited as having contravened Organisation for Economic Co-operation and Development (OECD, see p. 307) regulations through their involvement in mining operations in the country. Meanwhile, following continued ethnic hostilities near Bunia, most of the MONUC contingent had been dispatched to the region, and to the more southern town of Uvira, by the end of that month. In early December the new unified military was officially established, following the integration of former rebel combatants and Mai-Mai into the existing armed forces. In early February 2004 unidentified combatants attacked a MONUC convoy, killing a Kenyan military observer belonging to the contingent. In late March insurgents believed to be former members of a special presidential unit of Mobutu Sese Seko attacked four military garrisons in Kinshasa; the coup attempt was suppressed by government members, who arrested about 15 of the dissidents. In mid-May, following dialogue with the Government and MONUC, the ethnic rebel groups active in the Ituri region signed a peace agreement in Kinshasa.

At the end of May 2004 some 2,000 dissident troops, led by former RCD—Goma commanders who had been integrated into the national army, Brig.-Gen. Laurent Nkunda and Col Jules Mutebutsi, attacked forces loyal to the Government deployed in Bukavu, and by 2 June had seized control of the town. Both Banyamulenge officers claimed to have initiated military action in order to prevent further human rights' abuses being perpetrated by government forces in the region against their ethnic group. The failure of MONUC troops to prevent the capture of Bukavu caused protest riots in Kinshasa and several other towns, in which some 12 civilians were killed. The Rwandan Government denied accusations by Kabila that Rwandan troops had been redeployed on DRC territory. Rebel forces began to withdraw from Bukavu about two days later, and troops loyal to Kabila succeeded in regaining control of the town by 9 June. Nkunda, together with some 300 supporters, fled to Rwanda, and were subsequently disarmed. In mid-June Kabila dispatched some 10,000 troop reinforcements to the eastern border with Rwanda, prompting Kagame to warn that Rwanda would take any necessary measures to protect national security. (Later in June, however, the two Heads of State reached agreement to abide by the 2002 peace agreement.) Meanwhile, shortly after the anti-UN riots in Kinshasa, the national radio and television station in the capital was seized by about 20 disaffected members of the presidential guard, led by Maj. Eric Lenge. On 11 June 2004 Lenge broadcast an announcement that the transitional Government, which had failed to meet its commitments, had been overthrown, and suspended the capital's electricity supplies. (The coup attempt was, however, believed to have been largely precipitated by the Government's failure to pay the salaries of members of the armed forces.) Troops loyal to the Government rapidly regained control of Kinshasa, arresting 12 of the dissidents, and Lenge fled to the Republic of Congo (from

where he was subsequently extradited). In July Kabila reorganized the transitional Government, after several ministers relinquished portfolios in order to assume provincial governorships.

In August 2004 some 160 Banyamulenge, numbering among 20,000 who had fled from Bukavu in June to take refuge in Burundi, were massacred at a refugee camp at Gatumba, near the border between the two countries. A Burundian Hutu rebel faction, Forces nationales de libération, admitted responsibility for the atrocity, however, the Governments of Rwanda and Burundi believed that the Interahamwe militia operating within the DRC were also implicated and threatened to resume military engagement in the country. Nkunda denounced the massacre and also warned that he would take retaliatory action if the DRC Government failed to protect the Banyamulenge refugees. Ruberwa announced that RCD—Goma, in view of the collapse of the peace process, was to suspend participation in the transitional Government. At the end of August the Governments of the DRC, Uganda and Rwanda agreed to co-operate in the disarmament of the militia continuing to operate in the country, including the Interahamwe and members of the Ugandan rebel organization, the Alliance of Democratic Forces. At the beginning of September, following a visit by Mbeki to Kinshasa for mediation, Ruberwa announced that RCD—Goma had rejoined the Government. During that month the UN Security Council subsequently considered a proposal for the expansion of MONUC, then numbering some 10,800, to about 24,000 military personnel. Resolution 1565, approved on 1 October, authorized the expansion of the mission to 16,700 (while renewing the contingent's mandate for a further six months); the UN Secretary-General expressed concern that the approved increase in strength failed to meet his recommendations.

In late November 2004 Kabila suspended from office six cabinet ministers and 12 senior managers of state enterprises, who were accused of extensive financial malpractice. Reports also emerged in that month that Rwandan troops had entered DRC territory to suppress Hutu rebel activity. At the beginning of December, after MONUC troops confirmed the presence of Rwandan forces in the DRC, Kabila requested that the UN Security Council impose sanctions against Rwanda. Kagame protested that Rwandan forces had responded to rebel bombardments launched from DRC territory. Heavy fighting continued in Nord-Kivu province between government forces and dissident army units reportedly supported by Rwanda, and later in December MONUC announced that its troops were to establish a temporary 'buffer zone' between the factions engaged in conflict. A US-based humanitarian organization, the International Rescue Committee, issued estimates that some 3.8m. people had been killed in the DRC since August 1998, and that a further 31,000 civilians continued to die each month as a result of the conflict. In early January 2005 Kabila replaced the six ministers who had been suspended from office and reorganized the Government. Indications from the electoral commission that, owing to the intensified hostilities, the elections due to be conducted by the end of June would be postponed until later that year prompted opposition protests (which were violently dispersed by the security forces), while Bemba threatened to withdraw from the transitional administration in response to lack of progress in the peace process. (The Government, however, maintained that the elections would proceed as scheduled.)

The DRC Government has maintained strong relations with its former allies in the civil conflict, Zimbabwe, Angola and Namibia, but Zimbabwe's political and economic influence has been overtaken by that of South Africa, owing to President Mbeki's strong involvement in the domestic and regional peace process. Following Kabila's agreement with Kagame in Pretoria in July 2002, relations improved between the Rwandan and DRC Governments, although the two continued to support opposing forces engaged in hostilities in Nord-Kivu. The DRC Government's relations with Uganda also improved, despite ongoing tensions between Kabila and Uganda's main ally in the DRC, the MLC. Some 453,465 DRC refugees remained in neighbouring countries at the end of 2003 (150,160 in Tanzania, 81,004 in the Republic of Congo, 58,405 in Zambia, 40,568 in Burundi and 34,725 in Rwanda). The occupation of Bukavu by dissident troops in mid-2004 again increased concerns of conflict between the DRC and Rwanda and prompted the mass flight of civilians to neighbouring countries. Despite the significant financial support and military training pledged by the Belgian Government in 2004, Kabila recalled the DRC ambassador in

Belgium in October, after the Belgian Minister of Foreign Affairs strongly criticized the Kabila administration during a visit to Kinshasa. Following the massacre of Banyamulenge refugees from the DRC in Burundi in August (see above), MONUC confirmed later that year that Rwandan troops had re-engaged in hostilities in DRC territory.

Government

Following a comprehensive power-sharing agreement between the Government and rebel factions, reached in December 2002, a new Constitution was adopted on 4 April 2003, and Maj.-Gen. Joseph Kabila was inaugurated as President for a two-year transitional period on 7 April. A transitional Government of national unity was installed in July. On 22 August a bicameral Parliament, comprising a 500-member lower chamber, the National Assembly, and a 120-member upper chamber, the Senate, was inaugurated; the new transitional legislature included representatives of the former administration, political opposition and civil society, and the main rebel groups.

Defence

Following the overthrow of Mobutu's regime in May 1997, the former Zairean armed forces were disbanded. In August 2004 government forces, known as the Alliance des forces démocratiques pour la libération du Congo-Zaire (AFDL), were estimated to number 60,000, the navy 1,800 and the air force 3,000. A civil war began in August 1998 in the east of the country, with troops from a number of neighbouring countries becoming involved. Although peace was partially restored following a power-sharing agreement reached by the Government and rebel groups in December 2002, hostilities continued in the east of the country, and in late 2004 Rwandan troops were reported to have been redeployed in the region. As part of the power-sharing agreement between the Government and former rebel factions, a new unified armed forces, which incorporated former rebel combatants and militia, was officially established in December 2003. Under a military co-operation agreement, signed in June 2004, South Africa was to assist in the integration and training of the new armed forces; the Belgian Government was also to support the programme. At the end of 2004 the UN Mission in the Democratic Republic of the Congo (MONUC, see p. 75), which had been officially authorized in November 1999, comprised a total of 12,646 uniformed personnel, including 568 military observers, supported by 727 international and 1,125 local civilian staff; MONUC had a total authorized strength (increased in October) of 16,700 military personnel and 475 civilian police. The defence budget for 2002 was US $1,000m.

Economic Affairs

In 2003, according to estimates by the World Bank, the gross national income (GNI) of the DRC, measured at average 2001–03 prices, was US $5,314m., equivalent to $100 per head (or $640 per head on an international purchasing-power parity basis). During 1990–2003, it was estimated, the population increased at an average annual rate of 2.7%, while gross domestic product (GDP) per head declined, in real terms, by an average of 6.6% per year. Overall GDP decreased, in real terms, at an average annual rate of 3.9% in 1990–2003, however, it increased by an estimated 5.0% in 2003.

Agriculture (including forestry, livestock, hunting and fishing) contributed an estimated 57.9% of GDP in 2002. About 61.8% of the working population were employed in agriculture in mid-2003. The principal cash crops are coffee (which accounted for 8.8% of export earnings in 1999, although its contribution declined to an estimated 0.8% in 2000), palm oil and palm kernels, sugar, tea, cocoa, rubber and cotton. Agricultural GDP increased at an average annual rate of 0.4% in 1990–2002, declining by 5.4% in 2001, but increasing by 3.0% in 2002.

Industry (including mining, manufacturing, construction and public works, and power) contributed an estimated 19.3% of GDP in 2002. Some 15.9% of the working population were employed in industry in 1991. Industrial GDP declined at an average annual rate of 7.5% in 1990–2002, but increased, by 3.7% in 2002.

Mining (including mineral processing) contributed an esti-mated 9.8% of GDP in 2001. Mineral products accounted for at least 89.1% of export earnings in 2000. Diamonds, of which the DRC has rich deposits, are the most important source of foreign exchange, accounting for 49.8% of export earnings in 2000. Other main minerals are copper, cobalt (of which the country has 65% of the world's reserves) and zinc. Cadmium, cassiterite, gold and silver are also mined on a small scale. Columbite-

tantalite (coltan) has become a principal export in eastern regions previously under rebel control. By 2004 the partial restoration of peace and the adoption of new mining and invest-ment codes had prompted renewed investment interest in the sector. There are extensive offshore reserves of petroleum (rev-enue from petroleum accounted for 23.2% of export earnings in 2000). The sector's GDP (including the processing of minerals) decreased at an average annual rate of 22.5% in 1990–95, but increased by an average of 2.1% per year in 1996–2001; growth in 2001 was estimated at 7.5%.

Manufacturing contributed an estimated 4.0% of GDP in 2002. The most important sectors are textiles, building mate-rials, agricultural processing and industrial chemicals. In 2004 manufacturing plants were operated at far below capacity. Manufacturing GDP declined at an average annual rate of 12.4% in 1990–95 and of 8.0% in 1996–2001; an estimated decline of 12.5% was recorded in 2001.

Energy is derived principally from hydroelectric power. In 2001 an estimated 99.7% of electricity production was generated by hydroelectric plants. In 2000 imports of petroleum comprised 7.2% of the value of total merchandise imports.

The services sector contributed an estimated 22.8% of GDP in 2002, and employed some 19.0% of the working population in 1991. The GDP of the services sector decreased at an average annual rate of 10.1% in 1990–2002, but it increased by 4.9% in 2001 and by 3.0% in 2002.

In 2002 the DRC recorded an estimated trade surplus of US $27m., but there was a deficit of $159m. on the current account of the balance of payments. In 1995 the principal source of imports (an estimated 16.6%) was Belgium-Luxembourg; other major suppliers were South Africa, Nigeria, Ecuador, the United Kingdom and Germany. In that year South Africa was the principal market for exports (taking an estimated 29.6% of the total); the USA, Belgium-Luxembourg and Angola were also important markets for exports. In 2000 the principal exports were mineral products (mainly industrial diamonds, crude petroleum, cobalt and copper) and agricultural products (pri-marily coffee). The principal import was petroleum.

In 2003 the overall budget deficit (before interest resched-uling) was estimated at 88,947m. new Congolese francs, equiv-alent to 3.9% of GDP. At the end of 2002 external debt totalled US $8,726m., of which $7,391m. was long-term public debt. In 2001 the cost of debt-servicing was equivalent to 1.7% of the value of exports of goods and services. Annual inflation averaged 450.8% in 1993–2002. Consumer prices increased by 359.9% in 2001, by 31.5% in 2002, and by an estimated 12.8% in 2003.

The DRC maintains economic co-operation agreements with its neighbours, Burundi and Rwanda, through the Economic Community of the Great Lakes Countries (see p. 374). The DRC is also a member of the International Coffee Organization (see p. 370) and of the Common Market for Eastern and Southern Africa (COMESA, see p. 179). In September 1997 the DRC became a member of the Southern African Development Com-munity (SADC, see p. 345).

Potentially one of Africa's richest states, the DRC has exten-sive agricultural, mineral and energy resources. During the early 1990s, however, most foreign investment in the country was withdrawn, and by June 1994 government revenues had declined to such an extent that it was suspended from the IMF. The administration of Laurent-Désiré Kabila, which came to power in May 1997, secured foreign investment to revive the highly lucrative mining sector and subsequently succeeded in restoring some financial stability. However, the outbreak of civil war in August resulted in a further deterioration in the financial situation, with repeated depreciation of the Congolese franc, the resumption of hyperinflation and an increase in the budget deficit. Rebel factions gained control of much of the east of the country, where they systematically exploited mineral resources (thereby financing the continuing civil conflict). Ugandan and Rwandan forces supporting the rebels benefited significantly from gaining control of mineral concessions in the east, while Zimbabwe became involved in the conflict on behalf of the DRC Government, in return for significant control of the mining industry. Following the succession to the presidency of Joseph Kabila in January 2001, significant progress in peace negotia-tions was achieved, and a UN embargo on trade in unlicensed diamonds was imposed in May. In the same month the new Government implemented an IMF-monitored plan for the reha-bilitation of public finances, which included the introduction of an official 'floating' exchange rate. The IMF subsequently approved a three-year rehabilitation and reconstruction programme, supported by a Poverty Reduction and Growth Facility (PRGF) arrangement (officially commencing in April 2002). In January 2002, in response to Kabila's urgent appeals for aid, international donors pledged to release considerable development assistance to support the continuation of the peace process. The first year of the PRGF-supported programme resulted in considerable progress in post-conflict recovery, with a resumption in economic growth. The IMF announced that overall fiscal performance at the end of 2002 had exceeded targets, while consumer prices had declined sharply from hyperinflation levels. The authorities had also begun to implement structural reforms, including restructuring of the banking sector, and the introduction of new mining regulations. An extensive power-sharing accord, which incorporated the principal rebel factions, was reached in December, and a new transitional Government of national unity was installed in July 2003. After a further IMF review in July, it was decided that economic progress had been sufficient for the country to qualify for an 80% reduction in external debt under the enhanced initiative for heavily indebted poor countries. Government priorities were to reduce corruption, rehabilitate infrastructure and introduce further reform of government institutions and state-owned enterprises. The announcement of major mining projects in 2004 demonstrated a significant improvement in the private-investor confidence, despite continued fighting in the east of the country. In July the IMF, commending continuing government reforms, approved a further disbursement under the PRGF-supported programme; despite steadily increasing rates of growth and further success in imposing fiscal discipline, it was estimated that the country would not reach its 1990 level of development for 45 years. In November 2004, at a meeting of 'Paris Club' donors, convened under the auspices of the IMF and World Bank, the Kabila Government presented a new economic plan for 2005–07; the 'minimum partnership programme for transition and recovery', which was designed to consolidate the level of recovery reached under the poverty reduction strategy, received considerable pledges of financial support. Despite the Government's insistence that elections would be conducted by the end of June 2005, as scheduled, the intensified fighting in the east of the country in mid-2004 and subsequent political events increased the likelihood that completion of the transitional process would be delayed. Nevertheless, the Government's adherence to stabilization reforms, which were supported by rising levels of donor assistance, was viewed as remaining conducive to economic growth.

Education

Primary education, beginning at six years of age and lasting for six years, is officially compulsory. Secondary education, which is not compulsory, begins at 12 years of age and lasts for up to six years, comprising a first cycle of two years and a second of four years. In 1998/99, according to UNESCO estimates, primary enrolment included 32.6% of students in the relevant age-group (33.4% of boys; 31.8% of girls), while the comparable ratio for secondary enrolment was 11.7% (14.8% of boys; 8.6% of girls). The country has four universities, situated at Kinshasa, Kinshasa/Limete, Kisangani and Lubumbashi. In the budget for 1997 a total of 144,000m. new zaires (0.2% of total expenditure by the central Government) was allocated to education. In 2002 an emergency programme for education, with an estimated cost of US $101m., was introduced to restore access to basic education throughout the country.

Public Holidays

2005: 1 January (New Year's Day), 4 January (Commemoration of the Martyrs of Independence), 1 May (Labour Day), 24 June (Promulgation of the 1967 Constitution and Day of the Fishermen), 30 June (Independence Day), 1 August (Parents' Day), 14 October (Youth Day), 27 October (Naming Day), 17 November (Army Day), 24 November (Anniversary of the Second Republic), 25 December (Christmas Day).

2006: 1 January (New Year's Day), 4 January (Commemoration of the Martyrs of Independence), 1 May (Labour Day), 24 June (Promulgation of the 1967 Constitution and Day of the Fishermen), 30 June (Independence Day), 1 August (Parents' Day), 14 October (Youth Day), 27 October (Naming Day), 17 November (Army Day), 24 November (Anniversary of the Second Republic), 25 December (Christmas Day).

Weights and Measures

The metric system is in force.

Statistical Survey

Sources (unless otherwise stated): Département de l'Economie Nationale, Kinshasa; Institut National de la Statistique, Office Nationale de la Recherche et du Développement, BP 20, Kinshasa; tel. (12) 31401.

Area and Population

AREA, POPULATION AND DENSITY

Area (sq km)	2,344,885*
Population (census result)	
1 July 1984	
Males	14,543,800
Females	15,373,000
Total	29,916,800
Population (UN estimates at mid-year)†	
2001	49,785,000
2002	51,201,000
2003	52,771,000
Density (per sq km) at mid-2003	22.5

* 905,365 sq miles.

† Source: UN, *World Population Prospects: The 2002 Revision.*

REGIONS*

	Area (sq km)	Population (31 Dec. 1985)†
Bandundu	295,658	4,644,758
Bas-Zaïre	53,920	2,158,595
Equateur	403,293	3,960,187
Haut-Zaïre	503,239	5,119,750
Kasaï Occidental	156,967	3,465,756
Kasaï Oriental	168,216	2,859,220
Kivu	256,662	5,232,442
Shaba (formerly Katanga) . . .	496,965	4,452,618
Kinshasa (city)‡	9,965	2,778,281
Total	**2,344,885**	**34,671,607**

* In October 1997 a statutory order redesignated the regions as provinces. Kivu was divided into three separate provinces, and several of the other provinces were renamed. There are now 11 provinces: Bandundu, Bas-Congo, Equateur, Kasaï Occidental, Kasaï Oriental, Katanga (formerly Shaba), Kivu-Maniema, Nord-Kivu, Province Orientale (formerly Haut-Zaïre), Sud-Kivu, Kinshasa (city).

† Provisional.

‡ Including the commune of Maluku.

Source: Département de l'Administration du Territoire.

PRINCIPAL TOWNS
(population at census of July 1984)

Kinshasa (capital)	2,664,309	Likasi	213,862
Lubumbashi	564,830	Boma	197,617
Mbuji-Mayi	486,235	Bukavu	167,950
Kolwezi	416,122	Kikwit	149,296
Kisangani	317,581	Matadi	138,798
Kananga	298,693	Mbandaka	137,291

Source: UN, *Demographic Yearbook.*

Mid-2003: (UN estimate, including suburbs) Kinshasa 5,276,958 (Source: UN, *World Urbanization Prospects: The 2003 Revision*).

BIRTHS AND DEATHS
(UN estimates, annual averages)

	1985–90	1990–95	1995–2000
Birth rate (per 1,000)	48.5	48.7	49.5
Death rate (per 1,000)	18.9	20.3	25.0

Source: UN, *World Population Prospects: The 2002 Revision.*

Expectation of life (WHO estimates, years at birth): 43.5 (males 41.0; females 46.1) in 2002 (Source: WHO, *World Health Report*).

ECONOMICALLY ACTIVE POPULATION

Mid-2003 (estimates in '000): Agriculture, etc. 13,604; Total labour force 22,021 (Source: FAO).

Health and Welfare

KEY INDICATORS

Total fertility rate (children per woman, 2002)	6.7
Under-5 mortality rate (per 1,000 live births, 2003)	205
HIV/AIDS (% of persons aged 15–49, 2003)	4.2
Physicians (per 1,000 head, 1996)	0.07
Hospital beds (per 1,000 head, 1990)	1.43
Health expenditure (2001): US $ per head (PPP)	12
Health expenditure (2001): % of GDP	3.5
Health expenditure (2001): public (% of total)	44.4
Access to water (% of persons, 2002)	46
Access to sanitation (% of persons, 2002)	29
Human Development Index (2002): ranking	168
Human Development Index (2002): value	0.365

For sources and definitions, see explanatory note on p. vi.

Agriculture

PRINCIPAL CROPS
('000 metric tons)

	2001	2002	2003
Rice (paddy)	326	314	315
Maize	1,169	1,155	1,155
Millet	35	36	36
Sorghum	60*	60*	60†
Potatoes	91	91	92
Sweet potatoes	228	220	223
Cassava (Manioc)	15,436	14,929	14,945
Taro (Coco yam)	64	65	66
Yams*	290	320	330
Other roots and tubers*	59	70	70
Sugar cane	1,560	1,911	1,786
Dry beans	114	107	108
Dry peas*	65	68	68
Groundnuts (in shell)	368	355	360
Oil palm fruit	990*	1,150†	1,150†
Cabbages*	23	23	23
Tomatoes*	40	40	40
Onions (dry)*	53	53	53
Pumpkins*	39	39	39
Other vegetables*	295	295	295

— continued	2001	2002	2003
Bananas	313	313	315
Plantains	1,216	1,250*	1,250*
Oranges	178	180	180*
Grapefruit	10	10	10*
Avocados	61	60	61*
Mangoes	202	198	200*
Pineapples	192	192	193*
Papayas	206	210	211*
Other fruit*	67	67	67
Coffee (green)	37	32	40†
Cocoa beans	6	6	6*
Tea (made)	2	1	1*
Tobacco (leaves)	4	4	4†
Cotton (lint)	10	10	10*
Natural rubber (dry weight)*	7	7	7

* FAO estimate(s).
† Unofficial figure.
Source: FAO.

LIVESTOCK
('000 head, year ending September)

	2001	2002	2003*
Cattle	793	761	761
Sheep	911	897	897
Goats	4,067	4,004	4,004
Pigs	100	953	953
Poultry	20,552	19,592	19,600

* FAO estimates.
Source: FAO.

LIVESTOCK PRODUCTS
('000 metric tons)

	2001	2002	2003
Beef and veal	13.0	12.5	12.5
Goat meat	18.7	18.4	18.4
Pig meat	24.9	23.7	23.8
Poultry meat	11.1	10.5	10.6
Game meat	89.5	90.0*	90.0*
Other meat*	56.8	56.8	56.8
Cows' milk*	5.2	5.0	5.0
Hen eggs*	6.7	6.0	6.0

* FAO estimate(s).
Source: FAO.

Forestry

ROUNDWOOD REMOVALS
(FAO estimates, '000 cubic metres, excl. bark)

	2001	2002	2003
Sawlogs, veneer logs and logs for sleepers	170	170	170
Other industrial wood	3,483	3,483	3,483
Fuel wood	66,081	67,285	68,517
Total	69,734	70,938	72,170

Source: FAO.

SAWNWOOD PRODUCTION
('000 cubic metres, incl. railway sleepers)

	2001	2002	2003
Total (all broadleaved)	60	40	40*

* FAO estimate.
Source: FAO.

Fishing

('000 metric tons, live weight)

	2000	2001	2002
Capture*	209.3	214.6	220.0
Aquaculture	2.1	2.7	3.0
Total catch	211.4	217.3	223.0

* FAO estimates.

Source: FAO.

Mining

(metric tons, unless otherwise indicated)

	2000	2001	2002
Hard coal*	—	1,000	1,000
Crude petroleum ('000 barrels) .	8,500	8,500	8,500*
Copper ore†	21,000*	20,998	32,300
Zinc ore†	215	1,014	—
Tantalum and niobium (columbium) concentrates‡ . .	450	200*	100*
Cobalt concentrates*† . . .	10,000	13,000	12,500
Gold (kilograms)	69	19	20*
Diamonds ('000 carats)§ . . .	16,000	18,200	18,556

* Estimated production.
† Figures refer to output of mines.
‡ The estimated tantalum content was 130 metric tons in 2000, 60 metric tons in 2001 and 30 metric tons in 2002.
§ An estimated 20% of production is comprised of gemstones.

Source: US Geological Survey.

Industry

SELECTED PRODUCTS
('000 metric tons, unless otherwise indicated)

	1998	1999	2000
Maize flour	17	19	12
Wheat flour	113	89	117
Sugar	57	73	73
Cigarettes ('000 cartons) . .	3,848	3,200	3,712
Beer (million litres) . . .	161	145	171
Soft drinks (million litres) . .	78	75	81
Soaps	29	26	28
Acetylene	24	14	17
Tyres ('000 units)	56	38	—
Cement	145	173	169
Steel	118	87	159
Explosives	513	300	246
Bottles ('000 units) . . .	21	18	23
Gasoline ('000 barrels) . . .	434	431	431*
Kerosene ('000 barrels) . . .	340	340	340*
Jet fuel ('000 barrels) . . .	175	180	180*
Distillate fuel oil ('000 barrels) .	457	460	460*
Residual fuel oil ('000 barrels) . .	874	880	880*
Cotton fabrics ('000 sq metres) .	1,563	3,028	2,361
Printed fabrics ('000 sq metres) .	12,220	16,853	14,334
Footwear ('000 pairs) . . .	1,609	848	962
Blankets ('000 units) . . .	47	36	30
Matchets and wheels ('000 pieces)	245	207	n.a.
Sheet metal ('000 pieces) . .	86	75	65
Motor cars (units)	94	84	n.a.
Electric energy (million kWh) . .	4,519	5,100	5,813

* Estimate.

2001 (estimates, '000 metric tons unless otherwise indicated): Wheat flour 90; Beer (million litres) 155; Soft drinks (million litres) 64; Soaps 15; Acetylene 7; Cement 201; Bottles ('000 units) 17; Cotton ('000 sq metres) 2,353; Printed fabrics ('000 sq metres) 3,600; Footwear ('000 pairs) 32; Electric energy (million kWh) 5,798.

Note: Production for 2001 assumed to be unchanged from 2000 for gasoline, kerosene, jet fuel, distillate fuel oil and residual fuel oil.

Sources: IMF, *Democratic Republic of the Congo: Selected Issues and Statistical Appendix* (June 2003); US Geological Survey.

Finance

CURRENCY AND EXCHANGE RATES

Monetary Units
100 centimes = 1 new Congolese franc.

Sterling, Dollar and Euro Equivalents (30 September 2004)
£1 sterling = 770.86 new Congolese francs;
US $1 = 428.54 new Congolese francs;
€1 = 531.78 new Congolese francs;
1,000 new Congolese francs = £1.30 = $2.33 = €1.88.

Average Exchange Rate (new Congolese francs per US $)
2001   206.62
2002   346.49
2003   405.34

Note: In June 1967 the zaire was introduced, replacing the Congolese franc (CF) at an exchange rate of 1 zaire = CF 1,000. In October 1993 the zaire was replaced by the new zaire (NZ), equivalent to 3m. old zaires. On 30 June 1998 a new Congolese franc, equivalent to NZ 100,000, was introduced. The NZ was withdrawn from circulation on 30 June 1999. Some of the figures in this Survey are still given in terms of a previous currency.

BUDGET
('000 million new Congolese francs)*

Revenue†	2002	2003‡	2004§
Customs and excises	54,668	72,500	108,602
Direct and indirect taxes (excl. petroleum)	40,505	49,038	63,000
Petroleum royalties and taxes . .	31,507	36,386	36,907
Other	13,834	16,793	26,880
Non-budget revenue . . .	11,679	2,100	—
Total	152,193	176,817	235,389

Expenditure‖	2002	2003‡	2004§
Current expenditure	168,243	248,324	264,095
Wages and salaries . . .	39,287	57,104	88,828
Interest on public debt . . .	61,157	79,076	78,461
Transfers and subsidies . . .	6,674	19,867	14,225
Other current expenditure . .	61,125	92,277	82,581
Non-budget expenditure . . .	11,679	2,100	—
Capital expenditure	10,385	61,756	186,059
Externally financed investment	6,657	47,154	178,359
Domestically financed investment	3,728	14,603	7,700
Other operations	112	89	—
Total	190,419	312,270	450,154

* Figures refer to the consolidated accounts of the central Government.
† Excluding grants received ('000 million new Congolese francs): 7,447 in 2002; 46,506 in 2003 (estimate); 150,477 in 2004 (projection).
‡ Estimates.
§ Projections.
‖ Excluding lending minus repayments ('000 million new Congolese francs): 7,987 in 2002; 0 in 2003 (estimate); 0 in 2004 (projection). Also excluding expenditure related to the Highly Indebted Poor Countries (HIPC) initiative, introduced by the IMF and World Bank in 2003 ('000 million new Congolese francs): 0 in 2003 (estimate); 44,331 in 2004 (projection).

Source: IMF, *Democratic Republic of the Congo: Fourth Review Under the Three-Year Arrangement Under the Poverty Reduction and Growth Facility, Requests for Waiver of Performance Criteria and Additional Interim Assistance Under the Enhanced Initiative for Heavily Indebted Poor Countries—Staff Report; Staff Statement; Press Release on the Executive Board Discussion; and Statement by the Executive Director for the Democratic Republic of the Congo* (August 2004).

INTERNATIONAL RESERVES
(US $ million at 31 December)

	1993	1994	1995
Gold	8.59	10.71	10.83
Foreign exchange	46.20	120.69	146.60
Total	54.79	131.40	157.43

1996 (US $ million at 31 December): Foreign exchange 82.50.

1997 (US $ million at 31 December): Gold 15.80.

2002 (US $ million at 31 December): IMF special drawing rights 8.32.

2003 (US $ million at 31 December): IMF special drawing rights 7.96.

Source: IMF, *International Financial Statistics*.

MONEY SUPPLY
(million new Congolese francs at 31 December)

	2001	2002	2003
Currency outside banks . .	36,110	49,757	63,148
Demand deposits at deposit money banks	7,922	7,956	8,606
Total money (incl. others) . .	41,064	57,893	72,110

Source: IMF, *International Financial Statistics*.

COST OF LIVING
(Consumer Price Index for Kinshasa; base: August 1995 = 100)

	1998	1999	2000
Food	3,820.7	12,909.6	75,943.0
Rent	3,143.7	11,086.5	73,439.8
Clothing	3,498.7	17,225.7	113,520.0
All items (incl. others) . . .	3,259.0	12,069.0	78,899.0

Source: IMF, *Democratic Republic of the Congo: Selected Issues and Statistical Appendix* (July 2001).

All items (Consumer Price Index; base 2000 = 100): 459.9 in 2001; 604.9 in 2002 (Source: IMF, *International Financial Statistics*).

NATIONAL ACCOUNTS
('000 million new Congolese francs at current prices)

Expenditure on the Gross Domestic Product

	1999	2000	2001*
Government final consumption expenditure	3.1	22.3	84.6
Private final consumption expenditure	44.2	261.5	1,331.9
Gross capital formation	1.6	10.3	76.2
Total domestic expenditure .	48.9	294.1	1,492.7
Exports of goods and services . .	12.2	66.5	262.5
Less Imports of goods and services	9.1	63.5	291.2
GDP in purchasers' values . .	52.0	297.0	1,464.0
GDP at constant 1987 prices .	1.61	1.49	1.46

* Estimates.

Source: IMF, *Democratic Republic of the Congo: Selected Issues and Statistical Appendix* (June 2003).

Gross Domestic Product by Economic Activity

	1999	2000	2001*
Agriculture, forestry, livestock, hunting, and fishing	27.1	146.7	824.3
Mining†	4.6	30.5	142.0
Manufacturing	2.6	14.2	57.1
Construction and public works .	1.4	12.5	64.4
Electricity and water	1.1	2.4	11.7
Transportation and telecommunications	1.4	9.4	39.5
Trade and commerce	8.7	54.3	218.2
Public administration	2.1	7.1	26.4
Other services	2.6	16.7	60.2
GDP at factor cost	51.6	293.8	1,443.8
Import duties	0.4	3.2	20.2
GDP at market (purchasers') prices	52.0	297.0	1,464.0

* Estimates.
† Including processing.

Source: IMF, *Democratic Republic of the Congo: Selected Issues and Statistical Appendix* (June 2003).

BALANCE OF PAYMENTS
(US $ million)

	2000	2001	2002
Exports of goods f.o.b.	892	880	1,088
Imports of goods f.o.b.	−680	−807	−1,061
Trade balance	212	74	27
Services (net)	−169	−179	−252
Balance on goods and services	43	−105	−225
Income (net)	−388	−412	−297
Balance on goods, services and income	−345	−517	−522
Current transfers (net) . . .	146	268	363
Current balance	−199	−249	−159
Capital account (net)	−388	−315	148
Net errors and omissions . . .	−242	−144	−149
Overall balance	−829	−709	−161

Source: IMF, *Democratic Republic of the Congo: Enhanced Initiative for Heavily Indebted Poor Countries—Decision Point Document* (August 2003).

External Trade

PRINCIPAL COMMODITIES
(UN estimates, million old zaires)

Imports c.i.f.	1989	1990	1991
Food and live animals	63,380	121,824	2,172,956
Mineral fuels, lubricants, etc. . .	24,436	46,968	837,761
Chemicals	33,217	63,848	1,138,847
Basic manufactures	68,343	131,365	2,343,137
Machinery and transport equipment	102,706	197,414	3,521,243
Miscellaneous manufactured articles	16,418	31,557	562,877
Total (incl. others)	324,154	623,066	11,113,531

Exports f.o.b.	1989	1990	1991
Food and live animals	93,541	148,201	2,535,635
Mineral fuels, lubricants, etc. . .	36,064	57,138	977,599
Chemicals	49,024	77,672	1,328,924
Basic manufactures	100,866	159,807	2,734,207
Machinery and transport equipment	151,581	240,157	4,108,950
Miscellaneous manufactured articles	24,230	38,389	656,814
Total (incl. others)	478,409	757,967	12,968,384

Source: UN Economic Commission for Africa, *African Statistical Yearbook*.

1994 (US $ million): *Imports c.i.f.*: Mineral fuels 45.4; Total 628.8. *Exports f.o.b.*: Copper 42.8; Cobalt 140.3; Diamonds 293.6; Crude petroleum 123.5; Coffee 158.6; Total 1,271.6 (Source: IMF, *Zaire—Background Information and Statistical Data*, April 1996).

1996 (US $ million): *Imports c.i.f.*: Petroleum 79; Total 1,403. *Exports f.o.b.*: Copper 89; Cobalt 322; Diamonds 633; Crude petroleum 198; Coffee 263; Total 1,652 (Source: IMF, *Democratic Republic of the Congo: Selected Issues and Statistical Appendix*, July 2001).

1997 (US $ million): *Imports c.i.f.*: Petroleum 106; Total 1,133. *Exports f.o.b.*: Copper 83; Cobalt 119; Diamonds 611; Crude petroleum 177; Coffee 95; Total 1,189 (Source: IMF, *Democratic Republic of the Congo: Selected Issues and Statistical Appendix*, July 2001).

1998 (US $ million): *Imports c.i.f.*: Petroleum 126; Total 1,230. *Exports f.o.b.*: Copper 53; Cobalt 145; Diamonds 716; Crude petroleum 111; Coffee 67; Total 1,181 (Source: IMF, *Democratic Republic of the Congo: Selected Issues and Statistical Appendix*, July 2001).

1999 (US $ million): *Imports c.i.f.*: Petroleum 57; Total 458. *Exports f.o.b.*: Copper 48; Cobalt 80; Diamonds 579; Crude petroleum 116; Coffee 86; Total 974 (Source: IMF, *Democratic Republic of the Congo: Selected Issues and Statistical Appendix*, June 2003).

2000 (US $ million): *Imports c.i.f.*: Petroleum 49; Total 680. *Exports f.o.b.*: Copper 47; Cobalt 97; Diamonds 444; Crude petroleum 207; Coffee 7; Total 892 (Source: IMF, *Democratic Republic of the Congo: Selected Issues and Statistical Appendix*, June 2003).

SELECTED TRADING PARTNERS
(US $ million)

Imports c.i.f.	1995
Belgium-Luxembourg	147.2
Canada	9.8
China, People's Repub.	26.8
Côte d'Ivoire	35.5
Ecuador	65.1
Germany	48.2
India	9.9
Iran	10.3
Italy	26.5
Japan	11.8
Kenya	22.5
Morocco	9.2
Netherlands	36.5
Nigeria	72.5
South Africa	89.3
Togo	22.5
United Kingdom	50.2
Zambia	9.4
Total (incl. others)	889.2

Exports f.o.b.	1995
Angola	51.0
Belgium-Luxembourg	90.9
Canada	11.6
Germany	8.7
Irael	17.2
Italy	29.6
Philippines	30.2
Senegal	9.5
South Africa	219.7
Switzerland	29.7
United Kingdom	29.7
USA	107.6
Total (incl. others)	742.8

Source: UN, *International Trade Statistics Yearbook*.

Transport

RAILWAYS
(Total traffic, million)

	2000	2001	2002
Passenger-km	84	171	76
Freight (net ton-km)	85	228	307

Source: UN, *Statistical Yearbook*.

ROAD TRAFFIC
(motor vehicles in use at 31 December)

	1994	1995*	1996*
Passenger cars	698,672	762,000	787,000
Buses and coaches	51,578	55,000	60,000
Lorries and vans	464,205	495,000	538,000
Total vehicles	1,214,455	1,312,000	1,384,000

* Estimates.

Source: International Road Federation, *World Road Statistics*.

1999: Passenger cars 172,600; Commercial vehicles 34,600 (Source: UN, *Statistical Yearbook*).

SHIPPING
Merchant Fleet
(registered at 31 December)

	2001	2002	2003
Number of vessels	20	20	20
Total displacement ('000 grt)	12.9	12.9	12.9

Source: Lloyd's Register-Fairplay, *World Fleet Statistics*.

International Sea-borne Freight Traffic
(estimates, '000 metric tons)

	1988	1989	1990
Goods loaded	2,500	2,440	2,395
Goods unloaded	1,400	1,483	1,453

Source: UN, *Monthly Bulletin of Statistics*.

CIVIL AVIATION
(traffic on scheduled services)

	1999	2000	2001
Kilometres flown (million)	4	4	3
Passengers carried ('000)	132	128	95
Passenger-km (million)	263	245	157
Total ton-km (million)	39	34	22

Source: UN, *Statistical Yearbook*.

Tourism

FOREIGN TOURIST ARRIVALS BY ORIGIN

	1998	1999	2000
Africa	22,223	73,428	96,594
America	1,231	799	495
East Asia	1,333	1,400	—
Europe	7,975	4,295	5,681
Total (incl. others)	53,139	79,922	102,770

Tourism receipts (US $ million): 2 in 1998.

Source: World Tourism Organization.

Communications Media

	2000	2001	2002
Telephones ('000 main lines in use)*	9.8	10.0	10.0
Mobile cellular telephones ('000 subscribers)	15	150	560
Internet users ('000)	3	6	50

* Provisional or estimated figures.

Mobile cellular telephones ('000 subscribers): 1,000 in 2003.

Radio receivers ('000 in use): 18,030 in 1997.

Television receivers ('000 in use): 6,478 in 1997.

Facsimile machines (estimated number in use): 5,000 in 1996.

Personal computers ('000 in use): 200 in 1998; 500 in 1999.

Book production (titles published): 112 in 1996.

Daily newspapers: 9 in 1996.

Sources: International Telecommunication Union; UNESCO, *Statistical Yearbook*; UN Economic Commission for Africa, *African Statistical Yearbook*.

Education

(1998)

	Institu- tions	Teachers	Students Males	Females	Total
Primary . .	17,585	154,618	2,116,752	1,905,659	4,022,411
General secondary	6,007	89,461	554,895	307,830	862,725
Technical and vocational .			256,313	115,490	371,803
Tertiary . .	n.a.	3,788	n.a.	n.a.	60,341*

* Estimate.

Source: UNESCO, *Statistical Yearbook*.

Adult literacy rate (UNESCO estimates): 62.7% (males 74.2%; females 51.8%) in 2001 (Source: UN Development Programme, *Human Development Report*).

Directory

The Constitution

Following a power-sharing agreement between the Government of the Democratic Republic of Congo and rebel representatives, reached in December 2002 (see Recent History), a new Constitution, providing for the establishment of a two-year transitional authority, was officially adopted on 4 April 2003. The new document superseded the 15-point constitutional decree of the Democratic Republic of the Congo, which had been promulgated on 28 May 1997. On 7 April 2004 the incumbent President, Maj.-Gen. Joseph Kabila, was reinstalled for the transitional period. The transitional arrangements provide for the establishment of an interim Government of national unity, and bicameral Parliament, comprising a 500-member lower chamber, the National Assembly, and a 120-member upper chamber, the Senate. The new transitional organs of government comprise representatives of the former administration, political opposition and civil society, and the main rebel groups. The President is Commander-in-Chief of the armed forces, and has executive power to appoint and dismiss ministers and judges. The legislature does not have the power to overturn the Government through a vote of no confidence. Local government in each province is administered by a provincial Governor and Deputy Governor, who are appointed and dismissed by the President.

The Government

HEAD OF STATE

President: Maj.-Gen. JOSEPH KABILA (inaugurated 26 January 2001 and 7 April 2003).

CABINET
(April 2005)

Vice-President: JEAN-PIERRE BEMBA.

Vice-President: ABDOULAYE YERODIA NDOMBASI.

Vice-President: ARTHUR Z'AHIDI NGOMA.

Vice-President: AZARIAS RUBERWA.

Minister of the Interior, Decentralization and Security: THÉOPHILE MBEMBA FUNDU.

Minister of Foreign Affairs and International Co-operation: RAYMOND RAMAZANI BAYA.

Minister of Regional Co-operation: MBUSA NYAMWISI.

Minister of Defence, Demobilization and War Veterans' Affairs: ADOLPHE ONUSUMBA YEMBA.

Minister of Family and Women's Affairs: FAIDA MWANGILA.

Minister of Justice: HONORIUS KISIMBA NGOY.

Minister of Human Rights: MARIE MADELEINE KALALA.

Minister of Press and Information: HENRY MOVA SAKANYI.

Minister of Planning: ALEXIS THAMBWE-MWAMBA.

Minister of the Budget: FRANÇOIS MUAMBA TSISHIMBI.

Minister of Finance: PIERRE ANDRÉ FUTA.

Minister of the Economy: FLORIBERT BOKANGA.

Minister of Industry and Small- and Medium-sized Enterprises: JEAN MBUYU LUNYONGOLA.

Minister of Mining: INGELE IFOTO.

Minister of Energy: PIERRE MUZUMBA MWANA OMBE.

Minister of External Trade: CHANTAL NGALULA MULUMBA.

Minister of Parastatals: CÉLESTIN MVUNABANDI.

Minister of the Civil Service: ATHENASE MATENDA KYELU.

Minister of Agriculture: PAUL MUSAFIRI.

Minister of Rural Development: KALIBA MUNANGA.

Minister of Posts and Telecommunications: GERTRUDE KITEMBO.

Minister of Scientific Research: GÉRARD KAMANDA WA KAMANDA.

Minister of Public Works and Infrastructure: JOSE MAKILA.

Minister of Transport: EVA MAKASA.

Minister of the Environment: ANSELME ENERUNGA.

Minister of Tourism: JOSÉ ENGBANDA.

Minister of Land Affairs: VENANT TSHIPASA.

Minister of Town Planning: JOHN TIBASIMA.

Minister of Health: EMILE BONGELI YEKOLO.

Minister of Higher and University Education: JEAN-PIERRE LOLA KISANGA.

Minister of Primary and Secondary Education: CONSTANT NDOM NDA OMBEL.

Minister of Labour and Social Welfare: BALAMAGE NKOLO.

Minister of Social Affairs: LAURENT-CHARLES OTETE OMANGA.

Minister of Youth and Sports: ROGER NIMY.

Minister of Solidarity and Humanitarian Affairs: CATHERINE NZUZI WA MBOMBO.

Minister of Culture: CHRISTOPHE MUZUNGU.

MINISTRIES

All ministries are in Kinshasa.

Office of the President: Hôtel du Conseil Exécutif, ave de Lemera, Kinshasa-Gombe; tel. (12) 30892.

Ministry of Agriculture: Immeuble Sozacom, 3rd floor, blvd du 30 juin, BP 8722 KIN I, Kinshasa-Gombe; tel. (12) 31821.

Ministry of Defence, Demobilization and War Veterans' Affairs: BP 4111, Kinshasa-Gombe; tel. (12) 59375.

Ministry of the Economy: Immeuble Onatra, blvd du 30 juin, BP 8500 KIN I, Kinshasa-Gombe.

Ministry of Education: Enceinte de l'Institut de la Gombe, BP 3163, Kinshasa-Gombe; tel. (12) 30098.

Ministry of Energy: Immeuble Snel, 239 ave de la Justice, BP 5137 KIN I, Kinshasa-Gombe; tel. (12) 22570.

Ministry of Finance: blvd du 30 juin, BP 12998 KIN I, Kinshasa-Gombe; tel. (12) 31197.

Ministry of Foreign Affairs and International Co-operation: place de l'Indépendance, BP 7100, Kinshasa-Gombe; tel. (12) 32450.

Ministry of Health: blvd du 30 juin, BP 3088 KIN I, Kinshasa-Gombe; tel. (12) 31750.

Ministry of the Interior, Decentralization and Security: ave de Lemera, Kinshasa-Gombe; tel. (12) 23171.

Ministry of Justice: 228 ave de Lemera, BP 3137, Kinshasa-Gombe; tel. (12) 32432.

Ministry of Labour and Social Welfare: blvd du 30 juin, BP 3840, Kinshasa.

Ministry of Posts and Telecommunications: Immeuble Kilou, 4484 ave des Huiles, BP 800 KIN I, Kinshasa-Gombe; tel. (12) 24854.

Ministry of Public Works and Infrastructure: Immeuble Travaux Publics, Kinshasa-Gombe.

Ministry of Transport: Immeuble Onatra, blvd du 30 juin, BP 3304, Kinshasa-Gombe; tel. (12) 23660.

Ministry of Youth and Sports: 77 ave de la Justice, BP 8541 KIN I, Kinshasa-Gombe.

President

Following the assassination of President LAURENT-DÉSIRÉ KABILA on 16 January 2001, his son, Maj.-Gen. JOSEPH KABILA, was inaugurated as interim President on 26 January. On 7 April 2003 JOSEPH KABILA was inaugurated again as President, to head a transitional administration, in accordance with a power-sharing agreement reached in December 2002.

Legislature

A new transitional bicameral Parliament was inaugurated in Kinshasa by President JOSEPH KABILA on 22 August 2003. The 500-member lower chamber, or National Assembly, comprised a total of 94 members of RCD—Goma, the MLC, the former Government, opposition political parties and civil society, while the RCD—ML was allocated 15 deputies, Mai-Mai militia 10, and the RCD—N five. The 120-member upper chamber, or Senate, consisted of 22 representatives of the five main groups, four of the RCD—ML and Mai-Mai, and two of the RCD—N.

President of the National Assembly: OLIVIER KAMITATU ETSOU.

President of the Senate: PIERRE MARINI BODHO.

Political Organizations

In January 1999 a ban on the formation of political associations was officially ended, and in May 2001 remaining restrictions on the registration and operation of political parties were removed. Despite a peace agreement between the Government and rebel factions, reached in December 2002 and the subsequent installation of power-sharing institutions in 2003, heavy fighting continued in the east of the country.

Forces pour le salut du Congo (FSC): f. June 2000 by fmr supporters of Pres. Mobutu; Leader JÉRÔME TSHISHIMBI.

Front de l'intégration pour la pacification de l'Ituri (FIPI): Lendu militia group, supported by Ugandan forces in Ituri.

Front pour les nationalistes et intégrationistes (FNI): f. 2003 in Uganda; ethnic Lendu rebel group, in conflict with Union des patriotes congolais in north-east; Leader FLORIBERT NDJABU NGABU.

Mouvement pour la libération du Congo (MLC): f. 1998; fmr Ugandan-supported rebel movement; incl. in Govt in July 2003; Leader JEAN-PIERRE BEMBA; Sec.-Gen. THOMAS LUHAKA.

Mouvement populaire de la révolution (MPR): f. 1966 by Pres. Mobutu; sole legal political party until Nov. 1990; advocates national unity and opposes tribalism; Leader (vacant); Sec.-Gen. KITHIMA BIN RAMAZANI.

Organistes des progressistes du Congo (Madaraka ya wendeliza wa Kongo—MWENDEKO): Kinshasa; e-mail mwendeko@mail.chez .com; internet www.chez.com/mwendeko.

Parti démocrate et social chrétien (PDSC): 32B ave Tombalbaye, Kinshasa-Gombe; tel. (12) 21211; f. 1990; centrist; Pres. ANDRÉ BO-BOLIKO; Sec.-Gen. TUYABA LEWULA.

Parti populaire pour la reconstruction et le développement (PPRD): Kinshasa; Sec.-Gen. TSHIKEZ DIEMU.

Parti pour la réconciliation et le développement (PPRD): f. March 2002 by President Joseph Kabila.

Rassemblement congolais pour la démocratie (RCD—Goma): e-mail congorcd@congorcd.org; internet www.congorcd.org; f. 1998; rebel movement until Dec. 2002 peace agreement; incl. in Govt July 2003; main Ilunga faction; supported by Rwanda; Leader AZARIAS RUBERWA; Sec.-Gen. FRANCIS BEDY MAKHUBU MABELE.

Rassemblement congolais pour la démocratie—Mouvement de libération (RCD—ML): Bunia; broke away from main RCD in 1999; supported by Uganda; a number of groups were merged into the FLC (see above) in Jan. 2001; Pres. MBUSA NYAMWISI.

Rassemblement congolais pour la démocratie—National (RCD—N): Bafwasende; broke away from RCD—ML in Oct. 2000; Leader ROGER LUMBALA.

Rassemblement pour une nouvelle société (RNS): c/o 58 Hawthorne Court, Suite 1316, Washington, DC, 20017, USA; tel. (202) 4639373; fax (202) 4639374; e-mail info@congozaire.org.

Union des patriotes congolais (UPC): rebel group of Hema ethnic group, fmrly in conflict with Lendu in north-east; registered as political org. 2004, after peace agreement with Govt; Leader THOMAS LUBANGA.

Union pour la démocratie et le progrès social (UDPS): Twelfth St, Limete Zone, Kinshasa; e-mail udps@globalserve.net; internet www.udps.org/udps.html; f. 1982; Leader ETIENNE TSHISEKEDI WA MULUMBA; Sec.-Gen. Dr ADRIEN PHONGO KUNDA.

Union sacrée de l'opposition radicale (USOR): Kinshasa; f. 1991, comprising c. 130 movements and factions opposed to Pres. Mobutu, in which the UDPS was the dominant party; a radical internal faction, known as the **Union sacrée de l'opposition radicale et ses alliés (USORAL)**, emerged in 1994, led by FRÉDÉRIC KIBASSA MALIBA.

Diplomatic Representation

EMBASSIES IN THE DEMOCRATIC REPUBLIC OF THE CONGO

Angola: 4413–4429 blvd du 30 juin, BP 8625, Kinshasa; tel. (12) 32415; Ambassador MAWETE JOÃO BAPTISTA.

Belgium: Immeuble Le Cinquantenaire, place du 27 octobre, BP 899, Kinshasa; tel. (12) 20110; fax (12) 22120; e-mail kinshasa@diplobel.org; Ambassador RENIER NIJSKENS.

Benin: 3990 ave des Cliniques, BP 3265, Kinshasa-Gombe; tel. (98) 128659; e-mail abkin@raga.net; Ambassador GEORGES S. WHANNOU DE DRAVO.

Cameroon: 171 blvd du 30 juin, BP 10998, Kinshasa; tel. (12) 34787; Chargé d'affaires a.i. DOMINIQUE AWONO ESSAMA.

Canada: BP 8341, Kinshasa 1; tel. (88) 41277; e-mail knsha@dfait-maeci.gc.ca; Ambassador ROLAND GOULET.

Central African Republic: 11 ave Pumbu, BP 7769, Kinshasa; tel. (12) 30417; Ambassador SISSA LE BERNARD.

Chad: 67–69 ave du Cercle, BP 9097, Kinshasa; tel. (12) 22358; Ambassador MAITINE DJOUMBE.

Congo, Republic: 179 blvd du 30 juin, BP 9516, Kinshasa; tel. (12) 30220; Ambassador EDOUARD ROGER OKOULA.

Côte d'Ivoire: 68 ave de la Justice, BP 9197, Kinshasa; tel. (12) 21208; Ambassador GUILLAUME AHIPEAU.

Cuba: 4660 ave Cateam, BP 10699, Kinshasa; tel. (12) 8803823; Ambassador JOSÉ SIVILA DE LA TORRE.

Egypt: 519 ave de l'Ouganda, BP 8838, Kinshasa; tel. (12) 34368; Ambassador AZIZ ABDEL HAMID HAMZA.

Ethiopia: BP 8435, Kinshasa; tel. (12) 23327; Ambassador DIEUDEONNE A. GANGA.

France: 97 ave de la République du Tchad, BP 3093, Kinshasa; tel. (12) 21506; fax (762) 500044; Ambassador GEORGES SERRE.

Gabon: ave du 24 novembre, BP 9592, Kinshasa; tel. (12) 68325; Ambassador MICHEL MADOUNGOU.

Germany: 82 ave Roi Baudouin, BP 8400, Kinshasa-Gombe; tel. (89) 48201; fax (satellite) 871-68-2623227; e-mail amballemagne@ic.cd; Ambassador DORETTA LOSCHELDER.

Greece: Immeuble de la Communauté Hellénique, 3ème étage, blvd du 30 juin, BP 478, Kinshasa; tel. (88) 44862; fax (88) 01002; e-mail grembkin@ic.cd; Ambassador SPYROS THEOCHAROPOULOS.

Holy See: 81 ave Goma, BP 3091, Kinshasa; tel. (12) 33128; fax (12) 33346; e-mail nuntius@raga.net; Apostolic Nuncio Most Rev. GIOVANNI D'ANIELLO (Titular Archbishop of Paestum).

Israel: 141 blvd du 30 juin, BP 8343, Kinshasa; tel. (99) 87218; fax (88) 07494; e-mail kinshasa@israel.org; Ambassador JAMAR F. GOLAN.

Japan: Immeuble Citibank, 2ème étage, ave Colonel Lukusa, BP 1810, Kinshasa; tel. (88) 45305; fax (satellite) 871-761-21-41-42; e-mail ambj@ic.cd; Ambassador YASUO TAKANO.

Kenya: 4002 ave de l'Ouganda, BP 9667, Kinshasa; tel. (88) 06834; Chargé d'affaires J. K. CHUMBA.

Korea, Democratic People's Republic: 168 ave de l'Ouganda, BP 16597, Kinshasa; tel. (12) 31566; Ambassador HAN PON CHUN.

Korea, Republic: 2A ave des Orangers, BP 628, Kinshasa; tel. (88) 20722; Ambassador CHUN SOON-KYU.

Lebanon: 3 ave de l'Ouganda, Kinshasa; tel. (12) 82469; Chargé d'affaires a.i. CHEHADE MOUALLEM.

Liberia: 3 ave de l'Okapi, BP 8940, Kinshasa; tel. (12) 82289; Ambassador JALLA D. LANSANAH.

Mauritania: BP 16397, Kinshasa; tel. (12) 59575; Ambassador Lt-Col M'BARECK OULD BOUNA MOKHTAR.

Netherlands: 11 ave Zongo Ntolo, BP 10299, Kinshasa; tel. (12) 7800142; fax (12) 7800155; e-mail kss@minbuza; Ambassador B. W. SCHORTINGHUIS.

Nigeria: 141 blvd du 30 juin, BP 1700, Kinshasa; tel. (12) 43272; Ambassador AHMED MOHAMMED KELE.

Portugal: 270 ave des Aviateurs, BP 7775, Kinshasa; tel. (88) 01309; Ambassador FRANCISCO FALCAO MACHADO.

Russia: 80 ave de la Justice, BP 1143, Kinshasa 1; tel. (12) 33157; fax (12) 45575; Ambassador VALERII GAMAIVNE.

South Africa: 17 ave Ngongo Lutete, BP 7829, Kinshasa-Gombe; tel. (88) 48287; fax (88) 04152; e-mail ambasud@raga.net; Ambassador S. NGOMBANE.

Spain: blvd 30 juin, Bldg Communauté Hellénique, BP 8036, Kinshasa-Gombe; tel. (88) 43195; e-mail ambespcd@mail.mae.es; JOSÉ PASCUAL MARCO MARTÍNEZ.

Sudan: 24 ave de l'Ouganda, Kinshasa; tel. (99) 37396; Chargé d'affaires a.i. ABDEL RA'OUF AMIR.

Sweden: 89 ave Roi Baudouin, BP 11096, Kinshasa-Gombe; tel. (81) 82528; fax (satellite) 870-761-971069; e-mail ambasuede@ic.cd; Ambassador ROBERT RYDBERG.

Togo: 3 ave de la Vallée, BP 10117, Kinshasa; tel. (12) 30666; Ambassador MAMA GNOFAM.

Tunisia: 67–69 ave du Cercle, BP 1498, Kinshasa; tel. (88) 03901; e-mail atkinshasa@yahoo.fr; Ambassador AZOUZ ENNIFAR.

Turkey: 18 ave Pumbu, BP 7817, Kinshasa; tel. (88) 01207; fax (88) 04740; e-mail tckinsbe@raga.net; Ambassador DENIZ UZMEN.

United Kingdom: ave Roi Baudouin, BP 8049, Kinshasa; tel. (98) 169100; fax (88) 46102; e-mail ambrit@ic.cd; Ambassador ANDREW JAMES SPARKES.

USA: 310 ave des Aviateurs, BP 697, Kinshasa; tel. (88) 43608; fax (88) 43467; Ambassador ROGER A. MEECE.

Zambia: 54–58 ave de l'Ecole, BP 1144, Kinshasa; tel. (81) 9999437; fax (88) 45106; e-mail ambazambia@ic.cd; Ambassador TENS C. KAPOMA.

Judicial System

The Minister of Justice is responsible for the organization and definition of competence of the judiciary; civil, penal and commercial law and civil and penal procedures; the status of persons and property; the system of obligations and questions pertaining to nationality; international private law; status of magistrates; organization of the legal profession, counsels for the defence, notaries and of judicial auxiliaries; supervision of cemeteries, non-profit-making organizations, cults and institutions working in the public interest; the operation of prisons; confiscated property.

There is a Supreme Court in Kinshasa, and there are also nine Courts of Appeal and 36 County Courts. A presidential decree, signed in July 2000, provided for government decentralization, with the Supreme Court relocating to Kisangani.

The Head of State is empowered to appoint and dismiss magistrates.

Supreme Court
Cnr ave de la Justice and ave de Lemera, BP 3382, Kinshasa-Gombe; tel. (12) 25104.

President of the Supreme Court: BRUNO MBIANGO.

Procurator-General of the Republic: MONGULU T'APANGANE.

Religion

Many of the country's inhabitants follow traditional beliefs, which are mostly animistic. A large proportion of the population is Christian, predominantly Roman Catholic, and there are small Muslim, Jewish and Greek Orthodox communities.

CHRISTIANITY

The Roman Catholic Church
The Democratic Republic of the Congo comprises six archdioceses and 41 dioceses. An estimated 51% of the population are Roman Catholics.

Bishops' Conference
Conférence Episcopale de la République Démocratique du Congo, BP 3258, Kinshasa-Gombe; tel. (12) 34528; fax (88)44948; e-mail conf.episc.rdc@ic.cd.
f. 1981; Pres. Cardinal FRÉDÉRIC ETSOU-NZABI-BAMUNGWABI (Archbishop of Kinshasa).

Archbishop of Bukavu: Most Rev. CHARLES KAMBALE MBOGHA, Archevêché, BP 3324, Bukavu; tel. (761) 470721; fax (762) 141148; e-mail archevechebk@yahoo.fr.

Archbishop of Kananga: Most Rev. GODEFROID MUKENG'A KALOND, Archevêché, BP 70, Kananga; tel. 2477; e-mail procureka@yahoo.fr.

Archbishop of Kinshasa: Cardinal FRÉDÉRIC ETSOU-NZABI-BAMUNGWABI, Archevêché, ave de l'Université, BP 8431, Kinshasa 1; tel. (12) 3723546; e-mail archikin@ic.cd.

Archbishop of Kisangani: Most Rev. LAURENT MONSENGWO PASINYA,, Archevêché, ave Mpolo 10B, BP 505, Kisangani; tel. (761) 608334; fax (761) 608336.

Archbishop of Lubumbashi: Most Rev. FLORIBERT SONGASONGA MWITWA, Archevêché, BP 72, Lubumbashi; tel. (2) 48601.

Archbishop of Mbandaka-Bikoro: Most Rev. JOSEPH KUMUONDALA MBIMBA, Archevêché, BP 1064, Mbandaka; tel. 2234.

The Anglican Communion
The Church of the Province of the Congo comprises six dioceses.

Archbishop of the Province of the Congo and Bishop of Boga: Most Rev. PATRICE BYANKYA NJOJO, CAC-Boga, POB 25586, Nairobi, Kenya.

Bishop of Bukavu: Rt Rev. FIDÈLE BALUFUGA DIROKPA, CAC-Bukavu, POB 53435, Nairobi, Kenya.

Bishop of Katanga: Rt Rev. ISINGOMA KAHWA, BP 16482, Kinshasa; tel. (88) 06533; e-mail peac_isingoma@yahoo.fr.

Bishop of Kindu: Rt Rev. ZACHARIA MASIMANGE KATANDA, CAC-Kindu, POB 53435, Nairobi, Kenya; e-mail angkindu@antenna.nl.

Bishop of Kisangani: Rt Rev. SYLVESTRE MUGERA TIBAFA, CAC-Kisangani, BP 861, Kisangani.

Bishop of Nord Kivu: Rt Rev. METHUSELA MUNZENDA MUSUBAHO, CAC-Butembo, POB 21285, Nairobi, Kenya; fax (satellite) 871-166-1121.

Kimbanguist
Eglise de Jésus Christ sur la Terre par le Prophète Simon Kimbangu: BP 7069, Kinshasa; tel. (12) 68944; f. 1921; officially est. 1959; c. 5m. mems (1985); Spiritual Head HE SALOMON DIALUNGANA KIANGANI; Sec.-Gen. Rev. LUNTADILLA.

Protestant Churches
Eglise du Christ au Congo (ECC): ave de la Justice 75, BP 4938, Kinshasa-Gombe; f. 1902; a co-ordinating agency for all the Protestant churches, with the exception of the Kimbanguist Church; 62 mem. communities and a provincial org. in each province; c. 10m. mems (1982); Pres. Bishop MARINI BODHO; includes:

Communauté Baptiste du Congo-Ouest: BP 4728, Kinshasa 2; f. 1970; 450 parishes; 170,000 mems (1985); Gen. Sec. Rev. LUSAKWENO-VANGU.

Communauté des Disciples du Christ: BP 178, Mbandaka; tel. 31062; f. 1964; 250 parishes; 650,000 mems (1985); Gen. Sec. Rev. Dr ELONDA EFEFE.

Communauté Episcopale Baptiste en Afrique: 2 ave Jason Sendwe, BP 2809, Lubumbashi 1; tel. and fax (2) 348602; e-mail kitobokabwe@yahoo.fr; f. 1956; 1,300 episcopal communions and parishes; 150,000 mems (2001); Pres. Bishop KITOBO KABWEKA-LEZA.

Communauté Evangélique: BP 36, Luozi; f. 1961; 50 parishes; 33,750 mems (1985); Pres. Rev. K. LUKOMBO NTONTOLO.

Communauté Lumière: BP 10498, Kinshasa 1; f. 1931; 150 parishes; 220,000 mems (1985); Patriarch KAYUWA TSHIBUMBU WA KAHINGA.

Communauté Mennonite: BP 18, Tshikapa; f. 1960; 40,000 mems (1985); Gen. Sec. Rev. KABANGY DJEKE SHAPASA.

Communauté Presbytérienne: BP 117, Kananga; f. 1959; 150,000 mems (1985); Gen. Sec. Dr M. L. TSHIHAMBA.

Eglise Missionaire Apostolique: 375 ave Commerciale, BP 15859, Commune de N'Djili, Kinshasa 1; tel. (98) 165927; e-mail buzi4@hotmail.com; f. 1986; 5 parishes; 2,600 mems; Apostle for Africa Rev. LUFANGA-AYIMOU NANANDANA.

The Press

DAILIES

L'Avenir: Kinshasa; internet www.groupelavenir.net; owned by Groupe de l'avenir; Chair. PIUS MUABILU.

L'Analyste: 129 ave du Bas-Congo, BP 91, Kinshasa-Gombe; tel. (12) 80987; Dir and Editor-in-Chief BONGOMA KONI BOTAHE.

Boyoma: 31 blvd Mobutu, BP 982, Kisangani; Dir and Editor BADRIYO ROVA ROVATU.

Elima: 1 ave de la Révolution, BP 11498, Kinshasa; tel. (12) 77332; f. 1928; evening; Dir and Editor-in-Chief ESSOLOMWA NKOY EA LINGANGA.

Mjumbe: BP 2474, Lubumbashi; tel. (2) 25348; f. 1963; Dir and Editor TSHIMANGA KOYA KAKONA.

Le Palmarès: 220 ave Mpolo, BP 63, Kinshasa-Gombe; supports Union pour la démocratie et le progrès social; Editor MICHEL LADE-LUYA.

Le Phare: bldg du 29 juin, ave Col Lukusa 3392, BP 15662, Kinshasa-Gombe; tel. (12) 45896; e-mail info@le-phare.com; f. 1983; Editor POLYDOR MUBOYAYI MUBANGA; circ 4,000.

Le Potentiel: Immeuble Ruzizi, 873 ave du Bas-Congo, BP 11338, Kinshasa; tel. (12) 891053; e-mail potentiel@ic.cd; f. 1982; Editor MODESTE MUTINGA MUTUISHAYI; circ. 8,000.

La Référence Plus: BP 22520, Kinshasa; tel. (12) 45783; f. 1989; Dir ANDRÉ IPAKALA.

PERIODICALS

Afrique Editions: Kinshasa; tel. (88) 43202; e-mail bpongo@raga.net.

Allo Kinshasa: 3 rue Kayange, BP 20271, Kinshasa-Lemba; monthly; Editor MBUYU WA KABILA.

L'Aurore Protestante: Eglise du Christ au Congo, BP 4938, Kinshasa-Gombe; French; religion; monthly; circ. 10,000.

BEA Magazine de la Femme: 2 ave Masimanimba, BP 113380, Kinshasa 1; every 2 weeks; Editor MUTINGA MUTWISHAYI.

Bingwa: ave du 30 juin, zone Lubumbashi no 4334; weekly; sport; Dir and Editor MATEKE WA MULAMBA.

Cahiers Economiques et Sociaux: BP 257, Kinshasa XI, (National University of the Congo); sociological, political and economic review; quarterly; Dir Prof. NDONGALA TADI LEWA; circ. 2,000.

Cahiers des Religions Africaines: Faculté de Théologie Catholique de Kinshasa, BP 712, Kinshasa/Limete; tel. (12) 78476; f. 1967; English and French; religion; 2 a year; circ. 1,000.

Le Canard Libre: Kinshasa; f. 1991; Editor JOSEPH CASTRO MULEBE.

Circulaire d'Information: Association Nationale des Entreprises du Congo, 10 ave des Aviateurs, BP 7247, Kinshasa 1; tel. (12) 22565; f. 1959; French; legal and statutory texts for the business community; monthly.

La Colombe: 32B ave Tombalbaye, Kinshasa-Gombe; tel. (12) 21211; organ of Parti démocrate et social chrétien; circ. 5,000.

Congo-Afrique: Centre d'Etudes pour l'Action Sociale, 9 ave Père Boka, BP 3375, Kinshasa-Gombe; tel. (12) 34245; e-mail cepas@raga.net; f. 1961; economic, social and cultural; monthly; Editors FRANCIS KIKASSA MWANALESSA, RENÉ BEECKMANS; circ. 2,500.

Le Conseiller Comptable: 51 rue du Grand Séminaire, Quartier Nganda, BP 308, Kinshasa; tel. (88) 01216; fax (88) 00075; f. 1974; French; public finance and taxation; quarterly; Editor TOMENA FOKO; circ. 2,000.

Documentation et Information Protestante (DIP): Eglise du Christ au Congo, BP 4938, Kinshasa-Gombe; tel. and fax (88) 46387; e-mail eccm@ic.cd; French and English; religion.

Documentation et Informations Africaines (DIA): BP 2598, Kinshasa 1; tel. (12) 33197; fax (12) 33196; e-mail dia@ic.cd; internet www.peacelink.it/dia/index.html; Roman Catholic news agency reports; 3 a week; Dir Rev. Père VATA DIAMBANZA.

L'Entrepreneur Flash: Association Nationale des Entreprises du Congo, 10 ave des Aviateurs, BP 7247, Kinshasa 1; tel. (12) 22565; f. 1978; business news; monthly; circ. 1,000.

Etudes d'Histoire Africaine: National University of the Congo, BP 1825, Lubumbashi; f. 1970; French and English; history; annually; circ. 1,000.

Horizons 80: Société Congolaise d'Edition et d'Information, BP 9839, Kinshasa; economic affairs; weekly.

JuriCongo: coin des aves commerce et plateau, Galerie du 24 Novembre, Kinshasa; fax (12) 20320; e-mail cavas@ic.cd; guide to judicial affairs; Pres. EMERY MUKENDI WAFWANA.

Les Kasaï: 161 9e rue, BP 575, Kinshasa/Limete; weekly; Editor NSENGA NDOMBA.

Kin-Média: BP 15808, Kinshasa 1; monthly; Editor ILUNGA KASAMBAY.

KYA: 24 ave de l'Equateur, BP 7853, Kinshasa-Gombe; tel. (12) 27502; f. 1984; weekly for Bas-Congo; Editor SASSA KASSA YI KIBOBA.

Libération: Kinshasa; f. 1997; politics; supports the AFDL; weekly; Man. NGOYI KABUYA DIKATETA M'MIANA.

Mambenga 2000: BP 477, Mbandaka; Editor BOSANGE YEMA BOF.

Le Moniteur de l'Economie (Economic Monitor): Kinshasa; Man. Editor FÉLIX NZUZI.

Mwana Shaba: Générale des Carrières et des Mines, BP 450, Lubumbashi; monthly; circ. 25,000.

Ngabu: Société Nationale d'Assurances, Immeuble Sonas Sankuru, blvd du 30 juin, BP 3443, Kinshasa-Gombe; tel. (12) 23051; f. 1973; insurance news; quarterly.

Njanja: Société Nationale des Chemins de Fer Congolais, 115 place de la Gare, BP 297, Lubumbashi; tel. (2) 23430; fax (2) 61321; railways and transportation; annually; circ. 10,000.

NUKTA: 14 chaussée de Kasenga, BP 3805, Lubumbashi; weekly; agriculture; Editor NGOY BUNDUKI.

Post: Immeuble Linzadi, 1538 ave de la Douane, Kinshasa-Gombe; e-mail thepostrdc@yahoo.com; internet www.congoonline.com/thepost; 2 a week; Editor-in-Chief MUKEBAYI NKOSO.

Problèmes Sociaux Zaïrois: Centre d'Exécution de Programmes Sociaux et Economiques, Université de Lubumbashi, 208 ave Kasavubu, BP 1873, Lubumbashi; f. 1946; quarterly; Editor N'KASHAMA KADIMA.

Promoteur Congolais: Centre du Commerce International du Congo, 119 ave Colonel Tshatshi, BP 13, Kinshasa; f. 1979; international trade news; six a year.

Sciences, Techniques, Informations: Centre de Recherches Industrielles en Afrique Centrale (CRIAC), BP 54, Lubumbashi.

Le Sport Africain: 13è niveau Tour adm., Cité de la Voix du Congo, BP 3356, Kinshasa-Gombe; monthly; Pres. TSHIMPUMPU WA TSHIMPUMPU.

Taifa: 536 ave Lubumba, BP 884, Lubumbashi; weekly; Editor LWAMBWA MILAMBU.

Telema: Faculté Canisius, Kimwenza, BP 3724, Kinshasa-Gombe; f. 1974; religious; quarterly; edited by the Central Africa Jesuits; circ. 1,200.

Umoja: 23 Bunkeye Matonge, Kinshasa; weekly; Publr LÉON MOUKANDA LUNYAMA.

Vision: Kinshasa; 2 a week; independent; Man. Editor XAVIER BONANE YANGANZI.

La Voix des Sans-Voix: ave des Ecuries 3858, commune de Ngaliema, BP 11445, Kinshasa-Gombe; tel. (88) 40394; fax (88) 01826; e-mail vsv@ic.cd; internet www.congonline.com/vsv.

NEWS AGENCIES

Agence Congolaise de Presse (ACP): 44–48 ave Tombalbaye, BP 1595, Kinshasa 1; tel. (12) 22035; e-mail acpresse@rd-congo.com;

internet www.rd-congo.com/acp.html; f. 1957; state-controlled; Dir-Gen. ALI KALONGA.

Digital Congo: 3335 ave Kabasele Tshiamala, Kinshasa-Gombe; tel. (88) 06269; e-mail info@multimediacongo.net; internet www.digitalcongo.net; news service owned by Multimedia Congo.

Documentation et Informations Africaines (DIA): BP 2598, Kinshasa 1; tel. (12) 34528; f. 1957; Roman Catholic news agency; Dir Rev. Père VATA DIAMBANZA.

Foreign Bureaux

Agence France-Presse (AFP): Immeuble Wenge 3227, ave Wenge, Zone de la Gombe, BP 726, Kinshasa 1; tel. (12) 27009; Bureau Chief JEAN-PIERRE REJETTE.

Agenzia Nazionale Stampa Associata (ANSA) (Italy): BP 2790, Kinshasa 15; tel. (12) 30315; Bureau Chief (vacant).

Pan-African News Agency (PANA) (Senegal): BP 1400, Kinshasa; tel. (12) 23290; f. 1983; Bureau Chief ADRIEN HONORÉ MBEYET.

Xinhua (New China) News Agency (People's Republic of China): 293 ave Mfumu Lutunu, BP 8939, Kinshasa; tel. (12) 25647; Correspondent CHEN WEIBIN.

Press Association

Union de la Presse du Congo: BP 4941, Kinshasa 1; tel. (12) 24437.

Publishers

Aequatoria Centre: BP 276, Mbandaka; f. 1980; anthropology, biography, ethnicity, history, language and linguistics, social sciences; Dir HONORÉ VINCK.

CEEBA Publications: BP 246, Bandundu; f. 1965; humanities, languages, fiction; Man. Dir (Editorial) Dr HERMANN HOCHEGGER.

Centre de Linguistique Théorique et Appliquée (CELTA): BP 4956, Kinshasa-Gombe; tel. (81) 8129998; e-mail anyembwe@yahoo.fr; f. 1971; language arts and linguistics; Dir-Gen. ANDRÉ NYEMBWE NTITA.

Centre de Documentation Agricole: BP 7537, Kinshasa 1; tel. (12) 32498; agriculture, science; Dir PIERTE MBAYAKABUYI; Chief Editor J. MARCELLIN KAPUKUNGESA.

Centre de Recherches Pédagogiques: BP 8815, Kinshasa 1; f. 1959; accounting, education, geography, language, science; Dir P. DETIENNE.

Centre de Vulgarisation Agricole: BP 4008, Kinshasa 2; tel. (12) 71165; fax (12) 21351; agriculture, environment, health; Dir-Gen. KIMPIANGA MAHANIAH.

Centre International de Sémiologie: 109 ave Pruniers, BP 1825, Lubumbashi.

Centre Protestant d'Editions et de Diffusion (CEDI): 209 ave Kalémie, BP 11398, Kinshasa 1; tel. (12) 22202; fax (12) 26730; f. 1935; fiction, poetry, biography, religious, juvenile; Christian tracts, works in French, Lingala, Kikongo, etc.; Dir-Gen. HENRY DIRKS.

Commission de l'Education Chrétienne: BP 3258, Kinshasa-Gombe; tel. (12) 30086; education, religion; Man. Dir Abbé MUGADJA LEHANI.

Connaissance et Pratique du Droit Congolais Editions (CDPC): BP 5502, Kinshasa-Gombe; f. 1987; law; Editor DIBUNDA KABUINJI.

Facultés Catholiques de Kinshasa: 2 ave de l'Université, Kinshasa-Limete; tel. and fax (12) 46965; e-mail facakin@ic.cd; f. 1957; anthropology, art, economics, history, politics, computer science; Rector Prof. Mgr HIPPOLYTE NGIMBI NSEKA.

Editions Lokole: BP 5085, Kinshasa 10; state org. for the promotion of literature; Dir BOKEME SHANE MOLOBAY.

Editions Saint Paul: BP 8505, Kinshasa; tel. (12) 77726; fiction, general non-fiction, poetry, religion; Dir Sister FRANKA PERONA.

Les Editions du Trottoir: BP 1800, Kinshasa; tel. (12) 9936043; e-mail smuyengo@yahoo.fr; f. 1989; communications, fiction, literature, drama; Pres. CHARLES DJUNJU-SIMBA.

Librairie les Volcans: 22 ave Pres. Mobutu, BP 400, Goma, Nord-Kivu; f. 1995; social sciences; Man. Dir RUHAMA MUKANDOLI.

Presses Universitaires du Congo (PUC): 290 rue d'Aketi, BP 1800, Kinshasa 1; tel. (12) 9936043; e-mail smuyengo@yahoo.fr; f. 1972; science, arts and communications; Dir Abbé SÉBASTIEN MUYENGO.

GOVERNMENT PUBLISHING HOUSE

Imprimerie du Gouvernement Central: BP 3021, Kinshasa-Kalina.

Broadcasting and Communications

TELECOMMUNICATIONS

Comcell: Commune de la Gombe, 6 ave du Port, BP 614, Kinshasa; tel. (12) 20241; fax (satellite) 377-97-990026; e-mail comcell@raga.net; provides satellite communications network; 4,000 subscribers.

Office Congolais des Postes et des Télécommunications (OCPT): Hôtel des postes, blvd du 30 juin, BP 13798, Kinshasa; tel. (12) 21871; fax (88) 45010; e-mail ocpt@ic.cd; state-owned; 13,000 lines; 40,000 subscribers; Dir-Gen. KAPITAO MAMBWENI.

Telecel-Congo: ave de la Justice 25, Kinshasa; provides satellite communications network; largest private operator; 45% nationalized in 1998; 12,000 subscribers.

BROADCASTING

Radio-Télévision Nationale Congolaise (RTNC): BP 3171, Kinshasa-Gombe; tel. (12) 23171; state radio terrestrial and satellite television broadcasts; Dir-Gen. JOSE KAJANGUA.

Radio
Several private radio broadcasters operate in Kinshasa.

Radio Candip: Centre d'Animation et de Diffusion Pédagogique, BP 373, Bunia; state-controlled; under rebel control in late 1998.

La Voix du Congo: Station Nationale, BP 3164, Kinshasa-Gombe; tel. (12) 23175; state-controlled; operated by RTNC; broadcasts in French, Swahili, Lingala, Tshiluba, Kikongo; regional stations at Kisangani, Lubumbashi, Bukavu, Bandundu, Kananga, Mbuji-Mayi, Matadi, Mbandaka and Bunia.

Television
Several private television broadcasters operate in Kinshasa.

Antenne A: Immeuble Forescom, 2e étage, ave du Port 4, POB 2581, Kinshasa 1; tel. (12) 21736; private and commercial station; Dir-Gen. IGAL AVIVI NEIRSON.

Canal Z: ave du Port 6, POB 614, Kinshasa 1; tel. (12) 20239; commercial station; Dir-Gen. FRÉDÉRIC FLASSE.

Tele Kin Malebo (TKM): Kinshasa; private television station; nationalization announced 1997; Dir-Gen. NGONGO LUWOWO.

Télévision Congolaise: BP 3171, Kinshasa-Gombe; tel. (12) 23171; govt commercial station; operated by RTNC; broadcasts for 5 hours daily on weekdays and 10 hours daily at weekends.

Finance

(cap. = capital; res = reserves; dep. = deposits; m. = million; brs = branches; amounts in old zaires unless otherwise indicated)

BANKING

The introduction as legal tender of a new currency unit, the Congolese franc (CF), was completed on 30 June 1998. However, as a result of the civil conflict, its value immediately declined dramatically. In late 2003, following the restoration of relative peace and installation of new transitional authorities, the Central Bank introduced new notes in an effort to revive the national currency. In October Union des Banques Congolaises became the first bank to restore nation-wide operations. Reform of the national banking sector, which commenced in 2002, included the liquidation of five major loss-making institutions.

Central Bank

Banque du Congo: 513 blvd Colonel Tshatshi au nord, BP 2697, Kinshasa; tel. (12) 20704; fax (12) 8805152; e-mail cabgouv@bcc.cd; internet www.bcc.cd; f. 1964; res CF 1,030m. (2002); Gov. JEAN-CLAUDE MASANGU MULONGO; 8 brs.

Commercial Banks

Banque Commerciale du Congo SARL (BCDC): blvd du 30 juin, BP 488, Kinshasa; tel. (88) 21776; fax (12) 21770; e-mail dir@bcdc.cd; internet www.bcdc.cd; f. 1952 as Banque du Congo Belge, name changed as above 1997; cap. CF 3,279.9m., res CF 745.7m., dep. CF 31,668.8m. (Dec. 2003); Pres. NKEMA LILOO; Man. Dir YVES CUYPERS; 29 brs.

Banque Congolaise SARL: Immeuble Flavica 14/16, ave du Port, BP 9497, Kinshasa 1; tel. (99) 82003; fax (88) 46423; e-mail bank@rayventures.com; f. 1988; cap. and res NZ 3,000.2m., total assets NZ 9,579.1m. (Dec. 2003); Admistrator-Delegate Roger A. Yaghi.

Banque Internationale de Crédit SARL (BIC): 191 ave de l'Equateur, BP 1299, Kinshasa 1; tel. (88) 43790; fax (88) 01125; e-mail bic@ic.cd; f. 1994; cap. CF 54.4m., res CF 199.0m., dep. CF 4,283.6m. (Dec. 2001); Pres. Pascal Kinduelo Lumbu; Man. Dir Tharcisse K. M. Milembwe.

Banque Internationale pour l'Afrique au Congo (BIAC): Immeuble Nioki, ave de la Douane, Kinshasa 1; tel. (99) 17446; fax (88) 43501; e-mail chs@raga.net; cap. and res CF 657.6m., total assets CF 4,273.9m. (Dec. 2001); Pres. Robert Joncheray.

Citibank (Congo) SARL Congo: Immeuble Citibank Congo, angle aves Col Lukusa et Ngongo Lutete, BP 9999, Kinshasa 1; tel. (12) 20555; fax (12) 40015; e-mail singa.boyenge@citicorp.com; f. 1971; cap. and res NZ 199,425.2m., total assets NZ 1,928,804.9m. (Dec. 1996); Man. Dir Mabanza Meti; 1 br.

Nouvelle Banque de Kinshasa: 1 place du Marché, BP 8033, Kinshasa 1; tel. (12) 20562; fax (12) 496180043; f. 1969; nationalized 1975; control transferred to National Union of Congolese Workers in 1989; in liquidation in 1999; cap. NZ 2,000 (1990), res NZ 92,179.4m., dep. NZ 25,396.8m. (Dec. 1994); Pres. Dokolo Sanu; 15 brs.

Rawbank Sarl: 3487 blvd du 30 juin, Immeuble Concorde Commune de la Gombe, Kinshasa; tel. (88) 01001; fax (88) 11000; e-mail contact@rawbank.cd; internet www.rawbank.cd; f. 2002; cap. 635.0m., res 25.0m., dep. 3,435.9m. (2002); Mazhar Rawji.

Société Financière de Développement SARL (SOFIDE): Immeuble SOFIDE, 9–11 angle aves Ngabu et Kisangani, BP 1148, Kinshasa 1; tel. (12) 33760; fax (12) 20788; e-mail sofide2001@yahoo.fr; f. 1970; partly state-owned; provides tech. and financial aid, primarily for agricultural devt; cap. and res CF 198.7m., total assets CF 911.1m. (Dec. 2001); Pres. and Dir-Gen. Gabriel Mahele Wosongo; 4 brs.

Stanbic Bank Congo SARL: 12 ave de Mongala, BP 16297, Kinshasa 1; tel. (88) 48445; fax (88) 46216; e-mail sbiccongo@raga.net; internet www.stanbic.co.cd; f. 1973; subsidiary of Standard Bank Investment Corpn (South Africa); cap. and res CF 256.8m., total assets CF 4,390.8m. (Dec. 2001); Chair. C. Evans; Man. Dir Rebecca L. Gaskin; 1 br.

Union des Banques Congolaises SARL (UBC): angle ave de la Nation et ave des Aviateurs 19, BP 197, Kinshasa 1; tel. (88) 41333; fax (88) 46628; e-mail ubc@ic.cd; f. 1929; renamed as above in 1997; total assets US $59.3m. (Dec. 1997); Pres. Ntumba Mpoy; 13 brs.

INSURANCE

INTERAFF: Bldg Forescom, ave du Port 4, Kinshasa-Gombe; tel. (88) 01618; fax (320) 2091332; e-mail interaff@raga.net; internet www.ic.cd/interaff.

Société Nationale d'Assurances (SONAS): 3443 blvd du 30 juin, Kinshasa-Gombe; tel. (12) 5110503; e-mail sonask@hotmail.com; f. 1966; state-owned; cap. US $5m.;; 9 brs.

Trade and Industry

At November 1994 the Government's portfolio of state enterprises numbered 116, of which 56 were wholly owned by the Government.

DEVELOPMENT ORGANIZATIONS

Bureau pour le Développement Rural et Urbain: Mont Ngafula, Kinshasa; e-mail bdru_kin@yahoo.fr.

Caisse de Stabilisation Cotonnière (CSCo): BP 3058, Kinshasa-Gombe; tel. (12) 31206; f. 1978 to replace Office National des Fibres Textiles; acts as an intermediary between the Govt, cotton ginners and textile factories, and co-ordinates international financing of cotton sector.

La Générale des Carrières et des Mines (GÉCAMINES): 450 blvd Kamanyola, BP 450, Lubumbashi; tel. (2) 222118; fax (2) 223655; f. 1967 to acquire assets of Union Minière du Haut-Katanga; state-owned corpn engaged in mining and marketing of copper, cobalt, zinc and coal; also has interests in agriculture; Exec. Chair. Yuma Monga (acting).

Institut National pour l'Etude et la Recherche Agronomiques: BP 1513, Kisangani; f. 1933; agricultural research.

Office National du Café: ave Général Bobozo, BP 8931, Kinshasa 1; tel. (12) 77144; f. 1979; state agency for coffee and also cocoa, tea, quinquina and pyrethrum; Pres. Feruza wa Ghenda.

Pêcherie Maritime Congolaise: Kinshasa; DRC's only sea-fishing enterprise.

CHAMBER OF COMMERCE

Chambre de Commerce, d'Industrie et d'Agriculture du Congo: 10 ave des Aviateurs, BP 7247, Kinshasa 1; tel. (12) 22286.

INDUSTRIAL AND TRADE ASSOCIATION

Association Nationale des Entreprises du Congo: 10 ave des Aviateurs, BP 7247, Kinshasa; tel. (12) 24623; f. 1972; represents business interests for both domestic and foreign institutions; Man. Dir Edouard Luboya Diyoka; Gen. Sec. Athanase Matenda Kyelu.

EMPLOYERS' ASSOCIATION

Fédération des Entreprises du Congo (FEC): Kinshasa; e-mail feccongo@hotmail.com; Pres. Pascal Kinduel Lumbu; Sec.-Gen. Joseph Mukadula Kabue.

UTILITIES

Electricity

Société Nationale d'Electricité (SNEL): 2831 ave de la Justice, BP 500, Kinshasa; tel. (12) 26893; fax (12) 33735; f. 1970; state-owned; Dir-Gen. Muyumba Kalembe.

Water

Régie de Distribution d'Eau (REGIDESO): 65 blvd du 30 juin, BP 12599, Kinshasa; tel. (12) 22792; water supply admin; Pres. Lubungu Pene Shako.

TRADE UNIONS

The Union Nationale des Travailleurs was founded in 1967 as the sole trade-union organization. In 1990 the establishment of independent trade unions was legalized, and by early 1991 there were 12 officially recognized trade-union organizations.

Union Nationale des Travailleurs du Congo: BP 8814, Kinshasa; f. 1967; comprises 16 unions; Pres. Katalay Moleli Sangol.

Transport

Compagnie des Transports du Congo: ave Muzu 52/75, Kinshasa; tel. (88) 46249; fax (322) 7065718; e-mail ros@ic.cd; road transport; Dir Roger Senger.

Office National des Transports (ONATRA): BP 98, Kinshasa 1; tel. (12) 21457; fax (12) 1398632; e-mail onatradf@ic.cd; f. 1935; operates 10,077 km of waterways, 366 km of railways and road and air transport; administers ports of Kinshasa, Matadi, Boma and Banana; Pres. Jules Ibula Mwana Katakanga.

RAILWAYS

The main line runs from Lubumbashi to Ilebo. International services run to Dar es Salaam (Tanzania) and Lobito (Angola), and also connect with the Zambian, Zimbabwean, Mozambican and South African systems. In May 1997 the railway system was nationalized. In late 2003, under a major government programme, the rehabilitation of 500 km of railway linking northern and southern regions of the country commenced.

Kinshasa–Matadi Railway: BP 98, Kinshasa 1; 366 km operated by ONATRA; Pres. Jacques Mbelolo Bitwemi.

Société Nationale des Chemins de Fer du Congo (SNCC): 115 place de la Gare, BP 297, Lubumbashi; tel. (2) 46306; fax (2) 342254; e-mail sncc01aie-lubum-cd; f. 1974; 3,606 km (including 858 km electrified); administers all internal railway sections as well as river transport and transport on Lakes Tanganyika and Kivu; man. contract concluded with a Belgian-South African corpn, Sizarail, in 1995 for the man. of the Office des Chemins de Fer du Sud (OCS) and the Société des Chemins de Fer de l'Est (SFE) subsidiaries, with rail networks of 2,835 km and 1,286 km respectively; assets of Sizarail nationalized and returned to SNCC control in May 1997; Pres. and Gen. Man. Kibwe Mibuya Kakudji.

ROADS

In 1999 there were an estimated 157,000 km of roads, of which some 33,000 km were main roads. Following the installation of transitional authorities in July 2003, an extensive infrastructure rehabilitation programme, financed by external donors, including the World Bank, was initiated. Work on a principal road, connecting the south-western town of Moanda with Kinshasa and Lubumbashi, commenced late that year.

Office des Routes: Direction Générale, ave Ex-Descamp, BP 10899, Kinshasa-Gombe; tel. (12) 32036; construction and maintenance of roads.

INLAND WATERWAYS

The River Congo is navigable for more than 1,600 km. Above the Stanley Falls the Congo becomes the Lualaba, and is navigable along a 965-km stretch from Ubundu to Kindu and Kongolo to Bukama. The River Kasai, a tributary of the River Congo, is navigable by shipping as far as Ilebo, at which the line from Lubumbashi terminates. The total length of inland waterways is 14,935 km.

Régie des voies fluviales: 109 ave Lumpungu, Kinshasa-Gombe, BP 11697, Kinshasa 1; tel. (12) 26526; fax (12) 42580; administers river navigation; Gen. Man. NGIAM KIPOY.

Société Congolaise des Chemins de Fer des Grands Lacs: River Lualaba services: Bubundu–Kindu and Kongolo–Malemba N'kula; Lake Tanganyika services: Kamina–Kigoma–Kalundu–Moba–Mpulungu; Pres. and Gen. Man. KIBWE MBUYU KAKUDJI.

SHIPPING

The principal seaports are Matadi, Boma and Banana on the lower Congo. The port of Matadi has more than 1.6 km of quays and can accommodate up to 10 deep-water vessels. Matadi is linked by rail with Kinshasa. The country's merchant fleet numbered 20 vessels and amounted to 12,900 gross registered tons at 31 December 2003.

Compagnie Maritime du Congo SARL: USB Centre, place de la Poste, BP 9496, Kinshasa; tel. (88) 20396; fax (88) 26234; e-mail cmdckin@ic.cd; f. 1946; services: North Africa, Europe, North America and Asia to West Africa, East Africa to North Africa; Gen. Man. ALEX MUKENDI KAMAMA.

CIVIL AVIATION

International airports are located at Ndjili (for Kinshasa), Luano (for Lubumbashi), Bukavu, Goma and Kisangani. There are smaller airports and airstrips dispersed throughout the country.

Blue Airlines: BP 1115, Barumbu, Kinshasa 1; tel. (12) 20455; f. 1991; regional and domestic charter services for passengers and cargo; Man. T. MAYANI.

Business Aviation: 1345 ave de la Plaine, Kingabwa-Kinshasa; tel. (88) 45588; fax (99) 42260; e-mail businessaviation@ic.cd; internet www.businessaviation.cd; regional services.

Compagnie Africaine d'Aviation: 6ème rue, Limete, Kinshasa; tel. (88) 43072; fax (88) 41048; e-mail ltadek@hotmail.com; f. 1992; Pres. DAVID BLATTNER.

Congo Airlines: 1928 ave Kabambare, N'dolo-Kinshasa, BP 12847, Kinshasa; tel. (12) 43947; fax (12) 00235; e-mail cal-fih-dg@ic.cd; f. 1994 as Express Cargo, assumed present name in 1997; international, regional and domestic scheduled services for passengers and cargo; Pres. JOSÉ ENDUNO; CEO STAVROS PAPAIOANNOU.

Hewa Bora Airways: ave Kabambare 1928, BP 1284, Kinshasa; tel. (12) 20643; internet www.hba.cd; national and international services.

Lignes Aériennes du Congo (LAC): Air Terminus 4, ave du Port, Kinshasa-Gombe, BP 8552, Kinshasa 1; tel. (12) 20874; Pres. and Gen. Man. PAUL MUKANDILA MBAYABU.

Malila Airlift: ave Basoko 188, Kinshasa-Gombe; tel. (88) 46428; fax (satellite) 1-5304817707; e-mail malila.airlift@ic.cd; internet www.malila.cd; f. 1996; regional services; Man. VÉRONIQUE MALILA.

Waltair Aviation: 9ème rue 206, Limete, Kinshasa; tel. (88) 48439; fax (satellite) 1-3094162616; e-mail waltair.rdc@ic.cd; regional services; Dir VINCENT GILLET.

Zairean Airlines (Congo): 3555–3560 blvd du 30 juin, BP 2111, Kinshasa; tel. (88) 48103; f. 1981; international, regional and domestic services for passengers and cargo; Dir-Gen. Capt. ALFRED SOMMERAUER.

Tourism

The country offers extensive lake and mountain scenery, although tourism remains largely undeveloped. In 2000 tourist arrivals totalled 102,770, while receipts from tourism amounted to an estimated US $2m. in 1998.

Office National du Tourisme: 2A/2B ave des Orangers, BP 9502, Kinshasa-Gombe; tel. (12) 30070; f. 1959; Man. Dir BOTOLO MAGOZA.

Société Congolaise de l'Hôtellerie: Immeuble Memling, BP 1076, Kinshasa; tel. (12) 23260; Man. N'JOLI BALANGA.

THE REPUBLIC OF THE CONGO

Introductory Survey

Location, Climate, Language, Religion, Flag, Capital

The Republic of the Congo is an equatorial country on the west coast of Africa. It has a coastline of about 170 km on the Atlantic Ocean, from which the country extends northward to Cameroon and the Central African Republic. The Republic of the Congo is bordered by Gabon to the west and the Democratic Republic of the Congo (formerly Zaire) to the east, while in the south there is a short frontier with the Cabinda exclave of Angola. The climate is tropical, with temperatures averaging 21°C–27°C (70°F–80°F) throughout the year. The average annual rainfall is about 1,200 mm (47 ins). The official language is French; Kituba, Lingala and other African languages are also used. At least one-half of the population follow traditional animist beliefs and about 45% are Roman Catholics. There are small Protestant and Muslim minorities. The national flag (proportions 2 by 3) comprises a yellow stripe running diagonally from lower hoist to upper fly, separating a green triangle at the hoist from a red triangle in the fly. The capital is Brazzaville.

Recent History

Formerly part of French Equatorial Africa, Middle Congo became the autonomous Republic of the Congo, within the French Community, in November 1958, with Abbé Fulbert Youlou as the first Prime Minister, and subsequently as President when the Congo became fully independent on 15 August 1960. Youlou relinquished office in August 1963, following a period of internal unrest, and was succeeded by Alphonse Massamba-Débat, initially as Prime Minister, and from December as President. In July 1964 the Mouvement national de la révolution (MNR) was established as the sole political party. In August 1968 Massamba-Débat was overthrown in a military coup, led by Capt. (later Maj.) Marien Ngouabi, who was proclaimed President in January 1969. A new Marxist-Leninist party, the Parti congolais du travail (PCT), replaced the MNR, and in January 1970 the country was renamed the People's Republic of the Congo. In March 1977 Ngouabi was assassinated, and in April Col (later Brig.-Gen.) Jacques-Joachim Yhombi-Opango, the head of the armed forces, became the new Head of State. In February 1979 Yhombi-Opango surrendered his powers to a Provisional Committee appointed by the PCT. In March the head of the Provisional Committee, Col (later Gen.) Denis Sassou-Nguesso, became Chairman of the PCT Central Committee and President of the Republic.

In July 1989 Sassou-Nguesso, the sole candidate, was re-elected Chairman of the PCT and President of the Republic for a third five-year term. At legislative elections in September the PCT-approved single list of 133 candidates was endorsed by 99.2% of voters. The list included, for the first time, non-party candidates.

Progress towards political reform dominated the latter half of 1990. In August several political prisoners were released, among them Yhombi-Opango. In September the Central Committee of the PCT agreed to the immediate registration of new political parties. In December Poaty-Souchalaty resigned, the day before an extraordinary Congress of the PCT commenced. During the Congress the party abandoned Marxism-Leninism as its official ideology and formulated constitutional amendments legalizing a multi-party system, which took effect in January 1991. Gen. Louis Sylvain Goma was appointed Prime Minister (a position he had held between 1975 and 1984), to lead an interim Government.

A National Conference was convened in February 1991. Opposition movements were allocated seven of the 11 seats on the Conference's governing body. The Roman Catholic Bishop of Owando, Ernest N'Kombo, was elected as Chairman. Having voted to establish itself as a sovereign body, in April the Conference announced proposals to draft legislation providing for the abrogation of the Constitution and the abolition of the Assemblée nationale populaire and other national and regional institutions. In June a 153-member legislative Haut conseil de la République (HCR) was established, under the chairmanship of N'Kombo; this was empowered to supervise the implementation of the resolutions made by the Conference. From June the Prime

Minister replaced the President as Chairman of the Council of Ministers, and the country's official name reverted to the Republic of the Congo. A new Prime Minister, André Milongo (a former World Bank official), was appointed in June. In December the HCR adopted a draft Constitution, which provided for legislative power to be vested in an elected Assemblée nationale and Sénat and for executive power to be held by an elected President.

The draft Constitution was approved by 96.3% of voters at a national referendum in March 1992. In May Milongo appointed a new Council of Ministers. At elections to the new Assemblée nationale, held in June and July, the Union panafricaine pour la démocratie social (UPADS) won 39 of the 125 seats, the Mouvement congolais pour la démocratie et le développement intégral (MCDDI) 29 seats and the PCT 18 seats. At indirect elections to the Sénat, held in July, the UPADS again won the largest share (23) of the 60 seats, followed by the MCDDI, with 13 seats. At the first round of presidential voting, in August, Pascal Lissouba, the leader of the UPADS (and Prime Minister in 1963–66), won the largest share of the votes cast (35.9%); of the 15 other candidates, his closest rival was Bernard Kolelas of the MCDDI (22.9%). Sassou-Nguesso took 16.9% of the votes cast. At a second round of voting, two weeks later, Lissouba defeated Kolelas, with 61.3% of the votes cast.

Lissouba took office as President in August 1992. Maurice-Stéphane Bongho-Nouarra, of the UPADS, was appointed as Prime Minister. Meanwhile, the Union pour le renouveau démocratique (URD), a new alliance of seven parties, including the MCDDI, formed a coalition with the PCT (thereby establishing a parliamentary majority), which succeeded in winning a vote of 'no confidence' against the Government in October. In November the Government resigned, and shortly afterwards Lissouba dissolved the Assemblée nationale and announced that fresh legislative elections would be held in 1993. In December Claude Antoine Dacosta, a former World Bank official, was appointed Prime Minister and formed a transitional Government, comprising members of all the main political parties.

At the first round of elections to the Assemblée nationale, which took place in May 1993, the Mouvance présidentielle (MP), an electoral coalition of the UPADS and its allies, won 62 of the 125 seats, while the URD-PCT coalition secured 49. Protesting that serious electoral irregularities had occurred, the URD-PCT refused to contest the second round of elections in June (for seats where a clear majority had not been achieved in the first round) and demanded the repetition of some of the first-round polls. After the second round the MP had secured an absolute majority (69) of seats in the legislature. In June President Lissouba appointed a new Council of Ministers, with Yhombi-Opango as Prime Minister. During June Kolelas, now leader of the URD-PCT coalition, instigated a campaign of civil disobedience in an attempt to compel the Government to organize new elections. In late June the Supreme Court ruled that electoral irregularities had occurred at the first round of elections. By late July the Government and the opposition had negotiated a truce, and in August, following external mediation, the two sides agreed to refer the disputed first-round election results to impartial international arbitration and to rerun the second round of elections.

Following the repeated second round of legislative elections, which took place in October 1993, the MP had 65 seats, retaining an overall majority in the Assemblée nationale. The URD-PCT coalition, which now held 57 seats, agreed to participate in the new Assemblée. In September six opposition parties formed an alliance, the Forces démocratiques unies (FDU), headed by Sassou-Nguesso and affiliated with the URD. In December Lissouba and the two main opposition leaders—Sassou-Nguesso and Kolelas—signed an agreement seeking a permanent end to hostilities between their supporters.

In January 1995 the Government resigned, and a new coalition Council of Ministers was appointed, including members of the MCDDI and headed by Yhombi-Opango. In August 1996 Yhombi-Opango resigned as Prime Minister; he was replaced by David Charles Ganao, a former Minister of Foreign Affairs. In

September Ganao appointed representatives of the URD to an expanded Council of Ministers. In October elections were held for 23 of the 60 seats in the Sénat, following which the MP retained its majority in the upper chamber.

In February 1997 19 opposition parties issued a number of demands, including the expedited establishment of republican institutions, the creation of an independent electoral commission, the disarmament of civilians and the deployment of a multinational peace-keeping force. In May further unrest erupted, and in June an attempt by the Government, in preparation for legislative and presidential elections scheduled for July and August, to disarm the 'Cobra' militia group associated with Sassou-Nguesso precipitated a fierce national conflict along ethnic and political lines, involving the militias and opposing factions within the regular armed forces. Barricades were erected in Brazzaville, which was divided into three zones, controlled by supporters of Lissouba, Sassou-Nguesso and Kolelas, respectively. Despite mediation, none of the numerous cease-fire agreements signed during mid-1997 endured. In June French troops assisted in the evacuation of foreign residents from Brazzaville, and later in the month themselves departed. Fighting intensified in August and spread to the north. In September Lissouba appointed a Government of National Unity, under the premiership of Kolelas, thereby compromising the latter's role as a national mediator. Sassou-Nguesso refused the offer of five ministerial positions for his allies.

In October 1997 Sassou-Nguesso's forces, assisted by Angolan government troops, won control of Brazzaville and the strategic port of Pointe-Noire. Lissouba was ousted from the presidential palace, and, with Kolelas, found refuge in Burkina Faso. Sassou-Nguesso was inaugurated as President on 25 October, having retaken by force the office that he had lost at the 1992 presidential election, and appointed a new transitional Government in November. It was reported that some 10,000 people were killed during the civil war and that about 800,000 people were displaced, while the national infrastructure was severely disrupted.

A Forum for Unity and National Reconciliation was established in January 1998; notably, a grouping of political organizations loyal to Lissouba refused to participate. A Conseil national de transition (CNT) was to hold legislative power, pending the approval of a new constitution by referendum (scheduled for 2001), and subsequent legislative elections. Throughout 1998 clashes continued in the southern Pool region, a stronghold of the militia loyal to Kolelas, causing thousands to flee the area. Warrants were issued in November for the arrests of Lissouba, Kolelas and Yhombi-Opango, on charges of genocide and crimes against humanity.

Progress towards the restoration of democratic rule was impeded in December 1998, when a battle for control of Brazzaville broke out between forces loyal to Kolelas (who was in exile in the USA), reputedly supported by Angolan rebel groups, and Congolese government forces, augmented by Sassou-Nguesso's militia and Angolan government troops. More than 8,000 refugees were reported to have fled into the neighbouring Democratic Republic of the Congo (DRC). In late December government forces, aided by Angolan troops, launched offensives against Kolelas' forces in the south and west of the country.

By March 1999 the rebel militias had been obliged to withdraw to Pool, and by mid-1999 the further advance of government forces permitted residents to return to evacuated districts. In November the Government announced that it had reached agreement with the militias loyal to Lissouba and Kolelas, although the two rebel leaders rejected the agreement, which included provision for a cease-fire and for a general amnesty. In December the CNT adopted legislation providing for an amnesty for those militiamen who surrendered their weapons to the authorities before 15 January 2000. The Government announced its intention to continue to seek the prosecution of Lissouba and Kolelas for alleged war crimes.

In December 1999 President Omar Bongo of Gabon was designated the official mediator in negotiations between the Government and the militias; at the end of the month he hosted further discussions in Libreville, Gabon. Representatives of the armed forces and of the rebel militias subsequently signed a second peace agreement, in the presence of Bongo and Sassou-Nguesso. In late December a ceremony of reconciliation was held in Brazzaville between senior government figures and members of the previous Lissouba administration. In February 2000 the committee in charge of observing the implementation of the peace process announced, at a meeting with Bongo, that the civil war was definitively over. By that month it was estimated that around one-half of the estimated 810,000 people displaced by the conflict had returned to their homes.

In mid-November 2000 the Government adopted a draft Constitution, which included provisions for the institution of an executive presidency and a bicameral legislature. The Head of State would be elected for a term of seven years, renewable only once. In early December it was announced that some 13,000 weapons had been surrendered and 12,000 militiamen disarmed in the past year, although UN sources suggested that this represented less than one-half of the total number of militiamen in the Congo. Also in December, the PCT rejected demands by the MCDDI for an amnesty for Lissouba and Kolelas. In late December it was announced that the PCT had signed an agreement with the Rassemblement pour la démocratie et le progrès social, led by Jean-Pierre Thystère Tchicaya, to bring the latter party into the Government.

Internal and exiled opposition groups boycotted the opening ceremony of a period of national dialogue in mid-March 2001 and a series of regional debates, which took place later that month. Some 2,200 delegates from public institutions, civic associations and political parties attended the debates, reportedly reaching a consensus on the draft Constitution, despite concerns that the President would have the power to appoint and dismiss ministers at will, and that there would be no provision for a vote of censure against the Government. In April several returned exiles and opposition groups participated in a national convention in Brazzaville, although Kolelas and Lissouba were notably absent. The convention concluded, on 14 April, with the signature of a Convention for Peace and Reconstruction.

In July 2001 the families of some 353 missing Congolese citizens demanded a parliamentary inquiry into their disappearance from the Beach area of Brazzaville; it was reported that the missing people, former refugees from the civil war in the southern regions who had sought asylum in the DRC, had been arrested following their voluntary repatriation to the Congo in May 1999. In October–December, taking advantage of Belgian legislation permitting the country's courts to hear cases of international war crimes and crimes against humanity committed anywhere in the world, relatives of the missing filed three suits at courts in Belgium, accusing Sassou-Nguesso and other senior members of the Congolese Government of crimes against humanity with regard to the disappearances; following the introduction of amendments to this legislation in late 2003, it appeared unlikely that these cases would proceed. The Government announced in April 2004 that six of the people believed to have disappeared in 1999 had been identified among a group of refugees being repatriated from the DRC, and claimed that numerous others were still based in a camp in south-west DRC. Sassou-Nguesso ordered the establishment of a judicial inquiry into what had become known as the 'Beach affair', and in July 2004 four senior members of the Congolese armed forces, including Gen. Norbert Dabira (also sought in France, see below), were indicted for trial.

Meanwhile, in July 2001 a coalition of opposition parties, the Alliance pour la démocratie et le progrès (ADP), was formed under the leadership of Milongo, with the intention of fielding a single candidate in the presidential election due to be held in 2002. Meanwhile, the FDU was expanded to comprise some 29 parties, with the purpose of uniting behind Sassou-Nguesso in the election (although the PCT was to contest the subsequent legislative elections independently of the FDU).

In September 2001 the CNT approved the text of the proposed Constitution to be submitted to referendum, pending the compilation of an electoral census. Although the national convention had recommended that opposition parties participate in the electoral commission, only one such party, the ADP, was represented in the Commission nationale d'organisation des élections (CONEL), which was, moreover, to be responsible to the Ministry of the Interior, Security and Territorial Administration. In January 2002 a Congolese human rights organization urged the international community not to support the country's electoral process, citing numerous irregularities in the compilation of the electoral register.

The new Constitution was approved by some 84.5% of votes cast at the referendum, which took place on 20 January 2002, with a participation rate of some 77.5% of the electorate. In mid-February 10 presidential candidates were approved by the Supreme Court, including Sassou-Nguesso and Milongo. Six political parties supportive of Milongo, including Yhombi-Opango's Rassemblement pour la démocratie et le développement, formed an opposition alliance, the Convention pour la démocratie et le salut (CODESA), which effectively supplanted the ADP. None the less, in mid-February six of the 10 approved candidates, among them Milongo, threatened to withdraw from the polls unless the Supreme Court ruled that the electoral law conformed with the transitional fundamental law of 1997, which made no explicit provision for the holding of general elections. In early March 2002 three opposition candidates, including Milongo, who had been widely regarded as the sole credible challenger to Sassou-Nguesso, and who now headed the Union pour la démocratie et la République—Mwinda (UDR—Mwinda), withdrew from the election. Milongo urged his supporters to boycott the poll, stating that his concerns about the transparency of electoral procedures and the impartiality of the CONEL remained unresolved. With all the major opposition candidates thereby excluded, Sassou-Nguesso won an overwhelming victory at the presidential election, which was held on 10 March 2002, securing 89.41% of the votes cast. According to official figures, 69.36% of the electorate participated in the election.

Meanwhile, in late March 2002 renewed violence erupted in the Pool region, apparently instigated by members of a 'Ninja' militia group, led by Rev. Frédéric Bitsangou Ntumi (who had been a co-signatory of the peace agreement reached in 1999), which attacked the town of Kindamba, prompting several thousand civilians to flee. The conflict widened in early April, when two people were killed in an attack on a train on the Congo-Océan railway by members of the militia. By mid-April the unrest had spread to southern Brazzaville, and by late May some 50,000 people were reported to have been displaced. In late April government forces announced that they had regained control of the railway, facilitating a normalization in the supply of fuel and food to Brazzaville, although fighting continued in Pool. At the end of May government troops regained control of the rebel stronghold of Vindza, and in early June humanitarian assistance was finally permitted to reach the region.

The first round of elections to the 137-member Assemblée nationale, which was held on 26 May 2002, was contested by some 1,200 candidates from more than 100 parties; although more than one-half of the candidates had no party affiliation, it was reported than many of these nominally independent candidates were allies of Sassou-Nguesso. As a result of the unrest in Pool, voting was postponed indefinitely in eight constituencies, while disruption caused by protesters and administrative irregularities necessitated a rerun of polling in a further 12 constituencies on 28–29 May. Moreover, the CONEL subsequently announced the disqualification of 15 candidates. Turn-out in the first round, at which the PCT and its allies in the FDU won 38 of the 51 seats decided, was around 65%. Prior to the second round, the security situation in Brazzaville deteriorated markedly. In mid-June, while Sassou-Nguesso was in Italy, 'Ninja' rebels attacked the capital's main military base resulting in the deaths of 72 rebels, three army officers and 15 civilians. Despite requests by the UDR—Mwinda for a postponement of the elections in those areas where fighting had occurred, voting went ahead on 23 June, although the rate of participation, at an estimated 30% nation-wide, was appreciably lower than in the first round, and was as low as 10% in some constituencies in Brazzaville and in Pointe-Noire. Following the polls, supporters of Sassou-Nguesso held an absolute majority in the new Assemblée; the PCT emerged as the largest party, with 53 seats, while the FDU alliance held a total of 30 seats. The UDR—Mwinda became the largest opposition party, with six seats, while the UPADS held four seats. Notably, the MCDDI failed to secure representation in the Assemblée.

The local and municipal elections, held on 30 June 2002, were marked by a low turn-out and further entrenched Sassou-Nguesso's power; the success of the PCT and of constituent parties of the FDU ensured that supporters of the President held more than two-thirds of the elective seats. As the councillors elected on 30 June were those who would, in turn, elect the members of the Sénat on 7 July, the victory of those loyal to Sassou-Nguesso in the upper parliamentary chamber was also to be expected. Following these elections, the Sénat comprised 56 supporters of the President (44 from the PCT and 12 from the FDU), two representatives of civil society organizations, one independent and one member of the opposition. In early August Tchicaya was elected as President of the Assemblée nationale, and the Secretary-General of the PCT, Ambroise-Edouard Noumazalay was elected as President of the Sénat. Sassou-Nguesso

was inaugurated as elected President on 14 August; later in the month he announced the formation of a new Government, which, notably, included no representatives of the opposition (although several representatives from civil society were appointed to ministerial positions). The new Government stated that its priority was to combat corruption within the state and the public sector.

In late December 2002 Sassou-Nguesso announced the implementation of major structural and personnel changes in the military services; in particular, certain responsibilities that had formerly been held by the President, as the Supreme Commander of the Armed Forces, were to be transferred to a Deputy Chief of Defence Staff. In late January 2003 the 15 members of the High Court of Justice were named; among the eight parliamentarians appointed, there was one representative of the opposition, from the UPADS. Later in the month Gérard Bitsindou, a former cabinet director to Sassou-Nguesso, was appointed as the President of the Constitutional Court.

Meanwhile, during the second half of 2002 sporadic attacks by 'Ninja' militias in the Pool region, in particular against freight trains on the Congo-Océan railway, continued. In October unrest intensified, and several deaths of civilians were reported in clashes; up to 10,000 civilians were reported to have fled Pool, for Brazzaville, or the neighbouring Bouenza region, between early October and mid-November. In mid-November Sassou-Nguesso rejected the proposals of an *ad-hoc* presidential committee, which included the brokering of a cease-fire between government and 'Ninja' forces, and instead announced that a 'safe passage' would be provided from Pool to Brazzaville until mid-December for fighters who surrendered their arms, and reiterated that the terms of the peace agreement concluded in 1999 remained valid. Fighting subsequently intensified, however, and within one month only 371 rebels were reported to have surrendered (estimates of the number of rebels at large varied from 3,000–10,000). Although Sassou-Nguesso announced an extension of the amnesty, as a result of which a further 90 rebels surrendered in early January 2003, some 15 civilians were killed in an attack in Pool at the beginning of that month, and in early February the first outbreak of violence in the Bouenza region since 1999, in which a local police chief was killed, was reported. None the less, in mid-March 2003 the Government and Ntumi's 'Ninja' militia group signed a peace agreement. The rebels agreed to end hostilities and disarm, while the Government was to guarantee an amnesty for the rebels and integrate former combatants into the national armed forces. In April the European Commission announced that it was to extend a grant of €731,000 towards the demobilization and reintegration of former 'Ninja' rebels in the Pool region. (France, the USA and the People's Republic of China subsequently also provided substantial aid to assist the resettlement of displaced persons in Pool.) It was reported that at least 2,300 rebels had surrendered their weapons by the end of April. At the end of August the Assemblée nationale formally approved an amnesty for former 'Ninja' fighters, to cover the period from January 2000. By late September 2003 the situation in Pool had stabilized sufficiently to allow an electoral commission to be formed in the region; the delayed local and legislative elections were due to be held in 2005. None the less, in mid-October 2003 renewed clashes between 'Ninja' fighters and government forces near Mindouli, in Pool, resulted in at least 13 deaths. In mid-December, following reports that Kolelas had unsuccessfully attempted to re-enter the Congo under an assumed identity from the DRC, clashes were reported in Brazzaville between 'Ninja' groupings allied to Ntumi and Kolelas, although peace was soon restored.

In late January 2004 Ntumi announced a series of conditions for his return to Brazzaville from his base in the Pool region, including the installation of a government of national unity, the return of exiled former leaders, the definition of his status and an agreement on the number of his fighters to be integrated into the army, police and gendarmerie. Ntumi's demands were largely rejected by the Government in March, which insisted that the peace agreement signed a year earlier made no provision for any of his requirements

In April 2004 divisions emerged within the FDU after five constituent parties issued a statement denouncing the alliance's inaction and demanding that a convention be held in an effort to address issues such as state reform, the consolidation of peace, and combating corruption and fraud. In May the Government announced that it had closed seven sites for internally displaced persons that had been established south of Brazzaville in

October 2002 to shelter some 12,000 people who had fled fighting in Pool. Later that month the European Commission withdrew the €731,000 that it had granted in April 2003 to assist with the disarmament and reintegration of former 'Ninja' rebels in the Pool region, owing to the failure of the former combatants to surrender their weapons. However, in June 2004 the Commission extended a new grant of €2m. to finance a wider programme of disarmament and reintegration in all areas of the Congo affected by civil war, to be conducted over a period of between two and three years by the UN Development Programme. In August the Government announced its intention to allocate 201m. francs CFA for the disarmament, demobilization and reintegration of 450 former combatants. Also in that month some 20 opposition parties and associations, including the MCDDI, formed a coalition, the Coordination de l'opposition pour une alternance démocratique (CODE-A), with the stated aim of fostering non-violent political change in the Congo.

Meanwhile, in July 2004 the Congo was suspended from the Kimberley Process, an international initiative to eliminate the illegal trade in diamonds to fund conflicts, after a report identified irregularities in the country's diamond exports. Sassou-Nguesso subsequently pledged to halt diamond trading pending the implementation of reforms in the sector aimed at securing recertification by the Process.

In January 2005 President Sassou-Nguesso effected a reorganization of the Council of Ministers. The new Government comprised 35 ministers, all of whom were members of the PCT. Most notable was the creation of the post of Prime Minister, which was awarded to Isidore Mvouba, hitherto Minister of State, Minister of Transport and Privatization, responsible for the Co-ordination of Government Action. Roger Rigobert Andely was replaced as Minister for the Economy, Finance and the Budget by Pacifique Issoibeka, the deputy Governor of the Banque des Etats de l'Afrique Centrale, while Bruno Itoua, hitherto Managing Director of the Société Nationale des Pétroles du Congo, was appointed Minister of Energy and Hydraulics. Opposition figures, including the leader of CODE-A, Herve Ambroise Malonga, criticized the creation of the post of Prime Minister, claiming that it was in violation of the 2002 Constitution, which had enshrined presidential control over the executive.

Since the 1997 civil war the principal aim of Congolese foreign policy has been to gain international recognition for the legitimacy of the Sassou-Nguesso Government, and to ensure the continued support of the country's bilateral and multilateral donors. During the 1997 civil war President Lissouba accused France of favouring the rebel forces of Sassou-Nguesso (who was reported to have allied himself with French petroleum interests) over the elected administration. In May 1998 France extended its formal recognition to the Sassou-Nguesso Government, and in June resumed aid payments that had been suspended since the 1997 conflict. In September French military advisers were sent to Brazzaville to train the Congolese gendarmerie. Sassou-Nguesso made an official visit to Paris in September 2002, when he met President Jacques Chirac. However, relations between France and the Congo deteriorated from mid-2002, as a result of an investigation by a French court into several Congolese officials, including Sassou-Nguesso, in connection with the reported disappearance of 353 Congolese citizens, following their return from asylum in the DRC to the Congo in 1999 (see above). In December 2002 the Congo filed a case against France at the International Court of Justice (ICJ) at The Hague, Netherlands, claiming that the investigations represented a violation of Congolese sovereignty and disregarded Sassou-Nguesso's immunity as a Head of State. The ICJ ruled in June 2003 that investigations into the Inspector-General of the Congolese armed forces, Gen. Norbert Dabira, could continue, while noting that no action that warranted the intervention of the ICJ had yet been undertaken against Sassou-Nguesso or other government ministers. However, the ICJ was not expected to issue a ruling on the legitimacy of the jurisdiction of French courts over actions that were alleged to have occurred on Congolese territory; the ICJ also stated that the ruling would not prevent the Court conducting further investigations into the case. The head of Congo's national police force, Col Jean-François Ndenguet, was detained briefly during a visit to France at the beginning of April 2004 in connection with the investigation into the disappearances, but was released after claiming diplomatic immunity. In November the French investigation relating to the 'Beach affair' was annulled in its entirety by the Court of Appeal in Paris, which ruled that the French judiciary had no legitimate juris-

diction in the matter. The decision was denounced by French and Congolese human rights organizations as politically motivated, particularly in anticipation of Chirac's visit to Brazzaville in February 2005.

Prior to Sassou-Nguesso's seizure of power in 1997, relations with Angola were strained, as a result of the existence in the Congo of bases of an Angolan secessionist group, the Frente de Libertação do Enclave de Cabinda (FLEC). Angolan government troops facilitated Sassou-Nguesso's victory in the 1997 conflict by providing significant tactical support, and also played a role in the defeat of the rebel attack on Brazzaville in December 1998. In January 1999 the Heads of State of Angola, the Congo and the DRC met to agree a common policy on the conflicts in their countries. In December the interior ministers of the three countries met in Luanda, Angola, and signed a co-operation accord. The accord created a tripartite commission to ensure border security, the free movement of people and goods, the training of personnel, and the provision of assistance to displaced persons. Angolan troops assisted the Congolese Government in the renewed insurgency in the Pool region from early 2002, but the last contingent of Angolan soldiers was withdrawn from the Congo in December of that year.

Relations between the Republic of the Congo and the DRC steadily improved from the late 1990s. In December 1998 the two countries signed a non-aggression pact and agreed to establish a joint force to guarantee border security. In December 1999 Sassou-Nguesso met President Laurent-Désiré Kabila in order to discuss bilateral co-operation and the implementation of the tripartite Luanda accord, and further discussion on issues of common interest took place regularly between the two countries in 2000–02. In May 2001 19 DRC nationals suspected of involvement in the assassination of Laurent-Désiré Kabila in January were extradited from the Republic of the Congo to Kinshasa. In September 2002 Congolese authorities announced that, in accordance with a programme established in association with the International Organization for Migration (see p. 278), up to 4,000 soldiers from the DRC who had sought refuge or deserted in the Congo were to be repatriated. At a meeting in Brazzaville in May 2004 delegations from the Congo and the DRC discussed the urgent need to repatriate voluntarily and reintegrate former combatants who had taken refuge in their respective countries. In October a formal repatriation agreement for the 62,000 refugees from the DRC in the Congo was signed by representatives of both countries, in collaboration with the office of the UN High Commissioner for Refugees (UNHCR). Moreover, some 400 Congolese refugees were believed to have been repatriated from the Kimaza refugee camp in southwestern DRC during 2004.

Some 120 Congolese troops were dispatched to the Central African Republic (CAR) in March–April 2003, following the *coup d'état* in that country, to reinforce a peace-keeping force that had been deployed by the Communauté économique et monétaire de l'Afrique centrale in late 2002. In March 2004 some 200 refugees from the CAR, who had fled to the Congo following the failed *coup d'état* in May 2001 (see chapter on the CAR), were repatriated under the supervision of the UNHCR.

Government

Following the assumption of power by Gen. Denis Sassou-Nguesso on 15 October 1997, the 1992 Constitution was suspended. A Conseil national de transition was subsequently appointed, with 75 designated members, to act as an interim legislative body. A new Constitution, which was approved by referendum on 20 January 2002, took effect following a presidential election in March–April and legislative elections in May–June. Under the terms of the 2002 Constitution, executive power is vested in a President, who is directly elected for a seven-year term, renewable only once. The President appoints a Council of Ministers. Legislative power is vested in a bicameral Parliament, comprising a 137-member Assemblée nationale, which is directly elected for a five-year term, and a 66-member Sénat, which is indirectly elected by local councils for a six-year term (with one-half of the membership renewable every three years).

For administrative purposes the country is divided into 10 regions, consisting of 76 districts (sous-préfectures) and six municipalities (communes urbaines).

Defence

In August 2004 the army numbered 8,000, the navy about 800 and the air force 1,200. In addition, there was a 2,000-strong Gendarmerie. The estimated defence budget for 2004 was 70,000m. francs CFA.

Economic Affairs

In 2003, according to estimates by the World Bank, the Congo's gross national income (GNI), measured at average 2001–03 prices, was US $2,643m., equivalent to $640 per head (and $710 on an international purchasing-power parity basis). During 1990–2003, it was estimated, the population increased at an average annual rate of 3.2%, while gross domestic product (GDP) per head declined, in real terms, by an average of 1.4% per year. Overall GDP increased, in real terms, at an average annual rate of 1.8% in 1990–2003; growth in 2003 was 1.0%.

Agriculture (including forestry and fishing) contributed an estimated 6.5% of GDP in 2003, and employed about 38.1% of the total labour force in that year. The staple crops are cassava and plantains, while the major cash crops are sugar cane, oil palm, cocoa and coffee. Forests cover about 57% of the country's total land area, and forestry is a major economic activity. Sales of timber provided an estimated 8.4% of export earnings in 1995, but in February 1998, to encourage local processing of wood, forestry companies were prohibited from exporting rough timber. Following the implementation of liberalization measures in the sector, output of timber was expected to increase significantly in the early 2000s. In 2003 exports of wood provided 12.0% of export earnings, according to preliminary FAO figures. During 1990–2003 agricultural GDP increased at an average annual rate of 1.4%; growth in 2003 was 6.3%.

Industry (including mining, manufacturing, construction and power) contributed an estimated 63.4% of GDP in 2003, and employed an estimated 14.7% of the labour force in 1990. During 1990–2003 industrial GDP increased at an average annual rate of 2.1%; it grew by 3.7% in 2002 but declined by 2.2% in 2003.

Mining and manufacturing contributed an estimated 57.8% of GDP in 2003. The hydrocarbons sector is the only significant mining activity. In 2003 sales of petroleum and petroleum products provided 83.1% of export earnings, according to preliminary figures. Annual petroleum production (an estimated 87.6m. barrels in 2003, according to the US Geological Survey) was expected to continue to grow, as a result of major exploration and development planned at various offshore deposits, in particular near to the maritime border with Angola. Deposits of natural gas are also exploited. Lead, zinc, gold and copper are produced in small quantities, and the large-scale mining of magnesium was expected to commence in 2004. There are also exploitable reserves of diamonds, phosphate, iron ore, bauxite and potash. In October 2001 the Government issued the Portuguese company Escom a licence to prospect for diamonds in the far north of the country. The real GDP of the petroleum sector (extraction and refining) increased at an average annual rate of 4.9% in 1995–2001, but declined by an estimated 7.5% in 2001.

Manufacturing contributed 6.5% of GDP in 2003, according to the World Bank. The most important industries, the processing of agricultural and forest products, were adversely affected by the civil conflict in the late 1990s, but began to recover in the early 2000s, as political stability was restored. The textile, chemical and construction materials industries are also significant. During 1990–2003 manufacturing GDP increased at an average annual rate of 1.7%; growth of 10.0% was recorded in 2003.

In 2001 some 99.7% of total electricity production was generated by hydroelectric plants. Imports of fuel and energy comprised an estimated 23.7% of the value of total imports in 2000. The construction of a new hydroelectric dam at Imboulou, some 200 km north of Brazzaville, commenced in late 2003, with an anticipated completion date of 2009.

The services sector contributed 30.1% of GDP in 2003. During 1990–2003, it was estimated, the GDP of the services sector increased at an average annual rate of 1.6%; growth of 2.8% was recorded in 2003.

In 2003 the Congo recorded a visible trade surplus of an estimated 1,005,200m. francs CFA, but there was an estimated deficit of 1,200m. francs CFA on the current account of the balance of payments. In 1995 the principal source of imports (32.0%) was France, while the USA was the principal market for exports (22.6%). Italy and the Netherlands are also important trading partners. The principal exports in 2003 were petroleum and petroleum products, and wood. The principal imports in 1996 were machinery, chemical products, iron and steel and transport equipment.

The budget surplus for 2003, according to provisional figures, was 7,400m. francs CFA (equivalent to 0.4% of GDP). The country's external debt totalled US $5,152m. at the end of 2002, of which $3,974m. was long-term public debt. In that year the cost of debt-servicing was equivalent to 1.0% of the value of exports of goods and services. In December 2004 the African Development Bank approved a grant of $50m. to allow the Congo to clear one-third of its debt to that organization. The annual rate of inflation averaged 0.4% in 1997–2003. Consumer prices increased by an average of 4.4% in 2002, but declined by an estimated 0.6% in 2003.

The Republic of the Congo is a member of the Central African organs of the Franc Zone (see p. 267) and of the Communauté économique des états de l'Afrique centrale (CEEAC, see p. 373).

Civil conflict and ensuing instability adversely affected the Congo's economic performance in the late 1990s. The World Bank suspended relations with the Congo in November 1997 in response to the non-payment of debt arrears, while the outbreak of further hostilities in December 1998 led to the suspension of all donor activity. In recent years the high relative level of debt has remained a major impediment to the resumption of aid, and weaknesses in the implementation of reforms and a lack of strict budget control have prevented the Congo from qualifying for relief under the Bretton Woods institutions' initiative for heavily indebted poor countries. None the less, in November 2000 the IMF approved a credit of some US $14m. for the Congo in emergency post-conflict assistance, and in August 2001 the World Bank declared that the Congo had cleared all of its overdue service payments and was again eligible for credit. Major reforms, involving restructuring and privatization, were introduced in a number of important sectors in the early 2000s, including banking and petroleum. The Government's seven-year post-conflict economic reconstruction programme, introduced in 2003, emphasized major infrastructural improvements, including the construction of a year-round river port at Lékéti and a new international airport in the north of the country, while the restoration of peace in the Pool region, following the signing of a cease-fire agreement in March 2003, was expected to facilitate the eventual return to pre-conflict levels of international trade through the port at Pointe-Noire and the Congo-Océan railway line, although problems persisted in 2004 with numerous attacks on the section of the line passing through the Pool region (see Recent History). The Congo is the fourth-largest producer of petroleum in sub-Saharan Africa, and the Government's publication of an independent audit of the state-owned petroleum company, the Société Nationale des Pétroles du Congo, was a contributing factor in the IMF's decision, in December 2004, to approve a three-year Poverty Reduction and Growth Faciltity, equivalent to some $84.4m. The 2005 budget envisaged GDP growth of 9.1% in that year, compared with 4.1% in 2004, and also provided for increased expenditure on education, health and social protection. However, the IMF recommended that the Government improve fiscal transparency and the management of public finances in order to maintain economic progress.

Education

Education is officially compulsory for 10 years between six and 16 years of age. Primary education begins at the age of six and lasts for six years. Secondary education, from 12 years of age, lasts for seven years, comprising a first cycle of four years and a second of three years. Enrolment at primary schools in 2000/01 was equivalent to 97% of children in the relevant age-group (boys 101%; girls 93%). In that year, according to UNESCO estimates, enrolment at secondary schools was equivalent to 42% of children in the relevant age-group (boys 46%; girls 38%). In 1999/2000 13,403 students were attending tertiary institutions. In 2000 there were some 20,000 students enrolled in the Marien Ngouabi University in Brazzaville. Some Congolese students also attend further education establishments abroad. Expenditure on education by all levels of government was 52,274m. francs CFA in 1995. In September 2004 the World Bank approved a grant of US $20m. to assist with the reconstruction of the country's educational sector, which had been severely damaged by years of civil conflict.

Public Holidays

2005: 1 January (New Year's Day), 25 March (Good Friday), 28 March (Easter Monday), 1 May (Labour Day), 16 May (Whit

Monday), 15 August (Independence Day), 25 December (Christmas).

2006: 1 January (New Year's Day), 14 April (Good Friday), 17 April (Easter Monday), 1 May (Labour Day), 5 June (Whit

Monday), 15 August (Independence Day), 25 December (Christmas).

Weights and Measures
The metric system is in force.

Statistical Survey

Source (unless otherwise stated): Direction Générale, Centre National de la Statistique et des Etudes Economiques, BP 2031, Brazzaville; tel. and fax 81-59-09.

Area and Population

AREA, POPULATION AND DENSITY

Area (sq km)	342,000*
Population (census results)	
22 December 1984	1,909,248
30 July 1996	2,591,271
Population (UN estimates at mid-year)†	
2001	3,542,000
2002	3,633,000
2003	3,724,000
Density (per sq km) at mid-2003	10.9

* 132,047 sq miles.
† Source: UN, *World Population Prospects: The 2002 Revision.*

ETHNIC GROUPS

1995 (percentages): Kongo 51.4; Téké 17.2; Mbochi 11.4; Mbédé 4.7; Punu 2.9; Sanga 2.5; Maka 1.8; Pygmy 1.4; Others 6.7 (Source: La Francophonie).

REGIONS
(population at 1996 census)

	Area (sq km)	Population	Capital
Bouenza	12,260	189,839	Madingou
Cuvette . . . . }	74,850 {	112,946	Owando
Cuvette ouest . . }		49,422	Ewo
Kouilou	13,650	77,048	Pointe-Noire
Lékoumou . . .	20,950	75,734	Sibiti
Likouala	66,044	66,252	Impfondo
Niari	25,925	103,678	Loubomo (Dolisie)
Plateaux	38,400	139,371	Djambala
Pool	33,955	265,180	Kinkala
Sangha	55,795	39,439	Ouesso
Total*	341,829	1,118,909	

* Excluding the municipalities of Brazzaville (100 sq km, population 856,410), Pointe-Noire (45 sq km, population 455,131), Loubomo (Dolisie—18 sq km, population 79,852), Nkaya (8 sq km, population 46,727), Ouesso (population 17,784) and Mossendjo (population 16,458).

BIRTHS AND DEATHS
(UN estimates, annual averages)

	1985–90	1990–95	1995–2000
Birth rate (per 1,000)	43.8	44.2	44.4
Death rate (per 1,000)	11.2	12.7	15.0

Source: UN, *World Population Prospects: The 2002 Revision.*

Expectation of life (WHO estimates, years at birth): 53.1 (males 51.6; females 54.5) in 2002 (Source: WHO, *World Health Report*).

EMPLOYMENT
('000 persons at 1984 census)

	Males	Females	Total
Agriculture, etc.	105	186	291
Industry	61	8	69
Services	123	60	183
Total	289	254	543

Mid-2003 (FAO estimates, '000 persons): Agriculture, etc. 575; Total labour force 1,509 (Source: FAO).

Health and Welfare

KEY INDICATORS

Total fertility rate (children per woman, 2002)	6.3
Under-5 mortality rate (per 1,000 live births, 2003) . . .	108
HIV/AIDS (% of persons aged 15–49, 2003)	4.9
Physicians (per 1,000 head, 1995)	0.25
Hospital beds (per 1,000 head, 1990)	3.35
Health expenditure (2001): US $ per head (PPP)	22
Health expenditure (2001): % of GDP	2.1
Health expenditure (2001): public (% of total)	63.8
Access to water (% of persons, 2002)	46
Access to sanitation (% of persons, 2002)	9
Human Development Index (2002): ranking	144
Human Development Index (2002): value	0.494

For sources and definitions, see explanatory note on p. vi.

Agriculture

PRINCIPAL CROPS
('000 metric tons)

	2001	2002	2003*
Sweet potatoes	7.0*	5.4	6.0
Cassava (Manioc)	844.7	861.6	880.0
Yams	8.0*	10.9	12.0
Other roots and tubers* . . .	39.4	40.6	40.8
Sugar cane	454.4	458.6	460.0
Groundnuts (in shell)	23.4	23.7	23.7
Oil palm fruit*	90	90	90
Vegetables (incl. melons)* . . .	40.1	41.4	41.5
Bananas	82.7	84.4	85.0
Plantains*	71	71	71
Citrus fruit	12.6	10.4	10.5
Mangoes	23.5*	24.6	25.0
Other fruit*	31.6	32.5	32.5

* FAO estimate(s).

Source: FAO.

LIVESTOCK
('000 head, year ending September)

	2001	2002	2003*
Cattle	90	93*	122.4
Pigs	46.0*	46.2	46.3
Sheep*	96	98	97
Goats*	280.0	294.2	294.2
Poultry*	1,900	2,100	2,000

* FAO estimate(s).

Source: FAO.

LIVESTOCK PRODUCTS
(FAO estimates, '000 metric tons)

	2001	2002	2003
Beef and veal	1.7	1.7	2.0
Pig meat	2.1	2.1	2.1
Poultry meat	5.8	5.0	5.0
Game meat	16.0	18.0	18.0
Sheep and goat meat	1.1	1.1	1.1
Cows' milk	1.1	1.1	1.1
Hen eggs	1.2	1.2	1.2

Source: FAO.

Forestry

ROUNDWOOD REMOVALS
(FAO estimates, '000 cubic metres, excluding bark)

	2001	2002	2003
Sawlogs, veneer logs and logs for sleepers	520	520	520
Pulpwood	361	361	361
Other industrial wood	370	370	370
Fuel wood	1,169	1,186	1,202
Total	2,420	2,437	2,453

Source: FAO.

SAWNWOOD PRODUCTION
('000 cubic metres, including railway sleepers)

	2001	2002	2003
Total (all broadleaved)	126.0	169.7	314.5

Source: FAO.

Fishing

(FAO estimates, '000 metric tons, live weight)

	2000	2001	2002
Capture	44.7	42.2	43.0
Freshwater fishes	20.2	20.2	20.5
Sardinellas	10.5	9.5	9.7
Aquaculture	0.2	0.2	—
Total catch	44.9	42.4	43.0

Source: FAO.

Mining

	2001	2002*	2003*
Crude petroleum ('000 barrels)	98,920†	94,170†	87,600
Gold (kg)‡	10	10	30

* Estimates.
† Reported figure.
‡ Estimated metal content of ore.

Source: US Geological Survey.

Industry

SELECTED PRODUCTS
('000 metric tons, unless otherwise indicated)

	1998	1999	2000
Raw sugar	43	40	45
Veneer sheets ('000 cu metres)	52	19	10
Jet fuels*	17	17	38
Motor gasoline (petrol)	25	28	40
Kerosene	25*	28*	21
Distillate fuel oils	96*	85*	62
Residual fuel oils	272*	275*	206
Electric energy (million kWh)*	454	353	300

2001: Raw sugar ('000 metric tons) 42.9; Veneer sheets ('000 cu metres) 14.

2002: Raw sugar ('000 metric tons) 44.1; Veneer sheets ('000 cu metres) 21.

* Provisional figure(s).

Sources: UN, *Industrial Commodity Statistics Yearbook*; FAO.

Finance

CURRENCY AND EXCHANGE RATES

Monetary Units
> 100 centimes = 1 franc de la Coopération financière en Afrique centrale (CFA).

Sterling, Dollar and Euro Equivalents (31 December 2004)
> £1 sterling = 930.12 francs CFA;
> US $1 = 481.58 francs CFA;
> €1 = 655.96 francs CFA;
> 10,000 francs CFA = £10.75 = $20.77 = €15.24.

Average Exchange Rate (francs CFA per US $)
> 2002   696.99
> 2003   581.20
> 2004   528.29

Note: The exchange rate of 1 French franc = 50 francs CFA, established in 1948, remained in force until January 1994, when the CFA franc was devalued by 50%, with the exchange rate adjusted to 1 French franc = 100 francs CFA. The relationship to French currency remained in effect with the introduction of the euro on 1 January 1999. From that date, accordingly, a fixed exchange rate of €1 = 655.957 francs CFA has been in operation.

BUDGET
('000 million francs CFA)

Revenue*	2001	2002†	2003‡
Petroleum revenue	430.8	397.5	421.6
Royalties	430.8	395.7	381.1
Profit-sharing	0.0	0.0	0.0
Government share sold by SNPC	119.3	120.4	251.1
Other revenue	197.3	174.2	182.0
Domestic taxes	126.9	125.3	134.0
Direct	59.1	57.3	64.3
Indirect	67.8	68.0	69.7
Customs receipts	43.3	36.1	43.3
Domestic petroleum taxes	15.6	10.0	0.0
Non-tax revenue	11.5	2.8	4.7
Total	628.1	571.7	603.6

Expenditure§	2001	2002†	2003‡
Current expenditure . . .	440.6	563.1	470.5
Wages and salaries	118.1	120.4	120.2
Materials and supplies . . .	32.1	78.4	50.0
Transfers	72.7	104.9	130.8
Interest payments	152.0	176.7	117.8
External	144.3	162.3	94.4
Capital expenditure	205.4	181.7	134.8
Domestically financed . . .	200.4	158.1	111.0
Total	**645.9**	**744.8**	**605.3**

* Excluding grants received ('000 million francs CFA): 3.7 in 2001; 3.7 (estimate) in 2002; 9.9 (preliminary figure) in 2003.
† Estimates.
‡ Preliminary figures.
§ Excluding net lending ('000 million francs CFA): 0.0 in 2001; 1.6 (estimate) in 2002; 0.8 (preliminary figure) in 2003.
Sources: IMF, *Republic of Congo: Selected Issues and Statistical Appendix* (July 2004).

INTERNATIONAL RESERVES
(US $ million at 31 December)

	2001	2002	2003
Gold*	3.09	3.81	4.65
IMF special drawing rights . .	0.19	3.23	0.64
Reserve position in IMF . . .	0.67	0.73	0.80
Foreign exchange	68.05	27.67	33.36
Total	**72.00**	**35.44**	**39.45**

* National valuation.
Source: IMF, *International Financial Statistics.*

MONEY SUPPLY
('000 million francs CFA at 31 December)

	2001	2002	2003
Currency outside banks . .	142.91	129.00	131.92
Demand deposits at active commercial banks	81.36	129.77	89.50
Total money (incl. others) . .	**238.08**	**271.24**	**235.15**

Source: IMF, *International Financial Statistics.*

COST OF LIVING
(Consumer Price Index for Brazzaville and Pointe-Noire, unless otherwise indicated; base: December 1977 = 100)

	2001	2002*	2003†
Food	368.0	385.3	362.8
Clothing	465.2	488.6	439.1
Construction and rent . . .	551.8	562.2	567.1
Fuel and electricity	513.8	502.5	470.6
All items (incl. others)‡ . . .	**417.0**	**435.2**	**432.5**

* Estimates.
† Preliminary figures.
‡ Consumer Price Index for Brazzaville only.
Source: IMF, *Republic of Congo: Selected Issues and Statistical Appendix* (July 2004).

NATIONAL ACCOUNTS
('000 million francs CFA at current prices)
Expenditure on the Gross Domestic Product

	2001	2002	2003
Final consumption expenditure .	820.7	942.6	945.3
Households			
Non-profit institutions serving households	579.3	670.4	731.3
General government . . .	241.4	272.2	214.0
Gross capital formation . . .	629.3	549.2	624.5
Gross fixed capital formation .	579.3	599.2	599.5
Changes in inventories . .			
Acquisitions, less disposals, of valuables	50.0	−50.0	25.0

— continued	2001	2002	2003
Total domestic expenditure .	1,450.0	1,491.8	1,569.8
Exports of goods and services .	1,620.1	1,699.9	1,597.1
Less Imports of goods and services	1,125.4	1,088.4	1,084.2
Statistical discrepancy . . .	103.6	—	—
GDP in market prices . . .	**2,048.3**	**2,103.0**	**2,082.7**

Source: IMF, *International Financial Statistics.*

Gross Domestic Product by Economic Activity

	2001	2002*	2003†
Agriculture, hunting, forestry and fishing	118.8	131.8	128.0
Mining and quarrying‡ . . .	1,249.2	1,236.5	1,135.3
Manufacturing‡			
Electricity, gas and water . .	16.0	18.5	19.7
Construction	74.4	75.9	89.4
Trade, restaurants and hotels .	139.9	167.6	180.6
Transport, storage and communications	110.8	123.4	137.4
Government services	137.3	147.9	148.4
Other services	120.1	129.3	124.9
GDP at factor cost	**1,966.5**	**2,030.9**	**1,963.7**
Import duties	76.9	72.1	76.3
GDP in purchasers' values .	**2,043.4**	**2,103.0**	**2,040.0**

* Estimates.
† Preliminary figures.
‡ Including petroleum sector ('000 million francs CFA): 1,158.6 in 2001; 1,126.4 (estimate) in 2002; 1,003.4 (preliminary figure) in 2003.
Source: IMF, *Republic of Congo: Selected Issues and Statistical Appendix* (July 2004).

BALANCE OF PAYMENTS
('000 million francs CFA)

	2001	2002	2003*
Exports of goods f.o.b.	1,506.6	1,567.3	1,475.2
Imports of goods f.o.b.	−499.5	−492.2	−470.0
Trade balance	**1,007.1**	**1,075.1**	**1,005.2**
Balance on services	−462.8	−514.0	−496.8
Balance on goods and services	**544.3**	**561.1**	**508.4**
Other income	−611.3	−570.7	−513.3
Labour income	−19.2	−21.7	−13.2
Investment income	−592.0	−549.0	−500.1
Interest on public debt . .	−144.3	−162.3	−94.4
Balance on goods, services and income	**−67**	**−9.6**	**−4.9**
Current transfers (net)	2.3	2.7	3.8
Private transfers	−1.9	−1.7	−0.6
Public transfers	4.2	4.4	4.3
Current balance	**−64.6**	**−6.9**	**−1.2**
Capital account	69.2	10.7	11.1
Direct investment (net)	160.0	171.9	187.4
Direct investment in oil sector .	152.1	147.8	150.9
Portfolio investment	−5.3	−5.9	−3.7
Other investment	−262.0	−90.4	−174.6
Medium- and long-term . . .	−206.5	146.8	−61.1
Short-term	−55.4	−237.3	−113.5
Errors and omissions	−1.8	−104.2	−13.6
Overall balance	**−104.4**	**−24.8**	**5.5**

* Estimates.
Source: IMF, *Republic of Congo: Review of Performance Under the Staff-Monitored Program and Request for a Three-Year Arrangement Under the Poverty Reduction and Growth Facility—Staff Report; Staff Statement; Press Release on the Executive Board Discussion; and Statement by the Executive Director for the Republic of Congo* (January 2005).

External Trade

PRINCIPAL COMMODITIES

Imports c.i.f. (distribution by SITC, US $ million)	1993	1994	1995
Food and live animals . . .	59.6	87.9	108.5
Meat and meat preparations . .	15.8	23.7	28.1
Fresh, chilled or frozen meat and edible offals	15.0	21.7	26.8
Fish and fish preparations . . .	0.1	21.8	16.4
Cereals and cereal preparations .	27.5	23.8	36.7
Flour of wheat or meslin . . .	18.1	8.2	13.8
Mineral fuels, lubricants, etc. .	2.9	4.9	108.7
Petroleum, petroleum products, etc.	2.8	4.9	106.0
Refined petroleum products . .	2.7	3.1	105.5
Motor spirit (gasoline) and other light oils	—	—	38.4
Motor spirit (incl. aviation spirit)	—	—	30.7
Kerosene and other medium oils	—	—	19.2
Gas oils	—	—	44.4
Chemicals and related products	54.6	54.7	77.0
Medicaments (incl. veterinary) .	38.5	24.0	38.0
Basic manufactures	61.5	76.7	69.5
Iron and steel	17.8	20.5	15.6
Tubes, pipes and fittings . . .	14.6	17.6	9.7
'Seamless' tubes and pipes; blanks for tubes and pipes .	13.2	15.8	6.4
Iron or steel structures, etc. . .	0.2	21.6	1.0
Machinery and transport equipment	127.1	112.6	112.5
Machinery specialized for particular industries	10.7	17.3	17.2
Civil engineering and contractors' plant and equipment	7.2	11.9	10.0
General industrial machinery, equipment and parts	24.9	30.4	32.1
Electrical machinery, apparatus, etc.	11.7	23.7	19.0
Road vehicles and parts* . . .	20.4	20.7	21.1
Other transport equipment and parts*	47.1	6.5	3.8
Tugs, special-purpose vessels and floating structures . .	46.7	2.8	0.3
Light-vessels, fire-floats, dredgers, floating cranes, etc.	45.7	—	—
Miscellaneous manufactured articles	24.2	36.3	65.2
Professional, scientific and controlling instruments, etc. .	8.2	13.2	29.1
Measuring, checking, analysing and controlling instruments, etc.	7.5	11.6	26.3
Total (incl. others)	347.1	395.2	555.9

* Data on parts exclude tyres, engines and electrical parts.

Source: UN, *International Trade Statistics Yearbook*.

Exports f.o.b. ('000 million francs CFA)	2001	2002*	2003†
Wood	97.0	124.5	176.6
Petroleum, petroleum products, etc.	1,341.4	1,373.8	1,225.7
Crude petroleum	1,287.6	1,375.7	1,109.8
Refined products	3.3	17.5	0.0
Total (incl. others) . . .	1,506.6	1,567.3	1,475.6

* Estimates.
† Preliminary figures.

Source: IMF, *Republic of Congo: Selected Issues and Statistical Appendix* (August 2004).

Imports c.i.f. ('000 million francs CFA): 540.7 in 1997; 401.3 in 1998; 505.2 in 1999; 330.9 in 2000.

Source: IMF, *International Financial Statistics*.

PRINCIPAL TRADING PARTNERS
(US $ million)

Imports c.i.f.	1993	1994	1995*
Belgium-Luxembourg . . .	9.7	14.9	19.4
France (incl. Monaco) . . .	114.0	127.5	145.2
Germany	8.4	9.2	15.8
Hong Kong	4.5	4.0	3.7
Italy	66.2	17.1	20.8
Japan	11.1	10.2	12.3
Mauritania	—	0.7	5.9
Netherlands	27.5	24.6	30.7
Norway	1.7	4.0	2.4
Senegal	1.8	6.0	7.2
South Africa†	2.8	8.2	0.0
United Kingdom	9.0	12.7	16.6
USA	16.1	39.5	44.6
Total (incl. others)	347.1	395.2	555.9

Exports f.o.b.	1993	1994	1995
Angola	10.2	5.1	6.5
Brazil	0.1	14.0	—
Chile	—	15.6	—
France (incl. Monaco) . . .	79.5	56.3	107.3
Germany	2.6	8.1	11.5
Israel	12.8	11.8	—
Italy	226.3	191.8	189.6
Japan	14.4	3.2	3.4
Malta	—	—	31.3
Netherlands	16.6	11.0	130.7
Portugal	1.6	21.9	0.4
Spain	17.3	28.1	0.1
Switzerland-Liechtenstein . . .	12.3	—	—
USA	503.4	386.3	311.1
Total (incl others)	965.3	917.8	1,089.8

* Figures for individual countries exclude imports from free zones ($56.4 million) and stores and bunkers for ships and aircraft ($50.8 million).
† Including Botswana, Lesotho, Namibia and Swaziland.

Source: UN, *International Trade Statistics Yearbook*.

Transport

RAILWAYS
(traffic)

	1999	2000	2001
Passengers carried ('000) . . .	56.5	546.0	742.0
Freight carried ('000 metric tons) .	65.7	236.0	548.0
Passenger-km (million)	9	n.a.	n.a.
Freight ton-km (million) . . .	21	n.a.	n.a.

* Estimates.

Sources: UN, *Statistical Yearbook*; IMF, *Republic of Congo: Selected Issues and Statistical Appendix* (July 2004).

ROAD TRAFFIC
(estimates, '000 motor vehicles in use)

	1999	2000	2001
Passenger cars	26.2	29.7	29.7
Commercial vehicles	20.4	23.1	23.1

Source: UN, *Statistical Yearbook*.

SHIPPING

Merchant Fleet
(registered at 31 December)

	2001	2002	2003
Number of vessels	18	18	18
Total displacement ('000 grt) . .	3.4	3.4	3.4

Source: Lloyd's Register-Fairplay, *World Fleet Statistics*.

Freight Traffic at Pointe-Noire
(metric tons)

	1996	1997	1998
Goods loaded	670,150	708,203	n.a.
Goods unloaded	584,376	533,170	724,000*

* Rounded figure.

Source: mainly Banque des états de l'Afrique centrale, *Etudes et Statistiques*.

CIVIL AVIATION
(traffic on scheduled services)*

	1999	2000	2001
Kilometres flown (million) . .	4	4	3
Passengers carried ('000) . . .	132	128	95
Passenger-km (million) . . .	263	245	157
Total ton-km (million) . . .	39	34	22

* Including an apportionment of the traffic of Air Afrique.

Source: UN, *Statistical Yearbook*.

Tourism

	1998	1999	2000
Foreign tourist arrivals	25,082	4,753	26,000*
Tourism receipts (US $ million) .	9	12	12

* Rounded figure.

Tourism receipts (US $ million): 22 in 2001; 25 in 2002.

Source: World Tourism Organization.

Communications Media

	2001	2002	2003
Telephones ('000 main lines in use)	22	22	7
Mobile cellular telephones ('000 subscribers)	150.0	221.8	330.0
Personal computers ('000 in use)	12	13	15
Internet users ('000)	n.a.	15	15

Source: International Telecommunication Union.

Radio receivers ('000 in use): 341 in 1997 (Source: UNESCO, *Statistical Yearbook*).

Television receivers ('000 in use): 33 in 1997 (Source: UNESCO, *Statistical Yearbook*).

Daily newspapers: 6 in 1996 (Source: UNESCO, *Statistical Yearbook*).

Non-daily newspapers: 15 in 1995 (average circulation 38,000 copies) (Source: UNESCO, *Statistical Yearbook*).

Education
(1998/99)

	Institutions	Teachers	Students		
			Males	Females	Total
Pre-primary . .	95	606	2,338	3,695	6,033
Primary . . .	1,168	4,515	141,646	134,805	276,451
Secondary* . .	n.a.	5,094	71,169	43,281	114,450
Tertiary† . . .	n.a.	n.a.	11,804	1,599	13,403

* Figures refer to general secondary education only.
† 1999/2000 figures.

Sources: UNESCO Institute for Statistics; Ministry of Education, Brazzaville.

Adult literacy rate (UNESCO estimates): 82.8% (males 88.9%; females 77.1%) in 2002 (Source: UN Development Programme, *Human Development Report*).

Directory

The Constitution

The 1992 Constitution was suspended following the assumption of power by Gen. Denis Sassou-Nguesso on 15 October 1997. A new Constitution, which was approved by the Conseil national de transition (interim legislative body) on 2 September 2001 and endorsed by a public referendum on 20 January 2002, took effect following presidential and legislative elections in March–July 2002. Its main provisions are summarized below:

PREAMBLE
The Congolese people, having chosen a pluralist democracy as the basis for the development of the country, condemn the tyrannical use of power and political violence and declare that the fundamental principles proclaimed and guaranteed by the UN Charter, the Universal Declaration of Human Rights and other international treaties form an integral part of the present Constitution.

I. THE STATE AND SOVEREIGNTY
Articles 1–6: The Republic of the Congo is a sovereign, secular, social and democratic State. The principle of the Republic is government of the people, by the people and for the people. National sovereignty belongs to the people, who exercise it through universal suffrage by their elected representatives or by referendum. The official language of the Republic is French. The national languages of communication are Lingala and Kituba.

II. FUNDAMENTAL RIGHTS AND LIBERTIES
Articles 7–42: All citizens are equal before the law. Arbitrary arrest and all degrading forms of punishment are prohibited, and all accused are presumed innocent until proven guilty. Incitement to ethnic hatred, violence or civil war and the use of religion to political ends are forbidden. Equal access to education, which is compulsory until the age of 16, is guaranteed to all. The State is obliged to create conditions that enable all citizens to enjoy the right to work. All citizens, excluding members of the police and military forces, may participate in trade union activity. Slavery is forbidden, and forced labour permitted only as a judicial punishment.

III. DUTIES
Articles 43–50: All citizens have duties towards their family, society, the State and other legally recognized authorities. All citizens are obliged to conform to the Constitution, the laws of the Republic and to fulfil their obligations towards the State and society.

IV. POLITICAL PARTIES
Articles 51–55: Political parties may not be identified with an ethnic group, a region, a religion or a sect. They must protect and promote fundamental human rights, the rule of law, democracy, individual and collective freedoms, national territorial integrity and sovereignty, proscribe intolerance, ethnically based extremism, and any recourse to violence, and respect the secular form of the State.

V. EXECUTIVE POWER
Articles 56–88: The President of the Republic is the Head of State, Head of the Executive and Head of Government. The President is directly elected by an absolute majority of votes cast, for a term of seven years, renewable once. Presidential candidates must be of Congolese nationality and origin, aged between 40 and 70 years and have resided on national territory for at least 24 successive months prior to registering as a candidate. If required, a second round of voting takes place between the two highest-placed candidates in the first ballot. In the event of the death, resignation, or long-term incapacity of the President of the Republic, the President of the Sénat assumes limited executive functions for up to 90 days, pending an election, which he may not contest.

The President appoints ministers, senior civil servants, military staff and ambassadors. Ministers may not hold a parliamentary mandate or civic, public or military post, and their professional activity is restricted. The President of the Republic is the Supreme Head of the armed forces and the President of the Higher Council of Magistrates, and possesses the right of pardon. The President of the Republic chairs the Council of Ministers.

VI. LEGISLATIVE POWER

Articles 89–113: The Parliament is bicameral. Deputies are directly elected to the Assemblée nationale for a renewable term of five years. Senators are elected indirectly to the Sénat by local councils for a term of six years. One-half of the Sénat is elected every three years. Deputies and senators must be Congolese nationals, aged over 25 years in the case of deputies, or over 45 years in the case of senators, residing in national territory. A deputy or senator elected as a member of a political grouping may not resign from the grouping without simultaneously resigning his parliamentary position.

VII. RELATIONS BETWEEN THE LEGISLATIVE AND EXECUTIVE INSTITUTIONS

Articles 114–132: The President of the Republic may not dissolve the Assemblée nationale. The Assemblée nationale may not remove the President of the Republic. The legislative chambers consider proposed legislation in succession, with a view to adopting an identical text. If necessary, the President of the Republic may convene a joint commission to present a revised text to the two chambers. The President of the Republic may then call the Assemblée nationale to make a final decision. Special conditions apply to the passage of certain laws, including the national budget, and to a declaration of war or state of emergency.

VIII. JUDICIAL POWER

Articles 133–143: Judicial power is exercised by the Supreme Court, the Revenue and Budgetary Discipline Court, appeal courts and other national courts of law, which are independent of the legislature. The President of the Republic chairs a Higher Council of Magistrates, which guarantees the independence of the judiciary. The President of the Republic nominates judges to the Supreme Court and to the other courts of law, at the suggestion of the Higher Council of Magistrates. Judges of the Supreme Court may not be removed from office.

IX. CONSTITUTIONAL COURT

Articles 144–151: The Constitutional Court consists of nine members, each with a renewable mandate of nine years. One-third of the Court is renewed every three years. The President of the Republic nominates three members of the Constitutional Court independently, and the others at the suggestion of the President of each legislative chamber and of the Bureau of the Supreme Court. The President of the Republic nominates the President of the Constitutional Court. The Court ensures that laws, treaties and international agreements conform to the Constitution and oversees presidential elections.

X. HIGH COURT OF JUSTICE

Articles 152–156: The High Court of Justice is composed of an equal number of deputies and senators elected by their peers, and of members of the Supreme Court elected by their peers. It is chaired by the First President of the Supreme Court and is competent to try the President of the Republic in case of high treason. Members of the legislature, the Supreme Court and the Constitutional Court and government ministers are accountable to the High Court of Justice for crimes or offences committed in the execution of their duties, subject to a two-thirds' majority in a secret vote at a joint session of Parliament.

XI. ECONOMIC AND SOCIAL COUNCIL

Articles 157–160: The Economic and Social Council is a consultative assembly, which may become involved in any economic or social problem concerning the Republic, either of its own will or at the request of the President of the Republic or the President of either legislative chamber.

XII. HIGHER COUNCIL FOR THE FREEDOM OF COMMUNICATION

Articles 161–162: The Higher Council for the Freedom of Communication ensures freedom of information and communication, formulating recommendations on applicable issues.

XIII. MEDIATOR OF THE REPUBLIC

Articles 163–166: The Mediator of the Republic is an independent authority responsible for simplifying and humanizing relations between government and citizens, and may be addressed by any person dissatisfied with the workings of any public organization.

XIV. NATIONAL COMMISSION FOR HUMAN RIGHTS

Articles 167–169: The National Commission for Human Rights seeks to promote and protect human rights.

XV. POLICE AND MILITARY FORCES

Articles 170–173: The police and military bodies consist of the national police force, the national gendarmerie and the Congolese armed forces. These bodies are apolitical and subordinate to the civil authority. The creation of militia groups is prohibited.

XVI. LOCAL AUTHORITIES

Articles 174–177: The local administrative bodies of the Republic of the Congo are the department and the commune, and any others created by law.

XVII. INTERNATIONAL TREATIES AND AGREEMENTS

Articles 178–184: The President of the Republic negotiates, signs and, with the approval of Parliament, ratifies international treaties and agreements. Any proposed change to the territorial boundaries of the Republic must be submitted to popular referendum.

XVIII. ON REVISION

Articles 185–187: The Constitution may be revised at the initiative of the President of the Republic or members of Parliament. The territorial integrity of the Republic, the republican form of government, the secular nature of the State, the number of presidential terms of office permitted and the rights outlined in sections I and II (above) may not be the subject of any revision. Any constitutional amendments proposed by the President of the Republic are submitted directly to a referendum. Any constitutional changes proposed by Parliament must be approved by two-thirds of the members of both legislative chambers convened in congress, before being submitted to referendum. In both cases the Constitutional Court must have declared the acceptability of the proposals.

The Government

HEAD OF STATE

President: Gen. DENIS SASSOU-NGUESSO (assumed power 15 October 1997; inaugurated 25 October 1997; elected 10 March 2002).

COUNCIL OF MINISTERS
(March 2005)

Prime Minister, responsible for the Co-ordination of Government Action and Privatization: ISIDORE MVOUBA.

Minister of State, Minister of Foreign Affairs and the Francophonie: RODOLPHE ADADA.

Minister of Forestry and the Environment: HENRI DJOMBO.

Minister of Social Affairs, Solidarity, Humanitarian Action, Disabled Ex-servicemen and the Family: ÉMILIENNE RAOUL.

Minister of Agriculture, Livestock and Fishing: JEANNE DAMBENDZET.

Minister of Communication, responsible for Relations with Parliament, Government Spokesperson: ALAIN AKOUALA.

Minister of Trade, Consumption and Supplies: ADÉLAÏDE MOUNDELE-NGOLLO.

Minister of Construction, Town Planning, Living Conditions and Land Reform: CLAUDE ALPHONSE NTSILOU.

Minister of Security and Public Order: Div.-Gen. PAUL MBOT.

Minister of Culture and the Arts, responsible for Tourism: JEAN-CLAUDE GAKOSSO.

Minister at the Presidency, responsible for National Defence, Veterans and Disabled Ex-servicemen: JACQUES-YVON NDOULOU.

Minister of Higher Education and Scientific Research: HENRI OSSEBI.

Minister of Primary and Secondary Education, responsible for Literacy: ROSALIE KAMA.

Minister of Technical Education and Vocational Training: PIERRE-MICHEL NGUIMBI.

Minister of Finance, the Economy and the Budget: PACIFIQUE ISSOIBEKA.

Keeper of the Seals, Minister of Justice and Human Rights: GABRIEL ENTSA-EBIA.

Minister of State, Minister of Hydrocarbons: JEAN-BAPTISTE TATI-LOUTARD.

Minister of State, Minister of the Civil Service and State Reform: JEAN-MARTIN MBEMBA.

Minister of Energy and Hydraulics: BRUNO JEAN-RCHARD ITOUA.

Minister of State, Minister of Planning, Territorial Development, Economic Integration and NEPAD: PIERRE MOUSSA.

Minister of Industrial Development and the Promotion of the Private Sector: ÉMILE MABONDZOT.

Minister of Posts and Telecommunications, responsible for New Technologies: PHILIPPE MVOUO.

Minister of Land Reform and the Preservation of the Public Domain: LAMYR NGUELE.

Minister of Health and Population: Dr ALPHONSE GANDO.

Minister of Mines, Mining Industries and Geology: PIERRE OBA.

Minister of Sports and the Redeployment of Youth: MARCEL MBANI.

Minister of Territorial Administration and Decentralization: FRANÇOIS IBOVI.

Minister of Equipment and Public Works: FLORENT NTSIBA.

Minister of Transport and Civil Aviation: ANDRÉ OKOMBI-SAL-ISSA.

Minister at the Presidency, responsible for Development Co-operation: JUSTIN BALLAY MEGOT.

Minister of Labour, Employment and Social Security: GILBERT ONDONGO.

Minister of the Promotion and Integration of Women: JEANNE-FRANÇOISE LEKOMBA LOUMETO.

Minister of Scientific Reform and Technical Innovation: PIERRE-ERNEST ABANDZOUNOU.

Minister of the Maritime Economy and the Merchant Navy: LOUIS-MARIE NOMBO MAVOUNGOU.

Minister of Small- and Medium-sized Businesses, responsible for Handicrafts: PARFAIT AIMÉ COUSSOUD-MAVOUNGOU.

MINISTRIES

Office of the President: Palais du Peuple, Brazzaville; tel. 81-17-11; e-mail contact@presicongo.cg; internet www.presidence.cg.

Office of the Prime Minister: Brazzaville; tel. 81-10-67; internet www.gouv.cg.

Office of the Minister at the Presidency, responsible for Development Co-operation: Brazzaville; tel. 81-10-89.

Office of the Minister at the Presidency, responsible for National Defence, Veterans and Disabled Ex-servicemen: Brazzaville; tel. 81-22-31.

Ministry of Agriculture, Livestock and Fishing: BP 2453, Brazzaville; tel. 81-41-31; fax 81-19-29.

Ministry of the Civil Service and State Reform: BP 12151, Brazzaville; tel. 81-41-68; fax 81-41-49.

Ministry of Communication, responsible for Relations with Parliament: BP 114, Brazzaville; tel. 81-41-29; fax 81-41-28; e-mail depcompt@congonet.cg.

Ministry of Construction, Town Planning, Living Conditions and Land Reform: BP 1580, Brazzaville; tel. 81-34-48; fax 81-12-97.

Ministry of Culture, the Arts and Tourism: BP 20480, Brazzaville; tel. 81-02-35; fax 81-40-25.

Ministry of Energy and Hydraulics: Brazzaville.

Ministry of Equipment and Public Works: BP 2099, Brazzaville; tel. 81-59-41; fax 81-59-07.

Ministry of Finance, the Economy and the Budget: Centre Administratif, Quartier Plateau, BP 2083, Brazzaville; tel. 81-45-24; fax 81-43-69.

Ministry of Foreign Affairs and the Francophonie: BP 2070, Brazzaville; tel. 81-10-89; fax 81-41-61.

Ministry of Forestry and the Environment: Immeuble de l'Agriculture, Face à Blanche Gomez, BP 98, Brazzaville; tel. 81-41-41; fax 81-41-34; e-mail secretariat@minifor.com; internet www.minifor.com.

Ministry of Health and Population: BP 20101, Brazzaville; tel. 81-30-75; fax 81-14-33.

Ministry of Higher Education and Scientific Research: Ancien Immeuble de la Radio, BP 169, Brazzaville; tel. 81-08-15; fax 81-52-65.

Ministry of Hydrocarbons: BP 2120, Brazzaville; tel. 81-10-86; fax 81-10-85.

Ministry of Industrial Development and the Promotion of the Private Sector: Centre Administratif, Quartier Plateau, BP 2117, Brazzaville; tel. 81-30-09; fax 81-06-43.

Ministry of Justice and Human Rights: BP 2497, Brazzaville; tel. and fax 81-41-49.

Ministry of Labour, Employment and Social Security: Immeuble de la BCC, Av. Foch, BP 2075, Brazzaville; tel. 81-41-43; fax 81-05-50.

Ministry of Land Reform and the Preservation of the Public Domain: Brazzaville; tel. 81-34-48.

Ministry of the Maritime Economy and the Merchant Navy: Brazzaville; tel. 81-10-67; fax 82 -55-14.

Ministry of Mines, Mining Industries and Geology: BP 2124, Brazzaville; tel. 81-02-64; fax 81-50-77.

Ministry of Planning, Territorial Development and Economic Integration: BP 64, Brazzaville; tel. 81-06-56; fax 81-58-08.

Ministry of Posts and Telecommunications, responsible for New Technologies: BP 44, Brazzaville; tel. 81-41-18; fax 81-19-34.

Ministry of Primary and Secondary Education, responsible for Literacy: BP 5253, Brazzaville; tel. 81-24-52; fax 81-25-39.

Ministry of the Promotion of Women and the Integration of Women into Development: Brazzaville; tel. 81-19-29; fax ; .

Ministry of Scientific Reform and Technical Innovation: Ancien Immeuble de la Radio, Brazzaville; tel. 81-03-59.

Ministry of Security and Public Order: BP 2474, Brazzaville; tel. 81-41-73; fax 81-34-04.

Ministry of Small- and Medium-sized Businesses and Handicrafts: Brazzaville.

Ministry of Social Affairs, Solidarity, Humanitarian Action, Disabled Ex-servicemen and the Family: BP 2066, Brazzaville; tel. 81-53-39; fax 81-57-56.

Ministry of Sports and Youth Redeployment: BP 2061, Brazzaville; tel. 60-89-24.

Ministry of Technical Education and Vocational Training: BP 2076, Brazzaville; tel. 81-17-27; fax 81-56-82; e-mail metp_cab@yahoo.fr.

Ministry of Territorial Administration and Decentralization: BP 880, Brazzaville; tel. 81-40-60; fax 81-33-17.

Ministry of Trade, Consumption and Supplies: BP 2965, Brazzaville; tel. 81-41-16; fax 81-41-57; e-mail mougany@yahoo.fr.

Ministry of Transport and Civil Aviation: Immeuble Mafoua Virgile, BP 2066, Brazzaville; tel. 81-53-39; fax 81-57-56.

President and Legislature

PRESIDENT

Presidential Election, 10 March 2002

Candidate	Votes	% of votes
Denis Sassou-Nguesso	1,075,247	89.41
Joseph Kignoumbi Kia Mbougou	33,154	2.76
Angèle Bandou	27,849	2.32
Jean-Félix Demba Ntello	20,252	1.68
Luc Adamo Matéta	19,074	1.59
Côme Mankassa	15,054	1.25
Bonaventure Mizidi Bavouenza	11,981	1.00
Total	**1,202,611**	**100.00**

PARLEMENT

Assemblée nationale

Palais du Parlement, BP 2106, Brazzaville; tel. 81-11-12; fax 81-41-28; e-mail dsancongo@yahoo.fr.

President: JEAN-PIERRE THYSTÈRE TCHIKAYA.

General Election, 26 May and 23 June 2002*

Party	Seats
Parti congolais du travail (PCT)	53
Forces démocratiques unies (FDU)†	30
Union pour la démocratie et la République—Mwinda (UDR—Mwinda)	6
Union panafricaine pour la démocratie sociale (UPADS)	4
Independents	19
Others	17
Vacant‡	8
Total	**137**

* Including the results of voting in 12 constituencies where the elections were rerun on 28–29 May 2002, owing to procedural irregularities on 26 May.

† An alliance of 29 parties.

‡ Voting was postponed indefinitely in eight constituencies in the Pool region as a result of unrest.

Sénat

Palais du Parlement, Brazzaville.

President: Ambroise-Edouard Noumazalaye.

The upper chamber comprises 66 members, elected by representatives of local, regional and municipal authorities for a six-year term. After the first elections to the Sénat, held on 11 July 2002, the strength of the parties was as follows:

Party	Seats
Parti congolais du travail (PCT)	44
Forces démocratiques unies (FDU)*	12
Parti pour la reconstruction du Congo	1
Civil society organizations	2
Independent	1
Vacant†	6
Total	**66**

* An alliance of 29 parties.

† Six seats remained vacant, as unrest had led to the postponement, in June 2002, of local elections in the Pool region.

Advisory Council

Economic and Social Council: Brazzaville; f. 2003; 75 mems, appointed by the President of the Republic; Pres. Auguste-Célestin Gongarad Nkoua.

Political Organizations

In early 2004 there were more than 100 political parties and organizations in the Republic of the Congo, of which the following were among the most important:

Convention pour la démocratie et le salut (CODESA): Brazzaville; f. 2002; opposition alliance; Pres. André Milongo.

Convention nationale pour la République et la solidarité (CNRS): Brazzaville; f. 2001; Leader Martin Mberi.

Parti pour la reconstruction du Congo: Brazzaville.

Rassemblement pour la démocratie et le développement (RDD): Brazzaville; f. 1990; advocates a mixed economy; Pres. Joachim Yhombi-Opango; Chair. Saturnin Okabé.

Union pour la démocratie et le progrès social (UDPS): Brazzaville; f. 1994 by merger; Leader Jean-Michel Boukamba-Yangouma.

Union pour la démocratie et la République—Mwinda (UDR—Mwinda): Brazzaville; e-mail journalmwinda@presse-ecrite.com; internet www.mwinda.org; f. 1992; Leader André Milongo.

Coordination de l'opposition pour une alternance démocratique (CODE-A): Brazzaville; f. 2005; opposition alliance; Leader Herve Ambroise Malonga.

Forces démocratiques unies (FDU): Brazzaville; f. 1994; fmrly Forces démocratiques et patriotiques; 29 constituent parties in 2002; supports Govt of Pres. Sassou-Nguesso; Pres. Lékoundzou Itihi Ossé-toumba (acting).

Alliance pour le Congo (APC): Brazzaville; Leader Justin Coumba.

Alliance congolaise pour l'ouverture, le salut et la solidarité (ACOSS): Brazzaville; f. 1998; social-liberal; Pres. Dr Léon-Alfred Opimbat.

Club 2002: Brazzaville; f. 2002; Pres. Wilfrid Nguesso.

Rassemblement pour la démocratie et le progrès social (RDPS): Pointe-Noire; f. 1990; Pres. Jean-Pierre Thystère Tchi-kaya.

Rassemblement pour la démocratie et la République (RDR): Brazzaville; Leader Gen. (retd) Raymond Damase Ngollo.

Union patriotique pour la démocratie et le progrès (UPDP): Brazzaville; Pres. Auguste-Célestin Gongarad-Nkoua.

Union pour le progrès (UP): Brazzaville; Pres. Jean-Martin Mbemba; Sec.-Gen. Omer Defoundoux.

Union pour le redressement national (URN): Mpila, Brazzaville; f. 1999; Pres. Gabriel Bokilo.

Mouvement congolais pour la démocratie et le développement intégral (MCDDI): Brazzaville; e-mail info@mcddi.net; internet www.mcddi.org; f. 1990; Leader Bernard Kolelas (in exile); Pres. Michel Mampouya.

Parti congolais du travail (PCT): Mpila, Brazzaville; f. 1969; sole legal political party 1969–90; fmrly member of FDU; Pres. Gen. Denis Sassou-Nguesso; Sec.-Gen. Ambroise-Edouard Noumazalay.

Union congolaise des républicains (UCR): Brazzaville; Leader Côme Mankassa.

Union des forces démocratiques (UFD): Brazzaville; supports Govt; Pres. David Charles Ganou.

Union panafricaine pour la démocratie sociale (UPADS): Brazzaville; e-mail courrier@upads.org; internet www.upads.org; Pres. Pascal Lissouba (in exile); Leader Alphonse Ongako Datsou.

Diplomatic Representation

EMBASSIES IN THE REPUBLIC OF THE CONGO

Algeria: BP 2100, Brazzaville; tel. 81-54-77; fax 81-17-37; Ambassador Abdelah Laouari.

Angola: BP 388, Brazzaville; tel. 81-14-71; Chargé d'affaires a.i. Manuel Joâo.

Belgium: ave Patrice Lumumba, face Congo Pharmacie, BP 225, Brazzaville; tel. 81-07-65; fax 81-37-04; e-mail brazzaville@diplobel.org.

Cameroon: BP 2136, Brazzaville; tel. 81-10-08; fax 81-56-75; Chargé d'affaires a.i. Guillaume Nseke.

Central African Republic: BP 10, Brazzaville; tel. 83-40-14.

Chad: BP 386, Brazzaville; tel. 83-22-22; Ambassador Bintou Maloum.

China, People's Republic: blvd Lyauté, BP 213, Brazzaville; tel. 83-11-32; fax 81-11-35; Ambassador Wo Ruidi.

Congo, Democratic Republic: Brazzaville; tel. 83-29-38; Ambassador Félix Mumengui Otthuw.

Cuba: 28 rue Lacien Fourneaux, BP 80, Brazzaville; tel. 81-45-16; e-mail ambacuba@congonet.cg; Ambassador Sidenio Acosta Aday.

Egypt: Immeuble 15 Février, BP 917, Mpila, Brazzaville; tel. 83-44-28; Ambassador Medhat al-Kadi.

France: rue Alfassa, BP 2089, Brazzaville; tel. 81-55-41; e-mail webmestre@mail.com; internet www.ambafrance-cg.org; Ambassador Jean-Paul Taïx.

Guinea: Brazzaville; tel. 81-24-66.

Holy See: rue Colonel Brisset, BP 1168, Brazzaville; tel. 81-55-80; fax 81-55-81; e-mail nonapcg@yahoo.com; Apostolic Nuncio Most Rev. Andres Carras Cosa-Coso.

Italy: 2 blvd Lyauté, BP 2484, Brazzaville; tel. 81-58-41; fax 81-11-52; e-mail ambasciata.brazzaville@esteri.it; internet www.sedi.esteri.it/brazzaville; Ambassador Gaetano La Piana.

Korea, Democratic People's Republic: Brazzaville; tel. 83-41-98; Ambassador Kim Ryong Yong.

Libya: BP 920, Brazzaville.

Nigeria: 11 blvd Lyauté, BP 790, Brazzaville; tel. 83-13-16; Ambassador Greg Mbadiwe.

Russia: ave Félix Eboué, BP 2132, Brazzaville; tel. 81-19-23; fax 81-50-85; e-mail aamrussie@ic.cd; Ambassador Georgii Yu. Chepik.

Judicial System

The 2002 Constitution provides for the independence of the judiciary from the legislature. Judges are to be accountable to the Higher Council of Magistrates, under the chairmanship of the President of the Republic. The constituent bodies of the judiciary are the Supreme Court, the Revenue and Budgetary Discipline Court and the appeal courts. The High Court of Justice is chaired by the First President of the Supreme Court and is competent to try the President of the Republic in case of high treason, and to try members of the legislature, the Supreme Court, the Constitutional Court and government ministers for crimes or offences committed in the execution of their duties.

Supreme Court: BP 597, Brazzaville; tel. 83-01-32; First Pres. PLACIDE LENGA.

High Court of Justice: Brazzaville; f. 2003; Pres. PLACIDE LENGA (First Pres. of the Supreme Court); Chief Prosecutor GEORGES AKIERA.

Constitutional Court: Brazzaville; Pres. GÉRARD BITSINDOU; Vice-Pres. AUGUSTE ILOKI; Mems SIMON-PIERRE NGONIMBA-TSARI, THOMAS DELLOT, MARC MASSAMBA NDILOU, JACQUES BOMBÈTE, JEAN-PIERRE M'BÉRI, DELPHINE-EMMANUELLE ADOUKI, JEAN-BERNARD ANAËL SAMORY.

Religion

At least one-half of the population follow traditional animist beliefs. Most of the remainder are Christians (mainly Roman Catholics).

CHRISTIANITY

The Roman Catholic Church

The Congo comprises one archdiocese, five dioceses and an apostolic prefecture. At 31 December 2002 there were an estimated 2.3m. Roman Catholics in the Republic of the Congo, accounting for some 48.2% of the population.

Bishops' Conference

Conférence Episcopale du Congo, BP 200, Brazzaville; tel. 63-83-91; fax 81-18-28; e-mail confepiscongo@yahoo.fr.

f. 1992; Pres. Most Rev. KOMBO ERNEST (Bishop of Owando).

Archbishop of Brazzaville: Most Rev. ANATOLE MILANDOU, Archevêché, BP 2301, Brazzaville; tel. 81-53-63; fax 81-38-17; e-mail archebrazza@yahoo.fr.

Protestant Church

Eglise Evangélique du Congo: BP 3205, Bacongo-Brazzaville; tel. and fax 81-04-54 ; f. 1909; Presbyterian; autonomous since 1961; 135,811 mems (1993); 105 parishes (1998); Pres. Rev. ALPHONSE MBAMA.

ISLAM

In 1997 an estimated 2% of the population were Muslims. There were 49 mosques in the Congo in 1991.

Comité Islamique du Congo: 77 Makotipoko Moungali, BP 55, Brazzaville; tel. 82-87-45; f. 1988; Leaders HABIBOU SOUMARE, BACHIR GATSONGO, BOUILLA GUIBIDANESI.

BAHÁ'Í FAITH

Assemblée spirituelle nationale: BP 2094, Brazzaville; tel. 81-36-93; e-mail congolink1@aol.com.

The Press

In July 2000 legislation was adopted on the freedom of information and communication. The legislation, which confirmed the abolition of censorship and reduced the penalty for defamation from imprisonment to a fine, specified three types of punishable offence: the encouragement of social tension (including incitement to ethnic conflict), attacks on the authorities (including libels on the Head of State or on the judiciary), and libels against private individuals. The terms of the legislation were to be guaranteed by a regulatory body, the Higher Council for the Freedom of Communication.

DAILIES

ACI Actualité: BP 2144, Brazzaville; tel. and fax 81-01-98; publ. by Agence Congolaise d'Information; Dir-Gen. THÉODORE KIAMOSSI.

Aujourd'hui: Brazzaville; tel. and fax 83-77-44; f. 1991; Man. Dir and Editor-in-Chief FYLLA DI FUA DI SASSA.

Mweti: BP 991, Brazzaville; tel. 81-10-87; national news; Dir MATONGO AVELEY; Editor-in-Chief HUBERT MADOUABA; circ. 7,000.

PERIODICALS

L'Arroseur: Immeuble Boulangerie ex-Léon, BP 15021, Brazzaville; tel. 58-65-51; fax 58-37-60; e-mail larroseur@yahoo.fr; f. 2000; weekly; satirical; Dir GERRY-GÉRARD MANGONDO; Editor-in-Chief JEAN-MARIE KANGA.

L'Autre Vision: 48 rue Assiéné-Mikalou, BP 5255, Brazzaville; tel. 51-57-06; 2 a month; Dir JEAN PAULIN ITOUA.

Bulletin Mensuel de la Chambre de Commerce de Brazzaville: BP 92, Brazzaville; monthly.

Bulletin de Statistique: Centre National de la Statistique et des Etudes Economiques, BP 2031, Brazzaville; tel. and fax 81-59-09; f. 1977; quarterly; Dir-Gen. DOROTHÉE OUISSIKA.

Capital: 3 ave Charles de Gaulle, Plateau Centre Ville, BP 541, Brazzaville; tel. 58-95-10; fax 51-37-48; e-mail capital@hotmail.com; 2 a month; economics and business; Dir SERGE-DENIS MATONDO; Editor-in-Chief HERVÉ SAMPA.

Le Chemin: Brazzaville; f. 1983; evangelical Christian; Editor RAYMOND BITEMO.

Le Choc: BP 1314, Brazzaville; tel. 41-25-39; fax 82-04-25; weekly; Dir ROMUALD MBEPA; Editor-in-Chief JEAN-BAPTISTE BAKOUVOUKA.

Co Co Ri Co: 201 rue Dolisie-Ouenzé, Brazzaville; tel. 66-39-80; fax 58-59-22; weekly; satirical; Dir AIMÉ-SERGE BAZOUNGOULA BISSEMO TURBO; Editor-in-Chief MOKABI DAWA.

Le Coq: Brazzaville; f. 2000; weekly; Editor-in-Chief MALONGA BOUKA.

Les Dépêches de Brazzaville: Résidence Méridien, BP 15457, Brazzaville; tel. and fax 81-28-13; e-mail redaction@brazzaville-adiac.com; internet www.brazzaville-adiac.com; 6 a year; publ. by Agence d'Information de l'Afrique Centrale; Dir-Gen. JEAN-PAUL PIGASSE; Dir and Editor-in-Chief BELINDA AYESSA.

Les Echos du Congo: Immeubles Fédéraux 036, Centre-ville, Brazzaville; tel. 51-57-09; e-mail gam7@raga.net; weekly; pro-government; Dir-Gen. ADRIEN WAYI-LEWY; Editor-in-Chief INNOCENT OLIVIER TATY.

Le Flambeau: BP 1198, Brazzaville; tel. 66-35-23; e-mail congolink1@aol.com; weekly; independent; opposed to the Govt of Pres. Sassou-Nguesso; Dir and Man. Editor PRINCE-RICHARD NSANA.

Géopolitique Africaine: Brazzaville; f. 2000; quarterly; French- and English-language edns; Editor ANDRÉ SOUSSAN.

La Lettre de Brazzaville: Résidence Méridien, BP 15457, Brazzaville; tel. and fax 81-28-13; e-mail redaction@adiac.com; f. 2000; weekly; publ. by Agence d'Information de l'Afrique Centrale; Man. Dir JEAN-PAUL PIGASSE; Editor-in-Chief BELINDA AYESSA.

Le Monde du Travail: 45 rue Linzolo Talangai, BP 4020, Brazzaville; tel. 53-13-04; fax 56-74-44; 2 a month; Dir ANNE-MARIE NZILA; Editor-in-Chief MARC NKAZI-YANZINGA.

Le Nouveau Stade: BP 2159, Brazzaville; tel. 68-45-52; 2 a month; sports; Dir-Gen. LOUIS NGAMI; Editor-in-Chief S. F. KIMINA MAKUMBU.

La Nouvelle République: 3 ave des Ambassadeurs, BP 991, Brazzaville; tel. 81-00-20; pro-Govt; weekly; Dir-Gen. GASPARD NWAN; Editorial Dir HENRI BOUKOULOU.

L'Observateur: 165 ave de l'Amitié, BP 13370, Brazzaville; tel. 66-33-37; fax 81-11-81; weekly; independent; Dir GISLIN-SIMPLICE ONGOYUA.

Panorama: Brazzaville; tel. 66-15-07; fax 21-35-34; Editor FRANÇOIS OUDAÏ AKIÉRA.

Le Pays: BP 782, Brazzaville; tel. 61-06-11; fax 82-44-50; e-mail heblepays@yahoo.fr; f. 1991; weekly; Editorial Dir SYLVÈRE-ARSÈNE SAMBA.

La Référence: BP 13778, Brazzaville; tel. 56-11-37; fax 62-80-13; 2 a month; Dir PHILIPPE RICHET; Editor-in-Chief R. ASSEBAKO AMAIDJORE.

La Rue Meurt (Bala-Bala): BP 1258, Brazzaville; tel. 66-39-80; fax 81-02-30; f. 1991; weekly; satirical; opposes Sassou-Nguesso Govt; Publr MATTHIEU GAYELE; Editorial Dir JEAN-CLAUDE BONGOLO.

La Semaine Africaine: blvd Lyautey, face Chu, BP 2080, Brazzaville; tel. and fax 81-23-35; e-mail lasemaineafricaine@yahoo.fr; f. 1952; weekly; Roman Catholic; general news and social comment; circulates widely in francophone equatorial Africa; Dir JEAN-PIERRE GALLET; Editorial Dir JOACHIM MBANZA; circ. 7,500.

Le Soleil: f. 1991; weekly; organ of the Rassemblement pour la démocratie et le développement.

Le Stade: BP 114, Brazzaville; tel. 81-47-18; f. 1985; weekly; sports; Dir HUBERT-TRÉSOR MADOUABA-NTOUALANI; Editor-in-Chief LELAS PAUL NZOLANI; circ. 6,500.

Tam-Tam d'Afrique: 97 rue Moussana, Ouenzé, BP 1675, Brazzaville; tel. 51-03-95; e-mail tatafrique@yahoo.fr; weekly.

Le Temps: BP 2104, Brazzaville; weekly; owned by supporters of former Pres. Lissouba; Editor-in-Chief HENRI BOUKOULOU.

Vision pour Demain: 109 rue Bakongo Poto-Poto, BP 650, Brazzaville; tel. 41-14-22; 6 a year; Dir SAINT EUDES MFUMU FYLLA.

NEWS AGENCIES

Agence Congolaise d'Information (ACI): ave E. P. Lumumba, BP 2144, Brazzaville; tel. and fax 81-01-98; Gen. Man. THÉODORE KIAMOSSI.

Agence d'Information d'Afrique Centrale (ADIAC): Hôtel Méridien, BP 15457, Brazzaville; tel. and fax 81-28-13; e-mail belie@congonet.cg; internet www.brazzaville-adiac.com; f. 1997; Dirs JEAN-PAUL PIGASSE, BELINDA AYESSA; br. in Paris (France).

Foreign Bureaux

Agence France-Presse (AFP): c/o Agence Congolaise d'Information, BP 2144, Brazzaville; tel. 83-46-76.

Associated Press (AP) (USA): BP 2144, Brazzaville.

Inter Press Service (IPS) (Italy): POB 964, Brazzaville; tel. 810565.

Pan-African News Agency (PANA) (Senegal): BP 2144, Brazzaville; tel. 83-11-40; fax 83-70-15.

Xinhua (New China) News Agency (People's Republic of China): Brazzaville; tel. 83-44-01.

Publishers

Editions ADIAC—Agence d'Information d'Afrique Centrale: Hôtel Méridien, BP 15457, Brazzaville; tel. and fax 81-28-13; e-mail redaction@brazzaville-adiac.com; internet www.brazzaville-adiac .com; f. 1997; publishes chronicles of current affairs; Dirs JEAN-PAUL PIGASSE, BELINDA AYESSA.

Editions 'Héros dans l'Ombre': BP 1678, Brazzaville; tel. 650-51-52; e-mail leopold_mamo@yahoo.fr; f. 1980; literature, criticism, poetry, essays, politics, drama; Pres. LÉOPOLD PINDY-MAMONSONO.

Editions Lemba: BP 2351, Brazzaville; tel. 67-65-58; fax 81-00-17; e-mail editions_lemba@yahoo.fr; literature; Dir APOLLINAIRE SINGOU-BASSEHA.

Editions PAARI—Pan African Review of Innovation: BP 1622 Brazzaville; tel. 51-86-49; e-mail edpaari@yahoo.fr; f. 1991; social and human sciences, philosophy.

Editions Renaissance Congolaise: Brazzaville.

Imprimerie Centrale d'Afrique (ICA): BP 162, Pointe-Noire; f. 1949; Man. Dir M. SCHNEIDER.

Mokandart: BP 939, Brazzaville; tel. 68-46-69; e-mail mokandart@yahoo.fr; adult and children's literature; Pres. ANNICK VEYRINAUD MAKONDA.

GOVERNMENT PUBLISHING HOUSE

Imprimerie Nationale du Congo (INC): BP 58, Brazzaville; Dir JULES ONDZEKI.

Broadcasting and Communications

Higher Council for the Freedom of Communication: Brazzaville; f. 2003; 11 mems, nominated by the President of the Republic; Pres. JACQUES BANANGANZALA.

TELECOMMUNICATIONS

Celtel Congo: Celtel House, BP 1267, Pointe-Noire; Brazzaville; tel. 94-86-02; fax 94-88-75; e-mail celtelcongo@yahoo.fr; internet www.msi-cellular.com; f. 1999; mobile cellular telephone operator; network covers Brazzaville, Pointe-Noire, Loubomo (Dolisie), Ouesso, Owando and other urban areas; subsidiary of MSI Cellular (United Kingdom); Man. Dir ROB GELDERLOOS; 30,000 subscribers (Dec. 2000).

Cyrus International (CYRTEL): Brazzaville; mobile cellular telephone operator; operates as jt venture between Nexus International (70%), a subsidiary of France Telecom and SOTELCO.

Libertis: 22 rue Behagle, BP 1150, Brazzaville; tel. 81-47-70; fax 81-44-16; f. 2000; mobile cellular telephone operator; network covers Brazzaville and Pointe-Noire; subsidiary of Orascom Telecom (Egypt).

Société de Télécommunications du Congo (SOTELCO): BP 39, Brazzaville; tel. 81-16-66; f. 2001 by division of postal and telecommunications services of the fmr Office National des Postes et Télécommunications; mobile cellular telephone system introduced in 1996; majority Govt-owned, part-owned by Atlantic TeleNetwork; further transfer to private ownership pending; Dir-Gen. RENÉ-SERGE BLANCHARD OBA (acting).

RADIO AND TELEVISION

Radio Brazzaville: face Direction Générale, SOTELCO, Brazzaville; tel. 51-60-73; f. 1999; official station; Man. JEAN-PASCAL MONGO SLYM.

Canal FM: BP 60, Brazzaville; tel. 83-03-09; f. 1977 as Radio Rurales du Congo; present name adopted 2002; community stations established by the Agence de coopération culturelle et technique; transmitters in Brazzaville, Sembé, Nkayi, Etoumbi and Mossendjo; Dir ETIENNE EPAGNA-TOUA.

Radio Liberté: BP 1660, Brazzaville; tel. 81-57-42; f. 1997; operated by supporters of Pres. Sassou-Nguesso.

Radiodiffusion-Télévision Congolaise (RTC): BP 2241, Brazzaville; tel. 81-24-73; state-owned; Pres. JEAN-GILBERT FOUTOU; Dir-Gen. GILBERT-DAVID MUTAKALA.

Radio Congo: BP 2241, Brazzaville; tel. 81-50-60; radio programmes in French, Lingala, Kikongo, Subia, English and Portuguese; transmitters at Brazzaville and Pointe-Noire; Gen. Man. ALPHONSE BOUYA DIMI; Dir of Broadcasting THÉOPHILE MIETE LIKIBI.

Télévision congolaise (TVC): BP 975, Brazzaville; tel. 81-01-16; f. 1963; operates for 46 hours per week, with most programmes in French but some in Lingala and Kikongo; Gen. Man. WAMÉNE EKIAYE-ACKOLI.

Télédiffusion du Congo: BP 2912, Brazzaville; tel. 81-06-08; Gen. Man. MÉDARD BOKATOLA.

Finance

(cap. = capital; res = reserves; dep. = deposits; m. = million; br. = branch; amounts in francs CFA)

BANKING

Central Bank

Banque des Etats de l'Afrique Centrale (BEAC): BP 126, Brazzaville; tel. 81-10-73; fax 81-10-94; e-mail beacbzv@beac.int; internet www.beac.int; HQ in Yaoundé, Cameroon; f. 1973; bank of issue for mem. states of the Communauté économique et monétaire en Afrique centrale (CEMAC, fmrly Union douanière et économique de l'Afrique centrale); comprising Cameroon, the Central African Repub., Chad, the Repub. of the Congo, Equatorial Guinea and Gabon; cap. 45,000m., res 176,661m., total assets 2,144,626m. (Nov. 2003); Gov. JEAN-FÉLIX MAMALEPOT; Dir in Repub. of the Congo MATHIAS DZON; br. at Pointe-Noire.

Commercial Banks

BGFI Bank Congo: BP 14579, Angle rue Reims, face à Pairie de France, Brazzaville; tel. 81-40-50; fax 81-50-89; state-owned; cap. 1,000m. (2002); Pres. MATHIAS DZON; Dir-Gen. ALAIN MOUSSIROU MABIALA; 2 brs.

COFIPA—Compagnie de Financement et de Participation: ave Amílcar Cabral, BP 147, Brazzaville; tel. 81-58-34; fax 81-03-73; e-mail cofipabzv@caramail.com; f. 2001 on privatization of Union Congolaise de Banques; cap. 3,000m., total assets 54,668m. (Dec. 2002); Dir-Gen. TRAN VAN THANH; 14 brs.

Crédit pour l'Agriculture, l'Industrie et le Commerce (CAIC): ave Amílcar Cabral, BP 2889, Brazzaville; tel. 81-09-78; fax 81-09-77; e-mail caic20@calva.com; fmrly Crédit Rural du Congo; state-owned; transfer to private sector, as La Congolaise de Banques (LCB), pending; Dir-Gen. JEAN-PIERRE GRANGE; 4 brs.

Crédit Lyonnais-Congo (CL Co): ave Emmanuel Daddet, BP 1312, Pointe-Noire; tel. 94-24-00; fax 94-16-65; f. 2002 to replace Banque Internationale du Congo; 90% owned by Crédit Lyonnais (France), 10% state-owned; cap. 2,000m. (2002); Dir-Gen. LUCIEN ELSENSOHN; 2 brs.

Co-operative Banking Institution

Mutuelle Congolaise de l'Epargne et de Crédit (MUCODEC): BP 13237, Brazzaville; tel. 81-07-57; fax 81-01-68; f. 1994; Pres. and Dir-Gen. GERVAIS LETIER; 45 brs.

Development Bank

Banque de Développement des Etats de l'Afrique Centrale: BP 1177, Brazzaville; tel. 81-17-61; fax 81-18-80; cap. and res 25,528m., total assets 44,892m. (Dec. 2001); Chair. ERIC SORONGOPE; Gen. Man. ANICET G. DOLOGUÉLÉ.

Financial Institution

Caisse Congolaise d'Amortissement (CCA): ave Foch Beltrando, BP 2090, Brazzaville; tel. 81-57-35; fax 81-52-36; f. 1971; management of state funds; Dir-Gen. GEORGES NGUEKOUMOU.

INSURANCE

Assurances et Réassurances du Congo (ARC): BP 1033, Pointe-Noire; tel. 94-08-00; f. 1973; 50% state-owned; privatization pending; Dir-Gen. RAYMOND IBATA; brs at Brazzaville, Loubomo and Ouesso.

Gras Savoye Congo: 13 rue Germain Bikouma, angle Route de la Radio, Immeuble Guenin, BP 1901, Pointe Noire; tel. 94-79-72; fax 94-79-74; e-mail grassavoye.congo@cg.celtelplus.com; internet www .grassavoye.com; affiliated to Gras Savoye (France); insurance brokers and risk managers; Man. PHILIPPE BAILLÉ.

Société de Courtage d'Assurances et de Réassurances (SCDE): BP 13177, Immeuble Foch, ave Maréchal Foch, Brazzaville; tel. 81-17-63.

Trade and Industry

GOVERNMENT AGENCY

Comité des Privatisations et de Renforcement des Capacités Locales: Immeuble ex-SCBO, 7ème étage, BP 1176, Brazzaville; tel. 81-46-21; fax 81-46-09; e-mail privat@aol.com; oversees and co-ordinates transfer of state-owned enterprises to the private sector.

DEVELOPMENT ORGANIZATIONS

Agence Française de Développement (AFD): rue Béhagle, BP 96, Brazzaville; tel. 81-53-30; fax 81-29-42; e-mail afdbrazzaville@ yahoo.fr; internet www.afd.fr; French fund for economic co-operation; Dir ANDRÉ MEYER.

Mission Française de Coopération et d'Action Culturelle: BP 2175, Brazzaville; tel. 83-15-03; f. 1959; administers bilateral aid from France; Dir JEAN-BERNARD THIANT.

Société Nationale d'Elevage (SONEL): BP 81, Loutété, Massangui; f. 1964; development of semi-intensive stock-rearing; exploitation of cattle by-products; Man. Dir THÉOPHILE BIKAWA.

CHAMBERS OF COMMERCE

Chambre de Commerce, d'Agriculture, d'Industrie et des Métiers de Brazzaville: BP 92, Brazzaville; tel. and fax 81-16-08; f. 1935; Pres. PAUL OBAMBI; Sec.-Gen. GÉRARD DONGO.

Chambre de Commerce, d'Agriculture et d'Industrie de Kouilou: BP 665, Pointe-Noire; tel. 94-12-80; fax 94-07-13; f. 1948; fmrly Chambre de Commerce, d'Industrie et des Métiers de Pointe-Noire; Chair. NARCISSE POATY PACKA; Sec.-Gen. JEAN-BAPTISTE SOUMBOU.

Chambre de Commerce, d'Agriculture et d'Industrie de Loubomo: BP 78, Loubomo; tel. 91-00-17.

Chambre Nationale d'Industrie et d'Agriculture du Congo: BP 1119, Brazzaville; tel. 83-29-56; fmrly Conférence Permanente des Chambres de Commerce du Congo; Pres. PAUL OBAMBI.

EMPLOYERS' ORGANIZATIONS

Forum des Jeunes Entreprises du Congo (FJEC): BP 2080, Brazzaville; tel. 81-56-34; e-mail fjec@inmarsat.francetelecom.fr; f. 1996; Sec.-Gen. PAUL KAMPAKOL.

Union Nationale des Opérateurs du Congo (UNOC): BP 5187, Brazzaville; tel. 81-54-32; operates a professional training centre; Pres. El Hadj DJIBRIL ABDOULAYE BOPAKA.

Union Patronale et Interprofessionnelle du Congo (UNI-CONGO): BP 42, Brazzaville; tel. 81-47-68; fax 81-47-66; f. 1958; Nat. Pres. JEAN-CHRISTOPHE TRANCEPAIN; Sec.-Gen. JEAN-JACQUES SAMBA; membership of 10 federations, representing 400 enterprises, with a total work-force of 25,000 (2001).

UTILITIES

Electricity

Société Nationale d'Electricité (SNE): 95 ave Paul Doumer, BP 95, Brazzaville; tel. 81-38-58; f. 1967; transfer to private management proposed; operates hydroelectric plants at Bouenza and Djoué; Pres. JEAN BRUNO RICHARD ITOUA (acting); Dir-Gen. ALPHONSE BOUDONESA.

Water

Société Nationale de Distribution d'Eau (SNDE): rue du Sergent Malamine, BP 229, Brazzaville; tel. 83-73-26; fax 83-38-91; f. 1967; transferred to private-sector management by Bi-Water (United Kingdom) in 2002; water supply and sewerage; holds monopoly over wells and import of mineral water; Dir-Gen. AMBROISE BONGOUANDÉ.

TRADE UNION FEDERATIONS

Independent trade unions were legalized in 1991.

Confédération Générale des Travailleurs du Congo (CGTC): Brazzaville; f. 1995; Chair. PAUL DOUNA.

Confédération Nationale des Syndicats Libres (CNASYL): Brazzaville; f. 1994; Sec.-Gen. MICHEL KABOUL MAOUTA.

Confédération Syndicale Congolaise (CSC): BP 2311, Brazzaville; tel. 83-19-23; f. 1964; 80,000 mems.

Confédération Syndicale des Travailleurs du Congo (CSTC): BP 14743, Brazzaville; tel. 61-47-35; f. 1993; fed. of 13 trade unions; Chair. MICHEL SOUZA; 40,000 mems.

Confédération des Syndicats Libres Autonomes du Congo (COSYLAC): BP 14861, Brazzaville; tel. 82-42-65; fax 83-42-70; e-mail b.oba@congonet.cg; Pres. RENÉ BLANCHARD SERGE OBA.

Fédération nationale des travailleurs du Congo (FENATRAC): Brazzaville; f. 2001 by split from CSTC (q.v.); Sec. JULIEN NGOULOU.

Transport

RAILWAYS

In 1999 there were 1,152 km of railway track in the Congo. A 286-km section of privately owned line was used until 1991 to link the manganese mines at Moanda (in Gabon) with the main line to Pointe-Noire. Rail traffic has been severely disrupted since the 1997 civil war. The main line (of some 518 km) between Brazzaville and Pointe-Noire reopened briefly in November 1998 for freight traffic, but was subsequently closed following further unrest and sabotage. In early 2000 the Government signed two agreements with the Société Nationale des Chemins de fer Français (France) relating to the repair of the line and associated infrastructure, and to the management of the network. Freight services resumed in August 2000, followed by passenger services in January 2001, although there was further disruption to the railways during unrest in mid-2002. In May 2004 the rail service linking Brazzaville to the Pool region resumed operations.

Chemin de Fer Congo-Océan (CFCO): BP 651, Pointe-Noire; tel. 94-11-84; fax 94-12-30; f. 1969; entered partnership with Rail Afrique International in June 1998; transfer to private management proposed; Dir-Gen. JACKY TRIMARDEAU.

ROADS

In 2001 there were an estimated 17,244 km of roads, including 3,440 km of main roads and 4,150 km of secondary roads. Only about 7.0% of the total network was paved. The principal routes link Brazzaville with Pointe-Noire, in the south, and with Ouesso, in the north. A number of major construction projects initiated by President Sassou-Nguesso in 2000 and 2001 have involved the highways from Brazzaville to Kinkala, and from Brazzaville to the Pool region.

Régie Nationale des Transports et des Travaux Publics: BP 2073, Brazzaville; tel. 83-35-58; f. 1965; civil engineering, maintenance of roads and public works; Man. Dir HECTOR BIENVENU OUAMBA.

INLAND WATERWAYS

The Congo and Oubangui rivers form two axes of a highly developed inland waterway system. The Congo river and seven tributaries in the Congo basin provide 2,300 km of navigable river, and the Oubangui river, developed in co-operation with the Central African Republic, an additional 2,085 km.

Direction des Voies Navigables, Ports et Transports Fluviaux: BP 2048, Brazzaville; tel. 83-06-27; waterways authority; Dir MÉDARD OKOUMOU.

Transcap—Congo: BP 1154, Pointe-Noire; tel. 94-01-46; f. 1962; Chair. J. DROUAULT.

SHIPPING

The deep-water Atlantic seaport at Pointe-Noire is the most important port in Central Africa and Brazzaville is one of the principal ports on the Congo river. A major rehabilitation programme began in October 1999, with the aim of establishing Pointe-Noire as a regional centre for container traffic and as a logistics centre for offshore oil exploration. In 1997 708,203 metric tons of goods were loaded at the port of Pointe-Noire, and 533,170 tons were unloaded.

La Congolaise de Transport Maritime (COTRAM): Pointe-Noire; f. 1984; national shipping co; state-owned.

Maersk Congo: 10 rue Massabi, Zone Portuaire, Pointe-Noire; tel. 94-21-41; fax 94-23-25; e-mail pnrmkt@maersk.com; f. 1997; represents Maersk Sealand (Denmark).

Port Autonome de Brazzaville: BP 2048, Brazzaville; tel. 83-00-42; f. 2000; port authority; Dir JEAN-PAUL BOCKONDAS.

Port Autonome de Pointe-Noire: BP 711, Pointe-Noire; tel. 94-00-52; fax 94-20-42; e-mail info@congoport-papn.com ; internet www.congoport-papn.com; f. 2000; port authority; Dir-Gen. JEAN-MARIE ANIÉLÉ.

SAGA Congo: 18 rue du Prophète Lasse Zephirin, BP 674, Pointe Noire; tel. 94-10-16; fax 94-34-04; e-mail saga.congo@cg.dti.bollone.com.

Société Congolaise de Transports Maritimes (SOCOTRAM): BP 4922, Pointe Noire; tel. 94-49-21; fax 94-49-22; e-mail info@socotram.com; internet www.socotram.fr; f. 1990.

CIVIL AVIATION

There are international airports at Brazzaville (Maya-Maya) and Pointe-Noire (Agostinho Neto). There are also five regional airports, at Loubomo (Dolisie, Ngot-Nzounzoungou), Nkaye, Owando, Ouesso and Impfondo, as well as 12 smaller airfields. In early 2001 the construction of a new international airport at Ollombo, some 500 km north of Brazzaville, began; the airport was expected to open by 2008. The refurbishment of Brazzaville airport commenced in 2001.

Aéro-Service: ave Charles de Gaulle, BP 1138, Brazzaville; tel. 81-34-88; fax 83-09-47; e-mail info@aero-service.net; internet www.aero-service.net; f. 1967; scheduled and charter services; operates nationally and to regional destinations; Pres. and Dir-Gen. C. H. GRIESBAUM.

Trans Air Congo: Immeuble City Center, ave Amílcar Cabral, BP 2422, Brazzaville; tel. 81-10-46; fax 81-10-57; e-mail info@flytransaircongo.com; f. 1994; private airline operating internal scheduled and international charter flights; Pres. and Dir-Gen. BASSAM ELHAGE.

Tourism

The tourism sector has been severely disrupted by political instability and internal unrest. Tourist visitors numbered 4,753 in 1999 (compared with tourist arrivals of 25,082 in 1998). In 2000, however, the number of tourist arrivals increased to an estimated 26,000. In 2002 earnings from tourism were estimated at US $25m.

Direction Générale du Tourisme et des Loisirs: BP 456, Brazzaville; tel. 83-09-53; f. 1980; Dir-Gen. ANTOINE KOUNKOU-KIBOUILOU.

COSTA RICA

Introductory Survey

Location, Climate, Language, Religion, Flag, Capital

The Republic of Costa Rica lies in the Central American isthmus, with Nicaragua to the north, Panama to the south, the Caribbean Sea to the east and the Pacific Ocean to the west. The climate is warm and damp in the lowlands (average temperature 27°C (81°F)) and cooler on the Central Plateau (average temperature 22°C (72°F)), where two-thirds of the population live. The language spoken is Spanish. Almost all of the inhabitants profess Christianity, and the majority adhere to the Roman Catholic Church, the state religion. The national flag (proportions 3 by 5) has five horizontal stripes, of blue, white, red, white and blue, the red stripe being twice the width of the others. The state flag, in addition, has on the red stripe (to the left of centre) a white oval enclosing the national coat of arms, showing three volcanic peaks between the Caribbean and the Pacific. The capital is San José.

Recent History

Costa Rica was ruled by Spain from the 16th century until 1821, when independence was declared. The only significant interruption in the country's constitutional government since 1920 occurred in February 1948, when the victory of the opposition candidate, Otilio Ulate Blanco, in the presidential election was disputed. The legislature annulled the election in March but a civil war ensued. The anti-Government forces, led by José Figueres Ferrer, were successful, and a revolutionary junta took power in April. Costa Rica's army was abolished in December. After the preparation of a new Constitution, Ulate took office as President in January 1949.

Figueres, who founded the socialist Partido de Liberación Nacional (PLN), dominated national politics for decades, holding presidential office in 1953–58 and 1970–74. Under his leadership, Costa Rica became one of the most democratic countries in Latin America. Since the 1948 revolution, there have been frequent changes of power, all achieved by constitutional means. Figueres's first Government nationalized the banks and instituted a comprehensive social security system. The presidential election of 1958, however, was won by a conservative, Mario Echandi Jiménez, who reversed many PLN policies. His successor, Francisco Orlich Bolmarich (President from 1962 to 1966), was supported by the PLN but continued the encouragement of private enterprise. Another conservative, José Joaquín Trejos Fernández, held power in 1966–70. In 1974 the PLN candidate, Daniel Oduber Quirós, was elected President. He continued the policies of extending the welfare state and of establishing amicable relations with communist states. Communist and other left-wing parties were legalized in 1975. In 1978 Rodrigo Carazo Odio of the conservative Partido Unidad Opositora (PUO) coalition (subsequently the Coalición Unidad) was elected President. During Carazo's term of office increasing instability in Central America led to diplomatic tension, and in 1981 the President was criticized for his alleged involvement in illegal arms trafficking between Cuba and El Salvador.

At presidential and legislative elections in February 1982, Luis Alberto Monge Alvarez of the PLN won a comfortable majority when his party won 33 of the 57 seats in the Asamblea Legislativa (Legislative Assembly). Following his inauguration in May, President Monge announced a series of emergency economic measures, in an attempt to rescue the country from near-bankruptcy. A policy of neutrality towards the left-wing Sandinista Government of Nicaragua was continued. However, following a number of cross-border raids, a national alert was declared in May. The rebel Nicaraguan leader, Edén Pastora Gómez, was expelled in order to reduce Costa Rican involvement in the Nicaraguan conflict. Relations with Nicaragua deteriorated as guerrilla activity spread to San José. Thereafter Monge came under increasing pressure from liberal members of the Cabinet and PLN supporters to adopt a more neutral stance in foreign policy. Three leading members of the anti-Sandinista (Contra) movement were expelled from Costa Rica in May 1983, and 80 of Pastora's supporters were arrested in September. In addition, some 82 guerrilla camps were dismantled by the Civil Guard. In November Monge declared Costa Rica's neutrality in an attempt to elicit foreign support for his country. This declaration was opposed by the USA and led to the resignation of the Costa Rican Minister of Foreign Affairs.

In early 1984 there were increasing reports of incursions into Costa Rica by the Sandinista forces. Public opposition to any renunciation of neutrality was emphasized by a demonstration in support of peace and neutrality, held in San José and attended by over 20,000 people. An attempt was made to defuse the tension with the establishment of a commission, supported by the Contadora group (Colombia, Mexico, Panama and Venezuela), to monitor events in the border area. In late May, however, the attempted assassination of Pastora near the Costa Rican border exacerbated the rift within the Cabinet concerning government policy towards Nicaragua. In December, following an incident involving a Nicaraguan refugee at the Costa Rican embassy in Managua, diplomatic relations with Nicaragua were reduced to a minimal level. Reports of clashes between Costa Rican Civil Guardsmen and Sandinista forces along the joint border became increasingly frequent. In 1985 the Government's commitment to neutrality was disputed when it decided to establish an anti-guerrilla battalion, trained by US military advisers.

During 1983 there were signs of increasing urban unrest in response to the Government's austerity measures and to the agrarian crisis, which had produced high levels of unemployment, principally among workers on banana plantations. By August 1984 the Government's position was regarded as unstable. The division within the Cabinet over policy towards Nicaragua, coupled with the effects of the unpopular austerity programme and a protracted strike by banana plantation workers, which had resulted in two deaths, led to fears of a coup. At Monge's request, the Cabinet resigned, and in the subsequent reshuffle four ministers were replaced.

At presidential and legislative elections in February 1986 Oscar Arias Sánchez, the candidate of the PLN, was elected President, with 52% of the votes cast. The PLN also obtained a clear majority in the Asamblea Legislativa. The new Government was committed to the development of a welfare state, the renegotiation of the country's external debt, and the conclusion of a social pact with the trade unions. Furthermore, Arias was resolved to maintain and reinforce Costa Rica's policy of neutrality.

In February 1986 diplomatic relations with Nicaragua were fully restored, and it was decided to establish a permanent inspection and vigilance commission at the common border. In accordance with the Government's pledge to protect neutrality, Costa Rica objected to the allocation of US $100m. in US aid to the Contra forces in mid-1986. In addition, the Government embarked on a series of arrests and expulsions of Contras resident in Costa Rica. A degree of Costa Rican complicity in anti-Sandinista activity became apparent, however, in 1986, when the existence of a secret airstrip in Costa Rica, which was used as a supply base for the Contras, was made public. The airstrip had been constructed by the USA during President Monge's administration but had been closed on Arias's accession to power.

Throughout 1986 and 1987 Arias became increasingly involved in the quest for peace in Central America. In August 1987 the Presidents of El Salvador, Nicaragua, Guatemala, Honduras and Costa Rica signed a peace agreement based on proposals presented by Arias, who subsequently awarded the Nobel Peace Prize. In January 1988 Arias brought Nicaraguan government officials and Contra leaders together in San José for their first discussions concerning the implementation of a cease-fire. Prior to this meeting, Arias ordered three Contra leaders to leave Costa Rica or cease their military activities. Arias maintained his independent position by supporting discussions between the Contras and Sandinistas, held in Nicaragua in March, and by condemning any continuation of aid to the Contras. In November a border agreement was signed with Nicaragua.

In 1988 there were renewed indications of internal unrest as a result of the Government's economic policies. In March there were stoppages by public employees, to protest against concessions made to the IMF and the World Bank. In August there were strikes by farmers aggrieved at the Government's 'Agriculture for Change' policy of promoting the cultivation of cash crops, and thereby sacrificing the interests of many smallholders, to appease the IMF. Labour unrest increased throughout the country during 1989.

At presidential and legislative elections in February 1990, Rafael Angel Calderón Fournier, the candidate of the Partido Unidad Social Cristiana (PUSC), was elected President, with 51.3% of the votes cast. The PUSC obtained a clear majority in the Asamblea Legislativa, with 29 seats. On assuming office in May, Calderón inherited a large fiscal deficit and was therefore forced to renege on his pre-election promise of improvements in welfare and income distribution. In an attempt to reduce the deficit, the Government introduced an adjustment programme of austerity measures. In October 70,000–100,000 public- and private-sector employees participated in a one-day national strike to protest against the Government's economic policies. Later that month the Minister of Labour resigned, stating that his decision to do so reflected the rift between 'economic and social groups' within the Cabinet.

In August 1991 the Minister of Public Security and the Minister of National Planning and Economic Policy resigned, following disagreements with President Calderón. The Minister of the Interior and Police, Luis Fishman, was subsequently appointed acting Minister of Public Security. The Civil Guard and the Rural Guard (which had previously been responsible to the Ministry of Public Security and the Ministry of the Interior and Police, respectively) therefore came under the sole charge of Fishman. Opposition groups expressed concern at this concentration of power, in view of the continuing decline in popular support for Calderón and the level of public unrest. In November, in response to pressure from student and public-sector unions, Calderón abandoned austerity measures involving a reduction in the education budget and the dismissal of thousands of public employees. This decision prompted the resignation of the Minister of Finance, who claimed that the President's action would make it impossible to curb the rapidly increasing fiscal deficit and thus attain IMF-agreed targets.

In January 1992 Calderón was summoned before the Asamblea Legislativa's commission on drugs-trafficking to answer allegations that the PUSC had been the recipient of the proceeds of illegal drugs-trafficking during its election campaign in 1990. Calderón denied any knowledge of such payments. Following the decision made by the Government in March 1992 to remove foreign-exchange controls, there was mounting concern that Costa Rican banking institutions were being used increasingly for the purposes of laundering money obtained from illegal drugs-trafficking.

In March 1993 some 25 people, including the Nicaraguan Ambassador to Costa Rica, were taken hostage at the Nicaraguan embassy in San José. The demands of the hostage-takers included the dismissals of the head of the Nicaraguan armed forces and the Nicaraguan President's chief adviser. The hostages were later released unharmed in return for a ransom and safe passage out of the country. A similar incident, which took place in April and involved members of the Supreme Court being taken hostage, served to heighten concern about the security situation in Costa Rica.

Presidential and legislative elections were held in February 1994. The presidential ballot was narrowly won by José María Figueres Olsen, the PLN candidate. The PLN failed to obtain an outright majority in the Asamblea Legislativa, securing only 28 of the 57 seats, while the PUSC won 25 seats. Figueres assumed office in early May.

In May 1994 industrial action by employees of the Geest banana company resulted in violent clashes with the security forces. The strike was organized in protest at the dismissal of some 400 workers for attempting to join a union. The dispute, which was resolved following government intervention, came in the wake of allegations by the American Federation of Labor and Congress of Industrial Organizations, of violations of labour rights in Costa Rica. In late 1993 the Costa Rican authorities had avoided an investigation into the country's labour practices by the US trade representative office and the possible loss of trading benefits enjoyed under the Generalized System of Preferences by introducing legislation reforming the labour code.

In July 1995 some 50,000 teachers began strike action in protest at proposed reforms to the state pension system. Growing dissatisfaction among other public-sector employees at

government economic policy, in particular proposals for the deregulation and privatization of state enterprises, resulted in an escalation of the unrest, which culminated in a 100,000-strong demonstration in the capital in August. Following the protest, the Government reached an accord with the teachers, under which it agreed to establish a commission, to include representatives of the teachers' unions, to debate the proposed reform of the pension system and to review certain other of the Government's economic policies.

Presidential and legislative elections were held in February 1998. Miguel Angel Rodríguez Echeverría, again the candidate of the PUSC, secured a narrow victory over the PLN candidate, José Miguel Corrales Bolaños. The PUSC failed to obtain an outright majority in the legislature, securing only 27 of the 57 seats, while the PLN won 23. On 8 May Rodríguez was sworn in as President, and the new Cabinet was inaugurated.

The new President's attempts to alleviate the budget deficit through economic reform met with considerable opposition in 2000. In May of that year the Government was forced to withdraw proposed legislation on the privatization of the telecommunications and energy sectors, after the largest popular protests in the country in 30 years. In the same month a commission, comprising government, private-sector and trade-union representatives, was established to draft new proposals.

In June 2001 a constitutional commission was appointed to recommend a process of transformation from the presidential system of government to a semi-parliamentary one, in an attempt to improve the political decision-making process. In early July the Asamblea Legislativa approved legislation designed to improve tax efficiency: the new law would reduce tax on basic goods, while increasing duties on some luxury goods and services.

Presidential elections were held on 3 February 2002. Abel Pacheco, the candidate of the ruling PUSC, secured 38.5% of the votes cast. The second-placed candidate was Rolando Araya of the PLN, who attracted 30.9% of the ballot. Ottón Solís, representing the recently-formed Partido Acción Ciudadana (PAC), which campaigned against corruption, was third, with 26.3% of the votes. However, as no candidate gained 40% of the votes cast, for the first time in Costa Rican history a second round of voting was held between the two leading candidates, on 7 April. Pacheco won 58% of the votes cast in this round, while Araya attracted 42%. In legislative elections, also held on 3 February, the PAC again emerged as a strong third force in Costa Rican politics, securing 14 seats at the expense of the two main parties: the number of PUSC deputies in the 57-seat Asamblea Legislativa fell from 27 to 19, while the PLN's parliamentary representation fell from 23 to 17. The nationalist Movimiento Libertario obtained six seats, while the Partido Renovación Costarricense secured the remaining seat. The results, as well as the low voter turn-out (an estimated 67.3% in the first round presidential ballot) were a sign that the electorate had tired of two-party politics.

Pacheco was inaugurated as President on 8 May 2002. Upon assuming office, he pledged to reform the tax system and to seek ways to curb public-sector expenditure in order to reduce the budget deficit. In the previous month a report produced by a cross-party commission of former finance ministers concluded that higher taxes and reduced government spending were necessary to ensure the financial and social stability of the country by 2006. Among the proposals were the replacement of sales tax with value-added tax for some goods and services, the extension of profits tax to export zones and the removal of 160 administrative positions in the civil service. However, the Government announced in mid-May that 40% of its non-priority spending would be diverted to repair damage caused by heavy flooding earlier in that month, which had left an estimated 5,100 people homeless.

From mid-2002 a number of opposition groups made claims that the Pacheco electoral campaign had benefited from contributions from illegal sources. The President accused the opposition PLN of trying to discredit him; in September he renounced his presidential immunity from prosecution to allow the investigation of allegations that he had neglected to declare to the electoral tribunal some US $125,000 in cheque payments. A congressional commission, led by Luis Gerardo of the PLN, to examine the financing of election campaigns was due to report in 2005.

In January 2003 the first direct local authority elections in Costa Rica took place. However, voter participation was estimated to be only 40%, partly owing to further heavy storms, which isolated many communities and forced some 3,000 people to evacuate their homes. In April of that year the Constitutional Court voted 5–2 in favour of amending the restriction that prevented former presidents standing for re-election. It was widely believed that the ruling meant former President Arias would seek re-election to the presidency in 2006.

In November 2002 the Government intervened in the affairs of the state electricity and telecommunications company, the Instituto Costarricense de Electricidad (ICE), when the Comptroller-General ordered its directors to annul contracts awarded to an equipment supplier whose charges the Government considered to be too high. The following month the Government also announced that it would investigate a decision by the ICE to rescind a contract given to an Israeli company for the sale of telecommunications equipment. In mid-May 2003 employees at the ICE went on strike in an attempt to force the Government to issue a US $100m. bond to finance the company, after that year's budget had reduced funding to the electricity and telecommunications sector. An offer of $40m. by the Government was rejected by the strikers, who were joined in late May by teachers, protesting against, *inter alia*, salary underpayments and proposed pension reforms. In early June, following a mass demonstration in San José, the Government agreed to most of the ICE employees' demands, and as a result, the electricity-sector strikers returned to work. However, industrial action by teachers continued until the end of the month, when the Government agreed to revise proposed pension reforms. The industrial action led to the resignation of the Minister of Public Education, Astrid Fischel. She was succeeded by Manuel Bolaños.

Cabinet instability continued in July 2003 when Rogelio Pardo tendered his resignation as Minister of Science and Technology. He was replaced by Fernando Gutiérrez Ortiz. Furthermore, in September, Vilma Villalobos, the Minister of the Economy, Industry and Commerce, resigned from the Cabinet, citing personal reasons. She was succeeded by Gilberto Barrantes.

In October 2003 there was further conflict in the telecommunications sector as trade unions organized a demonstration in the capital to coincide with a further round of negotiations towards the proposed Central American Free Trade Agreement (CAFTA, for further details see Economic Affairs), in Houston, Texas, USA. The protesters were concerned that the Government would capitulate to US demands that the ICE's monopoly of the sector be ended. President Pacheco insisted his Government was opposed to such a move; however, in January 2004 the administration agreed to certain concessions on liberalization of the sector.

In August 2004 the deteriorating economic situation, combined with the perceived failure of the Government to address the issue, prompted public-sector unions to organize a week-long general strike. In particular, the industrial action was in protest at the Government's offer of a 4.5% salary increase, which was lower than the monthly rate of inflation (which reached 8.5% in that month). The unrest escalated later in the month when drivers' associations began protests around the country against the monopoly on vehicle inspections held by the Spanish company Riteve SyC. Farmers', teachers' and electricity-sector unions also joined the industrial action. Eight days of demonstrations and civil unrest were brought to an end on 31 August when the Government agreed to a 0.5% increase on the pay offer and to review Riteve SyC's contract. The concessions immediately provoked the resignation of the Minister of Finance, Alberto Dent, and his deputy, Selena Alvarado. The crisis in the Government deepened further early in the following month when, on 7 September, Ricardo Toledo, who had brokered the controversial increase, submitted his resignation as Minister of the Presidency. The following day Alberto Trejos, the Minister of Foreign Commerce, and Javier Chávez Bolaños, the Minister of Public Works and Transport, whose department had overseen the Riteve SyC negotiations, both also resigned.

As a result of the departures, in mid-September President Pacheco effected a cabinet reorganization. Federico Carrillo Zürcher was appointed Minister of Finance while Manuel Antonio González Sanz became Minister of Foreign Commerce. The portfolio of Vice-President Lineth Saborio was expanded to include the Ministry of the Presidency. Fernando Trejos was appointed Minister of Labour and Social Security, replacing Ovidio Pacheco who moved to the Ministry of Public Works and Transport. However, on 26 October Ovidio Pacheco tendered his resignation, citing grounds of ill health. His resignation followed media interest in a business linked to his family that lent money

at high rates of interest. Former Vice-Minister of the Presidency, Randall Quirós, was subsequently appointed his successor.

Throughout 2004 a series of disclosures of alleged corruption within the public sector tarnished the country's reputation for transparency. In May an investigation was begun into a US $39.2m. loan, made in 2001 by the Government of Finland to enable the Costa Rican health service to update its equipment. The inquiry revealed that a number of executives at the Costa Rican social security institute, the Caja Costarricense de Seguro Social (CCSS) had received payments from Corporación Fischel, the company contracted to supply the equipment. The former head of the CCSS and former PUSC deputy, Elisio Vargas, and the President of Corporación Fischel, Walter Reiche, were both subsequently imprisoned in connection with the case. Then, in September, former President Calderón was charged with accepting illegal payments from Corporación Fischel; he was arrested in October. His apprehension came just one week after another former PUSC President, Miguel Angel Rodríguez, had resigned as Secretary-General of the Organization of American States after being accused of accepting payments from a French communications company, Alcatel, in connection with a contract with the ICE. Rodríguez claimed he had no knowledge of the origin of the payment, which was made via an associate, José Antonio Lobo; he was later placed under house arrest. Earlier in the year, President Pacheco had dismissed Lobo and a fellow ICE board member following revelations that they had stayed in a Swiss hotel courtesy of the Swedish telecommunications company Ericsson, which was subsequently awarded a contract to supply cellular telephone lines. Furthermore, in late September Pacheco admitted to having received an illegal campaign contribution of $100,000 from Alcatel. In the following month it was also revealed that two Taiwanese firms had also donated $350,000 to the President's election campaign. Foreign contributions and those over $28,000 were prohibited by the electoral tribunal. In December the President was censured by the legislative committee charged with investigating campaign funding.

On 12 October 2004 thousands of people participated in a march in the capital in protest at the growing number of corruption scandals. Nevertheless, later that month another former President, this time from the PLN, José María Figueres, was accused of receiving illegal payments totalling US $900,000 from a sub-contractor of Alcatel. The former head of state, who lived in Switzerland, claimed the payments were legitimate earnings for his services as an adviser. However, he reneged a pledge to return to Costa Rica by December to appear before a congressional committee and was subsequently expelled from the PLN. On 12 November four other members of the PLN, including the Secretary-General, Carmen María Valverde Acosta, resigned from the party to avoid internal investigations into allegations of corruption.

Four days of torrential rain in January 2005 caused severe flooding that resulted in four deaths and severe damage to the country's infrastructure and to some 3,000 hectares of crops, principally banana and pineapple plantations. Reconstruction costs were estimated at US $20m., of which, approximately one-half would be incurred by the banana industry.

In August 1989, at a summit meeting in Honduras, the Presidents of Costa Rica, El Salvador, Guatemala, Honduras and Nicaragua ratified a plan, known as the Tela Agreement, to remove the Contra forces from base camps in Honduras, in exchange for the introduction of political reforms and the holding of free elections in Nicaragua. Peace proposals for El Salvador and Guatemala were also elaborated, as was an agreement on co-operation in the campaign against the trafficking and use of illicit drugs. In November, however, the conflicts in Nicaragua and El Salvador intensified. In December the deadline for the disbanding of Contra forces, agreed at Tela, passed unfulfilled, and the Presidents of the five Central American countries, meeting in Costa Rica, agreed on measures to revive the regional peace process. In February 1990, after being defeated in elections, Nicaragua's Sandinista Government decreed an immediate cease-fire. The Contras accepted this, and a cease-fire agreement was concluded in April.

In 1995 relations with Nicaragua became strained, following a series of incidents concerning immigration and the policing of the countries' joint border. A tightening of immigration policy in Costa Rica had led to the automatic expulsion of illegal immigrants who had previously been tolerated (providing, as they did, a source of cheap labour for agriculture and the construction industry). The change in government policy had been prompted by the excessive burden placed on Costa Rica's social services by a recent rapid increase in immigrant arrivals, and by a downturn in the country's economy. In January 1998 bilateral discussions were held regarding the continuing expulsion of Nicaraguan immigrants. Costa Rica demanded, as a condition for agreement on the issue, that Nicaragua grant concessions allowing Costa Rican artisan fishermen to operate in Nicaraguan territorial waters. Nicaragua, however, rejected the demand, and no agreement was reached. In July further antagonism developed between the two countries when Nicaragua prohibited Costa Rican civil guards from carrying arms while navigating the San Juan river, which forms the border between the two countries. According to a long-standing treaty, the river, which is Nicaraguan territory, was only to be used by Costa Rica for commercial purposes. In June 2000 both Governments agreed a procedure that would allow armed Costa Rican police officers to patrol the river. Nevertheless, in September 2001 Nicaragua disputed a ruling by the Costa Rican Constitutional Court that armed police officers were entitled to use the San Juan river without seeking prior permission from Nicaragua. Earlier, in May, a fresh dispute had arisen following the implementation of a US $25 charge for Costa Ricans using the river. In September 2002 the two countries appeared to have made some progress towards resolving the dispute. Nicaragua agreed to discontinue the $25 fee charged to Costa Ricans in exchange for the abolition of charges levied on visas and tourist permits required by Nicaraguans to enter Costa Rica. Costa Rica also announced that it would relinquish plans to refer the matter to the International Court of Justice. In July, however, the two Governments came into conflict over a separate issue when Nicaragua announced that it was to award concessions for petroleum exploration in an area of the Caribbean Sea and Pacific Ocean claimed by Costa Rica. Bilateral discussions aimed at solving the issue began in October.

In October 2000 Costa Rica ratified a maritime boundaries treaty with Colombia, recognizing their control over 500,000 sq km of the Pacific Ocean, including the Isla del Coco.

Government

Under the Constitution of 1949, executive power is vested in the President, assisted by two Vice-Presidents (or, in exceptional circumstances, one Vice-President) and an appointed Cabinet. The President is elected for a four-year term by compulsory adult suffrage, and a successful candidate must receive at least 40% of the votes. The legislative organ is the unicameral Asamblea Legislativa, with 57 members who are similarly elected for four years.

Defence

There have been no Costa Rican armed forces since 1948. In August 2004 Rural and Civil Guards totalled 2,000 and 4,400 men, respectively. In addition, there were 2,000 Border Security Police. There was also an Immediate Action Unit. In September 1999 legislation was approved providing for the establishment of a coastguard to participate in joint anti-drugs patrols with units of the US coastguard, under the terms of a co-operation agreement with the USA, which had received legislative approval in the previous month. Expenditure on the security forces totalled US $101m. in 2003.

Economic Affairs

In 2003, according to estimates by the World Bank, Costa Rica's gross national income (GNI), measured at average 2001–03 prices, was US $16,651m., equivalent to $4,280 per head (or $9,040 per head on an international purchasing-power parity basis). During 1990–2001, it was estimated, the population increased by an average of 2.1% per year, while gross domestic product (GDP) per head increased, in real terms, by an average of 2.6% per year. Overall GDP increased, in real terms, by an average annual rate of 4.7% in 1990–2003; GDP increased by 3.0% in 2002 and by 5.6% in 2003.

Agriculture (including hunting, forestry and fishing) contributed an estimated 8.4% of GDP in 2003 and employed 14.8% of the economically active population in the following year. In 2000 banana production employed some 40,000 people directly and a further 100,000 indirectly. The principal cash crops are bananas (which accounted for 9.0% of general export earnings in 2003), coffee (3.3% of general export earnings), flowers and tropical fruit. Seafood exports were also significant. Sugar cane, rice, maize and beans are also cultivated. According to the World Bank, the real GDP of the agricultural sector increased at an

average annual rate of 3.3% during 1990–2003. Real agricultural GDP declined by 2.0% in 2002, before increasing by an estimated 4.0% in 2003.

Industry (including mining, manufacturing, construction and power) employed 22.0% of the economically active population in 2004 and provided an estimated 27.4% of GDP in 2003. According to the World Bank, real industrial GDP increased at an average annual rate of 4.8% during 1990–2003. The real GDP of the sector increased by 2.3% in 2002 and by a further 4.5% in 2003. Mining employed only 0.5% of the economically active population in 2003 and contributed an estimated 0.1% of GDP. In June 2002 open-cast mining was banned by presidential decree in order to preserve the environment and the future of eco-tourism in Costa Rica.

The manufacturing sector employed 13.9% of the employed work-force in 2004 and contributed an estimated 20.4% of GDP in 2003. The principal branches of manufacturing were food products, chemical products, beverages and paper and paper products. Production of computer components by the US manufacturer Intel began in 1998, and by 2005 as many as 15 other high-technology manufacturers had opened factories in the country. By that year computer components accounted for some 15% of total export earnings. According to the World Bank, real GDP of the manufacturing sector increased at an average annual rate of 4.9% during 1990–2003. In 2002 the sector's GDP increased by 2.3% and in 2003 by 4.5%.

Energy is derived principally from petroleum and hydro-electric power. The Arenal hydroelectricity project was inaugurated in 1979; however, its full generating capacity of 1,974 MW did not fulfil Costa Rica's electricity requirements, and in 1993 the state electricity company, Instituto Costarricense de Electricidad (ICE) began its third electricity development programme. The programme included a US $300m. hydroelectric power project on the Río Reventazón, completed in 2000, and the country's first wind-generated power plant. In 2000 the ICE announced plans to build a 1,250 MW hydroelectric plant at Boruca by 2011. In 2001 hydroelectric power accounted for 81.5% of total electrical energy generation. Imports of mineral products accounted for an estimated 8.9% of the total value of imports in 2003.

The services sector employed 63.2% of the economically active population in 2004, and provided an estimated 64.1% of GDP in the previous year. According to the World Bank, the real GDP of this sector increased at an average annual rate of 4.6% during 1990–2003. Real GDP increased by 4.3% in 2002 and by 5.5% in 2003. Tourism is the country's most important source of foreign-exchange earnings and in 2000 the sector employed some 152,000 people. Receipts from tourism totalled an estimated US $1,199m. in 2003 and tourist arrivals numbered 1,238,692. Of these, some 41.2% originated from the USA. In December 2004 a second cruise-ship terminal was inaugurated at Puerto Limón to cater for the increasing number of visiting cruise ships.

In 2003 Costa Rica recorded a visible trade deficit of US $1,169.6m. and there was a deficit of $967.0m. on the current account of the balance of payments. In 2003 the principal source of imports (50.1%) was the USA; other major suppliers were Mexico (4.8%), Japan (4.1%) and Venezuela (3.6%). The USA was also the principal market for exports (46.7%); other significant purchasers were the Netherlands (5.8%), Guatemala (3.8%) and Malaysia (3.4%). The principal exports in 2003 were electrical components for microprocessors, bananas and medical transfusion equipment. The principal imports in that year were machinery and electrical equipment, food and live animals, and silk, cotton and textile fibres.

In 2002 there was an estimated budgetary deficit of 259,311.5m. colones (equivalent to some 4.2% of GDP). Costa Rica's estimated total external debt at the end of 2002 was US $4,834m., of which $3,335m. was long-term public debt. The cost of debt-servicing in that year was $670m., equivalent to 8.9% of exports of goods and services. The annual rate of inflation averaged 12.0% in 1995–2004. Consumer prices increased by 9.2% in 2003 and by 11.0% in 2004. Some 6.5% of the labour force were unemployed in 2004.

In May 2001 the Central American countries, including Costa Rica, agreed to establish, with Mexico, the 'Plan Puebla–Panamá'. This was a series of joint transport, industry and tourism projects intended to integrate the region.

Costa Rica is a member of the Central American Common Market (CACM, see p. 176) and the Inter-American Development Bank (IDB, see p. 268). In May 2000 legislation was passed enhancing the Caribbean Basin Initiative, first introduced in

1983, granting North American Free Trade Agreement (NAFTA) parity to products from 24 states, including Costa Rica. In April 2001 the Government concluded a free trade agreement with Canada, which was promulgated in November 2002. In late January 2003 the first round of talks on the establishment of a Central American Free Trade Agreement (CAFTA) with the USA were held in San José between representatives of the Governments of Costa Rica, El Salvador, Guatemala, Honduras, Nicaragua and the USA. In October 2003, during a round of talks in Houston, Texas, USA, disagreement emerged over US demands that Costa Rica liberalize its telecommunications industry, over which the ICE enjoyed a monopoly. The Costa Rican Government strongly resisted such a move; however, in December, at a final round of negotiations in the US capital, it agreed to open up certain parts of the industry. The USA countered these concessions with demands that Costa Rica also end the state monopoly of the insurance sector, prompting the Costa trade delegation to withdraw from the negotiations in protest. In January 2004, nevertheless, the two countries reached an agreement whereby the Costa Rican Government would partially privatize telecommunications and insurance sectors in return for agricultural subsidies. The agreement was signed in May, but had to be ratified by the Costa Rican legislature. Costa Rica was more successful in finalizing the terms of a free trade agreement with the Caribbean Community and Common Market (CARICOM). The agreement, reached in March 2003 and scheduled to take effect in January 2004, excluded just 58 of 6,000 locally produced products from free trade terms.

During the 1990s successive Governments adopted austerity measures aimed at addressing the country's high public-sector deficit. Measures promoting increased foreign investment and enabling private-sector participation in activities formerly confined to the state sector, including the deregulation of the banking system, were implemented in 1996. However, attempts by the Government of President Miguel Angel Rodríguez to end the state's monopoly in the telecommunications, energy and insurance sectors proved unsuccessful. Following the agreement reached with the USA in January 2004, as part of the ongoing CAFTA negotiations, partial and gradual liberalization of the telecommunications and insurance sectors were expected by 2006.

The agricultural sector was affected by fluctuations in the prices of coffee and bananas. In 2001 coffee exports totalled $163.4m., compared with $274.0m. in the previous year. There was a slight improvement in 2002, when exports stood at $165.3m. In late 2000 the situation in the banana industry became critical, with the three principal exporters, Chiquita Brands, Banana Development Corporation and Standard Fruits Company, cancelling contracts. Exports of bananas fell by US $100m. in 2000, to $553.2m. (10.1% of total exports). In April 2001, despite resistance from the multinationals, the Government fixed the price of a 40 lb box at $5.25. In July 2001 more than 1,000 ha of banana plantations were destroyed in an attempt to prevent the further spread of the 'sigatoka negra' blight. In early 1999, following the European Union's (EU, see p. 217) failure to satisfy the World Trade Organization that its banana-import regime complied with international trade regulations, the USA was permitted to impose compensatory tariffs on specific imports from the EU. These tariffs were removed, following an EU-USA accord in April 2001, under which the EU preferential market ended. From 1 July a transitional system, issuing licences according to historical trade patterns, was implemented, while the definitive tariff-only system was to enter into force on 1 January 2006. In May 2002 heavy rains destroyed banana crops worth some US $30m. on the country's Atlantic coast, causing revenue from banana exports to fall from $509m. in 2001 to an estimated $468m. in 2002.

In 2002 the new Pacheco Government pledged to reform the tax system and to seek ways to curb public-sector expenditure in order to reduce the budget deficit. Following the recommendations of an all-party commission earlier in the year, in December the Congreso approved further tax reforms aimed at eradicating the fiscal deficit by 2006. These included changes to the tax code and the levying of value-added tax on a wider range of goods and services. The reforms were to be accompanied by a 5.9% limit on any increases in government spending and the reduction of the budgets of the national electricity institution, social security departments and the state petroleum refinery. However, following the slow progress of the reforms through the legislature, in July 2003 the Government was forced to introduce a US $75m. spending cut. Failure to gain consensus on the details meant that the fiscal reform measures still awaited approval in early 2005. In October 2003 the IDB granted a loan of US $350m. to fund improvements to the nation's infrastructure and health and transport systems. An IMF report in September 2004 expressed concerns about the increasing dollarization of savings accounts and the large trade deficit. The trade deficit widened substantially in 2004, reaching US $1,450m. at the end of September. This was in large part owing to a substantial decline in exports by Intel, and was further exacerbated by high global petroleum prices. However, in November Intel announced plans to increase production by 50% in 2005. In 2004 inflation reached 13.1%, principally owing to steep rises in fuel and transport prices. Inflation was forecast to total some 12.5% in 2005; however, the Central Bank announced plans to tighten monetary policy in a bid to reduce it to 10%. GDP increased by 4.0% in 2004, and was expected to rise by 3.8% in 2005.

Education

Education at all levels is available free of charge, and is officially compulsory for children between six and 15 years of age. Primary education begins at six years of age and lasts for six years. Secondary education consists of a three-year basic course, followed by a more highly specialized course of two years. In 2001 primary enrolment included an estimated 90.6% of children in the relevant age-group (males 89.9%; females 91.4%), while the comparable ratio for secondary enrolment was 50.7% (males 48.2%; females 53.4%). There are four public universities, one of which is an open university and an increasing number of private ones. In 2001/02 total enrolment at primary, secondary and tertiary levels was 61% (males 60%; females 62%). Costa Rica has the highest adult literacy rate in Central America. Government expenditure on education in 1996 was 99,631m. colones (22.8% of total spending). In 2001 public expenditure on education represented 21.1% of total government spending.

Public Holidays

2005: 1 January (New Year's Day), 19 March (Feast of St Joseph, San José only), 24 March (Maundy Thursday), 25 March (Good Friday), 11 April (Anniversary of the Battle of Rivas), 2 May (for Labour Day), 26 May (Corpus Christi), 29 June (St Peter and St Paul), 26 July (Anniversary of the Annexation of Guanacaste Province), 2 August (Our Lady of the Angels), 15 August (Assumption), 15 September (Independence Day), 12 October (Columbus Day), 1 December (Abolition of the Armed Forces Day), 8 December (Immaculate Conception), 25 December (Christmas Day), 28–31 December (San José only).

2006: 1 January (New Year's Day), 19 March (Feast of St Joseph, San José only), 11 April (Anniversary of the Battle of Rivas), 13 April (Maundy Thursday), 14 April (Good Friday), 1 May (Labour Day), 15 June (Corpus Christi), 29 June (St Peter and St Paul), 26 July (Anniversary of the Annexation of Guanacaste Province), 2 August (Our Lady of the Angels), 14 August (Assumption), 15 September (Independence Day), 12 October (Columbus Day), 1 December (Abolition of the Armed Forces Day), 8 December (Immaculate Conception), 25 December (Christmas Day), 28–31 December (San José only).

Weights and Measures

The metric system is in force.

Statistical Survey

Sources (unless otherwise stated): Instituto Nacional de Estadística y Censos, de la Rotonda de la Bandera 450 metros oeste, sobre Calle Los Negritos, Edif. Ana Lorena, Mercedes de Montes de Oca, San José; tel. 280-9280; fax 224-2221; e-mail informacion@inec.go.cr; internet www.inec.go.cr; Banco Central de Costa Rica, Avdas Central y Primera, Calles 2 y 4, Apdo 10.058, 1000 San José; tel. 233-4233; fax 223-4658; internet www.bccr.fi.cr.

Area and Population

AREA, POPULATION AND DENSITY

Area (sq km)	
Land	51,060
Inland water	40
Total	51,100*
Population (census results)	
11 June 1984†	2,416,809
28 June 2000	
Males	1,996,350
Females	1,928,981
Total	3,925,331
Population (official estimate at mid-year)	
2002	4,045,837
2003	4,103,116
2004	4,159,757
Density (per sq km) at mid-2004	81.5

* 19,730 sq miles.
† Excluding adjustment for underenumeration.

PROVINCES
(official estimates, 1 July 2004)

	Area (sq km)	Population (estimates)	Density (per sq km)	Capital (with population)
Alajuela . .	9,757.5	783,116	80.3	Alajuela (242,769)
Cartago . .	3,124.7	469,982	150.4	Cartago (143,274)
Guanacaste .	10,140.7	288,448	28.4	Liberia (51,779)
Heredia . .	2,657.0	386,259	145.4	Heredia (113,189)
Limón . .	9,188.5	376,209	40.9	Limón (99,723)
Puntarenas .	11,265.7	393,226	34.9	Puntarenas (112,232)
San José . .	4,965.9	1,462,517	290.5	San José (336,829)
Total . .	51,100.0	4,159,757	83.8	—

PRINCIPAL TOWNS
(estimates, 28 June 2000)

San José	309,672	San Francisco . .	40,840
Limón	56,719	Cartago	38,363
Ipís	52,922	Cinco Esquinas . .	36,627
Desamparados . .	52,283	Liberia . . .	34,469
Alajuela	42,889	Puntarenas . . .	32,460

Source: Thomas Brinkhoff, *City Population* (internet www.citypopulation.de).

BIRTHS, MARRIAGES AND DEATHS

	Registered live births		Registered marriages		Registered deaths	
	Number	Rate (per 1,000)	Number	Rate (per 1,000)	Number	Rate (per 1,000)
1995	80,306	24.1	24,274	7.3	14,061	4.2
1996	79,203	23.3	23,574	6.9	13,993	4.1
1997	78,018	22.5	24,300	7.0	14,260	4.1
1998	76,982	21.8	24,831	7.0	14,708	4.2
1999	78,526	21.9	25,613	7.1	15,052	4.2
2000	78,178	20.5	24,436	6.2	14,944	3.9
2001	76,401	19.2	23,790*	6.0*	15,609	4.0
2002	71,144	17.6	n.a.	n.a.	15,004	3.7

* Provisional figure.

Expectation of life (WHO estimates, years at birth): 77.1 (males 74.9; females 79.5) in 2002 (Source: WHO, *World Health Report*).

ECONOMICALLY ACTIVE POPULATION*
('000 persons aged 12 years and over, household survey, July)

	2002	2003	2004
Agriculture, hunting and forestry	242.74	239.81	237.26
Fishing	8.77	8.57	8.07
Mining and quarrying	2.31	2.24	3.56
Manufacturing	226.28	230.06	229.48
Electricity, gas and water supply .	21.86	22.09	23.56
Construction	106.58	109.62	107.29
Wholesale and retail trade . . .	303.36	322.39	329.92
Hotels and restaurants	82.46	89.93	91.42
Transport, storage and communications	90.24	94.03	96.30
Financial intermediation . . .	32.02	35.54	36.69
Real estate, renting and business activities	103.19	101.23	101.98
Public administration activities .	71.87	76.26	78.50
Education	91.90	98.38	95.94
Health and social work	53.00	49.25	51.29
Other community, social and personal service activities . .	58.53	72.10	62.92
Private households with employed persons	83.41	79.28	90.79
Extra-territorial organizations and bodies	2.55	2.38	3.89
Not classifiable by economic activity	5.46	7.23	5.05
Total employed	1,586.49	1,640.39	1,653.88
Unemployed	108.53	117.19	114.88
Total labour force	1,695.02	1,757.58	1,768.76

* Figures for activities are rounded to the nearest 10 persons, and totals may not be equivalent to the sum of component parts as a result.

Health and Welfare

KEY INDICATORS

Total fertility rate (children per woman, 2002)	2.3
Under-5 mortality rate (per 1,000 live births, 2003) . . .	10
HIV/AIDS (% of persons aged 15–49, 2003)	0.6
Physicians (per 1,000 head, 1998)	0.9
Hospital beds (per 1,000 head, 1998)	1.68
Health expenditure (2001): US $ per head (PPP)	562
Health expenditure (2001): % of GDP	7.2
Health expenditure (2001): public (% of total)	68.5
Access to water (% of persons, 2002)	97
Access to sanitation (% of persons, 2002)	92
Human Development Index (2002): ranking	45
Human Development Index (2002): value	0.834

For sources and definitions, see explanatory note on p. vi.

Agriculture

PRINCIPAL CROPS
('000 metric tons)

	2001	2002	2003
Rice (paddy)	211.6	190.3	180.0
Potatoes	89.2	86.8	81.7
Cassava (Manioc)	106.3	94.2	94.2
Sugar cane	3,670.0	3,462.3	3,923.9
Watermelons*	77.0	77.0	77.0
Cantaloupes and other melons*	208.0	210.0	215.0
Oil palm fruit	666.1	692.4	700.0*
Bananas	1,739.3	1,612.0	1,863.0
Plantains*	65.0	67.0	70.0
Oranges	436.6	367.0	367.0
Pineapples	950.4	992.0	725.2
Coffee (green)	837.5	787.5	731.1

* FAO estimate(s).
Source: FAO.

LIVESTOCK
('000 head, year ending September)

	2001	2002	2003
Horses*	115	115	115
Mules*	5	5	5
Asses*	8	8	8
Cattle	1,289	1,220	1,150
Pigs*	525	535	500
Sheep*	3	3	3
Goats*	3	4	4
Chickens*	16,900	18,200	18,500

* FAO estimates.
Source: FAO.

LIVESTOCK PRODUCTS
('000 metric tons)

	2001	2002	2003
Beef and veal	76.0	68.3	74.1
Pig meat	35.7	36.0	35.8
Poultry meat	77.7	76.7	71.8
Cows' milk	737.2	761.9	788.6
Cheese*	7.3	9.1	9.1
Butter*	4.8	5.0	5.0
Hen eggs	46.5	47.7	47.1
Honey*	1.3	1.3	1.3
Cattle hides (fresh)*	11.0	9.6	9.4

* FAO estimates.
Source: FAO.

Forestry

ROUNDWOOD REMOVALS
(FAO estimates, '000 cubic metres, excl. bark)

	2001	2002	2003
Sawlogs, veneer logs and logs for sleepers	1,441	1,441	1,441
Other industrial wood	246	246	246
Fuel wood	3,474	3,463	3,454
Total	5,161	5,150	5,141

Source: FAO.

SAWNWOOD PRODUCTION
(FAO estimates, '000 cubic metres, incl. railway sleepers)

	1998	1999	2000
Coniferous (softwood)*	12	12	12
Broadleaved (hardwood)	768*	768*	800
Total*	780	780	812

* FAO estimate(s).
2001–03: Annual production as in 2000 (FAO estimates).
Source: FAO.

Fishing
('000 metric tons, live weight)

	2000	2001	2002
Capture	35.4	34.7	32.9
Freshwater fishes*	1.0	1.0	1.0
Clupeoids	1.6	2.2	4.2
Marlins, sailfishes, etc.	2.0	2.2	2.3
Tuna-like fishes	1.1	1.2	1.6
Common dolphinfish	8.4	11.2	7.8
Sharks, rays, skates, etc.	11.2	8.6	7.5
Other marine fishes	4.5	4.1	3.9
Aquaculture	9.7	10.5	17.9
Tilapias	8.1	8.5	13.2
Whiteleg shrimp	1.4	1.8	4.1
Total catch	45.1	45.3	50.8

* FAO estimates.
Source: FAO.

Industry

SELECTED PRODUCTS
('000 metric tons, unless otherwise indicated)

	1996	1997	1998
Cigarettes (million units)	16	n.a.	n.a.
Non-cellulosic continuous fibres	7.8	7.9	n.a.
Jet fuels	30	35	—
Motor spirit (gasoline)	77	81	n.a.
Naphthas	12	7	1
Kerosene	3	6	1
Distillate fuel oils	175	176	17
Residual fuel oils	310	325	149
Bitumen	23	26	12
Liquefied petroleum gas (refined)	2	2	n.a.
Cement	n.a.	n.a.	1,200
Electric energy (million kWh)	4,894	5,589	5,866

1999 ('000 metric tons, unless otherwise indicated): Raw sugar 366; Non-cellulosic continuous fibres 7.8; Kerosene 2; Distillate fuel oils 17; Bitumen 12; Cement 1,100; Electric energy 6,438 million kWh.

2000 ('000 metric tons, unless otherwise indicated): Raw sugar 369; Non-cellulosic continuous fibres 8.2; Kerosene 3; Bitumen 12; Cement 1,150; Electric energy 7,227 million kWh.

2001 ('000 metric tons): Raw sugar 365; Non-cellulosic continuous fibres 8.7; Distillate fuel oils 2; Bitumen 12; Cement 1,100.

Source: UN, *Industrial Commodity Statistics Yearbook*.

Finance

CURRENCY AND EXCHANGE RATES

Monetary Units
100 céntimos =1 Costa Rican colón.

Sterling, Dollar and Euro Equivalents (31 December 2004)
£1 sterling = 885.7596 colones
US $1 = 458.6100 colones
€1 = 624.6731 colones
1,000 Costa Rican colones = £1.13 = $2.18 = €1.60

Average Exchange Rate (colones per US $)
2002   359.8170
2003   398.6630
2004   437.9110

GENERAL BUDGET
(million colones)

Revenue	2000	2001	2002
Taxation	603,748	712,944	801,424.9
Income tax	133,090	163,059	185,600.3
Social security contributions .	18,677	21,151	23,090.8
Taxes on property . . .	15,374	17,397	22,054.3
Taxes on goods and services .	389,381	459,234	513,751.0
Taxes on international trade .	47,226	52,104	56,928.5
Other current revenue	2,755	6,875	4,636.2
Current transfers	2,035	2,273	2,689.6
Capital transfers	1,600	3,472	51.3
Total	610,138	725,563	808,802.0

Expenditure	2000	2001	2002
Current expenditure . . .	685,955	809,055	977,982.8
Wages and salaries	225,873	267,037	314,748.7
Social security contributions .	29,480	38,954	46,303.7
Other purchases of goods and services	22,837	26,625	36,146.0
Interest payments	175,653	213,866	259,416.6
Internal	149,549	174,019	211,223.4
External	26,104	39,847	48,193.2
Current transfers	232,111	262,573	321,367.8
Capital expenditure	75,351	73,217	90,130.5
Investment	23,414	16,100	21,729.2
Capital transfers	51,937	57,117	68,335.8
Total	761,306	882,272	1,068,113.5

INTERNATIONAL RESERVES
(US $ million at 31 December)

	2001	2002	2003
Gold*	0.02	0.02	0.02
IMF special drawing rights . .	0.09	0.09	0.05
Reserve position in IMF . . .	25.13	27.19	29.72
Foreign exchange	1,304.59	1,469.27	1,806.49
Total	1,329.83	1,496.57	1,836.29

* National valuation.

Source: IMF, *International Financial Statistics*.

MONEY SUPPLY
('000 million colones at 31 December)

	2001	2002	2003
Currency outside banks . . .	156.5	169.7	186.9
Demand deposits at commercial banks	542.3	662.6	779.0
Total money (incl. others) . .	724.2	843.1	970.1

Source: IMF, *International Financial Statistics*.

COST OF LIVING
(Consumer Price Index; base: January 1995 = 100)

	2002	2003	2004
Food, beverages and tobacco . .	235.5	255.9	287.0
Clothing and footwear	162.1	170.0	176.7
Housing	220.3	236.9	257.1
Medical care	275.5	307.6	349.2
Transport	259.1	294.8	338.5
Leisure and education	201.5	220.5	244.5
All items (incl. others)	228.0	248.9	276.4

NATIONAL ACCOUNTS
(million colones at current prices)

Expenditure on the Gross Domestic Product

	2001	2002	2003*
Government final consumption expenditure	772,575	900,615	1,013,482
Private final consumption expenditure	3,689,866	4,106,884	4,652,840
Increase in stocks	106,985	221,601	96,131
Gross fixed capital formation . .	987,279	1,143,140	1,332,290
Total domestic expenditure .	5,556,705	6,372,240	7,094,742
Exports of goods and services . .	2,236,332	2,569,619	3,260,847
Less Imports of goods and services	2,398,442	2,882,965	3,384,774
GDP in purchasers' values . .	5,394,595	6,058,895	6,970,815
GDP at constant 1991 prices .	1,438,695	1,480,666	1,577,362

* Preliminary figures.

Gross Domestic Product by Economic Activity

	2001	2002	2003*
Agriculture, hunting, forestry and fishing	429,098	467,695	551,239
Mining and quarrying	8,458	8,846	9,510
Manufacturing	1,066,499	1,179,164	1,344,992
Electricity, gas and water . . .	142,503	149,642	170,343
Construction	232,998	256,406	292,502
Trade, restaurants and hotels . .	963,027	1,050,096	1,205,774
Transport, storage and communications	413,057	494,186	595,209
Finance and insurance	254,554	308,798	374,685
Real estate	222,968	244,942	267,666
Other business services . . .	199,709	236,773	271,208
Public administration	201,267	239,941	269,464
Other community, social and personal services	927,254	1,079,933	1,243,560
Sub-total	5,061,392	5,716,422	6,596,151
Less Imputed bank service charge	185,670	239,214	274,699
GDP at basic prices	4,875,722	5,477,206	6,321,453
Taxes, *less* subsidies, on products	518,874	581,689	649,362
GDP in purchasers' values . .	5,394,595	6,058,895	6,970,815

* Preliminary figures.

BALANCE OF PAYMENTS
(US $ million)

	2001	2002	2003
Exports of goods f.o.b.	4,923.2	5,269.9	6,124.7
Imports of goods f.o.b.	−5,743.3	−6,537.1	−7,294.4
Trade balance	−820.1	−1,267.2	−1,169.6
Exports of services	1,900.6	1,869.9	2,027.0
Imports of services	−1,168.9	−1,182.1	−1,188.4
Balance on goods and services	−88.4	−579.5	−331.0
Other income received . . .	196.0	317.9	213.3
Other income paid	−975.6	−835.2	−1,061.9
Balance on goods, services and income	−867.9	−1,096.8	−1,179.9
Current transfers received . . .	266.4	296.9	368.6
Current transfers paid	−111.1	−116.2	−156.0
Current balance	−712.7	−916.1	−967.0
Capital account (net)	12.4	5.7	26.1
Direct investment abroad . .	−11.1	−34.1	−26.9
Direct investment from abroad .	453.6	661.9	576.7
Portfolio investment assets . .	−81.2	28.4	−91.6
Portfolio investment liabilities .	−57.9	−125.8	−304.5
Other investment assets . .	106.2	217.5	170.6
Other investment liabilities . .	−89.2	96.9	329.1
Net errors and omissions . .	243.9	28.2	68.0
Overall balance	−136.0	−37.4	−219.5

Source: IMF, *International Financial Statistics*.

External Trade

PRINCIPAL COMMODITIES
(US $ million)

Imports c.i.f.	2001	2002	2003
Food and live animals	276.0	342.4	355.5
Mineral products	484.8	620.5	700.1
Basic manufactures	194.4	231.9	240.6
Chemicals and related products .	724.9	777.0	845.6
Plastic materials and manufactures	452.3	468.4	487.4
Leather, hides and furs . . .	23.6	26.8	44.7
Paper, paperboard and manufactures	26.4	24.2	26.7
Wood pulp and other fibrous materials	325.7	319.6	351.8
Silk, cotton and textile fibres .	691.9	657.3	600.5
Footwear, hats, umbrellas, etc. .	46.8	49.2	51.7
Stone manufactures, etc. . .	82.4	89.3	89.7
Natural and cultured pearls . .	27.1	38.1	30.5
Common metals and manufactures	397.2	444.2	492.8
Machinery and electrical equipment	2,149.6	2,478.7	2,756.3
Transport equipment . . .	393.2	447.0	403.6
Optical and topographical apparatus and instruments etc.	128.8	184.9	306.1
Total (incl. others)	6,552.5	7,314.6	7,906.0

Exports f.o.b.	2001	2002	2003
Food and live animals	1,343.1	1,415.3	1,535.9
Mineral products	54.9	65.8	43.0
Basic manufactures	357.2	411.6	433.3
Chemicals and related products .	289.6	329.5	364.4
Plastic materials and manufactures	223.3	235.7	235.6
Leather, hides and furs . . .	44.9	39.9	51.9
Paper, paperboard and manufactures	31.7	33.5	30.1
Wood pulp and other fibrous materials	81.7	103.5	82.0
Silk, cotton and textile fibres .	676.4	692.0	584.7
Footwear, hats, umbrellas, etc. .	4.5	1.0	1.0
Stone manufactures, etc. . .	66.2	72.8	67.4
Natural and cultured pearls . .	27.3	35.4	31.3
Common metals and manufactures	116.9	126.8	134.6

Exports f.o.b.— *continued*	2001	2002	2003
Machinery and electrical equipment	1,315.5	1,423.9	1,955.8
Transport equipment . . .	34.1	19.4	28.8
Optical and topographical apparatus and instruments, etc..	333.6	404.1	533.3
Total (incl. others)	5,059.5	5,466.6	6,164.0

PRINCIPAL TRADING PARTNERS
(US $ million)

Imports c.i.f.	2001	2002	2003
Brazil	110.8	163.4	269.1
Canada	73.5	70.8	73.3
China, People's Republic . .	100.5	121.7	169.7
Colombia	154.2	164.9	213.3
El Salvador	92.0	108.1	101.9
France	76.3	66.7	195.5
Germany	137.1	162.7	170.6
Guatemala	140.9	149.7	153.5
Italy	72.6	85.6	112.5
Japan	230.1	378.7	325.3
Korea, Republic	138.6	139.8	103.4
Mexico	381.7	369.0	380.4
Netherlands	128.7	130.9	152.7
Panama	110.7	122.9	114.3
Spain	104.6	136.5	131.8
USA	3,504.1	3,598.9	4,002.0
Venezuela	298.5	379.3	280.7
Total (incl. others)	6,546.3	7,303.6	7,906.0

Exports f.o.b.	2001	2002	2003
Belgium*	90.9	85.7	98.4
El Salvador	151.8	135.4	160.9
Germany	117.5	169.8	208.2
Guatemala	211.4	226.7	232.7
Honduras	123.3	147.5	147.1
Italy	94.4	89.7	89.2
Malaysia	155.0	122.9	215.6
Mexico	87.3	129.5	150.4
Netherlands	275.2	319.4	375.7
Nicaragua	163.3	174.9	188.1
Panama	142.7	131.8	141.6
Puerto Rico	156.7	167.1	166.0
Sweden	46.1	59.1	72.8
United Kingdom	128.1	110.7	162.3
USA	2,504.8	2,726.7	2,977.2
Total (incl. others)	5,042.7	5,466.6	6,333.4

* Includes Luxembourg.

Transport

ROAD TRAFFIC
(motor vehicles in use at 31 December)

	2000	2001	2002
Private cars	341,990	354,394	367,832
Buses and coaches	11,983	12,419	12,891
Goods vehicles	177,875	184,326	191,315
Road tractors	24,027	24,898	25,842
Motorcycles and mopeds . . .	85,427	88,526	91,883

Source: IRF, *World Road Statistics*.

SHIPPING

Merchant Fleet
(registered at 31 December)

	2001	2002	2003
Number of vessels	12	13	14
Total displacement ('000 grt) . .	3.0	4.0	4.6

Source: Lloyd's Register-Fairplay, *World Fleet Statistics*.

International Sea-borne Freight Traffic
('000 metric tons)

	1996	1997	1998
Goods loaded	3,017	3,421	3,721
Goods unloaded	3,972	4,522	5,188

Source: Ministry of Public Works and Transport.

CIVIL AVIATION
(scheduled services)

	1999	2000	2001
Kilometres flown (million) . . .	27	20	24
Passengers carried ('000) . . .	1,055	878	738
Passenger-km (million)	2,145	2,358	2,152
Total ton-km (million)	245	252	179

Source: UN, *Statistical Yearbook*.

Tourism

FOREIGN TOURIST ARRIVALS BY COUNTRY OF ORIGIN

	2001	2002	2003
Canada	52,661	49,168	54,656
Colombia	47,547	35,220	26,645
El Salvador	35,054	33,531	33,892
France	15,558	18,309	23,606
Germany	23,995	23,848	29,151
Guatemala	32,574	33,150	35,174
Honduras	27,174	23,705	23,004
Italy	16,479	15,985	18,361
Mexico	36,841	37,870	46,113
Netherlands	18,922	19,938	24,665
Nicaragua	171,583	174,455	163,632
Panama	53,892	55,774	56,490
Spain	26,916	29,874	34,442
United Kingdom	18,922	19,037	23,019
USA	429,093	422,215	510,751
Total (incl. others) . . .	1,131,406	1,113,359	1,238,692

Tourism receipts (US $ million): 1,278 in 2001; 1,078 in 2002; 1,199 in 2003.

Hotels: 370 in 2001; 371 in 2002; 379 in 2003.

Communications Media

	2000	2001	2002
Telephones ('000 main lines in use)	1,003.4	945.0	1,038.0
Mobile cellular telephones ('000 subscribers)	209.1	311.3	459.8
Personal computers ('000 in use) .	n.a.	700.0	817.0
Internet users ('000)	228.0	384.0	800.0

Radio receivers ('000 in use): 3,045 in 1999.

Television receivers ('000 in use): 930 in 2000.

Facsimile machines (number in use): 8,500 in 1997.

Daily newspapers: 8 in 2000.

Non-daily newspapers: 27 in 2000.

Book production: 1,464 titles (excluding pamphlets) in 1998.

Sources: UNESCO, *Statistical Yearbook*, UN, *Statistical Yearbook*, International Telecommunication Union.

Education

(2001/02, unless otherwise indicated)

	Institu-tions*	Tea-chers*	Students		
			Males	Females	Total
Pre-primary . . .	1,821	3,604	47,804	45,929	93,733
Primary . . .	3,768	20,185	287,197	265,105	552,302
Secondary . . .	468	11,891	146,528	140,781	287,309
General . . .	386	8,908	111,683	116,242	227,925
Vocational . .	82	2,983	33,849	25,535	59,384
Tertiary	52	n.a.	37,460	41,722	79,182

* 1999.

Adult literacy rate (UNESCO estimates): 95.8% (males 95.7%; females 95.9%) in 2002 (Source: UN Development Programme, *Human Development Report*).

Directory

The Constitution

The present Constitution of Costa Rica was promulgated in November 1949. Its main provisions are summarized below:

GOVERNMENT

The government is unitary: provincial and local bodies derive their authority from the national Government. The country is divided into seven Provinces, each administered by a Governor who is appointed by the President. The Provinces are divided into Cantons, and each Canton into Districts. There is an elected Municipal Council in the chief city of each Canton, the number of its members being related to the population of the Canton. The Municipal Council supervises the affairs of the Canton. Municipal government is closely regulated by national law, particularly in matters of finance.

LEGISLATURE

The government consists of three branches: legislative, executive and judicial. Legislative power is vested in a single chamber, the Legislative Assembly (Asamblea Legislativa), which meets in regular session twice a year—from 1 May to 31 July, and from 1 September to 30 November. Special sessions may be convoked by the President to consider specified business. The Assembly is composed of 57 deputies elected for four years. The chief powers of the Assembly are to enact laws, levy taxes, authorize declarations of war and, by a two-thirds' majority, suspend, in cases of civil disorder, certain civil liberties guaranteed in the Constitution.

Bills may be initiated by the Assembly or by the Executive and must have three readings, in at least two different legislative periods, before they become law. The Assembly may override the presidential vote by a two-thirds' majority.

EXECUTIVE

The executive branch is headed by the President, who is assisted by the Cabinet. If the President should resign or be incapacitated, the executive power is entrusted to the First Vice-President; next in line to succeed to executive power are the Second Vice-President and the President of the Legislative Assembly.

The President sees that the laws and the provisions of the Constitution are carried out, and maintains order; has power to appoint and remove cabinet ministers and diplomatic representatives, and to negotiate treaties with foreign nations (which are, however, subject to ratification by the Legislative Assembly). The President is assisted in these duties by a Cabinet, each member of which is head of an executive department.

ELECTORATE

Suffrage is universal, compulsory and secret for persons over the age of 18 years.

DEFENCE

The Costa Rican Constitution has a clause outlawing a national army. Only by a continental convention or for the purpose of national defence may a military force be organized.

The Government

HEAD OF STATE

President: ABEL PACHECO DE LA ESPRIELLA (took office 8 May 2002).
First Vice-President: LINETH SABORÍO.
Second Vice-President: (vacant).

THE CABINET
(April 2005)

Minister of Finance: FEDERICO CARRILLO ZÜRCHER.

Minister of the Economy, Industry and Commerce: GILBERTO BARRANTES.

Minister of the Presidency: LINETH SABORÍO.

Minister of Planning and Economic Policy: JORGE POLINARIS.

Minister of Foreign Relations: ROBERTO TOVAR FAJA.

Minister of Foreign Commerce: MANUEL ANTONIO GONZÁLEZ SANZ.

Minister of the Interior, Police and Public Security: ROGELIO RAMOS MARTÍNEZ.

Minister of Agriculture and Livestock: RODOLFO COTO PACHECO.

Minister of the Environment and Energy: CARLOS MANUEL RODRÍGUEZ ECHANDI.

Minister of Justice: PATRICIA VEGA HERRERA.

Minister of Labour and Social Security: FERNANDO TREJOS.

Minister of Public Education: MANUEL ANTONIO BOLAÑOS SALAS.

Minister of Public Health: MARÍA DEL ROCÍO SÁENZ.

Minister of Housing: HELIO FALLAS VENEGAS.

Minister of Public Works and Transport: RANDALL QUIRÓS BUSTAMENTE.

Minister of Science and Technology: FERNANDO GUTIÉRREZ ORTIZ.

Minister of Culture, Youth and Sports: GUIDO SÁENZ GONZÁLEZ.

Minister of Tourism: RODRIGO CASTRO.

Minister of Women's Affairs: GEORGINA VARGAS PAGÁN.

Secretary-General of the Cabinet: HERMES NAVARRO DEL VALLE.

MINISTRIES

Ministry of Agriculture and Livestock: Antigüo Colegio La Salle, Sabana Sur, Apdo 10094, 1000 San José; tel. 231-2344; fax 232-2103; e-mail magweb@mag.go.cr; internet www.mag.go.cr.

Ministry of Culture, Youth and Sports: Avdas 3 y 7, Calles 11 y 15, frente al parque España, San José; tel. 255-3188; e-mail mincjd@costarricense.cr; internet www.mcjdcr.go.cr.

Ministry of the Economy, Industry and Commerce: Edif. IFAM, Moravia del Colegio Lincoln, San José; tel. 235-2700; fax 236-7281; e-mail info@meic.go.cr; internet www.meic.go.cr.

Ministry of the Environment and Energy: Avdas 8 y 10, Calle 25, Apdo 10.104, 1000 San José; tel. 233-4533; fax 257-0697; e-mail emiliarg@minae.go.cr; internet www.minae.go.cr.

Ministry of Finance: Edif. Antigüo Banco Anglo, Avda 2a, Calle 3a, San José; tel. 257-9333; fax 255-4874; e-mail WebMaster1@hacienda.go.cr; internet www1.hacienda.go.cr.

Ministry of Foreign Commerce: Montes de Oca, Apdo 96, 2050 San José; tel. 256-7111; fax 255-3281; e-mail info@comex.go.cr; internet www.comex.go.cr.

Ministry of Foreign Relations: Avda 7 y 9, Calle 11 y 13, Apdo 10027, 1000 San José; tel. 223-7555; fax 257-6597; e-mail despacho.ministro@rree.go.cr; internet www.rree.go.cr.

Ministry of Housing: Paseo de los Estudiantes, Apdo 222, 1002 San José; tel. 221-4411; fax 255-1976; internet www.mivah.go.cr.

Ministry of the Interior, Police and Public Security: Apdo 55, 4874 San José; tel. 227-4866; fax 226-6581; internet www.msp.go.cr.

Ministry of Justice: Zapote, frente a Price Mart, Registro Nacional, Edif. Administrativo, 4°, 1000 San José; tel. 280-9054; fax 234-7959; e-mail justicia@gobnet.go.cr; internet www.mj.go.cr.

Ministry of Labour and Social Security: Edif. Benjamín Núñez, 4°, Barrio Tournón, Apdo 10133, 1000 San José; tel. 257-8211; internet www.ministrabajo.go.cr.

Ministry of Planning and Economic Policy: Avdas 3 y 5, Calle 4, Apdo 10.127, 1000 San José; tel. 281-2700; fax 253-6243; e-mail pnd@ns.mideplan.go.cr; internet www.mideplan.go.cr.

Ministry of Public Education: Edif. Antigua Embajada, Apdo 10087, 1000 San José; tel. 233-9050; fax 233-0390; e-mail minieduc@sol.racsa.co.cr; internet www.mep.go.cr.

Ministry of Public Health: Calle 16, Avda 6 y 8, Apdo 10123, 1000 San José; tel. 223-0333; fax 255-4997; e-mail minsalud@netsalud.sa.cr; internet www.ministeriodesalud.go.cr.

Ministry of Public Works and Transport: Plaza González Víquez, C 9, Avda 20 y 22, Apdo 10176, 1000 San José; tel. 253-2000; fax 255-0242; internet www.mopt.go.cr.

Ministry of Science and Technology: 1.3 km al norte de la Embajada Americana, Apdo 5589, 1000 San José; tel. 290-1790; fax 290-4967; e-mail micit@micit.go.cr; internet www.micit.go.cr.

Ministry of Women's Affairs: San José.

President and Legislature

PRESIDENT

Elections, 3 February and 7 April 2002

Candidate	First round % of votes	Second round % of votes
Abel Pacheco de la Espriella (PUSC) .	38.5	58.0
Rolando Araya Monge (PLN) . . .	30.9	42.0
Ottón Solís (PAC)	26.3	—
Otto Guevara Guth (PML)	1.7	—
Total (incl. others)	100.0	100.0

ASAMBLEA LEGISLATIVA

General Election, 3 February 2002

Party	Seats
Partido Unidad Social Cristiana (PUSC)	19
Partido de Liberación Nacional (PLN)	17
Partido Acción Ciudadana (PAC)	14
Partido Movimiento Libertario (PML)	6
Partido Renovación Costarricense (PRC)	1
Total	57

Political Organizations

Alianza Nacional Cristiana (ANC): Calle Vargas Araya, Condominio UNI, 50 m norte Bazar Tere, Apdo 353, 2050 San José; tel. 253-2772; f. 1981; national party; Pres. VÍCTOR HUGO GONZÁLEZ MONTERO; Sec. SALVADOR ESTABAN BEATRIZ PORRAS.

Bloque Patriótico Parlamentario: San José; f. 2003 by dissident faction of the PAC.

Cambio 2000: 200 m al sur del Banco Popular de San José, Edif. esquinero, frente a la Sociedad de Seguros de Vida del Magisterio Nacional, San José; tel. 221-0694; f. 2000; Pres. WALTER COTO MOLINA; Sec. ROSA MARÍA ARTAVIA RODRÍGUEZ; Coalition comprising:

Acción Democrática Alajuelense: Frente al Liceo de San Carlos, Barrio San Roque, Ciudad Quesada, Alajuela; tel. 460-0075; f. 1978; provincial party; Pres. MARIANO BARQUERO FONSECA; Sec. JORGE ARROYO CASTRO.

Partido Pueblo Unido: 11 Calle Fallas, Ciudadela Cucubres de la plaza de deportes, Apdo 4.665, 1000 San José; tel. 224-1904; fax 224-2364; e-mail upvargas@sol.racsa.co.cr; f. 1995; national party; Pres. TRINO BARRANTES ARAYA; Sec. HUMBERTO VARGAS CARBONELL.

Independiente Obrero: Edif. Multifamiliares, Hatillo 5, Apdo 179, 1000 San José; tel. 254-5450; fax 283-7752; e-mail cuberopio@racsa.co.cr; f. 1971; national party; Pres. JOSÉ ALBERTO CUBERO CARMONA; Sec. LUIS FERNANDO SALAZAR VILLEGAS.

Movimiento Libertario (ML): Of. de Cabinas San Isidro, Barrio Los Yoses Sur, Apdo 4.674, 1000 San José; tel. 281-3767 ; fax 224-169222; e-mail infoo@libertario.org; internet www.libertario.org; f. 1994; national party; Pres. OTTO GUEVARA GUTH; Sec.-Gen. RAÚL COSTALES DOMÍNGUEZ.

Nuevo Partido Democrático: Central Barrio Naciones Unidas, detrás del Centro Comercial del Sur, Apdo 528, 2100 San José; tel. 227-1422; fax 283-4857; f. 1996; national party; Pres. RODRIGO GUTIÉRREZ SCHWANHAUSER; Sec. ROSA MARÍA ZELEDON GÓMEZ.

Partido Acción Ciudadana (PAC): 25 San Pedro, 425 metros sur del Templo Parroquial, San José; tel. 281-2727; fax 280-6640; e-mail pac2002@racsa.co.cr; internet www.pac.or.cr; f. 2000; centre party; Pres. OTTÓN SOLÍS; Sec. SADIE BRAVO PÉREZ.

Partido Acción Laborista Agrícola (PALA): 700m este y 50 norte del Palide Barva de Heredia, Apdo 698–1100 Tibás; tel. 236-6404; fax 240-6536; e-mail fmurillo66@hotmail.com; f. 1987; provincial party; Pres. FREDDY JESÚS MURILLO ESPINOZA; Sec. IRIS MARÍA RODRÍGUEZ VARGAS.

Partido Agrario Nacional: Frente al Banco Nacional, Guácimo, Apdo 14, 7210 Limón; tel. 710-0493; fax 710-0493; f. 1988; provincial party; Pres. LUIS FRANCISCO SÁNCHEZ MOREIR; Sec. PEDRO CAMPOS PICADO.

Partido Auténtico Limonense: 70 m Oeste de la Escuela Rafael Yglesias, Apdo 1046, Limón; tel. 758-3563; f. 1976; provincial party; Pres. MARVIN WRIGHT LINDO; Sec. DELROY SEINOR GRANT.

Partido Cambio Ya: Farmacia de la Cruz 2°, Ciudad Quesada, San Carlos, Alajuela; tel. 460-2501; fax 460-3855; f. 1995; provincial party; Pres. ANA PATRICIA GUILLÉN CAMPOS; Sec. MARÍA AURELIA ROJAS HERRERA.

Partido Convergencia Nacional: Del Restaurant Versalles, 50 m Oeste, Barrio Los Angeles, Cartago; tel. 551-4361; fax 552-3360; f. 1992; provincial party; Pres. EDUARDO CANTILLO ARIAS; Sec. SERGIO IZAGUIRRE CERDA.

Partido Demócrata (PD): Frente a las Oficinas del INVU, barrio Amón, contiguo a Restaurante La Criollita, Apdo 121, San José; tel. 256-4168; fax 256-0350; f. 1996; national party; Pres. ALVARO GONZÁLEZ ESPINOZA; Sec. ANA MARÍA PÉREZ GRANADOS.

Partido Fuerza Agraria de los Cartagineses: Comisión Campesina Asamblea Legislativa, Edif. Antiguo Sión, Cartago; tel. 551-8884; f. 1996; provincial party; Pres. ALICIA SOLANO BRAVO; Sec. JORGE ANGULO SOLANO.

Partido Fuerza Democrática (FD): Edif. Colón, Apdo 1129-1007, San José; tel. 258-7207; fax 258-7204; f. 1992 as coalition; later became national party; Pres. JUAN CARLOS CHAVES MORA; Vice-Pres. MARJORIE SANTAMARÍA MONGE.

Partido Guanacaste Independiente: Costado Norte de la Plaza de Fútbol, las Juntas, Guanacaste; tel. 662-0141; f. 1992; provincial party; Pres. JOSÉ ANGEL JARA CHAVARRÍA; Sec. TERESITA SALAS VINDAS.

Partido Integración Nacional (PIN): Apartamentos San Antonio, Contiguo a Banco Catay, San Pedro de Montes de Oca; tel. 225-5067; fax 280-7237; e-mail waltermunoz@costarricense.cr; f. 1996; national party; Pres. Dr WALTER MUÑOZ CÉSPEDES; Sec.-Gen. ANA LOURDES GÖLCHER GONZÁLEZ.

Partido Liberación Nacional (PLN): Mata Redonda, 125 m oeste del Ministerio de Agricultura y Ganadería, Casa Liberacionista José Figueres Ferrer, Apdo 10.051, 1000 San José; tel. 232-5133; fax 231-4097; e-mail palina@sol.racsa.co.cr; internet www.pln.or.cr; f. 1952; national social democratic party; affiliated to the Socialist International; 500,000 mems; Pres. FRANCISCO ANTONIO PACHECO FERNÁNDEZ; Sec.-Gen. OSCAR NÚÑEZ CALVO (acting).

Partido Patriótico Nacional: Curridabat, Residencial Hacienda Vieja, de la entrada principal 200 m al sur y 200 m al este, Casa esquinera, Apdo 1.525, San José; tel. 272-0835; fax 253-5868; f. 1971; national party; Pres. DANIEL ENRIQUE REYNOLDS VARGAS; Sec. ERICK DELGADO LEÓN.

Partido Renovación Costarricense (PRC): Centro Educativo Instituto de Desarrollo de Inteligencia, Hatillo 1, Avda Villanea, Apdo 31, 1300 San José; tel. 254-3651; fax 252-3270; f. 1995; national party; Pres. GERARDO JUSTO OROZCO ALVAREZ; First Vice-Pres. RAFAEL MATAMORO MESÉN.

Partido Rescate Nacional: De la Iglesia Católica de San Pedro de Montes de Oca 150 m al oeste, contiguo al restaurante El Farolito, San José; tel. 234-9569; fax 225-0931; f. 1996; national party; Pres. CARLOS VARGAS SOLANO; Sec. BUENAVENTURA CARLOS VILLALOBOS BRENES.

Partido Unidad Social Cristiana (PUSC): Del Restaurante Kentucky Fried Chicken 75 metros al sur, frente a la Embajada de España, Paseo Colón, Apdo 10.095, 1000 San José; tel. 248-2470; fax 248-2179; f. 1983; national party; Pres. LORENA VÁSQUEZ BADILLA; Sec. JORGE EDUARDO SÁNCHEZ SIBAJA.

Partido Unión Agrícola Cartagines: Costado Este de la Iglesia, Cervantes, Frente al Estanco del CNP Alvarado, Apdo 534-4024, Cartago; tel. 534-4024; fax 534-8305; f. 1969; provincial party; Pres. JUAN GUILLERMO BRENES CASTILLO; Sec. CAROLINA MÉNDEZ ZAMORA.

Partido Unión General (PUGEN): Casa 256, Centro de Pérez Zeledón, Frente al Edif. de la Cámara de Comercio, Apdo 440, 8000, Pérez Zeledón; tel. 771-0524; fax 771-0737; e-mail pugen@apc.c.co.cr; f. 1980; national party; Pres. Dr CARLOS A. FERNÁNDEZ VEGA; Sec. MARÍA LOURDES RODRÍGUEZ MORALES.

Diplomatic Representation

EMBASSIES IN COSTA RICA

Argentina: Curridabat, Apdo 1963, 1000 San José; tel. 234-6520; fax 283-9983; e-mail embarg@racsa.co.cr; Ambassador JUAN JOSÉ ARCURI.

Belgium: Los Yoses, 4a entrada, 25 m sur, Apdo 3725, 1000 San José; tel. 225-6633; fax 225-0351; e-mail sanjose@diplobel.be; internet www.diplobel.org/costarica; Ambassador ROBERT VANREUSEL.

Bolivia: Barrio Rohrmoser 669, Apdo 84810, 1000 San José; tel. 296-3747; fax 232-7292; e-mail embocr@racsa.co.cr; internet www.embajada-bolivia-costarica.com; Ambassador SUSANA PEÑARANDA DE DEL GRANADO.

Brazil: Edif. Torre Mercedes, 6°, Apdo 10.132, 1000 San José; tel. 295-6875; fax 295-6874; e-mail embbrsjo@yahoo.com; Ambassador FRANCISCO SOARES ALVIN NETODE SOUZA DE GOMES.

Canada: Oficentro Ejecutivo La Sabana, Edif. 5, 3°, detrás de la Contraloría, Centro Colón, Apdo 351, 1007 San José; tel. 242-4400; fax 242-4410; e-mail sjcra@dfait.maeci.gc.ca; internet www.dfait-maeci.gc.ca/sanjose; Ambassador MARIO LAGUÉ.

Chile: De Autos Subarú en Los Yoses, 200 m norte, Barrio Dent, San Pedro de Montes de Oca, Apdo 10102-1000 San José; tel. 280-0037; fax 253-7016; e-mail politica@embchile.co.cr; Ambassador GERMÁN GUERRERO PAREZ.

China (Taiwan): 300 m al norte y 150 m al este de la Iglesia Sta Teresita, Barrio Escalante, Apdo 676, 2010 San José; tel. 224-8180; fax 253-8333; e-mail embajroc@racsa.co.cr; Ambassador TZU-DAN WU.

Colombia: Barrio Dent de Taco Bell, San Pedro, Apdo 3.154, 1000 San José; tel. 283-6871; fax 283-6818; e-mail emsanjose@minrelext.gov.co; Ambassador JULIO ANIBAL RIAÑO VELANDIA.

Czech Republic: 75 m oeste de la entrada principal del Colegio Humboldt, Apdo 12.041, 1000 San José; tel. 296-5671; fax 296-5595; e-mail sanjose@embassy.mzv.cz; internet www.mzv.cz; Ambassador (vacant).

Dominican Republic: McDonald's de Curridabat 400 sur, 90 m este, Apdo 4746-1000 San José; tel. 283-8103; fax 280-7604; e-mail embdominicanacr@racsa.co.cr; Ambassador ADONAIDA MEDINA RODRÍGUEZ.

Ecuador: Edif. de la esquina sureste del Museo Nacional, 125 m al este, Avda 2, Calles 19 y 21, Apdo 1.374, 1000 San José; tel. 232-1503; fax 232-2086; e-mail embecuar@sol.racsa.co.cr; Ambassador Dr JUAN LEORO ALMEIDA.

El Salvador: Paseo Colón, Calle 30, Avda 1, No 53, Apdo 1.378, 1000 San José; tel. 257-7855; fax 257-7683; e-mail embasacr@sol.racsa.co.cr; Ambassador HUGO ROBERTO CARRILLO CORLETO.

France: Carretera a Curridabat, del Indoor Club 200 m sur y 25 m oeste, Apdo 10.177, 1000 San José; tel. 234-4167; fax 234-4195; e-mail sjfrance@sol.racsa.co.cr; internet www.ambafrance-cr.org; Ambassador NORBERT CARRASCO-SAULNIER.

Germany: Barrio Rohrmoser, de la Casa de Oscar Arias 200 m norte, 75 m este, Apdo 4.017, 1000 San José; tel. 232-5533; fax 231-6403; e-mail info@embajada-alemana-costarica.org; internet www.embajada-alemana-costarica.org; Ambassador VOLKER FINK.

Guatemala: De Pops Curridabat 500 m sur y 30 m este, 2a Casa Izquierda, Apdo 328, 1000 San José; tel. 283-2290; fax 283-2290; e-mail embcostarica@minex.gob.gt; Ambassador JORGE MARIO GARCÍA LAGUARDIA.

Holy See: Urbanización Rohrmoser, Sabana Oeste, Centro Colón, Apdo 992, 1007 San José (Apostolic Nunciature); tel. 232-2128; fax 231-2557; e-mail nuapcr@racsa.co.cr; Apostolic Nuncio Most Rev. OSVALDO PADILLA (Titular Archbishop of Pia).

Honduras: Los Yoses sur, del ITAN hacia la Presidencia la primera entrada a la izquierda, 200 m norte y 100 m este, Apdo 2.239, 1000 San José; tel. 234-9502; fax 253-2209; e-mail emhondcr@sol.racsa.co.cr; Ambassador ARISTIDES MEJÍA CASTRO.

Israel: Edif. Centro Colón, 11°, Calle 38 Paseo Colón, Apdo 5147, 1000 San José; tel. 221-6011; fax 257-0867; e-mail ambassador.sec@sanjose.mfa.gov.il; internet sanjose.mfa.gov.il; Ambassador ALEX BEN ZVI.

Italy: Los Yoses, 5a entrada, Apdo 1.729, 1000 San José; tel. 224-6574; fax 225-8200; e-mail ambiter@sol.racsa.co.cr; internet www.ambitcr.com; Ambassador GIOACCHINO CARLO TRIZZINO.

Japan: Oficentro Ejecutivo La Sabana, Edif. 7, 3°, detrás de la Contraloría, Sabana Sur, Apdo 501, 1000 San José; tel. 232-1255; fax 231-3140; e-mail embjapon@sol.racsa.co.cr; internet www.cr.emb-japan.go.jp; Ambassador TADANORI INOMATA.

Korea, Republic: Oficentro Ejecutivo La Sabana, Edif. 2, 3º, Sabana Sur, Apdo 838, 1007 San José; tel. 220-3160; fax 220-3168; e-mail koreasec@sol.racsa.co.cr; Ambassador IM CHANG-SOON.

Mexico: Avda 7, No 1371, Apdo 10.107, 1000 San José; tel. 257-0633; fax 258-2437; e-mail embamex@racsa.co.cr; internet www.embajadademexico.com; Ambassador MARÍA CARMEN OÑATE MUÑOZ.

Netherlands: Los Yoses, Avda 8, Calles 35 y 37, Apdo 10.285, 1000 San José; tel. 296-1490; fax 296-2933; e-mail nethemb@racsa.co.cr; internet www.nethemb.or.cr; Ambassador W. G. J. M. WESSELS.

Nicaragua: Edif. Trianón, Avda Central 250, Barrio la California, Apdo 1.382, 1000 San José; tel. 222-2373; fax 221-5481; e-mail embanic@sol.racsa.co.cr; Ambassador Dr FIALLOS NAVARRO.

Panama: Del Centro Colón 275 m norte, Calle 38, Avda 5 y 7, Apdo 94, 1000 San José; tel. 257-3241; fax 257-4864; Ambassador VIRGINIA I. BURGOA.

Peru: Del Colegio de Igenieros y Arquitctos, 350m al norte, Urb. Freses, Curridabat, Apdo 4248, 1000 San José; tel. 225-9145; fax 253-0457; e-mail embaperu@amnet.co.cr; internet www.embaperu-costarica.rree.gob.pe; Ambassador ALBERTO GUTIÉRREZ LA MADRID.

Poland: De la Iglesia Santa Teresita 300 m este, 3307, Barrio Escalante, Apdo 664, 2010 San José; tel. 225-1481; fax 225-1592; e-mail embajpolonia1@racsa.co.cr; internet www.polonia-emb-cr.com/indes.php; Ambassador RYSZARD SCHNEPF.

Russia: Curridabat, Lomas de Ayarco Sur, de la carretera a Cartago, 1a entrada, 100 m sur, Apdo 6.340, 1000 San José; tel. 272-1021; fax 272-0142; e-mail emrusa@sol.racsa.co.cr; Ambassador VLADIMIR N. KAZIMIROV.

Spain: Calle 32, Paseo Colón, Avda 2, Apdo 10.150, 1000 San José; tel. 222-1933; fax 222-4180; e-mail embespcr@correo.mae.es; Ambassador JUAN JOSÉ URTASUN ERRO.

Switzerland: Paseo Colón, Centro Colón, Apdo 895, 1007 San José; tel. 221-4829; fax 255-2831; e-mail vertretung@sjc.rep.admin.ch; Ambassador GABRIELA NÜTZI.

United Kingdom: Edif. Centro Colón, 11º, Apdo 815, 1007 San José; tel. 258-2025; fax 233-9938; e-mail britemb@sol.racsa.co.cr; internet www.britishembassycr.com; Ambassador GEORGINA BUTLER.

Uruguay: Avda 14, Calles 35 y 37, Apdo 3.448, 1000 San José; tel. 253-2755; fax 234-9909; e-mail embajrou@sol.racsa.co.cr; Ambassador ANTONIO RICARDO MORELL BORDOLI.

USA: Calle 120 Avda 0, Pavas, Apdo 920, 1200 San José; tel. 519-2000; fax 220-2305; e-mail sanjose@usembassy.or.cr; internet sanjose.usembassy.gov; Chargé d'affaires a.i. DOUGLAS M. BARNES.

Venezuela: Avda Central, Los Yoses, 5a entrada, Apdo 10.230, 1000 San José; tel. 225-8810; fax 253-1335; e-mail embaven@racsa.co.cr; Ambassador NORA URIBE TRUJILLO.

Judicial System

Ultimate judicial power is vested in the Supreme Court, the justices of which are elected by the Assembly for a term of eight years, and are automatically re-elected for an equal period, unless the Assembly decides to the contrary by a two-thirds vote. The Supreme Court justices sit in four courts, the First Court (civil, administrative, agrarian and commercial matters), the Second Court (employment and family), the Third Court (penal) and the Constitutional Court.

There are, in addition, appellate courts, criminal courts, civil courts and special courts. The jury system is not used. Judges of the lower courts are appointed by the Supreme Court's administrative body, the Supreme Council. The Supreme Council's five members are elected by the Supreme Court.

The Supreme Court
Barrio González Lahmann Avdas 6–8, Calles 17–19, Circuito Judicial 1, San José; tel. 295-3000; fax 257-0801.

President of the Supreme Court: LUIS PAULINO MORA MORA.

Supreme Council
Members: LUIS PAULINO MORA MORA, ALFONSO CHAVES RAMÍREZ, MIRIAM ANCHÍA PANIAGUA, MILENA CONEJO AGUILAR, LUPITA CHAVES CERVANTES, SILVIA NAVARRO ROMANINI, ALFREDO JONES LEÓN.

Justices of the First Court: Dr ANABELLE LEÓN FEOLI, Dr OSCAR GONZÁLEZ CAMACHO, Dr ROMÁN SOLÍS ZELAYA, CARMENMARÍA ESCOTO FERNÁNDEZ, LUIS GUILLERMO RIVAS LOÁICIGA.

Justices of the Second Court: ORLANDO AGUIRRE GÓMEZ, Dr BERNARDO VAN DER LAAT ECHEVERRÍA, ZARELA VILLANUEVA MONGE, JULIA VARELA ARAYA, Dr ROLANDO VEGA ROBERT.

Justices of the Third Court: Dr DANIEL GONZÁLEZ ALVAREZ, JOSÉ MANUEL ARROYO GUTIÉRREZ, JESÚS RAMÍREZ QUIRÓS, RODRIGO CASTRO MONGE, ALFONSO CHAVES RAMÍREZ.

Justices of the Constitutional Court: Dr LUIS FERNANDO SOLANO CARRERA, ANA VIRGINIA CALZADA MIRANDA, CARLOS ARGUEDAS RAMÍREZ, Dr GILBERT ARMIJO SANCHOL, ADRIÁN VARGAS BENAVIDES, LUIS PAULINO MORA MORA, ERNESTO JINESTA LOBO.

Religion

Under the Constitution, all forms of worship are tolerated. Roman Catholicism is the official religion of the country. Various Protestant churches are also represented.

CHRISTIANITY

The Roman Catholic Church
Costa Rica comprises one archdiocese and six dioceses. At 31 December 2002 Roman Catholics represented some 85% of the total population.

Bishops' Conference
Conferencia Episcopal de Costa Rica, Apdo 7288, 1000 San José; tel. 258-3053; fax 221-66-62; e-mail seccecor@racsa.co.cr.

f. 1977; Pres. Most Rev. JOSÉ FRANCISCO ULLOA ROJAS.

Archbishop of San José de Costa Rica: Most Rev. HUGO BARRANTES UREÑA, Arzobispado, Apdo 497, 1000 San José; tel. 258-1015; fax 221-2427; e-mail curiam@racsa.co.cr.

The Anglican Communion
Costa Rica comprises one of the five dioceses of the Iglesia Anglicana de la Región Central de América.

Bishop of Costa Rica: Rt Rev. HECTOR MONTERROSO, Apdo 10520, 1000 San José; tel. 225-0790; fax 253-8331; e-mail iarca@amnet.co.cr.

Other Churches

Federación de Asociaciones Bautistas de Costa Rica: Apdo 1.631, 2100 Guadalupe; tel. 253-5820; fax 253-4723; e-mail coven@racsa.co.cr; internet www.fabcr.org; f. 1946; represents Baptist churches; Pres. JOSÉ SOTO VILLEGAS.

Iglesia Evangélica Luterana de Costa Rica (Evangelical Lutheran Church of Costa Rica): Apdo 1512, Pavas, 1200 San José; tel. and fax 231-3345; e-mail evkirche@racsa.co.cr; internet www.ielcor.org; f. 1955; 600 mems; Pres. Rev. RENÉ LAMMER.

Iglesia Evangélica Metodista de Costa Rica (Evangelical Methodist Church of Costa Rica): Apdo 5481, 1000 San José; tel. 236-2171; fax 236-5921; e-mail semlfp@racsa.co.cr; autonomous since 1973; affiliated to the United Methodist Church; 6,000 mems; Pres. Bishop LUIS F. PALOMO.

BAHÁ'Í FAITH

Bahá'í Information Centre: Apdo 553, 1150 San José; tel. 231-0647; fax 296-1033; adherents resident in 242 localities.

National Spiritual Assembly of the Bahá'ís of Costa Rica: Apdo 553, 1150 La Uruca; tel. 231-0647; fax 296-1033; e-mail bahaiscr@sol.racsa.co.cr.

The Press

DAILIES

Al Día: Llorente de Tibás, Apdo 10.138, 1000, San José; tel. 247-4640; fax 247-4665; e-mail aldia@nacion.co.cr; internet www.aldia.co.cr; f. 1992; morning; independent; Dir ARMANDO M. GONZÁLEZ RODICIO; circ. 60,000.

Boletín Judicial: La Uruca, Apdo 5.024, San José; tel. 231-5222; internet www.boletinjudicial.go.cr; f. 1878; journal of the judiciary; Dir ISAÍAS CASTRO VARGAS; circ. 2,500.

Diario Extra: Calle 4, Avda 4, Apdo 177, 1009 San José; tel. 223-9505; fax 223-5921; internet www.diarioextra.com; f. 1978; morning; independent; Dir WILLIAM GÓMEZ VARGAS; circ. 120,000.

La Gaceta: La Uruca, Apdo 5.024, San José; tel. 231-5222; internet www.gaceta.go.cr; f. 1878; official gazette; Dir ISAÍAS CASTRO VARGAS; circ. 5,300.

El Heraldo: 400 m al este de las oficinas centrales, Apdo 1.500, San José; tel. 222-6665; fax 222-3039; e-mail info@elheraldo.net; internet www.elheraldo.net; f. 1994; morning; independent; Dir ERWIN KNOHR R; circ. 30,000.

La Nación: Llorente de Tibás, Apdo 10.138, 1000 San José; tel. 247-4747; fax 247-5002; e-mail cacortes@nacion.com; internet www .nacion.com; f. 1946; morning; independent; Pres. MANUEL F. JIMÉNEZ ECHEVERRÍA; circ. 120,000.

La Prensa Libre: Calle 4, Avda 4, Apdo 177.1009, San José; tel. 223-6666; fax 233-6831; e-mail plibre@prensalibre.co.cr; internet www.prensalibre.co.cr; f. 1889; evening; independent; Dir ANDRÉS BORRASÉ SANOU; circ. 56,000.

La República: Barrio Tournón, Guadalupe, Apdo 2130.1000, San José; tel. 223-0266; fax 257-0401; e-mail info@larepublica.co.cr; internet larepublica.terra.co.cr; f. 1950; reorganized 1967; morning; independent; Dir FRED BLASER; circ. 61,000.

PERIODICALS

Abanico: Calle 4, Avda 4, Apdo 177.1009, San José; tel. 223-6666; fax 223-4671; weekly supplement of *La Prensa Libre*; women's interests; Editor MARÍA DEL CARMEN POZO C; circ. 50,000.

Acta Médica Costarricense: Colegio de Médicos y Cirujanos de Costa Rica, Sabana Sur, Apdo 548-1000, San José; tel. 232-3433; fax 232-2406; e-mail medicos@racsa.co.cr; internet www.medicos.sa.cr; f. 1957; journal of the Colegio de Médicos; 4 issues per year; Publr Dr MARÍA PAZ LEÓN BRATTI; Editor Dr CARLOS SALAZAR VARGAS; circ. 5,000.

El Cafetalero: Calle 1, Avdas 18 y 20, Apdo 37, 1000 San José; tel. 222-6411; fax 223-6025; e-mail evilla@icafe.go.cr; f. 1964 as Noticiero del Café; changed name in 2000; bi-monthly; coffee journal; owned by the Instituto del Café de Costa Rica; Editor ERNESTO VILLALOBOS; circ. 10,000.

Contrapunto: La Uruca, Apdo 7, 1980 San José; tel. 231-3333; f. 1978; fortnightly; publication of Sistema Nacional de Radio y Televisión; Dir FABIO MUÑOZ CAMPOS; circ. 10,000.

Eco Católico: Calle 22, Avdas 3 y 5, Apdo 1.064, San José; tel. 222-6156; fax 256-0407; e-mail ecocatolico@rasca.co.cr; f. 1931; Catholic weekly; Dir ARMANDO ALFARO; circ. 20,000.

Mujer y Hogar: San José; f. 1943; weekly; women's journal; Editor and Gen. Man. CARMEN CORNEJO MÉNDEZ; circ. 15,000.

Perfil: Llorente de Tibás, Apdo 1.517, 1100 San José; tel. 247-4345; fax 247-5110; e-mail perfil@nacion.co.cr; f. 1984; fortnightly; women's interest; Dir CAROLINA CARAZO BARRANTES; circ. 16,000.

Polémica: San José; tel. 233-3964; f. 1981; every 4 months; left-wing; Dir GABRIEL AGUILERA PERALTA.

Rumbo: Llorente de Tibás, Apdo 10.138, 1000 San José; tel. 240-4848; fax 240-6480; f. 1984; weekly; general; Dir ROXANA ZÚÑIGA; circ. 15,000.

San José News: Apdo 7, 2730 San José; 2 a week; Dir CHRISTIAN RODRÍGUEZ.

Semanario Libertad: Calle 4, Avdas 8 y 10, Apdo 6.613, 1000 San José; tel. 225-9024; fax 253-2628; f. 1962; weekly; organ of the Partido del Pueblo Costarricense; Dir RODOLFO ULLOA B; Editor JOSÉ A. ZÚÑIGA; circ. 10,000.

Semanario Universidad: San José; tel. 207-5355; fax 207-4774; e-mail semana@cariari.ucr.ac.cr; internet cariari.ucr.ac.cr; f. 1970; weekly; general; Dir THAIS AGUILAR; circ. 15,000.

The Tico Times: Calle 15, Avda 8, Apdo 4.632, 1000 San José; tel. 258-1558; fax 223-6378; e-mail info@ticotimes.net; internet www .ticotimes.net; f. 1956; weekly; in English; Dir DERY DYER; circ. 15,210.

Tiempos de Costa Rica: 100m sur de Ferreterías El Mar, San Pedro, San José; tel. 280-2332; fax 280-6840; e-mail admin@tdm .com; internet www.tdm.com; f. 1996; Costa Rican edition of the international *Tiempos de Mundo*; Dir WILLIAM COOK.

PRESS ASSOCIATIONS

Colegio de Periodistas de Costa Rica: Sabana Este, Calle 42, Avda 4, Apdo 5.416, San José; tel. 233-5850; fax 223-8669; e-mail ejecutiva@colegiodeperiodistas.org; f. 1969; 1,447 mems; Pres. RAÚL SILESKY.

Sindicato Nacional de Periodistas: Sabana Este, Calle 42, Avda 4, Apdo 5.416, San José; tel. 222-7589; f. 1970; 200 mems; Sec.-Gen. SERGIO FERNANDEZ.

FOREIGN NEWS BUREAUX

ACAN-EFE (Central America): Costado Sur, Casa Matute Gómez, Casa 1912, Apdo 84.930, San José; tel. 222-6785; fax 233-7681; e-mail acanefe@sol.racsa.co.cr; Correspondent WILFREDO CHACÓN SERRANO.

Agence France-Presse (France): Barrio Escalante, Del Farolito 175m al Este, Casa 3361, Apdo 5.276, San José; tel. 280-1773; fax 280-1755; Correspondent DOMINIQUE PETTIT.

Agenzia Nazionale Stampa Associata (ANSA) (Italy): c/o Diario La República, Barrio Tournón, Guadalupe, Apdo 545, 1200 San José; tel. 231-1140; fax 231-1140; internet www.ansa.it; Correspondent LUIS CARTÍN S.

Deutsche Presse-Agentur (dpa) (Germany): Edif. 152, 3°, Calle 11, Avdas 1 y 3, Apdo 7.156, San José; tel. 233-0604; fax 233-0604; Correspondent ERNESTO RAMÍREZ.

Informatsionnoye Telegrafnoye Agentstvo Rossii—Telegrafnoye Agentstvo Suverennykh Stran (ITAR—TASS) (Russia): De la Casa Italia 1,000 m este, 50 m norte, Casa 675, Apdo 1.011, San José; tel. 224-1560; Correspondent ENRIQUE MORA.

Prensa Latina (Cuba): Avda 11, No 3185, Calles 31 y 33, Barrio Escalante (de la parrillada 25 m oeste), San José; tel. 253-1457; Correspondent FRANCISCO A. URIZARRI TAMAYO.

Rossiyskoye Informatsionnoye Agentstvo—Novosti (RIA—Novosti) (Russia): De la Casa Italiana 100 m este, 50 m norte, San José; tel. 224-1560; internet www.rian.ru.

Xinhua (New China) News Agency (People's Republic of China): Apdo 4.774, San José; tel. 231-3497; Correspondent XU BIHUA.

Publishers

Alef Editores: Apdo 146, 1017 San José 2000; tel. 255-0202; fax 222-7878; e-mail alefreading@racsa.co.cr; Dir JOSÉ SUCCAR.

Ediciones Farben, SA: De la Sylvania 500 oeste, Condominio Industrial Pavas 19, Apdo 592-1200 Pavas; tel. 290-7125; fax 290-0061; e-mail fvanderlaat@farben.co.cr; internet www.farben.co.cr; Dir FERNANDO VANDERLAAT.

Editorial Caribe: Apdo 1.307, San José; tel. 222-7244; e-mail info@editorialcaribe.com; internet www.editorialcaribe.com; f. 1949; division of Thomas Nelson Publrs; religious textbooks; Dir JOHN STROWEL.

Editorial Costa Rica: Costado oeste del cementerio, Guadalupe de Goicoechea, Apdo 10.010, San José; tel. 255-2323; fax 253-5091; e-mail editocr@racsa.co.cr; internet www.editorialcostarica.com; f. 1959; government-owned; cultural; Gen. Man. HABIB SUCCAR GUZMÁN.

Editorial Fernández Arce: 50 este de Sterling Products, la Paulina de Montes de Oca, Apdo 2.410, 1000 San José; tel. 224-5201; fax 225-6109; f. 1967; textbooks for primary, secondary and university education; Dir Dr MARIO FERNÁNDEZ LOBO.

Editorial de la Universidad Autónoma de Centro América (UACA): Apdo 7.637, 1000 San José; tel. 234-0701; fax 224-0391; e-mail info@uaca.ac.cr; f. 1981; Editor GUILLERMO MALAVASSI.

Editorial de la Universidad Estatal a Distancia (EUNED): Apdo 474, 2050 San Pedro; tel. 253-2121; fax 234-9138; e-mail editoria@uned.ac.cr; internet www.uned.ac.cr; f. 1979; Dir RENÉ MUIÑOS.

Editorial Universitaria Centroamericana (EDUCA): Ciudad Universitaria Rodrigo Facio, San Pedro, Montes de Oca, Apdo 64, 2060 San Pedro; tel. 224-3727; fax 253-9141; e-mail educa@sp.cusa .ac.cr; f. 1969; organ of the CSUCA; science, literature, philosophy; Dir ANITA DE FORMOSO.

Librería Lehmann, Imprenta y Litografía, Ltda: Calles 1 y 3, Avda Central, Apdo 10011, San José; tel. 524-0000; fax 233-0713; e-mail servicio@librerialehman.com; internet www.librerialehmann .com; f. 1896; general fiction, educational, textbooks; Man. Dir ANTONIO LEHMANN STRUVE.

Imprenta Nacional: San José; tel. 296-9570; Dir Gen. BIENVENIDO VENEGAS PORRAS.

Trejos Hermanos Sucesores, SA: Curridabat, Apdo 10.096, San José; tel. 224-2411; e-mail henry@trejoshnos.com; f. 1912; general and reference; Man. HENRY CHAMBERLAIN.

PUBLISHING ASSOCIATION

Cámara Costarricense del Libro: Paseo de los Estudiantes, Apdo 1571, 1002 San José; tel. 225-1363; fax 252-4297; e-mail ccl@libroscr .com; internet www.libroscr.com; f. 1978; Pres. OSCAR CASTILLO.

Broadcasting and Communications

TELECOMMUNICATIONS

In 2002 there were plans to expand and modernize the telecommunications sector. The French company Alcatel was to oversee the project.

Cámara Costarricense de Telecomunicaciones: Edif. Centro Colón, Apdo 591, 1007 San José; tel. and fax 255-3422; Pres. EVITA ARGUEDAS MAKLOUF.

Cámara Nacional de Medios de Comunicación Colectiva (CANAMECC): San José; tel. 222-4820; f. 1954; Pres. ANDRÉS QUINTANA CAVALLINI.

Instituto Costarricense de Electricidad (ICE): govt agency for power and telecommunications (see Trade and Industry: Utilities).

Radiográfica Costarricense, SA (RACSA): Avda 5, Calle 1, Frente al Edif. Numar, Apdo 54, 1000 San José; tel. 287-0087; fax 287-0379; e-mail mcruz@sol.racsa.co.cr; internet www.racsa.co.cr; f. 1921; state telecommunications co., owned by ICE; Dir-Gen. MARCO A. CRUZ MIRANDA.

RADIO

Asociación Costarricense de Información y Cultura (ACIC): Apdo 365, 1009 San José; f. 1983; independent body; controls private radio stations; Pres. JUAN FEDERICO MONTEALEGRE MARTÍN.

Cámara Nacional de Radio (CANARA): Paseo de los Estudiantes, Apdo 1.583, 1002 San José; tel. 233-1845; fax 255-4483; e-mail canara@sol.racsa.co.cr; internet www.canara.org; f. 1947; Exec. Dir LAURA ARRIETA VARGAS.

Control Nacional de Radio (CNR): Dirección Nacional de Comunicaciones, Ministerio de Gobernación y Policía, Apdo 10.006, 1000 San José; tel. 221-0992; fax 283-0741; e-mail cnradio@racsa.co.cr; f. 1954; governmental supervisory department; Dir MELVIN MURILLO ALVAREZ.

Non-commercial

Faro del Caribe: Apdo 2.710, 1000 San José; tel. 226-2573; fax 227-1725; e-mail juntadirectiva@farodelcaribe.org; internet www.farodelcaribe.org; f. 1948; religious and cultural programmes in Spanish and English; Man. GEOVANNY CALDERÓN CASTRO.

Radio Costa Rica: De Autos Bohío, en barrio Córdoba, 100 m sur y 100 m este, Apdo 6.462, 1000 San José; tel. 227-4690; fax 231-3408; e-mail canalcr@sol.racsa.co.cr; f. 1988; broadcasts Voice of America news bulletins (in Spanish) and locally-produced educational and entertainment programmes; Gen. Man. ANTONIO ALEXANDRE GARCÍA.

Radio Fides: Avda 4, Curia Metropolitana, Apdo 5.079, 1000 San José; tel. 258-1415; fax 233-2387; e-mail emiliom@radiofides.co.cr; internet www.radiofides.co.cr; f. 1952; Roman Catholic station; Dir EMILIO OTÁROLA.

Radio Nacional: 1 km oeste del Parque Nacional de Diversiones, La Uruca, Apdo 7, 1980 San José; tel. 231-7983; fax 220-0070; e-mail sinart@sol.racsa.co.cr; f. 1978; Dir RODOLFO RODRÍGUEZ.

Radio Santa Clara: Santa Clara, San Carlos, Apdo 221, Ciudad Quesada, Alajuela; tel. and fax 460-6666; e-mail radio@radiosantaclara.org; internet www.radiosantaclara.org; f. 1984; Roman Catholic station; Dir Rev. MARCO A. SOLÍS V.

Radio Universidad: Ciudad Universitaria Rodrigo Facio, San Pedro, Montes de Oca, Apdo 2.060, 1000 San José; tel. 207-5356; fax 207-5459; e-mail radioucr@cariari.ucr.ac.cr; internet cariari.ucr.ac.cr/~radioucr; f. 1949; classical music; Dir CARLOS MORALES.

Commercial

There are about 40 commercial radio stations, including:

89 Ya!: Costado sur del Parque Desamparados, Apdo 301, San José; tel. 259-3657; fax 250-2376; f. 1995; Dir ALEXANDER RAMOS RODRÍGUEZ.

Cadena de Emisoras Columbia: Apdo 1.708, San José; tel. 224-0808; fax 225-9275; e-mail columbia@columbia.co.cr; internet www.columbia.co.cr; operates Radio Columbia, Radio Dos, Radio 955 Jazz; Dir C. ARNOLDO ALFARO CHAVARRA.

Cadena Musical: Apdo 854, 1000, San José; tel. 257-2789; fax 233-9975; internet www.radiomusical.com; f. 1954; operates Radio Musical, Radio Bomba; Gen. Man. JORGE JAVIER CASTRO.

Grupo Centro: Apdo 6.133, San José; tel. 240-7591; fax 236-3672; f. 1971; operates Radio Centro 96.3 FM, Radio 820 AM, Televisora Guanacasteca Channels 16 and 28; Dir ROBERTO HERNÁNDEZ RAMÍREZ.

Radio Chorotega: Apdo 92, 5175 Santa Cruz de Guanacaste; tel. and fax 680-0447; f. 1983; Roman Catholic station; Dir Rev. EMILIO MONTES DE OCA CORDERO.

Radio Emaús: San Vito, Coto Brus; tel. and fax 773-3101; fax 773-4035; e-mail radioemaus@racsa.co.cr; f. 1962; Roman Catholic station; religious programmes; Dir Rev. MIGUEL ANGEL BERGANZA.

Radio Monumental: Avda Central y 2, Calle 2, Apdo 800, 1000 San José; tel. 222-0000; fax 222-8237; e-mail radio@monumental.co.cr; internet www.monumental.co.cr; f. 1929; all news station; Gen. Man. TERESA MARÍA CHÁVES ZAMORA.

Radio Sinaí: Apdo 262, 8000 San Isidro de El General; tel. 771-4367; fax 771-0598; f. 1957; Roman Catholic station; Dir Mgr ALVARO COTO OROZCO.

TELEVISION

Government-owned

Sistema Nacional de Radio y Televisión Cultural (SINART): 1 km al oeste del Parque Nacional de Diversiones La Uruca, Apdo 7, 1980 San José; tel. 231-3333; fax 231-6604; e-mail sinart@racsa.co.cr; f. 1977; cultural; Dir-Gen. GUIDO SÁENZ GONZÁLEZ.

Commercial

Alphavisión (Canal 19): Detrás Iglesia de Santa María y Griega, Carretera a Desamparados, Apdo 1.490, San José; tel. 226-9333; fax 226-9095; f. 1987; Gen. Man. CECILIA RAMÍREZ.

Canal 2: Apdo 1.585, Centro Colón, San José; tel. 220-0962; fax 290-6900; e-mail atena@conexionnetwork.com; internet conexionnetwork.com; f. 1983; Pres. ALEX TENA.

Canal 54: De Plaza Mayot, en Rohrmoser, 50 m oeste, 50 m sur, Apdo 640, San José; tel. 286-3344; fax 231-3408; e-mail canalcr@sol.racsa.co.cr; f. 1996; Pres. ANTONIO ALEXANDRE GARCÍA.

Multivisión de Costa Rica, Ltda (Canal 9): 150 m oeste del Centro Comercial de Guadalupe, Apdo 4.666, 1000 San José; tel. 233-4444; fax 221-1734; f. 1961; operates Radio Sistema Universal A.M. (f. 1956), Channel 9 (f. 1962), and FM (f. 1980); sold Channel 4 (f. 1964) to Repretel in 2000; Gen. Man. ARNOLD VARGAS.

Televisora de Costa Rica (Canal 7), SA (Teletica): Costado oeste Estadio Nacional, Apdo 3.876, San José; tel. 232-2222; fax 231-6258; e-mail info@teletica.com; internet www.teletica.com; f. 1960; operates Channel 7; Pres. OLGA COZZA DE PICADO; Gen. Man. RENÉ PICADO COZZA.

Repretel (Canales 4, 6 y 11): Apdo 2860, 1000 San José; tel. 290-6665; fax 232-4203; e-mail info@Repretel.com; internet www.repretel.com.

Finance

(cap. = capital; p.u. = paid up; res = reserves; dep. = deposits; m. = million; brs = branches; amounts in colones, unless otherwise indicated)

BANKING

Banco Central de Costa Rica: Avdas Central y Primera, Calles 2 y 4, Apdo 10.058, 1000 San José; tel. 243-3333; fax 243-4559; internet www.bccr.fi.cr; f. 1950; total assets 944,168.9m. (2003); scheduled for privatization; Pres. Dr FRANCISCO DE PAULA GUTIÉRREZ GUTIÉRREZ; Man. ROY GONZÁLEZ.

State-owned Banks

Banco de Costa Rica: Avdas Central y 2da, Calles 4 y 6, Apdo 10035, 1000 San José; tel. 287-9000; fax 255-0221; e-mail bancobcr@bancobcr.com; internet www.bancobcr.com; f. 1877; responsible for industry; cap. 32,537.4m., res 57,679.8m., dep.554,813.3m. (2003); Pres. MARIANO GUARDIA CAÑAS; Gen. Man. MARIO BARRENECHEA; 94 brs.

Banco Nacional de Costa Rica: Avda 1ra, Calle 2A, Apdo 10015, 1000 San José; tel. 221-2223; fax 2223-8054; e-mail bncr@bncr.fi.cr; internet www.bncr.fi.cr; f. 1914; responsible for the agricultural sector; cap. 30,042.7m., res 33,237.9m., dep. 873,049.6m. (2003); Pres. RODOLFO BRENES GÓMEZ; Gen. Man. GUILLERMO HEYDEN QUINTERO; 140 brs and agencies.

Banco Popular y de Desarrollo Comunal: Calle 1, Avda 2, Apdo 10190, San José; tel. 257-5797; fax 255-1966; e-mail relacionespublicas@bp.fi.cr; internet www.bancopopular.fi.cr; f. 1969; cap. 24,991.2m. (2003); Pres. FLORIBETH LÓPEZ UGALDE; Vice Pres. HILDA VALVERDE AVALOS.

Private Banks

Banco Banex SA: Barrio Tournón, Diagonal a Ulacit, Apdo 7983, 1000 San José; tel. 257-0522; fax 257-5967; e-mail interna@banex.co.cr; internet www.banex.co.cr; f. 1981 as Banco Agroindustrial y de Exportaciones, SA; adopted present name 1987; incorporated Banco

Metropolitano in May 2001 and Banco Bancrecen in December 2002; cap. 125,892.9m., res 2,640.7m., dep. 190,808.9m. (Dec. 2003); Pres. ALBERTO VALLARINO; Gen. Man. FEDERICO ALBERT; 36 brs.

Banco Bantec, SA: Calle Principalla Uruca, Antigua Cana, Apdo 1164, 1000 San José; tel. 290-8585; fax 290-2939; e-mail consorcio@ bantec.com.

Banco BCT, SA: Calle Central No. 160, Apdo 7698, San José; tel. 257-6010; fax 222-3706; e-mail banco@bct.fi.cr; f. 1984; total assets 13,794m. (1999); merged with Banco del Comercio, SA in 2000; Pres. ANTONIO BURGUÉS; Gen. Man. LEONEL BARUCH.

Banco de Crédito Centroamericano, SA (Bancentro): De la Rotonda la Bandera, Barrio Escalante, 50 m oeste, Apdo 5099, 1000 San José; tel. 280-5555; fax 280-5090; e-mail info@lafise.fi.cr; f. 1974; owned by Grupo Lafise; Pres. ROBERTO J. ZAMORA LLANES; Gen. Man CARLOS A. BRICEÑO RÍOS.

Banco Cuscatlan de Costa Rica, SA: De La Rotonda Juan Pablo II, 150 m norte, Canton Central, La Uruca, Apdo 6531, 1000 San José; tel. 299-0299; fax 220-0297; e-mail cuscatlan@cuscatlancr.com; internet www.bancocuscatlan.com; f. 1984 as Banco de Fomento Agrícola; changed name to Banco BFA in 1994; changed name to above in 2000; cap. 3,865.7m., res 750.8m., dep. 86,671.3m. (Dec. 2003); Pres. ERNESTO ROHRMOSER; Gen. Man. ALVARO ENRIQUE SABORIO LEGERS.

Banco Elca, SA: Del Centro Colón, 200 m norte, Paseo Colón, Apdo 1112, 1000 San José; tel. 258-3355; fax 233-8383; e-mail banelca@sol .racsa.co.cr; internet www.bancoelca.fi.cr; f. 1985 as Banco de la Industria; changed name to above in 2000; Pres. ROBERTO ALVARADO MOYA; Gen. Man. CARLOS ALVARADO MOYA.

Banco Improsa, SA: 2985 Calle 29 y 31, Avda 5, Carmen, San José; tel. 257-0689; fax 223-7319; e-mail banimpro@sol.racsa.co.cr.

Banco Interfin, SA: Calle 3, Avdas 2 y 4, Apdo 6899, San José; tel. 210-4000; fax 210–4510; e-mail webmaster@interfin.fi.cr; f. 1982; total assets 11,139m. (1999); Pres. Ing. LUIS LUKOWIECKI; Gen. Man. Dr LUIS LIBERMAN.

Banco Promérica, SA: Edif. Promérica, Sabana oeste canal 7, Mata Redonda, Apdo 1.289, 1200 San José; tel. 220-3090; fax 232-5727; e-mail solucion@promerica.fi.cr; internet www.promerica.fi.cr; 21 brs.

Banco BAC San José, SA: Calle Central, Avdas 3 y 5, Apdo 5.445, 1000 San José; tel. 295-9595; fax 222-7103; e-mail info@ bancosanjose.fi.cr; internet www.bacsanjose.com; f. 1968; fmrly Bank of America, SA; total assets US $505m. (2003); Pres. ERNESTO CASTEGNARO ODIO; Vice-Pres. GERARDO CORRALES BRENES.

Banco Uno, SA: Calle 28, Paseo Colón, Merced, Apdo 5884, 1000 San José; tel. 257-1344; fax 257-2215; e-mail bunocr@grupo-uno .com; internet www.bancouno.fi.cr.

Citibank (Costa Rica), SA: Edif. 3, Blvd Camino Real, Apdo 10277, San José; tel. 201-0800; fax 296-1496; e-mail citibab@sol .racsa.co.cr.

Scotiabank Costa Rica: Avda Primera, Calles Central y 2, Apdo 5395, 1000, San José; tel. 287-8700; fax 255-3076; e-mail scotiagg@ sol.racsa.co.cr; f. 1995; Gen. Man. BRIAN W. BRADY; 11 brs.

Banking Association

Asociación Bancaria Costarricense: San José; tel. 253-2889; fax 225-0987; e-mail abc@abc.fi.cr; internet www.abc.fi.cr; Pres. JORGE MONGE.

STOCK EXCHANGE

Bolsa Nacional de Valores, SA: Edif. Cartagena, 4°, Calle Central, Avda Primera, Santa Ana, Apdo 6.155, 1000 San José; tel. 204-4848; fax 204-4802; e-mail bnv@bnv.co.cr; internet www.bnv.co.cr; f. 1976; Chair. RODRIGO ARIAS SÁNCHEZ; CEO FEDERICO CARRILLO ZÜRCHER.

INSURANCE

In 1998 the Legislative Assembly approved legislative reform effectively terminating the state monopoly of all insurance activities.

Caja Costarricense de Seguro Social: Apdo 10.105, San José; tel. 257-9122; fax 222-1217; internet www.info.ccss.sa.cr; accident and health insurance, state-owned; Exec. Pres. Dr ELISEO VARGAS GARCÍA W.

Instituto Nacional de Seguros: Calles 9 y 9 bis, Avda 7, Apdo 10.061, 1000 San José; tel. 223-5800; fax 255-3381; internet www.ins .go.cr; f. 1924; administers the state monopoly of insurance; services of foreign insurance companies may be used only by authorization of the Ministry of the Economy, Industry and Commerce, and only after the Instituto has certified that it will not accept the risk; Exec. Pres. JORGE A. HERNÁNDEZ CASTAÑEDA; Gen. Man. ANA ROSS SALAZAR.

Trade and Industry

GOVERNMENT AGENCIES

Instituto Nacional de Vivienda y Urbanismo (INVU): Apdo 2.534, San José; tel. 221-5266; fax 223-4006; housing and town planning institute; Exec. Pres. ÁNGELO ALTAMURA; Gen. Man. PEDRO HERNÁNDEZ RUIZ.

Ministry of Planning and Economic Policy: See The Government (Ministries).

Promotora del Comercio Exterior de Costa Rica (PRO-COMER): Calle 40, Avdas Central y 3, Centro Colón, Apdo 1.278, 1007 San José; tel. 256-7111; fax 233-4655; e-mail info@procomer .com; internet www.procomer.com; f. 1968 to improve international competitiveness by providing services aimed at increasing, diversifying and expediting international trade.

DEVELOPMENT ORGANIZATIONS

Cámara de Azucareros: Calle 3, Avda Fernández Güell, Apdo 1.577, 1000 San José; tel. 221-2103; fax 222-1358; e-mail crazucar@ racsa.co.cr; f. 1949; sugar growers; Pres. RODRIGO ARIAS SÁNCHEZ.

Cámara Nacional de Bananeros: Edif. Urcha, 3°, Calle 11, Avda 6, Apdo 10.273, 1000 San José; tel. 222-7891; fax 233-1268; f. 1967; banana growers; Pres. JOSÉ ALVARO SANDOVAL; Exec. Dir JORGE MADRIGAL.

Cámara Nacional de Cafetaleros: Condominio Oroki 4D, La Uruca, Apdo 1.310, San José; tel. and fax 296-8334; e-mail camcafe@ racsa.co.cr; f. 1948; 70 mems; coffee millers and growers; Pres. RONALD PETER SEEVERS; Exec. Dir GABRIELA LOBO H.

Cámara Nacional de Ganaderos: Edif. Ilifilán, 4°, Calles 4 y 6, Avda Central, Apdo 5.539, 1000 San José; tel. 222-1652; cattle farmers; Pres. Ing. ALBERTO JOSÉ AMADOR ZAMORA.

Cámara Nacional de Artesanía y Pequeña Industria de Costa Rica (CANAPI): Calle 17, Avda 10, detrás estatua de San Martín, Apdo 1.783 Goicoechea, 2100 San José; tel. 223-2763; fax 255-4873; e-mail canapi@sol.racsa.co.cr; f. 1963; development, marketing and export of small-scale industries and handicrafts; Pres. and Exec. Dir RODRIGO GONZÁLEZ.

Corporación Bananera Nacional: Apdo 6504, 1000 San José; tel. 202-4700; fax 234-9421; e-mail corbana@racsa.co.cr; internet www .corbana.co.cr.

Costa Rican Investment and Development Board (CINDE): Edif. Los Balcones, Plaza Roble, 4°, Guachipelin, Ezcazú; tel. 201-2800; fax 201-2867; e-mail invest@cinde.org; internet www.cinde.or .cr; f. 1983; coalition for development of initiatives to attract foreign investment for production and export of new products; Chair. EMILIO BRUCE; CEO ENRIQUE EGLOFF.

Instituto del Café de Costa Rica: Calle 1, Avdas 18 y 20, Apdo 37, 1000 San José; tel. 222-6411; fax 222-2838; internet www.icafe.go.cr; e-mail achacon@icafe.go.cr; f. 1933 to develop the coffee industry, to control production and to regulate marketing; Pres. ALFREDO ANTONIO ROBERT POLINI.

Sistema de Información del Sector Agropecuario: San José; internet infoagro.go.cr.

CHAMBERS OF COMMERCE

Cámara de Comercio de Costa Rica: Urbanización Tournón, 150 m noroeste del parqueo del Centro Comercial El Pueblo, Apdo 1.114, 1000 San José; tel. 221-0005; fax 223-157; e-mail servicio@ camara-comercio.com; internet www.camara-comercio.com; f. 1915; 900 mems; Pres. EVITA ARGUEDAS MAKLOUF; Dirs JOSÉ SEGOVIA ATENCIA, DIETER FIEBERG SILAKOWSKI.

Cámara de Industrias de Costa Rica: 350 m sur de la Fuente de la Hispanidad, San Pedro de Montes de Oca, Apdo 10.003, San José; tel. 281-0006; fax 234-6163; e-mail cicr@cicr.com; internet www.cicr .com; Pres. JACK LIBERMAN GINSBURG; Vice-Pres. CHESTER ZELAYA GOEBEL.

Unión Costarricense de Cámaras y Asociaciones de la Empresa Privada (UCCAEP): 1002 Paseo de los Estudiantes, Apdo 539, San José; tel. 290-5595; fax 290-5596; internet www .uccaep.or.cr; f. 1974; business federation; Pres. Ing. SAMUEL YANKELEWITZ BERGER; Exec. Dir ALVARO RAMÍREZ BOGANTES.

INDUSTRIAL AND TRADE ASSOCIATIONS

Asociación de Empresas de Zonas Francas (AZOFRAS): La Uruca San José, Apdo 162, 3006 Barreal de Heredia; tel. 293-7073; fax 293-7094; e-mail azofras@racsa.co.cr; internet www.azofras.com; Pres. JORGE BRENES; Exec. Dir TIMOTHY SCOTT HALL.

Cámara Nacional de Agricultura y Agroindustria: Avda 10-10 bis, Cv. 23, Apdo 1.671, 1000 San José; tel. 225-8245; fax 280-0969; e-mail cnaacr@sol.racsa.co.cr; f. 1947; Pres. Ing. LEONEL PERALTA; Exec. Dir JOSÉ CARLOS BARQUERO ARCE.

Consejo Nacional de Producción: Calle 36 a 12, Apdo 2.205, San José; tel. 255-0056; fax 256-9625; e-mail sim@cnp.go.cr; internet www.mercanet.cnp.go.cr; f. 1948 to encourage agricultural and fish production and to regulate production and distribution of basic commodities; Pres. Ing. JAVIER FLORES GALAGARZA; Man. VIRGINIA VALVERDE DE MOLINA.

Instituto de Desarrollo Agrario (IDA): Apdo 5.054, 1000 San José; tel. 224-6066; internet www.ida.go.cr; Exec. Pres. WALTER CÉSPEDES SALAZAR.

Instituto Mixto de Ayuda Social (IMAS): Calle 29, Avdas 2 y 4, Apdo 6.213, San José; tel. 225-5555; fax 224-8783; internet www .imas.go.cr; Pres. MARTA LORA.

Instituto Nacional de Fomento Cooperativo: Apdo 10.103, 1000 San José; tel. 256-2944; fax 255-3835; e-mail info@infocoop.go.cr; internet www.infocoop.go.cr; f. 1973 to encourage the establishment of co-operatives and to provide technical assistance and credit facilities; Pres. RAFAEL ANGEL ROJAS JIMÉNEZ; Exec. Dir LUIS ANTONIO MONGE ROMÁN.

UTILITIES

Electricity

Cía Nacional de Fuerza y Luz, SA: Calle Central y Primera, Avda 5, Apdo 10.026, 1000 San José; tel. 296-4608; fax 296-3950; internet www.cnfl.go.cr; f. 1941; electricity company; member of ICE Group; Pres. PABLO COB.

Instituto Costarricense de Electricidad (ICE) (Costa Rican Electricity Institute): Apdo 10.032, 1000 San José; tel. 220-7720; fax 220-1555; e-mail ice-si@ice.co.cr; internet www.ice.co.cr; f. 1949; govt agency for power and telecommunications; Exec. Pres. Ing. PABLO COB SABORÍO.

JASEC (Junta Administrativa del Servicio Eléctrico Municipal de Cartago): Apdo 179-7050, Cartago; tel. 550-6800; fax 551-2115; e-mail agomez@jasec.co.cr; internet www.jasec.co.cr; f. 1964; Pres. ELÍAS CHAVEZ BRENES.

Servicio Nacional de Electricidad: Apdo 936, 1000 San José; tel. 220-0102; fax 220-0374; co-ordinates the development of the electricity industry; Chair. LEONEL FONSECA.

Water

Instituto Costarricense de Acueductos y Alcantarillados: Avda Central, Calle 2, Apdo 5.120, 1000 San José; tel. 257-8822; fax 222-2259; e-mail administrador@aya.go.cr; internet www.aya.go.cr; water and sewerage; Pres. EVERARDO RODRÍGUEZ BASTOS.

TRADE UNIONS

Asociación Nacional de Empleados Públicos (ANEP): Apdo 5152-1000, San José; tel. 257-8233; fax 257-8859; e-mail info@anep .or.cr; internet www.anep.or.cr; f. 1958; Sec.-Gen. ALBINO VARGAS.

Central del Movimiento de Trabajadores Costarricenses (CMTC) (Costa Rican Workers' Union): Calle 20, Avdas 3 y 5, Apdo 4.137, 1000 San José; tel. 221-7701; fax 221-3353; e-mail cmtccr@ solracsa.co.cr; internet cmtcr.org; Pres. DENNIS CABEZAS BADILLA.

Confederación Auténtica de Trabajadores Democráticos (Democratic Workers' Union): Calle 13, Avdas 10 y 12, Solera; tel. 253-2971; Pres. LUIS ARMANDO GUTIÉRREZ; Sec.-Gen. Prof. CARLOS VARGAS.

Confederación Costarricense de Trabajadores Democráticos (Costa Rican Confederation of Democratic Workers): Calles 3 y 5, Avda 12, Apdo 2.167, San José; tel. 222-1981; f. 1966; mem. ICFTU and ORIT; Sec.-Gen. LUIS ARMANDO GUTIÉRREZ R; 50,000 mems.

Confederación Unitaria de Trabajadores (CUT): Calles 1 y 3, Avda 12, Casa 142, Apdo 186, 1009 San José; tel. 233-4188; e-mail mcalde@racsa.co.cr; f. 1980 from a merger of the Federación Nacional de Trabajadores Públicos and the Confederación General de Trabajadores; 53 affiliated unions; Sec.-Gen. MIGUEL MARÍN CALDERÓN; *c*.75,000 mems.

Federación Sindical Agraria Nacional (FESIAN) (National Agrarian Confederation): Apdo 2.167, 1000 San José; tel. 233-5897; 20,000 member families; Sec.-Gen. JUAN MEJÍA VILLALOBOS.

The **Consejo Permanente de los Trabajadores**, formed in 1986, comprises six union organizations and two teachers' unions.

Transport

Ministry of Public Works and Transport: See The Government (Ministries); the Ministry is responsible for setting tariffs, allocating funds, maintaining existing systems and constructing new ones.

Cámara Nacional de Transportes: San José; national chamber of transport.

RAILWAYS

Instituto Costarricense de Ferrocarriles (INCOFER): Calle Central, Avda 22 y 24, Apdo 1, 1009 San José; tel. 222-8857; fax 222-6998; e-mail incofer@sol.racsa.co.cr; f. 1985; government-owned; Exec. Pres. LITTLETON BOLTON JONES; 471 km, of which 388 km are electrified.

INCOFER comprised:

División I: Atlantic sector running between Limón, Río Frío, Valle la Estrella and Siquirres. Main line of 109 km, with additional 120 km of branch lines, for tourists and the transport of bananas; services resumed in 1999.

División II: Pacific sector running from San José to Puntarenas and Caldera; 116 km of track, principally for transport of grain, iron and stone.

Note: In 1995 INCOFER suspended most operations, pending privatization, although some cargo transport continued.

ROADS

In 2000 there were 35,892 km of roads, of which 7,437 km were main roads and 28,455 km were secondary roads. An estimated 22% of the total road network was paved in that year. In 2001 the construction of four major roads across the country began; the first road to be built was 74 km long, running from San José to San Ramón.

SHIPPING

Local services operate between the Costa Rican ports of Puntarenas and Limón and those of Colón and Cristóbal in Panama and other Central American ports. The multi-million dollar project at Caldera on the Gulf of Nicoya is now in operation as the main Pacific port; Puntarenas is being used as the second port. The Caribbean coast is served by the port complex of Limón/Moín. International services are operated by various foreign shipping lines. The Caldera and Puntarenas ports were opened up to private investment and operation from 2002.

Junta de Administración Portuaria y de Desarrollo Económico de la Vertiente Atlántica (JAPDEVA): Calle 17, Avda 7, Apdo 5.330, 1000 San José; tel. 233-5301; state agency for the development of Atlantic ports; Exec. Pres. ALBERTO AMADOR.

Instituto Costarricense de Puertos del Pacífico (INCOP): Calle 36, Avda 3, Apdo 543, 1000 San José; tel. 223-7111; fax 223-4348; e-mail incoppe2@racsa.co.cr; f. 1972; state agency for the development of Pacific ports; Exec. Pres. ENRIQUE MONTELALEGRE MARTÍ.

CIVIL AVIATION

Costa Rica's main international airport is the Juan Santamaría Airport, 16 km from San José at El Coco. Following a report by the US Federal Aviation Administration, the aviation sector was to undergo expansion and modernization from 2001. There is a second international airport, the Daniel Oduber Quirós Airport, at Liberia and there are regional airports at Limón and Pavas (Tobías Bolaños Airport).

Nature Air: San José; tel. 535-8832; e-mail NatureAir@ centralamerica.com; flights from San José to 16 domestic destinations.

Líneas Aéreas Costarricenses, SA (LACSA) (Costa Rican Airlines): Edif. Lacsa, La Uruca, Apdo 1.531, San José; tel. 290-2727; fax 232-4178; internet www.flylatinamerica.com; f. 1945; operates international services within Latin America and to North America; Gen. Man. RICHARD KRUG.

Servicios Aéreos Nacionales, SA (SANSA): Paseo Colón, Centro Colón, Apdo 999, 1007 San José; tel. 233-2714; fax 255-2176; e-mail info@flysansa.com; subsidiary of LACSA; international, regional and domestic scheduled passenger and cargo services; Man. Dir CARLOS MANUEL DELGADO AGUILAR.

Servicios de Carga Aérea (SERCA): Aeropuerto Internacional Juan Santamaría, Apdo 6.855, San José; f. 1982; operates cargo service from San José.

Tourism

Costa Rica boasts a system of nature reserves and national parks unique in the world, which cover one-third of the country. The main tourist features are the Irazú and Poás volcanoes, the Orosí valley and the ruins of the colonial church at Ujarras. Tourists also visit San José, the capital, the Pacific beaches of Guanacaste and Puntarenas, and the Caribbean beaches of Limón. In 2001 there were numerous hotel and resort construction projects under way in the Guanacaste province. The projects were being undertaken by the Instituto Costarricense de Turismo. In May 2001 one of the country's principal tourist sites, La Casona de Santa Rosa, was almost completely destroyed by fire. Some 1,238,692 tourists visited Costa Rica in 2003, when tourism receipts totalled US $1,199m. Most visitors came from the USA (41.2%). There were 379 hotel in Costa Rica in 2003.

Cámara Nacional de Turismo (Canatur): tel. 234-6222; fax 253-8102; e-mail info@tourism.co.cr; internet www.costarica.tourism.co .cr.

Instituto Costarricense de Turismo (ICT): La Uruca, Costado Este del Puente Juan Pablo II, Apdo 777, 1000 San José; tel. 299-5880; fax 291-5675; internet www.visitcostarica.com; f. 1955; Exec. Pres. Rodrigo Castro Fonseca; Gen. Man. Guillermo Alvarado Herrera.

CÔTE D'IVOIRE
(THE IVORY COAST)

Introductory Survey

Location, Climate, Language, Religion, Flag, Capital

The Republic of Côte d'Ivoire lies on the west coast of Africa, between Ghana to the east and Liberia to the west, with Guinea, Mali and Burkina Faso to the north. Average temperatures vary between 21°C and 30°C (70°F and 86°F). The main rainy season, May–July, is followed by a shorter wet season in October–November. The official language is French, and a large number of African languages are also spoken. At the time of the 1998 census it was estimated that some 34% of the population were Christians (mainly Roman Catholics), 27% Muslims, 15% followed traditional indigenous beliefs, and 3% practised other religions, while 21% had no religious affiliation. (However, it was thought that the proportion of Muslims was, in fact, significantly higher, as the majority of unregistered foreign workers in Côte d'Ivoire were believed to be Muslims.) The national flag (proportions 2 by 3) has three equal vertical stripes, of orange, white and green. The political and administrative capital is Yamoussoukro, although most government ministries and offices remain in the former capital, Abidjan, which is the major centre for economic activity.

Recent History

Formerly a province of French West Africa, Côte d'Ivoire achieved self-government, within the French Community, in December 1958. Dr Félix Houphouët-Boigny, leader of the Parti démocratique de la Côte d'Ivoire—Rassemblement démocratique africain (PDCI—RDA), became Prime Minister in 1959. The country became fully independent on 7 August 1960; a new Constitution was adopted in October 1960, and Houphouët-Boigny became President in November.

Until 1990 the PDCI—RDA, founded in 1946, was Côte d'Ivoire's only legal political party, despite constitutional provision for the existence of other political organizations. A high rate of economic growth, together with strong support from France, contributed, until the late 1980s, to the stability of the regime. The announcement in early 1990 of austerity measures precipitated an unprecedented level of unrest. In April Houphouët-Boigny appointed Alassane Ouattara, the Governor of the Banque centrale des états de l'Afrique de l'ouest (BCEAO, the regional central bank), to chair a special commission to formulate economic and political reforms. From May it was announced that hitherto unofficial political organizations were to be formally recognized.

Côte d'Ivoire's first contested presidential election was held on 28 October 1990. Houphouët-Boigny—challenged by Laurent Gbagbo, the candidate of the socialist Front populaire ivoirien (FPI)—was re-elected for a seventh term with the support of 81.7% of votes cast. In November the legislature, the Assemblée nationale, approved two constitutional amendments. The first authorized the President of the legislature to assume the functions of the President of the Republic, in the event of the presidency becoming vacant, until the expiry of the previous incumbent's mandate (an arrangement that had existed, on an interim basis, since October 1985, following the abolition of the post of Vice-President of the Republic). The second amendment provided for the appointment of a Prime Minister, who would be accountable to the President; Ouattara was subsequently designated premier.

Almost 500 candidates, representing 17 political parties, contested legislative elections in November 1990. The PDCI—RDA returned 163 deputies to the 175-member Assemblée nationale; Gbagbo and eight other members of the FPI were elected, along with the leader of the Parti ivoirien des travailleurs (PIT), Francis Wodié, and two independent candidates. Henri Konan Bédié, who had held the presidency of the legislature since 1980, was re-elected to that post.

The Government's response to the report of a commission of inquiry into student disturbances in May–June 1991, in which one student died, provoked renewed violence in early 1992. The disturbances were led by the outlawed Fédération estudiantine et scolaire de Côte d'Ivoire (FESCI), which remained a significant force of protest against the Government throughout the 1990s. Houphouët-Boigny refused to subject the armed forces Chief of General Staff, Brig.-Gen. Robert Gueï, to disciplinary proceedings, despite the commission's conclusion that Gueï was ultimately responsible for violent acts perpetrated by forces under his command. In February Gbagbo was among more than 100 people arrested during a violent anti-Government demonstration in Abidjan, and in March was one of nine opposition leaders sentenced to two-year prison sentences under a new presidential ordinance that rendered political leaders responsible for violent acts committed by their supporters.

Houphouët-Boigny left Côte d'Ivoire in May 1993 to receive medical treatment in Europe. As the President's health failed, controversy arose over the issue of succession. Many senior politicians, including Ouattara and Gbagbo (both of whom were known to have presidential aspirations), asserted that the process defined in the Constitution effectively endorsed an 'hereditary presidency', since Bédié, like Houphouët-Boigny, was a member of the Akan ethnic group. Houphouët-Boigny died on 7 December. Later the same day Bédié announced that, in accordance with the Constitution, he was assuming the duties of President of the Republic with immediate effect. Ouattara initially refused to recognize Bédié's right of succession, but tendered his resignation two days later. Daniel Kablan Duncan, hitherto Minister-delegate to the Prime Minister, with responsibility for the Economy, Finance and Planning, was appointed as Prime Minister. Bédié's position was consolidated by his election to the chairmanship of the PDCI—RDA in April 1994, and by Ouattara's departure for the USA following his appointment to the post of Deputy Managing Director of the IMF. Disaffected members of the PDCI—RDA left the party in June to form what they termed a moderate, centrist organization, the Rassemblement des républicains (RDR); Ouattara formally announced his membership of the RDR in early 1995.

A new electoral code, adopted in December 1994, imposed new restrictions on eligibility for public office, notably stipulating that candidates for the presidency or for the Assemblée nationale be of direct Ivorian descent. The RDR protested that these restrictions would prevent Ouattara from contesting the presidency, since the former Prime Minister was of Burkinabè descent and would also be affected by the code's requirement that candidates have been continuously resident in Côte d'Ivoire for five years prior to seeking election.

In October 1995 the FPI (which was to have been represented by Gbagbo) and the RDR (whose Secretary-General, Djény Kobina, was to have replaced Ouattara as the party's candidate) announced their boycott of the forthcoming presidential election as long as the conditions were not 'clear and open'. Subsequent negotiations involving Bédié and opposition groups made no effective progress, and the presidential election took place, as scheduled, on 22 October 1995, following a week of violence in several towns. Bédié, with 95.25% of the valid votes cast, secured an overwhelming victory.

Prior to the legislative elections in November 1995, representatives of both the FPI and the RDR were appointed to the electoral commission, and both parties abandoned their threatened boycott of the poll. However, ongoing disturbances resulted in the postponement of polling in five constituencies, including the constituency that was to have been contested by Gbagbo; moreover, Kobina's candidacy was disallowed, on the grounds that he had been unable to prove direct Ivorian descent. In December the Constitutional Council annulled the results of the elections in three constituencies. The PDCI—RDA thus held 146 seats, the RDR 14, and the FPI nine, indicating a notable loss of support for the PDCI—RDA in the north in favour of the RDR.

In October 1995, shortly before the presidential election, Brig.-Gen. Gueï was replaced in his armed forces command and appointed as Minister of Employment and the Civil Service. Reports emerged in May of a coup attempt by members of the armed forces at the time of the civil unrest that preceded the 1995 presidential election. The departure of Gueï and the former Minister of Defence, Léon Konan Koffi, from the Government in August 1996 were interpreted as an indication of Bédié's desire to remove from positions of influence figures connected with the insecurity prior to the 1995 elections. In January 1997 Gueï was dismissed from the army, having been found to have committed serious disciplinary offences in the discharge of his duties.

In June 1998 RDR and FPI deputies boycotted a vote in the Assemblée nationale that approved substantial amendments to the Constitution. The opposition objected, in particular, to provisions conferring wider powers on the Head of State, whose mandate was to be extended to seven years. Henceforth, candidates for public office were required to be Ivorian by birth, or direct Ivorian descent, and to have been continuously resident in Côte d'Ivoire for 10 years. The amendments included provisions for the establishment of an upper legislative chamber, the Sénat. In September Gbagbo and Kobina led a demonstration in Abidjan to denounce the amendments. Following the death of Kobina in October, Henriette Dagba Diabaté assumed the post of Secretary-General of the RDR.

Alassane Ouattara returned to Côte d'Ivoire in July 1999 and, in August, was appointed to the newly created post of President of the RDR. Although Ouattara declared his intention to contest the 2000 presidential election, in October 1999 it was announced that his nationality certificate (which had been issued in September) had been annulled. In December a warrant was issued for Ouattara's arrest on charges of fraudulently procuring identity papers, although he had recently returned to France.

In late December 1999 a mutiny by soldiers demanding salary increases, the payment of outstanding arrears and the reinstatement of Gueï as armed forces Chief of General Staff rapidly escalated into a *coup d'état*. On 24 December Gueï announced that he had assumed power at the head of a Comité national de salut public (CNSP), and that the Constitution and its institutions had been suspended. Constitutional review and fresh legislative elections were promised, and opposition parties were invited to submit nominations for an interim government. In early January 2000 Bédié left Côte d'Ivoire; he subsequently sought refuge in France.

Gueï encountered considerable difficulty in achieving his stated objective of forming a broad-based government. The CNSP, having released the imprisoned RDR leaders, was at first perceived as being supportive of Ouattara, particularly as one prominent member, Intendant-Gen. Lassana Palenfo, had previously served in Ouattara's Government. Consequently, the FPI (which had become increasingly distanced from the RDR) withdrew its nominees from the coalition Government appointed in early January 2000, although subsequent negotiations resulted in the party attaining a larger number of ministerial posts than any other. The PDCI—RDA declined to approve Gueï's appointment of two ministers from the party.

In late January 2000 Gueï announced that presidential and legislative elections would be held by October, following a constitutional referendum in July. The draft Constitution, presented in May, provoked considerable controversy, as it demanded that presidential candidates be of only Ivorian nationality and parentage. Following protests from the RDR, Gueï dismissed all ministers of that party, with the exception of Diabaté. Seydou Elimane Diarra, an experienced diplomat and technocrat, and Minister of State, responsible for Governmental Co-ordination and the Planning of Development since January, was appointed as Prime Minister in mid-May. The revised Constitution was endorsed by 86.5% of votes cast in a referendum on 23–24 July, with turn-out estimated at 56%. Notably, all those involved in the *coup d'état* and members of the CNSP were granted immunity from prosecution.

In August 2000 Gueï announced that he would contest the forthcoming presidential election as an independent. In early October the Supreme Court announced that only five of the 19 candidates for the presidential election complied with the conditions of eligibility. Those whose candidacies were rejected included Ouattara, Emile Constant Bombet, the candidate of the PDCI—RDA, and several unofficial representatives of that party, including Bédié. Of the five candidates permitted to stand, only Gueï and Gbagbo were regarded as capable of eliciting popular support; allegations that the two men had undertaken a private agreement of co-operation had been encouraged by the increasingly prominent role of the FPI in Gueï's Council of Ministers. (In late September, following a further ministerial reorganization, the FPI had become the sole

political party to be represented in the Government.) Leaders of the PDCI—RDA and the RDR urged an electoral boycott in protest at the Supreme Court's decision.

The two weeks preceding the presidential election were characterized by heightened unrest, and a state of emergency was imposed. Nevertheless, voting proceeded generally without incident on 22 October 2000. Preliminary results indicated that Gbagbo had received a greater percentage of votes cast than Gueï. However, on 24 October the Ministry of the Interior and Decentralization announced the dissolution of the national electoral commission and declared Gueï the winner of the election. The Government claimed that certain, unspecified, political parties had perpetrated electoral fraud, and announced that, following the readjustment of the results, Gueï, with 52.7% of the votes cast, had defeated Gbagbo, with 41.0%. Prime Minister Diarra resigned in protest at alleged fraudulence on 23 October. Two days later the head of the presidential guard withdrew his support for Gueï, after demonstrations were held across the country to demand that Gueï step down in favour of Gbagbo. Following clashes between rival army factions in the military barracks in Abidjan, and a declaration of support for Gbagbo by the Chief of Staff of the Armed Forces, Gueï fled, and Gbagbo declared himself President.

According to official figures released by the electoral commission, and confirmed by the Supreme Court, Gbagbo had secured 59.4% of the valid votes cast, while Gueï had received 32.7%. However, a low rate of participation (an estimated 33.2% overall, but markedly lower in the largely Muslim and RDR-supporting regions in the north, as well as in Yamoussoukro and other strongholds of the PDCI—RDA) cast doubt on the legitimacy of Gbagbo's victory. Concern was raised that Gbagbo had voiced support, during his campaign, for the notion of strengthening national identity, or 'ivoirité', in potentially inflammatory terms, similar to those used previously by Bédié. Gbagbo was inaugurated as President on 26 October. In the three days following Gbagbo's accession to the presidency violent clashes between the security forces and RDR demonstrators demanding the annulment of the election resulted in 203 deaths, according to official figures. The discovery of a mass grave, containing the bodies of 57 people, in Yopougon, Abidjan, prompted the Government to announce an investigation into the violence. The UN subsequently established a commission of inquiry into the killings.

On 27 October 2000 Gbagbo appointed a new Council of Ministers, incorporating members of the FPI, the PDCI—RDA and the PIT. (The RDR stated that it would await legislative elections before participating in a coalition government.) Pascal Affi N'Guessan, the manager of Gbagbo's electoral campaign and a minister in the outgoing Government, was named as Prime Minister.

In early December 2000 the Supreme Court ruled that the candidacy of Ouattara in the forthcoming legislative elections was invalid. The RDR urged an 'active boycott' of the elections in protest. An estimated 30 people died in clashes between supporters of Ouattara and the police in early December, and several senior RDR officials were detained, as the Government accused the party of plotting a *coup d'état*. Following the death of his personal secretary, who had reportedly been beaten by police-officers, Ouattara fled to France. The UN, the Organization of African Unity (now the African Union—AU, see p. 144) and the European Union (EU, see p. 217) announced that they would withdraw their observers from the elections in response to the unrest and the exclusion of Ouattara. The legislative elections proceeded on 10 December, although violent clashes between RDR supporters and the security forces, in which 85 people were killed, prevented voting in 28 northern constituencies. Electoral turn-out was low, at 31.5%. The FPI secured 96 of the 225 seats in the Assemblée nationale, becoming the largest party. The PDCI—RDA won 77 seats, the PIT four, and independent candidates 17, while a 'moderate' faction of the RDR, which rejected the party's boycott of the elections, obtained one seat.

On the night of 7–8 January 2001 dissident soldiers seized control of the state radio and television station in Abidjan, in what was widely regarded as an attempted *coup d'état*. Troops loyal to the Government suppressed the uprising, in which 15 people were killed, within several hours. The Government accused unspecified neighbouring countries of having encouraged the failed coup, prompting attacks on properties owned by foreigners. (In mid-2002 nine people were convicted of involvement in the attempted coup and sentenced to terms of up to 20 years' imprisonment, while a further 19 defendants were acquitted.)

Meanwhile, at the remaining legislative elections, held in mid-January 2001, the PDCI—RDA secured 17 of the 26 contested seats, increasing its overall representation in the Assemblée nationale to 94 seats, only two less than the FPI. Independent candidates won five seats and the RDR faction four. Two seats in Kong, Ouattara's native town, remained uncontested. Only 13.3% of eligible voters participated in the elections. The legislative balance of power remained unclear. Mamadou Koulibaly of the FPI, hitherto Minister of the Economy and Finance, was elected President of the Assemblée nationale, with the support of both his own party and the PDCI—RDA. It soon emerged that seven of the 22 nominally independent deputies had been financed by the PDCI—RDA and were to return to the party. A further 14 independents, PDCI—RDA dissidents who had left the party to support Guei, formed a parliamentary alliance with the FPI and, in February, created a new centre-right party with some 50 other former members of the PDCI—RDA, the Union pour la démocratie et la paix de la Côte d'Ivoire (UDPCI).

N'Guessan was retained as Prime Minister in a new Council of Ministers appointed on 24 January 2001; of the 28 ministers, 18 were members of the FPI, while six were from the PDCI—RDA. Meanwhile, tensions between native Ivorians and Burkinabè migrants heightened, and, following a number of violent incidents, several thousand Burkinabè were reported to have returned to Burkina Faso from Côte d'Ivoire in January–February. In July N'Guessan was elected as President of the FPI, replacing Gbagbo. In the same month the UN commission of inquiry issued a report implicating members of the gendarmerie in the killings of the 57 people whose bodies had been found in a mass grave at Yopougon in October 2000. In early August 2001, however, eight gendarmes were acquitted by a military tribunal on charges of murder in relation to these killings, on grounds of lack of evidence; in April 2002 Gbagbo announced that a civil tribunal was to be convened to reopen investigations into the killings.

In late 2001 a national reconciliation forum, chaired by Diarra, was attended by some 700 representatives of political, religious and civil society organizations. Bédié returned to Côte d'Ivoire from France in late October to participate, while Guei also returned from self-imposed seclusion in the west of Côte d'Ivoire to address the forum, stating that Gbagbo had won the presidential election fraudulently, and that the two men had entered into a secret pact to determine the election result in Guei's favour, on condition that he contest no further elections. In mid-November Gbagbo admitted that certain clauses of the Constitution approved in July 2000 had been written in order to exclude Ouattara from future elections. At the beginning of December 2001 Ouattara addressed the forum, calling for the introduction of a new constitution, announcing his intention of remaining in Côte d'Ivoire and reiterating his determination to be elected to the presidency. When the forum closed, in mid-December, it recommended, *inter alia*, that Ouattara be granted a nationality certificate and that a committee of legal experts be created to examine certain clauses in the Constitution; proposals on land reform and the judicial system were also made. In late January 2002 a meeting took place in Yamoussoukro between Gbagbo, Bédié, Guei and Ouattara. In a joint statement, issued in mid-February, the four leaders reviewed the resolutions of the reconciliation forum and made further recommendations. In April Bédié was re-elected as President of the PDCI—RDA.

Ouattara was finally granted Ivorian citizenship in late June 2002, although, having held Burkinabè citizenship, he remained barred from contesting the presidency. In a further attempt at reconciliation, four RDR ministers were appointed to a reshuffled Government of National Unity, under N'Guessan's premiership, in early August. However, discontent at the composition of the Government became evident almost immediately; in particular, opposition parties expressed their dissatisfaction at the overruling of their preferred candidates for ministerial appointments by Gbagbo. Consequently, the UDPCI withdrew its support from the Government, although its sole minister remained in his post, in an independent capacity. Moreover, the PDCI—RDA alleged that Gbagbo had sought to portray the party as representing factional interests by overruling its nomination of seven ministerial candidates from various ethnic groups in favour of a list including six members of the Akan ethnic group, to which Bedié belonged.

In the early hours of 19 September 2002, while Gbagbo was on a state visit to Italy, an apparently meticulously planned armed rebellion broke out, almost simultaneously, in Bouaké, Korhogo and Abidjan. The unrest in Abidjan culminated in an attack on a military barracks and the assassination of Emile Boga Doudou, the Minister of State, Minister of the Interior and Decentralization. Guei, who had recently gained in prominence as a critic of the Government, was also killed, in an attack on his Abidjan residence. Although some 300 people were killed in the city, government troops rapidly regained control of Abidjan. However, two ministers were held hostage for several days in the north, which remained under rebel control. The exact motivation and identity of the rebels was initially obscure. Gbagbo, following his return to Côte d'Ivoire on 20 September, implied that an unnamed foreign country (widely understood to refer to Burkina Faso) was implicated in the insurgency, which he described as an attempted *coup d'état*.

Continuing unrest in the north, centred on Bouaké, prompted widespread concern across West Africa. In late September 2002 an emergency summit of the Economic Community of West African States (ECOWAS, see p. 205) resolved to dispatch a military mission to act as a 'buffer' between government and rebel troops, and mandated a 'contact group', comprising six Heads of State, to undertake negotiations between Gbagbo and the insurgents. In early October Master-Sgt Tuo Fozié, who had been sentenced to 20 years' imprisonment *in absentia* earlier in the year for his purported role in the January 2001 attempted coup, emerged as a spokesman for the rebels, who identified themselves as the Mouvement patriotique de la Côte d'Ivoire (MPCI) and stated as their principal demand the removal of Gbagbo from the presidency and the holding of fresh presidential and legislative elections. Negotiations between the MPCI and ECOWAS mediators took place in early October. Meanwhile, Gbagbo announced that the Government was prepared to enter into a cease-fire with the rebels, subject to their disarmament and the nation-wide restoration of government authority. However, the signature of the proposed cease-fire accord by the Government, initially scheduled for 5 October, was delayed on two occasions, and subsequently cancelled, precipitating the departure of the ECOWAS 'contact group' from Côte d'Ivoire. Meanwhile, government forces unsuccessfully attempted to recapture Bouaké.

In mid-October 2002 Gbagbo effectively assumed personal responsibility for defence, redesignating Moïse Lida Kouassi, hitherto Minister of State, Minister of Defence and Civil Protection, as Minister without Portfolio, Adviser to the Head of State. On the following day the MPCI gained control of Daloa, although, following several days of clashes, in which at least 17 people were killed, government forces recaptured the city. On 17 October Fozié signed a cease-fire agreement on behalf of the MPCI, to take effect from the following day; Gbagbo, speaking in a 'live' television broadcast, announced his acceptance of the accord. In late October, outside their base in Abidjan, French soldiers used tear gas to disperse pro-Government demonstrators, who were demanding the expulsion of Ouattara from the French embassy; both this demand, and calls for the rejection of government compromise with rebel groups, were increasingly expressed by the Coordination des jeunes patriotes (CJP), a movement led by Charles Blé Goudé, a former leader of the FESCI and an ally of Gbagbo. At the end of October the Government and the MPCI entered into further negotiations in Lomé, Togo, under the aegis of ECOWAS; another former leader of the FESCI, Guillaume Soro Kigbafori, now the Secretary-General of the recently formed political wing of the MPCI, led the rebel delegation.

In early November 2002 the Government announced an amnesty for the rebels and its acceptance of their eventual reintegration into the armed forces. Later in the month the four RDR representatives resigned from the Government, in protest at alleged human rights abuses in which the Government was implicated (including the purported existence of 'death squads', comprising elements close to the Government and the gendarmerie, the existence of which appeared to be subsequently confirmed in a report by the international human rights organization Amnesty International). At the end of the month Ouattara left Côte d'Ivoire and sought refuge in Gabon.

In late November 2002 national security deteriorated further, with the emergence of two new rebel groups, apparently unconnected to the MPCI, in western regions. The Mouvement populaire ivoirien du grand ouest (MPIGO) and the Mouvement pour la justice et la paix (MJP) both announced their intention of taking vengeance for the death of Gueï, and by the end of the month had gained control of the cities of Man and Danane, near the border with Liberia. It was reported that the western rebel groups included mercenaries from Liberia. At the end of November clashes between French troops and MJP fighters were reported near Man, the first offensive action taken by French troops during the conflict. In early December Ivorian government forces attacked Danane and Man; in the ensuing clashes more than 150 people were killed. In early December the MPCI demanded an international inquiry following the discovery of a mass grave, containing some 120 corpses, at Monoko-Zohi, in central Côte d'Ivoire, where the rebels had recently taken control; the authorities subsequently ordered an international inquiry. On 9 December the MPCI acknowledged the existence of a further communal grave, containing the corpses of some 86 people, reportedly pro-Government soldiers and gendarmes, near Bouaké. In mid-December the French Minister of Defence announced that French troops in Côte d'Ivoire were henceforth to be permitted to use force to enforce the cease-fire; earlier in the month it was announced that France was to increase its contingent of troops in the country to number some 2,500, while the deployment of the ECOWAS mission remained in abeyance. In early January 2003 the use of gunship helicopters by government troops to bombard rebel-controlled villages, resulting in the deaths of 24 civilians, provoked controversy.

During January 2003 French-led diplomatic efforts to broker and maintain an enduring cease-fire intensified; following a visit to Côte d'Ivoire by the French Minister of Foreign Affairs, Dominique de Villepin, it was announced that a summit was to be convened in Marcoussis, near Paris, France. Despite ongoing clashes in the west of Côte d'Ivoire, on 13 January a peace treaty was signed in Lomé by the leaders of the MPIGO and the MPJ, and, on behalf of the Government, by Laurent Dono Fologo, the President of the Economic and Social Council. Representatives of the Ivorian Government, seven political parties and the three rebel groups attended the Marcoussis summit, which commenced on 15 January. On 18 January the first contingent of the ECOWAS military mission (ECOMICI) arrived in Côte d'Ivoire. Although unrest continued, on 24 January unanimous agreement on a peace plan was reached by all parties involved in the negotiations. In accordance with this plan, Gbagbo was to remain as President until the expiry of his term of office in 2005, but was to share power with a new Prime Minister, appointed by consensus, at the head of a government of national reconciliation; the premier was to be forbidden from contesting the subsequent presidential election. Rebel groups and opposition parties were to receive government posts, while, under proposed constitutional reforms, candidates for public office were to be required to have only one Ivorian parent, rather than two, as had hitherto been the case. They were, however, to be of solely Ivorian nationality, and the minimum age qualification was to be reduced from 40 to 35 years. (These proposed constitutional amendments were subject to approval by a two-thirds' majority of the Assemblée nationale and by referendum.) Meanwhile, an amnesty was to be granted for those charged with 'anti-state' crimes, although this was not to extend to those suspected of human rights abuses. On 25 January it was announced that Diarra was to serve as Prime Minister in the government of national reconciliation.

The terms of the Marcoussis Accords, although welcomed internationally, provoked widespread protests in areas of Côte d'Ivoire under government control. Blé Goudé became a leading spokesman for those opposed to the sharing of power with rebel groups, and numerous attacks on French interests in Abidjan occurred. Moreover, the MPCI's assertion (which was not, however, substantiated by the text of the accords) that it was to gain control of the ministries responsible for defence and security was a particular source of grievance. Further delays in the formation of the proposed government of national reconciliation resulted from the deteriorating security situation; in particular, Diarra refused to return to Côte d'Ivoire from Senegal until his safety could be assured. At the end of January 2003 eight people were killed in inter-ethnic clashes in Agboville, north of Abidjan. Diarra was officially appointed as Prime Minister on 10 February. However, the formation of a new government continued to be delayed by the inability of all parties concerned to agree on acceptable candidates for the defence and security portfolios; in particular, it was reported that the FPI objected to the proposed appointment of Gaston Ouassen Koné, of the PDCI—RDA, as defence minister.

On 8 March 2003 an ECOWAS summit in Accra resulted in an agreement on the allocation of ministerial portfolios; the FPI was to be given 10 posts, the PDCI—RDA eight, the RDR and the MPCI seven each, and the MJP and the MPIGO one each, while four smaller parties were to receive a total of six posts. The defence and security portfolios were to be excluded from these arrangements. Instead, a 15-member Conseil de la securité nationale (CSN), comprising the President, the Prime Minister, the Chief of Staff of the Armed Forces, the leaders of the gendarmerie and the police force, and representatives of the political parties and groups in the Government of National Reconciliation, was to be established to monitor the operations of these ministries, and to approve Diarra's nominees to these posts.

Further difficulties were encountered prior to the inaugural session of the Council of Ministers on 13 March 2003. The RDR announced that insecurity in Côte d'Ivoire continued to prevent its ministerial candidates from returning to the country from abroad. The MPCI, the MPIGO and the MJP also announced that they would not attend the meeting. Following the session, the appointment of eight ministers of state and 15 ministers, from among those parties that attended, was announced. Prior to a further meeting of the Council of Ministers on 20 March, the appointees to 15 of the 18 unfilled posts were announced; however, representatives of the MPCI, the MPIGO and the MJP again failed to attend the meeting in Abidjan, and a delegation of the groups met the Prime Minister in Yamoussoukro to express their concerns regarding security and the functioning of the CSN. In late March Gbagbo issued a decree confirming a CSN decision that two existing ministers, from the FPI and the RDR, were to assume additional responsibilities for the security and defence ministries, on an interim basis. These interim appointments were denounced by the MPCI, which denied that its representative on the CSN had consented to the measures. In mid-April the first full meeting of the Council of Ministers was held; among the former rebels appointed to the Government were Soro, as Minister of State, Minister of Communication, and Fozié, as Minister of Youth and Public Service, while the military leader of the MPCI, Col Michel Gueu, was appointed as Minister of Sports and Leisure.

At the end of April 2003 Félix Doh, the leader of the MPIGO, was captured and killed. In early May the Chief of Staff of the Armed Forces, Gen. Mathias Doué, and Gueu signed a cease-fire agreement, which was intended to apply to all rebel groups operating within the country. However, violence continued, with more than 100 deaths reported in renewed clashes in western regions. Later in May Soro confirmed that the MPCI's military activities had ceased. In mid-June the national army and rebel forces agreed to the eventual confinement of troops, and by the end of the month it was reported that order had been restored in western regions. In late June the UN Mission in Côte d'Ivoire (MINUCI), authorized by the UN Security Council in May and charged with overseeing the implementation of the Marcoussis Accords, commenced operations in Abidjan, and on 4 July, in a ceremony held at the presidential palace, MPCI leaders formally announced the end of the conflict. In early August the Assemblée nationale approved legislation providing for an amnesty for those involved in political unrest between 17 September 2000 and 19 September 2002; those involved in abuses of human rights or violations of international humanitarian law were to be excluded from this amnesty. By the end of August more than 50 political prisoners had been released. Meanwhile, the MPCI effectively absorbed the MPIGO and MJP, and announced that the organization was henceforth to be known as the Forces nouvelles (FN).

In late August 2003 the French authorities announced that 16 people, including a former close ally of Gueï, Ibrahim Coulibaly, had been arrested in Paris, on suspicion of seeking to destabilize the Ivorian Government; rumours of a plot to assassinate Gbagbo also led to some 30 arrests in Côte d'Ivoire. (Coulibaly was released on bail by the French authorities in mid-September, pending further investigations; he subsequently declared himself to be the military leader of the former MPCI, although the nature of his relationship with activists of the group in Côte d'Ivoire remained obscure.) At the end of August some 50 people were arrested in Côte d'Ivoire, on suspicion of planning a *coup d'état*. Also in late August two French solders were killed in clashes with rebels in central Côte d'Ivoire, becoming the first peace-keeping troops to lose their lives in the conflict; the FN subsequently apologized for the incident, and the alleged perpetrators of the killings were captured and brought before a military tribunal in early September.

In mid-September 2003 appointments to the defence and security portfolios were finally announced: René Amani, a close associate of Diarra, was appointed as Minister of Defence, and Martin Bleou, a human rights activist and professor of law, was named as Minister of Security. However, the FN and the RDR stated that they would not accept these nominations. On 22 September the FN suspended its participation in the Government, accusing Gbagbo of delaying the process of reconciliation, although one of its nine ministers, Roger Banchi, the Minister of Small- and Medium-sized Enterprises, announced his intention to remain in his post. Moreover, the former rebels declared that they would not co-operate with the proposals for the disarmament and reintegration of former combatants. In late September, after an attack on a branch of the BCEAO and an outbreak of fighting in which at least 23 people were killed, French troops entered Bouaké and restored order, with the approval of the FN. In mid-October the Government prohibited demonstrations for a period of three months, and also resolved to dissolve the CJP; these measures followed several violent demonstrations in Abidjan, led by the CJP, which had demanded the expedited disarmament of the FN and had criticized the peace-keeping role of French troops in the conflict.

Ongoing diplomatic efforts, under the aegis of ECOWAS, to advance the peace process appeared to have little short-term success. Negotiations between Diarra and Soro, convened in Accra, Ghana, in mid-November 2003 by the Ghanaian President, John Kufuor, and attended by six heads of state from the region, failed to satisfy FN demands for greater security and increased devolution of powers from the President to the Prime Minister. At the end of the month several hundred supporters of the proscribed CJP attacked and besieged the French military base in Abidjan, demanding that French troops permit government forces to march into FN-controlled territory; although the French troops deployed tear-gas against the demonstrators, a peaceful protest outside the base, led by Blé Goudé, continued for several days.

In early December 2003 Gbagbo announced that the former rebel forces in the north of the country would commence disarmament later that month, several months later than had been initially planned. In the event the disarmament process was further delayed, although some 40 government soldiers that had been held as prisoners-of-war in FN-controlled areas were, none the less, released. Also that month the Council of Ministers approved proposed legislation that permitted presidential candidates to have only one parent of Ivorian origin, rather than two; as a constitutional amendment, this measure would require the approval of a two-thirds' majority of the Assemblée nationale and endorsement by public referendum before it could enter into force. Gbagbo announced that two other items of legislation, intended to grant greater security to migrant workers in Côte d'Ivoire, with regard to the right to apply for Ivorian citizenship, and to own agricultural land, would also be subject to approval by referendum, although without having been presented to the Assemblée nationale.

On 22 December 2003 the FN announced that its ministers were to resume their governmental responsibilities. In early January 2004 French peace-keeping troops began to enter regions of northern Côte d'Ivoire, with the agreement of the FN, reportedly in order to assist in the provision of humanitarian aid, although tensions persisted, particularly in Korhogo. In late February the UN Security Council established the UN Operation in Côte d'Ivoire (UNOCI, see p. 77); with an authorized military strength of 6,240, the peace-keeping operation was to be deployed for an initial period of 12 months from 4 April, on which date authority was to be transferred from MINUCI and ECOMICI to UNOCI. Nevertheless, the process of national reconciliation appeared to be stalling somewhat, with Soro's announcement, at the end of February, that former rebel fighters would not disarm prior to legislative and presidential elections scheduled for 2005. In early March 2004 the PDCI—RDA announced that its ministers were to suspend their participation in the Government, with immediate effect, in response to what it termed acts of humiliation and aggression against the party by supporters of Gbagbo; notably, all parties represented in the Government, with the exceptions of Gbagbo's FPI and the PIT, expressed support for the action of the PDCI—RDA.

In late March 2004 clashes occurred between members of the security forces and protesters following a demonstration in Abidjan, organized by seven of the 10 signatory parties of the Marcoussis Accords (known collectively as the G7). According to official figures, 37 people were killed, including two police-officers, although opposition sources estimated the number of deaths at more than 300. An inquiry, conducted by the office of the UN High Commissioner for Human Rights (UNHCR), later reportedly concluded that the security forces had been responsible for the killings of at least 120 civilians in a 'carefully planned operation' organized by 'the highest authorities of the state'. Following the outbreak of violence, the RDR, the FN and the Mouvement des forces d'avenir announced that they were to suspend their participation in the Government and refused to negotiate with Gbagbo. None the less, the first contingent of UNOCI forces arrived in Côte d'Ivoire in early April.

In mid-April 2004 President Gbagbo acceded to the G7's principal demands in an attempt to restore some stability, agreeing to allow equal access to the state media to all political organizations, to respect the right to demonstrate and to ensure the security of the people. The peace process remained stalled, however, and in mid-May Gbagbo dismissed three opposition ministers from the Government, including Soro, replacing them, in an acting capacity, with members of the FPI. Soro had previously urged FN ministers to return to Bouaké from Abidjan, after Gbagbo had threatened to suspend their salaries and restrict their freedom to travel in response to their boycott of government meetings. In early June the French embassy came under attack from the CJP and other Gbagbo loyalists, who accused France of favouring the rebel movements; UN vehicles were also vandalized during the attacks, which were condemned by Gbagbo. Later that month divisions within the rebel factions led to the deaths of 22 people in Bouaké and Korhogo as rival supporters of Soro and Ibrahim Coulibaly clashed. In mid-July a UN commission of inquiry, established by the UNHCR, commenced an investigation into human rights violations committed in Côte d'Ivoire between 19 September 2002 and 24 January 2003. In early August 2004 the UN announced the discovery of three mass graves containing the bodies of 99 people believed to have been killed in the rebel fighting in June.

In late July 2004 all parties to the conflict attended a meeting of West African heads of state in Accra, convened by the UN Secretary-General and the President of Ghana, at which they signed an agreement on means of implementing the Marcoussis Accords. The agreement, which was to be monitored by UNOCI, ECOWAS and the AU, stated that disarmament of the rebels was to commence by 15 October and progress on amending the Constitution as regards presidential eligibility and on other political reforms was to be made by the end of September. In mid-August, in accordance with the agreement, Gbagbo reinstated the three government ministers dismissed in May, and all ministers from opposition parties and rebel groups resumed participation in the Government. Shortly afterwards Gbagbo delegated some of his powers to the Prime Minister pending a presidential election scheduled for October 2005. However, the October 15 2004 disarmament deadline was not observed by the rebels, who declared that insufficient progress had been made towards the realisation of the proposed political reforms.

In early November 2004 the 18-month cease-fire was broken when the Ivorian Air Force launched bombing raids on Bouaké and other targets in the north of the country, reportedly resulting in the deaths of more than 80 civilians. On the third day of the renewed offensive, nine French troops from the Licorne peace-keeping contingent, together with an American aid consultant, were killed when a French military base in Bouaké was bombed. In retaliation French forces, acting on the direct orders of President Jacques Chirac, destroyed the Ivorian Air Force on the ground (see Defence, below). This precipitated several days of violence in Abidjan and elsewhere, with thousands of Ivorians, in particular members of Blé Goudé's pro-presidential Jeunes patriotes group, rioting, looting and attacking French and other foreign targets. French troops intervened to take control of Abidjan's airport and major thoroughfares and to protect French and other foreign nationals, clashing with rioters and protesters in the process (see below). On 15 November the UN Security Council voted unanimously in favour of imposing an arms embargo, drafted by France, on Côte d'Ivoire (the embargo was reinforced by a further Security Council resolution in February 2005, although additional sanctions regarding the assets and travel movements of specific political figures were not enforced). Meanwhile, Soro and eight other opposition ministers announced that they would not attend meetings of the Government, claiming that their security in Abidjan could not be guaranteed.

In November and December 2004 the South African President, Thabo Mbeki, designated as mediator by the AU, held talks with both the Ivorian Government and the FN aimed at re-establishing the Marcoussis Accords as the basis for solution of the crisis. Following concessions made by Gbagbo during these talks, a series of political reforms proposed by the Accords were submitted to the legislature for approval, and on 17 December the Assemblée nationale voted in favour of amending the Constitution to permit persons with only one, rather than two, Ivorian parents to contest the presidency (thus allowing Ouattara to stand against Gbagbo in the elections scheduled for October 2005). Gbagbo, however, insisted that any constitutional change would require ratification at a referendum, while the G7 objected that such a plebiscite, which could only effectively be organized if the country were united, was unnecessary. Soro and his fellow opposition ministers continued their boycott of government meetings in early 2005, declining to attend a special meeting arranged in Yamoussoukro at which Mbeki was also present, while the FN failed to observe yet another proposed disarmament deadline on 15 January.

Relations with France, the country's principal trading partner and provider of bilateral assistance, have been close since independence. French reaction to Gbagbo's election as President in October 2000 was divided, largely along party lines. President Chirac demanded that the election be rerun, incorporating those candidates who had been excluded from participating, while the leading party in the Government, the Parti socialiste, generally welcomed the accession to power of Gbagbo and the FPI. Following meetings between Gbagbo and Chirac in January 2001, France announced that full co-operation with Côte d'Ivoire, which had been suspended following the December 1999 *coup d'état*, would be restored. From late 2002 France dispatched additional troops to Côte d'Ivoire to supplement the 550 already stationed in the country and by late 2004 there were some 4,000 French troops stationed in Côte d'Ivoire, independent of the 6,000 UNOCI troops also deployed there. The French Government also played an active role in the diplomatic efforts that led to the signature of the Marcoussis Accords in late January 2003 (see above). However, France stated that it regarded the civil conflict as an internal Ivorian matter, disregarding Gbagbo's statements relating to the alleged involvement of external forces in the rebellion; such involvement would have resulted in the invocation of a clause in a defence treaty between the two countries, necessitating the active military support of France for the Ivorian authorities. None the less, there was widespread anti-French feeling, particularly in Abidjan, following the conclusion of the Marcoussis Accords, and several thousand French citizens resident in Côte d'Ivoire reportedly left the country.

Following the destruction of the Ivorian Air Force by the French military on 6 November 2004, in retaliation for an Ivorian bombing raid that had resulted in the deaths of nine French peacekeeping troops (see above), numerous French targets in Abidjan, including schools, businesses and homes, were attacked. French troops entered Abidjan to secure the international airport and protect French citizens, airlifting many of them out of the city. (In total it was estimated that 9,000 foreign citizens, the majority of them French, were evacuated from Abidjan during the crisis.) Some 600 French troops were dispatched to reinforce that country's military presence in Côte d'Ivoire, while diplomatic relations between the two countries remained tense. The French Government subsequently admitted that its forces had killed some 20 Ivorian civilians during clashes with rioters in Abidjan; the Ivorian authorities claimed the number was significantly higher.

The emphasis on '*ivoirité*', or national identity, in the domestic policies of Bédié, Gueï and Gbagbo, has strained Côte d'Ivoire's relations with other West African states, particularly Burkina Faso; Burkinabè migrants in Côte d'Ivoire increasingly suffered from discrimination and became the victims of inter-ethnic violence, causing several thousand to flee the country in early 2001. As the process of national reconciliation advanced, tensions eased somewhat, and Gbagbo made his first visit as President to Burkina in December. However, following the onset of widespread civil unrest in Côte d'Ivoire in September 2002, thousands of citizens of Burkina and Mali left the country, and the common border of Côte d'Ivoire and Burkina Faso was closed until early September 2003, when stability began to return to the region.

The protracted civil war in neighbouring Liberia resulted in the presence of large numbers of Liberian refugees in Côte d'Ivoire in the 1990s; the UNHCR estimated the total number at 327,288 at the end of 1996. The possible infiltration of refugee groups by Liberian fighters, together with sporadic incursions into eastern Côte d'Ivoire by Liberian armed factions, proved a significant security concern of the Ivorian authorities at this time. By 2002, following the installation of elected organs of state in Liberia in 1997, and the outbreak of civil conflict in Côte d'Ivoire in September 2002, the number of Liberian refugees in the country registered with the UNHCR had declined to 43,000, although it rose again to 74,180 over the course of 2003, following the deterioration of the security situation in eastern Liberia. Conversely, some 25,000 Ivorian nationals were thought by the UNHCR to have fled to Liberia in 2002 to escape fighting in western Côte d'Ivoire, while in 2004 some 10,000 Ivorians were reported to have sought refuge in Liberia following the renewed outbreak of violence in Côte d'Ivoire in November.

Government

Under the terms of the Constitution of July 2000, executive power is vested in the President, as Head of State, who is appointed by direct universal suffrage for a term of five years, renewable only once. The President appoints a Prime Minister, and on the latter's recommendation, a Council of Ministers. Legislative power is held by the Assemblée nationale, which is elected for a term of five years. The country is divided into 19 regions, and further sub-divided into 57 departments and 197 communes, each with its own elected council.

Defence

In August 2004 Côte d'Ivoire's active armed forces comprised an army of 6,500 men, a navy of about 900, an air force of 700, a presidential guard of 1,350 and a gendarmerie of 7,600. There was also a 1,500-strong militia. Reserve forces numbered 10,000 men. Military service is by selective conscription and lasts for 18 months. France supplies equipment and training, and had increased its military presence in Côte d'Ivoire from 550 to some 3,800 by August 2004, in order to monitor and enforce the cease-fire agreed in October 2002 between the Ivorian Government and rebels of the Mouvement patriotique de Côte d'Ivoire. The deployment by the Economic Community of West African States of a military mission (ECOMICI) commenced in Côte d'Ivoire in January 2003; by August an estimated 1,300 ECOMICI troops, of an authorized maximum of 3,411, were in Côte d'Ivoire. In June 2003 the UN Mission in Côte d'Ivoire (MINUCI) commenced operations in Abidjan, comprising 26 military liaison officers and 30 international civilian personnel. In late February 2004 the UN Security Council established the UN Operation in Côte d'Ivoire (UNOCI, see p. 77); with an authorized military strength of 6,240, the peace-keeping operation was deployed for an initial period of 12 months from early April, when authority was transferred from MINUCI and ECOMICI to UNOCI. The defence budget for 2004 was an estimated 80,000m. francs CFA. In November 2004, following the death of nine French troops in an airstrike conducted by Ivorian military aircraft, the entire Ivorian air force, reportedly consisting of two Sukhoi-25 warplanes and five helicopters, was destroyed on the ground by French retaliatory action. Later that month the UN imposed a 13-month arms embargo on Côte d'Ivoire.

Economic Affairs

In 2003, according to estimates by the World Bank, Côte d'Ivoire's gross national income (GNI), measured at average 2001–03 prices, was US $13,033m., equivalent to $660 per head (or $1,390 on an international purchasing-power parity basis). During 1990–2003, it was estimated, the population increased at an average annual rate of 2.8%, while gross domestic product (GDP) per head declined, in real terms, by an average of 1.3% per year. Overall GDP increased, in real terms, at an average annual rate of 1.4% in 1990–2003; however, real GDP declined by 1.6% in 2002 and by 3.8% in 2003.

Agriculture (including forestry and fishing) contributed 27.6% of GDP in 2003, and employed about 45.9% of the labour force in 2003. Côte d'Ivoire is the world's foremost producer of cocoa, responsible for some 37% of global cocoa bean production in 2003, and the contribution of exports of cocoa and related products to total export earnings was 27.8% in 2000, increasing to an estimated 44.2% in 2002. Côte d'Ivoire is also among the world's largest producers and exporters of coffee. Other major cash crops include cotton, rubber, bananas and pineapples. The principal subsistence crops are yams, cassava, plantains, rice (although large quantities of the last are still imported) and maize. Excessive exploitation of the country's forest resources has led to a decline in the importance of this sector, although measures have now been instigated to preserve remaining forests. Abidjan is among sub-Saharan Africa's principal fishing ports; however, the participation of Ivorian fishing fleets is minimal. During 1990–2002 agricultural GDP increased at an average annual rate of 2.7%. Agricultural GDP declined by 1.3% in 2003.

Industry (including mining, manufacturing, construction and power) contributed 20.8% of GDP in 2003. According to UN estimates, 11.5% of the labour force were employed in the sector in 1994. During 1990–2003 industrial GDP increased at an average annual rate of 2.1%, although industrial GDP declined by 4.6% in 2002 and by 3.5% in 2003.

Mining and quarrying contributed only 0.6% of GDP in 2002. Commercial exploitation of important offshore reserves of petroleum and natural gas commenced in the mid-1990s. Gold and diamonds are also mined, although illicit production of the latter has greatly exceeded commercial output. There is believed to be significant potential for the development of nickel deposits, and there are also notable reserves of manganese, iron ore and bauxite.

The manufacturing sector, which contributed 12.5% of GDP in 2003, is dominated by agro-industrial activities (such as the processing of cocoa, coffee, cotton, palm kernels, pineapples and fish). Crude petroleum is refined at Abidjan, while the tobacco industry uses mostly imported tobacco. During 1990–2003 manufacturing GDP increased by an average of 1.3% per year. However, the GDP of the sector declined by 6.5% in 2002 and by 5.5% in 2003.

Some 63.0% of Côte d'Ivoire's electricity generation in 2001 was derived from natural gas, while 36.7% was derived from hydroelectric installations, and 0.3% from petroleum (a major decline from 1992, when 85.2% of the country's electricity had been generated from petroleum combustion). Since 1995 the country has exploited indigenous reserves of natural gas, with the intention of becoming not only self-sufficient in energy, but also a regional exporter; the first stage of a major gas-powered turbine and power station in Abidjan commenced operations in 1999. Imports of fuel products accounted for some 21.5% of the value of total merchandise imports in 2002.

The services sector contributed 51.6% of GDP in 2003, and (according to UN estimates) employed 37.4% of the labour force in 1994. The transformation of Abidjan's stock market into a regional exchange for the member states of the Union économique et monétaire ouest-africaine (UEMOA, see p. 267) was expected to enhance the city's status as a centre for financial services. Abidjan's position as a major hub of regional communications and trade has been threatened by political unrest since the late 1990s, particularly following the rebel uprising of 2002–03. The GDP of the services sector increased by an average of 0.7% per year in 1990–2003. However, it declined by 0.1% in 2002 and by 5.1% in 2003.

In 2003 Côte d'Ivoire recorded a visible trade surplus of US $2,524.0m., and there was a surplus of $352.8m. on the current account of the balance of payments. In 2002 the principal source of imports was France (which, together with Monaco, supplied 21.4% of total imports); Nigeria (14.1%) and Singapore (5.4%) were also notable suppliers. The Netherlands was the principal market for exports in 2002 (taking 18.8% of total exports), followed by France, Nigeria and the USA. The principal exports in 2002 were cocoa and related products and petroleum and related products. The principal imports in the same year were petroleum and petroleum products, fresh fish, machinery, and rice.

Côte d'Ivoire recorded an overall budget deficit of 163,200m. francs CFA in 2002, excluding grants received and net lending (equivalent to 2.0% of GDP). The country's total external debt was US $11,816m. at the end of 2002, of which $9,110m. was long-term public debt. In that year the cost of debt-servicing was equivalent to 14.1% of the value of exports of goods and services. The annual rate of inflation averaged 2.7% in 1990–93. Consumer prices increased by an average of 26.1% in 1994 (following the devaluation of the currency at the beginning of the year); the inflation rate slowed to an annual average of 14.3% in 1995, and averaged 3.2% in 1996–2002. Consumer prices increased by 3.3% in 2003. Some 114,880 persons were registered as unemployed at the end of 1992.

Côte d'Ivoire is a member of numerous regional and international organizations, including the Economic Community of West African States (ECOWAS, see p. 205), the West African organs of the Franc Zone (see p. 267), the African Petroleum Producers' Association (APPA, see p. 369), the International Cocoa Organization (ICCO, see p. 370), the International Coffee Organization (see p. 370) and the Conseil de l'Entente (see p. 373). The African Development Bank (see p. 142) has its headquarters in Abidjan; however, in February 2003 contingency measures for a relocation to Tunisia for a period of at least two years were announced, as a result of heightened instability in Côte d'Ivoire.

In the late 1990s and early 2000s the economy of Côte d'Ivoire was adversely affected by international economic and domestic political developments, including a sharp fall in international prices for cocoa. By the time of the *coup d'état* of December 1999 Côte d'Ivoire's financial situation was precarious. In late 2000 the World Bank suspended assistance to Côte d'Ivoire, following a failure to repay debt totalling US $39.8m, and continuing political instability resulted in a decline in GDP in 2000. However, in September the IMF restored co-operation with Côte d'Ivoire, which had been suspended since late 1998. The World Bank resumed full co-operation in February 2002, after all outstanding debt had been paid, as did the European Union, which had suspended assistance in mid-1999, following revelations of the misappropriation of aid. An expected return to economic growth was largely inhibited by the consequences of the rebellion that commenced in September 2002 and the loss of government control over northern cotton-growing regions, although cocoa-growing regions remained largely under government control. A good cocoa crop and a sharp increase in international prices for the commodity at the end of 2002 were among the principal factors that prevented a dramatic economic decline in that year, despite heightened political instability from September. None the less, the international trade of the country was severely disrupted, particularly as a result of the closure of the border with Burkina Faso for a period of 12 months. Abidjan's status as an *entrepôt* for trade with land-locked neighbouring countries was challenged by the effects of this closure, and that of the Abidjan–Ouagadougou railway line, and consequently much trade was lost to Accra, Ghana; Cotonou, Benin; and Lomé, Togo. This trend continued following the renewed outbreak of violence in November 2004, and while this fresh deterioration of the political situation was not expected negatively to effect the cocoa industry, there were fears that the mass departure of foreign nationals would have a detrimental impact on the large number of French-owned businesses in Côte d'Ivoire. Meanwhile, in mid-2004 the World Bank again suspended assistance to Côte d'Ivoire and, despite predictions of a return to economic growth in 2005, any improvement in the economic position of Côte d'Ivoire remained largely dependent on the long-term restoration of political order.

Education

Education at all levels is available free of charge. Primary education, which is officially compulsory for six years between the ages of seven and 13 years, begins at six years of age and lasts for six years. Enrolment at primary schools in 2000/01 included 62% of children in the relevant age-group (males 71%; females 54%). The Ivorian Government's long-term objective is to provide primary education for all children by 2010. Secondary education, from the age of 12, lasts for up to seven years, comprising a first cycle of four years and a second cycle of three years. In 2000/01 total enrolment at secondary level was equivalent to only 23% of children in the relevant age-group (males 30%; females 17%), according to UNESCO estimates. The Université de Cocody (formerly the Université Nationale de Côte d'Ivoire), in Abidjan, has six faculties, and there are two other universities, at Abodo-Adjamé (also in Abidjan) and at Bouaké. Some 47,187 students were enrolled at university-level institutions in 1997/98. Expenditure on education in 1999 was estimated at 303,700m. francs CFA, equivalent to 25.3% of total government expenditure (excluding spending on the public debt). Education in the north of the country was badly disrupted following the failed coup in 2002.

Public Holidays

2005: 1 January (New Year's Day), 21 January* (Id al-Adha, Feast of the Sacrifice), 25 March (Good Friday), 28 March (Easter Monday), 1 May (Labour Day), 5 May (Ascension Day), 16 May (Whit Monday), 7 August (National Day), 15 August (Assumption), 1 November (All Saints' Day), 4 November* (Id al-

Fitr, end of Ramadan), 7 December (Félix Houphouët-Boigny Remembrance Day), 25 December (Christmas).

2006: 1 January (New Year's Day), 11 January* (Id al-Adha, Feast of the Sacrifice), 14 April (Good Friday), 17 April (Easter Monday), 1 May (Labour Day), 25 May (Ascension Day), 5 June (Whit Monday), 7 August (National Day), 15 August (Assumption), 24 October* (Id al-Fitr, end of Ramadan), 1 November (All

Saints' Day), 7 December (Félix Houphouët-Boigny Remembrance Day), 25 December (Christmas).

*These holidays are dependent on the Islamic lunar calendar and may vary by one or two days from the dates given.

Weights and Measures

The metric system is in force.

Statistical Survey

Source (unless otherwise stated): Institut National de la Statistique, BP V55, Abidjan; tel. 20-21-05-38; fax 20-21-44-01.

Area and Population

AREA, POPULATION AND DENSITY

Area (sq km)	322,462*
Population (census results)	
1 March 1988	10,815,694
20 December 1998	
Males	7,844,623
Females	7,522,049
Total	15,366,672
Population (UN estimates at mid-year)†	
2001	16,098,000
2002	16,365,000
2003	16,631,000
Density (per sq km) at mid-2003	51.6

* 124,503 sq miles.

† Source: UN, *World Population Prospects: The 2002 Revision*.

ETHNIC GROUPS

1998 census (percentages, residents born in Côte d'Ivoire): Akan 42*; Voltaïque 18†; Mandé du nord 17‡; Krou 11; Mandé du sud 10§; Naturalized Ivorians 1; Others 1.

* Comprising the Baoulé, Agni, Abrou, Ebrié, Abouré, Adioukrou and Appollonien groupings.

† Comprising the Sénoufo, Lobi, Koulango groupings.

‡ Comprising the Malinké and Dioula groupings.

§ Comprising the Yacouba and Gouro groupings.

NATIONALITY OF POPULATION
(numbers resident in Côte d'Ivoire at 1998 census)

Country of citizenship	Population	%
Côte d'Ivoire	11,366,625	73.97
Burkina Faso	2,238,548	14.57
Mali	792,258	5.16
Guinea	230,387	1.50
Ghana	133,221	0.87
Liberia	78,258	0.51
Other	527,375	3.43
Total	15,366,672	100.00

POPULATION BY REGION
(1998 census)

Region	Population
Centre	1,001,264
Centre-Est	394,758
Centre-Nord	1,189,424
Centre-Ouest	2,169,826
Nord	929,686
Nord-Est	696,292
Nord-Ouest	740,175
Ouest	1,445,279

Region— *continued*	Population
Sud	5,399,220
Sud-Ouest	1,400,748
Total	15,366,672

Note: In January 1997 the Government adopted legislation whereby Côte d'Ivoire's regions were to be reorganized. Further minor reorganizations were effected in April and July 2000. The new regions (with their regional capitals) are: Agnéby (Agboville), Bas-Sassandra (San-Pédro), Bafing (Touba), Denguélé (Odienné), 18 Montagnes (Man), Fromager (Gagnoa), Haut-Sassandra (Daloa), Lacs (Yamoussoukro), Lagunes (Abidjan), Marahoué (Bouaflé), Moyen-Cavally (Guiglo), Moyen-Comoé (Abengourou), N'zi-Comoé (Dimbokro), Savanes (Korhogo), Sud-Bandama (Divo), Sud-Comoé (Aboisso), Vallée du Bandama (Bouaké), Worodougou (Mankono) and Zanzan (Bondoukou).

PRINCIPAL TOWNS
(population at 1998 census)

Abidjan* . . .	2,877,948	Korhogo . . .	142,093
Bouaké	461,618	San-Pédro . . .	131,800
Yamoussoukro* . .	299,243	Man	116,657
Daloa	173,107	Gagnoa	107,124

* The process of transferring the official capital from Abidjan to Yamoussoukro began in 1983.

Mid-2003 (UN estimate, incl. suburbs): Abidjan 3,336,518 (Source: UN, *World Urbanization Prospects: The 2003 Revision*).

BIRTHS AND DEATHS
(UN estimates, annual averages)

	1985–90	1990–95	1995–2000
Birth rate (per 1,000)	46.0	40.4	37.1
Death rate (per 1,000)	14.7	15.7	18.5

Source: UN, *World Population Prospects: The 2002 Revision*.

Expectation of life (WHO estimates, years at birth): 45.3 (males 43.1; females 48.0) in 2002 (Source: WHO, *World Health Report*).

ECONOMICALLY ACTIVE POPULATION*
(persons aged 6 years and over, 1988 census)

	Males	Females	Total
Agriculture, hunting, forestry and fishing	1,791,101	836,574	2,627,675
Mining and quarrying . . .} Manufacturing . . . . . .}	78,768	6,283	85,051
Electricity, gas and water . .	13,573	1,092	14,665
Construction	82,203	2,313	84,516
Trade, restaurants and hotels .	227,873	302,486	530,359
Transport, storage and communications	114,396	3,120	117,516
Other services	434,782	156,444	591,226
Activities not adequately defined	998	297	1,295
Total labour force	2,743,694	1,308,609	4,052,303

* Figures exclude persons seeking work for the first time, totalling 210,450 (males 142,688; females 67,762).

Source: UN, *Demographic Yearbook*.

Mid-2003 (estimates in '000): Agriculture, etc. 3,118; Total labour force 6,792 (Source: FAO).

Health and Welfare

KEY INDICATORS

Total fertility rate (children per woman, 2002)	4.8
Under-5 mortality rate (per 1,000 live births, 2003) . . .	192
HIV/AIDS (% of persons aged 15–49, 2003)	7.0
Physicians (per 1,000 head, 1996)	0.09
Hospital beds (per 1,000 head, 1990)	0.8
Health expenditure (2001): US $ per head (PPP) . . .	127
Health expenditure (2001): % of GDP	6.2
Health expenditure (2001): public (% of total)	16
Access to water (% of persons, 2002)	84
Access to sanitation (% of persons, 2002)	40
Human Development Index (2002): ranking	163
Human Development Index (2002): value	0.399

For sources and definitions, see explanatory note on p. vi.

Agriculture

PRINCIPAL CROPS
('000 metric tons)

	2001	2002	2003†
Rice (paddy)	1,212.0	818.0*	820.0
Maize	573.0	550.0*	625.0
Millet*	73	70	70
Sorghum*	30	26	30
Sweet potatoes†	43	43	43
Cassava (Manioc)	1,688	1,700†	1,700
Taro (Coco yam)	369	370†	370
Yams	2,938	3,000†	3,000
Sugar cane†	1,155	1,155	1,045
Cashew nuts†	80	90	90
Kolanuts†	75	75	75
Groundnuts (in shell) . . .	145	150*	150
Coconuts†	240	240	240
Oil palm fruit†	1,400	1,400	1,400
Karité nuts (Sheanuts)† . . .	36	36	36
Cottonseed	162.0*	170.3*	176.0
Tomatoes†	170	170	170
Aubergines (Eggplants)† . . .	43	69	69
Chillies and green peppers† . . .	22.5	22.5	22.5
Green corn (Maize)†	240	240	240
Other vegetables†	115.7	115.7	115.7
Bananas†	270.0	270.0	270.0
Plantains†	1,410	1,420	1,420
Oranges†	30.0	30.0	30.0
Other citrus fruit†	31.3	31.3	31.3
Pineapples	235.0†	225.0*	225.0
Other fruit†	40.8	40.8	40.8
Cotton (lint)	124.5	152.0*	152.0*
Coffee (green)*	209.0	160.0	133.0
Cocoa beans	1,330.0†	1,225.0*	1,225.0
Natural rubber (dry weight) . .	127.9*	123.0*	123.0

* Unofficial figure(s).
† FAO estimate(s).

Source: FAO.

LIVESTOCK
('000 head, year ending September)

	2001	2002	2003
Cattle	1,442	1,341	1,201
Pigs	346	350	336
Sheep	1,487	1,522	1,523
Goats	1,162	1,191	1,192
Poultry	31,060	32,625	33,000*

* Estimate.

Source: FAO.

LIVESTOCK PRODUCTS
('000 metric tons)

	2001	2002	2003
Beef and veal	45.7	52.5	51.1
Mutton and lamb	5.0	5.1	5.1
Goat meat*	4.6	4.3	4.3
Pig meat*	10.6	14.3	12.3
Poultry meat*	64.9	69.3	69.3
Game meat	13†	13*	13*
Other meat	15†	15*	15*
Cows' milk	25.3	25.9	25.9*
Poultry eggs	32.5	31.2	31.2*
Cattle hides*	5.9	6.8	6.8
Sheepskins*	1.2	1.2	1.2
Goatskins*	1.2	1.1	1.1

* FAO estimate(s).
† Unofficial figure.

Source: FAO.

Forestry

ROUNDWOOD REMOVALS
('000 cubic metres, excluding bark)

	2001	2002	2003
Sawlogs, veneer logs and logs for sleepers	2,615	2,084	2,084*
Other industrial wood*	916	916	916
Fuel wood*	8,552	8,581	8,615
Total	12,083	11,581	11,615

* FAO estimate(s).
Source: FAO.

SAWNWOOD PRODUCTION
('000 cubic metres, including railway sleepers)

	2000	2001	2002
Total (all broadleaved)	603	630	620

2003: Figure assumed to be unchanged from 2002 (FAO estimate).
Source: FAO.

Fishing

('000 metric tons, live weight)

	2000	2001	2002
Capture*	75.8	73.6	79.7
Freshwater fishes	10.5	10.5	22.0
Bigeye grunt	5.2	1.7	2.8
Sardinellas	19.8	19.6	9.7
Bonga shad	11.0*	10.5*	9.4
Frigate and bullet tunas . .	6.8	n.a.	n.a.
Little tunny (Atlantic black skipjack)	2.8	n.a.	n.a.
Atlantic bumper	1.4	2.4	2.0
Aquaculture	1.2	1.0	0.8
Total catch*	77.0	74.6	80.5

* FAO estimate(s).

Source: FAO.

Mining

	2000	2001	2002*
Cement ('000 metric tons) . . .	650	650	650
Diamonds ('000 carats)	320.2	309.0†	306.5
Gold (kg)	3,154	3,100*	2,000
Natural gas (million cubic metres).	1,323	1,230*	1,350
Crude petroleum ('000 barrels) .	11,700	18,914†	18,000

* Estimate(s).
† Reported figure.

Source: US Geological Survey.

Industry

SELECTED PRODUCTS
('000 metric tons, unless otherwise indicated)

	1999	2000	2001
Beer of barley*†	240	230	250
Salted, dried or smoked fish* . .	15	15	15
Canned fish*	46.2	57.1	58.8
Palm oil—unrefined*	264.3	278.0	204.9
Raw sugar*	151.3	179.0‡	177.0‡
Cocoa powder and cake*† . . .	51.8	54.4	50.6
Cocoa butter*†	46.0	48.2	44.9
Plywood ('000 cubic metres) . .	59	80	81
Jet fuel	131	96	n.a.
Motor gasoline (petrol)	678	554	n.a.
Kerosene	905	536	n.a.
Gas-diesel (Distillate fuel) oils .	1,492	1,103	n.a.
Residual fuel oils	730	443	n.a.
Cement§	650	650	650
Electric energy (million kWh) . .	2,924	3,619	n.a.

Cotton yarn (pure and mixed, '000 metric tons): 24.7† in 1989.

* Data from FAO.
† Provisional or estimated figures.
‡ Unofficial figure.
§ Data from the US Geological Survey.

Source: mainly UN, *Industrial Commodity Statistics Yearbook*.

Finance

CURRENCY AND EXCHANGE RATES

Monetary Units
100 centimes = 1 franc de la Communauté financière africaine (CFA).

Sterling, Dollar and Euro Equivalents (31 December 2004)
£1 sterling = 930.12 francs CFA;
US $1 = 481.58 francs CFA;
€1 = 655.96 francs CFA;
10,000 francs CFA = £10.75 = $20.77 = €15.24.

Average Exchange Rate (francs CFA per US $)
2002   696.99
2003   581.20
2004   528.29

Note: An exchange rate of 1 French franc = 50 francs CFA, established in 1948, remained in force until January 1994, when the CFA franc was devalued by 50%, with the exchange rate adjusted to 1 French franc = 100 francs CFA. This relationship to French currency remained in effect with the introduction of the euro on 1 January 1999. From that date, accordingly, a fixed exchange rate of €1 = 655.957 francs CFA has been in operation.

BUDGET
('000 million francs CFA)

Revenue*	2000	2001	2002
Tax revenue	1,077.5	1,168.4	1,259.3
Direct taxes	334.4	327.2	333.1
Taxes on profits	143.3	115.8	111.5
Individual income taxes . .	128.2	133.5	145.8
Employers' contributions . .	23.6	24.8	24.7
Indirect taxes†	258.3	289.1	293.9
Value-added tax and			
withholding tax	142.5	167.3	174.7
Taxes on petroleum products .	95.5	93.6	94.4
Taxes on imports†	225.9	262.0	281.5
Value-added tax	109.1	127.3	129.0
Taxes on exports	163.4	196.5	256.4
Coffee and cocoa	156.1	188.0	246.9
Non-tax revenue	159.5	167.9	169.1
Social security contributions .	102.7	114.2	113.1
Total	1,237.0	1,336.3	1,428.4

Expenditure‡	2000	2001	2002
Current expenditure	1,148.6	1,154.0	1,264.2
Wages and salaries . . .	448.1	484.1	523.5
Other operating expenses . .	392.4	406.4	531.5
Interest due on public debt .	308.1	259.7	265.6
Internal	28.9	24.0	23.2
External	279.2	235.7	242.4
Capital expenditure	209.6	143.3	257.1
Domestically funded . . .	104.3	84.0	145.9
Funded from abroad . . .	105.3	59.3	111.2
Crisis-related expenditure . . .	—	—	57.5
Total	1,358.2	1,297.3	1,591.6

* Excluding grants received ('000 million francs CFA): 33.6 in 2000; 40.3 in 2001; 41.1 in 2002.
† Excluding taxes on petroleum products.
‡ Excluding net lending ('000 million francs CFA): 9.0 in 2000; 9.6 in 2001; 12.9 in 2002.

Sources: IMF, *Côte d'Ivoire: Statistical Appendix* (June 2004).

INTERNATIONAL RESERVES
(excluding gold, US $ million at 31 December)

	2001	2002	2003
IMF special drawing rights . .	0.7	1.2	0.3
Reserve position in IMF . . .	0.4	0.6	0.8
Foreign exchange	1,017.9	1,861.5	2,229.3
Total	1,019.0	1,863.3	2,230.4

Source: IMF, *International Financial Statistics*.

MONEY SUPPLY
('000 million francs CFA at 31 December)

	2001	2002	2003
Currency outside banks . . .	774.7	1,146.7	1,049.9
Demand deposits at deposit money			
banks*	507.8	571.6	563.3
Total money (incl. others) . .	1,324.8	1,750.5	1,626.3

* Excluding the deposits of public establishments of an administrative or social nature.

Source: IMF, *International Financial Statistics*.

COST OF LIVING
(Consumer Price Index for African households in Abidjan; base: 1996 = 100)

	2000	2001	2002
Food, beverages and tobacco . .	112.5	118.8	125.5
Clothing and footwear	109.4	113.4	110.4
Housing, water, electricity and gas	107.6	111.3	115.6
All items (incl. others)	112.3	117.3	121.0

Food, beverages and tobacco (Consumer Price Index for African households in Abidjan; base 2000=100): 125.6 in 2002; 130.6 in 2003 (Source: ILO).

All items (Consumer Price Index for African households in Abidjan; base 2000=100): 104.4 in 2001; 107.6 in 2002; 111.1 in 2003 (Source: ILO).

NATIONAL ACCOUNTS
('000 million francs CFA at current prices)

Expenditure on the Gross Domestic Product

	2000	2001	2002
Final consumption expenditure .	6,126.6	6,342.2	6,566.4
Households . . . . . }			
Non-profit institutions serving } households . . . . . }	5,076.6	5,241.7	5,275.8
General government . . .	1,050.0	1,100.5	1,290.6
Gross capital formation . . .	791.8	858.8	787.7
Gross fixed capital formation .	821.8	760.8	852.7
Changes in inventories . . }			
Acquisitions, less disposals, of } valuables . . . . . }	−30.0	98.0	−65.0
Total domestic expenditure .	6,918.4	7,201.0	7,354.1
Exports of goods and services .	3,010.0	3,163.0	3,390.8
Less Imports of goods and services	2,381.9	2,494.5	2,578.0
GDP in purchasers' values .	7,546.5	7,869.5	8,166.9

Source: IMF, *International Financial Statistics.*

Gross Domestic Product by Economic Activity

	2000	2001	2002
Agriculture, livestock-rearing, forestry and fishing	1,796.0	1,914.3	2,048.1
Mining and quarrying	28.7	27.1	45.5
Manufacturing	1,453.8	1,463.4	1,412.1
Electricity, gas and water . .	154.0	162.3	179.0
Construction and public works .	206.6	209.3	212.0
Transport, storage and communications	447.1	463.4	503.1
Trade	991.4	1,048.5	1,075.6
Non-market services . . .	924.8	979.7	1,063.4
Other services	1,036.5	1,068.8	1,059.6
Sub-total	7,038.9	7,336.8	7,598.4
Import duties and taxes . . .	507.6	532.7	568.5
GDP in purchasers' values . .	7,546.5	7,869.5	8,166.9

BALANCE OF PAYMENTS
(US $ million)

	2001	2002	2003
Exports of goods f.o.b.	3,945.9	5,274.8	5,844.1
Imports of goods f.o.b.	−2,417.7	−2,455.6	−3,320.0
Trade balance	1,528.2	2,819.3	2,524.0
Exports of services	577.8	585.3	712.5
Imports of services	−1,271.3	−1,544.7	−1,727.7
Balance on goods and services	834.8	1,859.9	1,508.9
Other income received . . .	137.3	141.2	167.0
Other income paid	−723.1	−770.9	−854.1
Balance on goods, services and income	249.0	1,230.2	821.7
Current transfers received . . .	88.5	131.9	150.7
Current transfers paid	−398.7	−593.8	−619.6
Current balance	−61.3	768.2	352.8
Capital account (net)	10.0	8.3	5.5
Direct investment from abroad .	272.7	212.6	179.9
Portfolio investment assets .	−12.0	−21.1	−35.0
Portfolio investment liabilities .	4.0	49.8	52.1
Financial derivatives assets . .	−3.8	−6.0	—
Other investment assets . . .	−129.1	−439.0	−413.0
Other investment liabilities .	−197.8	−828.6	−883.1
Net errors and omissions . .	31.1	−22.6	−17.1
Overall balance	−86.1	−278.4	−757.9

Source: IMF, *International Financial Statistics.*

External Trade

PRINCIPAL COMMODITIES
('000 francs CFA)

Imports c.i.f.	2000	2001	2002*
Fresh fish	92.5	107.7	123.6
Rice	69.6	95.4	93.2
Pharmaceutical products . . .	67.1	76.8	68.0
Plastic	73.7	90.1	80.4
Crude petroleum	484.6	396.0	290.9
Petroleum products	113.0	94.9	79.9
Chemicals	38.5	53.4	55.3
Iron	68.7	82.7	81.0
Paper and cardboard	51.9	55.1	52.8
Machinery	121.8	119.0	120.8
Electrical materials	83.6	76.7	63.0
Total (incl. others)	1,771.6	1,867.2	1,723.0

Exports f.o.b.	2000	2001	2002
Coffee beans	182.3	76.5	50.8
Cocoa beans	601.1	737.8	1,196.2
Cocoa, transformed	137.2	221.2	377.0
Petroleum products	522.9	396.1	405.7
Sawn wood	174.8	182.0	156.2
Cotton fibre	105.0	91.0	93.4
Total (incl. others)	2,654.9	2,770.5	3,561.3

* Estimates.

Source: IMF, *Côte d'Ivoire: Statistical Appendix* (June 2004).

PRINCIPAL TRADING PARTNERS
(percentage of total)

Imports c.i.f.	2000	2001	2002
Belgium-Luxembourg	4.0	2.4	2.4
Brazil	0.9	0.8	1.2
China, People's Republic . . .	2.7	3.0	2.4
France (incl. Monaco)	20.3	21.1	21.4
Germany	3.6	3.6	3.6
Italy	3.7	4.5	4.7
Japan	2.9	2.1	2.7
Netherlands	3.1	4.0	3.6
Nigeria	26.6	n.a.	14.1
Russian Federation	2.5	n.a.	3.0
Singapore	0.1	0.1	5.4
Spain	3.3	3.1	3.2
United Kingdom	2.3	3.3	2.5
USA	3.6	5.3	3.4

Exports f.o.b.	2000	2001	2002
Belgium-Luxembourg	3.9	2.2	2.6
Benin	1.2	0.8	0.8
Brazil	1.2	0.4	0.4
Burkina Faso	3.6	3.4	2.9
Cameroon	1.0	0.8	0.8
France (incl. Monaco)	15.2	13.9	13.1
Germany	3.1	4.0	2.8
Ghana	3.8	4.5	2.1
Indonesia	0.9	1.1	1.1
Italy	4.8	4.3	3.8
Mali	5.8	5.6	3.6
Netherlands	9.8	14.1	18.8
Niger	1.1	1.1	1.0
Nigeria	1.9	n.a.	9.4
Russian Federation	1.7	n.a.	2.8
Senegal	2.4	2.0	1.1
Spain	3.8	4.0	4.8
Togo	2.5	2.3	1.6
United Kingdom	2.5	2.2	2.6
USA	8.3	7.5	7.5

Sources: IMF, *Côte d'Ivoire: Statistical Appendix* (June 2004); World Tourism Organization, *Yearbook of Tourism Statistics*.

Transport

RAILWAYS
(traffic)

	1997	1998	1999
Passengers ('000)	379	269	243
Freight carried ('000 metric tons) .	596	643	806
Passenger-km (million)	154.6	118.8	93.1
Freight ton-km (million) . . .	504.8	527.2	537.6

Source: SITARAIL—Transport Ferroviaire de Personnel et de Marchandises, Abidjan.

ROAD TRAFFIC
('000 motor vehicles in use)

	1999	2000	2001
Passenger cars	109.6	113.9	113.9
Commercial vehicles	54.1	54.9	54.9

Source: UN, *Statistical Yearbook*.

SHIPPING
Merchant Fleet
(registered at 31 December)

	2001	2002	2003
Number of vessels	32	33	33
Total displacement ('000 grt) . .	8.6	8.9	8.9

Source: Lloyd's Register-Fairplay, *World Fleet Statistics*.

International Sea-borne Freight Traffic
(freight traffic at Abidjan, '000 metric tons)

	2001	2002	2003
Goods loaded	5,787	5,710	6,108
Goods unloaded	9,858	9,018	8,353

Source: Port Autonome d'Abidjan.

Freight traffic at San-Pédro ('000 metric tons, 1999): Goods loaded 851; Goods unloaded 365.

CIVIL AVIATION
(traffic on scheduled services)*

	1999	2000	2001
Kilometres flown (million) . . .	6	3	1
Passengers carried ('000) . . .	260	108	46
Passenger-km (million)	381	242	130
Total ton-km (million)	50	34	19

* Including an apportionment of the traffic of Air Afrique.

Source: UN, *Statistical Yearbook*.

Tourism

ARRIVALS BY COUNTRY OF RESIDENCE
('000)

	1996*	1997†	1998†
Belgium	4.3	4.2	4.5
Benin	12.5	11.1	14.3
Burkina Faso	11.0	11.9	17.1
Congo, Repub.	6.0	n.a.	7.6
France	66.7	69.0	73.2
Gabon	3.0	n.a.	5.4
Germany	3.2	3.8	3.9
Ghana	5.4	n.a.	6.7
Guinea	8.1	n.a.	12.5
Italy	5.0	14.0	7.6
Mali	10.7	n.a.	15.2
Niger	5.0	n.a.	5.4
Nigeria	7.9	n.a.	14.1
Senegal	13.0	12.1	16.6
Togo	8.7	8.2	10.8
United Kingdom	5.1	4.5	5.6
USA	15.3	17.0	18.8
Total (incl. others)	236.9	274.1	301.0

* Figures refer only to air arrivals at Abidjan—Félix Houphouët-Boigny airport.

† Figures refer to air arrivals at Abidjan—Félix Houphouët-Boigny airport and to arrivals at land frontiers.

Tourism receipts (US $ million): 93 in 1996; 90 in 1997; 98 in 1998; 100 in 1999; 49 in 2000; 53 in 2001; 50 in 2002.

Source: World Tourism Organization.

Communications Media

	2001	2002	2003
Telephones ('000 main lines in use)	293.6	336.1	328.0
Mobile cellular telephones ('000 subscribers)	728.5	1,027.1	1,236.0
Personal computers ('000 in use)	100	154	n.a.
Internet users ('000)	70	90	n.a.

Source: International Telecommunication Union.

Television receivers ('000 in use): 887 in 2000 (Source: UNESCO, *Statistical Yearbook*).

Radio receivers ('000 in use): 2,260 in 1997 (Source: UNESCO, *Statistical Yearbook*).

Daily newspapers: 12 in 1996 (average circulation 231,000 copies) (Source: UNESCO, *Statistical Yearbook*).

Non-daily newspapers: 15 in 1996 (average circulation 251,000 copies) (Source: UNESCO, *Statistical Yearbook*).

Education

(1997/98, unless otherwise indicated)

	Institu- tions	Teachers	Students		
			Males	Females	Total
Pre-primary . .	207*	829*	17,129	17,780	34,909
Primary . . .	7,599†	40,529	1,032,989	774,514	1,807,503
Secondary: General . .	428*	15,959*	355,796	183,328	539,124
Secondary: Teacher training‡ .	13§	538*	n.a.	n.a.	6,224*
Vocational¶ . .	n.a.	1,424	8,588	2,449	11,037
University level	n.a.	1,657¶	37,185	10,002	47,187

* 1995/96 figure.
† 1996/97 figure.
‡ Data refer only to schools attached to the Ministry of National Education.
§ 1993/94 figure.
¶ 1994/95 figure(s).

Source: Ministry of National Education, Abidjan.

1998/99: Primary: Students 1,910,820; General Secondary: Students 565,850.

2002/03: Primary: Students 2,118,501; General Secondary: Students 671,433.

Adult literacy rate (UNESCO estimates): 49.7% (males 60.3%; females 38.4%) in 2001 (Source: UN Development Programme, *Human Development Report*).

Directory

The Constitution

Following the *coup d'état* of 24 December 1999, the Constitution that had been in force, with amendments, since 1960 was suspended. A new Constitution was subsequently prepared by a consultative committee, and was approved by referendum in July 2000. The main provisions of the Constitution are summarized below:

PREAMBLE

The people of Côte d'Ivoire recognize their diverse ethnic, cultural and religious backgrounds, and desire to build a single, unified and prosperous nation based on constitutional legality and democratic institutions, the rights of the individual, cultural and spiritual values, transparency in public affairs, and the promotion of sub-regional, regional and African unity.

FREEDOMS, RIGHTS AND DUTIES

Articles 1–28: The State guarantees the implementation of the Constitution and guarantees to protect the rights of each citizen. The State guarantees its citizens equal access to health, education, culture, information, professional training, employment and justice. Freedom of thought and expression are guaranteed to all, although the encouragement of social, ethnic and religious discord is not permitted. Freedom of association and demonstration are guaranteed. Political parties may act freely within the law, however, parties must not be created solely on a regional, ethnic or religious basis. The rights of free enterprise, the right to join a trade union and the right to strike are guaranteed.

NATIONAL SOVEREIGNTY

Articles 29–33: Côte d'Ivoire is an independent and sovereign republic. The official language is French. Legislation regulates the promotion and development of national languages. The Republic of Côte d'Ivoire is indivisible, secular, democratic and social. All its citizens are equal. Sovereignty belongs to the people, and is exercised through referendums and the election of representatives. The right to vote freely and in secret is guaranteed to all citizens over 18 years of age.

HEAD OF STATE

Articles 34–57: The President of the Republic is the Head of State. The President is elected for a five-year mandate (renewable once only) by direct universal suffrage. Candidates must be aged between 40 and 65, and be Ivorian citizens holding no other nationality, and resident in the country, with Ivorian parents. If one candidate does not receive a simple majority of votes cast, a second round of voting takes place between the two most successful candidates. The President holds executive power, and appoints a Prime Minister to co-ordinate government action. The President appoints the Government on the recommendation of the Prime Minister. The President presides over the Council of Ministers, is the head of the civil service and the supreme head of the armed forces. The President may initiate legislation and call referendums. The President may not hold any other office or be a leader of a political party.

ASSEMBLÉE NATIONALE

Articles 58–83: The Assemblée nationale holds legislative power. The Assemblée nationale votes on the budget and scrutinizes the accounts of the nation. Deputies are elected for periods of five years by direct universal suffrage. Except in exceptional cases, deputies have legal immunity during the period of their mandate.

INTERNATIONAL AGREEMENTS

Articles 84–87: The President negotiates and ratifies treaties and international agreements. International agreements, which modify internal legislation, must be ratified by further legislation. The Constitution must be amended prior to the ratification of certain agreements if the Constitutional Council deems this necessary.

CONSTITUTIONAL COUNCIL

Articles 88–100: The Constitutional Council rules on the constitutionality of legislation. It also regulates the functioning of government. It is composed of a President, of the former Presidents of Côte d'Ivoire and of six councillors named by the President and by the President of the Assemblée nationale for mandates of six years. The Council supervises referendums and announces referendum and election results. It also examines the eligibility of candidates to the presidency and the legislature. There is no appeal against the Council's decisions.

JUDICIAL POWER

Articles 101–112: The judiciary is independent, and is composed of the High Court of Justice, the Court of Cassation*, the Council of State, the National Audit Court, and regional tribunals and appeals courts. The Higher Council of Magistrates examines questions relating to judicial independence and nominates and disciplines senior magistrates. The High Court of Justice judges members of the Government in cases relating to the execution of their duties. The

High Court, which is composed of deputies elected by the Assemblée nationale, may only judge the President in cases of high treason.

THE ECONOMIC AND SOCIAL COUNCIL

Articles 113–114: The Economic and Social Council gives its opinion on proposed legislation or decrees relating to its sphere of competence. The President may consult the Council on any economic or social matter.

THE MEDIATOR OF THE REPUBLIC

Articles 115–118: The Mediator is an independent mediating figure, appointed for a non-renewable six-year mandate by the President, in consultation with the President of the Assemblée nationale. The Mediator, who may not hold any other office or position, receives immunity from prosecution during the term of office.

OTHER ISSUES

Articles 119–133: Only the President or the Assemblée nationale, of whom a two-thirds' majority must be in favour, may propose amending the Constitution. Amendments relating to the nature of the presidency or the mechanism whereby the Constitution is amended must be approved by referendum; all other amendments may be enacted with the agreement of the President and of a four-fifths' majority of the Assemblée nationale. The form and the secular nature of the republic may not be amended. Immunity from prosecution is granted to members of the Comité national de salut public and to all those involved in the change of government of December 1999.

*Although the Constitution of 2000 refers to the highest court of appeal as the Court of Cassation, in early 2004 this court retained its previous designation, as the Supreme Court.

The Government

HEAD OF STATE

President of the Republic: LAURENT GBAGBO (took office 26 October 2000).

COUNCIL OF MINISTERS
(March 2005)

A Government of National Reconciliation, comprising members of the Front populaire ivoirien (FPI), the Forces nouvelles (FN), the Parti démocratique de la Côte d'Ivoire—Rassemblement démocratique africain (PDCI—RDA), the Rassemblement des républicains (RDR), the Parti ivoirien des travailleurs (PIT), the Union pour la démocratie et pour la paix de la Côte d'Ivoire (UDPCI), the Mouvement des forces d'avenir (MFA), the Union démocratique citoyenne (UDCY) and Independents (Ind.).

Note: In early March 2004 the PDCI—RDA announced that its ministers were to suspend their participation in the Government of National Reconciliation, with immediate effect, as did the FN, the MFA and the RDR later that month. The ministers of all of these groups resumed their participation in the Government in mid-August 2004; however, several ministers resumed their boycott following the resumption of hostilities in November 2004.

Prime Minister: SEYDOU ELIMANE DIARRA (Ind.).

Minister of State, Minister of Foreign Affairs: MAMADOU BAMBA (PDCI—RDA).

Minister of State, Keeper of the Seals, Minister of Justice: HENRIETTE DAGRI-DIABATÉ (RDR).

Minister of State, Minister of the Economy and Finance: PAUL-ANTOINE BOUABRÉ BOHOUN (FPI).

Minister of State, Minister of Defence: RENÉ AMANI (Ind.).

Minister of State, Minister of Internal Security: MARTIN BLÉOU (PIT).

Minister of State, Minister of Health and Population: MABRI TOIKEUSSE (UDPCI).

Minister of State, Minister of the Environment: ANGÈLE GNONSOA (PIT).

Minister of State, responsible for Territorial Administration: Col-Maj. ISSA DIAKITÉ (FN).

Minister of State, Minister of African Integration: THÉODORE MEL-EG (UDCY).

Minister of State, Minister of Transport: INNOCENT KOBENAN ANAKY (MFA).

Minister of State, Minister of Communication: GUILLAUME KIGBAFORI SORO (FN).

Minister of State, Minister of Mines and Energy: LÉON-EMMANUEL MONNET (FPI).

Minister of State, Minister of Agriculture: AMADOU GON COULIBALY (RDR).

Minister of State, Minister of Economic Infrastructure: PATRICK ACHI (PDCI—RDA).

Minister of the Civil Service and Labour, Government Spokesperson: HUBERT OULAÏ (FPI).

Minister of Religious Affairs: GNESSOA DÉSIRÉ GNONKONTÉ (PDCI—RDA).

Minister of Administrative Reform: ERIC KPLOHOUROU VICTOR KAHÉ (UDPCI).

Minister of Animal Production and Fisheries: KOBENAN KOUASSI ADJOUMANI (PDCI—RDA).

Minister of Relations with the Institutions of the Republic: ALPHONSE DOUATI (FPI).

Minister of Scientific Research: MAMADOU KONÉ (FN).

Minister of Construction and Town Planning: RAYMOND ABOUO-N'DORI (FPI).

Minister of Industry and the Development of the Private Sector: JEANNOT KOUADIO AHOUSSOU (PDCI—RDA).

Minister of Solidarity, Social Security and the Handicapped: CLOTILDE OHOUOCHI (FPI).

Minister of Tourism: MARCEL AMON TANOH (RDR).

Minister of National Education: MICHEL AMANI N'GUESSAN (FPI).

Minister of Higher Education: ZÉMOGO FOFANA (RDR).

Minister responsible for National Reconciliation: SÉBASTIEN DJÉDJÉ DANO (FPI).

Minister of Technical Education and Professional Training: YOUSSOUF SOUMAHORO (FN).

Minister of Trade: AHMADOU SOUMAHORO (RDR).

Minister of Water and Forestry: ADOU ASSOU (FPI).

Minister of Human Rights: VICTORINE DAILLY WODIÉ (PIT).

Minister of Culture and Francophone Affairs: MESSOU MALAN (PDCI—RDA).

Minister of New Information Technologies and Telecommunications: HAMED BAKAYOKO (RDR).

Minister of Small- and Medium-sized Enterprises: ROGER BANCHI (FN).

Minister of the Victims of War, the Displaced and the Exiled: Adjudant-chief MASSAMBA KONÉ (FN).

Minister of Planning and Development: BONIFACE NAMA BRITTO (PDCI—RDA).

Minister of Sports and Leisure: Col MICHEL GUEU (FN).

Minister of Crafts and the Training of the Informal Sector: MOUSSA DOSSO (FN).

Minister of the Struggle against AIDS: CHRISTINE NEBOUT ADJOBI (FPI).

Minister of Youth and Public Service: TUO FOZIÉ (FN).

Minister of Women, the Family and Children: JEANNE PEUHMOND-BROU (RDR).

MINISTRIES

Office of the President: 01 BP 1354, Abidjan 01; tel. 20-22-02-22; fax 20-21-14-25; e-mail lepresident@pr.ci; internet www.presidence.gov.ci.

Office of the Prime Minister: blvd Angoulvant, 01 BP 1533, Abidjan 01; tel. 20-31-50-00; fax 20-22-18-33; e-mail pm@primature.gov.ci; internet www.primature.gov.ci.

Ministry of Administrative Reform: Immeuble ex-Haut Commissariat à l'hydraulique, Plateau, Abidjan; tel. 20-32-14-48.

Ministry of African Integration: 5e–6e étages, Immeuble AMCI, 15 ave Joseph Anoma, Plateau, Abidjan; tel. 20-33-90-09.

Ministry of Agriculture: 25e étage, Immeuble Caisse de Stabilisation, BP V82, Abidjan; tel. 20-21-38-58; fax 20-21-46-18; e-mail minagra@cimail.net.

Ministry of Animal Production and Fisheries: 11e étage, Immeuble Caisse de Stabilisation, Plateau, Abidjan; tel. 20-21-33-94.

Ministry of the Civil Service and Labour: Immeuble Fonction Public, blvd Angoulvand, BP V93, Abidjan; tel. 20-21-42-90; fax 20-21-12-86.

Ministry of Communication: 22e étage, Tour C, Tours Administratives, Plateau, Abidjan; tel. 20-21-11-16.

Ministry of Construction and Town Planning: 26e étage, Tour D, Tours Administratives, 20 BP 650, Abidjan; tel. 20-21-82-35; fax 20-21-35-68.

Ministry of Crafts and the Training of the Informal Sector: 21e étage, Immeuble CCIA, rue Jean-Paul II, Plateau, Abidjan.

Ministry of Culture and Francophone Affairs: 22e étage, Tour E, Tours Administratives, BP V39, Abidjan; tel. 20-21-40-34; fax 20-21-33-59; e-mail culture.ci@ci.refer.org.

Ministry of Defence: Camp Galliéni, côté Bibliothèque nationale, BP V241, Abidjan; tel. 20-21-02-88; fax 20-22-41-75.

Ministry of Economic Infrastructure: 23e étage, Immeuble Postel 2001, BP V6, Plateau, Abidjan; tel. 20-34-73-01; fax 20-21-37-30; e-mail minie@aviso.ci.

Ministry of the Economy and Finance: 16e étage, Immeuble SCIAM, ave Marchand, BP V163, Abidjan; tel. 20-20-08-42; fax 20-21-32-08.

Ministry of the Environment: 10e étage, Tour D, Tours Administratives, BP V06, Abidjan; tel. 20-22-61-35; fax 20-22-20-50.

Ministry of Foreign Affairs: Bloc Ministériel, blvd Angoulvand, BP V109, Abidjan; tel. 20-22-71-50; fax 20-33-23-08.

Ministry of Health and Population: 16e étage, Tour C, Tours Administratives, Plateau, Abidjan; tel. 20-21-52-40.

Ministry of Higher Education: 20e étage, Tour C, Tours Administratives, BP V151, Abidjan; tel. 20-21-57-73; fax 20-21-22-25; internet www.mes.ci.

Ministry of Human Rights: 2e étage, Immeuble Nationale d'Assurance, Plateau, Abidjan; tel. 20-32-16-11.

Ministry of Industry and the Development of the Private Sector: 15e étage, Immeuble CCIA, rue Jean-Paul II, BP V65, Abidjan; tel. 20-21-64-73.

Ministry of Internal Security: Immeuble SETU, en face de la préfecture, BP V241, Abidjan; tel. 20-22-38-16; fax 20-22-36-48.

Ministry of Justice: Bloc Ministériel, blvd Angoulvand A-17, BP V107, Abidjan-Plateau; tel. 20-21-17-27; fax 20-33-12-59.

Ministry of Mines and Energy: 15e étage, Immeuble SCIAM, ave Marchand, BP V40, Abidjan; tel. 20-21-66-17; fax 20-21-37-30.

Ministry of National Education: 28e étage, Tour D, Tours Administratives, BP V120, Abidjan; tel. 20-21-85-27; fax 20-22-93-22; e-mail menfb@ci.refer.org.

Ministry of National Reconciliation: Cocody, 08 BP 590, Abidjan 08; tel. 22-48-89-82; fax 22-48-92-82; internet www.mirena-ci.org.

Ministry of New Information Technologies and Telecommunications: 21e étage, Immeuble Postel 2001, BP V138, Abidjan; tel. 22-34-73-65; fax 22-44-78-47.

Ministry of Planning and Development: 23e étage, Immeuble CCIA, rue Jean-Paul II, Abidjan; tel. 20-22-20-04.

Ministry of Relations with the Institutions of the Republic: Office of the Prime Minister, blvd Angoulvant, 01 BP 1533, Abidjan 01; tel. 20-22-00-20.

Ministry of Religious Affairs: 13e étage, Immeuble Postel 2001, Plateau, Abidjan; tel. 20-34-48-01.

Ministry of Scientific Research: 17e étage, Tour B, Tours Administratives, Plateau, Abidjan; tel. 20-21-36-20.

Ministry of Small- and Medium-sized Enterprises: 21e étage, Immeuble CCIA, rue Jean-Paul II, Abidjan; tel. 20-21-26-31.

Ministry of Solidarity, Social Security and the Handicapped: derrière ENA, Cocody-les-Deux-Plateau, BP V241, Abidjan; tel. 22-41-45-38.

Ministry of Sports and Leisure: 3e étage, Immeuble SOGEFIHA, Plateau, Abidjan; tel. 20-21-10-87.

Ministry of the Struggle against AIDS: 7e étage, Immeuble Caisse de Stabilisation, Plateau, Abidjan; tel. 20-21-08-46.

Ministry of Technical Education and Professional Training: 10e étage, Tour C, Tours Administratives, Plateau, Abidjan; tel. 20-21-17-02.

Ministry of Territorial Administration: Immeuble SETU, en face de la préfecture, Plateau, Abidjan; tel. 20-21-66-24.

Ministry of Tourism: 15e étage, Tour D, Tours Administratives, BP V184, Abidjan 01; tel. 20-34-79-13; fax 20-44-55-80.

Ministry of Trade: 26e étage, Immeuble CCIA, rue Jean-Paul II, BP V65, Abidjan; tel. 20-21-76-35; fax 20-21-64-74.

Ministry of Transport: 14e étage, Immeuble Postel 2001, BP V06, Abidjan; tel. 20-34-48-58; fax 20-21-37-30.

Ministry of the Victims of War, the Displaced and the Exiled: 14e étage, Tour B, Tours Administratives, Plateau, Abidjan; tel. 20-21-39-46.

Ministry of Water and Forestry: 19e étage, Tour D, Tours Administratives, Plateau, Abidjan; tel. 20-21-70-67.

Ministry of Women, the Family and Children: Tour E, Tours Administratives, BP V200, Abidjan; tel. 20-21-76-26; fax 20-21-44-61.

Ministry of Youth and Public Service: 8e étage, Tour B, Tours Administratives, BP V136, Abidjan; tel. 20-21-92-64; fax 20-22-48-21.

President and Legislature

PRESIDENT

Presidential Election, 22 October 2000

Candidate	Votes	% of votes
Laurent Gbagbo (FPI)	1,065,597	59.36
Robert Gueï (Ind.)	587,267	32.72
Francis Wodié (PIT)	102,253	5.70
Théodore Mel-Eg (UDCY)	26,331	1.47
Nicolas Dioulo (Ind.)	13,558	0.76
Total*	1,795,006	100.00

* Excluding invalid votes (25,413).

ASSEMBLÉE NATIONALE

Assemblée nationale: 01 BP 1381, Abidjan 01; tel. 20-21-60-69; fax 20-22-20-87.

President: MAMADOU KOULIBALY.

General Election, 10 December 2000*

Party	Seats
Front populaire ivoirien (FPI)	96
Parti démocratique de la Côte d'Ivoire—Rassemblement démocratique africain (PDCI—RDA)	94
Rassemblement des républicains (RDR)†	5
Parti ivoirien des travailleurs (PIT)	4
Union démocratique citoyenne (UDCY)	1
Mouvement des forces d'avenir (MFA)	1
Independents	22
Total‡	223

* These figures include the results of voting in 26 constituencies where elections were postponed until 14 January 2001, owing to unrest.
† The RDR officially boycotted the elections, and these seats were won by a faction within the party that did not participate in the boycott.
‡ Voting for the remaining two seats was postponed indefinitely.

Advisory Councils

Constitutional Council: Abidjan; tel. 20-21-31-65; fax 20-21-31-54; f. 1994; Pres. GEMAIN YANON YAPO.

Economic and Social Council: 04 BP 301, Abidjan 04; tel. 20-21-14-54; Pres. LAURENT DONA FOLOGO; Vice-Pres DIGBEU HILAIRE ANY, ETIENNE KOUDOU BOTI, NICOLE DEIGNA, MARTIN KOUAKOU N'GUESSA, VAKABA DEMOVALY TOURÉ; 120 mems.

Political Organizations

In early 2004 there were more than 102 registered political organizations.

Alliance pour la paix, le progrès et la souveraineté (APS): Abidjan; f. 2003 by fmr members of the UDPCI (q.v.); Pres. HILAIRE DIGBEU ANI.

Forces nouvelles: Bouaké; tel. 20-20-04-04; e-mail contact@nouvelleci.org; internet www.nouvelleci.org; f. 2003 by the Mouvement patriotique de Côte d'Ivoire (MPCI), following its absorption of the Mouvement populaire ivoirien du grand ouest (MPIGO) and the Mouvement pour la justice et la paix (MJP), both of which were based in Man, in the west of Côte d'Ivoire; representatives of these three 'politico-military' groups, which had emerged following the outbreak of civil conflict in September 2002, were included in the Government of National Reconciliation formed in March 2003; Sec.-Gen. GUILLAUME KIGBAFORI SORO.

Front populaire ivoirien (FPI): Marcory Zone 4C, 22 BP 302, Abidjan 22; tel. 21-24-36-76; fax 21-35-35-50; e-mail infoservice@fpi-ci.org; internet www.fpi-ci.org; f. 1990; socialist; Pres. PASCAL AFFI N'GUESSAN; Sec.-Gen. SYLVAIN MIAKA OURETO.

Mouvement des forces d'avenir (MFA): Adjamé, face Fraternité Matin, 01 BP 4137, Abidjan 01; tel. 07-57-47-13; f. 1995; Pres. INNOCENT KOBENA ANAKY.

Parti africain pour la renaissance ivoirienne (PARI): Abidjan; f. 1991; Sec.-Gen. DANIEL ANIKPO.

Parti démocratique de la Côte d'Ivoire—Rassemblement démocratique africain (PDCI—RDA): Maison du parti, Cocody, 01 BP 79, Abidjan 01; e-mail information@pdci-rda.org; internet www.pdcirda.org; f. 1946; Pres. HENRI KONAN BÉDIÉ; Sec.-Gen. ALPHONSE DJÉDJÉ MADY.

Parti ivoirien des travailleurs (PIT): 20 BP 43, Abidjan 20; e-mail pit@abc.ci; social-democratic; f. 1990; First Nat. Sec. FRANCIS WODIÉ.

Parti pour le progrès et le socialisme (PPS): Abidjan; f. 1993; Sec.-Gen. Prof. BAMBA MORIFÉRÉ.

Rassemblement des républicains (RDR): 8 rue Lepic, Cocody, 06 BP 1440, Abidjan 06; tel. 22-44-33-51; e-mail rdrci@rdrci.org; internet www.rdrci.org; f. 1994 following split from PDCI—RDA (q.v.); officially boycotted the general election of Dec. 2000, except for a faction of some 60 candidates, led by ALPHONSE OULAÏ TOUSSÉA; Pres. Dr ALASSANE DRAMANE OUATTARA; Sec.-Gen. HENRIETTE DAGRI-DIABATÉ.

Union démocratique citoyenne (UDCY): 37 bis rue de la Canebière—PISAM, 01 BP 1410, Abidjan 01; tel. 05-07-77-77; f. 2000 following split from PDCI—RDA (q.v.); Sec.-Gen. THÉODORE MEL-EG.

Union des sociaux-démocrates (USD): Abidjan; Sec.-Gen. Me JÉRÔME CLIMANLO COULIBALY.

Union pour la démocratie et pour la paix de la Côte d'Ivoire (UDPCI): Deux Plateaux, derrière SOCOCE, 06 BP 6647, Abidjan 06; tel. 22-41-31-21; fax 20-22-22-20; e-mail dougbo@voila.fr; f. 2001 following split from PDCI—RDA by supporters of fmr head of state Gen. Robert Guéï; Pres. PAUL AKOTO YAO; Sec.-Gen. ALASSANE SALIF N'DIAYE.

Diplomatic Representation

EMBASSIES IN CÔTE D'IVOIRE

Algeria: 53 blvd Clozel, 01 BP 1015, Abidjan 01; tel. 20-32-32-40; fax 20-22-37-12; Ambassador SALEH LEBDIOUI.

Angola: Lot 2461, rue des Jardins, Cocody-Deux-Plateaux, 01 BP 1734, Abidjan 01; tel. 22-41-38-79; fax 22-41-28-89; Ambassador BERNARDO MBALA NDOMBELE.

Austria: Immeuble N'Zarama, blvd Lagunaire, Plateau, 01 BP 1837, Abidjan 01; tel. 20-30-01-20; fax 20-22-19-23; e-mail abidjan-ob@bmaa.gv.at; Ambassador HEIDE KELLER.

Belgium: Immeuble Alliance, angle rue Lecoeur, 01 BP 1800, Abidjan 01; tel. 20-21-00-88; fax 20-22-41-77; e-mail Abidjan@diplobel.org; internet www.diplomatie.be/abidjan; Ambassador WILLY DE BUCK.

Benin: rue des Jasmins, Lot 1610, Cocody-Deux-Plateaux, 09 BP 283, Abidjan 09; tel. 22-41-44-13; fax 22-42-76-07; Ambassador OMER JEAN-GILLES DE SOUZA.

Brazil: Immeuble Alpha 2000, rue Gourgas, 01 BP 3820, Abidjan 01; tel. 20-22-23-41; fax 22-22-64-01; e-mail brascote@aviso.ci; Ambassador FAUSTO CARMELLO.

Burkina Faso: Immeuble SIDAM, 5e étage, 34 ave Houdaille, 01 BP 908, Abidjan 01; tel. 20-21-15-01; fax 20-21-66-41; Ambassador EMILE ILBOUDO.

Cameroon: Immeuble le Général, blvd Botreau Roussel, 06 BP 326, Abidjan 06; tel. 20-21-33-31; fax 20-21-66-11; Ambassador (vacant).

Canada: Immeuble Trade Centre, 23 ave Nogues, 01 BP 4104, Abidjan 01; tel. 20-21-20-09; fax 20-30-07-20; internet www.dfait-maeci.gc.ca/abidjan; e-mail abdjn@dfait-maeci.gc.ca; Ambassador MICHÈLE LEVESQUE.

Central African Republic: 9 rue des Jasmins, Cocody Danga Nord, 01 BP 3387, Abidjan 01; tel. 20-21-36-46; fax 22-44-85-16; Ambassador YAGAO-N'GAMA LAZARE.

China, People's Republic: Lot 45, ave Jacques Aka, Cocody, 01 BP 3691, Abidjan 01; tel. 22-44-59-00; fax 22-44-67-81; e-mail ambchine@aviso.ci; Ambassador MA ZHIXUE.

Colombia: 01 BP 3874, Abidjan 01; tel. 20-33-12-44; fax 20-32-47-31; e-mail emcoci@africaonline.co.ci; Ambassador (vacant).

Congo, Democratic Republic: Carrefour France-Amérique, RAN Treichville, ave 21, 01 BP 541, Abidjan 01; tel. 21-24-69-06; Ambassador ISABELLE I. NGANGELLI.

Czech Republic: Résidence Azur, 6e étage, 18 ave du Docteur Crozet, 01 BP 1349, Abidjan 01; tel. 20-21-20-30; fax 20-22-19-06; e-mail abidjan@embassy.mzv.cz; Chargé d'affaires a.i. VLADIMÍR HRADSKÝ.

Egypt: Immeuble El Nasr, rue du Commerce, 01 BP 2104, Abidjan 01; tel. 20-32-79-25; fax 20-22-30-53; e-mail amegypteci@afnet.net; Ambassador AHMED TEWFIK RAGEB.

Ethiopia: Immeuble Nour Al-Hayat, 01 BP 3712, Abidjan 01; tel. 20-21-33-65; fax 20-21-37-09; e-mail ambethio@africaonline.co.ci; Ambassador TADELECH HAÏLE MIKAEL.

France: rue Lecoeur, 01 BP 175, Abidjan 01; tel. 20-20-04-04; fax 20-20-04-47; e-mail Cad.ABIDJAN-FSLT@diplomatie.gouv.fr; internet www.ambafrance-ci.org; Ambassador GILDAS LE LIDEC.

Gabon: Immeuble Les Heveas, blvd Carde, 01 BP 3765, Abidjan 01; tel. 22-44-51-54; fax 22-44-75-05; Ambassador HENRI BEKALLE AKWE.

Germany: 39 blvd Hassan II, Cocody, 01 BP 1900, Abidjan 01; tel. and fax 22-44-20-41; e-mail d.bo.abj@africaonline.co.ci; internet www.abidjan.diplo.de; Ambassador Dr MARIUS HAAS.

Ghana: Lot 2393, rue J 95, Cocody-Deux-Plateaux, 01 BP 1871, Abidjan 01; tel. 20-33-11-24; fax 20-22-33-57; e-mail ghanaemb.abj@aviso.ci; Ambassador YAW SAFO BOAFO.

Guinea: Immeuble Duplessis, 08 BP 2280, Abidjan 08; tel. 20-22-25-20; fax 20-32-82-45; Ambassador (vacant).

Holy See: Apostolic Nunciature, rue Jacques Aka, 08 BP 1347, Abidjan 08; tel. 22-40-17-70; fax 22-40-17-74; e-mail nuntius@aviso.ci; Apostolic Nuncio Most Rev. ROBERTO CASSARI.

India: Cocody Danga Nord, 06 BP 318, Abidjan 06; tel. 22-42-37-69; fax 22-42-66-49; e-mail indeamadj@africaonline.co.ci; Ambassador T. SUSMITA GONGULEE.

Israel: Immeuble Nour Al-Hayat, 01 BP 1877, Abidjan 01; tel. 20-21-49-53; fax 20-21-87-04; e-mail info@abidjan.mfa.gov.il; Ambassador MICHAEL ARBEL.

Italy: 16 rue de la Canebière, Cocody, 01 BP 1905, Abidjan 01; tel. 22-44-61-70; fax 22-44-35-87; e-mail ambitali@aviso.ci; Ambassador PAOLO SANNELLA.

Japan: Immeuble Alpha 2000, 01 BP 1329, Abidjan 01; tel. 20-21-28-63; fax 20-21-30-51; Ambassador TETSUO SHIOGUCHI.

Korea, Republic: Immeuble le Mans, 8e étage, 01 BP 3950, Abidjan 01; tel. 20-32-22-90; fax 20-22-22-74; e-mail ambcoabj@mofat.go.kr; Ambassador KIM JONG-IL.

Lebanon: Immeuble Trade Center, ave Nogues, 01 BP 2227, Abidjan 01; tel. 20-33-28-24; fax 20-32-11-37; Ambassador MOSTAPHA ISSAM.

Liberia: Immeuble La Symphonie, ave Général de Gaulle, 01 BP 2514, Abidjan 01; tel. 20-22-23-59; fax 22-44-14-75; Ambassador KRONYANH M. WEEFUR.

Libya: Immeuble Shell, 01 BP 5725, Abidjan 01; tel. 20-22-01-27; fax 20-22-01-30; Ambassador FATHI NASHAD.

Mali: 46 blvd Lagunaire, 01 BP 2746, Abidjan 01; tel. 20-32-31-47; fax 20-21-55-14; Ambassador SADA SAMAKÉ.

Malta: 38 rue de la Canebière, Cocody, 01 BP 46, Abidjan 01; tel. 22-44-63-62; fax 22-44-19-78; Ambassador GÉRARD BLOHORN.

Mauritania: rue Pierre et Marie Curie, 01 BP 2275, Abidjan 01; tel. 22-41-16-43; fax 22-41-05-77; Ambassador ABDERRAHIM OULD HADRAMI.

Morocco: 24 rue de la Canebière, 01 BP 146, Abidjan 01; tel. 22-44-56-30; fax 22-44-60-58; e-mail khyate2001@aviso.ci; Ambassador (vacant).

Netherlands: Immeuble Les Harmonies, blvd Carde, 01 BP 1086, Abidjan 01; tel. 20-21-31-10; fax 20-21-17-61; e-mail nlgovabi@africaonline.co.ci; internet www.mfa.nl/abi; Ambassador J. W. G. JANSING.

Niger: 23 ave Angoulvant , 01 BP 2743, Abidjan 01; tel. 21-26-28-14; fax 21-26-41-88; Ambassador ADAM ABDOULAYE DAN MARADI.

Nigeria: Immeuble Maison du Nigéria, 35 blvd de la République, 01 BP 1906, Abidjan 01; tel. 20-22-30-82; fax 20-21-30-83; e-mail ebeolusan@hotmail.com; Ambassador EBENEZER OLUWADARE OLUSANMOKUN.

Norway: Immeuble N'Zarama, blvd Lagunaire, 01 BP 607, Abidjan 01; tel. 20-22-25-34; fax 20-21-91-99; e-mail emb.abidjan@mfa.no; internet www.abidjan.mfa.no; Ambassador ODD-EGIL ANDHØY.

Poland: Lot 57, CHU Cocody, 04 BP 308, Abidjan 08; tel. 22-44-10-67; fax 22-44-12-25; e-mail polska@polamb.ci; internet www.polamb .ci; Chargé d'affaires BOGUSŁAW NOWAKOWSKI.

Portugal: Immeuble N'Zarama, blvd Lagunaire, 01 BP 3669, Abidjan 01; tel. 20-21-92-41; fax 20-25-57-05; e-mail ambport@aviso .ci; Ambassador JOSÉ MANUEL PESSANHA VIEGAS.

Russia: Riviera Golf, face Grande Mosquée, 01 BP 7646, Abidjan 01; tel. 22-43-09-59; fax 22-43-11-66; e-mail ambrus@globeaccess.net; Ambassador ALEKSANDR M. TROFIMOV.

Saudi Arabia: Plateau, Abidjan; Ambassador (vacant).

Senegal: Immeuble Nabil, rue du Commerce, 08 BP 2165, Abidjan 08; tel. 20-33-28-76; fax 20-32-50-39; Ambassador MOUSTAPHA SÈNE.

South Africa: Villa Marc André, rue Mgr René Kouassi, Cocody, 08 BP 1806, Abidjan 08; tel. 22-44-59-63; fax 22-44-74-50; e-mail ambafsudpol@aviso.ci; Ambassador G. DUMISANI GWADISO.

Spain: impasse Abla Pokou Cocody, Danga Nord, 08 BP 876, Abidjan 08; tel. 22-44-48-50; fax 22-44-71-22; e-mail embespci@ correo.mae.es; Ambassador FRANCISCO ELIAS DE TEJADA LOZANO.

Sweden: Immeuble N'Zarama, blvd Lagunaire, Plateau, 04 BP 992, Abidjan 04; tel. 20-21-24-10; fax 20-21-21-07; e-mail ambassaden .abidjan@foreign.ministry.se; Ambassador INGA BJÖRK KLEVBY.

Switzerland: Immeuble Botreau Roussel, 28 ave Delafosse, 01 BP 1914, Abidjan 01; tel. 20-21-17-21; fax 20-21-27-70; Ambassador JOHANNES KUNZ.

Thailand: 13e étage, Tour CCIA, 01 BP 6471, Abidjan 01; tel. 20-21-19-59; fax 20-21-09-93; Ambassador PÖJ INDUWONGSE.

Tunisia: Immeuble Shell, ave Lamblin, 01 BP 3906, Abidjan 01; tel. 20-22-61-23; fax 20-22-61-24; Ambassador ZINE EL ABIDINE TERRAS.

United Kingdom: Immeuble Les Harmonies, angle blvd Carde et ave Dr Jamot, Plateau, 01 BP 2581, Abidjan 01; tel. 20-30-08-00; fax 20-30-08-34; e-mail britemb@aviso.ci; Ambassador DAVID COATES.

USA: 5 rue Jesse Owens, 01 BP 1712, Abidjan 01; tel. 20-21-09-79; fax 20-22-32-59; e-mail cca_ci@pd.state.gov; internet usembassy .state.gov/abidjan; Ambassador AUBREY HOOKS.

Judicial System

Since 1964 all civil, criminal, commercial and administrative cases have come under the jurisdiction of the courts of first instance, the assize courts and the Courts of Appeal, with the Supreme Court (referred to in the Constitution of 2000 as the Court of Cassation) as the highest court of appeal.

Supreme Court: rue Gourgas, Cocody, BP V30, Abidjan; tel. 20-22-73-72; fax 20-21-63-04; e-mail consetat@africaonline.co.ci; comprises three chambers: judicial, administrative and auditing; Pres. TIA KONÉ; Pres. of the Judicial Chamber KAMA YAO; Pres. of the Administrative Chamber GEORGES AMANGOUA.

Courts of Appeal: Abidjan: First Pres. MARIE-FÉLICITÉ ARKHUST HOMA YAO; Bouaké: First Pres. CHRISTIAN ANIBIÉ KAKRÉ ZÉPHIRIN; Daloa: First Pres. GONHI SAHI.

Courts of First Instance: Abidjan: Pres. ANTOINETTE MARSOUIN; Bouaké: Pres. KABLAN AKA EDOUKOU; Daloa: Pres. WOUNE BLEKA; there are a further 25 courts in the principal centres.

High Court of Justice: composed of deputies elected from and by the Assemblée nationale; has jurisdiction to impeach the President or other member of the Government.

Constitutional Council: blvd Carde, BP 4642, Abidjan 01; tel. 20-21-31-65; fax 20-21-31-54; f. 1998 to replace certain functions of the fmr Constitutional Chamber of the Supreme Court; Pres. YANON YAPO GERMAIN; Mems Prof. RENÉ DEGNI SÉGUI, ANDRÉ KOUASSI KOUAKOU, ABRAHAM AKENOU SOUGBRO, MARIE-AGATHE BAROUAN DIO-UMINCY LIKAGNÉNÉ , DOMINIQUE RÉGINE SUZANNE THALMAS TAYORO, LOUIS METAN AMANI.

Religion

The Constitution guarantees religious freedom, and this right is generally respected. Religious groups are required to register with the authorities, although no penalties are imposed on a group that fails to register. At the 1998 census it was estimated that about 34% of the population were Christians (mainly Roman Catholics), 27% of the population were Muslims, 15% followed traditional indigenous beliefs, 3% practised other religions, while 21% had no religious affiliation. It is, however, estimated that the proportion of Muslims

is in fact significantly higher, as the majority of unregistered foreign workers are Muslims. Muslims are found in greatest numbers in the north of the country, while Christians are found mostly in the southern, central, western and eastern regions. Traditional indigenous beliefs are generally prevalent in rural areas.

ISLAM

Conseil National Islamique (CNI): Mosquée d'Aghien les deux Plateaux, BP 174 Cédex 03, Abidjan 08; tel. and fax 22-42-67-79; e-mail cni@africaonline.co.ci; internet www.cni-cosim.ci; f. 1993; groups more than 5,000 local communities organized in 13 regional and 78 local organizations; Chair. Imam El Hadj IDRISS KOUDOUSS KONÉ.

Conseil Supérieur Islamique (CSI): 11 BP 71, Abidjan 11; tel. 21-25-24-70; fax 21-24-28-04; f. 1978; Chair. El Hadj MOUSTAPHA KOWEÏT DIABY.

CHRISTIANITY

The Roman Catholic Church

Côte d'Ivoire comprises four archdioceses and 10 dioceses. At 31 December 2002 there were approximately 2.7m. Roman Catholics in the country, comprising about 15.5% of the total population.

Bishops' Conference

Conférence Episcopale de la Côte d'Ivoire, BP 713, Abidjan-Riviera; tel. 22-47-20-00.

f. 1973; Pres. Most Rev. VITAL KOMENAN YAO (Archbishop of Bouaké).

Archbishop of Abidjan: Cardinal BERNARD AGRÉ, Archevêché, ave Jean Paul II, 01 BP 1287, Abidjan 01; tel. 20-21-23-08; fax 20-21-40-22.

Archbishop of Bouaké: Most Rev. VITAL KOMENAN YAO, Archevêché, 01 BP 649, Bouaké 01; tel. and fax 31-63-24-59; e-mail archebke@aviso.ci.

Archbishop of Gagnoa: Most Rev. JEAN-PIERRE KUTWÂ, Archevêché, BP 527, Gagnoa; tel. 32-77-25-68; fax 32-77-20-96.

Archbishop of Korhogo: Most Rev. MARIE-DANIEL DADIET, Archevêché, BP 12, Korhogo; tel. 36-86-01-18; fax 36-86-05-26.

Protestant Churches

CB International: BP 109, Korhogo; tel. 36-86-01-07; fax 36-86-11-50; f. 1947; fmrly Conservative Baptist Foreign Mission Society; active in evangelism, medical work, translation, literacy and theological education in the northern area and in Abidjan.

Eglise CMA—Christian and Missionary Alliance: BP 585, Bouaké 01; tel. 31-63-23-12; fax 31-63-54-12; f. 1929; 13 mission stations; Nat. Pres. Rev. CÉLESTIN COFFI.

Eglise du Nazaréen (Church of the Nazarene): 22 BP 623, Abidjan 22; tel. 22-41-07-80; fax 22-41-07-81; e-mail awfcon@compuserve .com; f. 1987; active in evangelism, ministerial training and medical work; Dir JOHN SEAMAN.

Eglise Evangélique des Assemblées de Dieu de Côte d'Ivoire: 04 BP 266, Abidjan 04; tel. 20-37-05-79; fax 20-24-94-65; f. 1960; Pres. JEAN-BAPTISTE NIELBIEN.

Eglise Harriste: Bingerville; f. 1913 by William Wade Harris; affiliated to World Council of Churches 1998; allows polygamous new converts; 100,000 mems, 1,400 preachers, 7,000 apostles; Sec.-Gen DOGBO JULES.

Eglise Protestante Baptiste Oeuvres et Mission: 03 BP 1032, Abidjan 03; tel. 23-45-20-18; fax 23-45-56-41; f. 1975; active in evangelism, teaching and social work; medical centre, 677 places of worship, 285 missionaries and 100,000 mems; Pres. YAYE ROBERT DION.

Eglise Protestante Méthodiste de Côte d'Ivoire: 41 blvd de la République, 01 BP 1282, Abidjan 01; tel. 20-21-17-97; fax 20-22-52-03; f. 1923; autonomous since 1985; c. 150,000 mems; Pres. BENJAMIN BONI.

Mission Evangélique de l'Afrique Occidentale (MEAO): BP 822, Bouaflé; tel. and fax 30-68-93-70; e-mail wirci@aviso.ci; f. 1934; 16 missionaries, 5 staff at mission school; Field Dirs HARRY EUVING, PAULINE EUVING; affiliated church: Alliance des Eglises Evangéliques de Côte d'Ivoire (AEECI); 260 churches, 68 full-time pastors; Pres. KOUASSI ALAINGBRÉ PASCAL.

Mission Evangélique Luthérienne en Côte d'Ivoire (MELCI): BP 196, Touba; tel. 33-70-77-11; e-mail melci@aviso.ci; f. 1984; active in evangelism and social work; Dir GJERMUND VISTE.

Union des Eglises Evangéliques du Sud-Ouest de la Côte d'Ivoire and Mission Biblique: 08 BP 20, Abidjan 08; f. 1927; c. 250 places of worship.

The Press

DAILIES

24 Heures: 2 résidence HALAMA, blvd Valéry Giscard d'Estaing, Koumassi, 07 BP 1014, Abidjan 07 ; tel. 21-56-39-06; fax 21-56-38-27; e-mail infos@24heures.net; internet www.24heuresci.com; f. 2002; Editor-in-Chief JOACHIM BEUGRÉ.

Actuel: Cocody-les-Deux-Plateaux, 06 BP 2868, Abidjan 06; tel. 22-42-63-27; fax 22-42-63-32; f. 1996; organ of the FPI; Dir EUGÈNE ALLOU WANYOU; Editor-in-Chief DIABATÉ A. SIDICK.

L'Aurore: 18 BP 418, Abidjan 18; tel. 05-61-65-75; Editor-in-Chief EHOUMAN KASSY.

Douze: rue Louis Lumière, zone 4c, 10 BP 2462, Abidjan 10; tel. 21-25-54-00; fax 21-24-47-27; e-mail douze@afnet.net; internet www .presseci.com/douze; publ. by Editions Olympe; f. 1994; sport; Dir MAZÉ SOUMAHORO; Editor-in-Chief FRANÇOIS BINI.

Fraternité Matin: blvd du Général de Gaulle, 01 BP 1807, Abidjan 01; tel. 20-37-06-66; fax 20-37-25-45; e-mail fratmat@africaonline.co .ci; internet www.fratmat.co.ci; f. 1964; official newspaper; Dir-Gen. HONORAT DÉ YÉDAGNE; Editorial Dir ALFRED DAN MOUSSA; circ. 32,000.

L'Intelligent d'Abidjan: Villa 12s, Bâtiment Star 4, 19 BP 1534, Abidjan 19; tel. 22-42-55-56; e-mail intelliabidjan@yahoo.fr; internet www.lintelligentdabidjan.org; f. 2003; Dir-Gen. W. ALAFÉ ASSÉ .

L'Inter: rue Louis Lumière, Zone 4c, 10 BP 2462, Abidjan 10; tel. 21-25-32-77; fax 21-24-47-27; e-mail inter@afnet.net; internet www .presseci.com/linter; f. 1998; publ. by Editions Olympe; independent; national and international politics and economics; Dir RAYMOND N'CHO NIMBA; Editor-in-Chief CHARLES A. D'ALMÉIDA; circ. 18,000 (2002).

Le JD (Jeune Démocrate): 23 BP 3842, Abidjan 23; tel. 23-51-62-45; fax 23-51-63-75; e-mail lejd@africaonline.co.ci; f. 1999; Dir IGNACE DASSOHIRI; Editor-in-Chief OCTAVE BOYOU.

Le Jour: 26 Cocody-les-Deux-Plateau, 25 BP 1082, Abidjan 25; tel. 20-21-95-78; fax 20-21-95-80; internet www.lejourplus.com; f. 1994; publ. by Editions Le Nere; independent; Dir of Publication KOUAMÉ KOUAKOU; Editor-in-Chief VICKY DELORE; circ. 15,000 (2002).

Le Journal: Abidjan; internet www.lejournalci.com; f. 2003; frmly *La Bombe*; supports PDCI—RDA; Dir of Publication NAZAIRE BREKA.

Le Libéral: 01 BP 6938, Abidjan 01; tel. and fax 22-52-21-41; e-mail leliberal@aviso.ci; internet www.leliberal.info; f. 1997; Dir YORO KONÉ; Editor-in-Chief BAKARY NIMAGA; circ. 15,000.

Le National: Angré, Cocody, 16 BP 165, Abidjan 16; tel. 22-52-27-43; fax 22-52-27-42; e-mail lenational@lenational.info; internet www .lenational.info; f. 1999; nationalist; Publr LAURENT TAPÉ KOULOU; Editor-in-Chief (vacant); circ. 20,000 (2002).

Notr'Aurore: Immeuble SICOGI, Bâtiment K, Appartement 124, Deux-Plateaux Aghien, blvd Latrille, Abidjan; tel. 22-42-08-21; fax 22-42-08-24; f. 2002; nationalist; Editor-in-Chief EMMANUEL GRIÉ.

Notre Chance: Immeuble SICOGI, 1er étage, porte escalier E, blvd du Gabon (Marcory), 10 BP 654, Abidjan 10; tel. 21-26-44-28; Dir MICHEL NAHOUA LEPREGNON.

Notre Voie: Cocody-les-Deux-Plateaux, 06 BP 2868, Abidjan 06; tel. 22-42-63-31; fax 22-42-63-32; e-mail gnh@africaonline.co.ci; internet www.notrevoie.ci; f. 1978; organ of the FPI; Dir WANYOU EUGÈNE ALLOU; Editor-in-Chief CÉSAR ÉTOU; circ. 20,000 (2002).

Le Nouveau Réveil: 220 Logements, Adjamé Sud-Tours SICOGI, face Frat-Mat, Bâtiment A, 2e étage P6, 04 BP 1947, Abidjan 04; tel. and fax 20-38-67-91; e-mail lenouveaureveil@yahoo.fr; internet www.lenouveaureveil.com; f. 2001 to replace weekly *Le Réveil-Hebdo*; supports PDCI—RDA; Dir of Publication DENIS KAH ZION; Editor-in-Chief EDDY PEHE; circ. 20,000 (2004).

Le Patriote: 23 rue Paul Langevin, Zone 4c, 22 BP 509, Abidjan 22; tel. 21-21-19-45; fax 21-35-11-83; e-mail info@lepatriote.net; internet www.lepatriote.net; organ of the RDR; Editor-in-Chief MOUSSA TOURÉ; circ. 40,000 (2002).

Le Populaire: 19 blvd Angoulvant, résidence Neuilly, Plateau, 01 BP 5496, Abidjan 01; tel. 21-36-34-15; fax 21-36-43-28; Dir RAPHAËL ORE LAKPÉ.

Soir Info: rue Louis Lumière, zone 4c, 10 BP 2462, Abidjan 10; tel. 21-25-32-77; fax 21-24-47-27; e-mail soirinfo@afnet.net; internet www.presseci.com/soirinfo; f. 1994; publ. by Editions Olympe; independent; Dir MAURICE FERRO BI BALI; Editor-in-Chief ZOROMÉ LOSS; circ. 22,000 (2002).

Tassouman: Abidjan-Cocody, 22 BP 400, Abidjan 22; tel. 05-70-21-68; e-mail tassouman@globeaccess.net; internet www.tassouman.ci; f. 2000; satirical; supports RDR; publication suspended Sept. 2002; Dir and Editor-in-Chief ABOUBAKAR S. KONE.

La Voie: face Institut Marie-Thérèse Houphouët-Boigny, 17 BP 656, Abidjan 17; tel. 20-37-68-23; fax 20-37-74-76; organ of the FPI; Dir ABOU DRAHAMANE SANGARÉ; Man. MAURICE LURIGNAN.

SELECTED BI-WEEKLIES AND WEEKLIES

L'Agora: Immeuble Nana Yamoussou, ave 13, rue 38, Treichville, 01 BP 5326, Abidjan 01; tel. 21-34-11-72; f. 1997; weekly; Dir FERNAND DÉDÉ; Editor-in-Chief BAMBA ALEX SOULEYMANE.

Argument: 09 BP 3328, Abidjan 09; tel. 20-37-63-96; f. 1998; weekly; Dir GUY BADIETO LIALY; Editor-in-Chief JEAN-LOUIS PÉHÉ.

Citypoche: Immeuble Nour al-Ayat, 18 BP 3136, Abidjan 18; tel. 20-21-91-89; f. 1997; weekly; Dir ÉLIANE STROEHLIN.

Le Démocrate: Maison du Congrès, ave 2, Treichville, 01 BP 1212, Abidjan 01; tel. 21-24-45-88; fax 21-24-25-61; f. 1991; weekly; organ of the PDCI—RDA; Dir NOËL YAO.

Le Front: Immeuble Mistral, 3e étage, 220 Logts, BP 11 26978 Abidjan 11; tel. 20-38-13-24; fax 20-38-70-83; e-mail quotidienlefront@yahoo.fr; internet www.lefront.com; two a week; Editorial Dir FATOUMATA COULIBALY; Editor KPOKPA BLÉ.

Gbich!: 10 BP 399, Abidjan 10; tel. and fax 21-26-31-94; e-mail gbich@assistweb.net; internet www.gbichonline.com; weekly; satirical; Editor-in-Chief MATHIEU BLEDOU.

Le Nouvel Horizon: 220 Logements, blvd du Général de Gaulle, Adjamé, 17 BP 656, Abidjan 17; tel. 20-37-68-23; f. 1990; weekly; organ of the FPI; Dir ABOU DRAHAMANE SANGARÉ; circ. 15,000.

La Nouvelle Presse: rue des Jardins, Cocody-les-Plateaux, 01 BP 8534, Abidjan 01; tel. 22-41-04-76; fax 22-41-04-15; e-mail jvieyra@africaonline.co.ci; f. 1992; weekly; publ. by Centre Africain de Presse et d'Edition; current affairs; Editors JUSTIN VIEYRA, JÉRÔME CARLOS; circ. 10,000.

Le Repère: 220 Logements, Adjamé Sud-Tours SICOGI, face Frat-Mat, Bâtiment A, 2e étage P6, 04 BP 1947, Abidjan 04; tel. and fax 20-38-67-91; supports PDCI—RDA; two a week; Dir of Publication DENIS KAH ZION; circ. 10,000 (2004).

Sports Magazine: Yopougon-SOGEFIHA, 01 BP 4030, Abidjan 01; tel. 23-45-14-02; f. 1997; weekly; Dir JOSEPH ABLE.

Téré: 220 Lgts, blvd du Général de Gaulle, Adjamé-Liberté, 20 BP 43, Abidjan 20; tel. and fax 20-37-79-42; weekly; organ of the PIT; Dir ANGÈLE GNONSOA.

Top-Visages: rue du Commerce, 23 BP 892, Abidjan 23; tel. 20-33-72-10; fax 20-32-81-05; e-mail contact@topvisages.net; internet www .topvisages.net; weekly; Editor-in-Chief E. TONGA BÉHI; circ. 40,000 (2004).

La Voie du Compatriote: Adjamé St-Michel; 09 BP 2008, Abidjan 09; tel. 20-37-50-13; f. 1998; weekly; Dir SINARI KAL.

SELECTED PERIODICALS

Côte d'Ivoire Magazine: Présidence de la République, 01 BP 1354, Abidjan 01; tel. 20-22-02-22; f. 1998; quarterly; Dir JEAN-NOËL LOUKO.

Juris-Social: Centre National de Documentation Juridique (CNDJ), villa 381 îlôt 43, face Polyclinique Saint Jacques, blvd Latrille, Cocody Deux-Plateaux, 01 BP 2757, Abidjan 01; tel. 20-22-74-85; fax 20-22-74-86; e-mail cndj@aviso-ci; internet www.cndj.ci; monthly; jurisprudence; CNDJ also publishes quarterly periodical *Juris OHADA*.

La Lettre de l'Afrique de l'Ouest: rue des Jardins, Cocody-les-Deux-Plateaux, 01 BP 8534, Abidjan 01; tel. 22-41-04-76; fax 22-41-04-15; e-mail jvieyra@africaonline.co.ci; f. 1995; publ. by Centre Africain de Presse et d'Edition; six a year; politics, economics, regional integration; Editors JUSTIN VIEYRA, JÉRÔME CARLOS.

Maisons et Matériaux: 08 BP 2150, Abidjan 08; tel. 22-42-92-17; monthly; Dir THIAM T. DJENEBOU.

Roots-Rock Magazine: Abidjan; tel. 22-42-84-74; f. 1998; monthly; music; Dir DIOMANDÉ DAVID.

RTI-Mag: 08 BP 663, Abidjan 08; tel. 20-33-14-46; fax 20-32-12-06; publ. by Radiodiffusion-Télévision Ivoirienne; listings magazine.

Sentiers: 26 ave Chardy, 01 BP 2432, Abidjan 01; tel. 20-21-95-68; fax 20-21-95-80; e-mail redaction@aviso.ci; Editor-in-Chief DIÉGOU BAILLY.

Stades d'Afrique: blvd du Général de Gaulle, 01 BP 1807, Abidjan 01; tel. 20-37-06-66; fax 20-37-25-45; e-mail fratmat@africaonline.co .ci; f. 2000; sports; monthly; Dir-Gen. EMMANUEL KOUASSI KOKORÉ; Editor-in-Chief HÉGAUD OUATTARA.

Le Succès: 21 BP 3748, Abidjan 21; tel. 20-37-71-64; monthly; Dir AKPLA PLAKATOU.

Univers jeunes: 01 BP 3713, Abidjan 01; tel. 20-21-20-00; fax 21-35-35-45; e-mail univers@africaonline.co.ci; monthly; Editor-in-Chief MOUSSA SY SAVANÉ.

La Voix d'Afrique: rue des Jardins, Cocody-les-Deux-Plateaux, 01 BP 8534, Abidjan 01; tel. 22-41-04-76; fax 22-41-04-15; e-mail jvieyra@africaonline.co.ci; publ. by Centre Africain de Presse et d'Edition; monthly; Editor-in-Chief GAOUSSOU KAMISSOKO.

NEWS AGENCIES

Agence Ivoirienne de Presse (AIP): ave Chardy, 04 BP 312, Abidjan 04; tel. 20-22-64-13; fax 20-21-35-39; e-mail aip@ci.refer.org; internet www.aip-ci.com; f. 1961; 14 regional bureaux; Dir DALLI DEBY.

Foreign Bureaux

Agence France-Presse (AFP): 18 ave du Docteur Crozet, 01 BP 726, Abidjan 01; tel. 20-21-90-17; fax 20-21-10-36; e-mail afp@aviso.ci; internet www.afp.com; Dir SERGE ARNOLD.

Associated Press (AP) (USA): 01 BP 5843, Abidjan 01; tel. 22-41-38-95; fax 22-41-28-94; e-mail iromauld@yahoo.fr; internet www.ap.org; Bureau Chief ELLEN KNICKMAYER.

PANA-Presse (Senegal): 09 BP 2744, Abidjan 09; tel. and fax 20-33-40-79; e-mail odji@bobley.africaonline.co.ci.

Reuters West Africa (United Kingdom): Résidence Les Acacias, 2e étage, appt 203–205, 20 blvd Clozel, 01 BP 2338, Abidjan 01; tel. 20-21-12-22; fax 20-21-30-77; e-mail abidjan.newsroom@reuters.com; West Africa Man. MICHEL CLÉMENT; Bureau Chief NICHOLAS PHYTHIAN.

Xinhua (New China) News Agency (People's Republic of China): Immeuble SGBCI, 4e étage, ave Lamblin, Plateau, 01 BP V321, Abidjan 01; tel. 20-32-52-20; fax 20-32-22-49; internet www.xinhua.org; Chief Correspondent LINGHU DAOCHENG.

PRESS ASSOCIATIONS

Association de la Presse Démocratique Ivoirienne (APDI): Abidjan; tel. 20-37-06-66; f. 1994; Chair. JEAN-BAPTISTE AKROU.

Union nationale des journalistes de Côte d'Ivoire (UNJCI): 06 BP 1675, Plateau, Abidjan 06; tel. 20-21-61-07; e-mail unjci@globeaccess.net; internet www.unjci.ci; f. 1991; Pres. HONORAT NDJOMOU DE YÉDAGNE; 200 mems.

Publishers

Centre Africain de Presse et d'Edition (CAPE): rue des Jardins, Cocody-les-Deux-Plateaux, 01 BP 8534, Abidjan 01; tel. 22-41-04-76; fax 22-41-04-15; e-mail jvieyra@africaonline.co.ci; Man. JUSTIN VIEYRA.

Centre d'Edition et de Diffusion Africaines (CEDA): 17 rue des Carrossiers, 04 BP 541, Abidjan 04; tel. 20-24-65-10; fax 21-25-05-67; e-mail infos@ceda-ci.com; internet www.ceda-ci.com; f. 1961; 20% state-owned; general non-fiction, school and children's books, literary fiction; Pres. and Dir-Gen. VENANCE KACOU.

Centre de Publications Evangéliques: 08 BP 900, Abidjan 08; tel. 22-44-48-05; fax 22-44-58-17; e-mail cpe@aviso.ci; f. 1970; reformed Christian; Dir JULES OUOBA.

Editions Bognini: 06 BP 1254, Abidjan 06; tel. 20-41-16-86; social sciences, literary fiction.

Editions Eburnie: 01 BP 1984, 01 Abidjan; tel. 20-21-64-65; fax 20-21-45-46; e-mail eburnie@aviso.ci; f. 2001; illustrated books for children, social sciences, poetry.

Editions Neter: 01 BP 7370, Abidjan 01; tel. 22-52-52-68; f. 1992; politics, culture, history, literary fiction; Dir RICHARD TA BI SENIN.

Nouvelles Editions Ivoiriennes: 1 blvd de Marseille, 01 BP 1818, Abidjan 01; tel. 21-24-07-66; fax 21-24-24-56; e-mail edition@nei-ci.com; internet www.nei-ci.com; f. 1972; literature, criticism, essays, drama, social sciences, history, in French and English; Dir GUY LAMBIN.

Presses Universitaires et Scolaires d'Afrique (PUSAF—Editions Cissé): 08 BP 177, Abidjan 08; tel. 22-41-12-71; mathematics, economics, medicine.

Université Nationale de Côte d'Ivoire: 01 BP V34, Abidjan 01; tel. 22-44-08-59; f. 1964; academic and general non-fiction and periodicals; Publications Dir GILLES VILASCO.

GOVERNMENT PUBLISHING HOUSE

Imprimerie Nationale: BP V87, Abidjan; tel. 20-21-76-11; fax 20-21-68-68.

Broadcasting and Communications

TELECOMMUNICATIONS

Regulatory Authorities

Agence des Télécommunications de Côte d'Ivoire (ATCI): Immeuble Postel 2001, 4e étage, rue Lecoeur, 18 BP 2203, Abidjan 18; tel. 20-34-43-74; fax 20-34-43-75; e-mail courrier@atci.ci; internet www.atci.ci; f. 1995; Man. Dir LESAN BASILE GNON.

Conseil des Télécommunications de Côte d'Ivoire: 17 BP 110, Abidjan 17; tel. 20-34-43-04; f. 1995; deals with issues of arbitration.

Service Providers

CORA de Comstar: Immeuble Alpha 2000, 11e étage, Plateau, Abidjan; tel. 20-22-81-01; fax 20-22-81-05; f. 1996 as Comstar Wireless, present name adopted 2000; mobile cellular telephone operator in Abidjan and surrounding region; operations suspended in Oct. 2003.

Côte d'Ivoire-Télécom (CI-Télécom): Immeuble Postel 2001, rue Lecoeur, 17 BP 275, Abidjan 17; tel. 20-34-40-00; fax 20-21-28-28; e-mail info@citelecom.ci; internet www.citelecom.ci; f. 1991; 51% owned by France Télécom; 49% state-owned; Pres. YAYA OUATTARA; Man. Dir ALAIN PETIT; 327,000 subscribers (June 2002).

Loteny Télécom—Télécel: 12 rue Crossons Duplessis, 01 BP 3685, Abidjan 01; tel. 20-32-32-32; fax 20-32-27-25; e-mail info@telecel.net; internet www.telecel.net; f. 1996; mobile cellular telephone operator in more than 60 urban centres; partnership between Telecel International, Access Télécom and Loteny Electronics; Pres. MIKO RWAYITARE; more than 300,000 subscribers (2002).

Orange Côte d'Ivoire: Immeuble Saha, blvd Valéry Giscard d'Estaing, Zone 4C, 11 BP 202, Abidjan 11; tel. 21-23-90-07; fax 21-23-90-11; internet www.orange.ci; f. 1996 as Société Ivoirienne de Mobiles (Ivoiris), present name adopted 2002; mobile cellular telephone operator in more than 60 urban centres; 85% owned by France Télécom; Man. Dir BERNARD CLIVET; 427,000 subscribers (June 2002).

BROADCASTING

Radio

In 1993 the Government permitted the first commercial radio stations to broadcast in Côte d'Ivoire; of the five licences initially granted, four were to foreign stations. Between 1998 and early 2001, a further 52 licences were granted, although strict regulations continue to restrict the operation of private radio stations.

Radiodiffusion-Télévision Ivoirienne (RTI): BP V 191, Abidjan 01; tel. 20-21-48-00; e-mail rti@rti.ci; f. 1962; state-owned; Pres. MAURICE BANDAMA; Dir-Gen. YACOUBA KÉBÉ.

    Fréquence 2: BP V 191, Abidjan 01; tel. 20-22-21-21; themed FM broadcasts to Abidjan and surrounding region; entertainment and youth; 147 hrs of programming weekly; transfer to private-sector management pending; Dir OULAÏ ELOI.

    Radio-CI: BP V 191, Abidjan 01; tel. 20-21-48-00; fmrly La Chaîne Nationale; general FM broadcasts; 280 hours of programmes weekly; also broadcasts regional news in national languages; 10 studios (eight in Abidjan and two in Bouaké); Dir OULAÏ ELOI.

Africa N° 1: 09 BP 951, Abidjan 09; tel. 07-83-62-09; fax 22-42-70-07; internet www.africa1.com; FM station; Dir NOËL YAO.

BBC Afrique: 04 BP 563, Abidjan 04; tel. 20-22-18-05; fax 20-21-21-01; e-mail bbcafrique@bbc.co.uk; internet www.bbc.co.uk/french; broadcasts commenced 1994; FM station operated by British Broadcasting Corpn.

City FM: Immeuble Alpha Cissé, avant la piscine d'Etat, Treichville, 01 BP 7207, Abidjan 01; tel. 21-25-10-28; internet www.assistweb.net/cityfm; f. 1999; Pres. and Man. Dir Me ALIOU SIBI.

Radio Espoir: 12 BP 27, Abidjan 12; tel. 21-75-68-02; fax 21-75-68-04; e-mail respoir@aviso.ci; internet www.radioespoir.ci; f. 1990; Roman Catholic; broadcasts in French, local and sub-regional languages; Dir Fr BASILE DIANÉ KOGNAN.

Radio France Internationale: Abidjan; tel. 05-60-92-00; e-mail biyack@hotmail.com; internet www.rfi.fr; Correspondent ALAIN BIYACK.

Radio Nostalgie: Abidjan; Dir-Gen. AHMED BAKAYOKO.

Radio Peleforo Gbon: Route Ferké km 2, BP 841, Korhogo; tel. 21-86-22-62; fax 21-86-20-33.

Radio Soleil: 16 BP 1179, Abidjan 16; tel. 21-99-17-64; fax 21-79-12-48; e-mail ebadouel@irisa.fr.

Television

Radiodiffusion-Télévision Ivoirienne (RTI): see above.

La Première Chaîne: 08 BP 331, Abidjan 08; tel. 22-44-90-39; general national and regional broadcasting; French and national languages; Dir Félicien Koffi.

TV 2: 08 BP 883, Abidjan 08; tel. 22-44-90-39; f. 1991; operates in Abidjan and the southern region; local news and current affairs; transfer to private-sector management pending; Dir Maixent Degney.

Canal Plus Horizons: Abidjan; e-mail abo.canal@aviso.ci; internet www.canalhorizons.com; broadcasts commenced 1994; subsidiary of Canal Plus (France); 15,000 subscribers (1995).

Finance

(cap. = capital; res = reserves; dep. = deposits; m. = million; br. = branch; amounts in francs CFA)

BANKING

Central Bank

Banque Centrale des Etats de l'Afrique de l'Ouest (BCEAO): 01 BP 1769, Abidjan 01; tel. 20-20-84-00; fax 20-22-28-52; internet www.bceao.int; f. 1962; HQ in Dakar, Senegal; bank of issue for the mem. states of the Union économique et monétaire ouest-africaine (UEMOA, comprising Benin, Burkina Faso, Côte d'Ivoire, Guinea-Bissau, Mali, Niger, Senegal and Togo); cap. and res 859,313m., total assets 5,671,675m. (Dec. 2002); Gov. Charles Konan Banny; Dir in Côte d'Ivoire Lansina Bakary; 5 brs.

Commercial Banks

Bank of Africa—Côte d'Ivoire (BOA—CI): ave Terrasson de Fougères, angle Rue Gourgas, 01 BP 4132, Abidjan 01; tel. 20-30-34-00; fax 20-30-34-01; e-mail boaci.dg@bkofafrica.com; internet www.bkofafrica.net/cote_d_ivoire.htm; f. 1980; 66.7% owned by Groupe African Financial Holding; cap. and res 3,061m., total assets 73,480m. (Dec. 2002); Dir-Gen. René Formey de Saint Louvent; 1 br.

Banque Atlantique—Côte d'Ivoire: Immeuble Atlantique, ave Nogues, Plateau, 04 BP 1036, Abidjan 04; tel. 20-31-59-50; fax 20-21-68-52; e-mail bacig@baci.ci; f. 1979; cap. 7,000.0m., res 237.2m., dep. 31,162.7m. (Dec. 2000); Pres. Kone Dossongui; Chair. Serge Guetta; Dir-Gen. Jean-Pierre Coti; 3 brs.

Banque de l'Habitat de Côte d'Ivoire (BHCI): 22 ave Joseph Anoma, 01 BP 2325, Abidjan 01; tel. 20-22-60-00; fax 20-22-58-18; f. 1993; cap. and res 1,755m., total assets 16,834m. (Dec. 1999); Chair. David Amuah; Man. Dir Lancina Coulibaly.

Banque Internationale pour le Commerce et l'Industrie de la Côte d'Ivoire SA (BICI-CI): ave Franchet d'Espérey, 01 BP 1298, Abidjan 01; tel. 20-20-16-00; fax 20-20-17-00; e-mail michel.lafont@africa.bnpparibas.com; internet www.bicici.org; f. 1962; 60.3% owned by BNP Paribas (France); cap. 16,666.7m., res 19,005.0m., dep. 231,005.4m. (Dec. 2002); Chair. Ange Koffy; 35 brs.

Banque Paribas Côte d'Ivoire (Paribas—CI): 17 ave Terrasson de Fougères, 17 BP 09, Abidjan 17; tel. 20-21-86-86; fax 20-21-88-23; f. 1984; 85% owned by BNP Paribas (France); cap. and res 2,938m., total assets 30,697m. (Dec. 1999); Pres. and Dir-Gen. François Dauge.

BIAO—Côte d'Ivoire (BIAO—CI): 8–10 ave Joseph Anoma, 01 BP 1274, Abidjan 01; tel. 20-20-07-20; fax 20-20-07-00; e-mail info@biao.co.ci; internet www.biao.co.ci; f. 1980; fmrly Banque Internationale pour l'Afrique de l'Ouest—Côte d'Ivoire; 70% owned by Banque Belgolaise (Belgium), 20% state-owned; cap. 10,000.0m., res 3,129.6m., dep. 164,659.6m. (Dec. 2003); Pres. Seydou Elimane Diarra; Vice-Pres. Daniel Cuylits; 31 brs.

Citibank Côte d'Ivoire: Immeuble Botreau-Roussel, 28 ave Delafosse, 01 BP 3698, Abidjan 01; tel. 20-20-90-00; fax 20-21-76-85; e-mail citibank@odaci.net; dep. 55,155m, total assets 127,630m. (Dec. 1999); Dir-Gen. Marc H. Wiesing.

Compagnie Bancaire de l'Atlantique Côte d'Ivoire (COBACI): Immeuble Atlantique, ave Nogues, 01 BP 522, Abidjan 01; tel. 20-21-28-04; fax 20-21-07-98; e-mail cobaci@africaonline.co.ci; 65% owned by Banque Atlantique–Côte d'Ivoire; cap. 3,274m., res 375m., dep. 17,515m. (Dec. 2001); Pres. Dossongui Koné; Dir-Gen. René M. Delafosse.

Compagnie Financière de la Côte d'Ivoire (COFINCI): Tour BICI-CI, 15e étage, rue Gourgas, 01 BP 1566, Abidjan 01; tel. 20-21-27-32; fax 20-21-26-43; e-mail y.kouassi@bicici.com; f. 1974; 72% owned by BICI-CI; cap. and res 2,425.0m., total assets 6,514.0m. (Dec. 2001); Chair. Ange Koffy.

Ecobank–Côte d'Ivoire: Immeuble Alliance, 1 ave Terrasson de Fougères, 01 BP 4107, Abidjan 01; tel. 20-21-10-41; fax 20-21-88-16; e-mail ecobankci@ecobank.com; internet www.ecobank.com; f. 1989; 94% owned by Ecobank Transnational Inc (Togo); cap. 3,226m., res −171m., dep. 86,404m. (Dec. 2002); Man. Dir Fogan Sossah; 1 br.

Omnifinance: 6e étage, Immeuble Alliance, 17 ave Terrasson de Fougères, 01 BP 6028, Abidjan 01; tel. 20-21-42-08; fax 20-21-42-58.

Société Générale de Banques en Côte d'Ivoire (SGBCI): 5–7 ave Joseph Anoma, 01 BP 1355, Abidjan 01; tel. 20-20-12-34; fax 20-20-14-92; e-mail drc.dir@sgbci.net; internet sgbci.groupe.socgen.com; f. 1962; 54.8% owned by Société Générale (France); cap. 15,333m., total assets 505,783m. (Dec. 2001); Pres. Tiémoko Yadé Coulibaly; Dir-Gen and Administrator Michel Miaille; 55 brs.

Société Générale de Financement et de Participations en Côte d'Ivoire (SOGEFINANCE): 5–7 ave Joseph Anoma, 01 BP 3904, Abidjan 01; tel. 20-22-55-30; fax 20-32-67-60; f. 1978; 58% owned by SGBCI; cap. and res 2,193m., total assets 6,285m. (Dec. 2001); Pres. Jean-Louis Mattei; Dir-Gen. Michel Miaille.

Société Ivoirienne de Banque (SIB): Immeuble Alpha 2000, 34 blvd de la République, 01 BP 1300, Abidjan 01; tel. 20-20-00-00; fax 221-97-41; e-mail info@sib.ci; internet www.sib.ci; f. 1962; 51% owned by Crédit Lyonnais (France), 49% state-owned; reduction of state holding to 19% proposed; cap. and res 15,733m., total assets 173,809m. (Dec. 2002); Man. Dir Pascal Fall; 14 brs.

Standard Chartered Bank Côte d'Ivoire (SCB—CI): 23 blvd de la République, face Commissariat du 1er arrondissement, 17 BP 1141, Abidjan 17; tel. 20-30-32-00; fax 20-30-32-01; internet www.standardchartered.com/ci/index.html; f. 2001; subsidiary of Standard Chartered Bank (United Kingdom); Dir-Gen. Christopher Knight; 4 brs.

Credit Institutions

Afribail—Côte d'Ivoire (Afribail—CI): 8–10 ave Joseph Anoma, 01 BP 1274, Abidjan 01; tel. 20-20-07-20; fax 20-20-07-00; 95% owned by BIAO—CI; cap. and res 776m., total assets 11,900m. (Dec. 1999); Chair. René Amany; Man. Dir Jacob Ahiwa Brou.

BICI Bail de Côte d'Ivoire: Tour BICI-CI, 5e étage, ave Franchet d'Espérey, 01 BP 6495, Abidjan 01; tel. 20-20-17-90; fax 20-22-93-95; e-mail m.djedjess@bicici.com; 75% owned by BICI-CI; cap. and res 1,463.5m., total assets 13,805.5m. (Dec. 2001); Pres. Ange Koffy; Man. Dir Martin Djedjes.

Coopérative Ivoirienne d'Epargne et de Crédit Automobile (CIECA): 04 BP 2084, Abidjan 04; tel. 20-22-77-13; fax 20-22-77-35; cap. and res 805m. (Dec. 1998), total assets 1,169m. (Dec. 1999); Dir-Gen. Dally Zabo.

Société Africaine de Crédit Automobilier (SAFCA): 1 rue des Carrossiers, Zone 3, 04 BP 27, Abidjan 04; tel. 21-21-07-07; fax 21-21-07-00; e-mail safca@aviso.ci; f. 1956; cap. and res 5,681.8m., total assets 22,511.1m. (Dec. 2001); Pres. and Dir-Gen. Diack Diawar.

Société Africaine de Crédit-Bail (SAFBAIL): Immeuble SAFCA, 1 rue des Carrossiers, Zone 3, 04 BP 27, Abidjan 04; tel. 21-24-91-77; fax 21-35-77-90; e-mail safca@aviso.ci; f. 1971; cap. and res 2,922m., total assets 13,414m. (Dec. 1999); Chair. and Man. Dir Diack Diawar.

SOGEFIBAIL—CI: 26 ave Delafosse, 01 BP 1355, Abidjan 01; tel. 20-32-85-15; fax 20-33-14-93; 35% owned by GENEFITEC, 35% by SOGEFINANCE, 25% by SGBCI; cap. and res 2,182m., total assets 7,046m. (Dec. 2001); Pres. Jean-Louis Mattei; Dir Pierre Gabriel Siby.

Bankers' Association

Association Professionnelle des Banques et Etablissements Financiers de Côte d'Ivoire (APBEFCI): 01 BP 3810, Abidjan 01; tel. 20-21-20-08; affiliated to Conseil National du Patronat Ivoirien (q.v.); Pres. Jean-Pierre Meyer.

Financial Institution

Caisse Autonome d'Amortissement de Côte d'Ivoire (CAA): Immeuble SCIAM, ave Marchand, 01 BP 670, Abidjan 01; tel. 20-20-98-00; fax 20-21-35-78; e-mail caadg@aviso.ci; f. 1959; management of state funds; cap. 10,000m., total assets 308,080m. (Dec. 2000); Chair. Abdoulaye Koné; Man. Dir Sékou Bamba.

STOCK EXCHANGE

Bourse Régionale des Valeurs Mobilières (BRVM): 18 ave Joseph Anoma, 01 BP 3802, Abidjan 01; tel. 20-32-66-85; fax 20-32-66-84; e-mail brvm@brvm.org; internet www.brvm.org; f. 1998 to succeed Bourse des Valeurs d'Abidjan; regional stock exchange serving mem. states of UEMOA; Dir-Gen. Jean-Paul Gillet.

BRVM (Antenne Nationale de Côte d'Ivoire): 18 ave Joseph Anoma, 01 BP 1541, Abidjan 01; tel. 20-31-55-50; fax 20-32-47-77;

e-mail tbah@brvm.org; Pres. Tiémoko Tade Coulibaly; Man. Tidiane Amadou Bah.

INSURANCE

Abidjanaise d'Assurances: Immeuble Woodin Center, ave Noguès, 01 BP 2909, Abidjan 01; tel. 20-22-46-96; fax 20-22-64-81; e-mail abjassur@africaonline.co.ci; Dir-Gen. Marc Richmond.

African American Insurance Co (AFRAM): Immeuble ex-Monopris, 2 ave Noguès, 01 BP 7124, Abidjan 01; tel. 20-31-30-44; fax 20-32-69-72; Dir-Gen. Christian Casel.

Alliance Africaine d'Assurances (3A): 17 BP 477, Abidjan 17; tel. 20-32-42-52; fax 20-32-54-90; Pres. Dam Sarr; Dir-Gen. Corinne Sarr.

AXA Assurances Côte d'Ivoire: ave Delafosse Prolongée, 01 BP 378, Abidjan 01; tel. 20-21-73-81; fax 20-22-12-43; f. 1981; fmrly l'Union Africaine—IARD; insurance and reinsurance; Chair. Joachim Richmond; Dir Alexandre Ahui Atte.

AXA Vie Côte d'Ivoire: 9 ave Houdaille, 01 BP 2016, Abidjan 01; tel. 20-22-25-15; fax 20-22-37-60; f. 1985; fmrly Union Africaine Vie; life assurance and capitalization; Chair. Joachim Richmond; Dir Patrice Desgranges.

Colina: Immeuble Colina, blvd Roume, 01 BP 3832, Abidjan 01; tel. 20-21-65-05; fax 20-22-59-05; e-mail c-dg@colina-sa.com; internet www.colina-sa.com; f. 1980; Chair. Michel Pharaon; Dir-Gen. Raymond Farhat.

Compagnie Nationale d'Assurances (CNA): Immeuble Symphonie, 30 ave du Général de Gaulle, 01 BP 1333, Abidjan 01; tel. 20-21-49-19; fax 20-22-49-06; f. 1972; cap. 400m.; insurance and reinsurance; transfer to private ownership pending; Chair. Sounkalo Djibo; Man. Dir Richard Coulibaly.

Gras Savoye Côte d'Ivoire: Immeuble Trade Center, ave Noguès, 01 BP 5675, Abidjan 01; tel. 20-25-25-00; fax 20-25-25-25; e-mail olivier.dubois@grassavoye.ci; internet www.grassavoye.com; affiliated to Gras Savoye (France); Man. Olivier Dubois.

Mutuelle Centrale d'Assurances: 15 Immeuble Ebrien, 01 BP 1217, Abidjan 01; tel. 20-21-11-24; fax 20-33-18-37.

Nouvelle Société Africaine d'Assurances (NSIA): Immeuble Manci, rue A43, 01 BP 1571 Abidjan 01; tel. 20-31-75-00; fax 20-31-98-00; e-mail nsia@africaonline.co.ci; f. 1995; Chair. and Man. Dir Jean Kacou Diagou.

NSIA-Vie: Immeuble Zandaman, ave Noguès, 01 BP 4092, Abidjan 01; tel. 20-31-98-00; fax 20-33-25-79; e-mail agci@africaonline.co.ci; f. 1988; fmrly Assurances Générales de Côte d'Ivoire—Vie (AGCI-Vie); life; Pres. and Dir-Gen. Jean Kacou Diagou.

Société Africaine d'Assurances et de Réassurances en République de Côte d'Ivoire (SAFARRIV): 01 BP 1741, Abidjan 01; tel. 20-21-91-57; fax 20-21-82-72; e-mail groupe-safarriv@safarriv.ci; internet www.safarriv.ci; f. 1975; affiliated to AGF Afrique; Pres. Tiémoko Yadé Coulibaly; Man. Dir Christian Arrault.

Trade and Industry

GOVERNMENT AGENCIES

Autorité pour la Régulation du Café et du Cacao: Abidjan; f. 2001; implements regulatory framework for coffee and cocoa trade.

Bureau National d'Etudes Techniques et de Développement (BNETD): ancien hôtel 'Le Relais', blvd Hassan II, Cocody, 04 BP 945, Abidjan 04; tel. 22-44-28-05; fax 22-44-56-66; e-mail info@bnetd .sita.net; f. 1978 as Direction et Contrôle des Grands Travaux; management and supervision of major public works projects; Man. Dir Don-Mello Ahoua.

Comité de Privatisation: 6 blvd de l'Indénié, 01 BP 1141, Abidjan 01; tel. 20-22-22-31; fax 20-22-22-35; e-mail cpct@africaonline.co.ci; state privatization authority; Pres. Paul Agodio; Dir-Gen. Ahoua Don Mello.

Compagnie Ivoirienne pour le Développement des Cultures Vivrières (CIDV): Abidjan; tel. 20-21-00-79; f. 1988; production of food crops; Man. Dir Benoît N'Dri Brou.

Nouvelle PETROCI: Immeuble les Hévéas, 14 blvd Carde, BP V194, Abidjan 01; tel. 20-20-25-00; fax 20-21-68-24; e-mail petrociholding@globeaccess.net; f. 1975 as Société Nationale d'Opérations Pétrolières de la Côte d'Ivoire (PETROCI); restructured 2000 to comprise three companies—Petroci Exploration Production, SA, Petroci Gaz and Petroci Industries Services; all aspects of hydrocarbons development; Pres. Paul Gui Dibo; Man. Dir Koffi Ernest.

Société pour le Développement Minier de la Côte d'Ivoire (SODEMI): 31 blvd des Martyrs, 01 BP 2816, Abidjan 01; tel. 22-44-

29-94; fax 22-44-08-21; e-mail sodemidg@aviso.cg; f. 1962; geological and mineral research; Pres. Nicolas Kouandi Angba; Man. Dir Jean-Yves Likane.

Société de Développement des Plantations Forestières (SODEFOR): blvd François Mitterrand, 01 BP 3770, Abidjan 01; tel. 22-44-46-16; fax 22-44-02-40; f. 1954; establishment and management of tree plantations, management of state forests, marketing of timber products; Man. Dir Jean-Claude Aneh.

Société pour le Développement des Productions Animales (SODEPRA): 01 BP 1249, Abidjan 01; tel. 20-21-13-10; f. 1970; rearing of livestock; Man. Dir Paul Lamizana.

DEVELOPMENT AGENCIES

Agence Française de Développement (AFD): blvd François Mitterrand, 01 BP 1814, Abidjan 01; tel. 22-44-53-05; fax 22-44-21-78; e-mail afdci@aviso.ci; internet www.afd.fr; fmrly Caisse Française de Développement; Dir in Côte d'Ivoire Guy Terracol.

Centre de Promotion des Investissements en Côte d'Ivoire (CEPICI): Tour CCIA, 5e étage, BP V152, Abidjan 01; tel. 20-21-40-70; fax 20-21-40-71; e-mail infocepici@bnetd.ci; internet www.cepici .net; f. 1993; investment promotion authority; Dir-Gen. Tchétché N'Guessan.

CHAMBERS OF COMMERCE

Chambre d'Agriculture de la Côte d'Ivoire: 11 ave Lamblin, 01 BP 1291, Abidjan 01; tel. 20-32-92-13; fax 20-32-92-20; Sec.-Gen. Gauthier N'Zi.

Chambre de Commerce et d'Industrie de Côte d'Ivoire: 6 ave Joseph Anoma, 01 BP 1399, Abidjan 01; tel. 20-33-16-00; fax 20-32-39-42; e-mail cci@africaonline.co.ci; f. 1992; Pres. Jean-Louis Billon; Dir-Gen. Yao Kouame.

TRADE ASSOCIATIONS

Bourse du Café et du Cacao (BCC): 04 BP 2576, Abidjan 04; tel. 20-20-27-20; fax 20-20-28-14; e-mail info@bcc.ci; internet www.bcc .ci; f. 2001 to replace marketing, purchasing and certain other functions of La Nouvelle Caistab (Caisse de Stabilisation et de Soutien des Prix des Productions Agricoles); Pres. Lucien Tapé Doh.

Fédération Ivoirienne des Producteurs de Café et de Cacao (FIPCC): Yamoussoukro; f. 1998; coffee and cocoa growers' asscn; Chair. Cissé Lociné; c. 3,000 mems.

Organisation de Commercialisation de l'Ananas et de la Banane (OCAB): Abidjan; pineapple and banana growers' asscn; Exec. Sec. Emmanuel Doli.

EMPLOYERS' ORGANIZATIONS

Association Nationale des Producteurs de Café-Cacao de Côte d'Ivoire (ANAPROCI): Pres. Henri Amouzou; Sec.-Gen. Thomas Eyimin.

Conseil National du Patronat Ivoirien: 01 BP 8666, Abidjan 01; tel. 20-32-17-97; fax 20-32-39-73; e-mail cnpi@aviso.ci; f. 1993; Pres. Diack Diawar; Sec.-Gen. Aboubakar Coulibaly; nine affiliated federations, including the following.

Fédération Maritime de la Côte d'Ivoire (FEDERMAR): 04 BP 723, Abidjan 04; tel. 20-21-25-83; f. 1958; Sec.-Gen. Vacaba Touré de Movaly.

Fédération Nationale des Industries et Services de Côte d'Ivoire (FNISCI): 01 BP 1340, Abidjan 01; tel. 20-21-71-42; fax 20-21-72-56; internet www.fnisci.org; f. 1993; Pres. Joseph-Desiré Biley; Dir-Gen. Daniel Teurquetil; 230 mems.

Syndicat des Commerçants Importateurs et Exportateurs (SCIMPEX): 01 BP 3792, Abidjan 01; tel. 20-21-54-27; fax 20-32-56-52; Pres. Jacques Rossignol; Sec.-Gen. M. Koffi.

Syndicat des Entrepreneurs et des Industriels de la Côte d'Ivoire (SEICI): Immeuble Jean Lefèbvre, 14 blvd de Marseille, 01 BP 464, Abidjan 01; tel. 20-21-83-85; f. 1934; Pres. Abdel Aziz Thiam.

Syndicat des Exportateurs et Négociants en Bois de Côte d'Ivoire: Immeuble CCIA, 11e étage, 01 BP 1979, Abidjan 01; tel. 20-21-12-39; fax 20-21-26-42; e-mail unemaf@africaonline.co.ci; Pres. Souleymane Coulibaly.

Syndicat des Producteurs Industriels du Bois (SPIB): Immeuble CCIA, 11e étage, 01 BP 318, Abidjan 01; tel. 20-21-12-39; fax 20-21-26-42; e-mail unemaf@africaonline.co.ci; f. 1943; Pres. Wilfried Birkenmaier.

Union des Entreprises Agricoles et Forestières: Immeuble CCIA, 11e étage, 01 BP 2300, Abidjan 01; tel. 20-21-12-39; fax 20-21-26-42; e-mail unemaf@africaonline.co.ci; f. 1952; Pres. Fulgence Koffy.

UTILITIES

Electricity

Compagnie Ivoirienne d'Electricité (CIE): ave Christiani, 01 BP 6932, Abidjan 01; tel. 21-23-33-00; fax 21-24-63-22; e-mail info@cie.ci; f. 1990; 71% controlled by Société Bouygues group (France); Pres. MARCEL ZADI KESSY; Dir-Gen. MARCEL PELISSOU.

Compagnie Ivoirienne de Production d'Electricité (CIPREL): Tour Sidom, 12e étage, ave Houdaille, 01 BP 4039, Abidjan 01; tel. 20-22-60-97; independent power production; Pres. OLIVIER BOUYGUES.

Gas

Gaz de Côte d'Ivoire (GDCI): 01 BP 1351, Abidjan; tel. 22-44-49-55; f. 1961; transfer to majority private ownership pending; gas distributor; Man. Dir LAMBERT KONAN.

Water

Société de Distribution d'Eau de la Côte d'Ivoire (SODECI): 1 ave Christiani, Treichville, 01 BP 1843, Abidjan 01; tel. 21-23-30-00; fax 21-24-20-33; f. 1959; production, treatment and distribution of drinking water; 46% owned by Groupe Bouygues (France), 51% owned by employees; Chair. MARCEL ZADI KESSY; Man. Dir PIERRE LE TAREAU.

TRADE UNIONS

Dignité: 03 BP 2031, Abidjan 03; tel. 21-39-26-02; fax 21-37-74-89; Sec.-Gen. BASILE MAHAN-GAHE; 10,000 mems (2001).

Fédération des Syndicats Autonomes de la Côte d'Ivoire (FESACI): Abidjan; breakaway group from the Union Générale des Travailleurs de Côte d'Ivoire; Sec.-Gen. MARCEL ETTÉ.

Union Générale des Travailleurs de Côte d'Ivoire (UGTCI): 05 BP 1203, Abidjan 05; tel. 20-21-26-65; f. 1962; Sec.-Gen. HYACINTHE ADIKO NIAMKEY; 100,000 individual mems; 190 affiliated unions.

Transport

RAILWAYS

The rail network in Côte d'Ivoire totalled 1,316 km in 1999, including 660 km of track from Abidjan to Niangoloko, on the border with Burkina Faso; from there, the railway extends to Kaya, via the Burkinabè capital, Ouagadougou.

SITARAIL—Transport Ferroviaire de Personnel et de Marchandises: Résidence Memanou, blvd Clozel, Plateau, 16 BP 1216, Abidjan 16; tel. 20-21-06-36; fax 20-22-48-47; f. 1995 to operate services on Abidjan–Ouagadougou–Kaya (Burkina Faso) line; Man. Dir ABDELAZIZ THIAM.

ROADS

There are about 68,000 km of roads, of which some 6,000 km are paved. Some 68,000m. francs CFA was invested in the road network in 1994–98; projects included the upgrading of 3,000 km of roads and 30,000 km of tracks. Tolls were introduced on some roads in the mid-1990s, to assist in funding the maintenance of the network.

Société des Transports Abidjanais (SOTRA): 01 BP 2009, Abidjan 01; tel. 21-24-90-80; fax 21-25-97-21; e-mail sotra@access.net; f. 1960; 60% state-owned; urban transport; Dir-Gen. PHILIPPE ATTEY.

SHIPPING

Côte d'Ivoire has two major ports, Abidjan and San-Pédro, both of which are industrial and commercial establishments with financial autonomy. Abidjan, which handled some 15.0m. metric tons of goods in 2001, is the largest container and trading port in West Africa. Access to the port is via the 2.7-km Vridi Canal. The port at San-Pédro, which handled 1.2m. tons of goods in 1999, remains the main gateway to the south-western region of Côte d'Ivoire. As a result of widespread civil unrest from September 2002, much international freight transport that formerly left or entered the West African region through ports in Côte d'Ivoire was transferred to neighbouring countries.

Port Autonome d'Abidjan (PAA): BP V85, Abidjan; tel. 21-23-80-00; fax 21-23-80-80; e-mail info@paa-ci.org; internet www.paa-ci.org; f. 1992; transferred to private ownership in 1999; Pres. ANGE-FRANÇOIS BARRY-BATTESTI; Man. Dir ALLAH ABOIDJÉ.

Port Autonome de San-Pédro (PASP): BP 339/340, San-Pédro; tel. 34-71-20-00; fax 34-71-27-15; e-mail pasp@pasp.ci; internet sanpedro-portci.com; f. 1971; Man. Dir OGOU ATTEMENE.

AMICI: Km 1, blvd de Marseille, 16 BP 643, Abidjan 16; tel. 21-35-28-50; fax 21-35-28-53; e-mail amici.abj@aviso.ci; internet www.amici-shipping.com; f. 1998; 45% owned by Ivorian interests, 25% by Danish interests, 20% by German interests and 10% by French interests.

Compagnie Maritime Africaine—Côte d'Ivoire (COMAF—CI): rond-point du Nouveau Port, 08 BP 867, Abidjan 08; tel. 20-32-40-77; f. 1973; navigation and management of ships; Dir FRANCO BERNARDINI.

SDV—Côte d'Ivoire (SDV—CI): 01 BP 4082, Abidjan 01; tel. 20-20-20-20; fax 20-20-21-20; f. 1943; sea and air transport; storage and warehousing; affiliated to Groupe Bolloré (France); Pres. GILLES CUCHE.

SAGA Côte d'Ivoire: rond-point du Nouveau Port, 01 BP 1727, Abidjan 01; tel. 21-23-23-23; fax 21-24-25-06; f. 1959; merchandise handling, transit and storage; privately owned; Pres. M. GEORGES; Dir-Gen. DAVID CHARRIER.

Société Agence Maritime de l'Ouest Africain—Côte d'Ivoire (SAMOA—CI): rue des Gallions, 01 BP 1611, Abidjan 01; tel. 20-21-29-65; f. 1955; shipping agents; Man. Dir CLAUDE PERDRIAUD.

Société Ivoirienne de Navigation Maritime (SIVOMAR): 5 rue Charpentier, zone 2B, Treichville, 01 BP 1395, Abidjan 01; tel. 20-21-73-23; fax 20-32-38-53; f. 1977; shipments to ports in Africa, the Mediterranean and the Far East; Dir SIMPLISSE DE MESSE ZINSOU.

Société Ouest-Africaine d'Entreprises Maritimes en Côte d'Ivoire (SOAEM–CI): 01 BP 1727, Abidjan 01; tel. 20-21-59-69; fax 20-32-24-67; f. 1978; merchandise handling, transit and storage; Chair. JACQUES PELTIER; Dir JACQUES COLOMBANI.

SOCOPAO–Côte d'Ivoire: Km 1, blvd de la République, 01 BP 1297, Abidjan 01; tel. 21-24-13-14; fax 21-24-21-30; e-mail socopao@africaonline.co.ci; shipping agents; Shipping Dir OLIVIER RANJARD.

CIVIL AVIATION

There are three international airports: Abidjan–Félix Houphouët-Boigny, Bouaké and Yamoussoukro. Work to expand and modernize Abidjan's airport began in mid-1996: the project, costing an estimated 14,000m. francs CFA, was scheduled for completion in late 2000. In addition, there are 25 domestic and regional airports, including those at Bouna, Korhogo, Man, Odienné and San-Pédro.

Agence Nationale de l'Aviation Civile: 07 BP 148, Abidjan 07; tel. 21-27-74-24; fax 21-27-63-46; civil aviation authority; Dir JEAN KOUASSI ABONOUAN.

Air Inter Ivoire: Aéroport de Port Boüet, 07 BP 62, Abidjan 07; tel. 21-27-84-65; internal flights.

Société Nouvelle Air Ivoire: Immeuble République, place de la République, 01 BP 7782, Abidjan 01; tel. 20-25-14-00; fax 20-25-14-25; e-mail info@airivoire.com; internet www.airivoire.com; f. 2000 to replace Air Ivoire (f. 1960); privatized in 2001; 76.42% owned by All Africa Airways, 23.58% state-owned; internal and regional flights.

Tourism

The game reserves, forests, lagoons, coastal resorts, rich ethnic folklore and the lively city of Abidjan are tourist attractions; Côte d'Ivoire also has well-developed facilities for business visitors, including golfing centres. Some 301,000 tourists visited Côte d'Ivoire in 1998; receipts from tourism in that year totalled US $108m. Tourism has been negatively affected by instability resulting from the *coup d'état* in December 1999, the disputed elections of October 2000, and the widespread civil unrest that commenced in September 2002. In 2002 receipts from tourism totalled $50m.

Office Ivoirien du Tourisme et de l'Hôtellerie: Immeuble ex-EECI, place de la République, 01 BP 8538, Abidjan 01; tel. 20-20-65-00; fax 20-20-65-31; e-mail oith@africaonline.co.ci; internet www.tourisme.ci; f. 1992; Dir CAMILLE KOUASSI.

CROATIA

Introductory Survey

Location, Climate, Language, Religion, Flag, Capital

The Republic of Croatia is situated in south-eastern Europe and has a long western coastline on the Adriatic Sea. It is bordered to the north-west by Slovenia, to the north-east by Hungary and to the east by the Vojvodina province of Serbia (Serbia and Montenegro). Bosnia and Herzegovina abuts into Croatia, forming a southern border along the Sava river and an eastern border within the Dinaric Alps. The Croatian territory of Dubrovnik (formerly Ragusa), which is situated at the southern tip of the narrowing stretch of Croatia (beyond a short coastal strip of Bosnia and Herzegovina), has a short border with Montenegro. The climate is continental in the hilly interior and Mediterranean on the coast. There is steady rainfall throughout the year, although summer is the wettest season. The average annual rainfall in Zagreb is 890 mm (35 ins). Both the ethnic Croats (who comprised 89.6% of the total population according to the 2001 census) and the Serb minority (4.5%) speak closely related languages of the Southern Slavonic group formerly referred to as variants of Serbo-Croat, but known, since the early 1990s, as Croatian and Serbian, respectively. Croatian is written in the Latin script, while Serbian is more commonly written in the Cyrillic script. There are, in addition, a number of small minority communities in Croatia, notably the Muslim community (which comprised 0.5% of the total population in 2001). The national flag (proportions 1 by 2) consists of three horizontal stripes, of red, white and dark blue, with the arms of Croatia (a shield of 25 squares, alternately red and white, below a blue crown composed of five shields) fimbriated in red and white and set in the centre of the flag, overlapping all three stripes. The capital is Zagreb.

Recent History

From the 16th century the territory of what is now the Republic of Croatia was divided between the Osmanlı (Ottoman—Turkish) and Habsburg (Austrian) Empires (although Dalmatia and Istria were dominated at different times by Venice and by France, while Ragusa—Dubrovnik was formerly an independent republic). After the Hungarian revolution of 1848–49, Croatia and Slavonia were made Austrian crown-lands. The Habsburg Empire became the Dual Monarchy of Austria-Hungary in 1867, and the territories were restored to the Hungarian Crown in the following year. Croatia gained its autonomy and was formally joined with Slavonia in 1881. However, Hungarian nationalism transformed traditional Croat-Serb rivalries into Southern Slav ('Yugoslav') solidarity. Following the collapse of the Austro-Hungarian Empire at the end of the First World War in October 1918, a Kingdom of Serbs, Croats and Slovenes (under the Serbian monarchy) was proclaimed on 4 December. The new Kingdom united Serbia, including Macedonia and Kosovo, with Montenegro and the Habsburg lands (modern Croatia, Slovenia and Vojvodina). The Kingdom was, however, dominated by the Serbs, and the Croats, as the second largest ethnic group, sought a greater share of power. Increasing unrest within the Kingdom culminated in the meeting of a separatist Croatian assembly in Zagreb in 1928. King Aleksandar imposed a royal dictatorship in January 1929, formally renaming the country Yugoslavia in October. In 1934 the King was assassinated in France by Croatian extremists.

Meanwhile, the Fascist Ustaša (Rebel) movement was gaining support among the discontented Croat peasantry. When German and Italian forces invaded Yugoslavia in 1941, many Croats welcomed the Axis powers' support for the establishment of an Independent State of Croatia. The new Croatian state, which included most of Bosnia and Herzegovina and parts of Serbia as well as modern-day Croatia, was proclaimed on 9 April 1941 and was led by the leader of the Ustaša, Ante Pavelić. During the Ustaša regime a vast number of Jews, Serbs, Roma (Gypsies) and political dissidents were murdered in extermination camps. At the same time fierce armed resistance was being waged by the Partisans, who were led by Josip Broz, known as Tito, the Croat-Slovene leader of the Communist Party of Yugoslavia (CPY). By 1943 Tito's forces were able to proclaim a provisional government in a number of areas. The Ustaša state collapsed in 1944, and Croatia was restored to Yugoslavia as one unit of a federal communist republic, which became the Socialist Federal Republic of Yugoslavia (SFRY) in 1963.

During the 1960s there was an increase in nationalism in Croatia. This 'mass movement' (*Maspok*) was supported by Croatian members of the ruling League of Communists (as the CPY had been renamed), as well as by non-communists. In December 1971 Tito committed himself to opposing the nationalist movement, and the Croatian communist leaders were obliged to resign. Together with others prominent in *Maspok*, they were arrested, and a purge of the League of Communists of Croatia (LCC) followed. In 1974, however, Tito introduced a new Constitution, which enshrined the federal (almost confederal) and collective nature of the Yugoslav state.

When the power of the LCC (which contained a high proportion of Serbs) began to decline, particularly from 1989, Croatian nationalism re-emerged as a significant force. Dissidents of the 1970s and 1980s were the main beneficiaries. Dr Franjo Tuđman, who had twice been imprisoned for publicly criticizing repression in Croatia, formed the Croatian Democratic Union (CDU) in 1990. This rapidly became the main challenger to the ruling party, which had changed its name to the League of Communists of Croatia—Party of Democratic Reform (LCC—PDR). The communists introduced a plurality ('first-past-the-post') voting system for the multi-party elections to the republican legislature in April–May 1990. Tuđman campaigned as a nationalist, prompting considerable concern among the Serbs by advocating a 'Greater Croatia' (to include Bosnia).

At the elections to the tricameral republican Sabor (Assembly), which took place on 24 April and 6–7 May 1990, the CDU obtained an absolute majority of seats in each of the three chambers, with 205 out of 351 seats in total. The next largest party was the LCC——PDR, with 73 seats. (Both the CDU and LCC—PDR won further seats in alliance with other parties.) Tuđman was elected President of Croatia, but he attempted to allay Serb fears by offering the vice-presidency of the Sabor to Dr Jovan Rašković, the leader of the Serbian Democratic Party. Although Rašković eventually refused the post, another Serb was appointed to it. However, Serb-dominated areas remained alienated by Tuđman's Croat nationalism. A 'Serb National Council', based at Knin (in Krajina), was formed in July and organized a referendum on autonomy for the Croatian Serbs. Despite attempts by the Croatian authorities to prohibit the referendum, it took place, amid virtual insurrection in some areas, in late August and early September. In October the Serb National Council announced the results of the referendum, and declared autonomy for the Krajina areas as the 'Serb Autonomous Region—SAR of Krajina'.

Meanwhile, in August 1990 the Socialist Republic of Croatia became the Republic of Croatia. In the same month the Sabor voted to dismiss the republican member of the federal State Presidency, Dr Stjepan (Stipe) Šuvar, and replace him with Stjepan (Stipe) Mesić, then President of the Government (premier) of Croatia. His appointment was confirmed in October. In December the Sabor enacted a new republican Constitution, which declared Croatia's sovereignty, its authority over its own armed forces and its right to secede from the SFRY. Tensions increased when in January 1991 the Croatian authorities refused to comply with an order by the federal State Presidency to disarm all paramilitary groups. The Croatian Minister of Defence was indicted on a charge of plotting armed rebellion, but the Croatian Government refused to arrest him and boycotted negotiations on the future of the federation. On 21 February Croatia asserted the primacy of its Constitution and laws over those of the SFRY and declared its conditions for participation in a confederation of sovereign states. Later that month the self-proclaimed SAR of Krajina declared its separation from Croatia and its intention of uniting with Serbia. In April the Croatian National Guard was formed, replacing the Territorial Defence Force, which had been under the jurisdiction of the Yugoslav People's Army (Jugoslovenska Narodna Armija—JNA). On 19 May some 94% of the voters participating in a referendum (which was largely boycotted by the Serb population) favoured

Croatia's becoming a sovereign entity, possibly within a confederal Yugoslavia, and 92% rejected a federal Yugoslavia.

On 25 June 1991 Croatia and Slovenia declared their independence and began the process of dissociation from the SFRY. (Two days later the SAR of Krajina declared its unification with the self-proclaimed Serb 'Community of Municipalities of Bosnian Krajina', based in Banja Luka, in Bosnia and Herzegovina.) During July war effectively began between the Croat and Serb communities in Croatia. In August an SAR of Western Slavonia was declared; the SAR of Slavonia, Baranja and Western Sirmium (known as Western Srem to Serbs) also proclaimed its autonomy later that month. In the same month Tuđman appointed a coalition Government, which was dominated by the CDU. The new Government continued to seek international recognition and to pursue negotiations at the EC-sponsored peace conference in The Hague, Netherlands. In September the UN placed an embargo on the delivery of all weapons and other military equipment to the territories that formerly comprised the SFRY. In October the Croatian Government refused to extend the three-month moratorium on the process of dissociation from the SFRY that had been agreed during the first round of EC peace negotiations in July. By November the JNA, supported by Serbian irregular troops, had secured about one-third of Croatian territory. The main area of conflict was Slavonia, in eastern Croatia, although Serbian and JNA attacks were also concentrated on the port of Zadar, in central Dalmatia. In November, in accordance with the principles formulated at The Hague, the Sabor declared its readiness to enact legislation guaranteeing minority rights, to allay the anxieties of the Serbs. However, there were increasing allegations of atrocities on both sides. The CDU came under mounting pressure from its more extreme nationalist groups to make no concessions to the Serbs. One of the most prominent of the nationalist parties was the Croatian Party of Rights (CPR), of which the armed wing, the Croatian Defence Association, was actively involved in the fighting and was implicated in other anti-Serb incidents. Meanwhile, in October the JNA attacked and besieged the coastal city of Dubrovnik; the eastern Slavonian town of Vukovar (where particularly intense fighting had taken place) finally surrendered on 18 November, after the 13th cease-fire agreement negotiated by the European Community (EC—later European Union, EU, see p. 217), which supervised the subsequent civilian evacuation. Both Croatia and Serbia indicated readiness to accept a UN peace-keeping force; military action continued, however, while negotiations on the terms for such a force (which was to be based in Sarajevo, Bosnia and Herzegovina) were conducted. The 14th cease-fire agreement, therefore, involved the UN, although it did not bring an end to all the fighting. In mid-December the UN Security Council's Resolution 724 provided for observers to be sent to the SFRY, in addition to a small team of civilian and military personnel to prepare for a possible peace-keeping force. In the same month a 'Republic of Serb Krajina' (RSK), formed by the union of the three SARs, was proclaimed.

In November 1991 the Supreme Council (a special war cabinet, chaired by the President of the Republic, which had been established in Croatia following the outbreak of civil conflict) ordered all Croatians to vacate any federal posts that they held and to place their services at the disposal of the Croatian state. On 5 December Mesić, Yugoslavia's nominal Head of State, resigned, followed by Ante Marković, the federal Prime Minister, on 19 December. On 23 December Germany announced its recognition of Croatia, and on 15 January 1992 the other members of the EC initiated general international recognition of Croatia, which culminated in its accession to the UN in May.

With more than 6,000 dead and 400,000 internally displaced in Croatia, a UN-sponsored unconditional cease-fire was signed by the Croatian National Guard and the JNA on 2 January 1992. In late February a 14,000-strong UN Protection Force (UNPROFOR) was entrusted with ensuring the withdrawal of the JNA from Croatia and the complete demilitarization of the three Serb-held enclaves, which were designated UN Protected Areas (UNPAs). In the same month UNPROFOR's mandate in Croatia was extended to cover the so-called 'pink zones' (areas occupied by JNA troops and with majority Serb populations, but outside the official UNPAs).

In mid-May 1992 the JNA began to withdraw from Croatia, in accordance with the UN demilitarization of Serb areas, and the siege of Dubrovnik ended on 28 May. Sporadic shelling continued, however, and UNPROFOR proved unable to prevent the expulsion of more than 1,000 non-Serbs by Serbian forces from

Eastern Slavonia, and had only limited success in its enforcement of the demilitarization of the UNPAs. In June Croatian forces launched a series of offensives in Serb-held areas, beginning with the shelling of Knin. This development provoked UN Security Council Resolution 762, adopted on 30 June, which required the Croat Government forces to withdraw to the positions that they had held prior to 21 June and to refrain from entering Serb-controlled areas.

In late July 1992 a military court in Split convicted 19 leading figures from the RSK for 'threatening the territorial integrity' of the Republic of Croatia. Shortly afterwards, however, as a precondition of their participation in the EC/UN peace conference on the former Yugoslavia, to be held in August, in London, United Kingdom, the leaders of the RSK renounced their claims to independence. In early September the Prime Minister of the Federal Republic of Yugoslavia (FRY, comprising Serbia and Montenegro), Milan Panić, announced Yugoslavia's willingness to recognize Croatia within the borders existing prior to the outbreak of civil war in mid-1991, on the condition that the Serbian enclaves be granted special status. During the London peace talks agreement was reached on economic co-operation between representatives of the Croatian Government and of the RSK, and at the end of September Presidents Tuđman of Croatia and Dobrica Ćosić of the FRY agreed to work towards a normalization of relations between their respective countries.

Presidential and legislative elections were held in Croatia on 2 August 1992, under the new Constitution (promulgated in December 1990), which provided for a bicameral legislature comprising a directly elected Zastupnički dom (Chamber of Representatives) and an indirectly elected Županijski dom (Chamber of Counties). Tuđman was re-elected, with 56% of the votes cast, more than twice the proportion obtained by his nearest rival, Dražen Budiša of the Croatian Social-Liberal Party (CSLP), while at the legislative elections the ruling CDU obtained an outright majority, securing 85 of the 138 seats contested in the lower Zastupnički dom. The new Government, under the premiership of Hrvoje Šarinić (hitherto head of the President's office), was appointed shortly thereafter. In late November the Zastupnički dom approved legislation providing for the reorganization of local government areas for electoral purposes, and in early January 1993 proportional representation was introduced to replace the former plurality electoral system. An election to the Županijski dom was held on 7 February. The CDU won 37 of the elective 63 seats, while the CSLP, together with allied parties, obtained 16 seats. (The CPR boycotted the election.)

In late January 1993 Croatian troops launched an offensive across the UN peace-keeping lines into Serb-held Krajina, in an effort to gain control of the Maslenica bridge, a vital communications link between northern Croatia and the Dalmatian coast. The Serbian forces in Krajina reclaimed weapons that they had earlier surrendered to UNPROFOR, in order to defend themselves. The UN responded by ordering Croatia to withdraw its troops and the Serb forces to return their weapons. As Croatian forces advanced towards the coastal town of Zadar on 26 January, President Ćosić of Yugoslavia warned the UN that, if UNPROFOR did not intervene, Yugoslavia would dispatch troops to defend the Serbs in Croatia. Two French members of UNPROFOR were killed in fighting around Zadar on the following day; consequently, the French Government dispatched an aircraft-carrier to the Adriatic Sea. The Croats regained control of the Maslenica bridge and Zemunik airport, and by the end of January the peace process in both Croatia and Bosnia and Herzegovina appeared to be in serious jeopardy.

There was extensive political unrest in Croatia throughout 1993. The issues of continuing civil strife in Krajina and of the quest for autonomy in the Istrian peninsula in the north-west of Croatia (see below) proved increasingly problematic for the Government and added to domestic dissatisfaction with the country's desperate economic circumstances and concern regarding Croatian involvement in the conflict in Bosnia and Herzegovina that had commenced in April 1992. In late March Šarinić's Government resigned, following a series of financial scandals and a rapid deterioration in the economic situation. A former executive of the Croatian state petroleum company, Nikica Valentić, was appointed Prime Minister. The new Government, which consisted only of members of the CDU, won a vote of confidence in the Zastupnički dom in late April. Despite growing opposition to his policies within the party, Tuđman was re-elected Chairman of the CDU in October.

At local elections in Istria in early February 1993, the Istrian Democratic Assembly (IDA), a party advocating Istrian autonomy, obtained 72% of the total votes cast. The IDA subsequently proposed that Istria become a transborder region comprising Croatian, Slovenian and Italian areas. Tuđman and his Government, however, strongly opposed any suggestion of Istrian autonomy. In early April a UN-sponsored agreement guaranteed the reconstruction and reopening of the Maslenica bridge, Zemunik airport and the Peruca hydroelectric plant (all situated in Krajina), under UNPROFOR supervision. The Croats decided to reconstruct the bridge themselves, however, and it was duly reopened by Tuđman in July. In the same month the Serbs, frustrated by the continued Croatian military presence in the area, launched an attack on Croatian forces. In mid-July the UN successfully negotiated the Erdut Agreement between the leaders of Croatia and Serbia, whereby Croat forces were to leave the Maslenica area (which would again be placed under the administration of UNPROFOR); in return, President Slobodan Milošević of Serbia was to dissuade Serb troops from attacking the bridge. However, the Croats failed to withdraw from Maslenica by the deadline of 31 July; the Croatian Government claimed that weapons belonging to Serb troops had not been surrendered to UNPROFOR, and fighting resumed. In August the Croatian Minister of Foreign Affairs, Dr Mate Granić, declared the Erdut Agreement invalid. In September a full-scale mobilization was undertaken among the Serbs of the SAR of Eastern Slavonia, Baranja and Western Sirmium, in response to the Croatian offensives in Krajina. Serb–Croat hostilities extended to Zagreb by mid-September. By this time most of the JNA had withdrawn from Croatia, and some Serb artillery had been placed under UN control, but UNPROFOR forces were not yet in effective control of Croatian borders.

On 4 October 1993, despite anti-UNPROFOR demonstrations in Croatia, the UN Security Council voted unanimously to extend UNPROFOR's mandate by Resolution 871, which also required the return to Croatian sovereignty of all 'pink zones', the restoration of all communications links between these regions and the remainder of Croatia, and the disarmament of Serb paramilitary groups. The UNPROFOR forces were empowered by the Resolution to act in self-defence while implementing the mandate. The Croat administration accepted the Resolution, but it was rejected by the assembly of the RSK, based in Beli Menastir, which proceeded to order the mobilization of all Serb conscripts in Krajina. Multi-party elections were held in the RSK in December, but these were declared illegal by the Constitutional Court of Croatia. In January 1994 Milan Martić, a candidate supported by President Milošević of Serbia, was elected to the post of 'President' of the RSK.

In mid-January 1994 Croatia and the FRY announced their intention to begin the normalization of relations, including the establishment of representative offices in Zagreb and Belgrade. (A parallel agreement was also signed between representatives of the Croat and Serb communities in Bosnia and Herzegovina.) In the same month the Croatian Government indicated the possibility of direct Croatian intervention in central Bosnia and Herzegovina, prompting the US Permanent Representative to the UN, Madeleine Albright, to threaten the imposition of international sanctions against Croatia. (Croatian army units had from 1992 supported the self-styled breakaway Croat state in Bosnia and Herzegovina, the 'Croat Community of Herzeg-Bosna'.) In late February President Tuđman approved proposals, advanced by the USA, for a Bosniak (Muslim)-Croat federation within Bosnia and Herzegovina, known as the Federation of Bosnia and Herzegovina, which would, it was declared, ultimately seek formal association with Croatia within a loose confederation. In the RSK, meanwhile, a cease-fire, which had been agreed between Croatia and the rebel Serbs in December 1993, was extended for a third time, until 31 March 1994. On 30 March a further cease-fire, agreed in Zagreb, provided for the establishment of a 'buffer' zone, to be monitored by UNPROFOR.

In April 1994 a long-standing public dispute between President Tuđman and Josip Manolić, the President of the Županijski dom and a leading member of the CDU, led to a division in the party. Manolić and other prominent liberals in the CDU (and in other parties) were displeased with Tuđman's perceived anti-Muslim views and his collusion with Gojko Šušak, the Minister of Defence, who was widely considered responsible for Croatia's involvement against the Bosniaks in the Bosnian conflict. Manolić demanded Šušak's resignation on the grounds that Tuđman could not hope to adhere to the accords creating the Federation of Bosnia and Herzegovina with Šušak as Minister of Defence. Tuđman responded by suspending Manolić from his position within the CDU. On 5 April it was announced that Manolić, together with Mesić (now the President of the Zastupnički dom), had left the CDU to form a new party, the Croatian Independent Democrats (CID). Formally established in late April, with Mesić as Chairman, the CID became the largest opposition party in the Sabor, with 18 deputies. In June the principal opposition parties commenced a boycott of the Sabor, in protest at the appointment of two CDU deputies as Presidents of the parliamentary chambers (Manolić and Mesić having agreed to resign from their posts in mid-May); opposition deputies only returned to the Sabor in September.

Meanwhile, the cease-fire in the RSK continued precariously. In late September 1994 the Zastupnički dom voted to end the existing mandate of UNPROFOR in Croatia, offering a renewed mandate, on the condition that UNPROFOR disarm Serb troops in Krajina, facilitate the return of Croat refugees to Krajina and protect Croatia's official borders. On 30 September, however, the Government withdrew its opposition to the continued presence of UN forces in Croatia, and on the same day the UN Security Council adopted a resolution renewing the UNPROFOR mandate in Croatia for a further six months. In mid-October a new negotiating forum was established in Zagreb with the aim of resolving the Krajina question; known as the 'Zagreb Group', it comprised two representatives of the EU and the US and Russian ambassadors to Croatia. The group initially proposed that the RSK be reintegrated into Croatia, but receive extensive autonomy. In late October, however, the RSK 'Prime Minister', Borislav Mikelić, rejected any notion of Krajina's reintegration.

On 12 January 1995 President Tuđman, encountering pressure from nationalist factions of the CDU and public dissatisfaction at the Government's perceived failure to assert control over Croatian territory, announced that the Government would not renew the UNPROFOR mandate in Croatia upon its expiry at the end of March, claiming that the UN presence had merely reinforced the Serbs' position. In late January the 'Zagreb Group' presented a fresh peace plan to Tuđman and the Krajina Serbs. The plan, which emphasized Croatia's territorial integrity, while affording rights to the Serb minority, envisaged the return of one-half of Serb-controlled territory to Croatia, in exchange for extensive regional autonomy for the Krajina Serbs. (The areas to be reintegrated into Croatia would be demilitarized, and administered by the UN for a minimum of five years.) The Krajina Serbs initially refused to consider the plan, but on 3 February Martić announced that the RSK would be willing to consider peace proposals if the UNPROFOR mandate were renewed and the RSK received guarantees of protection against Croat aggression. A few days later the RSK suspended an economic accord concluded with Croatia in December 1994 (providing for the re-establishment of basic infrastructural links between the RSK and Croatia), following Croatia's decision to terminate UNPROFOR's mandate. However, on 12 March 1995 Tuđman reversed his decision to expel UNPROFOR from Croatian territory, two weeks before the UN troops were due to begin their withdrawal. Croatia had agreed to a revised peace-keeping plan, following intensive diplomatic negotiations conducted by the international community (in particular, the USA), as a result of which a compromise UN mandate was to provide for a reduced peace-keeping force (to be known as the UN Confidence Restoration Operation—UNCRO), including several hundred troops to be deployed along Croatia's frontiers with Bosnia and Herzegovina and the FRY (effectively isolating Serb-occupied territory in Croatia from sources of military aid).

In early March 1995, following talks in Zagreb, a formal military alliance was announced between the Croatian, 'Herceg-Bosna' and (predominately Bosniak) Bosnian government armies. (A similar agreement establishing a military alliance between the Croatian Serbs and the Bosnian Serbs had been drawn up in Banja Luka, Bosnia and Herzegovina, in February.) UN relief supplies to Serb-held enclaves in Croatia were suspended in March, following the disruption of aid convoys by Croatian Serbs and their rebel Bosniak allies in the Bihać area of Bosnia and Herzegovina. On 13 April Dubrovnik and its airport were attacked by Bosnian Serb artillery, resulting in one death and prompting Mate Granić to lodge a formal protest with the UN. On 1–2 May Croatian government forces seized the SAR of Western Slavonia; large numbers of Serb troops fled the area during the offensive. Government sources claimed that the attack was necessary in order to restore the Zagreb–Belgrade motorway (which was reopened to civilian traffic on 3 May). The

Croatian Serbs retaliated with artillery attacks on Zagreb (where six civilians were killed), Karlovak and Sisak. The international community immediately intensified its efforts to achieve peace in Croatia, and on 3 May, under the mediation of the UN Special Envoy, Yasushi Akashi, the warring parties agreed a cease-fire, according to which Serb artillery was to be surrendered to the UN, in exchange for the safe passage of all Serb civilians and troops from Western Slavonia into Bosnia and Herzegovina (an evacuation was to be organized by the UN). Despite the ceasefire, sporadic fighting continued in the enclave.

In early June 1995, following the expiry of UNCRO's mandate in Croatia on 31 October 1994, Tudman threatened further offensives to seize Serb-held territories, prompting international criticism. In late July a joint offensive by Croatian government forces and 'Herceg-Bosna' troops resulted in the seizure of the strategic Serb-held town of Bosansko Grahovo, in western Bosnia and Herzegovina, thereby blocking the principal supply route from Serb-held areas of northern Bosnia and Herzegovina to Serb-held Krajina. On 4 August Croatian government troops launched a massive military operation and rapidly recaptured the Krajina enclave from the Croatian Serbs, prompting the largest exodus of refugees since the Yugoslav crisis began in 1991; about 150,000 Croatian Serbs either fled or were forcibly expelled from Krajina and took refuge in Serb-held areas in Bosnia and Herzegovina or in Serbia itself. Following the capture of Krajina, it was reported that Serbian troops had been stationed along the Serbian border with Croatia (thus strengthening the position of the Serb-held enclave of Eastern Slavonia against possible Croatian attack). In early September the UN announced that some 10,500 peace-keeping troops were to be withdrawn from Croatia, in view of the return of Krajina to control of the Croatian Government. On 20 September the Croatian Zastupnički dom voted to suspend sections of the law on minorities, which had provided the Krajina Serbs with special rights in areas where they had been a majority; this decision had been preceded two days earlier by a new electoral law reducing the guaranteed representation of the Serb minority in the Croatian legislature from 13 seats to three. The law also provided for 12 seats in the Zastupnički dom to represent some 470,000 Croatian emigrés, thus giving the right to vote to some 291,000 Bosnian Croats (many of whom supported the CDU's associated party in Bosnia and Herzegovina). At the end of September the Croatian Government, despite UN criticism, was reported to have resettled some 100,000 Bosnian refugees (both Croat and Muslim) in Krajina. In late September it was announced that elections to the Zastupnički dom would take place on 29 October.

During October 1995 fighting continued in parts of Croatia despite the UN-brokered cease-fire. Heavy clashes were reported between Croatian troops and Serb forces in Eastern Slavonia, and President Tudman continued to threaten the recapture of the Eastern Slavonian enclave by force, as part of the CDU's electoral manifesto. On 3 October, however, an 'agreement on basic principles' was signed between Croatian government officials and Serb leaders in Eastern Slavonia, following talks in the Serb-held town of Erdut, conducted under the mediation of the US ambassador to Croatia, Peter Galbraith, and UN negotiator Thorvald Stoltenberg. The 11-point agreement provided for a 'transitional period', during which authority over the enclave would be invested in an interim administration established by the UN, demilitarization of the area and creation of a joint Serb-Croat police force, and the safe return of refugees.

The electoral campaign in advance of elections to the Zastupnični dom was marred by widespread allegations of media bias; in early October 1995 the state-owned television network banned opposition broadcasts. At the elections on 29 October the CDU secured about 45% of the votes cast (although the party failed to obtain sufficient votes to achieve the two-thirds' parliamentary majority required to make constitutional amendments). A new Government was appointed in early November, under the premiership of the erstwhile Minister of the Economy, Zlatko Matesa.

On 12 November 1995 representatives of the Croatian Government and Eastern Slavonian Serbs signed an agreement in Erdut on the reintegration of the Eastern Slavonian enclave into Croatia. The signature of this accord followed peace negotiations between Tudman, Milošević and the President of the Presidency of Bosnia and Herzegovina, Dr Alija Izetbegović, conducted in Dayton, Ohio, USA (where the three leaders signed a comprehensive peace agreement, providing for the division of Bosnia and Herzegovina between a Muslim-Croat Federation and a

Serb Republic—see the chapter on Bosnia and Herzegovina). Under the terms of the accord, Eastern Slavonia was to be placed under the authority of a UN-appointed transitional administration for a period of up to two years prior to its full reintegration into Croatia. The interim administration and UN peace-keeping forces would supervise the demilitarization of the area and the return of refugees and displaced persons. Longstanding Serb demands for a referendum to be held at the end of the transitional period, in which citizens would vote for the region's integration into either Croatia or Serbia, were not included in the agreement. On 15 January 1996, under Resolution 1037, the UN Security Council established the UN Transitional Administration for Eastern Slavonia, Baranja and Western Sirmium (UNTAES), with an initial one-year mandate; UNTAES, comprising some 5,000 troops, replaced UNCRO, the mandate of which expired on that day. A US diplomat, Jacques Paul Klein, was subsequently appointed Transitional Administrator of the region. The UN Security Council also authorized the UN Mission of Observers in Prevlaka (UNMOP), comprising 28 military observers, to assume responsibility for monitoring the demilitarization of the Prevlaka peninsula, south-east of Dubrovnik, which was claimed by the FRY, on the grounds of its proximity to a naval base in Montenegro.

In April 1996 the Regional Executive Council of Eastern Slavonia appointed a former RSK 'President' (1992–94), Goran Hadžić, as President of the region. A new Regional Assembly (comprising representatives of Krajina and the five Eastern Slavonian municipalities) and Regional Executive Council were subsequently established. In the same month the Zastupnički dom approved legislation on co-operation between Croatia and the UN International Criminal Tribunal for the Former Yugoslavia (ICTY—based in The Hague), which provided for the transfer of authority to conduct criminal proceedings to the Tribunal and the extradition of the accused.

In early May 1996 Tudman dissolved the Zagreb City Assembly and appointed a Government Commissioner in its place (on the grounds that the Assembly had approved unconstitutional legislation), following a protracted dispute with an alliance of opposition parties that held a majority in the Assembly. In that month the Zastupnički dom adopted legislation granting amnesty for crimes committed during the civil conflict in Eastern Slavonia from August 1990 (excepting war crimes), with the aim of encouraging the return of displaced persons to the region. Later in May the demilitarization of Eastern Slavonia commenced; the process was completed within 30 days, as scheduled. In early July an international security force was installed in Eastern Slavonia for the transitional period.

In August 1996, following a meeting between Tudman and Milošević in Athens, Greece, an agreement was signed, providing for the establishment of full diplomatic relations between Croatia and the FRY; remaining issues of contention, most notably the territorial dispute over Prevlaka, were to be resolved by further negotiations. In October the Council of Europe (see p. 199) agreed to accept Croatia's application for membership, after the Government undertook to ratify the European Convention on Human Rights within one year of admission.

At the end of December 1996, following a meeting between Tudman and Klein, it was announced that local government elections in Eastern Slavonia were to take place in March 1997, concurrently with nationwide elections to the Županijski dom. (The elections were subsequently postponed until 13 April, apparently owing to difficulties in the organization of the voting in Eastern Slavonia.) In March the Independent Democratic Serb Party (IDSP), headed by Vojislav Stanimirović (the President of the Regional Council of Eastern Slavonia), was established to contest the elections in the enclave. In early April Serb officials in Eastern Slavonia conducted a referendum (which, however, the Croatian Government and UN officials declared to be illegitimate) regarding the future of the enclave; about 99.5% of the participating electorate voted in favour of Eastern Slavonia remaining a single administrative unit under Serb control after its return to Croatia. On 13 April elections to the Županijski dom and to a number of municipal and regional councils took place. Voting in the concurrent local government elections in Eastern Slavonia was extended for two days, owing to administrative irregularities. Nevertheless, election monitors from the Organization for Security and Co-operation in Europe (OSCE, see p. 314) declared that they had been largely 'free and fair'. The CDU secured 42 of the 63 elective seats in the Županijski dom, while the Croatian Peasants' Party took nine, the CSLP six, the Social Democratic Party (SDP, which had been reconstituted from the former LCC–PDR) four, and the IDA two seats. (A further five deputies were to be nominated by Tuđman, of whom two were to be members of the Serb community in Eastern Slavonia.) The IDSP obtained control of 11 of the 28 municipalities contested in the enclave. In May the CDU secured a narrow majority in the Zagreb City Assembly, following protracted negotiations.

In May 1997 the Government announced that the forthcoming presidential election was to take place on 15 June. Tuđman had been formally nominated as the presidential candidate of the CDU earlier that year (despite persistent reports, denied by government officials, that he was seriously ill). During a visit to Eastern Slavonia in early June Tuđman publicly offered reconciliation to all Serbs who were willing to accept Croatian citizenship, following continued pressure from Madeleine Albright, who had met Tuđman in late May. On 15 June Tuđman was re-elected with 61.4% of the votes cast; the SDP candidate, Zdravko Tomac, secured 21.0% of the votes cast and the CSLP leader, Vlado Gotovac, 17.6%. However, OSCE monitors declared that the election had not been conducted fairly, on the grounds that opposition parties had not been permitted coverage in the state-controlled media. Later in June the Constitutional Court endorsed the results of the election.

In early July 1997 the Government announced that the programme for the return of some 80,000 Croat refugees to Eastern Slavonia had commenced. In the same month, despite previous objections from the Croatian Government, the UN Security Council adopted a resolution to extend the mandate of UNTAES (which had already been renewed for an additional six months) until mid-January 1998, owing to UN concern over the continued stability of Eastern Slavonia. (However, the size of the contingent was reduced from about 5,000 to 2,800.) Also in July the Bretton Woods institutions temporarily suspended the disbursement of financial assistance to Croatia, as a result of pressure from the Governments of the USA, the United Kingdom and Germany, which continued to criticize, in particular, the slow progress in the resettlement of refugees, the Government's failure to comply with extradition orders on suspects issued by the ICTY and continued state control of the media.

On 5 August 1997 Tuđman was officially inaugurated for a second presidential term. In the same month the President of the CPR, Dobroslav Paraga, submitted a proposal at the ICTY that Tuđman, Šušak and a number of Bosnian Croats be charged in connection with the former conflict in Bosnia and Herzegovina. Paraga and a human rights activist, Ivan Zvonimir Čičak, were subsequently charged by the Croatian authorities with disseminating false information, after publishing claims in a national newspaper that Tuđman had been involved in initiating the conflict in Bosnia and Herzegovina. In November the legislature approved constitutional amendments, proposed by Tuđman, which, notably, prohibited the re-establishment of a union of Yugoslav states. In December Gotovac left the CSLP and formed a breakaway faction of the Party.

In mid-January 1998 the mandate of UNTAES expired and Eastern Slavonia was officially returned to Croatian authority, precipitating an increase in the number of ethnic Serbs leaving the former enclave. In February 1998 Tuđman was re-elected Chairman of the CDU. In April, following the violent suppression of protests at poor economic conditions earlier that year, the Government adopted legislation regulating public gatherings and demonstrations, which, it claimed, was in accordance with the standards of Western authorities. In May the Government announced a programme that relaxed conditions for the return of Serbian refugees to Croatia, following pressure from the international community (which had threatened to impose sanctions if the Croatian Government failed to allow the return of Serbs).

In early May 1998 Šušak died; Dr Andrija Hebrang (hitherto Minister of Health) was subsequently allocated the defence portfolio. In the same month the former Prime Minister, Hrvoje Sarinić, resigned from the post of head of the Office of the President, prompting speculation regarding increasing division within the CDU between moderates and nationalists.

In June 1998 Croatia submitted to the UN a proposal for a permanent settlement to the dispute over the Prevlaka peninsula; it was envisaged that a joint Croatian-FRY commission would demarcate the borders between the two countries and that a demilitarized zone would be established for a period of five years. In August Granić and the FRY Minister of Foreign

Affairs, meeting in Zagreb, agreed to conduct discussions on the issue of the Prevlaka peninsula. In September, following a meeting between Granić and the US ambassador in Croatia, it was agreed that joint Croatian-US commissions were to be established to further progress in the implementation of the Dayton peace agreement and Croatia's admission to the North Atlantic Treaty Organization's (NATO) 'Partnership for Peace' (see p. 303) programme.

In September 1998 the trial of three Croats, who were charged, together with a further six Croats *in absentia*, with the massacre of hundreds of ethnic Serbs in 1991, commenced in Zagreb (the first trial of Croats accused of perpetrating human rights violations against Serbs to take place in Croatia). In early October Sarinić tendered his resignation from his remaining government and party offices, including the post of presidential Chief of Staff, claiming that Tuđman had failed to support his allegations that CDU nationalists, with connections to members of the intelligence service, were campaigning against him and other moderate members of the party. In the same month Hebrang resigned from his posts of Minister of Defence and Vice-President of the CDU, also as a result of disagreement with Tuđman. Gen. Pavao Miljavac, hitherto Chief of Staff of the army, was subsequently appointed Minister of Defence.

In January 1999 the UN Security Council adopted a resolution on UNMOP, stating that violations of the demilitarized zone in the Prevlaka peninsula had continued and that negotiations on the normalization of relations between the FRY and Croatia had not resulted in any significant progress. In April Milan Ramljak resigned as Deputy Prime Minister and Minister of Justice, in protest at the Government's increasingly authoritarian stance. In July Croatia submitted an application at the ICTY to institute legal proceedings against the FRY for crimes of genocide committed by Yugoslav forces in Croatia in 1991–95. In August the Croatian Government complied with a request by the ICTY for the extradition of Vinko Martinović, who had been indicted for crimes committed during the Croatian–Muslim conflict in 1993–94. However, the authorities' reluctance to extradite Mladen Naletilić, who had also been indicted for crimes perpetrated during the Croatian–Muslim conflict, prompted severe criticism from the ICTY, while the US Government threatened to impose sanctions against Croatia. In early September the County Court in Zagreb ruled that there were no legal impediments to the extradition of Naletilić. In mid-October the Supreme Court rejected an appeal by Naletilić against the ruling, and he was finally extradited in March 2000.

In late October 1999 Tuđman announced that the elections to the Zastupnički dom would take place on 22 December. In early November, however, it was announced that Tuđman had undergone emergency medical treatment. He was consequently unable to confirm the election date, and on 26 November the Sabor provisionally transferred the powers of Head of State to the parliamentary Speaker, Vlatko Pavletić. On the following day the mandate of the Zastupnički dom expired, and Pavletić rescheduled the elections to take place on 3 January 2000. An alliance of six principal opposition parties, known as Opposition Six, pledged to establish a coalition government in the event of winning the parliamentary elections; of the Opposition Six parties, the SDP and CSLP were to present one joint candidate, while the Croatian Peasants' Party, the Liberal Party (LP), the Croatian People's Party (CPP) and the IDA were to submit a second joint candidate. Meanwhile, Tuđman's medical condition deteriorated, and he died on 10 December. Later that month the Government announced that the election for his successor would take place on 24 January 2000.

The elections to the Zastupnički dom, which took place on 3 January 2000 as scheduled, were contested by some 55 political associations. The coalition of the SDP and the CSLP (together with two minor parties) secured 47.0% of the votes cast and 71 of the 151 seats, defeating the CDU, with 30.5% of the votes cast and 45 seats; the alliance of the four other principal opposition parties, together with the Croatian Social Democrats' Action, won 15.9% of the total votes cast and 25 seats. The Chairman of the SDP, Ivica Račan, was subsequently designated as Prime Minister. Later in January nine candidates emerged to contest the forthcoming presidential election, including the CSLP leader, Dražen Budiša (who was to represent the SDP-CSLP alliance), and the former Yugoslav President Stipe Mesić, who was the joint candidate of the four other principal opposition parties. The CDU elected Mate Granić, hitherto Deputy Prime Minister and Minister of Foreign Affairs, as its presidential candidate, while Vladimir Šeks became acting leader, pending a party congress. In the first round of the election, which took place on 24 January, Mesić secured 41.1% of the votes cast, while Budiša won 27.7% and Granić 22.5%. Since no candidate received more than 50% of the votes, a second round between Mesić and Budiša was scheduled for 7 February. On 27 January Pavletić formally appointed Račan to the office of Prime Minister. Račan announced the establishment of a new coalition Government, comprising members of the Opposition Six parties. In the second presidential ballot Mesić achieved an outright majority, with 56.2% of the votes cast. On 9 February the Sabor adopted a motion expressing confidence in Račan's Government. Following his inauguration as President on 18 February, Mesić pledged to support the return of Serb refugees to Croatia.

In March 2000 the Government established a council for co-operation with the ICTY. In May, however, nationalists who had participated in the conflict of 1991–95 organized mass demonstrations in protest at the Government's policy of co-operation with the Tribunal. Meanwhile, in early April Granić left the CDU to form a new party, which became known as the Croatian Democratic Centre (CDC). In May a coalition of the SDP and the Croatian Pensioners' Party won the largest number of seats in the elections to Zagreb City Assembly. In the same month the Zastupnički dom approved constitutional amendments that guaranteed the educational and linguistic rights of minority groups, and representation in the legislature for those groups that constituted more than 8% of the total population.

Members of the armed forces and former supporters of Tuđman continued to condemn the Government's policy of co-operation with the ICTY, and in late September 2000 Mesić dismissed seven senior military officials who had publicly criticized the detention of war crimes suspects. In early November the Zastupnički dom adopted constitutional amendments that reduced the powers of the President and increased those of the legislature (which, henceforth, was to appoint the Government). In March 2001 the Government submitted a proposal to the Zastupnički dom for the abolition of the Županijski dom. Despite the strenuous opposition of the CDU, which held a majority of seats in the upper house, the Zastupnički dom accordingly approved a constitutional amendment converting the Sabor into a unicameral legislature. At local government elections, which took place on 20 May, the SDP-led coalition obtained control of 14 of the 21 County Assemblies. The CDU, despite receiving more votes than expected, secured a majority in only four County Assemblies (compared with 16 in the 1997 elections). In early June the IDA (which had held the European integration portfolio) withdrew from the Government, following differences with the other coalition parties, particularly with regard to the movement's aim to make Italian a second official language in Istria. The resignation of the Minister of Justice (an SDP representative) later that month was reported to be related to cabinet dissension over the Government's co-operation with the ICTY.

In early June 2001 the Rijeka County Court indicted a prominent Bosniak, Fikret Abdić (who had established an autonomous region in north-western Bosnia and Herzegovina in 1993), for crimes against humanity, including the killing of civilians in a detention camp in 1993. In accordance with a bilateral agreement between the Croatian and Bosnian authorities, the trial of Abdić, who had obtained Croatian citizenship in 1995, commenced in the Croatian town of Karlovac in July 2001. (He was sentenced to 20 years' imprisonment in July 2002.) In early July 2001, following protracted argument, the Government voted in favour of extraditing two Croatian generals suspected of war crimes to the ICTY, in compliance with a secret indictment issued by the Tribunal. Four ministers belonging to the CSLP subsequently resigned in protest at the Government's decision. In mid-July, however, Račan's administration won a motion of confidence in the Sabor, which also approved a statement reaffirming the Government's policy of co-operation with the ICTY. Following the forced resignation of Budiša (who had strongly opposed the extradition) from the leadership of the CSLP, the four representatives of that party rejoined the Government. Later in July one of the indicted suspects, Gen. (retd) Rahim Ademi, surrendered to the ICTY, where at his initial hearing he denied charges relating to the killing of Serb civilians during a Croatian offensive to regain control of Krajina in 1993. The other suspect, Gen. (retd) Ante Gotovina, who had been indicted on similar charges, pertaining to an offensive in 1995, remained at large, and the authorities subsequently declared that they believed him to have left the country. (In February 2002 it was

announced that Ademi was to be released provisionally from custody, pending his trial.)

In late September 2001 Milošević, who had been extradited to the ICTY in June on charges relating to Kosovo and Metohija (Kosovo—see the chapter on Serbia and Montenegro), was also formally indicted with crimes against humanity and violations of the Geneva Convention; Milošević was held responsible for the killing of large numbers of Croat civilians and the expulsion of some 170,000 non-Serbs from Croatian territory by Serb forces in 1991–92. In early October 2001 a former commander of the Yugoslav navy, together with three further Yugoslav military officers, were indicted by the ICTY for the killing of more than 40 civilians during the bombardment of Dubrovnik in 1991.

In February 2002 Budiša (who had continued to express open antagonism to Račan) was re-elected to the presidency of the CSLP, defeating the party General Secretary and incumbent Minister of Defence, Jozo Radoš. At the end of that month the CSLP leadership decided to remove the First Deputy Prime Minister, Goran Granić, and a further two CSLP ministers from the Government; it was reported that Budiša questioned their loyalty to the party, owing to their failure to support his apparent opposition to Račan's co-operation with the ICTY. The remaining three CSLP members in the Cabinet (including Radoš) subsequently tendered their resignations to demonstrate disagreement with the party leadership. In early March, following lengthy discussions, the coalition parties in the Government reached agreement on a cabinet reorganization. Budiša became First Deputy Prime Minister, while Granić (henceforth an independent) and three of the CSLP representatives were reappointed to the Government. The issue of co-operation with the ICTY remained under discussion. Following a long-standing power struggle within the CDU between the party leader, Ivo Sanader, and Tuđman's former close associate, Ivic Pasalić, Sanader was re-elected to the post in April.

In April 2002 the Ministers of Foreign Affairs of Croatia and the FRY signed a protocol on the principles that would be used to confirm the two countries' common border, including, notably, in the Prevlaka region. In May Milan Martić, the former President of the RSK, who had been indicted in 1996 for war crimes, in particular his alleged responsibility for the bombardment of Zagreb in 1995, surrendered to the ICTY. (The Yugoslav authorities had in April 2002 agreed to extradite Martić, then resident in Serbia, and a further 22 indicted suspects to the Tribunal.) He pleaded not guilty to all charges at the ICTY later in May. At the beginning of July Budiša finally withdrew the CSLP from the government coalition, after an agreement on joint ownership of the Krško nuclear power installation in Slovenia was ratified in the Sabor, despite the opposition of 17 of the CSLP's 23 deputies. He threatened to expel the six dissident CSLP deputies from the party. On 5 July Račan submitted his resignation to Mesić, following the collapse of his administration. Five days later, however, Račan was returned to the office of Prime Minister, after his nomination by Mesić was supported by 84 deputies in the Sabor. On 28 July Račan and the leaders of the other political parties belonging to the ruling coalition reached agreement on a new Council of Ministers, which was approved by the Sabor two days later.

In mid-July 2002 the Presidents of Croatia and the FRY met the members of the collective State Presidency of Bosnia and Herzegovina in Sarajevo (the first trilateral summit meeting since the dissolution of the SFRY). In September Gen. Janko Bobetko, the Croatian army Chief of Staff in 1991–95, was indicted by the ICTY on charges of crimes against humanity for his alleged involvement in the killing of some 100 Serbs in 1993. However, Račan rejected Bobetko's indictment, on the grounds that it violated the terms of the Constitution, thereby refusing for the first time to co-operate with the ICTY. In October 2002 the Chief Prosecutor at the ICTY, Carla Del Ponte, visited Croatia to urge the authorities to extradite Bobetko, and the imposition of UN sanctions against the country was envisaged. The Government declared Bobetko unfit to be extradited to the ICTY owing to ill health, but subsequently pledged to abide by the decision of UN medical experts. Bobetko died in April.

In December 2002 the Ministers of Foreign Affairs of Croatia and the FRY reached a provisional accord on the Prevlaka peninsula, thereby allowing the UN Security Council to end the mandate of UNMOP later that month; under the agreement, the peninsula was to remain demilitarized and joint maritime patrols were to be introduced. In early 2003, in response to continuing international pressure, the Government indicated that it was prepared to demonstrate its full co-operation with the ICTY, and in February Croatia submitted a formal application for membership of the EU. In March a former army commander, Gen. (retd) Mirko Norac (the most senior officer to be convicted by a Croatian court), was sentenced to 12 years' imprisonment for his involvement in the killing of some 50 Croatian Serb civilians in 1991; a further two defendants received terms of 15 years and 10 years, respectively. In September 2003 Mesić paid an official visit to Belgrade (the first to be made by a Croatian Head of State since 1991); he and Svetozar Marović, the Head of State of Serbia and Montenegro (which had been reconstituted from the FRY in February 2003), exchanged formal apologies for war crimes perpetrated against the citizens of the two states. In November the former leader of the self-proclaimed SAR of Krajina, Milan Babić, appearing before the ICTY, was charged with war crimes and crimes against humanity, in connection with the 'ethnic cleansing' of Croats from regions under his control in 1991–92. (At the end of January 2004 he pleaded guilty to one of the five charges against him, in the hope of receiving a lesser sentence from the Tribunal.) Meanwhile, the Government continued to insist that it was unable to locate and arrest Gotovina, despite pressure from the ICTY for his extradition (which was considered a precondition for expediting Croatia's accession to the EU).

Legislative elections were conducted on 23 November 2003. The CDU obtained 33.9% of the votes cast and 66 of the 152 seats in the Sabor, while the SDP, led by the incumbent Prime Minister, Ivica Račan (in alliance with the Liberal Party and the IDA), won only 22.6% of the votes and 43 seats. The CDU negotiated coalition agreements with the CDC (which led to the appointment of the newly elected party President, Vesna Škare Ožbolt, as Minister of Justice), the Croatian Peasants' Party and the CSLP, and gained the support of several independent deputies, thereby commanding a narrow parliamentary majority. On 23 December a new, 14-member Government, headed by Sanader and principally comprising CDU members, was approved by 88 votes in the Sabor, and conducted its first session in early January 2004. The administration included former members of the Tudman administration, notably: Hebrang, as Deputy Prime Minister and Minister of Health and Social Welfare; and a former ambassador to the USA, Miomir Žužul, as Minister of Foreign Affairs.

In March 2004 two retired generals, Ivan Cermak and Mladen Markac, who were charged with crimes relating to the seizure of Krajina by Croatian government forces in 1995, surrendered to the ICTY, following continued international pressure on the Croatian authorities. They subsequently both pleaded not guilty before the Tribunal. In April 2004 the European Commission announced that it favoured the opening of accession negotiations with Croatia, subject to the Government's continued compliance with the ICTY. In May the ICTY issued an indictment against Norac (who had been sentenced to a 12-year term of imprisonment by a Croatian court in March 2003) on a further five charges relating to an attack by Croatian troops in September 1993; it was ruled that the trials of both he and Gen. (retd) Rahim Ademi would be transferred to Croatia. Following a two-day EU summit meeting in Brussels, Belgium, in June 2004, Croatia was awarded the official status of candidate country for EU accession, with formal negotiations expected to commence in early 2005. (However, the Accession Strategy subsequently issued included a provision allowing for the suspension of negotiations if Croatia failed to meet international obligations.) At the end of June 2004 the ICTY imposed a custodial sentence of 13 years on Babić (a number of the charges against him having been abandoned following his guilty plea). Del Ponte commended the co-operation of the Croatian authorities with the ICTY and indicated that further numbers of outstanding cases would be transferred to the jurisdiction of courts in Croatia. In November the Minister of Defence, Berislav Rončević, announced that the Croatian Government had in July signed a military co-operation agreement with the USA, granting US forces greater access to Croatian airspace, territorial waters and training facilities; Rončević denied claims by Mesić that he, in his capacity as Supreme Commander of the Armed Forces, had not been informed of the bilateral accord.

In early January 2005 Žužul, who had been implicated by media reports in corrupt financial practices during the Tudman regime, announced his resignation (while strongly denying the allegations against him). A parliamentary motion expressing no confidence in Žužul had been defeated, but opposition parties strongly objected to his leading the forthcoming EU accession negotiations. (Sanader accepted his resignation, but requested that he remain provisionally in office, pending a government reorganization.) Meanwhile, the first round of the presidential election, which was contested by a total of 11 candidates, was conducted on 2 January; Mesić, who was supported by an alliance of centre-left parties, led by the SDP, secured 48.9% of votes cast, narrowly failing to secure an outright majority. His principal opponent, Jadranka Kosor, a Deputy Prime Minister and the CDU representative (who also received the support of women's organizations), won 20.3% and an independent candidate, Boris Mikšić, 17.8% of the votes. At the second round on 16 January Mesić was re-elected to the presidency, receiving 65.9% of votes cast.

In early February 2005 controversy emerged between Croatia and Serbia and Montenegro over the trial of three former Yugoslav generals indicted by the ICTY in connection with the 1991 Vukovar massacre. The Croatian Government claimed jurisdiction over the case, which was contested by the Serbian President. In the same month the French and German ministers responsible for European affairs, following a meeting with Croatian government leaders, maintained, while welcoming progress made towards EU integration by Croatia, that the accession negotiations, provisionally scheduled to commence on 17 March, remained dependent on the capture and extradition of Gotovina. The announcement coincided with intensified efforts by the Croatian security and intelligence services to locate Gotovina (who had indicated his readiness to surrender to the authorities if his trial was to be conducted in Croatia). Meanwhile, in mid-February Sanader announced a government reorganization, after Hebrang also tendered his resignation from the Council of Ministers, on grounds of ill health; the new appointments were confirmed by the Sabor on 17 February. Notably, a prominent business executive, Damir Polancec, was nominated to replace Hebrang as Deputy Prime Minister, while the Ministries of Foreign Affairs and European Integration were to be merged in reflection of Croatia's aspiration to join the EU, and the incumbent Minister of European Integration, Kolinda Grabar-Kitarović, was to assume the combined portfolio. Mesić (who had pledged to continue reforms towards EU accession) was inaugurated as President on 18 February. At the end of that month Sanader repeated appeals for Gotovina to surrender to the authorities, and refuted a statement by Del Ponte that the fugitive remained at large in Croatia. In March, following an official report by Del Ponte stating that the Croatian authorities had failed to demonstrate full co-operation with the ICTY, the EU announced the indefinite postponement of accession negotiations.

Government

According to the 1990 Constitution (amended in March 2001), legislative power is vested in the unicameral Sabor (Assembly), which has between 100 and 160 members and is elected for a four-year term. Executive power is held by the President, who is elected by universal adult suffrage for a period of five years. The Sabor appoints the Prime Minister and (upon the recommendation of the Prime Minister) the ministers. The country is divided, for electoral purposes, into 21 counties, 420 municipalities and 61 towns.

Defence

Military service is compulsory for men and lasts for a period of six months. In August 2004 the estimated total strength of the armed forces was 20,800 (the number of reservists totalled 108,200), including an army of an estimated 14,050, a navy of 2,500 and an air force of 2,300. The remainder comprised general staff. There were, in addition, 10,000 armed military police. In May 2000 Croatia was admitted to the North Atlantic Treaty Organization's (NATO) 'Partnership for Peace' (see p. 303) programme. Budgetary expenditure on defence by the central Government was estimated at US $596m. (2.1% of GDP) in 2003.

Economic Affairs

In 2003, according to estimates by the World Bank, Croatia's gross national income (GNI), measured at average 2001–03 prices, was US $27,227m., equivalent to $5,350 per head (or $10,710 per head on an international purchasing-power parity basis). During 1990–2003, it was estimated, the population declined at an average annual rate of 0.5%, while gross domestic product (GDP) per head increased, in real terms, by an average of 0.4% per year. Overall GDP declined, in real terms, at an average annual rate of 0.1% in 1990–2003; however, real GDP increased by 5.2% in 2002 and by 4.3% in 2003.

Agriculture (including hunting, forestry and fishing), according to preliminary estimates, contributed 8.0% of GDP in 2003. About 7.1% of the employed labour force were engaged in the sector in that year. The principal crops are maize, wheat, potatoes and sugar beet. In late 2003 the Croatian authorities declared a fishery and ecological zone in the Adriatic Sea, in an attempt to protect fish resources. The GDP of the agricultural sector declined, in real terms, at an average annual rate of 1.9% in 1990–2002; however, agricultural GDP increased by 2.0% in 2002.

Industry (including mining, manufacturing, construction and power) contributed an estimated 28.9% of GDP and engaged 31.0% of the employed labour force in 2003. Industrial GDP declined, in real terms, at an average annual rate of 3.6% during 1990–2002; however, GDP in the industrial sector increased by 5.7% in 2002.

The mining sector contributed 5.5% of GDP in 1998, and engaged just 0.5% of the employed labour force in 2002. Croatia has many exploitable mineral resources, including petroleum, coal and natural gas. The GDP of the mining sector declined by 2.4% in 1998; mining production increased by 1.9% in 1999.

The manufacturing sector contributed 20.2% of GDP and engaged 21.0% of the employed labour force in 2002. The GDP of the manufacturing sector declined, in real terms, at an average annual rate of 3.8% per year during 1990–2002; however, manufacturing GDP increased by 4.0% in 2002.

Of total electricity production in 2001, 52.7% was provided by hydroelectric power, 18.0% by petroleum, 15.4% by natural gas and 13.9% by coal. However, the country remains dependent on imported fuel, which accounted for some 10.9% of total imports in 2003.

Services provided an estimated 63.1% of GDP and engaged 61.9% of the employed labour force in 2003. The virtual elimination of tourism in Croatia (which in the late 1980s accounted for some 82% of the total tourism trade of the Socialist Federal Republic of Yugoslavia) represented the largest war-related economic loss. There was a significant recovery in the tourism sector from the late 1990s; by 2003 tourist arrivals had increased to 7,409,000 (compared with 3,805,000 in 1999). The GDP of the services sector increased, in real terms, at an average annual rate of 1.0% in 1990–2002; growth of 5.3% was recorded in 2002.

In 2003 Croatia recorded a visible trade deficit of US $7,908.3m., while there was a deficit of $2,084.7m. on the current account of the balance of payments. In 2003 the principal source of imports was Italy (18.2%); other major sources were Germany, Slovenia, Russia, Austria and France. The principal market for exports in that year was Italy (26.7%); other important purchasers were Bosnia and Herzegovina, Germany, Slovenia and Austria. The principal exports in 2003 were machinery and transport equipment, miscellaneous manufactured articles (particularly clothing and accessories), basic manufactures, chemical products, mineral fuels and food and live animals. The main imports in that year were machinery and transport equipment (most notably road vehicles), basic manufactures, mineral fuels (particularly petroleum and petroleum products), miscellaneous manufactured articles, chemical products and foodstuffs.

Croatia's overall budgetary deficit for 2002 was 3,680.5m. kuna (equivalent to 2.1% of GDP). In 2003, according to preliminary figures, the budgetary deficit was 2,186.6m. kuna (equivalent to 1.1% of GDP). The country's total external debt was US $15,347m. at the end of 2002, of which $7,679m. was long-term public debt. In that year the cost of debt-servicing was equivalent to 25.9% of the value of exports of goods and services. Consumer prices increased at an average annual rate of 68.8% in 1990–2003. However, the average rate of inflation was only 1.7% in 2002, and declined further in 2003, to 0.1%. The average annual rate of unemployment at the end of 2004 was estimated at 18.7%.

Croatia was admitted to the IMF in January 1993, and became a member of the European Bank for Reconstruction and Development (EBRD, see p. 212) in April of that year. In November 2000 Croatia was admitted to the World Trade Organization (WTO, see p. 357). In February 2003 Croatia made a formal application for membership of the European Union (EU, see p. 217). In early 2003 Croatia also joined the Central European Free Trade Association (CEFTA).

The outbreak of conflict in Croatia in the early 1990s resulted in a rapid deterioration of the economy. A new national currency, the kuna, was introduced in May 1994. In October of that year the IMF extended its first stand-by loan to Croatia, in support of an economic reform programme. The Government subsequently received reconstruction loans from other official creditors and concluded a rescheduling agreement with the 'Paris Club' of donor nations. In April 1996 an agreement was reached with the 'London Club' of commercial creditor banks, establishing Croatia's share of the foreign commercial bank debt incurred by the SFRY. In March 1997 the IMF approved a further three-year credit arrangement. Following the election of a new coalition Government in early 2000, relations with the USA and with western European Governments improved (resulting in increased financial aid). Having declared itself satisfied with Croatia's implementation of agreed structural reforms, the IMF in early 2003 approved a 14-month stand-by credit for Croatia (which, however, the Government viewed as precautionary), to support continued fiscal consolidation and structural reform. An IMF review in November commended progress made in fiscal discipline under the stand-by arrangement, concluding that real GDP growth had been higher and inflation lower than expected, while the current-account deficit had benefited from a strong increase in tourism revenue. Nevertheless, external debt also increased in that year, and was viewed as a potential threat to stability. A new centre-right Government, established in December, planned to continue the existing programme of reforms, particularly the rehabilitation of infrastructure and the privatization of public enterprises and remaining state-owned banks, with the ultimate aim of joining the EU. A further IMF progress review in November 2004 cited a slowing of growth in that year, and a gradual worsening of the external debt position, while urging the authorities to accelerate the programme of privatization and restructuring of public enterprises. In early 2005 the Government announced a campaign to suppress illicit financial activities, in an effort to strengthen official revenue levels. Following Croatia's application for membership of the EU (formally submitted in early 2003), it was awarded the official status of candidate country in mid-2004 (thereby gaining access to pre-accession funds). An EU Stabilization and Association Agreement for Croatia (which laid emphasis on fiscal restraint and the reduction of public-sector wage expenditure) entered into force in February 2005 as a framework for the country's process towards EU integration. The opening of accession negotiations had been provisionally scheduled for March, but, following the Government's continued failure to apprehend and extradite a war crimes suspect (see Recent History), was postponed indefinitely in that month.

Education

Pre-school education, for children aged from three to six years, is available free of charge. Education is officially compulsory for eight years, between seven and 15 years of age. Primary education, which is provided free, begins at the age of seven and continues for four years. Enrolment at primary schools in 1998 was equivalent to 77% of children in the appropriate age-group. Special education in foreign languages is provided for children of non-Croat ethnic origin, since all national minorities in Croatia have the right to learn their minority language. Secondary education is available free (although private schools also exist) and lasts for up to eight years, comprising two cycles of four years each. There are various types of secondary school: grammar, technical and specialized schools and mixed-curriculum schools. Enrolment at secondary schools in 1998 was equivalent to 81% of the relevant age-group. In 2003/04 there were 102 institutions of higher education in Croatia, including four universities (in Zagreb, Rijeka, Osijek and Split). In 2002/03 a total of 126,343 students were enrolled in higher education establishments. Projected budgetary expenditure on education by the central Government in 2002 was 6,314.8m. kuna (8.5% of total spending).

Public Holidays

2005: 1 January (New Year's Day), 6 January (Epiphany), 28 March (Easter Monday), 1 May (Labour Day), 26 May (Corpus Christi), 22 June (Anti-Fascism Day), 25 June (Statehood Day), 5 August (National Day), 15 August (Assumption), 8 October (Independence Day), 1 November (All Saints' Day), 25–26 December (Christmas).

2006: 1 January (New Year's Day), 6 January (Epiphany), 17 April (Easter Monday), 1 May (Labour Day), 15 June (Corpus Christi), 22 June (Anti-Fascism Day), 25 June (Statehood Day), 5 August (National Day), 15 August (Assumption), 8 October (Independence Day), 1 November (All Saints' Day), 25–26 December (Christmas).

Weights and Measures

The metric system is in force.

Statistical Survey

Source (unless otherwise stated): Central Bureau of Statistics of the Republic of Croatia, 10000 Zagreb, Ilica 3; tel. (1) 4806111; fax (1) 4806148; e-mail stat.info@dzs.hr; internet www.dzs.hr.

Area and Population

AREA, POPULATION AND DENSITY

Area (sq km)	56,594*
Population (census results)	
31 March 1991	4,784,265
31 March 2001†	
Males	2,135,900
Females	2,301,560
Total	4,437,460
Population (official estimates at mid-year)	
2001	4,437,000
2002	4,443,000
2003	4,442,000
Density (per sq km) at mid-2003	78.5

* 21,851 sq miles.

† Data are not directly comparable to those from the 1991 census, owing to a change in the definition used to calculate total population.

POPULATION BY ETHNIC GROUP
(census of 31 March 2001)

	Number ('000)	%
Croat	3,977.2	89.6
Serb	201.6	4.5
Muslim	20.8	0.5
Italian	19.6	0.4
Hungarian	16.6	0.4
Albanian	15.1	0.3
Slovenian	13.2	0.3
Czech	10.5	0.2
Roma	9.5	0.2
Montenegrin	4.9	0.1
Slovak	4.7	0.1
Macedonian	4.3	0.1
Others*	139.5	3.3
Total	**4,437.5**	**100.0**

* Including other groups, ethnically non-declared persons and unknown ethnicity.

COUNTIES

Županije (County)	Area (sq km)	Population (at census of March 2001)	Density (per sq km)
Bjelovar and Bilogora . .	2,640	133,084	50.4
Dubrovnik and Neretva . .	1,781	122,870	69.0
Istria	2,813	206,344	73.4
Karlovac	3,626	141,787	39.1
Koprivnica and Križevci . .	1,748	124,467	71.2
Krapina and Zagorje . . .	1,229	142,432	115.9
Lika and Senj	5,353	53,677	10.0
Međimurje	729	118,426	162.4
Osijek and Baranja . .	4,155	330,506	79.5
Požega and Slavonia . . .	1,823	85,831	47.1
Primorje and Gorski Kotar .	3,588	305,505	85.1
Sisak and Moslavina . .	4,468	185,387	41.5
Slavonski Brod and Posavina	2,030	176,765	87.1
Split and Dalmatia	4,540	463,676	102.1
Šibenik and Knin . . .	2,984	112,891	37.8
Varaždin	1,262	184,769	146.4
Virovitica and Podravina . .	2,024	93,389	46.1
Vukovar and Sirmium . .	2,454	204,768	83.4
Zadar	3,646	162,045	44.4
Zagreb City	641	779,145	1,215.5
Zagreb (County)	3,060	309,696	101.2
Total	**56,594**	**4,437,460**	**78.4**

PRINCIPAL TOWNS
(population at 2001 census)

Zagreb (capital) . .	691,724	Šibenik	37,060
Split	175,140	Sisak	36,785
Rijeka	143,800	Velika Gorica . .	33,339
Osijek	90,411	Vinkovci . . .	33,239
Zadar	69,556	Dubrovnik . . .	30,436
Slavonski Brod . .	58,642	Vukovar . . .	30,126
Pula	58,594	Bjelovar . . .	27,783
Karlovac	49,082	Koprivnica . . .	24,809
Sesvete	44,914	Požega	20,943
Varaždin	41,434	Đakovo	20,912

BIRTHS, MARRIAGES AND DEATHS

	Registered live births Number	Rate (per 1,000)	Registered marriages Number	Rate (per 1,000)	Registered deaths Number	Rate (per 1,000)
1996	53,811	12.0	24,596	5.5	50,636	11.3
1997	55,501	12.1	24,517	5.4	51,964	11.4
1998	47,068	10.5	24,243	5.4	52,311	11.6
1999	45,179	9.9	23,778	5.2	51,953	11.4
2000*	43,746	10.0	22,017	5.0	50,246	11.5
2001*	40,993	9.2	22,076	5.0	49,552	11.2
2002*	40,094	9.0	22,806	5.1	50,569	11.4
2003*	39,668	8.9	22,337	5.0	52,575	11.8

* Rates from 2000 onwards are calculated on the basis of the March 2001 census total of persons usually resident. Figures for earlier years were based on estimates of *de jure* population (permanent residents).

Expectation of life (WHO estimates, years at birth): 74.8 (males 71.0; females 78.6) in 2002 (Source: WHO, *World Health Report*).

EMPLOYMENT
(annual averages, '000 persons)

	2001	2002	2003
Agriculture, hunting and forestry	107.4	101.3	94.6
Fishing	3.8	4.2	4.4
Mining and quarrying	7.7	7.0	8.0
Manufacturing	287.0	285.1	288.4
Electricity, gas and water supply	27.7	27.1	26.8
Construction	90.2	98.3	108.1
Wholesale and retail trade; repair of motor vehicles, motorcycles and personal and household goods	205.8	213.9	226.9
Hotels and restaurants	76.4	77.4	78.5
Transport, storage and communications	96.8	96.2	97.6
Financial intermediation	29.8	30.3	31.2
Real estate, renting and business activities	69.6	71.8	77.0
Public administration and defence; compulsory social security	121.3	118.2	116.2
Education	83.8	85.3	86.9
Health and social work	82.4	82.6	84.0
Other community, social and personal service activities	44.0	46.9	50.7
Private households with employed persons	11.4	10.6	10.5
Total employed (incl. others)	**1,348.3**	**1,359.0**	**1,392.5**
Registered unemployed	380.2	389.7	329.8
Total labour force	**1,728.5**	**1,748.7**	**1,722.3**

Health and Welfare

KEY INDICATORS

Total fertility rate (children per woman, 2002)	1.6
Under-5 mortality rate (per 1,000 live births, 2003)	7
HIV/AIDS (% of persons aged 15–49, 2003)	<0.10
Physicians (per 1,000 head, 2001)	2.38
Hospital beds (per 1,000 head, 2001)	6.00
Health expenditure (2001): US $ per head (PPP)	726
Health expenditure (2001): % of GDP	9.0
Health expenditure (2001): public (% of total)	81.8
Human Development Index (2002): ranking	48
Human Development Index (2002): value	0.830

For sources and definitions, see explanatory note on p. vi.

Agriculture

PRINCIPAL CROPS
('000 metric tons)

	2001	2002	2003
Wheat	965.2	988.2	609.3
Barley	161.5	170.9	134.2
Maize	2,211.6	2,501.8	1,569.2
Oats	47.6	50.0*	34.1
Potatoes	670.2	736.2	375.1
Sugar beet	964.9	1,183.4	677.6
Dry beans	16.5	19.3	12.6
Soybeans (Soya beans)	91.8	129.5	82.6
Sunflower seed	43.0	63.0	69.3
Rapeseed	22.5	25.6*	28.6
Cabbages	123.7	127.6	97.8
Tomatoes	73.9	71.4	71.4†
Cucumbers and gherkins†	35.5	35.5	35.5
Green chillies and peppers	38.6	45.8	31.4
Dry onions	58.1	60.4	40.8
Garlic	9.9	10.1	6.9
Green beans	9.4	11.1	7.2
Green peas	10.4	11.5	8.9
Carrots	28.2	32.5	21.5
Watermelons	50.0	55.4	40.2

— *continued*	2001	2002	2003
Apples	32.5	59.1	58.1
Pears	6.7	7.6	7.8
Peaches and nectarines	9.0	10.1	6.6
Plums	39.6	20.5	42.8
Grapes	359.0	370.9	333.3
Tobacco (leaves)	10.5	10.9	9.7

* Unofficial figure.
† FAO estimate(s).

Source: FAO.

LIVESTOCK
('000 head at 31 December)

	2001	2002	2003
Horses	10	8	11*
Cattle	438	417	444*
Pigs	1,234	1,286	1,347
Sheep	539	580	587
Goats	93	97	86
Chickens	11,747	11,665	11,778
Ducks*	120	120	120
Geese*	120	120	120
Turkeys	710†	710*	710*

* FAO estimate(s).
† Unofficial figure.

Source: FAO.

LIVESTOCK PRODUCTS
('000 metric tons)

	2001	2002	2003*
Beef and veal	25.6	26.6	22.5
Mutton and lamb	2.0	2.4	1.5
Pigmeat	115.1	117.2	115.0
Poultry meat	33.7	42.6	42.6
Cows' milk	654.8	696.4	753.4
Sheep's milk	8.2	9.4	8.2
Butter	2.6	2.8*	2.8
Cheese (all kinds)	23.6	24.0*	23.9
Hen eggs	47.2	45.7	45.7
Honey	2.1	2.1	2.1

* FAO estimate(s).

Source: FAO.

Forestry

ROUNDWOOD REMOVALS
('000 cubic metres)

	2001	2002	2003
Sawlogs and veneer logs	1,938	1,969	2,055
Pulpwood	561	626	594
Other industrial wood	222	291	219
Fuel wood	747	755	979
Total	**3,468**	**3,641**	**3,847**

Source: FAO.

SAWNWOOD PRODUCTION
('000 cubic metres)

	2001	2002	2003
Coniferous (softwood)	118	122	103
Broadleaved (hardwood)	456	518	482
Total	**574**	**640**	**585**

Source: FAO.

Fishing

(metric tons, live weight)

	2001	2002	2003
Capture	20,215	24,224	21,836
European pilchard (sardine)	9,097	12,626	12,271
European anchovy	2,850	3,187	3,341
Atlantic bluefin tuna	3,045	3,971	3,028
Cephalopods	1,132	501	453
Aquaculture	10,166	8,416	7,605
Common carp	2,774	1,849	1,633
Rainbow trout	1,261	911	791
European seabass	1,520	1,800	803
Mediterranean mussel	2,870	2,400	1,900
Total catch	30,381	32,640	29,441

Mining

('000 metric tons, unless otherwise indicated)

	2000	2001	2002
Crude petroleum	1,214	1,121	1,108
Natural gas (million cu m)	1,659	2,010	2,122
Bentonite	10.0	10.6	11.2
Ceramic clay	6.1	6.0	6.0
Salt (unrefined)	33.7	32.6	36.9
Gypsum (crude)	150.8	130.9	145.0

Source: US Geological Survey.

Industry

SELECTED PRODUCTS

('000 metric tons, unless otherwise indicated)

	2001	2002	2003
Beer ('000 hectolitres)	3,799	3,624	3,679
Spirits ('000 hectolitres)	163	151	144
Cigarettes (million)	14,716	15,047	n.a.
Cotton fabrics and blankets ('000 sq metres)	14,059	14,083	12,321
Household linen ('000 sq metres)	6,502	6,700	n.a.
Ready-to-wear clothing ('000 sq metres)	24,468	19,591	17,710
Leather footwear ('000 pairs)	6,167	5,135	4,403
Paper and cardboard	234	240	n.a.
Cardboard packaging	184	198	196
Motor spirit (petrol)	1,250	1,184	n.a.
Gas oil (distillate fuels)	1,036	1,158	n.a.
Compound fertilizers	407	469	499
Synthetic materials and resin	64	65	75
Cement	3,246	3,378	3,654
Tractors (number)	2,386	4,524	n.a.
Tankers ('000 gross registered tons)	225	368	471
Cargo ships ('000 gross registered tons)	224	126	83
Chairs ('000)	1,834	2,051	2,059
Electric energy (million kWh)	12,674	12,725	13,247

Finance

CURRENCY AND EXCHANGE RATES

Monetary Unit
100 lipa = 1 kuna.

Sterling, Dollar and Euro Equivalents (31 December 2004)
£1 sterling = 10.887 kuna;
US $1 = 5.637 kuna;
€1 = 7.678 kuna;
1,000 kuna = £91.85 = $177.40= €130.24.

Average Exchange Rate (kuna per US $)
2002   7.869
2003   6.704
2004   6.036

Note: The Croatian dinar was introduced on 23 December 1991, replacing (and initially at par with) the Yugoslav dinar. On 30 May 1994 the kuna, equivalent to 1,000 dinars, was introduced.

STATE BUDGET
(million kuna)*

Revenue†	2001	2002	2003‡
Tax revenue	47,274.0	67,965.5	72,697.9
Taxes on personal income	3,404.4	3,363.3	3,114.6
Taxes on corporate income	1,987.2	2,659.1	3,074.5
Social security contributions	6,781.2	25,189.6	27,416.9
General sales, turnover or value-added taxes	23,422.3	26,465.6	28,800.2
Excises	7,698.9	7,474.2	7,851.0
Excises on petroleum products	4,194.4	3,329.9	3,345.9
Excises on tobacco products	2,098.6	2,193.0	2,349.4
Customs duties	3,215.4	2,050.6	1,810.9
Other current revenue	1,632.3	1,685.6	1,954.1
Capital revenue	4,597.3	218.0	3,597.6
Total	53,503.6	69,869.1	78,249.6

Expenditure§	2001	2002	2003
Current expenditure	52,819.2	68,923.5	75,041.4
Wages and employer contributions	14,877.9	19,896.9	21,780.4
Other purchases of goods and services	7,342.8	11,662.1	11,627.0
Interest payments	3,015.3	3,260.6	3,586.1
Domestic	1,043.1	1,373.6	1,683.1
Foreign	1,972.2	1,887.0	1,903.0
Subsidies	3,656.0	2,190.9	4,360.0
Other current transfers	23,927.1	31,913.0	33,688.0
Transfers to other levels of government	11,318.1	3,775.8	3,198.5
Transfers to non-profit institutions	663.5	819.3	881.0
Transfers to households	11,833.1	27,224.9	29,532.3
Transfers abroad	112.4	93.0	76.1
Capital expenditure	3,904.1	3,068.7	4,071.7
Total	56,723.3	71,992.1	79,113.1

* From July 2001 includes social security funds, but excludes revenue and expenditure from Croatian Roads Company and Croatian Motorways.
† Excluding grants received (million kuna): 10.4 in 2003.
‡ Preliminary.
§ Excluding lending minus repayments (million kuna): 1,089.5 in 2001; 1,377.5 in 2002; 1,333.5 in 2003.

INTERNATIONAL RESERVES
(US $ million at 31 December)

	2001	2002	2003
IMF special drawing rights	107.4	1.5	—
Reserve position in IMF	0.2	0.2	0.2
Foreign exchange	4,595.6	5,883.2	8,190.2
Total	4,703.2	5,884.9	8,190.5

Source: IMF, *International Financial Statistics*.

MONEY SUPPLY
(million kuna at 31 December)

	2001	2002	2003
Currency outside banks . . .	8,507.4	9,680.9	10,573.1
Demand deposits at deposit money banks	15,180.6	21,166.2	23,315.0
Total (incl. others)	23,703.6	30,866.3	33,888.7

Source: IMF, *International Financial Statistics*.

COST OF LIVING
(Consumer price index; base: 1990 = 100)

	2000	2001	2002
Food	62,506.7	63,813.3	64,320.0
Fuel and light	63,910.8	71,837.3	72,545.9
Clothing (incl. footwear) . . .	74,459.5	77,135.1	79,297.3
Housing	58,555.0	59,556.7	60,394.1
All items (incl. others)	70,519.5	73,714.3	75,168.8

Source: ILO.

NATIONAL ACCOUNTS
(million kuna at current prices)
Expenditure on the Gross Domestic Product

	2001	2002*	2003*
Government final consumption expenditure	37,956	37,741	39,789
Private final consumption expenditure	98,054	107,427	113,396
Change in inventories	2,665	6,822	5,508
Gross fixed capital formation . .	36,984	44,114	53,168
Total domestic expenditure .	175,659	196,104	211,861
Exports of goods and services . .	80,246	81,375	90,927
Less Imports of goods and services	90,265	98,089	109,721
GDP in purchasers' values . .	165,639	179,390	193,067

* Preliminary data.
Gross Domestic Product by Economic Activity

	2001	2002*	2003*
Agriculture, hunting, forestry and fishing	12,482	13,038	13,260
Mining and quarrying; manufacturing; electricity, gas and water supply	33,858	35,157	37,054
Construction	6,832	8,546	10,732
Wholesale and retail trade; repair of motor vehicles, motorcycles and personal and household goods	15,955	18,347	20,039
Hotels and restaurants	4,761	5,261	5,974
Transport, storage and communications	13,821	15,759	17,754
Financial intermediation; real estate, renting and business activities	21,260	24,355	27,493
Public administration and defence; compulsory social security; education; health and social work; other community, social and personal services; private households with employed persons	30,090	31,574	33,323
Sub-total	139,060	152,038	165,630
Less Financial intermediation services indirectly measured .	4,779	5,860	6,897
GDP at basic prices	134,281	146,178	158,733
Taxes, *less* subsidies, on products .	31,358	33,212	34,334
GDP in purchasers' values . .	165,639	179,390	193,067

* Preliminary data.

BALANCE OF PAYMENTS
(US $ million)

	2001	2002	2003
Exports of goods f.o.b.	4,758.7	5,003.6	6,307.7
Imports of goods f.o.b.	−8,860.0	−10,652.2	−14,216.0
Trade balance	−4,101.3	−5,648.6	−7,908.3
Exports of services	4,875.5	5,567.4	8,621.4
Imports of services	−1,948.1	−2,412.7	−2,980.0
Balance on goods and services	−1,173.9	−2,493.9	−2,266.9
Other income received . . .	418.9	428.4	482.2
Other income paid	−936.4	−930.5	−1,695.5
Balance on goods, services and income	−1,691.5	−2,996.0	−3,480.2
Current transfers received . . .	1,174.5	1,361.9	1,729.2
Current transfers paid	−208.8	−283.7	−333.7
Current balance	−725.8	−1,917.8	−2,084.7
Capital account (net)	133.0	443.4	83.6
Direct investment abroad . .	−154.6	−532.9	−92.6
Direct investment from abroad	1,558.7	1,124.0	1,998.2
Portfolio investment assets . .	−129.3	−626.5	155.1
Portfolio investment liabilities .	730.0	396.8	849.2
Other investment assets . .	360.4	358.8	−2,531.0
Other investment liabilities . .	149.9	2,365.2	4,248.6
Net errors and omissions . . .	−580.3	−785.1	−1,235.2
Overall balance	1,342.1	825.9	1,391.3

Source: IMF, *International Financial Statistics*.

External Trade

PRINCIPAL COMMODITIES
(distribution by SITC, US $ million)

Imports c.i.f.	2001	2002	2003
Food and live animals . . .	691.5	794.0	1,000.9
Mineral fuels, lubricants, etc. .	1,175.6	1,310.0	1,554.7
Petroleum and petroleum products	836.6	973.1	1,125.5
Chemicals and related products	1,038.5	1,214.6	1,560.8
Basic manufactures	1,786.5	2,082.3	2,661.6
Textile yarn, fabrics, etc. . . .	355.7	370.2	428.0
Iron and steel	315.8	376.4	522.4
Machinery and transport equipment	3,102.7	3,682.0	5,265.0
Machinery specialized for particular industries	286.5	428.2	562.7
General industrial machinery equipment and parts	398.2	525.3	742.2
Telecommunications and sound equipment	297.5	351.1	458.7
Electrical machinery, apparatus etc. (excl. telecommunications and sound equipment) . . .	427.5	568.5	836.3
Road vehicles and parts* . . .	943.0	1,136.9	1,571.7
Other transport equipment and parts*	357.2	214.6	527.0
Miscellaneous manufactured articles	1,042.9	1,249.0	1,646.8
Clothing and accessories (excl. footwear)	258.3	250.6	330.8
Total (incl. others)	9,147.1	10,722.0	14,209.0

Exports f.o.b.	2001	2002	2003
Food and live animals . .	322.5	392.7	560.4
Crude materials (inedible)			
except fuels	241.4	273.7	349.8
Cork and wood	148.0	162.0	202.9
Mineral fuels, lubricants, etc. .	476.6	458.4	595.3
Petroleum and petroleum products	349.1	327.9	422.1
Chemicals and related			
products	494.3	505.5	593.3
Medicinal and pharmaceutical			
products	174.3	192.7	203.0
Plastics in primary forms . .	102.1	107.1	126.1
Basic manufactures . . .	664.6	722.0	868.9
Non-metallic mineral			
manufactures	183.0	196.0	235.2
Machinery and transport			
equipment	1,368.4	1,395.0	1,823.3
Electrical machinery, apparatus			
etc. (excl. telecommunications			
and sound equipment) . .	243.7	316.2	462.9
Transport equipment and parts			
(excl. road vehicles)* . . .	719.8	610.3	772.7
Miscellaneous manufactured			
articles	968.1	1,009.2	1,211.3
Clothing and accessories (excl.			
footwear)	491.2	510.7	594.6
Footwear	165.7	148.0	157.3
Total (incl. others)	4,665.9	4,903.6	6,186.6

* Data on parts exclude tyres, engines and electrical parts.

PRINCIPAL TRADING PARTNERS
(US $ million)

Imports c.i.f.	2001	2002	2003
Austria	631.2	710.0	941.1
Belgium	132.5	156.0	179.6
Bosnia and Herzegovina . .	126.8	166.4	231.2
China, People's Republic . .	144.3	256.9	406.8
Czech Republic	209.3	266.2	353.9
France	397.6	554.8	749.2
Germany	1,583.2	1,742.3	2,221.0
Hungary	238.4	317.8	424.4
Italy	1,656.9	1,850.4	2,580.9
Japan	142.8	163.9	245.6
Korea, Republic	69.1	105.9	158.9
Netherlands	164.0	201.0	273.3
Russia	654.1	717.2	678.5
Slovenia	711.7	826.5	1,051.7
Spain	127.0	182.1	270.0
Sweden	110.4	130.4	193.0
Switzerland	153.4	167.6	182.5
United Kingdom	226.2	217.7	290.6
USA	297.3	310.2	365.8
Total (incl. others)	9,147.1	10,722.0	14,209.0

Exports f.o.b.	2001	2002	2003
Austria	267.9	365.7	479.4
Bosnia and Herzegovina . .	560.6	704.4	892.4
Cayman Islands	70.1	—	—
France	163.1	159.1	174.7
Germany	689.6	611.7	733.2
Greece	24.0	65.3	37.4
Hungary	56.9	82.9	80.5
Italy	1,105.4	1,113.6	1,649.9
Liberia	138.1	179.6	100.3
Macedonia, former Yugoslav			
republic	52.5	59.1	70.5
Malta	55.6	1.4	93.1
Netherlands	46.7	41.9	48.7
Poland	20.0	20.4	30.4
Russia	83.5	83.8	73.7
Slovenia	426.4	427.8	510.9
United Kingdom	67.3	62.6	72.1
USA	119.8	102.3	163.9
Yugoslavia*	149.2	172.4	190.8
Total (incl. others)	4,665.9	4,903.6	6,186.6

* Serbia and Montenegro from February 2003.

Transport

RAILWAYS
(traffic)

	2001	2002	2003*
Passenger journeys ('000) . .	36,964	36,239	35,980
Passenger-kilometres (million) .	1,241	1,195	1,163
Freight carried ('000 metric tons) .	10,807	10,654	11,723
Freight net ton-km (million) . .	2,074	2,206	2,487

* Provisional data.

ROAD TRAFFIC
(registered motor vehicles at 31 December)

	2001	2002	2003
Passenger cars	1,195,450	1,244,252	1,293,421
Buses	4,770	4,792	4,833
Registered goods vehicles . .	119,899	128,955	138,290
Motorcycles and mopeds . . .	73,766	85,295	n.a.

INLAND WATERWAYS
(vessels and traffic)

	2001	2002	2003
Tugs	32	24	25
Motor barges	4	5	5
Barges	95	71	69
Goods unloaded (million metric			
tons)	1	1	1

SHIPPING

Merchant Fleet
(registered at 31 December)

	2001	2002	2003
Number of vessels	243	256	259
Total displacement ('000 grt) . .	775.2	834.7	847.7

Source: Lloyd's Register-Fairplay, *World Fleet Statistics*.

International Sea-borne Freight Traffic

	2001	2002	2003
Vessels entered (million grt) . .	30.6	33.1	43.1
Goods loaded ('000 metric tons) .	5,847	4,597	4,053
Goods unloaded ('000 metric tons)	6,815	6,705	7,364
Goods in transit ('000 metric tons)	3,794	4,443	5,618

CIVIL AVIATION

	2001	2002	2003
Kilometres flown ('000)	13,225	14,929	16,445
Passengers carried ('000) . . .	1,245	1,356	1,582
Passenger-kilometres (million) .	922	1,027	1,228
Freight carried (metric tons) . .	6,007	6,105	6,247
Ton-kilometres ('000)	3,997	3,953	3,906

Tourism

FOREIGN TOURIST ARRIVALS BY COUNTRY OF ORIGIN
('000)

	2001	2002	2003
Austria	687	690	709
Bosnia and Herzegovina . . .	172	173	178
Czech Republic	742	698	699
Germany	1,300	1,482	1,552
Hungary	280	318	356
Italy	1,060	1,099	1,206
Poland	392	358	238
Slovakia	203	191	188
Slovenia	877	870	918
Total (incl. others)	6,544	6,944	7,409

Receipts from tourism (US $ million): 3,335 in 2001; 3,811 in 2002; 6,376 in 2003 (Sources: World Tourism Organization; Croatian National Bank).

Communications Media

	2001	2002	2003
Radio licences ('000)	1,150	1,163	1,168
Television licences ('000) . .	1,080	1,092	1,095
Telephone licences ('000) . . .	1,783	1,825	1,853
Mobile cellular telephones ('000 subscribers)*	1,755	2,340	2,553
Personal computers ('000 in use)*	620	760	n.a.
Internet users ('000)*	518	789	1,014
Book production (titles)	3,832	4,296	6,447
Daily newspapers (number) . .	14	13	12
Non-daily newspapers	251	252	269
Periodicals	2,211	2,255	2,422

* Source: International Telecommunication Union.

Facsimile machines (number in use): 50,237 in 1997 (Source: UN, *Statistical Yearbook*).

Education

(2003/04)

	Institutions	Teachers	Students
Pre-primary	1,067	7,020	89,212
Primary schools	2,138	28,335	393,421
Secondary schools	665	20,073	195,340
Higher education	102	7,917	126,343*

* Figure for 2002/03.

Adult literacy rate (UNESCO estimates): 98.1% (Males 99.3%; Females 97.1%) in 2002 (Source: UN Development Programme, *Human Development Report*).

Directory

The Constitution

The Constitution of the Republic of Croatia was promulgated on 21 December 1990. Croatia issued a declaration of dissociation from the Socialist Federal Republic of Yugoslavia in June 1991, and formal independence was proclaimed on 8 October. Constitutional amendments adopted in November 1997 included a prohibition on the re-establishment of a union of Yugoslav states. The Županijski dom (Chamber of Counties), the upper chamber of the hitherto bicameral legislature, was abolished by a constitutional amendment adopted in March 2001.

The following is a summary of the main provisions of the Constitution:

GENERAL PROVISIONS

The Republic of Croatia is a democratic, constitutional state where power belongs to the people and is exercised directly and through the elected representatives of popular sovereignty.

The Republic is an integral state, while its sovereignty is inalienable, indivisible and non-transferable. State power in the Republic is divided into legislative, executive and judicial power.

All citizens over the age of 18 years have the right to vote and to be candidates for election to public office. The right to vote is realized through direct elections, by secret ballot. Citizens of the Republic living outside its borders have the right to vote in elections for the Sabor (Assembly) and the President of the Republic.

In a state of war or when there is a direct threat to the independence and unity of the Republic, as well as in the case of serious natural disasters, some freedoms and rights that are guaranteed by the Constitution may be restricted. This is decided by the Sabor by a two-thirds' majority of its deputies and, if the Sabor cannot be convened, by the President of the Republic.

BASIC RIGHTS

The following rights are guaranteed and protected in the Republic: the right to life (the death sentence has been abolished), fundamental freedoms and privacy, equality before the law, the right to be presumed innocent until proven guilty and the principle of legality, the right to receive legal aid, the right to freedom of movement and residence, the right to seek asylum, inviolability of the home, freedom and secrecy of correspondence, safety and secrecy of personal data, freedom of thought and expression of opinion, freedom of conscience and religion (all religious communities are equal before the law and are separated from the State), the right of assembly and peaceful association, the right of ownership, entrepreneurship and free trade (monopolies are forbidden), the right to work and freedom of labour, the right to a nationality, the right to strike, and the right to a healthy environment.

Members of all peoples and minorities in the Republic enjoy equal rights. They are guaranteed the freedom to express their nationality, to use their language and alphabet and to enjoy cultural autonomy.

GOVERNMENT

Legislature

Legislative power resides with the unicameral Sabor, which has a minimum of 100 and a maximum of 160 members. The Sabor decides on the adoption and amendment of the Constitution, approves laws, adopts the state budgets, decides on war and peace, decides on the alteration of the borders of the Republic, calls referendums, supervises the work of the Government and other public officials responsible to the Sabor, in accordance with the Constitution and the law, and deals with other matters determined by the Constitution.

Members of the Sabor are elected by universal, direct and secret ballot for a term of four years, and their term is not mandatory. The

Sabor may be dissolved, with the approval of the majority of all the deputies. The Sabor has the power to appoint and dismiss the Prime Minister and (upon his recommendation) the ministers.

President of the Republic

The President of the Republic is the Head of State of Croatia. The President represents the country at home and abroad and is responsible for ensuring respect for the Constitution, guaranteeing the existence and unity of the Republic and the regular functioning of state power. The President is elected directly for a term of five years.

The President is the Supreme Commander of the Armed Forces. In the event of war or immediate danger, the President issues decrees having the force of law. The President may convene a meeting of the Government and place on its agenda items that, in his opinion, should be discussed. The President attends the Government's meetings and presides over them.

Ministers

Executive power in the Republic resides with the President, the Prime Minister and the Ministers. The Government of the Republic consists of the Ministers and the Prime Minister. The Government issues decrees, proposes laws and the budget, and implements laws and regulations that have been adopted by the Sabor. In its work, the Government is responsible to the President of the Republic and the Sabor.

JUDICATURE

Judicial power is vested in the courts and is autonomous and independent. The courts issue judgments on the basis of the Constitution and the law. The Supreme Court is the highest court and is responsible for the uniform implementation of laws and equal rights of citizens. Judges and state public prosecutors are appointed and relieved of duty by the State Judicial Council, which is elected by the Sabor for a term of eight years.

The Government

HEAD OF STATE

President of the Republic: STJEPAN MESIĆ (elected 7 February 2000; re-elected 16 January 2005; inaugurated 18 February 2005).

GOVERNMENT
(April 2005)

An administration principally comprising representatives of the Croatian Democratic Union (CDU).

Prime Minister: IVO SANADER (CDU).

Deputy Prime Minister, and Minister of the Family, Veterans' Affairs and Intergenerational Solidarity: JADRANKA KOSOR (CDU).

Deputy Prime Minister: DAMIR POLANCEC (CDU).

Minister of Finance: IVAN ŠUKER (CDU).

Minister of Defence: BERISLAV RONČEVIĆ (CDU).

Minister of Health: NEVEN LJUBICIĆ (CDU).

Minister of the Interior: MARIJAN MLINARIĆ (CDU).

Minister of Foreign Affairs and European Integration: KOLINDA GRABAR KITAROVIĆ (CDU).

Minister of the Economy, Labour and Entrepreneurship: BRANKO VUKELIĆ (CDU).

Minister of Agriculture, Forestry and Water Management: PETAR ČOBANKOVIĆ (CDU).

Minister of Maritime Affairs, Tourism, Transport and Development: BOŽIDAR KALMETA (CDU).

Minister of Justice: VESNA ŠKARE OŽBOLT (Democratic Centre).

Minister of Environmental Protection, Physical Planning and Construction: MARINA MATULOVIĆ DROPULIĆ (CDU).

Minister of Science, Education and Sport: DRAGAN PRIMORAC (Independent).

Minister of Culture: BOŽO BIŠKUPIĆ VUJIĆ (CDU).

MINISTRIES

Office of the President: 10000 Zagreb, Pantovčak 241; tel. (1) 4565191; fax (1) 4565299; e-mail ured@predsjednik.hr; internet www.predsjednik.hr.

Office of the Prime Minister: 10000 Zagreb, trg sv. Marka 2; tel. (1) 4569222; fax (1) 6303023; e-mail premijer@vlada.hr; internet www.vlada.hr.

Ministry of Agriculture, Forestry and Water Management: 10000 Zagreb, Ave Vukovar 78; tel. (1) 6133444; fax (1) 442070; internet www.mps.hr.

Ministry of Culture: 10000 Zagreb, Runjaninova 2; tel. (1) 4866666; fax (1) 4866280; internet www.min-kulture.hr.

Ministry of Defence: 10000 Zagreb, trg kralja Petra Krešimira IV 1; tel. (1) 4567111; e-mail infor@morh.hr; internet www.morh.hr.

Ministry of the Economy, Labour and Entrepreneurship: 10000 Zagreb, trg sv. Marka 2; tel. (1) 4569207; fax (1) 4550606; e-mail info@mingo.hr; internet www.mingo.hr.

Ministry of Environmental Protection, Physical Planning and Construction: 10000 Zagreb, Republike Austrije 20; tel. (1) 3782444; fax (1) 3772822; e-mail kabinet.ministra@zg.tel.hr; internet www.mzopu.hr.

Ministry of the Family, Veterans' Affairs and Intergenerational Solidarity: 10000 Zagreb, Park Stara Trešnjevka 4; tel. (1) 3657800; fax (1) 3657852; e-mail mobms@mobms.hr; internet www.mobms.hr.

Ministry of Finance: 10000 Zagreb, ul. Katančićeva 5; tel. (1) 4591333; fax (1) 4922583; e-mail kabinet@mfin.hr; internet www.mfin.hr.

Ministry of Foreign Affairs and European Integration: 10000 Zagreb, trg Nikole Šubića Zrinskog 7–8; tel. (1) 4569964; fax (1) 4569977; e-mail mvp@mvp.hr; internet www.mvp.hr.

Ministry of Health and Social Welfare: 10000 Zagreb, ul. Baruna Tranka 6; tel. (1) 431068; fax (1) 431067; internet www.miz.hr.

Ministry of the Interior: 10000 Zagreb, Savska cesta 39; tel. (1) 6122129; fax (1) 6122299; e-mail pitanja@mup.hr; internet www.mup.hr.

Ministry of Justice: 10000 Zagreb, Republike Austrije 14; tel. (1) 3710600; fax (1) 3710602; internet www.pravosudje.hr.

Ministry of Maritime Affairs, Tourism, Transport and Development: 10000 Zagreb, Prisavlje 14; tel. (1) 6169100; fax (1) 6196519; internet www.pomorstvo.hr.

Ministry of Science, Education and Sport: 10000 Zagreb, trg hrvatskih velikana 6; tel. (1) 4569009; fax (1) 4569087; e-mail office@mips.hr; internet www.mips.hr.

President

Presidential Election, First Ballot, 2 January 2005

	Votes	% of votes
Stjepan Mesić*	1,089,398	48.92
Jadranka Kosor (Croatian Democratic Union)	452,218	20.31
Boris Mikšić (Independent)	396,093	17.79
Đurđa Adlešić (Croatian Social-Liberal Party)	59,795	2.68
Slaven Letica (Independent)	57,748	2.59
Ljubo Ćesić (Independent)	41,216	1.85
Ivić Pašalić (Croatian Bloc—Movement for a Modern Croatia)	40,637	1.82
Anto Kovačević (Croatian Christian Democratic Union)	19,145	0.86
Miroslav Blažević (Party of Croatian Defenders)	17,847	0.80
Miroslav Rajh (Croatian Youth Party)	14,766	0.66
Doris Košta (Independent)	8,271	0.37
Mladen Kešer (Independent)	7,056	0.32
Tomislav Petrak (Croatian Popular Party)	2,614	0.12
Total	2,227,073	100.00

Presidential Election, Second Ballot, 16 January 2005

	Votes	% of votes
Stjepan Mesić*	1,454,451	65.93
Jadranka Kosor (Croatian Democratic Union)	751,692	34.07
Total	2,206,143	100.00

* Candidate of an alliance comprising the Social Democratic Party, the Croatian People's Party, the Croatian Peasants' Party, the Istrian Democratic Assembly, the Party of Liberal Democrats, the Liberal Party, the Primorian-Goranian Union and the Party of Democratic Action.

Legislature

Sabor
(Assembly)

10000 Zagreb, Trg sv. Marka 6; tel. (1) 4569222; fax (1) 6303018; e-mail sabor@sabor.hr; internet www.sabor.hr.

The unicameral Sabor comprises a minimum of 100 and a maximum of 160 members, who are elected directly for a term of four years.

President: VLADIMIR ŠEKS, 10000 Zagreb, Trg sv. Marka 6; tel. (1) 4569222; fax (1) 6303018; e-mail sabor@sabor.hr; internet www.sabor.hr.

General Election, 23 November 2003

	Votes	% of votes	Seats
Croatian Democratic Union . . .	840,692	33.91	66
Social Democratic Party . . . } Liberal Party . . . . } Istrian Democratic Assembly . . }	560,593	22.61	43
Croatian People's Party . . . } Croatian Party of Slavonia and Baranja . . . . } Primorje and Gorski Kotar Alliance of . . . . . . }	198,781	8.02	11
Croatian Peasants' Party . . .	177,359	7.15	9
Croatian Party of Rights . . } Zagorje Democratic Party . . }	157,987	6.37	8
Croatian Social-Liberal Party } Democratic Centre . . . . . }	100,335	4.05	3
Croatian Pensioners' Party . .	98,537	3.97	3
Croatian Democratic Peasants' Party	24,872	1.00	1
Others	319,811	12.92	—
Total	**2,478,967**	**100.00**	**152***

* Including eight seats reserved for representatives of ethnic minority groups.

Political Organizations

Croatian Bloc-Movement for a Modern Croatia (Hrvatski blok-pokret za modernu Hrvatsku): 10000 Zagreb, ul. kneza Mislava 11/1; f. 2002; Chair. IVIĆ PAŠALIĆ; 11,265 mems (2004).

Croatian Christian Democratic Party (Hrvatska kršćanska demokratska stranka—HKDS): 10000 Zagreb, Ilica 102; tel. and fax (1) 3771893; e-mail endom@inet.hr; f. 1990; Pres. IVAN KEGLEVIĆ.

Croatian Christian Democratic Union (CCDU) (Hrvatska kršćanska demokratska unija—HKDU): 10000 Zagreb, Tkalčićeva 4/1; tel. (1) 4883861; fax (1) 4816282; e-mail hkdu@inet.hr; internet www.hkdu.hr; f. 1992; Pres. PETAR ČURLIN.

Croatian Democratic Party (CDP) (Hrvatska demokratska stranka—HDS): 10000 Zagreb; tel. (1) 422062; fax (1) 424111; f. 1989; Pres. MATO BATINIĆ.

Croatian Democratic Peasant Party (Hrvatska demokratska seljačka stranka—HDSS): 40000 Čakovec, Strossmayerova 9; tel. (40) 364440; fax (40) 364964; f. 1994; Pres. IVAN MARTAN.

Croatian Democratic Union (CDU) (Hrvatska demokratska zajednica—HDZ): 10000 Zagreb, trg žrtava fašizma 4; tel. (1) 4553000; fax (1) 4552600; e-mail hdz@hdz.hr; internet www.hdz.hr; f. 1989; Christian Democrat; Chair. IVO SANADER; 432,000 mems (2001).

Croatian Independent Democrats (CID) (Hrvatski nezavisni demokrati—HND): 10000 Zagreb, Masarykova 22; tel. (1) 4848476; fax (1) 4849089; f. 1994 by split from CDU; Chair. IVICA GAŽI.

Croatian Party of the Right (CPR) (Hrvatska stranka prava—HSP): 10000 Zagreb, Primorska 5; tel. (1) 3778016; fax (1) 3778736; e-mail hsp@zg.tel.hr; internet www.hsp.hr; f. 1990 as revival of group originally founded in 1861; extreme right-wing nationalist; armed br. was the Croatian Defence Asscn or Hrvatske Obrambene Snage (HOS); Pres. ANTE ĐAPIĆ; 25,000 mems (2002).

Croatian Peasants' Party (Hrvatska seljačka stranka—HSS): 10000 Zagreb, ul. Kralja Zvonimira 17; tel. (1) 4553624; fax (1) 4553631; e-mail hss@hss.hr; internet www.hss.hr; f. 1989; Pres. ZLATKO TOMČIĆ; 51,000 mems (2003).

Croatian Pensioners' Party (Hrvatska stranka umirovljenika—HSU): 10000 Zagreb, Frankopanska 7/1; tel. (1) 4840058; fax (1) 4815324; e-mail strankahsu@hsu.hr; internet www.hsu.hr; f. 1996; Chair. VLADIMIR JORDAN.

Croatian People's Party—Liberal Democrats (CPP) (Hrvatska narodna stranka—Liberalni demokrati—HNS): 10000 Zagreb, Kneza Mislava 8; tel. (1) 4629111; fax (1) 4629110; e-mail hns@hns .hr; internet www.hns.hr; f. 1990; fmrly Croatian People's Party; Pres. VESNA PUSIĆ; 21,100 mems (2004).

Croatian Popular Party (Hrvatska pučka stranka—HPS): 10000 Zagreb, Ozaljska 93/2; tel. (1) 3633569; fax (1) 3633749; e-mail hps@ hps.hr; internet www.hps.hr; f. 1997; Pres. TOMISLAV MERČEPR; 22,980 mems (2003).

Croatian Republicans (Hrvatski republikanci): 10000 Zagreb, trg bana Josipa Jelačića 1/III; tel. (1) 4818780; fax (1) 4815021; e-mail republikanci@zg.tel.hr; f. 1998; Chair. TOMISLAV BOGDANIĆ.

Croatian Social-Liberal Party (CSLP) (Hrvatska socijalno-lib-eralna stranka—HSLS): 10000 Zagreb, trg N. Š. Zrinskog 17; tel. (1) 4810401; fax (1) 4810404; e-mail hsls@hsls.hr; internet www.hsls .hr; f. 1989; Pres. IVAN ČEHOK; 20,000 mems (2004).

Croatian Youth Party (Hrvatska stranka mladih—HSM): 10290 Zaprešić, Augusta Šenoe 174; e-mail info@konacnohsm.hr; internet www.konacnohsm.hr; f. 2004; Pres. MIROSLAV RAJH.

Democratic Centre (DC) (Demokratski Centar): 10000 Zagreb, Ilica 48/1; tel. (1) 4831111; fax (1) 4831045; e-mail demokratski-centar@demokratski-centar.hr; internet www .demokratski-centar.hr; f. 2000 by mems of Croatian Democratic Union; pro-European, moderate; Pres. VESNA ŠKARE OŽBOLT; 14,000 mems (2004).

Democratic Party of the Slavonian Plain (Demokratska stranka slavonske ravnice): 31000 Osijek, Hrvatske Republike 19; tel. (31) 696008; f. 1998; Pres. SLAVKO VUKŠIĆ; 4,000 mems (2004).

Democratic Party of Zagorje (Zagorska demokratska stranka—ZDS): 49210 Zabok, Matije Gupce 53/1; tel. and fax (49) 222359; e-mail zagorska-demokratska-stranka@kr.htnet.hr; internet www .zds.hr; f. 1997; Pres. STANKO BELINA; 5,500 mems (2002).

Independent Democratic Serb Party (Samostalna demokratska srpska stranka—SDSS): 32010 Vukovar, Radnički dom 1–3; tel. (32) 423211; fax (32) 424606; e-mail ivanasdss@yahoo.com; internet www.sdss.hr; f. 1995 by Serbs in Eastern Slavonia; Pres. Dr VOJISLAV STANIMIROVIĆ; 6,000 mems (2004).

Istrian Democratic Assembly (IDA) (Istarski demokratski sabor—IDS): 52100 Pula, Splitska 3; tel. (52) 380183; fax (52) 223316; e-mail ids-ddi@pu.tel.hr; internet www.ids-ddi.com; f. 1990; Pres. IVAN JAKOVČIĆ; 3,800 mems (2004).

Liberal Party (Liberalna stranka): 10000 Zagreb, Ilica 16/1; tel. (1) 4833896; fax (1) 4833799; e-mail liberali@bbm.hr; internet www .liberali.hr; f. 1998 by mems of the Croatian Social-Liberal Party; Pres. ZLATKO BENAŠIĆ; 5,400 mems (2004).

New Croatia (Nova Hrvatska—NH): 1000 Zagreb, Ksaver 200; tel. (1) 4677699; f. 1999; Pres. ANTE PRKAČIN; 5,000 mems (2003).

Olive—Dalmatian Autonomist Party (Maslina—Dalmatinska autonomaška stranka): 21000 Split, Kninska 1; tel. (98) 702107; f. 2003; Pres. NIKOLA ZOKIĆ; 7,000 mems (2003).

Party of Croatian Defenders (Stranka hrvatskih branitelja—SHB): 10000 Zagreb, Ozaljska 93/2; tel. (1) 3639214; e-mail stranka .hrvatski.branitelja@zg.htnet.hr; internet www.shb.hr; f. 2001; Pres. ŽELJKO GALEKOVIĆ.

Primorje and Gorski Kotar Alliance (Primorsko Goranski Savez): 51000 Rijeka, Ciottina 19; tel. and fax (51) 335359; e-mail pgs@kvarner.net; f. 1990; regionalist; Chair. NIKOLA IVANIŠ; 5,077 mems (2004).

Serb People's Party (SPP) (Srpska narodna stranka—SNS): 10000 Zagreb, trg Mažuranića 3; tel. and fax (1) 4855631; f. 2001; promotes cultural and individual rights for Serbs in Croatia; Pres. MILAN ĐUKIĆ.

Social Democratic Party (SDP) (Socijaldemokratska partija hrvatske—SPH): 10000 Zagreb, trg Iblerov 9; tel. (1) 4552658; fax (1) 4552842; e-mail sdp@sdp.hr; internet www.sdp.hr; f. 1990; fmrly the ruling League of Communists of Croatia (Party of Democratic Reform), renamed as above in 1993; Chair. IVICA RAČAN; 25,000 mems (2004).

Diplomatic Representation

EMBASSIES IN CROATIA

Albania: 10000 Zagreb, Jurišićeva 2A; tel. (1) 4810679; fax (1) 4810682; e-mail veleposlanstvo-albanije@zg.tel.hr; Ambassador ARBEN CICI.

Australia: 10000 Zagreb, Nova Ves 11, 3 Kaptol Centar; tel. (1) 4891200; fax (1) 4836606; e-mail australian.embassy@zg.htnet.hr; internet www.auembassy.hr; Ambassador ANNA CHRISTINA GEORGE.

Austria: 10000 Zagreb, Jabukovać 39; tel. (1) 4881050; fax (1) 4834461; e-mail agram.ob@bmaa.gv.at; internet www.bmaa.gv.at; Ambassador HANS KNITEL.

Belgium: 10000 Zagreb, Pantovčak 125; tel. (1) 4578901; fax (1) 4578903; e-mail ambabel@zg.htnet.hr; Ambassador MARIE-JOHANE ROCCAS.

Bosnia and Herzegovina: 10001 Zagreb, Torbarova 9; tel. (1) 4683761; fax (1) 4683764; e-mail ambasada-bh-zg@zg.tel.hr; Ambassador ZLATKO DIŽDAREVIĆ.

Bulgaria: 10000 Zagreb, Novi Goljak 25; tel. (1) 4823336; fax (1) 4823338; e-mail veleposlanstvo-bugarske1@zg.hinet.hr; Ambassador VICTOR VALKOV.

Canada: 10000 Zagreb, prilaz Đure Deželića 4; tel. (1) 4881200; fax (1) 4881230; e-mail zagreb@dfait-maeci.gc.ca; Ambassador STEFANIE BECK.

Chile: 10000 Zagreb, Smičiklasova 23/II; tel. (1) 4611958; fax (1) 4610328; e-mail embajada@echile.hr ; internet www.clembassy.hr; Ambassador MANUEL ATRIA RAWLINS.

China, People's Republic: 10000 Zagreb, Mlinovi 132; tel. (1) 4637011; fax (1) 4637012; Ambassador WU ZHENGLONG.

Czech Republic: 10000 Zagreb, Savska cesta 41; tel. (1) 6177239; fax (1) 6176630; e-mail czech.embassy@inet.hr; internet www.mzv.cz/zagreb; Ambassador PETR BURIANEK.

Egypt: 10000 Zagreb, Tuškanac 58A; tel. (1) 4834272; fax (1) 4834247; e-mail veleposlanstvo.a.r.egipat@zg.htnet.hr; Ambassador MOHAMED HAFEZ.

Finland: 10000 Zagreb, Berislavićeva 2/2; tel. (1) 4811662; fax (1) 4819946; e-mail embassy@finland.htnet.hr; internet www.finembassy.hr; Ambassador ILPO MANNINEN.

France: 10000 Zagreb, Hebrangova 2; tel. (1) 4893600; fax (1) 4893660; e-mail presse@ambafrance.hr; internet www.ambafrance.hr; Ambassador FRANÇOIS SAINT-PAUL.

Germany: 10000 Zagreb, ul. grada Vukovara 64; tel. (1) 6300100; fax (1) 6158103; e-mail deutsche.botschaft.zagreb@inet.hr; internet www.deutschebotschaft-zagreb.hr; Ambassador JÜRGEN ALFRED STAKS.

Greece: 10000 Zagreb, Opatička 12; tel. (1) 4810444; fax (1) 4810419; e-mail greece-embassy@grembassy.hr; internet www.grembassy.hr; Ambassador PANAYOTIS BAIZOS.

Holy See: 10000 Zagreb, Ksaverska cesta 10A; tel. (1) 4673996; fax (1) 4673997; e-mail apostolska.nuncijatura.rh@inet.hr; Apostolic Nincio Most Rev. FRANCISCO-JAVIER LOZANO (Titular Archbishop of Penafiel in Tripolitania).

Hungary: 10000 Zagreb, Pantovčak 255–257A; tel. (1) 4890900; fax (1) 4579301; e-mail secretary@hungemb.hr; internet www.hungemb.hr; Ambassador LÁSZLÓ MOHAI.

India: 10000 Zagreb, ul. Boškovićeva 7A; tel. (1) 4873240; fax (1) 4817907; e-mail embassy.india@zg.htnet.hr; internet www.ring.net/indija; Ambassador ANEIL MATHRANI.

Iran: 10000 Zagreb, Pantovčak 125C; tel. (1) 4578981; fax (1) 4578987; Ambassador JAFAR SHAMSIAN.

Italy: 10000 Zagreb, Medulićeva 22; tel. (1) 4846386; fax (1) 4846384; e-mail veleposlanstvo_italije@zg.tel.hr; internet www.ambitalia.hr; Ambassador ALESSANDRO GRAFINI.

Japan: 10000 Zagreb, Ksaver 211; tel. (1) 4677755; fax (1) 4677766; Ambassador KANAME IKEDA.

Libya: 10000 Zagreb, Gornje Prekrižje 51B; tel. (1) 4629250; fax (1) 4629279; Sec. of People's Bureau (Ambassador) SAID ABDULAATI MOHAMMED.

Macedonia, former Yugoslav republic: 10000 Zagreb, Petrinjska 29/1; tel. (1) 4922903; fax (1) 4922902; e-mail amb.makedonije.zgb@zg.tel.hr; Ambassador MAHI NESIMI.

Malaysia: 10000 Zagreb, Slavujevac 4A; tel. (1) 4834346; fax (1) 4834348; e-mail veleposlanstvo-malezije@zg.htnet.hr; Ambassador Dato AZMAN MUHAMMAD NAZIR.

Malta: 10000 Zagreb, Becićeve stube 2; tel. (1) 4677999; fax (1) 4677381; Ambassador NIKOLA barun ADAMOVICH ČEPINSKI.

Netherlands: 10000 Zagreb, Medvešćak 56; tel. (1) 4684880; fax (1) 4684582; e-mail nlgovzag@zg.tel.hr; internet www.netherlandsembassy.hr; Ambassador LIONEL S. VEER.

Norway: 10000 Zagreb, Petrinjska 9; tel. (1) 4922829; fax (1) 4922832; internet www.norwegianembassy.hr; Ambassador KNUT TORAASEN.

Poland: 10000 Zagreb, Krležin Gvozd 3; tel. (1) 4899444; fax (1) 4834577; e-mail ambasada-polska@zg.htnet.hr; internet www.ambasadapoljska.hr; Ambassador KAZIMIERZ KOPYRA.

Portugal: 10000 Zagreb, trg ban J. Jelačića 5/2; tel. (1) 4882210; fax (1) 4920663; e-mail emb.port.zagreb@zg.htnet.hr; Ambassador LUÍS BARREIROS.

Romania: 10000 Zagreb, Srebrnjak 150A; tel. (1) 2430137; e-mail roamb@zg.tel.hr; Ambassador MIHAIL DINUCU.

Russia: 10000 Zagreb, Bosanska 44; tel. (1) 3755038; fax (1) 3755040; e-mail veleposlanstvo-ruske-federacije@zg.tel.hr; Chargé d'affaires a.i. MIHAIL KONAROVSKI.

Serbia and Montenegro: 10000 Zagreb, Pantovčak 245; tel. (1) 4579067; fax (1) 4573338; e-mail ambasada@ambasada-srj.hr; Ambassador MILAN SIMURDIĆ.

Slovakia: 10000 Zagreb, prilaz Đure Deželića 10; tel. (1) 4848941; fax (1) 4848942; e-mail slovak.emb@zg.htnet.hr; Ambassador JÁN PETRÍK.

Slovenia: 10000 Zagreb, Savska cesta 41/II; tel. (1) 6311000; fax (1) 6177236; Ambassador PETER ANDREJ BEKEŠ.

Spain: 10000 Zagreb, Tuškanac 21A; tel. (1) 4848950; fax (1) 4848711; e-mail embajada.de.espana@zg.htnet.hr; Ambassador SEBASTIAN DE ERICE GOMEZ-ACEBO.

Sweden: 10000 Zagreb, Frankopanska 22; tel. (1) 4849322; fax (1) 4849244; e-mail swedish.embassy@zg.tel.hr; Ambassador STURE THEOLIN.

Switzerland: 10000 Zagreb, Bogovićeva 3; tel. (1) 4810891; fax (1) 4810890; e-mail swiemzag@zg.tel.hr; Ambassador MARCUS KAISER.

Turkey: 10000 Zagreb, Masarykova 3/II; tel. (1) 4855200; fax (1) 4855606; e-mail turembzag@zg.htnet.hr; Ambassador FATMA DICLE KOPUZ.

Ukraine: 10000 Zagreb, Voćarska 52; tel. (1) 4616296; fax (1) 4633726; e-mail ukr.emb@zg.htnet.hr; internet www.ukrembassy.hinet.hr; Ambassador VIKTOR A. KYRYK.

United Kingdom: 10000 Zagreb, Ivana Lucica 4; tel. (1) 6009100; fax (1) 6009111; e-mail british.embassyzagreb@fco.gov.uk; internet www.britishembassy.gov.uk/croatia; Ambassador Sir JOHN RAMSDEN.

USA: 10010 Zagreb, Thomasa Jeffersona 2; tel. (1) 6612200; fax (1) 6612373; e-mail irc@usembassy.hr; internet www.usembassy.hr; Ambassador RALPH FRANK.

Judicial System

The judicial system of Croatia is administered by the Ministry of Justice. The Constitutional Court consists of 11 judges, elected by the Assembly for a period of eight years. The Supreme Court is the highest judicial body in the country, comprising 26 judges, also elected for a period of eight years.

Supreme Court: 10000 Zagreb, trg Nikole Šubića Zrinskog 3; tel. (1) 4810022; fax (1) 4810035; e-mail vsrh@vsrh.hr; internet www.vsrh.hr; Pres. IVICA CRNIĆ.

Constitutional Court: 10000 Zagreb, Marka trg 4; tel. (1) 4550927; fax (1) 4551055; e-mail usud@usud.hr; internet www.usud.hr; Pres. Prof. PETAR KLARIĆ.

State Judicial Council: 10000 Zagreb, trg Nikole Šubića Zrinskog 3; tel. and fax (1) 4811501; Pres. MILAN GUDELJ.

Office of the Public Prosecutor: 10000 Zagreb, Gajeva 30A; tel. (1) 4591888; fax (1) 4591854; e-mail dorh@zg.htnet.hr; Public Prosecutor MLADEN BAJIĆ.

Religion

Most of the population are Christian, the largest denomination being the Roman Catholic Church, of which most ethnic Croats are adherents. The Archbishop of Zagreb is the most senior Roman Catholic prelate in Croatia. The Croatian Old Catholic Church, like other branches of the Old Catholic Church elsewhere in Europe, does not acknowledge the authority of the Vatican or various reforms, including, notably, the doctrine of papal infallibility, agreed at the First Vatican Council of 1869-1870. There is a significant Serbian Orthodox minority. According to the 2001 census, 87.8% of the population of Croatia were Roman Catholics, 4.4% were Eastern Orthodox, 1.3% Muslims, and there were small communities of Protestants and Jews.

CHRISTIANITY

The Roman Catholic Church

For ecclesiastical purposes, Croatia comprises four archdioceses (including one, Zadar, directly responsible to the Holy See) and 11 dioceses (including one for Catholics of the Byzantine rite). At 31 December 2002 there were an estimated 3.9m. adherents.

Latin Rite

Bishops' Conference

10000 Zagreb, Kaptol 22; tel. (1) 4811893; fax (1) 4811894; e-mail tanjnistvo@hbk.hr.

f. 1993; Pres. Cardinal JOSIP BOZANIĆ (Archbishop of Zagreb).

Archbishop of Rijeka: Dr IVAN DEVČIĆ, 51000 Rijeka, Slaviše Vajnera Čiče 2; tel. (51) 337999; fax (51) 215287; e-mail rijecka-nadbiskupija@ri.hinet.hr.

Archbishop of Split-Makarska: MARIN BARIŠIĆ, 21001 Split, ul. Zrinjsko-Frankopanska 14; tel. (21) 319523; fax (21) 319522; e-mail marin.barisic@hbk.hr.

Archbishop of Zadar: IVAN PRENDJA, 23000 Zadar, trg Zeleni 1; tel. (23) 315712; fax (23) 316299; e-mail nadbiskupija.zadarska@zd.te.hr.

Archbishop of Zagreb: Cardinal JOSIP BOZANIĆ, 10001 Zagreb,Kaptol 31; tel. (1) 4894802; fax (1) 4816094; e-mail uzgnadb@zg.hinet.hr.

Byzantine Rite

Bishop of Križevci: SLAVOMIR MIKLOVŠ, 10000 Zagreb, Kaptol 20; tel. (1) 270767; 48,975 adherents (1993).

Old Catholic Church

Croatian Catholic Church: 10000 Zagreb, ul. Kneza Branimira 11; tel. (1) 4841361; Bishop BERNHARD HEITZ.

Serbian Orthodox Church

Metropolitan of Zagreb and Ljubljana: Bishop JOVAN, Srpska Biskupija, 10000 Zagreb.

The Press

PRINCIPAL DAILIES

Osijek

Glas Slavonije (Voice of Slavonia): 31000 Osijek, Hrvatske Republike 20; tel. (31) 223200; fax (31) 223203; e-mail glas@glas-slavonije.tel.hr; internet www.glas-slavonije.hr; morning; independent; Editor SANJA MARKETIĆ; circ. 25,000.

Pula

Glas Istre (Voice of Istria): 52100 Pula, Riva 10; tel. (52) 212969; fax (52) 211434; morning; Dir ŽELJKO ŽMAK; circ. 20,000.

Rijeka

Novi List (New Paper): 51000 Rijeka, Zvonimirova 20A, POB 130; tel. (51) 32122; fax (51) 213654; internet www.novilist.hr; morning; Editor VELJKO VICEVIĆ; circ. 60,000.

La Voce del Popolo: 51000 Rijeka, Zvonimirova 20A; tel. (51) 211154; fax (51) 213528; e-mail lavoce@edit.hr; internet www.edit.hr/lavoce; f. 1944; morning; Italian; Editor-in-Chief ERROL SUPERINA; circ. 4,000.

Split

Nedjeljna Dalmacija (Weekly Dalmatia): 21000 Split, Gundulićeva 23; tel. (21) 362821; fax (21) 362526; f. 1972; weekly; politics and culture; Editor DRAŽEN GUDIĆ; circ. 45,000.

Slobodna Dalmacija (Free Dalmatia): 21000 Split, ul. Hrvatske mornarice 4; tel. (21) 513888; fax (21) 551220; internet www.slobodnadalmacija.com; morning; Editor JOSIP JOVIĆ; circ. 102,000.

Zagreb

Sportske novosti (Sports News): 10000 Zagreb, Slavonska Ave. 4; tel. (1) 341920; fax (1) 341950; morning; Editor DARKO TIRONI; circ. 55,000.

Večernji list (Evening Paper): 10000 Zagreb, Slavonska Ave. 4; tel. (1) 6500600; fax (1) 6500679; e-mail vecernji@vecernji.net.tel.hr; internet www.vecernji-list.hr; evening; Editor RUŽICA CIGLER; circ. 200,000.

Vjesnik (Herald): 10000 Zagreb, Slavonska Ave. 4, POB 104; tel. (1) 6161680; fax (1) 6161650; e-mail vjesnik@vjesnik.hr; internet www.vjesnik.com; morning; Editor IGOR MANDIĆ; circ. 8,000.

PERIODICALS

Arena: 10000 Zagreb, Slavonska Ave. 4; tel. (1) 6162795; fax (1) 6161572; e-mail arena@eph.hr; f. 1957; illustrated weekly; Editor MLADEN GEROVAĆ; circ. 135,000.

Feral Tribune: 21000 Split, Šetalište Bačvice 10; tel. (21) 488949; fax (21) 488941; e-mail info@feral.hr; internet www.feral.hr; f. 1984; weekly; satirical; Editor-in-Chief HENI ERCEG.

Glasnik (Speaker): 10000 Zagreb, trg hrvatskih velikana 4; tel. (1) 453000; fax (1) 453752; fortnightly; Editor ZDRAVKO GAVRAN; circ. 9,000.

Globus: 10000 Zagreb, Slavonska Ave. 4; tel. (1) 6162057; fax (1) 6162058; e-mail globus@eph.hr; internet www.globus.com.hr; f. 1990; political weekly; Editor MIRKO GALIĆ; circ. 110,000.

Gloria: 10000 Zagreb, Slavonska Ave. 2; tel. (1) 6161288; fax (1) 6182042; e-mail Fedja_Kalebic@eph.hr; internet www.gloria.com.hr; weekly; Editor DUBRAVKA TOMEKOVIĆ ARALICA; circ. 110,000.

Informator: 10000 Zagreb, Zelinska 3; tel. (1) 6111500; fax (1) 6111446; e-mail informator@informator.hr; internet www.informator.hr; f. 1952; economic and legal matters; Dir Dr FARUK REDŽEPAGIĆ.

Mila: 10000 Zagreb, Slavonska Ave. 4; tel. (1) 6161982; fax (1) 6162021; e-mail mila@eph.hr; weekly; Editor ZOJA PADOVAN; circ. 110,000.

OK: Croatia: 10000 Zagreb, Slavonska Ave. 4; tel. (1) 6162127; fax (1) 6162125; e-mail ok@eph.hr; f. 1989; illustrated monthly; Editor NEVEN KEPESKI; circ. 55,000.

Privredni vjesnik (Economic Herald): 10000 Zagreb, Kačićeva 9A; tel. (1) 4846661; fax (1) 4846656; e-mail redakcija@privredni-vjesnik.hr; internet www.privredni-vjesnik.hr; f. 1953; weekly; economics, finance; Editor-in-Chief FRANJO ŽILIĆ; circ. 10,000.

Republika: 10000 Zagreb, trg bana Josipa Jelačića; tel. (1) 274211; fax (1) 434790; f. 1945; monthly; published by Društvo hrvatskih književnika; literary review; Editor-in-Chief VELIMIR VISKOVIĆ.

Studio: 10000 Zagreb, Slavonska Ave. 4; tel. (1) 6162085; fax (1) 6162031; e-mail studio@eph.hr; f. 1964; illustrated weekly; Editor ROBERT NAPRTA; circ. 45,000.

Vikend (Weekend): 10000 Zagreb, Slavonska Ave. 4; tel. and fax (1) 6162064; 2 a week; Editor JOSIP MUŠNJAK; circ. 50,000.

NEWS AGENCIES

HINA News Agency—Hrvatska izvještajna novinska agencija (Croatian Information and News Agency): 10000 Zagreb, trg Marulidev 16; tel. (1) 4808700; fax (1) 4808820; e-mail newsline@hina.hr; internet www.hina.hr; f. 1990; Man. MIRKO BOLFEK.

IKA—Informativna katolička agencija (Catholic Press Agency): 10000 Zagreb, Kaptol 4; tel. (1) 4814951; fax (1) 4814957; e-mail ika-zg@zg.tel.hr; internet www.ika.hr; f. 1993; Man. Editor ANTON ŠULJIĆ.

Publishers

AGM Publisher: 10000 Zagreb, Mihanovićeva 28; tel. (1) 4856307; fax (1) 4856316; Croatian and foreign literature, arts, economics, science; Gen. Dir BOŽE ČOVIĆ.

Algoritam: 10000 Zagreb, Gajeva 12; tel. (1) 4803333; fax (1) 271541; e-mail mm@algoritam.hr; international bestsellers; Pres. NEVEN ANTIČEVIĆ.

August Cesarec: 10000 Zagreb, prilaz Đure Deželića 57; tel. (1) 171071; fax (1) 573695; Croatian and foreign literature.

Ceres: 10000 Zagreb, Tomašićeva 13; tel. (1) 4558501; fax (1) 4550387; e-mail ceres@zg.tel.hr; internet www.ceres.hr; poetry, fiction, and philosophical and scientific writings; Gen. Dir DRAGUTIN DUMANČIĆ.

Croatian Academy of Sciences and Arts Publishing Dept (Nakladni zavod Hrvatske Akademije Znanosti i Umjetnosti): 10000 Zagreb, trg Zrinski 11; tel. (1) 4819983; fax (1) 4819979; e-mail kabpred@hazu.hr; f. 1861; Pres. Prof. MILAN MOGUŠ.

Erasmus Publishing: 10000 Zagreb, Rakušina 4; tel. and fax (1) 433114; Croatian literature; Gen. Dir SREĆKO LIPOVČAN.

Europa Press: 10000 Zagreb, Slavonska ave. 4; tel. (1) 6190011; fax (1) 6190033; Dir MARJAN JURLEKA.

Hena Com: 10000 Zagreb, Horvaćanska 65; tel. and fax (1) 3750206; e-mail hena-com@hena-com.hr; internet www.hena-com.hr; children's books; Gen. Man. UZEIR HUSKOVIĆ.

Izvori: 10000 Zagreb, Trnjanska 64; tel. and fax (1) 6112576; e-mail info@izvori.com; internet www.izvori.com; scientific journalism, literature, classics, popular fiction, comic books.

Kršćanska Sadašnjost: 10001 Zagreb, trg Marulićev 14, POB 434; tel. (1) 4828219; fax (1) 4828227; e-mail ks@zg.tel.hr; internet www .ks.hr; theological publications.

M. Krleža Lexicographic Institute (Leksikografski zavod 'Miroslav Krleža'): 10000 Zagreb, Frankopanska 26; tel. (1) 4800333; fax (1) 4800399; f. 1951; encyclopedias, bibliographies and dictionaries; Pres. TOMISLAV LADAN.

Masmedia: 10000 Zagreb, ul. baruna Trenka 13; tel. (1) 4577400; fax (1) 4577769; e-mail masmedia@zg.tel.hr; business and professional literature; Gen. Dir STJEPAN ANDRAŠIĆ.

Matica Hrvatska (Croatian Matrix): 10000 Zagreb, trg Strossmayerov 2; tel. (1) 4819310; fax (1) 4819319; e-mail matica@matica .hr; internet www.matica.hr; arts and science, fiction, popular science, politics, economics, sociology, history; Chair. Prof. IGOR ZIDIĆ.

Mladost: 10000 Zagreb, Ilica 30; tel. (1) 453222; fax (1) 434878; f. 1947; fiction, science, art, children's books; Gen. Dir BRANKO VUKOVIĆ.

Mosta: 10000 Zagreb, Majevička 12A; tel. (1) 325196; fax (1) 327898; popular fiction; Gen. Dir NLADIMIR VUĆUR.

Mozaik Knjiga: 10000 Zagreb, Sauska 66; tel. (1) 6178910; fax (1) 6178911; e-mail zdranko.kafol@mozaik-knjiga.hr; internet www .mozaik-knjiga.hr; educational books; Gen. Dir ZDRANKO KAFOL.

Naprijed-Ljevak: 10000 Zagreb, Palmotićeva 30/1; tel. (1) 4804000; fax (1) e-mail naklada-ljevak@zg.htnet.hr; internet www.naklada-ljevak.hr; f. 1957; philosophy, psychology, religion, sociology, medicine, dictionaries, children's books, art, politics, economics, tourist guides; Exec. Dir IVANA LJEVAK.

Školska Knjiga (Schoolbooks): 10001 Zagreb, Masarykova 28, POB 1039; tel. (1) 4830511; fax (1) 4830510; e-mail skolska@ skolskaknjiga.hr; internet www.skolskaknjiga.hr; education, textbooks, art; Dir Dr DRAGOMIR MADERIĆ.

Školske Novine: 10000 Zagreb, Andrije Hebranga 40; tel. (1) 4855720; fax (1) 4855712; education, religion, poetry, textbooks; Gen. Man. IVAN RODIĆ.

Tehnička Knjiga: 10000 Zagreb, Jurišićeva 10; tel. (1) 278172; fax (1) 423611; f. 1947; technical literature, popular science, reference books; Gen. Man. ZVONIMIR VISTRIČKA.

Verbum: 21000 Split, Trumbićeva obala 12; tel. (21) 340260; fax (21) 340270; e-mail naklada@verbum.hr; internet www.verbum.hr; f. 1992; religion, philosophy and humanism; Gen. Man. MIRO RADALJ.

Znanje (Knowledge): 10000 Zagreb, Mandićeva 2; tel. (1) 3689534; fax (1) 3689531; e-mail znanje@zg.tel.hr; f. 1946; popular science, agriculture, fiction, poetry, essays; Pres. ŽARKO ŠEPETAVIĆ.

PUBLISHERS' ASSOCIATION

Croatian Publishers' and Booksellers' Asscn (Poslovna Zajednica Izdavača i Knjižara Hrvatske): 10000 Zagreb, Klaićeva 7; fax (1) 171624.

Broadcasting and Communications

TELECOMMUNICATIONS

Hrvatski Telekom—Hrvatske telekommunikacije (Croatian Telecom—HT): 10000 Zagreb, Savska cesta 32; tel. (1) 4911000; fax (1) 4911011; e-mail info@ht.hr; internet www.t.ht.hr; f. 1999; 51% owned by Deutsche Telekom (Germany); Pres. IVICA MUDRINIĆ.

T-Mobile Hrvatska (T-Mobile Croatia): 10000 Zagreb, ul. grada Vukovara 23; tel. (1) 4982000; fax (1) 4982011; e-mail web@t-mobile .hr; internet www.t-mobile.hr; subsidiary of Hravtski Telekom; provides mobile cellular telecommunications services.

VIPnet: 10000 Zagreb, trg Iblerov 10; tel. (1) 4691091; e-mail office@ vipnet.hr; internet www.vipnet.hr; 100% owned by Mobilkom Austria; f. 1998; provides mobile cellular telecommunications services.

BROADCASTING

Radio

Croatian Radio: 10000 Zagreb, HRT House, Dezmanova 6; tel. (1) 4807199; fax (1) 4807190; e-mail medjunrodni_hr@hrt.hr; internet www.hrt.hr; f. 1926; 3 radio stations; 8 regional stations (Sljeme, Osijek, Pula, Rijeka, Split, Zadar, Dubrovnik and Knin); broadcasts in Serbo-Croat, English and Spanish; Dir-Gen. MIRKO GALIĆ.

Otvoreni Radio: 10010 Zagreb, Cebini 28; tel. (1) 6623700; fax (1) 6623800; e-mail otvoreni@otvoreni.hr; internet www.otvoreni.hr; broadcasts popular music and entertainment programmes nationwide; Dirs ROBERT MILIČEVIĆ, DANIEL BERDAIS.

Radio 101: Zagreb; internet www.radio101.hr; independent radio station; Editor-in-Chief ZRINKA VRABEC-MOJZES.

Radio Baranja: 31300 Beli Manastir, trg Slobode 32/3; e-mail radio-baranja@zg.tel.hr; internet www.radio-baranja.hr; f. 1992; independent; Dir ZLATAR MARŠIĆ.

Television

Croatian Television (HRT): 10000 Zagreb, Prisavlje 3; tel. (1) 6342634; fax (1) 6343712; e-mail program@hrt.hr; internet www.hrt .hr; f. 1956; 2 channels; Dir-Gen. MIRKO GALIĆ; Dir MARIJA NEMČIĆ.

Finance

(cap. = capital; res = reserves; dep. = deposits; m. = million; amounts in kuna; brs = branches)

BANKING

At mid-2004 a total of 40 banking institutions were operating in Croatia, of which 18 were in majority foreign ownership. Total bank assets at this time amounted to 212,098m. kuna.

Central Bank

Croatian National Bank (Hrvatska Narodna Banka): 10000 Zagreb, trg hrvatskih velikana 3; tel. (1) 4564555; fax (1) 4550726; e-mail webmaster@hnb.hr; internet www.hnb.hr; in 1991 assumed the responsibilities of a central bank empowered as the republic's bank of issue; cap. 2,500.0m., res 2,407.0m., dep. 34,286.3m. (Dec. 2003); Gov. ŽELJKO ROHATINSKI.

Selected Banks

Croatia Banka: 10000 Zagreb, Kvaternikov trg 9; tel. (1) 2391111; fax (1) 2332470; e-mail intl.division@croatiabanka.hr; internet www .croatiabanka.hr; f. 1989; cap. 204.6m., res 73.8m., dep. 1,035.0m. (Dec. 2003); Chair. NIKO ŠEREMET; 23 brs.

Croatian Bank for Reconstruction and Development (Hrvatska Banka za Obnovu i Razvoj—HBOR): 10000 Zagreb, Strossmayerov trg 9; tel. (1) 4591666; fax (1) 4591790; e-mail mjuric@hbor.hr; internet www.hbor.hr; f. 1995; cap. 3,418.7m., res 513.8m., dep. 1,529.5m. (Dec. 2003); Pres. IVAN ŠUKER.

Dresdner Bank: 10000 Zagreb, Gajeva 1; tel. (1) 4866777; fax (1) 4866779; e-mail contact.croatia@dresdner-bank.com; internet www .dresdner-bank.hr; f. 1997; cap. 100.0m., res 5.0m., dep. 710.6m. (Dec. 2002); Pres. Dr HANS-JOACHIM GERSMANN.

Erste & Steiermärkische Bank: 51000 Rijeka, Jadranski trg 3A; tel. (62) 371000; fax (62) 372000; e-mail erstebank@erstebank.hr; internet www.erstebank.hr; f. 2000 by merger of Bjelovarska Banka, Cakoveka Banka and Trgovačka Banka; cap. 1,324.2m., res 51.3m., dep. 12,736.7m. (Dec. 2003); Chair. REINHARD ORTNER.

Hrvatska Poštanska Banka (Croatian Post Bank): 10000 Zagreb, Jurišićeva 4; tel. (1) 4804400; fax (1) 4810773; internet www.hpb.hr; f. 1991; cap. 584.8m., res 79.0m., dep. 4,360.0m. (Dec. 2003); Chair. JOSIP SLADE.

HVB Splitska Banka: 21000 Split, Boškovića 16; tel. (21) 312560; fax (21) 312586; e-mail info@splitskabanka.hr; internet www .splitskabanka.hr; f. 1966; cap. 455.3m., res 639.4m., dep. 12,333.8m. (Dec. 2003); Pres. ANTON KNETT.

Hypo Alpe-Adria-Bank: 10000 Zagreb, Koturaška 47; tel. (1) 6103666; fax (1) 6103555; e-mail bank.croatia@hypo-alpe-adria.com; internet www.hypo.hr; f. 1996; cap. 566.6m., res 129.3m., dep. 11,486.3m. (Dec. 2003); Chair. MAG KARL-HEINZ TRUSKALLER.

Istarska Kreditna Banka Umag (Istria Credit Bank Umag): 52470 Umag, Ernesta Miloša 1; tel. (52) 702300; fax (52) 741275; e-mail marketing@ikb.hr; internet www.ikb.hr; f. 1956; commercial and joint-stock bank; controlled by Dalmatinska Banka; cap. 64.9m., res 48.7m., dep. 1,293.5m. (Dec. 2003); Chair. MIRO DODIĆ; 16 brs.

Karlovačka Banka: 47000 Karlovac, Ivana Gorana Kovačića 1; tel. (47) 611540; fax (47) 614206; e-mail karlovacka.banka@hinet.hr; internet www.kaba.hr; f. 1955; cap. 68.1m., res 9.1m., dep. 979.7m. (2003); Pres. SANDA CVITEŠIĆ.

Kreditna Banka Zagreb (Credit Bank Zagreb): 10000 Zagreb, ul. grada Vukovara 74; tel. (1) 6167333; fax (1) 6116466; e-mail kbz-uprava@kbz.hr; internet www.kbz.hr; f. 1994; cap. 132.0m., res 19.9m., dep. 576.7m. (Dec. 2003); Pres. RUDO MIKULIĆ.

Međimurska Banka Čakovec (Međimurje Bank Čakovec): 40000 Čakovec, Valenta Morandinija 37; tel. (40) 370676; fax (40) 370505;

e-mail info@mb.hr; internet www.mb.hr; f. 1954; cap. 127.9m., res 31.0m., dep. 1,621.9m. (Dec. 2003); Pres. NENAD JEDUD.

Nova Banka: 10000 Zagreb, Divka Budaka 1D; tel. (1) 2352810; fax (1) 2352805; e-mail info@novabanka.hr; internet www.novabanka .hr; f. 1957 as Komunalna Banka Zadar; merged with Dubrovačka Banka Dubrovnik in 2004; cap. 455.3m., res 224.6m., dep. 4,322.4m. (Dec. 2003); Pres. ROBERT HANS VON GRIETHUYSEN.

Privredna Banka Zagreb: 10000 Zagreb, Račkoga 6, POB 1032; tel. (1) 4723344; fax (1) 4723131; e-mail pbz@pbz.hr; internet www .pbz.hr; f. 1966; commercial bank; cap. 1,666m., res 1,369m., dep. 36,742m. (Dec. 2003); Chief Exec. BOŽO PRKA; 28 brs.

Raiffeisenbank Austria: 10000 Zagreb, ul. Petrinjska 59, POB 651; tel. (1) 4566466; fax (1) 4811624; e-mail rba@rba.tel.hr; internet www.rba.hr; cap. 423.5m., res 422.2m., dep. 16,699.3m. (Dec. 2003); Chair. ZDENKO ADROVIĆ.

Slavonska Banka Osijek (Slavonian Bank): 31000 Osijek, Kapucinska 29, POB 108; tel. (31) 231231; fax (31) 201039; e-mail slbo@ slbo.hr; internet www.slbo.hr; f. 1989; cap. 356.5m., res 96.3m., dep. 3,275.6m. (Dec. 2003); Pres. IVAN MIHALJEVIĆ; 9 brs.

Štedbanka: 10000 Zagreb, Slavonska ave. 3; tel. (1) 6306666; fax (1) 6187015; e-mail stedbanka@zg.stedbanka.hr; internet www .stedbanka.hr; f. 1994; cap. 225.0m., res 2.7m., dep. 494.2m. (Dec. 2002); Pres. ŽELJKO UDOVIČIĆ.

Volksbank: 10000 Zagreb, Varšavska 9; tel. (1) 4801300; fax (1) 4801365; e-mail info@volksbank.tel.hr; internet www.volksbank.hr; f. 1997; cap. 140.2m., res 32.4m., dep. 1,211.4m. (Dec. 2003); Chair. TOMASZ TARABA.

Bankers' Organization

Croatian Banking Assn (Hrvatska udruga banaka): 10000 Zagreb, Centar Kaptol, Nova Ves 17; tel. (1) 4860080; fax (1) 4860081; e-mail info@hub.hr; internet www.hub.hr; Man. Dir Dr ZORAN BOHACEK.

STOCK EXCHANGE

Zagreb Stock Exchange (Zagrebačka Burza): 10000 Zagreb, Ksaver 208; tel. (1) 428455; fax (1) 420293; e-mail zeljko.kardum@ zse.hr; internet www.zse.hr; f. 1990; Gen. Man. MARINKO PAPUGA.

INSURANCE

Croatia Osiguranje: 10000 Zagreb, trg bana J. Jelačića 13; tel. (1) 4560111; fax (1) 4810516; e-mail informacije@zagreb.crosig.hr; internet www.crosig.hr; f. 1884; privatized 2002; Pres. HRVOJE VOJKOVIĆ.

Merkur Osiguranje: 10000 Zagreb, ul. grada Vukovara 237; tel. (1) 6308333; fax (1) 6157130; internet www.merkur.hr.

Trade and Industry

GOVERNMENT AGENCIES

Croatian Privatization Fund (Hrvatski fond za privatizaciju): 10000 Zagreb, Ivana Lučića 6; tel. (1) 4569111; fax (1) 4596294; e-mail hfp@hfp.hr; internet www.hfp.hr; f. 1994; Pres. DAMIR OSTOVIĆ.

Export and Investment-Promotion Agency (Agencija za promicanje izvoza i ulaganja): 10000 Zagreb, ul. grada Vukovara 78; tel. (1) 6109860; fax (1) 6109868; e-mail igor.maricic@mingosp.hr; Head of Agency IGOR MARIČIĆ.

CHAMBERS OF COMMERCE

Croatian Chamber of Economy (Hrvatska Gospodarska Komora): 10000 Zagreb, trg Rooseveltov 2; tel. (1) 4561555; fax (1) 4828380; e-mail hgk@alf.hr; internet www.hgk.hr; Pres. NADAN VIDOŠEVIĆ.

Croatian Chamber of Economy—Zagreb Chamber: 10000 Zagreb, Draškovićeva 45, POB 45; tel. (1) 4606777; fax (1) 4606813; e-mail hgkzg@hgk.hr; internet www.zg.hgk.hr; f. 1852; Pres. Dr ZLATAN FRÖHLICH.

Croatian Chamber of Trades and Crafts (Hrvatska obrtnička komora): 10000 Zagreb, Ilica 49/2; tel. (1) 4806666; fax (1) 4846610; e-mail hrvatska.obrtnicka.komora@zg.htnet.hr; internet www.hok .hr; Pres. STJEPAN ŠAFRAN.

EMPLOYERS' ASSOCIATION

Croatian Employers Association (Hrvatska udruga poslodavaca—HUP): 10000 Zagreb, Pavla Hatza 12; tel. (1) 4897555; fax (1)

4897556; e-mail hup@hup.hr; internet www.hup.hr; Gen. Dir ŽELJKO IVANČEVIĆ.

UTILITIES

Regulatory Authority

Croatian Energy Regulatory Council (Vijeće za regulaciju energetskih djelatnosti): 10000 Zagreb, Savska 163; tel. (1) 6326260; fax (1) 6326261; e-mail vred@vred.hr; internet www.vred.hr; Pres. Dr MIĆO KLEPO.

Electricity

HEP—Hrvatska Elektroprivreda (Croatian Electricity): 10000 Zagreb, Vukovara 37; tel. (1) 6322111; fax (1) 6170430; e-mail ivan .mravak@hep.hr; internet www.hep.hr; f. 1990; production and distribution of electricity; Dir IVAN MRAVAK.

Gas

Plinacro: 10000 Zagreb, Savska cesta 88A; tel. (1) 6301777; fax (1) 6301787; e-mail plinacro@plinacro.hr; internet www.plinacro.hr; f. 2001; distribution of natural gas; Chair. MARINA MATULOVIĆ DROPULIĆ.

Water

Hrvatske Vode (Croatian Water): 10000 Zagreb, Vukovara 220; tel. (1) 6307333; fax (1) 6155910; e-mail voda@voda.hr; internet www .voda.hr; f. 1995; state water-management organization; Dir DAVORIN ANDROŠIĆ.

TRADE UNIONS

Confederation of Independent Trade Unions of Croatia (Konfederacija nezavisnih sindikata Hrvatske—KNSH): 10000 Zagreb; f. 1990; 40,000 mems; Pres. DAVOR JURIĆ.

Union of Autonomous Trade Unions of Croatia (Savez samosalnih sindikata hrvatske—SSSH): 10000 Zagreb, trg kralja Petra Krešimira 2; tel. (1) 4655013; fax (1) 4655040; e-mail international-uatuc@sssh.hr; internet www.sssh.hr; f. 1990; 26 br. unions with 500,000 mems; Pres. DAVOR JURIĆ.

Workers' Trade Union Assn of Croatia (Udruga radničkih sindikata Hrvatske): 10000 Zagreb, Ilića Kralja Držislava 4/1; tel. (1) 4612896; fax (1) 4612896; e-mail ursh@inet.hr; internet www.ursh .hr; Pres. BORIS KUNST.

Transport

RAILWAYS

In 2001 there were an estimated 2,726 km of railway lines in Croatia, and 36% of the rail network was electrified in 1995. In mid-1996 the railway links between Eastern Slavonia, in Croatia and Serbia were reopened. In May 2000 the Government announced plans for the modernization of the track linking the port of Rijeka with Budapest, Hungary.

Croatian Railways (Hrvatske Željeznice): 10000 Zagreb, Mihanovićeva 12; tel. (1) 4577111; fax (1) 4577730; e-mail hrvatske .zeljeznice@hznet.hr; internet www.hznet.hr; f. 1990; state-owned; public railway transport, construction, modernization and maintenance of railway vehicles; Pres. Dr TOMISLAV JOSIP MLINARIĆ.

ROADS

The Road Fund is responsible for the planning, construction, maintenance and rehabilitation of all interurban roads in Croatia. In 2002 there were an estimated 28,344 km of roads in Croatia, of which 455 km were motorways. A 75-km motorway linking Dragonje, near the Slovenian border, with Pula in southern Istria was completed in the late 1990s. In June 2000 Croatia and Bosnia and Herzegovina signed a statement on the construction of the Ploče (Dalmatia)–Budapest transport corridor, to link Croatia with Hungary, by way of Bosnia and Herzegovina. The construction of this 'C5' corridor was intended to end the isolation of Croatia's southern areas and ensure the optimal use of Ploče's port capacity. More than 130 km of new and rehabilitated highway, connecting the northern borders of the country with the south, were opened in mid-2003. Further sections, including 338 km of road connecting Zagreb with Split, were scheduled for completion by mid-2005. The construction of a 146.5-km highway linking Zagreb with Rijeka, which was financed by the European Bank for Reconstruction and Development, was completed in mid-2004.

SHIPPING

Atlantska Plovidba: 20000 Dubrovnik, od sv. Mihajla 1; tel. (20) 352333; fax (20) 356148; internet www.atlant.hr; f. 1974; Dir ANTE JERKOVIĆ.

Croatia Line: 51000 Rijeka, Riva 18, POB 379; tel. (51) 205111; fax (51) 335811; e-mail erc.hr@croatialine.com; f. 1986; cargo and passenger services; chartering and tramping service; Gen. Man. DARIO VUKIĆ.

Jadrolinija Adriatic Shipping Line: 51000 Rijeka, Riva 16; tel. (51) 666111; fax (51) 213116; e-mail jadrolinija@jadrolinija.hr; internet www.jadrolinija.hr; f. 1872; regular passenger and car-ferry services between Croatian and Italian ports, and along the Adriatic coast of Dalmatia; Pres. SLAVKO LONČAR.

Jadroplov: 21000 Split, Obala kneza Branimira 16; tel. (21) 302666; fax (21) 342198; e-mail jadroplov@jadroplov.com ; internet www.jadroplov.com; f. 1984; fleet of 17 vessels and 1,500 containers engaged in linear and tramping service; Gen. Man. NIKŠA GIOVANELLI.

Slobodna Plovidba: 22000 Šibenik, Drage 2; tel. (22) 23755; fax (22) 27860; f. 1976; transport of goods by sea; tourism services; Dir VITOMIR JURAGA.

Tankerska Plovidba: 23000 Zadar, Božidara Petranovića 4; tel. (23) 202202; fax (23) 202375; internet www.tankerska.hr; f. 1976; Dir STANKO BANIĆ.

CIVIL AVIATION

There are 10 international airports in Croatia.

Croatia Airlines: 10000 Zagreb, Savska cesta 41; tel. (1) 6160066; fax (1) 6176845; e-mail pr@ctn.tel.hr; internet www.croatiaairlines.com; f. 1989 as Zagreb Airlines; name changed 1990; operates domestic and international services; Pres. IVAN MIŠETIĆ.

Tourism

The attractive Adriatic coast and the country's 1,185 islands made Croatia a very popular tourist destination before the 1990s. However, the conflict of the early 1990s greatly reduced tourist activity in the country. The industry showed signs of recovery after 1992, with foreign tourist arrivals reaching some 4.1m. in 1998. By 2003 foreign tourist arrivals had further recovered to 7.4m., and revenue from tourism had increased to US $6,376m.

Croatian Tourist Board (Hrvatska turistička zajednica): 10000 Zagreb, Ilberov trg 10/4; tel. (1) 4699333; fax (1) 4557827; e-mail info@htz.hr; internet www.croatia.hr; Pres. BOŽIDAR KALMETA.

CUBA

Introductory Survey

Location, Climate, Language, Religion, Flag, Capital

The Republic of Cuba is an archipelago of two main islands, Cuba and the Isla de la Juventud (Isle of Youth), formerly the Isla de Pinos (Isle of Pines), and about 1,600 keys and islets. It lies in the Caribbean Sea, 145 km (90 miles) south of Florida, USA. Other nearby countries are the Bahamas, Mexico, Jamaica and Haiti. The climate is tropical, with the annual rainy season from May to October. The average annual temperature is 25°C (77°F) and hurricanes are frequent. The language spoken is Spanish. Most of the inhabitants are Christians, of whom the great majority are Roman Catholics. The national flag (proportions 1 by 2) has five equal horizontal stripes, of blue, white, blue, white and blue, with a red triangle, enclosing a five-pointed white star, at the hoist. The capital is Havana (La Habana).

Recent History

Cuba was ruled by Spain from the 16th century until 1898, when the island was ceded to the USA following Spain's defeat in the Spanish–American War. Cuba became an independent republic on 20 May 1902, but the USA retained its naval bases on the island and, until 1934, reserved the right to intervene in Cuba's internal affairs. In 1933 an army sergeant, Fulgencio Batista Zaldivar, came to power at the head of a military revolt. Batista ruled the country, directly or indirectly, until 1944, when he retired after serving a four-year term as elected President.

In March 1952, however, Gen. Batista (as he had become) seized power again, deposing President Carlos Prío Socarrás in a bloodless coup. Batista's new regime soon proved to be unpopular and became harshly repressive. In July 1953 a radical opposition group, led by Dr Fidel Castro Ruz, attacked the Moncada army barracks in Santiago de Cuba. Castro was captured, with many of his supporters, but was later released. He went into exile and formed a revolutionary movement which was committed to Batista's overthrow. In December 1956 Castro landed in Cuba with a small group of followers, most of whom were captured or killed. However, 12 survivors, including Castro and the Argentine-born Dr Ernesto ('Che') Guevara, escaped into the hills of the Sierra Maestra, where they formed the nucleus of the guerrilla forces which, after a prolonged struggle, forced Batista to flee from Cuba on 1 January 1959. The Batista regime collapsed, and Castro's forces occupied Havana.

The assumption of power by the victorious rebels was initially met with great popular acclaim. The 1940 Constitution was suspended in January 1959 and replaced by a new 'Fundamental Law'. Executive and legislative power was vested in the Council of Ministers, with Fidel Castro as Prime Minister and his brother Raúl as his deputy. Guevara reportedly ranked third in importance. The new regime ruled by decree but promised to hold elections within 18 months. When it was firmly established, the Castro Government adopted a radical economic programme, including agrarian reform and the nationalization of industrial and commercial enterprises. These drastic reforms, combined with the regime's authoritarian nature, provoked opposition from some sectors of the population, including former supporters of Castro, and many Cubans went into exile.

All US business interests in Cuba were expropriated, without compensation, in October 1960, and the USA severed diplomatic relations in January 1961. A US-sponsored force of anti-Castro Cuban émigrés landed in April 1961 at the Bahía de Cochinos (Bay of Pigs), in southern Cuba, but the invasion was thwarted by Castro's troops. Later in the year, all pro-Government groups were merged to form the Organizaciones Revolucionarias Integradas (ORI). In December 1961 Fidel Castro publicly announced that Cuba had become a communist state, and he proclaimed a 'Marxist-Leninist' programme for the country's future development. In January 1962 Cuba was excluded from active participation in the Organization of American States (OAS). The USA instituted a full economic and political blockade of Cuba. Hostility to the USA was accompanied by increasingly close relations between Cuba and the USSR. In October 1962 the USA revealed the presence of Soviet missiles in Cuba but, after the imposition of a US naval blockade, the weapons were with-

drawn. The missile bases, capable of launching nuclear weapons against the USA, were dismantled, thus resolving one of the most serious international crises since the Second World War. In 1964 the OAS imposed diplomatic and commercial sanctions against Cuba.

The ORI was replaced in 1962 by a new Partido Unido de la Revolución Socialista Cubana (PURSC), which was established, under Fidel Castro's leadership, as the country's sole legal party. Guevara resigned his military and government posts in April 1965, subsequently leaving Cuba to pursue revolutionary activities abroad. In October 1965 the PURSC was renamed the Partido Comunista de Cuba (PCC). Although ostracized by most other Latin American countries, the PCC Government maintained and consolidated its internal authority, with little effective opposition. Supported by considerable aid from the USSR, the regime made significant progress in social and economic development, including improvements in education and public health. At the same time, Cuba continued to give active support to left-wing revolutionary movements in Latin America and in many other parts of the world. Guevara was killed in Bolivia, following an unsuccessful guerrilla uprising under his leadership, in October 1967.

In July 1972 Cuba's links with the Eastern bloc were strengthened when the country became a full member of the Council for Mutual Economic Assistance (CMEA—dissolved in 1991), a Moscow-based organization linking the USSR and other communist states. As a result of its admission to the CMEA, Cuba received preferential trade terms and more technical advisers from the USSR and Eastern European countries.

In June 1974 the country's first elections since the revolution were held for municipal offices in Matanzas province. Cuba's first 'socialist' Constitution was submitted to the First Congress of the PCC, held in December 1975, and came into force in February 1976, after being approved by popular referendum. As envisaged by the new Constitution, elections for 169 municipal assemblies were held in October 1976. These assemblies later elected delegates to provincial assemblies and deputies to the Asamblea Nacional del Poder Popular (National Assembly of People's Power), inaugurated in December 1976 as 'the supreme organ of state'. The National Assembly chose the members of a new Council of State, with Fidel Castro as President. The Second Congress of the PCC was held in December 1980, when Fidel and Raúl Castro were re-elected First and Second Secretaries, respectively. In December 1981 Fidel Castro was re-elected by the Assembly as President of the Council of State, and Raúl Castro re-elected as First Vice-President.

Cuba continued to be excluded from the activities of the OAS, although the Organization voted in favour of allowing members to normalize their relations with Cuba in 1975. Relations with the USA deteriorated because of Cuban involvement in Angola in 1976 and in Ethiopia in 1977. The relaxation of restrictions on emigration in April 1980 resulted in the departure of more than 125,000 Cubans for Florida, USA. Antagonism continued as Cuba's military and political presence abroad increased, threatening US spheres of influence.

In 1981 Cuba expressed interest in discussing foreign policy with the USA, and declared that the shipment of arms to guerrilla groups in Central America had ceased. High-level talks between the two countries took place in November 1981 but US hostility increased. Economic sanctions were strengthened, the major air link was closed, and tourism and investment by US nationals was prohibited in April 1982. Cuba's support of Argentina during the 1982 crisis concerning the Falkland Islands improved relations with the rest of Latin America, and the country's legitimacy was finally acknowledged when it was elected to the chair of the UN General Assembly Committee on Decolonization in September 1982, while continuing to play a leading role in the Non-aligned Movement (despite its firm alliance with the Soviet bloc).

An increase in US military activity in Honduras and the Caribbean region led President Castro to declare a 'state of national alert' in August 1983. The US invasion of Grenada in October, and the ensuing short-lived confrontation between US forces and Cuban personnel on the island, severely damaged hopes that the two countries might reach an agreement over the problems in Central America, and left Cuba isolated in the Caribbean, following the weakening of its diplomatic and military ties with Suriname in November.

In July 1984 official negotiations were begun with the USA on the issues of immigration and repatriation. In December agreement was reached on the resumption of Cuban immigration to the USA and the repatriation of 2,746 Cuban 'undesirables', who had accompanied other Cuban refugees to the USA in 1980. The repatriation of Cuban 'undesirables' began in February 1985, but, following the inauguration of Radio Martí (a radio station sponsored by the 'Voice of America' radio network, which began to broadcast Western-style news and other programmes to Cuba from Florida, USA), the Cuban Government suspended its immigration accord with the USA. Subsequently, all visits to Cuba by US residents of Cuban origin were banned. The US Government responded by restricting visits to the USA by PCC members and Cuban government officials. In September 1986, as a result of mediation by the Roman Catholic Church, more than 100 political prisoners and their families were permitted to leave Cuba for the USA.

Relations with the USA continued to deteriorate in 1987 when the US Government launched a campaign to direct public attention to violations of human rights in Cuba. In March a resolution to condemn Cuba's record on human rights was narrowly defeated at a meeting of the UN Commission on Human Rights. The Cuban Government subsequently allowed 348 current and former political prisoners to return to the USA. The restoration, in October 1987, of the 1984 immigration accord provoked rioting by Cuban exiles detained in US prisons. The accord allowed for the repatriation of 2,500 Cuban 'undesirables' in exchange for a US agreement to allow 23,000 Cubans to enter the USA annually. In 1988 the Government released some 250 political prisoners, and in the following January President Castro pledged to release the remaining 225 political prisoners acknowledged by the regime. In 1989 human rights activists formed a co-ordinating body and increased their operations. The Government responded in August by imprisoning leading activists for up to two years for having published allegedly false information. In September 1991 eight Cuban dissident organizations united to form a single democratic opposition group, the Concertación Democrática Cubana—CDC (Cuban Democratic Convergence), to campaign for political pluralism and economic reform.

In June 1989 President Castro was confronted by Cuba's most serious political crisis since the 1959 Revolution. It was discovered that a number of senior military personnel were not only involved in smuggling operations in Angola but were also aiding Colombian drugs-traffickers from the infamous Medellín cartel, by enabling them to use Cuban airstrips as refuelling points (en route from Colombia to the USA) in return for bribes. Following court-martial proceedings, Gen. Arnaldo Ochoa Sánchez, who had led the military campaign in Angola, was found guilty of high treason and was executed. Three other officers were also executed. A further purge led to the imposition of harsh sentences on 14 senior officials, including the head of civil aviation and the Ministers of the Interior and of Transport, who had been found guilty of corruption. President Castro insisted that the bureaucracy in Cuba needed to undergo a process of 'purification', but not reform. However, the scandal had clearly undermined the regime's credibility at the international, as well as the domestic, level.

In Angola, where Cuban troops numbered an estimated 50,000, the peace process gathered momentum in 1988. In May a large Cuban offensive almost succeeded in expelling South African forces from Angola and lent new impetus to the peace negotiations. A cease-fire was implemented, and at discussions held in New York, USA, in October, agreement was reached on a phased withdrawal of Cuban troops over a period of 24–30 months. The withdrawal was completed in May 1991.

In April 1989 President Gorbachev of the USSR undertook the first official visit to Cuba by a Soviet leader since 1974. The two Heads of State discussed Central American issues and ways in which Cuba's dependence on Soviet aid might be reduced, and the talks culminated in the signing of a treaty of friendship and economic co-operation. Although, ostensibly, relations remained good, tensions had arisen, owing to Castro's resistance to Soviet-style reforms. Gorbachev made it clear that, in future, general financial aid would be replaced by assistance for specific projects, thus giving the USSR greater power to influence policy

decisions in Cuba. In July President Castro strongly attacked the ideas of *perestroika* and *glasnost*, which he blamed for the 'crisis in socialism'. He pledged to eradicate all market forms of economic activity, despite the fact that Cuba's failure to integrate into the new supply-and-demand system of many Eastern European factories had led to delays in imports and acute shortages.

In October 1990 President Castro announced plans to reduce the PCC's bureaucracy by as much as 50%, including the reassignment of thousands of employees to more productive sectors. In November rationing was extended to all products. Cubans were told to prepare for the possibility of a 'special wartime period' by the Minister of the Revolutionary Armed Forces, Gen. Raúl Castro, who warned of a possible US military attack if the currently intensified US economic blockade should fail. In spite of the gravity of Cuba's political and economic situation, President Castro was defiant in his rejection of recommendations that, as a condition for the removal of the blockade, Cuba should adopt a market economy and political pluralism.

In September 1991 the USSR announced that it intended to withdraw the majority of its military personnel (some 3,000 troops and advisers) from Cuba. The decision, which was condemned by Cuba as presenting a major threat to its national security, came as the result of US demands that the USSR reduce its aid to Cuba as a precondition to the provision of US aid to the USSR. Cuba's subsequent demands that the USA withdraw its troops from the naval base at Guantánamo were rejected. The Soviet withdrawal was completed in June 1993.

In 1992 President Castro's efforts to quiet internal dissent and bolster the country against the perceived US threat revealed an increasingly militant attitude, as several death sentences were imposed on Cuban dissidents. In the same year the USA began to implement a series of measures tightening its economic blockade against Cuba. In April US President Bush issued an executive order barring ships that were engaged in trade with Cuba from entering US ports. In October the Cuban Democracy Act, also known as the 'Torricelli Law', was adopted, making it illegal for foreign subsidiaries of US companies to trade with Cuba. These measures encountered widespread international criticism, including protests by the European Community (EC, later European Union—EU) that they violated international law. In November the UN General Assembly adopted a non-binding resolution demanding the cessation of the trade embargo.

In July 1992 the National Assembly approved a number of amendments to the Constitution. Under the reforms, President Castro was granted the authority to declare a state of emergency and, in such an event, to assume full control of the armed forces at the head of a National Defence Council. An electoral reform, which had originally been proposed at the Fourth Congress of the PCC in October 1991, was formally adopted, providing for elections to the National Assembly to be conducted by direct vote. The constitutional revisions also included an updating of the business law, legitimizing foreign investment in approved state enterprises and recognizing foreign ownership of property in joint ventures.

On 24 February 1993 elections to the National Assembly and the 14 provincial assemblies were, for the first time, conducted by direct secret ballot. Only candidates nominated by the PCC were permitted to contest the elections. According to official results, there was an abstention rate of only 1.2%, and 87.3% of the electorate cast a 'united' ballot (a vote for the entire list of candidates). Only 7.2% of votes cast were blank or spoilt. All 589 deputies of the National Assembly were elected with more than the requisite 50% of the votes. In the following month Fidel Castro and Gen. Raúl Castro were unanimously re-elected by the National Assembly to their respective posts as President and First Vice-President of the Council of State.

In July 1993, with the economic crisis deepening and international reserves exhausted, Castro announced that a 30-year ban on Cuban citizens possessing foreign currency was to be lifted. The measure, which represented a significant departure from the country's centrally-planned socialist economy, was intended to attract the large sums of foreign currency (principally US dollars) in circulation on the black market into the economy, and to encourage remittances from Cuban exiles. Restrictions on Cuban exiles travelling to Cuba were also to be relaxed. Concerns that the measures were socially divisive, affording privileges to those receiving currency from relatives abroad, were acknowledged by the Government. In September, in a further move away from traditional economic policy, the Government authorized limited individual private enterprise in a range of 117 occupations. In the same month plans were announced for the introduction of agricultural reforms allowing for the decentralization and reorganization of state farms into 'Units of Basic Co-operative Production', to be managed and financed by the workers themselves.

In April 1994, in a reorganization of the Government, four new ministries were created and a number of state committees and institutes dissolved, reflecting a significant change in the economic management of the country. In early August, however, increasing discontent at deteriorating economic conditions resulted in rioting in the capital, precipitated by a confrontation between police and a large number of Cubans attempting to commandeer a ferry in order to take the vessel to the USA. In a public speech broadcast on the following day Castro indicated that, if the USA failed to halt the promotion of such illegal departures, Cuba would suspend its travel restrictions. The resultant surge of Cubans attempting to reach the USA by sea reached crisis proportions, and the US President, Bill Clinton, was forced to adopt measures to deter them. The automatic refugee status conferred on Cubans under the 1966 Cuban Adjustment Act was revoked, and Cubans were warned that those intercepted by the US Coast Guard would be transported to Guantánamo naval base and would not be allowed entry into the USA. Further measures imposed included the halting of cash remittances from Cuban exiles in the USA. However, these measures failed to stem the flow of Cubans seeking refuge in the USA, and in September 1994 the US and Cuban Governments held bilateral talks to resolve the crisis. As a result of the talks, the USA promised to grant visas allowing for the migration of a minimum of 20,000 Cubans annually (despite the 1984 immigration accord, a total of only 11,222 US entry visas had been granted to Cubans between December 1984 and July 1994). An additional 4,000–6,000 Cubans already on waiting lists for US visas would be granted them. In return, Cuba reintroduced border restrictions. More than 30,000 Cubans were estimated to have left the country during the period when travel restrictions were suspended, although the majority of these were detained by the US authorities and transported to camps in Guantánamo and the Panama Canal Zone. Talks continued with the USA throughout 1995. In May a further immigration accord was signed, bringing to an official end the automatic refugee status that had been revoked in August 1994. The accord also stated that all Cuban refugees intercepted at sea by the USA would thenceforth be repatriated. In addition, the USA agreed to grant visas to the majority of the approximately 20,000 Cuban refugees detained at Guantánamo, although the figure was to be deducted, over a period of four years, from the annual quota of visas granted under the September 1994 accord.

In early 1995 legislative proposals seeking to tighten the US embargo against Cuba were introduced to the US Congress by the Chairman of the Senate Foreign Relations Committee, Jesse Helms, and the Chairman of the House of Representatives Sub-Committee on the Western Hemisphere, Dan Burton. The proposals, referred to as the Helms-Burton bill, sought to impose sanctions on countries trading with or investing in Cuba, and threatened to reduce US aid to countries providing Cuba with financial assistance, notably Russia. The bill provoked international criticism, and a formal complaint was registered by the EU, which claimed that the legislation would be in violation of international law and the rules of the World Trade Organization (WTO, see p. 357). The legislation was approved by the House of Representatives in September but was considerably modified by the Senate.

In May 1995, following the first visit to Cuba by an international human rights mission since the 1959 Revolution, the Government authorized the release of six political prisoners. The mission had been co-ordinated by the human rights organization France-Libertés. According to Cuban human rights groups, however, more than 1,000 political prisoners remained in detention in the country.

In February 1996 Cuban MiG fighters shot down two US light aircraft piloted by members of the Cuban-American exile group Brothers to the Rescue, killing all four crew members. The action was vigorously condemned by the USA, which rejected Cuban claims that the aircraft had violated Cuban airspace. Further US sanctions were immediately implemented, including the indefinite suspension of charter flights to Cuba. In June the International Civil Aviation Organization confirmed US claims that the aircraft had been shot down over international waters. As a result of the incident, President Clinton

reversed his previous opposition to certain controversial elements of the Helms-Burton bill, and on 12 March he signed the legislation, officially entitled the Cuban Liberty and Solidarity Act, thus making it law. However, Clinton was empowered to issue executive orders, at six-monthly intervals, postponing the implementation of a section of the law, Title III, which allowed US citizens, including naturalized Cuban exiles, to prosecute through US courts any foreign corporation or investor with business dealings involving property that had been expropriated during the Castro regime. Title IV of the Act, which made executives of companies investing in Cuba (and their dependants) liable to exclusion from the USA, was implemented selectively. Approval of the Helms-Burton bill prompted strenuous criticism from Cuba's major trading partners. The EU announced its intention to challenge the extra-territorial provisions of the Act through the WTO, while Mexico and Canada sought to dispute the law under the provisions of the North American Free Trade Agreement. International opposition to the Helms-Burton bill increased following the issue, in May, by the US Department of State of letters to companies in Canada, Mexico and Italy, warning of possible prosecution. In June Canada initiated a series of legal measures to protect Canadian companies against the Act. Similar legislation was subsequently adopted by Mexico and the EU. In July Clinton imposed a six-month moratorium on Title III of the Act, which had been due to come into force in August. In November, in its annual vote on the US embargo, the UN General Assembly voted for its repeal with the largest majority to date. Notably, the United Kingdom, Germany and the Netherlands, which had all previously abstained on this question, voted in favour of a repeal. In the same month the WTO adopted a resolution to establish a disputes panel to rule on the legality of the Helms-Burton-sponsored Act.

In December 1996 agreement was reached by the members of the EU to make the extent of economic co-operation with Cuba contingent upon progress towards democracy in the country. In that month the Cuban Government adopted legislation to counteract the application of the Cuban Liberty and Solidarity (Helms-Burton) Act in an attempt to protect foreign investment in the country. The Government also expressed its readiness to negotiate with the USA regarding the compensation of US citizens with property claims in Cuba. In early February 1997 the EU requested that the WTO postpone the appointment of a disputes panel in order that further discussions be conducted with the USA in an effort to reach a negotiated settlement. However, these efforts were not successful, and on 20 February a disputes panel was appointed and given six months to reach a decision on whether the extra-territorial provisions of the Act contravened WTO rules on multilateral trade, or whether, as the USA maintained, the Act was a matter of national security and therefore not within the jurisdiction of the WTO. In March, in a further attempt to avoid confrontation, the EU and the USA resumed discussions concerning the Act, and in the following month agreement was reached in principle on a resolution of the dispute. Under the terms of the agreement, the USA was to continue deferring the implementation of Title III indefinitely, while the EU was to withdraw its petition to the WTO until October. In the interim, negotiations were to continue towards a multilateral accord defining investment principles, with particular emphasis on expropriated foreign assets. In a move widely interpreted as a concession to mounting domestic pressure to end restrictions on exports of food and medicines from the USA to Cuba, in March 1998 it was agreed that shipments of both commodities, via non-governmental organizations, were to be permitted. In addition, President Clinton announced an end to the ban on direct flights between the USA and Cuba (imposed in 1996) and on the transfer of cash remittances from the USA to Cuba. Henceforth, Cuban residents in the USA were to be permitted to send up to US $300 quarterly to relatives in Cuba. The process whereby applications for licences to sell medicines to Cuba were considered was also to be examined, with a view to accelerating procedures. However, the Cuban Government was extremely critical of a further outline agreement on extra-territorial legislation drafted by the US Government and the EU in May, which it considered to be highly concessionary on the part of the EU, at the expense of Cuban interests. Under the terms of the agreement, in return for a commitment from President Clinton to seek congressional consensus for a relaxation of the application of the Cuban Liberty and Solidarity Act, EU member states would participate in the compilation of a register of former US assets in Cuba (considered to have been illegally expropriated) and would observe firm US recommendations regarding their exclusivity. President Clinton repeatedly exercised his right to postpone the implementation of Title III. His successor, George W. Bush, continued to suspend the implementation of Title III at six-monthly intervals.

On 11 January 1998 elections to the National Assembly (enlarged from 589 to 601 seats) and to the 14 provincial assemblies were conducted. All 601 candidates who contested the legislative ballot were elected. Of the 7.8m. registered voters, 98.35% participated in the elections. Only 5% of votes cast were blank or spoilt. At the first meeting of the newly constituted National Assembly on 24 February, the new Council of State was announced, confirming Fidel and Raúl Castro, and the five incumbent Vice-Presidents, in their positions for a further five-year term. Of the remaining 23 ordinary members of the Council, 14 were new appointments.

In January 1998 Cuba received its first ever papal visit. During the visit Pope John Paul II was critical of the 'unjust and ethically unacceptable' US embargo against Cuba, and urged the reintegration of Cuba into the international community. In response, in late January, the Guatemalan Government announced that diplomatic relations were to be restored with Cuba, prompting a rebuke from the US Department of State. During February, moreover, it was announced that almost 300 Cuban prisoners were to be released, many as a result of a petition for clemency made by the papal delegation. In April, at a meeting of the UN Commission on Human Rights, the annual US-sponsored vote of censure against the Cuban Government for alleged abuses of human rights was defeated for the first time since 1991; the motion was supported by 16 countries and opposed by 19, while 18 abstained. Support for the annual UN General Assembly resolution urging an end to the US embargo against Cuba increased once again in October, receiving the support of 157 member nations. Twelve members abstained from the vote, while only two (the USA and Israel) voted against the resolution.

In mid-March 1999 the Provincial Court in Havana sentenced four prominent political dissidents to prison terms of between three and a half and five years' duration. The decision followed the introduction, in February, of uncompromising new legislation to combat increasing criminal activity and to curb subversion and dissent. The incarceration of the dissidents, together with the imposition of death sentences in March on two Salvadorean nationals (see below), drew criticism of Cuba's respect for human rights from the international community in general, and resulted in a significant deterioration in relations with Canada (Cuba's largest trading partner) and Spain in particular.

In March 1999 two Salvadorean nationals were convicted (and subsequently sentenced to death) on terrorism charges relating to a spate of bomb attacks in mid-1997, allegedly organized by the anti-Castro Cuban-American National Foundation (CANF, based in Florida, USA). In December 1999 the US Department of Justice acquitted five Cuban exiles, including a member of the CANF executive, accused of plotting to assassinate President Castro in Venezuela in 1997. Three Guatemalan nationals, arrested in March 1998, stood trial in November 2001 on charges of terrorist action, allegedly organized and financed by the CANF.

Despite a further easing of restrictions relating to the US embargo in August 1999, and well-publicized visits to Cuba by several prominent US politicians, attempts by the US Government to appease the increasingly influential anti-embargo lobby were largely frustrated by an exchange of legal challenges. In March a US judge ruled that payments owed to the Cuban national telecommunications company, which were currently being withheld by a number of US telecommunications companies by judicial request, could be used to help honour a compensation award of US $187m. against the Cuban authorities, made in the USA in 1997 to benefit relatives of four pilots shot down by the Cuban air force in 1996 (see above). The US Government had made known its objection to the ruling, claiming that the decision amounted to interference in foreign policy. In response, in early June a new lawsuit was brought to the Cuban courts by a number of government-sponsored organizations, which were seeking some $181,100m. in compensation for more than 3,000 deaths and more than 2,000 injuries allegedly inflicted on Cuban nationals since the 1959 Revolution by the 'aggressive' policies of the US Government. (In early 2001 the US Administration authorized the transfer of these payments, to compensate relatives of the four pilots.) In September 1999 a unanimous

declaration of the National Assembly condemned the US trade embargo as an act of 'genocide'. In October 2000 legislation was passed by the US Congress easing some aspects of the trade embargo, including the export of food and medicine. However, the Cuban Government declared that the conditions attached to the lifting of the restrictions were such that the legislation would tighten, rather than ease, the US embargo. In response, Cuba imposed a 10% tax on all telephone calls between the two countries and, in December, suspended telephone links with the USA, following the refusal of US telecommunications companies to pay the levy.

In the first six months of 2000 Cuban–US relations were dominated by the case of Elián González. In November 1999 Elián, a five-year-old Cuban boy, was rescued from the Atlantic Ocean off the coast of Florida, the sole survivor of a shipwrecked attempt to reach the USA, in which his mother had died. A dispute resulted between the boy's Miami-based relatives, who attempted to have him granted US citizenship, and his father in Cuba, who wanted his son repatriated. The US Department of Justice granted custody to Elián's father, but his Miami relatives refused to relinquish charge of the boy. In April armed Federal Bureau of Investigation (FBI) agents seized Elián from his Miami relatives and he eventually returned to Cuba in June. In Cuba the case prompted public demonstrations in protest at the USA's 'abduction' of the child.

In November 2000, during a visit to Panama to attend the Ibero-American Summit, an alleged plot to assassinate President Castro was uncovered. Anti-Castro activist Luis Posada Carriles was arrested, along with three others. Posada Carriles had escaped from custody in Venezuela, where he was indicted for the bombing of a Cuban aeroplane near Barbados in 1976, and was also implicated in a series of hotel bombings in Havana in 1997. The Cuban Government's request for Posada Carriles' extradition was subsequently refused. In April 2004 Posada Carriles was sentenced in Panama to an eight-year prison term. However, in August of that year, having been pardoned by the Panamanian President, Posada Carriles fled the country. In June 2001 President Castro collapsed from heat exhaustion during a public speech. Despite suffering no ill effects, he subsequently announced that his brother Raúl would have the authority and experience to assume the presidency, were it necessary.

In November 2001 'Hurricane Michelle' struck west-central Cuba. Five people were killed and thousands were evacuated from the coastal areas. The country suffered serious damage to its infrastructure and to the agricultural sector. The USA lifted temporarily the trade embargo, allowing Cuba to purchase food and medicines necessary for the reconstruction and aid effort.

In December 2001 the USA announced that it was to hold Afghan war detainees at its naval base at Guantánamo Bay. The first prisoners arrived at the new maximum-security prison in January 2002. In the same month Gen. Raúl Castro, the Minister of the Revolutionary Armed Forces, announced Cuba's support for the use of the base for this purpose. At the beginning of 2005 those being held at the gaol continued to await trial, while the conditions in which the prisoners were being held provoked criticism from several human rights organizations.

In May 2002 former US President Jimmy Carter visited Cuba; he was the most prominent US political figure to have travelled to the country since 1928. In an unprecedented televised address Carter criticized the human rights record of the Cuban Government but stated that he believed that the USA should initiate moves towards the lifting of the trade embargo. However, in a speech given on 20 May, the centenary of Cuban independence from Spain, US President George W. Bush affirmed that the embargo and travel restrictions would remain in place until Cuba installed a government that would respect political and civil rights. Cuban–US relations were further strained when, in the same month, the US Administration added Cuba to the list of states it claimed formed an 'axis of evil' that supported international terrorism. The US Under-Secretary of State for Arms Control and International Security, John Bolton, claimed that Cuba was engaged in limited biological warfare research and development and that it had provided biotechnology that could be used for civilian and military purposes by so-called 'rogue states'. In November Cuba finally acceded to the Treaty on the Non-Proliferation of Nuclear Weapons—NPT (see p. 93).

Also in May 2002 an 11,000-signature petition—part of a dissident initiative known as the 'Varela Project'—was submitted to the National Assembly; it called for a referendum on basic civil and political liberties. In the following month the

Government responded by initiating a drive to mobilize popular support for an amendment to the Constitution, declaring the socialist system to be 'untouchable' and ratifying that 'economic, diplomatic and political relations with any other state can never be negotiated in the face of aggression, threat or pressure from a foreign power'. The National Assembly subsequently voted unanimously to adopt a constitutional amendment declaring socialism in Cuba to be permanent and 'irrevocable'. In July, in an indication that the US legislature was moving towards a softening of its stance on Cuba, the US House of Representatives passed legislation easing both travel and trade restrictions to the country; the legislation was also approved by the Senate, although the Bush Administration stated its intention to veto any legislative provisions which might ease the embargo.

In November 2002 Vice-President Carlos Lage Dávila accused the US Government of encouraging 'terrorism against Cuba'. His remarks followed an incident in which eight Cuban citizens seized a government-owned aeroplane and flew it to Florida. Following an initial period of detention imposed by the US Immigration and Naturalization Service, the migrants were released. The Cuban Government then demanded that both the Cubans and the aircraft be returned to Cuba; the US Government, however, permitted the refugees to remain in the USA. In the same month a court in Florida ruled that the aeroplane could be sold as part of a US $27m. judgment against the Cuban Government that had been won by the ex-wife of a Cuban spy.

On 19 January 2003 elections took place to the National Assembly (enlarged from 601 to 609 seats) and the 14 provincial legislatures. All the candidates elected were unopposed and voter turn-out was 97.6%. Only 3.9% of ballot papers were either spoilt or left blank. Fidel Castro was subsequently re-elected as President for a sixth consecutive term.

In March 2003 relations with the USA worsened when James Cason, Principal Officer of the US Interests Section in Havana, was accused by the Cuban Government of attempting to incite a counter-revolution, having met with opponents of Fidel Castro during his short time in the country and, allegedly, disseminated anti-Government propaganda. Castro subsequently ordered that all those dissidents who had met with Cason be arrested, and imposed strict travel restrictions on all US diplomatic personnel resident in Cuba. The arrests provoked condemnation from international organizations and human rights groups. In April the trials of the dissidents began, prompting a further deterioration in US–Cuban relations. Seventy-five of those tried were found guilty of charges of subversion and treason and sentenced to prison terms of up to 28 years. Meanwhile, bilateral tensions were heightened further by government accusations that the USA was encouraging a spate of aeroplane hijackings by Cubans seeking asylum in the USA, owing to its lenient treatment of Cuban emigrants. In the same month, as the Government continued to adopt a more repressive stance towards the opposition, three men convicted of hijacking a ferry in an attempt to reach the USA were convicted of terrorism and executed following brief trials. In July, after the EU suspended Cuba's application to join its Cotonou Agreement (see below) in protest at the country's recent human rights record, President Castro announced that his Government would reject any aid offered by the EU and would terminate all political contact with the organization. Meanwhile, the EU stated that it would officially welcome Cuban dissidents into its embassies, while restricting contact with the Government.

In October 2003 US President Bush stated his intention to intensify the ban on US citizens travelling to Cuba. Although there were indications that the US Congress was softening its stance on the issue, in November it agreed to maintain the ban in return for additional federal funding. In December a US governmental commission, the Commission for Assistance to a Free Cuba, headed by US Secretary of State Colin Powell, held its inaugural meeting. The Commission's remit was to plan for the end of the Castro regime and the advent of democracy in Cuba. President Bush also reiterated his commitment to strengthening the US embargo on trade and tourism with the island.

In 2004 the Government continued to operate in an increasingly repressive manner. In January the Ministry of Computer Science and Communications announced new regulations prohibiting Cuban citizens from gaining unauthorized access to the internet through the state telephone system. As this was the only form of internet access available to most Cubans, the regulations further enforced state control over access to information on the island. In February the USA intensified its ban on

travel to Cuba when President Bush signed an order authorizing the US authorities to inspect any vessel sailing in US waters that did not have official permission to travel to Cuba. In the same month Col Manuel Marrero Cruz succeeded Ibrahim Ferradaz García as Minister of Tourism, following García's dismissal owing to the discovery of irregularities in the accounts of the state-owned tourism concern, Cubanacán. In April the UN Commission on Human Rights, at its annual session held in Geneva, Switzerland, passed a motion condemning human rights violations in Cuba and mandating the Commission to send a mission to the country in order that it could report on the situation. In response, the Cuban Government declared that it would not permit any human rights monitors to enter the country. Meanwhile, 10 dissidents were put on trial, in the first prosecution of anti-Government activists since 75 dissidents were imprisoned in the previous year. All were convicted of the charges against them and sentenced to custodial terms.

In May 2004 the USA announced that it would intensify its measures against Cuba, stating that it would place further restrictions on remittances into the country and that US military aircraft would be used to prevent Cuban radio stations from blocking pro-democracy broadcasts. In addition, Cuban Americans resident in the USA were only to be permitted to visit their relatives in Cuba once every three years. In response, President Castro orchestrated a protest march in Havana and restricted the quantity of goods available for purchase in US dollars within Cuba. In September it was reported that, contrary to statements made by US Under-Secretary of State for Arms Control and International Security John Bolton in 2002, Cuba actually possessed only a limited capability to manufacture biological weapons and did not appear to be doing so.

In October 2004 the Government announced that circulation of the US dollar in Cuba would not be permitted from the following month; a significant commission would also be imposed from then on when changing US dollars into local currency. In the same month the Minister of Basic Industry, Marcos Javier Portal León, was dismissed, largely owing to his failure to prevent a severe shortfall in the country's power supply following the breakdown of its largest power plant, in Matanzas province. He was replaced by Yadirá García Vera. In November the UN General Assembly passed its 13th resolution condemning the US embargo against Cuba; the USA, Israel, the Marshall Islands and Palau voted against the resolution, while Micronesia abstained. In December the journalist Jorge Olivera became the 14th dissident to be freed of the 75 that had been imprisoned in the previous year. Meanwhile, the largest military exercises to have been conducted on the island since 1986 took place. The so-called 'Bastión 2004' exercises, which were held over the course of one week, involved both Cuban citizens and the military.

Since 1985 Cuba has succeeded in establishing strong ties throughout Latin America and the Caribbean. Full diplomatic relations were restored with Colombia (suspended in 1981) in 1993, with Chile in 1995 and with Guatemala in 1998. Diplomatic relations were also re-established with the Dominican Republic in 1998 and with Honduras in 2002. In August 1998, during President Castro's first visit to the Dominican Republic, he attended a summit meeting of the Cariforum grouping of CARICOM (see p. 172) states and the Dominican Republic, at which the Statement of Santo Domingo was endorsed, envisaging full Cuban participation in any successor arrangement to Lomé IV. (Recent statements by the US and British Governments had indicated that pressure might be applied to EU member states to attach preconditions relating to human rights and democratic processes to Cuban participation in such an arrangement.) Cuba was afforded observer status to the Lomé Convention (which expired in February 2000 and was replaced by the Cotonou Agreement (see p. 262) in June) in 1998 and in 2001 the country restated its intention to request membership of the Africa, Caribbean and Pacific (ACP)-EU Joint Assembly. In June of that year Cuba signed an agreement with CARICOM designed to promote trade and co-operation. In November 1998 Cuba became the 12th full member of the Latin American Integration Association (LAIA, see p. 289), having enjoyed observer status since 1986. In December 2002 Cuba hosted a CARICOM summit meeting for the first time. In March 2003 the EU opened a legation office in Havana, and initially declared its support for Cuba's application to join the Agreement. However, following the Government's imprisonment of a large number of dissidents in the following month, the EU subsequently announced that it had downgraded relations with Cuba and indefinitely postponed the country's application to join the Cotonou Agreement. In January 2005, however, following the release of some of the jailed dissidents, the EU announced it would resume diplomatic relations with Cuba, for a six-month period.

Cuba traditionally enjoyed good relations with Mexico (which was the only Latin American country not to suspend diplomatic relations with the Castro regime in 1961). Although relations deteriorated during the presidency of Ernesto Zedillo Ponce de León (1994–2000), his successor, Vicente Fox Quesada, pledged to strengthen bilateral relations and, in February 2002, made an official visit to Cuba. However, in April bilateral relations were strained again when Mexico lent its support to a resolution sponsored by Uruguay condemning Cuba's human rights record at a meeting of the UN Human Rights Commission. Following the approval of the resolution (which also received support from the Governments of Argentina, Chile, Costa Rica, Guatemala and Peru) President Castro denounced the President of Uruguay, Jorge Batlle, as 'an abject Judas'; Uruguay subsequently severed diplomatic relations with Cuba (Batlle's successor, Tabaré Vázquez Rosas, pledged to restore relations once he took office in March 2005). In September the Mexican ambassador to Cuba, Ricardo Pascoe, resigned, citing his frustration at the deterioration of relations between the two countries. However, in November relations were improved somewhat when Mexico voted in favour of the annual UN resolution condemning the US trade embargo of Cuba. In 2003 efforts further to improve bilateral relations continued; in November Cuban Minister of Foreign Relations Felipe Ramón Pérez Roque met with his Mexican counterpart at the Ibero-American Summit meeting in Bolivia. However, in May 2004 Mexico recalled its ambassador and expelled the Cuban ambassador to Mexico after President Castro criticized Mexican policy towards Cuba. Peru also withdrew its ambassador from Cuba at the same time. In July, following talks between the ministers of foreign affairs of the two countries, it was announced that Mexico would return its ambassador to Cuba and permit the Cuban ambassador to return. Meanwhile, diplomatic relations with Argentina, which had been severed in 2001 following Argentina's support of a UN vote condemning Cuba's human rights record, were restored in October 2003. In August 2004 Cuba broke off diplomatic relations with Panama following that country's pardon of four Cuban exiles, including Luis Posada Carriles (see above), suspected of involvement in an attempt to assassinate President Castro in 2000. However, in November the two countries agreed to restore diplomatic links, following the denunciation of the pardon by Panama's new President, Martín Torrijos.

Government

Under the 1976 Constitution (the first since the 1959 Revolution, amended in July 1992), the supreme organ of state, and the sole legislative authority, is the Asamblea Nacional del Poder Popular (National Assembly of People's Power), with 609 deputies elected for five years by direct vote. The National Assembly elects 31 of its members to form the Council of State, the Assembly's permanent organ. The Council of State is the highest representative of the State, and its President is both Head of State and Head of Government. Executive and administrative authority is vested in the Council of Ministers, appointed by the National Assembly on the proposal of the Head of State. Municipal, regional and provincial assemblies have also been established. The Partido Comunista de Cuba (PCC), the only authorized political party, is 'the leading force of society and the State'. The PCC's highest authority is the Party Congress, which elects a Central Committee (150 members in 2005) to supervise the Party's work. To direct its policy, the Central Committee elects a Politburo (24 members in 2005).

Defence

Conscription for military service is for a two-year period, and conscripts also work on the land. In August 2003, according to Western estimates, the armed forces totalled 46,000 (including ready reserves serving 45 days per year to complete active and reserve units): the army numbered 35,000, the navy 3,000 and the air force 8,000. Army reserves were estimated to total 39,000. Paramilitary forces include 20,000 State Security troops, 6,500 border guards, a civil defence force of 50,000 and a Youth Labour Army of 70,000. A local militia organization (Milicias de Tropas Territoriales—MTT), comprising an estimated 1m. men and women, was formed in 1980. Expenditure on defence and internal security for 2002 was estimated at US $1,100m. Despite Cuban hostility, the USA maintains a base at Guantánamo Bay, with 590 naval, 165 marine and one air force personnel in 2003.

Economic Affairs

In 2003 Cuba's gross domestic product (GDP), measured at constant 1997 prices, was an estimated 28,393m. pesos. During 1991–2000, it was estimated, GDP declined, in real terms, at an average annual rate of 1.4%. GDP decreased by 6.2% in 2002, but increased by 2.4% in 2003. During 1990–2003 the population increased by an average of 0.5% per year.

Agriculture (including hunting, forestry and fishing) contributed 6.9% of GDP, measured at constant 1997 prices, in 2003 and employed 26.5% of the labour force in 2002. The principal cash crop has traditionally been sugar cane, with sugar and its derivatives accounting for 27.4% of export earnings in 2000. The sugar crop in 1998 was the worst in 50 years, reaching only some 3.3m. metric tons. It recovered slightly by 2000, amounting to 3.6m. tons, but fell short of expectations in 2001, to an estimated 3.2m. tons, owing to a drought and the destruction caused by 'Hurricane Michelle'. In 2002 sugar production reached only 3.5m. tons and it was estimated that production declined further in 2003, to only 2.3m. tons. In 2004 sugar production was estimated at 2.75m. tons, below the predicted level for that year. In 2002, as a result of the damage caused by the hurricane, together with the ongoing poor harvests, the Government announced that it would have to import sugar to meet domestic demand. In June the Government announced that, following recent production decreases, it intended to rationalize the sugar industry through a programme of restructuring—this would involve the closure of several sugar refineries and the loss of approximately 100,000 jobs in the sector. Approximately 60% of plantation area would be reallocated to other crops in an attempt to produce enough sugar to satisfy domestic needs, while sugar would only be exported while revenues continued to exceed production costs. In that year 70 of Cuba's sugar mills were closed down as the industry became increasingly unprofitable; 71 mills remained active. In 2000 Cuba produced some 30,600 tons of tobacco and in 2002 it produced 327.2m. cigars. Other important crops are rice, citrus fruits (819,500 tons in 2003), plantains and bananas. Fishing exports in 2000 reached 87.8m. pesos. Cuba's principal seafood export markets were Japan, France, Spain, Italy and Canada. In real terms, the GDP of the agricultural sector declined at an average rate of 0.5% per year during 1996–2002. Agricultural GDP decreased by 7.2% in 2002, but increased by 2.6% in 2003.

Industry (including mining, manufacturing, construction and power) contributed 26.4% of GDP, measured at constant 1997 prices, in 2003. The sector employed 20.4% of the labour force in 2002. Industrial GDP decreased, in real terms, at an average rate of 5.7% per year in 1996–2002. The sector's GDP declined by 5.3% in 2002 and by 0.9% in 2003.

Mining contributed 1.7% of GDP, measured at constant 1997 prices, in 2003 and employed 0.7% of the labour force in the previous year. Nickel is the principal mineral export. In 2003 nickel and cobalt output reached 71,700 metric tons, a decrease of some 4.5% compared with the previous year. In November 2004 Cuba signed several accords with the People's Republic of China, under which it agreed to provide 4,000 tons of nickel derivative to China annually from 2005. Cuba's state nickel company, Cubaniquel, was also to participate in a joint venture with the Chinese company Minmetal to construct the Las Cariocas nickel plant in Moa, which, once complete, would have an annual production capacity of 22,500 tons. Cuba also produces considerable amounts of chromium and copper, some iron and manganese, and there are workable deposits of gold and silver. The GDP of the mining sector increased by an average of 3.3% per year in 1996–2002; sectoral GDP increased by 6.6% in 2002 and by 3.1% in 2003.

Manufacturing contributed 16.7% of GDP, measured at constant 1997 prices, in 2003. The sector employed 14.0% of the labour force in 2002. The principal branches of manufacturing were food products, beverages and tobacco, machinery and industrial chemicals. In 2000 50% of the state citrus marketing company was purchased by a French-Spanish company, Altadis. During 1996–2002 manufacturing GDP increased, in real terms, at an average annual rate of 1.2%. The sector's GDP declined by 6.0% in 2002 and by 2.4% in 2003. The biomedical industry continued to expand in the 1990s, and in 1999 a joint venture was agreed with the pharmaceutical manufacturer SmithKline Beecham (later GlaxoSmithKline) to market the Cuban meningitis vaccine.

Energy is derived principally from petroleum and natural gas. In 2003 Cuba produced approximately 3.7m. metric tons of crude petroleum and 653.0m. cu m of natural gas. Petroleum production was expected to expand by up to 8% in 2004. Imports of mineral fuels accounted for 24.0% of the total cost of imports in 2000. Formerly, some 13m. tons of petroleum were imported annually from the USSR, with 2m. tons being re-exported, but following the dissolution of that country in 1991 imports were dramatically reduced. In 2003 the country generated its entire electricity requirement from domestically-produced petroleum and natural gas. Cuba expected to be self-sufficient in oil production by 2005. To this end, in 2001 Cuba began talks with Mexico on a possible bilateral agreement on energy efficiency, and in November Venezuela agreed to meet one-third of Cuba's petroleum requirements, on preferential terms, in exchange for medical and sports services. Despite some disruption to petroleum shipments from Venezuela in 2002, owing to domestic unrest in that country (see chapter on Venezuela), in 2003 Venezuela exported an average of 53,000 b/d to Cuba. In 1999 Cuba opened up 112,000 sq km of its waters to foreign exploration. Various foreign companies subsequently signed exploration contracts and in late 2003 the Spanish company Repsol YPF announced plans to install one of the world's largest deep-sea drilling rigs in the area. Drilling commenced in June 2004. In 2000 two oil-processing plants were planned for Santiago de Cuba and Cienfuegos, and two power-generation plants were being built by Sherritt Power of Canada. In February 2001 the Slovakian engineering company, SES Tlmace, won a contract to reconstruct the oil-burning power-station in Santa Cruz. In June the construction of a 25-km petroleum pipeline between Matanzas province and Puerto Escondido was being finalized. When complete, it was to be operated by the state petroleum company.

Services accounted for 66.7% of GDP, measured at constant 1997 prices, in 2003. The sector employed 53.2% of the labour force in that year. Tourism is one of the country's principal sources of foreign exchange, earning an estimated US $1,769m. in 2002, and development of the sector remains a priority of the Government. Following a downturn in tourist arrivals in late 2001 and 2002, attributable largely to the impact of the September 2001 terrorist attacks on the USA, the sector recovered in 2003, when arrivals reached an estimated 1.9m. The country's 21 airports were modernized and expanded through state and foreign investment during the late 1990s. In real terms, the GDP of the service sector increased at an average rate of 4.4% per year during 1996–2002. The GDP of services decreased by 6.5% in 2002, but increased by 3.8% in 2003.

In 1999 Cuba recorded a trade deficit of US $600m., and a deficit of $350m. on the current account of the balance of payments. In 2000 the principal source of imports was Venezuela (18.6%). In 2000 Russia was the principal market for exports, accounting for 19.4% of the total. Other major trading partners were Spain and Canada. The principal imports in 2000 were mineral fuels, machinery and transport equipment. The principal exports in that year were food and live animals, and crude materials (excluding fuels).

In 2003 Cuba recorded an estimated budget deficit of 1,074m. pesos. According to the Central Bank, the country's external debt totalled 10,893.3m. pesos in 2001. Cuba's debt to the former USSR was estimated to be $20,000m. in 2000. In December of that year the Russian Government proposed writing off 70% of this debt and renegotiating the remainder through the 'Paris Club' of Western government creditors. However, the Cuban Government refused to negotiate with the Paris Club and disputed the size of the debt owed to Russia. Bilateral discussions with Russia took place in 2000–01 and included the possible conversion of debt to equity through joint-venture contracts. According to official figures, some 3% of the labour force were unemployed at the end of 2003. Although no index of consumer prices is published, official estimates put inflation at 0.3% in 1999.

Cuba is a member of the Latin American Economic System (see p. 374) and of the Group of Latin American and Caribbean Sugar Exporting Countries (see p. 370).

In the early 1990s Cuba suffered severe economic decline, prompted by the collapse of the USSR and by the consequent termination of the favourable aid and trade arrangements that had supported the Cuban economy. Resultant shortages, particularly of petroleum and basic raw materials, seriously affected production in all sectors and necessitated wide-ranging austerity measures. In 1994, in a significant departure from the country's traditional command economy, a series of adjustment measures was introduced. The measures included the introduction of new taxes and the drastic reduction (by some 40%) of subsidies to loss-making state enterprises. In December 1994 a new 'convertible peso' was introduced to regulate the circulation of foreign currency. A new investment law, approved in September 1995, opened all sectors of the economy, with the exception of defence, health and education, to foreign participation and introduced the possibility of 100% foreign ownership.

In 1996 the USA intensified its sanctions against Cuba with the introduction of the Cuban Liberty and Solidarity (Helms-Burton) Act. Denied access to medium- and long-term loans, Cuba's indebtedness increased substantially as high-interest short-term loans were contracted in order to finance production, most notably in the sugar industry. In 1997 three free-trade zones were opened to attract foreign investment. During 1999 the Central Bank made known its intention henceforth to prefer to conduct international transactions in euros, hoping thus to weaken the stranglehold of the US dollar on the Cuban economy. In October 2001 the Government announced that, thenceforth, only US paper currency would be accepted, owing to the high cost of handling and exporting US coin currency. In July 2003 the Government announced that state-owned companies would be prohibited from using US dollars for transactions made within Cuba; these would have to be made in convertible pesos, as would import and debt payments and purchases from joint-venture companies, although the latter were exempted from the new regulations. In October 2004 the Government announced that, in response to the intensification of the US embargo earlier that year, from November the US dollar would no longer be permitted to circulate in Cuba. A significant commission would be charged on all transactions involving US dollars.

In 1999 the largest investments were in the mining (specifically nickel), tourism and telecommunications sectors. In December a 50% stake in Habanos, the state-owned cigar distributor, was sold for US $500m. In mid-2000 the EU called for a WTO disputes panel to rule on Section 211 of the 1998 US Omnibus Appropriations Act, under which trademarks used in connection with assets confiscated by the Cuban Government could not be registered without permission from the original owner. This followed a 1999 US court ruling against Havana Club International, a joint venture between Pernod Ricard of France and Cuba's Havana Rum and Liquors, concerning the use of the Havana Club rum brand name in the USA (the ruling was upheld by the US Supreme Court in October 2000). In response to the ruling, Cuba announced a new Bacardí brand, initiating a further dispute, this time with the Bacardí company in Bermuda. In January 2002 the WTO ruled that, in part, Section 211 violated the pact on protection of intellectual property and recommended that the USA bring its measures into conformity with the pact. In 2003 the US-Cuba Trademark Protection Act was passed by the US Congress, establishing procedures through which the Cuban Government's trademark registration and renewal process could be monitored, in order to ensure further protection for US trademarks in Cuba. In 2004 Cuba lobbied against legislation pending before the US Congress when it called for the USA to repeal Section 211, rather than merely amending it, as had been proposed.

In October 2000 the US Congress approved legislation allowing US food and medicine sales to Cuba, dependent on certain conditions. Imports of most Cuban goods remained illegal and other sanctions legislation remained operational. In July 2001 further regulations regarding US sales to Cuba were introduced. The Cuban Government responded by refusing to trade with the USA under what it considered 'discriminatory and humiliating terms'. In September 2002, although the trade and travel restrictions remained in operation, the first US food fair since 1959 was held in Havana as the business sector chose to take advantage of the easing of the embargo. According to the Government, by November 2003 Cuban businesses had signed food contracts worth US $510m. with US companies since the end of 2001. In late 2003 a report issued by the UN Economic Commission for Latin America and the Caribbean (ECLAC) identified Cuba's international isolation, bureaucratic inefficiency, shortage of foreign exchange and the ongoing US sanctions against the country as the main factors in the island's economic problems. The report stated that if Cuba was to effect a long-term economic recovery it would have to reduce state control over the economy and lift the restrictions on small businesses, essentially adopting a policy of greater liberalization. In 2004 the Cuban economy continued to stagnate, with

GDP expected to increase by only an estimated 2.4% in that year. It was feared that the ban imposed on circulation of the US dollar in the country from November would have an adverse effect on economic development, which had been further disrupted during the course of the year by an ongoing drought in the eastern half of the island and by the devastating effect of 'Hurricane Charley' in August. In addition, the Government's imposition of further restrictions upon private enterprises operating in Cuba was expected to make Cubans ever more dependent on remittances from relatives abroad.

Education

Education is universal and free at all levels. Education is based on Marxist-Leninist principles and combines study with manual work. Day nurseries are available for all children after their 45th day, and national schools at the pre-primary level are operated by the State for children of five years of age. Primary education, from six to 11 years of age, is compulsory, and secondary education lasts from 12 to 17 years of age, comprising two cycles of three years each. In 1998 primary enrolment included almost 100% of children in the relevant age-group, while secondary enrolment was equivalent to 87% of the population in the appropriate age-group. In 2002/03 there were an estimated 192,000 students in higher education. Workers attending university courses receive a state subsidy to provide for their dependants. Courses at intermediate and higher levels lay an emphasis on technology, agriculture and teacher training. In 2002 budgetary expenditure on education was estimated at 2,790m. pesos (16.4% of total spending).

Public Holidays

2005: 1 January (Liberation Day), 1 May (Labour Day), 25–27 July (Anniversary of the 1953 Revolution), 10 October (Wars of Independence Day), 25 December (Christmas Day).

2006: 1 January (Liberation Day), 1 May (Labour Day), 25–27 July (Anniversary of the 1953 Revolution), 10 October (Wars of Independence Day), 25 December (Christmas Day).

Weights and Measures

The metric system is in force.

Statistical Survey

Sources (unless otherwise stated): Cámara de Comercio de la República de Cuba, Calle 21, No 661/701, esq. Calle A, Apdo 4237, Vedado, Havana; tel. (7) 55-1321; fax (7) 33-3042; e-mail pdcia@camara.com.cu; internet www.camaracuba.cubaweb.cu; Oficina Nacional de Estadísticas, Calle Paseo 60, entre 3 y 5, Vedado, Havana; tel. (7) 30-0005; fax (7) 33-3083; internet www.cubagob.cu/otras_info/estadisticas.htm.

Area and Population

AREA, POPULATION AND DENSITY

Area (sq km)	110,860*
Population (census results)	
6 September 1970	8,569,121
11 September 1981	
Males	4,914,873
Females	4,808,732
Total	9,723,605
Population (official estimates at 31 December)	
2001	11,172,300
2002	11,200,400
2003	11,230,100
Density (per sq km) at mid-2003	101.3

* 42,803 sq miles.

PROVINCES
(31 December 2003)

	Population (estimates)
Camagüey	786,400
Ciego de Avila	415,300
Cienfuegos	398,000
Ciudad de la Habana	2,200,400
Granma	828,100
Guantánamo	510,300
La Habana	719,900
Holguín	1,027,800
Isla de la Juventud	86,600
Matanzas	674,600
Pinar del Rio	730,400
Sancti Spíritus	462,800
Santiago de Cuba	1,042,100
Las Tunas	529,200
Villa Clara	818,200
Total	11,230,100

PRINCIPAL TOWNS
(population in 1999)

La Habana (Havana, the capital) .	2,189,716	Pinar del Rio . .	148,500
Santiago de Cuba .	441,524	Bayamo . . .	143,600
Camagüey . .	306,049	Cienfuegos . . .	137,513
Holguín . . .	259,300	Las Tunas . . .	137,331
Santa Clara . .	210,100	Matanzas	124,754
Guantánamo . .	208,030	Sancti Spíritus* . .	103,591

* 1998 figure.

Source: UN Citydata.

Mid-2003 (UN estimate, incl. suburbs): La Habana (Havana) 2,188,919 (Source: UN, *World Urbanization Prospects: The 2003 Revision*).

BIRTHS, MARRIAGES AND DEATHS*

	Registered live births†		Registered marriages‡		Registered deaths	
	Number	Rate (per 1,000)	Number	Rate (per 1,000)	Number	Rate (per 1,000)
1996 . .	140,276	12.7	65,009	5.9	79,662	7.2
1997 . .	152,681	13.8	60,900	5.5	77,316	7.0
1998 . .	151,080	13.6	64,900	5.8	77,565	7.0
1999 . .	150,785	13.5	57,300	5.1	79,499	7.1
2000 . .	143,528	12.8	57,000	5.1	76,448	6.8
2001 . .	138,700	12.4	54,300	4.8	79,400	7.1
2002 . .	141,200	12.6	56,900	5.1	73,900	6.6
2003 . .	136,800	12.2	54,700	4.9	78,400	7.0

* Data are tabulated by year of registration rather than by year of occurrence.

† Births registered in the National Consumers Register, established on 31 December 1964.

‡ Including consensual unions formalized in response to special legislation.

Expectation of life (WHO estimates, years at birth): 77.1 (males 75.0; females 79.3) in 2002 (Source: WHO, *World Health Report*).

ECONOMICALLY ACTIVE POPULATION
(official estimates, '000 persons aged 15 years and over)

	2000	2001	2002
Agriculture, hunting, forestry and fishing	937.9	974.1	1,064.6
Mining and quarrying	50.5	33.1	28.3
Manufacturing	615.0	604.9	564.1
Electricity, gas and water	53.2	49.6	51.2
Construction	204.5	192.8	176.4
Trade, restaurants and hotels	473.6	470.6	507.9
Transport, storage and communications	194.9	207.1	201.7
Financing, insurance, real estate and business services	55.0	58.9	54.2
Community, social and personal services	1,258.4	1,377.8	1,375.7
Total labour force (incl. others)	3,843.0	3,968.9	4,024.1

Source: ILO.

CIVILIAN EMPLOYMENT IN THE STATE SECTOR
('000 persons)

	1998	1999	2000
Agriculture, hunting, forestry and fishing	733.1	714.4	714.2
Mining and quarrying	47.3	20.8	20.8
Manufacturing	458.9	512.7	512.6
Electricity, gas and water	46.0	51.0	51.0
Construction	178.9	167.1	167.8
Trade, restaurants and hotels	355.2	375.2	375.2
Transport, storage and communications	175.2	157.4	157.4
Financing, insurance, real estate and business services	47.6	54.3	54.3
Community, social and personal services	964.5	952.1	951.8
Total	3,006.7	3,005.0	3,005.1

Health and Welfare

KEY INDICATORS

Total fertility rate (children per woman, 2002)	1.6
Under-5 mortality rate (per 1,000 live births, 2003)	8
HIV/AIDS (% of persons aged 15–49, 2003)	0.10
Physicians (per 1,000 head, 1997)	5.30
Hospital beds (per 1,000 head, 1996)	5.13
Health expenditure (2001): US $ per head (PPP)	229
Health expenditure (2001): % of GDP	7.2
Health expenditure (2001): public (% of total)	86.2
Access to water (% of persons, 2002)	91
Access to sanitation (% of persons, 2002)	98
Human Development Index (2002): ranking	52
Human Development Index (2002): value	0.809

For sources and definitions, see explanatory note on p. vi.

Agriculture

PRINCIPAL CROPS
('000 metric tons)

	2001	2002	2003
Rice (paddy)	601.0	692.0	715.8
Maize	298.9	309.0	360.0
Potatoes	345.4	329.7	304.6
Sweet potatoes	360.3	392.4	503.4
Cassava (Manioc)	512.9	532.0	682.5
Yautia (Cocoyam)	102.2	122.5	125.0*
Sugar cane†	3,210	3,470	2,290
Dry beans	99.1	107.3	127.0
Groundnuts (in shell)*	10	10	10
Coconuts	88.7	108.6	108.6*
Cabbages	138.8	159.3	184.3
Tomatoes	452.7	496.0	643.7
Pumpkins, squash and gourds	351.8	416.6	481.8
Cucumbers and gherkins	248.0	300.2	347.2
Chillies and peppers, green	59.3	61.4	68.0
Dry onions	91.4	91.9	101.7
Garlic	40.3	31.7	36.6
Other vegetables*	1,229.8	1,725.2	1,932.7
Watermelons	66.0	64.5	74.6
Cantaloupes and other melons*	25	24	25
Bananas	318.1	206.9	315.4
Plantains	649.9	523.0	797.2
Oranges	608.2	296.6	492.2
Tangerines, mandarins, clementines and satsumas	28.2	27.7	46.0
Lemons and limes	18.2	16.1	26.7
Grapefruit and pomelos	302.5	137.3	227.8
Mangoes	211.8	207.8	232.9
Pineapples	29.3	36.2	40.5
Papayas	135.1	107.2	120.1
Other fruit*	281.4	322.1	365.9
Coffee (green)†	15.7	14.7	15.0
Fibre crops*	27.5	27.5	27.5
Tobacco (leaves)	31.8	34.5	34.5*

* FAO estimate(s).
† Unofficial figures.

Source: FAO.

LIVESTOCK
('000 head, year ending September)

	2001	2002	2003
Cattle	4,038.4	3,972.3	4,025.4
Horses*	400	400	400
Mules*	23	23	23
Pigs	1,313.2	1,554.5	1,683.6
Sheep†	2,991.1	3,080.3	3,120.7
Goats	291	400†	410†
Poultry	26,168	16,700*	23,210

* FAO estimate(s).
† Unofficial figure(s).

Source: FAO.

LIVESTOCK PRODUCTS
('000 metric tons)

	2001	2002	2003
Beef and veal	75.0	65.8	56.2
Pig meat	75.9	89.8	94.0
Chicken meat	54.8	35.1	33.7
Cows' milk	620.7	589.7	607.5
Cheese*	14.7	14.2	14.2
Butter*	7.1	7.0	7.0
Hen eggs	67.1	78.2	78.5
Honey	6.6	5.6	7.2
Hides and skins*	13.2	12.4	10.4

* FAO estimates.

Source: FAO.

Forestry

ROUNDWOOD REMOVALS
('000 cubic metres, excl. bark)

	2001	2002*	2003*
Sawlogs, veneer logs and logs for sleepers*	400	400	400
Other industrial wood	408	408	408
Fuel wood	888	2,810	2,789
Total	1,696	3,618	3,597

* FAO estimates.
Source: FAO.

SAWNWOOD PRODUCTION
('000 cubic metres, incl. railway sleepers, FAO estimates)

	1999	2000	2001
Coniferous (softwood)	66	101	107
Broadleaved (hardwood)	80	78	83
Total	146	179	190

2002–03: Figures assumed to be unchanged from 2001 (FAO estimates).
Source: FAO.

Fishing

('000 metric tons, live weight)

	2000	2001	2002
Capture	61.1	44.7	33.8
Blue tilapia	2.9	1.9	2.0
Lane snapper	2.1	1.9	1.8
Caribbean spiny lobster	7.5	6.8	8.0
Aquaculture*	31.1	24.1	25.7
Silver carp	17.5	13.0	12.8
Total catch*	92.2	68.8	59.6

* FAO estimates.
Note: Figures exclude sponges (metric tons): 57 in 2000; 51 in 2001; 54 in 2002.
Source: FAO.

Mining

('000 metric tons, unless otherwise indicated)

	2001	2002	2003
Crude petroleum	2,773.4	3,533.4	3,691.0
Natural gas (million cu metres)	594.6	584.7	653.0
Nickel and cobalt (metal content)	76.5	75.1	71.7
Crushed stone ('000 cu metres)*	3,300.0	n.a.	n.a.

* Source: US Geological Survey.

Industry

SELECTED PRODUCTS
('000 metric tons, unless otherwise indicated)

	2001	2002	2003
Crude steel	269.6	264.1	n.a.
Grey cement	1,324.1	1,326.9	1,331.0
Corrugated asbestos-cement tiles	2,023.3	5,954.2	4,400.0
Colour television sets ('000)	79.4	105.0	350.0
Fuel oil	903.1	773.9	1,105.0
Recapped tyres ('000)	140.1	107.8	n.a.
Woven textile fabrics (million sq metres)	46.9	n.a.	n.a.
Cigarettes ('000 million)	11.8	12.6	14.0
Cigars (million)	339.2	327.2	n.a.
Alcoholic beverages (excl. wines, '000 litres)	664.4	714.5	760.0
Beer ('000 hectolitres)	2,197.1	2,331.0	2,409.2
Soft drinks ('000 hectolitres)	2,873.4	3,090.6	n.a.
Electric energy (million kWh)	15,301.3	15,699.8	15,909.2

Finance

CURRENCY AND EXCHANGE RATES
Monetary Units
100 centavos = 1 Cuban peso.

Sterling, Dollar and Euro Equivalents (31 December 2004)
£1 sterling = 1.931 pesos;
US $1 = 1.000 pesos;
€1 = 1.362 pesos;
100 Cuban pesos = £51.78 = $100.00 = €73.42.

Note: The foregoing information relates to official exchange rates. For the purposes of foreign trade, the peso was at par with the US dollar during each of the 10 years 1987–96. A 'convertible peso' was introduced in December 1994. The free market rate of exchange in September 1998 was US $1 = 23 Cuban pesos.

STATE BUDGET
(million pesos)

	2001	2002	2003
Total revenue	15,033.5	16,196.7	17,250.0
Road tax	5,721.6	6,619.8	7,228.0
Social security contributions	1,247.8	1,336.3	1,405.0
Total expenditure	15,771.0	17,193.2	18,324.0
Entrepreneurial activity	2,622.2	3,285.8	3,473.0
Education	2,368.6	2,751.6	3,208.0
Health care	1,796.6	1,923.0	2,030.0
Social security	1,870.3	1,984.8	2,101.0
Management	565.2	611.1	602.9

Source: Ministry of Finance and Prices.

INTERNATIONAL RESERVES
(million pesos at 31 December)

	1987	1988
Gold and other precious metals	17.5	19.5
Cash and deposits in foreign banks (convertible currency)	36.5	78.0
Sub-total	54.0	97.5
Deposits in foreign banks (in transferable roubles)	142.5	137.0
Total	196.5	234.5

NATIONAL ACCOUNTS
Composition of Gross National Product
(million pesos at current prices)

	1998	1999	2000
Compensation of employees	10,328.3	11,146.9	11,965.8
Operating surplus	6,631.8	8,570.3	9,538.2
Consumption of fixed capital			
Gross domestic product (GDP) at factor cost	16,960.1	19,717.2	21,504.0
Indirect taxes *less* subsidies	6,940.7	5,786.4	6,130.7
GDP in purchasers' values	23,900.8	25,503.6	27,634.7
Less Factor income paid abroad (net)	599.2	514.1	693.0
Gross national product	23,301.6	24,989.5	26,941.7

Source: UN Economic Commission for Latin America and the Caribbean, *Statistical Yearbook*.

Expenditure on the Gross Domestic Product
(million pesos at current prices)

	1999	2000	2001
Government final consumption expenditure	5,986.5	6,686.9	7,731.0
Private final consumption expenditure	17,598.5	18,558.1	19,180.1
Increase in stocks	72.4	191.5	136.2
Gross fixed capital formation . .	3,290.8	3,630.2	3,225.8
Total domestic expenditure .	26,948.2	29,066.7	30,273.1
Exports of goods and services . .	4,123.5	4,318.9	4,232.0
Less Imports of goods and services	4,916.0	5,179.6	5,103.3
Statistical discrepancy	−9.0	—	—
GDP in purchasers' values .	26,146.7	28,206.0	29,401.8
GDP at constant 1997 prices .	24,956.4	26,482.1	27,273.7

Source: UN Economic Commission for Latin America and the Caribbean, *Statistical Yearbook*.

Gross Domestic Product by Economic Activity
(million pesos at constant 1997 prices)

	2001	2002	2003
Agriculture, hunting, forestry and fishing	2,021.2	1,875.7	1,923.9
Mining and quarrying	434.9	463.6	478.0
Manufacturing	5,091.2	4,787.8	4,671.8
Electricity, gas and water . . .	629.7	591.9	611.5
Construction	1,721.2	1,618.7	1,636.7
Wholesale and retail trade, restaurants and hotels . . .	8,053.7	7,788.7	8,163.8
Transport, storage and communications	2,951.2	2,716.6	2,712.4
Finance, insurance, real estate and business services	1,961.6	2,101.2	2,186.0
Community, social and personal services	6,289.3	5,403.4	5,625.4
Sub total	29,154.0	27,347.6	28,009.5
Import duties	403.0	338.6	383.6
Total	29,557.0	27,686.2	28,393.1

BALANCE OF PAYMENTS
(million pesos)

	1996	1997	1998
Exports of goods	1,866.2	1,823.1	1,444.4
Imports of goods	−3,656.5	−4,087.6	−4,229.7
Trade balance	−1,790.3	−2,264.5	−2,785.3
Services (net)	1,372.4	1,519.0	2,168.2
Balance on goods and services	−417.9	−745.5	−617.1
Other income (net)	−492.6	−482.9	−599.2
Balance on goods, services and income	−910.5	−1,228.4	−1,216.3
Current transfers (net)	743.7	791.7	820.0
Current balance	−166.8	−436.7	−396.3
Direct investment (net)	82.1	442.0	206.6
Other long-term capital (net) . .	225.8	344.9	426.1
Other capital (net)	−133.5	−329.5	−219.4
Overall balance	7.6	20.7	17.0

External Trade

PRINCIPAL COMMODITIES
('000 pesos)

Imports c.i.f.	1998	1999	2000
Food and live animals	704,200	722,396	671,801
Cereals and cereal preparations	348,260	313,755	285,541
Wheat and meslin (unmilled) .	178,590	122,979	112,187
Rice	99,382	141,163	100,772
Mineral fuels, lubricants, etc. . .	687,030	730,763	1,158,071
Petroleum and petroleum products	664,844	710,881	1,137,418
Crude petroleum oils, etc. .	65,358	88,087	279,901
Gas oils	151,819	198,056	301,551
Chemicals and related products .	419,720	428,938	418,765
Basic manufactures	628,672	687,889	673,195
Iron and steel	117,098	150,889	111,940
Manufactures of metal . .	141,184	152,491	162,428
Machinery and transport equipment	1,130,414	1,144,441	1,202,330
Power-generating machinery and equipment	208,992	129,110	131,725
General industrial machinery and equipment and machine parts	249,889	269,441	259,300
Total (incl. others)	4,181,192	4,349,090	4,829,050

Exports f.o.b.	1998	1999	2000
Food and live animals	776,262	659,992	657,305
Fish, crustaceans and molluscs and preparations thereof	102,786	96,055	87,830
Fresh, chilled or frozen fish . .	102,661	95,267	87,176
Fruit and vegetables	35,201	74,980	89,618
Sugar, sugar preparations and honey	605,494	470,680	458,427
Raw beet and cane sugars (solid)	593,694	458,210	447,677
Beverages and tobacco	202,562	218,471	179,719
Manufactured tobacco . . .	162,750	173,477	140,346
Crude materials (inedible) except fuels	358,781	436,808	623,089
Metalliferous ores and metal scrap	351,926	430,393	617,787
Nickel ores, concentrates, etc.	168,017	201,649	318,706
Petroleum, petroleum products and related materials	445	18,934	52,388
Chemicals and related products .	45,566	39,662	41,235
Basic manufactures	97,202	94,268	99,230
Iron and steel	45,985	43,430	61,484
Total (incl. others)	1,512,197	1,495,783	1,675,868

PRINCIPAL TRADING PARTNERS
('000 pesos)

Imports c.i.f.	1998	1999	2000
Argentina	108,827	129,938	106,424
Brazil	63,630	75,761	130,129
Canada	321,046	339,642	311,074
China, People's Republic . . .	336,496	432,241	445,769
Colombia	30,312	36,978	85,156
France	318,381	276,337	289,876
Germany	78,140	75,967	77,841
Italy	253,203	264,063	296,602
Mexico	342,796	321,772	298,527
Netherlands Antilles	74,397	84,312	25,788
Russia	134,881	124,545	111,300
Spain	608,210	721,771	743,589
United Kingdom	54,022	41,193	56,864
Venezuela	385,570	451,451	898,393
Total (incl. others)	4,181,192	4,349,090	4,829,050

Exports f.o.b.	1998	1999	2000
Belgium	41,407	43,978	48,289
Canada	230,169	229,185	277,728
China, People's Republic . . .	81,855	49,491	80,532
Colombia	20,610	5,853	18,941
Dominican Republic	31,272	44,580	19,823
France	43,110	50,517	42,411
Germany	67,859	72,596	120,882
Iran	14,442	19,620	14,179
Italy	27,979	39,283	34,198
Japan	19,478	49,506	29,374
Korea, Democratic People's Republic	24,609	35,157	43
Mexico	45,134	25,049	39,285
Netherlands	53,074	93,037	116,842
Portugal	14,562	26,424	17,844
Russia	355,254	302,776	324,577
Spain	141,069	159,409	149,656
Sweden	31,346	35,240	50,426
Switzerland	21,466	24,329	22,602
Taiwan	23,343	2,422	11,210
Ukraine	22,614	1,199	478
United Kingdom	24,687	30,206	38,101
Total (incl. others)	1,512,197	1,495,783	1,675,868

Transport

RAILWAYS

	2000	2001	2002
Passenger-kilometres (million) .	1,737	1,758	1,682
Freight ton-kilometres (million) .	808	842	814

Source: UN, *Statistical Yearbook*.

ROAD TRAFFIC
(motor vehicles in use at 31 December)

	1996	1997
Passenger cars	216,575	172,574
Buses and coaches	28,089	28,861
Lorries and vans	246,105	156,634

Source: International Road Federation, *World Road Statistics*.

SHIPPING
Merchant Fleet
(registered at 31 December)

	2001	2002	2003
Number of vessels	92	91	90
Total displacement ('000 grt) . .	101	103	90

Source: Lloyd's Register-Fairplay, *World Fleet Statistics*.

International Sea-borne Freight Traffic
('000 metric tons)

	1988	1989	1990
Goods loaded	8,600	8,517	8,092
Goods unloaded	15,500	15,595	15,440

Source: UN, *Monthly Bulletin of Statistics*.

CIVIL AVIATION
(traffic on scheduled services)

	1999	2000	2001
Kilometres flown (million) . . .	26	20	19
Passengers carried ('000) . . .	1,259	1,007	882
Passenger-kilometres (million) .	3,712	2,964	3,171
Total ton-kilometres (million) . .	421	335	361

Source: UN, *Statistical Yearbook*.

Tourism

ARRIVALS BY NATIONALITY*

	1999	2000	2001
Argentina	42,612	54,185	40,964
Canada	276,346	307,725	350,426
France	123,607	132,089	138,765
Germany	182,159	203,403	171,851
Italy	160,843	175,667	159,423
Mexico	70,983	86,540	98,495
Spain	146,978	153,197	140,125
United Kingdom	85,829	90,972	94,794
USA	62,345	76,898	78,789
Total (incl. others)	1,602,781	1,773,986	1,774,541

* Figures include same-day visitors (excursionists).

Source: World Tourism Organization, *Yearbook of Tourism Statistics*.

Tourist arrivals ('000): 1,686.1 in 2002.

Tourism receipts (US $ million): 1,948.2 in 2000; 1,840.4 in 2001; 1,769.1 in 2002.

Communications Media

	1999	2000	2001
Telephones ('000 main lines in use)	433.8	488.6	572.6
Mobile cellular telephones ('000 subscribers)	5.1	6.5	8.1
Personal computers ('000 in use) .	110	n.a.	220
Internet users ('000)	34.8	60.0	120.0
Book production (titles)	708	n.a.	1,004

Radio receivers ('000 in use): 3,900 in 1997.

Television receivers ('000 in use): 2,800 in 2000.

Facsimile machines (number in use): 392 in 1992.

Daily newspapers: 17 in 1996 (average estimated circulation 1.3m. copies).

Sources: UNESCO, *Statistical Yearbook*; UN, *Statistical Yearbook*; International Telecommunication Union.

Education
(2002/03)

	Institutions	Teachers	Students
Pre-primary	1,115	18,600	147,600
Primary	9,397	93,000	873,700
Secondary*	2,032	85,600	992,000
Universities	64	23,700	192,000

* According to results of 1981 population and housing census.

2003/04: Primary: 79,600 teachers; 856,500 students. Universities: 273,100 students.

Adult literacy rate (UNESCO estimates): 96.9% (males 97.0%; females 96.8%) in 2002 (Source: UN Development Programme, *Human Development Report*).

Directory

The Constitution

Following the assumption of power by the Castro regime, on 1 January 1959, the Constitution was suspended and a Fundamental Law of the Republic was instituted, with effect from 7 February 1959. In February 1976 Cuba's first socialist Constitution came into force after being submitted to the first Congress of the Communist Party of Cuba, in December 1975, and to popular referendum, in February 1976; it was amended in July 1992. The main provisions of the Constitution, as amended, are summarized below.

Note: On 27 July 2002 the Constitution was further amended to enshrine the socialist system as irrevocable and to ratify that economic, diplomatic and political relations with another state cannot be negotiated in the face of aggression, threat or pressure from a foreign power. A clause was also introduced making it impossible to remove these amendments from the Constitution.

POLITICAL, SOCIAL AND ECONOMIC PRINCIPLES

The Republic of Cuba is a socialist, independent, and sovereign state, organized with all and for the sake of all as a unitary and democratic republic for the enjoyment of political freedom, social justice, collective and individual well-being and human solidarity. Sovereignty rests with the people, from whom originates the power of the State. The Communist Party of Cuba is the leading force of society and the State. The State recognizes, respects and guarantees freedom of religion. Religious institutions are separate from the State. The socialist State carries out the will of the working people and guarantees work, medical care, education, food, clothing and housing. The Republic of Cuba bases its relations with other socialist countries on socialist internationalism, friendship, co-operation and mutual assistance. It reaffirms its willingness to integrate with and co-operate with the countries of Latin America and the Caribbean.

The State organizes and directs the economic life of the nation in accordance with a central social and economic development plan. The State directs and controls foreign trade. The State recognizes the right of small farmers to own their lands and other means of production and to sell that land. The State guarantees the right of citizens to ownership of personal property in the form of earnings, savings, place of residence and other possessions and objects which serve to satisfy their material and cultural needs. The State also guarantees the right of inheritance.

Cuban citizenship is acquired by birth or through naturalization.

The State protects the family, motherhood and matrimony.

The State directs and encourages all aspects of education, culture and science.

All citizens have equal rights and are subject to equal duties.

The State guarantees the right to medical care, education, freedom of speech and press, assembly, demonstration, association and privacy. In the socialist society work is the right and duty, and a source of pride for every citizen.

GOVERNMENT

National Assembly of People's Power

The National Assembly of People's Power (Asamblea Nacional del Poder Popular) is the supreme organ of the State and is the only organ with constituent and legislative authority. It is composed of deputies, over the age of 18, elected by free, direct and secret ballot, for a period of five years. All Cuban citizens aged 16 years or more, except those who are mentally incapacitated or who have committed a crime, are eligible to vote. The National Assembly of People's Power holds two ordinary sessions a year and a special session when requested by one-third of the deputies or by the Council of State. More than one-half of the total number of deputies must be present for a session to be held.

All decisions made by the Assembly, except those relating to constitutional reforms, are adopted by a simple majority of votes. The deputies may be recalled by their electors at any time.

The National Assembly of People's Power has the following functions:

to reform the Constitution;

to approve, modify and annul laws;

to supervise all organs of the State and government;

to decide on the constitutionality of laws and decrees;

to revoke decree-laws issued by the Council of State and the Council of Ministers;

to discuss and approve economic and social development plans, the state budget, monetary and credit systems;

to approve the general outlines of foreign and domestic policy, to ratify and annul international treaties, to declare war and approve peace treaties;

to approve the administrative division of the country;

to elect the President, First Vice-President, the Vice-Presidents and other members of the Council of State;

to elect the President, Vice-President and Secretary of the National Assembly;

to appoint the members of the Council of Ministers on the proposal of the President of the Council of State;

to elect the President, Vice-President and other judges of the People's Supreme Court;

to elect the Attorney-General and the Deputy Attorney-Generals;

to grant amnesty;

to call referendums.

The President of the National Assembly presides over sessions of the Assembly, calls ordinary sessions, proposes the draft agenda, signs the Official Gazette, organizes the work of the commissions appointed by the Assembly and attends the meetings of the Council of State.

Council of State

The Council of State is elected from the members of the National Assembly and represents that Assembly in the period between sessions. It comprises a President, one First Vice-President, five Vice-Presidents, one Secretary and 23 other members. Its mandate ends when a new Assembly meets. All decisions are adopted by a simple majority of votes. It is accountable for its actions to the National Assembly.

The Council of State has the following functions:

to call special sessions of the National Assembly;

to set the date for the election of a new Assembly;

to issue decree-laws in the period between the sessions of the National Assembly;

to decree mobilization in the event of war and to approve peace treaties when the Assembly is in recess;

to issue instructions to the courts and the Office of the Attorney-General of the Republic;

to appoint and remove ambassadors of Cuba abroad on the proposal of its President, to grant or refuse recognition to diplomatic representatives of other countries to Cuba;

to suspend those provisions of the Council of Ministers that are not in accordance with the Constitution;

to revoke the resolutions of the Executive Committee of the local organs of People's Power which are contrary to the Constitution or laws and decrees formulated by other higher organs.

For all purposes the Council of State is the highest representative of the Cuban state.

Head of State

The President of the Council of State is the Head of State and the Head of Government and has the following powers:

to represent the State and Government and conduct general policy;

to convene and preside over the sessions of the Council of State and the Council of Ministers;

to supervise the ministries and other administrative bodies;

to propose the members of the Council of Ministers to the National Assembly of People's Power;

to receive the credentials of the heads of foreign diplomatic missions;

to sign the decree-laws and other resolutions of the Council of State;

to exercise the Supreme Command of all armed institutions and determine their general organization;

to preside over the National Defence Council;

to declare a state of emergency in the cases outlined in the Constitution.

In the case of absence, illness or death of the President of the Council of State, the First Vice-President assumes the President's duties.

The Council of Ministers

The Council of Ministers is the highest-ranking executive and administrative organ. It is composed of the Head of State and

Government, as its President, the First Vice-President, the Vice-Presidents, the Ministers, the Secretary and other members determined by law. Its Executive Committee is composed of the President, the First Vice-President, the Vice-Presidents and other members of the Council of Ministers determined by the President.

The Council of Ministers has the following powers:

to conduct political, economic, cultural, scientific, social and defence policy as outlined by the National Assembly;

to approve international treaties;

to propose projects for the general development plan and, if they are approved by the National Assembly, to supervise their implementation;

to conduct foreign policy and trade;

to draw up bills and submit them to the National Assembly;

to draw up the draft state budget;

to conduct general administration, implement laws, issue decrees and supervise defence and national security.

The Council of Ministers is accountable to the National Assembly of People's Power.

LOCAL GOVERNMENT

The country is divided into 14 provinces and 169 municipalities. The provinces are: Pinar del Río, Habana, Ciudad de la Habana, Matanzas, Villa Clara, Cienfuegos, Sancti Spíritus, Ciego de Avila, Camagüey, Las Tunas, Holguín, Granma, Santiago de Cuba and Guantánamo.

Voting for delegates to the municipal assemblies is direct, secret and voluntary. All citizens over 16 years of age are eligible to vote. The number of delegates to each assembly is proportionate to the number of people living in that area. A delegate must obtain more than one-half of the total number of votes cast in the constituency in order to be elected. The Municipal and Provincial Assemblies of People's Power are elected by free, direct and secret ballot. Nominations for Municipal and Provincial Executive Committees of People's Power are submitted to the relevant assembly by a commission presided over by a representative of the Communist Party's leading organ and consisting of representatives of youth, workers', farmers', revolutionary and women's organizations. The President and Secretary of each of the regional and the provincial assemblies are the only full-time members, the other delegates carrying out their functions in addition to their normal employment.

The regular and extraordinary sessions of the local Assemblies of People's Power are public. More than one-half of the total number of members must be present in order for agreements made to be valid. Agreements are adopted by simple majority.

JUDICIARY

Judicial power is exercised by the People's Supreme Court and all other competent tribunals and courts. The People's Supreme Court is the supreme judicial authority and is accountable only to the National Assembly of People's Power. It can propose laws and issue regulations through its Council of Government. Judges are independent but the courts must inform the electorate of their activities at least once a year. Every accused person has the right to a defence and can be tried only by a tribunal.

The Office of the Attorney-General is subordinate only to the National Assembly and the Council of State and is responsible for ensuring that the law is properly obeyed.

The Constitution may be totally or partially modified only by a two-thirds' majority vote in the National Assembly of People's Power. If the modification is total, or if it concerns the composition and powers of the National Assembly of People's Power or the Council of State, or the rights and duties contained in the Constitution, it also requires a positive vote by referendum.

The Government

Head of State: Dr FIDEL CASTRO RUZ (took office 2 December 1976; re-elected December 1981, December 1986, March 1993, February 1998 and March 2003).

COUNCIL OF STATE
(April 2005)

President: Dr FIDEL CASTRO RUZ.

First Vice-President: Gen. RAÚL CASTRO RUZ.

Vice-Presidents: JUAN ALMEIDA BOSQUE, Gen. ABELARDO COLOMÉ IBARRA, CARLOS LAGE DÁVILA, JUAN ESTEBAN LAZO HERNÁNDEZ, JOSÉ RAMÓN MACHADO VENTURA.

Secretary: Dr JOSÉ M. MIYAR BARRUECOS.

Members: JOSÉ RAMÓN BALAGUER CABRERA, VILMA ESPÍN GUILLOIS DE CASTRO, Dr ARMANDO HART DÁVALOS, ORLANDO LUGO FONTE, NIDIA DIANA MARTÍNEZ PITI, MARÍA T. FERRER MADRAZO, MARTA HERNÁNDEZ ROMERO, Gen. JULIO CASAS REGUEIRO, PEDRO SÁEZ MONTEJO, Gen. ROBERTO IGNACIO GONZÁLEZ PLANAS, FRANCISCO SOBERÓN VALDÉS, PEDRO MIRET PRIETO, RAMIRO VALDÉS MENÉNDEZ, JULIO CRISTHIAN JIMÉNEZ MOLINA, ROBERTO FERNÁNDEZ RETAMAR, FELIPE RAMÓN PÉREZ ROQUE, MARCOS J. PORTAL LEÓN, LUIS S. HERRERA MARTÍNEZ, IRIS BETANCOURT TÉLLEZ, PEDRO ROSS LEAL, OTTO RIVERO TORRES, CARLOS MANUEL VALENCIAGA DÍAZ1 vacancy.

COUNCIL OF MINISTERS

President: Dr FIDEL CASTRO RUZ.

First Vice-President: Gen. RAÚL CASTRO RUZ.

Secretary: CARLOS LAGE DÁVILA.

Vice-Presidents: OSMANY CIENFUEGOS GORRIARÁN, PEDRO MIRET PRIETO, JOSÉ LUIS RODRÍGUEZ GARCÍA, JOSÉ RAMÓN FERNÁNDEZ ALVAREZ.

Minister of Agriculture: ALFREDO JORDÁN MORALES.

Minister of Foreign Trade: RAÚL DE LA NUEZ RAMÍREZ.

Minister of Domestic Trade: BARBARA CASTILLO CUESTA.

Minister of Computer Science and Communications: Gen. ROBERTO IGNACIO GONZÁLEZ PLANAS.

Minister of Construction: FIDEL FERNANDO FIGUEROA DE LA PAZ.

Minister of Culture: ABEL ENRIQUE PRIETO JIMÉNEZ.

Minister of Economy and Planning: JOSÉ LUIS RODRÍGUEZ GARCÍA.

Minister of Education: LUIS IGNACIO GÓMEZ GUTIÉRREZ.

Minister of Higher Education: FERNANDO VECINO ALEGRET.

Minister of the Revolutionary Armed Forces: Gen. RAÚL CASTRO RUZ.

Minister of Finance and Prices: GEORGINA BARREIRO FAJARDO.

Minister of the Food Industry: ALEJANDRO ROCA IGLESIAS.

Minister of Foreign Investment and Economic Co-operation: MARTHA LOMAS MORALES.

Minister of the Sugar Industry: Gen. ULISES ROSALES DEL TORO.

Minister of Light Industry: ESTELA MARTHA DOMINGUEZ ARIOSA.

Minister of the Fishing Industry: ALFREDO LÓPEZ VALDÉS.

Minister of the Iron, Steel and Engineering Industries: FERNANDO ACOSTA SANTANA.

Minister of Basic Industry: YADIRÁ GARCÍA VERA.

Minister of the Interior: Gen. ABELARDO COLOMÉ IBARRA.

Minister of Justice: ROBERTO T. DÍAZ SOTOLONGO.

Minister of Foreign Relations: FELIPE RAMÓN PÉREZ ROQUE.

Minister of Labour and Social Security: ALFREDO MORALES CARTAYA.

Minister of Public Health: JOSÉ RAMÓN BALAGUER CABRERA.

Minister of Science, Technology and the Environment: FERNANDO MARIO GONZÁLEZ BERMÚDEZ (acting).

Minister of Transportation: CARLOS MANUEL PAZO TORRADO.

Minister of Tourism: MANUEL MARRERO CRUZ.

Minister of Auditing and Control: LINA OLINDA PEDRAZA RODRÍGUEZ.

Minister, President of the Banco Central de Cuba: FRANCISCO SOBERÓN VALDÉS.

Ministers without Portfolio: RICARDO CABRISAS RUIZ, WILFREDO LÓPEZ RODRÍGUEZ.

MINISTRIES

Ministry of Agriculture: Avda Independencia, entre Conill y Sta Ana, Havana; tel. (7) 84-5770; fax (7) 33-5086.

Ministry of Auditing and Control: Havana; replaced the National Auditing Office in 2001.

Ministry of Basic Industry: Avda Salvador Allende 666, Havana; tel. (7) 70-7711; e-mail webmaster@one.gov.cu.

Ministry of Construction: Avda Carlos M. de Céspedes y Calle 35, Havana; tel. (7) 81-8385; fax (7) 33-5585; e-mail dirinter@ceniai.inf .cu.

Ministry of Culture: Calle 2, No 258, entre 11 y 13, Plaza de la Revolución, Vedado, CP 10400, Havana; tel. (7) 55-2260; fax (7) 66-2053; e-mail atencion@min.cult.cu; internet www.ministerio.cult.cu.

Ministry of Economy and Planning: 20 de Mayo y Ayestarán, Plaza de la Revolución, Havana; tel. (7) 881-8789; fax (7) 33-3387; e-mail mep@ceniai.inf.cu.

Ministry of Education: Obispo 160, Havana; tel. (7) 61-4888; internet www.rimed.cu.

Ministry of Finance and Prices: Calle Obispo 211, esq. Cuba, Havana; tel. (7) 867-1920; fax (7) 33-8050; e-mail sdinformacion@mfp.gov.cu; internet www.mfp.cu.

Ministry of the Fishing Industry: Avda 5, entre 246 y 248, No 24606, Barlovento, Playa, Havana; tel. (7) 209-7930; fax (7) 204-9168; e-mail info@fishnavy.inf.cu; internet www1.cubamar.cu.

Ministry of the Food Industry: Avda 41, No 4455, entre 48 y 50, Playa, Havana; tel. (7) 203-6801; fax (7) 204-0517; e-mail minal@minal.get.cma.net; internet www.minal.cubaindustria.cu.

Ministry of Foreign Relations: Calzada 360, esq. G, Vedado, Havana; tel. (7) 55-3537; fax (7) 33-3460; e-mail cubaminrex@minrex.gov.cu; internet www.cubaminrex.cu.

Ministry of Foreign Investment and Economic Co-operation: 512 calle 30, entre 22 y 24, Miramar, Havana; tel. (7) 202-3873; fax (7) 204-2105; e-mail cpinv@minvec.cu.

Ministry of Foreign Trade: Infanta 16, esq. 23, Vedado, Havana; tel. (7) 55-0428; fax (7) 55-0376; e-mail cepecdir@infocex.cu; internet www.infocex.cu/cepec.

Ministry of Higher Education: Calle 23, No 565, esq. a F, Vedado, Havana; tel. (7) 55-2314; fax (7) 33-3295; e-mail develop@reduniv.edu.cu; internet www.mes.edu.cu.

Ministry of Computer Science and Communications: Avdas Independencia y 19 de Mayo, Plaza de la Revolución, Havana; tel. (7) 81-7654; e-mail infosoc@mic.cu; internet www.mic.gov.cu.

Ministry of the Interior: Plaza de la Revolución, Havana; tel. (7) 30-1566; fax (7) 33-5261.

Ministry of Domestic Trade: Calle Habana 258, Havana; tel. (7) 62-5790.

Ministry of the Iron, Steel and Engineering Industries: Avda Rancho Boyeros y Calle 100, Havana; tel. (7) 45-3911; e-mail sime@sime.co.cu; internet www.disaic.cu/sime.

Ministry of Justice: Calle O, No 216, entre 23 y Humboldt, Vedado, Apdo 10400, Havana 4; tel. (7) 32-6319; internet www.minjus.cu.

Ministry of Labour and Social Security: Calle 23, esq. Calles O y P, Vedado, Havana; tel. (7) 55-0071; fax (7) 33-5816; e-mail mtssmin@ceniai.inf.cu.

Ministry of Light Industry: Empedrado 302, Havana; tel. (7) 67-0387; fax (7) 67-0329; e-mail ministro@minil.org.cu; internet www.ligera.cu.

Ministry of Public Health: Calle 23, No 301, Vedado, Havana; tel. (7) 32-2561; internet www.dne.sld.cu/minsap.

Ministry of the Revolutionary Armed Forces: Plaza de la Revolución, Havana; internet www.cubagob.cu/otras_info/minfar/far/minfar.htm.

Ministry of Science, Technology and the Environment: Industria y San José, Habana Vieja, Havana; tel. (7) 867-0606; fax (7) 33-8054; e-mail rosae@ceniai.inf.cu; internet www.cuba.cu/ciencia/citma/.

Ministry of Sugar: Calle 23, No 171, Vedado, Havana; tel. (7) 55-3194; fax (7) 55-3260; e-mail relint@ocentral.minaz.cu.

Ministry of Tourism: Calle 19, No 710, entre Paseo y A, Vedado, Havana; tel. (7) 33-0545; fax (7) 33-4086; e-mail promo@mintur.mit.cma.net; internet www.cubatravel.cu.

Ministry of Transportation: Avda Boyeros, esq. Tulipán, Plaza de la Revolución, Havana; tel. (7) 55-5030; e-mail raulito.pl@mitrans.transnet.cu; internet www.cubagob.cu/des_eco/mitrans.

Legislature

ASAMBLEA NACIONAL DEL PODER POPULAR

The National Assembly of People's Power was constituted on 2 December 1976. In July 1992 the National Assembly adopted a constitutional amendment providing for legislative elections by direct vote. Only candidates nominated by the Partido Comunista de Cuba (PCC) were permitted to contest the elections. At elections to the National Assembly conducted on 19 January 2003 all 609 candidates were elected. Of the 8.2m. registered voters, 97.61% participated in the elections. Only 3.86% of votes cast were blank or spoilt.

President: Ricardo Alarcón de Quesada.
Vice-President: Jaime Crombet Hernández Maurell.
Secretary: Dr Ernesto Suárez Méndez.

Political Organizations

Partido Comunista de Cuba (PCC) (Communist Party of Cuba): Havana; e-mail root@epol.cipcc.inf.cu; internet www.pcc.cu; f. 1961 as the Organizaciones Revolucionarias Integradas (ORI) from a fusion of the Partido Socialista Popular (Communist), Fidel Castro's Movimiento 26 de Julio and the Directorio Revolucionario 13 de Marzo; became the Partido Unido de la Revolución Socialista Cubana (PURSC) in 1962; renamed as the Partido Comunista de Cuba in 1965; 150-member Central Committee, Political Bureau (24 mems in 2004), and five Commissions; 706,132 mems (1994).

Political Bureau
Dr Fidel Castro Ruz; Gen. Raúl Castro Ruz; Juan Almeida Bosque; José Ramón Machado Ventura; Juan Esteban Lazo Hernández; Gen. Abelardo Colomé Ibarra; Pedro Ross Leal; Carlos Lage Dávila; Alfredo Jordán Morales; Gen. Ulises Rosales del Toro; Concepción Campa Huergo; Yadira García Vera; Abel Enrique Prieto Jiménez; Gen. Julio Casas Regueiro; Gen. Leopoldo Cintra Frías; Ricardo Alarcón de Quesada; José Ramón Balaguer Cabrera; Misael Enamorado Dager; Gen. Ramón Espinosa Martín; Marcos Javier Portal León; Juan Carlos Robinson Agramonte; Pedro Sáez Montejo; Jorge Luis Sierra López; Felipe Ramón Pérez Roque.

There are a number of dissident groups operating in Cuba. These include:

Arco Progresista: f. 2003; alliance of social-democratic groups in and outside Cuba.

Concertación Democrática Cubana (CDC): f. 1991; alliance of 11 dissident organizations campaigning for political pluralism and economic reform; Leader Elizardo Sánchez Santa Cruz.

Cuban Democratic Platform: f. 1990; alliance comprising three dissident organizations:

Coordinadora Social Demócrata.

Partido Demócrata Cristiano de Cuba (PDC): POB 558987, Miami, FL 33155, USA; tel. (305) 264-9411; fax (954) 489-1572; e-mail miyares@pdc-cuba.org; internet www.pdc-cuba.org; f. 1959 as Movimiento Demócrata Cristiano; name changed as above in 1991; Pres. Marcelino Miyares; Sec.-Gen. José Vazquez.

Unión Liberal Cubana: Menéndez y Pelayo 83, 28007 Madrid, Spain; fax (91) 5011342; e-mail cubaliberal@mercuryin.net; internet www.cubaliberal.org; mem. of Liberal International; Founder and Chair. Carlos Alberto Montaner.

Partido Cubano Ortodoxo: f. 1999; Leader Nelson Aguiar.

Partido Liberal Democrático de Cuba: Chair. Osvaldo Alfonso Valdés.

Partido pro-Derechos Humanos: f. 1988 to defend human rights in Cuba; Pres. Hiram Abi Cobas; Sec.-Gen. Tania Díaz.

Partido Social Revolucionario Democrático de Cuba: POB 351081, Miami, FL 33135, USA; tel. and fax (305) 649-2886; e-mail psrdc@psrdc.org; internet www.psrdc.org; f. 1992; Pres. Jorge Valls.

Partido Solidaridad Democrática (PSD): POB 310063, Miami, FL 33131, USA; tel. (305) 408-2659; e-mail gladyperez@aol.com; internet www.ccsi.com/~ams/psd; Pres. Fernando Sánchez López.

Solidaridad Cubana: Leader Fernando Sánchez López.

Diplomatic Representation

EMBASSIES IN CUBA

Algeria: Avda 5, No 2802, esq. 28, Miramar, Havana; tel. (7) 204-2835; fax (7) 204-2702; Ambassador Ahcene Kerman.

Angola: Avda 5, No 1012, entre 10 y 12, Miramar, Havana; tel. (7) 204-2474; fax (7) 204-0487; e-mail embangol@ceniai.inf.cu; Ambassador Antonio J. Condesse D. Carvahlo.

Argentina: Calle 36, No 511, entre 5 y 7, Miramar, Havana; tel. (7) 204-2565; fax (7) 204-2140; e-mail ecuba@enet.cu; Ambassador Darío Alessandro.

Austria: Calle 4, No 101, entre 1 y 3, Miramar, Havana; tel. (7) 204-2394; fax (7) 204-1235; e-mail havanna-ob@bmaa.gv.at; Ambassador Dr Helga Konrad.

Belarus: Avda 5, No 3802, entre 38 y 40, Miramar, Havana; tel. (7) 204-7330; fax (7) 204-7332; e-mail cuba@belembassy.org; Ambassador Poluyan Igor Ivanovich.

Belgium: Calle 8, No 309, entre 3 y 5, Miramar, Havana; tel. (7) 204-2410; fax (7) 204-1318; e-mail havana@diplobel.org; internet www.diplomatie.be/havana; Ambassador PIERRE-EMMANUEL DE BAUW.

Belize: Avda 5, No 3608, entre 36 y 36A, Miramar, Havana; tel. (7) 204-3504; fax (7) 204-3506; e-mail belize.embassy@ip.etecsa.cu; Ambassador ASSAH SHOMAN.

Benin: Calle 20, No 119, entre 1 y 3, Miramar, Havana; tel. (7) 204-2179; fax (7) 204-2334; e-mail ambencub@ceniai.inf.cu; Ambassador GEORGES B. N'KOUEI TIMANTY.

Bolivia: Calle 26, No 113, entre 1 y 3, Miramar, Havana; tel. (7) 204-2426; fax (7) 204-2127; e-mail emboliviahabana@cubacel.net; Ambassador ELSA GUEVARA AGUIRRE.

Brazil: Calle Lamparilla, No 2, 4°K, Habana Vieja, Havana; tel. (7) 66-9052; fax (7) 66-2912; e-mail brasil@ceniai.inf.cu; Ambassador TILDEN JOSÉ SANTIAGO.

Bulgaria: Calle B, No 252, entre 11 y 13, Vedado, Havana; tel. (7) 33-3125; fax (7) 33-3297; e-mail embulhav@ceniai.inf.cu; Chargé d'affaires a.i. LUBOMIR ILIEV IVANOV.

Burkina Faso: Calle 7, No 8401, Miramar, Havana; tel. (7) 204-2895; fax (7) 204-1942; e-mail ambfaso@ceniai.inf.cu; Ambassador SALIF NÉBIÉ.

Cambodia: Avda 5, No 7001, entre 70 y 72, Miramar, Havana; tel. (7) 204-1496; fax (7) 204-6400; e-mail cambodia@ceniai.inf.cu; Ambassador CHIM PRORNG.

Canada: Calle 30, No 518, entre 5 y 7, Miramar, Havana; tel. (7) 204-2516; fax (7) 204-2044; e-mail havan@dfait-maeci.gc.ca; internet www.dfait-maeci.gc.ca/cuba; Ambassador ALEXANDRA BUGAILISKIS.

Cape Verde: Calle 20, No 2001, esq. 7, Miramar, Havana; tel. (7) 204-2979; fax (7) 204-1072; e-mail ecvc@ceniai.inf.cu; Ambassador CRISPINA ALMEIDA GOMES.

Chile: Avda 33, No 1423, entre 16 y 18, Miramar, Havana; tel. (7) 204-1222; fax (7) 204-1694; e-mail echilecu@cubacel.net; internet www.embachilecu.cu; Ambassador MORENO LAVAL CELSO.

China, People's Republic: Calle 13, No 551, entre C y D, Vedado, Havana; tel. (7) 33-3005; fax (7) 33-3092; e-mail chinaemb_cu@mfa.gov.cn; Ambassador LI LIANTU.

Colombia: Calle 14, No 515, entre 5 y 7, Miramar, Havana; tel. (7) 204-1246; fax (7) 204-1249; e-mail elahabana@minrelext.gov.co; Ambassador LUIS HERNANDEZ OJEDA.

Congo, Republic: Avda 5, No 1003, Miramar, Havana; tel. and fax (7) 204-9055; Ambassador PASCAL ONGUEMBY.

Czech Republic: Avda Kohly, No 259, entre 41 y 43, Nuevo Vedado, Havana; tel. (7) 883-3201; fax (7) 883-3596; e-mail havana@embassy.mzv.cz; internet www.mzv.cz/havana; Chargé d'affaires a.i. PETR STIEGLER.

Dominican Republic: Avda 5, No 9202, entre 92 y 94, Miramar, Havana; tel. (7) 204-8429; fax (7) 204-8431; Ambassador RAFAEL A. BÁEZ PÉREZ.

Ecuador: Avda 5A, No 4407, entre 44 y 46, Miramar, Havana; tel. (7) 204-2034; fax (7) 204-2868; e-mail embecuad@ceniai.inf.cu; Ambassador ALBA COELLO MATUTE.

Egypt: Avda 5, No 1801, esq. 18, Miramar, Havana; tel. (7) 204-2441; fax (7) 204-0905; e-mail emegipto@enet.cu; Ambassador HAMDI MOHAMED ABDEL ELMONEIM EL SHAZLY.

France: Calle 14, No 312, entre 3 y 5, Miramar, Havana; tel. (7) 204-2132; fax (7) 204-1439; e-mail la-havane.amba@diplomatie.gouv.fr; internet www.ambafrance-cu.org; Ambassador JEAN LEVY.

Gambia: Calle 24, No 307, entre 3 y 5, Miramar, Havana; tel. (7) 204-5315; fax (7) 204-5316; Ambassador BALA GARBA-JAHUMPA.

Germany: Calle 13, No 652, esq. B, Vedado, Havana; tel. (7) 833-2539; fax (7) 833-1586; e-mail alemania@enet.cu; internet www.deutschebotschaft-havanna.cu; Ambassador Dr BERND WULFFEN.

Ghana: Avda 5, No 1808, esq. 20, Miramar, Havana; tel. (7) 204-2153; fax (7) 204-2317; e-mail eghana@ceniai.inf.cu; internet www.ghanaembassy.cu; Ambassador Dr ISAAC ANTWI-OMANE.

Greece: Avda 5, No 7802, esq. 78, Miramar, Havana; tel. (7) 204-2995; fax (7) 204-1784; e-mail gremb@enct.cu; Ambassador PETROS AVIERINOS.

Guatemala: Calle 16, No 505, entre 3 y 5, Miramar, Havana; tel. (7) 204-3417; fax (7) 204-3200; e-mail embagucu@ceniai.inf.cu; Ambassador HUGO RENÉ GUZMÁN MALDONADO.

Guinea: Calle 20, No 504, entre 5 y 7, Miramar, Havana; tel. (7) 204-2003; fax (7) 204-2380; Chargé d'affaires a.i. ALMAMY IBRAHIMA SECK.

Guinea-Bissau: Calle 14, No 313, entre 3 y 5, Miramar, Havana; tel. (7) 204-2689; fax (7) 204-2794; Chargé d'affaires a.i. TOMÁS SANCAS.

Guyana: Calle 18, No 506, entre 5 y 7, Miramar, Havana; tel. (7) 204-2249; fax (7) 204-2867; e-mail embguyana@enet.cu; Ambassador Dr TIMOTHY N. CRICHLOW.

Haiti: Avda 7, No 4402, entre 44 y 46, Miramar, Havana; tel. (7) 204-5421; fax (7) 204-5423; e-mail embhaiti@enet.cu; internet www.embhaiti.cu; Chargé d'affaires a.i. PIERRE MAX CHARLES.

Holy See: Calle 12, No 514, entre 5 y 7, Miramar, Havana (Apostolic Nunciature); tel. (7) 204-2700; fax (7) 204-2257; e-mail csa@pcn.net; Apostolic Nuncio Most Rev. LUIGI BONAZZI (Titular Archbishop of Atella).

Honduras: Interests Section: Casa Palhero 112, Planta Baja, Calle 30, entre 1 y 3, Miramar, Havana; tel. (7) 204-5497; fax (7) 204-5496; e-mail embhocu@ip.etecsa.cu; Chargé d'affaires a.i. REYNIERI DAVID AMADOR.

Hungary: Calle G, No 458, entre 19 y 21, Vedado, Havana; tel. (7) 833-3365; fax (7) 833-3286; e-mail embhuncu@ceniai.inf.cu; Ambassador JÓZSEF BALÁZS.

India: Calle 21, No 202, esq. a K, Vedado, Havana; tel. (7) 833-3777; fax (7) 833-3287; e-mail eoihav@ceniai.inf.cu; internet www.indembassyhavana.cu; Ambassador BHASKAR BALAKRISHNAN.

Indonesia: Avda 5, No 1607, esq. 18, Miramar, Havana; tel. (7) 204-9618; fax (7) 204-9617; e-mail indonhav@ceniai.inf.cu; internet www.indohav.cu; Ambassador INDRA TJAHJA SEMPURNAJAYA.

Iran: Avda 5, No 3002, esq. 30, Miramar, Havana; tel. (7) 204-2675; fax (7) 204-2770; e-mail embairan@ip.etecsa.cu; Ambassador AHMAD EDRISIAN.

Iraq: Avda 5, No 8201, entre 82 y 84, Miramar, Havana; tel. (7) 204-1607; fax (7) 204-2157; Chargé d'affaires a.i. MAZIN A. THIAB.

Italy: No 5, Avda 402, Calle 4, Miramar, Havana; tel. (7) 204-5615; fax (7) 204-5659; e-mail ambitcub@enet.cu; internet sedi.esteri.it/avana/; Ambassador ELIO MENZIONE.

Jamaica: Avda 5, No 3608, entre 36 y 36A, Miramar, Havana; tel. (7) 204-2908; fax (7) 204-2531; e-mail embjmcub@enet.cu; Ambassador ELINOR FELIX-SHERLOCK.

Japan: Centro de Negocios Miramar, Avda 3, No 1, 5°, esq. 80, Miramar, Havana; tel. (7) 204-3355; fax (7) 204-8902; Ambassador TATSUAKI IWATA.

Korea, Democratic People's Republic: Calle 17, No 752, Vedado, Havana; tel. (7) 66-2313; fax (7) 33-3073; Ambassador PAK DONG CHUN.

Laos: Avda 5, No 2808, esq. 30, Miramar, Havana; tel. (7) 204-1056; fax (7) 204-9622; e-mail embalao@ip.etecsa.cu; Ambassador PHOUANGKEO LANGSY.

Lebanon: Calle 17A, No 16403, entre 164 y 174, Siboney, Havana; tel. (7) 208-6220; fax (7) 208-6432; e-mail lbcunet@ceniai.inf.cu; Ambassador SLEIMAN C. RASSI.

Libya: Avda 7, No 1402, esq. 14, Miramar, Havana; tel. (7) 204-2192; fax (7) 204-2991; e-mail oficinalibia@ip.etecsa.cu; Ambassador RAJAB JABA-ALAH ALMOSHAITI.

Malaysia: Avda 5 y 68, No 6612, Miramar, Havana; tel. (7) 204-8883; fax (7) 204-6888; e-mail mwhavana@kln.gov.my; Ambassador Dato' MOHD KAMAL bin YAN YAHAYA.

Mali: Calle 36A, No 704, entre 7 y 9, Miramar, Havana; tel. (7) 204-5321; fax (7) 204-5320; e-mail ambamali@ceniai.inf.cu; Ambassador FIDELE DIARRA.

Mexico: Calle 12, No 518, Miramar, Playa, Havana; tel. (7) 204-2553; fax (7) 204-2717; e-mail embamex@ip.etecsa.cu; Ambassador MELBA PRIA.

Mongolia: Calle 66, No 505, esq. 5, Miramar, Havana; tel. (7) 204-2763; fax (7) 204-0639; e-mail monelch@ceniai.inf.cu; Ambassador GURJAV ERDENE.

Mozambique: Avda 7, No 2203, entre 22 y 24, Miramar, Havana; tel. (7) 204-2443; fax (7) 204-2232; e-mail embamoc@ceniai.inf.cu; Ambassador JERÓNIMO ROSA JOÃO CHIVAVI.

Namibia: Avda 5, No 4406, entre 44 y 46, Miramar, Havana; tel. (7) 204-1430; fax (7) 204-1431; e-mail embnamib@ceniai.inf.cu; Ambassador CLAUDIA YUSHONA.

Netherlands: Calle 8, No 307, entre 3 y 5, Miramar, Havana; tel. (7) 204-2511; fax (7) 204-2059; e-mail hav@minbuza.nl; Ambassador W. W. WILDEBOER.

Nicaragua: Calle 20, No 709, entre 7 y 9, Miramar, Havana; tel. (7) 204-1025; fax (7) 204-6323; e-mail embanicc@enet.cu; Chargé d'affaires a.i. CARLOS JOSÉ PÉREZ ROMAN.

Nigeria: Avda 5, No 1401, entre 14 y 16, Miramar, Havana; tel. (7) 204-2898; fax (7) 204-2202; e-mail enigera@ceniai.inf.cu; Ambassador NGAM NWACHUKWU.

Panama: Calle 26, No 109, entre 1 y 3, Miramar, Havana; tel. (7) 204-0858; fax (7) 204-1674; e-mail panembacuba@ip.etecsa.cu; Ambassador ABRAHAM BARCENAS ROSALES; relations suspended in Aug. 2004.

Paraguay: Calle 34, No 503, entre 5 y 7, Miramar, Havana; tel. (7) 204-0884; fax (7) 204-0883; e-mail cgphav@enet.cu; Chargé d'affaires a.i. AUGUSTO OCAMPOS CABALLERO.

Peru: Calle 30, No 107, entre 1 y 3, Miramar, Havana; tel. (7) 204-3570; fax (7) 204-2636; e-mail embaperu@ceniai.inf.cu; Chargé d'affaires a.i. FÉLIX VÁSQUEZ SOLÍS.

Philippines: Avda 5, No 2207, esq. 24, Miramar, Havana; tel. (7) 204-1372; fax (7) 204-2915; e-mail philhavpe@enet.cu; Ambassador REGINA IRENE P. SARMIENTO.

Poland: Calle G, No 452, esq. 19, Vedado, Havana; tel. (7) 833-2439; fax (7) 833-2442; e-mail ambhawpl@ceniai.inf.cu; internet www.embajadapolonia.cu; Ambassador TOMASZ TUROWSKI.

Portugal: Avda 7, No 2207, esq. 24, Miramar, Havana; tel. (7) 204-0149; fax (7) 204-2593; e-mail embport@enet.cu; Ambassador MARIO GODINHO DE MATOS.

Qatar: Hotel Nacional, Havana 211; tel. (7) 33-3564; fax (7) 73-4700; Ambassador ALI BIN SAAD AL-KHARJI.

Romania: Calle 21, No 307, Vedado, Havana; tel. (7) 33-3325; fax (7) 33-3324; e-mail erumania@ceniai.inf.cu; Ambassador CONSTANTIN SIMIRAD.

Russia: Avda 5, No 6402, entre 62 y 66, Miramar, Havana; tel. (7) 204-2686; fax (7) 204-1038; e-mail embrusia@ceniai.inf.cu; Ambassador ANDREI VIKTOROVICH DIMITRIEV.

Saudi Arabia: Avda 5, No 8206, entre 82 y 84, Miramar, Havana; tel. (7) 204-1045; fax (7) 204-6401; e-mail erasdcu@ceniai.inf.cu; Ambassador MOHAMED MUSTAFA TLEIMIDI.

Serbia and Montenegro: Calle 42, No 115, entre 1 y 3, Miramar, Havana; tel. (7) 204-2488; fax (7) 204-2982; e-mail embyuhav@ceniai.inf.cu; Ambassador LJILJANA KADIC.

Slovakia: Calle 66, No 521, entre 5B y 7, Miramar, Havana; tel. (7) 204-1884; fax (7) 204-1883; e-mail embeslovaca@enet.cu; Ambassador IVO HLAVACEK.

South Africa: Avda 5, No 4201, esq. 42, Miramar, Havana; tel. (7) 204-9671; fax (7) 204-1101; e-mail rsacuba@ceniai.inf.cu; internet www.sudafrica.cu; Ambassador THENJIWE ETHEL MTINTSO.

Spain: Cárcel No 51, esq. Zulueta, Havana; tel. (7) 866-8025; fax (7) 866-8006; e-mail embespcu@correo.mae.es; Ambassador CARLOS ALONSO ZALDIVAR.

Sri Lanka: Calle 32, No 307, entre 3 y 5, Miramar, Havana; tel. (7) 204-2562; fax (7) 204-2183; e-mail sri.lanka@ip.etecsa.cu; Ambassador PIYASIRI PREMACHANDRA VIJAYASEKERE.

Sweden: Calle 34, No 510, entre 5 y 7, Miramar, Havana; tel. (7) 204-2831; fax (7) 204-1194; e-mail ambassaden.havanna@foreign.ministry.se; Ambassador CHRISTER ELM.

Switzerland: Avda 5, No 2005, entre 20 y 22, Miramar, Havana; tel. (7) 204-2611; fax (7) 204-1148; e-mail swissem@enet.cu; Ambassador JEAN-CLAUDE RICHARD.

Syria: Avda 5, No 7402, entre 74 y 76, Miramar, Havana; tel. (7) 204-2266; fax (7) 204-2829; e-mail embsiria@ceniai.inf.cu; Ambassador CLOVIS KHOURY.

Turkey: Avda 5, No 3805, entre 36 y 40, Miramar, Havana; tel. (7) 204-1205; fax (7) 204-2899; e-mail turkemb@ip.etecsa.cu; Ambassador VEFAHAN OCAK.

Ukraine: Avda 5, No 4405, entre 44 y 46, Miramar, Havana; tel. (7) 204-2586; fax (7) 204-2341; e-mail cubukrem@ceniai.inf.cu; Ambassador VICTOR PASCHUK.

United Kingdom: Calle 34, No 702/4, esq. 7, Miramar, Havana; tel. (7) 204-1771; fax (7) 204-8104; e-mail embrit@ceniai.inf.cu; internet www.britishembassy.gov.uk/cuba; Ambassador JOHN ANTHONY DEW.

USA (Relations severed in 1961): Interests Section: Calzada, entre L y M, Vedado, Havana; tel. (7) 833-3551; fax (7) 833-1084; internet havana.usinterestsection.gov; Principal Officer JAMES C. CASON.

Uruguay: Calle 14, No 506, entre 5 y 7, Miramar, Havana; tel. (7) 204-2311; fax (7) 204-2246; e-mail urucub@ceniai.inf.cu; Ambassador (vacant); (diplomatic relations suspended in 2002).

Venezuela: Avda 1601, No 5, entre 16 y 18, Miramar, Havana; tel. (7) 204-2612; fax (7) 204-2773; e-mail vencuba@enet.cu; Ambassador ADÁN CHÁVEZ FRÍAS.

Viet Nam: Avda 5, No 1802, Miramar, Havana; tel. (7) 204-1502; fax (7) 204-1041; e-mail embaviet@ceniai.inf.cu; internet www.vietnamembassy.cu; Ambassador PHAM TIEN TU.

Yemen: Calle 16, No 503, entre 5 y 7, Miramar, Havana; tel. (7) 204-1506; fax (7) 204-1131; e-mail gamdan-hav@enet.cu; Ambassador AHMED AMIN MOHAMED ZAIDAN.

Zimbabwe: Avda 3, No 1001, esq. a 10, Miramar, Havana; tel. (7) 204-2857; fax (7) 204-2720; e-mail zimhavan@ip.etecsa.cu; Ambassador JEVANA BEN MASEKO.

Judicial System

The judicial system comprises the People's Supreme Court, the People's Provincial Courts and the People's Municipal Courts. The People's Supreme Court exercises the highest judicial authority.

PEOPLE'S SUPREME COURT

The People's Supreme Court comprises the Plenum, the six Courts of Justice in joint session and the Council of Government. When the Courts of Justice are in joint session they comprise all the professional and lay judges, the Attorney-General and the Minister of Justice. The Council of Government comprises the President and Vice-Presidents of the People's Supreme Court, the Presidents of each Court of Justice and the Attorney-General of the Republic. The Minister of Justice may participate in its meetings.

President: Dr RUBÉN REMIGIO FERRO.

Vice-Presidents: OSVALDO SÁNCHEZ MARTÍN, EMILIA GONZÁLEZ PÉREZ, EDUARDO RODRÍGUEZ GONZÁLEZ, PEDRO LUIS GONZÁLEZ CHÁVEZ.

Criminal Court
President: Dr JORGE L. BODES TORRES.

Civil and Administrative Court
President: CARLOS DÍAZ TENRREIRO.

Labour Court
President: Dr ANTONIO R. MARTÍN SÁNCHEZ.

Court for State Security
President: Dr GUILLERMO HERNÁNDEZ INFANTE.

Economic Court
President: NARCISO COBO ROURA.

Military Court
President: Col JUAN MARINO FUENTES CALZADO.

Attorney-General: JUAN ESCALONA REGUERA.

Religion

There is no established Church, and all religions are permitted, though Roman Catholicism predominates. The Afro-Cuban religions of Regla de Ocha (Santéria) and Regla Conga (Palo Monte) also have numerous adherents.

CHRISTIANITY

Consejo Ecuménico de Cuba (Ecumenical Council of Cuba): Calle 14, No 304, entre 3 y 5, Miramar, Playa, Havana; tel. (7) 33-1792; fax (7) 33-178820; f. 1941; 11 mem. churches; Pres. Rev. ORESTES GONZÁLEZ; Exec. Sec. Rev. JOSÉ LÓPEZ.

The Roman Catholic Church

Cuba comprises three archdioceses and eight dioceses. At 31 December 2002 there were 6,306,179 adherents, representing 51.2% of the total population.

Conferencia de Obispos Católicos de Cuba—COCC (Bishops' Conference)

Calle 26, No 314, entre 3 y 5, Miramar, Apdo 594, Havana; tel. (7) 29-2395; fax (7) 204-2168; e-mail adjunto@cocc.co.cu; internet www.celam.org/sitios/ce_cuba/COCC.htm.

f. 1983; Pres. Cardinal JAIME LUCAS ORTEGA Y ALAMINO (Archbishop of San Cristóbal de la Habana).

Archbishop of Camagüey: JUAN GARCÍA RODRÍGUEZ, Calle Luaces, No 55, Apdo 105, Camagüey 70100; tel. (322) 92268; fax (322) 87143; e-mail dei@cocc.co.cu.

Archbishop of San Cristóbal de la Habana: Cardinal JAIME LUCAS ORTEGA Y ALAMINO, Calle Habana No 152, esq. a Chacón, Apdo 594, Havana 10100; tel. (7) 62-4000; fax (7) 33-8109; e-mail cocc@brigadoo.com.

Archbishop of Santiago de Cuba: PEDRO CLARO MEURICE ESTÍU, Sánchez Hechevarría No 607, Apdo 26, Santiago de Cuba 90100; tel. (226) 25480; fax (226) 86186.

The Anglican Communion

Anglicans are adherents of the Iglesia Episcopal de Cuba (Episcopal Church of Cuba).

Bishop of Cuba: Rt Rev. JULIO CÉSAR HOLGUÍN KHOURY (acting), Calle 6, No 273, Vedado, Havana 10400; tel. (7) 832-1120; fax (7) 33-3293; e-mail episcopal@ip.etecsa.cu; internet www.cuba.anglican .org.

Protestant Churches

Convención Bautista de Cuba Oriental (Baptist Convention of Eastern Cuba): San Jerónimo, No 467, entre Calvario y Carnicería, Santiago de Cuba 90100; tel. (226) 62-0173; fax (226) 68-7010; e-mail maestra790@yahoo.com; internet www.cbcor.com; f. 1905; Pres. Rev. Dr ROY ACOSTA GARCÍA; Sec. Rev. IDALDO MATOS DELGADO.

Iglesia Metodista en Cuba (Methodist Church in Cuba): Calle K, No 502, 25 y 27, Vedado, Apdo 10400, Havana; tel. (7) 832-2991; fax (7) 833-3135; e-mail imecu@ip.etecsa.cu; autonomous since 1968; 6,000 mems; Bishop RICARDO PEREIRA DÍAZ.

Iglesia Presbiteriana Reformada en Cuba (Presbyterian-Reformed Church in Cuba): Salud 222, entre Lealtad y Campanario, Havana; tel. (7) 862-1219; fax (7) 833-8819; e-mail presbit@enet.cu; internet www.prccuba.org; f. 1890; 8,000 mems; Moderator Rev. Dr HÉCTOR MÉNDEZ.

Other denominations active in Cuba include the Apostolic Church of Jesus Christ, the Bethel Evangelical Church, the Christian Pentecostal Church, the Church of God, the Church of the Nazarene, the Free Baptist Convention, the Holy Pentecost Church, the Pentecostal Congregational Church and the Salvation Army.

The Press

DAILY

In October 1990 President Castro announced that, in accordance with other wide-ranging economic austerity measures, only one newspaper, *Granma*, would henceforth be published as a nation-wide daily. The other national dailies were to become weeklies or were to cease publication.

Granma: Avda Gen. Suárez y Territorial, Plaza de la Revolución, Apdo 6187, Havana; tel. (7) 881-3333; fax (7) 881-9854; e-mail correo@granma.cip.cu; internet www.granma.cubaweb.cu; f. 1965 to replace *Hoy* and *Revolución*; official Communist Party organ; Dir FRANK AGÜERO GÓMEZ; circ. 400,000.

PERIODICALS

Adelante: Avda A, Rpto Jayamá, Camagüey; e-mail adelante@ caonao.cmw.inf.cu; internet www.adelante.cu; f. 1959; Dir ZARITMA CARDOSO MORENO; circ. 42,000.

Ahora: Salida a San Germán y Circunvalación, Holguín; e-mail ahoraweb@ahora.cu; internet www.ahora.cu; f. 1962; Dir RADOBALDO MARTÍNEZ PÉREZ; circ. 50,000.

Alma Mater: Prado 553, esq. Teniente Ray, Habana Vieja, Havana; e-mail almamater@eabril.jovenclub.cu; internet www.almamater .cu; organ of the universities; Dir MARIO VIZCAÍNO SERRAT.

ANAP: Obispo 527, Apdo 605, Havana; f. 1961; monthly; information for small farmers; Editor RICARDO MACHADO; circ. 90,000.

Bastión: Territorial esq. a Gen. Suárez, Plaza de la Revolución, Havana; tel. (7) 79-3361; organ of the Revolutionary Armed Forces; Dir FRANK AGÜERO GÓMEZ; circ. 65,000.

Bohemia: Avda Independencia y San Pedro, Apdo 6000, Havana; tel. (7) 81-9213; fax (7) 33-5511; e-mail bohemia@bohemia.get.tur .cu; internet www.bohemia.cubaweb.cu; f. 1908; weekly; politics; Dir JOSÉ FERNÁNDEZ VEGA; circ. 100,000.

Boletín Alimentaria de Cuba: Amargura 103, 10100 Havana; tel. (7) 62-9245; f. 1996; quarterly; food industry; Dir ANTONIO CAMPOS; circ. 10,000.

El Caimán Barbudo: Paseo 613, Vedado, Havana; e-mail caiman@ eabril.jovenclub.cu; internet www.caimanbarbudo.cu; f. 1966; monthly; cultural; Dir FIDEL DÍAZ CASTRO; circ. 47,000.

Casa de las Américas: 3 y G Vedado, 10400 Havana; tel. (7) 55-2700; fax (7) 834-4554; e-mail camerica@camerica.co.cu; internet www.casa.cult.cu; f. 1959; 6 a year; cultural; Dir PABLO ARMANDO FERNÁNDEZ.

Cinco de Septiembre: Calle 63 y Circunvalación, 2°, Cienfuegos; tel. (7) 52-2636; e-mail cip219@cip.etecsa.cu; internet www .5septiembre.cu; f. 1980; Dir ALINA ROSELL CHONG; circ. 18,000.

Cómicos: Calle 28, No 112, entre 1 y 3, Miramar, Havana; tel. (7) 22-5892; monthly; humorous; circ. 70,000.

Cuba Internacional: Calle 21, No 406, entre F y G, Vedado, Havana; tel. (7) 832-3578; fax (7) 832-3268; e-mail cubainternac@ pubs.prensa-latina.cu; internet cubarevista.prensa-latina.cu; f. 1959; monthly; political; Editorial Dir ANA MARÍA RUIZ; circ. 30,000.

Dedeté: Territorial y Gen. Suárez, Plaza de la Revolución, Apdo 6344, Havana; tel. (7) 82-0134; fax (7) 81-8621; e-mail ddt@jrebelde .cip.cu; internet www.dedete.cubaweb.cu; f. 1969; monthly; Dir ALEN LAUZÁN; circ. 70,000.

La Demajagua: Amado Estévez, esq. Calle 10, Rpto R. Reyes, Bayamo; tel. (23) 42-4221; e-mail cip225@cip.enet.cu; internet www .lademajagua.co.cu; f. 1977; Dir LUIS CARLOS FRÓMETA AGÜERO; circ. 21,000.

El Deporte, Derecho del Pueblo: Vía Blanca y Boyeros, Havana; tel. (7) 40-6838; f. 1968; monthly; sport; Dir MANUEL VAILLANT CARPENTE; circ. 15,000.

El Economista: Asociación Nacional de Economistas de Cuba, Calle 22, No 901 esq. a 9, Miramar, Havana; tel. (7) 209-3303; fax (7) 202-3456; e-mail anec@info.get.cma.net; internet www.eleconomista .cubaweb.cu; monthly; business; Dir-Gen. ROBERTO VERRIER CASTRO.

Escambray: Adolfo del Castillo 10, Sancti Spíritus; tel. (41) 23003; e-mail cip220@cip.enet.cu; internet www.escambray.islagrande.cu; f. 1979; Dir JUAN ANTONIO BORREGO DÍAZ; circ. 21,000.

Girón: Avda Camilo Cienfuegos No 10505, P. Nuero, Matanzas; e-mail giron@ma.cc.cu; internet www.giron.co.cu; f. 1960; Dir CLOVIS ORTEGA CASTAÑEDA; circ. 25,000.

Guerrillero: Colón esq. Delicias y Adela Azcuy, Pinar del Río; e-mail cip216@cip.etecsa.cu; internet www.guerrillero.co.cu; f. 1969; Dir ERNESTO OSORIO ROQUE; circ. 33,000.

El Habanero: Gen. Suárez y Territorial, Plaza de la Revolución, Apdo 6269, Havana; tel. (7) 6160; e-mail internet@habanero.cip.cu; internet www.elhabanero.cubaweb.cu; f. 1987; Dir ANDRÉS HERNÁNDEZ RIVERO; circ. 21,000.

Industria Alimentica: Obispo 527, Apdo 605, Havana; tel. (7) 61-8453; f. 1968; quarterly; food industry; Editor CESAR VALDIVIA; circ. 10,000.

Invasor: Marcial Gómez 401, esq. Estrada Palma, Ciego de Avila; internet www.invasor.islagrande.cu; f. 1979; Dir MIGDALIA UTRERA PEÑA; circ. 10,500.

Juventud Rebelde: Avda Territorial y Gen. Suárez, Plaza de la Revolución, Apdo 6344, Havana; tel. (7) 882-0155; fax (7) 33-8959; e-mail cida@jrebelde.cip.cu; internet www.jrebelde.cubaweb.cu; f. 1965; organ of the Young Communist League; Dir ROGELIO POLANCO FUENTES; circ. 250,000.

Juventud Técnica: Prado 553, esq. Teniente Rey, Habana Vieja, Havana; tel. (7) 62-4330; e-mail jtecnica@eabril.jovenclub.cu; internet www.juventudtecnica.cu; f. 1965; every 2 months; scientific-technical; Dir MIRIAM ZITO VALDÉS; circ. 20,000.

Mar y Pesca: San Ignacio 303, entre Amargura y Teniente Rey, Habana Vieja, Havana; tel. (7) 861-5518; fax (7) 861-6280; e-mail marpesca@fishnavy.inf.cu; f. 1965; quarterly; fishing; Dir MARIO GUILLOT VEGA; circ. 20,000.

Moncada: Ministry of the Interior, Plaza de la Revolución, Havana; tel. (7) 830-1566; fax (7) 33-5261; f. 1966; monthly; government publication; Dir RICARDO MARTÍNEZ; circ. 70,000.

Muchacha: Galiano 264, esq. Neptuno, Havana; tel. (7) 861-5919; f. 1980; monthly; young women's magazine; Dir SILVIA MARTÍNEZ; circ. 120,000.

Mujeres: Galiano 264, entre Neptuno y Concordia, Havana; tel. (7) 861-5919; e-mail mujeres@teleda.get.tur.cu; internet www.mujeres .cubaweb.cu; f. 1961; monthly; women's magazine; Dir CAROLINA AGUILAR AYERRA; circ. 270,000.

El Muñe: Calle 28, No 112, entre 1 y 3, Miramar, Havana; tel. (7) 202-5892; weekly; circ. 50,000.

El Nuevo Fenix: Independencia 52, esq. a Honorato del Castillo, Sancti Spíritus; tel. (41) 27902; e-mail prelass@prensa-latina.cu; internet www.fenix.islagrande.cu; f. 1999; Dir YOLANDA BRITO.

Opciones: Territorial esq. Gen. Suárez, Plaza de la Revolucíon, Havana; tel. (7) 881-8934; fax (7) 881-8621; e-mail cida@jrebelde.cip .cu; internet www.opciones.cubaweb.cu; weekly; finance, commerce and tourism; Dir ROGELIO POLANCO FUENTES.

Opina: Edif. Focsa, M entre 17 y 19, Havana; f. 1979; 2 a month; consumer-orientated; published by Institute of Internal Demand; Dir EUGENIO RODRÍGUEZ BALARI; circ. 250,000.

Pablo: Calle 28, No 112, entre 1 y 3, Miramar, Havana; tel. (7) 22-5892; 16 a year; circ. 53,000.

Palante: Calle 21, No 954, entre 8 y 10, Vedado, Havana; tel. (7) 3-5098; e-mail palante@palan.cipcc.get.cma.net; f. 1961; weekly; humorous; Dir ROSENDO GUTIÉRREZ ROMÁN; circ. 235,000.

Periódico 26: Avda Carlos J. Finlay, Las Tunas; e-mail cip224@cip.enet.cu; internet www.periodico26.cu; Dir RAMIRO SEGURA GARCÍA.

Pionero: Calle 17, No 354, Havana; tel. (7) 32-4571; e-mail eabril@jcce.org.cu; internet www.pionero.cu; f. 1961; weekly; children's magazine; Editor PILAR DIGAT LANDROVE; circ. 210,000.

Prisma: Calle 21 y Avda G, No 406, Vedado, Havana; tel. (7) 832-3578; e-mail prisma@pubs.prensa-latina.cu; f. 1979; bimonthly; tourism; Man. Dir LUIS MANUEL ARCE; circ. 15,000 (Spanish), 10,000 (English).

RIL: O'Reilly 358, Havana; tel. (7) 62-0777; f. 1972; 2 a month; technical; Dir Exec. Council of Publicity Dept, Ministry of Light Industry; Chief Officer MIREYA CRESPO; circ. 8,000.

Sierra Maestra: Avda de Los Desfiles, Santiago de Cuba; tel. (7) 2-2813; e-mail cip226@cip.etecsa.cu; internet www.sierramaestra.cu; f. 1957; weekly; Dir ARNALDO CLAVEL CARMENATY; circ. 45,000.

Sol de Cuba: Calle 19, No 60, entre M y N, Vedado, Havana 4; tel. (7) 832-9881; f. 1983; every 3 months; Spanish, English and French editions; Gen. Dir ALCIDES GIRO MITJANS; Editorial Dir DORIS VÉLEZ; circ. 200,000.

Somos Jóvenes: Calle 17, No 354, esq. H, Vedado, Havana; tel. (7) 32-4571; e-mail eabril@jcce.org.cu; internet www.somosjovenes.cu; f. 1977; monthly; Dir YARELIS RICO; circ. 200,000.

Trabajadores: Territorial esq. Gen. Suárez, Plaza de la Revolución, Havana; tel. (7) 79-0819; fax (7) 55-5927; e-mail digital@trabaja.cip.cu; internet www.trabajadores.cubaweb.cu; f. 1970; organ of the trade-union movement; Dir JORGE LUIS CANELA CIURANA; circ. 150,000.

Tribuna de la Habana: Territorial esq. Gen. Suárez, Plaza de la Revolución, Havana; tel. (7) 881-8021; e-mail redac@tribuna.cip.cu; internet www.tribuna.islagrande.cu; f. 1980; weekly; Dir JESÚS ÁLVAREZ FERRER; circ. 90,000.

Vanguardia: Céspedes 5 (altos), Santa Clara, Matanzas; e-mail cip218@cip.enet.cu; internet www.vanguardia.co.cu; f. 1962; Dir PEDRO HERNÁNDEZ SOTO; circ. 24,000.

Venceremos: Avda Ernesto Che Guevara, Km 1½, Guantánamo; tel. (7) 32-5402; e-mail cip227@cip.enet.cu; internet www.venceremos.cubaweb.cu; f. 1962; economic, political and social publication for Guantánamo province; Dir ELIZABETH SANTIESTEBAN PÉREZ; circ. 33,500.

Ventiseis: Avda Carlos J. Finley, Las Tunas; f. 1977; Dir JOSÉ INFANTES REYES; circ. 21,000.

Verde Olivo: Avda de Rancho Boyeros y San Pedro, Havana; tel. (7) 79-8373; f. 1959; monthly; organ of the Revolutionary Armed Forces; Dir EUGENIO SUÁREZ PÉREZ; circ. 100,000.

Victoria: Carretera de la Fe, Km 1½, Plaza de la Revolución, Nueva Gerona, Isla de la Juventud; tel. (46) 32-4210; e-mail periodic@gerona.inf.cu; internet www.victoria.co.cu; f. 1967; Dir SERGIO RIVERO CARRASCO; circ. 9,200.

Zunzún: Obispo 527, Apdo 605, Havana; e-mail eabril@jcce.org.cu; internet www.zunzun.cu; f. 1990; children's magazine; Dir MARTHA RÍOS.

PRESS ASSOCIATIONS

Unión de Periodistas de Cuba: Avda 23, No 452, esq. I, Vedado, 10400 Havana; tel. (7) 32-4550; fax (7) 33-3079; e-mail cip307@cip.etecsa.cu; internet www.cubaperiodistas.cu; f. 1963; Pres. TUBAL PÁEZ HERNÁNDEZ.

Unión de Escritores y Artistas de Cuba: Calle 17, No 354, entre G y H, Vedado, Havana; tel. (7) 53-5081; fax (7) 33-3158; e-mail uneac@cubarte.cult.cu; internet www.uneac.com; Pres. RODULPHO VAILLANT; Exec. Vice-Pres. MIQUEL BARNET.

NEWS AGENCIES

Agencia de Información Nacional (AIN): Calle 23, No 358, esq. a J, Vedado, Havana; tel. (7) 32-5541; fax (7) 66-2049; e-mail web@ainch.ain.sld.cu; internet www.ain.cubaweb.cu; f. 1974; national news agency; Gen. Dir ESTEBAN RAMÍREZ ALONSO.

Prensa Latina (Agencia Informativa Latinoamericana, SA): Calle 23, No 201, esq. a N, Vedado, Havana; tel. (7) 55-3496; fax (7) 33-3069; e-mail dirdifu@prensa-latina.cu; internet www.prensa-latina.cu; f. 1959; Dir PEDRO MARGOLLES VILLANUEVA.

Foreign Bureaux

Agence France-Presse (AFP): Calle 17, No 4, 13°, entre N y O, Vedado, Havana; tel. (7) 33-3503; fax (7) 33-3034; e-mail mlsanz@ip.etecsa.cu; Bureau Chief MARIE SANZ.

Agencia EFE (Spain): Calle 36, No 110, entre 1 y 3, Miramar, Apdo 5, Havana; tel. (7) 204-2293; fax (7) 204-2272; e-mail efecuba@ip.etecsa.cu; Bureau Chief SOLEDAD MARÍN MARTÍN.

Agenzia Nazionale Stampa Associata (ANSA) (Italy): Edif. Someillán, Línea 5, Dpt 12, Vedado, Havana; tel. (8) 33-3542; e-mail ansacuba@enet.cu; internet www.ansa.it; Correspondent SILVINA SANTILLÁN.

Associated Press (AP) (USA): Lonja del Comercio, planta baja, Lamparilla 2, Local B, Habana Vieja, Havana; tel. (7) 33-0370; Correspondent ANITA SNOW.

Bulgarska Telegrafna Agentsia (BTA) (Bulgaria): Edif. Focsa, Calle 17, esq. M, Vedado, Apdo 22E, Havana; tel. (7) 32-4779; Bureau Chief VASIL MIKOULACH.

Česká tisková kancelář (ČTK) (Czech Republic): Edif. Fajardo, Calle 17 y M, Vedado, Apdo 3A, Vedado, Havana; tel. (7) 32-6101; Bureau Chief PAVEL ZOVADIL.

Deutsche Presse-Agentur (dpa) (Germany): Edif. Focsa, Calle 17 y M, Vedado, Apdo 2K, Havana; tel. (7) 33-3501; Bureau Chief VICTORIO COPA.

Informatsionnoye Telegrafnoye Agentstvo Rossii—Telegrafnoye Agentstvo Suverennykh Stran (ITAR—TASS) (Russia): Calle 96, No 317, entre 3 y 5, Miramar, Havana 4; tel. (7) 29-2528; Bureau Chief ALEKSANDR KANICHEV.

Inter Press Service (IPS) (Italy): Calle 36A, No 121 Bajos, esq. a 3, Miramar, Apdo 1, Havana; tel. (7) 22-1981; Bureau Chief CLAUDE JOSEPH HACKIN; Correspondent CARLOS BASTISTA MORENO.

Korean Central News Agency (Democratic People's Republic of Korea): Calle 10, No 613, esq. 25, Vedado, Apdo 6, Havana; tel. (7) 31-4201; Bureau Chief CHANG YON CHOL.

Magyar Távirati Iroda (MTI) (Hungary): Edif. Fajardo, Calle 17 y M, Apdo 2C, Havana; tel. (7) 32-8353; Bureau Chief ZOLTÁN TAKACS; Correspondent TIBOR CSÁSZÁR.

Novinska Agencija Tanjug (Serbia and Montenegro): Calle 5F, No 9801, esq. 98, Miramar, Havana; tel. (7) 22-7671; Bureau Chief DUŠAN DAKOVIĆ.

Polska Agencja Prasowa (PAP) (Poland): Calle 6, No 702, Apdo 5, entre 7 y 9, Miramar; Havana; tel. (7) 20-7067; Bureau Chief PIOTR SOMMERFED.

Reuters (United Kingdom): Edif. Someillán, Linea 5, 9°, Vedado, Havana; tel. (7) 33-3145; e-mail anthony.boadle@reuters.com; Bureau Chief ANTHONY BOADLE.

Rossiyskoye Informatsionnoye Agentstvo—Novosti (RIA—Novosti) (Russia): Calle 28, No 510, entre 5 y 7, Miramar, Havana; tel. (7) 22-4129; Bureau Chief YURII GOLOVIATENKO.

Viet Nam Agency (VNA): Calle 16, No 514, 1°, entre 5 y 7, Miramar, Havana; tel. (7) 32-4455; Bureau Chief PHAM DINH LOI.

Xinhua (New China) News Agency (People's Republic of China): Calle G, No 259, esq. 13, Vedado, Havana; tel. (7) 32-4616; Bureau Chief GAO YONGHUA.

Publishers

Artecubano Ediciones: Calle 3, No 1205, entre 12 y 14, Playa, Havana; tel. (7) 203-8581; fax (7) 204-2744; e-mail cnap@cubarte.cult.cu; Dir RAFAEL ACOSTA DE ARRIBA.

Casa de las Américas: Calle 3 y Avda G, Plaza de la Revolución, Vedado, 10400 Havana; tel. (7) 55-2716; fax (7) 832-7272; e-mail prensa@casa.cult.cu; internet www.casa.cult.cu; f. 1960; Latin American literature and social sciences; Dir PABLO ARMANDO FERNÁNDEZ.

Ediciones Creart: Calle 4, No 205, entre Línea y 11, Plaza de la Revolución, Vedado, Havana; tel. (7) 55-3496; fax (7) 33-3069; e-mail creart@cubarte.cult.cu; Dir TOMÁS VALDÉS BECERRA.

Ediciones Unión: Calle 17, No 354, entre G y H, Plaza de la Revolución, Vedado, 10400 Havana; tel. (7) 55-3112; fax (7) 33-3158; e-mail editora@uneac.co.cu; f. 1962; publishing arm of the Unión de Escritores y Artistas de Cuba; Cuban literature, art; Dir OLGA MARTA CABRERA.

Editora Abril: Prado 553, esq. Teniente Rey y Dragones, Habana Vieja, Havana; tel. (7) 862-7871; fax (7) 33-5282; e-mail eabril@jcce.org.cu; internet www.editoraabril.cu; f. 1980; attached to the Union of Young Communists; children's literature; Dir HERMINIO CAMACHO EIRANOVA.

Editora Política: Belascoaín No 864, esq. a Desagüe y Peñalver, Havana; tel. (7) 879-8553; fax (7) 881-1024; e-mail editora@epol .cipcc.get.cma.net; f. 1963; publishing institution of the Communist Party of Cuba; Dir Santiago Dórquez Pérez.

Editorial Academia: Industria y Barcelona, Capitolio Nacional, 4°, Habana Vieja, 10200 Havana; tel. and fax (7) 863-0315; e-mail editorial@gecyt.cu; f. 1963; attached to the Ministry of Science, Technology and the Environment; scientific and technical; Dir Gladys Hernández Herrera.

Editorial Arte y Literatura: Calle O' Reilly, No 4, esq. Tacón, Habana Vieja, Havana; tel. (7) 862-4326; fax (7) 33-8187; e-mail publicacions@icl.cult.cu; f. 1967; traditional Cuban literature and arts; Dir Elizabeth Díaz González.

Editorial Ciencias Médicas: Línea esq. 1, 10°, Vedado, 10400 Havana; tel. (7) 832-3863; fax (7) 33-3063; e-mail cnicm@infomed.sld .cu; attached to the Ministry of Public Health; books and magazines specializing in the medical sciences; Dir Guillermo Padrón González.

Editorial Ciencias Sociales: Calle 14, No 4104, entre 41 y 43, Miramar, Playa, Havana; tel. (7) 203-3959; fax (7) 33-3441; e-mail nuevomil@icl.cult.cu; f. 1967; attached to the Cuban Book Institute; social and political literature, history, philosophy, juridical sciences and economics; Dir Ernesto Escobar Soto.

Editorial Científico-Técnica: Calle 2, No 58, entre 3 y 5, Vedado, Havana; tel. (7) 3-9417; f. 1967; attached to the Ministry of Culture; technical and scientific literature; Dir Isidro Fernández Rodríguez.

Editorial Félix Varela: San Miguel No 1011, entre Mazón y Basarrate, Plaza de la Revolución, Vedado, 10400 Havana; tel. (7) 877-5617; fax (7) 73-5419; e-mail elsa@enpses.co.cu; Dir Elsa Rodríguez.

Editorial Gente Nueva: Calle 2, No 58, entre 3 y 5, Plaza de la Revolución, Vedado, 10400 Havana; tel. (7) 830-6548; fax (7) 33-8187; e-mail gentenueva@icl.cult.cu; internet www.cubaliteraria .com/icl/editoriales/gente_nueva; f. 1967; books for children; Dir Mirta González Gutiérrez.

Editorial José Martí: Calzada 259, entre I y J, Apdo 4208, Plaza de la Revolución, 10400 Havana; tel. (7) 832-9838; fax (7) 33-3441; e-mail editjmal@icl.cult.cu; f. 1983; attached to the Ministry of Culture; foreign-language publishing; Dir Lourdes González.

Editorial Letras Cubanas: Calle O'Reilly, No 4, esq. Tacón, Habana Vieja, 10100 Havana; tel. (7) 862-4378; fax (7) 33-8187; e-mail elc@icl.cult.cu; internet www.cubaliteraria.com/icl/ editoriales/letras_cubanas; f. 1977; attached to the Ministry of Culture; general, particularly classic and contemporary Cuban literature and arts; Dir Daniel García Santos.

Editorial Oriente: Santa Lucía 356, Santiago de Cuba; tel. (226) 22496; fax (226) 42387; e-mail edoriente@cultstgo.cult.cu; internet www.cubaliteraria.com; f. 1971; publishes works from the Eastern provinces; fiction, history, female literature and studies, art and culture, practical books and books for children; Dir Aida Bahr.

Editorial Pablo de la Torriente Brau: Calle 11, No 160, entre K y L, Plaza de la Revolución, Vedado, 10400 Havana; tel. (7) 832-7581; e-mail edpablo@eventos.cip.cu; f. 1985; publishing arm of the Unión de Periodistas de Cuba; Dir Irma de Armas Fonseca.

Editorial Pueblo y Educación: Avda 3A, No 4601, entre 46 y 60, Playa, Havana; tel. (7) 202-1490; fax (7) 204-0844; e-mail epe@ceniai .inf.cu; f. 1971; textbooks and educational publications; publishes Revista Educación three times a year (circ. 2,200); Dir Catalina Lajud Herrero.

Editorial Si-Mar: Calle 47, No 1210, entre 36 y Lindero, Plaza de la Revolución, Vedado, 10600 Havana; tel. (7) 881-8168; fax (7) 881-8523; e-mail edicion@simar.cu; Dir Elio Villareal Acevedo.

GOVERNMENT PUBLISHING HOUSES

Instituto Cubano del Libro: Palacio del Segundo Cabo, Calle O'Reilly, No 4, esq. a Tacón, Havana; tel. (7) 62-4789; fax (7) 33-8187; e-mail cclfilh@artsoft.cult.cu; internet www.cubaliteraria.com/icl; printing and publishing organization attached to the Ministry of Culture which combines several publishing houses and has direct links with others; presides over the National Editorial Council (CEN); Pres. Omar González Jiménez.

Oficina Publicaciones del Consejo de Estado: Calle 17, No 552, esq. a D, Plaza de la Revolución, Vedado, 10400 Havana; tel. (7) 55-1406; fax (7) 57-4578; e-mail palvarez@enet.cu; attached to the Council of State; books, pamphlets and other printed media on historical and political matters; Dir Pedro Alvarez Tabío.

Broadcasting and Communications

TELECOMMUNICATIONS

Empresa de Radiocomunicación y Radiodifusión (RADIO-CUBA): 406 entre Obispo y Obrapía, Habana Vieja, Havana; tel. (7) 860-7181; fax (7) 860-3107; e-mail dirgeneral@radiocuba.cu; internet www.radiocuba.cu; voice, mobile satellite and television radiocommunication services; Dir-Gen. Julio Antonio González García.

Empresa de Telecomunicaciones de Cuba, SA (ETECSA): Avda 5, entre 76 y 78, Edif. Barcelona, Miramar, Havana; tel. (7) 266-6203; fax (7) 860-5144; e-mail presidencia@etecsa.cu; internet www.etecsa.cu; f. 1991; 27% owned by Telecom Italia International, SpA; merged with Empresa de Telecomunicaciones Celulares del Caribe, SA (C-Com) and Teléfonos Celulares de Cuba, SA (CUBACEL) in 2003; Exec. Pres. José Antonio Fernández.

Instituto de Investigación y Desarrollo de las Telecomunicaciones (LACETEL): Avda Independencia, Km 14½, 1° de Mayo, Rancho Boyeros, Havana; tel. (7) 57-9265; fax (7) 33-5828; e-mail lacetel@lacetel.cu; internet www.lacetel.cu; Dir-Gen. Orlando Piñeira Oliva.

Ministerio de la Informática y las Comunicaciones (Dirección General de Telecomunicaciones): Avda Independencia y 19 de Mayo, Plaza de la Revolución, Havana; tel. (7) 81-7654; e-mail infosoc@mic.cu; internet www.mic.gov.cu; Dir Carlos Martínez Alburne.

Telecomunicaciones Móviles, SA (MOVITEL): Avda 47, No. 3405, Reparto Kohly, Havana; tel. (7) 204-8400; fax (7) 24-4264; e-mail asela@movitel.co.cu; internet www.movitel.co.cu; mobile telecommunications; Dir-Gen. Asela Fernández Lorenzo.

BROADCASTING

Ministerio de la Informática y las Comunicaciones (Dirección de Frecuencias Radioeléctricas): Avda Independencia y 19 de Mayo, Plaza de la Revolución, Havana; tel. (7) 81-7654; internet www.mic.gov.cu; Dir Carlos Martínez Alburne.

Instituto Cubano de Radio y Televisión (ICRT): Edif. Radiocentro, Avda 23, No 258, entre L y M, Vedado, Havana 4; tel. (7) 32-1568; fax (7) 33-3107; e-mail icrt@cecm.get.tur.cu; f. 1962; Pres. Ernesto López Domínguez.

Radio y Televisión Comercial: Calle 26, No 301, esq. 21, Vedado, Havana; tel. (7) 66-2719; fax (7) 33-3939; e-mail g.general@rtvc.com .cu; Dir René Duquesne López.

Radio

In 1997 there were five national networks and one international network, 14 provincial radio stations and 31 municipal radio stations, with a total of some 170 transmitters.

Radio Cadena Agramonte: Calle Cisneros, No 310, entre Ignacio Agramonte y General Gómez, Camagüey; tel. (322) 29-1195; e-mail cip240@cip.etecsa.cu; internet www.cadenagramonte.cubaweb.cu; digital radio; serves Camagüey; Dir Guillermo Pavón Pacheco.

Radio Enciclopedia: Calle N, No 266, entre 21 y 23, Vedado, Havana; tel. (7) 81-2809; e-mail enciclop@ceniai.inf.cu; internet www.radioenciclopedia.co.cu; f. 1962; national network; instrumental music programmes; 24 hours daily; Dir Edelsa Palacios Gordo.

Radio Habana Cuba: Infanta 105, Apdo 6240, Havana; tel. (7) 877-6628; fax (7) 881-2927; e-mail radiohc@enet.cu; internet www .radiohc.org; f. 1961; shortwave station; broadcasts in Spanish, English, French, Portuguese, Arabic, Esperanto, Quechua, Guaraní and Creole; Dir-Gen. Luis López.

CMBF (Radio Musical Nacional): Calle N, No 266, entre 21 y 23, Vedado, Plaza de la Revolución, Havana; tel. (7) 32-0085; e-mail musical@ceniai.inf.cu; f. 1948; national network; classical music programmes; 17 hours daily; Dir Luiz López-Quintana.

Radio Progreso: Infanta 105, esq. a 25, 6°, Apdo 3042, Havana; tel. (7) 70-4561; e-mail progreso@ceniai.inf.cu; internet www .radioprogreso.co.cu; f. 1929; national network; mainly entertainment and music; 24 hours daily; Dir Manuel E. Andrés Mazorra.

Radio Rebelde: Edif. ICRT, Avda 23, No 258, entre L y M, Vedado, Apdo 6277, Havana; tel. (7) 31-3514; fax (7) 33-4270; e-mail webrebelde@rrebelde.icrt.cu; internet www.radiorebelde.com.cu; f. 1958; merged with Radio Liberación in 1984; national network; 24-hour news and cultural programmes, music and sports; Dir-Gen. Gerardo Calderín Gaínza.

Radio Reloj: Edif. Radiocentro, Avda 23, No 258, entre L y M, Vedado, Havana; tel. (7) 55-4185; fax (7) 31-2706; e-mail radioreloj@ rreloj.icrt.cu; internet www.radioreloj.cu; f. 1947; national network; 24-hour news service; Dir Isidro Betancourt Silva.

Radio Taino: Edif. Radiocentro, Avda 23, No 258, entre L y M, Vedado, Havana; tel. (7) 55-4181; fax (7) 55-4490; e-mail radiotaino@89.1fm.cu; internet radiotaino.cubasi.cu; f. 1985; broadcasts in English and Spanish.

Television

Instituto Cubano de Radiodifusión (Televisión Nacional): Calle 23, No 258, Vedado, Havana; tel. (7) 55-4059; fax (7) 33-3107; f. 1950; broadcasts through four channels; Pres. ERNESTO LÓPEZ DOMÍNGUEZ.

Canal Educativo: Calle 23, No 258, Vedado, Havana; tel. (7) 55-4059; fax (7) 33-3107; f. 2002; broadcasts on channel 13; educational; Dir IVÁN BARRETO.

Cubavisión: Calle M, No 313, Vedado, Havana; e-mail info@cubavision.icrt.cu; internet www.cubavision.cubaweb.cu; broadcasts on channel 6.

Tele Rebelde: Mazón, No 52, Vedado, Havana; tel. (7) 32-3369; broadcasts on channel 2; Vice-Pres. GARY GONZÁLEZ.

CHTV: Habana Libre Hotel, Havana; f. 1990; subsidiary station of Tele-Rebelde; Dir ROSA MARÍA FERNÁNDEZ SOFÍA.

Finance

(cap. = capital; p.u. = paid up; res = reserves; dep. = deposits; m. = million; brs = branches)

BANKING

All banks were nationalized in 1960. Legislation establishing the national banking system was approved by the Council of State in 1984. A restructuring of the banking system, initiated in 1995, to accommodate Cuba's transformation to a more market-orientated economy, was proceeding in 2004. A new central bank, the Banco Central de Cuba (BCC), was created in 1997 to supersede the Banco Nacional de Cuba (BNC). The BCC was to be responsible for issuing currency, proposing and implementing monetary policy and the regulation of financial institutions. The BNC was to continue functioning as a commercial bank and servicing the country's foreign debt. The restructuring of the banking system also allowed for the creation of an investment bank, the Banco de Inversiones, to provide medium- and long-term financing for investment, and the Banco Financiero Internacional, SA, to offer short-term financing. A new agro-industrial and commercial bank was also to be created to provide services for farmers and co-operatives. The new banking system is under the control of Grupo Nueva Banca, which holds a majority share in each institution. In 2002 there were eight commercial banks, 18 non-banking financial institutions, 13 representative offices of foreign banks and four representative offices of non-banking financial institutions operating in Cuba.

Central Bank

Banco Central de Cuba (BCC): Calle Cuba, No 402, Aguiar 411, Habana Vieja, Havana; tel. (7) 860-4811; fax (7) 863-4061; e-mail plascncia@bc.gov.cu; internet www.bc.gov.cu; f. 1997; sole bank of issue; Pres. FRANCISCO SOBERÓN VALDEZ.

Commercial Banks

Banco de Crédito y Comercio (BANDEC): Amargura 158, entre Cuba y Aguiar, Habana Vieja, Havana; tel. (7) 861-4533; fax (7) 33-8968; e-mail ileana@oc.bandec.cu; Pres. ILEANA ESTÉVEZ.

Banco Exterior de Cuba: Calle 23, No 55, esq. a P, Vedado, Municipio Plaza, Havana; tel. (7) 55-0795; fax (7) 55-0794; e-mail bec@bec.co.cu; f. 1999; cap. 450m. pesos, res 2.8m. pesos, dep. 65.5m. pesos (Dec. 2002); Pres. JACOBO PEISON WEINER.

Banco Financiero Internacional, SA: Avda 5, No 9009, esq. 92, Miramar, Municipio Plaza, Havana; tel. (7) 267-5000; fax (7) 267-5002; e-mail bfi@bfi.com.cu; f. 1984; autonomous; finances Cuba's foreign trade; Pres. ERNESTO MEDINA; Gen. Man. (Int.) NIVALDO PULDÓN.

Banco Internacional de Comercio, SA: 20 de Mayo y Ayestarán, Apdo 6113, Havana 10600; tel. (7) 55-5482; fax (7) 66-6028; e-mail bicsa@bicsa.colombus.cu; f. 1993; cap. US $95.0m., res $11.3m., dep. $383.8m. (Dec. 2002); Chair. and Pres. MARCOS DÍAZ.

Banco Metropolitano: Avda 5 y Calle 112, Playa, Havana; tel. (7) 204-3869; fax (7) 204-9193; e-mail bm@banco-metropolitano.com; internet www.banco-metropolitano.com; f. 1996; offers foreign currency and deposit account facilities; Gen. Dir PEDRO DE LA ROSA GONZÁLEZ.

Banco Nacional de Cuba (BNC): Aguiar 456, entre Amargura y Lamparilla, Havana; tel. (7) 862-8896; fax (7) 66-9514; e-mail bancuba@bnc.cu; f. 1950; reorganized 1997; Chair. DIANA AMELIA FERNÁNDEZ VILA.

Foreign Banks

There are 13 foreign banks represented in Cuba, including Banco Bilbao Vizcaya Argentaria (Spain), Banco de Comercio Exterior de México, Banco Exterior de España, Banco Sabadell (Spain), ING Bank (Netherlands) and Société General de France.

Savings Bank

Banco Popular de Ahorro: Calle 16, No 306, entre 3 y 5, Miramar, Playa, Havana; tel. (7) 202-2545; fax (7) 204-1180; internet www.bancopopulardeahorro.com; f. 1983; savings bank; cap. 30m. pesos, dep. 5,363.7m. pesos; Pres. MANUEL VALE MARRERO; Sec. LOURDES PÉREZ SOLER; 520 brs.

Investment Bank

Banco de Inversiones, SA: Avda 5, No 6802, Miramar, Havana; ; tel. (7) 204-3373; fax (7) 204-3377; e-mail inversiones@bdi.cu; Pres. RAÚL RANGEL.

INSURANCE

State Organizations

Empresa del Seguro Estatal Nacional (ESEN): Calle 5, No 306, entre C y D, Vedado, Havana; tel. (7) 32-2500; fax (7) 33-8717; e-mail esen@esen.com.cu; internet www.esen.com.cu; f. 1978; motor and agricultural insurance; Dir-Gen. RAFAEL J. GONZALEZ PÉREZ.

Seguros Internacionales de Cuba, SA (Esicuba): Cuba No 314, entre Obispo y Obrapía, Habana Vieja, Havana; tel. (7) 33-8400; fax (7) 33-8038; e-mail esicuba@esicuba.cu; f. 1963; reorganized 1986; all classes of insurance except life; Pres. RAMÓN MARTÍNEZ CARRERA.

Trade and Industry

GOVERNMENT AGENCIES

Ministry of Foreign Investment and Economic Co-operation: 512 Calle 30, entre 22 y 24, Miramar, Havana; tel. (7) 202-3873; fax (7) 204-2105; e-mail epinv@minvec.cu.

Free-Trade Zones National Office: Calle 22, No 528, entre 3 y 5, Miramar, Havana; tel. (7) 204-7636; fax (7) 204-7637.

CHAMBER OF COMMERCE

Cámara de Comercio de la República de Cuba: Calle 21, No 661/701, esq. Calle A, Apdo 4237, Vedado, Havana; tel. (7) 55-1321; fax (7) 33-3042; e-mail pdcia@camara.com.cu; internet www.camaracuba.cu; f. 1963; mems include all Cuban foreign trade enterprises and the most important agricultural and industrial enterprises; Pres. BERTHA DELGADO GUANCHE GARCÍA; Sec.-Gen. FRANK ABEL PORTELA.

AGRICULTURAL ORGANIZATION

Asociación Nacional de Agricultores Pequeños (ANAP) (National Association of Small Farmers): Calle I, No 206, entre Linea y 13, Vedado, Havana; tel. (7) 32-4541; fax (7) 33-4244; f. 1961; 220,000 mems; Pres. ORLANDO LUGO FONTE; Vice-Pres. EVELIO PAUSA BELLO.

STATE IMPORT-EXPORT BOARDS

Alimport (Empresa Cubana Importadora de Alimentos): Infanta 16, 3°, Apdo 7006, Havana; tel. (7) 54-2501; fax (7) 33-3151; e-mail precios@alimport.com.cu; f. 1962; controls import of foodstuffs and liquors; Man. Dir PEDRO ALVAREZ BORREGO.

Autoimport (Empresa Central de Abastecimiento y Venta de Equipos de Transporte Ligero): Galiano 213, entre Concordia y Virtudes, Havana; tel. (7) 61-5322; fax (7) 66-6549; e-mail eric@autoimport.com.cu; imports cars, light vehicles, motor cycles and spare parts; Dir JOSÉ ARAÑABURU.

Aviaimport (Empresa Cubana Importadora y Exportadora de Aviación): Calle 182, No 126, entre 1 y 5, Rpto Flores, Playa, Havana; tel. (7) 33-0142; fax (7) 33-6234; e-mail aviaimport@avianet.cu; import and export of aircraft and components; Man. Dir MARCOS LAGO MARTÍNEZ.

Caribex (Empresa Exportadora del Caribe): Aparthotel Las Brisas, Apdo 3c23, Villa Panamericana, Havana; tel. (7) 95-1121; fax (7) 95-1120; e-mail acepex@acepex.telemar.cu; internet www1.cubamar.cu; export of seafood and marine products; Dir JACINTO FIERRO BAREFOOT.

Construimport (Empresa Central de Abastecimiento y Venta de Equipos de Construcción y sus Piezas): Carretera de Varona, Km 1½, Capdevila, Havana; tel. (7) 45-2567; fax (7) 66-6180; e-mail construimport@colombus.cu; f. 1969; controls the import and export of construction machinery and equipment; Man. Dir JESÚS SERRANO RODRÍGUEZ.

Consumimport (Empresa Cubana Importadora de Artículos de Consumo General): Calle 23, No 55, 9°, Apdo 6427, Vedado, Havana; tel. (7) 54-3110; fax (7) 54-2142; e-mail comer@consumimport .infocex.cu; f. 1962; imports and exports general consumer goods; Dir MERCEDES REY HECHAVARRÍA.

Copextel (Corporación Productora y Exportadora de Tecnología Electrónica): Calle 194 y 7A, Siboney, Havana; tel. (7) 21-8400; fax (7) 33-1414; e-mail copextel@copextel.com.cu; internet www.copextel .com.cu; f. 1986; exports LTEL personal computers and micro-computer software; Dir NORMA M. GARCÍA BRUZÓN.

Coprefil (Empresa Comercial y de Producciones Filatélicas): Avda 49, No 2831, Reparto Kohly, Havana; tel. (7) 204-9668; fax (7) 204-5077; e-mail coprefil@coprefil.cu; imports and exports postage stamps, postcards, calendars, handicrafts, communications equipment, electronics, watches, etc.; Dir NELSON IGLESIAS FERNÁNDEZ.

Cubaelectrónica (Empresa Importadora y Exportadora de Productos de la Electrónica): Calle 22, No 510, entre 5 y 7, Miramar, Havana; tel. (7) 204-0178; fax (7) 204-1233; e-mail mariaisabel@ columbus.cu; f. 1986; imports and exports electronic equipment and devices; Pres. MARÍA ISABEL MOREJÓN PÉREZ.

Cubaexport (Empresa Cubana Exportadora de Alimentos y Productos Varios): Calle 23, No 55, entre Infanta y P, 8°, Vedado, Apdo 6719, Havana; tel. (7) 54-3130; fax (7) 33-3587; e-mail cexport@ infocex.cu; export of foodstuffs and industrial products; Man. Dir MILDA PICOS RIVERS.

Cubafrutas (Empresa Cubana Exportadora de Frutas Tropicales): Calle 23, No 55, Apdo 6683, Vedado, Havana; tel. and fax (7) 79-5653; f. 1979; controls export of fruits, vegetables and canned foodstuffs; Dir JORGE AMARO MOREJÓN.

Cubalse (Empresa para Prestación de Servicios al Cuerpo Diplomático): Avda 3 y Final, Miramar, Havana; tel. (7) 204-2284; fax (7) 204-2282; e-mail cubalse@cm.cubalse.cma.net; internet www .cubalse.cu; f. 1974; imports consumer goods for the diplomatic corps and foreign technicians residing in Cuba; exports beverages and tobacco, leather goods and foodstuffs; other operations include real estate, retail trade, restaurants, clubs, automobile business, state-of-the-art equipment and household appliances, construction, investments, wholesale, road transport, freight transit, shipping, publicity, photography and video, financing, legal matters; Pres. REIDAL RONCOURT FONT.

Cubametales (Empresa Cubana Importadora de Metales, Combustibles y Lubricantes): Infanta 16, 4°, Apdo 6917, Vedado, Havana; tel. (7) 70-4225; fax (7) 33-3477; e-mail pedro@cubametal.infocex.cu; controls import of metals (ferrous and non-ferrous), crude petroleum and petroleum products; also engaged in the export of petroleum products and ferrous and non-ferrous scrap; Dir PEDRO PEREZ RODRÍGUEZ.

Cubaniquel (Empresa Cubana Exportadora de Minerales y Metales): Calle 23, No 55, 8°, Apdo 6128, Havana; tel. (7) 33-5334; fax (7) 33-3332; e-mail bcorrea@moa.minbas.cu; f. 1961; sole exporter of minerals and metals; Man. Dir RICARDO GONZÁLEZ.

Cubatabaco (Empresa Cubana del Tabaco): Calle O'Reilly, No 104, Apdo 6557, Havana; tel. (7) 861-5775; fax (7) 33-8214; e-mail juan@ cubatabaco.cu; f. 1962; controls export of leaf tobacco, cigars and cigarettes to France; Dir JUAN MANUEL DÍAZ TENORIO.

Cubatécnica (Empresa de Contratación de Asistencia Técnica): Calle 12, No 513, entre 5 y 7, Miramar, Havana; tel. (7) 22-3270; fax (7) 24-0923; e-mail info@cubatecnica.cu; internet www.cubatecnica .cu; f. 1976; controls export and import of technical assistance; Dir FÉLIX GONZÁLEZ NAVERÁN.

Cubatex (Empresa Cubana Importadora de Fibras, Tejidos, Cueros y sus Productos): Calle 23, No 55, Apdo 7115, Vedado, Havana; tel. (7) 70-2531; fax (7) 33-3321; controls import of fibres, textiles, hides and by-products and export of fabric and clothing; Dir LUISA AMPARO SESÍN VIDAL.

Cubazúcar (Empresa Cubana Exportadora de Azúcar y sus Derivados): Calle 23, No 55, 7°, Vedado, Apdo 6647, Havana; tel. (7) 54-2175; fax (7) 33-3482; e-mail producer@cubazucar.com; internet www.cubazucar.com; f. 1962; controls export of sugar, molasses and alcohol; Pres. JOSÉ LÓPEZ SILVERO.

Ecimact (Empresa Comercial de Industrias de Materiales, Construcción y Turismo): Calle 1C, entre 152 y 154, Miramar, Havana; tel. (7) 21-9783; controls import and export of engineering services and plant for industrial construction and tourist complexes; Dir OCTAVIO CASTILLA CANGAS.

Ecimetal (Empresa Importadora y Exportadora de Objetivos Industriales): Calle 23, No 55, esq. Plaza, Vedado, Havana; tel. (7) 55-0548; fax (7) 33-4737; e-mail ecimetal@infocex.cu; f. 1977; controls import and export of plant, equipment and raw materials for all major industrial sectors; Dir CONCEPCIÓN BUENO.

Ediciones Cubanas (Empresa de Comercio Exterior de Publicaciones): Obispo 527, Apdo 43, Havana; tel. (7) 863-1942; fax (7) 33-8943; e-mail ediuba@cubarte.cult.cu; controls import and export of books and periodicals; Dir NANCY MATOS LACOSTA.

Egrem (Estudios de Grabaciones y Ediciones Musicales): Avda 3, No 1008, entre 10 y 12, Miramar, Playa, Havana; tel. (7) 204-1925; fax (7) 204-2519; e-mail relaciones@egrem.cult.cu; f. 1964; controls the import and export of records, tapes, printed music and musical instruments; Dir Gen. JULIO BALLESTER GUZMÁN.

Emexcon (Empresa Importadora y Exportadora de la Construcción): Calle 25, No 2602, esq. a 26, Playa, Havana; tel. (7) 204-2263; fax (7) 204-1862; e-mail enrique@emexcon.com.cu; f. 1978; consulting engineer services, contracting, import and export of building materials and equipment; Dir ENRIQUE MARTÍNEZ DE LA FÉ.

Emiat (Empresa Importadora y Exportadora de Suministros Técnicos): Avda 47, No 2828, entre 28 y 34, Rpto Kohly, Havana; tel. (7) 203-0345; fax (7) 204-9353; e-mail emiat@enet.cu; f. 1983; imports technical materials, equipment and special products; exports furniture, kitchen utensils and accessories; Man. FIDEL GARCÍA HERNÁNDEZ.

Emidict (Empresa Especializada Importadora, Exportadora y Distribuidora para la Ciencia y la Técnica): Calle 16, No 102, esq. Avda 1, Miramar, Playa, 13000 Havana; tel. (7) 203-5316; fax (7) 204-1758; e-mail emidict@ceniai.inf.cu; internet www.emidict.com.cu; f. 1982; controls import and export of scientific and technical products and equipment, live animals; scientific information; Dir-Gen. CARLOS CANALES ENRÍQUEZ.

Energoimport (Empresa Importadora de Objetivos Electro-energéticos): Amenidad No 124, entre Nueva y 20 de Mayo, Municipio Cerro, 10600 Havana; tel. (7) 70-2501; fax (7) 66-6079; e-mail energoimport@energonet.com.cu; internet www.energonet.com.cu; f. 1977; controls import of equipment for electricity generation; Man. ANDRÉS MONTEZ PERRERA.

Eprob (Empresa de Proyectos para las Industrias de la Básica): Avda 31A, No 1805, entre 18 y 20, Edif. Las Ursulinas, Miramar, Playa, Apdo 12100, Havana; tel. (7) 202-5562; fax (7) 204-2146; f. 1967; exports consulting services and processing of engineering construction projects, consulting services and supplies of complete industrial plants and turn-key projects; Man. Dir GLORIA EXPÓSITO DÍAZ.

Eproyiv (Empresa de Proyectos para Industrias Varias): Calle 33, No 1815, entre 18 y 20, Playa, Havana; tel. (7) 24-2149; e-mail eproyiv@ceniai.inf.cu; f. 1967; consulting services, feasibility studies, development of basic and detailed engineering models, project management and turn-key projects; Dir MARTA ELENA HERNÁNDEZ DÍAZ.

Esi (Empresa de Suministros Industriales): Calle Aguiar, No 556, entre Teniente Rey y Muralla, Havana; tel. (7) 62-0696; fax (7) 33-8951; f. 1985; imports machinery, equipment and components for industrial plants; Dir-Gen. FRANCISCO DÍAZ CABRERA.

Fecuimport (Empresa Cubana Importadora y Exportadora de Ferrocarriles): Avda 7A, No 6209, entre 62 y 66, Apdo 6003, Miramar, Havana; tel. (7) 203-3764; f. 1968; imports and exports railway equipment; Pres. DOMINGOS HERRERA.

Ferrimport (Empresa Cubana Importadora de Artículos de Ferretería): Calle 23, No 55, 2°, Vedado, Apdo 6258, Havana; tel. (7) 870-6678; fax (7) 879-4417; f. 1965; importers of industrial hardware; Dir-Gen. ALEJANDRO MUSTELIER.

Fondo Cubano de Bienes Culturales: Calle 36, No 4702, esq. Avda 47, Reparto Kohly, Playa, Havana; tel. (7) 23-6523; fax (7) 24-0391; e-mail fcbc@cubarte.cult.cu; f. 1978; controls export of fine handicraft and works of art; Dir-Gen. JOSÉ GONZÁLEZ FERNÁNDEZ-LARREA.

Habanos, SA: Avda 3, No 2006, entre 20 y 22, Miramar, Havana; tel. (7) 204-0510; fax (7) 204-0490; e-mail habanos@habanos.cu; internet www.habanos.net; f. 1994; controls export of leaf and pipe tobacco, cigars and cigarettes to all markets; jt venture with Altadis, SA (Spain).

ICAIC (Instituto Cubano del Arte e Industria Cinematográficos): Calle 23, No 1155, Vedado, Havana 4; tel. (7) 55-3128; fax (7) 33-3032; f. 1959; production, import and export of films and newsreel; Dir ANTONIO RODRÍGUEZ RODRÍGUEZ.

Imexin (Empresa Importadora y Exportadora de Infraestructura): Avda 5, No 1007, esq. a 12, Miramar, Havana; tel. (7) 204-0658; fax (7) 204-0622; e-mail imexinsa@ceniai.inf.cu; f. 1977; controls import and export of infrastructure; Man. Dir RAÚL BENCE VIJANDE.

Imexpal (Empresa Importadora y Exportadora de Plantas Alimentarias, sus Complementos y Derivados): Calle 22, No 313, entre 3 y 5, Miramar, Havana; tel. (7) 29-1671; controls import and export of food-processing plants and related items; Man. Dir Ing. CONCEPCIÓN BUENO CAMPOS.

Maprinter (Empresa Cubana Importadora y Exportadora de Materias Primas y Productos Intermedios): Infanta 16, 2A, Apdo 2110, Havana; tel. (7) 854-2971; fax (7) 833-3535; e-mail direccion@maprinter.infocex.cu; f. 1962; controls import and export of raw materials and intermediate products; Dir-Gen. ODALYS ALDAMA.

Maquimport (Empresa Cubana Importadora de Maquinarias y Equipos): Calle 23, No 55, 6°, entre P y Infanta, Vedado, Apdo 6052, Havana; tel. (7) 55-0635; fax (7) 873-5443; e-mail maquimport@infocex.cu; imports industrial goods and equipment; Dir JORGE MIGUEL HERNÁNDEZ.

Marpesca (Empresa Cubana Importadora y Exportadora de Buques Mercantes y de Pesca): Conill No 580, esq. Avda 26, Nuevo Vedado, Havana; tel. (7) 881-1846; fax (7) 879-1010; f. 1978; imports and exports ships and port and fishing equipment; Pres. JOSÉ CEREIJO CASAS.

Medicuba (Empresa Cubana Importadora y Exportadora de Productos Médicos): Máximo Gómez 1, esq. a Egido, Havana; tel. (7) 62-4061; fax (7) 33-8516; e-mail alfonso@medicuba.sld.cu; enterprise for the export and import of medical and pharmaceutical products; Dir ALFONSO SÁNCHEZ DÍAZ.

Produimport (Empresa Central de Abastecimiento y Venta de Productos Químicos y de la Goma): Calle Consulado 262, entre Animas y Virtudes, Havana; tel. (7) 62-0581; fax (7) 62-9588; f. 1977; imports and exports spare parts for motor vehicles; Dir JOSÉ GUERRA MATOS.

Quimimport (Empresa Cubana Importadora y Exportadora de Productos Químicos): Calle 23, No 55, entre Infanta y P, Apdo 6088, Vedado, Havana; tel. (7) 33-3394; fax (7) 33-3190; e-mail global@quimimport.infocex.cu; controls import and export of chemical products; Dir ARMANDO BARRERA MARTÍNEZ.

Suchel (Empresa de Jabonería y Perfumería): Calzada de Buenos Aires 353, esq. a Durege, Apdo 6359, Havana; tel. (7) 649-8008; fax (7) 649-5311; e-mail direccion@suchel.co.cu; internet www.suchel.cu; f. 1977; imports materials for the detergent, perfumery and cosmetics industry, exports cosmetics, perfumes, hotel amenities and household products; Dir JOSÉ GARCÍA DÍAZ.

Tecnoazúcar (Empresa de Servicios Técnicos e Ingeniería para la Agro-industria Azucarera): Calle 12, No 310, entre 3 y 5, Miramar, Playa, Havana; tel. (7) 29-5441; fax (7) 33-1218; e-mail promocion@tecnoazucar.cu; imports machinery and equipment for the sugar industry, provides technical and engineering assistance for the sugar industry; exports sugar-machinery equipment and spare parts; provides engineering and technical assistance services for sugar-cane by-product industry; Gen. Man. VICTOR R. HERNÁNDEZ MARTÍNEZ.

Tecnoimport (Empresa Importadora y Exportadora de Productos Técnicos): Edif. La Marina, Avda del Puerto 102, entre Justiz y Obrapía, Habana Vieja, Havana; tel. (7) 861-5552; fax (7) 66-9777; e-mail celeste@ti.gae.com.cu; f. 1968; imports technical products; Dir ADEL IZQUIERDO RODRÍGUEZ.

Tecnotex (Empresa Cubana Exportadora e Importadora de Servicios, Artículos y Productos Técnicos Especializados): Avda 47, No 3419, Playa, Havana; tel. (7) 861-3536; fax (7) 66-6270; e-mail ailede@tecnotex.qae.com.cu; f. 1983; imports specialized technical and radiocommunications equipment, exports outdoor equipment and geodetic networks; Dir RENÉ ROJAS RODRÍGUEZ.

Tractoimport (Empresa Central de Abastecimiento y Venta de Maquinaria Agrícola y sus Piezas de Repuesto): Avda Rancho Boyeros y Calle 100, Apdo 7007, Havana; tel. (7) 45-2166; fax (7) 267-0786; e-mail direccion@tractoimport.colombus.cu; f. 1960 for the import of tractors and agricultural equipment; also exports pumps and agricultural implements; Dir ABDEL GARCÍA GONZÁLEZ.

Transimport (Empresa Central de Abastecimiento y Venta de Equipos de Transporte Pesados y sus Piezas): Calle 102 y Avda 63, Marianao, Apdo 6665, 11500 Havana; tel. (7) 260-0329; fax (7) 267-9050; e-mail direccion@transimport.co.cu; f. 1968; controls import and export of vehicles and transportation equipment; Dir-Gen. JUAN CARLOS TASSÉ BELLOT.

UTILITIES

Electricity

Unión Nacional Eléctrica (UNE): Havana; public utility.

Water

Instituto Nacional de Recursos Hidraulicos (INRH) (National Water Resources Institute): Virtudes 680, esq. Belascoain, Havana; regulatory body; Vice-Pres. AYMEE AGUIRRE HERNÁNDEZ.

TRADE UNIONS

All workers have the right to become members of a national trade union according to their industry and economic branch.

The following industries and labour branches have their own unions: Agriculture, Chemistry and Energetics, Civil Workers of the Revolutionary Armed Forces, Commerce and Gastronomy, Communications, Construction, Culture, Defence, Education and Science, Food, Forestry, Health, Light Industry, Merchant Marine, Mining and Metallurgy, Ports and Fishing, Public Administration, Sugar, Tobacco and Transport.

Central de Trabajadores de Cuba (CTC) (Confederation of Cuban Workers): Palacio de los Trabajadores, San Carlos y Peñalver, Havana; tel. (7) 78-4901; fax (7) 55-5927; e-mail digital@trabaja.cip.cu; internet www.trabajadores.cubaweb.cu; f. 1939; affiliated to WFTU and CPUSTAL; 19 national trade unions affiliated; Gen. Sec. PEDRO ROSS LEAL; 2,767,806 mems (1996).

Transport

The Ministry of Transportation controls all public transport.

RAILWAYS

The total length of railways in 1998 was 14,331 km, of which 9,638 km were used by the sugar industry. The remaining 4,520 km were public service railways operated by Ferrocarriles de Cuba. All railways were nationalized in 1960. In 2001 Cuba signed an agreement with Mexico for the maintenance and repair of rolling stock.

Ferrocarriles de Cuba: Edif. Estación Central, Egido y Arsenal, Havana; tel. (7) 70-1076; fax (7) 33-1489; f. 1960; operates public services; Dir-Gen. FERNANDO PÉREZ LÓPEZ; divided as follows:

División Occidente: serves Pinar del Río, Ciudad de la Habana, Havana Province and Matanzas.

División Centro: serves Villa Clara, Cienfuegos and Sancti Spíritus.

División Centro-Este: serves Camagüey, Ciego de Avila and Tunas.

División Oriente: serves Santiago de Cuba, Granma, Guantánamo and Holguín.

División Camilo Cienfuegos: serves part of Havana Province and Matanzas.

ROADS

In 1999 there were an estimated 60,858 km of roads, of which 4,353 km were highways or main roads. The Central Highway runs from Pinar del Río in the west to Santiago, for a length of 1,144 km. In addition to this paved highway, there are a number of secondary and 'farm-to-market' roads. A small proportion of these secondary roads is paved, but many can be used by motor vehicles only during the dry season.

SHIPPING

Cuba's principal ports are Havana (which handles 60% of all cargo), Santiago de Cuba, Cienfuegos, Nuevitas, Matanzas, Antilla, Guayabal and Mariel. Maritime transport has developed rapidly since 1959, and at 31 December 2003 Cuba had a merchant fleet of 90 ships (with a total displacement of 90,179 grt). In 2000 a US $100m. renovation and enlargement project for the port of Mariel was announced.

Coral Container Lines, SA: Calle Oficios 170, 1°, Habana Vieja, Havana; tel. (7) 67-0854; fax (7) 67-0850; e-mail info@coral.com.cu; internet www.coral.cubaweb.cu; f. 1994; liner services to Europe, Canada, Brazil and Mexico; 11 containers; Chair. and Man. Dir EVELIO GONZÁLEZ GONZÁLEZ.

Empresa Consignataria Mambisa: San José No 65, entre Prado y Zulueta, Habana Vieja, Havana; tel. (7) 862-2061; fax (7) 33-8111; e-mail mercedes@mambisa.transnet.cu; shipping agent, bunker suppliers; Man. Dir MERCEDES PÉREZ NEWHALL.

Empresa Cubana de Fletes (Cuflet): Calle Oficios No 170, entre Teniente Rey y Amargura, Apdo 6755, Havana; tel. (7) 61-2604; freight agents for Cuban cargo; Man. Dir CARLOS SÁNCHEZ PERDOMO.

Empresa de Navegación Caribe (Navecaribe): Calle San Martín, No 65, 4°, entre Agramonte y Pasco de Martí, Habana Vieja, Havana; tel. (7) 61-8611; fax (7) 33-8564; e-mail enccom@transnet.cu; f. 1966; operates Cuban coastal fleet; Dir RAMÓN DURÁN SUÁREZ.

Empresa de Navegación Mambisa: San Ignacio No 104, Apdo 543, Havana; tel. (7) 869-7901; fax (7) 61-0044; operates dry cargo, reefer and bulk carrier vessels; Gen. Man. GUMERSINDO GONZÁLEZ FELIÚ.

Naviera del Caribe (Carimar): Ofs 170, entre Amargura y Teniente Rey, 3°, Habana Vieja, Havana; tel. (7) 57-0925; fax (7) 204-8627; e-mail tbrito@coral.com.cu.

Naviera Frigorífica Marítima (Friomar): 5a Avda y 240, Barlovento, Playa, Havana; tel. (7) 209-8171; fax (7) 204-5864; e-mail friocom@fishnavy.inf.cu; specializes in shipping of refrigerated cargo; Dir JORGE FERNÁNDEZ.

Naviera Mar América: 5a Avda y 246, Edif. No 3, 1°, Barlovento, Playa, Havana; tel. (7) 204-8076; fax (7) 204-8889; e-mail nubia@maramerica.fishnavy.inf.eu.

Naviera Petrocost: 5a Avda y 246, Barlovento, Playa, Havana; tel. (7) 209-8067; fax (7) 204-5113; e-mail aleida@petrocost.fishnavy.inf.cu; transports liquid cargo to domestic and international destinations.

Naviera Poseidon: 5a Avda y 246, Edif. No 3, 2°, Barlovento, Playa, Havana; tel. (7) 209-8073; fax (7) 204-8627; e-mail yepe@poseidon.fishnavy.inf.cu.

Nexus Reefer: 5a Avda y 246, Edif. No 7, 1°, Barlovento, Playa, Havana; tel. (7) 204-8205; fax (7) 204-8490; e-mail sandra@antares.fishnavy.inf.cu; merchant reefer ships; Gen. Dir QUIRINO L. GUTIÉRREZ LÓPEZ.

CIVIL AVIATION

There are a total of 21 civilian airports, with 11 international airports, including Havana, Santiago de Cuba, Camagüey, Varadero and Holguín. Abel Santamaría International Airport opened in Villa Clara in early 2001. In January 2003 the King's Gardens International Airport in Cayo Coco was opened. The airport formed part of a new tourist 'offshore' centre. The international airports were all upgraded and expanded during the 1990s and a third terminal was constructed at the José Martí International Airport in Havana. In November 2001 three North American airlines were permitted to commence direct flights from Miami and New York to Havana.

Aerocaribbean: Calle 23, No 64 esq. a P, Vedado, Havana; tel. (7) 33-4543; fax (7) 33-5016; e-mail vpcr@cacsa.avianet.cu; f. 1982; international and domestic charter services; Chair. JULIÁN ALVAREZ INFIESTA.

Aerogaviota: Avda 47, No 2814, entre 28 y 34, Reparto Kolhy, Havana; tel. (7) 203-0668; fax (7) 204-2621; e-mail vpcom@aerogaviota.avianet.cu; f. 1994; operated by Cuban air force.

Empresa Consolidada Cubana de Aviación (Cubana): Calle 23, No 64, esq. a Infanta, Vedado, Havana; tel. (7) 33-4949; fax (7) 33-4056; e-mail vpcom@cubana.avianet.cu; internet www.cubana.cu; f. 1929; international services to North America, Central America, the Caribbean, South America and Europe; internal services from Havana to 14 other cities; Gen. Dir HERIBERTO PRIETO.

Instituto de Aeronáutica Civil de Cuba (IACC): Calle 23, No 64, Plaza de la Revolución, Vedado, Havana; tel. (7) 33-4949; fax (7) 33-4553; e-mail iacc@avianet.cu; internet www.cubagob.cu/des_eco/iacc/home.htm; f. 1985; Pres. ROGELIO ACEVEDO GONZÁLEZ.

Tourism

Tourism began to develop after 1977, with the easing of travel restrictions by the USA, and Cuba subsequently attracted European tourists. In 2000 the number of hotel rooms had increased to 34,000. In that year there were 189 hotels. A number of hotel tourism complexes were under construction in the early 2000s. In 2001 1,774,541 tourists visited the island. The number of tourists decreased to approximately 1,686,100 in 2002, when receipts from tourism totalled an estimated US $1,769m. In that year there were approximately 40,000 hotel rooms. It was feared that the tightening of restrictions on travel to Cuba by the USA in mid-2004 would have an adverse effect upon the continued development of the country's tourism sector.

Cubanacán: Calle 148, entre 11 y 13, Playa, Apdo 16046, Havana; tel. (7) 22-5512; fax (7) 22-8382; e-mail webmaster@coral.cha.cyt.cu; internet www.cubanacan.cu; f. 1987; Pres. MANUEL VILA.

Empresa de Turismo Internacional (Cubatur): Calle F, No 157, entre Calzada y Novena, Vedado, Havana; tel. (7) 33-4135; fax (7) 33-4037; e-mail casamatriz@cubatur.cu; internet www.cubatur.cu; f. 1968; Dir JOSÉ PADILLA.

Empresa de Turismo Nacional (Viajes Cuba): Calle 20, No 352, entre 21 y 23, Vedado, Havana; tel. (7) 30-0587; e-mail info@viajesmorella.com; internet www.viajes-cuba.com; f. 1981; Dir ANA ELIS DE LA CRUZ GARCÍA.

CYPRUS

Introductory Survey

Location, Climate, Language, Religion, Flag, Capital

The Republic of Cyprus is an island in the eastern Mediterranean Sea, about 100 km south of Turkey. The climate is mild, although snow falls in the mountainous south-west between December and March. Temperatures in Nicosia are generally between 5°C (41°F) and 36°C (97°F). About 75% of the population speak Greek and almost all of the remainder Turkish. The Greek-speaking community is overwhelmingly Christian, and nearly all Greek Cypriots adhere to the Orthodox Church of Cyprus, while most of the Turkish Cypriots are Muslims. The national flag of the Republic of Cyprus (proportions 3 by 5) is white, with a gold map of Cyprus, above two crossed green olive branches, in the centre. The national flag of the 'Turkish Republic of Northern Cyprus' (proportions 2 by 3) has a white field, with a red crescent and star to the left of centre between two narrow horizontal bands of red towards the upper and lower edges. The capital is Nicosia.

Recent History

A guerrilla war against British rule in Cyprus was begun in 1955 by Greek Cypriots seeking unification (*Enosis*) with Greece. Their movement, the National Organization of Cypriot Combatants (EOKA), was led politically by Archbishop Makarios III, head of the Greek Orthodox Church in Cyprus, and militarily by Gen. George Grivas. Archbishop Makarios was suspected by the British authorities of being involved in EOKA's campaign of violence, and in March 1956 he and three other *Enosis* leaders were deported. After a compromise agreement between the Greek and Turkish communities, a Constitution for an independent Cyprus was finalized in 1959. Makarios returned from exile and was elected the country's first President in December 1959. Cyprus became independent on 16 August 1960, although the United Kingdom retained sovereignty over two military base areas.

A constitutional dispute resulted in the withdrawal of the Turks from the central Government in December 1963, and there was serious inter-communal violence. In March 1964 a UN Peace-keeping Force in Cyprus (UNFICYP, see p. 77) was established to prevent a recurrence of fighting between the Greek and Turkish Cypriot communities. The effective exclusion of the Turks from political power led to the creation of separate administrative, judicial and legislative organs for the Turkish community. Discussions with a view to establishing a more equitable constitutional arrangement began in 1968; these continued intermittently for six years without achieving any agreement, as the Turks favoured some form of federation while the Greeks advocated a unitary state. Each community received military aid from its mother country, and officers of the Greek Army controlled the Greek Cypriot National Guard.

In 1971 Gen. Grivas returned to Cyprus, revived EOKA, and began a terrorist campaign for *Enosis*, directed against the Makarios Government and apparently supported by the military regime in Greece. Grivas died in January 1974, and in June Makarios ordered a purge of EOKA sympathizers from the police, National Guard and civil service, accusing the Greek regime of subversion. On 15 July Makarios was deposed in a military coup led by Greek officers of the National Guard, who appointed as President Nikos Sampson, an extremist Greek Cypriot politician and former EOKA militant. Makarios escaped from the island the following day and travelled to the United Kingdom. At the request of Rauf Denktaş, the Turkish Cypriot leader, the Turkish army intervened to protect the Turkish community and to prevent Greece from using its control of the National Guard to take over Cyprus. Turkish troops landed on 20 July and rapidly occupied the northern third of Cyprus, dividing the island along what became the Attila Line, which runs from Morphou through Nicosia to Famagusta. Sampson resigned on 23 July, and Glavkos Klerides, the President of the House of Representatives, became acting Head of State. The military regime in Greece collapsed the same day. In December Makarios returned to Cyprus and resumed the presidency. However, the Turkish Cypriots established a *de facto* Government in the north, and in February 1975 declared a 'Turkish Federated State of Cyprus' ('TFSC'), with Denktaş as President.

Makarios died in August 1977. He was succeeded as President by Spyros Kyprianou, a former Minister of Foreign Affairs and the President of the House of Representatives since 1976. Following a government reorganization in September 1980, the powerful communist party, the Anorthotiko Komma Ergazomenou Laou (AKEL—Progressive Party of the Working People), withdrew its support from the ruling Dimokratiko Komma (DIKO—Democratic Party), and Kyprianou lost his overall majority in the legislature. At the next general election, held in May 1981, AKEL and the Dimokratikos Synagermos (DISY—Democratic Rally) each won 12 seats in the House. DIKO, however, won only eight seats, so the President remained dependent on the support of AKEL.

In the 'TFSC' a new Council of Ministers was formed in December 1978 under Mustafa Çağatay, a former minister belonging to the Ulusal Bırlık Partisi (UBP—National Unity Party). At elections held in June 1981 President Denktaş was returned to office, but his party, the UBP, lost its legislative majority, and the Government that was subsequently formed by Çağatay was defeated in December. In March 1982 Çağatay formed a coalition Government, comprising the UBP, the Demokratik Halk Partisi (Democratic People's Party) and the Türkiye Bırlık Partisi (Turkish Unity Party).

In September 1980 UN-sponsored intercommunal peace talks were resumed. The constitutional issue remained the main problem: the Turkish Cypriots demanded equal status for the two communities, with equal representation in government and strong links with the mother country, while the Greeks, although accepting the principle of an alternating presidency, favoured a strong central government and objected to any disproportionate representation for the Turkish community, who constituted less than 20% of the population. Discussions on a UN plan involving a federal council, an alternating presidency and the allocation of 70% of the island to the Greek community faltered in February 1982, when the Greek Prime Minister, Andreas Papandreou, proposed the withdrawal of all Greek and Turkish troops and the convening of an international conference rather than the continuation of intercommunal talks. Meanwhile, in April 1981 it was agreed to establish a Committee on Missing Persons in Cyprus, comprising one representative of each community and a representative of the International Committee of the Red Cross (ICRC), to investigate the fate of 1,619 Greek Cypriots and 803 Turkish Cypriots listed as missing since the 1974 invasion. In May 1983 the UN General Assembly voted in favour of the withdrawal of Turkish troops from Cyprus, whereupon Denktaş threatened to boycott any further intercommunal talks and to seek recognition for the 'TFSC' as a sovereign state; simultaneously it was announced that the Turkish lira was to replace the Cyprus pound as legal tender in the 'TFSC'.

On 15 November 1983 the 'TFSC' made a unilateral declaration of independence as the 'Turkish Republic of Northern Cyprus' ('TRNC'), with Denktaş as President. Çağatay subsequently resigned the premiership and as leader of the UBP, and an interim Government was formed in December under Nejat Konuk (Prime Minister of the 'TFSC' during 1976–78 and President of the Legislative Assembly from 1981). Like the 'TFSC', the 'TRNC' was recognized only by Turkey, and the declaration of independence was condemned by the UN Security Council. The 'TRNC' and Turkey established diplomatic relations in April 1984, and the 'TRNC' formally rejected UN proposals for a suspension of its declaration of independence prior to further talks.

During 1984 a 'TRNC' Constituent Assembly drafted a new Constitution, which was approved by 70% of voters at a referendum in May 1985. At a presidential election in the 'TRNC' on 9 June Denktaş was returned to office, with more than 70% of votes cast. A general election followed on 23 June, at which the UBP, led by Dr Derviş Eroğlu, won 24 of the 50 seats in the Legislative Assembly. In July Eroğlu became 'TRNC' Prime Minister, leading a coalition Government formed by the UBP and the Toplumcu Kurtuluş Partisi (TKP—Communal Liberation Party).

In February 1983 Kyprianou was returned to the Greek Cypriot presidency for a further five-year term, taking 56.5% of the votes. In November 1985, following a debate on his leadership, the House of Representatives was dissolved. Elections to an enlarged legislature proceeded in December: Kyprianou's DIKO secured 16 seats, while DISY, which won 19 seats, and AKEL, with 15, did not reach the two-thirds' majority required to amend the Constitution and thus challenge the President's tenure of power. Kyprianou failed to secure a third presidential term in February 1988; the election was won at a second round of voting by Georghios Vassiliou, an economist who presented himself as an independent but who was unofficially supported by AKEL and the Socialistiko Komma Kyprou EDEK (EDEK—EDEK Socialist Party of Cyprus). Vassiliou undertook to restore a cross-party National Council (originally convened by President Makarios) to address the Cyprus issue.

Settlement plans proposed by the UN Secretary-General in July 1985 and in April 1986 were rejected by the Turkish Cypriots and the Greek Cypriots, respectively. Further measures concerning the demilitarization of the island, reportedly proposed by the Greek Cypriot Government, were rejected by Denktaş, who maintained that negotiations on the establishment of a two-zone, federal republic should precede any demilitarization. In March 1988 the new Greek Cypriot President rejected various proposals submitted by Denktaş, via the UN, including a plan to form committees to study the possibilities of intercommunal co-operation. Following a meeting with the revived National Council in June, however, Vassiliou agreed to a proposal by the UN Secretary-General that he and Denktaş should resume intercommunal talks, without pre-conditions, in their capacity as the leaders of two communities. Denktaş also approved the proposal, and a UN-sponsored summit meeting between the Greek and Turkish Cypriot leaders took place in Geneva, Switzerland, in August. Vassiliou and Denktaş subsequently began direct negotiations, under UN auspices, in September. No real progress was made, however, and, although Vassiliou and Denktaş resumed negotiations at the UN in February 1990, the talks were abandoned in March, chiefly because Denktaş demanded recognition of the right to self-determination for Turkish Cypriots.

In April 1988 Eroğlu resigned as 'TRNC' Prime Minister, following a disagreement between the UBP and its coalition partner (since September 1986), the Yeni Doğuş Partisi (New Dawn Party), which was demanding greater representation in the Government. At the request of Denktaş, Eroğlu formed a new Council of Ministers in May, comprising mainly UBP members but also including independents. In April 1990 Denktaş secured nearly 67% of the votes cast in an early presidential election. Eroğlu retained the office of Prime Minister, after the UBP won 34 of the 50 seats in the 'TRNC' Legislative Assembly at elections in May. (Following by-elections for 12 seats in October 1991, the UBP increased its representation in the Assembly to 45 members.)

In July 1990 the Government of Cyprus formally applied to join the European Community (EC, now European Union—EU, see p. 217). Denktaş condemned the application, on the grounds that the Turkish Cypriots had not been consulted, and stated that the action would prevent the resumption of intercommunal talks. In June 1993, none the less, the European Commission approved the eligibility of Cyprus for EC membership, although it insisted that the application should be linked to progress in the latest UN-sponsored talks concerning the island.

At the May 1991 general election for the Greek Cypriot seats in the House of Representatives, the conservative DISY, in alliance with the Komma Phileleftheron (Liberal Party), received 35.8% of the votes cast, thereby securing 20 of the 56 seats in the legislature. AKEL unexpectedly made the most significant gains, obtaining 30.6% of the votes and 18 seats.

Following unsuccessful attempts to promote the resumption of discussions between Vassiliou and Denktaş by the UN, the EC and the USA during 1990–91, the new UN Secretary-General, Dr Boutros Boutros-Ghali, made the resolution of the Cyprus problem a priority. UN envoys visited Cyprus, Turkey and Greece in February 1992, and in January and March Boutros-Ghali himself held separate meetings in New York, USA, with Vassiliou and Denktaş. However, no progress was achieved on the fundamental differences between the two sides concerning territory and displaced persons. In mid-1992 the UN Secretary-General conducted a second round of talks in New York with

Vassiliou and Denktaş, initially separately but subsequently involving direct discussions between the two leaders. The talks aimed to arrive at a draft settlement based on a 'set of ideas', compiled by Boutros-Ghali and endorsed by UN Security Council Resolution 750, advocating 'uninterrupted negotiations' until a settlement was reached. Discussions centred on UN proposals for the demarcation of Greek Cypriot and Turkish Cypriot areas of administration under a federal structure. However, following the publication of what was described as a 'non-map' in the Turkish Cypriot press, which showed the proposed area of Turkish administration as being about 25% smaller than the 'TRNC', Denktaş asserted that the UN's territorial proposals were totally unacceptable to the 'TRNC' Government, while political opinion in the Greek Cypriot area was divided. The five weeks of talks came to an end in August, again without having achieved significant progress. A third round of UN-sponsored talks, which commenced in New York in late October, were adjourned in the following month, owing to lack of progress.

At an election to the Greek Cypriot presidency in February 1993 the DISY leader, Glavkos Klerides, narrowly defeated the incumbent Vassiliou at a second round of voting. Vassiliou subsequently formed a new party, the Kinema ton Eleftheron Dimokraton (KED—Movement of Free Democrats). UN-sponsored negotiations were reconvened in New York in May, focusing on the Secretary-General's plan to introduce a series of what were termed 'confidence-building measures'. These included the proposed reopening, under UN administration, of the international airport at Nicosia, and the resettlement, also under UN directives, of a fenced suburb of Famagusta. Denktaş presented separate demands at the talks, among them the removal of the embargo against 'TRNC' airports, ports and sporting activities. The talks were abandoned in June, when the Turkish Cypriot negotiators declined to respond to the UN proposals.

In November 1993 Klerides and Andreas Papandreou, who had recently resumed the Greek premiership, agreed at a meeting in Athens that their countries would take joint decisions in negotiations for the settlement of the Cyprus problem. The two leaders also agreed on a common defence doctrine, whereby Greece was to provide Cyprus with a guarantee of air, land and naval protection.

An early general election was held in the 'TRNC' in December 1993, partly in response to increasing friction between President Denktaş and Prime Minister Eroğlu over the handling of the UN-sponsored peace talks. The UBP lost its majority in the Legislative Assembly, retaining only 17 of the 50 seats, and at the end of the month a coalition Government was formed by the Demokrat Parti (DP—Democrat Party), which had been supported by Denktaş, and the left-wing Cumhuriyetçi Türk Partisi (CTP—Republican Turkish Party). Together the DP and the CTP won 53.4% of the votes cast and 28 seats. The leader of the DP, Hakkı Atun (hitherto the Speaker of the Assembly), was appointed as Prime Minister of the new administration.

In February 1994, following the confirmation by both authorities of their acceptance, in principle, of the 'confidence-building measures', UN officials undertook what were designated 'proximity talks' separately with the Greek and Turkish Cypriot leaders. However, Denktaş considered that the proposals under discussion differed from the intention of the measures originally agreed, and therefore refused to accept the document that was presented to both sides in March. A report issued at the end of May by Boutros-Ghali for consideration by the UN Security Council held the 'TRNC' authorities responsible for the breakdown of the process. In the following month the UN conducted negotiations to reclarify the measures. Denktaş accepted certain proposed amendments, including the withdrawal of Turkish Cypriot troops from the access road to Nicosia international airport, but no substantive progress was made.

In July 1994 the UN Security Council adopted Resolution 939, advocating a new initiative on the part of the Secretary-General to formulate a solution for peace, based on a single nationality, international identity and sovereignty. In response, in the following month the 'TRNC' Legislative Assembly approved measures seeking to co-ordinate future foreign and defence policies with those of Turkey, asserting that no peace solution based on the concept of a federation would be acceptable, and demanding political and sovereign status equal to that of Greek Cyprus. No tangible progress was made at informal UN-sponsored meetings between Klerides and Denktaş during October.

The issue of Cyprus's bid to accede to the EU had, furthermore, greatly unsettled the progress of negotiations. In

June 1994 EU Heads of Government, meeting in Corfu, Greece, confirmed that Cyprus would be included in the next round of expansion of the Union. Denktaş remained adamant that any approach by the Greek Cypriots to the EU would prompt the 'TRNC' to seek further integration with Turkey. In early 1995 US officials commenced discussions with the two sides in an attempt to break the deadlock: while Denktaş insisted that the 'TRNC' would oppose Cyprus's application for EU membership until a settlement for the island had been reached, the Greek Cypriot Government demanded 'TRNC' acceptance of the application as a pre-condition to pursuing the talks. In March the EU agreed to consider Cyprus's membership application without discrimination based on the progress (or otherwise) of settlement talks. This was ratified in June by a meeting of the EU-Cyprus Association Council, at which it was agreed to commence pre-accession 'structured dialogue'.

Meanwhile, in February 1995 Hakkı Atun and the 'TRNC' Government resigned, following serious disagreements with Denktaş regarding the redistribution of Greek Cypriot-owned housing and land. However, the UBP failed to negotiate the formation of a new coalition, and in the following month Atun was reappointed Prime Minister. At a presidential election held in April Denktaş secured a conclusive victory only at a second round of voting (having taken 40.4% of votes cast in the first poll), winning 62.5% of the votes in a run-off contest with Eroğlu. Following protracted inter-party negotiations, a new coalition of the DP and CTP, under Atun's premiership, took office in June.

'Secret' negotiations between representatives of the two Cypriot communities, held in May 1995 in London, United Kingdom, on a joint US-British initiative, achieved little in furthering agreement on the island's future or in securing agreement for direct talks between Denktaş and Klerides. Allegations, which emerged in July, that Turkish Cypriot construction work in the capital was, in fact, part of efforts to fortify the buffer zone presented a new political obstacle to inter-communal negotiations.

In August 1995 the 'TRNC' Legislative Assembly adopted legislation concerning compensation for Greek-owned property in the north. At the end of October Özker Özgür resigned as Deputy Prime Minister, reportedly owing to his disapproval of Denktaş's uncompromising attitude regarding the Cyprus issue. In the following month Atun submitted the resignation of his entire Government, after Denktaş rejected a new list of CTP ministers. A new DP-CTP coalition, again under Atun's leadership and with Mehmet Ali Talat (of the CTP) replacing Özgür as Deputy Prime Minister, took office in December.

Elections for the Greek Cypriot seats in the House of Representatives in May 1996 produced little change in the composition of the legislature. DISY retained its 20 seats, with 34.5% of the votes cast; AKEL took 19 seats, an increase of one, with 33.0% of the votes, while DIKO held 10 seats, a loss of one compared with the 1991 election, with 16.4%.

Persistent policy differences within the 'TRNC' coalition caused the Government to resign in July 1996. Negotiations to establish a new administration were undertaken by the DP and the UBP, and in August the two parties signed a coalition agreement whereby UBP leader Eroğlu became Prime Minister.

In April 1996 the UN Security Council endorsed a US initiative (announced in late 1995) to promote a federal-based settlement for Cyprus. In May the United Kingdom appointed Sir David Hannay, a former Permanent Representative to the UN, as its first special representative to Cyprus. In June, in advance of a visit to the island by the UN Secretary-General's newly appointed Special Representative in Cyprus, Han Sung-Joo, Boutros-Ghali held discussions, separately, with Denktaş and Klerides, with the intention of generating support for future direct bilateral negotiations. However, international mediation efforts were diminished by a sharp escalation in intercommunal hostilities. At the end of October a UN-mediated military dialogue did commence, involving senior commanders of the Greek and Turkish Cypriot armed forces, to consider proposals for reducing intercommunal tension. Further mediation efforts were undermined in November by alleged violations of Greek Cypriot airspace by Turkish military aircraft, as well as by efforts by the Greek Cypriot community to prevent tourists from visiting the 'TRNC' and the continued opposition of the 'TRNC' to the Cypriot application to join the EU.

In December 1996 the European Court of Human Rights (ECHR) ruled that Turkey was in breach of the European Convention on Human Rights by, as a result of its occupation in the north, denying a woman access to her property. The ruling implicated Turkey as fully responsible for activities in the 'TRNC' and for the consequences of the military action in 1974.

In January 1997 an agreement signed by the Greek Cypriot Government and Russia regarding the purchase of an advanced anti-aircraft missile system became the focus of political hostilities between the Greek and Turkish Cypriots, and the cause of considerable international concern. The purchase agreement was condemned by the 'TRNC' as an 'act of aggression', and the potential for conflict over the issue increased when Turkey declared its willingness to use military force to prevent the deployment of the system. Greece in turn reiterated that it would defend Cyprus against any Turkish attack. US mediators sought urgent meetings with the Cypriot leaders, and were assured by the Greek Cypriot Government that the system would not be deployed until May 1998 at the earliest, and that its deployment would be dependent upon the progress made in talks. In addition, both sides approved UN-supported measures to reduce tension in the border area, although the Greek Cypriots rejected a US proposal for a ban on all military flights over the island. Later in January 1997 Turkey threatened to establish air and naval bases in the 'TRNC' if Greece continued to promote plans for the establishment of military facilities in the Greek Cypriot zone, and at the end of the month Turkish military vessels arrived in the 'TRNC' port of Famagusta. Turkey and the 'TRNC' also declared their commitment to a joint military concept whereby any attack on the 'TRNC' would be deemed a violation against Turkey.

In June 1997, following proximity talks between Klerides and Denktaş which had begun in March, the Cypriot leaders agreed to take part in direct UN-sponsored negotiations in the USA in July, under the chairmanship of the UN Special Envoy for Cyprus, Dr Diego Córdovez. The talks took place under the auspices of the new UN Secretary-General, Kofi Annan, and with the participation of Richard Holbrooke, who had been appointed US Special Envoy to Cyprus in June. Further private direct talks took place in Nicosia at the end of July, when agreement was reached to co-operate in efforts to trace persons missing since the hostilities in 1974. However, a second formal round of UN-sponsored negotiations, convened in Switzerland in August 1997, collapsed without agreement, after Denktaş demanded the suspension of Cyprus's application for EU membership, to which he remained opposed on the grounds that accession negotiations, scheduled to begin in 1998, were to be conducted with the Greek Cypriot Government, ignoring the issue of Turkish Cypriot sovereignty. (The EU had in the previous month formally agreed that Cyprus would be included in the next phase of the organization's enlargement.) An agreement by the 'TRNC' and Turkey, prior to the latest round of UN-sponsored talks, to create a joint committee to co-ordinate the partial integration of the 'TRNC' into Turkey was widely regarded as a response to the EU's decision to negotiate future membership with the Greek Cypriot Government while excluding Turkey from EU expansion. Although negotiations concerning security issues were held under UN auspices in Nicosia in September, US and UN efforts during October and November to promote progress in the talks, including visits to Cyprus by both Holbrooke and Córdovez, achieved little success, partly owing to the imminence of the Greek Cypriot presidential election. Denktaş rejected Holbrooke's attempts to persuade the 'TRNC' to join the Greek Cypriot Government at EU accession talks in 1998, insisting on EU recognition of the 'TRNC' and the simultaneous admission of Turkey to EU membership. Meanwhile, tension remained high, as Turkish fighter aircraft violated Greek Cypriot airspace in October 1997 in retaliation for Greek participation in Greek Cypriot military manoeuvres.

In November 1997 DIKO voted to leave the Greek Cypriot ruling coalition in advance of the presidential election, and the party's five government members resigned their posts. On 15 February 1998, at the second round of voting in the presidential election, Klerides defeated Georghios Iacovou, an independent candidate supported by AKEL and DIKO, taking 50.8% of the votes cast. A new coalition Government, composed of members of DISY, EDEK, the Enomeni Dimokrates (EDE—United Democrats—formed in 1996 by a merger of Vassiliou's KED and the Ananeotiko Dimokratiko Socialistiko Kinema) and independents, was sworn in at the end of the month.

The Greek Cypriot Government began accession talks with the EU in March 1998, and in the following month Cyprus confirmed its application for associate membership of Western European Union (WEU, see p. 352). In May Holbrooke visited Cyprus and held discussions with Klerides and Denktaş, with the aim of relaunching formal negotiations. However, no progress was made; Holbrooke cited the principal obstacles as Denktaş's demands for recognition of the 'TRNC' and for the withdrawal of the Cypriot application to join the EU, and the decision of the EU further to delay Turkey's application for membership. In August Denktaş rejected a UN plan for the reunification of Cyprus, proposing instead a confederation of equal status; this was deemed unacceptable by Klerides on the grounds that it would legitimize the status of the 'TRNC'. The UN Special Envoy travelled to Cyprus for individual meetings with Klerides and Denktaş in October, but the discussions were unsuccessful.

In June 1998 a number of Greek military aircraft landed at the Paphos airfield in southern Cyprus for the first time since the airfield's completion in January. Shortly afterwards Turkish military aircraft made reciprocal landings in the 'TRNC'. In July the Greek Cypriot Government condemned the arrival of Turkish military naval vessels and aircraft in the 'TRNC' for the celebrations of the anniversary of the Turkish invasion of the island. During the course of the year Turkish aircraft were accused of violating Greek Cypriot airspace on a number of occasions, and in October Turkish fighter planes allegedly harassed Greek military aircraft that were participating in joint exercises with Greek Cypriot forces. Earlier in the month, however, Denktaş had proposed a non-aggression treaty between the two sides. Joint Turkish-'TRNC' military exercises were held in November.

At the end of December 1998 it was formally announced that the contentious Russian missile system would not be deployed in Cyprus, following diplomatic pressure from Greece, the EU (which threatened to suspend Cypriot accession talks if the deployment proceeded), the USA and the UN. The decision was also influenced by the adoption earlier in the month of two resolutions by the UN Security Council (both of which were dismissed by Denktaş): the first renewed the UNFICYP mandate and appealed for the resumption of negotiations on reunification as a single sovereign state (apparently rejecting the 'TRNC' Government's proposed confederation), and the second expressed concern at the lack of progress towards a political settlement and advocated a phased reduction of military personnel and armaments on the island. The missiles were reportedly deployed in Crete, Greece, in March 1999, following the signature in February of an agreement by the Greek and Greek Cypriot Governments to the effect that Cyprus would own the missiles although they would be under Greek operational control. Klerides' reversal of policy regarding the missiles' deployment provoked intense domestic criticism, and prompted the withdrawal of EDEK (to which party the Minister of Defence belonged) from the Greek Cypriot governing coalition.

Meanwhile, at legislative elections held in the 'TRNC' on 6 December 1998 the UBP increased its representation to 24 seats (from 16 in 1993), while the DP held only 13 seats. The TKP won seven of the 50 seats and the CTP the remaining six. At the end of the month a new UBP-TKP Council of Ministers received presidential approval. Eroğlu remained as Prime Minister, and the TKP leader, Mustafa Akıncı, became Minister of State and Deputy Prime Minister.

In June 1999 the UN Security Council, extending the mandate of UNFICYP for a further six months, adopted a resolution urging the Greek and Turkish Cypriot authorities to participate in UN-sponsored negotiations in late 1999 without preconditions or proscribed issues. In November, despite his earlier reluctance to attend the proposed meeting, Denktaş confirmed that he would attend proximity talks with Klerides in New York under the auspices of the UN. UN Secretary-General Kofi Annan acted as a mediator in the indirect talks in the first half of December, which were, however, undermined by a decision taken at a summit meeting of EU Heads of State and Government in Helsinki, Finland, in that month that a political settlement for Cyprus was not a precondition to the accession of the Greek Cypriot Government to the EU. This decision was widely acknowledged to be a response to Greece's reversal of its opposition to Turkey's EU membership application, and the summit thus accorded Turkey formal status as a candidate for EU membership. Although Denktaş criticized the EU decision on Cyprus's accession, a second round of UN-mediated proximity talks began in Geneva at the end of January 2000, but again ended without any substantive progress.

A first round of presidential voting in the 'TRNC', conducted on 15 April 2000, was contested by eight candidates. Denktaş won 43.7% of the votes cast, thus failing to secure the majority necessary for outright victory. A second round was scheduled for 22 April, to be contested by Denktaş and his closest contender, Eroğlu (who had polled 30.1% at the first round), but was cancelled following Eroğlu's withdrawal on 19 April. Denktaş was consequently declared elected for a fourth term as President.

In mid-June 2000 the UN Security Council extended the mandate of UNFICYP for a further six months. Resolution 1303 notably excluded any reference to the authority of the 'TRNC', citing only the Government of Cyprus, and at the end of the month the 'TRNC' instituted a number of retaliatory measures against UNFICYP, including measures to impede the movement of UN forces and new tariffs for UN vehicles and for the use of utilities supplied by the north. 'TRNC' and Turkish forces also crossed into the buffer zone and established a check-point at a village inhabited by Greek Cypriots.

A third round of proximity talks (mediated by the UN Special Adviser on Cyprus, Alvaro de Soto, and focusing on what were termed 'core' issues of territory, constitutional arrangements, property rights and guarantees) took place in Geneva in July–August 2000. Again, there were no direct exchanges between the Greek Cypriot and Turkish Cypriot representatives, and the talks ended without progress. A further round of indirect negotiations began in New York in September. Klerides boycotted the early stages of the talks, in protest at a statement in which the UN Secretary-General had, in the view of the Greek Cypriots, implied that the 'TRNC' was equal in authority to the internationally recognized Cypriot Government, but the Greek Cypriot leader resumed attendance after he received assurances that the UN would act in accordance with earlier Security Council resolutions on the Cyprus issue. Nevertheless, the Greek and Turkish Cypriots remained apparently irreconcilable on the issue of a future structure for Cyprus, with the former advocating a reunified, bi-communal federation and the latter a looser confederation based on equal sovereignty. A fifth round of UN-sponsored proximity talks was convened in Geneva at the beginning of November. After separate meetings with both Klerides and Denktaş, Annan expressed his view that the negotiations had progressed, and both leaders were invited to a further round of contacts in January 2001. Later in November 2000, however, Denktaş stated that he would not return to the talks until such time as the 'TRNC' was accorded international recognition. His decision, taken with the support of the Government of Turkey, apparently reflected anger in the 'TRNC' that the UN Secretary-General had emphasized that any agreement on Cyprus must be based on the premise of a single sovereign entity, and in Turkey that the European Commission had, in a draft partnership agreement published earlier in November 2000, stipulated among preconditions for Turkish admission to the EU Turkey's willingness to promote a settlement for Cyprus based on UN resolutions. De Soto visited Cyprus in December in an effort to foster a resumption of contacts, but Denktaş reiterated that the 'TRNC' would not take part in any further talks unless its sovereignty was recognized; he warned, furthermore, that in the absence of such recognition UNFICYP would no longer be welcome in the 'TRNC'. In the same month the UN Security Council adopted Resolution 1331, extending the mandate of the force for a further six-month period; the resolution urged the 'TRNC' to revoke the restrictive measures imposed against UNFICYP in June, noting that these had undermined the operational effectiveness of the peace-keeping force.

In February 2001 Denktaş reiterated his determination not to participate in further UN proximity talks while the international community continued to regard the Greek Cypriot Government as the legitimate Government for the whole of Cyprus. He also criticized the EU for making a settlement to the Cyprus problem a condition for further progress on Turkey's application for EU membership. The divide between the two communities was further aggravated by an ECHR judgment in May that found Turkey guilty of extensive violations of human rights arising from its 1974 invasion and occupation of Northern Cyprus. Whereas the Greek Cypriot Government welcomed the ruling as 'historic', Denktaş claimed that it justified his refusal to participate in further talks.

At elections for the Greek Cypriot members of the House of Representatives on 27 May 2001, AKEL secured a narrow victory over DISY, taking 20 seats (with 34.7% of the votes cast), compared with the latter's 19 (34.0%). DIKO held nine seats (14.8%), one fewer than in 1996. In early June 2001 the AKEL leader, Demetris Christofias, was elected as the new President of the legislature, receiving crucial support from the DIKO members to defeat the DISY leader, Nicos Anastasiades.

The governing coalition of the 'TRNC' collapsed in late May 2001, following disagreement between the UBP and the TKP on the issue of whether to rejoin talks on the future status of the island. In June the UBP and the DP agreed to form a new coalition administration, with Eroğlu continuing as Prime Minister. The DP leader, Salih Coşar, became Minister of State and Deputy Prime Minister in a Government that was expected to be more supportive than its predecessor of President Denktaş's policy on the Cyprus question.

In September 2001 Alvaro de Soto announced that a new round of talks between Greek Cypriot and 'TRNC' representatives was to take place later in the month. However, Denktaş described the announcement as premature, and insisted that 'TRNC' representatives would not attend. In early December, none the less, Presidents Klerides and Denktaş met briefly for the first time in four years; following the meeting, de Soto stated that the two leaders had agreed to recommence direct talks on the future of the island in January 2002 'without preconditions'. On 5 December 2001 Klerides became the first Greek Cypriot leader to visit the Turkish Cypriot northern sector since the island's partition, when he travelled to the 'TRNC' to meet with Denktaş. The resumption of contacts was broadly welcomed in the 'TRNC', but Greek Cypriot opposition parties and representatives of Greek Cypriots whose relatives had been 'missing' since the invasion, or who had been forced from their homes in the north, were critical of Klerides' visit. Denktaş made a reciprocal visit to meet with his Greek Cypriot counterpart at the end of December 2001. Formal direct negotiations commenced on 21 January 2002; three sessions were scheduled to take place each week, with a view to reaching agreement by June. The talks were mediated by de Soto, who indicated that the focus of the discussions would be a power-sharing arrangement of Greek and Turkish regions within a proposed federal Cyprus. None the less, the political positions of the two parties remained apparently irreconcilable: the 'TRNC' continued to promote a solution based around a confederation of two separate states, while the Greek Cypriots (and the international community apart from Turkey) sought a united island with a high degree of communal autonomy. In mid-May, amid growing pessimism regarding the progress of the talks, Annan travelled to Cyprus, where he met separately with Klerides and Denktaş in an unsuccessful attempt to encourage a compromise before the scheduled date of the end of June.

Talks continued during the remainder of 2002. In September the UN Secretary-General hosted Klerides and Denktaş in Paris, France, with de Soto in attendance. A further such meeting was held in New York in early October, but was disrupted when Denktaş underwent emergency heart surgery while there. On 11 November the UN presented a comprehensive new peace plan (which became known as the 'Annan Plan') to Klerides and Denktaş. The plan envisaged the creation of a common federal state with two equal components, but a single international legal personality. The state would have a joint six-member presidential council, with members holding a 10-month rotating presidency, and a bicameral legislature, comprising a 48-member senate with an equal number of members from both sides, and a 48-member proportionally composed chamber of deputies. A common supreme court would have three judges from both sides, and three non-Cypriots. Dispossessed property owners would receive compensation, and the 'TRNC' would return territory to the Greek side, reducing the former's share of the island from 36% to 28.5%. This would allow 85,000 of the 162,000 Greek Cypriot refugees to return to their former homes, and would displace 42,000 Turkish Cypriots. Cyprus would be demilitarized, but both Greece and Turkey would be permitted to station up to 9,999 troops each on the island, and UNFICYP would retain its presence. The two leaders initially agreed to use the plan as a basis for future negotiations, but in early December Denktaş, who was in poor health, rejected a revised version of it.

The progress of EU accession talks meant that the need for a settlement to the Cyprus problem was increasingly urgent. At the EU summit held in Copenhagen, Denmark, in mid-December 2002, Cyprus was formally invited to join the EU in 2004. However, it was reiterated that if no peace agreement was forthcoming, only the Greek part of the island would be admitted. Meanwhile, Greece, which assumed the presidency of the EU in January 2003, had earlier emphasized that it would veto the admission of other EU candidate countries if Cyprus

was not admitted at the next round of expansion. Turkey, for its part, had warned in November 2001 that it might annex northern Cyprus if a divided island under a Greek Cypriot government was admitted to the EU.

Following the general election in Turkey in November 2002, Reçep Tayyip Erdoğan, the leader of the Justice and Development Party (AKP) which formed the new Government, stated that a peace agreement for Cyprus would accelerate his country's chances of joining the EU. Denktaş's stance on the issue of agreement on Cyprus was not only at odds with Erdoğan's, but also, increasingly, with that of the Turkish Cypriot population: up to 30,000 staged a protest to demand his resignation in late December, and some 50,000–70,000 Turkish Cypriots demonstrated in favour of the UN plan in mid-January 2003.

In the Greek Cypriot presidential election held on 16 February 2003 the DIKO leader, Tassos Papadopoulos (who was also supported by AKEL), was elected outright, with 51.5% of the votes cast. Klerides, who had sought a renewal of his mandate for 16 months, in order to oversee the peace process and Cyprus's accession, won 38.8% of the votes. There were concerns that Papadopoulos's victory would delay the implementation of the UN peace plan, as he was widely believed to favour a less compromising approach towards the Turkish Cypriots than his predecessor. The new President immediately demanded changes to the Annan Plan that would allow all Greek Cypriot refugees to return to the north. Annan extended, to 10 March, a deadline earlier set at 28 February for agreement on the island's future, which would thus allow a unified Cyprus to accede to the EU, and Papadopoulos and Denktaş held discussions in The Hague, Netherlands. However, the new deadline passed without agreement: Denktaş denounced the Annan Plan as unacceptable, and refused to continue discussions. The office of the UN Secretary-General's Special Adviser on Cyprus was subsequently closed down. In early April the Greek Cypriot Government rejected an offer by Denktaş to return the eastern town of Varosha, stating that the UN plan should be the principal basis for negotiation.

On 16 April 2003 President Papadopoulos signed Cyprus's Treaty of Accession to the EU in Athens, thereby confirming that Cyprus would join the organization on 1 May 2004. Under the terms of the treaty, only the Greek Cypriot south was to be admitted to the EU in the absence of a settlement on the divided status of the island. Later in that month the Turkish Cypriot authorities announced that they would open the 'TRNC' border to the Greek part of the island for the first time in 30 years, allowing Turkish Cypriots to visit that area for one-day trips and permitting Greek Cypriots to visit the north for up to three nights. The Greek Cypriot Government was hesitant in welcoming the move, stating that the opening of the border should not be regarded as a substitute for a settlement in accordance with UN resolutions. The leader of the Turkish Cypriot CTP, Mehmet Ali Talat, also expressed caution regarding the free movement of people across the border. Popular approval of the decision in both the north and south of the island was evident, however, and by July more than 900,000 people were reported to have crossed the border. However, the issue of the ownership of properties abandoned as a consequence of the 1974 division of the island remained largely unresolved. In June 2003 the UN Security Council extended the mandate of UNFICYP for a further six months. The Treaty of Accession was unanimously approved by the Greek Cypriot House of Representatives on 14 July and ratified by Papadopoulos on 28 July. In the same month Denktaş again declared that the UN plan for the reunification of Cyprus was unacceptable.

At legislative elections held in the 'TRNC' on 14 December 2003 the pro-EU CTP won the largest share of the votes, with 35.2%, narrowly defeating the ruling UBP, which secured 32.9%. However, parliamentary seats were distributed equally between pro-EU parties and parties that remained opposed to the reunification of Cyprus under the terms of the Annan Plan; thus the election results were inconclusive with regard to the issue of EU accession. On 16 December Eroğlu resigned and Talat was appointed as the new Turkish Cypriot Prime Minister. At the beginning of January 2004 Talat agreed to enter into a coalition with the DP (led by the President's son, Serdar Denktaş), despite differences of opinion between the CTP and the DP over the reunification issue. On 13 January President Denktaş approved a new coalition Government nominated by Talat, comprising six CTP ministers and four DP ministers. Serdar Denktaş was appointed Deputy Prime Minister and Minister of Foreign Affairs in the new administration.

The formation of a new Turkish Cypriot Government gave renewed impetus to the search for a political settlement. In early February 2004, under the aegis of Secretary-General Annan, Denktaş and Papadopoulos attended a further round of discussions in New York. On 13 February agreement was reached for the resumption of bilateral negotiations based on the Annan Plan (providing for a federation of two politically equal states), with a schedule for reaching a settlement prior to the island's accession to the EU on 1 May. In late February Papadopoulos and Denktaş resumed UN-sponsored negotiations in Nicosia, in an effort to finalize the details of a settlement, which was to be submitted for approval by both the Greek and Turkish Cypriot communities at concurrent referendums scheduled for 24 April. However, intensive discussions between the two leaders failed to resolve the remaining issues of disagreement and were relocated to Bürgenstock, Switzerland, in late March (where the Greek and Turkish Prime Ministers also joined the process). Denktaş, who continued to reject the UN plan, refused to continue his participation in the negotiations and was replaced by Talat as head of the Turkish Cypriot delegation. At the end of March Annan presented a finalized version of the peace plan, which was accepted by the 'TRNC' leadership and by the Greek and Turkish Governments; however, Papadopoulos (in a reversal of previous Greek Cypriot government policy) campaigned against this final settlement, which he strongly opposed on the grounds that it provided for the establishment of a recognized Turkish Cypriot state. (The Greek Cypriot Minister of Communications, Kikis Kazamias, resigned in protest at Papadopoulos's stance on the reunification plan.) At the referendums held on 24 April the Annan Plan was endorsed by Turkish Cypriots by 64.9% of votes cast, but rejected by Greek Cypriots by a decisive majority of 75.8% of the votes. Consequently, only the Greek Cypriot-administered part of the island was admitted to the EU on 1 May; the *acquis communautaire* was suspended in the 'TRNC', pending a future political settlement. Following appeals by Talat, the EU announced measures to alleviate the trade embargo in force against the 'TRNC' (whereby commodities produced in the 'TRNC' were to be exported via Greek Cypriot-administered Cyprus to EU member states); these entered into effect in August, with the resumption of direct trade between the two sides of the island.

At the end of April 2004 the 'TRNC' coalition Government lost its parliamentary majority, after two DP deputies withdrew their support and resigned from the Legislative Assembly. In May Papadopoulos reorganized the Greek Cypriot Council of Ministers, replacing Kazamias and the Minister of Finance, Iacovos Keravnos, who had resigned from his post to become Cyprus's first EU Commissioner. The 'TRNC' relaxed documentation requirements concerning travel to Turkish-administered Cyprus in that month, and ended time restrictions on visits by Greek Cypriots in June. In October the UN Security Council renewed the mandate of UNFICYP until mid-June 2005, but (despite opposition from the Greek Cypriot community) reduced the size of the contingent from about 1,262 to some 860. On 20 October Talat tendered his resignation, following the failure of his lengthy efforts to form a new 'TRNC' coalition administration. On the following day Denktaş invited Eroğlu (as leader of UBP, the strongest party in the Legislative Assembly) to nominate a new government; at the end of the month, however, Eroğlu returned the mandate to the President, after being unable to secure sufficient support from other parliamentary parties. In early November Denktaş redesignated Talat as Prime Minister, but he again failed to reach a coalition agreement and also returned the mandate later that month. Denktaş subsequently announced that early legislative elections would be conducted in the 'TRNC' on 20 February 2005 (while Talat's incumbent Government remained in office in an interim capacity).

The EU's provisional invitation to Turkey, made on 17 December 2004, to open accession negotiations in October 2005, again focused international attention on the necessity of reaching a political settlement in Cyprus. Erdoğan accepted a condition to sign a customs accord with EU member states by that date, but insisted that the protocol would not constitute official Turkish recognition of the authorities of Greek Cypriot-administered Cyprus, instead agreeing to a compromise arrangement, whereby Turkey made a commitment for future recognition.

At the elections to the 'TRNC' Legislative Assembly on 20 February 2005 Talat's CTP secured 44.5% of votes cast and 24 of the 50 seats in the chamber (a gain of seven seats), while the

UBP won 31.6% of the votes and 19 seats, the DP 13.4% and six seats, and the Barış ve Demokrasi Hareketi (BDH—Peace and Democracy Movement) 5.8% and one seat. The CTP was thus obliged to seek a renewed parliamentary alliance with Serdar Denktaş's anti-reunification DP to enable Talat to command a parliamentary majority. On 8 March President Denktaş approved a new 'TRNC' coalition Government (the composition of which was effectively unchanged from the previous administration), formed by Talat under a slightly amended power-sharing arrangement. However, Talat had been nominated by the CTP to contest the presidential election on 17 April, and it was expected that in the event that Talat was elected to the presidency, the Secretary-General of the CTP, Ferdi Sabit Soyer, would be designated premier. On 9 March Talat met with the Secretary-General of AKEL, Demetris Christofias, in the first discussions between 'TRNC' and Greek Cypriot leaders since the April 2004 referendums.

Nine candidates contested the 'TRNC' presidential election, held on 17 April 2005: Mehmet Ali Talat was elected outright, with 55.6% of votes cast, while Eroğlu, his closest rival, secured 22.7%. Talat, who pledged his commitment to achieving reunification of Cyprus, was inaugurated on 24 April. He duly nominated Soyer as Prime Minister, and a new CTP-DP coalition Government was approved by the Legislative Assembly on 28 April.

Government

The 1960 Constitution provided for a system of government in which power would be shared by the Greek and Turkish communities in proportion to their numbers. This Constitution officially remains in force, but since the ending of Turkish participation in the Government in 1963, and particularly since the creation of a separate Turkish area in northern Cyprus in 1974, each community has administered its own affairs, refusing to recognize the authority of the other's Government. The Greek Cypriot administration claims to be the Government of all Cyprus, and is generally recognized as such, although it has no Turkish participation. The northern area is under the *de facto* control of the 'Turkish Republic of Northern Cyprus' (for which a new Constitution was approved by a referendum in May 1985). Each community has its own President, Council of Ministers, legislature (the Greek Cypriot community continues to elect members to the House of Representatives, as established by the 1960 Constitution, while the 'TRNC' elects its own legislative assembly) and judicial system.

Defence

The formation of the National Guard was authorized by the House of Representatives in 1964, after the withdrawal of the Turkish members. Men between 18 and 50 years of age are liable to 25 months' conscription. At 1 August 2004 the National Guard comprised an army of 10,000 regulars, mainly composed of Cypriot conscripts (some 8,700) but with an estimated 200 seconded Greek Army officers and NCOs, and 60,000 reserves. A further 1,250 Greek army personnel were stationed in Cyprus at that time. There is also a Greek Cypriot paramilitary police force of some 750. In 2004 the defence budget for the Greek Cypriot area was some C£70m.

At 1 August 2004 the 'TRNC' had an army of an estimated 5,000 regulars and 26,000 reserves. There was also a para-military armed police force of about 150. Men between 18 and 50 years of age are liable to 24 months' conscription. The 'TRNC' forces were being supported by an estimated 36,000 Turkish troops. In 2002 the defence expenditure of the 'TRNC' was TL 67,500,000m.

A UN Security Council resolution adopted in October 2004 provided for the reduction of the UN Peace-keeping Force in Cyprus (UNFICYP, see p. 000) from 1,262 military and police personnel to about 860. At the end of January 2005 UNFICYP numbered 959 uniformed personnel, supported by 155 local and international civilian staff. There are British military bases (with personnel numbering 3,275 in August 2004) at Akrotiri, Episkopi and Dhekelia.

Economic Affairs

In 2001, according to estimates by the World Bank, Cyprus's gross national income (GNI), measured at average 1999–2001 prices, was US $9,097m., equivalent to $12,320 per head (or $18,080 per head on an international purchasing-power parity basis). During 1990–2003, it was estimated, the population increased at an average annual rate of 0.9%, while gross domestic product (GDP) per head increased, in real terms, by an average of 3.0% per year. Overall GDP increased, in real terms, by an annual average of 4.0% in 1990–2003; growth was 2.0% in 2002 and 4.0% in 2003. In the 'TRNC' GNI was officially estimated at $1,283.7m., or $5,949 per head, in 2003. GNI increased, in real terms, at an average annual rate of 4.0% in 1995–2003, while real GDP increased at an average annual rate of 4.8% in 1994–99. GDP declined by 5.4% in 2001, but increased by 6.2% in 2002 and by 10.6% in 2003.

In the Greek Cypriot area, according to provisional figures for 2003, agriculture (including hunting, forestry and fishing) contributed some 4.1% of GDP, while an estimated 7.6% of the employed labour force were engaged in the sector. The principal export crops of the area are potatoes (which accounted for 7.5% of domestic export earnings in 2001), citrus fruit (6.3%) and vegetables; grapes are cultivated notably for the wine industry, and barley is the principal cereal crop. In an effort to offset the island's vulnerability to drought, during the 1990s the Greek Cypriot Government granted concessions for the construction and operation of several desalination plants. The GDP of the area's agricultural sector increased by an average of 1.3% per year in 1995–2003; growth was an estimated 4.5% in 2003. In the 'TRNC' the agricultural sector contributed 10.3% of GDP and engaged 14.5% of the employed labour force in 2003. The principal crops of the 'TRNC' are citrus fruit, vegetables, potatoes, barley and wheat. The 'TRNC' imports water from Turkey in order to address the problem of drought. The GDP of the agricultural sector increased by an average of 1.0% per year in 1994–99. Agricultural GDP declined by 13.2% in 2000, but increased by 16.1% in 2001, by 18.9% in 2002 and by 7.3% in 2003.

Industry (comprising mining, manufacturing, construction and power) accounted for some 19.3% of GDP and engaged an estimated 21.3% of the employed labour force in the Greek Cypriot area in 2003, according to provisional figures. Industrial GDP increased by an average of 1.2% per year in 1995–2002; the sector grew by an estimated 1.9% in 2003. In the 'TRNC' the industrial sector contributed 16.7% of GDP and engaged 29.0% of the employed labour force in 2003. Industrial GDP in the 'TRNC' increased at an annual average rate of 2.0% in 1994–99. The GDP of the industrial sector (excluding construction) increased by 4.0% in 2000, declined by 6.5% in 2001, but rose by 5.0% in 2002 and by 7.7% in 2003.

In the Greek Cypriot area mining and quarrying, principally the extraction of material for the construction industry, provided only an estimated 0.3% of GDP and engaged only about 0.2% of the employed labour force, according to provisional figures for 2003. In 2001 it was announced that 25 foreign oil companies had expressed interest in acquiring exploration rights for potential petroleum and gas deposits in the eastern Mediterranean within Cyprus's economic zone. The GDP of the mining sector increased at an average annual rate of 6.3% in 1995–2003. Mining GDP rose by 7.0% in 2002, but declined by an estimated 0.5% in 2003. In the 'TRNC' mining and quarrying contributed 0.7% of GDP and engaged 1.3% of the employed labour force in 2003. The GDP of the 'TRNC' mining sector increased by an average of 1.3% per year in 1994–99. The sector's GDP increased by 11.8% in 2000, but decreased by 13.5% in 2001; however, mining GDP rose by 7.4% in 2002 and by 24.6% in 2003.

In the Greek Cypriot area manufacturing accounted for an estimated 9.0% of GDP and engaged about 10.8% of the employed labour force, according to provisional figures for 2003. Clothing represents the southern sector's main export commodity, providing 8.4% of domestic export earnings in 2001. The GDP of the manufacturing sector declined by an average of 0.2% per year in 1995–2003, decreasing by an estimated 0.9% in 2003. In the 'TRNC' the manufacturing sector provided 5.7% of GDP and engaged 6.6% of the employed labour force in 2003. The GDP of the 'TRNC' manufacturing sector increased at an average annual rate of 1.4% in 1994–99. Manufacturing GDP rose by 3.6% in 2000, declined by 6.9% in 2001, but increased by 5.7% in 2002 and by 7.3% in 2003.

Energy is derived almost entirely from imported petroleum, and mineral fuels comprised 10.1% of total imports (including goods for re-export) in the Greek Cypriot area in 2003. The Greek Cypriot Government is encouraging the development of renewable energy sources, including solar, wind and hydroelectric power. Mineral fuels and lubricants comprised 7.7% of total imports in the 'TRNC' in 2003.

The services sector in the Greek Cypriot area contributed an estimated 76.6% of GDP and engaged some 71.1% of the employed labour force in 2003, according to provisional figures. Within the sector, financial and business services provided an estimated 23.5% of overall GDP and generated some 10.3% of employment in 2003. In that year there were 29 'offshore' banking units in the Greek Cypriot area, and the number of registered 'offshore' enterprises was estimated to total more than 40,000. The Greek Cypriot authorities have also attempted to enhance the island's status as an entrepôt for shipping and trade throughout the Eastern Mediterranean, while Cyprus's shipping registry has developed rapidly, to become the world's sixth largest by the end of 2000. Tourist arrivals to the Greek Cypriot area declined by 10.3% in 2002 and by 4.8% in 2003, but increased by 2.0%, to about 2.3m., in 2004. Receipts from tourism in 2004 amounted to an estimated C£982.3m. In the Greek Cypriot zone the GDP of the services sector increased at an average annual rate of 4.1% in 1995–2003; the sector recorded growth of 1.7% in 2003. In the 'TRNC' the services sector contributed 73.0% of GDP and engaged 56.5% of the employed labour force in 2003. In that year a total of 469,867 tourists (340,083 of whom were from Turkey) visited the 'TRNC', and net tourism receipts were estimated at US $178.8m. Services GDP in the 'TRNC' increased by an average of 5.8% per year in 1994–99.

In 2003 the Greek Cypriot area recorded a visible trade deficit of US $3,134.4m. and a deficit of $441.8m. on the current account of the balance of payments. In 2003 the principal source of imports to the Greek Cypriot area was Greece (12.0%), followed by Italy, the United Kingdom, Germany and Japan. The United Kingdom was the principal purchaser of Greek Cypriot exports in that year, taking 32.0% of the total; Greece was also an important market. The principal exports from the Greek Cypriot zone in 2003 were vehicles and transport equipment, prepared foodstuffs, mineral products and chemicals. The principal imports in that year were machinery and electrical equipment, vehicles and transport equipment, mineral products, chemicals, textiles, metals and armaments. The 'TRNC' recorded a visible trade deficit in 2003 of $427.0m., while there was a surplus of $19.4m. on the current account of the balance of payments. In 2003 the principal imports to the 'TRNC' were machinery and transport equipment, basic manufactures, food and live animals, mineral fuels and lubricants, and beverages and tobacco; the principal exports were industrial products, food and live animals, and minerals. Turkey is by far the principal trading partner of the 'TRNC', supplying 62.6% of imports and taking 45.1% of exports in 2003 (although the United Kingdom purchased 23.4% of exports in that year).

In 2003 the Greek Cypriot Government recorded a budget deficit of an estimated C£427.7m., equivalent to 6.3% of GDP. External debt totalled C£1,796.0m. at the end of 1999, of which C£1,142.3m. was medium- and long-term public debt. In that year the cost of debt-servicing was equivalent to 5.8% of the value of exports of goods and services. General government consolidated debt totalled US $4,751.5m. (69.9% of GDP) in 2003. The annual rate of inflation averaged 3.6% in 1990–2002. Consumer prices increased by an average of 2.0% in 2001, by 2.7% in 2002 and by 4.2% in 2003. The rate of unemployment in the Greek Cypriot area was 4.7% of the labour force in January 2004. A budgetary deficit of US $176.9m. was recorded in the 'TRNC' in 2003. In the 'TRNC' the average increase in prices for the 12 months to December averaged 72.3% in 1994–99; the end-of-year rate of inflation was 53.2% in 2000, 76.8% in 2001, 24.5% in 2002 and 12.6% in 2003. According to official figures, 1.4% of the Turkish Cypriot labour force were unemployed in 2003.

Following an application by the Greek Cypriot Government in July 1990, the Greek-controlled southern sector of Cyprus officially acceded to the European Union (EU, see p. 217) on 1 May 2004 (see below). The 'TRNC' has guest status at the Economic Co-operation Organization (ECO, see p. 210).

The economy of Cyprus and its future development are inextricably linked to the continuing division of the island, which further intensive efforts by the UN and the EU in early 2004 failed to resolve. As a result of the Greek Cypriots' rejection of the Annan Plan in April, only the Greek Cypriot-administered part of the island joined the EU on 1 May 2004, with the EU's *acquis communautaire* being suspended in the Turkish Cypriot area, pending an eventual resolution of the political dispute. The Turkish Cypriot economy consequently remained heavily dependent on financial aid from Turkey, although, in recognition of the Turkish Cypriots' vote in favour of the Annan Plan for reunification, the EU declared its intention to develop economic relations with the 'TRNC' to reduce the wide economic disparities between the northern and southern parts of Cyprus. This aim was officially supported by the Greek Cypriot Government, on condition that any new arrangements would preserve its authority over trade between Cyprus and other countries and within the island. Having achieved EU accession, the Greek Cypriot administration was to continue efforts to reduce both its budget deficit and the level of public debt, with the aim of qualifying for membership of the single European currency, the euro, in 2007, and was expected, significantly, to join the EU's exchange-rate mechanism in 2005. Subdued economic growth in the Greek Cypriot area in 2002–03 regained momentum in 2004, as a result of increased investment in construction and a partial recovery in the vital tourism industry. The easing of restrictions on movement across the internal border from April 2003 brought considerable benefits to the Turkish Cypriot economy, in particular to the tourist sector, prompting large numbers of Greek Cypriots and foreign tourists to travel to the north. EU measures to alleviate the trade embargo in force against the 'TRNC' (whereby commodities produced in the Turkish Cypriot sector were to be exported via Greek Cypriot-administered Cyprus to EU member states) entered into effect in August 2004. The holiday property sector in the 'TRNC', adversely affected by uncertainty over the legal status of property owned by Greek Cypriots prior to the 1974 invasion, was revived following the Greek Cypriot rejection of the Annan Plan. The close connection with the Turkish economy, including the use of the Turkish lira as currency, has resulted in persistently high levels of inflation in the 'TRNC'; the new Turkish lira was introduced at the beginning of 2005, with the former currency to be withdrawn from circulation by the end of that year. In addition to EU pledges of financial assistance to the 'TRNC', the USA allocated substantial funds to support the development of Turkish Cypriot businesses, and in January 2005, in a significant move towards ending the 'TRNC's international isolation, a US business delegation visited the north of the island. Nevertheless, further possible initiatives with regard to reunification were likely to be impeded by differences in policy within both the Greek Cypriot and 'TRNC' governing coalitions.

Education

In the Greek Cypriot sector elementary education, which is compulsory and available free of charge, is provided in six grades for children between five-and-a-half and 12 years of age. Secondary education is free for all years of study and lasts for six years, with three compulsory years at the Gymnasium being followed by three non-compulsory years at a technical school or a Lyceum. Comprehensive secondary schools were introduced in 1995. There are five options of specialization at the Lyceums: classical, science, economics, commercial/secretarial and foreign languages. According to official estimates, enrolment in both primary and secondary education was equivalent to 98% of the relevant age-group in 2002/03. Technical and vocational colleges provide higher education for teachers, technicians, engineers, hoteliers and caterers, foresters, nurses and health inspectors. The University of Cyprus was established in September 1992, and there were a further 34 post-secondary institutions in 2002/03. In that year 3,658 students were enrolled at the University of Cyprus, while a total of 16,374 students from the Greek Cypriot area were studying at universities abroad. Public expenditure on education by the central Government in the Greek Cypriot area was estimated at C£449.0m. (equivalent to 6.7% of GDP) in 2003.

Education in the Turkish Cypriot zone is controlled by the 'TRNC'. Pre-primary education is provided by kindergartens for children of five and six years of age. Primary education is free and compulsory: it comprises elementary schools for the 7–11 age-group, and secondary-junior schools for the 12–14 age-group. Secondary education, for the 15–17 age-group, is provided by high schools and vocational schools, including colleges of agriculture, nursing and hotel management. It is free, but not compulsory. In 2003/04 30,605 students were enrolled at higher education establishments in the 'TRNC'. The Eastern Mediterranean University, established at Famagusta in 1986, is the principal tertiary institution, with 13,211 students in 2002/03; there are, in addition, six private universities, a teacher training college, a technological institute and a private business college.

Public Holidays

2005: 1 January (New Year's Day), 6 January (Epiphany)*, 21–24 January (Kurban Bayram—Feast of the Sacrifice)†, 14 March (Green Monday)*, 25 March (Greek Independence Day)*, 1 April (Anniversary of Cyprus Liberation Struggle), 21 April (Birth of the Prophet)†, 23 April (National Sovereignty and Children's Day)†, 29 April–2 May (Easter)*, 1 May (May Day), 19 May (Youth and Sports Day)†, 20 June (Pentecost)*, 20 July (Peace and Freedom Day, anniversary of the Turkish invasion in 1974)†, 1 August (Communal Resistance Day)†, 15 August (Assumption)*, 30 August (Victory Day)†, 1 October (Independence Day)*, 28 October (Greek National Day)*, 29 October (Turkish Republic Day)†, 4–6 November (Ramazam Bayram—end of Ramadan)†, 15 November (TRNC Day)†, 25–26 December (Christmas)*.

2006: 1 January (New Year's Day), 6 January (Epiphany)*, 11–14 February (Kurban Bayram—Feast of the Sacrifice)†, 6 March (Green Monday)*, 25 March (Greek Independence Day)*, 1 April (Anniversary of Cyprus Liberation Struggle), 11 April (Birth of the Prophet)†, 21–24 April (Easter)*, 23 April (National Sovereignty and Children's Day)†, 1 May (May Day), 19 May (Youth and Sports Day)†, 12 June (Pentecost)*, 20 July (Peace and Freedom Day, anniversary of the Turkish invasion in 1974)†, 1 August (Communal Resistance Day)†, 15 August (Assumption)*, 30 August (Victory Day)†, 1 October (Independence Day)*, 24–26 October (Ramazam Bayram—end of Ramadan)†, 28 October (Greek National Day)*, 29 October (Turkish Republic Day)†, 15 November (TRNC Day)†, 25–26 December (Christmas)*.

* Greek and Greek Orthodox.

† Turkish and Turkish Muslim.

Weights and Measures

Although the imperial and the metric systems are understood, Cyprus has a special internal system:

Weights

400 drams = 1 oke = 2.8 lb (1.27 kg).
44 okes = 1 Cyprus kantar.
180 okes = 1 Aleppo kantar.

Capacity

1 liquid oke = 2.25 pints (1.28 litres).
1 Cyprus litre = 5.6 pints (3.18 litres).

Length and Area

1 pic = 2 feet (61 cm).

Area

1 donum = 14,400 sq ft (1,338 sq m).

Statistical Survey

Source (unless otherwise indicated): Department of Statistics and Research, Ministry of Finance, Michalakis Karaolis St, 1444 Nicosia; tel. (2) 309301; fax (2) 661313; e-mail enquiries@cystat.mof.gov.cy; internet www.mof.gov.cy.

Note: Since July 1974 the northern part of Cyprus has been under Turkish occupation. As a result, some of the statistics relating to subsequent periods do not cover the whole island. Some separate figures for the 'TRNC' are also given.

AREA AND POPULATION

Area: 9,251 sq km (3,572 sq miles), incl. Turkish-occupied region; 5,896 sq km (2,276 sq miles), government-controlled area only.

Population: 703,529 (males 345,322, females 358,207), excl. Turkish-occupied region, at census of 1 October 2001; 793,100, incl. 87,600 in Turkish-occupied region, at 31 December 2001 (official estimate); 818,200, incl. estimates for the Turkish-occupied region, at 31 December 2003 (official estimate). Note: Figures for the Turkish-occupied region exclude settlers from Turkey, estimated at 115,000 in 2001.

Density (at 31 December 2003): 88.4 per sq km.

Ethnic Groups (estimates, 31 December 2001): Greeks 639,400 (80.6%), Turks 87,600 (11.1%), Others 66,100 (8.3%); Total 793,100.

Principal Districts (population, excl. Turkish-occupied region, at census of 1 October 2001): Levkosia 279,545; Ammochostos 38,371; Larnaka (Larnaca) 117,124, Lemesos (Limassol) 201,057, Pafos (Paphos) 67,432, *Total* 703,529.

Principal Towns (population at 1 October 2001): Nicosia (capital) 205,633 (excl. Turkish-occupied portion); Limassol 160,733; Larnaca 71,740; Paphos 47,198.

Births, Marriages and Deaths (government-controlled area, 2003): Registered live births 8,088 (birth rate 11.2 per 1,000); Registered marriages 10,810; Registered deaths 5,200 (death rate 7.2 per 1,000).

Expectation of Life (WHO estimates, years at birth): 77.3 (males 75.5; females 79.1) in 2002. Source: WHO, *World Health Report*.

Employment (government-controlled area, provisional figures, '000 persons aged 15 years and over, excl. armed forces, 2003): Agriculture, hunting, forestry and fishing 24.1 Mining and quarrying 0.6; Manufacturing 34.0; Electricity, gas and water 1.4; Construction 31.3; Trade, restaurants and hotels 88.4; Transport, storage and communications 21.6; Financing, insurance, real estate and business services 32.6; Community, social and other services 69.7; Private households 12.3; *Total* 316.0. Figures exclude employment on British sovereign bases.

HEALTH AND WELFARE

Key Indicators

Total Fertility Rate (children per woman, 2002): 1.9.

Under-5 Mortality Rate (per 1,000 live births, 2003): 5.

HIV/AIDS (% of persons aged 15–49, 2001): 0.25.

Physicians (per 1,000 head, 2001): 2.62.

Hospital Beds (per 1,000 head, 2001): 4.37.

Health Expenditure (2001): US $ per head (PPP): 941.

Health Expenditure (2001): % of GDP: 8.1.

Health Expenditure (2001): public (% of total): 47.7.

Human Development Index (2002): ranking: 30.

Human Development Index (2002): index: 0.883.
For sources and definitions, see explanatory note on p. vi.

AGRICULTURE

Principal Crops (government-controlled area, '000 metric tons, 2003): Wheat 13; Barley 128.5; Potatoes 120.0; Olives 17.5 (FAO estimate); Cabbages 4.8 (FAO estimate); Tomatoes 38.2 (FAO estimate); Cucumbers and gherkins 16 .5 (FAO estimate); Dry onions 7.0 (FAO estimate); Bananas 10.5 (FAO estimate); Oranges 35.0 (FAO estimate); Tangerines, mandarins, etc. 36.0 (FAO estimate); Lemons and limes 25.0 (FAO estimate); Grapefruit and pomelos 30.0 (FAO estimate); Apples 11.0 (FAO estimate); Grapes 80.9; Cantaloupes and other melons 11.0 (FAO estimate). Source: FAO.

Livestock (government-controlled area, '000 head, 2003): Cattle 58.3; Sheep 294.0; Goats 459.5; Pigs 491.4; Chickens 3.6; Asses 5.2 (FAO estimate). Source: FAO.

Livestock Products (government-controlled area, estimates, '000 metric tons, 2003): Beef and veal 4.4; Mutton and lamb 4.8; Goat meat 7.8; Pig meat 53.0; Poultry meat 36.7; Cows' milk 150.4; Sheep's milk 22.0; Goats' milk 40.0; Cheese 6.3; Hen eggs 12.3. Source: FAO.

Forestry (government-controlled area, '000 cubic metres, 2003): Roundwood removals (excl. bark) 12.0; Sawnwood production (incl. railway sleepers) 5.6. Source: FAO.

Fishing (government-controlled area, metric tons, live weight, 2002): Capture 1,978 (Bogue 162; Picarels 486); Aquaculture 1,862 (European seabass 422, Gilthead seabream 1,266); *Total catch* 3,840.

MINING AND QUARRYING

Selected Products (government-controlled area, provisional figures, metric tons, 2003): Sand and gravel 11,060,000; Gypsum 185,100; Bentonite 121,100; Umber 11,900.

INDUSTRY

Selected Products (government-controlled area, 2002 unless otherwise indicated): Wine 34.2m. litres; Beer 38.3m. litres; Soft drinks 62.3m. litres; Cigarettes 3,803m. (2001); Footwear 1,013,533 pairs; Bricks 60.8m.; Floor and wall tiles 319,000 sq m. (2001); Cement 1,657,289 metric tons; Electric energy 3,550 million kWh. (2001).

FINANCE

Currency and Exchange Rates: 100 cents = 1 Cyprus pound (Cyprus £). *Sterling, Dollar and Euro Equivalents* (31 December 2004): £1 sterling = 82.09 Cyprus cents; US $1 = 42.50 Cyprus cents; €1 = 57.89 Cyprus cents; Cyprus £100 = £121.82 sterling = $235.29 = €172.74. *Average Exchange Rate* (Cyprus £ per US dollar): 0.6107 in 2002; 0.5174 in 2003; 0.4686 in 2004.

Budget (government-controlled area, Cyprus £ million, 2002): *Revenue:* Taxation 1,760.1 (Direct taxes 647.7, Indirect taxes 808.9, Social security contributions 303.4); Other current revenue 422.2; Capital revenue 0.7; Total 2,183.0, excl. grants from abroad (2.8). *Expenditure:* Current expenditure 2,167.9 (Wages and salaries 598.5, Other goods and services 199.9, Social security payments 354.1, Subsidies 62.9, Interest payments 304.2, Other current expenditure 648.5); Capital expenditure 230.2 (Investments 173.0, Capital transfers 57.2); Total 2,398.1.

International Reserves (government-controlled area, US $ million at 31 December 2003): Gold (national valuation) 196.2; IMF special drawing rights 3.0; Reserve position in IMF 99.3; Foreign exchange 3,154.5; Total 3,453.0. Source: IMF, *International Financial Statistics*.

Money Supply (government-controlled area, Cyprus £ million at 31 December 2003): Currency outside banks 467.2, Demand deposits at deposit money banks 865.7; Total money (incl. others) 1,333.8. Source: IMF, *International Financial Statistics*.

Cost of Living (government-controlled area, Retail Price Index; base: 2000 = 100): 102.0 in 2001; 104.8 in 2002; 109.2 in 2003. Source: IMF, *International Financial Statistics*.

Gross Domestic Product in Purchasers' Values (government-controlled area, Cyprus £ million at current prices): 6,370.3 in 2002; 6,801.7 (provisional) in 2003; 7,252.6 (provisional) in 2004.

Expenditure on the Gross Domestic Product (government-controlled area, provisional, Cyprus £ million at current prices, 2003): Government final consumption expenditure 1,356.5; Private final consumption expenditure 4,336.7; Increase in stocks 49.9; Gross fixed capital formation 1,168.0; *Total domestic expenditure* 6,911.1; Exports of goods and services 3,176.3; *Less* Imports of goods and services 3,285.7; *GDP in purchasers' values* 6,801.7.

Gross Domestic Product by Economic Activity (government-controlled area, provisional, Cyprus £ million at current prices, 2003): Agriculture and hunting 251.1; Fishing 12.4; Mining and quarrying 20.9; Manufacturing 581.1; Electricity, gas and water supply 143.5; Construction 494.9; Wholesale and retail trade 772.7; Restaurants and hotels 516.8; Transport, storage and communications 542.8; Financial intermediation 381.7; Real estate, renting and business activities 1,130.3; Public administration and defence 639.1; Education 376.5; Health and social work 253.7; Other community, social and personal services 259.6; Private households with employed persons 44.0; *Sub-total* 6,421.1; Import duties 134.7; Value-added tax 523.1; *Less* Imputed bank service charges 277.2; *GDP in purchasers' values* 6,801.7.

Balance of Payments (government-controlled area, US $ million, 2003): Exports of goods f.o.b. 955.4, Imports of goods f.o.b.–4,089.8; *Trade balance* –3,134.4; Exports of services 5,213.7; Imports of services –2,277.9; *Balance on goods and services* –198.6; Other income received 491.9; Other income paid –879.0; *Balance on goods, services and income* –585.7; Current transfers received 387.0; Current transfers paid –243.0; *Current balance* –441.8; Capital account (net) 20.3; Direct investment abroad –538.5; Direct investment from abroad 1,025.1; Portfolio investment assets –482.5; Portfolio investment liabilities 802.5; Financial derivatives (net) 16.6; Other investment assets –2,479.2; Other investment liabilities 1,844.7; Net errors and omissions 45.2; *Overall balance* –187.6. Source: IMF, *International Financial Statistics*.

EXTERNAL TRADE

Total Trade (government-controlled area, Cyprus £ million): *Imports c.i.f.:* 2,528.7 in 2001; 2,486.6 in 2002; 2,304.0 in 2003. *Exports f.o.b. (incl. re-exports):* 628.0 in 2001; 511.3 in 2002; 476.8 in 2003.

Principal Commodities (government-controlled area, Cyprus £ '000, 2001): *Imports c.i.f.:* Consumer goods 793,230 (Food and beverages 145,038; Other non-durable 358,208; Semi-durable 173,717; Durable 116,267); Intermediate inputs 736,702 (Construction and mining 124,724; Manufacturing 443,190); Capital goods 269,552; Transport equipment and parts thereof 328,872 (Passenger motor vehicles 160,398; Motor vehicles for the transport of goods 85,864); Fuels and lubricants 302,471; Total (incl. others) 2,528,752. *Exports f.o.b.:* Potatoes 17,511; Citrus fruit 14,717; Cheese 8,558; Cigarettes 10,768; Cement 8,396; Pharmaceutical products 39,411; Clothing 19,700; Total (incl. others) 233,944. Figures for exports exclude re-exports (Cyprus £ '000): 381,039. Also excluded are domestic exports of stores and bunkers for ships and aircraft (Cyprus £ '000): 13,046.

Principal Trading Partners (government-controlled area, Cyprus £ million, 2003): *Imports c.i.f.:* China, People's Repub. 113.0; France 118.2; Germany 173.4; Greece 276.0; Israel 87.7; Italy 226.9; Japan 130.0; Netherlands 56.4; Russia 72.1; Spain 91.9; Syria 61.7; Taiwan 21.7; Thailand 20.2; United Kingdom 191.8; USA 96.2; Total (incl. others) 2,304.0. *Exports f.o.b.* (incl. re-exports): Egypt 11.8; France 5.6; Germany 18.7; Greece 43.8; Israel 4.3; Lebanon 16.2; Netherlands 12.3; Russia 7.9; Spain 5.4; Syria 8.8; United Arab Emirates 10.8; United Kingdom 152.4; USA 9.2; Total (incl. others) 476.8.

TRANSPORT

Road Traffic (government-controlled area, licensed motor vehicles, 31 December 2003): Private passenger cars 291,645; Taxis and self-drive cars 10,856; Buses and coaches 3,275; Lorries and vans 119,646; Motorcycles 41,516; Total (incl. others) 484,477.

Shipping (government-controlled area, freight traffic, '000 metric tons, 2003): Goods loaded 1,565, Goods unloaded 5,683. *Merchant Fleet:* At 31 December 2003 a total of 1,198 merchant vessels (combined displacement 22,054,166 grt) were registered in Cyprus (Source: Lloyd's Register-Fairplay, *World Fleet Statistics*).

Civil Aviation (government-controlled area, 2003): Overall passenger traffic 5,876,590; Total freight transported 32,115 metric tons.

TOURISM

Foreign Tourist Arrivals (government-controlled area, '000): 2,418.2 in 2002; 2,303.2 in 2003; 2,349.0 in 2004.

Arrivals by Country of Residence (government-controlled area, rounded figures, 2004): Germany 161,600; Greece 133,400; Norway 50,700; Russia 83,800; Sweden 84,000; Switzerland 41,300; United Kingdom 1,332,900; Total (incl. others) 2,349,000.

Tourism Receipts (government-controlled area, Cyprus £ million): 1,132.3 in 2002; 1,015.0 in 2003; 982.3 in 2004.

COMMUNICATIONS MEDIA

Radio Receivers (government-controlled area, 1997): 310,000 in use.

Television Receivers (government-controlled area, 2000): 122,000 in use.

Telephones (main lines in use, 2002): 492,000.

Facsimile Machines (provisional or estimated figure, number in use, 1993): 7,000.

Mobile Cellular Telephones (subscribers, 2002): 417,933.

Personal Computers ('000 in use, 2002): 193.

Internet Users ('000, 2002): 210.

Book Production (government-controlled area, 1999): 931 titles.

Newspapers (2000): 8 daily (circulation 87,000 copies); 38 non-daily (circulation 200,000 copies).

Periodicals (2000): 50 daily (circulation 372,000 copies).
Sources: mainly UNESCO, *Statistical Yearbook*, UN, *Statistical Yearbook,* and International Telecommunication Union.

EDUCATION

2002/03 (government-controlled area): Pre-primary: 638 institutions, 1,687 teachers, 25,298 pupils; Primary schools: 368 institutions, 4,121 teachers, 62,868 pupils; Secondary schools (Gymnasia and Lyceums): 149 institutions, 6,398 teachers, 64,711 pupils; Technical colleges: 11 institutions, 99 teachers, 328 pupils; University of Cyprus: 288 teachers, 3,658 students; Other post-secondary: 34 institutions, 957 teachers, 14,614 students.

Adult Literacy Rate: 96.8% (males 95.1%; females 98.6%) in 2002.
Source: UN Development Programme, *Human Development Report*.

'Turkish Republic of Northern Cyprus'

Sources: Statistics and Research Dept, State Planning Organization, Prime Ministry, Lefkoşa (Nicosia), Mersin 10, Turkey; tel. (22) 83141; fax (22) 85988; e-mail trnc-spo@management.emu.edu.tr; internet www.devplan.org; Office of the London Representative of the 'Turkish Republic of Northern Cyprus', 29 Bedford Sq., London WC1B 3EG; tel. (20) 7631-1920; fax (20) 7631-1948.

AREA AND POPULATION

Area: 3,355 sq km (1,295 sq miles).

Population (at census of 15 December 1996): 200,587 (males 105,978, females 94,609). *Mid-2003* (official estimate): 215,790.

Density (mid-2003): 64.3 per sq km.

Ethnic Groups (census, 15 December 1996): Turks 197,264, English 627, Greeks 384, Maronites 173, Russians 130, Germans 106, Others 1,903, *Total* 200,587.

Principal Towns (population within the municipal boundary, census of 15 December 1996): Lefkoşa (Nicosia) 42,767 (Turkish-occupied area only); Gazi Mağusa (Famagusta) 22,216; Girne (Kyrenia) 7,893.

Births, Marriages and Deaths (registered, 2001): Live births 2,550 (birth rate 15.0 per 1,000); Marriages 1,090 (marriage rate 5.2 per 1,000); Deaths 781 (death rate 8.0 per 1,000).

Expectation of life (years at birth, 2000): Males 70.9; Females 75.1.

Employment (2003): Agriculture, forestry and fishing 14,339; Industry 9,234; Construction 19,433; Trade and tourism 11,088; Transport and communications 8,550; Financial institutions 2,509; Business and personal services 15,089; Public services 18,618; *Total employed* 98,860. Total unemployed 1,375; *Total labour force* 100,235.

HEALTH AND WELFARE

Key Indicators

Physicians (per 1,000 head, 2002): 2.0.

Hospital Beds (per 1,000 head, 2003): 5.7.

AGRICULTURE

Principal Crops ('000 metric tons, 2001): Wheat 7.6; Barley 102.1; Potatoes 14.0; Legumes 2.5; Tomatoes 8.3; Onions 1.7; Artichokes 1.2; Watermelons 9.7; Melons 3.0; Cucumbers 2.1; Carobs 2.8; Olives 3.1; Lemons 10.7; Grapefruit 15.8; Oranges 61.6; Tangerines 2.0.

Livestock ('000 head, 2001): Cattle 34.2; Sheep 202.7; Goats 54.8; Chickens 4,238.

Livestock Products ('000 metric tons, unless otherwise indicated, 2001): Sheep's and goats' milk 11.4; Cows' milk 66.5; Mutton and lamb 3.3; Goat meat 0.8; Beef 2.1; Poultry meat 6.8; Wool 0.2; Eggs (million) 13.4.

Fishing (metric tons, 2001): Total catch 400.

FINANCE

Currency and Exchange Rates: Turkish currency: 100 kuruş = 1 Turkish lira (TL) or pound. *Sterling, Dollar and Euro Equivalents* (29 October 2004): £1 sterling = 2,699,673 liras; US $1 = 1,473,000 liras; €1 = 1,877,052 liras; 10,000,000 Turkish liras = £3.70 = $6.79 = €5.33. *Average Exchange Rate* (liras per US dollar): 1,225,590 in 2001; 1,507,230 in 2002; 1,501,170 in 2003.

Budget (provisional, '000 million Turkish liras, 2003): *Revenue:* Local revenue 580,586.7 (Direct taxes 160,000.0, Indirect taxes 165,000.0, Other income 108,000.0, Fund revenues 147,586.7); Foreign aid 175,700.0; Loans 328,827.8; Total 1,085,114.4. *Expenditure:* Personnel 278,567.6; Other goods and services 55,306.7; Transfers 552,540.2; Investments 131,200.0; Defence 67,500.0; Total 1,085,114.4.

Cost of Living (Retail Price Index at December; base: December of previous year = 100): 176.8 in 2001; 124.5 in 2002; 112.6 in 2003.

Expenditure on the Gross Domestic Product (provisional, '000 million Turkish liras at current prices, 2003): Government final consumption expenditure 482,674; Private final consumption expenditure 1,071,916; Increase in stocks 30,900; Gross fixed capital formation 300,218; *Total domestic expenditure* 1,885,707; Exports of goods and services, *less* Imports of goods and services –56,763; *GDP in purchasers' values* 1,828,944; *GDP at constant 1977 prices* (million liras) 9,523.6.

Gross Domestic Product by Economic Activity ('000 million Turkish liras, 2003): Agriculture, forestry and fishing 176,365.0; Industry 191,426.0 (Mining and quarrying 11,094.5, Manufacturing 97,153.6, Electricity and water 83,178.0); Construction 93,301.9; Wholesale and retail trade 180,438.0; Restaurants and hotels 120,441.8; Transport and communications 221,109.7; Finance 115,256.3; Ownership of dwellings 50,851.1; Business and personal services 152,767.6; Government services 404,604.2; *Sub-total* 1,706,561.6; Import duties 170,842.2; *GDP in purchasers' values* 1,877,403.7.

Balance of Payments (US $ million, 2003): Merchandise exports f.o.b. 50.8; Merchandise imports c.i.f. –477.8; *Trade balance* –427.0; Services and unrequited transfers (net) 446.4; *Current balance* 19.4; Capital movements (net) 178.7; Net errors and omissions 46.8; *Total* (net monetary movements) 244.9.

EXTERNAL TRADE

Principal Commodities (US $ million, 2003): *Imports c.i.f.:* Food and live animals 58.4; Beverages and tobacco 32.9; Mineral fuels, lubricants, etc. 36.6; Basic manufactures 100.4 Machinery and transport equipment 141.3; Miscellaneous manufactured articles 40.5; Total (incl. others) 477.8. *Exports f.o.b.:* Food and live animals 20.9; Industrial products 29.2; Minerals 0.7; Total 50.8.

Principal Trading Partners (US $ million, 2003): *Imports c.i.f:* Turkey 299.3; United Kingdom 49.3; USA 3.7; Total (incl. others) 477.8. *Exports f.o.b.:* Turkey 22.9; United Kingdom 11.9; USA 0.1; Total (incl. others) 50.8.

TRANSPORT

Road Traffic (registered motor vehicles, 2001): Saloon cars 76,850; Estate cars 9,168; Pick-ups 3,825; Vans 9,131; Buses 2,077; Trucks 1,593; Lorries 6,335; Motorcycles 16,424; Agricultural tractors 6,594; Total (incl. others) 134,454.

Shipping (2001): Freight traffic ('000 metric tons): Goods loaded 247.2, Goods unloaded 898.1; Vessels entered 3,220.

Civil Aviation: Passenger arrivals and departures 691,431 (2001); Freight landed and cleared (metric tons) 4,297 (2001).

TOURISM

Visitors (2003): 469,867 (including 340,083 Turkish).

Receipts (US $ million): 178.8 in 2003.

COMMUNICATIONS MEDIA

Radio Receivers (2001, provisional): 82,364 in use.

Television Receivers (2001, provisional): 70,960 in use.

Telephones (31 December 2001): 86,228 subscribers.

Mobile Cellular Telephones (31 December 2001): 143,178 subscribers.

EDUCATION

2003/04: *Primary and Pre-primary schools:* 242 institutions, 1,548 teachers, 20,252 pupils; *Secondary Schools:* 28 institutions, 939 teachers, 10,061 students; *General High Schools:* 22 institutions, 669 teachers, 6,430 students; *Vocational Schools:* 13 institutions, 440 teachers, 2,260 students; *Universities:* 8 institutions, 30,605 students (of which 9,922 Turkish Cypriots, 18,398 from Turkey, 2,285 from third countries; 2,150 'TRNC' students study abroad).

Adult Literacy Rate (census, 15 December 1996): 93.5%.

Directory

The Constitution

The Constitution, summarized below, entered into force on 16 August 1960, when Cyprus became an independent republic.

THE STATE OF CYPRUS

The State of Cyprus is an independent and sovereign Republic with a presidential regime.

The Greek Community comprises all citizens of the Republic who are of Greek origin and whose mother tongue is Greek or who share the Greek cultural traditions or who are members of the Greek Orthodox Church.

The Turkish Community comprises all citizens of the Republic who are of Turkish origin and whose mother tongue is Turkish or who share the Turkish cultural traditions or who are Muslims.

The official languages of the Republic are Greek and Turkish.

The Republic shall have its own flag of neutral design and colour, chosen jointly by the President and the Vice-President of the Republic.

The Greek and the Turkish Communities shall have the right to celebrate respectively the Greek and the Turkish national holidays.

THE PRESIDENT AND VICE-PRESIDENT

Executive power is vested in the President and the Vice-President, who are members of the Greek and Turkish Communities respectively, and are elected by their respective communities to hold office for five years.

The President of the Republic as Head of the State represents the Republic in all its official functions; signs the credentials of diplomatic envoys and receives the credentials of foreign diplomatic envoys; signs the credentials of delegates for the negotiation of international treaties, conventions or other agreements; signs the letter relating to the transmission of the instruments of ratification of any international treaties, conventions or agreements; confers the honours of the Republic.

The Vice-President of the Republic, as Vice-Head of the State, has the right to be present at all official functions; at the presentation of the credentials of foreign diplomatic envoys; to recommend to the President the conferment of honours on members of the Turkish Community, which recommendation the President shall accept unless there are grave reasons to the contrary.

The election of the President and the Vice-President of the Republic shall be direct, by universal suffrage and secret ballot, and

shall, except in the case of a by-election, take place on the same day but separately.

The office of the President and of the Vice-President shall be incompatible with that of a Minister or of a Representative or of a member of a Communal Chamber or of a member of any municipal council including a Mayor or of a member of the armed or security forces of the Republic or with a public or municipal office.

The President and Vice-President of the Republic are invested by the House of Representatives.

The President and the Vice-President of the Republic in order to ensure the executive power shall have a Council of Ministers composed of seven Greek Ministers and three Turkish Ministers. The Ministers shall be designated respectively by the President and the Vice-President of the Republic who shall appoint them by an instrument signed by them both. The President convenes and presides over the meetings of the Council of Ministers, while the Vice-President may ask the President to convene the Council and may take part in the discussions.

The decisions of the Council of Ministers shall be taken by an absolute majority and shall, unless the right of final veto or return is exercised by the President or the Vice-President of the Republic or both, be promulgated immediately by them.

The executive power exercised by the President and the Vice-President of the Republic conjointly consists of:

Determining the design and colour of the flag.

Creation or establishment of honours.

Appointment of the members of the Council of Ministers.

Promulgation by publication of the decisions of the Council of Ministers.

Promulgation by publication of any law or decision passed by the House of Representatives.

Appointments and termination of appointments as in Articles provided.

Institution of compulsory military service.

Reduction or increase of the security forces.

Exercise of the prerogative of mercy in capital cases.

Remission, suspension and commutation of sentences.

Right of references to the Supreme Constitutional Court and publication of Court decisions.

Address of messages to the House of Representatives.

The executive powers which may be exercised separately by the President and Vice-President include: designation and termination of appointment of Greek and Turkish Ministers respectively; the right of final veto on Council decisions and on laws concerning foreign affairs, defence or security; the publication of the communal laws and decisions of the Greek and Turkish Communal Chambers respectively; the right of recourse to the Supreme Constitutional Court; the prerogative of mercy in capital cases; and addressing messages to the House of Representatives.

THE COUNCIL OF MINISTERS

The Council of Ministers shall exercise executive power in all matters, other than those which are within the competence of a Communal Chamber, including the following:

General direction and control of the government of the Republic and the direction of general policy.

Foreign affairs, defence and security.

Co-ordination and supervision of all public services.

Supervision and disposition of property belonging to the Republic.

Consideration of Bills to be introduced to the House of Representatives by a Minister.

Making of any order or regulation for the carrying into effect of any law as provided by such law.

Consideration of the Budget of the Republic to be introduced to the House of Representatives.

THE HOUSE OF REPRESENTATIVES

The legislative power of the Republic shall be exercised by the House of Representatives in all matters except those expressly reserved to the Communal Chambers.

The number of Representatives shall be 50, subject to alteration by a resolution of the House of Representatives carried by a majority comprising two-thirds of the Representatives elected by the Greek Community and two-thirds of the Representatives elected by the Turkish Community.

Out of the number of Representatives 70% shall be elected by the Greek Community and 30% by the Turkish Community separately from amongst their members respectively, and, in the case of a contested election, by universal suffrage and by direct and secret ballot held on the same day.

The term of office of the House of Representatives shall be for a period of five years.

The President of the House of Representatives shall be a Greek, and shall be elected by the Representatives elected by the Greek Community, and the Vice-President shall be a Turk and shall be elected by the Representatives elected by the Turkish Community.

THE COMMUNAL CHAMBERS

The Greek and the Turkish Communities respectively shall elect from amongst their own members a Communal Chamber.

The Communal Chambers shall, in relation to their respective Community, have competence to exercise legislative power solely with regard to the following:

All religious, educational, cultural and teaching matters.

Personal status; composition and instances of courts dealing with civil disputes relating to personal status or to religious matters.

Imposition of personal taxes and fees on members of their respective Community in order to provide for their respective needs.

THE PUBLIC SERVICE AND THE ARMED FORCES

The public service shall be composed as to 70% of Greeks and as to 30% of Turks.

The Republic shall have an army of 2,000 men, of whom 60% shall be Greeks and 40% shall be Turks.

The security forces of the Republic shall consist of the police and gendarmerie and shall have a contingent of 2,000 men. The forces shall be composed as to 70% of Greeks and as to 30% of Turks.

OTHER PROVISIONS

The following measures have been passed by the House of Representatives since January 1964, when the Turkish members withdrew:

The amalgamation of the High Court and the Supreme Constitutional Court (see Judicial System section).

The abolition of the Greek Communal Chamber and the creation of a Ministry of Education.

The unification of the Municipalities.

The unification of the Police and the Gendarmerie.

The creation of a military force by providing that persons between the ages of 18 and 50 years can be called upon to serve in the National Guard.

The extension of the term of office of the President and the House of Representatives by one year intervals from July 1965 until elections in February 1968 and July 1970 respectively.

New electoral provisions; abolition of separate Greek and Turkish rolls; abolition of post of Vice-President, which was re-established in 1973.

The Government

HEAD OF STATE

President: TASSOS PAPADOPOULOS (took office 28 February 2003).

COUNCIL OF MINISTERS*
(April 2005)

A coalition Government, comprising the Dimokratiko Komma (DIKO), the Anorthotiko Komma Ergazomenou Laou (AKEL), the Kinima Sosialdimokraton (KISOS) and Independents (Ind.).

Minister of Foreign Affairs: GEORGIOS IACOVOU (Ind.).

Minister of Defence: KYRIAKOS MAVRONICOLAS (KISOS).

Minister of Finance: IACOVOS (MAKIS) KERAVNOS (DIKO).

Minister of the Interior: ANDREAS CHRISTOU (AKEL).

Minister of Justice and Public Order: DOROS THEODOROU (KISOS).

Minister of Commerce, Industry and Tourism: YIORGOS LILLIKAS (AKEL).

Minister of Education and Culture: PEFKIOS GEORGIADES (DIKO).

Minister of Health: ANDREAS GAVRIELIDES (AKEL).

Minister of Labour and Social Insurance: CHRISTOS TALIADOROS (DIKO).

Minister of Communications and Works: HARRIS THRASSOU (Ind.).

Minister of Agriculture, Natural Resources and the Environment: EFTHYMIOS EFTHYMIOU (Ind.).

Government Spokesman: KYPROS CHRYSOSTOMIDES (DIKO).

MINISTRIES

Office of the President: Presidential Palace, Dem. Severis Ave, 1400 Nicosia; tel. 22867400; fax 22867594; e-mail president@ presidency.gov.cy; internet www.pio.gov.cy/cygov/president.htm.

Ministry of Agriculture, Natural Resources and the Environment: Loukis Akritas Ave, 1411 Nicosia; tel. 22408307; fax 22781156; e-mail registry@moa.gov.cy.

Ministry of Commerce, Industry and Tourism: 6 Andreas Araouzos St, 1421 Nicosia; tel. 22867100; fax 22375120; e-mail perm .sec@mcit.gov.cy; internet www.cyprustrade.gov.cy.

Ministry of Communications and Works: 28 Achaion St, 1424 Nicosia; tel. 22800106; fax 22776248; e-mail permsec@mcw.gov.cy; internet www.mcw.gov.cy.

Ministry of Defence: 4 Emmanuel Roides Ave, 1432 Nicosia; tel. 22807622; fax 22676182; e-mail defense@mod.gov.cy.

Ministry of Education and Culture: Kimonos & Thoukydidou, Akropolis, 1434 Nicosia; tel. 22800600; fax 22427559; e-mail registry@moec.gov.cy; internet www.moec.gov.cy.

Ministry of Finance: Cnr M. Karaolis St and G. Afxentiou St, 1439 Nicosia; tel. 22601149; fax 22602747; e-mail registry@mof.gov.cy; internet www.mof.gov.cy.

Ministry of Foreign Affairs: Presidential Palace Ave, 1447 Nicosia; tel. 22401000; fax 22661881; e-mail minforeign1@mfa.gov .cy; internet www.mfa.gov.cy.

Ministry of Health: Byron Ave, 1448 Nicosia; tel. 22309526; fax 22305803; e-mail ministryofhealth@cytanet.com.cy; internet www .moh.gov.cy.

Ministry of the Interior: Dem. Severis Ave, Ex Secretariat Compound, 1453 Nicosia; tel. 22867625; fax 22671465; e-mail minint3@ cytanet.com.cy; internet www.moi.gov.cy.

---

*Under the Constitution of 1960, the vice-presidency and three posts in the Council of Ministers are reserved for Turkish Cypriots. However, there has been no Turkish participation in the Government since December 1963. In 1968 President Makarios announced that he considered the office of Vice-President in abeyance until Turkish participation in the Government is resumed, but the Turkish community elected Rauf Denktaş Vice-President in February 1973.

Ministry of Justice and Public Order: 125 Athalassa Ave, 1461 Nicosia; tel. 22805955; fax 22518356; e-mail registry@mjpo.gov.cy.

Ministry of Labour and Social Insurance: 7 Byron Ave, 1463 Nicosia; tel. 22401600; fax 22670993; e-mail administration@mlsi .gov.cy.

President and Legislature

PRESIDENT

Election, 16 February 2003

Candidate	Votes	%
Tassos Papadopoulos (DIKO, with AKEL, KISOS and KEP support)	213,353	51.5
Glavkos Klerides (DISY, with EDI and ADIK support)	160,724	38.8
Alecos Markides (Independent) .	27,404	6.6
Nikos Koutsou (NEO)	8,771	2.1
Costas Kyriakou (Independent) .	1,840	0.4
Andreas Efstratiou (Independent)	606	0.2
Adamos Katsantonis (Independent)	558	0.1
Christos Josephides (Independent)	391	0.1
Georgios Mavrogenis (Independent)	337	0.1
Pantelis Sofokleous (Independent)	209	0.1
Total	**431,690**	**100.0**

HOUSE OF REPRESENTATIVES

The House of Representatives originally consisted of 50 members, 35 from the Greek community and 15 from the Turkish community, elected for a term of five years. In January 1964 the Turkish members withdrew and set up the 'Turkish Legislative Assembly of the Turkish Cypriot Administration' (see below). At the 1985 elections the membership of the House was expanded to 80 members, of whom 56 were to be from the Greek community and 24 from the Turkish community (according to the ratio of representation specified in the Constitution).

President: DEMETRIS CHRISTOFIAS.

Elections for the Greek Representatives, 27 May 2001

Party	Votes	% of Votes	Seats
AKEL	142,648	34.7	20
DISY	139,721	34.0	19
DIKO	60,986	14.8	9
KISOS	26,767	6.5	4
NEO	12,333	3.0	1
EDI	10,635	2.6	1
ADIK	8,860	2.2	1
KEP	8,129	2.0	1
Independents	908	0.1	—
Total	**410,987**	**100.0**	**56**

Political Organizations

Agonistiko Dimokratiko Kinima (ADIK) (Fighting Democratic Movement): POB 216095, 80 Arch. Makariou III St, Flat 401, 1077 Nicosia; tel. 22765353; fax 22375737; e-mail info@adik.org.cy; internet www.adik.org.cy; f. 1999; centre-right; supports independent and united Cyprus and a settlement based on UN resolutions; Pres. DINOS MICHAELIDES; Gen. Sec. SPYROS STEFOU.

Anorthotiko Komma Ergazomenou Laou (AKEL) (Progressive Party of the Working People): POB 21827, 4 E. Papaioannou St, 1513 Nicosia; tel. 22761121; fax 22761574; e-mail k.e.akel@cytanet.com .cy; internet www.akel.org.cy; f. 1941; successor to the Communist Party of Cyprus (f. 1926); Marxist-Leninist; supports united, sovereign, independent, federal and demilitarized Cyprus; over 14,000 mems; Sec.-Gen. DEMETRIS CHRISTOFIAS.

Dimokratiko Komma (DIKO) (Democratic Party): POB 23979, 50 Grivas Dhigenis Ave, 1080 Nicosia; tel. 22666002; fax 22666488; e-mail diko@diko.org.cy; internet www.diko.org.cy; f. 1976; absorbed Enosi Kentrou (Centre Union, f. 1981) in 1989; supports settlement

of the Cyprus problem based on UN resolutions; Pres. TASSOS PAPA-DOPOULOS; Gen. Sec. ANDREAS ANGELIDES.

Dimokratikos Synagermos (DISY) (Democratic Rally): POB 25303, 25 Pindarou St, 1061 Nicosia; tel. 22883164; fax 22753821; e-mail epikinonia@disy.org.cy; internet www.disy.org.cy; f. 1976; absorbed Democratic National Party (DEK) in 1977, New Democratic Front (NEDIPA) in 1988 and Liberal Party in 1998; advocates market economy with restricted state intervention and increased state social role; 27,000 mems; Pres. NIKOS ANASTASIADES; Dir-Gen. GEORGE LIVERAS.

Enomeni Dimokrates (EDI) (United Democrats): POB 23494, 8 Iassonos St, 1683 Nicosia; tel. 22663030; fax 22664747; e-mail edicy@spidernet.com.cy; internet www.edi.org.cy; f. 1996 by merger of Ananeotiko Dimokratiko Socialistiko Kinema (ADISOK—Democratic Socialist Reform Movement) and Kinema ton Eleftheron Dimokraton (KED—Movement of Free Democrats); Pres. GEORGHIOS VASSILIOU; Gen. Sec. KOSTAS THEMISTOKLEOUS.

Epalxi Anasygrotisis Kentrou (EAK) (Political Forum for the Restructuring of the Centre): POB 22119, Lambousa St, 1095 Nicosia; tel. 22773564; fax 22779939; e-mail kchrysos@logos.cy.net; f. 1998; aims to achieve a wider grouping of all centrist social-democratic movements; supports a settlement to the Cyprus problem based on the principles of the Rule of Law, international law and respect for human rights for all citizens, and the establishment of a democratic federal system of government.

Gia tin Evropi (For Europe): Nicosia; f. by fmr mems of Dimokratikos Synagermos to contest European Parliament elections in 2004; announced est. of new party, European Democracy; Leader YIAN-NAKIS MATSIS.

Kinima Ekologon-Perivallontiston (KEP) (Movement of Ecologists and Environmentalists): POB 29682, 1722 Nicosia; tel. 22518787; fax 22512710; e-mail greenpar@cytanet.com.cy; internet www.cycentral.com/greens; f. 1996; opposed to any geographical division of the island; Gen. Co-ordinator SAVVAS PHILIPPOU.

Kinima Sosialdimokraton (KISOS) (Movement of Social Democrats): POB 21064, 40 Byron Ave, 1096 Nicosia; tel. 22670121; fax 22678894; e-mail info@kisos.org; internet www.kisos.org; f. 2000 as successor to Socialistico Komma Kyprou (EDEK—Socialist Party of Cyprus, f. 1969); supports independent, non-aligned, unitary, demilitarized Cyprus; Pres. Dr VASSOS LYSSARIDES; Dep. Pres. YIAN-NAKIS OMIROU.

Kinisi Politikou Eksychronismou (Movement for Political Reforms): 22 Stasikratous St, 1065 Nicosia; tel. 22668894; fax 22668892; f. 1995; supports settlement of the Cyprus problem based on UN resolutions.

Komma Evrodimokratikis Ananeosis (KEA) (Eurodemocratic Renewal Party): 176 Athalassa Ave, Office 402, 2025 Nicosia; tel. 22514551; fax 22513565; e-mail elpasco@cytanet.com.cy; f. 1998; supports federal settlement to the Cyprus problem based on UN resolutions; Pres. ANTONIS PASCHALIDES.

Neoi Orizontes (NEO) (New Horizons): POB 22496, 3 Trikoupi St, 1522 Nicosia; tel. 22761476; fax 22761144; e-mail neo@neoiorizontes .org; internet www.neoiorizontes.org; f. 1996; supports settlement of the Cyprus problem through political means and the establishment of a non-federal unitary state with single sovereignty throughout the island; Pres. NIKOS KOUTSOU; Gen. Sec. MARIA ROSSIDOU.

Diplomatic Representation

EMBASSIES AND HIGH COMMISSIONS IN CYPRUS

Australia: 4 Annis Komninis St, 2nd Floor, 1060 Nicosia; tel. 22753001; fax 22766486; e-mail auscomm@logos.cy.net; High Commissioner GARTH LESLIE HUNT.

Belgium: 2A Chilonos St, Office 402, 1101 Nicosia; tel. 22449020; fax 22774717; e-mail belgianembassy@cytanet.com.cy; Ambassador COLETTE TAQUET.

Bulgaria: POB 24029, 13 Konst. Paleologos St, 2406 Engomi, Nicosia; tel. 22672486; fax 22676598; e-mail bulgaria@cytanet.com .cy; Ambassador KRASSIMIR STEFANOV.

China, People's Republic: POB 4531, 28 Archimedes St, 2411 Engomi, Nicosia; tel. 22352182; fax 22353530; Ambassador ZHANG LIMIN.

Cuba: POB 28923, 1 Androcleous St, 1060 Nicosia; tel. 22769743; fax 22753820; e-mail embacuba@spidernet.com.cy; Ambassador PABLO RODRIGUEZ VIDAL.

Czech Republic: POB 5202, 48 Arsinois St, 1307 Nicosia; tel. 22421118; fax 22421059; e-mail nicosia@embassy.mzv.cz; internet www.mzv.cz/nicosia; Ambassador MARTIN VÁVRA.

Egypt: POB 21752, 14 Ayios Prokopios St, Engomi, 1512 Nicosia; tel. 22449050; fax 22449081; e-mail info@egyptianembassy.org.cy; internet www.egyptianembassy.org.cy; Ambassador MUHAMMAD ABD AL-HAKAM.

Finland: Arch. Makarios III Ave 9, Nicosia; tel. 22764222; Ambassador RISTO PIIPPONEN.

France: POB 21671, 12 Ploutarchou St, Engomi, 2406 Nicosia; tel. 22779910; fax 22781052; e-mail ambachyp@spidernet.com.cy; internet www.ambafrance-cy.org; Ambassador HADELIN DE LA TOUR DU PIN.

Germany: POB 25705, 1311 Nicosia, 10 Nikitaras St, Ay. Omoloyitae, 1080 Nicosia; tel. 22451145; fax 22665694; e-mail info@germanembassy-nicosia.org.cy; internet www.germanembassy-nicosia.org.cy; Ambassador Dr JOCHEN TREBESCH.

Greece: POB 21799, 8/10 Byron Ave, 1096 Nicosia; tel. 22445111; fax 22680649; e-mail grembnicosia@cytanet.com.cy; Ambassador CHRISTOS PANAGOPOULOS.

Holy See: POB 21964, Holy Cross Catholic Church, Paphos Gate, 1010 Nicosia (Apostolic Nunciature); tel. 22662132; fax 22660767; e-mail holcross@logos.cy.net; Apostolic Nuncio Most Rev. PIETRO SAMBI (Titular Archbishop of Belcastro—with residence in Jerusalem).

Hungary: 2 Pringipos Karolou St, Ayios Dhometios, 2373 Nicosia; tel. 22459130; fax 22459134; e-mail huembnic@cytanet.com.cy; Ambassador JANOS KISFALVI.

India: POB 25544, 3 Indira Gandhi St, Engomi, 2413 Nicosia; tel. 22351741; fax 22350402; e-mail hcoffice@cytanet.com.cy; High Commissioner MANOHAR RAM.

Iran: POB 8145, 42 Armenias St, Akropolis, Nicosia; tel. 22314459; fax 22315446; e-mail iranemb@cytanet.com.cy; Ambassador Dr SAYED REZA HADJ-ZARGARBASHI.

Ireland: 7 Aiantas St, St Omoloyites, 1082 Nicosia; POB 23848, 1686 Nicosia; tel. 22818183; fax 22660050; e-mail irishembassy@cytanet.com.cy; Ambassador JOHN F. SWIFT.

Israel: POB 25159, 4 I. Gryparis St, Nicosia; tel. 22369500; fax 22666338; e-mail ambass-sec@nicosia.mfa.gov.il; internet nicosia.mfa.gov.il; Ambassador ZUI COHEN-LITANT.

Italy: POB 27695, 11 25th March St, Engomi 2408, Nicosia; tel. 22357635; fax 22357616; e-mail ambnico@italianembassy.org.cy; internet www.italianembassy.org.cy; Ambassador GHERARDO LA FRANCESCA.

Lebanon: POB 21924, 6 Chiou St, Ayios Dhometios, 1515 Nicosia; tel. 22878282; fax 22878293; Ambassador MICHEL EL-KHOURY.

Libya: POB 22487, 7 Stassinos Ave, 1522 Nicosia; tel. 22460055; fax 22452710; e-mail lapbcy@cytanet.com.cy; Ambassador KHALIFA AHMAD BAZELYA.

Netherlands: 34 Demosthenis Severis Ave, 1080 Nicosia; tel. 22873666; fax 22872399; e-mail nlgovnic@globalsoftmail.com; Ambassador MAXIMILIAAN E.C. GEVERS.

Poland: 12–14 Kennedy Ave, POB 22743, 1087 Nicosia; tel. 22753784; fax 22751981; e-mail secretariat@polamb.org.cy; Ambassador ZBIGNIEW SZYMANSKI.

Romania: POB 22210, 27 Pireos St, Strovolos, 2023 Nicosia; tel. 22495333; fax 22517383; e-mail embrom@cytanet.com.cy; Chargé d'affaires MARIN GHETU.

Russia: Ay. Prokopias St and Archbishop Makarios III Ave, Engomi, Nicosia; tel. 22774622; fax 22774854; e-mail transl@cytanet.com.cy; Ambassador ANDREI A. NESTERENKO.

Serbia and Montenegro: 2 Vasilissis Olgas St, Engomi, 1101 Nicosia; tel. 22777511; fax 22775910; e-mail nicosia@scg.org.cy; internet www.scg.org.cy; Ambassador SVETISLAV BASARA.

Slovakia: POB 21165, 1503 Nicosia; tel. 22879681; fax 22311715; e-mail skembass@cytanet.com.cy; Ambassador JÁN VARŠO.

Spain: 32 Strovolos Ave, 2018 Strovolos, Nicosia; POB 28349, 2093 Nicosia; tel. 22450410; fax 22491291; e-mail enmora@cytanet.com.cy; Ambassador JOSÉ CERVERA DE GÓNGORA.

Sweden: Zenas Bldg, Second Floor, Theophani Theodotou and Princess Zena de Tyras Cnr, 1065 Nicosia; tel. 22672483; fax 22671783; Ambassador INGEMAR LINDAHL.

Switzerland: 46 Themistocles Dervis St, Medcon Tower, 1066 Nicosia; tel. 22466800; fax 22766008; e-mail vertretung@nic.rep.admin.ch; Chargé d'affaires a.i. MARIANNE ENGLER.

Syria: POB 21891, 24 Nikodimos Mylona St, Ay. Antonios, 1071 Nicosia; tel. 22817333; fax 22756963; e-mail syremb@cytanet.com.cy; Chargé d'affaires HAMZAH HAMZAH.

Ukraine: 5 Dositheou St, Lycavitos, 1071 Nicosia; tel. 22758069; fax 22758071; e-mail gccy@cytanet.com.cy; Ambassador BORYS HUMENIUK.

United Kingdom: POB 21978, Alexander Pallis St, 1587 Nicosia; tel. 22861100; fax 22861125; e-mail infobhc@cylink.com.cy; internet www.britain.org.cy; High Commissioner LYN PARKER.

USA: POB 24536, 7 Ploutarchou, 2407 Engomi, Nicosia; tel. 22776400; fax 22780944; e-mail amembass@spidernet.com.cy; internet www.americanembassy.org.cy; Ambassador MICHAEL KLOSSON.

Judicial System

Supreme Council of Judicature: Nicosia; The Supreme Council of Judicature is composed of the President and Judges of the Supreme Court. It is responsible for the appointment, promotion, transfer, etc., of the judges exercising civil and criminal jurisdiction in the District Courts, the Assize Courts, the Family Courts, the Military Court, the Rent Control Courts and the Industrial Dispute Court.

SUPREME COURT

Supreme Court
Char. Mouskos St, 1404 Nicosia; tel. 22865716; fax 22304500; e-mail chief.reg@sc.judicial.gov.cy.

The Constitution of 1960 provided for a separate Supreme Constitutional Court and High Court but in 1964, in view of the resignation of their neutral presidents, these were amalgamated to form a single Supreme Court.

The Supreme Court is the final appellate court in the Republic and the final adjudicator in matters of constitutional and administrative law, including recourses on conflict of competence between state organs on questions of the constitutionality of laws, etc. It deals with appeals from Assize Courts, District Courts and other inferior Courts as well as from the decisions of its own judges when exercising original jurisdiction in certain matters such as prerogative orders of *habeas corpus, mandamus, certiorari*, etc., and in admiralty cases.

President: CHRISTOS ARTEMIDES.

Judges: PETROS ARTEMIS, YIANNAKIS. CONSTANTINIDES, FRIXOS NICOLAIDES, GEORGIOS NIKOLAOU, MINOS. KRONIDES, TAKIS ELIADES, ANDREAS KRAMVIS, RALLIS GAVRIELIDES, DEMETRIS HADJICHAMBIS, EFI PAPADOPOULOU, MICHALIS PHOTIOU, MYRON NICOLATOS.

Attorney-General: SOLON NIKITAS.

OTHER COURTS
As required by the Constitution a law was passed in 1960 providing for the establishment, jurisdiction and powers of courts of civil and criminal jurisdiction, i.e. of six District Courts and six Assize Courts. In accordance with the provisions of new legislation, approved in 1991, a permanent Assize Court, with powers of jurisdiction in all districts, was established.

In addition to a single Military Court, there are specialized Courts concerned with cases relating to industrial disputes, rent control and family law.

'Turkish Republic of Northern Cyprus'

The Turkish intervention in Cyprus in July 1974 resulted in the establishment of a separate area in northern Cyprus under the control of the Autonomous Turkish Cypriot Administration, with a Council of Ministers and separate judicial, financial, police, military and educational machinery serving the Turkish community.

On 13 February 1975 the Turkish-occupied zone of Cyprus was declared the 'Turkish Federated State of Cyprus', and Rauf Denktaş declared President. At the second joint meeting held by the Executive Council and Legislative Assembly of the Autonomous Turkish Cypriot Administration, it was decided to set up a Constituent Assembly which would prepare a constitution for the 'Turkish Federated State of Cyprus' within 45 days. This Constitution, which was approved by the Turkish Cypriot population in a referendum held on 8 June 1975, was regarded by the Turkish Cypriots as a first step towards a federal republic of Cyprus. The main provisions of the Constitution are summarized below:

The 'Turkish Federated State of Cyprus' is a democratic, secular republic based on the principles of social justice and the rule of law. It shall exercise only those functions that fall outside the powers and functions expressly given to the (proposed) Federal Republic of Cyprus. Necessary amendments shall be made to the Constitution of the 'Turkish Federated State of Cyprus' when the Constitution of the Federal Republic comes into force. The official language is Turkish.

Legislative power is vested in a Legislative Assembly, composed of 40 deputies, elected by universal suffrage for a period of five years. The President is Head of State and is elected by universal suffrage for a period of five years. No person may be elected President for more than two consecutive terms. The Council of Ministers shall be composed of a prime minister and 10 ministers. Judicial power is exercised through independent courts.

Other provisions cover such matters as the rehabilitation of refugees, property rights outside the 'Turkish Federated State', protection of coasts, social insurance, the rights and duties of citizens, etc.

On 15 November 1983 a unilateral declaration of independence brought into being the 'Turkish Republic of Northern Cyprus', which, like the 'Turkish Federated State of Cyprus', was not granted international recognition.

The Constituent Assembly, established after the declaration of independence, prepared a new constitution, which was approved by the Turkish Cypriot electorate on 5 May 1985. The new Constitution is very similar to the old one, but the number of deputies in the Legislative Assembly was increased to 50.

HEAD OF STATE

President of the 'Turkish Republic of Northern Cyprus': MEHMET ALI TALAT (inaugurated 24 April 2005).

COUNCIL OF MINISTERS
(April 2005)

A coalition of the Cumhuriyetçi Türk Partisi (CTP) and the Demokrat Parti (DP).

Prime Minister: FERDI SABIT TASOYER (CTP).

Deputy Prime Minister and Minister of Foreign Affairs: SERDAR DENKTAŞ (DP).

Minister of Economy and Tourism: DERVIŞ KEMAL DENIZ (DP).

Minister of the Interior, Rural Affairs and Housing: ÖZKAN MURAT (CTP).

Minister of Finance: AHMET UZUN (CTP).

Minister of National Education and Culture: CANAN ÖZTOPRAK (DP).

Minister of Agriculture and Forestry: HÜSEYIN ÖZTOPRAK (DP).

Minister of Public Works and Transport: SALIH USAR (CTP).

Minister of Youth and Sports: ÖZKAN YORGANCIOĞLU (CTP).

Minister of Health and Social Welfare: EŞREF VAIZ (CTP).

Minister of Labour and Social Security: SONAY ADEM (CTP).

MINISTRIES

Prime Minister's Office: Selcuklu Rd, Lefkoşa (Nicosia), Mersin 10, Turkey; tel. 2283141; fax 2287280.

Deputy Prime Ministry and Ministry of Foreign Affairs: Selcuklu Rd, Lefkoşa (Nicosia), Mersin 10, Turkey; tel. 2283241; fax 2284290; e-mail pubinfo@trncinfo.org; internet www.trncinfo.org.

Ministry of Agriculture and Forestry: Lefkoşa (Nicosia), Mersin 10, Turkey; tel. 2283735; fax 2286945.

Ministry of Economy and Tourism: Lefkoşa (Nicosia), Mersin 10, Turkey; tel. 2289629; fax 2273976.

Ministry of Finance: Lefkoşa (Nicosia), Mersin 10, Turkey; tel. 2283116; fax 2278230.

Ministry of Health and Social Welfare: Lefkoşa (Nicosia), Mersin 10, Turkey; tel. 2283173; fax 2283893.

Ministry of the Interior, Rural Affairs and Housing: Lefkoşa (Nicosia), Mersin 10, Turkey; tel. 2283344; fax 2283043.

Ministry of Labour and Social Security: Lefkoşa (Nicosia), Mersin 10, Turkey; tel. 2275032; fax 2283776.

Ministry of National Education and Culture: Lefkoşa (Nicosia), Mersin 10, Turkey; e-mail meb@mebnet.net; internet www.mebnet .net.

Ministry of Public Works and Transport: Lefkoşa (Nicosia), Mersin 10, Turkey; tel. 2283666; fax 2281891.

Ministry of Youth and Sports: Lefkoşa (Nicosia), Mersin 10, Turkey; tel. 2275032; fax 2283776.

PRESIDENT

Election, 17 April 2005 (provisional results)

Candidates	Votes	%
Mehmet Ali Talat (Cumhuriyetçi Türk Partisi)	55,945	55.59
Dr Derviş Eroğlu (Ulusal Bırlık Partisi) .	22,874	22.73
Dr Mustafa Arabacioğlu (Demokrat Parti)	13,302	13.22
Nuri Cevikel (Yeni Partisi)	4,816	4.79
Zeki Besiktepeli (Independent) . . .	1,725	1.71
Huseyin Angolemli (Toplumcu Kurtulus Partisi)	1,054	1.05
Zehra Cengiz (Kıbrıs Sosyalist Partisi) .	439	0.44
Arif Salih Kirdag (Independent) . . .	309	0.30
Ayhan Kaymak (Independent)	168	0.17
Total	**100,632**	**100.00**

LEGISLATIVE ASSEMBLY

Speaker: FATMA EKENOĞLU (CTP).

General Election, 20 February 2005

Party	% of votes	Seats
Cumhuriyetçi Türk Partisi	44.5	24
Ulusal Bırlık Partisi	31.6	19
Demokrat Parti	13.4	6
Bariş ve Demokrasi Hareketi	5.8	1
Others	4.7	—
Total	**100.0**	**50**

POLITICAL ORGANIZATIONS

Bariş ve Demokrasi Hareketi (BDH) (Peace and Democracy Movement): 11 Osman Paşa Ave, Köşklüçiftlik,; tel. 2280108; fax 2287046; internet www.barisvedemokrasi.net; f. 2003 by merger of the Toplumcu Kurtuluş Partisi (TKP) with two smaller parties; democratic left party; Leader MUSTAFA AKINCI.

Çözüm ve AB Partisi (CABP) (Solution and European Union Party): Lefkoşa (Nicosia), Mersin 10, Turkey; Leader ALI EREL.

Cumhuriyetçi Türk Partisi (CTP) (Republican Turkish Party): 99A Şehit Salahi, Şevket Sok., Lefkoşa (Nicosia), Mersin 10, Turkey; tel. 2273300; fax 2281914; e-mail ctp@cypronet.net; internet www .ctpkibris.org; f. 1970 by members of the Turkish community in Cyprus; district organizations at Gazi Mağusa (Famagusta), Girne (Kyrenia), Güzelyurt (Morphou) and Lefkoşa (Nicosia); Leader MEHMET ALI TALAT; Gen. Sec. FERDI SABIT SOYER.

Demokrat Parti (DP) (Democrat Party): 9 Ilhan Savut St, Köşklüçiftlik, Lefkoşa (Nicosia), Mersin 10, Turkey; tel. 2283795; fax 2287130; e-mail yenidem@kktc.net; f. 1992 by disaffected UBP representatives; merged with the Yeni Doğuş Partisi (New Dawn Party; f. 1984) and Sosyal Demokrat Partisi (Social Democrat Party) in May 1993; Leader SERDAR DENKTAŞ.

Kıbrıs Adalet Partisi (KAP) (Cyprus Justice Party): 1 Osman Paşa Ave, Köşklüçiftlik, Lefkoşa (Nicosia), Mersin 10, Turkey; tel. 2270274; fax 2289938; Leader OĞUZ KALEIOĞLU.

Kıbrıs Sosyalist Partisi (KSP) (Cyprus Socialist Party): Lefkoşa (Nicosia), Mersin 10, Turkey; Leader ZEHRA CENGIZ.

Milliyetçi Bariş Partisi (MBP) (National Peace Party): Lefkoşa (Nicosia), Mersin 10, Turkey; f. 2003; Leader ERTUĞRUL HASIPOĞLU.

Serbest Düşünce Partisi (Free Thought Party): Lefkoşa (Nicosia), Mersin 10, Turkey; tel. ; fax ; e-mail ; internet ; f. 2004 by fmr mems of the DP; ; Chair. SALIH COSAR.

Toplumcu Kurtulus Partisi (TKP) (Communal Liberation Party): 44 Ikinci Selim Sok., Lefkoşa (Nicosia), Mersin 10, Turkey; tel. 2272555; e-mail info@toplumcukurtuluspartisi.org; internet www.toplumcukurtuluspartisi.org; f. 1976; Leader MUSTAFA AKINCI.

Ulusal Bırlık Partisi (UBP) (National Unity Party): 9 Atatürk Meydanı, Lefkoşa (Nicosia), Mersin 10, Turkey; tel. 2273972; f. 1975; right of centre; based on Atatürk's reforms, social justice, political equality and peaceful co-existence in an independent, bi-zonal, bi-communal, confederate state of Cyprus; Leader Dr DERVIŞ EROĞLU; Sec.-Gen. SUHA TURKOZ.

Yeni Partisi (New Party): Lefkoşa (Nikosia), Mersin 10, Turkey; f. 2004; Leader NURI CEVIKEL.

Yurtsever Bırlık Hareketi (YBH) (Patriotic Unity Movement): Lefkoşa (Nicosia), Mersin 10, Turkey; tel. 2274917; fax 2288931; e-mail ybh@north-cyprus.net; f. 1989 as New Cyprus Party (YKP); publishes weekly newsletter *Yeniçag*; Leader REMZI YEKTAOĞLU.

DIPLOMATIC REPRESENTATION

Embassy in the 'TRNC'

Turkey: Bedrettin Demirel Cad., T.C. Lefkoşa Büyükelçisi, Lefkoşa (Nicosia), Mersin 10, Turkey; tel. 2272314; fax 2285118; e-mail tclefkbe@cc.emu.edu.tr; Ambassador Aydan Karahan.

Turkey is the only country officially to have recognized the 'Turkish Republic of Northern Cyprus'.

JUDICIAL SYSTEM

Supreme Court: Lefkoşa (Nicosia), Mersin 10, Turkey; tel. 2287535; fax 2285265; e-mail mahkeme@kktc.net; The highest court in the 'TRNC' is the Supreme Court. The Supreme Court functions as the Constitutional Court, the Court of Appeal and the High Administrative Court. The Supreme Court, sitting as the Constitutional Court, has exclusive jurisdiction to adjudicate finally on all matters prescribed by the Constitution. The Supreme Court, sitting as the Court of Appeal, is the highest appellate court in the 'TRNC'. It also has original jurisdiction in certain matters of judicial review. The Supreme Court, sitting as the High Administrative Court, has exclusive jurisdiction on matters relating to administrative law.

The Supreme Court is composed of a president and seven judges.

President: Taner Erginel.

Judges: Celâl Karabacak, Taner Erginel, Metin A. Hakki, Nevvar Nolan, Mustafa Özkök, Gönül Erönen, Seyt A. Bensen.

Subordinate Courts: Judicial power other than that exercised by the Supreme Court is exercised by the Assize Courts, District Courts and Family Courts.

Supreme Council of Judicature

The Supreme Council of Judicature, composed of the president and judges of the Supreme Court, a member appointed by the President of the 'TRNC', a member appointed by the Legislative Assembly, the Attorney-General and a member elected by the Bar Association, is responsible for the appointment, promotion, transfer and matters relating to the discipline of all judges. The appointments of the president and judges of the Supreme Court are subject to the approval of the President of the 'TRNC'.

Attorney-General: Akın Sait.

Religion

Greeks form 77% of the population and most of them belong to the Orthodox Church, although there are also adherents of the Armenian Apostolic Church, the Anglican Communion and the Roman Catholic Church (including Maronites). Most Turks (about 18% of the population) are Muslims.

CHRISTIANITY

The Orthodox Church of Cyprus

The Autocephalous Orthodox Church of Cyprus, founded in AD 45, is part of the Eastern Orthodox Church; the Church is independent, and the Archbishop, who is also the Ethnarch (national leader of the Greek community), is elected by representatives of the towns and villages of Cyprus. The Church comprises six dioceses, and in 1995 had an estimated 600,000 members.

Archbishop of Nova Justiniana and all Cyprus: Archbishop Chrysostomos, POB 1130, Archbishop Kyprianos St, Nicosia; tel. 22430696; fax 22432470.

Metropolitan of Paphos: Bishop Chrysostomos.

Metropolitan of Kitium: Bishop Chrysostomos, POB 40036, 6300 Larnaca; tel. 24652269; fax 24655588; e-mail mlarnaca@logosnet.cy.net.

Metropolitan of Kyrenia: Bishop Paulus.

Metropolitan of Limassol: Bishop Athanasios.

Metropolitan of Morphou: Bishop Neophytios.

The Roman Catholic Church

Latin Rite

The Patriarchate of Jerusalem covers Israel, Jordan and Cyprus. The Patriarch is resident in Jerusalem (see the chapter on Israel).

Vicar Patriarchal for Cyprus: Fr Umberto Barato, Holy Cross Catholic Church, Paphos Gate, POB 21964, 1010 Nicosia; tel. 22662132; fax 22660767; e-mail holcross@logos.cy.net.

Maronite Rite

Most of the Roman Catholics in Cyprus are adherents of the Maronite rite. Prior to June 1988 the Archdiocese of Cyprus included

part of Lebanon. At 31 December 2002 the archdiocese contained an estimated 10,000 Maronite Catholics.

Archbishop of Cyprus: Most Rev. Boutros Gemayel, POB 22249, Maronite Archbishop's House, 8 Ayios Maronas St, Nicosia; tel. 22678877; fax 22668260.

The Anglican Communion

Anglicans in Cyprus are adherents of the Episcopal Church in Jerusalem and the Middle East, officially inaugurated in January 1976. The Church has four dioceses. The diocese of Cyprus and the Gulf includes Cyprus, Iraq and the countries of the Arabian peninsula.

Bishop in Cyprus and the Gulf, President Bishop of the Episcopal Church in Jeruselam and the Middle East: Most Rev. Clive Handford, c/o POB 22075, Diocesan Office, 2 Grigoris Afxentiou St, 1517 Nicosia; tel. 22671220; fax 22674553; e-mail georgia@spidernet.com.cy.

Other Christian Churches

Among other denominations active in Cyprus are the Armenian Apostolic Church and the Greek Evangelical Church.

ISLAM

Most adherents of Islam in Cyprus are Sunni Muslims of the Hanafi sect. The religious head of the Muslim community is the Mufti.

Mufti of Cyprus: Ahmet Cemal İlktaç (acting), PK 142, Lefkoşa (Nicosia), Mersin 10, Turkey.

The Press

GREEK CYPRIOT DAILIES

Alithia (Truth): POB 21695, 26A Pindaros and Androklis St, 1060 Nicosia; tel. 22763040; fax 22763945; e-mail alithia@spidernet.com.cy; f. 1952 as a weekly, 1982 as a daily; morning; Greek; right-wing; Dir Socratis Hasikos; Chief Editor Alekos Konstantinides; circ. 11,000.

Apogevmatini (Afternoon): POB 25603, 5 Aegaleo St, Strovolos, Nicosia; tel. 22353603; fax 22353223; f. 1972; afternoon; Greek; independent; Dirs Efthymios Hadjiefthimiou, Antonis Stavrides; Chief Editor Costakis Antonioy; circ. 8,000.

Cyprus Mail: POB 21144, 24 Vassilios Voulgaroktonos St, Nicosia; tel. 22818585; fax 22676385; e-mail mail@cyprus-mail.com; internet www.cyprus-mail.com; f. 1945; morning; English; independent; Dir Kyriacos Iakovides; Editor Kosta Pavlowitch; circ. 6,000.

Epilogi: 19 Nikitara St, Ay. Omologiles, Nicosia; tel. 22367345; fax 22367511; f. 1997; Greek; Chief Editor Costas Zachariades.

Haravgi (Dawn): POB 21556, ETAK Bldg, 6 Ezekia Papaioannou St, Nicosia; tel. 22766666; fax 22765154; e-mail haravgi@spidernet.com.cy; internet www.haravgi.com.cy; f. 1956; morning; Greek; organ of AKEL (Communist Party); Dir Nikos Katsourides; Chief Editor Androulla Giourof; circ. 10,000.

Machi (Combat): POB 27628, 4A Danaes, Engomi, Nicosia; tel. 22356676; fax 22356701; f. 1961; morning; Greek; right-wing; Dir Sotiris Sampson; Chief Editor Mina Sampson; circ. 4,750.

O Phileleftheros (Liberal): POB 21094, Commercial Centre, 1 Diogenous St, 3rd, 6th–7th Floor, Engomi, 1501 Nicosia; tel. 22744000; fax 22590122; e-mail artemiou@phileleftheros.com; internet www.phileleftheros.com.cy; f. 1955; morning; Greek; independent, moderate; Dir N. Pattichis; Editorial Dir Anthos Lykavgis; Chief Editor Takis Kounnafis; circ. 28,000.

Politis (Citizen): 12 Makhera St, Engomi, Nicosia; tel. 22861861; fax 22861871; e-mail info@politis-news.com; internet www.politis-news.com; f. 1999; morning; Greek; independent; Chief Editor Aristos Michaelides.

Simerini (Today): POB 21836, 31 Archangelos Ave, Strovolos, Nicosia; tel. 22353532; fax 22352298; internet www.simerini.com; f. 1976; morning; Greek; right-wing; supports DISY party; Dir Kostas Hadjikostis; Chief Editor Savvas Iakovides; circ. 17,000.

TURKISH CYPRIOT DAILIES

Afrika: Lefkoşa (Nicosia), Mersin 10, Turkey; tel. 2271338; fax 2274585; e-mail avrupa@cc.emu.edu.tr; frmly Avrupa; independent; Editor Şener Levent; circ. 3,000.

Bırlık (Unity): 43 Yediler Sok., PK 841, Lefkoşa (Nicosia), Mersin 10, Turkey; tel. 2272959; fax 2283959; f. 1980; Turkish; organ of UBP; Editor Lütfi Özter.

Halkın Sesi (Voice of the People): 172 Kyrenia Sok., Lefkoşa (Nicosia), Mersin 10, Turkey; tel. 2273141; f. 1942; morning;

Turkish; independent Turkish nationalist; Editor AKAY CEMAL; circ. 6,000.

Kıbrıs: Dr Fazil Küçük Bul., Lefkoşa (Nicosia), Mersin 10, Turkey; tel. 2252555; fax 2252934; e-mail kibris@cypronet.net; Editor MEHMET ALI AKPINAR; circ. 13,000.

Ortam (Political Conditions): 158A Girne Cad., Lefkoşa (Nicosia), Mersin 10, Turkey; tel. 2274872; Turkish; organ of the TKP; Editor ÖZAL ZIYA; circ. 1,250.

Vatan (Homeland): 46 Mufti Ziyai Sok., PK 842, Lefkoşa (Nicosia), Mersin 10, Turkey; tel. 2277557; fax 2277558; e-mail vatan@kktc .net; f. 1991; Editor ERTEN KASIMOĞLU.

Yeni Demokrat (New Democrat): 1 Cengiz Han Cad., Köşklüçiftlik, Lefkoşa (Nicosia), Mersin 10, Turkey; tel. 2281485; fax 2272558; Turkish; organ of the DP; Editor MUSTAFA OKAN; circ. 450.

Yeni Düzen (New System): Yeni Sanayi Sok., Lefkoşa (Nicosia), Mersin 10, Turkey; tel. 2256658; fax 2253240; e-mail yeniduzen@ defne.net; Turkish; organ of the CTP; Editor BURHAN ERASUAN; circ. 1,250.

GREEK CYPRIOT WEEKLIES

Athlitiki tis Kyriakis: 5 Epias, Engomi, Nicosia; tel. 22352966; fax 22348835; f. 1996; Greek; athletic; Dir PANAYIOTIS FELLOUKAS; Chief Editor SAWAS KOSHARIS; circ. 4,000.

Cyprus Financial Mirror: POB 24280, 80B Thermopylon St, 2007 Nicosia; tel. 22495790; fax 22495907; e-mail shavasb@ financialmirror.com; internet www.financialmirror.com; f. 1993; English (with Greek-language supplement); independent; Dirs MASIS DER PARTHOGH, SHAVASB BOHDJALIAN; circ. 3,500.

Cyprus Weekly: POB 24977, Suite 102, Trust House, Gryparis St, 1306 Nicosia; tel. 22666047; fax 22668665; e-mail weekly@spidernet .com.cy; internet www.cyprusweekly.com.cy; f. 1979; English; independent; Dirs GEORGES DER PARTHOGH, ALEX EFTHYVOULOS, ANDREAS HADJIPAPAS; Chief Editor MARTYN HENRY; circ. 18,000.

Ergatiki Phoni (Workers' Voice): POB 25018, SEK Bldg, 23 Alkeou St, Engomi, Nicosia; tel. 22441142; fax 22476360; f. 1947; Greek; organ of SEK trade union; Dir MICHALAKIS IOANNOU; Chief Editor XENIS XENOFONTOS; circ. 10,000.

Ergatiko Vima (Workers' Tribune): POB 21885, 31–35 Archemos St, Nicosia 1045; tel. 22349400; fax 22349382; f. 1956; Greek; organ of the PEO trade union; Chief Editor KOSTAS GREKOS; circ. 14,000.

Official Gazette: Printing Office of the Republic of Cyprus, Nicosia; tel. 22405811; fax 22303175; f. 1960; Greek; published by the Government of the Republic of Cyprus; circ. 5,000.

Paraskinio (Behind the Scenes): 6 Psichikou St, Strovolos, Nicosia; tel. 22322959; fax 22322940; f. 1987; Greek; Dir and Chief Editor D. MICHAEL; cir. 3,000.

Selides (Pages): POB 21094, 1501 Nicosia; tel. 22590000; fax 22590122; e-mail selides@phileleftheros.com; internet www .phileleftheros.com; f. 1991; Greek; Dir N. PATTICHIS; Chief Editor STAVROS CHRISTODOLOU; circ. 16,500.

Super Flash: POB 23647, 11 Kolokotronis St, Kaimakli, Nicosia; tel. 22316674; fax 22316582; f. 1979; youth magazine; Greek; Dir DEMETRIS ALONEFTIS; circ. 4,000.

Ta Nea (News): POB 4349, 40 Vyronos Ave, Nicosia; tel. 22476575; fax 22476512; f. 1968; Greek; organ of EDEK (Socialist Party); Chief Editor PHYTOS SOCRATOUS; circ. 3,000.

Tharros (Courage): POB 27628, 4A Danaes, Engomi, Nicosia; tel. 22356676; fax 22356701; f. 1961; Greek; right-wing; Dir SOTIRIS SAMPSON; Chief Editor MINA SAMPSON; circ. 5,500.

To Periodiko: POB 21836, Dias Bldg, 31 Archangelos Ave, Strovolos, Nicosia; tel. 22353646; fax 22352268; f. 1986; Greek; Dir KOSTAS HADJIKOSTIS; Chief Editor ANDREAS DEMETROPOULOS; circ. 16,000.

TURKISH CYPRIOT WEEKLIES

Cyprus Today: Dr Fazil Küçük Bul., PK 831, Lefkoşa (Nicosia), Mersin 10, Turkey; tel. 2252555; fax 2252934; e-mail cyprustoday@ yahoo.com; f. 1991; English; political, social, cultural and economic; Editor GILL FRASER; circ. 5,000.

Ekonomi (The Economy): Bedrettin Demirel Cad. No. 90, Lefkoşa (Nicosia), Mersin 10, Turkey; tel. 2283760; fax 2283089; f. 1958; Turkish; published by the Turkish Cypriot Chamber of Commerce; Editor-in-Chief SAMI TAŞARKAN; circ. 3,000.

Safak: PK 228, Lefkoşa (Nicosia), Mersin 10, Turkey; tel. 2271472; fax 2287910; f. 1992; Turkish; circ. 1,000.

Yeni Çağ: 28 Ramadan Cad., Lefkoşa (Nicosia), Mersin 10, Turkey; tel. 2274917; fax 2271476; e-mail yenicag@8m.com; internet www .north-cyprus.net/ybh; f. 1990; Turkish; publ. of the YBH; circ. 500.

OTHER WEEKLIES

The Blue Beret: POB 21642, HQ UNFICYP, 1590 Nicosia; tel. 22864550; fax 22864461; e-mail blueberetcyprus@hotmail.com; internet www.unficyp.org; English; f. 1964; circ. 1,500; Editor BRIAN KELLY.

Lion: 55 AEC Episkopi, British Forces Post Office 53; tel. 25962445; fax 25963181; e-mail lioncy@cytanet.com.cy; distributed to British Sovereign Base Areas, United Nations Forces and principal Cypriot towns; weekly; includes British Forces Broadcasting Services programme guide; Editor SARA WOOTTON; circ. 5,000.

Middle East Economic Survey: Middle East Petroleum and Economic Publications (Cyprus), POB 24940, 1355 Nicosia; tel. 22665431; fax 22671988; e-mail info@mees.com; internet www.mees .com; f. 1957 (in Beirut, Lebanon); weekly review and analysis of petroleum, finance and banking, and political developments; Publr BASIM W. ITAYIM; Editor GERALD BUTT.

GREEK CYPRIOT PERIODICALS

Cool: POB 8205, 86 Iphigenias St, 2091 Nicosia; tel. 22378900; fax 22378916; f. 1994; Greek; youth magazine; Chief Editor PROMETHEAS CHRISTOPHIDES; circ. 4,000.

Cypria (Cypriot Woman): POB 28506, 56 Kennedy Ave, 11th Floor, Strovolos, 2080 Nicosia; tel. 22494907; fax 22427051; e-mail pogo@ spidernet.com.cy; f. 1983; every 2 months; Greek; Owner MARO KARAYIANNI; circ. 7,000.

Cyprus P.C.: POB 24989, 6th Floor, 1 Kyriakou Matsi St, 1306 Nicosia; tel. 22765999; fax 22765909; e-mail pc@infomedia.cy.net; internet www.infomedia.com.cy; f. 1990; monthly; Greek; computing magazine; Dir LAKIS VARNAVA; circ. 5,000.

Cyprus Time Out: POB 3697, 4 Pygmalionos St, 1010 Nicosia; tel. 22472949; fax 22360668; f. 1978; monthly; English; Dir ELLADA SOPHOCLEOUS; Chief Editor LYN HAVILAND; circ. 8,000.

Cyprus Today: c/o Ministry of Education and Culture, 1434 Nicosia; tel. 22800933; fax 22518042; e-mail eioannou@culture.moec .gov.cy; f. 1963; quarterly; English; cultural and information review; published and distributed by Press and Information Office; Dir of Cultural Services Dr ELENI NIKITA; circ. 7,000.

Cyprus Tourism: POB 51697, Limassol; tel. 25337377; fax 25337374; f. 1989; bi-monthly; Greek; English; tourism and travel; Man. Dir G. EROTOKRITOU; circ. 250,000.

Dimosios Ypallilos (Civil Servant): 3 Dem. Severis Ave, 1066 Nicosia; tel. 22667260; fax 22665189; weekly; published by the Cyprus Civil Servants' Trade Union (PASYDY); circ. 14,000.

Enosis (Union): 71 Piraeus & Tombazis, Nicosia; tel. 22756862; fax 22757268; f. 1996; monthly; Greek; satirical; Chief Editor VASOS FTOCHOPOLILOS; circ. 2,000.

Eva: 6 Psichikou St, Strovolos, Nicosia; tel. 22322959; fax 22322940; f. 1996; Greek; Dir DINOS MICHAEL; Chief Editors CHARIS PONTIKIS, KATIA SAVVIDOU; circ. 4,000.

Hermes International: POB 24512, Nicosia; tel. 22570570; fax 22581617; f. 1992; quarterly; English; lifestyle, business, finance, management; Chief Editor JOHN VICKERS; circ. 8,500.

I Kypros Simera (Present Day Cyprus): Apellis St, 1456 Nicosia; tel. 22801183; fax 22666123; e-mail registry@pio.moi.gov.cy; internet www.mio.gov.cy; f. 1983; fortnightly; Greek; published by the Press and Information Office of the Ministry of the Interior; Principal Officers M. CHAVALAMPIDOU, A. LYRITSAS; circ. 3,500.

Nicosia This Month: POB 20365, Nikoklis Publishing House, Ledras and Pygmalionos St, Nicosia; tel. 22441922; fax 22519743; e-mail info@gnora.com; internet www.gnora.com; f. 1984; monthly; English; Chief Editor ELLADA SOPHOCLEOUS; circ. 4,000.

Omicron: POB 25211, 1 Commercial Centre Diogenous, 2nd Floor, 1307 Nicosia; tel. 22590110; fax 22590410; f. 1996; Greek; Dir NIKOS CHR. PATTICHIS; Chief Editor STAVROS CHRISTODOULOU; circ. 8,000.

Paediki Chara (Children's Joy): POB 136, 18 Archbishop Makarios III Ave, 1065 Nicosia; tel. 22817585; fax 22817599; e-mail poed@ cytanet.com.cy; f. 1962; monthly; for pupils; publ. by the Pancyprian Union of Greek Teachers; Editor SOFOCLES CHARALAMBIDES; circ. 15,000.

Synergatiko Vima (The Co-operative Tribune): Kosti Palama 5, 1096 Nicosia; tel. 22680757; fax 22660833; e-mail coop.confeder@ cytanet.com.cy; f. 1983; monthly; Greek; official organ of the Pancyprian Co-operative Confederation Ltd; circ. 5,000.

Synthesis (Composition): 6 Psichikou St, Strovolos, Nicosia; tel. 22322959; fax 22322940; f. 1988; every 2 months; Greek; interior decorating; Dir DINOS MICHAEL; circ. 6,000.

Tele Ores: POB 28205, 4 Acropoleos St, 1st Floor, 2091 Nicosia; tel. 22513300; fax 22513363; f. 1993; Greek; fortnightly; television guide; Chief Editor PROMETHEAS CHRISTOPHIDES; circ. 17,000.

Directory

TV Kanali (TV Channel): POB 25603, 5 Aegaleo St, Strovolos, Nicosia; tel. 22353603; fax 22353223; f. 1993; Greek; Dirs A. STAVR-IDES, E. HADJIEFTHYMIOU; Chief Editor CHARIS TOMAZOS; circ. 13,000.

TURKISH CYPRIOT PERIODICALS

Güvenlik Kuvvetleri Magazine: Lefkoşa (Nicosia), Mersin 10, Turkey; tel. 2275880; publ. by the Security Forces of the 'TRNC'.

Halkbilimi: Has-Der, PK 199, Lefkoşa (Nicosia), Mersin 10, Turkey; tel. 2283146; fax 2284125; e-mail mesan@north-cyprus.net; internet www.cypnet.com/ncyprus/gifs/halkbil.gif; f. 1986; annual; publ. of Folk Arts Assoc.; academic; Turkish; Chief Editor KANI KANOL; circ. 1,500 (2000).

Kıbrıs—Northern Cyprus Monthly: Ministry of Foreign Affairs and Defence, Lefkoşa (Nicosia), Mersin 10, Turkey; tel. 2283365; fax 2284847; e-mail pio@trncpio.org; internet www.trncpio.org; f. 1963; Editor GÖNÜL ATANER.

Kıbrıslı Türkün Sesi: 44 Mecidiye St, Lefkoşa (Nicosia), Mersin 10, Turkey; tel. 2278520; fax 2287966; internet www.medyatext.com/kibrisli/; monthly; political; Exec. Dir DOGAN HARMAN; Gen. Coordinator CEVDET ALPARSLAN.

Kültür Sanat Dergisi: Girne Cad. 92, Lefkoşa (Nicosia), Mersin 10, Turkey; tel. 2283313; e-mail info@turkishbank.com; internet www.turkishbank.com; publ. of Türk Bankası; circ. 1,000.

Kuzey Kıbrıs Kültür Dergisi (North Cyprus Cultural Journal): PK 157, Lefkoşa (Nicosia), Mersin 10, Turkey; tel. 2231298; f. 1987; monthly; Turkish; Chief Editor GÜNSEL DOĞASAL.

NEWS AGENCIES

Cyprus News Agency: POB 23947, 1687 Nicosia; tel. 22499662; fax 22492697; e-mail director@cna.org.cy; internet www.cna.org.cy; f. 1976; Greek, Turkish and English; Dir THEMIS THEMISTOCLEOUS.

Kuzey Kıbrıs Haber Ajansı (Northern Cyprus News Agency): Alirizin Efendi Cad., Vakiflar Işhani, Kat 2, No. 3, Ortaköy, Lefkoşa (Nicosia), Mersin 10, Turkey; tel. 2281922; fax 2281934; f. 1977; Dir-Gen. M. ALI AKPINAR.

Papyrus General Press Distribution Agency: POB 12669, 5 Arch. Kyprianou, Latsia, Nicosia; tel. 22488855; fax 22488883; e-mail papyrus@spidernet.com.cy.

TürkAjansı-Kıbrıs (TAK) (Turkish News Agency of Cyprus): POB 355, 30 Mehmet Akif Cad., Lefkoşa (Nicosia), Mersin 10, Turkey; tel. 22271818; fax 2271213; e-mail tak@emu.edu.tr; internet kktc.gov.nc.tr/tak; f. 1973; Dir EMIR HÜSEYN ERSOY.

Foreign Bureaux

Agence France-Presse (AFP) (France): POB 7242, Loizides Centre, 7th Floor, 36 Kypranoros St, Nicosia; tel. 22754050; fax 22768977; e-mail nicosie.redaction@afp.com; Bureau Chief PIERRE TAILLEFER.

Agencia EFE (Spain): 64 Metochiou St, Office 401, Nicosia; tel. 22775725; fax 22781662; Correspondent DOMINGO DEL PINO.

Agenzia Nazionale Stampa Associata (ANSA) (Italy): Middle East Office, 10 Katsonis St, Ayii Omoloyites, Nicosia; tel. 22491699; fax 22492732; Rep. VITTORIO FRENQUELLUCCI.

Associated Press (AP) (USA): POB 4853, Neoelen Marina, 10 Katsonis St, Nicosia; tel. 22492599; fax 22491617; Correspondent ALEX EFTY.

Athinaikon Praktorion Eidiseon (Greece): Flat 64, Tryfonos Bldg, Eleftherias Sq., 1011 Nicosia; tel. 22441110; fax 22457418; Rep. GEORGE LEONIDAS.

Informatsionnoye Telegrafnoye Agentstvo Rossii—Telegrafnoye Agentstvo Suverennykh Stran (ITAR—TASS) (Russia): POB 2235, 5–6 Evangelias St, Archangelos, Nicosia; tel. 22382486; Rep. ALEXEI YEROVTCHENKOV.

Iraqi News Agency: POB 1098, Flat 201, 11 Ippocratous St, Nicosia; tel. 22472095; fax 22472096.

Jamahiriya News Agency (JANA) (Libya): Flat 203, 12 Kypranoros, Nicosia; tel. 22361129; Rep. MUHAMMAD ALI ESHOWEIHIDI.

Reuters (United Kingdom): POB 25725, 5th Floor, George and Thelma Paraskevaides Foundation Bldg, 36 Grivas Dhigenis Ave, Nicosia; tel. 22469607; fax 22662487; Correspondent MICHELE KAMBAS.

Sofia-Press Agency (Bulgaria): 9 Roumeli St, Droshia, Larnaca; tel. 24494484; Rep. IONKA VERESIE.

Turkish News Agency (Anadolu Ajansı): Şehit Biray Mustafa Sok. 6, Yenişehir, Lefkoşa (Nicosia), Mersin 10, Turkey; tel. 2283125; fax 2285576; e-mail kktc@anadoluajansi.com.tr; internet www.anadoluajansi.com.tr.

United Press International (UPI) (USA): 24A Heroes Ave, Nicosia 171; tel. 22456643; fax 22455998; Rep. GEORGES DER PARTHOGH.

Xinhua (New China) News Agency (People's Republic of China): 12 Byzantiou St, Flat 201, Ayios Dhometios, Nicosia; tel. 22590133; fax 22590146; Rep. HUANG JIANMING.

Publishers

GREEK CYPRIOT PUBLISHERS

Andreou Chr. Publications: POB 22298, 67A Regenis St, 1520 Nicosia; tel. 22666877; fax 22666878; e-mail andreou2@cytanet.com.cy; f. 1979; biography, literature, history, regional interest.

Chrysopolitissa: 27 Al. Papadiamantis St, 2400 Nicosia; tel. 22353929; e-mail rina@spidernet.com.cy; f. 1973; theatre, literature.

Costas Epiphaniou: Ekdoseis Antiprosopies Ltd, POB 2451, 1521 Nicosia; tel. 22750873; fax 22759266; f. 1973; Dir COSTAS EPIPHANIOU.

Foundation 'Anastasios G. Leventis': 40 Gladstonos St, POB 22543, 1095 Nicosia; tel. 22667706; fax 22675002; e-mail leventcy@zenon.logos.cy.net; internet www.leventisfoundation.org.

KY KE M: POB 4108, Nicosia; tel. 22450302; fax 22463624; Pres. NIKOS KOUTSOU.

MAM Ltd (The House of Cyprus and Cyprological Publications): POB 21722, 1512 Nicosia; tel. 22753536; fax 22375802; e-mail mam@mam.com.cy; internet www.mam@mam.com.cy; f. 1965.

Nikoklis Publishing House: POB 23697, Nicosia; tel. 22672949; fax (22330218; ethnicity, travel; Man. ELLADA SOPHOCLEOUS.

Omilos Pnevmatikis Ananeoseos: 1 Omirou St, 2407 Engomi, Nicosia; tel. 22775854; literature.

Pierides Foundation: Larnaca; tel. 24651345; fax 24657227.

POLTE (Pancyprian Organization of Tertiary Education): c/o Higher Technical Institute, Nicosia; tel. 22305030; fax 22494953; Pres. KOSTAS NEOKLEOUS.

TURKISH CYPRIOT PUBLISHERS

Action Global Communications: POB 24676, 35 Ayiou Nicolaou St, Engomi, 1302 Lefkoşa (Nicosia), Mersin 10, Turkey; tel. 22818884; fax 22873632; e-mail chris.c@actionprgroup.com; internet www.actionprgroup.com; f. 1971; travel; Pres. TONY CHRISTODOULOU.

Bırlık Gazetesi: Yediler Sok., Lefkoşa (Nicosia), Mersin 10, Turkey; tel. 2272959; f. 1980; Dir MEHMET AKAR.

Bolan Matbaası: 35 Pençizade Sok., Lefkoşa (Nicosia), Mersin 10, Turkey; tel. 2274802.

Devlet Basımevi (Turkish Cypriot Government Printing House): Şerif Arzik Sok., Lefkoşa (Nicosia), Mersin 10, Turkey; tel. 2272010; Dir S. KÜRŞAD.

Halkın Sesi Ltd: 172 Girne Cad., Lefkoşa (Nicosia), Mersin 10, Turkey; tel. 2273141.

Kema Matbaası: 1 Tabak Hilmi Sok., Lefkoşa (Nicosia), Mersin 10, Turkey; tel. 2272785.

North Cyprus Research and Publishing Centre (CYREP): PK 327, Lefkoşa (Nicosia), Mersin 10, Turkey; tel. 8555179; fax 2272592; e-mail gazioglu@kktc.net; Man. Editor AHMET C. GAZIOĞLU.

K. Rüstem & Bro.: 22–24 Girne Cad., Lefkoşa (Nicosia), Mersin 10, Turkey; tel. 2271418.

Sebil International Press: PK 421, Lefkoşa (Nicosia), Mersin 10, Turkey; tel. 2246805; fax 2231804; e-mail ics@analiz.net; f. 1985; technical and scientific; Principal Officer E. BAŞARAN.

Tezel Matbaası: 35 Şinasi Sok., Lefkoşa (Nicosia), Mersin 10, Turkey; tel. 2271022.

Broadcasting and Communications

TELECOMMUNICATIONS

Cyprus Telecommunications Authority (CyTA): POB 24929, 1396 Nicosia; tel. 22701000; fax 22494940; e-mail pr@cyta.cytanet.com.cy; internet www.cyta.com.cy; provides national, international and cellular services in Cyprus.

Telekomünikasyon Diaresi Müdürlügü (Directorate of Telecommunications): Lefkoşa (Nicosia), Mersin 10, Turkey; tel. 2281888; fax 2288666; f. 1963; state-owned; responsible to Ministry of Communications and Works; admin. and operation of telecommunications services; Gen. Man. MUSTAFA BERKTUĞ.

BROADCASTING

Radio

British Forces Broadcasting Service, Cyprus: Akrotiri, British Forces Post Office 57; tel. 25968518; fax 25968580; e-mail info@bfbs .com; internet www.ssvc.com/bfbs/radio/cyprus; f. 1948; broadcasts a two-channel 24-hour radio service in English on VHF; Station Man. DUSTY MILLER; Engineering Man. JON FORDHAM.

Cyprus Broadcasting Corporation (CyBC): POB 24824, Broadcasting House, 1397 Nicosia; tel. 22422231; fax 22314050; e-mail rik@cybc.com.cy; internet www.cybc.com.cy; f. 1952; four 24-hour radio channels, two of which are mainly Greek; channel 2 broadcasts programmes in Turkish, English and Armenian; Chair. ANDREAS ALONEFTIS; Dir-Gen. MARIOS MAVRIKIOS; Head of Radio KYRIACOS CHARALAMBIDES.

Logos: Church of Cyprus, POB 27400, 1644 Nicosia; tel. 22355444; fax 22355737; e-mail director@logos.cy.net; Chair. ANDREAS PHILIPPOU; Dir-Gen. CHRISTODOULOS PROTOPAPAS.

Radio Astra: 145 Athalassas Ave, Strovolos, 2045 Nicosia; tel. 22313200; fax 22319261; e-mail info@astra.com.cy; internet www .astra.com.cy; Dir TAKIS HADJIGEORGIOU.

Radio Proto: POB 21836, 31 Archangelos St, Parissinos, 2054 Nicosia; tel. 22 353545; fax 22352266; e-mail pavlos@radioproto .com; internet www.radioproto.com; Chair. KOSTAS HADJIKOSTIS; Gen. Man. PAVLOS PAPACHRISTODOULOU.

Bayrak Radio and TV Corpn (BRTK): Atatürk Sq., Lefkoşa (Nicosia), Mersin 10, Turkey; tel. 2285555; fax 2281991; e-mail brt@ cc.emu.edu.tr; internet www.brt.gov.nc.tr; in July 1983 it became an independent Turkish Cypriot corpn, partly financed by the Govt; Radio Bayrak; f. 1963; home service in Turkish, overseas service in Turkish, Greek, English, Arabic and German; broadcasts 52.5 hours per day; Chair. VASFI CANDAN; Dir HÜSEYIN GÜRŞAN; Head of Radio PERAL AĞCATAŞ.

First FM and Interfirst FM: Lefkoşa (Nicosia), Mersin 10, Turkey; f. 1996.

Kıbrıs FM / Kıbrıs TV: Dr Fazil Küçük Blvd, Yeni Sanayi Bolgesi, Lefkoşa (Nicosia), Mersin 10, Turkey; tel. 2252555; fax 2253707; e-mail kibrisibrisgazetesi.com; Dir ERDINCH GUNDUZ.

Radio Emu: Gazi Mağusa (Famagusta), Mersin 10, Turkey; e-mail radioemu@cc.emu.edu.tr; internet www.emu.edu.tr/~radioemu.

Television

Greek Cypriot viewers have access to Greek television channels via satellite. Several Turkish channels are transmitted to the 'TRNC'.

Antenna TV: POB 20923, 1655 Nicosia; tel. 22311111; fax 22314959; Chair. LOUKIS PAPAPHILIPPOU; Man. Dir STELIOS MALEKOS.

British Forces Broadcasting Service, Cyprus: Akrotiri, British Forces Post Office 57; tel. 25952009; fax 25278580; e-mail dusty .miller@bfbs.com; f. 1948; broadcasts a daily TV service; Station Man. DUSTY MILLER; Engineering Man. DAVID GILL.

Cyprus Broadcasting Corporation (CyBC): POB 24824, Broadcasting House, 1397 Nicosia; tel. 22422231; fax 22314050; e-mail rik@cybc.com.cy; internet www.cybc.com.cy; television; f. 1957; **Pik 1 (CyBC 1)** one Band III 100/10-kW transmitter on Mount Olympus. **Pik 2 (CyBC 2)** one Band IV 100/10-kW ERP transmitter on Mount Olympus. **ET1** one Band IV 100/10-kW ERP transmitter on Mount Olympus for transmission of the ETI Programme received, via satellite, from Greece. The above three TV channels are also transmitted from 80 transposer stations; Chair. ANDREAS ALONEFTIS; Dir-Gen. MARIOS MAVRIKIOS.

Lumiere TV Ltd: POB 25614, 2063 Nicosia; tel. 22357272; fax 22354622; e-mail administration@ltv.com.cy; internet www .lumieretv.com; f. 1992; encoded signal; Chair. and Man. Dir AKIS AVRAAMIDES; Gen. Man. GEORGE XINARIS.

MEGA TV: POB 27400, 1644 Nicosia; tel. 22477777; fax 22477737; e-mail info@megatv.com.cy; Gen. Man. GEORGE MAMALAKIS.

Sigma Radio TV Ltd: POB 21836, 2054 Nicosia; tel. 22580100; fax 22358646; internet www.sigmatv.com; island-wide coverage; Chair. and Dir KOSTAS HADJICOSTIS; Man. DINOS ODYSSEOS; New Business Devt Dir ANDY HADJICOSTIS.

Bayrak Radio and TV Corpn (BRTK): Atatürk Sq., Lefkoşa (Nicosia), Mersin 10, Turkey; tel. 2255555; fax 2254581; e-mail brt@ cc.emu.edu.tr; internet www.brt.gov.nc.tr; in July 1983 it became an independent Turkish Cypriot corpn, partly financed by the Govt; Bayrak TV; f. 1976; transmits programmes in Turkish, Greek, English and Arabic on nine channels; Chair. VASFI CANDAN; Dir HÜSEYIN GÜRŞAN; Head of Television TÜLIN URAL.

Gene TV: Bevel Yusuf Cad. 8, Yenişehir, Lefkoşa (Nicosia), Mersin 10, Turkey; tel. 2280790; fax 2276363; Dir ERTAN BIRINCI.

Kanal T: Dr Fazıl Küçük Cad. Foto Filiz Binaları, Göçmenköy, Lefkoşa (Nicosia), Mersin 10, Turkey; tel. 2237678; fax 2234257; Owner ERSIN FATAR.

Finance

(brs = branches; cap. = capital; res = reserves; dep. = deposits; m. = million; amounts in Cyprus pounds, except for Turkish Cypriot banks)

BANKING

Central Banks

Central Bank of Cyprus: POB 25529, 80 Kennedy Ave, 1076 Nicosia; tel. 22714100; fax 22378153; e-mail cbcinfo@centralbank .gov.cy; internet www.centralbank.gov.cy; f. 1963; became fully independent from govt control in July 2002; cap. 15m., res 16.8m., dep. 2,032.0m. (Dec. 2004); Gov. CHRISTODOULOS CHRISTODOULOU.

Central Bank of the 'Turkish Republic of Northern Cyprus': Lefkoşa (Nicosia), Mersin 10, Turkey; e-mail info@kktcmb.trnc.net; internet www.kktcmb.trnc.net.

Greek Cypriot Banks

Alpha Bank Ltd: POB 21661, Yiorkion Bldg, 1 Prodromou St, 1596 Nicosia; tel. 22888798; fax 22773744; e-mail secretariat@alphabank .com.cy; internet www.alphabank.com.cy; f. 1960 as Lombard Banking (Cyprus) Ltd; name changed to Lombard NatWest Banking Ltd in 1989 and as above in 1998; locally incorporated although foreign-controlled; 100% owned by Alpha Bank, Athens; cap. 69.8m., res 29.4m., dep. 949.1m. (Dec. 2002); Chair. SPYROS N. FILARETOS; Man. Dir EMMANUEL ZALOUMIS; Gen. Man. C. KOKKINOS; 26 brs.

Bank of Cyprus Group: POB 21472, 51 Stassinos St, Ayia Paraskevi, 2002 Strovolos 140, 1599 Nicosia; tel. 22378000; fax 22378111; e-mail info@cy.bankofcyprus.com; internet www .bankofcyprus.com; f. 1899; reconstituted 1943 by the amalgamation of Bank of Cyprus, Larnaca Bank Ltd and Famagusta Bank Ltd; cap. 232.4m., res 290.7m., dep. 7,804.6m. (Dec. 2003); Chair. SOLON A. TRIANTAFYLLIDES; Group Chief Exec. CHR. S. PANTZARIS; 272 brs.

Co-operative Central Bank Ltd: POB 24537, 8 Gregoris Afxentiou St, 1389 Nicosia; tel. 22743000; fax 22670261; e-mail coopbank .gm@cytanet.com.cy; internet www.coopbank.com.cy; f. 1937 under the Co-operative Societies Law; banking and credit facilities to member societies, importer and distributor of agricultural requisites, insurance agent; cap. 9.9m., dep. 1,267.8m. (Dec. 2004); Chair. D. STAVROU; Sec.-Gen. E. CHLORAKIOTIS; 4 brs.

The Cyprus Popular Bank Ltd: POB 22032, Laiki HQ, 154 Limassol Ave, 1598 Nicosia; tel. 22752000; fax 22811496; e-mail laiki.telebank@laiki.com; internet www.laiki.com; f. 1901; full commercial banking; cap. 151.8m., res 123.3m., dep. 4,138.3m. (Dec. 2002); Chair. and Pres. KIKIS N. LAZARIDES; 120 brs.

Hellenic Bank Ltd: 200 cnr Limassol and Athalassa Ave, 2025 Nicosia; tel. 22500000; fax 22500050; e-mail hellenic@hellenicbank .com; internet www.hellenicbank.com; f. 1974; financial services group; cap. 59.1m., res 99.2m., dep. 2,169.2m. (Dec. 2003); Chair. and Chief Exec. PANOS CHR. GHALANOS; 103 brs.

Housing Finance Corpn: POB 23898, 41 Themistoklis Dervis St, Hawaii Tower, Nicosia; tel. 22761777; fax 22762870; f. 1980; provides long-term loans for home-buying; cap. 12m., dep. 213m. (June 2000); Gen. Man. CH. SHAMBARTAS; 6 brs.

National Bank of Greece (Cyprus) Ltd: 15 Arch. Makarios III Ave, 1065 Nicosia; tel. 22840000; fax 22840010; e-mail cloizou@nbg .com.cy; f. 1994 by incorporating all local business of the National Bank of Greece SA; full commercial banking; cap. 23m. (Nov. 2000); Chair. T. ARAPOGLOU; Man. Dir M. TSITSIRIDES; 30 brs.

Universal Bank: 6th Floor, Universal Tower, 85 Dhigenis Akritas Ave, 1070 Nicosia; tel. 22883333; fax 22358702; e-mail unimail@usb .com.cy; internet www.universalbank.com.cy; f. 1925 as Yialousa Savings Ltd (closed 1974, reopened 1990), renamed Universal Savings Bank Ltd, as above 2001; cap. 15.1m., res 12.4m., dep. 159.1m. (Dec. 2002); Chair. GEORGE SYRIMIS; Gen. Man. Dr SPYROS EPISKOPOU; 15 brs.

Turkish Cypriot Banks
(amounts in Turkish liras unless otherwise indicated)

Akdeniz Garanti Bankası Ltd: PK 149, 2–4 Celaliye Sok. Inönu Meydanı, Lefkoşa (Nicosia), Mersin 10, Turkey; tel. 2286742; fax 2286741; e-mail agbltd@superonline.com; internet www .akdenizgarantibank.com; f. 1989 as Mediterranean Guarantee

Bank; cap. and res 3,631,739m., dep. 173,800,479m. (Dec. 2004); Chair. BENGU SONYA.

Asbank Ltd: 8 Mecidiye Sok., PK 448, Lefkoşa (Nicosia), Mersin 10, Turkey; tel. 2283023; fax 2281244; e-mail asbank@kktc.net; internet www.asbank.com.tr; f. 1986; cap. 5,062,500m., res 2,607,667m. (Dec. 2003); Chair. ALTAY ADADEMIR; Gen. Man. T. M. ALTUNER; 7 brs.

First Merchant Bank OSH Ltd: 25 Serif Arzik Sok., Lefkoşa (Nicosia), Mersin 10, Turkey; tel. 2275373; fax 2275377; e-mail fmb@firstmerchantbank.com; internet www.firstmerchantbank.com; f. 1993; also provides offshore services; cap. US $10m., res US $8.6m., dep. US $1,562.3m. (Dec. 2002); Chair. and Gen. Man. Dr H. N. YAMAN.

Kıbrıs Altınbaş Bank Ltd (Cyprus Altınbaş Bank Ltd): PK 843, 2 Müftü Ziyai Efendi Sok., Lefkoşa (Nicosia), Mersin 10, Turkey; tel. 2288222; fax 2271623; e-mail kibrisaltinbasbank@yahu.com; internet www.altinbasbank.com.tr; f. 1993; cap. 748,100m., res 81,330m., dep. 7,822,563m. (Dec. 2000); Chair. VAKKAS ALTINBAŞ; Gen. Man. ÖZKAN TEKGUMUS.

Kıbrıs Continental Bank Ltd: 35–37 Girne Caddesi, Lefkoşa (Nicosia), Mersin 10, Turkey; tel. 2286961; fax 2286334; e-mail cbank_salim@kktc.net; internet www.kibriscontinentalbank.com; f. 1998; cap. 2,600,000m., res 2,605m., dep. 8,795,588m. (Dec. 2003); Chair. OSMAN KARAISMAILOĞLU; Gen. Man. SERACETTIN BAKTAY.

Kıbrıs Endüstri Bankası Ltd (Industrial Bank of Cyprus Ltd): Bedrettin Demirel Cad., Başbakanlık Kavşağı, Lefkoşa (Nicosia), Mersin 10, Turkey; tel. 2283770; fax 2271830.

Kıbrıs İktisat Bankası Ltd (Cyprus Economy Bank Ltd): 151 Bedreddin Demirel Cad., Lefkoşa (Nicosia), Mersin 10, Turkey; tel. 2285300; fax 2281311; e-mail info@iktisatbank.cc; internet www.iktisatbank.cc; f. 1990; cap. 4,080,000m., res 2,883,388m., dep. 71,342,099m. (Dec. 2003); Chair. and Gen. Man. METE ÖZMERTER; 12 brs.

Kıbrıs Türk Kooperatif Merkez Bankası Ltd (Cyprus Turkish Co-operative Central Bank): 49–55 Mahmut Paşa Sok., PK 823, Lefkoşa (Nicosia), Mersin 10, Turkey; tel. 2283207; fax 2276787; e-mail info@koopbank.com; internet www.koopbank.com; f. 1959; cap. and res 23,446,718m., dep. 698,296,063m. (Dec. 2004); banking and credit facilities to member societies and individuals; Chair. IBRAHIM BEYATLI; Gen. Man. NURI ERHAT; 14 brs.

Kıbrıs Vakiflar Bankası Ltd (Cyprus Vakiflar Bank Ltd): 58 Yediler Sok., PK 212, Lefkoşa (Nicosia), Mersin 10, Turkey; tel. 2275109; fax 2275169; e-mail kvb@kktc.net; f. 1982; cap. 3,700,000m., res 352,978m., dep. 133,751,255m. (Dec. 2002); Pres. and Chair. LATIF ARAN; Gen. Man. ALPAY R. ADANIR; 8 brs.

Limassol Turkish Co-operative Bank Ltd: 10 Orhaneli Sok., Kyrenia, PK 247, Mersin 10, Turkey; tel. 8150102; fax 8156959; e-mail libank@kktc.net; internet www.limasolbank.com; f. 1939; cap. 6,993,213.8m., res 601,679.6m, dep. 96,734,104.4m. (Dec. 2001); Chair. GÜZEL HALIM; Gen. Man. TANER EKDAL.

Türk Bankası Ltd (Turkish Bank Ltd): 92 Girne Cad., PK 242, Lefkoşa (Nicosia), Mersin 10, Turkey; tel. 2283313; fax 2282432; e-mail info@turkishbank.net; internet www.turkishbank.com; f. 1901; cap. 51,228,191m., res 33,687,177m., dep. 624,037,144m. (Dec. 2003); Chair. M. TANJU ÖZYOL; Gen. Man. C. YENAL MUSANNIF; 11 brs.

Universal Bank Limited: POB 658, 57 Mehmet Akif ave, Lefkoşa (Nicosia), Mersin 10, Turkey; tel. 2286262; fax 2287826; e-mail univers@kktc.net; internet www.bankunivers.com; f. 1997; cap. 2,747,500.0m., res 206,017.0m., dep. 21,539,621.0m. (Dec. 2002); Chair. ILHAN KÖSEOĞLU; Gen. Man. ERCAN ÖZGÜM.

Viyabank Ltd: Ataturk Cad., 16 Muhtar Yusuf Galleria, Lefkoşa (Nicosia), Mersin 10, Turkey; tel. 2288902; fax 2285878; e-mail viyabank@hotmail.com; internet www.viyabank.com; f. 1998; cap. US $2.5m., res US $0.5m., dep. US $4.2m. (Dec. 2002); Pres. SALVO TARAGANO; Chair. ERDOĞAN SEVINÇ; 2 brs.

Yakin Dogu Bank Ltd (Near East Bank Ltd): POB 47, 1 Girne Caddesi, Lefkoşa (Nicosia), Mersin 10, Turkey; tel. 2283834; fax 2284180; cap. 2,942,050.0m., res 986,567.3m., dep. 20,910,642.6m. (Dec. 2002); Chair. Dr SUAT I. GÜNSEL; Gen. Man. KAMIL NURI ÖZERK.

Yeşilada Bank Ltd: POB 626, 11 Atatürk Ave, Lefkoşa (Nicosia), Mersin 10, Turkey; tel. 2281999; fax 2281962; e-mail info@yesilada-bank.com; internet www.yesilada-bank.com; cap. 1,509,360.0m., res 231,530.0m., dep. 18,415,427.0m. (Dec. 2002); Chair. and Pres. ISMET KOTAK; Gen. Man. MUSTAFA UZUN.

Investment Organization

The Cyprus Investment and Securities Corpn Ltd: POB 20597, 1660 Nicosia; tel. 22881700; fax 22338800; e-mail info@cisco.bankofcyprus.com; internet www.cisco-online.com.cy; f. 1982 to promote the development of capital market; brokerage services, fund management, investment banking; member of Bank of Cyprus

Group; issued cap. 22m. (2004); Chair. S. A. TRIANTAFYLLIDES; Gen. Man. LOUIS POCHANIS.

Development Bank

The Cyprus Development Bank Ltd: POB 21415, Alpha House, 50 Archbishop Makarios III Ave, 1508 Nicosia; tel. 22846500; fax 22846603; e-mail info@cdb.com.cy; internet www.cyprusdevelopmentbank.com.cy; f. 1963; cap. 12.4m., res 5.4m., dep. 75m. (Dec. 2003); aims to accelerate the economic development of Cyprus by providing medium- and long-term loans for productive projects, developing the capital market, encouraging joint ventures and providing technical and managerial advice to productive private enterprises; Chair. ANDREAS MOUSKOS; Gen. Man. TAKIS TAOUSHANIS; 1 br.

Foreign Banks

Arab Bank PLC: POB 25700, 1 Spyrov Kyprianov Ave, 1393 Nicosia; tel. 22899100; fax 22760890; e-mail info@arabbank.com.cy; internet www.arabbank.com.cy; f. 1984; commercial; Man. JACK. BEIGHTON.

Emporiki Bank of Greece (Cyprus) Ltd: POB 25151, 1307 Nicosia; tel. 22663727; fax 22663923; e-mail info@combank.com.cy; internet www.combank.com.cy; f. 1992; fmrly Commercial Bank of Greece, renamed April 2003; Chair. G. MICHELIS.

Türkiye Cumhuriyeti Ziraat Bankası: Girnekapi Cad., Ibrahimpaşa Sok. 105, Lefkoşa (Nicosia), Mersin 10, Turkey; tel. 2283050; fax 2282041.

Türkiye Halk Bankası AŞ: POB 256, Lefkoşa (Nicosia), Mersin 10, Turkey; tel. 2288045; fax 2282900.

Türkiye İş Bankası AŞ: Girne Cad. 9, Lefkoşa (Nicosia), Mersin 10, Turkey; tel. 2283133; fax 2278315; e-mail S680001@isbank.com.tr; f. 1924; Man. ISMET DEMIRAĞ.

'Offshore' (International) Banking Units

In 2003 there were 29 Offshore Banking Units (OBUs) operating in Cyprus.

Agropromstroybank: POB 55297, Maximos Court B, 17 Leontiou St, Limassol; tel. 25384747; fax 25384858; Man. ALEXANDER MOKHONKO.

Allied Bank SAL: POB 54232, 3rd Floor, Flat 31, Lara Court, 276 Archbishop Makarios III Ave, Limassol; tel. 25363759; fax 25372711; Local Man. GEORGES ABI CHAMOUN.

Arab Bank PLC: POB 25700, 1 Santaroza Ave, 1393 Nicosia; tel. 22899100; fax 22760890; e-mail arabbank@spidernet.com.cy; OBU licence granted 1997; Area Exec. TOUFIC J. DAJAN.

Arab Jordan Investment Bank SA: POB 54384, Libra Tower, 23 Olympion St, Limassol; tel. 25351351; fax 25360151; e-mail ajib@c.cy .net; internet www.ajib.com; f. 1978; cap. and dep. US $388m., total assets US $410m. (Dec. 1999); Man. ABED ABU-DAYEH.

AVTOVAZBANK: POB 52270, Office 202, Lophitis Business Center, 249, 28th October Ave, 3035 Limassol; tel. 25354594; fax 25362582; e-mail avbkcy@cytanet.com.cy; internet www.avtovazbank.ru; Local Man. S. BONDARENKO.

Banca Română de Comerţ Exterior (Bancorex) SA: POB 22538, Margarita House, 5th Floor, 15 Them. Dervis St, 1309 Nicosia; tel. 22677992; fax 22677945; Local Man. GRIGORE IOAN BUDISAN.

Bank of Beirut and the Arab Countries SAL: POB 56201, Emelle Bldg, 1st Floor, 135 Archbishop Makarios III Ave, Limassol; tel. 25381290; fax 25381584; e-mail bbaccyp@spidernet.com.cy; Man. ELIE TABET.

Banque du Liban et d'Outre-Mer SAL: POB 53243, P. Lordos Centre Roundabout, Byron St, Limassol; tel. 25376433; fax 25376292; Local Man. S. FARAH.

Banque Nationale de Paris Intercontinentale SA: POB 50058, Kanika Business Centre, 319 28th October St, 3600 Limassol; tel. 25840840; fax 25840698; e-mail bnpi.cyprus@bnpparibas.com; internet www.bnpi.com.cy; Local Man. CHRISTIAN ARLOT.

Banque SBA: 8c Iris House, Kanika Enaerios Complex, John Kennedy St, Limassol; tel. 25588650; fax 25581643; e-mail sba.ibu@banque-sba.com; branch of Banque SBA (fmrly Société Bancaire Arabe), Paris; Local Man. ADNAN NUWAYHED.

Barclays Bank PLC: POB 27320, 88 Dhigenis Akritas Ave, 1644 Nicosia; tel. 22654400; fax 22754233; e-mail barclays@spidernet.com.cy; Cyprus Dir JONATHAN MILLS.

BEMO (Banque Européenne pour le Moyen-Orient SAL): POB 6232, Doma Court, 1st–2nd Floors, 227 Archbishop Makarios III Ave, Limassol; tel. 25583628; fax 25588611; e-mail bemolobu@spidernet.com.cy; Local Man. N. A. HCHAIME.

Byblos Bank SAL: POB 50218, Loucaides Bldg, 1 Archbishop Kyprianou St/St Andrew St, 3602 Limassol; tel. 25341433; fax 25367139; e-mail byblos@spidernet.com.cy; internet www.byblosbank.com.lb; Man. ANTOINE SMAIRA.

Crédit Libanais SAL: POB 53492, Chrysalia Court, 1st Floor, 206 Archbishop Makarios III Ave, 3030 Limassol; tel. 25376444; fax 25376807; e-mail clibhh@cytanet.com.cy; Local Man. HAYAT HARFOUCHE.

Crédit Suisse First Boston (Cyprus) Ltd: POB 57530, 199 Christodolou Hadsipavlou Ave, 3316 Limassol; tel. 25341244; fax 25817424; internet www.csfb.com; f. 1996; OBU status granted 1997; Gen. Man. ANTONIS ROUVAS.

DEPFA Investment Bank Ltd: POB 20909, 10 Diomidous St, 1665 Nicosia; tel. 22396300; fax 22396399; e-mail erol.riza@depfa.com; internet www.depfa.com; IBU licence granted 1998; Gen. Mans EROL RIZA, GEERT DECLERCK.

Emporiki Bank of Greece SA: 1 Iona Nicolaou, POB 27587, Engomi, 2431 Nicosia; tel. 22663686; fax 22663688; e-mail ibu@combank.com.cy; fmrly Commercial Bank of Greece, renamed April 2003; Man. K. RIALAS.

Federal Bank of the Middle East Ltd: POB 25566, J&P Bldg, 90 Archbishop Makarios III Ave, 1391 Nicosia; tel. 22888444; fax 22888555; e-mail mail@fbme.com; internet www.fbme.com; f. 1983; cap. US $46.0m., dep. $283.3m. (Dec. 2002); Chair. AYOUB-FARID M. SAAB; 2 brs.

First Investment Bank Ltd: POB 16023, cnr of Kennedy Ave & 39 Demoforitos St, 4th Floor, Flat 401, 2085 Nicosia; tel. 22760150; fax 22376560; Gen. Man. ENU NEDELE.

HSBC Bank (Cyprus) Ltd: POB 25718, Para Bldg. Block C, 7 Dositheou St, 1311 Nicosia; tel. 22376116; fax 22376121; internet www.hsbc.com; CEO ANDRI ANTONIADES; 1 br.

Karić Banka: POB 26522, Flat 22, Cronos Court, 66 Archbishop Makarios III Ave, Nicosia; tel. 22374980; fax 22374151; Man. Dir O. ERDELIJANOVIĆ.

Lebanon and Gulf Bank SAL International Banking Unit: POB 40337, Akamia Centre, 3rd Floor, Flat 309, cnr of G. Afxentiou and Archbishop Makarios III Ave, 6303 Larnaca; tel. 24620500; fax 24620708; e-mail lgbcy@logoscy.net; Local Man. F. SAADE.

Mega Euro Banka AD: c/o Tassos Papadopoulos and Co., Law Offices, 2 Safouli, Nicosia; OBU licence granted 1998.

Russian Commercial Bank (Cyprus) Ltd: POB 56868, 2 Amathuntos St, 3310 Limassol; tel. 25837300; fax 25342192; e-mail rcb@rcbcy.com; internet www.rcbcy.com; f. 1995; cap. US $10.8m., res US $9.8m., dep. US $1,371m. (Dec. 2004); CEO ANDREV A. SEREBRYAKOV.

Société Générale Cyprus Ltd: POB 25400, 7–9 Grivas Dhigenis Ave, 1309 Nicosia; tel. 22817777; fax 22765952; e-mail webmaster@sgcyprus.com; internet www.sgcyprus.com; cap. US $2.0m., res US $3.6m., dep. US $210.3m. (Dec. 2001); Chair. MAURICE SEHNAOUI; Gen. Man. JEAN-CLAUDE BOLOUX.

STOCK EXCHANGE

Cyprus Stock Exchange: POB 5427, 54 Grivas Dhigenis Ave, 1309 Nicosia; tel. 22668782; fax 22668790; e-mail cyse@zenon.logos.cy.net; internet www.cse.com.cy; official trading commenced in March 1996; 60 companies listed in 1999; Chair. AKIS KLEANTHOUS; Gen. Man. NONDAS METAXAS.

INSURANCE

Insurance Companies Control Service: Ministry of Finance, POB 23364, 1682 Nicosia; tel. 22303256; fax 22302938; e-mail insurance@mof.gov.cy; f. 1969 to control insurance companies, insurance agents, brokers and agents for brokers in Cyprus.

Greek Cypriot Insurance Companies

Aegis Insurance Co Ltd: POB 23450, 7 Klimentos St, Ayios Antonios, 1061 Nicosia; tel. 22343644; fax 22343866; Chair. ARISTOS KAISIDES; Principal Officer PANTELAKIS SOUGLIDES.

Aetna Insurance Co Ltd: POB 8909, 19 Stavrou St, 2035 Strovolos; tel. 22510933; fax 22510934; f. 1966; Chair. KONSTANTINOS L. PRODROMOU; Principal Officer KONSTANTINOS TSANGARIS.

Agrostroy Insurance Co Ltd: POB 6624, 89 Kennedy Ave, Office 201, 1077 Nicosia; tel. 22379210; fax 22379212; f. 1996; offshore captive company operating outside Cyprus; Chair. VALERIE V. USHAKOV; Principal Officer IOANNIS ELIA.

Akelius Insurance Ltd: POB 23415, 36 Laodikias St, 1683 Nicosia; tel. 22318883; fax 22318925; e-mail info@akelius.com; internet www.akelius.com; f. 1987; offshore company operating outside Cyprus;

Chair. ROGER AKELIOUS; CEO IOANNIS LOIZOU; Principal Officer DEMETRIS SYLLOURIS.

Allied Assurance & Reinsurance Co Ltd: POB 5509, 66 Grivas Dhigenis Ave, 1310 Nicosia; tel. 22672235; fax 22677656; f. 1982; offshore company operating outside Cyprus; Chair. HENRI J. G. CHALHOUB; Principal Officer DEMETRIOS DEMETRIOU.

Alpha Insurance Ltd: POB 26516, cnr Kennedy Ave and Stasinou St, 1640 Nicosia; tel. 22379999; fax 22379097; e-mail customer_service@alphainsurance.com.cy; f. 1993; Chair. DOUKAS PALEOLOGOS; Principal Officer and Sec. EVANGELOS ANASTASIADES.

Antarctic Insurance Co Ltd: POB 613, 199 Archbishop Makarios III Ave, Neokleou Bldg, 3030 Limassol; tel. 25362818; fax 25359262; offshore captive company operating outside Cyprus; Principal Officer ANDREAS NEOKLEOUS.

Apac Ltd: POB 25403, 5 Mourouzi St, Apt 1, 1055 Nicosia; tel. 22343086; fax 22343146; f. 1983; captive offshore company operating outside Cyprus; Chair. KYPROS CHRYSOSTOMIDES; Principal Officer GEORGHIOS POYATZIS.

Asfalistiki Eteria I 'Kentriki' Ltd: POB 25131, Kentriki Tower, 33 Clementos St, 1061 Nicosia; tel. 22745745; fax 22745746; e-mail kentriki@logosnet.com.cy; internet www.kentriki.com.cy; f. 1985; Chair. ARISTOS CHRYSOSTOMOU; Principal Officer GEORGHIOS GEORGALLIDES.

Aspis Pronia Insurance Co Ltd: POB 25183, 101 Acropolis Ave, 2012 Strovolos; tel. 22871087; fax 22492402; e-mail aspis@spidernet.com.cy; f. 1996; Chair. P. PSOMIADES; Principal Officer CHRISTAKIS ELEFTHERIOU.

Atlantic Insurance Co Ltd: POB 24579, 37 Prodromou St, 2nd Floor, 1090 Nicosia; tel. 22664052; fax 22661100; e-mail atlantic@spidernet.com.cy; f. 1983; Chair. and Man. Dir ZENIOS PYRISHIS; Principal Officer EMILIOS PYRISHIS.

Axioma Insurance (Cyprus) Ltd: POB 24881, 2 Ionni Klerides St, Demokritos No. 2 Bldg, Flat 83, 1070 Nicosia; tel. 22374197; fax 22374972; offshore company operating outside Cyprus; Principal Officer KONSTANTINOS KYAMIDES.

B & B Marine Insurance Ltd: POB 22545, 46 Gladstonos St, 1095 Nicosia; tel. 22666599; fax 22676476; f. 1996; offshore company operating outside Cyprus; Chair. DMITGRI MOLTCHANOV; Principal Officer GEORGHIOS YIANGOU.

Berytus Marine Insurance Ltd: POB 50132, 284 Archbishop Makarios III Ave, 3105 Limassol; tel. 25369404; fax 25377871; f. 1997; offshore company operating outside Cyprus; Principal Officer CHRIS GEORGHIADES.

Cathay Insurance Co Ltd: POB 54708, 21 Vasili Michailidi, 3727 Limassol; f. 1997; offshore captive company operating outside Cyprus; Principal Officer ARETI CHARIDEMOU.

Commercial Union Assurance (Cyprus) Ltd: POB 21312, Commercial Union House, 101 Archbishop Makarios III Ave, 1071 Nicosia; tel. 22377373; fax 22376155; e-mail mailbox@commercial-union.com.cy; internet www.commercial-union.com.cy; f. 1974; Chair. ANDREAS ARTEMIS; Man. Dir KONSTANTINOS P. DEKATRIS.

Cygnet Insurance Ltd: POB 58482, 56 Grivas Dhigenis Ave, Anna Tower, 4th Floor, Office 42, 3101 Limassol; tel. 25583253; fax 25584514; e-mail tcsl@logos.cy.net; f. 1997; offshore captive company operating outside Cyprus; Principal Officer MARIOS LOUKAIDES.

Cyprialife Ltd: POB 20819, 64 Archbishop Makarios III Ave and 1 Karpenisiou St, 1077 Nicosia; tel. 22887300; fax 22374450; e-mail cyprialife@cytanet.com.cy; f. 1995; Chair. KIKIS LAZARIDES; Principal Officer DIMIS MICHAELIDES.

Direct Insurance Company Ltd: POB 22274, 35–37 Byzantium St, 1585 Nicosia; tel. 22664433; fax 22665139; Chair. STAVROS DAVERONAS.

Emergency Market Insurance Ltd: POB 613, 199 Archbishop Makarios Ave, Neokleous Bldg, 3030 Limassol; tel. 25362818; fax 25359262; f. 1997; offshore captive company operating outside Cyprus; Principal Officer ANDREAS NEOKLEOUS.

Eurolife Ltd: POB 21655, Eurolife House, 4 Evrou, 1511 Nicosia; tel. 22474000; fax 22341092; internet www.bankofcyprus.com/eurolife; Chair. E. XENOPHONTOUS; Principal Officer ANDREAS KRITOTIS.

Eurosure Insurance Co Ltd: POB 21961, Eurosure Tower, 5 Limassol Ave, 2112 Aglantzia, 1515 Nicosia; tel. 22882500; fax 22882599; e-mail info@eurosure.com; internet www.eurosure.com; Chair. EFTHYVOULOS PARASKEVAIDES.

Excelsior General Insurance Co Ltd: POB 6106, 339 Ayiou Andreou St, Andrea Chambers, Of. 303, Limassol; tel. 25427021; fax 25312446; f. 1995; Chair. CLIVE E. K. LEWIS; Principal Officer MARIA HADJIANTONIOU.

FAM Financial and Mercantile Insurance Co Ltd: POB 50132, 284 Archbishop Makarios III Ave, Fortuna Bldg, Block 'B', 2nd Floor,

4007 Limassol; tel. 25362424; fax 25370055; f. 1993; offshore captive company operating outside Cyprus; Chair. VLADIMIR MOISSEEV; Principal Officer CHR. GEORGHIADES.

General Insurance of Cyprus Ltd: POB 21668, 2–4 Themistoklis Dervis St, 1066 Nicosia; tel. 22848700; fax 22671355; e-mail general@gic.bankofcyprus.com; f. 1951; Chair. V. ROLOGIS; Gen. Man. S. CHRISTODOULOU.

Geopolis Insurance Ltd: POB 8530, 6 Neoptolemou St, 2045 Strovolos, Nicosia; tel. 22490094; fax 22490494; f. 1993; Chair. MARIOS PROIOS; Principal Officer NIKOS DRYMIOTIS.

Granite Insurance Co Ltd: POB 613, 199 Archbishop Makarios III Ave, Neokleou Bldg, 3030 Limassol; tel. 25362818; fax 25359262; captive offshore company operating outside Cyprus; Chair. and Gen. Man. KOSTAS KOUTSOKOUMNIS; Principal Officer ANDREAS NEOKLEOUS.

Greene Insurances Ltd: POB 132, 4th Floor, Vereggaria Bldg, 25 Spyrou Araouzou St, 3036 Limassol; tel. 25362424; fax 25363842; f. 1987; Chair. GEORGHIOS CHRISTODOULOU; Principal Officer JOSIF CHRISTOU.

Hermes Insurance Ltd: POB 24828, 1st Floor, Anemomylos Bldg, 8 Michalakis Karaolis St, 1095 Nicosia; tel. 22666999; fax 22667999; e-mail cyprus-credit-insurance@cytanet.com.cy; f. 1980; Chair. and Man. Dir P. G. VOGAZIANOS.

I.G.R. Co Ltd: POB 21343, 20 Vasilissias Friderikis St, El Greco House, Office 104, 1066 Nicosia; tel. 22473688; fax 22455259; f. 1996; offshore company operating outside Cyprus; Principal Officer CHRISTODOULOS VASSILIADES.

Laiki Insurance Co Ltd: POB 22274, 45 Vyzantiou St, Strovolos, 1585 Nicosia; tel. 22664792; e-mail laiki.telebank@laiki.com; internet www.laiki.com; f. 1981; Chair. K. N. LAZARIDES; Gen. Man. STEPHIE DRACOS.

LCF Reinsurance Co Ltd: POB 60479, Abacus House, 58 Grivas Dhigenis Ave, 8103 Paphos, Nicosia; tel. 22555000; fax 22555001; f. 1984; Chair. ALAIN COPINE; Principal Officer SOPHIA XINARI.

Ledra Insurance Ltd: POB 23942, 66 Griva Dhigenis Ave, 1080 Nicosia; tel. 22743700; fax 22677656; f. 1994; Chair. CONSTANTINOS LOIZIDES; Principal Officer ALECOS PULCHERIOS.

Liberty Life Insurance Ltd: POB 26070, 75 Limassol Ave, 5th Floor, Nicosia; tel. 22319300; fax 22429134; f. 1994; Chair. KONSTANTINOS KITTIS; Principal Officer EURIPIDES NEOKLEOUS.

Marketrends Insurance Ltd: 34 Costi Palama, 1096 Nicosia; tel. 22558000; fax 22558100; e-mail markins@cytanet.com.cy; Man. Dir DEMETRIS ALETRARIS.

Medlife Insurance Ltd: POB 21675, Themistoklis Dervis-Florinis St, 1512 Nicosia; tel. 22675181; fax 22671889; e-mail office@medlife .net; internet www.medlife.net; f. 1995; Chair. Dr WOLFGANG GOSCHNIK.

Minerva Insurance Co Ltd: POB 20866, 8 Epaminondas St, 1684 Nicosia 137; tel. 22445134; fax 22455528; f. 1970; Chair. and Gen. Man. K. KOUTSOKOUMNIS.

Pancyprian Insurance Ltd: POB 21352, Pancyprian Tower, 66 Grivas Dhigenis Ave, 1080 Nicosia; tel. 22743743; fax 22677656; e-mail picl@pancyprian.com; f. 1993; Chair. CONSTANTINOS ST. LOIZIDES; Principal Officer SOCRATES DEMETRIOU.

Paneuropean Insurance Co Ltd: POB 553, 88 Archbishop Makarios III Ave, 1660 Nicosia; tel. 22377960; fax 22377396; f. 1980; Chair. N. K. SHACOLAS; Gen. Man. POLIS MICHAELIDES.

Philiki Insurance Co Ltd: POB 22274, 35–37 Byzantium St, 2026 Strovolos, 1585 Nicosia; tel. 22664433; fax 22665139; f. 1982; Chair. NIKOS SHAKOLAS; Principal Officer DOROS ORPHANIDES.

Progressive Insurance Co Ltd: POB 22111, 44 Kallipoleos St, 1071 Nicosia; tel. 22758585; fax 22754747; e-mail progressive@ cytanet.com.cy; Chair. ANDREAS HADJIANDREOU; Principal Officer TAKIS HADJIANDREOU.

Royal Crown Insurance Co Ltd: POB 24690, Royal Crown House, 20 Mnasiadou St, Nicosia 1302; tel. 22885555; fax 22670757; e-mail info@royalcrowninsurance.com; internet www.royalcrowninsurance .com; f. 1992; Chair. PHILIOS ZACHARIADES.

Saviour Insurance Co Ltd: POB 23957, 8 Michalakis Karaolis St, Anemomylos Bldg, Flat 204, 1687 Nicosia; tel. 22675085; fax 22676097; f. 1987; Chair. ROBERT SINCLAIR; Principal Officer KONSTANTINOS KITTIS.

Technolink Insurance Services Ltd: POB 7007, 70 Kennedy Ave, Papavasiliou House, 1076 Nicosia; tel. 22496000; fax 22493000; f. 1996; offshore captive company operating outside Cyprus; Principal Officer GEORGHIOS YIALLOURIDES.

Tercet Insurance Ltd: POB 2545, 46 Gladstones St, 1095 Nicosia; tel. 22466456; fax 22466476; f. 1994; Chair. ANDREAS STYLIANOU; Principal Officer MARIA PIPINGA.

Triada Insurance Ltd: POB 21675, corner Themistoklis Dervis & Florinis St, Stadyl Bldg, 6th Floor, 1512 Nicosia; tel. 22675182; fax 22675926; f. 1996; offshore captive company operating outside Cyprus; Principal Officer ANDREAS STYLIANOU.

Trust International Insurance Co (Cyprus) Ltd: POB 54857, 284 Archbishop Makarios III Ave, Fortuna Bldg, 2nd Floor, 4007 Limassol; tel. 25369404; fax 25377871; f. 1992; Chair. GHAZI K. ABU NAHL; Principal Officer CHR. GEORGHIADES.

Universal Life Insurance Company Ltd: POB 21270, Universal Tower, 85 Dhigenis Akritas Ave, 1505 Nicosia; tel. 22882222; fax 22882200; e-mail unilife@unilife.com.cy; internet www.universallife .com.cy; f. 1970; Chair. ANDREAS GEORGHIOU.

UPIC Ltd: POB 57237, Nicolaou Pentadromos Centre, 10th Floor, Ayias Zonis St, 3314 Limassol; tel. 25347664; fax 25347081; e-mail upic@spidernet.com.cy; f. 1992; Principal Officer POLAKIS SARRIS.

Veritima Insurance Ltd: POB 956, 2b Orpheus St, Office 104, 1070 Nicosia; tel. 22375646; fax 22375620; f. 1996; offshore captive company operating outside Cyprus; Principal Officer SANDROS DIKEOS.

VTI Insurance Co Ltd: POB 50613, 199 Archbishop Makarios III Ave, Neokleou Bldg, 4004 Limassol; tel. 25362818; fax 25359262; f. 1994; Chair. SOTERIS PITTAS; Principal Officer ANDREAS NEOKLEOUS.

Turkish Cypriot Insurance Companies

Akfinans Sigorta Insurance AŞ: 16 Osman Paşa Cad., Lefkoşa (Nicosia), POB 451, Mersin 10, Turkey; tel. 2284506; fax 2285713; e-mail akfinans@akfinans.com; internet www.akfinans.com; f. 1996; Gen. Man. MEHMET KADER.

Altınbaş Sigorta Ltd: Müftü Ziya Sok. 2, Lefkoşa (Nicosia), Mersin 10, Turkey; tel. 2288222; fax 2276648.

Anadolu Anonim: Memduh Asaf Sokak 8, Lefkoşa (Nicosia), Mersin 10, Turkey; tel. 2279595; fax 2279596; e-mail bolge50@ anadolusigorta.co.tr; internet www.anadolusigorta.com.tr.

Ankara Sigorta: PK 551, Bedrettin Demirel Cad., Lefkoşa (Nicosia), Mersin 10, Turkey; tel. 2285815; fax 2283099.

Başak Sigorta AŞ: Mehmet Akif Cad. 95, Lefkoşa (Nicosia), Mersin 10, Turkey; tel. 2280208; fax 2286160.

Bey Sigorta Ltd: Atatürk Cad. 5, Yenişehir, Lefkoşa (Nicosia), Mersin 10, Turkey; tel. 2288241; fax 2287362.

Gold Insurance Ltd: Salih Mecit Sok. 9, Lefkoşa (Nicosia), Mersin 10, Turkey; tel. 2286500; fax 2286300; e-mail ufahri@kibris.net.

Güneş Sigorta AŞ: Vakıflar İş Hanı 1C Girne Cad., Lefkoşa (Nicosia), Mersin 10, Turkey; tel. 2287333; fax 2281585.

Güven Sigorta (Kıbrıs) Sirketi AŞ: Mecidiye Sok. 8, Lefkoşa (Nicosia), Mersin 10, Turkey; tel. 2283023; fax 2281431.

İnan Sigorta TAŞ: Mehmet Akif Cad. 98, Kumsal, Lefkoşa (Nicosia), Mersin 10, Turkey; tel. 2283333; fax 2281976.

İsviçre Sigorta AŞ: Arkom Ltd, PK 693, Lefkoşa (Nicosia), Mersin 10, Turkey; tel. 2282125; fax 2288236; e-mail arkom@kktc.net.

Kıbrıs Sigorta: Osman Paşa Cad., Yağcıoğlu Işhanı 4, Lefkoşa (Nicosia), Mersin 10, Turkey; tel. 2283022; fax 2279277.

Ray Sigorta AŞ: Bedrettin Demirel Cad. Arabacıoğlu Apt. 7, Lefkoşa (Nicosia), Mersin 10, Turkey; tel. 2270380; fax 2270383.

Saray Sigorta: 182 Girne Cad., Lefkoşa (Nicosia), Mersin 10, Turkey; tel. 2272976; fax 2279001.

Şeker Sigorta (Kıbrıs) Ltd: Mahmut Paşa Sok. 14/A, PK 664, Lefkoşa (Nicosia), Mersin 10, Turkey; tel. 2285883; fax 2274074.

Zirve Sigorta Ltd: Gültekin Şengör Sok., Abahorlu Türk Apt. 9, Lefkoşa (Nicosia), Mersin 10, Turkey; tel. 2275633; fax 2283600.

Trade and Industry

GREEK CYPRIOT CHAMBERS OF COMMERCE AND INDUSTRY

Cyprus Chamber of Commerce and Industry: POB 21455, 38 Grivas Dhigenis Ave, 1509 Nicosia; tel. (22) 889800; fax (22) 669048; e-mail chamber@ccci.org.cy; internet www.ccci.org.cy; f. 1927; Pres. VASSILIS ROLOGIS; Sec.-Gen. PANAYIOTIS LOIZIDES; 8,000 mems, 100 affiliated trade asscns.

Famagusta Chamber of Commerce and Industry: POB 53124, 339 Ayiou Andreou St, Andrea Chambers Bldg, 2nd Floor, Office No. 201–202, 3300 Limassol; tel. (25) 370165; fax (25) 370291; e-mail chamberf@cytanet.com.cy; internet www.ccci.org.cy; f. 1952; Pres. ANDREAS MATSIS; Sec. and Dir IACOVOS HADJIVARNAVAS; 450 mems.

Larnaca Chamber of Commerce and Industry: POB 40287, 12 Gregoriou Afxentiou St, Skouros Bldg, Apt 43, 4th Floor, 6302 Larnaca; tel. (4) 655051; fax (4) 628281; e-mail lcci@spidernet.com.cy; Pres. ANDREAS LOUROUTZIATIS; Sec. GEORGE PSARAS; 450 mems.

Limassol Chamber of Commerce and Industry: POB 55699, 1st Floor, 166 Franklin Rossevelt, 3781 Limassol; tel. (25) 662556; fax (25) 661655; e-mail chamberl@cylink.com.cy; f. 1962; Pres. TONY ANTONIOU; Sec. and Dir CHRISTOS ANASTASSIADES; 770 mems.

Nicosia Chamber of Commerce and Industry: POB 21455, 38 Grivas Dhigenis Ave, Chamber Bldg, 1509 Nicosia; tel. (22) 889600; fax (22) 667433; e-mail ncci@ccci.org.cy; f. 1962; Pres. MANTHOS MAVROMATIS; Sec. SOCRATES HERACLEOUS; 1,200 mems.

Paphos Chamber of Commerce and Industry: POB 82, Athinon Ave & corner Alexandrou Papayou Ave, 8100 Paphos; tel. (6) 235115; fax (6) 244602; Pres. THEODOROS ARISTODEMOU; Sec. KENDEAS ZAMPIRINIS; 450 mems.

TURKISH CYPRIOT CHAMBERS OF COMMERCE AND INDUSTRY

Turkish Cypriot Chamber of Industry: 14 Osman Paşa Cad., PK 563, Köşklüçiftlik, Lefkoşa (Nicosia), Mersin 10, Turkey; tel. (22) 84596; fax (22) 84595; Pres. EREN ERTANIN.

Turkish Cypriot Chamber of Commerce: Bedrettin Demirel Cad., PK 718, Lefkoşa (Nicosia), Mersin 10, Turkey; tel. (22) 83645; fax (22) 83089; e-mail ktto@kibris.net; f. 1958; more than 6,000 regd mems; Chair. ALI EREL; Sec.-Gen. JANEL BURCAN.

GREEK CYPRIOT EMPLOYERS' ORGANIZATION

Cyprus Employers' & Industrialists' Federation: POB 21657, 30 Grivas Dhigenis Ave, 1511 Nicosia; tel. (22) 665102; fax (22) 669459; e-mail oeb@cytanet.com.cy; internet www.oeb-eif.org; f. 1960; 53 member trade associations, 400 direct and 3,000 indirect members; Dir-Gen. MICHAEL PILIKOS; Chair. BYRON KRANDIDIOTIS; The largest of the trade association members are: Cyprus Building Contractors' Association; Land and Building Developers' Association; Association of Cyprus Tourist Enterprises; Cyprus Shipping Association; Cyprus Footwear Manufacturers' Association; Cyprus Metal Industries Association; Cyprus Bankers Employers' Association; Cyprus Association of Business Consultants; Mechanical Contractors Association of Cyprus; Union of Solar Energy Industries of Cyprus.

TURKISH CYPRIOT EMPLOYERS' ORGANIZATION

Kıbrıs Türk şverenler Sendikası (Turkish Cypriot Employers' Association): PK 674, Lefkoşa (Nicosia), Mersin 10, Turkey; tel. (22) 73673; fax (22) 77479; Chair. HASAN SUNGUR.

GREEK CYPRIOT UTILITIES

Electricity

Electricity Authority of Cyprus (EAC): POB 24506, 1399 Nicosia; tel. (22) 845000; fax (22) 767658; e-mail eac@eac.com.cy; internet www.eac.com.cy; generation, transmission and distribution of electric energy in government-controlled area; also licensed to install and commercially exploit wired telecommunication network; total installed capacity 988 MW in 2003.

Water

Water Development Department: Dem. Severis Ave, 1413 Nicosia; tel. (22) 803100; fax (22) 675019; e-mail director@wdd.moa.gov.cy; internet www.pio.gov.cy/wdd; dam storage capacity 300m. cu m; Dir CHRISTODOULOS ARTEMIS.

TURKISH CYPRIOT UTILITIES

Electricity

Cyprus Turkish Electricity Corpn: Lefkoşa (Nicosia), Mersin 10, Turkey; tel. (22) 83648; fax (22) 83851.

TRADE UNIONS

Greek Cypriot Trade Unions

Cyprus Civil Servants' Trade Union: 3 Dem. Severis Ave, Nicosia; tel. (22) 844445; fax (22) 665199; e-mail pasydy@spidernet.com.cy; internet www.pasydy.org; f. 1949; registered 1966; restricted to persons in the civil employment of the Government and public authorities; 6 brs with a total membership of 15,383; Pres. ANDREAS CHRISTODOULOU; Gen. Sec. GLAFKOS HADJIPETROU.

Dimokratiki Ergatiki Omospondia Kyprou (DEOK) (Democratic Labour Federation of Cyprus): POB 21625, 40 Byron Ave, 1511 Nicosia; tel. (22) 676506; fax (22) 670494; e-mail deok@cytanet

.com.cy; f. 1962; 5 workers' unions with a total membership of 7,316; Gen. Sec. DIOMEDES DIOMEDOUS.

Pankypria Ergatiki Omospondia (PEO) (Pancyprian Federation of Labour): POB 21885, 31–35 Archermos St, Nicosia 1045; tel. (22) 886400; fax (22) 349382; e-mail peo@cytanet.com.cy; internet www.cytanet.com.cy/peo; f. 1946; registered 1947; previously the Pancyprian Trade Union Committee f. 1941, dissolved 1946; 8 unions and 176 brs with a total membership of 75,000; affiliated to the WFTU; Gen. Sec. PAMBIS KYRITSIS.

Pankyprios Omospondia Anexartition Syntechnion (Pancyprian Federation of Independent Trade Unions): 4B Dayaes St, 2369 Ay. Dhometios; POB 7521, 2430 Nicosia; tel. (22) 356414; fax (22) 354216; f. 1956; registered 1957; has no political orientations; 8 unions with a total membership of 798; Gen. Sec. KYRIACOS NATHANAEL.

Synomospondia Ergaton Kyprou (Cyprus Workers' Confederation): POB 25018, 11 Strovolos Ave, 2018 Strovolos, Nicosia; tel. (22) 849849; fax (22) 849850; e-mail sek@org.cy.net; f. 1944; registered 1950; 7 federations, 5 labour centres, 47 unions, 12 brs with a total membership of 65,000; affiliated to the ICFTU and the ETUC; Gen. Sec. DEMETRIS KITTENIS; Deputy Gen. Sec. NIKOS MOESEOS.

Union of Cyprus Journalists: POB 23495, Rik Ave 12, 1683 Nicosia; tel. 22446090; fax 22446095; e-mail cyjourun@logosnet.cy.net; f. 1959; Chair. ANDREAS KANNAOUROS.

Turkish Cypriot Trade Unions

In 1998 trade union membership totalled 24,864.

Devrimci İşçi Sendikaları Federasyonu (Dev-İş) (Revolutionary Trade Unions' Federation): 6 Serabioğlu Sok., 748 Lefkoşa (Nicosia), Mersin 10, Turkey; tel. (22) 86462; fax (22) 86463; e-mail devis@defne.net; f. 1976; four unions with a total membership of 1,850 (2002); affiliated to WFTU; Pres. ALI GULLE; Gen. Sec. MEHMET SEYIS.

Kıbrıs Türk İşçi Sendikaları Federasyonu (TÜRK-SEN) (Turkish Cypriot Trade Union Federation): POB 829, 7–7A Şehit Mehmet R. Hüseyin Sok., Lefkoşa (Nicosia), Mersin 10, Turkey; tel. (22) 72444; fax (22) 87831; e-mail turksen@north-cyprus.net; f. 1954; regd 1955; 12 unions with a total membership of 5,250 (1998); affiliated to ICFTU, ETUC, CTUC and the Confederation of Trade Unions of Turkey (Türk-İş); Pres. ARSLAN BIÇAKLI; Gen. Sec. ERKAN BIRER.

Transport

RAILWAYS

There are no railways in Cyprus.

ROADS

In 2002, according to the International Road Federation, there were 11,593 km of roads in the government-controlled areas, of which 268 km were motorway and 2,220 km were highways and other main roads; some 62.2% of the road network was paved. The Nicosia–Limassol four-lane dual carriageway, which was completed in 1985, was subsequently extended with the completion of the Limassol and Larnaca bypasses. Highways also connect Nicosia and Larnaca, Larnaca and Kophinou, Aradippo and Dhekelia, and Nicosia and Anthoupolis-Kokkinotrimithia. The first section of the Limassol–Paphos highway opened in 1997, and work on the remainder was completed in 2000. In 1997 work began on a Dhekelia–Ammochostos (Famagusta) highway. The north and south are now served by separate transport systems, and there are no services linking the two sectors.

SHIPPING

Until 1974 Famagusta, a natural port, was the island's most important harbour, handling about 83% of the country's cargo. Since its capture by the Turkish army in August 1974 the port has been officially declared closed to international traffic. However, it continues to serve the Turkish-occupied region.

The main ports that serve the island's maritime trade at present are Larnaca and Limassol, which were constructed in 1973 and 1974 respectively. Both ports have since been expanded and improved. There is also an industrial port at Vassiliko and there are three specialized petroleum terminals, at Larnaca, Dhekelia and Moni. A second container terminal became operational at Limassol in 1995.

In addition to serving local traffic, Limassol and Larnaca ports act as transhipment load centres for the Eastern Mediterranean, North Adriatic and Black Sea markets and as regional warehouse and assembly bases for the Middle East, North Africa and the Persian

(Arabian) Gulf. Containerized cargo handled at Cypriot ports amounted to 1,722,300 metric tons in 1998.

Both Kyrenia and Karavostassi are under Turkish occupation and have been declared closed to international traffic. Karavostassi used to be the country's major mineral port, dealing with 76% of the total mineral exports. However, since the war minerals have been passed through Vassiliko which is a specified industrial port. A hydrofoil service operates between Kyrenia and Mersin on the Turkish mainland. Car ferries sail from Kyrenia to Taşucu and Mersin, in Turkey.

At 31 December 2003 the Greek Cypriot shipping registry comprised 1,198 vessels, with an aggregate displacement of 22.1m. grt.

Department of Merchant Shipping: POB 56193, Kyllinis St, Mesk Geitonia, 4407 Limassol; tel. 25848100; fax 25848200; e-mail maritimeadmin@dms.mcw.com.cy; internet www.shipping.gov.cy; Dir SERGHIOS SERGHIOU.

Cyprus Ports Authority: POB 22007, 23 Crete St, 1516 Nicosia; tel. 22817200; fax 22765420; e-mail cpa@cpa.gov.cy; internet www.cpa.gov.cy; f. 1973; Chair. CHRYSIS PRENTZAS; Gen. Man. Dr YIANNAKIS KOKKINOS.

Cyprus Shipping Council: POB 56607, 3309 Limassol; tel. 25360717; fax 25358642; e-mail csc@csc-cy.org; internet www.csc-cy.org; Gen. Sec. THOMAS A. KAZAKOS.

Greek Cypriot Shipping Companies

Amer Shipping Ltd: POB 27363, 6th Floor, Ghinis Bldg, 58–60 Dhigenis Akritas Ave, 1061 Nicosia; tel. 22751707; fax 22751460; e-mail amer@spidernet.com.cy; internet www.amershipping.com; Man. Dir ANIL DESHPANDE.

C. F. Ahrenkiel Shipmanagement (Cyprus) Ltd: POB 53594, 4th Floor, O & A Tower, 25 Olympion St, 3033 Limassol; tel. 25854000; fax 25854001; Man. Dir VASSOS STAVROU.

Columbia Shipmanagement Ltd: POB 51624, Columbia House, Dodekanissou and Kolonakiou Corner, 3507 Limassol; tel. 25843100; fax 25320325; e-mail shipmanagement@csmcy.com; internet www.columbia.com.cy; f. 1978; Chair H. SCHOELLER; Man. Dir D. FRY.

Hanseatic Shipping Co Ltd: POB 50127, 3601 Limassol; ; tel. 25846400; fax 25745245; e-mail management@hanseatic.com.cy; internet www.hanseatic.com.cy; f. 1972; Man. Dir A. J. DROUSSIOTIS.

Interorient Navigation Co Ltd: POB 51309, 3 Thalia St, 3504 Limassol; tel. 25840300; fax 25575895; e-mail management@interorient.com.cy; internet www.interorient.com; Man. Dir JAN LISSOW.

Louis Cruise Lines: POB 21301, 1506 Nicosia; 20 Amphipoleos St, 2025 Strovolos; tel. 22588002; fax 22442848; e-mail kiliaris@louiscruises.com; internet www.louiscruises.com; Exec. Chair. COSTAKIS LOIZOU; Man. Dir STELIOS KILIARIS.

Marlow Navigation Co Ltd: POB 4077, Marlow Bldg, cnr 28th October St and Sotiris Michaelides St, Limassol; tel. 25348888; fax 25748222; e-mail marlow@marlow.com.cy; Gen. Man. ANDREAS NEOPHYTOU.

Oldendorff Ltd, Reederei 'Nord' Klaus E: POB 56345, Libra Tower, 23 Olympion St, 3306 Limassol; tel. 25841400; fax 25345077; e-mail mail@rnkeo.com.cy; internet www.rnkeo.com; Chair. and Man. Dir CHRISTIANE E. OLDENDORFF; Gen. Man. Capt. KEITH V. OBEYESEKERA.

Seatankers Management Co Ltd: POB 53562, Deana Beach Apartments, Block 1, 4th Floor, Promachon Eleftherias St, 4103 Limassol; tel. 25858300; fax 25323770; e-mail seatank@cytanet.com.cy; Dirs COSTAS PALLARIS, DIMITRIS HANNAS.

Turkish Cypriot Shipping Companies

Armen Shipping Ltd: Altun Tabya Yolu No. 10–11, Gazi Mağusa (Famagusta), Mersin 10, Turkey; tel. 3664086; fax 3665860; e-mail armen@armenshipping.com; Dir VARGIN VARER.

Compass Shipping Ltd: Seagate Court, Gazi Mağusa (Famagusta), Mersin 10, Turkey; tel. 3666393; fax 3666394.

Denko Koop Marine Cargo Department: PK 4, 12 Canbulat St, Gazi Mağusa (Famagusta), Mersin 10, Turkey; tel. 3665419; fax 3662773; e-mail info@koopbank.com; internet www.koopbank.com; Dir HASAN TRANSTURK.

Ertürk Ltd: Kyrenia (Girne), Mersin 10, Turkey; tel. 8155834; fax 8151808; Dir KEMAL ERTÜRK.

Fergun Maritime Co: Kyrenia (Girne), Mersin 10, Turkey; tel. 8154993; ferries to Turkish ports; Owner FEHIM KÜÇÜK.

Kıbrıs Türk Denizcilik Ltd, Şti (Turkish Cypriot Maritime Co Ltd): 3 Bülent Ecevit Bul., Gazi Mağusa (Famagusta), Mersin 10, Turkey; tel. 3665995; fax 3667840; e-mail cypship@superonline.com.

Medusa Marine Shipping Ltd: Aycan Apt, Gazi Mağusa (Famagusta), Mersin 10, Turkey; tel. 3663945; fax 3667800; Dir ERGÜN TOLAY.

Orion Navigation Ltd: Seagate Court, Gazi Mağusa (Famagusta), Mersin 10, Turkey; tel. 3662643; fax 3664773; e-mail orion@analiz.net; f. 1976; shipping agents; Dir O. LAMA; Shipping Man. L. LAMA.

Özari Shipping Ltd: Seagate Court, Gazi Mağusa (Famagusta), Mersin 10, Turkey; tel. 3666555; fax 3667098; Dir YALÇIN RUHI.

Tahsin Transtürk ve Oğlu Ltd: 11 Kizilkule Yolu, Gazi Mağusa (Famagusta), Mersin 10, Turkey; tel. 3665409.

CIVIL AVIATION

There is an international airport at Nicosia, which can accommodate all types of aircraft, including jet-engined airliners. It has been closed since 1974, following the Turkish invasion. A new international airport was constructed at Larnaca, from which flights operate to Europe, the USA, the Middle East and the Gulf. Another international airport at Paphos began operations in 1983. A C£210m. expansion and modernization of Larnaca and Paphos airports was proposed in late 2001 and was due for completion by 2010.

Avistar: POB 5532, Nicosia; tel. 22459533; fax 22477367; f. 1990; freight; Chief Exec. Dr WALDEMAR HAAS.

Cyprus Airways: 21 Alkeou St, Engomi 2404, POB 21903, 1514 Nicosia; tel. 22663054; fax 22663167; e-mail webcenter@cyprusairways.com; internet www.cyprusairways.com; f. 1947; jointly owned by Cyprus Government (69.62) and local interests; wholly-owned subsidiaries Cyprair Tours Ltd, Eurocypria Airlines Ltd, Duty Free Shops Ltd and Zenon NDC Ltd; Chair. CONSTANTINOS LOIZIDES; Gen. Man. CHRISTOS KYRIAKIDES (services throughout Europe and the Middle East).

Eurocypria Airlines (ECA): POB 970, 97 Artemidos Ave, Artemis Bldg, Larnaca; tel. 24658001; fax 24658008; services to European destinations from Larnaca and Paphos; Chair. HARIS LOIZIDES; Gen. Man. GEORGE SOUROULLAS.

In 1975 the Turkish authorities opened Ercan (formerly Tymbou) airport, and a second airport was opened at Geçitkale (Lefkoniko) in 1986.

Kıbrıs Türk Hava Yolları (Cyprus Turkish Airlines): Bedrettin Demirel Cad., PK 793, Lefkoşa (Nicosia), Mersin 10, Turkey; tel. 2283901; fax 2281468; e-mail info@kthy.net; internet www.kthy.net; f. 1974; jointly owned by the Turkish Cypriot Community Assembly Consolidated Improvement Fund and Turkish Airlines Inc; services to Turkey and five European countries; Gen. Man. M. ZEKI ZIYQ.

Tourism

In 2004 some 2,349,000 foreign tourists visited the Greek Cypriot area and receipts from tourism amounted to C£982.3m. In 2002 there were 94,466 hotel beds in the Greek Cypriot area. In 2003 469,867 tourists visited the Turkish Cypriot area, while revenue from tourism amounted to an estimated $178.8m.

Cyprus Tourism Organisation (CTO): POB 24535, 19 Limassol Ave, 2112 Nicosia; tel. 22691100; fax 22331644; e-mail cytour@cto.org.cy; internet www.visitcyprus.org.cy; Chair. PHOTIS PHOTIOU.

'TRNC' Ministry of Economy and Tourism: Lefkoşa (Nicosia), Mersin 10, Turkey; tel. 2289629; fax 2273976; e-mail info@holidayinnorthcyprus.com; internet www.holidayinnorthcyprus.com.

THE CZECH REPUBLIC

Introductory Survey

Location, Climate, Language, Religion, Flag, Capital

The Czech Republic lies in central Europe and comprises the Czech Lands of Bohemia and Moravia and part of Silesia. Its neighbours are Poland to the north, Germany to the north-west and west, Austria to the south and Slovakia to the east. The climate is continental, with warm summers and cold winters. The average mean temperature is 9°C (49°F). Czech, a member of the west Slavonic group, is the official language. There is a sizeable Slovak minority and also small Polish, German, Silesian, Roma, Hungarian and other minorities. The major religion is Christianity (about 40% of the population are Roman Catholics). The national flag (proportions 2 by 3) has two equal horizontal stripes, of white and red, on which is superimposed a blue triangle (half the length) at the hoist. The capital is Prague (Praha).

Recent History

In October 1918, following the collapse of the Austro-Hungarian Empire at the end of the First World War, the Republic of Czechoslovakia was established. The new state united the Czech Lands of Bohemia and Moravia, which had been incorporated into the Austrian Empire in the 16th and 17th centuries, and Slovakia, which had been under Hungarian rule for almost 1,000 years. After the Nazis came to power in Germany in 1933, there was increased agitation in the Sudetenland (an area in northern Bohemia that was inhabited by about 3m. German-speaking people) for autonomy within, and later secession from, Czechoslovakia. In 1938, to appease German demands, the British, French and Italian Prime Ministers concluded an agreement with the German leader, Adolf Hitler, whereby the Sudetenland was ceded to Germany, and other parts of Czechoslovakia were transferred to Hungary and Poland. The remainder of Czechoslovakia was invaded and occupied by Nazi armed forces in March 1939, and a German protectorate was established in Bohemia and Moravia. In Slovakia, which had been granted self-government in late 1938, a separate Slovak state was formed, under the pro-Nazi regime of Jozef Tiso.

After Germany's defeat in the Second World War (1939–45), the pre-1938 frontiers of Czechoslovakia were restored, although a small area in the east was ceded to the USSR in June 1945. Almost all of the German-speaking inhabitants of Czechoslovakia were expelled, and the Sudetenland was settled by Czechs from other parts of Bohemia. In response to Slovak demands for greater autonomy, a legislature (the Slovenská národná rada—Slovakian National Council) and an executive Board of Commissioners were established in Bratislava, the Slovak capital. At elections in 1946 the Communist Party of Czechoslovakia (CPCz) emerged as the leading party, winning 38% of the votes cast. The CPCz's leader, Klement Gottwald, became Prime Minister in a coalition Government. After ministers of other parties resigned, communist control became complete on 25 February 1948. A People's Republic was established on 9 June. Gottwald replaced Eduard Beneš as President, a position that he held until his death in 1953. The country aligned itself with the Soviet-led Eastern European bloc, joining the Council for Mutual Economic Assistance (CMEA) and the Warsaw Pact. Government followed a rigid Stalinist pattern, and in the early 1950s there were many political trials. Although these ended under Gottwald's successors, Antonín Zápotocký and, from 1956, Antonín Novotný, there was no relaxation of policy until 1963, when a new Government, with Jozef Lenárt as Prime Minister, was formed. Meanwhile, the country was renamed the Czechoslovak Socialist Republic, under a new Constitution, proclaimed in July 1960.

In January 1968 Alexander Dubček succeeded Novotný as CPCz Secretary, and in March Gen. Ludvík Svoboda succeeded Novotný as President. Oldřich Černík became Prime Minister in April. The new Government envisaged widespread reforms, including the introduction of a federal system of government, a more democratic electoral system, and a greater degree of separation between party and state. In August Warsaw Pact forces (numbering an estimated 600,000) invaded Czechoslovakia, occupying Prague and other major cities. Mass demonstrations

in protest at the invasion were held throughout the country, and many people were killed in clashes with occupation troops. The Soviet Government exerted heavy pressure on the Czechoslovak leaders to suppress their reformist policies and in April 1969 Dubček was replaced by a fellow Slovak, Dr Gustáv Husák, as First (subsequently General) Secretary of the Central Committee of the CPCz. Under Husák's leadership, there was a severe purge of the CPCz membership and most of Dubček's supporters were removed from the Government. All the reforms of 1968 were duly abandoned, with the exception of the federalization programme. This was implemented in January 1969, when the unitary Czechoslovak state was transformed into a federation, with separate Czech and Slovak Republics, each having its own legislature and Government. A Federal Government was established as the supreme executive organ of state power, and the country's existing legislature, the Národní shromáždění (National Assembly), was transformed into a bicameral Federální shromáždění (Federal Assembly). The first legislative elections since 1964 were held in November 1971, and 99.81% of the votes cast were in favour of candidates of the National Front (the communist-dominated organization embracing all the legal political parties in Czechoslovakia).

In May 1975 Husák was appointed to the largely ceremonial post of President of Czechoslovakia, retaining his positions of Chairman of the National Front and General Secretary of the CPCz. He held the latter post until December 1987, when he was replaced by Miloš Jakeš, an economist and member of the Presidium of the party's Central Committee. However, Husák remained as President of the Republic.

Although Jakeš affirmed his commitment to the moderate programme of reform initiated by his predecessor, repressive measures against the Roman Catholic Church and dissident groups continued. Of the latter, the most influential was Charter 77, which had been established in January 1977 by intellectuals, former politicians and others to campaign for the observance of civil and political rights. Despite the regime's continued attempts to suppress the movement, its sphere of influence broadened and it played a leading role in anti-Government demonstrations, which began in 1988. In February 1989, following one such demonstration, the Czech playwright, Václav Havel (a leader of Charter 77), was sentenced to nine months' imprisonment. (He was released in May, following international condemnation.) Anti-Government demonstrations followed in May, August and October 1989.

In November 1989 the protest actions of preceding months evolved into a process of dramatic, yet largely peaceful, political change, which subsequently became known as the 'velvet revolution'. On 17 November an anti-Government demonstration in Prague, the largest public protest for 20 years, was violently dispersed by the police; large numbers of demonstrators (who were mainly students) were injured. Large-scale protests continued in Prague and in other towns throughout the country. Later that month a new opposition group, Civic Forum, was established as an informal alliance, which united several existing opposition and human rights organizations, including Charter 77, and rapidly attracted widespread popular support. Meanwhile, Alexander Dubček addressed mass rallies in Bratislava and Prague, expressing his support for the opposition's demands for reform. On 24 November it was announced that Jakeš and the entire membership of the Presidium of the Central Committee had resigned. Karel Urbánek, a member of the Presidium, replaced Jakeš as General Secretary of the party, and a new Presidium was elected. The strength of Civic Forum and its Slovak counterpart, Public Against Violence (PAV), was demonstrated in discussions on reform, conducted between their leaders and the Federal Prime Minister, Ladislav Adamec. The opposition demands for the ending of censorship and the release of all political prisoners were accepted, and at the end of November the articles guaranteeing the CPCz's predominance were deleted from the Constitution.

In early December 1989 the Federal Government was reorganized. However, Civic Forum and PAV denounced the new Government, since the majority of its ministers had served in the previous administration, and it included only five non-communists. Adamec subsequently resigned as Prime Minister, and was replaced by Marián Čalfa, the newly appointed First Deputy Prime Minister. In the following week a new, interim Federal Government was formed, with a majority of non-communist members, including seven non-party supporters of Civic Forum. Husák resigned from the office of President of the Republic and at the end of December was replaced by Václav Havel. Alexander Dubček was elected Chairman of the Federální shromáždění. At an emergency congress of the CPCz, held in December, Urbánek was dismissed from the post of General Secretary of the Central Committee and this position was abolished. Adamec was appointed to the new post of Chairman of the party.

In April 1990 the Federální shromáždění voted to rename the country the Czech and Slovak Federative Republic (CzSFR). The decision, which followed intense controversy, satisfied Slovak demands that the new title should reflect the equal status of Slovakia within the federation. On 8–9 June the first democratic legislative elections since 1946 were held in Czechoslovakia. A total of 27 political associations contested representation to the Federální shromáždění (now numbering 300 seats) and to each republican legislature, with the participation of some 97% of the electorate. In the elections at federal level, the highest proportion of the total votes cast (about 46%) was secured by Civic Forum, in the Czech Lands, and by PAV, in Slovakia. The CPCz won a greater proportion of the votes (about 14%) than had been expected, obtaining the second highest representation in the Federální shromáždění. The Christian Democratic Union (a coalition of the Czechoslovak People's Party, the Christian Democratic Party—Chr.DP—and the Slovak-based Christian Democratic Movement—CDM) obtained approximately 12% of votes cast. Two parties that had campaigned for regional autonomy or secession secured more than the 5% minimum required for representation in the legislature: the Movement for Autonomous Democracy–Society for Moravia and Silesia (MAD–SMS) and the separatist Slovak National Party (SNP). The newly elected Federální shromáždění was to serve a transitional two-year term, during which time it was to draft new federal and republican constitutions and elect a new President of the Republic. In late June Dubček was re-elected Chairman of the Federální shromáždění. A new Federal Government, announced in that month, comprised 16 members: four from Civic Forum, three from PAV, one from the CDM and eight independents. In early July Havel was re-elected to the post of President.

In the latter half of 1990 there was increasing support in Slovakia for Slovak autonomy. A widening division emerged between the more moderate Slovak movements, such as PAV and the CDM, and a minority of more radical parties, which campaigned for full independence. In early March 1991 Vladimír Mečiar, the Slovak Prime Minister and a founding member of PAV, announced the formation of a minority faction within PAV (the Movement for a Democratic Slovakia—MDS), in support of greater Slovak autonomy. Meanwhile, disagreement over the direction of post-communist politics and economic management had led to a split within Civic Forum. Two main groups emerged in February 1991: the conservative Civic Democratic Party (CDP), led by Václav Klaus; and the liberal Civic Movement (CM). In late March representatives of all political forces in Czechoslovakia reached agreement on the framework of a new federal Constitution. Mečiar's policies and aggressive style of leadership were seen by many as detrimental to the future of Czech-Slovak relations, and in April the Slovenská národná rada voted to remove him from the Slovak premiership. Following this, the MDS was established as a separate political group. By late 1991 discussions in the Federální shromáždění on the new Constitution had reached an impasse. President Havel repeatedly proposed the holding of a referendum on the possible division of Czechoslovakia into two separate states, as the only democratic means of resolving the issue. The constitutional debate continued in the first half of 1992, with increasing Slovak support for the loosest possible confederation, comprising two nominally independent states. The majority of Czech politicians, however, were in favour of preserving the existing state structure, and rejected Slovak proposals as impracticable. In March it was agreed that the constitutional talks would be postponed until after the legislative elections due to take place in mid-1992.

The legislative elections of 5–6 June 1992 proved to be decisive in the eventual dismantling of Czechoslovakia, particularly as Mečiar's MDS emerged as the dominant political force in

Slovakia. With about 34% of the total Slovak votes cast, the party obtained 57 seats (the second largest representation) in the 300-member Federální shromáždění. The leading party in the Slovak Government, the CDM (which advocated a continued federation), won only 9% of the Slovak votes cast, securing 14 seats in the Federální shromáždění, one seat fewer than the separatist SNP. As had been expected, Václav Klaus's party, the CDP (in coalition with the Chr.DP), won the largest proportion (about 34%) of the total votes cast in the Czech Lands. The CDP was one of only two parties to contest the election in both republics, and in Slovakia it received 4% of the votes cast. In total, the CDP won 85 seats in the Federální shromáždění, thus becoming the largest party in the legislature. Two other splinter groups of the former Civic Forum—Dienstbier's CM and the Civic Democratic Alliance (CDA)—failed to win representation in the Federální shromáždění, as did the Civic Democratic Union (formerly PAV), in Slovakia. The successor organizations to the communist parties of the two republics achieved considerable success: the Left Bloc (which included the Communist Party of Bohemia and Moravia, CPBM) won a total of 34 seats in the Federální shromáždění, while the Slovak-based Party of the Democratic Left secured 23 seats. The representation of parties in the new republican legislatures did not differ greatly from that of the Federální shromáždění, although the CDA and the MAD–SMS succeeded in winning seats in the Česká národní rada (Czech National Council).

Negotiations on the formation of a new federal government were initiated by the CDP and the MDS, but only served to emphasize the two leading parties' fundamental divergence of opinion on the future of the CzSFR. Nevertheless, a transitional Federal Government, dominated by members of the CDP and the MDS, was appointed in early July 1992. The new Prime Minister was Jan Stráský of the CDP, who had served as a Deputy Prime Minister in the outgoing Czech Government. There was increasing recognition by Czech politicians that the constitutional talks on the future of Czechoslovakia were no longer viable and that a complete separation was preferable to the compromise measures that most Slovak parties favoured. The principal task of the new Federal Government, it was acknowledged, was to supervise the eventual dissolution of the CzSFR. Meanwhile, in late June the new Slovak Government was announced, with Mečiar as Prime Minister. All but one of the ministers were members of the MDS. A new coalition Czech Government, dominated by the CDP and with Klaus as Prime Minister, was appointed in early July. In three rounds of presidential elections, held in the same month, the Federální shromáždění failed to elect any of the candidates. Havel's re-election as President had effectively been blocked by the MDS and the SNP, and in mid-July he resigned from the post. Further rounds of voting in August and October were abandoned, since no candidates presented themselves.

The events of June and July 1992 had ensured that the emergence of two independent states was inevitable. On 17 July the Slovenská národná rada overwhelmingly approved a (symbolic) declaration of Slovak sovereignty, and in the following week the Czech and Slovak Prime Ministers agreed, in principle, to the dissolution of the CzSFR. In the following months extensive negotiations were conducted to determine the modalities of the division, which was to take effect from 1 January 1993. International observers expressed surprise not only that the dissolution of Czechoslovakia should be effected in so short a time, but also that the majority of Czechs and Slovaks (more than 60%, according to the results of public opinion polls) were still opposed to the country's division. Moreover, it appeared that Slovak leaders were less intent to leave the federation. Indeed, the failure of the Federální shromáždění, in early October 1992 and again in mid-November, to adopt legislation permitting the dissolution of the CzSFR was the result of opposition by (mainly) MDS deputies. However, the two republican Prime Ministers, supported by their respective governments, stressed that the process of partition was irreversible. In late October the Czech and Slovak Governments ratified a number of accords, including a customs union treaty to abolish trade restrictions between the two republics following their independence. Finally, on 25 November the Federální shromáždění adopted legislation providing for the constitutional disbanding of the federation, having secured the necessary three-fifths' majority by a margin of only three votes. Accordingly, the Federal Government accelerated the process of dividing the country's assets and liabilities as well as its armed forces. In most cases federal property was divided territorially.

It was agreed, however, that the two states would continue to share some federal infrastructure and would retain a single currency for the immediate future, although respective central banks were established. (Two separate currencies, the Czech and the Slovak koruna, were introduced in February 1993.)

On 17 December 1992 a treaty pledging cordial relations and co-operation was signed, followed by the establishment of diplomatic relations between the two republics. At midnight on 31 December all federal structures were dissolved and the Czech Republic and the Slovak Republic came into being. The dissolution of the CzSFR had thus been effected in an entirely peaceful fashion. As legal successors to Czechoslovakia, the two republics were quickly recognized by the states that had maintained diplomatic relations with the CzSFR, as well as by those international bodies of which the CzSFR had been a member. Existing treaties and agreements, to which the CzSFR had been a party, were to be honoured by both republics.

In anticipation of the establishment of the Czech Republic as an independent state, the existing legislature was replaced by a bicameral body, in accordance with the Czech Constitution (adopted in mid-December 1992); the Česká Národní rada was transformed into a Poslanecká sněmovna (Chamber of Deputies—lower house), which retained the Council's 200 members, and an upper house, the Senát (Senate), was to be elected at a later date. In late January 1993 the Poslanecká sněmovna elected Václav Havel to be the Czech Republic's first President. The composition of the Government remained largely unchanged. It included among its principal objectives the pursuance of the former Federal Government's economic reforms, including its programme of large-scale privatization.

Relations between the Czech Republic and Slovakia were troubled in early 1993 by disagreements over former Czechoslovak assets and property that still remained to be divided. In late 1993 there were also fears within the Czech Government that the restitution of property expropriated from Czech Jews during the period of Nazi occupation (1938–45) might lead to claims for compensation by those surviving Sudeten Germans who had been expelled from Czechoslovakia in 1945 (see below). Nevertheless, in April 1994 the Poslanecká sněmovna adopted legislation permitting the restitution of Jewish property. At local elections in November, the CDP was confirmed as the party with the broadest support (receiving some 31% of the total votes cast). Renewed controversy emerged in 1995 over the so-called 'lustration', or screening, law, which had been adopted by the Czechoslovak Federální shromáždění in October 1991. The law effectively banned former communist functionaries as well as members of the former state security service and the People's Militia (the CPCz's paramilitary force) from holding senior political, economic and judicial posts. In September 1995 the Poslanecká sněmovna voted to extend until 2000 the legislation on screening (which had been due to expire in late 1996). In the following month Havel rejected the decision, but the Chamber approved it for a second time, and the extension of the law entered into force.

The first general election since the dissolution of the CzSFR took place on 31 May and 1 June 1996. The CDP (which had merged with the Chr.DP in April) won 68 of the 200 seats in the Poslanecká sněmovna (with 29.6% of the total votes cast), while the Czech Social Democratic Party (CSDP), which had become a major force of the centre-left under the leadership of Miloš Zeman, almost quadrupled its parliamentary representation, winning 61 seats (26.4%). As a result, the coalition of the CDP, the Christian Democratic Union—Czechoslovak People's Party (CDU—CPP, which obtained 18 seats) and the CDA (13 seats) lost its overall majority, achieving a total of 99 seats. The CPBM and the Association for the Republic—Republican Party of Czechoslovakia were the only other parties to exceed the 5% minimum required for representation in the legislature, securing 22 seats and 18 seats, respectively. Despite losing its parliamentary majority, the governing coalition remained intact. The CSDP refused to join the coalition, but agreed to give tacit support on most issues to a minority government. In early July Václav Klaus formed a new Government; in a major concession to the CSDP, Miloš Zeman was appointed Chairman of the Poslanecká sněmovna. The Government survived a vote of confidence in late July, despite CSDP opposition to government proposals to return some 175,000 ha of land, appropriated by the communists, to the Roman Catholic Church, without seeking the approval of the legislature. Voter participation in the elections to the 81-seat Senát, which took place in mid-November

1996, was low, but the ruling coalition obtained a majority of the votes, winning 52 seats.

In August 1997 the Government had to address the problems of the Roma population (unofficially estimated at some 300,000), as hundreds of Roma, claiming to have suffered persecution in the Czech Republic, attempted to gain political asylum in Canada (which subsequently reimposed visa requirements for Czech visitors) and the United Kingdom. The Government established an interministerial commission for Roma community affairs in October and outlined further measures aimed at improving the situation of Roma in the Czech Republic. In early 1998 the Government formed a second commission, headed by Roma, to address issues affecting the Roma population, and a 40-year law restricting their nomadic way of life was revoked. None the less, a large number of Roma continued to seek political asylum abroad.

Meanwhile, three government ministers tendered their resignations in May 1997, as a result of economic problems and increasing divisions within the ruling coalition. Tension within the CDP and between the government coalition parties intensified in October, and Josef Zieleniec resigned from his position as Minister of Foreign Relations and as Deputy Chairman of the CDP. In early November a large demonstration of trade union members was staged in Prague, in protest against the Government's social welfare and economic policies. At the end of that month allegations of impropriety in the funding of the CDP led to the resignation of the Klaus administration (which denied the accusations), following the withdrawal of the CDU—CPP and the CDA from the coalition. In December Josef Lux, the Chairman of the CDU—CPP, was invited to lead talks on the formation of a new government. Josef Tošovský, hitherto Governor of the Czech National Bank, was designated Prime Minister in December, and a new, interim Government, comprising seven non-political ministers, four CDP members, three CDU—CPP members and three CDA members, was appointed in January 1998. The CDP was divided over its participation in the new administration, and the party's ministers subsequently defected to the Freedom Union (FU), a newly established breakaway party, which had 31 seats in the Poslanecká sněmovna by mid-February.

On 20 January 1998 Havel was narrowly re-elected to the presidency for a second five-year term. At the end of that month the Government won a vote of confidence when its policy statement was adopted in the Poslanecká sněmovna. In February Jiří Skalický resigned from the posts of Deputy Prime Minister and Minister of the Environment, and from the chairmanship of the CDA, after admitting that, prior to the 1996 elections (when the CDA controlled the ministries responsible for privatization and industry), the party had received donations from a number of companies. Two ministers subsequently resigned from the party. In April 1998 the Czech Republic's proposed membership of the North Atlantic Treaty Organization (NATO, see p. 301) was formally approved by the legislature, after the CSDP withdrew its demand for a referendum on the issue.

Early elections to the Poslanecká sněmovna were held on 19–20 June 1998. The CSDP retained its position (held since the earlier defection of the CDP deputies to the FU) as the largest party in the Poslanecká sněmovna, winning 74 seats (with 32.3% of the votes cast), while the CDP secured 63 seats (with 27.7%). The remaining seats were divided between the CPBM (with 24 seats), the CDU—CPP (20 seats) and the FU (19 seats). The rate of voter participation was 74%. As leader of the CSDP, Zeman was given the task of attempting to form a government, but the parliamentary parties failed to reach agreement on a coalition grouping. In July Zeman and Klaus signed an agreement whereby the CDP pledged not to initiate or support a motion expressing 'no confidence' in a minority CSDP government, in exchange for a number of senior parliamentary posts, including the chairmanship of the Poslanecká sněmovna (to which Klaus was later elected), and a commitment to early constitutional reform. On 17 July Zeman was formally appointed Prime Minister, and a new Council of Ministers was subsequently formed. Elections to renew one-third of the seats in the Senát were held in two rounds in November. The CSDP won only three of the 27 seats contested, while the CDP secured nine seats, and a four-party informal alliance, comprising the CDU—CPP, the CDA, the DU and the FU, won 13 seats. In local elections, also held in November, independent candidates, followed by the CDU—CPP, obtained the largest number of seats on municipal councils, owing to strong support in smaller, rural communities. In terms of votes, however, the CDP received the greatest endorsement.

In May 1999 a decision by the Council of Ministers to complete the construction of the controversial Temelín nuclear power plant in southern Bohemia, despite a resolution by the European Parliament opposing its completion, provoked international concern and strong criticism from President Havel and environmental groups. In July Ivo Svoboda was dismissed from the post of Minister of Finance. (In May 2002 he was charged with embezzlement during his term in office, and he was sentenced to five years' imprisonment in March 2004.) In September 1999 the Council of Ministers approved a number of proposals for constitutional change, which had been drafted by a joint CSDP-CDP commission. The amendments aimed to restrict presidential powers, including the right to appoint the Prime Minister and the heads of principal state institutions, and the right to grant amnesty. (The Poslanecká sněmovna approved the changes in January 2000, despite an opposition boycott of the vote.) On 17 November 1999 celebrations commemorating the 10th anniversary of the 'velvet revolution' coincided with a protest against the existing political system, organized by a group of former student leaders who had participated in the events of November 1989. Their appeal had been signed by some 150,000 supporters by early December 1999, when a large rally was staged in Prague. Jan Ruml subsequently resigned from the chairmanship of the FU. Meanwhile, Egon Lánský resigned from the post of Deputy Prime Minister for European Integration in December, citing ill health, although opposition parties had been demanding his resignation for several months, principally owing to dissatisfaction with preparations for entry to the European Union (EU, see p. 217). The Minister of Foreign Affairs, Jan Kavan, was subsequently elevated to the position of Deputy Prime Minister.

In late January 2000 the CSDP and the CDP extended their agreement on bilateral co-operation; the CSDP pledged to reorganize the Council of Ministers and to propose electoral reform measures, in return for the CDP's continued acceptance of the CSDP minority Government. The Council of Ministers was duly reorganized in March–April and four ministers were replaced. In early August, following the country's admission to NATO (see below), the Senát adopted a constitutional amendment permitting the Government to deploy peace-keeping forces abroad and to authorize the deployment of foreign troops on Czech territory without the prior approval of the legislature. At elections to one-third of seats in the Senát in November, the alliance of the CDU—CPP, the CDA, the DU and the FU secured 16 seats, thereby increasing its overall representation to 39 seats (although narrowly failing to obtain a majority in the chamber).

In early April 2001 Vladimír Špidla, the Deputy Prime Minister and Minister of Labour and Social Affairs, was elected unopposed to the chairmanship of the CSDP; Zeman had agreed to relinquish the party leadership (although he was to remain Prime Minister pending legislative elections, scheduled to take place in June 2002). Also in April 2001 the Deputy Prime Minister for Economic Policies and Minister of Finance, Pavel Mertlik, tendered his resignation, citing criticism by other ministers of a number of financial measures. He was replaced by Jiří Rusnok, hitherto Deputy Minister of Employment and Social Affairs. In early May the Minister of Defence, Vladimir Vetchý, was dismissed; he was replaced by Jaroslav Tvrdík. In November Lubomír Štrougal, the Prime Minister in 1970–88, was charged with having prevented investigations into secret police activities as Minister of the Interior in 1965; however, he was acquitted in February 2002, owing to lack of evidence.

Meanwhile, in late 2001 the FU and DU merged to form a single organization. In February 2002 it was announced that the electoral alliance of the CDU—CPP, CDA and FU—DU had been dissolved, owing to inter-party disagreement; however, the CDU—CPP and FU—DU subsequently formed a further grouping, known as the Coalition. At elections to the Poslanecká sněmovna on 14–15 June, the CSDP was the most successful party (with 30.2% of the votes cast); a low rate of voter participation appeared to confirm suggestions of widespread popular disenchantment with the political establishment. President Havel invited Špidla to commence negotiations to form a government, and on 9 July a formal agreement establishing the terms of the new coalition administration was signed by the leaders of the CSDP and the Coalition. In mid-July a 17-member coalition Government, headed by Špidla and dominated by the CSDP, was officially appointed by Havel. In early August the new administration was approved by a majority of 101 votes in the

Poslanecká sněmovna. (The three main parties shared the aim for the Czech Republic to join the EU, although divisions remained over economic and social welfare concerns.)

In September 2002 a former Prime Minister, Jozef Lenárt, and former leader of the CPCz, Miloš Jakeš, were acquitted of charges of collaborating with the Warsaw Pact troops that invaded Czechoslovakia in August 1968. Scheduled elections to 27 of the 81 seats in the Senát took place in October/November 2002: the representation of the government coalition parties in the chamber was reduced to 34 seats, while that of the CDP increased from 22 to 26 seats. Local elections also took place on 1–2 November, in which the CDP won the largest proportion of the votes cast.

Prior to the expiry of Havel's second term on 2 February 2003, voting took place in both legislative chambers to select a successor to the presidency. Following three inconclusive rounds in mid-January, later that month Klaus (who had relinquished the chairmanship of the CDP), contested further ballots against Zeman and Jaroslava Moserova of the CDA, in which no candidate received majority support. Klaus was finally elected President on 28 February, defeating the candidate of the ruling coalition, Jan Sokol, with 142 of the 281 votes cast in both chambers. Klaus was inaugurated on 7 March. Four days later the Government survived a vote of 'no confidence' in the Poslanecká sněmovna (which had been requested by the Prime Minister) by one vote; Špidla subsequently made efforts to assert his Government's tenuous command in the legislature, and replaced the Minister for Industry and Trade, Jiří Rusnok (who had supported Klaus).

The Minister of Defence, Jaroslav Tvrdík, resigned in late May 2003, in protest at reductions in military expenditure, resulting from reform of the defence sector. He was replaced in the following month by Lt-Gen. (retd) Miroslav Kostelka. In mid-June a referendum on the Czech Republic's proposed accession to the EU was held (see below). Differences in the attitudes of President Klaus and the governing coalition towards membership became evident when Klaus notably did not urge voters to support accession. In late July the governing coalition briefly lost its one-seat majority in the Poslanecká sněmovna, when CSDP deputy Josef Hojdar announced his intention to leave the grouping, in protest against plans to decrease government spending as part of a financial reform programme. (Hojdar rejoined the coalition in November.) In early August the Deputy Prime Minister and Minister of Justice, Pavel Rychetský, resigned his post, following the endorsement of his candidacy as Chairman of the Constitutional Court. Karel Čermák assumed the justice portfolio in mid-September. Later in September the Government narrowly survived a vote of 'no confidence' over its plans for fiscal reform, and the Poslanecká sněmovna subsequently adopted the reform proposals (see Economic Affairs). In the following month the Minister of Finance, Bohuslav Sobotka, was also appointed a Deputy Prime Minister, with responsibility for implementing the public-finance reform programme. In December 2003 Ratibor Majzlik, leader of the former Democratic Union which had merged with the Freedom Union in 2001 to form the FU—DU, announced his attention to leave the FU—DU; however, the FU—DU was not to change its name.

In April 2004 Marie Součková was dismissed as Minister of Health, in response to concerns at the existence of high levels of debt within the health service; CSDP deputy Jozef Kubinyi was appointed as her replacement later in the month. Also in April a Roma parliament was established in the Czech Republic. In the same month Viktor Kožený, a businessman living in exile who had been charged with fraud, established a new political party, the Viktor Kožený—Civic Federal Democracy Party. In June another new political party, the Democratic Union of the Czech Republic, was founded by members of the former Democratic Union. Former Democratic Union leader Majzlik (see above) was not instrumental in the founding of the party. Also in June Minister of Justice Karel Čermák resigned following a dispute over salaries in the judiciary.

At the end of June 2004 Prime Minister Vladimír Špidla resigned as head of the Government and as leader of the CSDP after narrowly surviving a vote of confidence in his leadership of the CSDP. Of 181 delegates, 103 voted against Špidla; although falling short of the three-fifths majority needed to remove him, the result indicated that Špidla had lost the support of the majority of his party. The vote followed a defeat for the CSDP in the Czech Republic's first elections to the European Parliament earlier in the month (following the accession of the country to the EU, with effect from 1 May), in which the CSDP had obtained only two of 24 seats contested. The resignation of Špidla, implying the departure of all members of his Government, was formally accepted at the beginning of July. President Klaus subsequently entrusted Stanislav Gross, hitherto First Deputy Prime Minister and Minister of the Interior and acting leader of the CSDP, with the task of forming a new Government. Gross was declared Prime Minister later in the month. In August a new Government was formally appointed, with six new ministerial appointments, including the appointment of Pavel Němec as Deputy Prime Minister and Minister of Justice. The new Government included members of the CDU—CPP and the FU—DU, as well as of the CSDP, as had the outgoing administration. Later in August the new Government narrowly survived a vote of confidence (as a result of the attendance of two deputies otherwise on long-term sick leave) in the Poslanecká sněmovna, with 101 deputies of a total 200 voting in favour of the Government. In October–November an election for one-third of seats in the Senát was held. The CSDP did not win any seats in this election, whilst the number of seats held by the opposition Civic Democratic Party increased substantially. In local elections held in the same month the Civic Democratic Party won the largest proportion of votes cast (36.4%).

In early 2005 Prime Minister Gross was the subject of allegations of corruption, particularly in connection with his purchase of an apartment in Prague. None the less, Gross was re-elected as leader of the CSDP at a conference of the party in late March. At the end of that month the CDU—CPP (which demanded Gross's resignation) withdrew from the governing coalition, as a result of which the Government lost its majority in the Poslanecká sněmovna. Following the announcement of several ministers that they no longer regarded themselves as part of the Government, Gross resigned on 25 April. On the same day President Klaus appointed the hitherto Minister of Regional Development, Jiří Paroubek, a member of the CSDP, as Prime Minister. The new Council of Ministers formed by Paroubek, which was substantially the same as the outgoing Government (with the renewed participation of the CDU—CPP), was, in accordance with the Constitution, to be confirmed in office by a vote of confidence in the Poslanecká sněmovna within 30 days; such a vote was expected to be held in mid-May.

An important focus of the Czech Republic's foreign policy is to maintain close relations with Slovakia and other neighbouring eastern European states. It is a member, with Slovakia, Hungary and Poland, of the Visegrad Group (established, following the collapse of communist rule, to promote economic, defence and other co-operation in the region). The Governments of the Czech Republic, Hungary and Poland agreed to co-ordinate preparations for accession to NATO and the EU (see below). Relations with Slovakia have been strained, mainly because of disagreements over the division of former federal property. In mid-September 1998, however, following talks between Miloš Zeman and Vladimír Mečiar, the Slovak Prime Minister, it was announced that a joint Czech-Slovak committee would meet in an attempt to further discussions on unresolved issues. The success of opposition parties in Slovak elections held at the end of that month, and the subsequent change of government, led to a further improvement in bilateral relations. Measures providing for dual Czech-Slovak citizenship became fully effective in October 1999, and in November an agreement on the division of former federal property was signed in Bratislava by Zeman and Mikuláš Dzurinda, the Slovak Prime Minister. The agreement provided for the exchange of shares between the Czech Republic's Komerční banka and Slovakia's Všeobecná úverová banka and the restitution of gold reserves to Slovakia. The gold had been held by the Czech Central Bank as collateral for debts owed by Slovakia to the Czech Republic. These debts, totalling some 26,000m. koruna, had proved to be a major obstacle during negotiations, as they had never been recognized by Slovakia. The Czech Government consequently opted effectively to relieve Slovakia of its debts by buying the Central Bank's claim for a symbolic one koruna, despite the opposition of several Czech politicians. In May 2000 Zeman and Dzurinda signed an agreement that resolved remaining problems associated with the division of jointly held assets.

Since the end of the Second World War Czech-German relations have been dominated by two issues: the question of compensation for Czech victims of Nazism, and demands for the restitution of property to the Sudeten Germans who were driven from Czechoslovakia in 1945–46. A joint declaration was finally signed by both Ministers of Foreign Affairs in December 1996,

and by Václav Klaus of the Czech Republic and Federal Chancellor Helmut Kohl of Germany in January 1997. In the declaration, Germany admitted that it was to blame for the Nazi occupation and the partition of Czechoslovakia in 1939, while the Czech Republic apologized for the abuses of human rights that were committed during the deportation of ethnic Germans. The declaration did not, however, entitle the expelled Sudeten Germans to make claims for compensation. A Czech-German fund was established in January 1998 to finance joint projects, in particular benefiting victims of the Nazis. Relations were strained somewhat in February and August, however, when the nomination of Sudeten Germans to a Czech-German advisory council was rejected by Miloš Zeman, who claimed that the nominees had opposed the January 1997 declaration that had provided for the establishment of the council. In January 2002 a comment by Zeman, which described the German-speakers expelled from the Sudetenland as supporters of the Nazi regime, provoked strong protests from both Sudeten Germans and the German Government. The ensuing strain in relations between the two countries resulted in the postponement of a visit to Prague (originally scheduled for March) by the German Chancellor, Gerhard Schröder. In February Zeman and his Slovakian counterpart, Mikuláš Dzurinda, announced that they would not be attending a summit meeting of the Visegrad countries, scheduled to take place on 1 March, following a demand by the Hungarian Prime Minister, Viktor Orbán, for the abolition of the Beneš Decrees, which had provided for the expulsion of ethnic Germans, as well as Hungarians, from the Sudetenland. In April the Poslanecká sněmovna unanimously approved a resolution stipulating the inviolability of the Beneš Decrees. Although the Decrees did not present an obstacle to Czech accession to the EU, during 2004 Germany made requests for the issue of the Decrees to be decided by European institutions. Following claims that the Decrees represented a human rights violation, EU member states in February 2005 concluded at a meeting in Geneva that discussion of the Decrees by the UN Human Rights Committee was not appropriate, and that the issue should be resolved within the Union.

The issue of the nuclear power installation at Temelín, in southern Bohemia, has impeded good relations between the Czech Republic and Austria. In September 2000 Austrian environmental protesters blockaded crossings at the Austrian–Czech border, following a decision by the Czech authorities that the power station was to commence operations; the demonstrations continued until mid-October. Despite pressure from the Austrian Government, which suspended imports of Czech electricity, the nuclear power plant commenced production in early October, after receiving authorization from the state nuclear safety office. In early November border protests were temporarily resumed, after discussions between Zeman and the Federal Chancellor of Austria, Wolfgang Schüssel, failed to resolve the ongoing dispute. In December, following further negotiations, the Czech Republic and Austria signed an agreement, whereby the plant was not to operate at commercial capacity until its safety and its environmental impact had been fully evaluated, under the supervision of the European Commission. In August 2001 the European Commission issued a controversial report: the Czech authorities maintained that the report demonstrated the safety of the plant and immediately commenced its reconnection with the national power network; however, Austrian anti-nuclear movements announced that they were to submit a legal challenge to the resumption of operations at the plant, which was also criticized by the Austrian authorities. In addition, the German Government expressed concern over safety at the nuclear installation. Later that year Schüssel threatened to veto the Czech Republic's accession to the EU unless the matter was satisfactorily resolved. Further safety issues were eventually agreed, and in April 2003 the Temelín installation commenced production at full capacity for an 18-month trial period. The plant became fully operational in October 2004.

In August 1993 the Czech Republic and Russia signed a treaty of friendship and co-operation (replacing the Russian-Czechoslovak treaty of 1992). In March 1994, despite Russia's apparent opposition, the Czech Republic joined NATO's 'Partnership for Peace' programme of military co-operation. In 1996 the Poslanecká sněmovna approved legislation prohibiting the storage of nuclear weapons on Czech territory, except where international treaties are concerned, thereby allowing for full membership of NATO. In July 1997 the Czech Republic, together with Hungary and Poland, was invited to commence membership negotiations. A protocol providing for the accession of the three states to NATO was signed in December and in March 1999 the Czech Republic, Hungary and Poland became full members of the Alliance. Associate membership of Western European Union (see p. 352) was subsequently granted. The Czech Republic is a member of the Council of Europe (see p. 199) and the Organization for Security and Co-operation in Europe (OSCE, see p. 314).

The Czech Republic was one of a number of central and eastern European states invited to commence negotiations in March 1998 on possible entry to the EU. In November more substantive talks commenced regarding the compliance of potential EU entrants with membership regulations. In December 2002, at an historic summit meeting in Copenhagen, Denmark, the Czech Republic was one of 10 nations that were formally invited to join the EU in May 2004. A plebiscite on EU membership was held in the Czech Republic on 13–14 June 2003. Of the 55.2% of the electorate who took part in the referendum, 77.3% voted in support of the Czech Republic's membership of the EU. The country became a full member on 1 May 2004.

Government

Legislative power is held by two chambers, the 200-member Poslanecká sněmovna (Chamber of Deputies) and the 81-member Senát (Senate). Members of the Poslanecká sněmovna and the Senate are elected for four and six years, respectively, by universal adult suffrage. The President of the Republic (Head of State) is elected for a term of five years by a joint session of the legislature. The President, who is also Commander of the Armed Forces, may be re-elected for a second consecutive term. He appoints the Prime Minister and, on the latter's recommendation, the other members of the Council of Ministers (the highest organ of executive power). For administrative purposes, the Czech Republic was divided into 14 self-governing units (regions) at the end of 2002. These replaced the 72 districts that had previously been in place.

Defence

In August 2004 total armed forces numbered 45,000 (including 6,000 conscripts): an army of 36,600 and an air force of 6,700; there were also some 1,700 troops attached to the Ministry of Defence and centrally controlled formations. In addition, there were 4,000 border guards and 1,600 internal security forces. In November 2004 new legislation was approved to abolish compulsory military service, and from 1 January 2005 the military became fully professional. In 2003 defence expenditure by the central Government totalled 52,600m. koruna. The budget for 2004 allocated 50,000m. koruna to defence. In March 1994 the Czech Republic joined the North Atlantic Treaty Organization's (NATO) 'Partnership for Peace' (see p. 303) programme of military co-operation, and it was formally admitted to the Alliance in March 1999.

Economic Affairs

In 2003, according to estimates by the World Bank, the Czech Republic's gross national income (GNI), measured at average 2001–03 prices, was US $81,306m., equivalent to $6,740 per head (or $15,650 per head on an international purchasing-power parity basis). During 1990–2003, it was estimated, the population decreased at an annual average rate of 0.1%, while gross domestic product (GDP) per head increased, in real terms, by an average of 0.8% per year. Overall GDP increased, in real terms, at an average annual rate of 0.7% in 1990–2003; annual growth was officially estimated at 1.5% in 2002 and 3.7% in 2003.

In 2003 agriculture (including hunting, forestry and fishing) contributed 2.8% of GDP and engaged an estimated 4.5% of the employed labour force. The principal crops are wheat, sugar beet, barley, potatoes and hops (the Czech Republic is a major beer producer and exporter). According to estimates by the World Bank, the GDP of the agricultural sector increased, in real terms, at an average annual rate of 4.9% in 1990–2002. However, agricultural GDP declined by 0.9% in 2001 and increased by 4.4% in 2002.

Industry (including manufacturing, mining, construction and power) contributed 38.1% of GDP and engaged an estimated 39.4% of the employed labour force in 2003. According to estimates by the World Bank, the GDP of the industrial sector declined, in real terms, at an average annual rate of 2.1% in 1990–2002. However, real industrial GDP declined by 0.8% in 2001 and by 1.2% in 2002.

In 2003 the mining sector contributed 1.3% of GDP and engaged an estimated 1.1% of the employed labour force. The principal minerals extracted are coal and lignite. According to the IMF, production of mining and quarrying increased, in real terms, by 1.4% in 1996, but declined by 2.9% in 1997, by 5.3% in 1998 and by 12.1% in 1999; however, growth in the sector was 9.2% in 2000, slowing to 1.9% in 2001 and 0.3% in 2002.

The manufacturing sector contributed 26.2% of GDP and engaged an estimated 27.3% of the employed labour force in 2003. Based on the value of output, the most important branches of manufacturing in 1999 were food products and beverages (accounting for 13.6% of the total), non-electric machinery and domestic appliances (8.5%), metal products (8.3%) and basic metals (7.8%). According to the IMF, manufacturing production increased, in real terms, by 3.0% in 1998, but declined by 2.6% in 1999; however, manufacturing output was estimated to have increased by 5.0% in 2000, by 7.5% in 2001 and by 5.4% in 2002.

In 2000 coal provided 73.3% of total electricity production and nuclear power 18.6%. Imports of mineral fuels comprised 7.5% of the value of total imports in 2003.

The services sector contributed 59.1% of GDP and engaged an estimated 56.0% of the employed labour force in 2003. Tourism is an important source of revenue, providing receipts of an estimated US $2,900m. in 2002. According to the World Bank, the GDP of the services sector increased, in real terms, at an average annual rate of 2.4% in 1990–2002. Real GDP in the services sector increased by 6.8% in 2001 and by 4.4% in 2002.

In 2003 the Czech Republic recorded a visible trade deficit of US $2,505m., and there was a deficit of $5,661m. on the current account of the balance of payments. In 2002 the principal source of imports (32.6%) was Germany; other major sources were Italy and Slovakia. Germany was also the principal market for exports (37.0%) in that year; other important purchasers were Slovakia, the United Kingdom and Austria. The principal exports in 2003 were machinery and transport equipment, basic manufactures, miscellaneous manufactured articles and chemical products. The principal imports in that year were machinery and transport equipment, basic manufactures, chemicals and related products, miscellaneous manufactured articles and mineral fuels.

In 2003 there was a budgetary deficit of 143,627m. koruna (equivalent to 5.6% of GDP). The Czech Republic's total external debt was US $26,419m. at the end of 2002, of which $6,904m. was long-term public debt. In that year the cost of debt-servicing was equivalent to 9.5% of the value of exports of goods and services. The annual rate of inflation averaged 6.0% in 1990–2002; consumer prices increased by 4.7% in 2001 and by 1.8% in 2002. In 2003 inflation was only 0.1%. In 2004 the average registered annual rate of unemployment was estimated at 10.2%.

The Czech Republic is a member of the IMF and the World Bank. It is also a member of the European Bank for Reconstruction and Development (EBRD, see p. 212), and in late 1995 became the first post-communist state in Eastern Europe to be admitted to the Organisation for Economic Co-operation and Development (OECD, see p. 307). In May 2004 the Czech Republic became a full member of the European Union (EU, see p. 217).

The Czech Republic was considered to have successfully undertaken the transition to a market economic system. In 1992–95 the country's programme of rapid privatization, price and currency stabilization and the establishment of a new banking system attracted widespread foreign investment. In 1996, however, economic growth decelerated and a budgetary deficit was recorded for the first time. Several banks ceased operations, and investor confidence was weakened by cases of embezzlement. In early 1999 the economy began to recover, following the Government's relaxation of monetary policies in late 1998 and significant progress in the restructuring of banks and state enterprises. The country subsequently benefited from strong export performance, and from a dramatic increase in foreign direct investment. Growth in GDP was recorded from 2000, although the restructuring process resulted in a rapidly increasing overall fiscal deficit and also contributed to a significant rise in the rate of unemployment. Preliminary figures indicated that GDP growth in 2004 was 3.8%, and for 2005 growth of more than 4% was predicted. The wider fiscal deficit was estimated to have reached some 4% of GDP in 2002, and deficit increased dramatically in 2003, reaching the equivalent of 12.6% of GDP. In May 2004, following the accession of the Czech Republic to the EU, it was reported that the budgetary deficit was the highest of any member state. In that month the Poslanecká sněmovna approved a convergence programme intended to prepare the Czech Republic for the eventual adoption of the euro, the common European currency, which would necessitate a reduction of the deficit to less than 3% of GDP. Preliminary figures indicated the deficit had been reduced to 5.2% in 2004, and for 2005 a deficit of 4.7% was predicted. It was hoped that the Czech Republic would be able to adopt the euro by 2010. In the long term EU membership was expected to provide greater opportunities for the development of enterprise, despite an anticipated increase in levels of both competition and regulation.

Education

Pre-school education is available for children aged between three and six years. Education is officially compulsory for children aged between six and 15 years, who attend basic school, covering both primary (grades 1–5) and lower secondary (grades 6–9) levels. In 1999/2000 90.4% of children in the relevant age-group were enrolled in primary schools (boys 90.4%; girls 90.4%). Education continues at upper secondary schools, of which there are three types: gymnasia (providing general education and preparing students mainly for university entry), secondary vocational schools and secondary technical schools. Students follow three- to four-year courses. In 1999/2000 84.3% of children in the appropriate age-group attended secondary schools (83.9% of boys; 84.8% of girls). After 1990 many private schools were established. Tertiary education comprises higher professional schools, which offer three-year courses, and universities, at which most courses last from five to six years. In 2003/04 some 233,442 students attended 24 universities. In 2002 total budgetary expenditure on education amounted to 86,202m. koruna.

Public Holidays

2005: 1 January (New Year's Day), 28 March (Easter Monday), 1 May (Labour Day), 8 May (Liberation Day), 5 July (Day of the Apostles SS Cyril and Methodius), 6 July (Anniversary of the Martyrdom of Jan Hus), 28 September (Czech Statehood Day), 28 October (Independence Day), 17 November (Freedom and Democracy Day), 24–25 December (Christmas), 26 December (St Stephen's Day).

2006: 1 January (New Year's Day), 17 April (Easter Monday), 1 May (Labour Day), 8 May (Liberation Day), 5 July (Day of the Apostles SS Cyril and Methodius), 6 July (Anniversary of the Martyrdom of Jan Hus), 28 September (Czech Statehood Day), 28 October (Independence Day), 17 November (Freedom and Democracy Day), 24–25 December (Christmas), 26 December (St Stephen's Day).

Weights and Measures

The metric system is in force.

Statistical Survey

Source: mainly Czech Statistical Office, Na padesátém 81, 100 82 Prague 10; tel. 274051111; internet www.czso.cz.

Area and Population

AREA, POPULATION AND DENSITY

Area (sq km)	78,866*
Population (census results)	
3 March 1991	10,302,215
1 March 2001	
Males	4,982,071
Females	5,247,989
Total	10,230,060
Population (official estimates at 31 December)	
2001	10,206,436
2002	10,203,269
2003	10,211,455
Density (per sq km) at 31 December 2003	129.5

* 30,450 sq miles.

POPULATION BY NATIONALITY
(census of 1 March 2001)

	Number	%
Czech (Bohemian)	9,249,777	90.4
Moravian	380,474	3.7
Slovak	193,190	1.9
Polish	51,968	0.5
German	39,108	0.4
Roma (Gypsy)	11,746	0.1
Silesian	10,878	0.1
Others and unknown	292,919	2.9
Total	**10,230,060**	**100.0**

REGIONS
(31 December 2003)

	Area (sq km)	Population	Density (per sq km)
Central Bohemia (Středočeský)	11,014	1,135,795	103.1
Highlands (Vysočina)	6,925	517,511	74.7
Hradec Králové (Královéhradecký)	4,757	547,563	115.1
Karlovy Vary (Karlovarský)	3,315	304,249	91.8
Liberec (Liberecký)	3,163	427,722	135.2
Moravia-Silesia (Moravskoslezský)	5,555	1,260,277	226.9
Olomouc (Olomoucký)	5,139	636,313	123.8
Pardubice (Pardubický)	4,519	505,486	111.9
Plzeň (Plzeňský)	7,560	550,113	72.8
Prague City (Praha)	496	1,165,581	2,350.0
South Bohemia (Jihočeský)	10,056	625,541	62.2
South Moravia (Jihomoravský)	7,067	1,122,570	158.8
Ústí nad Labem (Ústecký)	5,335	820,868	153.9
Zlín (Zlínský)	3,965	591,866	149.3
Total	**78,866**	**10,211,455**	**129.5**

PRINCIPAL TOWNS
(population at 31 December 2003)

Praha (Prague, the capital)	1,165,581	Pardubice	88,741
Brno	369,559	Havířov	84,914
Ostrava	313,088	Zlín	79,177
Plzeň (Pilsen)	164,180	Kladno	70,003
Olomouc	101,268	Most	67,905
Liberec	97,770	Karviná	63,677
České Budějovice (Budweis)	95,245	Frýdek-Místek	60,290
Hradec Králové	95,195	Opava	60,252
Ústí nad Labem	94,105		

BIRTHS, MARRIAGES AND DEATHS

	Registered live births		Registered marriages		Registered deaths	
	Number	Rate (per 1,000)	Number	Rate (per 1,000)	Number	Rate (per 1,000)
1996	90,446	8.8	53,896	5.2	112,782	10.9
1997	90,657	8.8	57,804	5.6	112,744	10.9
1998	90,535	8.8	55,027	5.3	109,527	10.6
1999	89,471	8.7	53,523	5.2	109,768	10.7
2000	90,910	8.8	55,321	5.4	109,001	10.6
2001	90,715	8.9	52,374	5.1	107,755	10.5
2002	92,786	9.1	52,732	5.2	108,243	10.6
2003	93,685	9.2	48,943	4.8	111,288	10.9

Expectation of life (WHO estimates, years at birth): 75.8 (males 72.4; females 79.0) in 2002 (Source: WHO, *World Health Report*).

ECONOMICALLY ACTIVE POPULATION
(persons aged 15 years and over)

	2001	2002	2003
Agriculture, hunting, forestry and fishing	225,200	227,900	213,200
Mining and quarrying	67,100	61,100	53,300
Manufacturing	1,310,400	1,318,200	1,294,300
Electricity, gas and water	87,300	83,800	77,100
Construction	427,700	425,200	438,700
Trade, restaurants and hotels	763,600	790,300	798,500
Transport, storage and communications	362,600	367,600	358,800
Finance, insurance, real estate and business activities	357,400	364,300	381,200
Public administration, defence and compulsory social security	339,300	325,700	331,900
Education	300,000	309,100	287,800
Health and social welfare	304,300	304,200	306,900
Other community, social and personal services	178,200	179,400	185,100
Total (incl. others)	4,727,700	4,764,900	4,733,200

Note: Figures are rounded to the nearest 100.

Health and Welfare

KEY INDICATORS

Total fertility rate (children per woman, 2003)	1.2
Under-5 mortality rate (per 1,000 live births, 2003)	4
HIV/AIDS (% of persons aged 15–49, 2003)	0.1
Physicians (per 1,000 head, 2003)	3.9
Hospital beds (per 1,000 head, 2000)	8.8
Health expenditure (2001): US $ per head (PPP)	1,129
Health expenditure (2001): % of GDP	7.4
Health expenditure (2001): public (% of total)	91.4
Human Development Index (2002): ranking	32
Human Development Index (2002): value	0.868

For sources and definitions, see explanatory note on p. vi.

Agriculture

PRINCIPAL CROPS
('000 metric tons)

	2001	2002	2003
Wheat	4,476	3,866	2,638
Barley	1,966	1,793	2,069
Maize	409	616	476
Rye*	149	119	159
Oats	136	168	233
Potatoes	1,131	901	682
Sugar beet	3,259	3,832	3,495
Dry peas	83	56	54
Rapeseed	973	710	388
Cabbages	104	73	75
Tomatoes	25	13	13
Cauliflowers	23	12	13
Cucumbers and gherkins	35	16	12

— continued	2001	2002	2003
Dry onions	84	45	34
Carrots	52	27	24
Apples	221	166	141
Pears	16	3	2
Peaches	5	6	6
Plums	23	2	2
Grapes	68	57	67
Hops	7	6	6

* Including mixed crops of wheat and rye.

LIVESTOCK
('000 head at 1 March)

	2001	2002	2003
Horses	27	20	20
Cattle	1,466	1,473	1,428
Pigs	3,348	3,363	3,127
Sheep	97	103	113
Goats	26	13	12
Chickens	18,767	21,785	18,406
Ducks	451	279	532
Geese	127	28	34
Turkeys	723	887	670

LIVESTOCK PRODUCTS
('000 metric tons, unless otherwise indicated)

	2001	2002	2003
Beef and veal	209	202	198
Pig meat	584	585	576
Poultry meat	313	317	304
Milk (million litres)	2,702	2,728	2,646
Hen eggs (millions)	3,190	1,829	1,859

Forestry

LOGGING
('000 cubic metres)

	2001	2002	2003
Coniferous (softwood)	12,680	13,010	13,660
Broadleaved (hardwood)	1,694	1,531	1,480
Total	14,374	14,541	15,140

Fishing*

(metric tons)

	2001	2002	2003
Common carp	20,981	20,505	20,950
Others	3,763	3,688	3,847
Total catch	24,744	24,193	24,797

* Figures refer only to fish caught by the Fishing Association (formerly State Fisheries) and members of the Czech and Moravian Fishing Union.

Mining

('000 metric tons)

	2000	2001	2002
Hard coal	14,855	15,138	14,469
Brown coal and lignite	50,307	50,968	48,892
Crude petroleum*	168	160	n.a.
Kaolin	1,242	1,140	1,125

* Source: US Geological Survey.

Industry

SELECTED PRODUCTS
('000 metric tons, unless otherwise indicated)

	2001	2002	2003
Wheat flour and meal	783	816	761
Refined sugar	482	517	521
Wine ('000 hectolitres) . . .	605	680	740
Beer ('000 hectolitres) . . .	17,734	17,987	18,216
Cotton yarn (metric tons) . .	65,124	69,775	60,550
Woven cotton fabrics ('000 metres)	231,917	210,333	182,286
Woollen fabrics ('000 metres) . .	13,517	13,268	16,073
Linen fabrics ('000 metres) . . .	16,377	13,835	12,071
Paper and paperboard	183	191	197
Footwear ('000 pairs)	2,937	1,776	1,202
Nitrogenous fertilizers* . . .	262	221	251
Soap	38	35	30
Motor spirit (petrol)	1,104	1,246	n.a.
Gas-diesel (distillate fuel) oil . .	2,250	2,412	n.a.
Residual fuel oils	773	667	n.a.
Coke	3,522	3,537	n.a.
Cement	3,591	3,249	3,502
Pig-iron	4,671	4,840	5,207
Crude steel	6,316	6,512	6,783
Trucks (number)	4,701	1,095	666
Motorcycles and mopeds (number)	10,602	13,488	n.a.
Bicycles (number)	236,574	53,985	n.a.
Electric energy (million kWh) . .	74,647	76,348	83,227

* Production in terms of nitrogen.

Finance

CURRENCY AND EXCHANGE RATES

Monetary Units

100 halérů (singular: halér—heller) = 1 Czech koruna (Czech crown or Kč.).

Sterling, Dollar and Euro Equivalents (31 December 2004)

£1 sterling = 43.20 koruna;
US $1 = 22.37 koruna;
€1 = 30.46 koruna;
1,000 koruna = £23.15 = $44.71 = €32.83.

Average Exchange Rate (koruna per US $)

2002   32.739
2003   28.209
2004   25.670

Note: In February 1993 the Czech Republic introduced its own currency, the Czech koruna, to replace (at par) the Czechoslovak koruna.

GENERAL BUDGET
(million koruna)*

Revenue†	2001	2002	2003
Tax revenue	782,021	833,045	894,677
Income, profits and capital gains	196,423	220,120	238,927
Social security contributions .	318,903	334,970	359,690
Domestic taxes on goods and services	245,486	255,624	271,856
General sales, turnover and value-added tax	150,939	154,439	164,388
Excises	76,281	79,493	84,171
Non-tax revenue	58,385	60,141	67,157
Capital revenue	9,652	11,152	11,236
Total	**850,058**	**904,338**	**973,070**

Expenditure‡	2001	2002	2003
General public services	54,243	57,866	60,802
Defence	37,158	40,558	46,156
Public order and safety . . .	43,425	48,608	53,252
Education	92,284	102,284	111,054
Health	145,443	155,356	167,687
Social security and welfare . .	309,107	331,613	346,098
Social security	288,354	297,719	322,789
Housing and community . . .	59,530	62,563	78,338
Recreation, cultural amenities and religious affairs and services .	22,708	24,980	26,500

Expenditure— *continued*‡	2001	2002	2003
Economic affairs and services . .	154,940	178,152	180,668
Transportation and communication	72,577	87,579	104,807
Roads	51,423	62,255	71,505
Other expenditures	55,497	69,692	58,820
Interest payments	21,819	15,711	19,862
Total §	**963,874**	**1,060,195**	**1,116,697**

* Figures represent a consolidation of the operations of the Government, comprising all central and local government funds and accounts.
† Excluding grants received (million koruna): 2,804 in 2001; 2,498 in 2002; 12,366 in 2003.
‡ Excluding lending minus repayments (million koruna): −58,845 in 2001; −141,611 in 2002; −1,055 in 2003.
§ Including adjustment for employer contributions at the same level of government (million koruna): −10,461 in 2001; −11,477 in 2002; −12,678 in 2003.

INTERNATIONAL RESERVES
(US $ million at 31 December)

	2001	2002	2003
Gold*	23	28	32
IMF special drawing rights . .	1	5	9
Reserve position in IMF . . .	151	236	468
Foreign exchange	14,189	23,315	26,294
Total	**14,364**	**23,584**	**26,803**

* National valuation.

Source: IMF, *International Financial Statistics*.

MONEY SUPPLY
('000 million koruna at 31 December)

	2001	2002	2003
Currency outside banks . . .	180.4	197.8	221.4
Demand deposits at deposit money banks	402.5	626.3	741.8
Total money (incl. others) . .	**583.6**	**827.0**	**964.2**

Source: IMF, *International Financial Statistics*.

COST OF LIVING
(Consumer Price Index; base: 1994 = 100)

	2001	2002	2003
Food, beverages and tobacco . .	131.2	128.6	125.8
Clothing and footwear . . .	136.1	132.5	126.0
Housing, water, fuel and light . .	250.3	265.4	270.8
Furnishings, household equipment and maintenance	126.0	125.8	123.9
All items (incl. others)	**158.4**	**161.3**	**161.4**

NATIONAL ACCOUNTS
('000 million koruna at current prices)

Expenditure on the Gross Domestic Product

	2001	2002	2003
Government final consumption expenditure	513.0	555.2	612.6
Private final consumption expenditure	1,192.3	1,234.7	1,298.2
Increase in stocks	30.0	30.9	18.1
Gross fixed capital formation . .	638.6	643.3	678.0
Total domestic expenditure .	**2,373.9**	**2,464.1**	**2,606.9**
Exports of goods and services . .	1,539.3	1,485.5	1,590.5
Less Imports of goods and services	1,598.0	1,535.0	1,646.6
GDP in purchasers' values (market prices)	**2,315.3**	**2,414.7**	**2,550.8**
GDP at constant 1995 prices	**1,617.9**	**1,642.0**	**1,703.0**

Source: IMF, *International Financial Statistics*.

Gross Domestic Product by Economic Activity

	2001	2002	2003
Agriculture, hunting, forestry and fishing	78.8	68.7	65.6
Mining and quarrying	30.1	31.1	30.8
Manufacturing	531.4	569.1	617.4
Electricity, gas and water	85.2	96.2	95.7
Construction	137.5	148.0	154.8
Wholesale and retail trade	274.1	272.1	276.4
Restaurants and hotels	49.4	49.4	49.5
Transport, storage and communications	224.5	248.2	253.8
Financial intermediation	67.6	78.6	77.2
Real estate, renting and business activities	321.4	309.8	343.7
Other services	333.4	360.5	391.2
Sub-total	2,133.4	2,231.7	2,356.1
Less Financial intermediation services indirectly measured	37.9	42.5	43.3
Gross value added in basic prices	2,095.4	2,189.2	2,312.8
Taxes on products	244.9	254.7	275.6
Less Subsidies on products	25.1	29.3	37.6
GDP in market prices	2,315.3	2,414.7	2,550.8

BALANCE OF PAYMENTS
(US $ million)

	2001	2002	2003
Exports of goods f.o.b.	33,404	38,480	48,736
Imports of goods f.o.b.	−36,482	−40,720	−51,242
Trade balance	−3,078	−2,240	−2,505
Exports of services	7,092	7,083	7,789
Imports of services	−5,567	−6,439	−7,320
Balance on goods and services	−1,554	−1,597	−2,035
Other income received	2,233	2,052	2,643
Other income paid	−4,422	−5,632	−6,809
Balance on goods, services and income	−3,743	−5,177	−6,201
Current transfers received	959	1,465	1,655
Current transfers paid	−489	−553	−1,115
Current balance	−3,273	−4,265	−5,661
Capital account (net)	−9	−4	−3
Direct investment abroad	−165	−211	−242
Direct investment from abroad	5,641	8,497	2,514
Portfolio investment assets	125	−2,373	−3,006
Portfolio investment liabilities	798	814	1,753
Financial derivatives assets	−254	−476	257
Financial derivatives liabilities	168	347	−114
Other investment assets	−1,199	4,015	2,279
Other investment liabilities	−544	9	2,414
Net errors and omissions	499	266	251
Overall balance	1,787	6,618	442

Source: IMF, *International Financial Statistics*.

External Trade

COMMODITY GROUPS
(distribution by SITC, million koruna)

Imports f.o.b.	2001	2002	2003
Food and live animals	53,662	54,177	57,087
Beverages and tobacco	7,272	6,594	7,530
Crude materials (inedible) except fuels	40,038	38,187	40,956
Mineral fuels, lubricants, etc.	125,774	100,241	107,789
Chemicals and related products	151,041	148,398	164,435
Basic manufactures	280,181	272,977	289,838
Machinery and transport equipment	585,007	561,815	616,258
Miscellaneous manufactured articles	139,885	140,027	152,708
Total (incl. others)	1,386,319	1,325,717	1,440,723

Exports f.o.b.	2001	2002	2003
Food and live animals	34,415	31,097	36,399
Beverages and tobacco	8,742	8,554	8,194
Crude materials (inedible) except fuels	38,603	35,078	38,422
Mineral fuels, lubricants, etc.	38,150	35,944	39,434
Chemicals and related products	81,679	74,677	80,579
Basic manufactures	309,107	293,727	316,410
Machinery and transport equipment	601,362	623,009	687,201
Miscellaneous manufactured articles	154,882	149,432	161,509
Total (incl. others)	1,269,634	1,254,394	1,370,930

PRINCIPAL TRADING PARTNERS
(million koruna)

Imports f.o.b.	2001	2002	2003
Austria	63,296	57,540	61,757
China, People's Republic	40,596	61,356	75,247
France	66,516	63,544	70,975
Germany	456,941	430,510	469,319
Hungary	24,025	26,026	29,298
Italy	72,841	71,604	76,501
Japan	25,670	27,447	32,780
Netherlands	32,777	31,266	31,548
Poland	52,015	53,176	59,809
Russia	75,966	59,988	65,834
Slovakia	74,569	69,324	74,713
Switzerland	21,897	20,848	23,122
United Kingdom	55,388	41,606	39,082
USA	55,196	43,271	44,933
Total (incl. others)	1,386,319	1,325,717	1,440,723

Exports f.o.b.	2001	2002	2003
Austria	73,075	69,424	85,617
France	54,396	58,443	64,884
Germany	484,424	457,020	507,154
Hungary	23,988	31,123	31,256
Italy	51,495	50,774	60,713
Netherlands	35,394	48,986	56,733
Poland	65,788	59,208	65,673
Russia	18,535	16,795	16,440
Slovakia	101,926	96,651	109,114
Switzerland	17,478	19,610	19,642
United Kingdom	69,359	72,791	73,907
USA	38,016	35,744	33,553
Total (incl. others)	1,269,634	1,254,394	1,370,930

Transport

RAILWAYS
(traffic)

	2001	2002	2003
Passenger-km (million)	7,299	6,597	6,518
Freight net ton-km (million)	16,882	15,810	15,847

ROAD TRAFFIC
(motor vehicles in use at 31 December)

	2001	2002	2003
Passenger cars*	3,529,791	3,647,067	3,706,012
Buses and coaches	18,384	21,340	20,627
Commercial vehicles	296,412	323,464	340,094
Special-purpose commercial vehicles	67,106	n.a.	n.a.
Motorcycles	755,482	760,219	751,634

* Including vans.

INLAND WATERWAYS
(freight carried, '000 metric tons)

	2001	2002	2003
Imports	481	384	240
Exports	515	418	375
Internal	750	761	558
Total (incl. others)	1,910	1,686	1,276

CIVIL AVIATION

	2001	2002	2003
Kilometres flown ('000)	63,949	68,683	70,522
Passengers carried ('000)	3,946	4,291	4,584
Freight carried (metric tons)	16,079	17,990	19,852
Passenger-km ('000)	6,398,920	6,894,961	7,096,292
Freight ton-km ('000)	29,209	31,776	41,563

Communications Media

	2001	2002	2003
Radio receivers ('000 subscribers)	2,832.3	2,773.9	2,707.7
Television receivers ('000 subscribers)	3,209.5	3,209.6	3,169.4
Telephones ('000 main lines in public networks)	10,808.0	12,285.6	13,335.0
Mobile cellular telephones ('000 subscribers)	6,947.2	8,610.2	9,708.7
Personal computers ('000 in use)	1,500*	1,500*	1,874
Internet users ('000)*	1,500*	1,500*	3,100
Book production (titles)	14,321	14,278	16,451
Daily newspapers (number)	105	93	96
Other periodicals (number)	3,364	3,543	3,276

* Source: International Telecommunication Union.

Tourism

FOREIGN TOURIST ARRIVALS*

Country of origin	2001	2002	2003
Austria	163,748	180,676	165,283
Denmark	137,927	96,501	105,273
France	187,118	185,192	193,215
Germany	1,551,353	1,394,581	1,439,124
Israel	183,438	105,281	71,602
Italy	309,517	253,992	281,420
Netherlands	270,930	190,887	238,564
Poland	369,883	318,272	291,344
Russia	n.a.	105,549	124,655
Slovakia	209,348	211,274	252,763
Spain	156,568	139,985	153,331
Sweden	96,559	71,526	80,443
United Kingdom	278,818	286,746	412,402
USA	218,139	187,837	221,311
Total (incl. others)	5,193,973	4,579,015	5,075,756

* Figures refer to visitors staying for at least one night at registered accommodation facilities.

Receipts from tourism (US $ million): 3,106 in 2001; 2,941 in 2002; 3,554 in 2003.

Education

(2003/04)

	Institutions	Teachers	Students
Pre-primary	4,822	23,244	280,491
Basic (primary and lower secondary)	3,870	65,615	956,324
Upper secondary:			
general	344	12,175	142,167
technical	806	20,791	219,963
vocational	538	11,083	179,561
Tertiary:			
higher professional schools	169	3,237	30,681
universities	24	14,221	233,442

Directory

The Constitution

The following is a summary of the main provisions of the Constitution of the Czech Republic, which was adopted on 16 December 1992 and entered into force on 1 January 1993:

GENERAL PROVISIONS

The Czech Republic is a sovereign, unified and democratic law-abiding state, founded on the respect for the rights and freedoms of the individual and citizen. All state power belongs to the people, who exercise this power through the intermediary of legislative, executive and judicial bodies. The fundamental rights and freedoms of the people are under the protection of the judiciary.

The political system is founded on the free and voluntary operation of political parties respecting fundamental democratic principles and rejecting force as a means to assert their interests. Political decisions derive from the will of the majority, expressed through the free ballot. Minorities are protected in decision-making by the majority.

The territory of the Czech Republic encompasses an indivisible whole, whose state border may be changed only by constitutional law. Procedures covering the acquisition and loss of Czech citizenship are determined by law. No one may be deprived of his or her citizenship against his or her will.

GOVERNMENT

Legislative Power

Legislative power in the Czech Republic is vested in two chambers, the Poslanecká sněmovna (Chamber of Deputies) and the Senát (Senate). The Poslanecká sněmovna has 200 members, elected for a term of four years. The Senát has 81 members, elected for a term of six years. Every two years one-third of the senators are elected. Both chambers elect their respective Chairman and Deputy Chairmen from among their members. Members of both chambers of the legislature are elected on the basis of universal, equal and direct suffrage by secret ballot. All citizens of 18 years and over are eligible to vote.

The legislature enacts the Constitution and laws; approves the state budget and the state final account; and approves the electoral law and international agreements. It elects the President of the Republic (at a joint session of both chambers), supervises the activities of the Government, and decides upon the declaration of war.

President of the Republic

The President of the Republic is Head of State. He or she is elected for a term of five years by a joint session of both chambers of the legislature. The President may not be elected for more than two consecutive terms.

The President appoints, dismisses and accepts the resignation of the Prime Minister and other members of the Government, dismisses the Government and accepts its resignation; convenes sessions of the Poslanecká sněmovna; may dissolve the Poslanecká sněmovna; names the judges of the Constitutional Court, its Chairman and Deputy Chairmen; appoints the Chairman and Deputy Chairmen of the Supreme Court; has the right to return adopted constitutional laws to the legislature; initials laws; and appoints members of the Council of the Czech National Bank. The President also represents the State in external affairs; is the Supreme Commander of the Armed Forces; receives heads of diplomatic missions; calls elections to the Poslanecká sněmovna and to the Senát; and has the right to grant amnesty.

Council of Ministers

The Council of Ministers is the highest organ of executive power. It is composed of the Prime Minister, the Deputy Prime Ministers and Ministers. It is answerable to the Poslanecká sněmovna. The President of the Republic appoints the Prime Minister, on whose recommendation he/she appoints the remaining members of the Council of Ministers and entrusts them with directing the ministries or other offices.

JUDICIAL SYSTEM

Judicial power is exercised on behalf of the Republic by independent courts. Judges are independent in the exercise of their function. The judiciary consists of the Supreme Court, the Supreme Administrative Court, high, regional and district courts.

The Constitutional Court is a judicial body protecting constitutionality. It consists of 15 judges appointed for a 10-year term by the President of the Republic with the consent of the Senát.

The Government

HEAD OF STATE

President: Václav Klaus (elected 28 February 2003; inaugurated 7 March 2003).

COUNCIL OF MINISTERS
(April 2005)

A coalition Government of the Czech Social Democratic Party (CSDP), Independents (Ind.) and the Coalition, comprising the Christian Democratic Union—Czechoslovak People's Party (CDU—CPP) and the Freedom Union—Democratic Union (FU-DU).

Note: Following the resignation of Stanislav Gross as Prime Minister, President Václav Klaus appointed the hitherto Minister of Regional Development, Jiří Paroubek, as premier on 25 April 2005. In accordance with the Constitution, the Council of Ministers appointed by Paroubek on that date was to be confirmed in office by a vote of confidence in the lower legislative chamber within 30 days.

Prime Minister: Jiří Paroubek (CSDP).

First Deputy Prime Minister and Minister of Finance: Bohuslav Sobotka (CSDP).

Deputy Prime Minister and Minister of Labour and Social Affairs: Zdeněk Škromach (CSDP).

Deputy Prime Minister and Minister of Justice: Pavel Němec (FU-DU).

Deputy Prime Minister and Minister of Transport: Milan Šimonovský (CDU—CPP).

Deputy Prime Minister, responsible for the Economy: Martin Jahn (Ind.).

Minister of Foreign Affairs: Cyril Svoboda (CDU—CPP).

Minister of Defence: Karel Kühnl (FU-DU).

Minister of the Interior: František Bublan (Ind.).

Minister of Industry and Trade: Milan Urban (CSDP).

Minister of Agriculture: Petr Zgarba (CSDP).

Minister of Health: Milada Emmerová (CSDP).

Minister of Education, Youth and Sport: Petra Buzková (CSDP).

Minister of the Environment: Libor Ambrozek (CDU—CPP).

Minister of Culture: Pavel Dostál (CSDP).

Minister of Regional Development: Radko Martínek (CSDP).

Minister of Information: Dana Bérová (FU-DU).

Minister without Portfolio, responsible for Legislation: Pavel Zářecký (Ind.).

MINISTRIES

Office of the President: Pražský hrad 119 08 Prague 1; tel. 224371111; fax 224373300; e-mail ladislav.jakl@hrad.cz; internet www.hrad.cz.

Office of the Government of the Czech Republic: nábř. E. Beneše 4, 118 01 Prague 1; tel. 224002111; fax 224003090; e-mail posta@vlada.cz; internet www.vlada.cz.

Ministry of Agriculture: Těšnov 17, 117 05 Prague 1; tel. 22181111; fax 224810478; e-mail info@mze.cz; internet www.mze.cz.

Ministry of Culture: Maltéské nám. 471/1, 118 11 Prague 1; tel. 257085111; fax 224318155; e-mail posta@mkcr.cz; internet www.mkcr.cz.

Ministry of Defence: Tychonova 1, 160 01 Prague 6; tel. 973201111; fax 973200149; e-mail info@army.cz; internet www.army.cz.

Ministry of Education, Youth and Sport: Karmelitská 8, 118 12 Prague 1; tel. 257193111; fax 257193790; e-mail info@msmt.cz; internet www.msmt.cz.

Ministry of the Environment: Vršovická 65, 100 10 Prague 10; tel. 267121111; fax 267310308; e-mail posta@env.cz; internet www.env.cz.

Ministry of Finance: Lětenská 15, 118 00 Prague 1; tel. 257041111; fax 257042788; e-mail podatelna@mfcr.cz; internet www.mfcr.cz.

Ministry of Foreign Affairs: Loretánské nám. 5, 118 00 Prague 1; tel. 224181111; fax 224182048; e-mail info@mzv.cz; internet www.mzv.cz.

Ministry of Health: Palackého nám. 4, 128 01 Prague 2; tel. 224971111; fax 224972111; e-mail mzcr@mzcr.cz; internet www.mzcr.cz.

Ministry for Industry and Trade: Na Františku 32, Politichýh věznů 20, 110 15 Prague 1; tel. 224851111; fax 224811089; e-mail mpo@mpo.cz; internet www.mpo.cz.

Ministry of Information: Havelkova 2, 130 00 Prague 3; tel. 221008111; fax 222721745; e-mail posta@micr.cz; internet www.micr.cz.

Ministry of the Interior: Nad štolou 3, 170 34 Prague 7; tel. 974811111; fax 261433552; e-mail posta@mvcr.cz; internet www.mvcr.cz.

Ministry of Justice: Vyšehradská 16, 128 10 Prague 2; tel. 2219977111; fax 224919927; e-mail msp@msp.justice.cz; internet www.justice.cz.

Ministry of Labour and Social Affairs: Na poříčním právu 1, 128 01 Prague 2; tel. 221921111; fax 221922664; e-mail posta@mpsv.cz; internet www.mpsv.cz.

Ministry for Regional Development: Staroměstské nám. 6, 110 15 Prague 1; tel. 221771617; fax 224861333; e-mail public@mmr.cz; internet www.mmr.cz.

Ministry of Transport: nábř. L. Svobody 12/1222, POB 9, 110 15 Prague 1; tel. 972211111; fax 972231184; e-mail posta@mdcr.cz; internet www.mdcr.cz.

Legislature

The Czech Constitution, which was adopted in December 1992, provided for the creation of a bicameral legislature as the highest organ of state authority in the Czech Republic (which was established as an independent state on 1 January 1993, following the dissolution of the Czech and Slovak Federative Republic). The lower house, the Poslanecká Sněmovna (Chamber of Deputies), retained the structure of the Czech National Council (the former republican legislature). The upper chamber, the Senát (Senate), was first elected in November 1996.

Poslanecká sněmovna
(Chamber of Deputies)

Sněmovní 4, 118 26 Prague 1; tel. 257171111; fax 257534469; e-mail posta@psp.cz; internet www.psp.cz.

Chairman: Lubomír Zaorálek.

General Election, 14–15 June 2002

Party	% of votes	Seats
Czech Social Democratic Party	30.2	70
Civic Democratic Party	24.5	58
Communist Party of Bohemia and Moravia .	18.5	41
Coalition*	14.3	31
Green Party	2.4	—
Others	10.1	—
Total	100.0	200

* An informal electoral alliance of the Christian Democratic Union—Czechoslovak People's Party and the Freedom Union—Democratic Union.

Senát
(Senate)

Valdštejnské nám. 4, 118 01 Prague 1; tel. 257071111; fax 257534499; e-mail webmaster@senat.cz; internet www.senat.cz.

Chairman: PREMYSL SOBOTKA.
One-third of the 81 seats of the Senát are renewed every two years.

Party	Seats after elections	
	Oct. 2002	Nov. 2004
Civic Democratic Party	26	36
Christian Democratic Union—		
Czechoslovak People's Party* . . .	16	14
Freedom Union—Democratic Union*† .	15	9
Czech Social Democratic Party . . .	11	7
Communist Party of Bohemia and		
Moravia	3	2
Others	8	5
Independents	2	8
Total	81	81

* Contested the 2000 and 2002 elections as an informal electoral alliance (in 2000 together with the Civil Democratic Alliance).
† One seat won in alliance with the Civic Democratic Alliance in 2004.

Political Organizations

Christian Democratic Union—Czechoslovak People's Party (CDU—CPP) (Křesťanská a demokratická uniei—Československá strana lidová): Palác Charitas, Karlovo náměstí 5, 12 801 Prague 2; tel. 226205111; fax 224917630; e-mail info@kdu.cz; internet www.kdu.cz; f. 1992; Chair. MIROSLAV KALOUSEK.

Civic Democratic Alliance (CDA) (Občanská demokratická aliance): Štefánikova 21, 150 00 Prague 5; tel. 257321791; fax 257327072; e-mail oda@oda.cz; internet www.oda.cz; f. 1991 as a formal political party, following a split in Civic Forum (f. 1989); fmrly an informal group within Civic Forum, conservative; Chair. JIŘINA NOVÁKOVÁ.

Civic Democratic Party (CDP) (Občanská demokratická strana): Jánský vršek 13, 118 00 Prague 1; tel. 234707111; fax 23470701; e-mail hk@ods.cz; internet www.ods.cz; f. 1991 following a split in Civic Forum (f. 1989); merged with Christian Democratic Party in 1996; liberal-conservative; Chair. MIREK TOPOLÁNEK.

Communist Party of Bohemia and Moravia (Komunistická strana Čech a Moravy): Politických vězňů 9, 111 21 Prague 1; tel. 222897331; fax 222897426; e-mail leftnews@kscm.cz; internet www.kscm.cz; f. 1991 as a result of the reorganization of the fmr Communist Party of Czechoslovakia; c. 95,500 mems; Leader MIROSLAV GREBENÍČEK.

Communist Party of Czechoslovakia (Komunistická strana Československa): Milánská 457, 100 00 Prague 10; e-mail ksc@ksc-uv.cz; internet www.ksc-uv.cz; f. 1995 as Party of Czechoslovak Communists renamed as above 1999; 19,980 mems; Sec.-Gen. ŠTĚPÁN MIROSLAV.

Conservative Party (Konzervativní strana): U Průhonu 6, 170 00 Prague 7; tel. and fax 220808572; e-mail info@konzervativnistrana.cz; internet www.konzervativnistrana.cz; f. 1994 by fmr mems of right-wing faction in CDA; Chair. JAN FOŘT.

Countryside Party (Strana venkova): Práčská 1881, 106 00 Prague 10; tel. 272652280; e-mail sv-sos@volny.cz; internet www.hlasvenkova.info; f. 1996; c. 3,000 mems; Chair. MARIE POLÁCHOVÁ.

Czech Right (Česká pravice): Slavojova 9, 128 00 Prague 2; e-mail cp-praha@ceskapravice.cz; tel. 224936232; internet www.ceskapravice.cz; f. 1994; conservative; Chair. MICHAL SIMKANIČ.

Czech Social Democratic Party (CSDP) (Česká strana sociálně demokratická): Lidový dům, Hybernská 7, 110 00 Prague 1; tel. and fax 296522111; e-mail info@socdem.cz; internet www.socdem.cz; f. 1878; prohibited 1948; re-established 1990; fmrly the Czechoslovak Social Democratic Party; Chair. STANISLAV GROSS.

Democratic Socialist Party (Strana demokratického socialismu): nám. W. Churchilla 2, 130 00 Prague 3; e-mail secret@sds.cz; internet www.sds.cz; f. 1997 by merger of Left Bloc and Party of the Democratic Left; c. 9,000 mems; Chair. MILAN NEUBERT.

Democratic Union of the Czech Republic (Demokratická Unie České Republiky—DEU-ČR): Všebořická 603, Ústí nad Labem, 400 01; tel. 737261969; fax 472742808; e-mail dorant@pvtnet.cz; internet www.deucr.cz; f. 2004 by mems of the fmr Democratic Union; Chair. JAN DORANT.

European Democrats (ED) (Evropští demokraté): Radlická 2, 150 00 Prague 5; tel. 257310334; fax 257310335; e-mail info@edemokrate.cz; internet www.edemokrate.cz; f. July 2002 by break-away mems of Civic Democratic Party; Chair. JAN KASL.

Free Democrats—Liberal National Social Party (Svobodní demokraté—Liberální strana národně sociální—SD—LSNS): Republiky nám. 7, 111 49 Prague 1; tel. 221618554; fax 224223443; e-mail sdlsns@mbox.vol.cz; internet www.ecn.cz/env/volby/sd/home.htm; f. 1995 by merger of Free Democrats (fmrly Civic Movement) and Liberal National Social Party (fmrly Czechoslovak Socialist Party); Chair. JIŘÍ DIENSTBIER.

Freedom Union-Democratic Union (FU-DU) (Unie svobody-Demokratická unie—Unie—US-DEU): Malostranské nám. 266/5, 110 00 Prague 1; tel. 257011411; fax 257011439; e-mail info@unie.cz; internet www.unie.cz; Freedom Union founded 1998 following a split in the Civic Democratic Party; merged with Democratic Union in 2001; Chair. PAVEL NÉMEC.

Green Party (Strana zelených): Murmanská 13/1246, 100 00 Prague 10; tel. and fax 272737592; e-mail predsednictvo@zeleni.cz; internet www.zeleni.cz; f. 1989; Pres. JAN BERÁNEK.

Liberal Reform Party (Librální reformní strana—LiRA): Bansko-bystrická 36, 621 00 Brno; tel. 777462817; e-mail info@liberalnistrana.cz; internet www.liberalnistrana.cz; Chair. MILAN HAMERSKÝ.

Party for Life Securities (Strana za životní jistoty): Trojická 20, 120 00 Prague 2; tel. 224919965; fax 222729785; e-mail szj@volny.cz; internet www.szj.cz; Chair. MARCELA KOZEROVÁ.

Party for Open Society (Strana pro otevřenou společnost—SOS): tř. Svornosti 79/1A, 779 00 Olomouc; tel. 585750664; e-mail info@stranaos.cz; internet www.stranaos.cz; promotes development of a political system based upon democratic and tolerant values and an active civil society; Chair. PAVEL NOVÁČEK.

Romany Civic Initiative (Romská občanská iniciativa): Pod Strašnickou vinicí 6, 100 00 Prague 10; f. 1990; Pres. ŠTEFAN LIČARTOVSKÝ.

Viktor Koženy—Civic Federal Democracy Party (Viktor Koženy—Občanská Federální Democracie): Prague; f. 2004; Chair. VIKTOR KOŽENÝ.

Diplomatic Representation

EMBASSIES IN THE CZECH REPUBLIC

Afghanistan: Na Kazance 634/7, 170 00 Prague 7; tel. 28544228; fax 28542009; e-mail afghanistan.ambasada@tiscali.cz; Ambassador AZIZULLAH KARZAI.

Albania: Pod kaštany 22, 160 00 Prague 6; tel. 233370594; fax 233377232; e-mail alembprg@mbox.vol.cz; Ambassador SHAQIR VUKAJ.

Algeria: V tišině 10/483, POB 204, 160 41 Prague 6; tel. 233371142; fax 233371144; e-mail ambalger@mbox.vol.cz; internet www.algerie.cz; Ambassador MOULAY MOHAMMED GUENDIL.

Argentina: Panská 6, 110 00 Prague 1; tel. 224212448; fax 222241246; e-mail embar@iol.cz; Ambassador JUAN EDUARDO FLEMING.

Austria: Viktora Huga 10, 151 15 Prague 5; tel. 257090511; fax 257316045; e-mail austrianembassy@vol.cz; internet www.austria.cz; Ambassador MARGOT KLESTIL-LOEFFLER.

Belarus: Sádky 626, 171 00 Prague 7; tel. 233540899; fax 233540925; Chargé d'affaires a.i. MIKALAI BARYSEVICH.

Belgium: Valdštejnská 6, 118 01 Prague 1; tel. 257533524; fax 257533750; e-mail prague@diplobel.org; Ambassador GUSTAAF DIERCKX.

Brazil: Praha Panská 5, 11000 Prague 1, Prague; tel. 224324965; fax 224312901; e-mail chebrem@mbox.vol.cz; Ambassador AFFONSO EMÍLIO DE ALENCASTRO MASSOT.

Bulgaria: Krakovská 6, 110 00 Prague 1; tel. 222211258; fax 222211728; e-mail bulvelv@mbox.vol.cz; Ambassador MARTIN TOMOV.

Canada: Muchova 6, 160 00 Prague 6; tel. 272101800; fax 272101890; e-mail canada@canada.cz; internet www.canada.cz; Ambassador BRUCE JUTZI.

Chile: U Vorlíků 4/623, 160 00 Prague 6; tel. 224315064; fax 224316069; e-mail echilecz@mbox.vol.cz; internet www.eol.cz/chile; Ambassador CARLOS KLAMMER.

China, People's Republic: Pelléova 18, 160 00 Prague 6; tel. 224311323; fax 224319888; e-mail chinaemb_cz@mfa.gov.cn; internet www.chinaembassy.cz; Ambassador TANG GUOQIANG.

Congo, Democratic Republic: Bošinská 25, 190 15 Prague 9; tel. and fax 286854665; e-mail ambrdcpraha@hotmail.com; Ambassador GOMEZ NDUBA KIMBAYA.

Croatia: V Průhledu 9, 162 00 Prague 6; tel. 233355695; fax 23123464; e-mail velrhprag@vol.cz; Ambassador VIKTOR BROŽ.

Cuba: Sibiřské nám. 1, 160 00 Prague 6; tel. 224311253; fax 23121029; Chargé d'affaires a.i. AYMÉE HERNÁNDEZ QUESADA.

Cyprus: Pod Hradbami 9, 160 00 Prague 6; tel. 224316833; fax 224317529; e-mail cyprusembass@mbox.vol.cz; Ambassador STAVROS AMVROSIOU.

Denmark: Maltézské nám. 5, POB 25, 118 01 Prague 1; tel. 257531600; fax 257531410; e-mail prgamb@um.dk; internet www.ambprag.um.dk; Ambassador JØRGEN RUD HANSEN BØJER.

Egypt: Pelléova 14, 160 00 Prague 6; tel. 224311506; fax 224311157; e-mail embassyegypt@iol.cz; Ambassador MUHAMMAD MOUSTAFA KAMAL.

Estonia: Na Kampě 1, 118 00 Prague 1; tel. 257011180; fax 257011181; e-mail embassy.prague@estemb.cz; Ambassador EVE-KÜLLI KALA.

Finland: Hellichova 1, 110 00 Prague 1; tel. 251177251; fax 251177241; e-mail sanomat.pra@formin.fi; Ambassador JORMA INKI.

France: Velkopřevorské nám. 2, POB 102, 118 00 Prague 1; tel. 251171711; fax 251171720; e-mail ambafrcz@vol.cz; internet www.france.cz; Ambassador JOËL DE ZORZI.

Germany: Vlašská 19, POB 88, 118 01 Prague 1; tel. 257113111; fax 257534056; e-mail zreg@prag.auswaertiges-amt.de; internet www.german-embassy.cz; Ambassador Dr MICHAEL LIBAL.

Ghana: V tišině 4, 160 00 Prague 6; tel. 233377236; fax 233375647; e-mail ghanaemb@mbox.vol.cz; Ambassador VERONICA SHARON BOAKYE KUFUOR.

Greece: Helénská 2, 120 00 Prague 2; tel. 222250943; fax 222253686; Ambassador VASSILIOS IKOSSIPENTARCHOS.

Holy See: Voršilská 12, 110 00 Prague 1; tel. 224999811; fax 224999833; e-mail nunciatgc@mbox.vol.cz; Apostolic Nuncio Most Rev. DIEGO CAUSERO (Titular Archbishop of Gradum).

Hungary: Českomalínská 20, 160 00 Prague 6; tel. 233324454; fax 233322104; e-mail huembprg@vol.cz; Ambassador ISTVÁN SZABÓ.

India: Valdštejnská 6, 118 00 Prague 1; tel. 257533490; fax 257533378; e-mail indembprague@bohem-net.cz; internet www.india.cz; Ambassador P. S. RAGHAVAN.

Indonesia: Nad Budánkami II/7, 150 21 Prague 5; tel. 257214388; fax 257212105; e-mail informace@indoneske-velvyslanectvi.cz; internet www.indoneske-velvyslanectvi.cz; Ambassador SANTOSO RAHARDJO.

Iran: Na Zátorce 18, 160 00 Prague 6; tel. 220570454; fax 233380255; Chargé d'affaires SEYED HUSSEIN REZVANI.

Iraq: Na Zátorce 10, 160 00 Prague 6; tel. 224326976; fax 224321715; e-mail iraqiembassy@volny.cz; Ambassador DHIA AL-DABBASS.

Ireland: Tržiště 13, 118 00 Prague 1; tel. 257530061; fax 257531387; e-mail irishembassy@iol.cz; Ambassador DONAL HAMILL.

Israel: Badeniho 2, 170 06 Prague 7; tel. 233325109; fax 233320092; e-mail ambassador-sec@prague.mfa.goo.il; internet www.prague.mfa.gov.il; Ambassador ARTHUR AVNON.

Italy: Nerudova 20, 118 00 Prague 1; tel. 233080111; fax 257531522; e-mail italemba@mbox.vol.cz; internet www.italianembassy.cz; Ambassador GIORGIO RADICATI.

Japan: Maltézské nám. 6, 118 01 Prague 1; tel. 257533546; fax 257532377; Ambassador KOICHI TAKAHASHI.

Kazakhstan: Romaina Rollanda 12, 160 00 Prague 6; tel. 233375642; fax 233375642; e-mail kzembas@bon.cz; Chargé d'affaires a.i. IGOR MUSSALIMOV.

Korea, Democratic People's Republic: Na Zátorce 6, 160 00 Prague 6; tel. 224320783; fax 224318817; Ambassador RI PYONG GAP.

Korea, Republic: Slavíčkova 5, 160 00 Prague 6; tel. 2234090411; fax 2234090450; Ambassador HAE JIN-CHUN.

Kuwait: Na Zátorce 26, 160 00 Prague 6; tel. 2205707781; fax 220570787; Ambassador KHALED MUTLAQ ZAYED AL-DUWAILAH.

Latvia: Hradešínská 3, POB 54, 101 00 Prague 10; tel. 255700881; fax 255700880; e-mail embassy.czech@mfa.gov.lv; internet www.prague.am.gov.lv; Ambassador IVETA ŠULCA.

Lebanon: Lazarská 6, 120 00 Prague 2; tel. 224930495; fax 224934534; Ambassador ZOUHEIR KAZZAZ.

Libya: Na baště sv. Jiří 7, 160 00 Prague 6; tel. 233324160; fax 233322173; Chargé d'affaires a.i. ABDELSALAM M. A. VALRGEI.

Lithuania: Pod Klikovkou 1916/2, 150 00 Prague 5; tel. 257210122; fax 257210124; e-mail ltembcz@mbox.vol.cz; internet www.ltembassycz.urrn.lt; Ambassador ROMUALDAS KOZYRROVIČIUS.

Luxembourg: Tržiště 13, 118 00 Prague 1; tel. 257181800; fax 257532537; e-mail renate.cech@mae.etat.lu; internet www.ambalux.cz; Ambassador PIERRE-LOUIS LORENZ.

Mexico: Nad Kazankou 8, 171 00 Prague 7; tel. 283061530; fax 233550477; e-mail embamex@rep-checa.cz; Ambassador FEDERICO SALAS.

Mongolia: Na Marně 5, 160 00 Prague 6; tel. 224311198; fax 224314827; e-mail monemb@bohem-net.cz; Ambassador SHIJEEKHUU ODONBAATAR.

Morocco: Komornická 25, 160 00 Prague 6; tel. 233325656; fax 233322634; e-mail sifamapragu@czn.cz; Chargé d'affaires ZOUHAIR JIBRAILI.

Netherlands: Gotthardská 6/27, 160 00 Prague 6; tel. 233015200; fax 233015254; e-mail nlgovpra@ti.cz; internet www.netherlandsembassy.cz; Ambassador IDA L. VAN VELDHUIZEN-ROTH-ENBÜCHER.

Norway: Hellichova 1/458, 118 00 Prague 1; tel. 257323737; fax 257326827; e-mail emb.prague@mfa.no; internet www.noramb.cz; Ambassador PETER RAEDER.

Peru: Muchova 9, 160 00 Prague 6; tel. 224316210; fax 224314749; e-mail embaperu.praga@post.cz; Chargé d'affaires a.i. CRISTINA RON-QUILLO DE BLÖDORN.

Philippines: Senovážné náměstí 8, 110 00 Prague 1; tel. 224216397; fax 224216390; e-mail praguepe@phembassy.cz; Ambassador CARMELITA RODRÍGUEZ SALAS.

Poland: Valdštejnská 8, 118 01 Prague 1; tel. 257530388; fax 257530135; e-mail ambrpczechy@mbox.vol.cz; internet www.ambpol.cz; Ambassador ANDRZEJ KRAWCZYK.

Portugal: Kinských nám. 7, 150 00 Prague 5; tel. 257311230; fax 257311234; e-mail embport@mbox.vol.cz; Ambassador FERNANDO MANUEL OLIVEIRA DE CASTRO BRANDÃO (designate).

Romania: Nerudova 5, POB 87, 118 01 Prague 1; tel. 257534210; fax 257531017; e-mail embrprg@mbox.vol.cz; internet www.rouemb.cz; Ambassador GHEORGHE TINCA.

Russia: Pod kaštany 1, 160 00 Prague 6; tel. 233374100; fax 233377235; e-mail rusembassy@cdnet.org; Ambassador ALEKSEI L. FEDOTOV.

Saudi Arabia: Na Hřebenkách 70, 150 00 Prague 5; tel. 257316597; fax 257316593; e-mail rse@saudi-embassy.cz; Ambassador Prince MANSOUR BIN KHALID BIN ABDULLAH AL-FARHAN AL-SAUD.

Serbia and Montenegro: Mostecká 15, 118 00 Prague 1; tel. 257532075; fax 257533948; e-mail yuambacz@mbox.vol.cz; Ambassador Dr ALEKSANDAR ILIĆ.

Slovakia: Pod hradbami 1, 160 00 Prague 6; tel. 233113051; fax 233113054; e-mail skembassy@mfa.sk; Ambassador LADISLAV BALLEK.

Slovenia: Pod hradbami 15, 160 41 Prague 6; tel. 233081211; fax 224314106; e-mail vpr@mzz-dkp.gov.si; Ambassador DRAGO MIROŠIČ.

South Africa: Ruská 65, POB 133, 100 00 Prague 10; tel. 267311114; fax 267311395; e-mail saprague@terminal.cz; Ambassador NOEL NOA LEHOKO.

Spain: Badeniho 4, 170 00 Prague 7; tel. 224311222; fax 233341770; e-mail embpraha@gts.cz; internet www.embajada-csp-praga.cz; Ambassador ANTONIO PEDAUYÉ Y GONZÁLEZ.

Sweden: Úvoz 13-Hradčany, POB 35, 160 12 Prague 612; tel. 220313200; fax 220313240; e-mail ambassaden.prag@foreign.ministry.se; Ambassador HARALD FÄLTH.

Switzerland: Pevnostní 7, POB 84, 162 01 Prague 6; tel. 220400611; fax 224311312; e-mail vertretung@pra.rep.admin.ch; Ambassador HANSRUDOLF HOFFMAN.

Syria: Juárezova 14, 160 00 Prague 6; tel. 224310952; fax 224317911; Ambassador NADRA FAYEZ SAYYAF.

Thailand: Romaina Rollanda 3, 160 00 Prague 6; tel. 220571435; fax 220570049; e-mail thaiemb@volny.cz; Chargé d'affaires a.i. NAT PINYOWATTANACHEEP.

Tunisia: Nad Kostelem 8, 147 00 Prague 4; tel. 244460652; fax 244460825; e-mail atprague@vol.cz; Ambassador MONCEF LARBI.

Turkey: Na Ořechovce 69, 162 00 Prague 616; tel. 224311402; fax 224311279; e-mail prag.be@worldonline.cz; Ambassador SABRI CENK DUATEPE.

Ukraine: Charlese de Gaulla 29, 160 00 Prague 6; tel. 233342000; fax 233344366; e-mail emb-cz@mfa.gov.ua; internet www .ukrembassy.cz; Ambassador IVAN KULEBA.

United Kingdom: Thunovská 14, 118 00 Prague 1; tel. 257402111; fax 257402296; e-mail info@britain.cz; internet www.britain.cz; Ambassador LINDA JOY DUFFIELD.

USA: Tržiště 15, 118 01 Prague 1; tel. 257530663; fax 257530583; internet www.usembassy.cz; Ambassador WILLIAM J. CABANISS.

Uruguay: Muchova 9, 160 00 Prague 6; tel. 224314755; fax 224313780; e-mail urupra@urupra.cz; Ambassador Dr PEDRO VIDAL SALABERRY.

Venezuela: Sněmovni 9, 110 00 Prague 1; tel. 257534256; fax 257534257; e-mail embaven@mbox.vol.cz; internet www.vol.cz/ embavenezuela; Chargé d'affaires a.i. MARÍA JOSÉ BÁEZ LORETO.

Viet Nam: Plzeňská 214, 150 00 Prague 5; tel. 257211540; fax 257211792; Ambassador KHAC BUT BUI.

Yemen: Pod hradbami 5, 160 00 Prague 6; tel. 233331568; fax 233332204; Ambassador SALEM YAHYA ALKHAREJAH.

Judicial System

The judicial system comprises the Supreme Court, the Supreme Administrative Court, chief, regional and district courts. There is also a 15-member Constitutional Court.

Supreme Court (Nejvyšší soud): Buresova 20, 657 37 Brno; tel. 541593111; fax 541213493; e-mail mbox@nsoud.cz; internet www .nsoud.cz; Chair. IVA BROZOVA.

Supreme Administrative Court (Nejvyšší správní soud): Masarykova 31, 657 40 Brno; tel. 542532311; fax 542532361; e-mail podatelna@nssoud.cz; internet www.nssoud.cz; Chair. JOSEF BAXA.

Office of the Chief Prosecutor: Jezuitska 4, 660 55 Brno; tel. 542512111; fax 542219621; e-mail posta@nsz.brn.justice.cz; Chief Prosecutor MARIE BENESOVA.

Constitutional Court (Ústavní soud): Joštova 8, 660 83 Brno; tel. 542161111; fax 542218326; e-mail podani@concourt.cz; internet www.concourt.cz; Chair. PAVEL RYCHETSKÝ.

Religion

According to the results of the March 2001 national census, about 60% of the population profess no religious belief. Among believers, the principal religion is Christianity, and the largest denomination the Roman Catholic Church.

CHRISTIANITY

Ecumenical Council of Churches in the Czech Republic (Ekumenická rada církví v České republice): Donská 5/370, 101 00 Prague 10; tel. and fax 271742326; e-mail ekumrada@iol.cz; internet www.ecumenicalcouncil.cz; f. 1955; 11 mem. churches; Pres. Bishop PAVEL ČERNÝ; Gen. Sec. JITKA KRAUSOVÁ.

The Roman Catholic Church

Latin Rite

The Czech Republic comprises two archdioceses and six dioceses. According to the results of the March 2001 national census, there were 2,740,780 adherents in the Czech Republic, equivalent to some 27% of the total population. The Roman Catholic Church estimated a total of 3,383,125 adherents in the country at 31 December 2002.

Czech Bishops' Conference: Thákurova 3, 160 00 Prague 6; tel. 220181421; fax 224310144; e-mail cbk2@ktf.cuni.cz; f. 1990; Pres. Most Rev. JAN GRAUBNER (Archbishop of Oloumouc).

Archbishop of Olomouc: Most Rev. JAN GRAUBNER, Wurmova 9, POB 193, 771 01 Olomouc; tel. 587405411; fax 585224840; e-mail arcibol@arcibol.cz; internet www.ado.cz.

Archbishop of Prague: Cardinal Dr MILOSLAV VLK, Hradčanské nám. 16, 119 02 Prague 1; tel. 220392111; fax 220514647; e-mail apha@apha.cz; internet www.apha.cz.

Byzantine Rite

Apostolic Exarch in the Czech Republic: Most Rev. Dr LADISLAV HUČKO (Titular Bishop of Orea,), Haštalské nám. 4, 110 00 Prague 1; tel. and fax 222312817; e-mail exarchat@volny.cz; internet www .exarchat.cz; 250,000 adherents (Dec. 2000).

The Eastern Orthodox Church

Orthodox Church in the Czech Lands and Slovakia (Pravoslavná církev v Českých zemích a na Slovensku): V jámě 6, 111 21 Prague 1; e-mail cilova@pravoslavnacirkev.cz; internet www .pravoslavnacirkev.cz; divided into two eparchies in the Czech Republic: Prague and Olomouc; Metropolitan of Prague and of the Czech Lands and Slovakia His Holiness Patriarch NIKOLAJ.

Protestant Churches

Baptist Union in the Czech Republic: Na Topolce 14, 140 00 Prague 4; tel. and fax 241434256; e-mail czechbaptist@iol.cz; internet www.baptist.cz; f. 1994; 2,395 mems; Pres. Rev. VLADISLAV DONÁT; Sec. Rev. JAN TITERA; 2,395 mems.

Brethren Church (Církev bratrská): Soukenická 15, 110 00 Prague 1; tel. and fax 22318131; e-mail pavel.cerny@cb.cz; internet www.cb .cz; f. 1880; 9,037 mems, 56 churches; Pres. PAVEL ČERNÝ; Sec. KAREL FOJTÍK.

Evangelical Church of Czech Brethren (Presbyterian) (Českobratrská církev evangelická): Jungmannova 9, 111 21 Prague 1; tel. 224999211; fax 224999219; e-mail srcce@srcce.cz; internet www .srcce.cz; f. 1781; united since 1918; active in Bohemia, Moravia and Silesia; 117,000 adherents (2001) and 262 parishes (2004); Pres. JOEL RUML; Synodal Curator MAHULENA ČEJKOVÁ.

Silesian Evangelical Church of the Augsburg Confession (Slezská církev evangelická a.v.): Na nivách 7, 737 01 Český Těšín; tel. 558731804; fax 558731815; e-mail sceav@sceav.cz; internet www .sceav.cz; Lutheran; 40,000 mems; Bishop VLADISLAV VOLNÝ.

United Methodist Church (Evangelická Církev Metodistická): Ječná 19, 120 00 Prague 2; tel. 2224919608; e-mail rada@umc.cz; internet www.umc.cz; 1,000 mems; 15 parishes; Supt JOSEF ČERVEŇÁK.

Unity of Brethren of the Czech Republic—Unitas Fratrum (Jednota bratrska ČR): Kollárova 456, 509 01 Nová Paka; tel. 326736274; e-mail urjb@cmail.cz; internet www.jbcr.info; f. 1457, reorganized 1862; widely known as the 'Moravian Church'; 2,447 mems; 21 parishes; Pres. Rev. JAROSLAV PLEVA.

Other Christian Churches

Apostolic Church in the Czech Republic (Apoštolská církev ČR): V Zídkách 402, 280 02 Kolín; tel. 321720457; fax 321727668; e-mail ustredi.kolin@apostolskacirkev.cz; internet www .apostolskacirkev.cz; f. 1989; 5,634 mems; Bishop RUDOLF BUBIK.

Church of the Seventh-day Adventists—Czech and Slovak Union (Církev adventistů sedmého dne—Česko-Slovenská Unie): Zálesí 50, 142 00 Prague 4; tel. 241471939; fax 244471863; e-mail unie@casd.cz; internet www.casd.cz; f. 1919; 7,744 mems; 138 congregations; Pres. PAVEL ŠIMEK.

Czechoslovak Hussite Church (Církev československá husitská): Wuchterlova 5, 166 26 Prague 6; tel. 220398111; fax 220398123; e-mail ustredni.rada@ccsh.cz; internet www.ccsh.cz; f. 1920; 100,000 mems; six dioceses, divided into 300 parishes; Chair. Patriarch Dr JAN SCHWARZ.

Old Catholic Church in the Czech Republic (Starokatolická cirkev v ČR): Na Bateriích 27, 162 00 Prague 6; tel. and fax 224319528; e-mail stkat@starokatolici.cz; internet starokatolici.cz; 1,700 mems, 17 parishes; Bishop Mgr DUŠAN HEJBAL.

JUDAISM

Federation of Jewish Communities in the Czech Republic (Federace židovských obcí v ČR): Maiselova 18, 110 01 Prague 1; tel. 224800824; fax 224810912; e-mail fedzid@vol.cz; internet www .fedzid.czweb.org; 3,000 mems in 10 registered communities; Pres. Dr JAN MUNK; Chief Rabbi EPHRAIM KAROL SIDON.

The Press

PRINCIPAL DAILIES

There were 90 national and regional daily newspapers published in 2004.

Brno

Brněnský večerník (Brno Evening Paper): Jakubské nám. 7, 658 44 Brno; tel. 542321227; fax 545215150; f. 1968; Editor-in-Chief PETR HOSKOVEC; circ. 16,000.

Rovnost (Equality): M. Horákové 9, 658 22 Brno; tel. 545321121; fax 545212873; internet www.rovnost.cz; f. 1885; morning; Editor-in-Chief PAVEL ŽÁRA; circ. 62,000.

České Budějovice

Českobudějovické listy (České Budějovice Paper): Vrbenská 23, 370 45 České Budějovice; tel. 387411993; fax 387411825; e-mail ceskobudejovicke.listy@denikybohemia.cz; internet www .ceskobudejovickelisty.cz; f. 1992; morning; Editor-in-Chief FRAN-TIŠEK LIPPL; circ. 53,000.

Hradec Králové

Hradecké noviny (Hradec Králové News): Kladská 17, 500 03 Hradec Králové; tel. 495800833; fax 495800889; e-mail j.zajickova@ vychod.denikybohemia.cz; internet www.hradeckenoviny.cz; f. 1992; Editor-in-Chief JITKA ZAJÍČKOVÁ; circ. 30,000.

Karlovy Vary

Karlovarské noviny (Karlovy Vary News): T.G. Masaryka 32, 360 21 Karlovy Vary; tel. 353224496; fax 353225115; e-mail karlovarske .noviny@denikybohemia.cz; internet www.karlovarskenoviny.cz; f. 1991; Editor-in-Chief IVANA KALINOVÁ; circ. 15,000.

Ostrava

Moravskoslezský deník (Moravia-Silesia Daily): Mlýnská 10, 701 11 Ostrava; tel. 596176311; fax 596176312; e-mail redakce@morava .vlp.cz; internet okresy.mojenoviny.cz/ostrava; f. 1991; Editor-in-Chief TOMÁŠ ŠIŘINA; circ. 130,000.

Svoboda (Freedom): Mlýnská 10, 701 11 Ostrava; tel. 592472311; fax 592472312; f. 1991; morning; Editor-in-Chief JOSEF LYS; circ. 100,000.

Pardubice

Pardubické noviny (Pardubice News): Třída Míru 60, 530 02 Pardubice; tel. 466613906; fax 466615640; e-mail j.korbel@vychod .denikybohemia.cz; internet www.pardubickenoviny.cz; f. 1992; Editor-in-Chief JAN KORBEL; circ. 15,000.

Plzeň

Plzeňský deník (Plzeň Daily): Kovářská 4, 304 83 Plzeň; tel. 377168321; fax 377221875; e-mail n.sedivcova@zapad .denikybohemia.cz; internet www.plzenskydenik.cz; f. 1992; (fmrly *Pravda—Truth*, f. 1919); Editor NATAŠA ŠEDIVCOVÁ; circ. 50,000.

Prague

Blesk (Lightning): Žerotinova 32, 130 50 Prague 3; tel. 225097616; fax 222714641; e-mail blesk@blesk.cz; internet www.blesk.cz; popular; Editor-in-Chief JIŘÍ FABIÁN; 300,000.

Hospodářské noviny (Economic News): Dobrovského 25, 170 55 Prague 7; tel. 233071111; fax 233072307; e-mail data@hn.economia .cz; internet www.ihned.cz; f. 1957; morning; Editor-in-Chief PETR ŠTĚPÁNEK; circ. 125,000 (2003).

Lidové noviny (People's News): Pobřežni 20/224, 186 21 Prague 8; tel. 267098700; fax 267098799; e-mail inzerce@lidovky.cz; internet www.lidovenoviny.cz; f. 1893, re-established 1988; morning; Editor-in-Chief PAVEL ŠAFR; circ. 80,000 (2003).

Mladá fronta Dnes (The Youth Front Today): Anděl Media Centrum, Karla Englíše 519/11, 150 00 Prague; tel. 225061111; fax 222062229; e-mail mfdnes@mfdnes.cz; internet www.mfdnes.cz; f. 1990; morning; independent; Editor-in-Chief PETR ŠABATA; circ. 350,000.

Právo (Right): Slezská 13, 120 00 Prague 2; tel. 221001111; fax 221001361; e-mail redakce@pravo.cz; internet www.pravo.cz; f. 1920 as *Rudé právo*: name changed as above 1995; morning; Editor-in-Chief ZDENĚK PORYBNÝ; circ. 250,000.

Večerník Praha (Evening Prague): Belgická 38, 120 85 Prague 2; tel. 221999111; fax 221999304; e-mail redakce@vecerka.cz; internet www.vecerka.cz; f. 1991; (fmrly *Večerní Praha*, f. 1955); evening; Editor-in-Chief JOSEF RICHTER; circ. 130,000.

Ústí nad Labem

Ústecký deník (Ústí nad Labem Daily): Klíšská 25, 400 01 Ústí nad Labem; tel. 475212022; fax 475211951; e-mail sefredaktor.ud@sever .vlp.cz; internet www.usteckydenik.cz; f. 1993; Editor-in-Chief ALENA VOLFOVÁ; circ. 95,000.

PRINCIPAL PERIODICALS

100+1 ZZ–Zahraniční zajímavost (100+1 ZZ–Foreign Interest): Karlovo nám. 5, 120 00 Prague 2; tel. 224914793; fax 224916922; e-mail sto@stoplus.cz; internet stoplusjedna.newtonit.cz; f. 1964; fortnightly foreign press digest; Editor-in-Chief VÁCLAV DUŠEK; circ. 85,000.

Amatérské radio: Zborovska 2, 150 00 Prague 5; tel. 257317311; e-mail pe@aradio.cz; internet www.aradio.cz; amateur radio technology and popular electronics; circ. 25,000 (2000).

Ateliér (Studio): Na Poříčí 30, 110 00 Prague 1; tel. and fax 221732338; e-mail atelier.art@volny.cz; f. 1988; visual arts; fortnightly; Editor-in-Chief BLANKA POLÁKOVÁ.

Auto Tip: Střelnična 1680/8, 182 21 Prague 8; tel. 266193173; fax 266193172; e-mail v.kodym@axelspringer.cz; f. 1990; fortnightly for motorists; Editor-in-Chief VÍTĚZSLAV KODYM; circ. 60,000.

Czech Business and Trade: V jirchářích 8, 110 00 Prague 1; tel. 221406623; fax 224934383; e-mail journal@ppagency.cz; f. 1928; monthly; publ. in English, German, Spanish, Russian and French; Editor-in-Chief Dr PAVLA PODSKALSKÁ; circ. 15,000.

Českomoravský profit (Bohemia and Moravia Profit): Vinohadská 230, 100 00 Prague 10; tel. 225010366; fax 225010377; e-mail profit@profit.cz; internet www.profit.cz; business, investment; weekly; f. 1991; Editor-in-Chief MARTIN SCHMARCZ.

Divadelní noviny (Theatre News): Celetná 7, 110 00 Prague 1; tel. 224809114; fax 222315912; e-mail divadelni.noviny@divadlo.cz; internet www.divadlo.cz/noviny; fortnightly; Editor-in-Chief JAN KOLÁŘ.

Ekonom (Economist): Dobrovského 25, 170 55 Prague 7; tel. 233071301; fax 233072002; e-mail ekonom@economia.cz; internet www.ekonom.cz; weekly; Editor-in-Chief ZBYNEK FIALA; circ. 30,000.

EURO: Holečkova 103/31, 150 000 Prague 5; tel. 251026111; fax 257328774; e-mail redakce@euro.cz; internet www.euro.cz; weekly; f. 1999; Editor-in-Chief ISTVÁN LÉKÓ.

Katolický týdeník (Catholic Weekly): Londýnská 44, 120 00 Prague 2; tel. 224250395; fax 224257041; e-mail redakce@ katolicky-tydenik.cz; internet www.katyd.cz; f. 1989; weekly; Editor-in-Chief ANTONÍN RANDA; circ. 70,000.

Květy (Flowers): Na Florenci 3, 117 14 Prague 1; tel. and fax 224219549; f. 1834; illustrated family weekly; Editor-in-Chief JIN-DŘICH MAŘAN; circ. 320,000.

Mladý svět (Young World): nám. dr. V Holého 16, 180 00 Prague 8; tel. 283106206; fax 283106230; e-mail redakce@mladysvet.cz; internet www.mladysvet.cz; f. 1959; illustrated weekly; Editor-in-Chief JAN HLAVÁC; circ. 110,000.

PC World: Seydlerova 2451/11, 158 00 Prague 5; tel. 257088111; fax 265208121; e-mail pcworld@idg.cz; internet www.pcworld.cz; monthly; Editor JANA PELIKÁNOVÁ.

Prager Wochenblatt (Prague Weekly): Vítkovická 373, 199 00 Prague 9; weekly; politics, culture, economy; in German; Editor-in-Chief FELIX SEEBAUER; circ. 30,000.

Prague Post: Štěpánská 20, 110 00 Prague 1; tel. 296334400; fax 296334450; e-mail office@praguepost.com; internet www .praguepost.com; f. 1991; political, economic and cultural weekly in English; Man. Editor MARK NESSMITH; circ. 15,000.

Reflex: Žerotínova 38, 130 50 Prague 3; tel. 225097111; fax 222582013; e-mail reflex@ringier.cz; internet www.reflex.cz; f. 1990; social, weekly; Editor-in-Chief PETR BÍLEK; circ. 60,000.

Respekt (Respect): Křemencova 10, 110 00 Prague 1; tel. 224930685; fax 224930792; e-mail redakce@respekt.cz; internet www.respekt.cz; f. 1990; political weekly; Editor-in-Chief JAROSLAV SPURNÝ (acting); circ. 25,000.

Romano Hangos (Romský hlas—Romany Voice): Francouzská 84, 602 00 Brno; tel. 545246674; e-mail rhangos@volny.vz; internet www.romanohangos.cz; f. 1999; weekly; in Romany and Czech; Editor-in-Chief KAREL HOLOMEK.

Romano Kurko (Romany Week): Černovické nábř. 7, 618 00 Brno; f. 1991; every two weeks; in Czech with Romany vocabulary; Dir M. SMOLEŇ; circ. 8,000.

Sondy (Soundings): W. Churchilla 2, 130 00 Prague 3; tel. 224462328; fax 224462313; e-mail sondy@cmkos.cz; internet www .tydenik-sondy.cz; f. 1990; weekly; journal of the Czech (Bohemian)-

Moravian Confederation of Trade Unions; Editor-in-Chief Jana Kašparová; circ. 40,000.

Tvar (Form): Na Florenci 3, 110 00 Prague 1; tel. 222828399; fax 222828397; e-mail tvar@ucl.cas.cz; internet www.dobraadresa.cz/tvar; fortnightly; literature.

Týden (The Week): Panská 7, 110 00 Prague 3; tel. 296827110; fax 224239408; internet www.tyden.cz; f. 1994; Editor-in-Chief Dalibor Balšínek; 30,000.

Týdeník Rozhlas (Radio Weekly): Jeseniova 36, 130 00 Prague 3; tel. 222715036; fax 222712616; internet www.radioservis-as.cz/tydenik; f. 1923; Editor-in-Chief Milan Šefl; circ. 170,000.

Vesmír (Universe): Na Florenci 3, 111 21 Prague 1; tel. 222828393; fax 222828396; e-mail redakce@vesmir.cz; internet www.vesmir.cz; f. 1871; monthly; popular science magazine; Editor Ivan M. Havel; circ. 10,500–11,000.

Vlasta: Žitná 18, 120 00 Prague 2; tel. 296162256; f. 1947; weekly; illustrated magazine for women; Editor-in-Chief Kateřina Smálková; circ. 380,000.

Výběr—Reader's Digest (Selection—Reader's Digest): K. Rotunde 89/4, 120 00 Prague 2; tel. 224232429; fax 224233283; internet www.vyber.cz; f. 1993; monthly; general interest; Editor-in-Chief Veronika Maxova.

Zora (Sight): Krakovská 21, 115 17 Prague 1; tel. 21462176; fax 21462175; e-mail zora@braillnet.cz; f. 1917; every two months; for the visually handicapped; Editor-in-Chief Dr Jiří Reichel.

NEWS AGENCIES

Česká tisková kancelář (ČTK) (Czech News Agency): Opletalova 5–7, 111 44 Prague 1; tel. 222098111; fax 224225376; e-mail ctk@mail.ctk.cz; internet www.ctk-online.cz; f. Nov. 1992, assuming control of all property and activities (in the Czech Lands) of the former Czechoslovak News Agency; news and photo-exchange service with all international and many national news agencies; maintains network of foreign correspondents; Czech and English general and economic news service; publishes daily bulletins in English; Gen. Dir Dr Milan Stibral.

Foreign Bureaux

Agence France-Presse (AFP): Ječná 15, 120 00 Prague 2; tel. 224921155; fax 224919155; e-mail afp@mbox.vol.cz; Bureau Chief René Pascal Biagi.

Agencia EFE (Spain): Uhříněveská 65, 100 00 Prague 10; tel. 267313620; e-mail efe@iol.cz; internet www.efe.es; Bureau Chief Miguel Fernández.

Agenzia Nazionale Stampa Associata (ANSA) (Italy): Prague; tel. and fax 224222793; internet www.ansa.it.

Allgemeiner Deutscher Nachrichtendienst (ADN) (Germany): Milevská 835, 140 00 Prague 4; tel. 241731111; Bureau Chief Steffi Gensicke.

Associated Press (AP) (Dow Jones News Service USA): Národní 25, 100 00 Prague 1; tel. 221085226; Correspondent Ondřej Hejma.

Deutsche Presse-Agentur (dpa) (Germany): Petrské nám. 1, 110 00 Prague 1; tel. 224810290; fax 222315196; Bureau Chief Wolfgang Jung.

ITAR-TASS (Information Telegraph Agency of Russia-Telegraphic Agency of the Sovereign Countries) (Russia): Pevnostní 5, 162 00 Prague 6; Bureau Chief Aleksandr Yakovlev.

Magyar Távirati Iroda (MTI) (Hungary): Prague; tel. and fax 266710131; e-mail tothenti@yahoo.com; internet www.mti.hu; Bureau Chief Laszlo Toth.

Novinska Agencija Tanjug (Serbia and Montenegro): Prague; Correspondent Branko Stošić.

Polska Agencja Prasowa (PAP) (Poland): Petrské nám. 1, 110 00 Prague 1; tel. and fax 224812205; internet www.pap.com.pl; Correspondent Zbygniew Krzystynjak.

RIA—Novosti (Russian Information Agency—News) (Russia): Italská 36, 130 00 Prague 3; tel. 222253095; e-mail riapraha@bohem-net.cz; Bureau Chief Valerij Enin.

Tlačová agentúra Slovenskej republiky (TASR) (Slovakia): Šlikova 1986/30, 160 00 Prague 6; tel. 233350088; e-mail tasr@tasr.sk; internet www.tasr.sk; Correspondent Bohdan Kopčák.

Xinhua (New China) News Agency (People's Republic of China): Pelléova 22, 169 00 Prague 6; tel. and fax 224311325; Correspondent San Xi-You.

PRESS ASSOCIATION

Syndicate of Journalists of the Czech Republic (Syndikát novinářů České republiky): Pařížská 9, 110 00 Prague 1; tel. (2) 2325109; fax (2) 2327782; e-mail sncr@mbox.vol.cz; internet www.syndikat-novinaru.cz; f. 1877; reorganized 1990; 5,000 mems; Chair. Irena Válová.

Publishers

Academia: Legerova 61, 120 00 Prague 2; tel. 224941976; fax 224941982; e-mail academia@academia.cz; internet www.academia.cz; f. 1953; scientific books, periodicals; Dir Alexander Tomský.

Akropolis: U Nikolajky 10, 150 00 Prague 5; tel. 251560234; e-mail tomas.akropolis@worldonline.cz; internet www.akropolis.info; f. 1990; Dir Jiří Tomáš.

Albatros: Na Pankraci 30, 140 00 Prague 4; tel. 234633271; fax 234633262; e-mail albatros@bonton.cz; internet www.albatros.cz; f. 1949; literature for children and young people, encyclopedias; Dir Martin Slavík.

Argo: Milíčova 13, 130 00 Prague 3; tel. 222781601; fax 222780184; e-mail argo@iargo.cz; internet www.argobooks.cz; f. 1992; Dir Milan Gelnar.

Atlantis: PS 374, Česká 15, 602 00 Brno; tel. and fax 542213221; e-mail atlantis-brno@volny.cz; internet www.volny.cz/atlantis; f. 1989.

BB Art: Bořivojova 85, 130 00 Prague 3; tel. 222721538; fax 222720525; e-mail bbart@bbart.cz; internet www.bbart.cz.

Beta: Květnového vítězství 332, 149 00 Prague 4; tel. 272910733; fax 271913830; e-mail info@dobrovsky.cz; internet www.dobrovsky.cz; f. 1990.

Brána: Hradešínská 30/1956, 101 00 Prague 10; tel. and fax 271740586; e-mail brana–praha@volny.cz; internet www.brana–knihy.cz.

Brázda: Braunerova 4, 180 00 Prague 8; tel. 284841098; e-mail nakladatelstvi.brazda@sendme.cz; internet www.nakladatelstvi-brazda.wz.cz; specialist and popular literature on agriculture, forestry, animals, hobbies, fishing, nature.

Dopravy a spojů (Transport and Communications) Publishers: Hybernská 5, 115 78 Prague 1; tel. (2) 2365774; fax (2) 2356772; Dir Ing. Alois Houdek.

Ekopress: U Líhní 100, 142 01 Prague 4; tel. 244471676; fax 244472649; e-mail expedice@ekopress.cz; internet www.ekopress.cz; economics, information technology, languages.

Epocha: Kaprova 12, 110 00 Prague 1; tel. 224810352; fax 224810353; e-mail epocha.praha@volny.cz.

Fragment: Radiová 1, 102 27 Prague 10; tel. 267008272; fax 267008273; e-mail fragment@fragment.cz; internet www.fragment.cz; f. 1991.

Grada Publishing: U Průhonu 22, 170 00 Prague 7; tel. 220386401; fax 220386400; e-mail obchod@gradapublishing.cz; internet www.gradapublishing.cz; f. 1991; Dir Milan Brunát.

Host: Přízova 12, 602 00 Brno; tel. 543216807; fax 543216809; e-mail redakce@hostbrno.cz; internet www.hostbrno.cz; f. 1990; fiction, literary criticism and theory.

Ivo Železný: U Libeňského pivovaru 10, 180 00 Prague 8; tel. 284825117; e-mail iz@iz.cz; internet www.iz.cz.

Kalich, nakladatelství a knihkupectví, s.r.o.: Jungmannova 9, 111 00 Prague 1; tel. 224947505; fax 224947504; e-mail kalichknih@volny.cz; internet www.kalich.evangnet.cz; f. 1920; Dirs Michal Plzák, Markéta Langouá.

Karolinum: Ovocný trh 3/5, 116 36 Prague 1; tel. 224491276; fax 224212041; e-mail cupress@cuni.cz; internet www.cuni.cz/uz/nk; Charles University in Prague publishing house; Dir Jaroslav Jirsa.

Kruh (Circle): Dlouhá 108, 500 21 Hradec Králové; tel. 49522076; f. 1966; regional literature, fiction and general; Dir Dr Jan Dvořák.

Labyrint (Labyrinth): Box 52, jablonecká 715, 190 00 Prague 9; tel. and fax 224922422; e-mail labyrint@wo.cz; internet labyrint.net; publishing house and cultural magazine; f. 1992.

Libri: Na Hutmance 7, 158 00 Prague 5; tel. 251612302; fax 251511013; e-mail libri@libri.cz; internet www.libri.cz; f. 1992; encyclopedias, specialist literature; Dir Karel Žaloudek.

Maťa: Lublaňská 34, 120 00 Prague 2; tel. and fax 222520765; e-mail mata@kosmas.cz; internet www.matapub.cz; f. 1993; fiction, poetry.

Melantrich: Václavské nám. 36, 112 12 Prague 1; tel. 222093215; fax 224213176; f. 1919; general, fiction, humanities, newspapers and magazines; Dir Milan Horský.

Mladá fronta (The Youth Front): Mezi Vodami 1952/9, 143 00 Prague 4; tel. 225276282; fax 225276278; e-mail prodej@mf.cz;

internet www.mf.cz; f. 1945; science fiction and fantasy literature, philosophy, sociology; Editor-in-Chief VLASTIMIL FIALA.

Motto: Spoluprá 4, 140 00 Prague 4; tel. and fax 261225619; e-mail erdakce@motto.cz; internet www.motto.cz.

Naše vojsko (Our Military): Vítězné nám. 4, 160 00 Prague 6; tel. 224313071; fax 224311204; e-mail info@nasevojsko.com; internet www.nasevojsko.com; f. 1945; military history and theory.

Odeon: Nádražní 32, 150 00 Prague 1; tel. 296536111; f. 1953; literature, poetry, fiction (classical and modern), literary theory, art books, reproductions; Dir MILUŠE SLAPNIČKOVÁ.

Olympia: Klimentská 1, 115 88 Prague 1; tel. 224810146; fax 22315192; e-mail olympia@mbox.vol.cz; f. 1954; sports, tourism, encyclopedias, fiction, illustrated books; Dir Ing. KAREL ZELNÍČEK.

Panton: Radlická 99, 150 00 Prague 5; tel. and fax (2) 548627; f. 1958; publishing house of the Czech Musical Fund; books on music, sheet music, records; Dir KAREL ČERNÝ.

Paseka: Chopinova 4, 120 00 Prague 2; tel. 222710752; fax 222718886; e-mail paseka@paseka.cz; internet www.paseka.cz; f. 1989; Owner LADISLAV HORÁČEK.

Portál: Klapkova 2, 182 00 Prague 8; tel. 283028111; fax 283028112; e-mail naklad@portal.cz; internet www.portal.cz; f. 1992; pedagogy, psychology, social work, dictionaries; Dir JAROSLAV KUCHAŘ; Editor-in-Chief JAROSLAV SCHROTTER.

Práce (Labour): Václavské nám. 17, 112 58 Prague 1; tel. 224009100; fax (2) 2320989; f. 1945; trade-union movement, fiction, general, periodicals; Dir JANA SCHMIDTOVÁ.

Rybka (Fish) Publishers: V Jirchářích 6, 110 00 Prague 1; tel. 224932263; fax 224932017; e-mail mrybka@mbox.vol.cz; internet www.rybkapub.cz; Dir MICHAL RYBKA.

Sagit: Horní 1, 700 30 Ostrava 3; tel. 596785999; fax 596786000; e-mail sagit@sagit.cz; internet www.sagit.cz; law, accounting, tax.

Scientia: Radimova 37/50, 169 00 Prague 6; tel. 233350199; fax 220513511; e-mail e.kesnerova@scientia.cz; internet www.scientia .cz; f. 1992; pedagogic literature.

Severočeské nakladatelství (North Bohemian Publishing House): Ústí nad Labem; tel. 4728581; regional literature, fiction and general; Dir JIŘÍ ŠVEJDA.

Slon (Elephant)—Sociologické Nakladatelství (Sociological Publishers): Jilská 1, 110 00 Prague 1; tel. and fax 222220025; e-mail redakce@slon-knihy.cz; internet slon-knihy.cz; f. 1991; sociology; Dir ALENA MILTOVÁ.

SPN pedagogické nakladatelství (SPN Pedagogical Publishing House): Ostrovní 30, 110 00 Prague 1; tel. and fax 224931451; e-mail spn@spn.cz; internet www.spn.cz; f. 1775; fmrly Státní pedagogické nakladatelství (State Pedagogical Publishing House); school and university textbooks, dictionaries, literature; Dir MARIE NOVOTNÁ.

Vyšehrad: Bartolomějská 9, 110 00 Prague 1; tel. and fax 224221703; e-mail info@vysehrad.cz; internet www.ivysehrad.cz; f. 1934; religion, philosophy, history, fiction; Dir PRAVOMIL NOVÁK; Chief Editor MARIE VÁLKOVÁ.

PUBLISHERS' ASSOCIATION

Association of Czech Booksellers and Publishers (Svaz českých knihkupců a nakladatelů): Jana Masaryka 56, 120 00 Prague 2; tel. 224219944; e-mail sckn@sckn.cz; internet www.sckn .cz; f. 1879; Chair. JITKA UHDEOVÁ.

Broadcasting and Communications

TELECOMMUNICATIONS

České Radiokomunikace: U Nákladového nádraži 3144, 130 00 Prague 3; tel. 242411111; fax 242417595; e-mail info@cra.cz; internet www.cra.cz; f. 1994; privatized 2000; Dir-Gen. MIROSLAV ČURÍN.

Český Telecom (Czech Telecom): Olšanská 5, 130 34 Prague 3; tel. 840114114; fax 266316666; e-mail jindrich.trpisovsky@ct.cz; internet www.telecom.cz; fmrly SPT Telecom, renamed 2000; monopoly operator of long-distance and international services; Chair. of Bd and Chief. Exec. GABRIEL BERDÁR.

EuroTel: Vyskočilova 1442/1B, PO Box 70, 140 21 Prague 4; tel. 267011111; fax 267011101; internet www.eurotel.cz; f. 1991; mobile cellular communications; 100 % owned by Český Telecom.

Oskar—Český Mobil: Vinoradská 167, 100 00 Prague 10; internet www.oskar.cz; 51% owned by Telesystem International Wireless (Canada); f. 2000; Man. Dir KARLA D. STEPHENS.

T-Mobile Czech Republic: Londýnská 730, 120 00 Prague 2; e-mail info@t-mobile.cz; internet www.t-mobile.cz; fmrly Radio-Mobil; 60.8% owned by C-Mobil, 39.2% by by České Radiokomuni-kace, a.s. (39.2%); f. 1996; Man. Dir ROLAND MAHLER.

RADIO

The Czech Republic has a dual state and private broadcasting system, with one publicly-owned radio broadcaster, Český rozhlas (Czech Radio), and two private nationwide radio broadcasters, Frek-vence 1, and Radio Impuls.

Local stations broadcast from Prague, Brno, České Budějovice, Hradec Králové, Ostrava, Plzeň, Ústí nad Labem and other towns. By the end of 2003 74 licences for local terrestrial radio broadcasting had been granted.

Český rozhlas (Czech Radio): Vinohradská 12, 120 99 Prague 2; tel. 221551111; fax 224222223; e-mail press@cro.cz; info@rozhlas.cz; internet www.rozhlas.cz; broadcasts nationwide programmes (including ČRo 1 Radiožurnál, ČRo 2 Praha, ČRo 3 Vlava) and Radio Praha's programme to foreign countries (ČRo 7).; Dir-Gen. VÁCLAV KASÍK.

Country Radio: Zenklová 34, 180 00 Prague 8; tel. 25102411; fax 251024224; e-mail info@countryradio.cz; internet www .countryradio.cz; commercial station; Man. Dir JAN ZILVAR.

Evropa 2: Wenzigova 4, 120 00 Prague 2; tel. 257001111; fax 257001807; e-mail info@evropa2.cz; internet www.evropa2.cz; com-mercial station; Pres. MICHAEL FLEISCHMANN.

Frekvence 1: Wenzigova 4, 120 00 Prague 2; tel. 257001111; fax 224262412; e-mail info@frekvence1.cz; internet www.frekvence1.cz; commercial station; Pres. MICHAEL FLEISCHMANN.

Radio FM Plus: Zikmunda Wintra, 320 90 Plzeň; tel. 377676111; fax 377422221; e-mail info@fmplus.cz; internet www.fmplus.cz; commercial station; Dir VÁCLAV JEŽEK.

Radio Free Europe/Radio Liberty: Vinohradská 1, 110 00 Prague 1; fax 221123420; internet www.rferl.org; non-profit corpn financed by the federal Govt of the USA; broadcasts c. 1,000 hours weekly in 28 languages to Eastern Europe, Eurasia and the Middle East; Chair. KENNETH Y. TOMLINSON; Dir of Broadcasting JEFF TRIMBLE.

Radio Impuls: Kovářská 15, 190 00 Prague 9; tel. 255700700; fax 255700727; e-mail impuls@radioimpuls.cz; internet www .radioimpuls.cz; f. 1999; Man. Dir. JIŘÍ HRABÁK.

TELEVISION

In 2000 there were five main terrestrial television stations: the two state-run channels, ČT1 and ČT2, reached 98% and 71% of the population, respectively, while two private commercial stations, Nova TV and Prima TV, were received by 99% and approximately 50%, respectively. At the end of 2003 there were 13 regional tele-vision broadcasters and 16 local television broadcasters.

Česká televize (Czech Television): Kavčí hory, 140 70 Prague 4; tel. 261131111; fax 26927202; e-mail jakub.puchalsky@czech-tv.cz; internet www.czech-tv.cz; f. 1992; state-owned; two channels (ČT1 and ČT2); studios in Prague, Brno and Ostrava; Dir JIŘÍ JANEČEK.

Nova TV: Kříženeckého nám. 322/5, 152 52 Prague 5; tel. 233100111; e-mail volejte.novu@nova.cz; internet www.nova.cz; f. 1994, through a joint venture with Central European Media Enter-prises (CME—of the USA) as the Czech Republic's first independent commercial station; majority owned by CME.

Prima TV: Na žertvách 24, 180 00 Prague 8; tel. 266700111; fax 266700201; e-mail informace@prima-tv.cz; internet www.prima-tv .cz; f. 1993; Gen. Dir MARTIN DVORÁK.

Finance

(cap. = capital; res = reserves; dep. = deposits; m. = million; brs = branches; amounts in Czech koruny)

BANKING

With the establishment of independent Czech and Slovak Republics on 1 January 1993, the State Bank of Czechoslovakia was divided and its functions were transferred to the newly created Czech National Bank and National Bank of Slovakia. The Czech National Bank is independent of the Government.

At 30 November 2004 35 banks were operating in the Czech Republic, nine of which were majority owned by Czech investors, 17 of which were majority owned by foreign investors and nine of which were branches of foreign banks.

Central Bank

Czech National Bank (Česká národní banka): Na Příkopě 28, 115 03 Prague 1; tel. 224411111; fax 224218522; e-mail info@cnb.cz; internet www.cnb.cz; f. 1993; bank of issue, the central authority of the Czech Republic in the monetary sphere, legislation and foreign exchange permission; central bank for directing and securing monetary policy, supervision of activities of other banks and savings banks; cap. 1,400m., res 5,861m., dep. 568,147m. (Dec. 2003); Gov. ZDENĚK TŮMA; 7 brs.

Commercial Banks

Bawag Bank CZ: Václavské nám. 40, 110 00 Prague 1; tel. 224406111; fax 224227333; e-mail info@bawag.cz; internet www.bawag.cz; f. 1991; fmrly Interbanka; cap. 1,708.7m. (Sept. 2004); res 1,597m., dep. 7,421m. (Sept. 2002); Chair. Dr IVAN ČERNOHORSKÝ.

BAWAG International Bank CZ: Vítězná 1/126, POB 229, 150 21 Prague 5; tel. 257006111; fax 257006200; internet www.bawag-bank.cz; f. 1992; 100% owned by BAWAG AG (Austria); fmrly Dresdner Bank (CZ); cap. 1,000m., res 1m., dep. 13,677m. (Dec. 2003); Chair. MARKUS HERMANN; 4 brs.

Calyon Bank Czech Republic: Ovocný trh 8, 117 19 Prague 1; tel. 222076111; fax 222076119; e-mail crlytre@mbox.vol.cz; internet www.creditlyonnais.cz; wholly owned subsidiary of Crédit Agricole Group (France); fmrly Crédit Lyonnais Bank Praha; cap. 600m. (Dec. 2003); res 555m., dep. 15,006m. (Dec. 2002); Chair. and Gen. Man. CHRISTIAN RAMANOEL.

Citibank Česká republika: Evropská 178, 166 40 Prague 6; tel. 844888844; fax 23061041; internet www.citibank.com/czech; f. 2001; 100%-owned subsidiary by Citibank Overseas Investment Corpn (USA); cap. 2,925m. (Dec. 2003), res 2,741m., dep. 44,557m. (Dec. 2002); Chair. ATIF BAJWA; 7 brs.

Česká exportní banka: Vodičkova 34, 111 21 Prague 1; e-mail ceb@ceb.cz; internet www.ceb.cz; f. 1995; cap. 1,650.0m. (Dec. 2003); res 303.8m., dep. 22,689.1m. (Dec. 2002); Chair. LADISLAV ZELINKA.

Česká spořitelna (Czech Savings Bank): Olbrachtova 1929/62, 140 00 Prague 4; tel. 261071111; fax 261073032; e-mail csas@csas.cz; internet www.csas.czhu; f. 1825; 97.9% holding owned by Erste Bank AG (Austria); cap. 15,200m. (Dec. 2003), res 22,152m., dep. 376,755m. (Dec. 2002); Chair. and Chief Exec. JOHN JAMES STACK; 647 brs.

Československá obchodní banka (CSOB) (Czechoslovak Commercial Bank): Na Příkopě 14, 115 20 Prague 1; tel. 224111111; fax 224225049; e-mail webmaster@csob.cz; internet www.csob.cz; f. 1965; 59.9% state holding purchased by KBC Bank (Belgium) September 2004; commercial and foreign-trade transactions; cap. 5,105m. (Dec. 2003), res 20,403m., dep. 432,125m. (Dec. 2002); Chair. and Gen. Man. PAVEL KAVÁNEK; 34 brs.

eBanka: Na Přikopě 19, 117 19 Prague 1; tel. 222115222; fax 222115500; internet www.ebanka.cz; f. 1990; cap. 1,042m., res 540m., dep. 9,582m. (Dec. 2003); Chair. LUBOŠ ČERNÝ.

GE Capital bank.: Vyskočilova 1422/1a, BB Centrum, 140 28 Prague 4; tel. 224443636; fax 224441500; internet www.gemoney.cz/ge/cz; f. 1998; 100% owned by GE Capital International Holdings Corpn (USA); cap. 510m. (Dec. 2003); res 2,422m., dep. 41,411m. (Dec. 2002); Chair. GERARD RYAN; 192 brs.

HVB Bank Czech Republic: Náměstí republiky 3A/2090, 110 00 Prague 1; tel. 221112111; fax 221112132; internet www.hvb.cz; f. 1999; subsidiary of Bayerische Hypo- und Vereinsbank (Germany); cap. 5,047m. (Dec. 2002), res 545m., dep. 90,011m. (Dec. 2001); Chair. DAVID GRUND.

J&T Banka: Pobřežní 297/14, 186 00 Prague 8; tel. 221710111; fax 221710211; e-mail info@jtbank.cz; internet www.jtbank.cz; f. 1992; cap. 501m. (Dec. 2003); res 576m., dep. 4,645m. (Dec. 2002); PATRIK TKÁČ.

Komerční banka: Na Příkopě 33, POB 839, 114 07 Prague 1; tel. 222432111; fax 224243020; e-mail profibanka@kb.cz; internet www.kb.cz; f. 1990; 49% state-owned; agreement to sell 60% state holding to Société Générale (France) reached in June 2001; cap. 19,005m. (Dec. 2003); res 14,960m., dep. 361,100m. (June 2003); Chair. and Chief Exec. ALEXIS RAYMOND JUAN; 335 brs.

Raiffeisenbank: Olbrachtova 2006/9, 140 21 Prague 4; tel. 272771111; fax 224231278; e-mail info@rb.cz; internet www.rb.cz; f. 1993; owned by Raiffesienbank (Austria); cap. 2,500m. (Dec. 2003), res 1,920m., dep. 53,398m. (Dec. 2001); Chair. and Gen. Man. Ing. LUBOR ŽALMAN.

Volksbank CZ: M-Palác Herspická 5, POB 226, 658 26 Brno; tel. 543525222; fax 543525553; e-mail brno.mpalac@volksbank.cz; internet www.volksbank.cz; cap. 750m. (Dec. 2003) res 365m., dep. 16,708m. (Sept. 2003); f. 1993; Chair. JOHANN LURF; 20 brs.

Živnostenská banka: Na Příkopě 20, POB 421, 113 80 Prague 1; tel. 224121111; fax 224125555; e-mail info@zivnobanka.cz; internet www.ziba.cz; f. 1868; 85.2%-owned by UniCredito Italiano S.p.A. (Italy) since Feb. 2003; cap. 1,360m. Dec. 2003), res 1,270.1m., dep. 47,102.2m. (Dec. 2002); Chair. JIŘÍ KUNERT; 8 brs.

Bankers' Organization

Czech Bankers' Association (Česká bankovni asociace): Vodičkova 30, 110 00 Prague 1; tel. 224225926; fax 224225957; e-mail cba@czech-ba.cz; internet www.czech-ba.cz; Pres. PAVEL KAVÁNEK.

STOCK EXCHANGE

Prague Stock Exchange (Burza cenných papírů Praha.): Rybná 14, 110 05 Prague 1; tel. 221831111; fax 221833040; e-mail info@pse.cz; internet www.pse.cz; f. 1992; Chair. PETR KOBLIC.

Regulatory Authority

Czech Securities Commission (Komise pro cenné papíry): Washingtonova 7, 111 21 Prague 1; tel. 221096111; fax 221096110; e-mail podatelna@sec.cz; internet www.sec.cz; f. 1998; Chair. PAVEL HOLLMANN.

INSURANCE

There were 40 companies providing insurance services in the Czech Republic in 2004, including seven foreign-owned institutions. Of these, 21 provided non-life insurance, three provided life insurance and 16 provided universal insurance.

Czech Co-operative Insurance Co (Kooperativa pojišťovna): Templová 747, 110 01 Prague 1; tel. 221000111; fax 22322562; e-mail info@koop.cz; internet www.koop.cz; life and non-life insurance; f. 1993; Chair. and Gen. Man. VLADIMÍR MRÁZ.

Czech Insurance Corpn (Česká pojišťovna): Na Pankráci 121, 140 21 Prague 4; tel. 224051111; fax 224052200; e-mail klient@cpoj.cz; internet www.cpoj.cz; f. 1827; issues life, accident, fire, aviation, industrial and marine insurance and all classes of reinsurance; Gen. Man. LADISLAV BARTONÍČEK.

Trade and Industry

GOVERNMENT AGENCIES

Czech Trade Promotion Agency (Česká agentura na podporu obchodu): Dittrichova 21, POB 76, 128 01 Prague 2; tel. 224907500; fax 224907503; e-mail info@czechtrade.cz; internet www.czechtradeoffices.cz; Gen. Dir MARTIN TLAPA.

Investment and Business Development Agency—CzechInvest (Agentura pro podporu podnikání a investic): Štěpánská 15, 120 00 Prague 2; tel. 296342500; fax 296342502; e-mail agentura@czechinvest.org; internet www.czechinvest.org; f. 1992; foreign investment agency; incorporates fmr Agency for the Development of Industry (CzechIndustry); Dir-Gen. RADOMIL NOVÁK.

National Property Fund of the Czech Republic (Fond národního majetku ČR): Rašínovo nábřeži 42, 128 00 Prague 2; tel. 224991111; fax 222718211; e-mail predseda@fnm.cz; internet www.fnm.cz; responsible for state property and state-owned companies in the period up to their privatization; Chair. JAN JUCHELKA.

CHAMBER OF COMMERCE

Economic Chamber of the Czech Republic (Hospodářská komora ČR): Freyova 27, 190 00 Prague 9; tel. 296696111; fax 296646221; e-mail office@komora.cz; internet www.komora.cz; f. 1850; has almost 15,000 members (trading corporations, industrial enterprises, banks and private enterprises); Pres. JAROMÍR DRÁBEK.

EMPLOYERS' ORGANIZATIONS

Association of Entrepreneurs of the Czech Republic (Sdružení podnikatelů ČR): Škrétova 6/44, 120 59 Prague 2; tel. and fax 222215373; e-mail spcr1989@volny.cz; internet www.sdruzenispcr.cz; Chair. BEDŘICH DANDA.

Confederation of Industry of the Czech Republic (Svaz průmyslu a dopravy ČR): Mikulandská 7, 113 61 Prague 1; tel. 224934088; fax 224934597; e-mail spcr@spcr.cz; internet www.spcr.cz; f. 1990; Dir-Gen. ZDENĚK LIŠKA; Pres. JAROSLAV MÍL.

UTILITIES

Electricity

České energetické závody Skupina (ČEZ) (Czech Power Co Group): Duhová 2/1444, 140 53 Prague 4; tel. 271131111; fax 271132001; e-mail info@mail.cez.cs; internet www.cez.cz; f. 1992; production and distributions co; 67.6%-owned by National Property Fund; merged with the following regional distribution cos in 2003: Severočeská energetika (North Bohemian Energy Co); Severomoravská energetika (North Moravian Energy Co); Středočeská energetická (Central Bohemian Energy Co); Východočeská energetika (East Moravian Energy Co); and Západočeská energetika (West Moravian Energy Co); also operates two nuclear-energy plants at Dukovany and Temelín; Gen. Man. MARTIN ROMAN; 7,600 employees.

Dalkia Česká republika: 28 října 3123/152, 709 74 Ostrava; tel. 596609111; fax 596609300; e-mail info@dalkia.cz; internet www.dalkia.cz; f. 1992; Chair. of Bd ZDENĚK DUBA; Dir-Gen. FRANÇOIS HABÈGRE.

E.ON Česká republika: Lannova 205/16, 370 49 České Budějovice; tel. 387312682; fax 386359803; e-mail info@eon.cz; internet www.eon.cz; f. 2005; comprises two subsidiary cos: E.ON Energie; and E.ON Distribuce; fmrly Jihočeská Energetika (South Bohemian Electricity) and Jihomoravska Energetika (South Moravian Electricity) distribution cos; Chair. MICHAL FEHN.

Opatovice Electricity (Elektrarny Opatovice): Pardubice 2, 532 13 Opatovice nad Labem; tel. 466843111; fax 466536030; e-mail info@eop.cz; internet www.eop.cz; f. 1905; generation and distribution co; 99.1% owned by International Power PLC (United Kingdom); Dir-Gen. RICHARD LAPPIN.

Pražská energetika (Prague Energy Co): Na Hroudé 4, 100 05 Prague 10; tel. 267051111; fax 267310817; internet www.pre.cz; distribution co to Prague city and surrounding area; Chair. and Gen. Man. Ing. DRAHOMÍR RUTA.

Gas

Jihomoravská plynárenská (JmP) (South Moravian Gas Co): Plynárenská 499/1, 657 02 Brno; tel. 545548111; fax 545578571; e-mail jmpas@jmpas.cz; internet www.jmpas.cz; distribution co; Chair. DAN TOK.

Severomoravsjká plynárenská (SmP) (North Moravian Gas Coi): Plynární 2748/6, 702 72 Ostrava; tel. 840111115; fax 596113985; e-mail info@smpas.cz; internet www.smpas.cz; f. 1994; distribution co; Chair. of Bd REINHOLD FRANK.

Transgas: Limuzská 12, 100 98 Prague 10; tel. 267971111; fax 267776965; e-mail info@transgas.cz; internet www.transgas.cz; f. 1971; majority-owned by RWE Energie AG (Germany); ; import and distribution co; Chair. of Bd Dr ULRICH JOBS.

Water

Pražské vodovody a kanalizace (Prague Water Supply and Sewerage Co): Pařížská 11, 110 00 Prague 1; tel. 221095111; fax 272172379; e-mail info@pvk.cz; internet www.pvk.cz; f. 1998; privatized in 2000; Dir-Gen. PHILIPPE GUITARD.

TRADE UNIONS

Czech (Bohemian)-Moravian Confederation of Trade Unions (Českomoravská konfederace odborových svazů): nám. W. Churchilla 2, 113 59 Prague 3; tel. 224461111; fax 222718994; e-mail cmkos@cmkos.cz; internet www.cmkos.cz; f. 1990; 33 affiliated unions (2005); Pres. MILAN ŠTĚCH.

Affiliated unions include the following:

Czech (Bohemian)-Moravian Trade Union of Workers in Education (Českomoravský odborový svaz školství): W. Churchilla nám. 2, 113 59 Prague 3; tel. 234461111; fax 222722685; e-mail cmos.skolstvi@cmkos.cz; internet www.skolskeodbory.cz; Pres. FRANTIŠEK DOBŠIK; 80,000 mems.

Trade Union of the Health Service and Social Care of the Czech Republic (Odborový svaz zdravotnictví a sociální péče ČR): Koněvova 54, 130 00 Prague 3; tel. 222714629; fax 222718211; e-mail osz_cr@cmkos.cz; internet osz.cmkos.cz; Pres. JIŘÍ SCHLANGER; 65,000 mems.

Trade Union of Workers in Textile, Clothing and Leather Industry of Bohemia and Moravia (Odborový svaz pracovníků textilního, oděvního a kožedělného průmyslu Čech a Moravy): W. Churchilla nám. 2, 113 59 Prague 3; tel. 222718931; fax 222721372; e-mail ostok@cmkos.cz; internet www.ostok.cz; Pres. MIROSLAVA PALEČKOVÁ; 79,600 mems.

Trade Union of Workers in Woodworking Industry, Forestry and Management of Water Supplies in the Czech Republic (Odborový svaz pracovníků dřevozpracujícího odvětví,

lesního a vodního hospodářství v České republice): W. Churchilla nám. 2, 113 59 Prague 3; tel. 234463091; fax 222716373; e-mail szopecha@cmkos.cz; internet osdlv.cmkos.cz; Pres. RUDOLF KYNCL; 43,000 mems.

UNIOS (Odborový svaz UNIOS): W. Churchilla nám. 2, 113 59 Prague 3; tel. 224463172; fax 224463185; e-mail unios@cmkos.cz; internet unios.cmkos.cz; f. 1994 to succeed Czech-Moravian Trade Union of Workers in Services (f. 1994); Pres. KAREL SLADKOVSKÝ; 38,000 mems.

Transport

RAILWAYS

In 2003 the total length of the Czech railway network was 9,520 km.

České dráhy (Czech Railways): nábř. L. Svobody 1222/12, 110 15 Prague 1; tel. 251432299; fax 222328784; e-mail infoservis@gr.cdrail.cz; internet www.cdrail.cz; f. 1993; Gen. Dir PETR KOUSAL.

Prague Public Transport Co (Dopravní podnik hl. m. Prahy): Sokolovska 217/42, 190 22 Prague 9; tel. 296192011; e-mail dpp@r.dpp.cz; internet www.dpp.cz; f. 1974; operates public transport services in Prague, including buses, trams, funicular cars, suburban train services and Prague underground railway (54 km and 53 stations operational in 2004); Gen. Dir MILAN HOUFEK.

ROADS

In 2003 there were an estimated 128,067 km of roads in the Czech Republic, including 518 km of motorways and 320 km of expressways

INLAND WATERWAYS

The total length of navigable waterways in the Czech Republic is 663.6 km. The Elbe (Labe) and its tributary, the Vltava, connect the Czech Republic with the North Sea via the port of Hamburg (Germany). The Oder provides a connection with the Baltic Sea and the port of Szczecin (Poland). The Czech Republic's river ports are Prague-Holešovice, Prague-Radotín, Kolín, Mělník, Ústí nad Labem and Děčín, on the Vltava and Elbe.

ČSPL Děčín: K. Čapka 211/1, 405 91 Děčín; tel. 412561111; fax 412510140; e-mail info@cspl.cz; internet www.cspl.cz; f. 1922; frmly Czechoslovak Elbe Navigation Co (Československá plavba labská); river transport of goods to Germany, Poland, the Netherlands, Belgium, Luxembourg, France and Switzerland; Chair. of Bd JIŘÍ KRATOCHVIL.

SHIPPING

Since August 1997 no ships have operated under the Czech flag. All Czech-owned ships operate under the Maltese and Cypriot flags.

Czech Ocean Shipping Co (Česká námořní plavba): Počernická 168, 100 99 Prague 10; tel. 267207111; e-mail mail@cos.cz; internet www.cos.cz; f. 1959; jt-stock co; six ships totalling 199,331 dwt; Man. Dir Capt. PAVEL TRNKA.

CIVIL AVIATION

There are main civil airports at Prague (Ruzyně), Brno, Karlovy Vary and Ostrava, operated by the Czech Airport Administration. The opening of a new terminal at Ruzyně in November 1997 increased the airport's capacity from 2.3m. passengers to 4.8m. In 2003 there were 7,737,431 international air passengers and 113,805 domestic air passengers.

ČSA—České aerolinie (Czech Airlines): Ruzyně Airport, 160 08 Prague 6; tel. 239007007; fax 224314273; e-mail call.centre@csa.cz; internet www.csa.cz; f. 1923; services to destinations in Europe, the Near, Middle and Far East, North Africa and North America; Pres. JAROSLAV TVRDIK.

Tourism

The Czech Republic has magnificent scenery, with summer and winter sports facilities. Prague, Kutna Hora, Olomouc, Český Krumlov and Telč are among the best known of the historic towns, and there are famous castles and cathedrals and numerous resorts, as well as spas with natural mineral springs at Karlovy Vary (Carlsbad) and Mariánské Lázně (Marienbad). In 2003 a total of almost 5,075,756 tourist arrivals were recorded. In the same year tourism receipts totalled US $3.6m.

Czech Tourist Authority: Vinohradská 46, POB 32, 120 41 Prague 2; tel. 221580111; fax 224247516; e-mail info@czechtourism.cz; internet www.visitczech.cz; f. 1993; Dir ROSTISLAV VONDRUSKA.

DENMARK

Introductory Survey

Location, Climate, Language, Religion, Flag, Capital

The Kingdom of Denmark is situated in northern Europe. It consists of the peninsula of Jutland, the islands of Zealand, Funen, Lolland, Falster and Bornholm, and 401 smaller islands. The country lies between the North Sea, to the west, and the Baltic Sea, to the east. Denmark's only land frontier is with Germany, to the south. Norway lies to the north of Denmark, across the Skagerrak, while Sweden, the most southerly region of which is separated from Zealand by a narrow strait, lies to the north-east. Outlying territories of Denmark are Greenland and the Faroe Islands in the North Atlantic Ocean. Denmark is low-lying and the climate is temperate, with mild summers and cold, rainy winters. The language is Danish. Almost all of the inhabitants profess Christianity: the Evangelical Lutheran Church, to which some 84% of the population belong, is the established Church, and there are also small communities of other Protestant groups and of Roman Catholics. The national flag (proportions 28 by 37) displays a white cross on a red background, the upright of the cross being to the left of centre. The capital is Copenhagen (København).

Recent History

In 1945, following the end of German wartime occupation, Denmark recognized the independence of Iceland, which had been declared in the previous year. Home rule was granted to the Faroe Islands in 1948 and to Greenland in 1979. Denmark was a founder member of the North Atlantic Treaty Organization (NATO, see p. 301) in 1949 and of the Nordic Council (see p. 296) in 1952. In January 1973, following a referendum, Denmark entered the European Communities (including the EEC), later more commonly referred to as simply the European Community (EC), and from 1993 restyled as the European Union (EU, see p. 217).

In 1947 King Frederik IX succeeded to the throne on the death of his father, Christian X. Denmark's Constitution was radically revised in 1953: new provisions allowed for female succession to the throne, abolished the upper house of the Folketing (parliament) and amended the franchise. King Frederik died in January 1972, and his eldest daughter, Margrethe, became the first queen to rule Denmark for nearly 600 years.

The system of proportional representation, which is embodied in the 1953 Constitution, makes it difficult for a single party to gain a majority in the Folketing. The minority Government of Venstre (Liberals), led by Poul Hartling and formed in 1973, was followed in 1975 by a minority Government of the Social-demokratiet (Social Democrats) under Anker Jørgensen. Jørgensen led various coalitions and minority Governments until 1982. General elections in 1977, 1979 and 1981 were held against a background of growing unemployment and attempts to tighten control of the economy. By September 1982 Jørgensen's economic policy, including attempts to reduce the budget deficit by introducing new taxes, had once more led to disagreements within the Cabinet, and the Government resigned.

Det Konservative Folkeparti (the Conservative People's Party), which had been absent from Danish coalitions since 1971, formed a centre-right four-party Government—with Venstre, the Centrum-Demokraterne (Centre Democrats) and the Kristeligt Folkeparti (Christian People's Party)—led by Poul Schlüter, who became Denmark's first Conservative Prime Minister since 1894. Holding only 66 of the Folketing's 179 seats, the coalition narrowly avoided defeat in October 1982, when it introduced stringent economic measures, and again in September 1983, when larger reductions in public spending were proposed. In December the right-wing Fremskridtspartiet (Progress Party) withdrew its support for further cuts in expenditure, and the Government was defeated. A general election to the Folketing was held in January 1984, and Schlüter's Government remained in office, with its component parties holding a total of 77 seats, and relying on the support of members of Det Radikale Venstre (Social Liberals).

In January 1986 the left-wing parties in the Folketing combined to reject the ratification by Denmark of the Single Euro-

pean Act (which amended the Treaty of Rome—the agreement that founded the EC—so as to establish the EC's single market and allow the EC Council of Ministers to take decisions by a qualified majority vote if a unanimous one was not achieved). Opponents of ratification, led by the Socialdemokratiet, argued that it would lead to a diminution of Denmark's power to maintain strict environmental controls. In a national referendum in February, however, 56.2% of the votes cast were in favour of ratification of the Act, and the Folketing formally approved it in May.

At a general election held in September 1987 Schlüter's coalition retained only 70 seats in the Folketing while the opposition Socialdemokratiet lost two of their 56 seats. Jørgensen later resigned as leader of the latter party. Several of the smaller and extremist parties made considerable gains, with the result that the outgoing coalition was weakened, while the main opposition parties were unable to command a working majority. Schlüter eventually formed a new Cabinet comprising representatives of the former four-party governing coalition. However, Det Radikale Venstre had earlier declared that they would not support any administration that depended on the support of the Fremskridtspartiet. This therefore left a precarious balance of power within the Folketing.

In April 1988 the Folketing adopted an opposition-sponsored resolution requiring the Government to inform visiting warships of the country's ban on nuclear weapons. The British and US Governments were highly critical of the resolution. Schlüter consequently announced an early general election for May 1988, on the issue of Denmark's membership of NATO and defence policy. For the main parties the election result was inconclusive, and negotiations lasting three weeks were necessary before Schlüter was appointed to seek a basis for viable government. At the beginning of June a new minority coalition, comprising members of Det Konservative Folkeparti, Venstre and Det Radikale Venstre, formed a Cabinet under Schlüter. The new Government restored good relations with its NATO allies by adopting a formula that requested all visiting warships to respect Danish law in its territorial waters, while making no specific reference to nuclear weapons.

The Government proposed large reductions in social welfare provision for 1989, and attacked demands by the Fremskridtspartiet for less taxation as unrealistic. The Fremskridtspartiet, however, continued to increase in popularity, and in November 1989 its share of the vote rose significantly in municipal elections, while Det Konservative Folkeparti lost support. The Government therefore proposed to reduce the rates of taxation in 1990, despite opposition on the part of the Socialdemokratiet to the accompanying decreases in welfare expenditure. An early general election was organized for December 1990. Although the Socialdemokratiet retained the largest share of the vote (winning an additional 14 seats to bring their total to 69), Schlüter formed a minority coalition Government, comprising Det Konservative Folkeparti, which had lost five seats in the election, and Venstre, which had gained an additional seven seats. As expected, Det Radikale Venstre, while no longer part of the Government, continued to support the majority of the new coalition Government's policies.

In May 1992 the Folketing voted, by 130 votes to 25, to approve the Treaty on European Union (the Maastricht Treaty), which further expanded the scope of the Treaty of Rome. In a national referendum held in Denmark in June, however, 50.7% of the votes cast were against ratification of the Treaty, compared with 49.3% in favour. This unexpected result caused consternation among Denmark's European partners, and during the rest of the year discussions took place among representatives of EC countries, who sought to establish a formula that, without necessitating the renegotiation of the Treaty, would allow the Danish Government to conduct a second referendum with some hope of success. In December EC heads of government agreed that Denmark should be allowed exemption from certain provisions of the Treaty, namely the final stage of European monetary union (including the adoption of a single currency); participation in a common defence policy; common

European citizenship; and co-operation in legal and home affairs: all provisions that had been regarded as a threat to national sovereignty by Danish opponents of ratification. Despite uncertainty as to how far these exemptions were legally binding, the agreement was endorsed by seven of the eight parties represented in the Folketing (the exception being the Fremskridtspartiet), and in a second referendum, held in May 1993, 56.7% of the votes cast were in favour of ratification and 43.3% against. In June 1994 the Government announced that it would seek an amendment to the Maastricht Treaty to ensure that environmental safety took precedence over European free-trade initiatives.

Meanwhile, in January 1993 Schlüter resigned from the premiership after a judicial inquiry disclosed that he had misled the Folketing in April 1989 over a scandal that had its origin in 1987, when the then Minister of Justice, Erik Ninn-Hansen, had illegally ordered civil servants to delay issuing entry visas to the families of Tamil refugees from Sri Lanka. In subsequent negotiations between political parties, Poul Nyrup Rasmussen, the leader of the Socialdemokratiet, obtained sufficient support to form a new government, and in late January 1993 a majority coalition Government (the first majority administration in Denmark for 11 years, controlling 90 of the 179 seats in the legislature) took office: it comprised members of the Socialdemokratiet and three small centre parties (Det Radikale Venstre, the Centrum-Demokraterne and the Kristeligt Folkeparti). The new Government gave priority to securing an affirmative vote for the Maastricht Treaty (see above).

In a general election in September 1994, three months earlier than scheduled, the Socialdemokratiet won a reduced number of seats, although they retained the largest share of the vote. Venstre, led by Uffe Ellemann-Jensen, gained an additional 13 seats, but the Kristeligt Folkeparti, a member of the outgoing coalition, failed to secure representation in the new legislature. None the less, Nyrup Rasmussen was able to form a minority Government with his two remaining coalition partners, Det Radikale Venstre and the Centrum-Demokraterne, and denied that the Government would be dependent for support on the left-wing Socialistik Folkeparti (Socialist People's Party). In December 1996, however, the Centrum-Demokraterne withdrew from the coalition, following the Government's decision to seek support from left-wing parties in order to achieve parliamentary approval for legislation relating to the 1997 budget.

In late October 1997 Thorkild Simonsen was appointed as the new Minister of the Interior and of Health, following mounting public concern at reports of increasingly high levels of immigration. As expected, a new government initiative was launched in December, enforcing stricter immigration policies.

The results of local elections conducted in November 1997 indicated that the Socialdemokratiet, who received some 33% of the votes cast, were continuing to attract the largest share of popular support. In February 1998 the Prime Minister, Nyrup Rasmussen, announced that an early general election would be conducted on 11 March, six months before the expiry of the mandate of the incumbent Government and in advance of a referendum on the Amsterdam Treaty on European integration (drafted at a meeting of EU members in the Netherlands in June 1997), which was scheduled to be held in late May. Despite the fact that the Centrum-Demokraterne supported an informal electoral alliance comprising Det Konservative Folkeparti and Venstre in the election, Nyrup Rasmussen's Government was returned to office with a narrow majority in the Folketing: the Socialdemokraterne, together with their coalition partner Det Radikale Venstre and other informal allies, secured a total of 90 of the 179 legislative seats, compared with 89 seats won by the centre-right opposition (led by Ellemann-Jensen). The right-wing Dansk Folkeparti (Danish People's Party), which campaigned for stricter immigration controls, performed strongly in its first general election, winning 7.4% of the total votes cast (13 seats). Following his defeat in the general election, Ellemann-Jensen resigned as leader of Venstre and was replaced by Anders Fogh Rasmussen.

On 28 May 1998 Danish voters narrowly endorsed the ratification of the Amsterdam Treaty by a margin of 55.1% in favour to 44.9% against. The referendum followed the rejection by the Danish Supreme Court early in the previous month of a legal challenge to the constitutional validity of the Maastricht Treaty, which had been brought by a group of private individuals who were opposed to further European integration.

In early November 1999 serious rioting erupted in a district of Copenhagen which housed a high concentration of immigrants.

The rioting, which was the most serious to occur in Denmark for six years, was reportedly provoked by the earlier announcement of a controversial judicial ruling, in accordance with which a man of Turkish origin became the first Danish-born person to receive an expulsion order from the country. (The man, convicted on charges of theft, had failed to apply for the Danish citizenship to which he was entitled.) The court decision was announced just days after the readmittance to the membership of the right-wing Fremskridtspartiet of the party's founder, Mogens Glistrup, who was renowned for his vociferous opposition to immigration; Glistrup's extreme racist sentiments, expressed following the court ruling, led, later in November, to the resignation from the party of all four of its representatives in the Folketing, leaving the Fremskridtspartiet with no parliamentary representation. (The four legislators subsequently founded a new political organization, Frihed 2000—Freedom 2000.)

On 28 September 2000 the Government held a national referendum to ascertain whether the population supported the adoption of the single European currency, the euro. Approval for the euro had been strong when the referendum was called in May, but had declined throughout the months preceding the vote, despite the support of the Government, the majority of the major political parties, the industrial sector, banks, trade unions, and the media. In the event Danish voters rejected membership of the single currency, with 53.1% opposed to the euro and 46.9% in favour; the rate of participation of the electorate was 87.5%. Immediately after the outcome of the referendum was revealed the central bank raised interest rates by 0.5% to defend the krone; opposition parties claimed the move was politically motivated in order to vindicate economic scaremongering by supporters of the euro prior to the referendum.

A government reorganization took place in December 2000, prompted by the resignation of Petersen from the foreign affairs portfolio in protest at the result of the referendum on the euro and by the need to replace the Minister of Defence, Hans Hækkerup, who had been appointed as head of the UN mission in Kosovo. Five new ministers were appointed, some of whom were relatively inexperienced, in an attempt to revitalize the Government.

Following the terrorist attacks in the USA in September 2001, the Prime Minister, Nyrup Rasmussen, announced that the general election, due to be held by mid-March 2002 at the latest, would be held early, on 20 November 2001, concurrently with local elections. He stated that, given the general unease and uncertainty generated by the attacks, and with major decisions to be made on security, four months of electoral campaigning would not be in the country's best interest. The Prime Minister also said that it was important to give the new government sufficient time to prepare to host the six-month rotating EU presidency, which Denmark was due to assume on 1 July 2002. There followed a brief period of uncharacteristically bitter campaigning, focusing mainly on the issue of immigration. At the general election the Socialdemokratiet won 52 of the 179 seats in the Folketing (with 29.1% of the valid votes cast), meaning that, for the first time since 1920, it was no longer the party with the largest representation in the legislature. Venstre won 56 seats (with 31.3% of the votes cast) and, under Anders Fogh Rasmussen, formed a minority coalition Government with Det Konservative Folkeparti, which secured 16 seats (9.0%). The Dansk Folkeparti performed well, winning 22 seats (12.0%); the leaders of Venstre stressed, however, that the far-right, anti-immigration party would not exert any influence over government policy. Nevertheless, by the end of November 2001 the Fogh Rasmussen Government had announced its intention to remove the legal right of refugees to bring their families to Denmark, to extend the period of residence required to obtain a residence permit from three to seven years, and to deport immediately all immigrants convicted of crimes—all of which was to be financed primarily by a privatization programme and a substantial reduction in development aid. A new Ministry of Refugees, Immigration and Integration Affairs was also created. The proposed legislation tightening the country's immigration and asylum regulations came into force, with the support of the Dansk Folkeparti, in July 2002. Following the 2001 general election there was a period of internecine struggle within the Socialdemokratiet, which culminated in Nyrup Rasmussen's resignation as party leader in November 2002 and his replacement by Mogens Lykketoft.

Following the publication of the draft new constitution of the EU in May 2003, which was intended to promote the smooth functioning of the organization following the accession of 10 new member states in May 2004, Fogh Rasmussen announced that Danish citizens would be granted a referendum on its contents. With other smaller members, the Danish Government was concerned to protect the role of less populous states within the EU. Of particular concern were plans for a permanent president for the Council of the EU to replace the existing system of a six-month rotating presidency, which gave equal status to all EU member states, and the proposal to limit the number of Commissioners in the future, both of which, it was feared, would diminish the role of smaller nations. In late February 2005, following his party's re-election to power, Fogh Rasmussen announced that a national referendum would be held on 27 September on whether to endorse the proposed EU constitution. Although the draft constitution was supported by more than four-fifths of the Folketing (including the governing Venstre), its ratification by the Danish people was by no means assured.

The Danish Government contributed a warship, a submarine and 160 troops to the US-led military operation in Iraq to oust the regime of Saddam Hussein in early 2003. There were deep public divisions over the Government's support for the invasion and these were reflected in the legislature, where the decision to approve the deployment of troops followed intense political debate. Only 93 of the 179 members of the Folketing voted in favour of the motion, which would not have been passed without the support of the far-right Dansk Folkeparti. Following the downfall of Saddam Hussein's regime in April, a 410-strong Danish peace-keeping force was dispatched to Iraq and was stationed near Basra (in southern Iraq) under British command. The Danish Government also helped to co-ordinate troop contributions from the Baltic republics. Despite the death of a member of the Danish armed forces in Iraq in August, the Government, claiming broad political support for humanitarian intervention, announced in September that it would send a further 90 soldiers to Iraq by the end of October and extended the duration of its military presence in Iraq until mid-2004. The Danish Government was also involved in plans for the post-war redevelopment of Iraq. In late April 2004 the Minister of Defence, Svend Aage Jensby, resigned amid allegations made by the opposition that the Danish military authorities had exaggerated the threat posed by Saddam Hussein in an attempt to justify the military action in Iraq; Jensby was replaced by Søren Gade.

At its national party congress in October 2003 the Kristeligt Folkeparti changed its name to the Kristeligtdemokraterne (Christian Democrats). The move, which was part of a strategy designed to improve the party's public image and was indicative of the strength of a youth movement within the party, was considered contentious and prompted the resignation of the Chairman, Jann Sjursen, who had opposed the change; he was replaced by Marianne Karlmose Nielsen.

Despite bitter opposition, the Government, with the support of the Dansk Folkeparti, proposed controversial legislation in the Folketing in June 2004 to abolish county authorities on 1 January 2007 and to replace them with five new administrative regions and 100 new councils. The new regions were to have responsibility for hospital administration, general urban planning, collective transportation and several social welfare institutions. Most of the remaining policy areas currently handled by counties were to be dealt with by municipal authorities. In October 2004 the opposition parties jointly submitted a resolution demanding that the Government reschedule the general election, which was due to be held in 2005, so that it took place prior to the parliamentary vote on the proposed reforms in the first half of 2005. The motion was defeated by 57 votes to 49.

In mid-January 2005, however, Prime Minister Fogh Rasmussen announced that the general election would indeed be held early, on 8 February, citing as his main reason for this the forthcoming ballot on the municipal reforms. There followed a brief period of campaigning during which the election was presented as a quasi-presidential contest between Fogh Rasmussen and Lykketoft. In the event, however, both Venstre and the Socialdemokratiet lost support to the other, smaller parties. At the election Venstre won 52 seats, constituting a loss of four seats, compared with the 2001 election, but enough to secure victory as the party with the largest representation in the Folketing; Fogh Rasmussen thus became the first ever Venstre Prime Minister to win a second term, and renewed his party's governing coalition with Det Konservative Folkeparti. The Socialdemokratiet won 47 seats, representing a loss of five seats; Lykketoft subsequently resigned as party leader and was

replaced by Helle Thorning-Schmidt. Det Radikale Venstre made the largest gain, of eight seats, and won 17 seats altogether.

In May 1999 the Danish Government signed a maritime boundary agreement with representatives of the Faroese Landsstýri and the British Government, thus ending a 30-year dispute over the location of the boundaries of a 42,000-sq km area in the North Sea, which was potentially rich in petroleum reserves.

In August 1991 Denmark and Sweden signed an agreement on the proposed construction of a 15.9-km road and rail system across the Oresund strait between Copenhagen and Malmö. Although construction was initially delayed, owing to objections raised by environmentalists in Sweden and Germany, the agreement was finally ratified by the Swedish Government in 1994 and the project was completed in July 2000 at a total cost of approximately 23,400m. kroner.

Following the dissolution of the USSR at the end of 1991, Denmark rapidly established diplomatic relations with (and began investing in) the former Soviet Baltic states of Estonia, Latvia and Lithuania, and was a founder member of the Council of Baltic Sea States (see p. 198), established in 1992.

Government

Denmark is a constitutional monarchy. Under the 1953 constitutional charter, legislative power is held jointly by the hereditary monarch (who has no personal political power) and the unicameral Folketing (parliament), which has 179 members, including 175 from metropolitan Denmark and two each from the Faroe Islands and Greenland. Members are elected for four years (subject to dissolution) on the basis of proportional representation. Executive power is exercised by the monarch through a Cabinet, which is led by the Prime Minister and is responsible to the Folketing. Denmark comprises 14 counties (amtskommuner), one city and one borough, all with elected councils. A proposed programme of municipal reform was presented to the Folketing in June 2004, under which the counties would be replaced by administrative regions and councils in 2007 (see Recent History).

Defence

In August 2004 Denmark maintained an army of 12,500 (including 5,200 conscripts), a navy of 3,800 (500 conscripts) and an air force of 4,200 (100 conscripts). There were, in total, 64,900 reservists, and a volunteer Home Guard numbering some 59,300. Military service is for 10 months (to be reduced to four months). Denmark abandoned its neutrality after the Second World War and has been a member of NATO since 1949. In 1992 Denmark assumed observer status in Western European Union (WEU, see p. 352). The defence budget for 2004 totalled 17,600m. kroner.

Economic Affairs

In 2003, according to estimates by the World Bank, Denmark's gross national income (GNI), measured at average 2001–03 prices, was US $209,604m., equivalent to $33,750 per head (or $31,210 per head on an international purchasing-power parity basis). During 1990–2003 Denmark's population grew at an average annual rate of 0.4%, while gross domestic product (GDP) per head increased, in real terms, at an average rate of 1.7% per year. Overall GDP increased, in real terms, at an average annual rate of 2.1% in 1990–2003; growth was 2.1% in 2002 and 0.4% in 2003.

Agriculture (including forestry and fishing) employed 3.0% of the economically active population in 2003, and contributed an estimated 2.2% of GDP, measured at current prices, in the same year. The principal activities are pig-farming and dairy farming; Denmark is a major exporter of pork products, and exports of live pigs and of pig meat accounted for an estimated 4.7% of total export revenue in 2003. Most of Denmark's agricultural production is exported, and the sector accounted for 16.8% of total exports in 2003 (including exports of manufactured goods of agricultural origin). The fishing industry accounted for 3.6% of total export earnings in that year. Agricultural GDP increased, in real terms, at an average annual rate of 2.3% in 1990–2002; the GDP of the sector grew by 2.2% in 2001, but declined by 4.5% in 2002.

Industry (including mining, manufacturing, construction, power and water) employed 23.8% of the working population and provided an estimated 25.1% of GDP in 2003. Industrial GDP increased, in real terms, at an average annual rate of 1.9% in 1990–2002; it grew by 1.2% in 2001 and by 0.8% in 2002.

Mining accounted for only 0.2% of employment and provided 2.6% of GDP in 2003. Denmark has few natural resources, but exploration for petroleum reserves in the Danish sector of the North Sea in the 1970s proved successful. Natural gas has also been extensively exploited. In 1989 it was established that there was a significant reserve of sand in north-western Jutland which could potentially be exploited for rich yields of titanium, zirconium and yttrium. The GDP of the mining sector increased, in real terms, at an average annual rate of 8.2% in 1990–99; the sector's GDP declined by 2.7% in 1998, but grew by 10.8% in 1999 and by 12.1% in 2000.

Manufacturing employed 16.4% of the working population and contributed 15.3% of GDP in 2003. Measured by value of output, in 1998 the most important manufacturing industries were food products (accounting for 22.0% of the total), non-electric machinery and domestic appliances (12.8%), chemicals and pharmaceuticals (8.1%), metal products (7.0%), and furniture (4.1%). Manufacturing GDP increased, in real terms, at an average annual rate of 1.9% in 1990–2001; it grew by 6.7% in 2000 and by 2.3% in 2001.

Energy is derived principally from petroleum and natural gas. Since 1996 Denmark has produced enough energy to satisfy its domestic consumption, and the degree of self-sufficiency in petroleum and natural gas production amounted to 203% and 160%, respectively, in 2000. In that year total petroleum production amounted to 21m. cu m and total gas output was 11,300m. cu m. In 2003 imports of mineral fuels accounted for 4.8% of the total cost of imports, while exports of mineral fuels contributed 7.3% of total export revenue. In 2001 47.3% of electricity was produced from coal, 24.6% from natural gas and 11.1% from petroleum (only 0.1% was provided by hydroelectric sources). The use of renewable sources of energy (including wind power) has been encouraged. In 2002 Denmark derived 17% of its energy from wind-turbines, and planned to increase the share to 50% by 2030.

Services engaged 73.1% of the employed population and provided 72.6% of GDP, measured at current prices, in 2003. In real terms, the combined GDP of the service sectors increased at an average rate of 2.4% per year in 1990–2002; it rose by 1.8% in 2001 and by 2.9% in 2002.

In 2003, according to the IMF, Denmark recorded a visible trade surplus of US $9,671m. and a surplus of $5,651m. on the current account of the balance of payments. Most Danish trade is with the other member states of the European Union (EU, see p. 217), which accounted for 70.8% of imports and 65.6% of exports in 2003. The principal source of imports in 2003 was Germany (contributing 23.1% of the total); other major suppliers were Sweden (12.9%), the United Kingdom (7.0%), the Netherlands (6.9%) and France (4.9%). Germany was also the principal market for exports (accounting for 18.6% of the total); other major purchasers included Sweden (12.8%), the United Kingdom (8.5%), the USA (6.1%) and Norway (5.7%). The principal exports in 2003 were machinery and transport equipment (accounting for 27.5% of total export revenue), food and live animals (17.5%), miscellaneous manufactured articles (16.7%) and chemicals and related products (14.0%). The principal imports in 2003 were machinery and transport equipment (accounting for 35.4% of total import costs), basic manufactures (16.1%), miscellaneous manufactured articles (15.5%), and chemicals and related products (11.2%).

In 2003 there was a budget surplus of 14,554m. kroner, equivalent to 1.0% of GDP, compared with a budgetary deficit equal to almost 4% of GDP in 1993. Public-sector debt was equivalent to 42% of GDP in 2002. The average annual rate of inflation was 2.0% in 1992–2003. Consumer prices increased by by 2.4% in 2002 and by 2.2% in 2003. The rate of unemployment was 5.5% in 2003.

Denmark is a member of the EU, the Nordic Council (see p. 296) and the Nordic Council of Ministers (see p. 297).

Denmark is a small open economy, which is highly dependent on trade with other countries. Foreign trade accounts for about two-thirds of GDP and about two-thirds of foreign trade is with other EU members. Owing to its reliance on trade, a principal objective of the country's foreign policy has been to maintain a stable exchange rate. Denmark did not, however, participate in the EU's programme of Economic and Monetary Union (EMU). Despite government support for entry into EMU, it was rejected in a referendum in 1993 and this was confirmed by a second plebiscite in September 2000. Denmark has, however, maintained a stable rate of exchange with the new common European currency, the euro. A buoyant rate of growth of GDP in 2004 was driven by an unexpectedly high rate of growth in exports, which was partly a result of the strength of the international economy, particularly outside Europe, during the first half of the year; this was supported by a low interest rate. An increase in domestic demand also contributed to the strong growth, driven mainly by private consumption, which was positively affected by a reduction in income tax and the suspension of the mandatory private savings scheme (Særlige pensionsordning). Private consumption was expected to grow by 3.5% in 2004 and by 3.0% in 2005. Greater disposable income coupled with a low interest rate led to an increase in real estate prices in 2004, thus fuelling investment and further increasing domestic demand. This led to a remarkable rise in Danish imports. Even though exports were expected to grow steadily during the next few years, the narrowing net balance of trade was expected to reduce total GDP growth up until 2006. Unemployment fell during 2004, and was expected to do so again in 2005, before levelling out in 2006–07 at around 5% of the labour force. GDP growth was forecast to stand at 2.5% in 2004, to reach more than 2.0% in 2005, and about 1.8% per year in 2006–07. As in many other EU countries in the mid-2000s, Denmark was faced with a serious challenge to the long-term prospects of its economy as a result of demographic changes, resulting in a smaller labour force and a larger elderly population, a combination which would affect the sustainability of public finances. The Government aimed to address this problem largely through the increased involvement of immigrants and refugees in the labour market, setting a target of 87,000 more people in employment by 2010. Denmark, which is attractive to foreign investors owing to its well-educated labour force and its stable economic conditions, was geographically well placed to benefit from the enlargement of the EU in May 2004. It was also expected that enlargement would contribute to the growth of Denmark's work-force. To avoid abuse of the benefit system, however, Denmark imposed conditions on potential workers from central and eastern European states for the first seven years following their countries' accession, limiting residence permits to those in full-time employment and excluding them from child-care leave and unemployment benefit.

Education

Education is compulsory for nine years between seven and 16 years of age. The State is obliged to offer a pre-school class and a tenth voluntary year. In 1999/2000 enrolment at pre-primary level was equivalent to 91.7% of children in the relevant age-group. State-subsidized private schools are available, but about 90% of pupils attend municipal schools. Primary and lower secondary education begins at seven years of age and lasts for nine (optionally 10) years. This includes at least six years at primary school. Enrolment at primary level included 99.3% of those in the relevant age-group in 1999/2000 (males 99.3%; females 99.4%). Secondary education is divided into two cycles of three years, the first beginning at 13 years of age, the second at the age of 16 or 17. Students may transfer to vocational courses at this stage. Total enrolment at secondary level in 1999/2000 included 89.5% of those in the relevant age-group (males 88.2%; females 90.8%). There are eight universities and many other institutions of further and higher education. The traditional folk high schools offer a wide range of further education opportunities, which do not confer any professional qualification. In 1999/2000 enrolment at tertiary level was equivalent to 56.1% of those in the relevant age-group (males 47.4%; females 65.2%). In 2003 general government expenditure on education totalled an estimated 114,714m. kroner, representing 15.0% of total budget spending.

Public Holidays

2005: 1 January (New Year's Day), 24–28 March (Easter), 22 April (General Prayer Day), 5 May (Ascension Day), 16 May (Whit Monday), 5 June (Constitution Day), 24–26 December (Christmas).

2006: 1 January (New Year's Day), 13–17 April (Easter), 12 May (General Prayer Day), 25 May (Ascension Day), 5 June (Whit Monday and Constitution Day), 24–26 December (Christmas).

Weights and Measures

The metric system is in force.

Statistical Survey

Note: The figures in this survey relate only to metropolitan Denmark, excluding the Faroe Islands (see p. 1485) and Greenland (see p. 1491), figures for which are dealt with in separate chapters.

Source (unless otherwise stated): Danmarks Statistik, Sejrøgade 11, POB 2550, 2100 Copenhagen Ø; tel. 39-17-39-17; fax 39-17-39-99; e-mail dst@dst.dk; internet www.dst.dk.

Area and Population

AREA, POPULATION AND DENSITY

Area (sq km)	43,098*
Population (census results)	
1 January 1991	5,146,469
1 January 2001	
Males	2,644,319
Females	2,704,893
Total	5,349,212
Population (official estimate at 1 January)	
2002	5,368,354
2003	5,383,507
2004	5,397,640
Density (per sq km) at 1 January 2004	125.2

* 16,640 sq miles.

Regions, Counties and Municipalities
(At 1 January 2004)

	Area (sq km)	Population	Density (per sq km)
Sjælland (Zealand)	7,451	2,273,215	305.1
København (Copenhagen):			
Municipality	88	501,664	5,684.6
County	528	618,407	1,170.6
Frederiksborg (Frederiksberg):			
Municipality	9	91,721	10,458.5
County	1,347	373,688	5,684.6
Roskilde	891	237,089	266.0
Vestsjælland (West Zealand) .	2,984	302,479	101.4
Lolland-Falster	1,795	113,717	63.3
Storstrøm*	3,398	261,884	77.1
Bornholm	589	43,774	74.4
Fyn (Funen)	3,486	475,082	136.3
Jylland (Jutland)	29,778	2,491,852	83.7
Sønderjylland (South Jutland) .	3,939	252,936	64.2
Ribe	3,131	224,595	71.7
Vejle	2,997	355,691	118.7
Ringkøbing	4,854	274,830	56.6
Århus (Aarhus)	4,561	653,472	143.3
Viborg	4,123	234,659	56.9
Nordjylland (North Jutland) .	6,173	495,669	80.3
Total	43,098	5,397,640	124.9

* Part of Storstrøm county lies on Sjælland.

Principal Towns
(city proper, population at 1 January 2004)

København				
(Copenhagen, the				
capital) . . .	501,664	Horsens	49,652
Århus (Aarhus) .	228,547	Roskilde	44,205
Odense . . .	145,554	Greve Strand . . .	41,313
Aalborg . . .	121,549	Næstved	40,533
Frederiksborg				
(Frederiksberg) .	91,721	Silkeborg	38,453
Esbjerg . . .	72,550	Fredericia	37,054
Randers . . .	55,739	Horsholm	36,027
Kolding . . .	54,941	Helsingør	35,002
Vejle	49,917	Køge	33,564

Births, Marriages and Deaths

	Registered live births		Registered marriages		Registered deaths	
	Number	Rate (per 1,000)	Number	Rate (per 1,000)	Number	Rate (per 1,000)
1996 .	67,638	12.9	35,953	6.8	61,043	11.6
1997 .	67,636	12.8	34,244	6.5	59,898	11.3
1998 .	66,170	12.5	34,733	6.6	58,453	11.0
1999 .	66,232	12.5	35,459	6.7	59,156	11.1
2000 .	67,081	12.6	38,844	7.3	57,986	10.9
2001 .	65,450	12.2	36,567	6.8	58,338	10.9
2002 .	64,149	11.9	37,210	6.9	58,610	10.9
2003 .	64,682	12.0	35,041	6.5	57,574	10.7

Expectation of life (WHO estimates, years at birth): 77.2 (males 74.8; females 79.5) in 2002 (Source: WHO, *World Health Report*).

Economically Active Population
(sample surveys, '000 persons aged 15 to 66 years, April–June)

	2001	2002	2003
Agriculture, hunting and forestry	84.9	80.4	77.0
Fishing	4.0	5.2	4.6
Mining and quarrying	2.6	4.5	5.7
Manufacturing	488.4	459.2	440.9
Electricity, gas and water supply	13.5	14.9	14.4
Construction	181.6	181.2	180.0
Wholesale and retail trade; repair			
of motor vehicles, motorcycles			
and personal and household			
goods	379.0	390.0	395.8
Hotels and restaurants	63.4	67.5	66.4
Transport, storage and			
communications	182.9	185.5	188.3
Financial intermediation . . .	84.3	85.6	81.8
Real estate, renting and business			
activities	257.4	252.4	248.8
Public administration and defence;			
compulsory social security . .	161.7	161.0	157.8
Education	202.4	208.6	208.5
Health and social work	483.0	481.8	477.7
Other community, social and			
personal service activities . .	128.3	128.3	136.0
Private households with employed			
persons	1.5	2.7	1.8
Extra-territorial organizations and			
bodies	0.7	1.1	2.3
Activities not adequately defined .	5.6	5.4	4.6
Total employed	2,725.1	2,715.3	2,692.5
Unemployed	137.0	134.0	157.6
Total labour force	2,862.0	2,849.3	2,850.1
Males	1,522.6	1,515.4	1,523.5
Females	1,339.4	1,333.9	1,326.4

Source: ILO.

Health and Welfare

KEY INDICATORS

Total fertility rate (children per woman, 2002)	1.8
Under-5 mortality rate (per 1,000 live births, 2003) . . .	4
HIV/AIDS (% of persons aged 15–49, 2003)	0.2
Physicians (per 1,000 head, 2001)	3.4
Hospital beds (per 1,000 head, 1998)	4.5
Health expenditure (2001): US $ per head (PPP) . . .	2,503
Health expenditure (2001): % of GDP	8.4
Health expenditure (2001): public (% of total)	82.4
Access to water (% of persons, 2002)	100
Human Development Index (2002): ranking	17
Human Development Index (2002): value	0.932

For sources and definitions, see explanatory note on p. vi.

Agriculture

PRINCIPAL CROPS
('000 metric tons)

	2001	2002	2003
Wheat	4,663.9	4,059.2	4,701.4
Barley	3,966.2	4,120.9	3,775.6
Rye	332.4	229.5	168.5
Oats	291.7	275.6	259.6
Triticale (wheat-rye hybrid) . .	169.0	121.6	145.8
Potatoes	1,543.0	1,504.2	1,412.2
Sugar beet	3,148.8	3,385.0	2,857.3
Dry peas	111.0	139.0	105.6
Other pulses	2.0	11.0	18.5
Rapeseed	211.6	218.0	354.2
Cabbages	33.0	31.0*	32.0*
Lettuce	9.8	9.8	11.6
Tomatoes	21.2	19.7	22.0*
Cucumbers and gherkins . .	13.7	15.0	14.0*
Dry onions	29.1	29.1	30.0*
Green peas*	40.0	40.0	40.0
Carrots	62.0	62.0	54.6
Other fresh vegetables* . . .	38.2	39.2	39.0
Apples	18.8	20.0*	33.0*
Other fresh fruit*	13.6	14.7	17.2

* FAO estimate(s).

Source: FAO.

LIVESTOCK
(at May)

	2001	2002	2003
Horses	43,143	38,136	42,707
Cattle	1,906,911	1,796,118	1,724,409
Pigs	12,607,545	12,732,035	12,948,944
Sheep	151,855	131,063	143,699
Chickens ('000 head) . . .	20,347	19,734	17,152
Turkeys ('000 head) . . .	547	552	576
Ducks ('000 head) . . .	337	291	230
Geese ('000 head) . . .	6	3	8

LIVESTOCK PRODUCTS
('000 metric tons)

	2001	2002	2003
Beef and veal	169	169	161
Pig meat	1,503	1,892	1,898
Poultry meat	218	219	205
Cows' milk	4,553	4,590	4,675
Butter	47	49	53
Cheese	318	320	326
Hen eggs	81	81	81

Forestry

ROUNDWOOD REMOVALS
('000 cu m, excl. bark)

	2001	2002	2003
Sawlogs, veneer logs and logs for sleepers	532	455	470
Pulpwood	466 {	153 }	340
Other industrial wood . . .		181	
Fuel wood	617	657	817
Total	1,615	1,446	1,627

SAWNWOOD PRODUCTION
('000 cu m, incl. railway sleepers)

	2001	2002	2003
Coniferous (softwood)	240	217	225
Broadleaved (hardwood) . . .	43	27	23
Total	283	244	248

Source: FAO.

Fishing

('000 metric tons, live weight)

	2000	2001	2002
Capture	1,534.1	1,510.4	1,442.1
Atlantic cod	57.0	46.2	37.9
Norway pout	150.0	62.9	78.2
Blue whiting (Poutassou) . .	62.1	65.1	51.0
Sandeels (Sandlances) . .	567.4	666.3	662.4
Atlantic herring	153.9	141.3	112.5
European sprat	276.9	256.5	237.4
Blue mussel	110.6	122.5	110.9
Aquaculture	43.6	41.6	32.0
Total catch	1,577.7	1,552.0	1,474.1

Note: Figures exclude aquatic mammals, recorded by number rather than weight. The number of harbour porpoises caught was: 4,149 in 2000; 3,887 in 2001; 0 in 2002.

Source: FAO.

2003 ('000 metric tons, live weight): Capture 1,035.6 (Atlantic cod 31.5; Norway pout 23.0; Blue whiting (Poutassou) 87.0; Sandeels (Sandlances) 283.7; Atlantic herring 114.7; European sprat 262.1; Blue mussel 92.5).

Mining

(sales-based estimates, '000 metric tons, unless otherwise indicated)

	2001	2002	2003
Crude petroleum (million barrels)*	88	88	n.a.
Natural gas (million cu m)*† . .	8,200	8,100	n.a.
Limestone	755	710	710
Chalk	333	348	387
Salt (unrefined)	605	584	586
Peat	337	367	322

* Source: US Geological Survey.

† Figures refer to gross output. Marketable production (estimates, million cu m) was: 7,330 in 2001; 7,300 in 2002; n.a. in 2003.

Industry

SELECTED PRODUCTS
('000 metric tons, unless otherwise indicated)

	2001	2002	2003
Pig meat:			
Fresh, chilled or frozen . . .	1,150	1,156	1,216
Salted, dried or smoked . . .	135	130	127
Poultry meat and offals	193	199	199
Fish fillets, etc.: fresh, chilled,			
frozen	63	63	65
Salami, sausages, etc	83	78	85
Beet and cane sugar (solid) . .	563	508	512
Beer ('000 hectolitres)	7,233	8,202	8,352
Flours, meals and pastes of fish .	408	385	258
Oil cake and meal	38	71	160
Cigarettes (million)	11,090	12,039	12,897
Cement	2,678	2,698	2,642
Motor spirit (petrol) (million litres)	2,814*	2,636	2,549
Gas oils	3,498*	3,418	3,482
Motor and fuel oils	1,647*	1,658	1,707
Asphalt for road surfaces . .	2,710	2,596	2,656
Washing powders, softeners, etc .	141	151	150
Refrigerators for household use			
('000)	86	50	42

* Including waste oils.

Finance

CURRENCY AND EXCHANGE RATES

Monetary Units
100 øre = 1 Danish krone (plural: kroner).

Sterling, Dollar and Euro Equivalents (31 December 2004)
£1 sterling = 10.5601 kroner;
US $1 = 5.4676 kroner;
€1 = 7.4474 kroner;
1,000 Danish kroner = £94.70 = $182.90 = €134.27.

Average Exchange Rate (kroner per US $)
2002   7.8947
2003   6.5877
2004   5.9911

GENERAL BUDGET
(million kroner, estimates)

Revenue	2001	2002	2003
Income taxes	391,009	392,551	400,301
Personal income tax	349,369	353,645	361,263
Corporation tax	41,640	38,906	39,065
Social security contributions . .	29,358	22,660	23,428
Current taxes on wealth and real			
property	24,762	26,077	27,243
Taxes on goods and services . .	209,439	217,071	219,855
VAT	128,550	132,484	135,437
Taxes on specific goods . . .	67,409	70,317	69,086
Stamp duty	4,964	5,480	6,214
Customs and import duties . .	0	0	0
Other taxes	4,686	4,739	8,477
Other current revenue	93,253	92,076	97,263
Capital revenue	4,066	8,463	5,089
Total	756,575	763,637	781,655

Expenditure	2001	2002	2003
General public services	58,681	61,404	63,093
Defence	21,995	22,440	22,535
Law and order	12,817	13,103	13,667
Education	107,491	110,515	114,714
Health	71,548	75,890	79,663
Social security and welfare . .	306,620	319,695	337,569
Housing and community amenities	12,970	13,127	13,192
Religious, recreational and cultural			
services	22,809	22,888	23,037
Economic services	50,035	50,509	51,265
Energy supplies	2,395	2,092	1,532
Unclassified functions	54,084	52,901	48,364
Total	719,050	742,473	767,101

INTERNATIONAL RESERVES
(US $ million at 31 December)*

	2001	2002	2003
Gold†	557	703	872
IMF special drawing rights . .	281	103	81
Reserve position in IMF . . .	712	982	1,020
Foreign exchange	16,117	25,901	36,004
Total	17,667	27,689	37,977

* Data referring to holdings of gold and foreign exchange exclude deposits made with the European Monetary Institute.
† National valuation.

Source: IMF, *International Financial Statistics.*

MONEY SUPPLY
(million kroner at 31 December*)

	2001	2002	2003
Currency outside banks . . .	39,210	38,980	40,990
Demand deposits at banks . . .	373,200	391,630	427,720
Total money (incl. others) . .	414,850	430,820	469,150

* Figures rounded to nearest ten million kroner.
Source: IMF, *International Financial Statistics.*

COST OF LIVING
(Consumer Price Index; base: 2000 = 100)

	2001	2002	2003
Food and non-alcoholic beverages	103.9	106.1	107.7
Alcoholic beverages and tobacco .	102.3	103.0	101.8
Clothing and footwear	98.5	100.8	101.8
Housing, water, electricity, gas and			
other fuels	102.9	105.9	108.5
Furnishings, household, etc. . .	101.9	103.8	104.9
Health	102.2	103.1	103.2
Transport	101.2	103.9	107.1
Communications	96.3	96.5	94.4
Recreation and culture	101.7	103.3	104.9
Education	103.8	110.4	134.1
Restaurants and hotels . . .	103.0	105.2	107.7
Miscellaneous goods and services .	104.6	109.7	114.0
All items	102.4	104.8	107.0

NATIONAL ACCOUNTS
(provisional, million kroner at current prices)

National Income and Product

	2001	2002	2003
Compensation of employees . .	714,646	734,918	754,518
Gross operating surplus and mixed			
income	416,563	424,608	437,390
Gross domestic income at			
factor cost	1,131,209	1,159,526	1,191,908
Taxes, *less* subsidies, on production	5,229	3,937	6,138
Gross value added	1,136,438	1,163,463	1,198,046
Taxes on products	207,943	215,688	218,565
Less Subsidies on products . . .	18,869	18,441	20,003
GDP in purchasers' values . .	1,325,512	1,360,709	1,396,608
Factor income from abroad . .	98,562	82,232	82,604
Less Factor income paid abroad .	116,888	102,971	93,068
Gross national income . . .	1,307,187	1,339,971	1,386,145
Current taxes on income, wealth,			
etc. abroad (net)	1,017	1,153	1,215
Other current transfers to and from			
abroad (net)	−27,751	−29,770	−30,995
Gross national disposable			
income	1,280,452	1,311,353	1,356,364

Expenditure on the Gross Domestic Product

	2001	2002	2003
Government final consumption expenditure	343,273	358,509	371,839
Private final consumption expenditure	624,483	641,856	659,259
Increase in stocks	272,233	283,409	279,413
Gross fixed capital formation			
Total domestic expenditure	1,239,989	1,283,774	1,310,511
Exports of goods and services	591,508	602,740	594,837
Less Imports of goods and services	505,985	525,805	508,741
GDP in purchasers' values	1,325,512	1,360,709	1,396,608
GDP at constant 1995 prices	1,170,719	1,182,628	1,187,865

Gross Domestic Product by Economic Activity

	2001	2002	2003
Agriculture and forestry	31,229	25,849	26,466
Fishing	2,521	2,688	1,463
Mining and quarrying	30,718	31,728	32,135
Manufacturing	184,473	188,384	189,980
Electricity, gas and water supply	24,814	26,988	27,662
Construction	58,674	60,063	62,020
Wholesale and retail trade, restaurants and hotels	160,059	163,188	168,259
Transport, storage and communication	93,822	92,738	97,803
Finance and insurance	60,154	62,382	67,113
Real estate and renting activities	132,202	139,349	146,660
Business services	90,738	91,496	88,800
Public administration and defence; compulsory social security	77,217	80,053	82,393
Education	63,046	66,350	68,648
Health care activities	49,840	52,194	54,390
Social work activities	67,966	71,559	74,222
Other community, social and personal service activities	49,123	50,456	53,880
Sub-total	1,176,595	1,205,465	1,241,894
Less Financial intermediation services indirectly measured	40,157	42,002	43,847
Gross value added at basic prices	1,136,438	1,163,463	1,198,046
Taxes on products	207,943	215,688	218,565
Less subsidies on products	18,869	18,441	20,003
GDP in purchasers' values	1,325,512	1,360,709	1,396,608

BALANCE OF PAYMENTS
(US $ million)

	2001	2002	2003
Exports of goods f.o.b.	50,466	55,473	64,537
Imports of goods f.o.b.	−43,048	−47,810	−54,840
Trade balance	7,418	7,662	9,697
Exports of services	25,134	26,667	31,672
Imports of services	−22,121	−24,305	−28,254
Balance on goods and services	10,431	10,024	13,116
Other income received	10,737	9,265	11,180
Other income paid	−13,748	−12,805	−13,796
Balance on goods, services and income	7,420	6,484	10,499
Current transfers received	3,719	3,466	4,615
Current transfers paid	−6,291	−6,489	−8,151
Current balance	4,848	3,460	6,963
Capital account (net)	14	152	−7
Direct investment abroad	−13,154	−2,650	−856
Direct investment from abroad	9,286	4,431	1,185
Portfolio investment assets	−14,772	−4,356	−21,930
Portfolio investment liabilities	10,510	4,843	6,010
Financial derivatives liabilities	694	390	−12
Other investment assets	9,054	−6,839	−9,314
Other investment liabilities	−7,331	8,000	19,789
Net errors and omissions	4,167	−1,887	2,846
Overall balance	3,317	5,546	4,674

Source: IMF, *International Financial Statistics.*

External Trade

PRINCIPAL COMMODITIES
(distribution by SITC, million kroner)

Imports c.i.f.	2001	2002	2003
Food and live animals	36,035	37,127	37,222
Crude materials (inedible) except fuels	12,787	12,704	12,898
Mineral fuels, lubricants, etc.	17,851	17,163	17,723
Petroleum, petroleum products, etc	14,383	13,369	13,563
Chemicals and related products	38,626	41,421	41,242
Basic manufactures	60,943	60,080	59,477
Machinery and transport equipment	130,373	144,583	130,923
Machinery specialized for particular industries	11,851	11,822	11,638
General industrial machinery, equipment and parts	16,345	17,100	17,559
Office machines and automatic data-processing equipment	17,412	19,083	19,246
Telecommunications and sound equipment	19,611	24,100	18,243
Other electrical machinery, apparatus, etc.	21,525	21,260	20,078
Road vehicles (incl. air-cushion vehicles) and parts*	24,037	26,939	24,257
Other transport equipment and parts*	10,654	14,693	11,944
Miscellaneous manufactured articles	57,419	57,281	57,368
Clothing and accessories (excl. footwear)	18,449	17,985	17,780
Total (incl. others)	369,852	384,709	369,701

Exports f.o.b.	2001	2002	2003
Food and live animals . . .	80,959	78,192	75,192
Meat and meat preparations . .	31,177	28,053	26,050
Dairy products and birds' eggs .	10,920	11,051	10,797
Fish (not marine mammals), crustaceans, molluscs and aquatic invertebrates . . .	16,773	16,250	15,365
Crude materials (inedible) except fuels	14,817	15,871	15,996
Mineral fuels, lubricants, etc.	29,082	30,758	31,528
Petroleum, petroleum products, etc.	23,417	24,672	25,330
Chemicals and related products	54,108	58,244	60,183
Medicinal and pharmaceutical products	28,161	30,374	32,190
Basic manufactures . . .	43,691	44,395	43,380
Machinery and transport equipment	117,368	129,700	118,240
Power generating machinery and equipment	16,219	15,040	14,885
Machinery specialized for particular industries . . .	16,004	15,599	15,642
General industrial machinery, equipment and parts*	27,526	29,552	29,062
Telecommunications and sound equipment	18,243	25,256	17,498
Other electrical machinery, apparatus, etc.	14,901	14,774	14,281
Miscellaneous manufactured articles	71,814	72,591	71,638
Furniture and parts	15,533	15,754	15,773
Clothing and accessories (excl. footwear)	14,751	14,931	15,048
Total (incl. others)	422,877	442,754	429,272

* Data on parts exclude tyres, engines and electrical parts.

PRINCIPAL TRADING PARTNERS
(million kroner)

Imports c.i.f.	2001	2002	2003
Austria	4,044.2	4,432,6	4,643.5
Belgium	12,499.7	13,825.7	1,281.5
China, People's Republic . . .	10,918.3	11,042.0	13,662.6
Finland	9,870.1	9,767.0	8,568.2
France (incl. Monaco)	21,405.9	25,119.2	17,926.7
Germany	80,613.4	84,766.6	85,582.6
Ireland	4,432.3	4,928.2	4,466.1
Italy	16,126.6	16,220.1	15,340.5
Japan	5,210.0	5,219.4	3,154.6
Korea, Republic	2,685.9	2,091.2	4,228.6
Netherlands	25,717.4	26,011.9	25,616.2
Norway	16,791.4	18,420.4	16,688.9
Poland	7,669.1	7,428.4	6,721.2
Spain	5,804.3	6,401.6	6,478.5
Sweden	43,987.2	45,677.5	47,708.6
Switzerland	4,704.3	4,385.9	4,184.0
Taiwan	2,659.0	2,548.3	2,828.9
United Kingdom	27,987.0	33,881.5	25,947.0
USA	16,311.2	15,253.9	11,988.6
Total (incl. others)	368,458.7	384,709.4	369,700.9

Exports f.o.b.	2001	2002	2003
Belgium	6,930.6	7,093.6	7,879.7
Finland	12,673.6	13,799.8	13,713.0
France (incl. Monaco)	21,711.4	20,653.3	21,706.6
Germany	84,064.4	85,364.6	79,685.1
Ireland	5,961.7	6,593.6	6,585.4
Italy	14,365.4	14,135.1	14,397.1
Japan	14,766.9	13,397.3	13,322.5
Netherlands	19,157.1	19,932.0	19,960.8
Norway	23,573.6	27,066.4	24,538.3
Poland	7,199.7	7,108.9	6,777.0
Russia	5,856.5	5,457.8	5,703.6
Spain	9,587.7	12,334.0	13,466.4
Sweden	48,722.1	51,551.7	54,381.0
Switzerland	5,306.0	5,583.3	4,882.7
United Kingdom	40,742.5	43,354.3	36,454.0
USA	29,323.1	28,610.2	26,178.0
Total (incl. others)	424,484.1	442,753.7	429,272.2

Transport

RAILWAYS
(traffic)

	2000	2001	2002
Number of journeys ('000) . . .	165,700	167,000	165,300
Passenger-kilometres (million) .	5,537	5,721	5,754
Goods carried ('000 tons) . . .	7,874	7,173	7,297
Ton-kilometres (million) . . .	2,025	1,961	1,906

ROAD TRAFFIC
(motor vehicles in use at 1 January)

	2002	2003	2004
Private cars	1,872,631	1,888,290	1,894,649
Vans	343,450	353,610	365,112
Buses, coaches	13,954	13,986	14,132
Lorries	36,801	35,752	34,896
Tractors	12,009	12,400	12,805
Motorcycles and mopeds . . .	146,365	151,322	155,740

SHIPPING

Merchant Fleet
(registered at 31 December)

	2001	2002	2003
Number of vessels	904	857	860
Total displacement ('000 grt) . .	6,913.5	7,403.1	7,567.0

Source: Lloyd's Register-Fairplay, *World Fleet Statistics.*

Sea-borne Freight Traffic at Danish Ports*
('000 metric tons loaded and unloaded)

	2001	2002	2003
Ålborg	2,581	2,652	2,756
Århus	9,980	9,621	9,983
Copenhagen	6,688	5,996	6,769
Fredericia	15,763	16,585	16,513
Kalundborg	8,530	7,613	8,342
Skaelskør	645	132	445
Others	49,785	51,684	59,146
Total	93,972	94,283	103,954

* Including domestic traffic and ferry traffic.

International Sea-borne Shipping*
(freight traffic, '000 metric tons)

	1999	2000	2001
Goods loaded	22,949	24,876	23,217
Goods unloaded	31,952	30,984	30,543

* Excluding international ferry traffic.

CIVIL AVIATION
(traffic on scheduled services)*

	1999	2000	2001
Kilometres flown (million) . .	82	85	92
Passengers carried ('000) . . .	5,971	5,923	6,382
Passenger-kilometres (million) .	5,883	6,128	6,952
Total ton-kilometres (million) . .	769	810	876

* Including an apportionment (2/7) of international operations by Scandinavian Airlines System (SAS).

Source: UN, *Statistical Yearbook*.

Tourism

FOREIGN TOURIST ARRIVALS
(at accommodation establishments)

Country of residence	1999	2000	2001
Finland	41,062	43,034	40,108
Germany	401,498	380,703	363,281
Italy	49,274	46,738	45,800
Netherlands	82,018	81,612	81,863
Norway	285,670	295,134	301,429
Sweden	597,102	648,036	564,769
United Kingdom	89,161	103,194	117,750
USA	84,151	93,616	97,264
Total (incl. others)	2,023,056	2,087,681	2,028,367

Tourism receipts (million US $): 3,836 in 1999; 4,038 in 2000; 4,600 in 2001; 5,785 in 2002.

Source: World Tourism Organization, mainly *Yearbook of Tourism Statistics*.

Communications Media

	2001	2002	2003
Radio licences ('000)*	2,247	2,247	n.a.
Television receivers (estimates, '000 in use) . . .	4,600	n.a.	n.a.
Book production: titles† . . .	14,319	14,154	14,843
Daily newspapers:			
Number	32	32	32
Average circulation ('000 copies)‡	1,453	1,430	1,378
Telephones ('000 main lines in use)	3,864.8	3,700.9	3,610.1
Mobile cellular telephones ('000 subscribers)	3,960.2	4,477.8	4,785.3
Personal computers (estimates, '000 in use)	2,900	3,100	n.a.
Internet users (estimates, '000) .	2,300	2,756	n.a.

* Includes combined radio and television licences.
† Including pamphlets (4,461 in 2001; 4,398 in 2002; 4,726 in 2003).
‡ On weekdays.

Facsimile machines ('000 in use): 250 in 1995.

Sources: partly International Telecommunication Union; UN, *Statistical Yearbook*.

Education

(1994/95)

	Institutions	Teachers	Students
Pre-primary	4,395	19,200	201,571
Primary	n.a.	33,100	328,875
Secondary:			
general	n.a.	37,000	321,448
vocational	n.a.	13,100	123,234
Higher	n.a.	9,600	169,783

2001/02: *Institutions*: Primary and secondary (general) 3,198; Secondary (vocational) 164; Higher 158. *Students*: Primary and secondary (general) 768,248; Secondary (vocational): 171,965; Higher 177,807.

2002/03: *Students*: Pre-primary 249,839; Primary 415,205; Secondary (general) 315,786; Secondary (vocational) 117,695; Higher 195,241.

Directory

The Constitution

The *Grundlov* (constitutional charter), summarized below, was adopted on 5 June 1953.

GOVERNMENT

The form of government is a limited (constitutional) monarchy. The legislative authority rests jointly with the Crown and the Folketing (parliament). Executive power is vested in the Crown, and the administration of justice is exercised by the courts. The Monarch can constitutionally 'do no wrong'. She exercises her authority through the Ministers appointed by her. The Ministers are responsible for the government of the country. The Constitution establishes the principle of Parliamentarism under which individual Ministers or the whole Cabinet must retire when defeated in the Folketing by a vote of 'no confidence'.

MONARCH

The Monarch acts on behalf of the State in international affairs. Except with the consent of the Folketing, she cannot, however, take any action that increases or reduces the area of the Realm or undertake any obligation, the fulfilment of which requires the co-operation of the Folketing or which is of major importance. Nor can the Monarch, without the consent of the Folketing, terminate any international agreement that has been concluded with the consent of the Folketing.

Apart from defence against armed attack on the Realm or on Danish forces, the Monarch cannot, without the consent of the Folketing, employ military force against any foreign power.

PARLIAMENT

The Folketing (parliament) is an assembly consisting of not more than 179 members, two of whom are elected in the Faroe Islands and two in Greenland. Danish nationals, having attained 18 years of age, with permanent residence in Denmark, have the franchise and are eligible for election. The members of the Folketing are elected for four years. Election is by a system of proportional representation, with direct and secret ballot on lists in large constituencies. A bill adopted by the Folketing may be submitted to referendum, when such referendum is claimed by not less than one-third of the members of the Folketing and not later than three days after the adoption. The bill is void if rejected by a majority of the votes cast, representing not less than 30% of all electors.

The Government

HEAD OF STATE

Queen of Denmark: HM Queen MARGRETHE II (succeeded to the throne 14 January 1972).

THE CABINET
(April 2005)

A coalition of Venstre (V—Liberals) and Det Konservative Folkeparti (DKF—Conservative People's Party).

Prime Minister: ANDERS FOGH RASMUSSEN (V).

Deputy Prime Minister and Minister of Economic Affairs, Business and Trade: BENDT BENDTSON (DKF).

Minister of Foreign Affairs: Dr PER STIG MØLLER (DKF).

Minister of Finance: THOR PEDERSEN (V).

Minister of Employment: CLAUS HJORT FREDERIKSEN (V).

Minister of Justice: LENE ESPERSEN (DKF).

Minister of Cultural Affairs: BRIAN MIKKELSEN (DKF).

Minister of Education and of Ecclesiastical Affairs: BERTEL HAARDER (V).

Minister of Transport and Energy: FLEMMING HANSEN (DKF).

Minister of Science, Technology and Innovation: HELGE SANDER (V).

Minister of Food, Agriculture and Fisheries: HANS CHRISTIAN SCHMIDT (V).

Minister of Interior Affairs and Health: LARS LØKKE RASMUSSEN (V).

Minister of Development Co-operation: ULLA TØRNÆS (V).

Minister of Defence: SØREN GADE JENSEN (V).

Minister of Social Affairs and Gender Equality: EVA KJER HANSEN (V).

Minister of the Environment and of Nordic Affairs: CONNIE HEDEGAARD (DKF).

Minister of Taxation: KRISTIAN JENSEN (V).

Minister of Refugees, Immigration and Integration Affairs: RIKKE HVILSHØJ (V).

Minister of Family and Consumer Affairs: LARS BARFOED (DKF).

MINISTRIES

Prime Minister's Office: Christiansborg, Prins Jørgens Gård 11, 1218 Copenhagen K; tel. 33-92-33-00; fax 33-11-16-65; e-mail stm@stm.dk; internet www.stm.dk.

Ministry of Culture: Nybrogade 2, POB 2140, 1015 Copenhagen K; tel. 33-92-33-70; fax 33-91-33-88; e-mail kum@kum.dk; internet www.kum.dk.

Ministry of Defence: Holmens Kanal 42, 1060 Copenhagen K; tel. 33-92-33-20; fax 33-32-06-55; e-mail fmn@fmn.dk; internet www.fmn.dk.

Ministry of Ecclesiastical Affairs: Frederiksholms Kanal 21, POB 2123, 1015 Copenhagen K; tel. 33-92-33-90; fax 33-92-39-13; e-mail km@km.dk; internet www.km.dk.

Ministry of Economic Affairs, Business and Trade: Slotsholmsgade 10–12, 1216 Copenhagen K; tel. 33-92-33-50; fax 33-12-37-78; e-mail oem@oem.dk; internet www.oem.dk.

Ministry of Education: Frederiksholms Kanal 21–25, 1220 Copenhagen K; tel. 33-92-50-00; fax 33-92-55-47; e-mail uvm@uvm.dk; internet www.uvm.dk.

Ministry of Employment: Ved Stranden 8, 1061 Copenhagen K; tel. 33-92-59-00; fax 33-12-13-78; e-mail bm@bm.dk; internet www.bm.dk.

Ministry of the Environment: Højbro Pl. 4, 1200 Copenhagen K; tel. 33-92-76-00; fax 33-32-22-27; e-mail mim@mim.dk; internet www.mim.dk.

Ministry of Finance: Christiansborg Slotspl. 1, 1218 Copenhagen K; tel. 33-92-33-33; fax 33-32-30-80; e-mail fm@fm.dk; internet www.fm.dk.

Ministry of Food, Agriculture and Fisheries: Holbergsgade 2, 1057 Copenhagen K; tel. 33-92-33-01; fax 33-14-50-42; e-mail fvm@fvm.dk; internet www.fvm.dk.

Ministry of Foreign Affairs: Asiatisk Pl. 2, 1448 Copenhagen K; tel. 33-92-00-00; fax 32-54-05-33; e-mail um@um.dk; internet www.um.dk.

Ministry of Justice: Slotsholmsgade 10, 1216 Copenhagen K; tel. 33-92-33-40; fax 33-93-35-10; e-mail jm@jm.dk; internet www.jm.dk.

Ministry of Refugees, Immigration and Integration Affairs: Holbergsgade 6, 1057 Copenhagen K; tel. 33-92-33-80; fax 33-11-12-39; e-mail inm@inm.dk; internet www.inm.dk.

Ministry of Science, Technology and Innovation: Bredgade 43, 1260 Copenhagen K; tel. 33-92-97-00; fax 33-32-35-01; e-mail vtu@vtu.dk; internet www.videnskabsministeriet.dk.

Ministry of Social Affairs and Gender Equality: Holmens Kanal 22, 1060 Copenhagen K; tel. 33-92-93-00; fax 33-93-25-18; e-mail sm@sm.dk; internet www.sm.dk.

Ministry of Taxation: Nicolai Eigtveds Gade 28, 1402 Copenhagen K; tel. 33-92-33-92; fax 33-14-91-05; e-mail skm@skm.dk; internet www.skat.dk.

Ministry of Transport: Frederiksholms Kanal 27, 1220 Copenhagen K; tel. 33-92-33-55; fax 33-12-38-93; e-mail trm@trm.dk; internet www.trm.dk.

Legislature

FOLKETING

Christiansborg, 1240 Copenhagen K; tel. 33-37-55-00; fax 33-32-85-36; e-mail folketinget@folketinget.dk; internet www.folketinget.dk.

President of the Folketing: CHRISTIAN MEJDAHL.

Secretary-General: HENRIK TVARNØ.

General Election, 8 February 2005
(metropolitan Denmark only)

Party	Votes	% of votes	Seats
Venstre (Liberals)	974,636	29.03	52
Socialdemokratiet (Social Democrats)	867,349	25.84	47
Dansk Folkeparti (Danish People's Party)	444,947	13.25	24
Det Konservative Folkeparti (Conservative People's Party) .	344,886	10.27	18
Det Radikale Venstre (Social Liberals)	308,212	9.18	17
Socialistik Folkeparti (Socialist People's Party)	201,047	5.99	11
Enhedslisten—De Rød-Grønne (Red-Green Alliance) . . .	114,123	3.40	6
Kristendemokraterne (Christian Democrats)	58,071	1.73	—
Centrum-Demokraterne (Centre Democrats)	33,880	1.01	—
Minoritetspartiet (Minority Party)	8,850	0.26	—
Independents	1,211	0.04	—
Total	3,357,212	100.00	175

The Folketing also includes two members from Greenland and two from the Faroe Islands.

Political Organizations

Arbejderpartiet Kommunisterne (APK) (Workers' Communist Party): Skibhusvej 100, 5000 Odense C; tel. 66-14-89-83; fax 66-19-19-83; e-mail apk@apk2000.dk; internet www.apk2000.dk; f. 2000; Marxist-Leninist.

Centrum-Demokraterne (Centre Democrats): Ny Vestergade 7, 1471 Copenhagen K; tel. 33-12-71-15; fax 33-12-01-15; e-mail landskontoret@centrumdemokraterne.dk; internet www.centrumdemokraterne.dk; f. 1973; opposes extreme ideologies, supports EU and NATO; Leader MIMI JAKOBSEN; Nat. Chair. PETER DUETOFT.

Danmarks Kommunistiske Parti (Danish Communist Party): Studiestræde 24, 1455 Copenhagen K; tel. 33-91-66-44; fax 33-32-03-72; e-mail dkp@dkp.dk; internet www.dkp.dk; f. 1919; Chair. HENRIK STAMER HEDIN.

Danmarks Kommunistiske Parti/Marxister Leninister (Marxist-Leninist Party): Griffenfeldsgade 26, 2200 Copenhagen K; tel. 35-35-60-69; fax 35-37-20-39; e-mail dkp-ml@dkp-ml.dk; internet www.dkp-ml.dk; Sec.-Gen. JØRGEN PETERSEN.

Danmarks Nationalsocialistike Bevægelse (DNSB) (Danish National Socialist Movement): Hundige Strandvej 153, POB 32, 2670 Greve; tel. 43-90-98-55; fax 43-90-72-71; internet www.dnsb.info.

Dansk Folkeparti (Danish People's Party): Christiansborg, 1240 Copenhagen K; tel. 33-37-51-99; fax 33-37-51-91; e-mail df@ft.dk; internet www.danskfolkeparti.dk; f. 1995 by defectors from the Progress Party; right-wing; Leader PIA KJAERSGAARD.

Enhedslisten—De Rød-Grønne (Red-Green Alliance): Studiestræde 24, 1455 Copenhagen K; tel. 33-93-33-24; fax 33-32-03-72; e-mail landskontoret@enhedslisten.dk; internet www.enhedslisten.dk; f. 1989 by three left-wing parties; membership of individual socialists; 21-mem. collective leadership.

Folkebevægelsen mod EU (People's Movement Against the European Union): Sigurdsgade 39A, 2200 Copenhagen N; tel. 35-82-18-00; fax 35-82-18-06; e-mail folkebevaegelsen@folkebevaegelsen.dk; internet www.folkebevaegelsen.dk; opposes membership of the EU, in favour of self-determination for Denmark and all European countries; 21-mem. collective leadership.

Fremskridtspartiet (Progress Party): POB 180, 2630 Taastrup; tel. 70-26-20-27; fax 70-26-23-27; e-mail frp@frp.dk; internet www .frp.dk; f. 1972; right-wing; advocates gradual abolition of income tax, disbandment of most of the civil service, and abolition of diplomatic service and about 90% of legislation; Chair. JOHANNES SØRENSEN; Leader KIRSTEN JACOBSEN; Sec.-Gen. MARTIN IPSEN.

De Grønne/Økologisk-realistik Alternativ (Green Party/The Realistic Ecological Alternative): Hjortekærbakken 10, 2800 Lyngby; tel. 45-88-94-79; e-mail grondebat@groenne.dk; internet www.groenne.dk; f. 1983; reformed 1991.

Grønne Demokrater (Green Democrats): Mejerivej 35, 8300 Odder; tel. 86-54-19-85; e-mail admin@groennedemokrater.dk; internet www.groennedemokrater.dk.

Det Humanistiske Parti (The Humanist Party): Copenhagen; tel. 31-24-70-60; pro-democratic, non-violent; Chair. CHRISTIAN ADAMSEN.

JuniBevægelsen (June Movement): Kronprinsensegade 2, 1114 Copenhagen K; tel. 33-93-00-46; fax 33-93-30-67; e-mail jb@ junibevaegelsen.dk; internet www.junibevaegelsen.dk; f. 1992; opposes EU federalism; Leaders JENS-PETER BONDE, HANNE DAHL, TRINE PERTOU-MACH.

Kommunistisk Parti i Danmark: Frederikssundsvej 82, 2400 Copenhagen NV; tel. 38-88-28-33; e-mail kpid@kpid.dk; internet www.kpid.dk; Chair. BETTY FRYDENSBJERG CARLSSON.

Det Konservative Folkeparti (Conservative People's Party): Nyhavn 4, 1051 Copenhagen K; tel. 33-13-41-40; fax 33-93-37-73; e-mail info@konservative.dk; internet www.konservative.dk; f. 1916; advocates free initiative and the maintenance of private property, but recognizes the right of the State to take action to keep the economic and social balance; Leader BENDT BENDTSEN; Sec.-Gen. MORTEN BANGSGAARD.

Kristendemokraterne (Christian Democrats): Allégade 24A, I., 2000 Frederiksberg; tel. 33-27-78-10; fax 33-21-31-16; e-mail kd@kd .dk; internet www.kd.dk; f. 1970 as Kristeligt Folkeparti (Christian People's Party), present name adopted 2003; emphasizes the need for political decisions based on Christian ethics; Chair. MARIANNE KARLMOSE NIELSEN; Sec.-Gen. BØRGE KLIT JOHANSEN.

Minoritetspartiet (Minority Party): Biblioteksvej 53A, 1., 2650 Hvidovre; tel. 36-49-03-00; e-mail info@minoritetspartiet.dk; internet www.minoritetspartiet.dk; f. 2000; centre-left party based on humanistic values; Chair. RUNE ENGELBRETH LARSEN.

Det Radikale Venstre (Social Liberals): Christiansborg, 1240 Copenhagen K; tel. 33-37-47-47; fax 33-13-72-51; e-mail radikale@ radikale.dk; internet www.radikale.dk; f. 1905; supports international *détente* and co-operation within regional and world organizations, social reforms without socialism, incomes policy, workers' participation in industry, state intervention in industrial disputes, state control of trusts and monopolies, strengthening private enterprise; Chair. SØREN BALD; Leader MARIANNE JELVED; Gen. Sec. ANDERS KLOPPENBORG.

Retsforbundet—Danmarks Retsforbund (Justice Party): Lyngbyvej 42, 2100 Copenhagen Ø; tel. 39-20-44-88; fax 39-20-44-50; e-mail sekretariat@retsforbundet.dk; internet www.retsforbundet .dk; f. 1919; programme is closely allied to Henry George's teachings (single tax, free trade); Chair. LARS BAEKGAARD.

Schleswigsche Partei/Slesvigsk Parti (SP) (Schleswig Party): Vestergade 30, 6200 Åbenrå; tel. 74-62-38-33; fax 74-62-79-39; e-mail sp@bdn.dk; internet www.schleswigsche-partei.dk; f. 1920; represents the German minority in North Schleswig; Chair. GERHARD D. MAMMEN.

Socialdemokratiet (Social Democrats): Danasvej 7, 1910 Frederiksberg C; tel. 70-30-08-00; fax 70-30-08-50; e-mail s@ socialdemokraterne.dk; internet www.socialdemokraterne.dk; f. 1871; finds its chief adherents among workers, employees and public servants; 50,000 mems; Leader HELLE THORNING-SCHMIDT; Gen. Sec. JENS CHRISTIANSEN.

Socialistisk Arbejderparti (Socialist Workers' Party): Studiestræde 24, o.g. 1. sal, 1455 Copenhagen K; tel. 33-33-79-48; fax 33-33-03-17; e-mail sap@sap-fi.dk; internet www.sap-fi.dk.

Socialistisk Folkeparti (Socialist People's Party): Christiansborg, 1240 Copenhagen K; tel. 33-37-44-44; fax 33-32-72-48; e-mail sf@sf .dk; internet www.sf.dk; f. 1959; socialist; Chair. VILLY SØVNDAL; Parliamentary Leader AAGE FRANDSEN; Sec. TURID LEIRVOLL.

Venstre (Liberals): Søllerødvej 30, 2840 Holte; tel. 45-80-22-33; fax 45-80-38-30; e-mail venstre@venstre.dk; internet www.venstre.dk; f. 1870; supports free trade, a minimum of state interference, and the adoption, in matters of social expenditure, of a modern general social security system; 72,850 mems (2004); Pres. ANDERS FOGH RASMUSSEN; Sec.-Gen. JENS SKIPPER RASMUSSEN.

Venstresocialisterne (VS) (Left Socialist Party of Denmark): Solidaritetshuset, Griffenfeldsgade 41, 2200 Copenhagen N; tel. and fax 35-35-06-08; internet www.venstresocialisterne.dk; f. 1968; revolutionary, Marxist, democratic, socialist party.

Diplomatic Representation

EMBASSIES IN DENMARK

Albania: Ny Østergade 7, 5th Floor, 1101 Copenhagen K; tel. 33-91-79-79; fax 33-91-79-69; e-mail embassyofalbania@mail.dk; Chargé d'affaires a.i. QEMAL MINXHOZI.

Algeria: Amaliegade 36, 1256 Copenhagen K; tel. 33-11-94-40; fax 33-11-58-50; e-mail ambalda@mail.tele.dk; Ambassador MALIKA SACI.

Argentina: Borgergade 16, I., 1300 Copenhagen K; tel. 33-15-80-82; fax 33-15-55-74; e-mail edina@mrecic.gov.ar; Ambassador JUAN CARLOS KRECKLER.

Australia: Dampfærgevej 26, 2100 Copenhagen Ø; tel. 70-26-36-76; fax 70-26-36-86; e-mail australian.embassy@mail.dk; internet www .denmark.embassy.gov.au; Ambassador RICHARD MATTHEW PEEK.

Austria: Sølundsvej 1, 2100 Copenhagen Ø; tel. 39-29-41-41; fax 39-29-20-86; e-mail kopenhagen-ob@bmaa.gv.at; Ambassador ERICH BUTTENHAUSER.

Belgium: Øster Allé 7, 2100 Copenhagen Ø; tel. 35-25-02-00; fax 35-25-02-11; e-mail copenhagen@diplobel.be; internet www.diplomatie .be/copenhagen; Ambassador MICHEL LASTCHENKO.

Bolivia: Amaliegade 16C, 2nd Floor, 1256 Copenhagen K; tel. 33-12-49-00; fax 33-12-49-03; e-mail embolivia.copenhague@tiscali.dk; Ambassador BARBARA CANDEO PATIÑO.

Bosnia and Herzegovina: H. C. Andersens Blvd 48, 2nd Floor, 1553 Copenhagen V; tel. 33-33-80-40; fax 33-33-80-17; e-mail ba-emb-dk-cph@mobilxnet.dk; internet www.embassybh.dk; Ambassador SEAD MASLO.

Brazil: Ryvangs Allé 24, 2100 Copenhagen Ø; tel. 39-20-64-78; fax 39-27-36-07; e-mail ambassade@brazil.dk; Ambassador MARCO CÉSAR MEIRA NASLAUSKY.

Bulgaria: Gamlehave Allé 7, 2920 Charlottenlund; tel. 39-64-24-84; fax 39-63-49-23; e-mail bg-embassy@mail.tdcadsl.dk; Ambassador Prof. DIMO VASSILEV DIMOV.

Burkina Faso: Svanemøllevej 20, 2100 Copenhagen Ø; tel. 39-18-40-22; fax 39-27-18-86; e-mail amba@ambaburkina.dk; internet www.ambaburkina.dk; Ambassador CÉLINE M. YODA.

Canada: Kr. Bernikowsgade 1, 1105 Copenhagen K; tel. 33-48-32-00; fax 33-48-32-20; e-mail copen@dfait-maeci.gc.ca; internet www .canada.dk; Ambassador FREDERICKA GREGORY.

Chile: Kastelsvej 15, 3rd Floor, 2100 Copenhagen Ø; tel. 35-38-58-34; fax 35-38-42-01; e-mail embassy@chiledk.dk; internet www .chiledk.dk; Ambassador JAIME LAGOS ERAZO.

China, People's Republic: Øregårds Allé 25, 2900 Hellerup; tel. 39-46-08-89; fax 39-62-54-84; e-mail mail@chinaembassy.dk; internet www.chinaembassy.dk; Ambassador ZHEN JIANGUO.

Côte d'Ivoire: Gersonsvej 8, 2900 Hellerup; tel. 39-62-88-22; fax 39-62-01-62; e-mail ambaivoire@mail.tele.dk; internet www.ambaci.dk; Ambassador DJEROU ROBERT LY.

Croatia: Frederiksgade 19, 1st Floor, 1265 Copenhagen K; tel. 33-91-90-95; fax 33-91-71-31; e-mail kopvel@mail.dk; Ambassador ANA MARIJA BESKER.

Cuba: Carolinevej 12, Ground Floor left, 2900 Hellerup; tel. and fax 39-40-15-10; e-mail ambadin@hotmail.com; internet www .cubaembassy.dk; Chargé d'affaires a.i. PEDRO PABLO PRADA.

Cyprus: Borgegade 28, 1st Floor, 1300 Copenhagen K; tel. 33-91-58-88; fax 33-91-58-77; e-mail consulate@cyprus-embassy.dk; Ambassador ANTONIS TOUMAZIS.

Czech Republic: Ryvangs Allé 14–16, 2100 Copenhagen Ø; tel. 39-29-18-88; fax 39-29-09-30; e-mail copenhagen@embassy.mzv.cz; internet www.czechembassy.dk; Ambassador MARIE KOSTÁLOVÁ.

Egypt: Kristianiagade 19, 2100 Copenhagen Ø; tel. 35-43-70-70; fax 35-25-32-62; Ambassador MONA OMAR ATTIA.

Eritrea: Rosbæksvej 11, 2100 Copenhagen Ø; tel. 39-27-69-91; fax 39-47-40-41; e-mail emberit@mail.dk; Chargé d'affaires BERKHET-AB HABTEMARIAM OGBAZGHI.

Estonia: Aurehøjvej 19, 2900 Hellerup; tel. 39-46-30-70; fax 39-46-30-76; e-mail embassy.copenhagen@mfa.ee; internet www.estemb .dk; Ambassador TAAVI TOOM.

Finland: Skt Annæ Pl. 24, 1250 Copenhagen K; tel. 33-13-42-14; fax 33-32-47-10; e-mail sanomat.kob@formin.fi; internet www.finlandembassy.dk; Ambassador PEKKA OJANEN.

France: Kongens Nytorv 4, 1050 Copenhagen K; tel. 33-67-01-00; fax 33-93-97-52; e-mail info@amba-france.dk; internet www.amba-france.dk; Ambassador RÉGIS DE BELENET.

Germany: Stockholmsgade 57, POB 2712, 2100 Copenhagen Ø; tel. 35-45-99-00; fax 35-26-71-05; e-mail tyskeamba@email.dk; internet www.kopenhagen.diplo.de; Ambassador JOHANNES DOHMES.

Ghana: Egebjerg Allé 13, 2900 Hellerup; tel. 39-62-82-22; fax 39-62-16-52; e-mail ghana@mail.dk; Ambassador EMMANUEL K. ADU.

Greece: Borgergade 16, 1300 Copenhagen K; tel. 33-11-45-33; fax 33-93-16-46; e-mail greekembcop@post.tele.dk; Ambassador STAVROS VASSILOPOULOS.

Hungary: Strandvejen 170, 2920 Charlottenlund; tel. 39-63-16-88; fax 39-63-00-52; e-mail huembcph@teliamail.dk; internet www.hungarianembassy.dk; Ambassador OTTÓ RÓNA.

Iceland: Strandgade 89, 1401 Copenhagen K; tel. 33-18-10-50; fax 33-18-10-59; e-mail icemb.coph@utn.stjr.is; Ambassador ÞORSTEINN PÁLSSON.

India: Vangehusvej 15, 2100 Copenhagen Ø; tel. 39-18-00-65; fax 39-27-02-18; e-mail indemb@euroconnect.dk; internet www.indian-embassy.dk; Ambassador HARSH KUNAR BHASIN.

Indonesia: Ørehøj Allé 1, 2900 Hellerup; tel. 39-62-44-22; fax 39-62-44-83; e-mail indon-dk@cybernet.dk; internet www.cybernet.dk/users/indon.dk; Ambassador PERWITORINI WIJONO.

Iran: Svanemøllevej 48, 2100 Copenhagen Ø; tel. 39-16-00-03; fax 39-16-00-75; e-mail iran-embassy@iran-embassy.dk; internet www.iran-embassy.dk; Ambassador AHMAD DANIALY.

Ireland: Østbanegade 21, 2100 Copenhagen Ø; tel. 35-42-32-33; fax 35-43-18-58; e-mail irlemb@email.dk; Ambassador JAMES BRENNAN.

Israel: Lundevangsvej 4, 2900 Hellerup; tel. 88-15-55-00; fax 88-15-55-55; e-mail info@copenhagen.mfa.gov.il; internet www.embassy-of-israel.dk; Ambassador DAVID WALZER.

Italy: Gammel Vartov Vej 7, 2900 Hellerup; tel. 39-62-68-77; fax 39-62-25-99; e-mail amba-info@italien-online.dk; internet www.italien-online.dk; Ambassador ROBERTO DI LEO.

Japan: Pilestræde 61, 1112 Copenhagen K; tel. 33-11-33-44; fax 33-11-33-77; e-mail info@embjapan.dk; internet www.embjapan.dk; Ambassador GOTARO OGAWA.

Korea, Republic: Svanemøllevej 104, 2900 Hellerup; tel. 39-46-04-00; fax 39-46-04-22; e-mail korembdk@post.tele.dk; internet www.koremb.dk; Ambassador HYO-SEUNG AHN.

Latvia: Rosbæksvej 17, 2100 Copenhagen Ø; tel. 39-27-60-00; fax 39-27-61-73; e-mail embassy.denmark@mfa.gov.lv; Ambassador INDULIS BERZINS.

Lesotho: Bøgevej 17, 2900 Hellerup; tel. 39-62-43-43; fax 39-62-15-38; e-mail lesotho.copenhagen@mail.dk; Ambassador Dr THEKISO GLADWIN KHATI.

Libya: Rosenvængets Hovedvej 4, 2100 Copenhagen Ø; tel. 35-26-36-11; fax 35-26-56-06; e-mail libyan-peoples-bureau@c.dk; Chargé d'affaires a.i. Dr MOHAMED ALI EL-FANDI.

Lithuania: Bernstorffsvej 214, 2920 Charlottenlund; tel. 39-63-62-07; fax 39-63-65-32; e-mail mail@lit-embassy.dk; internet www.lit-embassy.dk; Ambassador DEIVIDAS MATULIONIS.

Luxembourg: Fridtjof Nansens Pl. 5, 1st Floor, 2100 Copenhagen Ø; tel. 35-26-82-00; fax 35-26-82-08; e-mail copenhague.amb@mae.etat.lu; Ambassador GASTON STRONCK.

Macedonia, former Yugoslav republic: Kildergaardsvej 36, 2900 Hellerup; tel. 39-76-69-20; fax 39-76-69-23; e-mail makambas@post3.tele.dk; Ambassador Prof. Dr SAMI IBRAIMI.

Malta: Ny Østergade 7, 4th Floor, 1101 Copenhagen K; tel. 33-15-30-90; fax 33-15-30-91; e-mail maltaembassy.copenhagen@gov.mt; Ambassador CARMEL J. AQUILINA.

Mexico: Strandvejen 64E, 2900 Hellerup; tel. 39-61-05-00; fax 39-61-05-12; e-mail info@mexican-embassy.dk; internet www.mexican-embassy.dk; Ambassador MARTHA BARCENA-COQUI.

Morocco: Øregårds Allé 19, 2900 Hellerup; tel. 39-62-45-11; fax 39-62-24-49; e-mail sifamadk@mail.dk; Ambassador AÏCHA EL KABBAJ.

Netherlands: Toldbodgade 33, 1253 Copenhagen K; tel. 33-70-72-00; fax 33-14-03-50; e-mail nlgovkop@newmail.dk; internet www.nlembassy.dk; Ambassador HANS A. F. M. FÖRSTER.

Nicaragua: Kastelsvej 7, Ground Floor, 2100 Copenhagen Ø; tel. 35-55-48-70; fax 35-55-48-75; e-mail embajada@emb-nicaragua.dk; Ambassador Dr RICARDO JOSÉ ALVARADO NOGUERA.

Norway: Amaliegade 39, 1256 Copenhagen K; tel. 33-14-01-24; fax 33-14-06-24; e-mail emb.copenhagen@mfa.no; internet www.norsk.dk; Ambassador OLE PETER KOLBY.

Pakistan: Valeursvej 17, 2900 Hellerup; tel. 39-62-11-88; fax 39-40-10-70; e-mail parepcopenhagen@hotmail.com; Ambassador JARED A. QURESHI.

Poland: Richelieus Allé 12, 2900 Hellerup; tel. 39-46-77-00; fax 39-46-77-66; e-mail mail@ambpol.dk; internet www.ambpol.dk; Ambassador BARBARA TUGE-ERECINSKA.

Portugal: Toldbodgade 31, 2nd Floor, 1253 Copenhagen K; tel. 33-13-13-01; fax 33-14-92-14; e-mail embport@get2net.dk; Ambassador JOSÉ DE FREITAS FERRAZ.

Romania: Strandagervej 27, 2900 Hellerup; tel. 39-40-71-77; fax 39-62-78-99; e-mail roemb@mail.tele.dk; internet www.romanianembassy.dk; Ambassador Dr VLAD-ANDREI MOGA.

Russia: Kristianiagade 5, 2100 Copenhagen Ø; tel. 35-42-55-85; fax 35-42-37-41; e-mail embrus@mail.dk; internet www.denmark.mid.ru; Ambassador DMITRIY RYURIKOV.

Saudi Arabia: Lille Strandvej 27, 2900 Hellerup; tel. 39-62-12-00; fax 39-62-60-09; e-mail embassy@saudiemb.dk; Ambassador MOHAMMAD IBRAHIM AL-HEJAILAN.

Serbia and Montenegro: Svanevænget 36, 2100 Copenhagen Ø; tel. 39-29-77-84; fax 39-29-79-19; e-mail yuembdk@vip.cybercity.dk; Ambassador VLADIMIR RADULOVIĆ.

Slovakia: Vesterled 26–28, 2100 Copenhagen Ø; tel. 39-20-99-11; fax 39-20-99-12; e-mail embassy@copenhagen.mfa.sk; internet www.foreign.gov.sk; Ambassador ROMAN BUZEK.

Slovenia: Amaliegade 6, 1256 Copenhagen K; tel. 33-73-01-20; fax 33-15-06-07; e-mail slovenija@ofir.dk; Ambassador RUDOLF GABROVEC.

South Africa: Gammel Vartov Vej 8, POB 128, 2900 Hellerup; tel. 39-18-01-55; fax 39-18-40-06; e-mail sa.embassy@southafrica.dk; internet www.southafrica.dk; Ambassador STEPHEN P. GAWE.

Spain: Kristianiagade 21, 2100 Copenhagen Ø; tel. 35-42-47-00; fax 35-42-47-26; e-mail embespdk@mail.mae.es; Ambassador CARLOS BÁRCENA PORTOLÉS.

Swaziland: Kastelsvej 19, 2100 Copenhagen Ø; tel. 35-42-61-11; fax 35-42-63-00; e-mail embassy@swaziland.dk; Ambassador Prince DAVID DLAMINI.

Sweden: Skt Annæ Pl. 15A, 1250 Copenhagen K; tel. 33-36-03-70; fax 33-36-03-95; e-mail ambassaden.kopenhamn@foreign.ministry.se; internet www.sverigesambassad.dk; Ambassador CARL-MAGNUS HYLTENIUS.

Switzerland: Amaliegade 14, 1256 Copenhagen K; tel. 33-14-17-96; fax 33-33-75-51; e-mail vertretung@cop.rep.admin.ch; internet www.eda.admin.ch/copenh_emb; Ambassador ANDRÉ FAIVET.

Thailand: Norgesmindevej 18, 2900 Hellerup; tel. 39-62-50-10; fax 39-62-50-59; e-mail thai-dk@inet.uni2.dk; Ambassador ADISAK PANUPONG.

Turkey: Rosbæksvej 15, 2100 Copenhagen Ø; tel. 39-20-27-88; fax 39-20-51-66; e-mail turkembassy@internet.dk; internet www.turkembassy.dk; Ambassador FÜGEN OK.

Uganda: Sofievej 15, 2900 Hellerup; tel. 39-62-09-66; fax 39-61-01-48; e-mail ugandaembassy@mail.dk; internet www.ugandaembassy.dk; Ambassador OMAR MIGADDE LUBULWA.

Ukraine: Toldbodgade 37A, 1st Floor, 1253 Copenhagen K; tel. 33-16-15-35; fax 33-16-00-74; e-mail embassy.ua@mail.tele.dk; internet www.ukraine-embassy.dk; Chargé d'affaires a.i. YURII PAVLOV.

United Kingdom: Kastelsvej 36–40, 2100 Copenhagen Ø; tel. 35-44-52-00; fax 35-44-52-93; e-mail enquiry.copenhagen@fco.gov.uk; internet www.britishembassy.dk; Ambassador Sir NICHOLAS BROWNE.

USA: Dag Hammarskjølds Allé 24, 2100 Copenhagen Ø; tel. 35-55-31-44; fax 35-43-02-23; internet www.usembassy.dk; Ambassador STUART A. BERNSTEIN.

Venezuela: Tolbodgade 31, 3., 1253 Copenhagen K; tel. 33-93-63-11; fax 33-37-76-59; e-mail emvendk@mail.dk; internet www.ve-ambassade.dk; Ambassador VINCENTE EMILIO VALLENILLA.

Viet Nam: Gammel Vartov Vej 20, 2900 Hellerup; tel. 39-18-39-32; fax 39-18-41-71; e-mail info@vietnamemb.dk; internet www.vietnamemb.dk; Ambassador VU QUANG DIEM.

Judicial System

In Denmark the judiciary is independent of the Government. Judges are appointed by the Crown on the recommendation of the Minister of Justice and cannot be dismissed except by judicial sentence.

The ordinary courts are divided into three instances, the Lower Courts, the High Courts and the Supreme Court. There is one Lower Court for each of the 82 judicial districts in the country. These courts must have at least one judge trained in law and they hear the majority of minor cases. The two High Courts serve Jutland and the islands respectively. They serve as appeal courts for cases from the Lower Courts, but are also used to give first hearing to the more important cases. Each case must be heard by at least three judges. The Supreme Court, at which at least five judges must sit, is the court of appeal for cases from the High Courts. Usually only one appeal is allowed from either court, but in special instances the Board of Appeal may give leave for a second appeal, to the Supreme Court, from a case that started in a Lower Court. Furthermore, in certain minor cases, appeal from the Lower Courts to the High Courts is allowed only by leave of appeal from the Board of Appeal.

There is a special Maritime and Commercial Court in Copenhagen, consisting of a President and two Vice-Presidents with legal training and a number of commercial and nautical assessors; there is also a Labour Court, which deals with labour disputes.

An Ombudsman is appointed by Parliament after each general election, and is concerned with the quality and legality of the administration of the laws and administrative provisions. Although the Ombudsman holds no formal power to change decisions taken by the administration, he may, on a legal basis, express criticism of acts and decisions of administrative bodies. He is obliged to present an annual report to Parliament.

Supreme Court

Prins Jørgens Gård 13, 1218 Copenhagen K; tel. 33-63-27-50; fax 33-15-00-10; e-mail post@hoejesteret.dk; internet www.hoejesteret.dk.

President of the Supreme Court: TORBEN MELCHIOR.

President of the East High Court: SVEN ZIEGLER.

President of the West High Court: BJARNE CHRISTENSEN.

President of the Maritime and Commercial Court: JENS FEILBERG.

President of the Labour Court: BØRGE DAHL.

Ombudsman: HANS GAMMELTOFT-HANSEN.

Religion

CHRISTIANITY

Det Økumeniske Fællesraad i Danmark (Ecumenical Council of Denmark): Dag Hammarskjölds Allé 17/3, 2100 Copenhagen Ø; tel. 35-43-29-43; fax 35-43-29-44; e-mail oikoumene@oikoumene.dk; internet www.oikoumene.dk; f. 1939; associate council of the World Council of Churches; six mem. churches, one observer; Chair. Dr PETER LODBERG; Gen. Sec. HOLGER LAM.

The National Church

Den evangelisk-lutherske Folkekirke i Danmark (Evangelical Lutheran Church in Denmark)

Nørregade 11, 1165 Copenhagen K; tel. 33-47-65-00; fax 33-14-39-69.

The established Church of Denmark, supported by the State; no bishop exercises a presiding role, but the Bishop of Copenhagen is responsible for certain co-ordinating questions. Council on International Relations of the Evangelical Lutheran Church in Denmark (Peter Bangs Vej 1D, 2000 Frederiksberg; e-mail interchurch@interchurch.dk; internet www.interchurch.dk) is responsible for ecumenical relations. Membership in 2002 was 4,526,693 (84.3% of the population).

Bishop of Copenhagen: ERIK NORMAN SVENDSEN.

Bishop of Helsingør: LISE LOTTE REBEL.

Bishop of Roskilde: JAN LINDHARDT.

Bishop of Lolland-Falster: HOLGER JEPSEN.

Bishop of Odense: KRESTEN DREJERGAARD.

Bishop of Ålborg: SØREN LODBERG HVAS.

Bishop of Viborg: KARSTEN NISSEN.

Bishop of Århus: KJELD HOLM.

Bishop of Ribe: ELISABETH DONS CHRISTENSEN.

Bishop of Haderslev: NIELS HENRIK ARENDT.

The Roman Catholic Church

Denmark comprises a single diocese, directly responsible to the Holy See. At 31 December 2003 there were an estimated 35,745 adherents in the country. The Bishop participates in the Scandinavian Episcopal Conference (based in Sweden).

Bishop of Copenhagen: CZESLAW KOZON, Katolsk Bispekontor, Bredgade 69A, 1260 Copenhagen K; tel. 33-11-60-80; fax 33-14-60-86; e-mail bispekontor@katolsk.dk.

Other Churches

Apostolic Church in Denmark: Lykkegaardsvej 100, 6000 Kolding; tel. 79-32-16-00; fax 79-32-16-01; e-mail servicecenter@apostolic.dk; internet www.apostolic.dk; Nat. Leader JOHANNES HANSEN.

Baptistkirken i Danmark (Baptist Union of Denmark): Købnerhus, Lærdalsgade 7, 2300 Copenhagen S; tel. 32-59-07-08; fax 32-59-01-33; e-mail sekretariat@baptistkirken.dk; internet www.baptistkirken.dk; f. 1839; 5,100 mems; Pres. TORBEN ANDERSEN.

Church of England: St Alban's Church, Churchillparken 11, 1263 Copenhagen K; tel. 39-62-77-36; fax 39-62-77-35; e-mail chaplain@st-albans.dk; internet www.st-albans.dk; f. 1728; Chaplain MARK OAKLEY.

Church of Jesus Christ of Latter-day Saints (Mormons): Copenhagen; tel. 66-11-17-00; fax 99-11-17-25; e-mail noa@noa.dk; in Denmark 1850; c. 4,500 mems in 23 congregations.

Det Danske Missionsforbund (Danish Mission Covenant Church): Rosenlunden 17, 5000 Odense C; tel. 66-14-83-31; fax 66-14-83-00; e-mail ddm@email.dk; internet www.missionsforbundet.dk; Exec. Dir PALLE BYG.

First Church of Christ, Scientist, Copenhagen: Nyvej 7, 1851 Frederiksberg C; tel. 33-13-08-91; e-mail cs.rr@email.dk; also in Århus; tel. 86-16-22-78.

German Lutheran Church: Skt Petri Church Office, Larslejsstræde 11, 1451 Copenhagen K; tel. 33-13-38-33; fax 33-13-38-35; e-mail kirchenbuero@sankt-petri.dk; internet www.sankt-petri.dk.

Methodist Church: Metodistkirkens Social Arbejde, Rigensgade 21A, 1316 Copenhagen K; tel. 33-93-25-96; fax 33-93-65-39; e-mail msac@image.dk; f. 1910; Chair. FINN UTH.

Moravian Brethren: The Moravian Church, 6070 Christiansfeld; f. in Denmark 1773; Pastor JORGEN BØYTLER; Lindegade 26, 6070 Christiansfeld; tel. 74-56-14-20; fax 74-56-14-21; e-mail boeytler@post7.tele.dk.

Norwegian Seamen's Church: Kong Håkons Kirke, Ved Mønten 9, 2300 Copenhagen S; tel. 32-57-11-03; fax 32-57-40-05; e-mail kobenhavn@sjomannskirken.no; internet www.sjomannskirken.no; f. 1958.

Reformed Church: Reformed Synod of Denmark, Spindlerhus, Jyllandsgade 41, 7000 Fredericia; tel. 75-92-05-51; e-mail s.hofmeister@reformert.dk; internet www.reformert.dk; Rev. SABINE HOFMEISTER.

Russian Orthodox Church: Alexander Nevski Church, Bredgade 53, 1260 Copenhagen K; tel. 33-13-60-46; fax 33-13-28-85; e-mail ruskirke@vip.cybercity.dk; internet www.rusmedia.dk; f. 1883; Rector Fr SERGY PLEKHOV.

Seventh-day Adventists: Syvende Dags Adventistkirken, POB 15, Concordiavej 16, 2850 Nærum; tel. 45-58-77-77; fax 45-58-77-78; e-mail adventistkirken@adventist.dk; internet www.adventist.dk; f. 1863; Pres. OLE KENDEL; Sec. SVEN H. JENSEN.

Society of Friends: Danish Quaker Centre, Drejervej 17, 4., 2400 Copenhagen NV; tel. and fax 36-47-00-95; internet www.kvaekerne.dk.

Swedish Lutheran Church: Svenska Gustafskyrkan, Folke Bernadottes Allé, 2100 Copenhagen Ø; tel. 33-15-54-58; fax 33-15-02-94; e-mail info.danmark@skut.org; internet www.skut.org/danmark.

The Salvation Army and the Unitarians are also active in the country.

BAHÁ'Í FAITH

Bahá'í: Det Nationale Åndelige Råd, Sofievej 28, 2900 Hellerup; tel. 39-62-35-18; e-mail sekretariat@bahai.dk; internet www.bahai.dk.

ISLAM

The Muslim Community: Nusrat Djahan Mosque (and Ahmadiyya Mission), Eriksminde Allé 2, 2650 Hvidovre; tel. 36-75-35-02; fax 36-75-00-07.

JUDAISM

Jewish Community: Mosaisk Trossamfund, Ny Kongensgade 6, 1472 Copenhagen K; tel. 33-12-88-68; fax 33-12-33-57; e-mail mt@mosaiske.dk; internet www.mosaiske.dk; 2,500 mems; Chief Rabbi BENT LEXNER.

The Press

There are more than 220 separate newspapers, including some 32 principal dailies. The average total circulation of daily newspapers in 2003 was 1,378,000 on weekdays.

Most newspapers and magazines are privately owned and published by joint concerns, co-operatives or limited liability companies. The main concentration of papers is held by the Berlingske Group, which owns *Berlingske Tidende, Weekendavisen* and *B.T.*, and the provincial *Jydskevestkysten* and *Århus Stiftstidende*.

There is no truly national press. Copenhagen accounts for 20% of the national dailies and about one-half of the total circulation. No paper is directly owned by a political party, although all papers show a fairly pronounced political leaning.

PRINCIPAL DAILIES

Aabenraa

Der Nordschleswiger: Skibbroen 4, POB 1041, 6200 Aabenraa; tel. 74-62-38-80; fax 74-62-94-30; e-mail redaktion@nordschleswiger .dk; internet www.nordschleswiger.dk; f. 1946; German; Editor-in-Chief SIEGFRIED MATLOK; circ. 2,573.

Ålborg

Nordjyske Stiftstidende: Langagervej 1, POB 8000, 9220 Ålborg Øst; tel. 99-35-35-35; fax 99-35-33-75; e-mail central@nordjyske.dk; internet www.nordjyske.dk; f. 1767; adopted present name in 1999, following the merger of six regional dailies; mornings; Liberal independent; Publr and Editor-in-Chief PER LYNGBY; circ. weekdays 79,000, Sundays 90,541.

Århus

Århus Stiftstidende: Olof Palmes Allé 39, POB 1, 8200 Århus N; tel. 87-40-10-10; fax 87-40-14-04; e-mail redaktionen@stiften.dk; internet www.stiften.dk; f. 1794; evening and weekend mornings; Liberal independent; Editor-in-Chief ERIK FRODELUND; circ. weekdays 64,562, Sundays 74,422.

Copenhagen

Berlingske Tidende: Pilestræde 34, 1147 Copenhagen K; tel. 33-75-75-75; fax 33-75-20-20; e-mail redaktionen@berlingske.dk; internet www.berlingske.dk; f. 1749; morning; Conservative independent; Editor-in-Chief KARSTEN MADSEN; circ. weekdays 153,681, Sundays 184,944.

Børsen: Møntergade 19, 1140 Copenhagen K; tel. 33-32-01-02; fax 33-12-24-45; e-mail redaktionen@borsen.dk; internet www.borsen .dk; f. 1896; morning; independent; business news; Editor-in-Chief LEIF BECK FALLESEN; circ. 56,020.

B.T.: Kr. Bernikowsgade 6, POB 200, 1006 Copenhagen K; tel. 33-75-75-33; fax 33-75-20-33; e-mail bt@bt.dk; internet www.bt.dk; f. 1916; morning; Conservative independent; Editor-in-Chief KRISTIAN LUND; circ. weekdays 124,521, Sundays 170,929.

Dagbladet Arbejderen: Ryesgade 3F, 1. sal, 2200 Copenhagen N; tel. 35-35-21-93; fax 35-37-20-39; e-mail arbejderen@inform.dk; internet www.arbejderen.dk; Editor BIRTHE SØRENSEN.

Dagbladet Information: Store Kongensgade 40C, POB 188, 1006 Copenhagen K; tel. 33-69-60-00; fax 33-69-61-10; e-mail inf-dk@ information.dk; internet www.information.dk; f. 1943 (founded underground during occupation and then legally in 1945); morning; independent; Editor JØRGEN STEEN NIELSEN; circ. 20,834.

Ekstra Bladet: Rådhuspladsen 37, 1785 Copenhagen V; tel. 33-11-13-13; fax 33-14-10-00; e-mail post@ekstrabladet.dk; internet www .eb.dk; f. 1904; evening; Liberal independent; Editor-in-Chief HANS ENGELL; Man. Dir LARS HENRIK MUNCH; circ. weekdays 132,828, Sundays 158,151.

Kristeligt Dagblad: Rosengården 14, 1174 Copenhagen K; tel. 33-48-05-00; fax 33-48-05-01; e-mail kristeligt-dagblad@ kristeligt-dagblad.dk; internet www.kristeligt-dagblad.dk; f. 1896; morning; independent; Editor ERIK BJERAGER; circ. 20,000.

Politiken: Politikens Hus, Rådhuspladsen 37, 1785 Copenhagen V; tel. 33-11-85-11; fax 33-15-41-17; e-mail indland@pol.dk; internet www.politiken.dk; f. 1884; morning; Liberal independent; Editor-in-Chief TØGER SEIDENFADEN; circ. weekdays 138,177, Sundays 176,287.

Esbjerg

Jydskevestkysten: Banegårdspladsen, 6700 Esbjerg; tel. 75-12-45-00; fax 75-13-62-62; e-mail jydskevestkysten@jv.dk; internet www.jv.dk; f. 1917 as *Vestkysten*, merged with *Jydske Tidende* in 1991 to form present daily; morning; Liberal; Editor-in-Chief METTE BOCK; circ. weekdays 89,645, Sundays 101,595.

Helsingør

Helsingør Dagblad: Klostermosevej 101, 3000 Helsingør; tel. 49-22-21-10; fax 49-22-11-08; e-mail redaktionen@helsingordagblad.dk; internet www.helsingordagblad.dk; Editor-in-Chief JOHN BECH; circ. 6,738.

Herlev

Licitationen: Marienlundsvej 46D, POB 537, 2730 Herlev; tel. 70-15-02-22; fax 44-85-89-19; e-mail licitationen@licitationen.dk; internet www.licitationen.dk; Editor-in-Chief KLAUS TØTTRUP; circ. 5,495.

Herning

Herning Folkeblad: Østergade 25, 7400 Herning; tel. 96-26-37-00; fax 97-22-36-00; e-mail hf@herningfolkeblad.dk; internet www .herningfolkeblad.dk; f. 1869; evening; Liberal; Editor-in-Chief FLEMMING LARSEN; circ. 14,298.

Hillerød

Frederiksborg Amts Avis: Milnersvej 44–46, 3400 Hillerød; tel. 48-24-41-00; fax 42-25-48-40; f. 1874; morning; Liberal; Editor TORBEN DALLEY LARSEN; circ. weekdays 38,000, Sundays 35,800.

Holbæk

Holbæk Amts Venstreblad: Ahlgade 1, 4300 Holbæk; tel. 59-48-02-00; fax 59-44-50-34; e-mail redaktion@venstrebladet.dk; internet www.venstrebladet.dk; f. 1905; evening; Social Liberal; Editor-in-Chief MOGENS FLYVHOLM; circ. 19,087.

Holstebro

Dagbladet Holstebro-Struer: Lægårdvej 86, 7500 Holstebro; tel. 99-12-83-00; fax 97-41-03-20; e-mail holstebro@de-bergske.dk; internet www.bergske.dk; evening; Liberal independent; Man. Chief Editor ERIK MØLLER; circ. 11,801.

Horsens

Horsens Folkeblad: Søndergade 47, 8700 Horsens; tel. 76-27-20-00; fax 75-62-02-18; e-mail redaktionen@horsens-folkeblad.dk; internet www.horsens-folkeblad.dk; f. 1866; evening; Liberal; Editor JENS BEBE; circ. 19,375.

Kalundborg

Kalundborg Folkeblad: Skibbrogade 40, 4400 Kalundborg; tel. 56-21-24-60; fax 59-51-02-80; e-mail redaktion@kal-folkeblad.dk; internet www.kal-folkeblad.dk; Editor-in-Chief CLAUS SØRENSEN; circ. 8,637.

Kerteminde

Kjerteminde Avis: Ndr. Ringvej 54, 5300 Kerteminde; tel. 65-32-10-04; fax 65-32-39-04; e-mail info@kj-avis.dk; Editor JØRGEN WIND-HANSEN; circ. 1,693.

Næstved

Næstved Tidende: Dania 38, 4700 Næstved; tel. 72-45-11-00; fax 72-45-11-17; e-mail red@sj-medier.dk; internet www.sj-medier.dk; f. 1866; Liberal; 6 days a week; Editor SØREN BAUMANN; circ. 19,240.

Sjællands Tidende: Dania 38, 4700 Næstved; tel. 72-45-11-00; fax 72-45-11-17; e-mail red@sj-medier.dk; internet www.sj-medier.dk; f. 1815; morning; Liberal; for western part of Zealand; Editor SØREN BAUMANN; circ. 15,247.

Nykøbing

Lolland-Falsters Folketidende: Tværgade 14, 4800 Nykøbing F; tel. 54-88-02-00; fax 54-85-02-96; e-mail folketidende@indbakke.dk; internet www.folketidende.dk; f. 1873; evening; Liberal; Editor BO BISCHOFF; circ. 24,864.

Morsø Folkeblad: Elsøvej 105, 7900 Nykøbing M; tel. 97-72-10-00; fax 97-72-10-10; Editor-in-Chief LEIF KRISTIANSEN; circ. 6,021.

Odense

Fyens Stiftstidende: Blangstedgårdsvej 2–6, 5220 Odense SØ; tel. 66-11-11-11; fax 65-93-25-74; e-mail redaktion@fyens.dk; internet www.fyens.dk; f. 1772; morning; independent; Editor-in-Chief EGON TØTTRUP; circ. weekdays 63,349, Sundays 84,358.

Randers

Randers Amtsavis: Nørregade 7, 8900 Randers; tel. 87-12-20-00; fax 87-12-21-21; e-mail e-mail@amtsavisra.dk; f. 1810; evening; independent; Editor-in-Chief OLE C. JØRGENSEN; circ. 81,000.

Ringkøbing

Ringkøbing Amts Dagblad: Sankt Blichersvej 5, POB 146, 6950 Ringkøbing; tel. 99-75-73-00; fax 97-32-05-46; e-mail ringkoebing@de-bergske.dk; evening; Editor KRISTIAN SAND; circ. 15,389.

Rønne

Bornholms Tidende: Nørregade 11–13, 3700 Rønne; tel. 56-90-30-00; fax 56-90-30-92; e-mail redaktion@bhstid.dk; internet www.bornholmstidende.dk; f. 1866; evening; Liberal; Editor-in-Chief BJARNE PEDERSEN; circ. 13,904.

Silkeborg

Midtjyllands Avis: Vestergade 30, 8600 Silkeborg; tel. 86-82-13-00; fax 86-81-35-77; e-mail silkeborg@midtjyllandsavis.dk; internet www.midtjyllandsavis.dk; f. 1857; daily except Sundays; Editor-in-Chief STEFFEN LANGE; circ. 17,644.

Skive

Skive Folkeblad: Gemsevej 7–9, 7800 Skive; tel. 97-51-34-11; fax 97-51-28-35; e-mail skivefol@post6.tele.dk; internet www.skivefolkeblad.dk; f. 1880; Social Liberal; Editor OLE DALL; circ. 13,153.

Svendborg

Fyns Amts Avis: Sankt Nicolai Gade 3, 5700 Svendborg; tel. 62-21-46-21; fax 62-22-06-10; e-mail post@fynsamtsavis.dk; internet www.fynsamtsavis.dk; f. 1863; Liberal; Editor OLE C. JØRGENSEN; circ. 20,255.

Thisted

Thisted Dagblad: Thisted; tel. 99-19-93-00; fax 97-91-07-20; e-mail thisted@de-bergske.dk; Liberal independent; Editor HANS PETER KRAGH; circ. 9,188.

Vejle

Vejle Amts Folkeblad: Bugattivej 8, 7100 Vejle; tel. 75-85-77-88; fax 75-85-72-47; e-mail vaf-fd@vaf-fd.dk; internet www.vejleonline.dk; f. 1865; evening; Liberal; Editor ARNE MARIAGER; circ. 27,755.

Viborg

Viborg Stifts Folkeblad: Sankt Mathiasgade 7, 8800 Viborg; tel. 89-27-63-00; fax 89-27-63-70; e-mail viborg@de-bergske.dk; f. 1877; evening; Liberal Democrat; also published: *Viborg Nyt* (weekly); Editor PER V. SUNESEN; circ. 11,542.

Viby

Jyllands-Posten Morgenavisen: Grøndalsvej 3, 8260 Viby J; tel. 87-38-38-38; fax 87-38-31-99; e-mail jp@jp.dk; internet www.jp.dk; f. 1871; independent; Editor-in-Chief CARSTEN JUSTE; circ. weekdays 157,701, Sundays 214,823.

OTHER NEWSPAPERS

Den Blå Avis (East edition): Generatorvej 8D, 2730 Herlev; tel. 44-85-44-44; internet www.dba.dk; 2 a week; circ. 73,000.

Den Blå Avis (West edition): Marelisborg Havnevej 26, POB 180, 8100 Århus C; tel. 87-31-31-31; fax 86-20-20-02; internet www.dba.dk; Thursday; circ. 46,160.

Weekendavisen: Pilestræde 34, 3, 1147 Copenhagen K; tel. 33-75-25-33; fax 33-75-20-50; e-mail bwa@weekendavisen.dk; internet www.weekendavisen.dk; f. 1749; independent Conservative; Friday; Editor-in-Chief ANNE KNUDSEN; circ. 66,186.

POPULAR PERIODICALS

Ældre Sagen: Norregade 49, 1165 Copenhagen K; tel. 33-96-86-86; fax 33-96-86-87; e-mail aeldresagen@aeldresagen.dk; internet www.aeldresagen.dk; 6 a year; for senior citizens; Editor SANNA KJÆR HANSEN; circ. 360,000.

ALT for damerne: Hellerupvej 51, 2900 Hellerup; tel. 39-45-74-00; fax 39-45-74-80; e-mail alt@altfordamerne.dk; internet www.altfordamerne.dk; f. 1946; weekly; women's magazine; Editor-in-Chief HANNE HØIBERG; circ. 89,081.

Anders And & Co: Vognmagergade 11, 1148 Copenhagen K; tel. 33-30-50-00; fax 33-30-55-10; internet www.andeby.dk; weekly; children's magazine; Editor TOMMY MELLE; circ. 99,826.

Basserne: Hellerupvej 51, 2900 Hellerup; tel. 33-33-75-35; fax 33-33-75-05; fortnightly; children and youth; circ. 49,000.

Billed-Bladet: Vesterbrogade 16, 1620 Copenhagen V; tel. 31-23-16-11; fax 31-24-10-08; f. 1938; weekly; family picture magazine; Editor ANDERS THISTED; circ. 222,951.

Bo Bedre: Strandboulevarden 130, 2100 Copenhagen Ø; tel. 39-17-20-00; fax 39-17-23-02; e-mail bobedre@bp.bonnier.dk; monthly; homes and gardens; Editor-in-Chief ERIK RIMMER; circ. 99,894.

Camping: Silkeborg; tel. 86-82-55-00; fax 86-81-63-02; monthly; circ. 44,107.

Familie Journalen: Vigerslev Allé 18, 2500 Valby, Copenhagen; tel. 36-15-22-22; fax 36-15-22-99; e-mail redaktion@familiejournalen.dk; f. 1877; weekly; Editor-in-Chief PETER DALL; circ. 230,000.

Femina: Vigerslev Allé 18, 2500 Valby, Copenhagen; tel. 36-15-23-00; fax 36-15-23-99; f. 1873; weekly; Editor JUTTA LARSEN; circ. 93,866.

Gør Det Selv: Strandboulevarden 130, 2100 Copenhagen Ø; tel. 39-17-20-00; fax 39-17-23-07; e-mail gds@bp.bonnier.dk; internet www.goerdetselv.dk; f. 1975; every 3 weeks; do-it-yourself; Editor KÅRE OLOFSEN; circ. 150,000.

Helse—Familiens Lægemagasin: Hejrevej 37, 1. sal 2100 Copenhagen NV; tel. 35-25-05-25; fax 35-26-87-60; e-mail helse@helse.dk; internet www.helse.dk; monthly; family health; circ. 200,000.

Hendes Verden: Hellerupvej 51, 2900 Hellerup; tel. 39-45-75-50; fax 39-45-75-99; f. 1937; weekly; for women; Editor IBEN NIELSEN; circ. 58,302.

Hjemmet (The Home): Vognmagergade 10, 1145 Copenhagen K; tel. 39-45-76-00; fax 39-45-76-60; weekly; Editor-in-Chief BJARNE RAUNSTED; circ. 207,087.

I form: Strandboulevarden 130, 2100 Copenhagen Ø; tel. 39-17-20-00; fax 39-17-23-11; e-mail iform@iform.dk; internet www.iform.dk; 17 a year; sport, health, nutrition, sex, psychology; Editor KAREN LYAGER HORVE; circ. 70,766.

Idé-nyt: Gl. Klausdalsbrovej 495, 2730 Herlev; tel. 44-53-40-00; fax 44-92-11-21; e-mail idenyt@idenyt.dk; internet www.idenyt.dk; f. 1973; 9 a year; free magazine (regional editions); homes and gardens; circ. 1,679,655.

Illustreret Videnskab: Strandboulevarden 130, 2100 Copenhagen Ø; tel. 39-17-20-00; fax 39-17-23-12; internet www.illustreretvidenskab.dk; 17 a year; popular science; Editor JENS E. MATTHIESEN; circ. 88,132.

Mad og Bolig: Vigerslev Allé 18, 2500 Valby; tel. 36-15-20-00; fax 36-15-27-95; f. 1991; 10 a year; gastronomy, wine, interiors and travel; Editor JETTE ØSTERLUND; circ. 50,600.

Månedsmagasinet IN: Vigerslev Allé 18, 2500 Valby; tel. 36-15-20-00; fax 36-15-27-94; e-mail in@in.dk; internet www.in.dk; fashion magazine; Editor-in-Chief CAMILLA LINDEMANN; circ. 50,000.

Motor: Firskovvej 32, POB 500, 2800 Lyngby; tel. 45-27-07-07; fax 45-27-09-89; e-mail motor@fdm.dk; internet www.fdm.dk; monthly; cars and motoring; circ. 210,000.

Rapport: Marielundvej 46E, 2730 Herlev; tel. 44-85-88-66; fax 44-85-88-67; e-mail rap@rapport.dk; internet www.rapport.dk; f. 1971; men's weekly; Editor-in-Chief JAN SCHIWE NIELSEN; circ. 36,964.

Samvirke: FDB Samvirke, Fanøgade 15, 2100 Copenhagen Ø; tel. 39-47-00-00; fax 39-47-00-01; e-mail fdb@fdb.dk; f. 1928; consumer monthly; Publr and Editor-in-Chief POUL DINES; circ. 500,000.

Se og Hør: Vigerslev Allé 18, 2500 Valby; tel. 36-15-24-00; fax 36-15-24-99; e-mail redaktionen@seoghoer.dk; internet www.seoghoer.dk; f. 1940; news and TV; Editor HENRIK QVORTRUP; circ. 197,000.

Sofus' Lillebror: Copenhagen; tel. 33-33-75-35; fax 33-33-75-05; monthly; children and youth; circ. 44,000.

TIPS-bladet: Alsgarde Centret 2, 3140 Alsgarde; tel. 49-70-89-00; fax 49-70-88-30; weekly; sport; circ. 39,467.

Ud og Se: Allègade 8F, 2000 Frederiksberg; tel. 33-22-20-20; fax 33-22-99-59; e-mail ingo@jungersted.com; internet www.jungersted.com; travel monthly; circ. 230,000.

Ude og Hjemme: Vigerslev Allé 18, 2500 Valby, Copenhagen; tel. 36-15-25-25; fax 36-15-25-99; e-mail redaktionen@udeoghjemme.dk; internet www.udeoghjemme.dk; f. 1926; family weekly; Editor JØRN BAUENMAND; circ. 181,000.

Ugebladet Søndag: Otto Mønsteds Gade 3, 1505 Copenhagen V; tel. 36-15-34-00; fax 36-15-34-01; e-mail soendag@soendag.dk; f. 1921; weekly; family magazine; Editor JOHNNY JOHANSEN; circ. 103,603.

SPECIALIST PERIODICALS

ABF-Nyt: Carsten Ekström, Bagsværdhovedgade 296–298, 2880 Bagsværd; tel. 44-44-77-47; fax 44-44-67-47; e-mail abfnyt@announce-service.dk; 4 a year; Editor JAN HANSEN; circ. 60,185.

Aktive Kvinder: Niels Hemmingsensgade 10, 2. sal, 1153 Copenhagen K; tel. 33-13-12-22; fax 33-33-03-28; e-mail ddh@ddh-aktive-kvinder.dk; internet www.ddh-aktive-kvinder.dk; f.

1920; 6 a year; home management; Editor KIRSTEN WULFF; circ. 25,000.

Aktuel Elektronik: Naverland 35, 2600 Glostrup; tel. 43-24-26-28; fax 43-24-26-26; e-mail rsh@techmedia.dk; internet www.techmedia .dk/html/sites/elek.asp; 22 a year; computing and information technology; Editor-in-Chief ROLF SYLVESTER-HVID; circ. 21,642.

Alt om Data: St. Kongensgade 72, 1264 Copenhagen K; tel. 33-91-28-33; fax 33-91-01-21; e-mail redaktion@aod.dk; internet www.aod .dk/aod; f. 1983; monthly; Editor-in-Chief TORBEN OKHOLM; circ. 35,000.

Automatik: Algade 10, POB 80, 4500 Nykøbing; tel. 53-41-23-10; engineering; monthly; circ. 39,250.

Bådnyt: Marielundvej 46E, 2730 Herlev; tel. 44-85-89-55; fax 44-85-89-56; e-mail redaktionen@baadnyt.dk; internet www.baadnyt.dk; monthly; boats; Editor KNUT IVERSEN; circ. 18,500.

Beboerbladet: Allègade 8F, 2000 Frederiksberg; tel. 33-22-20-20; fax 33-22-99-59; e-mail info@jungersted.com; internet www .jungersted.com; quarterly; for tenants in public housing; circ. 540,000.

Beredskab: Meinungsgade 8D, 2200 Copenhagen N; tel. 35-24-00-00; fax 35-24-00-01; e-mail bf@beredskab.dk; internet www .beredskab.dk; f. 1934; 6 a year; civil protection and preparedness; publ. by the Danish Civil Protection League; circ. 4,000.

Bilsnak: Park Allé 355, 2605 Brøndby; tel. 43-28-82-00; fax 43-63-63-38; e-mail redaktion@bilsnak.dk; internet www.volkswagen.dk; f. 1976; 3 a year; cars; Editor JANNE DEGN SKALKAM; circ. 195,000.

Boligen: Studiestræde 50, 1554 Copenhagen V; tel. 33-76-20-21; fax 33-76-20-01; monthly; housing associations, architects; Editor HELGE MØLLER; circ. 30,000.

BygTek: Stationsparken 25, 2600 Glostrup; tel. 43-43-29-00; fax 43-43-13-28; e-mail odsgard@odsgard.dk; internet www.odsgard.dk; monthly; building and construction; circ. 25,000.

Computerworld: Carl Jacobsens Vej 25, 2500 Valby; tel. 77-30-03-00; fax 77-30-03-02; e-mail redaktionen@computerworld.dk; internet www.computerworld.dk; f. 1981; 2 a week; computing; Editors-in-Chief JAN HORSAGER, RUNE MICHAELSEN; circ. 28,000.

Cyklister: Dansk Cyklist Forbund, Rømersgade 7, 1362 Copenhagen K; tel. 33-32-31-21; fax 33-32-76-83; e-mail dcf@dcf.dk; internet www.dcf.dk; f. 1905; 6 a year; organ of Danish Cyclist Federation; Editor INGRID E. PETERSEN; circ. 19,000.

Effektivt Landbrug: Odensevej 29, 5550 Langeskov; tel. 70-15-12-37; fax 70-15-12-47; e-mail effektivt@landbrugnet.dk; internet www .landbrugnet.dk; 21 a year; farming; Editor BØJE ØSTERLUND; circ. 31,407.

FINANS: Langebrogade 5, 1411 Copenhagen K; tel. 32-96-46-00; internet www.finansforbundet.dk; 11 a year; for employees in the financial sector; circ. 53,000.

Folkeskolen: Vandkunsten 12, POB 2139, 1015 Copenhagen K; tel. 33-69-63-00; fax 33-69-64-26; e-mail folkeskolen@dlf.org; internet www.folkeskolen.dk; 43 a year; teaching; Editor THORKILD THEJSEN; circ. 87,275.

Foto Guiden: POB 239, 9900 Frederikshavn; tel. 98-42-90-60; fax 98-42-90-61; f. 1960; 2 a year; photography; Editor E. STEEN SØRENSEN; circ. 24,000.

Havebladet: Frederikssundsvej 304A, 2700 Brønshøj; tel. 38-28-87-50; fax 32-28-83-50; e-mail info@kolonihave.dk; internet www .kolonihave.dk; 5 a year; publ. by Kolonihaveforbundet for Danmark; gardening; circ. 40,500.

High Fidelity: Blegdamsvej 112A, 2100 Copenhagen Ø; tel. 70-23-70-01; fax 70-23-70-02; e-mail karen@hifi.dk; f. 1968; 8 a year; Editor-in-Chief MICHAEL MADSEN; circ. 24,833.

Hunden: Medichuset Wiegaarden, 9500 Hobro; tel. 98-51-20-66; fax 98-51-20-06; internet www.dansk-kennel-klub.dk; 10 a year; organ of the kennel club; circ. 30,000.

Ingeniøren: POB 373, Skelbækgade 4, 1503 Copenhagen V; tel. 33-26-53-00; fax 33-26-53-01; e-mail ing@ing.dk; internet www.ing.dk; f. 1892; weekly engineers' magazine; Editor-in-Chief PER WESTERGÅRD; circ. 70,011.

Jaeger: Hojnæsvej 56, 2610 Rødovre; tel. 36-72-42-00; fax 36-72-09-11; monthly except July; hunting; circ. 89,000.

Jern- og Maskinindustrien: Falkoner Allé 90, 2000 Frederiksberg; tel. 35-36-37-00; fax 35-36-37-90; e-mail jm@df-jm.dk; 22 a year; iron and metallic industries; circ. 25,295.

Kommunalbladet: Park Allé 9, 8000 Aarhus C; tel. 86-76-13-22; fax 86-76-13-10; e-mail redaktionen@kommunalbladet.dk; internet www.kommunalbladet.dk; 21 a year; municipal administration, civil servants; Editor LARS FRIIS HOLM; circ. 70,000.

Landsbladet Kvæg: Vester Farimagsgade 6, 1606 Copenhagen V; tel. 33-39-47-00; fax 33-39-47-49; e-mail kvaeg@dlmedier.dk; monthly; for cattle-breeders and dairy-farmers; related titles *Landsbladet Mark* for arable farmers (e-mail mark@dlmedier.dk), *Landsbladet Svin* for pig-farmers (e-mail svin@dlmedier.dk); circ. 15,000.

Lederne: Vermlandsgade 65, 2300 Copenhagen S; tel. 32-83-32-83; fax 32-83-32-84; e-mail lh@lederne.dk; internet www.lederne.dk; 11 a year; for managers; circ. 80,136.

Metal: Nyropsgade 38, 1602 Copenhagen V; tel. 33-63-20-00; fax 33-63-21-00; 16 a year; metal industries; circ. 150,571.

Produktion: Axelborg, Vesterbrogade 4A, 1503 Copenhagen; tel. 33-69-87-00; fax 33-69-87-87; e-mail info@dlg.dk; internet www.dlg .dk; 6 a year; farming; Editor ELSE DAMSGAARD; circ. 63,000.

Spejd: The Danish Guide and Scout Association, Arsenalvej 10, 1436 Copenhagen K; tel. 32-64-00-50; fax 32-64-00-75; e-mail dds@ dds.dk; internet www.dds.dk; 7 a year; organ of the Scout Movement; circ. 38,900.

Stat, Amt og Kommune Information: POB 162, 2600 Glostrup; tel. 43-43-31-21; fax 43-43-15-13; e-mail saki@saki.dk; internet www .saki.dk; monthly; public works and administration; circ. 21,000.

Sygeplejersken: Skt Annæ Pl. 30, POB 1084, 1008 Copenhagen K; tel. 33-15-15-55; fax 33-93-17-85; e-mail redaktionen@dsr.dk; internet www.tfs.dk; 50 a year; nursing; circ. 74,000.

Tidsskrift for Sukkersyge—Diabetes: Rytterkasernen 1, 5000 Odense C; tel. 66-12-90-06; fax 65-91-49-08; e-mail df@diabetes.dk; internet www.diabetes.dk; f. 1940; 6 a year; diabetes; Dirs FLEMMING KJERSGAARD JOHANSEN, KARIN MULVAD; circ. 62,000.

Ugeskrift for Læger: Trondhjemsgade 9, 2100 Copenhagen Ø; tel. 35-44-85-00; e-mail ufl@daol.dk; weekly; medical; Editors T. SCHROEDER, T. KITAJ; circ. 22,000.

NEWS AGENCY

Ritzaus Bureau I/S: Store Kongensgade 14, 1264 Copenhagen K; tel. 33-30-00-00; fax 33-30-00-01; e-mail ritzau@ritzau.dk; internet www.ritzau.dk; f. 1866; general, financial and commercial news; owned by all Danish newspapers; Chair. of Board of Dirs TORBEN DALBY LARSEN; Gen. Man. and Editor-in-Chief UFFE RIIS SØRENSEN.

Foreign Bureaux

Agence France-Presse (AFP): Store Kongensgade 14, 3rd floor, 1264 Copenhagen K; tel. 33-13-23-31; fax 33-14-32-06; e-mail afp@ nitzau.dk; Bureau Chief SLIM ALLAGUI.

Agencia EFE (Spain): Copenhagen; Correspondent MARÍA CAMINO SÁNCHEZ.

Agenzia Nazionale Stampa Associata (ANSA) (Italy): Vestergade 2, 1456 Copenhagen K; tel. 33-32-03-59; fax 33-32-03-69; Correspondent DANIELA ROMITI.

Allgemeiner Deutscher Nachrichtendienst (ADN) (Germany): Copenhagen; Bureau Chief HERBERT HANSCH.

Associated Press (AP) (USA): Copenhagen; tel. 33-11-15-04; fax 33-32-36-60; Bureau Chief ED McCULLOUGH.

Deutsche Presse-Agentur (dpa) (Germany): Store Kongensgade 14, 3rd Floor, 1264 Copenhagen K; tel. 33-14-22-19; fax 33-14-66-72; e-mail dpa@ritzau.dk; Chief Correspondent THOMAS BORCHERT.

Informatsionnoye Telegrafnoye Agentstvo Rossii— Telegrafnoye Agentstvo Suverennykh Stran (ITAR—TASS) (Russia): Uraniavej 9B, 1878 Frederiksberg C; tel. 31-31-88-48; Correspondent TARAS B. LARIOKHIN.

Reuters Danmark A/S (UK): Meldahlsgade 5, 1613 Copenhagen V; tel. 33-96-96-96; fax 33-12-32-72; e-mail copenhagen.newsroom@ reuters.com; Bureau Chief PER BECH THOMSEN.

PRESS ASSOCIATIONS

Dansk Fagpresse (Association of the Danish Specialized Press): Pressens Hus, Skindergade 7, 1159 Copenhagen K; tel. 33-97-40-00; fax 33-91-26-70; e-mail df@danskfagpresse.dk; internet www .danskfagpresse.dk; Man. Dir CHRISTIAN KIERKEGAARD.

Dansk Magasinpresses Udgiverforening (Danish Magazine Publishers' Association): Hammerensgade 6, 1267 Copenhagen K; tel. 33-11-88-44; fax 33-15-01-86; e-mail dmu-mags@internet.dk; internet www.dmu-mags.dk; Chair. PAAL THORE KROSBY; Dir FINN SKOVSGAARD.

Danske Dagblades Forening (Danish Newspaper Publishers' Association): Pressens Hus, Skindergade 7, 1159 Copenhagen K; tel. 33-97-40-00; fax 33-14-23-25; e-mail ddf@danskedagblade.dk; internet www.danskedagblade.dk; comprises managers and editors-in-chief of all newspapers; general representative for the Danish press; Man. Dir EBBE DAL.

Publishers

Aarhus Universitetsforlag: Langelandsgade 177, 8200 Aarhus N; tel. 89-42-53-70; fax 89-42-53-80; e-mail unipress@au.dk; internet www.unipress.dk; reference, non-fiction and educational; Man. Dir CLAES HVIDBAK.

Forlaget åløkke A/S: Porskærvej 15, Nim, 8700 Horsens; tel. 75-67-11-19; fax 75-67-10-74; e-mail alokke@get2net.dk; internet www.alokke.dk; f. 1977; educational, children's books, audio-visual and other study aids; Pres. BERTIL TOFT HANSEN; Man. Dir EVA B. HANSEN.

Akademisk Forlag A/S (Danish University Press): Pilestrade 52, 3. sal, POB 54, 1002 Copenhagen K; tel. 33-43-40-80; fax 33-43-40-99; e-mail akademisk@akademisk.dk; internet www.akademisk.dk; f. 1962; history, health, linguistics, university textbooks, educational materials; Dir ESBEN ESBENSEN.

Forlaget Amanda: Rathsacksvej 7, 1. Sal, 1862 Frederiksberg C; tel. 33-79-00-11; fax 33-27-60-79; e-mail forlag@dansklf.dk; internet www.danskfl.dk; art, culture, school books, non-fiction; Editorial Dir CHARLOTTE SVENDSTRUP.

Forlaget Apostrof ApS: Berggreensgade 24, 2100 Copenhagen Ø; tel. 39-20-84-20; fax 39-20-84-53; e-mail info@apostrof.dk; internet www.apostrof.dk; f. 1980; psychotherapy and contemporary psychology, fiction and non-fiction for children; Publrs MIA THESTRUP, OLE THESTRUP.

Arkitektens Forlag: Strandgade 27A, 1401 Copenhagen K; tel. 32-83-69-00; fax 32-83-69-41; e-mail eksp@arkfo.dk; internet www.arkfo.dk; architecture, planning; Dir KIM DIRCKINCK-HOLMFELD.

Forlaget Artia (Ars Audiendi ApS: Vognmagergade 9, 1120 Copenhagen K; tel. 33-12-28-98; fax 33-14-12-63; fiction, non-fiction, science fiction, music, horror; Publr ERIK LÆSSØE STILLING; Dir PETER SCHANTZ.

Aschehoug Dansk Forlag A/S: Landemærket 8, POB 2179, 1017 Copenhagen K; tel. 33-30-55-22; fax 33-30-58-22; e-mail info@ash.egmont.com; internet www.aschehoug.dk; imprints: Aschehoug (fiction), Aschehoug Fakta (non-fiction, reference, children's books), Sesam (educational, children's books, history); Man. Dir (Aschehoug) ANETTE WAD.

Peter Asschenfeldt's nye Forlag A/S: Ny Adelgade 8–10, 1104 Copenhagen K; tel. 33-37-07-60; fax 33-91-03-04; fiction; Publr PETER ASSCHENFELDT.

Blackwell Munksgaard: Rosenørns Allé 1, POB 227, 1502 Copenhagen V; tel. 77-33-33-33; fax 77-33-33-77; e-mail info@mks.blackwellpublishing.com; internet www.blackwellpublishing.com; f. 1917 as Munksgaard International Publishers Ltd, present name adopted 2000; scientific journals on medicine and dentistry; Man. Dir LISE BALTZER.

Thomas Bloms Forlag ApS: Skovenggaardsvej 8, 9490 Pandrup; tel. 98-24-85-25; fax 98-24-80-60; fiction, non-fiction, children's books, talking books; Publrs CONNIE BLOM, THOMAS BLOM.

Bogans Forlag: Kastaniebakken 8, POB 39, 3540 Lynge; tel. 48-18-80-55; fax 48-18-87-69; e-mail bogan@post.tele.dk; f. 1974; general paperbacks, popular science, non-fiction, humour, health; Publr EVAN BOGAN.

Borgens Forlag A/S: Valbygårdsvej 33, 2500 Valby; tel. 36-15-36-15; fax 36-15-36-16; e-mail post@borgen.dk; internet www.borgen.dk; f. 1948; fiction, poetry, children's books, humour, general non-fiction; Man. Dir NIELS BORGEN.

Børneugdstjeneste forlaget: Korskærvej 25, 7000 Fredericia; tel. 75-93-44-55; fax 75-92-42-75; religion, children's books; Dir THORKILD HØJVIG; Editorial Dir THOMAS B. MIKKELSEN.

Carit Andersens Forlag A/S: Upsalagade 18, 2100 Copenhagen Ø; tel. 35-43-62-22; fax 35-43-51-51; e-mail info@caritandersen.dk; internet www.caritandersen.dk; illustrated books, non-fiction, fiction, science fiction; Publr ERIK ALBRECHTSEN.

Forlaget Carlsen A/S: Krogshøjvej 32, 2880 Bagsværd; tel. 44-44-32-33; fax 44-44-36-33; e-mail carlsen@carlsen.dk; internet www.carlsen.dk; children's books; Man. Dir JESPER HOLM.

Cicero (Chr. Erichsens Forlag A/S): Vester Voldgade 83, 1552 Copenhagen V; tel. 33-16-03-08; fax 33-16-03-07; e-mail info@cicero.dk; internet www.cicero.dk; f. 1902; fiction, non-fiction, art, culture; Publrs NIELS GUDBERGSEN, ALIS CASPERSEN.

DA-Forlag/Dansk Arbejdsgiverforening: Vester Voldgade 113, 1552 Copenhagen V; tel. 33-38-94-63; fax 33-91-09-32; e-mail smh@da.dk; non-fiction and reference; Publishing Dir SØREN MELDORF HANSEN.

Dafolo A/S: Suderbovej 22–24, 9900 Frederikshavn; tel. 96-20-66-66; fax 98-42-97-11; e-mail dafolo@dafolo.dk; internet www.dafolo.dk; educational books; Publr MICHAEL SCHELDE.

Dansk BiblioteksCenter A/S: Tempovej 7–11, 2750 Ballerup; tel. 44-86-77-77; fax 44-86-78-91; e-mail dbc@dbc.dk; internet www.dbc.dk; bibliographic data, information services, library systems, media; Man. Dir MOGENS BRABRAND JENSEN.

Dansk Historisk Håndbogsforlag A/S: Buddingevej 87A, 2800 Lyngby; tel. 45-93-48-00; fax 45-93-47-47; e-mail genos@worldonline.dk; f. 1976; genealogy, heraldry, law, culture and local history, facsimile editions, microfiches produced by subsidiary co; Owners and Man. Dirs RITA JENSEN, HENNING JENSEN.

Dansk psykologisk Forlag: Kongvejen 155, 2830 Virum; tel. 35-38-16-55; fax 35-38-16-65; e-mail dk-psych@dpf.dk; internet www.dpf.dk; educational books, health, psychology; Man. Dir HANS GERHARDT.

Det Danske Bibelselskab/Det Kongelige Vajsenhus' Forlag: Frederiksborggade 50, 1360 Copenhagen K; tel. 33-12-78-35; fax 33-93-21-50; e-mail bibelselskabet@bibelselskabet.dk; internet www.bibelselskabet.dk; bibles, religious and liturgical books, children's books; Dir PETER BIRCH.

Christian Ejlers' Forlag ApS: Sølvgade 38/3, 1307 Copenhagen K; tel. 33-12-21-14; fax 33-12-28-84; e-mail liber@ce-publishers.dk; internet www.ejlers.dk; f. 1967; educational, academic and multimedia; Publr CHRISTIAN EJLERS.

Forlaget for Faglitteratur A/S: Biens Alle 6, 2300 Copenhagen S; tel. 32-59-79-07; medicine, technology.

Flachs: Øverødvej 98, 2840 Holte; tel. 45-42-48-30; fax 45-42-48-29; e-mail flachs@flachs.dk; internet www.flachs.dk; fiction, non-fiction, reference, educational and children's books; Publrs ALLAN FLACHS, ANETTE FLACHS.

Palle Fogtdal A/S: Østergade 22, 1100 Copenhagen K; tel. 33-15-39-15; fax 33-93-35-05; e-mail pallefogtdal@pallefogtdal.dk; Danish history, photography; Man. Dir PALLE FOGTDAL.

Forum: Købmagergade 62, 4th Floor, 1150 Copenhagen K; tel. 33-41-18-30; fax 33-41-18-31; f. 1940; history, fiction, biographies, quality paperbacks and children's books; Man. Dir TORBEN MADSEN.

Fremad: Købmagergade 62, POB 2252, 1019 Copenhagen K; tel. 33-41-18-10; fax 33-41-18-11; f. 1912; general trade, fiction, non-fiction, juveniles, reference, children's books; Man. Dir NIELS KØLLE.

G.E.C. Gad Publishers Ltd: Klosterstræde 9, 1157 Copenhagen K; tel. 77-66-60-00; fax 77-66-60-01; e-mail reception@gads-forlag.dk; internet www.gads-forlag.dk; f. 1855; biographies, history, reference, educational materials; Publ. Dir ULRIK HVILSHØJ.

Gyldendalske Boghandel, Nordisk Forlag A/S: Klareboderne 3, 1001 Copenhagen K; tel. 33-75-55-55; fax 33-75-55-56; e-mail gyldendal@gyldendal.dk; internet www.gyldendal.dk; f. 1770; fiction, non-fiction, reference books, paperbacks, children's books, textbooks; Man. Dir STIG ANDERSEN.

P. Haase & Søns Forlag A/S: Løvstræde 8, 1152 Copenhagen K; tel. 33-18-10-80; fax 33-11-59-59; e-mail haase@haase.dk; internet www.haase.dk; f. 1877; educational books, audio-visual aids, children's books, humour, fiction, non-fiction; imprints: Natur og Harmoni, Rasmus Navers Forlag; Man. Dir MICHAEL HAASE.

Edition Wilhelm Hansen A/S: Bornholmsgade 1, 1266 Copenhagen K; tel. 33-11-78-88; fax 33-14-81-78; e-mail ewh@ewh.dk; internet www.ewh.dk; f. 1857; music books, school and educational books; Man. Dir TINE BIRGER CHRISTENSEN.

Hernovs Forlag: Nørrebakken 25, 2820 Gentofte; tel. 32-96-33-14; fax 32-96-04-46; e-mail admin@hernov.dk; internet www.hernov.dk; f. 1941; fiction, non-fiction, classic literature and children's; Man. Dir Else HERNOV.

Holkenfeldt 3: Fuglevadsvej 71, 2800 Lyngby; tel. 45-93-12-21; fax 45-93-82-41; fiction, non-fiction, reference, sport, humour; Publr KAY HOLKENFELDT.

Høst & Søns Forlag: Købmagergade 62, POB 2212, 1018 Copenhagen K; tel. 33-38-28-88; fax 33-38-28-98; e-mail hoest@hoest.dk; internet www.hoest.dk; f. 1836; fiction, crafts and hobbies, languages, books on Denmark, children's books; Man. Dir ERIK C. LINDGREN.

Forlaget Hovedland: Elsdyvej 21, 8270 Højbjerg; tel. 86-27-65-00; fax 86-27-65-37; e-mail mail@hovedland.dk; internet www.hovedland.dk; fiction, non-fiction, environment, sport, health, crafts; Publr STEEN PIPER.

Forlaget Klematis A/S: Østre Skovvej 1, 8240 Risskov; tel. 86-17-54-55; fax 86-17-59-59; fiction, non-fiction, crafts, children's books; Dir CLAUS DALBY.

Forlaget Per Kofod ApS: Kompagnistræde 4B, 1208 Copenhagen K; tel. 33-32-70-27; fax 33-32-70-78; fiction, non-fiction, art and culture; Publr PER KOFOD.

Krak: Virumgaardsvej 21, 2830 Virum; tel. 45-95-65-00; fax 45-95-65-65; e-mail krak@krak.dk; internet www.krak.dk; f. 1770; business information, maps and yearbooks; Dir OVE LETH-SØRENSEN.

Egmont Lademann A/S: Gerdasgade 37, 2500 Valby; tel. 36-15-66-00; fax 36-44-11-62; internet www.lademann.dk; f. 1954; non-fiction, reference.

Lindhardt og Ringhof A/S: Frederiksborggade 1, 1360 Copenhagen K; tel. 33-69-50-00; fax 33-69-50-01; e-mail lr@lindhardt-og-ringhof.dk; internet www.lindhardt-og-ringhof.dk; general fiction and non-fiction; Dir TRINE LICHT.

Lohses Forlag (incl. Forlaget Korskaer): Korskærvej 25, 7000 Fredericia; tel. 75-93-44-55; fax 75-92-42-75; e-mail info@lohse.dk; internet www.lohse.dk; f. 1868; religion, children's books, biographies, devotional novels; Dir THORKILD HØJVIG; Editorial Dir THOMAS B. MIKKELSEN.

Forlaget Lotus: Ishøj; tel. 43-45-78-74; fax 43-45-97-71; e-mail fiolotus@post7.tele.dk; management, health, religion, the occult, educational; Publr FINN ANDERSEN.

Magnus Informatik A/S: Palægade 4, 1261 Copenhagen K; tel. 70-20-33-14; fax 33-96-01-01; e-mail magnus@magnus.dk; internet www.magnus.dk; f. 1962; guidebooks, journals, law; Man. Dir MORTEN ARNBERG.

Medicinsk Forlag ApS: Tranevej 2, 3650 Ølstykke; tel. and fax 47-17-65-92; e-mail anni@mediciniskforlag.dk; internet www.medicinskforlag.dk; astrology, medical and scientific books; Man. Dir ANNI LINDELØV.

Modtryk Forlaget: Anholtsgade 4, 8000 Århus C; tel. 87-31-76-00; fax 87-31-76-01; e-mail forlaget@modtryk.dk; internet www.modtryk.dk; f. 1972; children's and school books, fiction, thrillers and non-fiction; Man. Dir ILSE NØRR.

Nyt Nordisk Forlag-Arnold Busck A/S: Købmagergade 49, 1150 Copenhagen K; tel. 33-73-35-75; fax 33-73-35-76; e-mail nnf@nytnordiskforlag.dk; internet www.nytnordiskforlag.dk; f. 1896; textbooks, school books, guidebooks, fiction and non-fiction; Man. Dir OLE A. BUSCK; Dir JESPER T. FENSVIG.

Nyt Teknisk Forlag A/S: Bastbygningen, Ingerslevsgade 44, 1705 Copenhagen V; tel. 63-15-17-00; fax 33-43-66-77; e-mail info@nyttf.dk; internet www.nyttf.dk; f. 1948; computing, technical books, reference, business, educational, science; Man. Dir OLE SKALS PEDERSEN.

Jørgen Paludans Forlag ApS: 4 Straedet, 3100 Hornbæk; tel. 49-75-15-36; fax 49-75-15-37; language teaching, non-fiction, psychology, history, politics, economics, reference; Man. Dir JØRGEN PALUDAN.

C.A. Reitzels Boghandel og Forlag A/S: Nørregade 20, 1165 Copenhagen K; tel. 33-12-24-00; fax 33-14-02-70; f. 1819; reference books, philosophy, educational and academic books, Hans Christian Andersen, Kierkegaard; Dir SVEND OLUFSEN.

Hans Reitzels Forlag A/S: Østergade 13, POB 1073, 1008 Copenhagen K; tel. 33-38-28-00; fax 33-38-28-08; e-mail hrf@hansreitzel .dk; internet www.hansreitzel.dk; f. 1949; education, philosophy, psychology, sociology; Publ. Dir HANNE SALOMONSEN.

Rhodos, International Science and Art Publishers: Holtegaard, Hørsholmvej 17, 3050 Humelbæk; tel. 32-54-30-20; fax 32-54-30-22; e-mail rhodos@rhodos.dk; internet www.rhodos.dk; f. 1959; university books, art, science, fiction, poetry; Dir RUBEN BLAEDEL.

Samlerens Forlag A/S: POB 2252, Købmagergade 62, 1019 Copenhagen K; tel. 33-41-18-00; fax 33-41-18-01; e-mail torben_madsen@samleren.dk; internet www.samlerens.dk; Danish and foreign fiction, contemporary history and politics, biographies; Man. Dir TORBEN MADSEN.

Scandinavia Publishing House: Drejervej 11–21, 2400 Copenhagen NV; tel. 35-31-03-30; fax 35-31-03-34; e-mail jvo@scanpublishing.dk; internet www.scanpublishing.dk; f. 1973; children's books, religion, Hans Christian Andersen; Dir JØRGEN VIUM OLESEN.

Det Schønbergske Forlag A/S: Landemærket 5, 1119 Copenhagen K; tel. 33-73-35-85; fax 33-73-35-86; f. 1857; fiction, humour, psychology, biography, children's books, paperbacks, textbooks; Dir JOAKIM WERNER; Editor ARVID HONORÉ.

Spektrum: Købmagergade 62, POB 2252, 1019 Copenhagen K; tel. 33-41-18-30; fax 33-41-18-31; non-fiction, history, biographies, science, psychology, religion, philosophy, arts; Man. Dir OLE KNUDSEN.

Strandbergs Forlag ApS: 475 Vedbæk Strandvej, 2950 Vedbæk; tel. 42-89-47-60; fax 42-89-47-01; cultural history, travel; Publr HANS JØRGEN STRANDBERG.

Strubes Forlag og Boghandel ApS: Damhus Blvd 65, 2610 Rødovre; tel. 36-72-17-50; fax 36-72-17-52; health, astrology, philosophy, the occult; Man. Dir JONNA STRUBE.

Tiderne Skifter: Købmagergade 62, 1019 Copenhagen K; tel. 33-41-18-20; fax 33-41-18-21; e-mail tiderneskifter@tiderneskifter.dk; fiction, sexual and cultural politics, psychology, science, religion, arts; Man. Dir CLAUS CLAUSEN.

Forlaget Thomson: Nytorv 5, 1450 Copenhagen K; tel. 33-74-07-00; fax 33-93-30-77; textbooks, legal, economic, financial, management, business, accounting; Editorial Dir VIBEKE CHRISTIANSEN.

Unitas Forlag: Peter Bangs Vej 1D, 2000 Frederiksberg; tel. 36-16-64-81; fax 38-11-64-81; e-mail info@unitasforlag.dk; internet www .unitasforlag.dk; religion, fiction, education, children's books; Man. PEDER GUNDERSEN.

Forlaget Vindrose A/S: Valbygaardsvej 33, 2500 Valby; tel. 36-15-36-15; fax 36-15-36-16; f. 1980; general trade, fiction and non-fiction; Man. Dir NIELS BORGEN.

Vitafakta ApS: Vedbæk; tel. and fax 45-16-11-50; health books, nutrition, school books; Dir INGER MARIE HAUT.

Wisby & Wilkens: Vesterled 45, 8300 Odder; tel. 70-23-46-22; fax 70-23-47-22; e-mail mail@wisby-wilkens.com; internet www .wisby-wilkens.com; f. 1986; children's books, crafts, fiction, health, humour, science, religion; imprint: Mikro (drama, poetry, humour); Publr JACOB WISBY.

GOVERNMENT PUBLISHING HOUSE

Statens Information (State Information Service): Nørre Farimagsgade 65, POB 1103, 1009 Copenhagen K; tel. 33-37-92-00; fax 33-37-92-99; e-mail si@si.dk; internet www.si.dk; f. 1975; acts as public relations and information body for the public sector; publishes Statstidende (Official Gazette), etc.; Dir LEON ØSTERGAARD.

PUBLISHERS' ASSOCIATION

Den danske Forlæggerforening: Skindergade 7, 1159 Copenhagen K; tel. 33-15-66-88; fax 33-15-65-88; e-mail danishpublishers@danishpublishers.dk; internet www .danishpublishers.dk; f. 1837; 54 mems, 3 associate mems; Chair. ERIK C. LINDGREN; Man. Dir IB TUNE OLSEN.

Broadcasting and Communications

TELECOMMUNICATIONS

Telecommunications services are administered by the National IT and Telecom Agency.

Telecommunications links with the Faroe Islands are provided by satellite ground stations at Tórshavn and Herstedvester. The latter also provides international data communication links via the EUTELSAT system and the French Telecom 1 satellite system, while a station at Blåvand receives signals from INTELSAT.

Regulatory Organization

National IT and Telecom Agency: Holsteinsgade 63, 2100 Copenhagen Ø; tel. 45-35-00-00; fax 45-35-00-10; e-mail itst@itst.dk; internet www.itst.dk; f. 1991; under the Ministry of Science, Technology and Innovation, in charge of administration and regulation of the telecommunications sector as laid down in telecommunications legislation; works on legislation; government centre of expertise in telecommunications; Dir-Gen. JØRGEN ABILD ANDERSEN; Dep. Dir-Gens FINN PETERSEN, MICHAEL HENNEBERG PEDERSEN.

Major Service Providers

GN Great Nordic Ltd: Kongens Nytorv 26, POB 2167, 1016 Copenhagen; tel. 72-11-18-88; fax 72-11-18-89; e-mail info@gn.com; internet www.gn.com; Pres. and CEO JORGEN LINDEGAARD.

LASAT Networks A/S: Nibe; tel. 96-71-10-00; fax 96-71-10-99; e-mail lasat@lasat.com; internet www.lasat.com; f. 1982; CEO CLAUS CHRISTENSEN.

Telecom A/S: Telegade 2, 2630 Tåstrup; tel. 42-52-91-11; fax 42-52-93-31; Man. Dir GREGERS MOGENSEN.

TDC A/S: Norregade 21, 0900 Copenhagen; tel. 33-43-77-77; fax 33-43-73-89; e-mail teledanmark@tdk.dk; internet www.tdc.dk; f. as Tele Danmark A/S, present name adopted 2000; fmrly state-owned telecommunications company; transferred to private ownership in 1998; Chair. THORLEIF KRARUP.

BROADCASTING

Regulatory Authority

Mediesekretariatet: Vognmagergade 10, 1., 1120 Copengahen K; tel. 33-18-68-68; fax 33-18-68-69; e-mail rtv@mediesekretariat.dk; internet www.mediesekretariat.dk; f. 2001.

Broadcasting Association

Forende Danske Antenneanlæg (FDA) (Danish Cable Television Asscn): Annebergparken 21, POB 151, 4500 Nykøbing Sj; tel. 59-96-17-00; fax 59-96-17-17; e-mail fda@fda.dk; internet www.fda .dk; f. 1983; organizes 356 local networks, representing c. 417,000 connected households; Man. Dir SØREN BIRKSØ SØRENSEN.

Radio

DR RADIO: Radio House, Rosenørns Allé 22, 1999 Frederiksberg C; tel. 35-20-30-40; fax 35-20-26-44; e-mail webmaster@dr.dk; internet www.dr.dk; fmrly Danmarks Radio; independent statutory corpn; Dir-Gen. CHR. S. NISSEN; Dir of Radio Programmes LEIF LØNSMANN; operates a foreign service (Radio Denmark), nine regional stations and four national channels.

The four national channels are as follows:

Channel 1: broadcasts for 110 hours per week on FM, in Danish (Greenlandic programmes weekly); simulcast on DAB; Head FINN SLUMSTRUP.

Channel 2: a music channel, broadcasts on FM, for 45 hours per week nationally, in Danish, as well as regional and special (for foreign workers) programmes; Head STEED FREDERIKSEN.

Channel 3: broadcasts on FM for 24 hours per day, in Danish; primarily a popular music channel, it also broadcasts news in Greenlandic, Faroese and in English; simulcast on DAB; Head JESPER GRUNWALD.

Channel 4: broadcasts on FM for about 97 hours per week; news, entertainment and regional programmes; simulcast on DAB.

Radio 100FM: Rådhuspladsen 45, 1550 Copenhagen V; tel. 33-37-89-00; fax 33-37-89-67; e-mail info@radio100fm.dk; internet www .100fm.dk; f. 2003; owned by Talpa Radio International (Netherlands).

Sky Radio A/S: Lille Strandstræde 20, 1254 Copenhagen K; tel. 33-66-00-00; fax 33-66-00-01; internet www.sky.dk; f. 2003; music.

There are also some 250 operators licensed for low-power FM transmissions of local and community radio, etc.

Digital Radio

Digital audio broadcasting (DAB) began in Denmark in 2002, with 10 transmitters in operation covering the main cities of Copenhagen, Århus, Odense and Aalborg. The transmitter network has since expanded to cover 90% of the population. The main DAB operator is DR RADIO, which offers five music channels (DR Soft, DR Rock, DR Boogie Radio, DR Jazz and DR Klassisk), four news channels (DR Nyheder, DR Erhverv, DR Sport and DR Politik) and eight other channels (DR Plus, DR Litteratur, DR Kanon Kamelen, DR Event, DR Gyldne Genhør and simulcasts of Channel 1, Channel 3 and Channel 4.

Television

DR TV: TV-Byen, 2860 Søborg; tel. 35-20-30-40; fax 35-20-26-44; e-mail dr-kontakten@dr.dk; internet www.dr.dk; operates two services, DR 1 and DR 2; Dir-Gen. CHR. S. NISSEN; Man. Dir JØRGEN RAMSKOV; Dir (News) LISBETH KNUDSEN.

DR 1: terrestrial television channel; Controller JØRGEN RAMSKOV.

DR 2: satellite television channel; Controller TORBEN FRØLICH.

TV 2/DANMARK A/S: Rugaardsvej 25, 5100 Odense C; tel. 65-91-91-91; fax 65-91-33-22; e-mail tv2@tv2.dk; internet www.tv2.dk; began broadcasts in 1988; Denmark's first national commercial and public service TV station; changed to a state share co in December 2003; part-privatization pending; CEO PETER PARBO.

Viasat Broadcasting/TV 3: Wildersgade 8, 1408 Copenhagen K; tel. 35-25-90-00; fax 35-25-90-10; e-mail viasat@viasat.dk; internet www.tv3.dk; reaches 71% of the country via cable and satellite; Man. Dir LARS BO ANDERSEN; Dir of Programmes HENRIK RAVN.

There are some 50 operators licensed for local television transmission.

Digital Television

Canal Digital Danmark: Stationsparken 25, 2600 Glostrup; tel. 70-27-27-75; fax 70-27-27-63; e-mail info@canal-digital.dk; internet www.canaldigital.dk; f. 1997; wholly owned by Telenor AS (Norway).

Finance

(cap. = capital; res = reserves; dep. = deposits; m. = million; brs = branches; amounts in kroner or euros (€))

BANKING

The first Danish commercial bank was founded in 1846. In 1975 restrictions on savings banks were lifted, giving commercial and savings banks equal rights and status, and restrictions on the establishment of full branches of foreign banks were removed. In 1988 all remaining restrictions on capital movements were ended. In 1998 there were some 187 banks and savings banks in operation. All banks are under government supervision, and public representation is obligatory on all bank supervisory boards.

Supervisory Authority

Finanstilsynet (Danish Financial Supervisory Authority): Gammel Kongevej 74A, 1850 Frederiksberg C; tel. 33-55-82-82; fax 33-55-82-00; e-mail finanstilsynet@ftnet.dk; internet www.ftnet.dk; agency of the Ministry of Economic Affairs, Business and Trade; Man. Dir HENRIK BJERRE-NIELSEN.

Central Bank

Danmarks Nationalbank: Havnegade 5, 1093 Copenhagen K; tel. 33-63-63-63; fax 33-63-71-03; e-mail nationalbanken@ nationalbanken.dk; internet www.nationalbanken.dk; f. 1818; self-governing; sole right of issue; conducts monetary policy; administers reserves of foreign exchange; cap. 50m., res 50,195m., dep. 292,263m. (Dec. 2003); Gov. BODIL NYBOE ANDERSEN; Chairs TORBEN NIELSEN, JENS THOMSEN.

Commercial Banks

Alm. Brand Bank: Midtermolen 7, 2100 Copenhagen; tel. 35-47-48-49; fax 35-47-47-35; e-mail bank@almbrand.dk; internet www .almbrand-bank.dk; f. 1988; cap. 351m., dep. 10,217m. (Dec. 2003); Chair. CHRISTIAN N. B. ULRICH; Pres. and CEO HENRIK NORDAM; 42 brs.

Amagerbanken A/S: Amagerbrogade 25, 2300 Copenhagen S; tel. 32-66-66-66; fax 32-54-45-34; e-mail international@amagerbanken .dk; internet www.amagerbanken.dk; f. 1903; cap. 222m., res 47m., dep. 9,694m. (Dec. 2003); Chair. N. E. NIELSEN; CEO and Man. Dir KNUD CHRISTENSEN; 27 brs.

Arbejdernes Landsbank A/S: Panoptikonbygningen, Vesterbrogade 5, 1502 Copenhagen V; tel. 33-38-80-00; fax 33-38-89-60; e-mail info@albank.dk; internet www.albank.dk; f. 1919; cap. 300m., res 87m., dep. 12,467m. (Dec. 2003); Chair. POUL ERIK SKOV CHRISTENSEN; Gen. Mans E. MIDTGAARD, P. E. LETH, E. CASTELLA; 60 brs.

Danske Andelskassers Bank A/S: Baneskellet 1, Hammershøj, 8830 Tjele; tel. 87-99-33-00; fax 87-99-30-98; e-mail foreign@dabank .dk; internet www.dabank.dk; f. 1970; cap. 125m., res 131m., dep. 3,080m. (Dec. 2003); Chair. of Supervisory Bd KNUD LARSEN; Gen. Mans BENT HOEJGAARD JAKOBSEN, VAGN T. RAVN; 38 brs.

Danske Bank A/S: Holmens Kanal 2–12, 1092 Copenhagen K; tel. 33-44-00-00; fax 70-12-10-80; internet www.danskebank.com; f. 1871 as Danske Landmandsbank; merged with Copenhagen Handelsbank and Provinsbanken in 1990 to form Den Danske Bank A/S; present name adopted 2000; the bank acquired the insurance group Danica in 1995, the Norwegian Fokus Bank in 1999, Real Denmark in 2000 and Bikubanken Girobank A/S in 2001; cap. 7,117m., res 1,023m., dep. 1,549,111m. (Dec. 2003); Chair. PETER STRAARUP; 650 brs.

Forstædernes Bank A/S: Malervangen 1, 2600 Glostrup; tel. 43-96-17-20; fax 43-63-32-36; e-mail finans@forbank.dk; internet www .forbank.dk; f. 1902; cap. 374m., res 38m., dep. 9,883m. (Dec. 2003); subsidiary, Den Fri Bank (f. 1994), provides telephone banking service to individual customers; Chair. HELMER OLSEN; Man. Dir KJELD MOSEBO CHRISTENSEN; 20 brs.

Handelsbanken Midtbank A/S: Amaliegade 3, POB 1032, 1007 Copenhagen K; tel. 33-41-82-00; fax 33-41-82-60; internet www .handelsbanken.dk; f. 1965 as Midtbank A/S; wholly owned by Handelsbanken AB (Sweden); cap. 260m., res 552m., dep. 6,240m. (Dec. 2000); Chair. HANS CHRISTOFFERSEN; Gen. Man. STEEN HOVE; 23 brs.

Jyske Bank A/S: Vestergade 8–16, 8600 Silkeborg; tel. 89-22-22-22; fax 89-22-24-96; e-mail jyskebank@jyskebank.dk; internet www .jyskebank.dk; f. 1855; established in 1967; cap. 720m., res 1,187m., dep. 84,130m. (Dec. 2003); Chair. SVEN BUHRKALL; CEO ANDERS DAM; 124 brs.

Nordea Bank Danmark A/S: Stranddegade 3, 1401 Copenhagen V; tel. 33-33-33-33; fax 33-33-63-63; internet www.nordea.dk; f. 1990 as Unibank A/S by merger of Andelsbanken, Privatbanken and SDS; in 1999 the bank merged with the insurance co Tryg-Baltica Forsikring A/S, but remained part of the Unidanmark A/S group, which became part of Nordea Group (Finland) in 2000; cap. €1,160m., res €9,527m., dep. €188,689m. (Dec. 2003); Man. Dir PETER SCHÜTZE; 348 brs.

Nordjyske Bank A/S: Jernbanegade 4–8, POB 701, 9900 Frederikshavn; tel. 99-21-22-23; fax 96-33-50-67; e-mail email@ nordjyskebank.dk; internet www.nordjyskebank.dk; f. 1970 as Egnsbank Nord A/S, current name adopted 2002 following merger with Vendsyssel Bank A/S; cap. 84m., res 567m., dep. 3,482m. (Dec. 2003); Chair. HANS JOERGEN KAPTAIN; Man. Dirs JENS OLE JENSEN, HANS JØRN VINTHER; 17 brs.

Nørresundby Bank A/S: Torvet 4, 9400 Nørresundby; tel. 98-17-33-33; fax 98-19-18-78; e-mail nbudland@nrsbank.dk; internet www .noerresundbybank.dk; f. 1898; cap. 48m., res 8m., dep. 4,591m. (Dec. 2003); Chair. KJELD KOLIND JENSEN; Man. Dir and CEO ANDREAS RASMUSSEN; 18 brs.

Nykredit Bank A/S: Kalvebod Brygge 1–3, 1780 Copenhagen V; tel. 33-42-18-00; fax 33-42-18-01; e-mail nykredit-bank@nykredit.dk; internet www.nykredit.dk/bank; f. 1986; cap. 1,400m., res 1,109m., dep. 55,364m. (Dec. 2003); Chair. HENNING KRUSE PETERSEN; CEO and Man. Dir KIM DUUS.

Ringkjøbing Bank A/S: Torvet 2, 6950 Ringkjøbing; tel. 99-75-32-00; fax 97-32-15-41; e-mail info@ringkjoebing-bank.dk; internet www.ringkjoebing-bank.dk; f. 1872; cap. 32m., res 431m., dep. 3,067m. (Dec. 2003); Chair. POUL HJULMAND; Man. Dir PREBEN KNUDS-GAARD; 7 brs.

Ringkjøbing Landbobank A/S: Torvet 1, 6950 Ringkøbing; tel. 97-32-11-66; fax 97-32-18-18; e-mail post@landbobanken.dk; internet www.landbobanken.dk; f. 1886; cap. 26m., res 1,210m., dep. 7,780m. (Dec. 2004); Chair. JENS KJELDSEN; Gen. Mans BENT NAUR KRISTENSEN, JOHN BULL FISKER; 17 brs.

Roskilde Bank A/S: Algade 14, POB 39, 4000 Roskilde; tel. 46-35-17-00; fax 46-34-83-52; e-mail info@roskildebank.dk; internet www .roskildebank.dk; f. 1884; cap. 103m., res 291m., dep. 8,068m. (Dec. 2003); Chair. JENS WINTHER; Man. NIELS VALENTIN HANSEN; 20 brs.

Sparbank Vest: Adelgade 8, POB 505, 7800 Skive; tel. 97-52-33-11; fax 97-52-73-11; e-mail sp@rbankvest.dk; internet www .sparbankvest.dk; f. 1857; cap. 121m., res 974m., dep. 6,927m. (Dec. 2003); Chair. OLE BROENDUM JENSEN; CEO PREBEN RASMUSSEN; 36 brs.

Sydbank A/S: Peberlyk 4, POB 169, 6200 Åbenrå; tel. 74-36-36-36; fax 74-36-35-49; e-mail info@sydbank.dk; internet www.sydbank .com; f. 1970; cap. 750m., res 3,581m., dep. 59,328m. (Dec. 2003); Chair. KRESTEN PHILIPSEN; CEO CARSTEN ANDERSEN; 115 brs.

Savings Banks

Fionia Bank A/S: Vestre Stationsvej 7, POB 189, 5100 Odense C; tel. 65-20-40-60; fax 65-91-01-10; e-mail udland@fioniabank.dk; internet www.fioniabank.dk; f. 1974; fmrly Amtssparekassen Fyn A/S; cap. 181m., res 718m., dep. 14,394m. (Dec. 2003); Chair. CLAUS HANSEN; Man. Dir FINN B. SORENSEN; 37 brs.

Lån & Spar Bank: Højbro Pl. 9–11, POB 2117, 1014 Copenhagen K; tel. 33-14-87-48; fax 33-14-18-48; e-mail lsb@lsb.dk; internet www .lsb.dk; f. 1880; present name 1990; cap. 271m., res 85m., dep. 6,494m. (Dec. 2003); Chair. TOMMY AGERSKOV THOMSEN; Man. Dir and CEO PETER SCHOU; 14 brs.

Spar Nord Bank: Skelagervej 15, POB 162, 9100 Ålborg; tel. 96-34-40-00; fax 96-34-45-75; e-mail sparnord@sparnord.dk; internet www .sparnordbank.com; f. 1967; cap. 519m., res 261m., dep. 27,382m. (Dec. 2003); CEO LASSE NYBY; Man. Dirs LARS MØLLER, JOHN LUNDS-GAARD; 67 brs.

Bankers' Organization

Finansrådet: Finansrådets Hus, Amaliegade 7, 1256 Copenhagen K; tel. 33-70-10-00; fax 33-93-02-60; e-mail mail@finansraadet.dk; internet www.finansraadet.dk; f. 1990; 169 mems; Chair. PETER STRAARUP; Man. Dir JÖRGEN HORWITZ.

STOCK EXCHANGE

Københavns Fondsbørs (Copenhagen Stock Exchange): Nikolaj Pl. 6, POB 1040, 1007 Copenhagen K; tel. 33-93-33-66; fax 33-12-86-13; e-mail xcse@xcse.dk; internet www.xcse.dk; f. 1848; part of an alliance (Nordic Exchanges, Norex) with the Oslo, Reykjavík and Stockholm Stock Exchanges, launched June 1999; Pres. HANS-OLE JOCHUMSEN; Chair. HANS EJVIND HANSEN.

INSURANCE

Principal Companies

Alm. Brand af 1792: Lyngby Hovedgade 4, POB 1792, 2800 Lyngby; tel. 45-96-70-00; fax 45-93-05-46; e-mail almbrand@ almbrand.dk; internet www.almbrand.dk; f. 1792; subsidiaries:

finance, life, non-life and reinsurance; Chief Gen. Man. BENT KNIE-ANDERSEN.

Codan Forsikring A/S: Codanhus, Gl. Kongevej 60, 1790 Copenhagen V; tel. 33-55-55-55; fax 33-55-21-22; f. 1915 as Forsikringsselskabet Codan A/S; adopted present name 2000; controlled by Royal and Sun Alliance Group Ltd (UK); acquired insurance operations of Hafnia Holdings in 1993; accident, life; CEO JENS ERIK CHRISTENSEN.

Danica Liv I, Livsforsikringsaktieselskab: Parallelvej 17, 2800 Lyngby; tel. 45-23-23-23; fax 45-23-20-20; e-mail servicecentre@ danica.dk; internet www.danica.dk; f. 1842 as state insurance co; privatized 1990; pensions, life and non-life.

GE Frankona Reinsurance A/S: Grønningen 25, 1270 Copenhagen K; tel. 33-97-95-93; fax 33-97-94-41; f. 1894 as ERC Frankona Reinsurance A/S; present name adopted 2000; reinsurance, life and non-life, international; Gen. Man. WALTHER HAMMERSTROEM.

A/S Det Kjøbenhavnske Reassurance-Compagni (Copenhagen Re): Midtermolen 7, POB 325, 2100 Copenhagen Ø; tel. 35-47-45-45; fax 35-47-72-72; e-mail copre@copre.com; internet www .copre.com; f. 1915; reinsurance.

Købstædernes Forsikring: Grønningen 1, 1270 Copenhagen K; tel. 33-14-37-48; fax 33-32-06-66; e-mail kab@kab.dk; internet www .kab.dk; f. 1761; non-life; Chair. SVEND ERIK CHRISTENSEN; CEO MOGENS N. SKOV.

Kompas Rejseforsikring A/S: Klausdalsbrovej 601, 2750 Ballerup; tel. 44-68-81-00; fax 44-68-84-00; e-mail kompas@kompas.dk; internet www.kompas.dk; travel, health; Man. PER GULDBRANDSEN.

Max Levig & Cos Eft.: Klausdalsbrovej 601, 2750 Ballerup; tel. 44-20-39-60; fax 44-20-66-70; f. 1890; Gen. Man. HUGO ANDERSEN.

PFA Pension: Marina Park, Sundkrogsgade 4, 2100 Copenhagen Ø; tel. 39-17-50-00; fax 39-17-59-50; f. 1917; life; non-life, property; Gen. Mans HENRIK HEIDEBY, A. KÜHLE.

Skandia: Stamholmen 159, 2650 Hvidovre; tel. 36-87-47-47; fax 36-87-47-87; f. 1798 as Kgl. Brand A/S; adopted present name 2000; all branches; subsidiaries: workers' liability, life; Gen. Man. JAN SVENSSON.

Topdanmark Forsikring A/S: Borupvang 4, 2750 Ballerup; tel. 44-68-33-11; fax 44-68-19-06; e-mail topdanmark@topdanmark.dk; internet www.topdanmark.dk; f. 1985; all classes, with subsidiaries; CEO MICHAEL PRAM RASMUSSEN.

Tryg Vesta Group A/S: Klausdalsbrovej 601, 2750 Ballerup; tel. 70-11-20-20; fax 44-20-67-00; e-mail trygvesta@trygvesta.com; internet www.trygvesta.com; f. 1995 by merger of Tryg Forsikring A/S and Baltica Forsikring A/S; CEO STINE BOSSE.

Insurance Association

Forsikring & Pension: Amaliegade 10, 1256 Copenhagen K; tel. 33-43-55-00; fax 33-43-55-01; e-mail fp@forsikringenshus.dk; internet www.forsikringenshus.dk; f. 1918 as Assurandør-Societetet; present name adopted 1999; Chair. JENS ERIK CHRISTENSEN; Dir PER BREMER RASMUSSEN; 160 mems.

Trade and Industry

GOVERNMENT AGENCY

Dansk Industri (Confederation of Danish Industries): 1787 Copenhagen V; tel. 33-77-33-77; fax 33-77-33-00; e-mail di@di.dk; internet www.di.dk; f. 1992; Dir HANS SKOV CHRISTENSEN.

DEVELOPMENT ORGANIZATION

Det Økonomiske Råd (Danish Economic Council): Adelgade 13, 1304 Copenhagen K; tel. 33-13-51-28; fax 33-32-90-29; e-mail dors@ dors.dk; f. 1962 to supervise national economic development and help to co-ordinate the actions of economic interest groups; 26 members representing both sides of industry, the Government and independent economic experts; Co-Chairs Prof. TORBEN M. ANDERSEN, Prof. SØREN BO NIELSEN, Prof. JØRGEN BIRK MORTENSEN; Sec.-Gen. PEDER ANDERSEN.

CHAMBER OF COMMERCE

HTS (Handel, Transport og Serviceerhvervene): Børsen, 1217 Copenhagen K; tel. 70-13-12-00; fax 70-13-12-01; e-mail hts@hts.dk; internet www.hts.dk; f. 1742; Pres. KURT NYGAARD; Man. Dir LARS KROBÆK; approx. 2,000 mems.

INDUSTRIAL AND TRADE ASSOCIATION

Dansk Elvaerkers Forening (Association of Danish Energy Companies): Rosenørns Allé 9, 1970 Frederiksberg C; tel. 35-30-04-00; fax 35-30-04-01; e-mail de@danskenergi.dk; f. 1923; promotes the interests of Danish producers and suppliers of electricity; 100 mem. cos.

Landbrugsradet (Danish Agricultural Council): Axelborg, Axeltorv 3, 1609 Copenhagen V; tel. 33-39-40-00; fax 33-39-41-41; e-mail agriculture@agriculture.dk; internet www.agriculture.dk; f. 1919; Pres. PETER GAEMELKE; Dir KLAUS BUSTRUP; 41 mems.

Mejeriforeningen (Danish Dairy Board): Frederiks Allé 22, 8000 Århus; tel. 87-31-20-00; fax 87-31-20-01; e-mail ddb@mejeri.dk; f. 1912; Chair. KAJ OLE PEDERSEN; Man. Dir K. THAYSEN; 30 mems.

Oliebranchens Fællesrepræsentation (OFR) (Danish Petroleum Industry Association): Vognmagergade 7, POB 120, 1004 Copenhagen K; tel. 33-45-65-10; fax 33-45-65-11; e-mail ofr@oil-forum.dk; internet www.oil-forum.dk; representative organization for petroleum industry; Chair. K. M. OLESEN; Sec.-Gen. PETER STIGSGAARD.

EMPLOYERS' ORGANIZATION

Bryggeriforeningen (Danish Brewers' Association): Faxehus, Gamle Carlsberg Vej 16, 2500 Valby; tel. 72-16-24-24; fax 72-16-24-44; e-mail info@bryggeriforeningen.dk; internet www.bryggeriforeningen.dk; f. 1899; Chair. JOERN TOLSTRUP ROHDE; Dir NIELS HALD; 14 mems.

Dansk Arbejdsgiverforening (Confederation of Danish Employers): Vester Voldgade 113, 1790 Copenhagen V; tel. 33-38-90-00; fax 33-12-29-76; e-mail da@da.dk; internet www.da.dk; f. 1896; Chair. JØRGEN VORSHOLT; Dir-Gen. JØRN NEERGAARD LARSEN; 13 mem. orgs.

Dansk Landbrug (Danish Farmers): Axelborg, Vesterbrogade 4A 4., 1620 Copenhagen V; tel. 33-39-46-00; fax 33-39-46-06; e-mail dl@dansklandbrug.dk; internet www.dansklandbrug.dk; f. 2003 by merger of Danske Landboforeninger (f. 1893) and Dansk Familielandbrug (f. 1906); Chair. PETER GAEMELKE; Sec.-Gen. CARL AAGE DAHL; 60,000 mems.

Dansk Pelsdyravlerforening (DPF) (Danish Fur Breeders' Association): Langagervej 60, POB 1479, 2600 Glostrup; tel. 43-26-10-00; fax 43-26-11-26; e-mail cfc@cfc.dk; internet www.cfc.dk; co-operative of 2,300 mems.

Danske Maritime: Store Kongensgade 128, 1264 Copenhagen K; tel. 33-13-24-16; fax 33-11-10-96; e-mail mail@danishmaritime.org; internet www.danishmaritime.org; formerly Skibsværftsforeningen (Asscn of Danish Shipbuilders).

Håndværksrådet (Danish Federation of Small and Medium-sized Enterprises): Islands Brygge 26, 2300 Copenhagen S; tel. 33-93-20-00; fax 33-32-01-74; e-mail hvr@hvr.dk; internet www.hvr.dk; f. 1879; Chair. POUL ULSØE; Man. LARS JØRGEN NIELSEN; 110 asscns with 25,000 mems.

Industriens Arbejdsgivere i København (The Copenhagen Employers' Federation): 1787 Copenhagen V; tel. 33-77-33-77; fax 33-77-33-00; e-mail di@di.dk; internet www.di.dk; Chair. JØRGEN E. TANDRUP; Sec. H. ENGELHARDT; 420 mems.

Provinsindustriens Arbejdsgiverforening (Federation of Employers in Provincial Industry): 1787 Copenhagen V; tel. 33-77-33-77; fax 33-77-33-00; f. 1895; Chair. SVEND-AAGE NIELSEN; Sec. GLENN SØGÅRD.

Sammenslutningen af Landbrugets Arbejdsgiverforeninger (SALA) (Danish Confederation of Employers' Associations in Agriculture): Vester Farimagsgade 1, 1606 Copenhagen V; tel. 33-13-46-55; fax 33-11-89-53.

UTILITIES

Danish Energy Authority: Amaliegade 44, 1256 Copenhagen K; tel. 33-92-67-00; fax 33-11-47-43; e-mail ens@ens.dk; internet www.ens.dk; f. 1976; govt agency under Ministry of Economic Affairs, Business and Trade; Dir IB LARSEN.

Sikkerhedsstyrelsen (Danish Safety Technology Authority): Norregade 63, 6700 Esbjerg; tel. 33-73-20-00; fax 33-73-20-99; e-mail sik@sik.dk; internet www.sikkerhedsstyrelsen.dk; f. 1907; formerly Elektricitetsrådet (Electricity Council); current name adopted 2004; responsible for the legislation, and enforcement thereof, regarding safety of electrical and gas products and installations, ATEX products, toys and general products in Denmark; Pres. ULLA RÖTTIGER; Man. Dir SØREN KRØIGAARD.

Electricity

Elkraft Power Co Ltd: Lautruphøj 5, 2750 Ballerup; tel. 44-66-00-22; fax 44-65-61-04; e-mail elkraft@elkraft.dk; f. 1978; co-ordinates supply of electricity and co-generated heat to eastern Denmark; Man. Dir BENT AGERHOLM.

Københavns Belyningsvaesen (The Copenhagen Energy Department): Vognmagergade 8, 1149 Copenhagen K; tel. 33-12-72-90; fax 33-12-72-91; one of the largest distributors of electricity in Denmark; also supplier of gas, district-heating and public-lighting systems.

NESA A/S: Strandvejen 102, 2900 Hellerup; tel. 72-10-10-10; fax 72-10-10-11; e-mail nesa@nesa.dk; internet www.nesa.dk; f. 1902; largest distributor of electricity in Denmark; Man. Dir POUL LIND.

Gas

Dansk Gasteknisk Forening (Danish Technical Gas Association): Rønnehaven 12, 5320 Agedrup; f. 1911; promotes the use of gas; 680 mems.

DONG (Dansk Olie og Naturgas A/S): Agern Allé 24–26, 2970 Hørsholm; tel. 45-17-10-22; fax 45-17-10-44; e-mail dong@dong.dk; internet www.dong.dk; f. 1972; petroleum and natural gas exploration, production, storage and distribution; production and sale of electricity, wind power and geothermal energy; agreed, in June 2001, to establish consortium with POGC of Poland to build a new pipeline, BalticPipe, to transport natural gas from the North Sea to Poland; Chair. SVEN RISKÆR.

CO-OPERATIVE

Co-op Danmark A/S (Co-operative of Denmark): Roskildevej 65, 2620 Albertslund; tel. 43-86-43-86; fax 43-86-33-86; e-mail coop@coop.dk; internet www.coop.dk; f. 1896; fmrly Fællesforeningen for Danmarks Brugsforeninger; CEO H. C. MADSEN; 1,113,506 mems.

TRADE UNIONS

Landsorganisationen i Danmark (LO) (Danish Confederation of Trade Unions): Islands Brygge 32D, 2300 Copenhagen S; tel. 35-24-60-00; fax 35-24-63-00; e-mail lo@lo.dk; internet www.lo.dk; Pres. HANS JENSEN; Vice-Pres. TINE A. BRØNDUM; 1,386,370 mems (2004); 1,031 brs.

Blik og Rørarbejderforbundet i Danmark: Immerkær 42, 3650 Hvidovre; tel. 36-38-36-38; fax 36-38-36-39; e-mail forbund@blikroer.dk; internet www.blikroer.dk; f. 2002; Chair. KURT H. JAKOBSEN; c. 10,000 mems.

Dansk Artist Forbund (DAF): Vendersgade 24, 1363 Copenhagen K; tel. 33-32-66-77; fax 33-33-73-30; e-mail artisten@artisten.dk; internet www.artisten.dk; f. 1918; Chair. NICK OLANDER; c. 1,500 mems.

Dansk El-Forbund (Electricians' Union): Vodroffsvej 26, 1900 Frederiksberg C; tel. 33-29-70-00; fax 33-29-70-70; e-mail def@def.dk; internet www.def.dk; Pres. ERIK ANDERSSON; 30,311 mems.

Dansk Frisør og Kosmetiker Forbund (Danish Hairdressers' and Beauticians' Union): Lersø Parkallé 21, 2100 Copenhagen Ø; tel. 35-83-18-80; fax 35-82-14-62; e-mail dfkf@dfkf.dk; internet www.dfkf.dk; Chair. POUL MONGGAARD; c. 5,400 mems.

Dansk Funktionærforbund—Serviceforbundet (Danish Federation of Salaried Employees): Upsalagade 20, 2100 Copenhagen Ø; tel. 70-15-04-00; fax 70-15-04-05; e-mail dff-s@dff-s.dk; internet www.dff-s.dk; Pres. KARSTEN HANSEN; 22,001 mems (2003).

Dansk Jernbaneforbund (Railway Workers): Søndermarksvej 16, 2500 Valby; tel. 36-13-25-00; fax 36-13-25-01; e-mail djf@djf.dk; internet www.djf.dk; f. 2002; Chair. ULRIK SALMONSEN.

Dansk Metal (Metalworkers): Nyropsgade 38, POB 308, 1780 Copenhagen V; tel. 33-63-20-00; fax 33-63-21-50; e-mail metal@danskmetal.dk; internet www.danskmetal.dk; f. 1888; Pres. MAX BAHRING; c. 146,000 mems.

Fag og Arbejde (FOA): Staunings Pl. 1–3, POB 11, 1790 Copenhagen V; tel. 33-43-46-00; fax 33-13-40-42; e-mail foa@foa.dk; internet www.foa.dk; f. 2005 by merger of Forbundet af Offentligt Ansatte and Pædagogisk Medhjælper Forbund; c. 215,000 mems.

Fagligt Fælles Forbund (3F): Kampmannsgade 4, POB 392, 1790 Copenhagen V; tel. 70-30-03-00; fax 70-30-03-01; e-mail 3f@3f.dk; internet www.3f.dk; f. 2005 by merger of Kvindeligt Arbejderforbund and Specialarbejderforbundet i Danmark; Chair. POUL ERIK SKOV CHRISTENSEN; c. 360,000 mems.

Forbundet Trae-Industri-Byg i Danmark (Timber Industry and Construction Workers): Mimersgade 41, 2200 Copenhagen N; tel. 35-31-95-99; fax 35-31-94-50; e-mail tib@tib.dk; internet www.tib.dk; Pres. ARNE JOHANSEN; c. 70,000 mems.

Grafisk Forbund (Printing Workers): Lygten 16, 2400 Copenhagen; tel. 31-81-44-89; fax 31-81-02-07; f. 1993 by merger; Pres. TOM DURBING; 24,025 mems.

HK Danmark (Union of Commercial and Clerical Employees in Denmark): Weidekampsgade 8, 0900 Copenhagen C; tel. 33-30-43-

43; fax 33-30-40-99; e-mail hk@hk.dk; internet www.hk.dk; f. 1900; c. 375,000 mems.

Hærens Konstabel- og Korporalforening (Union of Enlisted Privates and Corporals in the Danish Army): Kronprinsensgade 8, 1114 Copenhagen K; tel. 33-93-65-22; fax 33-93-65-23; e-mail hkkf@hkkf.dk; internet www.hkkf.dk; f. 1959; Chair. FLEMMING D. V. NIELSEN; c. 4,500 mems.

Malerforbundet i Danmark (Painters): Lersø Parkallé 109, 2100 Copenhagen Ø; tel. 39-16-79-00; fax 39-19-79-10; e-mail maler@maler.dk; internet www.maler.dk; f. 1890; Pres. JØRN ERIK NIELSEN; c. 13,600 mems.

Nærings- og Nydelsesmiddelarbejder Forbundet (Food, Sugar Confectionery, Chocolate, Dairy Produce and Tobacco Workers): C. F. Richsvej 103, POB 1479, 2000 Frederiksberg; tel. 38-18-72-72; fax 38-18-72-00; e-mail nnf@nnf.dk; internet www.nnf.dk; Pres. HENRY HOLT JOCHUMSEN; c. 39,000 mems.

RestaurationsBranchens Forbund (Restaurant Workers): Thoravej 29–33, 2400 Copenhagen NV; tel. and fax 72-24-72-24; e-mail faglig@rbf.dk; internet www.rbf.dk; Chair. PREBEN RASMUSSEN; c. 22,500 mems.

Socialpædagogernes Landsforbund (National Federation of Social Educators in Denmark): Brolæggerstræde 9, 1211 Copenhagen K; tel. 33-96-28-00; fax 33-96-29-96; e-mail sl@sl.dk; internet www.sl.dk; Pres. KIRSTEN NISSEN; 33,000 mems (2004).

Spillerforeningen: Pilestræde 35, 1, 1112 Copenhagen K; tel. 33-12-11-28; fax 33-12-56-21; e-mail mail@spillerforeningen.dk; internet www.spillerforeningen.dk; f. 1977; Dir MADS ØLAND; c. 650 mems.

Teknisk Landsforbund (Professional Technicians): Nørre Voldgade 12, 1358 Copenhagen K; tel. 33-43-65-00; fax 33-43-66-77; e-mail tl@tl.dk; internet www.tl.dk; f. 1919; Pres. OLE SKALS PEDERSEN; c. 31,200 mems.

Akademikernes Centralorganisation (Danish Confederation of Professional Associations): Nørre Voldgade 29, POB 2192, 1017 Copenhagen K; tel. 33-69-40-40; fax 33-93-85-40; e-mail ac@ac.dk; internet www.ac.dk; 238,871 mems (2001).

Den Almindelige Danske Lægeforening (Danish Medical Association): Trondhjemsgade 9, 2100 Copenhagen Ø; tel. 35-44-85-00; fax 35-44-85-05; e-mail dadl@dadl.dk; internet www.dadl.dk; 20,469 mems (2001).

Civiløkonomerne (Association of Danish Business Economists): Søtorvet 5, POB 2043, 1012 Copenhagen K; tel. 33-14-14-46; fax 33-14-11-49; e-mail info@civiloekonomerne.org; internet www.civiloekonomerne.org; 16,500 mems (2001).

Danmark Jurist- og Økonomforbund (Association of Danish Lawyers and Economists): Gothersgade 133, POB 2126, 1015 Copenhagen K; tel. 33-95-97-00; fax 33-95-99-99; e-mail djoef@djoef.dk; internet www.djoef.dk; 39,446 mems (2001).

Dansk Magisterforening (Danish Association of Masters and PhDs): Nimbusparken, Peter Bangs Vej 32, 2000 Frederiksberg; tel. 38-15-66-00; fax 38-15-66-66; e-mail dm@magister.dk; internet www.magister.dk; 33,000 mems (2001).

Erhvervssprogligt Forbund (Danish Association of Business Language Graduates): Skindergade 45–47, POB 2246, 1019 Copenhagen K; tel. 33-91-98-00; fax 33-91-68-18; e-mail esf@esf.dk; internet www.esf.dk.

Gymnasieskolernes Lærerforening (Danish National Union of Upper Secondary School Teachers): Vesterbrogade 16, 1620 Copenhagen V; tel. 33-29-09-00; fax 33-29-09-01; e-mail gl@gl.org; internet www.gl.org; 11,490 mems (2005).

Ingeniørforeningen i Danmark (Society of Danish Engineers): Ingeniørhuset, Kalvebod Brygge 31–33, 1780 Copenhagen V; tel. 33-18-48-48; fax 33-18-48-99; e-mail ida@ida.dk; internet www.ida.dk; 60,000 mems (2003).

Funktionærernes og Tjenestemændenes Fællesråd (Civil Servants' and Salaried Employees' Confederation): Niels Hemmingsens Gade 12, POB 1169, 1010 Copenhagen K; tel. 33-36-88-00; fax 33-36-88-80; internet www.jtj.dk; f. 1952; Chair. BENTE SORGENTREY; 358,989 mems (2004).

Transport

In June 1998 an 18-km combined tunnel-and-bridge road and rail link across the Great Belt, linking the islands of Zealand and Funen, was completed, at a cost of US $6,500m.; the project incorporated the world's second longest suspension bridge. A 15.9-km road and rail link across the Øresund Strait, between Copenhagen and Malmö, was completed in July 2000 at a total cost of about 23,400m. kroner. In October 1992 a number of Danish railway companies, in con-

junction with the German and Swedish state railways, announced a plan to develop a high-speed rail system linking Stockholm and Oslo with Copenhagen, and Copenhagen with Berlin, Hamburg and Köln. The plan, which was estimated, at that time, to cost 40,000m.–50,000m. kroner, would include the bridge over the Øresund Strait and would require new track between Copenhagen and Hamburg and the construction of a fixed link across the Fehmern Belt. In 1996 contracts were signed for the construction of a 22-km underground light railway system in Copenhagen. The second section of the Copenhagen Metro, from Frederiksberg to Kongens Nytorv, was opened in May 2003, seven months after the opening of the first section, and three years later than originally planned.

RAILWAYS

Banestyrelsen (Danish National Railway Agency): Pakhusvej 10, 2100 Copenhagen Ø; tel. 82-34-00-00; fax 82-34-20-38; e-mail bane@bane.dk; internet www.bane.dk; f. 1997 to assume, from the DSB (see below), responsibility for the maintenance and development of the national rail network; controls 2,349 km of line, of which 602 km are electrified; also manages signalling and train control; CEO JENS ANDERSEN.

DSB (Danish State Railways): Sølvgade 40, 1349 Copenhagen K; tel. 33-14-04-00; fax 33-51-41-20; e-mail dsb@dsb.dk; internet www.dsb.dk; became an independent public corporation in Jan. 1999; operates passenger services; CEO KELD SENGELØV.

A total of 526 km, mostly branch lines, is run by 15 private companies.

ROADS

At 31 December 2002 Denmark had an estimated 71,847 km of paved roads, including 918 km of motorways, 701 km of national roads and 9,988 km of secondary roads.

SHIPPING

The Port of Copenhagen is the largest port in Denmark and the only one to incorporate a Free Port Zone. The other major ports are Århus, Fredericia, Ålborg and Esbjerg, all situated in Jutland. There are petroleum terminals, with adjacent refineries, at Kalundborg, Stigsnæs and Fredericia. Ferry services are provided by Scandlines (see below) and by various private companies.

Farvandsvæsenet (Royal Danish Administration of Navigation and Hydrography): Overgaden oven Vandet 62B, POB 1919, 1023 Copenhagen K; tel. 32-68-95-00; fax 31-57-43-41; e-mail frv@frv.dk; internet www.frv.dk.

Port Authorities

Århus: Port Authority of Århus, Mindet 2, POB 130, 8100 Århus; tel. 86-13-32-66; fax 86-12-76-62; e-mail port@aarhus.dk; Port Dir BJARNE MATHIESEN.

Associated Danish Ports A/S (ADP): Vesthavnsvej 33, 7000 Fredericia; tel. 79-21-50-00; fax 79-21-50-05; e-mail post@adp-as.dk; internet www.adp-as.dk; has authority for ports of Fredericia and Nyborg; Man. Dir JENS PETER PETERS.

Copenhagen: Copenhagen Malmö Port AB, Nordre Toldbod 7, POB 9, 1001 Copenhagen K; tel. 35-46-11-11; fax 35-46-11-64; e-mail cmport@cmport.com; internet www.cmport.com; f. by merger of ports of Copenhagen and Malmö; Man. Dir LARS KARLSSON; Port Capt. S. ANDERSEN.

Esbjerg: Port of Esbjerg, Hulvejen 1, POB 2, 6701 Esbjerg; tel. 75-12-41-44; fax 75-13-40-50; e-mail adm@portesbjerg.dk; internet www.portesbjerg.dk; Port Dir OLE INGRISCH; Head of Maritime Dept KARL-JOHAN MADSEN.

Frederikshavn: Frederikshavn Havn, Oliepieren 7, POB 129, 9900 Frederikshavn; tel. 96-20-47-00; fax 96-20-47-11; e-mail info@frederikshavnhavn.dk; internet www.frederikshavnhavn.dk; Man.Dir PREBEN REINHOLT; Harbour Captain JESPER G. THOMSEN.

Kalundborg: Kalundborg Port Authority, Vestre Haunepl. 7, 4400 Kalundborg; tel. 59-53-40-00; fax 59-53-40-03; e-mail info@portofkalundborg.dk; internet www.portofkalundborg.dk.

Sønderborg: Sønderborg Havn, Norrebro 1, 6400 Sønderborg; tel. 74-42-27-65; fax 74-43-30-19; internet www.sonderborg.dk; Harbour Master LASS ANDERSEN.

Principal Shipping Companies

Corral Line A/S: Havnevej 18, 6320 Egernsund; e-mail info@corralline.com; tel. 74-44-14-35; fax 74-44-14-75; formerly Sønderborg Rederiaktieselskab; 8 livestock carriers of 19,302 grt; shipowners, managers, chartering agents; world-wide; Man. Dir B. CLAUSEN.

Rederiet Otto Danielsen: Kongevejen 272A, 2830 Virum; tel. 45-83-25-55; fax 45-83-17-07; e-mail od@ottodanielsen.com; f. 1944; 7

general cargo vessels, totalling 20,793 grt, under foreign flags; general tramp trade, chartering, ship sales; Fleet Man. Jørn Staureby.

Dannebrog Rederi A/S: Rungsted Strandvej 113, 2960 Rungsted Kyst; tel. 45-17-77-77; fax 45-17-77-70; e-mail dbrog@dannebrog .com; f. 1883; 3 ro-ro vessels, product chemical tanker services; liner service USA–Europe, US Gulf–Caribbean, Mediterranean–Caribbean; CEO Johan Wedell-Wedellsborg.

DFDS A/S: Sundkrogsgade 11, 2100 Copenhagen Ø; tel. 33-42-33-42; fax 33-42-33-41; e-mail dfds@dfds.com; internet www.dfds.com; f. 1866; 8 car/passenger ships and 31 freight vessels; passenger and car ferry services between Denmark, Belgium, Germany, Latvia, Lithuania, the Netherlands, Norway, Sweden and the UK; J. Lauritzen Holding owns majority share; Man. Dir Ole Frie.

H. Folmer & Co: Fredericiagade 57, 1310 Copenhagen K; tel. 33-13-25-10; fax 33-13-54-64; f. 1955; 14 general cargo vessels of 14,100 grt; world-wide tramping; Man. Owners J. J. Folmer, Uffe Martin Jensen.

J. Lauritzen A/S: Skt Annæ Pl. 28, POB 2147, 1291 Copenhagen K; tel. 33-96-80-00; e-mail info@j-lauritzen.com; internet www.j-lauritzen.com; f. 1884; operates reefer ships, LPG/C carriers and bulk ships; Pres. Torben Janholt.

Mercandia Rederierne: Prags Blvd 94, 2300 Copenhagen S; tel. 32-83-01-55; fax 32-83-01-50; e-mail mercandia@vip.cybercity.dk; internet www.mercandia.dk; f. 1964; 24 ro-ro vessels and car ferries totalling 238,200 grt; tramp and liner services; Man. Owner Per Henriksen.

A. P. Møller: Esplanaden 50, 1098 Copenhagen K; tel. 33-63-33-63; fax 33-14-15-15; internet www.maersk.com; f. 1904; fleet of 38 container vessels, 13 products tankers, 5 crude petroleum tankers, 13 gas carriers, 26 offshore vessels and 7 drilling rigs, totalling 3,081,900 grt under the Danish flag; further tonnage owned by subsidiary cos in Singapore and the United Kingdom; world-wide liner and feeder services under the name of **Maersk Line**, and world-wide tanker, bulk, offshore and rig services; Man. Owner Jess Søderberg.

Dampskibsselskabet Norden A/S: Amaliegade 49, 1256 Copenhagen K; tel. 33-15-04-51; fax 33-15-61-99; e-mail mail@ds-norden .com; internet www.ds-norden.com; f. 1871; operates about 60 tankers and bulk carriers; world-wide tramping; Man. Dir Steen R. Krabbe.

Scandlines AG: Dampfaergevej 10, 2100 Copenhagen Ø; tel. 33-15-15-15; fax 35-29-02-01; e-mail scandlines@scandlines.dk; internet www.scandlines.dk; f. 1998 by merger of Scandlines A/S and Deutsche Fährgesellschaft Ostsee GmbH (Germany); maintains offices in Germany and Sweden; owned by Danish Govt and Deutsche Bahn; operates 20 ferry routes around Denmark and throughout the Baltic.

A/S Em. Z. Svitzer: Brøndby; tel. 43-43-43-71; fax 43-43-60-22; f. 1833; wholly-owned subsidiary of A. P. Møller; 22 tugs and salvage vessels and a barge fleet; salvage, towage and barge services; Gen. Man. Keld Balle Mortensen.

A/S Dampskibsselskabet Torm: Tuborg Havnevej 18, 2900 Hellerup; tel. 39-17-92-00; fax 39-17-93-93; e-mail mail@torm.dk; internet www.torm.dk; f. 1889; 16 product carriers of 617,772 grt, 7 bulk carriers of 199,507 grt, 2 multipurpose vessels of 27,376 grt and 2 AHTs (1999); operator of a time-chartered fleet; Man. Dir Klaus Kjærulff.

Shipping Association

Danmarks Rederiforening (Danish Shipowners' Asscn): Amaliegade 33, 1256 Copenhagen K; tel. 33-11-40-88; fax 33-11-62-10; e-mail info@shipowners.dk; internet www.danmarksrederiforening .dk; f. 1884; 21 mems, representing 6.7m. grt (Jan. 2002); Chair. of the Bd Knud Pontoppidan; Man. Dir Peter Bjerregaard.

CIVIL AVIATION

The main international airport is Copenhagen Airport, situated about 10 km from the centre of the capital. The following domestic airports have scheduled flights to European and Scandinavian destinations: Ålborg, Århus and Billund in Jutland. Other domestic airports include Roskilde (30 km south-west of Copenhagen); Esbjerg, Karup, Skrydstrup, Stauning, Sønderborg and Thisted in Jutland; Odense in Funen; and Bornholm Airport on the island of Bornholm.

Statens Luftfartsvæsen (Civil Aviation Administration): Luftfartshuset, POB 744, 2450 Copenhagen SV; tel. 36-18-60-00; fax 36-18-60-01; e-mail dcaa@slv.dk; internet www.slv.dk; Dir-Gen. Ole Asmussen.

Scandinavian Airlines System (SAS): Head Office: Hedegårdsvej 88, POB 150, 2770 Kastrup; tel. 32-32-00-00; internet www.sas.dk; f. 1946; the national carrier of Denmark, Norway and Sweden. It is a consortium owned two-sevenths by SAS Danmark A/S, two-sevenths by SAS Norge ASA and three-sevenths by SAS Sverige AB. Each parent organization is a limited company owned 50% by its respective government and 50% by private shareholders. The SAS group includes the consortium and the subsidiaries in which the consortium has a majority or otherwise controlling interest; the Board consists of two members from each of the parent companies and the chairmanship rotates among the three national chairmen on an annual basis. SAS absorbed Linjeflyg AB (domestic passenger, newspaper and postal services in Sweden) in January 1993; strategic alliance with Lufthansa (Germany) formed in 1995; Chair. Bo Berggren; Pres. and CEO Jan Stenberg.

National Airlines

Cimber Air Denmark: Sønderborg Airport, Lufthavnsvej 2, 6400 Sønderborg; tel. 74-42-22-77; fax 74-42-65-11; e-mail marketing@ cimber.dk; internet www.cimber.dk; f. 1950; operates domestic service in co-operation with Lufthansa and SAS; operates charter flights and total route systems for other cos throughout Europe; markets electronic data systems for airlines and industry; third party maintenance of AIR 42/72; Pres., CEO Jorgen Nielsen.

Maersk Air: Copenhagen Airport South, 2791 Dragør; tel. 32-31-44-44; fax 32-31-44-90; e-mail info@maersk-air.dk; internet www .maersk-air.com; f. 1969; provides charter flights for Scandinavian tour operators, operates international flights; owned by Møller Group (see under Shipping); subsidiary: Maersk Air Cargo; Chair. Bent Erik Carlsen; Pres. Finn Øelund.

Premiair: Copenhagen Airport South, Hangar 276, 2791 Dragør; tel. 32-47-72-00; fax 32-45-12-20; internet www.premiair.com; f. 1994 by merger of Conair A/S (Denmark) and Scanair (Sweden); controlling stake acquired by Airtours (United Kingdom) in 1996; flights to major destinations in Europe; Pres. Tom Clausen.

Star Air: Copenhagen Airport South, 2791 Dragør; tel. 32-31-43-01; fax 32-31-43-90; e-mail dcdq@starair.dk; internet www.maersk-air .com; f. 1987; operates cargo services in Europe; Pres. Finn Øelund.

SUN-AIR of Scandinavia A/S: Cumulusvej 10, 7190 Billund; tel. 76-50-01-00; fax 75-33-86-18; e-mail info@sunair.dk; internet www .sunair.dk; f. 1978; also maintains offices at Aalborg, Århus, Billund and Thisted Airports; operates charter flights, sells and leases aircraft and operates aircraft maintenance services, operates a franchise of scheduled flights throughout northern Europe in co-operation with British Airways since 1996; Dir Niels Sundberg.

Tourism

In 2001 tourist arrivals in Denmark totalled 2.03m.; in that year receipts from tourism totalled US $4,600m. Receipts from tourism increased to US $5,785m. in 2002.

Danmarks Turistråd (The Danish Tourist Board): Vesterbrogade 6D, 1620 Copenhagen V; tel. 33-11-14-15; fax 33-93-14-16; e-mail dt@ dt.dk; internet www.visitdenmark.com; f. 1967; Dir Lars Sandahl Sørensen.

DANISH EXTERNAL TERRITORIES

THE FAROE ISLANDS

Introductory Survey

Location, Climate, Language, Religion, Flag, Capital

The Faroe Islands are a group of 18 islands (of which 17 are inhabited) in the Atlantic Ocean, between Scotland and Iceland. The main island is Streymoy, where more than one-third of the population resides. The climate is mild in winter and cool in summer, with a mean temperature of 7°C (45°F). Most of the inhabitants profess Christianity: the majority of Faroese belong to the Evangelical Lutheran Church of Denmark. The principal language is Faroese, but Danish is a compulsory subject in all schools. The flag (proportions 16 by 22) displays a red cross, bordered with blue, on a white background, the upright of the cross being to the left of centre. The capital is Tórshavn, which is situated on Streymoy.

History and Government

The Faroe Islands have been under Danish administration since Queen Margrethe I of Denmark inherited Norway in 1380. The islands were occupied by the United Kingdom while Denmark was under German occupation during the Second World War, but they were restored to Danish control immediately after the war. The Home Rule Act of 1948 gave the Faroese control over all their internal affairs. The Faroe Islands did not join the European Community (now European Union—EU, see p. 217) with Denmark in 1973. There is a local parliament (the Løgting—Lagting in Danish), but the Danish legislature, the Folketing, to which the Faroese send two members, is responsible for defence and foreign policy, constitutional matters, and the judicial and monetary systems. The Faroes control fishing resources within their fisheries zone, and in September 1992 a long-standing dispute between Denmark and the Faroes was settled when the Danish Government agreed to give the Faroese authorities legislative and administrative power over mineral resources, including those beneath the bed of the sea in the area adjacent to the islands. This agreement removed one of the major obstacles to exploration for hydrocarbons off the Faroe Islands, where geologists consider that prospects for discovering reserves of petroleum and natural gas are favourable. In 1994 the Faroe Islands accordingly awarded a US company a licence to begin exploratory surveys, despite the existence of a long-standing dispute between Denmark and the United Kingdom over the demarcation of the continental shelf west of the Shetland Islands and south-east of the Faroe Islands, which had threatened to delay prospecting. This dispute was resolved in mid-1999, however, when representatives of the Faroese Government (the Landsstýri) signed an agreement with the Danish and British Governments regarding the location of the boundaries of the area concerned. The area, known as the 'golden corner' (formerly the White Zone), was believed to be potentially rich in petroleum reserves. Following the issue by the Faroese Government of a number of licences in mid-August 2000, exploratory drilling commenced in the 'golden corner' in mid-2001 (see Economy).

The centre-left coalition Government of the Social Democratic Party (SDP), Republicans and the People's Party, formed in 1975, collapsed in 1980 over a plan, opposed by the conservative People's Party, to extend through the winter months a government-owned ferry service linking the islands with Denmark, Norway and Scotland. At a general election, held in November, conservative political groups slightly increased their share of the popular vote. Although there was no material change in the balance of party representation in the Løgting, the Union Party formed a centre-right coalition with the People's Party and the Home Rule Party in January 1981. A general election was held in November 1984, and in December a four-party, centre-left coalition Government was formed under the premiership of Atli Dam, comprising his SDP, the Home Rule Party, the Republican Party and the Christian People's Party combined with the Progressive and Fishing Industry Party (CPP-PFIP).

Elections in 1988 demonstrated a shift to the right in the Faroes, to the benefit of the People's Party. Its one member in the Danish Folketing increased his support in the national elections of September 1987 and May 1988. At a Faroese general election in November 1988 the incumbent Government lost its majority, and the People's Party became the largest party in the Løgting. In January 1989, after 10 weeks of negotiations, a centre-right coalition, comprising the People's Party, the Republican Party, the Home Rule Party and the CPP-PFIP, and led by Jógvan Sundstein (Chairman of the People's Party), was formed. The coalition was committed to economic austerity and support for the fishing industry. In June, however, the CPP-PFIP and the Home Rule Party withdrew their support for the Government. After three weeks a new coalition was formed. Sundstein remained Prime Minister (Løgmaður), and his People's Party was supported by the Republican Party and the Union Party. In October 1990, however, these two parties withdrew their support for the coalition Government. As a result, an early general election was held in November. The SDP obtained the largest share of the vote, winning 10 seats (an increase of three), while the People's Party, which led the outgoing coalition, won seven seats (a loss of one seat).

In January 1991 a coalition between the SDP and the People's Party was formed, under the leadership of Atli Dam. He was replaced in January 1993 by Marita Petersen (also of the SDP). In April the People's Party withdrew from the coalition, and was replaced by the Republican Party and the Home Rule Party. At a general election, held in July 1994, the Union Party became the largest party in the Løgting, winning eight seats (an increase of two), while the SDP's allocation of seats was reduced from 10 to five. In September a coalition of the Union Party, the SDP, the Home Rule Party and the newly formed Labour Front took office. Edmund Joensen (Chairman of the Union Party) replaced Petersen as Prime Minister. In 1996 the People's Party replaced the SDP in the governing coalition. Joensen remained Prime Minister, while Anfinn Kallsberg succeeded Jóannes Eidesgaard as Minister of Finance and Economics. A general election was held on 30 April 1998, at which both the Republican Party and the People's Party each increased their allocation of seats to eight, while the number of seats secured by the SDP rose from five to seven; the parliamentary representation of the Union Party was reduced from eight seats to six. In mid-May a coalition Government was formed by members of the People's Party, the Republican Party and the Home Rule Party, under the premiership of Anfinn Kallsberg of the People's Party.

Tensions with the Danish Government in the early 1990s, the nationalistic persuasion of the new Government and the prospect of offshore petroleum discoveries revived Faroese ambitions for political and economic independence. (The Faroese had narrowly favoured independence from Denmark in a referendum in 1946, but the decision had been overturned by the Danish Folketing.) In October 1998 the Løgting adopted a resolution in support of the Government's intention (announced earlier that year) to seek status for the Faroe Islands as a 'sovereign nation' under the Danish monarchy, having a common monetary system with Denmark; it was envisaged by the Faroese Government that sovereignty for the islands would be most appropriately achieved through continued co-operation with Denmark within a new constitutional framework, based on a bilateral treaty between the two countries as equal, independent partners. A commission charged with the development of a proposal for a Faroese constitution was established by the Government in February 1999, and submitted its conclusions to the Løgting in June 2000. The Faroese envisaged retaining the Danish Queen Margrethe II as their Head of State and maintaining the link between their local currency and the Danish krone. The islands would seek to continue to co-operate with Denmark in social affairs, justice, health and air traffic control, and would also maintain present arrangements such as mutual rights of residence, employment and education. The Faroes would also seek to join NATO (see p. 301) and the UN.

Negotiations between the Danish and Faroese administrations concerning the future independence of the Faroe Islands began in March 2000, but swiftly stalled after the Danish Government confirmed that it would not oppose Faroese independence but would terminate annual subsidies (of about 1,000m. kroner) to the Faroes in four years time, compared with the 15 years envisaged by the Faroese. The Danish Prime Minister, Poul Nyrup Rasmussen, rejected an offer of mediation from the Icelandic premier, Davíð Oddsson. Discussions were resumed later in the year, but finally collapsed in late October, prompting Kallsberg to announce a plan to hold a referendum on independence in 2001. The Faroese had initially envisaged the successful negotiation of a treaty with the Danish Government prior to a referendum. The referendum, which in February was scheduled to be held on 26 May, was to include four issues: the full transfer of authority to the Faroese by 2012; the establishment of an economic fund to guarantee financial security during the transitional period; the gradual elimination of subsidies from Denmark; and the holding of a further referendum establishing the Faroe Islands as an independent state by 2012. The Danish Government reacted strongly to plans for a plebiscite, claiming that Denmark would regard it as a *de facto* referendum on sovereignty and that a vote in favour of the proposals for independence would result in the halting of Danish aid within four years. The reluctance of the Faroese population to lose Danish subsidies and disagreement within the Faroese coalition Government resulted in the cancellation of the referendum in early March 2001. Shortly afterwards agreement was reached within the Faroese Government on a plan for independence, which was subsequently submitted to the Danish authorities.

At the general election, held on 30 April 2002, the People's Party won seven seats in the Løgting; it subsequently formed a coalition Government with the Republican Party (which had secured eight seats), the Home Rule Party (one seat) and the Centre Party (one seat); the Union Party secured eight seats in the Løgting, and the Social Democratic Party won seven seats.

The Minister of Fisheries, Jørgen Niclasen, resigned in January 2003 following revelations of financial improprieties regarding loans he had made to prawn trawlers using public funds; Kallsberg assumed the portfolio.

On 26 June 2003 the Danish Prime Minister, Anders Fogh Rasmussen, made an official visit to the Faroe Islands. During his visit he and Kallsberg signed a bill providing a legal basis for the transfer of competencies from the Danish to the Faroese Governments. The legislation did not in itself transfer any powers (this was to be done subsequently, with a separate resolution required in the Løgting for each power to be transferred), but it did detail those powers which would remain with the Danish Folketing, namely: the Danish Constitution; Danish citizenship; the Danish Supreme Court; currency and monetary policy; and foreign, security and defence policy. As with other bilateral agreements, identical versions of the bill, in both Faroese and Danish, were to pass before the Løgting and the Folketing, respectively. The bill passed through the first of three readings in the Løgting in April 2005. It was expected that it would be enacted by 29 July (the Faroese National Day). Following its enactment the Faroese Government intended to transfer to its control powers covering civil emergency preparedness, company law, copyright law and industrial property rights, and the established church—all during its current term of office (which was due to last until 2008). The Government was also preparing to assume ownership of Vágar Airport from the Danish Government, and was reviewing the option to assume responsibility for civil aviation. Areas that remained to be transferred at a later stage were: the regulation of immigration and border control; criminal law; legislation and administration of the financial sector; health care; the judicial courts (excluding the Danish Supreme Court); the issuing of passports; the police and prosecution service; the prison service; and public pensions. Independently of this process, an additional piece of new legislation was presented to the Løgting and the Folketing to grant the Faroese Government authority to negotiate and conclude agreements under international law with other states and international organizations, and to allow (under certain circumstances) the Faroe Islands to become a member of international organizations in their own right. This bill was to be passed and enacted concurrently with the transfer of competencies bill.

In December 2003 the Republican Party withdrew from the ruling coalition, causing the collapse of the Government. The crisis was precipitated by the publication of a book that alluded to Kallsberg's past involvement in accounting fraud; he was accused of misappropriating 912,000 kroner between 1977 and 1981. Claiming that the money had subsequently been repaid

and that he had not personally gained from the affair, Kallsberg rejected demands by the leader of the Republican Party, Høgni Hoydal, to issue a public apology or to resign. Following the collapse of the Government Kallsberg called an early election.

At the general election, held on 20 January 2004, the Republican Party won eight seats, while the Union Party, the Social Democratic Party and the People's Party each won seven seats. A new coalition was agreed on 31 January and a new Government was officially formed on 3 February, with Jóannes Eidesgaard of the Social Democratic Party as Prime Minister. Whereas the previous coalition had been composed of only pro-independence parties and had thus favoured a swift severance of connections with Denmark, the new administration comprised the People's Party, which supported independence, and the Union Party and the Social Democratic Party, which both favoured continued union with Denmark. The new Government was expected to opt for the compromise arrangement of greater independence from Denmark without severing ties.

In January 2004 Eidesgaard dismissed the Minister of Fisheries, Jóhan Dahl, following allegations that Dahl had evaded a business debt years ago that his late business partner's widow had been obliged to pay. Bjørn Kalsø was appointed to replace Dahl the following day. In March the Government abolished the Ministry of Petroleum, which became the Faroese Petroleum Administration, part of the Ministry of Trade and Industry.

In March 2004 the Government proposed a resolution recognizing that, despite the Faroe Islands' long-standing policy of neutrality, they were a *de facto* member of NATO and had been so for some 50 years. Conservative members of the Løgting offered to support the Islands' formal accession to NATO.

In August 2004 the Danish Minister of Foreign Affairs, Per Stig Møller, paid a one-day visit to the Faroes during which he promised the islanders greater influence over Faroese foreign policy issues, and stated that the islands would be given 'full insight' into any issues affecting Faroese defence policy. The Faroe Islands would also be permitted to attend NATO meetings whenever relevant issues were under discussion.

In international affairs, the Faroe Islanders earned opprobrium for their traditional slaughter of pilot whales, an important source of food. After foreign journalists publicized the whaling in 1986, stricter regulations were imposed on whaling operations. In July 1992 the Faroese Government threatened to leave the International Whaling Commission (IWC, see p. 366), following the latter's criticism of whaling methods practised in the Faroe Islands. It was, however, claimed that the Faroese did not have the legal right to withdraw from the Commission independently of Denmark. In September the Faroe Islands, Greenland, Norway and Iceland agreed to establish the North Atlantic Marine Mammal Commission, in protest at what they viewed as the IWC's preoccupation with conservation. The Faroe Islands resumed commercial hunting of the minke whale in 1993 and began trading in whale meat in 2002 after a halt of 14 years. In March 2003 it was reported that the Faroe Islands were to begin importing whale meat from Norway.

Economic Affairs

In 1995 gross national product (GNP), estimated at 1990 prices, was US $829m., equivalent to $19,000 per head. Between 1973 and 1988, it was estimated, GNP increased, in real terms, at an average rate of 4.5% per year, with real GNP per head rising by 3.3% annually. Between 1989 and 1993, however, real GNP decreased dramatically, at an average rate of 9.4% per year. During 1994–95 real GNP increased by 4.2%. The population declined at an average annual rate of 1.6% in 1989–95, but increased by 1.1% per year in 1995–1999. Gross domestic product (GDP) increased, in real terms, by about 9.6% in 2002.

Agriculture (principally sheep-farming) and fishing contributed 20.5% of GDP in 2000. In 2002 the sector provided 13.9% of employment. Potatoes and other vegetables are the main crops. Only about 6% of the land surface is cultivated.

Fishing is the dominant industry. In 1999 fishing, aquaculture and fish-processing accounted for 25.1% of GDP; the sector employed 23% of the labour force in 1994. Fishing accounted for 96.3% of exports in 2003. Most fishing takes place within the 200-nautical-mile (370-km) fisheries zone imposed around the Faroes in 1977. In the 1980s fish farming began to be encouraged. By the early 2000s, however, the fish-farming industry was suffering from the effects of disease and low prices for farmed salmon. While vaccination of fry was legal in late 2004, the low prices paid to the fish farmers for their stock discouraged them from investing the necessary funds to carry this out. The traditional hunting of pilot whales continues to provide an important source of meat for the Faroese. The Faroe Islands resumed commercial hunting of the minke whale in 1993 and began trading in whale meat in 2002 after a halt of 14 years.

Industry (including mining, manufacturing, construction and power) contributed 19.0% of GDP in 2000. In 2002 the sector provided 21.6% of employment. The dominant sectors are fishing-related industries, such as fish-drying and -freezing, and ship maintenance and repairs.

Mining and quarrying contributed only 0.3% of GDP in 2000. 'Brown coal' (lignite) is mined on Suðuroy. The potential for petroleum production around the islands is believed to be significant. Following the resolution of a boundary dispute with the United Kingdom in May 1999, in mid-2000 the Ministry of Petroleum issued seven exploration licences (of six to nine years' duration) to 12 oil companies, organized into five groups, in the 'golden corner' (formerly the White Zone), an area south-east of the Faroe Islands; exploratory drilling commenced in mid-2001. In November the US company Amerada Hess announced that it had discovered petroleum in considerable quantities. It was expected, however, that, owing to Faroese tax laws, the islands would not derive any substantial income from the reserves for 12 years. The Danish authorities also stated that they intended to renegotiate Denmark's subsidy agreement with the Faroe Islands should the latter start to make a profit from the petroleum reserves. In January 2002 the Faroes Oil and Gas Company (FOGC—Føroya Kolvetni) became the first Faroese company to be listed on the London Stock Exchange. The Faroese Petroleum Administration (as the Ministry of Petroleum had become in early 2004) announced a second licensing round for offshore drilling in mid-2004.

Manufacturing contributed 11.4% of GDP in 2000. The dominant sector is fish-processing, which accounted for 5.7% of GDP in 1999. Technical repairs and shipyards contributed 2.1% of GDP in 1999, while exports of vessels accounted for 3.6% of exports in 2003. A small textile industry exports traditional Faroese woollens.

The energy sector contributed 2.1% of GDP in 2000. About 48% of the islands' energy requirements are provided by a hydroelectric power plant. In July 2003 Elfelagið SEV, the state electricity company, announced that it was to construct a power station in conjunction with a Scottish firm, Wavegen. The power station was to use tunnels built into cliffs on the shoreline to exploit energy from the sea. Imports of fuels and related products accounted for 9.8% of imports in 2003.

The services sector accounted for 60.6% of GDP in 2000. In 2002 the sector provided 64.5% of employment. In November 2003 an independent Faroese securities market was launched in co-operation with the Icelandic stock market.

In 2002 the Faroe Islands recorded a trade surplus of 518m. kroner, and there was a surplus of 1,339m. kroner on the current account of the balance of payments. Denmark was the Faroes' principal source of imports (27.1%) in 2003; other major suppliers were Germany (22.1%), Norway (20.5%) and Sweden (4.6%). Denmark was also the principal market for exports (23.3%) in that year; other major purchasers were the United Kingdom (22.1%), Spain (11.9%) and France (including Monaco) (9.4%). In 2003 the European Union (EU, see p. 217) as a whole took 79.0% of exports and supplied 66.7% of imports. The principal imports in 2003 were machinery and transport equipment (accounting for 41.5% of the total cost of imports), food and live animals (14.0%) and basic manufactures (12.4%). Principal exports in that year were frozen fish (contributing 35.0% of total export revenue), chilled fish (33.0%), and salted fish (16.4%).

Danish subsidies are an important source of income to the islands, and accounted for 16.7% of total government revenue in 2002. In that year, including the central government grant of 629.3m. kroner as revenue, the Faroese Government recorded a budget surplus of 175.9m. kroner. At the end of 1999 the net foreign debt was estimated at 447m. kroner. The annual rate of inflation was 4.3% in 2000 and 7.7% in 2001. In mid-2003 unemployment stood at 3% of the labour force (compared with 16% in mid-1995).

The Faroe Islands did not join the European Community (now EU) with Denmark in 1973, but did secure favourable terms of trade with Community members and special concessions in Denmark and the United Kingdom. Agreements on free trade were concluded between the Faroe Islands and Iceland, Norway, Sweden, Finland and Austria in 1992–93 and between the Faroe Islands and the EU in January 2004. In international fisheries organizations, where Denmark is represented by the EU, the Kingdom maintains separate membership in respect of the Faroe Islands (and Greenland). The Faroe Islands is also a member of the Nordic Council (see p. 296).

During the 1980s the Faroes' principal source of income, the fishing industry, was expanded with the help of substantial investment and official subsidies, financed by external borrowing. However, depletion of stocks and the resulting decline in catches, together with a fall in export prices, led to a reduction in export earnings and a financial crisis in the early 1990s (GDP was estimated to have declined by some 20% in 1993). The Danish Government attempted to stabilize the economy by restructuring the banking sector and by extending significant loans (by the end of 1997 it was estimated that the Faroes owed some 5,500m. kroner to the Danish Government, equivalent to 140,000 kroner per head). The report of an independent commission of inquiry into Denmark's response to the crisis in the Faroes, which had been established by the islanders in 1995, was published in early 1998 and levelled accusations of serious mismanagement at Danish government officials, and at the Danish Den Danske Bank. In June 1998 an agreement was reached by the Faroese and Danish Governments regarding a reduction of Faroese debt to Denmark as a form of compensation. Denmark's annual subsidy provides nearly one-third of the Faroes' budget. However, a number of petroleum companies commenced exploratory offshore drilling in Faroese waters during 2001, and initial results proved promising (see above). The discovery of substantial and commercially viable reserves of natural gas and petroleum would enable the Faroese economy to diversify, thereby reducing its overwhelming dependence on Danish subsidies as well as on the fisheries sector. From the end of the 1990s until the mid-2000s the Faroe Islands experienced a period of economic prosperity with high levels of growth and low unemployment. In May 2003, however, a nationwide strike began after the Government rejected a pay agreement reached between workers and management at the state-owned electricity company, Elfelagið SEV. About 12,000 members from five trade unions went on strike in sympathy with the electricity workers, closing schools, nurseries and shops and causing severe disruption to the docks, the postal service and public transport. The dispute was finally settled after 28 days. The strike, together with a sharp decline in fish prices, lower economic activity and tax reductions, contributed to a fall in GDP growth to an estimated 3.6% in 2003, compared with 9.5% in 2002. In late 2004 this downward trend continued as the fishing catch declined and the aquaculture industry struggled; a budget deficit was forecast for 2005. The Government proposed increasing domestic investment in order to encourage economic activity and employment, yet, despite this, overall investment was predicted to decline. Unemployment was reported to have increased in mid-2004, and was expected to rise further.

Education

The education system is similar to that of Denmark, except that Faroese is the language of instruction. Danish is, however, a compulsory subject in all schools. The Faroese Academy was upgraded to the University of the Faroe Islands in 1990.

In 2002 projected government expenditure on education, research and culture was set at 631.3m. kroner (representing 17.6% of total estimated budgetary spending).

Public Holidays

Public holidays in the Faroe Islands are the same as those for Denmark. In addition, the Faroese also celebrate Flag Day on 25 April and St Ólavsøka on 28–29 July each year. Various regional holidays are also observed in May–July.

Statistical Survey

Sources (unless otherwise stated): Statistics Faroe Islands, Traðagøta 39, POB 2068, 165 Argir; tel. 352028; fax 352038; e-mail hagstova@hagstova.fo; internet www.hagstova.fo; Faroese Government Office, Hovedvagtsgade 8, 2, 1103 Copenhagen K; tel. 33-14-08-66; fax 33-93-85-75; *Yearbook of Nordic Statistics*; Danmarks Statistik, Sejrøgade 11, POB 2550, 2100 Copenhagen Ø; tel. 39-17-39-17; fax 39-17-39-99; e-mail dst@dst.dk; internet www.dst.dk.

AREA AND POPULATION

Area: 1,398.9 sq km (540.1 sq miles).

Population: 47,704 at 31 December 2002; 48,812 (males 25,050, females 23,164) at 31 December 2003.

Density (31 December 2003): 34.9 per sq km.

Principal Towns (population at 31 December 2003): Tórshavn (capital) 12,657; Klaksvík 4,696; Hoyvík 2,806; Argir 1,852; Fuglafjørður 1,559.

Births, Marriages and Deaths (2003): Registered live births 704 (birth rate 14.7 per 1,000); Registered marriages 248 in 2002 (marriage rate 5.2 per 1,000); Registered deaths 407 (death rate 8.5 per 1,000).

Expectation of Life (years at birth, 2003): Males 76.5; Females 81.0.

Immigration and Emigration (2003): *Immigration:* Denmark 1,196; Greenland 30; Iceland 53; Norway 86; Sweden 12; Europe (unspecified) 117; Africa 8; Canada 2; USA 8; Americas (unspecified) 7; Asia 26; Oceania 3; Unknown 2; Total 1,550. *Emigration:* Denmark 1,056; Greenland 15; Finland 3; Iceland 40; Norway 52; Sweden 16; Europe (unspecified) 112; Africa 2; Canada 1; USA 5; Americas (unspecified) 12; Asia 4; Oceania 3; Total 1,321.

Economically Active Population ('000 persons, aged 15–64, 2002): Agriculture, hunting, forestry and fishing 4.3; Mining, manufacturing, and electricity and water supply 5.0; Construction 1.7; Wholesale and retail trade, restaurants and hotels 4.2; Transport and communication 2.5; Finance, insurance, real estate and business services 3.5; Other services 9.8; Unknown 0.4; *Total employed* 31.5.

HEALTH AND WELFARE

Key Indicators

Physicians (per 1,000 head, 2003): 1.7.

Hospital Beds (per 1,000 head, 2003): 5.9.

AGRICULTURE AND FISHING

Principal Crop (FAO estimate, 2003): Potatoes 1,500 metric tons. Source: FAO.

Livestock (FAO estimates, '000 head, year ending September 2003): Cattle 2; Sheep 68. Source: FAO.

Livestock Products (FAO estimates, metric tons, 2003): Beef and veal 77; Mutton and lamb 521; Sheepskins (fresh) 119. Source: FAO.

Fishing (FAO estimates, '000 metric tons, live weight, 2002): Capture 490.0 (Atlantic cod 38.1; Saithe (Pollock) 50.2; Blue whiting (Poutassou) 235.0; Capelin 35.0; Atlantic herring 35.2; Atlantic mackerel 24.0); Aquaculture 50.9 (Atlantic salmon 40.9); Total catch 540.9. Figures exclude aquatic mammals, recorded by number rather than by weight. Source: FAO.

INDUSTRY

Selected Products ('000 metric tons, unless otherwise indicated, 1996): Frozen or chilled fish 123; Salted and processed fish products 15; Aquaculture products 13; Oils, fats and meal of aquatic animals 124; Electric energy (million kWh) 182.

FINANCE

(Danish currency is in use)

Budget (million kroner, provisional, 2002): *Revenue:* Income taxes 1,675.3; Customs, excise and production duties 1,239.6; Interest, dividends 139.0; Share of net profit of Danmarks Nationalbank 21.0; Transfers from the Danish Government 629.3; Other revenue 57.9; Total 3,762.1. *Expenditure:* The Løgting 31.0; Central government 39.6; Financial matters 218.7; Fishing, shipping etc. 146.4; Economic services 376.1; Education and research, culture 631.3; Health and social welfare 1,670.3; Quarrying 23.7; Autonomy affairs 13.7; Interest paid and other expenditure 195.2; Investment 240.3; Total 3,586.2.

Cost of Living (Consumer Price Index at 1 January; base: 1 April 2001 = 100): All items 99.3 in 2002; 101.0 in 2003; 101.5 in 2004.

National Income and Product (million kroner at current prices, 2002): Compensation of employees 6,239; Gross operating surplus and mixed income 2,752; *Gross domestic product (GDP) at factor cost* 8,991; Taxes on products (net) 1,221; Other taxes on production (net) –44; *GDP in market prices* 10,168; Primary incomes received from abroad 705; *Less* Primary incomes paid abroad 345; *Gross national income (GNI)* 10,528; Current transfers from abroad 923; *Less* current transfers paid abroad 132; *Gross national disposable income* 11,319.

Expenditure on the Gross Domestic Product (million kroner at current prices, 2002): Government final consumption expenditure 2,570; Private final consumption expenditure 5,191; Increase in stocks –94; Gross fixed capital formation 2,322; *Total domestic expenditure* 9,989; Exports of goods and services 4,676; *Less* Imports of goods and services 4,497; GDP *in purchasers' values* 10,168.

Gross Domestic Product by Economic Activity (million kroner at current prices, 2000): Agriculture, fishing, etc. 1,551; Mining and quarrying 21; Manufacturing 867; Electricity, gas and water 161; Construction 388; Trade, restaurants and hotels 835; Transport, storage and communications 601; Financing 434; Dwellings 756; Business services 216; Domestic services, etc. 97; Government services 1,651; *Sub-total* 7,580; *Less* imputed bank service charges 401; *GDP at factor cost* 7,179; Indirect taxes 1,352; *Less* Subsidies 211; *GDP in purchasers' values* 8,320.

Balance of Payments (million kroner, 2002): Exports of goods f.o.b. 4,235; Imports of goods c.i.f. –3,717; *Trade balance* 518; Exports of services 522; Imports of services –866; *Balance on goods and services* 175; Other income received 705; Other income paid –345; *Balance on goods, services and income* 535; Current transfers received 860; Current transfers paid –56; *Current balance* 1,339.

EXTERNAL TRADE

Principal Commodities (million kroner, 2003): *Imports c.i.f.:* Food and live animals 651.4 (Feeding stuff for animals, excl. unmilled cereals 256.3); Crude materials (inedible) except fuels 151.3; Mineral fuels, lubricants, etc. 446.3 (Petroleum, petroleum products, etc. 444.9); Chemicals and related products 287.6 (Medicinal and pharmaceutical products 99.3); Basic manufactures 575.5 (Paper, paperboard and manufactures 96.7; Metal manufactures 243.4); Machinery and transport equipment 1,923.9 (Machinery specialized for particular industries 142.8; General industrial machinery, equipment and parts 143.4; Office machines and automatic data-processing equipment 94.6; Telecommunications and sound equipment 96.0; Other electrical machinery 110.7; Road vehicles (incl. air-cushion vehicles) 256.5; Other transport equipment 989.0); Miscellaneous manufactured articles 523.2 (Articles of apparel and clothing accessories, excl. footwear 111.1); Total (incl. others) 4,540.6. *Exports f.o.b.:* Frozen, chilled, salted, smoked and dried fish 3,764.4 (Cod 941.2; Haddock 331.0; Salmon 804.2; Trout 159.9; Blue whiting 127.5; Shrimps 221.4; Other species 860.5); Vessels 139.0; Total (incl. others) 3,908.0.

Principal Trading Partners (million kroner, 2003): *Imports c.i.f.:* China, People's Rep. 73; Denmark 1,256; France (incl. Monaco) 125; Germany 1,025; Iceland 132; Italy 60; Japan 81; Netherlands 65; Norway 950; Sweden 214; United Kingdom 170; USA 47; Total (incl. others) 4,641. *Exports f.o.b.:* Canada 107; China, People's Rep. 51; Denmark 909; France (incl. Monaco) 368; Germany 229; Iceland 110; Italy 124; Japan 159; Norway 201; Russia 39; Spain 467; Sweden 45; United Kingdom 864; USA 85; Total (incl. others) 3,908.

TRANSPORT

Road Traffic (registered motor vehicles, 31 December 2003): Private motor cars 17,085 (incl. 92 taxis); Buses 201; Lorries and vans 3,918; Motorcycles 378; Mopeds 844.

Shipping: *Merchant Fleet* (31 December 2003): 153 vessels, Total displacement 159,694 grt (Source: Lloyd's Register-Fairplay, *World Fleet Statistics*). *International Sea-borne Freight Traffic* (1996, '000 metric tons): Goods loaded 223, Goods unloaded 443.

TOURISM

Nationality of Overnight Guests at Guesthouses (2003): Faroe Islands 24,405; Denmark 31,571; Iceland 5,253; Norway 11,104; Sweden 2,052; Finland 681; United Kingdom and Ireland 4,820; Germany 4,149; Europe (unspecified) 2,474; USA and Canada 725; Austria and Switzerland 428; Total (incl. others) 89,969.

COMMUNICATIONS MEDIA

Radio Receivers (1997): 26,000 in use (Source: UNESCO, *Statistical Yearbook*).

Television Receivers (1997): 15,000 in use (Source: UNESCO, *Statistical Yearbook*).

Book Production (2003): 169 titles.

Newspapers (2003): 2 titles (circulation 17,000).

Telephones (main lines in use, 2000): 24,952 (Source: International Telecommunication Union).

Facsimile Machines (1993): 1,400 in use (Source: UN, *Statistical Yearbook*).

Mobile Cellular Telephones (subscribers, 2000): 16,971 (Source: International Telecommunication Union).

Internet Users ('000, 1999): 3 (Source: International Telecommunication Union).

EDUCATION

Institutions (2000/01): Basic schools 61 (Secondary schools 21); Upper secondary schools 3; Higher preparatory institutions 3.

Teachers (2002/03): 697 (full-time equivalent) in primary and secondary schools.

Students (2002/03, unless otherwise indicated): Pre-primary (1998/99) 59; Primary 5,567; Secondary 2,131; Upper secondary 600; Higher preparatory 165; Business schools 351; Fishery college 31; Social care and healthcare school 60; Technical schools 108; University 154; Total further education (1996/97) 2,166.

Directory

The Government

The legislative body is the Løgting (Lagting in Danish), which consists of 27 members, elected for four years on a basis of proportional representation in seven constituencies, with up to five supplementary seats dependent upon the discrepancy between the distribution of seats among the parties and the numbers of people voting. All Faroese over the age of 18 years have the right to vote. Based on the strength of the parties in the Løgting, a Government, the Landsstýri, is formed. This is the administrative body in certain spheres, chiefly relating to Faroese economic affairs. The Løgmaður (Prime Minister) has to ratify all Løgting laws. Power is decentralized and there are about 50 local authorities. The Ríkisumboðsmaður, or High Commissioner, represents the Danish Government, and has the right to address the Løgting and to advise on joint affairs. All Danish legislation must be submitted to the Landsstýri before becoming law in the Faroe Islands.

The Danish Folketing (parliament), to which the Faroese send two members, is responsible for defence and foreign policy, constitutional matters and the judicial and monetary systems.

LANDSSTÝRI
(April 2005)

A coalition of the Social Democratic Party (SDP), the People's Party (PP) and the Union Party (UP).

Prime Minister (with responsibility for Cabinet Affairs and International Relations): JÓANNES EIDESGAARD (SDP).

Deputy Prime Minister and Minister of Trade and Industry: BJARNI DJURHOLM (PP).

Minister of Finance: BÁRÐUR NIELSEN (UP).

Minister of Fisheries: BJØRN KALSØ (UP).

Minister of Education and Culture: JÓGVAN Á LAKJUNI (PP).

Minister of Social and Health Affairs: HANS PAULI STRØM (SDP).

Minister of the Interior: JÓGVAN VIÐ KELDU (PP).

Government Offices

Ríkisumboðsmaðurin (Danish High Commission): Amtmansbrekka 6, POB 12, 110 Tórshavn; tel. 351200; fax 310864; e-mail riomfr@fo.stm.dk; internet www.rigsombudsmanden.fo; High Commissioner BIRGIT KLEIS.

Løgtingsskrivstovan (Parliament Office): Tinghúsvegur 1–3, POB 208, 110 Tórshavn; tel. 310000; fax 310686; e-mail logting@logting .fo; internet www.logting.fo; Leader SUSANNA DANIELSEN.

Mission of the Faroes to Denmark: North Atlantic House, Strandgade 91, 4., 1401 Copenhagen K, Denmark; tel. 32-83-37-70; fax 32-83-37-75; e-mail faroes.mission.dk@tinganes.fo.

Løgmannsskrivstovan (Prime Minister's Office): Tinganes, POB 64, 110 Tórshavn; tel. 351010; fax 351015; e-mail info@tinganes.fo; internet www.tinganes.fo.

Ministry of Culture: Hoyvíksvegur 72, POB 3279, 110 Tórshavn; tel. 355050; fax 355055; e-mail mmr@mmr.fo; internet www.mmr.fo.

Ministry of Finance: Traðagøta 39, POB 2039, 165 Argir; tel. 352020; fax 352025; e-mail fmr@fmr.fo; internet www.fms.fo.

Ministry of Fisheries and Maritime Affairs: Yviri við Strond 17, POB 347, 110 Tórshavn; tel. 353030; fax 353035; e-mail fisk@fisk.fo; internet www.fisk.fo.

Ministry of Health and Social Affairs: Eirargarður 2, 110 Tórshavn; tel. 304050; fax 354045; e-mail ahr@ahr.fo; internet www.ahr .fo.

Ministry of the Interior: POB 159, 110 Tórshavn; tel. 358080; fax 358085; e-mail lmr@lmr.fo; internet www.lmr.fo.

Ministry of Trade and Industry: Tinganes, POB 377, 110 Tórshavn; tel. 356060; fax 356065; e-mail vmr@vmr.fo; internet www .vmr.fo.

LØGTING

The Løgting has between 27 and 32 members, elected by universal adult suffrage.

Speaker: EDMUND JOENSEN (Union Party).

Election, 20 January 2004

Party	Votes	% of votes	Seats
Tjóðveldisflokkurin (Republican Party) .	6,889	21.73	8
Sambandsflokkurin (Union Party) . . .	7,507	23.68	7
Javnaðarflokkurin (Social Democratic Party)	6,921	21.83	7
Fólkaflokkurin (People's Party) . . .	6,525	20.58	7
Miðflokkurin (Centre Party)	1,659	5.23	2
Sjálvstýrisflokkurin (Home Rule Party) .	1,461	4.61	1
Hin Stuttligi Flokkurin (The Funny Party)	745	2.35	—
Total	31,707	100.00	32

Political Organizations

Unless otherwise indicated, the address of each of the following organizations is: Áarvegur, POB 208, 110 Tórshavn; tel. 310850 fax 310686.

Fólkaflokkurin (People's Party): Jónas Broncksgøta 29, 100 Tórshavn; tel. 318210; fax 318260; e-mail xa@folkaflokkurin.fo; internet folkaflokkurin.fo; f. 1940; conservative-liberal party, favours free enterprise and wider political and economic autonomy for the Faroes; Chair. ÓLI BRECKMANN.

Hin Føroyski Flokkurin (The Faroese Party): f. 1994; seeks to abolish Home Rule and fully to re-integrate the Faroes into the Kingdom of Denmark; Chair. ÓLAVUR CHRISTIANSEN.

Hin Stuttligi Flokkurin (The Funny Party): Frammi við Garðar, 410 Kollafjørður; tel. 421698; f. 2004; seeks to lampoon the political establishment; Leader JOHAN DALSGAARD.

Javnaðarflokkurin (Social Democratic Party—SDP): tel. 312493; fax 319397; e-mail javnadarflokkarin@logting.fo; internet www .javnadarflokkurin.fo; f. 1928; Chair. JÓANNES EIDESGAARD.

Kristiligi Fólkaflokkurin, Føroya Framburðs- og Fiskivinnuflokkurin (Christian People's Party, Progressive and Fishing Industry Party—CPP-PFIP): à Brekku 5, 700 Klaksvík; tel. 457580; fax 457581; f. 1954; centrist party; Chair. NIELS PAULI DANIELSEN; Parliamentary Chair. LASSE KLEIN.

Miðflokkurin (Centre Party): POB 3237, 110 Tórshavn; tel. 314988; fax 312206; e-mail midflokk@post.olivant.fo; internet www .midflokkurin.fo; f. 1992; Chair. JENIS AV RANA.

Sambandsflokkurin (Union Party): Lucas Debersargøta 3, POB 1340, 110 Tórshavn; tel. 318870; fax 318910; e-mail samband@post .olivant.fo; internet www.samband.fo; f. 1906; favours the maintenance of close relations between the Faroes and the Kingdom of Denmark; conservative in internal affairs; Chair. EDMUND JOENSEN.

Sjálvstýrisflokkurin (Home Rule Party): Gamla Apotek, Tinghúsvegur, 100 Tórshavn; e-mail krossur@tingakrossur.fo; internet www.tingakrossur.fo/sfl; f. 1906; social-liberal party advocates eventual political independence for the Faroes within the Kingdom of Denmark; Chair. EYDUN ELTOR.

Tjóðveldisflokkurin (Republican Party): Kongagøta 11, POB 143, 100 Tórshavn; tel. 312200; e-mail loysing@post.olivant.fo; internet www.tjodveldi.fo; f. 1948; left-wing party, advocates the secession of the Faroes from Denmark; Chair. HØGNI HOYDAL.

Verkmannafylkingin (Labour Front): f. 1994 by trade union leaders and former members of the SDP.

Religion

CHRISTIANITY

The Faroes Church (Evangelical Lutheran Church of Denmark) regained its diocese in November 1990, and the suffragan bishop became Bishop of the Faroe Islands. The Church had 40,468 members in 2003, accounting for 84% of the population. The largest independent group is the 'Plymouth Brethren'. There is also a small Roman Catholic community.

Evangelical Lutheran Church

Føroya Biskupur (Bishop of the Faroe Islands): J. Paturssonargøta 20, POB 8, 110 Tórshavn; tel. 311995; fax 315889; HANS J. JOENSEN.

BAHÁ'Í FAITH

Bahá'í: POB 1095, 110 Tórshavn; tel. 315025; internet www.bahai .fo.

The Press

In 2003 there were two daily newspapers in the Faroe Islands, *Dimmalætting* and *Tíðindablaðið Sosialurin*, with a combined circulation of 18,000, and a further four general interest newspapers.

Dagblaðið: Reynagøta 9, 100 Tórshavn; tel. 319833; fax 319823; weekly; People's Party.

Dimmalætting: Smyrilsvegur 13, POB 3019, 110 Tórshavn; tel. 341200; fax 341201; e-mail post@dimma.fo; internet www.dimma.fo; f. 1878; 5 a week; Union Party; circ. 11,000.

FF/FA-Blaðið: Vágsbotnur, POB 58, 110 Tórshavn; tel. 312169; fax 318769; weekly; Editor VILMUND JACOBSEN; circ. 2,500.

Norðlýsið: á Hædd, POB 58, 700 Klaksvík; tel. 456285; fax 456498; weekly; circ. 1,200.

Oyggjatíðinði: R. C. Effersøesgøta 7, POB 3312, 110 Tórshavn; tel. 314411; fax 316410; 2 a week; circ. 4,500.

Tíðindablaðið Sosialurin: POB 76, 110 Tórshavn; tel. 341800; fax 341801; e-mail post@sosialurin.fo; internet www.sosialurin.fo; f. 1927; 5 a week; Social Democratic Party; Editor JAN MÜLLER; circ. 7,000.

NEWS AGENCY

Ritzaus Bureau: Gamli Vegur 3; tel. 316366; f. 1980; Man. RANDI MOHR.

Broadcasting and Communications

TELECOMMUNICATIONS

The Faroese telecommunications industry, formally a monopoly under Føroya Tele, was opened to competition in the early 2000s.

Post- og Fjarskiftiseftirlitið (Postal and Telecommunications Authority): POB 73, Skálatrøð 20, 110 Tórshavn; tel. 356020; fax 356035; e-mail fse@fse.fo; internet www.fse.fo; independent government agency with regulatory powers; Dir JÓGVAN THOMSEN.

Føroya Tele: POB 27, 110 Tórshavn; tel. 303030; fax 303031; e-mail ft@ft.fo; internet www.tele.fo.

Kall p/f: Óðinshædd 2, 100 Tórshavn; tel. 202020; fax 202021; e-mail kall@kall.fo; internet www.kall.fo; f. 1999; offers PSTN, ADSL and GSM services; CEO BJARNI ASKHAM BJARNASON.

RADIO

Útvarp Føroya (Radio Faroe Islands): Norðari Ringvegur, POB 328, 110 Tórshavn; tel. 342000; fax 342001; e-mail uf@uf.fo; internet www.uf.fo; f. 1957; Man. JÓGVAN JESPERSEN.

TELEVISION

Sjónvarp Føroya (Faroese Television): M. A. Winthersgøta 2, POB 21, 110 Tórshavn; tel. 340400; fax 340500; e-mail svf@svf.fo; internet www.svf.fo; f. 1984; Gen. Man. JÓGVAN JESPERSEN.

Finance

BANKS

(cap. = capital; res = reserves; dep. = deposits; m. = million; brs = branches; amounts in kroner)

Føroya Banki P/F: Húsagøta 3, POB 3048, 110 Tórshavn; tel. 311350; fax 315850; e-mail fbk@foroyabanki.fo; internet www .foroyabanki.fo; f. 1994 following merger of Føroya Banki (f. 1906) and Sjóvinnubankin (f. 1932); 99.4% state-owned through Finansieringsfonden af 1992 (Tórshavn); privatization pending; cap. 100m., res 4m., dep. 3,837m. (Dec. 2003); Chair. JÓHAN PÁLL JOENSEN; Man. Dir and CEO JØRN ASTRUP HANSEN; 20 brs.

Føroya Sparikassi (Faroese Savings Bank): Yviri við Strond 2, POB 34, 110 Tórshavn; tel. 348000; fax 348348; e-mail sparikassin@ sparikassin.fo; internet www.sparikassin.fo; f. 1832; 94.1% owned

by Sparikassagrunnurin; cap. 681m., res 73m., dep. 4,365m. (Dec. 2003); Chair. FRITLEIF OLSEN; Chief Man. Dir MARNER JACOBSEN.

Landsbanki Føroya: Müllers Hús, Gongin, POB 229, 110 Tórshavn; tel. 318305; fax 318537; e-mail landsbank@landsbank.fo; internet landsbank.fo; Man. SIGURÐ POULSEN.

Norðoya Sparikassi: Ósávegur 1, POB 149, 700 Klaksvík; tel. 475000; fax 476000; e-mail ns@ns.fo; internet www.ns.fo.

Suðuroya Sparikassi: POB 2, 900 Vágur; tel. 373064; fax 373340; e-mail sparsu@sparsu.fo; internet www.sparsu.fo; Man. SØREN L. BRUHN.

STOCK EXCHANGE

Virðisbrævamarknaður Føroya P/F (VMF): c/o Landsbanki Føroya, Gongin, POB 229, 110 Tórshavn; tel. 318305; fax 318537; internet vmf.fo; f. 2000; lists Faroese securities in co-operation with Kauphöll Íslands (Icelandic stock exchange); Chair. STEFÁN HALLDÓRSSON.

INSURANCE

Tryggingarfelagið Føroyar: Kongabrúgvin, POB 329, 110 Tórshavn; tel. 345600; fax 345601; e-mail tf@trigging.fr; internet www .trigging.fo; all non-marine; sole insurance co in islands; Man. GUNNAR Í LIÐA.

Trade and Industry

GOVERNMENT AGENCY

Fiskivinnuumsitingin (Fisheries Administration): POB 87, 110 Tórshavn; tel. 313068; fax 314942.

INDUSTRIAL AND TRADE ASSOCIATIONS

L/F Føroya Fiskasøla—Faroe Seafood P/F: POB 68, 110 Tórshavn; tel. 345345; fax 345300; e-mail faroe@faroe.com; f. 1948; restructured 1995; joint stock company of fish producers; exports all seafood products; Man. Dir ARNI AAGE.

Føroya Reiðarafelag (Faroe Fishing Vessel-Owners' Association): R. C. Effersøesgøta, POB 179, 110 Tórshavn; tel. 311864; fax 317278.

Menningarstovan (Faroe Islands Trade Council): Bryggjubakki 12, POB 259, 110 Tórshavn; tel. 353100; fax 353101; e-mail trade@ trade.fo; internet www.trade.fo; Man. KJARTAN KRISTIANSEN.

UTILITIES

Electricity

Elfelagið SEV: POB 319, 110 Tórshavn; tel. 346800; fax 346801; e-mail sev@sev.fo; internet www.sev.fo; state-owned.

EMPLOYERS' ORGANIZATION

Føroya Arbeiðsgevarafelag (Faroese Employers' Association): Vinnuhúsið, POB 1038, 110 Tórshavn; tel. 311864; fax 317278; e-mail industry@industry.fo; internet www.industry.fo; more than 600 mem. cos; organized in 12 sectoral feds, including Faroe Trade Masters Asscn, Faroe Fish Producers' Asscn, Faroe Fish Farming Asscn, Fed. of Faroes Industries, Faroe Merchant and Shopkeepers Asscn and Faroe Oil Industries Asscn.

TRADE UNION

Føroya Arbeiðarafelag (Faroese Labour Organization): Tjarnarðeild 5–7, POB 56, 110 Tórshavn; tel. 312101; fax 315374; e-mail fafelag@post.olivant.fo; internet www.fafelag.fo.

Transport

There are about 458 km of roads in the Faroe Islands. A 4.9-km tunnel running under the sea, linking Vágar to Streymoy, was opened in December 2002.

The main harbour is at Tórshavn; the other ports are at Fuglafjorður, Klaksvík, Skálafjorður, Tvøroyri, Vágur and Vestmanna. Between mid-May and mid-September, a summer roll-on, roll-off ferry service links the Faroe Islands with Iceland, Shetland (United Kingdom), Denmark and Norway.

There is an airport on Vágar.

Atlantic Airways Faroe Islands: Vágar Airport, 380 Sørvágur; tel. 341000; fax 341001; e-mail info@atlantic.fo; internet www .atlantic.fo; f. 1987; owned by Faroese Govt; scheduled and charter passenger and cargo services to Copenhagen, Reykjavík and Aberdeen; Man. Dir MAGNI ARGE.

Smyril Line: Jonas Broncksgøta 37, POB 370, 110 Tórshavn; tel. 345900; fax 345950; e-mail office@smyril-line.com; internet www.smyril-line.com; ferry service.

Tourism

Ferðaráð Føroya (Faroe Islands Tourist Board): Bryggjubakka 17, POB 118, 100 Tórshavn; tel. 316055; fax 310858; e-mail tourist@tourist.fo; internet www.tourist.fo; f. 1984.

GREENLAND

Introductory Survey

Location, Climate, Language, Religion, Flag, Capital

Greenland (Kalaallit Nunaat) is the world's largest island, with a total area of 2,166,086 sq km, and lies in the North Atlantic Ocean, east of Canada. Most of the territory is permanently covered by ice, but 410,449 sq km of coastland are habitable. Greenlandic, an Inuit (Eskimo) language, and Danish are the official languages. The majority of the population profess Christianity and belong mainly to the Evangelical Lutheran Church of Denmark. There are also small communities of other Protestant groups and of Roman Catholics. The flag (proportions 2 by 3) consists of two equal horizontal stripes (white above red), on which is superimposed a representation of the rising sun (a disc divided horizontally, red above white) to the left of centre. Nuuk (Godthåb) is the capital.

Recent History

Greenland first came under Danish rule in 1380. In the revision of the Danish Constitution in 1953, Greenland became part of the Kingdom and acquired the representation of two members in the Danish Folketing (Parliament). In October 1972 the Greenlanders voted, by 9,658 to 3,990, against joining the European Community (EC—now European Union—EU, see p. 217) but, as part of Denmark, were bound by the Danish decision to join. Resentment of Danish domination of the economy, education and the professions continued, taking expression when, in 1977, the nationalist Siumut movement formed a left-wing party. In 1975 the Minister for Greenland appointed a commission to devise terms for Greenland home rule, and its proposals were approved, by 73.1% to 26.9%, in a referendum among the Greenland electorate in January 1979. Siumut, led by a Lutheran pastor, Jonathan Motzfeldt, secured 13 seats in the 21-member Landsting (the local legislature) at a general election in April, and a five-member Landsstyre (Home Rule Government), with Motzfeldt as Prime Minister, took office in May. From 1979 the island gradually assumed full administration of its internal affairs.

In February 1982 a referendum was held to decide Greenland's continued membership of the EC. This resulted in a 53% majority in favour of withdrawal. Negotiations were begun in May, with the Danish Government acting on Greenland's behalf, and were concluded in March 1984 (with effect from 1 February 1985): Greenland was accorded the status of an overseas territory in association with the Community, with preferential access to EC markets.

At the April 1983 general election to the Landsting (enlarged, by measures adopted in 1982, to between 23 and 26 seats, depending on the proportion of votes cast), Siumut and the conservative Atassut party won 12 seats each, while the Inuit Ataqatigiit (IA) obtained two seats. Siumut once again formed a Government, led by Motzfeldt, dependent on the support of the IA members in the Landsting: this support was withdrawn in March 1984, when the IA members voted against the terms of withdrawal from the EC, and Motzfeldt resigned. In the ensuing general election, held in June, Siumut and Atassut won 11 seats each, while the IA took three seats. Motzfeldt again formed a coalition Government, comprising Siumut and the IA.

In March 1987 the coalition Government collapsed, following a dispute between Siumut and the IA over policy towards the modernization of the US radar facility at Thule, which was claimed by the IA to be in breach of the 1972 US-Soviet Anti-Ballistic Missile Treaty. A general election was held in May. Siumut and Atassut retained 11 seats each in the Landsting (which had been enlarged in 1986, to 27 seats—23 of which were

to be obtained by election in multi-member constituencies, while four were to be supplementary seats); the IA won four seats, and the remaining seat was secured by the newly formed Issittup Partiia, which was demanding the privatization of the trawler fleet. Motzfeldt eventually formed a new coalition Government with the IA. In May 1988, at elections to the Danish Folketing, Siumut was the most successful party. In June the coalition between Siumut and the IA collapsed, and Motzfeldt formed a new Siumut Government, with support from Atassut. In December 1990, when Atassut withdrew its support for the Siumut administration (following allegations that government ministers had misused public funds), Motzfeldt organized an early general election for March 1991, at which both Siumut and Atassut obtained a reduced share of the vote, while the IA's quota rose. Accordingly, Siumut retained 11 seats in the Landsting, while Atassut's representation decreased to eight seats and the IA's increased to five. A new party, the liberal Akulliit Partiiaat, won two seats, and the remaining place was taken by the Issittup Partiia. Siumut and the IA formed a coalition Government and elected the Chairman of Siumut, Lars Emil Johansen, as Prime Minister.

At the general election held in March 1995 Siumut increased its representation in the Landsting (enlarged to 31 seats) to 12 seats, while Atassut won 10 seats and the IA obtained six seats. A coalition Government was formed between Siumut and Atassut, following the withdrawal from negotiations of the IA, which failed to reach agreement with Siumut on the question of independence. Johansen retained the premiership, while Daniel Skifte, the leader of Atassut, was appointed Minister of Finance and Housing. In early 1997 Johansen asserted that Greenland could achieve economic independence from Denmark on the basis of its unexploited mineral resources. In September Motzfeldt replaced Johansen as Prime Minister at the head of the coalition. Johansen was reported to have taken a senior position with the Royal Greenland fishing group.

At the general election held in February 1999 Siumut received 35.3% of the votes cast, securing 11 seats in the Landsting. Atassut obtained 25.3% of the votes (eight seats), while the IA received 22.1% (seven seats). On 22 February a coalition Government was formed between Siumut and the IA; the two parties were to be represented in the Landsstyre by five and two ministers respectively. Jonathan Motzfeldt retained the premiership, while Josef Motzfeldt, the Chairman of the IA, was appointed Minister of Economy, Trade and Taxation.

In September 2001 Jonathan Motzfeldt was forced to resign as leader of Siumut during the party's annual congress, after he was held responsible for a deficit of 3,000m. kroner on the part of Royal Greenland (the island's main fish and seafood export company); Motzfeldt, however, retained his post as Prime Minister. In December the IA withdrew from the coalition Government, accusing Siumut of lacking direction in its policies. Siumut subsequently formed a new coalition Government with Atassut; the ministerial posts formerly held by the IA were taken over by members of Atassut, while there was no change in the ministries held by Siumut.

At the general election held on 3 December 2002 Siumut received 28.5% of the votes cast, winning 10 seats in the Landsting. The IA received 25.3% and won eight seats, Atassut 20.2% (seven seats) and Katusseqatigiit (Alliance of Independent Candidates) 6.6% (one seat); Demokraatit (the Democrats—a new party formed in October 2002) received 15.9% of the votes cast, securing five seats. Later that month Siumut and the IA formed a coalition Government, viewed by many as being strongly pro-independence, under the new Siumut Prime Minister, Hans Enoksen.

The Government was, however, extremely short-lived: the appointment to the top post of the civil service of Jens Lybeth,

Enoksen's electoral campaign manager and close personal friend, prompted accusations of favouritism. Lybeth then engaged the services of Maannguaq Berthelsen, an Inuit 'healer', to 'chase away evil spirits' from government offices, urging some 600 civil servants to use similar methods to promote harmony between Greenlanders and Danes. In the ensuing furore, Enoksen was obliged to dismiss Lybeth. Josef Motzfeldt, the Deputy Prime Minister and Chairman of the IA, remained unsatisfied with the situation, and approached the Demokraatit to discuss ousting Enoksen and forming a new Government. Enoksen, again compelled to act, dissolved the coalition in mid-January 2003 and formed a new Government in coalition with Atassut.

The new Government was dogged by political controversy, most notably the discord between the coalition partners concerning the revision of a commercial fishing agreement with the EU. In early September 2003 the leaders of Siumut called for a formal investigation into allegations that Augusta Salling, the Minister of Finance and Chairperson of Atassut, was involved in an accounting discrepancy amounting to some 97m. kroner. Salling threatened to withdraw Atassut from the coalition unless she received a guarantee that she would not face a motion of 'no confidence' when the Landsting assembled later that month. Siumut were unwilling to give her such a guarantee, and the governing coalition was consequently dissolved on 9 September. Siumut and the IA formed a new coalition Government, with Enoksen as Prime Minister, on 13 September.

In January 2004, following negotiations between Enoksen and the Danish Prime Minister, Anders Fogh Rasmussen, it was announced that the Danish Government and the Landsstyre were to appoint a joint commission in early 2004 to explore ways of granting greater devolution to Greenland, after civil servants had presented their recommendations. Greenland was to remain within the Danish commonwealth, however, and would continue receiving grants from Denmark. In March 2005, following a request by the joint commission to the Danish Ministry of Justice, Greenlanders were granted recognition as a separate people under international law. Whether this required recognition by the UN, and whether it granted Greenlanders sovereign rights, remained unresolved.

Denmark remains ultimately responsible for Greenland's foreign relations. Greenland does, however, have separate representation on the Nordic Council (see p. 296), and is a member of the Inuit Circumpolar Conference (see p. 374). Denmark, a member of NATO (see p. 301), retains its responsibility for defence, and Danish-US military co-operation in Greenland began in 1951, when Denmark signed a defence agreement with the US Government to allow four US bases in Greenland, including the Thule Air Base, near the Uummannaq Inuit settlement. Two years after the establishment of the base the indigenous Inuits, whose hunting grounds had been severely diminished by the development of the base, were forcibly resettled further north in Qaanaaq. Under a 1981 agreement on the defence of Greenland, two US radar bases were established on the island, at Thule and at Kangerlussuaq (Søndre Strømfjord). An agreement between the USA and Denmark for the reduction of the size of the bases from 325,000 ha to 160,000 ha took effect from October 1986, and the land thus available was returned to the Inuit. In March 1991 the USA agreed to transfer ownership and control of the base at Kangerlussuaq to the Greenland Government in September 1992, in exchange for the right to use it again in the future. In August 1999 the Danish High Court ordered the Danish Government to pay compensation of 500,000 kroner to Inuits who had been forced to leave their land in 1953 to allow for the expansion of the base at Thule. The Thule tribe appealed against the ruling, demanding 235m. kroner as compensation for lost living space and hunting grounds and arguing that the US-Denmark defence agreement was void under constitutional and international law. The Supreme Court rejected the tribe's appeal in November 2003, ruling that the agreement was still valid and approving the compensation recommended by the High Court.

Jonathan Motzfeldt and the Danish Minister of Foreign Affairs, Mogens Lykketoft, agreed in February 2001 not to adopt an official policy on the proposed US missile defence system, which would involve the upgrading of the early-warning radar station in the Thule base, pending an official request by the USA. Motzfeldt did, however, express personal concern at the plans, and called on the USA to discuss the proposals with its NATO allies. He added that Greenland would not accept the plans if they proved to be in breach of the 1972 Anti-Ballistic

Missile Treaty, or if Russia opposed them. Josef Motzfeldt and the opposition parties of the Danish Folketing were already expressing strong opposition to the proposals, claiming that they risked provoking another 'arms race'. Public opinion in Greenland was also strongly opposed to the plans; many feared that they would place Greenland at the centre of potential future conflicts.

In January 2001 the newly inaugurated US President, George W. Bush, stated in a letter to the Prime Minister, Motzfeldt, that Greenland 'should be open for dialogue' on the future of the Thule base. That the letter was sent directly to Motzfeldt rather than to Copenhagen caused consternation in Denmark, which still controlled Greenland's foreign policy. In September 2002 the USA returned the town of Dundas (also known as Uummannaq in Greenlandic) and its surroundings to Greenland; the USA had incorporated it into the Thule base some 50 years earlier. The US Administration formally submitted a request to upgrade the facilities at the Thule base in December 2002. In May 2003 Enoksen and the Danish Minister of Foreign Affairs, Dr Per Stig Møller, signed a Danish-Greenlandic principle agreement under which Greenland was to gain greater influence in foreign policy relating to the island, in return for its support for the modernization of the Thule base as part of the US missile defence programme. Henceforth Denmark was to consult Greenland on foreign policy matters in which Greenland was directly involved; the Landsstyre was to participate in future negotiations with Denmark on Greenland's foreign policy. Greenland was to be a co-signatory to future international agreements, provided they did not compromise local rights.

In May 2004 Greenland, Denmark and the USA reached an agreement on the upgrading of radar facilities at the Thule base as part of the US missile defence programme. The Landsstyre, the Foreign and Security Policy Committee of the Landsting and the Danish Folketing all approved the agreement unanimously, and it was signed on 6 August by the Deputy Prime Minister, Josef Motzfeldt, the US Secretary of State, Colin Powell, and the Danish Minister of Foreign Affairs, Dr Per Stig Møller. Under the agreement both Greenland and Denmark were to have representatives at the base, and Greenland's flag was to be flown there alongside those of the USA and Denmark. The USA was required both to consult with Greenland and Denmark on any further developments at the base and henceforth to notify the Landsstyre of any US aircraft landing outside the regular airports in Greenland. Agreements were also concluded on wider co-operation between Greenland and the USA, in areas such as research, energy, the environment and education.

In June 1980 the Danish Government declared an economic zone extending 200 nautical miles (370 km) off the east coast of Greenland. This, however, caused a dispute with Norway over territorial waters, owing to the existence of the small Norwegian island of Jan Mayen, 460 km off the east coast of Greenland. In 1988 Denmark requested the International Court of Justice (ICJ), based in The Hague, Netherlands, to arbitrate on the issue of conflicting economic zones. A delimitation line was established by the ICJ in June 1993. A subsequent accord on maritime delimitation, agreed between the Governments of Norway, Greenland and Iceland in November 1997, established the boundaries of a 1,934-sq km area of Arctic sea that had been excluded from the terms of the 1993 settlement. In January 2002 Greenland and the Faroe Islands renewed an agreement granting the mutual right to fish in each other's waters.

Government

Greenland is part of the Kingdom of Denmark, and the Danish Government, which remains responsible for foreign affairs, defence and justice, is represented by the Rigsombudsmand, or High Commissioner, in Nuuk (Godthåb). Most functions of government are administered by the 'Home Rule Government', the Landsstyre. The formation of this executive is dependent upon support in the local legislature, the Landsting. The Landsting has 31 members elected for a maximum term of four years, on a basis of proportional representation. Greenland also elects two members to the Danish Folketing (parliament). For administration purposes, Greenland is divided into 18 municipalities, of which the largest is Nuuk.

Defence

The Danish Government, which is responsible for Greenland's defence, co-ordinates military activities through its Greenland Command. The Greenland Command, which also undertakes fisheries control and sea rescues, is based at the Grønnedal naval base, in south-west Greenland. Greenlanders are not liable for military service. As part of the Kingdom of Denmark, Greenland belongs to NATO (see p. 301). The USA operates an air base, at Pituffik in Thule (see Recent History). In 2001 the Danish Government spent 260m. kroner (3.8% of total central government expenditure on Greenland) on the territory's defence (including the Fisheries Inspectorate).

Economic Affairs

In 1994, according to preliminary official estimates, Greenland's gross national product (GNP) was 6,381m. kroner, equivalent to some 114,800 kroner per head. The population increased at an average annual rate of 0.1% in 1990–2000. The economy enjoyed overall growth during the 1970s and 1980s, but gross domestic product (GDP) declined by 9%, in real terms, in 1990, and continued to decline significantly (owing to depleted fish stocks and the discontinuation of lead and zinc mining) until 1994 and 1995, when real growth rates of 5% and 3%, respectively, were recorded. GDP increased, in real terms, by 1.5% in 1996, by 1.4% in 1997 and by 7.8% in 1998.

Agriculture (including animal husbandry, fishing and hunting) employed 7.9% of the working population in 2000. Fishing dominates the commercial economy, as well as being important to the traditional way of life. In 2000 the fishing industry accounted for 95.6% of Greenland's total export revenue. The industry, including the processing of the catch, employed 25.3% of the paid labour force in 1996. The cod catch has declined substantially, however, since 1989. None the less, in 2002 202,800 metric tons of fish were landed in Greenland, compared with 147,300 tons in 1991. The traditional occupation of the Greenlanders is seal-hunting (for meat and fur), which remains important in the north. The only feasible agricultural activity in the harsh climate is livestock-rearing, and only sheep-farming has proved to be of any commercial significance. There are also herds of domesticated reindeer.

Industry (including mining, manufacturing, construction and public works) employed some 18.6% of those in paid employment in 2000. Mining earned 13.0% of total export revenue in 1990, but in 2000 employed less than 0.1% of the working population. A Swedish company extracted lead, zinc and some silver at the important mine at Marmorilik in the north-west. The mine was closed, however, in 1990. In November 2001 an Australian company announced that it was to establish a mine to extract niobium (a metal used in the manufacture of electronic components) in Greenland. In recent years there have been several discoveries of petroleum, natural gas and other mineral deposits (including gold and diamonds). In August 2004 NunaMinerals opened the Nalulaq Goldmine at Kirkspirdalen, in southern Greenland. Just one week later the same company announced that it had discovered further significant reserves of gold ore at Storøen, 40 km east of Nuuk. In April 2004 the Bureau of Minerals and Petroleum opened a new licensing round for petroleum exploration off the coast of Greenland; 10-year licences were offered for four selected offshore areas. Previously, however, only three companies had taken licences in the area, as drilling off Greenland was expensive, owing to the depth of the water and the climate. However, seismic analyses have indicated that there are significant reserves of petroleum and natural gas beneath the sea off the western coast of Greenland, and petroleum traces have been discovered in rocks in Disko Bay.

Manufacturing is mainly dependent upon the fishing industry. Water power (melt water from the ice-cap and glaciers) is an important potential source of electricity. All mineral fuels are imported. Mineral fuels accounted for 15.3% of total imports in 2001. Manufacturing employed 9.7% of the working population in 2000; 8.0% of the working population were employed in the fishing industries.

In 2001 Greenland recorded a trade deficit of 459.8m. kroner. The principal trading partner remains Denmark, although its monopoly on trade ceased in 1950. Denmark supplied 66.0% of imports and received 84.4% of exports in 2001. Trade is still dominated by companies owned by the Landsstyre. The principal exports are fish and fish products, and the principal imports are machinery and transport equipment.

Greenland is dependent upon large grants from the central Danish Government. In 2000 central government expenditure on Greenland included some 2,725m. kroner in the form of a direct grant to the Landsstyre. Greenland has few debts, and also receives valuable revenue from the European Union (EU, see p. 217), for fishing licences. The annual rate of inflation averaged 0.9% in 1995–99, and stood at 0.7% in 1999, 1.7% in

2000 and 2.8% in 2001. In 2002 an estimated 6.5% of the labour force were unemployed.

The services sector employed 73.6% of the working population in 2000; it is dominated by public administration, which alone employed 48.7% of the working population in that year.

Greenland, although a part of the Kingdom of Denmark, withdrew from the European Community (now EU) in 1985 (see Recent History). It remains a territory in association with the EU, however, and has preferential access to European markets. The loss of EU development aid has been offset by the annual payment for member countries to retain fishing rights in Greenlandic waters.

Greenland's economy is dominated by the fishing industry, but remains a subsistence, barter economy for a large part of the population. Migration to the towns and the rejection of a traditional life-style by many young people have, however, created new social and economic problems. Dependence on a single commodity leaves the economy vulnerable to the effects of depletion of fish stocks and fluctuating international prices. Any development or progress is possible only with Danish aid, which is already fundamental to Greenlandic finances. In an effort to generate revenue from the tourism industry, the Landsstyre undertook, in 1990, to achieve a target of 35,000 tourist arrivals (generating around 500m. kroner in tourism revenue) annually by 2005; by 1994 the campaign was showing positive results and tourist arrivals had doubled (to some 13,000) compared with levels in previous years. A national tourist board was founded in 1992, and concentrated primarily on sustainable tourism projects. In January 2005 the Government announced that (as in Canada) it was to allow tourists to hunt polar bears and keep their pelts as souvenirs. The Government envisaged an annual souvenir quota of 30 polar bear pelts. A similar quota already existed for musk oxen, which was set at 350 animals in early 2005.

Education

The educational system is based on that of Denmark, except that the main language of instruction is Greenlandic. Danish is, however, widely used. There is a school in every settlement. In 2001/02 there were 87 municipal primary and lower-secondary schools, with 11,368 pupils and 1,191 teachers (including 380 temporarily-employed teachers). In 1999/2000 there were three secondary schools with 571 pupils. There is a teacher-training college in Nuuk, and a university centre opened in 1987. In 2000 current expenditure on education by the Landsstyre amounted to 930m. kroner (representing 21.6% of total current budget spending—including allocations to the municipalities).

Public Holidays

Public holidays are the same as those for Denmark, with the exception of Constitution Day, which is not celebrated in Greenland. In addition, Greenlanders celebrate Mitaartut on 6 January, and Ullortuneq (Greenland's national day—literally: 'the longest day') on 21 June. Various regional holidays are also held to celebrate the return of the sun following the end of the long polar night; the timing of these vary according to latitude.

Statistical Survey

Sources: Statistics Greenland, *Statistical Yearbook;* Greenland Home Rule Government—Denmark Bureau, Pilestræde 52, POB 2151, 1122 Copenhagen K; tel. 33-13-42-24; fax 33-13-49-71; Statistics Greenland, POB 1025, 3900 Nuuk; tel. 345000; fax 322954; e-mail stat@gs.gh.gl; internet www.statgreen.gl.

AREA, POPULATION AND DENSITY

Area: Total 2,166,086 sq km (836,330 sq miles); Ice-free portion 410,449 sq km (158,475 sq miles).

Population: 56,676 (males 30,249, females 26,427) at 1 January 2003 (incl. 49,941 born in Greenland). *1 January 2004:* 56,854.

Density (1 January 2004, ice-free portion): 0.14 per sq km.

Principal Towns (population at 1 January 2003): Nuuk (Godthåb, the capital) 13,884; Sisimiut 5,263; Ilulissat 4,525; Aasiaat 3,142; Qaqortoq 3,129. *1 January 2004:* Nuuk 14,350.

Births, Marriages and Deaths (2001): Registered live births 937 (birth rate 16.6 per 1,000); Registered marriages (1999) 253 (marriage rate 4.5 per 1,000); Registered deaths 438 (death rate 7.8 per 1,000).

Expectation of Life (years at birth, 1997–2001): Males 62.8; Females 67.8.

Economically Active Population (2000): Animal husbandry, fishing and hunting 2,039; Quarrying 18; Manufacturing 2,508 (Fishing industries 2,072); Energy supply 467; Construction 1,808; Wholesale business 193; Retail trade 1,414; Hotels and restaurants 797; Transportation and tourism 1,622; Post and telecommunications service 573; Financial services, pensions and real estate 380; Other business services 374; Cleaning services 520; Public administration 12,588; Education 15; Social institutions, nurseries etc. 37; Organizations and institutions 179; Entertainment, sport and culture 300; Other services 31; International organizations 8; Activities not classified 724; Total 26,595*.
*Excludes 379 personnel employed from Danish mainland.

Labour Force (census of 26 October 1976): Males 14,234; Females 7,144; *Total* 21,378. *1 January 2004* (15–62 years, born in Greenland): Total 27,024.

HEALTH AND WELFARE
Key Indicators

Physicians (per 1,000 head, 2000): 1.6.

Health Expenditure (2000): million kroner: 792; % of current budgetary expenditure: 18.4.

AGRICULTURE AND FISHING

Livestock (2002): Sheep 18,967, Horses 148, Beehives 11, Poultry 166, Cattle 12, Reindeer 3,100.

Livestock Products (metric tons, 2000): Mutton and lamb 357; Other meat 2.

Hunting (2000): Fox skins 87, Polar bears 49.

Fishing ('000 metric tons, live weight, 2002): Greenland halibut 27.1; Atlantic cod 8.1; Capelin 30.2; Queen Crab 10.3; Northern prawn 109.5; Total catch (incl. others) 202.8. The total excludes aquatic mammals, which are recorded by number rather than by weight. In 2002 the number of aquatic mammals caught was: Minke whale 145; Fin whale 14; Humpback whale 5; Walrus 318; Harp seal 48,498; Harbour seal 123; Ringed seal 59,032; Bearded seal 1,329; Hooded seal 3,419 (Source: FAO).

INDUSTRY

Selected Products: Frozen fish (2001) 21,700 metric tons; Electric energy (2002) 311 million kWh (Source: UN, *Industrial Commodity Statistics Yearbook*).

FINANCE
(Danish currency is in use)

Central Government Expenditure (by Ministry, million kroner, 2000): *Current:* Finance 2,725 (Grant to Home Rule Government 2,725), Defence (incl. Fisheries Inspection) 268, Justice 165, Environment and Energy 58, Transport 38, Research 7, Prime Minister's Office 8, Labour 3, Agriculture and Fisheries 1, Business and Industry 2, Total 3,274. *Capital:* 0. *Total:* 3,274. *2003:* Grant to Home Rule Government 2,952m. kroner.

Home Rule Government Accounts (million kroner, 2000): *Revenue:* Current 5,054 (Income tax 866, Import and production duties 687, Interests 240, Fishing licences 285, Danish central govt grant 2,725); Capital 0; Total 5,054. *Expenditure:* Current 4,299 (Administration 294, Education 930, Church and culture 183, Social security and welfare 1,054, Health 792, Housing 326, Business and Trade 286, Industry 139, Transport and communication 198, Energy 104, Fisheries, hunting and agriculture 133; Other (incl. grants to municipalities) 443); Capital 583; Total 4,882.

Budget (million kroner, 2002, rounded): *Revenue:* 7,600; *Expenditure:* 7,500 (Capital expenditure 600).

Cost of Living (consumer price index; at July each year; base: July 1995 = 100): All items 105.3 in 2000; 108.2 in 2001; 112.9 in 2002.

Gross Domestic Product (provisional, million kroner at current market prices): 8,633 in 2000; 9,088 in 2001; 9,178 in 2002.

Gross National Product by Economic Activity (million kroner at factor cost, 1988): Agriculture and fisheries 971; Mineral resources 328; Manufacturing 171; Electricity, gas and heating 195; Construction 1,063, Other private services 1,989; Public sector 1,648; Total 6,365.

EXTERNAL TRADE

Principal Commodities (million kroner, 2001): *Imports c.i.f.:* Food and live animals 345; Beverages and tobacco 102; Mineral fuels, lubricants, etc. 413; Chemicals and related products 104; Basic manufactures 280; Machinery and transport equipment 749; Miscellaneous manufactured articles 340; Total (incl. others) 2,693. *Exports f.o.b.:* Flat fish, frozen 142.4; Fish fillets, frozen 197.5; Shrimp, frozen 727.5; Crustaceans, frozen 256.5; Total (incl. others) 2,232.8. *2003* (million kroner, provisional): Total imports c.i.f. 2,473; Total exports f.o.b. 2,267.

Principal Trading Partners (million kroner, 2001): *Imports c.i.f.:* Denmark 1,776.6; Norway 388.2; Total (incl. others) 2,692.6. *Exports f.o.b.:* Denmark 1,885.2, Japan 78.5; Norway 58.5; Thailand 28.2; USA 129.6; Total (incl. others) 2,232.8.

TRANSPORT

Road Traffic (registered motor vehicles excl. emergency services, 2002): Private cars 2,730 (incl. 210 taxis); Buses 72; Lorries 1,282; Motorcycles 10.

Shipping (2000): Number of vessels 162 (passenger ships 7, dry cargo ships 39, fishing vessels 110, others 6); Total displacement 59,938 grt (passenger ships 5,780 grt, dry cargo ships 6,411 grt, fishing vessels 47,046 grt, others 701 grt).

International Sea-borne Freight Traffic ('000 cubic metres, 2002): Goods loaded 245; Goods unloaded 355.

International Transport (passengers conveyed between Greenland, Denmark and Iceland): Ship (1983) 94; Aircraft (2002) 103,5622.

TOURISM

Occupancy of Registered Hotel Accommodation (nights, 2002): 179,349 (incl. 55,602 by Danish visitors).

COMMUNICATIONS MEDIA

Radio Receivers (1997): 27,000 in use.

Television Receivers (1997): 22,000 in use.

Telephones ('000 subscribers, 2002): 25.3.

Facsimile Machines (1992): 1,153 in use.

Mobile Cellular Telephones ('000 subscribers, 2002): 17.7.

Internet Users (2002): 9,071.

Book Publishing (titles, 2002): 139.
Sources: UNESCO, *Statistical Yearbook,* International Telecommunication Union and UN, *Statistical Yearbook.*

EDUCATION

(municipal primary and lower-secondary schools only, 2001/02)

Institutions: 87.

Teachers: 1,191 (incl. 380 temporarily-employed teachers and 202 non-Greenlandic-speaking teachers (2000/01)).

Students: 11,368.

Directory

The Government

The legislative body is the Landsting, with 31 members elected for four years, on a basis of proportional representation. Greenlanders and Danes resident in Greenland for at least six months prior to an election and over the age of 18 years have the right to vote. Based on the strength of the parties in the Landsting, an executive, the Landsstyre, is formed. Since 1979 the Landsstyre has gradually assumed control of the administration of Greenland's internal affairs. Jurisdiction in constitutional matters, foreign affairs and defence remains with the Danish Government, the highest representative of which, in Greenland, is the Rigsombudsmand or High Commissioner. Greenland sends two representatives to the Danish legislature, the Folketing.

LANDSSTYRE
(April 2005)

A coalition of Siumut (S) and Inuit Ataqatigiit (IA).

Prime Minister: HANS ENOKSEN (S).

Deputy Prime Minister, Minister of Finance and Foreign Affairs, Minister for Nordic Co-operation: JOSEF MOTZFELDT (IA).

Minister of Infrastructure, Housing and the Environment: JENS NAPÀTÒK (S).

Minister of Fisheries and Hunting: SIMON OLSEN (S).

Minister of Industry, Agriculture and the Labour Market: JOHAN LUND OLSEN (IA).

Minister of Family and Health: ASII CHEMNITZ NARUP (IA).

Minister of Self-governance, Justice and Petroleum: JØRGEN WÆVER JOHANSEN (S).

Minister of Culture, Education, Research and the Church: HENRIETTE RASMUSSEN (IA).

Government Offices

Rigsombudsmanden i Grønland (High Commission of Greenland): Indaleeqqap Aqq. 3, POB 1030, 3900 Nuuk; tel. 321001; fax 324171; e-mail riomgr@gl.stm.dk; internet www .rigsombudsmanden.gl; High Commissioner PETER LAVRITZEN.

Grønlands Hjemmestyre (Greenland Home Rule Government): POB 1015, 3900 Nuuk; Denmark Bureau, Pilestræde 52, POB 2151, 1016 Copenhagen K; tel. 345000; fax 325002; e-mail homerule@gh .gl; internet www.nanoq.gl.

LANDSTING

Chairman: DANIEL SKIFTE (Atassut).

Election, 3 December 2002

	Votes	% of votes	Seats
Siumut (Forward)	8,151	28.48	10
Inuit Ataqatigiit (Inuit Brotherhood) .	7,244	25.31	8
Atassut (Solidarity)	5,780	20.20	7
Demokraatit (Democrats)	4,558	15.93	5
Katusseqatigiit (Alliance of Independent Candidates) . . .	1,884	6.58	1
Arnat Partiiat (Women's Party) . .	686	2.40	—
Total (incl. others)	28,616	100.00	31

Political Organizations

Atassut (Solidarity): POB 399, 3900 Nuuk; tel. 323366; fax 325840; e-mail atassut.landsorganisation@partiit.centadm.gh.gl; f. 1978 and became political party in 1981; supports close links with Denmark and favours EU membership for Greenland; Leader DANIEL SKIFTE; Chair. AUGUSTA SALLING.

Demokraatit (Democrats—D): POB 164, 3900 Nuuk; tel. 345000; fax 346281; e-mail demokrat@greennet.gl; internet www.demokrat .gl; f. 2002; Chair. PER BERTHELSEN.

Inuit Ataqatigiit (Inuit Brotherhood—IA): POB 321, 3900 Nuuk; e-mail avm@gh.gl; f. 1978; socialist party, demanding that Greenland citizenship be restricted to those of Inuit parentage; advocates Greenland's eventual independence from Denmark; Chair. JOSEF MOTZFELDT.

Siumut (Forward): POB 357, 3900 Nuuk; tel. 322077; fax 322319; e-mail siumut@greennet.gl; f. 1971 and became political party in 1977; aims to promote collective ownership and co-operation, and to develop greater reliance on Greenland's own resources; favours greatest possible autonomy within the Kingdom of Denmark; social democratic party; Chair. HANS ENOKSEN.

Other registered parties include Arnat Partiiat (Women's Party) and Katusseqatigiit (Alliance of Independent Candidates).

Judicial System

The island is divided into 18 court districts and these courts all use lay assessors. For most cases these lower courts are for the first instance and appeal is to the Landsret, the higher court in Nuuk, which is the only one with a professional judge. This court hears the more serious cases in the first instance and appeal in these cases is to the High Court (Østre Landsret) in Copenhagen.

Religion

CHRISTIANITY

The Greenlandic Church, of which most of the population are adherents, forms an independent diocese of the Evangelical Lutheran Church in Denmark and comes under the jurisdiction of the Landsstyre and of the Bishop of Greenland. There are 17 parishes and in 1995 there were 23 ministers serving in Greenland.

Biskoppen over Grønlands Stift (Bishop of Greenland): SOFIE PETERSEN, Evangelical Lutheran Church, POB 90, 3900 Nuuk; tel. 321134; fax 321061; e-mail bispekontor@gh.gl.

There are also small groups of other Protestant churches and of Roman Catholics.

The Press

There are no daily newspapers in Greenland.

Atuagagdliutit/Grønlandsposten: POB 39, 3900 Nuuk; tel. 321083; fax 325483; e-mail redaktion@ag.gl; internet www.ag.gl; 2 a week; Editor JENS BRØNDEN.

Niviarsiaq: POB 357, 3900 Nuuk; tel. 322077; fax 322319; e-mail siumut@greennet.gl; organ of Siumut; monthly; Editor J. WÆVER JOHANSEN.

Sermitsiaq: Spindlers Bakke 10B, POB 150, 3900 Nuuk; tel. 321903; fax 322499; weekly; Editor POUL KRARUP.

Publishers

Atuakkiorfik A/S: Hans Egedesvej 3, POB 840, 3900 Nuuk; tel. 322122; fax 322500; e-mail editor@atuakkiorfik.gl; internet www .atuakkiorfik.gl; f. 1956; general fiction and non-fiction, children's and textbooks, public relations; Man. ÅGE RASMUSSEN.

Ilinniusiorfik Undervisningsmiddelforlag: POB 840, 3900 Nuuk; tel. 322122; fax 322500; e-mail ilinniusiorfik@ilinniusiorfik .gl; internet www.ilinniusiorfik.gl; state-owned; textbooks and teaching materials; non-profit-making organization; Man. EBBE MORTENSEN.

Broadcasting and Communications

TELECOMMUNICATIONS

TELE Greenland A/S: POB 1002, 3900 Nuuk; tel. 341255; fax 322255; e-mail tele@tele.gl; internet www.tele.gl; f. 1994; owned by Home Rule Govt.

BROADCASTING

Radio

Kalaallit Nunaata Radioa (KNR)—Grønlands Radio: POB 1007, 3900 Nuuk; tel. 325333; fax 325042; internet www.knr.gl; 5 AM stations, 45 FM stations; bilingual programmes in Greenlandic and Danish, 17 hours a day; Man. Dir PETER FREDERIK ROSING.

Avannaata Radioa: POB 223, 3952 Ilulissat; tel. 943633; fax 943618; e-mail avannaata@radio.knr.gl; regional station in north Greenland.

Kujataata Radioa: POB 158, 3920 Qaqortoq; regional station in south Greenland.

Radio—5 OZ 20: SPE BOX 139, 3970 Pituffik; FM/stereo, non-commercial station; broadcasts 21 hours a day; news, music, etc.; Station Man. INGRID KRISTENSEN.

Television

Kalaallit Nunaata Radioa TV: POB 1007, 3900 Nuuk; tel. 325333; fax 325042; internet www.knr.gl; broadcasts by VHF transmitter to all Greenland; commercial; most programmes in Danish; Man. Dir PETER FREDERIK ROSING.

Finance

BANK

(cap. = capital; res = reserves; dep. = deposits; m. = million; br. = branch; amounts in kroner)

The Bank of Greenland—GrønlandsBANKEN A/S: POB 1033, 3900 Nuuk; tel. 347700; fax 347706; e-mail banken@banken.gl; internet www.banken.gl; f. 1967 as The Bank of Greenland A/S; name changed as above following merger with Nuna Bank A/S in 1997; cap. 180.0m., res 352.2m., dep. 2,168.0m. (Dec. 2003); Pres. and Gen. Man. SVEND-ERIK DANIELSEN; Gen. Man. JESPER FLENSTED NIELSEN; Chair. JAKOB BROGAARD; 5 brs.

Trade and Industry

GOVERNMENT AGENCY

Government of Greenland, Bureau of Minerals and Petroleum: POB 930, 3900 Nuuk; tel. 346800; fax 324302; e-mail bmp@gh .gl; internet www.bmp.gl; f. 1998; performs the central administrative co-ordinating and regulatory tasks regarding exploration and production of mineral resources in Greenland; Dep. Min. HANS KRISTIAN SCHØNWANDT.

STATE-OWNED COMPANIES

Pilersuisoq A/S (KNI A/S)—Greenland Trade Service Ltd: POB 319, 3911 Sisimiut; tel. 862444; fax 866263; internet www .pilersuisoq.gl; f. 1993; statutory wholesale and retail trading co, petroleum and fuel supply; Chair. TØNNES BERTHELSEN; Pres. GERHARDT PETERSEN.

Pisiffik A/S Greenland TRADE RETAIL Ltd: POB 1009, 3911 Sisimiut; tel. 862600; fax 864175; e-mail mos@pisiffik.gl; f. 1993; statutory wholesale and retail trading co.; Chair. VILLY RASMUSSEN; Man. MICHAEL ØSTERGAARD.

Royal Greenland A/S: POB 1073, 3900 Nuuk; tel. 324422; fax 323349; internet www.royalgreenland.com; f. 1774; trade monopoly ended 1950; Home Rule Govt assumed control 1986; established as share company 1990 (all shares owned by Home Rule Govt); fishing group based in Greenland with subsidiaries in Japan, the United Kingdom, Scandinavia, the USA, Italy, France and Germany; main products are coldwater prawns and halibut; five trawlers; factories in Greenland, Denmark and Germany; Chair. UFFE ELLEMANN-JENSEN; Pres. and Chief Exec. KELD ASKÆR.

EMPLOYERS' ASSOCIATION

Grønlands Arbeijdsgiveforening (GA) (Greenland Employers' Association): Tjalfesvej 3, POB 73, 3900 Nuuk; c. 300 mem. orgs.

TRADE UNION

Sulinermik Inuussutissarsiutequartut Kattuffiat (SIK) (Greenland Workers' Union): POB 9, 3900 Nuuk; tel. 29922133; fax 29924939; internet www.randburg.com/gr/workersu.html; f. 1956 as Grønlands Arbejder Sammenslutning (GAS); Pres. JESS G. BERTHELSEN; Vice-Pres. OLE MAGNUSSEN; Sec. OLE KRISTIAN; c. 6,000 mems.

Transport

Owing to the long distances and harsh conditions there are no roads connecting towns in Greenland. Domestic traffic is mainly by air-craft (fixed-wing and helicopter), boat, snowmobile and dog-sled. There are airports or heliports in all towns for domestic flights.

The main port is at Nuuk; there are also all-year ports at Paamiut (Frederikshåb), Maniitsoq (Sukkertoppen) and Sisimiut (Holsteinsborg). In addition, there are shipyards at Nuuk, Qaqortoq, Paamiut, Maniitsoq, Sisimiut and Aasiaat. Coastal motor vessels operate passenger services along the west coast from Upernavik to Nanortalik.

SHIPPING COMPANY

Royal Arctic Line A/S: POB 1580, 3900 Nuuk; tel. 349100; fax 322450; e-mail info@ral.dk; internet www.ral.dk; f. 1993; owned by Home Rule Govt; four container vessels of 38,922 grt and one general cargo vessel of 4,209 grt; Pres. JENS ANDERSEN.

AIRLINE

Grønlandsfly A/S (Greenlandair Inc.): POB 1012, Nuuk Airport, 3900 Nuuk; tel. 343434; fax 327288; e-mail glahq@greenlandair.gl; internet www.greenlandair.gl; f. 1960; air services to the 19 principal centres in Greenland, and to Copenhagen (Denmark); supply, survey, ice-reconnaissance services and helicopter/fixed-wing charters; owned by Danish Govt, Greenland Home Rule Govt and SAS; Chair. PETER GRØNVOLD SAMUELSEN; Pres. FINN ØELUND.

Tourism

Tourist arrivals traditionally did not exceed 5,000–7,000 per year. In order to stimulate increased revenue, it was decided in 1990 to set a target of 30,000–35,000 tourist arrivals per year (generating annual income of some 500m. kroner) to be achieved by 2005. The national tourist board of Greenland, Greenland Tourism, was established in 1992 in order to develop tourism in Greenland, and concentrates primarily on developing sustainable tourism projects. In 2002 179,349 accommodation nights were recorded at registered hotels, including 55,602 by Danish visitors.

Greenland Tourism: POB 1615, Hans Egedesvej 29, 3900 Nuuk; tel. 342820; fax 322877; e-mail info@greenland.com; internet www .greenland.com; f. 1992; Chair. NILS WILHJELM; Man. Dir STIG RØMER WINTHER.

DJIBOUTI

Introductory Survey

Location, Climate, Language, Religion, Flag, Capital

The Republic of Djibouti is in the Horn of Africa, at the southern entrance to the Red Sea. It is bounded on the north by Eritrea, on the north, west and south-west by Ethiopia, and on the south-east by Somalia. The land is mainly volcanic desert, and the climate hot and arid. There are two main ethnic groups, the Issa, who are of Somali origin and comprise 50% of the population, and the Afar, who comprise 40% of the population and are of Ethiopian origin. Both groups are Muslims, and they speak related Cushitic languages. The official languages are Arabic and French. The flag has two equal horizontal stripes, of light blue and light green, with a white triangle, enclosing a five-pointed red star, at the hoist. The capital is Djibouti.

Recent History

In 1945 the area now comprising the Republic of Djibouti (then known as French Somaliland) was proclaimed an overseas territory of France, and in 1967 was renamed the French Territory of the Afars and the Issas. The Afar and the Issa have strong connections with Ethiopia and Somalia, respectively. Until the 1960s ethnic divisions were not marked; subsequently, however, internal tensions arose. Demands for independence were led by the Issa community, and, under pressure from the Organization of African Unity (OAU, now the African Union, see p. 144) to grant full independence to the territory, France acted to improve relations between the two communities. Following a referendum in May 1977, the territory became independent on 27 June. Hassan Gouled Aptidon, a senior Issa politician, became the first President of the Republic of Djibouti.

In March 1979 Gouled formed a new political party, the Rassemblement populaire pour le progrès (RPP), which was declared the sole legal party in October 1981. In June 1981 Gouled was elected to a further six-year term as President. Legislative elections were held in May 1982, when candidates were chosen from a single list approved by the RPP. At the next presidential and legislative elections, held in April 1987, Gouled was re-elected, while RPP-sponsored candidates for all 65 seats in the legislature were elected unopposed.

Until the mid-1980s there was little overt opposition to the RPP under Gouled's leadership. In May 1986 Aden Robleh Awalleh, a former political associate of Gouled, formed an opposition group, the Mouvement national djiboutien pour l'instauration de la démocratie (MNDID). Political tensions began to escalate during 1987, prompting Gouled to reorganize the Government. In April 1989 inter-tribal hostilities erupted in the capital and the Afar town of Tadjourah. Inter-ethnic tensions persisted, and in May 1990 fighting broke out between the Issa and the Gadabursi communities in the capital.

In April 1991 a new and powerful armed opposition group, the Front pour la restauration de l'unité et de la démocratie (FRUD), was formed by a merger of three insurgent Afar movements. In November the FRUD launched a full-scale insurrection against the Government and by late November the FRUD controlled many towns and villages in the north of the country. The Government introduced mass conscription and requested military assistance from France (see below) to repel what it described as 'external aggression' by soldiers loyal to the deposed President Mengistu of Ethiopia. The FRUD denied that it constituted a foreign aggressor, claiming that its aim was to secure fair political representation for all ethnic groups in Djibouti.

In early 1992, under pressure from the French Government to accommodate opposition demands for democratic reform, President Gouled appointed a commission to draft a new constitution, which was to restore the multi-party system and provide for free elections. The FRUD stated its willingness to negotiate with Gouled and undertook to observe a cease-fire, subject to satisfactory progress on democratic reforms. Gouled, however, reasserted that the FRUD was controlled by 'foreign interests' and accused France of failing to honour its defence agreement. By late January most of northern Djibouti was under FRUD control, although armed conflict between the FRUD and the Government continued. In June Ahmed Dini, who had been

Djibouti's first Prime Minister after independence, assumed the leadership of the FRUD.

President Gouled's constitutional plan, which was announced in April 1992, conceded the principle of political pluralism, but proposed few other changes and retained a strong executive presidency. The plan was rejected by the opposition parties and by the FRUD, although cautiously welcomed by France. A constitutional referendum, which was held in September, was boycotted by all the opposition groups; the Government, however, stated that, with 75% of the electorate participating, 97% of voters had endorsed the new Constitution. At the 30 September deadline for party registration, only the RPP and the Parti du renouveau démocratique (PRD), an opposition group formed earlier in 1992 under the leadership of Mohamed Djama Elabe, were granted legal status. The application for registration by the opposition Parti national démocratique (PND) was initially rejected, although it was allowed in October. Elections to the Assemblée nationale were held on 18 December, and all 65 seats were won by the RPP. More than 51% of the electorate abstained from voting, leading to charges from the PND that the legislature was unrepresentative.

Five candidates stood in Djibouti's first contested presidential election, which was held on 7 May 1993: Gouled, Elabe, Aden Robleh Awalleh (for the PND) and two independents. The election was again notable for a low level of participation (49.9%), but resulted in a clear victory for Gouled, who, according to official results, obtained 60.8% of the valid votes cast, compared with 22.0% for Elabe and 12.3% for Awalleh. The opposition alleged that there had been widespread electoral fraud.

In July 1993 the army launched a successful offensive on FRUD positions in the centre and north of the country, capturing the FRUD's headquarters, as well as other towns and areas held by the rebel group. Many of the rebels retreated into the mountains in the far north of the country. The FRUD continued its struggle, however, and began launching armed attacks on government forces. By July an estimated 80,000 civilians had been displaced by the fighting.

In March 1994 serious divisions emerged within the FRUD leadership. It was reported that the political bureau, led by Ahmed Dini, had been dissolved and that dissident members had formed an 'executive council', headed by Ougoureh Kifleh Ahmed. This dissident leadership (Ali Mohamed Daoud was subsequently declared President) sought support within the movement for a negotiated political settlement of the conflict. In June Kifleh Ahmed and the Government agreed terms for a cease-fire, and formal negotiations for a peace settlement began in July. Executive bodies of both FRUD factions continued to operate during the latter half of 1994, and parallel national congresses rejected the legitimacy of the opposing faction's leadership. In December an agreement signed by Kifleh Ahmed and the Minister of the Interior, Idris Harbi Farah, provided for a permanent cessation of hostilities, the incorporation of FRUD armed forces into the national force, the recognition of the FRUD as a legal political party, the multi-ethnic composition of a new council of ministers and the reform of electoral procedures prior to the next legislative elections. In accordance with the peace agreement, 300 members of the FRUD armed forces were integrated into the national army in March 1995. However, there was little further implementation of the accord, and there was considerable criticism of the agreement by the radical faction of the FRUD (which, under the leadership of Ahmed Dini, favoured a continuation of military operations and launched a number of small-scale attacks against government targets in late 1995) and other opposition groups. Nevertheless, Ali Mohamed Daoud and Kifleh Ahmed were appointed to posts in the Government in June. In March 1996 the Government granted legal recognition to the FRUD, which became the country's fourth and largest political party. However, Ibrahim Chehem Daoud, a former high-ranking official in the FRUD, who rejected the reconciliation between the Government and the group, formed a new group, FRUD-Renaissance.

In early 1996 President Gouled's prolonged hospitalization in France prompted a succession crisis within the RPP, between the President's nephew and principal adviser, Ismael Omar Gelleh, and his private secretary, Ismael Gedi Hared. In February a prison riot in the capital provoked a confrontation between the Minister of Justice and Islamic Affairs, Moumin Bahdon Farah, and the Minister of the Interior, Idris Harbi Farah. In March Bahdon Farah, who was opposed to Gelleh, was dismissed from the Council of Ministers, together with Ahmed Bulaleh Barreh, the Minister of Defence. Both ministers had openly opposed the December 1994 peace agreement with the FRUD, on the grounds that it strengthened the position of Gelleh and his followers. In April 1996 Bahdon Farah established a splinter group of the RPP, the Groupe pour la démocratie de la république (RPP—GDR), which included 13 of the 65 members of the Assemblée nationale. The President of the Assemblée subsequently claimed that the RPP—GDR would remain banned while Bahdon Farah continued to hold his position as Secretary-General of the RPP. In May Gouled expelled Gedi Hared from the RPP's executive committee, together with Bahdon Farah and former ministers Barreh and Ali Mahamade Houmed, all of whom opposed Gelleh. In June Gedi Hared formed an opposition alliance, the Coordination de l'opposition djiboutienne, embracing the PND, the Front uni de l'opposition djiboutienne (a coalition of internal opposition groups) and the RPP—GDR. In August Gedi Hared, Bahdon Farah and Barreh were among five people sentenced to six months' imprisonment and the suspension of their civil rights for five years for 'insulting the Head of State'. The accused had reportedly signed a document in May, alleging that President Gouled ruled by force and terror. The detainees were released from prison in January 1997, following a presidential pardon, although their civil rights were not restored. (In early September 2001 it was announced that the Government had proposed an amnesty for the five, under which their civil rights would be restored and they would be entitled to stand in the legislative elections of January 2003.)

In April 1997 the FRUD faction led by Ali Mohamed Daoud announced its intention to participate in the forthcoming legislative elections and to present joint electoral lists with the RPP. At the legislative elections, held on 19 December, the RPP-FRUD alliance won all the seats in the Assemblée nationale. The rate of voter participation was officially recorded at 63.8%. The PRD and the PND presented candidates in some districts, but neither succeeded in gaining representation. In late December President Gouled formed a new Council of Ministers; minor reshuffles had been effected in April and November.

In February 1999 President Gouled confirmed that he would not stand in the forthcoming presidential election; the RPP named Gelleh as its presidential candidate. At the election, held on 9 April, Gelleh won 74.4% of the votes cast, convincingly defeating his sole opponent, Moussa Ahmed Idris, who represented an opposition coalition, the Opposition djiboutienne unifiée (ODU), including the PND, the PRD and the Dini wing of the FRUD. Electoral participation was estimated at 60% of eligible voters. Following his inauguration as President on 7 May, Gelleh reappointed Barkad Gourad Hamadou as Prime Minister, at the head of a new Council of Ministers.

In early February 2000 the Government and the Dini wing of the FRUD signed a peace agreement in Paris, France. The accord provided for an end to hostilities, the reciprocal release of prisoners, the return of military units to positions held before the conflict, freedom of movement for persons and goods, the reintegration of FRUD insurgents into their previous positions of employment, and an amnesty for the rebels. In late March Dini returned to Djibouti from a self-imposed nine-year exile and announced his intention to assist in the implementation of the peace agreement. Meanwhile, earlier that month the RPP had convened its eighth congress, at which Gouled officially announced his retirement from active politics. Gelleh was elected to succeed him as President of the party. In April the commission for the implementation of the peace agreement between the Government and the Dini wing of the FRUD held its first meeting, during which four sub-commissions were established to organize disarmament and compensation, the rehabilitation of former combatants, the implementation of the decentralization programme and the strengthening of the democratic process. Meetings between the two sides continued during 2000. However, in October the FRUD issued a number of new demands and reports circulated that FRUD members were preparing to resume their armed struggle, if negotiations continued to be stalled.

In early February 2001 Barkad Gourad Hamadou resigned as Prime Minister on the grounds of ill health, after some 22 years in office. Dileita Mohamed Dileita, hitherto ambassador to Ethiopia, was appointed as Hamadou's replacement in March.

In May 2001 it was announced that an agreement bringing an official end to hostilities between the Government and the FRUD had been signed. The Government, for its part, pledged to establish a number of more representative local bodies and to introduce an 'unrestricted multi-party system' by September 2002. In early July 2001 President Gelleh effected a minor reorganization of the Council of Ministers, with moderate FRUD members allocated two portfolios.

On 4 September 2002, to coincide with the 10th anniversary of the approval of the new Constitution, the limit on the number of permitted political parties (previously fixed at four) was lifted. Henceforth, all parties would be recognized, subject to approval by the Ministry of the Interior and Decentralization, and, during the following months, a number of new parties registered with the intention of participating in the forthcoming legislative elections. At the elections, which were held on 10 January 2003, the Union pour la majorité présidentielle (UMP), a coalition comprising the RPP, the FRUD, the PND and the Parti populaire social démocrate, won 62.7% of the total votes cast; in accordance with the electoral laws, as it had won the majority of votes in each of the five constituencies, the UMP secured all 65 seats in the Assemblée nationale. Therefore, despite receiving 37.3% of votes cast, the opposition coalition, the Union pour l'alternance démocratique (UAD), comprising the Alliance républicaine pour la démocratie (ARD), the Mouvement du renouveau démocratique, the Parti djiboutien pour la démocratie, the Parti du renouveau démocratique and the Union djiboutienne pour la démocratie et la justice, failed to attain any legislative representation. However, for the first time in the country's history seven women were elected to the Assemblée nationale. According to official figures, the rate of voter participation was 48.4%. Later that month Idriss Arnaoud Ali, the deputy Secretary-General of the RPP, was appointed President of the Assemblée nationale; the Council of Ministers remained unaltered.

In late July 2003 the Djibouti Government announced that owing to 'security and economic' reasons all illegal immigrants would be required to leave Djibouti by the end of August. The deadline was subsequently extended until mid-September, by which time more than 80,000 immigrants, predominantly from Ethiopia and Somalia, had voluntarily left the country. The USA, which in August had warned of the possibility of terrorist attacks against Western targets in Djibouti, denied allegations that it had exerted pressure on the Djibouti Government to expel the illegal immigrants. Following the expiry of the deadline, security forces commenced operations to arrest and expel any remaining immigrants not in possession of identity papers.

In April 2004 widespread flooding occurred in Djibouti following torrential rains, which caused the banks of the River Ambouli to burst. Some 300 people were killed and 100,000 others were adversely affected as the floods devastated parts of the capital. The World Health Organization subsequently warned of the risk of a cholera outbreak. In September the World Bank approved a US $6.5m. project which would rehabilitate the country's social and economic infrastructure by rebuilding schools and health centres.

Concerns over the freedom of the press escalated during 2004 following the imprisonment in April of Daher Ahmad Farah, the editor-in-chief of *Le Renouveau*. Farah was released and reimprisoned several times throughout the year and in June the authorities prevented the publication of the newspaper. The international organization Reporters sans frontières denounced the Government's actions as an attempt to silence the opposition press.

In mid-September 2004 the death was announced of Ahmed Dini Ahmed, Djibouti's first Prime Minister following the country's independence from France. Ahmad Youssouf Houmed assumed the leadership of the ARD later that month.

At the presidential election held on 8 April 2005 Gelleh, who was unopposed following the withdrawal the previous month of the sole challenger, the PDD President Mohamed Daoud Chehem, was returned for a second term of office. Numerous opposition groups had appealed for a boycott of the election; however, official figures put the rate of voter participation at 78.9% and confirmed that Gelleh had received 100% of the votes cast.

Separate treaties of friendship and co-operation were signed in 1981 with Ethiopia, Somalia, Kenya and Sudan, with the aim of resolving regional conflicts. In August 1984 the Minister of Foreign Affairs reaffirmed Djibouti's policy of maintaining a neutral stance in the conflict between its neighbours in the Horn of Africa and expressed his Government's willingness to act as a mediator. A joint ministerial committee, which held its first session in mid-1985, was formed between Djibouti and Ethiopia, to strengthen existing relations and co-operation between the two countries. These relations, however, were overshadowed in 1986 by Ethiopia's support for the MNDID.

Djibouti's interest in promoting regional co-operation was exemplified by the creation, in February 1985, of the Intergovernmental Authority on Drought and Development (now the Intergovernmental Authority on Development (IGAD, see p. 270), with six (now seven) member states; Djibouti was chosen as the site of its permanent secretariat, and President Gouled became the first Chairman.

Following the overthrow of the Ethiopian President, Mengistu Haile Mariam, in May 1991, Djibouti established good relations with the successor transitional Government in that country. In June Djibouti hosted a preliminary conference of groups from southern Somalia, aimed at forming a transitional Somali government. In November 1997 Djibouti granted official recognition to the self-proclaimed 'Republic of Somaliland', which declared independence in 1991. In late 1999 President Gelleh drafted a peace plan aimed at reunifying Somali territory, to which the leaders of 'Somaliland' expressed their vehement opposition. Relations deteriorated further in April 2000 when the 'Somaliland' authorities closed the common border with Djibouti, following an incident in which a Djiboutian delegation was refused permission to leave its aircraft after landing at Hargeisa airport in 'Somaliland'. 'Somaliland' officials claimed that Djibouti was encouraging ethnic violence and had been responsible for a series of bomb attacks in Hargeisa. In response, Djibouti expelled three 'Somaliland' diplomats and closed the 'Somaliland' liaison office in Djibouti town. Furthermore, in May the 'Somaliland' authorities issued a ban on all flights from Djibouti to its territory; the Djibouti Government responded by prohibiting all flights to and from 'Somaliland'. The Djibouti-sponsored Somali national reconciliation conference, presided over by Gelleh, opened in May in Arta, about 40 km south of Djibouti town. The conference was attended by some 900 representatives of Somali clans and political and armed groups, and in August, following three months of extensive negotiations, the newly created Somali Transitional National Assembly elected Abdulkasim Salad Hasan President of Somalia. Relations between Djibouti and 'Somaliland' were further strained in April 2001 after the Djibouti authorities closed the common border and outlawed the transport of all goods and people between the two territories. In October a delegation from 'Somaliland', led by its minister responsible for foreign affairs, held talks with Djibouti officials in an attempt to improve relations; although several bilateral agreements were concluded, the common border remained closed. Following the death of President Mohamed Ibrahim Egal in May 2002, Gelleh moved swiftly to establish cordial relations with the new President of 'Somaliland', Dahir Riyale Kahin. At a meeting the following month they agreed to relocate the border crossing between the two countries and to strengthen bilateral relations.

In December 1995 the Djibouti Government protested to the Eritrean authorities about alleged incursions by Eritrean troops into north-eastern Djibouti. These allegations were vehemently denied by Eritrea. Relations between the two countries were strained in April 1996, when President Gouled rejected a map of Eritrea submitted by the Eritrean Minister of Foreign Affairs, which reportedly included a 20-km strip of territory belonging to Djibouti. In November 1998 Djibouti suspended diplomatic relations with Eritrea, following accusations by that country that it was supporting Ethiopia in the Eritrea–Ethiopia border dispute. Gouled had been actively involved in an OAU committee mediating on the dispute, which earlier in the month had proposed a peace plan that was accepted by Ethiopia, but not by Eritrea. In 1999 relations between Djibouti and Ethiopia continued to improve, while those between Djibouti and Eritrea deteriorated further. In November President Gelleh was praised by the Ethiopian President for his efforts in promoting a peace settlement in Somalia and in December the Djibouti and Ethiopian Governments signed a protocol of understanding on military co-operation, with the aim of establishing a further mutual defence pact. In March 2000, following Libyan mediation, Djibouti and

Eritrea announced that they had resumed diplomatic relations. In December relations between Djibouti and Ethiopia temporarily deteriorated after plans were announced to increase handling charges at Djibouti port by more than 150%, which the Ethiopian authorities maintained violated a 1999 trade agreement between the two countries. However, in February 2001 the Dubai Port Authority, which had assumed control of Djibouti port in May 2000, agreed to reduce the tariffs, and bilateral relations subsequently improved. In November 2004 it was announced that talks between Ethiopia and Djibouti would recommence in an attempt to resolve the issue of transporting goods imported by Ethiopia through Djibouti.

In August 1986 a new scheme for repatriating Ethiopian refugees, under the auspices of the UN High Commissioner for Refugees (UNHCR), was begun. The burden that 'official' refugees imposed on the economy was exacerbated by an influx of illegal immigrants from Somalia and Ethiopia, and in June 1987 the Djibouti Government announced tighter controls on border crossings and identity papers. Following discussions in February 1988, Djibouti and Ethiopia agreed to control movements across their common border and to curb the influx of refugees into Djibouti. Although the Government maintained that by early 1993 the number of Somali refugees in Djibouti had reached 120,000, UNHCR argued that many of these were economic migrants. In September 1994 UNHCR initiated a programme of voluntary repatriation for Ethiopian refugees in Djibouti. According to UNHCR, some 35,000 Ethiopians returned voluntarily to their homes between early 1995 and April 1996. UNHCR estimated that at 31 December 2003 there were 27,034 refugees in Djibouti, of whom 25,474 were Somali.

President Gouled consistently fostered cordial relations with France and encouraged the maintenance of French troops in Djibouti. However, the French military presence became more controversial following Iraq's invasion of Kuwait in August 1990 and the onset of the 'Gulf crisis', during which Djibouti became the base of operations connected with France's participation in the multinational force deployed in Saudi Arabia. By supporting the UN resolutions that were formulated against Iraq, Djibouti jeopardized its future relations with that country, which was emerging as an important supplier of economic and military aid. However, Djibouti's stance during the Gulf War of January–February 1991 strengthened its ties with France, and in February the Djibouti and French Governments signed defence treaties, extending military co-operation, although France refused to intervene militarily in the conflict between the Government and the FRUD. The failure of the Government to conclude a peace agreement with the FRUD strained relations with France in 1993–94. Relations improved as a result of the peace accord of December 1994, but tensions remained between the two countries. In April 1998, during a visit to Djibouti by the French Minister of Defence, it was announced that France planned to reduce its military presence in the country from 3,200 troops to 2,600 by 2000. However, in October 1999, the suspension of the troop reduction programme was announced and France confirmed its guarantees of Djibouti's territorial integrity. In July 2002, as part of a restructuring of the French forces in Djibouti, a new French army base was inaugurated, and in May 2003 the French Government agreed to provide Djibouti with €30m. per year of development aid over a 10-year period, of which €5m. would be used to maintain military bases and port facilities. France remained the leading donor of aid to Djibouti in 2004, granting €20m. of public development assistance.

The attacks on the World Trade Center in New York and the Pentagon in Washington, DC, on 11 September 2001 resulted in a significant enhancement of Djibouti's strategic importance to the USA and its allies. In early October Djibouti demonstrated its support for the US-led coalition against terrorism by establishing a seven-member Comité national de lutte contre le terrorisme to monitor security conditions in Djibouti. Djibouti agreed to grant access to its port and airfields, and coalition members stated their intention to use Djibouti as a base from where to monitor developments in Somalia, Sudan and other countries in the region. In December a German military delegation discussed the possibility of establishing a base camp for German naval forces participating in the war on terrorism with Djibouti officials, and in January 2002 Djibouti and Germany signed a memorandum of understanding on the status of German military and civilian personnel in Djibouti. The accord granted German military personnel access to Djibouti's port and airfields to conduct surveillance missions in the region, and some 1,200 German naval personnel were subsequently stationed in Djibouti, although this number had been reduced to 320 by early 2005. In December 2002 the US Secretary of Defense, Donald Rumsfeld, visited the 1,500 US troops based off the coast of Djibouti who formed the Combined Joint Task Force-Horn of Africa, which was to monitor ship movements in the Red Sea and along the East African coast. In mid-January 2003 Gelleh and several ministers met US President George W. Bush and other senior US officials during a visit to Washington, DC. According to Gelleh, the USA agreed to provide US $8m. over the following two years for education and health projects in Djibouti and pledged to reopen the office of the US Agency for International Development. In February Djibouti and the USA concluded an agreement that allowed US forces to use Djiboutian military installations, and in May the Combined Joint Task Force moved its headquarters on shore to a base in Djibouti. Throughout 2004 US military presence in Djibouti increased further with the construction of a new port at Doraleh and there were ongoing negotiations between the US Navy and the Emirates National Oil Company regarding the possible relocation of refuelling operations to Djibouti from Yemen. The USA also doubled its budget for training the Djibouti military to $325,000 in 2004. This training included courses in professionalizing officers, management of defence resources and coastal security.

Government

Executive power is vested in the President, who is directly elected by universal adult suffrage for a six-year term. Legislative power is held by the Assemblée nationale, consisting of 65 members elected for five years. The Council of Ministers, presided over by a Prime Minister, is responsible to the President. The Republic comprises five electoral districts.

Defence

Since independence, a large portion of the annual budget has been allocated to military expenditure, and defence absorbed an estimated 13.7% of total government budgetary expenditure in 2000. The total armed forces of Djibouti, in which all services form part of the army, was estimated at 9,850 in August 2004 (including 200 naval and 250 air force personnel, and 1,400 gendarmes), and there was a 2,500-strong national security force. At the same time there were about 2,850 French troops stationed in Djibouti, while the US-led Combined Joint Task Force-Horn of Africa also had its headquarters in the country. In January 2002 Djibouti and Germany signed a memorandum of understanding on the status of German military and civilian personnel in Djibouti, granting German military personnel access to Djibouti's port and airfields to conduct surveillance missions in the region; some 320 German naval personnel were stationed in Djibouti in early 2005. The defence budget for 2004 amounted to 4,500m. Djibouti francs.

Economic Affairs

In 2003, according to estimates by the World Bank, Djibouti's gross national income (GNI), measured at average 2001–03 prices, was US $641m., equivalent to $910 per head (or $2,200 on an international purchasing-power parity basis). During 1990–2003, it was estimated, the population increased at an average annual rate of 2.8%, owing partly to the influx of refugees from neighbouring Ethiopia and Somalia (although this figure was expected to decrease during 2004–05 due to the mass expulsion of foreign migrants), while gross domestic product (GDP) per head decreased, in real terms, by an average of 2.9% per year. Overall GDP declined, in real terms, at an average annual rate of 0.2% during 1990–2003; however, growth of 3.5% was recorded in 2003.

Agriculture (including hunting, forestry and fishing) provided only 3.5% of GDP in 2003, according to official figures, although some 77.9% of the labour force were engaged in the sector in mid-2002. There is little arable farming, owing to Djibouti's unproductive terrain, and the country is able to produce only about 10% of its total food requirements. More than one-half of the population are pastoral nomads, herding goats, sheep and camels. During 1990–2000, according to the World Bank, the real GDP of the agricultural sector increased at an average annual rate of 0.4%; agricultural GDP increased by 2.5% in 2000.

Industry (comprising manufacturing, construction and utilities) provided 16.1% of GDP in 2003, according to official figures, and engaged 11.0% of the employed labour force in 1991. Industrial activity is mainly limited to a few small-scale enter-

prises. During 1990–2000, according to the World Bank, industrial GDP declined at an average annual rate of 4.2%; however, industrial GDP increased by 1.1% in 2000.

The manufacturing sector contributed 3.4% of GDP in 2003. Almost all consumer goods have to be imported. Manufacturing GDP declined by an average of 7.5% per year in 1990–2000, according to the World Bank. However, the GDP of the sector increased by 0.9% in 2000.

In 1986 work commenced on a major geothermal exploration project, funded by the World Bank and foreign aid. In that year Saudi Arabia granted Djibouti US $21.4m. for the purchase and installation of three electricity generators, with a combined capacity of 15 MW. Total electricity generating capacity rose from 40 MW to 80 MW in 1988, when the second part of the Boulaos power station became operative. This figure continued to rise during the 1990s, and in 2003 Djibouti produced 263.6m. kWh of electricity. Nevertheless, imported fuels continued to satisfy a large proportion of Djibouti's energy requirements. Imports of petroleum products accounted for 18.5% of the value of total imports in 1999. In December 2004 Djibouti and Ethiopia agreed to connect their power generating facilities in an attempt to increase access to electricity.

Djibouti's economic viability is based on trade through the international port of Djibouti, and on the developing service sector, which accounted for 80.4% of GDP in 2003, according to official figures, and engaged 13.8% of the employed labour force in 1991. In May 2000 the Government and Dubai Ports International (DPI) signed an agreement providing DPI with a 20-year contract to manage the port of Djibouti. During 1990–2000, according to the World Bank, the GDP of the services sector declined at an average annual rate of 0.2%. Services GDP increased by 1.6% in 2000.

In 2002, Djibouti recorded a visible trade deficit of US $200.5m., and there was a deficit of $36.5m. on the current account of the balance of payments. According to the IMF, the principal sources of imports in 2002 were Ethiopia (11.1%) and France (7.6%). The principal markets for exports in that year were Somalia (57.2%) and Yemen (24.5%). The principal imports in 1999 were food and beverages, machinery and electrical appliances, qat (a narcotic leaf), petroleum products and vehicles and transport equipment. Most exports are unclassified.

Djibouti recorded a budget deficit of 839m. Djibouti francs in 2000 (equivalent to 0.9% of GDP). The country's total external debt was US $335.3m. at the end of 2002, of which $305.2m. was long-term public debt. In 2000 the cost of debt-servicing was equivalent to an estimated 5.5% of revenue from exports of goods and services. The annual rate of inflation averaged 4.8% during 1989–97. Consumer prices increased by an estimated 2.0% in 2003. In 1996 unemployment was estimated to affect some 58% of the labour force.

Djibouti is a member of the Intergovernmental Authority on Development (see p. 270) and numerous other international organizations, including the African Development Bank (see p. 142), the Arab Fund for Economic and Social Development (see p. 151) and the Islamic Development Bank (see p. 287). In 1995 Djibouti became a member of the World Trade Organization (see p. 357).

Djibouti has traditionally relied heavily on foreign assistance and in April 1996 the IMF approved Djibouti's first stand-by credit, equivalent to US $6.7m. In October 1999 the IMF agreed a $26.5m. loan to support the Government's three-year economic reform programme, and an initial payment of $3.8m. was released immediately. However, the payment of the balance was conditional on Djibouti implementing its 1999–2002 programme of economic and financial reform, which included reforms to tax, revenue administration and budget management; the completion of the army demobilization programme; the reform of the civil service; and the publication of a privatization programme for the six principal state-owned enterprises. Although there were continued delays in the army demobilization programme and the reform of the civil service, in November 2001 the IMF disbursed a further $5.0m., and in December 2002, following the completion of the third policy review, the IMF released funds totalling $6.0m. However, attempts by the Djiboutian authorities during 2004 to secure further assistance from the IMF proved unsuccessful, largely owing to the significant investment made in the economy by the USA and France. In May 2003 France had agreed to contribute €30m. per year over a 10-year period in order to maintain its military presence in the country, while the USA was to pay Djibouti $31m. for hosting its military base; when combined, these payments would cover more than 80% of the annual wage bill for the civil service. Moreover, in late 2003 the USA also announced that Djibouti would receive aid worth some $90m. during 2004, making Djibouti the largest recipient of US assistance in Africa. Despite the forced expulsion of more than 10% of the country's residents in late 2003 (see above), economic growth stalled in 2004, due in part to a sharp decrease in activity at Djibouti port, while progress towards implementing vital structural reforms remained slow. A sharp increase in government expenditure, particularly on health and education programmes, was also recorded in 2004, although this was offset slightly by higher taxation revenues, and the Government's most immediate priorities remained the creation of more employment opportunities and implementation of further measures to reduce poverty. Meanwhile, according to the central bank, inflation remained low, with price rises of just 1.5% and 2.0% recorded in 2002 and 2003, respectively.

Education

The Government has overall responsibility for education. Primary education generally begins at six years of age and lasts for six years. Secondary education, usually starting at the age of 12, lasts for seven years, comprising a first cycle of four years and a second of three years. In 1996 the total enrolment at primary and secondary schools was equivalent to 26% of the school-age population (31% of boys; 22% of girls). In 1999/2000 primary enrolment included 30.6% of pupils in the relevant age-group (34.9% of boys; 26.3% of girls), and secondary enrolment was equivalent to 14.7% of pupils in the relevant age-group (12.9% of boys; 16.6% of girls). Budgetary current expenditure on education in 2002 was 3,937m. Djibouti francs, equivalent to 12.8% of total government expenditure. The Pôle Universitaire de Djibouti, which opened in 1999, is the sole establishment for higher education with 1,181 students enrolled.

Public Holidays

2005: 1 January (New Year's Day), 21 January* (Id al-Adha, Feast of the Sacrifice), 10 February* (Muharram, Islamic New Year), 21 April* (Mouloud, Birth of the Prophet), 1 May (Workers' Day), 27 June (Independence Day), 4 November* (Id al-Fitr, end of Ramadan), 25 December (Christmas Day).

2006: 1 January (New Year's Day), 11 January* (Id al-Adha, Feast of the Sacrifice), 31 January* (Muharram, Islamic New Year), 11 April* (Mouloud, Birth of the Prophet), 1 May (Workers' Day), 27 June (Independence Day), 24 October* (Id al-Fitr, end of Ramadan), 25 December (Christmas Day).

*These holidays are dependent on the Islamic lunar calendar and may vary by one or two days from the dates given.

Weights and Measures

The metric system is in force.

Statistical Survey

Source (unless otherwise stated): Ministère de l'Economie, des Finances et de la Planification, chargé de la Privatisation, BP 13, Djibouti; tel. 353331; internet www.ministere-finances.dj.

AREA AND POPULATION

Area: 23,200 sq km (8,958 sq miles).

Population: 220,000 (1976 estimate), including Afars 70,000, Issas and other Somalis 80,000, Arabs 12,000, Europeans 15,000, other foreigners 40,000; 519,900 (including refugees and resident foreigners) at 31 December 1990 (official estimate); 703,000 (UN estimate) at mid-2003 (Source: UN, *World Population Prospects: The 2002 Revision*).

Density (mid-2003): 30.3 per sq km.

Principal Towns (estimated population in 2003): Djibouti (capital), 547,100; Ali-Sabieh 8,000; Tadjourah 7,500; Dikhil 6,500; Obock 5,000; Source: Stefan Helders, *World Gazetteer* (internet www.world-gazetteer.com).

Births and Deaths (UN estimates, 1995–2000): Average annual birth rate 42.3 per 1,000; Average annual death rate 17.2 per 1,000. Source: UN, *World Population Prospects: The 2002 Revision*.

Expectation of Life (WHO estimates, years at birth): 49.6 (males 48.6; females 50.7) in 2002. Source: WHO, *World Health Report*.

Economically Active Population (estimates, '000 persons, 1991): Agriculture, etc. 212; Industries 31; Services 39; *Total* 282 (males 167, females 115). Source: UN Economic Commission for Africa, *African Statistical Yearbook*. Mid-2003 ('000 persons, estimates): Agriculture, etc. 270; Total labour force 349. Source: FAO.

HEALTH AND WELFARE

Key Indicators

Total Fertility Rate (children per woman, 2002): 5.7.

Under-5 Mortality Rate (per 1,000 live births, 2003): 138.

HIV/AIDS (% of persons aged 15–49, 2003): 2.90.

Physicians (per 1,000 head, 2004): 0.13.

Hospital Beds (per 1,000 head, 1990): 2.54.

Health Expenditure (2001): US $ per head (PPP): 90.

Health Expenditure (2001): % of GDP: 7.0.

Health Expenditure (2001): public (% of total): 58.8.

Access to Water (% of persons, 2002): 80.

Access to Sanitation (% of persons, 2002): 50.

Human Development Index (2002): ranking: 154.

Human Development Index (2002): index: 0.454.
For sources and definitions, see explanatory note on p. vi.

AGRICULTURE, ETC.

Principal Crops (FAO estimates, '000 metric tons, 2003): Tomatoes 1.1; Other vegetables 23.4 (incl. melons); Lemons and limes 1.8; Other fruit 0.7. Source: FAO.

Livestock (FAO estimates, '000 head, 2003): Cattle 297; Sheep 466; Goats 512; Asses 9; Camels 69. Source: FAO.

Livestock Products (FAO estimates, '000 metric tons, 2003): Beef and veal 6.1; Mutton and lamb 2.2; Goat meat 2.4; Camel meat 0.7; Cows' milk 8.1; Camels' milk 5.9; Cattle hides 1.1; Sheepskins 0.4; Goatskins 0.5. Source: FAO.

Fishing (FAO estimates, metric tons, live weight, 2002): Groupers 100; Snappers and jobfishes 80; Porgies and seabreams 40; Barracudas 20; Carangids 20; Seerfishes 60; Other tuna-like fishes 15; Total catch (incl. others) 350. Source: FAO.

INDUSTRY

Electric Energy (million kWh): 235.3 in 2001; 246.8 in 2002; 263.6 in 2003.

FINANCE

Currency and Exchange Rates: 100 centimes = 1 Djibouti franc. *Sterling, Dollar and Euro Equivalents* (31 December 2004): £1 sterling = 343.25 Djibouti francs; US $1 = 177.72 Djibouti francs; €1 = 242.07 Djibouti francs; 1,000 Djibouti francs = £2.91 = $5.63= € 4.13. *Exchange Rate:* Fixed at US $1 = 177.721 Djibouti francs since February 1973.

Budget (million Djibouti francs, 2003): *Revenue:* Tax revenue 25,222 (Direct taxes 10,281; Indirect taxes 11,627; Registration fees, etc. 3,314); Other revenue (incl. property sales) 5,998; Total 31,220, excl. official grants (6,742). *Expenditure:* Current expenditure 34,061; Capital expenditure 6,429 (Foreign-financed 5,212); Total 40,490. Source: Banque Centrale de Djibouti, *Rapport Annuel 2003*.

International Reserves (US $ million at 31 December 2003): IMF special drawing rights 0.14; Reserve position in IMF 1.63; Foreign exchange 98.36; Total 100.13. Source: IMF, *International Financial Statistics*.

Money Supply (million Djibouti francs at 31 December 2003): Currency outside banks 11,113; Demand deposits at commercial banks 31,737; Total money 42,850. Source: IMF, *International Financial Statistics*.

Cost of Living (Consumer Price Index for expatriates; base: 1989 = 100): All items 137.2 in 1995; 142.9 in 1996; 145.8 (estimate) in 1997. Source: IMF, *Djibouti: Statistical Annex* (August 1998).

Expenditure on the Gross Domestic Product (provisional, million Djibouti francs at current purchasers' values, 2002): Government final consumption expenditure 26,420; Private final consumption expenditure 83,814; Gross capital formation 10,710; _Total domestic expenditure_ 120,944; Exports of goods and services 48,260; _Less_ Imports of goods and services 63,994; _GDP in purchasers' values_ 105,210. Source: IMF, _Djibouti: Statistical Appendix_ (March 2004).

Gross Domestic Product by Economic Activity (million Djibouti francs at current factor cost, 2003): Agriculture, hunting, forestry and fishing 3,445; Manufacturing (incl. mining) 3,334; Electricity and water 5,556; Construction and public works 6,778; Trade and hotels 15,557; Transport and communications 26,779; Finance and insurance 13,223; Public administration 20,890; Other services 1,889; _GDP at factor cost_ 97,451; Indirect taxes, _less_ subsidies 13,679; Statistical discrepancy –60; _GDP in purchasers' values_ 111,070. Source: Banque Centrale de Djibouti, _Rapport Annuel 2003_.

Balance of Payments (US $ million, 2002): Exports of goods f.o.b. 83.2; Imports of goods f.o.b. –283.7; _Trade balance_ –200.5; Exports of services and other income 189.9; Imports of services and other income –76.9; Statistical discrepancy 10.4; _Balance on goods, services and income_ –77.1; Official transfers (net) 44.4; Private transfers (net) –3.7; _Current balance_ –36.5; Foreign direct investment 5.0; Public sector (net) 29.9; Private capital (net) and net errors and omissions 54.7; _Overall balance_ 53.0. Source: IMF, _Djibouti: Statistical Appendix_ (March 2004).

EXTERNAL TRADE

Principal Commodities: _Imports c.i.f._ (million Djibouti francs, 1999): Food and beverages 6,796; Qat 3,300; Petroleum products 2,944; Chemical products 1,620; Clothing and footwear 1,251; Metals and metal products 1,355; Machinery and electrical appliances 3,399; Vehicles and transport equipment 2,781; Total (incl. others) 27,131. _Exports f.o.b._ (distribution by SITC, US $ '000, 1992): Food and live animals 3,292 (Rice 726, Coffee and coffee substitutes 1,773); Crude materials (inedible) except fuels 867; Basic manufactures 771; Machinery and transport equipment 1,260 (Road vehicles and parts 585, Other transport equipment 501); Commodities not classified according to kind 9,481; Total (incl. others) 15,919. Source: UN, _International Trade Statistics Yearbook_.

Principal Trading Partners: _Imports c.i.f._ (percentage of total trade, 2002): Ethiopia 11.1; France 7.6; Italy 3.1; Japan 2.5; Netherlands 4.4; Saudi Arabia 15.8; Singapore 2.2; United Kingdom 3.3; Yemen 1.3. _Exports f.o.b._ (percentage of total trade, 2002): Ethiopia 4.4; Somalia 57.2; Yemen 24.5. Source: IMF, _Djibouti: Statistical Appendix_ (March 2004).

TRANSPORT

Railways (traffic, 2002): Passengers ('000) 570; Freight ton-km (million) 201. Source: IMF, _Djibouti: Statistical Appendix_ (March 2004).

Road Traffic (estimates, motor vehicles in use, 1996): Passenger cars 9,200; Lorries and vans 2,040. Source: International Road Federation, _World Road Statistics_.

Shipping: _Merchant Fleet_ (registered at 31 December 2003): 12 vessels (displacement 4,060 grt) (Source: Lloyd's Register-Fairplay, _World Fleet Statistics_). _Freight Traffic_ ('000 metric tons, 2003): Goods loaded 1,067.2; Goods unloaded 4,900.3 (Source: Banque Centrale de Djibouti, _Rapport Annuel 2003_).

Civil Aviation: _Passengers Carried_ (2003) 180,452; _Freight Loaded and Unloaded_ (2003) 17,020 metric tons. Source: Banque Centrale de Djibouti, _Rapport Annuel 2003_.

TOURISM

Tourist Arrivals ('000): 20 in 1996; 20 in 1997; 20 in 1998.

Receipts from Tourism (US $ million): 4 in 1996; 4 in 1997; 4 in 1998 (Source: World Tourism Organization).

COMMUNICATIONS MEDIA

Newspapers (1995): 1 non-daily (estimated circulation 1,000).

Periodicals (1989): 7 (estimated combined circulation 6,000).

Radio Receivers (1997): 52,000 in use.

Television Receivers (2000): 45,000 in use.

Telephones (2003): 9,500 main lines in use.

Facsimile Machines (1999): 69 in use.

Mobile Cellular Telephones (2003): 23,000 subscribers.

Personal Computers (2003): 15,000 in use.

Internet Users (2003): 6,500.
Sources: mainly UNESCO, _Statistical Yearbook;_ UN, _Statistical Yearbook;_ International Telecommunication Union.

EDUCATION

Pre-primary (1996/97): 2 schools; 247 pupils.

Primary (2003/04): 82 schools; 42,156 pupils.

Secondary (2003/04): First cycle 15,119 pupils; Second cycle 5,992 pupils.

Higher (2003/04): 1,181 students; 94 teaching staff.
Sources: UNESCO, _Statistical Yearbook_; Ministère de l'éducation nationale et de l'enseignement supérieur; Pôle Universitaire de Djibouti.

Adult Literacy Rate (UNESCO estimates): 65.5% (males 76.1%; females 55.5%) in 2002. Source: UN Development Programme, _Human Development Report_.

Directory

The Constitution

A new Constitution was approved by national referendum on 4 September 1992 and entered into force on 15 September.

The Constitution of Djibouti guarantees the basic rights and freedoms of citizens; the functions of the principal organs of state are delineated therein.

The President of the Republic, who is Head of State and Head of Government, is directly elected, by universal adult suffrage, for a period of six years, renewable only once. The President nominates the Prime Minister and, following consultation with the latter, appoints the Council of Ministers. The legislature is the 65-member Assemblée nationale, which is elected, also by direct universal suffrage, for a period of five years.

The 1992 Constitution provided for the establishment of a maximum of four political parties. On 4 September 2002, however, this limit on the number of political parties was revoked.

The Government

HEAD OF STATE

President and Commander-in-Chief of the Armed Forces: ISMAEL OMAR GELLEH (inaugurated 7 May 1999, re-elected 8 April 2005).

COUNCIL OF MINISTERS
(April 2005)

Prime Minister: DILEITA MOHAMED DILEITA.

Minister of Justice, Muslim and Penal Affairs, and Human Rights: ISMAEL IBRAHIM HOUMED.

Minister of the Interior and Decentralization: ABOULKADER DOUALEH WAIS.

Minister of Defence: OUGOUREH KIFLEH AHMED.

Minister of Foreign Affairs, International Co-operation and Parliamentary Relations: ALI ABDI FARAH.

Minister of Economy, Finance and Planning, in charge of Privatization: YACIN ELMI BOUH.

Minister of Trade and Industry: SALEBAN OMAR OUDIN.

Minister of Agriculture, Livestock and Fishing: DINI ABDALLAH BILILIS.

Minister of Communication and Culture, in charge of Post and Telecommunications, and Government Spokesman: RIFKI ABDULKADER BAMAKHRAMA.

Minister of National and Higher Education: ABDI IBRAHIM ABSIEH.

Minister of Employment and National Solidarity: MOHAMED BARKAT ABDILLAHI.

Minister of Energy and Natural Resources: MOHAMED ALI MOHAMED.

Minister of Equipment and Transport: ELMI OBSIEH WAIS.

Minister of Health: Dr MOHAMED ALI KAMIL.

Minister of Presidential Affairs, in charge of Investment Promotion: OSMAN AHMED MOUSSA.

Minister of Urban Planning, Housing, the Environment, and National and Regional Development: ABDALLAH ABDILLAHI MIGUIL.

Minister of Youth, Sports, Leisure and Tourism: OTBAN GOITA MOUSSA.

Minister-delegate to the Prime Minister, in charge of the Promotion of Women's, Family and Social Affairs: HAWA AHMED YOUSSOUF.

Minister-delegate to the Minister of Foreign Affairs, International Co-operation and Parliamentary Relations, in charge of International Co-operation: MAHAMOUD ALI YOUSSOUF.

Minister-delegate to the Minister of Justice, Muslim and Penal Affairs, and Human Rights, in charge of Mosque Properties and Muslim Affairs: CHEIK MOGUEH DIRIR SAMATAR.

MINISTRIES

Office of the Prime Minister: BP 2086, Djibouti; tel. 351494; fax 355049.

Ministry of Agriculture, Livestock and Fishing: BP 453, Djibouti; tel. 351297.

Ministry of the Civil Service and Administrative Reform: BP 155, Djibouti; tel. 351464.

Ministry of Communication and Culture: 1 Rue de Moscou, BP 32, Djibouti; tel. 355672; fax 353957; internet www.mccpt.dj; e-mail mccpt@intnet.dj.

Ministry of Defence: BP 42, Djibouti; tel. 352034.

Ministry of the Economy, Finance and Planning: BP 13, Djibouti; tel. 353331; fax 356501; internet www.ministere-finances.dj; e-mail cabmefpp@intnet.dj.

Ministry of Employment and National Solidarity: Djibouti; tel. 351838; fax 357268; e-mail adetip@intnet.dj.

Ministry of Energy and Natural Resources: BP 175, Djibouti; tel. 350340.

Ministry of Equipment and Transport: Palais du Peuple, BP 2501, Djibouti; tel. 350990; fax 355975.

Ministry of Foreign Affairs, International Co-operation and Parliamentary Relations: Bd Cheick Osman, BP 1863, Djibouti; tel. 352471; fax 353049.

Ministry of Housing, Urbanization, Environment and National and Regional Development: BP 11, Djibouti; tel. 350006; fax 351618.

Ministry of Health: BP 296, Djibouti; tel. 353331; fax 356300.

Ministry of the Interior and Decentralization: BP 33, Djibouti; tel. 350791.

Ministry of Justice, Muslim and Penal Affairs, and Human Rights: BP 12, Djibouti; tel. 351506; fax 354012.

Ministry of Labour and Vocational Training: BP 170, Djibouti; tel. 350497.

Ministry of National and Higher Education: Cité Ministérielle, BP 16, Djibouti; tel. 350997; fax 354234; e-mail education.gov@intent.dj; internet www.education.gov.dj.

Ministry of Presidential Affairs: Djibouti.

Ministry of Trade and Industry: BP 1846, Djibouti; tel. 351682.

Ministry of Youth, Sports, Leisure and Tourism: BP 2506, Djibouti; tel. 355886; fax 356830.

President and Legislature

PRESIDENT

At the presidential election held on 8 April 2005 the incumbent Ismael Omar Gelleh of the Rassemblement populaire pour le progrès secured 100% of the valid votes cast. Gelleh was the sole candidate at the election following the withdrawal, in March, from the contest of Mohamed Daoud Chehem, the representative of the Parti djiboutien pour la démocratie.

ASSEMBLÉE NATIONALE

General Election, 10 January 2003

Party	Valid votes	% of votes	Seats
Union pour la majorité présidentielle* . . .	53,293	62.73	65
Union pour l'alternance démocratique† . . .	31,660	37.27	—
Total	84,953	100.00	65

* A coalition comprising the FRUD, the PND, the PPSD and the RPP.
† A coalition comprising the ARD, the MRD, the PDD, the PRD and the UDDJ.

Political Organizations

On 4 September 2002, to coincide with the 10th anniversary of the approval of the Constitution, restrictions on the number of legally permitted political parties (hitherto four) were formally removed. The following organizations contested the legislative elections of January 2003:

Alliance républicaine pour la démocratie (ARD): BP 1488 Marabout, Djibouti; tel. 250919; f. 2002; Leader AHMAD YOUSSOUF HOUMED; Sec.-Gen. ADAN MOHAMED ABDOU.

Front pour la restauration de l'unité et de la démocratie (FRUD): Djibouti; tel. 250279; f. 1991 by merger of three militant Afar groups; advocates fair representation in govt for all ethnic groups; commenced armed insurgency in Nov. 1991; split into two factions in March 1994; the dissident group, which negotiated a settlement with the Govt, obtained legal recognition in March 1996 and recognizes the following leaders; Pres. ALI MOHAMED DAOUD; Sec.-Gen. OUGOUREH KIFLEH AHMED; a dissident group, FRUD-Renaissance (led by IBRAHIM CHEHEM DAOUD), was formed in 1996.

Mouvement pour le renouveau démocratique et le développement (MRD): BP 3570, Avenue Nasser, Djibouti; internet www.mrd-djibouti.org; f. 2002; Pres. DAHER AHMED FARAH; Sec.-Gen. SOULEIMAN HASSAN FAIDAL.

Parti djiboutien pour la démocratie (PDD): Cité Einguela, Maison 22103, Djibouti; f. 2002; Pres. MOHAMED DAOUD CHEHEM; Sec.-Gen. ABDILLAHI MOHAMED SALAH.

Parti national démocratique (PND): BP 10204, Djibouti; tel. 342194; internet www.pnd-djibouti.org; f. 1992; seeks formation of a 'govt of national unity' to supervise implementation of democratic reforms; Pres. ADEN ROBLEH AWALLEH.

Parti populaire social democrate (PPSD): BP 434, Route Nelson Mandela; f. 2002; Pres. MOUMIN BAHDON FARAH; Sec.-Gen. HASSAN IDRISS AHMED.

Parti du renouveau démocratique (PRD): BP 2198, Djibouti; tel. 356235; fax 351474; f. 1992; seeks to establish democratic parliamentary govt; Pres. ABDILLAHI HAMAREITEH; Sec.-Gen. MAKI HOUMED GABA.

Rassemblement populaire pour le progrès (RPP): Djibouti; internet www.rpp.dj; f. 1979; sole legal party 1981–92; Pres. ISMAEL OMAR GELLEH; Sec.-Gen. IDRISS ARNAOUD ALI.

Union djiboutienne pour la démocratie et la justice (UDDJ): Djibouti.

The following organizations are banned:

Coordination de l'opposition djiboutienne: f. 1996; alliance of the PND, the FUOD and the RPP—GDR; Leader ISMAEL GEDI HARED.

Front des forces démocratiques (FFD): Leader OMAR ELMI KHAIREH.

Front de libération de la côte des Somalis (FLCS): f. 1963; Issas-supported; has operated from Somalia; Chair. ABDALLAH WABERI KHALIF; Vice-Chair. OMAR OSMAN RABEH.

Front uni de l'opposition djiboutienne (FUOD): f. 1992; based in Ethiopia; united front of internal opposition groups, incl. some fmr mems of the RPP; Leader MAHDI IBRAHIM A. GOD.

Groupe pour la démocratie de la république (RPP—GDR): f. 1996 by a dissident faction of the RPP; Leader MOUMIN BAHDON FARAH.

Mouvement de la jeunesse djiboutienne (MJD): Leader ABDOUL-KARIM ALI AMARKAK.

Mouvement pour l'unité et la démocratie (MUD): advocates political pluralism; Leader MOHAMED MOUSSA ALI 'TOURTOUR'.

Organisation des masses Afar (OMA): f. 1993 by mems of the fmr Mouvement populaire de libération; Chair. AHMED MALCO.

Parti centriste et des reformes démocratiques (PCRD): f. 1993 in Addis Ababa, Ethiopia, by a breakaway faction of the FRUD; seeks official registration as an opposition party; Chair. HASSAN ABDALLAH WATTA.

Parti populaire djiboutien (PPD): f. 1981; mainly Afar-supported; Leader MOUSSA AHMED IDRIS.

Union des démocrates djiboutiens (UDD): affiliated to the FUOD; Chair. MAHDI IBRAHIM AHMED.

Union démocratique pour le progrès (UDP): f. 1992; advocates democratic reforms; Leader FARAH WABERI.

Union des mouvements démocratiques (UMD): f. 1990 by merger of two militant external opposition groups; Pres. MOHAMED ADOYTA.

Diplomatic Representation

EMBASSIES IN DJIBOUTI

China, People's Republic: Djibouti; tel. 352246; Ambassador SHEN JIANG KUAN.

Egypt: BP 1989, Djibouti; tel. 351231; Ambassador IBRAHIM EL-CHOUMI.

Eritrea: BP 1944, Djibouti; tel. 354961; fax 351831; Ambassador MOHAMED ALI JABRA.

Ethiopia: ave Maréchal Joffre Foch, BP 230, Djibouti; tel. 350718; fax 354803; Ambassador SHEMSEDIN WORK ZEWDIE.

France: 45 blvd du Maréchal Foch, BP 2039, Djibouti; tel. 350963; fax 350272; e-mail ambfrdj@intnet.dj; Ambassador PHILIPPE SELZ.

Libya: BP 2073, Djibouti; tel. 350202; Ambassador KAMEL AL-HADI ALMARASH.

Oman: Djibouti; tel. 350852; Ambassador SAOUD SALEM HASSAN AL-ANSI.

Russia: BP 1913, Djibouti; tel. 350740; fax 355990; Ambassador MIKHAIL TSVIGOUN.

Saudi Arabia: BP 1921, Djibouti; tel. 351645; fax 352284; Ambassador ABDOULAZIZ MOHAMED AL-EIFAN.

Somalia: BP 549, Djibouti; tel. 353521; Ambassador ISE ALI AHMED.

Sudan: BP 4259, Djibouti; tel. 356404; fax 356662; Ambassador ISMAIL MOHAMED ABDELDAFI.

USA: Villa Plateau du Serpent, blvd du Maréchal Joffre, BP 185, Djibouti; tel. 353995; fax 353940; e-mail amembadm@bow.intnet.dj; Ambassador MARGUERITA DIANNE RAGSDALE.

Yemen: BP 194, Djibouti; tel. 352975; Ambassador ABDIL-RAB ALI AS-SLAH.

Judicial System

The Supreme Court was established in 1979. There is a high court of appeal and a court of first instance in Djibouti; each of the five administrative districts has a 'tribunal coutumier'.

President of the Court of Appeal: KADIDJA ABEBA.

Religion

ISLAM

Almost the entire population are Muslims.

Qadi of Djibouti: MOGUE HASSAN DIRIR, BP 168, Djibouti; tel. 352669.

CHRISTIANITY

The Roman Catholic Church

Djibouti comprises a single diocese, directly responsible to the Holy See. There were an estimated 7,000 adherents in the country at 31 December 2002.

Bishop of Djibouti: GIORGIO BERTIN, Evêché, blvd de la République, BP 94, Djibouti; tel. 350140; fax 354831; e-mail evechcat@intnet.dj.

The Anglican Communion

Within the Episcopal Church in Jerusalem and the Middle East, Djibouti lies within the jurisdiction of the Bishop in Egypt.

Other Christian Churches

Eglise Protestante: blvd de la République, BP 416, Djibouti; tel. 351820; fax 350706; e-mail eped@intnet.dj; f. 1957; Pastor JEAN-CLAUDE LEVEILLÉ.

Greek Orthodox Church: blvd de la République, Djibouti; tel. 351325; c. 350 adherents; Archimandrite STAVROS GEORGANAS.

The Ethiopian Orthodox Church is also active in Djibouti.

The Press

L'Atout: Palais du peuple, Djibouti; twice a year; publ. by the Centre National de la Promotion Culturelle et Artistique.

Carrefour Africain: BP 393, Djibouti; fax 354916; fortnightly; publ. by the Roman Catholic mission; circ. 500.

La Nation de Djibouti: place du 27 juin, BP 32, Djibouti; tel. 352201; fax 353937; internet www.lanation.dj; weekly; Dir ABDOUL-RASHID IDRISS; circ. 4,300.

Le Progrès: Djibouti; weekly; publ. by the RPP; Publr ALI MOHAMED HUMAD.

Le Renouveau: Djibouti; weekly; independent; Editor-in-Chief DAHER AHMED FARAH.

La République: Djibouti; weekly; independent; Editor-in-Chief AMIR ADAWEH.

Revue de l'ISERT: BP 486, Djibouti; tel. 352795; twice a year; publ. by the Institut Supérieur d'Etudes et de Recherches Scientifiques et Techniques (ISERT).

Le Temps: Djibouti; opposition newspaper; Owners MOUSSA AHMED IDRIS, ALI MEIDAL WAIS.

NEWS AGENCIES

Agence Djiboutienne d'Information (ADJI): 1 rue de Moscou, BP 32, Djibouti; tel. 354013; fax 354037; e-mail adi@intent.dj; internet www.adi.dj; f. 1978.

Foreign Bureau

Agence France-Presse (AFP): BP 97, Djibouti; tel. 352294; Correspondent KHALID HAIDAR ABDALLAH.

Broadcasting and Communications

TELECOMMUNICATIONS

Djibouti Telecom: 3 blvd G. Pompidou, BP 2105, Djibouti; tel. 351110; fax 355757; e-mail Djibouti_telecom@intent.dj; internet www.intent.dj; f. 1999 to replace Société des Télécommunications Internationales; 100% state-owned; Dir-Gen. MOHAMED KAMIL ALI.

BROADCASTING

Radio and Television

Djibnet: BP 1409, Djibouti; tel. 354288; e-mail webmaster@djibnet.com; internet www.djibnet.com.

Radiodiffusion-Télévision de Djibouti (RTD): BP 97, Djibouti; tel. and fax 352294; e-mail mo_hoche@hotmail.com; internet www.rtd.dj; f. 1957; state-controlled; programmes in French, Afar, Somali and Arabic; 17 hours radio and 5 hours television daily; Dir-Gen. (Radio) ABDI ATTEYEH ABDI; Dir-Gen. (Television) MOHAMED DJAMA ADEN.

Finance

(cap. = capital; res = reserves; dep. = deposits; m. = million; brs = branches; amounts in Djibouti francs)

BANKING

Central Bank

Banque Centrale de Djibouti: BP 2118, ave St Laurent du Var, Djibouti; tel. 352751; fax 356288; e-mail bndj@intnet.dj; internet www.banque-centrale.dj; f. 1977 as Banque Nationale de Djibouti; present name adopted 2002; bank of issue; cap. 805m., res 10,982m., dep. 2,698m. (Dec. 2002); Gov. DJAMA MAHAMOUD HAID; Gen.-Man. AHMED OSMAN.

Commercial Banks

Banque Indosuez—Mer Rouge (BIS—MR): 10 place Lagarde, BP 88, Djibouti; tel. 353016; fax 351638; e-mail indomr@intnet.dj; f. 1908 as Banque de l'Indochine; present name adopted 1977; owned by Calyon, Paris La Défense; cap. 1,500m., res 526.4m., dep. 28,668.8m. (Dec. 2003); Chair. and CEO JEAN-BERNARD ANGLADA.

Banque pour le Commerce et l'Industrie—Mer Rouge (BCI—MR): place Lagarde, BP 2122, Djibouti; tel. 350857; fax 354260; e-mail bcimr@intnet.dj; f. 1977; 51% owned by Banque Nationale de Paris Intercontinentale; cap. 3,000m. (Dec. 2001); Pres. JEAN-JACQUES SANTINI; Gen. Man. GUY CAZENAVE; 6 brs.

Investment Bank of Africa: Djibouti; f. 2000; subsidiary of AFH Holding (Luxembourg); cap. 300m.; CEO ILIA KARAS.

Development Bank

Banque de Développement de Djibouti: angle ave Georges Clemenceau et rue Pierre Curie, BP 520, Djibouti; tel. 353391; fax 355022; f. 1983; 39.2% govt-owned; cap. and res 1,233m., total assets 3,081m. (Dec. 1997); Dir-Gen. ABDOURAHMAN ISMAEL GELLEH.

Banking Association

Association Professionnelle des Banques: c/o Banque pour le Commerce et l'Industrie—Mer Rouge, place Lagarde, BP 2122, Djibouti; tel. 350857; fax 354260; Pres. MOHAMED ADEN.

INSURANCE

Les Assureurs de la Mer Rouge et du Golfe Arabe (AMERGA): Djibouti; f. 2000; Dirs THIERRY MARILL, LUC MARILL, ABDURAHMAN BARKAT ABDILLAHI, MOHAMED ADEN ABUBAKER.

Boucher Assurances: AGF—Assurances Générales de France, rue Marchand, BP 200, Djibouti; tel. 353636; fax 353056; Country Man. CHRISTIAN BOUCHER.

Ethiopian Insurance Corpn: rue de Marseille, BP 2047, Djibouti; tel. 352306.

Trade and Industry

CHAMBER OF COMMERCE

Chambre Internationale de Commerce et d'Industrie: BP 84, Place de Lagarde, Djibouti; tel. 351070; fax 350096; e-mail cicid@intent.dj; internet www.intnet.dj/public/cicid/index.html; f. 1906; 24 mems, 12 assoc. mems; Pres. SAID OMAR MOUSSA; First Vice-Pres. ABDOURAHMAN MAHAMOUD BOREH.

TRADE ASSOCIATION

Office National d'Approvisionnement et de Commercialisation (ONAC): BP 119, Djibouti; tel. 350327; Chair. MOHAMED ABDULKADER.

UTILITIES

Electricity

Electricité de Djibouti (EdD): c/o Ministry of Trade and Industry, BP 1846, Djibouti; tel. 351682; Dir-Gen. DJAMA ALI GELLEH.

Water

Office National des Eaux de Djibouti (ONED): c/o Ministry of Trade and Industry, BP 1846, Djibouti; tel. 351682.

Société des Eaux de Tadjourah: c/o Ministry of Trade and Industry, BP 1846, Djibouti; tel. 351682.

TRADE UNION

Union Djiboutienne du Travail: rue Pierre Pascal, BP 2767, Djibouti; tel. 823979; fax 355084; e-mail udt_djibouti@yahoo.fr; f. 1992 to succeed Union Générale des Travailleurs de Djibouti; confed. of 22 trade unions; Chair. HASSAN CHER HARED; Sec.-Gen. ADEN MOHAMED ABDOU.

Transport

RAILWAYS

Chemin de Fer Djibouti–Ethiopien (CDE): BP 2116, Djibouti; POB 1051, Addis Ababa; tel. 350280; fax 351256; tel. 517250; fax 513533; f. 1909; adopted present name in 1981; jtly-owned by Govts of Djibouti and Ethiopia; 781 km of track (121 km in Djibouti) linking Djibouti with Addis Ababa; Pres. SALEH OMAR HILDID; Dir-Gen. ALI ABDALLAH GADID.

ROADS

In 1996 there were an estimated 2,890 km of roads, comprising 1,090 km of main roads and 1,800 km of regional roads; some 12.6% of the roads were paved. Of the remainder, 1,000 km are serviceable throughout the year, the rest only during the dry season. About one-half of the roads are usable only by heavy vehicles. In 1981 the 40-km Grand Bara road was opened, linking the capital with the south. In 1986 the Djibouti–Tadjourah road, the construction of which was financed by Saudi Arabia, was opened, linking the capital with the north. In 1996 the Islamic Development Bank granted Djibouti a loan of US $3.6m. to finance road construction projects.

SHIPPING

Djibouti, which was established as a free port in 1981, handled 5,967,500 metric tons of freight in 2003.

Port Autonome International de Djibouti: BP 2107, Djibouti; tel. 352331; fax 356187; e-mail luc.deruyver@port.dj; internet www.port.dj; Man. Dir LUC DERUYVER.

Maritime and Transit Service: rue de Marseille, BP 680, Djibouti; tel. 353204; fax 354149.

Principal Shipping Agents

Almis Shipping Line & Transport Co: BP 85, Djibouti; tel. 356996; fax 356998; Man. Dir MOHAMED NOOR.

Cie Générale Maritime: 3 rue Marchand, BP 182, Djibouti; tel. 353825; fax 354778; Gen. Man. HENRI FERRAND.

Cie Maritime et de Manutention de Djibouti (COMAD): ave des Messageries Maritimes, BP 89, Djibouti; tel. 351028; fax 350466; e-mail comad@intnet.dj; internet www.intnet.dj/comad/index.htm; stevedoring; Man. Dir ALI A. HETTAM.

Global Shipping Services (GSS): POB 89, Djibouti; tel. 351028; fax 357091; e-mail gss@intnet.dj; shipping agents; Man. Dir ALI A. HETTAM.

Inchcape Shipping Services & Co (Djibouti) SA: 9–11 rue de Genève, BP 81, Djibouti; tel. 353844; fax 353294; e-mail iss@intnet.dj; f. 1942; Dir-Gen. AHMED OSMAN GELLEH.

International Transit Services: POB 1177; tel. 251155; fax 353258; e-mail its02@intnet.dj; Man. Dir ROBLEH MUHAMMAD.

J. J. Kothari & Co Ltd: rue d'Athens, BP 171, Djibouti; tel. 350219; fax 351778; e-mail kothari@intnet.dj; shipping agents; also ship managers, stevedores, freight forwarders; Dirs S. J. KOTHARI, NALIN KOTHARI.

Mitchell Cotts Djibouti SARL: blvd de la République, BP 85, Djibouti; tel. 351204; fax 355851; Dir FAHMY SAID CASSIM.

Société Maritime L. Savon et Ries: blvd Cheikh Osman, BP 2125, Djibouti; tel. 352351; fax 351103; Gen. Man. J. P. DELARUE.

CIVIL AVIATION

The international airport is at Ambouli, 6 km from Djibouti. There are six other airports providing domestic services.

Air Djibouti (Red Sea Airlines): BP 499, rue Marchand, Djibouti; tel. 356723; fax 356734; f. 1971; fmrly govt-owned, transferred to private ownership in 1997; internal flights and international services to destinations in Africa, the Middle East and Europe; Chair. SAAD BEN MOUSSA AL-JANAIBI.

Daallo Airlines: BP 2565, Djibouti; tel. 353401; fax 351765; internet www.daallo.com; f. 1992; operates services to Somalia, Saudi Arabia, the United Arab Emirates, France and the Netherlands; Man. Dir MOHAMED IBRAHIM YASSIN.

Djibouti Airlines (Puntavia Airline de Djibouti): BP 2240, place Lagarde, Djibouti; tel. 351006; fax 352429; f. 1996; scheduled and charter regional and domestic flights; Man. Dir M. VABERI.

Tourism

Djibouti offers desert scenery in its interior and watersport facilities on its coast. A casino operates in the capital. There were about 20,000 tourist arrivals in 1998, when receipts from tourism totalled US $4m.

Office National du Tourisme de Djibouti (ONTD): place du 27 juin, BP 1938, Djibouti; tel. 353790; fax 356322; e-mail onta@intnet.dj; internet www.office-tourisme.dj; Dir MOHAMED ABDILLAHI WAIS.

DOMINICA

Introductory Survey

Location, Climate, Language, Religion, Flag, Capital

The Commonwealth of Dominica is situated in the Windward Islands group of the West Indies, lying between Guadeloupe, to the north, and Martinique, to the south. The climate is tropical, though tempered by sea winds which sometimes reach hurricane force, especially from July to September. The average temperature is about 27°C (80°F), with little seasonal variation. Rainfall is heavy, especially in the mountainous areas, where the annual average is 6,350 mm (250 ins), compared with 1,800 mm (70 ins) along the coast. English is the official language, but a local French patois, or Creole, is widely spoken. In parts of the north-east an English dialect, known as Cocoy, is spoken by the descendants of Antiguan settlers. There is a small community of Carib Indians on the east coast. Almost all of the inhabitants profess Christianity, and about 83% are Roman Catholics. The national flag (proportions 1 by 2) has a green field, with equal stripes of yellow, white and black forming an upright cross, on the centre of which is superimposed a red disc containing a parrot surrounded by ten five-pointed green stars (one for each of the island's parishes). The capital is Roseau.

Recent History

Dominica was first settled by Arawaks and then Caribs. Control of the island was fiercely contested by the Caribs, British and French during the 17th and 18th centuries. The British eventually prevailed and Dominica formed part of the Leeward Islands federation until 1939. In 1940 it was transferred to the Windward Islands and remained attached to that group until the federal arrangement was ended in December 1959. Under a new Constitution, effective from January 1960, Dominica (like each other member of the group) achieved a separate status, with its own Administrator and an enlarged Legislative Council.

At the January 1961 elections to the Legislative Council, the ruling Dominica United People's Party was defeated by the Dominica Labour Party (DLP), formed from the People's National Movement and other groups. Edward LeBlanc, leader of the DLP, became Chief Minister. In March 1967 Dominica became one of the West Indies Associated States, gaining full autonomy in internal affairs, with the United Kingdom retaining responsibility for defence and foreign relations. The House of Assembly replaced the Legislative Council, the Administrator became Governor and the Chief Minister was restyled Premier. At elections to the House in October 1970, LeBlanc was returned to power as Premier.

In July 1974 LeBlanc retired, and was replaced as DLP leader and Premier by Patrick John, formerly Deputy Premier and Minister of Finance. At elections to the enlarged House of Assembly in March 1975 the DLP was returned to power. Following a decision in 1975 by the Associated States to seek independence separately, Dominica became an independent republic within the Commonwealth on 3 November 1978. John became Prime Minister, and Frederick Degazon, formerly Speaker of the House of Assembly, was eventually elected President.

In May 1979 two people were killed by the Defence Force at a demonstration against the Government's attempts to introduce legislation that would restrict the freedom of the trade unions and the press. The deaths fuelled increasing popular opposition to the Government, and a pressure group, the Committee for National Salvation (CNS), was formed to campaign for John's resignation. Government opponents organized a general strike which lasted 25 days, with John relinquishing power only after all his cabinet ministers had resigned and President Degazon had gone into hiding abroad (there was a succession of Acting Presidents; Degazon finally resigned in February 1980). Oliver Seraphin, the candidate proposed by the CNS, was elected Prime Minister, and an interim Government was formed to prepare for a general election after six months.

A general election was eventually held in July 1980, when the Dominica Freedom Party (DFP) achieved a convincing victory, winning 17 of the 21 elective seats in the House of Assembly. Eugenia Charles, the party's leader, became the Caribbean's first female Prime Minister. Both John, who contested the election as leader of the DLP, and Seraphin, who stood as leader of the newly-formed Democratic Labour Party (DEMLAB), lost their seats. The DLP and DEMLAB had both suffered from major political scandals prior to the election.

Fears for the island's security dominated 1981. In January the Government disarmed the Defence Force (which was officially disbanded in April), following reports that weapons were being traded for marijuana. Against a background of increasing violence and the declaration of a state of emergency, however, there were two coup attempts involving former Defence Force members. John, the former Prime Minister, was also implicated and imprisoned. In June 1982 John and his fellow prisoners were tried and acquitted, but the Government secured a retrial in October 1985. John and the former Deputy Commander of the Defence Force each received a prison sentence of 12 years (they were released in May 1990). In 1986 the former Commander of the Defence Force was hanged for the murder of a police officer during the second coup attempt. The death sentences on five other soldiers were commuted to life imprisonment.

After his release in June 1982, John attempted to form a new left-wing coalition party. By 1985 the DLP, DEMLAB, the United Dominica Labour Party and the Dominica Liberation Movement had united to form a left-wing grouping, known as the Labour Party of Dominica (LPD). The new leader, however, was Michael Douglas, a former Minister of Finance. At a general election in July 1985 the DFP was returned to power, winning 15 of the 21 elective seats in the House of Assembly. The opposition LPD won five seats, with the remaining seat being won by Roosevelt (Rosie) Douglas, the brother of the LPD leader, whose candidature was not officially endorsed by the LPD. Following the election, the LPD began an 18-month boycott of the House, in protest at the Government's decision to curtail live broadcasts of parliamentary proceedings. By July 1987, the DFP's strength in the House had increased to 17 seats, with four seats still being held by the LPD.

Dissatisfaction at continued government austerity measures was offset by the success of the land reform programme. Since independence, the Government had acquired nearly all the large estates, often in an attempt to forestall violence. In 1986 the first of the estates was divided, and tenure granted to the former workers. Despite the success of this programme, the opposition LPD and the Dominica United Workers' Party (UWP—formed in 1988) bitterly denounced many other government policies and criticized Charles's style of leadership. The two opposition parties failed to agree on the formation of an electoral alliance, however, and the DFP was returned for a third term in government at a general election in May 1990. The DFP won a total of 11 seats, the UWP became the official opposition (with six seats) and the LPD won four seats.

A programme, introduced in 1991, granting Dominican citizenship to foreigners in return for a minimum investment of US $35,000 in the country caused considerable controversy. The UWP expressed opposition to the policy, and in 1992 a pressure group, 'Concerned Citizens', organized protests demanding that the programme be modified. In response to such pressure, the Government announced in July that the minimum investment was to be increased substantially, the number of applications was to be limited to 800 and restrictions were to be placed on the investors' right to vote in Dominica. By early 1995 some 615 people (mainly Taiwanese) had been granted citizenship under the scheme, and about US $7.1m. had been invested in the country.

At a general election in June 1995 the DFP's 15-year tenure was finally ended as the UWP secured a narrow victory. The leader of the UWP, Edison James, was subsequently appointed as Prime Minister, and the LPD and DFP leaders agreed to occupy the position of Leader of the Opposition in alternate years, commencing with Brian Alleyne, Eugenia Charles's successor. In July a legal dispute arose concerning the eligibility to serve in the House of Assembly of one of the DFP's members, Charles Savarin, owing to a potential conflict of interests. As a result of the dispute, the position of Leader of the Opposition was transferred to the LPD leader, Rosie Douglas. In April 1996, however, Savarin was elected leader of the DFP following Alleyne's resignation.

In December 1997 the Government's citizenship programme again provoked controversy. *The Independent Newspaper* reported that, under the scheme, passports were being sold by agents for between US $15,000 and $20,000, and claimed that about 400 people had acquired citizenship in 1997. The opposition LPD accused the Government of undermining the credibility of Dominican citizenship, and in August 1998 Rosie Douglas demanded an inquiry into the programme, following an administrative error which had allowed an Australian, who was sought by investigators in connection with a business collapse, to acquire citizenship. In late 1999 it was announced that the Dominican Government had stopped granting citizenship to Russians, following reports that up to 300 Russians had paid $50,000 each to obtain a Dominican passport. In addition, there were complaints from the US Government that the trade in passports had increased 'suspicions of money-laundering' in Dominica.

In early October 1998 President Crispin Sorhaindo's five-year term in office ended. Following the failure of the Prime Minister and the Leader of the Opposition to agree on a joint nominee, the House of Assembly held a secret ballot to elect the new President. Vernon Shaw, a former cabinet secretary in the previous administration of Eugenia Charles, was duly elected and assumed the presidency on 6 October.

A general election was held on 31 January 2000. The UWP suffered a narrow electoral defeat, while the LPD was returned to power after two decades in opposition, winning 10 of the 21 elective seats in the House of Assembly and receiving 42.9% of total votes cast. The UWP secured nine seats (with 43.4% of the votes), and the DFP (which contested the election in alliance with the LPD) won two. The leader of the LPD, Rosie Douglas, was named as Prime Minister and formed a coalition Government with the DFP (which was allocated two ministerial portfolios).

On taking office, the new Government immediately suspended the controversial citizenship programme. However, following a review, in April 2000 the Government announced that the programme should be resumed, claiming that changes had been made to ensure that passports would not be granted to those with a criminal record. The programme was relaunched in June 2002, with a fee of US $100,000 for individual applicants.

In July 2000 Atherton Martin, the Minister for Agriculture, Planning and the Environment, resigned from his post after the Government voted against the establishment of a South Pacific whaling sanctuary at a meeting of the International Whaling Commission in Australia. The vote was reported to be contrary to a cabinet agreement to abstain. Martin claimed that Japan had threatened to withdraw funding for two fish processing plants in Dominica if the Government abstained, and accused the Japanese Government of 'international extortion'. Lloyd Pascal, hitherto Dominica's whaling commissioner, replaced Martin.

On 1 October 2000 the Prime Minister, Rosie Douglas, died suddenly of a heart attack. Two days later, following a vote in the House of Assembly, Pierre Charles, previously the Minister of Communications and Works, was sworn in as premier.

In December 2000 legislation was passed in the House of Assembly making the crime of money-laundering punishable by up to seven years' imprisonment and a fine of EC $1m. At the same time, the Government introduced stricter regulations governing its 'offshore' banking sector, following Dominica's inclusion on a blacklist published by the Financial Action Task Force (FATF) earlier in the year. Dominica was removed from the blacklist in October 2002, in light of the progress the Government had made in improving its anti-money-laundering measures. Part of these measures was the approval, in December 2001, of the Exchange of Information Bill, designed to give foreign authorities greater access to information about Dominica's 'offshore' banks.

In March 2001 Charles was confirmed as DLP leader at the party's annual conference. In November Charles placed Ambrose George, the Minister of Finance, on two weeks' leave of absence following the arrest on money-laundering charges of a businessman with whom he was travelling in Puerto Rico. Upon his return to government, and in the light of Dominica's place on the FATF blacklist, George was stripped of the finance portfolio, which passed to Charles, and given the post of Minister of Industry, Physical Planning and Enterprise Development.

In July 2002 the Public Service Union (PSU) organized a large-scale demonstration in the capital, Roseau, to protest against controversial tax increases introduced in a budget that was intended to engender economic recovery. In November a DFP deputy, dissatisfied with the Prime Minister's handling of the economic crisis, withdrew his support from the Government, leaving the governing coalition with a majority of one seat. Encouraged by this, the UWP attempted to force a vote of 'no confidence' in the Government; the motion failed, but the coalition's hold on power continued to look precarious. In February 2003 the PSU, objecting to Government proposals to reduce the size of the public-sector work-force and to compel workers to take two days of unpaid leave every month, organized a six-day strike. The strike ended after the Government agreed to review its proposal to reduce the public-sector wage bill. The industrial action further damaged the position of the embattled Government and possibly jeopardized the granting of a structural adjustment loan from the World Bank. In February 2004 new government plans to reduce public-sector salaries were denounced as 'unconstitutional' by — the PSU. However, in November the High Court ruled the IMF-endorsed government plans to be lawful.

On 1 October 2003 Nicholas Liverpool succeeded Vernon Shaw as President.

On 6 January 2004 Charles died from a heart attack at a hospital in Roseau. The LPD nominated Roosevelt Skerrit, hitherto Minister of Education, Youth and Sports, as his replacement. Skerrit was sworn in as Prime Minister on 8 January after his nomination had been endorsed by the coalition's other member, the DFP. On the same day, Skerrit, who added the planning portfolio to his new responsibilities as Prime Minister and Minister of Finance and Carib Affairs, appointed his first Cabinet; notable appointments included the return of Ambrose George (who had left the Cabinet in June 2002) to the Government, as Minister of Agriculture and the Environment. On 29 February Skerrit was elected leader of the LPD; George was appointed deputy leader. In spite of the country's economic difficulties and a stringent austerity programme, in early 2005 the LPD appeared to be well placed for the forthcoming election, which was scheduled for 5 May 2005. The Prime Minister officially launched the LPD's campaign for re-election on 16 January. In the early part of the year, however, the main priority of the Government was to rebuild the country in the wake of the earthquakes and landslides that afflicted Dominica in November 2004 and caused some US $19m.-worth of damage, according to official estimates.

In foreign policy, Dominica has close links with France and the USA. France helped in suppressing the coup attempts against the DFP Government in 1981, and Dominica was the first Commonwealth country to benefit from the French aid agency Fonds d'aide et de la co-opération (Fac). In 2001 Libya granted Dominica, in common with other eastern Caribbean islands, access to a US $2,000m. development fund. It was also reported in September that Libya had agreed to purchase Dominican bananas at high prices and would provide the island with an immediate grant of $4m. In February 2005 the Government announced that Libya was paying for the construction of two schools on the island and for 15 scholarships for Dominican students to attend university courses in Libya. In October 2001 Pierre Charles and the Cuban Minister of Foreign Affairs, Felipe Pérez Roque, signed a bilateral accord on tourism; they also agreed to co-operate further in trade and commerce.

Following a visit to the the Chinese capital, Beijing, Roosevelt Skerrit on 29 March 2004 announced that Dominica would establish diplomatic relations with the People's Republic of China in place of Taiwan. (China agreed to provide an estimated US $111m. in budgetary support, infrastructure grants and education exchanges.) A Chinese embassy was duly opened in Roseau in mid-June. Skerrit was heavily criticized by the opposition over the severing of relations with Taiwan. In January 2005 Skerrit accused the UWP of jeopardizing Dominica's nascent relations with China by accepting campaign funds from Taiwan. In February Edison James announced he was to commence legal action against Skerrit for slander; Skerrit had allegedly accused James of writing to the Chinese embassy requesting that China withdraw its funding for the construction of a new sports stadium before the impending election. Earlier in the year the Chinese embassy in Roseau courted further controversy by condemning the display of Taiwanese flags by UWP supporters and expressed strongly-worded dismay at local opposition to the 'one China principle'. Other recent criticism of

Dominica's perceived attachment to 'chequebook diplomacy' had occurred in December 2004 when Japan funded the construction of a EC $33m. fisheries complex on the island, allegedly in return for Dominica's support for the Japanese Government's pro-whaling stance on international bodies.

Government

Legislative power is vested in the unicameral House of Assembly, comprising 30 members (nine nominated and 21 elected for five years by universal adult suffrage). Executive authority is vested in the President, who is elected by the House, but in most matters the President is guided by the advice of the Cabinet and acts as the constitutional Head of State. He appoints the Prime Minister, who must be able to command a majority in the House, and (on the Prime Minister's recommendation) other ministers. The Cabinet is responsible to the House. The island is divided into 10 administrative divisions, known as parishes, and there is limited local government in Roseau, the capital, and in the Carib Territory.

Defence

The Dominican Defence Force was officially disbanded in 1981. There is a police force of about 300, which includes a coastguard service. The country participates in the US-sponsored Regional Security System.

Economic Affairs

In 2003, according to estimates by the World Bank, Dominica's gross national income (GNI), measured at average 2001–2003 prices, was US $238.1m., equivalent to $3,360 per head (or $5,090 per head on an international purchasing-power parity basis). Between 1990 and 2003 the population decreased by an average annual rate of 0.1%, while gross domestic product (GDP) per head increased, in real terms, by an average of 0.8% per year. Overall GDP increased, in real terms, by an average of 0.6% per year in 1990–2003; GDP decreased by 5.1% in 2002 and by a further 0.4% in 2003.

Agriculture (including forestry and fishing) is the principal economic activity, accounting for an estimated 16.5% of GDP in 2003. In 1997 the sector engaged 23.7% of the employed labour force. The principal cash crop is bananas. The banana industry, which was already experiencing difficulties (owing to a decline in prices), was adversely affected by a September 1997 ruling of the World Trade Organization (WTO, see p. 357) against Dominica's preferential access to the European (particularly the British) market. In 2000 and 2001 banana production increased slightly, to 31,000 metric tons and 33,000 tons, respectively. However, in 2002 banana output was estimated to have decreased to 29,000 tons, remaining at the same level in 2003. In 2002 receipts from banana exports totalled EC $25.7m. (some 22.7% of total domestic exports). Other important crops include coconuts (which provide copra for export as well as edible oil and soap), mangoes, avocados, papayas, ginger, citrus fruits and, mainly for domestic consumption, vegetables. Non-banana crops have grown in significance during recent years, from one-half of total crop production to about two-thirds in 2003. Livestock-rearing and fishing are also practised for local purposes. In December 2004 the construction of a EC $33m., Japanese-funded fisheries complex at Marigot was announced. Numerous other Japanese-funded fisheries projects have been donated to Dominica in recent years. Dominica has extensive timber reserves (more than 40% of the island's total land area is forest and woodland), and international aid agencies are encouraging the development of a balanced timber industry. The GDP of the agricultural sector decreased at an average annual rate of 1.8% in 1990–2003. In real terms, agricultural GDP declined by 0.7% in 2002 and by an estimated 3.7% in 2003.

Industry (comprising mining, manufacturing, construction and utilities) provided 20.8% of GDP in 2003, and employed 18.2% of the employed labour force in 1997. Real industrial GDP increased at an average rate of 1.2% per year during 1990–2003; the sector decreased by 12.2% in 2002 and increased by an estimated 4.6% in 2003. Manufacturing activity is mainly small-scale and dependent upon agriculture. The mining sector contributed only 0.7% of GDP in 2003. There is some quarrying of pumice, and there are extensive reserves of limestone and clay. Pumice is useful to the construction industry, which accounted for 7.3% of GDP in 2003, and employed 8.4% of the employed labour force in 1997. Extensive infrastructure development by the Government has maintained high levels of activity in the construction sector in recent years. The GDP of the construction sector increased at an average annual rate of

0.5%, in real terms, during 1990–2003; the sector's GDP declined by 25.6% in 2002, but increased by an estimated 11.3% in 2003. The Government has also encouraged the manufacturing sector in an attempt to diversify the economy. In 2003 manufacturing contributed 7.2% of GDP and, in 1997, employed 8.8% of the employed work-force. Real manufacturing GDP increased at an average rate of 0.2% per year during 1990–2003; the sector declined in 2001 and 2002 (by 13.6% and 2.3%, respectively), before recovering slightly in 2003, by 0.6%. There is a banana-packaging plant, a brewery and factories for the manufacturing and refining of crude and edible vegetable oils and for the production of soap, canned juices and cigarettes. Furniture, paint, cardboard boxes and candles are also significant manufactures.

In 2000 70% of Dominica's energy requirements were supplied by hydroelectric power. Investment in a hydroelectric development scheme and in the water supply system has been partially financed by the export of water, from Dominica's extensive reserves, to drier Caribbean islands such as Aruba. A hydroelectric power-station, with a generating capacity of 1.24 MW, began operation at Laudat in 1990. In 2002 Dominica's imports of mineral fuels totalled 9.5% of the cost of total imports. In 1998 a geothermal energy project in Soufrière began producing electricity, following investment of EC $25m. from a US company. In December 1996 the state-owned Dominica Electricity Services (Domlec) was privatized, with the British Government's overseas private finance institution, the Commonwealth Development Corporation (CDC), buying 72% of the company (in 2004 this share of the company was sold to the US-based WRB enterprises). Construction of a new 20-MW electric power plant, at an estimated cost of $80m., was completed in 2001.

Services engaged 53.8% of the employed labour force in 1997, and provided 62.7% of GDP in 2003. The combined GDP of the service sectors increased at an average rate of 2.1% per year during 1990–2003; however, in 2002 the sector declined by 2.9% and by an estimated further 1.3% in 2003. The tourist industry is of increasing importance to the economy and exploits Dominica's natural history and scenery. Successive Governments have placed considerable emphasis on the country's potential as an 'eco-tourism' destination, pursuing a development programme funded by the European Union (EU). The majority of tourists are cruise-ship passengers. Arrivals from cruise ships increased dramatically in 1990–2000, from 6,777 in 1990 to 239,544 in 2000. However, this figure decreased in 2001, to an estimated 207,627, and decreased further, to some 136,900, in 2002 when the US Government's 'war on terror' began to have a negative impact upon the region's tourism trade. Cruise-ship passengers began to return to the island in 2003 (when there were a total of 177,000), which helped to increase total tourism receipts by 11.4% (to US $50.9m.). In early 2004 the Government signed a three-year agreement with a cruise-ship operator, which, it was hoped, would increase revenue to the sector. In August 2004 the Government abandoned a long-standing plan to construct a new international airport; the earmarked funding was instead diverted towards the redevelopment of the existing Melville Hall Airport.

In 2002 Dominica recorded a visible trade deficit of US $171.62m. and a deficit of $93.71m. on the current account of the balance of payments. The principal source of imports in 2002 was the USA, which accounted for 36.7% of total imports, followed by Trinidad and Tobago (17.6%) and the United Kingdom (8.6%). The principal market for exports in 2002 was the United Kingdom, with 22.7% of the total, which receives a large proportion of Dominica's banana production. Jamaica was the second largest market; receiving 21.5% of total domestic exports. The principal imports in 2002 were machinery and transport equipment, food and live animals and basic manufactures (such as paper). The principal exports in the same year were fruit and nuts, soap and bananas.

In 2002, according to preliminary Eastern Caribbean Central Bank figures, there was an estimated budget deficit of EC $34m. At the end of 2002 Dominica's total external debt was US $206.7m., of which US $178.3m. was long-term public debt. In the same year the cost of debt-servicing was equivalent to 8.0% of the value of exports of goods and services. The annual rate of inflation averaged 1.1% in 1997–2003; consumer prices increased by an average of 0.3% in 2002 and by 1.5% in 2003. An estimated 23.1% of the labour force were unemployed in 1997.

Dominica is a member of the Organization of American States (see p. 319), the Caribbean Community and Common Market (CARICOM, see p. 172), the Organisation of Eastern Caribbean

States (see p. 384), and is a signatory of the Cotonou Agreement, the successor arrangement to the Lomé Conventions between the African, Caribbean and Pacific (ACP) countries and the European Union (see p. 217). Dominica is also a member of the Eastern Caribbean Securities Exchange (based in Saint Christopher and Nevis). Under the Charles administration, the island received considerable overseas aid.

The Dominican economy is heavily dependent on the production of coconut-based products and bananas, and their export to a limited market, and is thus vulnerable to adverse weather conditions, price fluctuations and economic conditions in its principal markets. The slowdown, and then contraction, in economic growth in 1999–2002 was largely attributable to the weak performance of the major productive sectors. Efforts to expand the country's economic base have been impeded by poor infrastructure and, in terms of tourism (and despite the Governments's success in promoting 'eco-tourism'), a paucity of desirable beaches. There was a decrease in both visitor arrivals and gross visitor expenditure in 2001 and 2002, although the sector recovered slightly in 2003 and, according to preliminary results, continued to improve in 2004. Banana exports decreased from the end of the 1990s, owing to drought, a fall in producer prices and uncertainties caused by the continuing dispute over the EU's banana import regime. The end to the banana trade dispute in April 2001 was expected to have further adverse effects on the sector in the early years of the 21st century (from 2006 the EU's import regime was to be replaced by a universal tariff system). In 2002 the Government announced the proposed privatization of the Banana Marketing Corporation (renamed Dominica Banana Producers Ltd in 2003). The industry was expected to record an increase in export revenue in 2004.

By the early 2000s the island's public finances had weakened considerably, owing to an increase in expenditure caused by a rising wage bill and debt-servicing obligations, as well as to a concurrent decrease in savings and foreign grants. In spite of the introduction in 1998 of value-added tax (VAT), Dominica's tax system remained inefficient, with its narrow base, collection difficulties and substantial exemptions contributing to stagnating revenues. From 2002 Dominica, under pressure from the IMF, introduced structural reforms in the areas of taxation policy and public administration, privatization and agricultural diversification. Austerity measures contained in the 2002/03 and 2003/04 budgets included a reduction in the number of cabinet ministers, increases in fuel, sales and telephone-service taxes, higher fees for passports and postage stamps, and public-sector salary cuts. In addition, in 2002 parliament approved an extra, reportedly temporary, 4% (reduced to 1% in July 2003) income tax, known as the 'Stabilization Levy', to be paid by virtually every earner. The predictably unpopular levy was repealed in the 2004/05 budget. In support of the reforms, significant funds were provided by the IMF, the World Bank, CARICOM and the EU. In February 2004 the Government announced that the public-sector wage bill would be further reduced by 10%. In a reflection of the Government's adherence to the IMF programme, in December 2003 the Government announced the sale of its controlling stake in the National Commercial Bank of Dominica, which henceforth became known as the National Bank of Dominica. Plans were also announced for the consolidation of the country's financial supervisory bodies into a single regulatory authority, the Financial Services Unit. The 2004/05 budget, presented in June 2004, forecast a rare fiscal surplus (although the country's external debt remained large). According to official estimates, 2004 saw a return to growth of around 2%, boosted by an improved performance by the banana and tourism industries. However, other sources predicted that, given the earthquake damage in November, growth for the year would be no more than 1%. Economic growth in 2005 was likely to be of a similar magnitude.

Education

Education is free and is provided by both government and denominational schools. There are also a number of schools for the mentally and physically handicapped. Education is compulsory for 10 years between five and 15 years of age. Primary education begins at the age of five and lasts for seven years. Enrolment of children in the primary age-group was 70.7% in 1992. Secondary education, beginning at 12 years of age, lasts for five years. A teacher-training college and nursing school provide further education, and there is also a branch of the University of the West Indies on the island. In 1997 the Government announced plans to invest EC $17.9m., mainly financed by a World Bank loan, in a Basic Education Reform project. In February 2005 the Government announced that funding provided by Libya would pay for the construction of a primary school in Portsmouth and a high school in Goodwill, near Roseau. Estimated budgetary expenditure on schools was $4.1m. in 2001/02 (equivalent to 1.5% of total expenditure).

Public Holidays

2005: 1 January (New Year's Day), 2 January (Merchants' Holiday), 7–8 February (Masquerade, Carnival), 25 March (Good Friday), 28 March (Easter Monday), 2 May (May or Labour Day), 16 May (Whit Monday), 1 August (Emancipation, August Monday), 3 November (Independence Day), 4 November (Community Service Day), 25–26 December (Christmas).

2006: 1 January (New Year's Day), 2 January (Merchants' Holiday), 27–28 February (Masquerade, Carnival), 14 April (Good Friday), 17 April (Easter Monday), 1 May (May or Labour Day), 5 June (Whit Monday), 7 August (Emancipation, August Monday), 3 November (Independence Day), 4 November (Community Service Day), 25–26 December (Christmas).

Weights and Measures

The metric system is replacing the imperial system of weights and measures.

Statistical Survey

Sources (unless otherwise stated): Eastern Caribbean Central Bank (internet www.eccb-centralbank.org).

AREA AND POPULATION

Area: 751 sq km (290 sq miles).

Population: 71,727 (males 36,434, females 35,293) at census of 12 May 2001. *2003* (mid-year estimate): 71,200 (Source: Caribbean Development Bank, *Social and Economic Indicators*).

Density (2003): 94.8 per sq km.

Population by Ethnic Group (*de jure* population, excl. those resident in institutions, 1981): Negro 67,272; Mixed race 4,433; Amerindian (Carib) 1,111; White 341; Total (incl. others) 73,795 (males 36,754, females 37,041). Source: UN, *Demographic Yearbook*.

Principal Town (population at 1991 census): Roseau (capital) 15,853. *Mid-2003* (UN estimate, incl. suburbs): Roseau 27,401 (Source: UN, *World Urbanization Prospects: The 2003 Revision*).

Births, Marriages and Deaths (registrations, 2002 unless otherwise indicated): Live births 1,081 (birth rate 15.3 per 1,000); Marriages (1998) 336 (marriage rate 4.4 per 1,000); Deaths 510 (death rate 7.3 per 1,000). Source: UN, *Demographic Yearbook*.

Expectation of Life (WHO estimates, years at birth): 73.3 (males 71.0; females 75.8) in 2002. Source: WHO, *World Health Report*.

Economically Active Population (rounded estimates, persons aged 15 years and over, 1997): Agriculture, hunting, forestry and fishing 6,000; Fishing 100; Manufacturing 2,250; Electricity, gas and water supply 280; Construction 2,150; Wholesale and retail trade 4,050; Hotels and restaurants 980; Transport, storage and communications 1,500; Financial intermediation 540; Real estate, renting and business activities 850; Public administration, defence and social security 1,530; Education 1,260; Health and social work 1,110; Other community, social and personal service activities 930; Private households with employed persons 1,080; Not classifiable by economic activity 1,090; *Total employed* 25,690; Unemployed 7,720; *Total labour force* 33,420 (males 18,120, females 15,300) (Source: ILO). *Mid-2003* (estimates): Agriculture, etc. 8,000; Total labour force 36,000 (Source: FAO).

HEALTH AND WELFARE
Key Indicators

Total Fertility Rate (children per woman, 2002): 1.8.

Under-5 Mortality Rate (per 1,000 live births, 2003): 14.

Physicians (per 1,000 head, 1996): 49.3.

Hospital Beds (per 1,000 head, 1996): 2.64.

Health Expenditure (2001): US $ per head (PPP): 312.

Health Expenditure (2001): % of GDP: 6.0.

Health Expenditure (2001): public (% of total): 71.3.

Access to Water (% of persons, 2002): 97.

Access to Sanitation (% of persons, 2002): 83.

Human Development Index (2002): ranking: 95.

Human Development Index (2002): value: 0.743.
For sources and definitions, see explanatory note on p. vi.

AGRICULTURE, ETC.

Principal Crops (FAO estimates, '000 metric tons, 2003): Sweet potatoes 1.9; Cassava 1.0; Yautia (Cocoyam) 4.6; Taro (Dasheen) 11.2; Yams 8.0; Sugar cane 4.4; Coconuts 11.5; Cabbages 0.7; Pumpkins 0.9; Cucumbers 1.7; Carrots 0.5; Other vegetables 2.7; Bananas 29.0; Plantains 5.7; Oranges 7.2; Lemons and limes 1.0; Grapefruit 17.0; Mangoes 1.9; Avocados 0.6; Other fruits 1.2. Source: FAO.

Livestock (FAO estimates, '000 head, year ending September 2003): Cattle 13.4; Pigs 5.0; Sheep 7.6; Goats 9.7; Poultry 190. Source: FAO.

Livestock Products (FAO estimates, '000 metric tons, 2003): Beef and veal 0.5; Pig meat 0.4; Poultry meat 0.3; Cows' milk 6.1; Hen eggs 0.2. Source: FAO.

Fishing (metric tons, live weight, 2002): Capture 1,217 (Skipjack tuna 55; Blackfin tuna 78; Yellowfin tuna 169; Marlins, sailfishes, etc. 72; Common dolphinfish 211); Aquaculture 3; *Total catch* 1,220. Source: FAO.

MINING

Pumice ('000 metric tons, incl. volcanic ash): Estimated production 100 per year in 1988–2000. Source: US Geological Survey.

INDUSTRY

Production (preliminary, 2001, metric tons, unless otherwise indicated): Laundry soap 6,444; Toilet soap 3,749; Dental cream 1,562; Hard surface cleansers 2,987; Crude coconut oil 855; Coconut meal 331; Electricity 77 million kWh (2000). Sources: IMF, *Dominica: Statistical Appendix* (October 2002), and UN, *Industrial Commodity Statistics Yearbook*.

FINANCE

Currency and Exchange Rates: 100 cents = 1 Eastern Caribbean dollar (EC $). *Sterling, US Dollar and Euro Equivalents* (31 December 2004): £1 sterling = EC $5.215; US $1 = EC $2.700; €1 = EC $3.678; EC $100 = £19.18 = US $37.04 = €27.19. *Exchange Rate:* Fixed at US $1 = EC $2.70 since July 1976.

Budget (preliminary, EC $ million, 2002): *Revenue:* Tax revenue 162.0 (Taxes on income and profits 41.6, Taxes on domestic goods and services 32.4, Taxes on international trade and transactions 85.4, Other taxes 2.6); Other current revenue 35.3; Capital revenue 1.8; Total 199.1, excl. grants received (25.6). *Expenditure:* Current expenditure 231.4 (Wages and salaries 123.9, Goods and services 29.9, Interest payments 39.5, Transfers and subsidies 38.0); Capital expenditure and net lending 27.2; Total 258.6.

International Reserves (US $ million at 31 December 2003): Reserve position in IMF 0.01; Foreign exchange 47.72; Total 47.73. Source: IMF, *International Financial Statistics*.

Money Supply (EC $ million at 31 December 2003): Currency outside banks 34.18; Demand deposits at commercial banks 97.23; Total money (incl. others) 131.54. Source: IMF, *International Financial Statistics*.

Cost of Living (Retail Price Index, base: 2000 = 100): All items 101.5 in 2001; 101.8 in 2002; 103.3 in 2003. Source: IMF, *International Financial Statistics*.

National Accounts (EC $ million at current prices): Gross domestic product in purchasers' values 718.6 in 2001; 689.9 in 2002; 707.5 (preliminary) in 2003.

Expenditure on the Gross Domestic Product (preliminary, EC $ million at current prices, 2003): Government final consumption expenditure 135.14; Private final consumption expenditure 480.45; Gross fixed capital formation (incl. increase in stocks) 177.31; *Total domestic expenditure* 792.90; Exports of goods and services 340.34; *Less* Imports of goods and services 425.79; *GDP in purchasers' values* 707.45.

Gross Domestic Product by Economic Activity (preliminary, EC $ million at current prices, 2003): Agriculture, hunting, forestry and fishing 103.85; Mining and quarrying 4.59; Manufacturing 45.50; Electricity and water 34.40; Construction 45.86; Wholesale and retail trade 73.32; Restaurants and hotels 17.01; Transport 47.45; Communications 28.69; Finance and insurance 66.62; Real estate and housing 22.26; Government services 127.57; Other services 10.89; *Sub-total* 628.01; *Less* imputed bank service charge 47.90; *GDP at factor cost* 580.11.

Balance of Payments (preliminary, EC $ million, 2003): Exports of goods f.o.b. 104.73; Imports of goods f.o.b. –276.35; *Trade balance* –171.62; Exports of services 235.61; Imports of services –149.44; *Balance on goods and services* –85.45; Other income received 7.50; Other income paid –62.33; *Balance on goods, services and income* –140.28; Current transfers received 65.34; Current transfers paid –18.77; *Current balance* –93.71; Capital account (net) 52.98; Direct investment from abroad 65.89; Portfolio investment assets –10.53; Portfolio investment liabilities 10.43; Other investment (net) –20.40; Net errors and omissions 2.68; *Overall balance* 7.34.

EXTERNAL TRADE

Principal Commodities (US $ million, 2002): *Imports c.i.f.:* Food products and live animals 21.9 (Meat and meat preparations 4.8; Cereals and cereal preparations 5.0); Beverages and tobacco 3.7; Mineral fuels, lubricants, etc. 11.0 (Refined petroleum products 9.5); Chemicals, etc. 14.2; Basic manufactures 19.6 (Paper products 5.7); Metal manufactures 4.7; Machinery and transport equipment 25.4 (Telecommunications and sound equipment 4.6; Road vehicles 6.8); Miscellaneous manufactured articles 15.1; Total (incl. others) 115.7. *Exports f.o.b.:* Food and live animals 15.9 (Roots and tubers 1.4; Fruit and nuts 12.2; Sauces, condiments and seasonings 1.5); Inedible crude materials 1.5 (Stone, sand and gravel 1.4); Chemicals, etc. 21.5 (Perfumes, cosmetics, toilet products, etc. 5.7; Soap 11.7; Disinfectants 1.6); Machinery and transport equipment 1.9; Total (incl. others) 41.9. Source: UN, *International Trade Statistics Yearbook*.

Principal Trading Partners (US $ million, 2002): *Imports c.i.f.:* Barbados 4.4; Canada 3.1; France 2.5; Guyana 1.4; Jamaica 1.6; Japan 4.7; Netherlands 2.2; Panama 1.3; Saint Lucia 4.1; Saint Vincent and the Grenadines 1.5; Trinidad and Tobago 20.4; United Kingdom 10.0; USA 42.5; Venezuela 1.5; Total (incl. others) 115.7. *Exports f.o.b.:* Antigua and Barbuda 3.5; Barbados 1.8; France 2.8; Grenada 0.6; Guyana 2.9; Jamaica 9.0; Netherlands Antilles 0.7; Saint Christopher and Nevis 1.4; Saint Lucia 1.2; Saint Vincent and the Grenadines 0.6; Trinidad and Tobago 1.9; United Kingdom 9.5; USA 3.9; Total (incl. others) 41.9. Source: UN, *International Trade Statistics Yearbook*.

TRANSPORT

Road Traffic (motor vehicles licensed in 1994): Private cars 6,491; Taxis 90; Buses 559; Motorcycles 94; Trucks 2,266; Jeeps 461; Tractors 24; Total 9,985. *2000* (motor vehicles in use): Passenger cars 8,700; Commercial vehicles 3,400. Source: partly UN, *Statistical Yearbook*.

Shipping: *Merchant Fleet* (registered at 31 December 2003): 29 vessels (total displacement 39,786 grt) (Source: Lloyd's Register-Fairplay, *World Fleet Statistics*); *International Freight Traffic* ('000 metric tons, estimates, 1993): Goods loaded 103.2; Goods unloaded 181.2.

Civil Aviation (1997): Aircraft arrivals and departures 18,672; Freight loaded 363 metric tons; Freight unloaded 575 metric tons.

TOURISM

Tourist Arrivals ('000): *Stop-overs:* 66.4 in 2001; 67.1 in 2002; 72.9 in 2003. *Cruise-ship passengers:* 207.6 in 2001; 136.9 in 2002; 177.0 in 2003.

Tourism Receipts (estimates, US $ million): 46.9 in 2001; 45.7 in 2002; 50.9 in 2003.
Source: Caribbean Development Bank, *Social and Economic Indicators*.

COMMUNICATIONS MEDIA

Radio Receivers (1997): 46,000 in use.

Television Receivers (1999): 17,000 in use.

Telephones (2002): 25,400 main lines in use.

Facsimile Machines (1996): 396 in use.

Mobile Cellular Telephones (2002): 9,400 subscribers.

Personal Computers (2001): 6,000 in use.

Internet Users (2002): 12,500.

Non-daily Newspapers (1996): 1.
Sources: mainly UNESCO, *Statistical Yearbook*, International Telecommunication Union and UN, *Statistical Yearbook*.

EDUCATION

Institutions (1994/95): Pre-primary 72 (1992/93); Primary 64; Secondary 14; Tertiary 2.

Teachers: Pre-primary 131 (1992/93); Primary 628 (1994/95); Secondary 269 (1994/95); Tertiary 34 (1992/93).

Pupils (1999): Pre-primary 3,000 (1992/93); Primary 12,885; Secondary 6,270; Tertiary 461 (1995/96).
Sources: UNESCO, *Statistical Yearbook*; Caribbean Development Bank, *Selected Indicators of Development*; UN Economic Commission for Latin America and the Caribbean, *Statistical Yearbook*.

Adult Literacy Rate (2001): 96.4%. Source: Secretariat of the Organisation of Eastern Caribbean States.

Directory

The Constitution

The Constitution came into effect at the independence of Dominica on 3 November 1978. Its main provisions are summarized below:

FUNDAMENTAL RIGHTS AND FREEDOMS

The Constitution guarantees the rights of life, liberty, security of the person, the protection of the law and respect for private property. The individual is entitled to freedom of conscience, of expression and assembly and has the right to an existence free from slavery, forced labour and torture. Protection against discrimination on the grounds of sex, race, place of origin, political opinion, colour or creed is assured.

THE PRESIDENT

The President is elected by the House of Assembly for a term of five years. A presidential candidate is nominated jointly by the Prime Minister and the Leader of the Opposition and on their concurrence is declared elected without any vote being taken; in the case of disagreement the choice will be made by secret ballot in the House of Assembly. Candidates must be citizens of Dominica aged at least 40 who have been resident in Dominica for five years prior to their nomination. A President may not hold office for more than two terms.

PARLIAMENT

Parliament consists of the President and the House of Assembly, composed of 21 elected Representatives and nine Senators. According to the wishes of Parliament, the latter may be appointed by the President—five on the advice of the Prime Minister and four on the advice of the Leader of the Opposition—or elected. The life of Parliament is five years.

Parliament has the power to amend the Constitution. Each constituency returns one Representative to the House who is directly elected in accordance with the Constitution. Every citizen over the age of 18 is eligible to vote.

THE EXECUTIVE

Executive authority is vested in the President. The President appoints as Prime Minister the elected member of the House who commands the support of a majority of its elected members, and other ministers on the advice of the Prime Minister. Not more than three ministers may be from among the appointed Senators. The President has the power to remove the Prime Minister from office if a resolution expressing 'no confidence' in the Government is adopted by the House and the Prime Minister does not resign within three days or advise the President to dissolve Parliament.

The Cabinet consists of the Prime Minister, other ministers and the Attorney-General in an ex officio capacity.

The Leader of the Opposition is appointed by the President as that elected member of the House who, in the President's judgement, is best able to command the support of a majority of the elected members who do not support the Government.

The Government

HEAD OF STATE

President: Dr NICHOLAS LIVERPOOL (assumed office 1 October 2003).

CABINET
(April 2005)

A coalition of the Labour Party of Dominica (LPD) and the Dominica Freedom Party (DFP).

Prime Minister and Minister of Finance, Planning and Carib Affairs: ROOSEVELT SKERRIT.

Minister of Communications, Works and Housing: REGINALD AUSTRIE (LPD).

Minister of Industry, Enterprise Development and Tourism: CHARLES SAVARIN (DFP).

Minister of Foreign Affairs and of Trade and Marketing: OSBORNE RIVIERE (LPD).

Minister of Community Development, Gender Affairs and Information: MATTHEW WALTER (LPD).

Minister of Agriculture and the Environment: AMBROSE GEORGE (LPD).

Minister of Education, Human Resource Development, Sports and Youth Affairs: VINCE HENDERSON (LPD).

Minister of Health and Social Security: Sen. HERBERT SABROACHE (DFP).

Attorney-General and Minister of Justice, Legal Affairs, Immigration and Labour: HENRY DYER (DFP).

MINISTRIES

Office of the President: Morne Bruce, Roseau; tel. 4482054; fax 4498366; e-mail presidentoffice@cwdom.dm.

Office of the Prime Minister: Government Headquarters, Kennedy Ave, Roseau; tel. 4482401; fax 4485200.

All other ministries are at Government Headquarters, Kennedy Ave, Roseau; tel. 4482401.

CARIB TERRITORY

This reserve of the remaining Amerindian population is located on the central east coast of the island. The Caribs enjoy a measure of local government and elect their chief.

Chief: GARNET JOSEPH.

Waitukubuli Karifuna Development Committee: Salybia, Carib Territory; tel. 4457336.

Legislature

HOUSE OF ASSEMBLY

Speaker: ALIX BOYD KNIGHT.

Clerk: ALEX F. PHILLIP.

Senators: 9.

Elected Members: 21.

General Election, 31 January 2000

Party	Votes cast	%	Seats
Labour Party of Dominica . .	15,362	42.9	10
Dominica United Workers'			
Party	15,555	43.4	9
Dominica Freedom Party . .	4,858	13.6	2
Independents	29	0.1	—
Total	35,804	100.0	21

Political Organizations

A Righteous Kingdom Party (ARK): Roseau; f. 2005; Christian; Leader HERMINA VALENTINE.

Dominica Freedom Party (DFP): Great George St, Roseau; tel. 4482104; Leader CHARLES SAVARIN.

Dominica United Workers' Party (UWP): 47 Cork St, Roseau; tel. 4485051; fax 4498448; e-mail uwp@cwdom.dm; internet www.uwp.dm; f. 1988; Leader EDISON JAMES; Pres. RON GREEN.

Labour Party of Dominica (LPD): Cork St, Roseau; tel. 4488511; f. 1985 as a merger and reunification of left-wing groups, incl. the Dominica Labour Party (DLP; f. 1961); Leader ROOSEVELT SKERRIT; Deputy Leader AMBROSE GEORGE.

Diplomatic Representation

EMBASSIES IN DOMINICA

China, People's Republic: Roseau; Ambassador YE DABO.

Venezuela: 20 Bath Rd, 3rd Floor, POB 770, Roseau; tel. 4483348; fax 4486198; e-mail embven@cwdom.dm; Ambassador CARMEN MARTÍNEZ DE GRIJALVA.

Judicial System

Justice is administered by the Eastern Caribbean Supreme Court (based in Saint Lucia), consisting of the Court of Appeal and the High Court. One of the six puisne judges of the High Court is resident in Dominica and presides over the Court of Summary Jurisdiction. The District Magistrate Courts deal with summary offences and civil offences involving limited sums of money (specified by law).

Religion

Most of the population profess Christianity, but there are some Muslims, Bahá'ís and Jews. The largest denomination is the Roman Catholic Church (with some 83% of the inhabitants in 2001).

CHRISTIANITY

The Roman Catholic Church

Dominica comprises the single diocese of Roseau, suffragan to the archdiocese of Castries (Saint Lucia). At 31 December 2002 there were an estimated 59,707 adherents in the country, representing a large majority of the inhabitants. The Bishop participates in the Antilles Episcopal Conference (currently based in Port of Spain, Trinidad).

Bishop of Roseau: Rt Rev. GABRIEL MALZAIRE, Bishop's House, Turkey Lane, POB 790, Roseau; tel. 4482837; fax 4483404; e-mail bishop@cwdom.dm.

The Anglican Communion

Anglicans in Dominica are adherents of the Church in the Province of the West Indies. The country forms part of the diocese of the North Eastern Caribbean and Aruba. The Bishop is resident in Antigua, and the Archbishop of the Province is the Bishop of the Bahamas and the Turks and Caicos Islands.

Other Christian Churches

Christian Union Church of the West Indies: District 1, Rose St, Goodwill; tel. 4482725.

Other denominations include Methodist, Pentecostal, Baptist, Church of God, Presbyterian, the Assemblies of Brethren, Moravian and Seventh-day Adventist groups, and the Jehovah's Witnesses.

BAHÁ'Í FAITH

National Spiritual Assembly: 79 Victoria St, POB 136, Roseau; tel. 4483881; fax 4488460; e-mail nsa_dominica@yahoo.com.

The Press

The Chronicle: Wallhouse, POB 1724, Roseau; tel. 4487887; fax 4480047; e-mail thechronicle@cwdom.dm; internet www.news-dominica.com/new-index.cfm; f. 1996; Friday; progressive independent; Editor RASCHID OSMAN; Gen. Man. J. ANTHONY WHITE; circ. 3,000 (1997).

The Independent Newspaper: POB 462, 9 Great Marlborough St, Roseau; tel. 4480221; fax 4484368; internet www.delphis.dm/indpub; weekly.

Official Gazette: Government Printery, Roseau; tel. 4482401, ext. 330; weekly; circ. 550.

The Sun: Sun Inc, 50 Independence St, POB 2255, Roseau; tel. 4484744; fax 4484764; e-mail acsun@cwdom.dm; internet www.dominicasun.com; f. 1998; Editor CHARLES JAMES.

The Times: Roseau; f. 2004; Friday.

The Tropical Star: POB 1998, Roseau; tel. 4484634; fax 4485984; e-mail tpl@cwdom.dm; weekly; circ. 3,000.

Broadcasting and Communications

TELECOMMUNICATIONS

Regulatory Authority

Eastern Caribbean Telecommunications Authority: POB 1886, Castries, St Lucia; tel. (758) 4581701; fax (758) 4581698; e-mail info@ectel.int; internet www.ectel.info; f. 2000 to regulate telecommunications in Dominica, Grenada, Saint Christopher and Nevis, Saint Lucia and Saint Vincent and the Grenadines.

Major Service Providers

Cable & Wireless Dominica: Hanover St, POB 6, Roseau; tel. 4481000; fax 4481111; e-mail pr@cwdom.dm; internet www.tod.dm; Gen. Man. CARL ROBERTS.

Telecommunications of Dominica (TOD): Mercury House, Hanover St, Roseau; tel. 4481024.

BROADCASTING

Radio

In 2001 there were three radio stations operating in Dominica.

Dominica Broadcasting Corporation: Victoria St, POB 148, Roseau; tel. 4483283; fax 4482918; e-mail dbsradio@cwdom.dm; internet www.dbcradio.net; government station; daily broadcasts in English; 2 hrs daily in French patois; 10 kW transmitter on the medium wave band; FM service; programmes received throughout Caribbean excluding Jamaica and Guyana; Gen. Man. MARIETTE WARRINGTON; Programme Dir SHERMAINE GREEN-BROWN.

Kairi FM: Island Communications Corpn, Great George St, POB 931, Roseau; tel. 4487330; fax 4487332; e-mail kairfm@tod.dm; internet www.delphis.dm/kairi.htm; f. 1994; Owner FRANKEY BELLOT.

Voice of Life Radio (ZGBC): Gospel Broadcasting Corpn, Loubiere, POB 205, Roseau; tel. 4487017; fax 4400551; e-mail volradio@cwdom.dm; internet www.voiceofliferadio.com; 112 hrs weekly AM, 24 hrs daily FM; Station Man. CLEMENTINA MONRO.

Television

There is no national television service, although there is a cable television network serving one-third of the island.

Marpin Telecom and Broadcasting Co Ltd: 5–7 Great Marlborough St, POB 2381, Roseau; tel. 4484107; fax 4482965; e-mail pubrel@marpin.dm; internet www.marpin.dm; f. 1982, present name adopted in 1996; commercial; cable service; went into receivership in 2004.

Finance

(cap. = capital; res = reserves; dep. = deposits; m. = million; amounts in East Caribbean dollars)

The Eastern Caribbean Central Bank, based in Saint Christopher, is the central issuing and monetary authority for Dominica.

Eastern Caribbean Central Bank—Dominica Office: Dorset House, cnr of Old St and Hodges Lane, POB 23, Roseau; tel. 4488001; fax 4488002; e-mail eccbdom@cwdom.dm.

BANKS

Bank of Nova Scotia—Scotiabank (Canada): 28 Hillsborough St, POB 520, Roseau; tel. 4485800; fax 4485805; e-mail scotia@cwdom.dm; Man. C. MONTE SMITH.

Banque Française Commerciale (France): Queen Mary St, Roseau; tel. 4484040; fax 4485335; e-mail bfc@cwd.dom.dm; Man. THIERRY FREY.

FirstCaribbean International Bank Ltd: Roseau; internet www.firstcaribbeanbank.com; f. 2002 following merger of Caribbean operations of Barclays Bank PLC and CIBC; Exec. Chair. MICHAEL MANSOOR; CEO CHARLES PINK.

National Bank of Dominica: 64 Hillsborough St, POB 271, Roseau; tel. 4484401; fax 4483982; e-mail nbd@cwdom.dm; internet www.ncbdominica.com; f. 1976, as the National Commercial Bank of Dominica; name changed as above after privatization in Dec. 2003; cap. 10.0m., res 10.0m., dep. 350.1m. (June 2003); 49% govt-owned; Chair. MILTON LAWRENCE; Gen. Man. VANS LEBLANC; 4 brs.

Royal Bank of Canada: Dame Mary Eugenia Charles Blvd, POB 19, Roseau; tel. 4482771; fax 4485398; Man. H. PINARD.

DEVELOPMENT BANK

Dominica Agricultural, Industrial and Development (DAID) Bank: cnr Charles Avenue and Rawles Lane, Goodwill, POB 215, Roseau; tel. 4482853; fax 4484903; e-mail aidbank@cwdom.dm; f. 1971; responsible to Ministry of Finance; planned privatization suspended in 1997; provides finance for the agriculture, tourism, housing, education and manufacturing sectors; cap. 9.5m. (1991); Chair. CRISPIN SORHAINDO; Man. PATRICIA CHARLES.

STOCK EXCHANGE

Eastern Caribbean Securities Exchange: based in Basseterre, Saint Christopher and Nevis; e-mail info@ecseonline.com; internet www.ecseonline.com; f. 2001; regional securities market designed to facilitate the buying and selling of financial products for the eight member territories—Anguilla, Antigua and Barbuda, Dominica, Grenada, Montserrat, Saint Christopher and Nevis, Saint Lucia and Saint Vincent and the Grenadines; Gen. Man. BALJIT VOHRA.

INSURANCE

In 2001 there were 19 insurance companies operating in Dominica. Several British, regional and US companies have agents in Roseau. Local companies include the following:

First Domestic Insurance Co Ltd: 19–21 King George V St, POB 1931, Roseau; tel. 4498202; fax 4485778; e-mail insurance@cwdom.dm.

Insurance Specialists and Consultants: 19–21 King George V St, POB 20, Roseau; tel. 4482022; fax 4485778.

J. B. Charles and Co Ltd: Old St, POB 121, Roseau; tel. 4482876.

Tonge Inc Ltd: 19–21 King George V St, POB 20, Roseau; tel. 4484027; fax 4485778.

Windward Islands Crop Insurance Co (Wincrop): Vanoulst House, Goodwill, POB 469, Roseau; tel. 4483955; fax 4484197; f. 1987; regional; coverage for weather destruction of, mainly, banana crops; Man. KERWIN FERREIRA; brs in Grenada, Saint Lucia and Saint Vincent.

Trade and Industry

DEVELOPMENT ORGANIZATIONS

National Development Corporation (NDC): Valley Rd, POB 293, Roseau; tel. 4482045; fax 4485840; e-mail ndc@cwdom.dm; internet www.ndcdominica.dm; f. 1988 by merger of Industrial Development Corpn (f. 1974) and Tourist Board; promotes local and foreign investment to increase employment, production and exports; promotes and co-ordinates tourism development; Chair. DESMOND CARLISLE; Gen. Man. VINCENT PHILBERT.

Eastern Caribbean States Export Development and Agricultural Diversification Unit (EDADU): POB 769, Roseau; tel. 4482240; fax 4485554; e-mail oecsedu@cwdom.dm; internet www.oecs-edu.org; f. 1990 as Eastern Caribbean States Export Development Agency; reformed as above in 1997; OECS regional development org.; Exec. Dir COLIN BULLY.

INDUSTRIAL AND TRADE ASSOCIATIONS

Dominica Association of Industry and Commerce (DAIC): POB 85, cnr Old St and Fields Lane, Roseau; tel. 4482874; fax 4486868; e-mail daic@marpin.dm; internet www.delphis.dm/daic.htm; f. 1972 by a merger of the Manufacturers' Association and the Chamber of Commerce; represents the business sector, liaises with the Government, and stimulates commerce and industry; 100 mems; Pres. ANTHONY BISCOMBE; CEO JEANILIA R. V. DE SMET.

Dominica Banana Producers Ltd (DBPL): Vanoulst House, POB 1620, Roseau; tel. 4482671; fax 4486445; e-mail dbmc@cwdom.dm; f. 1934 as Dominica Banana Growers' Association; restructured 1984 as the Dominica Banana Marketing Corpn; renamed as above in 2003; state-supported, scheduled for privatization; Chair. RICHARD CHARLES; Gen. Man. KERVIN STEPHENSON.

Dominica Export-Import Agency (DEXIA): Bay Front, POB 173, Roseau; tel. 4482780; fax 4486308; e-mail dexia@cwdom.dm; internet www.dexiaexport.com; f. 1986; replaced the Dominica Agricultural Marketing Board and the External Trade Bureau; exporter of Dominican agricultural products, trade facilitator and importer of bulk rice and sugar; Gen. Man. GREGOIRE THOMAS.

EMPLOYERS' ORGANIZATION

Dominica Employers' Federation: 14 Church St, POB 1783, Roseau; tel. 4482314; fax 4484474; e-mail def@cwdom.dm; Pres. ACKROYD BIRMINGHAM.

UTILITIES

Electricity

Dominica Electricity Services Ltd (Domlec): 18 Castle St, POB 1593, Roseau; tel. 4482681; fax 4485397; e-mail mansecdomlec@cwdom.dm; national electricity service; 72%-owned by the Commonwealth Development Corporation (United Kingdom); Gen. Man. MURRAY ROGERS.

Water

Dominica Water and Sewerage Co Ltd (DOWASCO): 3 High St, POB 185, Roseau; tel. 4484811; fax 4485813; e-mail dowasco@cwdom.dm; state-owned; Chair. DON CHRISTOPHER; Gen. Man. DAMIAN SHILLINGFORD.

TRADE UNIONS

Dominica Amalgamated Workers' Union (DAWU): 5 Hillsborough St, POB 137, Roseau; tel. 4483048; fax 4485787; f. 1960; Gen. Sec. FEDALINE M. MOULON; 500 mems (1996).

Dominica Association of Teachers: 7 Boyds Ave, Roseau; tel. 4488177; fax 4488177; e-mail dat@cwdom.dm; internet www.dateachers.4t.com; Pres. CELIA NICHOLAS; 630 mems (1996).

Dominica Trade Union: 70–71 Independence St, Roseau; tel. 4498139; fax 4499060; f. 1945; Pres. HAROLD SEALEY; Gen. Sec. LEO J. BERNARD NICHOLAS; 400 mems (1995).

Media Workers' Association: Roseau; Pres. MATTHIAS PELTIER.

National Workers' Union: Independence St, cnr Church St and Old Market Sq., POB 387, Roseau; tel. 4485209; fax 4481934; e-mail icss@cwdom.dm; f. 1977; Pres. RAWLINGS F. A. JEMMOTT; Gen. Sec. FRANKLIN FABIEN; 450 mems (1996).

Public Service Union: cnr Valley Rd and Windsor Lane, Roseau; tel. 4482102; fax 4488060; e-mail dcs@cwdom.dm; f. 1940; registered as a trade union in 1960; representing all grades of civil servants, including firemen, prison officers, nurses, teachers and postal workers; Pres. SONIA D. WILLIAMS; Gen. Sec. THOMAS LETANG; 1,400 mems.

Waterfront and Allied Workers' Union: 43 Hillsborough St, POB 181, Roseau; tel. 4482343; fax 4480086; e-mail wawu@cwdom.dm; f. 1965; Pres. LOUIS BENOIT; Gen. Sec. KERTIST AUGUSTIS; 1,500 mems.

Transport

ROADS

In 1999 there were an estimated 780 km (485 miles) of roads, of which about 50.4% was paved; there were also numerous tracks.

SHIPPING

A deep-water harbour at Woodbridge Bay serves Roseau, which is the principal port. Several foreign shipping lines call at Roseau, and there is a high-speed ferry service between Martinique and Guadeloupe which calls at Roseau eight times a week. Ships of the Geest Line call at Prince Rupert's Bay, Portsmouth, to collect bananas, and there are also cruise-ship facilities there. There are other specialized berthing facilities on the west coast.

Dominica Port Authority (DPA): POB 243, Roseau; tel. 4484431; fax 4486131; e-mail domport@cwdom.dm; f. 1972; responsible to the Ministry of Communications and Works; pilotage and cargo handling; Gen. Man. VINCENT ELWIN.

CIVIL AVIATION

Melville Hall Airport, 64 km (40 miles) from Roseau, and Canefield Airport, 5 km (3 miles) from Roseau, are the two airports on the island. A EC $15m. contract to upgrade Melville Hall Airport was signed with a French construction company in August 2004. It was hoped the project would be completed by 2006. The Government redirected the funds for the development, which had been partly provided by the European Union, from the previous (Dominica United Worker's Party) administration's plan to build a brand new international airport. The regional airline, LIAT (based in Antigua and Barbuda, and in which Dominica is a shareholder), provides daily services and, with Air Caraïbe, connects Dominica with all the islands of the Eastern Caribbean, including the international airports of Puerto Rico, Antigua, Guadeloupe and Martinique.

Tourism

The Government has designated areas of the island as nature reserves, to preserve the beautiful, lush scenery and the rich, natural heritage that constitute Dominica's main tourist attractions. Birdlife is particularly prolific, and includes several rare and endangered species, such as the Imperial parrot. There are also two marine reserves. Tourism is not as developed as it is among Dominica's neighbours, but the country is being promoted as an 'eco-tourism' and cruise destination. There were an estimated 249,900 visitors in 2003 (of whom 177,000 were cruise-ship passengers). Receipts from tourism totalled an estimated EC $137.4m. in 2003.

National Development Corporation (NDC)—Division of Tourism: Valley Rd, POB 293, Roseau; tel. 4482045; fax 4485840; e-mail ndctourism@cwdom.dm; internet www.ndcdominica.dm; f. 1988 following merger of Tourist Board with Industrial Devt Corpn; Dir of Tourism SHARON PASCAL.

Dominica Hotel and Tourism Association (DHTA): POB 384, Roseau; tel. 4486565; fax 4480299; e-mail dhta@cwdom.dm; Pres. ATHERTON MARTIN; Treas. MAXINE ALLEYNE.

THE DOMINICAN REPUBLIC

Introductory Survey

Location, Climate, Language, Religion, Flag, Capital

The Dominican Republic occupies the eastern part of the island of Hispaniola, which lies between Cuba and Puerto Rico in the Caribbean Sea. The country's only international frontier is with Haiti, to the west. The climate is sub-tropical, with an average annual temperature of 27°C (80°F). In Santo Domingo, temperatures are generally between 19°C (66°F) and 31°C (88°F). The west and south-west of the country are arid. Hispaniola lies in the path of tropical cyclones. The official language is Spanish. Almost all of the inhabitants profess Christianity, and some 89% are Roman Catholics. There are small Protestant and Jewish communities. The national flag (proportions 5 by 8) is blue (upper hoist and lower fly) and red (lower hoist and upper fly), quartered by a white cross. The state flag has, in addition, the national coat of arms, showing a quartered shield in the colours of the flag (on which are superimposed national banners, a cross and an open Bible) between scrolls above and below, at the centre of the cross. The capital is Santo Domingo.

Recent History

The Dominican Republic became independent in 1844, although it was occupied by US military forces between 1916 and 1924. General Rafael Leónidas Trujillo Molina overthrew the elected President, Horacio Vázquez, in 1930 and dominated the country until his assassination in May 1961. The dictator ruled personally from 1930 to 1947 and indirectly thereafter. His brother, Héctor Trujillo, was President from 1947 until August 1960, when he was replaced by Dr Joaquín Balaguer Ricardo, hitherto Vice-President. After Rafael Trujillo's death, President Balaguer remained in office, but in December 1961 he permitted moderate opposition groups to participate in a Council of State, which exercised legislative and executive powers. Balaguer resigned in January 1962, when the Council of State became the Provisional Government. A presidential election in December 1962, the country's first free election for 38 years, was won by Dr Juan Bosch Gaviño, the founder and leader of the Partido Revolucionario Dominicano (PRD), who had been in exile since 1930. President Bosch, a left-of-centre democrat, took office in February 1963 but was overthrown in the following September by a military coup. The leaders of the armed forces transferred power to a civilian triumvirate, led by Emilio de los Santos. In April 1965 a revolt by supporters of ex-President Bosch overthrew the triumvirate. Civil war broke out between pro-Bosch forces and military units headed by Gen. Elías Wessin y Wessin, who had played a leading role in the 1963 coup. The violence was eventually suppressed by the intervention of some 23,000 US troops, who were formally incorporated into an Inter-American peace force by the Organization of American States (OAS). The peace force withdrew in September 1965.

Following a period of provisional government under Héctor García Godoy, a presidential election in June 1966 was won by Balaguer, the candidate of the Partido Reformista Social Cristiano (PRSC). The PRSC, founded in 1964, also won a majority of seats in both houses of the new Congreso Nacional (National Congress). A new Constitution was promulgated in November. Despite his association with the Trujillo dictatorship, Balaguer initially proved to be a popular leader, and in May 1970 he was re-elected for a further four years. In February 1973 a state of emergency was declared when guerrilla forces landed on the coast. Captain Francisco Caamaño Deño, the leader of the 1965 revolt, and his followers were killed. Bosch and other opposition figures went into hiding. Bosch later resigned as leader of the PRD (founding the Partido de la Liberación Dominicana—PLD), undermining hopes of a united opposition in the May 1974 elections, when Balaguer was re-elected with a large majority.

In the May 1978 presidential election, Balaguer was defeated by the PRD candidate, Silvestre Antonio Guzmán Fernández. This was the first occasion in the country's history when an elected President yielded power to an elected successor. An attempted military coup in favour of Balaguer was prevented by pressure from the US Government. On assuming office in August, President Guzmán undertook to professionalize the armed forces by removing politically ambitious high-ranking officers. In June 1981 he declared his support for Jacobo Majluta Azar, his Vice-President, as his successor, but in November the PRD rejected Majluta's candidacy in favour of Dr Salvador Jorge Blanco, a left-wing senator, who was elected President in May 1982. In the congressional elections, held simultaneously, the PRD secured a majority in both the Senate and the Chamber of Deputies. Blanco assumed office in August. Although a member of the Socialist International, he maintained good relations with the USA (on which the country is economically dependent) and declared that he would not resume relations with Cuba.

In February 1985 a series of substantial price increases led to violent clashes between demonstrators and the security forces. Public unrest was exacerbated by the Government's decision in April to accept the IMF's terms for further financial aid. In June a 24-hour general strike was organized by trade unions, in protest at the Government's economic policy and its refusal to increase the minimum wage. In July, however, the threat of a 48-hour general strike prompted the Government to order an immediate increase in the minimum wage.

Further violence preceded the presidential and legislative elections of May 1986. The three principal candidates in the presidential election were all former Presidents: Balaguer of the PRSC; Majluta, who, having registered La Estructura, his right-wing faction of the PRD, as a separate political party in July 1985, nevertheless secured the candidacy of the ruling PRD; and Bosch of the PLD. The counting of votes was suspended twice, following allegations by Majluta of fraud by the PRSC and by the Junta Central Electoral (JCE—Central Electoral Board). Balaguer was finally declared the winner by a narrow margin of votes over Majluta, his closest rival. In the simultaneous legislative elections, the PRSC won 21 of the 30 seats in the Senate and 56 of the 120 seats in the Chamber of Deputies.

Upon taking office as President (for the fifth time) in August 1986, Balaguer initiated an investigation into alleged corrupt practices by members of the outgoing administration. Blanco, the outgoing President, was charged with embezzlement and the illegal purchase of military vehicles. (In August 1991 he was finally convicted of 'abuse of power' and misappropriation of public funds, and sentenced to 20 years' imprisonment. However, in September 1994 legislation granting him amnesty was approved by the Chamber of Deputies.) The financial accounts of the armed forces were examined, and the former Secretary of State for the Armed Forces was subsequently imprisoned. In September 1987 the Cabinet resigned, at the request of the President, to enable him to restructure the Government. Some 35,000 government posts were abolished, in an attempt to reduce public spending, and expenditure was to be redirected to a programme of public works projects, which were expected to create almost 100,000 new jobs. Nevertheless, the civil unrest continued.

In 1989 opposition to the Government's economic policies intensified. Popular discontent was aggravated by the deterioration of public utilities, particularly water and electricity. In June a 48-hour general strike to demand the doubling of the minimum wage, a reduction in the prices of staple commodities, and the ending of interruptions in the supplies of water and electricity resulted in the deaths of four people and the arrests of a further 3,000. In October, following a 66% rise in fuel prices, there were further violent demonstrations.

With presidential and legislative elections due to take place in May 1990, Balaguer's prospects for re-election were impeded considerably by the continuing deterioration of the economy. The principal contender for the presidency was the PLD candidate, Bosch, who concentrated his election campaign on seeking support from the private sector, promising privatization of state-owned companies. When the initial results indicated a narrow victory for Balaguer, Bosch accused the ruling PRSC and the JCE of fraud, necessitating a re-count, supervised by monitors from the OAS. Almost two months after the election, Balaguer was declared the official winner. The PRSC secured a narrow majority in the Senate, with 16 of the 30 seats. No party won an outright majority in the Chamber of Deputies, although this did not threaten seriously to impede government policies, in view of Balaguer's extensive powers to govern by decree.

In August 1990, in an attempt to reduce inflation, the Government announced a programme of austerity measures, almost doubling the price of petrol and essential foodstuffs. In response the trade unions called a 48-hour general strike and in the ensuing conflict with the security forces some 14 people were killed. The price increases were partially offset by an increase of 30% in the salaries of army personnel and civilian employees in the public sector. The trade unions, however, rejected an identical offer by the private sector and threatened further strike action if their demands for basic food subsidies and considerable wage increases were not satisfied. In September a three-day general strike was organized by the Organizaciones Colectivas Populares (OCP). In the following month another general strike was called by the OCP and the Central General de Trabajadores (CGT), with the stated aim of ousting Balaguer from power. Violent clashes with the security forces in Santo Domingo resulted in four deaths. In August 1991 the Government concluded a stand-by agreement with the IMF, in spite of trade-union and public opposition.

In January 1994 the PLD announced it had formed an alliance with the right-wing Fuerza Nacional Progresista (FNP) in order to contest the forthcoming general election. In the same month Balaguer officially announced his intention to contest the forthcoming presidential election; his nomination received the support of the majority of the PRSC. However, his decision prompted 20 members of the PRSC executive to withdraw from the party in order to support the presidential candidate of the Unidad Democrática (UD), Fernando Alvarez Bogaert, himself a defecting member of the PRSC. The UD subsequently signed an electoral pact with the PRD.

The official results of the presidential and legislative elections of 16 May 1994 were delayed, amid accusations of widespread voting irregularities. Interim results indicated a narrow victory for Balaguer in the presidential contest. However, the PRD claimed that the PRSC, which had effective control of the JCE, had removed the names of some 200,000 PRD supporters from the electoral rolls. A full recount was undertaken. In July an investigative commission confirmed that, as a result of serious irregularities, some 73,000 of the registered electorate had been denied a vote. Despite an atmosphere of growing political instability, Balaguer rejected opposition demands for the formation of a provisional government. Strike action in protest at the electoral irregularities was reported to have seriously affected several regions, including the capital, during that month. On 2 August the JCE announced the final election results, having apparently overlooked the findings of the electoral investigative commission. Balaguer was proclaimed the winner of the presidential election by a margin of less than 1% of the votes cast. In the Senate the alliance of the PRD and the UD secured 15 seats, while the PRSC won 14 and the PLD one seat. In the Chamber of Deputies the PRD/UD alliance obtained 57 seats, while the PRSC won 50 and the PLD 13 seats.

Talks aimed at ending the political crisis caused by the election were held in early August 1994, with the mediation of the OAS and the Roman Catholic Church, and resulted in the signing of the Pact for Democracy. Under the terms of the accord (agreed by all the major parties), a fresh presidential election was to be held in November 1995 and a series of constitutional reforms would be adopted, providing for the prohibition of the re-election of a president to a consecutive term, a new electoral system for the head of state (see below), and the reorganization of the judiciary. Additionally, the legislative and municipal elections were to be held mid-way through the presidential term. As a result of the accord, José Francisco Peña Gómez, the PRD leader, cancelled a series of planned strikes and demonstrations organized by his party. However, at a session of the National Congress, held on 14 August, the deputies of the PRSC, with the support of those of the PLD, voted to extend Balaguer's mandate from 18 months to two years. The PRD withdrew from the legislature in protest, and Peña Gómez announced that his party would boycott Congress and resume strike action. The OAS also criticized Congress for violating the terms of the Pact for Democracy. The constitutional amendments that the Pact envisaged were, however, approved by Congress. On 16 August Balaguer was inaugurated as President for a seventh term.

In April 1996 the energy shortfall again reached crisis proportions, with power cuts averaging between 14 and 20 hours per day. The crisis prompted renewed demands for Congress to expedite legislation enabling the privatization of the state elec-

tricity company, Corporación Dominicana de Electricidad (CDE), which, owing largely to inefficiency and corruption, operated at a considerable loss.

The presidential election of 16 May 1996, the first for some 30 years in which Balaguer was not a candidate, was conducted according to a new system, introduced since 1994, whereby a second round of voting would be conducted between the two leading candidates should no candidate secure an absolute majority in the initial ballot. In the first round Peña Gómez won 46% of the votes, while the candidate of the PLD, Leonel Fernández Reyna, obtained 39%. The candidate of the PRSC, Jacinto Peynado (who had received only nominal support from Balaguer), obtained just 15% of the votes. At the second round of the presidential election, conducted on 30 June, Fernández secured a narrow victory, winning 51.3% of the votes, while Peña Gómez obtained 48.8%. The establishment, earlier in the month, of an electoral alliance between the PLD and PRSC, entitled the Frente Nacional Patriótico, had ensured Fernández the support of the PRSC voters. While the PRSC failed to retain the presidency, Balaguer appeared to have succeeded in retaining considerable influence in the new administration, since the PLD's minority representation in Congress meant the party would be dependent on the support of the PRSC to implement planned institutional reforms. However, in early August relations between Fernández and Balaguer deteriorated when the PRSC signed an unexpected agreement with the PRD, which guaranteed the PRSC the presidency of the Senate while the PRD obtained that of the Chamber of Deputies. On 16 August Fernández was inaugurated, and the Cabinet, consisting almost exclusively of PLD members, was sworn in.

In 1997, as part of a campaign to eliminate deep-seated corruption in the country's institutions, Fernández restructured both the police and the judiciary. In August, in his role as Chairman of the Consejo Nacional de la Magistratura, Fernández also oversaw a restructuring of the Supreme Court, including the appointment of 15 new judges. Responsibility for appointing judges at all other levels of the judicial system was transferred from the Senate to the Supreme Court, principally to avoid appointments being influenced by political considerations.

Growing dissatisfaction with the continuing deterioration of public services and Fernández's failure to honour promises made during his election campaign provoked widespread disturbances and strike action throughout the country in 1997 and early 1998, with violent confrontations between demonstrators and the security forces resulting in several deaths. In October, in an effort to defuse the volatile social and political climate, Fernández introduced a recovery plan aimed at overcoming electricity and food shortages. However, in the following month a two-day general strike was organized by an 'umbrella' protest group, the Coordinadora Nacional de Organizaciones Populares (CNOP—National Confederation of Popular Organizations), in support of demands for pay increases, reductions in the price of fuel and basic foodstuffs and improved public services.

At legislative elections held on 16 May 1998 the PRD won 83 seats in the 149-seat Chamber of Deputies (enlarged from 120 seats), while the PLD obtained 49 seats and the PRSC secured the remaining 17 seats. In the Senate the PRD won 24 seats, while the PLD won four and the PRSC two seats. The number of registered voters who abstained from participating in the poll was, at some 48%, the highest on record. In July 1998 the outgoing Congress approved controversial legislation granting an amnesty to all public officials accused of corruption since 1978. The new legislature was inaugurated in August 1998. However, the PRD failed to secure the presidency of the Chamber of Deputies when a dissident group of PRD deputies joined forces with the PLD and the PRSC to re-elect the outgoing President of the Chamber, Héctor Rafael Peguero Méndez, to the post. Peguero had been expelled from the PRD in July, after refusing to accept the party's choice of candidate for the position.

Violent protests against electricity and water shortages and declining living standards continued in 1998 and 1999. In May 1999 the privatization of the CDE began.

In the first round of the presidential election, held on 16 May 2000, Rafael Hipólito Mejía Domínguez, the PRD candidate, received 49.9% of the votes cast, while the PRD candidate, Danilo Medina Sánchez, won 24.9%. Former President Joaquín Balaguer, standing as the PRSC's candidate for a potential eighth presidential term, won 24.6% of the ballot. Despite Mejía's failure to secure the constitutionally required 50%, a second ballot was not held and the JCE allowed Mejía to declare himself the winner. He was inaugurated as President on 16 August and a new Cabinet was officially appointed. The PRD crusade against the previous PLD administration's alleged corruption proved controversial, creating open hostility between the two parties. In November former President Fernández led a protest, following the arrest of various former senior government officials on corruption charges. Fernández himself was later similarly accused and arrested; however, they were all subsequently released, owing to lack of evidence. With only 73 PRD deputies in the 149-seat lower house (10 of the 83 elected in May 1998 had been expelled from the party), Mejía lacked a parliamentary majority, and was dependent for support on the PRSC.

In early 2001 President Mejía initiated a series of fiscal measures, increasing value-added tax (VAT), introducing taxes on luxury goods and obliging larger companies to pay corporation taxes in stages throughout the year. Petrol prices increased, following the implementation of a fixed tax on fuel, but there was no violent popular response. The Government also introduced a poverty mitigation programme, including training, infrastructural programmes and education, health and housing reforms. Social security legislation was introduced, aimed at providing employees with improved pensions and other benefits. The political programme also included decentralization of power and the restructuring of the public sector. There was some opposition to the measures, including a strike by hospital workers in protest at the proposed welfare reforms.

In December 2000 the Senate approved constitutional amendments to extend the presidential term to five years and the congressional term to six years, and to lower the minimum requirement of votes in a presidential election. The legislation was condemned by many politicians and, in order to appease opposition to the bill, Mejía subsequently appointed a Committee on Constitutional Reform to assess the situation. In October 2001 agreement was reached on the major clauses of a constitutional reform bill, which was then submitted to Congress. The proposed legislation included four principal points: a reduction in the proportion of votes needed to win a presidential election to 45% (or 40% if the leading candidate had at least a 10% majority); the abolition of 'closed' electoral stations; the election of representatives to the Central Andean Parliament to be decided by popular vote rather than by Congress; the establishment of a National Constituent Assembly to draft a new constitution. However, in November the Senate voted to include in the constitutional amendments a clause permitting the re-election of a President. Mejía opposed the inclusion of this reform, claiming that it distracted from the main issues (he declared he would not seek re-election in 2004). In December the Supreme Court ruled the proposed legislation to be unconstitutional. However, in January 2002 the Chamber of Deputies approved the formation of a National Constituent Assembly and in July, following re-examination, a bill of amendment permitting presidential re-election finally received assent from the National Assembly.

Legislative elections were held on 16 May 2002. The PRD secured 73 seats in the Chamber of Deputies, the PLD 41 (a reduction of its representation by eight seats) and the PRSC 36. The PRD also won 29 of 32 seats available in the Senate; the PLD obtained two and the PRSC the remaining seat. The failure of the PRD to secure an outright majority in the lower house ensured its continued dependence upon the support of the PRSC for the passage of legislation.

In July 2002 former President Joaquín Balaguer died at the age of 95. His death prompted speculation that there would be some political realignment within the legislature, following a formal proposal by the PLD that it enter into an alliance with the PRSC. However, in August the PRSC renewed its political alliance with the PRD, ensuring that the latter retained its dominance of the lower house. In November Col. Pedro Julio Goico, a member of the armed forces and the head of presidential security, was detained following fraud allegations. President Mejía became involved in the scandal when it was discovered that he had reinstated Goico to the armed forces following his suspension in 1997 and had subsequently promoted him, as well as appointing him head of security, despite the charges that he faced. Meanwhile, former President Leonel Fernández launched a new political movement, Frente Independiente Leonel al Poder (FILA), to support his candidacy in the 2004 presidential election.

In March 2003 President Mejía announced that, contrary to his previous statements on the subject, he did intend to seek re-election at the 2004 presidential election. The announcement prompted a split within the PRD between supporters and opponents of Mejía's re-election, including party Chairman Hatuey Decamps. In May the dissolution of the commercial bank Banco Intercontinental, SA (Baninter), following the exposure of huge losses at the bank owing to fraud, had serious political, as well as economic, implications. The President of Baninter, Ramón Báez Figueroa, allegedly had links to the PLD, thus damaging the reputation of that party as well as the Government. Figueroa and two other bank officials were later arrested on fraud charges. The Government's subsequent decision to guarantee all the deposits held at Baninter, at a cost of approximately US $2,200m., resulted in the onset of an economic crisis so severe that the Government was forced to request IMF assistance; in August a $618m. stand-by arrangement with the IMF was concluded. Meanwhile, the Government also took control of a media group linked to Baninter; its assets included the daily newspaper *Listín Diario*.

In October 2003 Mejía suffered a set-back to his hopes of re-election when, at an informal plebiscite of PRD members, his potential candidacy was rejected by 92% of those who voted. However, Mejía indicated that he still intended to seek the party's presidential nomination again. At the PRD's first primary election, held in December, Hatuey Decamps secured victory, although the JCE later declared the vote to have been illegal. In January 2004 President Mejía secured victory at a second PRD primary election. The election was, however, considered to be a farce, owing to the withdrawal from the contest of the three party members who presented the most credible challenge to Mejía: Vice-President Milagros Ortiz Bosch, former Secretary of State for Tourism Rafael Suberví Bonilla and Emmanuel Esquea Guerrero. They claimed to have withdrawn because they believed that Mejía's faction would use fraudulent methods to obtain victory. Mejía was, however, appointed the official PRD presidential candidate later in that month.

In November 2003 a 24-hour general strike took place, during which violent clashes occurred between the security forces and anti-Government protesters in several cities, resulting in the deaths of at least seven people. The strike was organized by the CNOP in protest at governmental mismanagement of the economy and, in particular, the failure to resolve the ongoing, and increasingly severe, power shortages. In late January 2004 a 48-hour general strike was held, during which at least nine people were killed and many more injured.

At the presidential election held in May 2004, which was contested by 11 candidates, Leonel Fernández of the PLD defeated the incumbent Mejía by a decisive margin, securing 57.11% of the votes cast, sufficient to ensure that no second round of voting would be necessary. Mejía attracted 33.65% of the ballot, while the PRSC candidate, Rafael Eduardo Estrella Virella, was third-placed with 8.65% of the votes. Fernández was inaugurated in August, together with his Vice-President, Rafael Alburqueque, and announced the composition of his new Cabinet shortly afterwards. Vicente Bengoa was appointed Secretary of State for Finance and Carlos Morales Troncoso Secretary of State for External Affairs.

In November 2004 it was reported that 10 high-ranking members of the Government of former President Mejía had been charged with embezzlement in connection with a scheme intended to promote the renewal of the country's car fleet. Those accused included the former Secretary of State for the Armed Forces and General Chief of Staff, Maj.-Gen. José Miguel Soto Jiménez, and the former Secretary of State for the Interior and Police, Dr Pedro Franco Badía. Meanwhile, President Fernández failed to make any significant progress in ending the country's ongoing electricity shortage.

The continuing illegal import of plantation labour into the Dominican Republic from Haiti was a major issue for successive Governments. In June 1991, in reaction to increasing criticism of the Dominican Republic's human rights record (and, in particular, the Government's apparent acquiescence in the exploitation of Haitian child labourers), President Balaguer ordered the repatriation of all Haitian residents aged under 16 or over 60 years. Protests made by the Haitian Government that such a unilateral measure contravened normal diplomatic procedure were rejected by Balaguer. Following the army coup of September 1991 in Haiti, tens of thousands of Haitians fled to the Dominican Republic. However, few were granted refugee status. In 1994 reports of large-scale smuggling from the Dominican Republic to Haiti, in defiance of UN sanctions against the Haitian military dictatorship, led to the establishment of a UN monitoring mission to observe the enforcement of the embargo until the lifting of UN sanctions (in October 1994). In 1997 the Dominican and Haitian Presidents agreed to put an immediate end to large-scale repatriations and for the repatriation process to be monitored by an international body to ensure the observance of human rights. In June 1998 Fernández became the first Dominican head of state to visit Haiti since 1936. At the meeting the two Presidents reached agreement on the establishment of joint border patrols to combat the traffic of drugs, arms and other contraband across the countries' joint border. In late 1999, following the summary deportation of some 8,000 Haitians, the two Governments signed a protocol limiting the repatriations.

In early 2001, following an increase in tensions in Haiti, a plan to protect Dominican territory was implemented; military forces deployed on the Dominican–Haitian border also were reinforced in an attempt to prevent both illegal immigration and drugs-trafficking. Relations improved during the presidency of Mejía, and there were proposals for joint Dominican-Haitian development programmes in the border region, to be financed by the European Union (EU). However, following the attempt by former Haitian police commissioners to take over the Haitian presidential palace, in December 2001, security along the Dominican–Haitian border was increased. In April the inauguration of an industrial park at Ouanaminthe, spanning the shared border, was perceived to signal the start of an improved bilateral relationship. In late 2002 the USA pledged weapons, technical assistance and joint military exercises in order to help the Dominican armed forces patrol the border area. In early 2004, in response to escalating political instability in Haiti, security in the border area was increased again. Following the overthrow of President Aristide in February 2004, Dominican relations with Haiti deteriorated when supporters of Aristide accused the Dominican authorities of having aided the insurgents who had led the rebellion against him.

Government

The Dominican Republic comprises 31 provinces, each administered by an appointed governor, and a Distrito Nacional (DN) containing the capital. Under the 1966 Constitution (as amended in 1994), legislative power is exercised by the bicameral National Congress, with a Senate of 32 members and a Chamber of Deputies (150 members). Members of both houses are elected for four years by universal adult suffrage. Executive power lies with the President, who is also elected by direct popular vote for four years. He is assisted by a Vice-President and a Cabinet comprising Secretaries of State.

Defence

Military service is voluntary and lasts for four years. In August 2003 the armed forces totalled 24,500 men: army 15,000, air force 5,500 and navy 4,000. Paramilitary forces numbered 15,000. The defence budget for 2003 was an estimated RD $3,100m.

Economic Affairs

In 2003, according to estimates by the World Bank, the Dominican Republic's gross national income (GNI), measured at average 2001–03 prices, was US $14,747m., equivalent to $2,070 per head (or $6,210 per head on an international purchasing-power parity basis). During 1990–2003, it was estimated, the population increased by an average of 1.7% per year, while gross domestic product (GDP) per head increased, in real terms, by an average of 3.2% per year. Overall GDP increased, in real terms, by an average of 5.1% per year in 1990–2003. Real GDP increased by 4.0% in 2001 and by 4.3% in 2002, but contracted by an estimated 0.4% in 2003.

Agriculture, including hunting, forestry and fishing, contributed an estimated 11.3% of GDP, at constant 1970 prices, in 2003, and employed 15.1% of the employed labour force in the previous year. The principal cash crops are sugar cane (sugar and sugar derivatives accounted for an estimated 9.5% of total export earnings in 2003), cocoa beans and tobacco. Agricultural GDP increased, in real terms, by an average of 3.8% per year during 1990–2003. Real agricultural GDP increased by 2.5% in 2002, but decreased by an estimated 2.9% in 2003. In 2001 the Government intended to implement a US $400m. development plan for fruit cultivation. In November 2002 it was reported that Japan was considering funding $400m. of agricultural and environmental projects in the country, including: a $70m. project to encourage the production of rice; a $10m. river basin reforestation project; and a $48m. loan intended to fund the sewer system in Santiago.

Industry (including mining, manufacturing, construction and power) employed 20.8% of the economically active population in 2002, and contributed an estimated 30.8% of GDP, at constant 1970 prices, in 2003. Industrial GDP increased, in real terms, by an average of 5.0% per year during 1990–2003. Real industrial GDP increased by 3.7% in 2002, but decreased by an estimated 4.9% in 2003.

Mining contributed an estimated 1.5% of GDP, at constant 1970 prices, in 2003, but employed only 0.3% of the economically active population in 2002. The major mineral export is ferro-nickel (providing approximately 22.9% of total export earnings in 2003). Gold and silver are also exploited, and there are workable deposits of gypsum, limestone and mercury. The slump in world prices forced the ferro-nickel mine at Bonao to close in late 1998. Following an increase in prices in early 2000, the mine was reopened; however, it was closed again temporarily in 2001 and 2002, owing to a decrease in demand and prices, before reopening in 2003. In February 2002 the Government reached agreement with Placer Dome of Canada on a 25-year concession to operate the Sulfuros de Pueblo Viejo mine. There were plans to develop other mines throughout the country. Real mining GDP decreased by an annual average of 0.8% during 1990–2003. The GDP of the mining sector decreased, in real terms, by 2.8% in 2002, but increased by an estimated 8.7% in 2003.

Manufacturing contributed an estimated 15.5% of GDP, at constant 1970 prices, in 2003, and employed 14.1% of the economically active population in 2002. Important branches of manufacturing included beer and cigarettes. The most dynamic sector in 1999 was construction, in particular cement production. At the end of 2003 there were 531 companies operating in 54 free-trade zones in the Dominican Republic, employing some 173,000 people. The passage of USA-Africa-Caribbean trade legislation in May 2000 gave Dominican apparel exports to the USA tariff-free status. The GDP of the manufacturing sector increased, in real terms, at an average rate of 3.9% per year during 1990–2003. Real manufacturing GDP increased by 4.0% in 2002, but decreased by an estimated 2.7% in 2003.

Energy is derived principally from petroleum; however, there is no domestic petroleum production. Imports of mineral fuels accounted for an estimated 13.2% of the total cost of imports in 1996. In the early 2000s construction was under way on a variety of energy projects, including: a 300 MW oil-fired power-station and a 300 MW gas-fired power-station, including a liquefied natural gas terminal; a regasification plant and a 500 MW gas-fired power-station; a hydroelectric dam in Altagracia, to supply drinking water and electricity to the province; and four mini-hydroelectric plants, together generating 16 MW. The Monción dam in Santiago Rodríguez, which included a 54 MW hydroelectric plant, was inaugurated in September 2001. York Caribbean Windpower, a subsidiary of York Research (USA), constructed a US $160m. wind park in Puerto Plata that became operational in mid-2002. In October 2000 the signing of the Caracas energy accord gave the Dominican Republic the option to buy petroleum from Venezuela under the preferential terms of the San José Agreement. However, in September 2003 Venezuela halted petroleum sales to the Dominican Republic, owing to a deterioration in diplomatic relations between the two countries.

The services sector contributed an estimated 57.9% of GDP, at constant 1970 prices, in 2003, and employed 64.0% of the economically active population in 2002. The tourism sector was the country's primary source of foreign-exchange earnings. In 2003 3,562,770 tourists visited the Dominican Republic; receipts from tourism totalled US $2,736m. in 2002. The GDP of the services sector expanded at an average annual rate of 5.5% during 1990–2003. Real services GDP increased by 5.0% in 2002 and by an estimated 2.6% in 2003.

In 2003 the Dominican Republic recorded a visible trade deficit of US $2,444.0m., and there was a surplus of $867.1m. on the current account of the balance of payments. In 2000 the principal source of imports was the USA (49.8%); other major suppliers were Venezuela, Mexico and Japan. In the same year the USA was the principal market for exports (43.1% of the total); other significant purchasers were Belgium-Luxembourg and Puerto Rico. The principal exports in 2003 were ferro-nickel and sugar and sugar derivatives. In 2003 exports from the free-trade zones amounted to $4,398.7m. The principal imports in 2003 were petroleum and petroleum products, and durable goods. In 2001 banana exports totalled $35m., compared with $23m. in 2000.

In 2003 there was an estimated budgetary deficit of RD \$19,310.7m. (equivalent to 3.8% of GDP). The Dominican Republic's total external debt at the end of 2002 was US \$6,256m., of which \$4,035m. was long term public debt. In that year the cost of debt-servicing was equivalent to 6.4% of total revenue from exports of goods and services. In 1990–2003 the average annual rate of inflation was 11.1%. Consumer prices increased by an average of 5.2% in 2002 and by 27.4% in 2003. An estimated 16.1% of the total labour force was unemployed in 2002.

In July 1984 the Dominican Republic was granted observer status in CARICOM (see p. 172). In December 1989 the country was accepted as a member of the ACP nations covered by the Lomé Convention (which expired in February 2000 and was replaced by the Cotonou Agreement (see p. 262) in June). In 1990 the Dominican Republic's application for full membership of CARICOM was threatened when ACP nations accused the Dominican Republic of breaking an agreement made under the Lomé Convention concerning the export of bananas to countries of the European Community (now the European Union). An agreement, originally signed in August 1998, establishing a free-trade area between CARICOM countries and the Dominican Republic, came into effect on 1 December 2001.

From the 1990s onwards the economy of the Dominican Republic was severely affected by the unstable nature of the country's electricity supply. Interruptions in the supply of electricity lasted up to 20 hours per day. The restructuring of the state electricity company (Corporación Dominicana de Electricidad—CDE) was repeatedly delayed, although in May 1999 the generating and distribution operations of the CDE were partially privatized. In July 2001 President Rafael Hipólito Mejía Domínguez approved legislation that provided a framework for the electricity industry. However, widespread protests became a regular occurrence from 2001, owing to continuing power cuts and the Government's failure to resolve the ongoing energy crisis. Trade unions called for the annulment of the privatization contracts that had been awarded to two electricity distribution companies—the US-owned company AES and the Spanish-owned Unión Fenosa—owing to allegations that since privatization the country's electricity service had become both more unreliable and more expensive. Following the accession of Leonel Fernández to the presidency in August 2004, the Government obtained credit in order to pay its debts to the various power companies in an attempt to end the country's frequent power failures. However, the ongoing power shortages soon recommenced.

On 1 January 2001 a programme of fiscal measures, including an increase in consumer taxes, a rise in tariffs on imported luxury goods, a tax increase on cars, insurance, advertising, flights, security, commercial rents, gambling, cigarettes and beer, and a corporation tax of 1.5%, came into effect. In 2002, despite several attempts by the Central Bank to stabilize the currency, the peso experienced significant devaluation. In mid-2003 the dissolution of the country's second largest commercial bank, Banco Intercontinental, SA (Baninter), forced the Government to seek financial assistance from the IMF in order to overcome the economic crisis that had resulted from massive misappropriation of funds at the bank (see Recent History). The IMF subsequently agreed a US \$618m. loan, the release of which was subject to the implementation of certain fiscal policies and structural measures. Further assistance from the World Bank and the Inter-American Development Bank brought the total of agreed loans to the country to approximately \$1,200m., to be disbursed over a period of two years. However, the IMF agreement was suspended in October, following the Government's announcement that it planned to buy back Unión Fenosa's stake in two of the country's power distribution companies, at an estimated cost of \$700m. The IMF stated that it intended to withhold the funds while it assessed the impact of the renationalization of the power companies. Meanwhile, the value of the Dominican currency continued to depreciate sharply throughout 2003. The Central Bank subsequently raised interest rates in an attempt to halt rising inflation and the

peso's continuing depreciation. The 2004 budget, approved by the Congreso Nacional in January of that year, put revenue at 120,000m. pesos, comprising 100,000m. pesos of regular income with the remainder in the form of international aid and donations. Following the approval of the budget, the IMF agreed to resume disbursement of funds, on condition that the Government implement tax reform. In the aftermath of the defeat of President Mejía at the May presidential election, the outgoing Government agreed upon a series of emergency tax reform measures with the incoming President, Leonel Fernández. The subsequent taxation increases, approved by the legislature in October, were widely perceived as being merely revenue raising measures. Following his inauguration in August 2004 President Fernández stressed that his Government would pursue an economic policy based on securing stability through the reduction of government spending and inflation. In the same month a free trade agreement with the USA was signed that would integrate the Dominican Republic into the Central American Free Trade Area (CAFTA). It was scheduled to come into effect on 1 January 2005. However, in November the USA stated that the Dominican Republic would be excluded from the CAFTA unless it lifted a tax that had recently been imposed on imports of beverages containing high fructose corn syrup as part of the package of tax reforms that had been approved in October. In the same month the Fernández Government concluded a preliminary agreement with the IMF that, it was hoped, would lead to a new stand-by arrangement. In the following month the Congreso Nacional voted to lift the controversial tariff on products containing corn syrup. Meanwhile, the peso appreciated significantly in value following the accession of Fernández to the presidency. The Government forecast that GDP would increase by 2.5% in 2005.

Education

Education is, where possible, compulsory for children between the ages of six and 14 years. Primary education begins at the age of six and lasts for eight years. Secondary education, starting at 14 years of age, lasts for four years. In 1999 the total enrolment in primary, secondary and tertiary education was equivalent to 72% of the relevant age group (males 69%; females 75%). In 1997 primary enrolment included an estimated 91.3% of children in the relevant age-group (males 89.0%; females 93.6%), while secondary enrolment included an estimated 78.5% of children in the relevant age-group (males 74.9%; females 82.1%). In 1994/95 there were 4,001 primary schools, and in 1996/97 there were an estimated 1,737 secondary schools. There are eight universities. In October 2001 the Government announced the investment of US \$52m. in the construction and repair of schools. Budgetary expenditure on education by the Secretariat of State for Education and Culture in 1997 was 5,114.7m. pesos, representing 14.3% of total government spending.

Public Holidays

2005: 1 January (New Year's Day), 6 January (Epiphany), 21 January (Our Lady of Altagracia), 26 January (Duarte), 27 February (Independence), 25 March (Good Friday), 14 April (Pan-American Day), 1 May (Labour Day), 16 July (Foundation of Sociedad la Trinitaria), 16 August (Restoration Day), 24 September (Our Lady of Mercedes), 12 October (Columbus Day), 24 October (United Nations Day), 1 November (All Saints' Day), 6 November (Constitution Day), 25 December (Christmas Day).

2006: 1 January (New Year's Day), 6 January (Epiphany), 21 January (Our Lady of Altagracia), 26 January (Duarte), 27 February (Independence), 14 April (Good Friday and Pan-American Day), 1 May (Labour Day), 16 July (Foundation of Sociedad la Trinitaria), 16 August (Restoration Day), 24 September (Our Lady of Mercedes), 12 October (Columbus Day), 24 October (United Nations Day), 1 November (All Saints' Day), 6 November (Constitution Day), 25 December (Christmas Day).

Weights and Measures

The metric system is officially in force but the imperial system is often used.

Statistical Survey

Sources (unless otherwise stated): Oficina Nacional de Estadística, Edif. de Oficinas Gubernamentales, Avda México, esq. Leopoldo Navarro, Santo Domingo; tel. 682-7777; fax 685-4424; e-mail direccion@one.gov.do; internet www.one.gov.do; Banco Central de la República Dominicana, Calle Pedro Henríquez Ureña, esq. Leopoldo Navarro, Apdo 1347, Santo Domingo; tel. 221-9111; fax 686-7488; e-mail info@bancentral.gov.do; internet www.bancentral.gov.do.

Area and Population

AREA, POPULATION AND DENSITY

Area (sq km)	
Land	48,072
Inland water	350
Total	48,422*
Population (census results)†	
24 September 1993	7,293,390
May 2002	
Males	4,297,326
Females	4,265,215
Total	8,562,541
Population (official estimates at mid-year)‡	
1999	8,324,945
2000	8,518,483
2001	8,528,000§
Density (per sq km) at census of May 2002	176.8

* 18,696 sq miles.
† Excluding adjustment for underenumeration.
‡ Not adjusted to take account of the results of the 1993 or 2002 census.
§ Preliminary figure.

PROVINCES*
(population at census of May 2002)

Santo Domingo†	1,822,028	Monseñor Nouel		153,213
Distrito Nacional†	916,398	Valverde		144,297
Santiago	810,462	Maria Trinidad		
		Sánchez		126,848
San Cristóbal	499,998	Monte Cristi		104,795
La Vega	378,523	Bahoruco		92,111
Puerto Plata	288,602	Samaná		92,102
San Pedro de Macorís	284,997	Salcedo		91,030
Duarte	274,858	El Seybo		81,326
San Juan	232,674	Hato Mayor		81,074
Espaillat	210,897	Elias Piña		59,669
Azua	202,565	San José de Ocoa		59,335
La Romana	202,320	Dajabón		58,150
La Altagracia	179,041	Santiago Rodríguez		54,629
Barahona	174,043	Independencia		46,870
Monte Plata	173,471	Pedernales		19,756
Peravía	160,328			
Sánchez Ramírez	154,312	**Total**		8,230,722

* Preliminary figures.
† Formerly formed the single province of Distrito Nacional.

PRINCIPAL TOWNS
(estimated population, 2000)

Santo Domingo DN			
(capital)	2,677,056	San Felipe de Puerto	
		Plata	150,237
Santiago de los			
Caballeros	580,745	Moca	142,780
Concepción de la			
Vega	241,917	San Juan de la	
		Maguana	136,822
San Cristóbal	199,693	Bonao	134,443
San Francisco de			
Macorís	198,068	Bajos de Haina	119,732
La Romana	189,900	Baní	110,353
San Pedro de Macorís	179,686	Cotuí	103,089

Mid-2003 (UN estimate, incl. suburbs): Santo Domingo 1,864,858 (Source: UN, *World Urbanization Prospects: The 2003 Revision*).

Births and deaths (1997): Registered live births 164,556 (birth rate 25.2 per 1,000); Registered deaths 26,301 (death rate 5.8 per 1,000).

Expectation of life (WHO estimates, years at birth): 68.0 (males 64.9; females 71.5) in 2002 (Source: WHO, *World Health Report*).

ECONOMICALLY ACTIVE POPULATION
('000 persons aged 10 years and over, national survey, April 2002)

	Males	Females	Total
Agriculture, hunting and forestry } Fishing	483.4	17.0	500.4
Mining and quarrying	8.7	0.0	8.7
Manufacturing	304.1	163.7	467.8
Electricity, gas and water supply	23.3	6.3	29.5
Construction	180.5	3.4	183.9
Wholesale and retail trade	461.3	255.0	716.3
Hotels and restaurants	74.7	117.7	192.4
Transport, storage and communications	222.0	20.6	242.6
Financial intermediation } Real estate, renting and business } activities	32.9	33.4	66.4
Public administration and defence	122.7	46.8	169.4
Education } Health and social work Other community, social and personal service activities }	258.7	473.0	731.6
Total employed	2,172.3	1,136.8	3,309.1
Unemployed	220.5	413.8	634.3
Total labour force	2,392.8	1,550.6	3,943.5

Health and Welfare

KEY INDICATORS

Total fertility rate (children per woman, 2002)	2.7
Under-5 mortality rate (per 1,000 live births, 2003)	35
HIV/AIDS (% of persons aged 15–49, 2003)	1.7
Physicians (per 1,000 head, 1997)	2.16
Hospital beds (per 1,000 head, 1996)	1.5
Health expenditure (2001): US $ per head (PPP)	353
Health expenditure (2001): % of GDP	6.1
Health expenditure (2001): public (% of total)	36.1
Access to water (% of persons, 2002)	93
Access to sanitation (% of persons, 2002)	57
Human Development Index (2002): ranking	98
Human Development Index (2002): value	0.738

For sources and definitions, see explanatory note on p. vi.

Agriculture

PRINCIPAL CROPS
('000 metric tons)

	2001	2002	2003
Rice (paddy)	721.7	730.7	609.2
Maize	36.5	30.3	39.2
Potatoes	64.7	48.6	45.9
Sweet potatoes	32.3	32.3	32.6
Cassava (Manioc)	123.9	120.2	123.9
Yautia (Cocoyam)	39.5	59.4	61.3
Sugar cane	4,645.3	4,846.5	5,036.3
Dry beans	30.3	29.4	29.1
Coconuts	169.1	171.8	177.7
Oil palm fruit*	153.0	155.0	155.0
Tomatoes	203.0	154.9	155.0*
Pumpkins, squash and gourds* .	23.0	23.5	23.5
Chillies and peppers, green . .	24.6	28.7	30.0*
Dry onions	41.2	42.7	43.0*
Garlic	4.1	7.0	7.0*
Carrots	26.7	20.8	21.0*
Cantaloupes and other melons* .	52.0	53.0	53.0
Other fresh vegetables* . . .	35.3	34.3	35.0
Bananas	442.0	502.9	481.0*
Plantains*	190.0	192.0	192.5
Oranges	66.7	86.1	88.0*
Mangoes*	185.0	185.5	185.5
Avocados	111.1	147.5	150.0*
Pineapples	136.9	108.6	110.0*
Papayas*	24.0	24.5	25.0
Other fresh fruit*	42.2	43.7	44.3
Coffee (green)	35.5	49.0	50.0*
Cocoa beans	44.9	49.7	50.0*
Tobacco (leaves)*	17.5	18.0	18.5

* FAO estimate(s).

Source: FAO.

LIVESTOCK
('000 head, year ending September)

	2001	2002	2003*
Horses*	340	342	343
Mules*	140	140	141
Asses*	150	150	151
Cattle	2,106.8	2,159.6	2,160.0
Pigs	565.5	577.0*	577.5
Sheep	106.0	121.3	122.0
Goats	187.4	188.0	188.5
Poultry	47,380	46,000*	46,500

* FAO estimate(s).

Source: FAO.

LIVESTOCK PRODUCTS
('000 metric tons)

	2001	2002	2003*
Beef and veal	70.8	71.7	72.0
Pig meat	63.1	64.0	65.0
Poultry meat	203.4	185.3	185.5
Cows' milk	420.3	517.7	520.0
Cheese	2.5*	3.7	3.7
Butter	1.5*	1.8	1.8
Hen eggs	77.0	82.4	83.0
Honey	1.4*	1.3	1.3
Cattle hides (fresh)*	8.8	8.9	8.9

* FAO estimate(s).

Source: FAO.

Forestry

ROUNDWOOD REMOVALS
('000 cubic metres, excl. bark)

	1983	1984	1985
Sawlogs, veneer logs and logs for sleepers	4	4	4
Other industrial wood	3	3	3
Fuel wood	531	543	556
Total	538	550	563

1986–2003: Annual production as in 1985 (FAO estimates).

Source: FAO.

Fishing

('000 metric tons, live weight)

	2000	2001	2002
Capture	11.0	13.2	18.3
Tilapia	—	0.5	1.2
Groupers, seabasses	0.9	0.9	1.1
Common carp	—	0.4	0.7
Snappers and jobfishes . . .	1.1	0.9	2.3
Grunts, sweetlips	0.3	0.4	0.3
Nurse shark	0.4	0.1	—
Caribbean spiny lobster . . .	1.3	1.2	3.0
Stromboid conchs	1.8	1.4	2.3
Aquaculture	2.1	2.6	3.6
Common carp	0.6	0.4	0.5
Total catch	13.2	15.9	21.9

Source: FAO.

Mining

	1999	2000	2001
Ferro-nickel ('000 metric tons) .	85	85	85*
Gold (kilograms)	651	—	—
Silver (kilograms)	3,140	—	—

* Estimate.

Source: US Geological Survey.

Industry

SELECTED PRODUCTS
('000 metric tons, unless otherwise indicated)

	1999	2000	2001
Wheat flour	391	245	272
Refined sugar	82	101	113
Cement	2,295	2,521	2,758
Beer ('000 hectolitres) . . .	3,484	3,666	3,176
Cigarettes (million)	4,005	n.a.	n.a.
Motor spirit (gasoline) . . .	303	345	n.a.
Electricity (million kWh) . . .	9,292	9,701	n.a.

Source: UN, *Industrial Commodity Statistics Yearbook*.

Finance

CURRENCY AND EXCHANGE RATES

Monetary Units
100 centavos = 1 Dominican Republic peso (RD $ or peso oro).

Sterling, Dollar and Euro Equivalents (31 December 2004)
£1 sterling = 60.085 pesos;
US $1 = 31.109 pesos;
€1 = 42.374 pesos;
1,000 Dominican Republic pesos = £16.64 = $32.14 = €23.60.

Average Exchange Rate (RD $ per US $)
2002   18.610
2003   30.831
2004   42.120

BUDGET
(RD $ million)

Revenue	2001	2002	2003*
Tax revenue	58,058.3	63,866.6	74,247.8
Taxes on income and profits	15,317.7	16,032.7	20,384.8
Taxes on goods and services	27,964.8	31,484.5	34,498.3
Taxes on international trade and transactions	13,415.1	14,773.4	17,573.0
Other current revenue	1,583.5	2,428.5	5,397.6
Capital revenue	213.9	782.9	39.3
Total	59,855.8	67,078.0	79,684.6

Expenditure	2001	2002	2003*
Current expenditure	43,419.3	48,383.6	59,421.5
Wages and salaries	21,496.2	24,925.4	26,107.7
Other services	2,075.5	3,275.1	4,325.9
Materials and supplies	4,048.7	4,477.5	5,288.7
Current transfers	12,157.3	10,650.9	14,072.6
Interest payments	2,989.9	4,386.5	7,844.1
Internal debt	726.8	1,534.9	2,336.6
External debt	2,263.2	2,851.6	5,507.4
Capital expenditure	15,444.1	18,993.8	16,325.7
Machines and equipment	994.5	1,241.7	854.7
Construction of works and agricultural plantations	7,624.7	8,309.8	7,286.2
Capital transfers	6,196.0	8,736.3	7,758.4
Total (incl. others)	58,863.4	67,377.4	75,747.2

* Preliminary figures.

INTERNATIONAL RESERVES
(US $ million at 31 December)

	2001	2002	2003
Gold*	5.1	5.2	7.6
IMF special drawing rights	0.4	0.3	0.1
Foreign exchange	1,099.0	468.1	253.0
Total	1,104.5	473.6	260.7

* Valued at market-related prices.

Source: IMF, *International Financial Statistics*.

MONEY SUPPLY
(RD $ million at 31 December)

	2001	2002	2003
Currency outside banks	16,628	18,265	29,631
Demand deposits at commercial banks	24,529	25,341	41,736
Total money (incl. others)	41,258	43,765	72,013

Source: IMF, *International Financial Statistics*.

COST OF LIVING
(Consumer Price Index; base: 2000 = 100)

	2001	2002	2003
Food	106.1	110.7	140.1
Clothing	104.7	108.4	117.1
Rent	106.7	120.6	165.0
All items (incl. others)	108.9	114.6	146.0

Source: ILO.

NATIONAL ACCOUNTS

National Income and Product
(RD $ million at current prices)

	2000	2001	2002
GDP in market prices	321,783	361,569	396,117
Net primary income from abroad	−17,047	−18,439	−21,041
Gross national income (GNI)	304,736	343,130	375,076
Less Consumption of fixed capital	19,307	21,694	23,767
Net national income	285,429	321,436	351,309

Source: IMF, *International Financial Statistics*.

Expenditure on the Gross Domestic Product
(RD $ million at current prices)

	2000	2001	2002
Final consumption expenditure	276,070	305,995	339,030
Households			
Non-profit institutions serving households	248,930	273,148	300,799
General government	27,140	32,847	38,231
Gross capital formation	77,091	83,695	91,869
Gross fixed capital formation	76,164	82,653	90,727
Changes in inventories			
Acquisitions, *less* disposals, of valuables	927	1,042	1,142
Total domestic expenditure	353,161	389,690	430,899
Exports of goods and services	146,094	141,583	152,286
Less Imports of goods and services	177,473	169,704	187,068
GDP in market prices	321,783	361,569	396,117
GDP at constant 1970 prices	6,611	6,823	7,105

Source: IMF, *International Financial Statistics*.

Gross Domestic Product by Economic Activity
(RD $ million at constant 1970 prices)

	2001	2002	2003*
Agriculture, hunting, forestry and fishing	816.0	836.1	811.7
Mining and quarrying	105.0	102.1	111.0
Manufacturing	1,096.5	1,140.6	1,109.6
Electricity and water	165.2	178.0	163.0
Construction	876.9	905.0	828.4
Wholesale and retail trade, restaurants and hotels	1,324.3	1,371.5	1,387.5
Transport, storage and communications	975.6	1,069.9	1,128.8
Finance, insurance and real estate	544.3	558.3	547.1
Community, social, personal and business services†	1,006.2	1,045.0	1,088.1
Total	6,910.0	7,206.7	7,175.3

* Preliminary figures.
† Including gas.

BALANCE OF PAYMENTS
(US $ million)

	2001	2002	2003
Exports of goods f.o.b	5,276.3	5,165.0	5,439.4
Imports of goods f.o.b.	−8,779.3	−8,837.7	−7,883.4
Trade balance	−3,503.0	−3,672.7	−2,444.0
Exports of services	3,110.3	3,070.8	3,435.3
Imports of services	−1,283.9	−1,313.5	−1,216.1
Balance on goods and services	−1,676.6	−1,915.4	−224.8
Other income received	271.2	300.4	343.7
Other income paid	−1,362.9	−1,452.2	−1,587.3
Balance on goods, services and income	−2,768.3	−3,067.2	−1,468.4
Current transfers received	2,232.0	2,451.9	2,510.3
Current transfers paid	−204.5	−182.6	−174.8
Current balance	−740.8	−797.9	867.1
Direct investment from abroad	1,079.1	916.8	309.9
Portfolio investment assets	123.5	−14.0	−20.1
Portfolio investment liabilities	480.2	−11.7	552.6
Other investment assets	−155.5	−1,402.2	−1,535.2
Other investment liabilities	180.1	894.1	−160.6
Net errors and omissions	−451.9	−139.3	−468.1
Overall balance	514.7	−554.2	−454.4

Source: IMF, *International Financial Statistics*.

External Trade

PRINCIPAL COMMODITIES

Imports f.o.b. (US $ million)*	2001	2002	2003
Consumer goods	2,875.0	3,107.6	2,532.8
Durable goods	576.0	784.9	348.2
Foodstuffs	258.6	288.4	260.3
Petroleum products	944.8	947.7	997.7
Raw materials	1,792.6	1,863.9	1,815.7
Artificial plastic materials	129.1	143.3	130.3
Petroleum and petroleum products	307.4	349.5	431.1
Cast iron and steel	173.8	188.3	163.6
Capital goods	1,285.3	1,265.9	917.4
For transport	184.3	237.8	131.8
For industry	311.0	232.7	192.8
Machinery	326.6	309.0	209.5
Total (incl. others)	5,952.9	6,237.3	5,265.8

* Figures exclude imports into free-trade zones.

Exports f.o.b. (US $ million)*	2001	2002	2003
Sugar and sugar cane derivatives	88.8	99.2	99.3
Raw cane sugar	64.6	74.0	75.3
Cocoa and cocoa manufactures	42.7	67.0	77.2
Cocoa beans	38.1	60.8	67.9
Tobacco and tobacco manufactures	30.4	25.5	25.0
Ferro-nickel	145.2	156.2	238.7
Other goods	334.2	374.2	432.2
Petroleum products	125.5	98.8	137.7
Total	794.7	847.7	1,040.7

* Figures exclude exports from free-trade zones, which totalled: US $4,481.6m. in 2001; US $4,317.3m. in 2002; US $4,398.7m. in 2003.

PRINCIPAL TRADING PARTNERS
(US $ '000)

Imports c.i.f.	1998	1999	2000
Argentina	60,697	40,687	24,808
Brazil	57,863	66,193	80,719
Canada	40,593	40,549	41,350
Colombia	45,434	65,040	75,199
Denmark	36,396	32,633	50,886
Germany	51,507	59,488	87,814
Italy	43,434	46,340	57,698
Japan	148,285	237,190	266,938
Korea, Democratic People's Republic	35,139	21,199	16,025
Mexico	245,284	265,894	436,254
Panama	80,808	124,101	157,221
Puerto Rico	131,209	72,388	88,813
Spain	125,141	143,688	243,198
Taiwan	46,847	72,018	79,221
USA	1,700,855	2,436,210	2,962,044
Venezuela	403,918	673,960	979,449
Total (incl. others)	3,446,603	4,635,545	5,953,829

Exports f.o.b.	1998	1999	2000
Belgium-Luxembourg	75,774	71,220	123,293
Canada	26,490	15,690	5,160
Cuba	2,422	4,604	10,114
France	10,805	11,930	11,227
Germany	30,236	28,467	26,908
Haiti	47,601	67,543	57,936
Italy	17,935	9,208	12,892
Japan	18,461	8,525	11,949
Korea, Republic	18,618	18,208	38,517
Mexico	9,356	4,897	3,343
Netherlands	12,526	11,668	17,340
Panama	9,960	17,923	18,879
Puerto Rico	74,012	91,948	97,505
Spain	17,262	16,931	15,300
United Kingdom	2,035	6,518	10,836
USA	448,509	327,875	373,462
Total (incl. others)	861,990	743,561	866,054

Source: Inter-American Development Bank.

Transport

ROAD TRAFFIC
(motor vehicles in use)

	1999	2000	2001
Passenger cars ('000)	445.9	455.6	561.3
Commercial vehicles ('000)	247.2	283.0	284.7

Source: UN, *Statistical Yearbook*.

SHIPPING

Merchant Fleet
(registered at 31 December)

	2001	2002	2003
Number of vessels	20	19	20
Total displacement ('000 grt)	9.4	9.2	12.8

Source: Lloyd's Register-Fairplay, *World Fleet Statistics*.

International Sea-borne Freight Traffic
('000 metric tons)

	1996	1997	1998
Goods loaded	112	152	139

Source: UN, *Monthly Bulletin of Statistics*.

CIVIL AVIATION
(traffic on scheduled services)

	1997	1998	1999
Kilometres flown (million) . . .	1	1	0
Passengers carried ('000)	34	34	10
Passengers-km (million)	16	16	5
Total ton-km (million)	1	1	0

Source: UN, *Statistical Yearbook*.

Tourism

ARRIVALS BY NATIONALITY

	2001	2002	2003
Canada	283,490	313,491	412,625
France	194,090	242,022	317,215
Germany	333,559	240,546	243,135
Italy	113,826	113,569	135,293
Spain	138,281	135,522	201,864
United Kingdom	139,582	146,257	171,696
USA	666,290	710,875	865,942
Total (incl. others)	3,088,548	3,104,709	3,562,770

Receipts from Tourism (US $ million): 2,860 in 2000; 2,798 in 2001; 2,736 in 2002 (Source: World Tourism Organization).

Communications Media

	1999	2000	2001
Telephones ('000 main lines in use)	826.7	894.2	955.1
Mobile cellular telephones ('000 subscribers)	424.4	705.4	1,270.1
Internet users ('000)	35.0	55.0	186.0

Daily newspapers: 10 in 1998 (average circulation 1.3m. copies).

Radio receivers ('000 in use): 1,440 in 1997.

Television receivers ('000 in use): 790 in 1998.

Facsimile machines (number in use): 2,300 in 1996.

Sources: UNESCO, *Statistical Yearbook*; UN, *Statistical Yearbook*; International Telecommunication Union.

Education

(1996/97)

	Institutions	Teachers	Students		
			Males	Females	Total
Pre-primary*	n.a.	8,571	96,252	94,289	190,541
Primary . . .	4,001†	39,860	691,675	668,369	1,360,044
Secondary: . .					
general . .	1,737	11,033	145,560*	184,384*	329,944*
teacher training† .	n.a.	86	549	743	1,292
vocational† .	n.a.	1,211	9,147	12,356	21,503
Higher . . .	n.a.	9,041	75,223	101,772	176,995

* 1997/98 figure(s).
† 1994/95 figure(s).

Source: UNESCO, *Statistical Yearbook*.

Adult literacy rate (UNESCO estimates): 84.4% (males 84.3%; females 84.4%) in 2002 (Source: UN Development Programme, *Human Development Report*).

Directory

The Constitution

The Constitution of the Dominican Republic was promulgated on 28 November 1966, and amended on 14 August 1994. Its main provisions are summarized below:

The Dominican Republic is a sovereign, free, independent state; no organizations set up by the State can bring about any act which might cause direct or indirect intervention in the internal or foreign affairs of the State or which might threaten the integrity of the State. The Dominican Republic recognizes and applies the norms of general and American international law and is in favour of and will support any initiative towards economic integration for the countries of America. The civil, republican, democratic, representative Government is divided into three independent powers: legislative, executive and judicial.

The territory of the Dominican Republic is as laid down in the Frontier Treaty of 1929 and its Protocol of Revision of 1936.

The life and property of the individual citizen are inviolable; there can be no sentence of death, torture nor any sentence which might cause physical harm to the individual. There is freedom of thought, of conscience, of religion, freedom to publish, freedom of unarmed association, provided that there is no subversion against public order, national security or decency. There is freedom of labour and trade unions; freedom to strike, except in the case of public services, according to the dispositions of the law.

The State will undertake agrarian reform, dedicating the land to useful interests and gradually eliminating the latifundios (large estates). The State will do all in its power to support all aspects of family life. Primary education is compulsory and all education is free. Social security services will be developed. Every Dominican has the duty to give what civil and military service the State may require. Every legally entitled citizen must exercise the right to vote, i.e. all persons over 18 years of age and all who are or have been married even if they are not yet 18.

GOVERNMENT

Legislative power is exercised by Congress which is made up of the Senate and Chamber of Deputies, elected by direct vote. Senators, one for each of the 31 Provinces and one for the Distrito Nacional, are elected for four years; they must be Dominicans in full exercise of their citizen's rights, and at least 25 years of age. Their duties are to elect the President and other members of the Electoral and Accounts Councils, and to approve the nomination of diplomats. Deputies, one for every 50,000 inhabitants or fraction over 25,000 in each Province and the Distrito Nacional, are elected for four years and must fulfil the same conditions for election as Senators.

Decisions of Congress are taken by absolute majority of at least half the members of each house; urgent matters require a two-thirds' majority. Both houses normally meet on 27 February and 16 August each year for sessions of 90 days, which can be extended for a further 60 days.

Executive power is exercised by the President of the Republic, who is elected by direct vote for a four-year term. No President may serve more than one consecutive term. The successful presidential candidate must obtain at least 50% plus one vote of the votes cast; if necessary, a second round of voting is held 45 days later, with the participation of the two parties that obtained the highest number of votes. The President must be a Dominican citizen by birth or origin, over 30 years of age and in full exercise of citizen's rights. The President must not have engaged in any active military or police service for at least a year prior to election. The President takes office on 16 August following the election. The President of the Republic is Head of the Public Administration and Supreme Chief of the armed forces and police forces. The President's duties include nominating Secretaries and Assistant Secretaries of State and other public officials, promulgating and publishing laws and resolutions of Congress and seeing to their faithful execution, watching over the collection and just investment of national income, nominating, with the approval of the Senate, members of the Diplomatic Corps, receiving foreign Heads of State, presiding at national functions, decreeing a State of Siege or Emergency or any other measures necessary during a public crisis. The President may not leave the country for more than 15 days without authorization from Congress. In the absence of the President, the Vice-President will assume power, or failing him, the President of the Supreme Court of Justice. The legislative and municipal elections are held two years after the presidential elections, mid-way through the presidential term.

LOCAL GOVERNMENT

Government in the Distrito Nacional and the Municipalities is in the hands of local councils, with members elected proportionally to the number of inhabitants, but numbering at least five. Each Province has a civil Governor, designated by the Executive.

JUDICIARY

Judicial power is exercised by the Supreme Court of Justice and the other Tribunals; no judicial official may hold another public office or employment, other than honorary or teaching. The Supreme Court is made up of at least 11 judges, who must be Dominican citizens by birth or origin, at least 35 years old, in full exercise of their citizen's rights, graduates in law and have practised professionally for at least 12 years. The National Judiciary Council appoints the members of the Supreme Court, who in turn appoint judges at all other levels of the judicial system. There are nine Courts of Appeal, a Lands Tribunal and a Court of the First Instance in each judicial district; in each Municipality and in the Distrito Nacional there are also Justices of the Peace.

Elections are directed by the Central Electoral Board. The armed forces are essentially obedient and apolitical, created for the defence of national independence and the maintenance of public order and the Constitution and Laws.

The artistic and historical riches of the country, whoever owns them, are part of the cultural heritage of the country and are under the safe-keeping of the State. Mineral deposits belong to the State. There is freedom to form political parties, provided they conform to the principles laid down in the Constitution. Justice is administered without charge throughout the Republic.

This Constitution can be reformed if the proposal for reform is supported in Congress by one-third of the members of either house or by the Executive. A special session of Congress must be called and any resolutions must have a two-thirds' majority. There can be no reform of the method of government, which must always be civil, republican, democratic and representative. Note: In July 2002 a National Constituent Assembly voted in favour of amending the Constitution to enable presidents to serve two consecutive terms; a further proposal to allow presidential candidates to win an election with less than 50% of votes cast was also under discussion.

The Government

HEAD OF STATE

President: LEONEL FERNÁNDEZ REYNA (took office 16 August 2004).
Vice-President: Dra RAFAEL ALBURQUEQUE.

CABINET
(April 2005)

Secretary of State to the Presidency: DANILO MEDINA.
Secretary of State for External Relations: CARLOS MORALES TRONCOSO.
Secretary of State for the Interior and Police: FRANKLIN ALMEYDA.
Secretary of State for the Armed Forces: Rear-Adm. SIGFRIDO PARED PÉREZ.
Secretary of State for Finance: VICENTE BENGOA.
Secretary of State for Education: ALEJANDRINA GERMÁN.
Secretary of State for Agriculture: ALMICAR ROMERO.
Secretary of State for Public Works and Communications: MANUEL DE JESÚS PÉREZ.
Secretary of State for Public Health and Social Welfare: SABINO BAÉZ.
Secretary of State for Industry and Commerce: FRANCISCO JAVIER GARCÍA.
Secretary of State for Labour: JOSÉ RAMÓN FADUL.
Secretary of State for Tourism: FELIX JIMÉNEZ.
Secretary of State for Sport, Physical Education and Recreation: FELIPE JAY PAYANO.

Secretary of State for Art and Culture: JOSÉ RAFAEL LANTIGUA.
Secretary of State for Higher Education, Science and Technology: LIGIA AMADA DE MELO.
Secretary of State for Women: GLADYS GUTIÉRREZ.
Secretary of State for Youth: MANUEL CRESPO.
Secretary of State for the Environment and Natural Resources: MAXIMILIAMO PUIG.
Technical Secretary of State to the Presidency: JUAN TEMISTOCLES MONTAS.
Administrative Secretary of State to the Presidency: LUIS MANUEL BONETTI.
Secretary of State without Portfolio: LUIS INCHAUSTI.
Secretary of State without Portfolio: BIENVENIDO PEREZ.

SECRETARIATS OF STATE

Administrative Secretariat of the Presidency: Palacio Nacional, Avda México, esq. Dr Delgado, Santo Domingo, DN; tel. 686-4771; fax 688-2100; e-mail prensa@presidencia.gov.do; internet www.presidencia.gov.do.
Technical Secretariat of the Presidency: Avda México, esq. Dr Delgado, Santo Domingo, DN; tel. 221-5140; fax 221-8627; internet www.stp.gov.do.
Secretariat of State for Agriculture: Autopista Duarte, Km 6.5, Los Jardines del Norte, Santo Domingo, DN; tel. 547-3888; fax 227-1268; e-mail sec.agric@codetel.net.do; internet www.agricultura.gov.do.
Secretariat of State for the Armed Forces: Plaza de la Independencia, Avda 27 de Febrero, esq. Luperón, Santo Domingo, DN; tel. 530-5149; fax 531-1309; internet www.secffaa.mil.do.
Secretariat of State for Art and Culture: Avda Máximo Gómez 10, esq. Santiago, Santo Domingo, DN; tel. 688-9700; fax 689-8907; e-mail decultura@hotmail.com; internet www.cultura.gov.do.
Secretariat of State for Education: Avda Máximo Gómez 10, esq. Santiago, Santo Domingo, DN; tel. 688-9700; fax 689-8907; e-mail sub-administrativo@see.gov.do; internet www.see.gov.do.
Secretariat of State for External Relations: Avda Independencia 752, Santo Domingo, DN; tel. 535-6280; fax 533-5772; e-mail correspondencia@serex.gov.do; internet www.serex.gov.do.
Secretariat of State for the Environment and Natural Resources: Santo Domingo, DN.
Secretariat of State for Finance: Avda México 45, esq. Leopoldo Navarro, Santo Domingo, DN; tel. 687-5131; fax 688-6561; e-mail webmaster@finanzas.gov.do; internet www.finanzas.gov.do.
Secretariat of State for Higher Education, Science and Technology: Centro de los Héroes, Avda Enrique Jiménez Moya, esq. Juan de Dios Ventura Simó, 5°, Santo Domingo, DN; tel. 533-3881; fax 535-4694; e-mail info@seescyt.gov.do; internet www.seescyt.gov.do.
Secretariat of State for Industry and Commerce: Edif. de Oficinas Gubernamentales, 7°, Avda Francia, esq. Leopoldo Navarro, Santo Domingo, DN; tel. 685-5171; fax 686-4741; e-mail ind.comercio@codetel.net.do; internet www.seic.gov.do.
Secretariat of State for the Interior and Police: Edif. de Oficinas Gubernamentales, 3°, Avda Francia, esq. Leopoldo Navarro, Santo Domingo, DN; tel. 686-6251; fax 221-8234.
Secretariat of State for Labour: Centro de los Héroes, Jiménez Moya 9, Santo Domingo, DN; tel. 535-4404; fax 535-4590; e-mail secret.trabajo@codetel.net.do; internet www.set.gov.do.
Secretariat of State for Public Health and Social Welfare: Avda Tiradentes, esq. San Cristóbal, Ensanche La Fe, Santo Domingo, DN; tel. 541-3121; fax 540-6445; e-mail saludp@saludpublica.gov.do; internet www.saludpublica.gov.do.
Secretariat of State for Public Works and Communications: Avda San Cristóbal, esq. Tiradentes, Ensanche La Fe, Santo Domingo, DN; tel. 565-2811; fax 562-3382; e-mail info.seopc@codetel.net.do; internet www.seopc.gov.do.
Secretariat of State for Sport, Physical Education and Recreation: Avda Ortega y Gasset, Centro Olímpico, Santo Domingo, DN; tel. 540-4010; fax 563-6586; internet www.sedefir.gov.do.
Secretariat of State for Tourism: Bloque D, Edif. de Oficinas Gubernamentales, Avda México, esq. 30 de Marzo, Apdo 497, Santo Domingo, DN; tel. 221-4660; fax 682-3806; e-mail sectur@codetel.net.do; internet www.dominicana.com.do.
Secretariat of State for Women: Bloque D, Edif. de Oficinas Gubernamentales, Avda México, esq. 30 de Marzo, Santo Domingo, DN; tel. 685-3755; fax 686-0911.

Secretariat of State for Youth: Avda John F. Kennedy, esq. Ortega y Gasset, Plaza Metro Politana, Santo Domingo, DN; tel. 732-7227; fax 472-8585; e-mail juventud@verizon.net.do.

President and Legislature

PRESIDENT

Election, 16 May 2004

Candidate	% of votes cast
Leonel Fernández Reyna (PLD)	57.11
Rafael Hipólito Mejía Domínguez (PRD) . . .	33.65
Rafael Eduardo Estrella Virella (PRSC)	8.65
Total (incl. others)	100.00

CONGRESO NACIONAL

The National Congress comprises a Senate and a Chamber of Deputies.

President of the Senate: ANDRES BAUTISTA (PRD).

President of the Chamber of Deputies: ALFREDO PACHECO (PRD).

General Election, 16 May 2002

	Seats	
	Senate	Chamber of Deputies
Partido Revolucionario Dominicano (PRD)	29	73
Partido de la Liberación Dominicana (PLD)	2	41
Partido Reformista Social Cristiano (PRSC)	1	36
Total	32	150

Political Organizations

Alianza por la Democracia (APD): Santo Domingo, DN; f. 1992 by breakaway group of the PLD; split into two factions (led, respectively, by Max Puig and Nélsida Marmolejos) in 1993; Sec.-Gen. VICENTE BENGOA.

Frente Independiente Leonel al Poder (FILA): Santo Domingo, DN; f. 2002; established by former Pres. Leonel Fernández to support his candidacy in 2004 presidential election; Pres. VICENTE BENGOA.

Fuerza Nacional Progresista (FNP): Santo Domingo, DN; right-wing; Leader MARIO VINICIO CASTILLO.

Fuerza de la Revolución: Avda Independencia 258, Apdo 2651, Santo Domingo, DN; e-mail fr@nodo50.ix.apc.org; internet www.nodo50.org/fr; f. 2000 by merger of the Partido Communista Dominicano, Movimiento Liberador 12 de Enero, Fuerza de Resistencia y Liberación Popular, Fuerza Revolucionaria 21 de Julio and other revolutionary groups; Marxist-Leninist.

Movimiento de Conciliación Nacional (MCN): Pina 207, Santo Domingo, DN; f. 1969; centre party; 659,277 mems; Pres. Dr JAIME M. FERNÁNDEZ; Sec. VÍCTOR MENA.

Movimiento de Integración Democrática (MIDA): Santo Domingo, DN; tel. 687-8895; centre-right; Leader Dr FRANCISCO AUGUSTO LORA.

Movimiento Popular Dominicano: Santo Domingo, DN; left-wing; Leader JULIO DE PEÑA VALDÉS.

Participación Ciudadana: Desiderio Arias 25, La Julia, Santo Domingo, DN; tel. 535-6200; fax 535-6631; e-mail p.ciudadana@codetel.net.do; internet www.pciudadana.com; f. 1993; Leaders JAVIER CABREJA POLANCO, RAMÓN TEJADA HOLGUÍN, JUAN BOLÍVAR DÍAZ.

Partido Demócrata Popular: Arz. Meriño 259, Santo Domingo, DN; tel. 685-2920; Leader LUIS HOMERO LÁJARA BURGOS.

Partido de la Liberación Dominicana (PLD): Avda Independencia 401, Santo Domingo, DN; tel. 685-3540; fax 687-5569; e-mail pldorg@pld.org.do; internet www.pld.org.do; f. 1973 by breakaway group of PRD; left-wing; Leader LEONEL FERNÁNDEZ REYNA; Sec.-Gen. REINALDO PARED PÉREZ.

Partido Quisqueyano Demócrata (PQD): Bolivar 51, esq. Uruguay, Santo Domingo, DN; tel. 565-0244; internet www.geocities

.com/CapitolHill/Senate/7090/; f. 1968; right-wing; 600,000 mems; Pres. Lic. PEDRO BERGÉS; Sec.-Gen. Dr ELÍAS WESSIN CHÁVEZ.

Partido Reformista Social Cristiano (PRSC): Avda San Cristóbal, Ensanche La Fe, Apdo 1332, Santo Domingo, DN; tel. 566-7089; f. 1964; centre-right party; Pres. RAFAEL BELLO ANDINO.

Partido Revolucionario Dominicano (PRD): Espaillat 118, Santo Domingo, DN; tel. 687-2193; e-mail prd@partidos.com; internet www.prd.partidos.com; f. 1939; democratic socialist; mem. of Socialist International; 400,000 mems; Chair. VICENTE SÁNCHEZ BARET; Sec.-Gen. RAFAEL SUBERVÍ BONILLA.

Partido Revolucionario Independiente (PRI): Santo Domingo, DN; f. 1985 after split by the PRD's right-wing faction; Pres. JOSÉ RAFAEL MOLINA UREÑA; Sec.-Gen. STORMI REYNOSO.

Partido Revolucionario Social Cristiano: Santo Domingo, DN; f. 1961; left-wing; Pres. Dr CLAUDIO ISIDORO ACOSTA; Sec.-Gen. Dr ALFONSO LOCKWARD.

Partido de los Trabajadores Dominicanos: Avda Duarte 69 (Altos), Santo Domingo, DN; tel. 685-7705; f. 1979; workers' party; Sec.-Gen. JOSÉ GONZÁLEZ ESPINOZA.

Unidad Democrática (UD): Santo Domingo, DN; Leader FERNANDO ALVAREZ BOGAERT.

Other parties include Unión Cívica Nacional (UCN), Partido Alianza Social Demócrata (ASD—Leader Dr JOSÉ RAFAEL ABINADER), Movimiento Nacional de Salvación (MNS—Leader LUIS JULIÁN PÉREZ), Partido Comunista del Trabajo de la República Dominicana (Sec.-Gen. RAFAEL CHALJUB MEJÍA), Partido de Veteranos Civiles (PVC), Partido Acción Constitucional (PAC), Partido Unión Patriótica (PUP—Leader ROBERTO SANTANA), Partido de Acción Nacional (right-wing) and Movimiento de Acción Social Cristiana (ASC).

Diplomatic Representation

EMBASSIES IN THE DOMINICAN REPUBLIC

Argentina: Avda Máximo Gómez 10, Apdo 1302, Santo Domingo, DN; tel. 682-2977; fax 221-2206; e-mail embarg@aster.com.do; Ambassador JORGE J. A. ROBALLO.

Belize: Carretera La Isabela, Calle Proyecto 3, Arroyo Manzano 1, Santo Domingo, DN; tel. 567-7146; fax 567-7159; e-mail embelize@codetel.net.do; Ambassador R. EDUARDO LAMA S.

Brazil: Avda Winston Churchill 32, Edif. Franco-Acra y Asociados, 2°, Apdo 1655, Santo Domingo, DN; tel. 532-0868; fax 532-0917; e-mail contacto@embajadadebrasil.org.do; internet www.embajadadebrasil.org.do; Ambassador P. G. VILAS-BÔAS CASTRO.

Canada: Apdo 2054, Santo Domingo, DN; tel. 685-1136; fax 682-2691; e-mail sdmgo@dfait-maeci.gc.ca; internet www.dfait-maeci.gc.ca/dominicanrepublic; Ambassador ADAM BLACKWELL.

Chile: Avda Anacaona 11, Mirador del Sur, Santo Domingo, DN; tel. 532-7800; fax 530-8310; e-mail embaj.chile@codetel.net.do; Ambassador RUBIO SANDOVAL CARLOS.

China (Taiwan): Edif. Palic, 1°, Avda Abraham Lincoln, esq. José Amado Soler, Apdo 4797, Santo Domingo, DN; tel. 562-5555; fax 563-4139; e-mail e.china@codetel.net.do; Ambassador CHI TAI FENG.

Colombia: Avda Abraham Lincoln 502, 2°, Santo Domingo, DN; tel. 562-1670; e-mail crdomini@minrelext.gov.co; Ambassador JORGE ENRIQUE GARAVITO DURÁN.

Costa Rica: Ensanche Serralles entre Abraham Lincoln y Lope de Vega, Calle Malaquías Gil 11 Altos, Santo Domingo, DN; tel. 683-7209; fax 565-6467; e-mail embarica@codetel.net.do; Ambassador EKHART PETERS SEEVERS.

Cuba: 808 Francisco Prats Ramírez, esq. El Millón, Santo Domingo, DN; tel. 537-2113; fax 537-9820; e-mail embadom@codetel.net.do; Ambassador OMAR R. CÓRDOVA RIVAS.

Ecuador: Calle Rafael Augusto Sánchez 17, Edif. Profesional Saint Michel, Of. 301, Ensanche Naco, Apdo 808, Santo Domingo, DN; tel. 563-8363; fax 563-8153; e-mail mecuador@codetel.net.do; Ambassador (vacant).

El Salvador: José A. Brea Peña 12, Ensanche Evaristo Morales, Santo Domingo, DN; tel. 565-4311; fax 541-7503; Ambassador Dr CARLOS ERNESTO MENDOZA C.

France: Las Damas 42, Zona Colonial, Santo Domingo, DN; tel. 657-5626; fax 657-5273; e-mail ambafrance@ambafrance-do.org; internet www.ambafrance-do.org; Ambassador JEAN-CLAUDE MOYRET.

Germany: Edif. Torre Piantini, 16°, Calle Gustavo Mejía Ricart, esq. Avda Abraham Lincoln, Santo Domingo, DN; tel. 542-8949; fax 542-8955; e-mail embal@verizon.net.do; Ambassador KARL KÖHLER.

Directory

Guatemala: Calle Santiago 359, Gazcue, Santo Domingo, DN; tel. 689-5327; fax 689-5146; e-mail embrepublicadominicana@minex .gob.gt; Ambassador Gen. BERNA RONALDO MÉNDEZ MARA.

Haiti: Avda Juan Sánchez Ramírez 33, Santo Domingo, DN; tel. 686-5778; fax 686-6096; e-mail amb.haiti@codetel.net.do; Chargé d'affaires a.i. JOSEPH MATHURIN BELONY.

Holy See: Avda Máximo Gómez 27, Apdo 312, Santo Domingo, DN (Apostolic Nunciature); tel. 682-3773; fax 687-0287; Apostolic Nuncio Most Rev. TIMOTHY BROGLIO (Titular Archbishop of Amiternum).

Honduras: Calle Arístides García Mella, esq. Dolores Rodríguez Objío, Edif. El Buen Pastor VI, Apt 1-B, 1°, Mirador del Sur, Santo Domingo, DN; tel. 482-7992; fax 482-7505; e-mail e.honduras@ codetel.net.do; Ambassador NERY MAGALY FÚNES.

Israel: Pedro Henríquez Ureña 80, Santo Domingo, DN; tel. 472-0774; fax 472-1785; e-mail info@santodomingo.mfa.gov.il; Ambassador YOAV BARON.

Italy: Rodríguez Objío 4, Santo Domingo, DN; tel. 682-0830; fax 682-8296; e-mail ambital@verizon.net.do; Ambassador GIORGIO SFARA.

Japan: Torre BHD, 8°, Avda Winston Churchill, esq. Luis F. Thomén, Santo Domingo, DN; tel. 567-3365; fax 566-8013; internet www.do.emb-japan.go.jp; Ambassador HARUO OKAMOTO.

Korea, Republic: Avda Sarasota 98, Santo Domingo, DN; tel. 532-4314; fax 532-3807; Ambassador LEE JOON-IL.

Mexico: Arzobispo Meriño No 265, esq. con las Mercedes, Zona Colonial, Santo Domingo, DN; tel. 687-6444; fax 687-7872; e-mail embamex@codetel.net.do; Ambassador ISABEL TÉLLEZ DE ORTEGA.

Nicaragua: Avda México 152, Condominio Elsa María, Apdo 1, La Esperilla, Santo Domingo, DN; tel. 563-2311; fax 565-7961; e-mail embnicaragua@codetel.net.do; Ambassador ALVARO SEVILLA SIERO.

Panama: Calle Enrique Henríquez 54, esq. Uruguay, Gazcue, Santo Domingo, DN; tel. 688-1043; fax 689-1273; e-mail emb.panam@ codetel.net.do; Ambassador MARIO GALVEZ.

Peru: Edif. Curvo Of., 485 Bella Vista, Pedro A. Bobea esq. Avda Anacaona, Santo Domingo, DN; tel. 532-6777; fax 532-6291; e-mail embaperu@codetel.net.do; Ambassador RAÚL GUTIÉRREZ.

Spain: Avda Independencia 1205, Santo Domingo, DN; tel. 535-6500; fax 535-1595; e-mail embespdo@mail.mae.es; Ambassador MARÍA JESÚS FIGA LÓPEZ-PALOP.

United Kingdom: Edif. Cominas Pepin, 7°, Avda 27 de Febrero 233, Santo Domingo, DN; tel. 472-7111; fax 472-7574; e-mail brit .emb.sadom@codetel.net.do; Ambassador ANDY ASHCROFT.

USA: César Nicolás Pensón, esq. Leopoldo Navarro, Santo Domingo, DN; tel. 541-2171; e-mail usis.ic@codetel.net.do; internet www .usemb.gov.do; Ambassador HANS H. HERTELL.

Uruguay: Baltasar Brum 7, Apt 1-B, Ensanche La Esperilla, Santo Domingo, DN; tel. 682-5565; fax 687-2167; e-mail embur@codetel .net.do; Ambassador CROCI DE MULA.

Venezuela: Avda Anacoana 7, Mirador del Sur, Santo Domingo, DN; tel. 537-8578; fax 537-8780; e-mail embvenezuela@codetel.net .do; Ambassador FRANCISCO ALBERTO BELISARIO LANDIS.

Judicial System

The Judicial Power resides in the Suprema Corte de Justicia (Supreme Court of Justice), the Cortes de Apelación (Courts of Appeal), the Juzgados de Primera Instancia (Tribunals of the First Instance), the municipal courts and the other judicial authorities provided by law. The Supreme Court is composed of at least 11 judges (16 in March 2005) and the Attorney-General, and exercises disciplinary authority over all the members of the judiciary. The Attorney-General of the Republic is the Chief of Judicial Police and of the Public Ministry which he represents before the Supreme Court of Justice. The Consejo Nacional de la Magistratura (National Judiciary Council) appoints the members of the Supreme Court, which in turn appoints judges at all other levels of the judicial system.

Corte Suprema
Centro de los Héroes, Calle Hipolito Herrera Billini, esq. Juan B. Perez, Santo Domingo, DN; tel. 533-3191; e-mail suprema.corte@ codetel.net.do; internet www.suprema.gov.do.

President: Dr JORGE SUBERO ISA.

Vice-President and President of First Court: Dr RAFAEL LUCIANO PICHARDO.

Second Vice-President: Dra EGLYS MARGARITA ESMURDOC.

President of Second Court: Dr HUGO ALVAREZ VALENCIA.

Justices: Dra MARGARITA A. TAVARES, VÍCTOR JOSÉ CASTELLANOS ESTRELLA, Dr JULIO IBARRA RÍOS, Dr EDGAR HERNÁNDEZ MEJÍA, Dra DULCE M. RODRÍGUEZ DE GORIS, Dra ANA ROSA BERGÉS DREYFOUS JUEZ, Dr JUAN LUPERÓN VÁSQUEZ, Dr JULIO ANÍBAL SUÁREZ, Dra ENILDA REYES PÉREZ, Dr JOSÉ ENRIQUE HERNÁNDEZ MACHADO, Dr PEDRO ROMERO CONFESOR, Dr DARÍO OCTAVIO FERNÁNDEZ ESPINAL.

Attorney-General: FRANCISCO DOMINGUEZ BRITO.

Religion

The majority of the inhabitants belong to the Roman Catholic Church, but freedom of worship exists for all denominations. The Baptist, Evangelist and Seventh-day Adventist churches and the Jewish faith are also represented.

CHRISTIANITY

The Roman Catholic Church
The Dominican Republic comprises two archdioceses and nine dioceses. At 31 December 2002 adherents represented about 89.0% of the population.

Bishops' Conference
Conferencia del Episcopado Dominicano, Apdo 186, Santo Domingo, DN; tel. 685-3141; fax 689-9454.

f. 1985; Pres. Cardinal NICOLÁS DE JESÚS LÓPEZ RODRÍGUEZ (Archbishop of Santo Domingo).

Archbishop of Santiago de los Caballeros: Most Rev. RAMÓN BENITO DE LA ROSA Y CARPIO, Arzobispado, Duvergé 14, Apdo 679, Santiago de los Caballeros; tel. 582-2094; fax 581-3580; e-mail arzobisp.stgo@codetel.net.do.

Archbishop of Santo Domingo: Cardinal NICOLÁS DE JESÚS LÓPEZ RODRÍGUEZ, Arzobispado, Isabel la Católica 55, Apdo 186, Santo Domingo, DN; tel. 685-3141; fax 688-7270; e-mail arzobispado@ codetel.net.do.

The Anglican Communion
Anglicans in the Dominican Republic are under the jurisdiction of the Episcopal Church in the USA. The country is classified as a missionary diocese, in Province IX.

Bishop of the Dominican Republic: Rt Rev. JULIO CÉSAR HOLGUÍN KHOURY, Santiago 114, Apdo 764, Santo Domingo, DN; tel. 688-6016; fax 686-6364; e-mail igelpidom@codetel.net.do.

BAHÁ'Í FAITH

National Spiritual Assembly of the Bahá'ís of the Dominican Republic: Cambronal 152, esq. Beller, Santo Domingo, DN; tel. 687-1726; fax 687-7606; e-mail bahai.rd.aen@codetel.net.do; f. 1961; 402 localities.

The Press

Dirección General de Información, Publicidad y Prensa: Santo Domingo, DN; f. 1983; government supervisory body; Dir-Gen. LUIS GONZÁLEZ FABRA.

DAILIES

Santo Domingo, DN

El Caribe: Calle Doctor Defilló 4, Los Prados, Apdo 416, Santo Domingo, DN; tel. 683-8100; fax 544-4003; e-mail editora@elcaribe .com.do; internet www.elcaribe.com.do; f. 1948; morning; circ. 32,000; Pres. LUIS GARCÍA RECIO; Dir VÍCTOR MANUEL TEJADA.

Diario Libre: Avda Abraham Lincoln, esq. Max Henriquez Ureña, Santo Domingo, DN; internet www.diariolibre.com.

Hoy: Avda San Martín 236, Santo Domingo, DN; tel. 565-5581; fax 567-2424; internet www.hoy.com.do; f. 1981; morning; Editor LUIS M. CARDENAS; circ. 40,000.

Listín Diario: Paseo de los Periodistas 52, Ensanche Miraflores, Santo Domingo, DN; tel. 686-6688; fax 686-6595; e-mail webmaster@listindiario.com.do; internet www.listin.com.do; f. 1889; morning; Dir-Gen. MIGUEL FRANJUL; Editor-in-Chief FABIO CABRAL; circ. 88,050.

La Nación: Calle San Antonio 2, Zona Industrial de Herrera, Santo Domingo, DN; tel. 537-2444; fax 537-4865; e-mail editor.nacion@ codetel.net.do; afternoon.

El Nacional: Avda San Martín 236, Santo Domingo, DN; tel. 565-5581; fax 565-4190; e-mail elnacional@codetel.net.do; internet www

.elnacional.com.do; f. 1966; evening and Sunday; Dir RADHAMÉS GÓMEZ PEPÍN; circ. 45,000.

El Nuevo Diario: Ensanche Gazcue, Santo Domingo, DN; tel. 687-6205; fax 688-0763; morning; Dir PERSIO MALDONADO.

El Siglo: Calle San Anton 2, Zona Industrial de Herrera, Apdo 20213, Santo Domingo, DN; tel. 518-4000; fax 518-4035; e-mail elsiglo@elsiglord.com; Editorial Dir OSVALDO SANTANA.

Santiago de los Caballeros, SD

La Información: Carretera Licey, Km 3, Santiago de los Caballeros, SD; tel. 581-1915; fax 581-7770; e-mail e.informacion@codetel.net.do; internet www.lainformacionrd.com; f. 1915; morning; Dir FERNANDO A. PÉREZ MEMÉN; circ. 15,000.

PERIODICALS AND REVIEWS

Agricultura: Autopista Duarte, Km 6.5, Los Jardines del Norte, Santo Domingo, DN; tel. 547-3888; fax 227-1268; organ of the Secretariat of State for Agriculture; f. 1905; monthly; Dir MIGUEL RODRÍGUEZ, Jr.

Agroconocimiento: Apdo 345-2, Santo Domingo, DN; monthly; agricultural news and technical information; Dir DOMINGO MARTE; circ. 10,000.

¡Ahora!: San Martín 236, Apdo 1402, Santo Domingo, DN; tel. 565-5581; e-mail revistaahora@internet.net.do; internet www.ahora.com.do; f. 1962; weekly; Editor RAFAEL MOLINA.

La Campiña: San Martín 236, Apdo 1402, Santo Domingo, DN; f. 1967; Dir Ing. JUAN ULISES GARCÍA B.

Carta Dominicana: Avda Tiradentes 56, Santo Domingo, DN; tel. 566-0119; f. 1974; monthly; economics; Dir JUAN RAMÓN QUIÑONES M.

Deportes: San Martín 236, Apdo 1402, Santo Domingo, DN; f. 1967; sports; fortnightly; Dir L. R. CORDERO; circ. 5,000.

Eva: San Martín 236, Apdo 1402, Santo Domingo, DN; f. 1967; fortnightly; Dir MAGDA FLORENCIO.

Horizontes de América: Santo Domingo, DN; f. 1967; monthly; Dir ARMANDO LEMUS CASTILLO.

Letra Grande, Arte y Literatura: Leonardo da Vinci 13, Mirador del Sur, Avda 27 de Febrero, Santo Domingo, DN; tel. 531-2225; f. 1980; monthly; art and literature; Dir JUAN RAMÓN QUIÑONES M.

Renovación: José Reyes, esq. El Conde, Santo Domingo, DN; fortnightly; Dir OLGA QUISQUEYA VIUDA MARTÍNEZ.

NEWS AGENCIES

La Noticia: Julio Verne 14, Santo Domingo, DN; tel. 535-0815; f. 1973; evening; Pres. JOSÉ A. BREA PEÑA; Dir BOLÍVAR BELLO.

Foreign Press Bureaux

Agence France-Presse (AFP) (France): Calle Roberto Pastoriza 220, Ensanche Naco, Santo Domingo, DN; tel. 566-0379.

Agencia EFE (Spain): Galerías Comerciales, 5°, Of. 507, Avda 27 de Febrero, Santo Domingo, DN; tel. 567-7617; Bureau Chief ANTONIO CASTILLO URBERUAGA.

Agenzia Nazionale Stampa Associata (ANSA) (Italy): Leopoldo Navarro 79, 3°, Sala 17, Apdo 20324, Huanca, Santo Domingo, DN; tel. 685-8765; fax 685-8765; Bureau Chief HUMBER ANDRÉS SUAZO.

Inter Press Service (IPS) (Italy): Cambronal, No. 4-1, Ciudad Nueva, Santo Domingo, DN; tel. 593-5153; Correspondent VIANCO MARTÍNEZ.

United Press International (UPI) (USA): Carrera A. Manoguaybo 16, Manoguaybo, DN; tel. 689-7171; Chief Correspondent SANTIAGO ESTRELLA VELOZ.

The Agence Haïtienne de Presse (AHP) is also represented.

Publishers

SANTO DOMINGO, DN

Arte y Cine, C por A: San Martín 45, Santo Domingo, DN; tel. 682-0342; fax 686-8354.

Editora Alfa y Omega: José Contreras 69, Santo Domingo, DN; tel. 532-5577.

Editora de las Antillas: Santo Domingo, DN; tel. 685-2197.

Editora Dominicana, SA: 23 Oeste, No 3 Lup., Santo Domingo, DN; tel. 688-0846.

Editora El Caribe, C por A: Calle Doctor Defilló 4, Los Prados, Apdo 416, Santo Domingo, DN; tel. 683-8100; fax 544-4003; e-mail

editora@elcaribe.com.do; internet www.elcaribe.com.do; f. 1948; Dir FERNANDO FERRÁN.

Editora Hoy, C por A: San Martín, 236, Santo Domingo, DN; tel. 566-1147.

Editora Listín Diario, C por A: Paseo de los Periodistas 52, Ensanche Miraflores, Apdo 1455, Santo Domingo, DN; tel. 686-6688; fax 686-6595; f. 1889; Pres. Dr ROGELIO A. PELLERANO.

Editorama, SA: Calle Eugenio Contreras, No. 54, Los Trinitarios, Apdo 2074, Santo Domingo, DN; tel. 596-6669; fax 594-1421; e-mail editorama@codetel.net.do; internet www.editorama.com; f. 1970; Pres. JUAN ANTONIO QUIÑONES MARTE.

Editorial Padilla, C por A: Avda 27 de Febrero, Santo Domingo, DN; tel. 379-1550; fax 379-2631.

Editorial Santo Domingo: Santo Domingo, DN; tel. 532-9431.

Editorial Stella: Avda 19 de Marzo 304, Santo Domingo, DN; tel. 682-2281; fax 687-0835.

Julio D. Postigo e Hijos: Santo Domingo, DN; f. 1949; fiction; Man. J. D. POSTIGO.

Publicaciones Ahora, C por A: Avda San Martín 236, Apdo 1402, Santo Domingo, DN; tel. 565-5580; fax 565-4190; Pres. JULIO CASTAÑO.

Publicaciones América: Santo Domingo, DN; Dir PEDRO BISONÓ.

SANTIAGO DE LOS CABALLEROS, SD

Editora el País, SA: Carrera Sánchez, Km 6½, Santiago de los Caballeros, SD; tel. 532-9511.

Broadcasting and Communications

Dirección General de Telecomunicaciones: Isabel la Católica 73, Santo Domingo, DN; tel. 682-2244; fax 682-3493; government supervisory body; Dir-Gen. RUBÉN MONTAS; Dir-Gen. of Television RAMON EMILIO COLOMBO.

Instituto Dominicano de las Telecomunicaciones (INDOTEL): Avda Abraham Lincoln, No 962, Edif. Osiris, Santo Domingo, DN; tel. 732-5555; fax 732-3904; e-mail info@indotel.org.do; internet www.indotel.org.do; Pres. Dr JOSÉ RAFAEL VARGAS.

TELECOMMUNICATIONS

Tricom Telecomunicaciones de Voz, Data y Video: Avda Lope de Vega 95, Santo Domingo, DN; tel. 476-4699; fax 567-4412; e-mail sc@tricom.com.do; internet www.tricom.net; f. 1992; Pres. and CEO CARL CARLSON; Chair. RICARDO VALDEZ ALBIZU.

Verizon Dominicana, C por A: Avda Lincoln 1101, Apdo 1377, Santo Domingo, DN; tel. 220-1212; fax 543-1301; e-mail ayuda@verizon.net.do; internet www.verizon.net.do; f. 1930; fmrly Compañia Dominicana de Teléfonos (Codetel); name changed as above in 2004; Pres. JORGE IVAN RAMÍREZ; Gen. Man. GUILLERMO AMORE.

BROADCASTING

Radio

There were some 130 commercial stations in the Dominican Republic. The government-owned broadcasting network, Radio Televisión Dominicana (see Television), operates nine radio stations.

Asociación Dominicana de Radiodifusoras (ADORA): Paul Harris 3, Centro de los Héroes, Santo Domingo, DN; tel. 535-4057; Pres. IVELISE DE TORRES.

Cadena de Noticias (CDN) Radio: Calle Doctor Defilló 4, Los Prados, Apdo 416, Santo Domingo, DN; tel. 683-8100; fax 544-4003; internet www.elcaribecdn.com.do/cdnradio.

Television

Antena Latina, Canal 7: Calle Gustavo Mejía Ricart, Santo Domingo, DN; internet www.antenalatina7.com; f. 1999; Pres. MIGUEL BONETTI DUBREIL; Editor-in-Chief MIGUEL ANGEL ORDONEZ.

Cadena de Noticias (CDN) Televisión: Calle Doctor Defilló 4, Los Prados, Santo Domingo, DN; tel. 262-2100; fax 567-2671; e-mail direccion@cdn.com.do; internet www.elcaribe.com.do/cdntv; broadcasts news on Channel 37.

Color Visión, Canal 9: San Martín, Avda Lope de Vega, Ensanche La Fe, Santo Domingo, DN; tel. 566-5876; fax 732-9347; e-mail colorvision@codetel.net.do; internet www.colorvision.com.do; f. 1969; majority owned by Corporación Dominicana de Radio y Televisión; commercial station; Dir-Gen. MANUEL QUIROZ MIRANDA.

Radio Televisión Dominicana, Canal 4: Dr Tejada Florentino 8, Apdo 869, Santo Domingo, DN; tel. 689-2120; e-mail rm.colombo@

codetel.net.do; internet www.rtvd.com; government station; Channel 4; Dir-Gen. Ramón Colombo; Gen. Man. Agustín Mercado.

Teleantillas, Canal 2: Autopista Duarte, Km 7½, Los Prados, Apdo 30404, Santo Domingo, DN; tel. 567-7751; fax 540-4912; e-mail vbaez@corripio.com.do; f. 1979; Gen. Man. Hector Valentín Báez.

Telecentro, Canal 13: Avda Pasteur 204, Santo Domingo, DN; tel. 687-9161; fax 542-7582; e-mail webmaster@telecentro.com.do; internet www.telecentro.com.do; Santo Domingo and east region; Pres. José Miguel Báez Figueroa.

Tele-Inde Canal 13: Avda Pasteur 101, Santo Domingo, DN; tel. 687-9161; commercial station; Dir Julio Hazim.

Telemicro, Canal 5: San Martín, Avda 27 de Febrero, Santo Domingo, DN; tel. 689-8151; fax 686-6528; e-mail programacion@telemicro.com.do; internet www.telemicro.com.do; f. 1982.

Telesistema, Canal 11: Avda 27 de Febrero 52, Sector Bergel, Santo Domingo, DN; tel. 563-6661; fax 472-1754; e-mail info@telesistema11.tv; internet www.telesistema11.tv; Pres. José L. Corripio.

Finance

(cap. = capital; dep. = deposits; m. = million; p.u. = paid up; res = reserves; amounts in pesos)

BANKING

Supervisory Body

Superintendencia de Bancos: 52 Avda México, esq. Leopoldo Navarro, Apdo 1326, Santo Domingo, DN; tel. 685-8141; fax 809-0859; e-mail administrativo@supbanco.gov.do; internet www.supbanco.gov.do; f. 1947; Superintendent Rafael Camilo Abréu.

Central Bank

Banco Central de la República Dominicana: Calle Pedro Henríquez Ureña, esq. Leopoldo Navarro, Apdo 1347, Santo Domingo, DN; tel. 221-9111; fax 687-7488; e-mail info@bancentral.gov.do; internet www.bancentral.gov.do; f. 1947; cap. 0.7m., res 92.3m., dep. 6,321.7m. (Dec. 1996); Gov. Hector Valdez Albizu; Vice-Gov. Félix E. Calvo Peralta.

Commercial Banks

Banco BHD, SA: Avda 27 de Febrero, esq. Avda Winston Churchill, Santo Domingo, DN; tel. 243-3232; fax 541-4949; e-mail servicio@bhd.com.do; internet www.bhd.com.do; f. 1972; total assets 11,902m. (1999); Exec. Pres. Luís Molina Achécar; 35 brs.

Banco Dominicano del Progreso, SA: Avda John F. Kennedy 3, Apdo 1329, Santo Domingo, DN; tel. 563-3233; fax 563-2455; internet www.progreso.com.do; f. 1974; merged with Banco Metropolitano, and Banco de Desarrollo Dominicano, SA, in 2000; cap. 1,004.4m., res 249.5m., dep. 11,433.5m. (Dec. 2002); Exec. Pres. Pedro E. Castillo L.; 20 brs.

Banco Gerencial y Fiduciario, SA: Avda 27 de Febrero 50, Santo Domingo, DN; tel. 473-9400; fax 565-7569; total assets 7,876m. (1999); f. 1983; Exec. Vice-Pres. George Manuel Hazoury Peña.

Banco Global, SA: Avda Rómulo Betancourt 1, esq. Avda A. Lincoln, Santo Domingo, DN; tel. 532-3000; fax 535-7070; total assets 11,486m. (1999); Pres. Oscar Lama.

Banco Industrial de Desarrollo e Inversión, SA: Avda San Martín 40, esq. Dr Delgado, Santo Domingo, DN; tel. 685-3194; fax 689-3485.

Banco Mercantil: Avda Pastoriza 303, Santo Domingo, DN; tel. 567-4444; fax 549-6509; e-mail info@mercantil.com.do; internet www.mercantil.com.do; f. 1985; total assets 9,579m. (1999); Pres. Andrés Aybar Báez; 21 brs.

Banco Multiple Leon, SA: Avda John F. Kennedy, esq. Tiradentes, Apdo 1408, Santo Domingo, DN; tel. 540-4441; fax 567-4854; e-mail info@leon.com.do; internet www.leon.com.do; f. 1981; fmrly Banco Nacional de Crédito, SA; became Bancrédito, in 2002; name changed as above Dec. 2003; cap. 686.8m., res 181.3m., dep. 7,911.3m. (Dec. 2000); Pres. and CEO Felipe J. Mendoza; 38 brs.

Banco Popular Dominicano: Avda John F. Kennedy 20, Torre Popular, Apdo 1441, Santo Domingo, DN; tel. 544-8000; fax 544-5899; e-mail contactenos@bpd.com.do; internet www.bpd.com.do; f. 1963; cap. 4,645.8m., res 1,270.4m., dep. 61,735.9m. (Dec. 2003); Pres., Chair. and Gen. Man. Manuel Alejandro Grullón; 184 brs.

Banco de Reservas de la República Dominicana: Isabel la Católica 201, Apdo 1353, Santo Domingo, DN; tel. 687-5366; fax 685-0602; e-mail sperdomo@brrd.com; internet www.banreservas.com.do; f. 1941; cap. 2,000.0m., res 1,326.3m., dep. 52,263.2m. (Dec.

2003); Dir Daniel Toribio; Pres. and Gen. Man. Manuel Antonio Lara Hernández; 112 brs.

Development Banks

Banco Agrícola de la República Dominicana: Avda G. Washington 601, Apdo 1057, Santo Domingo, DN; tel. 535-8088; fax 532-4645; e-mail bagricola.refor@codetel.net.do; f. 1945; government agricultural development bank; Pres. Lic. Rafael Angeles Suárez; Gen. Administrator Radhames Rodriguez Valerio.

Banco Continental de Desarrollo, SA: Edif. Continental, Avda Pedro Henríquez Ureña 126, Santo Domingo, DN; tel. 472-2228; fax 472-3027; internet www.banco-continental.com; Pres. Hugo Giliano; Man. Dir Anton Yelari.

Banco de Desarrollo Ademi, SA: Avda Rafael Augusto Sánchez 33, Plaza Intercaribe, Suite 203, Apdo 2887, Santo Domingo, DN; tel. 732-4411; fax 732-4401; e-mail banco.ademi@codetel.net.do; internet www.ademi.org.do; Pres. Margarita de Ferrari de Lluberes.

Banco de Desarrollo Agropecuario Norcentral, SA: Avda Independencia 801, esq. Avda Máximo Gómez, Santo Domingo, DN; tel. 686-0984; fax 687-0825.

Banco de Desarrollo de Exportación, SA: Fatino Falco, entre Avda Lope de Vega y Tiradentes 201, Santo Domingo, DN; tel. 566-5841; fax 565-1769.

Banco de Desarrollo Industrial, SA: Avda Sarasota 27, esq. La Julia, Santo Domingo, DN; tel. 535-8586; fax 535-6069.

Banco de Desarrollo Intercontinental, SA: Edif. Lilian, 5°, Avda Lope de Vega, esq. Gustavo Mejía Ricart, Santo Domingo, DN; tel. 544-0559; fax 563-6884.

Banco Nacional de la Construcción: Avda Alma Mater, esq. Pedro Henríquez Ureña, Santo Domingo, DN; tel. 685-9776; f. 1977; Gen. Man. Luis Manuel Pellerano.

Banco de la Pequeña Empresa, SA: Avda Bolivar 233, entre Avda Abraham Lincoln y Avda Winston Churchill, Santo Domingo, DN; tel. 534-8383; fax 534-8385.

Foreign Banks

Bank of Nova Scotia (Canada): Avda John F. Kennedy, esq. Lope de Vega, Apdo 1494, Santo Domingo, DN; tel. 544-1700; fax 567-5732; e-mail luis.zobors@scotiabank.com; f. 1920; signed agreement with Govt in July 2003 to acquire some operations of dissolved Banco Intercontinental, SA (Baninter); Vice-Pres. and Gen. Man. Luis F. Zobórs; 61 brs.

Citibank NA (USA): Avda John F. Kennedy 1, Apdo 1492, Santo Domingo, DN; tel. 566-5611; fax 685-7535; f. 1962; Gen. Man. Nicole Reich; 7 brs.

STOCK EXCHANGE

Santo Domingo Securities Exchange Inc: Edif. Empresarial, 1°, Avda John F. Kennedy, Apdo 25144, Santo Domingo, DN; tel. 567-6694; fax 567-6697; e-mail info@bolsard.com; internet www.bolsard.com; Pres. Marino Ginebra.

INSURANCE

Supervisory Body

Superintendencia de Seguros: Secretaría de Estado de Finanzas, Avda México, esq. Leopoldo Navarro, Santo Domingo, DN; tel. 688-1120; fax 685-0506; e-mail servicio@superseguro.gov.do; internet www.superseguro.gov.do; f. 1969; Superintendent Cesar Cabrera.

Insurance Companies

American Life and General Insurance Co, C por A: Edif. ALICO, 5°, Avda Abraham Lincoln, Apdo 131, Santo Domingo, DN; tel. 533-7131; fax 535-0362; e-mail caribalico@codetel.net.do; general; Gen. Man. Francisco Cabreja.

Angloamericana de Seguros, SA: Avda Gustavo Mejía Ricard 18, esq. Hermanos Roque Martínez, Ens. El Millón, Santo Domingo, DN; tel. 227-1002; fax 227-6005; e-mail anglo@angloam.com.do; internet www.angloam.com.do; f. 1996; Pres. Nelson Hedi Hernández P.; Vice-Pres. Esteban Betances Fabré.

Atlantica Insurance, SA: Avda 27 de Febrero 365A, 2°, Apdo 826, Santo Domingo, DN; tel. 565-5591; fax 565-4343; e-mail atlanticains@codetel.net.do; Dir-Gen. Lic. Rhina Ramírez de Peralta; Pres. Gamalier Peralta.

Bankers Security Life Insurance Society: Calle Gustavo Mejía Ricart 61, Apdo 1123, Santo Domingo, DN; tel. 544-2626; fax 567-9389; e-mail eizquierdo@bpd.com.do; Pres. Lic. Estela Ma. Fiallo T.

BMI Compañia de Seguros, SA: Avda Tiradentes 14, Edif. Alfonso Comercial, Apdo 916, Ens. Naco, Santo Domingo, DN; tel. 562-6660;

fax 562-6849; e-mail gerencia@bmi.com.do; Exec. Vice-Pres. PEDRO DA CUNHA.

Bonanza Compañía de Seguros, SA: Avda John F. Kennedy, Edif. Bonanza, Santo Domingo, DN; tel. 565-5531; fax 566-1087; e-mail bonanza.dom@codetel.net.do; internet www.bonanza.dominicana.com.do; Pres. Lic. DARIO LAMA.

Britanica de Seguros, SA: Max Henríquez Ureña 35, Apdo 3637, Santo Domingo, DN; tel. 542-6863; fax 544-4542; e-mail wharper@codetel.net.do; Pres. JOHN HARPER SALETA.

Centro de Seguros La Popular, C por A: Gustavo Mejía Ricart 61, Apdo 1123, Santo Domingo, DN; tel. 566-1988; fax 567-9389; f. 1965; general except life; Pres. Lic. ROSA FIALLO.

La Colonial, SA: Avda Sarasota 75, Bella Vista, Santo Domingo, DN; tel. 508-0707; fax 508-0608; e-mail info@lacolonial.com.do; internet www.lacolonial.com.do; f. 1971; general; Pres. Dr MIGUEL FERIS IGLESIAS.

Compañía de Seguros Palic, SA: Avda Abraham Lincoln, esq. José Amado Soler, Apdo 1132, Santo Domingo, DN; tel. 562-1271; fax 562-1825; e-mail cia.seg.palic2@codetel.net.do; Pres. JOSÉ ANTONIO CARO GINEBRA; Exec. Vice-Pres. MILAGROS DE LOS SANTOS.

Confederación del Canada Dominicana: Calle Salvador Sturla 17, Ens. Naco, Santo Domingo, DN; tel. 544-4144; fax 540-4740; e-mail confedom@codetel.net.do; f. 1988; Pres. Lic. MOISES A. FRANCO.

Federal Insurance Company: Edif. La Cumbre, 4°, Avda Tiradentes, esq. Presidente González, Santo Domingo, DN; tel. 567-0181; fax 567-8909; e-mail eizquierdo@bpd.com.do; Pres. LUIS AUGUSTO GINEBRA H.

General de Seguros, SA: Avda Sarasota 55, esq. Pedro A. Bobea, Apdo 2183, Santo Domingo, DN; tel. 535-8888; fax 532-4451; e-mail general.seg@codetel.net.do; f. 1981; general; Pres. Dr FERNANDO A. BALLISTA DÍAZ.

La Intercontinental de Seguros, SA: Plaza Naco, 2°, Avda Tiradentes, Apdo 825, Santo Domingo, DN; tel. 227-2002; fax 472-4111; e-mail fotero@lainter.com; internet www.lainter.com; general; Pres. Lic. RAMÓN BÁEZ ROMANO.

Magna Compañía de Seguros, SA: Edif. Magna Motors, Avda Abraham Lincoln, esq. John F. Kennedy, Apdo 1979, Santo Domingo, DN; tel. 544-1400; fax 562-5723; e-mail jvargas@segna.com.do; f. 1974; general and life; Pres. E. ANTONIO LAMA S.; Man. MILAGROS DE LOS SANTOS.

La Mundial de Seguros, SA: Avda Máximo Gómez, No 31, Santo Domingo, DN; tel. 685-2121; fax 682-3269; general except life and financial; Pres. PEDRO D'ACUNHA.

La Peninsular de Seguros, SA: Edif. Corp. Corominas Pepín, 3°, Avda 27 de Febrero 233, Santo Domingo, DN; tel. 472-1166; fax 563-2349; e-mail peninsu@aacr.net; general; Pres. Lic. ERNESTO ROMERO LANDRÓN.

Progreso Compañía de Seguros, SA (PROSEGUROS): Edif. Torre Progreso, 2°, Avda Winston Churchill, esq. Ludovino Fernández, Ens. Carmelita, Santo Domingo, DN; tel. 541-7182; fax 541-7915; e-mail JuanGa@progreso.com.do; Pres. VICENZO MASTROLILLI; Exec. Vice-Pres. Lic. JUAN GARRIGÓ.

Reaseguradora Hispaniola, SA: Avda Gustavo Mejía Ricart, Edif. 8, 2°, esq. Hermanos Roque Martínez, Ens. El Millón, Santo Domingo, DN; tel. 548-7171; fax 548-6007; e-mail rehsa@verizon.net.do; Pres. NELSON HEDI HERNÁNDEZ P.

SEGNA: Avda Máximo Gómez 31, Gazcue, Santo Domingo, DN; tel. 476-7100; fax 476-3427; e-mail info@segna.com.do; internet www.segna.com; f. 1964; general; fmrly Compañía Nacional de Seguros, C por A; name changed as above in 2001; Chair. Dr MÁXIMO A. PELLERANO.

Seguros La Antillana, SA: Avda Abraham Lincoln, esq. Max Henríquez Ureña, Apdo 27, Santo Domingo, DN; tel. 567-4481; fax 541-2927; e-mail seguros@seguroslaantilla.com; f. 1947; general and life; Pres. Lic. OSCAR LAMA.

Seguros BanReservas: Avda Gustavo Mejía Ricart, esq. Lope de Vega, Edif. Goico Castro, 3°, Santo Domingo, DN; tel. 960-7200; fax 563-4352; e-mail smahfoud@segbanreservas.com; internet www.segurosbanreservas.com; Pres. Lic. MANUEL LARA HERNÁNDEZ; Exec. Vice-Pres. SIMÓN MAHFOUD MIGUEL.

Seguros La Isleña, C por A: Edif. Centro Coordinador Empresarial, Avda Núñez de Cáceres, esq. Guarocuya, Santo Domingo, DN; tel. 567-7211; fax 565-1448; Pres. HUÁSCAR RODRIGUEZ; Exec. Vice-Pres. MARÍA DEL PILAR RODRÍGUEZ.

Seguros Pepín, SA: Edif. Corp. Corominas Pepín, Avda 27 de Febrero 233, Santo Domingo, DN; tel. 472-1006; fax 565-9176; general; Pres. Dr BIENVENIDO COROMINAS PEPIN.

Seguros Popular: Avda Winston Churchill 1100, Torre Universal América, Apdo 1052, Santo Domingo, DN; tel. 544-7200; fax 544-

7968; e-mail universal.seguros@codetel.net.do; internet www.universal.com.do; f. 1964 as La Universal de Seguros; merged with Grupo Asegurador América in 2000; general; Pres. ERNESTO IZQUIERDO.

Seguros San Rafael, C por A: Leopoldo Navarro 61, esq. San Francisco de Macorís, Edif. San Rafael, Apdo 1018, Santo Domingo, DN; fax 686-2628; e-mail sanrafael@codetel.net.do; general; Admin.-Gen. RAMÓN PERALTA.

El Sol de Seguros, SA: Torre Hipotecaria, 2°, Avda Tiradentes 25, Santo Domingo, DN; tel. 562-6504; fax 544-3260; general; Pres. ANTONIO ALMA.

Sudamericana de Seguros, SA: El Conde 105, frente al Parque Colón, Santo Domingo, DN; tel. 685-0141; fax 688-8074; Pres. VINCENZO MASTROLILLI.

Transglobal de Seguros, SA: Avda Lope de Vega 16, esq. Andres Julio Aybar y Ensanche Piantini, Apdo 1869, Santo Domingo, DN; tel. 541-3366; fax 567-9398; e-mail transglobal@codetel.net.do; internet www.transglobaldeseguros.com; Dirs JOSÉ MANUEL VARGAS, OSCAR LAMA.

Insurance Association

Cámara Dominicana de Aseguradores y Reaseguradores, Inc: Edif. Torre BHD, 5°, Luis F. Thomen, esq. Winston Churchill, Santo Domingo, DN; tel. 566-0014; fax 566-2600; e-mail cadoar@verizon.net.do; internet www.cadoar.org.do; f. 1972; Pres. SIMÓN MAHFOUD MIGUEL.

Trade and Industry

GOVERNMENT AGENCIES

Comisión Nacional de Energía (CNE): Calle Gustavo Mejía Ricart 73, esq. Agustín Lara, 3°, Ensanche Serralles, Santo Domingo, DN; tel. 732-2000; fax 547-2073; e-mail info@cne.gov.do; internet www.cne.gov.do; f. 2001; responsible for regulation and development of energy sector; Exec. Dir ANTONIO ALMONTE REYNOSO.

Comisión para la Reforma de la Empresa Pública: Gustavo Mejía Ricart 73, esq. Agustín Lara, Edif. Latinoamericana de Seguros, 6°, Ens. Serrallés, Santo Domingo, DN; tel. 683-3591; fax 683-3888; e-mail crepdom@codetel.net.do; internet www.crepdom.gov.do; commission charged with divestment and restructuring of state enterprises; Pres. RAFAEL MONTILLA MARTÍNEZ.

Consejo Estatal del Azúcar (CEA) (State Sugar Council): Centro de los Héroes, Apdo 1256/1258, Santo Domingo, DN; tel. 533-1161; fax 533-7393; internet www.crepdom.gov.do/CEA; f. 1966; management of operations contracted to private consortiums in 1999 and 2000; Dir-Gen. VÍCTOR MANUEL BÁEZ.

Corporación Dominicana de Empresas Estatales (CORDE) (Dominican State Corporation): Avda General Antonio Duvergé, Apdo 1378, Santo Domingo, DN; tel. 533-5171; f. 1966 to administer, direct and develop state enterprises; Dir-Gen. FERNANDO DURÁN.

Instituto de Estabilización de Precios (INESPRE): Plaza Independencia, Avda Luperon, esq. 27 de Febrero, Apdo 86-2, Santo Domingo, DN; tel. 537-0020; fax 531-0198; e-mail inespre.comp@codetel.net.do; internet www.inespre.gov.do; f. 1969; price commission; Exec. Dir JOSÉ FRANCISCO PENA GUABA.

Instituto Nacional de la Vivienda: Avda Tiredentes, esq. Pedro Henríquez Ureña, Santo Domingo, DN; tel. 732-0600; e-mail invi@codetel.net.do; internet www.invi.gov.do; f. 1962; low-cost housing institute; Dir-Gen. Ing. JUAN ANTONIO VARGAS.

DEVELOPMENT ORGANIZATIONS

Consejo Nacional para el Desarrollo Minero: Santo Domingo, DN; f. 2000; encourages the development of the mining sector; Exec. Dir MIGUEL PENA; Sec.-Gen. PEDRO VÁSQUEZ.

Departamento de Desarrollo y Financiamiento de Proyectos (DEFINPRO): c/o Banco Central de la República Dominicana, Pedro Henríquez Ureña, esq. Leopoldo Navarro, Apdo 1347, Santo Domingo, DN; tel. 221-9111; fax 687-7488; f. 1993; associated with AID, IDB, WB, KFW; encourages economic development in productive sectors of economy, excluding sugar; authorizes complementary financing to private sector for establishing and developing industrial and agricultural enterprises and free-zone industrial parks; Dir ANGEL NERY CASTILLO PIMENTEL.

Fundación Dominicana de Desarrollo (Dominican Development Foundation): Mercedes No 4, Apdo 857, Santo Domingo, DN; tel. 688-8101; fax 686-0430; f. 1962 to mobilize private resources for collaboration in financing small-scale development programmes; 384 mems; Dir Lic. ADA WISCOVITCH.

Instituto de Desarrollo y Crédito Cooperativo (IDECOOP): Centro de los Héroes, Apdo 1371, Santo Domingo, DN; tel. 533-8131; fax 535-5148; f. 1963 to encourage the development of co-operatives; Dir JAVIER PEÑA NÚÑEZ.

CHAMBERS OF COMMERCE

Cámara Americana de Comercio de la República Dominicana: Torre Empresarial, 6°, Avda Sarasota 20, Santo Domingo, DN; tel. 381-0777; fax 381-0286; e-mail amcham@codetel.net.do; internet www.amcham.org.do; Pres. JORGE IVÁN RAMÍREZ.

Cámara de Comercio y Producción de Santo Domingo: Arz. Nouel 206, Zona Colonial, Apdo 815, Santo Domingo, DN; tel. 682-2688; fax 685-2228; e-mail camara.sto.dgo@codetel.net.do; internet www.ccpsd.org.do; f. 1910; 1,500 active mems; Pres. JOSÉ MANUEL ARMENTEROS; Exec. Dir MILAGROS J. PUELLO.

There are official Chambers of Commerce in the larger towns.

INDUSTRIAL AND TRADE ASSOCIATIONS

Asociación Dominicana de Hacendados y Agricultores Inc: Santo Domingo, DN; tel. 565-0542; farming and agricultural org.; Pres. Lic. CESARIO CONTRERAS.

Asociación de Industrias de la República Dominicana Inc: Avda Sarasota 20, Torre Empresarial AIRD, 12°, Santo Domingo, DN; tel. 472-0000; fax 472-0303; e-mail aird@codetel.net.do; internet www.aird.org.do; f. 1962; industrial org.; Pres. YANDRA PORTELA.

Centro Dominicano de Promoción de Exportaciones (CEDOPEX): Plaza de la Bandera, Avda 27 de Febrero, Apdo 199-2, Santo Domingo, DN; tel. 530-5505; fax 531-5136; e-mail emartinez@cel-rd.gov.do; internet www.cei-rd.gov.do; promotion of exports and investments; Exec. Dir EDDY MARTÍNEZ MANZUETA.

Consejo Nacional de la Empresa Privada (CONEP): Avda Abraham Lincoln, esq. John F. Kennedy, Edif. Ambar, 4°, Santo Domingo, DN; tel. 562-1666; fax 540-5502; e-mail conep@conep.org .do; internet www.conep.org.do; Pres. Lic. ELENA VIYELLA DE PALIZA.

Consejo Nacional de Zonas Francas de Exportación: Leopoldo Navarro 61, Edif. San Rafael, 5°, Apdo 21430, Santo Domingo, DN; tel. 686-8077; fax 686-8079; e-mail webmaster@cnzfe.gov.do; internet www.cnzfe.gov.do; co-ordinating body for the free trade zones; Exec. Dir LUISA FERNÁNDEZ DURÁN.

Consejo Promotor de Inversiones (Investment Promotion Council): Avda Abraham Lincoln, Edif. Alico, 2°, Santo Domingo, DN; tel. 532-3281; fax 533-7029; Exec. Dir and CEO FREDERIC EMAM ZADÉ.

Corporación de Fomento Industrial (CFI): Avda 27 de Febrero, Plaza La Bandera, Apdo 1452, Santo Domingo, DN; tel. 530-0010; fax 530-1303; internet www.dominican-investment.com; f. 1962 to promote agro-industrial development; Dir-Gen. JOSÉ OVALLES.

Dirección General de Minería: Edif. de Oficinas Gubernamentales, 10°, Avda México, esq. Leopoldo Navarro, Santo Domingo, DN; tel. 685-8191; fax 686-8327; e-mail direc.mineria@codetel.net.do; internet www.dgm.gov.do; f. 1947; government mining and hydrocarbon org.; Dir-Gen. PEDRO VÁSQUEZ.

Instituto Agrario Dominicano (IAD): Avda 27 de Febrero, Santo Domingo, DN; tel. 530-8272; internet www.iad.gov.do; Dir-Gen. Ing. AGRON SALVADOR JIMÉNEZ A.

Instituto Dominicano de Tecnología Industrial (INDOTEC): Avda Núñez de Cáceres, esq. Olof Palme, Santo Domingo, DN; tel. 566-8121; fax 227-8808; e-mail indotec@codetel.net.do; internet www.indotec.gov.do; Exec. Dir SIXTO MANUEL BISONÓ PÉREZ.

Instituto Nacional del Azúcar (INAZUCAR): Avda Jiménez Moya, Apdo 667, Santo Domingo, DN; tel. 532-5571; fax 533-2402; e-mail inst.azucar@codetel.net.do; internet www.inazucar.gov.do; sugar institute; f. 1965; Exec. Dir SEVERO DE JS. OVALLE.

EMPLOYERS' ORGANIZATIONS

Confederación Patronal de la República Dominicana (COPARDOM): Avda Sarasota 20, Torre Empresarial AIRD, Suite 207, Santo Domingo, DN; tel. 381-4233; fax 381-4266; e-mail copardom@copardom.org.do; internet www.copardom.org.do; Pres. VIRGILIO ORTEGA NADAL.

Consejo Nacional de Hombres de Empresa Inc: Edif. Motorámbar, 7°, Avda Abraham Lincoln 1056, Santo Domingo, DN; tel. 562-1666; Pres. JOSÉ MANUEL PALIZA.

Federación Dominicana de Comerciantes: Carretera Sánchez Km 10, Santo Domingo, DN; tel. 533-2666; Pres. IVAN GARCÍA.

UTILITIES

Electricity

Corporación Dominicana de Empresas Eléctricas Estatales (CDEEE): Avda Independencia, esq. Fray C. de Utrera, Edif. Principal CDE, Centro de los Héroes, Santo Domingo, DN; tel. 535-1100; fax 533-7204; e-mail info@cde.gov.do; internet electricidad-rd.gov .do; f. 1955; state electricity company; partially privatized in 1999, renationalized in 2003; Dir-Gen. RAFAEL DE JESÚS PERELLÓ; Admin. Gen. Ing. RADHAMÉS SEGURA.

Superintendencia de Electricidad: Avda Gustavo Mejía Ricart 73, esq. Agustín Lara, Ensanche Serrallés, 5°, Edif. CREP, Santo Domingo, DN; tel. 683-2500; fax 732-2775; e-mail greinoso@sie.gov .do; internet www.sie.gov.do; f. 2001; Pres. GEORGE REINOSO.

There are three electricity distribution companies operating in the Dominican Republic. Empresa Distribuidora de Electricidad del Norte (Ede-Norte), responsible for distribution in the north of the country, and Empresa Distribuidora de Electricidad del Sur (Ede-Sur), in the south, are owned by the government, while Empresa Distribuidora de Electricidad del Este (Ede-Este), in the east, is jointly owned by the government and the US company AES. In early 2004 AES announced that it intended to divest its 50% stake in Ede-Este, owing to continued problems in the country's power sector.

Water

As part of the continuing programme of repair to the country's infrastructure, in 2001 construction began on aqueducts, intended to supply water to the provinces of Bahoruco, Barahona, Duarte, Espaillat, Independencia and Salcedo.

Instituto Nacional de Aguas Potables y Alcantarillado (INAPA): Calle Guarocuya, Santo Domingo, DN; tel. 567-1241; e-mail info@inapa.gov.do; internet www.inapa.gov.do; Exec. Dir JUAN ROBERTO RODRÍGUEZ HERNÁNDEZ.

Instituto Nacional de Recursos Hidráulicos: Avda Jiménez de Moya, Centro de los Héroes, Santo Domingo, DN; tel. 532-3271; internet www.indrhi.gov.do; f. 1965; Exec. Dir SILVIO CARRASCO.

TRADE UNIONS

Central General de Trabajadores (CGT): Santo Domingo, DN; tel. 688-3932; f. 1972; 13 sections; Sec.-Gen. FRANCISCO ANTONIO SANTOS; 65,000 mems.

Central de Trabajadores Independientes (CTI): Juan Erazo 133, Santo Domingo, DN; tel. 688-3932; f. 1978; left-wing; Sec.-Gen. RAFAEL SANTOS.

Central de Trabajadores Mayoritarias (CTM): Tunti Cáceres 222, Santo Domingo, DN; tel. 562-3392; Sec.-Gen. NÉLSIDA MARMOLEJOS.

Confederación Autónoma de Sindicatos Clasistas (CASC) (Autonomous Confederation of Trade Unions): J. Erazo 39, Santo Domingo, DN; tel. 687-8533; f. 1962; supports PRSC; Sec.-Gen. GABRIEL DEL RÍO.

Confederación Nacional de Trabajadores Dominicanos (CNTD) (National Confederation of Dominican Workers): José de Jesús Ravelo 56, Villa Juana, 5°, Santo Domingo, DN; tel. 221-2117; fax 221-3217; e-mail cntd@codetel.net.do; f. 1988 by merger; 11 provincial federations totalling 150 unions are affiliated; Sec.-Gen. MARIANO NEGRON TEJADA; 188,000 mems (est.).

Confederación de Trabajadores Unitaria (CTU) (United Workers' Confederation): Santo Domingo, DN; f. 1991; Pres. Dr EUGENIO PÉREZ CEPEDA.

Transport

RAILWAYS

In April 2001 plans were announced for the construction of a passenger and freight railway from the coastal port of Haina to Santiago, with the possibility of subsequent extension to Puerto Plata and Manzanillo.

Dirección General de Tránsito Terrestre: Avda San Cristóbal, Santo Domingo, DN; tel. 565-2811; e-mail dgttdom@hotmail.com; internet www.dgtt.gov.do; f. 1966; operated by Secretary of State for Public Works and Communications; Dir-Gen. Ing. RAFAEL T. CRESPO PEREZ.

Ferrocarriles Unidos Dominicanos: Santo Domingo, DN; government-owned; 142 km of track from La Vega to Sánchez and from Guayubín to Pepillo principally used for the transport of exports.

There are also a number of semi-autonomous and private railway companies for the transport of sugar cane, including:

Ferrocarril Central Río Haina: Apdo 1258, Haina; 113 km open.

Ferrocarril de Central Romana: La Romana; 375 km open; Pres. C. MORALES.

ROADS

In 2000 there were an estimated 17,000 km of roads, of which about 6,225 km were paved. There is a direct route from Santo Domingo to Port-au-Prince in Haiti. The Mejía administration undertook an extensive road-building programme from 2000, aiming primarily to reduce traffic congestion in Santo Domingo. In July 2001 the Government announced that a Colombian-led consortium, Consorcio Dominico-Colombiano Autopista del Nordeste, was to construct a toll road between Boca and San Pedro de Macorís. In early 2002 the Government announced the construction of two further bridges over the Ozama river, following the completion of the Juan Bosch Bridge.

Dirección General de Carreteras y Caminos Vecinales: Santo Domingo, DN; fax 567-5470; f. 1987; government supervisory body; Dir-Gen. ELIZABETH PERALTA BRITO.

Autoridad Metropolitana de Transporte (AMET): Avda Expreso V Centenario, esq. Avda San Martín, Santo Domingo, DN; tel. 686-6520; fax 686-3447; e-mail info@amet.gov.do; internet www.amet.gov.do; Dir-Gen. PEDRO DE JESUS CANDELIER.

SHIPPING

The Dominican Republic has 14 ports, of which Santo Domingo is by far the largest, handling about 80% of imports. In 2001 construction work was in progress on the conversion of Manzanillo port into a container terminal, and on Punta Caucedo and Haina ports. A new port and transhipment centre was being built near the Las Americas international airport, which was designed specifically for use by free-trade zone businesses.

A number of foreign shipping companies operate services to the island.

Agencias Navieras B&R, SA: Avda Abraham Lincoln 504, Apdo 1221, Santo Domingo, DN; tel. 544-2200; fax 562-3383; e-mail ops@navierasbr.com; internet www.navierasbr.com; f. 1919; shipping agents and export services; Man. JUAN PERICHE PIDAL.

Armadora Naval Dominicana, SA: Isabel la Católica 165, Apdo 2677, Santo Domingo, DN; tel. 689-6191; Man. Dir Capt. EINAR WETTRE.

Autoridad Portuaria Dominicana: Avda Máximo Gómez, Santo Domingo, DN; tel. 535-8462; Exec. Dir Prof. ARSENIO BORGES.

Líneas Marítimas de Santo Domingo, SA: José Gabriel García 8, Apdo 1148, Santo Domingo, DN; tel. 689-9146; fax 685-4654; Pres. C. LLUBERES; Vice-Pres. JUAN T. TAVARES.

CIVIL AVIATION

There are international airports at Santo Domingo (Aeropuerto Internacional de las Américas José Francisco Peña Gómez and Aeropuerto Internacional de Herrera), Puerto Plata, Punta Cana, Santiago, La Romana, Samaná and Barahona (Aeropuerto Internacional María Móntez). A new international airport (Aeropuerto Internacional La Isabela) at El Higuero, near Santo Domingo, intended to replace the Aeropuerto Internacional de Herrero, was scheduled to become operational in 2004. The international airports underwent privatization in 1999–2000. Most main cities have domestic airports.

Dirección General de Aeronáutica Civil: Avda México, esq. Avda 30 de Marzo, Apdo 1180, Santo Domingo, DN; tel. 221-7909; fax 221-8616; e-mail aeronautica.c@verizon.net.do; internet www.dgac.gov.do; f. 1955; government supervisory body; Dir-Gen. JORGE BOTELLO FERNÁNDEZ.

Aerochago: Aeropuerto Internacional de las Américas, Santo Domingo, DN; tel. 549-0709; fax 549-0708; f. 1973; operates cargo and charter service in Central America and the Caribbean; Gen. Man. PEDRO RODRÍGUEZ.

Aerolíneas Argo: Santo Domingo, DN; f. 1971; cargo and mail services to the USA, Puerto Rico and the US Virgin Islands.

Aerolíneas Dominicanas (Dominair): El Sol 62, Apdo 202, Santiago; tel. 581-8882; fax 582-5074; f. 1974; owned by Aeropostal (Venezuela); scheduled and charter passenger services.

Aerolíneas Santo Domingo: Edif. J. P., Avda 27 de Febrero 272, esq. Seminario, Santo Domingo, DN; e-mail reservas@airsantodomingo.com.do; internet www.airsantodomingo.com; f. 1996; operates scheduled and charter internal, regional and international flights; Pres. HENRY W. AZAR.

Aeromar Airlines: Avda Winston Churchill 71, esq. Desiderio Arias, Ensanche La Julia, Santo Domingo, DN; tel. 533-4447; fax 533-4550; e-mail customer_service@aeromarairlines.com; internet www.aeromarairlines.com; cargo and passenger services; Pres. RAYMUNDO POLANCO.

Compañía Dominicana de Aviación C por A: Avda Jiménez de Moya, esq. José Contreras, Apdo 1415, Santo Domingo, DN; tel. 532-8511; fax 535-1656; f. 1944; operates on international routes connecting Santo Domingo with the Netherlands Antilles, Aruba, the USA, Haiti and Venezuela; operations suspended 1995, privatization pending; Chair. Dr RODOLFO RINCÓN; CEO MARINA GINEBRA DE BONNELLY.

Tourism

Strenuous efforts were made to improve the tourism infrastructure, with 200m. pesos spent on increasing the number of hotel rooms by 50%, road improvements and new developments. In 2001 tourist developments were under way in the south-western province of Pedernales, in Monte Cristi and in Cap Cana. The total number of visitors to the Dominican Republic in 2003 was 3,562,770. In 2002 receipts from tourism totalled US $2,736m. There were 52,000 hotel rooms in the Dominican Republic in 2001, with a further 7,000 rooms under construction.

Secretaría de Estado de Turismo: Bloque D, Edif. de Oficinas Gubernamentales, Avda México, esq. 30 de Marzo, Apdo 497, Santo Domingo, DN; tel. 221-4660; fax 682-3806; e-mail sectur@sectur.gov.do; internet www.dominicana.com.do.

Asociación Dominicana de Agencias de Viajes: Apdo 2097, Calle Padre Billini 263, Santo Domingo, DN; tel. 687-8984; Pres. RAMÓN PRIETO.

Consejo de Promoción Turística: Avda México 66, Santo Domingo, DN; tel. 685-9054; fax 685-6752; e-mail cpt@codetel.net.do; Dir EVELYN PAIEWONSKY.

ECUADOR

Introductory Survey

Location, Climate, Language, Religion, Flag, Capital

The Republic of Ecuador lies on the west coast of South America. It is bordered by Colombia to the north, by Peru to the east and south, and by the Pacific Ocean to the west. The Galápagos Islands, about 960 km (600 miles) off shore, form part of Ecuador. The climate is affected by the Andes mountains, and the topography ranges from the tropical rainforest on the coast and in the eastern region to the tropical grasslands of the central valley and the permanent snowfields of the highlands. The official language is Spanish, but Quechua and other indigenous languages are very common. Almost all of the inhabitants profess Christianity, and almost 90% are Roman Catholics. The national flag (proportions 1 by 2) has three horizontal stripes, of yellow (one-half of the depth), blue and red. The state flag has, in addition, the national emblem (an oval cartouche, showing Mt Chimborazo and a steamer on a lake, surmounted by a condor) in the centre. The capital is Quito.

Recent History

Ecuador was ruled by Spain from the 16th century until 1822, when it achieved independence as part of Gran Colombia. In 1830 Ecuador seceded and became a separate republic. A long-standing division between Conservatives (Partido Conservador), whose support is generally strongest in the highlands, and Liberals (Partido Liberal, subsequently Partido Liberal Radical), based in the coastal region, began in the 19th century. Until 1948 Ecuador's political life was characterized by a rapid succession of presidents, dictators and juntas. Between 1830 and 1925 the country was governed by 40 different regimes. From 1925 to 1948 there was even greater instability, with a total of 22 heads of state.

Dr Galo Plaza Lasso, who was elected in 1948 and remained in power until 1952, was the first President since 1924 to complete his term of office. He created a climate of stability and economic progress. Dr José María Velasco Ibarra, who had previously been President in 1934–35 and 1944–47, was elected again in 1952 and held office until 1956. A 61-year-old tradition of Liberal Presidents was broken in 1956, when a Conservative candidate, Dr Camilo Ponce Enríquez, took office. He was succeeded in 1960 by Velasco, who campaigned as a non-party Liberal. In the following year, however, President Velasco was deposed by a coup, and was succeeded by his Vice-President, Dr Carlos Julio Arosemena Monroy. The latter was himself deposed in 1963 by a military junta, led by Capt. (later Rear-Adm.) Ramón Castro Jijón, the Commander-in-Chief of the Navy, who assumed the office of President. In 1966 the High Command of the Armed Forces dismissed the junta and installed Clemente Yerovi Indaburu, a wealthy business executive and a former Minister of Economics, as acting President. Yerovi was forced to resign when the Constituent Assembly, elected in October, proposed a new Constitution which prohibited the intervention of the armed forces in politics. In November he was replaced as provisional President by Dr Otto Arosemena Gómez, who held office until the elections of 1968, when Velasco returned from exile to win the presidency for the fifth time.

In 1970 Velasco, with the support of the army, suspended the Constitution, dissolved the Congreso Nacional (National Congress) and assumed dictatorial powers to confront a financial emergency. In 1972 he was overthrown for the fourth time by a military coup, led by Brig.-Gen. Guillermo Rodríguez Lara, the Commander-in-Chief of the Army, who proclaimed himself Head of State. In 1976 President Rodríguez resigned, and power was assumed by a three-man military junta, led by Vice-Adm. Alfredo Poveda Burbano, the Chief of Staff of the Navy. The new junta announced its intention to lead the country to a truly representative democracy. A national referendum approved a newly drafted Constitution in January 1978 and presidential elections took place in July. No candidate achieved an overall majority, and a second round of voting was held in April 1979, when a new legislature was also elected. Jaime Roldós Aguilera of the Concentración de Fuerzas Populares was elected President and he took office in August, when the Congreso was inaugurated and the new Constitution came into force. Roldós

promised social justice and economic development, and guaranteed freedom for the press, but he encountered antagonism from both the conservative sections of the Congreso Nacional and the trade unions. In 1981 Roldós died and was replaced by the Vice-President, Dr Osvaldo Hurtado Larrea. Hurtado encountered opposition from left-wing politicians and trade unions for his efforts to reduce government spending and from right-wing and commercial interests, which feared encroaching state intervention in the private economic sector. In January 1982 the heads of the armed forces resigned and the Minister of Defence was dismissed, when they opposed Hurtado's attempts to settle amicably the border dispute with Peru (see below).

In March 1983 the Government introduced a series of austerity measures, which encountered immediate opposition from the trade unions and private-sector employees. Discontent with the Government's performance was reflected in the results of the presidential and congressional elections of January 1984, when the ruling party, Democracia Popular–Unión Demócrata Cristiana (DP-UDC), lost support. At a second round of voting in May León Febres Cordero, leader of the Partido Social Cristiano (PSC) and presidential candidate of the conservative Frente de Reconstrucción Nacional, unexpectedly defeated Dr Rodrigo Borja Cevallos, representing the left-wing Izquierda Democrática (ID), with 52.2% of the votes cast.

The dismissal of the Chief of Staff of the Armed Forces, Lt-Gen. Frank Vargas Pazzos, brought about a military crisis in 1986. Vargas and his supporters barricaded themselves inside the Mantas military base until they had forced the resignation of both the Minister of Defence and the army commander, who had been accused by Vargas of embezzlement. Vargas then staged a second rebellion at the military base where he had been detained. Troops loyal to the President made an assault on the base, captured Vargas and arrested his supporters. In January 1987 President Febres Cordero was abducted and, after being held for 11 hours, was released in exchange for Vargas, who was granted an amnesty. In July 58 members of the air force were sentenced to up to 16 years' imprisonment for involvement in the abduction of the President.

In June 1986 President Febres Cordero lost the majority that his coalition of parties had held in the Congreso Nacional. In May 1988 Dr Rodrigo Borja Cevallos (of the ID) won the presidential election, securing 46% of the votes cast in a second round of voting, defeating Abdalá Bucaram Ortiz of the Partido Roldosista Ecuatoriano (PRE), who won 41%. Borja took office as President in August, promising to act promptly to address Ecuador's increasing economic problems and to change the country's isolationist foreign policy. However, large demonstrations in protest against the rise in the price of fuel and against other anti-inflationary economic measures swiftly followed.

In February 1989 the Government conducted a campaign to confiscate weapons belonging to paramilitary organizations. In March Alfaro Vive ¡Carajo! (AVC), a leading opposition (hitherto guerrilla) group, urged paramilitary forces across the political spectrum to surrender their weapons. The Government agreed to guarantee the civil rights of AVC members and promised to initiate a national dialogue in return for the group's demobilization. (The AVC concluded the process of demobilization in February 1991 and was absorbed by the ID in October 1991.) The guerrilla organization Montoneros Patria Libre dissociated itself from the agreement between the Government and the AVC and pledged to continue violent opposition.

At mid-term legislative elections in June 1990, the ID conceded control of the legislature to an informal alliance of the PSC and the PRE. In October a serious conflict arose between the Government and the legislature when the newly elected President of the Congreso Nacional, Dr Averroes Bucaram, attempted to stage a legislative coup against President Borja. Bucaram initially impeached several ministers, who were subsequently dismissed by the Congreso. The legislature then dismissed the Supreme Court justices and other high-ranking members of the judiciary, and appointed new courts with shortened mandates. Both the Government and the judiciary refused to recognize these actions, on the grounds that the Congreso had exceeded its constitutional powers. Bucaram then announced that the Congreso would initiate impeachment proceedings against Borja himself. However, this move was averted when three opposition deputies transferred their allegiance, so restoring Borja's congressional majority. Bucaram was subsequently dismissed as congressional President. None the less, impeachment proceedings against government ministers continued into 1991, and by August of that year a total of six ministers had been dismissed.

In May 1990 about 1,000 indigenous Indians marched into Quito to demand official recognition of the land rights and languages of the indigenous population and to win compensation from petroleum companies for environmental damage. In the following month the Confederación Nacional de Indígenas del Ecuador (CONAIE—National Confederation of the Indigenous Population of Ecuador) organized an uprising covering seven Andean provinces. Roads were blockaded, *haciendas* occupied, and supplies to the cities interrupted. Following the arrest of 30 Indians by the army, the rebels took military hostages. The Government offered to hold conciliatory negotiations with CONAIE, in exchange for the hostages. Discussions between CONAIE and President Borja collapsed in August but were resumed in February 1991, following the seizure by Indian groups in the Oriente of eight oil wells. As a result, the Government promised to consider the Indians' demands for stricter controls on the operations of the petroleum industry, and for financial compensation. In April 1992 several thousand Amazon Indians marched from the Oriente to Quito to demand that their historical rights to their homelands be recognized. In May President Borja agreed to grant legal title to more than 1m. ha of land in the province of Pastaza to the Indians.

At legislative elections in May 1992 the PSC gained the highest number of seats in the enlarged Congreso Nacional. The Partido Unidad Republicana (PUR), formed prior to the elections by the former PSC presidential candidate, Sexto Durán Ballén, in order to contest the presidential election, won the second highest number of seats, and was to govern with its ally, the PC. However, as the two parties' seats did not constitute a majority in the Congreso, support from other centre-right parties, particularly the PSC, was sought. In the second round of the presidential election, Durán secured 58% of the votes cast, defeating Nebot, who won 38%.

In September 1992 the Government's announcement of a programme of economic austerity measures, including the restructuring of the public sector, prompted violent demonstrations and several bomb attacks in Quito and Guayaquil and a general strike in May 1993. The 'Modernization Law', a crucial part of the controversial austerity programme (which was to provide for the privatization of some 160 state-owned companies and the reduction in the number of employees in the public sector by 100,000), was approved by the Congreso in August. In November striking teachers organized demonstrations throughout the country, demanding wage increases and reforms in the education system. During the protests two demonstrators were killed and many injured. Furthermore, the Government's decision in January 1994 to increase the price of fuel by more than 70% provoked violent demonstrations throughout the country and a general strike. In the following month the Tribunal of Constitutional Guarantees declared the rise to be unconstitutional, although President Durán refused to recognize the ruling. The unpopularity of Durán's PUR-PC governing alliance was demonstrated at mid-term congressional elections in May, when it won only nine of the 77 seats.

Environmental concerns regarding the exploitation of the Oriente by the petroleum industry continued to be expressed by national and international groups during 1993. In November five Amazon Indian tribes began legal proceedings against the international company Texaco to claim compensation totalling US $1,500m. for its part in polluting the rainforest. (It was estimated that some 17m. barrels of oil had been spilt during the company's 25 years of operations in the region.) Protests intensified in January 1994, when the Government initiated a round of bidding for petroleum-exploration licences for 10 hydrocarbon regions, including sites in the eastern Oriente, previously withheld because of opposition from environmentalists and indigenous communities.

In June 1994 the increasingly vociferous indigenous movement organized large-scale demonstrations across the country, in protest at a recently approved Land Development Law. The law, which allowed for the commercialization of Amerindian lands for farming and resource extraction, provoked serious

unrest and a general strike, during which a state of emergency was declared and the army mobilized. Seven protesters were killed, and many injured, in clashes with the security forces. The law was subsequently judged to be unconstitutional by the Tribunal of Constitutional Guarantees, although, again, President Durán refused to accept the ruling. In July the law was modified to extend the rights of landowners and those employed to work on the land.

In August 1994 a national referendum on constitutional reform finally took place, on President Durán's initiative, following much disagreement between the Government and the judiciary and opposition parties. All but one of the eight proposed reforms (which included measures to alter the electoral system and the role of the Congreso Nacional, and the establishment of a bicameral legislature) were approved; however, only some 50% of eligible voters participated, of whom some 20% returned void ballot papers.

Protests against the Government's economic programme of austerity measures and privatizations in January 1995 resulted in the deaths of two students in Quito during clashes with riot police. During May–July there was severe disruption as a result of further strikes. In July the country was plunged into a serious political crisis when Vice-President Alberto Dahik admitted giving funds from the state budget to opposition deputies (allegedly for use in local public-works projects) in return for their support for the Government's economic reform programme. Dahik refused to resign, despite the initiation of impeachment proceedings, and rejected the criminal charges against him. In a further development (believed by some observers to be an attempt to obstruct the case against Dahik) the President of the Supreme Court and two other justices were dismissed. Critics of the Government's action claimed that the dismissals themselves were unconstitutional, as they did not respect the separation of powers of the judiciary from the legislature and executive. In September impeachment proceedings began against the new Minister of Finance, Mauricio Pinto, for his role in various alleged financial irregularities. Impeachment proceedings against Dahik began in October, and on 11 October the Vice-President resigned.

In September 1995 troops were dispatched to the Galápagos Islands, following disturbances among the islanders, who were demanding the Government's acceptance of a special law granting increased political and financial autonomy to the islands, in addition to some US $16m. in priority economic aid. Concerned about the potentially disastrous effect of the protests on the country's important tourist industry, the Government quickly withdrew its opposition to the proposed legislation and agreed to establish a specialist commission to draft a new law acceptable to all parties. Moreover, in October petroleum workers resumed strike action in protest at the Government's privatization plans, and in one incident occupied the PETRO-ECUADOR building, taking two cabinet ministers hostage for several hours. The strike, together with a severe drought, which halted production at the Paute hydroelectric plant (which, under normal circumstances, provided 60%–70% of the country's electricity), resulted in serious energy shortages in late 1995.

A referendum on government proposals for constitutional reform was held in November 1995. All of the proposed changes were rejected in the plebiscite; the result was widely regarded as a reflection of the Government's continued unpopularity. Despite its decisive defeat, the Government announced its intention to pursue its programme of reforms. Widespread strikes and demonstrations by teachers and students in the same month led to the resignation of the Minister of Education. Industrial action among employees in the energy sector continued, and in January 1996 army units were deployed at prominent sites throughout the country in order to prevent further unrest. However, an industrial dispute by transport workers in March resulted in serious disruption in the capital and prompted a series of strikes in other sectors.

A presidential election, held in May 1996, failed to produce an outright winner, thus necessitating a second round of voting for the two leading contenders, Jaime Nebot Saadi of the PSC and Abdalá Bucaram Ortiz of the PRE. An increasingly vocal and politically-organized indigenous movement resulted in the strong performance of Freddy Ehlers, the candidate for the newly formed Movimiento Nuevo País-Pachakútik (MNPP), a coalition of Amerindian and labour groups. Ehlers secured 21% of the votes. At legislative elections held concurrently, the MNPP also emerged as a significant new force in the legislature, with a total of eight seats. At the second round of voting in the presidential election in July, Bucaram was the unexpected victor, receiving 54.5% of total votes. The success of Bucaram was widely interpreted as a rejection of the policies of the outgoing Government (which Nebot had promised to continue) and an expression of disenchantment with established party politics. Following his inauguration in August, Bucaram sought to allay the fears of the business community (prompted by his proposals for costly social reform) stating that existing economic arrangements would be maintained. Moreover, a team of prominent businessmen was assigned the role of advising the President on economic policy.

A 48-hour general strike began in January 1997, prompted by increases of up to 600% in the price of certain commodities and a climate of considerable dissatisfaction with the President's leadership. Protests intensified in early February when several hundred thousand demonstrators marched through Quito demanding Bucaram's resignation. The President responded by declaring a national holiday and a one-week closure of schools across the country, and stated his support for the strike. Meanwhile, troops were deployed in the capital as violent clashes erupted between protesters and security personnel and Bucaram was barricaded inside the presidential palace. On 6 February, at an emergency session, the Congreso Nacional voted by 44 votes to 34 to dismiss the President on the grounds of mental incapacity; by questioning the President's sanity, the Congreso was able to evade the normal impeachment requirements of a two-thirds' majority. A state of emergency was declared, and the erstwhile Speaker, Fabián Alarcón Rivera, who had assumed the presidency in an acting capacity, urged demonstrators to storm the presidential palace. Bucaram, however, refused to leave office and claimed that he would retain power by force if necessary. The situation was further complicated by the claim of the Vice-President, Rosalia Arteaga, to be the legitimate constitutional successor to Bucaram. Political confusion over the correct procedure led to fears of a military coup, despite a declaration of neutrality by the armed forces. Bucaram fled from the presidential palace on 9 February, and on the following day Arteaga was declared interim President. However, by 11 February Arteaga had resigned, amid continued constitutional uncertainty, and Alarcón was reinstated as President. Alarcón, who sought political reform and the restoration of economic confidence, announced a reorganization of cabinet portfolios (which included no members of the two largest parties in the Congreso, the PSC and the PRE) and the creation of a commission to investigate allegations of corruption against Bucaram and his administration. In March Bucaram's extradition from Panama (where he had been granted political asylum) was requested in order that he face charges of misappropriating some US $90m. of government funds. In the following month the President of the Supreme Court announced that extradition would only be possible once a prison sentence had been issued. Furthermore, in May Bucaram declared his intention to stand as a presidential candidate at Ecuador's next elections. As a result, the legislature voted almost unanimously in favour of a motion to impose an indefinite ban on Bucaram's candidacy in any future presidential election. (In January 1998 the Supreme Court issued a four-year prison sentence to Bucaram for libel and in April 2001 he was indicted on corruption charges.)

In May 1997 a national referendum sought public opinion on a variety of matters, including electoral reform, the modernization of the judiciary and the authenticity of Alarcón's position. Although 40.7% of the electorate did not participate, the vote revealed considerable support for the decision to remove Bucaram from office (75.7%) and for the appointment of Alarcón as interim President (68.3%). Some 64.5% of voters also favoured the creation of a national assembly to consider constitutional reform. Alarcón's apparent success in the referendum, however, was undermined in June by the launch of an official congressional inquiry into allegations that leading drugs-traffickers in the country had contributed to political party funds, and, particularly, to Alarcón's Frente Radical Alfarista.

The announcement in August 1997 that a national assembly to review the Constitution (as proposed in the referendum of May 1997) would not be installed until August 1998 was widely opposed, and provoked a 48-hour strike in protest, which virtually paralysed the country by means of numerous roadblocks. The strike was supported most strongly by Indian and peasant organizations, which insisted that an assembly should be convened as soon as possible in order to discuss indigenous rights and the proposed privatization of key areas of the economy. In

response to the apparent strength of public opinion, it was announced in September that elections for the 70 representatives to the assembly would take place in late November. However, 11 indigenous organizations demonstrated their lack of confidence in the Government to address their concerns by convening a mass rally in Quito to establish guide-lines for their own constitution.

In January 1998, following persistent pleas from international environmental and scientific organizations for greater protection of the Galápagos Islands, the Congreso Nacional approved a law which aimed to preserve the islands' unique environment more effectively. An element of the law, providing for an extension of the marine reserve around the islands from 15 to 40 nautical miles, attracted intense criticism from powerful fishing interests in the country and was, consequently, vetoed by Alarcón, prompting condemnation by environmentalists and small-scale fishing concerns, who claimed that the President had acceded to commercial pressures.

On 10 August 1998, following the conclusion of the discussions of the constituent assembly, a new Constitution came into force. Although it retained the majority of the provisions of the 1979 Constitution, a number of significant reforms were introduced, including the enlargement of the Congreso Nacional from 82 to 121 seats, the abolition of mid-term elections and the completion of a presidential term by the Vice-President in the case of the indefinite absence of the President.

At a presidential election on 31 May 1998 the DP candidate and mayor of Quito, Jamil Mahuad Witt, emerged as the strongest contender, securing 35.2% of total votes cast, while Alvaro Noboa Pontón for the PRE received 26.5% of votes. At the second round of voting in the presidential election on 12 July, Mahuad narrowly defeated Noboa. Noboa rejected the result, making allegations of widespread voting irregularities, none of which was upheld by the Supreme Electoral Tribunal or the international observers present in the country. Mahuad was sworn in on 10 August and appointed a Cabinet consisting predominantly of independent members. The new President's stated objectives focused on the stimulation of economic recovery following a series of serious reversals, including a decrease in world petroleum prices and the infrastructural and sociological damage caused by El Niño (a periodic warming of the tropical Pacific Ocean—see below). In addition, Mahuad proposed a number of social programmes (involving the creation of new jobs and the construction of low-cost homes), which prompted scepticism among observers, who doubted the feasibility of such plans.

A programme of severe adjustment measures, which included huge rises in the cost of domestic gas and electricity, as well as substantial increases in public transport fares and fuel prices, was introduced in September 1998, prompting the Frente Unitario de Trabajadores (FUT) and CONAIE to organize a general strike in the following month. Subsequent rioting and violent confrontation between demonstrators and security personnel resulted in the deaths of four people. In February 1999 disagreement over economic policy led to the resignation of the Minister of Finance, and severe disruption arising from extensive fuel shortages prompted the resignation of the Minister of Energy and Mines. In the same month the leader of the left-wing Movimiento Popular Democrático, Jaime Hurtado González, was assassinated in Quito. The killing was linked to a right-wing Colombian paramilitary group.

In March 1999 a substantial decrease in the value of the sucre led President Mahuad to declare a week-long bank holiday in an attempt to prevent the withdrawal of deposits and reduce the pressure on the currency. A few days later a 60-day state of emergency was declared by the Government in response to a two-day strike, organized by leaders of the main trade unions and Indian groups. In addition, the Government announced an economic retrenchment programme in an attempt to restore investor confidence and prevent economic collapse. Measures included an increase in fuel prices of up to 160%, a number of tax reforms (notably a rise in value-added tax—VAT), the partial 'freezing' of bank accounts, and the planned privatization of certain state-owned companies. These prompted a further series of protests and the resignation of the majority of the board of the central bank (citing differences over government financial policies). The main opposition party, the PSC, similarly refused to endorse the austerity programme, thus compelling the President to compromise with the proposal of less severe economic measures, which were narrowly approved by the Congreso, after which time Mahuad lifted the state of emergency. However, a further rise in prices and the collapse of a major bank (the Banco del Progreso) later in March led to renewed protests.

In April 1999 the Government announced an emergency plan entitled 'Ecuador 2000', which aimed to revive the economy and included a number of requisite measures to gain the support of the IMF. It incorporated numerous social and public works development schemes, tax reforms and moves towards less centralized government. The plan was approved by the IMF and it was hoped that the Fund would provide an estimated US $400m. in initial financing. However, in July taxi drivers and public transport workers took nation-wide industrial action in protest at increases in fuel prices and at the IMF's proposed economic retrenchment plan. In response to the ensuing massive disruption, the Government imposed a further state of emergency and called in the military. The state of emergency was lifted in mid-July, after President Mahuad agreed to 'freeze' fuel prices and allow co-operatives and transport companies access to 'frozen' bank deposits.

In August 1999 the Government announced its intention to default on US $96m. in interest payments on $6,000m. in outstanding foreign debt repayments (on so-called 'Brady bonds'—restructured commercial bank loans) for a period of 30 days, and to attempt to restructure its large external debts. The IMF-supported move was implemented owing to the country's inability to honour repayments on its foreign debt (which was equivalent to some 90% of GDP). At the end of September the IMF signed a preliminary agreement with Ecuador which was expected to provide up to $1,250m. in funding (comprising a $400m. stand-by loan from the IMF and $850m. in loans from other multilateral agencies).

In early January 2000, in an attempt to curb increasing unrest, amid indications that the economic crisis was deteriorating, President Mahuad imposed a state of emergency. However, on 21 January he was forced to flee from the presidential palace following large-scale protests in Quito by thousands of Indian demonstrators, who were supported by sections of the armed forces, over the President's perceived mismanagement of the economic crisis (including his controversial decision to replace the sucre with the US dollar). A three-man council was established to oversee the country. However, Gen. Carlos Mendoza, the Chief of Staff of the Armed Forces, disbanded the council within 24 hours of its creation, and announced the appointment of former Vice-President Gustavo Noboa Bejerano as President. This move followed talks with US officials, who had warned that foreign aid to Ecuador would be curtailed if power was not restored to the elected Government. The coup was widely condemned by governments around the world and by international organizations. Noboa, whose appointment as Head of State was endorsed by a large majority in the Congreso Nacional, promised to restore economic stability to the country. However, Indian activists who had supported the short-lived three-member council continued to demonstrate against the assumption of the presidency by Noboa, whom they viewed as ideologically similar to Mahuad. Noboa appointed Pedro Pinto Rubianes as the new Vice-President on 27 January and formed a new Cabinet, comprising members of the DP, the PSC and the PRE, in February.

In February 2000 four members of the armed forces, who allegedly participated in the events leading up to Mahuad's removal from office, were apprehended on charges of insurrection. It was later announced that as many as 113 army officers were to be charged in connection with the previous month's events. In May the entire military high command was replaced, even though later that month the Congreso approved an amnesty for military officers and civilians arrested in connection with the coup.

Congressional approval for a controversial economic reform programme, the Ley de Transformación Económica (Economic Transformation Law), which included the adoption of the US dollar as the official currency, as well as fiscal adjustments and an acceleration in the privatization process, was secured in February 2000. CONAIE, which had returned to prominence following its role in the removal of President Mahuad, organized a series of demonstrations in protest at the dollarization policy and to demand a referendum on the dissolution of the Congreso Nacional and the Supreme Court. Palliative measures introduced by the Government, including an increase in the minimum wage, were rejected by trade unions and indigenous organizations. Nevertheless, the process of dollarization formally began in March and in September the US dollar officially became Ecuador's sole currency. The announcement by the

Government in May of an IMF-approved economic adjustment package, which included a sharp increase in the price of fuel, provoked further antagonism between the Government and trade unions and indigenous organizations. However, in September CONAIE entered into renewed negotiations with the Government after its calls for mass demonstrations in the previous month had met with only moderate support.

Both the DP and the PSC performed well in municipal and provincial elections held throughout the country in May 2000, suggesting significant popular acceptance of the structural reforms. However, relations between the DP and the PSC were strained in August when the independent Susana González was controversially elected legislative President for the remaining two years of the current presidential term. The PSC claimed that, as the second largest party in the Congreso Nacional, its nominee should fill the position. At the end of the month a Constitutional Tribunal ruled that a new election should be held. In the same month the Government offered to resign in support of the President after the governing coalition lost its majority in the Congreso (divisions within the DP had resulted in several of its members aligning themselves with the centre-left opposition). The coalition's lack of a parliamentary majority endangered the proposed reform (also known as Trole 11) of the labour and petroleum sectors, as well as the privatization process. In late August President Noboa resorted to presidential decree to pass the proposed Trole 11 legislation, prompting CONAIE and trade unions to immediately launch an appeal to the Constitutional Tribunal on the legality of such a move. In January 2001 the Constitutional Tribunal upheld almost one-third of the objections against Trole 11, and, most notably, declared unconstitutional the clause concerning the proposed privatization of state-owned companies.

Popular resentment against the Government erupted in January 2001 after significant increases in fuel prices and transport costs were implemented. Thousands of Indian protesters occupied Quito and roadblocks were erected across the Andean highlands and the Amazon lowlands. In February the Government imposed a national state of emergency, which was lifted only after the Government acceded to the demands for a reduction in fuel prices in return for an end to the protests, which were marred by violence.

In February 2002 indigenous and civic groups in the northeast of the country occupied petroleum refineries, halted construction of a new oil pipeline and blocked major roads, prompting President Noboa to declare a state of emergency in the provinces of Sucumbíos and Orellana. In April, as a concession to the protesters, the Government pledged to direct funds to local infrastructure development. Meanwhile, the Government suffered an additional humiliation when it was forced to suspend the sale of state-owned electricity distribution facilities, owing to a lack of interested foreign buyers.

Presidential and legislative elections were held on 20 October 2002. In the congressional ballot, the PSC won 24 of the 100 contested seats, followed by the ID (15 seats), the PRE (14) and the right-wing Partido Renovador Institucional de Acción Nacional (PRIAN, 10 seats). The presidential election, held concurrently, was notable for a low rate of voter participation (62.9%) and for the electorate's rejection of candidates presented by traditional parties. None of the 11 candidates obtained sufficient votes to secure the presidency, and a second round of voting was held on 24 November, between Lucio Gutiérrez Borbua (a former colonel who had been imprisoned for participating in the coup against President Mahuad in 2000) and Álvaro Noboa Pontón (a banana magnate and founder of the PRIAN). Gutiérrez, who campaigned on a populist, anti-corruption platform, and whose own party (the Partido Sociedad Patriótica 21 de Enero) was supported by the MNPP, secured the presidency, winning 58.7% of the votes in the second round of the election, compared with Noboa's 41.3%.

As President-elect, Gutiérrez made clear his intention to honour Ecuador's debt obligations and continue negotiations with the IMF. Upon taking office in January 2003, he immediately decreed a series of measures intended to prevent a renewed fiscal crisis and to secure a new stand-by loan agreement with the IMF. These measures included a freeze on public-sector wages, a 35% increase in domestic petroleum prices and a 10% rise in electricity tariffs. In early February, following the IMF's approval of Ecuador's draft budget, the Government announced a new US $500m. package of multilateral loans. The new lending was conditional upon the implementation of a series of fiscal and administrative reforms, and the allocation of a higher proportion of oil revenues towards the country's estimated $17,000m. foreign debt. In late February, however, the opposition-controlled Congreso vetoed a tax reform law and reallocated intended debt repayments to health and education, in defiance of the President. Nevertheless, in March the IMF approved a US $205m. stand-by loan, which was followed by further lending from multilateral creditors.

During 2003 the new Government found it increasingly difficult to gain approval for any of its proposed reforms in the opposition-dominated legislature. In April further reforms to the customs service, a condition of the IMF stand-by agreement, were substantially amended by the Congreso before being passed. Proposed legislation to improve supervision of the financial sector was also rejected in May. In the same month teachers began a strike to demand that the Government pay outstanding backdated salaries. The industrial action ended in June after the Government agreed to pay increases in the sector. As a result of the legislative impasse, the governing coalition looked increasingly fragile throughout the year. In June when the President of CONAIE, Leonidas Iza, threatened to suspend its alliance with the Gutiérrez administration if the latter did not abandon its plans to increase fuel prices. Iza's stance gave weight to the demands of workers at the state oil company, PETROECUADOR, who withdrew their labour in June in protest at the proposed partial privatization of the company. The strike ended after the Government abandoned the production-sharing proposals and pledged to discuss future reform of the sector with trade unions. During July several smaller parties withdrew from the governing coalition, including the left-wing Movimiento Popular Democrático and the Ecuarunari. Then, in early August, the MNPP effectively left the Government, when party deputies walked out of a legislative vote on social security reform. The protest prompted President Gutiérrez to effect a cabinet reshuffle, in which all remaining MNPP ministers were replaced. In September President Gutiérrez secured a legislative alliance with the PSC, which resulted in the approval of far-reaching reforms to labour practices within the civil service.

Meanwhile, trade unions and indigenous groups continued to protest at the Government's decision to reduce fuel subsidies, and in November 2003 teaching unions declared an indefinite strike in objection to the level of funding in the sector. On 27 November indigenous groups organized a demonstration in the capital in protest at what they claimed was President Gutiérrez's failure to fulfil electoral pledges of social welfare reform. In the same month the Minister of Tourism, Nelson Herrera, resigned following accusations that he had used a private aeroplane belonging to César Fernández Cevallos, a former governor of Manabí who had been arrested in October on drugs-trafficking charges. Furthermore, the Congreso ordered an investigation into reports that Fernández Cevallos had contributed financially to the electoral campaign of President Gutiérrez. The scandal prompted a reallocation of government portfolios in December, in which seven cabinet members were replaced, although several senior ministers were reappointed to their posts. However, Gutiérrez's attempts to re-establish support for his Government suffered a set-back in early 2004 following a series of cabinet resignations; in early February the Minister of Agriculture, Sergio Seminario, resigned after it became clear that his proposed reforms were not going to be approved in the legislature, then in early March the housing and environment ministers also stepped down. Furthermore, in April, the Minister of Energy and Mines, Carlos Arboleda, resigned following opposition criticism of perceived plans to privatize PETRO-ECUADOR. He was replaced by Eduardo López, hitherto the presidential representative on PETROECUADOR's board.

On 1 February 2004 Iza was shot outside CONAIE's headquarters. The assassination attempt ended the uneasy truce between the Government and indigenous organizations and reignited calls for President Gutiérrez's resignation. However, in mid-February negotiations began between CONAIE and government representatives. In May the Confederación de las Nacionalidades Indígenas de la Amazonia Ecuatoriana (CONFENIAE—The Confederation of Amazonian Indigenous Peoples) withdrew its support for the Gutiérrez administration in favour of the opposition policies of CONAIE, accusing the Government of failing to fulfil its commitments.

Throughout 2004 the Gutiérrez Government was implicated in several corruption scandals. In March the former governor of the province of Manabí, who had been arrested on drugs-trafficking charges in October 2003, confirmed that he had contributed to the President's election campaign. Then in May the

Minister of Social Welfare, Patricio Acosta, was forced to resign after being implicated in a corruption investigation in the USA. He was replaced by Antonio Vargas. In the same month several oil companies accused the President of involvement in the bribing of officials at a PETROECUADOR subsidiary. Then, on 1 June the Minister of the Economy and Finance, Mauricio Pozo, resigned as congressional investigation got under way into his alleged use of social security funds to alleviate the budget deficit. The resignation of Pozo was a particular set-back for Gutiérrez, as not only was he a staunch ally of the President, but he was also the architect of the austere economic policy pursued by the Gutiérrez Government. Pozo's departure from government was preceded one day earlier by the resignation of the agriculture minister, Salomón Larrea, who had only been in the post since February.

At municipal and provincial elections held on 17 October 2004, the ruling PSP secured only two of 22 provincial mayoralties. Furthermore, in early November opposition parties, led by the PSC, began congressional proceedings to impeach the President on charges of misuse of public funds during the recent election campaign. However, support for the motion failed after the Government succeeded in assembling a so-called 'new majority' in the Congreso (a pro-Government bloc comprising the PSP, the PRE, the PRIAN, the Movimiento Popular Democrático, the Concentración de Fuerzas Populares, the Partido Socialist-Frente Amplio and independents). Nevertheless, opposition deputies did succeed in bringing a motion of censure against the Minister of Social Welfare, Antonio Vargas (he resigned in February 2005), and earlier in the month the Minister of the Interior, Raúl Baca Carbo, had also stepped down, apparently in a presidential bid to secure the PRE's support in the Congreso (Baca had called for the PRE's leader, former President Bucaram to be arrested if he returned to Ecuador).

In early December 2004 the Congreso voted to replace 27 of the 31 members of the Supreme Court, in which, President Gutiérrez alleged, the PSC exerted undue influence. Most of the new judges were allied with, or were sympathetic to, the pro-Government parties. The replacement of the Supreme Court judges was condemned by opposition groups, business leaders and foreign governments as unconstitutional. The dismissed judges subsequently established a 'Supreme Court-in-exile' in protest. In late January 2005 President Gutiérrez sought congressional approval for a proposed referendum on the composition of the Supreme Court, the Electoral Court and the Constitutional Court. Gutiérrez's proposal prompted the resignation, in late February, of the Minister of the Interior, Jaime Damerval, who instead favoured the establishment of an electoral council to designate replacements to the Supreme Court. He was replaced by Javier Ledesma. Opposition groups speculated that the purge of the Supreme Court was a preliminary step towards allowing former President Bucaram to end his exile in Panama without facing charges for misuse of public funds. Indeed, in early April former President Bucaram returned to Ecuador after the new President of the Supreme Court, Guillermo Castro, a staunch ally of Bucaram and a co-founder of the PRE, annulled his conviction. Castro claimed that Bucaram had been denied due process during his trial. Proceedings were also suspended against former President Noboa and former Vice-President Dahik on the same grounds.

In mid-February 2005 opposition parties organized a march in Quito in protest at the Government's increasingly authoritarian measures. It was estimated that as many as 150,000 people attended the demonstration. Well-supported opposition demonstrations in Quito and elsewhere were held throughout March and April. In response to the increasingly vociferous public protests, on 15 April President Gutiérrez announced the dissolution of the Supreme Court. None the less, on 19 April some 30,000 demonstrators surrounded the presidential palace to demand his resignation. On the following day the Congreso voted almost unanimously to dismiss Gutiérrez from office for 'abandonment of his post' (Gutiérrez fled to Brazil, where he claimed asylum). Alfredo Palacio Gonzales, hitherto Vice-President, was subsequently appointed head of state, pending new presidential elections. From 25 April Palacio began to make appointments to a new Cabinet composed largely of independent technocrats, and which included, notably, Rafael Correa Delgado as Minister of Economy and Finance. On 4 May Palacio appointed Alejandro Serrano as Vice-President. The new President announced his intention to honour Ecuador's international obligations, although he appealed for greater debt forgiveness from international creditors in order to increase social spending and restore stability to the country. Meanwhile, on 26 April the Congreso voted to dismiss the judges sitting on the Constitutional and Electoral Courts.

In April 1999 the World Trade Organization (WTO) upheld the complaint, put forward by the USA, Ecuador and four other Latin American countries, that the European Union (EU) unfairly favoured Caribbean banana producers, and authorized the USA to impose trade sanctions against EU goods. A two-tier tariff rate quota arrangement was agreed at a meeting between Ecuadorean government officials and leaders of Caribbean banana-producing countries in November, easing restrictions on Latin American banana exporters and consequently assisting Ecuadorean producers. In April 2001 the EU provided assurances to Ecuadorean producers over access to the EU market: quotas for Latin American producers were to be phased out by 2006 and replaced by a uniform tariff system. However, in January 2005 the Government expressed its strong opposition to the EU's proposed tariff of €230 per metric ton on Latin American banana imports, due to come into effect in January 2006. It was expected that the dispute would be submitted for the arbitration of the WTO.

The long-standing border dispute with Peru over the Cordillera del Cóndor erupted into war in January 1981. A cease-fire was declared a few days later under the auspices of the guarantors of the Rio Protocol of 1942 (Argentina, Brazil, Chile and the USA). The Protocol was not recognized by Ecuador as it awarded the area, which affords access to the Amazon river system, to Peru. Further clashes occurred along the border with Peru in December 1982 and January 1983. In January 1992 discussions on the border dispute were resumed. However, in January 1995 serious fighting broke out between the two sides, following reports of Peruvian incursions into Ecuadorean territory. Both Governments denied responsibility for instigating hostilities and issued contradictory reports concerning subsequent clashes. Following offers from the Organization of American States (OAS, see p. 319) and the four guarantor nations of the Rio Protocol, representatives of the two Governments met for negotiations in Rio de Janeiro, Brazil, and a cease-fire agreement was concluded in February. An observer mission, representing the four guarantor nations, was dispatched to the border, to oversee the separation of forces and demilitarization of the border area. Following intensive negotiations, agreement on the delimitation of the demilitarized zone in the disputed area was reached in July, and in October Ecuador finally repealed the state of emergency. A resumption of negotiations in September 1996 resulted in the signing of the Santiago Agreement by both sides in the following month, which was to provide a framework for a definitive solution on the border issue.

Following further negotiations in early 1998 a number of commissions were established to examine specific aspects of a potential agreement between Ecuador and Peru, including a trade and navigation treaty and the fixing of frontier markers on the ground in the Cordillera del Cóndor. Talks culminated in the signing of an accord in Brasília on 26 October by the Ministers of Foreign Affairs of Ecuador and Peru in the presence of the two countries' Presidents and of six other regional leaders. The accord confirmed Peru's claim regarding the delineation of the border, but granted Ecuador navigation and trading rights on the Amazon and its tributaries and the opportunity to establish two trading centres in Peru (although this was not to constitute sovereign access). Moreover, Ecuador was given 1 sq km of territory, as private property, at Tiwintza in Peru where many Ecuadorean soldiers, killed during the conflict in 1995, were buried. An official ceremony in May 1999 marked the transfer of Tiwintza from Peru to Ecuador, and both parties confirmed that two ecological parks were to be created along the common border, where military personnel would not be allowed access. Presidents Mahuad and Alberto Fujimori reiterated their intention to seek US $3,000m. in funding, over a 10-year period, to finance a number of development projects (including the construction of new roads and health and education centres) and to organize the removal of land mines in the border area.

Following the suspected involvement of Colombian paramilitaries in the murder of an Ecuadorean politician in Quito in February 1999 (see above) and reports of the presence of these troops in the country, Ecuador's military presence was strengthened at its border with Colombia. Nevertheless, criminal and military activities attributed to Colombian combatants continued on Ecuadorean territory. As the internal conflict in Colombia escalated from 2000, the number of Colombian refugees in Ecuador increased to an estimated 250,000 in 2003. In

April 2001 the US Administration of George W. Bush proposed a US $882.3m. package of economic and counter-narcotics assistance for Colombia, Peru, Bolivia, Ecuador, Brazil, Panama and Venezuela, known as the Andean Regional Initiative, under which Ecuador would receive some $76.5m. in aid for border-area development and security.

In March 2003 Colombian-Ecuadorean relations suffered after the new Ecuadorean Government of Lucio Gutiérrez ruled out the possibility of formally classifying the Fuerzas Armadas Revolucionarias de Colombia—Ejército del Pueblo (FARC—EP) as a terrorist organization. In October, however, allegations emerged that members of the Ecuadorean army had supplied a rocket used by the FARC—EP in an attack in the Colombian capital, Santafé de Bogotá. The Ecuadorean military protested the allegations and deployed some 7,000 troops to patrol the joint border. In November the Ecuadorean Government cancelled plans to allow the USA to construct three logistical centres in the country's northern provinces. In January 2004, following Ecuador's co-operation in the arrest of a senior FARC—EP operative in Quito, the Government announced that it would implement a so-called 'Plan Ecuador' to prevent the further spread of the Colombian conflict into Ecuadorean territory. In March the Colombian Government agreed to increase its military presence along the common border. However, following the initiation in April of the so-called 'Plan Patriota' offensive by the Colombian military against the FARC—EP, the Ecuadorean Government expressed concern at an increase in illegal incursions into its territory by the guerrilla grouping and by Colombian drugs-traffickers. In that month Ecuador increased its troop numbers on its border with Colombia. In October the head of the Colombian military, Carlos Alberto Ospina Ovalle, acknowledged the existence of such incursions from Colombia. In late February 2005 it was announced that 10 FARC—EP combatants had been captured in Quito in a joint operation by Colombian and Ecuadorean security forces.

Government

Executive power is vested in the President, who is directly elected by universal adult suffrage for a four-year term (starting from 15 January of the year following his election). The President is not eligible for re-election. Legislative power is held by the 100-member unicameral Congreso Nacional (National Congress), which is also directly elected for a four-year term. Ecuador comprises 21 provinces, composed of 193 cantons, 322 urban parishes and 757 rural parishes. Each province has a Governor, who is appointed by the President.

Defence

Military service, which lasts one year, is selective for men at the age of 20. In August 2004 there were 46,500 men in the armed forces: army 37,000, navy 5,500 (including 1,700 marines) and air force 4,000. Overall defence expenditure in 2004 was estimated to be US $588m.

Economic Affairs

In 2003, according to estimates by the World Bank, Ecuador's gross national income (GNI), measured at average 2001–2003 prices, was US $25,106m., equivalent to $1,790 per head (or $3,440 per head on an international purchasing-power parity basis). During 1990–2003, it was estimated, the population increased at an average annual rate of 1.9%, while gross domestic product (GDP) per head increased, in real terms, at an average annual rate of 0.4% in 1990–2003. Overall GDP increased, in real terms, at an average annual rate of 2.2% in 1990–2003; GDP increased by 2.6% in 2003.

Agriculture (including hunting, forestry and fishing) contributed 9.1% of GDP in 2003. According to census figures, some 9.2% of the active labour force were employed in the agricultural sector in 2003. Ecuador is the world's leading exporter of bananas, and coffee and cocoa are also important cash crops. The seafood sector, particularly the shrimp industry, was also a significant contributor to the economy. Ecuador's extensive forests yield valuable hardwoods, and the country is a leading producer of balsawood. Exports of cut flowers increased from US $0.5m. in 1985 to $283m. in 2002 (equivalent to 5.7% of the total value of exports). During 1990–2003 agricultural GDP decreased at an average annual rate of 1.7%. According to the World Bank, sectoral GDP grew by 7.2% in 2002 and by 2.5% in 2003.

Industry (including mining, manufacturing, construction and power) employed 21.7% of the active urban labour force, and provided 29.0% of GDP in 2003. During 1990–2003 industrial

GDP increased at an average annual rate of 2.9%. According to the World Bank, the sector grew by 0.1% in 2002 and by 4.0% in 2003.

Mining contributed 12.6% of GDP in 2003, although the mining sector employed only 0.6% of the urban labour force in that year. Petroleum and its derivatives remained the major exports in the early 21st century. Acording to the US Energy Information Administration, production averaged 421,000 barrels per day (b/d) in 2003; in April of that year the Government announced plans to increase production to some 613,000 b/d by 2007. In January 2004 proven petroleum reserves were estimated at 4,600m. barrels. Earnings from petroleum exports amounted to some US $2,060.9m. in 2002, equivalent to 41.0% of the total value of exports. Natural gas is extracted, but only a small proportion is retained. In January 2004 proven reserves of natural gas were 345,000m. cu ft, according to the US Energy Information Administration. Gold, silver, copper, antimony and zinc are also mined. In real terms, the GDP of the mining sector increased at an average rate of 4.1% per year during 1990–2001. According to the IMF, mining GDP increased by 1.7% in 2001, but decreased by 3.5% in 2002.

Manufacturing contributed 11.0% of GDP and employed 13.8% of the active force in urban areas in 2003. The most important branches of manufacturing were food, beverages and tobacco, textiles, clothing and leather and mineral and basic metallic products. Petroleum refining was also important. During 1990–2003 manufacturing GDP increased at an average annual rate of 0.9%, according to the World Bank. It increased by 0.7% in 2002 and by a further 2.5% in 2003.

Energy is derived principally from thermoelectric and hydroelectric plants. The country has an installed capacity of 3.2m. MW, one-half of which is produced domestically. Most domestic output comes from the Paute hydroelectricity plant. In 2004 plans were under way to build a hydroelectricity station at Mazar, south of Paute, to alleviate the effects of the frequent power shortages. The new plant was expected to produce a further 180 MW of electricity. Imports of fuels and lubricants comprised 4.5% of the value of total imports in 2002.

The services sector contributed 61.9% of GDP in 2003. Some 69.2% of the active urban labour force were employed in services in that year. The sector's GDP increased at an average annual rate of 2.9% during 1990–2003. It increased by 4.3% in 2002 and by a further 1.7% in 2003, according to the World Bank.

In 2003 Ecuador recorded a visible trade deficit of US $71m., and a deficit of $455m. on the current account of the balance of payments. In 2002 the principal source of imports was the USA (accounting for 23.0% of the total), which was also the principal market for exports (40.8%). Other major trading partners were the People's Republic of China, Colombia, Germany, Italy, Japan, the Republic of Korea, Panama and Peru. The principal exports in 2002 were petroleum and petroleum derivatives (41.0%), bananas (19.3%) and seafood products (13.7%). The principal imports in 2002 were machinery and transport equipment (40.7%), basic manufactures (17.9%) and chemicals (16.2%).

In 2002 there was a budgetary deficit of about US $185m. In 2002 some 28.7% of government expenditure was financed by revenue from petroleum. Ecuador's total external debt was US $16,452m. at the end of 2002, of which $13,828m. was long-term public debt. In that year the cost of debt-servicing was equivalent to 28.7% of the total value of exports of goods and services. In January 2005 President Gutiérrez led a government delegation to New York, USA, in a bid to persuade holders of government bonds due to mature in 2012 to exchange them for longer term bonds at lower rates of interest. The average annual rate of inflation in 1992–2003 was 34.0%; the rate averaged 12.4% in 2002 and 7.9% in 2003. The rate of unemployment decreased from an average of 14.0% in 1999 to 11.0% in late 2004.

Ecuador is a member of the Andean Community (see p. 148), the Organization of American States (OAS, see p. 319) and of the Asociación Latinoamericana de Integración (ALADI, see p. 289). In 1992 Ecuador withdrew from the Organization of the Petroleum Exporting Countries (OPEC, see p. 331) and announced its intention of seeking associate status. In 1995 Ecuador joined the World Trade Organization (WTO, see p. 357). In December 2004 Ecuador was one of the founder signatories to the agreement signed in Cusco, Peru, creating the South American Community of Nations (Comunidad Sudamericana de Naciones), intended to promote greater regional economic integration, due to become operational by 2007.

In the mid-1990s Ecuador's proven petroleum reserves almost tripled following discoveries in the Amazon region, and the Government signed contracts with numerous companies for further exploration and drilling. In late 1997 work to expand the capacity of the trans-Ecuadorean pipeline from 330,000 b/d to 410,000 b/d began. A new pipeline for heavy crudes (Oleoducto para Crudos Pesados—OCP), financed by a consortium of private companies at a cost of US $594m., became operative in September 2004, despite concerted protests from indigenous groups and environmental activists. From 2000 attempts to privatize a number of state-owned industries were repeatedly impeded by political turmoil, trade union opposition and a lack of interested investors. In April 2000 the IMF approved a 12-month stand-by credit of US $304m. to support the costly dollarization process. However, opposition from the Congreso Nacional, as well as from indigenous organizations and trade unions, delayed the release of the loan, which was conditional on implementation of several reforms, including a proposed increase in value-added tax (VAT). In January 2003 the new President, Lucio Gutiérrez, secured a further $500m. in IMF loans, following government pledges of fiscal reform. The IMF arrangement was conditional on the administration allocating a greater proportion of oil revenues towards debt repayment, which was projected at some 40% of the national budget in 2003. However, reports of a significant fall in petroleum production in that year led to fears that government revenues would not improve, despite high international oil prices and the completion of the new heavy-oil pipeline in September. Furthermore, by 2004 little progress had been made on IMF-mandated proposals to place the state telecommunications companies Andinatel and Pacifictel under private management. In December 2004 the IMF delivered a generally favourable assessment of Ecuador's macroeconomic performance, although it stressed the need for economic diversification and reforms to the financial, utility, petroleum and labour markets. In late 2004 the non-petroleum economy remained stagnant and some 60% of the population continued to live in poverty. Nevertheless, the IMF estimated growth of 5.4% in 2004 and predicted a further increase of 4.0% in 2005.

Education

Education is compulsory for 10 years, to be undertaken between five and 15 years of age, and all state schools are free. Private schools continue to play a vital role in the educational system. Primary education begins at six years of age and lasts for six years. Secondary education, in general and specialized technical or humanities schools, begins at the age of 12 and lasts for up to six years, comprising two equal cycles of three years each. In 1997 the total enrolment at primary and secondary schools was equivalent to 89.5% of the school-age population. In 1999/2000 there were 3,502 secondary schools and 18,033 primary schools. University courses extend for up to six years, and include programmes for teacher training. Total expenditure on education by the central Government was estimated at 1,957,051m. sucres (equivalent to 3.5% of GNP) in 1996. In many rural areas, Quechua and other indigenous Indian languages are used in education.

Public Holidays

2005: 1 January (New Year's Day), 6 January (Epiphany), 7–8 February (Carnival), 24 March (Holy Thursday), 25 March (Good Friday), 26 March (Easter Saturday), 1 May (Labour Day), 24 May (Battle of Pichincha), 26 May (Corpus Christi), 24 July (Birth of Simón Bolívar), 10 August (Independence of Quito), 9 October (Independence of Guayaquil), 12 October (Discovery of America), 1 November (All Saints' Day), 2 November (All Souls' Day), 3 November (Independence of Cuenca), 6 December (Foundation of Quito), 25 December (Christmas Day).

2006: 1 January (New Year's Day), 6 January (Epiphany), 27–28 February (Carnival), 13 April (Holy Thursday), 14 April (Good Friday), 15 April (Easter Saturday), 1 May (Labour Day), 24 May (Battle of Pichincha), 15 June (Corpus Christi), 24 July (Birth of Simón Bolívar), 10 August (Independence of Quito), 9 October (Independence of Guayaquil), 12 October (Discovery of America), 1 November (All Saints' Day), 2 November (All Souls' Day), 3 November (Independence of Cuenca), 6 December (Foundation of Quito), 25 December (Christmas Day).

Weights and Measures

The metric system is in force.

Statistical Survey

Sources (unless otherwise stated): Banco Central del Ecuador, Quito; Ministerio de Comercio Exterior, Industrialización, Pesca y Competitividad; Instituto Nacional de Estadística y Censos, Juan Larrea 534 y Riofrío, Quito; tel. (2) 529-858; e-mail inec1@ecnet.ec; internet www.inec.gov.ec.

Area and Population

AREA, POPULATION AND DENSITY

Area (sq km)	272,045*
Population (census results)†	
25 November 1990	9,648,189
25 November 2001	
Males	6,018,353
Females	6,138,255
Total	12,156,608
Population (UN estimate at mid-year)‡	
2002	12,810,000
2003	13,003,000
Density (per sq km) at mid-2003	47.8

* 105,037 sq miles.
† Excluding nomadic tribes of indigenous Indians and any adjustment for underenumeration, estimated to have been 6.3% in 1990; the 1990 total was subsequently revised to 9,697,979.
‡ Source: UN, *World Population Prospects: The 2002 Revision.*

PROVINCES
(2001 census)

	Population	Capital
Azuay	599,546	Cuenca
Bolívar	169,370	Guaranda
Cañar	206,981	Azogues
Carchi	152,939	Tulcán
Chimborazo . . .	403,632	Riobamba
Cotopaxi	349,540	Latacunga
El Oro	525,763	Machala
Esmeraldas . . .	385,223	Esmeraldas
Guayas	3,309,034	Guayaquil
Imbabura	344,044	Ibarra
Loja	404,835	Loja
Los Ríos	650,178	Babahoyo
Manabí	1,186,025	Portoviejo
Morona Santiago . .	115,412	Macas
Napo	79,139	Tena
Orellana	86,493	Puerto Francisco de Orellana (Coca)
Pastaza	61,779	Puyo
Pichincha	2,388,817	Quito
Sucumbíos . . .	128,995	Nueva Loja
Tungurahua . . .	441,034	Ambato
Zamora Chinchipe .	76,601	Zamora
Archipiélago de Colón (Galápagos)	18,640	Puerto Baquerizo (Isla San Cristóbal)
Total*	**12,156,608**	

* Including persons in unspecified areas, totalling 72,588.

PRINCIPAL TOWNS
(2001 census)

Guayaquil . .	1,985,379	Ambato . . .	154,095
Quito (capital) . .	1,399,378	Riobamba . . .	124,807
Cuenca . . .	277,374	Quevedo . . .	120,379
Machala . . .	204,578	Loja . . .	118,532
Santo Domingo de los Colorados . .	199,827	Milagro . . .	113,440
Manta . . .	183,105	Ibarra . . .	108,535
Portoviejo . .	171,847	Esmeraldas . .	95,124

Mid-2003 (UN estimate, incl. suburbs): Guayaquil 2,262,343 (Source: UN, *World Urbanization Prospects: The 2003 Revision*).

BIRTHS, MARRIAGES AND DEATHS
(excluding nomadic Indian tribes)*

	Registered live births†		Registered marriages		Registered deaths	
	Number	Rate (per 1,000)	Number	Rate (per 1,000)	Number	Rate (per 1,000)
1995	408,983	23.7	70,480	6.2	50,867	4.4
1996	302,217	23.1	72,094	6.2	52,300	4.5
1997	288,803	22.8	66,967	5.6	52,089	4.4
1998	364,684	22.7	69,867	n.a.	54,357	4.5
1999	368,659	24.6	77,593	n.a.	55,921	4.5
2000	345,715	23.4	74,875	n.a.	56,240	4.5
2001	332,776	n.a.	67,741	n.a.	55,214	4.5

* Registrations incomplete.
† Figures include registrations of large numbers of births occurring in previous years. The number of births registered in the year of occurrence was: 181,268 in 1995, 182,242 in 1996, 169,869 in 1997, 199,079 in 1998, 218,108 in 1999, 202,257 in 2000 and 192,786 in 2001.

Source: partly UN, *Demographic Yearbook.*

2002 (excluding nomadic Indian tribes): Live births registered in year of occurrence 183,792; Deaths 55,549 (Source: UN, *Population and Vital Statistics Report*).

Marriages: 66,208 in 2002.

Expectation of life (WHO estimates, years at birth): 70.6 (males 67.9; females 73.5) in 2002 (Source: WHO, *World Health Report*).

ECONOMICALLY ACTIVE POPULATION
(ISIC major divisions, urban areas only, '000 persons aged 10 years and over, at November of each year, unless otherwise indicated)

	2001*	2002	2003
Agriculture, hunting and forestry .	239.8	261.2	276.7
Fishing	42.3	35.6	46.0
Mining and quarrying . . .	18.3	22.3	20.4
Manufacturing	610.6	501.5	487.8
Electricity, gas and water . . .	27.8	14.0	17.0
Construction	234.9	240.5	239.9
Wholesale and retail trade; repair of motor vehicles, motorcycles and personal and household goods .	1,026.7	971.5	1,000.8
Hotels and restaurants . . .	158.2	147.4	131.3
Transport, storage and communications	244.6	222.3	233.2
Financial intermediation . .	33.5	46.4	51.8
Real estate, renting and business activities	158.2	155.0	154.9
Public administration and defence; compulsory social security . .	159.9	146.1	181.7
Education	211.4	238.8	234.4
Health and social work . . .	99.8	118.6	116.5
Other community, social and personal service activities . .	154.2	121.0	174.5
Private households with employed persons	232.1	217.0	163.4
Extra-territorial organizations and bodies	1.4	0.4	1.0
Activities not adequately defined . .	19.6	—	—
Total employed	**3,673.2**	**3,459.4**	**3,531.2**
Unemployed	451.0	352.9	461.1
Total labour force	**4,124.2**	**3,812.3**	**3,992.3**
Males	2,380.7	2,267.9	2,353.4
Females	1,743.6	1,544.4	1,638.9

* At July.

Source: ILO.

Health and Welfare

KEY INDICATORS

Total fertility rate (children per woman, 2002)	2.8
Under-5 mortality rate (per 1,000 live births, 2003) . . .	27
HIV/AIDS (% of persons aged 15–49, 2003)	0.6
Physicians (per 1,000 head, 1997)	1.70
Hospital beds (per 1,000 head, 1996)	1.55
Health expenditure (2001): US $ per head (PPP) . . .	177
Health expenditure (2001): % of GDP	4.5
Health expenditure (2001): public (% of total)	50.4
Access to water (% of persons, 2002)	86
Access to sanitation (% of persons, 2002)	72
Human Development Index (2002): ranking	100
Human Development Index (2002): value	0.735

For sources and definitions, see explanatory note on p. vi.

Agriculture

PRINCIPAL CROPS
('000 metric tons)

	2001	2002	2003
Rice (paddy)	1,256	1,285	1,236
Barley	26	29	27
Maize	337	602	677
Potatoes	441	485	397
Cassava (Manioc)	84	95	131
Sugar cane	5,654	5,670	5,691
Dry beans	30	48	49
Soybeans (Soya beans) . . .	113	109	109
Coconuts	25	22	21
Oil palm fruit*	1,424	1,506	1,450
Tomatoes	29	48	49
Pumpkins, squash and gourds* .	42	43	23
Onions and shallots (green) . .	101	98	70
Carrots	21	20	23
Watermelons	26	30	29
Other vegetables and melons* . .	93	108	112
Bananas	6,077	5,528	5,883
Plantains	813	542	651
Oranges	152	178	213
Tangerines, mandarins,			
clementines and satsumas . .	18	23	35
Grapefruit and pomelo . . .	4	32	31
Mangoes	89	101	89
Pineapples	47	77	90
Papayas	17	20	23
Other fresh fruit (excl. melons)* .	349	395	392
Coffee (green)	165	79	83
Cocoa beans	76	88	89
Abaca (Manila hemp)* . . .	25	26	26

* FAO estimates.

Source: FAO.

LIVESTOCK
('000 head, year ending September)

	2001	2002	2003
Cattle	4,657	4,794	4,977*
Sheep	2,249	2,381	2,645
Pigs*	2,897	2,959	3,007
Horses†	525	528	530
Goats	273	278	279†
Asses†	270	275	280
Mules†	158	160	160
Chickens	138,429	139,000†	142,000†
Ducks†	152	155	158
Geese†	50	50	50
Turkeys†	22	25	26

* Unofficial figure(s).
† FAO estimate(s).

Source: FAO.

LIVESTOCK PRODUCTS
('000 metric tons)

	2001	2002	2003
Beef and veal*	189.2	206.2	232.8
Mutton and lamb†	6.3	6.2	7.7
Pig meat	139.5*	144.9	154.0
Goat meat	1.3†	1.9	2.5
Poultry meat	202.9*	208.2	211.2
Cows' milk	2,431.1	2,433.2	2,456.5
Sheep's milk†	6.2	6.2	6.2
Goats' milk†	2.5	2.5	2.6
Butter†	5.1	5.3	4.9
Cheese†	7.7	8.2	7.3
Hen eggs	72.5	73.5	74.0
Wool: greasy†	2.2	2.4	2.6
Wool: scoured†	1.1	1.2	1.3
Cattle hides (fresh)†	31.6	34.4	34.4

* Unofficial figure(s).
† FAO estimate(s).

Source: FAO.

Forestry

ROUNDWOOD REMOVALS
('000 cubic metres, excluding bark)

	2001	2002	2003
Pulpwood	858	913	913
Fuel wood*	5,201	5,274	5,350
Total	6,059	6,187	6,263

* FAO estimates.

Source: FAO.

SAWNWOOD PRODUCTION
('000 cubic metres, including railway sleepers)

	2000	2001	2002
Coniferous (softwood) . . .	121	134	150
Broadleaved (hardwood) . .	594	660	600
Total	715	794	750

2003: Production as in 2002 (FAO estimates).

Source: FAO.

Fishing

('000 metric tons, live weight)

	2000	2001	2002
Capture	592.5	586.6	318.5*
Gurnards and searobins . .	27.1	1.4	1.5*
Chilean jack mackerel . .	7.1	134.0	0.6
South American pilchard . .	51.6	42.1	2.5
Pacific thread herring . . .	20.5	19.9	11.0
Anchoveta (Peruvian anchovy) .	—	2.1	71.0
Pacific anchoveta	13.8	73.5	18.3
Skipjack tuna	105.1	68.2	77.8
Yellowfin tuna	37.0	57.6	36.3
Bigeye tuna	29.4	23.4	21.3
Chub mackerel	84.3	85.4	17.1
Aquaculture	62.1	68.0	70.2*
Whiteleg shrimp	50.1	60.0	60.0*
Total catch	654.7	654.5	388.7*

* FAO estimate.

Source: FAO.

Mining

('000 barrels, unless otherwise indicated)

	1999	2000	2001
Crude petroleum	136,291	146,180	147,468
Natural gas (million cu m) . . .	964	1,057	1,050*
Natural gasoline	2,014	2,818	2,820*
Gold (kilograms)†	2,026	2,871	2,297

* Estimate.
† Metal content of ore only.

Source: US Geological Survey.

Industry

SELECTED PRODUCTS
('000 barrels, unless otherwise indicated)

	1999	2000	2001
Jet fuels	1,554	1,976	2,000*
Kerosene	716	575	600*
Motor spirit (gasoline) . . .	9,783	9,272	9,300*
Distillate fuel oils	8,361	12,161	12,000*
Residual fuel oils	20,833	16,327	16,300*
Liquefied petroleum gas . . .	3,000	2,600	2,800*
Crude steel ('000 metric tons) . .	53	58	61
Cement ('000 metric tons) . .	2,300	2,800*	2,850*
Electric energy (million kWh)† .	10,305	10,607	n.a.

* Provisional or estimated figure.
† Source: UN, *Industrial Commodity Statistics*.

Source (unless otherwise indicated): US Geological Survey.

Finance

CURRENCY AND EXCHANGE RATES

Monetary Units
United States currency is used: 100 cents = 1 US dollar ($).

Sterling and Euro Equivalents (31 December 2004)
£1 sterling = US $1.93;
€1 = US $1.36;
US $100 = £51.78 = €73.42.

Note: Ecuador's national currency was formerly the sucre. From 13 March 2000 the sucre was replaced by the US dollar, at an exchange rate of $1 = 25,000 sucres. Both currencies were officially in use for a transitional period of 180 days, but from 9 September sucres were withdrawn from circulation and the dollar became the sole legal tender.

BUDGET
(US $ million)

Revenue	2000	2001	2002
Petroleum revenue	1,396	1,280	1,363
Non-petroleum revenue . . .	1,854	2,566	3,209
Taxation	1,747	2,369	2,750
Taxes on income and profits .	458	475	531
Property taxes	14	23	49
Value-added tax	836	1,340	1,529
Selective excise taxes . . .	75	137	221
Taxes on international trade .	341	373	419
Import duties	321	354	414
Export duties	17	18	5
Other taxes	23	21	1
Non-tax revenue	107	158	338
Transfers	—	58	122
Statistical discrepancy . . .	—	–19	—
Total	3,250	3,846	4,572

Expenditure	2000	2001	2002
Wages and salaries	703	1,088	1,673
Purchases of goods and services .	169	122	318
Interest payments	1,009	938	823
Current transfers	145	183	366
Other current expenditure . . .	542	300	351
Capital expenditure	659	1,438	1,226
Fixed capital formation . .	425	645	611
Capital transfers	234	562	618
Other capital expenditure . .	—	232	–2
Total	3,227	4,068	4,757

Source: IMF, *Ecuador: Selected Issues and Statistical Appendix* (April 2003).

INTERNATIONAL RESERVES
(US $ million at 31 December)

	2001	2002	2003
Gold*	233.8	293.3	348.0
IMF special drawing rights . .	2.3	1.9	1.0
Reserve position in IMF . .	21.6	23.3	25.5
Foreign exchange	815.9	689.4	786.1
Total	1,073.6	1,007.9	1,160.6

* National valuation $277 per ounce at 31 December 2001; $347 per ounce at 31 December 2002; $412 per ounce at 31 December 2003.

Source: IMF, *International Financial Statistics*.

MONEY SUPPLY
(US $ million at 31 December)

	2002	2003
Currency outside banks	39.6	49.7
Demand deposits at deposit money banks . .	1,629.1	1,793.0
Total money (incl. others)*	1,794.8	1,985.3

* Includes private-sector deposits at the Central Bank.

Source: IMF, *International Financial Statistics*.

COST OF LIVING
(Consumer Price Index; base: 2000 = 100)

	2001	2002	2003
Food (incl. alcoholic beverages) .	131.2	141.7	145.8
Fuel (excl. light)	165.0	203.9	n.a.
Clothing	130.6	132.5	124.6
Rent	135.2	198.1	n.a.
All items (incl. others)	137.7	154.9	167.1

Source: ILO.

NATIONAL ACCOUNTS

Expenditure on the Gross Domestic Product
(US $ million at current prices)

	2000	2001	2002*
Government final consumption expenditure	1,564	2,134	3,044
Private final consumption expenditure	10,199	14,491	16,647
Changes in stocks	–60	854	780
Gross fixed capital formation . .	3,265	4,541	5,484
Total domestic expenditure	14,967	22,020	25,954
Exports of goods and services . .	5,906	5,613	6,054
Less Imports of goods and services	4,939	6,608	7,661
GDP at market prices . . .	15,934	21,024	24,347

* Provisional figures.

Source: IMF, *Ecuador: Selected Issues and Statistical Appendix* (April 2003).

Gross Domestic Product by Economic Activity
(US $ million at current prices)

	2000	2001	2002
Agriculture, hunting, forestry and fishing	1,466	1,647	1,873
Petroleum and other mining . .	3,430	2,590	2,735
Manufacturing	2,170	2,466	2,830
Oil	−1,360	−727	−799
Electricity, gas and water . . .	169	352	412
Construction	1,127	1,502	1,892
Trade	2,483	2,893	3,324
Transport and communications .	1,720	3,370	3,885
Financial services	301	584	636
Government services	835	1,133	1,414
Other services	376	554	656
Other	1,609	2,449	2,929
Sub-total	14,326	18,813	21,787
Import taxes and duties (net) . .	1,608	2,210	2,560
GDP in purchasers' values . .	15,934	21,024	24,347

Source: IMF, *Ecuador: Selected Issues and Statistical Appendix* (April 2003).

BALANCE OF PAYMENTS
(US $ million)

	2001	2002	2003
Exports of goods f.o.b.	4,781	5,198	6,197
Imports of goods f.o.b.	−5,179	−6,196	−6,268
Trade balance	−397	−998	−71
Exports of services	862	923	898
Imports of services	−1,434	−1,632	−1,590
Balance on goods and services	−969	−1,707	−763
Other income received	48	30	27
Other income paid	−1,412	−1,335	−1,492
Balance on goods, services and income	−2,333	−3,012	−2,227
Current transfers received . . .	1,686	1,712	1,794
Current transfers paid . . .	−47	−58	−22
Current balance	−695	−1,359	−455
Capital account (net)	−63	20	25
Direct investment from abroad .	1,330	1,275	1,555
Portfolio investment liabilities .	−148	—	8
Other investment assets . . .	−1,275	−1,394	−904
Other investment liabilities . .	868	1,240	−343
Net errors and omissions . . .	−276	−4	184
Overall balance	−258	−221	70

Source: IMF, *International Financial Statistics*.

External Trade

PRINCIPAL COMMODITIES
(distribution by SITC, US $ million)

Imports c.i.f.	2000	2001	2002
Food and live animals . . .	261.4	372.6	482.5
Cereals and cereal preparations .	109.1	139.7	165.9
Crude materials (inedible) except fuels	134.9	142.9	127.9
Mineral fuels, lubricants, etc. .	282.3	302.5	291.2
Petroleum, petroleum products, etc.	115.5	140.1	132.8
Liquefied petroleum gases, etc. .	166.1	161.5	157.5
Chemicals and related products	809.3	968.4	1,038.9
Medicinal and pharmaceutical products	198.7	258.8	289.1
Medicaments (incl. veterinary) .	167.4	220.7	246.3
Artificial resins, plastic materials etc.	145.0	161.9	183.3
Disinfectants, insecticides, fungicides, etc.	104.9	106.6	110.8
Basic manufactures	684.6	922.6	1,152.3
Paper, paperboard and articles thereof	109.0	122.3	146.7
Textile yarn, fabrics, etc. . . .	114.0	138.1	127.8
Iron and steel	191.5	274.5	454.3
Tubes, pipes and fittings . .	24.7	76.7	213.5
Machinery and transport equipment	914.9	1,964.6	2,614.6
Power-generating machinery and equipment	62.9	131.0	119.9
Machinery specialized for particular industries	133.0	292.3	269.2
General industrial machinery equipment and parts	182.9	292.3	444.0
Telecommunications and sound equipment	109.6	289.3	374.3
Other electrical machinery apparatus, etc.	146.5	226.1	281.7
Road vehicles and parts* . . .	184.3	620.3	923.2
Passenger motor cars (excl. buses)	72.6	248.0	399.2
Motor vehicles for goods transport and special purposes	43.7	188.0	299.0
Miscellaneous manufactured articles	266.5	241.7	304.9
Total (incl. others)	3,445.9	5,362.9	6,431.1

* Data on parts exclude tyres, engines and electrical parts.

Exports f.o.b.	2000	2001	2002
Food and live animals . . .	1,721.7	1,905.1	2,073.7
Fish, crustaceans and molluscs .	568.3	643.9	687.6
Fresh, chilled, frozen, salted or dried crustaceans and molluscs	274.3	282.7	254.7
Prepared or preserved fish, crustaceans and molluscs . .	213.3	268.0	342.0
Vegetables and fruit	938.2	987.5	1,121.6
Bananas and plantains . . .	820.6	846.7	969.4
Coffee, tea, cocoa and spices . .	123.0	132.2	171.2
Crude materials (inedible) except fuels	199.0	279.2	352.0
Cut flowers and foliage	155.6	229.3	291.1
Mineral fuels, lubricants, etc. .	2,442.3	1,899.8	2,060.9
Petroleum, petroleum products etc.	2,442.3	1,899.8	2,060.9
Crude petroleum oils, etc. . .	2,144.0	1,722.3	1,838.5
Refined petroleum products . .	231.5	134.6	171.1
Basic manufactures	177.6	198.1	188.6
Total (incl. others)	4,821.9	4,647.5	5,029.8

Source: UN, *International Trade Statistics Yearbook*.

PRINCIPAL TRADING PARTNERS
(US $ million)

Imports c.i.f.	2000	2001	2002
Argentina	55.7	95.0	169.1
Belgium	53.5	41.5	146.8
Brazil	136.4	200.2	405.9
Canada	68.2	127.4	72.6
Chile	200.4	259.0	300.9
China, People's Republic . . .	76.1	222.9	219.7
Colombia	488.2	762.7	902.3
Finland	2.6	3.7	71.3
France (incl. Monaco) . . .	30.4	56.5	59.2
Germany	117.4	209.4	181.5
Italy	54.1	112.5	142.6
Japan	123.6	376.4	391.6
Korea, Republic	55.2	181.0	149.7
Mexico	116.0	200.9	191.0
Netherlands	35.1	45.2	51.4
Panama	98.9	50.3	268.0
Peru	72.6	91.7	154.8
Russia	36.5	60.4	36.0
Spain	58.6	104.3	137.7
United Kingdom	38.7	47.5	64.2
USA	883.6	1,235.0	1,480.9
Venezuela	271.7	306.1	353.2
Total (incl. others)	3,445.9	5,362.9	6,431.1

Exports f.o.b.	2000	2001	2002
Argentina	92.7	70.9	15.1
Belgium	67.5	80.9	71.3
Chile	220.7	90.9	74.0
China, People's Republic . . .	57.7	9.2	14.6
Colombia	259.5	324.0	361.0
El Salvador	114.3	64.3	81.8
Germany	123.4	151.9	171.0
Italy	159.6	197.9	289.3
Jamaica	0.7	9.3	61.6
Japan	129.2	122.2	98.8
Korea, Republic	317.0	238.2	296.1
Mexico	49.8	49.9	25.3
Netherlands	82.5	76.4	89.6
Panama	293.3	297.2	170.5
Peru	288.5	341.4	373.7
Russia	119.7	134.2	219.6
Spain	70.5	70.5	65.2
USA	1,828.2	1,781.2	2,052.0
Venezuela	108.3	165.6	65.0
Total (incl. others)	4,821.9	4,647.5	5,029.8

Source: UN, *International Trade Statistics Yearbook*.

Transport

RAILWAYS
(traffic)

	1997	1998	1999
Passenger-kilometres (million) .	47	44	5
Net ton-kilometres (million) . .	—	14	—

Passenger-kilometres (million): 5 in 2000; 32 in 2001; 33 in 2002.

Source: UN, *Statistical Yearbook*.

ROAD TRAFFIC
(motor vehicles in use at 31 December)

	1999	2000	2001
Passenger cars	532,170	550,448	529,359
Buses and coaches	9,917	9,183	8,962
Lorries and vans	51,686	55,580	54,698
Road tractors	3,630	5,118	5,588
Motorcycles and mopeds . .	26,641	25,711	22,574

Source: IRF, *World Road Statistics*.

SHIPPING

Merchant Fleet
(registered at 31 December)

	2001	2002	2003
Number of vessels	175	182	211
Total displacement ('000 grt) . .	305.9	313.1	324.5

Source: Lloyd's Register-Fairplay, *World Fleet Statistics*.

International Sea-borne Freight Traffic
('000 metric tons)

	1988*	1989*	1990
Goods loaded	8,402	10,020	11,783
Goods unloaded	2,518	2,573	1,958

* Source: UN, *Monthly Bulletin of Statistics*.

CIVIL AVIATION
(traffic on scheduled services)

	1999	2000	2001
Kilometres flown (million) . .	16	12	8
Passengers carried ('000) . .	1,387	1,319	1,285
Passenger-km (million) . . .	1,388	1,042	715
Total ton-km (million) . . .	157	108	70

Source: UN, *Statistical Yearbook*.

Tourism

FOREIGN VISITOR ARRIVALS*

Country of residence	2000	2001	2002
Argentina	11,213	12,631	12,820
Chile	15,876	19,593	87,367
Colombia	191,501	182,316	186,927
France	12,560	12,161	13,080
Germany	18,824	17,733	18,640
Peru	90,727	84,794	87,367
Spain	13,175	15,400	15,483
United Kingdom	16,890	18,968	17,453
USA	139,333	148,100	149,612
Venezuela	11,891	14,089	14,160
Total (incl. others)	627,090	640,561	654,993

* Figures refer to total arrivals (including same-day visitors), except those of Ecuadorean nationals residing abroad.

Source: World Tourism Organization, *Yearbook of Tourism Statistics*.

Tourism receipts (US $ million): 402 in 2000; 430 in 2001; 447 in 2002 (Source: World Tourism Organization).

Communications Media

	2001	2002	2003
Television receivers ('000 in use) .	2,900	n.a.	n.a.
Telephones ('000 main lines in use)	1,335.8	1,426.2	1,549.0
Mobile cellular telephones ('000 subscribers)	859.2	1,560.9	2,394.4
Personal computers ('000 in use) .	300	403	n.a.
Internet users ('000)	333.0	537.9	569.7

Radio receivers ('000 in use): 5,040 in 1999.

Facsimile machines: 30,000 in use in 1996.

Daily newspapers: 36 in 2000 (average circulation 1,220,000).

Sources: UNESCO, *Statistical Yearbook*; UN, *Statistical Yearbook*; International Telecommunication Union.

Education

(1999/2000)

	Institutions	Teachers	Students
Pre-primary	5,244	14,686	209,334
Primary	18,203	86,598	1,982,636
Secondary	3,486	80,662	980,213
Higher*	n.a.	12,856	206,541

* 1990/91 figures.

Sources: UNESCO, *Statistical Yearbook*; Ministerio de Educación y Cultura.

Adult literacy rate (UNESCO estimates): 91.0% (males 92.3%; females 89.7%) in 2002 (Source: UN Development Programme, *Human Development Report*).

Directory

The Constitution

The 1945 Constitution was suspended in June 1970. In January 1978 a referendum was held to choose between two draft Constitutions, prepared by various special constitutional committees. In a 90% poll, 43% voted for a proposed new Constitution and 32.1% voted for a revised version of the 1945 Constitution. The new Constitution came into force on 10 August 1979. In November 1997 a National Constituent Assembly was elected for the purpose of reviewing the Constitution, and a new Constitution, which retained many of the provisions of the 1979 Constitution, came into force on 10 August 1998. The main provisions of the Constitution are summarized below:

CHAMBER OF REPRESENTATIVES

The Constitution of 1998 states that legislative power is exercised by the Chamber of Representatives, which sits for a period of 60 days from 10 August. The Chamber is required to set up four full-time Legislative Commissions to consider draft laws when the House is in recess. Special sessions of the Chamber of Representatives may be called.

Representatives are elected for four years from lists of candidates drawn up by legally recognized parties. Twelve are elected nationally; two from each Province with over 100,000 inhabitants, one from each Province with fewer than 100,000; and one for every 200,000 citizens or fractions of over 150,000. Representatives are eligible for re-election.

In addition to its law-making duties, the Chamber ratifies treaties, elects members of the Supreme and Superior Courts, and (from panels presented by the President) the Comptroller-General, the Attorney-General and the Superintendent of Banks. It is also able to overrule the President's amendment of a bill that it has submitted for Presidential approval. It may reconsider a rejected bill after a year or request a referendum, and may revoke the President's declaration of a state of emergency. The budget is considered in the first instance by the appropriate Legislative Commission and disagreements are resolved in the Chamber.

PRESIDENT

The presidential term is four years (starting from 15 January of the year following his election), and there is no re-election. The President appoints the Cabinet, the Governors of Provinces, diplomatic representatives and certain administrative employees, and is responsible for the direction of international relations. In the event of foreign invasion or internal disturbance, the President may declare a state of emergency and must notify the Chamber, or the Tribunal for Constitutional Guarantees if the Chamber is not in session.

As in other post-war Latin-American Constitutions, particular emphasis is laid on the functions and duties of the State, which is given wide responsibilities with regard to the protection of labour; assisting in the expansion of production; protecting the Indian and peasant communities; and organizing the distribution and development of uncultivated lands, by expropriation where necessary.

Voting is compulsory for every Ecuadorean citizen who is literate and over 18 years of age. An optional vote has been extended to illiterates (under 15% of the population by 1981). The Constitution guarantees liberty of conscience in all its manifestations, and states that the law shall not make any discrimination for religious reasons.

The Government

HEAD OF STATE

President: ALFREDO PALACIOS GONZALES (assumed office 20 April 2005).

Vice-President: ALEJANDRO SERRANO.

CABINET
(May 2005)

Minister of National Defence: Gen. (retd) ANÍBAL SOLÓN ESPINOSA.

Minister of Government and Police: OSCAR AYERVE.

Minister of Foreign Affairs: ANTONIO PARRA GIL.

Minister of the Economy and Finance: RAFAEL CORREA DELGADO.

Minister of Foreign Trade, Industrialization, Fishing and Competition: OSWALDO MOLESTINA ZABALA.

Minister of Labour and Human Resources: (vacant).

Minister of Energy and Mines: FAUSTO CORDÓVEZ CUIRIBOGA.

Minister of Urban Development and Housing: ARMANDO BRAVO.

Minister of Education and Culture: Dra CONSUELO YÉPEZ COSSÍO.

Minister of Public Health: Dr WELLINGTON SANDOVAL.

Minister of Agriculture: PABLO RIZZO.

Minister of the Environment: Dr ANITA ALBÁN MORA.

Minister of Tourism: MARÍA ISABEL SALVADOR.

Minister of Public Works and Communications: DERLIZ PALACIOS.

Minister of Social Welfare: ALBERTO RIGAIL.

The following are, *ex officio*, members of the Cabinet: the National Secretary of Administrative Development, the Co-ordinator of the Social Expenditure Fund (FISE), the State Comptroller-General, the State Procurator-General, the Chairman of the National Monetary Board, the General Manager of the State Bank, the General Manager of the Central Bank, the Secretary-General of the National Planning Council (CONADE), the President of the National Financial Corporation, the President of the National Modernization Council (CONAM), the Presidential Private Secretary, the Subsecretary-General of Public Administration and the Presidential Press Secretary.

MINISTRIES

Office of the President: Palacio Nacional, García Moreno 1043, Quito; tel. (2) 221-6300.

Office of the Vice-President: Manuel Larrea y Arenas, Edif. Consejo Provincial de Pichincha, 21°, Quito; tel. (2) 250-4953; fax (2) 250-3379.

Ministry of Agriculture: Avda Eloy Alfaro y Amazonas, Quito; tel. (2) 255-3472; fax (2) 256-4531; internet www.mag.gov.ec.

Ministry of Education and Cultures: Mejía 322, Quito; tel. (2) 221-6224; fax (2) 258-0116; internet www.mec.edu.ec.

Ministry of Energy and Mines: Juan León Mera y Orellana, 5°, Quito; tel. (2) 255-0041; fax (2) 255-0018; e-mail menergia2@andinanet.net; internet www.menergia.gov.ec.

Ministry of the Environment: Avda Eloy Alfaro y Amazonas, Edif. M.A.G., Quito; tel. (2) 256-3429; fax (2) 250-0041; e-mail mma@ambiente.gov.ec.

Ministry of the Economy and Finance: Avda 10 de Agosto 1661 y Jorge Washington, Quito; tel. (2) 254-4500; fax (2) 253-0703; internet minfinanzas.ec-gov.net.

Ministry of Foreign Affairs: Avda 10 de Agosto y Carrión, Quito; tel. (2) 223-0100; fax (2) 256-4873; e-mail webmast@mmrree.gov.ec; internet www.mmrree.gov.ec.

Ministry of Foreign Trade, Industrialization, Fishing and Competition: Avda Eloy Alfaro y Amazonas, Quito; tel. (2) 252-7988; fax (2) 250-3549.

Ministry of Government and Police: Espejo y Benalcázar, Quito; tel. (2) 295-5666; fax (2) 295-8360; e-mail informacion@mingobierno.gov.ec; internet www.mingobierno.gov.ec.

Ministry of Labour and Human Resources: Clemente Ponce 255 y Piedrahita, Quito; tel. (2) 256-6148; fax (2) 250-3122; e-mail mintrab@accessinter.net.

Ministry of National Defence: Exposición 208, Quito; tel. (2) 221-6150; fax (2) 256-9386; e-mail paginaweb@fuerzasarmadasecuador.org; internet www.fuerzasarmadasecuador.ec-gov.net.

Ministry of Public Health: Juan Larrea 444, Quito; tel. (2) 252-9163; fax 256-9786; e-mail msp@accessinter.net; internet www.msp.gov.ec.

Ministry of Public Works and Communications: Avda Juan León Mera y Orellana, Quito; tel. (2) 222-2749; fax (2) 222-3077; internet www.mop.gov.ec.

Ministry of Social Welfare: Quito.

Ministry of Tourism: Avda Eloy Alfaro 32 y Carlos Tobar, Quito; tel. (2) 250-7559; fax (2) 222-9330; e-mail promocion@turismo.gov.ec; internet www.vivecuador.com.

Ministry of Urban Development and Housing: Avda 10 de Agosto 2270 y Corotero, Quito; tel. (2) 223-8060; fax (2) 256-6785; e-mail mdesur2@ec-gov.net; internet www.miduvi.ec-gov.net.

Office for Public Administration: Palacio Nacional, García Moreno 1043, Quito; tel. (2) 251-5990.

President and Legislature

PRESIDENT

Elections, 20 October and 24 November 2002

Candidate	% of votes cast in first ballot	% of votes cast in second ballot
Col Lucio Edwin Gutiérrez Borbua (PSP-MNPP) .	20.3	58.7
Alvaro Fernando Noboa Pontón (PRIAN) .	17.4	41.3
León Roldos Aguilera (PS—FA-DP-CFP) . .	15.5	—
Rodrigo Borja Cevallos (ID)	14.0	—
Antonio Xavier Neira Menendez (PSC) . .	12.2	—
Total (incl. others)	100.0	100.0

CONGRESO

Cámara Nacional de Representantes

President: WILFREDO LUCERO BOLAÑOS.

Election, 20 October 2002

Political parties	Seats
Partido Social Cristiano (PSC)	24
Izquierda Democrática (ID)	15
Partido Roldosista Ecuatoriano (PRE)	14
Partido Renovador Institucional de Acción Nacional (PRIAN) .	10
Movimiento Nuevo País-Pachakútik (MNPP) . . .	8
Partido Sociedad Patriótica 21 de Enero (PSP) . .	8
Movimiento Popular Democrático (MPD)	7
Democracia Popular (DP)	5
Partido Socialista-Frente Amplio (PS—FA) . .	3
Independent	1
Total (incl. others)	100

Political Organizations

Acción Popular Revolucionaria Ecuatoriana (APRE): centrist; Leader Lt-Gen. FRANK VARGAS PAZZOS.

Coalición Nacional Republicana (CNR): Quito; f. 1986; fmrly Coalición Institucionalista Demócrata (CID).

Concentración de Fuerzas Populares (CFP): Quito; f. 1946; Leader GALO VAYAS; Dir Dr AVERROES BUCARAM SAXIDA.

Democracia Popular (DP): Calle Luis Saá 153 y Hermanos Pazmiño, Casilla 17-01-2300, Quito; tel. (2) 254-7654; fax (2) 250-2995; f. 1978 as Democracia Popular-Unión Demócrata Cristiana; Christian democrat; Leader Lic. ABSALÓN ROCHA.

Frente Futuro de Ecuador (FFE): f. 2002 to contest the October 2002 presidential and legislative elections; Leader ANTONIO VARGAS.

Frente Radical Alfarista (FRA): Quito; f. 1972; liberal; Leader IVÁN CASTRO PATIÑO.

Izquierda Democrática (ID): Polonia 161, entre Vancouver y Eloy Alfaro, Quito; tel. (2) 256-4436; fax (2) 256-9295; f. 1977; absorbed Fuerzas Armadas Populares Eloy Alfaro—Alfaro Vive ¡Carajo! (AVC) (Eloy Alfaro Popular Armed Forces—Alfaro Lives, Damn It!) in 1991; Leader GUILLERMO LANDAZURI; National Dir ANDRÉS VALLEJO.

Movimiento Independiente para una República Auténtica (MIRA): Quito; f. 1996; Leader Dra ROSALIA ARTEAGA SERRANO.

Movimiento Nuevo País-Pachakútik (MNPP/Pachakútik): Quito; political wing of CONAIE (q.v.); represents indigenous, environmental and social groups; Leader FREDDY EHLERS ZURITA; Nat. Dir GILBERTO TALAHUA.

Movimiento Popular Democrático (MPD): e-mail periodicopcion@andinanet.net; internet bloquempd.tripod.com; Stalinist; Dep. Leader STALIN VARGAS MEZA.

Partido Comunista Marxista-Leninista de Ecuador: e-mail pcmle@bigfoot.com; internet www.geocities.com/pcmle; Sec.-Gen. CAMILO ALMEYDA.

Partido Conservador (PC): Wilsón 578, Quito; tel. (2) 250-5061; f. 1855; incorporated Partido Unidad Republicano in 1995; centre-right; Leader SIXTO DURÁN BALLÉN.

Partido Demócrata (PD): Quito; Leader Dr FRANCISCO HUERTA MONTALVO.

Partido Liberal Radical (PLR): Quito; f. 1895; held office from 1895 to 1944 as the Liberal Party, which subsequently divided into various factions; perpetuates the traditions of the Liberal Party; Leader CARLOS JULIO PLAZA A.

Partido Renovador Institucional de Acción Nacional (PRIAN): Quito; right-wing, populist; Leader ALVARO FERNANDO NOBOA PONTÓN.

Partido Republicano (PR): Quito; Leader GUILLERMO SOTOMAYOR.

Partido Roldosista Ecuatoriano (PRE): Quito; f. 1982; populist; Dir ABDALÁ BUCARAM ORTIZ.

Partido Social Cristiano (PSC): Carrión 548 y Reina Victoria, Casilla 9454, Quito; tel. (2) 254-4536; fax (2) 256-8562; internet www.psc.org.ec; f. 1951; centre-right party; Pres. JAIME NEBOT SAADI; Leaders Dr LEÓN FEBRES CORDERO RIVADENEIRA, Lic. CAMILO PONCE GANGOTENA, HEINZ MOELLER FREILE, Lic. PASCUAL DEL CIOPPO ARAGUNDI.

Partido Socialista-Frente Amplio (PS-FA): Avda Gran Colombia y Yaguachi, Quito; tel. (2) 222-1764; fax (2) 222-2184; f. 1926; Pres. Dr MANUEL SALGADO TAMAYO.

Partido Sociedad Patriótica 21 de Enero (PSP): Quito; internet www.sociedadpatriotica.com; contested the 2002 elections in alliance with the MNPP; Leader Col LUCIO EDWIN GUTIÉRREZ BORBUA.

Unión Alfarista-FRA: Quito; f. 1998; centrist; Leader CÉSAR VERDUGA VÉLEZ.

The following guerrilla groups are active:

Grupo de Combatientes Populares (GCP): claims to defend human rights and to fight poverty.

Montoneros Patria Libre (MPL): f. 1986; advocates an end to authoritarianism.

Partido Maoísta-Comunista 'Puka Inti': Sec.-Gen. RAMIRO CELI.

OTHER ORGANIZATIONS

Confederación de las Nacionalidades Indígenas de la Amazonia Ecuatoriana (CONFENIAE): Avda 6 de Diciembre 159 y Pazmino, Of. 408, Apdo 17-01-4180, Quito; tel. (2) 543-973; fax (2) 220-325; e-mail confeniae@applicom.com; internet www.unii.net/confeniae; to represent indigenous peoples; mem. of CONAIE; Leader LUIS VARGAS.

Confederación de Nacionalidades Indígenas de Ecuador (CONAIE) (National Confederation of the Indigenous Population of Ecuador): Avda Los Granados 2553 y 6 de Diciembre, Quito; tel. (2) 245-2335; e-mail reincon@uio.telconet.net; internet conaie.org; f. 1986 to represent indigenous peoples; MNPP (q.v.) represents CONAIE in the legislature; Pres. LUIS MACAS; Vice-Pres. SANTIAGO DE LA CRUZ.

Coordinadora de las Organizaciones Indígenas de la Cuenca Amazónica (COICA): Quito; e-mail comunica@coica.org; internet www.coica.org; f. 1984; founded in Lima, Peru; moved to Quito in 1993; umbrella group of 9 orgs representing indigenous peoples of the Amazon Basin in Bolivia, Brazil, Colombia, Ecuador, French Guiana, Guyana, Suriname and Venezuela; Gen. Co-ordinator SEBASTIÃO HAJI ALVES RODRIGUES MANCHINERIS; Vice-Gen. Co-ordinator JOCELYN ROGER THERESE.

Federación de Pueblos Indígenas, Campesinas y Negros del Ecuador (Fedepicne): Quito; f. 1996 following split from CONAIE; formally recognized in 2003; Pres. LUIS PACHALA.

Frente Popular (FP): umbrella group of labour unions and other populist organizations; Pres. LUIS VILLACÍS.

Diplomatic Representation

EMBASSIES IN ECUADOR

Argentina: Avda Amazonas 22-147 y Roca, 8°, Quito; tel. (2) 256-2292; fax (2) 256-8177; e-mail embarge2@andinanet.net; Chargé d'affaires a.i. GONZALO TORRES CARIONI.

Belgium: Edif. Mansión Blanca, 10°, Avda República de El Salvador 1082 y Naciones Unidas; tel. (2) 227-6145; fax (2) 227-3910; e-mail quito@diplobel.org; Ambassador BEATRIX VAN HEMELDONCK.

Bolivia: Avda Eloy Alfaro 2432 y Fernando Ayarza, Casilla 17-210003, Quito; tel. (2) 244-4830; fax (2) 224-4833; e-mail embolivia-quito@andinanet.net; Ambassador Dr EDIL SANDOVAL MORÓN.

Brazil: Avda Amazonas 1429 y Colón, 9° y 10°, Apdo 17-01-231, Quito; tel. (2) 256-3142; fax (2) 250-4468; e-mail ebrasil@uio.satnet.net; Ambassador SERGIO AUGUSTO DE ABREU E LIMA FLORENCIO SOBRINHO.

Canada: Edif. Josueth Gonzales, Avda 6 de Diciembre 28-16 y Paul Rivet, 4°, Apdo 17-11-6512, Quito; tel. (2) 250-6162; fax (2) 250-3108; e-mail quito@dfait-maeci.gc.ca; internet www.dfait-maeci.gc.ca/ecuador; Ambassador BRIAN OAK.

Chile: Edif. Xerox, 4°, Juan Pablo Sanz 3617 y Amazonas, Quito; tel. (2) 224-9403; fax (2) 244-4470; e-mail embachileecu@trans-telco.net; Ambassador NELSON HADAD HERESY.

China, People's Republic: Avda Atahualpa 349 y Amazonas, Quito; tel. (2) 245-8927; fax (2) 244-4364; e-mail embchina@uio.telconet.net; Ambassador LIU YUQIN.

Colombia: Edif. Arista, Avda Colón 1133 y Amazonas, 7°, Apdo 17-07-9164, Quito; tel. (2) 222-8926; e-mail equito@minrelext.gov.co; Ambassador MARÍA PAULINA ESPINOZA DE LÓPEZ.

Costa Rica: Rumipamba 692 y República, 1°, Apdo 17-03-301, Quito; tel. (2) 225-4945; fax (2) 225-4087; e-mail embajcr@uiso.satnet.net; Ambassador LUZ ARGENTINA CALDERÓN GEI.

Cuba: Mercurio 365, entre La Razón y El Vengador, Quito; tel. (2) 245-6936; fax (2) 243-0594; e-mail embquito@uio.satnet.net; Ambassador ILEANA DÍAZ-ARGÜELLES ALASÁ.

Dominican Republic: Edif. Albatros, Avda de los Shyris 1240 y Portugal, 2°, Apdo 17-01-387-A, Quito; tel. (2) 243-4232; e-mail emrepdom@interactive.net.ec; Ambassador NESTOR JUAN CERÓN.

Egypt: Avda Tarqui 4-56 y Avda 6 de Diciembre, Apdo 9355, Quito; tel. (2) 222-5240; fax (2) 256-3521; Ambassador MOHAMED HANZA ELEISH.

El Salvador: Edif. Gabriela III, 3°, Avda República de El Salvador 733 y Portugal, Quito; tel. (2) 243-3070; fax (2) 224-2829; e-mail embelsal@uio.sdatnet.net; Ambassador RAFAEL ANGEL ALFARO PINEDA.

France: Calle Leonidas Plaza 107 y Avda Patria, CP 536, Quito; tel. (2) 256-0789; fax (2) 256-6424; e-mail francie@andinanet.net; internet www.ambafrance-ecu.org; Ambassador FRANÇOIS COUSIN.

Germany: Edif. Citiplaza, 13° y 14°, Avda Naciones Unidas y República de El Salvador, Casilla 17-17-536, Quito; tel. (2) 297-0820; fax (2) 297-0815; e-mail alemania@interactive.net.ec; internet www.embajada-quito.de; Ambassador SEPP JUERGEN WOELKER.

Guatemala: Edif. Gabriela III, 3°, Of. 301, Avda República de El Salvador 733 y Portugal, Apdo 17-03-294, Quito; tel. (2) 245-9700; e-mail embecuador@minex.gob.gt; Ambassador ANGELA GAROZ CABRERA.

Holy See: Avda Orellana 692, Apdo 17-07-8980, Quito; tel. (2) 250-5200; fax (2) 256-4810; e-mail nunapec@impsat.net.ec; Apostolic Nunciature; Apostolic Nuncio Most Rev. ALAIN PAUL LEBEAUPIN (Titular Archbishop of Vico Equense).

Honduras: Edif. World Trade Centre, Torre A, 5°, Of. 501, Avda 12 de Octubre 1942 y Luis Cordero, Apdo 17-03-4753, Quito; tel. (2) 222-3985; fax (2) 222-0441; e-mail embhquito@yahoo.com; Ambassador JORGE ALBERTO MILLA REYES.

Israel: Edif. Plaza 2000, Avda 12 de Octubre y General Francisco Salazar, Apdo 17-21-08, Quito; tel. (2) 223-7474; fax (2) 223-8055; e-mail israemb@interactive.net.ec; internet www.quito.mfa.il; Ambassador DANIEL SABAN.

Italy: Calle La Isla 111 y Humberto Albornoz, Casilla 17-03-72, Quito; tel. (2) 256-1077; fax (2) 250-2818; e-mail ambital@ambitalquito.org; internet www.ambitalquito.org; Ambassador GIULIO CESARE PICCIRILLI.

Japan: Juan León Mera 130 y Avda Patria, 7°, Quito; tel. (2) 256-1899; fax (2) 250-3670; e-mail japembec@uio.satnet.net; Ambassador HIROYUKI HIRAMATSU.

Korea, Republic: Edif. Citiplaza, 8°, Avda Naciones Unidas y Avda de El Salvador, Quito; tel. (2) 297-0625; fax (2) 297-0630; e-mail ecmco@interactive.net.ec; Ambassador SANG-WOOK NAM.

Mexico: Avda 6 de Diciembre 4843 y Naciones Unidas, Casilla 17-11-6371, Quito; tel. (2) 292-3770; fax (2) 244-8245; e-mail embajadamexico@embamex.org.ec; internet www.sre.gob.mx/ecuador; Ambassador ALMA PATRICIA SORIA AYUSO.

Netherlands: Edif. World Trade Centre, Torre 1, 1°, Avda 12 de Octubre 1942 y Luis Cordero, Quito; tel. (2) 222-9229; fax (2) 256-7917; e-mail nlgovqui@embajadadeholanda.com; internet www.embajadadeholanda.com; Ambassador FRANCISCUS GIJSBERTUS BIJVOET.

Panama: Edif. ESPRO, 6°, Alpallana 505 y Whimper, Quito; tel. (2) 250-8856; fax (2) 256-5234; e-mail panaembaecuador@hotmail.com; Ambassador MATEO CASTILLERO CASTILLO.

Paraguay: Edif. World Trade Center, Torre A, 9°, Of. 906, Avda 12 de Octubre 1942 y Luis Cordero, Apdo 17-03-139, Quito; tel. (2) 224-5871; fax (2) 225-1446; e-mail embapar@uio.telconet.net; Ambassador Dr CARLOS VILLAGRA MARSAL.

Peru: Avda República de El Salvador 495 e Irlanda, Apdo 17-07-9380, Quito; tel. (2) 246-8410; fax (2) 225-2560; e-mail embpeecu@uio.satnet.net; Ambassador LUIS MARCHAND STENS.

Russia: Reina Victoria 462 y Ramón Roca, Quito; tel. (2) 256-6361; fax (2) 256-5531; e-mail embrusia@accessinter.net; Ambassador MIKHAIL I. ORLOVETS.

Spain: La Pinta 455 y Amazonas, Casilla 9322, Quito; tel. (2) 256-4373; fax (2) 250-0826; e-mail embespec@correo.mae.es; Ambassador JUAN MARÍA ALZINA DE AGUILAR.

Switzerland: Edif. Xerox, 2°, Amazonas 3617 y Juan Pablo Sanz, Casilla 17-11-4815, Quito; tel. (2) 243-4949; fax (2) 244-9314; e-mail vertretung@qui.rep.admin.ch; internet www.eda.admin.ch/quito_emb/s/home.html; Ambassador ROBERT REICH.

United Kingdom: Edif. Citiplaza, 14°, Avda Naciones Unidas y República de El Salvador, Casilla 17-01-314, Quito; tel. (2) 297-0800; fax (2) 297-0809; e-mail britembq@interactive.net.ec; internet www.britembquito.org.ec; Ambassador RICHARD GEORGE LEWINGTON.

USA: Avda 12 de Octubre 1942 y Patria 120, Quito; tel. (2) 256-2890; fax (2) 250-2052; internet www.usembassy.org.ec; Ambassador KRISTIE ANNE KENNEY.

Uruguay: Edif. Josueth González, 9°, Avda 6 de Diciembre 2816 y Paul Rivet, Casilla 17-12-282, Quito; tel. (2) 256-3762; fax (2) 256-

3763; e-mail emburugl@emburuguay.int.ec; Ambassador JOSÉ LUIS ALDABALDE ARBURUAS.

Venezuela: Avda Los Cabildos 115, Apdo 17-01-688, Quito; tel. (2) 226-8636; fax (2) 246-6786; e-mail embavenecua@interactive.net.ec; Ambassador OSCAR NAVAS TORTOLERO.

Judicial System

Attorney-General: CECILIA ARMAS (acting).

Supreme Court of Justice: Palacio de Justicia, Avda 6 de Diciembre y Piedrahita 332, Quito; tel. (2) 290-0424; fax (2) 290-0425; e-mail dni-cnj@access.net.ec; internet www.justiciaecuador.gov.ec; f. 1830; Pres. (vacant).

Higher or Divisional Courts: Ambato, Azogues, Babahoyo, Cuenca, Esmeraldas, Guaranda, Guayaquil, Ibarra, Latacunga, Loja, Machala, Portoviejo, Quito, Riobamba and Tulcán; 90 judges.

Provincial Courts: There are 40 Provincial Courts in 15 districts; other courts include 94 Criminal, 219 Civil, 29 dealing with labour disputes and 17 Rent Tribunals.

Special Courts: National Court for Juveniles.

Religion

There is no state religion but nearly 90% of the population are Roman Catholics. There are representatives of various Protestant Churches and of the Jewish faith in Quito and Guayaquil.

CHRISTIANITY

The Roman Catholic Church

Ecuador comprises four archdioceses, 11 dioceses, seven Apostolic Vicariates and one Apostolic Prefecture. At 31 December 2002 there were an estimated 11,734,446 adherents in the country, equivalent to some 88.8% of the population.

Bishops' Conference

Conferencia Episcopal Ecuatoriana, Avda América 1805 y La Gasca, Apdo 17-01-1081, Quito; tel. (2) 255-8913; fax (2) 250-1429; e-mail dicuenca@etapa.com.ec.

f. 1939; statutes approved 1999; Pres. VICENTE RODRIGO CISNEROS DURÁN NAVAS (Archbishop of Cuenca).

Archbishop of Cuenca: VICENTE RODRIGO CISNEROS DURÁN NAVAS, Arzobispado, Manuel Vega 8-66 y Calle Bolívar, Apdo 01-01-0046, Cuenca; tel. (7) 831-651; fax (7) 844-436; e-mail dicuenca@etapa.com.ec.

Archbishop of Guayaquil: ANTONIO ARREGUI YARZA HOLGUÍN, Arzobispado, Calle Clemente Ballén 501 y Chimborazo, Apdo 09-01-0254, Guayaquil; e-mail marregui@q.ecua.net.ec; tel. (4) 232-2778; fax (4) 232-9695.

Archbishop of Portoviejo: JOSÉ MARIO RUIZ NAVAS, Arzobispado, Avda Universitaria s/n, Entre Alajuela y Ramos y Duarte, Casilla 13-01-0024, Portoviejo; tel. (5) 630-404; fax (5) 634-428; e-mail arzobis@ecua.net.ec.

Archbishop of Quito: RAÚL VELA CHIRIBOGA, Arzobispado, Calle Chile 1140 y Venezuela, Apdo 17-01-00106, Quito; e-mail raul.vela@andinanet.net; tel. (2) 228-4429; fax (2) 258-0973.

The Anglican Communion

Anglicans in Ecuador are under the jurisdiction of Province IX of the Episcopal Church in the USA. The country is divided into two dioceses, one of which, Central Ecuador, is a missionary diocese.

Bishop of Littoral Ecuador: Rt Rev. ALFREDO MORANTE, Calle Bogotá 1010, Barrio Centenario, Apdo 5250, Guayaquil.

Bishop of Central Ecuador: Rt Rev. JOSÉ NEPTALÍ LARREA MORENO, Apdo 17-11-6165, Quito; e-mail ecuacen@uio.satnet.net.

The Baptist Church

Baptist Convention of Ecuador: Casilla 3236, Guayaquil; tel. (4) 238-4865; Pres. Rev. HAROLT SANTE MATA; Sec. JORGE MORENO CHAVARRÍA.

The Methodist Church

United Evangelical Methodist Church: Evangelical United Church, Rumipamba 915, Casilla 17-03-236, Quito; tel. (2) 226-5158; fax (2) 243-9576; 800 mems, 2,000 adherents.

BAHÁ'Í FAITH

National Spiritual Assembly of the Bahá'ís: Apdo 869A, Quito; tel. (2) 256-3484; fax (2) 252-3192; e-mail ecua9nsa@uio.satnet.net; mems resident in 1,121 localities.

The Press

PRINCIPAL DAILIES

Quito

El Comercio: Avda Pedro Vicente Maldonado 11515 y el Tablón, Casilla 17-01-57, Quito; tel. (2) 267-0999; fax (2) 267-0466; e-mail contactenos@elcomercio.com; internet www.elcomercio.com; f. 1906; morning; independent; Proprs Compañía Anónima El Comercio; Pres. GUADALUPE MANTILLA DE ACQUAVIVA; Editor MARCO ARAUZ; circ. 160,000.

La Hora: Panamericana Norte Kilómetro 3½, Quito; tel. (2) 247-3724; fax (2) 247-5086; e-mail lahora@uio.satnet.net; internet www.lahora.com.ec; f. 1982; Nat. Pres. Dr FRANCISCO VIVANCO RIOFRÍO; Exec. Pres. FRANCISCO VIVANCO ARROYO; Gen. Editor JUANA LÓPEZ SARMIENTO.

Hoy: Avda Mariscal Sucre N-71345, Casilla 17-07-0969, Quito; tel. (2) 249-0888; fax (2) 249-1881; e-mail hoy@hoy.com.ec; internet www.hoy.com.ec; f. 1982; morning; independent; Man. JAIME MANTILLA ANDERSON; circ. 72,000.

El Tiempo: Avda América y Villalengua, Apdo 3117, Quito; f. 1965; morning; independent; Proprs Editorial La Unión, CA; Pres. ANTONIO GRANDA CENTENO; Editor EDUARDO GRANDA GARCÉS; circ. 35,000.

Ultimas Noticias: Avda Pedro Vicente Maldonado 11515 y el Tablón, Casilla 17-01-57, Quito; tel. (2) 267-0999; fax (2) 267-4923; f. 1938; evening; independent; commercial; Proprs Compañía Anónima El Comercio; Dir DAVID MANTILLA CASHMORE; circ. 60,000.

Guayaquil

Expreso: Avda Carlos Julio Arosemena, Casilla 5890, Guayaquil; tel. (4) 220-1100; fax (4) 220-0291; e-mail webmaster@granasa.com.ec; internet www.diario-expreso.com; f. 1973; morning; independent; Exec. Editor MARTÍN ULLOA; circ. 60,000.

El Extra: Avda Carlos Julio Arosemena, Casilla 5890, Guayaquil; tel. (4) 220-1100; fax (4) 220-0291; e-mail webmaster@granasa.com.ec; internet www.diario-extra.com; f. 1975; morning; Pres. ERROL CARTWRIGHT BETANCOURT; Editor HENRY HOLGUÍN; circ. 200,000.

La Razón: Avda Constitución y las Americas, Guayaquil; tel. (4) 228-0100; fax (4) 228-5110; e-mail cartas@larazonecuador.com; internet www.larazonecuador.com; f. 1965; morning; independent; Propr ROBERTO ISAÍAS DASSUM; Dir JORGE E. PÉREZ PESANTES; circ. 35,000.

La Segunda: Calle Colón 526 y Boyacá, Casilla 6366, Guayaquil; tel. (4) 232-0635; fax (4) 232-0539; f. 1983; morning; Propr CARLOS MANSUR; Dir VICENTE ADUM ANTÓN; circ. 60,000.

El Telégrafo: Avda 10 de Agosto 601 y Boyacá, Casilla 415, Guayaquil; tel. (4) 232-6500; fax (4) 232-3265; e-mail cartas@telegrafo.com.ec; internet www.telegrafo.com.ec; f. 1884; morning; independent; commercial; Proprs El Telégrafo CA; Dir CARLOS NAVARRETE CASTILLO; circ. 45,000 (weekdays), 55,000 (Sundays).

El Universo: Avda Domingo Comín y Alban, Casilla 09-01-531, Guayaquil; tel. (4) 249-0000; fax (4) 249-1034; e-mail editores@telconet.net; internet www.eluniverso.com; f. 1921; morning; independent; Pres. NICOLÁS PÉREZ LAPENTTI; Dir CARLOS PÉREZ BARRIGA; circ. 174,000 (weekdays), 290,000 (Sundays).

There are local daily newspapers of low circulation in other towns.

PERIODICALS

Quito

La Calle: Casilla 2010, Quito; f. 1956; weekly; politics; Dir CARLOS ENRIQUE CARRIÓN; circ. 20,000.

Cámara de Comercio de Quito: Avda Amazona y República, Casilla 202, Quito; tel. (2) 244-3787; fax (2) 243-5862; f. 1906; monthly; commerce; Pres. ANDRÉS PÉREZ ESPINOSA; Exec. Dir ARMANDO TOMASELLI; circ. 10,000.

Carta Económica del Ecuador: Toledo 1448 y Coruña, Apdo 3358, Quito; f. 1969; weekly; economic, financial and business information; Pres. Dr LINCOLN LARREA B.; circ. 8,000.

Chasqui: Avda Diego de Almagro 32-133 y Andrade Marín, Apdo 17-01-584, Quito; tel. (2) 254-8011; fax (2) 250-2487; e-mail chasqui@ciespal.net; internet ; f. 1997; monthly; media studies; publ. of the

Centro Internacional de Estudios Superiores de Comunicación para America Latina; Dir EDGAR JARAMILLO; Editor LUIS ELADIO PROAÑO.

El Colegial: Calle Carlos Ibarra 206, Quito; tel. (2) 221-6541; f. 1974; weekly; publ. of Student Press Association; Dir WILSON ALMEIDA MUÑOZ; circ. 20,000.

Cosas: Edif. Alpallana 2, 3°, Alpallana 289 y Diego Almagro, Quito; tel. (2) 250-8742; fax (2) 250-8747; e-mail ventasuio@cosas.com.ec; internet www.cosas.com.ec; women's interest; Editor CRISTA RODAS; Man. CARIDAD VELA.

Ecuador Guía Turística: Mejía 438, Of. 43, Quito; f. 1969; fortnightly; tourist information in Spanish and English; Propr Prensa Informativa Turística; Dir JORGE VACA O.; circ. 30,000.

Gestión: Avda González Suárez 335 y San Ignacio, 7°, Quito; tel. (2) 250-5524; fax (2) 250-5527; e-mail dinedi@andinanet.net.ec; internet www.gestion.dinediciones.com; f. 1999; economy and society; monthly; circ 15,000.

Integración: Solano 836, Quito; quarterly; economics of the Andean countries.

Letras del Ecuador: Casa de la Cultura Ecuatoriana, Avda 6 de Diciembre, Casilla 67, Quito; f. 1944; monthly; literature and art; non-political; Dir Dr TEODORO VANEGAS ANDRADE.

El Libertador: Olmedo 931 y García Moreno, Quito; f. 1926; monthly; Pres. Dr BENJAMÍN TERÁN VAREA.

Mensajero: Benalcázar 478, Apdo 17-01-4100, Quito; tel. (2) 221-9555; f. 1884; monthly; religion, culture, economics and politics; Man. OSWALDO CARRERA LANDÁZURI; circ. 5,000.

Quince Días: Sociedad Periodística Ecuatoriana, Los Pinos 315, Panamericana Norte Km 5½, Quito; tel. (2) 247-4122; fax (2) 256-6741; fortnightly; news and regional political analysis.

Guayaquil

Análisis Semanal: Elizalde 119, 10°, Apdo 4925, Guayaquil; tel. (4) 232-6590; fax (4) 232-6842; e-mail wspurrie@gye.satnet.net; internet www.ecuadoranalysis.com; weekly; economic and political affairs; Editor WALTER SPURRIER BAQUERIZO.

Ecuador Ilustrado: Guayaquil; f. 1924; monthly; literary; illustrated.

El Financiero: Casilla 6666, Guayaquil; tel. (4) 220-5051; e-mail elfinanciero@elfinanciero.com; internet www.elfinanciero.com; weekly; business and economic news; f. 1990; Dir DAVID PÉREZ MACCOLLUM.

Generación XXI: Aguirre 730 y Boyacá, Guayaquil; tel. (4) 232-7200; fax (4) 232-0499; e-mail flmerchan@vistazo.com; internet www .generacion21.com; youth; Gen. Editor SÉBASTIEN MELIÉRES.

Hogar: Aguirre 724 y Boyacá, Apdo 1239, Guayaquil; tel. (4) 232-7200; f. 1964; monthly; Man. Editor ROSA AMELIA ALVARADO; circ. 35,000.

Revista Estadio: Aguirre 730 y Boyacá, Apdo 1239, Guayaquil; tel. (4) 232-8505; fax (4) 232-0499; e-mail estadio@vistazo.com; internet www.estadio.com; f. 1962; fortnightly; sport; Editor LUIS SÁNCHEZ-ESPINAR; circ. 40,000.

Vistazo: Aguirre 730 y Boyacá, Casilla 09-01-1239, Guayaquil; tel. (4) 232-7200; fax (4) 232-0499; e-mail vistazo@vistazo.com; internet www.vistazo.com; f. 1957; fortnightly; general; Gen. Editor PATRICIA ESTUPIÑÁN DE BURBANO; circ. 85,000.

NEWS AGENCIES

Foreign Bureaux

Agencia EFE (Spain): Edif. La Fontana, 1°, Of. 1, Avda República de El Salvador 1058, y Naciones Unidas, Quito; tel. (2) 225-9682; fax (2) 225-5769; e-mail eferedaccion@andinanet.net; Bureau Chief EMILIO CRESPO.

Agenzia Nazionale Stampa Associata (ANSA) (Italy): Calle Venezuela 1013 y esq. Mejía, Of. 26, Quito; tel. (2) 258-0794; fax (2) 258-0782; Correspondent FERNANDO LARENAS.

Associated Press (AP) (USA): Edif. Sudamérica, 4°, Of. 44, Calle Venezuela 1018 y Mejía, Quito; tel. (2) 257-0235; Correspondent CARLOS CISTERNAS.

Deutsche Presse-Agentur (dpa) (Germany): Edif. Atrium, Of. 5-7, González Suárez 894 y Gonnessiat, Quito; tel. (2) 256-8986; Correspondent JORGE ORTIZ.

Informatsionnoye Telegrafnoye Agentstvo Rossii—Telegrafnoye Agentstvo Suverennykh Stran (ITAR—TASS) (Russia): Calle Roca 328 y 6 de Diciembre, 2°, Dep. 6, Quito; tel. (2) 251-1631; Correspondent VLADIMIR GOSTEV.

Inter Press Service (IPS) (Italy): Urbanización Los Arrayanes Manzanas 20, Casa 15, Calle León Pontón y Pasaje E, Casilla 17-01-1284, Quito; tel. (2) 266-2362; fax (2) 266-1977; e-mail jfrias@uio .telconet.net; Correspondent KINTTO LUCAS.

Prensa Latina (Cuba): Edif. Sudamérica, 2°, Of. 24, Calle Venezuela 1018 y Mejía, Quito; tel. (2) 251-9333; Bureau Chief ENRIQUE GARCÍA MEDINA.

Reuters (United Kingdom): Avda Amazonas 3655, 2°, Casilla 17-01-4112, Quito; tel. (2) 243-1753; fax (2) 243-2949; Correspondent JORGE AGUIRRE CHARVET.

Xinhua (New China) News Agency (People's Republic of China): Edif. Portugal, Avda Portugal y Avda de la República de El Salvador 730, 10°, Quito; Bureau Chief LIN MINZHONG.

Publishers

Artes Gráficas Ltda: Avda 12 de Octubre 1637, Apdo 533, Casilla 456A, Quito; Man. MANUEL DEL CASTILLO.

Casa de la Cultura Ecuatoriana: Avdas 6 de Diciembre y Patria; tel. (2) 222-3391; e-mail info@cce.org.ec; Dir JAIME PAREDES.

Centro de Educación Popular: Avda América 3584, Apdo 17-08-8604, Quito; tel. (2) 252-5521; fax (2) 254-2369; e-mail centro@cedep .ec; f. 1978; communications, economics; Dir DIEGO LANDÁZURI.

CEPLAES: Avda 6 de Diciembre 2912 y Alpallana, Apdo 17-11-6127, Quito; tel. (2) 254-8547; fax (2) 256-6207; f. 1978; agriculture, anthropology, education, health, social sciences, women's studies; Exec. Dir ALEXANDRA AYALA.

CIDAP: Hermano Miguel 3-23, Casilla 01-011-943, Cuenca; tel. (7) 282-9451; fax (7) 283-1450; e-mail cidapl@cidap.org.ec; internet www.cidap.org.ec; art, crafts, games, hobbies; Dir CLAUDIO MALO GONZALES.

CIESPAL (Centro Internacional de Estudios Superiores de Comunicación para América Latina): Avda Diego de Almagro 32-133 y Andrade Marín, Apdo 17-01-584, Quito; tel. (2) 254-8011; fax (2) 250-2487; e-mail ejaramillo@ciespal.net; internet www.ciespal.net; f. 1959; communications, technology; Dir EDGAR JARAMILLO.

Corporación de Estudios y Publicaciónes: Acuna 168 y J. Agama, Casilla 17-21-0086, Quito; tel. (2) 222-1711; fax (2) 222-6256; e-mail cep@accessinter.net; f. 1963; law, public administration.

Corporación Editora Nacional: Roca E9–59 y Tamayo, Apdo 17-12-886, Quito; tel. (2) 255-4358; fax (2) 256-6340; e-mail cen@ accessinter.net; f. 1977; archaeology, economics, education, geography, political science, history, law, literature, philosophy, social sciences; Pres. ERNESTO ALBÁN GOMEZ.

Cromograf, SA: Coronel 2207, Guayaquil; tel. (4) 234-6400; children's books, paperbacks, art productions.

Ediciones Abya-Yala: Avda 12 de Octubre 1430, CP 17-12-719, Quito; tel. (2) 250-6251; fax (2) 250-6267; e-mail admin-info@ abyayala.org; internet www.abyayala.org; f. 1975; anthropology, environmental studies, languages, education, theology; Pres. Fr JUAN BOTTASSO; Dir-Gen. P. XAVIER HERRÁN.

Ediciones Valladolid: Colón 818 y Santa Elena, Guayaquil; tel. (4) 232-9956; e-mail edival@andinanet.net; internet edival.ecuaemail .com; f. 1996; reference; Owner and Man. CÉSAR VALLADOLID.

Editorial Bueno: Avda República oeste 2-23 y Teresa de Cepeda (diagonal a los Puentes República); tel. (2) 225-8959; fax (2) 437-873; e-mail buenoeditores@yahoo.com; Man. CÉSAR FERNÁNDEZ BUENO.

Editorial Don Bosco: Vega Muñoz 10-68 y General Torres, Cuenca; tel. (7) 283-1745; fax (7) 284-2722; e-mail edibosco@bosco .org.ec; internet www.lns.com.ec; f. 1920; Gen. Man. P. EDUARDO SANDOVAL; Deputy Man. FANNY FAJARDO Z.

Editorial El Conejo: 6 de Diciembre 2309 y La Niña, Quito; tel. (2) 222-7948; fax (2) 250 1066; e-mail econejo@attglobal.net; internet www.editorialelconejo.com; non-profit publisher of educational and literary texts; Dir ABDÓN UBIDIA.

Editorial Edinacho SA: Bartolomé Sánchez Lote 6 y Calle C Lotización Muñoz Carvajal, Carcelén, 5932, Quito; tel. (2) 247-0429; fax (2) 247-0430; e-mail edinacho@ecnet.ec; f. 1985; Man. GERMÁN SEGURA; Editor Dr DALIA MARÍA NOBOA.

Eguez-Pérez en Nombre Colectivo/Abrapalabra Editores: América 5378, Casilla 464A, Quito; tel. and fax (2) 254-4178; f. 1990; drama, education, fiction, literature, science fiction, social sciences; Man. IVAN EGUEZ.

Libresa SA: Murgeon 364 y Ulloa, Quito; tel. (2) 223-0925; fax (2) 250-2992; e-mail info@libresa.com; internet www.libresa.com; f. 1979; education, literature, philosophy; Pres. FAUSTO COBA ESTRELLA; Man. JAIME PEÑA NOVOA.

Libros Técnicos Litesa Cía Ltda: Avda América 542, Apdo 456A, Quito; tel. (2) 252-8537; Man. MANUEL DEL CASTILLO.

Pontificia Universidad Católica del Ecuador, Centro de Publicaciones: Avda 12 de Octubre 1076 y Carrión, Apdo 17-01-2184, Quito; tel. (2) 252-9250; fax (2) 256-7117; e-mail puce@edu.ec; internet www.puce.edu.ec; f. 1974; literature, natural science, law, anthropology, sociology, politics, economics, theology, philosophy, history, archaeology, linguistics, languages and business; Rector Dr José Ribadeneira Espinosa; Dir Dr Marco Vinicio Rueda.

Trama Ediciones: Edif. Marinoar PB, entre Catalina Aldaz y El Batán, Eloy Alfaro 34-85, Quito; tel. (2) 224-6315; fax (2) 224-6317; e-mail trama@trama.ec; internet www.trama.com.ec; f. 1977; architecture, design, art and tourism; Dir-Gen. Rolando Moya Tasquer.

Universidad Central del Ecuador: Departamento de Publicaciones, Servicio de Almacén Universitario, Ciudad Universitaria, Avda América y A. Pérez Guerrero, POB 3291, Quito; tel. (2) 222-6080; fax (2) 250-1207.

Universidad de Guayaquil: Departamento de Publicaciones, Biblioteca General 'Luis de Tola y Avilés', Apdo 09-01-3834, Guayaquil; tel. (4) 251-6296; f. 1930; general literature, history, philosophy, fiction; Man. Dir Leonor Villao de Santander.

Broadcasting and Communications

TELECOMMUNICATIONS

Asociación Ecuatoriana de Radiodifusión (AER): Edif. Atlas, 8°, Of. 802, Calle Justino Cornejo con Francisco de Orellana, Guayaquil; tel. and fax (4) 229-1783; ind. asscn; Pres. Ing. Antonio Guerrero Onessa.

Consejo Nacional de Telecomunicaciones (CONATEL): Avda Diego de Almagro 31-95 y Alpallana, Casilla 17-07-9777, Quito; tel. (2) 222-5614; fax (2) 222-5030; e-mail comunicacion@conatel.gov.ec; internet www.conatel.gov.ec; Pres. Dr José Pileggi Véliz.

Secretaría Nacional de Telecomunicaciones: Avda Diego de Almagro 31-95 y Alpallana, Casilla 17-07-9777, Quito; tel. (2) 250-2197; fax (2) 290-1010; Secretario Nacional de Telecomunicaciones Ing. Carlos del Pozo Cazar.

Superintendencia de Telecomunicaciones (SUPTEL): Edif. Olimpo, Avda 9 de Octubre 1645 y Berlín, Casilla 17-21-1797, Quito; tel. (2) 222-2449; fax (2) 256-6688; e-mail supertel@server.supertel.gov.ec; internet www.supertel.gov.ec; Superintendente de Telecomunicaciones Iván Burbano.

Major Service Providers

Alegro PCS (Telecsa, SA): Edif. Vivaldi, Amazonas 3837 y Corea, Quito; tel. and fax (2) 299-0000; internet www.alegropcs.com; co-owned by Andinatel and Pacifictel; cellular telephone provider.

Andinatel: Edif. Zeta, Avda Amazonas y Veintimilla, Quito; tel. (2) 256-1004; fax (2) 256-2240; e-mail ventas@andinatel.com; internet www.andinatel.com; scheduled for privatization; Exec. Pres. Ing. Luis Recalde.

BellSouth Ecuador (OTECEL, SA): Edif. BellSouth, Avda República y Esq. La Pradera, Quito; tel. (2) 222-7700; internet www.bellsouth.com.ec; f. 1997; owned by Telefónica Móviles, SA (Spain); mobile telephone services.

Pacifictel: Calle Panamá y Roca, Guayaquil; tel. (4) 230-8724; internet www.pacifictel.net; scheduled for privatization; Exec. Pres. Ing. Mauricio Galindo.

BROADCASTING

Regulatory Authority

Consejo Nacional de Radiodifusión y Televisión (CONARTEL): Calle La Pinta 225 y Rábida, Quito; tel. (2) 223-3492; fax (2) 252-3188; Pres. Ing. Aloo Ottati Pino.

Radio

There are nearly 300 commercial stations, 10 cultural stations and 10 religious stations. The following are among the most important stations:

Emisoras Gran Colombia: Calle Galápagos 112 y Guayaquil, Quito; tel. (2) 244-2951; fax (2) 244-3147; f. 1943; Pres. Mario José Canessa Oneto.

Radio Católica Nacional: Avda América 1830 y Mercadillo, Casilla 17-03-540, Quito; tel. (2) 254-1557; fax (2) 256-7309; f. 1985; Pres. Antonio González.

Radio Centro: Avda República de El Salvador 836 y Portugal, Quito; tel. (2) 244-8900; fax (2) 250-4575; f. 1977; Pres. Édgar Yánez Villalobos.

Radio Colón: Avellanas E5-107 y Avda Eloy Alfaro, Casilla 17-07-9927, Quito; tel. 248-4574; fax (2) 248-5666; e-mail escucha@radiocolon.ec; internet www.radiocolon.ec; f. 1934; Pres. Dr Gerardo Castro; Dir Bernardo Nussbaum.

Radio CRE Satelital (CORTEL, SA): Edif. El Torreón, 9°, Avda Boyacá 642 y Padre Solano, Apdo 4144, Guayaquil; tel. (4) 256-4290; fax (4) 256-0386; e-mail administracion@cre.com.ec; Pres. Rafael Guerrero Valenzuela.

Radio La Luna: Quito; Owner Paco Velasco.

Radio Nacional del Ecuador: Mariano Echeverría 537 y Brasil, Casilla 17-01-82, Quito; tel. (2) 245-9555; fax (2) 245-5266; f. 1961; state-owned; Dir Ana Maldonado Robles.

Radio Quito: Avda 10 de Agosto 2441 y Colón, Casilla 17-21-1971, Quito; tel. (2) 250-8301; fax (2) 250-3311; f. 1940; Pres. Guadalupe Mantilla Mosquera.

Radio Sonorama (HCAEL): Eloy Alfaro 5400 y Los Granados, Casilla 130b, Quito; tel. (2) 244-8403; fax (2) 244-5858; f. 1975; Pres. Santiago Proaño.

Radio Sucre: Joaquin Orrantia y Miguel H. Alcivar (Casa de las Americas Kennedy Norte), Guayaquil; tel. (4) 268-0588; fax (4) 268-0592; e-mail info@radiosucretv.com; internet www.radiosucre.com.ec; f. 1983; Pres. Vicente Arroba Ditto; Dir Luis Sánchez Moreno.

Radio Zacaray: Avda Quito 1424 y Pasaje Aguavil, Santo Domingo de los Colorados; tel. (2) 275-0140; fax (2) 244-9207; e-mail admizar@uio.satnet.net; internet ecuadormedia.com; f. 1959; Pres. Hólger Velasteguí Domínguez.

La Voz de los Andes (HCJB): Villalengua 884 y Avda 10 de Agosto, Casilla 17-17-691, Quito; tel. (2) 226-6808; fax (2) 226-7263; e-mail helpdesk@hcjb.org.ec; f. 1931; operated by World Radio Missionary Fellowship; programmes in 11 languages (including Spanish and English) and 22 Quechua dialects; private, non-commercial, cultural, religious; Dir, Int. Radio Curt Cole; Gen. Man. John E. Beck.

Television

Corporación Ecuatoriana de Televisión—Ecuavisa Canal 2: Cerro El Carmen, Casilla 1239, Guayaquil; tel. (4) 230-0150; fax (4) 230-3677; f. 1967; Pres. Xavier Alvarado Roca; Gen. Man. Francisco Arosemena Robles.

Cadena Ecuatoriana de Televisión—TC Televisión Canal 10: Avda de las Américas, frente al Aeropuerto, Casilla 09-01-673, Guayaquil; tel. (4) 239-7664; fax (4) 228-7544; f. 1969; commercial; Pres. Roberto Isaías; Gen. Man. Jorge Kronfle.

Televisora Nacional—Ecuavisa Canal 8: Bosmediano 447 y José Carbo, Bellavista, Quito; tel. (2) 244-6472; fax (2) 244-5488; commercial; f. 1970; Pres. Patricio Jaramillo.

Televisión del Pacífico, SA—Gamavisión: Avda Eloy Alfaro 5400 y Río Coca, Quito; tel. (2) 226-2222; fax (2) 244-0259; e-mail nicovega@gamavision.com; internet www.gamavision.com; f. 1978; Pres. Nicolás Vega.

Teleamazonas Cratel, CA: Granda Centeno y Brasil, Casilla 17-11-04844, Quito; tel. (2) 245-1385; fax (2) 244-1620; e-mail contactenos@teleamazonas.com; f. 1974; commercial; Pres. Eduardo Granda Garcés.

Teleandina Canal 23: Avda de la Prensa 3920 y Fernández Salvador, Quito; tel. (2) 259-9403; fax (2) 259-2600; f. 1991; Pres. Humberto Ortiz Flores; Dir Patricio Aviles.

Finance

(cap. = capital; res = reserves; dep. = deposits; m. = million; brs = branches; amounts in US dollars unless otherwise indicated)

Junta Monetaria Nacional (National Monetary Board): Quito; tel. (2) 251-4833; fax (2) 257-0258; f. 1927; Pres. Francisco Swett.

SUPERVISORY AUTHORITY

Superintendencia de Bancos y Seguros: Avda 12 de Octubre 1561 y Madrid, Casilla 17-17-770, Quito; tel. (2) 255-4225; fax (2) 250-6812; e-mail alejo@e-mail.superban.gov.ec; internet www.superban.gov.ec; f. 1927; supervises national banking system, including state and private banks and other financial institutions; Superintendent Alejandro Maldonado García.

BANKING

Central Bank

Banco Central del Ecuador: Avda Amazonas y Atahualpa, Casilla 339, Quito; tel. (2) 225-5777; fax (2) 226-9064; internet www

.bce.fin.ec; f. 1927; cap. 2.5m., res 1,303.2m., dep. 1,529.0m. (Dec. 2003); Pres. POLIBIO CÓRDOVA; Gen. Man. LEOPOLDO R. BÁEZ CARRERA; 2 brs.

Other State Banks

Banco Ecuatoriano de la Vivienda: Avda l0 de Agosto 2270 y Cordero, Casilla 3244, Quito; tel. (2) 252-1311; f. 1962; Pres. Abog. JUAN PABLO MONCAGATTA; Gen. Man. Dr PATRICIO CEVALLOS MORÁN.

Banco del Estado (BDE): Avda Atahualpa 628 y 10 de Agosto, Casilla 17-01-00373, Quito; tel. (2) 225-0800; fax (2) 225-0320; f. 1979; Pres. Econ. CÉSAR ROBALINO; Gen. Man. LUIS MEJÍA MONTESDEOCA.

Banco Nacional de Fomento: Ante 107 y 10 de Agosto, Casilla 685, Quito; tel. (2) 256-0680; fax (2) 257-0286; internet www.bnf.fin.ec; f. 1928; Pres. HÉCTOR BALLESTEROS SEGARRA; 70 brs.

Corporación Financiera Nacional (CFN): Avda Juan León Mera 130 y Patria, Casilla 17-21-01924, Quito; tel. (2) 256-4900; fax (2) 222-3823; e-mail mbenitez@q.cfn.fin.ec; internet www.cfn.fin.ec; state-owned bank providing export credits, etc.; f. 1964; Pres. Ing. PEDRO KOHN; Financial Dir. HÉCTOR SAN ANDRÉS.

Commercial Banks

Quito

Banco Amazonas, SA: Avda Amazonas 4430 y Villalengua, Casilla 121, Quito; tel. (2) 226-0400; fax (2) 225-5123; e-mail basacomp@porta.net; internet www.bancoamazonas.com; f. 1976; affiliated to Banque Paribas; Pres. RAFAEL FERRETTI BENÍTEZ; Vice-Pres. ROBERTO SEMINARIO.

Banco Caja de Crédito Agrícola Ganadero, SA: Avda 6 de Diciembre 225 y Piedrahita, Quito; tel. (2) 252-8521; f. 1949; Man. HUGO GRIJALVA GARZÓN; Pres. NICOLÁS GUILLÉN.

Banco Consolidado del Ecuador: Avda Patria 740 y 9 de Octubre, Casilla 9150, Suc. 7, Quito; tel. (2) 256-0369; fax (2) 256-0719; f. 1981; cap. 2,874m., res 4,338m., dep. 5,545m. sucres (Oct. 1998); Chair. JAIME GILINSKI; Gen. Man. ANTONIO COY; 2 brs.

Banco General Rumiñahui: Avda República 720 y Eloy Alfaro, Quito; tel. (2) 250-9929; fax (2) 256-3786; e-mail bcainstitucional@bgr.com.ec; internet www.bgr.com.ec; total assets 192.0m. (Dec. 2004); Gen. Man. Gen. GUSTAVO HERRERA.

Banco Internacional, SA: Avda Patria E-421 y 9 de Octubre, Casilla 17-01-2114, Quito; tel. (2) 256-5547; fax (2) 256-5758; e-mail cromero@bancointernacional.com.ec; internet www.bancointernacional.com.ec; f. 1973; cap. 8,600m. (Dec. 2000); Pres. JOSÉ ENRIQUE FUSTER CAMPS; Gen. Man. RAÚL GUERRERO ANDRADE; 58 brs.

Banco del Pichincha, CA: Avda Amazonas 4560 y Pereira, Casilla 261, Quito; tel. (2) 298-0980; fax (2) 298-1226; internet www.pichincha.com; internet www.todo1.com; f. 1906; cap. 63.5m., res 76.4m., dep. 1,549.5m. (Dec. 2003); 61.82% owned by Exec. Pres. and Chair.; Exec. Pres. and Chair. Dr FIDEL EGAS GRIJALVA; Gen. Man. ANTONIO ACOSTA ESPINOSA; 127 brs.

Produbanco: Avda Amazonas 3775 y Japón, Casilla 17-03-38-A, Quito; tel. (2) 299-9000; fax (2) 244-7319; internet www.produbanco.com; f. 1978 as Banco de la Producción; name changed as above in 1996; cap. 60m., res 11.38m., dep. 542.36m. (Dec. 2004); filial of Grupo Financiero Producción; Pres. ABELARDO PACHANO BERTERO; Dir RODRIGO PAZ DELGADO; 55 brs.

UniBanco: Avda República 500 y Pasaje Carrión, Edif. Pucara, 1°, Quito; tel. (2) 290-7576; fax (2) 222-5000; f. 1964 as Banco de Cooperativas del Ecuador, name changed as above in 1995; Pres. SALVADOR PEDRERO; Treas. JUAN FERNANDO BERMEO.

Cuenca

Banco del Austro: Sucre y Borrero (esq.), Casilla 01-01-0167, Cuenca; tel. (7) 831-646; fax (7) 832-633; internet www.bancodelaustro.com; f. 1977; total assets 249.8m. (Sept. 2004); Pres. JUAN ELJURI ANTÓN; Gen. Man. PATRICIO ROBAYO IDROVO; 19 brs.

Guayaquil

Banco Bolivariano, CA: Junín 200 y Panamá, Casilla 09-01-10184, Guayaquil; tel. (4) 230-5000; fax (4) 256-6707; e-mail info@bolivariano.com; internet www.bolivariano.com; f. 1978; cap. 28.7m., res 6.4m., dep. 422.4m. (Dec. 2003); 61.2% owned by Tabos Investment SA; Chair. JOSÉ SALAZAR BARRAGÁN; Pres. and CEO MIGUEL BABRA LEÓN; 9 brs.

Banco del Pacífico: Francisco de P. Ycaza 200, Casilla 09-01-988, Guayaquil; tel. (4) 256-6010; fax (4) 232-8333; e-mail webadmin@pacifico.fin.ec; internet www.bp.fin.ec; f. 2000 by merger of Banco del Pacífico and Banco Continental; total assets 152.2m.; Exec. Pres. FÉLIX HERRERO BACHMEIER.

Banco Industrial y Comercial—Baninco: Pichincha 335 e Illingworth, Casilla 5817, Guayaquil; tel. (4) 232-3488; f. 1965; Pres. Ing. CARLOS MANZUR PERES; Gen. Man. GABRIEL MARTÍNEZ INTRIAGO; 2 brs.

Banco Territorial, SA: Panamá 814 y V. M. Rendón, Casilla 09-01-227, Guayaquil; tel. (4) 256-6695; fax (4) 256-6695; f. 1886; Pres. ROBERTO GOLDBAUM; Gen. Man. Ing. GUSTAVO HEINERT.

Loja

Banco de Loja: esq. Bolívar y Rocafuerte, Casilla 11-01-300, Loja; tel. (4) 757-1682; fax (4) 753-3019; internet www.bancodeloja.fin.ec; f. 1968; cap. 10,000m., res 4,207m., dep. 70,900m. sucres (Dec. 1996); Pres. Ing. STEVE BROWN HIDALGO; Man. Ing. LEONARDO BURNEO MULLER.

Machala

Banco de Machala, SA: Avda 9 de Mayo y Rocafuerte, Casilla 711, Machala; tel. (4) 256-6800; fax (4) 292-2744; internet www.bmachala.com; f. 1962; cap. 11.0m., res 0.4m., dep. 143.0; Pres. Dr ESTEBAN QUIROLA FIGUEROA; Exec. Pres. and Gen. Man. Dr MARIO CANESSA ONETO; 2 brs.

Portoviejo

Banco Comercial de Manabí, SA: Avda 10 de Agosto 600 y 18 de Octubre, Portoviejo; tel. (4) 265-3888; fax (4) 263-5527; f. 1980; Pres. Dr RUBÉN DARÍO MORALES; Gen. Man. ARISTO ANDRADE DÍAZ.

Foreign Banks

ABN AMBO Bank NV (Netherlands): República de El Salvador 1082, Edif. Mansión Blanca, Torre Londres, 5°, Quito; tel. (2) 243-4448; fax (2) 243-2163; e-mail juan.lopez@ec.abnamro.com; internet www.wholesale.abnamro.com; f. 1960; Country Rep. SANTIAGO HIDALGO; 6 brs.

Citibank, NA (USA): Juan León Mera 130 y Patria, Casilla 17-01-1393, Quito; tel. (2) 256-3300; fax (2) 256-6895; f. 1959; cap. 7,000m., res 1,000m., dep. 62,000m. (Dec. 1996); Gen. Man. BENJAMÍN FRANCO; 3 brs.

ING Bank NV (Netherlands): Edif. Centro Financiero, Avda Amazonas 4545 y Pereira, Quito; tel. (2) 298-1650; fax (2) 298-1665.

Lloyds TSB Bank Ltd (United Kingdom): Avda Amazonas 3428E entre Atahualpa y Núñez de Vela, Quito; tel. (4) 693-0000; fax (4) 693-0458; e-mail ltsbec@andinanet.net; internet www.lloydstsb.com.ec; f. 1988; in succession to the Bank of London and South America, f. 1936; Country Man. PAUL MCEVOY.

'Multibanco'

Banco de Guayaquil, SA: Plaza Ycaza 105 y Pichincha, Casilla 09-01-1300, Guayaquil; tel. (4) 251-7100; fax (4) 251-4406; e-mail servicios@bankguay.com; internet www.bancoguayaquil.com; f. 1923; absorbed the finance corpn, FINANSUR, in 1990 to become Ecuador's first 'multibanco', carrying out commercial and financial activities; cap. 145,000m., dep. 3,198,862m. sucres (Dec. 1998); Pres. DANILO CARRERA DROUET; Exec. Pres. GUILLERMO LASSO MENDOZA; 50 brs.

Finance Corporations

Corporación Financiera Nacional (CFN): Juan León Mera 130 y Avda Patria, Casilla 17-21-01924, Quito; tel. (2) 256-4900; fax (2) 222-3823; internet www.cfn.fin.ec; f. 1997; development finance agency; Chair. ROSA ELVIRA MANTILLA DE VELASCO.

Financiera Guayaquil, SA: Carchi 702 y 9 de Octubre, 6°, Casilla 2167, Guayaquil; f. 1976; cap. 900m., res 142m. (June 1987); Gen. Man. Dr MIGUEL BABRA LYON.

Associations

Asociación de Bancos Privados del Ecuador: Edif. Delta, 7°, Avda República de El Salvador 890 y Suecia, Casilla 17-11-6708, Quito; tel. (2) 246-6670; fax (2) 246-6702; e-mail echiribo@asobancos.org.ec; internet www.asobancos.org.ec; f. 1965; 36 mems; Pres. ÁNGELO CAPUTI; Exec. Pres. ERNESTO CHIRIBOGA BLONDET (acting).

Asociación de Compañías Financieras del Ecuador (AFIN): Robles 653 y Amazonas, 13°, Of. 1310-1311, Casilla 17-07-9156, Quito; tel. (2) 255-0623; fax (2) 256-7912; Pres. Ing. FRANCISCO ORTEGA.

STOCK EXCHANGES

Bolsa de Valores de Guayaquil: 9 de Octubre 110 y Pichincha, Guayaquil; tel. (4) 256-1519; fax (4) 256-1871; e-mail mmurillo@bvg.fin.ec; internet www.mundobvg.com; Pres. RODOLFO KRONFLE AKEL; Dir-Gen. ENRIQUE AROSEMENA BAQUERIZO.

Bolsa de Valores de Quito: Edif. Londres, 8°, Avda Amazonas 540 y Carrión, Casilla 17-01-3772, Quito; tel. (2) 222-1333; fax (2) 250-

0942; e-mail informacion@ccbvq.com; internet www.ccbvq.com; f. 1969; Pres. Patricio Peña; Exec. Pres. Mónica de Anderson.

INSURANCE

Instituto Ecuatoriano de Seguridad Social: Avda 10 de Agosto y Bogotá, Apdo 2640, Quito; tel. (2) 254-7400; fax (2) 250-4572; internet www.iess.gov.ec; f. 1928; various forms of state insurance provided; directs the Ecuadorean social insurance system; provides social benefits and medical service; Dir-Gen. Ing. Jorge Madera Castillo.

Principal National Companies

Bolívar Cía de Seguros del Ecuador, SA: Edif. Las Cámaras, 11° y 12°, Avda Francisco de Orellana, Guayaquil; tel. (2) 268-1777; fax (2) 268-3363; e-mail ssanmiguel@seguros-bolivar.com; internet www.seguros-bolivar.com; f. 1957; Gen. Man. Leonidas Ortega Amador.

Cía Reaseguradora del Ecuador, SA: Edif. Intercambios, 1°, Junín 105 y Malecón Simón Bolívar, Casilla 09-01-6776, Guayaquil; tel. (4) 256-4461; fax (4) 256-4454; e-mail oespinoz@ecuare.fin.ec; f. 1977; Man. Dir Ing. Omar Espinosa Romero.

Cía de Seguros Cóndor, SA: Plaza Ycaza 302, Apdo 09-01-5007, Guayaquil; tel. (4) 256-5300; fax (4) 256-0144; f. 1966; Gen. Man. Augusto Salame Arzubiaga.

Cía de Seguros Ecuatoriano-Suiza, SA: Avda 9 de Octubre 2101 y Tulcán, Apdo 09-01-0937, Guayaquil; tel. (4) 245-2444; fax (4) 245-3229; f. 1954; Gen. Man. Luis F. Salas Rubio.

Cía Seguros Unidos, SA: Edif. Urania, 4°, Avda 10 de Agosto 5133 y Naciones Unidas, Casilla 17-0373, Quito; tel. (2) 252-6466; fax (2) 245-0920; Gen. Man. Juan Rivas Domenech.

La Nacional Cía de Seguros Generales, SA: Panamá 809 y Rendón, Guayaquil; tel. (4) 256-0700; fax (4) 256-6327; f. 1940.

Panamericana del Ecuador, SA: Calle Portugal e-12-72 y Avda Eloy Alfaro, Quito; tel. (2) 246-8840; fax (2) 246-9650; f. 1973; Gen. Man. Germán Davila Leoro.

Seguros Rocafuerte, SA: Edif. Filanbanco, 15°, Plaza Carbo 505 y 9 de Octubre, Apdo 09-04-6491, Guayaquil; tel. (4) 232-6125; fax (4) 329-353; f. 1967; life and medical; Exec. Pres. Ing. Norman Pichardo Van Der Dijs.

La Unión Cía Nacional de Seguros: Urb. Los Cedros, Km 5½, Vía a la Costa, Apdo 09-01-1294, Guayaquil; tel. (4) 285-1500; fax (4) 285-1700; e-mail rgoldbaum@seguroslaunion.com; internet www .seguroslaunion.com; f. 1943; Exec. Pres. Roberto Goldbaum Morales; Gen. Man. David A. Goldbaum Morales.

Trade and Industry

GOVERNMENT AGENCIES

Consejo Nacional de Modernización del Estado (CONAM): Edif. CFN, 10°, Avda Juan León Mera 130 y Patria, Quito; tel. (2) 250-9432; fax (2) 222-8450; e-mail info@conam.gov.ec; internet www .conam.gov.ec; f. 1994; responsible for overseeing privatizations; Pres. Ing. Ricardo Noboa; Exec. Dir Ing. Antonio Peré Ycaza.

Empresa de Comercio Exterior (ECE): Quito; f. 1980 to promote non-traditional exports; State owns 33% share in company; share capital 25m. sucres.

Fondo de Promoción de Exportaciones (FOPEX): Juan León Mera 130 y Patria, Casilla 163, Quito; tel. (2) 256-4900; fax (2) 256-2519; f. 1972; export promotion; Dir Eliana Santamaría M.

Fondo de Solidaridad: Avda 6 de Diciembre 25–75 y Colón, Edif. Partenón, Quito; tel. (2) 220-0429; internet www.fondodesolidaridad .gov.ec; f. 1996; govt devt agency; responsibility for overseeing privatization of electricity sector; Pres. Jorge Burbano.

Instituto Ecuatoriano de Reforma Agraria y Colonización (IERAC): f. 1973 to supervise the Agrarian Reform Law under the auspices and co-ordination of the Ministry of Agriculture; Dir Luis Luna Gaybor.

Superintendencia de Compañías del Ecuador: Roca 660 y Amazonas, Casilla 687, Quito; tel. (2) 254-1606; fax (2) 256-6685; e-mail superintcias@q.supercias.gov.ec; internet www.supercias.gov .ec; f. 1964; responsible for the legal and accounting control of commercial enterprises; Supt Gonzalo Fabián Albuja Chaves.

DEVELOPMENT ORGANIZATIONS

Centro Nacional de Promoción de la Pequeña Industria y Artesanía (CENAPIA): Quito; agency to develop small-scale industry and handicrafts; Dir Econ. Edgar Guevara (acting).

Centro de Reconversión Económica del Azuay, Cañar y Morona Santiago (CREA): Avda México entre Unidad Nacional y las Américas, Casilla 01-01-1953, Cuenca; tel. (7) 817-500; fax (7) 817-134; f. 1959; development organization; Dir Dr Juan Tama.

Consejo Nacional de Desarrollo (CONADE): Juan Larrea y Arenas, Quito; fmrly Junta Nacional de Planificación y Coordinación Económica; aims to formulate a general plan of economic and social devt and supervise its execution; also to integrate local plans into the national; Chair. Galo Abril Ojeda; Sec. Pablo Lucio Paredes.

Fondo de Desarrollo del Sector Rural Marginal (FODERUMA): f. 1978 to allot funds to rural development programmes in poor areas.

Fondo Nacional de Desarrollo (FONADE): f. 1973; national development fund to finance projects as laid down in the five-year plan.

Instituto de Colonización de la Región Amazónica (INCREA): f. 1978 to encourage settlement in and economic development of the Amazon region; Dir Dr Dimas Guzmán.

Instituto Ecuatoriano de Recursos Hidráulicos (INERHI): undertakes irrigation and hydroelectric projects; Man. Ing. Eduardo García García.

Organización Comercial Ecuatoriana de Productos Artesanales (OCEPA): Carrión 1236 y Versalles, Casilla 17-01-2948, Quito; tel. (2) 254-1992; fax (2) 256-5961; f. 1964 to develop and promote handicrafts; Gen. Man. Marcelo Rodríguez.

Programa Nacional del Banano y Frutas Tropicales: Guayaquil; to promote the development of banana and tropical-fruit cultivation; Dir Ing. Jorge Gil Chang.

Programa Regional de Desarrollo del Sur del Ecuador (PREDESUR): Pasaje María Eufrasia 100 y Mosquera Narváez, Quito; tel. (2) 254-4415; f. 1972 to promote the development of the southern area of the country; Dir Ing. Luis Hernán Eguiguren Carrión.

CHAMBERS OF COMMERCE AND INDUSTRY

Cámara de Comercio de Ambato: Montalvo 630, Ambato; tel. and fax (3) 841-906; e-mail camcomam@uio.satnet.net; Pres. Pablo Vásconez.

Cámara de Comercio de Cuenca: Avda Federico Malo 1-90, 2°, Casilla 4929, Cuenca; tel. (7) 827-531; fax (7) 833-891; e-mail cccuenca@etapa.com.ec; internet www.cccuenca.com; f. 1919; 5,329 mems; Pres. Juan Pablo Vintimilla.

Cámara de Comercio Ecuatoriano-Americana (Amcham Quito-Ecuador): tel. (2) 250-7450; fax (2) 250-4571; e-mail info@ecamcham .com; internet www.ecamcham.com; f. 1974; promotes bilateral trade and investment between Ecuador and the USA; brs in Ambato, Cuenca and Manta; Pres. Mauricio Robalino; Vice-Pres. Alberto Sandoval.

Cámara de Comercio Ecuatoriano Canadiense (Ecuadorean-Canadian Chamber of Commerce): Quito; internet www .ecucanchamber.org; Exec. Dir Patricia Bustamante; Pres. Bill Ibbitson.

Cámara de Comercio de Guayaquil: Avda Francisco de Orellana y V. H. Sicouret, Centro Empresarial 'Las Cámaras', 2° y 3°, Guayaquil; tel. (4) 268-2771; fax (4) 268-2766; e-mail info@lacamara.org; internet www.lacamara.org; f. 1889; 31,000 affiliates; Pres. Eduardo Maruri Miranda.

Cámara de Comercio de Machala: Edif. Cámara de Comercio, 2°, Rocafuerte y Buenavista, CP 825, Machala; tel. (7) 930-640; fax (7) 934-454; e-mail ccomach@ecua.net.ec; internet ; Pres. José Mendieta E.

Cámara de Comercio de Manta: Edif. Banco del Pichincha, 1°, Avda 2, entre Calles 10 y 11, Manta; tel. and fax (5) 621-306; e-mail cacoma@manta.telconet.net; Pres. Mariano Zambrano S.

Cámara de Comercio de Quito: Edif. Las Cámaras, 6°, Avda República y Amazonas, 6°, Casilla 17-01-202, Quito; tel. (2) 244-3787; fax (2) 243-5862; e-mail ccq@ccq.org.ec; internet www.ccq.org .ec; f. 1906; 12,000 mems; Pres. Blasco Penaherrera Solah; Exec. Dir Miguel Chiriboga Torreo.

Cámara de Industrias de Cuenca: Edif. Cámara de Industrias de Cuenca, 12° y 13°, Avda Florencia Astudillo y Alfonso Cordero, Cuenca; tel. (7) 284-5053; fax (7) 284-0107; internet www .industriascuenca.org.ec; f. 1936; Pres. Ing. Marcejo Jaramillo Crespo.

Cámara de Industrias de Guayaquil: Avda Francisco de Orellana y M. Alcívar, Casilla 09-01-4007, Guayaquil; tel. (4) 268-2618; fax (4) 268-2680; e-mail caindgye@cig.org.ec; internet www.cig.ec; f. 1936; Pres. Alberto Dassum A.

Federación Nacional de Cámaras de Comercio del Ecuador: Avda Olmedo 414 y Boyacá, Guayaquil; tel. (4) 232-3130; fax (4) 232-

3478; Pres. BLASCO PEÑAHERRERA SOLAH; Exec. Vice-Pres. Dr ROBERTO ILLINGWORTH.

Federación Nacional de Cámaras de Industrias: Avda República y Amazonas, 10°, Casilla 2438, Quito; tel. (2) 245-2994; fax (2) 244-8118; e-mail camara@camindustriales.org.ec; internet www .camindustriales.org.ec; f. 1974; Pres. Ing. GUSTAVO PINTO.

INDUSTRIAL AND TRADE ASSOCIATIONS

Centro de Desarrollo Industrial del Ecuador (CENDES): Avda Orellana 1715 y 9 de Octubre, Casilla 2321, Quito; tel. (2) 252-7100; f. 1962; carries out industrial feasibility studies, supplies technical and administrative assistance to industry, promotes new industries, supervises investment programmes; Gen. Man. CLAUDIO CREAMER GUILLÉN.

Corporación de Desarrollo e Investigación Geológico-Minero-Metalúrgica (CODIGEM): Avda 10 de Agosto 5844 y Pereira, Casilla 17-03-23, Quito; tel. (2) 225-4673; fax (2) 225-4674; e-mail prodemi2@prodeminca.org.ec; f. 1991 to direct mining exploration and exploitation; Exec. Pres. Ing. JORGE BARRAGÁN G.

Corporación de Promoción de Exportaciones e Inversiones (CORPEI): Edif. Centro Empresarial Las Cámaras, Avda Francisco de Orellana y Miguel H. Alcívar, 2°, Guayaquil; tel. (4) 268-1550; fax (4) 268-1551; e-mail aissa@corpei.org.ec; internet www.corpei.org.ec; f. 1997 to promote exports and investment; CEO RICARDO E. ESTRADA.

Fondo Nacional de Preinversión (FONAPRE): Jorge Washington 624 y Amazonas, Casilla 17-01-3302, Quito; tel. (2) 256-3261; f. 1973 to undertake feasibility projects before investment; Pres. LUIS PARODÍ VALVERDE; Gen. Man. Ing. EDUARDO MOLINA GRAZZIANI.

EMPLOYERS' ORGANIZATIONS

Asociación de Atuneros: Malecón s/n, Muelle Portuario de Manta 1, Manta; tel. and fax (5) 262-6467; e-mail atunec@manta.ecua.net .ec; asscn of tuna producers; Pres. LUCÍA FERNÁNDEZ DE GENNA.

Asociación de Cafecultores del Cantón Piñas: García Moreno y Abdón Calderón, Quito; coffee growers' association.

Asociación de Comerciantes e Industriales: Avda Boyacá 1416, Guayaquil; traders' and industrialists' association.

Asociación de Compañías Consultoras del Ecuador: Edif. Delta 890, 4°, República de El Salvador y Suecia, Quito; tel. (2) 246-5048; fax (2) 245-1171; e-mail acce@acce.com.ec; internet www .consultoresecuador.com; asscn of consulting cos; Pres. RODOLFO RENDÓN.

Asociación de Industriales Gráficos de Pichincha: Edif. de las Cámaras, 8°, Amazonas y República, Quito; tel. (2) 292-3141; fax (2) 245-6664; e-mail aigquito@aig.org.ec; internet www.aig.org.ec; asscn of the graphic industry; Pres. ENRIQUE CORTÉZ.

Asociación Ecuatoriana de Industriales de la Madera: Edif. de las Cámaras, 7°, República y Amazonas, Quito; tel. (2) 226-0980; fax (2) 243-9560; e-mail secre@aima.org.ec; internet www.aima.org.ec; wood mafrs' asscn; Pres. CÉSAR ALVAREZ.

Asociación de Industriales Textiles del Ecuador (AITE): Edif. Las Cámaras, 8°, Avda República y Amazonas, Casilla 2893, Quito; tel. (2) 224-9434; fax (2) 244-5159; e-mail aite@aite.org.ec; internet www.aite.com.ec; f. 1938; textile mfrs' association; 40 mems; Pres. FERNANDO PÉREZ.

Asociación de Productores Bananeros del Ecuador (APRO-BANA): Guayaquil; banana growers' association; Pres. NICOLÁS CASTRO.

Asociación Nacional de Empresarios (ANDE): Edif. España, 6°, Of. 67, Avda Amazonas 25–23 y Colón, Casilla 17-01-3489, Quito; tel. (2) 223-8507; fax (2) 250-9806; e-mail ande@uio.satnet.net; internet www.ande.org.ec; national employers' asscn; Pres. PEDRO VILLAMAR; Vice-Pres. ERNESTO RIBADENEIRA TROYA.

Asociación Nacional de Exportadores de Cacao y Café (ANECAFE): Casilla 4774, Manta; tel. (2) 229-2782; fax (2) 229-2885; e-mail anacafe@uio.satnet.net; cocoa and coffee exporters' association.

Asociación Nacional de Exportadores de Camarones: Pres. LUIS VILLACÍS.

Asociación Nacional de Molineros: 6 de Diciembre 3470 e Ignacio Bossano, Quito; tel. (2) 246-5597; fax (2) 246-4754; Exec. Dir RAFAEL CALLEJAS.

Cámara de Agricultura: Casilla 17-21-322, Quito; tel. (2) 223-0195; Pres. ALBERTO ENRÍQUEZ PORTILLA.

Consorcio Ecuatoriano de Exportadores de Cacao y Café: cocoa and coffee exporters' consortium.

Corporación Nacional de Exportadores de Cacao y Café: Guayaquil; cocoa and coffee exporters' corporation.

Federación Nacional de Cooperativas Cafetaleras del Ecuador (FENACAFE): Jipijapa; tel. (4) 260-0631; e-mail orgcafex@mnb.satnet.net; coffee co-operatives federation.

Unión Nacional de Periodistas: Joaquín Auxe Iñaquito, Quito; national press association.

There are several other coffee and cocoa organizations.

STATE HYDROCARBON COMPANY

Empresa Estatal Petróleos del Ecuador (PETROECUADOR): Alpallana E-8-86 y Avda 6 de Diciembre, Casilla 17-11-5007, Quito; tel. (2) 256-3050; e-mail secdir@petroecuador.com.ec; internet www .petroecuador.com.ec; f. 1989; state petroleum co; operations in at least seven oilfields expected to be transferred to the private sector; Pres. PEDRO ESPÍN.

UTILITIES

Regulatory Authorities

Ministry of Energy and Mines: see section on The Government (Ministries).

Centro Nacional de Control de Energía (CENACE): Panamericana Sur Km 17.5, Sector Santa Rosa de Cutuglagua, Casilla 17-21-1991, Quito; tel. (2) 299-2030; fax (2) 299-2031; e-mail garguello@ cenace.org.ec; f. 1999; co-ordinates and oversees national energy system; Exec. Dir GABRIEL ARGÜELLO RÍOS.

Comisión Ecuatoriana de Energía Atómica: Juan Larrea 15-36 y Riofrío, Casilla 17-01-2517, Quito; tel. (2) 254-5861; fax (2) 256-3336; e-mail comecen1@comecenat.gov.ec; atomic energy commission; Exec. Dir CELIANO ALMEIDA; Head of Information HIPSY CIFUENTES.

Consejo Nacional de Electricidad (CONELEC): Avda Amazonas 33-299 e Inglaterra, Quito; tel. (2) 226-8746; fax (2) 226-8737; e-mail conelec@conelec.gov.ec; internet www.conelec.gov.ec; f. 1999; supervises electricity industry following transfer of assets of the former Instituto Ecuatoriano de Electrificación (INECEL) to the Fondo de Solidaridad; pending privatization as six generating companies, one transmission company and 19 distribution companies; Exec. Pres. DIEGO PÉREZ PALLARES.

Directorate of Renewable Energy and Energy Efficiency (Ministry of Energy and Mines): J. L. Mera y Orellana, Edif. MOP, 6°, Quito; tel. (2) 255-0018; fax (2) 255-0018; e-mail jvasconez@ menergia.gov.ec; internet www.menergia.gov.ec; f. 1995; research and development of new and renewable energy sources; Dir Ing. JOSÉ VASCONEZ E.

Directorate-General of Hydrocarbons: Avda 10 de Agosto 321, Quito; supervision of the enforcement of laws regarding the exploration and development of petroleum.

Electricity

Corporación Eléctrica de Guayaquil, SA: Urb. La Garzota, Sector 3, Manzana 47; tel. (4) 224-8006; fax (4) 224-8040; major producer and distributor of electricity, mostly using oil-fired or diesel generating capacity; partially privatized in 2003.

Empresa Eléctrica Quito, SA (EEQ): Avda 10 de Agosto y Las Casas, Quito; tel. (2) 254-3833; fax (2) 250-3817; internet www.eeq .com.ec; f. 1894; produces electricity for the region around Quito, mostly from hydroelectric plants; Gen. Man. HERNÁN ANDINO ROMERO.

Empresa Eléctrica Regional El Oro, SA (EMELORO): e-mail mandrad@emeloro.gov.ec; internet www.eeq.com.ec; electricity production and generation in El Oro province; Pres. WILSON LAPO.

Empresa Eléctrica Regional del Sur, SA (EERSSA): internet www.eeq.com.ec; f. 1973; electricity production and generation in Loja and Zamora Chinchipe provinces; Man. DANIEL MAHAUAD ORTEGA.

Empresa Eléctrica Riobamba, SA: Veloz 20-12 y Tarqui, Riobamba; tel. (3) 961-693; fax (3) 965-257; state-owned utility; Pres. OSWALDO GARCIA DAVALOS.

Water

Instituto Ecuatoriano de Obras Sanitarias: Toledo 684 y Lérida, Troncal, Quito; tel. (2) 252-2738.

TRADE UNIONS

Frente Unitario de Trabajadores (FUT): f. 1971; left-wing; 300,000 mems; Pres. JAIME ARCINIEGAS AGUIRRE; comprises:

Confederación Ecuatoriana de Organizaciones Clasistas (CEDOC): Calle Río de Janeiro 407 y Juan Larrea, Casilla 3207, Quito; tel. (2) 254-8086; f. 1938; affiliated to CMT and CLAT; humanist; Pres. RAMIRO ROSALES NARVÁEZ; Sec.-Gen. JORGE MUÑOZ; 150,000 mems (est.) organized in 20 provinces.

Confederación Ecuatoriana de Organizaciones Sindicales Libres (CEOSL): Casilla 17-01-1373, Quito; tel. (2) 252-2511; fax (2) 250-0836; e-mail ceosl@hoy.net; f. 1962; affiliated to ICFTU and ORIT; Pres. JAIME ARCINIEGAS AGUIRRE; Sec.-Gen. GUILLERMO TOUMA GONZÁLEZ.

Confederación de Trabajadores del Ecuador (CTE) (Confederation of Ecuadorean Workers): 9 de Octubre 26-106 y Marieta de Veintimilla, Casilla 17-014166, Quito; tel. (2) 252-0456; fax (2) 252-0445; e-mail cte@punto.net.ec; internet www.cte-ecuador.org; f. 1944; admitted to WFTU and CEPUSTAL; Pres. SANTIAGO YAGUAL YAGUAL; 1,200 affiliated unions, 76 national federations.

Central Católica de Obreros: Avda 24 de Mayo 344, Quito; tel. (2) 221-3704; f. 1906; craft and manual workers and intellectuals; Pres. CARLOS E. DÁVILA ZURITA.

A number of trade unions are not affiliated to the above groups. These include the Federación Nacional de Trabajadores Marítimos y Portuarios del Ecuador (FNTMPE—National Federation of Maritime and Port Workers of Ecuador) and both railway trade unions.

Transport

RAILWAYS

All railways are government-controlled. In 1997 the total length of track was 956 km.

Empresa Nacional de Ferrocarriles del Estado (ENFE): Calle Bolívar 443, Casilla 159, Quito; tel. (2) 221-6180; e-mail enfegg@ andinanet.net; national network currently has only 200 miles of track; Gen. Man. SERGIO COELLAR.

There are divisional state railway managements for the following lines: Guayaquil–Quito, Sibambe–Cuenca and Quito–San Lorenzo.

ROADS

There were 43,197 km of roads in 2000, of which 18.9% were paved. The Pan-American Highway runs north from Ambato to Quito and to the Colombian border at Tulcán and south to Cuenca and Loja. Major rebuilding projects were undertaken in late 1998 with finance from several development organizations to restore roads damaged by the effects of El Niño (a periodic warming of the tropical Pacific Ocean).

SHIPPING

The following are Ecuador's principal ports: Guayaquil, Esmeraldas, Manta and Puerto Bolívar.

Acotramar, CA: General Gómez 522 y Coronel Guayaquil, Casilla 4044, Guayaquil; tel. (4) 240-1004; fax (4) 244-4852.

Ecuanave, CA: Junin 415 y Córdova, 4°, Casilla 09-01-30H, Guayaquil; tel. (4) 229-3808; fax (4) 228-9257; e-mail ecuanav@ecua.net.ec; Chair. Ing. P. ERNESTO ESCOBAR; Man. Dir A. GUILLERMO SERRANO.

Flota Bananera Ecuatoriana, SA: Edif. Gran Pasaje, 9°, Plaza Ycaza 437, Guayaquil; tel. (4) 230-9333; f. 1967; owned by Govt and private stockholders; Pres. DIEGO SÁNCHEZ; Gen. Man. JORGE BARRIGA.

Flota Mercante Grancolombiana, SA: Guayaquil; tel. (4) 251-2791; f. 1946; with Colombia and Venezuela; on Venezuela's withdrawal, in 1953, Ecuador's 10% interest was increased to 20%; operates services from Colombia and Ecuador to European ports, US Gulf ports and New York, Mexican Atlantic ports and East Canada; offices in Quito, Cuenca, Bahía, Manta and Esmeraldas; Man. Naval Capt. J. ALBERTO SÁNCHEZ.

Flota Petrolera Ecuatoriana (FLOPEC): Edif. FLOPEC, Avda Amazonas 1188 y Cordero, Casilla 535-A, Quito; tel. (2) 256-4058; fax (2) 256-9794; e-mail g.general@flopec.com.ec; internet www .flopec.com.ec; f. 1972; Gen. Man. Vice-Adm. JORGE DONOSO MORAN.

Logística Marítima, CA (LOGMAR): Avda Córdova 812 y V. M. Rendón, 1°, Casilla 9622, Guayaquil; tel. (4) 230-7041; Pres. J. COELLOG; Man. IGNACIO RODRÍGUEZ BAQUERIZO.

Naviera del Pacífico, CA (NAPACA): El Oro 101 y La Ría, Casilla 09-01-529, Guayaquil; tel. (4) 234-2055; Pres. LUIS ADOLFO NOBOA NARANJO.

Servicios Oceánicos Internacionales, SA: Avda Domingo Comin y Calle 11, Casilla 79, Guayaquil; Pres. CARLOS VALDANO RAFFO; Man. FERNANDO VALDANO TRUJILLO.

Transfuel, CA: Junin 415 y Córdova, 4°, Casilla 09-01-30H, Guayaquil; tel. (4) 230-4142; Chair. Ing. ERNESTO ESCOBAR PALLARES; Man. Dir CARLOS MANRIQUE A.

Transportes Navieros Ecuatorianos (Transnave): Edif. Citibank, 4°–7°, Avda 9 de Octubre 416 y Chile, Casilla 4706, Guayaquil; tel. (4) 256-1455; fax (4) 256-6273; transports general cargo within the European South Pacific Magellan Conference, Japan West Coast South America Conference and Atlantic and Gulf West Coast South America Conference; Pres. Vice-Adm. YÉZID JARAMILLO SANTOS; Gen. Man. RUBÉN LANDÁZURI ZAMBRANO.

CIVIL AVIATION

There are two international airports: Mariscal Sucre, near Quito, and Simón Bolívar, near Guayaquil.

LAN Ecuador, SA: Avda de las Américas s/n, Guayaquil; tel. (4) 269-2850; fax (4) 228-5433; internet www.lanecuador.com; f. 2002; commenced operations in April 2003, following acquisition of assets of Ecuatoriana by LAN Chile; scheduled daily flights between Quito, Guayaquil, Miami and New York; Dir BRUNO ARDITO.

TAME Línea Aérea del Ecuador: Avda Amazonas 1354 y Colón, 6°, Casilla 17-07-8736, Sucursal Almagro, Quito; tel. (2) 250-9375; fax (2) 255-4907; e-mail tamejefv@impsat.net.ec; internet www.tame .com.ec; f. 1962; fmrly Transportes Aéreos Mercantiles Ecuatorianos, SA; removed from military control in 1990, state-owned; domestic scheduled and charter services for passengers and freight; Pres. JORGE CABEZAS; Gen. Man. BOLÍVAR MORA VINTIMILLA.

The following airlines also offer national and regional services:

Aerotaxis Ecuatorianos, SA (ATESA); Cía Ecuatoriana de Transportes Aéreos (CEDTA); Ecuastol Servicios Aéreos, SA; Ecuavia Cía Ltda; Aeroturismo Cía Ltda (SAVAC).

Tourism

Tourism has become an increasingly important industry in Ecuador, with 654,993 foreign arrivals (including same-day visitors) in 2002. Of total visitors in that year, some 29% came from Colombia, 13% were from Peru, 9% from other Latin American countries, 23% from the USA and 18% from Europe. In 2002 receipts from the tourism industry amounted to US $447m.

Asociación Ecuatoriana de Agencias de Viajes y Turismo (ASECUT): Edif. Banco del Pacífico, 5°, Avda Amazonas 22–94 y Veintimilla, Casilla 9421, Quito; tel. (2) 250-3669; fax (2) 250-0238; e-mail asecut@pi.pro.ec; f. 1953; Pres. ERIK RUGEL ROCA.

Federación Hotelera del Ecuador (AHOTEC): América 5378 y Diguja, Quito; tel. (2) 244-3425; fax (2) 245-3942; e-mail ahotec@ interactive.net.ec; internet www.hotelesecuador.com.ec; Pres. JOSÉ OCHOA; Exec. Dir DIEGO UTRERAS.

Ministry of Tourism: Avda Eloy Alfaro 32-300 y Carlos Tobar, Quito; tel. (2) 250-7559; fax (2) 250-7565; e-mail promocion@turismo .gov.ec; internet www.vivecuador.com; Minister of Tourism MARÍA ISABEL SALVADOR.

EGYPT

Introductory Survey

Location, Climate, Language, Religion, Flag, Capital

The Arab Republic of Egypt occupies the north-eastern corner of Africa, with an extension across the Gulf of Suez into the Sinai Peninsula, sometimes regarded as lying within Asia. Egypt is bounded to the north by the Mediterranean Sea, to the north-east by Israel, to the east by the Red Sea, to the south by Sudan, and to the west by Libya. The climate is arid, with a maximum annual rainfall of only 200 mm around Alexandria. More than 90% of the country is desert, and some 99% of the population live in the valley and delta of the River Nile. Summer temperatures reach a maximum of 43°C (110°F) and winters are mild, with an average day temperature of about 18°C (65°F). Arabic is the official language. More than 80% of the population are Muslims, mainly of the Sunni sect. The remainder are mostly Christians, principally Copts. The national flag (proportions 2 by 3) has three equal horizontal stripes, of red, white, and black; the white stripe has, in the centre, the national emblem (a striped shield superimposed on an eagle, with a cartouche beneath bearing the inscription, in Kufic script, 'Arab Republic of Egypt') in gold. The capital is Cairo (Al-Qahirah).

Recent History

Egypt, a province of Turkey's Ottoman Empire from the 16th century, was occupied by British forces in 1882. The administration was controlled by British officials, although Egypt remained nominally an Ottoman province until 1914, when a British protectorate was declared. The country was granted titular independence on 28 February 1922. Fuad I, the reigning Sultan, became King. He was succeeded in 1936 by his son, King Faruq (Farouk). The Anglo-Egyptian Treaty of 1936 recognized full Egyptian sovereignty, and after the Second World War British forces withdrew from Egypt, except for a military presence in the Suez Canal Zone. When the British mandate in Palestine was ended in 1948, Arab armies intervened to oppose the newly proclaimed State of Israel. A cease-fire was agreed in 1949, leaving Egyptian forces occupying the Gaza Strip.

On 23 July 1952 power was seized by a group of young army officers in a bloodless coup led by Lt-Col (later Col) Gamal Abd an-Nasir (Nasser). Farouk abdicated in favour of his infant son, Ahmad Fuad II, and went into exile. Gen. Muhammad Nagib (Neguib) was appointed Commander-in-Chief of the army and Chairman of the Revolution Command Council (RCC). In September Neguib was appointed Prime Minister and Military Governor, with Nasser as Deputy Prime Minister. In December the 1923 Constitution was abolished, and all political parties were dissolved in January 1953. The monarchy was abolished on 18 June 1953 and Egypt was proclaimed a republic, with Neguib as President and Prime Minister. In April 1954 Neguib was succeeded as Prime Minister by Nasser. In October Egypt and the United Kingdom signed an agreement providing for the withdrawal of all British forces from the Suez Canal by June 1956. President Neguib was relieved of all his remaining posts in November 1954, whereupon Nasser became acting Head of State.

The establishment of military rule was accompanied by wide-ranging reforms, including the redistribution of land, the promotion of industrial development and the expansion of social welfare services. In foreign affairs, the new regime was strongly committed to Arab unity, and Egypt played a prominent part in the Non-aligned Movement. In 1955, having failed to secure Western armaments on satisfactory terms, Egypt accepted military assistance from the USSR.

A new Constitution was approved by a national referendum in June 1956; Nasser was elected President unopposed, and the RCC was dissolved. In July, following the departure of British forces, the US and British Governments withdrew their offers of financial assistance for Egypt's construction of the Aswan High Dam. Nasser responded by announcing the nationalization of the Suez Canal Company, so that revenue from Canal tolls could be used to finance the dam's construction. The take-over of the Canal was a catalyst for Israel's invasion of the Sinai Peninsula on 29 October. British and French forces launched military operations against Egypt two days later. Intense pressure from

the UN and the USA resulted in a cease-fire on 6 November, and supervision by the UN of the invaders' withdrawal.

Egypt and Syria merged in February 1958 to form the United Arab Republic (UAR), with Nasser as President. The new nation strengthened earlier ties with the USSR and other countries of the communist bloc. In September 1961 Syria seceded from the UAR, but Egypt retained this title until September 1971.

In December 1962 Nasser established the Arab Socialist Union (ASU) as the country's only recognized political organization. In May 1967 he secured the withdrawal of the UN Emergency Force from Egyptian territory. Egypt subsequently reoccupied Sharm esh-Sheikh, on the Sinai Peninsula, and closed the Straits of Tiran to Israeli shipping. This precipitated the so-called Six-Day War, or June War, when Israel quickly defeated neighbouring Arab states, including Egypt. The war left Israel in control of the Gaza Strip and a large area of Egyptian territory, including the whole of the Sinai Peninsula. The Suez Canal was blocked, and remained closed until June 1975.

Nasser died suddenly in September 1970, and was succeeded by his Vice-President, Col Anwar Sadat. In September 1971 the UAR was renamed the Arab Republic of Egypt, and a new Constitution took effect. Egypt, Libya and Syria formed a Federation of Arab Republics in 1972, but this proved to be ineffective. In 1976 Egypt terminated its Treaty of Friendship with the USSR. Relations with the USA developed meanwhile, as President Sadat came to rely increasingly on US aid.

In October 1973 Egyptian troops crossed the Suez Canal to recover territory lost to Israel in 1967. After 18 days of fighting a cease-fire was achieved. In 1974–75 the US Secretary of State, Dr Henry Kissinger, negotiated disengagement agreements whereby Israel evacuated territory in Sinai and Israeli and Egyptian forces were separated by a buffer zone under the control of UN forces. In a dramatic peace-making initiative, opposed by many Arab countries, Sadat visited Israel in 1977 and addressed the Knesset (parliament). The leaders of Syria, Libya, Algeria, Iraq, the People's Democratic Republic of Yemen (PDRY) and the Palestine Liberation Organization (PLO) condemned Egypt, which responded by severing diplomatic relations with the five dissenting countries. In September 1978, following talks held at the US presidential retreat at Camp David, Maryland, Sadat and the Israeli Prime Minister, Menachem Begin, signed two agreements: the first provided for a five-year transitional period during which the inhabitants of the Israeli-occupied West Bank of Jordan and the Gaza Strip would obtain full autonomy and self-government; the second provided for a peace treaty between Egypt and Israel. The latter was signed in March 1979, whereafter Israel made phased withdrawals from the Sinai Peninsula, the last taking place in April 1982. The League of Arab States (the Arab League, see p. 290) expelled Egypt following the signing of the peace treaty, and imposed political and economic sanctions. Nevertheless, Egypt continued to forge relations with Israel, and in February 1980 the two countries exchanged ambassadors for the first time.

In 1974 Sadat began to introduce a more liberal political and economic regime. Political parties (banned since 1953) were allowed to participate in the 1976 elections for the Majlis ash-Sha'ab (People's Assembly), and in July 1978 Sadat formed the National Democratic Party (NDP), with himself as leader. In 1979 the special constitutional status of the ASU was ended. In October 1981 Sadat was assassinated by members of Islamic Jihad, a group of militant fundamentalist Islamists. Sadat was succeeded by Lt-Gen. Hosni Mubarak, his Vice-President and a former Commander-in-Chief of the air force. A new electoral law required parties to receive a minimum of 8% of the total vote in order to secure representation in the People's Assembly. This prompted opposition parties to boycott elections to local councils and to the Majlis ash-Shura (Advisory Council). At legislative elections in May 1984 the ruling NDP won 72.9% of the total vote. Of the four other participating parties, only the New Wafd Party, with 15.1%, achieved representation.

Meanwhile, a division in the Arab world between a 'moderate' grouping (including Jordan, Iraq and the Gulf states), which viewed the participation of Egypt as indispensable to any diplomatic moves towards solving the problems of the region, and a 'radical' grouping, led by Syria, became increasingly evident. The PLO leader, Yasser Arafat, visited President Mubarak for discussions in December 1983, signifying the end of estrangement between Egypt and the PLO, and in 1984 Jordan resumed diplomatic relations with Egypt. These two developments led to the profound involvement of Egypt in the pursuit of a negotiated settlement of the Palestinian question. In November 1987, at a summit conference in Jordan attended by the majority of Arab leaders, President Hafiz Assad of Syria obstructed proposals to readmit Egypt to the Arab League. However, recognizing Egypt's support for Iraq in the Iran–Iraq War and acknowledging the influence that Egypt could exercise on the problems of the region, the conference approved a resolution placing the establishment of diplomatic links with Egypt at the discretion of member states. Egypt was readmitted to the Arab League in May 1989.

The general election held in April 1987 resulted in a large majority for the ruling NDP. Of the 448 elective seats in the People's Assembly, the NDP won 346, the opposition parties together won 95, and independents seven. An electoral alliance of the Socialist Labour Party (SLP), the Liberal Socialist Party (LSP) and the Muslim Brotherhood won a combined total of 60 seats, of which the Brotherhood took 37 to become the largest single opposition group in the legislature. At a referendum held in October Mubarak was confirmed as President for a second six-year term of office by 97% of voters. In March 1988 the national state of emergency first declared after the assassination of President Sadat was renewed for a further three years.

Following Iraq's invasion and annexation of Kuwait in August 1990, Egypt convened an emergency summit meeting of Arab leaders at which 12 of the 20 Arab League states supported a resolution demanding the withdrawal of Iraqi forces from Kuwait and, in response to Saudi Arabia's request for international assistance to deter potential aggression by Iraq, voted to send an Arab force to the Persian (Arabian) Gulf region. The Egyptian contingent within the multinational force eventually amounted to 35,000 troops. Egypt emerged from the Gulf conflict with its international reputation enhanced, largely as a result of what was regarded as Mubarak's firm leadership of 'moderate' Arab opinion.

Legislative elections in November and December 1990 were boycotted by the principal opposition parties, in protest at the Government's refusal to concede to demands that the elections be removed from the supervision of the Ministry of the Interior and that the state of emergency be repealed. The credibility of the polls was further undermined by the low rate of participation by voters, estimated at 20%–30% of the registered electorate. Of the 444 elective seats in the new Assembly, the NDP won 348, the National Progressive Unionist Party (NPUP) six, and independent candidates (the majority of whom were affiliated to the NDP) 83. Voting for the remaining seven seats was suspended. The national state of emergency was renewed for a further three-year period in June 1991, in view of what the Government stated was the continued threat of internal and external subversion. The legislation was extended again in 1994, 1997 and 2000.

President Mubarak was formally proposed for a third term of office in July 1993, and in October his nomination was approved by some 94.9% of the valid votes cast at a national referendum. The opposition parties, none of which had endorsed Mubarak's candidature, demanded reforms including amendment of the Constitution to allow direct presidential elections, the unrestricted formation of political parties, and the introduction of a two-term limit to the presidency.

Legislative elections were held in November–December 1995, at which candidates of the NDP won 316 seats, thus retaining a decisive (albeit reduced) majority in the People's Assembly. The New Wafd Party took six seats, the NPUP five, and the LSP and the Nasserist Party one seat each. Of the 115 independent candidates elected, 99 were reported to have immediately joined or rejoined the NDP. Allegations of the intimidation of opposition supporters and of other electoral malpractices on the part of agents acting for the NDP were widespread. A new Council of Ministers was appointed in January 1996, with Kamal Ahmad al-Ganzouri, hitherto Minister of Planning, appointed Prime Minister (in place of Dr Atif Sidqi, who had held the post since 1986).

During 1998 domestic criticism of the Government resulted in the imposition of severe restrictions on the press (in place of more liberal legislation adopted in 1996). Dissenting editors of a number of newspapers were replaced with government supporters, while six journalists were imprisoned on charges of libel. Moreover, a new law was introduced whereby individuals were prohibited from owning publishing companies, and in June stringent printing restrictions were imposed on two leading independent English-language newspapers.

In June 1999 Mubarak was formally nominated for a fourth presidential term; his nomination was approved by 93.8% of the valid votes cast in a national referendum held on 26 September. Voter turn-out was reported to be 79.2%. Of the four main legal opposition parties, only the Nasserist Party had refused to endorse Mubarak's candidature. In October Mubarak appointed Dr Atif Muhammad Obeid, previously Minister of the Public Enterprise Sector and responsible for the Government's privatization programme, to succeed al-Ganzouri as Prime Minister. Obeid's appointment was widely interpreted as an indication that economic reforms would be accelerated. In March 2000 the Political Parties Committee approved the formation of a new political party, Hizb al-Wifaq al-Qawmi (or the National Accord Party).

In June 2000 the Government ordered the closure of the Ibn Khaldoun Center for Social and Development Studies, and the centre's director, Prof. Sa'adeddin Ibrahim (a prominent academic and pro-democracy activist), was arrested on suspicion of collecting funds without prior authority and defaming Egypt through his work. It was alleged that Ibrahim had accepted more than US \$220,000 from the European Commission to produce a video documentary on the electoral process in Egypt. Ibrahim was released on bail in August, but it was announced in September that he was to be tried on charges of receiving funds from abroad without permission. Furthermore, in November military prosecutors announced that they were to investigate charges of espionage against Ibrahim. In May 2001 Ibrahim was sentenced to seven years' imprisonment with hard labour, having been convicted of receiving unauthorized funding from overseas, embezzlement and forgery; 27 employees of the Ibn Khaldoun Center also received custodial terms ranging from one to five years. The verdicts were widely criticized by many Western governments and national and international human rights organizations. Ibrahim was released from detention in early February 2002, after a retrial at the Supreme State Security Court was ordered. In July, however, following the conclusion of the second trial, Ibrahim again received a seven-year gaol sentence. The verdict again provoked fierce international criticism and the USA subsequently announced that it would suspend new aid, worth US \$130m., to Egypt. In early December Ibrahim was released from prison after the Court of Cassation overturned his sentence and ordered a further retrial, and in mid-March 2003 Ibrahim and his 27 co-defendants were acquitted of all charges.

The Supreme Constitutional Court issued a judgment in July 2000 that the People's Assembly elected in 1995 was illegitimate (as was the Assembly elected in 1990), and that the existing electoral system was invalid since the constitutional requirement that the judiciary have sole responsibility for the supervision of elections had not been adhered to. President Mubarak subsequently convened an extraordinary session of the Assembly, at which two amendments to the existing electoral legislation were unanimously approved: these provided for judges to monitor voting in the impending general election.

Almost 4,000 candidates contested the 444 elective seats in the People's Assembly at polls conducted in three rounds, each of two stages, beginning on 18 October, 29 October and 8 November 2000. According to figures published by the Ministry of the Interior in mid-November, the NDP increased its majority, with candidates of the ruling party taking 353 seats. Independent candidates secured 72 seats, but it was reported that 35 of these had either joined or rejoined the NDP shortly after the elections. The New Wafd Party won seven seats, the NPUP six, the Nasserist Party three and the LSP one seat. The overall rate of participation by voters was officially stated to be between 15% and 40%. There were reports of outbreaks of violence in many parts of the country, primarily involving the security forces and members of the outlawed Muslim Brotherhood, and voting for the two seats in one constituency in Alexandria was postponed following the arrest of some 20 Muslim Brotherhood activists. At least 14 people were killed, and hundreds of others injured, during the polls, while large numbers of Islamists were arrested for public order offences.

The summit meeting of the Arab League held in Jordan in March 2001 appointed Amr Moussa, Egypt's Minister of Foreign Affairs since 1991, as the organization's Secretary-General. Ahmad Maher was appointed to replace Moussa in his government post in May 2001. At partial elections to the Advisory Council in that month 74 of the 88 contested seats were won by the NDP, while independent candidates took the remaining 14 seats. In mid-November President Mubarak effected a minor reorganization of the Council of Ministers. Most notably, the Ministry of Economics was abolished and responsibility for most of its functions was devolved to the new Governor of the Central Bank of Egypt.

Several high-profile court cases attracted considerable national and international attention from 2001. Early in the year a fundamentalist Islamist lawyer attempted to have a feminist writer, Nawal es-Sadawi, forcibly divorced from her husband on the grounds of apostasy after she had allegedly criticized aspects of orthodox Muslim beliefs in a newspaper interview. The case was, however, dismissed by the Prosecutor-General in April and by a family affairs tribunal in July. In September the editor of the independent weekly *An-Naaba* was sentenced to three years' imprisonment for undermining national security and inciting sectarian divisions. In June the newspaper had published an article in which it accused a former Coptic Christian monk of sexual misconduct and blackmail. The article, which was strongly criticized by President Mubarak, provoked days of angry protests in Cairo by several thousand Copts. The publication was prohibited the following month by the Administrative State Court. In mid-November 23 men, who had been among 52 individuals arrested as part of a campaign against homosexual activity following a police raid on a discothèque in May, were convicted by the State Security Court of engaging in immoral acts. Although homosexuality is not a crime under Egyptian law, the men were accused of practising 'habitual debauchery' and received terms of imprisonment ranging from one to five years. The remaining 29 defendants were acquitted. In May 2002, apparently in response to international pressure, President Mubarak overturned the sentences of 21 of the 23 men convicted of 'habitual debauchery' (on the grounds that they had been tried by the wrong court) and ordered the retrial of 50 of the 52 original defendants. However, Mubarak upheld gaol terms of five and three years, respectively, against two of the men, who had also been found guilty of 'scorning religion'. Upon completion of the retrial in March 2003, 21 of the accused were sentenced to three years' imprisonment; the other 29 defendants were again acquitted. In July 11 of those convicted were acquitted on appeal, owing to procedural errors at the retrial.

In February 2002 the worst rail disaster in Egypt's history, in which 373 people were killed after a train travelling from Cairo to Luxor caught fire, precipitated the resignation of the Minister of Transport and of the Chairman of Egyptian National Railways. New ministers of transport, health and civil aviation (responsibility for the last being devolved from the Ministry of Transport) were appointed in March.

At the eighth congress of the NDP held in Cairo in mid-September 2002, Mubarak was re-elected Chairman of the organization, while his son, Gamal, was elected Secretary-General for Policy, effectively making him the third most senior figure in the party and further fuelling speculation that he was being 'groomed' eventually to succeed his father. The Deputy Prime Minister and Minister of Agriculture and Land Reclamation, Dr Yousef Amin Wali, was replaced as the NPD's Secretary-General by the Minister of Information, Muhammad Safwat esh-Sharif, in a move widely regarded as an additional attempt to modernize the party.

In February 2003 the state of emergency was extended for a further three years; however, during 2003 the NDP appeared to acquiesce to demands for greater political liberalization and continued the modernization process instigated by Gamal Mubarak the previous year. In June the People's Assembly approved the creation of a National Council for Human Rights as well as the closure of a number of the State Security Courts; the power of judges to sentence offenders to imprisonment with hard labour was also abolished. At the NDP's first annual party conference held in late September, President Mubarak announced that all military orders issued under the emergency laws, which had been in place since the assassination of President Sadat in 1981, would be abolished, except those that were 'necessary to maintain public order and security'. However, a committee established by the Prime Minister to review the

existing emergency powers recommended that only six of the 13 military orders could be withdrawn. Nevertheless, restrictions and limitations pertaining to the formation of new political parties and the activities of existing political organizations were also to be reviewed, and Gamal Mubarak pledged to take steps to ensure that all Egyptians would receive the fundamental rights of participatory democracy and equality. In November 2003 the President was taken ill during a speech to the People's Assembly, prompting rumours that he would name a Vice-President. However, in January 2004 he publicly denied intensifying speculation that his son was being groomed to fill this position and assume the presidency in the event of his death.

Further partial elections took place to the 264-member Advisory Council in May and June 2004. The NDP won 70 of the 88 seats contested, while 17 of the remaining seats were secured by NDP members who had stood as independents; one seat was taken by the NPUP. A further 44 members of the Council were appointed by the President. In late June the Minister of Information and the Secretary-General of the NDP, Muhammad Safwat esh-Sharif, was elected Speaker of the Advisory Council, replacing Dr Mustafa Kamal Helmi. The Minister of Culture, Farouk Abd al-Aziz Hosni, assumed the information portfolio. In early July the death was announced of the Minister of Transport, Hamdy ash-Shayeb. Mubarak, who had delegated his constitutional and legal powers and jurisdictions to Prime Minister Obeid while he underwent surgery in Germany, was widely expected to announce an extensive reorganization of the Council of Ministers upon his return to Egypt. Indeed, on 9 July Obeid announced the resignation of his entire administration. Dr Ahmad Mahmoud Muhammad Nazif, the former Minister of Communications and Information Technology, was appointed Prime Minister and given the task of forming a new cabinet. The choice of a modern technocrat such as Nazif as Prime Minister signalled to many the President's desire to implement reform and boost the economy. On 14 July President Mubarak inaugurated a new 35-member Government, which was also reported to be of a technocratic, reformist nature, with the President instructing ministers that their principal task was to raise living standards and improve the performance of the administration. Notable changes intended to assist the process of economic reform included the creation of a Ministry of Investment and the merger of the Ministries of Foreign Trade and of Industry and Technological Development. Several appointees in the new Council of Ministers were regarded as having close links with Gamal Mubarak, including Ahmad Aboul Gheit, hitherto Egypt's Permanent Representative to the UN, who assumed the post of Minister of Foreign Affairs.

In October 2004 a new political party, al-Ghad, was approved by the Egyptian authorities after its fourth application. This decision was apparently prompted by criticism from the USA regarding the slow pace of democratic reform in the country, which had seen only two new political parties being licensed since 1977. The party, under the leadership of former New Wafd Party deputy Ayman an-Nour, set out its aims of combating poverty and improving the living conditions of Egypt's citizens. It brought to 18 the number of officially recognized parties. In late January 2005 an-Nour was arrested by the Egyptian authorities and charged with forgery.

Meanwhile, Egypt's first terrorist attack in seven years occurred in early October 2004, at the height of the Jewish holiday season, when three bombs exploded in the resorts of Taba, Ras Shitan and Nuweiba on the Sinai Peninsula, killing 34 people and injuring more than 100; many of the dead were Israelis. The militant Islamist al-Qa'ida (Base) organization of Osama bin Laden was initially believed to have been behind the attacks; however, blame soon began to focus on a previously unknown Egyptian militant group. In late October five Egyptians suspected of involvement in the bombings were arrested and the blame for the attacks was placed upon a Palestinian, Ayad Said Salah, who had been living in Egypt and who had died in the explosion in Taba. The Ministry of the Interior announced that Salah had acted to highlight the deteriorating situation in the Gaza Strip.

Opposition to Mubarak augmented towards the end of 2004, with the release in late October of a statement by more than 650 Egyptian activists, politicians and intellectuals urging a constitutional amendment to prevent the President from standing for another term in office. In December a demonstration by some 1,000 people took place in Cairo against the possibility that Mubarak might seek a fifth presidential term or that his son might succeed him. In January 2005 Mubarak again dismissed claims that he would not be running for President at the next election. In mid-February the Minister of Information, Dr Muhammad Mamdouh Ahmad el-Beltagi, was effectively demoted to the position of Minister of Youth, while the minister previously responsible for youth affairs, Anas el-Fiki, was named as his replacement.

In late February 2005 Mubarak announced plans for democratic reform in Egypt—specifically, the altering of the Constitution to allow multiple candidates in presidential elections. These measures were approved in principle by the People's Assembly in early March, and it was announced that the changes would be put to a referendum prior to the presidential election due to take place in September.

Since 1992 the Government's attempts to suppress Islamist fundamentalism has dominated the domestic political agenda. During the early 1990s fundamentalist violence increasingly targeted foreign tourists visiting Egypt, as well as foreign investors, and there were frequent confrontations between Islamist militants and the security forces. In May 1993 a report published by the human rights organization Amnesty International alleged that the Egyptian Government was systematically maltreating political detainees, and in November the organization accused the Government of breaching the UN Convention against Torture and Other Cruel, Inhuman or Degrading Treatment or Punishment.

In January 1994 the security forces were reported to have detained some 1,000 suspected fundamentalist activists in response to attacks on their members during that month. In March nine members of the Vanguards of Conquest (a faction of Islamic Jihad) were sentenced to death after having been convicted of conspiring to assassinate the Prime Minister in November 1993. In July 1994 a further five members of the militant group were sentenced to death for the attempted assassination of the Minister of the Interior in August 1993. Meanwhile, in April 1994 the chief of the anti-terrorist branch of the State Security Investigation Section was assassinated by members of Jama'ah al-Islamiyah (one of Egypt's principal militant Islamist groups), prompting retaliatory security operations.

In early 1995 the Government began to take steps to isolate the more moderate Muslim Brotherhood and to weaken its political influence in the approach to that year's legislative elections. Several leading members of the Brotherhood were arrested, and both President Mubarak and the Minister of the Interior claimed that there was evidence of links between the movement and Islamist extremists. The Government also acted to curb Islamist influence within professional organizations; in February the judiciary was accorded wide powers to intervene in union elections and to prevent Muslim Brotherhood members from standing. In January, meanwhile, clashes between extremists and security forces in Upper Egypt resulted in 87 deaths. In June Mubarak escaped an assassination attempt in Ethiopia while he was travelling to a summit meeting of the Organization of African Unity (OAU) in Addis Ababa; it was widely believed that the assailants were members of either Islamic Jihad or Jama'ah al-Islamiyah. Egypt's claim that the gunmen had been aided by Sudanese agents was denied by the Sudanese Government. (In September 1996 three Egyptians, reported to be members of unspecified Islamist groups, were sentenced to death by the Ethiopian Supreme Court for their involvement in the attempted assassination.)

In April 1996 12 prominent members of the Muslim Brotherhood were arrested and charged with attempting to revive the movement's activities and restore its links with extremist groups. For the first time the detainees included a member of the Brotherhood's Supreme Guidance Council. Three of those arrested were founder members of a new political organization, the Al-Wasat (Centre) Party, which the authorities claimed was serving as a 'front' for Brotherhood activities. The party's founders—who included Muslims, Christians, leftists and Nasserist activists—insisted, however, that they were seeking to create a political group that occupied the middle ground between the State and its fundamentalist Islamist opponents. (Twice in 1998 and again in June 1999 Al-Wasat was denied legal status by the authorities.)

In September 1997 a military court in Haekstep, north of the capital, conducted a military trial on an unprecedented scale of suspected Islamist militants; of 98 defendants convicted, four were sentenced to death and eight to life imprisonment. A few days later nine German tourists were killed, and 11 others injured, as a result of an attack on a tourist bus in Cairo. Although the perpetrators of the assault were widely believed to

be members of Jama'ah al-Islamiyah, the Egyptian Government claimed, in an apparent attempt to protect the country's vital tourism industry, that the attack was an isolated incident unconnected with terrorism. (In May 1998 two men were hanged, having been convicted in October 1997 of the attack.) In November 1997 the massacre near Luxor of 70 people, including 58 foreign tourists, by members of Jama'ah al-Islamiyah severely undermined both the crucial tourism sector and the claims of the Government to have suppressed Islamist violence. Mubarak criticized the security forces' failure to protect tourists, and dismissed the Minister of the Interior, who had formulated the Government's uncompromising policies aimed at eradicating Islamist militancy. Mubarak ordered a heightened security presence at all tourist sites and placed the Prime Minister at the head of a special committee charged with devising a plan to safeguard the tourism sector. In December a number of Jama'ah al-Islamiyah's exiled leaders claimed that the Luxor massacre had been perpetrated by a 'rogue' element acting without the authorization of the group's central leadership; furthermore, the leaders in exile announced that Jama'ah al-Islamiyah (at least, those members under their specific authority) would no longer target tourists in their conflict with the Government. (In May 1999 security officials in Switzerland alleged that the Saudi Arabian-born militant Islamist, Osama bin Laden, had financed the Luxor killings.)

New state security measures adopted by the Ministry of the Interior during 1998 included a relaxation of the criteria whereby affiliation to Islamist groups was assumed, and the release of some Islamist prisoners who had renounced connections with illegal organizations. By June 106 death sentences had been imposed upon Islamist fundamentalists since 1992, of which 72 had been exacted. In March 1998 Jama'ah al-Islamiyah declared a unilateral cease-fire and announced a new strategy of exerting maximum political pressure on the Government without the use of violence. Although the Government gave no formal acknowledgement of the apparent cease-fire, an acceleration in the release of imprisoned Islamist militants was subsequently evident. In April the Ministry of the Interior released some 1,200 Jama'ah al-Islamiyah detainees (reportedly among them two of the group's leaders who were involved in the assassination of President Sadat in 1981), and a further 1,200 were released in December. In February 1999 it was reported that three men suspected of involvement in the 1997 Luxor attack had been arrested on the Uruguayan–Brazilian border and were expected to stand trial in Cairo. In the same month proceedings began against 107 alleged members of Islamic Jihad who were charged with conspiring to overthrow the Government. In April 1999 nine of the defendants were sentenced to death; 78 received sentences ranging from one year to life imprisonment, all with hard labour, while 20 were acquitted. In June 20 members of Jama'ah al-Islamiyah were given custodial sentences, having been convicted by a military court of planning a bomb attack on President Mubarak's Alexandria residence in 1996; that death sentences were not imposed was interpreted by the organization's lawyers as a positive response to the recent cease-fire declaration.

The unofficial truce between the Government and Jama'ah al-Islamiyah was apparently jeopardized in September 1999, when security forces in Giza shot dead four alleged members of the organization, including the commander of its military wing. In November charges against 20 alleged members of the Muslim Brotherhood, who had been arrested in the previous month on charges of plotting to overthrow the Government and of infiltrating professional syndicates in order to undermine national security, were altered by the military court where they were standing trial from 'belonging' to the Muslim Brotherhood to 'participating in the founding and management' of the organization; any conviction under these charges was likely to result in much harsher sentences. The trial was initially postponed for procedural reasons but resumed in January 2000 (see below).

In January 2000 three days of violent clashes between Muslims and Copts in the southern village of el-Kosheh resulted in the deaths of an estimated 20 Christians and one Muslim. A subsequent inquiry conducted by the Egyptian Organization for Human Rights (EOHR) inferred that the primary cause of the violence was the 'economic inequalities' between the relatively prosperous Coptic majority and the poorer Muslim minority. There was a further outbreak of violence in el-Kosheh in late February. In February 2001 four Muslims were sentenced to custodial terms of up to 10 years for their part in the violence of early 2000; a further 92 defendants were acquitted. However,

after the Court of Cassation ordered a retrial of all 96 defendants, in February 2003 two men were sentenced to prison terms
of 15 years and three-and-a-half years, respectively; the
remainder were again acquitted. In June 2004 these sentences
were again reviewed, with three men receiving one and two-year
prison terms, and the fourth man's 15-year sentence being
reduced to 13 years. Again the other 92 defendants were
acquitted.

In February 2000 senior members of the leadership of Islamic
Jihad publicly urged the cessation of the organization's armed
activities, appealing to militants to concentrate their activities
on the liberation of the al-Aqsa Mosque in Jerusalem; this was
the first time that the group's leaders had called for a cease-fire.
Later in February eight prominent Islamists were arrested on
charges of seeking to revive the Muslim Brotherhood. In March,
none the less, between 500 and 1,000 Islamists, mostly members
of Jama'ah al-Islamiyah or Islamic Jihad, were reportedly
released from prison; a further 500 Islamists were freed in July.
Despite regular releases of large numbers of militants since
1998, human rights organizations maintained that more than
15,000 remained in Egyptian detention, many of whom were
being held without charge under the country's emergency laws.
Furthermore, during the approach to the 2000 legislative elections the authorities arrested increasing numbers of Muslim
Brotherhood members, in what was widely acknowledged as an
effort to prevent their standing as candidates for the People's
Assembly. In mid-November the Higher Military Court in Cairo
pronounced guilty verdicts on 15 of those arrested in late 1999
on charges of reviving the Brotherhood, sentencing them to
between three and five years' imprisonment; the five other
defendants were acquitted.

President Mubarak was swift to condemn the suicide attacks
on New York and Washington, DC, of 11 September 2001.
Several members of Egyptian Islamic Jihad were alleged to have
assumed significant roles in the suicide attacks, held to have
been perpetrated by Osama bin Laden's al-Qa'ida network. Dr
Ayman az-Zawahiri, the leader of Islamic Jihad who was said to
be one of bin Laden's closest associates, was presumed responsible for the organization of the attacks, and another Egyptian,
Muhammad Atef, who was reportedly killed by US forces in
Afghanistan in November, was, according to US intelligence,
believed to have been al-Qa'ida's chief military planner. Furthermore, an Egyptian national was suspected of having piloted
one of the hijacked aircraft that hit the World Trade Center in
New York. Following the events of 11 September more than 260
suspected Islamists were arrested in Egypt, and arrests of
Islamists continued on a large scale in mid-2002. In August 16
members of the Muslim Brotherhood were sentenced to terms of
imprisonment ranging from three to five years after being
convicted of inciting anti-Government demonstrations. In the
following month 51 militants, who had initially been arrested in
May 2001, were sentenced to up to 15 years' imprisonment for
conspiring to overthrow the Government. In August 2002,
meanwhile, a number of imprisoned senior members of Jama'ah
al-Islamiyah reiterated their commitment to the cease-fire
declared in 1998 and announced, in a series of interviews
published in the weekly *al-Mussawar*, that they had completely
renounced violence.

In May 2003 a recording apparently made by az-Zawahiri,
who was believed to be in hiding in the Afghan–Pakistani border
region, and broadcast by the Qatar-based satellite television
channel, Al-Jazeera, urged Muslims to launch attacks against
the foreign embassies of the USA, the United Kingdom, Australia and Norway. Az-Zawahiri also denounced a number of
Arab states, including Egypt, for hosting or assisting Western
forces involved in the campaign to oust the Iraqi regime of
Saddam Hussain (see below). In September Karam Zohdi, who
was imprisoned in 1981 for his role in the assassination of
President Sadat, was released from gaol, and in October 2003 a
further 900 members of Jama'ah al-Islamiyah were freed. In
January 2004 the Supreme Guide of the Muslim Brotherhood,
Mamoun al-Hodeibi, died suddenly; the organization subse-
quently appointed Muhammad Mahdi Akif as his successor.

In March 2004 26 people, including three British nationals,
were sentenced to prison terms of between one and five years for
membership of the illegal militant group Hizb at-Tahrir al-
Islami (Islamic Liberation Party), which aims to unite all
Muslim countries in a single Islamic state and which had been
banned in Egypt since 1974 following an attempted coup. Accusations of torture followed the verdict, and the British defendants claimed that they had been forced into signing confessions.

Meanwhile, the Egyptian authorities announced for the first
time in March 2004 that they were holding Ayman az-Zawahiri's
younger brother, Muhammad, and declared that he would be
tried in Egypt soon. Muhammad az-Zawahiri had been sentenced *in absentia* in 1999 for his alleged involvement in attacks
perpetrated by Islamic Jihad.

In May 2004, following a series of raids, 54 members of the
Muslim Brotherhood were arrested and several of their companies, including shops and publishing houses, were closed down.
The arrests were seen as the largest crack-down on the organization for many years, and represented the first campaign
against the group since Muhammad Mahdi Akif took over its
leadership in January.

Egyptian mediation was prominent in the Middle East peace
process throughout the 1990s. The country played an important
role in the efforts leading to the convening of the Middle East
peace conference in Madrid, Spain, in October 1991, and an
Egyptian delegation attended the first, symbolic session of the
conference. Egyptian mediators were influential in the secret
negotiations between Israel and the PLO that led to the signing
of the Declaration of Principles on Palestinian Self-Rule in
September 1993, and PLO and Israeli delegations subsequently
began to meet regularly in Cairo or at the Red Sea port of Taba
to discuss the detailed implementation of the Declaration of
Principles. In May 1994 an agreement on Palestinian self-rule in
the Gaza Strip and the Jericho area (for full details, see the
chapter on Israel) was signed in Cairo by the Israeli Prime
Minister, Itzhak Rabin, and the PLO Chairman, Yasser Arafat,
at a ceremony presided over by Mubarak. However, despite an
official visit to Egypt by President Ezer Weizman in December
(the first such visit by an Israeli Head of State), relations
between Egypt and Israel began to deteriorate. Egypt hosted
summit meetings of Arab leaders in December 1994 and February 1995, prompting censure from the Israeli Government,
and further tension arose when Mubarak reiterated his warning
that Egypt would not sign the Treaty on the Non-Proliferation of
Nuclear Weapons (or Non-Proliferation Treaty—NPT, see p. 93),
which was due for renewal in April 1995, unless Israel also
agreed to sign it; he urged other states to do likewise. In March
1995 Israel offered to sign the NPT once it had concluded peace
treaties with all of the Arab states and with Iran, and to allow
Egypt to inspect its research nuclear reactor at Nahal Shorek
(but not the nuclear facility at Dimona). Egypt rejected both
offers, but adopted a more conciliatory line on the issue. Meanwhile, Egypt's stance with regard to the NPT antagonized the
USA, which insisted that the continuation of US aid to Egypt depended on Egypt's signing the Treaty.

President Mubarak made his first visit to Jordan since the
Gulf crisis in January 1995, when he met King Hussein at
Aqaba. The visit was regarded as a sign of an improvement in
relations between the two countries, following Jordan's signing
of a peace treaty with Israel in July 1994.

Egypt continued its mediatory role in the complex negotiations that eventually led to the signing, in Washington, DC, of
the Israeli-Palestinian Interim Agreement on the West Bank
and the Gaza Strip in September 1995. In November Mubarak
made his first presidential visit to Israel to attend the funeral of
the assassinated Israeli Prime Minister, Itzhak Rabin. Egypt
also participated in meetings leading to the resumption of peace
negotiations between Israel and Syria at the end of 1995. In
March 1996, following a series of Palestinian suicide bomb
attacks in Israel, Egypt and the USA co-hosted a one-day
'Summit of Peacemakers' at the Red Sea resort of Sharm esh-
Sheikh. Egypt's relations with Israel deteriorated again in
April, as a consequence of Israeli military operations in Lebanon
(q.v.). In June, in response to the apparently rejectionist stance
of the new Israeli administration of Binyamin Netanyahu with
regard to the exchange of land for peace, Mubarak convened an
emergency summit meeting of the Arab League in Cairo—the
first such meeting for six years. The summit's final communiqué
reaffirmed the Arab states' commitment to peace, but warned
that peace and any further *rapprochement* between them and
Israel depended on Israel's returning all the Arab land that it
occupied in 1967.

President Mubarak cautiously welcomed the Wye River Memorandum signed by Netanyahu and Arafat in October 1998 (see
the chapter on Israel). However, in January 1999 Egypt suspended all contacts with the Israeli Government in protest
against its decision to suspend implementation of the agreement. The election, in May, of the leader of the One Israel
alliance, Ehud Barak, to the Israeli premiership was generally

welcomed in Egypt, but in July the Egyptian Minister of Foreign Affairs emphasized that there could be no normalization of Egyptian–Israeli relations prior to the resumption of comprehensive peace talks. Egyptian mediation was subsequently influential in discussions between Israeli and Palestinian negotiators that led to the signing of the Sharm esh-Sheikh Memorandum by Barak and Arafat in September 1999 (see the chapter on Israel).

In February 2000 Mubarak made his first ever visit to Lebanon. The main purpose of the visit was to demonstrate Egypt's solidarity with Lebanon following Israeli air attacks, condemned by Mubarak as 'criminal acts', on targets in Lebanon earlier in the month. None the less, Egypt continued to play an important role in the peace process during 2000. In March Arafat and Barak attended a summit meeting in Sharm esh-Sheikh, at which the two leaders agreed a formula for the resumption of peace talks, and Barak and Arafat both made brief visits to Cairo prior to the US-hosted summit at Camp David in July. Following the apparent failure of the summit, Mubarak emphasized that he would not pressure Arafat to make concessions regarding the central issue of the status of Jerusalem, and urged all Arab states to unite in support of the Palestinians until they regained all their legitimate rights in accordance with the pertinent UN resolutions.

Following the outbreak in Jerusalem in late September 2000 of violent clashes between Palestinians and Israeli security forces, which swiftly spread throughout the West Bank and Gaza, Mubarak assumed an important role in attempting to prevent the violence from escalating into a major regional crisis. Most notably, in mid-October, following mediation by UN Secretary-General Kofi Annan, Barak and Arafat agreed to lead delegations to a summit meeting at Sharm esh-Sheikh, brokered by US President Bill Clinton. Two days of intensive negotiations resulted in an agreement on the establishment of a fact-finding committee to investigate the causes of what had become known as the al-Aqsa *intifada* (uprising), but a tentative truce as part of the 'understanding' reached proved unviable and violence persisted. Later that month an emergency meeting of Heads of State of Arab League countries was convened in Cairo, at which Arab leaders held Israel solely to blame for the violence. In late November Egypt recalled its ambassador to Tel-Aviv, denouncing Israel's 'escalation of aggression and deliberate use of force against the Palestinian people'. Bilateral relations deteriorated further at the end of that month when an Egyptian engineer, Sherif Filali, was charged with having gathered information regarding Egyptian economic and military projects for the Israeli overseas intelligence service. In mid-June 2001 Filali was acquitted of the charges by the State Security Court; however, in September President Mubarak invoked emergency legislation to reverse the acquittal and ordered a retrial. In March 2002 Filali was convicted of providing information to Israel with the intent of harming Egypt's national interests, and was sentenced to 15 years' imprisonment with hard labour.

In the approach to the premiership election scheduled to take place in Israel in February 2001, Mubarak and outgoing US President Clinton intensified their diplomatic attempts to secure an accommodation between Israel and the Palestinians ahead of the expected electoral victory of the right-wing Likud leader, Ariel Sharon. Following his election, it was alleged that Sharon had requested that the USA decrease military assistance to Egypt. Mubarak subsequently warned Sharon that he would interpret any such demand as a 'hostile action' and that it would significantly alter Egypt's attitude towards Israel. Nevertheless, at an Arab League summit on the Palestinian situation, held in Jordan in late March, Mubarak deflected demands (as he had at the Cairo emergency summit in October 2000) from more radical Arab states that Egypt and Jordan should sever diplomatic relations with Israel entirely. In April 2001 a joint Egyptian-Jordanian peace plan urged an immediate halt to Israeli construction of settlements and a withdrawal of Israeli forces to pre-*intifada* positions. The plan was supported by the new US Republican Administration of President George W. Bush, the European Union (EU) and the Arab world; however, Mubarak's claim, following a meeting in Cairo in late April with the Israeli Deputy Prime Minister and Minister of Foreign Affairs, Shimon Peres, to have secured the agreement of both Israel and the Palestinians to the Egyptian-Jordanian proposal proved premature, and diplomatic progress stalled as violence continued to escalate in subsequent months. At an emergency meeting of Arab League ministers of foreign affairs in Cairo in mid-May it was agreed to suspend all political contacts with Israel until its

attacks on Palestinians were halted. In December Egypt and Syria issued a joint condemnation of the conduct of Israel's military forces in the Palestinian territories. Egypt suspended all non-diplomatic contacts with Israel in April 2002, and in the same month Mubarak demanded Israel's immediate and unconditional withdrawal from the West Bank.

In mid-July 2002, following an Israeli air force attack on Gaza City, which resulted in the death of a senior Hamas military figure and a further 15 civilians, Mubarak denounced the actions of the Israeli military and accused Sharon of deliberately ordering the attacks in order to sabotage Palestinian peace efforts. During late 2002 and early 2003 Egypt hosted a number of meetings between the main Palestinian factions, although optimism that militant groups would agree to cease attacks within Israeli territory for a period of one year proved unfounded. Mubarak strongly welcomed the publication, at the end of April, of the 'roadmap' peace plan drafted by the UN, the USA, the EU and Russia (see the chapter on Israel); however, Egyptian efforts to secure a cease-fire by armed Palestinian factions made no further progress, and in May Mubarak informed the visiting US Secretary of State, Colin Powell, that Egypt required evidence that Israel would accept the internationally sponsored roadmap before it would again attempt to broker a cease-fire agreement.

In early December 2003 representatives from the leading Palestinian factions attended further talks in Cairo, although attempts to secure a cease-fire proved unsuccessful; a unilateral truce agreed by the groups in June had collapsed in August. The Israeli Deputy Prime Minister and Minister of Foreign Affairs, Silvan Shalom, met with Mubarak in Geneva, Switzerland, later in December and the following week Egypt's Minister of Foreign Affairs, Ahmad Maher, travelled to Israel for discussions with Sharon and Shalom. The meeting was overshadowed, however, by an attack on Maher, perpetrated by Palestinian extremists, while he was visiting the al-Aqsa Mosque in Jerusalem. The assault, which resulted in Maher being taken to hospital, was condemned by both Israeli and Palestinian leaders. Seven Palestinians were detained for their roles in the incident. Further talks between Mubarak and Shalom were held in Cairo in mid-March 2004; the discussions reportedly focused on security arrangements in the event of an Israeli withdrawal from the Gaza Strip. In mid-April Mubarak travelled to the USA to discuss the 'roadmap' with President Bush; the US President also met with Sharon and endorsed Sharon's proposals for an Israeli 'disengagement' from Gaza, which also involved the consolidation of six Jewish settlements in the West Bank. It was envisaged that Egyptian forces would assume responsibility for border security in Gaza after Israel's unilateral withdrawal, which Sharon maintained would be completed by the end of 2005. In early December 2004, after talks held in Jerusalem between the Israeli Minister of Defence, Lt-Gen. Shaul Mofaz, and the Egyptian intelligence chief, Omar Suleiman, it was agreed that 750 Egyptian troops would be stationed on the border with Gaza ahead of the Israeli withdrawal, in a bid to prevent arms from being smuggled into the territory.

Following the terrorist attacks in the Sinai region of the country in October 2004 (see above), Egypt made clear its wish to send troops into the demilitarized buffer zone along the border with Israel, claiming that a military presence there could prevent further attacks. Diplomatic relations between Egypt and Israel generally improved in 2004, and in early December Egypt released an Israeli businessman who had been convicted of espionage in 1997, in exchange for the release of six Egyptian students from prison in Israel. Later in the month Ahmad Aboul Gheit, Egypt's Minister of Foreign Affairs, and Omar Suleiman visited Israel to confirm the deal and it was announced that Egypt would soon upgrade its diplomatic representation in Israel by returning an ambassador to Tel-Aviv. In mid-December 2004 a new trade deal between Egypt and Israel was signed allowing duty-free export between three newly established 'qualified industrial zones' and the USA, provided that at least 11.7% of the goods were manufactured in Israel. Despite being positively received within many Egyptian business circles, the protocol triggered angry demonstrations in Cairo among people who thought it would give Israel too much economic power over the country. In mid-February 2005 Egypt named its new ambassador to Israel as Muhammad Asim Ibrahim, the former ambassador to Sudan; Ibrahim took up his post in mid-March.

Although the USA announced in April 1996 that it would supply advanced military equipment to Egypt, including 21 F-16 fighter aircraft, in acknowledgement of the country's key role in the Middle East peace process, there have remained frequent tensions in relations between Egypt and the USA. In August 1998 Egypt was highly critical of US military air-strikes against targets in Afghanistan and Sudan held by the US authorities to be associated with Osama bin Laden. Tensions were further exacerbated by the air-strikes undertaken against Iraq by US and British forces in December, since Mubarak had consistently urged a diplomatic solution to the issue of weapons inspections. Differences persisted as the US Secretary of Defense, William Cohen, visited Cairo and other regional capitals in March 1999 to seek support for a renewed air campaign against Iraq. While in Egypt Cohen agreed to supply Egypt with US $3,200m. of US defence equipment, including a further 24 F-16 fighter aircraft. Following a further visit by Cohen, it was announced in April 2000 that the USA would supply short-range missiles in order to modernize Egypt's air-defence system. Meanwhile, Mubarak visited Washington in June 1999 and the two countries made significant progress on proposals for the resumption of Middle East peace talks, culminating in the signing of the Sharm esh-Sheikh Memorandum in September. In late 2000 the Egyptian and US leaders co-operated closely in their efforts to mediate in the Middle East crisis (see above). During a visit to the USA in early April 2001 President Mubarak met with President George W. Bush for the first time and urged the USA actively to support the Egyptian-Jordanian peace plan (see above). Meanwhile, Bush, who had indicated that Iraq would be his Administration's priority in terms of Middle East policy, expressed his unease at Egypt's lack of support for international sanctions against Saddam Hussain; he also urged Egypt to return its ambassador to Israel. Relations between Egypt and the USA deteriorated in mid-2002 following the imprisonment of Sa'adeddin Ibrahim (see above) and the subsequent announcement by the Bush Administration that it would suspend any additional foreign aid to Egypt in protest at what it considered to be the country's poor treatment of pro-democracy campaigners and human rights organizations. It was emphasized, however, that existing aid programmes would not be affected (the USA provides Egypt with annual assistance worth some US $2,000m.). Bilateral relations were further strained in late September after David Welch, the US ambassador to Egypt, writing in the daily *al-Ahram*, criticized a number of Egyptian publications for suggesting that al-Qa'ida had not been responsible for the previous year's attacks on the mainland USA. Welch was subsequently declared *persona non grata* in a widely published open letter signed by a number of prominent Egyptian intellectuals.

As the likelihood of a US-led military campaign to oust the Iraqi regime of Saddam Hussain increased during the second half of 2002, President Mubarak was one of a number of Arab leaders who expressed their concern at the effects of military intervention in Iraq on the Middle East as a whole, as well as its implications for the unity of Iraq. In August he stated that he did not believe that a single Arab state supported military action against Iraq. In September Mubarak received the Iraqi Minister of Foreign Affairs and requested that Iraq comply with pertinent UN resolutions and allow UN weapons inspectors to operate freely within the country. However, a series of Arab League meetings in early 2003 served to highlight the deepening divisions over the issue among Arab states.

Following the commencement of US-led hostilities against the Iraqi regime in mid-March 2003 there were a number of anti-war demonstrations in Cairo, resulting in the arrest of some 800 protesters. At the end of March Mubarak warned of the consequences that the conflict in Iraq would have on the Arab world and maintained that it would ignite Islamic fanaticism and create '100 new bin Ladens'. None the less, the ousting of Saddam Hussain in early April was met with considerable ambivalence by Egypt. In April 2004 Mubarak again highlighted his country's feeling of resentment towards the USA following its invasion of Iraq in an interview with the French newspaper *Le Monde*. He attributed this partly to the USA's support for Israel and its refusal to condemn the killing by Israeli forces of the newly appointed Hamas leader Abd al-Aziz ar-Rantisi in the Gaza Strip on 17 April.

Egypt's relations with Libya improved steadily during the 1990s, and Egypt joined the Community of Sahel-Saharan States (CEN-SAD, see p. 373), which was established in Tripoli in 1997. Meanwhile, bilateral links were dominated by the repercussions of the Lockerbie bombing (see the chapter on Libya), with Egypt actively seeking to avert a confrontation between Libya and the USA and its Western allies. Following the suspension of UN sanctions against Libya in April 1999, the national carrier, EgyptAir, resumed regular flights to Tripoli in July 2000; Libyan air services to Egypt resumed later that month.

Egypt has a long-standing border dispute with Sudan concerning the so-called Halaib triangle. Relations deteriorated sharply in mid-1995, after Egypt accused Sudan of complicity in the attempted assassination of President Mubarak in Addis Ababa (see above). Egypt strengthened its control of the Halaib triangle, and subsequently (in contravention of a bilateral agreement concluded in 1978) imposed visa and permit requirements on Sudanese nationals visiting or resident in Egypt. In September 1995 the OAU accused Sudan of direct involvement in the assassination attempt, and in December the organization demanded that Sudan extradite immediately three individuals sought in connection with the attack. (It was reported in mid-1999 that one of the suspects had been extradited to Cairo.) In February 1996 the Sudanese authorities introduced permit requirements for Egyptian nationals resident in Sudan. President Mubarak met with his Sudanese counterpart, Brig. Omar Hassan Ahmad al-Bashir, at the Arab League summit meeting in Cairo in May. In July, however, Egypt accused Sudan of harbouring Egyptian terrorists, contrary to an agreement concluded at the summit meeting. None the less, Egypt opposed the imposition by the UN of more stringent economic sanctions against Sudan (q.v.), on the grounds that they would harm the Sudanese people more than the regime. Bilateral security talks recommenced in August 1997 after a year-long suspension. In February 1998 river transport resumed between the Egyptian port of Aswan and Wadi Halfa in Sudan, and in April the two countries agreed to establish a joint ministerial committee. Although Sudan considered the presence of Sudanese opposition leaders in Egypt an obstacle to the normalization process, a meeting in Cairo, in May 1999, between representatives of the Sudanese Government and Sudan's former President Gaafar Mohammed Nimeri, to discuss arrangements for his return from exile, represented significant progress on this issue. In December Egypt and Sudan agreed to a full normalization of relations, and resolved to co-operate in addressing their border dispute. The new Egyptian ambassador to Sudan assumed his post in Khatoum in March 2000, and in September a number of bilateral co-operation accords were signed. In January 2004 Presidents Mubarak and al-Bashir signed what was termed the 'four freedoms' agreement, which allowed for freedom of movement, residence, work and property ownership between the two countries. The agreement was approved by both countries' legislatures in June and came into effect in September. At further talks between the two Presidents in December it was agreed that the construction of a road linking Egypt and Sudan would be intensified and that work would begin on joining the two rail networks.

In mid-December 2003 Mubarak held talks with the Iranian President, Dr Sayed Muhammad Khatami, in Geneva, representing the first meeting between the Heads of State of the two countries since bilateral diplomatic relations were severed following the Islamic Revolution in Iran in 1979. In January 2004 it was reported that they planned to restore diplomatic relations, although Egypt refused officially to confirm this. In early December Iran handed over to Egypt Moustafa Hamzah, a leader of Jama'ah al-Islamiyah and the alleged mastermind of a 1995 assassination attempt on President Mubarak, representing a significant step towards improving bilateral relations.

Meanwhile, in 2004 disputes over the Nile began to escalate as Tanzania confirmed that it intended to build a 170-km pipeline to draw water from Lake Victoria. This decision contravened the Nile Water Agreement drawn up in 1929 between Egypt and the United Kingdom, which states that Egypt has the right to veto any work which might threaten the flow of the river and allows the country to inspect the entire length of the Nile. Talks began in Uganda in March 2004 between the 10 countries that share the Nile's waters, and an agreement was reached whereby a permanent framework would be formulated to oversee management, planning and use of the river.

Government

Legislative power is held by the unicameral Majlis ash-Sha'ab (People's Assembly), which has 454 members: 10 nominated by the President and 444 directly elected for five years from 222 constituencies. The Assembly nominates the President, who is elected by popular referendum for six years (renewable). (In February 2005 plans were announced for a constitutional amendment to allow muliple candidates for the presidency.) The President, who is Head of State, has executive powers and appoints one or more Vice-Presidents, a Prime Minister and a Council of Ministers. There is also a 210-member advisory body, the Shura Council. The country is divided into 27 governorates.

Defence

In August 2004 Egypt had total armed forces of 450,000 (army 320,000, air defence command 80,000, navy 20,000, air force 30,000), with 410,000 reserves. There is a selective three-year period of national service. There are active paramilitary forces of an estimated 330,000. Budgeted defence expenditure for 2003 was forecast at £E9,900m.

Economic Affairs

In 2003, according to estimates by the World Bank, Egypt's gross national income (GNI), measured at average 2001–03 prices, was US $82,260m., equivalent to $1,390 per head (or $3,940 per head on an international purchasing-power parity basis). During 1990–2003, it was estimated, the population increased at an average annual rate of 2.0%, while gross domestic product (GDP) per head increased, in real terms, by 2.1% per year. Overall GDP increased, in real terms, at an average annual rate of 4.1% in 1990–2003. At factor cost, real GDP increased by 3.0% in 2002/03 and by 4.3% in 2003/04.

Agriculture (including forestry and fishing) contributed some 15.8% of GDP in 2003/04, and employed 27.5% of the economically active population in 2002. The principal crops include sugar cane, wheat, rice, maize and tomatoes. Exports of food and live animals accounted for 8.3% of total exports in 2002. During 1990–2003 agricultural GDP increased at an average annual rate of 3.1%. Agricultural GDP grew by an estimated 3.3% in 2003/04.

Industry (including mining, manufacturing, construction and power) provided an estimated 36.0% of GDP in 2003/04, and engaged 20.6% of the employed labour force in 2002. During 1990–2003 industrial GDP expanded at an average annual rate of 4.9%. Industrial GDP increased by an estimated 3.4% in 2003/04.

Mining contributed 8.9% of GDP in 2002/03. Egypt's mineral resources include petroleum, natural gas, phosphates, manganese, uranium, coal, iron ore and gold. Although the mining sector employed only 0.2% of the working population in 2002, petroleum and petroleum products accounted for 32.1% of total export earnings in that year. Petroleum production averaged an estimated 750,000 barrels per day in 2003, and at the end of that year Egypt's oil reserves were estimated to total 3,600m. barrels (sufficient to sustain production at 2003 levels for a little over 13 years). At the end of 2003 Egypt's proven natural gas reserves totalled 1,760,000m. cu m, sustainable for more than 70 years at constant production levels (totalling 25,000m. cu m in 2003). Until the early part of this century all the natural gas produced was consumed domestically, but the Government began exporting in 2003. In mid-2003 BP Egypt announced the largest petroleum discovery in the country for 14 years, and there were also major discoveries of natural gas and condensate in that year. Mining GDP increased by 2.8% in 2002/03.

Manufacturing contributed 19.3% of GDP in 2002/03, and engaged 11.6% of the employed labour force in 2002. Based on the value of output, the main branches of manufacturing in 1997 were food products (accounting for 19.6% of the total), petroleum refining (15.4%), chemicals (12.4%), textiles (12.2%), metals and metal products (9.3%) and non-metallic mineral manufactures (7.6%). In 2003 the Government announced major plans to develop the petrochemicals industry. During 1990–2002 the real GDP of the manufacturing sector increased by an average of 6.0% per year. Manufacturing GDP expanded by 2.6% in 2002/03.

Energy is derived principally from natural gas (which provided 68.2% of total electricity output in 2001), petroleum (14.7%) and hydroelectric power (17.1%). In 2002 fuel imports accounted for about an estimated 4.0% of the value of merchandise imports.

Services contributed an estimated 48.2% of GDP in 2003/04, and employed 51.9% of the working population in 2002. By the late 1980s tourism had become one of the most dynamic sectors of the Egyptian economy. For much of the 1990s, however, the sector was severely undermined by the campaign of violence aimed by fundamentalist Islamists at tourist targets, and visitor numbers and tourism revenues declined significantly. By 1999 there were signs of a recovery in the sector, although this was reversed as a result of the regional insecurity arising from the

Israeli–Palestinian violence from late 2000, the terrorist attacks against the USA in September 2001 and, temporarily, by the US-led intervention in Iraq in early 2003. The effect of the Sinai bombings on the tourist industry was not expected to be seen until mid-2005. In 1990–2003 the real GDP of the services sector increased by an average of 3.8% per year. Services GDP increased by an estimated 5.3% in 2003/04.

In 2003 Egypt recorded a visible trade deficit of US $4,201m., and there was a deficit of $3,743m. on the current account of the balance of payments. In 2002 the principal source of imports (13.5%) was the USA; other major suppliers were Germany, Italy, the People's Republic of China and France. The principal market for exports was Italy (10.7%), followed by India, the USA and the Netherlands. Egypt's principal exports in 2002 were petroleum and petroleum products, basic manufactures, food and live animals, chemicals and clothing. The principal imports were food and live animals, machinery and transport equipment, basic manufactures and chemicals.

For the financial year 2003/04 there was a projected deficit of £E28,700m. in the state public budget (equivalent to an estimated 7.0% of GDP). Egypt's external debt totalled US $30,750m. at the end of 2002, of which $27,282m. was long-term public debt. In that year the cost of servicing the foreign debt was equivalent to 10.3% of the value of exports of goods and services. The annual rate of inflation averaged 7.2% in 1990–2003. Consumer prices increased by an average of 2.7% in 2002, and by 4.2% in 2003. An estimated 10.2% of the total labour force were unemployed in 2002.

Egypt is a member of the Common Market for Eastern and Southern Africa (COMESA, see p. 179), the Council of Arab Economic Unity (see p. 196), the Organization of Arab Petroleum Exporting Countries (OAPEC, see p. 324), the African Petroleum Producers' Association (see p. 369), and the Co-operation Council for the Arab States of the Gulf (Arab Co-operation Council, see p. 193).

Following an impressive macro-economic performance during much of the 1990s, characterized by strong GDP growth and low inflation, Egypt's economy suffered a series of major reverses from the late 1990s and a serious liquidity crisis, resulting primarily from a depletion in the main sources of hard currency, prompted intervention by the Government and the Central Bank in mid-2000. The Egyptian pound's fixed exchange rate against the US dollar was informally abandoned, and in January 2001, under a series of fiscal reforms, control over the exchange rate was transferred to the Central Bank, which introduced a 'managed peg' system. Nevertheless, in 2001 the pound was devalued on a further three occasions and in January 2003, in anticipation of further economic difficulties resulting from a likely US-led military campaign against the regime of Saddam Hussain in Iraq, the Government abandoned the pound's peg to the US dollar and allowed the currency to float freely. The USA agreed to provide US $2,300m. worth of loan guarantees and economic grants to offset the expected economic repercussions of the conflict in Iraq, namely significantly decreased revenues from tourism and the Suez Canal. However, the tourism industry experienced a resurgence in 2003 and this was expected to continue in the coming years. Moreover, the Suez Canal saw an increase in revenue of US $77m. from the previous year. The discovery of major gas reserves and the commencement of gas exports in 2003 improved the country's trade balance, and was predicted to attract further overseas investment in development projects. Nevertheless, Egypt's external debt continued to rise during the year; the cost of servicing this debt, combined with the devaluation of the pound, increased inflationary pressures on the economy, resulting in a rapid rise in wholesale prices. The reorganization of the Council of Ministers in July 2004 was notable because of the inclusion for the first time of a large number of economists and technocrats. Indeed, in September the recently appointed Minister of Finance, Dr Yousuf Boutros-Ghali, set out his plans for comprehensive economic reform, which included measures to halve income and corporate taxes and to accelerate privatization of the banking sector and utilities. In August it was announced that a state-run chemical factory was to be sold, and in January 2005 that the Bank of Alexandria would be privatized later in that year. Although substantial economic growth was projected for 2005, this would remain insufficient to provide employment for the growing number of Egyptians entering the job market each year, and both the high level of unemployment and the widening budget deficit remained causes for concern.

Education

Education at all levels is available free of charge, and is officially compulsory for eight years between six and 14 years of age. Primary education, beginning at six years of age, lasts for five years. Secondary education, from 11 years of age, lasts for a further six years, comprising two cycles (the first being preparatory) of three years each. In 2001/02, according to UNESCO estimates, primary enrolment included 90% of children in the relevant age-group (males 92%; females 88%), while the comparable ratio for secondary enrolment was 81% (males 83%; females 79%). In 2001/02 there were an estimated 1,930,000 students enrolled in universities or other institutes of higher education. The Al-Azhar University and its various preparatory and associated institutes provide instruction and training in various disciplines, with emphasis on adherence to Islamic principles and teachings. Budget forecasts for 2000/01 allocated £E18,100m. (some 16.2% of total expenditure) to education.

Public Holidays

2005: 1 January (New Year), 21 January* (Id al-Adha, Feast of the Sacrifice), 10 February* (Muharram, Islamic New Year), 21 April* (Mouloud/Yum an-Nabi, Birth of Muhammad), 25 April (Sinai Day), 2 May (Sham an-Nessim, Coptic Easter Monday), 23 July (Revolution Day), 2 September* (Leilat al-Meiraj, Ascension of Muhammad), 6 October (Armed Forces Day), 24 October (Popular Resistance Day), 4 November* (Id al-Fitr, end of Ramadan), 23 December (Victory Day).

2006: 1 January (New Year), 11 January* (Id al-Adha, Feast of the Sacrifice), 31 January* (Muharram, Islamic New Year), 11 April* (Mouloud/Yum an-Nabi, Birth of Muhammad), 24 April (Sham an-Nessim, Coptic Easter Monday), 25 April (Sinai Day), 23 July (Revolution Day), 22 August* (Leilat al-Meiraj, Ascension of Muhammad), 6 October (Armed Forces Day), 24 October (Popular Resistance Day) (Id al-Fitr, end of Ramadan*), 23 December (Victory Day).

*These holidays are dependent on the Islamic lunar calendar and may vary by one or two days from the dates given.
Coptic Christian holidays include: Christmas (7 January), Palm Sunday and Easter Sunday.

Weights and Measures

The metric system is in force, but some Egyptian measurements are still in use.

Statistical Survey

Sources (unless otherwise stated): Central Agency for Public Mobilization and Statistics, POB 2086, Cairo (Nasr City); tel. (2) 4024632; fax (2) 4024099; internet www.capmas.gov.eg; Research Department, National Bank of Egypt, Cairo.

Area and Population

AREA, POPULATION AND DENSITY

Area (sq km)	1,002,000*
Population (census results)†	
17–18 November 1986	48,254,238
31 December 1996	
Males	30,351,390
Females	28,961,524
Total	59,312,914
Population (official estimates at 1 January)‡	
2003	67,313,045
2004	68,648,489
Density (per sq km) at 1 January 2004	68.5

* 386,874 sq miles. Inhabited and cultivated territory accounts for 55,039 sq km (21,251 sq miles).
† Excluding Egyptian nationals abroad, totalling an estimated 2,250,000 in 1986 and an estimated 2,180,000 in 1996.
‡ Excluding estimates of Egyptian nationals abroad, totalling 1,900,229 in 2004.

GOVERNORATES
(estimated population at 1 January 2004)

Governorate	Area (sq km)	Population	Density (per sq km)	Capital
Cairo	214.20	7,629,866	35,620.3	Cairo
Alexandria . .	2,679.36	3,755,901	1,401.8	Alexandria
Port Said . . .	72.07	529,684	7,349.6	Port Said
Ismailia . .	1,441.59	844,091	585.5	Ismailia
Suez	17,840.42	478,553	26.8	Suez
Damietta . .	589.17	1,056,324	1,792.9	Damietta
Dakahlia . .	3,470.90	4,839,359	1,394.3	El-Mansoura
Sharkia . .	4,179.55	5,009,690	1,198.6	Zagazig
Kalyoubia . .	1,001.09	3,804,188	3,800.0	Banha
Kafr esh-Sheikh	3,437.12	2,541,124	739.3	Kafr esh-Sheikh
Gharbia . .	1,942.21	3,859,378	1,987.1	Tanta
Menoufia . .	1,532.13	3,171,058	2,069.7	Shebien el-Kom
Behera . .	10,129.48	4,604,443	454.6	Damanhour
Giza . . .	85,153.56	5,535,498	65.0	Giza
Beni-Suef . .	1,321.50	2,208,082	1,670.9	Beni-Suef
Fayoum . .	1,827.10	2,371,780	1,298.1	El-Fayoum
Menia . .	2,261.70	3,960,656	1,751.2	El-Menia
Asyout . .	1,553.00	3,351,057	2,157.8	Asyout
Suhag . .	1,547.20	3,730,894	2,411.4	Suhag
Qena . . .	1,795.60	2,876,746	1,602.1	Qena
Luxor . . .	55.00	414,389	7,534.3	Luxor
Aswan . .	678.45	1,098,870	1,619.7	Aswan
Red Sea . . .	203,685.00	182,526	0.9	Hurghada
El-Wadi el-Gidid	376,505.00	166,211	0.4	El-Kharga
Matruh . .	212,112.00	262,210	1.2	Matruh
North Sinai .	27,574.00	302,077	11.0	El-Areesh
South Sinai .	33,140.00	63,834	1.9	Et-Tour
Total	997,738.40*	68,648,489	68.5*	—

* The official, rounded national total is 1,002,000 sq km.

PRINCIPAL TOWNS
(population at 1996 census)*

Cairo (Al-Qahirah, the capital)	6,789,479	Zagazig (Az-Zaqaziq)	267,351
Alexandria (Al-Iskandariyah)	3,328,196	El-Fayum (Al-Fayyum)	260,964
Giza (Al-Jizah)	2,221,868	Ismailia (Al-Ismailiyah)	254,477
Shoubra el-Kheima (Shubra al-Khaymah)	870,716	Kafr ed-Dawar (Kafr ad-Dawwar)	231,978
Port Said (Bur Sa'id)	469,533	Aswan	219,017
Suez (As-Suways)	417,610	Damanhour (Damanhur)	212,203
El-Mahalla el-Koubra (Al-Mahallah al-Kubra)	395,402	El-Menia (Al-Minya)	201,360
Tanta	371,010	Beni-Suef (Bani-Suwayf)	172,032
El-Mansoura (Al-Mansurah)	369,621	Qena (Qina)	171,275
Luxor (Al-Uqsor)	360,503	Suhag (Sawhaj)	170,125
Asyout (Asyut)	343,498	Shebien el-Kom (Shibin al-Kawn)	159,909

* Figures refer to provisional population. Revised figures include: Cairo 6,800,992; Alexandria 3,339,076; Port Said 472,335; Suez 417,527.

BIRTHS, MARRIAGES AND DEATHS

	Registered live births		Registered marriages		Registered deaths	
	Number	Rate (per 1,000)	Number	Rate (per 1,000)	Number	Rate (per 1,000)
1994	1,636,000	29.0	452,000	8.0	388,000	6.9
1995	1,605,000	27.9	471,000	8.2	385,000	6.7
1996	1,662,000	28.3	489,000	8.3	380,000	6.5
1997	1,655,000	27.5	493,000	8.2	389,000	6.5
1998	1,687,000	27.5	504,000	8.2	399,000	6.5
1999	1,693,000	27.0	520,000	8.3	401,000	6.4
2000	1,734,000	27.1	579,000	9.1	403,000	6.3
2001*	1,744,000	26.7	513,000	7.9	410,000	6.3

* Provisional figures.

2002: 26.3 (birth rate per 1,000).

2003: 1,775,804 registered live births (birth rate 26.1 per 1,000); 440,360 registered deaths (death rate 6.5 per 1,000).

Expectation of life (WHO estimates, years at birth): 67.1 (males 65.3; females 69.0) in 2002 (Source: WHO, *World Health Report*).

ECONOMICALLY ACTIVE POPULATION
(sample surveys, '000 persons aged 15 years and over)

	2000	2001	2002
Agriculture, hunting and forestry	5,000.5	4,901.5	4,800.4
Fishing	96.7	109.1	113.4
Mining and quarrying	47.4	59.5	44.5
Manufacturing	2,048.2	2,115.0	2,070.7
Electricity, gas and water supply	209.2	210.2	241.8
Construction	1,358.6	1,348.4	1,315.1
Wholesale and retail trade; repair of motor vehicles, motorcycles and personal and household goods	2,006.9	2,125.6	2,302.7
Hotels and restaurants	269.0	324.7	337.3
Transport, storage and communications	1,126.0	1,142.2	1,132.9
Financial intermediation	185.6	199.4	219.5
Real estate, renting and business activities	313.4	337.9	342.4
Public administration and defence; compulsory social security	1,825.1	1,886.8	1,945.5
Education	1,790.4	1,819.8	1,962.7
Health and social work	532.2	566.5	594.5
Other community, social and personal service activities	342.7	353.9	379.5

— continued	2000	2001	2002
Private households with employed persons	49.3	52.8	51.9
Activities not adequately defined	1.9	3.4	1.4
Total employed	17,203.3	17,556.7	17,856.2
Unemployed	1,698.0	1,696.3	2,020.6
Total labour force	18,901.3	19,253.0	19,876.8
Males	14,702.0	15,032.4	15,533.9
Females	4,199.3	4,220.6	4,342.9

Source: ILO.

Health and Welfare

KEY INDICATORS

Total fertility rate (children per woman, 2002)	3.3
Under-5 mortality rate (per 1,000 live births, 2003)	39
HIV/AIDS (% of persons aged 15–49, 2003)	<0.1
Physicians (per 1,000 head, 2002)	2.2
Hospital beds (per 1,000 head, 1997)	2.1
Health expenditure (2001): US $ per head (PPP)	153
Health expenditure (2001): % of GDP	3.9
Health expenditure (2001): public (% of total)	48.9
Access to water (% of persons, 2002)	98
Access to sanitation (% of persons, 2002)	68
Human Development Index (2002): ranking	120
Human Development Index (2002): value	0.653

For sources and definitions, see explanatory note on p. vi.

Agriculture

PRINCIPAL CROPS
('000 metric tons)

	2001	2002	2003
Wheat	6,254.6	6,183.2	6,844.7
Rice (paddy)	5,226.7	6,104.7	6,174.5
Barley	93.9	100.8	122.0*
Maize	6,842.3	5,676.5	5,681.8
Sorghum	862.3	887.7	942.8
Potatoes	1,903.1	1,985.3	2,039.4
Sweet potatoes	314.7	320.0*	307.6
Taro (Coco yam)	44.6	40.0*	40.0*
Sugar cane	15,571.5	16,016.0†	16,334.8†
Sugar beet	2,857.7	2,650.0*	2,691.5
Dry broad beans	439.5	400.9†	400.0*
Other pulses*	76.7	90.9	90.9
Groundnuts (in shell)	205.1	191.0†	191.0*
Olives	293.9	318.3	320.0*
Cottonseed	494.8	765.6†	550.0*
Cabbages	562.4	556.6†	560.0*
Artichokes	65.3	65.0*	65.0*
Lettuce	179.6	180.0*	180.0*
Tomatoes	6,328.7	6,777.9†	6,780.0*
Cauliflowers	109.9	110.0*	110.0*
Pumpkins, squash and gourds	706.8	707.0*	710.0*
Cucumbers and gherkins	567.6	629.0†	630.0*
Aubergines (Eggplants)	703.1	703.0*	710.0*
Chillies and green peppers	386.7	387.0*	390.0*
Dry onions	628.4	630.0*	630.0*
Garlic	215.4	216.0*	216.0*
Green beans	214.9	215.0†	215.0*
Green peas	227.1	352.3†	353.0*
Carrots	111.2	111.0*	111.0*
Okra	85.2	85.0*	85.0*
Other vegetables*	667.9	668.0	668.0
Bananas	849.3	877.6†	880.0*
Oranges	1,696.3	1,725.0†	1,740.0†
Tangerines, mandarins, clementines and satsumas	564.9	500.0*	505.0†
Lemons and limes	296.3	296.8*	300.0*
Apples	473.6	484.1	485.0*
Peaches and nectarines	247.3	257.0*	260.0*
Strawberries	68.1	68.0*	68.0*
Grapes	1,078.9	1,103.8	1,104.0*
Watermelons	1,446.9	1,600.0*	1,600.0*
Cantaloupes and other melons	856.5	860.0*	860.0*

— *continued*	2001	2002	2003
Figs	150.2	188.0	190.0*
Mangoes	325.5	326.1	327.0*
Dates	1,113.3	1,090.0†	1,100.0*
Other fruits and berries* . . .	491.0	493.9	496.0
Cotton (lint)†	330.0	285.0	200.0

* FAO estimate(s).
† Unofficial figure(s).

Source: FAO.

LIVESTOCK
('000 head, year ending September)

	2001	2002	2003*
Cattle	3,801	3,810*	3,810
Buffaloes	3,532	3,550*	3,560
Sheep	4,671	5,105†	4,672
Goats	3,497†	3,582†	3,470
Pigs	30	30*	30
Horses	53	62†	62
Asses*	3,050	3,070	3,070
Camels	134	127†	120
Rabbits*	9,250	9,250	9,250
Chickens*	91,000	92,000	92,000
Ducks*	9,100	9,200	9,200
Geese*	9,100	9,100	9,100
Turkeys*	1,850	1,890	1,900

* FAO estimate(s).
† Unofficial figure.

Source: FAO.

LIVESTOCK PRODUCTS
('000 metric tons)

	2001	2002	2003
Beef and veal	246.8*	252.4	294.1†
Buffalo meat†	303.0	306.5	306.5
Mutton and lamb†	75	80	75
Goat meat†	32.7	33.6	33.6
Pig meat	3.1*	3.1†	3.1†
Camel meat†	52	46	46
Rabbit meat†	69.8	69.8	69.8
Poultry meat	643.0	652.2†	652.2†
Other meat†	9.8	9.8	9.8
Cows' milk	1,617.7	1,997.2	2,597.6†
Buffaloes' milk	2,213.0	2,087.2	2,549.6
Sheep's milk	93	93†	93†
Goats' milk	15.0	15.1†	15.1†
Butter†	96.7	96.7	116.2
Cheese†	484.3	535.8	660.8
Hen eggs	199.6	200.0†	200.0†
Honey	8.5	8.7*	8.7†
Wool: greasy	7.6	7.6†	7.6†
Wool: scoured†	3.5	3.5	3.5
Cattle hides†	29.0	29.6	34.5
Buffalo hides†	26.3	26.6	35.0
Sheepskins†	9.0	9.6	9.0
Goatskins†	4.6	4.8	4.6

* Unofficial figure.
† FAO estimate(s).

Source: FAO.

Forestry

ROUNDWOOD REMOVALS
(FAO estimates, '000 cubic metres, excluding bark)

	2001	2002	2003
Industrial wood	134	134	134
Fuel wood	16,332	16,484	16,637
Total	16,466	16,618	16,771

Source: FAO.

SAWNWOOD PRODUCTION
('000 cubic metres, incl. railway sleepers)

	1998	1999	2000
Total (all broadleaved)	3	4	4

2001–03: Output assumed to be unchanged from 2000 (FAO estimates).

Source: FAO.

Fishing
('000 metric tons, live weight)

	2000	2001	2002
Capture	384.3	428.7	425.2
Nile tilapia	131.3	145.3	138.5
Mudfish	31.5	39.5	39.2
Other mullets	20.5	26.5	30.7
Sardinellas	25.4	24.4	17.5
Aquaculture	340.1	342.9	376.3
Grass carp	66.2	72.4	75.9
Nile tilapia	157.4	152.5	167.7
Flathead grey mullet	80.5	96.9	113.0
Total catch	724.4	771.5	801.5

Source: FAO.

Mining
(estimates, '000 metric tons, unless otherwise indicated, year ending 30 June)

	2000	2001	2002
Crude petroleum ('000 barrels) .	285,000	277,000	274,000
Natural gas (million cu m) . . .	25,000	25,000	31,000
Iron ore*	1,900	2,600	2,300
Salt (unrefined)	2,400	2,400	2,400
Phosphate rock	1,096	972	1,500
Gypsum (crude)	2,000	2,000	2,000
Kaolin	290	300	300

* Figures refer to gross weight. The estimated iron content is 50%.

Source: US Geological Survey.

Industry

SELECTED PRODUCTS
('000 metric tons, unless otherwise indicated, year ending 30 June)

	1997/98	1998/99	1999/2000
Cottonseed oil (refined)	306	290	260
Cigarettes (million)	52	51	53
Jute yarn	15	10	5
Jute fabrics	13	9	4
Wool yarn	12	12	15
Rubber tyres and tubes ('000)*	3,502	3,598	2,662
Caustic soda (Sodium hydroxide) .	51	58	44
Phosphate fertilizers†	365	378	390
Jet fuels	860	939	920
Kerosene	1,260	1,072	1,011
Distillate fuel oils	5,889	6,007	5,989
Residual fuel oil (Mazout) . . .	12,700	12,773	11,785
Petroleum bitumen (asphalt) . .	714	954	957
Cement	21,225	21,232	18,932
Passenger motor cars—assembly (number)	13,337	11,629‡	n.a.
Electric energy (million kWh) . .	62,300	62,300	70,600

* Tyres and inner tubes for road motor vehicles (including motorcycles) and bicycles.
† Production in terms of phosphoric acid.
‡ Estimate.

Finance

CURRENCY AND EXCHANGE RATES

Monetary Units
1,000 millièmes = 100 piastres = 5 tallaris = 1 Egyptian pound (£E).

Sterling, Dollar and Euro Equivalents (31 December 2004)
£1 sterling = £E11.841;
US $1 = £E6.131;
€1 = £E8.351;
£E100 = £8.44 sterling = $16.31 = €11.97

Note: From February 1991 foreign-exchange transactions were conducted through only two markets, the primary market and the free market. With effect from 8 October 1991, the primary market was eliminated, and all foreign-exchange transactions are effected through the free market. In January 2001 a new exchange-rate mechanism was introduced, whereby the value of the Egyptian pound would be allowed to fluctuate within narrow limits: initially, as much as 1% above or below a rate that was set by the Central Bank of Egypt, but would be adjusted periodically in response to market conditions. The trading band was widened to 3% in August, and in January 2003 the Government adopted a floating exchange rate.

Average Exchange Rate (Egyptian pound per US $)
2002   4.4997
2003   5.8509
2004   6.1963

STATE PUBLIC BUDGET
(£E million, year ending 30 June)

Revenue	1998/99	1999/2000*	2000/01†
Current revenue	67,207	71,898	86,294
Central Government	62,758	66,890	64,348
Tax revenue	48,096	50,869	62,909
Taxes on income and profits	15,641	17,550	27,788
Domestic taxes on goods and services	14,313	16,000	18,000
Customs duties	10,108	10,000	13,000
Stamp duties	3,342	3,324	4,121
Other current revenue	14,662	16,021	21,946
Profit transfers	9,802	10,856	13,406
Petroleum Authority	2,227	2,901	4,575
Suez Canal Authority	2,914	3,000	3,500
Central Bank of Egypt	3,222	3,500	3,200
Local government	4,449	2,879	1,404
Service authorities	1,576	2,129	35
Capital revenue	6,072	4,833	11,644
Total	**73,279**	**76,731**	**97,938**

Expenditure	1998/99	1999/2000*	2000/01†
Current expenditure	61,117	68,610	85,688
Wages	18,833	22,459	28,767
Pensions	5,009	6,228	8,090
Goods and services	3,888	3,946	3,884
Defence	8,290	8,321	3,727
Public debt interest	16,406	18,735	20,400
Local	14,081	16,435	18,400
Foreign	2,325	2,300	2,000
Subsidies	4,498	5,387	5,789
Capital expenditure (net)	24,892	20,452	26,011
Total	**86,009**	**89,062**	**111,699**

* Provisional figures.
† Projections.

INTERNATIONAL RESERVES
(US $ million at 31 December)

	2001	2002	2003
Gold*	488	571	631
IMF special drawing rights	35	91	189
Foreign exchange	12,891	13,151	13,400
Total	**13,414**	**13,813**	**14,220**

* Valued at market-related prices.

Source: IMF, *International Financial Statistics*.

MONEY SUPPLY
(£E million at 31 December)

	2001	2002	2003
Currency outside banks	40,548	45,281	52,475
Demand deposits at deposit money banks	23,515	27,021	36,627
Total money (incl. others)	**67,078**	**75,781**	**93,520**

Source: IMF, *International Financial Statistics*.

COST OF LIVING
(Consumer Price Index; base: 1990 = 100)

	1999	2000	2001
Food, beverages and tobacco	203.4	208.5	210.7
Fuel and light	313.6	336.1	338.2
Clothing and footwear	226.6	232.2	237.1
Rent	155.0	155.2	157.3
All items (incl. others)	**218.4**	**224.4**	**229.4**

Source: ILO, *Yearbook of Labour Statistics*.

2002: Food 219.6; All items 235.7 (Source: UN, *Monthly Bulletin of Statistics*).

2003: Food 238.9; All items 245.7 (Source: UN, *Monthly Bulletin of Statistics*).

NATIONAL ACCOUNTS
(£E million, year ending 30 June)

Expenditure on the Gross Domestic Product
(at current prices)

	2001	2002	2003
Government final consumption expenditure	40,600	47,200	52,000
Private final consumption expenditure	270,000	279,000	303,000
Increase in stocks	1,900	1,700	2,900
Gross fixed capital formation	63,600	67,500	68,100
Total domestic expenditure	**376,100**	**395,400**	**426,000**
Exports of goods and services	62,700	69,500	90,000
Less Imports of goods and services	80,100	86,4,000	101,000
GDP in purchasers' values	**358,700**	**378,500**	**415,000**

Source: IMF, *International Financial Statistics*.

Gross Domestic Product by Economic Activity
(at current factor cost)

	2001/02	2002/03	2003/04*
Agriculture, hunting, forestry and fishing	58,369.0	65,156.0	70,319.0
Manufacturing	70,084.2	110,176.3	133,696.3
Mining	29,359.5		
Electricity and water	7,455.2	8,020.9	8,690.0
Construction	16,560.0	16,710.0	17,880.0
Transport and communications	31,951.7	25,253.8	27,278.3
Tourism, restaurants and hotels	6,457.0	7,728.0	10,417.3
Trade, finance and insurance	73,226.9	79,273.0	86,381.0
Real estate	13,923.0	14,651.0	16,021.0
General government services	35,269.3	39,925.3	45,195.4
Other services	11,907.8	23,728.7	29,294.3
GDP at factor cost	**354,563.6**	**390,623.0**	**445,172.6**

* Provisional figures.

Source: Central Bank of Egypt.

BALANCE OF PAYMENTS
(US $ million)

	2001	2002	2003
Exports of goods f.o.b.	7,025	7,118	8,987
Imports of goods f.o.b.	−13,960	−12,879	−13,189
Trade balance	−6,935	−5,762	−4,201
Exports of services	9,042	9,320	11,073
Imports of services	−7,037	−6,629	−6,474
Balance on goods and services	−4,929	−3,071	−398
Other income received	1,468	698	578
Other income paid	−885	−965	−832
Balance on goods, services and			
income	−4,346	−3,338	145
Current transfers received . . .	4,056	4,002	3,708
Current transfers paid	−98	−42	−109
Current balance	−388	622	3,743
Direct investment abroad . . .	−12	−28	−21
Direct investment from abroad .	510	647	237
Portfolio investment assets . .	−2	−6	−25
Portfolio investment liabilities .	1,463	−672	−18
Other investment assets . . .	−1,261	−2,943	−4,651
Other investment liabilities . .	−509	−331	−1,248
Net errors and omissions . . .	−1,146	1,906	1,575
Overall balance	−1,345	−804	−407

Source: IMF, *International Financial Statistics*.

External Trade

Note: Figures exclude trade in military goods.

PRINCIPAL COMMODITIES
(distribution by SITC, US $ million)

Imports c.i.f.	1999	2001*	2002
Food and live animals . . .	2,917.5	2,741.4	2,949.9
Cereals and cereal preparations .	1,298.2	1,257.3	1,445.9
Wheat and meslin (unmilled) .	602.8	668.5	819.2
Maize (unmilled)	652.5	554.6	594.2
Crude materials (inedible)			
except fuels	1,068.3	951.8	952.6
Cork and wood	509.5	443.1	429.7
Simply worked wood and railway			
sleepers	473.2	422.8	408.7
Mineral fuels, lubricants, etc.	977.9	630.3	504.9
Petroleum, petroleum products,			
etc.	695.2	382.6	180.6
Animal and vegetable oils, fats			
and waxes	415.8	174.6	181.4
Chemicals and related			
products	1,830.9	1,518.4	1,511.6
Medicinal and pharmaceutical			
products	344.5	432.5	500.8
Artificial resins, plastic materials,			
etc.	584.4	465.9	374.0
Basic manufactures	2,876.5	2,131.0	1,897.4
Paper, paperboard and			
manufactures	452.8	340.6	251.8
Iron and steel	887.7	625.2	611.5
Machinery and transport			
equipment	4,187.6	2,853.1	2,497.9
Machinery specialized for			
particular industries	936.5	623.3	460.9
General industrial machinery,			
equipment and parts . . .	974.1	566.2	552.1
Electrical machinery, apparatus,			
etc.	676.8	532.2	488.8
Road vehicles and parts† . . .	582.9	340.1	330.8
Miscellaneous manufactured			
articles	664.6	593.6	578.0
Total (incl. others)	15,962.1	12,755.7	12,552.5

Exports f.o.b.	2000	2001	2002
Food and live animals . . .	379.5	390.1	387.3
Cereals and cereal preparations	106.9	152.9	111.0
Rice	104.6	143.0	106.0
Vegetables and fruit	201.7	174.2	196.5
Crude materials (inedible)			
except fuels	305.6	279.9	486.5
Textile fibres (excl. wool tops) and			
waste	29.4	197.5	345.7
Cotton	26.8	187.2	331.1
Mineral fuels, lubricants, etc.	2,949.3	1,686.7	1,572.5
Petroleum, petroleum products,			
etc.	2,773.0	1,565.6	1,507.7
Crude petroleum oils, etc. . .	616.8	297.6	316.7
Refined petroleum products .	2,138.1	1,255.7	1,181.0
Residual fuel oils	2,045.1	1,191.5	—
Chemicals and related			
products	350.7	323.4	304.0
Basic manufactures	340.2	763.6	998.1
Textile yarn, fabrics, etc. . . .	19.5	289.9	251.2
Textile yarn	12.5	126.2	112.3
Cotton yarn	12.1	122.8	107.8
Other textile articles	5.9	117.7	98.9
Iron and steel	147.8	137.2	237.4
Non-ferrous metals	21.2	135.0	117.2
Aluminium and aluminium			
alloys	20.6	134.5	115.5
Unwrought aluminium and			
alloys	16.4	104.1	102.2
Miscellaneous manufactured			
articles	302.3	354.4	398.8
Clothing and accessories (excl.			
footwear)	0.1	239.4	208.2
Cotton undergarments . . .	—	96.8	78.2
Total (incl. others)	4,640.7	4,164.9	4,691.6

* Figures for 2000 are not available.
† Excluding tyres, engines and electrical parts.
Source: UN, *International Trade Statistics Yearbook*.

PRINCIPAL TRADING PARTNERS
(countries of consignment, US $ million)

Imports c.i.f.	1999	2001*	2002
Argentina	196.3	258.0	305.2
Australia	435.0	525.6	483.8
Belgium	227.9	198.1	123.5
Brazil	318.2	252.7	366.1
China, People's Republic . . .	620.6	514.1	562.6
Denmark	121.6	139.5	73.8
Finland	206.1	151.9	165.4
France (incl. Monaco)	786.6	508.7	541.6
Germany	1,382.1	962.4	828.2
India	269.2	285.1	367.1
Indonesia	196.4	158.9	133.4
Ireland	214.1	78.2	47.0
Italy	1,049.3	643.9	632.7
Japan	520.9	366.7	334.8
Korea, Republic	349.9	270.0	210.0
Malaysia	196.5	112.1	130.9
Netherlands	373.6	259.0	222.9
Romania	211.7	131.6	108.7
Russia	402.5	291.6	430.4
Saudi Arabia	698.4	680.6	345.9
Spain	334.1	175.9	155.7
Sweden	310.4	194.1	148.8
Switzerland-Liechtenstein . . .	245.1	224.7	186.3
Turkey	356.6	244.2	223.7
Ukraine	224.0	211.9	242.8
United Kingdom	477.5	300.8	312.5
USA	2,295.8	1,837.2	1,691.9
Total (incl. others)	15,962.1	12,755.7	12,552.5

Exports f.o.b.	2000	2001	2002
Belgium	7.7	41.9	50.6
France (incl. Monaco)	317.2	164.1	117.9
Germany	63.3	111.3	96.1
Greece	65.9	47.4	79.4
India	206.7	253.6	413.6
Iraq	20.2	91.1	67.3
Israel	444.5	191.0	45.9
Italy	307.4	380.8	501.6
Japan	101.2	67.7	71.2
Korea, Republic	45.4	51.0	48.9
Lebanon	99.7	53.3	74.1
Libya	28.8	45.6	70.1
Netherlands	316.2	279.8	201.4
Romania	13.1	23.5	21.2
Saudi Arabia	119.9	147.7	134.2
Singapore	172.7	86.6	60.9
Spain	109.1	153.8	152.9
Syria	35.1	56.3	60.7
Turkey	110.8	77.0	78.2
United Arab Emirates . . .	55.3	59.4	79.1
United Kingdom	62.7	98.3	79.1
USA	257.4	346.6	388.5
Total (incl. others)	4,640.7	4,164.9	4,691.6

* Figures for 2000 imports are not available.

Source: UN, *International Trade Statistics Yearbook.*

Transport

RAILWAYS
(traffic, year ending 30 June)

	1998/99	1999/2000	2000/01
Passengers (million)	1,395	1,353	1,183
Passenger-km (million)	68,423	57,859	55,807
Freight ton-km (million) . . .	3,464	4,184	4,198

Source: UN, *Statistical Yearbook.*

ROAD TRAFFIC
(licensed motor vehicles in use at 31 December)

	1995*	1996	1997
Passenger cars	1,280,000	1,099,583	1,154,753
Buses and coaches	36,630	39,781	43,740
Lorries and vans	387,000	489,542	510,766
Motorcycles and mopeds . . .	397,000	427,864	439,756

* Estimates from IRF, *World Road Statistics.*

2002: Passenger cars ('000): 1,847.0; Commercial vehicles ('000): 650.0 (Source: UN, *Statistical Yearbook*).

SHIPPING
Merchant Fleet
(registered at 31 December)

	2001	2002	2003
Number of vessels	364	361	346
Displacement ('000 grt)	1,350.4	1,275.0	1,151.4

Source: Lloyd's Register-Fairplay, *World Fleet Statistics.*

International sea-borne freight traffic ('000 metric tons, incl. ships' stores, 1998): Goods loaded 23,868; Goods unloaded 31,152 (Source: UN, *Monthly Bulletin of Statistics*).

Suez Canal Traffic

	1998	1999	2000
Transits (number)	13,472	13,490	14,141
Displacement ('000 net tons) . .	386,069	384,994	438,962
Northbound goods traffic ('000 metric tons)	160,346	153,582	209,446
Southbound goods traffic ('000 metric tons)	118,107	153,088	158,535
Net tonnage of tankers ('000) . .	89,976	67,872	105,237

Source: Suez Canal Authority, *Yearly Report.*

CIVIL AVIATION
(traffic on scheduled services)

	1999	2000	2001
Kilometres flown (million) . . .	68	64	64
Passengers carried ('000) . . .	4,620	4,522	4,389
Passenger-km (million) . . .	9,074	8,828	8,893
Total ton-km (million)	1,097	1,085	1,051

Source: UN, *Statistical Yearbook.*

Tourism

ARRIVALS BY NATIONALITY
('000*)

	2000	2001	2002
France	379.9	290.6	280.2
Germany	786.3	715.1	730.3
Israel	326.5	109.4	146.7
Italy	752.2	594.5	701.2
Libya	152.5	165.8	225.2
Netherlands	142.1	122.6	117.3
Palestine	149.8	126.4	155.5
Russia	n.a.	210.2	382.5
Saudi Arabia	240.2	225.6	248.8
Switzerland	104.1	100.9	104.9
United Kingdom	378.4	324.8	357.5
USA	235.3	178.2	117.4
Total (incl. others)	5,506.2	4,648.5	5,191.7

* Figures refer to arrivals at frontiers of visitors from abroad. Excluding same-day visitors (excursionists), the total number of tourist arrivals (in '000) was: 5,116 in 2000; n.a. in 2001; n.a. in 2002.

Tourism receipts (US $ million): 4,345 in 2000; 3,800 in 2001; 3,764 in 2002.

Source: World Tourism Organization.

Communications Media

	2001	2002	2003
Telephones ('000 main lines in use)	6,650.0	6,688.4	8,735.7
Mobile cellular telephones ('000 subscribers)	2,793.8	4,412.0	5,797.5
Personal computers ('000 in use)	1,000	1,000	1,500
Internet users ('000)	600	600	2,700

1997: Radio receivers ('000 in use) 20,500.

1998: Book production 1,410 titles.

1999: Daily newspapers 16 (average circulation 2,080,000 copies); Other periodicals 45 (average circulation 1,371,000 copies); Facsimile machines ('000 in use) 34.2.

2000: Television receivers ('000 in use) 12,000.

Sources: UNESCO, *Statistical Yearbook*; International Telecommunication Union.

Education

(provisional figures, 1999/2000, unless otherwise indicated)

	Schools	Teachers*	Students
Pre-primary	3,172*	14,894	289,995†
Primary	15,533	314,528	7,224,989
Preparatory	7,544	193,469	4,345,356
Secondary:			
general	1,595	79,218	1,039,958
technical	1,826	145,050	1,913,022
Higher	356*‡	n.a.	1,316,491†

* 1998/99 figure(s).
† 1996/97 figure. Source: partly UNESCO, *Statistical Yearbook*.
‡ Official estimate.

Source: Ministry of Education.

2001/02: Total number of students ('000) 18,500; Number of students enrolled in university or higher education ('000) 1,930.

Al-Azhar (provisional figures, 1999/2000): Primary: 2,631 schools; 707,633 students. Preparatory: 1,805 schools; 316,108 students. Secondary: 1,081 schools; 269,469 students.

Adult literacy rate (UNESCO estimates): 55.6% (males 67.2%; females 43.6%) in 2002 (Source: UN Development Programme, *Human Development Report*).

Directory

The Constitution

A new Constitution for the Arab Republic of Egypt was approved by referendum on 11 September 1971.

THE STATE

Egypt is an Arab Republic with a democratic, socialist system based on the alliance of the working people and derived from the country's historical heritage and the spirit of Islam.

The Egyptian people are part of the Arab nation, who work towards total Arab unity.

Islam is the religion of the State; Arabic is its official language and the Islamic code is a principal source of legislation. The State safeguards the freedom of worship and of performing rites for all religions.

Sovereignty is of the people alone which is the source of all powers.

The protection, consolidation and preservation of the socialist gains is a national duty: the sovereignty of law is the basis of the country's rule, and the independence of immunity of the judiciary are basic guarantees for the protection of rights and liberties.

THE FUNDAMENTAL ELEMENTS OF SOCIETY

Social solidarity is the basis of Egyptian society, and the family is its nucleus.

The State ensures the equality of men and women in both political and social rights in line with the provisions of Muslim legislation.

Work is a right, an honour and a duty which the State guarantees together with the services of social and health insurance, pensions for incapacity and unemployment.

The economic basis of the Republic is a socialist democratic system based on sufficiency and justice in a manner preventing exploitation.

Ownership is of three kinds: public, co-operative and private. The public sector assumes the main responsibility for the regulation and growth of the national economy under the development plan.

Property is subject to the people's control.

Private ownership is safeguarded and may not be sequestrated except in cases specified in law nor expropriated except for the general good against fair legal compensation. The right of inheritance is guaranteed in it.

Nationalization shall only be allowed for considerations of public interest in accordance with the law and against compensation.

Agricultural holding may be limited by law.

The State follows a comprehensive central planning and compulsory planning approach based on quinquennial socio-economic and cultural development plans whereby the society's resources are mobilized and put to the best use.

The public sector assumes the leading role in the development of the national economy. The State provides absolute protection of this sector as well as the property of co-operative societies and trade unions against all attempts to tamper with them.

PUBLIC LIBERTIES, RIGHTS AND DUTIES

All citizens are equal before the law. Personal liberty is a natural right and no one may be arrested, searched, imprisoned or restricted in any way without a court order.

Houses have sanctity, and shall not be placed under surveillance or searched without a court order with reasons given for such action.

The law safeguards the sanctities of the private lives of all citizens; so have all postal, telegraphic, telephonic and other means of communication which may not therefore be confiscated, or perused except by a court order giving the reasons, and only for a specified period.

Public rights and freedoms are also inviolate and all calls for atheism and anything that reflects adversely on divine religions are prohibited.

The freedom of opinion, the Press, printing and publications and all information media are safeguarded.

Press censorship is forbidden, so are warnings, suspensions or cancellations through administrative channels. Under exceptional circumstances, as in cases of emergency or in wartime, censorship may be imposed on information media for a definite period.

Egyptians have the right to permanent or provisional emigration and no Egyptian may be deported or prevented from returning to the country.

Citizens have the right to private meetings in peace provided they bear no arms. Egyptians also have the right to form societies that have no secret activities. Public meetings are also allowed within the limits of the law.

SOVEREIGNTY OF THE LAW

All acts of crime should be specified together with the penalties for the acts.

Recourse to justice is a right of all citizens. Those who are financially unable will be assured of means to defend their rights.

Except in cases of *flagrante delicto* no person may be arrested or their freedom restricted unless an order authorizing arrest has been given by the competent judge or the public prosecution in accordance with the provisions of law.

SYSTEM OF GOVERNMENT

The President, who must be of Egyptian parentage and at least 40 years old, is nominated by at least one-third of the members of the People's Assembly, approved by at least two-thirds, and elected by popular referendum. His term is for six years and he 'may be re-elected for another subsequent term'. He may take emergency measures in the interests of the State but these measures must be approved by referendum within 60 days.

The People's Assembly, elected for five years, is the legislative body and approves general policy, the budget and the development plan. It shall have 'not less than 350' elected members, at least half of whom shall be workers or farmers, and the President may appoint up to 10 additional members. In exceptional circumstances the

Assembly, by a two-thirds' vote, may authorize the President to rule by decree for a specified period but these decrees must be approved by the Assembly at its next meeting. The law governing the composition of the People's Assembly was amended in May 1979 (see People's Assembly, below).

The Assembly may pass a vote of no confidence in a Deputy Prime Minister, a Minister or a Deputy Minister, provided three days' notice of the vote is given, and the Minister must then resign. In the case of the Prime Minister, the Assembly may 'prescribe' his responsibility and submit a report to the President: if the President disagrees with the report but the Assembly persists, then the matter is put to a referendum: if the people support the President the Assembly is dissolved; if they support the Assembly the President must accept the resignation of the Government. The President may dissolve the Assembly prematurely, but his action must be approved by a referendum and elections must be held within 60 days.

Executive Authority is vested in the President, who may appoint one or more Vice-Presidents and appoints all Ministers. He may also dismiss the Vice-Presidents and Ministers. The President has 'the right to refer to the people in connection with important matters related to the country's higher interests.' The Government is described as 'the supreme executive and administrative organ of the state'. Its members, whether full Ministers or Deputy Ministers, must be at least 35 years old. Further sections define the roles of Local Government, Specialized National Councils, the Judiciary, the Higher Constitutional Court, the Socialist Prosecutor-General, the Armed Forces and National Defence Council and the Police.

POLITICAL PARTIES

In June 1977 the People's Assembly adopted a new law on political parties, which, subject to certain conditions, permitted the formation of political parties for the first time since 1953. The law was passed in accordance with Article Five of the Constitution which describes the political system as 'a multi-party one' with four main parties: 'the ruling National Democratic Party, the Socialist Workers (the official opposition), the Liberal Socialists and the Unionist Progressive'. (The legality of the re-formed New Wafd Party was established by the courts in January 1984.)

1980 AMENDMENTS

On 30 April 1980 the People's Assembly passed a number of amendments, which were subsequently massively approved at a referendum the following month. A summary of the amendments follows:

(i) the regime in Egypt is socialist-democratic, based on the alliance of working people's forces.

(ii) the political system depends on multiple political parties; the Arab Socialist Union is therefore abolished.

(iii) the President is elected for a six-year term and can be elected for 'other terms'.

(iv) the President shall appoint a Consultative Council to preserve the principles of the revolutions of 23 July 1952 and 15 May 1971.

(v) a Supreme Press Council shall safeguard the freedom of the press, check government censorship and look after the interests of journalists.

(vi) Egypt's adherence to Islamic jurisprudence is affirmed. Christians and Jews are subject to their own jurisdiction in personal status affairs.

(vii) there will be no distinction of race or religion.

The Government

HEAD OF STATE

President: MUHAMMAD HOSNI MUBARAK (confirmed as President by referendum, 13 October 1981, after assassination of President Anwar Sadat; re-elected and confirmed by referendum 5 October 1987, 4 October 1993 and 26 September 1999).

COUNCIL OF MINISTERS
(April 2005)

Prime Minister: Dr AHMAD MAHMOUD MUHAMMAD NAZIF.

Minister of Agriculture and Land Reclamation: Eng. AHMAD ABD AL-MUNIM AL-LAITHY.

Minister of Defence and Military Production: Field Marshal MUHAMMAD HUSSAIN TANTAWI.

Minister of Foreign Affairs: AHMAD ABOUL GHEIT.

Minister of Justice: MAHMOUD ABOUL LEIL RASHED.

Minister of Information: ANAS EL-FIKI.

Minister of Culture: FAROUK ABD AL-AZIZ HOSNI.

Minister of Education: Dr AHMAD GAMAL ED-DIN MOUSSA.

Minister of Investment: Dr MAHMOUD MOHI ED-DIN.

Minister of Foreign Trade and Industry: Eng. RASHID MUHAMMAD RASHID.

Minister of Tourism: AHMAD AL-MAGHRABI.

Minister of Housing, Utilities and Urban Communities: Dr MUHAMMAD IBRAHIM SULAYMAN.

Minister of Labour and Migration: AHMAD AHMAD EL-AMAWI.

Minister of Awqaf (Islamic Endowments): Dr MAHMOUD HAMDI ZAKZOUK.

Minister of Health and Population: Dr MUHAMMAD AWAD AFIFI TAG ED-DIN.

Minister of Higher Education and Scientific Research: Dr AMR AZET SALAMA.

Minister of Irrigation and Water Resources: Dr MAHMOUD ABD AL-HALIM ABU ZEID.

Minister of the Interior: Maj.-Gen. HABIB IBRAHIM EL-ADLI.

Minister of Insurance and Social Affairs: Dr AMINA HAMZEH MAHMOUD AL-GUINDI.

Minister of International Co-operation: FAIZA MUHAMMAD ABOUL NAGA.

Minister of Electricity and Energy: Dr HASSAN AHMAD YOUNIS.

Minister of Transport: Dr ESSAM ABD AL-AZIZ SHARAF.

Minister of Youth: Dr MUHAMMAD MAMDOUH AHMAD EL-BELTAGI.

Minister of Supply and Internal Trade: Dr HASSAN ALI KHIDR.

Minister of Planning: Dr OSMAN MUHAMMAD OSMAN.

Minister of Finance: Dr YOUSUF BOUTROS-GHALI.

Minister of Communications and Information Technology: Dr TAREQ MUHAMMAD KAMEL.

Minister of Petroleum: Eng. AMIN SAMIH SAMIR FAHMI.

Minister of Civil Aviation: Gen. AHMAD MUHAMMAD SHAFIQ ZAKI.

Minister of State for Parliamentary Affairs: KAMAL MUHAMMAD ASH-SHAZLI.

Minister of State for Shura Council Affairs: Dr MUFID MAHMOUD SHEHAB.

Minister of State for Administrative Development: Dr AHMAD MAHMOUD DARWISH.

Minister of State for Environmental Affairs: MAGED GEORGE ELIAS.

Minister of State for Local Development: MUHAMMAD ABD AR-REHIM SHEHATA.

Minister of State for Military Production: Dr SAID ABDUH MOUSTAFA MESHAAL.

MINISTRIES

Office of the Prime Minister: Sharia Majlis ash-Sha'ab, Cairo; tel. (2) 7958014; fax (2) 7958016; e-mail primemin@idsc.gov.eg.

Ministry of Agriculture and Land Reclamation: Sharia Nadi es-Sayed, Cairo (Dokki), Giza; tel. (2) 3772566; fax (2) 3498128; e-mail sea@idsc.gov.eg; internet www.agri.gov.eg.

Ministry of Awqaf (Islamic Endowments): Sharia Sabri Abu Alam, Bab el-Louk, Cairo; tel. (2) 3929403; fax (2) 3900362; e-mail mawkaf@idsc1.gov.eg.

Ministry of Civil Aviation: Sharia Matar, Cairo; tel. (2) 3555566; fax (2) 3555564.

Ministry of Communications and Information Technology: Smart Village, km 28, Sharia Alexandria, Cairo; tel. (2) 5341300; e-mail webmaster@mcit.gov.eg; internet www.mcit.gov.eg.

Ministry of Culture: 2 Sharia Shagaret ed-Dor, Cairo (Zamalek); tel. (2) 7380761; fax (2) 7356449; e-mail mculture@idsc.gov.eg.

Ministry of Defence and Military Production: Sharia 23 July, Kobri el-Kobra, Cairo; tel. (2) 2602566; fax (2) 2916227; e-mail mod@idsc.gov.eg.

Ministry of Education: 4 Sharia Ibrahim Nagiv, Cairo (Garden City); tel. (2) 5787643; fax (2) 7962952; e-mail moe@idsc.gov.eg; internet www1.emoe.org.

Ministry of Electricity and Energy: Sharia Ramses, Abbassia, Cairo (Nasr City); tel. (2) 2616317; fax (2) 2616302; e-mail mee@idsc.gov.eg; internet www.moee.gov.eg.

Ministry of Finance: Justice and Finance Bldg, Sharia Majlis ash-Sha'ab, Lazoughli Sq., Cairo; tel. (2) 3541055; fax (2) 3551537; e-mail mofinance@idsc1.gov.eg.

Ministry of Foreign Affairs: Corniche en-Nil, Cairo (Maspiro); tel. (2) 5746861; fax (2) 5749533; e-mail minexter@idsc1.gov.eg; internet www.mfa.gov.eg.

Ministry of Foreign Trade and Industry: 8 Sharia Adly, Cairo; tel. (2) 3919661; fax (2) 3903029; e-mail moft@moft.gov.eg; internet www.moft.gov.eg.

Ministry of Health and Population: Sharia Majlis ash-Sha'ab, Lazoughli Sq., Cairo; tel. (2) 7941507; fax (2) 7953966; e-mail moh@idsc.gov.eg; internet www.mohp.gov.eg.

Ministry of Higher Education and Scientific Research: 101 Sharia Qasr el-Eini, Cairo; tel. (2) 7956962; fax (2) 7941005; e-mail mheducat@idsc.gov.eg; internet www.egy-mhe.gov.eg.

Ministry of Housing, Utilities and Urban Communities: 1 Ismail Abaza, Sharia Qasr el-Eini, Cairo; tel. (2) 3553468; fax (2) 3557836; e-mail mhuuc@idsc1.gov.eg.

Ministry of Information: Radio and TV Bldg, Corniche en-Nil, Cairo (Maspiro); tel. (2) 5748984; fax (2) 5748981; e-mail rtu@idsc.gov.eg; internet www.minfo.gov.eg.

Ministry of Insurance and Social Affairs: Sharia Sheikh Rihan, Bab el-Louk, Cairo; tel. (2) 3370039; fax (2) 3375390; e-mail msi@idsc.gov.eg; internet www.misaegy.com.

Ministry of the Interior: Sharia Sheikh Rihan, Bab el-Louk, Cairo; tel. (2) 3557500; fax (2) 5792031; e-mail moi2@idsc.gov.eg.

Ministry of Investment: 2 Sharia Latin America, Cairo (Garden City); tel. (2) 7959287; fax (2) 7959233; e-mail investment@investment.gov.eg; internet www.investment.gov.eg.

Ministry of Irrigation and Water Resources: Sharia Corniche en-Nil, Imbaba, Cairo; tel. (2) 5449440; fax (2) 5449410; e-mail minister@mwri.gov.eg; internet www.mwri.gov.eg.

Ministry of Justice: Justice and Finance Bldg, Sharia Majlis ash-Sha'ab, Lazoughli Sq., Cairo; tel. (2) 7951176; fax (2) 7955700; e-mail mojeb@idsc1.gov.eg.

Ministry of Labour and Migration: 96 Sharia Ahmad Orabi, Mohandessin, Embaba, Cairo; tel. (2) 3034438; fax (2) 3035332; e-mail info@mome.gov.eg; internet www.emigration.gov.eg.

Ministry of Military Production: 5 Sharia Ismail Abaza, Qasr el-Eini, Cairo; tel. (2) 3552428; fax (2) 3548739.

Ministry of Parliamentary Affairs: Sharia Majlis ash-Sha'ab, Lazoughli Sq., Cairo; tel. (2) 3557750; fax (2) 3557681.

Ministry of Petroleum: Sharia el-Mokhayem ed-Dayem, Cairo (Nasr City); tel. (2) 2626060; fax (2) 2636060; e-mail info-emp@emp.gov.eg; internet www.emp.gov.eg.

Ministry of Planning: Sharia Salah Salem, Cairo (Nasr City); tel. (2) 4014615; fax (2) 4014733; e-mail contact_mop@hotmail.co.uk; internet www.mop.gov.eg.

Ministry of Public Enterprise: Sharia Majlis ash-Sha'ab, Lazoughli Sq., Cairo; tel. (2) 3558026; fax (2) 3555882; e-mail mops@idsc.gov.eg; internet www.mpe-egypt.gov.eg.

Ministry of State for Administrative Development: Sharia Salah Salem, Cairo (Nasr City); tel. (2) 4022910; fax (2) 2614126.

Ministry of State for Environmental Affairs: 30 Sharia Helwan, Cairo; tel. (2) 5256452; fax (2) 5256490; e-mail eeaa@eeaa.gov.eg; internet www.eeaa.gov.eg.

Ministry of State for Local Development: Sharia Nadi es-Seid, Cairo (Dokki); tel. (2) 3497470; fax (2) 3497788; internet www.mld.gov.eg.

Ministry of Supply and Internal Trade: 99 Sharia Qasr el-Eini, Cairo; tel. (2) 3557598; fax (2) 3544973; e-mail msit@idsc.gov.eg.

Ministry of Tourism: Misr Travel Tower, Abbassia Sq., Cairo; tel. (2) 2828439; fax (2) 2859551; e-mail wwebmaster@visitegypt.gov.eg; internet www.visitegypt.gov.eg.

Ministry of Transport: 105 Sharia Qasr el-Eini, Cairo; tel. (2) 3555566; fax (2) 3555564; e-mail garb@idsc.gov.eg.

Legislature

MAJLIS ASH-SHA'AB
(People's Assembly)

There are 222 constituencies, which each elect two deputies to the Assembly. Ten deputies are appointed by the President, giving a total of 454 seats.

Speaker: Dr Ahmad Fathi Surur.

Deputy Speakers: Dr Abd al-Ahad Gamal ad-Din, Ahmad Abu Zeid, Dr Amal Uthman.

Elections, 18 and 29 October and 8 November 2000

	Seats
National Democratic Party*	353
New Wafd Party	7
National Progressive Unionist Party	6
Nasserist Party	3
Liberal Socialist Party	1
Independents	72
Total†	**442‡**

* Official candidates of the National Democratic Party (NDP) won 353 seats in the three rounds of voting. However, after the elections it was reported that 35 of the 72 candidates who had successfully contested the elections as independents had either joined or rejoined the NDP.

† There are, in addition, 10 deputies appointed by the President.

‡ The results for two seats in one constituency in Alexandria were annulled by a court ruling; elections were reheld there in mid-2002.

MAJLIS ASH-SHURA
(Advisory Council)

In September 1980 elections were held for a 210-member **Shura (Advisory) Council**, which replaced the former Central Committee of the Arab Socialist Union. Of the total number of members, 140 were elected and the remaining 70 appointed by the President. The opposition parties boycotted elections to the Council in October 1983, and again in October 1986, in protest against the 8% electoral threshold. In June 1989 elections to 153 of the Council's 210 seats were contested by opposition parties (the 'Islamic Alliance', consisting of the Muslim Brotherhood, the LSP and the SLP). However, all of the seats in which voting produced a result (143) were won by the NDP. NDP candidates won 88 of the 90 seats on the Council to which mid-term elections were held in June 1995. The remaining two elective seats were gained by independent candidates. On 21 June new appointments were made to 47 vacant, non-elective seats. Partial elections to the Council were held again in June 1998. The NDP won 85 of the 88 contested seats, while independent candidates won the remaining three seats. Most opposition parties chose not to contest the elections. In partial elections to the Council, held on 16 and 22 May 2001, the NDP won 74 of the 88 contested seats, while independent candidates won the remaining 14 seats. Further partial elections took place to the 264-member Council between 23 May and 19 June 2004, with the NDP winning 70 of the 88 seats contested and 17 of the remaining seats being taken by NDP members who had stood as independents; one seat was won by the National Progressive Unionist Party. A further 44 members of the Council were appointed by the President, so that one-half of its membership had been renewed or replaced.

Speaker: Muhammad Safwat esh-Sherif.

Deputy Speakers: Abderrahman Farag Mohsen, Muhammad Morsi.

Political Organizations

Democratic People's Party: f. 1992; Chair. Anwar Afifi.

Democratic Unionist Party: f. 1990; Pres. Ibrahim Abd al-Moneim Turk.

Al-Ghad (Tomorrow): f. 2004; aims to combat poverty and to improve the living conditions of Egypt's citizens; Founder Ayman an-Nour.

Green Party: e-mail awad@egyptiangreens.com; internet www.egyptiangreens.com; f. 1990; Pres. Dr Abd al-Moneim el-Asar; Gen. Sec. Muhammad Awad.

Hizb al-Wifaq al-Qawmi (National Accord Party): f. 2000.

Liberal Socialist Party (LSP): Cairo; f. 1976; advocates expansion of 'open door' economic policy and greater freedom for private enterprise and the press; Leader (vacant).

Misr el-Fatah (Young Egypt Party): f. 1990; Chair. Gamal Rabie.

Nasserist Party: Cairo; f. 1991; Chair. Diaa ed-Din Daoud.

National Democratic Party (NDP): Cairo; internet www.ndp.org.eg; f. 1978; government party established by Anwar Sadat; absorbed Arab Socialist Party; Leader Muhammad Hosni Mubarak; Sec.-Gen. Muhammad Safwat esh-Sharif; Political Bureau: Chair. Muhammad Hosni Mubarak.

National Progressive Unionist Party (Tagammu): 1 Sharia Karim ed-Dawlah, Cairo; f. 1976; left-wing; Leader Khaled Mohi ed-Din; Sec. Dr Rifa'at es-Said; 160,000 mems.

New Wafd Party (The Delegation): Cairo; internet www.alwafd.org; original Wafd Party; f. 1919; banned 1952; re-formed as New

Wafd Party Feb. 1978; disbanded June 1978; re-formed 1983; Leader NU'MAN JUM'AH; Sec.-Gen. IBRAHIM FARAG.

Social Justice Party: f. 1993; Chair. MUHAMMAD ABD AL-AAL.

Socialist Labour Party (SLP): 12 Sharia Awali el-Ahd, Cairo; f. 1978; official opposition party; pro-Islamist; Leader IBRAHIM SHUKRI.

Et-Takaful (Solidarity): f. 1995; advocates imposition of 'solidarity' tax on the rich in order to provide for the needs of the poor; Chair. Dr USAMA MUHAMMAD SHALTOUT.

The following organizations are proscribed by the Government:

Islamic Jihad (al-Jihad—Holy Struggle): militant Islamist grouping established following the imposition of a ban on the Muslim Brotherhood; Leader Dr AYMAN AZ-ZAWAHIRI.

Jama'ah al-Islamiyah (Islamic Group): militant Islamist group founded following the imposition of a ban on the Muslim Brotherhood; declared a cease-fire in March 1999; Spiritual Leader Sheikh OMAR ABD AR-RAHMAN; Chair. of the Shura Council MOUSTAFA HAMZAH; Mil. Cmmdr ALA ABD AR-RAQIL.

Muslim Brotherhood (Ikhwan al-Muslimun): internet www .ummah.org.uk/ikhwan; f. 1928, with the aim of establishing an Islamic society; banned in 1954; moderate; advocates the adoption of the *Shari'a*, or Islamic law, as the sole basis of the Egyptian legal system; Supreme Guide MUHAMMAD MAHDI AKIF.

Vanguards of Conquest: militant Islamist grouping; breakaway group from Islamic Jihad; Leader YASIR AS-SIRRI.

Diplomatic Representation

EMBASSIES IN EGYPT

Afghanistan: 59 Sharia el-Orouba, Cairo (Heliopolis); tel. (2) 4177236; fax (2) 4177238; Ambassador Dr M. RAHIM SHERZOY.

Albania: 29 Sharia Ismail Muhammad, Cairo (Zamalek); tel. (2) 3415651; fax (2) 3413732; Ambassador ARBEN PANDI CICI.

Algeria: 14 Sharia Bresil, Cairo (Zamalek); tel. (2) 3418527; fax (2) 3414158; Ambassador ABDELKADER HAGAR.

Angola: 12 Midan Fouad Mohi ed-Din, Mohandessin, Cairo; tel. (2) 3377602; fax (2) 708683; Ambassador HERMINO JOAQUIM ESCORCIO.

Argentina: 1st Floor, 8 Sharia es-Saleh Ayoub, Cairo (Zamalek); tel. (2) 7351501; fax (2) 7364355; e-mail argemb@idsc.gov.eg; Ambassador OSVALDO SANTIAGO PASCUAL.

Armenia: 20 Sharia Muhammad Mazhar, Cairo (Zamalek); tel. (2) 7374157; fax (2) 7374158; e-mail armenemb@idsc.gov.eg; Ambassador SERGEI MANASSARIAN.

Australia: 11th Floor, World Trade Centre, Corniche en-Nil, Cairo 11111 (Boulac); tel. (2) 5750444; fax (2) 5781638; e-mail cairo .austremb@dfat.gov.au; Ambassador VICTORIA OWEN.

Austria: 5th Floor, Riyadh Tower, 5 Sharia Wissa Wassef, cnr of Sharia en-Nil, Cairo 11111 (Giza); tel. (2) 5702975; fax (2) 5702979; e-mail aec@gega.net; Ambassador FERDINAND TRAUTTMANSDORFF.

Azerbaijan: 22 Sharia Hassan Assem, Cairo (Zamalek); tel. (2) 7351230; fax (2) 7351228; e-mail alakhv@link.com.eg; Ambassador FAIG BAGIROV.

Bahrain: 15 Sharia Bresil, Cairo (Zamalek); tel. (2) 3407996; fax (2) 3416609; Ambassador KHALIL IBRAHIM AZ-ZAWI.

Bangladesh: 47 Sharia Ahmad Heshmat, Cairo (Zamalek); tel. (2) 3412645; fax (2) 3402401; e-mail bdoot@wnet1.worldnet.com.eg; Ambassador RUHUL AMIN.

Belarus: 19–1 Sharia Muhammad el-Ghazali, Cairo (Dokki); tel. (2) 3375782; fax (2) 3375845; Ambassador IGOR LESHCHENYA.

Belgium: POB 37, 20 Sharia Kamal esh-Shennawi, Cairo 11511 (Garden City); tel. (2) 7947494; fax (2) 7943147; e-mail cairo@ diplobel.org; Ambassador PAUL PONJAERT.

Bolivia: 2 Sharia Hod el-Labban, Cairo (Garden City); tel. (2) 3546390; fax (2) 3550917; Ambassador HERNANDO VELASCO.

Bosnia and Herzegovina: 42 Sharia Sawra, Cairo (Dokki); tel. (2) 7499191; fax (2) 7499190; e-mail ambbih@link.net; Ambassador RADOMIR KOSIĆ.

Brazil: 1125 Corniche en-Nil, Cairo 11221 (Maspiro); tel. (2) 5773013; fax (2) 5774860; e-mail brasemb@soficom.com.eg; internet www.brazilembcairo.org; Ambassador ELIM SATURNINO FERREIRA DUTRA.

Brunei: 24 Sharia Hassan Assem, Cairo (Zamalek); tel. (2) 7360097; fax (2) 7386375; e-mail ebdic@mail.link.net; Ambassador Dato' Paduka Haji ALI BIN HAJI HASSAN.

Bulgaria: 6 Sharia el-Malek el-Ajdal, Cairo (Zamalek); tel. (2) 7363025; fax (2) 7363826; e-mail bulembcai@link.net; Ambassador ALEXANDAR OLSHEVSKI.

Burkina Faso: POB 306, Ramses Centre, 9 Sharia el-Fawakeh, Mohandessin, Cairo; tel. (2) 3758956; fax (2) 3756974; Ambassador SOPHIE SOW.

Burundi: 22 Sharia en-Nakhil, Madinet ed-Dobbat, Cairo (Dokki); tel. (2) 3373078; fax (2) 3378431; Ambassador GERVAIS NDIKUMAGNEGE.

Cambodia: 2 Sharia Tahawia, Cairo (Giza); tel. (2) 3489966; Ambassador IN SOPHEAP.

Cameroon: POB 2061, 15 Sharia Muhammad Sedki Soliman, Mohandessin, Cairo; tel. (2) 3441101; fax (2) 3459208; Ambassador MOUCHILI NJI MFOUAYO ISMAILA.

Canada: POB 1667, 6 Sharia Muhammad Fahmi es-Said, Cairo (Garden City); tel. (2) 7943110; fax (2) 7963548; e-mail cairo@ dfait-maeci.gc.ca; Ambassador PHILIP MACKINNON.

Central African Republic: 41 Sharia Mahmoud Azmy, Mohandessin, Cairo (Dokki); tel. (2) 3446873; Ambassador HENRY KOBA.

Chad: POB 1869, 12 Midan ar-Refaï, Cairo 11511 (Dokki); tel. (2) 3373379; fax (2) 3373232; Ambassador AMIN ABBA SIDICK.

Chile: El-Asmak Bldg, 1 Sharia Saleh Ayoub, Cairo (Zamalek); tel. (2) 7358711; fax (2) 7353716; e-mail embchile@link.net; Ambassador SAMUEL FERNÁNDEZ ILLAMES.

China, People's Republic: 14 Sharia Bahgat Ali, Cairo (Zamalek); tel. (2) 3411219; fax (2) 3409459; e-mail chinaemb@idsc.gov.eg; Ambassador WU SIKE.

Colombia: 6 Sharia Gueriza, Cairo (Zamalek); tel. (2) 3414203; fax (2) 3407429; e-mail colombemb@idsc.gov.eg; Ambassador JAIME GIRÓN DUARTE.

Congo, Democratic Republic: 5 Sharia Mansour Muhammad, Cairo (Zamalek); tel. (2) 3403662; fax (2) 3404342; Ambassador KAMIMBAYA WA DJONDO.

Côte d'Ivoire: 9 ave Shehab, rue Abdel Meguid Omar Mohandessine, Cairo; tel. (2) 3034373; fax (2) 3050148; e-mail ambaci@access .com.eg; internet www.ambaci-egypte.org; Ambassador KONAN N. MARCEL.

Croatia: 3 Sharia Abou el-Feda, Cairo (Zamalek); tel. (2) 7383155; fax (2) 7355812; e-mail croem@soficom.com.eg; Ambassador Dr IVICA TOMIĆ.

Cuba: Apartment 1, 13th Floor, 14 Sharia Kamel Muhammad, Cairo (Zamalek); tel. (2) 7360651; fax (2) 7360656; e-mail cubaemb@ link.net; Ambassador LUIS E. MARISY FIGUEREDO.

Cyprus: 17 Sharia Omar Tosson, Ahmed Orabi, Mohandessin, Cairo; tel. (2) 3455967; fax (2) 3455969; Ambassador PHAEDON ANASTASIOU.

Czech Republic: 1st Floor, 4 Sharia Dokki, Cairo 12511 (Giza); tel. (2) 7485759; fax (2) 7485892; e-mail cairo@embassy.mzv.cz; internet www.mfa.cz/cairo; Ambassador JAKUB KARFÍK.

Denmark: 12 Sharia Hassan Sabri, Cairo 11211 (Zamalek); tel. (2) 7396500; fax (2) 7396588; e-mail caiamb@um.dk; internet www .danemb.org.eg; Ambassador CHRISTIAN OLDENBURG.

Djibouti: 11 Sharia el-Gazaer, Aswan Sq., Cairo (Agouza); tel. (2) 3456546; fax (2) 3456549; Ambassador Sheikh MOUSSA MOHAMED AHMED.

Ecuador: Suez Canal Bldg, 4 Sharia Ibn Kasir, Cairo (Giza); tel. (2) 3496782; fax (2) 3609327; e-mail ecuademb@idsc.gov.eg; Ambassador FRANKLIN BAHAMONDE.

Ethiopia: 6 Sharia Abd ar-Rahman Hussein, Midan Gomhuria, Cairo (Dokki); tel. (2) 3353696; fax (2) 3353699; Ambassador GIRMA AMARE.

Finland: 13th Floor, 3 Sharia Abou el-Feda, 11511 Cairo (Zamalek); tel. (2) 7363722; fax (2) 7355170; e-mail fincairo@access.com.eg; internet www.finemb.org.eg; Ambassador HANNU MÄNTYVAARA.

France: POB 1777, 29 Sharia Giza, Cairo (Giza); tel. (2) 5703916; fax (2) 5710276; e-mail info@ambafrance-eg.org; internet www .diplo-france.org.eg; Ambassador JEAN-CLAUDE COUSSERAN.

Gabon: 17 Sharia Mecca el-Moukarama, Cairo (Dokki); tel. (2) 3379699; Ambassador JOSEPH MAMBOUNGOU.

Georgia: 28 Sharia Sad el-Aali, Cairo (Dokki); tel. (2) 3359024; fax (2) 3366129; e-mail geoembeg@link.com.eg; Ambassador APOLON SILAGADZE.

Germany: 8B Sharia Berlin (off Sharia Hassan Sabri), Cairo (Zamalek); tel. (2) 7399600; fax (2) 7360530; e-mail germemb@ tedata.net; internet www.cairo.diplo.de; Ambassador MARTIN KOBLER.

Ghana: 1 Sharia 26 July, Cairo (Zamalek); tel. (2) 3444455; fax (2) 3032292; Ambassador BON OHANE KWAPONG.

Greece: 18 Sharia Aicha at-Taimouria, Cairo (Garden City); tel. (2) 3551074; fax (2) 3563903; Ambassador PANAYOTIS VLASSOPOULOS.

Guatemala: POB 346, 11 Sharia 10, Maadi, Cairo; tel. (2) 3802914; fax (2) 3802915; e-mail guatemb@infinity.com.eg; Ambassador FLOR-IDALMA FRANCO PAIZ.

Guinea: 46 Sharia Muhammad Mazhar, Cairo (Zamalek); tel. (2) 7358109; fax (2) 7361446; Ambassador el Hadj OUSMANE CAMARA.

Guinea-Bissau: 37 Sharia Lebanon, Madinet el-Mohandessin, Cairo (Dokki).

Holy See: Apostolic Nunciature, Safarat al-Vatican, 5 Sharia Muhammad Mazhar, Cairo (Zamalek); tel. (2) 7352250; fax (2) 7356152; e-mail nunteg@yahoo.com; Apostolic Nuncio Most Rev. MARCO DINO BROGI (Titular Archbishop of Citta Ducale).

Honduras: 21 Sharia Aicha at-Taimouria, Cairo (Garden City); tel. (2) 3409510; fax (2) 3413835.

Hungary: 29 Sharia Muhammad Mazhar, Cairo (Zamalek); tel. (2) 7358659; fax (2) 7358648; e-mail huembcai@soficom.com.eg; Ambassador LÁSZLÓ KÁDÁR.

India: 5 Sharia Aziz Abaza, Cairo (Zamalek); tel. (2) 7360052; fax (2) 7364038; e-mail embassy@indembcairo.org; internet www .indembcairo.org; Ambassador R. SINGH; also looks after Iraqi interests at 5 Sharia Aziz Abaza, Cairo (Zamalek) (tel. (2) 3409815).

Indonesia: POB 1661, 13 Sharia Aicha at-Taimouria, Cairo (Garden City); tel. (2) 3547200; fax (2) 3562495; Ambassador Dr BOER MAUNA.

Iraq: Cairo; tel. (2) 7359815; fax (2) 7366956; e-mail caiemb@ iraqmofa.net; Ambassador SAFIYA AS-SUHAIL.

Ireland: POB 2681, 3 Sharia Abou el-Feda, Cairo (Zamalek); tel. (2) 7358264; fax (2) 7362863; e-mail irishemb@rite.com; Ambassador RICHARD O'BRIEN.

Israel: 6 Sharia Ibn el-Malek, Cairo (Giza); tel. (2) 7610380; fax (2) 7610414; Ambassador SHALOM COHEN.

Italy: 15 Sharia Abd ar-Rahman Fahmi, Cairo (Garden City); tel. (2) 7943194; fax (2) 7940657; e-mail ambcairo@brainy1.ie-eg.com; internet www.italembassy.org.eg; Ambassador ANTONIO BANDINI.

Japan: Cairo Centre Bldg, 2nd and 3rd Floors, 2 Sharia Abd al-Kader Hamza or 106 Sharia Qasr el-Eini, Cairo (Garden City); tel. (2) 7953962; fax (2) 7963540; e-mail center@embjapan.org.eg; internet www.mofa.go.jp/embjapan/egypt; Ambassador KUNIHIKO MAKITA.

Jordan: 6 Sharia Juhaini, Cairo; tel. (2) 3485566; fax (2) 3601027; Ambassador (vacant).

Kazakhstan: 4 Sharia Abay Kunanbayuli, New Maadi, Cairo; tel. and fax (2) 5194522; e-mail kazaemb@ids.gov.eg; Ambassador BOLAT-KHAN K. TAIZHANOV.

Kenya: POB 362, 7 Sharia el-Mohandes Galal, Cairo (Dokki); tel. (2) 3453628; fax (2) 3443400; Ambassador MUHAMMAD M. MAALIM.

Korea, Democratic People's Republic: 6 Sharia as-Saleh Ayoub, Cairo (Zamalek); tel. (2) 3408219; fax (2) 3414615; Ambassador JANG MYONG SON.

Korea, Republic: 3 Sharia Boulos Hanna, Cairo (Dokki); tel. (2) 3611234; fax (2) 3611238; Ambassador SHIM KYOUNG-BO.

Kuwait: 12 Sharia Nabil el-Wakkad, Cairo (Dokki); tel. (2) 3602661; fax (2) 3602657; Ambassador AHMED KHALID AL-KOLAIB.

Lebanon: 22 Sharia Mansour Muhammad, Cairo (Zamalek); tel. (2) 7382823; fax (2) 7382818; Ambassador ABDULLATIF MAMLOUK, (vacant).

Lesotho: 10 Sharia Bahr al-Ghazal, Sahafeyeen, Cairo; tel. (2) 3447025; fax (2) 3025495.

Liberia: 11 Sharia Bresil, Cairo (Zamalek); tel. (2) 3419864; fax (2) 3473074; Ambassador Dr BRAHIMA D. KABA.

Libya: 7 Sharia as-Saleh Ayoub, Cairo (Zamalek); tel. (2) 3401864; Ambassador SALEH OMAR AD-DAROUKI.

Lithuania: Cairo.

Malaysia: 29 Sharia Taha Hussein, Cairo (Zamalek); tel. (2) 3410863; fax (2) 3411049; Ambassador Dato RAJA MANSUR RAZMAN.

Mali: 3 Sharia al-Kawsar, Cairo (Dokki); tel. (2) 3371641; fax (2) 3371841; Ambassador MAMADOU KABA.

Malta: 25 Sharia 12, Maadi, Cairo; tel. (2) 3804451; fax (2) 3804452; e-mail maltaemb@link.net; Ambassador GAETAN NAUDI ACIS.

Mauritania: 114 Mohi ed-Din, Abou-el Ezz, Mohandessin, Cairo; tel. (2) 3490671; fax (2) 3489060; Ambassador MUHAMMAD LEMINE OULD.

Mauritius: 156 Sharia es-Sudan, Mohandessin, Cairo; tel. (2) 7618102; fax (2) 7618101; e-mail embamaur@thewayout.net; Ambassador SOOROOJDEV PHOKEER.

Mexico: 5th Floor, 17 Sharia Port Said, 11431 Cairo (Maadi); tel. (2) 3500258; fax (2) 3591887; e-mail oficial@embamexcairo.com; internet www.sre.gob.mx/egipto; Ambassador MIGUEL ANGEL OROZCO DEZA.

Mongolia: 3 Midan en-Nasr, Cairo (Dokki); tel. (2) 3460670; Ambassador SONOMDORJIN DAMBADARJAA.

Morocco: 10 Sharia Salah ed-Din, Cairo (Zamalek); tel. (2) 3409849; fax (2) 3411937; e-mail morocemb@idsc.gov.eg; Ambassador MUHAMMAD FARAJ EDOUKALI.

Mozambique: 9th Floor, 3 Sharia Abu el-Feda, Cairo (Zamalek); tel. (2) 3320647; fax (2) 3320383; e-mail emozcai@intouch.com; Ambassador DANIEL EDUARDO MONDLANE.

Myanmar: 24 Sharia Muhammad Mazhar, Cairo (Zamalek); tel. (2) 3404176; fax (2) 3416793; Ambassador U AUNG GYI.

Nepal: 9 Sharia Tiba, Madinet el-Kobah, Cairo (Dokki); tel. (2) 3603426; fax (2) 704447; Ambassador JITENDRA RAJ SHARMA.

Netherlands: 18 Sharia Hassan Sabri, Cairo (Zamalek); tel. (2) 7395500; fax (2) 7365349; e-mail az-cz@hollandemb.org.eg; internet www.hollandemb.org.eg; Ambassador TJEERD DE ZWAAN.

Niger: 101 Sharia Pyramids, Cairo (Giza); tel. (2) 3865607; Ambassador MOULOUD AL-HOUSSEINI.

Nigeria: 13 Sharia Gabalaya, Cairo (Zamalek); tel. (2) 3406042; fax (2) 3403907; Ambassador MOHAMMED GHALI OMAR.

Norway: 8 Sharia el-Gezirah, Cairo (Zamalek); tel. (2) 7353340; fax (2) 7370709; e-mail embcai@mfa.no; internet www.norway.org.eg; Ambassador BJØRN FRODE ØSTERN.

Oman: 52 Sharia el-Higaz, Mohandessin, Cairo; tel. (2) 3036011; fax (2) 3036464; Ambassador ABDULLAH BIN HAMED AL-BUSAIDI.

Pakistan: 8 Sharia es-Salouli, Cairo (Dokki); tel. (2) 7487806; fax (2) 7480310; Ambassador AREF AYUB.

Panama: POB 62, 4A Sharia Ibn Zanki, 11211 Cairo (Zamalek); tel. (2) 3400784; fax (2) 3411092; Chargé d'affaires a.i. ROY FRANCISCO LUNA GONZÁLEZ.

Peru: 8 Sharia Kamel esh-Shenawi, Cairo (Garden City); tel. (2) 3562973; fax (2) 3557985; Ambassador MANUEL VERAMENDI I. SERRA.

Philippines: 14 Sharia Muhammad Saleh, Cairo (Dokki); tel. (2) 7480396; fax (2) 7480393; e-mail cairope@dfa.gov.ph; Ambassador PETRNIL P. GARCIA.

Poland: 5 Sharia el-Aziz Osman, Cairo (Zamalek); tel. (2) 7367456; fax (2) 7355427; e-mail secretary@bolanda.org; internet www .bolanda.org; Ambassador JAN NATKAŃSKI.

Portugal: 1 Sharia es-Saleh Ayoub, Cairo (Zamalek); tel. (2) 7350779; fax (2) 7350790; e-mail embpcai@link.com.eg; Ambassador FERNANDO RAMOS MACHADO.

Qatar: 10 Sharia ath-Thamar, Midan an-Nasr, Madinet al-Mohandessin, Cairo; tel. (2) 3604693; fax (2) 3603618; Ambassador BADIR AD-DAFA.

Romania: 6 El-Kamel Muhammad, Cairo (Zamalek); tel. (2) 7360107; fax (2) 7360851; e-mail roembegy@link.net; Ambassador MARCEL DINU.

Russia: 95 Sharia Giza, Cairo (Giza); tel. (2) 3489353; fax (2) 3609074; Ambassador MIKHAIL BOGDANOV.

Rwanda: 23 Sharia Babel, Mohandessin, Cairo (Dokki); tel. (2) 3350532; fax (2) 3351479; Ambassador CÉLESTIN KABANDA.

San Marino: 5 Sharia Ramez, Mohandessin, Cairo; tel. (2) 3602718.

Saudi Arabia: 2 Sharia Ahmad Nessim, Cairo (Giza); tel. (2) 3490775; Ambassador ASSAD ABD AL-KAREM ABOU AN-NASR.

Senegal: 46 Sharia Abd al-Moneim Riad, Mohandessin, Cairo (Dokki); tel. (2) 3460946; fax (2) 3461039; Ambassador MAMADOU SOW.

Serbia and Montenegro: 33 Sharia Mansour Muhammad, Cairo (Zamalek); tel. (2) 3404061; fax (2) 3403913; Ambassador Dr IVAN IVEKOVIĆ.

Sierra Leone: *Interests served by Saudi Arabia.*

Singapore: 40 Sharia Babel, Cairo (Dokki); tel. (2) 7490468; fax (2) 7481682; e-mail singemb@link.com.eg; Ambassador TEE TUA BA.

Slovakia: 3 Sharia Adel Hussein Rostom, Dokki, Cairo (Giza); tel. (2) 3358240; fax (2) 3355810; e-mail zukahira@tedata.net.eg; Ambassador JOZEF CIBULA.

Slovenia: 5 es-Saraya el-Kobra Sq., Cairo (Garden City); tel. (2) 3555798; Ambassador ANDREJ ZLEBNIK.

Somalia: 27 Sharia es-Somal, Cairo (Dokki), Giza; tel. (2) 3374577; Ambassador ABDALLA HASSAN MAHMOUD.

South Africa: 18th Floor, Nile Tower Bldg, 21–23 Sharia Giza, Cairo (Giza); tel. (2) 5717238; fax (2) 5717241; e-mail saembcai@gega .net; Ambassador JUSTUS DE GOEDE.

Spain: 41 Sharia Ismail Muhammad, Cairo (Zamalek); tel. (2) 7356462; fax (2) 7352132; e-mail spainemb@startnet.com; Ambassador PEDRO LÓPEZ AGUIRREBENGOA.

Sri Lanka: POB 1157, 8 Sharia Sri Lanka, Cairo (Zamalek); tel. (2) 7350047; fax (2) 7367138; e-mail slembare@menanet.net; internet www.lankaemb-egypt.com; Ambassador W. HETTIARACHCHI.

Sudan: 4 Sharia el-Ibrahimi, Cairo (Garden City); tel. (2) 3545043; fax (2) 3542693; Ambassador MUHAMMAD HASSAN AL-HAJ.

Sweden: POB 131, 13 Sharia Muhammad Mazhar, Cairo (Zamalek); tel. (2) 3414132; fax (2) 3404357; e-mail sveamcai@link .com.eg; Ambassador CHRISTER SYLVÉN.

Switzerland: POB 633, 10 Sharia Abd al-Khalek Sarwat, Cairo; tel. (2) 5758284; fax (2) 5745236; e-mail vertretung@cai.rep.admin.ch; Ambassador BLAISE GODET.

Syria: 18 Sharia Abd ar-Rehim Sabry, POB 435, Cairo (Dokki); tel. (2) 3358806; fax (2) 3377020; Ambassador YUSUF AL-AHMAD.

Tanzania: 9 Sharia Abd al-Hamid Lotfi, Cairo (Dokki); tel. (2) 704155; Ambassador MUHAMMAD A. FOUM.

Thailand: 2 9 Sharia Tibba, Cairo (Zamalek); tel. (2) 76035533; fax (2) 7605076; e-mail royalthai@link.net; Ambassador CHARINAT SANTA-PUTRA.

Tunisia: 26 Sharia el-Jazirah, Cairo (Zamalek); tel. (2) 3418962; Ambassador CHEDLY NEFFATI.

Turkey: 25 Sharia Felaki, Cairo (Bab el-Louk); tel. (2) 3563318; fax (2) 3558110; Ambassador YAŞAR YAKIŞ.

Uganda: 9 Midan el-Messaha, Cairo (Dokki); tel. (2) 3486070; fax (2) 3485980; Ambassador IBRAHIM MUKIIBI.

Ukraine: 9 Sharia es-Saraya, Appt 31–32, Cairo (Dokki); tel. (2) 3491030; fax (2) 3360159; e-mail vlost@eis.com.eg; Ambassador ANDRIY VESELOVSKY.

United Arab Emirates: 4 Sharia Ibn Sina, Cairo (Giza); tel. (2) 3609721; e-mail uaeembassyca@online.com.eg; Ambassador AHMAD AL-MAHMOUD MUHAMMAD.

United Kingdom: 17 Sharia Ahmad Ragheb, Cairo (Garden City); tel. (2) 7940852; fax (2) 7940859; e-mail info@britishembassy.org.eg; internet www.britishembassy.org.eg; Ambassador DEREK PLUMBLY.

USA: 5 Sharia Latin America, Cairo (Garden City); tel. (2) 7973300; fax (2) 7973200; internet usembassy.egnet.net; Ambassador C. DAVID WELCH.

Uruguay: 6 Sharia Lotfallah, Cairo (Zamalek); tel. (2) 3415137; fax (2) 3418123; Ambassador JULIO CÉSAR FRANZINI.

Venezuela: 15A Sharia Mansour Muhammad, Cairo (Zamalek); tel. (2) 3413517; fax (2) 3417373; e-mail eov@idsc.gov.eg; Ambassador DARIO BAUDER.

Viet Nam: 39 Sharia Kambiz, Cairo (Dokki); tel. (2) 3371494; fax (2) 3496597; Ambassador DUONG HUYNH LAP.

Yemen: 28 Sharia Amean ar-Rafai, Cairo (Dokki); tel. (2) 3614224; fax (2) 3604815; Ambassador ABD AL-GHALIL GHILAN AHMAD.

Zambia: 6 Abd ar-Rahman Hussein, Mohandessin, Cairo (Dokki); tel. (2) 7610282; fax (2) 7610833; Ambassador Dr ANGEL ALFRED MWENDA.

Zimbabwe: 40 Sharia Ghaza, Mohandessin, Cairo; tel. (2) 3030404; fax (2) 3059741; e-mail zimcairo@thewayout.net; Ambassador Dr HENRY V. MOYANA.

Judicial System

The Courts of Law in Egypt are principally divided into two juridical court systems: Courts of General Jurisdiction and Administrative Courts. Since 1969 the Supreme Constitutional Court has been at the top of the Egyptian judicial structure.

THE SUPREME CONSTITUTIONAL COURT

The Supreme Constitutional Court is the highest court in Egypt. It has specific jurisdiction over: (i) judicial review of the constitutionality of laws and regulations; (ii) resolution of positive and negative jurisdictional conflicts and determination of the competent court between the different juridical court systems, e.g. Courts of General Jurisdiction and Administrative Courts, as well as other bodies exercising judicial competence; (iii) determination of disputes over the enforcement of two final but contradictory judgments rendered by two courts each belonging to a different juridical court system; (iv)

rendering binding interpretation of laws or decree laws in the event of a dispute in the application of said laws or decree laws, always provided that such a dispute is of a gravity requiring conformity of interpretation under the Constitution.

COURTS OF GENERAL JURISDICTION

The Courts of General Jurisdiction in Egypt are effectively divided into four categories, as follows: (i) The Court of Cassation; (ii) The Courts of Appeal; (iii) The Tribunals of First Instance; (iv) The District Tribunals; each of the above courts is divided into Civil and Criminal Chambers.

Court of Cassation

Is the highest court of general jurisdiction in Egypt. Its sessions are held in Cairo. Final judgments rendered by Courts of Appeal in criminal and civil litigation may be petitioned to the Court of Cassation by the Defendant or the Public Prosecutor in criminal litigation and by any of the parties in interest in civil litigation on grounds of defective application or interpretation of the law as stated in the challenged judgment, on grounds of irregularity of form or procedure, or violation of due process, and on grounds of defective reasoning of judgment rendered. The Court of Cassation is composed of the President, 41 Vice-Presidents and 92 Justices.

President: Hon. FATHI KHALIFA.

The Courts of Appeal: Each has geographical jurisdiction over one or more of the governorates of Egypt. Each Court of Appeal is divided into Criminal and Civil Chambers. The Criminal Chambers try felonies, and the Civil Chambers hear appeals filed against such judgment rendered by the Tribunals of First Instance where the law so stipulates. Each Chamber is composed of three Superior Judges. Each Court of Appeal is composed of President, and sufficient numbers of Vice-Presidents and Superior Judges.

The Tribunals of First Instance: In each governorate there are one or more Tribunals of First Instance, each of which is divided into several Chambers for criminal and civil litigations. Each Chamber is composed of: (a) a presiding judge, and (b) two sitting judges. A Tribunal of First Instance hears, as an Appellate Court, certain litigations as provided under the law.

District Tribunals: Each is a one-judge ancillary Chamber of a Tribunal of First Instance, having jurisdiction over minor civil and criminal litigations in smaller districts within the jurisdiction of such Tribunal of First Instance.

PUBLIC PROSECUTION

Public prosecution is headed by the Attorney-General, assisted by a number of Senior Deputy and Deputy Attorneys-General, and a sufficient number of chief prosecutors, prosecutors and assistant prosecutors. Public prosecution is represented at all levels of the Courts of General Jurisdiction in all criminal litigations and also in certain civil litigations as required by the law. Public prosecution controls and supervises enforcement of criminal law judgments.

Attorney-General: MAHIR ABD AL-WAHID.

Prosecutor-General: MUHAMMAD ABD AL-AZIZ EL-GINDI.

ADMINISTRATIVE COURTS SYSTEM (CONSEIL D'ETAT)

The Administrative Courts have jurisdiction over litigations involving the State or any of its governmental agencies. The Administrative Courts system is divided into two courts: the Administrative Courts and the Judicial Administrative Courts, at the top of which is the High Administrative Court. The Administrative Prosecutor investigates administrative crimes committed by government officials and civil servants.

President of Conseil d'Etat: Hon. MUHAMMAD HILAL QASIM.

Administrative Prosecutor: Hon. RIFA'AT KHAFAGI.

THE STATE COUNCIL

The State Council is an independent judicial body which has the authority to make decisions in administrative disputes and disciplinary cases within the judicial system.

THE SUPREME JUDICIAL COUNCIL

The Supreme Judicial Council was reinstituted in 1984, having been abolished in 1969. It exists to guarantee the independence of the judicial system from outside interference and is consulted with regard to draft laws organizing the affairs of the judicial bodies.

Religion

According to the 1986 census, some 94% of Egyptians are Muslims (and almost all of these follow Sunni tenets). According to government figures published in the same year, there are about 2m. Copts (a figure contested by Coptic sources, whose estimates range between 6m. and 7m.), forming the largest religious minority, and about 1m. members of other Christian groups. There is also a small Jewish minority.

ISLAM

There is a Higher Council for the Islamic Call, on which sit: the Grand Sheikh of al-Azhar (Chair.); the Minister of Awqaf (Islamic Endowments); the President and Vice-President of Al-Azhar University; the Grand Mufti of Egypt; and the Secretary-General of the Higher Council for Islamic Affairs.

Grand Sheikh of al-Azhar: Sheikh MUHAMMAD SAYED ATTIYAH TANTAWI.

Grand Mufti of Egypt: Sheikh ALI GOMAA.

CHRISTIANITY

Orthodox Churches

Armenian Apostolic Orthodox Church: POB 48, 179 Sharia Ramses, Cairo, Faggalah; tel. (2) 5901385; fax (2) 906671; Archbishop ZAVEN CHINCHINIAN; 7,000 mems.

Coptic Orthodox Church: St Mark Cathedral, POB 9035, Anba Ruess, 222 Sharia Ramses, Abbassia, Cairo; tel. (2) 2857889; fax (2) 2825683; e-mail coptpope@tecmina.com; internet www.copticpope.org; f. AD 61; Patriarch Pope SHENOUDA III; *c*.13m. followers in Egypt, Sudan, other African countries, the USA, Canada, Australia, Europe and the Middle East.

Greek Orthodox Patriarchate: POB 2006, Alexandria; tel. (3) 4868595; fax (3) 4875684; e-mail goptalex@tecmina.com; internet www.greekorthodox-alexandria.org; f. AD 43; Pope and Patriarch of Alexandria and All Africa THEODOROS II; 3m. mems.

The Roman Catholic Church

Armenian Rite

The Armenian Catholic diocese of Alexandria, with an estimated 1,276 adherents at 31 December 2002, is suffragan to the Patriarchate of Cilicia. The Patriarch is resident in Beirut, Lebanon.

Bishop of Alexandria: (vacant), Patriarcat Arménien Catholique, 36 Sharia Muhammad Sabri Abou Alam, 11121 Cairo; tel. (2) 3938429; fax (2) 3932025; e-mail pacal@gega.net.

Chaldean Rite

The Chaldean Catholic diocese of Cairo had an estimated 500 adherents at 31 December 2002.

Bishop of Cairo: Rt Rev. YOUSSEF IBRAHIM SARRAF, Evêché Chaldéen, Basilique-Sanctuaire Notre Dame de Fatima, 141 Sharia Nouzha, 11316 Cairo (Heliopolis); tel. and fax (2) 6355718.

Coptic Rite

Egypt comprises the Coptic Catholic Patriarchate of Alexandria and five dioceses. At 31 December 2002 there were an estimated 242,513 adherents in the country.

Patriarch of Alexandria: Cardinal STEPHANOS II (Andreas Ghattas), Patriarcat Copte Catholique, POB 69, 34 Sharia Ibn Sandar, Koubbeh Bridge, 11712 Cairo; tel. (2) 2571740; fax (2) 4545766.

Latin Rite

Egypt comprises the Apostolic Vicariate of Alexandria (incorporating Heliopolis and Port Said), containing an estimated 32,000 adherents at 31 December 2002.

Vicar Apostolic: Rt Rev. GIUSEPPE BAUSARDO (Titular Bishop of Ida in Mauretania), 10 Sharia Sidi el-Metwalli, Alexandria; tel. (3) 4876065; fax (3) 4838169; e-mail latinvic@link.net.

Maronite Rite

The Maronite diocese of Cairo had an estimated 5,000 adherents at 31 December 2002.

Bishop of Cairo: Rt Rev. JOSEPH DERGHAM, Evêché Maronite, 15 Sharia Hamdi, Daher, 11271 Cairo; tel. (2) 5939610; fax (2) 5892660.

Melkite Rite

His Beatitude Grégoire III Laham (resident in Damascus, Syria) is the Greek-Melkite Patriarch of Antioch and all the East, of Alexandria and of Jerusalem.

Patriarchal Exarchate of Egypt and Sudan: Patriarcat Grec-Melkite Catholique, 16 Sharia Daher, 11271 Cairo; tel. (2) 5905790; fax (2) 5935398; e-mail grecmelkitecath_egy@hotmail.com; 6,000 adherents (31 December 2004); Gen. Patriarchal Vicar for Egypt and Sudan Most Rev. JOSEPH-JULES ZEREY (Titular Archbishop of Damietta).

Syrian Rite

The Syrian Catholic diocese of Cairo had an estimated 1,739 adherents at 31 December 2002.

Bishop of Cairo: Rt Rev. CLÉMENT-JOSEPH HANNOUCHE, Evêché Syrien Catholique, 46 Sharia Daher, 11271 Cairo; tel. (2) 5901234.

The Anglican Communion

The Anglican diocese of Egypt, suspended in 1958, was revived in 1974 and became part of the Episcopal Church in Jerusalem and the Middle East, formally inaugurated in January 1976. The Province has four dioceses: Jerusalem, Egypt, Cyprus and the Gulf, and Iran, and its President is the Bishop in Egypt. The Bishop in Egypt has jurisdiction also over the Anglican chaplaincies in Algeria, Djibouti, Eritrea, Ethiopia, Libya, Somalia and Tunisia.

Bishop in Egypt: Rt Rev. Dr MOUNEER HANNA ANIS, Diocesan Office, POB 87, 5 Sharia Michel Lutfalla, 11211 Cairo (Zamalek); tel. (2) 7380829; fax (2) 7358941; e-mail diocese@intouch.com; internet www.geocities.com/dioceseofegypt.

Other Christian Churches

Coptic Evangelical Organization for Social Services: POB 162-11811, Panorama, Cairo; tel. (2) 2975901; fax (2) 2975878; e-mail gm@ceoss.org.eg.

Other denominations active in Egypt include the Coptic Evangelical Church (Synod of the Nile) and the Union of the Armenian Evangelical Churches in the Near East.

JUDAISM

The 1986 census recorded 794 Jews in Egypt.

Jewish Community: 13 Sharia Sebil el-Khazindar, Midan el-Guiesh, Abbassia, Cairo; tel. (2) 4824613; fax (2) 7369639; e-mail bassatine@yahoo.com; internet www.bassatine2yahoo.com; Office of the Community; President CARMEN WEINSTEIN.

The Press

Despite a fairly high illiteracy rate in Egypt, the country's press is well developed. Cairo is one of the region's largest publishing centres.

All newspapers and magazines are supervised, according to law, by the Supreme Press Council. The four major publishing houses of al-Ahram, Dar al-Hilal, Dar Akhbar al-Yawm and Dar at-Tahrir operate as separate entities and compete with each other commercially.

The most authoritative daily newspaper is the very long-established *Al-Ahram*.

DAILIES

Alexandria

Bareed ach-Charikat (Companies' Post): POB 813, Alexandria; f. 1952; Arabic; evening; commerce, finance, insurance and marine affairs; Editor S. BENEDUCCI; circ. 15,000.

Al-Ittihad al-Misri (Egyptian Unity): 13 Sharia Sidi Abd ar-Razzak, Alexandria; f. 1871; Arabic; evening; Propr ANWAR MAHER FARAG; Dir HASSAN MAHER FARAG.

Le Journal d'Alexandrie: 1 Sharia Rolo, Alexandria; French; evening; Editor CHARLES ARCACHE.

La Réforme: 8 Passage Sherif, Alexandria; French.

As-Safeer (The Ambassador): 4 Sharia as-Sahafa, Alexandria; f. 1924; Arabic; evening; Editor MUSTAFA SHARAF.

Tachydromos-Egyptos: 4 Sharia Zangarol, Alexandria; tel. (3) 35650; f. 1879; Greek; morning; liberal; Publr PENNY KOUTSOUMIS; Editor DINOS KOUTSOUMIS; circ. 2,000.

Cairo

Al-Ahram (The Pyramids): Sharia al-Galaa, Cairo 11511; tel. (2) 5801600; fax (2) 5786023; e-mail ahramdaily@ahram.org.eg; f. 1875; Arabic; morning, incl. Sundays; international edition published in London, United Kingdom; North American edition published in New York, USA; Chair. and Chief Editor IBRAHIM NAFEI; circ. 900,000 (weekdays), 1.1m. (Friday).

Al-Ahram al-Misaa' (The Evening Al-Ahram): Sharia al-Galaa, Cairo 11511; f. 1990; Arabic; evening; Editor-in-Chief MORSI ATALLAH.

Al-Ahrar: 58 Manshyet as-Sadr, Kobry al-Kobba, Cairo; tel. (2) 4823046; fax (2) 4823027; f. 1977; organ of Liberal Socialist Party; Editor-in-Chief SALAH QABADAYA.

Al-Akhbar (The News): Dar Akhbar al-Yawm, 6 Sharia as-Sahafa, Cairo; tel. (2) 5782600; fax (2) 5782520; f. 1952; Arabic; Chair. IBRAHIM ABU SADAH; Man. Editor GALAL DEWIDAR; circ. 780,000.

Arev: 3 Sharia Sulayman Halabi, Cairo; tel. (2) 5754703; e-mail arev@intouch.com; f. 1915; Armenian; evening; official organ of the Armenian Liberal Democratic Party; Editor ASSBED AZTINIAN.

The Egyptian Gazette: 24–26 Sharia Zakaria Ahmad, Cairo; tel. (2) 5783333; fax (2) 5781110; e-mail 100236.3241@compuserve.com; f. 1880; English; morning; Chair. SAMIR RAGAB; Editor-in-Chief MUHAMMAD ALI IBRAHIM; circ. 90,000.

Al-Gomhouriya (The Republic): 24 Sharia Zakaria Ahmad, Cairo; tel. (2) 5783333; fax (2) 5781717; f. 1953; Arabic; morning; mainly economic affairs; Chair. and Editor-in-Chief SAMIR RAGAB; circ. 900,000.

Al-Misaa' (The Evening): 24 Sharia Zakaria Ahmad, Cairo; tel. (2) 5781010; fax (2) 5784747; f. 1956; Arabic; evening; political, social and sport; Editor-in-Chief MUHAMMAD FOUDAH; Man. Dir ABD AL-HAMROSE; circ. 450,000.

Phos: 14 Sharia Zakaria Ahmad, Cairo; f. 1896; Greek; morning; Editor S. PATERAS; Man. BASILE A. PATERAS; circ. 20,000.

Le Progrès Egyptien: 24 Sharia Zakaria Ahmad, Cairo; tel. (2) (2) 5783333; fax (2) 5781110; f. 1890; French; morning including Sundays; Chair. SAMIR RAGAB; Editor-in-Chief KHALED ANWAR BAKIR; circ. 60,000.

Al-Wafd: 1 Sharia Boulos Hanna, Cairo (Dokki); tel. (2) 3482079; fax (2) 3602007; f. 1984; organ of the New Wafd Party; Editor-in-Chief GAMAL BADAWI; circ. 360,000.

PERIODICALS

Alexandria

Al-Ahad al-Gedid (New Sunday): 88 Sharia Said M. Koraim, Alexandria; tel. (3) 807874; f. 1936; Editor-in-Chief and Publr GALAL M. KORAITEM; circ. 60,000.

Alexandria Medical Journal: 4 G. Carducci, Alexandria; tel. (3) 4829001; fax (3) 4833076; e-mail alexmj@mail.com; internet www .who.sci.eg; f. 1922; English, French and Arabic; quarterly; publ. by Alexandria Medical Asscn; Editor Prof. TOUSSOUN ABOUL AZM.

Amitié Internationale: 59 ave el-Hourriya, Alexandria; tel. (3) 23639; f. 1957; publ. by Asscn Egyptienne d'Amitié Internationale; Arabic and French; quarterly; Editor Dr ZAKI BADAOUI.

L'Annuaire des Sociétés Egyptiennes par Actions: 23 Midan Tahrir, Alexandria; f. 1930; annually in Dec.; French; Propr ELIE I. POLITI; Editor OMAR ES-SAYED MOURSI.

L'Echo Sportif: 7 Sharia de l'Archevêché, Alexandria; French; weekly; Propr MICHEL BITTAR.

Egyptian Cotton Gazette: POB 1772, 12 Sharia Muhammad Tala'at Nooman, Alexandria 21111; tel. (3) 4806971; fax (3) 4873002; e-mail alcotexa@idsc.gov.eg; internet www.alcotexa.org; f. 1947; organ of the Alexandria Cotton Exporters' Association; English; 2 a year; Chief Editor GALAI EL REFAI.

Informateur des Assurances: 1 Sharia Sinan, Alexandria; f. 1936; French; monthly; Propr ELIE I. POLITI; Editor SIMON A. BARANIS.

La Réforme Illustré: 8 Passage Sherif, Alexandria; French; weekly; general.

Sina 'at en-Nassig (L'Industrie Textile): 5 rue de l'Archevêché, Alexandria; Arabic and French; monthly; Editor PHILIPPE COLAS.

Voce d'Italia: 90 Sharia Farahde, Alexandria; Italian; fortnightly; Editor R. AVELLINO.

Cairo

Al-Ahali (The People): Sharia Kareem ad-Dawli, Tala'at Harb Sq., Cairo; tel. (2) 7786583; fax (2) 3900412; f. 1978; weekly; publ. by the National Progressive Unionist Party; Chair. LOTFI WAKID; Editor-in-Chief ABD AL-BAKOURY.

Al-Ahram al-Arabi: Sharia al-Galaa, Cairo 11511; f. 1997; Arabic; weekly; political, social and economic affairs; Chair. IBRAHIM NAFIE; Editor-in-Chief OSAMA SARAYA.

Al-Ahram Hebdo: POB 1057, Sharia al-Galaa, Cairo 11511; tel. (2) 5783104; fax (2) 5782631; e-mail hebdo@ahram.org.eg; internet www.ahram.org.eg/hebdo; f. 1993; French; weekly; Editor-in-Chief MUHAMMAD SALMAWI.

Al-Ahram al-Iqtisadi (The Economic Al-Ahram): Sharia al-Galaa, Cairo 11511; tel. (2) 5786100; fax (2) 5786833; Arabic; weekly (Monday); economic and political affairs; owned by Al-Ahram publrs; Chief Editor ISSAM RIFA'AT; circ. 84,871.

Al-Ahram Weekly (The Pyramids): Al-Ahram Bldg, Sharia al-Galaa, Cairo 11511; tel. (2) 5786100; fax (2) 5786833; e-mail weeklyweb@ahram.org.eg; internet www.ahram.org.eg/weekly; f. 1989; English; weekly; publ. by Al-Ahram publications; Editor-in-Chief HOSNI GUINDY; circ. 150,000.

Akhbar al-Adab: 6 Sharia as-Sahafa, Cairo; tel. (2) 5795620; fax (2) 5782510; e-mail akhbarelyom@akhbarelyom.org; internet www .akhbarelyom.org.eg/eladab; f. 1993; literature and arts for young people; Editor-in-Chief GAMAL AL-GHITANI.

Akhbar al-Hawadith: 6 Sharia as-Sahafa, Cairo; tel. (2) 5782600; fax (2) 5782510; f. 1993; weekly; crime reports; Editor-in-Chief MUHAMMAD BARAKAT.

Akhbar an-Nogoome: 6 Sharia as-Sahafa, Cairo; tel. (2) 5782600; fax (2) 5782510; f. 1991; weekly; theatre and film news; Editor-in-Chief AMAL OSMAN.

Akhbar ar-Riadah: 6 Sharia as-Sahafa, Cairo; tel. (2) 5782600; fax (2) 5782510; f. 1990; weekly; sport; Editor-in-Chief IBRAHIM HEGAZY.

Akhbar al-Yom (Daily News): 6 Sharia as-Sahafa, Cairo; tel. (2) 5782600; fax (2) 5782520; internet www.akhbarelyom.org.eg; f. 1944; Arabic; weekly (Saturday); Chair. and Editor-in-Chief IBRAHIM ABU SEDAH; circ. 1,184,611.

Akher Sa'a (Last Hour): Dar Akhbar al-Yawm, Sharia as-Sahafa, Cairo; tel. (2) 5782600; fax (2) 5782530; f. 1934; Arabic; weekly (Sunday); independent; consumer and news magazine; Editor-in-Chief MAHMOUD SALAH; circ. 150,000.

Aqidaty (My Faith): 24–26 Sharia Zakaria Ahmad, Cairo; tel. (2) 5783333; fax (2) 5781110; weekly; Muslim religious newspaper; Editor-in-Chief ABD AR-RAOUF ES-SAYED; circ. 300,000.

Al-Arabi an-Nassiri: Cairo; f. 1993; publ. by the Nasserist Party; Editor-in-Chief MAHMOUD EL-MARAGHI.

Al-Azhar: Idarat al-Azhar, Sharia al-Azhar, Cairo; f. 1931; Arabic; Islamic monthly; supervised by the Egyptian Council for Islamic Research of Al-Azhar University; Dir MUHAMMAD FARID WAGDI.

Al-Bitrul (Petroleum): Cairo; monthly; publ. by the Egyptian General Petroleum Corporation.

Cairo Today: POB 2098, 1079 Corniche en-Nil, Cairo (Garden City); monthly.

Computerworld Middle East: World Publishing Ltd (Egypt), 41A Masaken al-Fursan Bldg, Sharia Kamal Hassan Ali, Cairo 11361; tel. (2) 3460601; fax (2) 3470118; English; monthly; specialist computer information.

Contemporary Thought: University of Cairo, Cairo; quarterly; Editor Dr Z. N. MAHMOUD.

Ad-Da'wa (The Call): Cairo; Arabic; monthly; organ of the Muslim Brotherhood.

Ad-Doctor: 8 Sharia Hoda Sharawi, Cairo; f. 1947; Arabic; monthly; Editor Dr AHMAD M. KAMAL; circ. 30,000.

Droit al-Haqq: Itihad al-Mohameen al-Arab, 13 Sharia Itihad, Cairo; publ. by the Arab Lawyers' Union; 3 a year.

Echos: 1–5 Sharia Mahmoud Bassiouni, Cairo; f. 1947; French; weekly; Dir and Propr GEORGES QRFALI.

The Egyptian Mail: 24–26 Sharia Zakaria Ahmad, Cairo; weekly; Sat. edn of *The Egyptian Gazette*; English; circ. 40,000.

El-Elm Magazine (Sciences): 24 Sharia Zakaria Ahmad, Cairo; tel. (2) 5781010; fax (2) 5784747; f. 1976; Arabic; monthly; publ. with the Academy of Scientific Research in Egypt; circ. 70,000.

Al-Fusoul (The Seasons): 17 Sharia Sherif Pasha, Cairo; Arabic; monthly; Propr and Chief Editor SAMIR MUHAMMAD ZAKI ABD AL-KADER.

Al-Garidat at-Tigariyat al-Misriya (The Egyptian Business Paper): 25 Sharia Nubar Pasha, Cairo; f. 1921; Arabic; weekly; circ. 7,000.

Hawa'a (Eve): Dar al-Hilal, 16 Sharia Muhammad Ezz el-Arab, Cairo 11511; tel. (2) 3625450; fax (2) 3625469; f. 1892; women's magazine; Arabic; weekly (Sat.); Chief Editor EKBAL BARAKA; circ. 210,502.

Al-Hilal Magazine: Dar al-Hilal, 16 Sharia Muhammad Ezz el-Arab, Cairo 11511; tel. (2) 3625450; fax (2) 3625469; f. 1895; Arabic; literary monthly; Editor MOUSTAFA NABIL.

Horreyati: 24 Sharia Zakaria Ahmad, Cairo; tel. (2) 5781010; fax (2) 5784747; f. 1990; weekly; social, cultural and sport; Editor-in-Chief MUHAMMAD NOUR ED-DIN; circ. 250,000.

Huwa wa Hiya (He and She): Middle East Foundation, POB 525, Cairo 11511; tel. (2) 5167400; fax (2) 5167325; e-mail editor@ huwawahiya.com; f. 1977; monthly; news, leisure, sport, health, religion, women's issues; Dir GEORGE TAWFIK.

Industrial Egypt: POB 251, 26A Sharia Sherif Pasha, Cairo; tel. (2) 3928317; fax (2) 3928075; f. 1924; quarterly bulletin and year book of the Federation of Egyptian Industries in English and Arabic; Editor ALI FAHMY.

Informateur Financier et Commercial: 24 Sharia Sulayman Pasha, Cairo; f. 1929; weekly; Dir HENRI POLITI; circ. 15,000.

Al-Iza'a wat-Television (Radio and Television): 16 Sharia Muhammad Ezz el-Arab, Cairo 11511; tel. (2) 3643314; fax (2) 3543030; f. 1935; Arabic; weekly; Man. Editor MAHMOUD ALI; circ. 80,000.

Al-Kerazeh (The Sermon): Cairo; Arabic; weekly newspaper of the Coptic Orthodox Church.

Al-Kawakeb (The Stars): Dar al-Hilal, 16 Sharia Muhammad Ezz el-Arab, Cairo 11511; tel. (2) 3625450; fax (2) 3625469; f. 1952; Arabic; weekly; film magazine; Editor-in-Chief RAGAA AN-NAKKASH; circ. 86,381.

Kitab al-Hilal: Dar al-Hilal, 16 Sharia Muhammad Ezz el-Arab, Cairo 11511; tel. (2) 3625450; fax (2) 3625469; monthly; Founders EMILE, SHOUKRI ZEIDAN; Editor MOUSTAFA NABIL.

Al-Kora wal-Malaeb (Football and Playgrounds): 24 Sharia Zakaria Ahmad, Cairo; tel. (2) 5783333; fax (2) 5784747; f. 1976; Arabic; weekly; sport; circ. 150,000.

Al-Liwa' al-Islami (Islamic Standard): 11 Sharia Sherif Pasha, Cairo; f. 1982; Arabic; weekly; govt paper to promote official view of Islamic revivalism; Propr AHMAD HAMZA; Editor MUHAMMAD ALI SHETA; circ. 30,000.

Lotus Magazine: 104 Sharia Qasr el-Eini, Cairo; f. 1992; English, French and Arabic; quarterly; computer software magazine; Editor BEREND HARMENS.

Magallat al-Mohandessin (The Engineer's Magazine): 28 Sharia Ramses, Cairo; f. 1945; publ. by The Engineers' Syndicate; Arabic and English; 10 a year; Editor and Sec. MAHMOUD SAMI ABD AL-KAWI.

Al-Magallat az-Zira'ia (The Agricultural Magazine): Cairo; monthly; agriculture; circ. 30,000.

Mayo (May): Sharia al-Galaa, Cairo; f. 1981; weekly; organ of National Democratic Party; Chair. ABDULLAH ABD AL-BARY; Chief Editor SAMIR RAGAB; circ. 500,000.

Medical Journal of Cairo University: Qasr el-Eini Hospital, Sharia Qasr el-Eini, Cairo; tel. and fax (2) 3655768; f. 1933; Qasr el-Eini Clinical Society; English; quarterly; Editor SALEH A. BEDIR.

MEN Economic Weekly: Middle East News Agency, 4 Sharia Hoda Sharawi, Cairo; tel. (2) 3933000; fax (2) 3935055.

The Middle East Observer: 41 Sharia Sherif, Cairo; tel. and fax (2) 3939732; e-mail meo@soficom.eg; internet www.meobserver.org; f. 1954; English; weekly; specializing in economics of Middle East and African markets; also publishes supplements on law, foreign trade and tenders; agent for IMF, UN and IDRC publications, distributor of World Bank publications; Man. Owner AHMAD FODA; Chief Editor HESHAM A. RAOUF; circ. 20,000.

Middle East Times Egypt: 2 Sharia el-Malek el-Afdal, Cairo (Zamalek); tel. (2) 3419930; fax (2) 3413725; e-mail met@ritsec1.com .eg; f. 1983; English; weekly; Man. Editor ROD CRAIG; circ. 6,000.

Al-Mussawar: Dar al-Hilal, 16 Sharia Muhammad Ezz el-Arab, Cairo 11511; tel. (2) 3625450; fax (2) 3625469; f. 1924; Arabic; weekly; news; Chair. and Editor-in-Chief MAKRAM MUHAMMAD AHMAD; circ. 130,423.

Nesf ad-Donia: Sharia al-Galaa, Cairo 11511; tel. (2) 5786100; f. 1990; weekly; women's magazine; publ. by Al-Ahram Publications; Editor-in-Chief SANAA AL-BESI.

October: Dar al-Maaref, 1119 Sharia Corniche en-Nil, Cairo; tel. (2) 5777077; fax (2) 5744999; f. 1976; weekly; Chair. and Editor-in-Chief RAGAB AL-BANA; circ. 140,500.

Al-Omal (The Workers): 90 Sharia al-Galaa, Cairo; publ. by the Egyptian Trade Union Federation: Arabic; weekly; Chief Editor AHMAD HARAK.

PC World Middle East: World Publishing Ltd (Egypt), 41A Masaken al-Fursan Bldg, Sharia Kamal Hassan Ali, Cairo 11361; tel. (2) 34606; fax (2) 3470118; monthly; computers.

Le Progrès Dimanche: 24 Sharia al-Galaa, Cairo; tel. (2) 5781010; fax (2) 5784747; French; weekly; Sunday edition of *Le Progrès Egyptien*; Editor-in-Chief KHALED ANWAR BAKIR; circ. 35,000.

Rose al-Yousuf: 89A Sharia Qasr el-Eini, Cairo; tel. (2) 3540888; fax (2) 3556413; f. 1925; Arabic; weekly; political; circulates throughout all Arab countries; Chair. of Board and Editor-in-Chief MUHAMMAD ABD AL-MONEIM; circ. 35,000.

As-Sabah (The Morning): 4 Sharia Muhammad Said Pasha, Cairo; f. 1922; Arabic; weekly (Thurs.); Editor RAOUF TAWFIK.

Sabah al-Kheir (Good Morning): 89A Sharia Qasr el-Eini, Cairo; tel. (2) 3540888; fax (2) 3556413; f. 1956; Arabic; weekly (Thurs.); light entertainment; Chief Editor RAOUF TAWFIK; circ. 70,000.

Ash-Shaab (The People): 313 Sharia Port Said, Sayeda Zeinab, Cairo; tel. (2) 3909716; fax (2) 3900283; e-mail elshaab@idsc.gov.eg; f. 1979; organ of Socialist Labour Party; bi-weekly (Tues. and Fri.); Editor-in-Chief MAGDI AHMAD HUSSEIN; circ. 130,000.

Shashati (My Screen): 24 Sharia Zakaria Ahmad, Cairo; tel. (2) 5781010; fax (2) 5784747; weekly; art, culture, fashion and television news.

As-Siyassa ad-Dawliya: Al-Ahram Bldg, 12th Floor, Sharia al-Galaa, Cairo 11511; tel. (2) 5786249; fax (2) 5792899; e-mail siyassa@ahram.org.eg; quarterly; politics and foreign affairs; Editor-in-Chief Dr OSAMA AL-GHAZALI.

Tabibak al-Khass (Family Doctor): Dar al-Hilal, 16 Sharia Muhammad Ezz el-Arab, Cairo; tel. (2) 3625473; fax (2) 3625442; monthly.

At-Tahrir (Liberation): 5 Sharia Naguib, Rihani, Cairo; Arabic; weekly; Editor ABD AL-AZIZ SADEK.

At-Taqaddum (Progress): c/o 1 Sharia Jarim ed-Dawlah, Cairo; f. 1978; weekly; organ of National Progressive Unionist Party.

Tchehreh Nema: 14 Sharia Hassan el-Akbar (Abdine), Cairo; f. 1904; Iranian; monthly; political, literary and general; Editor MANUCEHR TCHEHREH NEMA MOADEB ZADEH.

Up-to-Date International Industry: 10 Sharia al-Galaa, Cairo; Arabic and English; monthly; foreign trade journal.

Watani (My Country): 27 Sharia Abd al-Khalek Sarwat, Cairo; tel. (2) 3927201; fax (2) 3935946; e-mail watani@tecmina.com; internet www.watani.com.eg; f. 1958; Arabic and English; independent Sun. newspaper addressing Egyptians in general and the Christian Copts in particular; Editor-in-Chief YOUSSEF SIDHOM; circ. 60,000–100,000.

Yulio (July): July Press and Publishing House, Cairo; f. 1986; weekly; Nasserist; Editor ABDULLAH IMAM; and a monthly cultural magazine; Editor MAHMOUD AL-MARAGHI.

NEWS AGENCIES

Middle East News Agency (MENA): 17 Sharia Hoda Sharawi, Cairo; tel. (2) 3933000; fax (2) 3935055; e-mail newsroom@mena.org .eg; internet www.mena.org.eg; f. 1955; regular service in Arabic, English and French; Chair. and Editor-in-Chief MOUSTAFA NAGUIB.

Foreign Bureaux

Agence France-Presse (AFP): POB 1437-15511, 2nd Floor, 10 Misaha Sq., Cairo; tel. (2) 3481236; fax (2) 3603282; Chief SAMMY KETZ.

Agencia EFE (Spain): 35A Sharia Abou el-Feda, 4th Floor, Apt 14, Cairo (Zamalek); Correspondent DOMINGO DEL PIÑO.

Agenzia Nazionale Stampa Associata (ANSA) (Italy): 19 Sharia Abd al-Khalek Sarwat, Cairo; tel. (2) 3929821; fax (2) 3938642; Chief ANTONELLA TARQUINI.

Allgemeiner Deutscher Nachrichtendienst (ADN) (Germany): 17 Sharia el-Brazil, Apt 59, Cairo (Zamalek); tel. (2) 3404006; Correspondent RALF SCHULTZE.

Associated Press (AP) (USA): POB 1077, 1117 Sharia Corniche en-Nil, (Maspiro), Cairo 11221; tel. (2) 5784091; fax (2) 5784094; internet www.ap.org; Chief of Middle East Services EARLEEN FISHER.

Deutsche Presse-Agentur (dpa) (Germany): 1st Floor, 8 Sharia Dar esh-Shefaa, Cairo (Garden City); tel. (2) 7956842; fax (2) 7956318; e-mail dpa@tedata.net.eg; Chief ANN-BÉATRICE CLASMANN.

Informatsionnoye Telegrafnoye Agentstvo Rossii—Telegrafnoye Agentstvo Suverennykh Stran (ITAR—TASS) (Russia): 30 Sharia Muhammad Mazhar, Cairo (Zamalek); tel. (2) 3419784; fax (2) 3417268; Dir MIKHAIL I. KROUTIKHIN.

Jiji Press (Japan): 9 Sharia el-Kamal Muhammad, Cairo (Zamalek); tel. (2) 7356237; fax (2) 7355244; e-mail jijipresscairo@ yahoo.com; Chief TETSUYA KATAYAMA.

Kyodo News (Japan): Flat 301, 15 Sharia Hassan Sabri, Cairo 11211 (Zamalek); tel. (2) 7361756; fax (2) 7356105; e-mail kyodo@ link.net; Chief TOMOHIRO GIMA.

Reuters (United Kingdom): POB 2040, 21st Floor, Bank Misr Tower, 153 Sharia Muhammad Farid, Cairo; tel. (2) 5777150; fax (2) 5771133; e-mail cairo.newsroom@reuters.com; internet www .reuters.com; Chief ALISTAIR LYON.

United Press International (UPI) (USA): POB 872, 4 Sharia Eloui, Cairo; tel. (2) 3928106.

Xinhua (New China) News Agency (People's Republic of China): 2 Moussa Galal Sq., Mohandessin, Cairo; tel. (2) 3448950.

The Iraqi News Agency (INA) and the Saudi Press Agency (SPA) are also represented in Cairo.

PRESS ASSOCIATIONS

Egyptian Press Syndicate: Cairo; Chair. IBRAHIM NAFEH.

Foreign Press Association: Room 2037, Marriott Hotel, Cairo; tel. (2) 3419957.

Publishers

General Egyptian Book Organization: POB 1660, 117 Sharia Corniche en-Nil, Boulac, Cairo; tel. (2) 5779283; fax (2) 5754213; e-mail info@egyptianbook.org; internet www.egyptianbook.org; f. 1961; editing, publishing and distribution; organizer of Cairo International Book Fair; affiliated to the Ministry of Culture; Chair. Dr SAMIR SARHAN; Gen. Dir AHMAD SALAH ZAKI.

ALEXANDRIA

Alexandria University Press: Shatby, Alexandria.

Dar al-Matbo al-Gadidah: 5 Sharia St Mark, Alexandria; tel. (3) 4825508; fax (3) 4833819; agriculture, information sciences; social sciences.

Egyptian Printing and Publishing House: Ahmad es-Sayed Marouf, 59 Safia Zaghoul, Alexandria; f. 1947.

Maison Egyptienne d'Editions: Ahmad es-Sayed Marouf, Sharia Adib, Alexandria; f. 1950.

Maktab al-Misri al-Hadith li-t-Tiba wan-Nashr: 7 Sharia Noubar, Alexandria; also at 2 Sharia Sherif, Cairo; Man. AHMAD YEHIA.

CAIRO

Al-Ahram Establishment: Al-Ahram Bldg, 6 Sharia al-Galaa, Cairo 11511; tel. (2) 5786100; fax (2) 5786023; e-mail ahram@ahram .org.eg; internet www.ahram.org.eg; f. 1875; publ. newspapers, magazines and books, incl. *Al-Ahram*; Chair. and Chief Editor IBRAHIM NAFEI; Dep. Chair. and Gen. Man. ALI GHONEIM.

Boustany's Publishing House: 29 Sharia Faggalah, Cairo 11271; tel. (2) 5915315; fax (2) 2623085; e-mail boustany@boustanys.com; internet www.boustanys.com; f. 1900; fiction, poetry, history, biography, philosophy, language, literature, politics, religion, archaeology, Egyptology; Chief Exec. FADWA BOUSTANY.

Cairo University Press: Al-Giza, Cairo; tel. (2) 846144.

Dar Akhbar al-Yawm: 6 Sharia as-Sahafa, Cairo; tel. (2) 5748100; fax (2) 5748895; e-mail akhbarelyom@akhbarelyom.org; internet www.akhbarelyom.org; f. 1944; publ. *Al-Akhbar* (daily), *Akhbar al-Yawm* (weekly), and colour magazine *Akher Sa'a* (weekly); Pres. IBRAHIM SAAD.

Dar al-Gomhouriya: 24 Sharia Zakaria Ahmad, Cairo; tel. (2) 5781010; fax (2) 5784747; affiliate of At-Tahrir Printing and Publishing House; publications include the dailies, *Al-Gomhouriya, Al-Misaa', Egyptian Gazette* and *Le Progrès Egyptien*; Pres. SAMIR RAGAB.

Dar al-Hilal Publishing Institution: 16 Sharia Muhammad Ezz el-Arab, Cairo 11511; tel. (2) 3625450; fax (2) 3625469; f. 1892; publ. *Al-Hilal, Riwayat al-Hilal, Kitab al-Hilal, Tabibak al-Khass* (monthlies); *Al-Mussawar, Al-Kawakeb, Hawaa, Samir, Mickey* (weeklies); Chief Exec. MAKRAN MUHAMMAD AHMAD.

Dar al-Kitab al-Masri: POB 156, 33 Sharia Qasr en-Nil, Cairo 11511; tel. (2) 3922168; fax (2) 3924657; e-mail daralkitabalmasri@ hotmail.com; f. 1929; publishing, printing and distribution; publishers of books on Islam and history, as well as dictionaries, encyclopaedias, textbooks, children's books and books of general interest; Pres. and Man. Dir HASSAN ez-ZEIN.

Dar al-Maaref: 1119 Sharia Corniche en-Nil, Cairo; tel. (2) 5777077; fax (2) 5744999; e-mail maaref@idselgov.eg; internet www .octobermag.com; f. 1890; publishing, printing and distribution of wide variety of books in Arabic and other languages; publishers of *October* magazine; Chair. and Man. Dir RAGAB AL-BANA.

Dar an-Nahda al-Arabia: 32 Sharia Abd al-Khalek Sarwat, Cairo; tel. (2) 3926931; f. 1960; literature, law.

Dar an-Nashr (formerly Les Editions Universitaires d'Egypte): POB 1347, 41 Sharia Sherif, Cairo 11511; tel. (2) 3934606; fax (2) 3921997; f. 1947; university textbooks, academic works, encyclopaedia.

Dar ash-Shorouk Publishing House (Egyptian Publishers Association): 8 Sharia Sebaweh el-Masri, Rabaa el-Adawia; Nasr City, Cairo 11371; tel. (2) 4023399; fax (2) 4037567; e-mail imoallem@shorouk.com; f. 1968; publishing, printing and distribution; publishers of books on politics, history, Islamic studies, economics, literature, art and children's books; Chair. IBRAHIM EL-MOALLEM.

Dar ath-Thakafah al-Gadidah: 32 Sharia Sabry Abou Alam, Cairo; tel. (2) 42718; f. 1968; Pres. MUHAMMAD YOUSUF ELGUINDI.

Editions le Progrès: 6 Sharia Sherif Pasha, Cairo; Propr WADI SHOUKRI.

Egyptian Co for Printing and Publishing: 40 Sharia Noubar, Cairo; tel. (2) 21310; Chair. MUHAMMAD MAHMOUD HAMED.

Elias Modern Publishing House: 1 Sharia Kenisset ar-Rum el-Kathulik, Daher, Cairo; tel. (2) 5903756; fax (2) 5880091; e-mail eliaspub@tedata.net.eg; internet www.eliaspublishing.com; f. 1913; publishing, printing and distribution; publs dictionaries, children's books and books on linguistics, poetry and arts; Man. Dir LAURA KFOURY; Gen. Man. NADIM ELIAS.

Al-Khira Press: 8 Sharia Soliman el-Halabi, Cairo; tel. and fax (2) 5744809; Owner ABD AL-MEGUID MUHAMMAD.

Lagnat at-Taalif wat-Targama wan-Nashr (Committee for Writing, Translating and Publishing Books): 9 Sharia el-Kerdassi (Abdine), Cairo.

Librairie La Renaissance d'Egypte (Hassan Muhammad & Sons): POB 2172, 9 Sharia Adly, Cairo; f. 1930; religion, history, geography, medicine, architecture, economics, politics, law, philosophy, psychology, children's books, atlases, dictionaries; Man. HASSAN MUHAMMAD.

Maktabet Misr: POB 16, 3 Sharia Kamal Sidki, Cairo; tel. (2) 5898553; fax (2) 7870051; e-mail info@misrbookshop.com; internet www.misrbookshop.com; f. 1932; publs wide variety of fiction, biographies and textbooks for schools and universities; Man. AMIR SAID GOUDA es-SAHHAR.

Middle East Book Centre: 45 Sharia Qasr en-Nil, Cairo; tel. (2) 910980; f. 1954; biography, fiction, history, language, literature, religion, philosophy, sciences; Man. Dir Dr A. M. MOSHARRAFA.

National Centre for Educational Research and Development: 12 Sharia Waked, el-Borg el-Faddy, POB 836, Cairo; tel. (2) 3930981; f. 1956; formerly Documentation and Research Centre for Education (Ministry of Education); bibliographies, directories, information and education bulletins; Dir Prof. ABD EL-FATTAH GALAL.

National Library Press (Dar al-Kutub): Midan Ahmad Maher, Cairo; bibliographic works.

Senouhy Publishers: 54 Sharia Abd al-Khalek Sarwat, Cairo; f. 1956; history, poetry, regional interests, religion, non-fiction; Man. Dir LEILA A. FADEL.

At-Tahrir Printing and Publishing House: 24 Sharia Zakaria Ahmad, Cairo; tel. (2) 5781222; fax (2) 2784747; e-mail eltahrir@ eltahrir.net; internet www.eltahrir.net; f. 1953; affil. to Shura (Advisory) Council; Pres. and Chair. of Bd SAMIR RAGAB.

Watani (My Country): 27 Sharia Abd al-Khalek Sarwat, Cairo; tel. (2) 3927201; fax (2) 3935946; e-mail watani@tecmina.com; internet www.watani.com.eg; f. 1958; Arabic and English; Editor-in-Chief YOUSSEF SIDHOM.

Broadcasting and Communications

TELECOMMUNICATIONS

Telecommunications Regulatory Authority (TRA): 27 Sharia Mohi ed-Din Abuelezz, Dokki, Cairo (Giza); tel. (2) 3377711; fax (2) 3373300; e-mail tra@tra.gov.eg; internet www.tra.gov.eg; f. 2000; Chair. Dr AHMAD MAHMOUD MUHAMMAD NAZIF; Exec. Dir Dr ALAA ED-DIN MUHAMMAD FAHMY.

Telecom Egypt: POB 2271, Sharia Ramses, Cairo 11511; tel. (2) 5793444; fax (2) 5744244; e-mail telecomegypt@telecomegypt.com .eg; internet www.telecomegypt.com.eg; f. 1957; provider of fixed-line telephone services; Chair. AKIL HAMED BESHIR.

Egyptian Company for Mobile Services (MobiNil): Cairo; e-mail customercare@mobinil.com; internet www.mobinil.com; began operation of the existing state-controlled mobile telecommunications network in early 1998; owned by France Telecom and Orascom Telecom; CEO OSMAN SULTAN.

Orascom Telecom: 160 Sharia 26 July, POB 1191, Cairo (Agouza); tel. (2) 3026930; fax (2) 3440201; e-mail info@orascom.com; internet www.orascom.com; Chair. and CEO NAGUIB SAWARIS.

Vodafone Egypt: 7A Corniche en-Nil, Maadi, 11431 Cairo; tel. (2) 5292000; e-mail customer-service@vodafone.com.eg; internet www .vodafone.com/eg; f. 1998 by the MisrFone consortium; mobile telephone service provider; majority-owned by Vodafone International (UK); Chair. MUHAMMAD NOSSAIR; CEO and Man. Dir IAN GRAY.

BROADCASTING

Radio

Egyptian Radio and Television Union (ERTU): POB 11511, Cairo 1186; tel. (2) 5787120; fax (2) 746989; e-mail ertu@ertu.gov.eg; internet www.ertu.gov.eg; f. 1928; home service radio programmes in Arabic, English and French; foreign services in Arabic, English, French, Swahili, Hausa, Bengali, Urdu, German, Spanish, Armenian, Greek, Hebrew, Indonesian, Malay, Thai, Hindi, Pashtu, Farsi, Turkish, Somali, Portuguese, Fulani, Italian, Zulu, Shona, Sindebele, Lingala, Afar, Amharic, Yoruba, Wolof, Bambara; Pres. AMIN BASSIOUNI.

Middle East Radio: Société Egyptienne de Publicité, 24–26 Sharia Zakaria Ahmad, Cairo; tel. (2) 5781010; fax (2) 5784747; internet www.tahriv.net.

Television

Egypt has two direct television broadcast satellites. The second satellite, Nilesat 102, was launched in August 2000.

Egyptian Radio and Television Union (ERTU): see Radio.

Finance

(cap. = capital; res = reserves; dep. = deposits; m. = million; brs = branches; amounts in Egyptian pounds unless otherwise stated)

BANKING

Central Bank

Central Bank of Egypt: 31 Sharia Qasr en-Nil, Cairo; tel. (2) 3931514; fax (2) 3926361; e-mail research@cbe.org.eg; internet www.cbe.org.eg; f. 1961; controls Egypt's monetary policy and supervises the banking and insurance sectors; cap. 1,000m., res 1,690.0m., dep. 177,361.5m. (June 2004); Gov. and Chair. FAROUK EL-OKDAH; Dep. Govs TAREK HASSAN ALI AMER, MAHMOUD ABD AL-AZIZ MAHMOUD; 3 brs.

Commercial and Specialized Banks

Alexandria Commercial and Maritime Bank, SAE: POB 2376, 85 ave el-Hourriya, Alexandria 21519; tel. (3) 3921237; fax (3) 3913706; internet www.acmb.com.eg; f. 1981; cap. 112.1m., res 59.1m., dep. 1,956.0m. (Dec. 2003); Chair. and Man. Dir ESSAM MUHAMMAD ABOU HAMID; 7 brs.

Bank of Alexandria: 49 Sharia Qasr en-Nil, Cairo; tel. (2) 3913822 (Cairo); fax (2) 3910481 (Cairo); e-mail foreign@alexbank.com; internet www.alexbank.com; f. 1957; privatization pending; cap. 800m., res 605.3m., dep. 29,914.3m. (June 2003); Chair. MAHMOUD SAYED ABD AL-LATIF; 184 brs.

Bank of Commerce and Development (At-Tegaryoon): POB 1373, 13 Sharia 26 July, Mohandessin, Cairo (Agouza); tel. (2) 3472063; fax (2) 3023963; f. 1980; cap. 151.6m., res 0.7m., dep. 722.6m. (Dec. 2002); Man. Dir FATHI YASSIN MUHAMMAD ALI; 6 brs.

Banque du Caire, SAE: POB 9022, Banque du Caire Tower, 6 Sharia Dr Moustafa Abu Zahra, Nasr City, Cairo 11371; tel. (2) 2647400; fax (2) 403725; e-mail intl.division@bdc.com.eg; internet www.bdc.com.eg; f. 1952; state-owned; cap. 1,600.0m., res 779.5m., dep. 38,699.4m. (June 2003); Chair. AHMAD MUNIR EL-BARDAI; Vice-Chair. MONA YASSINE; 216 brs in Egypt, 5 abroad.

Banque Misr, SAE: 151 Sharia Muhammad Farid, Cairo; tel. (2) 3912711; fax (2) 3919779; internet www.banquemisr.com.eg; f. 1920; merger with Misr Exterior Bank in 2004; privatization pending; cap. 1,800m., res 1,192.4m., dep. 77,719.9m. (Dec 2003); Chair. MUHAMMAD KAMAL AD-DIN BARAKAT; 438 brs.

Commercial International Bank (Egypt), SAE: POB 2430, Nile Tower Bldg, 21–23 Sharia Charles de Gaulle, Cairo (Giza); tel. (2) 5703164; fax (2) 5703172; e-mail info@cibeg.com; internet www.cibeg.com; f. 1975 as Chase National Bank (Egypt) SAE; adopted present name 1987; National Bank of Egypt has 19.91% interest, Bankers Trust Co (USA) 18.76%, International Finance Corpn 5%; cap. 1,300m., res 438.0m., dep. 21,023.8m. (Dec. 2003); Exec. Chair. and Man. Dir HISHAM EZZ AL-ARAB; 69 brs.

Egyptian Arab Land Bank: 78 Sharia Gamet ad-Duwal al-Arabia, Mohandessin, Cairo (Giza); tel. (2) 3383691; fax 3383561; e-mail ealb@eal-bank.com; internet www.eal-bank.com; f. 1880; cap. 1,000m., res 172.6m., dep. 17,072.4m. (June 2003); Chair. MUHAMMAD FATHY ES-SEBAAI MANSOUR; 26 brs in Egypt, 14 abroad.

Export Development Bank of Egypt (EDBE): 108 Mohyee el-Din Abou al-Ezz, Cairo 12311 (Dokki); tel. (2) 7480578; fax (2) 3385940; f. 1983 to replace National Import-Export Bank; cap.

500.0m., res 295.1m., dep. 6,528.9m. (June 2003); Chair. MUHAMMAD SHERIF SHARAF; Vice-Chair. OLA ABD AL-AZIZ GADALLAH; 10 brs.

HSBC Bank Egypt, SAE: POB 126, Abou el-Feda Bldg, 3 Sharia Abou el-Feda, Cairo (Zamalek); tel. (2) 3409186; fax (2) 3414010; e-mail hsbcegypt@hsbc.com; internet www.hsbc.com; f. 1982 as Hongkong Egyptian Bank; changed name to Egyptian British Bank in 1994; changed name to above in 2001; the Hongkong and Shanghai Banking Corporation has a 90% shareholding, other interests 10%; cap. 351.6m., res 71.6m., dep. 7,054.5m. (Dec. 2003); Chair. and Man. Dir ABD AS-SALAM EL-ANWAR; 14 brs.

Mohandes Bank: 3–5 Sharia Mossadek, Cairo; tel. (2) 3362760; fax (2) 3362741; internet www.mohandesbank.com; f. 1979; cap. 161.0m., res 5.9m., dep. 4,588.1m. (Dec. 2002); Pres. and Man. Dir MOUSTAFA MOUSTAFA MARZOUK; 9 brs.

National Bank for Development (NBD): POB 647, 5 Sharia el-Borsa el-Gedida, Cairo 11511; tel. (2) 3907784; fax (2) 3936039; e-mail nbd@internetegypt.com; internet www.nbdegypt.com; f. 1980; cap. 281.9m., res 183.5m., dep. 7,295.0m. (Dec. 2003); Chair. and Man. Dir ALI I. SHAKER; 67 brs; there are affiliated National Banks for Development in 16 governorates.

National Bank of Egypt: POB 11611, National Bank of Egypt Tower, 1187 Corniche en-Nil, Cairo; tel. (2) 5749101; fax (2) 5762672; e-mail nbe@nbe.com.eg; internet www.nbe.com.eg; f. 1898; privatization pending; handles all commercial banking operations; cap. 2,250.0m., res 3,298.0m., dep. 106,797.0m. (June 2003); Chair. HUSSEIN ABD AL-AZIZ HUSSEIN; 343 brs.

Principal Bank for Development and Agricultural Credit: POB 11669, 110 Sharia Qasr el-Eini, Cairo; tel. (2) 7951204; fax (2) 7948337; f. 1976 to succeed former credit organizations; state-owned; cap. 1,406m., res 275m., dep. 7,293m. (June 2001); Chair. Dr YOUSSEF A. RAHMAN HOSNI; 167 brs.

Société Arabe Internationale de Banque (SAIB): POB 54, 56 Sharia Gamet ed-Dowal al-Arabia, Mohandessin, Cairo (Giza); tel. (2) 7499464; fax (2) 3603497; f. 1976; the Arab International Bank has a 41.1% share, other interests 58.9%; cap. US $48.0m., res US $48.0m., dep. US $338.2m. (Dec. 2003); Chair. Dr HASSAN ABBAS ZAKI; Man. Dir MUHAMMAD NOUR; 6 brs.

United Bank of Egypt (UBE): Cairo Center, 106 Sharia Kasr el-Eini, Cairo; tel. (2) 7920146; fax (2) 7920153; e-mail info@ube.net; internet www.ube.net; f. 1981 as Dakahlia National Bank for Development; current name adopted in 1997; cap. 200m., res 51.4m., dep 3,700m. (Sept. 2003); Chair. and Man. Dir MUHAMMAD ADEL ES-SANHOURY; 9 brs.

Social Bank

Nasser Social Bank: POB 2552, 35 Sharia Qasr en-Nil, Cairo; tel. (2) 3924484; fax (2) 3921930; f. 1971; state-owned; interest-free savings and investment bank for social and economic activities, participating in social insurance, specializing in financing co-operatives, craftsmen and social institutions; cap. 20m.; Chair. NASSIF TAHOON.

Multinational Banks

Arab African International Bank: 5 Midan as-Saray al-Koubra, POB 60, Majlis esh-Sha'ab, Cairo 11516 (Garden City); tel. (2) 7945094; fax (2) 7958493; internet www.aaibank.com; f. 1964 as Arab African Bank, renamed 1978; cap. US $100.0m., res US $43.7m., dep. US $961.5m. (Dec. 2003); commercial investments and retail banking; shareholders are Govts of Kuwait, Egypt, Algeria, Jordan and Qatar, Bank Al-Jazira (Saudi Arabia), Rafidain Bank (Iraq), individuals and Arab institutions; Chair. Dr FAHED MOHAMMED AR-RASHED; Vice-Chair. and Man. Dir HASSAN E. ABDALLA; 10 brs in Egypt, 3 abroad.

Arab International Bank: POB 1563, 35 Sharia Abd al-Khalek Sarwat, Cairo; tel. (2) 3918794; fax (2) 3916233; internet www.aib-eg.com; f. 1971 as Egyptian International Bank for Foreign Trade and Investment, renamed 1974; cap. US $278.0m., res US $136.9m., dep. US $2,948.3m. (June 2003); offshore bank; aims to promote trade and investment in shareholders' countries and other Arab countries; owned by Egypt, Libya, UAE, Oman, Qatar and private Arab shareholders; Chair. Dr MUSTAFA KHALIL; Man. Dir ALI GAMAL AD-DIN DABBOUS; 7 brs.

Commercial Foreign Venture Banks

Alwatany Bank of Egypt: POB 63, 13 Sharia Semar, Dr Fouad Mohi ed-Din Sq., Gameat ed-Dewal al-Arabia, Mohandessin, Cairo 12655; tel. (2) 3388816; fax (2) 3379302; e-mail watany@alwatany.com.eg; internet www.alwatany.com.eg; f. 1980; cap. 250.0m., res 78.0m., dep. 5,421.6m. (Dec. 2003); Chair. and Man. Dir AHMAD HASSAN KOURA; 16 brs.

BNP PARIBAS Le Caire: POB 2441, 3 Latin America St, Cairo (Garden City); tel. (2) 7948323; fax (2) 7958156; e-mail bcpegypt@

bcpegypt.com; internet www.egypt.bnpparibas.net; f. 1977 as Banque du Caire et de Paris SAE; name changed in 2001; BNP Group Paribas has 76% interest and Banque du Caire 19.8%; cap. 53.0m., res 148.8m., dep. 2,219.8m. (Dec. 2003); Chair. JEAN THOMA-ZEAU; Man. Dir JEAN-MARC TORRE; 7 brs.

Cairo Barclays Bank, SAE: POB 110, 12 Midan esh-Sheikh Yousuf, Cairo (Garden City); tel. (2) 3662600; fax (2) 3662810; f. 1975 as Cairo Barclays Int. Bank; name changed to Banque du Caire Barclays International in 1983; renamed in 1999; Barclays Bank has 60%, Banque du Caire 40%; cap. 240.0m., res 46.6m., dep. 3,414.9m. (Dec. 2003); Chair. ELIE KHOURI; Man. Dir COLIN PLOWMAN; 7 brs.

Cairo Far East Bank, SAE: POB 757, 104 Corniche en-Nil, Cairo (Dokki); tel. (2) 3362516; fax (2) 3483818; f. 1978; cap. 62.5m., res 13.9m., dep. 188.5m. (Dec. 2003); Chair. MONA FAHMY YASSINE; Man. Dir AHMAD G. HAMDI; 4 brs.

Crédit Agricole Indosuez (Egypt), SAE: 46 Sharia el-Batal Ahmad Abd al-Aziz, Mohandessin, Cairo; tel. (2) 3361897; fax (2) 3608673; e-mail caie@eg.ca-indosuez.com; internet www .ca-indosuez.com; f. 1978 as Crédit International d'Egypte; renamed in 2001; Crédit Agricole Indosuez has 75% interest, el-Mansour & el-Maghraby for Financial Investment 25%; cap. 60.2m., res 51.4m., dep. 1,215.0m. (Dec. 2003); Chair. MUHAMMAD LOTFI MANSOUR; Man. Dir ADRIAN PHARES; 3 brs.

Delta International Bank: POB 1159, 1113 Corniche en-Nil, Cairo; tel. (2) 5753484; fax (2) 5743403; e-mail info@ deltainternationalbank.com; internet www.deltainternationalbank .com; f. 1978; cap. 500.0m., res 42.8m., dep. 2,463.0m. (Dec. 2003); Chair. and Man. Dir ALY MUHAMMAD NEGM; 18 brs.

Egyptian American Bank: POB 1825, 4 & 6 Sharia Hassan Sabri, Cairo (Zamalek); tel. (2) 7380126; fax (2) 7380609; e-mail ebarakat@ eab-online.com; internet www.eab-online.com; f. 1976; Amex Holdings Inc has 40.8% interest, Bank of Alexandria 32.5%, others 26.7%; cap. 144.0m., res 369.7m., dep. 9,142.6m. (Dec. 2003); Chair. MAH-MOUD ABD AL-LATIF; Man. Dir RODERICK RICHARDS; 31 brs.

Egyptian Commercial Bank: POB 92, 4th Floor, Evergreen Bldg, 10 Sharia Talaat Harb, Majlis ash-Sha'ab, Cairo; tel. (2) 5764644; fax (2) 5799862; internet www.ecb.com.eg; f. 1978 as Alexandria-Kuwait International Bank, name changed as above in 1997; cap. 150m., res 23.5m., dep. 2,417.9m. (Dec. 2003); Chair. MUHAMMAD ABD AL-WAHAD; Gen. Man. MUHAMMAD GAMAL MOHARAM; 12 brs.

Egyptian Gulf Bank: POB 56, El-Orman Plaza Bldg, 8–10 Sharia Ahmad Nessim, Cairo (Giza); tel. (2) 7606640; fax (2) 7606512; e-mail h.r.egb@mst1.mist.com.eg; internet www.egbbank.com.eg; f. 1981; Misr Insurance Co has 24.9% interest; cap. 217.7m., res 43.0m., dep. 2,315.3m. (Dec. 2003); Chair. KHALDOUN BAKRY BARAKAT; Man. Dir HISHAM RAMEZ ABD AL-HAFEZ; 5 brs.

Egyptian-Saudi Finance Bank: POB 455, 60 Sharia Mohy ad-Din Abu al-Ezz, Cairo (Dokki); tel. (2) 7481777; fax (2) 7611436; e-mail centeral@esf-bank.com; internet www.esf-bank.com; f. 1980 as Pyramids Bank; cap. 150.0m., res 18.5m., dep. 3,875.4m. (Sept. 2004); Chair. Sheikh SALEH ABDULLAH KAMEL; Man. Dir ASHRAF AHMAD EL-GHAMRAWY; 14 brs.

Faisal Islamic Bank of Egypt, SAE: POB 2446, 3 26 Sharia July, Cairo 11511; tel. (2) 7868939; fax (2) 7866744; e-mail foreigndept@ faisalbank.com.eg; internet www.faisalbank.com.eg; f. 1977; all banking operations conducted according to Islamic principles; cap. 263.7m., res 60.0m., dep. 12,879.7m. (Dec. 2003); Chair. Prince MUHAMMAD AL-FAISAL AS-SA'UD; 16 brs.

Misr-America International Bank: POB 1003, 12 Sharia Nadi es-Seid, Cairo 11511 (Dokki); tel. (2) 7616623; fax (2) 7616610; e-mail headoffice@maib.com.eg; internet www.maib.com.eg; f. 1977; Misr Insurance Co has 50% interest, Banque du Caire 33%, Industrial Development Bank of Egypt 17%, S.A. for Investments, Luxembourg 1.2%; cap. 100.0m., res 21.4m., dep. 1,471.0m. (Dec. 2003); Chair. and Man. Dir AHMAD MOUNIR EL-BARDAIE; 9 brs.

Misr International Bank, SAE: POB 218, 54 Sharia el-Batal Ahmad Abd al-Aziz, Mohandessin, Cairo 12411; tel. (2) 7497255; fax (2) 3489796; internet www.mibank.com.eg; f. 1975; the Banque Misr has 26.0% interest, Banco di Roma 10%, UBAF London 8.5%, Europartners 7.9%; cap. 140.6m., res 969.0m., dep. 14,590.0m. (Dec. 2003); Chair. HATEM SADEK; 18 brs.

Misr Romanian Bank: 54 Sharia Lebanon, Mohandessin, Cairo (Giza); tel. (2) 3039825; fax (2) 3039804; e-mail mrbeg@ie-eg.com; internet www.mrb.com.eg; f. 1977; Banque Misr has 33% interest, Romanian Commercial Bank (Bucharest) 19%, Raiffeisen Bank (Bucharest) 15%, and Romanian Bank for Development (Groupe Societe Générale Bucharest) 15%; cap. 182.3m., res 53.7m., dep. 3,187.4m. (Dec. 2003); Chair. ABD AR-RAHMAN BARAKA; 7 brs in Egypt, 3 in Romania.

Mohandes Bank: POB 170, 3–5 Sharia Mossadek, Cairo (Dokki); tel. (2) 3373110; fax (2) 3362741; internet www.mohandesbank.com;

f. 1979; cap. 161.0m., res 5.9m., dep. 5,049.1m. (Dec. 2002); Chair. and Man. Dir MOUSTAFA MOUSTAFA MARZOUK; 8 brs.

Nile Bank, SAE: POB 2741, 35 Sharia Ramses, Abd al-Moneim Riad Sq., Cairo; tel. (2) 5741417; fax (2) 5756296; e-mail nilebank@ egyptonline.com; f. 1978; cap. 32.2m., res 93.8m., dep. 2,045.5m. (Dec. 2003); Chair. and Man. Dir MUHAMMAD ES-SABAGH; 18 brs.

Suez Canal Bank, SAE: POB 2620, 7 Abd el-Kader Hamza St, Cairo (Garden City); tel. (2) 7943433; fax (2) 7942526; e-mail int-div@scbank.com.eg; internet www.scbank.com.eg; f. 1978; cap. 287.5m., res 499.9m., dep. 11,318.7m. (Dec. 2003); Chair. and Man. Dir WAGDY YOUSUF RABBAT; 25 brs.

Non-Commercial Banks

Arab Banking Corporation—Egypt: 1 Sharia el-Saleh Ayoub, Cairo (Zamalek); tel. (2) 7362684; fax (2) 7363643; e-mail abcegypt@ arabbanking.com.eg; internet www.arabbanking.com.eg; f. 1982 as Egypt Arab African Bank; acquired by Arab Banking Corporation (Bahrain) in 1999; Arab Banking Corporation has 93% interest, other interests 7%; cap. 100m., res 82.1m., dep. 2,041.5m. (Dec. 2003); commercial and investment bank; Chair. GHAZI ABD AL-JAWAD; Vice-Chair. EISSA AS-SUWAIDI; 9 brs.

Arab Investment Bank: POB 826, Cairo Sky Center Bldg, 8 Sharia Abd al-Khalek Sarwat, Cairo; tel. (2) 5768097; fax (2) 5770329; e-mail arinbank@mst1.mist.com.eg; internet www.aib.com.eg; f. 1978 as Union Arab Bank for Development and Investment; Egyptian/Syrian/Libyan joint venture; cap. 85.8m., res 2.5m., dep. 1,923.0m. (Dec. 2002); Chair. Prof. Dr MUHAMMAD AHMAD AR-RAZAZ; 13 brs.

Housing and Development Bank, SAE: POB 234, 12 Sharia Syria, Mohandessin, Cairo (Giza); tel. (2) 7492013; fax (2) 7600712; e-mail hdbank@internetegypt.com; internet www.hdb-egy.com; f. 1979; cap. 90.2m., res 241.5m., dep. 3,246.7m. (Dec. 2003); Chair. and Man. Dir FATHY ES-SEBAIE MANSOUR; 24 brs.

Islamic International Bank for Investment and Development: POB 180, 4 Sharia Ali Ismail, Mesaha Sq., Cairo (Dokki); tel. (2) 7489983; fax (2) 3600771; e-mail ibid@infinitycom.eg; internet www.iibid.com; f. 1980; cap. 133.8m., res –58.4m., dep. 3,720.1m. (Dec. 2002); Chair. BADAWY HASSAN HASSANAIN; Gen. Man. SAYED MUHAMMAD EL-MENSHAWY; 8 brs.

Misr Iran Development Bank: POB 219, Nile Tower Bldg, 21 Charles de Gaulle Ave, Cairo 12612 (Giza); tel. (2) 5727311; fax (2) 5701185; e-mail midb@mst1.mist.com.eg; internet www.midb.com .eg; f. 1975; the Bank of Alexandria has 29.93% interest, Misr Insurance Co 29.93%, Iran Foreign Investment Co 40.14%; cap. 433.7m., res 135.8m., dep. 2,646.7m. (Dec. 2003); Chair. and Man. Dir ISMAIL HASSAN MUHAMMAD; 10 brs.

National Société Générale Bank, SAE: POB 2664, 5 Sharia Champollion, 11111 Cairo; tel. (2) 7707000; fax (2) 7707799; e-mail info@nsgb.com.eg; internet www.nsgb.com.eg; f. 1978; the Société Générale de Paris has 54.33% interest, National Bank of Egypt 19.32%, other interests 26.35%; cap. 500.0m., res 172.8m., dep. 9,272.5m. (Dec. 2003); Chair. MUHAMMAD MADBOULY; Man. Dir GUY POUPET; 26 brs.

STOCK EXCHANGES

Capital Market Authority: POB 618, 20 Sharia Emad ed-Din, Cairo 11111; tel. (2) 5779696; fax (2) 5755339; e-mail cmaegypt@cma .gov.eg; internet www.cma.gov.eg; f. 1979; Chair. ABDELHAMID MUHAMMAD IBRAHIM; Dep. Chair. AHMAD SAAD ABD AL-LATIF.

Cairo and Alexandria Stock Exchanges (CASE): 4 Sharia esh-Sherifein, 11513 Cairo; 11 Sharia Talaat Harb, Menshia, Alexandria; tel. (2) 3921447; fax (2) 3928526; tel. (3) 4835432; fax (3) 4823039; e-mail webmaster@egyptse.com; internet www.egyptse .com; f. 1861; Chair. Dr SAMEH AT-TORGOMAN.

INSURANCE

Al-Ahly Insurance: Cairo; state-owned; scheduled for privatization.

Arab International Insurance Co: POB 2704, 28 Sharia Talaat Harb, Cairo; tel. (2) 5746322; fax (2) 5760053; e-mail aiic@aiic.com .eg; internet www.aiic.co.eg; f. 1976; a joint-stock free zone company established by Egyptian and foreign insurance companies; Chair. and Man. Dir HASSAN MUHAMMAD HAFEZ.

Ach-Chark Insurance Co: 15 Sharia Qasr en-Nil, Cairo; tel. (2) 5740455; fax (2) 5753316; e-mail ins_chark@frcu.eun.eg; f. 1931; scheduled for privatization; general and life; Chair. ANWAR ZEKRY.

Egyptian Reinsurance Co, SAE: POB 950, 7 Sharia Abd al-Latif Boltia, Cairo (Garden City); tel. (2) 7918300; fax (2) 7954360; e-mail egyptre@egyptre.com; internet www.egyptre.com.eg; f. 1957; scheduled for privatization; Chair. GAMAL HAMZA.

Al-Iktisad esh-Shabee, SAE: 11 Sharia Emad ed-Din, Cairo; f. 1948; Man. Dir and Gen. Man. W. KHAYAT.

Misr Insurance Co: POB 261, 44A Sharia Dokki, Cairo (Dokki); tel. (2) 3355350; fax (2) 3370428; e-mail micfin@frcu.eun.eg; internet www.frcu.eun.eg; f. 1934; all classes of insurance and reinsurance; scheduled for privatization; Chair. MOAWAD HASSANEIN.

Mohandes Insurance Co: POB 62, 3 El-Mesaha Sq., Cairo (Dokki); tel. (2) 3352162; fax (2) 3352697; e-mail mohandes@mist1.mist.com .eg; f. 1980; privately-owned; insurance and reinsurance; Chair. and Man. Dir SAMIR MOUSTAFA METWALLI.

Al-Mottahida: POB 804, 9 Sharia Sulayman Pasha, Cairo; f. 1957.

National Insurance Co of Egypt, SAE: POB 592, 41 Sharia Qasr en-Nil, Cairo; tel. (2) 3910731; fax (2) 3909133; e-mail omr-nice@eis .co.eg; f. 1900; cap. 100m.; scheduled for privatization; Chair. MUHAMMAD ABUL-YAZEED.

Provident Association of Egypt, SAE: POB 390, 9 Sharia Sherif Pasha, Alexandria; f. 1936; Man. Dir G. C. VORLOOU.

Trade and Industry

GOVERNMENT AGENCY

Egyptian Geological Survey and Mining Authority (EGSMA): 3 Tarik Salah Salem, Abbassia, Cairo; tel. (2) 6828013; fax (2) 4820128; e-mail egsma@idsc.gov.eg; internet www.egsma.gov.eg; f. 1896; state supervisory authority concerned with geological mapping, mineral exploration and other mining activities; Chair. ABU EL-HASSAN ABD AR-RAOUF.

DEVELOPMENT ORGANIZATION

General Authority for Investment and Free Zones (GAFI): POB 1007, 8 Sharia Adly, Cairo; tel. (2) 3906163; fax (2) 3907315; e-mail gafi@idsc.gov.eg; internet www.gafi.gov.eg; Chair. Eng. Dr MUHAMMAD EL-GHAMRAWI DAWOUD.

CHAMBERS OF COMMERCE

Federation of Chambers of Commerce: 4 el-Falaki Sq., Cairo; tel. (2) 3551164; fax (2) 3557940; Pres. MAHMOUD EL-ARABY.

Alexandria

Alexandria Chamber of Commerce: 31 Sharia el-Ghorfa Altogariya, Alexandria; tel. (3) 809339; fax (2) 808993; Pres. MOUSTAFA EN-NAGGAR.

Cairo

American Chamber of Commerce in Egypt: 33 Sharia Sulayman Abaza, Cairo (Dokki); tel. 3381050; fax (2) 3381060; e-mail web@amcham.org.eg; internet www.amcham.org.eg; Pres. Dr TAHER HELMY; Exec. Dir HISHAM FAHMY.

Cairo Chamber of Commerce: 4 el-Falaki Sq., Cairo; tel. (2) 3558261; fax (2) 3563603; f. 1913; Pres. MAHMOUD EL-ARABY; Sec.-Gen. MOSTAFA ZAKI TAHA.

In addition, there are 20 local chambers of commerce.

EMPLOYERS' ORGANIZATION

Federation of Egyptian Industries: 1195 Corniche en-Nil, Ramlet Boulal, Cairo; and 65 Gamal Abd an-Nasir Ave, Alexandria; tel. (2) 5796950; fax (2) 5796953 (Cairo); tel. and fax (3) 4916121 (Alexandria); e-mail feind@idsc.net.eg; internet www.fei.org.eg; f. 1922; Pres. MUHAMMAD FARID KHAMIS; represents the industrial community in Egypt.

PETROLEUM AND GAS

Arab Petroleum Pipelines Co (SUMED): POB 158, Es-Saray, 431 El-Geish Ave, Louran, Alexandria; tel. (3) 5864138; fax (3) 5871295; f. 1974; Suez–Mediterranean crude oil transportation pipeline (capacity: 117m. metric tons per year) and petroleum terminal operators; Chair. and Man. Dir Eng. HAZEM AMIN HAMMAD.

Belayim Petroleum Co (PETROBEL): POB 7074, Sharia el-Mokhayam, Cairo (Nasr City); tel. (2) 2621738; fax (2) 2609792; f. 1977; capital equally shared between EGPC and International Egyptian Oil Co, which is a subsidiary of ENI of Italy; petroleum and gas exploration, drilling and production; Chair. and Man. Dir FAROUK KENAWY.

Egyptian General Petroleum Corporation (EGPC): POB 2130, 4th Sector, Sharia Palestine, New Maadi, Cairo; tel. (2) 7065956; fax (2) 7028813; e-mail info@egpc.com.eg; internet www.egpc.com.eg; state supervisory authority generally concerned with the planning of

policies relating to petroleum activities in Egypt with the object of securing the development of the petroleum industry and ensuring its effective administration; Chair. MOUSTAFA SHAARAWI; Dep. Chair. HASAB EN-NABI ASAL.

General Petroleum Co (GPC): POB 743, 8 Sharia Dr Moustafa Abou Zahra, Cairo (Nasr City); tel. (2) 4030975; fax (2) 4037602; f. 1957; wholly-owned subsidiary of EGPC; operates mainly in Eastern Desert; Chair. HUSSEIN KAMAL.

Egyptian Natural Gas Holding Co (EGAS): 85C Sharia Nasr, Nasr City, Cairo; tel. (2) 4055845; fax (2) 4055876; e-mail egas@egas .com.eg; internet www.egas.com.eg; f. 2001 as part of a restructuring of the natural gas sector; Chair. MUHAMMAD TAWILA.

GASCO: Sheraton Heliopolis, 6A Sharia Moustafa Rifaat, Cairo (Heliopolis); tel. (2) 2666458; fax (2) 2666469; e-mail gasco@gasco .com.eg; internet www.gasco.com.eg; f. 1997; Gen. Man. Eng. MUHAMMAD IBRAHIM.

Gulf of Suez Petroleum Co (GUPCO): POB 2400, 4th Sector, Sharia Palestine, New Maadi, Cairo 11511; tel. (2) 3520985; fax (2) 3531286; f. 1965; partnership between EGPC and BP Egypt (UK/USA); developed the el-Morgan oilfield in the Gulf of Suez, also holds other exploration concessions in the Gulf of Suez and the Western Desert; Chair. AHMAD SHAWKY ABDINE; Man. Dir L. D. McVAY.

Western Desert Petroleum Co (WEPCO): POB 412, Borg eth-Thagr Bldg, Sharia Safia Zagloul, Alexandria; tel. (3) 4928710; fax (3) 4934016; f. 1967 as partnership between EGPC (50% interest) and Phillips Petroleum (35%) and later Hispanoil (15%); developed Alamein, Yidma and Umbarka fields in the Western Desert and later Abu Qir offshore gasfield in 1978 followed by NAF gas field in 1987; Chair. Eng. MUHAMMAD MOHI ED-DIN BAHGAT.

UTILITIES

Electricity

In 1998 seven new electricity generation and distribution companies were created, under the direct ownership of the Egyptian Electricity Authority (EEA). In 2000 the EEA was restructured into a holding company controlling five generation and seven distribution companies. A specialized grid company was to manage electricity transmission. The Government commenced partial privatizations of the generation and distribution companies in 2001–02, while retaining control of the hydroelectric generation and grid management companies.

Egypt Electricity Holding Co: Sharia Ramses, Cairo (Nasr City); tel. (2) 2616301; fax (2) 2616512; formerly the Egyptian Electricity Authority, renamed as above in 2000; Chair. NABIL YOUNES.

Alexandria Electricity Distribution: 9 Sharia Sidi el-Liban, Alexandria; tel. (3) 4935726; fax (3) 4933223.

Cairo Electricity Co: 53 Sharia 26 July, Cairo; tel. (2) 766612.

Cairo Electricity Distribution: 53 Sharia 26 July, Cairo; tel. (2) 766612; fax (2) 760383; Gen. Man. LOFTY EL-MOSHTLY.

Gas

Egypt Gas Company: Corniche en-Nil, 2 Geziret Muhammad, Warak-Imbaba, Cairo; tel. and fax (2) 3126081; e-mail egyptgas@ hotmail.com; f. 1983; Chair and Man. Dir NABIL HASHEM.

Water

National Association for Potable Water and Sanitary Drainage (NOPWASD): 6th Floor, Mogamma Bldg, et-Tahrir Sq., Cairo; tel. (2) 3557664; fax (2) 3562869; f. 1981; water and sewerage authority; Chair. MUHAMMAD KHALED MOUSTAFA.

TRADE UNIONS

Egyptian Trade Union Federation (ETUF): 90 Sharia al-Galaa, Cairo; tel. (2) 5740362; fax (2) 5753427; f. 1957; 23 affiliated unions; 5m. mems; affiliated to the International Confederation of Arab Trade Unions and to the Organization of African Trade Union Unity; Pres. MUHAMMAD ES-SAYED RASHID; Gen. Sec. MUHAMMAD ES-SAYED MORSI.

General Trade Union of Air Transport: G2, Osman Ibn Affoun, Sofin Sq., Cairo; tel. (2) 2413165; fax (2) 6336149; 11,000 mems; Pres. Eng. CHEHATA MUHAMMAD CHEHATA; Gen. Sec. MUHAMMAD HUSSEIN.

General Trade Union of Banks and Insurance: 2 Sharia el-Kady el-Fadel, Cairo; 56,000 mems; Pres. MAHMOUD MUHAMMAD DABBOUR; Gen. Sec. ABDOU HASSAN MUHAMMAD ALI.

General Trade Union of Building and Wood Workers: 9 Sharia Emad ed-Din, Cairo; tel. (2) 5913486; fax (2) 5915849; e-mail gtubww@hotmail.com; 500,000 mems; Pres. SAYED TAHA HASSAN; Gen. Sec. MUHAMMAD BAHAA.

General Trade Union of Chemical Workers: 90 Sharia al-Galaa, Cairo; fax (2) 5750490; 120,000 mems; Pres. IBRAHIM EL-AZHARY; Gen. Sec. GAAFER ABD EL-MONEM.

General Trade Union of Commerce: 54D Sharia el-Gomhouriya, Alfy Borg, Cairo; tel. (2) 5903159; fax (2) 5914144; f. 1903; 120,000 mems; Pres. FOUAD TOMA; Gen. Sec. SAMIR A. SHAFI.

General Trade Union of Food Industries: 3 Sharia Housni, Hadaek el-Koba, Cairo; 111,000 mems; Pres. SAAD M. AHMAD; Gen. Sec. ADLY TANOUS IBRAHIM.

General Trade Union of Health Services: 22 Sharia esh-Sheikh Qamar, es-Sakakiny, Cairo; 56,000 mems; Pres. IBRAHIM ABOU EL-MUTI IBRAHIM; Gen. Sec. AHMAD ABD AL-LATIF SALEM.

General Trade Union of Hotels and Tourism Workers: POB 606, 90 Sharia al-Galaa, Cairo; tel. and fax (2) 773901; 70,000 mems; Pres. MUHAMMAD HILAL ESH-SHARKAWI.

General Trade Union of Maritime Transport: 36 Sharia Sharif, Cairo; 46,000 mems; Pres. THABET MUHAMMAD ES-SEFARI; Gen. Sec. MUHAMMAD RAMADAN ABOU TOR.

General Trade Union of Military Production: 90 Sharia al-Galaa, Cairo; 64,000 mems; Pres. MOUSTAFA MUHAMMAD MOUNGI; Gen. Sec. FEKRY IMAM.

General Trade Union of Mine Workers: 5 Sharia Ali Sharawi, Hadaek el-Koba, Cairo; 14,000 mems; Pres. ABBAS MAHMOUD IBRAHIM; Gen. Sec. AMIN HASSAN AMER.

General Trade Union of Petroleum Workers: 5 Sharia Ali Sharawi, Hadaek el-Koba, Cairo; tel. (2) 4820091; fax (2) 4834551; 60,000 mems; Pres. FAUZI ABD AL-BARI; Gen. Sec. AMIR ABD ES-SALAM.

General Trade Union of Postal Workers: 90 Sharia al-Galaa, Cairo; 80,000 mems; Pres. HASSAN MUHAMMAD EID; Gen. Sec. SALEM MAHMOUD SALEM.

General Trade Union of Press, Printing and Information: 90 Sharia al-Galaa, Cairo; tel. (2) 740324; 55,000 mems; Pres. MUHAMMAD ALI EL-FIKKI; Gen. Sec. AHMAD ED-DESSOUKI.

General Trade Union of Public and Administrative Workers: 2 Sharia Muhammad Haggag, Midan et-Tahrir, Cairo; tel. (2) 5742134; fax (2) 5752044; e-mail mostommmostafa@hotmail.com; 250,000 mems; Pres. Dr AHMAD ABDELZAHER; Gen. Sec. MUKHTAR HAMOUDA.

General Trade Union of Public Utilities Workers: POB 194, 6 Sharia Ramsis, Cairo; tel. (2) 5799614; fax (2) 5799616; e-mail rostommostafa@hotmail.com; 290,000 mems; Pres. MUHAMMAD ES-SAYED MORSI ALY; Gen. Sec. USAMA GAMAL ABDUL SAMIEE.

General Trade Union of Railway Workers: POB 84 (el-Faggalah), 15 Sharia Emad ed-Din, Cairo; tel. (2) 5930305; fax (2) 5917776; 90,000 mems; Pres. SABER AHMAD HUSSAIN; Gen. Sec. YASIN SOLUMAN.

General Trade Union of Road Transport: 90 Sharia al-Galaa, Cairo; tel. (2) 5752955; fax (2) 5754919; 245,000 mems; Pres. SABRY EL-GUERIDI; Gen. Sec. SAYED RADURAN.

General Trade Union of Telecommunications Workers: POB 651, Cairo; 60,000 mems; Pres. KHAIRI HACHEM; Sec.-Gen. IBRAHIM SALEH.

General Trade Union of Textile Workers: 327 Sharia Shoubra, Cairo; 244,000 mems; Pres. ALI MUHAMMAD DOUFDAA; Gen. Sec. HASSAN TOULBA MARZOUK.

General Trade Union of Workers in Agriculture and Irrigation: 31 Sharia Mansour, Cairo (Bab el-Louk); tel. (2) 3541419; 150,000 mems; Pres. MUKHTAR ABD AL-HAMID; Gen. Sec. FATHI A. KURTAM.

General Trade Union of Workers in Engineering, Metal and Electrical Industries: 90 Sharia al-Galaa, Cairo; tel. (2) 742519; 160,000 mems; Pres. SAID GOMAA; Gen. Sec. MUHAMMAD FARES.

Transport

RAILWAYS

The area of the Nile Delta is well served by railways. Lines also run from Cairo southward along the Nile to Aswan, and westward along the coast to Salloum.

Egyptian National Railways: Station Bldg, Midan Ramses, Cairo 11794; tel. (2) 5751000; fax (2) 5740000; f. 1852; length 8,600 km; 42 km electrified; a 346-km line to carry phosphate and iron ore from the Bahariya mines, in the Western Desert, to the Helwan iron and steel works in south Cairo, was opened in 1973, and the Qena–Safaga line (length 223 km) came into operation in 1989; Chair. EID ABDELKADER.

Alexandria Passenger Transport Authority: POB 466, Aflaton, esh-Shatby, Alexandria 21111; tel. (3) 5975223; fax (3) 5971187; e-mail chrmapta@cns-egypt.com; f. 1860; controls City Tramways (28 km), Ramleh Electric Railway (16 km), suburban buses and minibuses (1,688 km); 121 tram cars, 42 light railway three-car sets; Chair. and Tech. Dir Eng. MEDHAT HAFEZ.

Cairo Metro: National Authority for Tunnels, POB 466, Ramses Bldg, Midan Ramses, Cairo 11794; tel. (2) 5742968; fax (2) 5742950; construction of the first electrified, 1,435-mm gauge underground transport system in Africa and the Middle East began in Cairo in 1982. Line 1 has a total of 35 stations (5 underground), connects el-Marg el Gedida with Helwan and is 44 km long with a 4.2-km tunnel beneath central Cairo; Line 2 links Shoubra el-Kheima with Giza at el-Monib station, totalling 21.6km. (13 km in tunnel), and with 20 stations (12 underground), two of which interconnect with Line 1; the fifth phase of Line 2, from Um el-Masnien to el-Monib stations was inaugurated in January 2005; construction of Line 3 which will connect Imbaba and Mohandeseen with Cairo International Airport and will total 34.2 km (30.3 km in tunnel) with 29 stations (27 underground) was due to commence in the near future; Chair. Eng. SAAD HASSAN SHEHATA.

Cairo Transport Authority: POB 254, Madinet Nasr, Cairo; tel. (2) 830533; length 78 km (electrified); gauge 1,000 mm; operates 16 tram routes and 24 km of light railway; 720 cars; Chair. M. E. ABD ES-SALAM.

Lower Egypt Railway: El-Mansoura; f. 1898; length 160 km; gauge 1,000 mm; 20 diesel railcars.

ROADS

There are good metalled main roads as follows: Cairo–Alexandria (desert road); Cairo–Banha–Tanta–Damanhour–Alexandria; Cairo–Suez (desert road); Cairo–Ismailia–Port Said or Suez; Cairo–Fayoum (desert road); in 1997 there were some 41,300 km of roads, including 22,000 km of highways. The estimated total length of the road network at mid-2001 was 48,260 km. The Ahmad Hamdi road tunnel (1.64 km) beneath the Suez Canal was opened in 1980. A 320-km macadamized road linking Mersa Matruh, on the Mediterranean coast, with the oasis town of Siwa was completed in 1986. A second bridge over the Suez Canal was completed in mid-2001.

General Authority for Roads, Bridges and Land Transport—Ministry of Transport: 105 Sharia Qasr el-Eini, Cairo; tel. (2) 7957429; fax (2) 7950591; e-mail garblt@garblt.com; Chair. Eng. ADEL MUHAMMAD YOUSSEF.

SHIPPING

Egypt's principal ports are Alexandria, Port Said and Suez. A port constructed at a cost of £E315m., and designed to handle up to 16m. metric tons of grain, fruit and other merchandise per year (22% of the country's projected imports by 2000) in its first stage of development, was opened at Damietta in 1986. The second stage will increase handling capacity to 25m. tons per year. A ferry link between Nuweibeh and the Jordanian port of Aqaba was opened in 1985.

Alexandria Port Authority: 106 ave el-Horreia, Alexandria; Head Office: 106 Sharia el-Hourriya, Alexandria; tel. (3) 4871640; fax (3) 4869714; e-mail alexportinfo@internetalex.com; internet www .alexandriaportauthority.com; f. 1966; Chair. R. Adm. MUHAMMAD FARAG LOTRY; Vice-Chair. R. Adm. MUHAMMAD M. ZAKI.

Major Shipping Companies

Alexandria Shipping and Navigation Co: POB 812, 557 ave el-Hourriya, Alexandria; tel. (3) 62923; services between Egypt, N. and W. Europe, USA, Red Sea and Mediterranean; 5 vessels; Chair. Eng. MAHMOUD ISMAIL; Man. Dir ABD AL-AZIZ QADRI.

Arab Maritime Petroleum Transport Co (AMPTC): POB 143, 9th Floor, Nile Tower Bldg, 21 Sharia Giza, 12211 Giza; tel. (2) 5701311; fax (2) 3378080; e-mail amptc.cairo@amptc.net; internet www.amptc.net; 11 vessels; Chair. Dr RAMADAN ES-SANOUSSI BELHAG; Gen. Man. SULAYMAN AL-BASSAM.

Egyptian Navigation Co: POB 82, 2 Sharia en-Nasr, Alexandria 21511; tel. (3) 4800050; fax (3) 4871345; e-mail enc@dataxprs.com .eg; internet www.enc.com.eg; f. 1930; owners and operators of Egypt's mercantile marine; international trade transportation; 24 vessels; Chair. ABDALLA ALI FAHIM; Man. Dir ABU ZID ES-SAADANY.

Memnon Tours Co: POB 2533, 18 Sharia Hoda Sharawi, Cairo; tel. (2) 3930195; fax (2) 3917410; 7 vessels.

Misr Petroleum Co: POB 228, Misr Petroleum House, 6 Sharia Orabi, Cairo; tel. (2) 5755000; fax (2) 5745436; 8 vessels; Chair. Eng. SALAH ED-DIN HASSAN.

Misr Shipping Co: POB 157, 13 Sharia Masgid en-Nasr, Soumoha, Sidi Gaber, Alexandria; tel. (3) 4270227; fax (3) 4288425; e-mail insp@misrshipping.com; internet www.misrshipping.com; 9 vessels; Chair. and Man. Dir Adm. YOUSRI HANAFY.

National Navigation Co: 4 Sharia Ehegaz, Cairo (Heliopolis); tel. (2) 4525575; fax (2) 4526171; 11 vessels; Chair. and Man. Dir MUHAMMAD SHAWKI YOUNIS.

Pan-Arab Shipping Co: POB 39, 404 ave el-Hourriya, Rushdi, Alexandria; tel. (3) 5468835; fax (3) 5469533; f. 1974; Arab League Co; 5 vessels; Chair. Adm. MUHAMMAD SHERIF ES-SADEK; Gen. Man. Capt. MAMDOUH EL-GUINDY.

As-Salam Shipping & Trading Establishment: Apartment 203, 24 Sharia Ahmad Talceer, Cairo (Heliopolis); tel. (2) 908535; fax (2) 4175390; 6 vessels.

Samatour Shipping Co: As-Salam Bldg, 4 Sharia Naguib er-Rihani, Rami Station, Alexandria; tel. (3) 4822028; fax (3) 4832003; 5 vessels; Chair. SALEM A. SALEM.

Sayed Nasr Navigation Lines: 5 Sharia Dr Ahmad Amin, Cairo (Heliopolis); tel. (2) 2457643; fax (2) 2457736; 6 vessels.

Société Cooperative des Pétroles: Cooperative Bldg, 94 Sharia Qasr el-Eini, Cairo; tel. (2) 7360623; fax (2) 7956404; Chair. Dr TAMER ABU BAKR; Gen. Dir OSAMA IBRAHIM.

THE SUEZ CANAL

In 2000 a total of 14,141 vessels, with a net displacement of 439m. tons, used the Suez Canal, linking the Mediterranean and Red Seas.

Length of canal 190 km; maximum permissible draught: 17.68 m (58 ft); breadth of canal at water level and breadth between buoys defining the navigable channel at −11 m: 365 m and 225 m, respectively, in the northern section and 305 m and 205 m in the southern section.

Suez Canal Authority (Hay'at Canal as-Suways): Irshad Bldg, Ismailia; Cairo Office: 6 Sharia Lazoughli, Cairo (Garden City); tel. (64) 9100000; fax (64) 914784; e-mail scanalb@idsc.net.eg; f. 1956; Chair. Adm. AHMAD ALI FADEL.

Suez Canal Container Handling Company: Cairo; f. 2000; with 30-year concession to operate the East Port Said container terminal, scheduled to begin operations in late 2002.

CIVIL AVIATION

The main international airports are at Heliopolis (23 km from the centre of Cairo) and Alexandria (7 km from the city centre). An international airport was opened at Nuzhah in 1983. In early 2001 the Ministry of Transport announced the restructuring and modernization of the civil aviation sector. In that year airports were under construction at el-Alamein, west of Alexandria, and at Asyout; however, plans for the construction of a new airport in west Cairo were suspended in late 2001. The existing Cairo airport was to be expanded, with a third terminal and a new runway, while the Sharm esh-Sheikh airport was also scheduled for expansion. Further expansion plans were announced in late 2003, including the construction of a new international airport at Borg al-Arab and the expansion of airports at Luxor, Sharm esh-Sheikh and Hurghada.

In 2000 19.5m. passengers and 188,783 metric tons of cargo passed through Egypt's airports.

EgyptAir: Administration Complex, Cairo International Airport, Cairo (Heliopolis); tel. (2) 2674700; fax (2) 2663773; internet www.egyptair.com.eg; f. 1932 as Misr Airwork; known as United Arab Airlines 1960–1971; operates internal services in Egypt and external services throughout the Middle East, Far East, Africa, Europe and the USA; Chair. ATEF ABD AL-HAMID; CEO SHERIF GALAL.

Egyptian Civil Aviation Authority: ECAA Complex, Sharia Airport, Cairo 11776; tel. (2) 2677610; fax (2) 2470351; e-mail egoca@idsc.gov.eg; f. 2000; Chair. Dr IBRAHIM MUHAMMAD MUTAWALLI AD-DUMEIRI.

Egyptian Holding Co for Airports and Air Traffic: Cairo; f. 2001; responsible for management and development of all Egyptian airports; Pres. ABD AL-FATTAH KATTU.

Cairo Airport Authority (CAA): Cairo International Airport, Cairo (Heliopolis); tel. (2) 2474245; fax (2) 2432522; under management of Egyptian Holding Co since 2003.

Egyptian Airports Co: Cairo; f. 2001; responsible for new airport projects; Pres. NAGI SAMUEL.

Tourism

Tourism is currently Egypt's second largest source of revenue, generating US $3,764m. in 2002. Traditionally the industry has attracted tourists to the country's pyramids and monuments. However, recently the industry has diversified; the Red Sea coastline has 1,000 km of beaches along which developments, including two international airports at Taba and Suba Bay, are under construction and where scuba diving is a popular pursuit. A new luxury resort was planned for Port Ghaleb, equipped with a marina for 1,000 yachts and an airport. In 2001 the Biblioteca Alexandrina opened in Alexandria. The tourism industry was adversely affected in the mid-1990s by the campaign of violence by fundamentalist Islamists; although some recovery in tourist numbers was recorded by the end of the decade, the sector was again adversely affected by the crisis in Israeli–Palestinian relations from late 2000, and by the repercussions of the suicide attacks on the USA in September 2001. In 2002 tourist arrivals decreased to 2.1m., compared with more than 5m. (including excursionists) in 2000. Nevertheless, a reported 6.0m. tourists visited Egypt during 2003.

Ministry of Tourism: Misr Travel Tower, Abbassia Sq., Cairo; tel. (2) 2828439; fax (2) 2859551; e-mail wwebmaster@visitegypt.gov.eg; internet www.visitegypt.gov.eg; f. 1965; brs at Alexandria, Port Said, Suez, Luxor and Aswan; Minister of Tourism AHMAD AL-MAGHRABI.

Egyptian General Authority for the Promotion of Tourism: Misr Travel Tower, Abbassia Sq., Cairo; tel. (2) 2853576; fax (2) 2854363; e-mail contact@touregypt.net; internet www.touregypt.net; Chair. ADEL ABD AL-AZIZ.

Egyptian General Co for Tourism and Hotels (EGOTH): 4 Sharia Latin America, Cairo (Garden City); tel. (2) 7942914; fax (2) 7964830; e-mail info@egoth.com.eg; internet www.egoth.com.eg; f. 1961; affiliated to the holding co for Housing, Tourism and Cinema; Chair. NABIL ALI SELIM.

EL SALVADOR

Introductory Survey

Location, Climate, Language, Religion, Flag, Capital

The Republic of El Salvador lies on the Pacific coast of Central America. It is bounded by Guatemala to the west and by Honduras to the north and east. The climate varies from tropical on the coastal plain to temperate in the uplands. The language is Spanish. About 74% of the population are Roman Catholics, and other Christian churches are represented. The civil flag (proportions 2 by 3) consists of three equal horizontal stripes, of blue, over white, over blue. The state flag differs by the addition, in the centre of the white stripe, of the national coat of arms. The capital is San Salvador.

Recent History

El Salvador was ruled by Spain until 1821, and became independent in 1839. Since then the country's history has been one of frequent coups and outbursts of political violence. General Maximiliano Hernández Martínez became President in 1931, and ruthlessly suppressed a peasant uprising, with an alleged 30,000 killings (including that of Farabundo Martí, the leader of the rebel peasants), in 1932. President Hernández was deposed in 1944, and the next elected President, Gen. Salvador Castañeda Castro, was overthrown in 1948. His successor as President, Lt-Col Oscar Osorio (1950–56), relinquished power to Lt-Col José María Lemus, who was deposed by a bloodless coup in 1960. He was replaced by a military junta, which was itself supplanted by another junta in January 1961. Under this Junta, the conservative Partido de Conciliación Nacional (PCN) was established and won all 54 seats in elections to the Asamblea Legislativa (Legislative Assembly) in December. A member of the Junta, Lt-Col Julio Adalberto Rivera, was elected unopposed to the presidency in 1962. He was succeeded by the PCN candidate, Gen. Fidel Sánchez Hernández, in 1967.

In the 1972 presidential election Col Arturo Armando Molina Barraza, candidate of the ruling PCN, was elected. His rival, José Napoleón Duarte, the leader of the left-wing coalition party, Unión Nacional de Oposición, staged an abortive coup in March, and Col Molina took office in July, despite allegations of massive electoral fraud. Similar allegations were made during the 1977 presidential election, after which the PCN candidate, Gen. Carlos Humberto Romero Mena, took office.

Reports of violations of human rights by the Government were widespread in 1979. The polarization of left and right after 1972 was characterized by an increase in guerrilla activity. In October 1979 President Romero was overthrown and replaced by a Junta of civilians and army officers. The Junta, which promised to install a democratic system and to organize elections, declared a political amnesty and invited participation from the guerrilla groups, but violence continued between government troops and guerrilla forces, and elections were postponed. In January 1980 an ultimatum from progressive members of the Government resulted in the formation of a new Government, a coalition of military officers and the Partido Demócrata Cristiano (PDC). In March the country moved closer to full-scale civil war following the assassination of the Roman Catholic Archbishop of San Salvador, Oscar Romero y Galdames, an outspoken supporter of human rights.

In December 1980 José Napoleón Duarte, the 1972 presidential candidate and a member of the Junta, was sworn in as President. In January 1981 the guerrillas launched their 'final offensive' and, after initial gains, the opposition front, Frente Democrático Revolucionario—FDR (allied with the guerrilla front, the Frente Farabundo Martí para la Liberación Nacional—FMLN), proposed negotiations with the USA. The US authorities referred them to the Salvadorean Government, which refused to recognize the FDR while it was linked with the guerrillas. The USA affirmed its support for the Duarte Government and provided civilian and military aid. During 1981 the guerrilla forces unified and strengthened their control over the north and east of the country. Attacks on economic targets continued, while the army retaliated by acting indiscriminately against the local population in guerrilla-controlled areas. By December there were an estimated 300,000 Salvadorean refugees, many of whom had fled to neighbouring countries.

At elections to a National Constituent Assembly, conducted in March 1982, the PDC failed to win an absolute majority against the five right-wing parties, which, together having obtained 60% of the total votes, formed a Government of National Unity. Major Roberto D'Aubuisson Arrieta, leader of the extreme right-wing Alianza Republicana Nacionalista (ARENA), became President of the National Constituent Assembly. In April a politically independent banker, Dr Alvaro Magaña Borja, was elected interim President of El Salvador, after pressure from the armed forces. However, the Assembly voted to award itself considerable power over the President. Military leaders then demanded that five ministerial posts be given to members of the PDC, fearing that, otherwise, US military aid would be withdrawn. A presidential election was scheduled for 1983, and a new constitution was to be drafted. During 1982 about 1,600 Salvadorean troops were trained in the USA, and US military advisers were reported to be actively participating in the conflict.

The presidential election was postponed until March 1984, as a result of disagreement in the National Constituent Assembly over the new Constitution, which finally became effective in December 1983. The issue of agrarian reform caused a serious dispute between Maj. D'Aubuisson's ARENA party and the PDC, and provoked a campaign by right-wing 'death squads' against trade unionists and peasant leaders. (In 1980 the governing Junta had nationalized some 60% of the country's prime arable land as part of a three-phase agrarian reform initiative, which envisaged the eventual redesignation of 90% of El Salvador's farmland. However, subsequent phases of the expropriation and reallocation programme had been suspended in March 1981 and May 1982, prompting US Government threats to withdraw financial and military assistance.) In December 1983 ARENA secured the support of the Assembly for the reactivation of a severely compromised reform programme, which provided for a maximum permissible landholding of 245 ha (rather than 100 ha as originally envisaged). This represented an important victory for the ARENA party, which had been isolated in the Assembly following the collapse of its alliance with the PCN in February.

Following a period of intense activity by 'death squads' in late 1983, when the weekly total of murders exceeded 200, the US Government urged the removal of several high-level officials, military officers and political figures who were linked to the murders. The failure of the US-trained 'rapid reaction' battalions and frequent reports of army atrocities undermined both public confidence in the Government and US President Ronald Reagan's efforts to secure further US aid for El Salvador. In February 1984, following a number of strategic territorial advances, the FDR-FMLN proposed the formation of a broadly-based provisional government, as part of a peace plan without preconditions. The plan was rejected by the Government. The guerrillas refused to participate in the presidential election, conducted in March 1984, and attempted to prevent voting in various provinces. As no candidate emerged with a clear majority, a second round of voting was held in May, when José Napoleón Duarte, the candidate of the PDC, defeated Maj. D'Aubuisson, the ARENA candidate.

Following his inauguration in June 1984, President Duarte instituted a purge of the armed forces and the reorganization of the police force, including the disbanding of the notorious Treasury Police. Both the FDR-FMLN and the President expressed their willingness to commence peace negotiations. Following pressure from the Roman Catholic Church and trade unions, the Government opened discussions with guerrilla leaders in Chalatenango in October. A second round of negotiations, held in November, ended amid accusations of intransigence from both sides.

At legislative and municipal elections in March 1985 the PDC won a convincing victory over the ARENA-PCN electoral alliance, thereby securing a clear majority in the new Asamblea Nacional (National Assembly). The PDC's victory, coupled with internal divisions within the right-wing grouping, precipitated a decline in the popularity and influence of the alliance, which culminated in the resignation of ARENA's leader, Roberto D'Aubuisson, in September.

Despite a perceived decline in political violence and abuses of human rights in 1985–86, the failure of the Government and the rebels to agree an agenda for renewed negotiations during this period prompted speculation that a military solution would be sought to end the civil war. Such speculation was supported by reports of the armed forces' growing domination of the conflict and by the success of the army's 'Unidos para reconstruir' campaign, a social and economic programme, launched in July 1986, to recover areas that had been devastated by the protracted fighting.

In March 1987 guerrillas carried out a successful attack on the army garrison at El Paraíso, which enabled them to take the military initiative in the civil war. Later in the year, however, the Salvadorean Government's participation in a peace plan for Central America, which was signed on 7 August in Guatemala City, encouraged hopes that a peaceful solution could be found to the conflict. Discussions between the Government and the FDR-FMLN were eventually held in October, when agreement was reached on the formation of two committees to study the possibility of a cease-fire and an amnesty.

Despite the inauguration, in September 1987, of a National Reconciliation Commission, appointed by the President in August, and the Government's proclamation, in November, of a unilateral cease-fire, no long-term cessation of hostilities was maintained by either side. The political situation deteriorated further in late 1987, following President Duarte's public denunciation of Roberto D'Aubuisson's complicity in the murder of Archbishop Romero y Galdames in March 1980. Furthermore, in 1988 there were increasing reports of the resurgence of 'death squads', and it was suggested that abuses of human rights were rapidly returning to the level reached at the beginning of the internal conflict.

In February 1988 the FMLN launched a campaign of bombings and transport disruptions, in order to undermine preparations for the forthcoming legislative and municipal elections. At the elections, in March, ARENA secured control of more than 200 municipalities, including San Salvador, hitherto held for more than 20 years by the PDC. The party also resumed an overall majority in the Asamblea.

By the end of 1988 it was estimated that as many as 70,000 Salvadoreans had died in the course of the civil war, while the US Administration had provided some US $3,000m. in aid to the Government. Moreover, by early 1989 many areas appeared to be without government, following the resignations of some 75 mayors and nine judges, purportedly because of death threats by the FMLN. In late January, however, radical new peace proposals were announced by the FMLN, which, for the first time, expressed its willingness to participate in the electoral process. The FMLN proposed that the presidential election be postponed from March to September, and offered a 60-day cease-fire (30 days on each side of a September election date). However, negotiations about this proposal failed to produce agreement. The FMLN advocated a boycott of the election, to be held on 19 March, and intensified its campaign of violence, resulting in the deaths of more than 40 people on election day alone. The election resulted in victory for the ARENA candidate, Alfredo Cristiani Burkard. The level of abstention was estimated at almost 50%. Cristiani took office on 1 June 1989.

In August 1989 the Heads of State of five Central American countries signed an agreement in Tela, Honduras. The accord included an appeal to the FMLN to abandon its military campaign and to 'initiate dialogue' with the Salvadorean Government. In the spirit engendered by the Tela agreement, representatives of the Government and the FMLN began negotiations in Mexico City in September. A second round of discussions took place in October. However, a planned third round of talks was abandoned following a bomb attack in late October, allegedly perpetrated by the Salvadorean army, on the headquarters of the Salvadorean Workers' National Union Federation (FENAS-TRAS), in which 10 people were killed. On 7 November, in accordance with the Tela agreement, the UN Security Council authorized the creation of the UN Observer Group for Central America (ONUCA), a multinational military force, to monitor developments in the region.

On 11 November 1989 the FMLN launched a military offensive, and throughout the month the fiercest fighting for nine years took place. The Government declared a state of siege, and stability was further undermined when, on 16 November, gunmen murdered the head of a San Salvador Jesuit university

and five other Jesuit priests. On 12 January 1990, however, the FMLN announced that it would accept an offer made by the Salvadorean Government whereby the UN Secretary-General, Javier Pérez de Cuéllar, was to arrange the reopening of peace talks. In March President Cristiani announced that he was willing to offer a comprehensive amnesty, territorial concessions and the opportunity to participate fully in political processes to members of the FMLN, as part of a broad-based peace proposal. Later in the year, however, hopes for the successful negotiation of a peaceful settlement were frustrated by the failure of the two sides to reach a consensus, at a series of UN-sponsored discussions, on the crucial issue of the future role, structure and accountability of the armed forces.

In May 1990 guerrilla forces had launched their first major offensive since November 1989. By the end of September all hopes for a cease-fire had been abandoned. A renewed FMLN offensive was undertaken by the newly-proclaimed National Army for Democracy (the establishment of which marked the reorganization of the FMLN's previous divisions into a more conventional army structure) in several departments in November. The conflict was considered to have entered into a new phase when, in the same month, a government aircraft was shot down by guerrilla forces armed with surface-to-air missiles (supplied by Nicaraguan military personnel).

Negotiations between the Government and the FMLN continued throughout 1991, interspersed by violent exchanges between the guerrillas and the security forces. On 10 March elections to the Asamblea (enlarged from 60 to 84 seats) and to 262 municipalities were conducted. While guerrilla forces refrained from disrupting the proceedings (the FMLN announced a three-day cease-fire), it was reported that many voters were intimidated by an escalation in military operations, and more than 50% of the electorate failed to cast a vote. The final results revealed that ARENA had lost its majority in the Asamblea, but continued to command considerable support, with 44.3% of the votes and 39 seats. The party also retained significant support in the local elections, with victories in 175 of the 262 municipalities.

In late March 1991 a new initiative for the negotiation of a peace settlement was presented by the FMLN in Managua, Nicaragua, following a meeting between foreign affairs ministers from Central America and the European Community (EC, now European Union—EU). This new proposal dispensed with previous stipulations put forward by the guerrillas that military and constitutional reforms should be effected prior to any cease-fire, and suggested that concessions on both sides could be adopted simultaneously. The constitutional requirement that amendments to the Constitution be ratified by two successive legislative assemblies lent impetus to negotiations in April, the current Asamblea being scheduled to dissolve at the end of the month. Despite the attempts of uncompromising right-wing members of the Asamblea to sabotage the proceedings, a last-minute agreement on human rights (including the creation of a three-member 'truth commission', to be appointed by the UN Secretary-General) and on judicial and electoral reform was reached by the Government and the FMLN, and was swiftly approved by the Asamblea, prior to its dissolution. The working structure of a cease-fire and the detailed reform and purge of the armed forces were set aside for negotiation at a later date.

In May 1991 the UN Security Council voted to create an observer mission to El Salvador (ONUSAL), to be charged with the verification of accords reached between the Government and the FMLN. Initially the mission was to be resident in six regional centres for a 12-month period, and was expected to participate in any future cease-fire and peaceful reintegration programme. The creation of ONUSAL was denounced by right-wing groups within El Salvador as unwarranted interference and as an insult to national sovereignty.

In August 1991 both sides attended a round of discussions in New York, USA, where a new framework for peace was agreed. A National Commission for the Consolidation of Peace (COPAZ) was to be created (comprising representatives of both sides, as well as of all major political parties), which would supervise the enforcement of guarantees for the political integration of guerrillas. The FMLN also secured guaranteed territorial rights for peasants settled in guerrilla-controlled areas, and the participation of former FMLN members in a National Civilian Police, which was to be under the control of a new Ministry of the Interior and Public Security. At the same time, the Asamblea approved constitutional reforms, whereby the Central Electoral Commission would be replaced by a Supreme Electoral Tribunal, composed of five magistrates (one from each of the five most successful parties at the previous presidential election), to be elected by the Asamblea.

In December 1991, following renewed discussions between the Government and the guerrilla leaders in New York, a new peace initiative was announced. Under the terms of the agreement, a formal cease-fire was to be implemented on 1 February 1992, under the supervision of some 1,000 UN personnel. The FMLN was to begin a process of disarmament, to be implemented in five stages (simultaneous with the dissolution of the notorious, military-controlled, 17,000-strong rapid deployment battalions), leading to full disarmament by 31 October. The success of the cease-fire agreement was expected to be dependent upon the adequate implementation, by the Government, of previously agreed reforms to the judiciary, the electoral system, guarantees of territorial rights, human rights, and guerrilla participation in civil defence, and of newly agreed reforms whereby the armed forces would be purged of those most responsible for abuses of human rights during the previous 12 years, and would be reduced in size by almost one-half, over a 22-month period.

On 16 January 1992, at Chapultepec Castle in Mexico City, the formal peace accord was ratified and was witnessed by the new UN Secretary-General, Boutros Boutros-Ghali, the US Secretary of State, James Baker, Heads of State from Central America, South America and Europe, representatives of El Salvador's military high command and all 84 members of the Asamblea. On 1 February some 30,000 Salvadoreans gathered in San Salvador to celebrate the first day of the cease-fire and to attend the formal installation of COPAZ.

Although mutual allegations of failure to comply with the terms of the peace accord persisted during 1992, prompting the temporary withdrawal, in May, of the FMLN from COPAZ, and resulting in further UN mediation and the negotiation of a revised timetable for disarmament, the cease-fire was carefully observed by both sides. In San Salvador on 15 December (declared National Reconciliation Day), at a ceremony attended by President Cristiani, FMLN leaders, the UN Secretary-General and Central American Heads of State and government representatives, the conflict was formally concluded, the terms of the December 1991 agreement having been fulfilled to the satisfaction of both sides. On the same day the FMLN was officially registered and recognized as a legitimate political party.

In November 1992, in accordance with the terms of the December 1991 peace accord, the Comisión de la Verdad (Truth Commission) announced the names of more than 200 military personnel alleged to have participated in abuses of human rights during the civil war. By early 1993, however, despite the urgences of the UN Secretary-General, the reluctance of the Government to comply with the conditions of the peace accord, relating to the removal from the armed forces of those personnel (particularly officers) identified by the Commission, threatened the further successful implementation of the process of pacification, and prompted the FMLN to delay the demobilization of its forces and the destruction of its remaining arsenals. The situation was exacerbated in March by the publication of the report of the Commission, which attributed responsibility for the vast majority of the war's 75,000 fatalities to the counter-insurgency measures of the armed forces, including the systematic eradication, by the security forces, of civilians thought to harbour left-wing sympathies. Some 400 murders were attributed to the FMLN. Forty military personnel, identified by name as those responsible for various human rights atrocities, included the late ARENA founder Roberto D'Aubuisson Arrieta, who was identified as the authority behind the organization of 'death squads' in the early 1980s, and the murder of the Archbishop Romero y Galdames; also identified was the Minister of Defence and Public Security, Gen. René Emilio Ponce, his deputy, Gen. Orlando Zepeda, and the former air force chief, Gen. Juan Rafael Bustillo, who were believed to have ordered the murder of six prominent Jesuits in 1989. (In September 1991 Col Guillermo Benavides and an army lieutenant were found guilty of murder and sentenced to a maximum of 30 years' imprisonment; the seven other men charged were acquitted, on the grounds that they were simply following orders. In September 2004 air force Captain Alvaro Rafael Saravia was found guilty of planning and facilitating the murder of Archbishop Romero y Galdames in a civil case brought in a US court. He was ordered, *in absentia*, to pay US $2.5m. in compensation and $7.5m. in punitive damages.) The report recommended that the judiciary should be reorganized, and that all individuals identi-

fied by the report should be permanently excluded from all institutions of national defence and public security, and should be barred from holding public office for a period of 10 years.

While the conclusions of the report were welcomed by the FMLN, representatives of the Government and the armed forces challenged the legal validity of the document, despite the insistence of UN officials that the recommendations of the report were mandatory under the terms of the peace accord. However, later in March 1993, the strength of ARENA's representation in the Asamblea overcame opposition from the PDC, the Convergencia Democrática (CD, a left-wing alliance comprising two of the leading groups within the FDR-FMLN and the Partido Social Demócrata) and the Movimiento Nacional Revolucionario (MNR), and secured the approval of an amnesty law to extend to all political crimes committed before 1992, prompting widespread public outrage, which was compounded, in April 1993, by the release of the two prisoners sentenced for the murder of the six Jesuits. In June 1993 the Government compromised to some extent, by announcing the compulsory retirement of several veteran military officers, including Gen. Ponce, although their immunity from prosecution was guaranteed.

The findings of the Truth Commission, together with the disclosure of information following the declassification by the US Administration, in November 1993, of hitherto confidential documents relating to the Administrations of former US Presidents Ronald Reagan and George Bush, Sr, suggested that detailed knowledge of abuses of human rights was suppressed by US officials in order to continue to secure congressional funding for the Government in El Salvador in the 1980s. Evidence also emerged that US military training had been provided, in at least one instance, for a civilian group in El Salvador operating as a 'death squad'. In June 1998 three members of the National Guard, convicted in 1984 of the murder, in 1980, of three US nuns and a US lay worker, were granted a conditional release from prison on the grounds that they were simply following orders.

Meanwhile, in June 1993 the FMLN had agreed to comply with an ultimatum issued by the UN, that the location and destruction of all remaining arms caches in El Salvador and neighbouring countries should be swiftly implemented. In December, bowing to pressure from the UN, President Cristiani inaugurated a four-member commission of investigation (the Joint Group for the Investigation of Illegal Armed Groups), to examine allegations of political motivation behind an escalation in violent attacks against members of the FMLN in late 1993. The conclusions of the commission claimed that officials from numerous government departments, together with current and former members of the security forces, were continuing to participate in organized crime and in politically motivated acts of violence.

Voting to elect a new president, vice-president, legislature, 262 mayors and 20 members of the Central American parliament took place on 20 March 1994. ARENA's presidential candidate, Armando Calderón Sol, failed to secure the clear majority needed for outright victory in the first poll, and was forced to contest a second round of voting against the second-placed candidate, Rubén Zamora Rivas, the joint CD-FMLN-MNR nominee, on 24 April, which Calderón Sol won. ARENA candidates also achieved considerable success in the legislative elections and in the municipal poll. FMLN candidates were also considered to have performed well in the party's first electoral contest, winning 21 seats in the Asamblea and a number of rural municipalities. Calderón Sol was inaugurated on 1 June and a new Cabinet was installed.

Meanwhile, serious divisions emerged within the FMLN during 1994, and in December two constituent parties, the Resistencia Nacional (RN) and the Expresión Renovadora del Pueblo (ERP—formerly the Fuerzas Armadas de la Resistencia Nacional and the Ejército Revolucionario Popular guerrilla groups, respectively) announced their withdrawal from the FMLN, owing to a divergence of political interests. In March 1995 the Secretary-General of the ERP, Joaquín Villalobos (who had been highly critical of the predominance of political extremism), announced the formation of a new centre-left political force, the Partido Demócrata (PD), comprising the ERP, the RN, the MNR and a dissident faction of the PDC. The new party demonstrated an immediate willingness to co-operate with the country's most prominent political forces.

In September 1994 and January 1995, in protest at the Government's failure to honour the terms of the 1992 peace accord with regard to financial compensation and other benefits for demobilized military personnel, retired soldiers occupied the Asamblea and took a number of deputies hostage. On both occasions the occupation was ended swiftly and peacefully following the Government's agreement to enter into direct negotiations with the former soldiers. The Association of the Demobilized Armed Forces had earlier threatened to sabotage the economy by disrupting transport communications and foreign businesses throughout the country if the Government failed to meet its obligations, and had organized a series of co-ordinated protests throughout the country in January 1995. Further demonstrations by army veterans during March and November were forcibly curtailed by the security forces, prompting concern that such incidents might provoke a renewed escalation of armed conflict.

In May 1994 the UN Security Council voted to extend the ONUSAL mandate for a further six months in order to supervise the full implementation of the outstanding provisions of the peace agreement. Of particular concern were delays in the reform of the judiciary, the initiation of the land reform programme and the full integration and activation of the National Civilian Police. In September the UN Secretary-General appealed to the Government and to the international community for increased financial commitment to the peace process. In the same month, in the context of increasing levels of crime and social unrest, the ONUSAL mandate was further extended, pending the effective habilitation of the National Civilian Police; a further extension, until the end of April 1995, was approved by the UN Security Council in November. A small contingent of UN observers, MINUSAL, was mandated to remain in El Salvador until April 1996 (the revised deadline for the fulfilment of the outstanding terms of the peace accord). By this date, however, full implementation of those terms of the accord relating to land allocation for refugees and former combatants, and to the reform of the judiciary and the electoral code, had yet to be achieved. A reduced MINUSAL contingent was further mandated to oversee Government efforts to fulfil the outstanding terms of the agreement, and the mission was formally terminated on 31 December 1996.

The results of the congressional and municipal elections of 16 March 1997 demonstrated a significant increase in support for the FMLN, particularly in the capital, where the party won seven of the 16 contested seats and secured the mayorality. The results of the legislative poll revealed a considerable erosion of ARENA's predominance in the Asamblea, with the party securing 29 seats, just one more than the FMLN. Widespread concern was expressed at the high level of voter abstention, estimated to be some 60%.

The presidential election of 7 March 1999 was won by Francisco Flores Pérez, the candidate of ARENA, who obtained 52% of the votes, thereby obviating the need for a second round of voting. Despite contesting the election in alliance with the Unión Social Cristiana, the candidate of the FMLN, Facundo Guardado, received only 29%. Voter participation was the lowest recorded in the country's history, with more than 60% of the 3.2m. registered voters abstaining. President Flores was inaugurated on 1 June, when a new council of ministers was installed. Flores stated that his Government's priority was to address the problem of violent crime, and an initiative, named 'Mano Dura' (Iron Fist), was unveiled that included provision for the restructuring of the National Civilian Police force and a revision of the penal code. However, economic measures announced later that month, which included the rationalization of public bodies, prompted a succession of strikes by public-sector workers. Furthermore, the Government was embarrassed by allegations that foreign funds, donated for disaster relief following the impact of 'Hurricane Mitch' in November 1998, had been diverted by ARENA to former paramilitaries in an attempt to buy votes for Flores in the presidential election.

Dissatisfaction with the ARENA Government was demonstrated in the results of the legislative elections of 12 March 2000, in which the FMLN became the largest single party in the Asamblea Nacional, winning 31 of the 84 seats. ARENA secured 29 seats, followed by the PCN. Voter turn-out was only 33%. On 21 March the FMLN proposed a governability pact with ARENA, but relations between the two parties immediately became strained, and on 1 May ARENA formed an alliance with the PCN and the PDC in order to prevent the FMLN claiming the presidency of the Asamblea. Although the party gaining the most seats was, traditionally, given the presidency, in order to prevent a political impasse it was decided that the post was to be rotated annually among the three largest parties, the PCN, ARENA and the FMLN.

On 22 November 2000 President Flores unexpectedly announced that, from 1 January 2001, the US dollar would be introduced as an official currency alongside the colón, anchored to the colón at a fixed rate of exchange. The 'dollarization' was an attempt to stabilize the economy, lower interest rates, and stimulate domestic and foreign investment. The so-called Law of Monetary Integration was approved by the Asamblea Nacional in December, and from 1 January 2001 the US dollar circulated freely with the colón at a fixed rate of 8.75.

On 13 January 2001 an earthquake, measuring 7.6 on the Richter scale, hit El Salvador. President Flores immediately declared a state of emergency. Besides numerous aftershocks, a second earthquake, measuring 6.6 on the Richter scale, struck on 12 February. More than 1,100 people were killed, an estimated 4,000 people were injured, and a further 1.5m. people were left homeless by the two earthquakes. Reconstruction costs were estimated at US $1,900m., representing around 14% of gross domestic product (GDP). In March the Inter-American Development Bank (IDB, see p. 268) pledged some US $1,278.5m. in aid, mainly for economic, social and environmental development projects, and in September the IDB announced a $70m. loan to help rebuild the country's infrastructure. In the same month the US immigration authorities granted a one-year protective status (later extented to two) to Salvadorean illegal immigrants residing in the USA and released those held in custody.

During 2001 internal divisions deepened between the more orthodox and the reformist elements of the FMLN. In October the FMLN leader, Facundo Guardado, a reformist, was expelled from the party after being accused of failing to support the party executive and of supporting government policies, such as the dollarization of the economy. In November, following internal elections, Salvador Sánchez Cerón, from the party's orthodox wing, became the new FMLN leader. Following Sánchez's appointment, in January 2002 six reformist FMLN deputies left the party, thus reducing the FMLN's legislative representation to 25 seats. ARENA, led by Roberto Murray Meza, became the largest parliamentary bloc, with 29 seats. In April the six FMLN dissidents joined with Guardado to form a new party, the Movimiento Renovador (Renewal Movement).

In June 2002 two former army generals and defence ministers, Gen. (retd) Carlos Eugenio Vides Casanova and Gen. (retd) José Guillermo García, were convicted by a US court of 'crimes against humanity'. The case was brought by three El Salvadorean civilians who had been tortured by troops under the generals' commands during the civil war. In November 2000 Vides Casanova and García had been acquitted of charges of involvement in the 1980 murder of three US nuns and a US lay worker.

In September 2002 doctors at a hospital in San Salvador began a strike in protest at President Flores' plans to privatize sections of the health service, as well as in support of 10 colleagues who had been dismissed and a further 300 whose pay had been docked following their participation in earlier industrial action. The strikes spread to 11 other hospitals throughout the country and on 23 October medical workers organized a demonstration in San Salvador. The strike led to a dispute in the Asamblea Legislativa: in October deputies approved legislation that prevented the privatization of the social services, but in the following month President Flores presented his own bill, which would allow private-sector participation in the health care industry. The President emphasized that his legislation would constitute reform of the health service, not privatization; nevertheless, the proposed law was subsequently rejected by the Asamblea. Meanwhile, protests intensified: strikers erected road blocks in the capital in late October and in November doctors announced that the strike would continue indefinitely until the Government abandoned privatization plans. In December an estimated 100,000 people attended a demonstration in San Salvador in protest at the proposed privatization. In mid-June 2003 the strike was eventually brought to an end after the Government agreed to halt privatization of the health service. All employees who took part in the industrial action, including those who were dismissed, were fully reinstated. A commission, comprising representatives of the Government, trade unions and civil society, was established to reform to the health system. However, the FMLN remained sceptical of the agreement and in September organized a demonstration in the capital to protest at what it called government attempts to privatize the sector 'by stealth'.

In legislative elections held on 16 March 2003 the FMLN won 33.8% of votes cast and retained its 31 seats in the Asamblea Nacional. The ARENA performed less well than expected, securing 32.0% of votes and 27 seats, two fewer than in the last legislature. The PCN won 13.1% of votes and increased its number of seats from 14 to 16, while the PDC retained its five seats. Support for the ARENA also faltered in the concurrently held local elections, with the ruling party retaining control of 109 of the country's 262 municipalities (from 126). The poor electoral performance prompted the Government to propose a series of populist measures, such as an increase in pensions and a reduction in electricity prices, aimed at regaining voter support in advance of the 2004 presidential elections.

A presidential election was held on 21 March 2004. The ARENA candidate, businessman Elías Antonio (Tony) Saca, secured an overwhelming victory, obtaining 57.7% of the votes cast. Schafik Jorge Handal, the former guerrilla who was the nominee of the FMLN, attracted some 35.6% of the ballot, while Héctor Silva Argüello, representing a coalition of the PDC and the Centro Democrático Unido, and the PCN candidate, José Rafael Machuca Zelaya, secured 3.9% and 2.7% of the votes cast, respectively. The voter turn-out was 60.2%. President Saca was inaugurated on 1 June and he appointed a new Cabinet, largely comprising ARENA members. The new Government's stated priorities were to reduce violent crime and to increase employment through development of the tourism industry and promotion of foreign investment, particularly in the free zones. To this end, President Saca created a Ministry of Tourism, headed by Luis Cardenal, and announced plans to liberalize the sugar and pharmaceutical sectors. The new President also promised reform in four spheres—public health, public education, fiscal administration and electoral procedure.

Saca assumed the presidency with a clear popular mandate. None the less, he adopted a consensus-building approach in an attempt to improve relations with the opposition FMLN, who held the largest number of seats in the Asamblea Legislativa. He established a permanent multi-party commission to encourage debate on issues of national importance. In his first month in office Saca gained FMLN approval of the long-delayed 2004 budget of US $2,790m. by agreeing to increase the allocations to health and education. However, the consensus was short-lived: the Government's decision to send a replacement contingent of 380 troops to Iraq in August met with criticism from the opposition party, and in October the FMLN withdrew from the multiparty commission.

Upon taking office President Saca proposed stringent new legislation to reduce gang-related crime. However, a commission formed to review the proposals concluded, in July 2004, that, instead of implementing new legislation, existing laws relating to violent crime and juvenile delinquency should be tightened. An initiative, known as 'Súper Mano Dura' (Super Iron Fist), that was launched in September gained widespread support. The initiative was an extension of President Flores's 'Mano Dura' campaign, which had met with limited success. Despite resulting in 19,275 arrests, only 964 suspected gang members had been committed for trial. The new campaign included proposals to appoint prosecutors dedicated to bringing charges against gang members. There was also provision for the rehabilitation of gang members and their reinsertion into society. In mid-August some 31 inmates had died as a result of fighting between gang members in the La Esperanza prison. The Government's new initiative also included proposals to reduce crime and violence within prisons, such as the segregation of gang members. In addition, it was suggested that army barracks be used to relieve overcrowding in the country's gaols, which in 2004 contained 12,000 inmates, twice the intended capacity.

In an attempt to resolve a territorial dispute between El Salvador and Honduras over three islands in the Gulf of Fonseca and a small area of land on the joint border, President Duarte and President Azcona of Honduras submitted the dispute to the International Court of Justice (ICJ) for arbitration in December 1986. In September 1992 both countries accepted the ruling of the ICJ, which awarded one-third of the disputed mainland and two of the three disputed islands to El Salvador. Following prolonged negotiations, the two parties signed a convention in January 1998 specifying the rights and obligations of those affected, including the right to choose between Honduran and Salvadorean citizenship. In July 2001 El Salvador and Honduras signed a development plan for the border area between

the two countries. In September 2003, however, the El Salvadorean Government asked the ICJ to review its 1992 decision, claiming that evidence had been discovered that potentially undermined the ruling.

Government

Executive power is held by the President, assisted by the Vice-President and the Cabinet. The President is elected for a five-year term by universal adult suffrage. Legislative power is vested in the Asamblea Nacional (National Assembly), with 84 members elected by universal adult suffrage for a three-year term.

Defence

Military service is by compulsory selective conscription of men between 18 and 30 years of age for one year. In August 2004 the armed forces totalled 15,500 men, of whom an estimated 13,850 were in the army, 700 were in the navy and the 950 were in the air force. The National Civilian Police force, created in 1991, numbered around 12,000 personnel by 2000 and there were plans for it to total some 16,000. Defence expenditure in 2003 totalled an estimated US $106m.

Economic Affairs

In 2003, according to estimates by the World Bank, El Salvador's gross national product (GNI), measured at average 2001–03 prices, was US $14,084m., equivalent to $2,200 per head (or $4,890 per head on an international purchasing-power parity basis). In 1990–2003 the population increased at an average annual rate of 1.9%, while gross domestic product (GDP) per head increased, in real terms, by an average of 2.0% per year. Overall GDP increased, in real terms, at an average annual rate of 4.0% in 1990–2003. GDP grew by 2.1% in 2002 and by 1.8% in 2003.

Agriculture (including hunting, forestry and fishing) contributed an estimated 9.4% of GDP in 2003 and employed some 19.6% of the employed labour force in 2002. The principal cash crops are coffee and sugar cane. Maize, beans, rice and millet are the major subsistence crops. During 1990–2002 agricultural GDP increased at an average annual rate of 1.2%. The sector's GDP decreased by 0.5% in 2002, before increasing by 6.0% in 2003. The agricultural sector was badly affected by the earthquakes that struck the country in early 2001. In March of that year the Inter-American Development Bank (IDB) pledged some US $1,278.5m. in emergency assistance, of which US $132.6m. was intended for rehabilitation and development of agriculture; a further US $101.0m. was made available for redevelopment of the coffee industry, which had been particularly badly affected. The coffee sector decreased by an estimated 13% in 2001. In 2000 coffee accounted for 22.4% of export earnings, excluding *maquila* zones; this fell to a preliminary 5.2% in 2003. The 2003/04 coffee harvest produced 1.36m. 60 kg sacks, 6% less than the previous year. In October 2002 the Government announced that it would loan some US $192m. to the coffee industry over the next three years. Despite this, many producers dismissed their workers or began to cultivate other crops. El Salvador's fishing catch was relatively small; however, in mid-2003 a Spanish firm, Grupo Calvo, opened a tuna-processing plant at Punta Gorda, which aimed to export 25,000 metric tons of tuna per year.

Industry (including mining, manufacturing, construction and power) contributed an estimated 31.8% of GDP in 2003, and the sector engaged 24.2% of the employed labour force in 2002. During 1990–2003 industrial GDP increased at an average annual rate of 4.8%. The sector's GDP increased by an estimated 2.8% in 2002 and by an estimated 4.8% in 2003.

El Salvador has no significant mineral resources, and the mining sector employed less than 0.2% of the economically active population and contributed only 0.5% of GDP in 2002. Small quantities of gold, silver, sea-salt and limestone are mined or quarried. The mining sector increased by 3.0% in 2000.

Manufacturing contributed an estimated 24.5% of GDP in 2003 and employed 18.0% of the active labour force in 2002. The most important branches of manufacturing (excluding the in-bond industry) were food products, chemical products, petroleum products, textiles, apparel (excluding footwear) and beverages. During 1990–2003 manufacturing GDP increased at an average annual rate of 4.8%. The sector's GDP increased by an estimated 2.5% in 2002 and by an estimated 4.0% in 2003. By the late 1990s manufacturing had become the highest-earning export sector, generating the equivalent of 58% of total exports in 2001. There is a thriving offshore (*maquila*) manufacturing sector, which in 2003 generated more than one-half (an estimated 60%) of the country's total exports. In 1995–2000 *maquila* exports increased at an average annual rate of 20%. However, as a consequence of the natural disasters in El Salvador, the faltering US economy and competition from the People's Republic of China, growth decreased substantially after 2000; the sector expanded by 2.5% in 2001, rising to 6.5% in 2002. Following the earthquakes in early 2001, the IDB pledged some US $62.2m. to the industry and commerce sector and a further $574.7m. to the housing sector to fund a renovation and reconstruction programme. In September the IDB announced a loan of $70m. and in December the World Bank pledged $270m. over three years, to help reconstruction efforts.

Energy is derived principally from imported fuel. Fuel imports accounted for an estimated 13% of the cost of merchandise imports in 2002. In 2003 El Salvador derived almost one-half (48.1%) of its electricity from petroleum, compared with just 6.8% in 1990. An estimated further 28.5% of total electricity production in 2003 was contributed by hydroelectric installations. In 2001 construction began on an electricity interconnection between El Salvador and Honduras, part of a planned Central American regional power network.

The services sector contributed an estimated 58.7% of GDP in 2003 and employed 55.7% of the economically active population in 2002. The GDP of the services sector increased by an average of 4.3% per year in 1990–2003. The sector grew by an estimated at 10.7% in 2002, before declining by an estimated 0.2% in 2003. In 2002 receipts from tourism totalled US $342m., a significant increase on the previous year, when revenue totalled $235m.

In 2003 El Salvador recorded a visible trade deficit of US $2,273.6m., while there was a deficit of $733.6m. on the current account of the balance of payments. Following the earthquakes in 2001, remittances from workers abroad increased, with payments from the USA alone totalling some US $1,935m. in that year. Remittances in 2004 were equivalent to about 16% of annual GDP and totalled about $2,547.6m. In 2003 almost one-half of total imports (an estimated 49.8%) was provided by the USA; other major suppliers were Guatemala, Costa Rica and Honduras. The USA was also the principal market for exports (taking an estimated 67.6% of exports, mostly from the *maquila* sector, in 2003); other significant purchasers were Guatemala, Honduras and Costa Rica. In 2002 the main exports were food and live animals (of which coffee comprised almost one-third), chemicals and related products and wood and paper products. In the same year the principal imports were chemicals and related products, minerals and foodstuffs.

In 2001 there was an estimated budgetary deficit of 426.4m. colones, equivalent to some 3.1% of GDP. El Salvador's external debt totalled US $5,828m. at the end of 2002, of which $4,837m. was long-term public debt. In that year the cost of debt-servicing was $453m., equivalent to 7.7% of exports of goods and services. The average annual rate of inflation was 6.9% in 1990–2003; consumer prices rose by 2.5% in 2003, before increasing to 5.4% in 2004, according to the Central Bank. Some 6.2% of the labour force were unemployed in 2002.

El Salvador is a member of the Central American Common Market (CACM, see p. 176), which aims to increase trade within the region and to encourage monetary and industrial co-operation.

In March 2001 the free trade agreement with Mexico was implemented. In May the Central American countries, including El Salvador, reached the basis of a deal with Mexico, the 'Plan Puebla–Panamá', to integrate the region through joint transport, industry and tourism projects. In November El Salvador, Guatemala, Honduras and Nicaragua (known as the CA-4 group of countries) began negotiations with Canada on a free trade agreement. Negotiations towards a further free trade agreement, to be known as the Central American Free Trade Agreement (CAFTA), were concluded between the CA-4 group of countries and the USA in December 2003. The Agreement entailed the gradual elimination of tariffs on most industrial and agricultural products over the next 10 and 20 years, respectively. The Agreement was ratified by the legislature in December 2004.

Considerable progress in reducing financial imbalances and in addressing the problem of widespread poverty was achieved from the mid-1990s. The administration of President Calderón Sol also made advances in the divestment of state assets in the sectors of electricity distribution and telecommunications. The introduction, in January 2001, of the US dollar as an official currency alongside the colón, anchored to the colón at a fixed rate of exchange, was intended to stabilize the economy, to lower interest rates, and to stimulate domestic and foreign investment. Following the 2001 earthquakes, in February 2002 the Flores Pérez Government announced plans to increase public investment by 23% in that year. The extra funds were intended to rebuild schools and roads and were expected to generate some 30,000 jobs. Economic growth of 2.1% and 1.8% was recorded in 2002 and 2003, respectively. Economic growth was less than expected in 2004, partly owing to a 3.7% decline in *maquila* exports. However, effective diversification was demonstrated by a 19.2% increase in non-traditional exports. Overall, the economy expanded by an estimated 1.8% in that year and was forecast to grow by 2.3% in 2005. However, FMLN opposition to Government debt proposals were expected to delay approval of the budget, which would, in turn, inhibit government expenditure.

Education

There are two national universities and more than 30 private universities. Education is provided free of charge in state schools, and there are also numerous private schools. Pre-primary education, beginning at four years of age and lasting for three years, and primary education, beginning at seven years of age and lasting for nine years, are officially compulsory. In 2002 enrolment at pre-primary institutions was equivalent to 43.3% of children in the relevant age-group, while enrolment at primary schools was equivalent to 86.9% of children in the relevant age-group. Secondary education begins at the age of 16 and lasts for two years for an academic diploma or three years for a vocational one. In 2002 enrolment at secondary schools was equivalent to just 25.5% of students in the relevant age-group. In the same year combined enrolment in pre-primary, primary and secondary education was equivalent to 66.2% of students in the relevant age-group. Following the 2001 earthquakes the IDB pledged some US $43.6m. for infrastructure reconstruction and child protection. Budgetary expenditure on education by the central Government in 2001 was US $459.1m., equivalent to 23.3% of total expenditure.

Public Holidays

2005: 1 January (New Year's Day), 25–28 March (Easter), 1 May (Labour Day), 10 May (Mothers' Day), 5–6 August* (El Salvador del Mundo Festival), 15 September (Independence Day), 12 October (Discovery of America), 2 November (All Souls' Day), 5 November (First Call of Independence), 24–25 December (Christmas), 31 December (New Year's Eve).

2006: 1 January (New Year's Day), 14–17 April (Easter), 1 May (Labour Day), 10 May (Mothers' Day), 5–6 August* (El Salvador del Mundo Festival), 15 September (Independence Day), 12 October (Discovery of America), 2 November (All Souls' Day), 5 November (First Call of Independence), 24–25 December (Christmas), 31 December (New Year's Eve).

* 1–6 August in San Salvador.

Weights and Measures

The metric system is officially in force. Some old Spanish measures are also used, including:

25 libras = 1 arroba;
4 arrobas = 1 quintal (46 kg);
1 manzana = 0.699 ha.

Statistical Survey

Sources (unless otherwise stated): Banco Central de Reserva de El Salvador, Alameda Juan Pablo II y 17 Avda Norte, Apdo 01-106, San Salvador; tel. 271-0011; fax 271-4575; internet www.bcr.gob.sv; Dirección General de Estadística y Censos, Edif. Centro de Gobierno, Alameda Juan Pablo II y Calle Guadalupe, San Salvador; tel. 286-4260; fax 286-2505; internet www.minec.gob.sv.

Area and Population

AREA, POPULATION AND DENSITY

Area (sq km)	
Land	20,721
Inland water	320
Total	21,041*
Population (census results)†	
28 June 1971	3,554,648
27 September 1992	
Males	2,485,613
Females	2,632,986
Total	5,118,599
Population (official estimates at mid-year)	
2001	6,396,890
2002	6,517,800
2003	6,638,200
Density (per sq km) at mid-2003	320.4

* 8,124 sq miles.

† Excluding adjustments for underenumeration.

PRINCIPAL TOWNS
(official population estimates at mid-2001)*

San Salvador					
(capital)	. . .	485,847	Mejicanos	. . .	193,400
Soyapango	. .	287,034	Apopa .	. . .	179,122
Santa Ana	. .	253,037	Nueva San Salvador.		163,794
San Miguel	. .	245,428	Ciudad Delgado .	.	157,094

* Figures refer to municipios, which may each contain rural areas as well as an urban centre.

Mid-2003 (UN estimates, incl. suburbs): San Salvador 1,423,915 (Source: UN, *World Urbanization Prospects: The 2003 Revision*).

BIRTHS, MARRIAGES AND DEATHS

	Registered live births		Registered marriages		Registered deaths	
	Number	Rate (per 1,000)	Number	Rate (per 1,000)	Number	Rate (per 1,000)
1994 . . .	160,772	29.0	27,761	5.0	29,407	5.3
1995 . . .	159,336	28.1	25,308	4.5	29,130	5.1
1996 . . .	163,007	28.2	27,130	4.7	28,904	5.0
1997 . . .	164,143	27.8	23,561	4.0	29,118	4.9
1998 . . .	158,350	26.3	25,937	4.3	29,919	5.0
1999 . . .	153,636	25.0	34,306	5.6	28,056	4.6
2000 . . .	150,176	23.9	28,231	4.5	28,154	4.5
2001* . .	138,354	21.6	29,216	4.6	29,559	4.6

* Provisional figures.

2002 (official estimates): Live births 168,300 (birth rate 25.8 per 1,000); deaths 38,900 (death rate 6.0 per 1,000).

Expectation of life (WHO estimates, years at birth): 69.7 (males 66.5; females 72.8) in 2002 (Source: WHO, *World Health Report*).

ECONOMICALLY ACTIVE POPULATION
(ISIC major divisions, '000 persons aged 10 years and over)

	2000	2001	2002
Agriculture, hunting, forestry and fishing	501.8	534.3	474.4
Mining and quarrying	1.5	3.0	3.5
Manufacturing	433.5	431.6	434.0
Electricity, gas and water . . .	8.8	10.9	10.7
Construction	118.8	133.0	136.2
Trade, restaurants and hotels .	610.9	667.4	688.5
Transport, storage and communication	109.4	113.4	103.4
Financing, insurance, real estate and business services . . .	87.8	100.5	98.0
Public administration, defence and social security	123.8	97.5	100.5
Education	69.8	88.0	94.5
Other community, social and personal services	154.9	155.3	155.4
Private households with employed persons	100.4	115.0	103.2
Other activities not adequately defined	1.2	1.5	10.4
Total employed	2,322.7	2,451.3	2,412.8
Unemployed	173.7	183.5	160.2
Total labour force	2,496.4	2,634.8	2,573.0

Source: ILO.

Health and Welfare

KEY INDICATORS

Total fertility rate (children per woman, 2002) . . .	2.9
Under-5 mortality rate (per 1,000 live births, 2003) . . .	36
HIV/AIDS (% of persons aged 15–49, 2003) . . .	0.7
Physicians (per 1,000 head, 1997)	1.07
Hospital beds (per 1,000 head, 1996)	1.65
Health expenditure (2001): US $ per head (PPP) . . .	376
Health expenditure (2001): % of GDP	8.0
Health expenditure (2001): public (% of total)	46.7
Access to water (% of persons, 2002)	82
Access to sanitation (% of prsons, 2002)	63
Human Development Index (2002): ranking	103
Human Development Index (2002): value	0.720

For sources and definitions, see explanatory note on p. vi.

Agriculture

PRINCIPAL CROPS
('000 metric tons)

	2001	2002	2003
Rice (paddy)	37.7	29.1	28.4
Maize	571.5	644.4	618.0
Sorghum	150.5	140.8	144.3
Yautia (Cocoyam)*	52.0	52.0	52.0
Sugar cane	4,877.2	4,528.2	4,531.5
Dry beans	74.9	82.6	78.1
Coconuts	88.3	24.3	24.3
Vegetables*	58.4	58.4	58.4
Watermelons*	75.0	75.0	75.0
Bananas*	65.0	65.0	65.0
Plantains*	66.0	66.0	66.0
Other fruit*	156.2	156.2	156.2
Coffee (green)	112.2	91.5	91.5*

* FAO estimate(s).

Source: FAO.

LIVESTOCK
('000 head, year ending September)

	2001	2002	2003
Horses*	96	96	96
Asses*	3	3	3
Mules*	24	24	24
Cattle	1,216	1,100*	1,000*
Pigs	150	153	153
Sheep*	5	5	5
Goats*	15	11	11
Chickens*	7,200	8,100	8,100

* FAO estimate(s).

Source: FAO.

LIVESTOCK PRODUCTS
('000 metric tons)

	2001	2002	2003
Beef and veal	35.1	30.3	32.5*
Pig meat*	8.7	8.7	8.7
Chicken meat	74.1	78.5	78.6*
Cows' milk	383.5	408.0	170.0
Cheese*	2.4	2.4	2.4
Hen eggs	61.3	65.9	65.9*
Fresh cattle hides*	6.7	6.7	6.7

* FAO estimate(s).

Source: FAO.

Forestry

ROUNDWOOD REMOVALS
('000 cubic metres, excl. bark)

	2001	2002	2003
Sawlogs, veneer logs and logs for sleepers	682	682	682*
Fuel wood	4,518	4,518	4,147
Total	5,200	5,200	4,829*

* FAO estimate.

Source: FAO.

SAWNWOOD PRODUCTION
(FAO estimates, '000 cubic metres, incl. railway sleepers)

	1995	1996	1997
Coniferous (softwood)	57	57	—
Broadleaved (hardwood) . . .	14	14	58
Total	70	70	58

1998–2003: Annual production as in 1997 (FAO estimates).

Source: FAO.

Fishing

('000 metric tons, live weight)

	2000	2001	2002
Capture	9.6	19.0	34.5
Nile tilapia	1.2	0.6	1.2
Other freshwater fishes . .	1.6	1.1	1.5
Croakers and drums . . .	0.3	0.6	0.8
Skipjack tuna	—	4.5	6.8
Yellowfin tuna	—	2.2	3.4
Bigeye tuna	—	2.1	4.6
Sharks, rays, skates, etc. . .	0.4	0.8	1.0
Other marine fishes . . .	1.9	1.7	3.4
Whiteleg shrimp	0.5	0.5	0.9
Pacific seabobs	1.5	1.5	0.9
Marine molluscs	1.1	0.8	0.8
Aquaculture	0.3	0.4	0.8
Total catch	9.9	19.4	35.2

Source: FAO.

Mining

(metric tons, unless otherwise specified)

	1999	2000	2001
Gold (kg)	71	—	—
Gypsum	5,600	5,600	5,600
Limestone ('000 metric tons) . .	3,200	3,200	3,200
Salt (marine)	741,500	715,260	710,00*
Silver (kg)	20	—	—

2002: Gypsum 5,600 metric tons; Limestone 3,200,000 metric tons; Salt (marine) 715,000 metric tons*.

* Estimate.

Source: US Geological Survey.

Industry

SELECTED PRODUCTS
('000 metric tons, unless otherwise indicated)

	1998	1999	2000
Raw sugar	474	457	524
Motor gasoline (petrol) . . .	134	135	140
Distillate fuel oils	146	199	163
Residual fuel oils	497	519	537
Liquefied petroleum gas (refined) .	16	18	14
Cement*	1,020	24,250	25,036
Electric energy (million kWh) . .	3,821	3,769	3,456

2001: Raw sugar 504; Cement 25,000*.

* Source: US Geological Survey.

Source: UN, *Industrial Commodity Statistics Yearbook*.

Finance

CURRENCY AND EXCHANGE RATES

Monetary Units
  100 centavos = 1 Salvadorean colón.

Sterling, Dollar and Euro Equivalents (31 December 2004)
  £1 sterling = 16.8998 colones;
  US $1 = 8.7500 colones;
  €1 = 11.9184 colones;
  1,000 Salvadorean colones = £59.17 = $114.29 = €83.90.

Note: The foregoing information refers to the principal exchange rate, applicable to official receipts and payments, imports of petroleum and exports of coffee. In addition, there is a market exchange rate, applicable to other transactions. The principal rate was maintained at 8.755 colones per US dollar from May 1995 to December 2000. However, in January 2001, with the introduction of legislation making the US dollar legal tender, the rate was adjusted to $1 = 8.750 colones. Both currencies were to be accepted for a transitional period.

BUDGET
(million colones until 2000; US $ million from 2001)

Revenue*	1999	2000	2001
Current revenue	12,009.2	13,486.1	1,481.3
Taxation	11,723.8	12,484.9	1,387.3
Taxes on income, profits and capital gains	3,574.4	3,683.8	367.1
Individual	1,436.5	1,361.6	170.3
Corporate	2,137.9	2,322.2	196.8
Domestic taxes on goods and services	6,328.1	7,428.8	857.9
General sales or turnover taxes	5,795.7	7,003.8	808.6
Excises	453.2	425.0	49.3
Taxes on international trade and transactions . . .	1,315.3	1,230.4	148.8
Customs duties	1,296.7	1,229.9	144.9
Other taxes	386.4	44.6	1.9
Non-tax revenue	253.2	1,001.2	93.6
Adjustment	32.2	—	0.2
Capital revenue	6.6	7.0	0.2
Total	12,015.8	13,493.1	1,481.5

Expenditure†	1999	2000	2001
General public services	1,419.3	1,613.5	250.2
Defence	872.9	839.3	250.2
Public order and safety	2,272.3	2,401.8	309.6
Education	2,380.4	2,775.0	459.1
Health	569.8	578.2	217.9
Social security and welfare . .	299.4	163.8	116.3
Housing and community services .	62.8	194.4	149.0
Recreational, cultural and religious affairs	235.3	242.9	66.0
Economic affairs and services . .	1,525.2	2,074.0	289.0
Agriculture	169.4	644.9	48.3
Transportation and communications	1,072.2	1,122.6	193.1
Total (incl. others)	10,979.5	11,452.2	1,968.6
Adjustment		22.6	−834.4	−184.7
Current‡	9,579.3	10,262.9	1,681.9
Capital	1,377.6	2,023.7	471.4

* Excluding grants received: 18.9m. colones in 1999; 532.9m. colones in 2000; US $18.1m. in 2001.
† Excluding lending minus repayments: −31.7m. colones in 1999; −134.1m. colones in 2000; US $ −42.8m. in 2001.
‡ Including interest payments: 1,319.5m. colones in 1999; 1,360.2m. colones in 2000; US $165.3m. in 2001.
Source: IMF, *Government Finance Statistics Yearbook*.

INTERNATIONAL RESERVES
(US $ million at 31 December)

	2001	2002	2003
Gold*	19.8	19.8	19.8
IMF special drawing rights . .	31.4	34.0	37.1
Foreign exchange	1,709.6	1,588.8	1,905.8
Total	1,741.0	1,622.8	1,962.7

* Valued at US $42.22 per troy ounce.
Source: IMF, *International Financial Statistics*.

MONEY SUPPLY
(US $ million at 31 December)

	2001	2002	2003
Currency outside banks . . .	220.2	60.6	36.4
Demand deposits at deposit money banks	977.7	1,027.1	1,085.6
Total money (incl. others) . .	1,198.1	1,090.4	1,198.6

Source: IMF, *International Financial Statistics*.

COST OF LIVING
(Consumer Price Index; base: 1992 = 100)

	2001	2002	2003
Food and non-alcoholic beverages	167.9	169.2	176.4
Rent, water, electricity, gas and other fuels	175.9	184.5	184.4
Clothing	114.2	111.2	110.2
Health	180.9	188.8	195.4
Transport	116.1	119.8	121.6
All items (incl. others) . . .	162.3	166.8	171.0

NATIONAL ACCOUNTS
National Income and Product
(million colones at current prices)

	2000	2001	2002
Gross domestic product (GDP) at factor cost	106,857.9	111,355.1	115,137.4
Indirect taxes	8,136.4	8,887.1	9,869.1
Less Subsidies	26.8	26.8	22.8
GDP in purchasers' values	114,967.5	120,215.4	124,983.7
Less Factor income from abroad (net)	2,214.6	2,324.9	2,513.0
Gross national product (GNP)	112,752.9	117,890.5	122,470.7

Source: UN Economic Commission for Latin America and the Caribbean, *Statistical Yearbook*.

Expenditure on the Gross Domestic Product
(million colones at current prices)

	2001	2002	2003
Government final consumption expenditure	12,609	11,943	12,193
Private final consumption expenditure	107,331	110,857	118,541
Increase in stocks	308	—	—
Gross fixed capital formation . .	19,857	20,554	21,440
Total domestic expenditure .	140,105	143,354	152,174
Exports of goods and services . .	31,152	33,240	35,501
Less Imports of goods and services	50,475	51,610	56,457
GDP in purchasers' values .	120,783	124,984	131,219
GDP at constant 1990 prices .	58,297	59,532	60,604

Source: IMF, *International Financial Statistics*.

Gross Domestic Product by Economic Activity
(million colones at current prices)

	2000	2001	2002
Agriculture, hunting, forestry and fishing	11,253.7	11,387.5	10,865.0
Mining and quarrying	460.7	497.6	548.4
Manufacturing	26,518.9	27,921.0	29,328.4
Construction	5,005.9	5,658.9	5,902.0
Electricity, gas and water . .	1,944.2	2,076.9	2,106.5
Transport, storage and communications	9,767.0	10,489.9	11,189.4
Wholesale and retail trade, restaurants and hotels . . .	22,275.2	23,271.7	24,043.0
Finance, insurance, real estate and business services	9,665.6	10,239.3	10,633.6
Owner-occupied dwellings . .	9,026.7	9,061.3	9,700.8
Community, social, domestic and personal services	7,716.1	8,283.9	8,773.5
Government services	8,506.3	8,601.9	8,470.8
Sub-total	112,140.4	117,489.9	121,561.4
Import duties	1,229.9	1,333.7	1,320.2
Value-added tax	6,312.2	7,008.7	7,251.2
Less Imputed bank service charge	4,758.7	5,049.6	5,149.1
Total	114,923.8	120,782.7	124,983.7

BALANCE OF PAYMENTS
(US $ million)

	2001	2002	2003
Exports of goods f.o.b.	2,890.8	3,020.8	3,162.4
Imports of goods f.o.b.	−4,796.0	−4,891.7	−5,436.0
Trade balance	−1,905.2	−1,870.9	−2,273.6
Exports of services	696.2	781.9	824.1
Imports of services	−999.4	−1,022.2	−993.5
Balance on goods and services	−2,208.4	−2,111.2	−2,443.0
Other income received	168.9	159.1	140.4
Other income paid	−434.6	−482.5	−548.1
Balance on goods, services and income	−2,474.1	−2,434.6	−2,850.7
Current transfers received . . .	2,359.2	2,110.6	2,197.1
Current transfers paid	−75.2	−87.8	−80.0
Current balance	−190.1	−411.8	−733.6
Capital account (net)	197.7	208.9	112.9
Direct investment abroad . . .	9.7	25.7	−18.6
Direct investment from abroad .	250.2	470.0	103.7
Portfolio investment assets . .	−126.5	−289.2	−263.7
Portfolio investment liabilities .	160.6	554.8	452.7
Other investment assets . . .	−630.9	−224.8	19.8
Other investment liabilities . .	464.2	150.4	795.6
Net errors and omissions . . .	−312.6	−607.5	−152.6
Overall balance	−177.7	−123.5	316.2

Source: IMF, *International Financial Statistics*.

External Trade

PRINCIPAL COMMODITIES
(distribution by SITC, US $ million)

Imports c.i.f.*	2000	2001	2002
Food and live animals chiefly for food	515.40	545.3	578.5
Crude materials, inedible, except fuels	92.7	112.1	101.7
Mineral products	595.6	502.6	504.7
Crude petroleum oils . . .	210.4	168.8	175.3
Petroleum products, refined .	292.0	262.6	260.2
Chemicals and related products	554.1	588.4	603.5
Medicinal and pharmaceutical products	153.3	148.2	162.1
Manufactured goods classified chiefly by materials . . .	595.4	709.2	658.8
Wood pulp, paper, paperboard and articles thereof . . .	129.0	150.3	142.0
Machinery and transport equipment	1,002.7	943.0	909.8
Road vehicles	233.9	241.0	274.4
Miscellaneous manufactured articles	338.5	359.0	413.5
Total (incl. others)	3,795.2	3,865.6	3,907.3

* Excluding imports into *maquila* zones (US $ million): 1,153 in 2000; 1,161 in 2001; 1,283 in 2002.

Exports f.o.b.*	2000	2001	2002
Food and live animals, chiefly for food	536.2	387.9	368.3
Coffee, including roasted and decaffeinated coffee . . .	301.5	118.7	109.2
Unrefined sugar	40.0	70.3	44.4
Mineral products	66.4	71.5	64.6
Petroleum products, refined .	58.5	67.6	60.5
Chemical products	169.7	173.5	178.1
Woodpulp, paper, paperboard and articles thereof . . .	83.2	92.8	118.8
Textiles and textile articles .	78.8	71.9	69.9
Miscellaneous manufactured articles	173.0	173.5	188.9
Total (incl. others)	1,341.4	1,213.5	1,233.8

* Excluding exports from *maquila* zones (US $ million): 1,609 in 2000; 1,650 in 2001; 1,758 in 2002 .

PRINCIPAL TRADING PARTNERS
(US $ million)

Imports c.i.f.	2000	2001	2002
Brazil	40.2	52.0	79.7
Colombia	27.5	35.0	40.2
Costa Rica	143.2	163.4	149.0
Ecuador	151.4	127.4	152.5
Finland	61.1	29.3	13.9
France	37.9	32.0	29.7
Germany	75.8	89.0	81.0
Guatemala	488.2	435.4	418.6
Honduras	119.9	134.7	156.5
Italy	35.6	41.8	44.5
Japan	122.5	124.4	137.2
Korea, Republic	39.0	40.8	46.9
Mexico	255.7	312.4	293.1
Netherlands Antilles . . .	175.6	42.5	64.1
Nicaragua	69.8	87.9	97.5
Panama	130.9	135.1	156.2
Russia	38.2	48.5	25.4
Spain	55.6	54.8	62.5
USA	1,322.0	1,324.4	1,313.3
Venezuela	63.0	82.3	78.7
Total (incl. others)	3,795.2	3,865.6	3,907.3

Exports f.o.b.*	2000	2001	2002
Belgium	13.8	4.7	5.0
Costa Rica	85.6	94.6	106.6
Dominican Republic	12.2	12.4	20.8
France	12.2	10.2	10.6
Germany	94.4	48.8	36.4
Guatemala	322.5	323.2	344.0
Honduras	225.1	184.3	176.2
Japan	9.5	5.6	6.1
Mexico	10.8	24.6	31.9
Netherlands	4.2	1.1	2.9
Nicaragua	107.5	120.3	112.5
Panama	39.0	48.9	45.0
Russia	17.5	48.9	18.5
United Kingdom	14.5	6.5	6.3
USA	322.8	227.4	249.9
Total (incl. others)	1,341.4	1,213.5	1,233.8

* Excluding *maquila* zones.

Source: UN, *International Trade Statistics Yearbook*.

Transport

RAILWAYS
(traffic)

	1999	2000
Number of passengers ('000)	543.3	687.3
Passenger-kilometres (million)	8.4	10.7
Freight ('000 metric tons)	188.6	136.2
Freight ton-kilometres (million)	19.4	13.1

Source: Ferrocarriles Nacionales de El Salvador.

ROAD TRAFFIC
(motor vehicles in use at 31 December)

	1998	1999	2000
Passenger cars	187,440	197,374	207,259
Buses and coaches	34,784	36,204	37,554
Lorries and vans	166,065	177,741	189,812
Motorcycles and mopeds	32,271	35,021	37,139

Source: Servicio de Tránsito Centroamericano (SERTRACEN).

SHIPPING

Merchant Fleet
(registered at 31 December)

	2001	2002	2003
Number of vessels	12	14	14
Total displacement ('000 grt)	1.5	5.6	5.6

Source: Lloyd's Register-Fairplay, *World Fleet Statistics*.

CIVIL AVIATION
(traffic on scheduled services)

	1999	2000	2001
Kilometres flown (million)	28	30	26
Passengers carried ('000)	1,624	1,960	1,692
Passenger–km (million)	5,091	2,829	2,907
Total ton-km (million)	502	284	308

Source: UN, *Statistical Yearbook*.

Tourism

TOURIST ARRIVALS BY COUNTRY OF ORIGIN
(excluding Salvadorean nationals residing abroad)

	1999	2000	2001
Canada	12,722	11,543	10,901
Costa Rica	23,257	29,046	22,689
Guatemala	205,559	273,543	285,749
Honduras	113,268	151,919	113,911
Mexico	21,007	22,427	19,302
Nicaragua	60,727	72,746	59,426
Panama	6,938	9,045	2,267
Spain	9,810	9,881	9,893
USA	143,614	142,962	130,128
Total (incl. others)	658,191	794,678	734,627

Receipts from tourism (US $ million): 254 in 2000; 235 in 2001; 342 in 2002.

Sources: World Tourism Organization, *Yearbook of Tourism Statistics*, World Bank, *World Development Indicators*.

Communications Media

	2000	2001	2002
Telephones ('000 main lines in use)	625	650	668
Mobile cellular telephones ('000 subscribers)	744	858	889
Personal computers ('000 in use)	100	140	163
Internet users ('000)	70	150	300

Radio receivers ('000 in use): 2,940 in 1999.

Television receivers ('000 in use): 1,260 in 2000.

Daily newspapers: 4 in 1998 (circulation 171,000).

Non-daily newspapers: 6 in 1996 (circulation 52,000).

Book Production: 663 in 1998.

Sources: UNESCO, *Statistical Yearbook*, International Telecommunication Union.

Education
(2002, unless otherwise indicated)

	Institutions	Teachers*	Students Males	Females	Total†
Pre-primary	4,838	5,116	112,718	115,129	228,064
Primary	5,414	31,921	659,896	621,141	1,281,693
Secondary	757	5,647	77,573	80,293	157,959
Tertiary: University level*	28	6,908	57,734	49,984	107,718
Tertiary: Other higher*	15	593	3,643	3,314	6,957

* 2000.
† Including unspecified gender.

Source: Ministry of Education.

Adult literacy rate (UNESCO estimates): 79.7% (males 82.4%; females 77.1%) in 2002 (Source: UN Development Programme, *Human Development Report*).

Directory

The Constitution

The Constitution of the Republic of El Salvador came into effect on 20 December 1983.

The Constitution provides for a republican, democratic and representative form of government, composed of three Powers—Legislative, Executive, and Judicial—which are to operate independently. Voting is a right and duty of all citizens over 18 years of age. Presidential and congressional elections may not be held simultaneously.

The Constitution binds the country, as part of the Central American Nation, to favour the total or partial reconstruction of the Republic of Central America. Integration in a unitary, federal or confederal form, provided that democratic and republican principles are respected and that basic rights of individuals are fully guaranteed, is subject to popular approval.

LEGISLATIVE ASSEMBLY

Legislative power is vested in a single chamber, the Asamblea Nacional, whose members are elected every three years and are eligible for re-election. The Asamblea's term of office begins on 1 May. The Asamblea's duties include the choosing of the President and Vice-President of the Republic from the two citizens who shall have gained the largest number of votes for each of these offices, if no candidate obtains an absolute majority in the election. It also selects the members of the Supreme and subsidiary courts; of the Elections Council; and the Accounts Court of the Republic. It determines taxes; ratifies treaties concluded by the Executive with other States and international organizations; sanctions the Budget; regulates the monetary system of the country; determines the conditions under which foreign currencies may circulate; and suspends and reimposes constitutional guarantees. The right to initiate legislation may be exercised by the Asamblea (as well as by the President, through the Cabinet, and by the Supreme Court). The Asamblea may override, with a two-thirds majority, the President's objections to a Bill which it has sent for presidential approval.

PRESIDENT

The President is elected for five years, the term beginning and expiring on 1 June. The principle of alternation in the presidential office is established in the Constitution, which states the action to be taken should this principle be violated. The Executive is responsible for the preparation of the Budget and its presentation to the Asamblea; the direction of foreign affairs; the organization of the armed and security forces; and the convening of extraordinary sessions of the Asamblea. In the event of the President's death, resignation, removal or other cause, the Vice-President takes office for the rest of the presidential term; and, in case of necessity, the Vice-President may be replaced by one of the two Designates elected by the Asamblea.

JUDICIARY

Judicial power is exercised by the Supreme Court and by other competent tribunals. The Magistrates of the Supreme Court are elected by the Legislature, their number to be determined by law. The Supreme Court alone is competent to decide whether laws, decrees and regulations are constitutional or not.

The Government

HEAD OF STATE

President: ELÍAS ANTONIO (TONY) SACA (assumed office 1 June 2004).

Vice-President: ANA VILMA DE ESCOBAR.

CABINET
(April 2005)

Minister of the Treasury: GUILLERMO LÓPEZ SUÁREZ.

Minister of Foreign Affairs: FRANCISCO LAÍNEZ RIVAS.

Minister of Government: RENÉ MARIO FIGUEROA.

Minister of the Economy: YOLANDA MAYORA DE GAVIDIA.

Minister of Education: DARLYN MEZA.

Minister of National Defence: Gen. OTTO ROMERO ORELLANDA.

Minister of Labour and Social Security: JOSÉ ROBERTO ESPINAL ESCOBAR.

Minister of Public Health and Social Welfare: Dr JOSÉ GUILLERMO MAZA BRIZUELA.

Minister of Agriculture and Livestock: MARIO SALAVERRÍA NOLASCO.

Minister of Public Works: DAVID GUTIÉRREZ MIRANDA.

Minister of the Environment and Natural Resources: HUGO CÉSAR BARRERA GUERRERO.

Minister of Tourism: LUIS CARDENAL.

MINISTRIES

Ministry for the Presidency: Avda Cuba, Calle Darío González 806, Barrio San Brizinto, San Salvador; tel. 221-8483; fax 771-0950; e-mail casapres@casapres.gob.sv; internet www.casapres.gob.sv.

Ministry of Agriculture and Livestock: Final 1a, Avda Norte y Avda Manuel Gallardo, Nueva San Salvador; tel. 228-4443; fax 229-9271; e-mail direccion.dgsva@mag.gob.sv; internet www.mag.gob.sv.

Ministry of the Economy: Edif. C1–C2, Centro de Gobierno, Alameda Juan Pablo II y Calle Guadalupe, San Salvador; tel. 281-1122; fax 221-5446; internet www.minec.gob.sv.

Ministry of Education: Edif. A, Centro de Gobierno, Alameda Juan Pablo II y Calle Guadalupe, San Salvador; tel. 281-0044; fax 281-0077; e-mail educacion@mined.gob.sv; internet www.mined.gob.sv.

Ministry of the Environment and Natural Resources: Carretera a Nueva San Salvador 5.5km, Calle y Col. Las Mercedes, San Salvador; tel. 223-0444; fax 260-3115; e-mail medioambiente@marn.gob.sv; internet www.marn.gob.sv.

Ministry of Foreign Affairs: Calle Circunvalación 227, Col. San Benito, San Salvador; tel. 243-9648; fax 243-9656; e-mail webmaster@rree.gob.sv; internet www.rree.gob.sv.

Ministry of Government: Centro de Gobierno, Edif. B-1, Alameda Juan Pablo II y Avda Norte 17, San Salvador; tel. 221-3688; fax 221-3956; e-mail DT@gobernacion.gob.sv; internet www.gobernacion.gob.sv.

Ministry of Labour and Social Security: Paseo Gen. Escalón 4122, San Salvador; tel. 209-3700; fax 209-3728; e-mail informacion@mtps.gob.sv; internet www.mtps.gob.sv.

Ministry of National Defence: Alameda Dr Manuel Enrique Araújo, Km 5, Carretera a Santa Tecla, San Salvador; tel. 223-0233; fax 998-2005; internet www.fuerzaarmada.gob.sv.

Ministry of Public Health and Social Welfare: Calle Arce 827, San Salvador; tel. 221-0966; fax 221-0991; e-mail webmaster@mspas.gob.sv; internet www.mspas.gob.sv.

Ministry of Public Works: Carretera a Santa Tecla 5.5 km, San Salvador; tel. 223-8040; fax 279-3723; internet www.mop.gob.sv.

Ministry of Tourism: San Salvador.

Ministry of the Treasury: 1231 Blvd Los Héroes, San Salvador; tel. 244-3000; fax 244-6408; e-mail webmaster@mh.gob.sv; internet www.mh.gob.sv.

President and Legislature

PRESIDENT

Election, 21 March 2004

Candidates	% of votes cast
Elías Antonio (Tony) Saca (ARENA)	57.71
Schafik Jorge Handal (FMLN)	35.68
Héctor Silva Argüello (PDC/CDU)	3.90
José Rafael Machuca Zelaya (PCN)	2.71
Total	100.00

ASAMBLEA NACIONAL

President: CIRO CRUZ ZEPEDA.

General Election, 16 March 2003

Party	% of votes cast	Seats
Frente Farabundo Martí para la Liberación Nacional (FMLN) . . .	33.8	31
Alianza Republicana Nacionalista (ARENA)	32.0	28
Partido de Conciliación Nacional (PCN)	13.1	15
Partido Demócrata Cristiano (PDC) . .	7.3	5
Centro Democrático Unido (CDU)* . .	6.4	5
Other parties	7.4	—
Total	100.0	84

*Electoral alliance comprising the Movimiento Nacional Revolucionario (MNR), the Movimiento Popular Social Cristiano (MPSC) and the Partido Social Demócrata (PSD).

Political Organizations

Alianza Republicana Nacionalista (ARENA): Prolongación Calle Arce 2423, entre 45 y 47 Avda Norte, San Salvador; tel. 260-4400; fax 260-5918; internet www.arena.com.sv; f. 1981; right-wing; Pres. ELÍAS ANTONIO (TONY) SACA.

Centro Democrático Unido (CDU): Blvd Tutunichapa y Calle Roberto Masferrer 1313, Urb. Médica, San Salvador; tel. 226-1752; fax 225-5883; e-mail hsilva@asamblea.gob.sv; f. 1987 as Convergencia Democrática (CD); electoral alliance of the Movimiento Nacional Revolucionario (MNR), the Movimiento Popular Social Cristiano (MPSC) and the Partido Social Demócrata (PSD); changed name as above in 2000; became political party in 2001; Leader VINICIO PEÑATE; Sec.-Gen. RUBÉN IGNACIO ZAMORA.

Concertación Socialdemócrata (CSD): San Salvador; f. November 2004 by Facundo Guardado, Francisco Jovel and other fmr mems of the FMLN; moderate left-wing movt.

Frente Farabundo Martí para la Liberación Nacional (FMLN): 29 Calle Poniente 1316, Col. Layco, San Salvador; tel. 226-5236; internet www.fmln.org.sv; f. 1980 as the FDR (Frente Democrático Revolucionario-FMLN) as a left-wing opposition front to the PDC-military coalition Government; the FDR was the political wing and the FMLN was the guerrilla front; military operations were co-ordinated by the Dirección Revolucionaria Unida (DRU); achieved legal recognition 1992; comprised various factions, including Communist (Leader SCHAFIK JORGE HANDAL), Renewalist (Leader OSCAR ORTIZ) and Terceristas (Leader MANUEL MELGAR); Co-ordinator-Gen. MEDARDO GONZÁLEZ.

Partido de Conciliación Nacional (PCN): 15 Avda Norte y 3a Calle Poniente 244, San Salvador; tel. 221-3752; fax 281-9272; e-mail czepeda@asamblea.gob.sv; f. 1961; right-wing; Leader RAFAEL MACHUCA; Sec.-Gen. CIRO CRUZ ZEPEDA.

Partido Demócrata Cristiano (PDC): 3a Calle Poniente 924, San Salvador; tel. 222-6320; fax 998-1526; e-mail pdcsal@navegante.com.sv; f. 1960; 150,000 mems; anti-imperialist, advocates self-determination and Latin American integration; Sec.-Gen. RODOLFO ANTONIO PARKER SOTO.

Partido Nacional Liberal (PNL): 5a Calle Poniente y 3a Avda Norte 226, San Salvador; tel. 222-6511; Leader OSCAR SILDER CHÁVEZ HERNÁNDEZ.

Partido Social Demócrata (PSD).

Partido Unificación Cristiana Democrática (UCD): 7a Calle Ote. 52, Col. Los Andes, San Marcos; tel. 213-0759; Sec.-Gen. JOSÉ ALEJANDRO DUARTE.

Partido Unionista Centroamericana (PUCA): San Salvador; advocates reunification of Central America; Pres. Dr GABRIEL PILOÑA ARAÚJO.

Diplomatic Representation

EMBASSIES IN EL SALVADOR

Argentina: 79 Avda Norte y 11 Calle Poniente 704, Col. Escalón, Apdo 384, San Salvador; tel. 263-3638; fax 263-3580; e-mail argensalv@saltel.net; Ambassador SILVIO HÉCTOR NEUMAN.

Belize: Calle el Bosque Norte y Calle Lomas de Candelaria, Col. Jardines de la Primera Etapa, San Salvador; tel. 248-1423; fax 273-6244; e-mail embelguat@guate.net; Ambassador DARWIN GABOUREL.

Brazil: Blvd de Hipódromo 132, Col. San Benito, San Salvador; tel. 298-1993; fax 279-3934; e-mail brasemb@es.com.sv; Ambassador MARÍA LUCÍA SANTOS POMPEU.

Canada: Centro Financiero Gigante, Torre A, Lobby 2, Alameda Roosevelt y 65 Avda Sur, Col. Escalón, San Salvador; tel. 279-4655; fax 279-0765; e-mail sal@dfait-maeci.gc.ca; internet www.dfait-maeci.gc.ca/elsalvador; Ambassador JAMES LAMBERT (resident in Guatemala).

Chile: Pasaje Bellavista 121, 9a Calle Poniente, Col. Escalón, San Salvador; tel. 263-4285; fax 263-4308; e-mail conchile@conchileelsalvador.com.sv; internet www.conchileelsalvador.com.sv; Ambassador RAQUEL MORALES ETCHEVERS.

China (Taiwan): Avda La Capilla 716, Col. San Benito, Apdo 956, San Salvador; tel. 263-1330; fax 263-1329; e-mail sinoemb3@sv.intercomnet.net; Ambassador HOU PING-FU.

Colombia: Calle El Mirador 5120, Col. Escalón, San Salvador; tel. 263-1936; fax 263-1942; e-mail elsalvador@minrelext.gov.co; Ambassador FABIO TORRIJOS QUINTERO.

Costa Rica: 85 Avda Sur y Calle Cuscatlán 4415, Col. Escalón, San Salvador; tel. 264-3863; fax 264-3866; e-mail embaricasal@sgsica.org; Ambassador JOSÉ DE JESÚS CONEJO AMADOR.

Dominican Republic: Avda República Federal de Alemania 163, Col. Escalón, San Salvador; tel. 263-1816; fax 263-1816; Ambassador HECTOR PEREYRA ARIZA.

Ecuador: 77 Avda Norte 208, Col. Escalón, San Salvador; tel. 263-5323; fax 263-5258; e-mail ecuador@integra.com.sv; Ambassador Dr FRANCISCO PROAÑO ARANDI.

Egypt: 9a Calle Poniente y 93 Avda Norte 12-97, Col. Escalón, San Salvador; tel. 211-5788; fax 263-2411; e-mail emebgip@telesal.net; Chargé d'affaires a.i. MEDHAT MOURSSI ELBANAN.

France: 1 Calle Poniente 3718, Col. Escalón, Apdo 474, San Salvador; tel. 279-4016; fax 298-1536; e-mail ambafrance@es.com.sv; internet www.embafrancia.com.sv; Ambassador FRANCIS ROUDIÈRE.

Germany: 7a Calle Poniente 3972, esq. 77a Avda Norte, Col. Escalón, Apdo 693, San Salvador; tel. 247-0000; fax 247-0099; e-mail zreg@sans.diplo.de; internet www.san-salvador.diplo.de; Ambassador Dr JOACHIM NEUKIRCH.

Guatemala: 15 Avda Norte 135, San Salvador; tel. 271-2225; fax 221-3019; Ambassador CARLOS ARTURO GONZÁLEZ ESTRADA.

Holy See: 87 Avda Norte y 7a Calle Poniente, Col. Escalón, Apdo 01-95, San Salvador (Apostolic Nunciature); tel. 263-2931; fax 263-3010; e-mail nunels@telesal.net; Apostolic Nuncio Most Rev. GIACINTO BERLOCO (Titular Archbishop of Fidene).

Honduras: 89 Avda Norte, entre 7 y 9 Calle Poniente, Col. Escalón, San Salvador; tel. 263-2808; fax 263-2296; Ambassador JAIME GÜELL BOGRÁN.

Israel: Centro Financiero Gigante, Torre B, 11°, Alameda Roosevelt y Avda Sur 63, San Salvador; tel. 211-3434; fax 211-3443; Ambassador YOSEF LIVNÉ.

Italy: Calle la Reforma 158, Col. San Benito, Apdo 0199, San Salvador; tel. 223-4806; fax 298-3050; e-mail ambitalia@ambasciatait.org.sv; internet www.ambasciatait.org.sv; Ambassador ROBERTO FALASCHI.

Japan: Calle Loma Linda 258, Col. San Benito, San Salvador; tel. 224-4740; fax 298-6685; Ambassador AKIO HOSONO.

Korea, Republic: 5a Calle Poniente 3970, entre 75 y 77 Avda Norte, Col. Escalón, San Salvador; tel. 263-9145; fax 263-0783; e-mail embcorea@mofat.go.kr; Ambassador CHOO YEON-GON.

Mexico: Calle Circunvalación y Pasaje 12, Col. San Benito, Apdo 432, San Salvador; tel. 243-3190; fax 243-0437; e-mail embamex@sv.intercom.com.sv; Ambassador PABLO RUIZ LIMÓN.

Nicaragua: 71 Avda Norte y 1a Calle Poniente 164, Col. Escalón, San Salvador; tel. 263-8770; fax 263-2292; Ambassador CECILE SABORIO COZE.

Panama: Avda Bungamilias 21, Col. San Francisco, San Salvador; tel. and fax 298-0773; e-mail embpan@telesal.net; Ambassador RODERICK GUERRA BIANCO.

Peru: 7 Calle Poniente 4111, Col. Escalón, San Salvador; tel. 263-3326; fax 263-3310; e-mail embperu@telesal.net; Ambassador SERGIO KOSTRITSKY PEREIRA.

Spain: Calle La Reforma 167, Col. San Benito, San Salvador; tel. 257-5700; fax 298-0402; e-mail embespsv@correo.mae.es; Ambassador JORGE HEVIA SIERRA.

USA: Blvd Santa Elena Sur, Antiguo Cuscatlán, San Salvador; tel. 278-4444; fax 278-1815; internet www.usinfo.org.sv; Ambassador HUGH DOUGLAS BARCLAY.

Uruguay: Edif. Gran Plaza 405, Blvd del Hipódromo, Col. San Benito, San Salvador; tel. 279-1627; fax 279-1626; Ambassador ROBERTO PABLO TOURIÑO.

Venezuela: 7a Calle Poniente, entre 75 y 77 Avda Norte, Col. Escalón, San Salvador; tel. 263-3977; fax 211-0027; e-mail venesal@amnetsal.com; Chargé d'affaires a.i. MARÍA EUGENIA SILVA.

Judicial System

Supreme Court of Justice

Frente a Plaza José Simeón Cañas, Centro de Gobierno, San Salvador; tel. 271-8888; fax 271-3767; internet www.csj.gob.sv.

f. 1824; composed of 15 Magistrates, one of whom is its President. The Court is divided into four chambers: Constitutional Law, Civil Law, Criminal Law and Litigation; Pres. AGUSTÍN GARCÍA CALDERÓN.

Courts of Original Jurisdiction: 201 courts throughout the country.

Courts of Appeals: 34 chambers composed of two Magistrates.

Courts of Peace: 322 courts throughout the country.

Attorney-General of the Republic: MARCOS GREGORIO SÁNCHEZ TREJO.

Attorney-General for the Defence of Human Rights: BEATRICE ALAMANNI DE CARRILLO.

Religion

Roman Catholicism is the dominant religion, but other denominations are also permitted. In 2003 21.2% of the population belonged to Protestant churches. The Baptist Church, Seventh-day Adventists, Jehovah's Witnesses, and the Church of Jesus Christ of Latter-day Saints (Mormons) are represented.

CHRISTIANITY

The Roman Catholic Church

El Salvador comprises one archdiocese and seven dioceses. At 31 December 2002, according to the Vatican, Roman Catholics represented some 74% of the total population.

Bishops' Conference

Conferencia Episcopal de El Salvador, 15 Avda Norte 1420, Col. Layco, Apdo 1310, San Salvador; tel. 226 6344; fax 226-4979; e-mail arzfsl@vip.telesal.net.

f. 1974; Pres. Most Rev. FERNANDO SÁENZ LACALLE (Archbishop of San Salvador).

Archbishop of San Salvador: Most Rev. FERNANDO SÁENZ LACALLE, Arzobispado, Avda Dr Emilio Alvarez y Avda Dr Max Bloch, Col. Médica, Apdo 2253, San Salvador; tel. 225-8997; fax 226-5330; e-mail arzfsl@vip.telesal.net.

The Anglican Communion

El Salvador comprises one of the five dioceses of the Iglesia Anglicana de la Región Central de América. The Iglesia Anglicana has some 5,000 members.

Bishop of El Salvador: Rt Rev. MARTÍN DE JESÚS BARAHONA PASCACIO, 47 Avda Sur, 723 Col. Flor Blanca, Apdo 01-274, San Salvador; tel. 223-2252; fax 223-7952; e-mail martinba@gbm.net; internet www.cristosal.org.

The Baptist Church

Baptist Association of El Salvador: Avda Sierra Nevada 922, Col. Miramonte, Apdo 347, San Salvador; tel. 226-6287; e-mail asociacionbautistaabes@latinmail.com; f. 1933; Pres. Rev. MIGUEL ÁNGEL DUARTE RECINOS.

Other Churches

Sínodo Luterano Salvadoreño (Salvadorean Lutheran Synod): Final 49 Avda Sur, Calle Paralela al Bulevar de los Próceres, San Salvador; tel. 225-2843; fax 248-3451; e-mail comunicaciones@sinodoluterano.org.sv; Pres. Bishop MEDARDO E. GÓMEZ SOTO; 12,000 mems.

The Press

DAILY NEWSPAPERS

San Miguel

Diario de Oriente: Avda Gerardo Barrios 406, San Miguel.

San Salvador

Co Latino: 23a Avda Sur 225, Apdo 96, San Salvador; tel. 271-0671; fax 271-0971; e-mail info@diariocolatino.com; f. 1890; evening; Editor FRANCISCO ELÍAS VALENCIA; circ. 15,000.

El Diario de Hoy: 11 Calle Oriente 271, Apdo 495, San Salvador; tel. 271-0100; fax 271-2040; e-mail comedh@es.com.sv; internet www.elsalvador.com; f. 1936; morning; independent; Dir ENRIQUE ALTAMIRANO MADRIZ; circ. 115,000.

Diario Oficial: 4a Calle Poniente y 15e, Avda Sur 829, San Salvador; tel. 233-7821; fax 222-4936; e-mail diariooficial@imprentanacional.gob.sv; f. 1875; Dir RENÉ ORLANDO SANTAMARÍA COBOS; circ. 1000.

El Mundo: 15 Calle Poniente y 7a Avda Norte 521, San Salvador; tel. 225-3300; fax 222-1490; e-mail mercadeo@elmundo.com.sv; internet www.elmundo.com.sv; f. 1967; evening; Exec. Dir ERNESTO BORJA PAPINI; Gen. Man. ARTURO ARGUELLO OERTEL; circ. 40,215.

La Prensa Gráfica: 3a Calle Poniente 130, San Salvador; tel. 271-1010; fax 271-4242; e-mail lpg@gbm.net; internet www.laprensagrafica.com.sv; f. 1915; general information; conservative, independent; Editor RODOLFO DUTRIZ; circ. 97,312 (weekdays), 115,564 (Sundays).

Santa Ana

Diario de Occidente: 1a Avda Sur 3, Santa Ana; tel. 441-2931; f. 1910; Editor ALEX E. MONTENEGRO; circ. 6,000.

PERIODICALS

Cultura: Concultura, Ministerio de Educación, 17 Avda Sur 430, San Salvador; tel. 222-0665; fax 271-1071; quarterly; educational; Dir Dr RICARDO ROQUE BALDOVINOS.

Orientación: 1a Calle Poniente 3412, San Salvador; tel. 998-6838; fax 224-5099; f. 1952; Catholic weekly; Dir P. FABIAN AMAYA TORRES; circ. 8,000.

Proceso: Universidad Centroamericana, Apdo 01-575, San Salvador; tel. 224-0011; fax 273-3556; f. 1980; weekly newsletter, published by the Documentation and Information Centre of the Universidad Centroamericana José Simeón Cañas; Dir LUIS ARMANDO GONZÁLEZ.

Revista del Ateneo de El Salvador: 13a Calle Poniente, Centro de Gobierno, San Salvador; tel. 222-9686; f. 1912; 3 a year; official organ of Salvadorean Athenaeum; Pres. Lic JOSÉ OSCAR RAMÍREZ PÉREZ; Sec.-Gen. Lic. RUBÉN REGALADO SERMEÑO.

Revista Judicial: Centro de Gobierno, San Salvador; tel. 222-4522; organ of the Supreme Court; Dir Dr MANUEL ARRIETA GALLEGOS.

PRESS ASSOCIATIONS

Asociación de Periodistas de El Salvador (Press Association of El Salvador): Edif. Casa del Periodista, Paseo Gen. Escalón 4130, San Salvador; tel. 263-5335; e-mail info@apes.org.sv; internet www.apes.org.sv; Pres. HERMINIA FÚNES.

FOREIGN NEWS AGENCIES

Agencia EFE (Spain): San Salvador; Bureau Chief CRISTINA HASBÚN DE MERINO.

Agenzia Nazionale Stampa Associata (ANSA) (Italy): Edif. 'Comercial 29', 29 Calle Poniente y 11 Avda Norte, San Salvador; tel. 226-8008; fax 774-5512; Bureau Chief RENÉ ALBERTO CONTRERAS.

Associated Press (AP) (USA): San Salvador; Correspondent ANA LEONOR CABRERA.

Deutsche Presse-Agentur (dpa) (Germany): San Salvador; Correspondent JORGE ARMANDO CONTRERAS.

Inter Press Service (IPS) (Italy): San Salvador; e-mail ipslatam@ipsnews.net; Correspondent PABLO IACUB.

Publishers

Centro de Paz (CEPAZ): Col. Libertad, Avda Washington 405, San Salvador; tel. and fax 226-2117; e-mail cepaz@cepaz.org.sv; internet www.cepaz.org.sv; social history.

Clásicos Roxsil, SA de CV: 4a Avda Sur 2–3, Nueva San Salvador; tel. 228-1832; fax 228-1212; e-mail roxanabe@navegante.com.sv; f. 1976; textbooks, literature; Dir ROSA VICTORIA SERRANO DE LÓPEZ.

Editorial Universitaria: Universidad 'Dr José Matías Delgado', Km 8.5, Carretera a Santa Tecla, Ciudad Merliot; tel. 278-1011; e-mail jalas@ujmd.edu.sv; internet www.ujmd.edu.sv/seditorial .html; f. 1984.

Distribuidora de Textos Escolares (D'TEXE): Edif. C, Col., Paseo y Condominio Miralvalle, San Salvador; tel. 274-2031; f. 1985; educational; Dir JORGE A. LÓPEZ HIDALGO.

Dirección de Publicaciones e Impresos: Ministerio de Educación, 17a Avda Sur 430, San Salvador; tel. 271-1806; fax 271-1071; e-mail direccion@dpi.gov.sv; f. 1953; literary and general; Dir MIGUEL ANGEL RIVERA LARIOS.

UCA Editores: Apdo 01-575, San Salvador; tel. 273-4400; fax 273-3556; e-mail distpubli@ued.uca.edu.sv; internet www.uca.edu.sv; f. 1975; social science, religion, economy, literature and textbooks; Dir RODOLFO CARDENAL.

PUBLISHERS' ASSOCIATION

Cámara Salvadoreña del Libro: Col. Flor Blanca, 47 Avda Norte y 1a Calle Poniente, Apdo 3384, San Salvador; tel. 261-0293; fax 261-2231; e-mail camsalibre@terra.com.sv; f. 1974; Pres. ANA MOLINA DE FAUVET.

Broadcasting and Communications

TELECOMMUNICATIONS

Regulatory Authority

Superintendencia General de Electricidad y Telecomunicaciones (SIGET): Sexta Décima Calle Poniente y 37 Avda Sur 2001, Col. Flor Blanca, San Salvador; tel. 257-4438; internet www.siget .gob.sv; f. 1996; Supt Lic. JORGE NIETO.

Major Service Providers

Digicel: San Salvador; internet www.digicel.com.sv; provider of mobile telecommunications; owned by Digicel (USA).

Telecom El Salvador: Alameda Manuel Enrique Araujo y Calle Nueva 1, 40°, Edif. Palic, San Salvador; tel. 800-8155; internet www .telecom.com.sv; terrestrial telecommunications network, fmrly part of Administración Nacional de Telecomunicaciones (Antel), which was divested in 1998; changed name from CTE Antel Telecom in 1999; became subsidiary of France Télécom in 2002; Pres. DOMINIQUE ST JEAN.

> **Telecom Personal:** Alameda Manuel Enrique Araujo y Calle Nueva 1, 40°, Edif. Palic, San Salvador; internet www.personal .com.sv; provider of mobile telecommunications; subsidiary of Telecom El Salvador.

Telefónica El Salvador: San Salvador; e-mail telefonica .empresas@telefonicamail.com.sv; internet www.telefonica.com.sv; manages sale of telecommunications frequencies; fmrly Internacional de Telecomunicaciones (Intel), which was divested in 1998; controlling interest owned by Telefónica, SA (Spain); Pres. CÉSAR ALIERTA.

> **Telefónica Movistar:** Torre Telefónica (Torre B de Centro Financiero Gigante), Alameda Roosevelt y 63 Avda Sur, Col. Escalón, San Salvador; tel. 257-4000; internet www.telefonica.com.sv/ movistar; provider of mobile telecommunications; 92% owned by Telefónica Móviles, SA (Spain), part of Telefónica, SA.

Telemóvil: Avda Roosevelt, Centro Financiero, Gigante Torre D, 9°, San Salvador; tel. 246-9977; fax 246-9999; e-mail servicioalcliente@ tigo.com.sv; internet www.telemovil.com; provider of mobile telecommunications; subsidiary of Millicom International Cellular (Sweden).

Tricom, SA: San Salvador; provider of mobile telecommunications; owned by Tricom, SA (Dominican Republic).

RADIO

Asociación Salvadoreña de Radiodifusores (ASDER): Avda Izalco, Bloco 6 No 33, Residencial San Luis, San Salvador; tel. 222-0872; fax 274-6870; e-mail asder@ejje.com; internet www.asder .sv; f. 1965; Pres. Dr JOSÉ LUIS SACA MELÉNDEZ.

YSSS Radio Nacional de El Salvador: Dirección General de Medios, Calle Monserrat, Plantel Ex-IVU, San Salvador; tel. 773-4170; e-mail radio.elsalvador@gobernacion.gob.sv; internet www .radioelsalvador.com.sv; f. 1926; non-commercial cultural station; Dir-Gen. JAIME VILANOVA.

There are 64 commercial radio stations. Radio Venceremos and Radio Farabundo Martí, operated by the former guerrilla group FMLN, were legalized in April 1992. Radio Mayavisión (operated by FMLN supporters), began broadcasting in November 1993.

TELEVISION

Canal 2, SA: Carretera a Nueva San Salvador, Apdo 720, San Salvador; tel. 223-6744; fax 998-6565; internet www.teledos.com; commercial; Pres. BORIS ESERSKI; Gen. Man. SALVADOR I. GADALA MARÍA.

Canal 4, SA: Carretera a Nueva San Salvador, Apdo 720, San Salvador; tel. 224-4555; owned by Telecorporación Salvadoreña (TCS); commercial; Pres. BORIS ESERSKI; Man. RONALD CALVO.

Canal 6, SA: Km 6, Carretera Panamericana a Santa Tecla, San Salvador; tel. 209-5068; fax 209-2033; e-mail director@elnoticiero .com.sv; internet www.elnoticiero.com.sv; f. 1972; owned by Telecorporación Salvadoreña (TCS); commercial; Exec. Dir JUAN CARLOS ESERSKI; Man. Dr PEDRO LEONEL MORENO MONGE.

Canal 8 (Agape TV): 1511 Calle Gerardo Barrios, Col. Cucumacuyán, San Salvador; tel. 281-2828; fax 271-3414; e-mail info@ agapetv8.com; internet www.agapetv8.com; catholic, family channel; Pres. FLAVIÁN MUCCI.

Canal 12: Urb. Santa Elena 12, Antiguo Cuscatlán, San Salvador; tel. 278-0622; fax 278-0722; internet www.canal12.com.sv; f. 1984; Dir ALEJANDRO GONZÁLEZ.

Canal 15: 4a Avda Sur y 5a Calle Oriente 301, San Miguel; tel. 661-3298; fax 661-3298; f. 1994; Gen. Man. JOAQUÍN APARICIO.

Canal 19: Final Calle Los Abetos 1, Col. San Francisco, San Salvador; e-mail serviciosmegavision@salnet.net; owned by Grupo Megavisión; children's channel; Gen. Man. MARIO CAÑAS.

Canal 21 (Megavisión): Primera Calle Poniente entre 85 y 87 Avda Norte, Apdo 2789, San Salvador; tel. 283-2121; fax 283-2132; e-mail serviciosmegavision@salnet.net; internet www.canal21tv.com.sv; f. 1993; Pres. OSCAR ANTONIO SAFIE; Dir HUGO ESCOBAR.

Fundación Canal 25: Final Calle Libertad 100, Ciudad Merliot, Nueva San Salvador; tel. 248-2525; fax 278-8526; f. 1997; commercial; Gen. Man. JORGE MIRA.

Tecnovisión Canal 33: Calle Arce 1120, San Salvador; tel. 275-8888; e-mail jgomez@utec.edu.sv; internet www.utec.edu.sv; owned by the Universidad Tecnológica de El Salvador; Pres. MAURICIO LOUCEL.

Finance

(cap. = capital; p.u. = paid up; res = reserves; dep. = deposits; m. = million; brs = branches; amounts in colones unless otherwise stated)

BANKING

The banking system was nationalized in March 1980. In 1994 the transfer to private ownership of six banks and seven savings and loans institutions, as part of a programme of economic reform begun in 1991, was completed.

Supervisory Bodies

Superintendencia del Sistema Financiero: 7a Avda Norte 240, Apdo 2942, San Salvador; tel. 281-2444; fax 281-1621; internet www .ssf.gob.sv; Pres. LUIS ARMANDO MONTENEGRO.

Superintendencia de Valores: Antiguo Edif. BCR, 1a Calle Poniente y 7a Avda Norte, San Salvador; tel. 281-8900; fax 221-3404; e-mail info@superval.gob.sv; internet www.superval.gob.sv; Pres. Lic. OMAR ERNESTO RODRÍGUEZ ALEMÁN.

Central Bank

Banco Central de Reserva de El Salvador: Alameda Juan Pablo II y 17 Avda Norte, Apdo 01-106, San Salvador; tel. 281-8000; fax 281-8011; e-mail comunicaciones@bcr.gob.sv; internet www.bcr.gob .sv; f. 1934; nationalized Dec. 1961; entered monetary integration process 1 Jan. 2001; cap. US $115.0m., res $29.2m., dep. $1,556.3m. (Dec. 2003); Pres. LUZ MARÍA DE PORTILLO.

Commercial and Mortgage Banks

Banco Agrícola: Blvd Constitución 100, San Salvador; tel. 267-5787; fax 267-5775; e-mail info@bancoagricola.com; internet www .bancoagricola.com; f. 1955; dep. US $2,456.6m., total assets $2,9991.5m. (Dec. 2003); merged with Banco Desarrollo in July 2000; acquired Banco Capital in November 2001; Pres. RODOLFO SCHILDKRECHT; 150 brs world-wide.

Banco Americano: World Trade Center, Torre II, Local 109, 89 Avda Norte y Calle al Mirador, San Salvador; tel. 245-0651; fax 298-5251; e-mail presidencia@bamericano.com; internet www .bamericano.com; privately owned; formerly Unibanco; cap. US $13.0m., res $0.2m., dep. $78.5m. (Dec. 2003); Pres. Ing. RONALD A. LACAYO.

Banco de Comercio: Centro Financiero, 25 Avda Norte y 23 Calle Poniente, San Salvador; tel. 226-4577; fax 225-7767; e-mail informacion@banco.com.sv; internet www.banco.com.sv; f. 1949; privately owned; scheduled to merge with Scotiabank in July 2005; total assets 9,074m. (1999); Pres. JOSÉ GUSTAVO BELISMELIS VIDES; 48 brs.

Banco Cuscatlán de El Salvador, SA: Edif. Pirámide Cuscatlán, Km 10, Carretera a Santa Tecla, Apdo 626, San Salvador; tel. 212-3333; fax 228-5700; e-mail cuscatlan@bancocuscatlan.com; internet www.bancocuscatlan.com; f. 1972; privately owned; cap. 90m., res 123.6m., dep. 1,531.6m. (Sept. 2003); Pres. MAURICIO SAMAYOA RIVAS; Vice-Pres. ROBERTO ORTIZ; 31 brs.

Banco Hipotecario: Pasaje Senda Florida Sur, Col. Escalón, Apdo 999, San Salvador; tel. 250-7101; fax 250-7039; internet www .bancohipotecario.com.sv; f. 1935; cap. 104.0m., dep. 1,852m. (Dec. 1998); Pres. Ing. JOSÉ ROBERTO NAVARRO ESCOBAR; Exec. Dir BRUNO GUSTAVO WYLD BERG; 12 brs.

Banco Promérica: 71 Avda Sur y Paseo Gen. Escalón 3669, Col. Escalón, San Salvador; tel. 243-3344; fax 245-2979; e-mail baprosal@promerica.com.sv; internet www.promerica.com.sv; privately owned; Pres. Lic. RAMIRO ORTIZ GURDIÁN.

Banco Salvadoreño, SA (BANCOSAL): Edif. Centro Financiero, Avda Manuel Enrique Araujo y Avda Olímpica 3550, Apdo 06-73, San Salvador; tel. 298-4444; fax 298-0102; e-mail info@bancosal .com; internet www.bancosal.com; f. 1885; privately-owned commercial bank; cap. US $90m., dep. 1,130.2m. (Jun. 2004); merged with Banco de Construcción y Ahorro, SA (BANCASA) in July 2000; Pres. and Chair. Lic. MARÍA EUGENIA BRIZUELA DE ÁVILA; Vice-Pres. Ing. MOISÉS CASTRO MACEDA; 78 brs.

Banco UNO: Paseo Gen. Escalón y 69 Avda Sur 3563, Col. Escalón, San Salvador; tel. 245-0055; fax 245-0080; internet www.bancouno .com.sv; cap. US $11.4m., res $9.9m., dep. $150.6m. (Dec 2002); Pres. Ing. ALBINO ROMÁN.

Financiera Calpiá: Paseo General Escalón 5438, San Salvador; tel. 264-1194; fax 264-1647; e-mail financiera@calpia.com.sv; Pres. PEDRO DALMAU GORRITA.

Foreign Banks

Citibank, NA (USA): Edif. Palic, Calle Nueva 1, Col. Escalón, San Salvador; tel. 211-2484; fax 211-1842; e-mail bert.veltman@ citigroup.com; internet www.citibank.com/elsalvador; Pres. ROBERT B. WILLUMSTAD; CEO CHARLES PRINCE.

First Commercial Bank (USA): Centro Comercial Gigante, Torre Telefónica, 3°, 63 Avda Sur y Alameda Roosevelt, San Salvador; tel. 211-2121; fax 211-2130; e-mail fcb971@saltel.net; Vice-Pres. PETER MING-FUNG LAN.

Scotiabank (Canada): Edif. Torre Scotiabank, Avda Olímpica 129, San Salvador; tel. 245-1211; fax 224-2884; internet www.scotiabank .com.sv; f. 1972; total assets 3,970.8m.; Pres. Ing. LUIS IVANDIC.

Public Institutions

Banco de Fomento Agropecuario: Km 10.5, Carretera al Puerto de la Libertad, Nueva San Salvador; tel. 228-5188; fax 228-5199; f. 1973; state-owned; cap. 605.0m., dep. 872.0m. (Oct. 1997); Pres. Lic. RAÚL GARCÍA PRIETO; 27 brs.

Banco Multisectorial de Inversiones: Edif. Century Plaza, Alameda Manuel E. Araujo, San Salvador; tel. 267-0000; fax 267-0011; e-mail bmigada@es.com.sv; internet www.bmi.gob.sv; f. 1994; Pres. Dr NICOLA ANGELUCCI.

Federación de Cajas de Crédito (FEDECREDITO): 25 Avda Norte y 23 Calle Poniente, San Salvador; tel. 225-5922; fax 226-7059; internet www.fedecredito.com.sv; f. 1943; Pres. Lic. MARCO TULIO RODRÍGUEZ MENA.

Fondo Social Para la Vivienda: Calle Rubén Darío, entre 15 y 17 Avda Sur, San Salvador; tel. 271-2774; e-mail comunicaciones@fsv .gob.sv; internet www.fsv.gob.sv; Pres. Lic. ENRIQUE OÑATE.

Banking Association

Asociación Bancaria Salvadoreña (ABANSA): Alameda Roosevelt 2511, entre 47 y 49 Avda Sur, San Salvador; tel. 298-6938; fax 223-1079; internet www.abansa.org.sv; Pres. Ing. JOSÉ GUSTAVO BELISMELIS.

STOCK EXCHANGE

Mercado de Valores de El Salvador, SA de CV (Bolsa de Valores): Urb. Jardines de la Hacienda, Blvd Merliot y Avda Las Carretas, Antiguo Cuscatlán, La Libertad, San Salvador; tel. 212-6400; fax 278-4377; e-mail info@bves.com.sv; internet www.bves .com.sv; f. 1992; Pres. ROLANDO DUARTE SCHLAGETER.

INSURANCE

AIG Unión y Desarrollo, SA: Calle Loma Linda 265, Col. San Benito, Apdo 92, San Salvador; tel. 298-5455; fax 298-5084; e-mail aig.elsalvador@uni-desa.com; f. 1998; following merger of Unión y Desarrollo, SA and AIG; Pres. FRANCISCO R. DE SOLA.

Aseguradora Agrícola Comercial, SA: Alameda Roosevelt 3104, Apdo 1855, San Salvador; tel. 260-3344; fax 260-5592; e-mail informacion@acasal.com.sv; internet www.acasal.com.sv; f. 1973; Pres. LUIS ALFREDO ESCALANTE SOL; Gen. Man. LUIS ALFONSO FIGUEROA.

Aseguradora Popular, SA: Paseo Gen. Escalón 5338, Col. Escalón, San Salvador; tel. 263-0700; fax 263-1246; e-mail aseposapresi@ telesal.net; f. 1975; Pres. Dr CARLOS ARMANDO LAHÚD; Gen. Man. HERIBERTO PÉREZ AGUIRRE.

Aseguradora Suiza Salvadoreña, SA (ASESUISA): Alameda Dr M. E. Araujo, Plaza Suiza, Apdo 1490, San Salvador; tel. 209-5000; fax 209-5001; e-mail info@asesuisa.com; internet www.asesuisa .com; f. 1969; Pres. MAURICIO MEYER COHEN; Gen. Man. RICARDO COHEN.

La Central de Seguros y Fianzas, SA: Avda Olímpica 3333, Apdo 01-255, San Salvador; tel. 279-3544; fax 223-7647; e-mail hroque@ lacentral.com.sv; internet www.lacentral.com.sv; f. 1983; Pres. EDUARDO ENRIQUE CHACÓN BORJA; Man. HECTOR ROQUE RUBALLO.

La Centro Americana, SA: Alameda Roosevelt 3107, Apdo 527, San Salvador; tel. 223-6666; fax 223-7203; internet www.lacentro .com; f. 1915; Pres. RUFINO GARAY AYALA; Gen. Man. ANTONIO PENEDO.

Compañía Anglo Salvadoreña de Seguros, SA: Paseo Gen. Escalón 3848, San Salvador; tel. 263-0009; fax 263-0106; f. 1976; Pres. JOSÉ ARTURO GÓMEZ; Vice-Pres. LETICIA FARFÁN DE GÓMEZ.

Compañía General de Seguros, SA: Calle Loma Linda 223, Col. San Benito, Apdo 1004, San Salvador; tel. 279-3777; fax 223-0719; f. 1955; Pres. JOSÉ GUSTAVO BELISMELIS VIDES; Gen. Man. ERIC PRADO.

Internacional de Seguros, SA (Interseguros): Centro Financiero Banco Salvadoreño, 5°, Avda Olímpica 3550, Col. Escalón, San Salvador; tel. 238-0202; fax 238-5727; e-mail interseguros@ interseguros.com.sv; internet www.interseguros.com.sv; f. 1958; Merged with Seguros Universales in 2004; Pres. Dr ENRIQUE GARCÍA PRIETO; Gen. Man. ALEJANDRO CABRERA RIVAS.

Seguros e Inversiones, SA (SISA): 10.5 km Carretera Panamericana, Santa Tecla; tel. 229-8888; fax 229-8187; f. 1962; Pres. ALFREDO FÉLIX CRISTIANI BURKARD; Pres. EDUARDO MONTENEGRO.

Trade and Industry

GOVERNMENT AGENCIES AND DEVELOPMENT ORGANIZATIONS

Consejo Nacional de Ciencia y Tecnología (CONACYT): Col. Médica, Avda Dr Emilio Alvarez, Pasaje Dr Guillermo Rodríguez Pacas 51, San Salvador; tel. 226-2800; fax 225-6255; internet www .conacyt.gob.sv; f. 1992; formulation and guidance of national policy on science and technology; Exec. Dir CARLOS ROBERTO OCHOA CORDOBA.

Corporación de Exportadores de El Salvador (COEXPORT): Condomínios del Mediterráneo, Edif. 'A', No 23, Col. Jardines de Guadalupe, San Salvador; tel. 243-1328; fax 243-3159; e-mail info@ coexport.com; internet www.coexport.com; f. 1973 to promote Salvadorean exports; Exec. Dir Lic. SILVIA M. CUÉLLAR.

Corporación Salvadoreña de Inversiones (CORSAIN): 1a Calle Poniente, entre 43 y 45 Avda Norte, San Salvador; tel. 224-4242; fax 224-6877; e-mail audisjus@cortedecuentas.gob.sv; Pres. ERNESTO HAREM.

Fondo de Financiamiento y Garantía para la Pequeña Empresa (FIGAPE): 9a Avda Norte 225, Apdo 1990, San Salvador; tel. 771-1994; f. 1994; government body to assist small-sized industries; Pres. Lic. MARCO TULIO GUARDADO.

Fondo Social para la Vivienda (FSV): Calle Rubén Darío y 17 Avda Sur 455, San Salvador; tel. 271-1662; fax 271-2910; internet www.fsv.gob.sv; f. 1973; Pres. EDGAR RAMIRO MENDOZA JEREZ; Gen. Man. FRANCISCO ANTONIO GUEVARA.

Instituto Salvadoreño de Transformación Agraria (ISTA): Km 5½, Carretera a Santa Tecla, San Salvador; tel. 224-6000; fax

224-0259; f. 1976 to promote rural development; empowered to buy inefficiently cultivated land; Pres. José Roberto Molina Morales.

CHAMBER OF COMMERCE

Cámara de Comercio e Industria de El Salvador: 9a Avda Norte y 5a Calle Poniente, Apdo 1640, San Salvador; tel. 244-2000; fax 271-4461; e-mail camara@camarasal.com; internet www .camarasal.com; f. 1915; 2,000 mems; Pres. Eduardo Oñate Muyshondt; Exec. Dir Alberto Padilla Aquino; brs in San Miguel, Santa Ana and Sonsonate.

INDUSTRIAL AND TRADE ASSOCIATIONS

Asociación Azúcarera de El Salvador: 103 Avda Norte y Calle Arturo Ambrogi 145, Col. Escalón, San Salvador; tel. 263-0378; fax 263-0361; e-mail asosugar@sal.gbm.net; internet www .asociacionazucarera.com; national sugar association, fmrly Instituto Nacional del Azúcar; Pres. Mario Salaverria; Exec. Dir Dr Francisco Armando.

Asociación Cafetalera de El Salvador (ACES): 67 Avda Norte 116, Col. Escalón, San Salvador; tel. 223-3024; fax 223-7471; e-mail acafesal@sal.gbm.net; f. 1930; coffee growers' asscn; Pres. Ing. Eduardo E. Barrientos.

Asociación de Ganaderos de El Salvador: 1a Avda Norte 1332, San Salvador; tel. 225-7208; f. 1932; livestock breeders' asscn; Pres. Lic. Carlos Arturo Muyshondt.

Asociación Salvadoreña de Beneficiadores y Exportadores de Café (ABECAFE): 87a Avda Norte 720, Col. Escalón, San Salvador; tel. 263-2834; fax 263-2833; e-mail abecafe@intersal.com; coffee producers' and exporters' asscn; Pres. Carlos Borgonovo.

Asociación Salvadoreña de Industriales: Calles Roma y Liverpool, Col. Roma, Apdo 48, San Salvador; tel. 279-2488; fax 279-1880; e-mail asi@asi.com.sv; internet www.asi.com.sv; f. 1958; 400 mems; manufacturers' asscn; Pres. Napoleón Guerrero Berrios; Exec. Dir Lic. Jorge Arriaza.

Consejo Salvadoreño del Café (CSC): 75 Avda Norte y 7a Calle Poniente 3876, Col. Escalón, San Salvador; tel. 263-3787; fax 263-3833; e-mail csc@consejocafe.org.sv; internet www.consejocafe.org .sv; f. 1989 as successor to the Instituto Nacional del Café; formulates policy and oversees the coffee industry; Exec. Dir Ricardo Espitia.

Cooperativa Algodonera Salvadoreña, Ltda (COPAL): 6a y 10a Calle Poniente y 43 Avda Sur 2305, Col. Flor Blanca, San Salvador; tel. 298-9330; fax 298-9331; f. 1940; 185 mems; cotton growers' asscn; Pres. Luiz Méndez Novoa; Vice-Pres. Lic. José Ramiro Parada Díaz.

UCAFES: Avda Río Lempa, Calle Adriático 44, Jardines de Guadalupe, San Salvador; tel. 243-2238; fax 298-1504; union of coffee-growing co-operatives; Pres. Joaquín Salaverría.

EMPLOYERS' ORGANIZATION

There are several business associations, the most important of which is the Asociación Nacional de Empresa Privada.

Asociación Nacional de Empresa Privada (ANEP) (National Private Enterprise Association): 1a Calle Pte y 71a Avda Norte 204, Col. Escalón, Apdo 1204, San Salvador; tel. 224-1236; fax 223-8932; e-mail communicaciones.anep@telesal.net; internet www.anep.org .sv; national private enterprise association; Pres. Federico Colorado; Exec. Dir Lic. Luis Mario Rodríguez.

UTILITIES

Electricity

Comisión Ejecutiva Hidroeléctrica del Río Lempa (CEL): 9a Calle Poniente 950, San Salvador; tel. 211-6000; fax 222-9359; e-mail naguilar@cel.gob.sv; internet www.cel.gob.sv; f. 1948; state energy agency dealing with electricity generation and transmission, and non-conventional energy sources; scheduled for privatization; Pres. Guillermo A. Sol Bang.

Superintendencia General de Electricidad y Telecomunicaciones (SIGET): Col. Flor Blanca, Sexta Décima Calle Poniente 2001, San Salvador; tel. 257-4438; e-mail jtrigueros@siget.gob.sv; internet www.siget.gob.sv; f. 1996; Supt Lic. José Luis Trigueros.

Electricity Companies

In order to increase competition, the electricity-trading market was opened up in October 2000. Four companies (two domestic and two foreign) subsequently applied for licences to trade electricity in the wholesale market, from SIGET.

AES Aurora: Operates three distribution companies in El Salvador:

CLESA: 23 Avda Sur y 5a Calle Oriente, Barrio San Rafael, Santa Ana; tel. 447-6000; fax 447-6155.

Compañía de Alumbrado Electric (CAESS): Calle El Bambú, Col. San Antonio, Ayutuxtepeque, San Salvador; tel. 207-2011; fax 232-5012.

EEO: Final 8a, Calle Poniente, Calle a Ciudad Pacífico, Plantel Jalacatal, San Miguel.

CONEC-ES, SA de CV: Edif. Gran Plaza 204, Blvd del Hipódromo, San Benito, San Salvador; subsidiary of Energia Global (USA); provides electricity from sustainable sources, imported from Costa Rica; Gen. Man. Vicente Machado.

Geotérmica Salvadoreña, SA (GESAL): Col. Utila Santa Tecla, San Salvador; tel. 275-9385; fax 263-9505; e-mail info@gesal.com; internet www.gesal.com.sv; electricity generation; two geothermic stations; joint US-Chilean owned; Gen. Man. José Antonio Rodríguez.

Water

Administración Nacional de Acueductos y Alcantarillados (ANDA): Edif. ANDA, Final Avda Don Bosco, Col. Libertad, San Salvador; tel. 225-3534; fax 225-3152; internet www.anda.gob.sv; f. 1961; maintenance of water supply and sewerage systems; Pres. Manuel Enrique Arrieta.

TRADE UNIONS

Asociación de Sindicatos Independientes (ASIES) (Association of Independent Trade Unions): San Salvador.

Central de Trabajadores Democráticos (CTD) (Democratic Workers' Confederation): 1a Avda Norte y 19 Calle Poniente 12, San Salvador; tel. and fax 235-8043; e-mail comuctd@netcomsa.com; Sec.-Gen. Amadeo García Espinoza.

Central de Trabajadores Salvadoreños (CTS) (Salvadorean Workers' Confederation): 224A Pasaje Espínola, Col. Manzano, San Jacinto, San Salvador; tel. 270-5246; fax 270-1703; f. 1966; Christian Democratic; 35,000 mems.

Confederación General de Sindicatos (CGS) (General Confederation of Unions): 3a Calle Oriente 226, San Salvador; tel. and fax 222-3527; f. 1958; admitted to ICFTU/ORIT; Sec.-Gen. José Israel Huiza Cisneros; 27,000 mems.

Confederación General del Trabajo (CGT) (General Confederation of Workers): 4a Avda Sur y 8a Calle Oriente 240, San Salvador; tel. and fax 222-6182; f. 1983; 20 affiliated unions; Sec.-Gen. José René Pérez; 85,000 mems.

Confederación Unitaria de Trabajadores Salvadoreños (CUTS) (United Salvadorean Workers' Federation): 141 Avda A, Col. San José, San Salvador; tel. and fax 225-3756; e-mail proyectocuts@salnet.net; left-wing; Sec.-Gen. Noé Nerio.

Coordinadora Sindical de los Trabajadores Salvadoreños (CSTS) (Salvadorean Workers' Union): Col. San José, Blvd Universitario 2226, San Salvador; conglomerate of independent left-wing trade unions; Co-ordinator Victor Aguilar.

Federación Campesina Cristiana de El Salvador-Unión de Trabajadores del Campo (FECCAS-UTC) (Christian Peasant Federation of El Salvador—Union of Countryside Workers): Universidad Nacional, Apdo 4000, San Salvador; allied illegal Christian peasants' organizations.

Federación Nacional Sindical de Trabajadores Salvadoreños (FENASTRAS) (Salvadorean Workers' National Union Federation): 10a Avda Norte 120, San Salvador; f. 1975; left-wing; 35,000 mems in 16 affiliates.

Unión Comunal Salvadoreña (UCS) (Salvadorean Communal Union): 2a Calle Oriente y Avda Melvyn Jones, Santa Tecla, San Salvador; tel. 228-2023; fax 229-1111; peasants' association; 100,000 mems; Gen. Sec. Guillermo Blanco.

Unidad Nacional de Trabajadores Salvadoreños (UNTS) (National Unity of Salvadorean Workers): Calle 27 Poniente 432, Col. Layco, Apdo 2479, Centro de Gobierno El Salvador, San Salvador; tel. 225-7811; fax 225-0558; f. 1986; largest trade union conglomerate; Leader Marco Tulio Lima; affiliated unions include.

Unidad Popular Democrática (UPD) (Popular Democratic Unity): San Salvador; f. 1980; led by a committee of 10; 500,000 mems.

Unión Nacional Obrera-Campesina (UNOC) (Worker-Peasant National Union): Blvd María Cristina 165, San Salvador; tel. 225-6981; fax 228-1434; f. 1986; centre-left labour organization; 500,000 mems.

Some unions, such as those of the taxi drivers and bus owners, are affiliated to the Federación Nacional de Empresas Pequeñas Salvadoreñas—Fenapes, the association of small businesses.

Transport

Comisión Ejecutiva Portuaria Autónoma (CEPA): Edif. Torre Roble, Blvd de Los Héroes, Apdo 2667, San Salvador; tel. 224-1133; fax 224-0907; internet www.cepa.gob.sv; f. 1952; operates and administers the ports of Acajutla (on Pacific coast) and Cutuco (on Gulf of Fonseca) and the El Salvador International Airport, as well as Ferrocarriles Nacionales de El Salvador; Pres. Ruy César Miranda; Gen. Man. Lic. Arturo Germán Martínez.

RAILWAYS

In 1998 there were 547 km of railway track in the country. The main track links San Salvador with the ports of Acajutla and Cutuco and with San Jerónimo on the border with Guatemala. The 429 km Salvadorean section of the International Railways of Central America runs from Anguiatú on the El Salvador–Guatemala border to the Pacific ports of Acajutla and Cutuco and connects San Salvador with Guatemala City and the Guatemalan Atlantic ports of Puerto Barrios and Santo Tomás de Castilla. A project to connect the Salvadorean and Guatemalan railway systems between Santa Ana and Santa Lucía (in Guatemala) is under consideration.

Ferrocarriles Nacionales de El Salvador (FENADESAL): Avda Peralta 903, Apdo 2292, San Salvador; tel. 271-5632; fax 271-5650; 562 km open; in 1975 Ferrocarril de El Salvador and the Salvadorean section of International Railways of Central America (429 km open) were merged and are administered by the Railroad Division of CEPA (q.v.); Gen. Man. Tulio O. Vergara.

ROADS

The country's highway system is well integrated with its railway services. There were some 10,029 km of roads in 1999, including: the Pan-American Highway (306 km). Following the earthquakes of early 2001, the Inter-American Development Bank (IDB) pledged some US $106.0m. to the transport sector for the restoration and reconstruction of roads and bridges.

SHIPPING

The port of Acajutla is administered by CEPA (see above). Services are also provided by foreign lines. The port of Cutuco has been inactive since 1996; however, it was being considered for privatization.

CIVIL AVIATION

The El Salvador International Airport is located 40 km (25 miles) from San Salvador in Comalapa. An expansion of the airport was completed in 1998, with a second expansion phase of hotel and commercial space to be completed early in the 21st century. The former international airport at Ilopango is used for military and private civilian aircraft; there are an additional 88 private airports, four with permanent-surface runways.

TACA International Airlines: Edif. Caribe, 2°, Col. Escalón, San Salvador; tel. 339-9155; fax 223-3757; internet www.taca.com; f. 1939; passenger and cargo services to Central America and the USA; Pres. Federico Bloch; Gen. Man. Ben Baldanza.

United Airlines: Centro Comercial, Galerías, Paseo Escalón, San Salvador; tel. 279-3900; fax 298-5539; e-mail patricia.mejia@ual .com; internet www.unitedelsalvador.com; f. 1910.

Tourism

El Salvador was one of the centres of the ancient Mayan civilization, and the ruined temples and cities are of great interest. The volcanoes and lakes of the uplands provide magnificent scenery, while there are fine beaches along the Pacific coast. The civil war, from 1979 to 1992, severely affected the tourism industry. However, the number of tourist arrivals increased from 282,835 in 1996 to 795,000 in 2000. Tourism receipts in 2000 were US $254m. Following the earthquakes of early 2001, the IDB pledged some $3.6m. to the tourism and historical and cultural heritage sectors, for the reconstruction and renovation of recreational centres, the promotion of tourism, and the development of culture and heritage. In 2001 tourist arrivals decreased to 734,627 and tourism receipts fell to $235m. Receipts increased in 2002 to $342m.

Asociación Salvadoreña de Hoteles: San Salvador; tel. 298-3629; fax 298-3628; e-mail asocdehoteles@telesal.net; internet www .elsalhoteles.com; f. 1996; Pres. Carlos Alberto Delgado Z.; Sec. Bellyni Siguenza.

Buró de Convenciones de El Salvador: Edif. Olimpic Plaza, 73 Avda Sur 28, 2°, San Salvador; tel. 224-0819; fax 223-4912; internet www.convencioneselsalvador.com.sv; f. 1973; assists in organization of national and international events; Pres. Alfredo Morales; Exec. Dir Adriana de Gale.

Cámara Salvadoreña de Turismo (CASATUR): Alameda Manuel Enrique Araujo y Pasaje Carbonel 2A, San Salvador; tel. 279-2156; fax 223-9775; e-mail casatur@telesal.net; internet www .casatur.com; f. 1978; non-profit org. concerned with promotion of tourism in El Salvador; Pres. Carlos Alberto Delgado; Exec. Dir Ena López Portillo.

Corporación Salvadoreña de Turismo (CORSATUR): Avda El Espino 68, Urb. Madre Selva, Santa Elena, Antigua Cuscatlán, La Libertad, San Salvador; tel. 243-7835; fax 243-7844; e-mail corsatur@salnet.net; internet www.elsalvadorturismo.gob.sv; f. 1997; Pres. Manuel Avilés; Tourism Man. Ana N. Ochoa.

Feria Internacional de El Salvador (FIES): Avda La Revolución 222, Col. San Benito, Apdo 493, San Salvador; tel. 243-0244; fax 243-3161; e-mail feria@fies.gob.sv; internet www.fies.gob.sv; f. 1965; Pres. Manuel Arrieta.

Instituto Salvadoreño de Turismo (ISTU) (National Tourism Institute): Calle Rubén Darío 619, San Salvador; tel. 222-5727; fax 222-1208; e-mail informacion@istu.gob.sv; internet www.istu.gob .sv; f. 1950; Pres. Manuel Avilés; Man. Dir Rolando Gutiérrez Oriani.

EQUATORIAL GUINEA

Introductory Survey

Location, Climate, Language, Religion, Flag, Capital

The Republic of Equatorial Guinea consists of the islands of Bioko (formerly Fernando Póo and subsequently renamed Macías Nguema Biyogo under the regime of President Macías), Corisco, Great Elobey, Little Elobey and Annobón (previously known also as Pagalu), and the mainland region of Río Muni (previously known also as Mbini) on the west coast of Africa. Cameroon lies to the north and Gabon to the east and south of Río Muni, while Bioko lies off shore from Cameroon and Nigeria. The small island of Annobón lies far to the south, beyond the islands of São Tomé and Príncipe. The climate is hot and humid, with average temperatures higher than 26°C (80°F). The official languages are Spanish and French. In Río Muni the Fang language is spoken, as well as those of coastal tribes such as the Combe, Balemke and Bujeba. Bubi is the indigenous language on Bioko, although Fang is also widely used, and Ibo is spoken by the resident Nigerian population. An estimated 90% of the population are adherents of the Roman Catholic Church, although traditional forms of worship are also followed. The national flag (proportions 2 by 3) has three equal horizontal stripes, of green, white and red, with a blue triangle at the hoist and the national coat of arms (a silver shield, containing a tree, with six yellow stars above and a scroll beneath) in the centre of the white stripe. The capital is Malabo (formerly Santa Isabel).

Recent History

Portugal ceded the territory to Spain in 1778. The mainland region and the islands were periodically united for administrative purposes. In July 1959 Spanish Guinea, as the combined territory was known, was divided into two provinces: Río Muni, on the African mainland, and Fernando Póo (now Bioko), with other nearby islands. From 1960 the two provinces were represented in the Spanish legislature. In December 1963 they were merged again, to form Equatorial Guinea, with a limited measure of self-government.

After 190 years of Spanish rule, independence was declared on 12 October 1968. Francisco Macías Nguema, Equatorial Guinea's first President, formed a coalition Government from all the parties represented in the new National Assembly.

In February 1970 the President outlawed all existing political parties and formed the Partido Unico Nacional (PUN), which later became the Partido Unico Nacional de los Trabajadores (PUNT). Macías appointed himself Life President in July 1972. A new Constitution, giving absolute powers to the President was adopted in July 1973. Macías controlled both radio and press and all citizens were forbidden to leave the country, although many fled during his rule. During 1975–77 there were many arrests and executions. The Macías regime maintained close relations with the Soviet bloc.

In August 1979 President Macías was overthrown in a coup led by his nephew, Lt-Col (later Gen.) Teodoro Obiang Nguema Mbasogo, hitherto the Deputy Minister of Defence. (Obiang Nguema subsequently ceased to use his forename.) Macías was found guilty of treason, genocide, embezzlement and violation of human rights, and was executed in September. The Spanish Government, which admitted prior knowledge of the coup, was the first to recognize the new regime, and remained a major supplier of financial and technical aid. Obiang Nguema appointed civilians to the Government for the first time in December 1981. In August 1982 he was reappointed President for a further seven years, and later that month a new Constitution, which provided for an eventual return to civilian government, was approved by 95% of voters in a referendum. At legislative elections held in August 1983 some 41 candidates, who had been nominated by the President, were elected (unopposed) to a new House of Representatives.

The imposition, from 1979 to 1991, of a ban on organized political activity within Equatorial Guinea, and persistent allegations against the Obiang Nguema regime of human rights abuses and corruption, resulted in the development of a substantial opposition-in-exile.

During the 1980s Obiang Nguema's rule was threatened on a number of occasions. A series of attempted coups were reported and in January 1986 the President reinforced his control by assuming the post of Minister of Defence. An attempt in July by senior civilian and military officials to occupy the presidential palace in Malabo was quelled by loyalist forces. In the following month the alleged leader of the coup attempt, Eugenio Abeso Mondu (a former diplomat and a member of the House of Representatives), was sentenced to death and executed, while prison sentences were imposed on 12 others who had been convicted of complicity in the plot. In August 1987 Obiang Nguema announced the establishment of a 'governmental party', the Partido Democrático de Guinea Ecuatorial (PDGE), while continuing to reject demands for the legalization of opposition parties. At legislative elections held in July 1988, 99.2% of voters endorsed a single list of candidates who had been nominated by the President.

In June 1989, at the first presidential election to be held since independence, Obiang Nguema, the sole candidate, reportedly received the support of more than 99% of the electorate. Opposition groupings criticized the conduct of the election and declared the result invalid. Following his success, the President appealed to dissidents to return to Equatorial Guinea and declared an amnesty for political prisoners. However, Obiang Nguema reiterated his opposition to the establishment of a multi-party system, and in December 1990 it was reported that about 30 advocates of the introduction of a plural political system had been imprisoned. The human rights organization Amnesty International has frequently reiterated accusations against the Equato-Guinean authorities of detaining and torturing political opponents.

A new Constitution, containing provisions for a multi-party political system, was approved by an overwhelming majority of voters at a national referendum in November 1991. However, opposition movements rejected the Constitution, owing to the inclusion of clauses exempting the President from any judicial procedures arising from his tenure of office and prohibiting citizens who had not been continuously resident in Equatorial Guinea for 10 years from standing as election candidates, while requiring all political parties to submit a large deposit (which could not be provided by funds from abroad) as a condition of registration. In January 1992 a transitional Government (comprising only members of the PDGE) was formed, and a general amnesty was extended to all political exiles. The UN published a report in January that criticized the human rights record of the Equato-Guinean authorities and some of the provisions incorporated in the new Constitution. Throughout 1992 the security forces continued to arrest members of opposition parties. In November a new alliance of opposition organizations, the Plataforma de la Oposición Conjunta (POC), was created.

In January 1993 an electoral law was promulgated. In February the UN released another report in which it alleged a serious disregard for human rights by the Obiang Nguema regime. During February and March the Government and several opposition organizations negotiated a national pact that established conditions for the conduct of legislative elections due to take place in 1993. However, the Government was accused of violating the pact, and further arrests and mistreatment of its political opponents were reported. During August violent clashes occurred on the island of Annobón between anti-Government demonstrators and the security forces. Accusations by the Equato-Guinean authorities that Spain had incited the unrest were strongly denied by the Spanish Government.

Multi-party legislative elections took place in November 1993. The elections were, however, boycotted by most of the parties in the POC, in protest at Obiang Nguema's refusal to review contentious clauses of the electoral law or to permit impartial international observers to inspect the electoral register. The UN declined a request by the Equato-Guinean authorities to monitor the elections, contending that correct electoral procedures were evidently being infringed. Representatives of the OAU were present and estimated that 50% of the electorate participated. The PDGE won 68 of the 80 seats in the House of Representatives, while, of the six opposition parties that presented candidates, the Convención Socialdemócrata Popular obtained six seats, the Unión Democrática y Social de Guinea Ecuatorial (UDS) won five seats and the Convención Liberal Democrática (CLD) secured one. Widespread electoral irregularities were alleged to have occurred and, prior to the elections, opposition politicians were reportedly subjected to intimidation by the security forces. In early December the Government announced that all party political gatherings would henceforth be subject to prior official authorization. In December Silvestre Siale Bileka, hitherto Prime Minister of the interim Government, was appointed Prime Minister of the new administration, which included no opposition representatives.

In April 1994 Severo Moto Nsa, the founding leader of one of the most influential exiled opposition parties, the Partido del Progreso de Guinea Equatorial (PPGE), based in Spain, returned to Equatorial Guinea. In June, in response to pressure from international aid donors, the Government agreed to amend the controversial electoral law and to conduct a preliminary electoral census prior to local elections. In September, however, the authorities began to compile a full population census, instead of preparing for the local elections, which had been scheduled for November. The census was boycotted by opposition parties, and many people were arrested in ensuing clashes with the security forces. The local elections were postponed.

In early 1995 the Constitution and electoral law were amended to reduce from 10 to five the minimum number of years required for candidates to have been resident in Equatorial Guinea. In February several leading members of the PPGE, including Moto Nsa, were arrested for allegedly plotting to overthrow Obiang Nguema; in April they were found guilty by a military court and sentenced to terms of imprisonment. (Moto Nsa received a sentence of 28 years.) The convictions and sentences were widely condemned by foreign Governments and in August, following representations by President Jacques Chirac of France, Obiang Nguema unexpectedly pardoned all the convicted PPGE members.

Local elections were staged, on a multi-party basis, in September 1995. According to the official results, the ruling PDGE won an overall victory, securing a majority of the votes cast in two-thirds of local administrations. Allegations by the opposition (which claimed to have obtained 62% of the votes) that serious electoral malpractice had occurred were supported by the Spanish ambassador to Equatorial Guinea. A monitoring team of international observers agreed that some electoral irregularities had taken place.

At a presidential election held in February 1996 Obiang Nguema was returned to office, reportedly securing more than 90% of the votes cast. However, influential opposition leaders boycotted the contest, in protest at alleged electoral irregularities and official intimidation. In March Obiang Nguema appointed a new Prime Minister, Angel Serafin Seriche Dougan (hitherto a Deputy Minister); an enlarged Council of Ministers was announced in April. Representatives of opposition parties had declined a presidential invitation to participate in the new administration. During March the POC was dissolved.

In April 1997 representatives of the Government and of 13 opposition parties concluded a new national pact. During the following month Moto Nsa was arrested by the Angolan authorities with a consignment of arms, which were reportedly intended for use in a planned coup in Equatorial Guinea. Following his release in June, Moto Nsa was granted refuge in Spain. Meanwhile, the PPGE was banned; the party subsequently divided into two factions, one of which was led by Moto Nsa. In August Moto Nsa and 11 others were convicted *in absentia* of treason; Moto Nsa was sentenced to 101 years' imprisonment. In September the Government protested strongly to Spain for granting political asylum to Moto Nsa. Shortly afterwards French was declared the second official national language. In January 1998 the Government resigned. Seriche Dougan was reappointed as Prime Minister, and a new, enlarged Council of Ministers was formed. In the following month the House of Representatives approved a new electoral law, which banned political coalitions.

In January 1998 armed protesters launched three successive attacks against military targets on Bioko, killing four soldiers and three civilians. The terrorist action was alleged to have been perpetrated by members of the secessionist Movimiento para la Autodeterminación de la Isla de Bioko (MAIB), which was founded in 1993 by ethnic Bubis (the original inhabitants of the island, who, following independence, had become outnumbered by the mainland Fang). Subsequently hundreds of Bubis and resident Nigerians were arrested; many were reportedly also

severely tortured. In May 1998 some 116 detainees were tried by a military court in connection with the January attacks, on charges including terrorism and treason. Fifteen of the defendants were found guilty of the most serious charges and sentenced to death; in response to international pressure, however, the death sentences were commuted to sentences of life imprisonment in September.

During early 1999 six unregistered opposition parties exiled in Spain, including the MAIB and Moto Nsa's faction of the PPGE, formed a new alliance, the Coordinadora de la Oposición Conjunta. Equatorial Guinea's second multi-party legislative elections took place in early March, amid allegations of electoral malpractice and of the systematic intimidation of opposition candidates by the security forces. The elections were contested by 13 parties (excluding the divided PPGE, which had been banned in 1997—see above), and some 99% of the electorate was estimated to have voted. According to the official results, the ruling PDGE obtained more than 90% of the votes, increasing its representation from 68 to 75 of the 80 seats in the House of Representatives. Two opposition parties, the Unión Popular (UP) and the Convergencia para la Democracia Social (CPDS), secured four seats and one seat, respectively. Both parties, however, refused to participate in the new administration, in protest at alleged violations of the electoral law. (This policy subsequently led to an internal crisis within the UP and a change of leadership was instigated in August 2000.) The UP, the CPDS and five other opposition organizations campaigned, without success, to have the election results annulled. Following the election, Seriche Dougan was reappointed to the premiership, and in late July a new Council of Ministers was announced.

The new administration dismissed hundreds of civil servants, including a number of high-ranking officials, during its first three months in office, as part of efforts to eradicate corruption. Furthermore, in January 2000 a number of judicial officials, including the President of the Supreme Tribunal and the President of the Constitutional Court, were dismissed. Former Prime Minister Silvestre Siale Bileka was appointed to the presidency of the Supreme Tribunal. Nevertheless, in March 2000 the new Special Representative for Equatorial Guinea at the UN Human Rights Commission condemned the Equato-Guinean authorities for systematic and serious human rights violations. The Special Representative further stated that, despite some minor advances, real democracy did not exist in the country and accused the Government of refusing to authorize the formation of human rights non-governmental organizations. Following intense lobbying by several African countries, the mandate of the Special Representative was terminated in April 2002. However in December a new UN Human Rights Rapporteur arrived in Equatorial Guinea, with a mandate to investigate claims of human rights violations.

In October 2000 Obiang Nguema reportedly urged Seriche Dougan to resign after the House of Representatives severely criticized the Prime Minister for failing to address adequately the problem of corruption in government. In November six opposition parties, including the CPDS, the UP and the ADP, formed the Frente de la Oposición Democrática in order to create a common front to promote democracy. Another coalition was created in March 2001 by eight opposition parties in exile in Spain (including the PPGE and the MAIB) and the CPDS and the UP in Equatorial Guinea.

In late February 2001 Seriche Dougan announced the resignation of his Government, in response to further pressure from the President and the legislature. Cándido Muatetema Rivas, formerly Deputy Secretary-General of the PDGE, was subsequently appointed as Prime Minister and formed a new Council of Ministers. Five members of the opposition were appointed to the new Government, including Jeremías Ondo Ngomo, the President of the UP, as Minister-delegate for Communications and Transport. In July Obiang Nguema was nominated as the PDGE candidate for the 2003 presidential election. In the same month the President made overtures to exiled political groups, urging them to legalize their political movements in Equatorial Guinea. In late July 2001 Florentino Ecomo Nsogo, the President of the Partido de Reconstrucción y Bienestar Social, became the first opposition leader to return from Spain in response to Obiang Nguema's request. In August the Government announced a programme of modernization for the army, to be financed by increased petroleum revenues.

In May and June 2002 some 144 members of opposition parties were tried on charges relating to an alleged plot to oust Obiang Nguema, following their arrest in March. In June 68 of the defendants received sentences of up to 20 years' imprisonment; those convicted included the Secretary-General of the CPDS, Plácido Micó Abogo, and Felipe Ondo Obiang, the Chairman of the Fuerza Demócrata Republicana (FDR). International concern regarding Equatorial Guinea's treatment of opposition groups increased further in July, following the death of Juan Ondo Nguema, a police-officer who had been convicted in June; opposition parties alleged that Ondo Nguema's death had resulted from injuries sustained during torture while in custody. None the less, also in July, the Secretary-General of the UP, Fabián Nsué Nguema, was imprisoned on charges of insulting the Head of State. In October, however, Nsué Nguema was released, along with some 120 others; it was reported 30 of those convicted in June were included in the presidential pardon.

In early November 2002 President Obiang Nguema announced that the presidential election would be brought forward to 15 December (from February 2003). A National Electoral Council was created, although international bodies were unwilling to monitor voting in view of the apparent weakness of the country's electoral institutions. Nevertheless, several leading members of both the exiled and resident opposition— including Celestino Bonifacio Bacale of the CPDS and Tomás Mecheba Fernández of the Partido Socialista de Guinea Ecuatorial—declared their intention to contest the election, albeit without agreeing to sign a written guarantee of their candidacy. Alfonso Nsué Mokuy of the CLD also agreed to participate in the election, as did the Deputy Minister of Public Works, Housing and Urban Affairs, Carmelo Modú Acusé Bindang (the President of the UDS), and the Deputy Minister of Communications and Transport, Ondo Ngomo (of the UP).

On 15 December 2002, with voting already under way, Bacale and other opposition candidates announced their withdrawal from the election, alleging widespread irregularities in voting procedures. Their claims related to the apparent lack of secrecy in voting, the insufficient number of ballot papers for opposition candidates and voter intimidation. According to the official results, Obiang Nguema was re-elected to the presidency, with 97.1% of the votes cast. The conduct of the election was condemned by the European Union (EU), which urged the Government to grant an amnesty to opposition members. Despite the newly re-elected President's call for the opposition leaders to join the PDGE in a government of national unity, 'radical' opposition parties continued to refuse to participate in Obiang Nguema's administration. In February 2003 a new Government was formed, again headed by Prime Minister Cándido Muatetema Rivas. Meanwhile, the CPDS continued to demand the release of all the opposition members imprisoned in June 2002, including Micó Abogo. Micó Abogo was granted a conditional presidential pardon in August 2003, and was released along with some 17 other political opponents of the regime sentenced in the previous year. However, the Government denied claims that Ondo Obiang had died in custody, stating that he had been transferred to another prison on the mainland. Also in August, Moto Nsa and the leaders of two other Equato-Guinean opposition parties announced that they had formed a government-in-exile in Madrid, Spain.

Rumours of a possible coup plot in November 2003 prompted the arrest and eight-day detention of a journalist employed by the French news agency Agence France-Presse. The reports appeared to arise from speculation over Obiang Nguema's eventual successor, especially in view of the President's purported ill health, with several government ministers and military officers said to be concerned about the possibility of Obiang Nguema's son, Theodoro (Teodorín) Nguema Obiang Mangue, the Minister of State in charge of Infrastructure and Forests, succeeding his father to the presidency. A significant number of army personnel were arrested in December, although the Government denied that those detained had been involved in an alleged coup attempt, stating that the arrests were related to the misappropriation of military funds. In January 2004 the President of the Supreme Tribunal resigned, claiming that the implementation of judicial reform in Equatorial Guinea had not proceeded as envisaged. In February secret trials of those arrested in December were under way in Bata, according to reports citing opposition sources.

In mid-March 2004 the Government announced that a group of 15 suspected mercenaries had been arrested on suspicion of planning a *coup d'état*, which President Obiang Nguema subsequently claimed had been funded by multinational companies and organized by Moto Nsa with the collusion of the Spanish Government. Following the death in custody of one of the

accused, in November the remaining 14 defendants were found guilty of involvement in the coup attempt and received lengthy custodial sentences. Although Moto Nsa denied any involvement in the affair, he was sentenced *in absentia* by the court in Malabo to 63 years' imprisonment, while Nick du Toit, a former South African special forces officer who was alleged to have been the leader of the group in Equatorial Guinea, was sentenced to 34 years' imprisonment. Human rights groups condemned the trial for grave abuses of procedure. Meanwhile, in August 66 men, who had been detained by the Zimbabwean authorities at Harare airport in mid-March on suspicion of involvement in the coup attempt, were handed down gaol sentences ranging from 12 to 16 months for contravening immigration laws. They had been acquitted of any connection with those arrested in Equatorial Guinea in March for conspiring to overthrow the Equato-Guinean Government, owing to a lack of evidence. However, Simon Mann, a South African-based British security consultant and the alleged leader of the coup plot, was convicted in September of attempting illegally to procure weapons and was sentenced to seven years' imprisonment (subsequently reduced to four). Also in August Sir Mark Thatcher (a businessman and son of the former British Prime Minister Baroness Thatcher) was arrested in Cape Town, South Africa, on suspicion of having provided financial support for the alleged coup attempt. Thatcher initially denied any involvement in the affair, however, in January 2005 he admitted contravening South African anti-mercenary legislation by agreeing to finance the use of a helicopter and was fined R3m. (more than US $500,000) and given a four-year suspended sentence.

Legislative and municipal elections were held concurrently on 25 April 2004. The PDGE won 68 of the 100 seats in an expanded House of Representatives, while a coalition of eight parties allied to Obiang Nguema, styled the 'democratic opposition', secured a further 30 seats. International observers and the CPDS, which took the remaining two seats, denounced the results as fraudulent. The PDGE and its allies also won 237 of the 244 council seats in the country's 30 municipalities. The rate of participation by eligible voters was estimated at 97%. In mid-June Prime Minister Rivas announced the resignation of his Government and Obiang Nguema subsequently appointed a new PDGE-dominated Council of Ministers, headed by Miguel Abia Biteo Boricó, hitherto Minister of State for Parliamentary Relations and Judicial Affairs.

Meanwhile, in May 2004 the authorities claimed to have averted another attempt to overthrow the Government (this time originating in Gabon) and linked it to an opposition politician exiled in the USA since the 1970s. Five people were killed and five more captured by Equato-Guinean security forces following an attack on a military garrison on the island of Corisco. In response to this suspected coup attempt there followed several arrests in Bata and Libreville, Gabon, of persons linked to the PPGE.

Equatorial Guinea enjoyed exceptionally high revenues from petroleum exports from the late 1990s; allegations emerged, however, that members of the Obiang Nguema regime were accruing private profits from national petroleum exports. In May 2003 controversy arose when the US-based Riggs Bank acknowledged that some US $500m. had been paid into an account to which President Obiang Nguema was the sole signatory; international petroleum companies were alleged to be the source of the funds. In January 2005 Riggs Bank admitted criminal liability in assisting Obiang Nguema in improper financial transactions. Meanwhile, in February 2004 Obiang Nguema issued a decree providing for the creation of a National Commission for Personal Ethics, which would oblige all public employees to declare their assets. However, in July a US Senate report concluded that to secure contracts and co-operation petroleum companies made substantial payments to government officials, their families or entities owned by them. Also in late January 2005 the Equato-Guinean authorities announced the discovery of chronic and systematic fraud in several government ministries.

While Spain (the former colonial power) has traditionally been a major trading partner and aid donor, Equatorial Guinea's entry in 1983 into the Customs and Economic Union of Central Africa (replaced in 1999 by the Communauté économique et monétaire de l'Afrique centrale, see p. 267) represented a significant move towards a greater integration with neighbouring francophone countries. In 1985 Equatorial Guinea joined the Franc Zone (see p. 266), with financial assistance from France. Obiang Nguema has regularly attended Franco-African summit meetings. In 1989 the Spanish Government agreed to cancel one-third of Equatorial Guinea's public debt to Spain and in 1991 cancelled a further one-third of the bilateral debt. From mid-1993, however, Equato-Guinean-Spanish relations deteriorated, and in January 1994 the Spanish Government withdrew one-half of its aid to Equatorial Guinea in retaliation for the expulsion in December 1993 of a Spanish diplomat whom the Equato-Guinean authorities had accused of interfering in the country's internal affairs. In September 1997 the Obiang Nguema administration protested strongly to the Spanish Government over Spain's offer of political asylum to the opposition leader Severo Moto Nsa (see above). On several occasions in 1998 the Equato-Guinean Government accused Spain of attempting to destabilize Equatorial Guinea by providing funds to opposition organizations. However, in October 1999 the Spanish Government agreed to resume full assistance to its former colony, and during a visit to Madrid in March 2001 Obiang Nguema held talks with Spanish Prime Minister José María Aznar, who agreed to normalize relations with Equatorial Guinea in the economic field. Spain was willing to help strengthen the Equatorial Guinean institutions, in order to promote economic development, in exchange for the promotion and protection of human rights within Equatorial Guinea and legal guarantees for foreign investment. In 2003 relations improved further following Spain's support for Equatorial Guinea's territorial claims to the island of Mbagne (see below), and the Spanish Ministers of Health and Consumer Affairs and of Foreign Affairs visited Malabo in November. In February 2004 the two Governments signed a new two-year agreement on development co-operation, worth some €34m. In April the Spanish Government cancelled 50% of Equatorial Guinea's debt, estimated at some €70m. Relations were strained, however, following accusations made in September by Boricó that the previous Spanish administration of José María Aznar had actively colluded with the alleged coup attempt directed by Moto Nsa uncovered earlier in March (see above) and that the incumbent Spanish Government, led by Prime Minister José Luis Rodríguez Zapatero, had withheld information regarding this alleged collusion. The Zapatero administration denied the claims.

In late Febraury 2005 Obiang Nguema held talks in Bata with the Spanish Minister of Foreign Affairs and Co-operation, Miguel Ángel Moratinos Cuyaubé, during which both parties expressed their desire to maintain cordial relations and high levels of co-operation between the two countries. Although Moratinos reassured Obiang Nguema that the Spanish Government would act forcefully to prevent any preparations being made in Spanish territory to destabilize or overthrow the Obiang Nguema administration, he reiterated that the extradition of Moto Nsa was a judicial matter, in which the Spanish Government would not intervene.

In 1999 the medical aid agency Médecins sans frontières withdrew its mission from Equatorial Guinea in protest against the alleged manipulation of humanitarian aid by the Government. During the 1990s the EU withdrew financial aid to Equatorial Guinea, and the UN Development Programme suspended some projects.

Equatorial Guinea contributed 31 troops to CEMAC's peacekeeping mission in the Central African Republic in January 2003, but withdrew its contingent shortly after the coup that took place in that country in March.

In November 1999 Equatorial Guinea, Angola, Cameroon, the Republic of the Congo, Gabon, Nigeria and São Tomé and Príncipe established an international committee to demarcate maritime borders in the Gulf of Guinea. The development of petroleum reserves in the region during the 1990s had revived long-standing frontier disputes. In September 2000 Equatorial Guinea and Nigeria formally resolved their maritime border dispute, reaching an agreement (signed in December 2001) on the demarcation of the border, which was expected to encourage further petroleum exploration and development in that area.

In March 2003 relations between Equatorial Guinea and Gabon were strained following the occupation of the small island of Mbagne by a contingent of Gabonese troops. Both countries had long claimed ownership of Mbagne and two smaller islands, which lie in potentially oil-rich waters in Corisco Bay, north of the Gabonese capital, Libreville, and south-west of the Equato-Guinean mainland. In June Equatorial Guinea rejected a Gabonese proposal to share any petroleum revenues from the island, and discussions between the two sides ended without agreement in December. However, in January 2004 Equatorial Guinea and Gabon issued a joint communiqué, accepting the appointment of a UN mediator in the dispute. In July a provisional agreement was reached to explore jointly for petroleum in the disputed territories. At a meeting in Libreville in January 2005 the Presidents of both countries expressed optimism that an amicable agreement would soon be finalized.

Government

In November 1991 a new Constitution was approved in a referendum, providing for the introduction of multi-party democracy. Executive power is vested in the President, whose seven-year term of office is renewable indefinitely. The President is immune from prosecution for offences committed before, during or after his tenure of the post. Legislative power is held by a 100-member House of Representatives, which serves for a term of five years. Both the President and the House of Representatives are directly elected by universal adult suffrage. The President appoints a Council of Ministers, headed by a Prime Minister, from among the members of the House of Representatives.

Defence

In August 2004 there were 1,100 men in the army, 120 in the navy and 100 in the air force. There was also a paramilitary force, trained by French military personnel. Military service is voluntary. The estimated defence budget for 2004 was 3,600m. francs CFA. Spain has provided military advisers and training since 1979, and military aid has also been received from the USA.

Economic Affairs

In 2001, according to estimates by the World Bank, Equatorial Guinea's gross national income (GNI), measured at average 1999–2001 prices, was US $454m., equivalent to $930 per head. During 1990–2003, it was estimated, the population increased at an average annual rate of 2.6%, while gross domestic product (GDP) per head increased, in real terms, by an average of 17.7% per year. Overall GDP increased, in real terms, at an average annual rate of 20.7% in 1990–2003. Real GDP increased by 15.6% in 2003.

Agriculture (including hunting, forestry and fishing) contributed 6.8% of GDP in 2003 (compared with 51.6% of GDP in 1995). The sector employed an estimated 69.1% of the labour force in 2003. The principal cash crop is cocoa, which, according to the Banque de France, provided an estimated 0.2% of total export earnings in 2003. The Government is encouraging the production of bananas, spices (vanilla, black pepper and coriander) and medicinal plants for export. The main subsistence crops are cassava and sweet potatoes. Exploitation of the country's vast, but rapidly diminishing, forest resources (principally of okoumé and akoga timber) provided an estimated 1.8% (or 31,100m. francs CFA) of export revenue in 2003, according to the Banque de France. Almost all industrial fishing activity is practised by foreign fleets, notably by those of countries of the European Union. During 1990–2003, according to the World Bank, the real GDP of the agricultural sector increased at an average annual rate of 4.2%. Agricultural GDP increased by 4.9% in 2002 but declined by 11.7% in 2003.

Industry (including mining, manufacturing, construction and power) contributed 88.9% of GDP in 2003 (compared with 27.2% of GDP in 1995). During 1990–2003, according to the World Bank, industrial GDP increased at an average annual rate of 42.2%. Industrial GDP rose by 21.8% in 2003.

Extractive activities were minimal during the 1980s, and the mining sector employed less than 0.2% of the working population in 1983. However, the development of onshore and offshore reserves of petroleum and of offshore deposits of natural gas led to unprecedented economic growth during the 1990s. Exports of petroleum commenced in 1992 and provided an estimated 92.0% of total export earnings in 2003, according to the Banque de France. The petroleum sector contributed 87.2% of GDP in 2002 (compared with 18.2% of GDP in 1995). Petroleum production increased from 56,601 barrels per day (b/d) in 1997 to 237,500 b/d in 2003 (of which 206,000 b/d was crude oil), increasing further in the first half of 2004 to 350,000 b/d, according to the US Energy Information Administration. Proven reserves of petroleum were some 1,100m. barrels in 2004. Natural gas extraction also increased rapidly from the 1990s. Proven reserves at the country's largest gas field, Alba, were some 1,300,000m. cu ft in late 2004. The existence of deposits of gold, uranium, iron ore, titanium, tantalum and manganese has also been confirmed. During 1997–2002 the GDP of the petroleum sector increased at an average annual rate of 32.9%, according to the IMF; growth in 2002 was 21.4%.

The manufacturing sector contributed only 0.1% of GDP in 2002. Wood-processing constitutes the main commercial manufacturing activity. During 1997–2002 manufacturing GDP increased at an average annual rate of 7.4%, according to the IMF; growth in 2002 was 12.4%.

An estimated total of 23m. kWh of electric energy was generated in 2000. According to the US Energy Information Administration, in 2004 Equatorial Guinea had 15.4 MW of proven installed capacity and 5 MW–30 MW of estimated additional capacity. There was about 4 MW of oil-fired thermal capacity and 1 MW of hydroelectric capacity on the mainland. Bioko was supplied by one hydroelectric plant (on the Riaba river) with an estimated capacity of 3.6 MW and two thermal plants, including the 10.4-MW Punta Europa gas-fired plant located at the northern end of the island. Also in that year, there was a further 4 MW–6 MW of generation capacity at the AMPCO complex on Bioko. Imports of fuel products comprised 8.6% of the value of total imports in 2003.

The services sector contributed 4.3% of GDP in 2003. The dominant services are trade, restaurants and hotels, and government services. During 1990–2003, according to the World Bank, the GDP of the services sector increased at an average annual rate of 9.4%, It grew by 12.0% in 2002, however, in 2003 it declined by 4.0%.

In 2002 there was a visible trade surplus of 778,100m. francs CFA, while the deficit on the current account of the balance of payments was 127,400m. francs CFA. In 2002 the Federal Republic of Yugoslavia (now Serbia and Montenegro) was the principal source of imports (29.1%), while the USA was the principal destination of exports (28.3%). Other major trading partners were Spain, the People's Republic of China, the United Kingdom and France. In 2002 petroleum and timber constituted the principal sources of export revenue, while in 1990 the principal imports were ships and boats, petroleum and related products and food and live animals.

In 2003 the budget surplus was estimated at 213,100m. francs CFA (equivalent to 12.3% of GDP). Equatorial Guinea's external debt was US $260.4m. at the end of 2002, of which $209.1m. was long-term public debt. In that year, it was estimated, the cost of debt-servicing was equivalent to 0.5% of the value of exports of goods and services. The rate of inflation averaged 7.5% per year in 1990–98. Following the devaluation of the CFA franc in January 1994, consumer prices rose by an estimated 38.9% in that year. The annual average rate of inflation was 7.5% in 2002 and an estimated 7.3% in 2003.

Equatorial Guinea is a member of the Central African organs of the Franc Zone (see p. 267), including the Communauté économique et monétaire de l'Afrique centrale (CEMAC, see p. 267).

Equatorial Guinea suffered a severe economic decline under the Macías regime. The Obiang Nguema administration has achieved some success in rehabilitating and diversifying the primary sector, although the significance of the country's traditional industries has declined substantially since the commencement of petroleum exports in 1992. Petroleum production led to exceptional economic growth from the late 1990s. In 1996, however, the IMF suspended its activities in Equatorial Guinea, following the largely unsuccessful implementation of an economic development programme, and the Fund subsequently urged the Government to increase transparency in the management of petroleum contracts and revenue. Despite a largely favourable IMF assessment released in December 2003, con-

cerns remained that an inefficient taxation system and insufficient budgetary discipline were undermining revenue from the profitable petroleum and timber sectors. Equatorial Guinea is burdened by a large and growing external debt, although a protocol on debt conversion was signed with Spain, the country's largest creditor, in November 2003. Economic relations with the USA have also strengthened in recent years as a result of major investments in the development of Equato-Guinean oilfields by US energy companies. However, although construction and infrastructure projects proliferated from the 1990s, the levels of extreme poverty have not been addressed. The absence of any visible improvement in living standards among the general population since the early 1990s has been variously attributed to corruption, the disadvantageous terms of many contracts negotiated by the state petroleum company, Guinea Ecuatorial de Petróleo (GEPetrol), and reduced international aid. None the less, the minimum private-sector wage was increased by 20% in early 2003. In order to increase government non-petroleum receipts, a value-added tax, a reduction in the number of duty-exempt imports and a new tax-payer coding system were to be introduced in 2005–06. Equatorial Guinea's petroleum output increased to approximately 350,000 b/d in the first half of 2004, with GDP growth of 26.6% recorded in that year. Despite these recent positive trends, there remained a need to improve the competitiveness of the economy and to develop the non-petroleum sectors, while increasing the transparency of petroleum-related transactions, in order to ensure that the population's social and development requirements were satisfied.

Education

Education is officially compulsory and free for five years between the ages of six and 11 years. Primary education starts at six years of age and normally lasts for five years. Secondary education, beginning at the age of 12, spans a seven-year period, comprising a first cycle of four years and a second cycle of three years. In 1982 the total enrolment at primary and secondary schools was equivalent to 81% of the school-age population. In 2000/01 total enrolment at primary schools included 72% of children in the relevant age-group (males 76%; females 68%). In 1999/2000, according to UNESCO estimates, secondary enrolment included 26% of children in the relevant age-group (males 37%; females 16%). In 1998/99 there were 890 pupils in higher education.Since 1979, assistance in the development of the educational system has been provided by Spain. Two higher education centres, at Bata and Malabo, are administered by the Spanish Universidad Nacional de Educación a Distancia. The French Government also provides considerable financial assistance. In September 2002 a new National Plan for Education was ratified. The initiative aimed to improve basic literacy and introduce education on health-related topics. In 1993 budgetary expenditure on education by the central Government amounted to an estimated 9.3% of total expenditure.

Public Holidays

2005: 1 January (New Year's Day), 5 March (Independence Day), 25–28 March (Easter), 1 May (Labour Day), 25 May (AU Day), 10 December (Human Rights Day), 25 December (Christmas).

2006: 1 January (New Year's Day), 5 March (Independence Day), 14–17 April (Easter), 1 May (Labour Day), 25 May (AU Day), 10 December (Human Rights Day), 25 December (Christmas).

Weights and Measures

The metric system is in force.

Statistical Survey

Source (unless otherwise stated): Dirección Técnica de Estadística, Secretaría de Estado para el Plan de Desarrollo Económico, Malabo.

AREA AND POPULATION

Area: 28,051 sq km (10,831 sq miles): Río Muni 26,017 sq km, Bioko 2,017 sq km, Annobón 17 sq km.

Population: 300,000 (Río Muni 240,804, Bioko 57,190, Annobón 2,006), comprising 144,268 males and 155,732 females, at census of 4–17 July 1983 (Source: Ministerio de Asuntos Exteriores, Madrid); 406,151 at census of 4 July 1994 (provisional). *Mid-2003* (UN

estimate): 494,000 (Source: UN, *World Population Prospects: The 2002 Revision*).

Density (mid-2003): 17.6 per sq km.

Provinces (population, census of July 1983): Kié-Ntem 70,202; Litoral 66,370; Centro-Sur 52,393; Wele-Nzas 51,839; Bioko Norte 46,221; Bioko Sur 10,969; Annobón 2,006.

Principal Towns (population at 1983 census): Bata 24,100; Malabo (capital) 15,253. *Mid-2003* (UN estimate, incl. suburbs): Malabo

95,450 (Source: UN, *World Urbanization Prospects: The 2003 Revision*).

Births and Deaths (UN estimates, annual averages): Birth rate 43.1 per 1,000 in 1995–2000; Death rate 17.3 per 1,000 in 1995–2000. Source: UN, *World Population Prospects: The 2002 Revision*.

Expectation of Life (WHO estimates, years at birth): 53.4 (males 51.9; females 54.8) in 2002. Source: WHO, *World Health Report*.

Economically Active Population (persons aged 6 years and over, 1983 census): Agriculture, hunting, forestry and fishing 59,390; Mining and quarrying 126; Manufacturing 1,490; Electricity, gas and water 224; Construction 1,929; Trade, restaurants and hotels 3,059; Transport, storage and communications 1,752; Financing, insurance, real estate and business services 409; Community, social and personal services 8,377; Activities not adequately defined 984; *Total employed* 77,740 (males 47,893, females 29,847); Unemployed 24,825 (males 18,040, females 6,785); *Total labour force* 102,565 (males 65,933, females 36,632). Note: Figures are based on un-adjusted census data, indicating a total population of 261,779. The adjusted total is 300,000 (Source: ILO, *Yearbook of Labour Statistics*). *Mid-2003* (FAO estimates, '000 persons): Agriculture, etc. 141; Total labour force 204 (Source: FAO).

HEALTH AND WELFARE

Key Indicators

Total Fertility Rate (children per woman, 2002): 5.9.

Under-5 Mortality Rate (per 1,000 live births, 2003): 146.

HIV/AIDS (% of persons aged 15–49, 2001): 3.38.

Physicians (per 1,000 head, 1990–99): 24.6.

Hospital Beds (per 1,000 head, 1988): 2.8.

Health Expenditure (2001): US $ per head (PPP): 106.

Health Expenditure (2001): % of GDP: 2.0.

Health Expenditure (2001): public (% of total): 60.4.

Access to Water (% of persons, 2002): 44.

Access to Sanitation (% of persons, 2002): 53.

Human Development Index (2002): ranking: 109.

Human Development Index (2002): value: 0.703.
For sources and definitions, see explanatory note on p. vi.

AGRICULTURE, ETC.

Principal Crops (FAO estimates, '000 metric tons, 2003): Sweet potatoes 36; Cassava 45; Coconuts 6; Oil palm fruit 35; Bananas 20; Plantains 31; Cocoa beans 2; Green coffee 4. Source: FAO.

Livestock (FAO estimates, '000 head, year ending September 2003): Cattle 5; Pigs 6; Sheep 38; Goats 9. Source: FAO.

Forestry (FAO estimates, 2003): Roundwood removals ('000 cubic metres): Fuel wood 447 (assumed to be unchanged since 1983); Sawlogs, veneer logs and logs for sleepers 364; Total 811. Source: FAO.

Fishing (FAO estimates, metric tons, live weight, 2002): Freshwater fishes 1,000; Clupeoids 1,900; Sharks, rays, skates, etc. 100; Total catch (incl. others) 3,500. Source: FAO.

MINING

Production (estimates, 2002): Crude petroleum 69 million barrels; Natural gas 1,050 million cubic metres. Source: US Geological Survey.

INDUSTRY

Palm Oil ('000 metric tons): 3.5 in 2002; 3.5 in 2003 (FAO estimate). Source: FAO.

Veneer Sheets (FAO estimates, '000 cubic metres): 15 in 2000; 15 in 2001; 15 in 2002. Source: FAO.

Electric Energy (estimates, million kWh): 21 in 1998; 21 in 1999; 23 in 2000. Source: UN, *Industrial Commodity Statistics Yearbook*.

FINANCE

Currency and Exchange Rates: 100 centimes = 1 franc de la Coopération financière en Afrique centrale (CFA). *Sterling, Dollar and Euro Equivalents* (31 December 2004): £1 sterling = 930.12 francs CFA; US $1 = 481.58 francs CFA; €1 = 655.96 francs CFA; 10,000 francs CFA = £10.75 = $20.77 = €15.24. *Average Exchange Rate* (francs CFA per US dollar): 696.99 in 2002; 581.20 in 2003; 528.29 in 2004. *Note:* An exchange rate of 1 French franc = 50 francs CFA, established in 1948, remained in force until January 1994, when the CFA franc was devalued by 50%, with the exchange rate adjusted to 1 French franc = 100 francs CFA. This relationship to French currency remained in effect with the introduction of the euro on 1 January 1999. From that date, accordingly, a fixed exchange rate of €1 = 655.957 francs CFA has been in operation.

Budget (estimates, million francs CFA, 2002): *Revenue:* Petroleum sector 338,268; Taxation 63,529 (Taxes on income and profits 38,866, Taxes on domestic goods and services 14,237, Taxes on international trade 9,281, Other taxes 1,145); Other revenue 12,687; Total revenue 414,484. *Expenditure:* Current expenditure 100,602 (Wages and salaries 26,047, Other goods and services 50,854, Subsidies and transfers 19,779, Interest payments 3,922); Capital expenditure 126,634; Total expenditure 227,236. Source: IMF, *Equatorial Guinea: Selected Issues and Statistical Appendix* (December 2003).

International Reserves (US $ million at 31 December 2003): IMF special drawing rights 0.04; Foreign exchange 237.65; Total 237.69. Source: IMF, *International Financial Statistics*.

Money Supply ('000 million francs CFA at 31 December 2003): Currency outside deposit money banks 35.12; Demand deposits at deposit money banks 78.53; *Total money* (incl. others) 114.45. Source: IMF, *International Financial Statistics*.

Cost of Living (Consumer Price Index; base: 2000 = 100): 108.8 in 2001; 117.0 in 2002. Source: IMF, *Equatorial Guinea: Selected Issues and Statistical Appendix* (December 2003).

Expenditure on the Gross Domestic Product ('000 million francs CFA at factor cost, 2002): Government final consumption expenditure 135.4; Private final consumption expenditure 485.2; Gross capital formation 434.8; *Total domestic expenditure* 1,055.4; Exports of goods and non-factor services 1,551.4; *Less* Imports of goods and services –1,126.0; *GDP at factor cost* 1,480.8. Source: IMF, *Equatorial Guinea: Selected Issues and Statistical Appendix* (December 2003).

Gross Domestic Product by Economic Activity ('000 million francs CFA, 2002): Agriculture, hunting, forestry and fishing 73.7; Petroleum sector 1,291.6; Manufacturing 1.6; Electricity 5.2; Construction 32.2; Trade 24.6; Transport and communications 4.9; Finance and housing 7.2; Government services 31.1; Other services 8.9; *Sub-total* 1,480.8; Import duties 4.7; *GDP at market prices* 1,485.5. Source: IMF, *Equatorial Guinea: Selected Issues and Statistical Appendix* (December 2003).

Balance of Payments ('000 million francs CFA, 2002): Exports of goods f.o.b. 1,547.0; Imports of goods c.i.f. –768.9; *Trade balance* 778.1; Exports of services –505.0; Imports of non-factor services –357.1; Interest payments –44.1; *Balance on goods, services and income* –128.1; Official transfers (net) 0.7; *Current balance* –127.4; Direct foreign investment 312.4 (of which, petroleum-related direct foreign investment 305.5); Amortization –5.8; *Overall balance* 179.2. Source: IMF, *Equatorial Guinea: Selected Issues and Statistical Appendix* (December 2003).

EXTERNAL TRADE

Principal Commodities (distribution by SITC, US $ '000, 1990): *Imports c.i.f.:* Food and live animals 4,340; Beverages and tobacco 3,198, (Alcoholic beverages 2,393); Crude materials (inedible) except fuels 2,589 (Crude fertilizers and crude minerals 2,102); Petroleum and petroleum products 4,738; Chemicals and related products 2,378; Basic manufactures 3,931; Machinery and transport equipment 35,880 (Road vehicles and parts 3,764, Ships, boats and floating structures 24,715); Miscellaneous manufactured articles 2,725; Total (incl. others) 61,601. *Exports f.o.b.:* Food and live animals 6,742 (Cocoa 6,372); Beverages and tobacco 3,217 (Tobacco and tobacco manufactures 2,321); Crude materials (inedible) except fuels 20,017 (Sawlogs and veneer logs 12,839, Textile fibres and waste 7,078); Machinery and transport equipment 24,574 (Ships, boats and floating structures 23,852); Total (incl. others) 61,705. Source: UN, *International Trade Statistics Yearbook*. *2002* ('000 million francs CFA): Imports c.i.f. 768.9; Exports 1,547.0 (Petroleum 1,468.0; Timber 67.2). Source: IMF, *Equatorial Guinea: Selected Issues and Statistical Appendix* (December 2003).

Principal Trading Partners ('000 million francs CFA, 2002; figures are approximate): *Imports c.i.f.:* Yugoslavia, Fed. Repub. 224; United Kingdom 122; USA 114; France 80; Netherlands 37; Italy 36; Total (incl. others) 769. *Exports f.o.b.:* USA 438; Spain 391; China, People's Repub. 269; Cameroon 76; Italy 40; Germany 22; Total (incl. others) 1,547. Source: IMF, *Equatorial Guinea: Selected Issues and Statistical Appendix* (December 2003).

TRANSPORT

Road Traffic (estimates, motor vehicles in use at 31 December 1996): Passenger cars 1,520; Lorries and vans 540. Source: IRF, *World Road Statistics*.

Shipping: *Merchant Fleet* (at 31 December 2003): Vessels 43; Total displacement 31,299 grt (Source: Lloyd's Register-Fairplay, *World Fleet Statistics*). *International Sea-borne Freight Traffic* ('000 metric tons, 1990): Goods loaded 110; Goods unloaded 64 (Source: UN, *Monthly Bulletin of Statistics*).

Civil Aviation (traffic on scheduled services, 1998): Passengers carried ('000) 21; Passenger-km (million) 4. Source: UN, *Statistical Yearbook*.

COMMUNICATIONS MEDIA

Radio Receivers (1997): 180,000 in use.

Television Receivers (1997): 4,000 in use.

Newspaper (1996): 1 daily (estimated circulation 2,000).

Book Production (1998): 17 titles.

Telephones (2003): 9,600 main lines in use.

Facsimile Machines (1998): 65 in use.

Mobile Cellular Telephones (2003): 41,500 subscribers.

Personal Computers (2002): 4,000 in use.

Internet Users (2002): 1,700.
Sources: UNESCO, *Statistical Yearbook;* UN, *Statistical Yearbook;* International Telecommunication Union.

EDUCATION

Pre-primary (1998): Schools 180; Teachers 387; Pupils 16,645.

Primary (1998): Schools 483; Teachers 1,322; Pupils 74,940.

Secondary (1998): Teachers 763; Pupils 18,802.

Higher (1990/91): Teachers 58; Pupils 578.
Source: UNESCO Institute for Statistics.

Adult Literacy Rate (UNESCO estimates): 84.2% (males 92.8%; females 76.0%) in 2001. Source: UN Development Programme, *Human Development Report*.

Directory

The Constitution

The present Constitution was approved by a national referendum on 16 November 1991 and amended in January 1995. It provided for the introduction of a plural political system and for the establishment of a legislative House of Representatives (Cámara de Representantes del Pueblo). The term of office of the President is seven years, renewable on an indefinite number of occasions. The President is immune from prosecution for offences committed before, during or after his tenure of the post. The Cámara de Representantes serves for a term of five years. Both the President and the Cámara de Representantes are directly elected by universal adult suffrage. The President appoints a Council of Ministers, headed by a Prime Minister.

The Government

HEAD OF STATE

President and Supreme Commander of the Armed Forces: Gen. (Teodoro) Obiang Nguema Mbasogo (assumed office 25 August 1979; elected President 25 June 1989; re-elected 25 February 1996 and 15 December 2002).

COUNCIL OF MINISTERS
(April 2005)

The three parties represented in the Government are the Partido Democrático de Guinea Ecuatorial (PDGE), the Convención Liberal Democrática (CLD) and the Unión Democrática y Social de Guinea Ecuatorial (UDS).

Prime Minister and Head of Government: Miguel Abia Biteo Boricó (PDGE).

First Deputy Prime Minister in charge of Internal Affairs: Marcelino Oyono Ntutumu (PDGE).

Second Deputy Prime Minister in charge of Public Administration, Social Affairs and Human Rights: Ricardo Mangue Obama Nfubea (PDGE).

Minister of State for Presidential Missions: Alejandro Evuna Owono Asangono (PDGE).

Minister, Secretary-General of the Government in charge of Administrative Co-ordination and Parliamentary Relations: Antonio Martin Ndong Ntutumu (PDGE).

Minister of Foreign Affairs, International Co-operation and Francophone Affairs: Pastor Michá Ondo Bilé (PDGE).

Minister of Justice, Worship and Prisons: Angel Masie Mibuy (PDGE).

Minister of the Interior and Local Corporations: Clemente Ngonga Nguema (PDGE).

Minister of National Defence: Gen. Antonio Mba Nguema (Ind.).

Minister of National Security: Col Manuel Nguema Mba (Ind.).

Minister of Transport, Technology, Posts and Telecommunications: Demetrio Elo Ndong Nsefumu (PDGE).

Minister of Infrastructure and Town Planning: Aniceto Ebiaka Mohete (PDGE).

Minister of the Economy, Trade and Business Development: Jaime Ela Ndong (PDGE).

Minister of Planning, Economic Development and Public Investment: Carmelo Modú Acuse Bindang (UDS).

Minister of Finance and the Budget: Marcelino Owono Edú (PDGE).

Minister of Mines, Industry and Energy: Atanasio Ela Ntugu Nsa (PDGE).

Minister of Education, Science and Sports: Cristóbal Mañana Ela (PDGE).

Minister of Health and Social Welfare: Justino Obama Nvé (PDGE).

Minister of Labour and Social Security: Enrique Mercader Costa (PDGE).

Minister of Agriculture and Forests: Teodoro (Teodorín) Nguema Obiang Mangue (PDGE).

Minister of Women's Development: Jesusa Obono Engono (PDGE).

Minister of Fishing and the Environment: Dr Fortunato Ofa Mbo (PDGE).

Minister of Information, Culture and Tourism, Government Spokesperson: Alfonso Nsue Mokuy (CLD).

In addition, there are 12 Deputy Ministers and 15 Secretaries of State.

MINISTRIES

All ministries are in Malabo.

Ministry of Agriculture and Forests: Apdo 504, Malabo.

Ministry of the Economy, Trade and Business Development: BP 404, Malabo; tel. (09) 31-05; fax (09) 20-43.

Ministry of Foreign Affairs, International Co-operation and Francophone Affairs: Malabo; tel. (09) 32-20; fax (09) 31-32.

Ministry of the Interior and Local Corporations: Malabo; fax (09) 26-83.

Ministry of Justice, Worship and Prisons: Malabo; fax (09) 21-15.

Ministry of Mines, Industry and Energy: Calle 12 de Octubre s/n, Malabo; tel. (09) 35-67; fax (09) 33-53; e-mail d.shaw@ecqc.com; internet www.equatorialoil.com.

President and Legislature

PRESIDENT

Gen. (Teodoro) Obiang Nguema Mbasogo was re-elected to the presidency unopposed on 15 December 2002, securing 97.1% of votes cast, following the withdrawal of all other candidates.

CÁMARA DE REPRESENTANTES DEL PUEBLO
(House of Representatives)

Speaker: Dr SALOMON NGUEMA OWONO.

General Election, 25 April 2004

Party	Seats
Partido Democrático de Guinea Ecuatorial (PDGE) .	68
Democratic opposition*	30
Convergencia para la Democracia Social (CPDS) . .	2
Total	100

*A coalition of eight parties allied to President Obiang Nguema, including the Convención Socialdemócrata Popular (CSDP), the Partido de la Convergencia Social Democráta (PCSD) and the Unión Popular (UP).

Political Organizations

Alianza Democrática Progresista (ADP): Pres. FRANCISCO MBÁ OLÚ BAHAMONDE.

Alianza Nacional para la Restauración Democrática de Guinea Ecuatorial (ANRD): 95 Ruperto Chapi, 28100 Madrid, Spain; tel. (91) 623-88-64; f. 1974; Sec.-Gen. LUIS ONDO AYANG.

Alianza Popular de Guinea Ecuatorial (APGE): pro-Government party; Pres. CARMELO MBA; Vice-Pres. TOMÁS BUEICHEKÚ.

Convención Liberal Democrática (CLD): Pres. ALFONSO NSUE MOKUY.

Convención Socialdemócrata Popular (CSDP): Leader SECUNDINO OYONO.

Convergencia para la Democracia Social (CPDS): Calle Tres de Agosto, Apdo 72, 2° andar, 1 Malabo; tel. (09) 20-13; e-mail cpds@intnet.gq; internet www.cpds-gq.org; Pres. SANTIAGO OBAMA NDONG; Sec.-Gen. PLÁCIDO MICÓ ABOGO.

Coordinación Democrática de los Partidos de Oposición de Guinea Ecuatorial: coalition based in Libreville, Gabon; f. 1991.

Frente Democrático para la Reforma: Sec.-Gen. BIYONGO BI-TUNG.

Movimiento Nacional para la Nueva Liberación de Guinea Ecuatorial.

Partido Republicano.

Partido de Reunificación (PR).

Unión para la Democracia y el Desarrollo Social (UDDS): f. 1990; Sec.-Gen. ANTONIO SIBACHA BUEICHEKU.

Foro-Democracia Guinea Ecuatorial (FDGE).

Fuerza Demócrata Republicana (FDR): f. 1995; clandestine; Chair. FELIPE ONDO OBIANG.

Movimiento para la Autodeterminación de la Isla de Bioko (MAIB): e-mail info@maib.org; internet www.maib.org; f. 1993 by Bubi interests seeking independence of Bioko; clandestine; Gen. Coordinator WEJA CHICAMPO (arrested on 4 March 2004); Spokesman Dr ENRIQUE BONEKE.

Movimiento Nacional de Liberación de Guinea Ecuatoriana: POB 1484, Brooklyn, New York 11202-1484, USA; e-mail monalige@equatorialguinea-monalige.com; internet www.equatorialguinea-monalige.com; clandestine opposition party based in USA.

Partido de la Convergencia Social Demócrata (PCSD): Pres. BUENAVENTURA MESUY.

Partido Democrático de Guinea Ecuatorial (PDGE): Malabo; f. 1987; sole legal party 1987–92; Chair. Gen. (TEODORO) OBIANG NGUEMA MBASOGO; Sec.-Gen. FILISBERTO NTUTUMU MBA.

Partido para el Desarrollo (PPD): based in Spain; f. June 2001; Pres. ELOY ELO MVE MBENGOMO.

Partido del Progreso de Guinea Ecuatorial (PPGE): e-mail ppge@telepolis.com; internet www.guinea-ecuatorial.org; f. 1983; Christian Democrat faction led by SEVERO MOTO NSA; based in Spain.

Partido de Reconstrucción y Bienestar Social (PRBS): Pres. FLORENTINO ECOMO NSOGO.

Partido Social Demócrata (PSD): Pres. BENJAMÍN BALINGA.

Partido Socialista de Guinea Ecuatorial (PSGE): Sec.-Gen. TOMÁS MECHEBA FERNÁNDEZ-GALILEA.

Resistencia Nacional de Guinea Ecuatorial (RENAGE): Apdo de Correos 40, 28930 Móstoles, Madrid, Spain; internet www.renage.org; f. 2000; alliance of seven opposition groups; Leader DANIEL M. OYONO.

Unión Democrática Independiente (UDI): Leader DANIEL M. OYONO.

Unión Democrática Nacional (UDEMA): Pres. JOSÉ MECHEBA.

Unión Democrática y Social de Guinea Ecuatorial (UDS): Pres. CARMELO MODÚ ACUSÉ BINDANG.

Unión Popular (UP): f. 1992; conservative; Pres. JEREMÍAS ONDO NGOMO.

Unión Popular—Progresista (UP—Progresista): Leader PEDRO EKONG.

Unión para la Reconciliación y el Progreso (URP).

Diplomatic Representation

EMBASSIES IN EQUATORIAL GUINEA

Algeria: Malabo.

Angola: Malabo.

Cameroon: 37 Calle Rey Boncoro, Apdo 292, Malabo; tel. and fax (09) 22-63; Ambassador JOHN NCHOTU AKUM.

China, People's Republic: Carretera del Aeropuerto, Apdo 44, Malabo; tel. (09) 35-05; fax (09) 23-81; e-mail chinaemb_gq@mfa.gov.cn; Ambassador WANG XIAOYUAN.

France: Carretera del Aeropuerto, Apdo 326, Malabo; tel. (09) 20-05; fax (09) 23-05; internet www.ambafrance-gq.org; Ambassador HENRI DENIAUD.

Gabon: Calle de Argelia, Apdo 18, Malabo; Ambassador JEAN-BAPTISTE MBATCHI.

Guinea: Malabo.

Korea, Democratic People's Republic: Malabo; Ambassador HWANGBO UNG BOM.

Morocco: Avda Enrique, Apdo 329, Malabo; tel. (09) 26-50; fax (09) 26-55; e-mail sifamambo@intnet.gq; Chargé d'affaires a.i. MOHAMED MOUNIR BENHAMMOU.

Nigeria: 4 Paseo de los Cocoteros, Apdo 78, Malabo; tel. (09) 23-86; Chargé d'affaires a.i. EDWARD NWADA.

Russia: Malabo; Ambassador LEV ALEKSANDROVICH VAKHRAMEYEV.

Spain: Parque de las Avenidas de Africa s/n, Malabo; tel. (09) 20-20; fax (09) 26-11; e-mail embespgq@correo.mae.es; Ambassador CARLOS ROBLES FRAGA.

USA: Malabo; e-mail usembassymalabo@yahoo.com; internet usembassy.state.gov/malabo; Chargé d'affaires a.i. A. JAMES PANOS.

Judicial System

The structure of judicial administration was established in 1981. The Supreme Tribunal in Malabo, consisting of a President of the Supreme Tribunal, the Presidents of the three chambers (civil, criminal and administrative), and two magistrates from each chamber, is the highest court of appeal. There are Territorial High Courts in Malabo and Bata, which also sit as courts of appeal. Courts of first instance sit in Malabo and Bata, and may be convened in the other provincial capitals. Local courts may be convened when necessary.

President of the Supreme Tribunal: SERGIO ABESO TOMO.

Attorney-General: ANTONIO NZAMBI.

Religion

An estimated 94% of the population are adherents of the Roman Catholic Church. Traditional forms of worship are also followed.

CHRISTIANITY

The Roman Catholic Church

Equatorial Guinea comprises one archdiocese and two dioceses. There were an estimated 388,534 adherents in the country at 31 December 2001.

Bishops' Conference

Arzobispado, Apdo 106, Malabo; tel. (09) 29-09; fax (09) 21-76; e-mail arzobispadomalabo@hotmail.com.
f. 1984; Pres. Most Rev. ILDEFONSO OBAMA OBONO (Archbishop of Malabo).

Archbishop of Malabo: Most Rev. ILDEFONSO OBAMA OBONO, Arzobispado, Apdo 106, Malabo; tel. (09) 29-09; fax (09) 21-76; e-mail arzobispadomalabo@hotmail.com.

Protestant Church

Iglesia Reformada Evangélica de Guinea Ecuatorial (Evangelical Reformed Church of Equatorial Guinea): Apdo 195, Malabo; f. 1960; c. 8,000 mems.

The Press

Ebano: Malabo; f. 1940; weekly; government-controlled.

El Patio: Apdo 180, Malabo; tel. (09) 27-20; fax (09) 27-22; Spanish; cultural review; 6 a year; publ. by Centro Cultural Hispano-Guineano; Editor JUAN-TOMÁS ÁVILA LAUREL.

Hoja Parroquial: Malabo; weekly.

La Gaceta: Malabo; f. 1996; bi-weekly.

La Verdad: Talleres Gráficos de Convergencia para la Democracia Social, Calle Tres de Agosto 72, Apdo 441, Malabo; publ. by the Convergencia para la Democracia Social; 5 annually; Editor PLÁCIDO MICÓ ABOGO.

Poto-poto: Bata; f. 1940; weekly; government-controlled.

Voz del Pueblo: Malabo; publ. by the Partido Democrático de Guinea Ecuatorial.

FOREIGN NEWS BUREAU

Agencia EFE (Spain): 50 Calle del Presidente Nasser, Malabo; tel. (09) 31-65; Bureau Chief DONATO NDONGO-BIDYOGO.

PRESS ASSOCIATION

Asociación para la Libertad de Prensa y de Expresión en Guinea Ecuatorial (ASOLPEGE Libre): Calle Isla Cabrera 3, 5°, 46026 Valencia, Spain; tel. (660) 930629; e-mail asopge_ngo@hotmail.com; f. 1997; name changed as above following relocation to Spain in 2003; Pres. PEDRO NOLASCO NDONG OBAMA.

Publisher

Centro Cultural Hispano-Guineano: Apdo 180, Malabo; tel. (09) 27-20; fax (09) 27-22; Spanish support withdrawn 2002.

Broadcasting and Communications

TELECOMMUNICATIONS

Dirección General de Correos y de Telecomunicaciones: Malabo; tel. (09) 28-57; fax (09) 25-15; Man. Dir M. DAUCHAT.

Guinea Ecuatorial de Telecomunicaciones, SA (GETESA): Calle Rey Boncoro 27, Apdo 494, Malabo; tel. (09) 28-15; fax (09) 33-13; e-mail contact@getesa.gq; internet www.getesa.gq; f. 1987; 60% state-owned, 40% owned by France Telecom; Man. FRANCISCO NVE NSOGO.

RADIO

Radio Africa and Radio East Africa: Apdo 851, Malabo; e-mail pabcomain@aol.com; commercial station; owned by Pan American Broadcasting; music and religious programmes in English.

Radio Nacional de Guinea Ecuatorial: Apdo 749, Barrio Comandachina, Bata; Apdo 195, 90 Avda 30 de Agosto, Malabo; tel. (08) 25-92; fax (08) 20-93; tel. (09) 22-60; fax (09) 20-97; govt-controlled; commercial station; programmes in Spanish, French and vernacular languages; Dir (Bata) SEBASTIÁN ELÓ ASEKO; Dir (Malabo) JUAN EYENE OPKUA NGUEMA.

Radio Santa Isabel: Malabo; Spanish and French programmes.

Radio Televisión Asonga: Bata; private.

TELEVISION

Televisión Nacional: Malabo; broadcasts in Spanish and French; Dir ANTONIO NKULU OYE.

Finance

(cap. = capital; res = reserves; dep. = deposits; m. = million; br. = branch; amounts in francs CFA)

BANKING

Central Bank

Banque des Etats de l'Afrique Centrale (BEAC): Apdo 501, Malabo; tel. (09) 20-10; fax (09) 20-06; e-mail beacmal@beac.int; HQ in Yaoundé, Cameroon; agency also in Bata; f. 1973; bank of issue for mem. states of the Communauté économique et monétaire de l'Afrique centrale (CEMAC, fmrly Union douanière et économique de l'Afrique centrale), comprising Cameroon, the Central African Repub., Chad, the Repub. of the Congo, Equatorial Guinea and Gabon; cap. 45,000m., res 176,661m., total assets 2,144,626m. (Nov. 2003); Gov. JEAN-FÉLIX MAMALEPOT; Dir in Equatorial Guinea FRANCISCO GARCÍA BERNICO; 2 brs in Equatorial Guinea.

Commercial Banks

BGFIBANK Guinea Ecuatorial: Calle de Bata s/n, Apdo 749, Malabo; tel. (09) 63-52; fax (09) 63-73; e-mail bgfi.ge@internet.gq; internet www.bgfi.com/htm/en/bgfibank/branch-malabo.html; 55% owned by BGFIBANK, 35% owned by private shareholders, 10% state-owned; incorporated June 2001; total assets 1,500m. (Dec. 2003); Pres. ESONO EDJO MELCHOR; Dir-Gen. JEAN MINKO M'OBAME.

Caisse Commune d'Epargne et d'Investissement Guinea Ecuatorial (CCEI-GE): Calle del Presidente Nasser, Apdo 428, Malabo; tel. (09) 22-03; fax (09) 33-11; e-mail geccei@hotmail.com; 51% owned by Afriland First Bank (Cameroon), 13% owned by local investors, 10% state-owned; f. 1995; cap. 3,500m. (Dec. 2004); Pres. BÁLTASAR ENGONGA EDJO'O; Dir-Gen. JOSEPH CÉLESTIN TINDJOU DJAMENI.

Commercial Bank Guinea Ecuatorial (CBGE): Carretera de Luba, Apdo 189, Malabo; e-mail cbgebank@cbc-bank.com; internet www.cbc-bank.com; f. 2003; cap. 1,500m. (Jan. 2003).

Société Générale des Banques GE (SGBGE): Calle Argelia # 6, Apdo 686, Malabo; tel. (09) 33-37; fax (09) 67-95; e-mail jmjgarcia@yahoo.fr; internet groupe.socgen.com/bhfm/sgbge/home_f.htm; f. 1986; present name adopted 1998; 57.24% owned by Société Générale SA (France), 31.80% state-owned, 10.95% owned by local investors; cap. 1,740m. (Dec. 2004); Pres. MARCELINO OWONO EDU; Dir-Gen. CHRISTIAN DELMAS; Man. Dir JEAN-CLAUDE ROBERT; brs in Bata and Malabo.

Development Banks

Banco de Fomento y Desarrollo (BFD): Malabo; f. 1998; 30% state-owned; cap. 50m.

Banque de Développement des Etats de l'Afrique Centrale: see Franc Zone.

Financial Institution

Caja Autónoma de Amortización de la Deuda Pública: Ministry of the Economy, Apdo 404, Malabo; tel. (09) 31-05; fax (09) 20-43; management of state funds; Dir-Gen. RAFAEL TUN.

INSURANCE

Equatorial Guinean Insurance Company, SA (EGICO): Avda de la Libertad, Malabo; state-owned.

Trade and Industry

GOVERNMENT AGENCIES

Cámaras Oficiales Agrícolas de Guinea: Bioko and Bata; purchase of cocoa and coffee from indigenous planters, who are partially grouped in co-operatives.

Empresa General de Industria y Comercio (EGISCA): Malabo; f. 1986; parastatal body jtly operated with the French Société pour l'Organisation, l'Aménagement et le Développement des Industries Alimentaires et Agricoles (SOMDIA); import-export agency.

Oficina para la Cooperación con Guinea Ecuatorial (OCGE): Malabo; f. 1981; administers bilateral aid from Spain.

DEVELOPMENT ORGANIZATIONS

Agencia Española de Cooperación Internacional (AECI): Parque de la Avda de Africa, Malabo; tel. (09) 16-21; fax (09) 29-32; e-mail ucemalabo@intnet.gq; internet www.aeci.es.

Asociación Bienestar Familiar de Guinea Ecuatorial: BP 984, Malabo; tel. and fax (09) 33-13; e-mail abifage1@hotmail.com; family welfare org.

Asociación Hijos de Lommbe (A Vonna va Lommbe): Malabo; e-mail avvl@bisa.com; internet www.bisala.com/avvl.html; f. 2000; agricultural development org.

Centro de Estudios e Iniciativas para el Desarrollo de Guinea Ecuatorial (CEIDIGE): Malabo; e-mail ceidbata@intnet.gq; internet www.eurosur.org/CEIDGE/portada.html; umbrella group of development NGOs; Pres. JOSÉ ANTONIO NSANG ANDEME.

Family Care Guinea Ecuatorial (FGCE): Malabo; f. 2000; health and education development; Dir LAUREN TAYLOR STEVENSON.

Instituto Nacional de Promoción Agropecuaria (INPAGE): Malabo; govt agricultural development agency; reorganized 2000.

Sociedad Anónima de Desarrollo del Comercio (SOADECO–Guinée): Malabo; f. 1986; parastatal body jtly operated with the French Société pour l'Organisation, l'Aménagement et le Développement des Industries Alimentaires et Agricoles (SOMDIA); development of commerce.

CHAMBER OF COMMERCE

Cámara de Comercio, Agrícola y Forestal de Malabo: Avda de la Independencia, Apdo 51, Malabo; tel. (09) 23-43; fax (09) 44-62; Dir ENRIQUE MERCADER COASTA.

INDUSTRIAL AND TRADE ASSOCIATIONS

Guinea Ecuatorial de Petróleo (GEPetrol): Calle Acacio Mane 39, BP 965, Malabo; tel. (09) 67-69; fax (09) 66-92; e-mail bonifacio .monsuy@ge-petrol.com; internet www.equatorialoil.com/pages/ GEPetrol%20page.htm; f. 2001; state-owned petroleum company; National Dir CÁNDIDO NSUE OKOMO.

INPROCAO: Malabo; production, marketing and distribution of cocoa.

Total Ecuatoguineana de Gestión (GE—Total): Malabo; f. 1984; 50% state-owned, 50% by Total (France); petroleum marketing and distribution.

Unión General de Empresas Privadas de la República de Guinea Ecuatorial (UGEPRIGE): Apdo 138, Malabo.

Utilities

Electricity

ENERGE: Malabo; state-owned electricity board.

Sociedad de Electricidad de Guinea Ecuatorial (SEGESA): Apdo 139, Malabo; tel. (09) 27-37; fax (09) 33-29; state-owned electricity distributor; Man. Dir BENITO ONDO.

TRADE UNIONS

A law permitting the establishment of trade unions was introduced in 1992.

Transport

RAILWAYS

There are no railways in Equatorial Guinea.

ROADS

In 1999 there were an estimated 2,880 km of roads and tracks.

Bioko: a semi-circular tarred road serves the northern part of the island from Malabo down to Batete in the west and from Malabo to Bacake Grande in the east, with a feeder road from Luba to Moka and Bahía de la Concepción.

Río Muni: a tarred road links Bata with the town of Mbini (Río Benito) in the west; another road, partly tarred, links Bata with the frontier post of Ebebiyín in the east and then continues into Gabon; other earth roads join Acurenam, Mongomo and Anisok.

SHIPPING

The main ports are Bata (general cargo and most of the country's export timber), Malabo (general), Luba (bananas, timber and petroleum), Mbini and Cogo (timber).

CIVIL AVIATION

There are two international airports, at Malabo (Santa Isabel Airport) and Bata. The national carrier, EGA—Ecuato Guineana de Aviación (which has been in liquidation since 1990), continues to provide limited regional and domestic services, as well as a weekly service to Madrid, Spain. Scheduled services between Malabo and Madrid are operated by Iberia and Líneas Aéreas de España. Direct flights to Paris, France, London, United Kingdom, and Zürich, Switzerland, are also available. SONAGESA, jointly operated by GEPetrol and SONAIR of Angola, offers direct connections between Malabo and Houston, Texas, USA.

EGA—Ecuato Guineana de Aviación: Apdo 665, Malabo; tel. (09) 23-25; fax (09) 33-13; internet www.ecuatoguineana.com/ega/ega .htm; regional and domestic passenger and cargo services; Pres. MELCHOR ESONO EDJO.

Tourism

Tourism remains undeveloped. Future interest in this sector would be likely to focus on the unspoilt beaches of Río Muni and Bioko's scenic mountain terrain.

ERITREA

Introductory Survey

Location, Climate, Language, Religion, Flag, Capital

The State of Eritrea, which has a coastline on the Red Sea extending for almost 1,000 km, is bounded to the north-west by Sudan, to the south and west by Ethiopia, and to the south-east by Djibouti. Its territory includes the Dahlak islands, a low-lying coralline archipelago off shore from Massawa. Rainfall is less than 500 mm per year in lowland areas, increasing to 1,000 mm in the highlands. The temperature gradient is similarly steep: average annual temperatures range from 17°C (63°F) in the highlands to 30°C (86°F) in Massawa. The Danakil depression in the south-east, which is more than 130 m below sea-level in places, experiences some of the highest temperatures recorded, frequently exceeding 50°C (122°F). The major language groups in Eritrea are Afar, Bilien, Hedareb, Kunama, Nara, Rashaida, Saho, Tigre and Tigrinya. English is rapidly becoming the language of business and is the medium of instruction at secondary schools and at university. Arabic is also widely spoken. The population is fairly evenly divided between Tigrinya-speaking Christians (mainly Orthodox), the traditional inhabitants of the highlands, and the Muslim communities of the western lowlands, northern highlands and east coast; there are also systems of traditional belief adhered to by a small number of the population. The national flag (proportions 1 by 2) consists of a red triangle with its base corresponding to the hoist and its apex at the centre of the fly, in which is situated, towards the hoist, an upright gold olive branch with six clusters of three leaves each, framed by a wreath of two gold olive branches; the remainder of the field is green at the top and light blue at the base. The capital is Asmara.

Recent History

The Treaty of Ucciali, which was signed in 1889 between Italy and Ethiopia, gave the Italian Government control over what is today the State of Eritrea. Italian exploitation of the colony continued until the defeat of the Axis powers by the Allied powers in East Africa during the Second World War. During 1941–52 Eritrea was under British administration. The Eritrean national identity, which was established during the Italian colonial period, was further subjugated under British rule. As the Allied powers and the UN discussed the future of the former Italian colony, Ethiopian territorial claims helped to foment a more militant nationalism among the Eritrean population. In 1952 a compromise agreement was reached, whereby a federation was formed between Eritrea and Ethiopia. However, the absence of adequate provisions for the creation of federal structures allowed Ethiopia to reduce Eritrea's status to that of an Ethiopian province by 1962.

Resistance to the Ethiopian annexation was first organized in the late 1950s, and in 1961 the Eritrean Liberation Front (ELF) launched an armed struggle. In the mid-1970s a reformist group broke away from the ELF and formed the Popular Liberation Forces (renamed the Eritrean People's Liberation Front, EPLF, in 1977), and the military confrontation with the Ethiopian Government began in earnest. A major consequence of the split between the two groups was the civil war of 1972–74. After two phases of desertion from the ELF to the EPLF, firstly in 1977–78 and secondly in 1985 (following a second civil war), the ELF was left without a coherent military apparatus.

Following the 1974 revolution in Ethiopia and the assumption of power by Mengistu Haile Mariam in 1977, thousands of new recruits joined the EPLF, and the armed struggle transformed into full-scale warfare. The numerically and materially superior Ethiopian forces achieved significant victories over the EPLF, and, following defeat in the highlands, the EPLF was forced to retreat to its stronghold in the north of Eritrea. The EPLF launched counter-attacks throughout the late 1980s and slowly drove back the Ethiopian forces on all fronts. By 1989 the EPLF had gained control of the north and the west of the country, and in late 1989 the EPLF captured Massawa port, thereby severing a major supply-route to the Ethiopian forces, who were by now besieged in Asmara. In May 1991 units of the EPLF entered Asmara, after the Ethiopian troops had fled, and immediately established an interim EPLF administration.

Following the liberation of Asmara by the EPLF, and of Addis Ababa by the Ethiopian People's Revolutionary Democratic Front (EPRDF), a conference was convened in London, United Kingdom, in August 1991. Both the USA and the Ethiopian delegation accepted the EPLF administration as the legitimate provisional Government of Eritrea, and the EPLF agreed to hold a referendum on independence in 1993. The provisional Government, which was to administer Eritrea during the two years prior to the referendum, drew most of its members from the EPLF. The Government struggled to rehabilitate and develop Eritrea's war-torn economy and infrastructure, and to feed a population of whom 80% remained dependent on food aid. The agricultural sector had been severely disrupted by the war, and urban economic activity was almost non-existent.

At the UN-supervised referendum on independence, held in April 1993, 99.8% of Eritreans who voted endorsed national independence. The anniversary of the liberation of Asmara, 24 May, was proclaimed Independence Day, and on 28 May Eritrea formally attained international recognition. In June Eritrea was admitted to the Organization of African Unity (OAU, now the African Union—AU, see p. 144). Following Eritrea's accession to independence, a four-year transitional period was declared, during which preparations were to proceed for establishing a constitutional and pluralist political system. At the apex of the transitional Government were three state institutions: the Consultative Council (the executive authority formed from the ministers, provincial administrators and heads of government authorities and commissions); the National Assembly (the legislative authority formed from the Central Committee of the EPLF, together with 30 members from the Provincial Assemblies and 30 individuals selected by the Central Committee); and the judiciary. One of the National Assembly's first acts was the election as Head of State of Issaias Afewerki, the Secretary-General of the EPLF, by a margin of 99 votes to five.

In February 1994 the EPLF transformed itself into a political party, the People's Front for Democracy and Justice (PFDJ). An 18-member Executive Committee and a 75-member Central Committee were elected; President Afewerki was elected Chairman of the latter. In March the National Assembly adopted a series of resolutions whereby the former executive body, the Consultative Council, was formally superseded by a State Council. Other measures adopted included the creation of a 50-member Constitutional Commission and the establishment of a committee charged with the reorganization of the country's administrative divisions. It was decided that the National Assembly would henceforth comprise the 75 members of the PFDJ Central Committee and 75 directly elected members. However, no mechanism was announced for their election. All but eight of the 50 members of the Constitutional Commission were government appointees, and there was no provision for any opposition participation in the interim system.

A draft constitution was discussed at international conventions held by the Constitutional Commission in July 1994 and January 1995. In May the National Assembly approved proposals to create six administrative regions to replace the 10 regional divisions that had been in place since colonial rule. In November the Assembly approved new names for the regions and finalized details of their exact boundaries and sub-divisions.

In early 1997 the Government established a Constituent Assembly, comprising 527 members (150 from the National Assembly, with the remainder selected from representatives of Eritreans residing abroad or elected by regional assemblies), to discuss and ratify the draft constitution. On 23 May the Constituent Assembly adopted the Constitution, authorizing 'conditional' political pluralism and instituting a presidential regime, with a President elected for a maximum of two five-year terms. The President, as Head of State, would appoint a Prime Minister and judges of the Supreme Court; his or her mandate could be revoked should two-thirds of the members of the National Assembly so demand. The Constituent Assembly was disbanded, and a Transitional National Assembly (consisting of the 75 members of the PFDJ Central Committee, 60 members of the Constituent Assembly and 15 representatives of Eritreans residing abroad) was empowered to act as the legislature until the holding of elections to a new National Assembly.

It was initially announced that Eritrea's first post-independence elections, which were scheduled to have been held in 1998, but were postponed indefinitely following the outbreak of hostilities with Ethiopia (see below), would take place in December 2001. However, during 2001 the likelihood of elections taking place in that year diminished, as President Afewerki assumed an increasingly authoritarian position. In February he dismissed the Minister of Local Government, Mahmoud Ahmed Sherifo and dissolved the electoral commission, which Sherifo had been appointed to head. In June Afewerki replaced the Ministers of Trade and Industry and of Maritime Resources. They were among a group of 15 senior PFDJ officials, including 11 former government ministers, who, in May, had signed a letter publicly accusing Afewerki of working in an 'illegal and unconstitutional manner'. In August the Chief Justice of the Supreme Court was dismissed after he openly expressed his disapproval of Afewerki's continued interference in court operations. In mid-September six of the G-15, as the 15 signatories of the letter criticizing Afewerki had become known, were arrested, and the Government announced the 'temporary suspension' of the independent press. A few days later a further five members of the G-15 were detained. The Government justified the arrests on the grounds that the 11 were involved in 'illegal activities which endangered the country'. In early October the Eritrean authorities expelled the Italian ambassador after he expressed concern at recent events in Eritrea on behalf of the European Union. The Italian Government responded by expelling the Eritrean ambassador in Rome, and later that month Denmark, France, Germany and the Netherlands recalled their ambassadors from Eritrea for consultations. The four returned to their posts in Asmara in mid-November, although Italy initially refused to reinstate its ambassador. In June 2002 Italy and Eritrea resumed diplomatic contacts and, following a meeting between Afewerki and the Italian Prime Minister, Silvio Berlusconi, agreed to the return of both countries' ambassadors.

Although no formal postponement of the legislative elections was announced, the failure of the National Assembly to convene to ratify legislation on the electoral system and on political pluralism by December 2001 made further delay inevitable. In late January 2002 the National Assembly ratified the electoral law, but failed to set an election date. Meanwhile, President Afewerki replaced the Ministers of Information, Tourism, and Transport and Communications in September, October and November 2001, respectively. In January 2002 dissident members of the ruling PFDJ, including several members of the G-15, announced the formation, in exile, of a new political party, the Eritrean People's Liberation Front—Democratic Party (EPLF—DP).

During 2004 several Eritrean opposition parties took steps to form a viable opposition movement to the PFDJ. In February, following talks in Germany, the EPLF—DP announced that it would reform as the Eritrean Democratic Party (EDP), while remaining under the leadership of Mesfin Hagos. In May numerous former members of the ELF and the PFDJ combined to establish the Eritrean Popular Movement (EPM). In August two new coalitions were formed; the first united the EPM and four smaller parties under the umbrella of the Eritrean National Alliance (ENA), while the second brought the EDP, the ELF and the Eritrean Liberation Front—Revolutionary Council together. In late December representatives of these two alliances met in Khartoum, Sudan for talks with the Ethiopian Prime Minister, Meles Zenawi, and the Sudanese President, Omar Hassan Ahmad al-Bashir, aimed at settling issues surrounding the border conflict with Ethiopia (see below). In January 2005 Hiruy Tedla Bairu was elected leader of the ENA and an opposition conference was scheduled for later that month.

Hopes that national legislative elections would finally take place were raised in 2004 as elections for the regional assemblies were held in May with some 92% of registered voters casting their ballots. The National Election Committee praised the high level of participation and overall fairness of the election process and indicated that the success of these elections paved the way for free national elections in the future. However, some analysts maintained that the regional elections had been unfairly influenced by the PFDJ and stated that it was unlikely that a general election would take place under the prevailing political conditions. Indeed, by early 2005 no date had been set for the holding of elections.

Relations between the transitional Government and Sudan, which had supported the EPLF during the war, deteriorated in December 1993, following an incursion by members of an Islamist group, the Eritrean Islamic Jihad (EIJ), into Eritrea from Sudan, during which all the members of the group, and an Eritrean army commander, were killed. In response to the incident, President Afewerki stressed the links between the EIJ and the Sudanese National Islamic Front, led by Dr Hassan at-Turabi, implying that the latter had prior knowledge of the incursion. However, following a swift denial by the Sudanese Government that it would interfere in the affairs of neighbouring states, Afewerki reaffirmed his support for the Sudanese authorities and his commitment to improving bilateral relations.

In August 1994 Eritrea and Sudan signed an agreement concerning borders, security and the repatriation of refugees, and in November the office of the UN High Commissioner for Refugees (UNHCR) initiated a repatriation programme for Eritrean refugees currently in Sudan. Some 500,000 Eritreans had taken refuge in Sudan in the early 1990s as a result of separatist conflicts, although by 1995 an estimated 125,000 had returned spontaneously, particularly following Eritrea's accession to independence.

Relations between Eritrea and Sudan deteriorated in November 1994, when the Eritrean authorities accused Sudan of training 400 terrorists since August. Sudan accused Eritrea of training some 3,000 Sudanese rebels in camps within Eritrea. In December Eritrea severed diplomatic relations with Sudan. Further destabilization was provoked in early 1995 by attacks and infiltration in Barka Province by commandos of the military wing of the EIJ. The Eritrean authorities subsequently claimed to have identified six training camps on the Sudanese side of the border and also alleged that large numbers of Eritrean refugees in Sudan had been arrested by Sudanese security forces. Sudan responded by proposing Eritrea's suspension from the Intergovernmental Authority on Drought and Development (IGADD, now the Intergovernmental Authority on Development—IGAD, see p. 270), which had been attempting to mediate in Sudan's civil war. The Sudanese Government protested strongly against Eritrea's growing support for the Sudanese opposition grouping, the National Democratic Alliance (NDA), which held a number of conferences in Asmara in the mid-1990s. In February 1996 Eritrea granted Sudanese opposition leaders permission to use Sudan's embassy in Asmara as their headquarters. In February 1998 Sudan closed the border with Eritrea in an attempt to prevent incursions into Sudan. In November the Ministers of Foreign Affairs of the two countries attended a mediation meeting in Qatar, at the conclusion of which they signed a memorandum of understanding to normalize relations. Tensions remained, however, and mutual recriminations regarding border incidents continued.

In early 1999 Sudan took steps to resolve its differences with Ethiopia, thus increasing the tension between Eritrea and Sudan. In April, however, Sudan indicated its willingness also to improve relations with Eritrea, and in May a reconciliatory agreement was signed in Qatar, which, *inter alia*, restored diplomatic relations between the two countries. In January 2000 President al-Bashir of Sudan visited Afewerki in Asmara, where they pledged further to improve bilateral relations between the two countries. Following the renewed outbreak of hostilities between Eritrea and Ethiopia in May (see below), some 94,000 Eritreans fleeing the Ethiopian advances crossed the border into Sudan. After the cessation of fighting in June, many Eritrean refugees were repatriated with the assistance of UNHCR, and by January 2002 some 36,500 Eritreans had returned to their home country. In January 2003 refugee status was withdrawn from more than 320,000 Eritreans in Sudan, although UNHCR maintained that its repatriation programme would continue until all those registered with the agency had been returned to their homeland. Meanwhile, during 2000 the Eritrean Government assumed a mediatory role in the conflict between the Sudanese Government and opposition groups based in Eritrea. In August 2000 the two countries exchanged ambassadors, and in September al-Bashir travelled to Asmara where he met with the leader of the opposition NDA for the first time since 1989. In July 2001 Eritrea and Sudan signed an agreement on border security, which aimed to eradicate smuggling and illegal infiltration, as well as ensure the safe passage of people and goods across the common border. In October 2002 relations between the two countries again deteriorated after the Sudanese Government claimed that Eritrean forces had been involved in the

NDA's capture of Hanashkoreb in eastern Sudan. Although Eritrea strenuously denied any involvement in the incident, Sudan closed the countries' common border with immediate effect. Following a meeting with the Yemeni President, Ali Abdullah Saleh, and the Ethiopian Prime Minister, Meles Zenawi, in December 2003, President al-Bashir accused Eritrea of arming and training rebels in the Darfur region of Sudan and maintained that Eritrea was a destabilizing force in the region. Eritrea refuted the allegations. In early March 2004 two explosions in Tesseney, close to the Sudanese border, resulted in the deaths of at least three people and seven more people were killed in an explosion in Barentu in late May. The Eritrean authorities accused Sudanese groups of carrying out the attacks, however, Sudan strongly denied any involvement in the incidents and stated that the explosions had been the work of Eritrean opposition forces. Relations between the two countries showed little sign of improvement during 2004.

In November 1995 there were reports that Eritrean troops had attempted to land on the Red Sea island of Greater Hanish, one of three islands (the others being Lesser Hanish and Zuqar) claimed by both Eritrea and Yemen. The disputed islands had been used by Eritrea (with apparent Yemeni approval) during its struggle for independence from Ethiopia. Yemen had subsequently resumed its claims to the islands, because of both their strategic importance (located close to a principal shipping lane) and the possible existence of exploitable petroleum reserves in their surrounding waters. Negotiations in Eritrea and Yemen failed to defuse the crisis, and in mid-December fighting erupted between the two sides, resulting in several deaths. Two days later Eritrea and Yemen agreed to a cease-fire, but fighting resumed on the following day, and Eritrean forces succeeded in occupying Greater Hanish. The cease-fire was adhered to thenceforth, and some 180 captured Yemeni soldiers were released at the end of the month. In May Eritrea and Yemen signed an arbitration accord in Paris, France, whereby the two sides agreed to submit the dispute to an international tribunal and France subsequently undertook to observe and supervise military movements in the area around the disputed islands. In August, despite the accord, Eritrean troops occupied Lesser Hanish; however, later in the month Eritrea withdrew its soldiers after mediation by France and a UN Security Council instruction to evacuate the island forthwith. In October Eritrea and Yemen confirmed that they would submit the dispute to an international tribunal. In October 1998 the tribunal ruled that Yemen had sovereignty over Greater and Lesser Hanish, and all islands to their north-west, while Eritrea had sovereignty over the Mohabaka islands. The court recommended that the fishing traditions around the islands be maintained, thereby granting access to the Hanish islands to Eritrean and Yemeni fishermen. Both countries accepted the ruling, and shortly afterwards agreed to establish a joint committee to strengthen bilateral co-operation.

In November 1995 Eritrea and Djibouti pledged to enhance bilateral co-operation, following a meeting between Eritrea's Minister of Foreign Affairs, Petros Solomon, and Djibouti's President Gouled. Nevertheless, relations between the two countries were strained in April 1996, when Gouled reportedly rejected a map (produced by Italy in 1935) submitted by Solomon, which apparently indicated that a 20-km strip of land claimed by Djibouti was, in fact, Eritrean territory. Meanwhile, Eritrea denied reports of an attempted occupation of a border post in Djibouti (within the disputed territory) by Eritrean troops. Relations between the two countries subsequently improved; however, in November 1998 Djibouti suspended diplomatic relations with Eritrea, following allegations by the Eritrean authorities that it was supporting Ethiopia in the Eritrea–Ethiopia border conflict (see below). The two countries re-established diplomatic relations in March 2000, following Libyan mediation.

In September 1993 the first meeting of the Ethiopian-Eritrean joint ministerial commission was held in Asmara, during which agreement was reached on measures to allow the free movement of nationals between each country, and on co-operation regarding foreign affairs and economic policy. Meetings held between President Afewerki and the Ethiopian President, Meles Zenawi, in December underlined the good relations prevailing between the two Governments.

Relations with Ethiopia deteriorated in late 1997, following Eritrea's adoption of a new currency (the nakfa) to replace the Ethiopian birr and the subsequent disruption of cross-border trade. In May 1998 fighting erupted between Eritrean and Ethiopian troops in the border region after both countries accused the other of having invaded their territory. Hostilities escalated in June in areas around Badme, Zalambessa and Assab, resulting in numerous casualties for both sides. A peace plan devised by the USA and Rwanda in early June was unsuccessful, although later that month Eritrea and Ethiopia agreed to an aerial cease-fire, following mediation by the USA and Italy. In August an OAU mediation committee presented its report to the Ministers of Foreign Affairs of Eritrea and Ethiopia at an OAU meeting in Ouagadougou, Burkina Faso. The proposals, which endorsed the US-Rwandan peace plan, were rejected by Eritrea, which maintained that it would not withdraw its troops from the disputed territory prior to negotiations. In November President Afewerki and Prime Minister Meles of Ethiopia were present at different sessions of a special meeting of the OAU mediation committee in Ouagadougou, which was also attended by the Heads of State of Burkina Faso, Zimbabwe and Djibouti. The committee's peace proposals, which again stressed the need to demilitarize and demarcate the disputed territory, were accepted by Ethiopia, but rejected by Eritrea. Eritrea, moreover, demanded that Djibouti withdraw from the committee, accusing it of providing assistance to Ethiopia in the conflict. Djibouti suspended diplomatic relations with Eritrea, in protest at the allegations. Other international mediation attempts in late 1998 (including that of Anthony Lake, a former US national security adviser) failed to resolve the dispute, and in February 1999 the aerial cease-fire was broken and intense fighting resumed in the border region. In April both sides claimed that they were now prepared to accept and implement the OAU peace proposals, and at the OAU summit held in Algiers, Algeria, in July they confirmed their commitment to the OAU's Framework Agreement. Afewerki announced that Eritrean troops would be withdrawn from all territory captured from Ethiopia since 6 May 1998. Under the agreement, Ethiopia was also required to withdraw from all Eritrean territory captured since 6 February 1999, which, in effect, would see both sides return to their positions before the war. After requesting clarification of technical arrangements to end the war, Ethiopia informed the OAU in September that it had rejected the peace agreement, owing to inconsistencies contained therein. Eritrea accused Ethiopia of deliberately stalling proceedings, while secretly preparing for a fresh offensive.

Throughout late 1999 and early 2000 there were reports of numerous clashes between Eritrean and Ethiopian troops, and both countries continued to promote and assist opposition groups hostile to their foe. In late April 2000 delegations from both countries agreed to attend OAU-sponsored talks in Algiers, although they refused to meet directly, forcing Algerian diplomats to act as mediators. However, the talks collapsed, and in mid-May hostilities between the two countries broke out again; Ethiopia launched a major offensive near the disputed towns of Badme and Zalambessa and succeeded in repulsing the Eritrean forces. The UN Security Council subsequently unanimously approved the imposition of a 12-month arms embargo on Eritrea and Ethiopia. Ethiopian forces captured the strategically important Eritrean town of Barentu and took control of the western front. By late May Ethiopian forces had seized Zalambessa and the Eritrean authorities had announced that they would withdraw troops from the disputed areas, although Afewerki maintained that this was merely a 'gesture of goodwill' designed to revive the peace talks, which resumed in Algiers on 29 May. Two days later the Ethiopian Prime Minister, Meles Zenawi, stated that the war was over and that his troops had withdrawn from most of the territory it had captured from Eritrea. Following extensive negotiations in early June, both sides expressed their readiness, in principle, to accept the OAU's cease-fire agreement, and on 18 June the Ethiopian and Eritrean Ministers of Foreign Affairs signed an agreement, which provided for an immediate cease-fire and the deployment of a UN peace-keeping force in a 25-km temporary security zone (TSZ) inside Eritrea until the issue of the demarcation of the border had been settled. It was estimated that some 100,000 people had been killed and up to 1.5m. Eritreans displaced since the conflict had begun in 1998. Indirect negotiations to discuss the technical issues of the peace accord, involving representatives from both countries, took place in Washington, DC, USA, in early July 2000 and continued in Algiers in October. Meanwhile, in September the UN Security Council approved the deployment of the UN Mission in Ethiopia and Eritrea (UNMEE, see p. 73), a 4,200-strong peace-keeping force, which was placed under the command of the Special Representative of the UN Secretary-General, Legwaila Joseph Legwaila. On 12 December Eritrea and Ethiopia signed an agreement in Algiers, which formally ended the conflict between the two countries. The agreement provided for a permanent cessation of all hostilities, the immediate return of all prisoners of war, the demarcation of the common border by an independent commission and the establishment of a Claims Commission to assess the issues of compensation and reparations. Furthermore, both countries pledged to co-operate with an independent investigation, which aimed to determine the origins of the conflict.

By late January 2001 the UNMEE force had been fully deployed and began making provisions for the establishment of a TSZ in a 25-km area along the Ethiopia–Eritrea border. On 22 February the Ethiopian Government notified UNMEE that it had completed the redeployment of its troops; UNMEE verified the withdrawal as complete on 7 March. However, at the fourth meeting of the Military Co-ordination Commission (MCC), in late February, the Eritrean delegation had registered its objections to adjustments made to the original boundaries of the future TSZ, on which agreement had been provisionally reached at a previous MCC meeting. The Eritrean authorities subsequently informed UNMEE that they had suspended the withdrawal of their forces. In mid-March UNMEE's mandate was extended until September, and in early April, following intensive negotiations, Eritrea recommenced the redeployment of its troops. Nevertheless, Eritrea reiterated its dissatisfaction regarding the southern boundary of the prospective TSZ. On 16 April it was announced that the withdrawal of Eritrea's forces was complete, and two days later UNMEE declared the establishment of the TSZ, marking the formal separation of the Eritrean and Ethiopian forces. In late June UNMEE presented the final map of the TSZ to Eritrea and Ethiopia, although it emphasized that it would not influence the work of the neutral boundary commission charged with determining the border between the two countries. Despite this announcement, the Ethiopian Government expressed its dissatisfaction with the map. Also that month UNMEE complained that Eritrea was refusing to grant unrestricted movement to its members, thus impeding its ability to undertake its duties effectively. At the eighth MCC meeting in August both countries reiterated their objections to the current boundaries of the TSZ. In mid-September UNMEE's mandate was extended for a further six months, although Legwaila acknowledged that the mission faced an extremely difficult task in achieving lasting peace, as the two countries remained 'polarized', and also admitted that neither country had fully adhered to the terms of the agreement on the cessation of hostilities. In mid-December the two countries began presenting their cases for border demarcation to the five-member Boundary Commission (BC) at the International Court of Justice (see p. 19) at The Hague, Netherlands. In mid-March 2002 UNMEE's mandate was extended until mid-September.

The BC delivered its findings in April 2002. Both Ethiopia and Eritrea had committed themselves in advance to the acceptance of the Commission's report. However, the Commission did not identify on which side of the boundary line Badme lay, stating that it was awaiting delineation on the ground, which was expected to take up to one year. In the absence of any decision by the BC, both countries immediately claimed to have been awarded Badme. When UNMEE invited journalists to visit Badme in late April by entering through Eritrea, Ethiopia reacted by closing the border to UNMEE and demanding the removal of the UNMEE commander, Maj.-Gen. Patrick Cammaert. The border was reopened to UN personnel in early May. Later that month Ethiopia formally requested 'interpretation, correction and consultation' of the Boundary Commission's report, but this was rejected by the Commission in late June.

Meanwhile, in early March 2003 the BC reported to the UN Security Council that Ethiopia's requests for changes to the border ruling, in order to 'take better account of human and physical geography', threatened to undermine the peace process as a whole. Despite Ethiopia's claims that it had been promised that demarcations could be refined, later in March the BC categorically ruled Badme to be Eritrean territory. Meles subsequently complained that the decision was 'wrong and unjust' and vowed to continue to contest the ruling. The demarcation of the border, which had originally been scheduled to take place in May, was postponed until July, and then delayed again until October; both the MCC and the UN expressed their frustration at the slow progress being made towards the resolution of the matter. In October, in a letter to the UN Security Council, Meles

called for a new body to be established to resolve the crisis and again denounced the BC's ruling as 'unacceptable'. However, the Security Council stated that Ethiopia had committed itself under the 2000 Algiers agreement to accept the BC's decision as 'final and binding' and urged it to accept and implement the border ruling. Both Legwaila and the Chairman of the BC, Elihu Lauterpacht, were critical of Ethiopia's lack of compliance with its obligations under the terms of the peace accord, and the ongoing impasse was further compounded by the BC's announcement in late October that the demarcation of the border had been delayed indefinitely. Ethiopia maintained that it had agreed to allow demarcation to take place in the eastern sector of the border region, but that it refused to accept the ruling in other areas and had expressed grave concerns about the competency of the BC. Eritrea continued, however, to insist that the ruling be fully implemented.

The process suffered a further reverse in mid-November 2003, when Eritrea withdrew its ambassador to the AU and accused the organization of neglecting its responsibilities over the dispute with Ethiopia. However, in the following month both countries agreed to establish three Sector Military Co-ordination Committees, under the chairmanship of UNMEE's Sector Commanders, in order to improve the mechanism for dealing with incidents in the border areas; it was hoped that the committees would prevent any minor border incidents from escalating into wider conflict. Later in December Lloyd Axworthy, a former Canadian Minister of Foreign Affairs, was appointed as the UN's special envoy to the region, tasked with resolving the stalled peace process between Eritrea and Ethiopia. While Ethiopia welcomed the appointment and pledged to work closely with Axworthy, the Eritrean Government expressed its opposition to the appointment, as it feared that it would result in amendments to the BC's ruling.

UN concerns over the lack of progress on the part of both Eritrea and Ethiopia to implement the border ruling continued during 2004. In March UNMEE's mandate was extended by a further six months and the UN Security Council urged the two countries to co-operate with each other and with Axworthy. In April Legwaila highlighted the difficulties faced by UN peacekeepers in the region owing to continuing travel restrictions placed upon them by the Eritrean authorities, who closed the road from Asmara to Barentu to all UNMEE vehicles for over a month. Following accusations by Eritrean officials in May of serious malpractice on the part of the UN forces, Legwaila issued an ultimatum to Eritrea that it should either co-operate with the UN peace-keeping forces or ask its troops to leave. In September UNMEE's mandate was extended until March 2005 and it was announced that the peace-keeping mission would be reduced with 550 Kenyan troops stationed on the eastern part of the border being replaced by helicopter patrols by the end of January. Meanwhile, in November 2004, Ethiopia stated that it had, in principle, accepted the BC's ruling of April 2002 and was prepared to re-enter into talks with Eritrea regarding the demarcation of the border. However, Eritrea dismissed this announcement as little more than a further attempt by Ethiopia to buy time. By mid-April 2005 there had been no agreement between the two countries to re-establish talks and the border remained disputed.

The repatriation of prisoners of war began in December 2000. By October 2001 856 Eritrean and 653 Ethiopian prisoners of war had been repatriated; however, it was reported that some 400 prisoners of war remained in Eritrea, and an estimated 1,800 Eritreans were still being held in Ethiopia. In November 2002 it was announced that Ethiopia had released all Eritrean prisoners of war and that their repatriation had commenced. All Ethiopian prisoners of war had been released in August. Other difficulties remained for the Eritrean authorities, primarily the need to repatriate the vast numbers of Eritreans who had been displaced during the conflict and the severe food shortages still affecting the nation, with relief agencies estimating that more than 1m. Eritreans (about one-quarter of the population) required food aid. In early 2004 the UN announced that there were still 58,953 internally displaced persons in Eritrea, and that in 2005 2.3m. Eritreans would require humanitarian assistance, mainly in the form of food aid, following poor rainfall in 2004.

Government

In May 1991 the Eritrean People's Liberation Front (EPLF, restyled as the People's Front for Democracy and Justice—PFDJ—in February 1994) established a provisional Government to administer Eritrea, pending the holding of a national referendum on the issue of independence. The EPLF did not invite other organizations to participate, although it promised that free elections would be held following the referendum. The referendum was held in April 1993, and Eritrea was proclaimed an independent state in the following month. A transitional Government was established, at the apex of which were three state institutions: the Consultative Council (the executive authority formed from the ministers, provincial administrators and heads of government authorities and commissions); the National Assembly (the legislative authority comprising the Central Committee of the EPLF, 30 additional members from the Provincial Assemblies and 30 individuals selected by the Central Committee); and the judiciary. In March 1994 the Consultative Council was superseded by a State Council. At independence a four-year transitional period was declared, during which preparations were to proceed for the establishment of a constitutional and pluralist political system. Meanwhile, in March 1994 the National Assembly voted to alter its composition: it would thenceforth comprise the 75 members of the PFDJ Central Committee and 75 directly elected members. In May 1997, following the adoption of the Constitution, the Constituent Assembly empowered a Transitional National Assembly (comprising the 75 members of the PFDJ Central Committee, 60 members of the former Constituent Assembly and 15 representatives of Eritreans residing abroad) to act as the legislature until elections were held for a new National Assembly.

Defence

Eritrea's armed forces increased rapidly during the 1999–2000 border conflict with Ethiopia and in August 2004, despite the cessation of hostilities in June 2000, were estimated to number 201,750, including an army of about 200,000 (of which some 60,000 were scheduled to be demobilized), a navy of 1,400 and an air force of about 350. In July 2000 the UN Security Council adopted a resolution (No. 1312) establishing the UN Mission in Ethiopia and Eritrea (UNMEE, see p. 73), which was to supervise the cease-fire and the implementation of a peace agreement. At the end of December 2004 UNMEE numbered 3,705 troops, 213 military observers, and 208 international and 254 local civilian personnel; UNMEE had a total authorized strength of 4,200 troops (including 220 military observers). National service is compulsory for all Eritrean citizens between 18 and 40 years of age (with certain exceptions), for a 16-month period, including four months of military training. Budgeted expenditure on defence (including the demobilization of ex-combatants) in 2004 was estimated at 74m. nakfa.

Economic Affairs

In 2003, according to estimates by the World Bank, Eritrea's gross national income (GNI), measured at average 2001–03 prices, was US $851m., equivalent to $190 per head (or $1,110 per head on an international purchasing-power parity basis). During 1990–2003, it was estimated, the population increased at an average annual rate of 2.6%, while gross domestic product (GDP) per head increased, in real terms, by an average of 2.4% per year during 1992–2003. Overall GDP increased, in real terms, at an average annual rate of 5.1% in 1992–2003; growth in 2003 was 5.0%.

By far the most important sector of the economy is agriculture, which, despite a reduction in food production of roughly 40% between 1980 and 1990, still sustains 90% of the population. In 2003 agriculture (including forestry and fishing) accounted for an estimated 15.4% of GDP and employed an estimated 76.6% of the economically active population. Most sedentary agriculture is practised in the highlands, where rainfall is sufficient to cultivate the main crops: teff (an indigenous grain), sorghum, potatoes, millet, barley and wheat.As a result of serious environmental degradation (caused directly and indirectly by the war of independence), water scarcity and unreliable rainfall, projects have been undertaken to build water reservoirs and small dams, while badly eroded hillsides have been terraced and new trees planted in order to prevent soil erosion. Although fishing activity is on a very small scale, the total catch increased considerably in the first half of the 1990s, reaching 3,267 metric tons in 1996. The total catch subsequently declined, but rose to 12,612 tons in 2000, before falling again, to 8,820 tons, in 2001 and to 7,832 in 2002. According to the UN, sustainable yields of as much as 70,000 tons per year may be possible. In real terms, the GDP of the agricultural sector decreased at an average annual rate of 1.2% in 1992–2003.

Agricultural GDP fell by 35.5% in 2002, but grew by 38.7% in 2003.

In 2003 industrial production (comprising mining, manufacturing, construction and utilities) accounted for an estimated 23.8% of GDP. Some 5.0% of the labour force were employed in the industrial sector in 1990. Eritrea's industrial base traditionally centred on the production of glass, cement, footwear and canned goods, but most industrial enterprises were badly damaged during the war of independence. Industrial GDP increased, in real terms, at an average annual rate of 11.8% in 1992–2003. Industrial GDP increased by 0.9% in 2003.

Eritrea's mineral resources are believed to be of significant potential value, although in 2002 mining and quarrying accounted for less than 0.1% of GDP. Of particular importance, in view of Eritrea's acute energy shortage, is the possibility of large reserves of petroleum and natural gas beneath the Red Sea. Production-sharing agreements for the exploration of petroleum and gas were signed with the Anadarko Petroleum Corpn of the USA in 1995 and 1997. However, Anadarko's first three deep drills were dry, and in May 1999 the company began reducing operations by removing most of its operational staff. Other mineral resources include potash, zinc, magnesium, copper, iron ore, marble and gold. New legislation on mining, adopted in 1995, declared all mineral resources to be state assets, but recognized an extensive role for private investors in their exploitation. Following the discovery in August 2004 of high-grade gold and copper in Western Eritrea, the Eritrean authorities prohibited all mining exploration by foreign companies in September while it reassessed its mining legislation. The ban was lifted in January 2005 with the Government announcing the possibility of increasing its option to buy into mining projects from the current maximum of 20% to 30%.

The manufacturing sector provided an estimated 11.0% of GDP in 2003. Until mid-1997 imported petroleum was processed at the Assab refinery, whose entire output of petroleum products was delivered to Ethiopia. The authorities announced that they would import refined petroleum for the immediate future. Eritrea purchases its own petroleum requirements from Ethiopia under a quota arrangement; however, trade between the two countries was disrupted by the outbreak of hostilities in May 1998. In late 2004 the Government suspended the sale of petrol to the public following fuel rationing precipitated by the rising cost of petroleum on world markets. The GDP of the sector increased, in real terms, at an average annual rate of 7.9% in 1992–2003, but declined by 1.1% in 2003.

Most electric energy is provided by four thermal power stations, largely dependent on imported fuel. Imports of fuel and energy comprised an estimated 8.9% of the total cost of imports in 2000. However, electricity is provided to only some 10% of the population, the remainder relying on fuelwood and animal products. In mid-1999 the discovery of geothermal potential at the Alid volcanic centre raised hopes that Eritrea's energy problems could be alleviated.

The services sector contributed an estimated 60.8% of GDP in 2003. The dominant services are trade, public administration and transport. The GDP of the services sector increased, in real terms, at an average annual rate of 5.7% in 1992–2003. Services GDP increased by 1.0% in 2003.

In 2002, according to estimates by the IMF, Eritrea recorded a trade deficit of US $481.7m., and there was a deficit of $99.6m. on the current account of the balance of payments. In 2001 the principal sources of non-petroleum imports were Italy (accounting for an estimated 18.7% of the total), Saudi Arabia and the United Arab Emirates. Exports in that year were mostly to Sudan (48.9%) and Italy. Eritrea's principal exports in 2002 were food and live animals (73.2% of the total), crude materials and basic manufactures. The main non-petroleum imports in that year were machinery and transport equipment (29.6% of the total), food and live animals, and basic manufactures.

In 2002 it was estimated that Eritrea's budget deficit reached 2,728.5m. nakfa, equivalent to 30.2% of GDP. Eritrea's external debt at the end of 2002 totalled US $527.6m., of which $496.4m. was long-term public debt. The cost of debt-servicing represented 4.7% of the value of exports of goods and services in that year. The annual rate of inflation averaged 8.9% in 1996–2002. Consumer prices increased by an estimated average of 14.6% in 2001 and by 16.9% in 2002. Unemployment and underemployment are estimated to affect as many as 50% of the labour force.

In 1993 Eritrea was admitted to the group of African, Caribbean and Pacific (ACP) countries party to the Lomé Convention; in September 2001 Eritrea ratified the Cotonou Agreement (see p. 262), the successor of the Lomé Convention. Eritrea became a member of the IMF in 1994.

Since independence the Eritrean Government has placed emphasis on improving agricultural productivity, promoting export-orientated industries, developing financial and tourism services, and restructuring the public administration. However, the country has experienced severe difficulties and many of the Government's initial aims have not been realised. In November 1997 the introduction of the nakfa as the national currency (Eritrea had retained the Ethiopian birr as its monetary unit since independence), initially at par with the birr, led to the outbreak of hostilities with Ethiopia. Cross-border trade was adversely affected and in May 1998 Ethiopia re-routed its maritime commerce via Djibouti. The conflict, which ended in December 2000, had a devastating effect on the Eritrean economy. Trade with Ethiopia, which previously accounted for two-thirds of Eritrean exports, virtually ceased, and Eritrea was estimated to have spent at least US $1m. per day on the war. This expenditure, coupled with the failure of successive harvests, increased Eritrea's already considerable reliance on donations from aid organizations, and the need to feed, clothe and shelter the vast numbers of people displaced during the war has placed a further strain on government finances. The planned demobilization of large numbers of the Eritrean armed forces has proceeded only slowly, and President Afewerki's increasingly repressive tendencies during the early 2000s resulted in the cancellation and suspension of some $400m. of development funding, on which the country remains heavily dependent. With the March–May rains failing to materialize Eritrea suffered severe drought and food shortages during 2004 and by early 2005 it was estimated that some 2.3m. Eritreans were in need of humanitarian assistance. The situation in 2005 was not expected to improve and a number of serious economic challenges remained for Eritrea, including the reduction of its large budget and trade deficits. Furthermore, GDP growth in that year was projected at just 0.7%, while the country was also facing the possibility of a second consecutive year with levels of inflation over 20%.

Education

Education is provided free of charge in government schools and at the University of Asmara. There are also some fee-paying private schools. Education is officially compulsory for children between seven and 13 years of age. Primary education begins at the age of seven and lasts for five years. Secondary education, beginning at 12 years of age, lasts for up to six years, comprising a first cycle of two years and a second of four years. In 1996 the total enrolment at primary and secondary schools was equivalent to 37% of the school-age population (males 41%; females 33%). In 2001 primary enrolment included 42.5% of children in the relevant age-group, while the comparable ratio for secondary enrolment was only 21.3%). Total government expenditure on education and training in 2002 was an estimated 467.2m. nakfa (7.6% of total spending). In 1997/98 there were 3,096 students enrolled at the University of Asmara or at equivalent level institutions.

Public Holidays

2005: 1 January (New Year's Day), 6 January (Epiphany), 21 January* (Id al-Adha/Arafat), 24 May (Independence Day), 20 June (Martyrs' Day), 1 September (anniversary of the start of the armed struggle), 4 November* (Id al-Fitr, end of Ramadan), 25 December (Christmas).

2006: 1 January (New Year's Day), 6 January (Epiphany), 11 January* (Id al-Adha/Arafat), 24 May (Independence Day), 20 June (Martyrs' Day), 1 September (anniversary of the start of the armed struggle), 24 October* (Id al-Fitr, end of Ramadan), 25 December (Christmas).

*These holidays are dependent on the Islamic lunar calendar and may vary by one or two days from the dates given.

Weights and Measures

The metric system is in force.

Statistical Survey

Source (unless otherwise stated): Ministry of Trade and Industry, POB 1844, Asmara; tel. (1) 118386; fax (1) 120586.

Area and Population

AREA, POPULATION AND DENSITY*

Area (sq km)	121,144†
Population (census results)	
9 May 1984	
Males	1,374,452
Females	1,373,852
Total	2,748,304
Population (UN estimates at mid-year)‡	
2001	3,847,000
2002	3,991,000
2003	4,141,000
Density (per sq km) at mid-2003	34.2

* Including the Assab district.
† 46,774 sq miles.
‡ Source: UN, *World Population Prospects: The 2002 Revision.*

PRINCIPAL TOWNS
(estimated population at January 2005)

Asmara (capital) .	563,948	Keren	58,080
Assab	78,018	Mitsiwa (Massawa) .	39,098

Source: Stefan Helders, *World Gazetteer* (internet www.world-gazetteer.com).

BIRTHS AND DEATHS
(UN estimates, averages per year)

	1985–90	1990–95	1995–2000
Birth rate (per 1,000)	44.2	43.2	42.1
Death rate (per 1,000)	16.3	14.2	12.6

Source: UN, *World Population Prospects: The 2002 Revision.*

Expectation of life (WHO estimates, years at birth): 57.6 (males 55.8; females 59.3) in 2002 (Source: WHO, *World Development Report*).

Health and Welfare

KEY INDICATORS

Total fertility rate (children per woman, 2002)	5.5
Under-5 mortality rate (per 1,000 live births, 2003) . . .	85
HIV/AIDS (% of persons aged 15–49, 2003)	2.70
Physicians (per 1,000 head, 1996)	0.03
Health expenditure (2001): US $ per head (PPP)	36
Health expenditure (2001): % of GDP	5.7
Health expenditure (2001): public (% of total)	65.1
Access to water (% of persons, 2002)	57
Access to sanitation (% of persons, 2002)	9
Human Development Index (2002): ranking	156
Human Development Index (2002): value	0.439

For sources and definitions, see explanatory note on p. vi.

Agriculture

PRINCIPAL CROPS
('000 metric tons)

	2001	2002	2003
Wheat	25.4	13.0	3.4
Barley	44.9	9.7	8.6
Maize	9.1	3.0	4.5
Millet	30.3	5.8	16.9
Sorghum	78.8	28.4	64.1
Potatoes	17.4	15.3	10.9
Other roots and tubers*	90.0	85.0	85.0
Dry beans	4.0	0.4	0.6
Dry broad beans*	1.8	1.8	1.8
Dry peas	1.1	2.8	1.0*
Chick-peas	8.2	1.8	1.4
Lentils*	3.0	3.0	3.0
Vetches*	5.0	4.5	4.5
Other pulses*	32.0	25.0	25.0
Groundnuts (in shell)	1.4	1.2	1.0*
Sesame seed	1.9	1.4	7.0
Linseed	0.6	0.2*	0.2*
Vegetables*	28.0	23.0	23.0
Fruits and berries*	3.8	2.0	2.0

* FAO estimate(s).

Source: FAO.

LIVESTOCK
(FAO estimates, '000 head, year ending September)

	2001	2002	2003
Cattle	2,200	1,900	1,927
Sheep	2,150	2,000	2,100
Goats	1,700	1,700	1,700
Camels	75	75	75
Poultry	1,370	1,370	1,370

Source: FAO.

LIVESTOCK PRODUCTS
(FAO estimates, '000 metric tons)

	2001	2002	2003
Beef and veal	16.7	14.2	16.7
Mutton and lamb	5.7	5.5	5.6
Goat meat	5.8	5.8	5.8
Poultry meat	2.1	2.1	2.1
Camels' milk	5.1	5.1	5.1
Cows' milk	52.0	39.2	39.2
Goats' milk	8.5	8.5	8.5
Sheep's milk	3.9	3.9	3.9
Hen eggs	2.0	2.0	2.0
Wool: greasy	0.8	0.8	0.8
Wool: scoured	0.4	0.4	0.4
Cattle hides	3.2	2.7	3.2
Sheepskins	0.6	0.6	0.6
Goatskins	0.7	0.7	0.7

Source: FAO.

Fishing

(metric tons, live weight)

	2000	2001	2002
Lizardfishes	3,177	2,574	3,274
Sea catfishes	851	436	273
Threadfin breams	1,757	1,115	675
Silver grunts	472	199	152
Grunts and sweetlips	536	435	198
Emperors (Scavengers)	443	345	164
Barracudas	684	2	455
Carangids	2,026	1,014	730
Narrow-barred Spanish mackerel	217	280	177
Penaeus shrimps	519	790	508
Total catch (incl. others)	12,612	8,820	7,832

Source: FAO.

Mining

(estimates, '000 metric tons, unless otherwise indicated)

	2001	2002	2003
Gold (kilograms)	107	n.a.	n.a.
Marble (sq m)	17,656	12,851	12,900
Limestone	3	3	3
Salt	78	116	117

Source: US Geological Survey.

Finance

CURRENCY AND EXCHANGE RATES

Monetary Units
100 cents = 1 nakfa.

Sterling, Dollar and Euro Equivalents (31 December 2004)
£1 sterling = 26.63 nakfa;
US $1 = 13.79 nakfa;
€1 = 18.78 nakfa;
1,000 nakfa = £37.55 = $72.53 = €53.25.

Note: Following its secession from Ethiopia in May 1993, Eritrea retained the Ethiopian currency, the birr. An exchange rate of US $1 = 5.000 birr was introduced in October 1992 and remained in force until April 1994, when it was adjusted to $1 = 5.130 birr. Further adjustments were made subsequently. In addition to the official exchange rate, the Bank of Eritrea applied a marginal auction rate (determined at fortnightly auctions of foreign exchange, conducted by the National Bank of Ethiopia) to aid-funded imports and to most transactions in services. A more depreciated preferential rate applied to remittances of foreign exchange by Eritreans abroad, to proceeds from exports and to most payments for imports. On 1 April 1997 Eritrea unified the official and preferential exchange rates at $1 = 7.20 birr (which had been the preferential rate since January 1996). In November 1997 the Government introduced a separate national currency, the nakfa, replacing (and initially at par with) the Ethiopian birr. The exchange rate in relation to the US dollar was initially set at the prevailing unified rate, but from 1 May 1998 a mechanism to provide a market-related exchange rate was established.

AVERAGE EXCHANGE RATE (nakfa per US $)

2002	13.9582
2003	13.8779
2004	13.7875

BUDGET
(million birr/nakfa)

Revenue*	2000	2001†	2002‡
Tax revenue	982.7	1,278.8	1,538.2
Direct taxes	473.5	572.9	552.8
Taxes on personal income	122.7	136.9	159.6
Taxes on business profits	299.9	387.5	337.2
Rehabilitation tax	10.4	2.9	1.8
Domestic sales tax (incl. stamp duties)	238.1	297.0	368.3
Import duties and taxes	271.0	409.0	617.1
Port fees and charges	59.4	103.3	148.5
Other current revenue	743.4	429.4	575.6
Extraordinary revenue	322.9	174.9	29.2
Total	2,108.3	1,986.4	2,291.4

Expenditure	2000	2001†	2002‡
Current expenditure	4,333.8	4,160.4	4,147.2
General services	2,722.2	2,444.7	2,619.5
Internal affairs	25.9	36.4	46.9
Regional administration . .	328.8	326.7	164.8
Foreign affairs	102.7	103.6	179.1
Defence§	2,220.3	1,883.6	2,104.4
Economic services	55.7	64.6	71.1
Agriculture and natural resources	32.9	34.3	37.5
Mining and energy	2.9	3.1	3.4
Construction and urban development	7.8	9.2	13.7
Transport and communications	5.6	5.7	6.7
Social services	361.8	345.6	394.8
Education and training . .	163.8	182.0	182.9
Health	99.3	97.6	110.8
Demobilization of ex-combatants	—	6.9	7.8
Capital expenditure	1,064.9	2,005.0	1,991.1
General services	117.4	241.2	227.8
Economic development . . .	581.4	1,359.0	955.6
Agriculture and natural resources	116.2	164.7	131.3
Trade, industry and tourism .	1.2	4.7	5.8
Construction, transport and communications	262.7	551.2	378.4
Social development	366.1	404.8	807.7
Education	262.2	231.2	284.3
Health	85.9	143.2	478.2
Total	5,398.7	6,165.4	6,138.3

* Excluding grants received (million nakfa): 1,204.8 in 2000 (current 1,165.5, capital 39.3); 1,375.6 (estimate) in 2001 (current 913.6, capital 462.0); 1,118.4 (preliminary) in 2002 (current 510.0, capital 608.4).
† Preliminary figures.
‡ Estimates.
§ Including some demobilization costs.
Source: IMF, *Eritrea: Selected Issues and Statistical Appendix* (June 2003).

MONEY SUPPLY
(million nakfa at 31 December)

	2001	2002	2003
Currency outside banks . . .	1,868	2,279	2,765
Demand deposits at banks . . .	3,081	3,667	4,036
Total money (incl. others) . .	5,035	5,982	6,927

Source: IMF, *International Financial Statistics.*

COST OF LIVING
(Consumer Price Index for Asmara at December; base: 1996 = 100)

	2000	2001*	2002*
Food	190.4	200.3	236.0
Beverages and tobacco	144.5	178.4	184.7
Clothing and footwear	133.0	143.0	181.4
Energy, water and building materials	153.4	178.1	224.1
Furniture and housing equipment	166.7	170.7	222.8
Medical care	124.1	126.5	135.3
Transport and communications .	107.0	112.3	247.8
Recreation and education . . .	152.3	149.5	175.6
Personal care	147.3	177.2	196.5
All items	147.6	169.2	197.8

* Preliminary figures.

Source: African Development Bank.

NATIONAL ACCOUNTS
(million birr/nakfa at current prices)
Gross Domestic Product by Economic Activity

	2000	2001*	2002*
Agriculture, forestry and fishing .	871.1	1,279.2	941.3
Mining and quarrying	5.8	2.8	3.3
Manufacturing†	644.2	772.6	939.1
Electricity and water	68.4	80.8	100.8
Construction	607.8	746.3	954.0
Wholesale and retail trade . . .	1,136.2	1,369.5	1,672.6
Transport and communications .	727.8	877.0	1,071.3
Financial services	189.2	228.0	278.5
Dwellings and domestic services .	121.9	143.5	169.5
Public administration and services	1,037.7	1,197.7	1,387.6
Other services	362.7	436.6	528.0
GDP at factor cost	5,772.8	7,134.0	8,045.8
Indirect taxes, *less* subsidies . .	427.7	637.0	985.4
GDP in purchasers' values . .	6,200.5	7,771.0	9,031.2

* Preliminary figures.
† Including handicrafts and small-scale industry.

Source: IMF, *Eritrea: Selected Issues and Statistical Appendix* (June 2003).

BALANCE OF PAYMENTS
(US $ million)

	2000	2001*	2002†
Exports of goods f.o.b.	36.7	19.9	51.8
Imports of goods c.i.f.	−470.3	−536.7	−533.4
Trade balance	−433.5	−516.7	−481.7
Exports of services	60.7	127.5	132.6
Imports of services	−28.3	−33.4	−30.3
Balance on goods and services	−401.1	−422.6	−379.4
Other income (net)	−1.4	−4.6	−6.1
Balance on goods, services and income	−402.5	−427.2	−385.5
Private unrequited transfers (net)	195.7	175.0	205.6
Official unrequited transfers (net)	102.4	120.8	80.3
Current balance	−104.5	−131.4	−99.6
Capital account (net)	—	7.3	3.6
Financial account	98.7	94.8	64.6
Short-term capital (net) . . .	−14.7	18.7	15.9
Net errors and omissions . . .	−9.5	36.5	−7.6
Overall balance	−15.2	7.2	−39.0

* Preliminary figures.
† Estimates.
Source: IMF, *Eritrea: Selected Issues and Statistical Appendix* (June 2003).

External Trade
PRINCIPAL COMMODITIES
(million nakfa)

Imports c.i.f. (excl. petroleum)	2000	2001*	2002†
Food and live animals	1,125.7	1,677.1	1,439.1
Animal and vegetable oils, fats and waxes	111.1	156.0	85.2
Chemicals and related products .	111.2	156.0	85.2
Basic manufactures	726.7	818.0	1,230.3
Machinery and transport equipment	771.2	994.0	1,610.4
Miscellaneous manufactured articles	245.3	346.0	501.3
Total (incl. others)	3,344.0	4,355.7	5,447.3

Exports f.o.b.	2000	2001*	2002†
Food and live animals	109.8	89.8	422.6
Crude materials (inedible) except fuels	37.7	31.0	62.6
Chemicals and related products .	6.3	7.1	4.6
Basic manufactures	26.1	57.1	56.0
Miscellaneous manufactured articles	4.7	5.3	19.2
Total (incl. others)	188.7	193.4	577.6

* Preliminary figures.
† Estimates.

Source: IMF, *Eritrea: Selected Issues and Statistical Appendix* (June 2003).

PRINCIPAL TRADING PARTNERS
(million nakfa)

Imports c.i.f.	1999	2000	2001*
Belgium	76.8	118.1	121.6
Germany	125.0	103.4	120.9
Italy	480.9	436.3	806.0
Netherlands	88.2	103.7	141.3
Saudi Arabia	521.8	374.2	714.3
United Arab Emirates . .	603.5	637.0	659.0
United Kingdom	108.5	155.0	98.4
USA	90.9	177.5	207.7
Total (incl. others)	3,128.6	3,344.0	4,313.4

Exports f.o.b.	1999	2000	2001*
Djibouti	28.3	—	0.3
Germany	5.6	4.6	6.7
Italy	8.6	7.4	15.9
Netherlands	2.6	9.8	2.3
Saudi Arabia	12.9	17.4	3.1
Sudan	54.9	94.8	94.6
United Arab Emirates . . .	7.4	0.5	1.1
Total (incl. others)	163.6	188.7	193.4

* Preliminary figures.

Source: IMF, *Eritrea: Selected Issues and Statistical Appendix* (June 2003).

Transport

ROAD TRAFFIC
(motor vehicles in use)

	1996	1997	1998
Number of registered vehicles . .	27,013	31,276	35,942

SHIPPING
Merchant Fleet
(registered at 31 December)

	2001	2002	2003
Number of vessels	12	12	12
Displacement (grt)	20,686	20,686	21,092

Source: Lloyd's Register-Fairplay, *World Fleet Statistics*.

CIVIL AVIATION

	1996	1997	1998
Passengers ('000)	168.1	173.8	105.2

Tourism

ARRIVALS BY COUNTRY OF ORIGIN

	2000	2001	2002
Belgium, Luxembourg and Netherlands	1,435	1,444	373
Germany	469	958	1,015
India	562	2,231	2,549
Italy	1,691	2,934	2,859
Japan	1,214	1,237	701
Sudan	2,875	5,517	6,262
USA	1,464	1,736	1,693
Total (incl. others)	70,355	113,024	100,828

Tourism receipts (US $ million): 36 in 2000; 74 in 2001; 73 in 2002.

Source: World Tourism Organization.

Communications Media

	2001	2002	2003
Telephones ('000 main lines in use)	32.0	35.9	38.1
Personal computers ('000 in use) .	7	9	12
Internet users ('000)	10.0	10.0	9.5

Mobile cellular telephones (subscribers): 12,000 in 2004.

Radio receivers ('000 in use): 345 in 1997.

Book production (1993): 106 titles (including 23 pamphlets) and 420,000 copies (including 60,000 pamphlets). Figures for books, excluding pamphlets, refer only to school textbooks (64 titles; 323,000 copies) and government publications (19 titles; 37,000 copies).

Television receivers ('000 in use): 100 in 2000.

Facsimile machines (number in use): 1,771 in 2000.

Sources: mainly UNESCO, *Statistical Yearbook*; International Telecommunication Union.

Education

(1996/97)

	Institutions	Teachers	Pupils
Pre-primary	61	207	7,443
Primary	549	5,476	240,737
Secondary: General	n.a.	1,959	88,054
Secondary: Teacher-training . .	n.a.	33	359
Secondary: Vocational . . .	n.a.	79	674
University and equivalent level* .	n.a.	198	3,096

* Figures refer to 1997/98.

Source: UNESCO, *Statistical Yearbook*.

Adult literacy rate (UNESCO estimates): 56.7% (males 68.2%; females 45.6%) in 2001 (Source: UN Development Programme, *Human Development Report*).

Directory

The Constitution

On 23 May 1997 the Constituent Assembly unanimously adopted the Eritrean Constitution. A presidential regime was instituted, with the President to be elected for a maximum of two five-year terms. The President, as Head of State, has extensive powers and appoints, with the approval of the National Assembly (the legislature), the ministers, the commissioners, the Auditor-General, the President of the central bank and the judges of the Supreme Court. The President's mandate can be revoked if two-thirds of the members of the National Assembly so demand. 'Conditional' political pluralism is authorized. Pending the election of a new National Assembly, legislative power was to be held by a Transitional National Assembly, comprising the 75 members of the PFDJ Central Committee, 60 members of the former Constituent Assembly and 15 representatives of Eritreans residing abroad.

The Government

HEAD OF STATE

President: Issaias Afewerki (assumed power May 1991; elected President by the National Assembly 8 June 1993).

CABINET
(April 2005)

President: Issaias Afewerki.

Minister of Defence: Gen. Sebhat Ephrem.

Minister of Justice: Fawzia Hashim.

Minister of Foreign Affairs: Ali Sayyid Abdullah.

Minister of Information: Naizghi Kiflu.

Minister of Finance: Berhane Abrehe.

Minister of Trade and Industry: Dr Giorgis Teklemikael.

Minister of Agriculture: Arefaine Berhe.

Minister of Labour and Human Welfare: Askalu Menkerios.

Minister of Marine Resources: Ahmed Haji Ali.

Minister of Construction: Abraha Asfaha.

Minister of Energy and Mines: Tesfai Gebreselassie.

Minister of Education: Osman Salih Muhammad.

Minister of Health: Dr Salih Mekki.

Minister of Transport and Communications: Woldemikael Abraha.

Minister of Tourism: Amna Nur Husayn.

Minister of Land, Water and the Environment: Tesfai Ghirmazion.

MINISTRIES AND COMMISSIONS

Office of the President: POB 257, Asmara; tel. (1) 122132; fax (1) 125123.

Ministry of Agriculture: POB 1048, Asmara; tel. (1) 181499; fax (1) 181415.

Ministry of Construction: POB 841, Asmara; tel. (1) 119077; fax (1) 120661.

Ministry of Defence: POB 629, Asmara; tel. (1) 115493; fax (1) 124920.

Ministry of Education: POB 5610, Asmara; tel. (1) 113044; fax (1) 113866.

Ministry of Energy and Mines: POB 5285, Asmara; tel. (1) 116872; fax (1) 127652.

Ministry of Finance: POB 896, Asmara; tel. (1) 118131; fax (1) 127947.

Ministry of Fisheries: POB 923, Asmara; tel. (1) 120400; fax (1) 122185; e-mail mofisha@eol.com.er.

Ministry of Foreign Affairs: POB 190, Asmara; tel. (1) 127838; fax (1) 123788; e-mail tesfai@wg.eol.

Ministry of Health: POB 212, Asmara; tel. (1) 117549; fax (1) 112899.

Ministry of Information: POB 242, Asmara; tel. (1) 117111; fax (1) 124647.

Ministry of Justice: POB 241, Asmara; tel. (1) 127739; fax (1) 126422.

Ministry of Labour and Human Welfare: POB 5252, Asmara; tel. (1) 181846; fax (1) 181649; e-mail mlhw@eol.com.er.

Ministry of Land, Water and the Environment: POB 976, Asmara; tel. (1) 118021; fax (1) 123285.

Ministry of Local Government: POB 225, Asmara; tel. (1) 127734.

Ministry of Tourism: POB 1010, Asmara; tel. (1) 126997; fax (1) 126949; e-mail eritrea_tourism@cts.com.er; internet www.shaebia.org/mot.html.

Ministry of Trade and Industry: POB 1844, Asmara; tel. (1) 118386; fax (1) 110586.

Ministry of Transport and Communications: POB 6465, Asmara; tel. (1) 123681; fax (1) 127048; e-mail motc.rez@eol.com.er.

Eritrean Relief and Refugee Commission: POB 1098, Asmara; tel. (1) 182222; fax (1) 182970; e-mail john@errec.er.punchdown.org.

Land and Housing Commission: POB 348, Asmara; tel. (1) 117400.

Provincial Administrators

There are six administrative regions in Eritrea, each with regional, sub-regional and village administrations.

Anseba Province: Abdalla Musa.

Debub Province: Mesfin Hagos.

Debubawi Keyih Bahri Province: Musa Rab'a.

Gash-Barka Province: Mustafa Nur Hussein.

Maakel Province: Semere Rusom.

Semenawi Keyih Bahri Province: Ibrahim Idris Totil.

Legislature

NATIONAL ASSEMBLY

In accordance with transitional arrangements formulated in Decree No. 37 of May 1993, the National Assembly consists of the Central Committee of the People's Front for Democracy and Justice (PFDJ) and 60 other members: 30 from the Provincial Assemblies and an additional 30 members, including a minimum of 10 women, to be nominated by the PFDJ Central Committee. The legislative body 'outlines the internal and external policies of the government, regulates their implementation, approves the budget and elects a president for the country'. The National Assembly is to hold regular sessions every six months under the chairmanship of the President. In his role as Head of the Government and Commander-in-Chief of the Army, the President nominates individuals to head the various government departments. These nominations are ratified by the legislative body. In March 1994 the National Assembly voted to alter its composition: it would henceforth comprise the 75 members of the Central Committee of the PFDJ and 75 directly elected members. In May 1997, following the adoption of the Constitution, the Constituent Assembly empowered a Transitional National Assembly (comprising the 75 members of the PFDJ, 60 members of the former Constituent Assembly and 15 representatives of Eritreans residing abroad) to act as the legislature until elections were held for a new National Assembly.

Chairman of the Transitional National Assembly: Issaias Afewerki.

Political Organizations

Afar Federal Alliance.

Democratic Movement for the Liberation of Eritrea: opposition group; Leader Hamid Turky.

Democratic Movement for the Liberation of Eritrean Kunama.

Eritrean Democratic Party (EDP): e-mail mdeasfrica@eritrea1.org; internet eritrea1.org; f. 2001 as the Eritrean People's Liberation Front—Democratic Party (EPLF-DP); breakaway group from the PFDJ; name changed to above in 2004; Leader Mesfin Hagos.

Eritrean Islamic Jihad (EIJ): radical opposition group; in Aug. 1993 split into a mil. wing and a political wing, led by Sheikh Mohamed Arafa.

Eritrean Islamic Party for Justice and Development (EIPJD) (Al-Hezb Al-Islami Al-Eritree Liladalah Wetenmiya): internet www.alkhalas.org; founded as Al-Khalas; Leader Khalil Muhammad Amer.

Eritrean Liberation Front (ELF): f. 1958; commenced armed struggle against Ethiopia in 1961; subsequently split into numerous factions (see below); mainly Muslim support; opposes the PFDJ; principal factions:

Eritrean Liberation Front—Central Command (ELF—CC): f. 1982; Chair. Abdallah Idriss.

Eritrean Liberation Front—National Council (ELF—NC): Leader Hassan Ali Assad.

Eritrean Liberation Front—Revolutionary Council (ELF—RC): Pres. Seyoum Ogbamichael; Leader Ahmed Mohamed Nasser.

Eritrean National Alliance (ENA): f. 1999 as the Alliance of Eritrean National Forces, adopted present name in 2002; Chair. Hiruy Tedla Bairu; Sec.-Gen. Husayn Khalifa.

Eritrean Popular Movement (EPM): f. 2004; Transitional leaders Adhanom Gebremariam, Abdallah Adem, Muhammad Ibrahim.

Gash Setit Organization: Leader Ismail Nada.

Movement for Democratic Change: Leader Dr Tesfai Brinji.

People's Democratic Front for the Liberation of Eritrea.

People's Front for Democracy and Justice (PFDJ): POB 1081, Asmara; tel. (1) 121399; fax (1) 120848; internet www.shaebia.org; f. 1970 as the Eritrean Popular Liberation Forces, following a split in the Eritrean Liberation Front; renamed the Eritrean People's Liberation Front in 1977; adopted present name in Feb. 1994; Christian and Muslim support; in May 1991 took control of Eritrea and formed provisional Govt; formed transitional Govt in May 1993; Chair. ISSAIAS AFEWERKI; Sec.-Gen. ALAMIN MOHAMED SAID.

Red Sea Afar Democratic Organization: Afar opposition group; Sec.-Gen. AMIN AHMMAD.

Diplomatic Representation

EMBASSIES IN ERITREA

China, People's Republic: 16 Ogaden St, POB 204, Asmara; tel. (1) 185271; fax (1) 185275; Ambassador HUANG YONGAN.

Denmark: Ras Dashan St 11, POB 6300, Asmara; tel. (1) 124346; fax (1) 124343; e-mail asmamb@um.dk; Chargé d'affaires a.i. PETER TRUELSEN.

Djibouti: POB 5589, Asmara; tel. (1) 354961; fax (1) 351831; Ambassador AHMAD ISSA.

Egypt: POB 5577, Asmara; tel. (1) 123603; fax (1) 123294; Ambassador Dr RIFAT AL-ANSARI.

Ethiopia: Franklin D. Roosevelt St, POB 5688, Asmara; tel. (1) 116365; fax (1) 116144; Ambassador AWALOM WOLDU (recalled May 1998).

France: POB 209, Asmara; tel. (1) 126599; fax (1) 121036; e-mail af@gemel.com.er; Ambassador GÉRARD SAMBRANA.

Germany: 24 Ogaden Ave, POB 5589, Asmara; tel. (1) 182670; fax (1) 182900; Ambassador ELMAR TIMPE.

Israel: POB 5600, Asmara; tel. (1) 185626; fax (1) 185550; e-mail isremb@eol.com.er; Ambassador URI SAVIR.

Italy: POB 220, Asmara; tel. (1) 120160; fax (1) 121115; e-mail iea@eol.com.er; Ambassador EMANUELE PIGNATELLI.

Japan: Asmara; Ambassador MAKOTO ASSAMI.

Libya: Asmara.

Russia: POB 5667, Asmara; tel. (1) 127172; fax (1) 127164; e-mail rusemb@eol.com.er; Ambassador ALEXANDER OBLOV.

Saudi Arabia: POB 5599, Asmara; tel. (1) 120171; fax (1) 121027; Ambassador ABDUL R. IBRAHIM AT-TOELMI.

Sudan: Asmara; tel. (1) 202072; fax (1) 200760; e-mail sudanemb@eol.com.er; Ambassador Dr MAHJOUB AL-BASHA.

United Kingdom: 24 Emperor Yohannes Ave, POB 5584, Asmara; tel. (1) 120145; fax (1) 120104; e-mail alembca@gemel.com.er; Ambassador MICHAEL MURRAY.

USA: Franklin D. Roosevelt St, POB 211, Asmara; tel. (1) 120004; fax (1) 127584; Ambassador SCOTT DELISI.

Yemen: POB 5566, Asmara; tel. (1) 114434; fax (1) 117921; Ambassador Dr AKRAM ABD AL-MARIK AL-QABRI.

Judicial System

The judicial system operates on the basis of transitional laws which incorporate pre-independence laws of the Eritrean People's Liberation Front, revised Ethiopian laws, customary laws and post-independence enacted laws. The independence of the judiciary in the discharge of its functions is unequivocally stated in Decree No. 37, which defines the powers and duties of the Government. It is subject only to the law and to no other authority. The court structure is composed of first instance sub-zonal courts, appellate and first instance zonal courts, appellate and first instance high courts, a panel of high court judges, presided over by the President of the High Court, and a Supreme Court presided over by the Chief Justice, as a court of last resort. The judges of the Supreme Court are appointed by the President of the State, subject to confirmation by the National Assembly.

Supreme Court: Asmara.

High Court: POB 241, Asmara; tel. (1) 127739; fax (1) 201828; e-mail prshict@eol.com.er.

Religion

Eritrea is almost equally divided between Muslims and Christians. Most Christians are adherents of the Orthodox Church, although there are Protestant and Roman Catholic communities. A small number of the population follow traditional beliefs.

CHRISTIANITY

The Eritrean Orthodox Church

In September 1993 the separation of the Eritrean Orthodox Church from the Ethiopian Orthodox Church was agreed by the respective church leaderships. The Eritrean Orthodox Church announced that it was to create a diocese of each of the country's then 10 provinces. The first five bishops of the Eritrean Orthodox Church were consecrated in Cairo in September 1994. In May 1998 Eritrea's first Patriarch (Abune) was consecrated in Alexandria.

Patriarch (Abune): Archbishop ANTONIOS.

The Roman Catholic Church

At 31 December 2002 there were an estimated 144,640 adherents in the country.

Bishop of Asmara: Rt Rev. ABBA MENGHISTEAB TESFAMARIAM, 19 Gonder St, POB 244, Asmara; tel. (1) 120206; fax (1) 126519; e-mail kimehret@gemel.com.er.

Bishop of Barentu: Rt Rev. THOMAS OSMAN, POB 9, Barentu; tel. and fax (1) 127283.

Bishop of Keren: Rt Rev. KIDANE YEBIO, POB 460, Keren; tel. (1) 401907; fax (1) 401604; e-mail cek@gemel.com.er.

The Anglican Communion

Within the Episcopal Church in Jerusalem and the Middle East, Eritrea lies within the jurisdiction of the Bishop in Egypt.

Leader: ASFAHA MAHARY.

ISLAM

Eritrea's main Muslim communities are concentrated in the western lowlands, the northern highlands and the eastern coastal region.

Leader: Sheikh AL-AMIN OSMAN AL-AMIN.

The Press

Business Perspective: POB 856, Asmara; tel. (1) 121589; fax (1) 120138; monthly; Tigrinya, Arabic and English; publ. by Eritrean National Chamber of Commerce; Editor MOHAMMED-SFAF HAMMED.

Chamber News: POB 856, Asmara; tel. (1) 120045; fax (1) 120138; monthly; Tigrinya, Arabic and English; publ. by Asmara Chamber of Commerce.

Eritrea Profile: POB 247, Asmara; f. 1994; weekly; English; publ. by the Ministry of Information.

Hadas Eritra (New Eritrea): Asmara; f. 1991; six times a week; in English, Tigrinya and Arabic; govt publ.; Editor PAULOS NETABAY ABRAHAM; circ. 49,200.

Meqahil: Asmara; Editor MATHEWOS HABEAB.

Newsletter: POB 856, Asmara; tel. (1) 121589; fax (1) 120138; e-mail encc@aol.com.er; monthly; Tigrinya, Arabic and English; publ. by Eritrean National Chamber of Commerce; Editor MOHAMMED-SFAF HAMMED.

Broadcasting and Communications

Ministry of Transport and Communications (Communications Department): POB 4918, Asmara; tel. (1) 115847; fax (1) 126966; e-mail motc.rez@eol.com.er; Dir-Gen. ESTIFANOS AFEWERKI.

TELECOMMUNICATIONS

Eritrea Telecommunication Services Co. (EriTel): 11 Semaetat St, POB 234, Asmara; tel. (1) 124655; fax (1) 120938; e-mail eritel@tse.com.er; f. 1991; Gen. Man. TESFASELASSIE BERHANE.

Ericel: Asmara; f. 2001; operates mobile cellular telephone network.

BROADCASTING

Radio

Voice of the Broad Masses of Eritrea (Dimtsi Hafash): POB 242, Asmara; tel. (1) 120426; fax (1) 126747; govt-controlled; programmes in Arabic, Tigrinya, Tigre, Saho, Oromo, Amharic, Afar, Bilien, Nara, Hedareb and Kunama; Dir-Gen. TESFAI KELETA; Technical Dir BERHANE GEREZGIHER.

Television

ERI-TV: Asmara; f. 1992; govt station providing educational, tech. and information service; broadcasting began in 1993 in Arabic, Tigre and Tigrinya; transmissions limited to Asmara and surrounding areas; Dir-Gen. ALI ABDU.

Finance

(cap. = capital; dep. = deposits; m. = million; brs = branches; amounts in Ethiopian birr)

In November 1997 Eritrea adopted the nakfa as its unit of currency, replacing the Ethiopian birr, which had been Eritrea's monetary unit since independence.

BANKING

Central Bank

Bank of Eritrea: POB 849, 21 Victory Ave, Asmara; tel. (1) 123036; fax (1) 123162; e-mail tekieb@boe.gov.er; f. 1993; bank of issue; Gov. TEKIE BEYENE.

Other Banks

Commercial Bank of Eritrea: POB 219, 208 Liberty Ave, Asmara; tel. (1) 121844; fax (1) 124887; e-mail gm.cber@gemel.com.er; f. 1991; dep. 5,100m. (Dec. 1996); Gen. Man. YAMANE TESFAI; 15 brs.

Eritrean Development and Investment Bank: POB 1266, Asmara; tel. (1) 126777; e-mail edib@gemel.com.er; f. 1996; cap. 60m., total assets 290m. (2003); provides medium- to long-term credit; Gen. Man. Dr GOITOM W. MARIAM; 4 brs.

Housing and Commerce Bank of Eritrea: POB 235, Asmara; tel. (1) 120350; fax (1) 120401; e-mail hcb@gemel.com.er; f. 1994; cap. 33m., total assets 1,824.7m. (Dec. 1999); finances residential and commercial construction projects and commercial loans; CEO Dr ARAIA TSEGGAI; 7 brs.

INSURANCE

National Insurance Corporation of Eritrea (NICE): NICE Bldg, POB 881, Asmara; tel. (1) 123000; fax (1) 123240; e-mail nice@eol.com.er; Gen. Man. ZERU WOLDEMICHAEL.

Trade and Industry

CHAMBER OF COMMERCE

Eritrean National Chamber of Commerce: POB 856, Asmara; tel. (1) 121388; fax (1) 120138; e-mail encc@aol.com.er.

TRADE ASSOCIATION

Red Sea Trading Corporation: 29/31 Ras Alula St, POB 332, Asmara; tel. (1) 127846; fax (1) 124353; f. 1983; import and export services; operated by the PFDJ; Gen. Man. KUBROM DAFLA.

UTILITIES

Electricity

Eritrean Electricity Authority (EEA): POB 911, Asmara; fax (1) 121468; e-mail eeahrg@eol.com.er.

Water

Dept of Water Resources: POB 1488, Asmara; tel. (1) 119636; fax (1) 124625; e-mail wrdmlwe@eol.com.er.

Transport

Eritrea's transport infrastructure was severely damaged during the three decades of war prior to independence. International creditors have since provided loans for the repair and reconstruction of the road network and for the improvement of port facilities.

RAILWAYS

The 306-km railway connection between Agordat, Asmara and the port of Massawa was severely damaged during the war of independence and ceased operation in 1975. However, in 1999 an 81-km section of the Asmara–Massawa line (between Massawa and Embatkala) became operational, and in 2001 a further 18-km section of the railway, connecting Embatkala and Ghinda, was completed. In February 2003 the reconstruction of the entire Asmara–Massawa line was completed.

Eritrean Railway: POB 6081, Asmara; tel. (1) 123365; fax (1) 201785; Co-ordinator, Railways Rehabilitation Project AMANUEL GEBRESELLASIE.

ROADS

In 1999 there were an estimated 4,010 km of roads in Eritrea, of which some 874 km were paved. Roads that are paved require considerable repair, as do many of the bridges across seasonal water courses destroyed in the war. Road construction between Asmara and the port of Massawa was given particular priority in the Recovery and Rehabilitation Programme.

SHIPPING

Eritrea has two major seaports: Massawa, which sustained heavy war damage in 1990, and Assab, which has principally served Addis Ababa, in Ethiopia. Under an accord signed between the Ethiopian and Eritrean Governments in 1993, the two countries agreed to share the facilities of both ports. Since independence, activity in Massawa has increased substantially; however, activity at Assab declined following the outbreak of hostilities with Ethiopia in May 1998. In 1998 a total of 463 vessels docked at Massawa, handling 1.2m. metric tons of goods; 322 vessels docked at Assab, which handled 1.0m. tons of goods. At 31 December 2003 Eritrea's registered merchant fleet numbered 12 vessels, with a total displacement of 21,092 grt.

Dept of Maritime Transport: POB 679, Asmara; tel. (1) 121317; fax (1) 121316; e-mail motc.rez@eol.com.er; Dir-Gen. ALEM TZEHAIE.

Port and Maritime Transport Authority: POB 851, Asmara; tel. (1) 111399; fax (1) 113647; Dir WELDE MIKAEL ABRAHAM.

Eritrean Shipping Lines: 80 Semaetat Ave, POB 1110, Asmara; tel. (1) 120359; fax (1) 120331; f. 1992; provides shipping services in Red Sea and Persian (Arabian) Gulf areas and owns and operates four cargo ships; Gen. Man. TEWELDE KELATI.

CIVIL AVIATION

The international airport is at Asmara.

Civil Aviation Department: POB 252, Asmara; tel. (1) 124335; fax (1) 124334; e-mail motc.rez@eol.com.er; handles freight and passenger traffic for eight scheduled carriers which use Asmara airport; Dir-Gen. PAULOS KAHSAY.

Eri-Air: Asmara; weekly charter flights to Italy; Man. Dirs TEWOLDE TESFAMARIAM, HAILEMARIAM GEBRECHRISTOS.

Eritrean Airlines: POB 222, Asmara; tel. (1) 181822; fax (1) 181255; Man. Dir ABRAHA GHIRMAZION.

Tourism

The Ministry of Tourism is overseeing the development of this sector, although its advance since independence has been inhibited by the country's war-damaged transport infrastructure, and by subsequent conflicts with Ethiopia and other regional tensions. Eritrea possesses many areas of scenic and scientific interest, including the Dahlak Islands (a coralline archipelago rich in marine life), offshore from Massawa, and the massive escarpment rising up from the coastal plain and supporting a unique ecosystem. In 2002 tourist arrivals in Eritrea totalled 100,828 and tourism receipts amounted to US $73m.

Eritrean Tourism Service Corporation: Asmara; operates govt-owned hotels.

ESTONIA

Introductory Survey

Location, Climate, Language, Religion, Flag, Capital

The Republic of Estonia (formerly the Estonian Soviet Socialist Republic) is situated in north-eastern Europe. The country is bordered to the south by Latvia, and to the east by Russia. Estonia's northern coastline is on the Gulf of Finland and its territory includes more than 1,520 islands, mainly off its western coastline in the Gulf of Rīga and the Baltic Sea. The largest of the islands are Saaremaa and Hiiumaa, in the Gulf of Rīga. The climate is influenced by Estonia's position between the Eurasian land mass and the Baltic Sea and the North Atlantic Ocean. The mean January temperature in Tallinn is –0.6°C (30.9°F); in July the mean temperature is 17.1°C (62.8°F). Average annual precipitation is 568 mm. The official language is Estonian, which is a member of the Baltic-Finnic group of the Finno-Ugric languages; it is written in the Latin script and is closely related to Finnish. Many of the Russian residents, who comprise over 25% of the total population, do not speak Estonian. Most of the population profess Christianity and, by tradition, Estonians belong to the Evangelical Lutheran Church. Smaller Protestant sects and the Eastern Orthodox Church are also represented. The national flag (proportions 7 by 11) consists of three equal horizontal stripes, of blue, black and white. The capital is Tallinn.

Recent History

The Russian annexation of Estonia, formerly under Swedish rule, was formalized in 1721. During the latter half of the 19th century, as the powers of the dominant Baltic German nobility declined, Estonians experienced a national cultural revival, which culminated in political demands for autonomy during the 1905 Russian Revolution, and for full independence after the beginning of the First World War. On 30 March 1917 the Provisional Government in Petrograd (St Petersburg), which had taken power after the abdication of Tsar Nicholas II in February, approved autonomy for Estonia. A Maapäev (Provisional Council) was elected as the country's representative body. However, in October the Bolsheviks staged a coup in Tallinn, and declared the Estonian Soviet Executive Committee as the sole government of Estonia. As German forces advanced towards Estonia in early 1918, the Bolshevik troops were forced to leave. The major Estonian political parties united to form the Estonian Salvation Committee, and on 24 February an independent Republic of Estonia was proclaimed. A Provisional Government, headed by Konstantin Päts, was formed, but Germany refused to recognize Estonia's independence and the country was occupied by German troops until the end of the First World War. Following the capitulation of Germany in November, the Provisional Government assumed power. After a period of armed conflict between Soviet and Estonian troops, the Republic of Estonia and Soviet Russia signed the Treaty of Tartu on 2 February 1920, under the terms of which the Soviet Government recognized Estonia's independence and renounced any rights to its territory. Estonian independence was recognized by the major Western powers in January 1921, and Estonia was admitted to the League of Nations.

Independence lasted until 1940. During most of this time the country had a liberal-democratic political system, in which the Riigikogu (State Assembly) was the dominant political force. Significant social, cultural and economic advances were made in the 1920s, including radical land reform. However, the decline in trade with Russia and the economic depression of the 1930s, combined with the political problems of a divided parliament, caused public dissatisfaction. In March 1934 Prime Minister Päts seized power in a bloodless coup and introduced a period of authoritarian rule. The Riigikogu and political parties were disbanded, but in 1938 a new Constitution was adopted, which provided for a presidential system of government, with a bicameral legislature. In April 1938 Päts was elected President.

In August 1939 the USSR and Germany signed a non-aggression treaty (the Nazi-Soviet or Molotov-Ribbentrop Pact). The 'Secret Protocols' to the treaty provided for the occupation of Estonia (along with various other territories) by the USSR. In September Estonia was forced to sign an agreement that per-mitted the USSR to base Soviet troops there. In June 1940 the Government, in accordance with a Soviet ultimatum, resigned, and a new administration was appointed by the Soviet authorities, with Johannes Vares-Barbarus as Prime Minister. In July elections were held, in which only candidates approved by the Soviet authorities were permitted to participate. On 21 July the Estonian Soviet Socialist Republic was proclaimed by the new legislature, and on 6 August the republic was formally incorporated into the USSR. Soviet rule in Estonia lasted less than one year. In that short period, however, Soviet policy resulted in mass deportations of Estonians, the expropriation of property, severe restrictions on cultural life and the introduction of Soviet-style government.

German forces entered Estonia in July 1941 and remained in occupation until September 1944. Thereafter, following a short-lived attempt to reinstate Estonian independence, Soviet troops occupied the whole of the country, and the process of 'sovietiza-tion' was resumed. By the end of 1949 most Estonian farmers had been forced to join collective farms. Heavy industry was expanded, with investment concentrated on electricity generation and the chemicals sector. Structural change in the economy was accompanied by increased political repression, with deportations of Estonians continuing until the death of Stalin (Iosif V. Dzhugashvili) in 1953. The most overt form of opposition to Soviet rule was provided by the 'forest brethren' (*metsavennad*), a guerrilla movement, which continued to conduct armed operations against Soviet personnel and institutions until the mid-1950s. In the late 1960s, as in other Soviet republics, more traditional forms of dissent appeared, concentrating on cultural issues, provoked by the increasing domination of the republic by immigrant Russians and other Slavs.

During the late 1970s and the 1980s the issues of 'russification' and environmental degradation became subjects of intense debate in Estonia. The policy of *glasnost*, introduced by the Soviet leader, Mikhail Gorbachev, in 1986, allowed such discussion to spread beyond dissident groups. The success of the first major demonstrations of the 1980s, organized to oppose plans to increase open-cast phosphorite mining in north-eastern Estonia, prompted further protests. In August 1987 a demonstration attended by some 2,000 people commemorated the anniversary of the signing of the Nazi-Soviet Pact, and an Estonian Group for the Publication of the Molotov-Ribbentrop Pact (MRP-AEG) was subsequently formed. During 1988 the Nazi-Soviet Pact was duly published, and the MRP-AEG reformed as the Estonian National Independence Party (ENIP), proclaiming the restoration of Estonian independence as its political objective. Another opposition group, the Estonian Popular Front (EPF), was formally constituted at its first congress in October, and included many members of the ruling Communist Party of Estonia (CPE). The EPF was more cautious than the ENIP in its approach, advocating the transformation of the USSR into a confederal system; the CPE was forced to adapt its policies to retain a measure of public support. On 16 November the Estonian Supreme Soviet (Supreme Council—legislature) adopted a declaration of sovereignty, which included the right to annul all-Union (USSR) legislation. The Presidium of the USSR Supreme Soviet declared the sovereignty legislation unconstitutional, but the Estonian Supreme Soviet affirmed its decision in December.

The adoption of Estonian as the state language was accepted by the Supreme Soviet in January 1989, and the tricolour of independent Estonia was reinstated as the official flag. Despite the successes of the opposition, differing political tactics were employed by the radical ENIP and the EPF. The ENIP refused to nominate candidates for elections to the all-Union Congress of People's Deputies in March. Instead, the ENIP leadership announced plans for the registration by citizens' committees of all citizens of the 1918–40 Republic of Estonia and their descendants. Voters on an electoral register, thus compiled, would elect a Eesti Kongress (Congress of Estonia) as the legal successor to the pre-1940 Estonian legislature. The EPF, however, participated in the elections to the Congress of People's Deputies and won 27 of the 36 contested seats. Five seats were won by the International Movement (Intermovement), a political group composed predominantly of ethnic Russians, which was established in July 1988 to oppose the growing influence of the Estonian opposition movements in the republic. In October 1989 delegates at the second congress of the EPF voted to adopt the restoration of Estonian independence as official policy. In November the Estonian Supreme Soviet voted to annul the 1940 decision of its predecessor to enter the USSR, declaring that the decision had been reached under coercion from Soviet armed forces.

On 2 February 1990 a mass rally was held to commemorate the anniversary of the 1920 Treaty of Tartu. Deputies attending the rally later met to approve a declaration urging the USSR Supreme Soviet to begin negotiations on restoring Estonia's independence. On 22 February 1990 the Estonian Supreme Soviet approved the declaration, and on the following day it voted to abolish the constitutional guarantee of power enjoyed by the CPE. This formal decision permitted largely free elections to take place to the Estonian Supreme Soviet in March. The EPF won 43 of the 105 seats, and 35 were won by the Association for a Free Estonia and other pro-independence groups. The remainder were won by members of the Intermovement. Candidates belonging to the CPE, which was represented in all these groups, won 55 seats. At the first session of the new legislature, Arnold Rüütel, previously Chairman of the Presidium of the Supreme Soviet, was elected to the new post of Chairman of the Supreme Soviet, in which was vested those state powers that had been the preserve of the First Secretary of the CPE. On 30 March the Supreme Soviet adopted a declaration that proclaimed the beginning of a transitional period towards independence and denied the validity of Soviet power in the republic.

In late February and early March 1990 some 580,000 people (excluding those who had migrated to Estonia after the Soviet invasion of 1940 and their descendants) took part in elections to the rival parliament to the Supreme Soviet, the Eesti Kongress. The Congress convened on 11–12 March and declared itself the constitutional representative of the Estonian people. The participants adopted resolutions demanding the restoration of Estonian independence and the withdrawal of Soviet troops from Estonia.

In early April 1990 the Supreme Soviet elected Edgar Savisaar, a leader of the EPF, as Prime Minister and on 8 May it voted to restore the first five articles of the 1938 Constitution, which described Estonia's independent status. The formal name of pre-1940 Estonia, the Republic of Estonia, was also restored, as were the state emblems, flag and anthem. On 16 May 1990 a transitional system of government was approved. Although formal economic sanctions were not imposed on Estonia (as was the case with Lithuania), relations with the Soviet authorities were severely strained. In mid-May President Gorbachev annulled the republic's declaration of independence, declaring that it violated the USSR Constitution. The Estonian leadership's request for negotiations on the status of the republic was refused by Gorbachev, who insisted that the independence declaration be rescinded before negotiations could begin. There was also opposition within the republic, mostly from ethnic Russians affiliated to the Intermovement.

When troops of the USSR's Ministry of Internal Affairs attempted military intervention in Latvia and Lithuania in January 1991, the Estonian leadership anticipated similar confrontation. Barricades and makeshift defences were erected, but no military action was taken. However, events in the other Baltic republics (Latvia and Lithuania) intensified popular distrust of Estonian involvement in a new union, which was being negotiated by other Soviet republics. Consequently, Estonia refused to participate in a referendum on the future of the USSR, which took place in nine of the republics in March 1991. The Estonian authorities had conducted a poll on the issue of independence earlier in the same month. According to the official results, 82.9% of the registered electorate took part, of which 77.8% voted in favour of Estonian independence.

When the conservative communist 'State Committee for the State of Emergency' announced that it had seized power in the USSR on 19 August 1991, Estonia, together with the other Baltic republics, expected military intervention to overthrow the pro-independence governments. Gen. Fyodor Kuzmin, the Soviet commander of the Baltic military district, informed Arnold Rüütel, the Chairman of the republican legislature, that he was taking full control of Estonia. Military vehicles entered Tallinn on 20 August, and troops occupied the city's television station. However, the military command did not prevent a session of the Estonian Supreme Council from convening on the same day. Deputies adopted a resolution declaring the full and immediate independence of Estonia, thus ending the transitional period that had begun in March 1990. Plans were also announced for the formation of a government-in-exile, should the Government and the Supreme Council be disbanded by Soviet troops. After it became evident, on 22 August 1991, that the Soviet coup had collapsed, the Government began to take measures against persons who had allegedly supported the coup. The anti-Government movements, the Intermovement and the Communist Party of the Soviet Union were banned in Estonia.

As the Estonian Government moved to assert its authority over former Soviet institutions, other countries quickly began to recognize its independence. On 6 September the USSR State Soviet finally recognized the re-establishment of Estonian independence. Later in the month Estonia, together with the other Baltic states, was admitted to the UN, as well as to the Conference on Security and Co-operation in Europe (CSCE), later the Organization for Security and Co-operation in Europe (OSCE, see p. 314). During the remainder of 1991 Estonia re-established diplomatic relations with most major states and was offered membership of leading international organizations. In internal politics there was hope for a cessation of conflict between the radical Eesti Kongress and the Supreme Council, with the establishment of a Constitutional Assembly, composed of equal numbers of delegates from each body, which was to draft a new constitution.

In January 1992, following a series of disputes with the Supreme Council, Savisaar resigned as Prime Minister and was replaced by the erstwhile Minister of Transport, Tiit Vähi. A new Council of Ministers, which included seven ministers from the previous Government, was approved by the Supreme Council at the end of the month.

The draft Constitution that had been prepared by the Constitutional Assembly was approved by some 91% of the electorate in a referendum held in late June 1992. Under the recently adopted Citizenship Law, only citizens of pre-1940 Estonia and their descendants, or those who had successfully applied for citizenship, were entitled to vote. This ruling drew strong criticism from Russian leaders, concerned that the rights of the large Russian minority in Estonia, most of whom had not been granted citizenship and who were thus disenfranchised, were being violated. The new Constitution, which entered into force in early July 1992, provided for a parliamentary system of government, with a strong presidency. An election to the new legislature, the Riigikogu, was to be held in September, concurrently with a direct presidential election (although subsequent presidents would be elected by the Riigikogu).

Legislative and presidential elections were duly held on 20 September 1992, with the participation of some 67% of the electorate. The country's Russian and other ethnic minorities, who represented 42% of the total population, were again barred from voting (with the exception of those whose applications for citizenship had been granted). The elections to the 101-seat Riigikogu were contested by some 40 parties and movements, largely grouped into eight coalitions. The nationalist Fatherland (Isamaa, or Pro Patria) alliance emerged with the largest number of seats (29). The centrist Popular Front alliance (led by the EPF) won an unexpectedly low total of 15 seats. The Secure Home alliance, which comprised some former communists, obtained 17 seats. The Moderates electoral alliance obtained 12 seats and the ENIP, which was not part of a coalition, won 10 seats. None of the four candidates in the presidential election won an overall majority of the votes. It thus fell to the Riigikogu to choose from the two most successful candidates, Arnold Rüütel, now a leading member of the Secure Home alliance, and Lennart Meri, a former Minister of Foreign Affairs, who was supported by Fatherland. In early October the Fatherland-dominated Riigikogu elected Meri as Estonia's President.

A new coalition Government, with a large representation of Fatherland members, as well as members of the Moderates and the ENIP, was announced in mid-October 1992. Earlier in the month Mart Laar, a 32-year-old historian and the leader of Fatherland, had been chosen as Prime Minister. Laar indicated that the principal objectives of his administration would be to negotiate the withdrawal of all Russian troops remaining in Estonia, as well as to accelerate the country's privatization programme. In late November four of the five constituent parties of the Fatherland alliance united to form the National Fatherland Party (NFP), with Laar as its Chairman. In the same month the CPE was renamed the Estonian Democratic Labour Party.

In November 1993 Laar survived a vote of 'no confidence' in the Riigikogu. In January 1994 Laar reshuffled four key portfolios in the Council of Ministers, overcoming initial opposition by President Meri to two of the nominees. Meanwhile, in November 1993 the EPF was disbanded. In May–June four members of the Council of Ministers resigned. Defections from the Fatherland faction within the Riigikogu resulted in Laar's supporters retaining control of only 19 seats in the legislature by early September. Following the revelation in that month that Laar had secretly contravened an agreement with the IMF, a vote of 'no confidence' in the Prime Minister was endorsed by the Riigikogu. In late October Andres Tarand, hitherto Minister of the Environment, was appointed to replace Laar. A new Council of Ministers, which included representatives of Fatherland and the Moderates, the ENIP and liberal and right-wing parties, was announced in the following month.

The results of the legislative elections, held on 5 March, reflected widespread popular dissatisfaction with the parties of the governing coalition. The largest number of seats in the Riigikogu (41 of the total of 101) was won by an alliance of the centrist Estonian Coalition Party (ECP, led by the former Prime Minister, Tiit Vähi) and the Rural Union (comprising various agrarian parties, most prominently Rüütel's Estonian Country People's Party). A coalition of the newly established Estonian Reform Party (ERP, led by Siim Kallas, the President of the Bank of Estonia) and liberal groups obtained 19 seats, followed by Edgar Savisaar's Estonian Centre Party (16). The NFP (in coalition with the ENIP) won only eight seats, while the Moderates alliance (which included Andres Tarand) obtained six seats. The 'Estonia is Our Home' alliance (which represented the Russian-speaking minority) won six seats; this development was broadly welcomed as a potentially stabilizing factor in both the domestic and foreign affairs of the country. The participation rate was almost 70%.

Tiit Vähi was confirmed as Prime Minister by the legislature in early April 1995, and the new Government—a coalition of the ECP/Rural Union and the Estonian Centre Party—was appointed later in the month. The Government survived only until early October, when it was revealed that Edgar Savisaar, the Minister of the Interior, had made clandestine recordings of conversations that he had held with other politicians concerning the formation of a new coalition government. The Estonian Centre Party subsequently refused to accept his dismissal by Vähi. As a result of the effective collapse of the coalition, Vähi and the remaining members of the Council of Ministers tendered their resignations. In mid-October President Meri reappointed Vähi as Prime Minister and charged him with the formation of a new Government. This emerged in late October, and represented a coalition of the ECP/Rural Union and the ERP. Meanwhile, Savisaar resigned as Chairman of the Estonian Centre Party. In December the NFP and the ENIP, which had campaigned jointly for the legislative elections in March, merged to form the Pro Patria (Fatherland) Union.

A presidential election was held in the Riigikogu on 26 August 1996, contested by the incumbent, Lennart Meri, and Arnold Rüütel, now of the Estonian Country People's Party. Following two further inconclusive rounds of voting, a larger electoral college, comprising the 101 deputies of the legislature and 273 representatives of local government (as provided for by the Constitution), was convened on 20 September. As none of the five candidates contesting the election on this occasion secured an overall majority of the votes, a further round of voting was held to choose between the leading candidates, Meri and Rüütel. The election was won by Meri, with 52% of the votes cast, and in October he was duly sworn in as President for a second term.

In October 1996 local government elections were held, in which the ERP gained control of the Tallinn city government. In November the ECP concluded a co-operation agreement with the Estonian Centre Party, which had held no representation in the Government since October 1995. Disagreements among the coalition partners led to the collapse of the Tallinn city leadership, and Savisaar was appointed as the new Chairman of the Council, replacing the newly elected ERP candidate. The ERP threatened to leave the Government unless the co-operation agreement with the Estonian Centre Party was cancelled, and in late November 1996 six ministers, including Kallas (hitherto the Minister for Foreign Affairs) resigned, thus causing the collapse of the ruling coalition. Following the failure of negotiations between the ECP, the Estonian Centre Party and the Develop-

ment Party, a minority Government, comprising the ECP, the Rural Union and independent members, was appointed, in early December. In early 1997 a series of allegations of abuse of office were made against Tiit Vähi. Although a legislative motion of 'no confidence', presented by the leaders of four opposition parties, was defeated by a narrow margin, Vähi tendered his resignation at the end of February. Mart Siimann, the leader of the ECP parliamentary faction, was appointed Prime Minister, and was asked to form a new Government. In mid-March a new minority Government, which comprised a coalition of the ECP, the Rural Union and independent members was appointed. In September Vähi announced his resignation from the ECP and his retirement from political life. His position as Chairman of the ECP was assumed by Siimann.

At the legislative elections, held on 7 March 1999, the Estonian Centre Party won 28 of the 101 seats; the ERP and the Pro Patria (Fatherland) Union each secured 18 seats, the Moderates (in alliance with the People's Party) 17, the Estonian Country People's Party seven and the United People's Party of Estonia six. Just 57.4% of the electorate participated. Although the Estonian Centre Party obtained the largest number of seats, it was unable to form a majority coalition. A centre-right coalition Government was thus formed by the ERP, the Pro Patria Union and the Moderates, with each party receiving five ministerial posts; Mart Laar, leader of the Pro Patria Union, was appointed Prime Minister (the post he had held in 1992–94). In May 1999 it was announced that some 300,000 non-citizens permanently resident in Estonia (principally comprising ethnic Russians) were to be allowed to participate in local elections to be held in October.

At the local elections of October 1999 the governing ERP-Pro Patria (Fatherland) Union-Moderates alliance obtained control of 13 of Estonia's 15 county governments. The alliance joined four members of the People's Trust Party and one member of the People's Choice bloc (both representing the Russian-speaking population), to take control of Tallinn city government. Jüri Mõis was appointed Mayor of Tallinn, after resigning as Minister of Internal Affairs. In November the Moderates' Party and the People's Party merged to form the People's Party Moderates. In June 2000 a new party, the Estonian People's Union (EPU), was formed by the merger of the Estonian Rural People's Party, the Rural Union and the Pensioners' and Families' Party.

In April 2001 a vote of 'no confidence', brought against Prime Minister Laar, was narrowly defeated. In May Jüri Mõis resigned as Mayor of Tallinn, after being threatened with a fifth confidence vote. A member of the Pro Patria (Fatherland) Union, Tõnis Palts, was elected as his successor, following a 'run-off' election, which was contested by Savisaar.

Inconclusive rounds of voting in the presidential election took place in the Riigikogu on 27–28 August 2001. The terms of the Constitution prevented the incumbent, Lennart Meri, from standing for a third term of office, and the first round of the election was contested by Andres Tarand of the People's Party Moderates and Peeter Kreitzberg of the opposition Estonian Centre Party. Tarand was replaced as the candidate of the ruling coalition by Peeter Tulviste of the Pro Patria (Fatherland) Union in the second and third rounds of voting, but neither candidate emerged as the victor. An Electoral Body, composed of the 101 parliamentary deputies, and 266 representatives of local government, was therefore convened on 21 September. Toomas Savi of the governing ERP (members of which had, hitherto, abstained from voting), and Arnold Rüütel, now the honorary Chairman of the opposition EPU, also participated at this stage, progressing to a second round, as the candidates with the greatest number of votes. Rüütel eventually emerged as the victor in the 'run-off' election, in which he secured 186 votes. He was sworn in as President on 8 October. The protracted electoral process had led to renewed demands for electoral reform, and some Estonians expressed concern at the election of a former communist official as President.

In late September 2001, satisfying long-standing opposition demands, Mikhel Pärnoja tendered his resignation as Minister of Economic Affairs, citing the unpopularity of decisions he had made regarding the privatization of the railway network and the planned divestment of the Narva Power Plants. In early December the ERP announced that it was to leave the Tallinn City Government. It subsequently signed a coalition agreement with the Estonian Centre Party, in what was widely regarded as an attempt to distance itself from the increasingly unpopular national Government of which it remained a part. Tõnis Palts was forced to resign as Mayor, when a censure motion, brought by members of the Estonian Centre Party, was passed by a significant majority. His Pro Patria (Fatherland) Union left the city government, and Savisaar was elected as Mayor of Tallinn in mid-December. These developments prompted Prime Minister Mart Laar and his Government to resign on 8 January 2002.

On 17 January 2002 the Estonian Centre Party and the ERP signed an agreement on the formation of an interim, coalition government, despite their contrasting political ideals; eight ministers were to be appointed from the Estonian Centre Party and six from the ERP. The parties of the coalition held fewer than one-half of the seats in the Riigikogu and, therefore, required the support of the EPU. On 22 January Kallas of the ERP was approved as Prime Minister, despite failing to obtain the support of his former government allies, the Pro Patria (Fatherland) Union and the People's Party Moderates.

In July 2002, following a ruling by the Supreme Court prohibiting the formation of electoral blocs, the Riigikogu voted to permit their continued existence until 2005, in order to avoid a delay in holding the forthcoming local elections. The local elections duly took place on 20 October. Parties represented in the national Government won the majority of the votes cast. At the beginning of November 2002 Savisaar was re-elected as Mayor of Tallinn. Meanwhile, in response to their parties' poor performance in the elections, in late October Toomas Hendrik Ilves resigned as Chairman of the People's Party Moderates, to be succeeded by Ivari Padar, and Mart Laar resigned the chairmanship of the Pro Patria (Fatherland) Union, with Tunne Kelam elected as his successor. In late January 2003 the EPU absorbed the New Estonia Party. Meanwhile, in mid-December 2002 the Riigikogu had scheduled a referendum on membership of the European Union (EU, see p. 217) for 14 September 2003 (see below); voters were to be asked whether they supported Estonia's proposed accession to the EU in 2004, and the adoption of legislation amending the country's Constitution. In February 2003 the Riigikogu approved an extension of the terms of local councils, from three years to four, in the first amendment to be made to the Constitution since its adoption. In early February the Minister of Internal Affairs, Ain Seppik of the Estonian Centre Party, resigned, following severe criticism of his actions as a judge at the Supreme Court during the Soviet era.

Eleven parties participated in the parliamentary elections held on 2 March 2003, in which the Estonian Centre party received 25.4% of the votes cast and 28 seats in the 101-member Riigikogu, the right-wing Union for the Republic Res Publica (founded in 2001) obtained 24.6% and 28 seats, and the ERP took 17.7% and 19 seats; the Estonian People's Union, the Pro Patria (Fatherland) Union and the People's Party Moderates also secured more than the 5% of the votes required to achieve representation in the Riigikogu. The level of participation by the electorate was 58.2%. Although the Estonian Centre Party secured the largest number of votes cast, Union for the Republic Res Publica refused to initiate talks with it on the formation of a new government, and instead invited the ERP, the Estonian People's Union and the Pro Patria (Fatherland) Union to join it in a four-member coalition. However, the ERP and the Estonian People's Union objected to the inclusion of the Pro Patria (Fatherland) Union, and on 27 March agreement was reached on the formation of a three-party government. After Savisaar declined the President's offer to form a government, on 2 April Juhan Parts, the leader of Union for the Republic Res Publica and a former chief auditor at the Bank of Estonia, was nominated as Prime Minister. The new coalition Government, approved on 9 April, consisted of five members of that party, five members of the ERP and four representatives of the Estonian People's Union.

In mid-September 2003 the Minister of Finance, Tõnis Palts, resigned, after an investigation was initiated into allegations of tax evasion dating from before his appointment to the Council of Ministers; Taavi Veskimägi was appointed as his successor. In the national referendum, held as scheduled on 14 September, 66.8% of votes were cast in favour of Estonia's accession to the EU, which was, thereby, to take effect from 1 May 2004. (The rate of participation was 64.1%.) In February 2004 a congress of the People's Party Moderates voted formally to change the party's name to the Social Democratic Party.

President Rüütel accepted the resignation of Tiit Tammsaar as Minister of Agriculture in early April 2004, after it had emerged that nearly one-third of the state grain reserve was unaccounted for. In September Meelis Atonen resigned as Minister of the Economy and Communications, having failed to

obtain government support for proposed changes to a ferry service. In Estonia's first elections to the European Parliament, held in June 2004, two of the parties of the ruling coalition failed to obtain any representation in that body (the ERP received one seat, out of the total of six allocated to representatives of Estonia), while the opposition Social Democratic Party obtained three mandates; the Estonian Centre Party and the Pro Patria (Fatherland) Union each obtained one seat. In October Savisaar of the Estonian Centre Party was forced to resign as Mayor of Tallinn, as the result of a vote of 'no confidence' by the city council, following accusations of an autocratic style of leadership and financial mismanagement. He was replaced by the former Mayor and former Minister of Finance, Tõnis Palts of Union for the Republic Res Publica. Meanwhile, the Estonian Centre Party increasingly took measures regarded as seeking to increase its support among the ethnic Russian population of Estonia, at the end of the year controversially signing a co-operation agreement with the *de facto* ruling party of Russia, Unity and Fatherland-United Russia. One consequence of these measures was that members of the party who supported closer co-operation and integration with the EU either left the party or distanced themselves from the party's organization; by the end of January 2005 the party's faction in the Riigikogu had diminished from 28 to 19 members.

Meanwhile, in November 2004 Margus Hanson resigned as Minister of Defence following the theft from his home of classified documents; subsequently, he was the subject of a criminal investigation into the matter. Also in November the new Minister of the Economy and Communications, Andrus Ansip, was elected Chairman of the ERP, replacing Kallas, who had been appointed as the country's representative to the European Commission. The Estonian Social-Democratic Labour Party was renamed the Estonian Left Party in December, and Sirje Kingsepp was elected as its leader, in place of Tiit Toomsalu. In February 2005 the long-standing Minister of Foreign Affairs, Kristiina Ojuland, was dismissed from office (following her refusal to resign), after a security audit found that 91 classified documents had disappeared from the Ministry in 1996–2004. It was observed that this crisis threatened the stability of the ruling coalition, with the ERP reluctant to agree to Ojuland's removal, particularly given the premier's lack of consultation on the matter. The ERP ultimately accepted the appointment of Rein Lang as her successor, but many commentators doubted that the coalition would endure a full term until 2007, especially in light of the coalition's conflicting financial commitments. Municipal elections were scheduled to be held in October 2005.

Since the restoration of Estonian independence in 1991, the republic's relations with its eastern neighbour, Russia, have been strained by a number of issues, most notably the presence of former Soviet troops (under Russian jurisdiction) and the rights of the large Russian minority in Estonia (equivalent to 25.6% of the population, according to the 2000 census, with a significantly higher proportion being recorded in Tallinn). Under the Citizenship Law of 1992 (a modified version of that adopted in 1938), non-ethnic Estonians who settled in the republic after its annexation by the USSR in 1940, and their descendants, were obliged to apply for naturalization. Many of the requirements for naturalization—including an examination in the Estonian language—were criticized by the Russian Government as being excessively stringent, and discriminatory against the Russian-speaking minority. A new citizenship law, adopted in January 1995, gave non-citizens until 12 July to apply for residence and work permits, by which time almost 330,000 people (more than 80% of the total) had submitted applications. The deadline was extended until 30 November 1996, and by October of that year some 110,000 people had taken Russian citizenship, while continuing to reside in Estonia. In May 1997 the Ministry of Internal Affairs announced that Soviet passports were no longer valid in Estonia. In December 1998 the Riigikogu approved legislation requiring elected officials to demonstrate sufficient command of Estonian to participate in the basic bureaucratic procedures of office. (Legislation specifying more stringent language requirements, approved by the Riigikogu in the previous year, had been vetoed by President Meri.) The legislation became effective in May 1999, and on 1 July a further amendment to the Language Law, pertaining to those employed in the services sector, came into force. In April 2000, following a statement by the OSCE High Commissioner on National Minorities that the language legislation contradicted international standards on freedom of expression, the law was amended, to make knowledge of Estonian compulsory only where it was deemed necessary for the sake of public interest (for example, in areas such as public health and security). In November 2001 the requirement that electoral candidates be able to speak Estonian was abolished, although legislation adopted in same month made Estonian the official language of parliament.

With the dissolution of the USSR in 1991, several thousand former Soviet troops remained stationed (under Russian command) on Estonian territory. Their withdrawal was commenced in 1992, but the Russian leadership increasingly linked the progress of the troop withdrawals with the question of the citizenship, and other rights, of the Russian-speaking minority in Estonia. In July 1994 a bilateral agreement was reached, awarding civil and social guarantees to all Russian military pensioners in Estonia. The withdrawal of former Soviet troops was completed on 29 August.

A further cause of tension in Estonian-Russian relations concerned Estonia's demand for the return of some 2,000 sq km (770 sq miles) of territory that had been ceded to Russia in 1944. In June 1994 Russian President Boris Yeltsin ordered the unilateral demarcation of Russia's border with Estonia according to the post-1944 boundary, although no agreement with Estonia had been concluded. During 1995 Estonia abandoned its demand for the return of the disputed territories. Instead, the Estonian Government appealed only for minor amendments to be made to the existing line of demarcation, in order to improve border security; more importantly, it insisted that Russia recognize the Treaty of Tartu of 1920 (in which Russia recognized Estonia's independence) as the basis of future relations between the two countries. However, the Russian Government maintained that the Treaty had lost its legal force, having been superseded by the declaration on bilateral relations signed by Russia and Estonia in 1991. In November 1996 the Estonian authorities announced that they were prepared to omit references to the Treaty of Tartu from the border agreement, and declared that it would be signed by Estonia and Russia at a summit of the OSCE in December. However, the Russian Government continued to refuse to sign the agreement. Relations between Estonia and Russia remained strained, and in September 2000 Estonia decreed that from 2001 a full visa regime would come into effect between the two countries (as part of Estonia's preparations for EU membership), despite Russian misgivings. Further tensions arose in December 2003, when the Riigikogu approved amendments to legislation on foreign nationals, which prevented Russian military pensioners from obtaining permanent residency in Estonia. The Russian Government warned that any abrogation of the bilateral agreement of July 1994 would be likely severely to damage Estonian-Russian relations. In 2005 the ratification of a border treaty between the two countries became a viable topic once more, following an informal meeting between President Rüütel and President Vladimir Putin of Russia in January, and owing to the need for Russia to resolve visa agreements with member states of the recently expanded EU.

Estonia pursues close relations with its Baltic neighbours, Latvia and Lithuania. In late 1991 the three states established a consultative interparliamentary body, the Baltic Assembly, with the aim of developing political and economic co-operation. In early 1992 it was agreed to abolish almost all trade restrictions between the three countries and to introduce a common visa policy, and a tripartite agreement on free trade and regional security was signed in late 1993. A customs agreement came into force in June 1996, which constituted the first stage of the establishment of a unified customs system. In November 1997 the three countries agreed to remove all non-tariff customs barriers between them and to reject Russian overtures to provide unilateral security guarantees. In January 1998 the Presidents of the three states met President Clinton of the USA in Washington, DC, and all parties signed a Charter of Partnership. The Baltic Assembly also maintains close links with the Nordic Council. Estonia is a member of the Council of Baltic Sea States (see p. 198), established in March 1992. In July 1999 the Estonian, Latvian and Lithuanian Prime Ministers agreed to develop the Baltic Common Economic Area and to remove obstacles to the further implementation of trilateral agreements on free trade.

An important focus of Estonia's foreign policy was the attainment of full membership of the EU. In July 1995 Estonia became an associate member, and in December it officially applied for full membership; formal accession negotiations began on 31 March 1998. In October 2002 the European Commission approved a report, which identified 10 countries, including Estonia, as ready to join the EU on 1 May 2004, when Estonia duly acceded to membership. In June 2004 Estonia was one of three new EU member states (alongside Lithuania and Slovenia) to be admitted to the exchange rate mechanism (ERM 2) as a precursor to adopting the common European currency, the euro. The proposed EU Constitutional Treaty was not to be put to a further referendum unless it was found by a parliamentary committee to contravene the existing national Constitution, and was to be ratified by the vote of the Riigikogu. Estonia also pursued membership of North Atlantic Treaty Organization (NATO, see p. 301). The country joined NATO's 'Partnership for Peace' programme of military co-operation in 1994. In November 2002, at a NATO summit meeting held in Prague, Czech Republic, Estonia was one of seven countries to be invited formally to accede to the Alliance in 2004. Estonia became a full member of NATO on 29 March 2004. Estonia is also a member of the Council of Europe (see p. 199).

Government

Legislative authority resides with the Riigikogu (State Assembly), which has 101 members, elected by universal adult suffrage for a four-year term. The Riigikogu elects the President (Head of State) for a term of five years. The President is also Supreme Commander of Estonia's armed forces. Executive power is held by the Council of Ministers, which is headed by the Prime Minister, who is nominated by the President. For administrative purposes, Estonia is divided into 15 counties (*maakonds*), which in turn are subdivided into cities, rural municipalities and towns.

Defence

Before regaining independence in 1991, Estonia had no armed forces separate from those of the USSR. Following the establishment of its own Ministry of Defence in April 1992, Estonia began to form a national army. By August 2004 its total armed forces numbered an estimated 4,980 (army 4,450, navy 335, air force 195). There was also a reserve militia of some 24,000. There is a paramilitary border guard numbering 2,600 troops, under the command of the Ministry of Internal Affairs. In July 2000 the standard duration of military service was reduced from 12 to eight months. Also in 2000 a plan for the reform of the armed forces was approved. In February 1994 Estonia joined the North Atlantic Treaty Organization's (NATO) 'Partnership for Peace' (see p. 303) programme of military co-operation. In 1998 the Baltic states agreed to establish a joint airspace observation system (BALTNET), a defence college and a peace-keeping battalion (BALTBAT), which was to be divided into three national battalions from 2001. A Baltic naval unit (BALTRON) was established in mid-1998. In November 2002 Estonia was invited to join NATO, and it became a full member on 29 March 2004. In early April BALTNET was formally absorbed into NATO's Integrated Air Defence System. Estonia had implemented measures to increase its defence expenditure, in compliance with NATO requirements that countries aspiring to membership should allocate at least 2.0% of annual GDP to defence. The budget for 2004 assigned 2,600m. kroons to defence.

Economic Affairs

In 2003, according to World Bank estimates, Estonia's gross national income (GNI), measured at average 2000–03 prices, was US $7,839m., equivalent to $4,960 per head (or $12,480 per head on an international purchasing-power parity basis). During 1990–2003, it was estimated, the population declined at an average annual rate of 1.1%, while gross domestic product (GDP) per head increased, in real terms, by an average of 1.3% per year. Overall GDP increased, in real terms, at an average annual rate of 0.2% during 1990–2003. However, real GDP increased by 6.0% in 2002 and by 4.7% in 2003.

Agriculture (including hunting, forestry and fishing) contributed 4.4% of GDP in 2003. In that year the sector provided 6.2% of employment. Animal husbandry is the main activity in the agricultural sector. Some 27.4% of Estonia's land is cultivable. The principal crops are grains, potatoes and fruits and vegetables. Forestry products are also important. During 1990–2003, according to the World Bank, agricultural GDP declined, in real terms, at an average annual rate of 3.0%. The GDP of the sector increased by 4.2% in 2002, but decreased by 2.9% in 2003.

Industry (including mining and quarrying, manufacturing, construction and power) contributed 28.1% of GDP in 2003. In that year the sector provided 32.5% of employment. The sector is dominated by machine-building, electronics and electrical engineering. During 1990–2003, according to the World Bank, industrial GDP declined, in real terms, at an average annual rate of 1.5%. However, industrial GDP increased by 9.7% in 2002 and by 5.0% in 2003.

Mining and quarrying contributed 1.0% of GDP in 2003, when it provided 1.0% of employment. Estonia's principal mineral resource is oil-shale, and there are also deposits of peat and phosphorite ore. There are total estimated reserves of oil-shale of some 4,000 metric tons. However, annual extraction of oil-shale had declined to some 11.7m. tons by 2000, compared with some 31m. tons in 1980. Phosphorite ore is processed to produce phosphates for use in agriculture, but development of the industry has been accompanied by increasing environmental problems. According to official figures, the GDP of the mining and quarrying sector increased by 15.8% in 2002 and by 7.2% in 2003.

In 2003 the manufacturing sector accounted for 17.7% of GDP and engaged an estimated 22.6% of the employed labour force. The sector is based on products of food- and beverage-processing (especially dairy products), textiles and clothing, fertilizers and other chemical products, and wood and timber products (particularly furniture). The World Bank estimated that in 1993–2003 the GDP of the manufacturing sector increased, in real terms, at an average annual rate of 6.6%. Real manufacturing GDP increased by 10.0% in 2002 and by 5.0% in 2003.

The country relies on oil-shale for over 90% of its energy requirements. In 2003 imports of mineral fuels accounted for 6.1% of total imports.

The services sector accounted for 67.5% of GDP in 2003, and engaged 61.3% of the employed population. During 1990–2003, according to the World Bank, the GDP of the services sector increased, in real terms, by an annual average of 1.9%. The GDP of the sector increased by 4.4% in 2002 and by 2.8% in 2003.

In 2003 Estonia recorded a visible trade deficit of US $1,579.5m., while there was a deficit of $1,199.2m. on the current account of the balance of payments. After 1991 trade with the West, particularly Scandinavia, increased considerably, while trade with former Soviet republics declined from about 90% of the pre-1991 total to some 30% by 1995. In 2003 Finland was Estonia's principal trading partner, accounting for 15.9% of imports and 21.9% of exports. Other important sources of imports were Germany, Russia and Sweden; Sweden, Russia, Germany and Latvia were important purchasers of exports. In 2003 the principal exports were machinery and electrical goods (23.4% of total export revenue), wood and wood products (12.2%), textiles (8.9%), base metals (8.1%), miscellaneous manufactured articles (8.1%), foodstuffs, beverages and tobacco (6.2%), transport vehicles (6.0%) and chemicals (5.9%). The principal imports were machinery and electrical goods (27.4%), transport vehicles (13.8%), base metals (9.8%), chemical products (7.5%), foodstuffs, beverages and tobacco (7.1%), mineral products (6.4%), and textiles (6.0%).

In 2003, according to preliminary figures, there was a general consolidated budgetary surplus of 1,572m. kroons (equivalent to 1.2% of GDP). Estonia's external debt totalled US $4,741m. at the end of 2002, of which $482m. was long-term public debt. In the same year the cost of debt-servicing was equivalent to 13.7% of the value of exports of goods and services. The annual rate of inflation reached 1,069% in 1992. However, in 1993, following a programme of radical monetary reform, the average annual rate of inflation was reduced to 89%. During 1992–2002 the annual rate of inflation averaged 20.1%. Consumer prices increased by 3.5% in 2002 and by 1.3% in 2003. Some 32,306 people (approximately 4.9% of the labour force) were officially registered as unemployed at December 2004.

In 1992 Estonia became a member of the IMF and the World Bank. It also joined the European Bank for Reconstruction and Development (see p. 212). In November 1999 Estonia became a member of the World Trade Organization (WTO, see p. 357). Estonia signed a free-trade agreement with the European Union (EU, see p. 217) in 1994. It became an associate member of the EU in June 1995, and acceded as a full member in May 2004.

Even before it regained independence in mid-1991, Estonia had begun a transition to a market economy, and far-reaching economic reforms were continued thereafter. However, despite Estonia's relative prosperity during the Soviet period, the collapse of the USSR and its internal economic system resulted in serious economic difficulties. In June 1992 Estonia introduced a new currency, the kroon, pegged at a rate of 8:1 against the German Deutsche Mark, enhancing international financial confidence in the country. The economy was adversely affected by the Russian financial crisis of 1998, but it recovered in 2000, and Estonia's final stand-by arrangement with the IMF expired in 2001. Strong growth was recorded in 2002 and 2003, with domestic investment and consumption stimulated by Estonia's anticipated membership of the EU from May 2004, and the rate of consumer-price inflation was the lowest to be recorded since independence. The Government adopted a modified programme in November 2003 for the gradual diminution of the rate of personal income tax in 2004–06 (the income-tax rate was 26% in 2003), according to which the rate of income tax was to decline by 1% in 2004 and 2007, and by 2% in the intervening years. Membership of the EU, which took effect in May 2004, entailed increased public spending by the Government (on projects such as infrastructural development) and the general government budget was expected to generate a deficit in 2005/06 for the first time in that decade; the country was also to fund increased security measures along the border with Russia, in preparation for Estonian participation in the so-called Schengen accords on the free movement of people between EU member-states with effect from 2007. Following the country's accession to the EU in May 2004, Estonia also joined the exchange rate mechanism (ERM 2) in June 2004 (three of the 10 new EU members qualified), a precursor to the future adoption of the common European currency, the euro. It was possible that Estonia could meet the final adoption criteria (which included the requirement that the annual government budgetary deficit remain less than 3% of GDP) from 2007. The deficit on the current account of the balance of payments remained Estonia's largest ongoing economic challenge, having reached some 14% of GDP in 2004, although economic development, in general, remained strong. Growth of some 5%–6% was forecast for 2005 and 2006, supported by a recovery in the global telecommunications industry, which has a significant investment in Estonia.

Education

Compulsory education begins at the age of seven and lasts for nine years: primary school (Grades 1–6) and lower secondary (Grades 7–9). Students may then attend either general secondary school (Grades 10–12) or vocational school. In 2003/04 there were 47 higher-education institutions, including Tartu University (founded in 1632) and the Tallinn Technical University, with a total of 59,025 students enrolled. The language of instruction at all levels is either Estonian or Russian. In 2003/04 24% of students at primary and secondary schools took classes with Russian as the language of instruction, and in 2000/01 11.6% of students enrolled in higher education received tuition in Russian. In November 2003 the Riigikogu rejected a proposal to introduce Estonian as the language of instruction in all secondary schools by 2007/08. In 2003 enrolment at primary schools was equivalent to 99.3% of the corresponding age group. At secondary school level, enrolment was equivalent to 94.9% of the school-age population, and in tertiary education it was equivalent to 63.5% of those aged 19 and 38.6% of those aged 19–25. Central government expenditure on education totalled 2,875.5m. kroons in 1999; local government expenditure amounted to 2,791.2m. kroons. Total public-sector expenditure on education in that year was equivalent to an estimated 7% of GDP.

Public Holidays

2005: 1 January (New Year's Day), 24 February (Independence Day), 25 March (Good Friday), 1 May (Spring Day), 23 June (Victory Day, anniversary of the Battle of Võnnu in 1919), 24 June (Midsummer Day, Jaanipäev), 20 August (Restoration of Independence Day), 25–26 December (Protestant and Catholic Christmas).

2006: 1 January (New Year's Day), 24 February (Independence Day), 14 April (Good Friday), 1 May (Spring Day), 23 June (Victory Day, anniversary of the Battle of Võnnu in 1919), 24 June (Midsummer Day, Jaanipäev), 20 August (Restoration of Independence Day), 25–26 December (Protestant and Catholic Christmas).

Weights and Measures

The metric system is in force.

Statistical Survey

Source (unless otherwise stated): Statistical Office of Estonia (Statiskaamet), Endla 15, Tallinn 0100; tel. 625-9202; fax 625-9370; e-mail stat@stat.ee; internet www.stat.ee.

Area and Population

AREA, POPULATION AND DENSITY

Area (sq km)	45,227*
Population (census results)†	
12 January 1989	1,565,662
31 March 2000	
Males	631,851
Females	738,201
Total	1,370,052
Population (official estimates at 1 January)†	
2002	1,361,242
2003	1,356,045
2004	1,351,000
Density (per sq km) at 1 January 2004	29.9

* 17,462 sq miles.
† Figures refer to permanent inhabitants. The *de facto* total was 1,572,916 at the 1989 census and 1,356,931 at the 2000 census.

POPULATION BY NATIONALITY
(1 January 2003)

	Number	%
Estonian	927,293	68.4
Russian	349,227	25.7
Ukrainian	28,820	2.1
Belarusian	16,891	1.2
Finnish	11,371	0.8
Tatar	2,562	0.2
Latvian	2,276	0.2
Polish	2,147	0.2
Lithuanian	2,100	0.2
Jewish	2,046	0.2
German	1,900	0.1
Others	9,412	0.7
Total	1,356,045	100.0

POPULATION BY COUNTY
(official estimates, 1 January 2003)

County	Area (sq km)*	Population	Density (per sq km)	County town (with population)
Harju	4,333	522,252	120.5	Tallinn (397,150)
Hiiu	1,023	10,348	10.1	Kärdla (3,767)
Ida-Viru . .	3,364	176,181	52.4	Jõhvi (11,743)
Järva . . .	2,623	38,408	14.6	Paide (9,648)
Jõgeva . . .	2,604	37,886	14.6	Jõgeva (6,410)
Lääne . . .	2,383	28,232	11.8	Haapsalu (11,922)
Lääne-Viru .	3,465	67,052	19.4	Rakvere (16,913)
Pärnu . . .	4,807	90,127	18.8	Pärnu (44,781)
Põlva . . .	2,165	32,121	14.8	Põlva (6,483)
Rapla . . .	2,980	37,270	12.5	Rapla (5,742)†
Saare . . .	2,922	35,584	12.2	Kuressaare (14,951)
Tartu . . .	2,993	148,992	49.8	Tartu (101,190)
Valga . . .	2,044	35,242	17.2	Valga (14,120)
Viljandi . .	3,423	57,148	16.7	Viljandi (20,509)
Võru . . .	2,305	39,202	17.0	Võru (14,750)
Total . . .	43,432	1,356,045	31.2	

* Excluding that part of Lake Peipsi which belongs to Estonia, and the area of Lake Võrtsjärv.
† Estimated population at 1 January 2002.

PRINCIPAL TOWNS
(estimated population, excluding suburbs, at 1 January 2003)

Tallinn (capital) . .	397,150	Kohtla-Järve . . .	46,765
Tartu	101,190	Pärnu	44,781
Narva	67,752	Viljandi	20,509

BIRTHS, MARRIAGES AND DEATHS*

	Registered live births		Registered marriages		Registered deaths	
	Number	Rate (per 1,000)	Number	Rate (per 1,000)	Number	Rate (per 1,000)
1995	13,509	9.4	7,006	4.8	20,828	14.5
1996	13,242	9.3	5,517	3.9	19,020	13.4
1997	12,577	8.9	5,589	3.9	18,572	13.2
1998	12,167	8.7	5,430	3.9	19,445	14.0
1999	12,425	9.0	5,590	4.1	18,447	13.4
2000	13,067	9.5	5,485	4.0	18,403	13.4
2001	12,632	9.3	5,647	4.1	18,516	13.6
2002	13,001	9.6	5,853	4.3	18,355	13.5

* Revised figures, based on the results of the 1989 and 2000 population censuses.

Expectation of life (WHO estimates, years at birth): 71.1 (males 65.1; females 77.1) in 2002 (Source: WHO, *World Health Report*).

EMPLOYMENT
(annual averages, '000 persons aged 15–74 years)

	2001	2002	2003
Agriculture, hunting and forestry	37.3	38.8	34.4
Fishing	2.7	1.9	2.3
Mining and quarrying	5.8	5.7	5.7
Manufacturing	134.1	128.2	134.1
Electricity, gas and water supply	11.4	10.5	10.2
Construction	39.3	38.9	42.9
Wholesale and retail trade . . .	83.6	86.3	80.8
Hotels and restaurants . . .	17.4	17.9	17.4
Transport, storage and communications	53.7	54.5	56.2
Financial intermediation . . .	7.2	7.9	7.6
Real estate, renting and business activities	38.2	44.3	44.4
Public administration and defence; compulsory social security . .	34.8	33.2	34.5
Education	51.0	55.6	56.9
Health and social work . . .	30.9	31.6	36.4
Activities not adequately defined	30.4	30.1	30.4
Total employed	577.7	585.5	594.3

Unemployed (annual averages, '000 persons aged 15–74): 83.1 in 2001; 67.2 in 2002; 66.2 in 2003.

Health and Welfare

KEY INDICATORS

Total fertility rate (children per woman, 2002)	1.2
Under-5 mortality rate (per 1,000 live births, 2003) . .	9
HIV/AIDS (% of persons aged 15–49, 2001)	1.00
Physicians (per 1,000 head, 2001)	3.13
Hospital beds (per 1,000 head, 2001)	6.72
Health expenditure (2001): US $ per head (PPP)	562
Health expenditure (2001): % of GDP	5.5
Health expenditure (2001): public (% of total)	77.8
Human Development Index (2002): ranking	36
Human Development Index (2002): value	0.853

For sources and definitions, see explanatory note on p. vi.

Agriculture

PRINCIPAL CROPS
('000 metric tons)

	2001	2002	2003
Wheat	132.9	148.4	144.9
Barley	270.0	249.4	253.6
Rye	42.9	41.5	23.3
Oats	91.4	61.7	63.3
Triticale (wheat-rye hybrid)	9.0	12.9	9.9
Other cereals	12.2	10.9	10.6
Potatoes	343.1	210.9	244.4
Dry peas	5.0	4.8	4.8
Rapeseed	41.3	63.9	69.2
Cabbages	16.7	9.4	17.3
Cucumbers and gherkins	11.5	8.1	6.7
Carrots	11.6	11.0	19.6
Other vegetables	21.6	15.0	20.4
Apples	15.1	17.2	17.2*
Other fruits*	13.3	12.6	9.6

* FAO estimate(s).

Source: FAO.

LIVESTOCK
('000 head, year ending September)

	2001	2002	2003
Cattle	253	261	254
Pigs	300	345	341
Sheep	29	29	30
Chickens	2,366	2,295	2,096
Ducks*	20	20	20
Geese*	8	8	8
Turkeys*	20	20	20
Rabbits	55	45*	43*

* FAO estimate(s).

Source: FAO.

LIVESTOCK PRODUCTS
('000 metric tons, unless otherwise indicated)

	2001	2002	2003
Beef and veal	14.2	16.5	13.1
Pig meat	33.6	39.9	39.5
Poultry meat	9.2	11.5	14.4
Cows' milk	684.0	611.6	611.5
Butter	6.7	7.3	7.3*
Cheese	17.1	15.0	15.1*
Hen eggs	17.3	15.6	14.6
Honey (metric tons)	291	771	535

* FAO estimate.

Source: FAO.

Forestry

ROUNDWOOD REMOVALS
('000 cubic metres, excl. bark)

	2001	2002	2003*
Sawlogs, veneer logs and logs for sleepers	3,260	3,940	3,870
Pulpwood	3,910	3,480	3,520
Other industrial wood	1,150	1,180	910
Fuel wood	1,880	1,900	1,900
Total	10,200	10,500	10,200

* Unofficial figures.

Source: FAO.

SAWNWOOD PRODUCTION
('000 cubic metres, incl. railway sleepers)

	2001	2002	2003*
Coniferous (softwood)	1,505	1,656	1,770
Broadleaved (hardwood)	118	169	180
Total	1,623	1,825	1,950

* Unofficial figures.

Source: FAO.

Fishing

('000 metric tons, live weight)

	2000	2001	2002
Capture	113.1	105.2	101.5
Atlantic redfishes	8.7	0.8	0.0
Atlantic herring	41.7	41.7	36.3
European sprat	41.4	40.8	40.7
Northern prawn	12.8	11.2	14.2
Aquaculture	0.2	0.5	0.3
Total catch	113.4	105.7	101.7

Source: FAO.

Mining

('000 metric tons)

	2000	2001	2002
Oil-shale	11,727	11,837	12,400
Peat	760	844	1,508

Source: US Geological Survey.

Industry

SELECTED PRODUCTS
('000 metric tons, unless otherwise indicated)

	2000	2001	2002
Distilled spirits ('000 hectolitres)	86.4	115.2	142.4
Wine ('000 hectolitres)	32.6	30.4	34.3
Beer ('000 hectolitres)	950.1	1,015.2	1,044.1
Soft drinks ('000 hectolitres)	698.5	725.1	810.6
Woven cotton fabric ('000 sq metres)	121,409	120,704	119,199
Linen fabric ('000 sq metres)	7,100*	n.a.	n.a.
Carpets ('000 sq metres)	1,866	2,069	1,834
Footwear ('000 pairs)	1,443	1,345	1,811
Plywood ('000 cubic metres)	18.4	29.2	38.5
Particle board ('000 cubic metres)	175.8	185.9	187.2
Fibreboard (million sq metres)	17.7	17.3	18.3
Chemical wood pulp	54.4	51.7	65.3
Paper	52.4	53.3	63.5
Nitrogenous fertilizers†	38.0	39.0	23.4
Building bricks (million)	16.9	20.3	22.9
Cement	329.1	404.6	465.9
Electric energy (million kWh)	8,513	8,483	8,527

* Rounded figure; source: UN, *Industrial Commodity Statistics Yearbook*.
† In terms of nitrogen.

Electric energy (million kWh): 10,143 in 2003.

Finance

CURRENCY AND EXCHANGE RATES

Monetary Units
100 cents = 1 kroon

Sterling, Dollar and Euro Equivalents (31 December 2004)
£1 sterling = 22.16 kroons;
US $1 = 11.47 kroons;
€1 = 15.62 kroons;
1,000 kroons = £45.14 = $87.18 = €64.00.

Average Exchange Rate (kroons per US $)
2002   16.612
2003   13.856
2004   12.596

Note: In June 1992 Estonia reintroduced its national currency, the kroon, replacing the rouble of the former USSR, initially at a rate of one kroon per 10 roubles.

BUDGET
(million kroons)*

Revenue†	2001	2002	2003
Tax revenue	32,022.5	37,172.8	41,323.8
Taxes on income, profits and			
capital gains	7,847.4	9,154.4	10,974.6
Individual	7,099.1	7,806.4	8,818.2
Corporate	748.3	1,348.0	2,156.4
Social security contributions	11,529.9	12,759.8	14,297.5
Taxes on property . . .	384.7	372.5	440.6
Domestic taxes on goods and			
services	12,220.5	14,347.1	15,611.1
General sales, turnover or			
value-added taxes . .	8,642.5	10,172.0	11,186.7
Excises	3,434.1	3,937.5	4,161.6
Other	154.1	206.5	227.9
Non-tax revenue	4,266.4	4,900.5	5,594.6
Total	**36,288.9**	**42,073.3**	**46,918.4**

Expenditure‡	2001	2002	2003
Expenditure on goods and services	18,748.1	20,628.3	18,266.8
Wages and salaries	5,606.1	6,343.7	7,512.7
Employers' social contributions .	1,775.1	2,002.6	2,604.1
Other purchases of goods and			
services	11,366.9	12,282.0	8,150.0
Subsidies and other current			
transfers	14,171.3	16,519.6	22,513.3
Subsidies	805.0	1,137.7	1,403.6
Social benefits	10,678.6	11,791.2	13,683.8
Transfers abroad	40.7	49.8	131.4
Acquisition of fixed assets . .	3,315.7	4,219.0	3,855.4
Other expenditure	14.8	135.4	710.9
Total	**36,249.9**	**41,502.3**	**45,346.4**

* Figures represent a consolidation of the operations of the Government, comprising all central and local government accounts.
† Excluding grants received (million kroons): 629.5 in 2001; 712.8 in 2002; 1,494.2 in 2003.
‡ Excluding lending minus repayments (million kroons): –271.3 in 2001; –131.7 in 2002; n.a. in 2003.

INTERNATIONAL RESERVES
(US $ million at 31 December)

	2001	2002	2003
Gold*	2.29	2.83	3.44
IMF special drawing rights . .	0.03	0.07	0.08
Reserve position in IMF . . .	0.01	0.01	0.01
Foreign exchange	820.20	1,000.30	1,373.27
Total	**822.53**	**1,003.21**	**1,376.80**

* National valuation.

Source: IMF, *International Financial Statistics*.

MONEY SUPPLY
(million kroons at 31 December)

	2001	2002	2003
Currency outside banks . .	6,951.9	6,994.9	7,139.7
Demand deposits at banks . . .	17,967.9	20,225.5	23,603.3
Total money (incl. others) . .	**24,948.2**	**27,274.5**	**30,806.6**

Source: IMF, *International Financial Statistics*.

COST OF LIVING
(Consumer Price Index; base: 1997 = 100)

	2001	2002	2003
Food (incl. beverages)	111.9	115.3	113.3
Alcohol and tobacco	127.3	129.1	132.9
Clothing (incl. footwear) . . .	128.6	133.9	135.7
Housing	135.9	147.1	151.6
All items (incl. others) . . .	**123.0**	**127.3**	**129.0**

NATIONAL ACCOUNTS
(million kroons at current prices)

Expenditure on the Gross Domestic Product

	2001	2002	2003
Final consumption expenditure . .	78,505.9	88,853.8	95,097.8
Households	57,351.9	65,135.3	69,201.7
Non-profit institutions serving			
households	1,322.5	1,762.6	2,038.3
General government	19,831.5	21,955.9	23,857.8
Gross capital formation	30,470.1	37,164.9	39,172.7
Gross fixed capital formation . .	28,134.3	33,554.7	35,749.7
Changes in inventories . . ⎫			
Acquisitions, less disposals, of ⎬	2,335.8	3,610.2	3,423.0
valuables . . ⎭			
Total domestic expenditure . .	**108,976.0**	**126,018.7**	**134,270.5**
Exports of goods and services			
f.o.b.	87,533.6	86,613.3	94,348.3
Less Imports of goods and			
services f.o.b.	91,157.3	94,931.5	104,449.3
Statistical discrepancy	–1,014.6	–831.5	1,662.6
GDP in market prices	**104,337.7**	**116,869.0**	**125,832.1**
GDP at constant 2000 prices . .	**98,644.9**	**105,791.2**	**111,233.6**

Gross Domestic Product by Economic Activity

	2001	2002	2003
Agriculture and hunting	2,953.7	2,946.8	2,930.0
Forestry	1,776.2	1,999.2	1,880.2
Fishing	204.2	194.8	182.2
Mining and quarrying	891.8	987.8	1,097.2
Manufacturing	16,137.9	18,383.6	20,029.9
Electricity, gas and water supply .	2,756.1	2,999.0	3,170.8
Construction	5,406.8	6,672.0	7,392.8
Wholesale and retail trade; repair of motor vehicles, motorcycles and personal and household goods	12,227.6	13,698.9	14,161.2
Hotels and restaurants . . .	1,341.4	1,503.1	1,604.7
Transport, storage and communications	14,320.6	15,366.6	16,969.1
Financial intermediation	16,432.1	17,932.4	18,822.6
Real estate, renting and business activities	3,606.0	4,406.7	4,797.5
Public administration and defence; compulsory social security	4,487.1	4,946.3	5,514.3
Education	4,762.6	5,347.0	5,786.1
Health and social work	2,758.8	3,077.6	3,507.2
Other community, social and personal service activities . . .	4,193.7	4,680.7	5,119.5
Sub-total	94,256.6	105,142.5	112,965.3
Less Financial intermediation services indirectly measured	1,450.4	1,632.2	1,690.9
Gross value added in basic prices	92,806.2	103,510.3	111,274.4
Taxes on products . . . . .⎫ *Less* Subsidies on products . .⎭	11,531.5	13,358.7	14,557.7
GDP in market prices	104,337.7	116,869.0	125,832.1

BALANCE OF PAYMENTS
(US $ million)

	2001	2002	2003
Exports of goods f.o.b.	3,359.7	3,532.2	4,603.4
Imports of goods f.o.b.	−4,148.4	−4,621.3	−6,183.0
Trade balance	−788.7	−1,089.2	−1,579.5
Exports of services	1,649.3	1,712.7	2,233.6
Imports of services	−1,069.2	−1,126.1	−1,382.9
Balance on goods and services	−208.6	−502.5	−728.8
Other income received . . .	171.3	203.1	244.9
Other income paid	−453.5	−530.2	−821.6
Balance on goods, services and income	−490.8	−829.6	−1,305.5
Current transfers received . . .	181.4	174.3	207.7
Current transfers paid	−29.4	−61.3	−101.4
Current balance	−338.8	−716.6	−1,199.2
Capital account (net)	5.1	19.0	39.7
Direct investment abroad . . .	−200.1	−131.9	−148.2
Direct investment from abroad .	542.5	284.5	890.8
Portfolio investment assets . .	−118.8	−192.0	−394.3
Portfolio investment liabilities .	84.7	344.9	558.2
Financial derivatives assets .	−0.1	−2.6	−9.9
Financial derivatives liabilities .	−2.1	−1.4	8.1
Other investment assets . . .	−220.3	50.5	−127.3
Other investment liabilities .	183.6	399.4	560.0
Net errors and omissions . . .	22.3	15.3	−8.6
Overall balance	−41.9	69.3	169.4

Source: IMF, *International Financial Statistics*.

External Trade

PRINCIPAL COMMODITIES
(million kroons)

Imports c.i.f.	2001	2002	2003
Prepared foodstuffs; beverages, spirits and vinegar; tobacco and manufactured substitutes . .	5,496.1	6,987.8	7,784.0
Mineral products	6,452.5	7,483.7	7,039.5
Mineral fuels, mineral oils and products of their distillation; bituminous substances, etc. .	6,171.4	7,050.4	6,696.6
Products of chemical or allied industries	7,130.6	7,597.1	8,278.8
Plastics, rubber and articles thereof	4,246.2	4,775.4	5,606.3
Plastics and articles thereof . .	3,362.9	3,600.5	4,085.5
Paper-making material; paper and paperboard and articles thereof .	3,015.8	2,744.3	2,706.7
Textiles and textile articles . .	6,378.1	6,851.2	6,631.8
Base metals and articles of base metal	8,026.3	9,305.2	10,779.7
Iron and steel	2,515.1	2,693.9	3,576.4
Articles of iron and steel . . .	2,149.4	2,569.7	4,196.2
Machinery and mechanical appliances; electrical equipment; sound and television apparatus .	28,434.2	26,795.6	30,141.9
Nuclear reactors, boilers machinery and mechanical appliances; parts thereof . .	9,283.7	10,988.4	11,365.1
Vehicles, aircraft, vessels and associated transport equipment	8,407.0	10,224.4	15,196.5
Railway or tramway locomotives, rolling-stock and parts thereof	396.4	769.0	4,153.3
Vehicles other than railway or tramway rolling-stock, and parts and accessories . . .	7,624.9	8,953.3	10,343.6
Total (incl. others)	91,355.1	96,878.7	109,905.1

Exports f.o.b.	2001	2002	2003
Live animals and animal products	2,748.3	2,804.5	2,749.9
Prepared foodstuffs; beverages, spirits and vinegar; tobacco and manufactured substitutes . .	3,707.8	4,887.5	4,819.8
Cocoa and cocoa preparations .	1,455.2	2,377.6	2,049.2
Mineral products	3,038.1	4,081.4	3,563.3
Mineral fuels, mineral oils and products of their distillation .	2,750.8	3,827.0	3,296.5
Products of chemical or allied industries	3,634.0	3,698.3	4,556.8
Plastics, rubber and articles thereof	1,577.6	2,019.0	2,539.5
Wood and articles thereof; wood charcoal	7,744.4	8,677.0	9,499.2
Paper-making material; paper and paperboard and articles thereof .	1,742.6	2,335.4	2,613.8
Textiles and textile articles . .	7,130.9	7,151.3	6,912.5
Non-knitted clothing and accessories	2,771.3	3,027.3	2,779.6
Base metals and articles of base metal	5,733.0	6,340.6	6,278.5
Iron and steel	1,515.0	1,470.8	2,581.0
Articles of iron or steel . . .	2,070.5	2,279.7	2,140.6
Machinery and mechanical appliances; electrical equipment; sound and television apparatus .	20,406.9	15,783.5	18,181.2
Nuclear reactors, boilers machinery and mechanical appliances; parts thereof . .	2,846.1	3,140.2	3,255.6
Electrical machinery equipment and parts; sound and television apparatus parts and accessories	17,560.8	12,643.3	14,925.6
Vehicles, aircraft, vessels and associated transport equipment	3,496.9	3,898.4	4,685.7
Miscellaneous manufactured articles	4,851.5	5,533.4	6,260.8
Furniture; bedding, mattresses cushions, etc.; lamps and lighting fittings; prefabricated buildings	4,252.6	5,023.1	5,683.4
Total (incl. others)	70,119.3	71,752.5	77,573.4

PRINCIPAL TRADING PARTNERS
(million kroons)

Imports c.i.f.	2001	2002	2003
Belarus	1,077.4	292.0	1,520.6
Belgium	1,520.3	1,865.8	1,794.0
China, People's Repub.	6,679.9	4,491.5	4,572.1
Côte d'Ivoire	1,068.0	1,404.9	1,101.9
Czech Republic	1,369.5	214.9	1,480.9
Denmark	2,126.0	2,200.1	2,171.5
Finland	14,637.5	15,058.3	17,451.3
France	2,218.4	2,542.8	3,386.8
Germany	9,324.8	10,769.4	12,156.1
Italy	2,908.3	4,010.7	3,869.2
Japan	4,000.3	3,713.8	4,499.6
Latvia	1,938.8	2,227.2	2,633.5
Lithuania	2,059.8	2,718.9	3,144.7
Netherlands	2,062.7	2,388.4	2,226.5
Norway	1,095.5	1,152.0	1,159.7
Poland	1,832.9	2,351.0	2,760.5
Russia	11,416.0	11,673.4	11,212.7
Spain	185.4	552.9	1,213.7
Sweden	7,572.4	8,172.3	8,423.2
Ukraine	1,207.1	1,268.2	4,674.1
United Kingdom	2,246.2	2,241.3	2,450.5
USA	2,122.3	2,730.8	3,191.1
Total (incl. others)	91,355.1	96,878.7	109,905.1

Exports f.o.b.	2001	2002	2003
Belgium	649.1	599.4	1,048.3
Denmark	2,067.6	2,776.7	2,480.6
Finland	19,949.5	14,591.9	16,993.5
France	725.4	833.6	1,177.4
Germany	4,359.7	5,946.4	6,473.6
Hungary	546.0	721.1	793.5
Italy	640.0	701.1	868.3
Latvia	5,227.0	5,537.3	5,765.3
Lithuania	2,513.4	2,965.1	3,122.1
Netherlands	1,789.5	2,144.4	2,222.5
Norway	1,829.5	2,170.9	2,354.9
Russia	6,022.8	7,140.8	8,862.4
Sweden	8,303.8	8,922.8	9,676.7
Ukraine	2,103.1	2,133.8	2,758.8
United Kingdom	2,566.4	3,060.8	2,760.2
USA	1,527.2	1,540.3	1,799.8
Total (incl. others)	70,116.5	71,752.5	77,573.4

Transport

RAILWAYS
(traffic)

	2001	2002	2003
Passengers carried ('000)	5,478	5,187	5,066
Passenger-kilometres (million)	182.4	177.7	181.5
Freight carried ('000 metric tons)	64,560	71,021	72,228
Freight ton-kilometres (million)	8,525.7	9,736.1	9,685.4

ROAD TRAFFIC
('000 motor vehicles in use at 31 December)

	2001	2002	2003
Passenger cars	407.3	400.7	434.0
Buses and coaches	5.5	5.3	5.4
Lorries and vans	80.5	80.2	83.4
Motorcycles	6.8	7.3	8.1

SHIPPING

Merchant Fleet
(registered at 31 December)

	2001	2002	2003
Number of vessels	191	181	178
Total displacement ('000 grt)	346.6	357.4	358.2

Source: Lloyd's Register-Fairplay, *World Fleet Statistics*.

International Sea-borne Freight Traffic
('000 metric tons)

	2001	2002	2003
Goods loaded	37,435	41,835	42,604
Goods unloaded	4,084	5,439	5,060

CIVIL AVIATION
(traffic on scheduled services)

	2001	2002	2003
Passengers carried ('000)	362.3	433.3	633.1
Passenger-km (million)	310.0	354.6	488.8
Freight carried ('000 tons)	7.8	5.9	4.4
Total ton-km (million)	3.5	5.3	4.5

Tourism

FOREIGN TOURIST ARRIVALS BY COUNTRY OF ORIGIN*

	2001	2002	2003
Finland	611,895	647,866	706,473
Germany	43,617	52,794	68,151
Latvia	25,219	33,511	29,230
Norway	16,298	22,875	29,842
Russia	24,989	31,754	37,320
Sweden	55,943	61,305	66,751
United Kingdom	23,513†	28,307†	30,151
Total (incl. others)	908,072	1,003,383	1,112,746

* Figures refer to arrivals at registered accommodation establishments.
† Including Ireland.

Receipts from tourism (US $ million): 506 in 2000; 507 in 2001; 555 in 2002 (Source: World Tourism Organization).

Communications Media

	2001	2002	2003
Television receivers ('000 in use)	900	n.a.	n.a.
Telephones ('000 main lines in use)	504	475	n.a.
Mobile cellular telephones ('000 subscribers)	651	881	n.a.
Personal computers ('000 in use)	250	285	n.a.
Internet users ('000)	430	560	n.a.
Book production: titles	3,506	3,458	3,727
Book production: copies ('000) . .	5,456	5,362	5,607
Daily newspapers: number . . .	14	13	14
Non-daily newspapers: number .	95	114	114
Other periodicals: number . . .	1,088	1,143	1,180
Other periodicals: average annual circulation ('000 copies) . . .	20,378	21,782	19,832

1996: Radio receivers in use 221,000.

Sources: partly UN, *Statistical Yearbook*, and International Telecommunication Union.

Education

(2003/04)

	Institutions	Teachers	Students
Pre-primary	597	8,070*	51,300
Primary	386		92,000
General secondary	239	17,986†	101,000
Special	48		6,000
Vocational and professional .	71	1,779†	28,183‡
Universities, etc.	377	3,052§	59,025‡

* Figure refers to 1997/98. Including staff in child care and pre-school institutions. (Source: UNESCO, *Statistical Yearbook*).
† Figures refer to 2000/01.
‡ Including students enrolled in evening and correspondence courses.
§ Figure refers to 1996/97.

Adult literacy rate (estimates based on census data): 99.8% (males 99.8%; females 99.8%) in 2002 (Source: UN Development Programme, *Human Development Report*).

Directory

The Constitution

A new Constitution, based on that of 1938, was adopted by a referendum held on 28 June 1992. It took effect on 3 July. The following is a summary of its main provisions.

FUNDAMENTAL RIGHTS, LIBERTIES AND DUTIES

Every child with one parent who is an Estonian citizen has the right, by birth, to Estonian citizenship. Anyone who, as a minor, lost his or her Estonian citizenship has the right to have his or her citizenship restored. The rights, liberties and duties of all persons, as listed in the Constitution, are equal for Estonian citizens as well as for citizens of foreign states and stateless persons who are present in Estonia.

All persons are equal before the law. No one may be discriminated against on the basis of nationality, race, colour, sex, language, origin, creed, political or other persuasions. Everyone has the right to the protection of the state and the law. Guaranteeing rights and liberties is the responsibility of the legislative, executive and judicial powers, as well as of local government. Everyone has the right to appeal to a court of law if his or her rights or liberties have been violated.

The state organizes vocational education and assists in finding work for persons seeking employment. Working conditions are under state supervision. Employers and employees may freely join unions and associations. Estonian citizens have the right to engage in commercial activities and to form profit-making associations. The property rights of everyone are inviolable. All persons legally present in Estonia have the right to freedom of movement and choice of abode. Everyone has the right to leave Estonia.

Everyone has the right to health care and to education. Education is compulsory for school-age children. Everyone has the right to instruction in Estonian.

The official language of state and local government authorities is Estonian. In localities where the language of the majority of the population is other than Estonian, local government authorities may use the language of the majority of the permanent residents of that locality for internal communication.

THE PEOPLE

The people exercise their supreme power through citizens who have the right to vote by: i) electing the Riigikogu (legislature); ii) participating in referendums. The right to vote belongs to every Estonian citizen who has attained the age of 18 years.

THE RIIGIKOGU

Legislative power rests with the Riigikogu (State Assembly). It comprises 101 members, elected every four years in free elections on the principle of proportionality. Every citizen entitled to vote who has attained 21 years of age may stand as a candidate for the Riigikogu.

The Riigikogu adopts laws and resolutions; decides on the holding of referendums; elects the President of the Republic; ratifies or rejects foreign treaties; authorizes the candidate for Prime Minister to form the Council of Ministers; adopts the national budget and approves the report on its execution; may declare a state of emergency, or, on the proposal of the President, declare a state of war, order mobilization and demobilization.

The Riigikogu elects from among its members a Chairman (Speaker) and two Deputy Chairmen to direct its work.

THE PRESIDENT

The President of the Republic is the Head of State of Estonia. The President represents Estonia in international relations; appoints and recalls, on the proposal of the Government, diplomatic representatives of Estonia and accepts letters of credence of diplomatic representatives accredited to Estonia; declares regular (and early) elections to the Riigikogu; initiates amendments to the Constitution; nominates the candidate for the post of Prime Minister; and is the Supreme Commander of Estonia's armed forces.

The President is elected by secret ballot of the Riigikogu for a term of five years. No person may be elected to the office for more than two consecutive terms. Any Estonian citizen by birth, who is at least 40 years of age, may stand as a candidate for President.

Should the President not be elected after three rounds of voting, the Speaker of the Riigikogu convenes, within one month, an Electoral Body to elect the President.

THE GOVERNMENT

Executive power is held by the Government of the Republic (Council of Ministers). The Government implements national, domestic and foreign policies; directs and co-ordinates the work of government institutions; organizes the implementation of legislation, the resolutions of the Riigikogu, and the edicts of the President; submits draft legislation to the Riigikogu, as well as foreign treaties; prepares a draft of the national budget and presents it to the Riigikogu; administers the implementation of the national budget; and organizes relations with foreign states.

The Government comprises the Prime Minister and Ministers. The President of the Republic nominates a candidate for Prime Minister, who is charged with forming a new government.

JUDICIAL SYSTEM

Justice is administered solely by the courts. They are independent in their work and administer justice in accordance with the Constitution and laws. The court system is comprised of rural and city, as well as administrative, courts (first level); district courts (second level); and the Supreme Court of the Republic of Estonia (the highest court in the land).

The Government

HEAD OF STATE

President: ARNOLD RÜÜTEL (elected 21 September 2001; inaugurated 8 October 2001).

COUNCIL OF MINISTERS
(April 2005)

A coalition of the Estonian Centre Party, the Estonian Reform Party (ERP) and the Estonian People's Union.

Prime Minister: ANDRUS ANSIP (ERP).

Minister of Internal Affairs: KALLE LAANET (Estonian Centre Party).

Minister of Foreign Affairs: URMAS PAET (ERP).

Minister of Justice: REIN LANG (ERP).

Minister of Economic Affairs and Communications: EDGAR SAVISAAR (Estonian Centre Party).

Minister of Finance: AIVAR SÕERD (Estonian People's Union).

Minister of the Environment: VILLU REILJAN (Estonian People's Union).

Minister of Culture: RAIVO PALMARU (Estonian Centre Party).

Minister of Education and Science: MAILIS REPS (Estonian Centre Party).

Minister of Agriculture: ESTER TUIKSOO (Estonian People's Union).

Minister of Social Affairs: JAAK AAB (Estonian Centre Party).

Minister of Defence: JAAK JÕERÜÜT (ERP).

Minister of Population and Ethnic Affairs: PAUL-EERIK RUMMO (ERP).

Minister of Regional Affairs: JAAN ÕUNAPUU (Estonian People's Union).

MINISTRIES

Office of the President: A. Weizenbergi 39, Tallinn 15050; tel. 631-6202; fax 631-6250; e-mail sekretar@vpk.ee; internet www.president.ee.

Office of the Prime Minister: Stenbocki maja, Rahukohtu 3, Tallinn 15161; tel. 631-6701; fax 631-6704; e-mail peaminister@rk.ee; internet www.peaminister.ee.

Ministry of Agriculture: Lai 39/41, Tallinn 15056; tel. 625-6101; fax 625-6200; e-mail pm@agri.ee; internet www.agri.ee.

Ministry of Culture: Suur Karja 23, Tallinn 15076; tel. 628-2222; fax 628-2200; e-mail info@kul.ee; internet www.kul.ee.

Ministry of Defence: Sakala 1, Tallinn 10141; tel. 640-6012; fax 640-6001; e-mail info@kmin.ee; internet www.mod.gov.ee.

Ministry of Economic Affairs and Communications: Harju 11, Tallinn 15072; tel. 625-6342; fax 631-3660; e-mail info@mkm.ee; internet www.mkm.ee.

Ministry of Education and Science: Munga 18, Tartu 50088; tel. 735-0222; fax 735-0250; e-mail hm@hm.ee; internet www.hm.ee.

Ministry of the Environment: Toompuiestee 24, Tallinn 15172; tel. 626-2800; fax 626-2801; e-mail min@ekm.envir.ee; internet www.envir.ee.

Ministry of Finance: Suur-Ameerika 1, Tallinn 15006; tel. 611-3558; fax 696-6810; e-mail info@fin.ee; internet www.fin.ee.

Ministry of Foreign Affairs: Islandi Väljak 1, Tallinn 15049; tel. 631-7000; fax 631-7099; e-mail vminfo@vm.ee; internet www.vm.ee.

Ministry of Internal Affairs: Pikk 61, Tallinn 15065; tel. 612-5001; fax 612-5087; e-mail sisemin@sisemin.gov.ee; internet www.sisemin.gov.ee.

Ministry of Justice: Tõnismägi 5A, Tallinn 15191; tel. 620-8100; fax 620-8109; e-mail sekretar@just.ee; internet www.just.ee.

Ministry of Population and Ethnic Affairs: Rahukohtu 1, Tallinn 15161; tel. 693-5709; fax 693-5904; e-mail rahmin@riigikantselei.ee; internet www.rahvastikuminister.ee.

Ministry of Social Affairs: Gonsiori 29, Tallinn 15191; tel. 626-9700; fax 626-9802; e-mail smin@sm.ee; internet www.sm.ee.

President and Legislature

PRESIDENT

In a first round of voting by members of the Riigikogu (State Assembly), held on 27–28 August 2001, neither candidate (Andres Tarand and Peeter Kreitzberg) was successful in obtaining the requisite two-thirds' majority (68 votes) to be elected. Tarand was subsequently replaced by Peeter Tulviste, while Kreitzberg retained his candidacy. However, neither candidate secured the requisite majority after two further rounds of voting. In accordance with the Constitution, a larger electoral college, comprising the 101 parliamentary deputies and 266 representatives of local government

organs, was convened on 21 September. Four candidates contested the first round of the election and, as no candidate achieved the necessary 185 votes, the leading two candidates, Toomas Savi and Arnold Rüütel, proceeded to a further round of voting. The election was won by Arnold Rüütel, with 186 votes; Savi received 155.

LEGISLATURE

Riigikogu
(State Assembly)

Lossi plats 1A, Tallinn 15165; tel. 631-6331; fax 631-6334; e-mail riigikogu@riigikogu.ee; internet www.riigikogu.ee.

Speaker: ENE ERGMA.

General Election, 2 March 2003

Parties	% of votes	Seats
Estonian Centre Party	25.4	28
Union for the Republic Res Publica	24.6	28
Estonian Reform Party	17.7	19
Estonian People's Union	13.0	13
Pro Patria (Fatherland) Union	7.3	7
People's Party Moderates*	7.0	6
Others	5.0	0
Total	**100.0**	**101**

*Renamed the Social Democratic Party in 2004.

Political Organizations

Democrats–Estonian Democratic Party (Demokraadid–Eesti Demokraatlik Partei): Tallinn 10611, Telliskivi 22/1; tel. 661-6199; fax 625-9810; e-mail demokraatlik@hot.ee; internet www.demokraadid.ee; fmrly Estonian Blue Party; Chair. JAAN LAAS.

Estonian Centre Party (Eesti Keskerakond): Toom-Rüütli 3/5, Tallinn 10130; POB 3737, Tallinn 0090; tel. 627-3460; fax 627-3461; e-mail keskerakond@keskerakond.ee; internet www.keskerakond.ee; f. 1991; absorbed the Estonian Green Party in mid-1998; Chair. EDGAR SAVISAAR; Gen. Sec. KADRI MUST; 5,000 mems.

Estonian Christian People's Party (Eesti Kristlik Rahvapartei): Narva mnt. 51, Tallinn 10152; tel. 504-5760; fax 678-2311; e-mail ekrp@ekrp.ee; internet www.ekrp.ee; f. 1998; Chair. ALDO VINKEL.

Estonian Conservative Party: Järva 19, Pärnu 80023; tel. 561-6207; fax 642-2969; e-mail konservatiivid@hot.ee; internet www.hot.ee/konservatiivid; Leader ANDRO ROOS.

Estonian Independence Party (Eesti Iseseisvuspartei): Tallinna mnt 39, Haapsalu 90509; e-mail iseseisvuspartei@iseseisvuspartei.ee; internet www.iseseisvuspartei.ee; opposes European Union membership; planned merger with the National Conservative Party-Farmers' Assembly; Chair. VELLO LEITO; 1,047 mems (2002).

Estonian Left Party (Eesti Vasakpartei): Rävala puiestee 8, POB 4102, Tallinn 10143; tel. 661-2406; fax 661-2402; e-mail esdtp@solo.ee; internet www.esdtp.ee; f. 1920 as the Communist Party of Estonia; renamed Estonian Democratic Labour Party in 1992 and Estonian Social-Democratic Labour Party in 1997; renamed as above in 2004; Chair. SIRJE KINGSEPP; 1,250 mems (2003).

Estonian People's Union (Eestimaa Rahvaliit): Pärnu mnt. 30–6, Tallinn 10141; tel. 644-8578; fax 648-5053; e-mail erl@erl.ee; internet www.erl.ee; f. 2000 by merger of the Estonian Pensioners' and Families' Party and the Estonian Rural People's Union; merged with the New Estonia Party in Jan. 2003; right-wing; Hon. Chair. ARNOLD RÜÜTEL; Chair. VILLU REILJAN; 9,000 mems (2005).

Estonian Reform Party (ERP) (Eesti Reformierakond): Tõnismagi 3A–15, Tallinn 0001; tel. 640-8740; fax 640-8741; e-mail info@reform.ee; internet www.reform.ee; f. 1994; liberal; Gen. Sec. HEIKI KRANICH; Chair. ANDRUS ANSIP.

Estonian United People's Party (Eestimaa Ühendatud Rahvapartei/Obyedinennaya Narodnaya Partiya Estonii): Estonia pst. 3/5, Tallinn 10143; tel. 645-5335; fax 645-5336; e-mail eurp@eurp.ee; internet www.eurp.ee; f. 1994; represents the Russian-speaking minority in Estonia; Chair. VIKTOR ANDREYEV.

National Conservative Party-Farmers' Assembly (Rahvuslik Konservatiivne Partei-Pollumeeste Kogu): Aardla 6B, Tartu 50113; tel. 671-7060; f. 2002 by former mems of the Pro Patria (Fatherland) Union; Chair. MART HELME; approx. 1,700 mems (2002).

Pro Patria (Fatherland) Union (Isamaaliit): Wismari 11, Tallinn 10136; tel. 669-1070; fax 660-1071; e-mail info@isamaaliit.ee; internet www.isamaaliit.ee; f. 1995 by merger of the National Fatherland Party Isamaa; f. 1992; and the Estonian National Independence Party; right-wing party; f. 1988; Chair. TŌNIS LUKAS; Sec.-Gen. AIMAR ALTOSAAR; 2,900 mems.

Progressive Party (Arengupartei): Tallinn; e-mail arengupartei@online.ee; internet www.arengupartei.ee; f. 1996 following a split in the Estonian Centre Party; Chair. ANDRA VEIDEMANN; Sec.-Gen. TOIVO KEVA; 1,300 mems.

Republican Party (Vabariiklik Partei): Kuperjanovi 56-5, Tartu 50409; tel. 521-4512; e-mail leping.vp@mail.ee; internet www.vabariiklikpartei.ee; f. 1999; Chair. KRISTJAN-OLARI LEPING.

Russian Party in Estonia: Tallinn; f. 1994; merged with the Russian People's Party of Estonia in early 1996; represents the Russian-speaking minority in Estonia; opposed to North Atlantic Treaty Organization (NATO) membership; absorbed the Estonian Unity Party, the Russian-Baltic Party and the Russian Unity Party in Dec. 2002; Chair. STANISLAV CHEREPANOV.

Social Democratic Party (Sotsiaaldemokraatlik Erakond): Ahtri 10A, Tallinn 10151; tel. 611-6040; e-mail kantselei@sotsdem.ee; internet www.sotsdem.ee; f. 1999 as the People's Party Moderates, by merger of the People's Party and the Moderates' Party; name changed in 2004; Chair. IVARI PADAR; Sec.-Gen. REIN ORG.

Union for the Republic Res Publica (Ühendus Vabariigi Eest Res Publica): Narva mnt. 7, Tallinn 10117; tel. 610-9244; fax 610-9243; e-mail respublica@respublica.ee; internet www.respublica.ee; f. 2001; right-wing; Chair. JUHAN PARTS; 2,500 mems.

Diplomatic Representation

EMBASSIES IN ESTONIA

Austria: Vambola 6, Tallinn 14114; tel. 627-8740; fax 631-4365; Ambassador Dr JAKUB FORST-BATTAGLIA.

China, People's Republic: Narva mnt. 98, Tallinn 15009; tel. 601-5830; fax 601-5833; e-mail office@chinaembassy.ee; internet www.chinaembassy.ee; Ambassador HONG JIUYIN.

Czech Republic: Lahe 4, Tallinn 10150; tel. 627-4400; fax 631-4716; e-mail tallinn@embassy.mzv.cz; internet www.mfa.cz/tallinn; Ambassador MILOŠ LEXA.

Denmark: Wismari 5, Tallinn 15047; tel. 630-6400; fax 630-6421; e-mail tllamb@um.dk; internet www.denmark.ee; Ambassador JØRGEN MUNK RASMUSSEN.

Finland: Kohtu 4, Tallinn 15180; tel. 610-3200; fax 610-3281; e-mail sanomat.tal@formin.fi; internet www.finland.ee; Ambassador JAAKKO BLOMBERG.

France: Toom-Kuninga 20, Tallinn 15185; tel. 631-1492; fax 631-1385; e-mail france@datanet-ee.org; internet www.ambafrance-ee.org; Ambassador CHANTAL DE BOURMONT.

Germany: Toom-Kuninga 11, Tallinn 15048; tel. 627-5300; fax 627-5304; e-mail deutschland@online.ee; internet www.germany.ee; Ambassador JÜRGEN DRÖGE.

Hungary: Narva mnt. 122, Tallinn 10127; tel. 605-1880; fax 605-4088; e-mail huembtal@mfa.neti.ee; internet www.huembtal.ee; Ambassador LÁSZLÓ NIKICSER.

Ireland: Demini Bldg, Viru 1/Vene 2, Tallinn 10123; tel. 681-1888; fax 681-1889; e-mail embassytallinn@eircom.net; Ambassador SEAN FARRELL.

Italy: Vene 2, Tallinn 10123; tel. 627-6160; fax 631-1370; e-mail italemb1@online.ee; internet www.italembtallinn.ee; Ambassador RUGGERO VOZZI.

Japan: Harju 6, Tallinn 10130; tel. 631-0531; fax 631-0533; e-mail jaapansk@online.ee; Chargé d'affaires a.i. KEIICHI HASEGAWA.

Latvia: Tōnismägi 10, Tallinn 10119; tel. 627-7850; fax 625-7855; e-mail embassy.estonia@mfa.gov.lv; Ambassador EDGARS SKUJA.

Lithuania: Uus 15, Tallinn 15070; tel. 631-4030; fax 641-2013; e-mail amber@anet.ee; internet www.hot.ee/lietambasada; Ambassador ANTANAS VINKUS.

Netherlands: Harju 6, Tallin 10130; tel. 631-0580; fax 631-0583; e-mail neth.gov@online.ee; internet www.netherlandsembassy.ee; Ambassador JOANNA M. P. F. VAN VLIET.

Norway: Harju 6, Tallinn 15054; tel. 627-1000; fax 627-1001; e-mail emb.tallinn@mfa.no; Ambassador PER K. PEDERSEN.

Poland: Pärnu mnt. 8, Tallinn 10503; tel. 627-8206; fax 644-5221; e-mail ambrptal@netexpress.ee; internet www.poola.ee; Ambassador WOJCIECH WRÓBLEWSKI.

Russia: Pikk 19, Tallinn 10133; tel. 646-4175; fax 646-4178; e-mail vensaat@online.ee; internet www.estonia.mid.ru; Ambassador KONSTANTIN PROVALOV.

Spain: Liivalaia 13/15, Tallinn 10118; tel. 667-6651; fax 631-3767; e-mail emb.tallinn@mae.es; Ambassador MIGUEL BAUZÁ MORE.

Sweden: Pikk 28, Tallinn 15055; tel. 640-5600; fax 640-5695; e-mail swedemb@neti.ee; internet www.sweden.ee; Ambassador DAG HARTELIUS.

Turkey: Narva mnt. 30, Tallinn 10152; tel. 627-2880; fax 627-2885; e-mail tallinn.be@mfa.gov.tr; Ambassador ÖMER ALTUG.

Ukraine: Lahe 6, Tallinn 15170; tel. 601-5815; fax 601-5816; e-mail embukr@eol.ee; internet www.uninet.ee/~embukra; Ambassador MYKOLA MAKAREVYCH.

United Kingdom: Wismari 6, Tallinn 10136; tel. 667-4700; fax 667-4755; e-mail information@britishembassy.ee; internet www.britishembassy.ee; Ambassador NIGEL HAYWOOD.

USA: Kentmanni 20, Tallinn 15099; tel. 668-8100; fax 668-8134; e-mail tallinn@usemb.ee; internet www.usemb.ee; Ambassador ALDONA WOS.

Judicial System

Supreme Court
(Riigikohus)

Lossi 17, Tartu 50093; tel. 730-9002; fax 730-9003; e-mail nc@nc.ee; internet www.nc.ee.

Chief Justice and Chairman of the Constitutional Review Chamber: MÄRT RASK.

Chairman of the Civil Chamber: ANTS KULL.

Chairman of the Criminal Chamber: HANNES KIRIS.

Chairman of the Administrative Law Chamber: TŌNU ANTON.

Office of the Chancellor of Justice (Õiguskantsleri): Kohtu 8, Tallinn 15193; tel. 693-8400; fax 693-8401; e-mail info@oiguskantsler.ee; internet www.oiguskantsler.ee; f. 1993; reviews general application of legislative and executive powers and of local governments for conformity with the Constitution, supervises activities of state agencies in guaranteeing constitutional rights and freedoms; Chancellor of Justice ALLAR JÕKS.

Public Prosecutor's Office (Riigiprokuratuur): Wismari 7, Tallinn 15188; tel. 631-3002; fax 645-1475; e-mail info@prokuratuur.ee; internet www.prokuratuur.ee; State Prosecutor-Gen. NORMAN AAS.

Religion

CHRISTIANITY

Protestant Churches

Consistory of the Estonian Evangelical Lutheran Church (Eesti Evangeelne Luterlike Kirik): Kiriku plats 3, Tallinn 10130; tel. 627-7350; fax 627-7352; e-mail konsistoorium@eelk.ee; internet www.eelk.ee; Archbishop JAAN KIIVIT.

Estonian Conference of Seventh-day Adventists (Seitsmenda Päeva Adventistide Kogudus Eesti Liit): Lille 18, Tartu 51010; tel. 734-3211; fax 734-3389; e-mail office@advent.ee; internet www.advent.ee; f. 1917; Chair. ÜLO PÄRNA.

Union of Free Evangelical Christian and Baptist Churches of Estonia (Eesti Evangeeliumi Kristlaste ja Baptistide Koguduste Liit): Jakobsoni 14, Tallinn 10128; tel. 670-0698; fax 650-6008; e-mail eekbl@ekklesia.ee; internet www.ekklesia.ee; Pres. JOOSEP TAMMO.

United Methodist Church in Estonia (Eesti Metodisti Kirik): EMK Kirikuvalitsus, Narva mnt. 51, Tallinn 10152; tel. 668-8477; fax 631-3482; e-mail keskus@metodistikirik.ee; internet www.metodistikirik.ee; f. 1907; forms part of the Northern European Area of the United Methodist Church; Superintendent OLAV PÄRNAMETS.

The Eastern Orthodox Church

Between 1923 and 1940 the Estonian Apostolic Orthodox Church (EAOC) was under the jurisdiction of the Ecumenical Patriarchate of Constantinople (based in Istanbul, Turkey). Following the Soviet occupation of Estonia in 1940, the EAOC was banned and its churches and communities were placed under the jurisdiction of the Moscow Patriarchate. The leaders of the EAOC went into exile in Stockholm, Sweden. After the restoration of Estonian independence, in 1993 Estonia recognized the EAOC as the legal successor of the Orthodox Church in operation before the Second World War, and in February 1996 the Ecumenical Patriarchate restored the EAOC to its jurisdiction. The Estonian Orthodox Church of the Moscow Patriarchate was officially registered in April 2002.

Estonian Apostolic Orthodox Church (Eesti Apostlik Õigeusu Kirik): Wismari 32, Tallinn 10136; tel. 660-0780; fax 660-0782; e-mail eaok@eaok.ee; internet www.eoc.ee; Metropolitan of Tallinn and All Estonia STEPHANOS; 60 congregations.

Estonian Orthodox Church (Moscow Patriarchate) (Moskva Patriarhaadi Eesti Õigeusu Kirik/Estonskaya Pravoslavnaya Tserkov Moskovskogo Patriarkhata): Pikk 64/4, Tallinn 10133; tel. 641-1301; fax 641-1302; e-mail mpeok@hot.ee; internet www.orthodox.ee; Metropolitan of Tallinn and All Estonia KORNELIUS; 32 congregations.

The Roman Catholic Church

At 31 December 2002 there were an estimated 5,000 Roman Catholic adherents (of both the Latin and Byzantine rites) in Estonia.

Office of the Apostolic Administrator: Jaan Poska 47, Tallinn 10150; tel. 601-3079; fax 601-3190; e-mail admapost@online.ee; Apostolic Administrator Most Rev. PETER STEPHAN ZURBRIGGEN (Titular Archbishop of Glastonia (Glastonbury) and Apostolic Nuncio to Lithuania, Estonia and Latvia—resident in Vilnius, Lithuania).

ISLAM

Estonian Islamic Congregation: Sütiste 52–76, Tallinn 0034; tel. 652-2403; f. 1928; Chair. of Bd TIMUR SEIFULLEN.

JUDAISM

In the early 2000s there were an estimated 3,000 Jews resident in Estonia, principally in Tallinn.

Jewish Community of Estonia (Eesti Juudi Kogukond/Yevreiskaya Obshchina Estonii): Karu 16, Tallinn; POB 3576, Tallinn 10507; tel. and fax 662-3034; e-mail community@jewish.ee; internet www.jewish.ee; Chair. CILJA LAUD.

The Press

In 2003 there were 14 officially registered daily newspapers and 114 non-daily newspapers published in Estonia. In that year 11 daily newspapers and in 2002 91 non-daily newspapers were published in Estonian. In 2003 1,180 periodicals were published, 948 of which were published in Estonian.

PRINCIPAL NEWSPAPERS

In Estonian except where otherwise stated.

Äripäev (Business Daily): Pärnu mnt. 105, Tallinn 19094; tel. 667-0222; fax 667-0165; e-mail mbp@mbp.ee; internet www.mbp.ee; f. 1989; five days a week; business and finance; Editor-in-Chief IGOR RÕTOV; circ. 17,200.

Den za Dnem (Day After Day): Pärnu mnt. 130, Tallinn 11313; tel. 678-8288; fax 678-8290; e-mail ambre@dd.ee; internet www.dd.ee; f. 1991; weekly; in Russian; circ. 18,500.

Eesti Ekspress (Estonian Express): Narva mnt. 11E, Tallinn 10151; tel. 669-8080; fax 669-8154; e-mail ekspress@ekspress.ee; internet www.ekspress.ee; f. 1989; weekly; Editor-in-Chief AAVO KOKK; circ. 49,300.

Eesti Kirik (Estonian Church): Ülikooli, Tartu 51003; tel. 743-1437; fax 743-3243; f. 1923; weekly; Editor-in-Chief SIRJE SEMM; circ. 2,100.

Eesti Päevaleht (Estonian Daily): Pärnu mnt. 67A, POB 433, Tallinn 10151; tel. 614-4498; fax 614-4334; e-mail mail@epl.ee; internet www.epl.ee; f. 1905; daily; Editor-in-Chief PRIIT HÕBEMÄGI; circ. 37,000.

Maaleht (Country News): Toompuiestee 16, Tallinn 10137; tel. 661-3718; fax 662-2292; e-mail ml@maaleht.ee; internet www.maaleht.ee; f. 1987; weekly; problems and aspects of politics, culture, agriculture and country life; Editor-in-Chief SULEV VALNER; circ. 42,000.

Meie Meel (Our Mind): POB 104, Tallinn 0090; tel. 681-253; fax 646-1625; e-mail meiemeel@zzz.ee; f. 1991; weekly; youth paper; Editor-in-Chief MARE VETEMAA; circ. 20,700.

Molodezh Estonii (Youth of Estonia): Narva mnt. 13A, Tallinn 10502; tel. 614-3400; fax 613-3406; e-mail ilja@moles.ee; internet www.moles.ee; f. 1991; in Russian; Editor-in-Chief ILYA NIKOFOROV.

Postimees (Postman): Maakri 23A, Tallinn 10145; tel. 666-2302; fax 666-2301; e-mail erik.roose@postimees.ee; internet www.postimees.ee; f. 1857; daily; Editor-in-Chief URMAS KLAAS; circ. 60,200.

Sirp: POB 388, Tallinn 10503; tel. 640-5770; fax 640-5771; e-mail sirp@sirp.ee; internet www.sirp.ee; f. 1940; weekly; the arts; Editor-in-Chief MIHKEL MUTT; circ. 3,500.

SL Õhtuleht (Evening Gazette): Narva mnt. 13, POB 106, Tallinn 10501; tel. 614-4805; fax 614-4001; e-mail priit@sloleht.ee; internet www.sloleht.ee; f. 2000; daily; Editor-in-Chief VÄINO KOORBERG; circ. 67,200.

Vesti dnya (News of the Day): Madala 16, Tallinn 10315; tel. 665-1100; fax 665-1111; e-mail vnews@vesti.ee; internet www.vesti.ee; five days a week in Russian; also *Vesti nedeli* (*News of the Week*), Fridays; Editor-in-Chief PAVEL IVANOV; circ. 6,100.

PRINCIPAL PERIODICALS

Akadeemia: Ülikooli 21, Tartu 51007; tel. 742-3050; fax 742-3146; e-mail akadeemia@akad.ee; internet www.akad.ee; f. 1989; monthly; journal of the Union of Writers; Editor-in-Chief TOOMAS KIHO; circ. 2,500.

Eesti Arst (Estonian Physician): Pepleri 32, Tartu 51010; tel. and fax 742-7825; e-mail eestiarst@eestiarst.ee; internet www.eestiarst.ee; f. 1922; monthly; Editor-in-Chief VÄINO SINISALU; circ. 3,800–4,200.

Eesti Loodus (Estonian Nature): Veski 4, POB 110, Tartu 50002; tel. 742-1186; fax 742-1143; e-mail toimetus@el.loodus.ee; internet www.loodusajakiri.ee/eesti_loodus; f. 1933; monthly; popular science; illustrated; Editor-in-Chief TOOMAS KUKK; circ. 5,200.

Eesti Naine (Estonian Woman): Maakri 23A, Tallinn 10145; tel. 666-2627; fax 666-2557; e-mail katrin.streimann@kirjastus.ee; internet www.kirjastus.ee/eestinaine; f. 1924; monthly; Editor-in-Chief KATRIN STREIMANN; circ. 24,000.

Hea Laps (Good Kid): Harju 1, Tallinn 10146; tel. 631-4428; e-mail hea.laps@mail.ee; internet kommikas.kalev.ee/healaps; monthly; for children; Editor-in-Chief LEELO TUNGAL.

Horisont (Horizon): Narva mnt. 5, Tallinn 0117; tel. 661-6163; fax 641-8033; e-mail horisont@horisont.ee; f. 1967; 6 a year; popular scientific; Editor-in-Chief INDREK ROHTMETS; circ. 3,000.

Keel ja Kirjandus (Language and Literature): Roosikrantsi 6, Tallinn 10119; tel. 644-9228; fax 644-1800; e-mail kk@eki.ee; internet www.eki.ee/keeljakirjandus; f. 1958; monthly; publ. by Academy of Sciences and Union of Writers; Editor-in-Chief MART MERI; circ. 900.

Kodukiri (Your Home): Maakri 23A, Tallinn 10145; tel. 666-2550; fax 666-2558; e-mail velve.saar@kirjastus.ee; f. 1992; monthly; Editor-in-Chief KATRIN KUUSEMÄE; circ. 50,000.

Linguistica Uralica: Roosikrantsi 6, Tallinn 10119; tel. 644-0745; e-mail lu@eki.ee; internet www.kirj.ee/l-u.htm; f. 1965; academic journal; Editor-in-Chief VÄINO KLAUS; circ. 300.

Looming (Creation): Harju 1, Tallinn 10146; tel. 627-6420; e-mail looming@hot.ee; f. 1923; journal of the Union of Writers; fiction, poetry, literary criticism; Editor-in-Chief UDO UIBO; circ. 1,800.

Loomingu Raamatukogu (Library of Creativity): Harju 1, Tallinn 10146; tel. 627-6425; e-mail lr@looming.ee; f. 1957; publ. by Union of Writers; poetry, fiction and non-fiction by Estonian and foreign authors; Editor-in-Chief TOOMAS HAUG; circ. 1,400.

Maakodu (Country Home): Toompuiestee 16, Tallinn 10137; tel. 660-5306; fax 662-2292; e-mail meelim@maaleht.ee; internet www.maaleht.ee; f. 1989; monthly; Editor-in-Chief MEELI MÜÜRIPEAL; circ. 12,000.

Maamajandus (Country Economy): Toompuiestee 16, Tallinn 10137; tel. 661-3381; fax 661-3344; e-mail ylo.kalm@maaleht.ee; internet www.maaleht.ee; f. 2000; monthly; Editor-in-Chief ÜLO KALM; circ. 2,000.

Oil Shale: Kohtu 6, Tallinn 10130; tel. 646-7512; fax 646-6026; e-mail aili@kirj.ee; internet www.kirj.ee/oilshale; f. 1984; quarterly; geology, chemistry, mining, oil-shale industry; Editor-in-Chief ANTO RAUKAS; circ. 350.

Põllumajandus (Agriculture): Lai 39, Tallinn 0001; tel. 641-1161; f. 1932; monthly; Editor-in-Chief ARVO SIRENDI; circ. 1,000.

Täheke (Little Star): Roosikrantsi 6, Tallinn 10119; tel. 646-3697; e-mail taheke@taheke.ee; f. 1960; monthly; illustrated; for 5–10-year-olds; Editor-in-Chief ILONA MARTSON; circ. 6,000.

Teater, Muusika, Kino (Theatre, Music, Cinema): Voorimehe 9, Tallinn 10146; tel. and fax 646-4742; f. 1982; monthly; Editor-in-Chief MADIS KOLK; circ. 1,500.

Vikerkaar (Rainbow): Voorimehe 9, Tallinn 10146; tel. 646-4059; e-mail vikerkaar@teleport.ee; f. 1986; monthly; fiction, poetry, critical works; in Estonian and Russian; Editor-in-Chief MÄRT VÄLJATAGA; circ. 1,500.

NEWS AGENCY

BNS (Baltic News Service): Pärnu mnt. 105, Tallinn 15043; tel. 610-8800; fax 610-8811; e-mail bns@bns.ee; internet www.bns.ee; f. 1990; Chief Exec. GEORGE SHABAD.

PRESS ORGANIZATIONS

Estonian Journalists' Union (Eesti Ajakirjanike Liit): Gonsiori 21/409, Tallinn 10147; tel. and fax 646-3699; e-mail eal@eal.ee; internet www.eal.ee; f. 1919; Dir. MERIKE VIILUP.

Estonian Newspaper Association (Eesti Ajalehtede Liit): Pärnu mnt. 67A, Tallinn 10134; tel. 646-1005; fax 631-1210; e-mail eall@eall.ee; internet www.eall.ee; f. 1990; 41 mem. newspapers; Chair. AGU VEETAMM.

Estonian Press Council (Avaliku Sõna Nõukogu): Gonsiori 21, Tallinn 15020; tel. and fax 646-3699; e-mail asn@asn.org.ee; internet www.asn.org.ee; Chair. URMAS LOIT.

Publishers

Eesti Raamat (Estonian Book): Laki 26, Tallinn 12915; tel. and fax 658-7889; e-mail georg.grynberg@mail.ee; f. 1940; fiction for children and adults; Dir ANNE-ASTRI KASK.

Estonian Encyclopedia Publishers (Eesti Entsüklopeediakirjastus): Narva mnt. 4, Tallinn 10117; tel. 699-9620; fax 699-9621; e-mail ene@ene.ee; internet www.ene.ee; f. 1991; Man. Dir HARDO AASMÄE.

Huma: Vene 14, Tallinn 10123; tel. and fax 644-0955; e-mail info@huma.ee; internet www.huma.ee; f. 1990; fiction, non-fiction, children's books, art, calendars; Dir LIIVI KESKPAIK.

Ilmamaa: Vanemuise 19, Tartu 51014; tel. 742-7290; fax 742-7320; e-mail ilmamaa@ilmamaa.ee; internet www.ilmamaa.ee; f. 1992; general fiction, philosophy, cultural history, electronic publishing; Dir MART JAGOMÄGI.

Ilo: Madara 14, Tallinn 10612; tel. 661-0550; fax 661-0556; e-mail ilo@ilo.ee; internet www.ilo.ee; dictionaries, reference books, text books, history, management, psychology, law and children's books; Dir RAUL KILGAS.

Koolibri: Pärnu mnt. 10, Tallinn 10148; tel. 644-5223; fax 644-6813; e-mail koolibri@koolibri.ee; internet www.koolibri.ee; f. 1991; textbooks, dictionaries, children's books; Dir ANTS LANG.

Kunst (Fine Art): Lai 34, Tallinn 10133; POB 105, Tallinn 10502; tel. 641-1764; fax 641-1762; e-mail kunst.lai@mail.ee; f. 1957; fine arts, fiction, tourism, history, biographies; Dir SIRJE HELME.

Kupar: Tallinn; tel. 628-6174; fax 646-2076; e-mail kupar@netexpress.ee; f. 1987; contemporary fiction; Dir IVO SANDRE.

Logos: Narma mnt. 51, Tallinn 10152; tel. and fax 661-3712; e-mail logos@logos.ee; internet www.logos.ee; f. 1991; Christian; Chair. INGMAR KURG.

Monokkel: POB 311, Tallinn 10503; tel. 501-6307; fax 656-9176; e-mail monokkel@hot.ee; internet www.hot.ee/monokkel; f. 1988; history, fiction; Dir ANTS ÖÖBIK.

Olion: Laki 26, Tallinn 12915; tel. 655-0175; fax 655-0173; e-mail olion@hot.ee; internet www.kirjastused.com/olion/; f. 1989; politics, reference, history, biographies, children's books; Dir HÜLLE UNT.

Õllu: Harju 1, Tallinn 10146; tel. 652-2038; fiction; Chair. of Bd HEINO KIIK.

Olympia OÜ: Gonsiori 12–15, Tallinn 10117; tel. 661-2853; e-mail olympia@online.ee; sports; Editor-in-Chief PAAVO KIVINE.

Perioodika (Periodicals): Voorimehe 9, Tallinn 10146; tel. 644-1252; fax 644-2484; f. 1964; newspapers, guidebooks, periodicals, fiction, children's books in foreign languages; Dir UNO SILLAJÕE.

Tartu University Press: Tiigi 78, Tartu 50410; tel. 737-5961; fax 737-5944; e-mail tyk@psych.ut.ee; f. 1958; science, textbooks, etc; Chair. VAIKO TIGANE.

Tiritamm: Laki 26, Tallinn 12915; tel. and fax 656-3570; e-mail tiritamm@tiritamm.ee; internet www.eestikirjastused.com/tiritamm/; f. 1991; children's books; Dir SIRJE SAIMRE.

Valgus: Tulika 19, Tallinn 10613; tel. 650-5025; fax 650-5104; e-mail info@kirjastusvalgus.ee; internet www.kirjastusvalgus.ee; f. 1965; scientific literature, resource materials and textbooks; Editor-in-Chief EVA KOLLI.

PUBLISHERS' ASSOCIATION

Estonian Publishers' Assocn (Eesti Kirjastuste Liit): Roosikrantsi 6/207,10119 Tallinn; tel. 644-9866; fax 641-1443; e-mail kirjastusteliit@eki.ee; internet www.estbook.com; f. 1991; Dir-Gen. KRISTIINA RAID.

Broadcasting and Communications

TELECOMMUNICATIONS

Regulatory Authorities

National Communications Board: Ädala 2, Tallinn 10614; tel. 693-1154; fax 693-1155; e-mail postbox@sa.ee; internet www.sa.ee; Dir JÜRI JÕEMA.

Service Providers

Eesti Telekom AS (Estonian Telecom Ltd): Roosikrantsi 2, Tallinn 10119; tel. 631-1212; fax 631-1224; e-mail mailbox@telekom.ee; internet www.telekom.ee; f. 1992 as Eesti Telefon (subsequently a subsidiary, renamed Elion in 2003); privatized in 1999; subsidiaries include Eesti Mobiltelefon AS (EMT—q.v.) and Elion Enterprises; Chair. and Chief Exec. JAAN MÄNNIK.

Eesti Mobiltelefon AS (EMT): Lasnamäe 64, Tallinn 19095; tel. 639-7111; fax 611-1897; e-mail emt@emt.ee; internet www.emt.ee; f. 1991; owned by Eesti Telekom AS; Pres. PEEP AAVIKSOO.

BROADCASTING

Supervisory Authority

Broadcasting Council: Gonsiori 21, Tallinn 15020; tel. 611-4305; fax 611-4457; e-mail rhn@er.ee; mems appointed by Riigikogu (State Assembly).

Radio

In 2003 there were 26 private radio broadcasters operating in Estonia (one with an international broadcasting licence, 15 with regional licences and 11 with local licences), in addition to the public broadcaster, Eesti Raadio (Estonian Radio).

Eesti Raadio (Estonian Radio): Gonsiori 21, Tallinn 15020; tel. 611-4115; fax 611-4457; e-mail raadio@er.ee; internet www.er.ee; f. 1926; five 24-hour channels (three in Estonian, one in Russian and one in English, French and German); external service in English; Chair. and Dir-Gen. MARGUS ALLIKMAA.

Raadio Elmar: Õpetaja 9A, Tartu 51003; tel. 742-7520; fax 774-2044; e-mail elmar@elmar.ee; internet www.elmar.ee; Dir JAAN HABICHT.

Raadio Kuku: Narva mnt. 63, Tallinn 20606; tel. 630-7660; fax 601-5759; internet www.kuku.ee; Chair. of Bd REIN LANG.

Raadio Sky Plus: Pärnu mnt. 139C, Tallinn 11317; tel. 678-8777; fax 678-8710; e-mail sky@sky.ee; internet www.skyplus.fm; Chief Exec. ILMAR KOMPUS.

Raadio Uuno: Narva mnt. 63, Tallinn 20606; tel. 630-7080; fax 630-7085; e-mail uuno@uuno.ee; internet www.uuno.ee; Chair. of Bd REIN LANG.

Star FM: Peterburi tee 81, Tallinn 11415; tel. 622-0288; fax 622-0294; e-mail info@starfm.ee; internet www.starfm.ee; Chair. SVEN NUTMANN.

Tartu Pereraadio (Tartu Family Radio): Annemõisa 8, Tartu 50718; tel. and fax 748-8458; e-mail tartu@pereraadio.ee; internet www.pereraadio.ee; f. 1994; Christian; Pres. JOEL LUHAMETS.

Television

There are three national commercial television stations and one public broadcaster in Estonia. In addition, five cable television licences have been issued. The commercial stations are:

Eesti Televisioon (Estonian Television): Faehlmanni 12, Tallinn 15029; tel. 628-4113; fax 628-4155; e-mail etv@etv.ee; internet www.etv.ee; f. 1955; state-owned; one channel; programmes in Estonian and Russian; Chair. ILMAR RAAG.

Kanal 2 (Channel 2): Maakri 23A, Tallinn 10145; tel. 666-2450; fax 666-2451; e-mail info@kanal2.ee; internet www.kanal2.ee; f. 1993; commercial; Chair. HANS ERIK MATRE.

TV3: Peterburgi tee 81, Tallinn 11415; tel. 622-0200; fax 622-0201; e-mail tv3@tv3.ee; internet www.tv3.ee; f. 1996; Exec. Dir TOOMAS VARA.

Broadcasting Association

Association of Estonian Broadcasters (AEB) (Eesti Ringhäälingute Liit): Ülemiste tee 3A, Tallinn 11415; tel. and fax 606-1701; e-mail erl@online.ee; internet www.ringhliit.ee; f. 1992; 16 mems; Man. Dir URMAS LOIT.

Finance

(cap. = capital; res = reserves; dep. = deposits; m. = million; brs = branches; amounts in kroons)

BANKING

Central Bank

Bank of Estonia (Eesti Pank): Estonia pst. 13, Tallinn 15095; tel. 668-0719; fax 668-0836; e-mail info@epbe.ee; internet www .bankofestonia.info; f. 1918; re-established 1990; bank of issue; cap. and res 3,228.5m., dep. 5,616.4m. (Dec. 2003); Pres. VAHUR KRAFT.

Commercial Banks

Estonian Credit Bank (Eesti Krediidipank): Narva mnt. 4, Tallinn 15014; tel. 669-0900; fax 661-6037; e-mail info@krediidipank.ee; internet www.krediidipank.ee; f. 1992; 28.2% owned by Latvijas Biznesa banka (Latvia); cap. 85.3m., res 0.3m., dep. 1,456.4m. (Dec. 2003); Pres. AIN SOIDLA; Chair. of Bd ANDRUS KLUGE; 12 brs.

Hansapank: Liivalaia 8, Tallinn 15040; tel. 631-0310; fax 631-0410; e-mail hansa@hansa.ee; internet www.hansa.ee; f. 1991; merged with Estonian Savings Bank (Eesti Hoiupank) in 1998; 59.7% owned by ForeningsSparbanken AB (Sweden); cap. €50.7m., res €207.9m., dep. €2,963.0m. (Dec. 2003); Chair. of Council ANDERS EK; Chair. of Bd INDREK NEIVELT; 93 brs (in Estonia).

Nordea Panga Eesti filiaal (Nordea Bank, Estonian branch): Hobujaama 4, Tallinn 15068; tel. 628-3200; fax 628-3201; e-mail tallinn@nordea.com; internet www.nordea.ee; f. 1995; subsidiary of Nordea Bank Finland.

Sampo Bank: Narva mnt. 11, POB 19, Tallinn 15015; tel. 680-0800; fax 630-2200; e-mail info@sampopank.ee; internet www.sampo.ee; f. 1992; present name adopted 2000; wholly owned by Sampo Bank (Finland); cap. 323.1m., res 21.8m., dep. 6,160.7m. (Dec. 2003); Chair. HÄRMO VÄRK; 13 brs.

Tallinn Business Bank (Tallinna Äripanga): Estonia pst. 3–5, Tallinn 15097; tel. 668-8000; fax 668-8001; e-mail info@tbb.ee; internet www.tbb.ee; f. 1991; cap. 104.4m., res 12.3m., dep. 260.2m. (Dec. 2003); Chair. of Bd VALERII HARITONOV.

Union Bank of Estonia (Eesti Ühispank): Tornimäe 2, Tallinn 15010; tel. 665-5100; fax 665-5102; e-mail postkast@eyp.ee; internet www.eyp.ee; f. 1992; 100% owned by Scandinaviska Enskilda Banken (Sweden); cap. 665.6m., res 1,815.4m., dep. 21.335.3m. (Dec. 2003); Pres. AIN HANSCHMIDT; 90 brs.

Banking Association

Estonian Banking Association (Eesti Pangaliit): Ahtri 12, Tallinn 10151; tel. 611-6567; fax 611-6568; e-mail post@pangaliit.ee; internet www.pangaliit.ee; f. 1992; Chair. INDREK NEIVELT; Man. Dir KATRIN TALIHÄRM.

STOCK EXCHANGE

Tallinn Stock Exchange (Tallinna Börs): Pärnu mnt. 12, Tallinn 10148; tel. 640-8840; fax 640-8801; e-mail hex@hex.ee; internet www .hex.ee; f. 1995; 61.6% owned by the OMHEX group (Finland); Chair. GERT TIIVAS.

INSURANCE

At the end of 2003 there were five insurance organizations providing life insurance, and eight providing non-life insurance, operating in Estonia. The following were among the principal companies operating at that time.

Estonian Insurance Asscn (Eesti Kindlustusseltside Liit): Kiriku 6, Tallinn 10130; tel. 620-1903; fax 646-6527; e-mail info@eksl.ee; internet www.eksl.ee; f. 1993; Chair. INDREK HOLST.

Insurance Companies

ERGO: Lauteri 5, Tallinn 10114; tel. 610-6500 ; fax 610-6501; internet www.ergo-kindlustus.ee; provides non-life insurance (as ERGO Kindlustuse) and life insurance (ERGO Elukindlustrus); Chair. of Bd OLGA REZNIK.

Hansa Elukindlustus (Hansa Life Insurance): Liivalaia 12, Tallinn 15036; tel. 613-1120; fax 613-1130; e-mail hek@hansa.ee; internet www.hansa.ee; 100% owned by Hansapank; fmrly Hansa-panga Elukindlustuse; present name adopted 2004; life insurance; Chair. of Council PRIIT PÕLDOJA.

If Eesti Kindlustus (If Estonia Insurance): Pronksi 19, 10124 Tallinn; tel. 667-1099; fax 667-1016; e-mail info@if.ee; internet www .if.ee; f. 1999; non-life; Chief Exec. OLAVI LAIDO.

Nordicum Kindlustus Eesti: Liivalaia 13/15, Tallinn 10118; tel. 667-1400; fax 667-1401; e-mail sekretar@nordicum.ee; internet www.nordicum.ee; owned by QBE International (Australia); fmrly Nordea Kindlustus Eesti.

Salva Kindlustuse (Salva Insurance): Pärnu mnt 16, Tallinn 10141; tel. 680-0500; fax 680-0501; e-mail salva@salva.ee; internet www.salva.ee; non-life insurance.

Seesam: Roosikrantsi 11, Tallinn 10119; tel. 610-3000; fax 610-3010; e-mail info@seesam.ee; internet www.seesam.ee; wholly owned by Keskinäinen Henkivakuutusosakeyhtiö Suomi (Suomi Mutual Life Assurance Co—Finland); provides life insurance (as Seesam Elukindlustuse) and non-life insurance (Seesam Rahvusvaheline Kindlustuse); Chair. of Bd ERKI KILU.

Ühispanga Elukindlustuse (Union Bank Life Insurance): Tornimäe 2, Tallinn 10145; tel. 665-6840; fax 665-6847; e-mail elukindlustus@eyp.ee; internet www.kindlustan.com; wholly owned by Union Bank of Estonia; life; Chair. of Council AIN HANSCHMIDT.

Trade and Industry

GOVERNMENT AGENCIES

Consumer Protection Board (Tarbijakaitseametist): Kiriku 4, Tallinn 15071; tel. 620-1700; fax 620-1701; e-mail info@consumer .ee; internet www.consumer.ee; f. 1994; Dir-Gen. HELLE ARUNIIT.

Enterprise Estonia (Ettevõtluse Arendamise Sihtasutus): Liivalaia 13/15, Tallinn 10118; tel. 627-9700; fax 627-9427; e-mail eas@ eas.ee; internet www.eas.ee; Chair. TEA VARRAK.

Estonian Centre for Standardization (Eesti Standardikeskus) (EVS): Aru 10, Tallinn 10317; tel. 605-5050; fax 605-5070; e-mail info@evs.ee; internet www.evs.ee; f. 1999; Man. Dir SVEN KASEMAA.

Estonian Competition Board (Kohkurentsiamet): Lõkke 4, Tallinn 15184; tel. 680-3942; fax 680-3943; e-mail compet@ konkurentsiamet.ee; internet www.konkurentsiamet.ee; Dir-Gen. PEETER TAMMISTU.

Estonian Investment Agency: Roosikrantsi 11, Tallinn 10119; tel. 627-9420; fax 627-9427; e-mail info@eas.ee; internet www .investinestonia.com; Dir ANDRUS VIIRG.

CHAMBERS OF COMMERCE

Estonian Chamber of Agriculture and Commerce (Eesti Põllumajandus-Kaubanduskoda): Vilmsi 53B, Tallinn 10147; tel. 600-9349; fax 600-9350; e-mail info@epkk.ee; internet www.epkk.ee; Chair. ALAR OPPAR.

Estonian Chamber of Commerce and Industry (ECCI) (Eesti Kaubandus-Tööstuskoda): Toom-Kooli 17, Tallinn 10130; tel. 646-0244; fax 646-0245; e-mail koda@koda.ee; internet www.koda.ee; f. 1925; brs in Tartu, Jõhvi, Pärnu and Kuressaare; Pres. TOOMAS LUMAN.

INDUSTRIAL AND TRADE ASSOCIATIONS

Asscn of Construction Material Producers of Estonia (Eesti Ehitusmaterjalide Tootjate Liit): Kiriku 6, Tallinn 10130; tel. 648-1918; fax 648-9062; e-mail eetl@hot.ee; internet www.hot.ee/eetl; Pres. VIKTOR VALKIAINEN.

Asscn of Estonian Electrotechnical and Electronic Industry: Pirita 20, Tallinn 0001; tel. 623-8981; fax 623-7827; Pres. GUNNAR TOOMSOO.

Asscn of Estonian Food Industry: Saku 15–105, Tallinn 11314; tel. 648-6073; fax 631-2718; e-mail info@toiduliit.ee; internet www .toiduliit.ee; f. 1993; Man. Dir HELVE REMMEL.

Asscn of Estonian International Road Carriers (Eesti Rahvusvaheliste Autovedajate Assotsiatsioon—ERAA): Narva mnt. 91, Tallinn 10127; tel. 606-2040; fax 606-2041; e-mail info@eraa.ee; internet www.eraa.ee; Sec.-Gen. TOIVO KULDKEPP.

Estonian Agricultural Producers Central Union (Eestimaa Pollumajandustootjate Keskliit): Lai 39/41, Tallinn 10133; tel. and fax 641-1113; e-mail epk.epk@mail.ee; Chair. of Bd VIKTOR SARTAKOV.

Estonian Asscn of Construction Entrepreneurs (Eesti Ehitusettevõtjate Liit): Kiriku 6, Tallinn 10130; tel. and fax 648-9005; fax 641-0071; e-mail eeel@eeel.ee; internet www.eeel.ee; Man. Dir TARMO LIGE.

Estonian Asscn of Fisheries: Gonsiori 29-502, Tallinn 10147; tel. 648-4537; fax 641-9006; e-mail kalaliit@online.ee; Chair. JAAN JALAKAS; Man. Dir VALDUR NOORMÄGI.

Estonian Assocn of Small and Medium-sized Enterprises (EVEA) (Eesti Väike-Ja Keskmiste Ettevõtjate Assotsiatsioon): Pronksi 3, Tallinn 10124; tel. 640-3935; fax 631-2451; e-mail sme@ evea.ee; internet www.evea.ee; f. 1988; Pres. RIIVO SINIJÄRV; Man. Dir MARGIT KALLASTE.

Estonian Business Assen: Liivalaia 9, 10118 Tallinn; tel. 646-2030; fax 646-2031; e-mail easa@esea.ee; internet www.esea.ee; f. 1996; Pres. URMAS SOORUMAA; Man. Dir JAAK SAARNIIT.

Estonian Clothing and Textile Assen (Eesti Rõivaja Tekstiililiit): Tartu mnt. 63, Tallinn 10115; tel. 611-5567; fax 611-5568; e-mail ertl@online.ee; Chair. MADIS VÕÕRAS.

Estonian Dairy Assen (Eesti Piimaliit): Vilmsi 53, Tallinn 10147; tel. 600-9357; fax 600-9355; e-mail eestipl@online.ee; Chair. of Bd ENN SOKK; Man. Dir REIN REISSON.

Estonian Forest Industries Federation (Eesti Metsatööstuse Liit): Marja 9, Tallinn 10617; tel. 656-7643; fax 656-7644; e-mail info@emtl.ee; internet www.forestindustries.ee; Man. Dir ANDRES TALIJÄRV.

Estonian Gas Assen (Eesti Gaasiliit): Liivalaia 9, Tallinn 0001; tel. 646-1571; fax 631-4340; Chair. of Bd ANDRES SAAR.

Estonian Hotel and Restaurant Assen (Eesti Hotellide ja Restoranide Liit): Kiriku 6, Tallinn 10130; tel. 641-1428; fax 641-1425; e-mail info@ehrl.ee; Chair. of Bd TARMO SUMBERG.

Estonian Meat Assen (Eesti Lihaliit): Lai 39/41, Tallinn 10133; tel. 641-1179; fax 641-1035; e-mail lihaliit@hot.ee; f. 1989; 18 mem. companies (2002); Chair. of Bd AIGAR PINDMAA; Man. Dir PEETER GRIGORJEV.

Estonian Oil Assen (Eesti Õliühing): Kiriku 6, Tallinn 10130; tel. 620-1930; fax 620-1935; e-mail maimu@oilunion.ee; internet www.oilunion.ee; f. 1993; represents more than 70% of the fuel market; Chair. RAIVO VARE.

Estonian Society of Merchants: Kiriku 6, Tallinn 10130; tel. 620-1914; fax 620-1935; e-mail info@kaupmeesteliit.ee; internet www.kaupmeesteliit.ee; Chair. of Bd PEETER RAUDSEPP; Man. Dir MARIKA MERILAI.

Estonian Trade Council (Eesti Väliskaubanduse Liit): Liimi 1, Tallinn 10621; tel. 656-3299; fax 656-3923; e-mail etc@etc.ee; internet www.etc.ee; f. 1991; non-profit non-govt org; promotes export trade; Chair. of Bd ANDRES TAMM.

Estonian Woodworking Federation: Pärnu mnt. 158B, Tallinn 11317; tel. 655-8525; fax 655-8524; e-mail info@furnitureindustry.ee; internet www.furnitureindustry.ee; Chair. AIN SAARMANN; Man. Dir MÄRT RAHAMÄGI.

ETK Managers' Club: Narva mnt. 7, Tallinn 10117; tel. 630-2324; fax 630-2333; f. 1991; Pres. GEORG ILVEST.

Federation of the Estonian Chemical Industry: Kiriku 6, Tallinn 10130; tel. and fax 648-9004; e-mail info@keemia.ee; internet www.keemia.ee; f. 1991; 32 mem. enterprises; Chair. ILMAR VESIALIIK; Man. Dir HALLAR MEIBAUM.

Federation of the Estonian Engineering Industry: Mustamäe 4, Tallinn 10621; tel. 611-5893; fax 656-6640; e-mail emliit@emliit.ee; f. 1991; 80 mem. enterprises; Chair. of Bd JÜRI RIIVES.

Union of Estonian Automobile Enterprises (Eesti Autoettevõtete Liit): Magasini 31, Tallinn 10138; tel. 643-9476; fax 644-3345; e-mail al@autoettevoteliit.ee; Pres. MATI MÄGI.

Union of Estonian Breweries (Eesti Õlletootjate Liit): Tähtvere 58/62, Tartu 2400; tel. 743-4330; fax 743-1193; Chair. of Bd MADIS PADDAR.

Union of Estonian Paper Manufacturers (Eesti Paberitööstuse Liit): Tööstuse 19, Kohila 3420; tel. 483-3564; fax 483-2132; e-mail kohilapv@netexpress.ee; Chair. of Bd HENNO PAVELSON.

Union of Estonian Wine Producers (Eesti Veinitootjate Liit): Karksi, Karksi vald, Vilijandi mk. 69104; tel. and fax 435-4022; e-mail veinilitt@hot.ee; Chair. of Bd JÜRI KERT.

EMPLOYERS' ORGANIZATION

Estonian Employers' Confederation (Eesti Tööandjate Kesliit): Kiriku 6, Tallinn 10130; tel. 699-9301; fax 699-9310; e-mail ettk@ettk.ee; internet www.ettk.ee; f. 1991 as Confederation of Estonian Industry; Chair. of Bd MEELIS VIRKEBAU; Man. Dir TIIT LAJA.

UTILITIES

Electricity

Eesti Energia (Estonian Energy Co): Laki 24, Tallinn 12915; tel. 715-2222; fax 715-2200; e-mail info@energia.ee; internet www.energia.ee; f. 1939; producer, transmitter and distributor of thermal and electric energy; manufacture of electric motors; electrical engineering; Chair. GUNNAR OKK; 8,000 employees.

Gas

Eesti Gaas (Estonian Gas Co): Liivalaia 9, Tallinn 10118; tel. 630-3003; fax 631-3884; e-mail info@gaas.ee; internet www.gaas.ee; f.

1993; purchases and distributes natural gas; constructs pipelines; calibrates gas meters; Chair. AARNE SAAR; 255 employees.

Water

Tallinn Water Co (Tallinna Vesi): Ädala 10, Tallinn 10614; tel. 626-2200; fax 626-2300; e-mail tvesi@tvesi.ee; internet www.tallinnavesi.ee; f. 1997; supply and treatment of water; collection and treatment of waste water; 50.4% owned by United Utilities Tallinna (a subsidiary of United Utilities International, United Kingdom), 49.6% by Tallinn City Governent; Chair. and Chief Exec. BOB GALLIENE; Dir-Gen. ENNO PERE; 359 employees.

TRADE UNIONS

Assen of Estonian Chemical Industry Workers' Trade Unions: Kohtla-Järve; tel. 334-7828; fax 334-5798; f. 1990; Chair. MIHKEL ISKÜL.

Assen of Estonian Radio- and Electronics-Industry Workers' Trade Unions: Rävala 4, Tallinn 0100; tel. 643-2318; Chair. LYUBOV SEROVA.

Confederation of Estonian Employee Unions (TeenistujateAmetiliitude Keskorganisatsioon): Gonsiori 21, Tallinn 10147; tel. 641-9800; e-mail talo@online.ee; internet www.talo.ee; f. 1992; comprises 13 member unions from the broadcasting, cultural, customs, education, engineering, journalism, radiology and scientific sectors; Chair. TOIVO ROOSIMAA.

Confederation of Estonian Food and Landworkers' Unions: 32 Raua Str, Tallinn 10152; tel. and fax 641-0249; e-mail aare.etmk@mail.ee; f. 1989; Chair. AARE-LEMBIT NEEVE.

Confederation of Estonian Trade Unions (Eesti Ametiühingute Kesskliit): Pärnu mnt 41A , Tallinn 10119; tel. 641-2800; fax 641-2802; e-mail eakl@eakl.ee; internet www.eakl.ee; f. 1990; 26 branch and professional trade union members; Chair. KADI PARNITS; estimated 95,000 individual mems.

Estonian Communication Workers' Trade Union (Eesti Sidetöötajate Ametiühingute Liit—ESAL): Masti 2/5, Tallinn 11911; tel. 601-1124; e-mail esal@uninet.ee; internet www.esal.org.ee; Chair. ÕIE VÄLJAS.

Estonian Light Industry Workers' Trade Union: Rävala 4, Tallinn 0100; tel. and fax 643-1640; Chair. EVI JAAGURA.

Estonian Transportation and Roadworkers' Union (Eesti Transpordi-ja Teetöötajate Ametiühing—ETTA): Kalju 7–1, Tallinn 10414; tel. 641-3131; fax 641-3129; e-mail etta@etta.ee; internet www.etta.ee; Chair. PEEP PETERSON.

Society of Estonian Economy Workers' Trade Unions: Rävala 4, Tallinn 10143; tel. and fax 661-2414; e-mail emal@online.ee.

Trade Union of Oil-Shale Industry Workers (Põlevkivitootjate Ametiühingu Liit): Jaama 10, Jõhvi 415033; tel. 336-4821; fax 336-4810; e-mail eptal@ep.ee; Chair. MAIDO AGUR.

Transport

RAILWAYS

In 2003 there were 967 km of railway track in use, of which 131 km were electrified. Main lines link Tallinn with Narva and St Petersburg (Russia), Tartu and Pskov (Russia). Passenger services, except for the suburban services around Tallinn, are relatively limited, however. In December 2001 the World Bank disbursed a loan of 870m. kroons to Estonian Railways for the upgrading of engines and infrastructure repairs.

Estonian Railway Administration: Lastekodu 31, Tallinn 10113; tel. 605-7401; fax 605-7410; e-mail raudteeamet@rdtamet.ee; internet www.rdtamet.ee; f. 1999; Dir-Gen. OLEG EPNER.

Edelaraudtee: Kaare 25, Türi 72213; tel. 57-123; fax 57-121; e-mail info@edel.ee; internet www.edel.ee; f. 1997; owned by GB Railways (United Kingdom); operates intercity passenger services on the routes: Tallinn–Tartu; Tallinn–Narva; Tartu–Varga; Tallinn–Vijandi–Pärnu; and Tartu–Orava; Dir KALVI PUKKA.

Eesti Raudtee (Estonian Railways): Pikk 36, Tallinn 15073; tel. 615-8610; fax 615-8710; e-mail raudtee@evr.ee; internet www.evr.ee; f. 1918; privatized in 2001; freight carriers; Chair. of Supervisory Bd EDWARD A. BURKHARDT; 4,000 employees.

Elektriraudtee (Electric Railways): Vabaduse pst. 176, Tallinn 10917; tel. 673-7400; fax 673-7440; e-mail info@elektriraudtee.ee; internet www.elektriraudtee.ee ; f. 1998; suburban passenger services in Tallinn region.

EVR Ekspress: Toompuiestee 37, Tallinn 10133; e-mail evrekspress@evrekspress.ee; internet www.evrekspress.ee; f. 1998;

100%-owned subsidiary of Eesti Raudtee; operates international passenger services on Tallinn–Narva–Tver–Moscow (Russia) line.

ROADS

In 2002 Estonia had a total road network of 51,410 km, of which 1,455 km were main roads, 12,442 km were secondary roads, 2,496 were basic roads and 34,975 km were local roads. The motorway network totalled 87 km in 1999. In the early 2000s there were plans to construct an international motorway, to be known as the Via Baltica, between Tallinn and Warsaw, Poland. The project was to be partly funded by the European Union. In 2000 51.5% of the total road network was asphalted.

Estonian Road Administration (Maanteeamet): Pärnu mnt. 463A, Tallinn 10916; tel. 611-9300; fax 611-9360; e-mail estroad@ mnt.ee; internet www.mnt.ee; f. 1990; six regional road offices; 15 county offices; Gen. Dir RIHO SÖRMUS.

INLAND WATERWAYS

In 2003 there were 320 km of navigable inland waterways.

SHIPPING

Tallinn is the main port for freight transportation. There are regular passenger services between Tallinn and Helsinki, Finland. A service between Tallinn and Stockholm, Sweden, was inaugurated in 1991.

Estonian Maritime Administration (EMA) (Veeteede Amet): Valge 4, Tallinn 114113; tel. 620-5500; fax 620-5506; e-mail eva@vta .ee; internet www.vta.ee; f. 1990; govt org.; administers and implements state maritime safety policies, ship-control, pilot, lighthouse and hydrography services; Gen. Dir ANDRUS MAIDE; 375 employees.

Principal Shipping Companies

Eesti Merelaevandus (ESCO) (Estonian Shipping Co): Sadama 4, Tallinn 10111; tel. 640-9500; fax 640-9595; e-mail online@eml.ee; internet www.eml.ee; f. 1940; owned by Tschudi and Eitzen (Norway); liner services, ship chartering and cargo shipping; Man. Dir TOM STAGE PETERSEN; 500 employees.

Saaremaa Laevakompanii (Saaremaa Shipping Co): Kohtu 1, Kuressaare 93812; tel. 452-4350; fax 452-4350; e-mail slk@ laevakompanii.ee; internet www.laevakompanii.ee; f. 1992; passenger and cargo services between mainland Estonia and Saaremaa, Hiiumaa, Vormsi islands; Dir-Gen. TÕNIS RIHVK.

Shipowners' Association

Estonian Shipowners' Association (Eesti Laevaomanike Liit): Luise 1A, Tallinn 10142; tel. and fax 646-0109; e-mail reeder@ teleport.ee; Pres. REIN MERISALU.

Port Authority

Port of Tallinn (Tallinna Sadam): Sadama 25, Tallinn 15051; tel. 631-8555; fax 631-8166; e-mail portoftallinn@portoftallinn.com; internet www.portoftallinn.com; f. 1991; Chair. of Bd RIHO RASMANN; Harbour Master E. HUNT; 990 employees.

CIVIL AVIATION

There are direct regular passenger air services linking the international airport at Tallinn with several countries in northern, central and western Europe.

Civil Aviation Administration (Lennuamat): Rävala pst. 8, Tallinn 10143; tel. 694-9666; fax 694-9667; e-mail info@ecaa.ee; internet www.ecaa.ee; f. 1990; Dir-Gen. KOIT KASKEL.

Air Livonia: Eametsa küla, Sauga vald, Pärnu maakond 80044; tel. 447-5007; fax 447-5006; e-mail info@airlivonia.ee; internet www .airlivonia.ee; f. ; scheduled and charter passenger and cargo flights between Pärnu and several Estonian islands in the Baltic Sea; Dir ANTS ARINGO.

Avies: Lennujaama 2, Tallinn 11101; tel. 605-8022; fax 621-2951; e-mail info@avies.ee; internet www.avies.ee; f. 1991; domestic passenger services between Tallinn and Saaremaa and Hiiumaa islands, international scheduled and charter passenger and cargo services.

Estonian Air: Lennujaama 13, Tallinn 11101; tel. 640-1101; fax 601-6092; e-mail ov@estonian-air.ee; internet www.estonian-air.ee; f. 1991; passenger and cargo flights to Europe, the CIS and North Africa; Pres. and Bd BØRGE THORNBECH.

Pakker Avio: Väike-sõjamäe 9, Tallinn 11415; tel. 509-8627; e-mail pakkeravio@hot.ee; internet www.pakkeravio.ee; provides an 'air taxi' service on the routes: Tallinn–Helsinki; Tallinn–Stockholm; Tallinn–Copenhagen; and Tallinn–Rīga; Dir-Gen. ALBERT KALJU.

Tourism

Estonia has a wide range of attractions for tourists, including the historic towns of Tallinn and Tartu, extensive nature reserves and coastal resorts. In 1990 the National Tourism Board was established to develop facilities for tourism in Estonia. In 2003 there were 1,112,746 visitors to Estonia (measured by arrivals at registered accommodation establishments), with Finland the main source of tourists. In that year receipts from tourism totalled US $507m.

Estonian Tourist Board (Turismiarenduskeskus): Roosikrantsi 11, Tallinn 10119; tel. 627-9770; fax 627-9777; e-mail info@ visitestonia.com; internet www.visitestonia.com; f. 1990; Dir MAARIKA LIIVAMÄGI.

ETHIOPIA

Introductory Survey

Location, Climate, Language, Religion, Flag, Capital

The Federal Democratic Republic of Ethiopia is a land-locked country in eastern Africa; it has a long frontier with Somalia near the Horn of Africa. Sudan lies to the west, Eritrea to the north, Djibouti to the north-east and Kenya to the south. The climate is mainly temperate because of the high plateau terrain, with an average annual temperature of 13°C (55°F), abundant rainfall in some years and low humidity. The lower country and valley gorges are very hot and subject to recurrent drought. The official language is Amharic, but many other local languages are also spoken. English is widely used in official and commercial circles. The Ethiopian Orthodox (Tewahido) Church, an ancient Christian sect, has a wide following in the north and on the southern plateau. In much of the south and east the inhabitants include Muslims and followers of animist beliefs. The national flag (proportions 1 by 2) has three equal horizontal stripes, of green, yellow and red, superimposed in the centre of which is a blue disk bearing a yellow pentagram, resembling a star, with single yellow rays extending outwards from the inner angles of the star. The capital is Addis Ababa.

Recent History

In September 1974 Emperor Haile Selassie was deposed by the armed forces. The imperial regime was replaced by the Provisional Military Administrative Council (PMAC), known popularly as the Dergue (Committee), led by Brig.-Gen. Teferi Benti and in December Ethiopia was declared a socialist state. A radical programme of social and economic reforms led to widespread unrest, however, and in February 1977 Lt-Col Mengistu Haile Mariam executed Teferi and his closest associates, and replaced him as Chairman of the PMAC and as Head of State.

During 1977–78, in an attempt to end opposition to the regime, the Government imprisoned or killed thousands of its opponents. Political power was consolidated in a Commission for Organizing the Party of the Working People of Ethiopia (COPWE), largely dominated by military personnel. In September 1984, at the COPWE's third congress, the Workers' Party of Ethiopia (WPE) was formally inaugurated. Mengistu was unanimously elected Secretary-General of the party, which modelled itself on the Communist Party of the Soviet Union. In February 1987, at a referendum, some 81% of the electorate endorsed a new Constitution and in June national elections were held to an 835-seat legislature, the National Shengo (Assembly). In September, at the inaugural meeting of the new legislature, the PMAC was abolished, and the People's Democratic Republic of Ethiopia was declared. The National Shengo unanimously elected Mengistu as President of the Republic, and a 24-member Council of State was also elected, to act as the Shengo's permanent organ.

Numerous groups, encouraged by the confusion resulting from the 1974 revolution, launched armed insurgencies against the Government. Of these, the most effective were based in the Ogaden, Eritrea and Tigrai regions. Somalia laid claim to the Ogaden, which is populated mainly by ethnic Somalis. Somali troops supported incursions by forces of the Western Somali Liberation Front, and in 1977 the Somalis made major advances in the Ogaden. In 1978, however, they were forced to retreat, and by the end of 1980 Ethiopian forces had gained control of virtually the whole of the Ogaden region.

The former Italian colony of Eritrea was merged with Ethiopia, in a federal arrangement, in September 1952, and annexed to Ethiopia as a province in November 1962. A secessionist movement, the Eritrean Liberation Front (ELF), was founded in Egypt in 1958. In the late 1960s and early 1970s the ELF enjoyed considerable success against government troops, but eventually split into several rival factions, the largest of which was the Eritrean People's Liberation Front (EPLF). In 1978 government troops re-established control in much of Eritrea, and the EPLF retreated to the northern town of Nakfa. In 1982 an offensive by government troops failed to capture Nakfa, and in 1984 the EPLF made several successful counter-attacks. In mid-1986 government forces abandoned the north-east coast to the rebels.

An insurgent movement also emerged in Tigrai province in the late 1970s. The Tigrai People's Liberation Front (TPLF) was armed and trained by the EPLF, but relations between the two groups deteriorated sharply in the mid-1980s. The TPLF was weakened by conflict with other anti-Government groups, and in 1985 and 1986 government forces had considerable success against the TPLF.

The conflict in the north of the country during 1984–85 compounded difficulties being experienced in areas of Ethiopia already severely affected by famine. In 1984 the rains failed for the third consecutive crop season, and in May it was estimated that 7m. people could suffer starvation. Emergency food aid was received from many Western nations, but distribution was hampered, both by the continuing conflict and by the inadequacy of Ethiopia's infrastructure.

In September 1987 the newly elected National Shengo announced that five areas, including Eritrea and Tigrai, were to become 'autonomous regions' under the new Constitution. Eritrea was granted a considerable degree of self-government, but both the EPLF and the TPLF rejected the proposals. In March 1988 EPLF forces captured the town of Afabet; the TPLF took advantage of the movement of government forces from Tigrai to Eritrea and overran all the garrisons in north-western and north-eastern Tigrai. In May the Government declared a state of emergency in Eritrea and Tigrai, and in June government troops regained control of some of the captured garrison towns in Tigrai, suffering heavy losses in the process. However, in early 1989, following major defeats in north-west Tigrai, government forces abandoned virtually the whole region to the TPLF.

Following the capture of Massawa port by the EPLF in February 1990 (presenting a direct threat to the continued survival of the Ethiopian army in Eritrea), President Mengistu was obliged to make a number of concessions. In March Ethiopian socialism was virtually abandoned, when the WPE was renamed the Ethiopian Democratic Unity Party, and membership was opened to non-Marxists. Mengistu began introducing elements of a market economy and dismantling many of the economic structures that had been established after the 1974 revolution. However, heavy defeats of government forces continued during 1990 and early 1991.

By late April 1991, troops of the Ethiopian People's Revolutionary Democratic Front (EPRDF)—an alliance of the TPLF and the Ethiopian People's Democratic Movement (EPDM)—had captured Ambo, a town 130 km west of Addis Ababa, while EPLF forces were 50 km north of Assab, Ethiopia's principal port. On 21 May, faced with the prospect of the imminent defeat of his army, Mengistu fled the country. Lt-Gen. Tesfaye, the Vice-President, assumed control. On 28 May, following the failure of negotiations in the United Kingdom, and with the public support of the USA, units of the EPRDF entered Addis Ababa. They encountered little resistance, and the EPRDF established an interim Government, pending the convening, in July, of a multi-party conference, which was to elect a transitional government. Meanwhile, the EPLF had gained control of the Eritrean capital, Asmara, and announced the establishment of a provisional Government to administer Eritrea until the holding of a referendum, within two years, on the issue of independence.

In July 1991 a national conference adopted amendments to a national charter, presented by the EPRDF, and elected an 87-member Council of Representatives, which was to govern for a transitional period of two years, after which free national elections were to be held. The national charter provided guarantees for freedom of association and expression, and for self-determination for Ethiopia's various ethnic groups. The EPLF was not officially represented at the conference, but came to an agreement with the EPRDF, whereby the EPRDF accepted the formation of the EPLF's provisional Government of Eritrea and the determination by referendum of the future of the region. In late July the Council of Representatives established a commission to draft a new constitution and elected Meles Zenawi, the leader of the EPRDF (and of the TPLF), as Chairman of the Council, a position that made him President of the transitional Government and Head of State, and in August it appointed a Council of Ministers.

In November 1991, in accordance with the national charter's promise of self-determination for Ethiopia's peoples, the transitional Government announced the division of the country into 14 regional administrations, which would have autonomy in matters of regional law and internal affairs. A transitional economic policy, designed to accelerate economic reform, was also approved.

In early 1992 skirmishes continued between forces of the EPRDF and the Oromo Liberation Front (OLF) in the south and east of the country, severely hampering the distribution of food aid to some 6.5m. people affected by drought and to a further 1.4m. people displaced during the continuing conflict. In April a cease-fire between the two sides was agreed, under the auspices of the USA and the EPLF. Local elections were held in many parts of the country in April and May, and regional elections in June. An international observer group, including representatives of the UN, the Organization of African Unity (OAU, now the African Union—AU, see p. 144) and the European Community (EC, now the European Union—EU, see p. 217), indicated that claims of electoral malpractice at the regional polls by the EPRDF in many areas were, at least in part, justified. Shortly after the elections, in which the EPRDF and associated parties obtained 90% of the votes cast, the OLF withdrew its support from the transitional Government. In July 10 political organizations that were signatories to the national charter of July 1991 demanded the annulment of the results of the regional elections. The transitional Government established a board 'to correct election errors' at the end of the month, but by late August the regional councils were functioning in all parts of the country except the Afar and Somali areas, where the elections had been postponed.

In November 1992 the provisional Government of Eritrea announced that a UN-supervised referendum on the area's status would be held in April 1993. The Sudanese Government expressed its readiness to assist the Eritrean Referendum Commission in conducting a plebiscite among some 250,000 Eritrean refugees still residing in Sudan. The referendum revealed overwhelming support for Eritrean independence, which was duly proclaimed on 24 May 1993.

Elections to a Constituent Assembly were conducted in Ethiopia in June 1994, in which the EPRDF won 484 of the 547 seats. The Constituent Assembly was inaugurated in October to debate a draft Constitution, which it ratified in December. The new Constitution provided for the establishment of a federal government and the division of the country (renamed the Federal Democratic Republic of Ethiopia) into nine states and two chartered cities. It provided for regional autonomy, including the right of secession. A new legislature, the Federal Parliamentary Assembly, was to be established, comprising two chambers: the House of People's Representatives (consisting of no more than 550 directly elected members) and the House of the Federation (composed of 117 deputies, elected by the new state assemblies).

The EPRDF and its allies won an overwhelming victory in elections to the House of People's Representatives and state assemblies in May 1995. Most opposition parties boycotted the poll. International observers accepted that the elections were conducted in a largely free and fair manner.

On 21 August 1995 legislative power was transferred from the transitional Council of Representatives to the Federal Parliamentary Assembly. On 22 August the transitional administration was terminated, and the country's new Constitution and designation as the Federal Democratic Republic of Ethiopia were formally instituted. Later that day Dr Negasso Gidada (formerly the Minister of Information), a member of the Oromo People's Democratic Organization (OPDO, which was in alliance with the EPRDF) and the nominee of the EPRDF, was elected President of the Federal Republic. A new Prime Minister, ex-President Meles Zenawi, was elected from among the members of the House of People's Representatives; Meles nominated a 17-member Council of Ministers, which was duly approved by the Federal Parliamentary Assembly.

During late 1995 and early 1996 the Meles administration was criticized for its harsh treatment of opposition activists. In June 1996 Dr Taye Wolde Semayat, the Secretary-General of the Ethiopian Teachers' Association, was arrested with several associates and accused of leading a clandestine political organization (the Ethiopian National Patriotic Front—ENPF), which had allegedly been responsible for several terrorist acts.

The arrests were strongly criticized by human rights groups, which claimed that the detainees were guilty only of expressing discontent at certain government policies. Meanwhile, the Somali-based al-Ittihad al-Islam (Islamic Union Party—which sought independence for Ethiopia's Ogaden province) claimed responsibility for bomb explosions at hotels in Addis Ababa and Dire Dawa in early 1996, and for the attempted assassination in July of the Minister of Transport and Communications. Government forces launched reprisal attacks on al-Ittihad bases in Somalia on numerous occasions during 1996–98, resulting in the deaths of several hundred al-Ittihad members.

In September 1998 some 30 delegates attended a meeting in Paris, France, of Ethiopian opposition movements, during which eight groups agreed to establish a new bloc, the Coalition of Ethiopian Opposition Political Organizations (CEOPO).

Meanwhile, the trial of 69 former government officials, including Mengistu, opened in Addis Ababa in December 1994, although proceedings were adjourned on numerous occasions. The defendants, 23 of whom were being tried *in absentia* (including Mengistu, who was in exile in Zimbabwe) and five of whom had died while awaiting trial, were accused of crimes against humanity and of genocide, perpetrated during 1974–91. In February 1997 the office of the Special Prosecutor announced that an additional 5,198 people would be indicted for war crimes and genocide, of whom nearly 3,000 would be tried *in absentia*. In November 1999 South Africa refused a request from the Ethiopian Government to extradite ex-President Mengistu, after it emerged that he was receiving medical treatment in that country. In March 2001 Mengistu was granted permanent residence in Zimbabwe, thus removing any possibility of his extradition to Ethiopia. In April the Ethiopian High Court found 37 people (13 *in absentia*) guilty of crimes against humanity and genocide; they were sentenced to up to 20 years' 'rigorous' imprisonment. The trial of Mengistu (who remained in Zimbabwe) resumed in Addis Ababa in November 2003, with defence lawyers commencing the presentation of their case. According to official figures, some 6,426 defendants were still awaiting trial, including almost 3,000 *in absentia*, although Ethiopian judicial sources maintained that all trials would be completed during 2004. More than 1,569 verdicts had been reached by late 2003, with 1,017 resulting in convictions.

Elections to the House of People's Representatives and the House of the Federation were held concurrently on 14 May 2000, except in the Somali regional state, where voting was postponed until 31 August, owing to severe drought. Voting was also repeated in several constituencies after accusations of irregularities were upheld by the National Electoral Board (NEB). According to results published by the NEB in September, the OPDO won the largest number of seats in the House of People's Representatives, taking 178 of the 546 available. The OPDO's major partners in the EPRDF coalition, the Amhara National Democratic Movement (as the EPDM had been renamed in 1994) and the TPLF, gained 134 and 38 seats, respectively, while a number of smaller groups in the EPRDF won a further 19 seats. The EPRDF thus comfortably retained its large majority in the lower chamber. In mid-October the new legislature was sworn in, and Meles was re-elected as Prime Minister.

In March 2001 Prime Minister Meles dismissed numerous high-ranking TPLF members, including Siye Abraha, a former Minister of Defence, and Gebru Asrat, President of Tigrai regional state, from their party posts. (Asrat was also dismissed as President of Tigrai in April.) This followed the emergence of major divisions within the TPLF between pro-Meles reformists and conservatives critical of the Prime Minister's handling of the conflict with Eritrea (see below) and of the country's economy. It was claimed later in April that several dissident members of the TPLF were being detained in the capital and that Abraha had been accused of illicitly obtaining commission from weapons-handling and siphoning hard currency into foreign bank accounts.

During 2001 the Meles administration suffered a number of internal set-backs. In May Ethiopia's Head of Security and Intelligence, Kinfe Gebremedhin, a staunch supporter of the Prime Minister, was assassinated in Addis Ababa. In late June President Gidada was dismissed from the executive committee of the OPDO, after it was alleged that he had refused to accept the party's programme of reform and was providing support to dissidents opposed to Meles. Gidada, in turn, accused the Government of embarking on a campaign of propaganda against him. Gidada was also expelled from the EPRDF, however, he remained insistent that he would complete his presidential term, which was scheduled to end in October. In August relations between the Prime Minister and the President were further strained by Gidada's criticism of the appointment of the army Chief-of-Staff, Abedula Gemeda, to the leadership of the OPDO. Earlier that month the Speaker of the House of the Federation, Almaz Meko, had accused the Tigraian-dominated Government of persecuting the Oromo people and the TPLF of plundering the resources of the Oromo people in order to develop the Tigrai region. She subsequently resigned from her post, relinquished her membership of both the OPDO and the central committee of the EPRDF, and defected to the OLF. Nevertheless, by mid-September it appeared that Meles had succeeding in re-establishing control over the TPLF, and therefore the EPRDF, following his re-election as Chairman of the party.

On 8 October 2001 Lt Girma Wolde Giorgis, a former President of the parliament during Haile Selassie's reign and a member of the House of People's Representatives since 1995, was elected by the legislature to replace Gidada as President of Ethiopia. Later that month Prime Minister Meles effected a major reorganization of the Council of Ministers and created several new ministries, including a Ministry of Federal Affairs; only eight of the members of the previous Council of Ministers were retained.

In mid-March 2002 violence erupted in the Tepi region of the Southern Nations, Nationalities and Peoples State between rival ethnic groups and the security forces, following a series of protests regarding the outcome of local elections, held in December 2001. According to official figures, 128 people were killed in the disturbances, although opposition sources claimed the number was as high as 1,000, and there were reports that a number of villages had been razed to the ground. The EU subsequently demanded a 'transparent, public and open' inquiry into the incidents and expressed its concern that a large number of those killed were the victims of 'revenge attacks' by local police-officers. In May as many as 38 people were killed in Awasa after police violently suppressed a demonstration. Human rights organizations condemned the actions of the security forces, claiming that they had fired indiscriminately on unarmed civilians. In August some 90 state employees, including 41 police-officers and 11 administrative officials, were arrested by the state authorities for their roles in the March riots and charged with human rights violations, instigation of violence and abuses of office.

During 2003 a number of new political parties and coalition organizations were formed with the intention of challenging the ruling EPRDF at the legislative elections scheduled for mid-2005. Meles also intended to reorganize the EPRDF, in order to transform it into a national, non-ethnic party, of which the TPLF, the ANDM and the OPDO would form regional branches. The most significant of the new groupings were the United Ethiopian Democratic Party, which was created by the merger of the Ethiopian Democratic Unity Party and the Ethiopian Democratic Party, and the United Ethiopian Democratic Forces (UEDF), under the leadership of Dr Beyene Petros.

In January 2004 Petros wrote to the Prime Minister requesting that he review and reform the electoral law and begin negotiations, with the aim of legalizing all opposition parties. In May several thousand supporters of four opposition parties gathered in Addis Ababa to protest against the lack of a neutral election board to oversee the legislative elections, which were scheduled to be contested on 15 May 2005, and to voice their concerns about the situation in the Gambela region (see below). In November the ruling EPRDF held its first ever meeting with opposition groups and announced its intention to review existing electoral legislation. However, despite unveiling a number of amendments to the electoral law in January 2005, which included granting opposition groups access to state-controlled media and the provision for opposition parties to call meetings and organize demonstrations, the Government did not adhere to earlier pledges to alter the composition of the NEB. Also in that month it was announced that elections in the Somali regional state would be delayed until July.

Meanwhile, from December 2003 clashes between the Anuak and Nuer communities over disputed land in the Gambela region of the country escalated. The increase in violence was precipitated by the killing of eight officials from the office of the UN High Commissioner for Refugees (UNHCR) and the Federal Agency for Refugee and Returnee Affairs, reportedly committed by the Anuak, who had been angered by the proposed construction on their land of a camp to house Nuer refugees. The

Anuak community was the target of a number of revenge attacks, which resulted in the death of some 100 people (although opposition sources indicated that the actual casualty figures were much higher), and it was alleged that the Government had actively encouraged reprisals against the Anuak community. As the violence escalated some 15,000 Anuak, including the President of the region Okelo Akuai, sought refuge in Sudan. In late January 2004 some 200 people were killed after Anuak militants attacked a gold mine where many new settlers to the region were working. In March the Government released a statement apologizing for its inadequate response towards the escalating violence in the Gambela region, and pledged to bring the perpetrators to justice. By mid-2004 the situation had calmed significantly and about 8,000 of those who had fled in January had returned to Gambela. In December the UNHCR resumed operations in the region.

Attempts by the Government to reduce the country's reliance on foreign food aid intensified in March 2004 when Prime Minister Meles announced proposals to relocate up to 2m. people from the dry highlands to more fertile areas along the border with Sudan. It was estimated that some 15m. Ethiopians were dependent on food aid, however, the three-year plan was criticized by several international aid agencies that warned that the land set aside for the relocation was notorious for diseases, such as malaria, and lacked the necessary infrastructure to host those being resettled. Indeed, in June the UN was forced to intervene and provide emergency assistance for some 250,000 people who had been relocated, while UNICEF provided medication and mosquito nets to combat the spread of malaria.

Ethiopia's foreign affairs after Mengistu's coup in 1977 were dominated by relations with the USSR, which replaced the USA as the principal supplier of armaments to Ethiopia and provided military advisers and economic aid. In the late 1980s, however, changes in Soviet foreign policy weakened the relationship, and the Soviet Government began to urge a political, rather than military, solution to Ethiopia's regional conflicts.

Relations with Somalia have been problematic since the Ogaden War of 1977–78. However, in April 1988 Ethiopia and Somalia agreed to re-establish diplomatic relations, to withdraw troops from their common border and to exchange prisoners of war. During 1988–91 an estimated 600,000 Somali refugees entered Ethiopia from northern Somalia, of whom more than 150,000 arrived in the first half of 1991. The transitional Government of Ethiopia declared a policy of non-interference in the affairs of neighbouring states and adopted a neutral stance in Somalia's civil conflict. In November 2000 the President of Somalia, Abdulkassim Salad Hasan, visited Ethiopia for the first time since his election in August. This followed a visit to Ethiopia by the President of the self-proclaimed 'Republic of Somaliland' earlier that month. During his visit Hasan held talks with senior Ethiopian officials, but, although relations between the two countries were reported to have improved as a result of the discussions, the Ethiopian authorities continued to refuse to recognize officially the Hasan administration and urged it to reach agreements with its opponents. In January 2001 relations between the countries deteriorated after the Somali Prime Minister accused Ethiopia of continuing to assist the Somali-based Rahawin Resistance Army (RRA), which had taken control of a number of towns in south-west Somalia, and maintained that Ethiopia was behind an assassination attempt on the Speaker of Somalia's transitional legislature. The accusations were strenuously denied by the Ethiopian authorities, which stated that no Ethiopian troops were in Somali territory. Later in the year Ethiopia agreed to mediate between the Somali Transitional National Government (TNG) and the Somali Reconciliation and Restoration Council, which had been established in Ethiopia in March to rival the TNG. In April 2002 five members of al-Ittihad were sentenced to death by an Ethiopian court for their roles in a series of terrorist attacks in Ethiopia in 1995, in which 27 people were killed and a further 16 injured. The Ethiopian Prime Minister, Meles Zenawi, claimed that Ethiopia had obtained proof of links between al-Ittihad and the al-Qa'ida (Base) organization, which was believed to have been responsible for the devastating suicide attacks of 11 September 2001 in the USA. In February 2003 Meles admitted that Ethiopian troops had, on occasion, been dispatched into Somali territory in pursuit of suspected members of al-Ittihad. Relations between Somalia and Ethiopia were further strained by Meles' claim that a number of al-Ittihad members were represented in the Somali TNG; the accusation was, however, strenuously denied by Hasan.

Following the military coup in Sudan in April 1985, full diplomatic relations were restored between Ethiopia and Sudan. Relations between the two countries were strained, however, by the influx into Ethiopia, in the late 1980s, of thousands of Sudanese refugees, fleeing from famine and civil war in southern Sudan. The vast majority of an estimated 380,000 refugees were reported to have returned to Sudan by early 1991, as a result of the civil war in Ethiopia. The change of government in Ethiopia in May 1991 led to a considerable improvement in relations between Ethiopia and Sudan, and in October President Meles and Sudan's leader, Lt-Gen. al-Bashir, signed an agreement on friendship and co-operation. In September 1995 the Ethiopian administration adopted a number of sanctions against Sudan, including the suspension of air flights between the two countries and a reduction in Sudanese diplomatic representation in Ethiopia, after the Sudanese authorities refused to extradite to Ethiopia three men allegedly involved in an assassination attempt on President Mubarak of Egypt in Addis Ababa in June. Accusations of border incursions intensified during 1996–97. Although attacks against Sudanese positions were known to have been launched by the Sudan People's Liberation Army (SPLA), operating from Ethiopia, the Ethiopian authorities denied any knowledge of their activities. Relations between the two countries subsequently improved, and in October 1998 Ethiopia reportedly resumed air flights to Sudan. The Ethiopian authorities were also reported to have closed the SPLA offices in western Ethiopia, while Sudan closed the OLF base in Khartoum. In November 1999 Prime Minister Meles received Lt-Gen. al-Bashir in Addis Ababa, where they announced their intent to form closer economic ties between the two countries. In November 2004 the two countries finalized the demarcation of their common border on paper and requested financial assistance from international organizations in order to demarcate the border on the ground.

In November 1991 the leaders of Ethiopia and Kenya signed a co-operation agreement, although in October 1992 it was reported that the Kenyan Government was secretly giving asylum to Ethiopian dissidents. In April 1997 the two countries agreed to strengthen border controls following an attack by Ethiopian tribesmen in Kenya's frontier region, in which 41 civilians and 16 security personnel were killed. Additional security measures were agreed in late 1998, following an incursion by Ethiopian tribesmen into Kenya, which resulted in some 140 fatalities. In March 1999 Kenyan security forces exchanged fire with Ethiopian troops pursuing OLF rebels across the border. Kenya accused Ethiopia of violating international law, and relations between the two countries became further strained after Ethiopian soldiers attacked villages along the border. Bilateral relations deteriorated yet further during late 2000 and early 2001 after it was reported that some 50 Kenyans had been killed by Ethiopian militia forces. In January 2001 representatives from both countries met in Nairobi, Kenya, and agreed to take steps aimed at ending disputes along the common border.

After May 1991 the EPLF governed Eritrea as a *de facto* independent state and conducted its affairs with foreign countries accordingly. Ethiopia and the newly independent Eritrea signed a treaty of co-operation during a visit by the Eritrean President, Issaias Afewerki, to Addis Ababa in July 1993. The agreement included provisions on the joint utilization of resources and co-operation in the energy, transport, defence and education sectors. A further agreement, signed in late 1994, provided for the free movement of goods between the two countries without payment of customs dues.

In late 1997 relations with Eritrea deteriorated, following that country's adoption of a new currency (to replace the Ethiopian birr) and the subsequent disruption of cross-border trade. Fighting between Ethiopian and Eritrean troops erupted in early May 1998, with both countries accusing the other of having invaded their territory. In mid-June the USA and Italy successfully mediated an aerial cease-fire, but a resolution passed by the UN Security Council later that month, demanding that Ethiopia and Eritrea cease hostilities forthwith, was ignored. The OAU established a mediation committee in June in an attempt to end the dispute, and in July an OAU delegation visited the two countries. The committee presented its report to the Ethiopian and Eritrean Ministers of Foreign Affairs at a meeting in Ouagadougou, Burkina Faso, in August; however, its proposals were rejected by Eritrea, necessitating the convening of a special meeting of the mediation committee in Ouagadougou in November. Ethiopia welcomed the committee's proposals,

which stressed the need to demilitarize and demarcate the disputed region, but Eritrea rejected the plans.

In February 1999, after two weeks of intense fighting, Ethiopia recaptured the disputed town of Badme, and the Eritrean Government announced that it had accepted the OAU peace plan that it had rejected in late 1998. However, Ethiopia appeared eager to maximize its opportunity to secure access to the coast, ignoring appeals by the UN Security Council for an immediate cease-fire. Fighting erupted again in March 1999, as the two sides continued to blame each other for obstructing the OAU's peace efforts.

In July 1999 the deadlock between Ethiopia and Eritrea appeared to have been broken at the OAU summit meeting in Algiers, when the two warring countries confirmed their commitment to the OAU peace proposals, under which both sides would withdraw from all territory captured since the outbreak of the conflict, thus effectively returning both sides to their pre-war frontiers. However, the situation was complicated by Eritrean demands for war reparations and Ethiopian requests for clarification of the technical arrangements regarding the withdrawal of troops from the disputed territory. In August Eritrea formally accepted the latest OAU peace plan; however, in the following month Ethiopia announced that it had rejected the proposals, as the technical arrangements did not guarantee a return to the *status quo ante*. In February 2000 former US national security adviser Anthony Lake and Prime Minister Ahmed Ouyahia of Algeria, the OAU's special envoy, visited Addis Ababa and Asmara, but failed to persuade the two warring parties to accept the OAU's peace proposals. In April it was announced that some 8m. people in Ethiopia were in danger of starvation, and both the Ethiopian and Eritrean Governments were strongly criticized by aid agencies for continuing to spend vast amounts on funding their war efforts, while millions of their citizens endured severe food shortages.

In mid-May 2000 Ethiopian troops launched a major offensive near the disputed towns of Badme and Zalambessa, repelling the Eritrean forces. An announcement by the UN Security Council that it would impose sanctions and an embargo on the sale of all military supplies to the two countries, if fighting did not cease within three days, provoked violent protests outside the British and US embassies in Addis Ababa. However, hostilities continued, and on 18 May the UN Security Council unanimously approved the imposition of a 12-month arms embargo on Ethiopia and Eritrea. Shortly afterwards Ethiopian forces captured the strategically vital town of Barentu, thus taking control of the western front. Zalambessa subsequently fell to the Ethiopian forces, and on 25 May the Eritrean Government announced the withdrawal of its troops from all disputed areas. On 31 May Prime Minister Meles stated that Ethiopia had no territorial claims over Eritrea and that the war between the two countries was over; nevertheless, sporadic fighting continued to take place. Following extensive indirect negotiations in Algiers during early June, both sides expressed their willingness, in principle, to accept the OAU's peace proposals. On 18 June the Ethiopian and Eritrean Ministers of Foreign Affairs signed an agreement, which provided for an immediate cease-fire and the establishment of a 25-km temporary security zone (TSZ) on the Eritrean side of the common border until the issue of the final demarcation of the border had been settled. It was estimated that as many as 120,000 people had been killed since the beginning of the conflict in 1998, and that more than 350,000 Ethiopians had been internally displaced. Indirect negotiations involving representatives from both countries, at which the technical issues of the peace agreement were to be discussed, commenced in Washington, DC, USA, in early July and continued in Algiers in October. Meanwhile, in mid-September the UN Security Council approved the deployment of a 4,200-strong UN Mission in Ethiopia and Eritrea (UNMEE, see p. 73).

In December 2000 Ethiopia and Eritrea signed an agreement in Algiers, which formally brought an end to the conflict. The agreement provided for a permanent cessation of all hostilities, the return of all prisoners of war, the demarcation of the common border by an independent commission, and the establishment of a Claims Commission to assess the issues of compensation and reparations. Furthermore, both countries pledged to co-operate with an independent investigation into the origins of the conflict. Later that month the first exchange of prisoners of war between the two countries took place. By late January 2001 the UNMEE force had arrived in the region, and, in compliance with the provisions for the establishment of a TSZ along the Ethiopia–Eritrea border, Ethiopian troops commenced their withdrawal from the territory they had captured from Eritrea. In March UNMEE's mandate was extended until September. Despite Eritrea's dissatisfaction at the southern boundary of the prospective TSZ, on 16 April it was announced that the withdrawal of its forces was complete. Two days later UNMEE declared the establishment of the TSZ, marking the formal separation of the Eritrean and Ethiopian forces. In mid-May the arms embargo imposed on the two countries by the UN in May 2000 was lifted. In late June 2001 UNMEE presented the final map of the TSZ to Ethiopia and Eritrea, although it emphasized that it would not influence the work of the neutral Boundary Commission charged with determining the border between the two countries. Despite this announcement, the Ethiopian Government expressed its dissatisfaction with the map, and at the eighth Military Co-ordination Committee (MCC) meeting in August both countries again stated their objections to the current boundaries of the TSZ. In mid-September UNMEE's mandate was extended for a further six months, although the head of the mission, Legwaila Joseph Legwaila, acknowledged that UNMEE faced an extremely difficult task in achieving lasting peace.

In mid-December 2001 Ethiopia and Eritrea began presenting their cases for border demarcation to the five-member Boundary Commission (BC) at the International Court of Justice (see p. 19) at The Hague, Netherlands. In mid-March 2002 UNMEE's mandate was extended until mid-September. The BC delivered its findings in April. Both Ethiopia and Eritrea had committed themselves in advance to the acceptance of the report, which was carefully balanced, thus allowing both sides to claim success. However, the Commission did not identify on which side of the boundary line Badme lay, stating that it was awaiting delineation on the ground, which was expected to take up to one year, as extensive demining was required prior to placing boundary markers. In the absence of any decision by the BC, both countries immediately claimed to have been awarded Badme. When UNMEE invited journalists to visit Badme in late April by entering through Eritrea, Ethiopia reacted by closing the border to UNMEE and demanding the removal of the UNMEE commander, Maj.-Gen. Patrick Cammaert. The border was reopened to UN personnel in early May. Later that month Ethiopia formally requested 'interpretation, correction and consultation' of the BC's report, but this was rejected by the Commission in late June.

In early March 2003 the BC reported to the UN Security Council that Ethiopia's requests for changes to the border ruling, in order to 'take better account of human and physical geography', threatened to undermine the peace process as a whole. Despite Ethiopia's claims that it had been promised that demarcations could be refined, later in March the BC categorically ruled Badme to be Eritrean territory, thus rejecting Ethiopia's territorial claim over the town. Meles subsequently complained that the decision was 'wrong and unjust' and vowed to continue to contest the ruling.

The demarcation of the border, which had originally been scheduled to take place in May 2003, was postponed until July, and then further delayed until October. In a letter to the UN Security Council in October, Prime Minister Meles requested the establishment of a new body to resolve the crisis and again denounced the BC's ruling as 'unacceptable'. However, the Security Council stated that Ethiopia had, under the 2000 Algiers accord, committed itself to accept the BC's decision as 'final and binding' and urged it to accept and implement the border ruling. The Chairman of the BC, Elihu Lauterpacht, and Legwaila criticized Ethiopia's lack of compliance with its obligations under the terms of the peace agreement and the ongoing impasse was further compounded by the BC's announcement in late October that the demarcation of the border had been delayed indefinitely.

The process suffered a further reverse in mid-November 2003, when Eritrea withdrew its ambassador to the AU and accused the organization of neglecting its responsibilities over the dispute with Ethiopia. However, in the following month both countries agreed to establish three Sector Military Co-ordination Committees, under the chairmanship of UNMEE's Sector Commanders, in order to improve the mechanism for dealing with incidents in the border areas; it was hoped that the committees would prevent any minor border incidents from escalating into wider conflict. Later in December Lloyd Axworthy, a former Canadian Minister of Foreign Affairs, was appointed as the UN's special envoy to the region, tasked with resolving the stalled peace process between Eritrea and

Ethiopia. While Ethiopia welcomed the appointment and pledged to work closely with Axworthy, the Eritrean Government expressed its opposition to the appointment, as it feared that it would result in amendments to the BC's ruling.

In 2004 the UN was again critical of the failure of Ethiopia and Eritrea to reach an agreement on the border ruling. Despite this, UNMEEs mandate was extended by a further six months in March and again in September. In November Ethiopia indicated that it would co-operate with UNMEE when Meles announced a five-point plan aimed at resolving the disputed border issue and declared that Ethiopia had, in principle, accepted the BC's ruling of April 2002. Meles' statement was dismissed by the Eritrean authorities as an attempt by Ethiopia to further stall the process and also provoked demonstrations by some 100,000 people in Addis Ababa in January 2005 opposed to the Government's intention of resuming peace talks with Eritrea. In mid-December 2004 the UN withdrew some 550 Kenyan troops from the TSZ in an attempt to reduce the costs of its military presence in the area. By mid-April 2005 no agreement between the two countries on the re-establishment of talks had been reached and the border remained disputed.

In 1984 some 13,000 Falashas, a Jewish group in Ethiopia, reached Israel, from where they were flown to Israel in a secret airlift. In May 1991 Israel evacuated a further 14,000 Falashas from Addis Ababa; some 10,000 Falashmura (Ethiopian Christians whose forefathers had converted from Judaism) were subsequently granted Israeli citizenship on humanitarian grounds. In March 1999 Israel pledged to examine the possibility of bringing the estimated 19,000 Jews remaining in Ethiopia to Israel, and in April 2000 the Israeli Minister of the Interior visited Ethiopia to investigate the claims of some 26,000 Ethiopians who maintained that they belonged to the Falashmura community and were thus eligible to settle in Israel under Israeli law. In February 2003 the Israeli Government ruled that the Falashmura had been forced to convert to Christianity to avoid religious persecution and that they had the right to settle in Israel. In January 2005 Israel announced that it would accelerate the emigration process and that the remaining 20,000 Ethiopian Falashas and Falashmura would arrive in Israel by 2007.

Government

In August 1995 the Council of Representatives, a body established in 1991 to govern the country during the transitional period after the overthrow of the Mengistu regime, formally transferred power to a newly elected legislature, the Federal Parliamentary Assembly. Under the provisions of a new Constitution, adopted in December 1994, the country became a federation, consisting of nine states and two chartered cities, the capital, Addis Ababa, and Dire Dawa. The states have their own parliamentary assemblies, which also elect representatives to the House of the Federation, the upper chamber of the Federal Parliamentary Assembly. The lower chamber, the House of People's Representatives, consists of no more than 550 directly elected deputies. The Federal Parliamentary Assembly elects a President as Head of State. However, the President fulfils mainly ceremonial functions, executive power being the preserve of the Prime Minister. The Prime Minister, who is elected by the House of People's Representatives, appoints the Council of Ministers (subject to approval by the legislature), and acts as Commander-in-Chief of the armed forces.

Defence

In December 1991 Ethiopia's transitional Government announced that a 'national defence army', based on already active EPRDF troops, would constitute Ethiopia's armed forces during the transitional period. In October 1993 the Minister of Defence announced that preparations were under way to create a 'multi-ethnic defence force', comprising members of all the different ethnic groups in Ethiopia. Extensive demobilization of former members of the TPLF has since taken place. In September 1996 the Government sold its naval assets. Owing to the war with Eritrea during 1999–2000, there was a large increase in the size of the armed forces and in defence expenditure. In August 2004 Ethiopia's active armed forces numbered an estimated 182,500, comprising an army of about 180,000 and an air force of some 2,500. The defence budget for 2004 was estimated at 2,500m. birr. In July 2000 the UN Security Council adopted a resolution (No. 1312) establishing the UN Mission in Ethiopia and Eritrea (UNMEE, see p. 73), which was to supervise the cease-fire and the implementation of a peace agreement between the two countries. At the end of December 2004

UNMEE numbered 3,705 troops, 213 military observers, and 208 international and 254 local civilian personnel; UNMEE had a total authorized strength of 4,200 troops (including 220 military observers).

Economic Affairs

In 2003, according to estimates by the World Bank, Ethiopia's gross national income (GNI), measured at average 2001–03 prices, was US $6,583m., equivalent to $90 per head (or $710 per head on an international purchasing-power parity basis): one of the lowest recorded levels of GNI per head for any country in the world. During 1990–2003, it was estimated, the population increased at an average annual rate of 2.3%, while gross domestic product (GDP) per head increased, in real terms, by an average of 0.6% per year. Overall GDP increased, in real terms, at an average annual rate of 2.8% during 1990–2003; it grew by 1.9% in 2002, but decreased by 3.9% in 2003.

Agriculture (including forestry and fishing) contributed 41.8% of GDP in 2003, and employed an estimated 81.1% of the economically active population in 2003. The principal cash crop is coffee (which accounted for 38.5% of export earnings in 2002). The principal subsistence crops are cereals (maize, sorghum, wheat, barley, and teff) and sugar cane. During 1990–2003 agricultural GDP increased at an average annual rate of 0.8%. Agricultural GDP decreased by 12.2% in 2003.

Industry (including mining, manufacturing, construction and power) employed 2.0% of the labour force in 1995, and provided 11.0% of GDP in 2003. During 1990–2003 industrial GDP increased by an average of 2.0% per year. It rose by 4.9% in 2003.

Mining contributed only an estimated 0.5% of GDP (at constant 1980/81 prices) in 2000/01, and employed less than 0.1% of the labour force in 1995. Ethiopia has reserves of petroleum, although these have not been exploited, and there are also deposits of copper and potash. Gold, tantalite, soda ash, kaolin, dimension stones, precious metals and gemstones, salt, and industrial and construction materials are mined. In April 2000 a US company discovered large petroleum deposits in the west of the country, and in June 2003 the Ethiopian Government granted an exploration licence to Petronas of Malaysia. During 1996/97–2000/01 mining GDP increased by an estimated average of 7.4% per year; growth in 2000/01 was an estimated 8.4%.

Manufacturing employed only 1.6% of the labour force in 1995, and contributed 7.0% of GDP in 2002. During 1990–2001 manufacturing GDP increased at an average annual rate of 2.6%. It increased by 7.9% in 2001.

In years of normal rainfall, energy is derived principally from Ethiopia's massive hydroelectric power resources. In 2001 98.7% of Ethiopia's electricity was produced by hydroelectric power schemes. Imports of mineral fuels accounted for 12.4% of the cost of total imports in 2002. In 1993 agreement was reached with the World Bank on the financing of a project to construct a liquefied gas unit to exploit gas reserves in the Ogaden. In late 1995 the Government announced plans to develop geothermal energy sources at 15 sites in various regions of the country. Ethiopia's electricity generating capacity was expected to reach 713 MW by 2005.

Services, which consisted mainly of wholesale and retail trade, public administration and defence, and transport and communications, employed 9.5% of the labour force in 1995, and contributed 47.2% of GDP in 2003. The combined GDP of the service sectors increased, in real terms, at an average rate of 4.6% per year during 1990–2003. It rose by 2.0% in 2003.

In 2002 Ethiopia recorded a visible trade deficit of US $974.8m., and there was a deficit of $149.5m. on the current account of the balance of payments. In 2002 the principal source of imports (9.1%) was the People's Republic of China; other major suppliers were Italy, the USA, the United Arab Emirates, Japan, Saudi Arabia, Germany and India. The principal market for exports in that year were Djibouti (13.1%), Germany, Italy, Japan and Saudi Arabia. The principal exports in 2002 were food and live animals, coffee, crude materials and leather and leather products. The principal imports in that year were machinery and transport equipment, basic manufactures, chemicals and related products, mineral fuels and related products and food and live animals.

In the fiscal year 2002/03 it was estimated that Ethiopia's budgetary deficit reached 4,239m. birr. Ethiopia is the principal African recipient of concessionary funding, and the largest recipient of EU aid. At the end of 2002 Ethiopia's total external debt was $6,522m., of which $6,313m. was long-term public debt. In that year the cost of debt-servicing was equivalent to an esti-

mated 9.7% of total earnings from the export of goods and services. The annual rate of inflation averaged 2.2% in 1995–2003. Consumer prices increased by 1.5% in 2002, and by 17.8% in 2003. 25,690 people were registered as unemployed in 1999.

Ethiopia is a member of the African Development Bank (see p. 142) and the Common Market for Eastern and Southern Africa (see p. 179). In July 2001 Ethiopia ratified the Cotonou Agreement (see p. 262), the successor of the Lomé Convention of the EU.

Ethiopia remains one of the poorest countries in the world, and the country's economy continues to suffer from the effects of recurrent, catastrophic drought, which severely disrupts agricultural production (the country's economic base). The rapidly expanding population has further highlighted structural deficiencies in this sector, which, coupled with the scarcity of land and the lack of agricultural development, have resulted in massive environmental degradation and, in turn, widespread poverty and famine. The Ethiopian economy is also heavily dependent on assistance and grants from abroad, particularly in times of drought. A number of donors suspended aid during the war with Eritrea, however, following the cessation of fighting in mid-2000 (see above), the World Bank agreed to resume development assistance to Ethiopia. From early 2001 Ethiopia also benefited from significant IMF assistance under the Poverty Reduction and Growth Facility and qualified for additional debt relief from the initiative for heavily indebted poor countries (HIPC). In May 2004 Ethiopia reached the completion point of the HIPC initiative and was granted debt relief totalling some $1,300m. In October the 'Paris Club' of donor nations cancelled $758m. of debt, and later that year Germany, Italy and the USA cancelled some or all of the debt owed to them by Ethiopia. The Ethiopian Government introduced value-added tax on certain goods at a rate of 10% in January 2003, which was expected to increase government revenues, thus enabling greater expenditure on health, education and infrastructural projects. Despite a successful harvest in 2003/04 resulting in GDP growth of 11.6% in that year, some 5m. people remained in critical need of food aid in 2004 and in early 2005, as part of its highly ambitious goal of achieving food self-sufficiency by 2007, the Government launched a project which aimed to improve agricultural and economic infrastructures. Plans were also announced, in conjunction with the World Bank, to upgrade the country's road network in order to secure the swifter distribution of emergency food assistance. Nevertheless, further structural reforms were necessary if economic growth was to continue.

Education

Education in Ethiopia is available free of charge up to grade 10, and, after a rapid growth in numbers of schools, it became compulsory between the ages of seven and 13 years. Since 1976 most primary and secondary schools have been controlled by local peasant associations and urban dwellers' associations. In 1994 Ethiopia adopted a new Education and Training Policy and Strategy, which restructured the education system and aimed to improve the quality of education. Primary education begins at seven years of age and lasts for eight years. Secondary education, beginning at 15 years of age, lasts for a further four years, comprising two cycles of two years each, the second of which provides preparatory education for entry to the tertiary level. A system of vocational and technical education also exists parallel to the preparatory programme. In 2000/01 total enrolment at primary schools included 47% of children in the appropriate age-group (53% of boys; 41% of girls); according to UNESCO estimates, enrolment at secondary schools included 13% of children in the relevant age-group (15% of boys; 10% of girls). There are 21 institutions of higher education in Ethiopia, including six universities (in Addis Ababa, Bahir Dar, Alemanya, Jimma, Awassa and Makele). A total of 67,682 students were enrolled in higher education in 1999/2000. The 1999/2000 budget allocated an estimated 11.3% (2,304m. birr) of total expenditure to education.

Public Holidays

2005: 7 January* (Christmas), 19 January* (Epiphany), 21 January† (Id al-Adha/Arafat), 2 March (Battle of Adowa), 21 April† (Mouloud, Birth of the Prophet), 29 April* (Good Friday), 1 May (May Day), 2 May* (Easter Monday), 5 May (Patriots' Victory Day), 28 May (Downfall of the Dergue), 11 September (New Year's Day), 27 September* (Feast of the True Cross), 4 November† (Id al-Fitr, end of Ramadan).

2006: 7 January* (Christmas), 11 January† (Id al-Adha/Arafat), 19 January* (Epiphany), 2 March (Battle of Adowa), 11 April† (Mouloud, Birth of the Prophet), 21 April* (Good Friday), 24 April* (Easter Monday), 1 May (May Day), 5 May (Patriots' Victory Day), 28 May (Downfall of the Dergue), 11 September (New Year's Day), 27 September* (Feast of the True Cross), 24 October† (Id al-Fitr, end of Ramadan).

* Coptic holidays.

† These holidays are dependent on the Islamic lunar calendar and may vary by one or two days from the dates given.

Note: Ethiopia uses its own solar calendar; the Ethiopian year 1997 began on 11 September 2004.

Weights and Measures

The metric system is officially in use. There are also many local weights and measures.

Statistical Survey

Source (unless otherwise stated): Central Statistical Authority, POB 1143, Addis Ababa; tel. (1) 553010; fax (1) 550334.

Note: Unless otherwise indicated, figures in this Survey refer to the territory of Ethiopia after the secession of Eritrea in May 1993.

Area and Population

AREA, POPULATION AND DENSITY

Area (sq km)	1,133,380*
Population (census results)	
9 May 1984†	39,868,501
11 October 1994	
Males	26,910,698
Females	26,566,567
Total	53,477,265
Population (official estimates at mid-year)	
2000	63,495,000
2001	65,370,000
2002	67,220,000
Density (per sq km) at mid-2002	59.3

* 437,600 sq miles.

† Including an estimate for areas not covered by the census.

ADMINISTRATIVE DIVISIONS
(estimated population at mid-1999)

	Population ('000)		
	Males	Females	Total
Regional States			
1 Tigrai	1,767	1,826	3,593
2 Afar	667	521	1,188
3 Amhara	7,938	7,912	15,850
4 Oromia	10,833	10,861	21,694
5 Somali	1,952	1,650	3,602
6 Benishangul/Gumuz	264	259	523
7 Southern Nations, Nationalities and Peoples	6,029	6,103	12,132
8 Gambela	105	101	206
9 Harari	78	76	154
Chartered Cities			
1 Dire Dawa	154	152	306
2 Addis Ababa	1,169	1,255	2,424
Total	30,956	30,716	61,672

PRINCIPAL TOWNS
(estimates, 2001)

Addis Ababa (capital)	2,570,000	Mekele . . .		134,996
Dire Dawa	227,494	Bahir Dar . . .		134,062
Nazret	180,537	Jimma		125,569
Gondar	156,087	Debre Zeit . . .		103,569
Dessie	135,529	Harar		101,000

Source: UN, *Demographic Yearbook*.

BIRTHS AND DEATHS
(UN estimates, annual averages)

	1985–90	1990–95	1995–2000
Birth rate (per 1,000)	48.9	47.0	44.8
Death rate (per 1,000)	19.8	18.4	17.8

Source: UN, *World Population Prospects: The 2002 Revision*.

Expectation of life (WHO estimates, years at birth): 48.0 (males 46.8; females 49.4) in 2002 (Source: WHO, *World Health Report*).

ECONOMICALLY ACTIVE POPULATION
(official estimates, ISIC major divisions, persons aged 10 years and over, mid-1995)*

	Males	Females	Total
Agriculture, hunting, forestry and fishing	12,681,037	8,924,280	21,605,317
Mining and quarrying	12,114	4,426	16,540
Manufacturing	224,106	160,889	384,995
Electricity, gas and water . . .	14,799	2,267	17,066
Construction	55,906	5,326	61,232
Trade, restaurants and hotels . .	335,353	600,584	935,937
Transport, storage and communications	87,975	15,179	103,154
Financing, insurance, real estate and business services . . .	14,513	4,938	19,451
Community, social and personal services	777,907	474,317	1,252,224
Total labour force	14,203,710	10,192,206	24,395,916

* The figures exclude persons seeking work for the first time, totalling 210,184 (males 100,790; females 109,394), but include other unemployed persons.

Source: ILO, *Yearbook of Labour Statistics*.

Mid-2003 (estimates in '000): Agriculture, etc. 25,056; Total labour force 30,896 (Source: FAO).

Health and Welfare

KEY INDICATORS

Total fertility rate (children per woman, 2002)	6.2
Under-5 mortality rate (per 1,000 live births, 2003) . . .	169
HIV/AIDS (% of persons aged 15–49, 2003)	4.40
Physicians (per 1,000 head, 1994)	0.03
Hospital beds (per 1,000 head, 1990)	0.24
Health expenditure (2001): US $ per head (PPP)	14
Health expenditure (2001): % of GDP	3.6
Health expenditure (2001): public (% of total)	40.5
Access to water (% of persons, 2002)	22
Access to sanitation (% of persons, 2002)	6
Human Development Index (2002): ranking	170
Human Development Index (2002): value	0.359

For sources and definitions, see explanatory note on p. vi.

Agriculture

PRINCIPAL CROPS
('000 metric tons)

	2001	2002	2003
Wheat	1,596	1,478	1,400*
Barley	1,017	1,093	850*
Maize	3,298	2,968	3,000*
Oats	57	43	50*
Millet (Dagusa)	316	308	350*
Sorghum	1,541	1,566	1,600*
Other cereals	1,737	1,640	1,700*
Potatoes	415†	385	390†
Sweet potatoes	200†	339	340†
Yams†	280	300	300
Other roots and tubers†	3,550	3,700	3,700
Sugar cane	2,232	2,232	2,235†
Dry beans	211.0	115.7	116.0†
Dry broad beans	453.8	447.1	448.0†
Dry peas	146.6	153.3	155.0†
Chick-peas	175.7	180.4	181.0†
Lentils	65.3	38.4	39.0†
Vetches	99.4	92.3	93.0†
Other pulses	8.0	16.0	16.0†
Tree nuts†	75	72	72
Soybeans (Soya beans)†	26	27	27
Groundnuts (in shell)	15.2	13.3	13.5†
Castor beans†	15.0	15.0	15.0
Rapeseed	14.7	16.9	17.0†
Safflower seed†	38	38	38
Sesame seed	18.9	38.9	39.0†
Cottonseed	45.5*	45.5†	45.5†
Cotton (lint)	14*	14†	14†
Linseed	64.1	51.1	52.0†
Cabbages	130†	150	150†
Tomatoes†	55	55	55
Green onions and shallots†	19	19	19
Dry onions	120†	140	140†
Garlic	50†	70	71†
Other vegetables†	420	420	420
Bananas†	82	82	82
Oranges†	15	15	15
Mangoes	156.8	159.6	163.3
Avocados	78.9	80.0	81.3
Papayas	223.0	226.0	230.5
Other fruit†	161.6	163.3	166.8
Coffee (green)	228.0*	220†	220†
Pimento and allspice†	115	115	115

* Unofficial figure.
† FAO estimate(s).
Source: FAO.

LIVESTOCK
('000 head, year ending September)

	2001	2002*	2003*
Cattle	35,383	35,500	35,500
Sheep	11,438	11,438	11,450
Goats	9,621	9,622	9,623
Asses	3,414	3,430	3,430
Horses	1,254	1,300	1,300
Mules	256	260	260
Camels	326	326	326
Pigs*	26	26	26
Poultry	37,764	38,000	39,000

* FAO estimates.
Source: FAO.

LIVESTOCK PRODUCTS
(FAO estimates, '000 metric tons)

	2001	2002	2003
Beef and veal	304	304	304
Mutton and lamb	37.8	37.8	37.8
Goat meat	28.6	28.7	28.7
Pig meat	1.5	1.5	1.5
Poultry meat	49.8	50.2	50.2
Game meat	74	74	74
Other meat	53.0	53.1	53.1
Cows' milk	1,450	1,450	1,450
Goats' milk	17.1	17.1	17.1
Sheep's milk	28.6	28.6	28.6
Butter	2.0	2.0	2.0
Ghee	15.6	15.6	15.6
Cheese	5.9	5.9	5.9
Hen eggs	37.8	37.8	37.8
Honey	29.0	29.0	29.0
Wool: greasy	12.0	12.0	12.0
Wool: scoured	3.1	3.1	3.1
Cattle hides	58.8	58.9	58.9
Sheepskins	6.8	6.8	6.8
Goatskins	6.1	6.1	6.1

Source: FAO.

Forestry

ROUNDWOOD REMOVALS
('000 cubic metres, excl. bark)

	2001	2002	2003
Sawlogs, veneer logs and logs for sleepers	6*	8	6
Pulpwood*	7	7	7
Other industrial wood*	2,445	2,445	2,444
Fuel wood*	88,825	90,202	91,603
Total	91,283	92,662	94,060

* FAO estimate(s).
Source: FAO.

SAWNWOOD PRODUCTION
('000 cubic metres, incl. railway sleepers)

	2001	2002	2003
Coniferous (softwood)	25*	1	0
Broadleaved (hardwood)	35*	13	17
Total	60	14	17

* FAO estimate.
Source: FAO.

Fishing

(metric tons, live weight)

	2000	2001	2002
Rhinofishes	3,451	3,387	2,303
Other cyprinids	860	843	759
Tilapias	7,000	6,870	4,603
North African catfish	4,000	3,926	4,318
Total catch (incl. others)	15,681	15,390	12,300

Source: FAO.

Mining

(estimates, '000 metric tons, unless otherwise indicated, year ending 7 July)

	2000/01	2001/02	2002/03
Gold (kilograms)	5,200	5,300	5,300
Limestone	1,300	1,300	1,300
Gypsum and anhydrite	51	51	62
Pumice	169	170	170

Source: US Geological Survey.

Industry

SELECTED PRODUCTS

('000 metric tons, unless otherwise indicated, year ending 7 July)

	1998/99	1999/2000	2000/01
Wheat flour	168	185	165
Macaroni and pasta	24	30	26
Raw sugar	235	251	251
Wine ('000 hectolitres) . . .	18	23	25
Beer ('000 hectolitres) . . .	921	1,111	1,605
Mineral waters ('000 hectolitres) .	421	400	395
Soft drinks ('000 hectolitres) . .	667	616	677
Cigarettes (million)	1,829	1,931	1,904
Cotton yarn	3.4	4.0	5.7
Woven cotton fabrics ('000 sq m) .	43,000	38,000	45,000
Nylon fabrics ('000 sq m) . . .	4,000	2,900	1,300
Footwear (excluding rubber, '000 pairs)	n.a.	5,022	6,358
Soap	13.1	17.2	14.8
Tyres ('000)	148	119	209
Clay building bricks ('000) . . .	19	20	20
Quicklime	7	9	11
Cement	767	816	819

Source: UN, *Industrial Commodity Statistics Yearbook*.

Beer of millet ('000 metric tons): 220.7 in 2001; 208.0 in 2002; 244.1 in 2003 (Source: FAO).

Beer of barley ('000 metric tons): 388.2 in 2001; 411.7 in 2002; 322.0 in 2003 (Source: FAO).

Finance

CURRENCY AND EXCHANGE RATES

Monetary Units
100 cents = 1 birr.

Sterling, Dollar and Euro Equivalents (29 October 2004)
£1 sterling = 15.840 birr;
US $1 = 8.647 birr;
€1 = 11.013 birr;
1,000 birr = £63.13 = $115.65 = €90.80.

Average Exchange Rate (birr per US $)
2001   8.4575
2002   8.5678
2003   8.5997

GENERAL BUDGET

(preliminary, rounded figures, million birr, year ending 7 July)

Revenue*	2000/01	2001/02	2002/03
Taxation	7,440	7,927	8,243
Taxes on income and profits .	2,143	2,439	2,472
Personal income	686	760	833
Business profits	1,457	1,679	1,639
Domestic indirect taxes . . .	1,381	1,498	1,668
Import duties	3,231	3,280	3,564
Export duties	93	28	1
Other revenue	2,738	2,482	2,907
Government investment income	1,353	1,017	1,102
Reimbursements and property sales	203	288	204
Sales of goods and services . .	340	338	330
Total	10,178	10,409	11,150

* Excluding grants received from abroad (million birr): 2,628 in 2000/01; 2,425 in 2001/02; 3,012 in 2002/03.

Expenditure	2000/01	2001/02	2002/03
Current expenditure	10,379	10,551	12,305
General services	5,071	4,630	4,679
Economic services	943	1,049	1,328
Social services	2,234	2,800	3,183
Interest and charges	1,080	1,005	1,042
External assistance (grants)*	978	1,006	1,844
Capital expenditure	5,003	6,130	5,817
Economic development . .	3,163	3,330	3,341
Social development . . .	1,330	995	1,331
General services and compensation	510	693	444
External assistance (grants)* .	—	1,113	701
Special programs	404	971	279
Total	15,786	17,652	18,401

* Imputed value of goods and services provided mainly in kind.

Source: National Bank of Ethiopia.

INTERNATIONAL RESERVES

(US $ million, at 31 December)

	2001	2002	2003
Gold*	0.3	0.3	n.a.
IMF special drawing rights . .	0.2	0.1	0.1
Reserve position in IMF . . .	9.0	9.7	10.7
Foreign exchange	424.1	871.9	944.8
Total	433.6	882.0	955.6

* National valuation.

Source: IMF, *International Financial Statistics*.

MONEY SUPPLY

(million birr, at 31 December)

	2001	2002	2003
Currency outside banks . . .	4,870.3	5,686.3	6,874.3
Demand deposits at commercial banks	8,484.8	10,185.4	11,659.4
Total money (incl. others) . .	13,865.2	16,557.9	18,595.1

Source: IMF, *International Financial Statistics*.

COST OF LIVING

(Consumer Price Index; base: 1995 = 100)

	2001	2002	2003
All items	99.5	101.0	119.0

Sources: IMF, *International Financial Statistics*.

NATIONAL ACCOUNTS

(million birr at current prices; year ending 7 July)

Expenditure on the Gross Domestic Product

	1998/99	1999/2000	2000/01
Government final consumption expenditure	9,105	12,029	9,065
Private final consumption expenditure	38,999	40,566	43,416
Statistical discrepancy . . .	420	−497	12
Gross capital formation	7,790	7,995	8,747
Total domestic expenditure .	56,314	60,093	61,240
Exports of goods and services . .	7,258	8,086	8,106
Less Imports of goods and services	14,884	16,105	16,335
GDP in purchasers' values . .	48,688	52,074	53,011

Source: IMF, *International Financial Statistics*.

Gross Domestic Product by Economic Activity
(at constant 1980/81 factor cost; year ending 7 July)

	1998/99	1999/2000	2000/01*
Agriculture, hunting, forestry and fishing . . .	6,874	7,025	7,831
Mining and quarrying	75	83	90
Manufacturing	982	1,015	1,068
Electricity, gas and water . . .	226	235	243
Construction	418	399	431
Trade, hotels and restaurants . .	1,344	1,397	1,469
Transport, storage and communications	910	1,027	1,081
Finance, insurance and real estate	1,046	1,144	1,207
Public administration and defence	2,138	2,449	2,513
Education	356	388	427
Health	188	187	202
Domestic and other services . .	738	766	795
Total	**15,294**	**16,112**	**17,357**

* Estimated figures.

Source: IMF, *Ethiopia: Statistical Appendix* (September 2002).

Total GDP at factor cost (at constant 1980/81 prices, revised figures; year ending 7 July): 15,461 in 1998/99; 16,303 in 1999/2000; 17,583 in 2000/01 (Source: IMF, *International Financial Statistics*).

BALANCE OF PAYMENTS
(US $ million)

	2000	2001	2002
Exports of goods f.o.b.	486.0	455.6	480.2
Imports of goods f.o.b.	–1,131.4	–1,625.8	–479.9
Trade balance	**–645.4**	**–1,170.3**	**–974.8**
Exports of services	506.2	522.9	585.4
Imports of services	–490.7	–525.6	–582.6
Balance on goods and services	**–629.9**	**–1,172.9**	**–972.0**
Other income received . . .	16.2	16.3	14.3
Other income paid	–52.0	–48.3	–36.9
Balance on goods, services and income	**–665.7**	**–1,204.9**	**–994.6**
Current transfers received . . .	697.9	774.6	865.5
Current transfers paid	–17.6	–24.0	–20.5
Current balance	**14.6**	**–454.3**	**–149.5**
Investment assets	116.1	25.1	–4.1
Investment liabilities	–93.2	–200.3	–75.0
Net errors and omissions . . .	–233.0	–141.7	–858.4
Overall balance	**–195.6**	**–771.3**	**–1,087.0**

Source: IMF, *International Financial Statistics*.

External Trade

PRINCIPAL COMMODITIES
(distribution by SITC, US $ '000)

Imports c.i.f.	2000	2001	2002
Food and live animals . . .	57.1	218.9	151.8
Cereals and cereal preparations .	39.5	199.5	136.0
Unmilled wheat and meslin . .	18.1	136.4	107.1
Unmilled durum wheat . .	9.6	47.6	52.8
Mineral fuels, lubricants, etc. .	253.4	316.9	197.8
Refined petroleum products . .	247.2	308.8	187.2
Chemicals and related products	142.6	205.2	204.5
Manufactured fertilizers . . .	27.8	44.6	66.1
Basic manufactures	243.8	350.4	302.6
Textile yarn, fabrics, etc. . . .	55.9	71.6	66.1
Iron and steel	70.8	105.0	101.7
Universals, plates and sheets .	40.8	57.0	51.2
Machinery and transport equipment	402.0	503.3	514.1
Machinery specialized for particular industries	67.0	70.9	73.6
General industrial machinery equipment and parts . . .	44.4	63.8	52.8
Telecommunications, sound recording and reproducing equipment	41.1	45.2	47.4
Electrical machinery, apparatus, etc.*	48.7	67.3	65.9
Road vehicles and parts† . . .	151.4	169.3	191.7
Passenger motor cars (excl. buses)	39.9	53.5	69.5
Lorries and special purposes motor vehicles	72.2	73.3	75.4
Motor vehicles for goods transport, etc.	70.3	66.3	72.3
Miscellaneous manufactured articles	109.8	135.6	162.4
Total (incl. others)	**1,260.4**	**1,811.0**	**1,593.5**

* Excluding telecommunications and sound equipment.
† Excluding tyres, engines and electrical parts.

Exports f.o.b.	2000	2001	2002
Food and live animals . . .	291.0	203.1	244.1
Unmilled cereals	3.4	18.1	12.0
Vegetables and fruit	13.8	29.6	41.5
Beans, peas and other leguminous vegetables, dried and shelled	8.9	20.8	30.5
Raw sugar beet and cane, solid .	10.3	0.9	20.4
Coffee, not roasted, coffee husks and skins	255.4	145.1	159.8
Crude materials (inedible) except fuels	114.0	140.7	107.3
Raw hides and skins (excl. furs) .	6.5	27.9	8.7
Oil seeds and oleaginous fruit . .	28.7	37.7	40.0
Sesame seeds	22.1	24.5	31.3
Miscellaneous manufactured articles	47.4	50.4	57.1
Leather	41.0	46.7	53.4
Sheep and lamb skin leather .	31.7	26.5	29.0
Commodities and transactions not elsewhere specified . .	27.7	4.5	3.6
Non-monetary gold, unwrought or semi-manufactured	27.7	4.5	3.5
Total (incl. others)	**482.0**	**402.6**	**414.9**

Source: UN *International Trade Statistics Yearbook*.

PRINCIPAL TRADING PARTNERS
(US $ million)

Imports c.i.f.	2000	2001	2002
Belgium	18.2	38.0	41.0
China, People's Republic . . .	96.7	134.8	144.8
Denmark	12.3	21.0	10.3
Djibouti	3.3	48.9	60.3
Egypt	16.2	17.8	19.4
France (incl. Monaco)	39.7	58.2	25.9
Germany	65.3	87.1	83.7
Greece	6.1	15.1	16.2
India	65.6	91.1	83.6
Indonesia	23.6	28.2	26.1
Italy	111.6	135.3	140.6
Japan	103.0	78.5	113.0
Jordan	11.0	8.0	16.4
Kenya	20.4	15.1	17.4
Korea, Republic	39.2	42.8	21.5
Malaysia	14.2	12.1	7.3
Netherlands	16.0	41.9	39.0
Russia	13.8	8.8	15.8
Saudi Arabia	20.6	201.2	111.1
Sweden	30.7	38.5	30.1
Turkey	23.1	22.8	35.1
United Arab Emirates	29.6	112.2	114.3
United Kingdom	54.8	61.7	73.1
USA	60.9	167.6	126.6
Yemen	240.6	132.4	7.9
Total (incl. others)	1,260.4	1,811.0	1,593.5

Exports f.o.b.	2000	2001	2002
Belgium	16.8	7.3	12.4
China, People's Republic . . .	0.9	4.5	7.4
Djibouti	51.4	71.4	54.4
Egypt	6.4	2.6	4.9
France	14.2	11.6	11.1
Germany	94.3	23.1	49.5
Greece	1.9	2.9	4.8
Iceland	—	11.8	2.3
India	7.9	17.4	11.0
Indonesia	5.8	3.4	2.4
Israel	15.5	14.0	15.1
Italy	32.2	42.6	41.0
Japan	56.3	37.2	37.3
Malaysia	3.0	1.9	4.3
Netherlands	10.1	4.6	4.2
Pakistan	3.6	2.1	13.8
Saudi Arabia	38.9	37.8	28.1
Somalia	29.3	13.4	9.6
Switzerland	28.8	8.4	10.2
Thailand	0.6	9.8	1.1
United Arab Emirates	2.8	6.4	8.1
United Kingdom	10.4	15.8	17.3
USA	17.6	19.6	16.7
Yemen	6.2	8.0	7.6
Total (incl. others)	482.0	402.6	414.9

Source: UN, *International Trade Statistics Yearbook*.

Transport

RAILWAYS
(traffic, year ending 7 July)*

	1996/97	1997/98	1998/99
Addis Ababa–Djibouti:			
Passenger-km (million) . . .	157	167	150
Freight (million net ton-km) .	106	90	116

* Including traffic on the section of the Djibouti–Addis Ababa line which runs through the Republic of Djibouti. Data pertaining to freight include service traffic.

Source: former Ministry of Transport and Communications, Addis Ababa.

ROAD TRAFFIC
(motor vehicles in use, year ending 7 July)

	2000	2001	2002
Passenger cars	59,048	59,737	67,614
Buses and coaches	9,334	11,387	18,067
Lorries and vans	34,355	43,375	34,102
Motorcycles and mopeds . . .	n.a.	2,198	2,575
Road tractors	6,809	1,275	1,396
Total	109,546	117,972	123,754

Source: IRF, *World Road Statistics*.

SHIPPING
Merchant Fleet
(registered at 31 December)

	2001	2002	2003
Number of vessels	9	9	9
Displacement (grt)	81,933	81,933	81,933

Source: Lloyd's Register-Fairplay, *World Fleet Statistics*.

International Sea-borne Shipping
(freight traffic, '000 metric tons, year ending 7 July)

	1996/97	1997/98	1998/99
Goods loaded	242	201	313
Goods unloaded	777	1,155	947

Source: former Ministry of Transport and Communications, Addis Ababa.

CIVIL AVIATION
(traffic on scheduled services)

	1999	2000	2001
Kilometres flown (million) . . .	29	29	32
Passengers carried ('000) . . .	861	945	1,028
Passenger-km (million)	2,458	2,753	2,953
Total ton-km (million)	371	383	402

Source: UN, *Statistical Yearbook*.

Tourism

TOURIST ARRIVALS BY COUNTRY OF ORIGIN

	2000	2001	2002
Canada	2,597	3,076	3,895
Djibouti	14,512	31,289	26,447
France	5,856	3,834	4,270
Germany	4,665	4,515	4,499
India	3,480	3,244	3,778
Italy	4,395	4,349	4,297
Japan	1,193	1,936	1,857
Kenya	3,437	3,899	3,726
Netherlands	2,717	3,038	2,544
Saudi Arabia	1,967	3,001	2,610
Sudan	4,723	4,231	3,091
United Kingdom	7,074	5,858	6,123
USA	11,318	11,009	14,972
Yemen	3,897	2,567	2,651
Total (incl. others)*	135,954	148,438	156,327

* Including Ethiopian nationals residing abroad.

Receipts from tourism (US $ million): 68 in 2000; 75 in 2001; n.a. in 2002.

Source: World Tourism Organization.

Communications Media

	2001	2002	2003
Telephones ('000 main lines in use)	310.0	368.2	435.0
Mobile cellular telephones ('000 subscribers)	27.5	50.4	97.8
Personal computers ('000 in use) .	75	100	150
Internet users ('000)	25	50	75

Book production: 444 titles in 1999.

Non-daily newspapers: 78 in 1998 (average combined circulation 402,000).

Daily newspapers: 2 in 1998 (average circulation 23,000 copies).

Radio receivers ('000 in use): 11,340 in 2000.

Television receivers ('000 in use): 1,260 in 2000.

Facsimile machines (number in use): 3,594 in 2000.

Sources: UNESCO, *Statistical Yearbook*; UN, *Statistical Yearbook*; International Telecommunication Union.

Education

(1999/2000)

	Institutions	Teachers	Students
Pre-primary	834	2,877	99,710
Primary	11,490	115,777	6,462,503
Secondary: general	410	13,154	571,719
Secondary: teacher training . .	12	294	4,813
Secondary: skill development centres	25	367	2,474
Secondary: technical and vocational (government) . . .	16	523	3,427
Secondary: technical and vocational (non-government) .	9	125	1,837
University level	6	1,779	40,894
Other higher:			
Government	11	578	18,412
Non-government	4	140	8,376

Source: Ministry of Education, Addis Ababa.

Adult literacy rate (UNESCO estimates): 41.5% (males 49.2%; females 33.8%) in 2002 (Source: UN Development Programme, *Human Development Report*).

Directory

The Constitution

The Constitution of the Federal Democratic Republic of Ethiopia was adopted by the transitional Government on 8 December 1994. The following is a summary of the main provisions of the Constitution, which came into force on 22 August 1995.

GENERAL PROVISIONS

The Constitution establishes a federal and democratic state structure and all sovereign power resides in the nations, nationalities and peoples of Ethiopia. The Constitution is the supreme law of the land. Human rights and freedoms, emanating from the nature of mankind, are inviolable and inalienable. State and religion are separate and there shall be no state religion. The State shall not interfere in religious matters and vice versa. All Ethiopian languages shall enjoy equal state recognition; Amharic shall be the working language of the Federal Government.

FUNDAMENTAL RIGHTS AND FREEDOMS

All persons are equal before the law and are guaranteed equal and effective protection, without discrimination on grounds of race, nation, nationality, or other social origin, colour, sex, language, religion, political or other opinion, property, birth or other status. Everyone has the right to freedom of thought, conscience and religion and the freedom, either individually or in community with others, and in public or private, to manifest his religion or belief in worship, observance, practice and teaching. Every person has the inviolable and inalienable right to life, privacy, and the security of person and liberty.

DEMOCRATIC RIGHTS

Every Ethiopian national, without discrimination based on colour, race, nation, nationality, sex, language, religion, political or other opinion, or other status, has the following rights: on the attainment of 18 years of age, to vote in accordance with the law; to be elected to any office at any level of government; to freely express oneself without interference; to hold opinions without interference; to engage in economic activity and to pursue a livelihood anywhere within the national territory; to choose his or her means of livelihood, occupation and profession; and to own private property.

Every nation, nationality and people in Ethiopia has the following rights: an unconditional right to self-determination, including the right to secession; the right to speak, to write and to develop its own language; the right to express, to develop and to promote its culture, and to preserve its history; the right to a full measure of self-government which includes the right to establish institutions of government in the territory that it inhabits. Women shall, in the enjoyment of rights and protections provided for by this Constitution, have equal right with men.

STATE STRUCTURE

The Federal Democratic Republic of Ethiopia shall have a parliamentarian form of government. The Federal Democratic Republic shall comprise nine States. Addis Ababa shall be the capital city of the Federal State.

STRUCTURE AND DIVISION OF POWERS

The Federal Democratic Republic of Ethiopia comprises the Federal Government and the member States. The Federal Government and the States shall have legislative, executive and judicial powers. The House of People's Representatives is the highest authority of the Federal Government. The House is responsible to the people. The State Council is the highest organ of state authority. It is responsible to the people of the State. State government shall be established at state and other administrative levels deemed necessary. Adequate power shall be granted to the lowest units of government to enable the people to participate directly in the administration of such units. The State Council has legislative power on matters falling under state jurisdiction. Consistent with the provisions of this Constitution, the Council has the power to draft, adopt and amend the state constitution. The state administration constitutes the highest organ of executive power. State judicial power is vested in its courts. The States shall respect the powers of the Federal Government. The Federal Government shall likewise respect the powers of the States. The Federal Government may, when necessary, delegate to the States powers and functions granted to it by the Constitution.

THE FEDERAL HOUSES

There shall be two Federal Houses: the House of People's Representatives and the House of the Federation.

Members of the House of People's Representatives shall be elected by the people for a term of five years on the basis of universal suffrage and by direct, free and fair elections held by secret ballot. Members of the House, on the basis of population and special representation of minority nationalities and peoples, shall not exceed 550; of these, minority nationalities and peoples shall have at least 20 seats. The House of People's Representatives shall have legislative power in all matters assigned by this Constitution to federal jurisdiction. The political party or coalition of political parties that has the greatest number of seats in the House of People's Representatives shall form and lead the Executive. Elections for a new House shall be concluded one month prior to the expiry of the House's term.

The House of the Federation is composed of representatives of nations, nationalities and peoples. Each nation, nationality and people shall be represented in the House of the Federation by at least one member. Each nation or nationality shall be represented by one additional representative for each one million of its population. Members of the House of the Federation shall be elected by the State Councils. The State Councils may themselves elect representatives to the House of the Federation, or they may hold elections to have the representatives elected by the people directly. The House of the Federation shall hold at least two sessions annually. The term of mandate of the House of the Federation shall be five years. No one may be a member of the House of People's Representatives and of the House of the Federation simultaneously.

PRESIDENT OF THE REPUBLIC
The President of the Federal Democratic Republic of Ethiopia is the Head of State. The House of People's Representatives shall nominate the candidate for President. The nominee shall be elected President if a joint session of the House of People's Representatives and the House of the Federation approves his candidacy by a two-thirds' majority vote. The term of office of the President shall be six years. No person shall be elected President for more than two terms. The President's duties include the opening of the Federal Houses; appointing ambassadors and other envoys to represent the country abroad; granting, upon recommendation by the Prime Minister and in accordance with law, high military titles; and granting pardons.

THE EXECUTIVE
The highest executive powers of the Federal Government are vested in the Prime Minister and in the Council of Ministers. The Prime Minister and the Council of Ministers are responsible to the House of People's Representatives. In the exercise of state functions, members of the Council of Ministers are collectively responsible for all decisions they make as a body. Unless otherwise provided in this Constitution, the term of office of the Prime Minister is the duration of the mandate of the House of People's Representatives. The Prime Minister is the Chief Executive, the Chairman of the Council of Ministers, and the Commander-in-Chief of the national armed forces. The Prime Minister shall submit for approval to the House of People's Representatives nominees for ministerial posts from among members of the two Houses or from among persons who are not members of either House and possess the required qualifications. The Council of Ministers is responsible to the Prime Minister and, in all its decisions, is responsible to the House of People's Representatives. The Council of Ministers ensures the implementation of laws and decisions adopted by the House of People's Representatives.

STRUCTURE AND POWERS OF THE COURTS
Supreme Federal judicial authority is vested in the Federal Supreme Court. The House of People's Representatives may, by a two-thirds' majority vote, establish nation-wide, or in some parts of the country only, the Federal High Court and First-Instance Courts it deems necessary. Unless decided in this manner, the jurisdictions of the Federal High Court and of the First-Instance Courts are hereby delegated to the state courts. States shall establish State Supreme, High and First-Instance Courts. Judicial powers, both at federal and state levels, are vested in the courts. Courts of any level shall be free from any interference of influence of any governmental body, government official or from any other source. Judges shall exercise their functions in full independence and shall be directed solely by the law. The Federal Supreme Court shall have the highest and final judicial power over federal matters. State Supreme Courts shall have the highest and final judicial power over state matters. They shall also exercise the jurisdiction of the Federal High Court.

MISCELLANEOUS PROVISIONS
The Council of Ministers of the Federal Government shall have the power to decree a state of emergency in the event of an external invasion, a breakdown of law and order that endangers the constitutional order and cannot be controlled by the regular law enforcement agencies and personnel, a natural disaster or an epidemic. State executives can decree a state-wide state of emergency should a natural disaster or an epidemic occur.

A National Election Board independent of any influence shall be established, to conduct free and fair elections in federal and state constituencies in an impartial manner.

The Government

HEAD OF STATE
President: Lt GIRMA WOLDE GIORGIS (took office 8 October 2001).

COUNCIL OF MINISTERS
(April 2005)

Prime Minister: MELES ZENAWI.

Deputy Prime Minister and Minister of Rural Development: ADDISO LEGGESE.

Minister of Foreign Affairs: SEYOUM MESFIN.

Minister of Health: Dr KEBEDE TADESSE.

Minister of Capacity Building: TEFERA WALWA.

Minister of Infrastructure: Dr KASSA YLALA.

Minister of Defence: Gen ABEDULA GEMEDA.

Minister of Energy and Mines: MOHAMMED DIRIR.

Minister of Finance and Economic Development and Co-operation: SUFYAN AHMED.

Minister of Information: BEREKET SIMEON.

Minister of Education: GENET ZEWDE.

Minister of Agriculture: Dr MULATU TESHOME.

Minister of Trade and Industry: GIRMA BIRU.

Minister of Justice: HARIKA HAROYE.

Minister of Federal Affairs: ABBAY TSEHAYE.

Minister of Labour and Social Affairs: HASAN ABDELA.

Minister of Water Resources: SHIFERAW JARSO.

Minister of Revenues: GETACHEW BELAY.

Minister of Youth, Culture and Sport: TESHOME TOGA.

MINISTRIES
Office of the President: POB 1031, Addis Ababa; tel. (1) 122473; fax (1) 522041.

Office of the Prime Minister: POB 1013, Addis Ababa; tel. (1) 552044; fax (1) 522020.

Ministry of Agriculture and Rural Development: POB 62347, Addis Ababa; tel. (1) 538134; fax (1) 530776; e-mail moav@telecom.net.et.

Ministry of Capacity Building: Addis Ababa; tel. (1) 552800; fax (1) 553338.

Ministry of Defence: POB 1373, Addis Ababa; tel. (1) 511777; fax (1) 516053.

Ministry of Education: POB 1367, Addis Ababa; tel. (1) 553133; fax (1) 5160299.

Ministry of Energy and Mines: POB 486, Addis Ababa; tel. (1) 463166; fax (1) 4633644; e-mail mm&e@telecom.net.et.

Ministry of Federal Affairs: POB 5718, Addis Ababa; tel. (1) 512766.

Ministry of Finance, Economic Development and Co-operation: POB 1037, Addis Ababa; tel. (1) 552800; fax (1) 550118; e-mail meda2@telecom.net.et.

Ministry of Foreign Affairs: POB 393, Addis Ababa; tel. (1) 517345; fax (1) 514300; e-mail mfa.addis@telecom.net.et; internet www.mfa.gov.et.

Ministry of Health: POB 1234, Addis Ababa; tel. (1) 517011; fax (1) 519366; e-mail moh@telecom.net.et.

Ministry of Information: Addis Ababa; tel. (1) 551100; fax (1) 569678.

Ministry of Infrastructure: POB 1238, Addis Ababa; tel. (1) 516166; fax (1) 515665.

Ministry of Justice: POB 1370, Addis Ababa; tel. (1) 517950; fax (1) 517755; e-mail justice@telecom.net.et.

Ministry of Labour and Social Affairs: POB 2056, Addis Ababa; tel. (1) 517080; fax (1) 518396; e-mail moisa-comt@telecom.net.et.

Ministry of Revenues: POB 2559, Addis Ababa; tel. (1) 511066; fax (1) 512555.

Ministry of Rural Development: POB 1031, Addis Ababa; tel. (1) 564790; fax (1) 552030.

Ministry of Trade and Industry: POB 704, Addis Ababa; tel. (1) 518025; fax (1) 514288.

Ministry of Water Resources: POB 5744, Addis Ababa; tel. (1) 611111; fax (1) 611700; e-mail mowrl@telecom.net.et.

Ministry of Youth, Culture and Sport: POB 1364, Addis Ababa; tel. (1) 517020.

Regional Governments
Ethiopia comprises nine regional governments, one chartered city (Addis Ababa) and one Administrative Council (Dire Dawa), which are vested with authority for self-administration. The executive bodies are respectively headed by Presidents (regional states) and Chairmen (Addis Ababa and Dire Dawa).

PRESIDENTS
Tigrai: TSEGAYE BERHE.

Afar: ESMAEL ALISERO.

Amhara: YOSEF RETA.

Oromia: JUNEIDI SADO.

Somali: ABDIJIBRIL ABUBEKER.

Benishangul/Gumuz: YAREGAL AYSHESHIM.

Southern Nations, Nationalities and Peoples: HAILEMARIAM DESALEGNE.

Gambela: KEAT TUACH BITHOW (acting).

Harari: FUAD IBRAHIM.

CHAIRMEN

Dire Dawa: SOLOMON HAILU.

Addis Ababa: ARKEBE OQUBAY MITIKU.

Legislature

FEDERAL PARLIAMENTARY ASSEMBLY

The legislature comprises an upper house, the House of the Federation (Yefedereshn Mekir Bet), with 108 seats (members are selected by state assemblies and are drawn one each from 22 minority nationalities and one from each professional sector of the remaining nationalities, and serve for a period of five years), and a lower house of no more than 550 directly elected members, the House of People's Representatives (Yehizbtewekayoch Mekir Bet), who are also elected for a five-year term.

Speaker of the House of the Federation: MULATU TESHOME.

Yehizbtewekayoch Mekir Bet
(House of People's Representatives)

Speaker: DAWIT YOHANES.

Deputy Speaker: PETROS OLANGO.

General Election, 14 May and 31 August* 2000

Party	Seats
Oromo People's Democratic Organization (OPDO)	178
Amhara National Democratic Movement (ANDM)	134
Tigrai People's Liberation Front (TPLF)	38
Walayta, Gamo, Gofa, Dawro, and Konta People's Democratic Organization (WGGPDO)	30
Ethiopian People's Revolutionary Democratic Front (EPRDF)	19
Somali People's Democratic Party (SPDP)	19
Sidama People's Democratic Organization (SPDO)	18
Gurage Nationalities' Democratic Movement (GNDM)	15
Kafa Shaka People's Democratic Organization (KSPDO)	10
Afar National Democratic Party (ANDP)	8
Gedeyo People's Revolutionary Democratic Front (GPRDF)	7
South Omo People's Democratic Movement (SOPDM)	7
Benishangul Gumuz People's Democratic Unity Front (BGPDUF)	6
Kembata, Alabaa and Tembaro (KAT)	6
Bench Madji People's Democratic Organization (BMPDO)	5
Hadiya Nation Democratic Organization (HNDO)	5
Gambela People's Democratic Front (GPDF)	3
South Ethiopia People's Democratic Front (SEPDF)	3
Council of Alternative Forces for Peace and Democracy in Ethiopia (CAFPDE)	2
Derashe People's Democratic Organization (DPDO)	2
Ethiopian Democratic Party (EDP)	2
Hadiya People's Democratic Organization (HPDO)	2
Southern Ethiopian People's Democratic Union (SEPDU)	2
All Amhara People's Organization (AAPO)†	1
Argoba People's Democratic Movement (APDM)	1
Burgi People's Democratic Union (BPDU)	1
Gambella People's Democratic Congress (GPDC)	1
Konso People's Democratic Organization (KPDO)	1
Kore Nationality Democratic Organization (KNDO)	1
Oromo Liberation Unity Front (OLUF)	1
Oromo National Congress (ONC)	1
Oyda Nationality Democratic Organization (ONDO)	1
Sidama Hadicho People's Democratic Organization (SHPDO)	1

Party— *continued*	Seats
Silte People's Democratic Unity Party (SPDUP)	1
Yem People's Democratic Unity Party (YPDUP)	1
Independents	13
Total*	**546**

*Owing to irregularities and violence at some polling stations, voting was reheld in 16 constituencies. Furthermore, voting in the Somali Regional State was postponed until 31 August because of severe drought affecting the area.
† Now the All Ethiopia Unity Party (AEUP).

Political Organizations

Afar People's Democratic Organization (APDO): fmrly Afar Liberation Front (ALF); based in fmr Hararge and Wollo Admin. Regions; Leader ISMAIL ALI SIRRO.

Afar Revolutionary Democratic Front (ARDF): f. 2004.

All Ethiopia Unity Party (AEUP): e-mail info@aeup.com; internet www.aeup.com; fmrly the All Amhara People's Organization; Pres. HAILU SHAWEL; Sec.-Gen. MEKONEN BISHAW.

Coalition of Ethiopian Democratic Forces (COEDF): f. 1991 in the USA by the Ethiopian People's Revolutionary Party—EPRP (the dominant member), together with a faction of the Ethiopian Democratic Union (EDU) and the Ethiopian Socialist Movement (MEISON); opposes the EPRDF; Chair. MERSHA YOSEPH.

Coalition of Ethiopian Opposition Political Organizations (CEOPO): f. 1998 in France as a coalition of groups opposing the EPRDF; Chair. NEGEDE GOBEZIE; Chair. (Ethiopia) KIFLEH TIGNEH ABATE.

Dal-Webi Democratic Movement: f. 2004.

Ethiopian Democratic League (EDL): f. 2004.

Ethiopian National Congress (ENC): USA-based organization; aims to form a unified opposition among anti-Govt parties; Chair. GEBEYEHU IJUGU.

Ethiopian National Democratic Party (ENDP): f. 1994 by merger of five pro-Govt orgs with mems in the Council of Representatives; comprises: the Ethiopian Democratic Organization, the Ethiopian Democratic Organization Coalition (EDC), the Gurage People's Democratic Front (GPDF), the Kembata People's Congress (KPC), and the Wolaita People's Democratic Front (WPDF); Chair. FEKADU GEDAMU.

Ethiopian People's Revolutionary Democratic Front (EPRDF): Addis Ababa; f. 1989 by the TPLF as an alliance of insurgent groups seeking regional autonomy and engaged in armed struggle against the EDUP Govt; Chair. MELES ZENAWI; Vice-Chair. ADDISO LEGGESE; in May 1991, with other orgs, formed transitional Govt.

  Amhara National Democratic Movement (ANDM): based in Tigrai; represents interests of the Amhara people; fmrly the Ethiopian People's Democratic Movement (EPDM); adopted present name in 1994; Sec.-Gen. TEFERA WALWA.

  Oromo People's Democratic Organization (OPDO): f. 1990 by the TPLF to promote its cause in Oromo areas; based among the Oromo people in the Shoa region; Leader Gen. ABEDULA GEMEDA.

  Tigrai People's Liberation Front (TPLF): f. 1975; the dominant org. within the EPRDF; Chair. MELES ZENAWI; Vice-Chair. SEYOUM MESFIN.

Ethiopian Rainbow Movement for Democracy and Justice: f. 2004.

Gambela People's Democratic Front (GPDF): pro-Govt group based in the Gambela region; Chair. AKILO NIGILIO.

Joint Action for Democracy in Ethiopia (JADE): Addis Ababa; f. 2003 by the CAFPDE, the AEUP and the ONC as a common forum to enable them to co-ordinate their opposition to the EPRDF.

  All Ethiopia Unity Party (AEUP): e-mail info@aeup.com; internet www.aeup.com; fmrly the All Amhara People's Organization; Pres. HAILU SHAWEL; Sec.-Gen. MEKONEN BISHAW.

  Council of Alternative Forces for Peace and Democracy in Ethiopia (CAFPDE): e-mail cafpde@smtp.cafpde.org; internet www.cafpde.org; f. 1993 as a broadly-based coalition of groups opposing the EPRDF; Chair. Dr BEYENE PETROS.

  Oromo National Congress (ONC): Leader MERERA GUDINA.

Oromo Liberation Front (OLF): internet www .oromoliberationfront.org; seeks self-determination for the Oromo people; participated in the Ethiopian transitional Govt until June

1992; Chair. KATABE MAYU (acting); Vice-Chair. ABDULFATTAH A. MOUSSA BIYYO.

Somali Abo Liberation Front (SALF): operates in fmr Bale Admin. Region; has received Somali military assistance; Sec.-Gen. MASURAD SHU'ABI IBRAHIM.

Somali People's Democratic Party: f. 1998 by merger of Ogaden National Liberation Front (ONLF) and the Ethiopian Somali Democratic League (ESDL—an alliance comprising the Somali Democratic Union Party, the Issa and Gurgura Liberation Front, the Gurgura Independence Front, the Eastern Gabooye Democratic Organization, the Eastern Ethiopian Somali League, the Horyal Democratic Front, the Social Alliance Democratic Organization, the Somali Abo Democratic Union, the Shekhash People's Democratic Movement, the Ethiopian Somalis' Democratic Movement and the Per Barreh Party); Chair. MOHAMOUD DIRIR GHEDDI; Sec.-Gen. SULTAN IBRAHIM.

Southern Ethiopian People's Democratic Coalition (SEPDC): opposition alliance; Chair. Dr BEYENE PETROS.

Southern Ethiopian People's Democratic Union (SEPDU): f. 1992 as an alliance of 10 ethnically-based political groups from the south of the country; was represented in the transitional Council of Representatives, although five of the participating groups were expelled from the Council in April 1993.

United Ethiopian Democratic Forces (UEDF): Addis Ababa; f. 2003; Chair. Dr MERERE GUDINA.

United Ethiopian Democratic Party (UEDP): Addis Ababa; f. 2003 by the merger of Ethiopian Democratic Unity Party and the Ethiopian Democratic Party; Sec.-Gen. Dr ADMASSU GEBREYEHU.

United Oromo Liberation Forces (UOLF): f. 2000 in Asmara, Eritrea, as a common Oromo Front seeking to overthrow the Ethiopian Government; Chair. WAQO CUTU; Sec.-Gen. GALASA DILBO; alliance comprises:

  Islamic Front for the Liberation of Oromia: Leader ABDEL-KARIM IBRAHIM HAMID.

  Oromo Liberation Council (OLC).

  Oromo Liberation Front (OLF): see above.

  Oromo People's Liberation Front (OPLF).

  Oromo People's Liberation Organization (OPLO).

  United Oromo People's Liberation Front (UOPLF): Chair. WAQO CUTU.

Western Somali Liberation Front (WSLF): POB 978, Mogadishu, Somalia; f. 1975; aims to unite the Ogaden region with Somalia; maintains guerrilla forces of c. 3,000 men; has received support from regular Somali forces; Sec.-Gen. ISSA SHAYKH ABDI NASIR ADAN.

The following parties all have parliamentary representation: **Afar National Democratic Party (ANDP); Argoba People's Democratic Movement (APDM); Bench Madji People's Democratic Organization (BMPD); Benishangul Gumuz People's Democratic Unity Front (BGPDUF); Burgi People's Democratic Union (BPDU); Derashe People's Democratic Organization (DPDO); Gambela People's Democratic Congress (GPDC); Gedeyo People's Revolutionary Democratic Front (GPRDF); Gurage Nationalities' Democratic Movement (GNDM); Hadiya Nation Democratic Organization (HNDO); Hadiya People's Democratic Organization (HPDO); Kafa Shaka People's Democratic Organization (KSPDO); Kembata Alabaa and Tembaro (KAT); Konso People's Democratic Organization (KPDO); Kore Nationality Democratic Organization (KNDO); Oromo Liberation Unity Front (OLUF); Oyda Nationality Democratic Organization (ONDO); Sidama Hadicho People's Democratic Organization (SHPDO); Sidama People's Democratic Organization (SPDO); Silte People's Democratic Unity Party (SPDUP); South Ethiopia People's Democratic Front (SEPDF); South Omo People's Democratic Movement (SOPDM); Southern Ethiopian People's Democratic Union (SEPDU); Walayta, Gamo, Gofa, Dawro, and Konta People's Democratic Organization (WGGPDO); Yem People's Democratic Organization Unity Party (YPDUP).**

Diplomatic Representation

EMBASSIES IN ETHIOPIA

Algeria: POB 5740, Addis Ababa; tel. (1) 652300; fax (1) 650187; e-mail algemb@telecom.net.et; Ambassador SMAIL CHERGUI.

Angola: Kebele 18, House No. 26, POB 2962, Addis Ababa; tel. (1) 710118; fax (1) 514922; e-mail angola.embassy@telecom.net.et; Ambassador MIGUEL NETO.

Austria: POB 1219, Addis Ababa; tel. (1) 712144; fax (1) 712140; e-mail addis-abeba-ob@bmaa.gv.at; Ambassador BRIGGITTE ÖPPINGER-WALCHSHOFER.

Belgium: POB 1239, Addis Ababa; tel. (1) 611813; fax (1) 613646; e-mail embel.et@telecom.net.et; Ambassador CHRISTIAAN VAN DRIESSCHE.

Benin: Addis Ababa; Ambassador JEAN-MARIE EHOUZOU.

Bulgaria: POB 987, Addis Ababa; tel. (1) 610032; fax (1) 613373; Chargé d'affaires a.i. MIROSLAV KOMAROV.

Burkina Faso: POB 19685, Addis Ababa; tel. (1) 615863; fax (1) 612094; e-mail ambfet@telecom.net.et; Ambassador BRUNO ZIDOUEMBA.

Burundi: POB 3641, Addis Ababa; tel. (1) 651300; e-mail burundi.emb@telecom.net.et; Ambassador MELCHIOR BWAKIRA.

Cameroon: Bole Rd, POB 1026, Addis Ababa; tel. and fax (1) 504488; Ambassador JEAN-HILAIRE MBÉA MBÉA.

Canada: Old Airport Area, Higher 23, Kebele 12, House No. 122, POB 1130, Addis Ababa; tel. (1) 713022; fax (1) 713033; Ambassador JOHN R. SCHRAM.

Chad: POB 5119 Addis Ababa; tel. (1) 613819; fax (1) 612050; Ambassador MAHAMAT ABDELKERIM.

China, People's Republic: POB 5643, Addis Ababa; tel. (1) 711960; fax (1) 712457; e-mail chinesembassy@telecom.net.et; Ambassador LIN LIN.

Congo, Democratic Republic: Makanisa Rd, POB 2723, Addis Ababa; tel. (1) 710111; fax (1) 713466; e-mail rdca@telecom.net.et; Chargé d'affaires a.i. MARGRET RASHID KABAMBA.

Congo, Republic: POB 5639, Addis Ababa; tel. (1) 514188; Chargé d'affaires a.i. CASIMIR MPIERA.

Côte d'Ivoire: POB 3668, Addis Ababa; tel. (1) 712178; e-mail coted.aa@telecom.net.et; Ambassador DALO GBOUAGBRÉ.

Cuba: Jimma Rd, POB 5623, Addis Ababa; tel. (1) 620459; fax (1) 620460; Ambassador RICARDO GARCÍA.

Czech Republic: POB 3108, Addis Ababa; tel. (1) 516132; fax (1) 513471; e-mail addisabeba@embassy.mzv.cz; internet www.mzv.cz/addisabeba; Ambassador MIROSLAV KŘENEK.

Djibouti: POB 1022, Addis Ababa; tel. (1) 613200; fax (1) 612786; Ambassador (vacant).

Egypt: POB 1611, Addis Ababa; tel. (1) 553077; fax (1) 552722; Ambassador SHAMEL NASSER.

Equatorial Guinea: POB 246, Addis Ababa; tel. (1) 615973; Ambassador APLINAR MOIHE ECHEK.

Eritrea: POB 2571, Addis Ababa; tel. (1) 512844; fax (1) 514911; Chargé d'affaires a.i. SAHIH OMER.

Finland: Higher 17, Kebele 19, House No. 163, POB 1017, Addis Ababa; tel. (1) 611575; fax (1) 615964; e-mail finland.embassy@telecom.net.et; Chargé d'affaires a.i. KARI TOIVIAINEN.

France: Kabana, POB 1464, Addis Ababa; tel. (1) 550066; fax (1) 551441; e-mail ambfrance@telecom.net.et; Ambassador STÉPHANE GOMPERTZ.

Gabon: POB 1256, Addis Ababa; tel. (1) 611090; fax (1) 613760; Ambassador EMMANUEL MENDOUME-NZE.

Germany: Kabana, POB 660, Addis Ababa; tel. (1) 550433; fax (1) 551311; Ambassador HELGA GRAFIN STRACHWITZ.

Ghana: POB 3173, Addis Ababa; tel. (1) 711402; fax (1) 712511; e-mail ghmfa24@telecom.net.et; Ambassador JOHN EVONLAH AGGREY.

Greece: off Debre Zeit Rd, POB 1168, Addis Ababa; tel. (1) 654911; fax (1) 654883; e-mail greekembassy@telecom.net.et; internet www.telecom.net.et/~greekemb; Ambassador SPYROS ALIAGAS.

Guinea: POB 1190, Addis Ababa; tel. (1) 651308; fax (1) 651250; Ambassador MAMADI DIAWARA.

Holy See: POB 588, Addis Ababa (Apostolic Nunciature); tel. (1) 712100; fax (1) 711499; e-mail vatican.embassy@telecom.net.et; Apostolic Nuncio Most Rev. SILVANO M. TOMASI (Titular Archbishop of Asolo).

Hungary: Abattoirs Rd, POB 1213, Addis Ababa; tel. (1) 651850; Ambassador Dr SÁNDOR ROBEL.

India: Kabena, POB 528, Addis Ababa; tel. (1) 552394; fax (1) 552521; e-mail indembassy@podis.gn.apc.org; Ambassador KADAKATH PATHROSE ERNEST.

Indonesia: Mekanisa Rd, POB 1004, Addis Ababa; tel. (1) 710122; fax (1) 710873; e-mail kbriadis@telecom.net.et; Ambassador HADITMO HARSOJO.

Iran: POB 70488, Addis Ababa; tel. (1) 200794; fax (1) 711915; e-mail csiri@telecom.net.et; internet www.telecom.net.et/~iranet; Ambassador ABABA KIUMARS FOTOUHI QIYAM.

Ireland: POB 9585, Addis Ababa; tel. (1) 665050; fax (1) 665020; e-mail ireland.emb@telecom.net.et; Chargé d'affaires a.i. PAULINE CONWAY.

Israel: POB 1266, Addis Ababa; tel. (1) 610998; fax (1) 612456; e-mail info@addisababa.mfa.gov.il; Ambassador (vacant).

Italy: Villa Italia, POB 1105, Addis Ababa; tel. (1) 553042; fax (1) 550218; e-mail italembadd@telecom.net.et; Ambassador MARCELLO RICOVERI.

Jamaica: National House, Africa Ave, POB 5633, Addis Ababa; tel. (1) 613656; Ambassador OWEN A. SINGH.

Japan: Sunshine Bldg, Bole Rd, POB 5650, Addis Ababa; tel. (1) 511088; fax (1) 511350; e-mail japan-embassy@telecom.net.et; Ambassador HIROYOSHI IHARA.

Kenya: Fikre Mariam Rd, POB 3301, Addis Ababa; tel. (1) 610033; fax (1) 611433; e-mail kenya.embassy@telecom.net.et; Ambassador BOAZ K. MBAYA.

Korea, Democratic People's Republic: POB 2378, Addis Ababa; tel. (1) 182828; fax (1) 625417; Ambassador O NAM JUNG.

Korea, Republic: Jimma Rd, Old Airport Area, POB 2047, Addis Ababa; tel. (1) 655230; Ambassador JA CHOL-HAHN.

Kuwait: Addis Ababa; tel. (1) 615411; fax (1) 612621; Ambassador MUHAMMAD AL-AWADHI.

Lesotho: POB 7483, Addis Ababa; tel. (1) 614368; fax (1) 612837; Ambassador MASHULA H. LETEKA.

Liberia: POB 3116, Addis Ababa; tel. (1) 513655; Ambassador MARCUS M. KOFA.

Libya: POB 5728, Addis Ababa; tel. (1) 511077; fax (1) 511383; Ambassador ALI ABDALLA AWIDA.

Madagascar: POB 60004, Addis Ababa; tel. (1) 612555; fax (1) 610127; e-mail amba.mad.addis@telecom.net.et; Ambassador HER-INIAINA RAZAFIMAHEFA RAKOTOBE.

Malawi: POB 2316, Addis Ababa; tel. (1) 615866; fax (1) 615436; e-mail malemb@telecom.net.et; Ambassador WILLIE CHAKANI.

Mali: POB 4561, Addis Ababa; tel. (1) 201528; fax (1) 712601; Ambassador AL MAAMOUN KEITA.

Mexico: Tsige Mariam Bldg 292/21, 4th Floor, Churchill Rd, POB 2962, Addis Ababa; tel. (1) 443456; Ambassador CARLOS FERRER.

Morocco: 210 Bole Rd, POB 60033, Addis Ababa; tel. (1) 531700; fax (1) 511828; e-mail morocco.emb@telecom.net.et; Ambassador SIDI MUHAMMAD RAHHALI.

Mozambique: POB 5671, Addis Ababa; tel. (1) 710020; fax (1) 613824; e-mail embamoc-add@telecom.net.et; Ambassador ALEX-ANDRE ZANDAMELA.

Namibia: Higher 17, Kebele 19, House No. 002, POB 1443, Addis Ababa; tel. (1) 611966; fax (1) 612677; e-mail embassy@telecom.net .et; Ambassador GEORGE OBANGA.

Netherlands: POB 1241, Addis Ababa; tel. (1) 711100; fax (1) 711577; e-mail netherlands.emb@telecom.net.et; internet www .telecom.net.et/~nethemb/body.htm; Ambassador PIETER J. T. MARRES.

Niger: Debrezenit Rd, Higher 18, Kebele 41, House No. 057, POB 5791, Addis Ababa; tel. (1) 651305; Ambassador ASSANE IGODOE.

Nigeria: POB 1019, Addis Ababa; tel. (1) 552307; Ambassador J. K. SHINKAYE.

Norway: POB 8383, Addis Ababa; tel. (1) 710799; fax (1) 711255; e-mail ambassade-addis@telecom.net.et; Ambassador S. OSKARSSON.

Romania: 17 Woreda, Kebele 19, 10 Bole Rd, POB 2478, Addis Ababa; tel. (1) 610156; fax (1) 611191; e-mail roembaddis@telecom .net.et; Chargé d'affaires a.i. MARIUS NICOLESCU.

Russia: POB 1500, Addis Ababa; tel. (1) 612060; fax (1) 613795; e-mail russemb@telecom.net.et; Ambassador VALERY N. LIPNYAKOV.

Rwanda: Africa House, Higher 17, Kebele 20, POB 5618, Addis Ababa; tel. (1) 610300; fax (1) 610411; e-mail rwanda.emb@telecom .net.et; Ambassador Dr NGOGA PASCAL.

Saudi Arabia: Old Airport Area, POB 1104, Addis Ababa; tel. (1) 712952; fax (1) 711799; Ambassador SAOUD A. M. AL-YAHAYA.

Senegal: Africa Ave, POB 2581, Addis Ababa; tel. (1) 611376; fax (1) 610020; Ambassador MAME BALLA SY.

Serbia and Montenegro: POB 1341, Addis Ababa; tel. (1) 517804; fax (1) 514192; e-mail yugoslav.embassy@telecom.net.et; Ambassador VOJISLAV VUCIEVIC.

Sierra Leone: POB 5619, Addis Ababa; tel. (1) 710033; fax (1) 711911; e-mail sleon.et@telecom.net.et; Ambassador MELVIN H. CHA-LOBAH.

Somalia: Addis Ababa; Ambassador ABRAHIM HAJI NUR.

South Africa: POB 1091, Addis Ababa; tel. (1) 713034; fax (1) 711330; e-mail sa.embassy.addis@telecom.net.et; Ambassador JER-EMIAH N. MAMABOLO.

Spain: Entoto St, POB 2312, Addis Ababa; tel. (1) 550222; fax (1) 551131; e-mail embespet@mail.mae.es; Ambassador MARIA DEL CARMEN DE LA PENA.

Sudan: Kirkos, Kebele, POB 1110, Addis Ababa; tel. (1) 516477; fax (1) 518141; e-mail sudan.embassy@telecom.net.et; Ambassador OSMAN AS-SAYED.

Swaziland: Addis Ababa; Ambassador SOLOMON DLAMINI.

Sweden: Ras Kebele 53, House No. 891, Tessema Sefer, Woreda 3, POB 1142, Addis Ababa; tel. (1) 511255; fax (1) 515408; e-mail ambassaden.addis.abeba@sida.se; Ambassador HÅKAN ÅKESSON.

Switzerland: Jimma Rd, Old Airport Area, POB 1106, Addis Ababa; tel. (1) 711107; fax (1) 712177; e-mail swissemadd@telecom .net.et; Ambassador PAOLO BROGINI.

Tanzania: POB 1077, Addis Ababa; tel. (1) 511063; fax (1) 517358; Ambassador CHARLES S. KILEO.

Togo: Addis Ababa; Ambassador KATI OHARA KORGA.

Tunisia: Wereda 17, Kebele 19, Bole Rd, POB 100069, Addis Ababa; tel. (1) 612063; fax (1) 614568; e-mail embassy.tunisia@telecom.net .et; Ambassador ZOUHEIR ALLAGUI.

Turkey: POB 1506, Addis Ababa; tel. (1) 613161; fax (1) 611688; e-mail turk.emb@telecom.net.et; Ambassador KENAN TEPEDELEN.

Uganda: Addis Ababa; tel. (1) 513088; fax (1) 514355; Ambassador Dr ALEX KAMUGISHA.

United Kingdom: POB 858, Addis Ababa; tel. (1) 612354; fax (1) 610588; e-mail britishembassy.addisababa@fco.gov.uk; internet www.britishembassy.gov.uk/ethiopia; Ambassador ROBERT DEWAR.

USA: Entoto St, POB 1014, Addis Ababa; tel. (1) 550666; fax (1) 551328; e-mail usembassy@telecom.net.et; internet www.telecom .net.et/~usemb-et; Ambassador AURELIA E. BRAZEAL.

Venezuela: Debre Zeit Rd, POB 5584, Addis Ababa; tel. (1) 654790; Chargé d'affaires a.i. ALFREDO HERNÁNDEZ-ROVATI.

Viet Nam: POB 1288, Addis Ababa; Ambassador NGUYEN DUY KINH.

Yemen: POB 664, Addis Ababa; Ambassador MANSUR ABD AL-JALIL ABD AL-RAB.

Zambia: POB 1909, Addis Ababa; tel. (1) 711302; fax (1) 711566; Ambassador SIMATAA AKAPELWA.

Zimbabwe: POB 5624, Addis Ababa; tel. (1) 613877; fax (1) 613476; e-mail zimbabwe.embassy@telecom.net.et; Ambassador NEVILLE NDONDO.

Judicial System

The 1994 Constitution stipulates the establishment of an independent judiciary in Ethiopia. Judicial powers are vested in the courts, both at federal and state level. The supreme federal judicial authority is the Federal Supreme Court. This court has the highest and final power of jurisdiction over federal matters. The federal states of the Federal Democratic Republic of Ethiopia can establish Supreme, High and First-Instance Courts. The Supreme Courts of the federal States have the highest and the final power of jurisdiction over state matters. They also exercise the jurisdiction of the Federal High Court. According to the Constitution, courts of any level are free from any interference or influence from government bodies, government officials or any other source. In addition, judges exercise their duties independently and are directed solely by the law.

Federal Supreme Court: Addis Ababa; tel. (1) 448425; comprises civil, criminal and military sections; its jurisdiction extends to the supervision of all judicial proceedings throughout the country; the Supreme Court is also empowered to review cases upon which final rulings have been made by the courts (including the Supreme Court) where judicial errors have occurred; Pres. KEMAL BEDRI.

Federal High Court: POB 3483, Addis Ababa; tel. (1) 751911; fax (1) 755399; e-mail fedhc@telecom.net.et; hears appeals from the state courts; has original jurisdiction; Pres. WOUBISHET KIBRU.

Awraja Courts: regional courts composed of three judges, criminal and civil.

Warada Courts: sub-regional; one judge sits alone with very limited jurisdiction, criminal only.

Religion

About 45% of the population are Muslims and about 40% belong to the Ethiopian Orthodox (Tewahido) Church. There are also significant Evangelical Protestant and Roman Catholic communities. The Pentecostal Church and the Society of International Missionaries carry out mission work in Ethiopia. There are also Hindu and Sikh religious institutions. Virtually all of Ethiopia's small Jewish population had been evacuated by the Israeli Government by mid-1999. It has been estimated that 5%–15% of the population follow animist rites and beliefs.

CHRISTIANITY

Ethiopian Orthodox (Tewahido) Church

The Ethiopian Orthodox (Tewahido) Church is one of the five oriental orthodox churches. It was founded in AD 328, and in 1989 had more than 22m. members, 20,000 parishes and 290,000 clergy. The Supreme Body is the Holy Synod and the National Council, under the chairmanship of the Patriarch (Abune). The Church comprises 25 archdioceses and dioceses (including those in Jerusalem, Sudan, Djibouti and the Western Hemisphere). There are 32 Archbishops and Bishops. The Church administers 1,139 schools and 12 relief and rehabilitation centres throughout Ethiopia.

Patriarchate Head Office: POB 1283, Addis Ababa; tel. (1) 116507; Patriarch (Abune) Archbishop PAULOS; Gen. Sec. L. M. DEMTSE GEBRE MEDHIN.

The Roman Catholic Church

At 31 December 2002 Ethiopia contained an estimated 52,218 adherents of the Alexandrian-Ethiopian Rite and 423,452 adherents of the Latin Rite.

Bishops' Conference: Ethiopian and Eritrean Episcopal Conference, POB 21322, Addis Ababa; tel. (1) 550300; fax (1) 553113; f. 1966; Pres. Most Rev. BERHANEYESUS DEMEREW SOURAPHIEL (Archbishop of Addis Ababa).

Alexandrian-Ethiopian Rite

Adherents are served by one archdiocese (Addis Ababa) and two dioceses (Adigrat and Emdeber).

Archbishop of Addis Ababa: Most Rev. BERHANEYESUS DEMEREW SOURAPHIEL, Catholic Archbishop's House, POB 21903, Addis Ababa; tel. (1) 111667; fax (1) 553113.

Latin Rite

Aherents are served by the five Apostolic Vicariates of Awasa, Harar, Meki, Nekemte and Soddo-Hosanna, and by the Apostolic Prefectures of Gambela and Jimma-Bonga.

Other Christian Churches

The Anglican Communion: Within the Episcopal Church in Jerusalem and the Middle East, the Bishop in Egypt has jurisdiction over seven African countries, including Ethiopia.

Armenian Orthodox Church: St George's Armenian Church, POB 116, Addis Ababa; f. 1923; Deacon VARTKES NALBANDIAN.

Ethiopian Evangelical Church (Mekane Yesus): POB 2087, Addis Ababa; tel. (1) 531919; fax (1) 534148; e-mail eecmy.co@telecom.net.et; Pres. Rev. ITEFFA GOBENA; f. 1959; affiliated to Lutheran World Fed., All Africa Conf. of Churches and World Council of Churches; c. 4.16m. mems (2004).

Greek Orthodox Church: POB 571, Addis Ababa; Metropolitan of Axum Most Rev. PETROS YIAKOUMELOS.

Seventh-day Adventist Church: POB 145, Addis Ababa; tel. (1) 511319; e-mail sdaeum@telecom.net.et; f. 1907; Pres. TINSAE TOLESSA; 130,000 mems.

ISLAM

Leader: Haji MOHAMMED AHMAD.

JUDAISM

A phased emigration to Israel of about 27,000 Falashas (Ethiopian Jews) took place during 1984–91. In February 2003 the Israeli Government ruled that the Falashmura (Ethiopian Christians whose forefathers had converted from Judaism) had been forced to convert to Christianity to avoid religious persecution and that they had the right to settle in Israel. In January 2004 Ethiopia and Israel agreed to allow the Falashmura to be flown to Israel; some 17,000 Falashmura and a further 3,000 Falashas were expected to arrive in Israel by 2007.

The Press

DAILIES

Addis Zemen: POB 30145, Addis Ababa; f. 1941; Amharic; publ. by the Ministry of Information; Editor-in-Chief (vacant); circ. 40,000.

The Daily Monitor: POB 22588, Addis Ababa; tel. (1) 611880; fax (1) 518409; f. 1993; English; Editor-in-Chief LULLIT MICKAEL; circ. 6,000.

Ethiopian Herald: POB 30701, Addis Ababa; tel. (1) 119050; f. 1943; English; publ. by the Ministry of Information; Editor-in-Chief KIFLOM HADGOI; circ. 37,000.

PERIODICALS

Abyotawit Ethiopia: POB 2549, Addis Ababa; fortnightly; Amharic.

Addis Tribune: Tambek International, POB 2395, Addis Ababa; tel. (1) 615228; fax (1) 615227; e-mail tambek@telecom.net.et; internet www.addistribune.ethiopiaonline.com; f. 1993; weekly; English; Editor-in-Chief (vacant); circ. 6,000.

Addis Zimit: POB 2395, Addis Ababa; tel. (1) 118613; fax (1) 552110; f. 1993; weekly; Amharic; Editor-in-Chief (vacant); circ. 8,000.

Al-Alem: POB 30232, Addis Ababa; tel. (1) 158046; fax (1) 516819; f. 1941; weekly; Arabic; publ. by the Ministry of Information; Editor-in-Chief TELSOM AHMED; circ. 2,500.

Berisa: POB 30232, Addis Ababa; f. 1976; weekly; Oromogna; publ. by the Ministry of Information; Editor BULO SIBA; circ. 3,500.

Beza: Addis Ababa; weekly; Editor-in-Chief YARED KEMFE.

Birhan Family Magazine: Addis Ababa; monthly; women's magazine.

Birritu: National Bank of Ethiopia, POB 5550, Addis Ababa; tel. (1) 517430; fax (1) 514588; e-mail nbe.excd@telecom.net.et; internet www.nbe.gov.et; f. 1982; quarterly; Amharic and English; banking, insurance and macroeconomic news; circ. 2,000; Editor-in-Chief SEMENEH ADGE; Dep. Editor-in-Chief ATO ABEBE DEMISSE.

Ethiopis Review: Editor-in-Chief TESFERA ASMARE.

Mabruk: Addis Ababa; weekly; Editor-in-Chief TESAHALENNE MENGESHA.

Maebel: Addis Ababa; weekly; Amharic; Editor-in-Chief ABERA WOGI.

Meskerem: Addis Ababa; quarterly; theoretical politics; circ. 100,000.

Negarit Gazzetta: POB 1031, Addis Ababa; irregularly; Amharic and English; official gazette.

Nigdina Limat: POB 2458, Addis Ababa; tel. (1) 513882; fax (1) 511479; e-mail aachamber1@telecom.net.et; monthly; Amharic; publ. by the Addis Ababa (Ethiopia) Chamber of Commerce; circ. 6,000.

Press Digest: POB 12719, Addis Ababa; tel. (1) 504200; fax (1) 513523; e-mail phoenix.universal@telecom.net.et; internet pressdigest.phoenixuniversal.com; f. 1993; weekly.

Tequami: Addis Ababa; weekly; Editor-in-Chief SAMSON SEYUM.

Tinsae (Resurrection): Addis Ababa; tel. (1) 116507; Amharic and English; publ. by the Ethiopian Orthodox Church.

Tobia Magazine: POB 22373, Addis Ababa; tel. (1) 556177; fax (1) 552654; e-mail akpac@telecom.net.et; monthly; Amharic; Man. GOSHU MOGES; circ. 30,000.

Tobia Newspaper: POB 22373, Addis Ababa; tel. (1) 556177; fax (1) 552654; e-mail akpac@telecom.net.et; weekly; Amharic; Man. GOSHU MOGES; circ. 25,000.

Tomar: Benishangul; weekly; Amharic; Editor-in-Chief BEFEKADU MOREDA.

Wetaderna Alamaw: POB 1901, Addis Ababa; fortnightly; Amharic.

Yezareitu Ethiopia (Ethiopia Today): POB 30232, Addis Ababa; weekly; Amharic and English; publ. by the Ministry of Information; Editor-in-Chief IMIRU WORKU; circ. 30,000.

NEWS AGENCIES

Ethiopian News Agency (ENA): Patriot St, POB 530, Addis Ababa; tel. (1) 550011; fax (1) 551609; e-mail ena@telecom.net.et; internet www.telecom.net.et/~ena; Chair NETSANET ASFAW.

Foreign Bureaux

Agence France-Presse (AFP): POB 3537, Addis Ababa; tel. (1) 511006; Chief SABA SEYOUM.

Agenzia Nazionale Stampa Associata (ANSA) (Italy): POB 1001, Addis Ababa; tel. (1) 111007; Chief BRAHAME GHEBREZGHI-ABIHER.

Associated Press (AP): Addis Ababa; tel. (1) 161726; Correspondent ABEBE ANDUALAM.

Deutsche Presse-Agentur (dpa) (Germany): Addis Ababa; tel. (1) 510687; Correspondent GHION HAGOS.

Informatsionnoye Telegrafnoye Agentstvo Rossii—Telegrafnoye Agentstvo Suverennykh Stran (ITAR—TASS) (Russia): Addis Ababa; tel. (1) 181255; Bureau Chief GENNADII G. GABRIELYAN.

Prensa Latina (Cuba): Gen. Makonnen Bldg, 5th Floor, nr Ghion Hotel, opp. National Stadium, Addis Ababa; tel. (1) 519899; Chief HUGO RIUS BLEIN.

Reuters (UK): Addis Ababa; tel. (1) 156505; Correspondent TSEGAYE TADESSE.

Rossiiskoye Informatsionnoye Agentstvo—Novosti (RIA—Novosti) (Russia): POB 239, Addis Ababa; Chief VITALII POLIKARPOV.

Xinhua (New China) News Agency (People's Republic of China): POB 2497, Addis Ababa; tel. (1) 515676; fax (1) 514742; Correspondent CHEN CAILIN.

PRESS ASSOCIATIONS

Ethiopian Free Press Journalists' Association (EFJA): POB 31317, Addis Ababa; tel. (1) 555021; fax (1) 922939; e-mail efja@telecom.net.et; internet www.ifex.org/members/efja; f. 1993; granted legal recognition in 2000; activities suspended in late 2003; Pres. KIFLE MULAT.

Ethiopian Journalists' Association: POB 30288, Addis Ababa; tel. (1) 117852; fax (1) 513365; Pres. KEFALE MAMMO.

Publishers

Addis Ababa University Press: POB 1176, Addis Ababa; tel. (1) 119148; fax (1) 550655; e-mail aau.pres@telecom.net.et; f. 1968; educational and reference works in English, general books in English and Amharic; Editor MESSELECH HABTE.

Berhanena Selam Printing Enterprise: POB 980 Addis Ababa; tel. (1) 553233; fax (1) 553939; e-mail bspe@telecom.net.et; f. 1921; fmrly Government Printing Press; publishes and prints newspapers, periodicals, books, security prints and other miscellaneous commercial prints; Gen. Man. MULUWORK G. HIWOT.

Ethiopia Book Centre: POB 1024, Addis Ababa; tel. (1) 116844; f. 1977; privately-owned; publr, importer, wholesaler and retailer of educational books.

Kuraz Publishing Agency: POB 30933, Addis Ababa; tel. (1) 551688; state-owned.

Broadcasting and Communications

TELECOMMUNICATIONS

Ethiopian Telecommunications Corpn (ETC): POB 1047, Addis Ababa; tel. (1) 510500; fax (1) 515777; e-mail etc-hq@telecom.net.et; internet www.telecom.net.et; Pres. GETACHEW BELAY; Man. Dir TESFAYE BIRU.

BROADCASTING

Radio

Radio Ethiopia: POB 1020, Addis Ababa; tel. (1) 121011; f. 1941; Amharic, English, French, Arabic, Afar, Oromifa, Tigre, Tigrinya and Somali; Gen. Man. KASA MILOKO.

Radio Torch: Addis Ababa; f. 1994; Amharic; autonomous station; Gen. Man. SEIFU TURE GETACHEW.

Radio Voice of One Free Ethiopia: Amharic; broadcasts twice a week; opposes current Govts of Ethiopia and Eritrea.

Voice of the Revolution of Tigrai: POB 450, Mekele; tel. (4) 410545; fax (4) 405485; e-mail vort@telecom.net.et; f. 1985; Tigrinya and Afargna; broadcasts 57 hours per week; supports Tigrai People's Liberation Front.

Television

Ethiopian Television: POB 5544, Addis Ababa; tel. (1) 155326; fax (1) 512685; f. 1964; semi-autonomous station; accepts commercial advertising; programmes transmitted from Addis Ababa to 26 regional stations; Chair. BEREKET SIMON; Gen. Man. SELOME TADDESSE.

Finance

(cap. = capital; res = reserves; dep. = deposits; m. = million; brs = branches; amounts in birr)

BANKING

Central Bank

National Bank of Ethiopia: POB 5550, Addis Ababa; tel. (1) 517430; fax (1) 514588; e-mail nbe.vgov@telecom.net.et; internet www.nbe.gov.et; f. 1964; bank of issue; cap. 50.0m., res 2,356.4m., dep. 12,138.4m. (June 2002); Gov. TEKLEWOLD ATNAFU; Vice-Gov. ALEMSEGED ASSEFA; 1 br.

Other Banks

Awash International Bank SC: Africa Ave, POB 12638, Addis Ababa; tel. (1) 614482; fax (1) 614477; e-mail awash.bank@telecom.net.et; internet www.awash-bank.com; f. 1994; cap. 110.1m., res 20.4m., dep. 1,042.9m. (Dec. 2002); Chair. BULCHA DEMEKSA; 25 brs.

Bank of Abyssinia: POB 12947, Addis Ababa; tel. (1) 530663; fax (1) 510409; e-mail abyssinia@telecom.net.et; internet www.bankofabyssinia.com; f. 1905; closed 1935 and reopened 1996; commercial banking services; cap. and res 139m., dep. 795m. (Jan. 2002); Chair. ADDIS ANTENEH; CEO KEBEDE TEMESGEN; 15 brs.

Commercial Bank of Ethiopia: Unity Sq., POB 255, Addis Ababa; tel. (1) 511271; fax (1) 514522; e-mail cbe.plng@telecom.net.et; internet www.combanketh.com; f. 1943; reorg. 1996; state-owned; cap. 619.7m., res 606.5m., dep. 19,514.9m. (June 2003); Pres. GEZAHEGN YILMA; 171 brs.

Construction and Business Bank: Higher 21, Kebele 04, POB 3480, Addis Ababa; tel. (1) 512300; fax (1) 515103; e-mail cbb@telecom.net.et; f. 1975 as Housing and Savings Bank; provides credit for construction projects and a range of commercial banking services; state-owned; total assets 933.1m. (June 2001); Chair. HAILE ASEGIDE; Gen. Man. ADMASSU TECHANE; 20 brs.

Dashen Bank: POB 12752, Garad Bldg, Debre Zeit Rd, Addis Ababa; tel. (1) 661380; fax (1) 653037; e-mail dashen.bank@telecom.net.et; internet www.dashenbanksc.com; cap. 75.0m., res 24.7m., dep. 1,621.4m. (June 2003); Pres. LULSEGED TEFERI; 22 brs.

Development Bank of Ethiopia: POB 1900, Addis Ababa; tel. (1) 511188; fax (1) 511606; e-mail dbe@telecom.net.et; provides devt finance for industry and agriculture, technical advice and assistance in project evaluation; state-owned; cap. and res 385.2m., dep. 727.7m. (March 1999); Chair. GIRMA BIRRU; Gen. Man. MOGES CHEMERE; 32 brs.

NIB International Bank SC: POB 2439, Africa Avenue, Dembel City Centre, Addis Ababa; tel. (1) 503288; fax (1) 504349; e-mail nibbank@telecom.net.et; internet www.addischamber.com/nibbank.htm; f. 1999; cap. 129.1m., res 18.9m., dep. 832.3m. (June 2004); Chair. DEMBEL BALCHA; Gen. Man. LEGESSE TICKEHER.

United Bank: POB 19963, Addis Ababa; tel. (1) 655222; fax (1) 655243; e-mail hibretbank@telecom.net.et; f. 1998; commercial banking services; cap. and res 96m., dep. 532.7m. (June 2004); Chair. EYESSUS W. ZAFU; Pres. ADMASSU TECHANE; 14 brs.

Wegagen Bank: POB 1018, Addis Ababa; tel. (1) 532800; fax (1) 523521; e-mail wegagen@telecom.net.et; f. 1997; commercial banking services; cap. 95.4m., total assets 1,660m. (Feb. 2004); Chair. SEEYE ABRAHA; CEO KIDANE NIKODIMOS; 23 brs.

Bankers' Association

Ethiopian Bankers' Association: Addis Ababa; f. 2001; Pres. LEIKUN BERHANU.

INSURANCE

Africa Insurance Co: POB 12941, Addis Ababa; tel. (1) 517861; fax (1) 510376; Gen. Man. ALEM TESFATSION.

Awash Insurance Co: POB 12637, Addis Ababa; tel. (1) 614420; fax (1) 614419; Gen. Man. TSEGAYE KEMAS.

Ethiopian Insurance Corpn: POB 2545, Addis Ababa; tel. (1) 512400; fax (1) 517499; e-mail eic.mdxvs@telecom.net.et; internet www.eic.com.et; f. 1976; life, property and legal liabilities insurance cover; Man. Dir Tewodros Tilahun.

Global Insurance SC: POB 180112, Addis Abba; tel. (1) 567400; fax (1) 566200; e-mail globalinsu@telecom.net.et; f. 1997; Gen. Man. Masresha G. Meskel.

Lion Insurance SC: POB 661, Addis Ababa; tel. (1) 513305; fax (1) 534799; e-mail daniel@telecom.net.et; f. 1998; Gen. Man. Tesfaye Natnael.

National Insurance Co of Ethiopia: POB 12645, Addis Ababa; tel. (1) 661129; fax (1) 650660; e-mail nice@telecom.net.et; Man. Dir and CEO Habtematiam Shumgizaw.

Nile Insurance Co: POB 12836, Addis Ababa; tel. (1) 537709; fax (1) 514592; e-mail nileinsu@mail.telecom.net.et; f. 1995; Gen. Man. Mahtsentu Feleke.

Nyala Insurance SC: POB 12753, Mickey Leland St, Addis Ababa; tel. (1) 626667; fax (1) 626706; e-mail nisco@telecom.net.et; internet www.nyalainsurance.com; Man. Dir Nahu-Senaye Araya.

United Insurance Co SC: POB 1156, Addis Ababa; tel. (1) 515656; fax (1) 513258; e-mail united.insurance@telecom.net.et; Chair. Getachew Kassaye; Man. Dir Iyesuswork Zafu.

Trade and Industry

CHAMBERS OF COMMERCE

Ethiopian Chamber of Commerce: Mexico Sq., POB 517, Addis Ababa; tel. (1) 518240; fax (1) 517699; e-mail ethchamb@telecom.net .et; f. 1947; city chambers in Addis Ababa, Asella, Awasa, Bahir Dar, Dire Dawa, Nazret, Jimma, Gondar, Dessie, Mekele and Shashemene; Pres. Aschalew Haile; Sec.-Gen. Andu Alem Tegegne.

Addis Ababa Chamber of Commerce: POB 2458, Addis Ababa; tel. (1) 513882; fax (1) 511479; e-mail AAchamber1@telecom.net.et; internet www.addischamber.com; Chair. Berhane Mewa; Sec.-Gen. Semunesh Demetros.

INDUSTRIAL AND TRADE ASSOCIATIONS

Ethiopian Beverages Corpn: POB 1285, Addis Ababa; tel. (1) 186185; Gen. Man. Menna Tewahede.

Ethiopian Cement Corpn: POB 5782, Addis Ababa; tel. (1) 552222; fax (1) 551572; Gen. Man. Redi Gemal.

Ethiopian Chemical Corpn: POB 5747, Addis Ababa; tel. (1) 184305; Gen. Man. Asnake Sahlu.

Ethiopian Coffee Export Enterprise: POB 2591, Addis Ababa; tel. (1) 515330; fax (1) 510762; f. 1977; Chair. Sufian Ahmed; Gen. Man. Derga Gurmessa.

Ethiopian Food Corpn: Addis Ababa; tel. (1) 518522; fax (1) 513173; f. 1975; produces and distributes food items, including edible oil, ghee substitute, pasta, bread, maize, wheat flour, etc.; Gen. Man. Bekele Haile.

Ethiopian Fruit and Vegetable Marketing Enterprise: POB 2374, Addis Ababa; tel. (1) 519192; fax (1) 516483; f. 1980; sole wholesale domestic distributor and exporter of fresh and processed fruit and vegetables, and floricultural products; Gen. Man. Kaknu Pewonde.

Ethiopian Grain Trade Enterprise: POB 3321, Addis Ababa; tel. (1) 653166; fax (1) 652792; e-mail egte@telecom.net.et; Gen. Man. Girma Bekele.

Ethiopian Handicrafts and Small-Scale Industries Development Agency: Addis Ababa; tel. (1) 157366; f. 1977.

Ethiopian Import and Export Corpn (ETIMEX): Addis Ababa; tel. (1) 511112; fax (1) 515411; f. 1975; state trading corpn under the supervision of the Ministry of Trade and Industry; import of building materials, foodstuffs, stationery and office equipment, textiles, clothing, chemicals, general merchandise, capital goods; Gen. Man. Aschenaki G. Hiwot.

Ethiopian National Metal Works Corpn: Addis Ababa; fax (1) 510714; Gen. Man. Alula Berhane.

Ethiopian Oil Seeds and Pulses Export Corpn: POB 5719, Addis Ababa; tel. (1) 550597; fax (1) 553299; f. 1975; Gen. Man. Abdouruhman Mohammed.

Ethiopia Peasants' Association (EPA): f. 1978 to promote improved agricultural techniques, home industries, education, public health and self-reliance; comprises 30,000 peasant asscns with c. 7m. mems; Chair. (vacant).

Ethiopian Petroleum Enterprise: POB 3375, Addis Ababa; fax (1) 512938; e-mail ethpetroleum@telecom.net.et; f. 1976; Gen. Man. Yigzaw Mekonnen.

Ethiopian Pharmaceuticals and Medical Supplies Corpn (EPHARMECOR): POB 21904, Addis Ababa; tel. (1) 134577; fax (1) 752555; f. 1976; manufacture, import, export and distribution of pharmaceuticals, chemicals, dressings, surgical and dental instruments, hospital and laboratory supplies; Gen. Man. Girma Bepasso.

Ethiopian Sugar Corpn: POB 133, Addis Ababa; tel. (1) 519700; fax (1) 513488; Gen. Man. Abate Lemengh.

Green Star Food Co LLC: POB 5579, Addis Ababa; tel. (1) 526588; fax (1) 526599; e-mail greenstar@telecom.net.et; f. 1984; fmrly the Ethiopian Livestock and Meat Corpn; production and marketing of canned and frozen foods; Gen. Man. Dawit Bekele.

National Leather and Shoe Corpn: POB 2516, Addis Ababa; tel. (1) 514075; fax (1) 513525; f. 1975; produces and sells semi-processed hides and skins, finished leather, leather goods and footwear; Gen. Man. Girma W. Aregai.

National Textiles Corpn: Addis Ababa; tel. (1) 157316; fax (1) 511955; f. 1975; production of yarn, fabrics, knitwear, blankets, bags, etc.; Gen. Man. Fikre Hugiane.

Natural Gum Processing and Marketing Enterprise: POB 62322, Addis Ababa; tel. (1) 527082; fax (1) 518110; e-mail natgum@ telecom.net.et; f. 1976; Gen. Man. Teklehaimanot Nigatu.

UTILITIES

Electricity

Ethiopian Electric Power Corpn (EEPCO): De Gaulle Sq., POB 1233, Addis Ababa; tel. (1) 111443; fax (1) 551324; Chair. Haile Selassie Asegide; Gen. Man. Mihret Debebe.

Water

Addis Ababa Water Sewerage Authority: POB 1505; Addis Ababa; tel. (1) 550422; fax (1) 553793; e-mail aawsa.ha@telecom.net .et.

Water Resources Development Authority: POB 1045, Addis Ababa; tel. (1) 612999; fax (1) 611245; Gen. Man. Getachew Gizaw.

TRADE UNIONS

Ethiopian Trade Union (ETU): POB 3653, Addis Ababa; tel. (1) 514366; f. 1975; comprises nine industrial unions and 22 regional unions with a total membership of 320,000 (1987); Chair. (vacant).

Transport

RAILWAYS

Djibouti-Ethiopian Railway (Chemin de Fer Djibouti-Ethiopien) (CDE): POB 1051, Addis Ababa; tel. (1) 517250; fax (1) 513533; e-mail cde@telecom.net.et; f. 1909; adopted present name in 1981; jtly-owned by Govts of Ethiopia and Djibouti; 781 km of track (681 km in Ethiopia), linking Addis Ababa with Djibouti; Pres. Saleh Omar Hildid; Dir-Gen. Ali Abdallah Gadid.

ROADS

In 2000 the total road network comprised an estimated 31,571 km of primary, secondary and feeder roads, of which 3,789 km were paved, the remainder being gravel roads. In addition, there are some 30,000 km of unclassified tracks and trails. A highway links Addis Ababa with Nairobi in Kenya, forming part of the Trans-East Africa Highway. In mid-2003 work commenced on the second phase of the Road Sector Development Programme, which aimed to upgrade 80% and 63% of paved and gravel roads, respectively, to an acceptable condition by 2007.

Comet Transport SC: POB 2402, Addis Ababa; tel. (1) 423962; fax (1) 426024; e-mail cometrans@telecom.net.et; f. 1994; Gen. Man. Feleke Yimer.

Ethiopian Freight Transport Corpn: Addis Ababa; restructured into five autonomous enterprises in 1994.

Ethiopian Road Transport Authority: POB 2504, Addis Ababa; tel. (1) 510244; fax (1) 510715; e-mail kasahun_khmariam@yahoo .com; enforces road transport regulations, promotes road safety, registers vehicles and issues driving licences; Gen. Man. Kasahun H. Mariam.

Ethiopian Roads Authority: POB 1770, Addis Ababa; tel. (1) 517170; fax (1) 514866; f. 1951; construction and maintenance of roads, bridges and airports; Gen. Man. Zaid Wolde Gebreal.

Public Transport Corpn: POB 5780, Addis Ababa; tel. (1) 153117; fax (1) 510720; f. 1977; urban bus services in Addis Ababa and Jimma, and services between towns; restructured into three autonomous enterprises in 1994 and scheduled for privatization; Man. Dir AHMED NURU.

SHIPPING

The formerly Ethiopian-controlled ports of Massawa and Assab now lie within the boundaries of the State of Eritrea (q.v.). Although an agreement exists between the two Governments allowing Ethiopian access to the two ports, which can handle more than 1m. metric tons of merchandise annually, in mid-1998 Ethiopia ceased using the ports, owing to the outbreak of hostilities. Ethiopia's maritime trade currently passes through Djibouti (in the Republic of Djibouti), and also through the Kenyan port of Mombasa. An agreement was also signed in July 2003, to allow Ethiopia to use Port Sudan (in Sudan). At 31 December 2003 Ethiopia's registered merchant fleet numbered nine vessels, with a total displacement of 81,933 grt.

Ethiopian Shipping Lines Corpn: POB 2572, Addis Ababa; tel. (1) 518280; fax (1) 519525; e-mail esl@telecom.net.et; f. 1964; serves Red Sea, Europe, Mediterranean, Gulf and Far East with its own fleet and chartered vessels; Chair. G. TSADKAN GEBRE TENSAY; Gen. Man. AMBACHEW ABRAHA.

Marine Transport Authority: Ministry of Infrastructure, POB 1238, Addis Ababa; tel. (1) 158227; fax (1) 515665; e-mail ketecom@telecom.net.et; f. 1993; regulates maritime transport services; Dept Head ASKAL W. GEORGIS.

Maritime and Transit Services Enterprise: POB 1186, Addis Ababa; tel. (1) 517564; fax (1) 518197; e-mail mtse@telecom.net.et; internet www.telecom.net/~mtse; f. 1979; services include stevedoring, storehandling, bagging, forwarding and trucking; Chair. GETACHEW GEBRE; Gen. Man. AHMED YASSIN.

CIVIL AVIATION

Ethiopia has two international airports (at Addis Ababa and Dire Dawa) and around 40 airfields. Bole International Airport in the capital handles 95% of international air traffic and 85% of domestic flights. A programme to modernize the airport, at an estimated cost of 819m. birr (US $130m.), was undertaken during 1997–2001. Construction of airports at Axum, Lalibela and Gondar was completed in April 2000.

Ethiopian Airlines: Bole International Airport, POB 1755, Addis Ababa; tel. (1) 612222; fax (1) 611474; e-mail publicrelations@ethiopianairlines.com; internet www.ethiopianairlines.com; f. 1945; operates regular domestic services and flights to 47 international destinations in Africa, Europe, Middle East, Asia and the USA; Chair. SEYOUM MESFIN; CEO GIRMA WAKE.

Ethiopian Civil Aviation Authority: POB 978, Addis Ababa; tel. (1) 610277; fax (1) 612533; e-mail civil.aviation@telecom.net.et; regulatory authority; provides air navigational facilities; Dir-Gen. TEFERA MEKONEN (acting).

Tourism

Ethiopia's tourist attractions include the early Christian monuments and churches, the ancient capitals of Gondar and Axum, the Blue Nile (or Tississat) Falls and the National Parks of the Simien and Bale Mountains. Tourist arrivals in 2002 totalled 156,327, and receipts from tourism amounted to US $75m. in that year.

Ethiopian Tourism Commission: POB 2183, Addis Ababa; tel. (1) 517470; fax (1) 513899; e-mail info@tourismethiopia.org; internet tourismethiopia.org; f. 1964; formulates national tourism policy, publicizes tourist attractions and regulates standards of tourist facilities; Commr YOUSUF ABDULLAHI SUKKAR.

FIJI

Introductory Survey

Location, Climate, Language, Religion, Flag, Capital

The Republic of Fiji comprises more than 300 islands, of which 100 are inhabited, situated about 1,930 km (1,200 miles) south of the equator in the Pacific Ocean. The four main islands are Viti Levu (on which almost 70% of the country's population lives), Vanua Levu, Taveuni and Kadavu. The climate is tropical, with temperatures ranging from 16°C to 32°C (60°F–90°F). Rainfall is heavy on the windward side. Fijian and Hindi are the principal languages but English is also widely spoken. In 1996 about 58% of the population were Christians (mainly Methodists), 34% Hindus and 7% Muslims. The national flag (proportions 1 by 2) is light blue, with the United Kingdom flag as a canton in the upper hoist. In the fly is the main part of Fiji's national coat of arms: a white field quartered by a red upright cross, the quarters containing sugar canes, a coconut palm, a stem of bananas and a dove bearing an olive branch; in chief is a red panel with a yellow crowned lion holding a white cocoa pod. The capital is Suva, on Viti Levu.

Recent History

The first Europeans to settle on the islands were sandalwood traders, missionaries and shipwrecked sailors, and in October 1874 Fiji was proclaimed a British possession. In September 1966 the British Government introduced a new Constitution for Fiji. It provided for a ministerial form of government, an almost wholly elected Legislative Council and the introduction of universal adult suffrage. Rather than using a common roll of voters, however, the Constitution introduced an electoral system that combined communal (Fijian and Indian) rolls with cross-voting. In September 1967 the Executive Council became the Council of Ministers, with Ratu Kamisese Mara, leader of the multiracial (but predominantly Fijian) Alliance Party (AP), as Fiji's first Chief Minister. Following a constitutional conference in April–May 1970, Fiji achieved independence, within the Commonwealth, on 10 October 1970. The Legislative Council was renamed the House of Representatives, and a second parliamentary chamber, the nominated Senate, was established. The British-appointed Governor became Fiji's first Governor-General, while Ratu Sir Kamisese Mara (as he had become in 1969) took office as Prime Minister.

Fiji was, however, troubled by racial tensions. Although the descendants of indentured Indian workers who were brought to Fiji in the late 19th century had grown to outnumber the native inhabitants, they were discriminated against in political representation and land ownership rights. A new electoral system was adopted in 1970 to ensure a racial balance in the legislature.

At the general election held in March and April 1977 the National Federation Party (NFP), traditionally supported by the Indian population, won 26 of the 52 seats in the House of Representatives, but was unable to form a government and subsequently split into two factions. The AP governed in a caretaker capacity until the holding of a further general election in September, when it was returned with its largest-ever majority. While the two main parties professed multiracial ideas, the Fijian Nationalist Party campaigned in support of its 'Fiji for the Fijians' programme in order to foster nationalist sentiment.

In 1980 Ratu Sir Kamisese Mara's suggestion that a Government of National Unity be formed was overshadowed by renewed political disagreement between the AP and the NFP (whose two factions had drawn closer together again) over land ownership. Fijians owned 83% of the land and were strongly defending their traditional rights, while the Indian population was pressing for greater security of land tenure. The general election held in July 1982 was also dominated by racial issues. The AP retained power after winning 28 seats, but its majority had been reduced from 20 to four. The NFP won 22 seats and the Western United Front (WUF), which professed a multiracial outlook, took the remaining two seats.

A meeting of union leaders in May 1985 represented the beginning of discussions that culminated in the founding of the Fiji Labour Party (FLP), officially inaugurated in Suva in July. Sponsored by the Fiji Trades Union Congress (FTUC), and

under the presidency of Dr Timoci Bavadra, the new party was formed with the aim of presenting a more effective parliamentary opposition, and declared the provision of free education and a national medical scheme to be among its priorities. The FLP hoped to work through farmers' organizations to win votes among rural electorates, which traditionally supported the NFP. During 1985–86 disagreements between the Government and the FTUC over economic policies became increasingly acrimonious, leading to an outbreak of labour unrest and the withdrawal, in June 1986, of government recognition of the FTUC as the unions' representative organization.

At a general election in April 1987 a coalition of the FLP and NFP won 28 seats (19 of which were secured by ethnic Indian candidates) in the House of Representatives, thus defeating the ruling AP, which won only 24 seats. The new Government, led by Bavadra, was therefore the first in Fijian history to contain a majority of ministers of Indian, rather than Melanesian, origin. Bavadra, himself, was of Melanesian descent. On 14 May, however, the Government was overthrown by a military coup, led by Lt-Col (later Maj.-Gen.) Sitiveni Rabuka. The Governor-General, Ratu Sir Penaia Ganilau, responded by declaring a state of emergency and appointed a 19-member advisory council, including Bavadra and Rabuka. However, Bavadra refused to participate in the council, denouncing it as unconstitutional and biased in its composition.

Widespread racial violence followed the coup, and there were several public demands for Bavadra's reinstatement as Prime Minister. In July 1987 the Great Council of Fijian Chiefs, comprising the country's 70 hereditary Melanesian leaders, approved plans for constitutional reform. In September negotiations began, on the initiative of Ganilau, between delegations led by the two former Prime Ministers, Bavadra and Mara, to resolve the political crisis. On 22 September it was announced that the two factions had agreed to form an interim bipartisan Government.

On 25 September 1987, however, before the new plan could be implemented, Rabuka staged a second coup and announced his intention to declare Fiji a republic. Despite Ganilau's refusal to recognize the seizure of power, Rabuka revoked the Constitution on 1 October and proclaimed himself Head of State, thus deposing the Queen. Ganilau conceded defeat and resigned as Governor-General. At a meeting in Canada, Commonwealth Heads of Government formally declared that Fiji's membership of the Commonwealth had lapsed. An interim Cabinet, comprising mainly ethnic Fijians, was installed by Rabuka. In late October Rabuka announced that he would resign as Head of State as soon as he had appointed a new President of the Republic. Several cases of violations of human rights by the Fijian army were reported, as the regime assumed powers of detention without trial and suspended all political activity.

On 6 December 1987 Rabuka resigned as Head of State. Although he had previously refused to accept the post, Ganilau, the former Governor-General, became the first President of the Fijian Republic. Mara was reappointed Prime Minister, and Rabuka became Minister of Home Affairs. A new interim Cabinet was announced on 9 December, containing 11 members of Rabuka's administration, but no member of Bavadra's deposed Government.

In February 1988 Rotuma (the only Polynesian island in the country), which lies to the north-west of Vanua Levu, declared itself politically independent of Fiji, whose newly acquired republican status it refused to recognize. Fijian troops were dispatched to the island, however, and soon quelled the dissent.

A new draft Constitution was approved by the interim Government in September 1988. The proposed Constitution was rejected, however, by a multiracial constitutional committee, which considered unnecessary the specific reservation of the principal offices of state for ethnic Fijians. In September 1989 the committee published a revised draft, which was still, however, condemned by Bavadra and the FLP-NFP coalition. In November Bavadra died and was replaced as leader of the FLP-NFP coalition by his widow, Adi Kuini Bavadra.

In January 1990 Rabuka resigned from the Cabinet and returned to his military duties. Mara agreed to remain as Prime Minister until the restoration of constitutional government. In June the Great Council of Chiefs approved the draft Constitution. At the same time, the Great Council of Chiefs stated its intention to form a new party, the Soqosoqo ni Vakavulewa ni Taukei (SVT) or Fijian Political Party, to advocate the cause of ethnic Fijians. The new Constitution was finally promulgated on 25 July by President Ganilau, and was immediately condemned by the FLP-NFP coalition, which announced that it would boycott any elections held in accordance with the Constitution's provisions. Angered by the fact that a legislative majority was guaranteed to ethnic Fijians (who were reserved 37 of the 70 elective seats, compared with 27 Indian seats), and that the Great Council of Chiefs was to nominate ethnic Fijians to 24 of the 34 seats in the Senate and to appoint the President of the Republic, the opposition organized anti-Constitution demonstrations. The new Constitution was similarly condemned for its racial bias by India, New Zealand and Australia at the UN General Assembly, meeting in New York in October. In May 1991 the Commonwealth stated that Fiji would not be re-admitted to the organization until it changed its Constitution.

In July 1991 Rabuka resigned as Commander of the Armed Forces in order to rejoin the Cabinet as Deputy Prime Minister and Minister of Home Affairs, although towards the end of 1991, he relinquished the post in order to assume the leadership of the SVT.

Disagreements between the Government and the FTUC re-emerged at the beginning of 1991. In February a strike by more than 900 members of the Fijian Miners' Union over union recognition, pay and poor working conditions led to the dismissal of some 400 of the workers. In May the Government announced a series of reforms to the labour laws, including the abolition of the minimum wage, restrictions on strike action and derecognition of unions that did not represent at least two-thirds of the work-force. A significant political development announced by the Government in late 1992 was the official recognition of the FTUC (withheld since 1986) as the sole representative of workers in Fiji.

At legislative elections in May 1992 the SVT secured 30 of the 37 seats reserved for ethnic Fijians, while the NFP won 14 and the FLP 13 of the seats reserved for Indian representatives. Following the election, the FLP agreed to participate in Parliament and to support Rabuka in his campaign for the premiership, in return for a guarantee from the SVT of a full review of the Constitution and of trade union and land laws. Rabuka was, therefore, appointed Prime Minister and formed a coalition Government (consisting of 14 members of the SVT and five others).

Remarks made by the Prime Minister in an Australian television interview in October 1992, expressing his implicit support for the repatriation of Fijian Indians, attracted controversy and prompted renewed fears that any reform of the Constitution would be merely superficial. Nevertheless, in December Rabuka formally invited the opposition leaders, Jai Ram Reddy of the NFP and Mahendra Chaudhry of the FLP (formerly the National Secretary of the FTUC), to form a Government of National Unity. The move was largely welcomed, but Indian politicians expressed reluctance to take part in a government whose political control remained fundamentally vested with ethnic Fijians. Rabuka was criticized equally by nationalist extremists of the Taukei Solidarity Movement, who accused him of conceding too much political power to Fijian Indians. Following the appointment of a new Cabinet in June, all 13 of the FLP legislative members began an indefinite boycott of Parliament, in protest at Rabuka's failure to implement the reforms, which he had agreed to carry out in return for their support for his election to the premiership in June 1992.

In December 1993 President Ganilau died, following a long illness, and was replaced by Ratu Sir Kamisese Mara, who took office on 18 January 1994 (re-elected on 18 January 1999).

At legislative elections held in February 1994 the SVT increased the number of its seats in the House of Representatives to 31, while the Fijian Association Party (FAP, established in January by former members of the SVT) secured only five seats, of a total of 37 reserved for ethnic Fijians. Of the 27 seats reserved for ethnic Indian representatives, 20 were secured by the NFP. The SVT subsequently formed a governing coalition with the General Voters' Party (GVP, which represented the interests of the General Electors—i.e. the minority Chinese and European communities and people from elsewhere in the Pacific

region resident in Fiji) and an independent member, under the premiership of Rabuka, who announced the formation of a new Cabinet composed entirely of ethnic Fijians. In response to international concern regarding the continued existence of Fiji's racially-biased Constitution, Rabuka announced in June that a Constitutional Review Commission had been established, which, it was hoped, would have completed a review of the Constitution by 1997.

In January 1995 the Government announced that it was to recommend that Parliament vote to repeal the Sunday observance law (imposed after the coups of 1987), which prohibited work, organized entertainment and sport on that day. It was believed that the law had become increasingly unpopular, particularly among the Indian community. However, the announcement aroused intense opposition from nationalist politicians and Methodist church leaders, who organized demonstrations in three cities, attended by more than 12,000 people. In February, however, the House of Representatives voted in favour of removing the regulations. The Senate narrowly rejected the proposal, thus effectively delaying the implementation of any changes. The Sunday observance law was finally repealed in November.

The issue of independence for the island of Rotuma was revived in September 1995 with the return of the King of Rotuma from exile in New Zealand. King Gagaj Sa Lagfatmaro, who had fled to New Zealand following death threats made against him during the military coups of 1987, appeared before the Constitutional Review Commission to petition for the island's independence within the Commonwealth, reiterating his view that Rotuma remained a British colony rather than a part of Fiji.

In September 1995 the Government decided to transfer all state land (comprising some 10% of Fiji's total land area), hitherto administered by the Government Lands Department, to the Native Land Trust Board. The decision was to allow the allocation of land to indigenous Fijians on the basis of native custom. However, concern among the Fijian Indian population increased following reports in early 1996 that many would not be able to renew their land leases (most of which were due to expire between 1997 and 2024) under the Agricultural Landlords and Tenants Act (ALTA). The reports were strongly denied by the Government, despite statements by several Fijian land-owning clans that Indians' leases would not be renewed. Moreover, a recently-formed sugar cane growers' association solely for ethnic Fijians, the Taukei Cane Growers' Association, announced its intention to campaign for ethnic Fijian control of the sugar industry, largely by refusing to renew land leases to ethnic Indians (who held some 85% of sugar farm leases). Concern was expressed that mounting tensions between land-owners and tenants could lead to violence, and that the situation was affecting investor confidence. By the end of 2000 almost 2,000 land leases had expired, leaving many tenant farmers and their families homeless. Some 70 farmers, who had expressed a wish not to be resettled, received rehabilitation grants of $F28,000 in December 2000, although the authorities were criticized for their apparent slowness in processing the applications. In January 2001 the administration of native land leases was transferred from ALTA to the Native Lands Trust Act (NLTA), prompting fears of increased bias in favour of ethnic Fijian landowners and further instability in the sugar industry. A further 1,500 leases expired during 2001.

Meanwhile, racial tension intensified in October 1995, following the publication of the SVT's submission to the Constitutional Review Commission. In its report the party detailed plans to abandon the present multiracial form of government, recommending instead the adoption of an electoral system based on racial representation, in which each ethnic group would select its own representatives. The expression of numerous extreme anti-Indian sentiments in the document was widely condemned (by both ethnic Fijians and ethnic Indians) as offensive.

A rift within the GVP in early 1996, which resulted in two of the four GVP members of the House of Representatives withdrawing their support for the Government, prompted Rabuka to seek alternative coalition partners from among the opposition, in an attempt to establish a more secure majority. However, the Prime Minister was unsuccessful in persuading parliamentary members of the FAP (which had strongly criticized the SVT's submission to the Constitutional Review Commission the previous year) to join the Government. The administration's troubles during 1996 contributed to the defeat of the SVT in virtually every municipality at local elections which took place in September.

Existing divisions within the Government were further exacerbated by the presentation to the House of Representatives, in September 1996, of the Constitutional Review Commission's report. The report included recommendations to enlarge the House of Representatives to 75 seats, with 25 seats reserved on a racial basis (12 for ethnic Fijians, 10 for Fijian Indians, two for General Electors and one for Rotuma Islanders), and also proposed that the size of the Senate should be reduced from 34 to 32 members (and the number of nominated ethnic Fijian senators be reduced from 24 to 15), and that the Prime Minister should be a Fijian of any race, while the President should continue to be an indigenous Fijian. Rabuka and Mara both endorsed the findings of the report, while several nationalist parties, including the Vanua Independent Party, the Fijian Nationalist United Front Party (FNUFP) and the Taukei Solidarity Movement, expressed extreme opposition to the proposals, and formed a coalition in an attempt to further their influence within Parliament. In addition, a number of SVT members of the House of Representatives aligned themselves with the nationalists, and in early 1997 were reported to be responsible for a series of political manoeuvres within the Cabinet, aimed at undermining Rabuka's position. The parliamentary committee reviewing the report agreed on a majority of the 700 recommendations, but proposed that the House of Representatives be enlarged to only 71 seats, with 46 seats reserved on a racial basis (23 for ethnic Fijians, 19 for Indians, three for General Electors and one for Rotuma Islanders) and 25 seats open to all races. The committee's modified proposals were presented in May to the Great Council of Chiefs, which officially endorsed the recommendations in early June. The Constitution Amendment Bill was approved unanimously by the House of Representatives and the Senate in the following month. Rabuka was anxious to reassure extremist nationalist Fijians, who had vociferously opposed the reforms throughout the debate, that their interests would be protected under the amended Constitution (which was not due to take effect until July 1998) and that indigenous Fijians would continue to play a pre-eminent role in the government of the country.

Despite opposition from both the FLP and the nationalist parties, Fiji was readmitted to the Commonwealth at a meeting of member states in October 1997. In the same month Rabuka was granted an audience with Queen Elizabeth II in London, at which he formally apologized for the military coups of 1987. Events in early 1998 were dominated by political reaction to the imminent promulgation of the new Constitution. An extremist nationalist group of former SVT supporters, including senior church, military and police officials, were rumoured to be planning to overthrow Rabuka's Government. Meanwhile, it was reported that opponents of the Constitution were discussing the establishment of several new political parties. The new Constitution, none the less, came into effect on 27 July 1998.

A dispute between tribal landowners and the Government over compensation payments for land flooded by the Monosavu hydroelectric power station erupted into violence in July 1998. Landowners, who had been demanding compensation worth some $A30m. since the plant was constructed in 1983, seized control of the station (which supplies 90% of Fiji's electricity) and carried out a series of arson attacks on Fiji Electricity Authority property. In October the Government agreed to pay the landowners compensation totalling some $A12m., although many involved in the dispute rejected the offer and announced their intention of pursuing a legal claim against the Government.

The prospect of legislative elections, to be held in early May 1999, prompted reports of political manoeuvring as parties sought to increase their influence by forming alliances. In addition, a number of changes in the country's political organizations occurred in late 1998. Following the death of Josefata Kamikamica, Adi Kuini Vuikaba Speed (widow of ex-President Bavadra) was elected leader of the FAP. Meanwhile, the GVP and the General Electors' Party merged to form the United General Party (UGP) under the leadership of the Minister for Tourism, Transport and Civil Aviation, David Pickering, and Rabuka was re-elected leader of the SVT (despite the party being required to amend its constitution in order for this to be possible). The formation of a new party, the Veitokani ni Lewenivanua Vakarisito (VLV, Christian Democratic Alliance), by several senior church and military leaders and former members of the nationalist Taukei Solidarity Movement, was widely criticized for its extremist stance and refusal to accept the newly formed, multiracial Constitution.

At legislative elections held on 8–15 May 1999, the first to be held under the new Constitution, Rabuka's coalition Government was defeated by Mahendra Chaudhry, leader of the Indian-dominated FLP, who thus became Fiji's first ethnic Indian Prime Minister. Chaudhry's broad-based Government (a coalition of the FLP, FAP, VLV and the Party of National Unity—PANU) initially seemed threatened by the reluctance of FAP members to serve under an Indian Prime Minister. The leaders were persuaded to remain in the coalition in the interests of national unity, after the intervention of President Mara. Political stability after the elections was further marred by demands for Chaudhry's resignation by the Fijian Nationalist Vanua Takolavo Party (NVTLP), and by a number of arson attacks, allegedly linked to the outgoing SVT (although these allegations were denied by Rabuka). Following the SVT's decisive defeat in the elections, Rabuka resigned as party leader; he was replaced by Ratu Inoke Kubuabola, the former Minister for Communications, Works and Energy. Rabuka was later appointed the first independent Chairman of the newly autonomous Great Council of Chiefs. The NVTLP was widely suspected to have been responsible for three bomb explosions in Suva in August 1999. In the same month a parliamentary vote of 'no confidence' against Prime Minister Chaudhry was overwhelmingly defeated. In the latter half of 1999 there were persistent demands by various nationalist groups (including the SVT) that Chaudhry be replaced by a leader of indigenous Fijian descent, and a number of demonstrations were organized, expressing disillusionment with the Government. In October the opposition coalition was successful in gaining control of a majority of councils in local elections, while the FLP won control of four municipal councils (having previously been in charge of none).

The Government's decision to disband the Fiji Intelligence Service from December 1999 was criticized by the opposition as 'foolish' and racially motivated. An announcement by the Chief Justice in December of a project to amend a number of laws that did not comply with the terms of the new Constitution, together with reports that the Government was planning to withdraw state funds previously provided to assist indigenous Fijian business interests, prompted further accusations of racism by the Government against ethnic Fijians. Consequently, the SVT and the VLV held talks to discuss ways of consolidating the ethnic Fijian political base. Proposed legislation, which would alter the distribution of power between the President and the Prime Minister, attracted further criticism from the opposition, and in February 2000 a faction of the FAP announced its withdrawal from the governing coalition, citing dissatisfaction with Chaudhry's leadership. Of greater significance, however, was the announcement in April that the extremist nationalist Taukei Movement (which had been inactive for several years) had been revived with the sole intention of removing the Prime Minister from office. The group subsequently publicized a campaign of demonstrations and civil disobedience, prompting the army to issue a statement distancing itself from any anti-Government agitation and pledging loyalty to Chaudhry. The campaign attracted considerable public support, however, and culminated in a march through Suva by some 5,000 people in early May.

On 19 May 2000 a group of armed men, led by businessman George Speight, invaded the parliament building and ousted the Government, taking hostage Chaudhry and 30 other members of the governing coalition. President Mara condemned the coup and declared a state of emergency as Speight's supporters rampaged through the streets of Suva, looting and setting fire to Indian businesses. Speight declared that he had reclaimed Fiji for indigenous Fijians and had dissolved the Constitution. Moreover, he threatened to kill the hostages if the military intervened. On 22 May Mara formally invited Rabuka, in his role as chairman of the Great Council of Chiefs, to seek a resolution of the crisis. In the following days the Great Council of Chiefs convened to discuss the situation and proposed the replacement of Chaudhry's Government with an interim administration, an amnesty for Speight and the rebels, and the amendment of the Constitution. Speight rejected the proposals, demanding that Mara also be removed from office. Meanwhile, violent clashes erupted at the headquarters of Fiji Television when the rebels stormed the building following the broadcast of an interview with an opponent of the coup. A police-officer was shot dead, television equipment was destroyed and the station's employees were taken hostage. On 29 May Mara resigned and the Commander of the Armed Forces, Frank Bainimarama, announced the imposition of martial law and a curfew, in an attempt to restore calm and stability to the country. In an expression of his apparent reluctance to assume the role, Bainimarama gave Mara a whale's tooth, a traditional Fijian symbol of regret.

Negotiations between the newly installed Military Executive Council and the Great Council of Chiefs continued throughout June 2000. Failure to reach a conclusive outcome seemed to be the result of inconsistencies in Speight's demands and an ambivalent attitude on the part of the military towards the coup. Regular patrols by the security forces curbed rioting in Suva, although outbreaks of violence in rural areas (mostly in the form of attacks on Indian Fijians, the looting and burning of Indian-owned farms and the occupation of several tourist resorts) were reported. On 25 June the four female hostages were released from the parliament building. The Military Executive Council announced its intention to appoint an interim government without consulting Speight and demanded that the rebel leader release the remaining hostages. Speight reiterated his threat to kill all those held if any rescue attempts were made.

An interim administration of 19 indigenous Fijians led by Laisenia Qarase (the former managing director of the Merchant Bank of Fiji) was sworn in on 4 July 2000. Minutes after the ceremony a gun battle erupted outside the parliament building in which four civilians and one rebel were injured; the rebel subsequently died. Speight announced that he not recognize the interim authority, and most of Fiji's mainstream political parties similarly denounced it, although the Methodist Church declared its support for the body. On 12 July a further nine hostages were released and on the following day the remaining 18, including Chaudhry, were liberated. In accordance with Speight's wishes, Ratu Josefa Iloilo, hitherto the First Vice-President, was then installed as President. In the same month Chandrika Prasad, a farmer, quickly brought a legal challenge to the abrogation of the 1997 Constitution in the High Court of Fiji. Chaudhry launched an international campaign to reinstate both the Constitution and the People's Coalition Government.

Incidents of civil unrest (including the occupation of the hydroelectric dam at Monosavu and of the army barracks on Vanua Levu) continued throughout July 2000 as Speight sought to manipulate existing grievances, particularly disputes over land ownership, in order to mobilize additional support. On 29 July, however, Speight was finally arrested, along with dozens of his supporters, for breaking the terms of his amnesty by refusing to relinquish weapons. Armed rebels responded violently to the arrest, and in Labasa Indian Fijians were rounded up and detained in army barracks by supporters of Speight. In early August more than 300 rebels appeared in court on a variety of firearms and public order offences. Speight was similarly charged with several minor offences. On 11 August Speight and 14 of his supporters were formally charged with treason. During September Speight made several applications for bail, all of which were refused. Meanwhile, the suspended police commissioner, Isikia Savua, revealed that police were conducting an investigation into a commercial deal involving the Fijian mahogany trade, which, it was believed, might have precipitated the coup; Speight had been chairman of both Fiji Pine Corporation and Fiji Hardwood Corporation before being dismissed in 1999. This view was reiterated by the deposed Prime Minister on an overseas tour during October, when Chaudhry expressed his commitment to the restoration of democracy and constitutional rule and stated his belief that the coup had been motivated by commercial vested interests rather than by concern over indigenous rights.

In early November 2000 about 40 soldiers staged a mutiny at army headquarters in Suva. Troops loyal to Bainimarama, who narrowly escaped capture, retook the barracks following an eight-hour assault in which five rebels and four loyal soldiers were killed. It was later revealed that a number of the rebel soldiers had been involved in the coup in May and speculation spread that the mutiny had been another attempted coup. The chairman of the Great Council of Chiefs, Sitiveni Rabuka, denied allegations by New Zealand's Minister of Foreign Affairs and Trade, Phil Goff, that he had been involved in the mutiny. In November 2002 Capt. Shane Stevens was sentenced to life imprisonment after he was found guilty of leading the mutiny two years earlier. Fourteen other soldiers received lesser sentences for their part in the uprising. Bainimarama criticized the majority of the sentences for being too lenient.

On 15 November 2000 the High Court ruled that the existing Constitution remained valid and that the elected Parliament, ousted in the coup, remained Fiji's legitimate governing authority. Laisenia Qarase responded by lodging an appeal against the ruling and by declaring that the interim authority, of which he was leader, would continue as the country's national government until new elections could be organized and a new constitution drafted within 18 months.

In mid-December 2000 Chaudhry's campaign to re-establish his Government suffered a significant set-back when the ministers of foreign affairs of Australia and New Zealand announced that they were abandoning their appeal for its reinstatement, although they would continue to support a return to the 1997 Constitution. However, within Fiji, supporters of a return to democracy formed the Fiji First Movement, which aimed to consolidate opposition to the post-coup regime. The group organized a series of protests across the country in late 2000 and early 2001.

In February 2001 an international panel of judges at the Court of Appeal began the hearing against the November 2000 ruling, which found the abrogation of the 1997 Constitution to be illegal. In its final judgment the court ruled that the 1997 Constitution remained the supreme law of Fiji, that the interim civilian government could not prove that it had the support of a majority of Fijian people and was therefore illegal and that, following Mara's resignation, the office of President remained vacant. The ruling was welcomed by many countries in the region, including Australia and New Zealand, and appeared to be accepted by the interim authority, which announced that it would organize elections as soon as possible. However, on 14 March Iloilo informed Chaudhry in a letter that he had been dismissed as Prime Minister, claiming that by advising Iloilo to dissolve the authority in preparation for elections he had accepted that he no longer had the mandate of Parliament. Chaudhry rejected the decision as unconstitutional and unlawful. Ratu Tevita Momoedonu was appointed Prime Minister on the same day. On the following day, however, Iloilo dismissed Momoedonu, on the advice of the Great Council of Chiefs, and reinstated Laisenia Qarase as head of the interim authority. It was announced that a general election would be held in August–September 2001, and would be conducted under the preferential voting system, similar to that of Australia, as used in Fiji's 1999 election.

There followed a period of factionalism and fragmentation among Fiji's political parties. George Speight had already been appointed President of the new Matanitu Vanua (MV—Conservative Alliance Party), despite facing the charge of treason for his part in the 2000 coup. In May 2001 Qarase formed the Soqosoqo Duavata ni Lewenivanua (SDL—Fiji United Party), a new contender for the indigenous Melanesian vote, thus rivalling the established SVT. Another indigenous party, the Bai Kei Viti, was launched in June. Tupeni Baba, former Deputy Prime Minister in Chaudhry's Government, left the FLP and formed the New Labour United Party (NLUP). The election took place between 25 August and 1 September. Qarase's SDL was victorious, but failed to obtain an overall majority. The SDL secured 31 seats in the House of Representatives (increasing to 32 of the 71 seats after a by-election on 25 September). The FLP won 27 seats, the MV six seats and the NLUP two seats. International monitors were satisfied that the election had been contested fairly.

Following the election, however, by refusing to allow the FLP any representation in his new Cabinet, Qarase was accused of contravening a provision of the Constitution whereby a party winning more than 10% of the seats in the House of Representatives was entitled to a ministerial post. Two members of George Speight's MV were included in the Cabinet. Qarase claimed that Mahendra Chaudhry had not accepted that the Government should be based fundamentally on nationalist Fijian principles. In October 2001, when members of the House of Representatives were sworn in, Chaudhry refused to accept the position of Leader of the Opposition, a title that consequently fell to Prem Singh, leader of the NFP. In December Parliament approved the Social Justice Bill, a programme of affirmative action favouring Fijians and Rotumans in education, land rights and business-funding policies.

The Prime Minister defended himself against demands for his resignation in January 2002 following allegations that he had broken the Electoral Act by pledging some $F25m. of funds from the Ministry of Agriculture to pro-indigenous Fijian businesses during the 2001 election campaign. In February 2002, furthermore, an appeal court ruled that the Prime Minister had violated the Constitution by failing to incorporate any member of the opposition FLP in his Cabinet. Qarase had previously declared that he would resign if the legal challenge against him were to be successful. (The newly appointed Chief Justice, Daniel Fatiaki, was himself under scrutiny in mid-2002—the Chief Justice being appointed on the advice of the Prime Minister and the Leader of the Opposition, and being responsible for assembling the Supreme Court.) In September the High Court ruled that Prem Singh, the NFP leader, was not entitled to retain his parliamentary seat (the validity of certain votes cast at the 2001 election having been questioned). The disputed seat was therefore allocated to a member of the FLP. Also in September, in advance of the ruling by the Supreme Court on the issue of the inclusion of the FLP in the Cabinet, the Prime Minister effected a ministerial reorganization, assuming personal responsibility for a number of additional portfolios. In April 2003 the Commander of the Armed Forces, Frank Bainimarama, intervened in the ongoing dispute, stating that if the judicial ruling went against Qarase then he should resign. Meanwhile, rumours circulated that a further coup might be attempted if the Government were ordered to include FLP members in the Cabinet. The Supreme Court finally delivered its ruling on 18 July, finding in favour of Chaudhry and declaring that, in order to uphold the Constitution, Qarase should form a new cabinet including eight members of the FLP. Qarase responded by proposing to retain his current 22-member Cabinet and to add 14 FLP members. Both the opposition and the SVT leader, Sitiveni Rabuka, criticized the proposal, which would result in more than one-half of all members of the House of Representatives serving as cabinet ministers, and would give Fiji the largest cabinet in the world, in proportion to its population. Chaudhry expressed dissatisfaction with the suggestion, claiming that the positions offered to his party were too junior. However, Qarase remained defiant, his intransigence resulting in several more weeks of political impasse. At the end of August Qarase formally nominated a cabinet which included 14 FLP members (although Chaudhry was not among those named). The opposition, however, continued to resist the proposal, claiming that they should be consulted over the composition of the Cabinet. The ransacking of the FLP office in Lautoka at the beginning of September, in which records and property were destroyed, was believed by many observers to be an act of intimidation against the party. The Supreme Court was expected to rule on the matter in a sitting due to take place in early 2004.

Meanwhile, in June 2002 the Prime Minister and the FLP leader co-operated briefly in addressing the issue of expiring land leases that were threatening Fiji's sugar industry. A committee, comprising members of both the SDL and FLP, was established to try to negotiate land leases that would satisfy both Indian Fijian tenants and their predominantly ethnic Fijian landowners. Most of the 30-year leases drawn up under the ALTA (see above) were expiring, and both tenants and the FLP were opposed to its replacement by the Native Land Trust Act (NLTA), which they saw as disproportionately favouring landowners. Two parliamentary bills had been approved by the Senate in April, reducing the land under state control to around 1% of the total and increasing the amount under the Native Land Trust Board to over 90%. During 2003 more than 1,100 tenants on Vanua Levu were evicted following the expiry of their land leases.

In August 2002, however, the FLP abandoned a second round of land lease discussions and announced that it would boycott most of the proceedings in the current session of Parliament. Chaudhry accused the Government of attempting to accelerate the passage of six bills through Parliament without regard for the mandatory 30 days' notice of a bill being tabled. He also complained that the Government had not given the FLP the full details of the proposed NLTA. The Prime Minister protested that this would compel the Government to accept the decision of the Great Council of Chiefs regarding the leases. Tensions between the ruling SDL and the FLP and, furthermore, between Fijians and Indian Fijians had been further exacerbated by anti-Indian comments made by the Minister for Women, Social Welfare and Land Resettlement, Asenaca Caucau, which the Prime Minister had not denounced. In September Qarase effected a reorganization of cabinet portfolios in which he assumed direct responsibility for the reform of the sugar industry and restated his commitment to resolve the long-standing issue of land leases.

The trial of George Speight and his accomplices on charges of treason opened in May 2001. (Speight was refused bail to enable him to occupy the seat that he won in the legislative election later in the year.) All the accused pleaded guilty to their involvement in the coup of May 2000, and at the conclusion of the trial in February 2002 Speight received the death sentence. Within hours of the verdict, however, President Iloilo signed a decree commuting the sentence to life imprisonment. Prison sentences of between 18 months and three years were imposed on 10 of Speight's accomplices, the charges of treason having been replaced by lesser charges of abduction. The trial of two other defendants on charges of treason began in July and, after being suspended as a result of technical problems, resumed in November, following the rejection of protests from the defendants that they were protected by an Immunity Decree promulgated by the Commander of the Fiji Military Forces, Frank Bainimarama. Both were found guilty in March 2003, when a further 23 people were arrested on charges relating to the coup. In April 2004 an additional 61 soldiers were charged with various crimes concerning their involvement in the coup. Moreover, in the following month Vice-President Ratu Jope Seniloli was charged with having attempted to usurp President Mara during the coup, in addition to the existing charges against him. Also in May George Speight made a further court appearance on charges of hostage-taking during the 2000 coup. The leader of the FLP, Mahendra Chaudhry, and member of Parliament, Ganesh Chand, were claiming US $3.6m. in compensation for the 56 days they were held hostage in the government buildings by Speight and his accomplices. In July 2004 a group of 21 soldiers (the second such group) was found guilty of mutiny for their role in the plot to assassinate military commander Bainimarama and to liberate coup leader George Speight. Moreover, in November paramount chief Ratu Inoke Takiveikata was sentenced to life imprisonment after being found guilty on several charges relating to the mutiny. Meanwhile, in August Seniloli was found guilty of treason and sentenced to four years' imprisonment. His appeal against his conviction was rejected in November; however, he was unexpectedly released from prison later that month on medical grounds, which were widely disputed. Upon his release Seniloli resigned as Vice-President at the insistence of the military.

In June 2003 during a public reconciliation ceremony the High Chief of a district of Vanua Levu publicly apologized for his involvement in the coup and announced a ban, in his locality, on words that differentiate ethnic Fijians from their Indian Fijian neighbours. Almost one year later the Great Council of Chiefs issued a historic public apology to all Indian Fijians for injustices committed against them during the coups of 1987 and 2000. Moreover, when, in July 2004, Adi Litia Cakobau (a senator appointed by the Great Council of Chiefs) proposed a motion in the upper house to outlaw the use of the terms Indian Fijian and Indo-Fijian, claiming that they were insulting to ethnic Fijians, the Great Council expressed outrage at her position.

Fears that Fiji was becoming a haven for criminal organizations proved well founded in June 2004 when drugs and the chemicals associated with their production, valued at an estimated US $500m., were discovered during a raid by Fijian police on three warehouses near the capital, Suva. The warehouses were believed to be the largest laboratory producing the illegal drug methamphetamine in the southern hemisphere. Seven people were arrested during the raid, of whom six were Chinese. In the same month the Pacific Transnational Crime Centre opened in Suva in response to an increase in crime in the region, in particular the activities of criminal networks from outside the Pacific region, which were believed to be establishing operations in the Pacific islands.

In late September 2004 the Minister for National Reconciliation and Multi-Ethnic Affairs and the Cabinet's only ethnic Indian member, George Shiu Raj, resigned following accusations that he had overspent government money while on an official trip to India during 2003.

In mid-December 2004 (following the resignation of Ratu Jope Seniloli—see above) the Great Council of Chiefs approved President Iloilo's proposal of Ratu Joni Madraiwiwi as the country's next Vice-President. Madraiwiwi took up the post in January 2005.

In November 1989, meanwhile, the Fijian Government expelled the Indian ambassador to Fiji for allegedly interfering in Fiji's internal affairs, and the status of the Indian embassy was downgraded to that of a consulate. Relations between Fiji and India deteriorated following the coup of May 1987, when many ethnic Indians emigrated. In January 1989 statistical information, released by the interim Government, indicated that the islands' ethnic Fijians were in a majority for the first time since 1946. Following the adoption of significant constitutional reforms in 1997 diplomatic relations improved considerably, and in October the Indian Government invited Fiji to open a High Commission in New Delhi. In February 1999 India lifted its trade embargo against Fiji (which had been in force for 10 years), and in May India reopened its High Commission in Suva. However, Fiji's relations with the international community suffered a major reversal following the coup of May 2000, which was condemned by the UN, the Commonwealth, the United Kingdom, Australia, New Zealand and several other nations in the region. In June Fiji was partially suspended from the Commonwealth (having been readmitted in October 1997 following its expulsion after the coups of 1987) and a delegation of ministers of foreign affairs from the organization visited the islands to demand the reinstatement of the 1997 Constitution. Australia, New Zealand and the Commonwealth withheld formal recognition of Qarase's Government when Parliament opened in October 2001, but in December the Commonwealth Ministerial Action Group recommended that Fiji be readmitted to meetings of the Commonwealth. In November 2002 Qarase's Government confirmed its intention to reopen the Fijian High Commission in India, claiming that it was needed to cater for the new business and diplomatic links being fostered by the administration. (The mission was reopened in April 2004.) It was reported that Indian business concerns had expressed interest in reviving Fiji's kava industry and that Indian film companies were interested in using Fiji as a location for filming. The sanctions imposed by the European Union (EU) remained in place until early 2002. In late 2003 the EU announced the resumption of development aid to Fiji (suspended since 2000) and stated its willingness to discuss further co-operation with the Fijian Government.

Relations with France, meanwhile, were severely strained from 1995 by that country's decision to resume nuclear testing in the region. In January 2002 the French Government removed its sanctions against Fiji, following the islands' democratic election of the previous year.

Government

Fiji has a parliamentary form of government with a bicameral legislature, comprising the elected 71-seat House of Representatives and the appointed Senate, with 32 members. The Constitution states that 46 seats in the House are reserved on a racial basis (23 for ethnic Fijians, 19 for Indians, three for other races—General Electors—and one for Rotuma Islanders) and 25 seats are open to all races. The Senate is appointed by the President of the Republic, 14 members on the advice of the Great Council of Chiefs (a 70-member traditional body comprising every hereditary chief (Ratu) of a Fijian clan), nine on the advice of the Prime Minister, eight on the advice of the Leader of the Opposition and one on the advice of the Rotuma Island Council. In November 2002 the Prime Minister announced that he supported attempts by the Great Council of Chiefs to acquire legislative powers.

Defence

The Fiji Military Forces consist of men in the regular army, the Naval Squadron, the conservation corps and the territorials. The conservation corps was created in 1975 to make use of unemployed labour in construction work. As the country is a member of the Commonwealth, Fijians are entitled to work in the British armed forces and in late 2004 more than 2,000 Fijian soldiers were serving in Iraq with the British army, while a further 500 were working as mercenaries in the region. In August 2004 the total armed forces in Fiji numbered 3,500 men: 3,200 in the army and 300 in the navy. Budgetary expenditure on defence in 2004 was US $36m.

Economic Affairs

In 2003, according to estimates by the World Bank, Fiji's gross national income (GNI), measured at average 2001–03 prices, was US $2,207m, equivalent to $2,360 per head (or $5,410 on an international purchasing-power parity basis). During 1990–2003, it was estimated, the population increased at an average annual rate of 1.0%, while gross domestic product (GDP) per head increased, in real terms by an average of 1.6%. According to figures from the Asian Development Bank (ADB), overall GDP increased, in real terms, at an average annual rate of 2.7%

in 1990–2003. The ADB estimated that Fiji's GDP increased by 4.3% in 2002 and by 3.0% in 2003. The organization estimated an increase of 3.8% in 2004.

In 2003 agriculture (including forestry and fishing) contributed an estimated 13.9% of GDP. In 2003, according to FAO, the sector engaged 38.4% of the economically active population. The principal cash crop is sugar cane, which normally accounts for about 80% of total agricultural production and 30% of the country's GDP. Following the successful implementation of a crop rehabilitation programme in the late 1990s, the sugar industry subsequently experienced a sharp decline in output owing to problems arising from the coup in May 2000 and from the issue of expiring land leases (see above). Sugar production declined by 25.9% in 2001 but increased by 41.7% in 2002. In 2003 production of the crop again declined owing to the effects of a prolonged drought and the continued issue of the non-renewal of land leases. In 2003 sugar accounted for 18.1% of total export earnings. Other important export crops are coconuts and ginger, while the most significant subsistence crop is paddy rice. Fishing became an increasingly important activity from the mid-1990s. In 2003 fish products earned some $F85m in export revenue (6.7% of domestic export receipts). During 1990–2003, according to ADB estimates, agricultural GDP rose by an average annual rate of just 0.2%. The sector's GDP was estimated to have contracted by 3.9% in 2003 and to have increased by 3.7% in 2004.

Industry (including mining, manufacturing, construction and utilities) engaged 33.8% of the total number of paid employees in 1998, and provided an estimated 25.0% of GDP in 2003. The GDP of the industrial sector, according to the ADB, increased at an average rate of 3.5% per year during 1990–2003. The industrial sector's GDP was estimated to have increased by 5.1% in 2003 and by 7.5% in 2004.

Mining contributed an estimated 2.1% of GDP in 2003, and engaged 1.8% of those in paid employment in 1999. Gold and silver are the major mineral exports. Production of gold totalled 3,517 kg in 2003, when exports earned $F76.5m, equivalent to 6.0% of total export earnings. A copper-mining project in Namosi, central Viti Levu, began operations in 1997. In December 2004 an Australian prospecting company announced that it expected to be granted a licence to conduct deep-sea exploration for gold, zinc and copper in Fijian waters. The mining sector's GDP, however, remained almost constant in real terms (increasing at an average annual rate of less than 0.05%) between 1990 and 2002, a particularly sharp decrease of 14.1% being recorded in 2000. Following a slight contraction in 2002, growth was estimated at almost 1.0% in 2003.

Manufacturing contributed an estimated 13.8% of GDP in 2003 and engaged 26.0% of paid employees in 1999. The sector's GDP increased at an estimated average annual rate of 3.3% during 1990–2003. Compared with the previous year, manufacturing GDP rose by 11.6% in 2001 but contracted by 4.0% in 2002, before expanding by an estimated 5.2% in 2003. The most important branch of the sector is food-processing, in particular sugar, molasses and coconut oil. The bottling of mineral water for export was becoming increasingly important in the early 2000s. The ready-made garment industry is also important and has particularly benefited from the tax-exemption scheme implemented by the Government in 1987. Garments represented 19.8% of export earnings in 2003. However, the loss of preferential access to the US market in 2005 was expected severely to affect the garment industry and the economy as a whole. The Fijian Government estimated that some 5,000 jobs in the industry would be lost as a result. The predicted impact on the industry was expected to be mitigated slightly by Australia's announcement in December 2004 that it would extend its agreement with Fiji allowing garment export quotas to continue for a further seven years.

Energy is derived principally from hydroelectric power, which provided some 90% of Fiji's electricity in the late 1990s. The electricity, gas and water sector accounted for an estimated 4.4% of GDP in 2003. Imports of mineral fuels represented 14.7% of the total cost of imports in 2003.

The services sector contributed an estimated 61.1% of GDP in 2003. During 1990–2003 the sector's GDP rose by an average annual rate of 2.9%, according to estimated figures from the ADB. The GDP of the services sector increased by an estimated 3.2% in 2003 and by 1.9% in 2004. Tourism is Fiji's largest source of foreign exchange. In 2000, however, arrivals fell to 294,070 and earnings to $F413.5m., as a result of the events surrounding the coup of May of that year. In 2001 the industry earned $F495.5m. By 2002 tourist numbers had recovered to 397,859. Arrivals were reported to have totalled an estimated 430,800 in 2003, providing revenue of $F615.4m. in that year. An increase in tourist arrivals was expected in 2004 with the introduction of budget airline services from Australia and New Zealand. Most visitors are from Australia (31.1% of total arrivals in 2002), followed by New Zealand (17.2%), the USA (14.8%), the United Kingdom (10.9%) and Japan (6.6%).

Fiji consistently records a trade deficit. According to the ADB, this amounted to US $340m. in 2003, when the country also recorded a deficit of US $171m. on the current account of the balance of payments. Export earnings increased from $F1,194.8m. in 2002 to $F1,273.1 in 2003. Imports rose from $F1,953.2m. in 2002 to $F2,214.6 in 2003. The principal sources of imports in 2003 were Australia (34.9%), New Zealand (17.1%) and Singapore (19.5%). The principal markets for exports were Australia (19.6%), the USA (23.7%) and the United Kingdom (13.6%). The principal imports in 2003 were machinery and transport equipment (30.0% of total costs in that year). Fiji's principal domestic exports are clothing, sugar, gold and fish. Fiji also re-exports mineral fuels (including bunkers for ships and aircraft).

In 2004 there was a projected budgetary deficit equivalent to 3.9% of GDP, compared with a similar figure for 2003. In 2003/04 Fiji received financial assistance from New Zealand totalling $NZ4.1m. Australian assistance for 2004/05 was projected at $A25.1m. In late 2003 the European Union (EU) announced its decision to release development aid withheld since the coup of 2000. Assistance was resumed with a payment of US $27m. for education. Fiji's total external debt was US $258m. at the end of 2003. In that year the external debt was equivalent to 4.2% of GDP and the cost of debt-servicing was equivalent to 2.5% of the revenue from goods and services. The average annual rate of inflation was 3.4% in 1990–2000. According to the ADB, the inflation rate increased to 4.3% in 2001, but declined to 0.7% in the following year, before rising to 4.2% in 2003 and decreasing to an estimated 3.5% in 2004. An estimated 14.1% of the total labour force were unemployed in 2002. Since 1987 Fiji has suffered a very high rate of emigration, particularly of skilled and professional personnel. Although the rate of emigration of professional and technical workers decreased by 2.8% in 2001, the number of emigrants from the services sector increased by 28.2%. An increase of some 6% in the number of emigrants was recorded in 2003, a disproportionate percentage of whom were professionals from the health and education sectors.

Fiji is a member of the UN Economic and Social Commission for Asia and the Pacific (ESCAP, see p. 31), the Pacific Islands Forum (see p. 339), the Pacific Community (see p. 337), the Colombo Plan (see p. 373) and the International Sugar Organization (see p. 371). Fiji is also a signatory of the South Pacific Regional Trade and Economic Co-operation Agreement—SPARTECA (see p. 341) and the Lomé Conventions and successor Cotonou Agreement (see p. 262) with the European Union (EU). In 1996 Fiji was admitted to the Melanesian Spearhead Group.

The overthrow of the Government during a coup in May 2000 and the subsequent installation of an unelected authority had a severe impact on Fiji's economy. A significant amount of that year's excellent sugar crop was not harvested, and a large proportion of tourist bookings was cancelled. In addition, the islands lost a considerable sum of revenue owing to cancellation of foreign aid and investment, and the Government was unable to collect taxes worth more than $F90m. Moreover, the country faced further hardship through the imposition of economic sanctions and trade union boycotts from abroad (which particularly affected the mining sector and garment manufacture). It was

estimated that 6,700 people lost their jobs in the second half of 2000, the overwhelming majority of these having been engaged either in tourist-related activities or in manufacturing. In response to the economic difficulties following the coup, the Government introduced an emergency interim budget in July 2000, including austerity measures which were successful in keeping government debt at a manageable level. The 2001 budget, reduced business taxes, as a way of stimulating investment in the economy. In 2002 the Government established the Fiji Investment Corporation to manage and promote investment in tourism, forestry, fisheries and inter-island shipping services. Economic growth in 2003 resulted largely from a significant increase in tourist arrivals, partly prompted by the country's recent hosting of the South Pacific Games, and by an expansion of the construction sector, following the launch of several large private-sector projects and a number of important public infrastructure programmes. A slower rate of growth was predicted for 2004 owing to ongoing problems related to the issue of land-ownership, the increasing shortage of skilled workers and the collapse of the sugar industry. The end of preferential access to the US market for Fijian garment exports in 2005 was also expected to have a negative impact on the economy. In mid-2003 the Fiji Manufacturers' Association protested that the Melanesian Free Trade Agreement (of which Fiji was a member) was harming the country's economy by restricting the export of certain goods from Fiji to other member countries. In April 2003 the Government announced that the restructuring of Fiji's important sugar industry would be postponed for at least a further year because of disagreement among stakeholders. It was hoped that sugar farmers would be given assistance to diversify their activities before 2007 when the EU protocol governing sugar prices (under which Fiji had been guaranteed the sale of its sugar at preferential rates) was due to expire.

Education

Education in Fiji is compulsory at primary level. The Government planned to extend the duration of compulsory free education in 2002. Primary education begins at six years of age, lasts for eight years and is provided free of charge. Secondary education, beginning at the age of 14, lasts for a further three years. State subsidies are available for secondary and tertiary education in cases of hardship. In 2003 there were 719 primary schools (with a total enrolment of 142,781 pupils), 157 secondary schools (with an enrolment of 68,178 pupils), and in 1998 there were 33 vocational and technical institutions (with 915 enrolled students in 2002). In 1999 Fiji had four teacher-training colleges (with 1,003 students in 2000). In 2003 a total of 15,393 students were enrolled at the University of the South Pacific. Budgetary expenditure on education by the central Government in 2002 was projected at $F168.4m., representing 14.4% of total spending.

Public Holidays

2005 : 1 January (New Year's Day), 25–28 March (Easter), 25 April* (Birth of the Prophet Muhammad), 6 May (National Youth Day), 30 May (Ratu Sir Lala Sukuna Day), 13 June (Queen's Official Birthday), 10 October (Fiji Day), 1 November (Diwali), 25–26 December (Christmas).

2006 (provisional): 1 January (New Year's Day), 14–17 April (Easter), 11 April* (Birth of the Prophet Muhammad), 5 May (National Youth Day), May/June (Ratu Sir Lala Sukuna Day), 12 June (Queen's Official Birthday), 9 October (Fiji Day), 1 November (Diwali), 25–26 December (Christmas).

*This Islamic holiday is dependent on the lunar calendar and may vary by one or two days from the dates given.

Weights and Measures

The metric system is in force.

Statistical Survey

Sources (unless otherwise stated): Bureau of Statistics, POB 2221, Government Bldgs, Suva; tel. 315144; fax 303656; internet www.spc.int/ prism/country/fj/stats ; Reserve Bank of Fiji, POB 1220, Suva; tel. 313611; fax 301688; e-mail rbf@reservebank.gov.fj; internet www .reservebank.gov.fj.

AREA AND POPULATION

Area (incl. the Rotuma group): 18,376 sq km (7,095 sq miles). Land area of 18,333 sq km (7,078 sq miles) consists mainly of the islands of Viti Levu (10,429 sq km—4,027 sq miles) and Vanua Levu (5,556 sq km—2,145 sq miles).

Population: 715,375 at census of 31 August 1986; 775,077 (males 393,931, females 381,146) at census of 25 August 1996; 826,281 (official estimate) at 31 December 2002.

Density (31 December 2002): 45.0 per sq km.

Principal Towns (population at 1996 census): Suva (capital) 77,366; Lautoka 36,083; Nadi 9,170; Labasa 6,491; Ba 6,314. *Mid-2003* (UN estimate, incl. suburbs): Greater Suva 210,472 (Source: UN, *World Urbanization Prospects: The 2003 Revision*).

Ethnic Groups (1996 census): Fijians 393,575; Indians 338,818; Part-European 11,685; European 3,103; Rotuman 9,727; Chinese 4,939; Other Pacific Islanders 10,463; Others 2,767; Total 775,077. *2002* (official estimates at 31 December): Fijians 441,092; Indians 327,667; Others 57,522; Total 826,281.

Births, Marriages and Deaths (registrations, 1999 unless otherwise indicated): Live births 16,916 (birth rate 21.0 per 1,000); Marriages (1998) 8,058 (marriage rate 10.1 per 1,000); Deaths 3,603 (death rate 4.5 per 1,000). Source: UN, *Demographic Yearbook*.

Expectation of Life (WHO, estimates years at birth): 67.3 (males 64.6; females 70.3) in 2002. Source: WHO, *World Health Report*.

Economically Active Population (persons aged 15 years and over, census of 31 August 1986): Agriculture, hunting, forestry and fishing 106,305; Mining and quarrying 1,345; Manufacturing 18,106; Electricity, gas and water 2,154; Construction 11,786; Trade, restaurants and hotels 26,010; Transport, storage and communications 13,151; Financing, insurance, real estate and business services 6,016; Community, social and personal services 36,619; Activities not adequately defined 1,479; *Total employed* 222,971 (males 179,595, females 43,376); Unemployed 18,189 (males 10,334, females 7,855); *Total labour force* 241,160 (males 189,929, females 51,231). *1999* (total labour force, provisional): 330,800 (unemployed 25,100). *2000* (total labour force, provisional): 341,700 (unemployed 41,700). *Mid-2003* (estimates in '000): Agriculture, etc. 133; Total labour force 346 (Source: FAO).

HEALTH AND WELFARE

Key Indicators

Total Fertility Rate (children per woman, 2002): 2.9.

Under-5 Mortality Rate (per 1,000 live births, 2003): 20.

HIV/AIDS (% of persons aged 15–49, 2003): 0.1.

Physicians (per 1,000 head, 1997): 0.48.

Health Expenditure (2001): US $ per head (PPP): 224.

Health Expenditure (2001): % of GDP: 4.0.

Health Expenditure (2001): public (% of total): 67.1.

Access to Sanitation (% of persons, 2002): 98.

Human Development Index (2002): ranking: 81.

Human Development Index (2002): value: 0.758.
For sources and definitions, see explanatory note on p. vi.

AGRICULTURE, ETC.

Principal Crops (FAO estimates, '000 metric tons, 2003): Sugar cane 3,300; Coconuts 170; Copra 9; Cassava 33; Rice (paddy) 16; Sweet potatoes 6; Bananas 7; Yams 5; Taro 38. Source: FAO.

Livestock (FAO estimates, '000 head, year ending September 2003): Cattle 320; Pigs 139; Goats 248; Horses 44; Chickens 3,800. Source: FAO.

Livestock Products (FAO estimates, metric tons, 2003): Poultry meat 8,884; Beef and veal 8,550; Goat meat 960; Pig meat 3,938; Hen eggs 2,700; Cows' milk 57,500; Butter and ghee 1,850; Honey 103. Source: FAO.

Forestry ('000 cubic metres, 2003): *Roundwood Removals* (excl. bark): Sawlogs and veneer logs 181; Fuel wood 37; Pulpwood 159; Total 377. *Sawnwood Production* (incl. sleepers): 84. Source: FAO.

Fishing (FAO estimates, '000 metric tons, live weight, 2002): Capture 42.8 (Groupers 1.5; Snappers 1.7; Emperors 2.9; Barracudas 2.8; Mullets 2.9; Narrow-barred Spanish mackerel 2.1; Albacore 8.0; Freshwater molluscs 5.2; Anadara clams 2.9; Other marine molluscs 3.2); Aquaculture 1.7; *Total catch* 44.5. Figures exclude aquatic plants ('000 metric tons): 0.8 (capture 0.5, aquaculture 0.3). Also excluded are trochus shells (150 metric tons), pearl oyster shells (10 tons) and corals (1,000 tons). Source: FAO.

MINING

Production (kg, 2003): Gold 3,517; Silver 1,247.

INDUSTRY

Production (metric tons, 2001, unless otherwise indicated): Sugar 496,000 (2003); Molasses 142,000 (1997); Coconut oil 8,000 (2003); Flour 64,000 (2003); Soap 3,000 (2003); Cement 100,000 (2003); Paint ('000 litres) 2,789; Beer ('000 litres) 18,000; Soft drinks ('000 litres) 24,160; Cigarettes 442; Matches ('000 gross boxes) 128; Electric energy (million kWh) 545 (2000 estimate); Ice cream ('000 litres) 1,257; Toilet paper ('000 rolls) 20,225. Source: UN, *Industrial Commodity Statistics Yearbook*, and ADB, *Key Indicators of Developing Asian and Pacific Countries*.

FINANCE

Currency and Exchange Rates: 100 cents = 1 Fiji dollar ($F). *Sterling, US Dollar and Euro Equivalents* (31 December 2004): £1 sterling = $F3.1772; US $1 = $F1.6450; €1 = $F2.2407; $F100 = £31.47 = US $60.79 = €44.63. *Average Exchange Rate ($F per US $)*: 2.1869 in 2002; 1.8958 in 2003; 1.7331 in 2004.

General Budget ($F million, 2002): *Revenue:* Current revenue 949.4 (Taxes 796.5, Non-taxes 152.9); Capital revenue 80.7; Total 1,030.1. *Expenditure:* General public services 149.5; Defence 56.2; Education 168.4; Health 82.0; Social security and welfare 3.4; Housing and community amenities 7.53; Economic services 73.7 (Agriculture 6.5, Industry 31.4, Electricity, gas and water 11.3, Transport and communications 24.5); Other purposes 632.5; Total 1,173.2 (Current 971.8, Capital 201.4). Source: Asian Development Bank, *Key Indicators of Developing Asian and Pacific Countries*. *2003:* Total current revenue 1,079.1; Total current expenditure 1,083.4.

International Reserves (US $ million at 31 December 2003): Gold (valued at market-related prices) 0.35; IMF special drawing rights 7.70; Reserve position in IMF 22.57; Foreign exchange 393.35; Total 423.97. Source: IMF, *International Financial Statistics*.

Money Supply ($F million at 31 December 2003): Currency outside banks 226.2; Demand deposits at commercial banks 666.0; Total money (incl. others) 900.6. Source: IMF, *International Financial Statistics*.

Cost of Living (Consumer Price Index; base: 1993 = 100): 124.7 in 2001; 125.6 in 2002; 130.9 in 2003.

Expenditure on the Gross Domestic Product ($F million at current prices, 2001): Government final consumption expenditure 655.4; Private final consumption expenditure 2,188.0; Increase in stocks 40.0; Gross fixed capital formation 516.8; *Total domestic expenditure* 3,400.2; Exports of goods and services 2,136.0; *Less* Imports of goods and services 2,327.0; Statistical discrepancy 626.64; *GDP in purchasers' values* 3,835.8. Source: Asian Development Bank, *Key Indicators of Developing Asian and Pacific Countries*.

Gross Domestic Product by Economic Activity ($F million at constant 1989 prices, 2003, preliminary): Agriculture, forestry and fishing 335.4; Mining and quarrying 50.6; Manufacturing 333.3; Electricity, gas and water 105.8; Building and construction 111.3; Wholesale and retail trade 448.6; Transport and communications 339.2; Finance, real estate, etc. 254.9; Public administration 409.9; Other services 17.8; *Sub-total* 2,406.8; *Less* Imputed bank service charges 129.2; *GDP at factor cost* 2,277.6. Source: Asian Development Bank, *Key Indicators of Developing Asian and Pacific Countries*.

Balance of Payments (US $ million, 1999): Exports of goods f.o.b. 537.7; Imports of goods f.o.b. –653.3; *Trade balance* –115.6; Exports of services 525.1; Imports of services –389.8; *Balance on goods and services* 19.7; Other income received 47.3; Other income paid –82.8; *Balance on goods, services and income* –15.8; Current transfers received 42.7; Current transfers paid –14.2; *Current balance* 12.7; Capital account (net) 14.0; Direct investment abroad –53.0; Direct investment from abroad –33.2; Other investment assets –62.2; Other investment liabilities 44.4; Net errors and omissions 32.5; *Overall balance* –44.9. Source: IMF, *International Financial Statistics*.

EXTERNAL TRADE

Principal Commodities ($F million, 2002): *Imports c.i.f.* (distribution by SITC): Food and live animals 297.0; Mineral fuels, lubricants, etc. 336.0; Chemicals and related products 131.8; Basic manufactures 95.8; Machinery and transport equipment 446.8; Miscellaneous manufactured articles 31.1; Total (incl. others) 1,953.2. *Exports f.o.b.:* Food and live animals 137.09; Beverages and tobacco 339.9; Basic manufactures 79.2; Machinery and transport equipment 42.7; Total (incl. others) 1,194.8. Source: Asian Development Bank, *Key Indicators of Developing Asian and Pacific Countries*. *2003:* Total imports c.i.f. 2,214.6; Total exports f.o.b. 1,273.1.

Principal Trading Partners (US $ million, 2003): *Imports c.i.f.:* Australia 341.0; China, People's Republic 28.6; Hong Kong 25.8; India 18.7; Indonesia 17.8; Japan 44.0; New Zealand 167.1; Singapore 190.0; Thailand 21.9; USA 21.6; Total (incl. others) 976.1. *Exports:* Australia 139.8; Japan 45.3; Kiribati 11.5; New Zealand 27.9; Samoa 38.3; Tonga 18.6; United Kingdom 96.9; USA 168.7; Total (incl. others) 712.6. Source: Asian Development Bank, *Key Indicators of Developing Asian and Pacific Countries*.

TRANSPORT

Road Traffic (motor vehicles registered at 31 December 2003): Passenger cars 66,028; Goods vehicles 38,025; Buses 2,019; Taxis 3,729; Rental vehicles 5,511; Motorcycles 4,670; Tractors 5,619; Total (incl. others) 130,878.

Shipping: *Merchant Fleet* (registered at 31 December 2003): Vessels 49; Total displacement ('000 grt) 23.1 (Source: Lloyd's Register-Fairplay, *World Fleet Statistics*). *International Freight Traffic* ('000 metric tons, 1990): Goods loaded 568; Goods unloaded 625 (Source: UN, *Monthly Bulletin of Statistics*).

Civil Aviation (traffic on scheduled services, 2001): Passengers carried 613,000; Passenger-kilometres 2,391 million; Total ton-kilometres 306 million. Source: UN, *Statistical Yearbook*.

TOURISM

Foreign Visitors by Country of Residence (excluding cruise-ship passengers, 2002): Australia 123,606; Canada 9,802; Japan 26,382; New Zealand 68,293; Pacific Islands 24,051; United Kingdom 43,393; USA 58,815; Total (incl. others) 397,859. *2003:* Total arrivals 430,800.

Tourism Receipts ($F million): 413.5 in 2000; 495.5 in 2001; 615.4 in 2003.

COMMUNICATIONS MEDIA

Radio Receivers (1999): 545,000 in use*.

Television Receivers (2000): 92,000 in use†.

Telephones (2003): 102,000 main lines in use†.

Facsimile Machines (1999): 2,815 in use†.

Mobile Cellular Telephones (2003): 109,900 subscribers†.

Personal Computers (2002): 40,000 in use†.

Internet Users (2003): 55,000†.

Book Production (1980): 110 titles (84 books, 26 pamphlets); 273,000 copies (229,000 books, 44,000 pamphlets).

Daily Newspapers (2001): 3 (estimated combined circulation 49,124)‡.

Non-daily Newspapers (provisional, 1988): 7 (combined circulation 99,000)*.

* Source: UNESCO, *Statistical Yearbook*.
† Source: International Telecommunication Union.
‡ Source: Audit Bureau of Circulations, Australia.

EDUCATION

Pre-Primary (2002): 569 schools; 264 teachers; 7,076 pupils.

Primary (2003): 719 schools; 5,107 teachers; 142,781 pupils.

General Secondary (2003): 157 schools; 3,935 teachers; 68,178 pupils.

Vocational and Technical (2002): 33 institutions (1998); 1,024 teachers (including special schools—2000); 915 students.

Teacher Training (2000): 4 institutions (1999); 97 teachers; 1,003 students.

Medical (1989): 2 institutions; 493 students.

University (2003): 1 institution; 277 teachers (1991); 10,161 students.
Source: mainly UNESCO, *Statistical Yearbook*, and UN, *Statistical Yearbook for Asia and the Pacific*.

Adult Literacy Rate (UNESCO estimates): 92.9% (males 94.5%, females 91.4%) in 2002. Source: UN Development Programme, *Human Development Report*.

Directory

The Constitution

On 1 March 2001 President Iloilo reinstated the 1997 Constitution, after the Great Council of Chiefs (Bose Levu Vakaturaga—a traditional body, with some 70 members, consisting of every hereditary chief or Ratu of each Fijian clan) had approved the draft. The Constitution Amendment Bill that was approved in July 1997 included provisions to ensure of a multi-racial Cabinet. The following is a summary of the main provisions:

The Constitution, which declares Fiji to be a sovereign, democratic republic, guarantees fundamental human rights, a universal, secret and equal suffrage and equality before the law for all Fijian citizens. Citizenship may be acquired by birth, descent, registration or naturalization and is assured for all those who were Fijian citizens before 6 October 1987. Parliament may make provision for the deprivation or renunciation of a person's citizenship. Ethnic Fijians, and the Polynesian inhabitants of Rotuma, receive special constitutional consideration. The Judicial and Legal Services Commission, the Public Service Commission and the Police Service Commission are established as supervisory bodies.

THE GREAT COUNCIL OF CHIEFS

The Great Council of Chiefs (Bose Levu Vakaturaga) derives its authority from the status of its members and their chiefly lineage. The Great Council appoints the President of the Republic and selects the 14 nominees for appointment to the Senate, the upper chamber of the Parliament.

The Great Council became fully independent of the Government in mid-1999.

THE EXECUTIVE

Executive authority is vested in the President of the Republic, who is appointed by the Great Council of Chiefs, for a five-year term, to be constitutional Head of State and Commander-in-Chief of the armed forces. The Presidential Council advises the President on matters of national importance. The President, and Parliament, can be empowered to introduce any necessary measures in an emergency or in response to acts of subversion which threaten Fiji.

In most cases the President is guided by the Cabinet, which conducts the government of the Republic. The Cabinet is led by the Prime Minister, who is a Fijian of any ethnic origin and is appointed by the President from among the members of Parliament, on the basis of support in the legislature. The Prime Minister selects the other members of the Cabinet (the Attorney-General, the minister responsible for defence and security and any other ministers) from either the House of Representatives or the Senate on a multi-party and multiracial basis. The Cabinet is responsible to Parliament.

THE LEGISLATURE

Legislative power is vested in the Parliament, which comprises the President, the appointed upper house or Senate and an elected

House of Representatives. The maximum duration of a parliament is five years.

The Senate has 32 members, appointed by the President of the Republic for the term of the Parliament. A total of 14 senators are nominated by the Great Council of Chiefs, nine are appointed on the advice of the Prime Minister, eight on the advice of the Leader of the Opposition, and one on the advice of the Rotuma Island Council. The Senate is a house of review, with some powers to initiate legislation, but with limited influence on financial measures. The Senate is important in the protection of ethnic Fijian interests, and its consent is essential to any attempt to amend, alter or repeal any provisions affecting ethnic Fijians, their customs, land or tradition.

The House of Representatives has 71 elected members, who themselves elect their presiding officials and the Speaker from outside the membership of the House, and Deputy Speaker from among their number (excluding ministers). Voting is communal, with universal suffrage for all citizens of the Republic aged over 21 years. Seats are reserved on a racial basis: 23 for ethnic Fijians, 19 for Indians, three for other races (General Electors), one for Rotuma Islanders and 25 open seats. Elections must be held at least every five years and are to be administered by an independent Supervisor of Elections. An independent Boundaries Commission determines constituency boundaries.

THE JUDICIARY

The judiciary is independent and comprises the High Court, the Fiji Court of Appeal and the Supreme Court. The High Court and the Supreme Court are the final arbiters of the Constitution. The establishment of Fijian courts is provided for, and decisions of the Native Lands Commission (relating to ethnic Fijian customs, traditions and usage, and on disputes over the headship of any part of the Fijian people, with the customary right to occupy and use any native lands) are declared to be final and without appeal.

The Government

HEAD OF STATE

President: Ratu JOSEFA ILOILO (appointed 12 July 2000 by an interim authority established following the coup of 19 May 2000).

Vice-President: Ratu JONI MADRAIWIWI (appointed 15 December 2004).

THE CABINET
(April 2005)

Prime Minister, Minister for Fijian Affairs, Culture and Heritage, National Reconciliation and Unity, Multi-Ethnic Affairs and Reform of the Sugar Industry: LAISENIA QARASE.

Minister for Foreign Affairs and External Trade: KALIOPATE TAVOLA.

Minister for Finance and National Planning: Ratu JONE KUBUABOLA.

Attorney-General and Minister for Justice: QORINIASI BALE.

Minister for Lands and Mineral Resources: MANASA LUQIA.

Minister for Works and Energy: SAVENACA DRAUNIDALO.

Minister for Education: RO TEIMUMU VUIKABA KEPA.

Minister for Tourism: PITA NACUVA.

Minister for Regional Development: TED YOUNG.

Minister for Transport and Civil Aviation: JOSEFA VOSANIBOLA.

Minister for Labour, Industrial Relations and Productivity: KENNETH ZINCK.

Minister for Commerce, Business Development and Investment: TOMASI VUETILOVONI.

Minister for Information, Communications and Media Relations: AHMED ALI.

Minister for Local Government, Housing, Squatter Settlement and Environment: PIO WONG.

Minister of Health: SOLOMONE NAIVALU.

Minister for Agriculture, Sugar and Land Resettlement: JONETANI GALUINADI.

Minister for Women, Social Welfare and Poverty Alleviation: Adi ASENACA CAUCAU.

Minister for Youth, Employment Opportunities and Sports: ISIRELI LEWENIQILA.

Minister for Home Affairs and Immigration: JOKETANI COKANASIGA.

Minister for Fisheries and Forests: KONISI YABAKI.

Minister for Public Enterprises and Public Sector Reform: IRAMI MATAIRAVULA.

MINISTRIES

Office of the President: Government Bldgs, POB 2513, Suva; tel. 3314244; fax 3301645.

Office of the Prime Minister: Government Bldgs, POB 2353, Suva; tel. 3211201; fax 3306034; e-mail pmsoffice@is.com.fj; internet www.fiji.gov.fj.

Office of the Attorney-General and Ministry of Justice: Government Bldgs, Victoria Parade, POB 2213, Suva; tel. 3309866; fax 3305421.

Ministry of Agriculture, Sugar and Land Resettlement: PMB, POB 358, Raiwaqa; tel. 3384233; fax 3385048; e-mail maffinfo@is.com.fj.

Ministry of Commerce, Business Development and Investment: Government Bldgs, POB 2131, Suva; tel. 3305411; fax 3302617.

Ministry of Education: Marela House, Thurston St, PMB, Suva; tel. 3314477; fax 3303511.

Ministry of Finance and National Planning: Government Bldgs, POB 2212, Suva; tel. 3307011; fax 3300834.

Ministry of Fisheries and Forests: POB 2218, Government Bldgs, Suva; tel. 3301611; fax 3300435; e-mail forestry-hq@mff.net.fj.

Ministry of Foreign Affairs and External Trade: Government Bldgs, POB 2220, Suva; tel. 3309628; fax 3301741; e-mail info@foreignaffairs.gov.fj; internet www.foreignaffairs.gov.fj.

Ministry of Health: Government Bldgs, POB 2223, Suva; tel. 3306177; fax 3306163; e-mail info@health.gov.fj.

Ministry of Home Affairs and Immigration: Government Bldgs, POB 2349, Suva; tel. 3211401; fax 3317721; e-mail inforhomeaff@govnet.gov.fj.

Ministry of Information, Communications and Media Relations: Government Bldgs, POB 2225, Suva; tel. 3211700; fax 3303146; e-mail info@fiji.gov.fj.

Ministry of Labour, Industrial Relations and Productivity: Government Bldgs, POB 2216, Suva; tel. 3211640; fax 3304701; e-mail minlabour@is.com.fj.

Ministry of Lands and Mineral Resources: Government Bldgs, POB 2118, Suva; tel. 3211556; fax 3302730; e-mail mbaravilala@lands.gov.fj.

Ministry of Local Government, Housing, Squatter Settlement and Environment: *National Planning*: Government Bldgs, POB 2351, Suva; *Local Government*: Government Bldgs, POB 2131; *Environment*: Government Bldgs, POB 2131; tel. 3313411; fax 3304809; tel. 3211310; fax 3303515; tel. 3311069; fax 3312879; e-mail msovaki@govnet.gov.fj.

Ministry of Information, Communications and Media Relations: Government Bldgs, POB 2225, Suva; tel. 3211700; fax 3303146; e-mail info@fiji.gov.fj.

Ministry of Public Enterprise and Public Sector Reform: Government Bldgs, POB 2278, Suva; tel. 3315577; fax 3315035; e-mail mshareem@govnet.gov.fj; internet www.publicenterprises.gov.fj.

Ministry of Regional Development: POB 2219, Government Bldgs, Suva; tel. 3313400; fax 3303256.

Ministry of Tourism: Government Bldgs, POB 2278, Suva; tel. 3312788; fax 3302060; e-mail infodesk@fijivb.gov.fj; internet www.bulafiji.com.

Ministry of Transport and Civil Aviation: Private Mail Bag, Samabula; tel. 3316866; fax 3307839; e-mail infodesk@fijifvb.gov.fj; internet www.bulafiji.com.

Ministry of Women, Social Welfare and Poverty Alleviation: POB 14068, Suva; tel. 3312199; fax 3303829; e-mail slomaloma@govnet.gov.fj.

Ministry of Works and Energy: POB 2493, Government Bldgs, Suva; tel. 3384111; fax 3383198.

Ministry of Youth, Employment Opportunities and Sports: Government Bldgs, POB 2448, Suva; tel. 3315960; fax 3305348.

Legislature

PARLIAMENT

Senate

The Senate is also known as the House of Review. The upper chamber comprises 32 appointed members (see The Constitution).

House of Representatives

The lower chamber comprises 71 elected members: 23 representing ethnic Fijians, 19 representing ethnic Indians, three representing other races (General Electors), one for Rotuma Islanders and 25 seats open to all races.

Speaker: Ratu EPELI NAILATIKAU.

General Election, 25 August–1 September 2001

	Fijian	Indian	Other*	Open Seats	Total Seats
Fiji United Party (SDL) . .	18	—	1	13	32
Fiji Labour Party (FLP) . .	—	19	—	8	27
Conservative Alliance Party (MV)	5	—	—	1	6
New Labour Unity Party (NLUP)	—	—	1	1	2
National Federation Party (NFP)	—	0	—	1	1
United General Party (UGP)	—	—	1	—	1
Independents	—	—	1	1	2
Total	**23**	**19**	**4**	**25**	**71**

*One Rotuman and three General Electors' seats.

Notes: The total includes one seat won by the Fiji United Party in a by-election held on 25 September 2001. In September 2002, following a court ruling, the one NFP seat was awarded to the FLP, thus bringing the latter's representation to 28 seats.

Political Organizations

Bai Kei Viti: Suva; f. 2001; Sec. Ratu TEVITA MOMOEDONU.

Fiji Indian Congress: POB 3661, Samabula, Suva; tel. 3391211; fax 3340117; f. 1991; Gen. Sec. VIJAY RAGHWAN.

Fiji Indian Liberal Party: Rakiraki; f. 1991; represents the interests of the Indian community, particularly sugar-cane farmers and students; Sec. SWANI KUMAR.

Fiji Labour Party (FLP): POB 2162, Government Bldgs, Suva; tel. 3305811; fax 3305317; e-mail flp@connect.com.fj; internet www.flp .org.fj; f. 1985; Pres. JOKAPECI KOROI; Sec.-Gen. MAHENDRA PAL CHAUDHRY.

Fijian Association Party (FAP): Suva; f. 1995 by merger of Fijian Association (a breakaway faction of the SVT) and the multiracial All Nationals Congress; Leader Adi KUINI SPEED; Pres. Ratu INOKE SERU.

Fijian Conservative Party: Suva; f. 1989 by former mems of the Fiji Nationalist Party and the Alliance Party; Leader ISIRELI VUIBAU.

Fijian Nationalist United Front Party (FNUFP): POB 1336, Suva; tel. 3362317; f. 1992 to replace Fijian Nationalist Party; seeks additional parliamentary representation for persons of Fijian ethnic origin, the introduction of other pro-Fijian reforms and the repatriation of ethnic Indians; Leader SAKEASI BAKEWA BUTADROKA.

Janata Party: Suva; f. 1995 by former mems of NFP and FLP.

Matanitu Vanua (MV) (Conservative Alliance Party): c/o House of Representatives, Suva; f. 2001; Leader GEORGE SPEIGHT.

National Federation Party (NFP): POB 13534, Suva; tel. 3305811; fax 3305317; f. 1960 by merger of the Federation Party, which was multiracial but mainly Indian, and the National Democratic Party; Leader ATTAR SINGH; Pres. JOGINDRA SINGH.

Nationalist Vanua Takolavo Party (NVTLP): c/o House of Representatives, Suva; Leader SAULA TELAWA.

New Labour Movement: Suva; Gen. Sec. MICHAEL COLUMBUS.

New Labour United Party (NLUP): Suva; f. 2001 ; Leader Dr TUPENI BABA; Pres. Ratu MELI VESIKULA.

Party of National Unity (PANU): Ba; f. 1998 to lobby for increased representation for the province of Ba; Leader MELI BOGI-LEKA.

Soqosoqo Duavata ni Lewenivanua (SDL) (Fiji United Party): c/o House of Representatives, Suva; f. 1990; Leader LAISENIA QARASE; Gen. Sec. JALE BABA.

Soqosoqo ni Vakavulewa ni Taukei (SVT) (Fijian Political Party): Suva; f. 1990 by Great Council of Chiefs; supports constitutional dominance of ethnic Fijians but accepts multiracialism; Pres. Ratu SITIVENI RABUKA; Gen. Sec. EMA DRUAVESI.

Taukei Movement: POB 505, Lautoka; f. 1987, following merger of Taukei Liberation Front and Domo Ni Taukei group; right-wing indigenous Fijian nationalist group; Pres. Ratu TEVITA BOLOBOLO; Vice-Pres. Ratu INOKE KUBUABOLA; Gen. Sec. APISAI TORA.

United General Party (UGP): Suva; f. 1998 by the merger of the General Electors' Party and the General Voters' Party (fmrly the General Electors' Association, one of the three wings of the Alliance Party—AP, the ruling party 1970–87); represents the interests of the minority Chinese and European communities and people from other Pacific Islands resident in Fiji, all of whom are classed as General Electors under the 1998 Constitution; Pres. DAVID PICK-ERING.

Vanua Independent Party: Leader ILIESA TUVALOVO; Sec. URAIA TUISOVISOVI.

Veitokani ni Lewenivanua Vakarisito (VLV) (Christian Democratic Alliance): c/o House of Representatives, Suva; f. 1998 in opposition to constitutional reforms and to defend Christian and Melanesian interests; Leader POESCI WAQALEVU BUNE; Sec. TANIELA TABU.

Other minor parties that contested the 2001 election included the Justice and Freedom Party, the Dodonu ni Taukei Party, the Girmit Heritage Party, the General Voters Party, the Lio'on Famor Rotuma Party and the Party of the Truth.

Supporters of secession are concentrated in Rotuma.

Diplomatic Representation

EMBASSIES AND HIGH COMMISSIONS IN FIJI

Australia: 37 Princes Rd, POB 214, Suva; tel. 3382211; fax 3382065; e-mail public-affairs-suva@dfat.gov.au; High Commissioner JENNIFER RAWSON.

China, People's Republic: 147 Queen Elizabeth Dr., PMB, Nasese, Suva; tel. 3300215; fax 3300950; e-mail chinaemb@is.com.fj; Ambassador CAI JINBIAO.

France: Dominion House, 7th Floor, Thomson St, Suva; tel. 3312233; fax 3301894; e-mail eugene.berg@diplomatie.gouv.fr; Ambassador EUGENE BERG.

India: POB 471, Suva; tel. 3301125; fax 3301032; e-mail hicomindsuva@is.com.fj; High Commissioner ISHWAR SINGH CHAUHAN.

Japan: Dominion House, 2nd Floor, POB 13045, Suva; tel. 3304633; fax 3302984; e-mail eojfiji@is.com.fj; Ambassador HISATO MURAYAMA.

Korea, Republic: Vanua House, 8th Floor, PMB, Suva; tel. 3300977; fax 3303410; Ambassador LIM DAE-TAEK.

Malaysia: Pacific House, 5th Floor, POB 356, Suva; tel. 3312166; fax 3303350; e-mail mwsuva@is.com.fj; High Commissioner MOHAMMED TAKWIR DIN.

Marshall Islands: 41 Borron Rd, Government Bldgs, POB 2038, Suva; tel. 3387899; fax 3387115; Ambassador MACK KAMINAGA.

Micronesia, Federated States: 37 Loftus St, POB 15493, Suva; tel. 304566; fax 3300842; e-mail fsmsuva@sopacsun.sopac.org.fj; Ambassador KODARO MARTIN GALLEN.

Nauru: Ratu Sukuna House, 7th Floor, Government Bldgs, POB 2420, Suva; tel. 3313566; fax 3302861; High Commissioner Dr LUDWIG KEKE.

New Zealand: Reserve Bank of Fiji Bldg, 10th Floor, Pratt St, POB 1378, Suva; tel. 3311422; fax 3300842; e-mail nzhc@connect.com.fj; High Commissioner ADRIAN SIMCOCK.

Papua New Guinea: Credit Corporation House, 3rd Floor, Government Bldgs, POB 2447, Suva; tel. 3304244; fax 3300178; e-mail kundufj@is.com.fj; High Commissioner ALEXIS OAENGO MAINO.

Tuvalu: 16 Gorrie St, POB 14449, Suva; tel. 3301355; fax 3308479; High Commissioner TAUKELINA FINIKASO.

United Kingdom: Victoria House, 47 Gladstone Rd, POB 1355, Suva; tel. 3229100; fax 3229132; e-mail publicdiplomacysuva@fco .gov.uk; internet www.britishhighcommission.fco.gov.uk/fiji; High Commissioner CHARLES F. MOCHAN.

USA: 31 Loftus St, POB 218, Suva; tel. 3314466; fax 3300081; e-mail usembsuva@is.com.fj; internet www.amembassy-fiji.gov; Ambassador DAVID LYON.

Judicial System

Justice is administered by the Supreme Court, the Fiji Court of Appeal, the High Court and the Magistrates' Courts. The Supreme Court of Fiji is the superior court of record presided over by the Chief Justice. The 1990 Constitution provided for the establishment of Fijian customary courts and declared as final decisions of the Native Lands Commission in cases involving Fijian custom, etc.

Supreme Court
Suva; tel. 3211524; fax 3300674.

Chief Justice: DANIEL FATIAKI.

President of the Fiji Court of Appeal: JAI RAM REDDY.

Director of Public Prosecutions: PETER RIDGWAY.

Solicitor-General: NAINENDRA NAND.

Religion

CHRISTIANITY

Most ethnic Fijians are Christians. Methodists are the largest Christian group, followed by Roman Catholics. In the census of 1996 about 58% of the population were Christian (mainly Methodists, who comprised 36.2% of the total population).

Fiji Council of Churches: POB 2300, Government Bldgs, Suva; tel. (1) 3313798; f. 1964; nine mem. churches; Pres. Rev. APIMELEKI QILIO; Gen. Sec. Rev. IFREREIMI CAMA; (acting).

The Anglican Communion

In April 1990 Polynesia, formerly a missionary diocese of the Church of the Province of New Zealand, became a full and integral diocese. The diocese of Polynesia is based in Fiji but also includes Wallis and Futuna, Tuvalu, Kiribati, French Polynesia, Cook Islands, Tonga, Samoa and Tokelau. There were an estimated 6,325 adherents in 1996.

Bishop of Polynesia: Rt Rev. Jabez Leslie Bryce, Bishop's Office, 8 Desvoeux Rd, Suva; e-mail episcopus@connect.com.fj; tel. 3304716; fax 3302687.

The Roman Catholic Church

Fiji comprises a single archdiocese. At 31 December 2002 there were an estimated 85,518 adherents in the country.

Bishops' Conference: Episcopal Conference of the Pacific Secretariat (CEPAC), 14 Williamson Rd, POB 289, Suva; tel. 3300340; fax 3303143; e-mail cepac@connect.com.fj; f. 1968; 17 mems; Pres. Most Rev. APURON ANTHONY SABLAN (Archbishop of Agaña, Guam); Admin. Officer THOMAS TAVUTONIVALU.

Regional Appeal Tribunal for CEPAC
14 Williamson Rd, POB 289, Suva; tel. 300340; fax 3303143; e-mail cepac@is.com.fj.

f. 1980; 17 mems; Judicial Vicar Rev. THEO KOSTER.

Archbishop of Suva: Most Rev. PETERO MATACA, Archdiocesan Office, Nicolas House, 35 Pratt St, POB 109, Suva; tel. 3301955; fax 3301565; e-mail cabajog@yahoo.com.

Other Christian Churches

Methodist Church in Fiji (Lotu Wesele e Viti): Epworth Arcade, Nina St, POB 357, Suva; tel. 3311477; fax 3303771; f. 1835; autonomous since 1964; 211,550 mems (2003); Gen. Sec. Rev. JIONE LANGI; Pres. Rev. LAISIASA RATABACACA.

Other denominations active in the country include the Assembly of God (with c. 7,000 mems), the Baptist Mission, the Congregational Christian Church and the Presbyterian Church.

HINDUISM

Most of the Indian community are Hindus. According to the census of 1996, some 34% of the population were Hindus.

ISLAM

In 1996 some 7% of the population were Muslim. There are several Islamic organizations:

Fiji Muslim League: POB 3990, Samabula, Suva; tel. 3384566; fax 3370204; e-mail fijimuslim@is.com.fj; f. 1926; Nat. Pres. HAFIZUD DEAN KHAN; Gen. Sec. NISAR AHMAD ALI; 26 brs and 3 subsidiary orgs.

SIKHISM

Sikh Association of Fiji: Suva; Pres. HARKEWAL SINGH.

BAHÁ'Í FAITH

National Spiritual Assembly: National Office, POB 639, Suva; tel. 3387574; fax 3387772; e-mail nsafijiskm@suva.is.com.fj; mems resident in 490 localities; national headquarters for consultancy and co-ordination.

The Press

NEWSPAPERS AND PERIODICALS

Coconut Telegraph: POB 249, Savusavu, Vanua Levu; f. 1975; monthly; serves widely-scattered rural communities; Editor LEMA LOW.

Fiji Calling: POB 12095, Suva; tel. 3305916; fax 3301930; publ. by Associated Media Ltd; every 6 months; English; Publr YASHWANT GAUNDER.

Fiji Cane Grower: POB 12095, Suva; tel. 3305916; fax 3305256.

Fiji Daily Post: 10–16 Toorak Rd, POB 2071, Govt Bldgs, Suva; f. 1987 as *Fiji Post* , daily from 1989; English; 100% govt-owned since Sept. 2003; Chair. MALAKAI NAIYAGA; Editor FRED WESLEY.

Fiji Magic: POB 12095, Suva; tel. 3305916; fax 3302852; e-mail fijimagic@fijilive.com; internet www.fijilive.com/fijimagic; publ. by Associated Media Ltd; monthly; English; Publr YASHWANT GAUNDER; circ. 15,000.

Fiji Republic Gazette: Printing Dept, POB 98, Suva; tel. 3385999; fax 3370203; f. 1874; weekly; English.

Fiji Sun: 12 Amra St, Walubay, Suva; tel. 3307555; fax 3311455; e-mail fijisun@sun.com.fj; re-established 1999; daily; Editor LEONE CABENATABUA; Publr MICHAEL RICHARDS.

Fiji Times: 20 Gordon St, POB 1167, Suva; tel. 3304111; fax 3301521; f. 1869; publ. by Fiji Times Ltd; daily; English; Man. Dir TONY YIANNI; Editor SAMISONI KAKAIUALU; circ. 34,000.

Fiji Trade Review: The Rubine Group, POB 12511, Suva; tel. 3313944; monthly; English; Publr GEORGE RUBINE; Editor MABEL HOWARD.

Islands Business Magazine: 46 Gordon St, POB 12718, Suva; tel. 3303108; fax 3301423; e-mail editor@ibi.com.fj; internet www.pacificislands.cc; fmrly *Pacific Magazine*; regional monthly news and business magazine featuring the Fiji Islands Business supplement; English; Publr ROBERT KEITH-REID; Editor-in-Chief LAISA TAGA; circ. 8,500.

Na Tui: 422 Fletcher Rd, POB 2071, Govt Bldgs, Suva; f. 1988; weekly; Fijian; Publr TANIELA BOLEA; Editor SAMISONI BOLATAGICI; circ. 7,000.

Nai Lalakai: 20 Gordon St, POB 1167, Suva; tel. 3304111; fax 3301521; e-mail fijitimes@is.com.fj; f. 1962; publ. by Fiji Times Ltd; weekly; Fijian; Editor SAMISONI KAKAIVALU; circ. 18,000.

Pacific Business: POB 12095, Suva; tel. 3305916; fax 3301930; publ. by Associated Media Ltd; monthly; English; Publr YASHWANT GAUNDER.

Pacific Telecom: POB 12095, Suva; tel. 3300591; fax 3302852; e-mail review@is.com.fj; publ. by Associated Media Ltd; monthly; English; Publr YASHWANT GAUNDER.

Pactrainer: PMB, Suva; tel. 3303623; fax 3303943; e-mail pina@is.com.fj; monthly; newsletter of Pacific Journalism Development Centre; Editor PETER LOMAS.

PINA Nius: Pacific Islands News Association, 46 Gordon St, PMB, Suva; tel. 3303623; fax 3303943; e-mail pina@is.com.fj; internet www.pinarius.org; monthly newsletter of Pacific Islands News Association; Editor NINA RATULELE.

The Review: POB 12095, Suva; tel. 3305916; fax 3301930; e-mail review@is.com.fj; publ. by Associated Media Ltd; monthly; English; Publr YASHWANT GAUNDER.

Sartaj: John Beater Enterprises Ltd, Raiwaqa, POB 5141, Suva; f. 1988; weekly; Hindi; Editor S. DASO; circ. 15,000.

Shanti Dut: 20 Gordon St, POB 1167, Suva; f. 1935; publ. by Fiji Times Ltd; weekly; Hindi; Editor NILAM KUMAR; circ. 12,000.

Top Shot: Suva; f. 1995; golf magazine; monthly.

Volasiga: 10–16 Toorak Rd, POB 2071, Suva; f. 1988; weekly; Fijian; Gen. Man. ANURA BANDARA (acting); Editor SAMISONI BOLATA-GICI.

The Weekender: 2 Dension Rd, POB 15652, Suva; tel. 3315477; fax 3305346; publ. by Media Resources Ltd; weekly; English; Publr JOSEFATA NATA.

PRESS ASSOCIATIONS

Fiji Islands Media Association: c/o Vasiti Ivaqa, POB 12718, Suva; tel. 3303108; fax 3301423; national press asscn; operates Fiji Press Club and Fiji Journalism Training Institute; Sec. NINA RATULELE.

Pacific Islands News Association: 46 Gordon St, PMB, Suva; tel. 3303623; fax 3303943; e-mail pina@is.com.fj; internet www.pinarius .org; regional press asscn; defends freedom of information and expression, promotes professional co-operation, provides training and education; Administrator NINA RATULELE; Pres. JOHNSON HONIMAE.

Publishers

Fiji Times Ltd: POB 1167, Suva; tel. 3304111; fax 3302011; e-mail tyianni@fijitimes.com.fj; f. 1869; Propr News Corpn Ltd; largest newspaper publr; also publrs of books and magazines; Man. Dir TONY YIANNI.

Lotu Pasifika Productions: POB 2401, Suva; tel. 3301314; fax 3301183; f. 1973; cookery, education, poetry, religion; Gen. Man. SERU L. VEREBALAVU.

University of the South Pacific: University Media Centre, POB 1168, Suva; tel. 3313900; fax 3301305; e-mail austin_l@usp.ac.fj; f. 1986; education, natural history, regional interests.

GOVERNMENT PUBLISHING HOUSE

Printing and Stationery Department: POB 98, Suva; tel. 3385999; fax 3370203.

Broadcasting and Communications

TELECOMMUNICATIONS

Fiji International Telecommunicatons Ltd (FINTEL): 158 Victoria Parade, POB 59, Suva; tel. 3312933; fax 3300750; e-mail prichards@fintelfiji.com; 51% govt-owned; 49% C&W plc; CEO SAKARAIA TUILAKEPA.

Telcom Fiji Ltd: Private Mail Bag, Suva; tel. 3304019; fax 3301765; internet www.tfl.com.fj/; Chair. LIONEL YEE; CEO WINSTON THOMPSON.

Vodafone Fiji Ltd: Private Mail Bag, Suva; tel. 3312000; fax 3312007; e-mail aslam.khan@vodafone.com.fj; 51% owned by Telecom Fiji, 49% by Vodafone International Holdings BV; Man. Dir ASLAM KHAN.

BROADCASTING

Radio

Fiji Broadcasting Commission—FBC (Radio Fiji): Broadcasting House, POB 334, Suva; tel. 3314333; fax 3301643; f. 1954; statutory body; jointly funded by govt grant and advertising revenue; Chair. DANIEL WHIPPY; CEO SIRELI KINI.

Radio Fiji 1 broadcasts nationally on AM in English and Fijian;

Radio Fiji 2 broadcasts nationally on AM in English and Hindi;

Radio Fiji Gold broadcasts nationally on AM and FM in English;

104 FM and Radio Rajdhani 98 FM, mainly with musical programmes, broadcast in English and Hindi respectively, but are received only on Viti Levu;

Bula FM, musical programmes, broadcasts in Fijian, received only on Viti Levu.

Communications Fiji Ltd: 231 Waimanu Rd, PMB, Suva; tel. 3314766; fax 3303748; e-mail cfl@fm96.com.fj; f. 1985; operates three commercial stations; Man. Dir WILLIAM PARKINSON; Gen. Man. IAN JACKSON.

FM 96, f. 1985, broadcasts 24 hours per day, on FM, in English;

Navtarang, f. 1989, broadcasts 24 hours per day, on FM, in Hindi;

Viti FM, f. 1996, broadcasts 24 hours per day, on FM, in Fijian.

Radio Light/Radio Naya Jiwan: Shop 11A & B, Pacific Harbour Culture Centre, POB 319, Pacific Harbour; tel. and fax 3450007; fax 3450096; e-mail radiolight@connect.com.fj; internet www.radiolight .org; f. 1990; non-profit religious organization; broadcasts in English (Radio Light) and Hindi (Radio Naya Jiwan)on FM 106, FM 93.6 and FM 94.8; Station Man. and Programmes Dir DOUGLAS ROSE.

Radio Pasifik: POB 1168, University of the South Pacific, Suva; tel. 3313900; fax 3312591; e-mail schuster@usp.ac.fj; Gen. Man. ALFRED SCHUSTER.

Television

Film and Television Unit (FTU): c/o Ministry of Information and Communications, Govt Bldgs, POB 2225, Suva; tel. 3314688; fax 3300196; video library; production unit established by Govt and Hanns Seidel Foundation (Germany); a weekly news magazine and local documentary programmes.

Fiji Television Ltd: 20 Gorrie St, POB 2442, Govt Bldgs, Suva; tel. 3305100; fax 3305077; e-mail fijitv@is.com.fj; internet www.fijitv .com; f. 1994; operates two services, Fiji 1, a free channel, and Sky Fiji, a three-channel subscription service; Chair. OLOTA ROKOVUNISEI; CEO KEN CLARK; Head of Programming RICHARD BROADBRIDGE.

In 1990 two television stations were constructed at Suva and Monsavu, with aid from the People's Republic of China. A permanent television station became operational in July 1994.

Finance

In 1996 the Ministry of Finance announced that it had secured financial assistance for the undertaking of a study to investigate the possibility of developing an 'offshore' financial centre in Fiji.

BANKING

(cap. = capital; res = reserves; dep. = deposits; m. = million; brs = branches; amounts in Fiji dollars)

Central Bank

Reserve Bank of Fiji: 1 Pratt St, PMB, Suva; tel. 3313611; fax 3301688; e-mail rbf@reservebank.gov.fj; internet www.reservebank .gov.fj; f. 1984 to replace Central Monetary Authority of Fiji; bank of issue; administers Insurance Act; cap. 2.0m., res 70.8m., dep. 351.0m. (Dec. 2003); Chair. and Gov. SAVENACA NARUBE.

Commercial Bank

Colonial National Bank : 3 Central St, POB 1166, Suva; tel. 3314400; fax 3302190; f. 1974 as National Bank of Fiji; 51% acquired from Fiji Govt by Colonial Ltd in 1999; 51% owned by Commonwealth Bank of Australia, 49% owned by Govt of Fiji; cap. 15.0m., res 0.3m., dep. 262.9m. (June 2003), dep. 317.2m. (June 2004); Chair. MALAKAI NAIYAGA; Gen. Man. MIKE UPPERTON; 15 brs; 45 agencies.

Development Bank

Fiji Development Bank: 360 Victoria Parade, POB 104, Suva; tel. 3314866; fax 3314886; f. 1967; finances the development of natural resources, agriculture, transportation and other industries and enterprises; statutory body; applied for a commercial banking licence in Nov. 2004; cap. 50.8m., res 14.0m., dep. 182.6m. (June 1993); Chair. DAVID AIDNEY; 9 brs.

Merchant Banks

Merchant Finance and Investment Company Ltd: 91 Gordon St, POB 14213, Suva; tel. 3314955; fax 3300026; e-mail merchantfi@ connect.com.fj; f. 1986; fmrly Merchant Bank of Fiji Ltd; owned by Fijian Holdings Ltd (80%), South Pacific Trustees (20%); Man. Dir S. WELEILAKEBA; 3 brs.

National MBf Finance (Fiji) Ltd: Burns Philp Bldg, 2nd Floor, POB 13525, Suva; tel. 302232; fax 3305915; e-mail mbf@is.com.fj; f. 1991; 51% owned by the National Bank of Fiji, 49% by MBf Asia Capital Corpn Holding Ltd (Hong Kong); Chief Operating Officer SIEK KART; 4 brs.

Foreign Banks

Agence Française de Développement (ADF) (France): Suva; licensed to operate in Fiji in 1997.

Australia and New Zealand (ANZ) Banking Group Ltd: ANZ House, 25 Victoria Parade, POB 179, Suva; tel. 3213000; fax 3312527; bought Bank of New Zealand in Fiji (8 brs) in 1990; Gen. Man. (Fiji) JOHN VELEGRINIS; 17 brs; 9 agencies.

Bank of Baroda (India): Bank of Baroda Bldg, Marks St, POB 57, Suva; tel. 3311400; fax 3302510; e-mail bobsuva@is.com.fj; f. 1908; CEO S. K. BAGCHI; 7 brs; 2 agencies.

Bank of Hawaii (USA): 67–69 Victoria Parade, POB 273, Suva; tel. 3312144; fax 3312464; f. 1993; Gen. Man. BRIAN BLISS; 3 brs.

Habib Bank (Pakistan): Narsey's Bldg, Renwick Rd, POB 108, Suva; tel. 3304011; fax 3304835; e-mail hblfibas@is.com.fj; Chief Man. (Fiji) ABDUL MATIN; licensed to operate in Fiji 1990; 3 brs.

Westpac Banking Corporation (Australia): 1 Thomson St, Suva; tel. 3300666; fax 3301813; Chief Man. (Pacific Islands region) TREVOR WISEMANTEL; 12 brs; 9 agencies.

STOCK EXCHANGE

South Pacific Stock Exchange: Level 2, Plaza One, Provident Plaza, 33 Ellery St, POB 11689, Suva; tel. 3304130; fax 3304145; e-mail suvastockex@is.com.fj; internet www.suvastockex.com; formerly Suva Stock Exchange; name changed as above in 2000; Chair. FOANA T. NEMANI; Man. MESAKE NAWARI.

INSURANCE

Blue Shield (Pacific) Ltd: Parade Bldg, POB 15137, Suva; tel. 3311733; fax 3300318; Fijian co; subsidiary of Colonial Mutual Life Assurance Society Ltd; medical and life insurance; Chief Exec. SIALENI VUETAKI.

Colonial Mutual Life Assurance Society Ltd: Colonial Bldg, PMB, Suva; tel. 314400; fax 3303448; f. 1876; inc in Australia; life; Gen. Man. SIMON SWANSON.

Dominion Insurance Ltd: Civic House, POB 14468, Suva; tel. 3311055; fax 3303475; partly owned by Flour Mills of (Fiji) Ltd; general insurance; Man. Dir GARY S. CALLAGHAN.

FAI Insurance (Fiji) Ltd: Suva.

Fiji Reinsurance Corpn Ltd: RBF Bldg, POB 12704, Suva; tel. 3313471; fax 3305679; 20% govt-owned; reinsurance; Chair. Ratu JONE Y. KUBUABOLA; Man. PETER MARIO.

Fijicare Mutual Assurance: 41 Loftus St, POB 15808, Suva; tel. 3302717; fax 3302119; f. 1992; CEO JEFF PRICE.

Insurance Trust of Fiji: Loftus St, POB 114, Suva; tel. 3311242; fax 3302541; Man. SAMUEL KRISHNA.

National Insurance Co of (Fiji) Ltd: McGowan Bldg, Suva; tel. 3315955; fax 3301376; owned by New Zealand interests; Gen. Man. GEOFF THOMPSON.

New India Assurance Co Ltd: Harifam Centre, POB 71, Suva; tel. 3313488; fax 3302679; Man. MILIND A. KHARAT.

Queensland Insurance (Fiji) Ltd: Queensland Insurance Center, Victoria Parade, POB 101, Suva; tel. 3315455; fax 3300285; e-mail info.fiji@qbe.com; internet www.qbe.com/asiapacific; owned by Australian interests; Gen. Man. JOHN HUNT.

There are also two Indian insurance companies operating in Fiji.

Trade and Industry

GOVERNMENT AGENCIES

Fiji National Training Council (FNTC): Beaumont Rd, POB 6890, Nasinu; tel. 3392000; fax 3340184; e-mail gen-enq@fntc.ac.fj; internet www.tpaf.ac.fj; Dir-Gen. JONE USAMATE.

Fiji Trade and Investment Board: Civic House, 6th Floor, Victoria Parade, Suva; tel. 3315988; fax 3301783; e-mail ftibinfo@ftib.org.fj; internet www.ftib.org.fj; f. 1980, restyled 1988, to promote and stimulate foreign and local economic development investment; Chair. JAMES DATTA; CEO JESONI VITUSAGAVULU.

Mineral Resources Department: Private Mail Bag, Suva; tel. 3381611; fax 3370039; e-mail director@mrd.gov.fj; internet www.mrd.gov.fj/index.html.

DEVELOPMENT ORGANIZATIONS

Fiji Development Company Ltd: POB 161, FNPF Place, 350 Victoria Parade, Suva; tel. 3304611; fax 3304171; e-mail hfc@is.com.fj; f. 1960; subsidiary of the Commonwealth Development Corpn; Man. F. KHAN.

Fiji-United States Business Council: CI-FTIB; POB 2303; Suva; f. 1998 to develop and expand trade links between the two countries; Pres. RAMENDRA NARAYAN.

Fijian Development Fund Board: POB 122, Suva; tel. 3312601; fax 3302585; f. 1951; funds derived from payments of $F20 a metric ton from the sales of copra by indigenous Fijians; deposits receive interest at 2.5%; funds used only for Fijian development schemes; Chair. Minister for Fijian Affairs; CEO VINCENT TOVATA.

Land Development Authority: c/o Ministry for Agriculture, Sugar and Land Resettlement, POB 5442, Raiwaqa; tel. 33384900; fax 33384058; f. 1961 to co-ordinate development plans for land and marine resources; Chair. JONETANI GALUINADI.

CHAMBERS OF COMMERCE

Ba Chamber of Commerce: POB 99, Ba; tel. 6670134; fax 6670132; Pres. DIJENDRA SINGH.

Labasa Chamber of Commerce: POB 992, Labasa; tel. 8811467; fax 8813009; Pres. JAIWANT KRISHNA.

Lautoka Chamber of Commerce and Industry: POB 366, Lautoka; tel. 6661834; fax 6662379; e-mail vaghco@connect.com.fj; Pres. NATWARLAL VAGH.

Levuka Chamber of Commerce: POB 85, Levuka; tel. 3440248; fax 3440252; Pres. ISHRAR ALI.

Nadi Chamber of Commerce: POB 2735, Nadi; tel. 6701704; fax 6702314; e-mail arunkumar@is.com.fj; Pres. VENKAT RAMANI AIYER.

Nausori Chamber of Commerce: POB 228, Nausori; tel. 3478235; fax 3400134; Pres. ROBERT RAJ KUMAR.

Sigatoka Chamber of Commerce: POB 882, Sigatoka; tel. 6500064; fax 6520006; Pres. NATWAR SINGH.

Suva Chamber of Commerce and Industry: 37 Viria Rd, Vatuwaqa Industrial Estate, POB 337, Suva; tel. 3380975; fax 3380854; f. 1902; Joint Sec. VERONIKA HANSRAJ; 150 mems.

Tavua-Vatukoula Chamber of Commerce: POB 698, Tavua; tel. 6680390; fax 6680390; Pres. SOHAN SINGH.

INDUSTRIAL AND TRADE ASSOCIATIONS

Fiji Forest Industries (FFI): Suva; Deputy Chair. Ratu SOSO KATONIVERE.

Fiji Kava Council: Suva; Chair. Ratu JOSATEKI NAWALOWALO.

Fiji National Petroleum Co Ltd: Suva; f. 1991; govt-owned, distributor of petroleum products.

Fiji Sugar Corporation Ltd: Western House, 3rd Floor, Cnr of Bila and Vidilo St, PMB, Lautoka; tel. 6662655; fax 6664685; nationalized 1974; buyer of sugar-cane and raw sugar mfrs; Chair. HAFIZUD D. KHAN; Man. Dir JOHN MCFADDEN.

Fiji Sugar Marketing Co Ltd: Dominion House, 5th Floor, Thomson St, POB 1402, Suva; tel. 3311588; fax 3300607; Man. Dir JONETANI GALUINADI.

Mining and Quarrying Council: 42 Gorrie St, Suva; tel. 33313188; fax 3302183; e-mail employer@is.com.fj; Chief Exec. K. A. J. ROBERTS.

National Trading Corporation Ltd: POB 13673, Suva; tel. 3315211; fax 3315584; f. 1992; a govt-owned body set up to develop markets for agricultural and marine produce locally and overseas; processes and markets fresh fruit, vegetables and ginger products; CEO APIAMA CEGUMALINA.

Native Lands Trust Board: POB 116, Suva; tel. 3312733; e-mail info@nltb.com.fj; internet www.nltb.com.fj; manages holdings of ethnic Fijian landowners; Gen. Man. KALIVATI BAKANI.

Pacific Fishing Co: Suva; fish-canning; govt-owned.

Sugar Cane Growers' Council: Canegrowers' Bldg, 3rd Floor, 75 Drasa Ave, Lautoka; tel. 6650466; fax 6650624; e-mail canegrower@is.com.fj; f. 1985; aims to develop the sugar industry and protect the interests of registered growers; CEO JAGANNATH SAMI; Gen. Man. BALA DASS; Chair. RUSIATE MUSUDROKA.

Sugar Commission of Fiji: POB 5993, Lautoka; tel. 6664866; fax 6664051; e-mail scof@is.com.fj; Chair. GERALD BARRACK.

EMPLOYERS' ORGANIZATIONS

Fiji Employers' Federation: 42 Gorrie St, POB 575, Suva; tel. 3313188; fax 3302183; e-mail employer@fef.com.fj; represents 230 major employers; Pres. HAFIZ U. KHAN; CEO KENNETH A. J. ROBERTS.

Fiji Manufacturers' Association: POB 1308, Suva; tel. 3318811; fax 3318811; e-mail fma@connect.com.fj; internet www.fijimanufacturers.com; f. 1971; CEO DESMOND WHITESIDE; 68 mems.

Local Inter-Island Shipowners' Association: POB 152, Suva; fax 3303389; e-mail consortship@connect.com.fj; Pres. GEORGE PATTERSON; Sec. LEO B. SMITH.

Textile, Clothing and Footwear Council: POB 10015, Nabua; tel. 3384777; fax 3370446; Sec. R. DUNSTAN.

UTILITIES

Electricity

Fiji Electricity Authority (FEA): PMB, Suva; tel. 3311133; fax 3311882; e-mail ceo@fea.com.fj; f. 1966; govt-owned; responsible for the generation, transmission and distribution of electricity throughout Fiji; CEO ROKOSERU NABALARUA.

Water

Water and Sewerage Section: Public Works Dept, Ministry of Works and Energy, Nasilivata House, Kings Rd, PMB, Samabula; tel. 3384111; fax 3383013; e-mail rsshandil@fijiwater.gov.fj; Dir RAM SUMER SHANDIL.

TRADE UNIONS

Fiji Trades Union Congress (FTUC): 32 Des Voeux Rd, POB 1418, Suva; tel. 3315377; fax 3300306; e-mail ftucl@is.com.fj; f. 1951; affiliated to ICFTU and ICFTU—APRO; 35 affiliated unions; more than 42,000 mems; Pres. DANIEL URAI; Gen. Sec. FELIX ANTHONY.

Principal affiliated unions:

Association of USP Staff: POB 1168, Suva; tel. 3313900; fax 3301305; f. 1977; Pres. GANESH CHAND; Sec. D. R. RAO.

Federated Airline Staff Association: Nadi Airport, POB 9259, Nadi; tel. 6722877; fax 6720068; e-mail fasa@ats.com.fj; Sec. RAJESH SHARMA.

Fiji Aviation Workers' Association: FTUC Complex, 32 Des Voeux Rd, POB 5351, Raiwaqa; tel. 3303184; fax 3311805; Pres. VALENTINE SIMPSON; Gen. Sec. ATTAR SINGH.

Fiji Bank and Finance Sector Employees' Union: 101 Gordon St, POB 853, Suva; tel. 3301827; fax 3301956; e-mail fbeu@connect.com.fj; Nat. Sec. DIWAN C. SHANKAR.

Fiji Electricity and Allied Workers Union: POB 1390, Lautoka; tel. 6666353; e-mail feawu@is.com.fj; Pres. LEONE SAKETA; Sec. J. A. PAUL.

Fiji Garment, Textile and Allied Workers' Union: c/o FTUC, Raiwaqa; f. 1992.

Fiji Nursing Association: POB 1364, Suva; tel. 3305855; e-mail fna@connect.com.fj; Gen. Sec. KUINI LUTUA.

Fiji Public Service Association: 298 Waimanu Rd, POB 1405, Suva; tel. 3311922; fax 3301099; e-mail fpsags@connect.com.fj; f. 1943; 4,000 mems; Pres. REIJIELI NAVUMA; Gen. Sec. RAJESHWAR SINGH.

Fiji Sugar and General Workers' Union: 84 Naviti St, POB 330, Lautoka; tel. 6660746; fax 664888; 25,000 mems; Pres. SHIU LINGAM; Gen. Sec. FELIX ANTHONY.

Fiji Teachers' Union: 1–3 Berry Rd, Govt Bldgs, POB 2203, Suva; tel. 3314099; fax 3305962; e-mail ftu@is.com.fj; f. 1930; 3,200 mems; Pres. BALRAM; Gen. Sec. AGNI DEO SINGH.

Fijian Teachers Association: POB 14464, Suva; tel. 3315099; fax 3304978; e-mail fta@connect.com.fj; Pres. TEVITA KOROI; Gen. Sec. MAIKA NAMUDU.

Insurance Officers' Association: POB 71, Suva; tel. 3313488; Pres. JAGDISH KHATRI; Sec. DAVID LEE.

Mineworkers' Union of Fiji: POB 876, Tavua; f. 1986; Pres. HENNESY PETERS; Sec. KAVEKINI NAVUSO.

National Farmers' Union: POB 522, Labasa; tel. 8811838; 10,000 mems (sugar-cane farmers); Pres. DEWAN CHAND; Gen. Sec. M. P. CHAUDHRY; CEO MOHAMMED LATIF SUBEDAR.

National Union of Factory and Commercial Workers: POB 989, Suva; tel. 3311155; 3,800 mems; Pres. CAMA TUILEVEUKA; Gen. Sec. JAMES R. RAMAN.

National Union of Hotel and Catering Employees: Nadi Airport, POB 9426, Nadi; tel. 670906; fax 6700181; Pres. EMOSI DAWAI; Sec. TIMOA NAIVAHIWAQA.

Public Employees' Union: POB 781, Suva; tel. 3304501; 6,752 mems; Pres. SEMI TIKOICINA; Gen. Sec. FILIMONE BANUVE.

Transport and Oil Workers' Union: POB 903, Suva; tel. 3302534; f. 1988 following merger of Oil and Allied Workers' Union and Transport Workers' Union; Pres. J. BOLA; Sec. MICHAEL COLUMBUS.

There are several independent trade unions, including Fiji Registered Ports Workers' Union (f. 1947; Pres. JIOJI TAHOLOSALE).

Transport

RAILWAYS

Fiji Sugar Corporation Railway: Rarawai Mill, POB 155, Ba; tel. 6674044; fax 670505; for use in cane-harvesting season, May–Dec.; 595 km of permanent track and 225 km of temporary track (gauge of 600 mm), serving cane-growing areas at Ba, Lautoka and Penang on Viti Levu and Labasa on Vanua Levu; Gen. Man. ADURU KUVA.

ROADS

At the end of 1996 there were some 3,440 km of roads in Fiji, of which 49.2% were paved. A 500-km highway circles the main island of Viti Levu.

SHIPPING

There are ports of call at Suva, Lautoka, Levuka and Savusavu. The main port, Suva, handles more than 800 ships a year, including large passenger liners. Lautoka handles more than 300 vessels and liners and Levuka, the former capital of Fiji, mainly handles commercial fishing vessels. In 1996 a feasibility study into the possible establishment of a free port at Suva was commissioned. In May 1997 the Government approved 14 new ports of entry in the northern, western and central eastern districts of Fiji.

Maritime and Ports Authority of Fiji (MPAF): Administration Bldg, Princes Wharf, POB 780, Suva; tel. 3312700; fax 3300064; corporatized in 1998; Chair. DANIEL ELISHA; Port Master Capt. GEORGE MACOMBER.

Ports Terminals Ltd: POB S13, Suva; tel. 3304725; fax 3304769; e-mail herbert@suv.ptl.com.fj; f. 1998; stevedore, pilotage, storage and warehousing; CEO H. HAZELMAN; Port Manager E. KURUSIGA.

Burns Philp Shipping (Fiji) Ltd: Rodwell Rd, POB 15832, Suva; tel. 3315444; fax 3302754; e-mail info@pacshipfiji.com.fj; shipping agents, customs agents and international forwarding agents, crew handling; Gen. Man. DANNY REES.

Consort Shipping Line Ltd: Muaiwalu Complex, Rona St, Walubay, POB 152, Suva; tel. 3313344; fax 3303389; CEO HECTOR SMITH; Man. Dir JUSTIN SMIT.

Fiji Maritime Services Ltd: c/o Fiji Ports Workers and Seafarers Union, 36 Edinburgh Drive, Suva; f. 1989 by PAF and the Ports Workers' Union; services between Lautoka and Vanua Levu ports.

Inter-Ports Shipping Corpn Ltd: 25 Eliza St, Walu Bay; POB 152, Suva; tel. 3313638; f. 1984; Man. Dir JUSTIN SMITH.

Transcargo Express Fiji Ltd: POB 936, Suva; f. 1974; Man. Dir LEO B. SMITH.

Wong's Shipping Co Ltd: Suite 647, Epworth House, Nina St, POB 1269, Suva; tel. 3311867.

CIVIL AVIATION

There is an international airport at Nadi (about 210 km from Suva), a smaller international airport at Nausori (Suva) and 15 other airfields. Nadi is an important transit airport in the Pacific and in 1990 direct flights to Japan also began.

Airports Fiji Ltd: Nadi International Airport, Nadi; tel. 6725777; fax 6725 161; e-mail info@afl.com.fj; Chair. VILIAME LEQA; CEO Ratu SAKIUSA TUISOLIA.

Air Fiji Ltd: 219 Victoria Parade, POB 1259, Suva; tel. 3314666; fax 3300771; internet www.airfiji.net; operates 65 scheduled services daily to 15 domestic destinations; daily service to Tonga and Tuvalu and direct flights to Auckland and Sydney commenced in 1999; charter operations, aerial photography and surveillance also conducted; partly owned by the Fijian Govt, which was expected to sell a majority of its shares in 2001; Chair. DOUG HAZARD; CEO KEN MACDONALD.

Air Pacific Ltd: Air Pacific Centre, POB 9266, Nadi International Airport, Nadi; tel. 6720777; fax 6720512; internet www.airpacific .com; f. 1951 as Fiji Airways, name changed in 1971; domestic and international services from Nausori Airport (serving Suva) to Nadi and international services to Tonga, Solomon Islands, Cook Islands, Vanuatu, Samoa, Japan, Australia, New Zealand and the USA; 51% govt-owned, 46.05% owned by Qantas (Australia); Chair. GERALD BARRACK; Man. Dir MICHAEL MCQUAY; CEO JOHN CAMPBELL.

Fijian Airways International: POB 10138, Nadi International Airport, Nadi; tel. 6724702; fax 6724654; f. 1997; service to London via Singapore and Mumbai (India) planned; Chair. NEIL UNDERHILL; CEO ALAN LINDREA.

Hibiscus Air Ltd: Nadi International Airport, Nadi; domestic airline operating charter and non-scheduled flights around Fiji.

Sunflower Airlines Ltd: POB 9452, Nadi International Airport, Nadi; tel. 6723555; fax 6720085; e-mail sun@is.com.fj; internet www .fiji.to; f. 1980; scheduled flights to domestic destinations, also charter services; Man. Dir DON IAN COLLINGWOOD.

Vanua Air Charters: Labasa; f. 1993; provides domestic charter and freight services; Propr CHARAN SINGH.

Tourism

Scenery, climate, fishing and diving attract visitors to Fiji, where tourism is an important industry. The number of foreign tourist arrivals increased from 348,014 in 2001 (excluding cruise-ship passengers who numbered 6,858 in 2001) to 397,859 in 2002 and to an estimated 430,800 in 2003. In 2002 some 31.1% of visitors came from Australia, 17.2% from New Zealand, 14.8% from the USA, 10.9% from the United Kingdom and 6.6% from Japan. A total of 5,542 rooms in 187 hotels were available in 2001. Receipts from tourism increased from $F495.5m. in 2001 to an estimated $F615.4m. in 2003. The South Pacific Tourism Organization (formerly the Tourism Council of The South Pacific) is based in Suva. In 1998 the Government announced its intention further to develop the tourist industry in Fiji through the establishment of the Fiji Tourism Development Plan: 1998–2005. In April 1999 construction began on a new luxury resort at Korotoga, situated half-way between Suva and Nadi. The industry was severely affected by the coup of May 2000. However, tourism expanded significantly during 2002–03 and was expected to contribute substantially to high economic growth rates in the following years.

Fiji Hotel Association (FHA): 42 Gorrie St, GPOB 13560, Suva; tel. 3302980; fax 3300331; e-mail fha@connect.com.fj; represents 85 hotels; Pres. DIXON SEETO; Chief Exec. OLIVIA PARETI.

Fiji Visitors' Bureau: POB 92, Suva; tel. 3302433; fax 3300986; e-mail infodesk@fijifvb.gov.fj; internet www.bulafiji.com; f. 1923; Chair. SITIVENI WELEILAKEBA; Chief Exec. VILIAME GAVOKA; Dir of Tourism ERONI LUVENIYALI.

FINLAND

Introductory Survey

Location, Climate, Language, Religion, Flag, Capital

The Republic of Finland lies in northern Europe, bordered to the far north by Norway and to the north-west by Sweden. Russia adjoins the whole of the eastern frontier. Finland's western and southern shores are washed by the Baltic Sea. The climate varies sharply, with warm summers and cold winters. The mean annual temperature is 5°C (41°F) in Helsinki and –0.4°C (31°F) in the far north. There are two official languages: more than 93% of the population speak Finnish and 6% speak Swedish. There is a small Sámi (Lapp) population in the north. Almost all of the inhabitants profess Christianity, and about 85% belong to the Evangelical Lutheran Church. The national flag (proportions 11 by 18) displays an azure blue cross (the upright to the left of centre) on a white background. The state flag has, at the centre of the cross, the national coat of arms (a yellow-edged red shield containing a golden lion and nine white roses). The capital is Helsinki.

Recent History

Finland formed part of the Kingdom of Sweden until 1809, when it became an autonomous Grand Duchy under the Russian Empire. During the Russian revolution of 1917 the territory proclaimed its independence. Following a brief civil war, a democratic Constitution was adopted in 1919. The Soviet regime that came to power in Russia attempted to regain control of Finland but acknowledged the country's independence in 1920.

Demands by the USSR for military bases in Finland and for the cession of part of the Karelian isthmus, in south-eastern Finland, were rejected by the Finnish Government in November 1939. As a result, the USSR attacked Finland, and the two countries fought the 'Winter War', a fiercely contested conflict lasting 15 weeks, before Finnish forces were defeated. Following its surrender, Finland ceded an area of 41,880 sq km (16,170 sq miles) to the USSR in March 1940. In the hope of recovering the lost territory, Finland joined Nazi Germany in attacking the USSR in 1941. However, a separate armistice between Finland and the USSR was concluded in 1944.

In accordance with a peace treaty signed in February 1947, Finland agreed to the transfer of about 12% of its pre-war territory (including the Karelian isthmus and the Petsamo area on the Arctic coast) to the USSR, and to the payment of reparations, which totalled about US $570m. when completed in 1952. Meanwhile, in April 1948 Finland and the USSR signed the Finno-Soviet Treaty of Friendship, Co-operation and Mutual Assistance (the YYA treaty), which was extended for periods of 20 years in 1955, 1970 and again in 1983. A major requirement of the treaty was that Finland repel any attack made on the USSR by Germany, or its allies, through Finnish territory. (The treaty was replaced by a non-military agreement in 1992, see below.)

Since independence in 1917, the politics of Finland have been characterized by coalition governments (including numerous minority coalitions) and the development of consensus between parties. The Social Democratic Party (Sosialidemokraattinen Puolue, SDP) and the Centre Party (Keskusta—Kesk) have usually been the dominant participants in government. The conservative opposition gained significant support at a general election in March 1979, following several years of economic crises. A new centre-left coalition Government was formed in May, however, by Dr Mauno Koivisto, a Social Democratic economist and former Prime Minister. This four-party Government, comprising Kesk, the SDP, the Swedish People's Party (Svenska Folkpartiet, SFP) and the Finnish People's Democratic League (Suomen Kansan Demokraattinen Liitto, SKDL—an electoral alliance, which included the communists), continued to pursue deflationary economic policies, although there were disagreements within the Cabinet (Valtioneuvosto) in 1981, over social welfare policy and budgetary matters.

Dr Urho Kekkonen, who had been President since 1956, resigned in October 1981. Dr Koivisto was elected President in January 1982. He was succeeded as head of the coalition by a former Prime Minister, Kalevi Sorsa, a Social Democrat. Towards the end of 1982 the SKDL refused to support austerity measures or an increase in defence spending. This led to the reformation of the coalition in December, without the SKDL, until the general election of March 1983.

At this election the SDP won 57 of the 200 seats in the Parliament (Eduskunta), compared with 52 in the 1979 election; while the conservative opposition National Coalition Party (Kansallinen Kokoomus—Kok) lost three seats. In May Sorsa formed another centre-left coalition, comprising the SDP, the SFP, Kesk and the Finnish Rural Party (Suomen Maaseudun Puolue, SMP): the coalition parties held a total of 122 parliamentary seats.

At a general election held in March 1987, the combined non-socialist parties gained a majority in the Eduskunta for the first time since the election of 1945. Although the SDP remained the largest single party, losing one seat and retaining 56, the system of modified proportional representation enabled Kok to gain an additional nine seats, winning a total of 53, while increasing its share of the votes cast by only 1%. President Koivisto eventually invited Harri Holkeri, a former Chairman of Kok, to form a coalition Government comprising Kok, the SDP, the SFP and the SMP, thus avoiding a polarization of the political parties within the Eduskunta. The four parties controlled 131 of the 200 seats. Holkeri became the first conservative Prime Minister since 1946, and Kesk joined the opposition for the first appreciable length of time since independence.

In February 1988 Koivisto retained office after the first presidential election by direct popular vote (in accordance with constitutional changes adopted in the previous year), following his campaign for a reduction in presidential power. He did not win the required absolute majority, however, and an electoral college was convened. Koivisto was re-elected after an endorsement by the Prime Minister, Holkeri, who had also contested the presidency and who had received the third highest number of direct votes (behind Paavo Väyrynen, the leader of Kesk).

At a general election held in March 1991, Kesk obtained 55 of the 200 seats in the Eduskunta, the SDP gained 48 seats, and Kok 40 seats. In April a coalition Government, comprising Kesk, Kok, the SFP and the Finnish Christian Union (Suomen Kristillinen Liitto, SKL), took office. The new coalition constituted the country's first wholly non-socialist Government for 25 years. The Chairman of Kesk, Esko Aho, was appointed Prime Minister. In March 1993 President Koivisto announced that he would not present himself as a candidate for a third term in the forthcoming presidential election. In the first stage of the election, which took place in January 1994, the two most successful candidates were Martti Ahtisaari (the SDP candidate and a senior United Nations official), with 25.9% of the votes cast, and Elisabeth Rehn (the SFP candidate and Minister of Defence), with 22%. The Kesk candidate (Paavo Väyrynen) obtained 19.5% of the votes cast, and the Kok candidate 15.2%. Both of the leading candidates were firm supporters of Finland's application for membership of the European Union (EU, see p. 217), as the European Community (EC) had been restyled in late 1993. In accordance with constitutional changes adopted since the previous election (stipulating that, if no candidate gained more than 50% of the votes cast, the electorate should choose between the two candidates with the most votes), a second stage of the election took place in February 1994. It was won by Ahtisaari (with 53.9% of the votes cast), who took office in March.

At a general election held in March 1995, the SDP obtained 63 of the 200 seats in the Eduskunta, Kesk secured 44 seats, Kok 39 seats, and the Vasemmistoliitto (Left Alliance), formed in 1990 by a merger of the communist parties and the SKDL, 22 seats. A new coalition Government was formed in April, comprising the SDP, Kok, the SFP, the Vasemmistoliitto and the Vihreä Liitto (VL—Green League). Paavo Lipponen, the leader of the SDP, replaced Aho as Prime Minister, and Sauli Niinistö, the Chairman of Kok, was appointed Deputy Prime Minister.

Following a general election held in March 1999, the SDP remained the largest party in the Eduskunta, gaining 51 of the 200 seats. Kesk won 48 seats and Kok 46 in an election that was characterized by the second lowest rate of voter participation—

68%—since 1945. In April the five parties of the outgoing Government—the SDP, Kok, the SFP, the Vasemmistoliitto and the VL—agreed to form a new coalition. The terms of the new coalition agreement stipulated that the SDP leader, Paavo Lipponen, should remain in office as Prime Minister, while the leader of Kok, Sauli Niinistö, was reappointed as Minister of Finance. The remaining portfolios of the Cabinet were redistributed among the coalition partners. Another element of the coalition agreement was that there should be no increase (in real terms) in public expenditure during the term in office of the new legislature.

Presidential elections were held in January and February 2000, at which Ahtisaari did not seek re-election, following his failure to secure the nomination of the SDP. In mid-January seven candidates contested the first round of the ballot, which was won by Tarja Halonen (the SDP candidate and Minister of Foreign Affairs), who received 40% of the votes cast; the second largest share of the vote (34.4%) was obtained by Esko Aho (the Kesk candidate). As Halonen had failed to win 50% of the vote, a second round of voting was held on 6 February, contested by Halonen and Aho. This second stage of the election was won by Halonen (with 51.6% of the votes cast), who took office as the first female President of Finland on 1 March. Following the conclusion of the elections, a minor reorganization of the Cabinet was effected, in which Halonen was replaced as Minister of Foreign Affairs by Erkki Tuomioja, the former Minister of Trade and Industry.

A new Constitution entered into force on 1 March 2000, under the provisions of which the executive power of the President was significantly reduced while the real authority of the Eduskunta was increased, with the power of decision-making being divided more equally between the Eduskunta, the Cabinet and the President. According to the 1919 Constitution, the President had appointed the Prime Minister and the other ministers; however, under the new Constitution, the Eduskunta elected the Prime Minister (who was then officially appointed by the President) and the other government ministers were appointed by the President on the basis of nominations by the Prime Minister. In addition, according to new constitutional provisions, the President was to co-operate more closely with the Cabinet with regard to issues of foreign policy.

Following his defeat in the presidential election, the Chairman of the opposition Kesk, Aho, took leave from domestic politics for one year from August 2000 to lecture at Harvard University in the USA. His decision was believed to reflect the perceived stability of the coalition, which, despite its disparate composition, seemed likely to complete its full four-year term in government. Anneli Jäätteenmäki, a former Minister of Justice, was elected to replace Aho during his sabbatical. At municipal elections that were held on 22 October 2000, however, the two principal parties in the coalition (the SDP and Kok) suffered losses, while Kesk, under the leadership of Jäätteenmäki, secured the largest gains, winning 23.8% of the votes cast to become the largest municipal party. Voter participation in the local elections was only 55.8% of the electorate (compared with 61.3% in 1996). Popular support for Jäätteenmäki's leadership of Kesk prompted Aho's resignation in mid-2002 and the election of Jäätteenmäki as Chairperson.

In November 2000 the stability of the coalition Government was threatened by a controversial proposal by a Finnish electricity company to build a fifth nuclear reactor in Finland, the first such proposal in western Europe since the mid-1980s. The Government was divided over the issue; the SDP Minister of Trade and Industry, Sinikka Mönkäre, was in favour of the proposal, while the VL was strongly opposed to nuclear expansion and threatened to leave the coalition should the proposal be accepted. In January 2002 the construction of the new reactor was approved by the Cabinet, despite the opposition of seven ministers, led by the Chairman of the VL and Minister of Health and Social Services, Osmo Soininvaara. The Eduskunta approved the proposal in May, by 107 votes to 92, prompting the resignation of the VL from the coalition Government; the coalition retained a majority in the Eduskunta, however, with 130 seats.

In November 2002 the opposition proposed a motion of 'no confidence' in the Government over its role in the seriously unprofitable investments of the telecommunications company Sonera. The latter, which was 53% owned by the Government, had invested €8,400m. in a German third-generation mobile telephone licence in 2000; in July 2002 the company had announced its intention to write off a debt of €4,300m. A government inquiry into the affair, which was launched in August, published its findings in October, exonerating the Prime Minister and the Cabinet from any responsibility for the corporate error. The Government survived the motion of 'no confidence' by 106 votes to 64.

A general election was held on 16 March 2003; 69.6% of the electorate participated in the poll. The opposition Kesk, which had campaigned on a platform of improving public health care, promoting employment by lowering social contributions and income taxes for low-paid jobs, and relaxing legislation for small businesses, won the largest representation in the new Eduskunta, with 24.7% of the votes cast, securing 55 seats. The SDP secured 24.5% of the votes cast and 53 seats, an increase of two seats compared with the last election. Although the SDP made gains, the three other members of the former government coalition lost seats, with Kok suffering the worst reverse, with the loss of six seats (winning 18.5% of the votes and 40 seats). Lipponen's coalition tendered its resignation to the President, but continued as a caretaker administration pending the formation of a new government. The Eduskunta met at the end of March and named Jäätteenmäki as its Speaker. Under the new Constitution the party with the largest representation was to lead negotiations regarding the formation of a coalition government. Accordingly, in early April Kesk formed a coalition Government with the SDP and the SFP (which had obtained 4.6% of the votes in the election and, thus, 8 seats) with Jäätteenmäki as Prime Minister (her role as Speaker of the Eduskunta was assumed by Paavo Lipponen). Jäätteenmäki was the country's first female Prime Minister, and, with her appointment, Finland became the only country in Europe with women simultaneously holding the posts of Prime Minister and President.

Jäätteenmäki's premiership, however, was extremely short-lived. On 18 June 2003, just 63 days after her inauguration, she resigned following allegations that she had improperly used classified foreign ministry information to discredit the outgoing Prime Minister, Paavo Lipponen, and secure victory for Kesk in the general election. The leaked documents, one of which recorded exchanges between Lipponen and the US President, George W. Bush, in December 2002, were reportedly used by Jäätteenmäki to portray Lipponen as being overly supportive of US policy regarding Iraq; the majority of Finns were opposed to the US-led military action launched in Iraq in March 2003 to remove the regime of Saddam Hussain. Jäätteenmäki's subsequent claims made to the Eduskunta that the documents were unsolicited were contradicted by the presidential aide responsible for divulging their contents. The Deputy Chairman of Kesk, Matti Vanhanen, who had been assigned the post of Minister of Defence in the new Government, was appointed to replace Jäätteenmäki as Prime Minister. Jäätteenmäki, whilst continuing to reject allegations of any wrongdoing on her part, also stood down from her position as Chairperson of Kesk; Vanhanen was elected to replace her at a special party convention held on 4 October. Jäätteenmäki was subsequently questioned by police officials who were investigating the allegations, and in December was charged with inciting or assisting the former presidential aide publicly to divulge official secrets. Jäätteenmäki and the former aide, Martti Manninen (who was charged with violating official secrecy), stood trial in early March 2004; Jäätteenmäki was acquitted but Manninen was found guilty and fined 80 days' salary.

In November 2003 the Government announced that it would launch an investigation into claims that during the Second World War the Finnish authorities handed over nearly 3,000 Jews and communists to the Nazi regime in Germany rather than the officially acknowledged total of 27.

In April 2004 the Eduskunta approved, by 135 votes to 53, legislation limiting the employment rights of nationals from eight of the 10 countries due to accede to the EU on 1 May. The legislation required citizens of these countries (the Czech Republic, Estonia, Hungary, Latvia, Lithuania, Poland, Slovakia and Slovenia) to apply for work permits, which would be granted only if the position they sought could not be filled by a Finnish citizen. The restrictions were to remain in place for two years but could thereafter be renewed on an annual basis; citizens of the other two accession states, Cyprus and Malta, were exempt from the legislation.

In August 2004 the Prime Minister, Vanhanen, confirmed that as the Treaty establishing a Constitution for Europe commanded widespread popular support in Finland a referendum would not be necessary. The constitutional treaty, which aimed to facilitate the smooth functioning of the EU following its enlargement in May 2004, had been signed by the EU Heads of State or of Government in October 2004 but remained subject to ratification by a vote in the national legislature or by referendum in each of the 25 member states by October 2006. The Eduskunta was expected to ratify the constitutional treaty in late 2005 or early 2006.

A central topic of political discourse in 2004 was Finland's defence policy. The debate was partly prompted by the establishment of EU rapid deployment forces (see below) but was also focused on the compilation of the latest Government Security and Defence Policy report, determining Finland's future security strategies. The report, which was approved by the Government and the President, confirmed that Finland's defence would continue to be based on the maintenance and development of a credible defence capability as a militarily neutral and non-aligned country but also retained as a 'possibility' the option of a future application for membership of NATO (see p. 301). The report was submitted to the Eduskunta for discussion in late 2004. The opposition Kok criticized the report, arguing that the EU's intensifying co-operation on defence, notably the security guarantees contained in the constitutional treaty, meant that Finland was effectively militarily aligned. Despite overwhelming support in the Eduskunta for the security policy, the leader of Kok, Jyrki Katainen, demanded an unprecedented parliamentary vote to confirm that Finland could no longer be considered a non-aligned country. The Government defeated the motion by a comfortable margin in December 2004, with the Eduskunta voting to remain non-aligned. The timetable of Finland's accession to the Ottawa Convention, prohibiting anti-personnel landmines, was also agreed in December; Finland would sign the convention in 2012 and destroy its landmines by 2016.

The Government announced its decision in October and November 2004 to contribute to two battle groups as part of the EU rapid deployment force; the first with Sweden and possibly Norway as partners (although Norway was not a member of the EU) and the second with Germany and the Netherlands. Participation in the battle groups, which were to be deployed to international crisis areas from 2007, raised the issue of the potential reform of the Finnish Peacekeeping Act to permit Finnish contributions to military operations authorized by the EU alone, rather than the present requirement for authorization by the UN or the Organization for Security and Co-operation in Europe (see p. 314).

Local elections were held in October 2004 at which the SDP won 24.1% of the votes cast, compared with 23.0% in the previous elections, making it the largest party at local level, while Kesk's share of the vote declined from 23.8% to 22.8%; the participation rate at the elections was relatively high at 58.6% of the electorate. Of the main opposition parties, Kok increased its share of the votes from 20.8% to 21.8% of the votes cast, while the Vasemmistoliitto won 9.6% and the VL 7.4%. In March 2005 Lipponen announced that he would resign as leader of the SDP at the party conference in June.

Finland has traditionally maintained a neutral stance in foreign affairs. It joined the United Nations and the Nordic Council (see p. 296) in 1955, but became a full member of the European Free Trade Association (EFTA, see p. 214) only in 1986. In 1989 Finland joined the Council of Europe (see p. 199). A free-trade agreement between Finland and the EC took effect in 1974. In March 1992 the Finnish Government formally applied to join the EC, despite opposition from farmers, who feared the impact of membership on Finland's strongly-protected agricultural sector. In a referendum on the question of Finland's accession to membership of the EU, which was held on 16 October 1994, 56.9% of the votes cast were in favour of membership, and in November the treaty of accession was ratified after protracted debate in the Eduskunta. Opponents of EU membership highlighted the benefits of Finland's traditional policy of neutrality, particularly with regard to Russian national security considerations, and warned that the country would now be increasingly forced to identify with Western security policy. The Government declared, however, that Finland's neutral stance would not be compromised either by joining the EU or by its stated intention to participate in NATO's 'Partnership for Peace' programme, and announced that it would not seek full membership of NATO or Western European Union (WEU, see p. 352). Finland left EFTA and joined the EU, as scheduled, on 1 January 1995. Finland has proved its commitment to European integration, joining Economic and Monetary Union (EMU), which commenced on 1 January 1999.

In July 1999 Finland assumed the presidency of the EU for the first time. During its six-month incumbency the Government had intended to promote economic and cultural links in the so-called 'Northern Dimension'—the Nordic countries, the Baltic states and Russia. In the event, this agenda was superseded by the conflict over the Serbian region of Kosovo and Metohija in Yugoslavia (now Serbia and Montenegro), which led to Western military intervention from March. Finland was deemed to have distinguished itself through its diplomacy, in particular the role of the Finnish President, which was important in securing an end to the hostilities in Yugoslavia. Finland contributes 800 troops to the Kosovo Force (KFOR), an international NATO-led force responsible for establishing and maintaining security in Kosovo since 1999 and continues its commitment to peace-keeping in Bosnia and Herzegovina by contributing 200 troops to the EU Force (EUFOR), which assumed responsibility for operations there in December 2004.

Following the terrorist attacks of 11 September 2001 in the USA, Finland did not participate in the US-led retaliatory military action against the Taliban regime in Afghanistan. Finnish military personnel did, however, take part in the subsequent peace-keeping operation in Afghanistan as part of a wider UN-authorized multinational body (the International Security Assistance Force—ISAF) including NATO forces. Finland was opposed to military action against the regime of Saddam Hussein in Iraq in early 2003 without a UN Security Council resolution, but indicated that it would be prepared to take part in military action under UN auspices and in possible humanitarian and peace-keeping operations. In the event, Finland pledged US $5.1m. for reconstruction in Iraq but did not send any troops.

The pursuance of friendly relations with the USSR, and latterly Russia, has generally been regarded as a priority in Finnish foreign affairs. In October 1989 Mikhail Gorbachev became the first Soviet Head of State to visit Finland since 1975, and recognized Finland's neutral status. The 1948 Finno–Soviet Treaty of Friendship, Co-operation and Mutual Assistance, which bound Finland to a military defence alliance with the USSR and prevented the country from joining any international organization (including the EC) whose members posed a military threat to the USSR, was replaced in January 1992 by a 10-year agreement, signed by Finland and Russia, which involved no military commitment. The agreement was to be automatically renewed for five-year periods unless annulled by either signatory. The new treaty also included undertakings by the two countries not to use force against each other and to respect the inviolability of their common border and each other's territorial integrity. Amicable Finno–Russian relations continued in the early 2000s, with President Halonen and the Russian President, Vladimir Putin, meeting on a number of occasions.

In October 2004 President Halonen met the Japanese Prime Minister, Junichiro Koizumi. They agreed to work together towards UN reforms; in particular Halonen agreed to support Japan's bid for a permanent seat on the UN Security Council. In January and February 2005 Finland hosted peace negotiations between the Indonesian Government and separatist rebels from the Indonesian province of Aceh. A third round of negotiations were scheduled for April.

A joint Finnish-Norwegian survey of the two countries' border in Arctic Lapland concluded in January 2002 that the Inarijoki River, the deepest point of which is taken to mark the border, had changed its course. Consequently, an unnamed island in the middle of the river, which had previously been Norwegian, was found to be part of Finland. Norway accordingly transferred the island to Finland.

Government

Finland has a republican Constitution, under the provisions of which executive power is divided between the Eduskunta (Parliament), the Valtioneuvosto (Cabinet) and the President. The unicameral Eduskunta has 200 members, elected by universal adult suffrage for four years on the basis of proportional representation. The President is elected for six years by direct popular vote. Legislative power is exercised by the Eduskunta. The Eduskunta elects the Prime Minister, who is then appointed by the President. The other government ministers are appointed by the President on the basis of nominations by the Prime Minister. Finland is divided into 452 municipalities, which are guaranteed self-government and are entitled to levy taxes. The province of Ahvenanmaa (the Åland Islands) has rights of legislation in internal affairs.

Defence

In August 2004 the armed forces of Finland numbered 27,000 (of whom 18,500 were conscripts serving up to 12 months), comprising an army of 19,200 (14,800 conscripts), an air force of 2,800 (1,000 conscripts) and a navy of 5,000 (2,700 conscripts). There were also some 435,000 reserves (to be reduced to 340,000) and a 3,100-strong frontier guard (under the Ministry of the Interior). The proposed defence budget for 2004 was 2,066m. euros (equivalent to 5.6% of total proposed budgetary expenditure). Finland announced in October and November its participation in the creation of two European Union (EU) battle groups as their contribution to the EU's rapid reaction force; one with Sweden and perhaps Norway and the second with Germany and the Netherlands. Finland's total contribution would number 330 troops and the units were to be ready for international deployment to crisis areas from 2007.

Economic Affairs

In 2003, according to estimates by the World Bank, Finland's gross national income (GNI), measured at average 2001–03 prices, was US $160,625m., equivalent to $27,020 per head (or $27,100 per head on an international purchasing-power parity basis). During 1990–2003, it was estimated, the population increased at an average annual rate of 0.3%, while gross domestic product (GDP) per head increased, in real terms, by an average of 1.5% per year. Overall GDP increased, in real terms, at an average annual rate of 1.9% per year in 1990–2003; growth was 11.9% in 2003 and 3.7% in 2004.

Agriculture (including hunting, forestry and fishing) contributed an estimated 3.4% of GDP in 2003 and employed 5.1% of the working population in that year. Forestry is the most important branch of the sector, with products of the wood and paper industries providing about 20.7% of export earnings in 2003. Animal husbandry is the predominant form of farming. The major crops are barley, oats and sugar beet. During 1990–2002 agricultural GDP increased, in real terms, by an average of 0.7% per year; agricultural GDP declined by 4.9% in 2001 and increased by 2.1% in 2002.

Industry (including mining, manufacturing, construction and power) provided 30.4% of GDP in 2003 and employed 26.2% of the working population in that year. Industrial GDP increased, in real terms, by an average of 2.9% per year during 1990–2002; industrial GDP declined by 0.4% in 2001 and increased by 1.0% in 2002.

Mining and quarrying contributed 0.3% of GDP in 2003 and employed 0.2% of the working population in the same year. The GDP of the mining sector increased, in real terms, at an average rate of 3.4% per year during 1995–99; mining GDP declined by 17.8% in 1998, but increased by 18.0% in 1999. Gold is the major mineral export, and zinc ore, copper ore and lead ore are also mined in small quantities.

Manufacturing provided 22.6% of GDP in 2003, and in the same year employed 18.8% of the working population. The most important branches of manufacturing are the electronics industry (particularly mobile telephones), transport equipment, metal products and food and beverages. The GDP of the manufacturing sector increased, in real terms, at an average rate of 6.1% per year during 1995–2001; the sector's GDP increased by 12.4% in 2000 and declined by 0.5% in 2001.

Of total energy generated in 2001 30.6% was derived from nuclear energy, 23.5% from coal, 17.7% from hydroelectric power, 15.5% from natural gas and 0.9% from petroleum. In early 2005 there were four nuclear reactors in operation. Construction of a fifth nuclear plant, a 1,600-MW nuclear reactor in Olkiluoto in south-west Finland, was scheduled for completion in 2009 at an estimated cost of €3,000m. Imports of mineral fuels comprised 12.2% of the total cost of imports in 2003.

Services provided 66.2% of GDP in 2003 and engaged 68.7% of the employed labour force in the same year. In real terms, the combined GDP of the services sector increased at an average rate of 1.7% per year during 1990–2002; growth in the sector's GDP was recorded at 1.9% in 2001 and 1.8% in 2002.

In 2003 Finland recorded a visible trade surplus of US $12,646m., and there was a surplus of $6,829m. on the current account of the balance of payments. In 2003 the principal source of imports was Germany (providing 15.0% of total imports); other major sources were Russia (11.9%), Sweden (11.1%) and the United Kingdom (5.3%). Germany was also the principal market for exports in the same year (accounting for 11.8% of total exports); other major purchasers were Sweden (9.9%), the United Kingdom and the USA (both 8.1%). The

European Union (EU, see p. 217) accounted for 53.0% of exports and 55.0% of imports in 2003. The principal exports in that year were machinery and transport equipment (mainly electronic products, notably mobile telephones), basic manufactures (mainly paper, paperboard and manufactures) and chemicals and related products. The principal imports were machinery and transport equipment, basic manufactures, chemicals and related products, and mineral fuels and lubricants.

In 2003 Finland recorded an overall budget deficit of €484m. (equivalent to 0.3% of GDP). In 2002 Finland's gross public debt amounted to some €4,634m. The average annual rate of inflation was 1.4% during 1992–2003. Consumer prices increased by 1.6% in 2002 and by 0.9% in 2003. The rate of unemployment declined from 15.4% in 1995 to 8.8% in 2004.

Finland is a member of the Nordic Council (see p. 296) and the Organisation for Economic Co-operation and Development (see p. 307). In January 1995 it left the European Free Trade Association (see p. 214) and joined the EU.

Finland's economy has consistently achieved higher growth rates than the European average following a sharp recession at the beginning of the 1990s. At 3.7% in 2004 its GDP growth was the second fastest rate in the euro zone, after Greece. Finland's competitiveness stems from providing a favourable environment for large international companies, with highly skilled employees and transparent and predictable economic policy. However, its dependence on the narrow base of the high technology industry, particularly its reliance on telecommunications, notably the largest company in the economy, Nokia, leaves the Finnish economy exposed to global fluctuations in this sector. The significant forestry sector is also vulnerable to external market forces. Investment was a key issue for the Finnish economy: companies have been slow to invest in production equipment, apart from the electronics industry, and this was reflected in the modest export figures for 2004. The low levels of investment were due, at least in part, to the disappointingly low levels of turnover on the Helsinki Stock Exchange (apart from the electronics firm Nokia and the forest industry). However, owing to increased levels of investment, domestic consumption and foreign trade, the official growth forecast of 2.8% for 2005 was increased to 3.3% as the economy began to expand earlier than expected. The Government was committed to reforming the labour market to improve employment levels (unemployment remains consistently high at about 9%). One such measure was a pension reform programme, which was to be phased in from 2005 and was expected to increase employment by encouraging older workers to remain in the workforce and to lower the cost of pensions by reducing the currently generous pension entitlements. These measures, together with regular substantial budgetary surpluses, would serve to prepare for the impact of an ageing population on public pensions and health care. Finland's future development was also threatened by the accession to the EU of neighbouring Estonia in May 2004, where wages and corporate tax rates were far lower than in Finland. In response to this competition, Finland, where both taxes and wages were above the European average, cut corporate tax from 29% to 26% from January 2005 and was gradually to reduce income tax.

Education

Compulsory education was introduced in 1921. By the 1977/78 school year, the whole country had transferred to a new comprehensive education system. Tuition is free and the core curriculum is the same for all students. Compulsory attendance lasts for nine years, and is divided into a six-year lower stage, beginning at the age of seven, and a three-year upper stage (or lower secondary stage), beginning at the age of 13. After comprehensive school, the pupil may continue his or her studies, either at a general upper secondary school, or a vocational upper secondary school. The upper secondary school curriculum is designed for three years but may be completed in two or four years. Courses leading to basic vocational qualifications take three years to complete. The matriculation examination taken at the end of three years of general upper secondary school gives eligibility for higher education as do three-year vocational diplomas. Higher education is provided by 20 universities and 25 polytechnics. Of total proposed budgetary expenditure by the central Government in 2005, €6,147m. (equivalent to 16.3% of total proposed expenditure) was allocated to the Ministry of Education.

Public Holidays

2005: 1 January (New Year's Day), 6 January (Epiphany), 25 March (Good Friday), 28 March (Easter Monday), 1 May (May

Day), 5 May (Ascension Day), 15 May (Whitsun), 25 June (Midsummer Day), 5 November (All Saints' Day), 6 December (Independence Day), 24–26 December (Christmas).

2006: 1 January (New Year's Day), 6 January (Epiphany), 14 April (Good Friday), 17 April (Easter Monday), 1 May (May

Day), 25 May (Ascension Day), 4 June (Whitsun), 24 June (Midsummer Day), 4 November (All Saints' Day), 6 December (Independence Day), 24–26 December (Christmas).

Weights and Measures

The metric system is in force.

Statistical Survey

Source (unless otherwise specified): Statistics Finland, 00022 Helsinki; tel. (9) 17342220; fax (9) 17342279; e-mail kirjasto@tilastokeskus.fi; internet www .tilastokeskus.fi.

Note: Figures in this Survey include data for the autonomous Åland Islands.

Area and Population

AREA, POPULATION AND DENSITY

Area (sq km)	
Land	304,473
Inland water	33,672
Total	338,145*
Population (census results)	
31 December 1995	5,116,826
31 December 2000	
Males	2,529,341
Females	2,651,774
Total	5,181,115
Population (official estimate at 31 December)	
2002	5,206,295
2003	5,219,732
2004	5,236,118
Density (per sq km) at 31 December 2004	17.2†

* 130,559 sq miles.
† Land area only.

REGIONS
(estimated population at 31 December 2003)*

	Land area (sq km)†	Population	Density (per sq km)†
Uusimaa (Nyland)	6,366	1,338,180	210.2
Itä-Uusimaa (Östra Nyland) . .	2,747	91,689	33.4
Varsinais-Suomi (Egentliga Finland)	10,624	452,444	42.6
Satakunta	8,290	234,777	28.3
Kanta-Häme (Egentliga Tavastland)	5,204	166,648	32.0
Pirkanmaa (Birkaland) . .	12,272	457,317	37.3
Päijät-Häme (Päijänne-Tavastland)	5,133	198,434	38.7
Kymenlaakso (Kymmenedalen) .	5,106	185,662	36.4
Etelä-Karjala (Södra Karelen) .	5,618	136,301	24.3
Etelä-Savo (Södra Savolax) .	14,137	162,296	11.5
Pohjois-Savo (Norra Savolax) . .	16,808	251,356	15.0
Pohjois-Karjala (Norra Karelen) .	17,782	169,129	9.5
Keski-Suomi (Mellersta Finland) .	16,582	266,082	16.0
Etelä-Pohjanmaa (Södra Österbotten)	13,458	193,954	14.4
Pohjanmaa (Österbotten) . . .	7,675	173,111	22.6
Keski-Pohjanmaa (Mellersta Österbotten)	5,286	70,584	13.4
Pohjois-Pohjanmaa (Norra Österbotten)	35,290	371,931	10.5
Kainuu (Kajanaland)	21,567	86,573	4.0
Lappi (Lappland)	93,004	186,917	2.0
Ahvenanmaa (Åland)	1,527	26,347	17.3
Total	304,473	5,219,732	17.1

* According to the regional division of 1 January 2004.
† Excluding inland waters, totalling 33,672 sq km.

PRINCIPAL TOWNS
(estimated population at 31 December 2003)*

Helsinki (Helsingfors) (capital) . .	559,330	Kuopio	88,250
Espoo (Esbo) . . .	224,231	Jyväskylä . . .	82,409
Tampere (Tammerfors) . .	200,966	Pori (Björneborg) .	76,189
Vantaa (Vanda) . .	184,039	Lappeenranta (Villmanstrand) .	58,897
Turku (Åbo) . . .	175,059	Vaasa (Vasa) . .	56,953
Oulu (Uleåborg) . .	125,928	Kotka	54,618
Lahti	98,253	Joensuu	52,659

* According to the regional division of 1 January 2004.

BIRTHS, MARRIAGES AND DEATHS

	Registered live births*		Registered marriages†		Registered deaths*	
	Number	Rate (per 1,000)	Number	Rate (per 1,000)	Number	Rate (per 1,000)
1996 . .	60,723	11.8	24,464	4.8	49,167	9.6
1997 . .	59,329	11.5	23,444	4.6	49,108	9.6
1998 . .	57,108	11.1	24,023	4.7	49,262	9.6
1999 . .	57,574	11.1	24,271	4.7	49,345	9.6
2000 . .	56,742	11.0	26,150	5.1	49,339	9.5
2001 . .	56,189	10.8	24,830	4.8	48,550	9.4
2002 . .	55,555	10.7	26,969	5.2	49,418	9.5
2003 . .	56,630	10.9	25,815	5.0	48,996	9.4

* Including Finnish nationals temporarily outside the country.
† Data relate only to marriages in which the bride was domiciled in Finland.

Expectation of life (WHO estimates, years at birth): 78.2 (males 74.8; females 81.5) in 2002 (Source: WHO, *World Health Report*).

ECONOMICALLY ACTIVE POPULATION*
(annual averages, '000 persons aged 15 to 74 years)

	2001	2002	2003
Agriculture, forestry and fishing .	135	127	120
Mining and quarrying	3	5	5
Manufacturing	472	466	444
Electricity, gas and water . . .	22	20	20
Construction	145	148	151
Trade, restaurants and hotels . .	357	363	363
Transport, storage and communications	174	169	173
Finance, insurance, real estate and business services	301	308	313
Community, social and personal services	750	759	767
Activities not adequately defined .	7	7	8
Total employed	2,367	2,372	2,365
Unemployed	238	237	235
Total labour force	2,605	2,610	2,600

* Excluding persons on compulsory military service (21,000 in 2001; 20,000 in 2002; 20,000 in 2003).

Health and Welfare

KEY INDICATORS

Total fertility rate (children per woman, 2002)	1.7
Under-5 mortality rate (per 1,000 live births, 2003) . . .	5
HIV/AIDS (% of persons aged 15–49, 2003)	0.1
Physicians (per 1,000 head, 2001)	3.10
Hospital beds (per 1,000 head, 2000)	7.5
Health expenditure (2001): US $ per head (PPP) . . .	1,845
Health expenditure (2001): % of GDP	7.0
Health expenditure (2001): public (% of total)	75.6
Access to water (% of persons, 2002)	100
Access to sanitation (% of persons, 2002)	100
Human Development Index (2002): ranking	13
Human Development Index (2002): value	0.935

For sources and definitions, see explanatory note on p. vi.

Agriculture

PRINCIPAL CROPS

('000 metric tons; farms with arable land of 1 hectare or more)

	2001	2002	2003
Wheat	489	569	679
Barley	1,786	1,739	1,697
Rye	64	73	73
Oats	1,287	1,508	1,295
Mixed grain*	44	48	44
Potatoes	733	780	617
Rapeseed*	101	103	94
Sugar beet	1,105	1,066	892

* Source: FAO.

LIVESTOCK

('000 head at 1 May; farms with arable land of 1 hectare or more)

	2001	2002	2003
Horses*	58.6	59.1	60.2
Cattle	1,037.4	1,025.4	1,000.2
Sheep	96.0	95.9	98.4
Reindeer	186.0	200.0	197.0
Pigs†	1,260.8	1,315.0	1,374.9
Poultry	4,244.7	3,984.8	3,947.1

* Including horses not on farms.
† Including piggeries of dairies.

LIVESTOCK PRODUCTS

('000 metric tons)

	2001	2002	2003
Beef	89.6	90.6	95.7
Veal	0.2	0.1	0.1
Pig meat	173.7	184.2	193.2
Poultry meat	75.7	82.6	83.7
Cows' milk*	2,378.0	2,376.2	2,323.3
Butter†	61.0	60.6	58.4
Cheese‡	97.8	98.6	97.5
Hen eggs	56.5	54.7	56.2

* Millions of litres.
† Including amount of butter in vegetable oil mixture.
‡ Excluding curd.

Forestry

ROUNDWOOD REMOVALS

('000 cu m, excl. bark)

	2001	2002	2003
Sawlogs, veneer logs and logs for sleepers	23,359	23,835	24,577
Pulpwood	24,368	24,694	24,669
Fuel wood	4,483	4,482	4,533
Total	52,210	53,011	53,779

Source: FAO.

SAWNWOOD PRODUCTION

('000 cu m, incl. railway sleepers)

	2001	2002	2003
Coniferous (softwood)	12,670	13,280	13,645
Broadleaved (hardwood) . . .	100	110	100
Total	12,770	13,390	13,745

Source: FAO.

Fishing

('000 metric tons, live weight)

	2000	2001	2002
Capture	156.5	150.1	144.8
Roaches	5.4	5.5	5.5
Northern pike	10.4	10.4	10.5
European perch	13.4	13.4	13.5
Vendace	5.0	5.0	5.0
Atlantic herring	81.6	82.9	76.5
European sprat	23.2	15.9	17.4
Aquaculture	15.4	15.7	15.1
Rainbow trout	15.3	15.5	14.9
Total catch	171.9	165.8	159.9

Note: Figures exclude aquatic mammals, recorded by number rather than by weight. The catch of grey seals was 62 in 2000; 73 in 2001; 86 in 2002.

Source: FAO.

Mining

('000 metric tons, unless otherwise indicated)

	2000	2001	2002
Copper ore*†	14.4	13.7	14.4
Nickel ore (metric tons)* . . .	2,600	2,000	2,500†
Zinc ore*†	30.5	36.3	61.6
Chromium ore‡	630	575†	566
Cobalt (metric tons)†§ . . .	3,864	3,908	4,292
Mercury (metric tons)† . . .	76	71	51
Silver (metric tons)†§ . . .	25.4	24.0	29.4
Gold (kilograms)†§ . . .	4,951	5,552	4,666
Platinum (kilograms)†§ . . .	441	510	508
Phosphate rock (incl. apatite)∥ .	750	750	760
Peat: for fuel†	3,932	5,368	6,450
Peat: for horticulture† . . .	1,174	834	770

* Figures refer to the metal content of ores.
† Estimated production.
‡ Figures refer to the gross weight of chromite. The estimated chromic oxide content (in '000 metric tons) was: 235 in 2000; 210 in 2001; 205 in 2002.
§ Figures refer to production of metal and (for cobalt) powder and salts.
∥ Figures refer to gross weight. The phosphoric acid content (in '000 metric tons) was: 277 in 2000; 277 in 2001; 280 in 2002.

Source: US Geological Survey.

Industry

SELECTED PRODUCTS
('000 metric tons, unless otherwise indicated)

	2001	2002	2003*
Cellulose	6,481	7,503	7,421
Newsprint	1,480	1,189	946
Other paper, boards and			
cardboards	11,497	11,362	12,113
Plywoods and veneers ('000 cubic			
metres)	1,086	1,135	1,139
Cement	1,325	1,198	1,150
Pig iron and ferro-alloys . . .	2,852	2,829	3,091
Electricity (net, million kWh) . .	71,454	71,617	80,015
Sugar	110	161	136
Rolled steel products (metric tons)	3,857	3,975	4,090
Cigarettes (million)	3,999	4,130	n.a.

* Preliminary data.

Finance

CURRENCY AND EXCHANGE RATES

Monetary Units
100 cent = 1 euro (€).

Sterling and Dollar Equivalents (31 December 2004)
£1 sterling = 1.4180 euros;
US $1 = 0.7342 euros;
100 euros = £70.52 = $135.21.

Average Exchange Rate (euros per US $)
2002   1.0626
2003   0.8860
2004   0.8054

Note: The national currency was formerly the markka (Finnmark). From the introduction of the euro, with Finnish participation, on 1 January 1999, a fixed exchange rate of €1 = 5.94573 markkaa was in operation. Euro notes and coins were introduced on 1 January 2002. The euro and local currency circulated alongside each other until 28 February, after which the euro became the sole legal tender.

BUDGET
(€ million)*

Revenue	2003	2004†	2005‡
Taxes and other levies	30,263	30,343	31,573
Taxes on income and property .	12,439	12,894	12,997
Taxes on turnover	10,769	10,735	11,604
Excise duties	4,858	4,524	4,565
Other taxes	2,178	2,167	2,383
Other levies	19	23	24
Miscellaneous revenues . . .	3,920	4,281	4,570
Sub-total	34,183	34,624	36,143
Interest on investments and profits			
received	994	1,022	928
Loans receivable	1,236	1,419	540
Total	36,413	37,065	37,611

Expenditure	2003	2004†	2005‡
President of the Republic . . .	7	8	9
Parliament	111	101	97
Council of State	45	48	49
Ministry of Foreign Affairs . . .	709	766	822
Ministry of Justice	641	671	662
Ministry of the Interior	1,419	1,443	1,504
Ministry of Defence	2,006	2,073	2,137
Ministry of Finance	4,987	5,345	5,566
Ministry of Education	5,786	6,054	6,147
Ministry of Agriculture and			
Forestry	2,544	2,687	2,722
Ministry of Transport and			
Communications	1,755	1,778	1,761
Ministry of Trade and Industry .	914	964	972
Ministry of Social Affairs and			
Health	8,571	9,364	9,868
Ministry of Labour	2,092	2,305	2,164
Ministry of the Environment . .	657	676	683
Public debt	4,653	2,782	2,447
Total	36,897	37,065	37,611

* Figures refer to the General Budget only, excluding the operations of the Social Insurance Institution and of other social security funds with their own budgets.
† Projections.
‡ Proposals.

INTERNATIONAL RESERVES
(US $ million at 31 December)

	2001	2002	2003
Gold*	436.0	540.5	658.0
IMF special drawing rights . .	234.1	199.9	194.6
Reserve position in IMF . . .	551.7	648.3	775.8
Foreign exchange	7,197.6	8,436.8	9,544.5
Total	8,419.4	9,825.5	11,172.9

* Valued at market-related prices.

Source: IMF, *International Financial Statistics*.

MONEY SUPPLY
(€ million at 31 December)

	2001	2002	2003
Currency in circulation	2,687	6,258*	7,215*
Demand deposits at banking			
institutions	39,014	40,952	44,445

* Of which €3,446m. in 2002, and €3,918 in 2003, were put into circulation by the Bank of Finland.

Source: IMF, *International Financial Statistics*.

COST OF LIVING
(Consumer Price Index; base: 2000 = 100)

	2001	2002	2003
Food and non-alcoholic beverages .	104.4	107.4	108.1
Alcoholic beverages and tobacco .	101.8	103.6	104.7
Clothing and footwear	100.9	100.0	99.8
Housing, water, electricity, gas and			
other fuels	103.0	103.4	104.8
Furniture, household equipment .	102.4	103.9	104.4
Health	102.3	107.3	110.7
Transport	100.9	102.1	102.0
Communication	99.8	100.4	97.0
Recreation and culture	103.1	105.3	106.5
Education	103.3	106.6	113.0
Restaurants and hotels	102.3	104.7	107.7
Miscellaneous goods and services .	104.4	105.5	106.3
All items	102.6	104.2	105.1

NATIONAL ACCOUNTS

National Income and Product
(€ million at current prices)

	2001	2002	2003*
Compensation of employees . .	66,481	68,422	70,625
Operating surplus	30,736	32,467	31,078
Domestic factor incomes . .	97,217	100,889	101,703
Consumption of fixed capital .	22,348	22,585	23,037
Gross domestic product at factor cost	119,565	123,474	124,740
Indirect taxes	18,721	19,639	20,581
Less Subsidies	2,818	2,829	2,803
GDP in purchasers' values . .	135,468	140,284	142,518
Factor income received from abroad . . . . . } *Less* Factor income paid abroad . }	−853	−223	−545
Gross national product . .	134,615	140,061	141,973
Less Consumption of fixed capital	22,348	22,585	23,037
National income in market prices	112,267	117,476	118,936

* Provisional figures.

Expenditure on the Gross Domestic Product
(€ '000 million at current prices)

	2001	2002	2003
Government final consumption expenditure	28.39	30.30	31.81
Private final consumption expenditure	67.92	71.14	74.55
Increase in stocks	0.14	0.55	0.97
Gross fixed capital formation . .	27.73	26.58	25.90
Total domestic expenditure .	124.18	128.57	133.23
Exports of goods and services . .	54.07	54.12	53.05
Less Imports of goods and services	42.78	42.37	43.76
GDP in purchasers' values . .	135.47	140.32	142.52

Source: IMF, *International Financial Statistics.*

Gross Domestic Product by Economic Activity
(€ million at current prices)

	2001	2002	2003*
Agriculture, hunting, forestry and fishing	4,225	4,393	4,269
Mining and quarrying	308	329	373
Manufacturing	29,618	28,915	28,465
Electricity, gas and water . . .	2,214	2,475	2,850
Construction	6,829	6,598	6,703
Trade, restaurants and hotels . .	13,957	14,777	14,983
Transport, storage and communication	12,811	13,356	13,557
Finance, insurance and business services	12,863	12,528	11,742
Owner-occupied dwellings . . .	10,269	10,945	11,499
Public administration and welfare	21,099	22,255	23,113
Other community, social and personal services	6,991	8,211	8,533
Sub-total	121,184	124,782	126,087
Less Imputed bank service charge	3,078	2,757	2,787
GDP in basic values . . .	118,106	122,025	123,300
Commodity taxes	18,423	19,329	20,249
Less Commodity subsidies . . .	1,061	1,070	1,031
GDP in purchasers' values . .	135,468	140,284	142,518

* Provisional figures.

BALANCE OF PAYMENTS
(US $ million)

	2001	2002	2003
Exports of goods f.o.b.	42,980	44,856	52,516
Imports of goods f.o.b.	−30,321	−31,974	−39,870
Trade balance	12,659	12,882	12,646
Exports of services	5,832	6,490	7,829
Imports of services	−8,105	−8,009	−10,349
Balance on goods and services	10,386	11,363	10,190
Other income received . . .	8,568	8,657	9,985
Other income paid	−9,573	−9,259	−12,338
Balance on goods, services and income	9,381	10,761	7,837
Current transfers received . . .	1,562	1,732	2,002
Current transfers paid	−2,239	−2,344	−3,010
Current balance	8,704	10,148	6,829
Capital account (net)	83	89	99
Direct investment abroad . . .	−8,458	−7,801	2,583
Direct investment from abroad .	3,739	8,156	3,436
Portfolio investment assets . .	−11,594	−13,432	−10,922
Portfolio investment liabilities .	5,985	8,899	9,494
Financial derivatives liabilities .	38	−325	1,715
Other investment assets . . .	−10,117	−1,328	−15,734
Other investment liabilities . .	9,465	−2,773	−1,931
Net errors and omissions . . .	2,565	−1,747	3,921
Overall balance	410	−113	−508

Source: IMF, *International Financial Statistics.*

External Trade

PRINCIPAL COMMODITIES
(distribution by SITC, € million)

Imports c.i.f.	2001	2002	2003
Food and live animals . . .	1,587.1	1,678.6	1,747.1
Crude materials (inedible) except fuels	2,375.9	2,283.4	2,578.9
Metalliferous ores and metal scrap	1,021.5	930.6	1,212.3
Mineral fuels, lubricants, etc. .	4,153.7	4,045.7	4,480.8
Petroleum, petroleum products, etc.	3,008.1	2,978.4	3,145.5
Crude petroleum oils, etc. . .	2,163.0	2,269.2	2,241.9
Chemicals and related products	3,958.6	4,173.8	4,306.0
Basic manufactures	4,365.9	4,296.9	4,419.5
Iron and steel	1,118.5	1,075.8	1,141.5
Machinery and transport equipment	14,583.7	14,159.0	13,889.5
Non-electric machinery . . .	5,133.4	4,913.5	4,642.2
Electrical machinery, apparatus, etc.	6,395.7	6,063.4	5,697.1
Transport equipment	3,054.6	3,182.1	3,550.2
Road vehicles and parts* . .	2,405.9	2,814.5	3,189.8
Passenger motor cars (excl. buses)	1,076.2	1,362.1	1,823.7
Miscellaneous manufactured articles	3,731.2	3,801.3	3,825.5
Total (incl. others)	35,890.7	35,611.1	36,775.0

* Excluding tyres, engines and electrical parts.

Exports f.o.b.	2001	2002	2003
Crude materials (inedible) except fuels	3,024.1	3,126.6	3,080.0
Wood, lumber and cork	1,531.3	1,568.1	1,585.8
Shaped or simply worked wood	1,463.5	1,490.3	1,510.0
Sawn coniferous lumber . .	1,407.8	1,433.2	1,451.8
Pulp and waste paper . . .	874.0	927.3	951.2
Mineral fuels, lubricants, etc. .	1,504.9	1,606.9	1,824.9
Petroleum, petroleum products, etc.	1,452.1	1,524.9	1,570.4
Refined petroleum products . .	1,436.3	1,506.0	1,543.3
Chemicals and related products	3,045.1	3,308.3	3,325.9
Basic manufactures	14,853.4	14,610.6	14,547.6
Paper, paperboard and manufactures	8,954.7	8,573.8	8,029.3
Paper and paperboard . . .	8,297.4	8,075.5	7,572.8
Printing and writing paper in bulk	5,101.0	5,069.8	4,812.6
Iron and steel	1,920.8	2,022.7	2,593.7
Non-ferrous metals	1,187.6	1,151.3	1,119.5
Machinery and transport equipment	21,382.0	20,595.6	19,506.3
Non-electric machinery	6,455.4	6,237.6	5,961.4
Electrical machinery, apparatus, etc.	11,319.2	11,195.6	10,602.3
Transport equipment	3,607.5	3,162.4	2,942.6
Ships and boats	1,751.3	1,504.9	1,574.0
Miscellaneous manufactured articles	2,715.4	2,689.9	2,630.2
Total (incl. others)	47,800.4	47,245.2	46,378.0

PRINCIPAL TRADING PARTNERS
(€ million)*

Imports c.i.f.	2001	2002	2003
Belgium	826.4	876.4	872.3
China, People's Republic . . .	1,101.7	1,251.5	1,581.6
Denmark	1,302.4	1,539.1	1,541.2
Estonia	1,178.1	958.5	1,032.4
France	1,608.1	1,505.7	1,777.2
Germany	5,188.4	5,425.3	5,513.3
Italy	1,270.2	1,385.6	1,376.1
Japan	1,538.5	1,553.6	1,506.7
Netherlands	1,313.9	1,381.5	1,466.2
Norway	1,178.3	1,160.5	1,012.0
Russia	3,427.2	3,566.0	4,367.0
Spain	664.9	556.2	603.6
Sweden	3,671.1	4,051.5	4,063.7
United Kingdom	2,302.3	2,094.3	1,936.1
USA	2,453.0	2,339.6	1,710.6
Total (incl. others)	35,890.7	35,611.1	36,775.0

Exports f.o.b.	2001	2002	2003
Belgium	1,178.4	1,291.4	1,295.6
China, People's Republic . . .	1,258.9	1,215.4	1,283.2
Denmark	1,167.5	1,149.0	1,029.9
Estonia	1,058.4	1,230.5	1,137.6
France	2,202.4	2,178.3	1,731.9
Germany	2,903.1	5,621.3	5,491.2
Italy	1,741.1	1,617.5	1,845.0
Netherlands	1,870.2	2,179.0	2,168.8
Norway	1,211.9	1,133.3	1,117.9
Russia	2,806.1	3,128.3	3,476.6
Spain	1,195.8	1,222.0	1,296.9
Sweden	1,033.5	4,125.3	4,590.4
United Kingdom	4,596.9	4,563.4	3,740.4
USA	4,639.9	4,207.2	3,759.8
Total (incl. others)	47,800.4	47,245.2	46,378.0

* Imports by country of production; exports by country of consumption.

Transport

RAILWAYS
(traffic)

	2001	2002	2003
Passengers ('000 journeys) . . .	54,987	57,695	59,909
Passenger-km (million)	3,282	3,318	3,338
Freight carried ('000 metric tons)	41,678	41,679	43,503
Freight ton-km (million) . . .	9,857	9,664	10,047

ROAD TRAFFIC
(registered motor vehicles at 31 December)

	2001	2002	2003
Passenger cars	2,160,603	2,194,683	2,274,577
Buses and coaches	9,769	10,005	10,358
Lorries and vans	312,557	319,699	327,122
Motorcycles	102,811	116,021	129,670
Snowmobiles*	93,486	96,442	97,936

* Excluding Åland Islands.

SHIPPING

Merchant Fleet
(registered at 31 December)

	2001	2002	2003
Number of vessels	284	283	280
Total displacement ('000 grt) . .	1,595.4	1,545.2	1,452.1

Source: Lloyd's Register-Fairplay, *World Fleet Statistics*.

International Sea-borne Freight Traffic

	2001	2002	2003
Number of vessels entered . . .	29,246	30,065	30,037
Goods ('000 metric tons):			
loaded	39,638	41,478	41,563
unloaded	44,904	45,468	51,836

CANAL TRAFFIC

	2001	2002	2003
Vessels in transit*	41,411	42,116	43,000
Goods carried ('000 metric tons) .	4,926	4,665	4,509

* Excludes vessels on self-service lock canals.

CIVIL AVIATION
(traffic on scheduled services, '000)

	2001	2002	2003
Kilometres flown	108,000	116,000	123,000
Passenger-kilometres	13,211,000	13,396,000	14,008,000
Cargo ton-kilometres	179,180	219,964	258,178

Tourism

FOREIGN TOURIST ARRIVALS
(at accommodation establishments)

Country of residence	2001	2002	2003
Denmark	55,603	55,063	54,287
Estonia	54,519	51,796	54,577
France	67,345	73,536	81,065
Germany	233,351	247,143	256,049
Italy	65,484	67,663	72,500
Japan	82,317	74,173	69,063
Netherlands	82,078	104,260	110,847
Norway	110,231	110,291	101,478
Russia	204,459	215,159	194,388
Sweden	352,980	344,115	341,100
Switzerland	48,730	46,585	53,701
United Kingdom	161,457	152,022	167,817
USA	101,035	90,272	82,822
Total (incl. others)	1,999,298	2,042,540	2,047,444

Tourism receipts (US $ million): 1,441 in 2001; 1,573 in 2002; n.a. in 2003.

Source: World Tourism Organization.

Communications Media

	2001	2002	2003
Newspapers:			
number*	208	206	203
total circulation ('000 copies)	3,246	3,261	3,217
Other periodicals: number	5,158	5,017	5,042
Book production: titles	12,090	12,069	12,309
Telephones ('000 main lines in use)†	2,806.2	2,725.6	2,567.6
Mobile cellular telephones ('000 subscribers)†	4,175.6	4,516.8	4,747.1
Personal computers (estimates, '000 in use)†	2,200	2,300	n.a.
Internet users ('000 aged 15 years and over)†	2,432	2,654	2,786

* Comprising 54 dailies and 154 non-dailies in 2001; 54 dailies and 156 non-dailies in 2002; 53 dailies and 150 non-dailies in 2003.
† Source: International Telecommunication Union.

Radio receivers ('000 in use): 7,700 in 1997 (Source: UNESCO, *Statistical Yearbook*).

Television receivers ('000 in use): 3,580 in 2000 (Source: International Telecommunication Union).

Facsimile machines ('000 in use): 198 in 1997 (Source: UN, *Statistical Yearbook*).

Education

(2003)

	Institutions	Teachers†	Students
Comprehensive schools*	3,808	43,783	606,500
Senior secondary schools	440	7,480	127,900
Vocational and professional institutions	309	13,854	203,900
Polytechnics	31	5,844	140,800
Universities	20	7,728	168,800

* Comprising six-year primary stage and three-year lower secondary stage.
† 2002 figures.

Directory

The Constitution

The Constitution of Finland entered into force on 1 March 2000, amending the Constitution of July 1919. Its main provisions are summarized below:

FUNDAMENTAL PROVISIONS

Finland is a sovereign republic. The powers of the State are vested in the people, who are represented by the Eduskunta (Parliament). Legislative power is exercised by the Eduskunta, which also decides on state finances; governmental power is held by the President of the Republic and the Cabinet; and judicial power is exercised by independent courts of law. The basic rights and liberties of the individual are guaranteed in the Constitution.

PARLIAMENT

The unicameral Eduskunta comprises 200 representatives, who are elected for a term of four years by a direct, proportional and secret vote. For the parliamentary elections the country is divided, on the basis of the number of Finnish citizens, into at least 12 and at most 18 constituencies. In addition, the Åland Islands form their own constituency for the election of one representative. Registered political parties, and groups of persons who have the right to vote, are entitled to nominate candidates in parliamentary elections. The President of the Republic, in response to a proposal by the Prime Minister, may order that extraordinary parliamentary elections be held. The Eduskunta elects from among its members a Speaker and two Deputy Speakers for each parliamentary session. The proposal for the enactment of legislation is initiated in the Eduskunta either by the Government or through a motion submitted by a representative.

PRESIDENT

The President of the Republic is elected by a direct vote for a term of six years (with the same person restricted to a maximum of two consecutive terms in office). The President will be a native-born Finnish citizen. The candidate who receives more than one-half of the votes cast in the election will be elected President. If none of the candidates receives a majority of the votes cast, a further election will be held between the two candidates who have received the most votes. The right to nominate a candidate in the presidential election is held by any registered political party from which at least one representative was elected to the Eduskunta in the most recent elections, as well as by any group of 20,000 persons who have the right to vote. The President of the Republic makes decisions on the basis of proposals submitted by the Cabinet. The foreign policy of Finland is directed by the President of the Republic in co-operation with the Cabinet.

CABINET

The Cabinet comprises the Prime Minister and the necessary number of ministers. The Eduskunta elects the Prime Minister, who is thereafter appointed to the office by the President of the Republic. The President appoints the other ministers on the basis of nominations made by the Prime Minister.

JUDICIARY

The Supreme Court, the Courts of Appeal and the District Courts are the general courts of law. The Supreme Administrative Court and the regional Administrative Courts are the general courts of administrative law. Justice in civil, commercial and criminal matters in the final instance is administered by the Supreme Court, while justice in administrative matters in the final instance is administered by the Supreme Administrative Court. The High

Court of Impeachment deals with charges brought against a member of the Government, the Chancellor of Justice, the Parliamentary Ombudsman or a member of the supreme courts for unlawful conduct in office. Tenured judges are appointed by the President of the Republic.

ADMINISTRATION AND SELF-GOVERNMENT

In addition to the Government, the civil administration of the State may consist of agencies, institutions and other bodies. The Åland Islands are guaranteed self-government. Finland is divided into municipalities, which are guaranteed self-government, and are entitled to levy tax. In their native region the Sámi have linguistic and cultural autonomy.

The Government

HEAD OF STATE

President: TARJA HALONEN (took office 1 March 2000).

CABINET
(Valtioneuvosto)
(April 2005)

A coalition of Keskusta (Centre Party—Kesk), the Sosialidemokraattinen (Social Democratic Party—SDP) and the Svenska Folkpartiet (Swedish People's Party—SFP).

Prime Minister: MATTI VANHANEN (Kesk).

Deputy Prime Minister and Minister of Finance: ANTTI KALLIOMÄKI (SDP).

Minister of Foreign Affairs: ERKKI TUOMIOJA (SDP).

Minister of Foreign Trade and Development: PAULA LEHTOMÄKI (Kesk).

Minister of Justice: JOHANNES KOSKINEN (SDP).

Minister of the Interior: KARI RAJAMÄKI (SDP).

Minister of Regional and Municipal Affairs: HANNES MANNINEN (Kesk).

Minister of Defence: SEPPO KÄÄRIÄINEN (Kesk).

Co-ordinate Minister for Finance: ULLA-MAJ WIDEROOS (SFP).

Minister of Education: TUULA HAATAINEN (SDP).

Minister of Culture: TANJA KARPELA (Kesk).

Minister of Agriculture and Forestry: JUHA KORKEAOJA (Kesk).

Minister of Transport and Communications: LEENA LUHTANEN (SDP).

Minister of Trade and Industry: MAURI PEKKARINEN (Kesk).

Minister of Social Affairs and Health: SINIKKA MÖNKÄRE (SDP).

Minister of Health and Social Services: LIISA HYSSÄLÄ (Kesk).

Minister of Labour: TARJA FILATOV (SDP).

Minister of the Environment: JAN-ERIK ENESTAM (SFP).

MINISTRIES

Prime Minister's Office: Snellmaninkatu 1A, 00170 Helsinki; POB 23, 00023 Government; tel. (9) 16001; fax (9) 16022165; e-mail registry@vnk.fi; internet www.vnk.fi.

Ministry of Agriculture and Forestry: Hallituskatu 3A, 00170 Helsinki; POB 30, 00023 Government; tel. (9) 16001; fax (9) 16054202; e-mail tiedotus@mmm.fi; internet www.mmm.fi.

Ministry of Defence: Eteläinen Makasiinikatu 8, POB 31, 00131 Helsinki; tel. (9) 16001; fax (9) 16088244; e-mail puolustusministerio@plm.vn.fi; internet www.defmin.fi.

Ministry of Education: Meritullinkatu 10, 00171 Helsinki; POB 29, 00023 Government; tel. (9) 16004; fax (9) 1359335; e-mail opmkirjaamo@minedu.fi; internet www.minedu.fi.

Ministry of the Environment: Kasarmikatu 25, 00131 Helsinki; POB 35, 00023 Government; tel. (9) 16007; fax (9) 16039545; e-mail kirjaamo.ym@ymparisto.fi; internet www.ymparisto.fi.

Ministry of Finance: Snellmaninkatu 1A, 00170 Helsinki; POB 28, 00023 Government; tel. (9) 16001; fax (9) 16033123; e-mail valtiovarainministerio@vm.fi; internet www.vm.fi.

Ministry of Foreign Affairs: Merikasarmi, Laivastokatu 22, Merikasarminkatu 5F, POB 176, 00161 Helsinki; tel. (9) 16005; fax (9) 629840; e-mail kirjaamo.um@formin.fi; internet formin.finland.fi.

Ministry of the Interior: Kirkkokatu 12, 00170 Helsinki; POB 26, 00023 Government; tel. (9) 16001; fax (9) 16044635; e-mail sm .kirjaamp@sm.intermin.fi; internet www.intermin.fi.

Ministry of Justice: Korkeavuorenkatu 37, 00150 Helsinki; POB 25, 00023 Government; tel. (9) 16003; fax (9) 16067730; e-mail om-tiedotus@om.fi; internet www.om.fi.

Ministry of Labour: Eteläesplanadi 4, 00101 Helsinki; POB 34, 00023 Government; tel. (9) 16006; fax (9) 16048990; e-mail kirjaamo .tyoministerio@mol.fi; internet www.mol.fi.

Ministry of Social Affairs and Health: Meritullinkatu 8, 00170 Helsinki; POB 33, 00023 Government; tel. (9) 16001; fax (9) 16074126; e-mail kirjaamo.stm@stm.fi; internet www.stm.fi.

Ministry of Trade and Industry: Aleksanterinkatu 4, 00171 Helsinki; POB 32, 00023 Government; tel. (9) 16001; fax (9) 16063666; e-mail tiedotus@ktm.fi; internet www.ktm.fi.

Ministry of Transport and Communications: Eteläesplanadi 16–18, 00131 Helsinki; POB 31, 00023 Government; tel. (9) 16002; fax (9) 16028596; e-mail kirjaamo@mintc.fi; internet www.mintc.fi.

President and Legislature

PRESIDENT

Elections of 16 January and 6 February 2000

	Popular vote (%)	
	First Round	Second Round
Tarja Halonen (SDP)	40.0	51.6
Esko Aho (Kesk)	34.4	48.4
Riitta Uosukainen (Kok)	12.8	—
Märta Elisabeth Rehn (SFP)	7.9	—
Heidi Hautala (VL)	3.3	—
Ilkka Hakalehto (PS)	1.0	—
Risto Kuisma (REM)	0.6	—
Total	100.0	100.0

EDUSKUNTA
(Parliament)

Suomen Eduskunta

Mannerheimintie 30, 00102 Helsinki; tel. (9) 4321; fax (9) 4322274; e-mail parliament@parliament.fi; internet www.eduskunta.fi.

Speaker: PAAVO LIPPONEN (SDP).

Secretary-General: SEPPO TIITINEN.

General Election, 16 March 2003

Party	Votes	% of votes	Seats
Keskusta (Kesk— Centre Party)	689,147	24.70	55
Sosialidemokraattinen Puolue (SDP— Social Democratic Party)	682,819	24.48	53
Kansallinen Kokoomus (Kok— National Coalition Party) . .	517,171	18.54	40
Vasemmistoliitto (V—Left Alliance)	276,756	9.92	19
Vihreä Liitto (Green League) .	223,267	8.00	14
Svenska Folkpartiet (SFP— Swedish People's Party) . .	186,587	6.69	9*
Kristillisdemokraatit (Christian Democrats)	148,965	5.34	7
Perussuomalaiset/Sannfinländarna (PerusS—True Finns) . . .	43,791	1.57	3
Suomen Kommunistinen Puolue (Finnish Communist Party) .	21,111	0.76	—
Total	2,789,614	100.00	200

*Including a representative of the Åland Islands.

Political Organizations

Kansallinen Kokoomus (Kok) (National Coalition Party): Pohjoinen Rautatiekatu 21B, 00100 Helsinki; tel. and fax (0) 207488402; fax (9) 6938206; e-mail jori.arvonen@kokoomus.fi; internet www .kokoomus.fi; f. 1918; moderate conservative political ideology; Chair. JYRKI KATAINEN; Sec.-Gen. HARRI JASKARI; Chair. Parliamentary Group BEN ZYSKOWICZ; 50,000 mems.

Keskusta (Kesk) (Centre Party): Apollonkatu 11A, 00100 Helsinki; tel. (9) 75144200; fax (9) 75144240; e-mail puoluetoimisto@keskusta

.fi; internet www.keskusta.fi; f. 1906; a radical centre party founded to promote the interests of the rural population, now a reformist movement favouring individual enterprise, equality and decentralization; Chair. MATTI VANHANEN; Sec.-Gen. EERO LANKIA; Chair. Parliamentary Group TIMO KALLI; 200,000 mems.

Kristillisdemokraatit (KD) (Christian Democrats): Karjalankatu 2c, 7 krs, 00520 Helsinki; tel. (9) 34882200; fax (9) 34882228; e-mail kd@kd.fi; internet www.kd.fi; f. 1958 as Suomen Kristillinen Liitto, present name adopted 2001; Chair. PÄIVI RÄSÄNEN; Sec. ANNIKA KOKKO; Chair. Parliamentary Group SARI ESSAYAH; 14,700 mems.

Liberaalit (Liberals): Vehkatie 29, 01300 Vantaa; tel. (9) 85168401; fax (9) 85168402; e-mail liberaalit@liberaalit.fi; internet www.liberaalit.fi; f. 1965 as a coalition of the Finnish People's Party and the Liberal Union; Chair. TOMI RIIHIMÄKI; Sec.-Gen. KIMMO ERIKSSON; 4,000 mems.

Perussuomalaiset/Sannfinländarna rp (PerusS) (True Finns): Mannerheimintie 40B 56, 00100 Helsinki; tel. (9) 4540411; fax (9) 4540466; e-mail peruss@perussuomalaiset.fi; internet www.perussuomalaiset.fi; f. 1995; Chair. TIMO SOINI; Sec. HANNU PURHO.

Sosialidemokraattinen Puolue (SDP) (Social Democratic Party): Saariniemenkatu 6, 00530 Helsinki; tel. (9) 478988; fax (9) 712752; e-mail palaute@sdp.fi; internet www.sdp.fi; f. 1899; constitutional socialist programme; mainly supported by the urban working and middle classes; Chair. PAAVO LIPPONEN; Gen. Sec. EERO HEINÄLUOMA; Chair. Parliamentary Group JOUNI BACKMAN; 59,000 mems.

Suomen Kommunistinen Puolue (SKP) (Finnish Communist Party): Petter Wetterin tie 1A, 00810 Helsinki; tel. (09) 77438150; fax (09) 77438160; e-mail skp@skp.fi; internet www.skp.fi; f. 1918; refounded by breakaway group after the SKP formed the Vasemmistoliitto (Left Alliance) with other left-wing groups in 1990.

Svenska Folkpartiet (SFP) (Swedish People's Party): Simonsgatan 8A, 00100 Helsinki; tel. (9) 693070; fax (9) 6931968; internet www.sfp.fi; f. 1906; a liberal party representing the interests of the Swedish-speaking minority; Chair. JAN-ERIK ENESTAM; Sec. BERTH SUNDSTRÖM; Chair. Parliamentary Group CHRISTINA GESTRIN; 35,700 mems.

Vasemmistoliitto (V) (Left Alliance): Viherniemenkatu 5A, 00530 Helsinki; tel. (9) 774741; fax (9) 77474200; e-mail vas@vasemmistoliitto.fi; internet www.vasemmistoliitto.fi; f. 1990 as a merger of the Finnish People's Democratic League (f. 1944), the Communist Party of Finland (f. 1918), the Democratic League of Finnish Women, and left-wing groups; Chair. SUVI-ANNE SIIMES; Sec.-Gen. AULIS RUUTH; Chair. Parliamentary Group MARTTI KORHONEN; 10,000 mems.

Vihreä Liitto (VL) (Green League): Frederikinkatu 33A, 00120 Helsinki; tel. (9) 58604160; fax (9) 58604161; e-mail vihreat@vihrealiitto.fi; internet www.greens.fi; f. 1988; Chair. OSMO SOININVAARA; Sec. ARI HEIKKINEN.

Diplomatic Representation

EMBASSIES IN FINLAND

Argentina: Bulevardi 5A 11, 00120 Helsinki; tel. (9) 42428700; fax (9) 42428701; e-mail embassy@embargentina.fi; internet www.embargentina.fi; Ambassador ALFREDO CORTI.

Austria: Keskuskatu 1A, 00100 Helsinki; tel. (9) 6818600; fax (9) 665084; e-mail helsinki-ob@bmaa.gv.at; Ambassador Dr CHRISTOPH QUERNER.

Belgium: Kalliolinnantie 5, 00140 Helsinki; tel. (9) 170412; fax (9) 628842; e-mail ambel.helsinki@kolumbus.fi; Ambassador JOHAN VAN DESSEL.

Brazil: Itäinen puistotie 4B 1, 00140 Helsinki; tel. (9) 177922; fax (9) 650084; e-mail brasemb.helsinki@kolumbus.fi; Ambassador LUIZ HENRIQUE PEREIRA DA FONSECA.

Bulgaria: Kuusisaarentie 2B, 00340 Helsinki; tel. (9) 4584055; fax (9) 4584550; e-mail bulembfi@icon.fi; Chargé d'affaires a.i. KIRIL DIMITROV.

Canada: Pohjoisesplanadi 25B, 00100 Helsinki; tel. (9) 228530; fax (9) 601060; internet www.canada.fi; Ambassador ADÈLE DION.

Chile: Erottajankatu 11, 00130 Helsinki; tel. (9) 6126780; fax (9) 61267825; e-mail echilefi@kolumbus.fi; Ambassador IGNACIO GONZALEZ SERRANO.

China, People's Republic: Vanha Kelkkamäki 9–11, 00570 Helsinki; tel. (9) 22890110; fax (9) 22890168; Ambassador ZHANG ZHIJIAN.

Colombia: Ratakatu 1B A1, 00120 Helsinki; tel. (9) 6802799; fax (9) 6802180; e-mail emcolhel.emba@kolumbus.fi; Chargé d'affaires a.i. CARMEN LUCIA TRISTANCHO-CEDIEL.

Croatia: Eteläesplanadi 12, 1, 00130 Helsinki; tel. (9) 6222232; fax (9) 6222221; e-mail croatia@embassy.inet.fi; Ambassador MARIN AUDRIJASEVIĆ.

Cuba: Uudenmaankatu 26A 3, 00120 Helsinki; tel. (9) 6802022; fax (9) 643163; e-mail cuba@embacuba.inet.fi; internet personal.inet.fi/business.cuba; Chargé d'affaires MANUEL VIÑAS BARREDO.

Cyprus: Bulevardi 5A 19, 00120 Helsinki; tel. (9) 6962820; fax (9) 69628230; e-mail mail@cyprusembassy.fi; internet www.cyprusembassy.fi; Ambassador LORIA MARKIDES.

Czech Republic: Armfeltintie 14, 00150 Helsinki; tel. (9) 171169; fax (9) 630655; e-mail helsinki@embassy.mzv.cz; Ambassador ALENA PROUZOVÁ.

Denmark: Keskuskatu 1A, POB 1042, 00101 Helsinki; tel. (9) 6841050; fax (9) 68410540; e-mail helamb@um.dk; internet www.denmark.fi; Ambassador NIELS HELSKOV.

Egypt: Munkkiniemen puistotie 25, 00330 Helsinki; tel. (9) 4777470; fax (9) 47774721; Ambassador SOAD MAHMOUD SHALABY.

Estonia: Itäinen puistotie 10, 00140 Helsinki; tel. (9) 6220260; fax (9) 62202610; e-mail sekretar@estemb.fi; internet www.estemb.fi; Ambassador MATTI MAASIKAS.

France: Itäinen puistotie 13, 00140 Helsinki; tel. (9) 618780; fax (9) 618783923; e-mail ambassade.france@kolumbus.fi; Ambassador JEAN-JACQUES SUBRENAT.

Germany: POB 5, 00331 Helsinki; tel. (9) 458580; fax (9) 45858258; e-mail info@deutschland.fi; internet www.helsinki.diplo.de; Ambassador Dr HANNS H. SCHUMACHER.

Greece: Maaneesikatu 2A 4, 00170 Helsinki; tel. (9) 6229790; fax (9) 2781200; e-mail gr@greekembassy.fi; internet www.greekembassy.fi; Ambassador LYSANDER MIGLIARESSIS-PHOCAS.

Hungary: Kuusisaarenkuja 6, 00340 Helsinki; tel. (9) 484144; fax (9) 480497; e-mail office@unkari.fi; Ambassador Dr GÁBOR ZUPKÓ.

Iceland: Pohjoisesplanadi 27C, 00100 Helsinki; tel. (9) 6122460; fax (9) 61224620; e-mail icemb.helsinki@utn.stjr.is; internet www.islanti.fi; Ambassador JÓN BALDVINN HANNIBALSSON.

India: Satamakatu 2A 8, 00160 Helsinki; tel. (9) 608927; fax (9) 6221208; e-mail eoihelsinki@indianembassy.fi; Ambassador OM PRAKASH GUPTA.

Indonesia: Kuusisaarentie 3, 00340 Helsinki; tel. (9) 4470370; fax (9) 4582882; e-mail info@indonesian-embassy.fi; internet www.indonesian-embassy.fi; Ambassador AHMAD FAUZIE GANI.

Iran: Kulosaarentie 9, 00570 Helsinki; tel. (9) 6869240; fax (9) 68692410; e-mail embassy@iran.fi; internet www.iran.fi; Ambassador JAVAD KAJOUYAN FINI.

Iraq: Lars Sonckin tie 2, 00570 Helsinki; tel. (9) 6849177; fax (9) 6848977.

Ireland: Erottajankatu 7A, 00130 Helsinki; tel. (9) 646006; fax (9) 646022; e-mail embassy.ireland@welho.com; Ambassador ANTÓIN MACUNFRAIDH.

Israel: Vironkatu 5A, 00170 Helsinki; tel. (9) 6812020; fax (9) 1356959; e-mail embassy@israel.fi; internet www.mfa.gov.il; Ambassador SHEMI TZUR.

Italy: Itäinen puistotie 4, 00140 Helsinki; tel. (9) 6811280; fax (9) 6987829; e-mail info@italia.fi; internet www.italia.fi; Ambassador PIETRO LONARDO.

Japan: Eteläranta 8, 00130 Helsinki; tel. (9) 6860200; fax (9) 633012; e-mail webmaster@jpnembassy.fi; internet www.fi.emb-japan.go.jp; Ambassador NORIMASA HASEGAWA.

Korea, Republic: Fabianinkatu 8A, 00130 Helsinki; tel. (9) 2515000; fax (9) 25150055; e-mail koreanembassy@kolumbus.fi; Ambassador JUNG-PYO HONG.

Latvia: Armfeltintie 10, 00150 Helsinki; tel. (9) 47647244; fax (9) 47647288; e-mail embassy.finland@mfa.gov.lv; Ambassador VALDIS KRASTINŠ.

Lithuania: Rauhankatu 13A, 00170 Helsinki; tel. (9) 608210; fax (9) 608220; e-mail embassylt@kolumbus.fi; internet fi.urm.lt; Ambassador AUDRIUS BRŪZGA.

Mexico: Simonkatu 12A, 00100 Helsinki; tel. (9) 5860430; fax (9) 6949411; e-mail mexican.embassy@welho.com; Ambassador JOSÉ GONZALO E. AGUIRRE ENRILE.

Morocco: Mikonkatu 8A–9, 00100 Helsinki; tel. (9) 61224840; fax (9) 635160; e-mail embassyofmorocco@co.inet.fi; Chargé d'affaires a.i. ABDELLAH M'SAHI.

Netherlands: Eteläesplanadi 24A, 00130 Helsinki; tel. (9) 661737; fax (9) 654734; e-mail nlgovhel@kolumbus.fi; internet www.netherlands.fi; Ambassador NIEK PETER VAN ZUTPHEN.

Norway: Rehbinderintie 17, 00150 Helsinki; tel. (9) 6860180; fax (9) 657807; e-mail emb.helsinki@mfa.no; Ambassador HAAKON B. HJELDE.

Peru: Annankatu 31–33C 44, 00100 Helsinki; tel. (9) 6933681; fax (9) 6933682; e-mail embassy.peru@peruemb.inet.fi; Ambassador MANUEL PICASSO BOTTO.

Poland: Armas Lindgrenin tie 21, 00570 Helsinki; tel. (9) 618280; fax (9) 6847477; e-mail amb.poland@helsinki.inet.fi; internet www .embassyofpoland.fi; Ambassador STANISŁAW STEBELSKI.

Portugal: Itäinen puistotie 11B, 00140 Helsinki; tel. (9) 68243715; fax (9) 663550; e-mail emb.port@portugal.fi; Ambassador JOÃO SILVA LEITÃO.

Romania: Stenbackinkatu 24, 00250 Helsinki; tel. (9) 2414414; fax (9) 2413272; e-mail romamb@clinet.fi; internet www.romania.fi; Ambassador NEAGU UDROIU.

Russia: Tehtaankatu 1B, 00140 Helsinki; tel. (9) 661876; fax (9) 661006; e-mail rusembassy@co.inet.fi; Ambassador VLADIMIR M. GRININ.

Serbia and Montenegro: Kulosaarentie 36, 00570 Helsinki; tel. (9) 6848522; fax (9) 6848783; e-mail info@ambascghki@kolumbus.fi; Chargé d'affaires a.i. DJORDJE LUKIĆ.

Slovakia: Annankatu 25, 00100 Helsinki; tel. (9) 68117810; fax (9) 68117820; e-mail skemb.hels@sci.fi; Ambassador VIERA ŠTUPÁKOVÁ.

Slovenia: Eteläesplanadi 24A, 00130 Helsinki; POB 9, 00101 Helsinki; tel. (9) 2289940; fax (9) 6944775; e-mail vhe@mzz-dkp.gov.si; Chargé d'affaires a.i. ALAIN BERGANT.

South Africa: Rahapajankatu 1A 5, 00160 Helsinki; tel. (9) 68603100; fax (9) 68603160; e-mail saembfin@welno.com; internet www.southafricanembassy.fi; Ambassador BUKELWA HANS.

Spain: Kalliolinnantie 6, 00140 Helsinki; tel. (9) 6877080; fax (9) 170923; e-mail embespfi@mail.mae.es; Ambassador ANTONIO GARÍA ABAD.

Sweden: Pohjoisesplanadi 7B, 00171 Helsinki; tel. (9) 6877660; fax (9) 655285; e-mail ambassaden.helsingfors@foreign.ministry.se; internet www.sverige.fi; Ambassador ULF HJERTONSSON.

Switzerland: Uudenmaankatu 16A, 00120 Helsinki; tel. (9) 6229500; fax (9) 62295050; e-mail vertretung@hel.rep.admin.ch; Ambassador PIERRE CHRZANOVSKI.

Turkey: Puistokatu 1B A 3, 00140 Helsinki; tel. (9) 6811030; fax (9) 655011; e-mail turkish.embassy@welho.com; Ambassador ILHAN YIGITBASIOGLU.

Ukraine: Vähäniityntie 9, 00570 Helsinki; tel. (9) 2289000; fax (9) 2289001; e-mail ukrainian.embassy@kolumbus.fi; Ambassador OLEKSANDR MAIDANNYK.

United Kingdom: Itäinen puistotie 17, 00140 Helsinki; tel. (9) 22865100; fax (9) 22865262; e-mail info@ukembassy.fi; internet www.ukembassy.fi; Ambassador MATTHEW KIRK.

USA: Itäinen puistotie 14A, 00140 Helsinki; tel. (9) 616250; fax (9) 174681; e-mail webmaster@usembassy.fi; internet www.usembassy .fi; Ambassador EARLE I. MACK.

Venezuela: Bulevardi 1A, POB 285, 00101 Helsinki; tel. (9) 641522; fax (9) 640971; e-mail embavene.finland@dlc.fi; Ambassador JOSÉ E. LÓPEZ CONTRERAS.

Judicial System

The administration of justice is independent of the Government and judges can be removed only by judicial sentence. The compulsory retirement age for judges is 67.

SUPREME COURT

Korkein oikeus/Högsta domstolen

Pohjoisesplanadi 3, POB 301, 00171 Helsinki; tel. (9) 12381; fax (9) 1238354; e-mail korkein.oikeus@om.fi; internet www.kko.fi.

Consists of a President and at least 15 Justices appointed by the President of the Republic. Final court appeal in civil and criminal cases, supervises judges and executive authorities.

President: LEIF SEVÓN.

SUPREME ADMINISTRATIVE COURT

Korkein hallinto-oikeus/Högsta förvaltningsdomstolen

Unioninkatu 16, POB 180, 00131 Helsinki; tel. (9) 18531; fax (9) 1853382; e-mail korkein.hallinto-oikeus@om.fi; internet www.kho .if.

Consists of a President and 20 Justices appointed by the President of the Republic. Highest tribunal for appeals in administrative cases.

President: PEKKA HALLBERG.

COURTS OF APPEAL

There are Courts of Appeal at Turku, Vaasa, Kuopio, Helsinki, Kouvola, and Rovaniemi, consisting of a President and an appropriate number of members.

ADMINISTRATIVE COURTS

There are eight Administrative Courts, which hear the appeals of private individuals and corporate bodies against the authorities in tax cases, municipal cases, construction cases, social welfare and health-care cases and other administrative cases. In certain of these, the appeal must be preceded by a complaint to a separate lower appellate body. The State and municipal authorities also have a right of appeal in certain cases.

DISTRICT COURTS

Courts of first instance for almost all suits. Appeals lie to the Court of Appeal, and then to the Supreme Court. The composition of the District Court is determined by the type of case to be heard. Civil cases and 'ordinary' criminal cases can be considered by one judge. Other criminal cases and family law cases are heard by a judge and a panel of three lay judges (jurors). Other civil cases are heard by three legally-qualified judges. There are 66 District Courts.

SPECIAL COURTS

In addition there are a number of special courts with more restricted jurisdictions. These are: the High Court of Impeachment, the Insurance Court, the Labour Court and the Market Court. There is no constitutional court in Finland, but the Constitutional Committee of Parliament has been entrusted with the process of verifying the compatibility of new legislation with the Constitution.

CHANCELLOR OF JUSTICE

The Oikeuskansleri is responsible for ensuring that authorities and officials comply with the law. He is the chief public prosecutor, and acts as counsel for the Government.

Chancellor of Justice: PAAVO NIKULA.

Chancellor of Justice's Office: Snellmaninkatu 1A, 00170 Helsinki; POB 20, 00023 Government; tel. (9) 16001; fax (9) 16023975; e-mail kirjaamo@okv.vn.fi; internet www.vn.fi/okv.

PARLIAMENTARY OMBUDSMAN

The Eduskunnan Oikeusasiamies is the Finnish Ombudsman appointed by the Eduskunta to supervise the observance of the law.

Parliamentary Ombudsman: Riitta-Leena PAUNIO.

Parliamentary Ombudsman's Office: Arkadiankatu 3, 00102 Helsinki; tel. (9) 4321; fax (9) 4322268; e-mail eoa-kirjaamo@ eduskunta.fi; internet www.ombudsman.fi.

In addition to the Chancellor of Justice and the Parliamentary Ombudsman, there are also specialized authorities that have similar duties in more limited fields. These include the Consumer Ombudsman, the Ombudsman for Equality, the Data Protection Ombudsman, the Ombudsman for Aliens and the Bankruptcy Ombudsman.

Religion

CHRISTIANITY

Suomen ekumeeninen neuvosto/Ekumeniska rådet i Finland (Finnish Ecumenical Council): Katajanokankatu 7, POB 185, 00161 Helsinki; tel. (9) 1802369; fax (9) 174313; e-mail sen@ekumenia.fi; internet www.ekumenia.fi; f. 1917; 12 mem. churches; Pres. Archbishop JUKKA PAARMA (Archbishop of Karelia and All Finland, Evangelical Lutheran Church of Finland); Gen. Sec. Rev. JAN EDSTRÖM.

National Churches

Suomen evankelis-luterilainen kirkko (Evangelical Lutheran Church of Finland): Dept for International Relations, Satamakatu 11, POB 185, 00161 Helsinki; tel. (9) 18021; fax (9) 1802230; about 84.6% of the population are adherents; Leader Archbishop Dr JUKKA PAARMA.

Suomen Ortodoksinen Kirkko (Orthodox Church of Finland): Karjalankatu 1, 70110 Kuopio; tel. (17) 2872230; fax (17) 2872231; e-mail info@ort.fi; internet www.ort.fi; 60,000 mems; Leader LEO (Archbishop of Karelia and all Finland).

The Roman Catholic Church

Finland comprises the single diocese of Helsinki, directly responsible to the Holy See. At 31 December 2003 there were 8,438 adherents in the country. The Bishop participates in the Scandinavian Episcopal Conference (based in Sweden).

Bishop of Helsinki: JÓZEF WRÓBEL, Rehbinderintie 21, 00150 Helsinki; tel. (9) 6877160; fax (9) 639820; e-mail curia@catholic.fi.

Other Churches

Finlands svenska baptistmission (Finland Swedish Baptist Union): POB 54, 65101 Vasa; tel. (6) 3464500; fax (6) 3464510; e-mail fsb@baptist.fi; internet www.baptist.fi; f. 1856; 1,353 mems; Gen. Sec. NILS ERIK VIKSTRÖM.

Jehovan Todistajat (Jehovah's Witnesses): Puutarhatie 60, 01300 Vantaa; tel. (9) 825885; fax (9) 82588285; internet www.watchtower.org; 19,630 mems.

Myöhempien Aikojen Pyhien Jeesuksen Kristuksen Kirkko (Church of Jesus Christ of Latter-day Saints—Mormon): Neitsytpolku 3A, 00140 Helsinki; tel. (9) 6962750; fax (9) 69627510; e-mail 2015803@ldschurch.org; internet www.mormonit.fi; 4,504 mems.

Suomen Adventtikirkko (Seventh-day Adventist Church in Finland): POB 94, 33101 Tampere; tel. (3) 3611111; fax (3) 3600454; e-mail advent@sdafin.org; internet www.adventtikirkko.fi; f. 1894; 5,469 mems; Pres. ATTE HELMINEN; Sec. ANNE LESKINEN.

Suomen Baptistiyhdyskunta (Baptists—Finnish-speaking): Kissanmaankatu 19, 33530 Tampere; tel. (3) 2530901; fax (3) 2530913; e-mail kharis@sci.fi; 1,821 mems; Pres. Rev. JORMA LEMPINEN.

Suomen Vapaakirkko (Evangelical Free Church of Finland): POB 198, 13101 Hämeenlinna; tel. (3) 6445150; fax (3) 6122153; e-mail svk@svk.fi; internet www.svk.fi; f. 1923; 14,100 mems; Pres. Rev. OLAVI RINTALA.

Svenska Kyrkan i Finland (Church of Sweden in Finland): Minervagatan 6, 00100 Helsinki; tel. (9) 443831; fax (9) 4546059; e-mail forsamlingen@olauspetri.inet.fi; f. 1919; 1,300 mems; Rector Dr JARL JERGMAR.

Finlands svenska metodistkyrka (United Methodist Church in Finland—Swedish-speaking): Apollonkatu 5, 00100 Helsinki; tel. (9) 449874; e-mail kyrkostyrelsen@metodistkyrkan.fi; internet www.metodistkyrkan.fi; 1,000 mems; District Superintendents Rev. FREDRIK WEGELIUS, Rev. HANS VÄXBY.

Suomen Metodistikirkko (United Methodist Church—Finnish-speaking): Punavuorenkatu 2, 00120 Helsinki; tel. (9) 628135; e-mail suomen@metodistikirkko.fi; 782 mems; District Superintendent Rev. TIMO VIRTANEN.

The Anglican Church and the Salvation Army are also active in the country.

BAHÁ'Í FAITH

Suomen Bahá'í-yhteisö (Bahá'í Community of Finland): POB 423, 00600 Helsinki; tel. (9) 790875; fax (9) 790058; e-mail secretariat@bahai.fi; f. 1953; 600 mems.

JUDAISM

Helsingin Juutalainen Seurakunta (Jewish Community of Helsinki): Synagogue and Community Centre, Malminkatu 26, 00100 Helsinki; tel. (9) 5860310; fax (9) 6948916; e-mail srk@jchelsinki.fi; internet www.jchelsinki.fi; 1,200 mems; Pres. GIDEON BOLOTOWSKY; Exec. Dir DAN KANTOR.

ISLAM

Suomen Islamilainen Yhdyskunta (Islamic Community of Finland): POB 87, 00101 Helsinki; tel. (9) 3512190; fax (9) 6121156; 936 mems; Imam ENVER YILDIRIM.

The Press

In 2003 there were 53 daily newspapers in Finland; the total circulation for all types of newspaper was some 3.2m. A number of dailies are printed in Swedish. The most popular daily papers are *Helsingin Sanomat*, *Ilta-Sanomat*, *Aamulehti* and *Iltalehti*. Most respected for its standard of news coverage and commentary is *Helsingin Sanomat*, an independent paper.

PRINCIPAL DAILIES

Espoo

Hevosurheilu: Tulkinkuja 3, 02600 Espoo; tel. (9) 51100300; fax (9) 51100390; e-mail hevosurheilu@hevosurheilulehti.fi; internet www

.hippos.fi/hu; independent; Man. Dir JUKKO AHONEN; Editor-in-Chief JORMA KEMILÄINEN; circ. 27,589.

Helsinki

Helsingin Sanomat: Töölönlahdenkatu 2, POB 77, 00089 Sanomat; tel. (9) 1221; fax (9) 605709; e-mail janne.virkkunen@sanomat.fi; internet www.helsinginsanomat.fi; f. 1889; independent; Publr SEPPO KIEVARI; Senior Editor-in-Chief JANNE VIRKKUNEN; circ. 441,325.

Hufvudstadsbladet: Mannerheimvägen 18, POB 217, 00101 Helsinki; tel. (9) 12531; fax (9) 642930; e-mail nyheter@hbl.fi; internet www.hbl.fi; f. 1864; Swedish language; independent; Editors-in-Chief MAX ARHIPPAINEN, BARBRO TEIR; circ. 50,649.

Iltalehti: Aleksanterinkatu 9, 4, 00100 Helsinki; tel. (9) 507721; fax (9) 177313; e-mail il.toimitus@iltalehti.fi; internet www.iltalehti.fi; f. 1981; afternoon; independent; Man. Dir VELI-MATTI ASIKAINEN; Editor-in-Chief PETRI HAKALA; circ. 132,836 weekdays, 165,528 Saturday.

Ilta-Sanomat: POB 45, 00089 Sanomat; tel. (9) 1221; fax (9) 1223419; e-mail iltasanomat@sanoma.fi; internet www.iltsanomat .fi; f. 1932; afternoon; independent; Man. Dir PEKKA HARJU; Editor-in-Chief ANTTI-PEKKA PIETILA; circ. 198,693 weekdays, 230,949 weekend.

Kansan Uutiset: Fabianinkatu 7, 00131 Helsinki; tel. (9) 759601; f. 1957; organ of the Left Alliance; Editor YRJÖ RAUTIO; circ. 9,749.

Kauppalehti (The Commercial Daily): POB 189, 00101 Helsinki; tel. (9) 50781; fax (9) 5078419; internet www.kauppalehti.fi; f. 1898; morning; Man. Dir JUHA BLOHSTER; Editor-in-Chief HANNU LEINONEN; circ. 84,626.

Maaseudun Tulevaisuus: Simonkatu 6, POB 440, 00100 Helsinki; tel. (9) 204132100; fax (9) 6944766; internet www .maaseuduntulevaisuus.fi; f. 1916; independent; Man. Dir HEIKKI LAURINEN; Editor-in-Chief LAURI KONTRO; circ. 84,000.

Uutispöivä Demari: Haapaniemenkatu 7–9B, POB 338, 00531 Helsinki; tel. (9) 701041; fax (9) 7010567; e-mail toimitus@demari.fi; internet www.demari.fi; f. 1895; chief organ of the Social Democratic Party; Man. Dir HEIKKI NYKANEN; Editor-in-Chief KARI AROLA; circ. 23,021.

Hämeenlinna

Hämeen Sanomat: Vanajantie 7, POB 530, 13111 Hämeenlinna; tel. (3) 61511; fax (3) 6151492; internet www.hameensanomat.fi; f. 1879; independent; Man. Dir MATTI VIHERVUORI; Editor-in-Chief OLLI-PEKKA BEHM; circ. 30,076.

Joensuu

Karjalainen: Kosti Aaltosentie 9, POB 99, 80141 Joensuu; tel. (13) 2551; fax (13) 2552363; e-mail toimitus@karjalainen.fi; internet www.karjalainen.fi; f. 1874; independent; Man. Dir RAIMO PUUSTINEN; Editor PEKKA SITARI; circ. 47,636.

Jyväskylä

Keskisuomalainen: Aholaidantie 3, POB 159, 40101 Jyväskylä; tel. (14) 622000; fax (14) 622272; e-mail tietopalvelu@keskisuomalainen.fi; internet www.keskisuomalainen.fi; f. 1871; Man. Dir ERKKI PORANEN; Editor ERKKI LAATIKAINEN; circ. 75,836.

Kajaani

Kainuun Sanomat: Viestitie 2, POB 150, 87101 Kajaani; tel. (8) 61661; fax (8) 6166307; e-mail toimitus@kainuunsanomat.fi; internet www.kainuunsanomat.fi; f. 1918; independent; Man. Dir JUHA RUOTSALAINEN; Editor-in-Chief MATTI PIIRAINEN; circ. 23,454.

Kemi

Pohjolan Sanomat: Sairaalakatu 2, 94100 Kemi; tel. (16) 2911; fax (16) 291300; e-mail ps.toimitus@pohjolansanomat.fi; internet www .pohjolansanomat.fi; f. 1915; Man. Dir MARTTI NIKKANEN; Editor-in-Chief HEIKKI LÄÄKKÖLÄ; circ. 23,483.

Kokkola

Keskipohjanmaa: Kosila, POB 45, 67101 Kokkola; tel. (6) 8272000; fax (6) 8220208; internet www.keskipohjanmaa.net; f. 1917; independent; Man. Dir EINO LAUKKA; Editor LASSI FRANNALA; circ. 28,057.

Kotka

Kymen Sanomat: POB 27, 48101 Kotka; tel. (5) 210015; fax (5) 21005206; e-mail uutiset@kymensanomat.fi; internet www .kymensanomat.fi; f. 1902; independent; Man. Dir ANTTI MÄKELÄ; Editor MARKKU ESPO; circ. 27,408.

Kouvola

Kouvolan Sanomat: POB 40, 45101 Kouvola; tel. (5) 280014; fax (5) 28004206; e-mail toimitus@kouvolansanomat.fi; internet www .kouvolansanomat.fi; f. 1909; independent; Man. Dir JUHA OKSANEN; Editor-in-Chief VILLE POHJONEN; circ. 29,600.

Kuopio

Savon Sanomat: POB 68, 70101 Kuopio; tel. (17) 303111; fax (17) 303347; e-mail lukijansanomat@iwn.fi; internet www .savonsanomat.fi; f. 1907; independent; Man. Dir HEIKKI AURASMAA; Editor-in-Chief TAPANI LEPOLA; circ. 67,185.

Lahti

Etelä-Suomen Sanomat: Ilmarisentie 7, POB 80, 15101 Lahti; tel. (3) 75751; fax (3) 7575466; internet www.ess.fi; f. 1900; independent; Man. Dir JUKKA OTTELA; Editor-in-Chief HEIKKI HAKALA; circ. 61,277.

Lappeenranta

Etelä-Saimaa: POB 3, 53501 Lappeenranta; tel. (5) 538815; fax (5) 53883205; internet www.esaimaa.fi; f. 1885; independent; Man. Dir ANTERO JUNTTILA; Editor JORMA HERNESMAA; circ. 34,419.

Mikkeli

Länsi-Savo: POB 6, 50101 Mikkeli; tel. (15) 3501; fax (15) 350337; e-mail toimitus@lansi-savo.fi; internet www.lansi-savo.fi; independent; Man. Dir JUKKA TIKKA; Editor-in-Chief KARI JUUTILAINEN; circ. 26,149.

Oulu

Kaleva: POB 170, 90401 Oulu; tel. (8) 5377111; fax (8) 5377195; e-mail kaleva@kaleva.fi; internet www.kaleva.fi; f. 1899; independent; Man. Dir TAISTO RISKI; Editor-in-Chief RISTO UIMONEN; circ. 81,689.

Pori

Satakunnan Kansa: POB 58, 28101 Pori; tel. (2) 6228111; fax (2) 6228392; e-mail sk.toimitus@satakunnankansa.fi; internet www .satakunnankansa.fi; f. 1873; independent; Man. Dir TUOMO SAARINEN; Editor-in-Chief JOUKO JOKINEN; circ. 56,781.

Rauma

Länsi-Suomi: Susivuorentie 2, 26100 Rauma; tel. (2) 83361; fax (2) 8420959; f. 1905; independent; Man. Dir and Editor-in-Chief PAULI UUSI-KILPONEN; circ. 17,171.

Rovaniemi

Lapin Kansa: Veitikantie 2–8, 96100 Rovaniemi; tel. (16) 320011; fax (16) 3200345; e-mail lktoimitus@lapinkansa.fi; internet www .lapinkansa.fi; f. 1928; independent; Man. Dir JUHA RUOTSALAINEN; Editor-in-Chief HEIKKI TUOMI-NIKULA; circ. 35,887.

Salo

Salon Seudun Sanomat: Örninkatu 14, POB 117, 24101 Salo; tel. (2) 77021; fax (2) 7702300; internet www.sss.fi; independent; Man. Dir KIRSTI KIRJONEN; Editor-in-Chief JARMO VÄHÄSILTA; circ. 21,913.

Savonlinna

Itä-Savo: POB 101, 57101 Savonlinna; tel. (15) 51740; Man. Dir (vacant); Editor KYÖSTI PIENIMÄKI; circ. 20,821.

Seinäjoki

Ilkka: POB 60, 60101 Seinäjoki; tel. (6) 4186555; fax (6) 4186500; e-mail ilkka.toimitus@ilkka.fi; internet www.ilkka.fi; f. 1906; independent; Man. Dir MATTI KORKIATUPA; Editor-in-Chief KARI HOKKANEN; circ. 54,976.

Tampere

Aamulehti: POB 327, 33101 Tampere; tel. (3) 2666111; fax (3) 2666259; internet www.aamulehti.fi; f. 1881; Editor MATTI APUNEN; circ. 136,028 weekdays, 142,701 Sunday.

Turku

Turun Sanomat: POB 95, 20101 Turku; tel. (2) 2693311; fax (2) 2693274; e-mail ts.toimitus@ts-group.fi; internet www .turunsanomat.fi; f. 1904; independent; Man. Dir KEIJO KETONEN; Editors-in-Chief ARI VALJAKKA, RAIMO VAHTERA, AIMO MASSINEN; circ. 114,086 weekdays, 125,318 Sunday.

Tuusula

Keski-Uusimaa: POB 52, 04301 Tuusula; tel. (9) 273000; fax (9) 27300205; e-mail toimitus@keskiuusimaa.fi; internet www

.keskiuusimaa.fi; independent; Man. Dir JORMA HÄMÄLÄINEN; Editor-in-Chief EERO LEHTINEN; circ. 21,851.

Vaasa

Pohjalainen: Pitkäkatu 37, POB 37, 65101 Vaasa; tel. (6) 3249111; fax (6) 3249351; e-mail kari.mantila@pohjalainen.fi; internet www .pohjalainen.fi; f. 1903; independent; Man. Dir MATTI KORKIATUPA; Editor MARKU MANTILA; circ. 33,491.

Vasabladet: Sandögatan 6, POB 52, 65101 Vaasa; tel. (6) 3260211; fax (6) 3129003; e-mail tips@vasabladet.fi; internet www.vasabladet .fi; f. 1856; Swedish language; Liberal independent; Man. Dir HANS BOIJE; Editor-in-Chief DENNIS RUNDT; circ. 26,500.

PRINCIPAL PERIODICALS

7 päivää: POB 124, 00151 Helsinki; tel. (9) 177777; fax (9) 177477; weekly; television and radio; circ. 127,810.

Ahjo: POB 107, 00531 Helsinki; tel. (9) 77071; fax (9) 7707400; e-mail ahjo@metalliliitto.fi; fortnightly; for metal industry employees; Editor-in-Chief JUKKA RIKSMAN; circ. 175,000.

Aku Ankka (Donald Duck): POB 40, 00040 Helsinki; tel. (9) 1201; fax (9) 1205569; f. 1951; weekly; children's; Editor-in-Chief MARKKU KIVEKÄS; circ. 283,334.

Apu: Hitsaajankatu 10, 00081 Helsinki; tel. (9) 75961; fax (9) 781911; e-mail matti.saari@apu.fi; internet www.apu.fi; f. 1933; weekly; family journal; Editor-in-Chief MATTI SAARI; circ. 254,696.

Avotakka: Risto Rytintie 33, 00081 A-lehdet, Helsinki; tel. (9) 75961; fax (9) 75983110; e-mail avotakka@a-lehdet.fi; internet www .a-lehdet.fi/avotakka; f. 1967; monthly; interior decorating; Editor-in-Chief SOILI UKKOLA; circ. 102,162.

Birka: Köydenpunojankatu 2A, 00180 Helsinki; tel. (9) 15668510; fax (9) 15668525; 10 a year; trade; in Swedish; circ. 64,189.

Diabetes: Kirjoniementie 15, 33680 Tampere; tel. (3) 2860111; fax (3) 3600462; e-mail lehdet@diabetes.fi; internet www.diabetes.fi; f. 1949; monthly; health; circ. 58,758.

Eeva: Hitsaajankatu 7/7, 00081 A-lehdet, Helsinki; tel. (9) 75961; fax (9) 786858; e-mail eeva@a-lehdet.fi; internet www.a-lehdet.fi/ eeva; f. 1933; monthly; women's; Editor-in-Chief LIISA JÄPPINEN; circ. 99,678.

Erä: Esterinportti 1, 00015 Kuvalehdet, Helsinki; tel. (9) 15661; fax (9) 15666210; e-mail era@kuvalehdet.fi; internet www.eralehti.fi; monthly; sport, fishing and outdoor leisure; Editor SEPPO SUURONEN; circ. 52,088.

ET-lehti: POB 100, 00040 Helsinki; tel. (9) 1201; fax (9) 1205428; e-mail kaisa.larmela@helsinkimedia.fi; monthly; over-50s magazine; Editor-in-Chief KAISA LARMELA; circ. 250,000.

Gloria: POB 100, 00040 Helsinki; tel. (9) 1201; fax (9) 1205427; e-mail gloria@helsinkimedia.fi; monthly; women's; Editor-in-Chief RIITTA LINDEGREN; circ. 64,000.

Hippo: POB 308, 00101 Helsinki; tel. (9) 4041; fax (9) 4042165; 4 a year; Editor-in-Chief STINA SUOMINEN; circ. 188,141.

Hymy: Maistraatinportti 1, 00240 Helsinki; tel. (9) 15661; fax (9) 15666206; monthly; family journal; Editor ESKO TULUSTO; circ. 94,527.

Hyvä Terveys: POB 100, 00040 Sanoma Magazines; tel. (9) 1201; fax (9) 1205456; e-mail hyva.terveys@sanomamagazines.fi; internet www.hyvaterveys.fi; 11 a year; health; Editor-in-Chief MAIJA TOPPILA; circ. 104,094.

IT-Invalidityö: Kumpulantie 1A, 00520 Helsinki; tel. (9) 613191; fax (9) 2722142; e-mail it-lehti@invalidiliitto.fi; internet www .it-lehti.fi; 12 a year; for handicapped people; Editor-in-Chief SINIKKA RANTALA; circ. 44,207.

Kaksplus: Maistraatinportti 1, 00015 Kuvalehdet; tel. (9) 1566591; fax (9) 1566550; e-mail kaksplus@kuvalehdet.fi; internet www .kaksplus.fi; f. 1969; monthly; for families with young children; Editor-in-Chief MARI IKONEN; circ. 39,974.

Katso: Hitsaajankatu 7/5, 00081 A-lehdet, Helsinki; tel. (9) 75961; fax (9) 7583102; e-mail katso@a-lehdet.fi; internet www.a-lehdet.fi/ katso; f. 1960; weekly; TV, radio, film and video; Editor-in-Chief MARKKU VEIJALAINEN; circ. 70,388.

Kauneus ja terveys: Hitsaajankatu 10, 00081 Helsinki; tel. (9) 75961; fax (9) 786858; monthly; health and beauty; circ. 61,647.

Kirkko ja kaupunki: POB 137, 00201 Helsinki; tel. (9) 41552000; fax (9) 41552347; internet www.usko.net; weekly; church and community; Editor-in-Chief SEPPO SIMOLA; circ. 209,247.

Kodin Kuvalehti: POB 100, 00040 Helsinki; tel. (9) 1201; fax (9) 1205468; e-mail kodin.kuvalehti@helsinkimedia.fi; fortnightly; family magazine; Editor LEENA KARO; circ. 180,068.

Kotilääkäri: Maistraatinportti 1, 00240 Helsinki; tel. (9) 15661; fax (9) 1566507; e-mail kotilaakari@kuvalehdet.fi; f. 1889; monthly; health and beauty; Editor-in-Chief Tarja Hurme; circ. 64,769.

Kotiliesi: Maistraatinportti 1, 00240 Helsinki; tel. (9) 15661; fax (9) 147724; f. 1922; fortnightly; women's; Editor-in-Chief Elina Simonen-Hyvärinen; circ. 200,474.

Kotivinkki: Kalevankatu 56, 00180 Helsinki; tel. (9) 773951; fax (9) 77395399; e-mail ritva.kaarakainen@forma.fi; internet www.kotivinkki.fi; monthly; women's; Editor-in-Chief Anneli Myller; circ. 207,550.

Me Naiset: POB 100, 00040 Helsinki; tel. (9) 1201; fax (9) 1205414; internet www.menaiset.fi; f. 1952; weekly; women's; Editor Ulla-Maija Paavilainen; circ. 115,000.

Metsälehti: Soidinkj 4, 00700 Helsinki; tel. (9) 1562333; fax (9) 1562335; e-mail paavo.seppanen@metsalehti.mailnet.fi; internet www.metsalehti.fi; f. 1933; fortnightly; forestry; Editor Paavo Seppänen; circ. 37,606.

MikroPC: POB 920, 00101 Helsinki; tel. (9) 148801; fax (9) 6856631; 20 a year; computers; circ. 39,000.

Nykyposti: Maistraatinportti 1, 00240 Helsinki; tel. (9) 15661; fax (9) 144595; f. 1977; monthly; family journal; Editor Jaana Laukkanen; circ. 107,375.

Partio: Kylänvanhimmantie 29, 00640 Helsinki; tel. (9) 25331100; fax (9) 25331160; e-mail jaana.kivipelto@sp.partio.fi; six a year; the Scout movement; circ. 57,188.

Pellervo: POB 77, 00101 Helsinki; tel. (9) 4767501; fax (9) 6948845; e-mail finncoop@pellervo.fi; internet www.pellervo.fi; f. 1899; monthly; agricultural and co-operative, home and country life journal; organ of the central organization of co-operatives; Editors-in-Chief Martti Seppänen, Kaisu Räsänen; circ. 32,000.

PerusSuomalainen: Mannerheimintie 40B 56, 00100 Helsinki; tel. (9) 4540411; fax (9) 4540466; e-mail peruss@perussuomalaiset.fi; internet www.perussuomalaiset.fi; f. 1996; 12 a year; organ of the Perussuomalaiset/Sannfinländarna rp (PerusS—True Finns); Editor Rolf (Fred) Sormo; circ. 100,000.

Pirkka: Köydenpunojank 2A D, 00180 Helsinki; tel. (9) 15668510; fax (9) 15668525; 10 a year; Swedish; trade; Editor-in-Chief Riitta Korhonen; circ. 1,383,482.

Reserviläinen: Döbelninkatu 2, 00260 Helsinki; tel. (9) 40562018; fax (9) 499875; e-mail reservilainen@maanpuolustusyhtio.fi; nine a year; military; circ. 60,000.

Sähköviesti/Elbladet: POB 1427, 00101 Helsinki; tel. (9) 53052700; fax (9) 53052801; e-mail ari.vesa@energia.fi; f. 1939; quarterly; publ. by Finnish Electricity Asscn; Editor-in-Chief Ari J. Vesa; circ. 101,575.

Sampovisio: POB 2, 00040 Helsinki; tel. (9) 1205964; fax (9) 1205999; six a year; business, finance; circ. 65,000.

Seura: Maistraatinportti 1, 00240 Helsinki; tel. (9) 15661; fax (9) 1496472; f. 1934; weekly; family journal; Editor-in-Chief Jouni Flinkkilä; circ. 268,553.

STTK—lehti: POB 248, 00171 Helsinki; tel. (9) 131521; fax (9) 652367; e-mail matti.hynynen@sttk.fi; eight a year; organ of Finnish Confederation of Salaried Employees; Editor-in-Chief Matti Hynynen; circ. 40,000.

Suomen Kuvalehti: Maistraatinportti 1, 00015 Kuvalehdet; tel. (9) 15661; fax (9) 144076; e-mail suomen.kuvalehti@kuvalehdet.fi; internet www.suomenkuvalehti.fi; f. 1916; weekly; illustrated news; Editor-in-Chief Tapani Ruokanen; circ. 100,967.

Suosikki: Maistraatinportti 1, 00015 Yhtyneet Kuvalehdet; tel. (9) 1566553; fax (9) 144595; e-mail suosikki@kuvalehdet.fi; internet www.suosikki.fi; f. 1961; monthly; youth magazine, pop-music, movies, fashion; Editor-in-Chief Katja Ståhl; circ. 52,410.

Suuri Käsityölehti: POB 100, 00040 Helsinki; tel. (9) 1201; fax (9) 1205428; f. 1974; monthly; needlework, knitting and dress-making magazine; Editor Kristina Tötterman; circ. 126,858.

Talouselämä: Malminkatu 30, POB 920, 00101 Helsinki; tel. (9) 2044240; fax (9) 204424108; e-mail te@talentum.fi; internet www.talouselama.fi; f. 1938; 43 a year; economy, business; Man. Dir Harri Roschier; Editor-in-Chief Pekka Seppänen; circ. 78,804.

Tekniikan Maailma: Esterinportti 1, 00240 Helsinki; tel. (9) 15661; fax (9) 15666313; e-mail tekniikan.maailma@kuvalehdet.fi; internet www.tekniikanmaailma.fi; f. 1953; 22 a year; technical review; Editor-in-Chief Martti J. Merilinna; circ. 143,104.

Trendi: Kalevankatu 56A, 00180 A-lehdet, Helsinki; tel. (9) 773951; fax (9) 77395399; 10 a year; women's lifestyle; circ. 62,063.

Tuulilasi: 00081 A-lehdet; tel. (9) 75961; fax (9) 75983103; e-mail tuulilasi@a-lehdet.fi; internet www.tuulilasi.fi; f. 1963; monthly; motoring; Editor-in-Chief Lauri Larmela; circ. 93,614.

Työ Terveys Turvallisuus: Topeliuksenkatu 41A, 00250 Helsinki; tel. (30) 4741; fax (30) 4742478; f. 1971; 12 a year; occupational safety and health; Editor-in-Chief Matti Tapiainen; circ. 72,525.

Valitut Palat: POB 46, 00441 Helsinki; tel. (9) 503441; fax (9) 5034499; internet www.valitutpalat.fi; monthly; Finnish Reader's Digest; Editor-in-Chief Raimo Möysä; circ. 226,297.

Voi Hyvin: Risto Rytin tie 33, 00081 A-lehdet, Helsinki; tel. (9) 75961; fax (9) 75983109; e-mail voihyvin@a-lehdet.fi; internet www.a-lehdet.fi/voihyvin; six a year; health; circ. 60,000.

Yhteishyvä: Fleminginkatu 34, POB 171, 00511 Helsinki; tel. (9) 1882621; fax (9) 1882626; e-mail elo@sok.fi; internet www.yhteiashyva.fi; f. 1905; monthly; free to members of co-operative group; Editor-in-Chief Pentti Törmälä; circ. 848,000.

NEWS AGENCIES

Oy Suomen Tietotoimisto-Finska Notisbyrån Ab (STT-FNB): Albertinkatu 33, POB 550, 00101 Helsinki; tel. (9) 695811; fax (9) 69581335; e-mail toimitus@stt.fi; internet www.stt.fi; f. 1887; nine provincial branches; independent national agency distributing domestic and international news in Finnish and Swedish; Chair. Seppo Kievari; Gen. Man. and Editor-in-Chief Mikael Pentikaïnen.

Foreign Bureaux

Agence France-Presse (AFP) (France): Hämeentie 101B, 38, 00500 Helsinki; tel. (9) 737693; fax (9) 27095339; Correspondent Pascal Zerling.

Agenzia Nazionale Stampa Associata (ANSA) (Italy): Albertinkatu 33, 00180 Helsinki; tel. 503075115; fax (9) 69581335; e-mail anna.torvalds@stt.fi; Correspondent Anna Torvalds.

Associated Press (AP) (USA): Erottasankatu 9B, 00130 Helsinki; tel. (9) 6802394; fax (9) 6802310; e-mail aphelsinki@ap.org; Correspondent Matti Huuhtanen.

Informatsionnoye Telegrafnoye Agentstvo Rossii—Telegrafnoye Agentstvo Suverennykh Stran (ITAR—TASS) (Russia): Ratakatu 1A B 10, 00120 Helsinki; tel. (9) 601877; fax (9) 601151; e-mail ryhels@hotmail.com; internet www.itar-tass.com; Dir Yuri Romantsov.

Inter Press Service (IPS) (Italy): Helsinki; tel. (9) 7536954; fax (9) 7536964; e-mail ips@kaapeli.fi; Editor Milla Sundström.

Reuters (UK): Yrjönkatu 23B 7, POB 550, 00110 Helsinki; tel. (9) 68050247; fax (9) 6802284; Correspondent Adam Jasser.

Rossiyskoye Informatsionnoye Agentstvo—Novosti (RIA—Novosti) (Russia): Lönnrotinkatu 25A, 00180 Helsinki; tel. (9) 6820580; fax (9) 6942357; Dir Leonid Laakso; Correspondent Rudolf Hiltunen.

Xinhua (New China) News Agency (People's Republic of China): Hopeasalmentie 14, 00570 Helsinki; tel. (9) 6847587; fax (9) 6848629; Correspondents Zheng Huanging, Qie Shuangtao.

PRESS ASSOCIATIONS

Aikakauslehtien Liitto (Periodical Publishers' Association): Lönnrotinkatu 11, 00120 Helsinki; tel. (9) 22877280; fax (9) 603478; internet www.aikakauslehdet.fi; f. 1946; aims to further the interests of publishers of magazines and periodicals, to encourage co-operation between publishers, and to improve standards; Man. Dir Matti Ahtomies.

Suomen Journalistiliitto—Finlands Journalistförbund r.y. (Union of Journalists): Hietalahdenkatu 2B 22, 00180 Helsinki; tel. (9) 6122330; fax (9) 644120; e-mail eila.hypponen@journalistiliitto.fi; internet www.journalistiliitto.fi; f. 1921; 13,500 mems; Pres. Pekka Laine; Sec.-Gen. Eila Hyppönen.

Sanomalehtien Liitto—Tidningarnas Förbund (Finnish Newspapers' Association): Lönnrotinkatu 11, 00100 Helsinki; tel. (9) 22877300; fax (9) 607989; e-mail info@sanomalehdet.fi; internet www.sanomalehdet.fi; f. 1908; represents the press in relations with Government and advertisers; undertakes technical research; promotes newspaper advertising; 204 mems; Dir Kristiina Markkula.

Publishers

Art House Oy: Bulevardi 19C, 00120 Helsinki; tel. (9) 6932727; fax (9) 6949028; f. 1975; Finnish and foreign fiction, non-fiction, popular science, horror, fantasy, science fiction, detective fiction; Publr Paavo Haavikko.

Gummerus Kustannus Oy: Arkadiankatu 23B, POB 749, 00101 Helsinki; tel. (9) 584301; fax (9) 58430200; e-mail publisher@gummerus.fi; internet www.gummerus.fi; f. 1872; fiction, non-fiction, encyclopaedias, dictionaries; Man. Dir Ilkka Kylmälä.

Karisto Oy: Paroistentie 2, POB 102, 13101 Hämeenlinna; tel. (3) 63151; fax (3) 6161565; f. 1900; non-fiction and fiction, the printing industry; Man. Dir Simo Moisio.

Kirjapaja: POB 137, 00201 Helsinki; tel. (9) 613021; fax (9) 61302341; e-mail mira.pitkanen@kirjapaja.fi; internet www .kirjapaja.fi; f. 1942; Christian literature, general fiction, non-fiction, reference, juvenile; Man. Dir Mira Pitkänen.

Kustannus-Mäkelä Oy: POB 14, 03601 Karkkila; tel. (9) 2257995; fax (9) 2257660; f. 1971; juvenile, fiction; Man. Dir Orvo Mäkelä.

Oy Like Kustannus Ltd: Meritullinkatu 21, 00170 Helsinki; tel. (9) 1351385; fax (9) 1351372; e-mail likekustannus@dlc.fi; f. 1987; film literature, fiction, non-fiction, comics; Man. Dir Hannu Paloviita.

Otava Publishing Co Ltd: Uudenmaankatu 10, 00120 Helsinki; tel. (9) 19961; fax (9) 643136; e-mail otava@otava.fi; internet www .otava.fi; f. 1890; non-fiction, fiction, the printing industry, science, juvenile, and textbooks; Man. Dir Antti Reenpää.

Schildts Förlags Ab: Rusthållargatan 1, 02270 Espoo; tel. (9) 8870400; fax (9) 8043257; e-mail schildts@schildts.fi; f. 1913; subjects mainly in Swedish; Man. Dir Johan Johnson.

Söderström & Co Förlags Ab: Georgsgatan 29A, 00100 Helsinki; tel. (9) 68418620; fax (9) 68418621; e-mail soderstrom@soderstrom .fi; internet www.soderstrom.fi; f. 1891; all subjects in Swedish only; Man. Dir Marianne Bargum.

Suomalaisen Kirjallisuuden Seura, SKS (Finnish Literature Society): POB 259, 00171 Helsinki; tel. (9) 131231; fax (9) 13123220; e-mail books@finlit.fi; internet www.finlit.fi; f. 1831; Finnish and other Finno-Ugric languages, Finnish literature, literary scholarship, folklore, comparative ethnology and history; Publishing Dir Päivi Vallisaari.

Tammi Publishers: Urho Kekkosen katu 4–6E, 00100 Helsinki; tel. (9) 6937621; fax (9) 69376266; e-mail tammi@tammi.net; internet www.tammi.net; f. 1943; fiction, non-fiction, juvenile; Man. Dir Pentti Molander.

Weilin & Göös Oy: Kappelitie 8, 02200 Espoo; tel. (9) 43771; fax (9) 4377270; e-mail weegee@wg.fi; internet www.wg.fi; f. 1872; non-fiction, encyclopaedias.

Werner Söderström Corpn (WSOY): Bulevardi 12, 00120 Helsinki; tel. (9) 61681; fax (9) 61683560; internet www.wsoy.fi; f. 1878; fiction and non-fiction, science, juvenile, textbooks, reference, comics, the printing industry; Pres. Jorma Kaimio.

PUBLISHERS' ASSOCIATION

Suomen Kustannusyhdistys (Finnish Book Publishers' Association): POB 177, 00121 Helsinki; tel. (9) 22877258; fax (9) 6121226; e-mail veikko.sonninen@skyry.net; internet www.skyry.net; f. 1858; Chair. Leena Majander; Man. Dir Veikko Sonninen; 100 mems.

Broadcasting and Communications

REGULATORY AUTHORITY

Finnish Communications Regulatory Authority (FICORA): Itämerenkatu 3A, POB 313, 00181 Helsinki; tel. (9) 69661; fax (9) 6966410; e-mail info@ficora.fi; internet www.ficora.fi; affiliated to Ministry of Transport and Communications; CEO Rauni Hagman.

TELECOMMUNICATIONS

Elisa Corpn: Kutomotie 18, POB 1, 00061 Elisa; tel. (0) 1026000; fax (0) 1026060; internet www.elisa.com; Pres. and CEO Veli-Matti Mattila.

Finnet International Ltd: Itämerenkatu 1, POB 999, 00181 Helsinki; tel. (9) 695500; fax (9) 69550300.

Nokia Oyj: Keilalahdentie 4, 02150 Espoo; POB 226, 00045 Nokia Group; tel. (0)718008000; fax (0)718038226; internet www.nokia .com; Pres. and CEO Jorma Ollila.

Telecon Ltd: POB 110, Teollisuuskatu 15, 00511 Helsinki; tel. (9) 20405390; fax (9) 20405389; e-mail telecon@telecon.fi; Man. Dir Yrjö Sirkeinen.

TeliaSonera Finland Oyj: Teollisuuskatu 15, POB 106, 00051 Sonera; tel. (800) 17000; fax (800) 188111; e-mail yritysasiakaspalvelu@sonera.com; internet www.teliasonera.fi; f. 2002; merger of Telia AB (Sweden) and Sonera Ltd; Pres. and CEO Anni Vepsäläinen.

RADIO

The first commercial radio stations were introduced in 1985 and stations proliferated rapidly to reach 59 by 1990. The global eco-

nomic recession of the early 1990s led to the collapse of many commercial stations but the industry began to recover in the late 1990s, notably with the launch of the first national commercial radio station, Radio Nova, in May 1997. In 2003 there were 71 radio stations; Radio Nova remained the only national commercial station. In 1999 RAB Finland was established to promote and develop the Finnish private radio industry by providing extensive information services free of charge to media planners, buyers and advertisers.

In May 1999 the first part of the national Digital Audio Broadcast (DAB) network was launched by Yleisradio (Finnish Broadcasting Company—YLE) with 10 transmitters (rising to 11 in 2001), covering 2m. people (approximately 40% of the population). YLE currently broadcasts its five existing analogue channels and has added five new 24–hour services (a news/talk service, classical music channel, young adult lifestyle channel, multilingual foreign language news service, English news service) and four part-time services (YLE Parliament, Swedish language extra news, Swedish language extra sports, educational radio). On 14 November 2002 the Government granted Digita Oy a network operating licence.

RAB Finland: Lönnrotinkatu 11A, 00121 Helsinki; tel. (9) 22877341; fax (9) 648221; e-mail tomo.savola@rabfinland.fi; internet www.rabfinland.fi; f. 1999; promotes Finnish private radio industry by providing extensive information services free of charge; Man. Dir Timo Savola.

Classic FM: Lintulahdenkatu 10, 00500 Helsinki; tel. (9) 6126911; fax (9) 61269130; e-mail tom.bussman@mediasalesfinland.fi; internet www.classicfm.fi.

Groove FM: Lintulahdenkatu 10, 00500 Helsinki; tel. (9) 6126911; fax (9) 61269130; e-mail tom.bussman@mediasalesfinland.fi; internet www.groovefm.fi.

Iskelmä: Tallberginkatu 1C, 00180 Helsinki; tel. (9) 680960; fax (9) 68096521; e-mail erkka.jaakkola@sbs.fi; internet www.iskelma.fi.

Kiss FM: Tallberginkatu 1C, 00180 Helsinki; tel. (9) 68096501; fax (9) 68096521; e-mail juha.mellin@kiss.fi; internet www.kiss.fi.

NRJ: Kiviaidankatu 2I, 00210 Helsinki; tel. (9) 681900; fax (9) 68190102; e-mail marko.lintussari@nrj.fi; internet www.nrj.fi.

Radio Nova: Ilmalankatu 2C, 00241 Helsinki; tel. (9) 88488700; fax (9) 88488720; e-mail leena.rotko@radionova.fi; internet www .radionova.fi; largest commercial radio station; 74% owned by Alma Media; Marketing Dir Päivi Nurmesniemi.

Radio SuomiPOP: Lintulahdenkatu 10, 00500 Helsinki; tel. (9) 6126911; fax (9) 61269130; e-mail tom.bussman@mediasalesfinland .fi.

Sport FM: Areenakuja 1, 00240 Helsinki; tel. (9) 2041997; fax (9) 2041994; e-mail tapio.karimies@sport.fm.

Sävelradio: Hankasuontie 3, 00390 Helsinki; tel. (9) 56156900; fax (9) 56156902; e-mail kari.kuorikoski@janton.fi; internet www .savelradio.fi.

Yleisradio Oy (YLE) (Finnish Broadcasting Company): POB 90, 00024 Yleisradio; tel. (9) 14801; fax (9) 14803216; e-mail fbc@yle.fi; internet www.yle.fi/fbc; f. 1926; 99.9% state-owned, with management appointed by the Administrative Council; Dir-Gen. Mikael Jungner; Dir of Radio and Deputy Dir-Gen. Seppo Härkönen; Dir of Television Olli-Pekka Heinonen; Dir of Swedish-language Radio and Television Programmes Ann Sandelin.

Digita Oy: POB 135, 00521 Helsinki; tel. (9) 20411711; fax (9) 204117234; e-mail pauli.heikkila@digita.fi; internet www.digita .fi; f. 1999; Man. Dir Pauli Heikkilä.

YLE R1 (Radio Ylen Ykkönen): 24-hour arts and culture in Finnish; Dir Antti Pajamo.

YLE R2 (Radiomafia): 24-hour popular culture for young people in Finnish; Dir Jukka Haarma.

YLE R3 (Radio Suomi): 24-hour news, current affairs, sport, regional programmes in Finnish; Dir Raimo Vanninen.

YLE R4 (Radio Extrem): Swedish-language channel for young people; Dir Richard Nordgren.

YLE R5 (Radio Vega): news, current affairs, art, culture and regional programmes in Swedish; Dir Peik Henrichson.

YLE Radio Finland: POB 78, 00024 Yleisradio; tel. (9) 14804320; fax (9) 14801169; e-mail rfinland@yle.fi; internet www .yle.fi/rfinland; broadcasts in Finnish, Swedish, English, German, French, Russian and Classical Latin; Head of International Radio Juhani Niinisto.

YLE Sámi Radio: 99870 Inari; tel. (16) 671261; fax (16) 671265; internet www.yle.fi/samiradio; Sámi-language network covering northern Lapland.

www.europaworld.com   1693

TELEVISION

Yleisradio (YLE): (see above) operates two national networks, TV 1 and TV 2, and leases the third network to the commercial company MTV Finland (see below).

YLE/TV 1: POB 97, 00024 Yleisradio; tel. (9) 14801; fax (9) 14803424; internet www.yle.fi/tv1; f. 1957; programmes in Finnish; Head of Programming RIITTA JALONEN.

YLE/TV 2: POB 196, 33101 Tampere; tel. (3) 3456111; fax (3) 3456892; internet www.yle.fi/tv2; f. 1964; programmes in Finnish and Swedish; Dir PÄIVI KÄRKKÄINEN.

YLE/TV 4: relays programmes from Sweden for coastal areas in southern Finland.

MTV Finland: 00033 MTV3; 00240 Helsinki; tel. (9) 15001; fax (9) 1500707; e-mail palaute@mtv3.fi; internet www.mtv3.fi; f. 1957; independent nation-wide commercial television company producing programmes on the third national network (MTV3), leased from YLE, the state broadcasting company (see above); became part of Alma Media Corpn in 1998; broadcasts about 120 hours per week; Pres. and CEO PEKKA KARHUVAARA.

Oy Ruutunelonen Ab: POB 40, 00521 Helsinki; tel. (9) 45451; fax (9) 1482323; e-mail juha-pekka.louhelainen@nelonen.fi; internet www.nelonen.fi; independent commercial television co reaching 81% of households via terrestrial, satellite and cable broadcasting; 90.6% owned by Swelcom Oy; CEO JUHA-PEKKA LOUHELAINEN.

DIGITAL TELEVISION

Digital Video Broadcasting (DVB) began in Finland in 2001. Analogue networks will be closed down on 31 August 2007. As a result of international agreements, Finland has DVB channels for three terrestrial networks. Frequencies can also be allocated to a fourth network covering about 70% of the population. The Finnish Communications Regulatory Authority (FICORA) is responsible for the frequency plan for distribution networks and grants the radio licences required for transmitters. FICORA is also responsible for international co-operation related to frequency usage.

Canal Digital Finland Oy: POB 866, 33101 Tampere; tel. (0) 207699000; fax (0) 207699006; e-mail asiakaspalvelu@canaldigital.fi; internet www.canaldigital.fi.

Finance

The Bank of Finland is the country's central bank and the centre of Finland's monetary and banking system. It functions 'under guarantee and supervision of the Eduskunta (Parliament) and the Bank supervisors delegated by the Eduskunta'.

At the end of 2003 there were a total of 335 domestic banks operating in Finland, of which eight were commercial banks. There were 244 co-operative banks belonging to the OKO Bank Group, 42 local co-operative banks and 39 savings banks. There were eight foreign credit institutions.

In addition to the above, there were finance and credit card companies, mortgage banks and special credit institutions. Insurance companies also grant credit.

BANKING

(cap. = capital; res = reserves; dep. = deposits; m. = million; brs = branches; amounts in euros (€))

Supervisory Authority

Financial Supervision Authority: Snellmaninkatu 1, POB 159, 00101 Helsinki; tel. (9) 18351; fax (9) 1835328; e-mail rahoitustarkastus@bof.fi; internet www.rata.bof.fi; f. 1993; maintains confidence in the financial markets by supervising the markets and the bodies working within them. It functions administratively in connection with the Bank of Finland, but operates as an independent decision-making body; Dir-Gen. KAARLO JÄNNÄRI.

Central Bank

Suomen Pankki/Finlands Bank (The Bank of Finland): Snellmaninaukio, POB 160, 00101 Helsinki; tel. (9) 1831; fax (9) 174872; e-mail info@bof.fi; internet www.bof.fi; f. 1811; Bank of Issue under the guarantee and supervision of the Eduskunta; cap. €841m., res €545m., dep. €2,395m. (Dec. 2003); Gov. ERKKI LIIKANEN; 4 brs.

Commercial Banks

Nordea Bank Finland PLC: Aleksanterinkatu 36B, 00100 Helsinki; tel. (9) 1651; fax (9) 16554500; internet www.nordea.fi; cap. €1,160m., res €9,527m., dep. €188,689m. (Dec. 2003); CEO LARS G. NORDSTRÖM; 416 brs.

Sampo Bank PLC: Unioninkatu 22, Helsinki, 00075 Sampo; tel. 1051515; fax 105140051; e-mail viestinta@sampo.fi; internet www.sampo.fi; subsidiary of financial holding co Sampo PLC (formed by merger of Leonia Bank PLC—f. 1886 as Postipankki Ltd—with insurance company Sampo PLC in 2001); cap. €106m., res €635m., dep. €14,505m. (Dec. 2003); CEO BJÖRN WAHLROOS; 63 brs.

Co-operative Banks

Association of Finnish Local Co-operative Banks: Yrjöninkatu 23A, POB 1290, 00101 Helsinki; tel. (9) 6811700; fax (9) 68117070; internet www.paikallisosuuspankit.fi; f. 1997; central organization of local co-operative banking group, which comprises 43 local co-operatives; cap. €200m., dep. €1,600m., total assets €2,062m. (Dec. 2000); 241 brs.

OKO Osuuspankkien Keskuspankki Oyj (OKO Bank): Teollisuuskatu 1B, POB 308, 00101 Helsinki; tel. 10252011; fax 102522002; internet www.okobank.com; f. 1902; cap. €202m., res €404m., dep. €12,917m. (Dec. 2003); Chair. and CEO ANTTI TANSKANEN; Pres. MIKAEL SILVENNOINEN; 682 brs.

Savings Bank

Aktia Sparbank Abp (Aktia Savings Bank PLC): Mannerheimintie 14, 00100 Helsinki; tel. 102475000; fax 102476356; e-mail aktia@aktia.fi; internet www.aktia.fi; f. 1852 as Helsingfors Sparbank; current name adopted 1997; cap. €71m., res €69m., dep. €3,111m. (Dec. 2003); Chair. STIG STENDAHL; Man. Dir MIKAEL INGBERG; 62 brs.

Mortgage Banks

OP-Asuntoluottopankki: POB 308, 00101 Helsinki; tel. (9) 4041; fax (9) 4042620; f. 2000; part of OKO Bank Group.

Suomen Asuntoluottopankki (Housing Loan Bank of Finland): Unioninkatu 22, 00075 Sampo; tel. 105135789; fax 105134616; f. 2000; part of Sampo Group; cap. €6m., total assets €25m. (Dec. 2000).

Investment Bank

Nordiska Investeringsbanken (Nordic Investment Bank): Fabianinkatu 34, POB 249, 00171 Helsinki; tel. (9) 18001; fax (9) 1800210; e-mail info@nib.int; internet www.nib.int; f. 1975; owned by Govts of Denmark (22%), Finland (19%), Iceland (1%), Norway (20%) and Sweden (38%); cap. €404m., res €1,094m., dep. €13,453m. (Dec. 2003); Pres. and CEO JON SIGURÐSSON.

Banking Associations

Säästöpankkiliitto (Finnish Savings Banks Association): Linnoitustie 9, POB 68, 02601 Espoo; tel. (9) 548051; fax (0) 206029108; internet www.savings-banks.fi; f. 1906; 40 mems; Chair. JUSSI HAKALA; Man. Dir MARKKU RUUTU; 256 brs.

Suomen Hypoteekkiyhdistys (Mortgage Society of Finland): Yrjönkatu 9, POB 509, 00101 Helsinki; tel. (9) 228361; fax (9) 647443; e-mail hypo@hypoteekkiyhdistys.fi; internet www.hypoteekkiyhdistys.fi; f. 1860; cap. €36m., total assets €336m. (Dec. 2000); Pres. MATTI INHA.

Suomen Pankkiyhdistys r.y. (The Finnish Bankers' Association): Museokatu 8A, POB 1009, 00101 Helsinki; tel. (9) 4056120; fax (9) 40561291; e-mail info@fba.fi; internet www.fba.fi; f. 1914; Chair. MIKA IHAMUOTILA; Man. Dir MARKUS FOGELHOLM.

Suomen Rahoitusyhtiöiden Yhdistys r.y. (Finnish Finance Houses' Association): Museokatu 8A, POB 1009, 00101 Helsinki; tel. (9) 4056120; fax (9) 40561291; internet www.rahoitusyhtiot.fi; f. 1974; Chair. ILKKA KANSANNIVA.

STOCK EXCHANGE

HEX Helsinki: Fabianinkatu 14, POB 361, 00131 Helsinki; tel. (9) 616671; fax (9) 61667366; e-mail info@hex.fi; internet www.hex.com; f. 1912; owned by OMX AB; total market cap. €159,000m. (Dec. 2004); 137 listed cos, 44 mems; forms group with stock exchanges in Helsinki, Rīga, Tallinn and Vilnius; Chair. of Bd of Dirs JUSSI LAITINEN; CEO JUHANI ERMA.

INSURANCE

In May 2004 there were 46 licensed insurance companies, 26 specializing in non-life business and reinsurance and seven in statutory pension insurance. In February 2004 22 foreign insurance companies had branches in Finland.

A-Vakuutus keskinäinen yhtiö (A-Vakuutus Mutual Insurance Co): Hietalahdenranta 3, POB 165, 00151 Helsinki; tel. 105040; fax 105045200; non-life; Man. Dir ESKO RINKINEN.

Aurum Life Insurance Co. Ltd: POB 308, 00101 Helsinki; tel. (9) 4042528; fax (9) 4043501; Man. Dir JUKKA RUUSKANEN.

Eurooppalainen Insurance Co Ltd: Lapinmäentie 1, 00013 Pohjola; tel. 1055911; fax 105592205; non-life; Man. Dir JOUNI AALTONEN.

Garantia Insurance Co Ltd: Salomonkatu 17A, POB 600, 00101 Helsinki; tel. (9) 685811; fax (9) 68581301; internet www.garantia.fi; non-life; Man. Dir MIKAEL ENGLUND.

Henkivakuutusosakeyhtiö Pohjola (Pohjola Life Assurance Co Ltd): POB 1068, 00101 Helsinki; tel. 1055911; fax 105596799; internet www.pohjola.fi; Man. Dir JARMO KUISMA.

Henkivakuutusosakeyhtiö Veritas (Veritas Life Insurance Co Ltd): Olavintie 2, POB 133, 20101 Turku; tel. 1055010; fax 105501690; internet www.veritas.fi; Pres. MATTI RUOHONEN.

Keskinäinen Eläkevakuutusyhtiö Ilmarinen (Ilmarinen Mutual Pension Insurance Co): Porkkalankatu 1, 00018 Ilmarinen; tel. 1028411; fax 102843445; e-mail info@ilmarinen.fi; internet www.ilmarinen.fi; f. 1961; statutory employment pensions; Man. Dir KARI PURO.

Keskinäinen Eläkevakuutusyhtiö Tapiola (Tapiola Mutual Pension Insurance Co): 02010 Tapiola; tel. (9) 4531; fax (9) 4532146; internet www.tapiola.fi; Pres. ASMO KALPALA; Man. Dir OLLI-PEKKA LAINE.

Keskinäinen työeläkevakuutusyhtiö Varma (Varma Mutual Pension Insurance Co): POB 1, 00098 Varma; tel. (0) 1051513; fax (0) 105144752; e-mail info@varma.fi; internet www.varma.fi; formerly Varma-Sampo; Man. Dir PAAVO PITKÄNEN.

Keskinäinen Henkivakuutusosakeyhtiö Suomi (Suomi Mutual Life Assurance Co): Lönnrotinkatu 5, 00120 Helsinki; tel. 1055911; fax 105596799; Man. Dir JUKKA RANTALA.

Keskinäinen Henkivakuutusyhtiö Tapiola (Tapiola Mutual Life Assurance Co): 02010 Tapiola; tel. (9) 4531; fax (9) 4532146; internet www.tapiola.fi; Pres. ASMO KALPALA; Man. Dir JUHA-PEKKA HALMEENMAKI.

Keskinäinen Vakuutusyhtiö Fennia (Fennia Mutual Insurance Co): Asemamiehenkatu 3, 00520 Helsinki; tel. (0) 105031; fax (0) 105035300; non-life; Man. Dir HANNU KETOLA.

Keskinäinen Vakuutusyhtiö Kaleva (Kaleva Mutual Insurance Co): Bulevardi 56, 00075 Sampo; tel. 10515225; fax 105767501; internet www.sampo.fi; Man. Dir MATTI RANTANEN.

Keskinäinen Vakuutusyhtiö Tapiola (Tapiola General Mutual Insurance Co): 02010 Tapiola; tel. (9) 4531; fax (9) 4532146; internet www.tapiola.fi; non-life; Pres. ASMO KALPALA; Man. Dir JUHA SEPPÄNEN.

Lähivakuutus Keskinäinen Yhtiö (Local Insurance Mutual Co): Lintuvaarantie 2, POB 50, 02601 Espoo; tel. (9) 511011; fax (9) 51101335; e-mail myynti@lahivakuutus.fi; internet www.lahivakuutus.fi; non-life; Man. Dir HARRI KAINULAINEN.

Merita Henkivakaatus Oy (Merita Life Assurance Ltd): Asemakuja 2, 00020 Merita; tel. (9) 16527601; fax (9) 8594622; internet www.merita.fi/selekta; Man. Dir SEPPO ILVESSALO.

Palonvara Mutual Insurance Co: Saimaankatu 20, 15140 Lahti; tel. (3) 873300; fax (3) 8733050; e-mail palvelu@palonvara.fi; internet www.palonvara.fi; f. 1912; non-life; Man. Dir JUKKA HERTTI.

Pankavara Insurance Co Ltd: Kanavaranta 1, POB 309, 00101 Helsinki; tel. 2046131; fax 204621447; non-life; Man. Dir JUKKA KÄHKÖNEN.

Pohjantähti Keskäinen Vakuutusyhtiö (Pohjantähti Mutual Insurance Co): Keinusaarentie 2, POB 164, 13101 Hämeenlinna; tel. (3) 62671; fax (3) 6169303; e-mail polvelu@pohjantahti.fi; internet www.pohjantahti.fi; f. 1895; non-life; Man. Dir EERO YLÄ-SOININMÄKI.

Spruce Insurance Ltd: POB 330, 00101 Helsinki; tel. 108611; fax 108621107; e-mail jaana.dromberg@kemira.com; non-life; Man. Dir DRAANA DROMBERG.

Teollisuusvakuutus Oy (Industrial Insurance Co Ltd): Vattuniemenkuja 8A, 00035 Helsinki; tel. 1051512; fax 105145232; internet www.sampo.fi; non-life; Man. Dir JUHA TOIVOLA.

Vakuutusosakeyhtiö Pohjola (Pohjola Insurance Co Ltd): Lapinmäentie 1, 00013 Pohjola; tel. 1055911; fax 105592205; non-life; Man. Dir JOUKKO BERGIUS.

Insurance Associations

Federation of Accident Insurance Institutions: Bulevardi 28, POB 275, 00121 Helsinki; tel. (9) 680401; fax (9) 68040389; internet www.tvl.fi; f. 1920; Man. Dir TAPANI MIETTINEN.

Federation of Finnish Insurance Companies: Bulevardi 28, 00120 Helsinki; tel. (9) 680401; fax (9) 68040216; e-mail esko.kivisaari@vakes.fi; internet www.vakes.fi/svk; f. 1942; Chair. KARI STADIGH; Man. Dir ESKO KIVISAARI; 49 mems.

Finnish Motor Insurers' Centre: Bulevardi 28, 00120 Helsinki; tel. (9) 680401; fax (9) 68040391; e-mail lvk@vakes.fi; internet www.vakes.fi/lvk; f. 1938; Man. Dir ULLA NIKU-KOSKINEN.

Finnish Pension Alliance TELA: Lastenkodinkuja 1, 00180 Helsinki; tel. (9) 695560; fax (9) 69556200; f. 1964; Man. Dir ESA SWANLJUNG.

Nordic Nuclear Insurers: Ratakatu 9, 00120 Helsinki; tel. (9) 6801490; Man. Dir PETER GRANQVIST.

Trade and Industry

GOVERNMENT AGENCIES

Finpro: Porkkalankatu 1, POB 358, 00181 Helsinki; tel. (0) 2046951; fax (0) 204695200; e-mail info@finpro.fi; internet www.finpro.fi; f. 1919 as Finnish Foreign Trade Association; Chair., Supervisory Bd MATTI HONKALA; Chair. of Bd of Dirs ANTTI HERLIN; Pres. and CEO TAPANI KASKEALA.

Invest in Finland Bureau: Aleksanterinkatu 17, POB 800, 00101 Helsinki; tel. (9) 6969125; fax (9) 69692530; e-mail investinfinland@wtc.fi; internet www.investinfinland.fi.

DEVELOPMENT ORGANIZATION

Altia Group: Salmisaarenranta 7, POB 350, 00101 Helsinki; tel. (9) 13311; fax (9) 1333361; e-mail viestinta@altiagroup.com; internet www.altiagroup.com; f. 1932; development, manufacture, import, export, wholesale and marketing of alcoholic beverages; 100% state-owned; Pres. and CEO VEIKKO KASURINEN.

CHAMBERS OF COMMERCE

Helsinki Chamber of Commerce: Kalevankatu 12, 00100 Helsinki; tel. (9) 228601; f. 1917; Pres. KURT NORDMAN; Man. Dir HEIKKI HELIÖ; 4,100 mems.

Keskuskauppakamari (The Central Chamber of Commerce of Finland): Aleksanterinkatu 17, POB 1000, 00101 Helsinki; tel. (9) 696969; fax (9) 650303; internet www.chamber.fi; f. 1918; Gen. Man. KARI JALAS; represents 21 regional chambers of commerce.

INDUSTRIAL AND TRADE ASSOCIATIONS

Kalatalouden Keskusliitto (Federation of Finnish Fisheries Associations): Köydenpunojankatu 7B 23, 00180 Helsinki; tel. (9) 6844590; fax (9) 68445959; e-mail kalastus@ahven.net; internet www.ahven.net; f. 1891; Sec. M. MYLLYLÄ; 616,000 mems.

Kaukomarkkinat Oy: Kutojantie 4, 02630 Espoo; tel. (9) 5211; fax (9) 5216641; e-mail kari.ansio@kaukomarkkinat.fi; internet www.kaukomarkkinat.fi; f. 1947; export, import and international trade; Pres. KARI ANSIO.

Kaupan Keskusliitto (Federation of Finnish Commerce and Trade): Mannerheimintie 76A, 00250 Helsinki; tel. (9) 43156122; fax (9) 43156302; e-mail e-mail@kaupankl.fi; internet www.kaupankl.fi; f. 1992; Man. Dir GUY WIRES; 36 mem. asscns with more than 12,000 firms.

Kesko Oyj (Retailers' Wholesale Co): Satamakatu 3, 00160 Helsinki; tel. (0) 105311; fax (9) 174398; internet www.kesko.fi; f. 1941; retailer-owned wholesale corporation, trading in foodstuffs, textiles, shoes, consumer goods, hardware, agricultural and builders' supplies, and machinery; Pres. MATTI HONKALA.

Maa- ja metsataloustuottajain Keskusliitto MTK r.y. (Central Union of Agricultural Producers and Forest Owners): Simonkatu 6, 00100 Helsinki; tel. (0) 204131; fax (0) 204132425; e-mail paavo.makinen@mtk.fi; internet www.mtk.fi; f. 1917; Chair. of Bd of Dirs ESA HÄRMÄLÄ; Sec.-Gen. PAAVO MÄKINEN; 179,000 mems.

Metsäteollisuus r.y. (Finnish Forest Industries' Federation): Snellmaninkatu 13, POB 336, 00171 Helsinki; tel. (9) 13261; fax (9) 1324445; e-mail timo-poranen@forestindustries.fi; internet www.forestindustries.fi; f. 1918; Man. Dir TIMO PORANEN; mems: 120 cos in the forestry industry and sales or trade asscns.

Sähköenergialiitto r.y. (Finnish Electricity Association): POB 100, 00101 Helsinki; tel. (9) 530520; fax (9) 53052100; internet www.energia.fi; f. 1926; 100 mems; development of technical, economic and administrative functions of utilities; consultant services in electricity supply; educational activities; research and advice on electrical applications; collection and publication of electricity statistics; publishes consumer magazine *Sähköviesti/Elbladet*; domestic and international co-operation; safety at work and environmental conservation.

Suomalaisen Työn Liitto (Association for Finnish Work): Mikonkatu 17, POB 429, 00101 Helsinki; tel. (9) 6962430; fax (9) 69624333; e-mail stl@avainlippu.fi; internet www.avainlippu.fi; f. 1978; public relations for Finnish products and for Finnish work; Chair. of Council MAURI PEKKARINEN; Chair., Bd of Dirs PEKKA SAIRANEN; Man. Dir LARS COLLIN; c. 1,200 mems.

Suomen Betonitieto (Finnish Concrete Industry Asscn): Helsinki; tel. (9) 12991; fax (9) 1299291; internet www.betoni.com; f. 1929; Chair. HANNU MARTIKAINEN; Man. Dir OLLI HÄMÄLÄINEN; 51 mems.

Suomen Osuuskauppojen Keskusliitto (SOKL) r.y. (Finnish Co-operative Union): POB 171, 00511 Helsinki; tel. (9) 1882222; fax (9) 1882580; f. 1908; Chair. JUKKA HUISKONEN; Man. Dir TAAVI HEIK-KILÄ; 44 mems.

Svenska lantbruksproducenternas centralförbund (Central Union of Swedish-speaking Agricultural Producers): Fredriksgatan 61A, 00100 Helsinki; tel. (9) 5860460; fax (9) 6941358; internet www .slc.fi; f. 1945; Chair. H. FALCK; 16,000 mems.

Teknisen Kaupan Liitto (Association of Finnish Technical Traders): Sarkiniementie 3, 00210 Helsinki; tel. (9) 6824130; fax (9) 68241310; e-mail tekninen.kauppa@tkl.fi; internet www.tkl.fi; f. 1918; organization of the main importers dealing in steel and metals, machines and equipment, heavy chemicals and raw materials; Chair. HEIMO AHO; Man. Dir KLAUS KATARA; 225 mems.

EMPLOYERS' ORGANIZATIONS

Autoliikenteen Työnantajaliitto r.y. (Employers' Federation of Road Transport): Nuijamiestentie 7A, 00400 Helsinki; tel. (9) 47899480; fax (9) 5883995; internet www.altnet.fi; Chair. MIKKO VÄHÄLÄ; Man. Dir HANNU PARVELA; c. 1,000 mems.

Kultaseppien Työnantajaliitto r.y. (Employers' Association of Goldsmiths): Eteläranta 10, 00130 Helsinki; tel. (9) 172841; fax (9) 179588; e-mail sari.vannela@ryhma.ttliitot.fi; Chair. ILKKA RUOHOLA; Exec. Dir SARI VANNELA.

Palvelutyönantajat r.y. (Employers' Confederation of Service Industries): Eteläranta 10, 00130 Helsinki; tel. (9) 172831; fax (9) 655588; internet www.palvelutyonantajat.fi; f. 1945; 13 mem. asscns consisting of about 8,900 enterprises with 362,200 employees; Man. Dir ARTO OJALA.

Suomen Tiiliteollisuusliitto r.y. (Finnish Brick Industry Association): POB 381, 00131 Helsinki; tel. (9) 12991; fax (9) 1299214; e-mail juha.luhanka@rakennusteollisuus.fi; Chair. LARS-ERIK NYSTRÖM.

Teollisuuden ja Työnantajain Keskusliitto (TT) (Confederation of Finnish Industry and Employers): Eteläranta 10, POB 30, 00131 Helsinki; tel. (9) 68681; fax (9) 68682812; e-mail tt@tt.fi; internet www.tt.fi; f. 1907; renamed 1992; aims to promote co-operation between cos and mem. organizations and to protect the interests of mems in employment issues; 30 asscns consisting of about 5,600 enterprises with 500,000 employees; Chair. JURKI JUUSELA; Dir-Gen. (vacant).

Elintarviketeollisuusliitto r.y. (Finnish Food and Drink Industries' Federation): Pasilankatu 2, 00240 Helsinki; tel. (9) 148871; fax (9) 14887201; e-mail info@etl.fi; internet www.etl.fi; Chair. BERTEL PAULIG; Dir-Gen. HEIKKI JUUTINEN.

Kemianteollisuus (KT) r.y. (Chemical Industry Federation): Eteläranta 10, POB 4, 00131 Helsinki; tel. (9) 172841; fax (9) 630225; internet www.chemind.fi; Chair. LASSE KURKILAHTI; Man. Dir HANNU VORNAMO.

Kenkä- ja Nahkateollisuus r.y. (Association of Finnish Shoe and Leather Industries): Eteläranta 10, 00130 Helsinki; tel. (9) 172841; fax (9) 179588; e-mail sari.vannela@ryhma.ttliitot.fi; Chair. OLAVI VILJANMAA; Exec. Dir SARI VANNELA.

Kumiteollisuus r.y. (Rubber Manufacturers' Association): Eteläranta 10, 00130 Helsinki; tel. (9) 6220410; fax (9) 176135; e-mail tuula.rantalaiho@kumi.ttliitot.fi; internet www.kumiteollisuus.fi; Chair. KIM GRAN; Man. Dir TUULA RANTALAIHO.

Lääketeollisuus r.y. (Pharma Industry Finland—PIF): Sörnä isten rantatie 23, POB 108, 00501 Helsinki; tel. (9) 5842400; fax (9) 58424728; e-mail pif@pif.fi; internet www.pif.fi; Chair. LASSE SAVONEN; Man. Dir JARMO LEHTONEN.

Muoviteollisuus r.y. (Finnish Plastics Industries Federation): Eteläranta 10, 00130 Helsinki; tel. (9) 172841; fax (9) 171164; internet www.plastics.fi; Chair. KARI KALLONEN; Man. Dir KARI TEPPOLA.

Palvelualojen Toimialaliitto r.y. (Association of Support Service Industries): Eteläranta 10, 00130 Helsinki; tel. (9) 172841; fax (9) 176877; internet www.palvelualojentoimialaliitto.com; Chair. PYRY LAUTSUO; Man. Dir PETER FORSSTRÖM.

PT Työnantajaliitto r.y. (PT Employers' Federation): Mannerheiminaukio 1A, 00100 Helsinki; tel. (9) 613151; fax (9) 61315082; Chair. PEKKA VENNAMO; Man. Dir JUHA KIVINEN.

Puusepänteollisuuden Liitto r.y. (Association of the Finnish Furniture and Joinery Industries): Snellmaninkatu 13, POB 336,

00171 Helsinki; tel. (9) 13261; fax (9) 1324447; e-mail jukka .nevala@forestindustries.fi; internet www.finfurniture.org; f. 1917; Chair. PEKKA SAIRANEN; Man. Dir JUKKA NEVALA; 90 mems.

Rakennusteollisuus RT r.y. (Confederation of Finnish Construction Industries): Unioninkatu 14 VI, 00130 Helsinki; tel. (9) 12991; fax (9) 628264; e-mail rt@rakennusteollisuus.fi; internet www.rakennusteollisuus.fi; f. 2001; Chair. LAURI RATIA; Man. Dir TERHO SALO.

Rannikko- ja Sisävesiliikenteen Työnantajaliitto (RASILA) r.y. (Coastal and Inland Waterway Employers' Association): Satamakatu 4A, 00160 Helsinki; tel. (9) 62267312; fax (9) 669251; Chair. STEFAN HÅKANS; Man. Dir HENRIK LÖNNQVIST.

Satamaoperaattorit r.y. (Federation of Finnish Master Stevedores): POB 268, Köydenpunojankatu 8, 00180 Helsinki; tel. (9) 6949800; fax (9) 6944585; f. 1906; formerly Suomen Lastauttajain Liitto (SLL) r.y.; Chair. HANS MARTIN; Man. Dir JOUKO SANTALA.

Suomen Kiinteistöliitto r.y. (Finnish Real-Estate Association): Annankatu 24, 00100 Helsinki; tel. (9) 166761; fax (9) 16676400; internet www.kliitto.fi; f. 1907; Chair. ASKO SALMINEN; Man. Dir UKKO LAURILA.

Suomen Varustamoyhdistys r.y. (Finnish Shipowners' Association): see under Shipping.

Suunnittelu- ja konsulttitoimistojen liitto (SKOL) r.y. (Finnish Association of Consulting Firms—SKOL): Tapiolan Keskustorni, 02100 Espoo; tel. (0) 205955100; fax (0) 205955111; e-mail skolry@skolry.fi; internet www.skolry.fi; Chair. MARKKU KASKIMIES; Man. Dir TIMO MYLLYS; 255 mems.

Teknokemian Yhdistys r.y. (Finnish Cosmetic, Toiletry and Detergent Association): Eteläranta 10, 00130 Helsinki; tel. (9) 172841; fax (9) 666561; e-mail stig.granqvist@ty.ttliitot.fi; internet www.teknokem.fi; Chair. KIRSI-MARJA KOSKELO; Man. Dir STIG GRANQVIST.

Teknologiateollisuus r.y. (Technology Industries of Finland): Eteläranta 10, POB 10, 00131 Helsinki; tel. (9) 19231; fax (9) 624462; internet www.techind.fi; f. 1903 as Metalliteollisuuden Keskusliitto r.y.; Chair. MATTI ALAHUHTA; Man. Dir MARTTI MÄENPÄÄ.

Tieto- ja tekniikka-alojen työnantajaliitto TIKLI r.y. (Asscn of Electrical and Telecommunications Employers): Yrjönkatu 13A, 00120 Helsinki; tel. (0) 205955000; fax (0) 205955001; formerly Sähkö- ja telealan työnantajaliitto r.y.; Chair. JUKKA ALHO; Dir-Gen. HARRI HIETALA; 200 mems.

Toimistoteknisen Kaupan Yhdistys (TTK) r.y. (Finnish Association of Office Technology Traders): Särkiniementie 3, 00210 Helsinki; tel. (9) 6824130; fax (9) 68241310; e-mail ttk@tkl .fi; internet www.ttkry.com; Chair. PER-OLOF ÅSTEDT; Man. Dir KLAUS KATARA.

Tupakkateollisuusliitto r.y. (Finnish Tobacco Industries' Federation): POB 115, 00241 Helsinki; tel. (9) 644373; fax (9) 14887201; e-mail asta.morsky@etl.fi; Chair. PAUL CROMPTON.

Työnantajain Yleinen Ryhmä r.y. (Finnish Employers' General Group): Eteläranta 10, 00130 Helsinki; tel. (9) 172841; fax (9) 179588; e-mail sari.vannela@ryhma.ttliitot.fi; Chair. MARKKU JOKINEN; Exec. Dir SARI VANNELA.

Viestintätyönantajat VTA (Media Employers' Association): Lönnrotinkatu 11A, 00120 Helsinki; tel. (9) 22877200; fax (9) 603527; Chair. KEIJO KETONEN; Dir JOHANNA VARIS.

Yleinen Teollisuusliitto r.y. (General Industry Association): Eteläranta 10, 00130 Helsinki; tel. (9) 6220410; fax (9) 176135; Chair. MARKKU TALONEN; Man. Dir MARKKU KÄPPI.

UTILITIES

Electricity

Fortum Oyj: POB 1, 00048 Fortum; tel. 104511; fax 104524798; internet www.fortum.fi; f. 1998 following merger of the Imatran Voima Group and the Neste Group; 60.5% state-owned; member of Fortum Corpn, international energy co with core businesses in oil, gas, power and heat; listed on the Helsinki exchanges in Dec. 1998; Exec. Chair. PETER FAGERNÄS; CEO MIKAEL LILIUS.

Kemijoki Oy: Valtakatu 9–11, POB 8131, 96101 Rovaniemi; tel. (16) 7401; fax (16) 7402325; e-mail info@kemijoki.fi; internet www .kemijoki.fi; f. 1954; electric power; 66.99% state-owned; Chair. of Supervisory Bd KALERVO NURMIMÄKI; Chair. of Bd of Management TAPIO KUULA; 344 employees.

Pohjolan Voima Oy (PVO): Töölönkatu 4, POB 40, 00101 Helsinki; tel. (9) 693061; fax (9) 69306335; e-mail info@pvo.fi; internet www.pohjolanvoima.fi; Pres. and CEO TIMO RAJALA.

Regional electricity providers operate, of which the largest is Helsingin Energia.

Helsingin Energia (Helsinki Energy): 00090 Helen; tel. (9) 6171; fax (9) 6172360; e-mail helsingin.energia@helsinginenergia.fi; internet www.helsinginenergia.fi; f. 1909; municipal undertaking; generates and distributes electrical power and district heating; distributes natural gas; Man. Dir Seppo Ruohonen.

Gas

Gasum Oy: POB 21, 02151 Espoo; tel. (0) 204471; fax (0) 204478639; e-mail tuomo.saarni@gasum.fi; internet www.gasum.fi; 31% owned by Fortum Oyj, 25% owned by OAO Gazprom (Russia), 24% state-owned and 20% owned by E.ON Ruhrgas AG (Germany); imports and sells natural gas, owns and operates natural gas transmission system; operates three subsidiaries, Helsinkikaasu, Suomen Kaasuenergia and Kaasupörssi.

Water

Helsinki Water: Iimalankuja 2A, 00240 Helsinki; POB 1100, 00099 Helsinki; tel. (9) 47371; fax (9) 47342010; responsible for water supply and sewerage of the greater Helsinki area.

CO-OPERATIVES

Pellervo (Confederation of Finnish Co-operatives): Simonkatu 6, POB 77, 00101 Helsinki; tel. (9) 4767501; fax (9) 6948845; e-mail toimisto@pellervo.fi; internet www.pellervo.fi; f. 1899; central organization of co-operatives; CEO Samuli Skurnik; 430 mem. societies (incl. 7 central co-operative societies).

Munakunta (Co-operative Egg Producers' Association): POB 6, 20761 Piispanristi; tel. 2214420; fax 22144222; internet www.kultamuna.fi; f. 1921; Man. Dir Jan Lähde; 500 mems.

Valio Ltd (Finnish Co-operative Dairies' Association): POB 10, 00039 Valio; tel. 10381121; fax 103812059; internet www.valio.com; f. 1905; production and marketing of dairy products; Pres. and CEO Harry Salonaho.

TRADE UNIONS

AKAVA (Confederation of Unions for Academic Professionals): Rautatieläisenkatu 6, 00520 Helsinki; tel. (0) 207489400; fax (9) 142595; internet www.akava.fi; f. 1950; 32 affiliates, incl. asscns of doctors, engineers, social workers and teachers; total membership 448,000; Pres. Risto Piekka.

Suomen Ammattiliittojen Keskusjärjestö (SAK) r.y. (Central Organization of Finnish Trade Unions): Siltasaarenkatu 3A, POB 157, 00531 Helsinki; tel. (9) 77211; fax (9) 7721447; internet www.sak.fi; f. 1907; 25 affiliated unions; 1,110,000 mems (1996); Pres. Lauri Ihalainen; Dirs Tuulikki Kannisto, Pekka Ahmavaara.

Principal affiliated unions:

Auto- ja Kuljetusalan Työntekijäliitto (AKT) r.y. (Transport Workers): John Stenbergin ranta 6, POB 313, 00531 Helsinki; tel. (9) 613110; fax (9) 739287; e-mail juhani.koivunen@akt.fi; internet www.akt.fi; f. 1948; Pres. Timo Räty; Secs Juhani Salmela, Juhani Koivunen; 50,836 mems.

Kemianliitto-Kemifacket r.y. (Chemical Workers): Siltasaarenkatu 2, POB 324, 00531 Helsinki; tel. (9) 773971; fax (9) 7538511; internet www.kemianliitto.fi; f. 1993; incorporated Tekstiili- ja vaatetustyöväen liitto Teva r.y. (Textile and Garment Workers' Union) in 2004; Pres. Timo Vallittu; Sec. Seppo Wikström; 50,000 mems.

Kunta-alan Ammattiliitto (KTV) r.y. (Municipal Sector): Kolmas linja 4, POB 101, 00531 Helsinki; tel. (0) 1077031; fax (0) 107703397; internet www.ktv.fi; f. 1931; Pres. Tuire Santamäki-Vuori; 211,031 mems.

Metallityöväen Liitto r.y. (Metalworkers): Siltasaarenkatu 3–5A, POB 107, 00531 Helsinki; tel. (9) 77071; fax (9) 7707277; internet www.metalliliitto.fi; f. 1899; Pres. Per-Erik Lundh; Sec. Erik Lindfors; 164,000 mems.

Palvelualojen ammattiliitto PAM r.y. (Service Union United): Paasivuorenkatu 4–6, POB 54, 00531 Helsinki; tel. (9) 77074002; fax 207742039; internet www.pam.fi; f. 1987 as Liikealan ammattiliitto r.y.; present name adopted 2000; Pres. Ann Selin; Vice-Pres Anssi Vuorio, Kaarlo Julkunen; 200,000 mems.

Paperiliitto r.y. (Paperworkers): Paasivuorenkatu 4–6A, POB 326, 00531 Helsinki; tel. (9) 70891; fax (9) 7012279; f. 1906; Pres. Jouko Ahonen; Gen. Sec. Petri Vanhala; 48,569 mems.

Puu- ja erityisalojen Liitto r.y. (Wood and Allied Workers): Haapaniemenkatu 7–9B, POB 318, 00531 Helsinki; tel. (9) 615161; fax (9) 736069; e-mail puuliitto@puuliitto.fi; internet www.puuliitto.fi; f. 1993 by merger of two unions; Pres. Kalevi Vanhala; 50,000 mems.

Rakennusliitto r.y. (Construction Workers): Siltasaarenkatu 4, POB 307, 00531 Helsinki; tel. (9) 77021; fax (9) 7702241; e-mail info@rakennusliitto.fi; internet www.rakennusliitto.fi; f. 1930; Pres. Pekka Hynönen; 89,000 mems.

Sähköalojen ammattiliitto r.y. (Electrical Workers): Aleksanterinkatu 15, POB 747, 33101 Tampere; tel. (3) 2520111; fax (3) 2520210; e-mail lauri.lyly@sahkoliitto.fi; internet www.sahkoliitto.fi; f. 1955; Pres. Martti Alakoski; Sec. Heimo Rinne; 32,000 mems.

Suomen Elintarviketyöläisten Liitto (SEL) r.y. (Food Workers): Siltasaarenkatu 6, POB 213, 00531 Helsinki; tel. (0) 20774004; fax (0) 207740604; internet www.selry.fi; f. 1905; Pres. Ritva Savtschenko; 41,000 mems.

Suomen Merimies-Unioni r.y. (Seamen): Uudenmaankatu 16B, POB 249, 00121 Helsinki; tel. (9) 6152020; fax (9) 61520227; e-mail erkki.ukkonen@smury.fi; internet www.smury.fi; f. 1916; Pres. Pekka Tervaväinen; Sec. Erkki Ukkonen; 11,158 mems.

Viestintäalan ammattiliitto r.y. (Media Union): Siltasaarenkatu 4, POB 303, 00531 Helsinki; tel. (9) 616581; fax (9) 61658333; e-mail pertti.raitoharju@viestintaliitto.fi; internet www.viestintaliitto.fi; f. 1894; Pres. Pertti Raitoharju; Sec. Irene Hämäläinen; 32,000 mems.

STTK (Finnish Confederation of Salaried Employees): Pohjoisranta 4A, POB 248, 00171 Helsinki; tel. (9) 131521; fax (9) 652367; internet www.sttk.fi.

The principal independent trade unions (formerly affiliated to the now-dissolved Confederation of Salaried Employees—TVK, f. 1922) include the following:

Ammattiliitto SUORA r.y.: Ratamestarinkatu 12, 00520 Helsinki; tel. (9) 229141; fax (9) 22914301; f. 1931; Suomen Rahoitus- ja Erityisalojen ammattiliitto r.y. (Financial Sector Union); Pres. Tarja Lankila; Sec.-Gen. Simo Leivo; 37,000 mems.

Erityisalojen Toimihenkilöliitto ERTO r.y. (Special Service and Clerical Employees): Asemamiehenkatu 4, 00520 Helsinki; tel. (0) 201130200; fax (0) 201130201; e-mail info.erto@erto.fi; internet www.erto.fi; f. 1968; Chair. Antti Rinne; 27,000 mems.

Hallintovirkailijoiden Keskusliitto (HVK) (Civil Servants): Ratamestarinkatu 11, 00520 Helsinki; tel. (9) 1551; f. 1992; Chair. Heikki Kujanpää; 12,500 mems.

Kunnallisvirkamiesliitto r.y. (KVL) (Municipal Officers): Asemamiehenkatu 4, 00520 Helsinki; tel. (9) 1551; fax (9) 1552333; f. 1918; Chair. Markku Jalonen; 74,000 mems.

Maanpuolustuksen ja Turvallisuuden Ammattijärjestöt (MTAJ) r.y. (Defence and Security Employees): Ratamestarinkatu 11, 00520 Helsinki; tel. (9) 1551; f. 1992; Chair. Pirkko Mattila; 7,800 mems.

Suomen Perushoitajaliitto (Enrolled Nurses): Asemamiehenkatu 2, 00520 Helsinki; tel. (9) 141833; f. 1948; Chair. Kaarina Muhli; 36,000 mems.

Suomen Poliisijärjestöjen Liitto (Police): Asemamiehenkatu 2, 00520 Helsinki; tel. (9) 1551; f. 1990; Chair. Matti Krats; 13,600 mems.

Tehy (Union of Health and Social-Care Professionals): POB 10, 00060 Helsinki; tel. (9) 1551; fax (9) 1483038; e-mail tehy.international@tehy.fi; f. 1982; Chair. Jaana Laitinen-Pesola; 110,000 mems.

Vakuutusväen Liitto r.y. (Insurance Employees): Asemamiehenkatu 2, 00520 Helsinki; tel. (9) 85672400; fax (9) 85672401; e-mail sirpa.spoljari@jttpalvelut.fi; internet www.vvl.fi; f. 1945; Chair. Sirpa Komonen; Gen. Sec. Sirpa Spoljari; 11,000 mems.

Valtion Laitosten ja Yhtiöiden Toimihenkilöliitto (Employees in State-owned Institutions and Companies): Topparikuja 7, 00520 Helsinki; tel. (9) 348050; fax (9) 145135; e-mail joan.vingisar@vty.fi; f. 1945; Gen. Sec. Pekka Eloranta; 10,000 mems.

Transport

RAILWAYS

Finland had 5,851 km of railways in 2003, providing internal services and connections with Sweden and Russia. As part of an initiative to upgrade the existing rail network a high-speed rail link was planned between Helsinki and St Petersburg, Russia; it was scheduled to be operational in 2008. An underground railway service has been provided by Helsinki City Transport since 1982.

Ratahallintokeskus (RHK) (Finnish Rail Administration): POB 185, 00101 Helsinki; tel. (9) 58405111; fax (9) 58405100; e-mail info@rhk.fi; internet www.rhk.fi; f. 1995; civil service department under the Ministry of Transport and Communications; owns the rail network, together with its equipment, structures and land holdings; wide gauge (1,524 mm); 2,372 km of route are electrified; responsible for management, maintenance and development of railways; Chief Dir O. NIEMIMUUKKO.

Karhula Railway: Ratakatu 8, 48600 Karhula; tel. (5) 298221; fax (5) 298225; f. 1937; goods transport; operates 10 km of railway (1,524 mm gauge); Man. PERTTI HONKALA.

VR Group: Vilhonkatu 13, POB 488, 00101 Helsinki; tel. (307) 10; fax (307) 21500; internet www.vr.fi; began operating 1862; joint-stock co since 1995; operates 5,854 km of railways; Pres. and CEO HENRI KUITUNEN; Exec. Vice-Pres. JUHANI KOPPERI.

ROADS

Finland had 78,650 km of public roads in 2002, of which 591 km were motorways, 13,262 km other main roads, 28,447 km secondary or regional roads and 36,350 other roads.

In early 2001 Tielaitos (National Road Administration) was divided into the following organizations:

Tiehallinto (Finnish Road Administration): POB 33, 00521 Helsinki; tel. (204) 2211; fax (204) 222202; e-mail info@tiehallinto.fi; internet www.tiehallinto.fi; f. 1799; government agency; divided into nine road districts; manages the public road network, including bridges and ferries; organizes bids for road construction and maintenance; Dir-Gen. EERO KARJALUOTO.

Tieliikelaitos (Finnish Road Enterprise): POB 73, 00521 Helsinki; tel. (204) 4411; internet www.tieliikelaitos.fi; unincorporated state enterprise; provides transport infrastructure and transport environment services; Man. Dir HEIKKI KOIVISTO.

INLAND WATERWAYS

Lakes cover 33,672 sq km. The inland waterway system comprises 7,842 km of buoyed-out channels, 40 open canals and 37 lock canals. The total length of canals is 116 km. In 2000 cargo vessel traffic on inland waterways amounted to 2.3m. metric tons (including traffic on the Saimaa Canal), timber floating amounted to 1m. tons and passenger traffic to 480,000 passengers.

In 1968 the southern part of the Saimaa Canal, which was leased to Finland by the USSR for 50 years, was opened for vessels. In 2000 a total of 1.8m. metric tons of goods were transported along the canal.

SHIPPING

The chief port of export is Kotka. Reclamation of land was carried out to build a second container port in Kotka. It opened in 2001 and has the capacity to handle 500,000 20-ft equivalent units (TEUs) of cargo per year. The main port of import is Helsinki, which has three specialized harbours. The West Harbour handles most of the container traffic, the North Harbour cargo ferry (ro-ro) traffic and the South Harbour passenger traffic. Other important international ports are Turku (Åbo), Rauma and Hamina.

Port Authority Association

Suomen Satamaliitto (Finnish Port Association): Toinen Linja 14, 00530 Helsinki; tel. (9) 7711; fax (9) 7530474; e-mail matti.aura@satamaliitto.fi; internet www.finnports.com; f. 1923; 29 mems; Man. Dir MATTI AURA.

Port Authorities

Hamina: POB 14, 49401 Hamina; tel. (5) 2255400; fax (5) 22554101; e-mail office@portofhamina.fi; internet www.portofhamina.fi; Port Man. SEPPO HERRALA; Harbour Master MARKKU KOSKINEN.

Helsinki: Port of Helsinki, POB 800, 00099 Helsinki; tel. (9) 173331; fax (9) 17333232; e-mail port.helsinki@hel.fi; internet www.portofhelsinki.fi; Man. Dir HEIKKI NISSINEN; Harbour Master KARI NOROVIITA.

Kotka: Port of Kotka Ltd, Laivurinkatu 7, 48100 Kotka; tel. (5) 2344280; fax (5) 2181375; e-mail marketing@portofkotka.fi; internet www.portofkotka.fi; Man. Dir KIMMO NASKI.

Rauma: Port of Rauma, Hakunintie 19, 26100 Rauma; tel. (2) 8344712; fax (2) 8226369; e-mail harbour.office@portofrauma.com; internet www.portofrauma.com; Dir HANNU ASUMALAHTI.

Turku: Turku Port Authority, Linnankatu 90, 20100 Turku; tel. (2) 2674111; fax (2) 2674125; e-mail pekka.rasanen@turku.fi; internet www.port.turku.fi; Harbour Master PEKKA RÄSÄNEN.

Shipowners' Association

Suomen Varustamoyhdistys r.y. (Finnish Shipowners' Association): Satamakatu 4, POB 155, 00161 Helsinki; tel. (9) 6226730; fax

(9) 669251; e-mail office@varustamoyhdistys.fi; internet www.varustamoyhdistys.fi; f. 1932; Chair. JUKKA LAAKSOVIRTA; Man. Dir MIKA NYKÄNEN; 6 mems.

Principal Companies

ESL Shipping Oy: Suolakivenkatu 10, 00810 Helsinki; tel. (9) 7595777; fax (9) 787315; world-wide tramp services; Man. Dir E. YRJOLA.

Finnlines PLC: Porkkalainkatu 20A, POB 197, 00181 Helsinki; tel. 1034350; fax 103435200; e-mail info@finnlines.fi; internet www.finnlines.fi; f. 1949; liner and contract services between Finland and other European countries; overland and inland services combined with direct sea links; Pres. and CEO ANTTI LAGERROOS; 85 cargo ferries.

Fortum Oil and Gas Oy: POB 100, 00048 Fortum Keilaniemi, 02150 Spoo; tel. 104511; fax 104524777; internet www.fortum.com; Senior Vice-Pres. JUKKA LAAKSOVIRJA.

Alfons Håkans Oy Ab: Linnankatu 36C, 20100 Turku; tel. (2) 515500; fax (2) 2515873; e-mail office.turku@alfonshakans.fi; 30 tugs.

Nurminen Maritime Oy: POB 124, 00241 Helsinki; tel. 1054500; fax 105452000; e-mail info@johnnurminen.com; internet www.johnnurminen.com; liner and port agency services; Man. Dir JAN LÖNNBLAD.

Rederi Ab Engship: Linnankatu 33B, 20100 Turku; tel. (2) 5125500; fax (2) 2502087; e-mail engship@engship.fi; internet www.engship.fi; Man. Dir BENGT ENGBLOM; 11 dry cargo vessels; 96,800 dwt.

Rettig Oy Ab Bore: Veistämönaukio 1–3, POB 144, 20101 Turku; tel. (2) 2813600; fax (2) 2534036; e-mail info@boret.com; internet www.boreship.com; f. 1897; Man. Dir KAJ ERIKSSON; 4 cargo ferries; 32,751 dwt.

RG Line Oy Ab: Vaskiluodon Satama, 65170 Vaasa; tel. (6) 3200300; fax (6) 3194545; e-mail info@rgline.com; internet www.rgline.com; operates ferry services across the Gulf of Bothnia from Vaasa to Umeå.

Silja Oy Ab: 02060 Silja; Keilaranta 9, Espoo; tel. (9) 18041; fax (9) 1804484; internet www.silja.com; f. 1883; passenger and cargo services in the Baltic; Man. Dir ANTTI PANKAKOSKI; 12 vessels.

CIVIL AVIATION

An international airport is situated at Helsinki-Vantaa, 19 km from Helsinki. International and domestic services also operate to and from airports at Ivalo, Joensuu, Jyväskylä, Kajaani, Kemi-Tornio, Kruunupyy, Kuopio, Lappeenranta, Mariehamn, Oulu, Pori, Rovaniemi, Savonlinna, Tampere-Pirkkala, Turku, Vaasa and Varkaus. Domestic services are available at airports at Enontekiö, Kittilä, Kuusamo and Mikkeli.

In 2001 13.8m. passengers passed through Finnish airports.

Ilmailulaitos (Civil Aviation Administration): POB 50, 01531 Vantaa; tel. (9) 82771; fax (9) 82772099; e-mail ilmailulaitos@fcaa.fi; internet www.ilmailulaitos.fi; Dir-Gen. MIKKO TALVITIE.

Principal Airlines

Air Botnia: POB 168, 01531 Vantaa; tel. (9) 61512900; fax (9) 61512919; e-mail airbotnia@sas.se; internet www.airbotnia.fi; f. 1994; intra-nordic services; acquired by Scandinavian Airlines System in 1998; Pres. and CEO KJELL FREDHEIM.

Finnair Oyj: Tietotie 11A, POB 15, 01053 Vantaa; tel. (9) 81881; fax (9) 8184979; internet www.finnair.com; f. 1923; 58.4% state-owned; 16 domestic services, 38 European services and 9 international services (to Asia and North America); Pres. and CEO KEIJO SUILA.

Tourism

Europe's largest inland water system, vast forests, magnificent scenery and the possibility of holiday seclusion are Finland's main attractions. Most visitors come from other Nordic countries, Germany, Russia, the United Kingdom and the USA. Registered accommodation establishments recorded 4,290,288 overnight stays by foreigners in 2002.

Matkailun edistämiskeskus (Finnish Tourist Board): Töölönkatu 11, POB 625, 00101 Helsinki; tel. (9) 4176911; fax (9) 41679333; e-mail mek@mek.fi; internet www.mek.fi; f. 1973; Chair. BO GÖRAN ERIKSSON; Dir JAAKKO LEHTONEN.

FINNISH EXTERNAL TERRITORY

THE ÅLAND ISLANDS

Introductory Survey

Location, Language, Religion, Flag, Capital

The Åland Islands are a group of 6,554 islands (of which some 60 are inhabited) in the Gulf of Bothnia, between Finland and Sweden. About 93% of the inhabitants are Swedish-speaking, and Swedish is the official language; the remaining 5% are Finnish-speaking. The majority profess Christianity, and 91% belong to the Evangelical Lutheran Church of Finland. The flag displays a red cross, bordered with yellow, on a blue background, the upright of the cross being to the left of centre. The capital is Mariehamn, which is situated on Åland, the largest island in the group.

History and Government

For geographical and economic reasons, the Åland Islands were traditionally associated closely with Sweden. In 1809, when Sweden was forced to cede Finland to Russia, the islands were incorporated into the Finnish Grand Duchy. However, following Finland's declaration of independence from the Russian Empire in 1917, the Ålanders demanded the right to self-determination and sought to be reunited with Sweden. Their demands were supported by the Swedish Government and people. In 1920 Finland granted the islands autonomy but refused to acknowledge their secession, and in 1921 the Åland question was referred to the League of Nations. In June the League granted Finland sovereignty over the islands, while directing that certain conditions pertaining to national identity be included in the autonomy legislation offered by Finland and that the islands should be a neutral and non-fortified region. Elections were held in accordance with the new legislation, and the new provincial parliament (Landsting) held its first plenary session on 9 June 1922. The revised Autonomy Act of 1951 provided for independent rights of legislation in internal affairs and for autonomous control over the islands' economy. This Act could not be amended or repealed by the Finnish Eduskunta (Parliament) without the consent of the Åland Landsting.

In 1988 constitutional reform introduced the principle of a majority parliamentary government, to be formed by the Lantrådskandidat, the member of the Landsting nominated to conduct negotiations between the parties. These negotiations may yield two alternative outcomes: either the nominee will submit a proposal to create a new government or the nominee will fail to reach agreement on a new government (in which case renewed negotiations will ensue). The first formal parliamentary government and opposition were duly established. The governing coalition consisted of the three largest parties that had been elected to the Landsting in October 1987 (the Centre Party, the Liberals and the Moderates), which together held 22 seats in the 30-member legislature.

At a general election held in October 1991 the Centre Party increased its share of the seats in the Landsting to 10, while the Liberal Party secured seven seats and the Moderates and Social Democrats won six and four seats respectively. The parties forming the new coalition Government included the Centre and Moderate Parties, as before, while the Liberal Party was replaced by the Social Democratic Party.

A revised Autonomy Act, providing Åland with a greater degree of autonomous control, was adopted in 1991 and took effect on 1 January 1993. The rules regarding legislative authority were modernized, and the right of the Åland legislature (henceforth known as the Lagting) to enact laws was extended. Åland was given greater discretion with respect to its budget, and the revised Act also introduced changes in matters such as right of domicile, land-ownership regulations and administrative authority. The Autonomy Act contains a provision that, in any treaty which Finland may conclude with a foreign state and to which Åland is a party, the Lagting must consent to the statute implementing the treaty in order for the provision to enter into force in Åland. This procedure gave Åland the opportunity not to consent to membership of the European Union (EU, see p. 217). A referendum on the issue of Åland's proposed accession to membership of the EU in 1995 was held in November 1994, immediately after similar referendums in Finland and Sweden had shown a majority in favour of membership. (A small majority of Åland citizens had supported Finland's membership.) Despite low participation in the referendum, 73.7% of the votes cast supported membership and Åland duly joined the EU, together with Finland and Sweden, on 1 January 1995. Under the terms of the treaty of accession, Åland was accorded special exemption from tax union with the EU in order to stimulate the ferry and tourism industries. (In 1998 two of Europe's largest ferry operators, Silja and Viking—both Finnish—re-routed their major services via Åland in order to continue to conduct duty-free sales, which were later abolished within the rest of the EU.)

A general election was held in October 1995. The Centre Party secured nine seats and the Liberal Party won eight seats, while the Moderates and Social Democrats maintained the representation that they had achieved in the previous parliament. The new coalition Government was composed of members of the Centre and Moderate Parties and one independent.

At a general election held in October 1999 the Centre Party and the Liberal Party each won nine seats. The Moderate Party, meanwhile, secured only four seats, compared with six at the previous election, while the Social Democrats maintained their level of representation, with three seats. Independents grouped together in the Obunden samling won four seats. A coalition Government was formed comprising the Centre Party, the Moderate Party and the Independents. In March 2001, following a 'no-confidence' motion in the Lagting, the Chairman (Lantråd) of the Government, Roger Nordlund of the Centre Party, dissolved the coalition and formed a new administration comprising members of the Centre Party and the Liberal Party.

A general election was held on 19 October 2003, at which the Centre Party and the Liberal Party each won seven seats. The two parties formed a new Government in coalition with the Social Democrats (who had secured six seats) and the Moderate Party (with four seats), with Roger Nordlund again being appointed as Lantråd. The other parties represented in the Lagting obtained just six seats between them.

In August 2004 the Finnish Government agreed new, more stringent regulations securing the islands' demilitarized status, following reports that this had been violated by troop movements over the past two decades.

In January 2005, following a motion of 'no confidence' in the Lagting, the governing coalition was dissolved and Nordlund formed a new administration comprising members of the Centre Party, the Social Democrats and the Moderate Party.

Economic Affairs

In 2001 the gross domestic product (GDP) of the Åland Islands, measured at current prices, was €891m. In 2002 4.8% of the working population were employed in the agriculture sector. Forests covered 57.4% of the islands in 2001, and in 2003 only 9.0% of the total land area was arable. The principal crops are cereals, sugar beet, potatoes and fruit. Dairy-farming and sheep-rearing are also important.

Since 1960 the economy of the islands has expanded and diversified. Fishing has declined as a source of income, and shipping (particularly the operation of ferry services between Finland and Sweden), trade and tourism have become the dominant economic sectors. In 2002 services engaged 77.7% of the employed labour force. The transport sector, including shipping, employed 18.6%. The political autonomy of the islands and their strategic location between Sweden and Finland have contributed to expanding banking and trade sectors; financial services engaged 3.7% of the employed labour force in 2002, while trade and hotels employed 13.7%. Tourist arrivals totalled 1,769,955 in 2003.

The Finnish State collects taxes, duties and fees from the Åland Islands, which receives 0.45% of total Finnish government income in return. If the taxes raised in the Åland Islands exceeds 0.5% of corresponding Finnish tax revenues, the islands receive the excess amount in the form of a tax redemption. A tax redemption of €11.84m. was paid to the islands in 2003 relating to the fiscal year 2001. Consumer prices increased at an average annual rate of 3.4% in 1990–2003; prices rose by 3.2% in 2002 and by 1.0% in 2003. The unemployment rate stood at 2.6% in February 2005, compared with 5.2% in 1996. The Finnish currency, the markka, was used by the islands until the end of 2001. Euro notes and coins were introduced on 1 January 2002, and, as in Finland as a whole, the common European currency, the euro, became the sole legal tender from 1 March 2002. In March 2004 it was reported that residents of the Åland Islands enjoyed the highest average net income in Finland; the difference between regions was, however, not very pronounced.

Education

The education system is similar to that of Finland, except that Swedish is the language of instruction and Finnish an optional subject.

Statistical Survey

Source: Statistics Åland, POB 1187, 22111 Mariehamn; tel. (18) 25490; fax (18) 19495; internet www.asub.aland.fi.

AREA AND POPULATION

Area (according to regional division of 1 January 2004, under which the Åland Islands' territorial waters were extended; figures are provisional): 13,346 sq km (5,125 sq miles), of which 1,527 sq km (589 sq miles) is land and 11,820 sq km (4,563 sq miles) is water.

Population (31 December 2003): 26,347 (males 12,957, females 13,390).

Density (land area only, 31 December 2003): 17.3 per sq km.

Principal Towns (31 December 2002): Mariehamn (capital) 9,824; Godby 832; Prästgården 465; Storby 462; Ödkarby 306; Söderby 291.

Births, Marriages and Deaths (2003): Registered live births 262 (birth rate 10.0 per 1,000); Marriages 110 (marriage rate 4.2 per 1,000); Deaths 268 (death rate 10.2 per 1,000).

Expectation of Life (years at birth): 81.8 (males 79.2; females 84.4) in 2002.

Employment (2002): Agriculture 613; Fishing and aquaculture 89; Mining 3; Manufacturing 1,180; Energy 117; Construction 875; Trade 1,347; Hotels and restaurants 421; Transport 2,395; Financial services 475; Real estate, etc. 640; Public services 1,151; Education 961; Health and social care 1,948; Other services 670; Activities not classified 384; Total employed 13,269.

HEALTH AND WELFARE

Physicians (2003): 59.

Hospital Beds (2003): 148.

AGRICULTURE

Agricultural Production (metric tons, unless otherwise stated, 2003): Milk ('000 litres) 14,249; Beef 615; Pork 118; Mutton 50; Poultry 1,497 (2002); Horse meat 2; Eggs 236; Wheat 3,845; Rye 693; Triticale (wheat-rye hybrid) 81; Barley 1,389; Oats 3,005; Peas 43; Turnip rape 42; Sugar beet 34,054; Potatoes 13,497; Onions 8,347; Cucumbers 149; Leeks 247; Chinese cabbage 1,077; Apples 1,794; Strawberries ('000 litres) 16; Tomatoes 78; Parsley ('000 bunches) 118; Dill ('000 bunches) 108; Lettuce 591; Celery 63; Carrots 68 177.

Livestock (2003): Cattle 7,651; Pigs 880; Hens 14,142; Sheep 4,995; Horses 253.

FORESTRY

Forestry Production (cu m, roundwood, 2002): Logs 67,950; Pulp 117,120.

FISHING

Fishing (metric tons, live weight, 2003): Capture 3,645 (Baltic herring 2,620, Cod 575; Other fish 450); Aquaculture 3,866; *Total catch* 7,511.

FINANCE

Currency: Finnish currency was used until the end of 2001. Euro notes and coins were introduced on 1 January 2002, and the euro became the sole legal tender from 1 March.Some of the figures in this Survey are still in terms of Finnish markkaa. For details of exchange rates, see the chapter on Finland.

Budget (€ '000, 2002): Revenue 240,549; Expenditure 240,882.

Cost of Living (consumer price index; base: 1995 = 100): All items 106.8 in 2000; 109.3 in 2001; 111.5 in 2002.

Expenditure on the Gross Domestic Product (€ million at current prices, 2001): Wages and salaries 339; Employers' contribution to social security 68; Operating surplus 221; Fixed capital depreciation 180; *Total domestic expenditure* 808; Indirect taxes 108; *Less* Subsidies 25; *GDP in market prices* 891.

Gross Domestic Product by Economic Activity (€ million at current prices, 2001): Agriculture, hunting, forestry and fishing 29; Manufacturing 61; Construction 31; Trade, restaurants and hotels 72; Transport, storage and communications 338; Financing, insurance, real estate and business services 115; Government services 157; Other community, social and personal services 22; Non-profit institutions 10; *Sub-total* 835; *Less* Imputed bank service charge 28; *GDP at factor cost* 807; Indirect taxes 108; *Less* Subsidies 25; *GDP in purchasers' values* 891.

EXTERNAL TRADE

2003 (€ '000): Imports 311,083; Exports 118,370Note: Figures include imports from Finland (208,475), and exports to Finland (70,427).

TRANSPORT

Road Traffic (registered motor vehicles, 31 December 2003): Private motor cars 15,194; Vans 2,968; Lorries 463; Buses 40; Motorcycles 777; Tractors 3,398.

Shipping (2003): Merchant fleet 55 vessels; Total displacement 886,661 grt. Note: Figures include 16 vessels registered under flags other than Åland or Finland, total displacement 518,440 grt.

TOURISM

Tourist Arrivals (2003): 1,769,955.

EDUCATION

Primary and Secondary Schools (2003): Institutions 27 (Comprehensive schools 26, of which 8 also offer upper-stage education, Upper-stage only 1); Pupils 3,094 (Comprehensive schools 2,031, Upper-stage schools 1,063).

Pupils Enrolled in Education After Comprehensive Schools (2003): Preparatory study programme 422 (males 174, females 248); Vocational 100 (males 54, females 46); Vocational programme 558 (males 312, females 246); Advanced vocational programme 384 (males 237, females 147); Other 66 (males 43, females 23).

Directory

Government and Legislature

The legislative body is the Lagting, comprising 30 members, elected every four years on a basis of proportional representation. All Ålanders over the age of 18 years, possessing Åland regional citizenship, have the right to vote and to seek election. An Executive Council (Landskapsregeringen), consisting of five to seven members, is elected by the Lagting, and its Chairman (Lantråd) is the highest-ranking politician in Åland after the Speaker (Talman) of the Lagting. The President has the right to veto Lagting decisions only when the Lagting exceeds its legislative competence, or when there is a threat to the security of the country. The Governor of Åland represents the Government of Finland and is appointed by the Finnish President (with the agreement of the Speaker of the Åland legislature).

Governor: PETER LINDBÄCK.

LANDSKAPSREGERINGEN
(Executive Council)
(April 2005)

The governing coalition comprises members of the Centre Party, the Social Democrats and the Moderate Party.

Chairman (Lantråd): ROGER NORDLUND (Centre Party).

Deputy Chairman (Vicelantråd): Jörgen Strand (Moderate Party).

Members: Camilla Gunell (Social Democrats), Runar Karlsson (Centre Party), Harriet Lindeman (Moderate Party), Britt Lundberg (Centre Party), Lasse Wiklöf (Social Democrats).

LAGTING
(Parliament)

Speaker (Talman): Viveka Eriksson (Liberal Party) 2005–2007.

Election, 19 October 2003

	Votes	% of votes	Seats
Åländsk Center (Centre Party)	2,980	24.14	7
Liberalerna på Åland (Liberal Party)	2,970	24.06	7
Ålands socialdemokrater (Social Democrats)	2,340	18.95	6
Frisinnad samverkan (Moderate Party)	1,677	13.58	4
Obunden samling (Independents)	1,163	9.42	3
Ålands Framtid (Åland's Future)	800	6.48	2
Ålands Framstegsgrupp (Progress Group)	416	3.37	1
Total	12,346	100.00	30

Political Organizations

Unless otherwise indicated, the address of each of the following organizations is: Ålands Lagting, POB 69, 22101 Mariehamn; tel. (18) 25000; fax (18) 13302; internet www.lagtinget.aland.fi.

Åländsk Center (Centre Party): e-mail centern@lagtinget.aland.fi; internet www.centern.aland.fi; Chair. Roger Nordlund; Leader Jan-Erik Mattsson; Sec. Robert Branér.

Ålands Framstegsgrupp (Progress Group): e-mail ronald.boman@lagtinget.aland.fi; internet www.afg.aland.fi; Chair. and Leader Ronald Boman.

Ålands socialdemokrater (Social Democrats): e-mail socialdemokraterna@lagtinget.aland.fi; internet www.socialdemokraterna.aland.fi; Chair. Barbro Sundback.

Frisinnad samverkan (Moderate Party): e-mail fs@lagtinget.aland.fi; internet www.fs.aland.fi; Chair. Roger Jansson; Leader Jörgen Strand; Sec.-Gen. Nina Danielsson.

Liberalerna på Åland (Liberal Party): tel. (18) 25362; fax (18) 16075; e-mail liberalerna@lagtinget.aland.fi; internet www.liberalerna.aland.fi; Chair. Olof Erland; Leader Leo Sjöstrand; Gen. Sec. Solveig Gestberg.

Ålands Framtid r.f. (Åland's Future): tel. (18) 25366; e-mail framtid@aland.fi; internet www.alandsframtid.com; f. 2003; separatist; Leader Anders Eriksson.

Obunden samling (Independents): tel. (18) 25368; fax (18) 16370; e-mail info@obundet.nu; internet www.obundet.nu; f. 1987; Chair. Gun-Mari Lindholm; Leader Bert Häggblom.

Religion

The majority of the islands' population are Christian. In 2003 there were 23,985 adherents of the Lutheran National Church, accounting for 91.0% of the population. There were also small numbers of Roman Catholics, Greek Orthodox Christians, Adventists and Jehovah's Witnesses; 109 people practised other religions.

The Press

Ålandstidningen: POB 50, Strandgatan 16, 22100 Mariehamn; tel. (18) 26026; fax (18) 15505; e-mail nyheter@tidningen.aland.net; internet www.tidningen.aland.net; 5 a week; f. 1891; Editor-in-Chief Niklas Lampi; circ. 10,876.

Nya Åland: POB 21, 22101 Mariehamn; tel. (18) 23444; fax (18) 23450; e-mail vd@nyan.aland.fi; internet www.nyan.aland.fi; f. 1981; 5 a week; Man. Dir D.-J. Dahlblom; circ. 7,179.

Broadcasting and Communications

TELECOMMUNICATIONS

Ålands Mobiltelefon Ab: e-mail info@gsm.aland.fi; internet www.gsm.aland.fi; f. 1989; licensed to operate both GSM- and UMTS-networks on the islands.

Ålands Telefonandelslag: POB 22, 22411 Godby; tel. (18) 41053; fax (18) 41299; e-mail godby@altel.aland.fi; internet www.altel.aland.fi; f. 1910.

Mariehamns Telefon Ab: Ålandsvägen 52, POB 1228, 22111 Mariehamn; tel. (18) 27044; fax (18) 15900; e-mail telefon@mtel.aland.fi; internet www.mtel.aland.fi; f. 1892; Dir Stig Selander.

RADIO AND TELEVISION

Ålands Radio och TV Ab: Ålandsvägen 24, POB 140, 22101 Mariehamn; tel. (18) 26060; fax (18) 26520; e-mail info@radiotv.aland.fi; internet www.radiotv.aland.fi; f. 1996; broadcasts radio programmes in Swedish, 115.5 hours a week; operates three analogue and five digital television channels; Man. Dir Pia Rothberg-Olofsson; Editor-in-Chief Astrid Olhagen.

Steel FM: Strandgränd 2, 22100 Mariehamn; tel. (018) 16200; fax (018) 22079; e-mail mail@steelfm.net; internet www.steelfm.net.

TV Åland: POB 171, 22101 Mariehamn; tel. (18) 14035; fax 18) 14037; e-mail redaktion@tv.aland.fi; internet www.tv.aland.fi; f. 1984; broadcasts to 70% of islands.

Finance

BANKS
(cap. = capital; res = reserves; dep. = deposits; m. = million; amounts in euros; brs = branches)

Ålandsbanken Abp (Bank of Åland PLC): Nygatan 2, POB 3, 22101 Mariehamn; tel. (204) 29011; fax (204) 29228; e-mail info@alandsbanken.fi; internet www.alandsbanken.fi; f. 1919 as Ålands Aktiebank; name changed to Bank of Åland Ltd 1980, changed as above in 1998; merged with Ålands Hypoteksbank Ab in November 1995; cap. 22m., res 60m., dep. 1,666m. (Dec. 2003); Man. Dir Peter Grönlund; 28 brs.

Andelsbanken för Åland: POB 34, 22101 Mariehamn; tel. (18) 26000; Dirs Håkan Clemes, Roland Karlsson.

Lappo Andelsbank: 22840 Lappo; tel. (18) 56621; fax (18) 56699; Dir Torsten Nordberg.

Merita Bank: Torggatan 10, 22100 Mariehamn; tel. (18) 5330; fax (18) 12499; Dirs Erling Gustafsson, Jan-Erik Rask.

INSURANCE

Alandia Group: Ålandsvägen 31, POB 121, 22101 Mariehamn; tel. (18) 29000; fax (18) 12290; e-mail mhamn@alandiabolagen.com; internet www.alandiabolagen.com; f. 1938; life, non-life and marine; comprises three subsidiaries; Gen. Man. Johan Dahlman.

Ålands Ömsesidiga Försäkringsbolag (Åland Mutual Insurance Co): Köpmansgatan 6, POB 64, 22101 Mariehamn; tel. (18) 27600; fax (18) 27610; f. 1866; property; Man. Dir Bjarne Olofsson.

Cabanco Insurance Co Ltd: Köpmansgatan 6, POB 64, 22101 Mariehamn; tel. (18) 27690; fax (18) 27699; Man. Dir Bo-Sture Sjölund.

Hamnia Reinsurance Co Ltd: Köpmansgatan 6, POB 64, 22101 Mariehamn; tel. (18) 27690; fax (18) 27699; Man. Dir Bo-Sture Sjölund.

Trade and Industry

CHAMBER OF COMMERCE

Ålands Handelskammare: Torggatan 5, 22100 Mariehamn; tel. (18) 29029; fax (18) 21129; e-mail info@hk.aland.fi; internet www.hk.aland.fi; f. 1945; Chair. Anders Nordlund; Man. Dir Johan Eriksson.

TRADE ASSOCIATION

Ålands Företagareförening (Åland Business Asscn): Skarpansvägen 17, 22100 Mariehamn; tel. (18) 23277; fax (18) 23288; e-mail ombudsman@aff.aland.fi; internet www.aff.aland.fi; f. 1957; Chair. Christer Kullman; Sec. Jonny Mattsson.

EMPLOYERS' ORGANIZATIONS

Ålands Arbetsgivareförening (Åland Employers' Asscn): Torggatan 5, 22100 Mariehamn; tel. (18) 291474; fax (18) 21129; f. 1969; Chair. KJELL CLEMES.

Ålands Fiskodlarförening (Åland Fish Farmers' Asscn): Fischamnen, 22100 Mariehamn; tel. (18) 17834; fax (18) 17833; e-mail info@fiskodlarna.aland.fi; internet www.fiskodlarna.aland.fi; Chair. MARCUS ERIKSSON; Sec. ANDREAS ENQUIST.

Ålands köpmannaförening (Åland Businessmen's Asscn): Ålandsvägen 34, 22100 Mariehamn; tel. (18) 13650; fax (18) 12145; e-mail kopmannaforeningen@aland.net; f. 1927; Chair. TOM FORSBOM; Sec. STEFAN BLOMQVIST.

Ålands producentförbund (Åland Agricultural Producers' Asscn): Ålands Landsbygdscentrum, 22150 Jomala; tel. (18) 329640; fax (18) 329631; e-mail henry.lindstrom@landsbygd.aland.fi; f. 1946; Chair. ANDERS ENGLUND; Man. Dir HENRY LINDSTROM.

Fraktfartygsföreningen r.f. (Cargo Ship's Asscn): Norragatan 7A, 22100 Mariehamn; tel. (18) 23662; fax (18) 23644; e-mail small.ton@aland.net; internet www.fraktfartygsforeningen.fi; f. as Utrikesfartens Småtonnageförening; present name adopted 2000; Man. Dir OLOF WIDÉN.

TRADE UNIONS

AKAVA-Åland (Professional Asscn): Storagatan 14, 22100 Mariehamn; tel. (18) 16348; fax (18) 12125; e-mail akava-a@aland.net; Chair. PEKKA ERÄMETSÄ; Gen. Sec. MARIA HAGMAN.

Fackorgan för offentliga arbetsomraden på Åland (FOA-Å) (Joint Organization of Civil Servants and Workers (VTY) in Åland): Norragatan 7A 1, 22100 Mariehamn; tel. (18) 16976; e-mail info@foa.inet.fi; Chair. ULLA ANDERSSON; Gen. Sec. ULLA BRITT DAHL.

FFC-facken på Åland: POB 108, 22101 Mariehamn; tel. (18) 16207; fax (18) 17207; e-mail kurt.gustafsson@sak.fi; internet www.facket.aland.fi; Chair. PER-ÅKE ASPBÄCK; Gen. Sec. KURT GUSTAFSSON.

Tjänstemannaorganisationerna på Åland, TCÅ r.f. (Union of Salaried Employees in Åland): Strandgatan 23, 22100 Mariehamn; tel. (18) 16210; e-mail tca@aland.net; Chair. ANNE SJÖLUND; Dir TUULA MATTSSON.

Transport

The islands are linked to the Swedish and Finnish mainlands by ferry services and by air services from Mariehamn airport.

Ålandstrafiken: Strandgatan 25, 22100 Mariehamn; tel. (18) 25155; fax (18) 17815; e-mail info@alandstrafiken.aland.fi; internet www.alandstrafiken.aland.fi; operates buses on the islands and ferry services between the islands.

ROADS

In 2002 there was a road network of 912 km, of which 683 km was paved. There were 426 km of main roads, 215 km of local roads and 271 km of municipal roads. There was also a bicycle route network of 350 km, which included 25 km of paved bicycle routes in Mariehamn.

SHIPPING

Ferry services operate from the Åland Islands to Sweden and the Finnish mainland and a new service to Estonia was introduced in 2004.

Ålands Redarförening r.f. (Åland Shipowners' Association): Hamngatan 8, 22100 Mariehamn; tel. (18) 13430; fax (18) 22520; e-mail info@alship.aland.fi; f. 1934; Chair. WIKING JOHANSSON; Man. Dir HANS AHLSTRÖM; seven mems.

Principal Companies

Birka Line Abp: POB 175, 22101 Mariehamn; tel. (18) 27027; fax (18) 27343; e-mail info@birkaline.com; internet www.birkaline.com; f. 1971; shipping service; Man. Dir WIKING JOHANSSON.

Birka Cargo Ab Ltd: Storagatan 11, POB 175, 22101 Mariehamn; tel. (18) 27320; fax (18) 23223; e-mail info@birkacargo.com; internet www.birkacargo.com; f. 1990 as United Shipping Ltd Ab; 7 ro-ro vessels; Man. Dir STEFAN AXBERG.

Lundqvist Rederierna: Norra Esplanadgatan 9B, 22100 Mariehamn; tel. (18) 26050; fax (18) 26428; e-mail info@lundqvist.aland.fi; f. 1927; tanker and ro-ro services; Pres. BEN LUNDQVIST; total tonnage 1.0m. dwt.

Rederiaktiebolaget Eckerö (Eckerö Linjen): Torggatan 2, POB 158, 22101 Mariehamn; tel. (18) 28000; fax (18) 12011; e-mail info@eckerolinjen.fi; internet www.eckerolinjen.fi; f. 1980; operates ferry routes between the Åland Islands and Sweden, and between Finland and Estonia; Man. Dir BJÖRN BLOMGVIST.

Rederi Ab Lillgaard: Nygatan 5, POB 136, 22101 Mariehamn; tel. (18) 13120; fax (18) 17220.

Rederiaktiebolaget Gustaf Erikson: POB 49, 22101 Mariehamn; tel. (18) 27070; fax (18) 12670; e-mail gustaf.erikson@geson.aland.fi; f. 1913; Man. Dir GUN ERIKSON-HJERLING; manages dry cargo and refrigerated vessels.

Viking Line Abp: Norragatan 4, 22100 Mariehamn; tel. (18) 27000; fax (18) 16977; e-mail nn@vikingline.fi; internet www.vikingline.fi; f. 1963; operates cruise and ferry services between Finland and Sweden and throughout the Baltic Sea; Chair. BEN LUNDQVIST; Man. Dir NILS-ERIK EKLUND; 7 car/passenger vessels; total tonnage 212,474 grt.

CIVIL AVIATION

The islands' airport is at Mariehamn. In 2003 the airport handled 58,505 passengers, 132 metric tons of freight and 277 tons of post. It is served by Finnair.

Tourism

The Åland archipelago has numerous bays, inlets, islands and open stretches of water, and is an area of great natural beauty. Cycling, canoeing, kayaking and hiking attract tourists to the islands. Most visitors are from the Nordic countries, and particularly from mainland Finland and Sweden. In 2003 tourist arrivals totalled 1,769,955.

Ålands Turist Förbund (Åland Tourist Asscn): Storagatan 8, 22100 Mariehamn; tel. (18) 24000; fax (18) 24265; e-mail info@visitaland.com; internet www.visitaland.com; f. 1989; Chair. MAGNUS LUNDBERG; Man. Dir GUNILLA G. NORDLUND.

Ålands Turist och Konferens Ab: Hotell Arkipelag, Strandgatan 31, 22100 Mariehamn; tel. (18) 15349; fax (18) 21077; e-mail info@turist-konferens.aland.fi; internet www.turist-konferens.aland.fi.

FRANCE

Introductory Survey

Location, Climate, Language, Religion, Flag, Capital

The French Republic is situated in western Europe. It is bounded to the north by the English Channel (la Manche), to the east by Belgium, Luxembourg, Germany, Switzerland and Italy, to the south by the Mediterranean Sea and Spain, and to the west by the Atlantic Ocean. The island of Corsica is part of metropolitan France, while 10 overseas possessions (French Guiana, Guadeloupe, Martinique, Réunion, Mayotte, Saint Pierre and Miquelon, French Polynesia, French Southern and Antarctic Territories, Wallis and Futuna Islands and New Caledonia) also form an integral part of the Republic. The climate is temperate throughout most of the country, but in the south it is of the Mediterranean type, with warm summers and mild winters. The principal language is French, which has numerous regional dialects, and small minorities speak Breton and Basque. A majority of French citizens profess Christianity, and about 73% of the population are adherents of the Roman Catholic Church. Other Christian denominations are represented, and there are also Muslim and Jewish communities. The national flag (proportions 2 by 3) has three equal vertical stripes, of blue, white and red. The capital is Paris.

Recent History

In September 1939, following Nazi Germany's invasion of Poland, France and the United Kingdom declared war on Germany, thus entering the Second World War. In June 1940 France was forced to sign an armistice, following a swift invasion and occupation of French territory by German forces. After the liberation of France from German occupation in 1944, a provisional Government took office under Gen. Charles de Gaulle, leader of the 'Free French' forces during the wartime resistance. The war in Europe ended in May 1945, when German forces surrendered at Reims. In 1946, following a referendum, the Fourth Republic was established and Gen. de Gaulle announced his intention to retire from public life.

France had 26 different Governments from 1946 until the Fourth Republic came to an end in 1958 with an insurrection in Algeria (then an overseas department) and the threat of civil war. In May 1958 the President, René Coty, invited Gen. de Gaulle to form a government. In June the Assemblée nationale (legislature) invested de Gaulle as Prime Minister, with the power to rule by decree for six months. A new Constitution, approved by referendum in September, was promulgated in October; thus the Fifth Republic came into being, with Gen. de Gaulle taking office as President in January 1959. The new system provided for a strong presidency, the authority of which would be strengthened by national referendums and a stable executive.

France was a founder member of the European Community (EC—now European Union—EU, see p. 217) and of the North Atlantic Treaty Organization (NATO, see p. 301).

The early years of the Fifth Republic were overshadowed by the Algerian crisis. De Gaulle granted Algeria independence in 1962, withdrew troops and repatriated French settlers. In May 1968 students and workers joined in a revolt against the Government's authoritarian education and information policies, low wage rates and lack of social reform. For a time the republic appeared threatened, but the student movement collapsed and the general strike was settled by large wage rises. In April 1969 President de Gaulle resigned following his defeat in a referendum on regional reform.

Georges Pompidou, who had been Prime Minister from 1962–68, was elected President in June 1969. The Gaullist government coalition was returned at a general election in March 1973. Pompidou died in April 1974. In the presidential election held in May, Valéry Giscard d'Estaing, formerly leader of the centre-right Républicains Indépendants (RI) narrowly defeated François Mitterrand, the First Secretary of the Parti Socialiste (PS). A coalition Government was formed from members of the RI, the Gaullist Union des Démocrates pour la Republique (UDR) and the centrist parties. In August 1976 Jacques Chirac resigned as Prime Minister and subsequently undertook to transform the UDR into a new party, the Rassemblement pour la République (RPR). In February 1978 the governing non-Gaullist parties formed the Union pour la Démocratie Française (UDF) to compete against RPR candidates in the Assemblée nationale elections held in March, when the governing coalition retained a working majority.

In the April/May 1981 presidential elections Mitterrand defeated Giscard d'Estaing. At elections for a new Assembly, held in June, the PS and associated groups, principally the Mouvement des Radicaux de Gauche (MRG), won an overall majority of seats, following which four members of the Parti Communiste Française (PCF) were appointed to the Council of Ministers. The new Government introduced a programme of social and labour reforms, including the transfer of several major industrial enterprises and financial institutions to state control.

A legislative election took place in March 1986, using a party-list based system of proportional representation for the first time. Although the PS remained the largest single party in the new Assemblée nationale, the centre-right parties, led by the RPR-UDF alliance, commanded a majority of seats. The PCF suffered a severe decline in support, while the far-right Front National (FN) won legislative seats for the first time. A period of political 'cohabitation' ensued as Mitterrand invited the RPR leader, Chirac, to form a new Council of Ministers.

In April 1986 Chirac introduced legislation that allowed his Government to legislate by decree on economic and social issues and on the proposed reversion to a voting system comprising single-member constituencies for legislative elections. However, Mitterrand insisted on exercising the presidential right to withhold approval of decrees that reversed the previous Government's social reforms. In July Chirac thus resorted to the 'guillotine' procedure (setting a time-limit for consideration of legislative proposals) to gain parliamentary consent for legislation providing for the transfer to the private sector of 65 state-owned companies, which, since it had been approved by the predominantly right-wing Sénat (Senate) and the Constitutional Council, the President was legally bound to approve.

Mitterrand was re-elected as President in May 1988, defeating Chirac. The PS-dominated Government under the premiership of Michel Rocard failed to command a reliable majority in the 577-seat Assemblée nationale. A general election took place in June, with a reintroduced single-seat majority voting system. An alliance of the PS and the MRG secured 276 seats, whilst an alliance of the RPR, the UDF and other right-wing candidates won 272. The PCF won 27 seats, and the FN one (compared with the 35 deputies it held in the previous legislature). Rocard was reappointed as Prime Minister. Rocard resigned in May 1991, and was succeeded by Edith Cresson, France's first female Prime Minister, who had resigned eight months previously from her post as Minister of European Affairs. In April 1992 Mitterrand replaced Cresson as Prime Minister, appointing Pierre Bérégovoy, hitherto the Minister of State for the Economy, Finance and the Budget, as her successor. In June the Assemblée nationale approved constitutional changes allowing the ratification of the EC's Treaty on European Union (the Maastricht Treaty), subject to approval by referendum. In the referendum, held in September, 69.7% of the electorate voted, of whom 51.1% were in favour of the ratification of the Treaty.

At elections to the Assemblée nationale, held in March 1993, the RPR won 247 of the 577 seats in the Assemblée, the UDF 213 and the PS 54. Chirac, as the leader of the largest party in the new legislature, had made it known that he intended to concentrate on his candidacy in the 1995 presidential election, and consequently was not available for the post of Prime Minister. Mitterrand therefore asked another RPR member, Edouard Balladur, a former Minister of Finance, to form a government.

In the first round of voting in the presidential election, on 23 April 1995, Lionel Jospin, the candidate of the PS, obtained 23% of the votes, while Chirac and Balladur, both representing the RPR, took 21% and 19% respectively. Jean-Marie Le Pen, the leader of the FN, won 15%. In the second round, on 7 May, Chirac (with 53% of the votes) defeated Jospin. Balladur resigned as Prime Minister, and Chirac appointed Alain Juppé (Minister of Foreign Affairs in the previous Government) as his successor. Juppé formed an administration in which the principal portfolios were evenly shared between the RPR and the UDF. In October Juppé was elected President of the RPR, while Jospin was elected First Secretary of the PS, a position he had held in 1981–88.

In April 1997 Chirac announced that legislative elections would take place in May–June, some 10 months earlier than required. In the first round of voting, held on 25 May, the PS secured 23.5% of total votes cast, the RPR 15.7%, the FN 14.9% and the UDF 14.2%. Following the second round of voting, held on 1 June, the PS secured 241 seats, the RPR 134, the UDF 108 and the PCF 38. Despite its strong performance in the first round, the FN won only one seat. The unexpected victory of the PS, which began a further period of 'cohabitation', was widely attributed to dissatisfaction with Juppé's administration and the imposition of economic austerity measures necessitated under the terms of Economic and Monetary Union (EMU, see p. 251) within the EU. Jospin, leader of the PS, became Prime Minister, and formed a 'plural left' coalition.

In October 1997 the trial of Maurice Papon, a former civil servant and senior official in the pro-Nazi Vichy regime (1940–44), prior to his involvement in the anti-Nazi resistance movement, and who served as a government minister at various times between 1935–81, opened in Bordeaux. Papon was accused of deporting some 1,560 Jews to Germany, where almost all were killed in Nazi concentration camps, in 1943–44. In April 1998 Papon was sentenced to 10 years' imprisonment, having been found guilty of complicity in crimes against humanity, although he was exempt from imprisonment, on the grounds of ill health. In October 1999, however, on the eve of his appeal, it became clear that Papon, who had been due to surrender into custody, had absconded, and had thus forfeited any right to appeal. An international warrant was issued for his arrest, and Papon was subsequently apprehended, expelled from Switzerland, and returned to begin sentence in France. In June 2001 the European Court of Human Rights dismissed an appeal for Papon's release, stating that both the general health and state of mind of the detainee did not warrant an end to his detention. Following his release from imprisonment, on the grounds of ill health, in September 2002, the Ministry of Justice sought to return Papon to prison, stating that his release constituted a threat to public order. However, in February 2003 the Court of Cassation ruled that there were no legal grounds for Papon's renewed incarceration. (In February 2004, following a ruling by the European Court of Human Rights that Papon had been illegally denied the right to appeal, a commission of judges at the Court of Cassation rejected an appeal by Papon's lawyers for a retrial, but granted a review of his conviction; however, this final appeal was rejected by the Court of Cassation in June.)

At regional council elections held in March 1998, the governing socialist coalition won 39.4% of the total vote, the centre-right opposition secured 35.6%, and the FN 15.5%. A subsequent offer by the FN to form alliances with the RPR and the UDF in order to secure control of a number of councils caused much controversy. Both parties instructed their members to ignore the proposal; however, five members of the UDF defied their leadership and consequently obtained council presidencies. Two later resigned, while the remaining three were expelled from the party. A further two senior UDF members left the party in protest at the expulsions, amid serious criticism of the management of the crisis by party President, François Léotard; moreover, one of the constituent parties of the UDF, Démocratie Libérale (DL—formerly the Parti Républicain—PR), announced its departure from the Union, partly as a result of its agreement to form alliances with the FN in regional councils, and partly as a result of its support for a more market-orientated economic policy. Later in the year the UDF reconstituted itself as a unified party. In late June the Assemblée nationale voted to reform the system of regional elections, to take effect from the elections scheduled for 2004, largely as a result of the problems experienced following the elections in March. The changes, which aimed to ensure coherent majorities in the regional councils, included the replacement of the previous one-round system with a two-round poll in which a party with an outright majority in the first round of voting would automatically receive 25% of the seats available.

At a by-election in May 1998 the FN lost its only seat in the Assemblée nationale. Meanwhile, in April a court banned Le Pen from holding or seeking public office for two years (reduced to one year on appeal) and gave him a three-month suspended prison sentence after finding him guilty of physical assault on a PS candidate in the 1997 general election. The selection of a potential replacement for Le Pen, necessitated by the ban, to lead the FN list of candidates in the following year's elections to the European Parliament (of which the FN leader was a member), resulted in a major dispute within the party and the creation of two rival factions. Deepening divisions between supporters of Le Pen and those of Bruno Mégret, the party's second-in-command, led to the expulsion of Mégret, and that of six other senior party officials. In January 1999 Mégret launched his own party, which subsequently became known as the Mouvement National Républicain (MNR), and which appeared to follow harsher anti-immigrant policies than the FN. In October 2000 Le Pen was expelled from his seat in the European Parliament, following the rejection of his final appeal against his 1998 conviction in the European Court of Human Rights. However, in January 2001 Le Pen lodged an appeal at the Court of First Instance of the European Communities, stating that his exclusion from the legislature was illegal on the grounds that the decision to withdraw his legislative mandate had been taken by the President of the European Parliament, rather than by a parliamentary vote; pending the result of this appeal Le Pen was permitted to resume his responsibilities in the Parliament. In April 2003 the Court upheld the ban, and Le Pen's period of suspension formally began in mid-May.

In March 1999 Roland Dumas took leave of absence from the presidency of the Constitutional Council, following the reopening that month of a judicial inquiry into his involvement in the corruption scandals at the formerly state-owned petroleum company, Elf Aquitaine. (Dumas resigned in March 2000 when it was announced that he would stand trial for his alleged participation in reputedly corrupt practices at Elf Aquitaine; the trial was subsequently postponed until January 2001.) Also in March 1999 a Paris public prosecutor upheld a ruling of the Constitutional Court, issued in January, that the President of the Republic enjoyed immunity from prosecution for all crimes, other than high treason, for the duration of his presidential term. This decision, which was confirmed by an appeal court ruling in January 2000, followed the disclosure of documentation purporting to show that Chirac had been aware of the existence of at least 300 fictitious employees, reputedly including RPR members or supporters, on the payroll of the Paris city council under his tenure as mayor.

At elections to the European Parliament held in June 1999, the RPR, in alliance with DL, gained only 12.8% of the votes cast, less than the PS, which won 22.0% of votes cast, and a breakaway Gaullist group, opposed to the terms of the Maastricht Treaty, the Rassemblement pour la France (RPF), led by Charles Pasqua, which gained 13.1% of the votes cast. In December Michèle Alliot-Marie was elected President of the RPR.

In March 2000 Jospin carried out the first major reorganization of the Council of Ministers since taking office. Laurent Fabius, Prime Minister in 1984–86, returned to office as Minister of the Economy, Finance and Industry. The hitherto First Vice-President of the Assemblée nationale, Raymond Forni, replaced Fabius as its President. Jack Lang, a former Minister of Culture under President Mitterrand, returned to senior office as Minister of National Education. In August 2000 the Minister of the Interior, Jean-Pierre Chevènement, the leader and sole minister of the Mouvement des Citoyens (MDC), resigned in protest at government policy towards Corsica (see below). Daniel Vaillant of the PS was appointed in his place. A further ministerial reshuffle was implemented in October.

Evidence of Chirac's apparent knowledge and tolerance of corrupt practice within government deepened in September 2000, when a transcript of a video cassette made by Jean-Claude Méry, a former RPR official who had been imprisoned on charges of embezzlement in the mid-1990s, was published posthumously in Le Monde. In the recording Méry stated that Chirac had personally ordered him to arrange for funds of the Paris city council to be diverted to political parties. In December 2000 Michel Roussin, who had been Chirac's principal private secretary from 1989–93, was arrested, while the former unofficial treasurer for the RPR was remanded for questioning. Their testimony, which was leaked to the press, included details of the systematic levying of an illegal 2% commission on public works contracts awarded by the Paris administration. The RPR, the PR and the PS were all reportedly implicated in this scheme.

Throughout 2000 the tensions caused by a prolonged period of 'cohabitation' promoted moves towards constitutional change. In May Valéry Giscard d'Estaing submitted proposals to reduce the presidential term from seven to five years, in order to bring it into line with the life of a parliament. In June 2000 the Assemblée nationale voted conclusively in favour of the proposed constitutional amendment. Amid concerns that the more conservative Sénat might not support the bill by the two-thirds' majority required for a constitutional change to be approved, Chirac called for a referendum, to be held on 24 September. The referendum attracted only a 30.6% participation rate, by far the lowest in any constitutional referendum held in metropolitan France. Of those who voted, 73.2% were in favour of the change, which was thereby enacted, to take effect from the 2002 presidential elections. Meanwhile, a proposal previously raised by the UDF leader, François Bayrou, to the effect that presidential elections be held in advance of the parliamentary elections due in May 2002, gained in popularity, as it was felt that the proposed arrangement would be more likely to prevent a further period of 'cohabitation'. Following a series of votes in the two legislative chambers, the Constitutional Council approved the proposal in May 2001. Following inconclusive municipal and cantonal elections in March 2001, several ministers resigned from the mayorships that they had won in these elections and two Secretaries of State resigned from their government positions, following Jospin's insistence that henceforth members of the Government would not be permitted simultaneously to hold more than one elected position. In April officials from the RPR, UDF, and DL, although not including the senior leadership of the two latter parties, announced their intention to form a unified centre-right platform, which subsequently became known as the Union en Mouvement (UEM), prior to the legislative elections of 2002. (A previous attempt to form a loose umbrella organization of the centre right, the Alliance pour La France, in 1998–99 had been abandoned after several months.)

In early April 2001 Chirac refused to attend court to give evidence pertaining to the reputedly illegal use of funds in the Paris city council. At the end of the month the investigating judge in the case, Eric Halphen, announced the existence of consistent evidence implicating Chirac, but stated that the doctrine of presidential immunity prevented Chirac from being brought to trial. Although Jospin and the hierarchy of the PS opposed bringing Chirac to trial, the socialist deputy Arnaud Montebourg launched a campaign to bring the case against Chirac to the High Court of Justice, which was the only court constitutionally able to bring charges against the President.

Meanwhile, the trial of Dumas on charges of having misappropriated public funds was further delayed, in February 2001, following the extradition to France, from the Philippines, in relation to further charges of corruption within Elf Aquitaine, of the company's former Deputy Chairman, Alfred Sirven, who refused to co-operate with the trial when brought to court in March 2001, and who had reportedly swallowed the memory chip of a mobile phone believed to contain evidence pertaining to the case following his capture. At the end of May Dumas and Sirven were among four people found guilty on charges relating to fraudulent practice within Elf Aquitaine; Dumas was sentenced to six months in prison, while Sirven received a sentence of four years; none-the-less all four were released on bail, pending an appeal, which was expected to necessitate the investigation of further alleged instances of corruption within Elf Aquitaine.

In June 2001 new revelations concerning Chirac's alleged involvement in financial malpractice emerged, including the first implications that Chirac had personally benefited from malpractice; the President was alleged to have spent up to 2.4m. francs (a figure subsequently increased to 3.1m. francs) of state 'secret funds'—issued annually by the Office of the Prime Minister for the security services, to pay bonuses to staff, and as a contingency fund—on airline tickets and luxury hotel bills for himself and his family in 1992–95, although suspicions were voiced that the finance for these holidays may have originated from the alleged illicit commission payments made by building firms to the Paris city council. In mid-June 2001 the Assemblée nationale approved a bill, supported by the PS, that proposed removing judicial immunity from the President for acts committed outside his official role; however, the bill was regarded as having a purely symbolic function, as it was unlikely to gain the support of the Sénat or the President. In a television interview broadcast on 14 July, President Chirac declared himself innocent of all charges made against him, and confirmed that he would not participate in any court case. At the end of the month a parliamentary committee agreed to a demand by magistrates to see the statements of personal financial wealth made by Chirac between 1988 and 1995; these statements made no reference to the large sums of money with which Chirac had purchased the holidays. Additional revelations concerning Chirac's reputed malpractice as the treasurer of a charity in the late 1970s also emerged at this time.

In August 2001 Jospin announced changes to a law that shortened the maximum working week from 39 to 35 hours, which had been regarded as central to the Government's policy of creating some 700,000 new jobs. The amendments permitted companies with up to 20 employees legally to institute a longer working week, apparently in response to protests by employers at the restrictions engendered by the law. Previous concessions had already been made, after the implementation of the first stage of the legislation was greeted with widespread protests in February 2000.

In September 2001 the Appeal Court dismissed Halphen as the leading investigator into the case regarding the illicit transfer of funds from building contractors to political parties at the Paris city council; Halphen was ruled to have exceeded his powers by calling the President as a witness, and by introducing certain items of evidence, including the video cassette of Méry. Although the case could be tried again, under a different judge, this decision effectively ruled out any development in the case so long as Chirac remained President. (Halphen announced his retirement from the judiciary in January 2002, stating his dissatisfaction with the judicial system.) In mid-October 2001 the Court of Cassation confirmed the Constitutional Court's ruling that an incumbent President could not be prosecuted; additionally, the court ruled that a Head of State could not undergo formal investigation while in power, even for offences allegedly committed prior to taking office. The court also suspended the statute of limitations, as a consequence of which Montebourg ended his campaign to bring Chirac to trial. In the same month, in response to an investigation instigated by Jospin, the President of the Audit Court presented a report which recommended that henceforth, unspent funds from the Prime Minister's Office should be returned to the state budget each year, that bonuses paid to staff should be subject to taxation, and that the 'secret funds', as such, should be reserved solely for the secret security services. (In January 2005 it was reported that supporters of Chirac were planning to introduce amendments to the Constitution, which would protect Chirac from prosecution on these and other potential charges of political corruption, by conferring on presidents at the end of their term of office the position of senator for life with immunity from prosecution.)

The first round of the presidential election, held on 21 April 2002, was contested by an unprecedented 16 candidates. Prior to the first round, Chirac and Jospin had been widely expected to progress to second round. However, apparently partly as a result of the wide choice of candidates, a relatively low rate of participation (only 69.2% of the electorate cast valid votes), and a campaign focus on issues related to 'insecurity' and law and order, Jospin polled only 16.2% of the valid votes cast, while Chirac accounted for 19.9% and Le Pen 16.9%. The splintering of the governmental 'plural left' coalition was to prove detrimental for Jospin, as four of the parties hitherto represented in that coalition, other than the PS, presented individual candidates for the presidency, obtaining 16.3% of votes cast in total. Moreover, three Trotskyite candidates together polled some 10.4% of votes cast. The unexpected qualification of the FN leader for the second-round poll precipitated widespread demonstrations, and the majority of the defeated candidates rallied around Chirac as a candidate that represented 'republican values', although Chirac's first-round vote, in both percentage and actual terms, had been the lowest of any outgoing President of the Fifth Republic. In the second round, on 5 May, the turn-out increased slightly— 75.4% of the electorate cast valid votes. Although Le Pen's share of the vote rose marginally, Chirac's victory, with 82.2% of the valid votes cast, was widely interpreted as a resounding defeat for the far-right. On 6 May, following Jospin's resignation as Prime Minister, Chirac appointed Jean-Pierre Raffarin, of the DL, and latterly President of Poitou–Charantes regional council, as Prime Minister. On 7 May Raffarin appointed an interim Government; among the principal appointments were Nicolas Sarkozy as Minister of the Interior, Interior Security and Local Freedoms, Alliot-Marie as Minister of Defence and Dominique de Villepin as Minister of Foreign Affairs. In the period between the presidential elections and those to the Assemblée nationale, Chirac was instrumental in the organization of a new centre-right electoral alliance to replace the RPR, and to build on the informal alliances forged within the UEM; this alliance was initially titled the Union pour la Majorité Présidentielle (UMP), and was provisionally led by Juppé.

At the elections to the Assemblée nationale held on 9 and 16 June 2002 the UMP, which incorporated the greater part of the RPR and DL, and significant elements of the UDF, succeeded in becoming the largest grouping in the new Assemblée, with 355 of the 577 seats, whilst a further 43 representatives of other parties of the centre-right and right were elected, thus ensuring a clear working majority for the pro-presidential grouping in the assembly. Of the 176 seats awarded to parties of the broad left, the PS was the most successful, with 140 deputies. The FN obtained 11.34% of votes cast in the first round of polling, but did not receive any deputies. The new Government, which was appointed shortly after the conclusion of the legislative elections, retained substantially the same members as the interim Government appointed in May and cited law and order, a programme of decentralization, and further privatizations among its principal concerns. Concern about the degree of support for the far-right in France, which had heightened following Le Pen's progression to the second round of the presidential election, intensified further, following an attempt, on the national day, July 14, to assassinate President Chirac during a procession in Paris; it subsequently emerged that the assailant, Maxime Brunerie, was a member of a small neo-fascist grouping, Unité Radicale (UR), and had, moreover, contested a municipal election as a candidate of the MNR in 2001; UR was formally proscribed in early August, and Brunerie was subsequently interned in a psychiatric hospital. (Brunerie was brought to trial in late 2004, and sentenced in December to 10 years' imprisonment.)

In the aftermath of the legislative elections, the UMP consolidated its position, formally constituting itself as the Union pour un Mouvement Populaire in November 2002, absorbing the RPR and DL, in addition to factions of the UDF and the RPF; Juppé was elected as President of the party. In mid-December a UMP group was formed in the Sénat; with 166 of 321 seats, the group had an absolute majority in the chamber. Meanwhile, the future ideological direction of the PS became a subject of intense debate within the party; none the less, François Hollande, the First Secretary of the party since 1997, was re-elected to that position, with a clear majority of votes, in May 2003.

Meanwhile, in late January 2003 Dumas was cleared of all charges against him in the Elf Aquitaine case; although his conduct was described as 'blameable', he was not charged with any crime. However, the former Elf employees charged alongside Dumas were found guilty on appeal; the former President of Elf, Loïk Le Floch-Prigent was sentenced to 30 months' imprisonment, Sirven received three years' imprisonment, whilst Dumas's former mistress, Christine Deviers-Joncour, was sentenced to 18 months' imprisonment, with an additional suspended sentence of 12 months. In mid-March a further court case into allegations of corruption in the company, investigations for which had commenced in 1995, began in Paris. Some 37 former executives and managers, including Le Floch-Prigent, Sirven and the former director of the company's operations in Africa, André Tarallo, faced charges of permitting the embezzlement of the equivalent of some €300m. of funds in the late 1980s and early 1990s. The case, which was described as the largest judicial investigation into corporate corruption in French history, revealed that funding from the company had been diverted illicitly, by means of secret bank accounts, in order to provide illegal funding to the heads of states of several African countries in which the company operated, and to several political parties and senior politicians in France and in other European countries. It was reported, moreover, that this funding had sought to enhance not only the commercial interests of Elf, but also the foreign-policy interests of France. (The court, however, did not establish whether named politicians had received bribes, and these allegations were, in several cases, publicly denied by those implicated.) In mid-November Le Floch-Prigent and Sirven were each sentenced to a further five years' imprisonment; Le Floch-Prigent was fined €375,000, and Sirven was fined €1m., while Tarallo was sentenced to four years' imprisonment and fined €2m. However, Tarallo and Le Floch-Prigent were both released from prison in January and April 2004, respectively, on the grounds of ill health, and in May Sirven also managed to secure

his release from imprisonment, under judicial control, pending appeal proceedings later in the year, during which the prosecution requested harsher sentences for Sirven and Tarallo (Le Floch-Prigent declined to appeal his sentence). The court was expected to announce its verdict on 31 March 2005; Sirven, however, died in February of that year.

Further concerns at the extent of corrupt practices in public life, meanwhile, were raised following the announcement, in early May 2003, that Juppé, alongside 26 other defendants, was to face trial on charges that the Paris city council and private companies had illegally paid staff of the RPR during Juppé's tenure as Secretary-General of the Party (in 1988–95) and as Deputy Mayor of Paris (1983–95). The trial commenced in late September 2003, and in late January 2004 Juppé was found guilty and given an 18 months' suspended prison sentence, and banned from holding public office for a period of 10 years. However, Juppé was permitted to remain in office as Mayor of Bordeaux, and as a parliamentary deputy, pending an appeal. Although the constitutional immunity of the President of the Republic from prosecution and investigation prevented any investigation into Chirac's behaviour, the judges ruled that Juppé had been directly subordinate to Chirac in his capacity as President of the RPR. (Moreover, Chirac was the Mayor of Paris for the entire duration of Juppé's service as the Deputy Mayor.) 13 other business executives also received suspended prison sentences in the case. Following Juppé's conviction, several leading figures in the UMP (of which he remained the President) rallied to Juppé's support; notably, Chirac praised what he described as Juppé's honesty, humanity and competence. Chirac also ordered that a judicial investigation be launched into an alleged campaign of intimidation against the judges in the case. However, Juppé's decision to remain in public office pending an appeal appeared to contradict an earlier statement that he would resign from public office in the event of being found guilty; it also appeared possible that Chirac could face charges related to the case following the expiry of his presidential mandate, in 2007. Meanwhile, in late January 2004 the Secretary of State for Property Programmes of Justice, Pierre Bédier, resigned from the Government, following the opening of a judicial investigation into allegations that he had illegally received funds from building contracts in the municipality of Mantes-la-Jolie, near Paris; Bédier denied the allegations against him. In mid-February François Léotard, Minister of National Defence in 1993–95, was found guilty of the illicit transfer of funds to the former PR (which, as the DL, had now been subsumed into the UMP), and given a 10 months' suspended jail sentence.

On 17 March 2003 the two houses of Parliament, meeting in congress, approved several constitutional changes. One of these amendments related to the implementation of the European arrest warrant, while the remainder of the amendments related to the proposed decentralization programme; the latter amendments provided for the eventual possibility of territorial units receiving varying degrees of autonomy and powers, to be decided in each case by law, for the institution of deliberative assemblies and for the holding of local referendums in such territories. Moreover, the amendments permitted the introduction of legislation pertaining to decentralization on a temporary, or experimental, basis. Notably, the first article of the Constitution was amended to assert that the organization of the Republic was decentralized. Later in the month the Constitutional Council rejected an appeal for a ruling by 60 socialist Senators that the amendments violated existing provisions of the Constitution. However, attempts to implement policies that utilized the new constitutional provisions initially proved unsuccessful—on 6 July, in the first instance of the holding of a local referendum under these provisions, voters in Corsica rejected proposals to reorganize the administration of the island by a narrow majority (see below), and on 7 December voters in the overseas departments of Guadeloupe (see p. 1760) and Martinique (see p. 1767) rejected proposals to restructure and simplify their territorial administration. Meanwhile, in mid-January 2004 the Assemblée nationale approved an organic law and an ordinary law, the combined effect of which was to grant autonomous status to the overseas country of French Polynesia (see p. 1798); this legislation was finally approved, with minor amendments, in mid-February, by the Constitutional Council.

In July 2003 several reforms to senatorial elections were approved by Parlement; henceforth, senators were to be elected for a term of six years (instead of nine), and one-half (rather than one-third) of the seats were to be renewable every three years. Moreover, with effect from 2010, the number of senators was to be increased from 321 to 346, and the minimum age for eligible candidates to the Sénat was to be reduced from 35 to 30 years.

A major topic of political debate in 2003 and early 2004 concerned the wearing of the *foulard* or other types of veil by female Muslim schoolchildren and students during classes at state educational establishments. Although a 1989 ruling of the Conseil d'état declared that the wearing of religious symbols in state schools did not violate the principle of the secularity of the State, formalized in 1905, so long as they were deemed to be of a 'non-ostentatious' nature, the ruling had subsequently been used to exclude a number of Islamic students from educational establishments. In mid-December 2003 a presidential commission, chaired by the national ombudsman, Bernard Stasi, to investigate measures to ensure that the secular form of the republic be protected, recommended that legislation explicitly to forbid the wearing of the veil, and other conspicuous religious symbols, including Jewish skullcaps and large Christian crosses in state-run schools and colleges be introduced; Chirac expressed support for such a measure, and legislation to that end was approved by the Assemblée nationale in mid-February 2004, and by the Sénat in early March. The law came into effect at the beginning of the new school year in early September. More than 600 students defied the ban but following mediation with their families this was reduced to 72. By 20 January 2005 a total of 48 Muslim schoolgirls had been expelled for violating the new law by wearing Islamic headscarves.

Widespread public discontent with the Government of Raffarin was reflected in the results of regional and cantonal elections, held in two rounds on 21 and 28 March 2004, following which the parties of the centre-right lost control of 13 regions to parties of the left and centre-left, which thereby controlled all of the regions of metropolitan France excluding Alsace and Corsica. In response to these results, Raffarin tendered his resignation as Prime Minister on 30 March, but was immediately reappointed to that position by President Chirac. The formation of a new Government was announced on 31 March, in which several of the principal members of the former administration changed roles. Sarkozy was appointed as Minister of State, Minister of the Economy, Finance and Industry, and was replaced as Minister of the Interior, Internal Security and Local Freedoms by de Villepin. Michel Barnier, hitherto EU Commissioner for Regional Policy and Institutional Reform, who had previously held government office in 1993–97, was appointed as Minister of Foreign Affairs. However, in the European parliamentary elections held on 13 June, the UMP suffered another serious defeat, obtaining only 16.6% of votes cast, whereas the PS received 28.9%. Voter participation in the election was unprecedentedly low at only 43.1%.

The UMP's electoral performance did not improve at the partial indirect elections to the Sénat held on 26 September 2004. The PS and its allies made considerable gains, achieving a net increase of 14 seats, while the UMP lost its outright majority in the chamber, with a net loss of six seats. However, the centre-right parties together retained control of the Sénat. Raffarin, whose decision to contest the senatorial elections was widely attributed to the insecurity of his premiership owing to popular dissatisfaction with the Government, was duly elected to the Sénat but was unable to assume his seat while he remained in the Government. The first stage of the reforms to the senatorial elections approved in July 2003 took effect at this poll, when the number of senators was increased from 321 to 331.

During 2004 concern was expressed by Chirac and others at the rising number of anti-Jewish and anti-Muslim attacks, attributed largely to extremist Muslim groups and the far right respectively. The Government announced the establishment of security monitoring committees in each department with the aim of preventing anti-semitic attacks. A report commissioned by the Government was published in October warning that an increase in racism and anti-semitism in France posed a threat to the democratic system. Recorded racist and anti-Semitic offences increased by 82% in 2004 compared with 2003, to 1,513, of which 361 were described as violent. In December 2004 new initiatives were introduced to promote the integration of Muslim population in France. The aim was to combat growing fundamentalism among young Muslims through the encouragement of a moderate 'French Islam'. The measures announced by the Minister of the Interior, de Villepin, included funding for the building of mosques and courses on French law, customs and language for Islamic religious leaders, *imams*. Meanwhile, the

reduction of economic inequality along ethnic lines in French society was a central aim of the Plan for Social Cohesion presented in 2004 by Jean-Louis Borloo, Minister of Employment, Labour and Social Cohesion (a survey conducted by the Institut national de la statistique et des études économiques in that year suggested that 30% of immigrants of Algerian origin and 28% of Moroccan origin were unemployed).

In August 2004 two French journalists, Christian Chesnot and Georges Malbrunot, were kidnapped and held hostage in Iraq. It was reported that their captors were demanding the repeal of the law prohibiting the wearing of the veil and other religious symbols in schools; however, the ban came into effect as planned in September. A failed attempt by a UMP deputy, Didier Julia, in September to negotiate the release of the hostages provoked widespread media attention and speculation, particularly with regard to the degree to which Julia had acted independently from the Government, and also concerning the reported involvement of Laurent Gbagbo, the President of Côte d'Ivoire, who had allegedly lent Julia a plane in which to fly to Iraq. (An investigation into the matter was launched in December.) The journalists were eventually released in December, while the conditions of their release remained unclear. A further French journalist, Florence Aubenas, was taken hostage in Iraq in January 2005.

In July 2004 Juppé resigned as President of the UMP, in anticipation of the findings of an appeal against his conviction earlier in the year. In its verdict in December, the appeal court upheld the conviction but reduced the length of the ban on holding public office from 10 years to one (following the verdict Juppé also resigned as mayor of Bordeaux). Meanwhile, in November 2004 Sarkozy was elected President of the UMP, winning 85.1% of votes cast. There was widespread speculation that Sarkozy intended to use the leadership of the ruling party as a platform from which to launch his candidature in the presidential elections due in 2007. Following the insistence of President Chirac that the head of the UMP would not be permitted simultaneously to hold ministerial office, Sarkozy resigned as Minister of the Economy, Finance and Industry; in a subsequent minor reshuffle, Chirac appointed Hervé Gaymard, formerly Minister of Agriculture, Food, Fisheries and Rural Affairs, as Sarkozy's replacement, though without the additional designation of Minister of State that Sarkozy had held. On 25 February 2005, however, following a scandal over the high cost of his apartment financed by the State, Gaymard resigned from this position and was replaced by the chief executive of France Télécom, Thierry Breton.

A central topic of political discourse in France in 2004 was the issue of ratification of the Treaty establishing a Constitution for Europe. On 14 July , following considerable political pressure, notably from within the UMP, Chirac announced that the constitutional treaty would be ratified by means of a national referendum, to be held in the following year. The PS split into two factions over the issue, with one faction, led by the First Secretary, François Hollande, supporting the constitution, while the other, led by the former premier, Laurent Fabius, opposed it. In an internal party referendum held on 1 December to decide the official policy of the PS, 58% of votes cast were in favour of ratification. In February 2005 Parlement adopted an amendment to the country's Constitution to conform with the EU constitutional treaty. The amendment was necessitated by a ruling by the Constitutional Council that the European constitutional treaty could not legally coexist with the French Constitution under current law. Subsequently, on 4 March Chirac announced that the referendum on the EU constitutional treaty would take place on 29 May.

In December 2004 Raffarin announced legislative proposals intended to relax further the regulations controlling the 35-hour working week, notably including a proposed increase in the annual quota of supplementary working hours. Left-wing parties denounced the proposals, as did trade unions, which organized large-scale demonstrations across France on 5 February 2005 in protest against the reforms. Nevertheless, the proposals were adopted at the first reading by the Assemblée nationale on 9 February 2005. Meanwhile, in late February the Government announced that the rate of unemployment had reached the politically significant level of 10% of the population for the first time since February 2000.

Demands for the independence of Corsica increased markedly during the 1960s and 1970s, with particular discontent being expressed at the resettlement there of French citizens displaced from Algeria following its independence in 1962. In 1972 the status of Corsica was upgraded to that of a Province, administered by a centrally appointed *Préfet*. (It had hitherto formed an administrative department within the Province of Provence–Côte d'Azur.) The assassination of two gendarmes at Aléria, in eastern Corsica, in August 1975, marked a significant escalation in the campaign for Corsican independence; from 1976 the clandestine Fronte di Liberazione Naziunale di a Corsica (FLNC) was regarded as the leading pro-independence organization. Also in 1976 the Government, led by the Prime Minister, Chirac, subdivided the province of Corsica into two departments, Corse-du-Sud and Haute-Corse. However, demands for greater autonomy or independence persisted, with intermittent bombing campaigns conducted by separatists both in Corsica and in continental France. As a result of decentralization legislation of 1982, the status of Corsica was elevated to that of a 'collectivité territoriale' (territorial community), with its own directly-elected 61-seat Assembly, and an administration with augmented executive powers. In April 1991 the Assemblée nationale adopted legislation that granted greater autonomy to Corsica; a seven-member executive council was to be formed, chosen from a 51-member Assemblée de Corse, which would be elected in 1992. In early February 1998, in the most serious act of violence committed by separatist militants to date, the Préfet of Corsica, Claude Erignac, was assassinated. The killing was condemned by the FLNC. In June 2003 the trial of eight suspected accomplices in the assassination of Erignac commenced in Paris, although the primary suspect, Yvan Colonna, remained in hiding. In mid-July all eight received custodial sentences; two of the accused received life sentences, and two others were sentenced to 30 years' imprisonment. Meanwhile, in July Colonna was unexpectedly captured in southern Corsica and arrested; he was transferred to Paris later in the month, and placed under judicial investigation on suspicion of murder and association with a terrorist organization, although he denied having killed Erignac. His provisional custody was extended for a further year in July 2004. An arson attack on a bar in the provincial capital, Ajaccio, in April 1999 led to the arrest and dismissal of the Préfet, Bernard Bonnet, and the disbandment of the security unit that had been established after the murder of Erignac. Bonnet's arrest was made in response to allegations that the head of the unit, Henri Mazères, had ordered the attack on the bar; Bonnet, Mazères and an aide, Gerard Pardini, received custodial sentences in January 2002 for ordering the arson attacks, although Bonnet denied any involvement and announced that he would appeal. (Bonnet's sentence was upheld at the appeal, which concluded in Bastia in January 2003.)

Meanwhile, negotiations, supported by the Prime Minister, Jospin, that involved the Government and representatives of Corsica commenced in Paris in December 1999. Four groups of Corsican militants called an unconditional cease-fire, and pledged to disarm should their aims, including the recognition of the Corsican people as a nation, and the granting of official status to the Corsican language on the island, be achieved. The peace process resulted in agreement on a number of proposals known as the Matignon Accords. In July 2000 the proposals were approved in the Assemblée de Corse by an overwhelming majority. Under the proposals, subject to the maintenance of peace on Corsica, and the approval of the Assemblée nationale, a referendum would be held on eventual revisions to the Constitution in 2004, prior to the introduction of a single political and administrative body for the island with formal, but limited, legislative powers, replacing the two existing administrative departments. The proposals also provided for instruction in the Corsican language to take place in all primary schools. The Minister of the Interior, Jean-Pierre Chevènement, resigned in protest over the proposals, while President Chirac and other leading figures in the RPR also expressed their opposition to this proposed act of decentralization. Although most dissident groups maintained a cease-fire following the signature of the Matignon Accords, increasing concern was expressed at the prevalence of organized crime in Corsica, while sporadic, low-level attacks by dissident groups continued. On 22 May 2001 the Assemblée nationale approved a more moderate version of the bill to amend the status of Corsica than that which had initially been envisaged, with the view to presenting a text that would be acceptable to the Constitutional Council; consequently, Corsican language instruction at primary schools was to be optional, rather than compulsory, and the French Parliament would be required to pass enabling legislation before local legislation approved by the Assemblée de Corse could take effect. Corsican separatists expressed disapproval of the amend-

ments. By September the process envisaged by the Matignon Accords appeared to be stalling; the moderate nationalist leader, Jean-Guy Talamoni, who had been involved in negotiating the Matignon Accords, announced that the moderate separatist Corsica Nazione had decided, by an almost unanimous vote of its militants and representatives, to withdraw from the provisions of the Accords. The final bill on greater autonomy, which had been subject to further amendments, had, none the less, received the approval of both legislative houses by mid-December. The Gaullist parties, which generally opposed the legislation, announced that they would bring the bill before the Constitutional Council. In mid-January 2002 the Constitutional Council ruled that the section of the bill that permitted the Assemblée de Corse to amend national legislation on the island was illegitimate, although the section of the law that permitted the optional use of Corsican language in primary schools was approved.

Following the defeat of Jospin in the first round of presidential elections in April 2002, and a statement by Chirac to the effect that Corsican aspirations for greater autonomy were insignificant, nationalists on the island announced their withdrawal from the Matignon process. In early May the FLNC-Union des Combatants (FLNC-UDC—as the main faction of the organization was now known) announced that it was to resume its dissident campaign, although the group stated its preference for a negotiated settlement. In June the new centre-right Government, led by Raffarin, unexpectedly announced that it was to seek several amendments to the Constitution that would permit the eventual decentralization of a number of powers, and that, moreover, Corsica would be one region which could be expected to be affected by these measures. In late July Sarkozy visited Corsica, where he spoke to the Assemblée de Corse and announced efforts to relaunch a dialogue with nationalists. Following the generally positive reception of these efforts, Raffarin also travelled to the island. However, amid scepticism regarding the Government's intentions, the number of small-scale bomb attacks on the island increased sharply in 2002, to reach the highest annual total recorded (in excess of 220) since 1997. In February 2003 the Assemblée de Corse voted in favour of a proposal, supported by Sarkozy, whereby the two administrative departments in Corsica were to be replaced by a single *collectivité*, subject to the approval of these measures by a referendum to be held in Corsica. Following the approval, on 17 March, by the Assemblée nationale of various constitutional changes that permitted, *inter alia*, local referendums, it was announced that such a plebiscite was to be held in July on the future administrative structure of the island. Although several separatist groups, including the FLNC-UDC, Corsica Nazione, and the political wing of the FLNC-UDC, Indipendenza, announced their support for the proposals, other more radical groups expressed concern that plans to devolve limited legislative and additional tax-raising powers to the new *collectivité*, which had been included in the Matignon Accords, had not been revived. The referendum went ahead as planned on 6 July. Expectations that the poll would be very closely contested were, in the event, fulfilled, and the proposal was narrowly defeated, with 50.98% of the votes against the restructuring. A relatively high turn-out of 60.52% was reported at the plebiscite.

Following the defeat of the Government's proposals for restructuring the administration of Corsica, there was an escalation of violence by Corsican separatist groups, both in Corsica and in continental France; in late July 2003 two bombs in Nice injured 16 people. The FLNC-UDC, which had announced that it was to end its cease-fire earlier in the month, claimed responsibility for these attacks and for a series of bombings in Corsica; a more militant separatist faction, known as the FLNC des anonymes, also ended its cease-fire and announced its merger with the FLNC-UDC. Moreover, in mid-July deputies of the moderate separatist faction, Corsica Nazione, announced that they were to suspend participation in the Assemblée de Corse, in protest against what they described as the iniquitous verdict of the trial against the eight accomplices in the murder of Erignac. Corsica Nazione also announced that they were to appeal to the Conseil d'état against the result of the referendum, citing instances of alleged electoral fraud. In mid-September the nationalist deputies resumed their duties at the Assemblée de Corse, and in mid-October the Conseil d'état ruled that, despite having found evidence of some irregularities, the result of the referendum was valid. In late October Sarkozy made his 10th visit as Minister of the Interior, Interior Security and Local Freedoms to Corsica, when he announced that any reopening of

withdrew from these duties in December 1998 and criticized aerial raids on Iraq by US and British forces in February 2001. In that month France also announced that it was opposed to the continuation of UN sanctions against Iraq implemented in connection with that country's alleged possession of weapons of mass destruction. In June France recommended to the UN Security Council that foreign investment be permitted in the Iraqi petroleum industry, but, none the less, declared its full support for the 'smart sanctions' proposed by the USA and the United Kingdom at this time. In the aftermath of the attacks in New York and Washington, DC, attributed to the al-Qa'ida (Base) organization, on 11 September 2001, France offered full military and logistical support, including the dispatch to Afghanistan of marines, engineers and members of the Special Forces to the USA in its campaign against al-Qa'ida. However, France remained a prominent critic of several aspects of the foreign policy of the administration of the US President, George W. Bush. Although France supported the UN Security Council Resolution 1441 (presented by the USA and the United Kingdom) in November 2002, which demanded the expedited admittance of UN weapons inspectors to Iraq, the French Minister of Foreign Affairs, de Villepin, maintained opposition to any UN Security Council resolution that would authorize any automatic resort to force against Iraq. Moreover, as Spain, the USA and the United Kingdom sought to gain support for a further UN Security Council resolution regarding Iraq's non-compliance with the requirements of Resolution 1441, in March 2003, President Chirac reiterated that France would, at that stage, veto any resolution that would have the effect of legitimizing military action against that country, and was a prominent opponent of the US-led military action that commenced later that month. However, following the conclusion of large-scale hostilities in Iraq, France gave full approval to UN Security Council Resolution 1483, approved in late May, which recognized the Coalition Provisional Authority as the legal occupying power in Iraq.

In May 1992 France and Germany announced that they would establish a joint defence force of 50,000 troops, the 'Eurocorps', which was intended to provide a basis for a European army under the aegis of Western European Union (WEU, see p. 352), and which became operational in November 1995. Belgium, Spain and Luxembourg also agreed to participate in the force. In January 1993 an agreement was signed between NATO and the French and German Governments, establishing formal links between the corps and NATO's military structure. In late 2000 it was announced that France would contribute 12,000 troops, of a total of more than 60,000 that would form a European rapid reaction force, to participate in peace-keeping missions from 2003. Proposals for a new autonomous European military command headquarters near Brussels, with the capacity to plan and execute European operations autonomously, was put forward by Belgium, France, Germany and Luxembourg (the EU states most opposed to the US-led military campaign in Iraq to remove the regime of Saddam Hussain), following a meeting in Brussels at the end of April 2003. The proposal was opposed by several EU states, notably the United Kingdom, which feared that NATO would be undermined. A compromise was reached in December, under which a small cell of planning staff would be created, situated in NATO's military headquarters in Belgium, which would only be used if NATO declined involvement and national European headquarters needed support. Under a new European plan devised to compensate for the inadequacies of the rapid reaction force, which although theoretically declared ready for action in May 2003, in practice was adversely affected by shortfalls in equipment, a series of battle groups were to be established for deployment to crisis areas by 2007. France (as well as Italy, Spain and the United Kingdom) agreed to create its own battle group.

Government

Under the 1958 Constitution, legislative power is held by the bicameral Parliament, comprising a Sénat (Senate) and an Assemblée nationale (National Assembly). The Sénat currently has 331 members (304 for metropolitan France, 15 for the overseas possessions, and 12 for French nationals abroad). Previously, senators were elected for a nine-year term by an electoral college composed of the members of the Assemblée nationale, delegates from the Councils of the Departments and delegates from the Municipal Councils. One-third of the Sénat was renewable every three years, and election is by a system of proportional representation in those constituencies represented by four or more senators (five or more prior to the elections held

in September 2001). A law approved by Parlement in July 2003 introduced a number of reforms to senatorial elections; henceforth, senators were to be elected for a term of six years, with one-half of the seats renewable every three years. With effect from 2010, the number of senators was to be increased from 321 to 346, and the minimum age for eligible candidates to the Senate was to be reduced from 35 to 30 years. (The first stage of reform, whereby the number of senators increased from 321 to 331, took place at the partial senatorial elections held in September 2004.) The Assemblée nationale has 577 members, with 555 for metropolitan France and 22 for the overseas possessions. Members of the Assemblée are elected by universal adult suffrage, under a single-member constituency system of direct election, using a second ballot if the first ballot failed to produce an absolute majority for any one candidate. The term of the Assemblée is five years, subject to dissolution. Executive power is held by the President. Since 1962 the President had been directly elected by popular vote (using two ballots if necessary) for seven years, although a constitutional amendment passed on 2 October 2000 shortened the term of office to five years. The President appoints a Council of Ministers, headed by the Prime Minister, which administers the country and is responsible to Parliament. Under constitutional amendments and legislation instituted in 1998–2000, political parties are penalized financially if they do not ensure parity of men and women in candidatures for elections.

Metropolitan France comprises 22 administrative regions containing 96 departments. Under the decentralization law of March 1982, administrative and financial power in metropolitan France was transferred from the Préfets, who became Commissaires de la République, to locally-elected departmental assemblies (Conseils généraux) and regional assemblies (Conseils régionaux). Corsica has its own directly-elected legislative assembly (the Assemblée de Corse). The 10 overseas possessions comprise: four Overseas Departments (French Guiana, Guadeloupe, Martinique and Réunion); one overseas 'collectivité départementale' (Mayotte), one overseas 'collectivité territoriale' (St Pierre and Miquelon), two Overseas Territories (the French Southern and Antarctic Territories and the Wallis and Futuna Islands) and two Overseas Countries (New Caledonia and French Polynesia), all of which are integral parts of the French Republic. Amendments to the Constitution, approved in March 2003, which described the organization of the Republic as decentralized, provide for the eventual possibility of territorial units receiving varying degrees of autonomy and powers, to be decided in each case by law, for the institution of deliberative assemblies and for the holding of local referendums in such territories. Moreover, the amendments permitted the introduction of legislation pertaining to decentralization on a temporary, or experimental, basis.

Defence

French military policy is decided by the Supreme Defence Council. Military service was compulsory, and lasted for a period of 10 months, until November 2001, when proposals to create fully professional armed forces, which were submitted to the Assemblée nationale in 1996, took effect. In August 2004 the total active armed forces numbered 259,050, including an army of 137,000, a navy of 44,250, an air force of 64,000, central service staff numbering 5,200 and a medical corps of 8,600. In addition, there was a paramilitary gendarmerie of 101,399. Total reserves stood at 100,000 (army 28,000; navy 6,500; air force 8,000, gendarmerie 50,000, medical service 7,000, others 500) in August 2003. Government expenditure on defence in 2004 amounted to €41,565m. Defence expenditure was budgeted at €42,424m. for 2005. Although a member of NATO, France withdrew from its integrated military organization in 1966, and possesses its own nuclear weapons. In 1995, however, it was announced that France was to rejoin NATO's defence committee, and in 1996 President Chirac declared France's intention to rejoin NATO's integrated military command; by early 2005, however, there had been no firm indication as to when or if this latter move was likely to occur. In mid-2000 France announced that it would be the third largest contributor of troops, behind Germany and the United Kingdom, to the European rapid reaction force, which was to enter service, primarily on peace-keeping missions, in 2003. Under a new European plan approved in November 2004, France agreed to establish one of up to 13 battle groups, comprising 1,000–1,500 troops, for deployment to crisis areas by 2007.

Economic Affairs

In 2003, according to estimates by the World Bank, France's gross national income (GNI), measured at average 2001–03 prices, was US $1,756,551m., equivalent to $24,770 per head (or $27,460 on an international purchasing-power parity basis). During 1990–2003, it was estimated, the population increased by an average of 0.4% per year, while gross domestic product (GDP) per head increased, in real terms, by an average of 1.3% per year. Overall GDP increased, in real terms, at an average rate of 1.7% per year in 1990–2003. Real GDP increased by 1.2% in 2002 and by 0.1% in 2003, the lowest annual growth since an annual decline in GDP was recorded in 1993.

Agriculture (including forestry and fishing) contributed 2.7% of GDP in 2002, and engaged 4.1% of the economically active population in 2003. The principal crops are wheat, sugar beet, maize and barley. Livestock, dairy products and wine are also important. Agricultural GDP increased, in real terms, by an average of 1.4% per year in 1990–2001; it declined by 0.8% in 2000 and by 0.6% in 2001. The sector was adversely affected in 2000–01 by the outbreak of bovine spongiform encephalopathy (BSE—'mad cow disease') and its human variant, Creutzfeldt-Jakob disease, v-CJD). Following the imposition of *post mortem* screening procedures and stringent measures, including the slaughter of all animals in a herd found to contain BSE (until February 2002 when it was limited to cattle born before January 2001), the incidence of confirmed cases in France declined from 276 in 2001, to 239 in 2002 and 137 in 2003.

Industry (including mining, manufacturing, construction and power) provided 24.9% of GDP in 2002, and employed 21.6% of the working population in 2003. Industrial GDP increased, in real terms, by an average of 1.5% per year during 1990–2001; it increased by 4.4% in 2000 and by 1.6% in 2001.

Mining and quarrying contributed 0.2% of GDP in 2001, and employed 0.3% of the working population in 1994. Petroleum and natural gas are extracted and metallic minerals, including iron ore, copper and zinc, are mined. The production of coal, an industry which used to dominate the sector, finished in April 2004 with the closure of France's last operating coal mine, at Creutzwald in Lorraine. In real terms, the GDP of the mining sector increased by 7.4% in 2001.

Manufacturing provided 18.4% of GDP in 2001, and employed 18.8% of the working population in 1994. Measured by the value of output, the most important branches of manufacturing in 1995 were machinery and transport equipment (accounting for 31% of the total), food, beverages and tobacco (17%), chemicals (10%) and fabricated metal products (6%). According to the World Bank, manufacturing GDP increased, in real terms, at an average annual rate of 2.3% in 1990–2000; growth in 2000 was 4.2%.

France has only limited fossil fuel resources, and in the early 2000s was the world's largest producer of nuclear power per head of population. In 2001 nuclear power provided 77.1% of total electricity production and hydroelectric power 13.6%. In October 2004 Électricité de France announced that construction of a new nuclear power station in Normandy would commence in 2007 at a projected cost of €3,000m. In 2005 France had 58 nuclear power stations, many of which would need to be replaced in around 2020. Imports of fuel products comprised 9.2% of the value of total merchandise imports in 2002; in the early 2000s the major sources of petroleum imported to France were Saudi Arabia and Norway. In late 1998 the NorFra pipeline, which connected Norway's Troll gas field in the North Sea to the French national gas grid, opened, becoming the first pipeline to link a foreign production field to France. By 2005 it was anticipated that this pipeline would supply one-third of France's total national gas requirements The GDP of the energy sector increased, in real terms, at an average rate of 1.5% per year in 1990–99.

Services accounted for 72.4% of GDP in 2002, and employed 74.3% of the working population in 2003. In the late 1990s and early 2000s France was consistently the country with the largest quantity of tourist visitors in the world; there were an estimated 77,012,000 tourist arrivals in 2002, and tourism receipts in that year totalled US $32,329m., according to the World Tourism Organization. The combined GDP of all service sectors increased, in real terms, at an average rate of 2.1% per year in 1990–2001; it increased by 3.7% in 2000 and by 2.6% in 2001.

In 2003 France recorded a trade surplus of US $1,100m. and there was a surplus of $4,400m. on the current account of the balance of payments. In 2002+ the principal source of imports (providing 17.2% of the total) was Germany; other major sources were Italy (9.0%), the USA (8.0%), and the United Kingdom (7.3%). Germany was also the principal market for exports in that year (accounting for 14.5% of the total); other major trading partners were the United Kingdom (10.3%), Spain (9.7%), Italy (9.1%) and the USA (8.1%). The EU as a whole provided 59.6% of imports in 2002 and took 62.0% of exports. The principal exports in 2002 were machinery and transport equipment, chemicals, basic manufactures, and miscellaneous manufactured articles. The principal imports were machinery and transport equipment, basic manufactures and miscellaneous manufactured articles.

The budget deficit for 2004 was equivalent to 3.7% of GDP. In 2004 gross state debt was €1,066,000m. equivalent to 65.6% of annual GDP. The average annual rate of inflation in 1990–2003 was 1.8%. Consumer prices increased by 1.7% in 2001, 1.9% in 2002 and 2.1% in 2003. The rate of unemployment declined from 12.3% in 1997 to 8.8% in 2001, but had risen again, to 9.7% in 2003. Unemployment was estimated at 10.0% in January 2005.

France is a member of the European Union (EU, see p. 217), and of the Organisation for Economic Co-operation and Development (see p. 307), and presides over the Franc Zone (see p. 266).

France adopted the euro in January 1999 as a single currency unit for transactions throughout the euro zone and as an internationally traded currency, and as legal tender in cash from 1 January 2002. After a period of strong growth from 1997 to 2000, the expansion of the French economy slowed in 2001–02, and GDP growth in 2003 was evaluated by the World Bank at only 0.1%, the lowest since an overall decline in GDP was recorded in 1996. However, an increase in consumer spending in late 2004 was expected to result in an improved growth rate for that year. Legislation introduced by the Jospin administration in January 2000, which reduced the duration of the working week from 39 to 35 hours, was initially regarded as contributing to an appreciable reduction in unemployment. However, in response to concerns that this restriction exerted a negative impact on the competitiveness of the French economy and necessitated additional costs, the Raffarin administration introduced a series of amendments increasing the flexibility of the system; the second set of proposed amendments, which was passed in its first reading by the Assemblée nationale in February 2005, notably increased the annual number of supplementary working hours. The proposed elimination of the 3% surcharge on corporate taxes during 2005–06, announced by the Raffarin Government in 2004, was seen as another policy intended to increase business freedom and stimulate employment. Unemployment, meanwhile, reached the politically symbolic figure of 10.0% in January 2005. Under considerable pressure from the European Commission to open markets to competition and restrict state subsidies—in 2001 France remained the euro zone country with the highest general government expenditure and revenue (in both cases in excess of 50%) as a share of GDP—the Raffarin administration made the increased privatization of France's last major state-owned companies a priority from 2002. In July 2002 Raffarin announced that the capital of the state-owned energy utilities Electricité de France (EdF) and Gaz de France was progressively to be opened to private investors, although both companies would remain within the public sector. Despite protests organized by workers and trade unions, in mid-2004 Parlement passed legislation providing for the transformation of EdF and Gaz de France into limited liability companies, with the State maintaining a 70% holding in their share capital and voting rights. In February 2005 Hervé Gaymard, at that time still Minister of the Economy, Finance and Industry, announced that he intended the sale of 30% of Gaz de France to be completed by mid-year, with the sale of 30% of EdF following before the end of 2005. (The partial sale of EdF was, however, expected to present significant difficulties: the company's net debt was reported at €24,000m. and its pension liabilities were estimated at €65,000m.) Meanwhile, in November 2004 the outgoing Minister of Finance, Nicolas Sarkozy announced plans for the sale into private ownership of 35% of Areva, the world's largest nuclear energy group; the sale was expected to be completed in the first half of 2005. Previously, in July 2003, the Government had announced proposals for the state-controlled telecommunications company, France Télécom, to be transferred to majority private ownership; this was accomplished in September 2004, with the State becoming a minority shareholder following the sale of 11.8% of its holding. A major motivating factor behind the privatization programme of the Raffarin administration was thought to be the ongoing problem of France's public deficit, which at 3.7% in 2004 exceeded, for the third consecutive year, the limit of 3.0% of national GDP permitted by the euro zone Stability and Growth Pact. (In 2003, when the public deficit had been equivalent to 4.2% of GDP, the European Commission had launched its excessive debt procedure against France, under which the country could have been fined up to 0.5% of its GDP; however, the procedure had been suspended in November, on condition that the French Government implement various reforms intended to reduce the deficit to under 3.0% in 2005.) In early 2005 the Ministry of Finance predicted that it would succeed in lowering the public deficit to 2.9% in 2005; fears were expressed, however, that this prediction was too heavily dependent on optimistic predictions for continued growth and government revenue from the potentially complicated privatization of EdF. Also uncertain in early 2005 was the success or otherwise of the health insurance reform programme formulated by Philippe Douste-Blazy, then Minister of Health and Social Protection, and approved by Parlement in August 2004, which sought to reduce the public health insurance deficit, evaluated at an unprecedented €11,900m. in 2003. Public debt also continued to rise in 2004, exacerbating the difficulty of reducing the budget deficit, since 20% of total budget expenditure in 2004 comprised interest payments on the debt. However, continued low interest rates in the euro zone helped prevent further increased in the debt.

Education

France is divided into 27 educational districts, called Académies, each responsible for the administration of education, from primary to higher levels, in its area. Education is compulsory and free for children aged six to 16 years. Primary education begins at six years of age and lasts for five years. At the age of 11 all pupils enter the first cycle of the Enseignement secondaire, with a four-year general course. At the age of 15 they may then proceed to the second cycle, choosing a course leading to the baccalauréat examination after three years or a course leading to vocational qualifications after two or three years, with commercial, administrative or industrial options. From 1963 junior classes in the Lycées were gradually abolished in favour of new junior comprehensives, called Collèges. Alongside the collèges and lycées, technical education is provided in the Lycées professionnels and the Lycées techniques. About 17% of children attend France's 10,000 private schools, most of which are administered by the Roman Catholic Church.

Educational reforms, introduced in 1980, aimed to decentralize the state school system: the school calendar now varies according to three zones, and the previously rigid syllabus has been replaced by more flexibility and choice of curricula. Further decentralization measures included, from 1986, the transfer of financial responsibility for education to the local authorities.

The minimum qualification for entry to university faculties is the baccalauréat. There are three stages of university education. The first level, the Diplôme d'études universitaires générales (DEUG), is reached after two years of study, and the first degree, the Licence, is obtained after three years. The master's degree (Maîtrise) is obtained after four years of study, while the doctorate requires six or seven years' study and the submission of a thesis. The prestigious Grandes Ecoles complement the universities; entry to them is by competitive examination, and they have traditionally supplied France's administrative élite. The 1968 reforms in higher education aimed to increase university autonomy and to render teaching methods less formal. Enrolment at schools in 1996 included 100% of children in the relevant age-group for primary education and 95% (males 94%; females 95%) for secondary education. Expenditure on education by all levels of government in 1999 totalled an estimated €92,600m. (7.2% of GDP). Budgetary expenditure on national education by the central Government amounted to €59,166m. in 2001 (equivalent to 22.7% of total budgetary expenditure).

Public Holidays

2005: 1 January (New Year's Day), 28 March (Easter Monday), 1 May (Labour Day), 5 May (Ascension Day), 8 May (Liberation Day), 14 July (National Day, Fall of the Bastille), 15 August (Assumption), 1 November (All Saints' Day), 11 November (Armistice Day), 25 December (Christmas Day).

2006: 1 January (New Year's Day), 17 April (Easter Monday), 1 May (Labour Day), 25 May (Ascension Day), 8 May (Liberation Day), 14 July (National Day, Fall of the Bastille), 15 August (Assumption), 1 November (All Saints' Day), 11 November (Armistice Day), 25 December (Christmas Day).

Weights and Measures

The metric system is in force.

Statistical Survey

Unless otherwise indicated, figures in this survey refer to metropolitan France, excluding the Overseas Possessions

Source (unless otherwise stated): Institut national de la statistique et des études économiques, 18 boulevard Adolphe Pinard, 75675 Paris Cédex 14; tel. 1-45-17-50-50; internet www.insee.fr.

Area and Population

AREA, POPULATION AND DENSITY

Area (sq km)	543,965*
Population (census results, *de jure*)†	
5 March 1990	56,615,155
8 March 1999‡	
Males	28,419,419
Females	30,101,269
Total	58,520,688
Population (provisional official data at mid-year)	
2002	59,678,252
2003	60,027,912
2004	60,380,600
Density (per sq km) at mid-2004	111.0

* 210,026 sq miles.

† Excluding professional soldiers and military personnel outside the country with no personal residence in France.

‡ Data are provisional. The revised total is 58,518,395. Figures include double counting.

NATIONALITY OF THE POPULATION
(numbers resident in France at 1999 census, revised figures)

Country of citizenship	Population	%
France	55,257,502	94.42
Portugal	553,663	0.95
Morocco	504,096	0.86
Algeria	477,482	0.82
Turkey	208,049	0.36
Italy	201,670	0.34
Spain	161,762	0.28
Tunisia	154,356	0.26
Germany	78,381	0.31
Belgium	66,666	0.11
Yugoslavia*	50,543	0.09
Poland	33,758	0.06
Others	772,760	1.32
Total	58,520,688	100.00

* The successor states of the former Socialist Federal Republic of Yugoslavia, comprising Bosnia and Herzegovina, Croatia, the former Yugoslav republic of Macedonia, Slovenia and the Federal Republic of Yugoslavia (now Serbia and Montenegro).

REGIONS

(estimated population at 1 January 2002, provisional figures)

	Area (sq km)	Population	Density (per sq km)	Principal city
Alsace	8,280.2	1,768,079	213.5	Strasbourg
Aquitaine . . .	41,308.4	2,966,556	71.8	Bordeaux
Auvergne . . .	26,012.9	1,312,954	50.5	Clermont-Ferrand
Basse-Normandie .	17,589.3	1,432,409	81.4	Caen
Bourgogne (Burgundy) . .	31,582.0	1,608,447	50.9	Dijon
Bretagne (Brittany) .	27,207.9	2,959,497	108.8	Rennes
Centre	39,150.9	2,457,516	62.8	Orléans
Champagne–Ardenne . . .	25,605.8	1,338,500	52.3	Châlons-sur-Marne
Corse (Corsica) .	8,679.8	264,448	30.5	Ajaccio
Franche-Comté .	16,202.3	1,125,980	69.5	Besançon
Haute-Normandie .	12,317.4	1,787,269	145.1	Rouen
Ile-de-France . .	12,012.3	11,078,266	922.2	Paris
Languedoc–Roussillon .	27,375.8	2,375,615	86.8	Montpellier
Limousin . . .	16,942.3	709,747	41.9	Limoges
Lorraine . . .	23,547.4	2,316,936	98.4	Nancy
Midi–Pyrénées .	45,347.9	2,612,707	57.6	Toulouse
Nord–Pas-de-Calais . . .	12,414.1	4,017,414	323.6	Lille
Pays de la Loire .	32,081.8	3,289,811	102.5	Nantes
Picardie (Picardy) .	19,399.5	1,866,428	96.2	Amiens
Poitou–Charentes .	25,809.5	1,660,788	64.3	Poitiers
Provence–Alpes–Côte d'Azur . .	31,399.6	4,625,512	147.3	Marseille
Rhône–Alpes . .	43,698.2	5,767,242	132.0	Lyon
Total	543,965.4	59,342,121	109.1	

PRINCIPAL TOWNS*

(population at 1999 census, revised figures)

Paris (capital) . .	2,125,246	Brest	149,634
Marseille (Marseilles) . .	798,430	Le Mans	146,105
Lyon (Lyons) . . .	445,452	Clermont-Ferrand .	137,140
Toulouse	390,350	Amiens	135,501
Nice	342,738	Aix-en-Provence . .	134,222
Nantes	270,251	Limoges	133,968
Strasbourg . . .	264,115	Nîmes	133,424
Montpellier . . .	225,392	Tours	132,820
Bordeaux	215,363	Villeurbanne . . .	124,215
Rennes	206,229	Metz	123,776
Le Havre	190,905	Besançon . . .	117,733
Reims (Rheims) . .	187,206	Caen	113,987
Lille	184,493	Orléans	113,126
Saint-Etienne . .	180,210	Mulhouse	110,359
Toulon	160,639	Rouen	106,592
Grenoble	153,317	Boulogne-Billancourt	106,367
Angers	151,279	Perpignan . . .	105,115
Dijon	149,867	Nancy	103,605

* Figures refer to the population of communes (municipalities).

BIRTHS, MARRIAGES AND DEATHS*

	Registered live births		Registered marriages		Registered deaths	
	Number	Rate (per 1,000)	Number	Rate (per 1,000)	Number	Rate (per 1,000)
1997 . .	726,768	12.5	283,984	4.9	530,319	9.1
1998 . .	738,080	12.6	271,361	4.6	534,005	9.1
1999 . .	744,791	12.7	286,191	4.9	537,661	9.2
2000 . .	774,782	13.1	297,922	5.1	530,864	9.0
2001 . .	770,945	13.0	288,255	4.9	531,073	9.0
2002† . .	761,630	12.8	279,087	4.7	534,183	9.0
2003† . .	761,464	12.7	275,963	4.6	549,987	9.2
2004† . .	764,700	12.7	259,400	4.3	508,500	8.4

* Including data for national armed forces outside the country.
† Provisional figures.

Expectation of life (WHO estimates, years at birth): 79.7 (males 75.9; females 83.5) in 2002 (Source: WHO, *World Health Report*).

ECONOMICALLY ACTIVE POPULATION

(annual averages, '000 persons aged 15 years and over)

	2001	2002	2003
Agriculture, forestry and fishing .	1,028.3	1,014.6	1,012.1
Food products, beverages and tobacco	637.0	640.7	641.5
Consumer goods industries . .	718.2	699.6	677.9
Automobile industry	265.7	263.5	261.1
Equipment goods industries . .	780.8	765.9	744.1
Intermediate goods industries . .	1,418.4	1,387.3	1,348.8
Energy	225.6	223.2	220.1
Construction	1,470.7	1,492.6	1,501.8
Commerce	3,396.3	3,450.2	3,489.3
Transportation	1,084.4	1,098.5	1,104.2
Financial activities	798.6	812.2	808.1
Real estate and renting activities .	300.5	306.3	306.5
Business services	3,495.1	3,520.7	3,504.0
Domestic and personal services .	2,328.2	2,374.0	2,437.9
Education, health and social work	3,972.7	3,997.9	4,029.0
General government and non-profit institutions serving households .	2,799.1	2,840.2	2,847.1
Total	24,719.6	24,887.4	24,933.5

2001 (annual averages, '000 persons aged 15 years and over, incl. Overseas Possessions): Total employed 24,966.4; Unemployed 2,523.4; Total labour force 27,489.9.

2002 (annual averages, '000 persons aged 15 years and over, incl. Overseas Possessions): Total employed 25,111.0; Unemployed 2,623.5; Total labour force 27,734.5.

Health and Welfare

KEY INDICATORS

Total fertility rate (children per woman, 2002)	1.9
Under-5 mortality rate (per 1,000 live births, 2003) . . .	5
HIV/AIDS (% of persons aged 15–49, 2003)	0.4
Physicians (per 1,000 head, 2001)	3.30
Hospital beds (per 1,000 head, 2000)	8.2
Health expenditure (2001): US $ per head (PPP)	2,567
Health expenditure (2001): % of GDP	9.6
Health expenditure (2001): public (% of total)	76.0
Human Development Index (2002): ranking	16
Human Development Index (2002): value	0.932

For sources and definitions, see explanatory note on p. vi.

Agriculture

PRINCIPAL CROPS
('000 metric tons)

	2001	2002	2003
Wheat	31,540.3	38,939.2	30,474.7
Rice (paddy)	102.8	105.2	106.7
Barley	9,799.1	10,976.0	9,844.2
Maize*	16,408.2	16,440.0	11,990.9
Rye	116.0	139.2	112.1
Oats	484.8	756.1	554.9
Sorghum	397.7	458.9	231.4
Triticale (wheat-rye hybrid)	1,122.1	1,491.0	1,281.8
Potatoes	6,077.9	6,874.4	6,348.1
Sugar beet	26,841	33,464	29,358
Pulses†	1,877.4	2,035.0	1,948.8
Soybeans (Soya beans)	309.7	208.5	149.0
Sunflower seed	1,584.0	1,493.3	1,505.1
Rapeseed	2,877.7	3,320.2	3,361.2
Cabbages	243.1	252.4	215.3
Artichokes	59.5	71.7	50.3
Lettuce	490.9	488.0	460.5
Spinach	112.5	114.0	117.2
Tomatoes	859.3	802.5	825.4
Cauliflowers	401.6	399.9	413.7
Pumpkins, squash and gourds	213.7	223.9	203.1
Cucumbers and gherkins	127.4	137.2	135.8
Onions (dry)	404.6	451.2	374.0
Beans (green)	104.5	104.2	97.7
Peas (green)	474.0	447.2	420.7
String beans	359.6	371.6	351.7
Carrots	649.5	727.6	688.4
Canteloupes and other melons	318.3	283.4	298.8
Apples	2,397.0	2,432.2	2,136.9
Pears	259.5	246.0	199.5
Apricots	103.2	169.4	123.8
Peaches and nectarines	458.1	455.5	347.2
Plums	271.6	246.4	250.2
Strawberries‡	52.7	49.0	45.0
Grapes	7,225.4	6,853.5	6,307.1
Kiwi fruit	78.9	77.4	74.1
Tobacco (leaves)	23.9	24.3	25.5

* Figures refer to main, associated and catch crops.
† FAO estimates.
‡ Unofficial figures.
Source: FAO.

LIVESTOCK
('000 head, year ending 30 September)

	2001	2002	2003
Cattle	20,462	20,116	19,596
Pigs	15,382	15,327	15,138
Sheep	9,443	9,336	9,256
Goats	1,231	1,232	1,223
Horses	343	345	350
Asses*	16	15	15
Mules*	15	15	15
Chickens	219,435	202,742	200,841
Ducks	25,644	25,781	24,163
Turkeys	38,293	35,765	34,721

* FAO estimates.
Source: FAO.

LIVESTOCK PRODUCTS
('000 metric tons)

	2001	2002	2003
Beef and veal	1,566.0	1,640.0	1,631.0*
Mutton and lamb	133.8	128.4	130.8
Pig meat	2,315.2	2,346.0	2,321.0
Chicken meat	1,230.1	1,148.0	1,132.7
Duck meat	231.1	253.9	253.9
Turkey meat	746.7	695.3	634.7
Other meat†	311.4	309.5	307.9
Cows' milk	24,903.3	25,197.3	24,614.1
Sheep's milk	255.8	256.8	263.7
Goats' milk	511.6	536.1	545.7
Butter	448.8	449.8	434.6
Cheese	1,770.0	1,782.5	1,809.6
Honey	15.4	15.0†	15.0†
Hen eggs	1,016.4	998.8	998.2
Wool: greasy†	22	22	22
Wool: scoured†	12	12	12
Cattle hides†	150	160	162
Sheepskins†	15.2	15.2	15.5

* Unofficial figure.
† FAO estimate(s).
Source: FAO.

Forestry

ROUNDWOOD REMOVALS
('000 cubic metres, excluding bark)

	2001	2002	2003
Sawlogs, veneer logs and logs for sleepers	25,372	21,578	22,000
Pulpwood	11,645	10,709	11,500
Other industrial wood	454	449	450
Fuel wood	2,360	2,713	2,900
Total	39,831	35,449	36,850

Source: FAO.

SAWNWOOD PRODUCTION
('000 cubic metres, including railway sleepers)

	2001	2002	2003
Coniferous (softwood)	7,714	7,486	7,200
Broadleaved (hardwood)	2,804	2,329	2,405
Total	10,518	9,815	9,605

Source: FAO.

Fishing*

('000 metric tons, live weight)

	2000	2001	2002
Capture	623.8	605.6	620.1
Pollocks	26.9	28.5	30.1
Atlantic herring	25.4	27.6	26.6
European pilchard (Sardine)	29.2	29.1	34.4
Skipjack tuna	58.1	48.6	70.6
Yellowfin tuna	67.5	63.6	67.9
Crustaceans	20.5	21.8	20.2
Molluscs	77.5	72.1	74.3
Aquaculture	266.7	251.6	249.7
Rainbow trout	41.1	46.5	45.2
Pacific cupped oyster	133.5	107.4	107.0
Blue mussel	60.8	55.2	55.0
Total catch	890.5	857.2	869.8

* Figures exclude aquatic plants ('000 metric tons): 68.2 (capture 68.2, aquaculture 0.0) in 2000; 66.3 (capture 66.3; aquaculture 0.0) in 2001; 80.4 (capture 80.4; aquaculture 0.0) in 2002; coral (metric tons): 3.6 in 2000; 3.7 in 2001; 5.6 in 2002; and sponges (metric tons, FAO estimates): 3.0 in 2000; 2.0 in 2001; 1.4 in 2002. Also excluded are aquatic mammals, recorded by number rather than by weight. The number of toothed whales caught was: 224 in 2000; 154 in 2001; 238 in 2002.

Source: FAO.

Mining

('000 metric tons, unless otherwise indicated)

	2000	2001	2002*
Hard coal	3,805	2,364	1,900
Brown coal (incl. lignite) . .	297	324	300
Crude petroleum ('000 barrels) .	11,591	10,082	10,000
Natural gas (million cu metres) .	1,873	1,810	1,850
Silver (kilograms)*†	720	800	600
Uranium (metric tons)† . . .	318	182	175
Gold (kilograms)†	2,632	2,510	2,600
Kaolin and kaolinitic clay‡ . . .	380	375	360
Potash salts‡§	321	257	130
Fluorspar‡	105	115	105
Barite (Barytes)‖	91	81	80
Salt*	7,116	7,097	7,000
Gypsum and anhydrite (crude)*	4,500	4,500	4,500
Pozzolan and lapilli*	450	400	400
Mica*	10	10	10
Talc (crude)	376	367	370

* Estimate(s).
† Figures refer to the metal content of ores and concentrates.
‡ Figures refer to marketable production.
§ Figures refer to potassium oxide (K_2O) content.
‖ Figures refer to barium sulphite ($BaSO_3$) content.

Source: US Geological Survey.

Industry

SELECTED PRODUCTS

('000 metric tons, unless otherwise indicated)

	1999	2000	2001
Margarine	130	n.a.	n.a.
Wheat flour	6,152	6,371	6,225
Raw sugar*	4,914	4,602	4,238
Wine*	6,294	5,977	5,538
Beer of barley*	1,662	1,599	1,572
Cigarettes (million)	42,405	42,398	41,787
Cotton yarn (pure)	103.0	89.5	86.6
Woven cotton fabrics (million sq metres)	702	579	548
Wool yarn (pure)	10.3	7.6	6.5
Woven woollen fabrics (metric tons)	4,032	3,684	3,168
Artificial or synthetic fibres (metric tons)	73,320	66,036	n.a.
Woven fabrics of artificial or synthetic fibres (metric tons) .	111,252	111,936	n.a.
Mechanical and semi-chemical wood pulp	885	764	741
Chemical wood pulp	1,704	1,817	1,817
Newsprint	1,099	1,039	1,033
Other printing and writing paper .	3,247	3,435	3,298
Other paper and paperboard . .	5,257	5,532	5,299
Synthetic rubber	592.4	639.0	667.0
Rubber tyres ('000)†	66,960	67,714	63,790
Sulphuric acid	2,177	2,181	2,051
Caustic soda (Sodium hydroxide) .	1,601	1,690	n.a.
Fertilizers	3,845	3,710	n.a.
Liquefied petroleum gas‡ . . .	2,613	3,005	n.a.
Motor gasolene (petrol) . . .	17,786	17,231	n.a.
Naphthas	4,642	5,776	n.a.
Jet fuels	6,426	6,030	n.a.
Kerosene	84	82	n.a.
Gas-diesel oil (Distillate fuel oil) .	32,684	34,596	n.a.
Residual fuel oils	10,821	11,090	n.a.
Petroleum bitumen (asphalt) . .	3,660.	3,733	n.a.
Coke-oven coke	5,418	5,234	n.a.
Cement (excl. clinker)	20,302	20,000	20,652
Pig-iron	13,852	14,293	12,870
Crude steel	22,100	21,001	20,000
Aluminium (unwrought—primary)	455.0	441.1	459.8
Lead (unwrought)	131.0	258.0	238.0
Zinc (unwrought)	331.0	337.4	345.3
Radio receivers ('000)	2,961	3,831	n.a.
Television receivers ('000) . .	4,705	5,079	n.a.
Merchant ships launched ('000 gross reg. tons)	108	194	330

— continued	1999	2000	2001
Passenger motor cars ('000)§ . .	4,265	4,652	3,182
Lorries and vans ('000)§ . . .	627.6	741.8	n.a.
Electric energy (million kWh) . .	530,728	546,707	n.a.

* Data from FAO. Data refer to production during crop year ending 30 September.
† Rubber tyres for passenger motor vehicles and similar.
‡ Excluding production in natural gas processing plants ('000 metric tons): 256 in 1999.
§ Including manufactured components, to be assembled in other territories.

Source: mainly UN, *Industrial Commodity Statistics Yearbook*.

Finance

CURRENCY AND EXCHANGE RATES

Monetary Units
100 cent = 1 euro (€).

Sterling and Dollar Equivalents (31 December 2004)
£1 sterling = 1.4180 euros;
US $1 = 0.7342 euros;
100 euros = £70.52 = $136.21.

Average Exchange Rate (euros per US $)
2002   1.0626
2003   0.8860
2004   0.8054

Note: The national currency was formerly the French franc. From the introduction of the euro, with French participation, on 1 January 1999, a fixed exchange rate of €1 = 6.5596 French francs was in operation. Euro notes and coins were introduced on 1 January 2002. The euro and local currency circulated alongside each other until 17 February, after which the euro became the sole legal tender.

GENERAL BUDGET

(€ million)

Revenue	2000	2001
Tax revenue	236,482	248,823
Income tax	51,496	52,445
Corporation tax	40,757	42,814
Other direct taxation	22,245	23,985
Domestic tax on petroleum products . . .	25,480	25,305
Value-added tax	103,855	108,967
Stamp duty, etc.	16,161	15,803
Non-tax revenue	27,951	29,077
Sub-total	250,522	277,900
Deductions for local communities	−28,894	−31,669
Deductions for EU	−15,016	−15,169
Total	220,522	231,062

Expenditure*	2000	2001
General non-salary disbursements (net) . . .	53,916	51,050
Agriculture and fisheries	4,427	5,107
Culture and communications	2,452	2,549
Defence	37,019	37,309
Economy, finance and industry	13,834	14,143
Employment and solidarity	32,673	31,947
Equipment, transport and housing . .	20,945	21,363
Foreign affairs	3,196	3,368
Interior	13,175	16,980
Justice	4,162	4,435
National education	55,030	59,166
Overseas territories, etc.	972	1,040
Research and technology	6,077	6,157
War veterans	3,672	3,627
Total (incl. others)	253,806	260,900

* Expenditure by ministry, according to initial budgetary law.

Source: Ministry of the Economy, Finance and Industry, Paris.

Revised totals (€ million): *Total revenue:* 229,970 in 2000; 234,410 in 2001; 227,470 in 2002; 221,560 in 2003. *Total expenditure:* 259,310 in 2000; 266,030 in 2001; 277,460 in 2002; 278,270 in 2003.

INTERNATIONAL RESERVES
(US $ million at 31 December)

	2001	2002	2003
Gold*	26,888	33,331	40,576
IMF special drawing rights . .	492	622	761
Reserve position in IMF . . .	4,894	5,778	6,303
Foreign exchange	26,363	21,965	23,122
Total	58,637	61,696	70,762

* Valued at market-related prices.

Source: IMF, *International Financial Statistics*.

MONEY SUPPLY
(€ million at 31 December)

	2001	2002	2003
Currency outside banks . . .	34,575	74,153*	84,978*
Demand deposits at banking institutions	305,546	295,536	350,139

* Currency put into circulation by the Banque de France totalled €41,636m. in 2002 and €43,250m. in 2003.

Source: IMF, *International Financial Statistics*.

COST OF LIVING
(Consumer Price Index, average of monthly figures; base: 1998 = 100)

	2000	2001	2002
Food (incl. beverages and tobacco)	103.4	108.6	112.0
Fuel and light	113.3	111.3	109.5
Clothing and household linen . .	100.2	100.7	101.5
Rent, water and domestic services	102.1	102.6	105.1
All items (incl. others)	102.2	103.9	105.9

NATIONAL ACCOUNTS

National Income and Product
(€ '000 million at current prices)

	1999	2000	2001
Gross domestic product in purchasers' values . . .	1,355.1	1,420.1	1,475.6
Factor income received from abroad	64.5	75.0	85.5
Less Factor income paid abroad	50.0	63.3	74.0
Gross national product (GNP) .	1,369.7	1,431.8	1,487.1
Less Consumption of fixed capital	185.0	196.5	205.5
National income in market prices	1,184.6	1,235.3	1,281.7
Other current transfers from abroad	13.1	13.9	14.5
Less Other current transfers paid abroad	22.9	25.1	26.8
National disposable income	1,174.9	1,224.0	1,269.4

Source: UN, *National Accounts Statistics*.

Expenditure on the Gross Domestic Product
(€ '000 million at current prices)

	2001	2002	2003
Final consumption expenditure .	1,150.3	1,200.1	1,243.2
Households	797.6	825.5	854.2
Non-profit institutions serving households	9.9	10.3	10.7
General government	342.8	364.3	378.3
Gross capital formation	301.8	298.2	294.8
Gross fixed capital formation .	296.9	295.8	298.7
Changes in inventories . . .	3.4	1.1	−5.2
Acquisitions, less disposals, of valuables	1.5	1.3	1.3
Total domestic expenditure .	1,452.1	1,498.3	1,537.0
Exports of goods and services . .	412.1	412.6	401.9
Less Imports of goods and services	388.7	384.0	382.6
GDP in purchasers' values	1,475.6	1,526.8	1,557.2
GDP at constant 1995 prices .	1,377.1	1,393.4	1,399.9

Gross Domestic Product by Economic Activity
(€ million at current prices; figures rounded to nearest €10m.)

	1999	2000	2001
Agriculture, hunting, forestry and fishing	36,700	35,530	36,860
Mining and quarrying	2,230	2,570	2,760
Manufacturing	223,950	234,290	243,090
Electricity, gas and water . . .	26,870	25,650	26,270
Construction	54,540	60,670	65,110
Trade, restaurants and hotels . .	160,010	167,000	174,700
Transport, storage and communications	79,820	82,200	88,150
Finance, insurance, real estate and business services*	362,960	390,980	402,030
Public administration and defence; compulsory social security . .	105,270	108,990	114,070
Education, health and social work; other community, social and personal services	180,510	188,340	195,830
Private households with employed persons	8,940	9,430	10,030
Sub-total	1,241,790	1,305,680	1,358,920
Less Financial intermediation services indirectly measured .	35,230	37,320	36,520
Gross value added in market prices	1,206,560	1,268,3600	1,322,390
Taxes, *less* subsidies on products .	148,540	151,780	153,190
GDP in market prices . . .	1,355,100	1,420,140	1,475,580

* Including imputed rents of owner-occupied dwellings.

Source: UN, *National Accounts Statistics*.

BALANCE OF PAYMENTS
(US $ '000 million)*

	2001	2002	2003
Exports of goods f.o.b.	294.6	307.7	361.9
Imports of goods f.o.b.	−291.8	−300.7	−360.8
Trade balance	2.8	6.9	1.1
Exports of services	82.3	86.6	99.7
Imports of services	−56.9	−69.3	−84.8
Balance on goods and services	28.3	24.2	16.0
Other income received	74.1	64.8	88.6
Other income paid	−59.0	−60.9	−81.0
Balance on goods, services and income	43.3	28.2	23.6
Current transfers received . . .	17.3	19.9	23.6
Current transfers paid	−31.9	−34.3	−42.8
Current balance	28.8	13.8	4.4
Capital account (net)	−0.3	−0.2	−8.2
Direct investment abroad . . .	−87.0	−49.7	−57.4
Direct investment from abroad .	50.4	49.4	47.8
Portfolio investment assets . .	−85.5	−84.7	−147.5
Portfolio investment liabilities .	106.9	67.9	136.2
Financial derivatives liabilities .	2.3	5.3	−7.1
Other investment assets . . .	−59.2	−36.4	−20.0
Other investment liabilities . .	38.8	24.3	47.4
Net errors and omissions . . .	−0.8	6.3	5.8
Overall balance	−5.6	−4.0	1.3

* Figures refer to transactions of metropolitan France, Monaco and the French Overseas Departments and Territories with the rest of the world.

Source: IMF, *International Financial Statistics*.

External Trade

(Note: Figures refer to the trade of metropolitan France, French Overseas Departments (French Guiana, Guadeloupe, Martinique and Réunion) and Monaco with the rest of the world, excluding trade in war materials, goods exported under the off-shore procurement programme, war reparations and restitutions and the export of sea products direct from the high seas. The figures include trade in second-hand ships and aircraft, and the supply of stores and bunkers for foreign ships and aircraft.)

PRINCIPAL COMMODITIES
(distribution by SITC, US $ million)

Imports c.i.f.	2000	2001	2002
Food and live animals . . .	20,424.6	19,725.0	21,354.5
Mineral fuels, lubricants, etc. (incl. electric current) . . .	30,878.2	28,032.0	27,974.5
Petroleum, petroleum products, etc.	24,547.3	21,005.8	20,862.2
Crude petroleum oils, etc. . .	17,997.3	15,435.5	14,731.4
Chemicals and related products	37,154.3	36,596.2	39,262.4
Medicinal and pharmaceutical products	7,972.3	9,272.6	10,781.1
Basic manufactures	45,855.5	42,659.7	43,391.8
Machinery and transport equipment . . .	121,673.4	113,110.5	114,457.1
Power-generating machinery and equipment	10,085.5	10,444.4	10,410.2
General industrial machinery, equipment and parts . .	12,918.8	12,743.0	13,103.1
Office machines and automatic data-processing equipment . .	15,982.0	14,322.4	13,211.2
Automatic data-processing machines and units . .	9,393.0	8,054.8	7,873.2
Telecommunications and sound equipment	10,914.6	10,150.0	9,372.0
Other electrical machinery, apparatus, etc. . . .	23,920.7	19,242.7	19,056.3
Road vehicles and parts* . .	30,205.5	29,905.2	32,625.1
Passenger motor cars (excl. buses)	16,815.5	16,121.6	17,488.9
Miscellaneous manufactured articles	42,087.6	41,635.2	44,582.9
Clothing and accessories (excl. footwear)	11,484.7	11,698.4	12,456.1
Total (incl. others)	310,896.8	293,869.0	303,774.4

* Data on parts exclude tyres, engines and electrical parts.

Exports f.o.b.	2000	2001	2002
Food and live animals . . .	23,628.3	21,888.8	24,051.2
Beverages and tobacco . . .	8,479.2	7,994.8	9,059.3
Beverages	8,103.6	7,599.9	8,562.4
Chemicals and related products	40,769.6	41,265.2	45,499.1
Medicinal and pharmaceutical products	10,321.2	12,635.7	14,941.4
Medicaments (incl. veterinary medicaments)	8,259.0	10,593.2	12,578.9
Basic manufactures . . .	43,299.7	40,624.9	41,976.3
Iron and steel	9,892.6	9,264.9	9,751.7
Machinery and transport equipment . . .	135,692.9	129,696.3	133,049.3
Power-generating machinery and equipment	10,470.0	11,009.6	10,503.3
General industrial machinery, equipment and parts . .	12,991.9	12,815.9	13,956.1
Office machines and automatic data-processing equipment . .	10,079.7	8,332.8	7,161.0
Telecommunications and sound equipment	13,917.7	11,057.0	10,479.2
Other electrical machinery, apparatus, etc. . . .	22,700.4	20,590.2	20,158.0
Road vehicles and parts* . .	37,740.1	37,567.5	42,643.2
Passenger motor cars (excl. buses)	19,388.3	21,046.3	24,862.8
Parts and accessories for cars, buses, lorries, etc.* . . .	12,479.1	11,229.1	12,203.5

Exports f.o.b.— *continued*	2000	2001	2002
Other transport equipment and parts*	19,500.6	20,176.7	19,788.8
Aircraft, associated equipment and parts*	16,605.5	17,209.6	17,169.7
Miscellaneous manufactured articles	29,136.5	29,032.1	31,108.0
Total (incl. others)	302,248.0	289,586.1	304,893.4

* Data on parts exclude tyres, engines and electrical parts.

Source: UN, *International Trade Statistics Yearbook*.

PRINCIPAL TRADING PARTNERS
(US $ million)

Imports c.i.f.	2000	2001	2002
Belgium	20,772.0	19,280.7	20,007.2
China, People's Republic . . .	9,866.6	9,704.9	10,691.3
Germany	50,388.3	48,949.4	52,213.8
Ireland	6,389.4	5,328.9	6,139.6
Italy	27,050.6	26,300.2	27,415.1
Japan	11,750.9	9,858.9	9,862.3
Netherlands	14,896.3	13,954.1	14,405.6
Norway	7,246.5	6,283.6	5,711.4
Portugal	2,935.0	2,856.7	3,145.4
Russia	4,428.8	4,543.4	4,942.5
Saudi Arabia	3,244.7	2,187.7	2,117.1
Spain	21,120.1	19,993.6	21,818.9
Sweden	4,370.2	3,912.3	4,081.2
Switzerland-Liechtenstein . .	7,018.7	6,814.7	6,773.3
United Kingdom	24,762.6	22,047.4	22,194.7
USA	27,364.3	26,289.4	24,260.1
Total (incl. others)	310,896.8	293,869.0	303,774.4

Exports f.o.b.	2000	2001	2002
Algeria	2,718.5	3,031.5	3,543.1
Austria	3,146.3	2,892.0	2,853.7
Belgium	20,955.5	20,428.1	22,019.1
Canada	2,426.8	2,582.3	2,534.2
China, People's Republic . .	3,039.5	2,940.3	3,272.4
Germany	45,500.2	41,518.0	44,216.7
Greece	2,404.1	2,343.7	2,480.4
Hong Kong	2,210.3	3,511.4	2,580.5
Italy	26,944.5	25,425.9	27,620.9
Japan	5,099.4	4,849.6	5,244.2
Netherlands	13,223.0	11,634.5	12,180.3
Poland	2,903.8	3,111.1	3,575.2
Portugal	4,436.7	4,113.6	4,431.2
Spain	29,234.4	27,907.3	29,565.1
Sweden	4,659.7	4,326.0	4,374.7
Switzerland-Liechtenstein . .	10,075.2	9,792.5	9,895.7
Turkey	3,456.8	1,981.5	2,728.4
United Kingdom	29,755.2	28,479.5	31,330.2
USA	26,543.2	25,614.7	24,666.1
Total (incl. others)	302,248.0	289,586.1	304,893.4

Source: UN, *International Trade Statistics Yearbook*.

Transport

RAILWAYS
(traffic)

	2001	2002	2003
Paying passengers ('000 journeys)	874,000	890,000	n.a.
Freight carried ('000 metric tons)	126,300	127,600	n.a.
Passenger-km (million)	71,340	73,170	71,840
Freight ton-km (million)* . . .	50,400	50,000	46,800

* Including passengers' baggage.

Source: Société Nationale des Chemins de fer Français, Paris.

ROAD TRAFFIC
('000 motor vehicles in use at 31 December)

	2000	2001	2002
Passenger cars	28,060	28,700	29,160
Lorries and vans . . .	5,673	5,816	5,903
Buses and coaches	80	81	81

Source: International Road Federation, *World Road Statistics*.

INLAND WATERWAYS

	2000	2001	2002
Freight carried ('000 metric tons)	58,671	56,169	56,788
Freight ton-km (million) . . .	7,261	6,716	6,939

Source: Voies navigables de France.

SHIPPING

Merchant Fleet
(registered at 31 December)

	2001	2002	2003
Number of vessels	699	707	711
Total displacement ('000 grt) . .	1,406.8	1,541.2	1,459.8

Source: Lloyd's Register-Fairplay, *World Fleet Statistics*.

Sea-borne Freight Traffic
('000 metric tons)

	1998	1999	2000
Goods loaded (excl. stores) . . .	96,000	99,900	100,300
International	86,000	n.a.	n.a.
Coastwise	10,000	n.a.	n.a.
Goods unloaded (excl. fish) . . .	240,700	233,100	245,400
International	226,700	n.a.	n.a.
Coastwise	14,000	n.a.	n.a.

Source: Ministère de l'Equipement, du Logement, des Transports et du Tourisme.

CIVIL AVIATION
(revenue traffic on scheduled services)*

	2001	2002	2003
Passengers carried ('000) . . .	55,249	57,263	54,860
Passenger-km (million)	126,208	131,373	130,563
Total ton-km (million)	4,386	4,473	4,697

* Including data for airlines based in French Overseas Departments and Territories.

Source: Direction générale d'aviation civile.

Tourism

FOREIGN TOURIST ARRIVALS BY COUNTRY OF ORIGIN
('000, estimates)

	2000	2001	2002
Belgium and Luxembourg . . .	8,326	8,238	8,472
Germany	15,008	13,880	14,346
Italy	7,869	7,058	7,874
Netherlands	10,774	11,776	12,631
Spain	2,995	2,858	2,965
Switzerland	3,463	3,296	3,074
United Kingdom and Ireland . .	14,304	14,885	14,958
USA	3,816	3,539	2,996
Total (incl. others)	77,190	75,202	77,012

Sources: World Tourism Organization, *Yearbook of Tourism Statistics*, and Secretariat of State for Tourism, Ministry of Capital Works, Housing, Tourism and the Sea, Paris.

Tourism receipts (US $ million): 30,754 in 2000; 29,979 in 2001; 32,329 in 2002 (Source: World Tourism Organization).

Communications Media

	2001	2002	2003
Telephones ('000 main lines in use)	34,032.9	34,124.2	33,905.4
Mobile cellular telephones ('000 subscribers)	35,922.3	38,585.3	41,683.1
Personal computers ('000 in use) .	20,000	20,700	n.a.
Internet users ('000)	15,653	18,716	21,900

Television receivers ('000 in use): 37,000 in 2000.

Radio receivers ('000 in use): 55,300 in 1997.

Facsimile machines ('000 in use): 2,800 in 1997.

Book production: 51,837 titles in 2000.

Daily newspapers (1999): 93 titles (combined circulation 2,895.1m.).

Non-daily newspapers (1995): 278 titles (circulation 1,714,000 copies).

Other periodicals (1993): 2,683 titles (circulation 120,018,000 copies in 1991).

Sources: mainly UN, *Statistical Yearbook*; UNESCO, *Statistical Yearbook*; International Telecommunication Union.

Education

(2003/04, public and private, metropolitan France and Overseas Territories, unless otherwise indicated)

	Institu-tions	Tea-chers*	Students Males	Students Females	Students Total
Pre-primary . .	18,147		1,330,063‡	1,268,628‡	2,598,691‡
Primary . .	}	}	1,998,521‡	1,901,459‡	3,899,980‡
Integration and adaption schooling . .	39,040	362,936†	32,117	21,186	53,303
Secondary:					
Lower . .	6,987	243,608	1,650,617	1,593,963	3,244,580
Upper— Professional .	1,716	} 255,257	383,031	323,857	706,888
Upper— Gen./Technical	2,620		677,696	833,285	1,501,981
Higher:					
Universities§ . .	257	} 86,986‖	622,000¶	804,000¶	1,426,000¶
Other	4,099		n.a.	n.a.	829,199

* Excludes trainee teachers.
† Of which 16,333 were teachers of integration and adaption schooling.
‡ Estimate.
§ Includes University Institutes of Technology and Schools of Engineering attached to universities.
‖ Figure for 2002/03.
¶ Approximate figure.

Source: Ministère de l'éducation nationale, de l'enseignement et de la recherche.

Directory

The Constitution

The Constitution of the Fifth Republic was adopted by referendum on 28 September 1958, promulgated on 6 October 1958 and subsequently amended as indicated below.

PREAMBLE

The French people hereby solemnly proclaims its attachment to the Rights of Man and to the principles of national sovereignty as defined by the Declaration of 1789, confirmed and complemented by the Preamble of the Constitution of 1946.

By virtue of these principles and that of the free determination of peoples, the Republic hereby offers to the Overseas Territories that express the desire to adhere to them, new institutions based on the common ideal of liberty, equality and fraternity and conceived with a view to their democratic evolution.

Article 1. (As amended by legislation of 4 August 1995 and 17 March 2003.) France shall be a Republic, indivisible, secular, democratic and social. It shall ensure the equality of all citizens before the law, without distinction of origin, race or religion. It shall respect all beliefs. Its organization shall be decentralized.

I. ON SOVEREIGNTY

Article 2. (As amended by legislation of 25 June 1992.) The language of the Republic shall be French.

The national emblem shall be the tricolour flag, blue, white and red.

The national anthem shall be the 'Marseillaise'.

The motto of the Republic shall be 'Liberty, Equality, Fraternity'.

Its principle shall be government of the people, by the people, and for the people.

Article 3. (As amended by legislation of 8 July 1999.) National sovereignty belongs to the people, who shall exercise this sovereignty through their representatives and through the referendum.

No section of the people, nor any individual, may arrogate to themselves or himself the exercise thereof.

Suffrage may be direct or indirect under the conditions stipulated by the Constitution. It shall always be universal, equal and secret.

All French citizens of both sexes who have reached their majority and who enjoy civil and political rights may vote under the conditions to be determined by law.

The law shall promote equal access by women and men to elective offices and positions.

Article 4. (As amended by legislation of 8 July 1999.) Political parties and groups are instrumental in the exercise of suffrage. They may form and carry on their activities freely. They must respect the principles of national sovereignty and of democracy. They shall contribute to the implementation of the principle set out in the last paragraph of Article 3 as provided by the law.

II. THE PRESIDENT OF THE REPUBLIC

Article 5. (As amended by legislation of 4 August 1995.) The President of the Republic shall see that the Constitution is respected. He shall ensure, by his arbitration, the regular functioning of the governmental authorities, as well as the continuity of the State.

He shall be the guarantor of national independence, of the integrity of the territory, and of respect for treaties.

Article 6. (As amended by legislation of 6 November 1962 and 2 October 2000.) The President of the Republic shall be elected for five years by direct universal suffrage. The method of implementation of the present Article shall be determined by an organic law.

Article 7. (As amended by legislation of 6 November 1962, 18 June 1976 and 17 March 2003.) The President of the Republic shall be elected by an absolute majority of the votes cast. If such a majority is not obtained at the first ballot, a second ballot shall take place 14 days later. Those who may stand for the second ballot shall be only the two candidates who, after the possible withdrawal of candidates with more votes, have gained the largest number of votes on the first ballot.

Voting shall begin at the summons of the Government. The election of the new President of the Republic shall take place not less than 20 days and not more than 35 days before the expiry of the powers of the President in office. In the event that the Presidency of the Republic has been vacated for any reason whatsoever, or impeded in its functioning as officially declared by the Constitutional Council, after the matter has been referred to it by the Government and which shall give its ruling by an absolute majority of its members, the functions of the President of the Republic, with the exception of those covered by Articles 11 and 12 hereunder, shall be temporarily exercised by the President of the Sénat (Senate) or, if the latter is in his turn unable to exercise his functions, by the Government.

In the case of vacancy or when the impediment is declared to be permanent by the Constitutional Council, the voting for the election of the new President shall take place, except in case of *force majeure* officially noted by the Constitutional Council, not less than 20 days and not more than 35 days after the beginning of the vacancy or of the declaration of the final nature of the impediment.

If, in the seven days preceding the latest date for the lodging of candidatures, one of the persons who, at least 30 days prior to that date, publicly announced his decision to be a candidate dies or is impeded, the Constitutional Council may decide to postpone the election.

If, before the first ballot, one of the candidates dies or is impeded, the Constitutional Council orders the postponement of the election.

In the event of the death or impediment, before any candidates have withdrawn, of one of the two candidates who received the greatest number of votes in the first ballot, the Constitutional Council shall declare that the electoral procedure must be repeated in full; the same shall apply in the event of the death or impediment of one of the two candidates standing for the second ballot.

All cases shall be referred to the Constitutional Council under the conditions laid down in paragraph 2 of Article 61 below, or under those determined for the presentation of candidates by the organic law provided for in Article 6 above.

The Constitutional Council may extend the periods stipulated in paragraphs 3 and 5 above provided that polling shall not take place more than 35 days after the date of the decision of the Constitutional Council. If the implementation of the provisions of this paragraph results in the postponement of the election beyond the expiry of the powers of the President in office, the latter shall remain in office until his successor is proclaimed.

Articles 49 and 50 and Article 89 of the Constitution may not be put into application during the vacancy of the Presidency of the Republic or during the period between the declaration of the final nature of the impediment of the President of the Republic and the election of his successor.

Article 8. The President of the Republic shall appoint the Prime Minister. He shall terminate the functions of the Prime Minister when the latter presents the resignation of the Government.

At the suggestion of the Prime Minister, he shall appoint the other members of the Government and shall terminate their functions.

Article 9. The President of the Republic shall preside over the Council of Ministers.

Article 10. The President of the Republic shall promulgate laws within 15 days following the transmission to the Government of the finally adopted law.

He may, before the expiry of this time limit, ask Parliament for a reconsideration of the law or of certain of its Articles. This reconsideration may not be refused.

Article 11. (As amended by legislation of 4 August 1995.) The President of the Republic, on the proposal of the government during [Parliamentary] sessions, or on joint motion of the two Assemblies published in the *Journal Officiel*, may submit to a referendum any bill dealing with the organization of the governmental authorities, with reforms related to the economic or social policy of the nation and to the public services contributing thereto or providing for authorization to ratify a treaty that, without being contrary to the Constitution, might affect the functioning of the institutions.

Where the referendum is held in response to a proposal by the Government, the latter shall make a statement before each Assembly, which shall be followed by a debate.

Where the referendum decides in favour of the government bill, the President of the Republic shall promulgate the law within 15 days following the proclamation of the results of the vote.

Article 12. (As amended by legislation of 4 August 1995.) The President of the Republic may, after consultation with the Prime Minister and the Presidents of the Assemblies, declare the dissolution of the Assemblée nationale (National Assembly).

A general election shall take place 20 days at the least and 40 days at the most after the dissolution.

The Assemblée nationale shall convene by right on the second Thursday following its election. If this meeting takes place between the period provided for the ordinary session, a session shall, by right, be opened for a 15-day period.

There may be no further dissolution within a year following this election.

Article 13. (As amended by legislation of 17 March 2003) The President of the Republic shall sign the ordinances and decrees decided upon in the Council of Ministers.

He shall make appointments to the civil and military posts of the State.

Councillors of State, the Grand Chancellor of the Legion of Honour, Ambassadors and Envoys Extraordinary, Master Councillors of the Audit Court, prefects, representatives of the State in the Overseas communities governed by Article 74 and in New Caledonia, general officers, rectors of academies [regional divisions of the public educational system] and directors of central administrations shall be appointed in meetings of the Council of Ministers.

An organic law shall determine the other posts to be filled by decision of the Council of Ministers, as well as the conditions under which the power of the President of the Republic to make appointments to office may be delegated by him to be exercised in his name.

Article 14. The President of the Republic shall accredit Ambassadors and Envoys Extraordinary to foreign powers; foreign Ambassadors and Envoys Extraordinary shall be accredited to him.

Article 15. The President of the Republic shall be commander of the armed forces. He shall preside over the higher councils and committees of national defence.

Article 16. When the institutions of the Republic, the independence of the nation, the integrity of its territory or the fulfilment of its international commitments are threatened in a grave and immediate manner and the regular functioning of the constitutional governmental authorities is interrupted, the President of the Republic shall take the measures required by these circumstances, after official consultation with the Prime Minister and the Presidents of the Assemblies, and the Constitutional Council.

He shall inform the nation of these measures in a message.

These measures must be prompted by the desire to ensure to the constitutional governmental authorities, in the shortest possible time, the means of accomplishing their mission. The Constitutional Council shall be consulted with regard to such measures.

Parliament shall meet by right.

The Assemblée nationale may not be dissolved during the exercise of exceptional powers.

Article 17. The President of the Republic shall have the right of pardon.

Article 18. The President of the Republic shall communicate with the two Assemblies of Parliament by means of messages, which he shall cause to be read, and which shall not be the occasion for any debate.

Between sessions, the Parliament shall be convened especially to this end.

Article 19. Official decisions of the President of the Republic, other than those provided for under Articles 8 (first paragraph), 11, 12, 16, 18, 54, 56 and 61, shall be counter-signed by the Prime Minister and, where applicable, by the appropriate ministers.

III. THE GOVERNMENT

Article 20. The Government shall determine and conduct the policy of the nation.

It shall have at its disposal the administration and the armed forces.

It shall be responsible to the Parliament under the conditions and according to the procedures stipulated in Articles 49 and 50.

Article 21. The Prime Minister shall direct the operation of the Government. He shall be responsible for national defence. He shall ensure the execution of the laws. Subject to the provisions of Article 13, he shall have regulatory powers and shall make appointments to civil and military posts.

He may delegate certain of his powers to the ministers.

He shall replace, should the occasion arise, the President of the Republic as the Chairman of the councils and committees provided for under Article 15.

He may, in exceptional instances, replace him as the chairman of a meeting of the Council of Ministers by virtue of an explicit delegation and for a specific agenda.

Article 22. The official decisions of the Prime Minister shall be counter-signed, when circumstances so require, by the ministers responsible for their execution.

Article 23. The functions of Members of the Government shall be incompatible with the exercise of any parliamentary mandate, with the holding of any office, at the national level, in business, professional or labour organizations, and with any public employment or professional activity.

An organic law shall determine the conditions under which the holders of such mandates, functions or employments shall be replaced.

The replacement of the members of Parliament shall take place in accordance with the provisions of Article 25.

IV. THE PARLIAMENT

Article 24. The Parliament shall comprise the Assemblée nationale and the Sénat.

The deputies to the Assemblée nationale shall be elected by direct suffrage.

The Sénat shall be elected by indirect suffrage. It shall ensure the representation of the territorial communities of the Republic. French nationals living outside France shall be represented in the Sénat.

Article 25. An organic law shall determine the term for which each Assembly is elected, the number of its members, their emoluments, the conditions of eligibility, and the offices incompatible with membership of the Assemblies.

It shall likewise determine the conditions under which, in the case of a vacancy in either Assembly, persons shall be elected to replace the deputy or senator whose seat has been vacated until the holding of new complete or partial elections to the Assembly concerned.

Article 26. (As amended by legislation of 4 August 1995.) No Member of Parliament may be prosecuted, subjected to inquiry, arrested, detained or tried as a result of the opinions expressed or votes cast by him in the exercise of his functions.

No Member of Parliament shall be subjected, in regard to any criminal or correctional matter, to arrest or any other custodial or semi-custodial measures other than with the authorization of the Assembly of which he is a member. Such authorization shall not be required in the case of a serious crime or other major offence committed *in flagrante delicto* or a final conviction.

The detention, subjection to custodial or semi-custodial measures, or prosecution of a Member of Parliament shall be suspended for the duration of the session if the Assembly of which he is a member so requires.

The Assembly concerned shall convene as of right for additional sittings in order to permit the preceding paragraph to be applied should circumstances so require.

Article 27. Any compulsory vote shall be null and void.

The right to vote of the members of Parliament shall be personal.

An organic law may, under exceptional circumstances, authorize the delegation of a vote. In this case, no member may be delegated more than one vote.

Article 28. (As amended by legislation of 4 August 1995.) Parliament shall convene by right in one ordinary session a year, which shall start on the first working day of October and shall end on the last working day of June.

The number of days for which each Assembly may sit during the ordinary session shall not exceed one hundred and twenty. The sitting weeks shall be determined by each Assembly.

The Prime Minister, after consulting the President of the Assembly concerned, or the majority of the members of each Assembly, may decide to meet for additional sitting days.

The days and hours of sittings shall be determined by the rules of procedure of each Assembly.

Article 29. Parliament shall convene in extraordinary session at the request of the Prime Minister or of the majority of the members comprising the Assemblée nationale, to consider a specific agenda.

When an extraordinary session is held at the request of the members of the Assemblée nationale, the closure decree shall take effect as soon as the Parliament has exhausted the agenda for which it was called, and at the latest 12 days from the date of its meeting.

Only the Prime Minister may ask for a new session before the end of the month following the closure decree.

Article 30. Apart from cases in which Parliament meets by right, extraordinary sessions shall be opened and closed by decree of the President of the Republic.

Article 31. The members of the Government shall have access to the two Assemblies. They shall be heard when they so request.

They may call for the assistance of Commissioners of the Government.

Article 32. The President of the Assemblée nationale shall be elected for the duration of the legislature. The President of the Sénat shall be elected after each partial re-election [of the Sénat].

Article 33. The meetings of the two Assemblies shall be public. An *in extenso* report of the debates shall be published in the *Journal Officiel.*

Each Assembly may sit in secret committee at the request of the Premier or of one-tenth of its members.

V. ON RELATIONS BETWEEN PARLIAMENT AND THE GOVERNMENT

Article 34. (As amended by legislation of 22 February 1996 and 17 March 2003.) Laws shall be voted by Parliament.

Legislation shall establish the regulations concerning:

Civil rights and the fundamental guarantees granted to the citizens for the exercise of their public liberties; the obligations imposed by the national defence upon the person and property of citizens;

Nationality, status and legal capacity of persons; marriage contracts, inheritance and gifts;

Determination of crimes and misdemeanours as well as the penalties imposed therefor; criminal procedure; amnesty; the creation of new juridical systems and the status of magistrates;

The basis, the rate and the methods of collecting taxes of all types; the issue of currency.

Legislation likewise shall determine the regulations concerning:

The electoral system of the Parliamentary Assemblies and the local assemblies;

The establishment of categories of public institutions;

The fundamental guarantees granted to civil and military personnel employed by the State;

The nationalization of enterprises and the transfers of the property of enterprises from the public to the private sector.

Legislation shall determine the fundamental principles of:

The general organization of national defence;

The free administration of territorial communities, of their competencies and their resources;

Education;

Property rights, civil and commercial obligations;

Legislation pertaining to employment unions and social security.

The financial laws shall determine the financial resources and obligations of the State under the conditions and with the reservations to be provided for by an organic law.

Social security finance bills shall determine the general conditions for the financial balance of social security and, taking account of their revenue forecasts, shall determine expenditure targets in the manner and under the reserves provided for by an organic law.

Laws pertaining to national planning shall determine the objectives of the economic and social action of the State.

The provisions of the present Article may be detailed and supplemented by an organic law.

Article 35. Parliament shall authorize the declaration of war.

Article 36. Martial law shall be decreed in a meeting of the Council of Ministers.

Its extension beyond 12 days may be authorized only by Parliament.

Article 37. Matters other than those that fall within the domain of law shall be of a regulatory character.

Legislative texts concerning these matters may be modified by decrees issued after consultation with the Council of State. Those legislative texts which shall be passed after the entry into force of the present Constitution shall be modified by decree only if the Constitutional Council has stated that they have a regulatory character as defined in the preceding paragraph.

Article 37–1. (Appended by legislation of 17 March 2003). Law and regulations may include, for a limited duration and object, dispositions of an experimental character.

Article 38. The Government may, in order to carry out its programme, ask Parliament for authorization to take through ordinances, during a limited period, measures that are normally within the domain of law.

The ordinances shall be enacted in meetings of Ministers after consultation with the Council of State. They shall come into force upon their publication but shall become null and void if the bill for their ratification is not submitted to Parliament before the date set by the enabling act.

At the expiry of the time limit referred to in the first paragraph of the present Article, the ordinances may be modified only by the law in respect of those matters which are within the legislative domain.

Article 39. (As amended by legislation of 22 February 1996 and 17 March 2003.) The Prime Minister and the Members of Parliament alike shall have the right to initiate legislation.

Government bills shall be discussed in the Council of Ministers after consultation with the Council of State and shall be filed with the secretariat of one of the two Assemblies. Finance bills shall be submitted first to the Assemblée nationale. Finance bills and social security finance bills shall be submitted first to the Assemblée nationale. Without prejudice to the first paragraph of Article 44, projects of law having for their principal object the organization of territorial communities, and projects of law related to the representative authorities of French nationals living outside France shall be submitted in the first instance to the Sénat.

Article 40. Private members' bills and amendments shall be inadmissible when their adoption would have as a consequence either a diminution of public financial resources or an increase in public expenditure.

Article 41. If it shall appear in the course of the legislative procedure that a Parliamentary bill or an amendment is not within the domain of law or is contrary to a delegation granted by virtue of Article 38, the Government may declare its inadmissibility.

In case of disagreement between the Government and the President of the Assembly concerned, the Constitutional Council, upon the request of one or the other, shall rule within a time limit of eight days.

Article 42. The discussion of bills shall pertain, in the first Assembly to which they have been referred, to the text presented by the Government.

An Assembly given a text passed by the other Assembly shall deliberate on the text that is transmitted to it.

Article 43. Government and private members' bills shall, at the request of the Government or of the Assembly concerned, be sent for study to committees especially designated for this purpose.

Government and private members' bills for which such a request has not been made shall be sent to one of the permanent committees, the number of which is limited to six in each Assembly.

Article 44. Members of Parliament and of the Government have the right of amendment.

After the opening of the debate, the Government may oppose the examination of any amendment which has not previously been submitted to committee.

If the Government so requests, the Assembly concerned shall decide, by a single vote, on all or part of the text under discussion, retaining only the amendments proposed or accepted by the Government.

Article 45. Every government or private member's bill shall be considered successively in the two Assemblies of Parliament with a view to the adoption of an identical text.

When, as a result of disagreement between the two Assemblies, it has been impossible to adopt a Government or private member's bill after two readings by each Assembly, or, if the Government has declared the matter urgent, after a single reading by each of them, the Prime Minister shall have the right to bring about a meeting of a joint committee composed of an equal number from both Assemblies charged with the task of proposing a text on the matters still under discussion.

The text elaborated by the joint committee may be submitted by the Government for approval of the two Assemblies. No amendment shall be admissible except by agreement with the Government.

If the joint committee does not succeed in adopting a common text, or if this text is not adopted under the conditions set forth in the preceding paragraph, the Government may, after a new reading by the Assemblée nationale and by the Sénat, ask the Assemblée nationale to rule definitively. In this case, the Assemblée nationale may reconsider either the text elaborated by the joint committee, or the last text voted by it, modified when circumstances so require by one or several of the amendments adopted by the Sénat.

Article 46. The laws that the Constitution characterizes as organic shall be passed and amended under the following conditions:

A Government or private member's bill shall be submitted to the deliberation and to the vote of the first Assembly notified only at the expiration of a period of 15 days following its introduction;

The procedure of Article 45 shall be applicable. Nevertheless, lacking an agreement between the two Assemblies, the text may be adopted by the Assemblée nationale on final reading only by an absolute majority of its members;

The organic laws relative to the Sénat must be passed in the same manner by the two Assemblies;

The organic laws may be promulgated only after a declaration by the Constitutional Council on their constitutionality.

Article 47. The Parliament shall pass finance bills under the conditions to be stipulated by an organic law.

Should the Assemblée nationale fail to reach a decision on first reading within a time limit of 40 days after a bill has been filed, the Government shall refer it to the Sénat, which must rule within a time limit of 15 days. The procedure set forth in Article 45 shall then be followed.

Should Parliament fail to reach a decision within a time limit of 70 days, the provisions of the bill may be enforced by ordinance.

Should the finance bill establishing the resources and expenditures of a fiscal year not be filed in time for it to be promulgated before the beginning of that fiscal year, the Government shall urgently request Parliament for authorization to collect taxes and shall make available by decree the funds needed to meet the Government commitments already voted.

The time limits stipulated in the present Article shall be suspended when the Parliament is not in session.

The Audit Court shall assist Parliament and the Government in supervising the implementation of the finance laws.

Article 47–1. (Appended by legislation of 22 February 1996.) Parliament shall pass social security finance bills in the manner provided for by an organic law.

Should the Assemblée nationale fail to reach a decision on first reading within twenty days following the introduction of a bill, the Government shall refer the bill to the Sénat, which must rule within fifteen days. The procedure set out in Article 45 shall then apply.

Should Parliament fail to reach a decision within fifty days, the provisions of the bill may be implemented by ordinance.

The time limits set by this Article shall be suspended when Parliament is not in session and, as regards each assembly, during the weeks when it has decided not to sit in accordance with the second paragraph of Article 28.

The Audit Court shall assist Parliament and the Government in monitoring the implementation of social security finance Acts.

Article 48. (As amended by legislation of 4 August 1995.) Without prejudice to the application of the last three paragraphs of Article 28, the discussion of the bills tabled or agreed upon by the Government shall have priority on the agenda of the Assemblies in the order determined by the Government.

At least one meeting a week shall be reserved, by priority, for questions asked by Members of Parliament and for answers by the Government.

One meeting a month shall be reserved, by priority, for the agenda determined by each Assembly.

Article 49. (As amended by legislation of 4 August 1995.) The Prime Minister, after deliberation by the Council of Ministers, shall make the Government responsible, before the Assemblée nationale, for its programme or, should the occasion arise, for a declaration of general policy.

The Assemblée nationale may challenge the responsibility of the Government by a motion of censure. Such a motion is admissible only if it is signed by at least one-tenth of the members of the Assemblée nationale. The vote may not take place before 48 hours after the motion has been filed. Only the votes that are favourable to a motion of censure shall be counted; the motion of censure may be adopted only by a majority of the members comprising the Assembly. Except as provided for in the following paragraph, a Deputy shall not sign more than three motions of censure during a single ordinary session and more than one during a single extraordinary session.

The Prime Minister may, after deliberation by the Council of Ministers, make the Government responsible before the Assemblée nationale for the adoption of a bill. In this case, the text shall be considered as adopted unless a motion of censure, filed during the twenty-four hours that follow, is carried under the conditions provided for in the preceding paragraph.

The Prime Minister shall have the right to request the Sénat for approval of a declaration of general policy.

Article 50. When the Assemblée nationale adopts a motion of censure, or when it disapproves the programme or a declaration of general policy of the Government, the Prime Minister must hand the resignation of the Government to the President of the Republic.

Article 51. (As amended by legislation of 4 August 1995.) The closure of the ordinary or of extraordinary sessions shall by right be delayed, should the occasion arise, in order to permit the application of Article 49. Additional sittings shall by right be held for the same purpose.

VI. ON TREATIES AND INTERNATIONAL AGREEMENTS

Article 52. (As amended by legislation of 4 August 1995.) The President of the Republic shall negotiate and ratify treaties.

He shall be informed of all negotiations leading to the conclusion of an international agreement not subject to ratification.

Article 53. Peace treaties, commercial treaties, treaties or agreements relative to international organization, those that commit the finances of the State, those that modify provisions of a legislative nature, those relative to the status of persons, those that call for the cession, exchange or addition of territory may be ratified or approved only by a law.

They shall go into effect only after having been ratified or approved.

No cession, no exchange, or addition of territory shall be valid without the consent of the populations concerned.

Article 53–1. (Appended by legislation of 25 November 1993.) The Republic may conclude, with European states that are bound by commitments identical with its own in the matter of asylum and the protection of human rights and fundamental liberties, agreements determining their respective competence in regard to the consideration of requests for asylum submitted to them.

However, even if the request does not fall within their competence under the terms of these agreements, the authorities of the Republic shall remain empowered to grant asylum to any foreigner who is persecuted for his action in pursuit of liberty or who seeks the protection of France for some other reason.

Article 53–2. (Appended by legislation of 8 July 1999.) The Republic may recognize the jurisdiction of the International Criminal Court as provided for by the treaty signed on 18 July 1998.

Article 54. (As amended by legislation of 25 June 1992.) If the Constitutional Council, the matter having been referred to it by the President of the Republic, by the Prime Minister, by the President of one or the other Assembly, or by any 60 Deputies or 60 Senators, shall declare that an international commitment contains a clause contrary to the Constitution, the authorization to ratify or approve the commitment in question may be given only after amendment of the Constitution.

Article 55. Treaties or agreements duly ratified or approved shall, upon their publication, have an authority superior to that of laws, subject, for each agreement or treaty, to its application by the other party.

VII. THE CONSTITUTIONAL COUNCIL

Article 56. The Constitutional Council shall consist of nine members, whose mandates shall last nine years and shall not be renewable. One-third of the membership of the Constitutional Council shall be renewed every three years. Three of its members shall be appointed by the President of the Republic, three by the President of the Assemblée nationale, three by the President of the Sénat.

In addition to the nine members provided for above, former Presidents of the Republic shall be members *ex officio* for life of the Constitutional Council.

The President shall be appointed by the President of the Republic. He shall have the deciding vote in case of a tie.

Article 57. The office of member of the Constitutional Council shall be incompatible with that of minister or Member of Parliament. Other incompatibilities shall be determined by an organic law.

Article 58. The Constitutional Council shall ensure the regularity of the election of the President of the Republic.

It shall examine complaints and shall announce the results of the vote.

Article 59. The Constitutional Council shall rule, in the case of disagreement, on the regularity of the election of deputies and senators.

Article 60. (As amended by legislation of 17 March 2003 and 28 February 2005.) The Constitutional Council shall ensure the regularity of the referendum procedure, as provided for in Articles 11 and 89, and in Title XV. It shall announce the results thereof.

Article 61. (As amended by legislation of 29 October 1974.) Organic laws, before their promulgation, and regulations of the Parliamentary Assemblies, before they come into application, must be submitted to the Constitutional Council, which shall rule on their constitutionality.

To the same end, laws may be submitted to the Constitutional Council, before their promulgation, by the President of the Republic, the Prime Minister, the President of the Assemblée nationale, the President of the Sénat, or any 60 deputies or 60 senators.

In the cases provided for by the two preceding paragraphs, the Constitutional Council must make its ruling within a time limit of one month. Nevertheless, at the request of the Government, in case of urgency, this period shall be reduced to eight days.

In these same cases, referral to the Constitutional Council shall suspend the time limit for promulgation.

Article 62. A provision declared unconstitutional may not be promulgated or implemented.

The decisions of the Constitutional Council may not be appealed to any jurisdiction whatsoever. They shall be binding on the governmental authorities and on all administrative and juridical authorities.

Article 63. An organic law shall determine the rules of organization and functioning of the Constitutional Council, the procedure to be followed before it, and in particular of the periods of time allowed for laying disputes before it.

VIII. ON JUDICIAL AUTHORITY

Article 64. The President of the Republic shall be the guarantor of the independence of the judicial authority.

He shall be assisted by the High Council of the Judiciary.

An organic law shall determine the status of the judiciary.

Judges may not be removed from office.

Article 65. (As amended by legislation of 27 July 1993.) The High Council of the Judiciary shall be presided over by the President of the Republic. The Minister of Justice shall be its Vice-President *ex officio*. He may preside in place of the President of the Republic.

The High Council of the Judiciary shall consist of two sections, one with competence for judges, the other for public prosecutors.

The section with competence for judges shall include, in addition to the President of the Republic and the Minister of Justice, five judges and one public prosecutor, one senior member of the Council of State appointed by the Council of State, and three prominent citizens who are neither members of Parliament nor the judiciary, appointed respectively by the President of the Republic, the President of the Assemblée nationale and the President of the Sénat.

The section with jurisdiction for public prosecutors shall include, in addition to the President of the Republic and the Minister of Justice, five public prosecutors and one judge, the senior member of the Council of State and the three prominent citizens referred to in the preceding paragraph.

The section of the High Council of the Judiciary with jurisdiction for judges shall make nominations for the appointment of judges in the Court of Cassation, for the First Presidents of the courts of appeal and the presidents of the tribunaux de grande instance. Other judges shall be appointed with its assent.

It shall serve as the disciplinary council for judges. When acting in that capacity, it shall be presided over by the First President of the Court of Cassation.

The section of the High Council of the Judiciary with jurisdiction for public prosecutors shall give its opinion on the appointment of public prosecutors, with the exception of posts to be filled in the Council of Ministers. It shall give its opinion on disciplinary penalties with regard to public prosecutors. When acting in that capacity, it shall be presided over by the Chief Public Prosecutor at the Court of Cassation.

An organic law shall determine the manner in which this Article is to be implemented.

Article 66. No one may be arbitrarily detained.

The judicial authority, guardian of individual liberty, shall ensure the respect of this principle under the conditions stipulated by law.

IX. THE HIGH COURT OF JUSTICE

Article 67. A High Court of Justice shall be instituted.

It shall be composed, in equal number, of members elected, from among their membership, by the Assemblée nationale and by the Sénat after each general or partial election to these Assemblies. It shall elect its President from among its members.

An organic law shall determine the composition of the High Court, its rules, as well as the procedure to be applied before it.

Article 68. (As amended by legislation of 27 July 1993.) The President of the Republic shall not be held accountable for actions performed in the exercise of his office except in the case of high treason. He may be indicted only by the two Assemblies ruling by identical vote in open balloting and by an absolute majority of the members of said Assemblies. He shall be tried by the High Court of Justice.

X. ON THE CRIMINAL LIABILITY OF MEMBERS OF GOVERNMENT
(Title and section appended by legislation of 27 July 1993)

Article 68–1. The members of the Government shall be criminally liable for actions performed in the exercise of their office and rated as crimes or misdemeanours at the time they were committed.

They shall be tried by the Court of Justice of the Republic.

The Court of Justice of the Republic shall be bound by such definition of serious crimes and other major offences and such determination of penalties as are laid down by the law.

Article 68–2. The Court of Justice of the Republic shall consist of 15 members: 12 Members of Parliament, elected in equal number from among their ranks by the Assemblée nationale and the Sénat after each general or partial election to these Assemblies, and three judges of the Court of Cassation, one of whom shall preside over the Court of Justice of the Republic.

Any person claiming to be a victim of a crime or misdemeanour committed by a member of the Government in the exercise of his duties may lodge a complaint with a commission of requests.

This commission shall order either the closure of the case or that it be forwarded to the chief public prosecutor at the Court of Cassation for referral to the Court of Justice of the Republic.

The Chief Public Prosecutor at the Court of Cassation may also make a reference *ex officio* to the Court of Justice of the Republic with the assent of the commission of requests.

An organic law shall determine the manner in which this Article is to be implemented.

Article 68–3. (Appended by legislation of 4 August 1995.) The provisions of this title shall apply to acts committed before its entry into force (on 27 July 1993).

XI. THE ECONOMIC AND SOCIAL COUNCIL

Article 69. The Economic and Social Council, at the referral of the Government, shall give its opinion on the Government bills, draft ordinances and decrees, as well as on the private members' bills submitted to it.

A member of the Economic and Social Council may be designated by the Council to present, before the Parliamentary Assemblies, the opinion of the Council on the Government or private members' bills that have been submitted to it.

Article 70. (As amended by legislation of 4 August 1995.) The Economic and Social Council may likewise be consulted by the Government on any problem of an economic or social character. Any plan, or any bill dealing with a plan, of an economic or social character shall be submitted to it for advice.

Article 71. The composition of the Economic and Social Council and its rules of procedure shall be determined by an organic law.

XII. ON TERRITORIAL COMMUNITIES

Article 72. (As amended by legislation of 17 March 2003.) The territorial communities of the Republic shall be the communes, the departments, regions, communities granted a particular status and overseas communities regulated by Article 74. Any other territorial community shall be created by law, if need be, at the place of one or more of the communities mentioned in this paragraph.

The territorial communities shall serve the purpose of taking decisions for the entirety of competencies which may be best made at their level of jurisdiction.

In conditions provided for by law, these communities shall administer themselves freely by means of elected councils and dispose of a regulatory power for the exercise of their competencies.

In conditions provided for by organic law, and provided that the essential conditions exist for the exercise of a public liberty or a constitutionally guaranteed right, territorial communities or groupings thereof may, depending on the case, as provided for by law or regulations, exercise, in an experimental manner and for a limited object and duration, legislative or regulatory dispositions which govern the exercise of their competencies.

No territorial community may exercise any tutelage over any other. However, when the exercise of a competency necessitates the participation of several territorial units, the law may authorize one of the communities, or one grouping thereof, to organize the modalities of their common action.

In the territorial communities of the Republic, the representative of the State, representative of each member of the Government, shall be responsible for national interests, administrative control and the respect of the law.

Article 72–1. (Appended by legislation of 17 March 2003.) Law shall determine the conditions under which voters of each territorial community may, by exercising the right of petition, demand the inclusion in the agenda of the Deliberative Assembly of that community a question relating to its competencies.

In conditions provided for by organic law, projects of deliberation or of an act relating to the competency of a territorial community may, at the initiative of that community, be submitted, by means of a referendum, to the decision of the voters of that same community.

When the creation of a territorial community granted with a particular status or the modification of the organization thereof is envisaged, the law may approve the consultation of voters registered in the communities concerned. The modification of the boundaries of territorial communities may also follow from the consultation of voters in conditions provided for by law.

Article 72-2. (Appended by legislation of 17 March 2003.) Territorial communities shall benefit from resources which they may dispose of freely in conditions determined by law.

They may receive all or part of the product of taxation of every kind. The law may authorize them to set the basis and levels of taxation within limits determined by law.

The fiscal receipts and other resources belonging to the territorial communities shall represent, for each category of community, a determining share of the sum of their resources. Organic law shall determine the conditions under which this rule is implemented.

Any transfer of competencies between the State and territorial communities shall be accompanied by the attribution of equivalent resources to those which were dedicated to their exercise. Any creation or extension of competencies which necessitates an increase in expenditure by territorial communities shall be accompanied by resources determined by law.

The law shall provide for mechanisms of adjustment intended to promote equality between territorial communities.

Article 72-3. (Appended by legislation of 17 March 2003.) The Republic recognizes, among the French people, the overseas populations, sharing a common ideal of liberty, equality and fraternity.

Guadeloupe, French Guiana, Martinique, Réunion, Mayotte, St Pierre and Miquelon, Wallis and Futuna and French Polynesia shall be governed by Article 73 with regard to Overseas Departments and Regions, and for the territorial communities created by the application of the last paragraph of Article 73, and by Article 74 with regard to other communities.

The status of New Caledonia shall be governed by Title XIII.

The law shall determine the legislative regime and the particular organization of the French Southern and Antarctic Territories.

Article 72–4. (Appended by legislation of 17 March 2003.) No change, for part or the whole of any of the communities referred to in the second paragraph of Article 72-3, from one to the other of the regimes provided for in Articles 73 and 74, may take place without the prior consent having been obtained of the voters of the community, or of that part of the community concerned, in conditions determined by the following paragraph. Any such change of regime shall be determined by organic law.

The President of the Republic, on the proposal of the Government during [Parliamentary] sessions, or on joint motion of the two Assemblies published in the *Journal Officiel*, may decide to consult the voters of a territorial community located overseas on a matter related to its organization, its competencies or its legislative regime. When this consultation relates to a proposed change as provided for in the previous paragraph and is organized in response to the request of the Government, the President shall make a declaration to that end before each Assembly, which shall be followed by a debate.

Article 73. (As amended by legislation of 17 March 2003.) In the overseas departments and regions, laws and regulations shall be fully applicable. They may be subject to adaptations which take account of the particular characteristics and constraints of these communities.

These adaptations may be decided by the communities with regard to subjects in which they exercise competency and should they be so authorized by the law.

By special dispensation referred to in the first paragraph, and in order to take account of their specific qualities, the communities governed by the present Article may be authorized by law to themselves determine the rules applicable on their territory, in a limited number of subjects which fall under the domain of the law.

These rules may not concern nationality, civic rights, guarantees of public liberties, the State and the capacity of persons, the organization of justice, penal law, the penal procedure, foreign policy, defence, security and public order, money, credit and exchange, or electoral law. This list may be clarified and completed by an organic law.

The dispositions provided for in the previous two paragraphs shall not be applicable to either the Department or the Region of Réunion.

The authorizations provided for in the second and third paragraphs shall be decided, at the request of the community concerned, under conditions and reserves provided for in an organic law. They may not be applied should the essential conditions for the exercise of a public liberty or of a constitutionally guaranteed right be brought into question.

The creation by law of a community in replacement of an overseas department or region, or the institution of a single Deliberative Assembly for these two communities shall not occur without the prior consent, received in the form provided for in the second paragraph of Article 72-4, of the voters registered in the totality of those communities.

Article 74. (As amended by legislation of 25 June 1992 and 17 March 2003.) The overseas communities governed by the present Article shall have a status which takes account of their proper interests within the Republic

This status shall be defined by an organic law, adopted after the advice of the Deliberative Assembly, which shall determine:

the conditions under which the laws and regulations shall be applicable in that community;

the competencies of that community; excepting those already so exercised, the transfer of competencies from the State shall not include those subjects enumerated in the fourth paragraph of Article 73, clarified and completed, if need be, by an organic law;

the rules of the organization and functioning of institutions of the community, and the electoral regime of its Deliberative Assembly;

the conditions under which the institutions of that community shall be consulted upon projects and propositions of law and projects of edict or of decree including dispositions particular to that community, as well as regarding the ratification or approval of international engagements concluded within subjects relating to its competency.

Organic law may also determine, for those communities granted with autonomy, the conditions under which:

the Council of State shall exercise judicial control specific to certain categories of acts of the Deliberative Assembly intervening in the scope of activities exercised by the assembly within the domain of the law;

the Deliberative Assembly may modify a law promulgated prior to the entry into force of the status of the community, when the Constitutional Council, referred by the authorities of the community, has stated that the law has intervened in the domain of the competency of this community;

measures justified by local necessities may be taken by the community in favour of its population, with regard to the access to employment, the right of establishment for the exercise of a professional activity or for the protection of property;

the community may participate, under the control of the State, in the exercise of the competencies it maintains, with respect to guarantees accorded to the entirety of the national territory for the exercise of public liberties.

Article 74–1. (Appended by legislation of 17 March 2003.) In those overseas communities to which Article 74 applies and in New Caledonia, the Government may, within those areas which remain within the competence of the State, extend by the means of edicts, with any necessary adaptations, the dispositions of a legislative nature in force in metropolitan France, except where the law shall expressly preclude, for the dispositions concerned, the recourse to this procedure.

Any such edicts shall be taken to the Council of Ministers following the advice of the Deliberative Assemblies concerned and of the Council of State. They enter into force from the time of their publication. They become null and void should they not be ratified by Parliament within a period of eighteen months following this publication.

Article 75. Citizens of the Republic who do not have ordinary civil status, the only status referred to in Article 34, may keep their personal status as long as they have not renounced it.

XIII. TRANSITIONAL PROVISIONS RELATING TO NEW CALEDONIA
(Section appended by legislation of 20 July 1998)

Article 76. The population of New Caledonia is called upon to vote by 31 December 1998 on the provisions of the agreement signed at Nouméa on 5 May 1998, and published in the *Journal Officiel* of the French Republic on 27 May 1998.

Persons satisfying the requirements laid down in Article 2 of Act No. 88-1028 of 9 November 1988 shall be eligible to take part in the vote.

The measures required to organize the ballot shall be taken by decree adopted after consultation with the Council of State and discussion in the Council of Ministers.

Article 77. After approval of the agreement by the vote provided for in Article 76, the organic law passed after consultation with the Deliberative Assembly of New Caledonia shall determine, in order to ensure the development of New Caledonia in accordance with the guidelines set out in that agreement and as required for its implementation:

the competencies of the State which are to be transferred definitively to the institutions of New Caledonia, at what time and in what manner such transfers are to be made, and how the costs incurred thereby are to be apportioned;

the rules for the organization and operation of the institutions of New Caledonia, including the circumstances in which certain categories of instrument passed by the Deliberative Assembly may be referred to the Constitutional Council for review before publication;

the rules concerning citizenship, the electoral system, employment, and ordinary civil status;

the circumstances and the time limits within which the population concerned in New Caledonia is to vote on the attainment of full sovereignty.

Any other measures required to give effect to the agreement referred to in Article 76 shall be determined by law.

[A former Article 76, permitting Overseas Territories to retain their former status within the Republic and a section 'On the Community' (Articles 77–87), providing for a community of autonomous states of common citizenship, were repealed by legislation of 4 August 1995.]

XIV. ON AGREEMENTS OF ASSOCIATION

Article 88. The Republic may make agreements with States that wish to associate themselves with it in order to develop their own civilizations.

XV. ON THE EUROPEAN COMMUNITIES AND THE EUROPEAN UNION
(Section appended by legislation of 25 June 1992 and 28 February 2005)

Article 88–1. (Amended by legislation of 28 February 2005.) The Republic shall participate in the European Communities and in the European Union constituted by States that have freely chosen, by virtue of the treaties that established them, to exercise some of their powers in common.

It may participate in the European Union under the conditions envisaged by the treaty establishing a Constitution for Europe, signed on 29 October 2004.

Article 88–2. (Amended by legislation of 25 January 1999 and 17 March 2003.) Subject to reciprocity and in accordance with the terms of the Treaty on European Union signed on 7 February 1992, France agrees to the transfer of competencies necessary for the establishment of European economic and monetary union.

Subject to the same reservation and in accordance with the terms of the Treaty establishing the European Community, as amended by the treaty signed on 2 October 1997, the transfer of competencies necessary for the determination of rules concerning freedom of movement for persons and related areas may be agreed.

The law shall determine the rules relative to the European mandate of arrest with regard to acts taken on the basis of the treaty of the European Union.

Article 88–3. Subject to reciprocity and in accordance with the terms of the Treaty on European Union signed on 7 February 1992, the right to vote and stand as a candidate in municipal elections shall be granted only to citizens of the Union residing in France. Such citizens shall neither exercise the office of mayor or deputy mayor nor participate in the designation of Sénat electors or in the election of Senators. An organic law passed in identical terms by the two Assemblies shall determine the manner of implementation of this Article.

Article 88–4. (Amended by legislation of 25 January 1999.) The Government shall present to the Assemblée nationale and the Sénat any proposals for or drafts of acts of the European Communities or the European Union containing provisions of a legislative nature as soon as they have been transmitted to the Council of the European Union. It may also present to them other proposals or drafts of acts or any document emanating from a European Union institution.

In the manner laid down by the rules of procedure of each Assembly, resolutions may be passed, even if Parliament is not in session, on the drafts, proposals or documents referred to in the preceding paragraph.

Article 88–5 (appended by legislation of 28 February 2005.) Any bill authorizing the ratification of a treaty concerning the adhesion of a State to the European Union or the European Communities shall be submitted to a referendum by the President of the Republic.

[Article 88-5, in the wording which shall be in force until the treaty establishing a Constitution for Europe enters into force, does not apply to adhesions made following an intergovernmental conference convened on the decision of the Council of Europe prior to 1 July 2004.]

XVI. ON AMENDMENT

Article 89. The initiative for amending the Constitution shall belong both to the President of the Republic on the proposal of the Prime Minister and to the Members of Parliament.

The Government or private member's bill for amendment must be passed by the two Assemblies in identical terms. The amendment shall become definitive after approval by a referendum.

Nevertheless, the proposed amendment shall not be submitted to a referendum when the President of the Republic decides to submit it to Parliament convened in Congress; in this case, the proposed amendment shall be approved only if it is accepted by a three-fifths majority of the votes cast. The Secretariat of the Congress shall be that of the Assemblée nationale.

No amendment procedure may be undertaken or followed if it is prejudicial to the integrity of the territory.

The republican form of government shall not be the object of an amendment.

ELECTORAL LAW, JULY 1986

The 577 Deputies of the Assemblée nationale are to be directly elected under the former single-member constituency system (in force before the implementation of a system of proportional representation imposed by the electoral law of 1985). Participating parties can nominate only one candidate and designate a reserve candidate, who can serve as a replacement if the elected Deputy is appointed a Minister or a member of the Constitutional Council, or is sent on a government assignment scheduled to last more than six months, or dies. A candidate must receive an absolute majority and at least one-quarter of registered votes in order to be elected to the Assemblée nationale. If these conditions are not fulfilled, a second ballot will be held a week later, for voters to choose between all candidates receiving 12.5% of the total votes on the first ballot. The candidate who receives a simple majority of votes on the second ballot will then be elected. Candidates polling less than 5% of the votes will lose their deposit.

The Government

HEAD OF STATE

President: Jacques Chirac (took office 17 May 1995; re-elected 5 May 2002).

COUNCIL OF MINISTERS
(April 2005)

Prime Minister: Jean-Pierre Raffarin.

Minister of the Economy, Finance and Industry: Thierry Breton.

Minister of National Education, Higher Education and Research: François Fillon.

Minister of the Interior, Internal Security and Local Freedoms: Dominique de Villepin.

Minister of Employment, Labour and Social Cohesion: Jean-Louis Borloo.

Keeper of the Seals, Minister of Justice: Dominique Perben.

Minister of Defence: Michèle Alliot-Marie.

Minister of Foreign Affairs: Michel Barnier.

Minister of Solidarity, Health and the Family: Philippe Douste-Blazy.

Minister of Capital Works, Transport, Land Management, Tourism and the Sea: Gilles de Robien.

Minister of the Civil Service and the Reform of the State: Renaud Dutreil.

Minister of Agriculture, Food, Fishing and Rural Affairs: Dominique Bussereau.

Minister of Ecology and Sustainable Development: Serge Lepeltier.

Minister of Culture and Communication: Renaud Donnedieu de Vabres.

Minister of Small- and Medium-sized Enterprises, Trade, Crafts, the Liberal Professions and Consumption: Christian Jacob.

Minister of the Overseas Possessions: Brigitte Girardin.

Minister of Youth, Sports and Social Associations: Jean-François Lamour.

Minister of Sexual and Professional Equality: Nicole Ameline.

Minister-Delegate attached to the Prime Minister:

Relations with Parliament: Henri Cuq.

Ministers-Delegates attached to the Minister of the Economy, Finance and Industry:

Industry: Patrick Devedjian.

External Trade: François Loos.

The Budget and Budgetary Reform, and Government Spokesperson: Jean-François Copé.

Minister-Delegate attached to the Minister of National Education, Higher Education and Research:

Research: François d'Aubert.

Minister-Delegate attached to the Minister of the Interior, Internal Security and Local Freedoms:

The Interior: Marie-Josée Roig.

Ministers-Delegate attached to the Minister of Employment, Labour and Social Cohesion:

Labour Relations: Gérard Larcher.

Integration, Equal Opportunities and the Battle Against Exclusion: Nelly Olin.

Accommodation and Towns: Marc-Philippe Daubresse.

Minister-Delegate attached to the Minister of Defence:

Veterans: Hamlaoui Mekachera.

Ministers-Delegate attached to the Minister of Foreign Affairs:

European Affairs: Claudie Haigneré.

Co-operation, Development and French-speaking Peoples: Xavier Darcos.

Minister-Delegate attached to the Minister of Capital Works, Transport, Land Management, Tourism and the Sea:

Tourism: Léon Bertrand.

SECRETARIES OF STATE

Attached to the Minister of Ecology and Sustainable Development:

Sustainable Development: Tokia Saïfa.

Attached to the Minister of Health and Social Protection:

Handicapped Persons: Marie-Anne Montchamp;

Elderly Persons: Catherine Vautrin;

Health Insurance: Xavier Bertrand.

Attached to the Minister of Employment, Labour and Social Cohesion:

Professional Training of the Young: Laurent Henart.

Attached to the Keeper of the Seals, Minister of Justice:

The Rights of Victims: Nicole Guedj.

Attached to the Minister of Foreign Affairs:

Foreign Affairs: Renaud Muselier.

Attached to the Minister of the Civil Service and the Reform of the State:

The Reform of the State: ERIC WOERTH.

Attached to the Minister of Capital Works, Transport, Land Management, Tourism and the Sea:

Transport and the Sea: FRANÇOIS GOULARD;

Land Management: FRÉDÉRIC DE SAINT-SERNIN.

Attached to the Minister of Agriculture, Food, Fishing and Rural Affairs:

Agriculture, Food, Fishing and Rural Affairs: NICOLAS FORISSIER.

MINISTRIES

Office of the President: Palais de l'Elysée, 55–57 rue du Faubourg Saint Honoré, 75008 Paris; tel. 1-42-92-81-00; fax 1-47-42-24-65; internet www.elysee.fr.

Office of the Prime Minister: Hôtel Matignon, 57 rue de Varenne, 75007 Paris; tel. 1-42-75-80-00; fax 1-42-75-75-04; e-mail premier-ministre@premier-ministre.gouv.fr; internet www .premier-ministre.gouv.fr.

Ministry of Agriculture, Food, Fishing and Rural Affairs: 78 rue de Varenne, 75349 Paris 07; tel. 1-49-55-49-55; fax 1-49-55-40-39; e-mail webmaster@agriculture.gouv.fr; internet www .agriculture.gouv.fr.

Ministry of Capital Works, Transport, Land Management, Tourism and the Sea: 246 blvd Saint-Germain, 75007 Paris; tel. 1-40-81-31-59; fax 1-40-81-31-64; e-mail webmestre@equipement.gouv .fr; internet www.equipement.gouv.fr.

Ministry of the Civil Service and the Reform of the State: 72 rue de Varenne, 75007 Paris; tel. 1-42-75-80-00; fax 1-42-75-89-70; e-mail laurent.fleuriot.fpre.gouv.fr; internet www.fonction-publique .gouv.fr.

Ministry of Culture and Communication: 3 rue de Valois, 75001 Paris; tel. 1-40-15-80-00; fax 1-42-61-35-77; e-mail atelier-internet .dic@culture.gouv.fr; internet www.culture.gouv.fr.

Ministry of Defence: 14 rue Saint Dominique, 75007 Paris; tel. 1-42-19-30-11; fax 1-47-05-40-91; internet www.defense.gouv.fr.

Ministry of Ecology and Sustainable Development: 20 ave de Ségur, 75302 Paris Cédex 07; tel. 1-42-19-20-21; e-mail ministere@ environnement.gouv.fr; internet www.environnement.gouv.fr.

Ministry of the Economy, Finance and Industry: 139 rue de Bercy, 75572 Paris Cédex 12; tel. 1-40-04-04-04; fax 1-43-43-75-97; internet www.minefi.gouv.fr.

Ministry of Employment, Labour and Social Cohesion: 127 rue de Grenelle, 75007 Paris; tel. 1-44-38-38-38; fax 1-44-38-20-10; internet www.emploi-solidarite.gouv.fr.

Ministry of the Family and Childhood: Hôtel de Clermont, 69 rue de Varenne, 75007 Paris; tel. 1-42-75-80-80; internet www .famille.gouv.fr.

Ministry of Foreign Affairs: 37 quai d'Orsay, 75007 Paris; tel. 1-43-17-53-53; fax 1-43-17-52-03; internet www.diplomatie.gouv.fr.

Ministry of Health and Social Protection: 8 ave de Ségur, 75007 Paris; tel. 1-40-56-60-00; internet www.sante.gouv.fr.

Ministry of the Interior, Internal Security and Local Freedoms: place Beauvau, 75008 Paris; tel. 1-49-27-49-27; fax 1-43-59-89-50; e-mail sirp@interieur.gouv.fr; internet www.interieur.gouv .fr.

Ministry of Justice: 13 place Vendôme, 75042 Paris Cédex 01; tel. 1-44-77-60-60; fax 1-44-77-70-20; e-mail cyberjustice@justice.gouv .fr; internet www.justice.gouv.fr.

Ministry of National Education, Higher Education and Research: 110 rue de Grenelle, 75357 Paris 07; tel. 1-55-55-10-10; fax 1-45-51-53-63; internet www.education.gouv.fr.

Ministry of the Overseas Possessions: 27 rue Oudinot, 75007 Paris; tel. 1-53-69-20-00; internet www.outre-mer.gouv.fr.

Ministry of Sexual and Professional Equality: 101 rue de Grenelle, 75007 Paris; tel. 1-55-55-10-10.

Ministry of Youth, Sports and Social Associations: 95 ave de France, 75650 Paris Cédex 13; tel. 1-40-45-90-00; fax 1-42-50-42-49; e-mail arnaud.beuron@jeunesse-sports.gouv.fr; internet www .jeunesse-sports.gouv.fr.

President and Legislature

PRESIDENT

Presidential Election, First Ballot, 21 April 2002

Candidates	Votes	% of votes
Jacques Chirac (Rassemblement pour la République)	5,665,855	19.88
Jean-Marie Le Pen (Front National)	4,804,713	16.86
Lionel Jospin (Parti Socialiste)	4,610,113	16.18
François Bayrou (Union pour la Démocratie Française)	1,949,170	6.84
Arlette Laguiller (Lutte Ouvrière)	1,630,045	5.72
Jean-Pierre Chevènement (Mouvement des Citoyens)	1,518,528	5.33
Noël Mamère (Les Verts)	1,495,724	5.25
Olivier Besancenot (Ligue Communiste Révolutionnaire)	1,210,562	4.25
Jean Saint-Josse (Chasse Pêche Nature Traditions)	1,204,689	4.23
Alain Madelin (Démocratie Libérale)	1,113,484	3.91
Robert Hue (Parti Communiste Français)	960,480	3.37
Bruno Mégret (Mouvement National Républicain)	667,026	2.34
Christiane Taubira (Parti guyanais de centre-gauche/Parti Radical de Gauche)	660,447	2.32
Corinne Lepage (Citoyenneté, Action, Participation pour le 21ème siècle)	535,837	1.88
Christine Boutin (Forum des républicains sociaux)	339,112	1.19
Daniel Gluckstein (Parti des Travailleurs)	132,686	0.47
Total	28,498,471	100.00

Presidential Election, Second Ballot, 5 May 2002

Candidate	Votes	% of votes
Jacques Chirac (Rassemblement pour la République)	25,537,956	82.21
Jean-Marie Le Pen (Front National)	5,525,032	17.79
Total	31,062,988	100.00

PARLEMENT
(Parliament)

Assemblée nationale
(National Assembly)

126 rue de l'Université, 75355 Paris Cédex 07; tel. 1-40-63-60-00; fax 1-45-55-75-23; e-mail infos@assemblee-nat.fr; internet www .assemblee-nationale.fr.

President: JEAN-LOUIS DEBRÉ.

General Election, 9 June and 16 June 2002

Party	% of votes cast in first ballot	% of votes cast in second ballot*	Seats
Union pour la Majorité Présidentielle	33.30	47.26	355†
Parti Socialiste (PS)	24.11	35.26	140
Union pour la Démocratie Française (UDF)	4.85	3.92	29†
Parti Communiste Français (PCF)	4.82	3.26	21
Parti Radical de Gauche (PRG)	1.54	2.15	8
Les Verts	4.51	3.19	3
Démocratie Libérale (DL)	0.41	—	2†
Rassemblement pour la France (RPF)	0.37	0.29	3
Mouvement pour la France (MPF)	0.80	—	2
Front National (FN)	11.34	1.85	—
Pôle Républicain (PR)	1.19	0.06	—
Chasse Pêche Nature Traditions (CPNT)	1.67		—
Ligue Communiste Révolutionnaire (LCR)	1.27	—	—
Lutte Ouvrière (LO)	1.20	—	—
Mouvement National Républicain (MNR)	1.09		—

Party— *continued*	% of votes cast in first ballot	% of votes cast in second ballot*	Seats
Various right-wing candidates‡	3.65	1.29	7
Various left-wing candidates .	1.09	1.27	5
Regionalist candidates . . .	0.26	0.14	1
Various ecologist candidates§ .	1.17	—	—
Various far-left candidates‖ .	0.32	—	—
Various far-right candidates¶	0.24	—	—
Others**	0.77	0.06	1
Total	**100.00**	**100.00**	**577**

* Held where no candidate had won the requisite overall majority in the first ballot, between candidates who had received at least 12.5% of the votes in that round. The total number of valid votes cast was 25,246,045 in the first round, and 21,221,026 in the second round.

† In November 2002 the Union pour un Mouvement Populaire (UMP) was formed on the basis of the Union pour la Majorité Présidentielle, Démocratie Libérale and other right-wing and centrist factions, including elements of the Union pour la Démocratie Française.

‡ Including, notably, candidates of the Droite Libérale Chrétienne and the Centre National des Indépendants et Paysans.

§ Including, notably, candidates of Génération Ecologie-Les Bleus and the Mouvement Ecologiste Indépendant.

‖ Including, notably, candidates of the Parti des Travailleurs, Les Motivé-e-s and Les Alternatifs.

¶ Including, notably, candidates of the Parti National Républicain, La France aux Français and the Parti Nationaliste Français.

** Including, notably, candidates of the Rassemblement des Contribuables Français, the Parti de la Loi Naturelle and the Union pour la Semaine de Quatre Jours.

Sénat
(Senate)

15 rue de Vaugirard, 75291 Paris Cédex 06; tel. 1-42-34-20-00; fax 1-42-34-26-77; e-mail communication@senat.fr; internet www.senat.fr.

President: CHRISTIAN PONCELET.

Prior to mid-2003 members of the Senate were indirectly elected for a term of nine years, with one-third of the seats renewable every three years. A law approved by Parlement in July 2003 introduced a number of reforms to senatorial elections; henceforth, senators were to be elected for a term of six years, with one-half of the seats renewable every three years, and seats were to be allocated through a combination of majority voting and proportional representation. With effect from 2010, the number of senators was to be increased to 346, and the minimum age for eligible candidates to the Senate was to be reduced from 35 to 30 years.

A partial election to the Senate took place on 26 September 2004. Following this election, the number of seats in the Senate was increased from 321 to 331: 304 for metropolitan France; 15 for the overseas departments and territories; and 12 for French nationals abroad. The strength of the parties at 1 May 2005 was as follows:

Grouping	Seats
Groupe Union pour un Mouvement Populaire	155*†
Groupe Socialiste	97
Groupe de l'Union Centriste	33
Groupe Communiste Républicain et Citoyenne . . .	23
Groupe du Rassemblement Démocratique et Social Européen	15
Non-attached	7
Total	**330†‡**

* The Groupe Union pour un Mouvement Populaire was formed on 11 December 2002 on the basis of the Groupe du Rassemblement pour la République and the Groupe de l'Union des Républicains et des Indépendants, both of which thereby ceased to exist; a number of senators from the Groupe de l'Union Centriste, the Groupe du Rassemblement Démocratique et Social Européen, and one hitherto non-attached senator also joined the new grouping. On that date, the strength of the groupings was as follows: Groupe Union pour un Mouvement Populaire 167, Groupe Socialiste 82, Groupe de l'Union Centriste 27, Groupe Communiste Républicain et Citoyen 23, Groupe du Rassemblement Démocratique et Social Européen 17, Non-attached 5.

† In the senatorial elections held in September 2004, the Prime Minister, Jean-Pierre Raffarin, was elected as a senator for the department of Vienne, representing the Groupe Union pour un Mouvement Populaire. However, he was unable to take up his seat in the Senate while he retained his position in the Government, and consequently the strength of the Groupe Union pour un Mouvement Populaire was reduced from 156 to 155, while the overall number of active senators was reduced to 330.

‡ On 25 November 2004 the Constitutional Council annulled the results of the September senatorial elections in the department of Bas-Rhin. Consequently the Groupe Union pour un Mouvement Populaire lost four representatives and the Groupe Socialiste one, while the total number of active senators was temporarily reduced from 331 to 326. A new poll was held in Bas-Rhin on 20 February 2005, at which the same five senators were elected as at the original, subsequently annulled election.

Political Organizations

Les Alternatifs: 40 rue de Malte, 75011 Paris; tel. 1-43-57-44-80; fax 1-43-57-64-50; e-mail contact@alternatifs.org; internet www.alternatifs.org; f. 1998; socialist, ecologist.

Association pour une Gauche Républicaine (AGR): 32 rue des Ormeaux, 70400 Hericourt; tel. 6-08-25-11-17; e-mail info@a-g-r.com; internet www.a-g-r.org; f. 2002 by mems of fmr Mouvement des Citoyens; left-wing, opposed to economic liberalism and to the terms of the Maastricht treaty; Pres. JEAN-PIERRE MICHEL; Sec.-Gen. PIERRE PERTUS.

Chasse Pêche Nature Traditions (CPNT): Centre d'Affaires Praxis, 245 blvd de la Paix, 64000 Pau; tel. 5-59-14-71-71; fax 5-59-14-71-72; e-mail cpnt@cpnt.asso.fr; internet www.cpnt.asso.fr; f. 1989 as Chasse-Pêche-Traditions; emphasizes defence of rural traditions and the sovereignty of the State within Europe; Pres. JEAN SAINT-JOSSE; Sec.-Gen. JEAN-LOUIS BERNIÉ.

Front National (FN): 4 rue Vauguyon, 92210 Saint-Cloud; tel. 1-41-12-10-00; fax 1-41-12-10-86; e-mail vizier@frontnational.com; internet www.frontnational.com; f. 1972; extreme right-wing nationalist; Pres. JEAN-MARIE LE PEN; Sec.-Gen. CARL LANG.

Génération Ecologie-Les Bleus: 25 ave Jean Jaurès, 75019 Paris; tel. 1-56-53-53-73; fax 1-56-53-53-70; e-mail generation.ecologie@wanadoo.fr; internet www.generation-ecologie.com; f. 1990; ecologist; Pres. FRANCE GAMERRE.

Ligue Communiste Révolutionnaire (LCR): 2 rue Richard Lenoir, 93100 Montreuil; tel. 1-48-70-42-30; fax 1-48-59-39-59; e-mail lcr@lcr-rouge.org; internet www.lcr-rouge.org; f. 1974; Trotskyist; 3,000 mems (2004); Leaders ALAIN KRIVINE, OLIVIER BESANCENOT, ROSELINE VACHETTA.

Lutte Ouvrière (LO): BP 233, 75865 Paris Cédex 18; tel. 1-48-43-65-22; fax 1-48-43-69-94; e-mail contact@lutte-ouvriere.org; internet www.lutte-ouvriere.org; f. 1968; Trotskyist; Leaders ARLETTE LAGUILLER, F. DUBURG, GEORGES KALDY, ROBERT BARCIA HARDY.

Mouvement Ecologiste Indépendant (MEI): 26 rue Nicolaï, 75012 Paris; tel. 2-33-45-37-82; e-mail contact@mei-fr.org; internet www.mei-fr.org; f. 1994; ecologist; 1,000 mems; Pres. ANTOINE WAECHTER; Nat. Sec. DOMINIQUE BAUDUIN.

Mouvement National Républicain (MNR): 15 rue de Cronstadt, 75015 Paris; tel. 1-56-56-64-34; fax 1-56-56-52-47; e-mail m-n-r@m-n-r.com; internet www.m-n-r.com; f. 1999 by breakaway faction of FN; extreme right-wing nationalist; Pres. BRUNO MÉGRET.

Mouvement pour la France (MPF): 35 ave de la Motte-Piquet, 75007 Paris; tel. 1-44-42-02-42; fax 1-44-42-02-43; e-mail mpf@mpf-villiers.org; internet www.mpf-villiers.org; f. 1994; right-wing, nationalist; Pres. PHILIPPE DE VILLIERS.

Mouvement Républicain et Citoyen (MRC): 9 rue du Faubourg Poissonière, 75009 Paris; tel. 1-44-83-83-00; fax 1-44-83-83-10; e-mail contact@mrc-france.org; internet mrc-france.org; f. 2002 as Pôle Républicain on the basis of the Mouvement des Citoyens; present name adopted 2003; socialist; sceptical of increased European integration or devolution of powers from the nation-state; Hon. Pres. JEAN-PIERRE CHEVÈNEMENT; First Sec. JEAN-LUC LAURENT; Spokesperson GEORGES SARRE; 4,000 mems (2002).

Parti Communiste Français (PCF): 2 place du Colonel Fabien, 75019 Paris; tel. 1-40-40-12-12; fax 1-40-40-13-56; e-mail pcf@pcf.fr; internet www.pcf.fr; subscribed to the common programme of the United Left (with the Parti Socialiste) until 1977; advocates independent foreign policy; Nat. Sec. MARIE-GEORGE BUFFET.

Parti Radical de Gauche (PRG): 13 rue Duroc, 75007 Paris; tel. 1-45-66-67-68; fax 1-45-66-47-93; e-mail pascalcedan@prg.com.fr; internet www.planeteradicale.org; f. 1972 as the Mouvement des Radicaux de Gauche; left-wing; Pres. JEAN-MICHEL BAYLET; Sec.-Gen. ELISABETH BOYER.

Parti Socialiste (PS): 10 rue de Solférino, 75333 Paris Cédex 07; tel. 1-45-56-77-00; fax 1-47-05-15-78; e-mail infops@parti-socialiste

.fr; internet www.parti-socialiste.fr; f. 1971; First Sec. FRANÇOIS HOLLANDE; 147,300 mems (2002).

Le Rassemblement pour la France et l'Indépendance de l'Europe (Le Rassemblement): 120 ave Charles de Gaulle, 92522 Neuilly-sur-Seine Cédex; tel. 1–72–92–05–03; fax 1-72-92-05-13; e-mail infos@charles-pasqua.com; internet www.rpfie.org; f. 1999 as Rassemblement pour la France—RPF; present name adopted 2003; right-wing, nationalist; Pres. CHARLES PASQUA.

Union pour la Démocratie Française (UDF): 133 bis rue de l'Université, 75007 Paris; tel. 1-53-59-20-00; fax 1-53-59-20-59; e-mail internet@udf.org; internet www.udf.org; f. 1978 to unite for electoral purposes non-Gaullist 'majority' candidates; frequently formed electoral alliances with Gaullist Rassemblement des Républicains; reconstituted as a unified party in 1998; in 2002 elections to Assemblée nationale some elements formed electoral alliances with UMP, and subsequently were absorbed into that party; Pres. FRANÇOIS BAYROU.

Union pour un Mouvement Populaire (UMP): 55 rue La Boétie, 75384 Paris Cédex 08; tel. 1-40-76-60-00; e-mail ump@u-m-p.org; internet www.u-m-p.org; f. 2002; founded as Union pour la Majorité Presidentielle by members of the former Rassemblement pour la République and Démocratie Liberale parties, in conjunction with elements of the UDF (q.v.); centre-right grouping formed to ensure that President Jacques Chirac had a majority grouping in the Assemblée nationale; Pres. NICOLAS SARKOZY; Sec.-Gen. PIERRE MÉHAIGNERIE.

Associated organizations include:

Centre National des Indépendants et Paysans (CNI): 6 rue Quentin Bauchart, 75008 Paris; tel. 1-47-23-47-00; fax 1-47-23-47-03; e-mail contact@cni.asso.fr; internet www.cnip.asso.fr; f. 1949; right-wing; Pres. ANNICK DU ROSCOAT; Sec.-Gen. BERNARD BEAUDET.

Parti Radical: 1 place de Valois, 75001 Paris; tel. 1-42-61-56-32; fax 1-42-61-49-65; e-mail radical@partiradical.net; internet www.partiradical.net; f. 1901; democratic socialist; fmrly affiliated to UDF, associate mem. of UMP since Nov. 2002; Pres. ANDRÉ ROSSINOT; Sec.-Gen. ARLETTE FRUCTUS.

Unione Naziunale: Assemblée de Corse, 22 Cours Grandval, BP 215, 21087 Ajaccio Cédex 01; tel. 4-95-51-64-85; fax 4-95-50-08-22; e-mail unione.naziunale-ctc@wanadoo.fr; f. 1992 as Corsica Nazione; current name adopted 2004; supports the establishment of an independent state in Corsica; Leader JEAN-GUY TALAMONI.

Les Verts: 247 rue du Faubourg Saint-Martin, 75010 Paris; tel. 1-53-19-53-19; fax 1-53-19-03-93; e-mail verts@les-verts.org; internet www.les-verts.org; f. 1984; ecologist; Spokespersons MARIE-HÉLÈNE AUBERT, YVES CONTASSOT, MIREILLE FERRI, YANN WEHRLING; Nat. Sec. GILLES LEMAIRE; 7,000 mems (2003).

Diplomatic Representation

EMBASSIES IN FRANCE

Afghanistan: 32 ave Raphaël, 75016 Paris; tel. 1-45-25-05-29; fax 1-45-24-60-68; e-mail ambafghane@wanadoo.fr; internet www.ambafghane-paris.com; Ambassador Prof ZALMAÏ HAQUANI.

Albania: 57 ave Marceau, 75116 Paris; tel. 1-70-71-92-25; fax 1-47-23-59-85; e-mail ambassade.albanie@wanadoo.fr; internet www.amb-albanie-paris.com; Ambassador FERIT HOXHA.

Algeria: 50 rue de Lisbonne, 75008 Paris; tel. 1-53-93-20-20; fax 1-42-25-10-25; e-mail ambassadealgerie@free.fr; Ambassador MOHAMED GHOUALMI.

Andorra: 51 bis rue de Boulainvilliers , 75016 Paris; tel. 1-40-06-03-30; fax 1-40-06-03-64; e-mail ambaixada@andorra.ad; internet www.amb-andorre.fr; Ambassador IMMA TOR FAUS.

Angola: 19 ave Foch, 75116 Paris; tel. 1-45-01-58-20; fax 1-45-00-33-71; e-mail barreira.ramiro_manuel_ @libertysurf.fr; internet www.amb-angola.fr; Ambassador AMBROSIO LUKOKI.

Antigua and Barbuda: 43 ave de Friedland, 75008 Paris; tel. 1-53-96-93-96; fax 1-53-96-93-97; e-mail carl.roberts@antigua-barbuda.com; Ambassador Dr CARL ROBERTS.

Argentina: 6 rue Cimarosa, 75116 Paris; tel. 1-44-05-27-00; fax 1-45-53-46-33; e-mail efranpol@noos.fr; Ambassador JUAN ARCHIBALDO LANÚS.

Armenia: 9 rue Viète, 75017 Paris; tel. 1-42-12-98-00; fax 1-42-12-98-03; e-mail ambarmen@wanadoo.fr; Ambassador EDWARD NALBANDIAN.

Australia: 4 rue Jean Rey, 75724 Paris Cédex 15; tel. 1-40-59-33-00; fax 1-40-59-33-10; e-mail information.paris@dfat.gov.au; internet www.france.embassy.gov.au; Ambassador PENELOPE ANNE WENSLEY.

Austria: 6 rue Fabert, 75007 Paris; tel. 1-40-63-30-63; fax 1-45-55-63-65; e-mail paris-ob@bmaa.gv.at; internet www.amb-autriche.fr; Ambassador ANTON PROHASKA.

Azerbaijan: 209 rue de l'Université, 75007 Paris; tel. 1-44-18-60-20; fax 1-44-18-60-25; e-mail ambazer@wanadoo.fr; internet www.amb-azerbaijan.fr; Ambassador TARIK ISMAÏL OGLOU ALIYEV.

Bahrain: 3 bis place des Etats-Unis, 75116 Paris; tel. 1-47-23-48-68; fax 1-47-20-55-75; e-mail ambassade@ambarhein-france.com; Chargé d'affaires KHALED AL-TAMIMI.

Bangladesh: 39 rue Erlanger, 75016 Paris; tel. 1-46-51-90-33; fax 1-46-51-90-35; e-mail bdootpar@club-internet.fr; Ambassador JAHANGIR SAADAT.

Belarus: 38 blvd Suchet, 75016 Paris; tel. 1-44-14-69-79; fax 1-44-14-69-70; e-mail france@belembassy.org; Ambassador VIKTAR SHYKH.

Belgium: 9 rue de Tilsitt, 75017 Paris; tel. 1-44-09-39-39; fax 1-47-54-07-64; e-mail paris@diplobel.org; internet www.diplomatie.be/paris; Ambassador PIERRE-ETIENNE CHAMPENOIS.

Benin: 87 ave Victor Hugo, 75116 Paris; tel. 1-45-00-98-82; fax 1-45-01-82-02; e-mail ambassade@ambassade-benin.org; internet www.ambassade-benin.org; Ambassador EDGAR YVES MONNOU.

Bolivia: 12 ave Président Kennedy, 75016 Paris; tel. 1-42-24-93-44; fax 1-45-25-86-23; e-mail embolivia.paris@wanadoo.fr; Ambassador FLORENCIA BALLIVIAN DE ROMERO.

Bosnia and Herzegovina: 174 rue de Courcelles, 75017 Paris; tel. 1-42-67-34-22; fax 1-40-53-85-22; Ambassador ZELJANA ZOVKO.

Brazil: 34 cours Albert 1er, 75008 Paris; tel. 1-45-61-63-00; fax 1-42-89-03-45; e-mail imprensa@bresil.org; internet www.bresil.org; Ambassador SERGIO SILVIA DO AMARAL.

Brunei: 7 rue de Presbourg, 75116 Paris; tel. 1-53-64-67-60; fax 1-53-64-67-83; e-mail ambassade.brunei@wanadoo.fr; Ambassador Dato' Paduka ZAINIDI bin Haji SIDUP.

Bulgaria: 1 ave Rapp, 75007 Paris; tel. 1-45-51-85-90; fax 1-45-51-18-68; e-mail bulgamb@wanadoo.fr; Ambassador MARIN RAYKOV.

Burkina Faso: 159 blvd Haussmann, 75008 Paris; tel. 1-43-59-90-63; fax 1-42-56-50-07; e-mail amba.burkina.faso@wanadoo.fr; internet www.ambaburkinafrance.org; Ambassador FILIPPE SAWADOGO.

Burundi: 24 rue Raynouard, 75016 Paris; tel. 1-45-20-15-16; fax 1-45-20-02-54; e-mail ambabu.paris@wanadoo.fr; Ambassador LIBOIRE NGENDAHAYO.

Cambodia: 4 rue Adolphe Yvon, 75116 Paris; tel. 1-45-03-47-20; fax 1-45-03-47-40; e-mail ambcambodgeparis@mangoosta.fr; Ambassador UCH KIMAN.

Cameroon: 73 rue d'Auteuil, 75116 Paris; tel. 1-47-43-98-33; fax 1-46-51-24-52; Ambassador PASCAL BILOA TANG.

Canada: 35 ave Montaigne, 75008 Paris; tel. 1-44-43-29-00; fax 1-44-43-29-99; e-mail paris_webmaster@international.gc.ca; internet www.amb-canada.fr; Ambassador CLAUDE LAVERDURE.

Cape Verde: 80 rue Jouffroy d'Abbans, 75017 Paris; tel. 1-42-12-73-50; fax 1-40-53-04-36; e-mail ambassade-cap-vert@wanadoo.fr; Ambassador JOSÉ FERREIRA DUARTE.

Central African Republic: 30 rue des Perchamps, 75116 Paris; tel. 6-15-68-78-33; fax 1-42-88-00-13; Ambassador NESTOR KOMBOT-NAGUEMON.

Chad: 65 rue des Belles Feuilles, 75116 Paris; tel. 1-45-53-36-75; fax 1-45-53-16-09; e-mail ambatchad-paris@libertysurf.fr; Ambassador MAHMOUD HISSEIN MAHMOUD.

Chile: 2 ave de la Motte-Picquet, 75007 Paris; tel. 1-44-18-59-60; fax 1-44-18-59-61; e-mail echile@amb-chili.fr; internet www.amb-chili.fr; Ambassador HERNAN SANDOVAL ORELLANA.

China, People's Republic: 11 ave George V, 75008 Paris; tel. 1-47-23-36-77; fax 1-47-20-24-22; e-mail xinwen@clubobs.com; internet www.amb-chine.fr; Ambassador ZHAO JINJUN.

Colombia: 22 rue de l'Elysée, 75008 Paris; tel. 1-42-65-46-08; fax 1-42-66-18-60; e-mail eparis@minrelext.gov.co; internet www.embcolfrancia.com; Ambassador MIGUEL GÓMEZ MARTÍNEZ.

Comoros: 20 rue Marbeau, 75116 Paris; tel. 1-40-67-90-54; fax 1-40-67-72-96; Ambassador SULTÁN CHOUZOUR.

Congo, Democratic Republic: 32 cours Albert 1er, 75008 Paris; tel. 1-42-25-57-50; fax 1-43-59-30-21; e-mail amb.rdc.paris@wanadoo.fr; Ambassador EDDYI ANGULU MABENGI.

Congo, Republic: 37 bis rue Paul Valéry, 75116 Paris; tel. 1-45-00-60-57; fax 1-40-67-17-33; Ambassador HENRI LOPES.

Costa Rica: 78 ave Emile Zola, 75015 Paris; tel. 1-45-78-96-96; fax 1-45-78-99-66; e-mail embcr@wanadoo.fr; Ambassador ANI RAMOS DE ANAYA SAGREDA.

Côte d'Ivoire: 102 ave Raymond Poincaré, 75116 Paris; tel. 1-53-64-62-62; fax 1-45-00-47-97; e-mail bureco-fr@cotedivoire.com; Ambassador HYACINTHE MARCEL KOUASSI.

Croatia: 39 ave Georges Mandel, 75116 Paris; tel. 1-53-70-02-80; fax 1-53-70-02-90; e-mail secretariat@amb-croatie.fr; internet www.amb-croatie.fr; Ambassador BOŽIDAR GAGRO.

Cuba: 16 rue de Presles, 75015 Paris; tel. 1-45-67-55-35; fax 1-45-66-80-92; e-mail internet.la-havane-amba@diplomatie.fr; internet www.ambafrance-cu.org; Ambassador ROGELIO PLACIDO SANCHEZ LEVIS.

Cyprus: 23 rue Galilée, 75116 Paris; tel. 1-47-20-86-28; fax 1-40-70-13-44; e-mail ambrechypre@wanadoo.fr; Ambassador MINAS A. HADJIMICHAEL.

Czech Republic: 15 ave Charles Floquet, 75007 Paris; tel. 1-40-65-13-00; fax 1-40-65-13-13; e-mail paris@embassy.mzv.cz; internet www.mzv.cz/paris; Ambassador PAVEL FISCHER.

Denmark: 77 ave Marceau, 75116 Paris; tel. 1-44-31-21-21; fax 1-44-31-21-88; e-mail paramb@um.dk; internet www.amb-danemark.fr; Ambassador NIELS EGELUND.

Djibouti: 26 rue Emile Ménier, 75116 Paris; tel. 1-47-27-49-22; fax 1-45-53-50-53; e-mail ambassadeur@ambdjibouti.org; Ambassador RACHAD FARAH.

Dominican Republic: 45 rue de Courcelles, 75008 Paris; tel. 1-53-53-95-95; fax 1-45-63-35-63; e-mail embajadom@amba-dominicaine-paris.com; internet www.amba-dominicaine-paris.com; Chargé d'affaires a.i. GABRIELLA BONETTI ZELLER.

Ecuador: 34 ave de Messine, 75008 Paris; tel. 1-45-61-10-21; fax 1-42-56-06-64; e-mail embajadaenfrancia@ambassade-equateur.fr; internet www.ambassade-equateur.fr; Ambassador JUAN SALAZAR SANCISI.

Egypt: 56 ave d'Iéna, 75116 Paris; tel. 1-53-67-88-30; fax 1-47-23-06-43; e-mail ambassadedegypteaparis@hotmail.com; internet www.ambassade-egypte.com; Ambassador HATEM AZIZ SEIF EL-NASR.

El Salvador: 12 rue Galilée, 75116 Paris; tel. 1-47-20-42-02; fax 1-40-70-01-95; e-mail embparis@wanadoo.fr; Ambassador JOAQUIN RODEZNO MUNGUIA.

Equatorial Guinea: 29 blvd de Courcelles, 75008 Paris; tel. 1-56-88-54-54; fax 1-56-88-10-75; e-mail embarege_paris@hotmail.com; Ambassador NARCISO NTUGU ABESO OYANA.

Eritrea: 1 rue de Staël, 75015 Paris; tel. 1-43-06-15-56; fax 1-43-06-07-51; Ambassador HANNA SIMON.

Estonia: 46 rue Pierre Charron, 75008 Paris; tel. 1-56-62-22-00; fax 1-49-52-05-65; e-mail embassy.paris@mfa.ee; internet www.est-emb.fr; Ambassador ANDRES TALVIK.

Ethiopia: 35 ave Charles Floquet, 75007 Paris; tel. 1-47-83-83-95; fax 1-43-06-52-14; e-mail embeth@frce.fr; Ambassador SAHLE-WORK ZEWDE.

Finland: 1 pl. de Finlande, 75007 Paris; tel. 1-44-18-19-20; fax 1-45-55-51-57; e-mail sanomat.par@formin.fi; internet www.amb-finlande.fr; Ambassador ESKO HAMILO.

Gabon: 26 bis ave Raphaël, 75016 Paris; tel. 1-44-30-22-30; fax 1-42-24-62-42; Ambassador JEAN-MARIE ADZÉ.

The Gambia: 117 rue St Lazare, 75008 Paris; tel. 1-72-74-82-61; fax 1-53-04-05-99; e-mail ambgambia-france@hotmail.com; Ambassador WILLIAM JOHN JOOF.

Georgia: 104 ave Raymond Poincaré, 75116 Paris; tel. 1-45-02-16-16; fax 1-45-02-16-01; e-mail sophieko@cybercable.fr; Ambassador NATIA JAPARIDZE .

Germany: 13–15 ave Franklin D. Roosevelt, 75008 Paris; tel. 1-53-83-45-00; fax 1-43-59-74-18; e-mail ambassade@amb-allemagne.fr; internet www.amb-allemagne.fr; Ambassador KLAUS NEUBERT.

Ghana: 8 Villa Saïd, 75116 Paris; tel. 1-45-00-09-50; fax 1-45-00-81-95; e-mail embassy.of.ghana1@libertysurf.fr; Ambassador Prof. ALBERT OWUSU-SARPONG.

Greece: 17 rue Auguste Vacquerie, 75116 Paris; tel. 1-47-23-72-28; fax 1-47-23-73-85; e-mail ambgrpar@wanadoo.fr; internet www.amb-grece.fr/presse; Ambassador DIMITRIS KARAÏTIDIS.

Guatemala: 2 rue Villebois-Mareuil, 75017 Paris; tel. 1-42-27-78-63; fax 1-47-54-02-06; e-mail embguatefrancia@wanadoo.fr; Ambassador ANAISABEL PRERA FLORES.

Guinea: 51 rue de la Faisanderie, 75116 Paris; tel. 1-47-04-81-48; fax 1-47-04-57-65; e-mail ambagiu.paris@laposte.net; Ambassador LANSANA KÉITA.

Guinea-Bissau: 94 rue Saint Lazare, 75009 Paris; tel. 1-45-26-18-51; fax 1-45-26-60-59; Ambassador JOÃO SOARES DA GAMA.

Haiti: 10 rue Théodule Ribot, BP 275, 75017 Paris; tel. 1-47-63-47-78; fax 1-42-27-02-05; e-mail haiti01@francophonie.org; Chargé d'affaires FRITZNER GASPARD.

Holy See: 10 ave du Président Wilson, 75116 Paris (Apostolic Nunciature); tel. 1-53-23-01-50; fax 1-47-23-65-44; e-mail noncapfr@wanadoo.fr; Apostolic Nuncio Most Rev. FORTUNATO BALDELLI (Titular Archbishop of Bevagna).

Honduras: 8 rue Crevaux, 75116 Paris; tel. 1-47-55-86-45; fax 1-47-55-86-48; e-mail ambassade.honduras@noos.fr; Ambassador MARIO CARIAS ZAPATA.

Hungary: 7 sq. Vergennes, 75015 Paris; tel. 1-56-36-07-54; fax 1-56-36-02-68; e-mail ambassade-de-hongrie@amb-hongrie.fr; internet www.hongrie.org; Ambassador ANDRÉ ERDÖS.

Iceland: 8 ave Kléber, 75116 Paris; tel. 1-44-17-32-85; fax 1-40-67-99-96; e-mail icemb.paris@utn.stjr.is; internet www.iceland.org/fr; Ambassador TÓMAS INGI OLRICH.

India: 15 rue Alfred Dehodencq, 75016 Paris; tel. 1-40-50-70-70; fax 1-40-50-09-96; e-mail eiparis.admin@wanadoo.fr; internet www.amb-inde.fr; Ambassador DILIP LAHIRI.

Indonesia: 47–49 rue Cortambert, 75116 Paris; tel. 1-45-03-07-60; fax 1-45-04-50-32; e-mail kasubpen@amb-indonesie.fr; internet www.amb-indonesie.fr; Ambassador ADIAN SILALAHI.

Iran: 4 ave d'Iéna, 75116 Paris; tel. 1-40-69-79-00; fax 1-40-70-01-57; e-mail contact@amb-iran.fr; internet www.amb-iran.fr; Ambassador SEYED MOHAMMAD SADEGH KHARAZI.

Iraq: 53 rue de la Faisanderie, 75016 Paris; tel. 1-45-53-33-70; fax 1-45-53-33-80; e-mail paris@embassyiraq.com; internet www.embassyiraq.com; Ambassador MOUAFAK MEHDI ABOUD HAMOUD.

Ireland: 4 rue Rude, 75116 Paris; tel. 1-44-17-67-00; fax 1-44-17-67-60; e-mail paris@dfa.ie; Ambassador ANNE ANDERSON (delegate).

Israel: 3 rue Rabelais, 75008 Paris; tel. 1-40-76-55-00; fax 1-40-76-55-55; e-mail ambassade@par.mfa.gov.il; internet www.amb-israel.fr; Ambassador NISSIM ZVILI.

Italy: 51 rue de Varenne, 75343 Paris Cédex 07; tel. 1-49-54-03-00; fax 1-45-54–04-10; e-mail ambasciata@amb-italie.fr; internet www.amb-italie.fr; Ambassador GIOVANNI DOMINEDÒ.

Japan: 7 ave Hoche, 75008 Paris; tel. 1-48-88-62-00; fax 1-42-27-50-81; e-mail info-fr@amb-japon.fr; internet www.fr.emb-japan.go.jp; Ambassador HIROSHI HIRABAYASHI.

Jordan: 80 blvd Maurice Barres, 92200 Neuilly sur Seine; tel. 1-55-62-00-00; fax 1-55-62-00-06; e-mail amjo.paris@wanadoo.fr; Ambassador DINA KAWAR.

Kazakhstan: 59 rue Pierre Charron, 75008 Paris; tel. 1-45-61-52-00; fax 1-45-61-52-01; e-mail vk001@dial.oleane.com; internet www.amb-kazakhstan.fr; Ambassador DULAT O. KUANYSHEV.

Kenya: 3 rue Freycinet, 75116 Paris; tel. 1-56-62-25-25; fax 1-47-20-44-41; e-mail paris@amb-kenya.fr; internet www.kenyaembassyparis.org; Ambassador RAYCHELLE A. OMAMO.

Korea, Republic: 125 rue de Grenelle, 75007 Paris; tel. 1-47-53-01-01; fax 1-47-53-00-41; e-mail koremb-fr@mofat.go.kr; internet www.amb-coreesud.fr; Ambassador JU CHUL-KI.

Kuwait: 2 rue de Lübeck, 75116 Paris; tel. 1-47-23-54-25; fax 1-47-20-33-59; Ambassador AHMAD al-EBRAHIM.

Laos: 74 ave Raymond Poincaré, 75116 Paris; tel. 1-45-53-02-98; fax 1-47-57-27-89; e-mail ambalaoparis@wanadoo.fr; Ambassador SOUTSAKHONE PATHAMMAVONG.

Latvia: 6 villa Saïd, 75116 Paris; tel. 1-53-64-58-10; fax 1-53-64-58-19; e-mail embassy.france@mfa.gov.lv; internet www.paris.am.gov.lv; Ambassador ROLANDS LAPPUĶE.

Lebanon: 3 villa Copernic, 75116 Paris; tel. 1-40-67-75-75; fax 1-40-67-16-42; e-mail ambliban@club-internet.fr; Ambassador SYLVIE FADLALLAH.

Liberia: 12 place du Général Catroux, 75017 Paris; tel. 1-47-63-58-55; fax 1-42-12-76-14; e-mail libem.paris@wanadoo.fr; Ambassador (vacant).

Libya: 2 rue Charles Lamoureux, 75116 Paris; tel. 1-47-04-71-60; fax 1-47-55-96-25; Sec. of the People's Bureau Dr MOHAMED EL-HARARI.

Lithuania: 22 blvd de Courcelles, 75017 Paris; tel. 1-40-54-50-50; fax 1-40-54-50-75; e-mail amb.lituanie@magic.fr; internet www.amb-lituanie-paris.fr; Ambassador GIEDRIUS ČEKUOLIS.

Luxembourg: 33 ave Rapp, 75007 Paris; tel. 1-45-55-13-37; fax 1-45-51-72-29; e-mail paris.amb@mae.etat.lu; Ambassador HUBERT WURTH.

Macedonia, former Yugoslav republic: 5 rue de la Faisanderie, 75116 Paris; tel. 1-45-77-10-50; fax 1-45-77-14-84; e-mail ambassade@fr.olee.com; Ambassador JORDAN PLEVNEŠ.

Madagascar: 4 ave Raphaël, 75016 Paris; tel. 1-45-04-62-11; fax 1-45-03-58-70; e-mail info@ambassade-madagascar.fr; internet www.ambamad-france.com; Ambassador JEAN-PIERRE RAZAFY-ANDRIAMI-HAINGO.

Malawi: 20 rue Euler, 75008 Paris; tel. 1-40-70-18-46; fax 1-47-23-62-48; e-mail malawi.embassy@libertysurf.fr; Ambassador Dr AHMED I. KHARODIA.

Malaysia: 2 bis rue Bénouville, 75116 Paris; tel. 1-45-53-11-85; fax 1-47-27-34-60; e-mail mwparis@wanadoo.fr; Ambassador Dato' HAMIDAH YUSOFF.

Mali: 89 rue du Cherche-Midi, 75263 Paris Cédex 06; tel. 1-45-48-58-43; fax 1-45-48-55-34; Ambassador MOHAMED SALIA SOKONA.

Malta: 92 ave des Champs Elysées, 75008 Paris; tel. 1-56-59-75-90; fax 1-45-62-00-36; e-mail maltaembassy.paris@gov.mt; Ambassador Dr VICKY-ANN CREMONA.

Mauritania: 5 rue de Montévidéo, 75116 Paris; tel. 1-45-04-88-54; fax 1-40-72-82-96; e-mail ambassade.mauritanie@wanadoo.fr; Ambassador SIDNEY SOKHONA.

Mauritius: 127 rue de Tocqueville, 75017 Paris; tel. 1-42-27-30-19; fax 1-40-53-02-91; e-mail ambassade.maurice@online.fr; Ambassador Dr MOHAMMAD HOUSSEIN ISMAËL DILMAHOMED.

Mexico: 9 rue de Longchamp, 75116 Paris; tel. 1-53-70-27-70; fax 1-47-55-65-29; e-mail embfrancia@sre.gob.mx; internet www.sre.gob.mx/francia; Ambassador CLAUDE HELLER.

Moldova: 1 rue de Sfax, 75116 Paris; tel. 1-40-67-11-20; fax 1-40-67-11-23; e-mail ambassade.moldavie@wanadoo.fr; Ambassador ANDREI NEGUTA.

Monaco: 22 blvd Suchet, 75116 Paris; tel. 1-45-04-74-54; fax 1-45-04-45-16; Ambassador CHRISTIAN ORSETTI.

Mongolia: 5 ave Robert Schuman, 92100 Boulogne-Billancourt; tel. 1-46-05-28-12; fax 1-46-05-30-16; e-mail esyam@ambassademongolie.fr; Ambassador TSEND BATBUYAN.

Morocco: 5 rue Le Tasse, 75016 Paris; tel. 1-45-20-69-35; fax 1-45-20-22-58; e-mail affgeneral@amb-maroc.fr; Ambassador FATHALLAH SIJILMASSI.

Mozambique: 82 rue Laugier, 75017 Paris; tel. 1-47-64-91-32; fax 1-44-15-90-13; e-mail embamocparis@compuserve.com; Ambassador FERNANDA EUGÉNIO LICHALE.

Myanmar: 60 rue de Courcelles, 75008 Paris; tel. 1-42-25-56-95; fax 1-42-56-49-41; e-mail me-paris@wanadoo.fr; internet www.myanmarembassyparis.com; Ambassador U WUNNA MAUNG LWIN.

Namibia: 80 ave Foch, 75016 Paris; tel. 1-44-17-32-65; fax 1-44-17-32-73; e-mail namparis@club-internet.fr; Ambassador WILFRIED I. EMVULA.

Nepal: 45 bis rue des Acacias, 75017 Paris; tel. 1-46-22-48-67; fax 1-42-27-08-65; e-mail ambassadedunepal@noos.fr; internet www.nepalembassy.org; Chargé d'affaires a.i. NIRANJAN MAN SINGH BASNYAT.

Netherlands: 7–9 rue Eblé, 75007 Paris; tel. 1-40-62-33-00; fax 1-40-62-34-56; e-mail ambassade@amb-pays-bas.fr; internet www.amb-pays-bas.fr; Ambassador CHRISTIAAN MARK JOHAN KRÖNER.

New Zealand: 7 ter rue Léonard de Vinci, 75116 Paris; tel. 1-45-01-43-43; fax 1-45-01-43-44; e-mail nzembassy-paris@fr.oleane.com; internet www.nzembassy.com/France; Ambassador ADRIAN HENRY MACEY.

Niger: 154 rue de Longchamp, 75116 Paris; tel. 1-45-04-80-60; fax 1-45-04-79-73; Ambassador ADAMOU SEYDOU.

Nigeria: 173 ave Victor Hugo, 75116 Paris; tel. 1-47-04-68-65; fax 1-47-04-47-54; e-mail embassy@nigeriafrance.com; internet www.nigeriafrance.com; Ambassador GODFREY BAYOUR PREWARE.

Norway: 28 rue Bayard, 75008 Paris; tel. 1-53-67-04-00; fax 1-53-67-04-40; e-mail emb.paris@mfa.no; internet www.norvege.no; Ambassador SVEN ERIK SVEDMAN.

Oman: 50 ave d'Iéna, 75116 Paris; tel. 1-47-23-01-63; fax 1-47-23-77-10; Ambassador JAIFER SALIM AL-SAID.

Pakistan: 18 rue Lord Byron, 75008 Paris; tel. 1-45-62-23-32; fax 1-45-62-89-15; e-mail pakemb_paris@yahoo.com; Ambassador MUSA JAVED CHONAN.

Panama: 145 ave de Suffren, 75015 Paris; tel. 1-45-66-42-44; fax 1-45-67-99-43; e-mail panaemba.francia@wanadoo.fr; Ambassador OMAR JAÉN SUÁREZ.

Paraguay: 1 rue St Dominique, 75007 Paris; tel. and fax 1-45-44-84-09; e-mail embapar@eybereable.fr; Ambassador LUIS FERNANDO AVALOS GIMENEZ.

Peru: 50 ave Kléber, 75116 Paris; tel. 1-53-70-42-00; fax 1-47-04-32-55; e-mail perou.ambassade@amb-perou.fr; internet www.amb-perou.fr; Chargé d'affaires a.i. THIERRY ROCA-REY.

Philippines: 4 Hameau de Boulainvilliers, 75016 Paris; tel. 1-44-14-57-00; fax 1-46-47-56-00; e-mail ambaphiliparis@wanadoo.fr; Ambassador HECTOR K. VILLARROEL.

Poland: 1–3 rue de Talleyrand, 75343 Paris Cédex 07; tel. 1-43-17-34-05; fax 1-43-17-35-07; e-mail info@ambassade.pologne.net; internet www.ambassade.pologne.net; Ambassador JAN TOMBINSKI.

Portugal: 3 rue de Noisiel, 75116 Paris; tel. 1-47-27-35-29; fax 1-44-05-94-02; e-mail mailto@embaixada-portugal-fr.org; internet www.embaixada-portugal-fr.org; Ambassador JOAO ROSA LÁ.

Qatar: 57 quai d'Orsay, 75007 Paris; tel. 1-45-51-90-71; fax 1-45-51-77-07; e-mail paris@mofa.gov.qa; Ambassador MOHAMED JAHAM ABDUL AZIZ AL-KUWARI.

Romania: 5 rue de l'Exposition, 75007 Paris; tel. 1-47-05-10-46; fax 1-45-56-97-47; e-mail secretariat@amb-roumanie.fr; internet www.amb-roumanie.fr; Ambassador SABIN POP.

Russia: 40–50 blvd Lannes, 75116 Paris; tel. 1-45-04-05-50; fax 1-45-04-17-65; e-mail ambrus@wanadoo.fr; internet www.france.mid.ru; Ambassador ALEKSANDR A. AVDEYEV.

Rwanda: 12 rue Jadin, 75017 Paris; tel. 1-42-27-36-31; fax 1-42-27-74-69; Ambassador EMMANUEL NDAGIJIMANA.

San Marino: 4 rue de Cerisoles, 75116 Paris; tel. and fax 1-47-23-04-75; e-mail amb.rsm.f@wanadoo.fr; Ambassador Countess ISA CORINALDI DE BENEDETTI.

Saudi Arabia: 5 ave Hoche, 75008 Paris; tel. 1-56-79-40-00; fax 1-56-79-40-01; e-mail fremb@mofa.gov.sa; Ambassador Dr MOHAMMED AL ASHEKH.

Senegal: 14 ave Robert Schuman, 75007 Paris; tel. 1-47-05-39-45; fax 1-45-56-04-30; e-mail repsen@wanadoo.fr; internet perso.wanadoo.fr/ambassenparis/sarrsitecult.html; Ambassador DOUDOU DIOP SALLA.

Serbia and Montenegro: 54 rue de la Faisanderie, 75116 Paris; tel. 1-40-72-24-24; fax 1-40-72-24-11; e-mail ambasadapariz@wanadoo.fr; Ambassador RADOMIR DIKLIĆ.

Seychelles: 51 ave Mozart, 75016 Paris; tel. 1-42-30-57-47; fax 1-42-30-57-40; e-mail ambsey@aol.com; Ambassador CALLIXTE D'OFFAY.

Singapore: 12 sq. de l'ave Foch, 75116 Paris; tel. 1-45-00-33-61; fax 1-45-00-61-79; e-mail ambsing@wanadoo.fr; internet www.mfa.gov.sg/paris; Ambassador CHEW TAI SOO.

Slovakia: 125 rue du Ranelagh, 75016 Paris; tel. 1-44-14-56-00; fax 1-42-88-76-53; e-mail paris@amb-slovaquie.fr; internet www.amb-slovaquie.fr; Ambassador MÁRIA KRASNOHORSKÁ.

Slovenia: 28 rue Bois-le-Vent, 75116 Paris; tel. 1-44-96-50-71; fax 1-45-24-67-05; e-mail vpa@mzz-dkp.gov.si; Ambassador MAGDALENA TOVORNIK.

Somalia: 26 rue Dumont d'Urville, 75116 Paris; tel. 1-45-00-88-98; Ambassador Said Hajgi MOHAMOUD FARAH.

South Africa: 59 quai d'Orsay, 75343 Paris Cédex 07; tel. 1-53-59-23-23; fax 1-53-59-23-33; e-mail saembassyparis@compuserve.com; internet www.afriquesud.net; Ambassador NOMASONTO MARY SIBANDA-THUSI.

Spain: 22 ave Marceau, 75008 Paris; tel. 1-44-43-18-00; fax 1-47-23-59-55; e-mail ambespfr@mail.mae.es; internet www.amb-espagne.fr; Ambassador FRANCISCO VILLAR Y ORTIZ DE URBINA.

Sri Lanka: 16 rue Spontini, 75016 Paris; tel. 1-55-73-31-31; fax 1-55-73-18-49; e-mail sl.france@wanadoo.fr; Ambassador ANANDA CHANDRAKUMARA GOONASEKERA.

Sudan: 56 ave Montaigne, 75008 Paris; tel. 1-42-25-55-71; fax 1-54-63-66-73; e-mail ambassade-du-soudan@wanadoo.fr; internet www.ambassade-du-soudan.org; Ambassador ABDELBASIT BADAWI ALI ELSANOUSI.

Sweden: 17 rue Barbet-de-Jouy, 75007 Paris; tel. 1-44-18-88-00; fax 1-44-18-88-40; e-mail info@amb-suede.fr; internet www.amb-suede.fr; Ambassador FRANK BELFRAGE.

Switzerland: 142 rue de Grenelle, 75007 Paris; tel. 1-49-55-67-00; fax 1-49-55-67-67; e-mail vertretung@par.rep.admin.ch; internet www.amb-suisse.fr; Ambassador FRANÇOIS NORDMANN.

Syria: 20 rue Vaneau, 75007 Paris; tel. 1-40-62-61-00; fax 1-47-05-92-73; e-mail ambassade-syrie@wanadoo.fr; Ambassador SIBA NASSER.

Tanzania: 13 ave Raymond Poincaré, 75116 Paris; tel. 1-53-70-63-66; fax 1-47-55-05-46; e-mail ambtanzanie@wanadoo.fr; internet amb-tanzanie.fr; Ambassador JUMA V. MWAPACHU.

Thailand: 8 rue Greuze, 75116 Paris; tel. 1-56-26-50-50; fax 1-56-26-04-45; e-mail thaipar@wanadoo.fr; Ambassador VIRASAKDI FUTRAKUL.

Togo: 8 rue Alfred Roll, 75017 Paris; tel. 1-43-80-12-13; fax 1-43-80-06-05; Ambassador KONDI CHARLES MADJOME AGBA.

Tunisia: 25 rue Barbet-de-Jouy, 75007 Paris; tel. 1-45-55-95-98; fax 1-45-56-02-64; e-mail atn.paris@wanadoo.fr; internet amb-tunisie.fr; Ambassador MONCER ROUISSI.

Turkey: 16 ave de Lamballe, 75016 Paris; tel. 1-53-92-71-12; fax 1-45-20-41-91; e-mail paris.be@mfa.gov.tr; Ambassador ULUÇ ÖZÜLKER.

Turkmenistan: 13 rue Picot, 75116 Paris; tel. 1-47-55-05-36; fax 1-47-55-05-68; e-mail turkmenamb@aol.com; Ambassador (vacant).

Ukraine: 21 ave de Saxe, 75007 Paris; tel. 1-43-06-07-37; fax 1-43-06-02-94; e-mail ambassade-ukraine@wanadoo.fr; Ambassador YURIY A. SERGEYEV.

United Arab Emirates: 3 rue de Lota, 75116 Paris; tel. 1-44-34-02-00; fax 1-47-55-61-04; e-mail ambassade.emirats@wanadoo.fr; Ambassador SAIF SULTAN MUBARAK AL-ARYANI.

United Kingdom: 35 rue du Faubourg Saint Honoré, 75383 Paris Cédex 08; tel. 1-44-51-31-00; fax 1-44-51-41-27; internet www.amb-grandebretagne.fr; Ambassador Sir JOHN HOLMES.

USA: 2 ave Gabriel, 75382 Paris Cédex 08; tel. 1-43-12-22-22; fax 1-42-66-97-83; internet www.amb-usa.fr; Ambassador HOWARD H. LEACH.

Uruguay: 15 rue Le Sueur, 75116 Paris; tel. 1-45-00-81-37; fax 1-45-01-25-17; e-mail urugali@fr.inter.net; internet www.amb-uruguay-france.com; Ambassador JORGE TALICE.

Uzbekistan: 22 rue d'Aguesseau, 75008 Paris; tel. 1-53-30-03-53; fax 1-53-30-03-54; e-mail ambassade.ouzbekistan@fr.oleane.com; internet www.oaric.com/ouzbekistan.htm; Ambassador KHAMIDULLA S. KARAMATOV.

Venezuela: 11 rue Copernic, 75116 Paris; tel. 1-45-53-29-98; fax 1-47-55-64-56; e-mail info@amb-venezuela.fr; internet www.embavenez-paris.com; Ambassador ROY CHADERTON-MATOS.

Viet Nam: 62–66 rue Boileau, 75016 Paris; tel. 1-44-14-64-00; fax 1-45-24-39-48; e-mail vnparis@wanadoo.fr; Ambassador NGUYÊN ĐINH BIN.

Yemen: 25 rue Georges Bizet, 75116 Paris; tel. 1-53-23-87-87; fax 1-47-23-69-41; Ambassador MOHAMED AHMED BA-SALAMA.

Zimbabwe: 12 rue Lord Byron, 75008 Paris; tel. 1-56-88-16-00; fax 1-56-88-16-09; e-mail zim.paris@wanadoo.fr; Ambassador KELEBERT NKOMANI.

Judicial System

The Judiciary is independent of the Government. Judges of the Court of Cassation and the First President of the Court of Appeal are appointed by the executive from nominations of the High Council of the Judiciary.

Subordinate cases are heard by Tribunaux d'instance, of which there are 471, and more serious cases by Tribunaux de grande instance, of which there are 181. Parallel to these Tribunals are the Tribunaux de commerce, for commercial cases, composed of judges elected by traders and manufacturers among themselves. These do not exist in every district. Where there is no Tribunal de commerce, commercial disputes are judged by Tribunaux de grande instance.

The Conseils de Prud'hommes (Boards of Arbitration) consist of an equal number of workers or employees and employers ruling on the differences that arise over Contracts of Work.

The Tribunaux correctionnnels (Correctional Courts) for criminal cases correspond to the Tribunaux de grande instance for civil cases. They pronounce on all graver offences (délits), including those involving imprisonment. Offences committed by juveniles of under 18 years go before specialized tribunals for children.

From all these Tribunals appeal lies to the Cours d'appel (Courts of Appeal).

The Cours d'assises (Courts of Assize) have no regular sittings, but are called when necessary to try every important case, such as murder. They are presided over by judges who are members of the Cours d'appel, and are composed of elected judges (jury). Their decision is final, except where shown to be wrong in law, and then recourse is had to the Cour de cassation (Court of Cassation). The Cour de cassation is not a supreme court of appeal but a higher authority for the proper application of the law. Its duty is to see that judgments are not contrary either to the letter or to the spirit of the law; any judgment annulled by the Court involves the trying of the case anew by a court of the same category as that which made the original decision.

A programme of extensive reforms in the judicial system, which aimed to reduce political control of the Judiciary and to increase citizens' rights, was introduced in stages between 1997 and 2001. A notable innovation introduced by these reforms was the introduction of the convention that a person accused of a crime is presumed innocent unless otherwise proven.

COUR DE CASSATION
5 quai de l'Horloge, 75055 Paris RP; tel. 1-44-32-50-50; fax 1-44-32-78-29; e-mail webmstre@courdecassation.fr; internet www.courdecassation.fr.

First President: GUY CANIVET.

Presidents of Chambers: JEAN-PIERRE ANCEL (1ère Chambre civile), JEAN-PIERRE DINTILHAC (2ème Chambre civile), JEAN-FRANÇOIS WEBER (3ème Chambre civile), DANIEL TRICOT (Chambre commerciale), PIERRE SARGOS (Chambre sociale), BRUNO COTTE (Chambre criminelle).

Solicitor-General: JEAN-LOUIS NADAL.

There are 12 Counsellors, two First Attorneys-General and 29 Attorneys-General.

Chief Clerk of the Court: MARLÈNE TARDI.

President of the Council of Advocates at the Cour de Cassation: EMMANUEL PIWNICA.

COUR D'APPEL DE PARIS
34 quai des Orfèvres, 75001 Paris; tel. 1-44-32-52-52; internet www.ca-paris.justice.fr.

First President: RENAUD CHAZAL DE MAURIAC.

There are also 61 Presidents of Chambers.

Solicitor-General: YVES BOT.

There are also 124 Counsellors, 22 Attorneys-General and 36 Deputies.

TRIBUNAL DE GRANDE INSTANCE DE PARIS
4 blvd du Palais, 75055 Paris RP; tel. 1-44-32-51-51; fax 1-43-29-12-55; internet www.tgi-paris.justice.fr.

President: JEAN-CLAUDE MAGENDIE.

Solicitor of the Republic of Paris: JEAN-CLAUDE MARIN .

TRIBUNAL DE COMMERCE DE PARIS
1 quai de Corse, 75181 Paris Cédex 04; tel. 8-91-01-75-75; e-mail eric.labonne@greffe-tc-paris.fr; internet www.greffe-tc-paris.fr.

President: PERRETTE REY.

TRIBUNAUX ADMINISTRATIFS
Certain cases arising between civil servants (when on duty) and the Government, or between any citizen and the Government are judged by special administrative courts.

The Tribunaux administratifs, of which there are 22, are situated in the capital of each area; the Conseil d'Etat (see below) has its seat in Paris.

TRIBUNAL DES CONFLITS
Decides whether cases shall be submitted to the ordinary or administrative courts.

President: The Minister of Justice, Keeper of the Seals.

Vice-President: YVES ROBINEAU.

There are also four Counsellors of the Cour de cassation and three Counsellors of State.

COUR DES COMPTES
13 rue Cambon, 75100 Paris RP; tel. 1-42-98-95-00; fax 1-42-60-01-59; e-mail international@ccomptes.fr; internet www.ccomptes.fr.

An administrative tribunal (Audit Court) competent to judge the correctness of public accounts. It is the arbiter of common law of all public accounts laid before it. The judgments of the Court may be annulled by the Conseil d'Etat.

First President: PHILIPPE SÉGUIN.

Presidents of Chambers: FRANÇOIS DELAFOSSE, BERTRAND FRAGONARD, JEAN PICQ, ALAIN PICHON, JEAN-FRANÇOIS CARREZ, BERNARD CIEUTAT, JEAN-FRANÇOIS BÉRNARD.

Solicitor-General: HÉLÈNE GISSEROT.

CHAMBRES RÉGIONALES DES COMPTES
In 1983 jurisdiction over the accounts of local administrations (Régions, Départements and Communes) and public institutions (hospitals, council housing, etc.) was transferred from the Cour des comptes to local Chambres régionales. The 26 courts are autonomous but under the jurisdiction of the State. Appeals may be brought before the Cour des comptes.

CONSEIL D'ETAT
Place du Palais-Royal, 75100 Paris 01 SP; tel. 1-40-20-80-00; fax 1-40-20-80-08; e-mail webmestre@conseil-etat.fr; internet www.conseil-etat.fr.

The Council of State is a council of the central power and the supreme administrative court, with 201 members in active service.

As the consultative organ of the Government, it gives opinions in the legislative and administrative domain (interior, finance, public works and social sections). In administrative jurisdiction it has three functions: to judge in the first and last resort such cases as appeals against excess of power laid against official decrees or individuals; to judge appeals against judgments made by Tribunaux administratifs, Cours administratives d'appel and resolutions of courts of litigation; and to annul decisions made by various specialized administrative authorities that adjudicate without appeal, such as the Cour des comptes.

President: The Prime Minister.

Vice-President: RENAUD DENOIX DE SAINT-MARC.

Presidents of Sections: MARIE-EVE AUBIN, JEAN-MICHEL BELORGEY, RAPHAËL HADAS-LEBEL, OLIVER FOUQUET, BRUNO GENEVOIS, YVES ROBINEAU.

General Secretary: PATRICK FRYDMAN.

CONSEIL CONSTITUTIONNEL
2 rue de Montpensier, 75001 Paris; tel. 1-40-15-30-00; fax 1-40-20-93-27; e-mail info@conseil-constitutionnel.fr; internet www.conseil-constitutionnel.fr.

President: PIERRE MAZEAUD.

Members: VALÉRY GISCARD D'ESTAING (ex officio), SIMONE VEIL, JEAN-CLAUDE COLLIARD, OLIVIER DUTHEILLET DE LAMOTHE, DOMINIQUE SCHNAPPER, PIERRE JOXE, PIERRE STEINMETZ, JACQUELINE DE GUILLENSCHMIDT, JEAN-LOUIS PEZANT.

Religion

CHRISTIANITY

Conseil d'Eglises Chrétiennes en France: 80 rue de l'Abbé-Carton, 75014 Paris; tel. 1-53-90-25-50; fax 1-45-42-03-07; e-mail unite.chretiens.revue@wanadoo.fr; f. 1987; ecumenical organization comprising representatives from all Christian denominations to express opinions on social issues; 21 mems; Pres. Pastor JEAN-ARNOLD DE CLERMONT, Most Rev. JEAN-PIERRE RICARD, Most Rev. EMMANUEL ADAMAKIS; Secs Pastor GILL DAUDÉ, Fr MICHEL MALLÈVRE, Archbishop GRIGORIOS PAPATHOMAS.

The Roman Catholic Church
For ecclesiastical purposes, France comprises nine Apostolic Regions, together forming 22 archdioceses (of which one, Strasbourg, is directly responsible to the Holy See), 70 dioceses (including one, Metz, directly responsible to the Holy See) and one Territorial Prelature. The Archbishop of Paris is also the Ordinary for Catholics of Oriental Rites. At 31 December 2002 an estimated 73.3% of the population were adherents of the Roman Catholic Church.

Bishops' Conference
Conférence des Evêques de France, 106 rue du Bac, 75341 Paris Cédex 07; tel. 1-45-49-69-70; fax 1-45-48-13-39; e-mail sg@cef.fr; internet www.cef.fr.

Pres. Most Rev. JEAN-PIERRE RICARD (Archbishop of Bordeaux); Sec.-Gen. Rev. STANISLAS LALANNE.

Latin Rite:

Archbishop of Lyon and Primate of Gaul: Cardinal PHILIPPE BARBARIN, Archevêché, 1 place de Fourvière, 69321 Lyon Cédex 05; tel. 4-72-38-80-90; fax 4-78-36-06-00; e-mail dioceselyon@wanadoo.fr; internet catholique-lyon.cef.fr.

Archbishop of Aix: Most Rev. CLAUDE FEIDT.

Archbishop of Albi: Most Rev. PIERRE-MARIE CARRÉ.

Archbishop of Auch: Most Rev. MAURICE GARDÈS.

Archbishop of Avignon: Most Rev. JEAN-PIERRE CATTENOZ.

Archbishop of Besançon: Most Rev. ANDRÉ JEAN RENÉ LACRAMPE.

Archbishop of Bordeaux: Most Rev JEAN-PIERRE RICARD.

Archbishop of Bourges: Most Rev. HUBERT BARBIER.

Archbishop of Cambrai: Most Rev. FRANÇOIS GARNIER.

Archbishop of Chambéry: Most Rev. LAURENT ULRICH.

Archbishop of Clermont: Most Rev. HIPPOLYTE SIMON.

Archbishop of Dijon: Most Rev ROLAND MINNERATH.

Archbishop of Marseille: Cardinal BERNARD PANAFIEU.

Archbishop of Montpellier: Most Rev. GUY THOMAZEAU.

Archbishop of Paris: Most Rev. ANDRÉ VINGT-TROIS.

Archbishop of Reims: Most Rev. THIERRY JORDAN.

Archbishop of Rennes: Most Rev. FRANÇOIS SAINT-MACARY.

Archbishop of Rouen: Most Rev. JEAN-CHARLES DESCUBES.

Archbishop of Sens-Auxerre: Most Rev. YVES PATENÔTRE.

Archbishop of Strasbourg: Most Rev. JOSEPH DORÉ.

Archbishop of Toulouse: Most Rev. EMILE MARCUS.

Archbishop of Tours: Most Rev. ANDRÉ VINGT-TROIS.

Armenian Rite:

Bishop of Sainte-Croix-de-Paris: GRÉGOIRE GHABROYAN, 10 bis rue Thouin, 75005 Paris; tel. 1-40-51-11-90; fax 1-40-51-11-99; e-mail epaparis@francenet.fr.
30,000 adherents (2002).

Ukrainian Rite:

Apostolic Exarch in France: Most Rev. MICHEL HRYNCHYSHYN (Titular Bishop of Zygris), 186 blvd Saint-Germain, 75006 Paris; tel. 1-45-48-48-65; fax 1-48-08-34-05.
16,000 adherents (1989).

Protestant Churches
There are some 950,000 Protestants in France.

Eglise méthodiste: 3 rue Paul Verlaine, 30100 Alès; tel. 4-66-86-20-72; the total Methodist community was estimated at 1,000 mems in 2001.

Fédération protestante de France: 47 rue de Clichy, 75311 Paris Cédex 09; tel. 1-44-53-47-00; fax 1-48-74-66-31; e-mail fpf@protestants.org; internet www.protestants.org; f. 1905; Pres. Pastor JEAN-ARNOLD DE CLERMONT; Gen. Sec. Pastor PIERRE-ANDRÉ SCHAECHTELIN.

The Federation includes:

Armée du Salut (Foundation and Congregation): 60 rue des Frères Flavien, 75976 Paris Cédex 20; tel. 1-43-62-25-95; fax 1-43-62-25-98; e-mail info@armeedusalut.fr; internet www.armeedusalut.fr; f. 1881; Pres. Lt–Col ALAIN DUCHÊNE.

Communauté protestante évangélique de Vannes: 18 blvd Edouard Herriot, 56000 Vannes; tel. 2-97-47-16-75; fax 2-97-42-44-93; Pres. JEAN-MARC THOBOIS.

Eglise de la Confession d'Augsbourg d'Alsace et de Lorraine: 1b quai St Thomas, BP 80022, 67081 Strasbourg Cédex; tel. 3-8825-90-05; fax 3-88-25-90-99; e-mail epal-media@epal.fr; internet www.epal.fr; 200,000 mems; Pres. Prof. JEAN-FRANÇOIS COLLANGE.

Eglise protestante évangélique: 30 Quéreux de la Laiterie, 17300 Rochefort.

Eglise évangélique luthérienne de France: 16 rue Chauchat, 75009 Paris; tel. 1-44-79-04-73; fax 1-44-79-05-81; e-mail usynparis@aol.com; internet www.eelf.org; 40,000 mems; f. 1872; Pres. Pastor JEAN TARTIER; Sec. JEANNIE FAVRE.

Eglise réformée d'Alsace et de Lorraine: 1 quai St Thomas, BP 80022, 67081 Strasbourg Cédex; tel. 3-88-25-90-10; fax 3-88-25-90-99; e-mail eral@protestants.org; internet www.protestants.org/epal; 33,000 mems; Pres. Pastor JEAN-PAUL HUMBERT.

Eglise réformée de France: 47 rue de Clichy, 75311 Paris Cédex 09; tel. 1-48-74-90-92; fax 1-42-81-52-40; internet www.eglise-reformee-fr.org; 350,000 mems; Pres. Nat. Council Pastor MARCEL MANOËL; Gen. Sec. Pastor BERTRAND DE CAZENOVE.

Fédération des Eglises évangéliques baptistes de France: 47 rue de Clichy, 75311 Paris Cédex 09; tel. 1-53-20-15-40; fax 1-53-20-15-41; e-mail secretariat@feebf.com; internet www.feebf.com; 6,000 mems; f. 1910; Pres. Pastor DANIEL LHERMENAULT; Gen. Sec. Pastor ETIENNE LINKOWSKI.

Mission évangélique tzigane de France: 'Les Petites Brosses', 45500 Neuvoy; tel. 2-38-67-03-18; 100,000 mems; f. 1946; Pres. Pastor GEORGES MEYER; Sec. FERRET WASSO.

Mission populaire évangélique de France: 47 rue de Clichy, 75009 Paris Cédex 09; tel. 1-48-74-98-58; fax 1-48-78-52-37; e-mail mpefr@wanadoo.fr; internet www.missionpopulaire.org; 4,000 mems; f. 1871; Pres. Pastor BERTRAND VERGNIOL.

Union des Eglises évangeliques libres de France: 12 rue Claude-Perrault, 31500 Toulouse; tel. 5-61-26-06-18; internet www.ueel.org; 2,500 mems; Pres. Pastor PIERRE LACOSTE; Sec. RAYMOND CHAMARD.

Union Nationale des Eglises réformées évangéliques indépendantes de France: 74 rue Henri Revoil, 30900 Nîmes; tel. 4-66-23-95-05; e-mail unerei@wanadoo.fr; internet erei.free.fr; f. 1938; 12,000 mems; Pres. ANTOINE SCHLUCHTER; Sec.-Gen. GÉRARD FINES.

Scots Kirk Paris (Church of Scotland): 17 rue Bayard, 75008 Paris; tel. and fax 1-48-78-47-94; e-mail scotskirk@wanadoo.fr; internet www.scotskirkparis.com; Minister (vacant).

The Orthodox Church

There are about 200,000 Orthodox believers in France, of whom 100,000 are Russian Orthodox and 50,000 Greek Orthodox. There are 85 parishes and eight monasteries.

Administration of Russian Orthodox Churches in Western Europe (Jurisdiction of the Ecumenical Patriarchate): Cathédrale St Alexandre-Nevski, 12 rue Daru, 75008 Paris; tel. 1-46-22-38-91; internet www.russie.net/orthodoxie/nevsky.htm; Pres. Most Rev. GABRIEL (DE WYLDA) (Archbishop of Russian Orthodox Churches in Western Europe and Exarch of the Ecumenical Patriarch).

Assembly of the Orthodox Churches of France (Greek Orthodox Church): Cathédrale St Stéphane, 7 rue Georges Bizet, 75116 Paris; tel. 1-47-20-82-35; fax 1-47-20-83-15; e-mail eglise .orthodoxe.grecque@wanadoo.fr; f. 1997; Pres. Most Rev. EMMANUEL (ADAMAKIS) (Metropolitan of France).

Russian Orthodox Church (Moscow Patriarchate): Metochie des Trois Docteurs a Paris, 75015 Paris; tel. 1-48-28-99-90; fax 1-48-28-74-54; e-mail korsoun@free.fr; internet e.korsoun.free.fr; the diocese of Chersonesus covers France, Portugal, Spain and Switzerland; Archbishop of Chersonesus INNOCENT (VASILIYEV).

The Anglican Communion

Within the Church of England, France forms part of the diocese of Gibraltar in Europe. The Bishop is resident in London (United Kingdom).

Archdeacon of France: Ven. ANTHONY WELLS, St. Michael's Church, 5 rue d'Aguesseau, 75008 Paris; tel. 1-47-42-70-88; fax 1-47-42-74-75; e-mail office@saintmichaelsparis.org; internet www .saintmichaelsparis.org.

Other Christian Denominations

Société Religieuse des Amis (Quakers, Assemblée de France)/Centre Quaker International: 114 rue de Vaugirard, 75006 Paris; tel. 1-45-48-74-23; e-mail quaker.paris@tiscali.fr; internet quaker.chez.tiscali.fr; f. 1920; 10 meetings nationwide; Clerk JEANNE-HENRIETTE LOUIS, AXEL JENSEN.

ISLAM

In numerical terms, Islam is the second most important religion in France; in 2001 there were about 5m. adherents, of whom some 35% resided in the Ile-de-France region. In early 2002 there were an estimated 1,500 Islamic places of worship in France.

Conseil français du culte musulman: Paris; f. 2003 to represent Islamic interests to the public authorities; Pres. Dr DALIL BOUBAKEUR; Vice-Pres MOHAMED BECHARI, FOUAD ALAOUI; Sec.-Gen. HAYDAR DEMIRYUREK.

Fédération Nationale des Musulmans de France (FNMF): Paris; f. 1985; 20 asscns; Pres. DANIEL YOUSSOF LECLERQ.

Institut Musulman de la Grande Mosquée de Paris: 2 bis place du Puits de l'Ermite, 75005 Paris; tel. 1-45-35-97-33; fax 1-45-35-16-23; e-mail rectorat@mosquee-de-paris.net; internet www .mosquee-de-paris.com; f. 1926; cultural, diplomatic, social, judicial and religious sections; research and information and commercial annexes; Rector Dr DALIL BOUBAKEUR.

Ligue nationale des Musulmans de France: BP 39, 91103 Corbeil-Essones Cédex; tel. 8-92-68-18-30; e-mail inscription@lnmf.net; internet www.lnmf.net.

JUDAISM

There are about 650,000 Jews in France.

Conseil représentatif des institutions juives de France (CRIF): 39 rue Broca, 75005 Paris; tel. 1-42-17-11-11; e-mail info@ crif.org; internet www.crif.org; 61 asscns; Pres. ROGER CUKIERMAN.

Consistoire Central—Union des Communautés Juives de France: 19 rue Saint Georges, 75009 Paris; tel. 1-49-70-88-00; fax 1-42-81-03-66; e-mail consis@wanadoo.fr; f. 1808; 230 asscns; Chief Rabbi of France JOSEPH SITRUK; Pres. JEAN KAHN; Dir-Gen. FRÉDÉRIC ATTALI.

Consistoire Israélite de Paris: 17 rue Saint Georges, 75009 Paris; tel. 1-40-82-76-76; internet www.consistoire.org; f. 1808; 40,000 mems; Pres. MOÏSE COHEN; Chief Rabbi of Paris DAVID MESSAS; Chief Rabbi of the Consistoire Israélite de Paris ALAIN GOLDMANN.

Fonds social juif unifié (FSJU): Espace Rachi, 39 rue Broca, 75005 Paris; tel. 1-42-17-10-62; fax 1-42-17-10-45; e-mail info@fsju .org; internet www.fsju.org; f. 1950; unites the principal organizations supporting Jewish cultural, educational and social activity in

France, and seeks to establish closer links between French Jewry and Israel; Pres. DAVID DE ROTHSCHILD; Dir DAVID SAADA.

BAHÁ'Í FAITH

Centre National Bahá'í: 45 rue Pergolèse, 75116 Paris; tel. 1-45-00-90-26; e-mail info@bahai.fr; internet www.bahai-fr.org.

BUDDHISM

World Federation of Buddhists, French Regional Centre: 98 chemin de la Calade, 06250 Mougins; Sec. TEISAN PERUSAT STORK.

The Press

Most major daily newspapers are owned by individual publishers or by the powerful groups that have developed round either a company or a single personality. The major groups are as follows:

Amaury Group: 25 ave Michelet, 93408 Saint Ouen Cédex; tel. 1-40-10-30-30; fax 1-40-11-15-26; owns *Le Parisien*, *Aujourd'hui en France*, the sports daily *L'Equipe*, the weeklies *L'Equipe Magazine* and *France-Football*, and the monthly *Vélo Magazine*; Man. Dir PHILIPPE AMAURY.

Bayard Presse: 3–5 rue Bayard, 75393 Paris Cédex 08; tel. 1-44-35-60-60; fax 1-44-35-61-61; e-mail communication@bayard-presse .com; internet www.bayardpresse.fr; f. 1873; Roman Catholic press group; owns 100 publs world-wide (43 within France), incl. the national *La Croix*, *Pèlerin*, *Panorama*, *Notre Temps* magazines for young people and the over 50s, and several specialized religious publications; Pres. ALAIN CORDIER.

Emap France: 19–21 rue Emile Duclaux, 92284 Suresnes Cédex; tel. 1-41-33-50-01; fax 1-41-33-57-19; internet www.emapfrance .com; fmrly Editions Mondiales; acquired Groupe Excelsior in 2003; owns several popular magazines, incl. *Nous Deux*, *FHM*, *Science et Vie*, *Studio*, *Télé-Star*, *Top Santé*, *Télépoche*, *Auto Plus* and also specialized magazines; Man. Dir ARNAUD DE PUYFONTAINE.

Hachette Filipacchi Médias (HFM): 149 rue Anatole-France, 92534 Levallois-Peret Cédex; tel. 1-41-34-60-00; internet www .hachette-filipacchi.com; f. 1999 by merger of Filipacchi Groupe and Hachette Groupe Presse; controls 48 magazines in France incl. *Paris-Match*, *Echo des Savanes*, *Pariscope*, *Jeune et Jolie*, *Photo*, *France-Dimanche*, *Elle*, *Télé 7 Jours* and holds stake in 10 regional daily newspapers; also owns 184 magazines world-wide; Pres. and Dir-Gen. GÉRALD DE ROQUEMAUREL.

Socpresse: 12 rue de Presbourg, 75116 Paris; one of the largest of the provincial daily press groups; fmrly Hersant Group; owns 20 dailies, numerous weeklies, fortnightlies and periodicals; dailies incl. *Le Progrès*, *Le Figaro*, *France-Soir*, *Le Dauphiné Libéré*, *Nord-Matin* and *Nord-Eclair*; acquired Groupe Express-Expansion in 2003; Pres. and Dir-Gen. SERGE DASSAULT.

DAILY PAPERS (PARIS)

La Croix: 3–5 rue Bayard, 75393 Paris Cédex 08; tel. 1-44-35-60-60; fax 1-44-35-60-01; e-mail lecteurs.lacroix@bayard-presse.com; internet www.la-croix.com; f. 1883; Roman Catholic; Dir BRUNO FRAPPAT; circ. in France 91,506 (2002).

Les Echos: 46 rue la Boétie, 75381 Paris Cédex 08; tel. 1-49-53-65-65; fax 1-45-61-48-92; internet www.lesechos.fr; f. 1908; owned by Pearson; economic and financial; Dir of Publication DAVID GUIRAUD; Editorial Dir (vacant); circ. in France 119,370 (2004).

L'Equipe: 4 rue Rouget-de-l'Isle, 92130 Issy-les-Moulineaux Cédex; tel. 1-40-93-20-20; fax 1-40-93-20-08; e-mail courrierdeslecteurs@ lequipe.presse.fr; internet www.lequipe.fr; f. 1946; sport; owned by Manchette Sports; Chair. LOUIS GILLET; Editorial Dir CLAUDE DROUSSENT; circ. in France 321,153 (2002).

Le Figaro: 37 rue du Louvre, 75002 Paris; tel. 1-42-21-62-00; fax 1-42-21-64-05; e-mail contact@lefigaro.fr; internet www.lefigaro.fr; f. 1828; morning; news and literary; magazine on Saturdays; three weekly supplements; Pres. SERGE DASSAULT; Dir-Gen. FRANCIS MOREL; Editorial Dir NICOLAS BEYTOUT; circ. 365,682 (2002).

France-Soir: 37 rue du Louvre, 75002 Paris; tel. 1-44-82-87-00; internet francesoir.quotidiano.net; f. 1941 as *Défense de la France*; present title adopted 1944; Dir PHILIPPE BOUVARD; circ. 87,000 (2001).

L'Humanité: 32 rue Jean Jaurès, 93528 Saint-Denis Cédex; tel. 1-49-22-72-72; fax 1-49-22-73-00; internet www.humanite.presse.fr; f. 1904 by Jean Jaurès; communist; morning; Dir PATRICK LE HYARIC; Editor-in-Chief PIERRE LAURENT.

International Herald Tribune: 6 bis rue des Graviers, 92521 Neuilly-sur-Seine Cédex; tel. 1-41-43-93-00; fax 1-41-43-93-38; e-mail iht@iht.com; internet www.iht.com; f. 1887; present name adopted 1966; 100% owned by The New York Times Co (USA);

English language; Publr MICHAEL GOLDEN; Exec. Editor WALTER WELLS; circ. 245,223 in 180 countries (2002).

Le Journal Officiel de la République Française: 26 rue Desaix, 75727 Paris Cédex 15; tel. 1-40-58-75-00; fax 1-45-79-17-84; e-mail info@journal-officiel.gouv.fr; internet www.legifrance.gouv.fr; f. 1870; official journal of the Government; publishes laws, decrees, parliamentary proceedings, and economic bulletins; Dir JEAN-PAUL BOLUFER.

Libération: 11 rue Béranger, 75154 Paris Cédex 03; tel. 1-42-76-17-89; fax 1-42-72-94-93; internet www.liberation.com; f. 1973; 37% owned by Edouard de Rothschild; Pres. and Dir of Publication SERGE JULY; Dir-Gen. (vacant); Editorial Dir ANTOINE DE GAUDEMAR; circ. in France 156,507 (2002).

Le Monde: 21 bis rue Claude-Bernard, 75242 Paris Cédex 05; tel. 1-42-17-20-00; fax 1-42-17-21-21; e-mail lemonde@lemonde.fr; internet www.lemonde.fr; f. 1944; independent; Chair. of Supervisory Bd ALAIN MINC; Pres. and Dir of Publication JEAN-MARIE COLOMBANI; Editorial Dir GÉRARD COURTOIS; circ. in France 345,231 (2003).

Paris-Turf: Société des Editions France Libre, 65 rue de Bercy, 75012 Paris; e-mail info@paris-turf.com; internet www.paris-turf.com; horse-racing; Editorial Dir FRANÇOIS HALLOPÉ; circ. 105,000 (2000).

Le Parisien: 25 ave Michelet, 93405 Saint-Ouen Cédex; tel. 1-40-10-30-30; fax 1-40-10-35-16; e-mail courriers@leparisien.com; internet www.leparisien.fr; f. 1944; morning; sold in Paris area and surrounding départements; Man. Dir JACQUES GUERIN; Editorial Dir CHRISTIAN DE VILLENEUVE; circ. 366,814 (2002).

Aujourd'hui en France: f. 1994; national version of *Le Parisien*; Editor in Chief CAROLINE BRUN; circ. in France 147,143 (2002).

Le Quotidien du Médecin: 21 rue Camille Desmoulins, 92789 Issy-les-Moulineaux Cédex; tel. 1-73-28-12-70; fax 1-73-28-13-85; e-mail redaction@quotimed.com; internet www.quotimed.com; medical journal; Pres. and Dir-Gen. Dr GÉRARD KOUCHNER; Editorial Dir RICHARD LISCIA; circ. 82,000.

La Tribune: 51 rue Vivienne, 75095 Paris Cédex 02; tel. 1-44-82-16-16; fax 1-44-82-17-92; e-mail directiondelaredaction@latribune.fr; internet www.latribune.fr; economic and financial; Editorial Dir FRANÇOIS-XAVIER PIETRI; circ. in France 80,042 (2002).

SUNDAY PAPERS (PARIS)

Le Journal du Dimanche: 149 rue Anatole France, 92534 Levallois-Perret Cédex; tel. 1-41-34-60-00; fax 1-41-34-97-16; e-mail jcmaurice@hfp.fr; Dir JEAN-CLAUDE MAURICE; Editors-in-Chief CHRISTIAN SAUVAGE, PATRICE TRAPIER; circ. 303,000 (2002).

Le Parisien Dimanche: 25 ave Michelet, 93405 Saint Ouen Cédex; tel. 1-40-10-30-30; fax 1-40-10-35-16; e-mail infoat@leparisien.fr; internet www.leparisien.fr.

PRINCIPAL PROVINCIAL DAILY PAPERS

Amiens

Le Courrier Picard: 29 rue de la République, BP 1021, 80010 Amiens Cédex 01; tel. 3-22-82-60-00; fax 3-22-82-60-12; e-mail jquemere@courrier-picard.fr; internet www.courrier-picard.fr; f. 1944; Chair./Man. DOMINIQUE FONTAINE; Editor-in-Chief FRANÇOIS PERRIER; circ. 69,779 (2002).

Angers

Le Courrier de l'Ouest: 4 blvd Albert Blanchoin, BP 728, 49007 Angers Cédex 01; tel. 2-41-68-86-88; fax 2-41-44-31-43; f. 1944; acquired in 2005 by Ouest-France group; Pres. and Man. Dir CHRISTIAN COUSTAL; Editor-in-Chief JACQUES BOSSEAU; circ. 101,188 (2002).

Angoulême

La Charente Libre: 16903 Angoulême Cédex 09; tel. 5-45-94-16-00; fax 5-45-94-16-19; e-mail charente@charentelibre.fr; internet www.charentelibre.com; Pres. JEAN-CLAUDE BONNAUD; Editorial Dir JACQUES GUYON; Editor-in-Chief JEAN-LOUIS HERVOIS; circ. 39,971 (2002).

Auxerre

L'Yonne Républicaine: 8-12 ave Jean Moulin, 89025 Auxerre; tel. 3-86-49-52-00; fax 3-86-46-52-35; e-mail direction@lyonne-republicaine.fr; internet www.lyonne-republicaine.fr; f. 1944; Dir-Gen. JOËL LOUBERT; Editor-in-Chief GÉRARD DELORME; circ. 44,496 (2001).

Bordeaux

Sud-Ouest: 101 place J. Lemoine, 33094 Bordeaux Cédex; tel. 5-56-00-33-33; fax 5-56-00-33-01; e-mail contact@sudouest.com; internet www.sudouest.com; f. 1944; independent; Pres. and Man. Dir PIERRE JEANTET; Editor-in-Chief PATRICK VENRIES; circ. 329,271 (2002).

Bourges

Le Berry Républicain: 1–3 place Berry, 18023 Bourges Cédex; tel. 2-48-27-63-63; fax 2-48-48-17-19; e-mail redaction.berry@centrefrance.com; internet www.centrefrance.com; Editor-in-Chief BERNARD STEPHAN; circ. 34,069 (2002).

Chalon-sur-Saône

Le Journal de Saône-et-Loire: 9 rue des Tonneliers, BP 134, 71100 Chalon-sur-Saône; tel. 3-85-44-68-68; fax 3-85-93-02-96; e-mail jslmediatheque@le-journal-de-saone-et-loire.fr; internet jsl.sdv.fr; f. 1826; Dir FRANÇOIS PRETET; circ. 83,000 (2000).

Chartres

L'Echo Républicain: 37 rue de Châteaudun, BP 189, 28000 Chartres; f. 1929; Pres. and Dir-Gen. JACQUES CAMUS; Sec.-Gen. J. P. COUSIN; circ. 35,000.

Clermont-Ferrand

La Montagne: 28 rue Morel Ladeuil, BP 83, 63000 Clermont-Ferrand Cédex 1; tel. 4-73-17-17-17; fax 4-73-17-18-19; e-mail lamontagne@centrefrance.com; internet www.centrefrance.com; f. 1919; independent; Man. Dir JEAN-PIERRE CAILLARD; circ. 215,468 (2002).

Dijon

Le Bien Public-Les Dépêches: 7 blvd du Chanoine Kir, BP 550, 21015 Dijon Cédex; tel. 3-80-42-42-23; fax 3-80-42-42-10; e-mail redaction@lebienpublic.fr; internet www.bienpublic.fr; f. 1850 as Le Bien Public; merged with Les Dépêches 2001; Pres. FRANÇOIS PRETET; Editor-in-Chief JEAN-LOUIS PIERRE; circ. 54,303 (2002).

Epinal

Liberté de l'Est: 40 quai des Bons Enfants, 88026 Epinal Cédex 07; tel. 3-29-82-98-00; fax 3-29-82-99-29; e-mail contact@lalibertedelest.fr; internet www.lalibertedelest.fr; f. 1945; Chair./Man. Dir ALAIN GARROUY; Editor-in-Chief GÉRARD NOEL; circ. 30,630 (1998).

Grenoble

Le Dauphiné Libéré: Les Iles-Cordées, 38913 Veurey-Voroize Cédex; tel. 4-76-88-71-00; fax 4-76-88-70-96; e-mail redaction@ledauphine.com; internet www.ledauphine.com; f. 1945; Pres., Dir-Gen. and Editor-in-Chief HENRI-PIERRE GUILBERT; circ. 260,582 (2002).

Lille

La Voix du Nord: 8 place du Général de Gaulle, BP 549, 59023 Lille Cédex; tel. 3-20-78-40-40; fax 3-20-78-42-44; e-mail webvdn@lavoixdunord.fr; internet www.lavoixdunord.fr; f. 1944; Pres. and Dir-Gen. MICHEL NOZIÈRE; Editor-in-Chief JEAN-MICHEL BRETONNIER; circ. 317,616 (2002).

Limoges

L'Echo du Centre: 29 rue Claude-Henri Gorceix, 87022 Limoges Cédex 09; tel. 5-55-04-49-99; fax 5-55-04-49-78; f. 1943; five edns; Communist; Man. Dir CHRISTIAN AUDOUIN; Editor-in-Chief BERNARD CUNY.

Le Populaire du Centre: 7 rue du Général Catroux, BP 541, 87011 Limoges Cédex; tel. 5-55-58-59-60; fax 5-55-58-69-79; e-mail lepopulaire@centrefrance.com; internet www.centrefrance.com; f. 1905; Chair. MARCEL TOURLONIAS; Dir FRANÇOIS GILARDI; circ. 48,334 (2003).

Lyon

Le Progrès: 93 ave du Progrès, 69682 Chassieu; tel. 4-72-22-23-23; fax 4-78-90-52-40; internet www.leprogres.fr; f. 1859; Pres. and Dir-Gen. CHRISTIAN COUSTAL; Editor-in-Chief JEAN PAUL LARDY; circ. 263,246 (2002).

Le Mans

Le Maine Libre: 28–30 place de l'Eperon, BP 299, 72013 Le Mans Cédex; tel. 2-43-83-72-50; fax 2-43-83-72-59; acquired in 2005 by the Ouest-France group; Pres. and Dir-Gen. GÉRARD CHOL; Editor-in-Chief RAYMOND MAUDET; circ. 49,288 (2002).

Marseille

La Marseillaise: 19 cours Honoré d'Estienne d'Orves, BP 1862, 13222 Marseille Cédex 01; tel. 4-91-57-75-00; fax 4-91-57-75-25; f. 1944; Communist; Man. Dir PAUL BIAGGINI; Editor-in-Chief CHRISTIAN DIGNE.

MarseillePlus: 248 ave Roger-Salengro, 13015 Marseille; tel. 4-91-84-00-00; e-mail redaction@marseilleplus.com; internet www.marseilleplus.com; f. 2002; Mon.–Fri. mornings; distributed free of charge.

La Provence: 248 ave Roger-Salengro, 13902 Marseille Cédex 02; tel. 4-91-84-45-45; fax 4-91-84-49-95; e-mail redaction@laprovence-presse.fr; internet www.laprovence-presse.fr; f. 1996 following merger of *Le Provençal* with *Le Méridional*; Pres. and Dir-Gen. GHISLAIN LELEU; Editor-in-Chief LAURENT GILARDINO; circ. 168,662 (2002).

Metz

Le Républicain Lorrain: 3 ave des Deux Fontaines, 57777 Metz Cédex 09; tel. 3-87-34-17-89; fax 3-87-33-28-18; e-mail pm.pernet@republicain-lorrain.fr; internet www.republicain-lorrain.fr; f. 1919; independent; Chair. CLAUDE PUHL; Editor-in-Chief MAURICE PADIOU; circ. 161,871 (2002).

Montpellier

Midi-Libre: Mas de Grille, 34923 Montpellier Cédex 09; tel. 4-67-07-67-07; fax 4-67-07-68-13; internet www.midilibre.com; f. 1944; Pres. and Dir-Gen. JEAN-PAUL LOUVEAU; Editor-in-Chief ROGER ANTECH; circ. 164,580 (2002).

Morlaix

Le Télégramme: 7 voie d'Accès au Port, BP 243, 29205 Morlaix Cédex; tel. 2-98-62-11-33; fax 2-98-88-76-65; e-mail telegramme@bretagne-online.com; internet www.letelegramme.com; f. 1944; fmrly Le Télégramme de Brest et de l'Ouest; Pres. and Man. Dir EDOUARD COUDURIER; Editor-in-Chief JEAN-CLAUDE CASSENAC; circ. 194,072 (2002).

Mulhouse

L'Alsace: 18 rue de Thann, 68945 Mulhouse Cédex 09; tel. 3-89-32-70-00; fax 3-89-32-11-26; e-mail redaction@alsapresse.com; internet www.alsapresse.com; f. 1944; Chair. JEAN-DOMINIQUE PRETET; Editor-in-Chief JEAN-MARIE HAEFFELLE; circ. 115,027 (2002).

Nancy

L'Est Républicain: rue Théophraste-Renaudot, Nancy Houdemont, 54185 Heillecourt Cédex; tel. 3-83-59-80-54; fax 3-83-59-80-13; e-mail er-secretariat-general@wanadoo.fr; internet www.estrepublican.fr; f. 1889; Pres. and Dir-Gen. GÉRARD LIGNAC; Editor-in-Chief PIERRE TARIBO; circ. 212,677 (2002).

Nantes

Presse Océan: 5 rue du Santeuil, BP 22418, 44024 Nantes Cédex 01; tel. 2-40-44-24-00; fax 2-40-44-24-59; f. 1944; acquired in 2005 by the Ouest-France group; Chair. CHRISTIAN COUSTAL; Editor-in-Chief JEAN-PIERRE CHAMPIAT; circ. 57,361 (2002).

Nevers

Le Journal du Centre: 3 rue du Chemin de Fer, BP 106, 58001 Nevers; tel. 3-86-71-45-00; fax 3-86-71-45-20; e-mail lejournalducentre@centrefrance.com; internet www.centrefrance.com; f. 1943; Man. Dir LOUIS COTTIER; Editor-in-Chief DANIEL RUIZ; circ. 32,754 (2003).

Nice

Nice-Matin: 214 route de Grenoble, BP 4, 06290 Nice Cédex 03; tel. 4-93-18-28-38; fax 4-93-83-93-97; internet www.nicematin.fr; f. 1945; Chair./Man. Dir MICHEL COMBOUL; Editor-in-Chief HUBERT PERRIN; circ. 273,324 (2001, including regional editions, *Corse-Matin* and *Var-Matin*.

Orléans

La République du Centre: 31 rue de la Hatte, BP 93035, 45403 Fleury-les-Aubrais Cédex; tel. 2-38-78-79-80; fax 2-38-78-79-79; e-mail dleger@larep.com; f. 1944; Pres. and Dir-Gen. JACQUES CAMUS; Editor-in-Chief DENIS LEGER; circ. 56,327 (2002).

Perpignan

L'Indépendant: 'Le Mas de la Garrigue', 2 ave Alfred Sauvy, 66605 Rivesaltes Cédex; tel. 4-68-64-88-88; fax 4-68-64-88-38; e-mail redaction.steno@lindependant.com; internet www.lindependant.com; f. 1846; daily; also *Indépendant-Dimanche* (Sunday); Dir-Gen. ANDRÉ LAURENS; circ. 82,595.

Reims

L'Union: 5 rue de Talleyrand, 51083 Reims Cédex; tel. 3-26-50-50-50; fax 3-26-50-51-69; e-mail dirgen@journal-lunion.fr; internet www.lunion.presse.fr; f. 1944; Chair. DANIEL HUTIER; Editor-in-Chief THIERRY DE CABARRUS; circ. 120,947 (2002).

Rennes

Ouest-France: 10 rue du Breil, 35051 Rennes Cédex 09; tel. 2-99-32-60-00; fax 2-99-32-60-25; internet www.ouest-france.fr; f. 1944; publ. by non-profit making Société civile pour le soutien des principes de la démocratie humaniste; 42 local editions (weekdays), 9 editions (Sundays); the largest circulation of any daily newspaper in France; Chair./Man. Dir FRANÇOIS-RÉGIS HUTIN; Editor-in-Chief DIDIER PILLET; circ. 785,113 (weekdays—2002), 252,010 (Sundays—2001).

Roubaix

Nord-Eclair: 42 rue du Général Sarrail, 59052 Roubaix Cédex 1; tel. 3-20-25-02-50; fax 3-20-25-62-98; e-mail rosa.cassaro@nord-eclair.com; f. 1944; Pres. JACQUES HARDOIN; Dir-Gen. and Editorial Dir JEAN-RENÉ LORE; circ. 53,339 (2002).

Rouen

Paris-Normandie: 19 place du Général de Gaulle, BP 563, 76187 Rouen Cédex; tel. 2-35-14-56-56; fax 2-35-14-56-15; e-mail redaction.web@paris-normandie.fr; internet www.paris-normandie.com; f. 1944; Pres. and Dir-Gen. PHILIPPE HERSANT; Editor-in-Chief GILLES DAUXERRE; circ. 81,551 (2002).

Strasbourg

Les Dernières Nouvelles d'Alsace: 17–21 rue de la Nuée Bleue, BP 406/R1, 67077 Strasbourg Cédex; tel. 3-88-21-55-00; fax 3-88-21-56-41; e-mail dnasug@sdv.fr; internet www.dna.fr; f. 1877; non-party; Pres. and Dir-Gen. GÉRARD LIGNAC; Editor-in-Chief ALAIN HOWILLER; circ. 203,345 (2002).

Toulon

Var Matin: 214 route de Grenoble, BP 4, 06290 Nice Cédex 3; tel. 4-94-06-91-91; fax 4-94-63-49-98; internet www.varmatin.com; f. 1975; Pres. and Dir-Gen. MICHEL COMBOUL; Editorial Dir PATRICK ANDRIEU; circ. 93,000.

Toulouse

La Dépêche du Midi: ave Jean Baylet, 31095 Toulouse Cédex; tel. 5-62-11-33-00; fax 5-61-44-74-74; internet www.ladepeche.fr; f. 1870; Pres. and Dir-Gen JEAN-MICHEL BAYLET; Editors-in-Chief GUY-MICHEL EMPOCIELLO, HENRI AMAR; circ. 207,348 (2002).

Tours

La Nouvelle République du Centre-Ouest: 232 ave de Grammont, 37048 Tours Cédex; tel. 2-47-31-70-00; fax 2-47-31-70-70; e-mail nr.redactionenchef@nrco.fr; internet www.lanouvellerepublique.fr; f. 1944; non-party; Pres. OLIVIER SAINT-CRICQ; Editor-in-Chief PASCAL ARNAUD; circ. 240,772 (2003).

Troyes

L'Est-Eclair: 71 ave du Maréchal Leclerc, 10120 St André les Vergers; tel. 3-25-71-75-75; fax 3-25-79-58-54; e-mail redaction@lest-eclair.fr; f. 1945; Dir FRANÇOIS LE SACHÉ; circ. 33,000.

SELECTED PERIODICALS

General, Current Affairs and Politics

Annales—Histoire, Sciences sociales: 54 blvd Raspail, 75006 Paris; tel. 1-49-54-23-77; fax 1-49-54-26-88; e-mail annales@ehess.fr; f. 1929; every 2 months.

Armées d'Aujourd'hui: Délégation à l'Information et à la Communication de la Défense, BP 33, 00445 Armées; tel. 1-56-77-23-03; fax 1-56-77-23-04; e-mail journalistes@dicod.defense.gouv.fr; 10 a year; military and technical; produced by the Délégation à l'Information et à la Communication de la Défense; circ. 100,000.

Le Canard Enchaîné: 173 rue Saint Honoré, 75051 Paris Cédex 01; tel. 1-42-60-31-36; fax 1-42-27-97-87; internet www.canardenchaine.com; f. 1915; weekly; satirical; Dir MICHEL GAILLARD; circ. 446,331 (2002).

Commentaire: 116 rue du Bac, 75007 Paris; tel. 1-45-49-37-82; fax 1-45-44-32-18; e-mail infos@commentaire.fr; internet www.commentaire.fr; f. 1978; quarterly; Dir JEAN-CLAUDE CASANOVA.

Courrier International: 64–68 rue du Dessous-des-Berges, 75647 Paris Cédex 13; tel. 1-46-46-16-00; fax 1-46-46-16-01; e-mail communication@courrierinternational.com; internet www .courrierinternational.com; f. 1990; weekly; current affairs and political; Pres. and Editorial Dir. PHILIPPE THUREAU-DANGIN; circ. 143,000 (2001).

L'Evénement: 32 rue René Boulanger, 75467 Paris Cédex 10; tel. 1-53-72-00-00; f. 1984 as L'Evénement du jeudi; weekly; current affairs; Dir JEAN-FRANÇOIS KAHN; Editor-in-Chief BERNARD POULET; circ. 169,820 (1998).

L'Express: 17 rue de l'Arrivée, 75733 Paris Cédex 15; tel. 1-53-91-11-11; fax 1-53-91-12-05; e-mail dired@lexpress.fr; internet www .lexpress.fr; f. 1953; weekly, Mondays; Editorial Dir DENIS JEAMBAR; circ. 432,000 (2002).

L'Humanité Hebdo: 32 rue Jean Jaurès, 93528 Saint-Denis Cedex; tel. 1-49-22-72-72; fax 1-49-22-73-00; internet www.humanite .presse.fr; current affairs; Editor MARTINE BULARD.

Ici-Paris: 10 rue Thierry le Luron, 92592 Levallois-Perret Cédex; tel. 1-41-34-88-10; fax 1-41-34-89-34; f. 1945; weekly; Dir GHISLAIN LE LEU; Editor JOEL LAFFAY; circ. 411,281 (2003).

Marianne: 32 rue René Boulanger, 75484 Paris Cédex 10; tel. 1-53-72-29-00; fax 1-53-72-29-72; e-mail s.marty@journal-marianne.com; internet www.marianne-en-ligne.fr; f. 1997; weekly; current affairs; Dir ROBERT ASSERAF; circ. 75,000 (2003).

Le Monde Diplomatique: 1 ave Stephen Pichon, 75013 Paris; tel. 1-53-94-96-15; fax 1-53-94-96-26; e-mail secretariat@ monde-diplomatique.fr; internet www.monde-diplomatique.fr; f. 1954; international affairs; Dir IGNACIO RAMONET; circ. 210,000 (2001).

Le Nouvel Observateur: 10–12 place de la Bourse, 75002 Paris; tel. 1-44-88-34-34; e-mail direction@nouvelobs.com; internet permanent.nouvelobs.com; f. 1964; weekly; left-wing political and literary; Chair. CLAUDE PERDRIEL; Dir JEAN DANIEL; circ. 432,433.

Paris-Match: 151 rue Anatole-France, 92598 Levallois-Perret Cédex; tel. 1-41-34-62-43; fax 1-41-34-75-29; e-mail lesommire@ parismatch.com; internet www.parismatch.com; f. 1949; weekly; magazine of French and world affairs; Gen. Dir. ALAIN GENESTAR; Editor-in-Chief GILLES MARTIN CHAUFFIER; circ. 776,700.

Passages: 17 rue Simone Weil, 75013 Paris; tel. 1-45-86-30-02; fax 1-44-23-98-24; e-mail passages@club-internet.fr; internet www .penso.club-internet.fr/passages; f. 1987; 6 a year; multidisciplinary discussions of geostrategic issues, seeking to present major contemporary events in an ethical and historical perspective; Dir EMILE MALET; circ. 75,000.

Le Peuple: 263 rue de Paris, Case 432, 93514 Montreuil Cédex; tel. 1-48-18-83-05; fax 1-48-59-28-31; e-mail lepeuple@cgt.fr; internet www.lepeuple-cgt.fr; f. 1921; fortnightly; official organ of the Confédération Générale du Travail (trade union confederation); Dir DANIEL PRADA; Editor-in-Chief FRANÇOISE DUCHESNE.

Le Point: 74 ave du Maine, 75014 Paris; tel. 1-44-10-10-10; fax 1-43-21-43-24; e-mail courrier@lepoint.tm.fr; internet www.lepoint.fr; f. 1972; weekly; politics and current affairs; Man. Dir BERNARD WOUTS; Editor-in-Chief MICHEL COLOMES; circ. 339,331.

Point de Vue: 142 rue du Bac, 75007 Paris; tel. 1-44-39-11-11; fax 1-42-84-17-34; e-mail contact@pointdevue.fr; internet www .pointdevue.fr; weekly; general illustrated; Dir and Editor LAURE BOULAY DE LA MEURTHE; circ. 215,308 (2002).

Politique Internationale: 11 rue du Bois de Boulogne, 75116 Paris; tel. 1-45-00-15-26; fax 1-45-00-38-79; f. 1978; quarterly; Dir and Editor-in-Chief PATRICK WAJSMAN.

Regards: 120 rue Lafayette, 75010 Paris; tel. 1-47-70-01-90; e-mail regards@regards.fr; internet www.regards.fr; monthly; communist, politics, current affairs, culture; Editor-in-Chief CLÉMENTINE AUTAIN.

Revue 'Défense Nationale': Ecole Militaire, BP 86-07, 75325 Paris Cédex 07; tel. 1-44-42-38-23; fax 1-44-42-31-89; e-mail redac@defnat .com; internet www.defnat.com; f. 1939; 11 a year; publ. by Committee for Study of National Defence; military, economic, political and scientific problems; Dir. Gen. CHRISTIAN QUESNOT; Editor Adm. GIRARD.

Revue des Deux Mondes: 97 rue de Lille, 75007 Paris; tel. 1-47-53-61-94; fax 1-47-53-61-99; e-mail contact@revuedesdeuxmondes.fr; internet www.revuedesdeuxmondes.fr; f. 1829; monthly; current affairs; Pres. MARC LADREIT DE LACHARRIÈRE; Editor-in-Chief MICHEL CREPU.

Rivarol: 1 rue St Hauteville, 75010 Paris; tel. 1-53-34-97-97; fax 1-53-34-97-98; e-mail galic@rivarol.com; internet www.rivarol.com; f. 1951; weekly; conservative, political, literary and satirical; Dir and Editor-in-Chief CAMILLE-MARIE GALIC; circ. 12,000.

Technikart: 156/2 rue de la Roquette, 75011 Paris; tel. 1-43-14-36-08; e-mail rturcat@technikart.com; internet www.technikart.com; monthly; cultural review; Editor-in-Chief RAPHAËL TURCAT.

La Vie: 163 blvd Malesherbes, 75859 Paris Cédex 17; tel. 1-48-88-46-00; fax 1-48-88-46-01; e-mail vie.forum@mp.com.fr; internet www .lavie.presse.fr; f. 1945; acquired by Le Monde SA in 2003; weekly; general, Christian; President and Dir-Gen. JEAN-CLAUDE PETIT; circ. 218,000 (2001).

VSD (Vendredi-Samedi-Dimanche): 15 rue Galvani, 75809 Paris Cédex 17; tel. 1-56-99-47-00; fax 1-56-99-51-28; e-mail lecteurs@vsd .fr; internet www.vsd.fr; f. 1977; weekly; current affairs, leisure; Editors-in-Chief MARC DOLISI, CHRISTIAN MOGUEROU; circ. 225,238 (1999).

The Arts

L'Architecture d'Aujourd'hui: 6 rue Lhomond, 75005 Paris; tel. 1-44-32-18-66; e-mail sowa@jmplace.com; f. 1930; publ. by Editions J-M. Place; Editor-in-Chief AXEL SOWA; circ. 16,000.

Art et Décoration: 16–18 rue de l'Amiral Mouchez, 75686 Paris Cédex 14; tel. 1-45-65-48-48; e-mail info@art-decoration.fr; internet www.art-decoration.fr; f. 1897; 8 a year; Dir JEAN MASSIN; Editor-in-Chief DANIEL SOUBEYRAND; circ. 451,443.

Critique: 7 rue Bernard Palissy, 75006 Paris; tel. 1-45-44-23-16; fax 1-42-84-08-63; f. 1946; nine a year; general review of French and foreign literature, philosophy, art, social sciences and history; Dir PHILIPPE ROGER; Editor LAURE DEFIOLLLES.

Diapason: Paris; tel. 1-46-62-20-00; fax 1-46-62-25-33; f. 1956; monthly; classical music; Pres. and Dir-Gen. CLAUDE POMMEREAU; Editor-in-Chief YVES PETIT DE VOIZE; circ. 70,000.

Esprit: 212 rue St. Martin, 75003 Paris; tel. 1-48-04-92-90; fax 1-48-04-50-53; e-mail redaction@esprit.presse.fr; internet www.esprit .presse.fr; f. 1932; 10 a year; philosophy, history, sociology; Dir OLIVIER MONGIN; Editor-in-Chief MARC-OLIVIER PADIS.

Gazette des Beaux-Arts: 140 rue du Faubourg Saint Honoré, 75008 Paris; tel. 1-45-61-61-70; fax 1-45-61-61-71; e-mail gazette.des .beaux.arts@wanadoo.fr; f. 1859; monthly; the oldest review of the history of art; Dir GUY WILDENSTEIN.

Les Inrockuptibles: 144 rue du Rivoli, 75001 Paris; tel. 1-42-44-16-16; fax 1-42-44-16-00; e-mail laurent.lafou@inrocks.com; internet www.lesinrocks.com; f. 1986; weekly; music, cinema, literature and television; Editorial Dir CHRISTIAN FEVRET; circ.42,000.

Lire: 14 blvd Poissonnière, 75308 Paris Cédex 09; tel. 1-53-24-40-40; fax 1-53-24-41-16; e-mail fbusnel@lire.fr; internet www.lire.fr; f. 1975; monthly; literary review; Editorial Dir FRANÇOIS BUSNEL; circ. 120,000 (2001).

Livres de France: 35 rue Grégoire de Tours, 75006 Paris; tel. 1-44-41-28-00; fax 1-43-29-77-85; f. 1979; 11 a year; Dir JEAN-MARIE DOUBLET.

Livres-Hebdo: 35 rue Grégoire-de-Tours, 75006 Paris; tel. 1-44-41-28-00; fax 1-43-29-77-85; e-mail livreshebdo@electre.com; f. 1979; 46 a year; Editor-in-Chief CHRISTINE FERRAND.

Magazine Littéraire: 4 rue du Texel, 75014 Paris; tel. 1-40-47-44-900; fax 1-40-47-44-98; e-mail magazine@magazine-litteraire.com; internet www.magazine-litteraire.com; f. 1966; monthly; literature; Dir BERNARD WOUTS; Editor JEAN-LOUIS HUE.

Le Matricule des Anges: BP 225, 34004 Montpellier Cédex; tel. and fax 4-67-92-29-33; e-mail lmda@lmda.net; internet www.lmda .net; f. 1992; monthly; literary criticism; Editor-in-Chief PHILIPPE SAVARY.

Le Monde de l'Education: 46 rue du Fer à Moulin, 75005 Paris; tel. 1-44-08-79-11; fax 1-44-08-79-12; e-mail mangin@lemonde.fr; internet www.lemonde.fr/mde; f. 1974; monthly; education; Editor-in-Chief BRIGITTE PERUCCA; circ. 40,000.

La Quinzaine Littéraire: 135 rue Saint-Martin, 75194 Paris Cédex 04; tel. 1-48-87-75-87; fax 1-48-87-13-01; e-mail selis@ wanadoo.fr; internet www.quinzaine-litteraire.net; f. 1966; fortnightly; Dir MAURICE NADEAU; circ. 20,000.

La République Internationale des Lettres: 11 Rue du Clos, 75020 Paris; e-mail editeur@republique-des-lettres.com; internet www.republique-des-lettres.com; f. 1994; monthly; literature; Dir and Editor NOËL BLANDIN; circ. 20,000.

Les Temps Modernes: 26 rue de Condé, 75006 Paris; tel. 1-43-29-08-47; fax 1-40-51-83-38; f. 1945 by J.-P. Sartre; four a year; literary review; publ. by Gallimard; Dir CLAUDE LANZMANN.

Economic and Financial

Challenges: 10–12 place de la Bourse, 75002 Paris; tel. 1-44-88-34-34; e-mail redaction@challenges.fr; internet www.challenges-eco .com; fortnightly; economics and politics; Chair. CLAUDE PERDRIEL.

L'Expansion: 14 blvd Poissonnière, 75308 Paris Cédex 09; tel. 1-53-24-40-40; fax 1-53-24-41-05; internet www.lexpansion.com; f. 1967; monthly; economics and business; Editorial Dir GEORGES VALANCE; circ. 147,602 (2000).

Marchés Tropicaux: 11 rue du Faubourg Poissonnière, 75009 Paris; tel. 1-49-49-07-49; fax 1-49-49-07-45; e-mail info@marches-tropicaux.com; internet www.moreux.fr; f. 1945; weekly; analysis and information on Africa and the Indian Ocean and on tropical products; Pres. MILUTINA RADIC; Publr STEPHANE RICHARD; Editor BENEDICTE CHATEL.

Mieux Vivre Votre Argent: 32 rue Notre-Dame-des-Victoires, 75002 Paris; tel. 1-53-00-20-00; fax 1-42-33-44-98; e-mail jpviallon@mieuxvivre.fr; internet www.mieuxvivre.fr; monthly; f. 1918; investment, economics; Editorial Dir JEAN-ANTOINE BOUCHEZ; Editor-in-Chief JEAN-FRANÇOIS FILLIATRE; circ. 257,994 (2001).

Le Monde-Initiatives: 1–3 ave Stephen Pichon, 75013 Paris; tel. 1-53-94-96-60; fax 1-53-94-96-80; e-mail initiatives@lemonde.fr; f. 2002; monthly; Dir ALAIN LEBAUBE; circ. 50,000 (2002).

Le Nouvel Economiste: 10 rue du Faubourg Montmartre, 75009 Paris; tel. 1-55-33-30-00; fax 1-55-33-30-31; f. 1975; two a month; Pres. and Dir-Gen.. CLAUDE POSTERNAK; Editorial Dir YANNICK LE BOURDONNEC; circ. 117,090.

L'Usine Nouvelle: 12–14 rue Médéric 75815 Paris Cédex 17; tel. 1-56-79-41-00; fax 1-56-79-42-34; internet www.usinenouvelle.com; f. 1945; weekly; technical and industrial journal; Dir JEAN-LÉON VANDOOME; Editor-in-Chief JEAN-LOUIS MARROU; circ. 63,100 (2002).

Valeurs Actuelles: 10 place du Général Catroux, 75858 Paris Cédex 17; tel. 1-40-54-11-00; fax 1-40-54-12-85; internet www.valeursactuelles.com; f. 1966; weekly; politics, economics, international affairs; Editor MICHEL KEMPINSKI; circ. 100,000.

La Vie Financière: 14 blvd Poissonnière, 75308 Paris Cédex 09; tel. 1-53-24-40-40; fax 1-53-24-41-10; e-mail jl.champetier@laviefinanciere.com; internet www.laviefinanciere.com; f. 1945; weekly; economics and finance; Publishing Dir DENIS JEAMBAR; Editorial Dir NASSER OUZEGDOUH; circ. 98,623 (2001).

History and Geography

Annales de Géographie: 21 rue de Montparnasse, 75298 Paris Cédex 15; tel. 1-44-39-51-24; fax 1-40-46-62-21; e-mail info@editions-sedes.com; f. 1891; every 2 months.

Cahiers de Civilisation Médiévale: 24 rue de la Chaine, 86022 Poitiers; tel. 5-49-45-45-63; fax 5-49-45-45-73; e-mail marie-helene.debies@mshs-univ-poitiers.fr; f. 1958; quarterly; pluri-disciplinary medieval studies, concentrating on the 10th–12th centuries; Dir MARTIN AURELL; circ. 1,500 (2002).

La Géographie: 184 blvd Saint Germain, 75006 Paris; tel. 1-45-48-54-62; fax 1-42-22-40-93; e-mail socgeo@socgeo.org; internet www.socgeo.org; f. 1821; quarterly of the Société de Géographie; Chair. Prof. JEAN BASTIÉ.

L'Histoire: 4 rue de Texel, 75014 Paris; tel. 1-40-47-44-00; fax 1-40-47-44-03; e-mail courrier@histoire.presse.fr; internet www.histoire.presse.fr; f. 1978; monthly; Dir-Gen. STÉPHANE KHÉMIS; Editor-in-Chief VALÉRIE HANNIN.

Historia: 74 ave du Maire, 75014 Paris; tel. 1-44-10-12-90; fax 1-44-10-12-94; e-mail pczete@tallandier.fr; internet www.historia.presse.fr; f. 1909; monthly; Dir BERNARD WOUTS; circ. 104,097.

Revue d'Histoire Diplomatique: 13 rue Soufflot, 75005 Paris; tel. 1-43-54-05-97; fax 1-46-34-07-60; f. 1887; quarterly; Dirs MAURICE VAISSE, GEORGES-HENRI SOUTOU.

Revue Historique: Archives Nationales, 60 rue des Francs Bourgeois, 75003 Paris; f. 1876; quarterly; Dirs CLAUDE GAUVARD, JEAN-FRANÇOIS SIRINELLI.

Revue de Synthèse: Centre International de Synthèse, 4 rue Lhomond, 75005 Paris; tel. 1-55-42-83-11; fax 1-55-42-83-19; e-mail revuedesynthese@ens.fr; internet www.ehess.fr/acta/synthese; f. 1900; two a year; anthropology, economics, social sciences; Dir ERIC BRIAN.

Leisure Interests and Sport

Cahiers du Cinéma: 9 passage de la Boule-Blanche, 75012 Paris; tel. 1-53-44-75-75; fax 1-43-43-95-04; e-mail courrier@cahiersducinema.com; f. 1951; monthly; film reviews; Editors-in-Chief CHARLES TESSON, JEAN-MARC LALANNE; circ. 30,000 (2002).

Le Chasseur Français: 39 rue du Gouverneur Général Eboué, 92130 Issy-les-Moulineaux Cédex; tel. 1-41-33-22-01; fax 1-41-33-22-90; internet www.lechasseurfrancais.com; f. 1885; monthly; hunting, shooting, fishing; Dir DENIS NOËL; circ. 517,140 (2002).

France-Football: 4 rue Rouget de Lisle, 92793 Issy-les-Moulineaux Cédex 9; tel. 1-40-93-20-20; fax 1-40-93-24-05; f. 1947; twice weekly;

owned by Amaury Group; Editor GÉRARD ERNAULT; circ. 230,000 (Tues.), 135,000 (Fri.—2002).

Pariscope: 149 ave Anatole France, 92534 Levallois-Perret Cédex; tel. 1-41-34-73-47; fax 1-41-34-78-30; f. 1965; listings and reviews of events in Paris and Ile-de-France; weekly; Dir-Gen. ANNE-MARIE COUDERC; Editorial Dir PASCALE DACBERT-LEMAIRE; circ. 150,000 (2003).

Photo: 149 rue Anatole France, 92534 Levallois-Perret; tel. 1-41-34-73-27; fax 1-41-34-71-52; e-mail photo@hfp.fr; internet www.photo.fr; f. 1967; monthly; specialist photography magazine; Editorial Dir ERIC COLMET-DAAGE; circ. 87,400.

Télépoche: 150 rue Gallieni, 92644 Boulogne-Billancourt Cédex; tel. 1-41-33-50-02; fax 1-41-33-57-48; e-mail pierreyves.simon@emapfrance.com; internet www.telepoche.fr; f. 1966; weekly; publ. by EMAP France; television; Pres. and Dir-Gen. ARNAUD ROY DE PUYFONTAINE; Editor PIERRE-YVES SIMON; circ. 1,027,240 (2002).

Vélo Magazine: 4 rue Rouget de Lisle, 92793 Issy-les-Moulineaux; tel. 1-40-93-20-20; fax 1-40-93-20-09; e-mail velomag@lequipe.presse.fr; monthly; cycling; Editorial Dir CLAUDE DROUSSENT.

Voiles et Voiliers: 13 rue du Breil, 35063 Rennes Cédex; tel. 2-99-32-58-80; fax 2-99-41-89-57; internet www.voilesetvoiliers.com; monthly; sailing and nautical sports; publ. by Ouest-France group; Dir. CHARLES DE FREMINVILLE; circ. 70,388 (2001).

Maritime

Le Droit Maritime Français: 190 blvd Haussmann, 75008 Paris; tel. 1-44-95-99-50; fax 1-42-89-08-72; f. 1949; monthly; maritime law; Editor STÉPHANE MIRIBEL.

Le Journal de la Marine Marchande et du Transport Multimodal: 1 ave Edouard Belion, 92500 Rueil-Malmaison; tel. 1-41-29-75-95; fax 1-41-29-75-98; e-mail marine-marchande@groupeliaisons.fr; f. 1919; weekly shipping publication; Pres. S. TSCHANZ; Editor-in-Chief M. AYSONNAVE.

Le Marin: 13 rue du Breil, 35063 Rennes Cédex; tel. 2-99-32-58-80; fax 2-99-41-89-57; e-mail y.bessoule@infomer.fr; internet www.lemarin.fr; f. 1946; weekly; publ. by Infomer; subsidiary of Ouest-France group; Dir-Gen. RODOLPHE DE LOYNES; Editor-in-Chief YANN BESSOULE; circ. 13,203 (2001).

Religion and Philosophy

Actualité Juive: 14 rue Raymond Salez, 93260 Les Lilas; tel. 1-43-60-20-20; fax 1-43-60-20-21; e-mail a-j-presse@actuj.com; internet www.actuj.net; weekly; Dir SERGE BENATTAR; circ. 17,000 (2004).

Etudes: 14 rue d'Assas, 75006 Paris; tel. 1-44-39-48-48; fax 1-44-39-48-17; e-mail francoise.le-corre@ser-sa.com; internet perso.wanadoo.fr/assas-editions; f. 1856; monthly; general interest; Editor-in-Chief FRANÇOISE LE CORRE.

France Catholique: 60 rue de Fontenay, 92350 Le Plessis Robinson; tel. 1-46-30-79-01; fax 1-46-30-04-64; e-mail francecath@aol.com; internet www.france-catholique.fr; weekly; Dir FRÉDÉRIC AIMARD; Editor-in-Chief GÉRARD LECLERC; circ. 20,000.

Le Monde des Religions: 163 blvd Malesherbes, 78859 Paris Cédex 17; tel. 1-48-88-46-00; fax 1-42-27-04-19; e-mail le.monde.des.religions@mp.com.fr; internet www.lavie.presse.fr/MDR/sommaire.php; f. 2003 to replace *Actualité des Religions*; six a year; Dir JEAN-PAUL GUETNY.

Pèlerin: 3–5 rue Bayard, 75008 Paris; tel. 1-44-35-60-60; fax 1-44-35-60-21; e-mail rene.poujol@bayard-presse.com; internet www.pelerin.info; f. 1873; weekly; Dir ALAIN CORDIER; Editor-in-Chief RENÉ POUJOL; circ. 317,800 (1999).

Prier: 163 blvd Malesherbes, 75017 Paris; tel. 1-48-88-46-00; fax 1-42-27-29-03; e-mail o.sauvaget@mp.com.fr; internet www.prier.org; f. 1978; monthly; review of modern prayer and contemplation; Editor ELISABETH MARSHALL; circ. 62,611.

Réforme: 53–55 ave du Maine, 75014 Paris; tel. 1-43-20-32-67; fax 1-43-21-42-86; e-mail reforme@reforme.net; internet www.reforme.net; f. 1945; weekly; considers current affairs from a protestant Christian perspective; Dir JEAN-LUC NOUTON; Editor-in-Chief NATHALIE DE SENNVILLE-LEENHARDT; circ. 6,000 (2003).

Revue des Sciences Philosophiques et Théologiques: Librairie J. Vrin, 6 place de la Sorbonne, 75005 Paris; tel. 1-43-54-03-47; fax 1-43-54-48-18; e-mail contact@vrin.fr; internet www.vrin.fr; f. 1907; quarterly.

Silence: Ecologie, Alternatives, Non-violence: 9 rue Dumenge, 69317 Lyon Cédex 04; tel. 4-78-39-55-33; internet www.revuesilence.net; f. 1982; monthly; circ. 7,500.

Témoignage Chrétien: 49 rue du Faubourg Poissonnière, 75009 Paris; tel. 1-44-83-82-75; fax 1-44-83-82-88; e-mail lecteurs@temoignagechretien.fr; internet www.temoignagechretien.fr; f.

1941; weekly; Christianity and politics; Pres. and Dir of Publication JACQUES MAILLOT; Editorial Dir MICHEL COOL.

La Voix Protestante: 14 rue de Trévise, 75009 Paris; tel. 1-47-70-23-53; fax 1-48-01-09-13; e-mail la.voix.protestante@wanadoo.fr; monthly review of Protestant churches; Editor DIDIER WEIL.

Science and Technology

Action Auto-Moto: 149 rue Anatole France, 92534 Levallois-Perret Cédex; tel. 1-41-34-95-25; fax 1-41-34-95-26; internet www .auto-moto.com; monthly; cars; Dir BRUNO LESOUËF; Editorial Dir JEAN SAVARY.

Air et Cosmos: 1 bis ave de la République, 75011 Paris; tel. 1-49-29-30-00; fax 1-49-29-32-01; e-mail aerospacemedia@aerospacemedia .com; internet www.air-cosmos.com; f. 1962; weekly; aerospace; Pres. and Dir-Gen. PIERRE CONDOM; Editor-in-Chief JEAN—PIERRE CASAMAYOU.

Annales de Chimie—Science des Matériaux: Lavoisier SAS, 14 rue de Provigny, 94236 Cachan Cedex; tel. 1-47-40-67-00; fax 1-47-40-67-02; e-mail info@lavoisier.fr; f. 1789; six a year; chemistry and material science.

L'Argus de l'Automobile: 1 place Boieldieu, 75082 Paris Cédex 02; tel. 1-53-29-11-00; fax 1-49-27-09-50; internet www.argusauto.com; f. 1927; motoring weekly; Dir ALEXANDRINE BRETON DES LOŸS.

Astérisque: Société Mathématique de France, Institut Henri Poincaré, 11 rue Pierre et Marie Curie, 75231 Paris Cédex 05; tel. 1-44-27-67-99; fax 1-40-46-90-96; e-mail revues@smf.ens.fr; internet smf .emath.fr/Publications/Asterisque; f. 1973; 7–9 a year; mathematics; Editor-in-Chief Y. ANDRÉ; Sec. NATHALIE CHRISTIAËN.

L'Astronomie: 3 rue Beethoven, 75016 Paris; tel. 1-42-24-13-74; fax 1-42-30-75-47; e-mail ste.astro.france@wanadoo.fr; internet www .iap.fr/saf; f. 1887; monthly; publ. by Société Astronomique de France; Chair. PATRICK GUIBERT.

L'Auto Journal: 37–43 rue du Colonel Pierre Avia, 75015 Paris; tel. 1-41-33-50-00; fax 1-41-33-57-04; e-mail olivier.bernis@emapfrance .com; internet www.autojournal.fr; fortnightly; cars; Editor-in-Chief OLIVIER BERNIS.

Biochimie: Centre universitaire des Saints Pères, 45 rue des Saints Pères, 75270 Paris Cédex 06; tel. 1-40-20-04-12; fax 1-40-20-04-22; e-mail redaction.biochimie@ibpc.fr; f. 1914; monthly; biochemistry; Editor-in-Chief M. GRUNBERG-MANAGO.

Electronique Pratique: 2–12 rue de Bellevue, 75940 Paris Cédex 19; tel. 1-44-84-84-84; fax 1-44-84-85-45; e-mail redaction@ electroniquepratique.com; internet www.electroniquepratique.com; monthly; electronics; Editorial Dir BERNARD FIGHIERA.

Industries et Techniques: 12–14 rue Médéric, 75017 Paris; tel. 1-56-79-41-00; fax 1-45-58-15-19; e-mail webmaster-it@ industries-techniques.com; internet www.industries-techniques .com; monthly; Editorial Dir PAUL WAGNER.

Ingénieurs de l'Automobile: Editions VB, 15 rue du 19 Janvier, 92380 Garches; tel. 1-47-01-44-74; fax 1-47-01-48-25; e-mail didier .rose@lcda.fr; internet www.lcda.fr/html/ingenieurs.htm; f. 1927; 8 a year; technical automobile review, in French and English; Editor-in-Chief DIDIER ROSE.

Matériaux et Techniques: SIRPE Editeur, 76 rue de Rivoli, 75004 Paris; tel. 1-42-78-52-20; fax 1-42-74-40-48; e-mail sirpe@noos.fr; internet www.sirpe.com; f. 1913; monthly; review of engineering research and progress on industrial materials; publ. by La Société d'Ingénierie, de Recherche, de Prospective et d'Edition; Editor-in-Chief R. DROUHIN.

Le Monde Informatique: IDG Communications France, 5 rue Chantecoq, 92808 Puteaux Cédex; tel. 1-41-97-61-61; fax 1-49-04-79-04; e-mail lmihebdo@idg.fr; internet www.weblmi.com; weekly; information science; Publr MICHEL CRESTIN; Editor-in-Chief FRANÇOIS JEANNE.

Le Moniteur des Travaux Publics et du Bâtiment: 17 rue d'Uzès, 75108 Paris Cédex 02; tel. 1-40-13-30-30; fax 1-40-41-94-95; e-mail redac@groupemoniteur.fr; internet www.lemoniteur-expert .com; f. 1903; weekly; construction; Chair. JACQUES GUY; Editor-in-Chief BERTRAND FABRÉ; circ. 67,000.

Psychologie Française: Université Nancy II, BP 3397, 54015 Nancy Cédex; e-mail nicole.dubois@univ-nancy2.fr; internet perso .wanadoo.fr/sfpsy/psy_fr.htm; f. 1956; quarterly; review of the Société Française de Psychologie; Editor NICOLE DUBOIS.

La Recherche: 4 rue de Texel, 75014 Paris; tel. 1-40-47-44-00; fax 1-40-47-44-02; e-mail courrier@larecherche.fr; internet www .larecherche.fr; monthly; review of the Société d'éditions scientifiques; Dir. STÉPHANE KHÉMIS; Editor-in-Chief ALINE RICHARD.

Science et Vie: 1 rue du Colonel Pierre Avia, 75015 Paris; tel. 1-46-48-48-48; fax 1-46-48-48-67; e-mail svmems@excelsior.fr; internet www.science-et-vie.com; f. 1913; monthly; Dir of Publication JEAN-LUC BREYSSE; circ. 350,000.

Women's, Home and Fashion

Cosmopolitan: 10 blvd des Frères Voisin, 92792 Issy-les-Moulineaux Cédex 9; tel. 1-41-46-88-88; fax 1-41-48-84-93; f. 1973; Editor SYLVIE OVERNOY; circ. 204,789 in France (2002).

Côté Femme: 3–5 rue Bayard, 75393 Paris Cédex 08; tel. 1-44-35-60-60; fax 1-44-35-60-37; e-mail micheline.noel@bayard-presse.com; f. 1922; weekly; Editor-in-Chief CLAUDINE LITAUD; circ. 234,637 (2002).

Elle: 11 rue de Cambrai, 75019 Paris; tel. 1-41-34-60-11; fax 1-41-34-74-94; e-mail ellemagazine@hfp.fr; internet www.elle.fr; f. 1945; monthly; Dir ANNE-MARIE PÉRIER-SARDOU; Editor-in-Chief VALÉRIE TORANIAN; circ. 358,400.

Femme Actuelle: 73–75 rue La Condamine, 75854 Paris Cédex 17; tel. 1-44-90-67-50; fax 1-44-90-67-14; e-mail femactu@prisma-presse .com; internet www.femmeactuelle.fr; f. 1984; weekly; Editor-in-Chief MARYSE BONNET; circ. 1,500,000 (2003).

Le Journal de la Maison: 20 rue de Billancourt, BP 406, 92103 Boulogne-Billancourt Cédex; tel. 1-41-10-13-55; fax 1-41-10-13-01; e-mail ccorvaisier@hfp.fr; monthly; home; Editor CAROLINE CORVAISIER.

Marie-Claire: 10 blvd des Frères Voisin, 92792 Issy-les-Moulineaux Cédex 9; tel. 1-41-46-88-88; fax 1-41-46-86-86; e-mail webgmc@gmc.tm.fr; internet www.groupemarieclaire.com; f. 1954; monthly; Editor-in-Chief TINA KIEFFER; circ. 403,171 in France (2002); also *Marie-France.*

Marie-France: 10 blvd des Frères Voisin, 92792 Issy-Les-Moulineaux; f. 1944; Editor-in-Chief MARIE-FRANCE LEPOUTRE; circ. in France 184,441 (2002).

Modes et Travaux: 1 rue du Colonel Pierre Avia, 75015 Paris; tel. 1-46-48-48-48; f. 1919; monthly; publ. by Emap France; Editor JEANNE THIRIET; circ. 512,167 (2002).

Notre Temps: 3–5 rue Bayard, 75393 Paris Cédex 08; tel. 1-44-35-60-60; fax 1-44-35-60-31; e-mail redaction@notretemps.com; internet www.notretemps.com; monthly; for retired people; Dir PATRICK DARDE; Editor RÉMY MICHEL.

Nous Deux: 152 rue Galliéni, 92644 Boulogne-Billancourt Cédex; tel. 1-41-86-86-86; fax 1-41-86-84-02; e-mail nous-deux@emapfrance .com; f. 1947; weekly; Editor MARION MINUIT; circ. 348,582 (2003).

Parents: 10 rue Thierry-le-Luron, 92592 Levallois-Perret Cédex; tel. 1-41-34-61-88; fax 1-41-34-70-79; magazine for parents; Editorial Dir. CATHERINE LILIÈVRE; circ. 378,100.

Pleine Vie: 152 rue Galliéni, 92644 Boulogne-Billancourt Cédex; tel. 1-41-86-84-15; fax 1-41-86-85-63; e-mail annick.alombert@ emapfrance.com; f. 1997; monthly; intended for women aged 50 and over; Dir ANNICK ALOMBERT; circ. 1,083,980 (2003).

Questions de Femmes: 117 rue de la Tour, 75116 Paris; tel. 1-45-03-80-00; fax 1-45-03-80-20; e-mail gleroy@groupe-ayache.com; internet www.questionsdefemmes.com; f. 1996; monthly; Editor-in-Chief GENEVIÈVE LEROY.

Santé Magazine: 110 rue Marius Aufan, BP 318, 92304 Levallois-Perret Cédex; tel. 1-41-49-41-49; fax 1-40-89-04-30; e-mail direction@santemagazine.fr; internet santemagazine.fr; f. 1976; monthly; health; Editor ANDRÉ GIOVANNI.

Vogue: 56A rue du Faubourg Saint Honoré, 75008 Paris; tel. 1-53-43-50-00; fax 1-53-43-60-60; internet www.vogueparis.com; monthly; Publr DIDIER SUBERBIELLE; Editor-in-Chief CARINE ROITFELD.

NEWS AGENCIES

Agence France-Presse (AFP): 13 place de la Bourse, 75002 Paris; tel. 1-40-41-46-46; fax 1-40-41-73-99; e-mail contact@afp.com; internet www.afp.fr; f. 1944; 24-hour service of world political, financial, sporting news, and photographs; 165 agencies and 2,000 correspondents world-wide; Pres.and Dir-Gen. BERTRAND EVENO; Editor-in-Chief ERIC WISHART.

Agence Parisienne de Presse: 18 rue Saint Fiacre, 75002 Paris; tel. 1-42-36-95-59; fax 1-42-33-83-24; f. 1949; Man. Dir MICHEL BURTON.

Infomedia M.C.: 8 rue de la Michodière, 75002 Paris; tel. 1-47-42-14-33; fax 1-47-42-14-39; f. 1988; economic and financial news; Dir FRANÇOIS COUDURIER.

Foreign Bureaux

Agence Maghreb Arabe Presse (MAP) (Morocco): 9 blvd la Madeleine, 75001 Paris; tel. 1-42-44-24-30; fax 1-42-44-24-40; e-mail hasna.daoudi@wanadoo.fr; internet www.map.co.ma; f. 1959; Correspondent HASNA DAOUDI.

Agence de Presse Xinhua (People's Republic of China): 27 rue Médéric, 92110 Clichy-la-Garenne; tel. 1-41-06-97-33; fax 1-42-70-65-38; internet www.xinhua.org; Bureau Chief QI YANG.

Agencia EFE (Spain): 10 rue Saint-Marc, 75002 Paris; tel. 1-44-82-65-40; fax 1-40-39-91-78; e-mail efeparis@wanadoo.fr; internet www.efe.es; f. 1939; Bureau Chief ANNE LEROUX.

Agenzia Nazionale Stampa Associata (ANSA) (Italy): 29 rue Tronchet, 75008 Paris; tel. 1-42-65-55-16; fax 1-42-65-12-11; e-mail ansa.paris@noos.fr; internet www.ansa.it; Bureau Chief FRANCESCO BIANCHINI.

Anadolu Ajansi (Anatolian News Agency) (Turkey): 90 blvd Garibaldi, 75015 Paris; tel. (1) 42-19-99-25; fax (1) 43-06-17-98; e-mail paris@anadoluajansi.com.tr.

Associated Press (AP) (USA): 162 rue du Faubourg Saint Honoré, 75008 Paris; tel. 1-43-59-86-76; fax 1-40-74-00-45; e-mail apmail@associatedpress.fr; internet www.ap.org; Bureau Chief KEVIN COSTELLOE.

Deutsche Presse-Agentur (dpa) (Germany): 30 rue Saint Augustin, 75002 Paris; tel. 1-47-42-95-02; fax 1-47-42-51-75; e-mail paris@dpa.com; Bureau Chief HANNS-JOCHEN KAFFSACK.

ITAR-TASS (Information Telegraph Agency of Russia-Telegraphic Agency of the Sovereign Countries) (Russia): 27 ave Bosquet, 75007 Paris; tel. 1-44-11-31-80; fax 1-47-05-33-98; internet www.itar-tass.com; Chief Correspondent and Head of ITAR-TASS Western European Regional Office VITALII MAKARCHEV.

IPS—Inter Press Service: Paris; tel. 1-45-49-81-62; e-mail rameshjaura@visto.com; internet www.ips.org; European Co-ordinator RAMESH JAURA.

Jiji Tsushin (Jji Press Ltd) (Japan): 27 blvd des Italiens, 75002 Paris; tel. 1-42-66-96-57; fax 1-42-66-96-61; internet www.jiji.co.jp; Bureau Chief YUKIO YOSHINAGA.

Magyar Távirati Iroda (MTI) (Hungary): 365 rue de Vaugirard, 75015 Paris; tel. 1-45-33-22-59; fax 1-45-33-32-06; e-mail mtiparis@yahoo.fr; internet hirek.mti.hu; Correspondent ANSAF HILU.

Middle East News Agency (Egypt): Paris; tel. 1-47-42-16-03; fax 1-47-42-44-52; internet www.mena.org.eg; f. 1956; Dir MOHAMED EL-SHAMY.

Reuters (UK): 6–8 blvd Haussmann, 75457 Paris Cédex 09; tel. 1-49-49-50-00; fax 1-53-34-02-60; internet www.reuters.fr; Dir CHRISTIAN LEVESQUE; Editor-in-Chief G. REGENSTREIF.

RIA-Novosti (Russian News and Information Agency) (Russia): 14 place du Général Catroux, 75017 Paris; tel. 1-42-27-79-21; fax 1-43-80-96-83; internet www.rian.ru; Bureau Chief VIKTOR ONUCHKO.

United Press International (UPI) (USA): Paris; tel. 1-42-60-23-68; fax 1-42-60-30-98; internet www.upi.com.

PRESS ASSOCIATIONS

Comité de Liaison de la Presse: Paris; tel. 1-53-20-90-56; liaison organization for press, radio and cinema.

Fédération Française des Agences de Presse (FFAP): Paris; tel. 1-42-93-42-57; fax 1-42-93-15-32; e-mail info@agencesdepresse.fr; internet www.ffap.fr; comprises five syndicates (news, photographs, television, general information and multimedia) with a total membership of 109 agencies; Pres. ARNAUD HAMELIN; Dir JACQUES MORANDAT.

Fédération Nationale de la Presse Française (FNPF): 13 rue La Fayette, 75009 Paris; tel. 1-53-20-90-50; fax 1-53-20-90-51; e-mail fnpf@portail-presse.com; internet www.portail-presse.com; f. 1944; mems: Syndicat de la Presse Parisienne, Syndicat Professionnel de la Presse, Magazine et d'Opinion, Syndicat de la Presse Quotidienne Régionale, Syndicat de la Presse Quotidienne Départementale, Fédération de la Presse Périodique Régionale, Fédération Nationale de la Presse d'Information Spécialisée; Pres. FRANÇOIS D'ORCIVAL.

Fédération Nationale de la Presse d'Information Spécialisée: 37 rue de Rome, 75008 Paris; tel. 1-44-90-43-60; fax 1-44-90-43-72; e-mail contact@fnps.fr; internet www.fnps.fr; comprises Syndicat National de la Presse Agricole et Rurale (SNPAR), Syndicat National de la Presse Médicale et des Professions de Santé (SNPM), Syndicat de la Presse Culturelle et Scientifique (SPCS), Syndicat de la Presse Economique, Juridique et Politique (SPEJS), Syndicat de la Presse Professionnelle (SP—PRO, Syndicat de la Presse d'Informations Spécialisées (SPIS) and Syndicat de la Presse Sociale (SPS), representing some 1,350 specialised or professional publications.; CEO JEAN-MICHEL HUAN.

Fédération de la Presse Périodique Régionale: 72 rue d'Hauteville, 75010 Paris; tel. 1-45-23-98-00; fax 1-45-23-98-01; e-mail sphr@sphr.fr; internet www.sphr.fr; f. 1970; present name adopted 1992; mems: Syndicat de la Presse Hebdomadaire Régionale, Syndicat National des Publications Régionales, Syndicat de la Presse Judiciaire de Province, Syndicat National de la Presse Judiciaire; represents 250 regional periodical publications; Pres. BERNARD BIENVENU; Sec.-Gen. WILLIAMS CAPTIER.

Syndicat de la Presse Quotidienne Régionale: 17 place des Etats-Unis, 75116 Paris; tel. 1-40-73-80-20; fax 1-47-20-48-94; internet www.spqr.fr; f. 1986; regional dailies; Pres. MICHEL COMBOUL; Dir-Gen. BRUNO HOCQUART DE TURTOT.

PRESS INSTITUTE

Institut Français de Presse et des Sciences de l'Information: 92 rue d'Assas, 75006 Paris; tel. 1-44-41-57-93; fax 1-44-41-59-49; e-mail ifp@u-paris2.fr; f. 1951; studies and teaches all aspects of communication and the media; maintains research and documentation centre; open to research workers, students, journalists; Dir JOSIANE JOUËT.

Publishers

Actes Sud: Le Méjan, place Nina-Berberova, BP 38, 13633 Arles; tel. 4-90-49-86-91; fax 4-90-96-95-25; e-mail contact@actes-sud.fr; internet www.actes-sud.fr; f. 1978; French and translated literature, music, theatre, studies of Arabic and Islamic civilisations; Pres. FRANÇOISE NYSSEN; Editorial Dir BERTRAND PY.

Editions Albin Michel: 22 rue Huyghens, 75014 Paris Cédex 14; tel. 1-42-79-10-00; fax 1-43-27-21-58; e-mail virginie.caminade@albin-michel.fr; internet www.albin-michel.fr; f. 1901; general, fiction, history, classics; Pres. FRANCIS ESMÉNARD; Man. Dir RICHARD DUCOUSSET.

Armand Colin Editeur: 21 rue du Montparnasse, 75283 Paris Cédex 06; tel. 1-44-39-54-47; fax 1-44-39-51-10; e-mail infos@armand-colin.com; internet www.armand-colin.com; f. 1870; imprint of Hachette Livre; literature, history, human and social sciences, university textbooks; Dir-Gen. GUILLAUME DERVIEUX.

Assouline: 26-28 rue Danielle Casanova, 75002 Paris; tel. 1-42-60-33-84; e-mail contact@assouline.com; internet www.assouline.com; f. 1994; art, fashion, design, lifestyle; Dir PROSPER ASSOULINE.

Editions de l'Atelier/Editions Ouvrières: 12 ave Soeur Rosalie, 75013 Paris; tel. 1-44-08-95-15; fax 1-44-08-95-00; e-mail editions.atelier@wanadoo.fr; f. 1929; religious, educational, political and social, including labour movement; Dir-Gen. BERNARD STEPHAN.

Editions Aubier: 13 quai Conti, 75006 Paris; tel. 1-40-51-31-00; fax 1-43-29-71-04; internet editions.flammarion.com/editeurs/?aubier; f. 1925; psychoanalysis, literature, philosophy, history and sociology; Man. Dir M. AUBIER-GABAIL.

Editions Balland: 33 rue Saint André des Arts, 75006 Paris; tel. 1-43-25-74-40; fax 1-46-33-56-21; e-mail balland@club-internet.fr; internet www.balland.fr; f. 1967; literature, non-fiction; Chair. and Man. Dir DENIS BOURGEOIS.

Bayard Editions—Centurion: 3–5 rue Bayard, 75393 Paris Cédex 08; tel. 1-44-35-60-60; fax 1-44-35-61-61; e-mail communication@bayardpresse.com; internet www.bayardpresse.com; f. 1870; children's books, religion, human sciences; Pres. ALAIN CORDIER; Man. Dir PATRICK ZAGO.

Beauchesne Editeur: 7 Cité du Cardinal Lemoine, 75005 Paris; tel. 1-53-10-08-18; fax 1-53-10-85-19; e-mail beauchesne2@wanadoo.fr; internet www.editions-beauchesne.com; f. 1850; scripture, religion and theology, philosophy, religious history, politics, encyclopaedias; Man. Dir JEAN-ETIENNE MITTELMANN.

Editions Belfond: 12 ave d'Italie, 75627 Paris Cédex 13; tel. 1-44-16-05-00; fax 1-44-16-05-06; internet www.belfond.fr; f. 1963; fiction, poetry, documents, history, arts; Chair. JÉRÔME TALAMON; Man. Dir FABIENNE DELMOTE.

Berger-Levrault: 17 rue Rémy Dumoncel, 75014 Paris; tel. 1-40-64-42-53; fax 1-40-64-42-30; e-mail francoise.lelouvier@berger-levrault.fr; internet www.berger-levrault.fr; f. 1976; fine arts, health, social and economic sciences, law; Chair. MARC FRIEDEL; Man. Dir BERNARD AJAC.

Bordas: 89 blvd Blanqui, 75013 Paris; tel. 1-44-39-54-45; fax 1-43-22-85-18; e-mail mvrignaud@bordas.tm.fr; internet www.editions-bordas.com; f. 1946; encyclopaedias, dictionaries, history, geography, arts, children's and educational; Dir-Gen. MARIE-FRANÇOISE ENSLEN.

Editions Bornemann: 62 rue Blanche, 75009 Paris; tel. 1-42-82-08-16; fax 1-48-74-14-88; f. 1829; art, fiction, sports, nature, easy readers; Chair. and Man. Dir PIERRE C. LAHAYE.

Buchet-Chastel: 7 rue des Canettes, 75006 Paris; tel. 1-44-32-05-60; fax 1-44-32-05-61; e-mail buchet_chastel@buchet_chastel.fr; f. 1929; literature, music, crafts, religion, practical guides; Chair. VERA MICHALSKI; Gen. Man. FRANÇOISE DILLEMANN.

Calmann-Lévy: 31 rue de Fleurus, 75006 Paris ; tel. 1-49-54-36-00; f. 1836; French and foreign literature, history, social sciences, economics, sport, leisure; Chair. JEAN-ETIENNE COHEN-SEAT.

Editions Casterman: 36 rue du Chemin Vert, 75011 Paris; tel. 1-55-28-12-00; fax 1-55-28-12-60; e-mail info@casterman.com; internet www.casterman.com; f. 1857; juvenile, comics, fiction, education, leisure, art; Chair. and Man. Dir SIMON CASTERMAN.

Editions du Cerf: 29 blvd de Latour Maubourg, 75340 Paris Cédex 07; tel. 1-44-18-12-12; fax 1-45-56-04-27; e-mail cerf.diffusion@wanadoo.fr; internet www.editionsducerf.fr; f. 1929; religion, social science; Chair. MICHEL BON; Man. Dir NICOLAS SED.

Editions Champ Vallon: rue Gérin, 01420 Seyssel; tel. 4-50-56-15-51; fax 4-50-56-15-64; e-mail info@champ-vallon.com; internet www.champ-vallon.com; f. 1980; social sciences, literary history, literary criticism; Dirs MYRIAM MONTEIRO-BRAZ, PATRICK BEAUNE.

Editions Chiron: 10 rue Léon-Foucault, 78184 Saint-Quentin-en-Yveline; tel. 1-30-14-19-30; fax 1-30-14-19-46; e-mail info@editionschiron.com; internet www.editionschiron.com; f. 1907; sport, education, fitness, health, dance, games; Dir MARINUS VISSER.

Editions Climats: 470 chemin des Pins, 34170 Castelnau-le Lez; tel. 4-99-58-30-91; fax 4-99-58-30-92; e-mail contact@editions-climats.com; internet www.editions-climats.com; f. 1988; literature, arts, political science; Dir ALAIN MARTIN.

Editions Dalloz: 31–35 rue Froidevaux, 75685 Paris Cédex 14; tel. 1-40-64-54-54; fax 1-40-64-54-97; e-mail ventes@dalloz.fr; internet www.dalloz.fr; f. 1824; law, philosophy, political science, business and economics; imprint of Editis; Pres. and Dir-Gen. CHARLES VALLÉE.

Dargaud: 15–27 rue Moussorgski, 75895 Paris Cédex 18; tel. 1-53-26-32-32; fax 1-53-26-32-00; e-mail contact@dargaud.fr; internet www.dargaud.fr; f. 1943; juvenile, cartoons, comics, video, graphic novels; Chair. and Man. Dir CLAUDE DE SAINT-VINCENT.

De Boccard, Edition-Diffusion: 11 rue de Médicis, 75006 Paris; tel. 1-43-26-00-37; fax 1-43-54-85-83; e-mail deboccard@wanadoo.fr; internet www.deboccard.com; f. 1866; history, archaeology, religion, orientalism, medievalism; Man. Dir DOMINIQUE CHAULET.

La Découverte: 9 bis rue Abel Hovelacque, 75013 Paris; tel. 1-44-08-84-00; fax 1-44-08-84-39; e-mail ladecouverte@editionsladecouverte.com; internet www.editionsladecouverte.fr; f. 1959; imprint of Editis; economic, social and political science, literature, history; Man. Dir FRANÇOIS GÈZE.

Editions Denoël: 9 rue du Cherche-Midi, 75278 Paris Cédex 06; tel. 1-44-39-73-73; fax 1-44-39-73-90; internet www.gallimard.fr/catalog/html/grp/denoel.htm; f. 1930; imprint of Editions Gallimard; general literature, science fiction, crime, history; Dir-Gen. OLIVIER RUBINSTEIN.

Desclée De Brouwer (DDB): 76 bis rue des Saints Pères, 75007 Paris; tel. 1-45-49-61-92; fax 1-42-22-61-41; e-mail direction@descleedebrouwer.com; internet www.descleedebrouwer.com; f. 1877; religion, philosophy, arts, human sciences; Dir MARC LEBOUCHER.

Diderot Editeur: 22 rue Malher, 75004 Paris; tel. 1-48-04-91-45; f. 1995; science, fine arts, history of art and culture.

La Documentation Française: 29 quai Voltaire, 75344 Paris Cédex 07; tel. 1-40-15-70-00; fax 1-40-15-72-30; e-mail depcom@ladocumentationfrancaise.fr; internet www.ladocumentationfrancaise.fr; f. 1945; government publs; politics, law, economics, culture, science; Man. Dir OLIVIER CAZENAVE.

Dunod: 5 rue Laromiguière, 75005 Paris Cédex; tel. 1-40-46-35-00; fax 1-40-46-49-95; e-mail infos@dunod.com; internet www.dunod.com; f. 1800; science, computer science, electronics, economics, accountancy, management, psychology and humanities; imprint of Hachette Group; Dir-Gen. NATHALIE DE BAUDRY D'ASSON.

Edilarge Editions Ouest-France: 13 rue du Breil, 35063 Rennes Cédex; tel. 2-99-32-58-27; fax 2-99-32-58-30; internet www.edilarge.com; history, guides; subsidiary of Ouest-France group; fmrly Editions Ouest-France; Chair. FRANÇOIS-XAVIER HUTIN; Dir-Gen. SERVANE BIGUAIS.

Edisud: 3120 Route d'Avignon, 13090 Aix-en-Provence; tel. 4-42-21-61-44; fax 4-42-21-56-20; e-mail info@edisud.com; internet www.edisud.com; f. 1971; Dir CHARLY-YVES CHAUDOREILLE.

Editis: 31 rue du Colisée, 75383 Paris Cédex 08; tel. 1-53-53-30-00; fax 1-53-53-37-37; e-mail benoit.liva@vupublishing.net; internet www.editis.com; f. 1835 as Havas; renamed Vivendi Universal Publishing 2001, then VUP-Investima 10 in 2003; present name adopted Oct. 2003; education, literature, reference; imprints include Bordas, Dunod, Fleuve Noir, Harrap, Laffont, Larousse-Bordas, Le Robert; Dir of Publishing ALAIN KOUCK.

Eyrolles: 61 blvd Saint Germain, 75005 Paris; tel. 1-44-41-11-11; fax 1-44-41-11-44; e-mail librairie@eyrolles.com; internet www.eyrolles.com; f. 1918; science, computing, technology, electronics, management, law; Man. Dir JEAN-PIERRE TISSIER.

Fayard: 75 rue des Saints Pères, 75279 Paris Cédex 06; tel. 1-45-49-82-00; fax 1-42-22-40-17; e-mail rights@editions-fayard.fr; internet www.editions-fayard.fr; f. 1857; literature, biography, history, religion, essays, music; Pres. and Dir-Gen. CLAUDE DURAND.

Editions des Femmes Antoinette Fouque: 6 rue de Mézières, 75006 Paris; tel. 1-42-22-60-74; fax 1-42-22-62-73; e-mail info@desfemmes.fr; internet www.desfemmes.fr; f. 1973; mainly women authors; fiction, essays, art, history, politics, psychoanalysis, talking books; Dir ANTOINETTE FOUQUE.

Flammarion (Librairie Ernest Flammarion): 26 rue Racine, 75006 Paris; tel. 1-40-51-31-00; fax 1-43-29-76-44; e-mail basquin@easynet.fr; internet editions.flammarion.com; f. 1875; general literature, art, human sciences, sport, children's books, medicine; Chair. CHARLES-HENRI FLAMMARION; Man. Dir FRÉDÉRIC MOREL.

Editions Fleurus: 15–27 rue Moussorgski, 75895 Paris Cédex 18; tel. 1-53-26-33-35; fax 1-53-26-33-36; e-mail m.daigne@fleurus-mame.fr; f. 1944; arts, education, leisure; Chair. VINCENT MONTAGNE; Man. Dir PIERRE-MARIE DUMONT; also Fleurus Idées, Fleurus Enfants, Fleurus Jeunesse, Mame, Tardy, Critérion, Desclée, Droguet et Ardant.

Fleuve Noir: 12 ave d'Italie, 75627 Paris Cédex 13; tel. 1-44-16-05-00; fax 1-44-16-05-07; e-mail beatrice.duval@universpoche.com; imprint of Editis; crime and science fiction; Chair. JEAN-CLAUDE DUBOST; Man. Dir BÉATRICE DUVAL.

Editions Foucher: 31 rue du Fleurus, 75278 Paris Cédex 06; tel. 1-49-54-35-35; fax 1-49-54-35-00; e-mail cfages@editions-foucher.fr; internet www.editions-foucher.fr; f. 1936; science, economics, law, medicine textbooks; Chair. and Man. Dir BERNARD FOULON.

Editions Gallimard: 5 rue Sébastien-Bottin, 75328 Paris Cédex 7; tel. 1-49-54-42-00; fax 1-45-44-94-03; e-mail pub@gallimard.fr; internet www.gallimard.fr; f. 1911; general fiction, literature, history, poetry, children's, philosophy; Dir ANTOINE GALLIMARD; Editorial Dir TERESA CREMISI.

Editions Grasset et Fasquelle: 61 rue des Saints-Pères, 75006 Paris; tel. 1-44-39-22-00; fax 1-42-22-64-18; e-mail afarges@grasset.fr; internet www.grasset.fr; f. 1907; contemporary literature, criticism, general fiction and children's books; Pres. OLIVIER NORA.

Librairie Gründ: 60 rue Mazarine, 75006 Paris; tel. 1-43-29-87-40; fax 1-43-29-49-86; internet www.grund.fr; f. 1880; art, natural history, children's books, guides; Chair. ALAIN GRÜND.

Hachette Livre: 43 quai de Grenelle, 75905 Paris Cédex 15; tel. 1-43-92-30-00; fax 1-43-92-30-30; internet www.hachette.com; f. 1826; fifth-largest publisher in profit terms worldwide in 2004; group comprises over 40 publishing houses in France and abroad, particularly in the UK and Spain; Pres. and Dir-Gen. ARNAUD NOURRY.

L'Harmattan Edition: 7 rue de l'Ecole Polytechnique, 75005 Paris; tel. 1-40-46-79-20; fax 1-43-25-82-03; e-mail harmat@worldnet.fr; internet www.editions-harmattan.fr; f. 1975; politics, human sciences, developing countries; Dir DENIS PRYEN.

Editions Hatier: 8 rue d'Assas, 75278 Paris Cédex 06; tel. 1-49-54-49-54; fax 1-40-49-00-45; e-mail mnmalapert@editions-hatier.fr; internet www.editions-hatier.fr; f. 1880; children's books, fiction, history, science, nature guides; Chair. BERNARD FOULON.

Hermann: 293 rue Lecourbe, 75015 Paris; tel. 1-45-57-45-40; fax 1-40-60-12-93; e-mail hermann.sa@wanadoo.fr; f. 1870; sciences and art, humanities; Chair. PIERRE BERÈS.

Editions Ibolya Virag: 11 rue du Grand-Prieuré, 75011 Paris; tel. and fax 1-43-38-56-05; fax 1-43-38-43-14; e-mail iboya_virag@hotmail.com; f. 1996; fiction, history, Central and Eastern Europe, Russia and Central Asia; Dir IBOLYA VIRAG.

J'ai Lu: 84 rue de Grenelle, 75007 Paris; tel. 1-44-39-34-70; fax 1-45-44-65-52; e-mail ajasmin@jailu.com; internet www.jailu.com; f. 1958; fiction, paperbacks; subsidiary of Flammarion; Chair. CHARLES-HENRI FLAMMARION; Man. Dir BERTRAND LOBRY.

Editions Julliard: 24 ave Marceau, 75008 Paris; tel. 1-53-67-14-00; fax 1-53-67-14-14; internet www.laffont.fr/julliard/index.htm; f. 1931; general literature, biography, essays; imprint of Editions Robert Laffont/Editis.

Editions du JurisClasseur: 141 rue de Javel, 75747 Paris Cédex 15; tel. 1-45-58-93-76; fax 1-45-58-94-00; e-mail editorial@juris-classeur.com; internet www.juris-classeur.com; member of Groupe Lexis-Nexis (ReedElsevier); imprints include Litec and Légisoft; law, economics, taxation; Dirs ANJER HOLL, MARIELLE BERNARD.

Karthala Editions: 22–24 blvd Arago, 75013 Paris; tel. 1-43-31-15-59; fax 1-45-35-27-05; e-mail karthala@wanadoo.fr; internet www.karthala.com; politics, history, developing countries.

Jeanne Laffitte: 25 Cours d'Estienne d'Orves, BP 1903, 13225 Marseille Cédex 01; tel. 4-91-59-80-49; fax 4-91-54-76-33; e-mail librairie@jeanne-laffitte.com; internet www.jeanne-laffitte.com; f. 1972; art, geography, culture, medicine, history; Chair. and Man. Dir JEANNE LAFFITTE.

Editions Robert Laffont: 24 ave Marceau, 75381 Paris Cédex 08; tel. 1-53-67-14-00; fax 1-53-67-14-14; e-mail bvernet@robert.laffont .fr; internet www.laffont.fr; f. 1941; literature, history, translations; imprint of Editis; Dirs LEONELLO BRANDOLINI, NICOLE LATTES.

Larousse: 21 rue du Montparnasse, 75283 Paris Cédex 06; tel. 1-44-39-44-00; fax 1-44-39-43-43; internet www.larousse.net; f. 1852; general, specializing in dictionaries, illustrated books on scientific subjects, encyclopaedias, classics; imprint of Hachette Livre; Pres. and Dir-Gen. PHILIPPE MERLET.

Editions J.-C. Lattès: 17 rue Jacob, 75006 Paris; tel. 1-44-41-74-00; fax 1-43-25-30-47; e-mail mpageix@editions-jclattes.fr; internet www.editions-jclattes.fr; f. 1968; imprint of Hachette Livre; general fiction and non-fiction, biography; Man. Dir ISABELLE LAFFONT.

Letouzey et Ané: 87 blvd Raspail, 75006 Paris; tel. 1-45-48-80-14; fax 1-45-49-03-43; e-mail letouzey@free.fr; f. 1885; theology, religion, archaeology, history, ecclesiastical encyclopaedias and dictionaries, biography; Man. Dir FLORENCE LETOUZEY.

LGDJ—Montchrestien: 31 rue Falguière, 75741 Paris Cédex 15; e-mail info@eja.fr; internet www.lgdj.fr; tel. 1-56-54-16-00; fax 1-56-54-16-49; f. 1836; law and economy; Chair. LIONEL GUÉRIN; Dir VINCENT MARTY.

Le Livre de Poche: 31 rue de Fleurus, 75006 Paris; tel. 1-49-54-37-00; fax 1-49-54-37-01; internet www.livredepoche.com; f. 1953; general literature, dictionaries, encyclopaedias; Gen.-Man. DOMINIQUE GOUST.

Editions Magnard: 20 rue Berbier-du-Mets, 75647 Paris Cédex 13; tel. 1-44-08-85-85; fax 1-44-08-49-79; e-mail contact@magnard.fr; internet www.magnard.fr; f. 1933; children's and educational books; subsidiary of Editions Albin Michel; Man. Dir JEAN-MANUEL BOURGOIS.

Masson Editeur: 120 blvd Saint Germain, 75006 Paris; tel. 1-40-46-60-00; fax 1-40-46-60-01; e-mail infos@masson.fr; internet www .masson.fr; f. 1804; medicine and science, books and periodicals; publrs for various academies and societies; subsidiary of Medimedia; Pres. GÉRARD KOUCHNER.

Mercure de France: 26 rue de Condé, 75006 Paris; tel. 1-55-42-61-90; fax 1-43-54-49-91; internet www.mercuredefrance.fr; f. 1893; general fiction, history, biography, sociology; Pres. and Man. Dir ISABELLE GALLIMARD; Editor NICOLAS BREHAL.

Editions de Minuit: 7 rue Bernard Palissy, 75006 Paris; tel. 1-44-39-39-20; fax 1-45-44-82-36; e-mail contact@leseditionsdeminuit.fr; internet www.leseditionsdeminuit.fr; f. 1945; general literature; Man. Dir IRÈNE LINDON.

Nathan Education: 9 rue Méchain, 75014 Paris; tel. 1-45-87-50-00; fax 1-47-07-57-57; internet www.nathan.fr; f. 1881; educational books for all levels; Chair. BERTRAND EVENO; Man. Dir JEAN-PAUL BAUDOIN.

Editions Payot-Rivages: 106 blvd Saint Germain, 75006 Paris; tel. 1-44-41-39-90; fax 1-44-41-39-69; e-mail payotrivages@wanadoo .com; f. 1917; literature, human sciences, philosophy; Chair. and Dir JEAN-FRANÇOIS LAMUNIÈRE.

A. et J. Picard: 82 rue Bonaparte, 75006 Paris; tel. 1-43-26-96-73; fax 1-43-26-42-64; e-mail livres@librairie-picard.com; internet www .abebooks.com/home/libpicard; f. 1869; archaeology, architecture, history of art, history, pre-history, auxiliary sciences, linguistics, musicological works, antiquarian books; Chair. and Man. Dir CHANTAL PASINI-PICARD.

Plon-Perrin: 76 rue Bonaparte, 75284 Paris Cédex 06; tel. 1-44-41-35-00; fax 1-44-41-35-01; e-mail stephane.billerey@plon-perrin.com; internet www.editions-perrin.fr; f. 1884; imprint of Editis; fiction, travel, history, anthropology, human sciences, biography; Chair. OLIVIER ORBAN.

Editions P.O.L: 33 rue Saint-André-des-Arts, 75006 Paris; tel. 1-43-54-21-20; fax 1-43-54-11-31; e-mail pol@pol-editeur.fr; internet www.pol-editeur.fr; literature; arts; Dir-Gen. PAUL OTCHAKOVSKI-LAURENS.

Presses de la Cité: 12 ave d'Italie, 75625 Paris Cédex 13; tel. 1-44-16-05-00; internet www.pressesdelacite.com; f. 1944; fiction and factual literature for general audience; Dir JEAN ARCACHE.

Presses de Sciences Po: 44 rue du Four, 75006 Paris; tel. 1-44-39-39-60; fax 1-45-48-04-41; e-mail info.presses@sciences-po.fr; internet www.sciences-po.fr/edition; f. 1975; history, politics, linguistics, economics, sociology; Dir MARIE-GENEVIÈVE VANDESANDE.

Presses Universitaires de France: 6 ave Reille, 75014 Paris; tel. 1-58-10-31-00; fax 1-58-10-31-80; e-mail info@puf.com; internet www.puf.com; f. 1921; philosophy, psychology, psychoanalysis, psychiatry, education, sociology, theology, history, geography, economics, law, linguistics, literature, science; Chair. MICHEL PRIGENT.

Presses Universitaires de Grenoble: Saint Martin-d'Héres, 38040 Grenoble Cédex 09; tel. 4-76-82-56-51; fax 4-76-82-78-35; e-mail pug@pug.fr; internet www.pug.fr; f. 1972; psychology, law, economics, management, history, statistics, literature, medicine, science, politics; Man. Dir BERNARD WIRBEL.

Presses Universitaires de Nancy: 42–44 ave de la Libération, BP 3347, 54014 Nancy Cédex; tel. 3-83-96-84-30; fax 3-83-96-84-39; e-mail pun@univ-nancy2.fr; internet www.univ-nancy2.fr/PUN; f. 1976; literature, history, law, social sciences, politics; Administrator EDWIGE HELMER.

Editions Privat: 10 rue des Arts, BP 828, 31080 Toulouse Cédex 06; tel. 5-34-31-81-81; fax 5-34-31-64-44; e-mail info@editions-privat .com; f. 1839; regional, national and international history, heritage, health; Dir PASCAL GALODÉ.

Le Serpent à Plumes: 20 rue des Petits Champs, 75002 Paris; tel. 1-55-35-95-85; fax 1-42-61-17-46; e-mail contact@serpentaplumes .com; internet www.serpentaplumes.com; f. 1993; acquired by Editions du Rocher in 2004; world literature; Dir PIERRE ASTIER.

Editions du Seuil: 27 rue Jacob, 75261 Paris Cédex 06; tel. 1-40-46-50-50; fax 1-40-46-43-00; e-mail contact@seuil.com; internet www .seuil.com; f. 1936; acquired by La Martinière in 2003; modern literature, fiction, illustrated books, non-fiction; Pres. CLAUDE CHERKI.

Editions du Signe: 1 rue Alfred Kastler, BP 94, Eckbolsheim, 67038 Strasbourg Cédex 02; tel. 3-88-78-91-91; fax 3-88-78-91-99; e-mail info@editionsdusigne.fr; internet www.editionsdusigne.fr; f. 1987; Christianity; Chair. and Man. Dir CHRISTIAN RIEHL.

Editions Stock: 31 rue de Fleurus, 75006 Paris; tel. 1-49-54-36-55; fax 1-49-54-36-62; e-mail hamalric@editions-stock.fr; internet www .editions-stock.fr; f. 1710; literature, translations, biography, human sciences, guides; Chair. and Editorial. Dir JEAN-MARC ROBERTS; Dir-Gen. HELENE AMALRIC.

Succès du Livre: 60 rue St André des Arts, 75006 Paris; tel. 1-43-29-82-82; fax 1-43-29-60-75; f. 1987; fiction, biography; Chair. JACQUES DOMAS.

Editions de la Table Ronde: 7 rue Corneille, 75006 Paris; tel. 1-43-26-03-95; fax 1-44-07-09-30; f. 1944; fiction, essays, religion, travel, theatre, youth; Pres. DENIS TILLINAC.

Editions Tallandier: 18 rue Dauphine, 75006 Paris; tel. 1-40-46-43-88; fax 1-40-46-43-98; e-mail atalland@st2.tallandier.fr; internet www.tallandier.com; f. 1865; history, reference; Dir HENRI BOVET.

Editions Vigot: 23 rue de l'Ecole de Médecine, 75006 Paris; tel. 1-43-29-54-50; fax 1-46-34-05-89; f. 1890; medicine, pharmacology, nature, veterinary science, sport, fitness, tourism, cookery; Chair. CHRISTIAN VIGOT; Man. Dir DANIEL VIGOT.

Librairie Philosophique J. Vrin: 6 place de la Sorbonne, 75005 Paris; tel. 1-43-54-03-47; fax 1-43-54-48-18; e-mail contact@vrin.fr; internet www.vrin.fr; f. 1911; university textbooks, philosophy, education, science, law, religion; Chair. and Man. Dir A. PAULHAC-VRIN.

Librairie Vuibert: 20 rue Berbier-du-Mets, 75647 Paris Cédex 13; tel. 1-44-08-49-00; fax 1-44-08-49-39; e-mail laurence.brunel@ vuibert.fr; internet www.vuibert.com; f. 1877; school and university textbooks, psychology, law; subsidiary of Editions Albin Michel.

PUBLISHERS' AND BOOKSELLERS' ASSOCIATIONS

Cercle de la Librairie (Syndicat des Industries et Commerces du Livre): 35 rue Grégoire de Tours, 75006 Paris Cédex; tel. 1-44-41-28-00; fax 1-44-41-28-40; f. 1847; a syndicate of the book trade, grouping the principal asscns of publishers, booksellers and printers; Chair. DENIS MOLLAT; Man. Dir JEAN-MARIE DOUBLET.

Chambre Syndicale des Editeurs de Musique de France: 4–6 place de la Bourse, 75080 Paris Cédex 02; tel. 1-44-88-73-74; fax 1-44-88-73-89; e-mail cemf@bmg.com; f. 1873; music publishers' asscn; Chair. BERNARD BROSSOLLET; Sec. NELLY QUEROL.

Chambre Syndicale de l'Edition Musicale (CSDEM): 62 rue Blanche, 75009 Paris; tel. 1-48-74-09-29; fax 1-42-81-19-87; e-mail csdem@club-internet.fr; internet www.csdem.org; f. 1978 by merger; music publishers.

Fédération Française Syndicale de la Librairie: 24 place de la République, 14100 Lisieux; tel. 2-31-62-16-87; fax 2-31-63-97-37; f. 1892; booksellers' asscn; Chair. COLETTE HEDOU.

Syndicat National de l'Edition: 115 blvd Saint-Germain, 75006 Paris; tel. 1-44-41-40-50; fax 1-44-41-40-77; internet www.sne.fr; f. 1892; publishers' asscn; 550 mems; Chair. SERGE EYROLLES; Man. Dir JEAN SARZANA.

Syndicat National de la Librairie Ancienne et Moderne: 4 rue Gît-le-Cœur, 75006 Paris; tel. 1-43-29-46-38; fax 1-43-25-41-63; e-mail slam-livre@wanadoo.fr; internet www.slam-livre.fr; f. 1914; booksellers' asscn; 220 mems; Pres. ALAIN MARCHISET.

Broadcasting and Communications

TELECOMMUNICATIONS

Regulatory Authorities

Agence Nationale des Fréquences (ANFR): 78 ave du Général de Gaulle, BP 400, 94704 Maisons-Alfort Cédex; tel. 1-45-18-72-72; fax 1-45-18-72-00; e-mail parmentier@anfr.fr; internet www.anfr.fr; Pres. JEAN-CLAUDE GUIGUET; Gen. Man. JEAN-MARC CHADUC.

Autorité de Régulation des Télécommunications (ART): 7 sq. Max Hymans, 75730 Paris Cédex 15; tel. 1-40-47-70-00; fax 1-40-47-71-98; internet www.art-telecom.fr; Pres. JEAN-MICHEL HUBERT; Gen. Man. JEAN MARIMBERT.

Direction des Postes et Télécommunications (DPT): 20 ave de Ségur, 75354 Paris 07; tel. 1-43-19-19-39; fax 1-43-19-63-00; e-mail emmanuel.gabla@industrie.gouv.fr; Dir PATRICK DE GUERRE.

Major Service Providers

Bouygues Telecom: Arcs de Seine, 20 quai du Point du Jour, 92100 Boulogne-Billancourt; tel. 8-10-63-01-00; internet www.bouygtel .com; f. 1994; mobile cellular telecommunications; Pres. PHILIPPE MONTAGNER; Dir-Gen. GILLES PÉLISSON.

Cegetel: 1 place Carpeaux, Tour Séquoia, 92915 Paris La Défense Cédex; tel. 1-71-07-07-07; fax 1-71-07-75-22; internet www .cegetel-entreprises.fr; f. 1996; Pres. and Dir-Gen. FRANK ESSER; Dir-Gen. OLIVIER HUART.

France Telecom: 6 place d'Alleray, 75505 Paris Cédex 15; tel. 1-44-44-22-22; fax 1-44-44-29-30; e-mail infos.groupe@francetelecom .com; internet www.francetelecom.fr; 42.2% state-owned, following privatization in 2004; acquired Orange (UK) in 2000; Chief Exec. DIDIER LOMBARD.

OrangeFrance: 41–45 blvd Romain Rolland, 92120 Montrouge; tel. 1-55-22-22-22; fax 1-55-22-25-50; internet www.orange.fr; f. 1992 as Itineris; present name adopted 2001; mobile cellular telecommunications; 19.2m. subscribers (Dec. 2002); Pres. THIERRY BRETON; Pres. and Dir-Gen. SANJIV AHUJA.

SFR: 1 place Carpeaux, Tour Séquoia, 92915 Paris La Défense Cédex; tel. 8-05-77-66-66; internet www.sfr.fr; f. 1993; mobile cellular telecommunications; Pres. and Dir-Gen FRANK ESSER; Dir-Gen. PIERRE BARDON; 13.5m. subscribers (Dec. 2002).

BROADCASTING

Conseil Supérieur de l'Audiovisuel (CSA): Tour Mirabeau, 39–43 quai André Citroën, 75739 Paris Cédex 15; tel. 1-40-58-38-00; fax 1-45-79-00-06; internet www.csa.fr; f. 1989 as replacement for the Commission Nationale de la Communication et des Libertés (CNCL); supervises all French broadcasting; awards licences to private radio and television stations, allocates cable networks and frequencies, appoints heads of state-owned radio and television cos, monitors programme standards; consists of nine members, appointed for six years: three nominated by the Pres. of the Republic; three by the Pres. of the National Assembly; and three by the Pres. of the Senate; Pres. DOMINIQUE BAUDIS; Gen. Man. DENIS RAPONE.

Institut National de l'Audiovisuel: 4 ave de l'Europe, 94366 Bry-sur-Marne Cédex; tel. 1-49-83-26-74; fax 1-49-83-23-89; e-mail dtixiergallix@ina.fr; internet www.ina.fr; f. 1975; research and professional training in the field of broadcasting; radio and TV archives, TV production; Publ. *Les Nouveaux Dossiers de l'Audiovisuel*; (6 a year); Pres. EMMANUEL HOOG.

Télédiffusion de France (TDF): 10 rue d'Oradour-sur-Glane, 75732 Paris Cédex 15; e-mail e-tdf@tdf.fr; internet www.tdf.fr; f. 1975; partly privatized 1987; restructured in 2002; responsible for broadcasting programmes produced by the production companies, for the organization and maintenance of the networks, for study and research into radio and television equipment; operates a cable television network; broadcasts digital terrestial television.

Radio

State-controlled Radio

Public radio services are provided by three entities: Radio France for the domestic audience; Réseau France Outre-Mer for the French overseas departments and territories; and Radio France Internationale for foreign countries (and those of foreign origin in France). Radio France began the digital broadcasting of certain of its channels in early 2000.

Société Nationale de Radiodiffusion (Radio France: 116 ave du Président Kennedy, 75786 Paris Cédex 16; tel. 1-56-40-29-07; fax 1-42-30-14-88; internet www.radio-france.fr; f. 1975; planning and production of radio programmes; provides five national services, 47 local stations and two European services; Chair. JEAN-PAUL CLUZEL; Man. Dir CLAUDE NOREK.

France Bleu: tel. 1-56-40-37-86; internet www.francebleu.com; f. 1980, restructured 2000; network of domestic services; for older people; Dir MICHEL MEYER.

France Culture: tel. 1-56-40-27-91; internet franceculture.com; domestic, nation-wide service; Dir LAURE ADLER.

France Culture Europe: European service, broadcast by TDF1/TDF2 satellite; cultural and information; Dir LAURE ADLER.

France-Info : tel. 1-56-40-20-43; internet www.france-info.com; domestic, nation-wide service; continuous news and information; f. 1987; Dir MICHEL POLACCO.

France Inter: tel. 1-56-40-37-57; internet www.franceinter.com; domestic, nation-wide service; general programmes, for entertainment and information; Dir GILLES SCHNEIDER.

France Musiques: tel. 1-56-40-36-12; internet www .francemusiques.com; domestic, nation-wide service; Dir THIERRY BEAUVERT.

Hector: tel. 1-56-40-31-83; internet www.rfhector.com; European service, broadcast by TDF1/TDF2 satellite; mainly classical music.

Le Mouv': tel. 5-62-30-70-16; internet www.lemouv.com; domestic, nation-wide service; music and general interest for people aged 18–35; f. 1997; Dir MARC GARCIA.

Réseau FIP: tel. 1-56-40-16-15; internet www.radiofrance.fr/ chaines/fip/radio; f. 1971; comprises nine local stations; continuous music; Dir DOMINIQUE PENSEC.

Radio France Internationale (RFI): 116 ave du Président Kennedy, BP 9516, 75786 Paris Cédex 16; tel. 1-56-40-12-12; fax 1-56-40-47-59; internet www.rfi.fr; f. 1975; broadcasts on MW and FM transmitters, mainly to Africa, Eastern Europe, North America, the Caribbean, South-East Asia and the Middle East, in French and 19 other languages; Pres.and Dir-Gen. ANTOINE SCHWARZ.

Réseau France Outre-mer (RFO): 35–37 rue Danton, 92240 Malakoff; tel. 1-55-22-71-00; fax 1-55-22-74-76; e-mail rfo@rfo.fr; internet www.rfo.fr; controls broadcasting in the French overseas territories; 10 local stations providing two radio networks, two television channels, the latter broadcasting material from various state and private channels as well as local programmes, and one satellite television channel; Pres. ANDRÉ-MICHEL BESSE.

Independent Radio

BFM: 12 rue d'Oradour sur Glane, 75015 Paris; tel. 1-71-19-11-81; fax 1-71-19-11-80; e-mail nrepa@radiobfm.com; internet www .radiobfm.com; f. 1992; broadcasts on cable and 14 FM frequencies; politics, economics; Pres. ALAIN WEILL.

Europe 1: 11 rue de Cambrai, 75945 Paris Cédex 19; tel. 1-53-35-72-60; e-mail courrier@europe1.fr; internet www.europe1.fr; owned by Groupe Lagardère, which also owns Europe 2 (for younger listeners) and RFM; broadcasting on long wave and 99 FM frequencies; Chair. ARNAUD LAGARDÈRE; Dir-Gen. JÉRÔME BELLAY.

Radio Monte-Carlo (RMC): 12 rue d'Oradour sur Glane, 75015 Paris; tel. 1-71-19-11-91; fax 1-71-19-11-90; internet www.rmcinfo .fr; broadcasting on long wave and 148 FM frequencies; information, talk and sports programmes; Pres. ALAIN WEILL.

RTL: 22 rue Bayard, 75008 Paris; tel. 1-40-70-40-70; fax 1-40-70-42-72; internet www.rtl.fr; broadcasting on long wave and 150 FM frequencies; Chair. and Man. Dir RÉMY SAUTTER.

Television

State-controlled Television

France Télévisions: 7 esplanade Henri de France, 75907 Paris; tel. 1-56-22-60-00; fax 1-47-20-24-54; internet www.francetelevisions.fr; f. 1992 as supervisory authority for the national public television networks (France 2, France 3 and France 5: see below); Pres. MARC TESSIER; Sec.-Gen. FRANÇOIS GUILBEAU.

France 2: 7 Esplanade Henri de France, 75907 Paris Cédex 15; tel. 1-56-22-42-42; e-mail contact@france2.fr; internet www .france2.fr; f. 1975; general programmes for a nation-wide audience; Pres. MARC TESSIER; Dir-Gen. CHRISTOPHER BALDELLI.

France 3 (F3): 7 Esplanade Henri de France, 75907 Paris Cédex 15; tel. 1-56-22-30-30; internet www.france3.fr; f. 1975 as France Régions 3 (FR3); general programmes for a nation-wide audience (with a larger proportion of cultural and educational programmes than F2), and regional programmes transmitted from 13 regional stations; Pres. MARC TESSIER; Dir-Gen. RÉMY PFLIMLIN.

France 5 (F5): 10 rue Horace Vernet, 92785 Issy-les-Moulineaux Cédex 09; tel. 1-56-22-93-93; e-mail telespectateurs@france5.fr; internet www.france5.fr; f. 1994 as La Cinquième; present name adopted 2002; educational programmes and documentaries; Pres. MARC TESSIER; Dir-Gen. DANIEL GOUDINEAU.

Arte France: 8 rue Marceau, 92785 Issy-les-Moulineaux Cédex 09; tel. 1-55-00-77-77; fax 1-55-00-77-00; internet www.arte-tv.com; f. 1992 to replace La Sept; arts, cultural programmes, in French and German; Pres. JÉRÔME CLÉMENT; Dir-Gen. JEAN ROZAT.

Television programmes for France's overseas departments and territories are provided by Réseau France Outre-mer (see under Radio).

Independent Television

Canal Plus: 85–89 quai André Citroën, 75711 Paris Cédex 15; tel. 1-44-25-10-00; fax 1-44-25-12-34; e-mail contact_web@cplus.fr; internet www.cplus.fr; f. 1984; 100% owned by Vivendi Universal; coded programmes financed by audience subscription; uncoded programmes financed by advertising sold by Canal Plus; specializes in drama (including cinema films) and sport; launched a 'pay-per-view' service for sports events 1996; produces 21 theme channels in six countries; Pres. and Dir-Gen BERTRAND MÉHEUT.

Demain!: 1 rue Patry, 92220 Bagneux; fax 1-45-36-889-01; internet www.demain.fr; e-mail v.schmidt@demain.fr; f. 1997; information about employment for job-seekers; Dir-Gen. JEAN-FRANÇOIS DION.

LCI (La Chaîne Info): 54 ave de la Voie Lactée, 92656 Boulogne-Billancourt Cédex; tel. 1-41-41-37-37; e-mail comm-lci@lci.fr; internet www.lci.fr; f. 1994; news, information; Pres. ETIENNE MOUGEOTTE; Dir-Gen. JEAN-CLAUDE DASSIER.

M6: 89 ave Charles de Gaulle, 92575 Neuilly-sur-Seine Cédex; tel. 1-41-92-66-66; fax 1-41-92-66-10; e-mail pholl@m6.fr; internet www.m6.fr; f. 1986 as TV6, re-formed as M6 1987; 46% owned by RTL Group, 37% by Groupe Suez; specializes in drama, music and magazines; Chair. of Bd JEAN DRUCKER; CEO NICOLAS DE TAVERNOST.

Télévision Française 1 (TF1): 1 quai du Point du Jour, 92656 Boulogne-Billancourt Cédex; tel. 1-41-41-12-34; fax 1-41-41-28-40; internet www.tf1.fr; f. 1975 as a state-owned channel, privatized 1987; 40.1% owned by Bouygues SA, 3.0% by Société Générale, and smaller percentages by other shareholders, including 2.4% by TF1 employees; general programmes; Pres. and Dir-Gen. PATRICK LE LAY.

Cable Television

Est Vidéocommunication: 26 blvd du Président Wilson, 67954 Strasbourg Cédex 9; tel. 3-88-76-44-60; fax 3-88-76-44-69; e-mail estvideo@evc.net; internet www.evc.net; f. 1988; 137,500 subscribers (2001); affiliated to Electricité de Strasbourg; Dir-Gen. FRANÇOIS HOLVECK.

France Télécom Cable: 3 rue Danton, 92240 Malakoff; tel. 1-55-58-34-00; fax 1-55-58-34-06; e-mail ftc.communication@wanadoo.fr; internet www.francetelecomcable.fr; f. 1993; 753,900 subscribers (1998); Chair. PATRICK PINOCHET.

NC Numéricâble: 12–16 rue Guynemer, 92445 Issy-les-Moulineaux; tel. 1-55-92-46-00; fax 1-55-92-46-90; e-mail communication@ncnumericable.com; internet www.ncnumericable.com; f. 1997; affiliated to Canal Plus; 602,937 subscribers (1998); Pres. BERNARD COTTIN; Dir-Gen. CHRISTIAN KOZAR.

Noos: 20 place des Vins de France, 75614 Paris Cédex 12; tel. 1-53-44-81-81; fax 1-53-44-80-98; e-mail webmaster@noos.com; internet www.noos.com; f. 1986 as Lyonnaise Communications; affiliated to Groupe Suez; 633,405 subscribers (1998); Chair. FRANÇOIS JACLOT; Dir-Gen. FRANÇOIS GUICHARD.

Finance

(cap. = capital; res = reserves; dep. = deposits; m. = million; brs = branches; amounts in euros)

BANKING

Central Bank

Banque de France: 1 rue la Vrillière, 75001 Paris; tel. 1-42-92-42-92; fax 1-42-92-45-00; internet www.banque-france.fr; f. 1800; nationalized 1946; became independent 1994; acts as banker to the Treasury, issues bank notes, controls credit and money supply and administers France's gold and currency assets; in 1993 the National Assembly approved legislation to make the Banque de France an independent central bank, with a General Council to supervise activities and appoint the principal officials, and a nine-member monetary policy committee, independent of government control, to be in charge of French monetary policy; a member of the European

System of Central Banks since June 1998; cap. and res 26,391.0m., dep. 31,501.0m., total assets 158,351.5m. (Dec. 2003); Gov. CHRISTIAN NOYER; First Dep. Gov. HERVÉ HANNOUN; Second Dep. Gov. JEAN-PAUL REDOUIN; 211 brs; restructuring and closure of 115 branches proposed in 2004–06.

State Savings Bank

Caisse des depôts et consignations: 56 rue de Lille, 75356 Paris Cédex 07; tel. 1-58-50-00-00; fax 1-58-50-02-46; internet www.caissedesdepots.fr; f. 1816; manages state savings system, holds widespread investments in industrial cos; res 11,959m., dep. 241,655m., total assets 379,506m. (Dec. 2003); Pres. and Dir-Gen FRANCIS MAYER; 1 br.

Other Savings Banks

Caisse d'Epargne Ile de France Paris: BP 9401, 19 rue du Louvre, 75021 Paris Cédex 01; tel. 1-40-41-30-31; fax 1-42-33-45-18; internet www.caisse-epargne.fr; f. 1818; cap. 266.6m., res 556.4m., dep. 24,364.3m. (Dec. 2003); Pres. NICOLE MOREAU; Chair. BERNARD COMOLET; 301 brs.

Caisse Nationale des Caisses d'Epargne et de Prevoyance (CNCEP): BP 540, 77 blvd Saint-Jacques, 75673 Paris Cédex 14; tel. 1-58-40-41-42; fax 1-58-40-48-00; internet www.caisse-epargne.com; f. 1999 by merger; 65% owned by Caisses d'Epargne, 35% by Caisse des Dépôts et Consignations; cap. 2,905m., res 1,013m., dep. 118,052m. (Dec. 2002); Chair., Supervisory Bd JACQUES MOUTON; Chair., Management Bd CHARLES MILHAUD.

Commercial Banks

Banca Intesa (France): 23 rue Linois, 75725 Paris Cédex 15; tel. 1-45-23-72-22; fax 1-45-23-70-90; e-mail hoff@bcif.fr; internet www.bcif.fr; f. 1918 as Banca Commerciale Italiana (France); present name adopted 2003; 99.99% owned by IntesaBci SpA (Italy); cap. 160.3m, res 54.8m., dep. 1,627.2m. (Dec. 2003); Chair. GENNAZO STAMMATI; Gen. Man. EUGENIO GUICCIARDI.

Banque AGF: 87 rue de Richelieu, 75002 Paris; tel. 1-53-24-48-48; fax 1-53-24-48-41; e-mail serviceclient@banqueagf.fr; internet www.banqueagf.fr; f. 1991 by merger as Banque du Phénix; affiliated to Group Allianz; cap. 202.0m. (Dec. 2001); Pres. PHILIPPE TOUSSAINT.

Banque de Bretagne: 18 quai Duguay-Trouin, 35084 Rennes Cédex; tel. 2-99-01-75-75; fax 2-99-01-75-00; internet www.banque-de-bretagne.com; f. 1909; 100% owned by BNP Paribas; cap. 52.9m., res 13.6m., dep. 1,408.9m. (Dec. 2003); Pres. GERARD UZEL; 70 brs.

Banque CIAL—Crédit Industriel d'Alsace et de Lorraine (CIC Banque CIAL): 31 rue Jean Wenger-Valentin, 67000 Strasbourg; tel. 3-88-37-61-23; fax 3-88-37-71-81; internet www.banquecial.fr; f. 1919; 99.99% owned by Crédit Industriel et Commercial; cap. 26.8m., dep. 13,009m., total assets 58,363m. (Dec. 2003); Chair. PHILIPPE VIDAL; Gen. Man. PIERRE JACHEZ; 151 brs and sub-brs.

Banque Commerciale pour l'Europe du Nord—Eurobank (BCEN—Eurobank): 79–81 blvd Haussmann, 75382 Paris Cédex 08; tel. 1-40-06-43-21; fax 1-40-06-48-48; f. 1921; present name adopted 1972; 87% owned by Central Bank of the Russian Federation; cap. 185.3m., res −110.6m., dep. 418.3m. (Dec. 2003); Chair. KONSTANTIN KORISCHENKO.

Banque Commerciale pour le Marché de l'Entreprise: 32 rue Mirabeau, 29480 Le Relecq-Kerhuon Cédex; tel. 2-98-34-68-80; fax 2-98-43-83-03; e-mail contacts@bcme.fr; f. 1985; present name adopted 2000; cap. 120.0m., res 14.5m., dep. 2,310.4m. (Dec. 2003); Pres. MARCEL GARNIER; Dir-Gen. GILBERT RICHARD.

Banque de l'Economie du Commerce et de la Monétique: 34 rue du Wacken, 67913 Strasbourg Cédex 9; tel. 3-88-14-74-74; fax 3-88-14-75-10; e-mail becm@becm.creditmutuel.fr; internet www.becm.fr; f. 1992 as Banque de l'Economie—Crédit Mutuel; cap. 219.5m., dep. 1,010.2m. (Dec. 2003), total assets 5,716.7m. (Dec. 2001); Chief Exec. BERNARD BARTELMANN; 34 brs.

Banque Espírito Santo et de la Vénétie: 45 ave Georges Mandel, 75116 Paris; tel. 1-44-34-48-00; fax 1-44-34-48-48; e-mail besv@besv.fr; internet www.besv.fr; f. 1945; present name adopted 1998; absorbed Via Banque in 2002; 42% owned by Espirito Santo Financial Group SA (Luxembourg); cap. 52.2m., res 10.5m., dep. 1,673.1m. (Dec. 2003); Chair. CHRISTIAN MENARD.

Banque Fédérative du Crédit Mutuel: 34 rue du Wacken, 67000 Strasbourg; tel. 3-88-14-88-14; fax 3-88-14-67-00; internet www.bfcm.creditmutuel.fr; f. 1895; cap.1,302.2m., res 2,187.5m., dep. 170,306.2m. (Dec. 2003); Pres. and Chair. ETIENNE PFLIMLIN; Dir-Gen. MICHEL LUCAS; 16 brs.

Banque Hervet: 1 Place de la Préfecture, 18004 Bourges; tel. 1-57-66-52-58; fax 1-57-66-52-51; e-mail marketing@banque-hervet.fr; internet www.banque-hervet.fr; f. 1830; 97.9% owned by CCF; dep.

1,854m., total assets 5,266m. (Dec. 2000); Chair.of Bd and Pres. FRANÇOIS MORLAT; CEO FLORENT LE GRELLE; 86 brs.

Banque Intercontinentale Arabe: 67 ave Franklin D. Roosevelt, 75008 Paris; tel. 1-53-76-62-62; fax 1-42-89-09-59; e-mail contact@ bia-paris.fr; internet www.bia-paris.fr; f. 1975; 50% owned by Banque Extérieure d'Algérie, 50% by Libyan Arab Foreign Bank; cap. 158.1m., res 2.4m., dep. 430.2m. (Dec. 2003); Pres. MOHAMED TERBECHE.

Banque Nationale de Paris Intercontinentale: 1 rue Taitbout, 75009 Paris; tel. 1-40-14-22-11; fax 1-40-14-69-34; internet www .bnpgroup.com; f. 1940; present name adopted 1972; 100% owned by BNP Paribas; cap. 30.5m., res. 4.0m., dep. 679.7m. (Dec. 2003); Chair.and CEO JEAN-JACQUES SANTINI.

Banque de Neuflize (Banque NSMD): 3 ave Hoche, 75008 Paris; tel. 1-56-21-70-00; fax 1-56-21-84-60; e-mail webmaster@fr.abnamro .com; internet www.banquedeneuflize.fr; f. 1966 by merger; became Banque de Neuflize, Schlumberger, Mallet, Demachy in 1999; name changed as above April 2004; 96.5% owned by ABN AMRO France; cap. 197.2m., res 103.6m., dep. 4,971.2m. (Dec. 2002); Pres. and Chair. Man. Bd JEAN-LOUIS MILIN; 18 brs.

Banque de Réescompte et de Placement (BAREP): 3 rue Lafayette, 75009 Paris; tel. 1-53-32-90-00; fax 1-53-32-90-19; internet www.barep.com; f. 1974; 100% owned by Société Générale; cap. 10.7m., res 28.7m., dep. 6,865.0m. (Dec. 2001); CEO SERGE MERVAUD; Dir-Gen. LAURENT BERHOLET-THOMAS.

Banque OBC—Odier Bungener Courvoisier: 57 ave d'Iéna, BP 195, 75783 Paris Cédex 16; tel. 1-45-02-40-00; fax 1-45-00-77-79; e-mail severine.cheyppe@fr.abnamro.com; internet www.obc.fr; f. 1960 by merger; present name adopted 1987; 99.99% owned by ABN AMRO France; cap. 60.0m., res 12.3m., dep. 900.1m. (Dec. 2002); Chair. and Chief Exec. MAGGIEL SCALOGNE.

Banque Régionale de l'Ouest: BP 49, 7 rue Gallois, 41003 Blois; tel. 2-54-56-54-56; fax 2-54-56-54-00; e-mail brostoi@bro.cic.fr; internet www.bro.fr; f. 1913; 100% owned by Crédit Industriel et Commercial; cap. 34.8m., res 57.1m., dep. 2,221.2m. (Dec. 2003); Chair. MICHEL MICHENKO; Dir-Gen JEAN-PIERRE BICHON; 95 brs.

Banque Sanpaolo: 52 ave Hoche, 75008 Paris Cédex 08; tel. 1-47-54-40-22; fax 1-47-54-47-91; e-mail info@sanpaolo.fr; internet www .sanpaolo.fr; f. 1971 by merger; 60% owned by Caisse Nationale des Caisses d'Epargne et de Prevoyance, 40% owned by Sanpaolo IMI SpA (Italy); cap. 350.0m., res 38.9m., dep. 6,227.0m. (Dec. 2003); Chair.of Bd. and Pres NICOLAS MERINDOL; 60 brs.

Banque Scalbert-Dupont: 33 ave le Corbusier, BP 567, 59800 Lille; tel. 3-20-12-64-64; fax 3-20-12-64-05; e-mail bsdinter@bsd.cic .fr; internet www.bsd.tm.fr; f. 1977 by merger; 100% owned by Crédit Industriel et Commercial; cap. 101.6m., res 140.6m., dep. 4,708.2m. (Dec. 2003); Chair. GÉRARD ROMEDEMME; Gen. Man. STELLI PREMAIR; 146 brs.

Banque Sudameris: 4 rue Meyerbeer, 75009 Paris; tel. 1-48-01-77-77; fax 1-42-46-32-13; e-mail webmaster@sudameris.com; internet www.sudameris.com; f. 1910; present name adopted 1978; holding bank; cap. 545.2m., res 1,117.8m., dep. 16,500.9m. (Dec. 2001); active principally in South America; Chair. L. BENASSI.

Banque Worms: Le Voltaire, 1 place des Degrés, Puteaux, 92059 Paris La Défense Cédex; tel. 1-49-07-50-50; fax 1-49-07-59-11; internet www.banque-worms.fr; f. 1928; 100% owned by Deutsche Bank; cap. 335.3m., res −87.5m., dep. 4,250.1m. (Dec. 2000); Chair. JÉRÔME MEYSSONNIER; 18 brs.

Barclays Bank PLC France: 183 ave Daumesnil, 75575 Paris Cédex 12; tel. 1-55-78-78-78; fax 1-55-78-70-00; e-mail contact.fr@ barclays.co.uk; internet www.barclays.fr; f. 1968; subsidiary of Barclays Bank PLC (United Kingdom); Gen. Man. PASCAL ROCHE; 43 brs.

BNP Paribas: 16 blvd des Italiens, 75009 Paris; tel. 1-40-14-45-46; fax 1-40-14-69-40; internet www.bnpparibas.com; f. 2000 by merger of Banque Nationale de Paris and Paribas; cap. 1,806m., res 22,754m., dep. 484,976m. (Dec. 2003); Pres. MICHEL PÉBEREAU; Dir-Gen. BAUDOIN PROT.

CCF: 103 ave des Champs Elysées, 75419 Paris Cédex 08; tel. 1-40-70-70-40; fax 1-40-70-70-09; internet www.ccf.com; 99.99% owned by HSBC Bank PLC (United Kingdom); f. 1894; fmrly Crédit Commercial de France; present name adopted 2002; cap. 371.8m., res 2,056.3m., dep. 46,153.3m. (Dec. 2003); Chair. and CEO CHARLES DE CROISSET; 184 brs in France.

Cetelem: 5 ave Kléber, 75116 Paris; tel. 1-55-43-55-43; fax 1-55-43-55-30; internet www.cetelem.fr; f. 1953; cap. 340.0m., res 1,412.7m., dep. 22,215.1m. (Dec. 2003); Chair., Supervisory Bd BERNARD MÜLLER; Exec. Chair., Management Bd MARC MANGEZ.

Compagnie Financière Edmond de Rothschild Banque: 47 rue du Faubourg Saint Honoré, 75401 Paris Cédex 08; tel. 1-40-17-25-25; fax 1-40-17-24-02; internet www.lcf-rothschild.fr; f. 1971; present name adopted 1986; cap. 68.6m., res 92.9m., dep. 1,912.2m.

(Dec. 2002); Chair., Exec. Bd MICHEL CICUREL; Dir-Gen. GUY GRYM-BERG.

CPR: 30 rue Saint Georges, 75312 Paris Cédex 09; tel. 1-45-96-20-00; fax 1-45-96-25-55; e-mail dircom@cpr.fr; internet www.cpr.fr; f. 1928 as Compagnie Parisienne de Réescompte; present name adopted 1997; discount bank; 88.53% owned by Crédit Agricole Indosuez; cap. 93.9m., res 350.7m., dep. 6,538.2m. (Dec. 2000); Chair. ROBERT RAYMOND; Gen. Man. ALEC DE LEZARDIÈRE; 2 brs.

Calyon (Calyon Corporate and Investment Bank): 9 quai Paul Doumer, 92920 Paris La Défense Cédex; tel. 1-41-89-00-00; fax 1-41-89-15-22; internet www.calyon.com; f. 1975 as Banque Indosuez, subsequently Crédit Agricole Indosuez; name changed to above 2004 following transfer of Crédit Lyonnais Corporate and Investment Banking Division to Crédit Agricole Insdosuez; 100% owned by Crédit Lyonnais from June 2003; merchant and offshore banking; cap. 1,137.0m., res 1,846.0m., dep. 122,507.0m. (Dec. 2002); Pres. JEAN LAURENT; 13 brs in France, 44 outside France.

Crédit Foncier de France: 19 rue des Capucines, 75001 Paris Cédex 01; tel. 1-42-44-80-00; fax 1-42-44-86-99; e-mail communication@creditfoncier.fr; internet www.creditfoncier.fr; f. 1852; 90.6% owned by Caisses d'Epargne et de Prévoyance; mortgage banking; cap. 394.8m., res 405.6m., dep. 42,151.7m. (Dec. 2003); Gov. FRANÇOIS LEMASSON.

Crédit Industriel et Commercial (CIC): 6 ave de Provence, 75452 Paris Cédex 09; tel. 1-45-96-96-96; fax 1-45-96-96-66; internet www.cic-banques.fr; f. 1990 by merger; present name adopted 2000; 70.47% owned by Banque Fédérative du Crédit Mutuel; cap. 563m., res 3,207m., dep. 123,295m. (Dec. 2003); Pres. ETIENNE PFIMLIN; Chair. MICHEL LUCAS.

Crédit Industriel de Normandie (Banque CIN): BP 3026X, 15 place de la Pucelle d'Orléans, 76041 Rouen; tel. 2-35-08-64-00; fax 2-35-08-64-38; internet www.cin.fr; f. 1932; 100% owned by Crédit Industriel et Commercial; cap. 100.0m., res 16.7m., dep. 2,541.2m. (Dec. 2003); Chair. GÉRARD ROMEDENNE; Gen. Man. STELLI PREMAOR; 7 brs and 71 sub-brs.

Crédit Industriel de l'Ouest (Banque CIO): BP 84001, 2 ave Jean-Claude Bonduelle, 44040 Nantes Cédex 1; tel. 2-40-12-91-91; fax 2-40-12-92-07; e-mail cio-international@cio.cic.fr; internet www .cio.fr; f. 1957; 100% owned by Crédit Industriel et Commercial; cap. 56.7m., res 241.4m., dep. 6,880.7m. (Dec. 2003); Chair. MICHEL MICHENKO; Man. Dir GÉRARD GOULET; 13 brs and 181 sub-brs.

Crédit Lyonnais: 19 blvd des Italiens, 75002 Paris; tel. 1-42-95-70-00; fax 1-42-95-33-24; internet www.creditlyonnais.fr; f. 1863; privatized 1999; acquired Crédit Agricole in June 2003; cap. 3,978m., res 4,401m., dep. 179,751m. (Dec. 2003); Chair.of Bd JEAN LAURENT; Chief Exec. GEORGES PAUGET; 2,100 brs.

Crédit du Nord: 28 place Rihour, BP 569, 59800 Lille Cédex; tel. 1-40-22-40-22; fax 3-20-57-74-05; internet www.credit-du-nord.fr; f. 1974 by merger; 80% owned by Société Générale; cap. 740.3m., res 248.5m., dep. 18,478.6m. (Dec. 2003); Pres. ALAIN PY; Gen. Man. BERNARD BEAUFILS; 614 brs.

Entenial: 33–37 blvd Vauban, Guyancourt, 78066 St Quentin-en-Yvelines Cédex; tel. 1-39-41-10-10; fax 1-39-41-10-55; internet www .entenial.com; f. 2000 by merger of Banque La Henin, COCEFI and Comptoir de Banque; 98.66% owned by Crédit Foncier de France; cap. 180.5m., res 190.9m., dep. 13,391.6m. (Dec. 2003); Pres. JACQUES LEBHAR.

Fortis Banque France: 29–30 Quai de Dion Bouton, 92824 Puteaux; tel. 1-55-67-89-00; e-mail courrier@fr.fortisbanque.com; internet www.fr.fortisbank.com; f. 1920; 99.94% owned by Fortis Bank (Belgium); cap. 35.2m., res 180.4, dep. 3,922.2m. (Dec. 2003); Pres. and Chair. of Bd LUCAS WILLEMYNS; 87 brs.

HSBC Private Bank France: 20 Place Vendôme, 75332 Paris Cédex 07; tel. 1-44-86-18-61; fax 1-42-60-05-62; f. 1966; 100% owned by HSBC Holdings plc; present name adopted 2003, following merger of HSBC Bank France with three other private banking entities of CCF Group; Chair. GÉRARD DE BARTILLAT.

ING Bank (France): Cœur Défense A, La Défense 4, 110 Esplanade Général de Gaulle, 92931 Paris La Défense Cédex; tel. 1-56-39-39-39; internet www.ingbank.fr; f. 1953; present name adopted 2000; 100% owned by ING Belgium; cap. 320.0m., res 166.7m., dep. 3,156.8m. (Dec. 2003); Chair. LUC VANDWALLE; 1 br.

Lyonnaise de Banque: 8 rue de la République, 69001 Lyon; tel. 4-78-92-02-12; fax 4-78-92-03-00; e-mail ddi@lb.cicomore.fr; internet www.l-b.fr; f. 1865; 100% owned by Crédit Industriel et Commercial; cap. 228.3m., res 265.9m., dep. 11,442.7m. (Dec. 2003); Chair. and Chief Exec. RÉMY WEBER; 368 brs.

Natexis Banques Populaires: 45 rue Saint-Dominique, 75007 Paris; tel. and fax 1-58-32-30-00; internet www.nxbp .banquepopulaire.fr; f. 1999; 73% owned by Banque Fédérale des

Banques Populaires; cap. 769m., res 2,879m., dep. 93,308m. (Dec. 2003); Chair. PHILIPPE DUPONT; Chief Exec. FRANÇOIS LADAM.

Société Bordelaise de CIC: 42 cours du Chapeau Rouge, 33000 Bordeaux; tel. 5-57-85-55-00; fax 5-57-85-57-50; internet www.sb.cic .fr; f. 1880; 100% owned by Crédit Industrial et Commercial; cap. 84.3m., res 25.3m., dep. 2,699.3m. (Dec. 2003); Chair. and Dir-Gen. JEAN-JACQUES TAMBURINI; 93 brs.

Société Générale: Tour Société Générale, 17 Cours Valmy, 92972 Paris La Défense; tel. 1-42-14-20-00; fax 1-40-98-20-99; internet www.socgen.com; f. 1864; cap. 548m., res 13,837m., dep. 365,442m. (Dec. 2003); Chair. and Chief Exec. DANIEL BOUTON; 2,000 brs in France.

Société Marseillaise de Crédit: 75 rue Paradis, 13006 Marseille; tel. 4-91-13-33-33; fax 4-91-13-55-15; e-mail infos@smc.fr; internet www.smc.fr; f. 1865; 96.99% owned by Compagnie Financière Ile du Rhône; cap. 16.0m., res 104.6m., dep. 2,672.5m. (Dec. 2003); Chair. JOSEPH PEREZ; CEO EMMANUEL BARTHELEMY; 160 brs.

Société Nancéienne Varin-Bernier (CIC Banque SNVB): 4 place André Maginot, 54074 Nancy; tel. 3-83-34-50-00; fax 3-83-34-50-99; e-mail snvbinter@snvb.cic.fr; internet www.snvb.fr; f. 1881; 100% owned by Crédit Industriel et Commercial; cap. 60.0m., res 222.4m., dep. 7,342.0m. (Dec. 2003); Chair. PHILIPPE VIDAL; Gen. Man. LUC DYMARSKI; 148 brs.

Union de Banques à Paris: 184 ave Frédéric et Irène Joliot Curie, 92729 Nanterre Cédex; tel. 1-57-66-60-00; fax 1-57-66-67-17; internet www.ubp.fr; f. 1935; 99.4% owned by Crédit Industriel et Commercial; cap. 51.0, res 29.8, dep. 1,830.4 (Dec. 2001); Chair. PIERRE JAMMES; Chief Exec. and Gen. Man. JEAN-FRANÇOIS LE TREIS; 55 brs.

Union de Banques Arabes et Françaises (UBAF): 190 ave Charles de Gaulle, 92523 Neuilly-sur-Seine; tel. 1-46-40-61-01; fax 1-47-38-13-88; e-mail info@ubafrance.com; internet www.ubaf.fr; f. 1970; 43.9% owned by Crédit Lyonnais, 56.1% by Arab interests; commercial, Islamic and merchant banking; cap. 228.3m., res 104.9m., dep. 1,608.9m. (Dec. 2003); Chair. PATRICK LEGAIT.

Co-operative Banks

Banque Populaire d'Alsace: BP 401 R/1, 5–7 rue du 22 novembre, 67001 Strasbourg; tel. 3-88-62-77-11; fax 3-88-62-70-35; internet www.alsace.banquepopulaire.fr; f. 2003 by merger of Banque Populaire de la Région Economique de Strasbourg and Banque Populaire du Haut Rhin; cap. 159.7m., res 153.5m., dep. 3,808.5m. (Dec. 2003); Pres. THIERRY CAHN; Dir-Gen. DOMINIQUE DIDON; 94 brs.

Banque Populaire Bourgogne Franche-Comté: 14 blvd de la Trémouille, BP 310, 21008 Dijon Cédex; tel. 8-20-33-75-00; fax 8-20-20-36-20; internet www.bpbfc.banquepopulaire.fr; f. 2002 by merger of Banque Populaire de Bourgogne and Banque Populaire de Franche-Comté, du Mâconnais et de l'Ain; cap. 151.1m., res 236.4m., dep. 5,772.5m. (Dec. 2003); Pres. JEAN-PHILIPPE GIRARD; Dir-Gen. BERNARD JEANNIN; 151 brs.

Banque Populaire de la Côte d'Azur (BPCA): BP 241, 457 Promenade des Anglais, 06024 Nice; tel. 4-93-21-52-00; fax 4-93-21-54-45; e-mail contact@cotedazur.banquepopulaire.fr; internet www .cotedazur.banquepopulaire.fr; f. 1986; cap. 66.9m., res 54.6m., dep. 2,627.8m. (Dec. 2002); Pres BERNARD FLEURY; Gen. Man. JEAN-FRANÇOIS COMAS; 67 brs.

Banque Populaire Loire et Lyonnais: 141 rue Garibaldi, 69003 Lyon; tel. 4-89-95-55-55; fax 4-78-71-03-99; e-mail contact@bp21 .banquepopulaire.fr; internet www.loirelyonnais.banquepopulaire .fr; f. 2000 by merger of Banque Populaire de Lyon and Banque Populaire de la Loire; cap. 149.5m., res 124.7m., dep. 3,264.1m. (Dec. 2003); Chair. HENRÉ GENTY; Gen.-Man. DANIEL DUQUESNE.

Banque Populaire du Massif Central: BP 53, 18 blvd Jean Moulin, 63002 Clermont-Ferrand; tel. 4-73-23-46-23; fax 4-73-23-47-99; internet www.massifcentral.banquepopulaire.fr; f. 1920; cap. 90.8m., res 94.0m., dep. 1,988.9m. (Dec. 2002); Chair. of Bd PHILIPPE HOSPIÇAL; Gen. Man. CHRISTIAN DU PAYRAT.

Banque Populaire du Sud-Ouest: 5 place Jean Jaurès, BP 516, 33000 Bordeaux; tel. 5-56-01-86-86; fax 5-56-48-99-39; internet www.sudouest.banquepopulaire.fr; f. 1920; cap. 68.4m., res 69.2m., dep. 2,067.9m. (Dec. 2002); Chair. JEAN-LOUIS D'ANGLADE.

BRED Banque Populaire: 18 quai de la Rapée, 75604 Paris Cédex 12; tel. 1-48-98-60-00; fax 1-40-04-71-57; e-mail webmaster@bred.fr; internet www.bred.fr; f. 1919; present name adopted 1994; cap. 220.0m., res 444.3m., dep. 17,354.8m. (Dec. 2003); Chair. STEVE GENTILI; Gen. Man. and CEO JEAN MICHEL LATY; 244 brs (including 52 in the French Overseas).

Caisse Centrale du Crédit Mutuel: 88–90 rue Cardinet, 75847 Paris Cédex 17; tel. 1-44-01-10-10; fax 1-44-01-12-30; internet www .creditmutuel.fr; f. 1963; central organization of 16 autonomous banks (Caisses Fédérales); cap. 101.5m., res 110.9m., dep.

8,276.9m.m. (Dec. 2003); Chair. ETIENNE PFIMLIN; Gen.-Man. MICHEL LUCAS.

Compagnie Financière du Crédit Mutuel (CFCM): 32 rue Mirabeau, 29480 Le Relecq-Kerhuon; tel. 2-98-00-22-22; fax 2-98-60-27-24; e-mail pierrette.jouanique@cfcm.fr; internet www.cmb.fr; f. 1960; present name adopted 2001; 100% owned by Caisse Inter-federale de Credit Mutuel; cap. 715.0m., res 178.3m., dep. 12,731.4m. (Dec. 2003); Chair. CHRISTIAN TOUZALIN; Exec. Man.-Dir LOUIS ECHELARD; 300 brs.

Crédit Agricole: 91–93 blvd Pasteur, 75015 Paris; tel. 1-43-23-52-02; fax 1-43-23-20-28; internet www.credit-agricole.fr; f. 1920; central institution for co-operative banking group comprising 53 Caisses Regionales and a central bank (CNCA); emphasis on agribusiness; 52% acquired by Crédit Lyonnais in June 2003; cap. 4,418m., res 18,127m., dep. 526,899m. (Dec. 2003); Pres. RENÉ CARRON; Chief Exec. JEAN LAURENT; 7,971 brs.

Crédit Coopératif: BP 211, 33 rue des Trois Fontanot, 92002 Nanterre; tel. 1-47-24-85-00; fax 1-47-24-89-25; e-mail din@coopanet .com; internet www.credit-cooperatif.coop; f. 1893; present name adopted 2001; merged with Caisse Centrale de Crédit Coopératif in October 2003; cap. 190.4m., res 118.8m., dep. 6,258.8m. (Dec. 2003); Chair JEAN-CLAUDE DETILLEUX; Dir-Gen. PIERRE LAJUGIE; 63 brs.

Investment Banks

Caisse Centrale de Réescompte (CCR): 44 rue Washington, 75008 Paris; tel. 1-49-53-20-00; fax 1-42-25-60-48; internet www .groupe-ccr.com; f. 1938; cap. 108.2m., res 57.0m., dep. 3,099.4m. (Dec. 2003); 97.5% owned by Commerzbank AG (Germany); Chair., Supervisory Bd KLAUS PATIG; Chair., Management Bd DANIEL TERMINET.

Dresdner Bank Gestions France: 108 blvd Haussmann, 75008 Paris; tel. 1-44-70-80-80; fax 1-42-93-03-30; e-mail webmaster-paris@dresdner-bank.de; f. 1979; fmrly Dresdner Kleinwort Benson (Marchés); present name adopted 2001; Chair. ALEXIS PILLET-WILL; Dir KONSTANTIN VON SCHWEINITZ.

Supervisory Body

Association Française des Etablissements de Crédit (AFEC): 36 rue Taitbout, 75009 Paris; tel. 1-48-24-34-34; fax 1-48-24-13-31; f. 1983; advises Govt on monetary and credit policy and supervises the banking system; Pres. MICHEL FREYCHE; Gen. Man. ROBERT PELLETIER.

Banking Association

Fédération Bancaire Française: 18 rue La Fayette, 75440 Paris Cédex 09; tel. 1-48-00-52-52; fax 1-42-46-76-40; e-mail fbf@fbf.fr; internet www.fbf.fr; f. 1941; 430 mems; Pres. DANIEL BOUTON; Dir-Gen. ARIANE OBOLENSKY.

STOCK EXCHANGES

The Paris Stock Exchange (Bourse) was established in 1725. There are provincial exchanges at Bordeaux, Lille, Lyon, Marseille, Nancy and Nantes. During the 1980s the Paris Bourse underwent extensive changes and deregulation and a fully computerized clearing and settlement system, called Relit, was installed. The reforms allowed member firms to open their capital to banks, insurance companies and other financial institutions.

In September 2000 Euronext, the largest stock exchange in the euro zone, was formed by the merger of the stock exchanges of Paris (Bourse de Paris), Brussels, Belgium (Brussels Exchanges) and Amsterdam, the Netherlands (Amsterdam Exchanges); in February 2002 the Bolsa de Valores de Lisboa e Porta in Lisbon, Portugal, merged with Euronext, and adopted the name Euronext Lisbonne and Euronext acquired LIFFE (London International Financial Futures and Options Exchange).

Euronext Paris: 39 rue Cambon, 75001 Paris; tel. 1-49-27-10-00; fax 1-49-27-14-33; e-mail d.lande@euronext.fr; internet www .euronext.fr; Pres. and Dir-Gen. JEAN-FRANÇOIS THÉODORE.

Marché à Terme International de France (MATIF): 39 rue Cambon, 75001 Paris; tel. 1-49-27-10-00; fax 1-49-27-11-15; e-mail n.devilaine@euronext.fr; internet www.matif.fr; f. 1986; financial and commodities futures exchange.

Le Marché des Options Négociables de Paris (MONEP): 39 rue Cambon, 75001 Paris; e-mail monep@euronext.com; internet www.monep.fr; f. 1987; derivatives and options trading.

Stock Exchange Associations

Autorité des Marchés Financiers (AMF): 17 place de la Bourse, 75082 Paris Cédex 2; tel. 1-53-45-60-00; fax 1-53-45-61-00; e-mail centrededoc@amf-france.org; internet www.amf-france.org; f. 2003 by merger of Commission des Opérations de Bourse and Conseil des Marchés Financiers; 330 mems; Pres. MICHEL PRADA; Sec.-Gen. GÉRARD RAMEIX.

Fédération Française des Clubs d'Investissement (FFCI): 39 rue Cambon, 75001 Paris; tel. 1-42-60-12-47; fax 1-42-60-10-14; e-mail info@clubinvestissement.com; internet www .clubinvestissement.com; f. 1968; fmrly Fédération Nationale des Associations de Clubs d'Investissement (FNACI); represents investment clubs in matters concerning public and political institutions; Pres. DOMINIQUE LEBLANC; Sec.-Gen. ALDO SICURANI.

INSURANCE

Assurances du Crédit Mutuel IARD, SA: BP 373 R 10, 34 rue du Wacken, 67010 Strasbourg Cédex; tel. 3-88-14-90-90; fax 3-88-14-90-01; internet www.creditmutuel.fr; Pres. MICHEL LUCAS; Dir ALAIN SCHMITTER.

Assurances Générales de France (AGF): 87 rue de Richelieu, 75002 Paris Cédex 02; tel. 1-44-86-20-00; fax 1-44-86-27-90; internet www.agf.fr; f. 1968 by merger; affiliated to Groupe Allianz (Germany); insurance and reinsurance; Pres. JEAN-PHILIPPE THIERRY; Dirs-Gen. LAURENT MIGNON, FRANÇOIS THOMAZEAU, LOUIS DE MONTFERRAND, JEAN-FRANÇOIS LEQUOY.

Aviva: 52 rue de la Victoire, 75009 Paris; e-mail veronique_eriaud@ aviva.fr; internet www.aviva.fr; f. 1998 as CGU France by merger to incorporate fmr Abeille Assurances; present name adopted 2002; affiliated to CGNU Group (United Kingdom); Pres. BRUNO ROSTAIN.

AXA Assurances IARD: 21 rue de Châteaudun, 75441 Paris Cédex 09; tel. 1-53-21-16-00; fax 1-53-21-17-96; internet www.axa.com; Chair. of Supervisory Bd CLAUDE BÉBÉAR; Chair. of Management Bd HENRI DE CASTRIES.

Caisse Centrale des Assurances Mutuelles Agricoles: 8 rue d'Astorg, 75383 Paris Cédex 08; tel. 1-44-56-77-77; fax 1-44-56-79-46; internet www.groupama.com; affiliated to Groupama; Dir STÉPHANE GIN.

Caisse Nationale de Prévoyance-Assurances (CNP): 4 place Raoul Dautry, 75716 Paris Cédex 15; tel. 1-42-18-88-88; fax 1-42-34-70-14; internet www.cnp.fr; general insurance; Pres GILLES BENOIST, EDMOND ALPHANDERY.

Cardif: 4 rue des Frères Caudron, 92858 Rueil-Malmaison Cédex; tel. 1-41-42-83-00; fax 1-41-42-84-17; internet www.cardif.fr; general insurance; Pres. PAUL VILLEMAGNE; Dir-Gen ERIC LOMBARD.

Ecureuil Vie: 5 rue Masseran, 75007 Paris; tel. 1-58-40-64-00; fax 1-58-40-64-01; life insurance; Pres. PIERRE CARLI; Dir GÉRARD LUNEL.

ERISA: Immeuble Ile de France, 4 pl. de la Pyramide, 92800 Paris La Défense; tel. 1-41-02-40-40; fax 1-41-02-49-84; life insurance; affiliated to HSBC France; Pres. PATRICK POLLET; Dir JOËLLE DURIEUX.

La Fédération Continentale: 11 blvd Haussmann, 75009 Paris; tel. 1-55-32-74-00; fax 1-55-32-74-01; e-mail webmastre@ federation-continentale.fr; internet www.federation-continentale.fr; f. 1961; life insurance; member of Groupe Generali (Italy); Pres. HENRI MOULARD; Dir-Gen. DANIEL COLLIGNON.

Garantie Mutuelle des Fonctionnaires: 76 rue de Prony, 75857 Paris Cédex 17; tel. 1-47-54-10-10; fax 1-47-54-18-97; internet www .gmf.fr; f. 1934; Pres. YVES CAZAUX; Dir CHRISTIAN SASTRE.

Generali France Assurances: 5 rue de Londres, 75456 Paris Cédex 09; tel. 1-55-32-40-00; fax 1-55-32-40-05; e-mail webmaster@ agence.generali.fr; internet www.assurances.generali.fr; Pres. CLAUDE TENDIL; Dir ERIC LE GENTIL.

GPA Assurances—Groupe Generali: 7 blvd Haussmann, 75447 Paris Cedex 09; tel. 1-58-34-15-15; fax 1-58-34-10-90; internet www .gpa.fr; Pres. CLAUDE TENDIL; Dir-Gen. JEAN-YVES HERMENIER.

Groupama Vie: 5 rue du Centre, 93199 Noisy Le Grand Cédex; tel. 1-49-31-31-31; fax 1-49-31-31-98; e-mail webmaster@groupama.fr; internet www.groupama.com; life insurance; Dir PIERRE BEAUMIN.

Groupe des Assurances Nationales (GAN): 8–10 rue d'Astorg, Paris 75008; tel. 1-42-47-50-00; fax 1-42-47-67-66; e-mail gan .rimbault.philippe@wanadoo.fr; internet www.gan.fr; f. 1820; fire; f. 1830; life; f. 1865; accident; affiliated to Groupama; Pres. JEAN-FRANÇOIS LEMOUX; Dir HENRI GUS.

La Mondiale: 32 ave Emile Zola, Mons en Baroeul, 59896 Lille Cédex 9; tel. 3-20-67-37-00; fax 3-20-47-70-90; internet www .lamondiale.com; f. 1905; life insurance; Pres. and Dir-Gen. PATRICK PEUGEOT.

La Mutuelle d'Assurances du Commerce et de l'Industrie (MACI): BP 609, 8 rue de Dammartin, 59671 Roubaix Cédex 1; tel. 3-20-45-72-00; fax 3-20-45-72-36; Pres. GILBERT TOULEMONDE; Dir LUCIEN CATRY.

Mutuelles du Mans Assurances: 10 blvd Alexandre Oyon, 72030 Le Mans Cédex 09; tel. 2-43-41-72-72; fax 2-43-41-72-26; internet www.mma.fr; f. 1828; life and general insurance; comprises three companies: MMA-IARD, DAS and MMA-VIE; Pres. and Dir-Gen JEAN-CLAUDE SEYS; Dir-Gen. JACQUES LENORMAND.

Predica: 50 rue de la Procession, 75724 Paris Cédex 15; tel. 1-43-23-58-00; fax 1-43-23-03-47; internet www.ca-predica.fr; affiliated to Crédit Agricole; general insurance; Pres. JEAN-CLAUDE PICHON; Dir-Gen. MICHEL VILLATTE.

Previposte: BP 7162, 4 Place Raoul Dautry, 75716 Paris Cédex 15; tel. 1-42-18-91-80; fax 1-42-18-94-94; life insurance; Pres. JACQUES OUVAROFF; Dir GILLES ARTAUD.

Socapi: 42 rue des Mathurins, 75008 Paris; tel. 1-44-71-52-00; fax 1-40-17-02-33; internet www.socapi.fr; f. 1985; 100% owned by Groupe des Assurances du Crédit Mutuel; life insurance; Pres. ALAIN SCHMITTER.

Suravenir: BP 103, 232 rue Général Paulet, 29802 Brest Cédex 09; tel. 2-98-34-65-00; fax 2-98-34-65-11; e-mail relations-client@ suravenir.fr; internet www.suravenir.fr; f. 1984; general insurance; Pres., Bd MARCEL BARON; Pres., Management LOUIS ECHELARD.

Union des Assurances Fédérales (UAF): 27 ave Claude Vellefaux, 75499 Paris Cédex 10; tel. 1-40-03-10-00; fax 1-40-18-36-93; internet www.uafdirect.fr; life insurance; affiliated to Crédit Lyonnais; Chair. and CEO JEAN-PIERRE WIEDMER.

Insurance Associations

Fédération des Agents Généraux d'Assurances (AGEA): 104 rue Jouffroy d'Abbans, 75847 Paris Cédex 17; tel. 1-44-01-18-00; fax 1-43-18-72-60; e-mail regis.devaux@agea.fr; internet www.agea.fr; Pres. GUY BAQUÉ.

Fédération Française des Courtiers d'Assurances et de Réassurances (FCA): 91 rue Saint Lazare, 75009 Paris; tel. 1-48-74-19-12; fax 1-42-82-91-10; e-mail ffca@wanadoo.fr; internet www.ffca.fr; f. 1991; Chair. RÉGIS FABRE; c. 700 mems.

Fédération Française des Sociétés d'Assurances (FFSA): 26 blvd Haussmann, 75009 Paris; tel. 1-42-47-90-00; fax 1-42-47-93-11; internet www.ffsa.fr; f. 1937; Chair. GÉRARD DE LA MARTINIÈRE; Sec.-Gen. GILLES WOLKOWITSCH.

Syndicat Français des Assureurs-Conseils: 14 rue de la Grange Batelière, 75009 Paris; tel. 1-55-33-51-51; fax 1-48-00-93-01; e-mail sfac2@wanadoo.fr; internet www.sfac-assurance.fr; Pres. HERVÉ DE WAZIÈRES.

Trade and Industry

GOVERNMENT AGENCIES

Conseil du Commerce de France: 14 rue de Castiglione, 75001 Paris; tel. 1-40-15-03-03; fax 1-40-15-97-22; Pres. BAUDOUIN MONNOYEUR.

UBIFRANCE—l'Agence Française pour le développement international des entreprises: 10 ave d'Iéna, 75116 Paris; tel. 1-40-73-30-00; fax 1-40-73-39-79; e-mail Claire.rocheteau@ubifrance .fr; internet www.ubifrance.fr; f. 2004 through merger of the Centre Français du Commerce Extérieur and the association UBIFrance; Minister-delegate for External Trade FRANÇOIS LOOS.

DEVELOPMENT ORGANIZATIONS

Agence pour la Création d'Entreprises (APCE): 14 rue Delambre, 75682 Paris Cédex 14; tel. 1-42-18-58-58; fax 1-42-18-58-00; e-mail info@apce.com; internet www.apce.com; Pres. MICHEL HERVÉ.

Groupe IDI: 18 ave Matignon, 75008 Paris; tel. 1-55-27-80-00; fax 1-40-17-04-44; f. 1970 as Institut de Développement Industriel; provides venture capital, takes equity shares in small and medium-sized businesses; Chair. CHRISTIAN LANGLOIS MEURINNE; CEO F. MARMISSOLE.

CHAMBERS OF COMMERCE

There are Chambers of Commerce in all the larger towns for all the more important commodities produced or manufactured.

Assemblée des Chambres Françaises de Commerce et d'Industrie: 45 ave d'Iéna, 75116 Paris; tel. 1-40-69-37-00; e-mail contactsweb@acfci.cci.fr; internet www.acfci.cci.fr; f. 1964; unites 160 local and 20 regional chambers of commerce and industry; Pres. JEAN-FRANÇOIS BERNARDIN.

Chambre de Commerce et d'Industrie de Paris: 27 ave de Friedland, 75382 Paris Cédex 08; tel. 1-55-65-55-65; fax 1-55-65-78-68; e-mail michel.franck@ccip.fr; internet www.ccip.fr; f. 1803; 307,000 mems in Paris and surrounding regions (Hauts de Seine, Seine-Saint-Denis and Val de Marne); Pres. MICHEL FRANCK.

INDUSTRIAL AND TRADE ASSOCIATIONS

Armateurs de France: 47 rue de Monceau, 75008 Paris; tel. 1-53-89-52-52; fax 1-53-89-52-53; e-mail info@armateursdefrance.org;

internet www.armateursdefrance.org; f. 1903; fmrly Comité Central des Armateurs de France; shipping; Pres. PATRICK DECAVELE; Delegate-Gen. ANNE BARTHE; 110 mems.

Assemblée Permanente des Chambres d'Agriculture (APCA): 9 ave George V, 75008 Paris; tel. 1-53-57-10-10; fax 1-53-57-10-05; e-mail accueil@apca.chambagri.fr; internet paris.apca.chambagri.fr; f. 1929; Pres. LUC GUYAU; Dir-Gen. ROLAND BAUD.

Association Nationale des Industries Alimentaires (ANIA): 155 blvd Haussmann, 75008 Paris; tel. 1-53-83-86-00; fax 1-45-61-96-64; e-mail infos@ania.net; internet www.ania.net; f. 1971; food produce; Pres. VICTOR SCHERRER.

Chambre Syndicale de l'Ameublement, Négoce de Paris et de l'Ile de France: 15 rue de la Cerisaie, 75004 Paris; tel. 1-42-72-13-79; fax 1-42-72-02-36; e-mail info@meubleparis.net; internet www.meubleparis.net; f. 1860; furnishing; Chair. NICOLE PHILIBERT; 350 mems.

Chambre Syndicale des Céramistes et Ateliers d'Art de France: 4 passage Roux, 75017 Paris; tel. 1-44-01-08-30; fax 1-44-01-08-35; e-mail info@ateliersdart.com; internet www.ateliersdart.com; f. 1886; craft and design trades; Chair. VICTOR DESCHANG.

Chambre Syndicale des Constructeurs de Navires: 47 rue de Monceau, 75008 Paris; tel. 1-53-89-52-01; fax 1-53-89-52-15; e-mail cscn@club-internet.fr; internet www.cscn.fr; shipbuilding; Chair. PATRICK BOISSIER; Gen. Man. FABRICE THEOBALD.

Comité des Constructeurs Français d'Automobiles: 2 rue de Presbourg, 75008 Paris; tel. 1-49-52-51-00; fax 1-47-23-74-73; internet www.ccfa.fr; f. 1909; motor manufacturing; Chair. MANUEL GOMEZ; 8 mems.

Comité National des Pêches Maritimes et des Elevages Marins (CNPMEM): 134 ave de Malakoff, 75116 Paris; tel. 1-72-71-18-00; fax 1-72-71-18-50; e-mail cnpmem@comite-peches.fr; internet www.comite-peches.fr; marine fisheries.

Comité Professionnel du Pétrole: 212 ave Paul Doumer, 92508 Rueil-Malmaison Cédex; tel. 1-47-16-94-60; fax 1-47-08-10-57; e-mail webmestre@cpdp.org; internet www.cpdp.org; f. 1950; petroleum industry; 80 mems; Pres. JACQUES CHAUMAS.

Commissariat à l'Energie Atomique (CEA) (Atomic Energy Commission): 31–33 rue de la Fédération, 75752 Paris Cédex 15; tel. 1-40-56-10-00; fax 1-40-56-29-70; e-mail dcom@aramis.cea.fr; internet www.cea.fr; f. 1945; promotes the uses of nuclear energy in science, industry and national defence; involved in research of nuclear materials; reactor development; fundamental research; innovation and transfer of technologies; military applications; biotechnologies; robotics; electronics; new materials; radiological protection and nuclear safety; Gen. Administrator PASCAL COLOMBANI; High Commissioner RENÉ PELLAT.

Confédération des Industries Céramiques de France: 3 rue La Boétie, 75008 Paris; tel. 1-58-18-30-40; fax 1-42-66-09-00; e-mail cicf@ceramique.org; f. 1937; ceramic industry; Chair. JACQUES RUSSEIL; Man. Dir FRANÇOIS DE LA TOUR; 85 mems, 5 affiliates.

Les Entreprises du Medicament (LEEM): 88 rue de la Faisanderie, 75782 Paris Cédex 16; tel. 1-45-03-88-70; fax 1-45-03-39-25; e-mail dei@leem.org; internet www.leem.org; fmrly Syndicat National de l'Industrie Pharmaceutique; pharmaceuticals; Chair. JEAN-PIERRE CASSAN.

Fédération des Chambres Syndicales de l'Industrie du Verre: 3 rue la Boétie, 75008 Paris; tel. 1-42-65-60-02; fax 1-42-66-23-88; e-mail fedeverre@wanadoo.fr; internet www.verre-avenir.org; f. 1874; glass industry; Pres. JACQUES DEMARTY.

Fédération des Chambres Syndicales des Minerais, Minéraux Industriels et Métaux non-Ferreux (FEDEM): 17 rue Hamelin, 75016 Paris; tel. 1–40–76–44–50; e-mail contact@fedem.fr; internet www.fedem.fr; f. 1945; minerals and non-ferrous metals; Chair. YVES RAMBAUD; Delegate-Gen. CHRISTOPHE BAULINET; 16 affiliated syndicates.

Fédération des Exportateurs des Vins et Spiritueux de France: 95 rue de Monceau, 75008 Paris; tel. 1-45-22-75-73; fax 1-45-22-94-16; e-mail contact@fevs.com; f. 1921; exporters of wines and spirits; Pres. PATRICK RICARD; Delegate-Gen. LOUIS RÉGIS AFFRE; 450 mems.

Fédération Française de l'Acier: Immeuble Pacific, 11-13 Cours Valmy, 92070 Paris La Défense Cédex; tel. 1-41-25-58-00; fax 1-41-25-59-81; e-mail svp.clients@ffa.fr; internet www.ffa.fr; f. 1945; steel-making; Pres. GUY DOLLÉ; Vice-Pres. and Delegate-Gen. BERNARD ROGY.

Fédération Française du Bâtiment: 33 ave Kléber, 75784 Paris Cédex 16; tel. 1-40-69-51-00; fax 1-45-53-58-77; e-mail ffbbox@ffb.fr; internet www.ffbatiment.fr; f. 1906; building trade; Pres. CHRISTIAN BAFFY; 50,000 mems.

Fédération Française des Industries Lainière et Cotonnière (FFILC): BP 121, 37–39 rue de Neuilly, 92113 Clichy Cédex; tel. 1-47-56-30-40; fax 1-47-37-06-20; e-mail ffilc@fedcoton-laine.com; internet www.fedcoton-laine.com; f. 1902; manufacturing of wool, cotton and associated textiles; Pres. CAMILLE AMALRIC; 400 mems.

Fédération Française du Négoce de Bois (FFNB): 215 bis blvd St Germain, 75007 Paris; tel. 1-45-48-28-44; fax 1-45-48-42-89; e-mail contact@bois-mat.com; internet www.bois-mat.com; timber trade; Pres. GÉRAUD SPIRE; Dir-Gen. LAURENT MARTIN-SAINT-LÉON.

Fédération Française de la Tannerie-Mégisserie: 122 rue de Provence, 75008 Paris; tel. 1-45-22-96-45; fax 1-42-93-37-44; e-mail fftm@leatherfrance.com; internet www.leatherfrance.com; f. 1885; leather industry; 100 mems.

Fédération de l'Imprimerie et de la Communication Graphique: 68 blvd Saint Marcel, 75005 Paris; tel. 1-44-08-64-46; fax 1-43-36-09-51; e-mail pressecom@ficg.fr; printing, communication and design; Pres. JACQUES CHIRAT.

Fédération des Industries de la Parfumerie (France): 33 Champs Elysées, 75008 Paris; tel. 1-56-69-67-89; fax 1-56-69-67-90; makers of perfume, cosmetics and toiletries; Pres. ALAIN GRANGÉ CABANE.

Fédération des Industries Electriques, Electroniques et de Communication (FIEEC): 11–17 rue Hameline, 75783 Paris Cédex 16; tel. 1-45-05-70-70; fax 1-45-53-03-93; e-mail comm@fieec.fr; internet www.fieec.fr; f. 1925; electrical and electronics industries; Chair. HENRI STARCK; Delegate-Gen. JEAN-CLAUDE KARPELÈS; c. 1,000 mems.

Fédération des Industries Mécaniques: 39–41 rue Louis Blanc, 92400 Courbevoie; tel. 1-47-17-60-27; fax 1-47-17-64-37; e-mail ppoisson@fimeca.com; internet www.fim.net; f. 1840; mechanical and metal-working; Pres. YVON JACOB; Dir-Gen. ALAIN POIX.

Fédération des Industries Nautiques: Port de Javel Haut, 75015 Paris; tel. 1-44-37-04-00; fax 1-45-77-21-88; e-mail info@fin.fr; internet www.fin.fr; f. 1965; pleasure-boating; Pres. ANNETTE ROUX; Man. Dir TIBOR SILLINGER; 600 mems.

Fédération Nationale du Bois: 6 rue François 1er, 75008 Paris; tel. 1-56-69-52-00; fax 1-56-69-52-09; e-mail infos@fnbois.com; internet www.fnbois.com; f. 1884; timber and wood products; Chair. LAURENT DENORMANDIE; 1,850 mems.

Fédération Nationale des Chambres Syndicales des Horlogers, Bijoutiers, Joailliers et Orfèvres (HBJO): 249 rue Saint Martin, 75003 Paris; tel. 1-44-54-34-00; fax 1-44-54-34-07; e-mail fedhbjo@wanadoo.fr; internet www.fedehbjo.com; jewellery, watch-and clock-making; Pres. GÉRARD ATLAN; 1,200 mems.

Fédération Nationale de l'Industrie Hôtelière (FNIH): 22 rue d'Anjou, 75008 Paris; tel. 1-44-94-19-94; fax 1-42-65-16-21; e-mail fnih@imagenet.fr; Chair. ANDRÉ DAGUIN.

Fédération Nationale de l'Industrie Laitière: 42 rue de Châteaudun, 75314 Paris Cédex 09; tel. 1-49-70-72-86; fax 1-42-80-63-94; e-mail fnil@atla.asso.fr; f. 1946; dairy products; Pres. XAVIER PAUL-RENARD; Sec.-Gen. HUGUES TRIBALLAT.

Fédération Nationale des Industries Électrométallurgiques, Électrochimiques et Connexes: 30 ave de Messine, 75008 Paris; tel. 1-45-61-06-63; fax 1-45-63-61-54; Chair. JACQUES GANI.

Fédération Nationale de la Musique: 62 rue Blanche, 75009 Paris; tel. 1-48-74-09-29; fax 1-42-81-19-87; f. 1964; includes Chambre Syndicale de la Facture Instrumentale, Syndicat National de l'Edition Phonographique and other groups; musical instruments, publications and recordings; Chair. PIERRE HENRY; Sec.-Gen. FRANÇOIS WELLEBROUCK.

Les Fondeurs de France: 45 rue Louis Blanc, 92038 Paris La Défense Cédex; tel. 1-43-34-76-30; fax 1-43-34-76-31; e-mail contact@fondeursdefrance.org; internet www.fondeursdefrance.org; f. 1897; metal casting; Pres. ANDRÉ ROBERT-DEHAULT; Dir-Gen. OLIVIER DUCRU; 300 mems.

Groupe Intersyndical de l'Industrie Nucléaire (GIIN): 92038 Paris La Défense Cedex; tel. 1-47-17-62-78; fax 1-47-17-68-91; e-mail contact@giin.fr; internet www.giin.fr; f. 1959; aims to promote the interests of the French nuclear industry; 200 member firms.

Groupement des Industries Françaises Aéronautiques et Spatiales (GIFAS): 4 rue Galilée, 75782 Paris Cédex 16; tel. 1-44-43-17-00; fax 1-40-70-91-41; e-mail infogifas@gifas.asso.fr; internet www.gifas.asso.fr; aerospace industry; Pres. PHILIPPE CAMUS.

Syndicat Général des Cuirs et Peaux: Bourse de Commerce, 2 rue de Viarmes, 75040 Paris Cédex 01; tel. 1-45-08-08-54; fax 1-40-39-97-31; e-mail cuirsetpeaux@wanadoo.fr; f. 1977; untreated leather and hides; Chair. PIERRE BONEFANT; 30 mems.

Syndicat Général des Fabricants d'Huile et de Tourteaux de France: 118 ave Achille Peretti, 92200 Neuilly-sur-Seine; tel. 1-46-

37-22-06; fax 1-46-37-15-60; f. 1928; edible oils; Pres. HENRI RIEUX; Sec.-Gen. JEAN-CLAUDE BARSACQ.

Syndicat National des Industries de la Communication Graphique et de l'Imprimerie Francaises (SICOGIF): 48 blvd des Batignolles, 75017 Paris; tel. 1-40-08-18-18; fax 1-40-08-00-24; e-mail info@sicogif.com; internet www.sicogif.com; f. 1991; printers' asscn; 310 mems; Chair. JEAN-RAOUL ROSAY; Sec.-Gen. PHILIPPE QUEINEC.

Union des Armateurs à la Pêche de France: 59 rue des Mathurins, 75008 Paris; tel. 1-42-66-32-60; fax 1-47-42-91-12; e-mail uapf75@wanadoo.fr; f. 1945; fishing-vessels; Chair. PATRICE LEDUC; Delegate-Gen. MICHEL DION.

Union des Fabricants de Porcelaine de Limoges: 7 bis rue du Général Cérez, 87000 Limoges; tel. 5-55-77-29-18; fax 5-55-77-36-81; e-mail ufpl@porcelainelimoges.org; porcelain manufacturing; Chair. BERTRAND RAYNAUD; Sec.-Gen. MARIE-THÉRÈSE PASQUET.

Union des Industries Chimiques (UIC): Le Diamant A, 14 rue de la République, 92800 Paris La Défense Cédex 10; tel. 1-46-53-11-00; fax 1-46-96-00-59; e-mail uicgeneral@uic.fr; internet www.uic.fr; f. 1860; chemical industry; Pres. M. RIVIÈRE; 58 affiliated unions.

Union des Industries Métallurgiques et Minières (UIMM): 56 ave de Wagram, 75017 Paris; tel. 1-40-54-20-20; fax 1-47-66-22-74; e-mail uimm@uimm.fr; internet www.uimm.fr; metallurgy and mining; Chair. DANIEL DEWAVRIN; 223 mems.

Union des Industries Papetières pour les Affaires Sociales (UNIPAS): 154 blvd Haussmann, 75008 Paris; tel. 1-53-89-25-25; fax 1-53-89-25-26; e-mail contact@unipas.org; internet www.unipas.org; f. 1864; paper, cardboard and cellulose; Chair. JEAN-PIERRE QUÉRÉ; Sec.-Gen. BRIGITTE MILLART.

Union des Industries Textiles: BP 121, 37–39 rue de Neuilly, 92113 Clichy Cédex; tel. 1-47-56-31-00; fax 1-47-30-25-28; e-mail thierry_noblot.uit@textile.fr; internet www.textile.fr; f. 1901; Chair. GUILLAUME SARKOZY; 2,500 mems.

Union professionnelle artisanale (UPA): 53 rue Ampère, 75017 Paris; tel. 1-47-63-31-31; fax 1-47-63-31-10; e-mail UPA@wanadoo .fr; internet www.upa.fr; f. 1975; unites crafts and other manual workers in three trade bodies and more than 100 regional organizations; Chair. PIERRE PERRIN.

EMPLOYERS' ORGANIZATIONS

Association Française des Entreprises Privées (AGREF): Paris; represents the interests of 81 of the largest enterprises in France; Chair. BERTRAND COLLOMB.

Centre des Jeunes Dirigeants d'Entreprise (CJD): 19 ave Georges V, 75008 Paris; tel. 1-53-23-92-50; fax 1-40-70-15-66; e-mail cjd@cjd.net; internet www.cjd.net; f. 1938; asscn for young entrepreneurs (under 45 years of age); Pres. FRANÇOISE COURELLE; 2,400 mems (2004).

Confédération Générale des Petites et Moyennes Entreprises (CGPME): 10 Terrasse Bellini, 92806 Puteaux Cédex; tel. 1-47-62-73-73; fax 1-47-73-08-86; e-mail contact@cgpme.org; internet www .cgpme.org; small and medium-sized cos; Chair. JEAN-FRANÇOIS ROUBAUD; 1,600,000 mems (2001).

Les Entrepreneurs et Dirigeants Chrétiens (Les EDC): 24 rue Hamelin, 75116 Paris; tel. 1-45-53-09-01; fax 1-47-27-43-32; e-mail lesedc@lesedc.org; internet www.lesedc.org; fmrly Centre Français du Patronat Chrétien; asscn of Christian employers; Nat. Pres. PIERRE LECOCQ.

Entreprise et Progrès: 11 rue Anatole de la Forge, 75017 Paris; tel. 1-45-74-52-62; fax 1-45-74-52-63; e-mail progres@noos.fr; internet www.entreprise-progres.net; f. 1970; represents 110 enterprises; Pres. PAUL DUBRULE; Sec.-Gen. ODILE DELORT-MAIXANDEAU.

Entreprises de Taille Humaine Indépendants et de Croissance (ETHIC): 6 Villa Thoréton, 75015 Paris; tel. 1-56-82-20-75; fax 1-56-82-20-37; e-mail l.michon@ethic.fr; internet www.ethic.fr; f. 1976; represents small enterprises and promotes ethical values in business; Pres. SOPHIE DE MENTHON.

Mouvement des Entreprises de France (MEDEF): 55 ave Bosquet, 75330 Paris Cédex 07; tel. 1-53-59-19-19; fax 1-45-51-20-44; internet www.medef.fr; f. 1998 to replace Conseil National du Patronat Français; employers' asscn grouping 700,000 cos from all sectors of activity in 85 professional feds and 152 regional orgs; Chair. ERNEST-ANTOINE SEILLIÈRE DE LABORDE.

UTILITIES

Electricity

Alcatel: 54 rue la Boétie, 75008 Paris; tel. 1-40-76-10-10; fax 1-40-76-14-00; internet www.alcatel.com; f. 1898; telecommunications and business systems, broadband access, terrestrial and submarine optical networks; 60,000 employees; Chair. and CEO SERGE TCHURUK; Pres.. PHILIPPE GERMOND.

Charbonnages de France (CdF): 100 ave Albert 1er, BP 220, 92503 Rueil-Malmaison Cédex; tel. 1-47-52-35-00; fax 1-47-51-30-75; e-mail cdf.com@groupecharbonnages.fr; internet www .groupecharbonnages.fr; f. 1946; responsible for coal mining, sales and research in metropolitan France; there are also engineering and electricity divisions; 9,957 employees; Pres. and Dir-Gen. PHILIPPE DE LADOUCETTE.

Electricité de France (EdF): 22–30 ave de Wagram, 75382 Paris Cédex 8; tel. 1-40-42-46-37; fax 1-40-42-72-44; e-mail masteredf@ edfgdf.fr; internet www.edf.fr; established under the Electricity and Gas Industry Nationalization Act of 1946; responsible for generating and supplying electricity for distribution to consumers in metropolitan France; plans were announced in November 2004 to part-privatize EdF, with the state maintaining a 70% holding in its share capital and voting rights; 167,000 employees (2003); Chair. and CEO PIERRE GADONNEIX.

Gas

Gaz de France: 23 rue Philibert Delorme, 75840 Paris Cédex 17; tel. 1-47-54-24-35; fax 1-47-54-74-42; internet www.gdf.fr; established under the Electricity and Gas Industry Nationalization Act of 1946; responsible for distribution of gas in metropolitan France; plans were announced in November 2004 to part-privatize Gaz de France, with the state maintaining a 70% holding in its share capital and voting rights; natural gas reserves: 77,184m. cu m, natural gas production: 4,600m. cu m (2003); 38,100 employees (2003); Chair. and CEO JEAN-FRANCOIS CIRELLI.

Water

Générale des Eaux: 38 ave Kléber, 75799 Paris Cédex 16; tel. 1-71-75-00-00; fax 1-71-75-03-05; e-mail anne.froger@generale-des-eaux .net; internet www.generale-des-eaux.com; f. 1853; subsidiary of Veolia Water; provides water and other environmental services, as well as telecommunications and construction; Pres. and Dir-Gen. HENRI PROGLIO.

Lyonnaise des Eaux: 1 rue d'Astorg, 75008 Paris; internet www .lyonnaise-des-eaux.fr; f. 1858; fmrly Suez-Lyonnaise des Eaux; present name adopted 2001; subsidiary of Ondeo (Groupe Suez); Pres. and CEO GÉRARD MESTRALLET.

TRADE UNIONS

In late 1995 it was estimated that some 8% of the French labour force belonged to trade unions (compared with 18% in 1980).

There are three major trade union organizations:

Confédération Générale du Travail (CGT): Complexe Immobilier Intersyndical CGT, 263 rue de Paris, 93516 Montreuil Cédex; tel. 1-48-18-80-00; fax 1-49-88-18-57; e-mail info@cgt.fr; internet www.cgt.fr; f. 1895; National Congress is held every three years; Sec.-Gen. BERNARD THIBAULT; 700,000 mems.

Affiliated federations:

CGT-Agro-Alimentaire et Forestière (FNAF): 263 rue de Paris, Case 428, 93514 Montreuil Cédex; tel. 1-48-18-83-27; fax 1-48-51-57-49; e-mail fnaf@fnaf-cgt.com; Sec.-Gen. FREDDY HUCK.

CGT-Bois Ameublement (Fédération Nationale des Travailleurs et Travailleuses des Industries du Bois de l'Ameublement et Connexes) (Woodworkers): 263 rue de Paris, Case 414, 93514 Montreuil Cédex; tel. 1-48-18-81-61; fax 1-48-51-59-91; e-mail cgt.bois1@wanadoo.fr; Sec.-Gen. HENRI SANCHEZ.

CGT-Cheminots (Railway Workers): 263 rue de Paris, Case 546, 93515 Montreuil Cédex; tel. 1-49-88-61-00; fax 1-48-57-95-65; e-mail coord@cheminotcgt.fr; internet www.cheminotcgt.fr; Sec.-Gen. DIDIER LERESTE.

CGT-Commerce: 263 rue de Paris, Case 425, 93514 Montreuil Cédex; tel. 1-48-18-83-11; fax 1-48-18-83-19; e-mail fd.commerce .services@cgt.fr; Sec.-Gen. EVELYNE PETIT.

CGT-Construction (Building): 263 rue de Paris, Case 413, 93514 Montreuil Cédex; tel. 1-48-18-81-60; fax 1-48-59-10-37; e-mail construction@cgt.fr; internet www.construction.cgt.fr; Sec.-Gen. ERIC AUBIN.

CGT-Education Recherche Culture (CGT-FERC): 263 rue de Paris, Case 544, 93515 Montreuil Cédex; tel. 1-48-18-82-44; fax 1-49-88-07-43; e-mail ferc@cgt.fr; internet www.ferc.cgt.fr; Sec.-Gen. RICHARD BERAUD.

CGT-Equipement (Capital Works): 263 rue de Paris, Case 543, 93515 Montreuil Cédex; tel. 1-48-18-82-81; fax 1-48-51-62-50; e-mail equipement.cgt@wanadoo.fr; Sec.-Gen. DANIEL SALANDRI.

CGT-Finances: 263 rue de Paris, Case 540, 93515 Montreuil Cédex; tel. 1-48-18-82-21; fax 1-48-18-82-52; e-mail finances@cgt.fr; internet www.finances.cgt.fr; Sec.-Gen. CHRISTOPHE DELECOURT.

CGT-Fonctionnaires (CGT-UGFF) (Civil Servants): 263 rue de Paris, Case 542, 93514 Montreuil Cédex; tel. 1-48-18-82-31; fax 1-48-18-82-11; e-mail ugff.cgt@wanadoo.fr; internet www.ugff.cgt.fr; groups National Education, Finance, Technical and Administrative, Civil Servants, Police, etc.; comprises some 70 national unions and six professional federations; Sec.-Gen. BERNARD LHUBERT.

CGT-Industries Chimiques (Chemical Industries): 263 rue de Paris, Case 429, 93514 Montreuil Cédex; tel. 1-48-18-80-36; fax 1-48-18-80-35; e-mail fnic@cgt.fr; internet www.fnic.cgt.fr; Sec.-Gen. JEAN-MICHEL PETIT.

CGT-Industries du Livre, du Papier et de la Communication (FILPAC) (Printing, Paper Products and Media): 263 rue de Paris, Case 426, 93514 Montreuil Cédex; tel. 1-48-18-80-24; fax 1-48-51-99-07; e-mail filpac@filpac-cgt.fr; internet www.filpac-cgt.fr; Sec.-Gen. MICHEL MULLER.

CGT-Ingénieurs, Cadres et Techniciens (CGT-UGICT) (Engineers, Managerial Staff and Technicians): 263 rue de Paris, Case 408, 93514 Montreuil Cédex; tel. 1-48-18-81-25; fax 1-48-51-64-57; e-mail ugict@cgt.fr; internet www.ugict.cgt.fr; f. 1963; Secs-Gen. MARIE-JO KOTLICKI, JEAN-FRANÇOIS BOLZINGER.

CGT-Intérimaires (Temporary Workers): 263 rue de Paris, Case 460, 93514 Montreuil Cédex; tel. 1-48-18-84-16; fax 1-48-18-82-59; e-mail contact@interim.cgt.fr; internet www.interim.cgt.fr; Pres. LE NOUAIL MARLIÈRE.

CGT-Journalistes: 263 rue de Paris, Case 570, 93514 Montreuil Cédex; tel. 1-48-18-81-78; fax 1-48-51-58-08; e-mail snj@cgt.fr; Sec.-Gen. MICHEL DIARD.

CGT-Marine Marchande (Merchant Marine): Cercle Franklin, 119 Cours de la République, 76000 Le Havre; tel. 2-35-25-04-81; fax 2-35-24-23-77; e-mail fedeoffmarmarugict.cgt@wanadoo.fr; Sec.-Gen. CHARLES NARELLI.

CGT-Maritimes (Seamen): 263 rue de Paris, Case 420, 93514 Montreuil Cédex; tel. 1-48-18-84-21; fax 1-48-51-59-21; e-mail fnsm-cgt@wanadoo.fr; Sec.-Gen. ALAIN MERLET.

CGT-Métallurgie (FTM) (Metalworkers): 263 rue de Paris, Case 433, 93514 Montreuil Cédex; tel. 1-48-18-21-21; fax 1-48-59-80-66; e-mail metaux@cgt.fr; internet www.ftm-cgt.fr; f. 1891; Sec.-Gen. DANIEL SANCHEZ.

CGT-Mines-Energie: 263 rue de Paris, Case 535, 93515 Montreuil Cédex; tel. 1-56-93-26-50; fax 1-56-93-27-49; e-mail fnme@fnme-cgt.fr; internet www.fnme-cgt.fr; Sec.-Gen. FRÉDÉRIC IMBRECHT.

CGT-Organismes Sociaux (Social Services): 263 rue de Paris, Case 536, 93515 Montreuil Cédex; tel. 1-48-18-83-56; fax 1-48-59-24-75; e-mail fede@orgasociaux.cgt.fr; internet www.orgasociaux.cgt.fr; Sec.-Gen. PHILIPPE HOURCADE.

CGT-Pénitentiaires (Prison workers): 263 rue de Paris, Case 542, 93514 Montreuil Cédex; tel. 1-48-18-82-42; fax 1-48-18-82-50; e-mail ugsp-cgt2@wanadoo.fr; internet www.ugsp-cgt.org; Sec-Gen. CÉLINE VERZELETTI.

CGT-Police: 263 rue de Paris, Case 550, 93514 Montreuil Cédex; tel. 1-48-51-14-40; fax 1-48-51-14-43; e-mail cgt.police@wanadoo.fr; f. 1906; Sec.-Gen. MICHEL GASTALDI.

CGT-Ports et Docks: 263 rue de Paris, Case 424, 93514 Montreuil Cédex; tel. 1-48-18-82-96; fax 1-48-18-82-94; e-mail portsetdocks-cgt@wanadoo.fr; Sec.-Gen. DANIEL LEFÈVRE.

CGT-Postes et Télécommunications (CGT-PTT): 263 rue de Paris, Case 545, 93515 Montreuil Cédex; tel. 1-48-18-54-00; fax 1-48-59-25-22; e-mail fede@cgt-ptt.fr; internet www.cgt-ptt.fr; Sec.-Gen. ALAIN GAUTHERON.

CGT-Professionnels de la Vente (Sales Workers): Bourse du Travail, 3 rue du Château d'eau, 75010 Paris; tel. 1-42-39-02-99; fax 1-42-39-09-11; e-mail fede.proventecgt@libertysurf.fr; Sec.-Gen. ALAIN SERRE.

CGT-Santé, Action Sociale (Health and Social Services): 263 rue de Montreuil, Case 538, 93514 Montreuil Cédex; tel. 1-48-18-20-99; fax 1-48-18-29-80; e-mail santeas@cgt.fr; internet www.cgt.fr/santeas; f. 1907; Sec.-Gen. NADINE PRIGENT.

CGT-Secteurs Financiers: 263 rue de Paris, Case 537, 93515 Montreuil Cédex; tel. 1-48-18-83-40; fax 1-49-88-16-36; e-mail fnpsf@cgt.fr; internet www.fnpsf.cgt.fr; Sec.-Gen. PHILIPPE BOURGALE.

CGT-Services Publics (Community Services): 263 rue de Paris, Case 547, 93514 Montreuil Cédex; tel. 1-48-18-83-74; fax 1-48-51-98-20; e-mail fdsp@cgt.fr; internet www.spterritoriaux.cgt.fr; Sec.-Gen. MAÏTÉ LASSALLE.

CGT-Sociétés d'études (Research, Service-sector Workers, Translators, Accountants, Notaries): 263 rue de Paris, Case 421, 93514 Montreuil Cédex; tel. 1-48-18-84-34; fax 1-48-18-84-86; e-mail fsetud@cgt.fr; internet www.soc-etudes.cgt.fr; Pres. NOËL LECHAT.

CGT-Spectacle, Audio-Visuel et Action Culturelle (Theatre, Media and Culture): 14–16 rue des Lilas, 75019 Paris; tel. 1-48-03-87-60; fax 1-42-40-90-20; e-mail cgtspectacle@fnsac-cgt.com; internet www.fnsac-cgt.com; Sec.-Gen. JEAN VOIRIN.

CGT-Tabac et Allumettes (Tobacco and Matches): 263 rue de Paris, Case 422, 93514 Montreuil Cédex; tel. 1-48-18-84-19; fax 1-48-51-54-53; e-mail tabacs.allumettes@cgt.fr; Sec.-Gen. FRÉDÉRIQUE BARTLETT.

CGT-Textiles, Habillement, Cuir (Textiles): 263 rue de Paris, Case 415, 93514 Montreuil Cédex; tel. 1-48-18-82-98; fax 1-48-18-83-01; e-mail thc@cgt.fr; Sec.-Gen. MAURAD RABHI.

CGT-Transports: 263 rue de Paris, Case 423, 93514 Montreuil Cédex; tel. 1-48-18-80-82; fax 1-48-18-82-54; e-mail transports@cgt.fr; Sec.-Gen. ALAIN RENAULT.

CGT-Travailleurs de l'Etat (State Employees): 263 rue de Paris, Case 541, 93515 Montreuil Cédex; tel. 1-48-18-86-86; fax 1-48-18-86-87; e-mail trav-etat@cgt.fr; Sec.-Gen. JEAN-LOUIS NAUDET.

CGT-Verre-Céramique (Glassworkers, Ceramics): 263 rue de Paris, Case 417, 93514 Montreuil Cédex; tel. 1-48-18-80-13; fax 1-48-18-80-11; e-mail ver-ceram@cgt.fr; Sec.-Gen. MOHAMMED OUSSEDIK.

Force Ouvrière: 141 ave du Maine, 75680 Paris Cédex 14; tel. 1-40-52-82-00; fax 1-40-52-82-02; internet www.force-ouvriere.fr; f. 1948 by breakaway from the more left-wing CGT (above); mem. of ICFTU and of the European Trade Union Confederation; Sec.-Gen. JEAN-CLAUDE MAILLY; c. 1m. mems.

Affiliated federations:

FO-Action Sociale: 7 passage Tenaille, 75680 Paris Cédex 14; tel. 1-40-52-85-80; fax 1-40-52-85-79; e-mail mpinaud@force-ouvriere.fr; Sec.-Gen. MICHEL PINAUD.

FO-Administration Générale de l'État: 46 rue des Petites Ecuries, 75010 Paris; tel. 1-42-46-40-19; fax 1-42-46-19-57; e-mail flamarque@force-ouvriere.fr; internet www.fage-fo.com; f. 1948; Sec.-Gen. JEAN-CLAUDE LE BOURSICAUD; 20,000 mems.

FO-Agriculture, Alimentation et Tabacs (Agriculture, Food and Tobacco): 7 passage Tenaille, 75680 Paris Cédex 14; tel. 1-40-52-85-10; fax 1-40-52-85-12; e-mail rafael.nedzynski@fgta-fo.org; internet www.fgtafo.fr; Sec.-Gen. RAFAËL NEDZYNSKI.

FO-Cadres et Ingénieurs (UCI) (Managers, Engineers): 2 rue de la Michodière, 75002 Paris; tel. 1-47-42-39-69; fax 1-47-42-03-53; e-mail hbouchet@force-ouvriere.fr; internet www.uci-fo.com; Sec.-Gen. HUBERT BOUCHET.

FO-Cheminots (Railway Workers): 61 rue de la Chapelle, 75018 Paris; tel. 1-55-26-94-00; fax 1-55-26-94-01; e-mail federation@fo-cheminots.com; internet www.fo-cheminots.com; f. 1948; Sec.-Gen. ERIC FALEMPIN; 10,000 mems.

FO-Coiffure, Esthétique, Parfumerie (Hairdressers, Beauticians and Perfumery): 3 rue de la Croix Blanche, 18350 Nerondes; tel. 2-48-78-89-32; fax 2-48-74-81-26; e-mail fcoiffure@force-ouvriere.fr; Sec.-Gen. GUY MARIN.

FO-Communications (Post and Telecommunications): 60 rue Vergniaud, 75640 Paris Cédex 13; tel. 1-40-78-31-50; fax 1-40-78-30-58; e-mail federation@fo-com.com; internet www.fo-com.com; f. 1947; Sec.-Gen. JACQUES LEMERCIER.

FO-Cuirs, Textiles, Habillement (Leather, Textiles and Clothing): 7 passage Tenaille, 75680 Paris Cédex 14; tel. 1-40-52-83-00; fax 1-40-52-82-99; e-mail fvanderosieren@force-ouvriere.fr; Sec.-Gen. FRANCIS VAN DE ROSIEREN.

FO-Défense, Industries de l'Armement et Secteurs Assimilés (Defence and Arms Manufacture): 46 rue des Petites Ecuries, 75010 Paris; tel. 1-42-46-00-05; fax 1-45-23-12-89; e-mail fediasa@force-ouvriere.fr; Sec.-Gen. CHARLES SISTACH.

FO-Employés et Cadres (Office Workers and Private Sector Managerial Staff): 28 rue des Petits Hôtels, 75010 Paris; tel. 1-48-01-91-91; fax 1-48-01-91-92; e-mail fecfo@wanadoo.fr; internet www.fecfo.fr; Sec.-Gen. ROSE BOUTARIC.

FO-Energie et Mines (Energy and Mines): 60 rue Vergniaud, 75640 Paris Cédex 13; tel. 1-44-16-86-20; fax 1-44-16-86-32; e-mail federation@fnem-fo.fr; internet www.fnem-fo.fr; Sec.-Gen. GABRIEL GAUDY.

FO-Enseignement, Culture et Formation Professionnelle (Teaching): 6–8 rue Gaston-Lauriau, 93513 Montreuil Cédex; tel. 1-56-93-22-22; fax 1-56-93-22-20; e-mail fchaintron@force-ouvriere.fr; Sec.-Gen. FRANÇOIS CHAINTRON; 50,000 mems.

FO-Equipements, Transports et Services (Transport and Public Works): 46 rue des Petites Ecuries, 75010 Paris; tel. 1-44-83-86-20; fax 1-48-24-38-32; e-mail yveyrier@force-ouvriere.fr; internet www.fets-fo.fr; f. 1932; Sec.-Gen. YVES VEYRIER; 50,000 mems.

FO-Fédéchimie (Chemical Industries): 60 rue Vergniaud, 75640 Paris Cédex 13; tel. 1-45-80-14-90; fax 1-45-80-08-03; e-mail mdecayeux@force-ouvriere.fr; f. 1948; Sec.-Gen. MICHEL DECAYEUX.

FO-Finances: 46 rue des Petites Ecuries, 75010 Paris; tel. 1-42-46-75-20; fax 1-47-70-23-92; e-mail fo.finances@wanadoo.fr; internet financesfo.fr; Sec.-Gen. MICHEL MONTEIL.

FO-Fonctionnaires (Civil Servants): 46 rue des Petites Ecuries, 75010 Paris; tel. 1-44-83-65-55; fax 1-42-46-97-80; e-mail fofonctionnaires@force-ouvriere.fr; internet www.fo-fonctionnaires.fr; Sec.-Gen. GÉRARD NOGUÈS.

FO-Générale (Building, Public Works, Wood, Ceramics, Paper, Cardboard and Building Materials): 170 ave Parmentier, 75010 Paris; tel. 1-42-01-30-00; fax 1-42-39-50-44; e-mail mdaudigny@force-ouvriere.fr; internet www.federationgeneralefo.com; Sec.-Gen. MICHEL DAUDIGNY.

FO-Livre (Printing Trades): 7 passage Tenaille, 75680 Paris Cédex 14; tel. 1-40-52-85-00; fax 1-40-52-85-01; e-mail livre.fo@wanadoo.fr; Sec.-Gen. PATRICE SACQUÉPÉE.

FO-Métaux (Metals): 9 rue Baudouin, 75013 Paris; tel. 1-53-94-54-00; fax 1-45-83-78-87; e-mail contact@fo-metaux.fr; internet www.fo-metaux.com; Sec.-Gen. FRÉDÉRIC HOMEZ.

FO-Mineurs, Miniers et Similaires (Mine Workers): 7 passage Tenaille, 75014 Paris; tel. 1-40-52-85-50; fax 1-40-52-85-48; e-mail bfraysse@force-ouvriere.fr; Sec.-Gen. BERNARD FRAYSSE.

FO-Pharmacie, Officine-Industrie VM, Drogurie-Répartition, Laboratoire d'Analyse (Pharmacists, Druggists and Analytical Laboratories): 7 passage Tenaille, 75680 Paris Cédex 14; tel. 1-40-52-85-60; fax 1-40-52-85-61; e-mail fopharma@wanadoo.fr; internet www.fo-pharmacie.com; Sec.-Gen. GILBERT LEBRUMENT.

FO-Police: 146–148 rue Picpus, 75012 Paris; tel. 1-53-46-11-00; fax 1-44-68-07-41; e-mail xbeugnet@force-ouvriere.fr; internet www.fsgp-fo.com; f. 1948; Sec.-Gen. XAVIER BEUGNET; 11,000 mems.

FO-Services des Départements et Régions (Local and Regional Government): 46 rue des Petits Ecuries, 75010 Paris; tel. 1-42-46-50-52; fax 1-47-70-26-06; e-mail msimonnin@force-ouvriere.fr; Sec.-Gen. MICHÈLE SIMONNIN.

FO-Services Publics et de Santé (Health and Public Services): 153–155 rue de Rome, 75017 Paris; tel. 1-44-01-06-00; fax 1-42-27-21-40; e-mail fedespsfo@wanadoo.fr; internet www.fo-publics-sante.org; f. 1947; Sec.-Gen. JEAN-MARIE BELLOT; 130,000 mems (2002).

FO-Fédération des Syndicats des Arts, des Spectacles, de l'Audiovisuel, de la Presse et du Multimedia (FASAPFO): 2 rue de la Michodière, 75002 Paris; tel. 1-47-42-35-86; fax 1-47-42-39-45; e-mail fasap-fo@wanadoo.fr; Sec.-Gen. FRANÇOISE CHAZAUD.

FO-Transports: 7 passage Tenaille, 75680 Paris Cédex 14; tel. 1-40-52-85-45; fax 1-40-52-85-09; e-mail fotransports@force-ouvriere.fr; Gen. Sec. GÉRARD APRUZZESE.

Confédération Française Démocratique du Travail (CFDT): 4 blvd de la Villette, 75955 Paris Cédex 19; tel. 1-42-03-80-00; fax 1-42-03-81-44; e-mail confederation@cfdt.fr; internet www.cfdt.fr; f. 1919 as Confédération Française des Travailleurs Chrétiens—CFTC, present title and constitution adopted 1964; moderate; co-ordinates 1,500 trade unions, 95 departmental and overseas unions, 3 confederal unions and 17 affiliated professional federations, all of which are autonomous. There are also 22 regional orgs; 873,877 mems (2003); affiliated to European Trade Union Confederation and to ICFTU; Sec.-Gen. FRANÇOIS CHÉRÈQUE.

Affiliated federations:

CFDT-Agroalimentaire (FGA-CFDT): 47–49 ave Simon Bolivar, 75950 Paris Cédex 19; tel. 1-56-41-50-50; fax 1-56-41-50-30; e-mail fga@cfdt.fr; internet www.fga-cfdt.fr; f. 1980; Sec.-Gen. HERVÉ GARNIER; 50,000 mems (2001).

CFDT-Banques et Sociétés Financières: 47–49 ave Simon Bolivar, 75950 Paris Cédex 19; tel. 1-56-41-54-50; fax 1-56-41-54-51; e-mail federation@cfdt-banques.fr; internet www.cfdt-banques.fr; Sec.-Gen. JEAN-CLAUDE BRANCHEREAU.

CFDT-Chimie-Energie (FCE-CFDT): 47–49 ave Simon Bolivar, 75950 Paris Cédex 19; tel. 1-56-41-53-00; fax 1-56-41-53-01; e-mail fce@fce.cfdt.fr; internet www.fce.cfdt.fr; f. 1946; Sec.-Gen. PATRICK PIERRON; 57,000 mems (1996).

CFDT-Communication et Culture: 47–49 ave Simon Bolivar, 75950 Paris Cédex 19; tel. 1-56-41-53-80; fax 1-56-41-53-90; e-mail contact@fcc-cfdt.net; internet www.fcc-cfdt.net; Sec.-Gen. DANIÈLE RIVED.

CFDT-Construction-Bois (FNCB-CFDT) (Builders, Woodworkers, Architects, Town-planners): 47–49 ave Simon Bolivar, 75950 Paris Cédex 19; tel. 1-56-41-55-60; fax 1-56-41-55-61; e-mail fncb@cfdt.fr; internet www.cfdt-construction-bois.fr; f. 1934; Sec.-Gen. JOSEPH MURGIA.

CFDT-Education Nationale (SGEN-CFDT) (National Education): 47–49 ave Simon Bolivar, 75950 Paris Cédex 19; tel. 1-56-41-51-00; fax 1-56-41-51-11; e-mail fede@sgen-cfdt.org; internet www.sgen-cfdt.org; f. 1937; Sec.-Gen. JEAN-LUC VILLENEUVE.

CFDT-Etablissements et Arsenaux de l'Etat: 47–49 ave Simon Bolivar, 75950 Paris Cédex 19; tel. 1-56-41-56-80; fax 1-56-41-56-89; e-mail feae@cfdt.fr; Sec.-Gen. JACQUES LEPINARD.

CFDT-Finances et Affaires Economiques (Finance): 47–49 ave Simon Bolivar, 75950 Paris Cédex 19; tel. 1-56-41-55-55; fax 1-56-41-55-59; e-mail federation@cfdt-finances.fr; internet www.cfdt-finances.fr; f. 1936; civil servants and workers within government financial departments; Sec.-Gen. PHILIPPE LECLEZIO.

CFDT-Fonctionnaires et Assimilés (UFFA) (Civil Servants): 47–49 ave Simon Bolivar, 75950 Paris Cédex 19; tel. 1-56-41-54-40; fax 1-56-41-54-44; e-mail uffa@uffa.cfdt.fr; f. 1932; Sec.-Gen. MARIE-CLAUDE KERVELLA.

CFDT-Formation et Enseignement Privés (Independent education): 47–49 ave Simon Bolivar, 75950 Paris Cédex 19; tel. 1-56-41-54-70; fax 1-56-41-54-71; e-mail contact@fep-cfdt.fr; internet www.fep-cfdt.fr; Sec.-Gen. XAVIER NAU.

CFDT-Habillement, Cuir et Textile (HACUITEX) (Clothing Industry): 47–49 ave Simon Bolivar, 75950 Paris Cédex 19; tel. 1-56-41-55-90; fax 1-56-41-55-95; e-mail hacuitex@cfdt.fr; f. 1963; Sec.-Gen. MARTIAL VIDET.

CFDT-Ingénieurs et Cadres (Managers, Professionals, Engineers): 47–49 ave Simon Bolivar, 75950 Paris Cédex 19; tel. 1-56-41-55-00; fax 1-56-41-55-01; e-mail contact@cfdt-cadres.fr; internet www.cadres-plus.net; Sec.-Gen. FRANÇOIS FAYOL.

CFDT-Interco (Local Government Workers): 47–49 ave Simon Bolivar, 75950 Paris Cédex 19; tel. 1-56-41-52-52; fax 1-56-41-52-51; e-mail interco@cfdt.fr; internet www.interco-cfdt.fr; Sec.-Gen. ALEXIS GUÉNÉGO.

CFDT-Métallurgie et Mines (Miners, Machinery and Metal Workers): 47–49 ave Simon Bolivar, 75950 Paris Cédex 19; tel. 1-56-41-50-70; fax 1-56-41-50-96; e-mail mines_metallurgie@fgmm.cfdt.fr; internet www.fgmm.cfdt.fr; Sec.-Gen. MARCEL GRIGNARD.

CFDT-Postes et Télécoms (FUPT) (Post and Telecommunications Workers): 47–49 ave Simon Bolivar, 75950 Paris Cédex 19; tel. 1-56-41-54-00; fax 1-56-41-54-01; e-mail fupt@cfdt.fr; internet www.cfdt-postes-telecoms.org; Sec.-Gen. HERVÉ MORLAND.

CFDT-Protection Sociale, Travail, Emploi (Social Security): 47–49 ave Simon Bolivar, 75950 Paris Cédex 19; tel. 1-56-41-51-50; fax 1-56-41-51-51; e-mail pste@cfdt.fr; internet www.pste-cfdt.org; Sec.-Gen. JEAN-LOUIS TARDIVAUD.

CFDT-Retraités (UCR) (Retired People): 47–49 ave Simon Bolivar, 75950 Paris Cédex 19; tel. 1-56-41-55-20; fax 1-56-41-55-21; e-mail union-retraites@cfdt.fr; Sec.-Gen. JACQUES SENSE.

CFDT-Services (Trade, Insurance, Legal, Property and other Service Sector Professions): Tour Essor, 14 rue Scandicci, 93508 Pantin Cédex; tel. 1-48-10-65-90; fax 1-48-10-65-95; e-mail services@cfdt.fr; internet www.cfdt-services.fr; Sec.-Gen. DIDIER BRULÉ.

CFDT-Services de Santé et Services Sociaux (Health and Social Workers): 47–49 ave Simon Bolivar, 75950 Paris Cédex 19; tel. 1-56-41-52-00; fax 1-42-02-48-08; e-mail santesociaux@cfdt.fr; internet www.fed-cfdt-sante-sociaux.org; Sec.-Gen. YOLANDE BRIAND.

CFDT-Transports-Equipement (Transport, Public Works and Housing—FGTE): 47–49 ave Simon Bolivar, 75950 Paris Cédex 19; tel. 1-56-41-56-03; fax 1-42-02-49-96; e-mail lecoq@fgte-cfdt.org; internet www.fgte.org; f. 1977; Sec.-Gen. JOËL LECOQ.

Confédération Française de l'Encadrement (CFE—CGC): 59–63 rue du Rocher, 75008 Paris; tel. 1-55-30-12-12; fax 1-55-30-13-13; e-mail presse@cfecgc.fr; internet www.cfecgc.fr; f. 1944; organizes managerial staff, professional staff and technicians; co-ordinates unions in every industry and sector; Nat. Pres. JEAN-LUC CAZETTES; Sec-Gen. JEAN-LOUIS WALTER; 140,000 mems (2004).

Confédération Française des Travailleurs Chrétiens (CFTC): 13 rue des Ecluses Saint Martin, 75483 Paris Cédex 10; tel. 1-44-52-49-00; fax 1-44-52-49-18; e-mail eurint@cftc.fr; internet www.cftc.fr; f. 1919; present form in 1964 after majority CFTC became CFDT (see above); mem. European Trade Union Confederation, World Confederation of Labour; Chair. JACQUES VOISIN; Gen. Sec. JACKY DINTINGER; 130,000 mems (2003).

Confédération des Syndicats Libres (CSL): 37 rue Lucien Sampaix, 75010 Paris; tel. 1-55-26-12-12; fax 1-55-26-12-00; e-mail csl@ifrance.com; internet www.ifrance.com/csl; f. 1947; fmrly Confédération française du Travail; Sec.-Gen. GEORGES LENGLET; 250,000 mems.

Fédération Nationale des Syndicats Autonomes: Paris; f. 1952; groups unions in the private sector; Sec.-Gen. MICHEL-ANDRÉ TILLIÈRES.

Fédération Nationale des Syndicats d'Exploitants Agricoles (FNSEA) (National Federation of Farmers' Unions): 11 rue de la Baume, 75008 Paris; tel. 1-53-83-47-47; fax 1-53-83-48-48; e-mail fnsea@fnsea.fr; internet www.fnsea.fr; f. 1946; comprises 92 departmental federations and 32,000 local unions; Chair. JEAN-MICHEL LEMÉTAYER; Dir-Gen. PATRICK FERRÈRE; 600,000 mems.

Fédération Syndicale Unitaire (FSU): 3–5 rue de Metz, 75010 Paris; tel. 1-44-79-90-30; fax 1-48-01-02-52; e-mail webmaster@fsu.fr; internet www.fsu.fr; f. 1993; federation of civil service and education workers' unions; Sec.-Gen. GÉRARD ASCHIERI; 180,000 mems (2004).

> **Syndicat National Unitaire des Instituteurs (SNUIPP):** 128 blvd Blanqui, 75013 Paris; tel. 1-44-08-69-30; fax 1-44-08-69-40; e-mail snuipp@snuipp.fr; internet www.snuipp.fr; f. 1993; primary-school teachers; Sec-Gen. NICOLE GENEIX.

UNSA Education: 87 bis ave Georges Gosnat, 94853 Ivry-sur-Seine Cédex; tel. 1-56-20-29-52; fax 1-56-20-29-89; e-mail national@unsa-education.org; internet www.unsa-education.org; f. 1948; federation of teachers' unions; fmrly Fédération de l'Education Nationale; Sec.-Gen. PATRICK GONTHIER.

Transport

RAILWAYS

Most of the French railways are controlled by the Société Nationale des Chemins de fer Français (SNCF), established in 1937, and the Réseau Ferré de France (f. 1997) manages track and infrastructure. The SNCF is divided into 22 régions (areas). In 2003 the SNCF operated 31,385 km of track, of which 14,464 km were electrified. High-speed services (trains à grande vitesse—TGV) operate between Paris and various other destinations: Lyon (TGV Sud-Est), extending to Marseille or Nîmes (TGV Méditerranée), Bordeaux or Nantes (TGV Atlantique), and Lille (TGV Nord Europe). The TGV network covered 1,540 km of track in 2003. A further TGV line, linking Paris with Strasbourg (TGV Est), was expected to open in 2006. The Parisian transport system is controlled by a separate authority, the Régie Autonome des Transports Parisiens (RATP). A number of small railways in the provinces are run by independent organizations. In 1994 a rail link between France and the United Kingdom was opened, including a tunnel under the English Channel (la Manche), from Calais to Folkestone.

Réseau Ferré de France (RFF): 92 ave de France, 75648 Paris Cédex; tel. 1-53-94-30-00; fax 1-53-94-38-00; internet www.rff.fr; f. 1997 to assume ownership and financial control of national rail infrastructure; state-owned; Pres. JEAN-PIERRE DUPORT; Gen. Man. JEAN-MARIE BERTRAND.

Société Nationale des Chemins de fer Français (SNCF): 34 rue du Commandant Mouchotte, 75699 Paris Cédex 14; tel. 1-53-25-60-00; fax 1-53-25-61-08; e-mail webcom@sncf.fr; internet www.sncf.fr; f. 1937; Pres. LOUIS GALLOIS; Sec.-Gen. PAUL MINGASSON.

Channel Tunnel (Le Tunnel sous la Manche)

Groupe Eurotunnel: BP 69, Coquelles Cédex; tel. 3-21-00-65-43; internet www.eurotunnel.fr; Anglo-French consortium contracted to design, finance and construct the Channel Tunnel under a concession granted for a period up to 2052 (later extended to 2086); receives finance exclusively from the private sector, including international commercial banks; the Channel Tunnel was formally opened in May 1994; operates a series of road vehicle 'shuttle' trains and passenger and freight trains through the Channel Tunnel; Group Chair. JACQUES MAILLOT; Chief Exec. JEAN-LOUIS RAYMOND.

Metropolitan Railways

Régie Autonome des Transports Parisiens (RATP): 54 quai de la Rapée, 75599 Paris Cédex 12; tel. 1-58-78-20-20; fax 1-58-78-31-70; internet www.ratp.fr; f. 1949; state-owned; operates the Paris underground (comprising 16 lines totalling 214 km, and 297 stations in 2003), RER suburban railways (totalling 327 km in 2001), 2 suburban tram lines, and 261 bus routes; Chair. and Dir-Gen. ANNE-MARIE IDRAC.

Four provincial cities also have underground railway systems: Marseille, Lyon, Lille and Rennes.

ROADS

At 31 December 2000 there were 11,500 km of motorways (autoroutes). There were also 27,500 km of national roads (routes nationales), 355,000 km of secondary roads and 500,000 km of major local roads.

Fédération Nationale des Transports Routiers (FNTR): 6 rue Ampère, 75017 Paris; tel. 1-44-29-04-29; fax 1-44-29-04-01; e-mail fntr@fntr.fr; internet www.fntr.fr; road transport; Co-Chair. FRANÇOIS BRANCHE, GEORGES CAUSSE, BERNARD LIEBART, GÉRARD PERRIN.

INLAND WATERWAYS

At 31 December 2000 there were 8,500 km of navigable waterways, of which 1,686 km were accessible to craft of 3,000 metric tons.

Voies navigables de France: 175 rue Ludovic Boutleux, BP 820, 62408 Béthune Cédex; tel. 3-21-63-24-42; e-mail direction-generale@vnf.fr; internet www.vnf.fr; f. 1991; management and development of France's inland waterways; responsible for 3,800 km of navigable canals and 2,900 km of navigable rivers; Pres. FRANÇOIS BORDRY; Dir-Gen. GUY JANIN.

SHIPPING

In 2000 the principal ports, in terms of quantity of cargo, were Marseille, Le Havre and Dunkerque, and the principal passenger port was Calais. The six major seaports (Marseille, Le Havre, Dunkerque, Nantes-Saint-Nazaire, Rouen, and Bordeaux) are operated by autonomous authorities, although the State retains supervisory powers.

Conseil National des Communautés Portuaires: Paris; tel. 1-40-81-86-11; f. 1987; central independent consultative and co-ordinating body for ports and port authorities; more than 50 mems, including 10 trade union mems; Pres. JACQUES DUPUY-DAUBY; Sec.-Gen. M. DE ROCQUIGNY DU FAYEL.

Direction du Transport Maritime, des Ports et du Littoral (DTMPL): 22 rue Monge, 75005 Paris; tel. 1-40-81-72-10; f. 1997; Govt body responsible for the economic development of port and civil maritime activities and the protection of the littoral; Dir DIDIER SIMMONET.

Port Autonome Atlantique—Nantes-Saint Nazaire: Nantes; tel. 2-40-44-20-26; fax 2-40-44-21-81; e-mail ser.com@nantes.port.fr; internet www.nantes.port.fr; f. 1966; Pres. MICHEL QUIMBERT; Dir-Gen. FRANÇOIS MARENDET.

Port Autonome de Bordeaux: 3 pl. Gabriel, 33075 Bordeaux; tel. 5-56-90-58-00; fax 5-56-90-58-80; e-mail postoffice@bordeaux-port.fr; internet www.bordeaux-port.fr; Pres. MICHEL SAMMARCELLI; Dir-Gen. PHILIPPE DEISS.

Port Autonome de Dunkerque: terre-plein Guillain, 59386 Dunkerque Cédex 01; tel. 3-28-28-78-78; fax 3-28-28-78-77; e-mail info@portdedunkerque.fr; internet www.portdedunkerque.fr; Pres. JO DAIRIN; Dir-Gen. JEAN-CLAUDE TERRIER.

Port Autonome de Marseille: 23 pl. de la Joliette, BP 1965, 13226 Marseille Cédex 02; tel. 4-91-39-40-00; fax 4-91-39-57-00; e-mail pam@marseille-port.fr; internet www.marseille-port.fr; Pres. CHRISTIAN GARIN; Dir-Gen. ERIC BRASSART.

Port Autonome du Havre: BP 1413, 76067 Le Havre Cédex; tel. 2-32-74-74-00; fax 2-32-74-74-29; e-mail pahmail@havre-port.fr; internet www.havre-port.fr; Chair. JEAN-PIERRE LECOMTE; Dir.-Gen. JEAN-MARC LACAVE.

Port Autonome de Rouen: 34 blvd de Boisguilbert, BP 4075, 76022 Rouen Cédex 03; tel. 2-35-52-54-56; fax 2-35-52-54-13; e-mail dg@rouen.port.fr; internet www.rouen.port.fr; Pres. GHISLAIN DE BOISSIEU; Dir-Gen. MARTINE BONNY.

Port de Calais: pl. de l'Europe, 62226 Calais Cédex; tel. 3-21-96-31-20; fax 3-21-34-08-92; e-mail ccic@calais.cci.fr; internet www.calais-port.com; Pres. HENRI RAVISSE.

Principal Shipping Companies

Note: Not all the vessels belonging to the companies listed below are registered under the French flag.

Brittany Ferries: Port du Bloscon, BP 72, 29688 Roscoff Cédex; tel. 2-98-29-28-00; fax 2-98-29-27-00; e-mail compay@brittany-ferries.fr; internet www.brittany-ferries.fr; f. 1972 as BretagneAngleterreIrlande (BAI); transport between France, Ireland, Spain and the United Kingdom; Chair. ALEXIS GOURVENNEC; Man. Dir MICHEL MARAVAL.

Broström Tankers, SA: 5 ave Percier, 75008 Paris; tel. 1-42-99-66-66; fax 1-42-99-66-20; e-mail brotank.paris@brostrom.fr; internet www.brostroms.se/tankers; subsidiary of Broström AB (Sweden); fmrly Van Ommeren Tankers; oil product and chemical coastal tankers and tramping.

Compagnie Maritime Marfret: 13 quai de la Joliette, 13002 Marseille; tel. 4-91-56-91-00; fax 4-91-56-91-01; e-mail mfmedsea@marfret.fr; internet www.marfret.fr; freight services to the Mediterranean, South America, the Caribbean, Canada and northern Europe; Dir-Gen. BERNARD VIDIL.

Consortium Européen de Transports Maritimes (CETRAMAR): 87 ave de la Grande Armée, 75782 Paris Cédex 16; tel. 1-40-66-11-11; fax 1-45-00-77-35; Chair. PHILIPPE POIRIER D'ANGÉ D'ORSAY; Man. Dir ANDRÉ MAIRE; displacement 564,291 grt.

Corsica Ferries: 5 bis rue Chanoine Leschi, 20296 Bastia; tel. 4-95-32-95-95; fax 4-95-32-14-71; internet www.corsicaferries.com; affiliated to Groupe Lota Maritime; passenger and freight ferry services between Corsica, Sardinia, mainland France, and mainland Italy; Pres. PASCAL LOTA.

Esso France: 2 rue des Martinets, 92569 Rueil-Malmaison Cédex; tel. 1-47-10-60-00; fax 1-47-10-60-44; internet www.esso.com/eaff/essofrance; f. 1952; merged with Mobil Oil Française in 2003; Chair. and Man. Dir PATRICK HEINZLE.

Groupe CMA—CGM: 4 quai d'Arenc, BP 2409, 13215 Marseille Cédex 02; tel. 4-91-39-30-00; fax 4-91-39-30-95; e-mail webmaster@cma-cgm.com; internet www.cma-cgm.com; f. 1996 by merger of Compagnie Générale Maritime and Compagnie Maritime d'Affrètement; freight services to USA, Canada, the Caribbean, Central and South America, the Mediterranean, the Middle East, the Far East, India, Australia, New Zealand, Indonesia, East Africa and other Pacific and Indian Ocean areas; 25 ships owned; Chair. JACQUES R. SAADÉ; Dir-Gens FARID T. SALEM, ALAIN WILS; displacement 1,900,000 grt (2001).

Louis Dreyfus Armateurs (LDA): 87 ave de la Grande Armée, 75782 Paris Cédex 16; tel. 1-40-66-11-11; fax 1-45-00-23-97; e-mail gehannep@lda.fr; internet www.lda.fr; gas and bulk carriers; Pres. PHILIPPE LOUIS-DREYFUS; Chief Exec. P. GEHANNE.

Navale Française SA: 8 blvd Victor Hugo, 34000 Montpellier; tel. 4-67-58-82-12; fax 4-67-92-98-34; Chair. MARC CHEVALLIER.

SeaFrance: Nouveau Terminal Car Ferry, 62100 Calais; tel. 8-03-04-40-45 ; e-mail presse@seafrance.net; internet www.seafrance.fr; wholly-owned subsidiary of Société Nationale des Chemins de Fer Français; f. 1996 to replace Société Nouvelle d'Armement Transmanche (SNAT); vehicle and passenger services between France and the United Kingdom, Ireland and the Channel Islands; Man. Dir EUDES RIBLIER.

Société d'Armement et de Transport (Socatra): 9 allées de Tourny, 33000 Bordeaux; tel. 5-56-00-00-56; fax 5-56-48-51-23; e-mail direction@socatra.com; internet www.socatra.com; f. 1977; Chair. F. BOZZONI; Man. Dir M. DUBOURG.

Société Européenne de Transport Maritime: 9 allées de Tourny, 33000 Bordeaux; tel. 5-56-00-00-56; fax 5-56-48-51-23; Man. Dirs GILLES BOUTHILLIER, FERNAND BOZZONI; displacement 53,261 grt.

Société Nationale Maritime Corse-Méditerranée: 61 blvd des Dames, BP 1963, 13226 Marseille Cédex 02; tel. 4-91-56-32-00; fax 4-91-56-34-94; e-mail info@sncm.fr; internet www.sncm.fr; passenger and roll on/roll off ferry services between France and Corsica, Sardinia, North Africa; also subsidiary *Corsica Maritima*; Chair. PIERRE VIEU; displacement 141,454 grt.

Société Navale Caennaise: Caen; tel. 2-31-72-54-00; fax 2-31-78-04-94; e-mail veluma@mail.cpod.fr; internet perso.normandnet.fr/navale; f. 1901; cargo services to Europe and West Africa; Chair. and Man. Dir A. LABAT; displacement 59,680 grt.

Société Services et Transports: route du Hoc Gonfreville-L'Orcher, 76700 Harfleur; tel. 2-35-24-72-00; fax 2-35-53-36-25; petroleum and gas transport, passenger transport; Chair. YVES ROUSIER; Man. Dir JACQUES CHARVET; displacement 118,274 grt.

CIVIL AVIATION

There are international airports at Orly and Roissy-Charles de Gaulle (Paris), Bordeaux, Lille, Lyon, Marseille, Nice, Strasbourg and Toulouse.

Aéroports de Paris: 291 blvd de Raspail, 75675 Paris Cédex 14; tel. 1-43-35-70-00; fax 1-43-35-74-27; e-mail webmaster@adp.fr; internet www.adp.fr; state authority in charge of Paris airports at Orly and Roissy-Charles de Gaulle, 12 runways for light aircraft, including Le Bourget, and a heliport at Issy-les-Moulineaux; Pres. PIERRE GRAFF; Man. Dir HUBERT DU MESNIL.

Airlines

Air France: 45 rue de Paris, 95747 Roissy Cédex; tel. 1-41-56-78-00; fax 1-41-56-70-29; internet www.airfrance.net; f. 1933; 25.8% state-owned; merger with KLM (Netherlands) approved 2004; internal, international, European and inter-continental services; Chair. JEAN-CYRIL SPINETTA.

Brit Air: Aéroport, CS 27925-29679 Morlaix; tel. 2-98-62-10-22; fax 2-98-62-77-66; internet www.britair.com; f. 1973; domestic and European flights; 99% owned by Air France; Pres. and Dir-Gen. MARC LAMIDEY.

Corsair: 2 rue Charles Lindbergh, 94636 Rungis Cédex; tel. 1-49-79-49-59; tel. www.corsair.fr; f. 1981; scheduled flights between metropolitan France and Italy, Madagascar, Morocco, Kenya, and the French overseas possessions, and chartered flights to other medium- and long-range destinations; Pres. and Dir-Gen. PIERRE CHESNEAU.

Hex Air: Aéroport Le Puy, 43320 Loudes; tel. 4-71-08-62-28; fax 4-71-08-04-10; f. 1991; domestic services; Pres. BERNARD GUICHON.

Regional CAE: Aéroport Nantes Atlantique, 44345 Bougenais Cédex; tel. 2-40-13-53-00; fax 2-40-13-53-08; e-mail contact@regional.com; internet www.regional.com; f. 2001 by merger of Flandre Air, Proteus and Regional Airlines; operates European and domestic flights; 100% owned by Air France; Pres. and Dir-Gen. JACQUES BANKIR.

Star Airlines: Immeuble Horizon, 10 allée Bienvenue, 93885 Noisy-le-Grand Cédex; tel. 1-33-48-15-90-00; internet www.star-airlines.fr; f. 1995; charter and scheduled flights between France and the Bahamas, Cuba, the Maldives, Mauritius, Mexico and Sri Lanka; Pres. and Dir-Gen. CÉDRIC PASTOUR.

TAT European Airlines: 47 rue Christiaan-Huygens, BP 7237, 37072 Tours Cédex 02; tel. 2-47-42-30-00; fax 2-47-54-29-50; f. 1968; wholly-owned by British Airways; Pres. RODOLPHE MARCHAIS; Chair. MARC ROCHET.

Airlines Association

Fédération Nationale de l'Aviation Marchande (FNAM): 28 rue de Châteaudun, 75009 Paris; tel. 1-45-26-23-24; fax 1-45-26-23-95; e-mail info@fnam.fr; internet www.fnam.fr; f. 1991; Delegate-Gen. JEAN-PIERRE LE GOFF.

Chambre Syndicale du Transport Aérien (CSTA): 28 rue de Châteaudun, 75009 Paris; tel. 1-45-26-23-24; fax 1-45-26-23-95; e-mail info@fnam.fr; internet www.fnam.fr/syndicats/csta.asp; f. 1947 to represent French airlines at national level; Pres. LIONEL GUERIN.

Tourism

France attracts tourists from all over the world. Paris is famous for its boulevards, historic buildings, theatres, art treasures, fashion houses, restaurants and night clubs. The Mediterranean and Atlantic coasts and the French Alps are the most popular tourist resorts. Among other attractions are the many ancient towns, the châteaux of the Loire, the fishing villages of Brittany and Normandy, and spas and places of pilgrimage, such as Vichy and Lourdes. The theme park, Disneyland Paris, also attracts large numbers of tourists. There were an estimated 77,012,000 tourist arrivals in 2002; estimated tourist receipts in 2002 totalled US $32,329m. Most visitors are from the United Kingdom, Germany, Belgium, the Netherlands and Italy.

Direction du Tourisme: 2 rue Linois, 75740 Paris Cédex 15; tel. 1-44-37-36-00; fax 1-44-37-36-36; internet www.tourisme.gouv.fr; Dir BRUNO FARENIAUX.

Maison de la France: 20 ave de l'Opéra, 75041 Paris Cédex 01; tel. 1-42-96-70-00; fax 1-42-96-70-11; internet www.franceguide.com; f. 1987; Pres. GÉRARD BRÉMOND; Dir-Gen. JEAN-PHILIPPE PEROL.

Observatoire National du Tourisme: 8 ave de l'Opéra, 75001 Paris; tel. 1-44-77-95-40; fax 1-44-77-95-50; e-mail isabelle.chevassut@ont-tourisme.com; internet www.ont-tourisme.com; f. 1991; conducts studies and publishes information on all aspects of tourism in France; Pres. MAURICE BERNADET; Dir ALAIN MONFERRAND.

There are Regional Tourism Committees in the 23 regions and 4 overseas départements. There are more than 3,200 Offices de Tourisme and Syndicats d'Initiative (tourist offices operated by the local authorities) throughout France.

FRENCH OVERSEAS POSSESSIONS

Ministry of Overseas Departments, Territories and Country: 27 rue Oudinot, 75007 Paris, France; tel. 1-53-69-20-00; internet www .outre-mer.gouv.fr.

Minister of the Overseas Possessions: BRIGITTE GIRARDIN.

The national flag of France, proportions two by three, with three equal vertical stripes, of blue, white and red, is used in the Overseas Possessions.

French Overseas Departments

The four Overseas Departments (départements d'outre-mer) are French Guiana, Guadeloupe, Martinique and Réunion. They are integral parts of the French Republic. Each Overseas Department is administered by a Prefect (Préfet), appointed by the French Government, and the administrative structure is similar to that of the Departments of metropolitan France. Overseas Departments, however, have their own Courts of Appeal (Cours d'Appel). In 1974 each of the Overseas Departments was granted the additional status of a Region (a unit devised for the purpose of economic and social planning, presided over by a Conseil régional—Regional Council). Under the decentralization law of March 1982, the executive power of the Prefect in each Overseas Department was transferred to the locally-elected Conseil général (General Council). As a compromise between autonomy and complete assimilation into France, the responsibility of the Conseil régional for economic, social and cultural affairs was increased in 1983. In February of that year the first direct elections for the Conseils régionaux were held. Government proposals regarding the institutional future and socio-economic development of the Departments were definitively approved by the Assemblée nationale in November 2000 and by the Cour Constitutionnel (Constitutional Council) in December. These changes provided for the establishment on French Guiana, Guadeloupe and Martinique of congresses of the Conseils régionaux and généraux;

the transfer to the Regions of responsibilities in areas such as roads, territorial development, water resources and housing; and measures to increase the Departments' autonomy in conducting relations with neighbouring countries and territories; a proposal to create a second department on Réunion, was however, withdrawn. However, in the event, the full implementation of the other measures was delayed, and the new, centre-right Government that assumed office following the general election held in June 2002 introduced new proposals for the restructuring and decentralization of the Republic. Constitutional changes, approved by parliament in March 2003, and which described the Government of the French Republic as decentralized, permitted the holding of local referendums on the changing of the status of a territorial unit, the establishment of local consultative assemblies, and the devolution of powers on a temporary or experimental basis to territorial communities within the Republic. Proposals to replace the Conseils régionaux and généraux in Guadeloupe and Martinique in each case with a unified territorial authority were the subject of local referendums in December 2003. However, in both cases, the proposals were rejected and the status of both territories was to remain unchanged. The Overseas Departments continue to send elected representatives to the Assemblée nationale and to the Sénat in Paris, and also to the European Parliament.

FRENCH GUIANA

Introductory Survey

Location, Climate, Language, Religion, Capital

French Guiana (Guyane) lies on the north coast of South America, with Suriname to the west and Brazil to the south and east. The climate is humid, with a season of heavy rains from April to July and another short rainy season in December and January. Average temperature at sea-level is 27°C (85°F), with little seasonal variation. French is the official language, but a Creole patois is also spoken. The majority of the population belong to the Roman Catholic Church, although other Christian churches are represented. The capital is Cayenne.

Recent History

French occupation commenced in the early 17th century. After brief periods of Dutch, English and Portuguese rule, the territory was finally confirmed as French in 1817. The colony steadily declined, after a short period of prosperity in the 1850s as a result of the discovery of gold in the basin of the Approuague river. French Guiana, including the notorious Devil's Island, was used as a penal colony and as a place of exile for convicts and political prisoners before the practice was halted in 1937. The colony became a Department of France in 1946.

French Guiana's reputation as an area of political and economic stagnation was dispelled by the growth of pro-independence sentiments, and the use of violence by a small minority, compounded by tensions between the Guyanais and large numbers of immigrant workers. In 1974 French Guiana was granted regional status, as part of France's governmental reorganization, thus acquiring greater economic autonomy. In that year, none the less, demonstrations against unemployment, the worsening economic situation and French government policy with regard to the Department led to the detention of leading trade unionists and pro-independence politicians. In 1975 the French

Government announced plans to increase investment in French Guiana, but these were largely unsuccessful, owing partly to the problems of developing the interior (about 90% of the territory is covered by forest). Further industrial and political unrest in the late 1970s prompted the Parti Socialiste Guyanais (PSG), then the strongest political organization, to demand greater autonomy for the Department. In 1980 there were several bomb attacks against 'colonialist' targets by an extremist group, Fo nou Libéré la Guyane. Reforms introduced by the French Socialist Government in 1982–83 devolved some power over local affairs to the new Conseil régional (Regional Council). In the February 1983 elections to the Conseil régional the left-wing parties gained a majority of votes, but not of seats, and the balance of power was held by the separatist Union des Travailleurs Guyanais (UTG), the political wing of which became the Parti National Populaire Guyanais (PNPG) in November 1985. At elections to the Conseil général (General Council) held in March 1985, the PSG and left-wing independents secured 13 seats out of a total of 19.

For the general election to the Assemblée nationale in March 1986, French Guiana's representation was increased from one to two deputies. The incumbent PSG deputy was re-elected, the other seat being won by the Gaullist Rassemblement pour la République (RPR). The PSG increased its strength on the Conseil régional following simultaneous elections to that body, and Georges Othily of the PSG was re-elected President of the Conseil.

Of the votes cast in the Department at the 1988 French presidential election, the incumbent François Mitterrand of the Parti Socialiste (PS) defeated Jacques Chirac of the RPR. In the legislative elections held in June, the RPR none the less retained a seat in the Assemblée nationale. In September–October the left-wing parties won a majority of seats at elections to the Conseil général. In September 1989 Othily, the President of the Conseil régional, was elected to take French Guiana's seat in the French Sénat (Senate). Othily had recently been expelled from the PSG for having worked too closely with the opposition parties. However, he attracted support from those who regarded the party's domination of French Guiana as corrupt, and his victory over the incumbent senator, a PSG member, was believed to reflect the level of dissatisfaction within the party.

In March 1992 elections were held to both the Conseil général and the Conseil régional. In the former, the PSG retained 10 seats, while other left-wing candidates took five seats. The PSG leader, Elie Castor, retained the presidency of the Conseil général. The party also won 16 seats in the Conseil régional, and the PSG Secretary-General, Antoine Karam, was subsequently elected as the body's President. In a referendum in September, 67.3% of voters in French Guiana approved ratification of the Treaty on European Union (see p. 217), although a high abstention rate was recorded.

At the March 1993 elections to the Assemblée nationale Léon Bertrand of the RPR was re-elected, along with Christiane Taubira-Delannon, the founder of the independent left-wing Walwari movement and an outspoken critic of existing policies for the management of French Guiana's natural resources; she subsequently joined the République et liberté grouping in the Assemblée nationale.

The PSG's representation in the Conseil général declined to eight seats following the March 1994 cantonal elections; none the less, one of its members, Stéphan Phinéra-Horth, was subsequently elected President of the Conseil (Elie Castor having left the party). Taubira-Delannon, defeated by Karam, failed to secure election, although another member of the Walwari movement did enter the Conseil. Taubira-Delannon was elected to the European Parliament in June, as a representative of the Energie radicale grouping—which secured the greatest percentage of the votes (36.3%) in the Department, ahead of the government list and a combined list of the parties of the left of the four Overseas Departments.

At the first round of voting in the 1995 presidential elections, on 23 April, there was a considerable increase in support in French Guiana for Chirac, who took 39.8% of the votes cast, at the expense of the candidate of the PS, Lionel Jospin, who received the support of 24.2% of voters. The level of support for Jean-Marie Le Pen, of the extreme right-wing Front National, almost doubled (to 8.1%), compared with that at the 1988 election. At the second round, on 7 May, Chirac won 57.4% of the valid votes cast.

Beginning in late October 1996 a boycott of classes by secondary-school pupils, who were demanding improved conditions of study, escalated in the following month into a crisis that was regarded as exemplifying wider social tensions between the Department and metropolitan France. The refusal of the Prefect, Pierre Dartout, to receive schools' representatives prompted protests in Cayenne, which swiftly degenerated into rioting and looting, apparently as the protesters were joined by disaffected youths from deprived areas. Considerable material damage was caused to government and commercial property during two nights of violence. The central Government dispatched anti-riot police to assist the local security forces, and it was announced that the Secretary of State for Overseas Departments and Territories, Jean-Jacques de Peretti, and the Minister of National Education, François Bayrou, would visit French Guiana. However, the conviction, shortly afterwards, of several people implicated in the rioting provoked further protests and clashes with security forces, and a one-day general strike in Cayenne, organized by the UTG, resulted in the closure of most businesses and government departments. The extent of the security forces' actions in suppressing the demonstrations was criticized, while the competence of the Department's administrators in their approach to the crisis was the focus of considerable scrutiny. Local officials, meanwhile, denounced the role in the violence not only of unemployed youths but also of separatist groups, alleging that the latter were seeking to exploit the crisis for their own ends. Bayrou and de Peretti subsequently arrived in Cayenne to meet those involved in the crisis. Local administrators and schools' representatives had already reached agreement on the students' material demands, but, to considerable local acclaim, the ministers announced the establishment, effective from the beginning of 1997, of separate Academies for French Guiana, Guadeloupe and Martinique. The creation was also announced of additional primary educational facilities, and a programme was declared to improve academic standards in secondary schools. In all, the measures were to cost the French Government more than 500m. francs.

In April 1997 violent incidents followed the arrest of five pro-independence activists suspected of setting fire to the home of the public prosecutor during the disturbances of November 1996. Five others, including leading members of the UTG and the PNPG, were subsequently detained in connection with the arson incident. The transfer of all 10 detainees to Martinique prompted further violent protests in Cayenne. Police reinforcements were dispatched by the central Government to help suppress the violence, as nine gendarmes reportedly received gunshot wounds during two nights of rioting. In July one of the detainees, Jean-Victor Castor, a prominent member of the UTG and the pro-independence Mouvement pour la Décolonisation et l'Emancipation Sociale (MDES), who had been released the previous month, was rearrested and accused of assaulting a policeman during the April riots. Following the announcement, in August, that Castor was to remain in custody, some 200 demonstrators clashed with riot police in Cayenne. Castor was released shortly afterwards, and in September a further four separatists, who had been held on remand since April, were also freed.

In late May and early June 1997 Léon Bertrand and Christiane Taubira-Delannon were both re-elected to the Assemblée nationale in elections that were marked by a high rate of abstention. Candidates from pro-independence parties notably gained increased support, winning slightly more than 10% of the votes cast in both constituencies.

Elections to the Conseil régional and the Conseil général were held in March 1998. The PSG's representation in the former declined to 11 seats, with other left-wing candidates securing a further 11 seats (including two won by Walwari). Antoine Karam was re-elected to the presidency of the Conseil. The PSG also lost seats in the Conseil général, retaining only five of the 19 seats, while other left-wing candidates took a further five, and independent candidates won seven seats. André Lecante, an independent left-wing councillor, was elected as the body's President, defeating the incumbent, Phinéra-Horth. In late September 1998 Othily was re-elected to the Sénat.

In January 1999 representatives of 10 separatist organizations from French Guiana, Guadeloupe and Martinique, including the MDES and the PNPG, signed a joint declaration denouncing 'French colonialism', in which they stated their intention to campaign for the reinstatement of the three Caribbean Overseas Departments on a UN list of territories to be decolonized. In February members of the Conseil régional and the Conseil général held a congress to discuss the political, economic and social future of French Guiana; the participants proposed the replacement of the two Conseils with a single body, to which responsibility in several areas, such as economic development, health and education, would be transferred. Several RPR councillors boycotted the meeting. In October, however, Lionel Jospin, the Prime Minister, precluded from future legislation any merger of the Conseil régional and Conseil général. Following a series of meetings held in late 1999, in December the Presidents of the regional councils of French Guiana, Guadeloupe and Martinique signed a joint declaration in Basse-Terre, Guadeloupe, affirming their intention to propose, to the President and the Government, a legislative amendment, possibly constitutional, aimed at creating a new status of overseas region. The declaration, however, was dismissed by the Secretary of State for Overseas Departments and Territories, Jean-Jack Queyranne, in February 2000 as unconstitutional and exceeding the mandate of politicians responsible. In March, during a visit to the Department by Queyranne, rioting broke out following Queyranne's refusal to meet a delegation of separatist organizations. Later that month the Conseil régional overwhelmingly rejected reforms proposed by Queyranne in February, which included the creation of a Congress in French Guiana, as well as the extension of the Departments' powers in areas such as regional co-operation. Nevertheless, the proposals were provisionally accepted by the Assemblée nationale in May, and were subsequently adopted, by a narrow margin, by the Sénat, following a number of modifications. In November the Assemblée nationale approved the reforms, and in December they were ratified by the Constitutional Council. At a referendum held in September, French Guiana voted overwhelmingly in favour (80%) of reducing the presidential mandate from seven years to five.

In late November 2000 several people were injured following riots in Cayenne. The demonstrations followed a march, organized by the UTG, demanding greater autonomy for French Guiana, as well as immediate negotiations with the new Secretary of State for Overseas Departments and Territories, Christian Paul. Protesters claimed they had been excluded from talks on French Guiana's status (Paul had invited leaders of various political parties in French Guiana to attend a meeting to be held in France in December, but the offer was rejected by MDES activists, who demanded the meeting be held in Cayenne). Nevertheless, discussions were held in mid-December in Paris at which Paul, various senior politicians from French Guiana and representatives from the PSG, the RPR, Walwari, and the Forces Démocratiques Guyanaises (FDG) were present. It was agreed that further talks were to be held between the Conseil régional and the Conseil général of French Guiana before the end of 2001, eventually to be followed by a referendum in the Department. In early January 2001, following further consultations, it was agreed that a document detailing proposals for increased autonomy for French Guiana was to be drawn up by local officials and was to be presented to the French Government for approval. Following a meeting of members of both Conseils in late June 2001, a series of proposals on greater autonomy, to be presented to the French Government, was agreed upon. These included: the division of the territory into four districts; the creation of a 'collectivité territoriale' (territorial community), governed by a 41-member Assembly elected for a five-year term; and the establishment of an independent executive council. Furthermore, the proposals included a request that the territory be given control over legislative and administrative affairs, as well as legislative authority on matters concerning French Guiana alone. In November the French Government announced itself to be in favour of the suggested constitutional developments, although no further steps had been effected by early 2005. Referendums held in December 2003 in Guadeloupe and Martinique on the question of legislative reform prompted renewed demands by pro-independence campaigners for a referendum to address the issue of greater autonomy for French Guiana.

At municipal elections held in March 2001, the PSG candidate for the mayorship of Cayenne, Jean-Claude Lafontaine, defeated the Walwari candidate, Christiane Taubira-Delannon. At concurrently held elections to the presidency of the Conseil général the left-wing independent candidate Joseph Ho-Ten-You defeated André Lecante. In regional elections in March 2004 the PSG won 17 of the 31 seats on the Conseil régional; the remaining 14 seats were divided equally between a joint list presented by the FDG and Walwari, and the right-wing Union pour la Majorité Présidentielle (UMP).

In September 2001 Christian Paul announced the establishment of a number of measures designed to improve security in the Department. Plans included a 20% increase in the police force, the creation of a small 'peace corps' and a continuous police presence in the town of Maripasoula and its surrounding region, following concerns over the security of gold prospectors in the area. In the first round of the presidential election, held on 21 April 2002, Taubira-Delannon received 52.7% of the votes cast in the Department, followed by Chirac, who attracted 19.0%. In the second round, held on 5 May, Chirac overwhelmingly defeated Jean-Marie Le Pen, receiving 89.1% of the vote and thereby winning a second presidential term. At the legislative elections held in June, Taubira-Delannon was re-elected to the Assemblée nationale with 65.3% of the vote, and Bertrand with 64.0%; about two-thirds of registered voters abstained. In July 2002 Ange Mancini was appointed Prefect, replacing Henri Masse. In elections to the Conseil régional held in March 2004 the PSG won 17 of the council's 31 seats with 37.7% of the votes cast, while the FDG and the UMP (reconstituted as the Union pour un Mouvement Populaire) each won seven seats, with 31.2% and 31.1% of the ballot, respectively. Antoine Karam was duly re-elected as President of the Conseil régional.

In mid-2001 the French President, Jacques Chirac, rejected a joint request by French Guiana, Guadeloupe and Martinique that they be permitted to join, as associate members, the Association of Caribbean States (see p. 372).

Government

France is represented in French Guiana by an appointed Prefect. There are two councils with local powers: the Conseil général, with 19 members, and the Conseil régional, with 31 members. Both are elected by universal adult suffrage for a period of six years. French Guiana elects two representatives to the Assemblée nationale in Paris, and sends one elected representative to the Sénat. French Guiana is also represented at the European Parliament.

Defence

At 1 August 2004 France maintained military forces of 3,100 and a gendarmerie in French Guiana.

Economic Affairs

In 2001 French Guiana's gross domestic product (GDP), measured at current prices, was US $1,308m., equivalent to $7,737 per head. Between 1990 and 2001, according to UN estimates, GDP increased, in real terms, at an average rate of 3.1% per year; growth in 2001 was 1.6%. Between the censuses of 1990 and 1999, according to provisional figures, the population increased at an average annual rate of 3.5%.

According to FAO estimates, agriculture (including fishing) engaged 17.1% of the economically active population in 2003. In 2000 the sector contributed 5.1% of GDP. In 2000 agricultural products accounted for some 22% of total export earnings, at €27m. The dominant activities are fisheries and forestry, although the contribution of the latter to export earnings has declined in recent years. In 2003 exports of shrimps totalled some €13m. and accounted for 11.7% of export earnings. The principal crops for local consumption are cassava, vegetables and rice, and sugar cane is grown for making rum. Rice, pineapples and citrus fruit are cultivated for export. According to UN estimates, agricultural GDP decreased at an average annual rate of 0.8% in 1990–98; in 1998 agricultural GDP increased by an estimated 0.3%.

Industry, including construction, engaged about 15.6% of the employed labour force in 1999 and, according to official sources, contributed 18.7% of GDP. The mining sector is dominated by the extraction of gold, which involves small-scale alluvial operations as well as larger local and multinational mining concerns. Exploration activity intensified in the mid-1990s, and the proposed construction of a major new road into the interior of the Department was expected to encourage further development. Officially-recorded gold exports were estimated at 4,857 kg in 1999 (actual production levels and sales are believed to be higher than published levels). In 2002 2,971 kg of gold were mined. In 2003 exports of gold were worth more than €55m., accounting for some 49.9% of export earnings. Crushed rock for the construction industry is the only other mineral extracted in significant quantities, although exploratory drilling of known diamond deposits began in 1995. Deposits of bauxite, columbotantalite and kaolin are also present. There is little manufacturing activity, except for the processing of fisheries products (mainly shrimp-freezing) and the distillation of rum. In 1990–98 industrial GDP (excluding construction) increased at an average annual rate of 7.8%. The construction sector expanded at an average of 2.0% per year in the same period.

French Guiana was heavily dependent on imported fuels for the generation of energy prior to the flooding of the Petit-Saut hydroelectric dam, on the River Sinnamary, in 1994. Together with existing generating plants, the 116-MW dam was expected to satisfy the territory's electrical energy requirements for about 30 years. Refined petroleum imports accounted for 10.0% of total imports in 2003.

The services sector engaged 77.7% of the employed labour force in 1999 and, according to official sources, contributed 76.1% of GDP. The European Space Agency's satellite-launching centre at Kourou (established in 1964 and expanded during the 1990s) has provided a considerable stimulus to the economy, most notably the construction sector (which engaged 7.5% of the employed labour force in 1999). In 2003 the space centre was estimated to contribute approximately one-quarter of French Guiana's GDP and approximately one-half of its tax revenues. The tourist sector expanded in the last two decades of the 20th century, although its potential is limited by the lack of infrastructure away from the coast. In 2002 some 65,000 visitor arrivals were recorded. In early 2003 the French Minister of the Overseas Possessions announced plans to stimulate the economies of French Guiana, Guadeloupe and Martinique that included the introduction of tax incentives for the hotel sector.

In 2003 the principal source of imports was metropolitan France (which supplied 47.5% of total imports); the Department's other major suppliers were Trinidad and Tobago (9.6%), Italy and Japan. Metropolitan France was also the principal market for exports in that year (62.8%); other important purchasers were Switzerland (11.5%), Martinique and Guadeloupe. The principal imports in 2003 were road vehicles, refined petroleum products and pharmaceutical products; the principal exports were gold, shrimps and boats. In 2003 French Guiana recorded a trade deficit of more than €523.9m. The value of exports in that year was some €110.8m., less than one-fifth of the total value of imports, worth some €634.7m.

Under the 1998 regional budget it was envisaged that expenditure would total €67m., while revenue was €63m. By September 1988 French Guiana's external debt had reached US $1,200m. The annual rate of inflation averaged 1.5% in 1994–2003; consumer prices increased by an average of 1.5% in 2002 and by 1.1% in 2003. Unemployment in 2003 was estimated at 24.5% of the total labour force. However, there is a shortage of skilled labour, offset partly by immigration.

As an integral part of France, French Guiana is a member of the European Union (EU, see p. 217).

Economic development in French Guiana has been hindered by the Department's location, poor infrastructure away from the coast and lack of a skilled indigenous labour force, although there is considerable potential for further growth in the fishing, forestry and tourism (notably 'eco-tourism') sectors. A particular concern was the high rate of unemployment. French Guiana's geographical characteristics—large parts of the territory are accessible only by river—have resulted in difficulties in regulating key areas of the economy, such as gold-mining and forestry. Considerable concern has been expressed regarding the ecological consequences of such a lack of controls; moreover, the flooding of a large area of forest (some 340 sq km), as part of the Petit-Saut barrage project, prompted disquiet among environmental groups, as did uncertainty regarding the ecological implications of the satellite-launching programme at Kourou. Proposals for the creation of a national park, covering 2.5m. ha of the south of French Guiana, with the aim of protecting an expanse of equatorial forest, were still being hindered in 2004 by the need to reconcile ecological concerns with economic priorities and the needs of the resident communities, notably the demands of gold prospectors. The budget deficit represents a significant obstacle to growth, while high demand for imported consumer goods (much of which is generated by relatively well-remunerated civil servants, who constitute about two-thirds of the working population) undermines progress in reducing the trade deficit. In 2000 there was a projected deficit of some €14m. on the departmental budget.

Education

Education is modelled on the system in metropolitan France, and is compulsory for 10 years between the ages of six and 16 years. Primary education begins at six years of age and lasts for five years. Secondary education, beginning at 11 years of age, lasts for up to seven years, comprising a first cycle of four years and a second of three years. Education at state schools is provided free of charge. In 2002/03 there were 43 pre-primary schools and 97 primary schools; there were 35 secondary schools in 2000/01. There were 35,759 students in pre-primary and primary education in 2002/03, while in secondary education there were 22,003 (including 3,073 students in vocational education), of whom some 92% attended state schools. Higher education in law, administration and French language and literature is provided by a branch of the Université des Antilles et de la Guyane in Cayenne (the university as a whole had some 12,000 enrolled students in 2004), and one department of a technical institute opened at Kourou in 1988. There is also a teacher-training college and an agricultural college. Total government expenditure on education amounted to 851m. French francs in 1993. The French Government announced its decision to increase expenditure in the education sector in 2000–06, including €71m. on the construction of new school buildings. An Academy for French Guiana was established in January 1997.

Public Holidays

2005: 1 January (New Year's Day), 7–8 February (Lenten Carnival), 9 February (Ash Wednesday), 25–28 March (Easter), 1 May (Labour Day), 5 May (Ascension Day), 16 May (Whit Monday), 10 June (Slavery Day), 14 July (National Day), 11 November (Armistice Day), 25 December (Christmas Day).

2006: 1 January (New Year's Day), 27–28 February (Lenten Carnival), 1 March (Ash Wednesday), 14–17 April (Easter), 1 May (Labour Day), 25 May (Ascension Day), 5 June (Whit Monday), 10 June (Slavery Day), 14 July (National Day), 11 November (Armistice Day), 25 December (Christmas Day).

Weights and Measures

The metric system is in use.

Statistical Survey

Sources (unless otherwise stated): Institut National de la Statistique et des Etudes Economiques (INSEE), Service Régional de Guyane, ave Pasteur, BP 6017, 97306 Cayenne Cédex; tel. 5-94-29-73-00; fax 5-94-29-73-01; internet www.insee.fr/fr/insee_regions/guyane; Chambre de Commerce et d'Industrie, Hôtel Consulaire, pl. de l'Esplanade, BP 49, 97321 Cayenne Cédex; tel. 5-94-29-96-00; fax 5-94-29-96-34; internet www.guyane.cci.fr.

AREA AND POPULATION

Area: 83,534 sq km (32,253 sq miles).

Population: 114,808 (males 59,799, females 55,009) at census of 15 March 1990; 157,213 at census of 8 March 1999. *2004* (official estimate at 1 January, rounded figure): 184,000.

Density (at 1 January 2004): 2.2 per sq km.

Principal Towns (population at 1999 census, provisional): Cayenne (capital) 50,594; Saint-Laurent-du-Maroni 19,211; Kourou 19,107; Matoury 18,032; Rémire-Montjoly 15,555; Mana 5,445; Macouria 5,050; Maripasoula 3,710. *Mid-2003* (UN estimate, incl. suburbs): Cayenne 56,081 (Source: UN, *World Urbanization Prospects: The 2003 Revision*).

Births, Marriages and Deaths (1999): Registered live births 4,907 (birth rate 31.0 per 1,000); Registered marriages 548 (marriage rate 3.5 per 1,000); Registered deaths 648 (death rate 4.1 per 1,000). *2001:* Registered marriages 553. *2002:* Registered live births 5,249; Registered deaths 656 (Source: UN, *Population and Vital Statistics Report*).

Expectation of Life (years at birth, 1999): Males 71.7; Females 79.2.

Economically Active Population (persons aged 15 years and over, 1999): Agriculture, forestry and fishing 2,888; Construction 3,256; Industry 3,524; Trade 4,573; Transport 1,616; Education, health and social services 8,990; Public administration 10,337; Other services 8,259; Total employed 43,443 (males 25,703; females 17,740). *Mid-2003* (estimates): Agriculture, etc. 13,000; Total labour force 76,000 (males 50,000, females 26,000) (Source: FAO). *December 2003:* Unemployed 12,042.

HEALTH AND WELFARE

Key Indicators

Access to Water (% of persons, 2002): 84.

Access to Sanitation (% of persons, 2002): 78.
For sources and definitions, see explanatory note on p. vi.

AGRICULTURE, ETC.

Principal Crops (FAO estimates, '000 metric tons, 2003): Rice (paddy) 24.2; Cassava 10.4; Sugar-cane 5.4; Cabbages 6.4; Tomatoes 3.8; Cucumbers and gherkins 3.7; Green beans 3.3; Other fresh vegetables 7.5; Bananas 4.5; Plantains 3.2. Source: FAO.

Livestock (FAO estimates, '000 head, 2003): Cattle 9.2; Pigs 10.5; Sheep 2.6. Source: FAO.

Livestock Products (FAO estimates, metric tons, 2003): Beef and veal 460; Pig meat 1,245; Poultry meat 560; Cows' milk 270; Hen eggs 460. Source: FAO.

Forestry (FAO estimates, '000 cubic metres, 2003): *Roundwood Removals* (excl. bark): Sawlogs, veneer logs and logs for sleepers 51; Other industrial wood 9; Fuel wood 89; Total 149. *Sawnwood Production* (incl. railway sleepers): Total 15. Source: FAO.

Fishing (metric tons, live weight, 2002): Capture 5,568 (Marine fishes 2,500—FAO estimate, Shrimps 3,068); Aquaculture 38; *Total catch* 5,606. Source: FAO.

MINING

Production ('000 metric tons unless otherwise indicated, estimates, 2002): Cement 62,000; Gold (metal content of ore, kilograms) 2,971; Sand 1,500. Source: US Geological Survey.

INDUSTRY

Production: Rum 3,072 hl in 2000; Electric energy 455 million kWh in 2000 (estimate). Source: partly UN, *Industrial Commodity Statistics Yearbook*.

FINANCE

Currency and Exchange Rates: 100 cent = 1 euro (€). *Sterling and Dollar Equivalents* (31 December 2004): £1 sterling = €1.4180; US $1 = €0.7341; €1,000 = £705.24 = $1,362.10. *Average Exchange Rate* (euros per US dollar): 1.0626 in 2002; 0.8860 in 2003; 0.8054. Note: The national currency was formerly the French franc. From the introduction of the euro, with French participation, on 1 January 1999, a fixed exchange rate of €1 = 6.55957 French francs was in operation. Euro notes and coins were introduced on 1 January 2002. The euro and French currency circulated alongside each other until 17 February, after which the euro became the sole legal tender. Some of the figures in this Survey are still in terms of francs.

Budget (million French francs, 1992): *French Government:* Revenue 706; Expenditure 1,505. *Regional Government:* Revenue 558; Expenditure 666. *Departmental Government:* Revenue 998; Expenditure 803. *Communes:* Revenue 998; Expenditure 982. *1998* (€ million): *Regional Budget:* Revenue 63; Expenditure 67. *Departmental Budget:* Revenue 137; Expenditure 15.

Money Supply (million French francs at 31 December 1996): Currency outside banks 3,000; Demand deposits at banks 1,621; Total money 4,621.

Cost of Living (Consumer Price Index; base: 2000 = 100): 101.6 in 2001; 103.1 in 2002; 104.2 in 2003. Source: ILO.

Expenditure on the Gross Domestic Product (million French francs at current prices, 1995): Government final consumption expenditure 4,042; Private final consumption expenditure 5,898; Increase in stocks 121; Gross fixed capital formation 2,542; *Total domestic expenditure* 12,603; Exports of goods and services 7,746; *Less* Imports of goods and services 9,577; *GDP in purchasers' values* 10,772.

Gross Domestic Product by Economic Activity (million French francs at current prices, 1995): Agriculture, hunting, forestry and fishing 572; Mining, quarrying and manufacturing 988; Electricity, gas and water 139; Construction 858; Trade, restaurants and hotels 1,895; Transport, storage and communications 1,241; Finance, insurance, real estate and business services 815; Public administration 1,492; Other services 2,451; *Sub-total* 10,449; *Less* Imputed bank service charge 310; *GDP at basic prices* 10,139; Taxes, less subsidies, on products 633; *GDP in purchasers' values* 10,772.

EXTERNAL TRADE

Principal Commodities: *Imports* (€ million, 2003): Road vehicles 72.8; Refined petroleum products 64.3; Pharmaceutical products 27.8; Water and non-alcoholic beverages 16.5; Milk and dairy products 16.2; Road vehicle parts 14.9; Mining or construction equipment 13.2; Computers and data-processing equipment 12.3 ; Radios, televisions and communication equipment 11.7; Total (incl. others) 640.7. *Exports f.o.b.:* (€ million, 2003): Gold 55.3; Shrimps 13.0; Boats 9.0; Instruments of measurement and control 7.3; Metal products 4.3; Frozen fish 3.3; Rice 3.2; Wood, cut or shaped barks 2.6; Total (incl. others) 110.8. Source: Direction nationale du commerce extérieur.

Principal Trading Partners (€ million, 2000): *Imports c.i.f.:* Belgium-Luxembourg 10; France (metropolitan) 346; Germany 15; Italy 18; Japan 18; Martinique 11; Netherlands 12; Spain 9; Trinidad and Tobago 66; USA 12; Total (incl. others) 620. *Exports f.o.b.:* Brazil 5; France (metropolitan) 77; Guadeloupe 6; Italy 2; Martinique 4; Netherlands 3; Spain 3; Switzerland 6; USA 9; Total (incl. others) 121.

TRANSPORT

Road Traffic ('000 motor vehicles in use, 2001): Passenger cars 32.9; Commercial vehicles 11.9. (Source: UN, *Statistical Yearbook*). *2002:* 50,000 motor vehicles in use.

International Sea-borne Shipping (traffic, 2002 unless otherwise indicated): Vessels entered 385; Goods loaded 39,047 metric tons; Goods unloaded 492,193 metric tons; Passengers carried 275,300 (1998).

Civil Aviation (traffic, 2002 unless otherwise indicated): Freight carried 8,167 metric tons; Passengers carried 383,889 (2003).

TOURISM

Tourist Arrivals (2002): 65,000.

Receipts from Tourism (US $ million): 51 in 1998; 50 in 1999. Source: World Tourism Organization.

COMMUNICATIONS MEDIA

Radio Receivers ('000 in use): 104 in 1997.

Television Receivers ('000 in use): 37 in 1998.

Telephones ('000 main lines in use): 49.2 in 1999.

Facsimile Machines (number in use): 185 in 1990.

Mobile Cellular Telephones ('000 subscribers): 81.8 in 2001.

Personal Computers ('000 in use): 23 in 1999.

Internet Users ('000): 10.1 in 2002.

Daily Newspaper: 1 in 1996 (average circulation 2,000 copies). Sources: UNESCO, *Statistical Yearbook*; UN, *Statistical Yearbook*; International Telecommunication Union.

EDUCATION

Pre-primary (2002/03): 43 institutions; 12,274 students.

Primary (2002/03): 97 institutions; 2,751 teachers (2,506 state, 245 private); 23,485 students.

Secondary (2002/03, unless otherwise indicated): 35 institutions (2000/01); 4,553 teachers (4,178 state, 375 private); 22,003 students.

Higher (2000/01): 666 students (1998/99); 42 teachers. Source: Ministère de l'Education Nationale, de l'Enseignement Supérieur et de la Recherche, *Repères et Références Statisques sur les Enseignements, la Formation et la Recherche 2003*.

Directory

The Government

(April 2005)

Prefect: ANGE MANCINI, Préfecture, rue Fiedmont, BP 7008, 97307 Cayenne Cédex; tel. 5-94-39-45-00; fax 5-94-30-02-77; e-mail sgaer1 .prefect.guyane@wanadoo.fr; internet www.guyane.pref.gouv.fr.

President of the General Council: PIERRE DESERT, Hôtel du Département, pl. Léopold Héder, BP 5021, 97305 Cayenne Cédex; tel. 5-94-29-55-00; fax 5-94-29-55-25.

President of the Economic and Social Committee (CESR): (vacant), 35 ave Léopold Héder, 97300 Cayenne; tel. 5-94-28-96-81; fax 5-94-30-73-65; e-mail cesr@cr-guyane.fr.

President of the Culture, Education and Environment Committee (CCEE): AUXENCE CONTOUT, 47 rue du XIV juillet , 97300 Cayenne; tel. 5-94-25-66-84; fax 5-94-37-94-24; e-mail ccee@ cr-guyane.fr.

Deputies to the French National Assembly: CHRISTIANE TAUBIRA (Walwari), JULIANA RIMANE (UMP).

Representative to the French Senate: GEORGES OTHILY (Rassemblement Démocratique et Social Européen).

Conseil Régional

66 ave du Général de Gaulle, BP 7025, 97300 Cayenne Cédex; tel. 5-94-29-20-20; fax 5-94-31-95-22; e-mail cabcrg@cr-guyane.fr.

President: ANTOINE KARAM (PSG).

Elections, 21 and 28 March 2004

	Seats
Parti Socialiste Guyanais (PSG)	17
Forces Démocratiques Guyanaises-Walwari	7
UMP	7
Total	**31**

Political Organizations

Forces Démocratiques Guyanaises (FDG): Cayenne; e-mail g .othily@senat.fr; f. 1989 by a split in the PSG; Leader GEORGES OTHILY.

Mouvement pour la Décolonisation et l'Emancipation Sociale (MDES): 21 rue Maissin, 97300 Cayenne; tel. 5-94-30-55-97; fax 5-94-30-97-73; e-mail mdes.parti@wanadoo.fr; internet www .mdes.org; f. 1991; pro-independence party; Sec.-Gen. MAURICE PINDARD.

Parti Socialiste (PS): 7 rue de l'Adjudant Pindard, 97334 Cayenne Cédex; tel. 5-94-37-81-33; fax 5-94-37-81-56; Leader LÉON JEAN BAPTISTE EDOUARD; Sec. PAUL DEBRIETTE; departmental br. of the metropolitan party.

Parti Socialiste Guyanais (PSG): 1 Cité Césaire, Cayenne; f. 1956; left-wing; Sec.-Gen. ANTOINE KARAM.

Union pour la Démocratie Française (UDF): Cayenne; tel. 5-94-31-17-10; f. 1979; local br. of the national party; centre-right; Leader GEORGES HABRAN-MERY.

Union pour un Mouvement Populaire (UMP): 42 rue du Docteur Barrat, 97300 Cayenne; tel. 5-94-25-24-08; fax 5-94-24-66-80; e-mail ump973@nplus.gf; internet www.u-m-p.org; f. 2002; centre-right; local br. of the metropolitan party; Leader Léon Bertrand; Sec. Louis-Rémy Budoc.

Les Verts Guyane: 64 rue Madame Payé, 97300 Cayenne; tel. 5-94-40-97-27; e-mail tamanoir.guyane@wanadoo.fr; internet guyane.lesverts.fr; local br. of national green party; Leader Brigitte Wyngaarde.

Walwari: Cayenne; f. 1993; left-wing; Leader Christiane Taubira.

Judicial System

Courts of Appeal: see Judicial System, Martinique.

Tribunal de Grande Instance: Palais de Justice, 9 ave du Général de Gaulle, 97300 Cayenne; Pres. J. Fahet; Procurator-Gen. Anne Kayanakis.

Religion

CHRISTIANITY

The Roman Catholic Church

French Guiana comprises the single diocese of Cayenne, suffragan to the archdiocese of Fort-de-France, Martinique. At 31 December 2002 there were an estimated 150,000 adherents in French Guiana, representing some 75% of the total population. French Guiana participates in the Antilles Episcopal Conference, currently based in Port of Spain, Trinidad and Tobago.

Bishop of Cayenne: Rt Rev. Louis Sankalé, Evêché, 24 rue Madame Payé, BP 378, 97328 Cayenne Cédex; tel. 5-94-28-98-48; fax 5-94-30-20-33; e-mail louisankale@wanadoo.fr.

The Anglican Communion

Within the Church in the Province of the West Indies, French Guiana forms part of the diocese of Guyana. The Bishop is resident in Georgetown, Guyana. There were fewer than 100 adherents at mid-2000.

Other Churches

At mid-2000 there were an estimated 7,000 Protestants and 7,200 adherents professing other forms of Christianity.

Assembly of God: 1051 route de Raban, 97300 Cayenne; tel. 5-94-35-23-04; fax 5-94-35-23-05; e-mail jacques.rhino@wanadoo.fr; internet www.addguyane.com; Pres. Jacques Rhino.

Church of Jesus Christ of Latter-day Saints (Mormons): Route de la Rocade, 97305 Cayenne; Br. Pres. François Pratique.

Seventh-day Adventist Church: Mission Adventiste de la Guyane, 39 rue Schoëlcher, BP 169, 97324 Cayenne Cédex; tel. 5-94-25-64-26; fax 5-94-37-93-02; e-mail mission.adventiste@wanadoo.fr; f. 1949; Pres. and Chair. Max-Réné Laurent; 1,936 mems (March 2003).

The Jehovah's Witnesses are also represented.

The Press

France-Guyane: 88 bis ave du Général de Gaulle, 97300 Cayenne; tel. 5-94-31-48-80; fax 5-94-31-11-57; daily; Publishing Dir Philippe Hersant; Local Dir Jean-Noël Bire; circ. 5,500.

La Presse de Guyane: pl. Léopold Héder, 97300 Cayenne; tel. 5-94-29-55-55; fax 5-94-29-55-54; Editor Tchisséka Lobelt; 4 a week; circ. 1,000.

La Semaine Guyanaise: 6 ave Pasteur, 97300 Cayenne; tel. 5-94-31-09-83; fax 5-94-31-95-20; e-mail semaine.guyanaise@nplus.gf; weekly; Dir Alain Chaumet.

Ròt Kozé: 21 rue Maissin, 97300 Cayenne; tel. 5-94-30-55-97; fax 5-94-30-97-73; internet www.mdes.org; f. 1990; monthly; Dir Maurice Pindard; left-wing organ of the MDES party.

NEWS AGENCIES

Agence France Presse: 22 réseau St Antoine, 97300 Cayenne; tel. and fax 5-94-29-34-72; Rep. Alexandre Roziga.

Foreign Bureau

Reuters (United Kingdom): Impasse du 8 Mai 1945, 97300 Cayenne; tel. 5-94-30-44-26; fax 5-94-31-93-24; Rep. Alexander Miles.

Broadcasting and Communications

TELECOMMUNICATIONS

France Telecom: 76 ave Voltaire, BP 8080, 97000 Cayenne; tel. 5-94-39-91-08; fax 5-94-39-91-95; local br. of national telecommunications co.

BROADCASTING

Réseau France Outre-mer (RFO): ave le Grand Boulevard, Z.A.D. Moulin à Vent, 97354 Rémire-Montjoly; tel. 5-94-25-67-00; fax 5-94-25-67-64; e-mail rfosaf@nplus.gf; internet www.rfo.fr; fmrly Société Nationale de Radio-Télévision Française d'Outre-mer, renamed as above 1999; Radio-Guyane Inter: broadcasts 18 hours daily; accounts for 46.6% of listeners (2003); Téléguyane: 2 channels, 32 hours weekly; accounts for 59.5% of viewers (2003); Pres. André-Michel Besse; Regional Dir Anastasie Bourquin.

Radio

Seven private FM radio stations are in operation.

Radio Gabrielle: rue Montravel, 97311 Roura; tel. 5-94-27-00-47; fax 5-94-28-01-28.

Radio Ouassaille: rue Maurice Demongeot, 97360 Mana; tel. 5-94-34-80-96.

Radio Pagani: ave Justin Catayee, 97355 Macouria Tonate; tel. 5-94-38-85-90.

Radio Tout'Moun: rue des Mandarines, 97300 Cayenne; tel. 5-94-31-80-79; fax 5-94-30-91-19; f. 1982; broadcasts 24 hours a day.

Radio U.D.L. (Union Défense des Libertés): ave Félix Eboué, 97323 Saint-Laurent-du-Maroni; tel. 5-94-34-27-90.

RCI Guyane: 33 rue Madame Payé, 97300 Cayenne; tel. 5-94-30-50-00; fax 5-94-30-60-00.

RFM 90: Annexe Hôtel des Roches, Le Manguier, 97310 Kourou; tel. 5-94-32-07-90.

Television

Antenne Guyane Créole: 31 ave Louis Pasteur, 97300 Cayenne; tel. 5-94-28-82-88; fax 5-94-29-13-08; e-mail acg@nplus.gf; internet www.acg.gf; private television station; accounts for 25.4% of viewers (2003); Pres. Marc Ho-A-Chuck; Gen. Man. Wladimir Mangachoff.

Finance

(cap. = capital; res = reserves; dep. = deposits; m. = million; brs = branches; amounts in French francs)

BANKING

Central Bank

Institut d'Emission des Départements d'Outre-mer (IEDOM): 8 rue Christophe Colomb, BP 6016, 97306 Cayenne Cédex; tel. 5-94-29-36-50; fax 5-94-30-02-76; e-mail iedomguyane@wanadoo.fr; internet www.iedom.com; f. 1959; Dir Didier Grebert.

Commercial Banks

Banque Française Commerciale Antilles-Guyane (BFC Antilles-Guyane): 8 pl. des Palmistes, BP 111, 97345 Cayenne; tel. 5-94-29-11-11; fax 5-94-30-13-12; e-mail f.aujoulat@bfc-ag.com; internet www.bfc-ag.com; see chapter on Guadeloupe; f. 1985; Regional Dir Philippe Bissainte.

BNP Paribas Guyane SA: 2 pl. Victor Schoëlcher, BP 35, 97300 Cayenne; tel. 5-94-39-63-00; fax 5-94-30-23-08; e-mail bnpg@bnpparibas.com; internet www.bnpparibas.com; f. 1964 following purchase of BNP Guyane (f. 1855); name changed July 2000; owned by BNP Paribas SA, 94%; BNP Paribas Martinique, 3%; BNP Paribas Guadeloupe, 3%; cap. 71.7m., res 100.0m., dep. 2,007m. (Dec. 1994); Dir and Gen. Man. François du Peuty; Gen. Sec. Georges Cloute-Cazaala; 5 brs.

BRED-Banque Populaire (BRED-BP): 5 ave du Général de Gaulle, 97300 Cayenne; tel. 5-94-25-56-80; fax 5-94-31-98-40; 3 brs.

Development Bank

Société Financière pour le Développement économique de la Guyane (SOFIDEG): PK 3, 700 route de Baduel, BP 860, 97339 Cayenne Cédex; tel. 5-94-29-94-29; fax 5-94-30-60-44; e-mail sofideg@nplus.gf; f. 1982; bought from the Agence Française de Développement (AFD—q.v.) by BRED-BP in 2003; Dir François Chevillotte.

Trade and Industry

GOVERNMENT AGENCIES

Conseil Economique et Social: 66 rue du Général de Gaulle, BPC 25, 97300 Cayenne; tel. 5-94-30-81-00; fax 5-94-30-73-65; e-mail cesrccee@netplus.gf; Pres. ROGER-MICHEL LOUPEC.

Direction de l'Agriculture et de la Forêt (DAF): Parc Rebard, BP 5002, 97305 Cayenne Cédex; tel. 5-94-29-63-74; fax 5-94-29-63-63; e-mail daf973@agriculture.gouv.fr; internet daf.guyane.agriculture.gouv.fr.

Direction Régionale de l'Industrie, de la Recherche et de l'Environnement (DRIRE): Pointe Buzaré, BP 7001, 97307 Cayenne; tel. 5-94-29-75-30; fax 5-94-29-07-34; e-mail drire-antilles-guyane@industrie.gouv.fr; internet www.ggm.drire.gouv.fr; active in industry, business services, transport, public works, tourism and distribution; Regional Dir PHILIPPE COMBE.

Direction Régionale et Départementale des Affaires Maritimes (DRAM): 2 bis rue Mentel, BP 6008, 97306 Cayenne Cédex ; tel. 5-94-29-36-15 ; fax 5-94-29-36-16; e-mail stephane.gatto@equipement.gouv.fr; responsible for shipping, fishing and other maritime issues at a national and community level.

DEVELOPMENT ORGANIZATIONS

Agence Française de Développement (AFD): Lotissement les Héliconias, route de Baduel, BP 1122, 97345 Cayenne Cédex; tel. 5-94-29-90-90; fax 5-94-30-63-32; e-mail afd.cayenne@gf.groupe-afd.org; fmrly Caisse Française de Développement; Man. GENEVIÈVE JAVALOYES.

Agence pour la Création et le Développement des Entreprises en Guyane (ACREDEG): pl. Schoelcher, BP 235, 97300 Cayenne; tel. 5-94-25-66-66; fax 5-94-25-43-19; e-mail acredeg@nplus.gf ; internet www.acredeg.gf; f. 1998; Pres. JEAN CLAUDE SIMONEAU; Dir RAYMOND CHARPENTIER-TITY.

CHAMBERS OF COMMERCE

Chambre d'Agriculture: 8 ave du Général de Gaulle, Cayenne; tel. 5-94-29-61-95; fax 5-94-31-00-01; e-mail chambre.agriculture.973@wanadoo.fr; Pres. PATRICK LABRANCHE.

Chambre de Commerce et d'Industrie: Hôtel Consulaire, pl. de l'Esplanade, BP 49, 97300 Cayenne Cédex; tel. 5-94-29-96-00; fax 5-94-29-96-34; e-mail contact@guyane.cci.fr; internet www.guyane.cci.fr; Pres. JEAN-PAUL LE PELLETIER.

Chambre de Métiers: Jardin Botanique, blvd de la République, BP 176, 97324 Cayenne Cédex; tel. 5-94-30-21-80; fax 5-94-30-54-22; e-mail cmg@nplus.fr; Pres. SYLVAIN LEMKI.

Jeune Chambre Economique de Cayenne: 1 Cité A. Horth, route de Montabo, BP 1094, Cayenne; tel. 5-94-31-62-99; fax 5-94-31-76-13; f. 1960; Pres. FRANCK VERSET.

EMPLOYERS' ORGANIZATIONS

Coopérative des Céréales et Oléagineux de Guyane (COCEROG): PK 24, chemin départemental 8, Sarcelles, 97360 Mana; tel. 5-94-34-20-82; fax 5-94-34-02-08.

Groupement Régional des Agriculteurs de Guyane (GRAGE): PK 15 route nationale 1, Domaine de Soula, 97355 Macouria; tel. 5-94-38-71-26; fax ; e-mail grage@wanadoo.fr; affiliated to the Confédération Paysanne; Pres ALBÉRIC BENTH.

Ordre des pharmaciens du département Guyane: ave Hector Berlioz, 97310 Kourou; tel. 5-94-32-17-62 ; fax 5-94-32-17-66; Pres. LOUISE AREL-GOLITIN.

Syndicat des Exploitants Forestiers et Scieurs de Guyane (SEFSG): Macouria; tel. 5-94-35-26-66; fax 5-94-35-29-92; f. 1987; timber processers; Man. M. POMIES.

Union Patronale de Guyane (UPDG): 27A Résidence Gustave Stanislas, Source de Baduel, BP 820, 97338 Cayenne Cédex; tel. 5-94-31-17-71; fax 5-94-30-32-13; e-mail updg@nplus.gf; Pres. JOËL IBOS.

UTILITIES

Electricity

Électricité de France Guyane (EDF): blvd Jubelin, BP 6002, 97306 Cayenne; tel. 5-94-39-64-00; fax 5-94-30-10-81; state-owned; Gen. Man. MARC GIRARD.

Water

Société Guyanaise des Eaux (SGDE): 2738 route de Montabo, 97305 Cayenne; tel. 5-94-30-32-32; fax 5-94-30-59-60; Pres. FRANÇOIS MARTIN; Gen. Man. JACQUES FOURNET.

TRADE UNIONS

Centrale Démocratique des Travailleurs de la Guyane (CDTG): 99–100 Cité Césaire, BP 383, 97328 Cayenne Cédex; tel. 5-94-31-02-32; fax 5-94-31-81-05; e-mail sg.cdtg@wanadoo.fr; Sec.-Gen. JEAN-MARC BOURETTE.

Union Départementale Confédération Française des Travailleurs Chrétiens Guyane (UD CFTC Guyane): BP 763, 97337 Cayenne Cédex; tel. 5-94-35-63-14; fax 5-94-35-77-30; e-mail lydie.leneveu@wanadoo.fr.

Union Départementale Force Ouvrière de Guyane (FO): 25 Cité Mirza, rue des Acajous, 97300 Cayenne; tel. 5-94-31-62-55; e-mail jmbilquez@force-ouvriere.fr; Sec.-Gen. CHRISTIAN DESFLOTS.

Union des Travailleurs Guyanais (UTG): 14 bis rue Digue Ronjon, 97300 Cayenne; tel. 5-94-30-17-67; fax 5-94-35-47-74; Sec.-Gen. CHRISTIAN RAVIN.

Union Régionale Guyane: 52 rue François Arago, BP 807, 97300 Cayenne; tel. 05-94-21-67-61; fax 05-94-30-89-70.

UNSA Education Guyane: 46 rue Vermont Polycarpe, 97300 Cayenne; tel. and fax 5-94-30-89-70; e-mail unsa-education-guyane@wanadoo.fr; Sec.-Gen. MARTINE NIVOIX.

Transport

RAILWAYS

There are no railways in French Guiana.

ROADS

In 2004 there were 1,300 km (miles) of roads in French Guiana, of which 397 km were main roads. Much of the network is concentrated along the coast, although proposals for a major new road into the interior of the Department were under consideration.

SHIPPING

Dégrad-des-Cannes, on the estuary of the river Mahury, is the principal port, handling 80% of maritime traffic in 1989. There are other ports at Le Larivot, Saint-Laurent-du-Maroni and Kourou. Saint-Laurent is used primarily for the export of timber, and Le Larivot for fishing vessels. There are river ports on the Oyapock and on the Approuague. There is a ferry service across the Maroni river between Saint-Laurent and Albina, Suriname. The rivers provide the best means of access to the interior, although numerous rapids prevent navigation by large vessels.

Société des Transports Maritimes Guyanaise (STMG): 515 chemin St Antoine, 97300 Cayenne; Man. ANTOINE PORRY.

SOMARIG (Société Maritime et Industrielle de la Guyane): Z. I. de Dégrad-des-Cannes, Rémire, BP 81, 97322 Cayenne Cédex; tel. 5-94-35-42-00; fax 5-94-35-53-44; e-mail cay.genmbox@cma-cgm.com; Man. Dir PHILIPPE BABLON.

CIVIL AVIATION

Rochambeau International Airport, situated 17.5 km (11 miles) from Cayenne, is equipped to handle the largest jet aircraft. Access to remote inland areas is frequently by helicopter.

Air Guyane: Aéroport de Rochambeau, 97300 Matoury; tel. 5-94-35-03-07; fax 5-94-30-54-37; e-mail resa@airguyane.com; internet www.airguyane.com; f. 1980; operates internal and international services; Pres. CHRISTIAN MARCHAND.

Tourism

The main attractions are the natural beauty of the tropical scenery and the Amerindian villages of the interior. In 2002 there were 28 hotels with some 1,300 rooms. In that year some 65,000 tourist arrivals were recorded.

Comité du Tourisme de la Guyane: 12 rue Lallouette, BP 801, 97338 Cayenne Cédex; tel. 5-94-29-65-00; fax 5-94-29-65-01; e-mail ctginfo@tourisme-guyane.com; internet www.tourisme-guyane.com; Pres. JEAN-ELIE PANELLE; Dir GEORGES EUZET.

Délégation Régionale au Tourisme, au Commerce et à l'Artisanat pour la Guyane: 9 rue Louis Blanc, BP 7008, 97307 Cayenne Cédex; tel. 5-94-28-92-90; fax 5-94-31-01-04; e-mail drtca973@nplus .gf; Delegate PAUL RENAUD.

Fédération des Offices de Tourisme et Syndicats d'Initiative de la Guyane (FOTSIG): 12 rue Lallouette, 97300 Cayenne; tel. 5-94-30-96-29; fax 5-94-31-23-41; e-mail fotsig@nplus.gf; internet www.guyanetourisme.com; Pres. ARMAND HILDAIRE.

Office Culturel de la Région Guyane: 82 ave du Général de Gaulle, BP 6007, 97306 Cayenne Cédex; tel. 5-94-28-94-00; fax 5-94-28-94-04; e-mail ocrg@nplus.gf; internet www.ocrg.gf; f. 1998 following the dissolution of the Association Régionale de Développement Culturel; Pres. MYRIAM KEREL.

GUADELOUPE

Introductory Survey

Location, Climate, Language, Religion, Capital

Guadeloupe is the most northerly of the Windward Islands group in the West Indies. Dominica lies to the south, and Antigua and Montserrat to the north-west. Guadeloupe is formed by two large islands, Grande-Terre and Basse-Terre, separated by a narrow sea channel (but linked by a bridge), with a smaller island, Marie-Galante, to the south-east, and another, La Désirade, to the east. There are also a number of small dependencies, mainly Saint-Barthélemy and the northern half of Saint-Martin (the remainder being part of the Netherlands Antilles), among the Leeward Islands. The climate is tropical, with an average temperature of 26°C (79°F), and a more humid and wet season between June and November. French is the official language, but a Creole patois is widely spoken. The majority of the population profess Christianity, and belong to the Roman Catholic Church. The capital is the town of Basse-Terre; the other main town and the principal commercial centre is Pointe-à-Pitre, on Grande-Terre.

Recent History

Guadeloupe was first occupied by the French in 1635, and has remained French territory, apart from a number of brief occupations by the British in the 18th and early 19th centuries. It gained departmental status in 1946.

The deterioration of the economy and an increase in unemployment provoked industrial and political unrest during the 1960s and 1970s, including outbreaks of serious rioting in 1967. Pro-independence parties (which had rarely won more than 5% of the total vote at elections in Guadeloupe) resorted, in some cases, to violence as a means of expressing their opposition to the economic and political dominance of white, pro-French landowners and government officials. In 1980 and 1981 there was a series of bomb attacks on hotels, government offices and other targets by a group called the Groupe de Libération Armée, and in 1983 and 1984 there were further bombings by a group styling itself the Alliance Révolutionnaire Caraïbe (ARC). The Government responded by outlawing the ARC and reinforcing the military and police presence throughout Guadeloupe. (The ARC merged with the Mouvement Populaire pour une Guadeloupe Indépendante—MPGI—in 1984.) Further sporadic acts of violence continued in 1985–87, and in January 1988 responsibility for bomb explosions in various parts of the territory was claimed by a previously unknown pro-independence group, the Organisation Révolutionnaire Armée.

In 1974 Guadeloupe was granted the status of a Region, and an indirectly-elected Conseil régional (Regional Council) was formed. In direct elections to a new Conseil régional in February 1983, held as a result of the recent decentralization reforms, the centre-right coalition succeeded in gaining a majority of the seats and control of the administration. In January 1984 Lucette Michaux-Chevry, the President of the Conseil général (General Council), formed a new conservative centre party, Le Parti de la Guadeloupe, which remained in alliance with the right-wing Rassemblement pour la République (RPR). However, at the elections for the Conseil général held in March 1985, the left-wing combination of the Parti Socialiste (PS) and the Parti Communiste Guadeloupéen (PCG) gained a majority of seats on the enlarged Conseil, and the PS leader, Dominique Larifla, was elected its President. In July demonstrations and a general strike, organized by pro-separatist activists in order to obtain the release of a leading member of the MPGI, quickly intensified into civil disorder and rioting in the main commercial centre, Pointe-à-Pitre.

For the March 1986 general election to the Assemblée nationale, Guadeloupe's representation was increased from three to four deputies. The local branches of the RPR and the centre-right Union pour la Démocratie Française (UDF), which had campaigned jointly at the 1981 general election and the 1983 regional elections, presented separate candidates. Ernest Moutoussamy and Frédéric Jalton, respectively the incumbent PCG and PS members of the Assemblée, were re-elected, but the UDF deputy was not; the two remaining seats were won by RPR candidates (Michaux-Chevry and Henri Beaujean). In the concurrent elections for the 41 seats on the Conseil régional, the two left-wing parties together won a majority of seats. As a result, José Moustache of the RPR was replaced as President of the Conseil by Félix Proto of the PS. At the 1988 French presidential elections the incumbent President François Mitterrand of the PS defeated Jacques Chirac of the RPR. At elections to the Assemblée nationale in June, Larifla (for the PS) defeated Beaujean, while the three other deputies to the Assemblée retained their seats. In September–October the left-wing parties won 26 of the 42 seats at elections to the Conseil général, and Larifla was re-elected President of the Conseil.

In April 1989 the separatist Union Populaire pour la Libération de la Guadeloupe (UPLG) organized protests in Port Louis to demand the release of 'political prisoners', which led to violent clashes with the police. A number of activists of the now disbanded ARC (including its leader, Luc Reinette) staged a hunger strike while awaiting trial in Paris, accused in connection with politically-motivated offences in the Overseas Departments. In the following month the Comité Guadeloupéen de Soutien aux Prisonniers Politiques united 11 organizations in demonstrations against the Government. Demands included the release of the prisoners held in France, a rejection of the Single European Act and the granting of a series of social measures. In June the Assemblée nationale approved legislation granting an amnesty for crimes that had taken place before July 1988, and that were intended to undermine the authority of the French Republic in the Overseas Departments. The agreement of those seeking greater independence in Guadeloupe to work within the democratic framework had gained parliamentary support for the amnesty. However, when the freed activists returned to Guadeloupe in July 1989, they urged increased confrontation with the authorities in order to achieve autonomous rule. In March 1990 the UPLG declared that it would henceforth participate in elections, and would seek associated status (rather than full independence) for Guadeloupe.

In March 1992 concurrent elections were held to the Conseil général and the Conseil régional. Larifla was re-elected as President of the former, despite his refusal to contest as part of the local official PS list of candidates and his leadership of a group of 'dissident' PS members. (The division was not recognized at national level.) In the elections to the Conseil régional the official PS list (headed by Jalton) secured nine seats and the dissident PS members seven. Former members of the PCG, who had formed a new organization, the Parti Progressiste Démocratique Guadeloupéen (PPDG), won five seats. The RPR, the UDF and other right-wing candidates formed an electoral alliance, Objectif Guadeloupe, to contest the elections, together securing 15 of the 41 seats in the Conseil régional. Jalton's refusal to reach an agreement with the 'dissident' PS members prompted Larifla's list to support the presidential candidacy of Michaux-Chevry. Thus, despite an overall left-wing majority in the Conseil régional, the right-wing Michaux-Chevry was elected as President. In December 1992, however, the French

Conseil d'état declared the election to the Conseil régional invalid, owing to the failure of Larifla's list to pay a deposit on each seat prior to the registration of its candidates. Other heads of lists were subsequently found to have submitted incomplete documents to the election commission, and (although malpractice was discounted) the electoral code necessitated that they be declared ineligible for election to the Conseil régional for one year. Fresh elections took place in January 1994, at which Objectif Guadeloupe took 22 seats, while the PS and 'dissident' PS retained a total of only 10 seats.

In a referendum on 20 September 1992 67.5% of voters in Guadeloupe endorsed ratification of the Treaty on European Union (see p. 217), although a high abstention rate was recorded.

The persistence of divisions between the socialists was evident at the March 1993 elections to the Assemblée nationale. Michaux-Chevry of the RPR was re-elected, as were Moutoussamy (for the PPDG) and Jalton (representing the anti-Larifla faction of the PS). Larifla, meanwhile, was defeated by Edouard Chammougon, a candidate of the independent right, who was elected (despite his implication in several corruption scandals—see below) with the assistance of votes in the second round of those socialists who resented Larifla's support for Michaux-Chevry in 1992. Michaux-Chevry was appointed to the position of Minister-Delegate, with responsibility for human rights and humanitarian action, in Edouard Balladur's centre-right coalition Government.

The left retained control of the Conseil général following cantonal elections in March 1994. Larifla was subsequently re-elected President of the Conseil. At elections to the European Parliament in June, a combined list of parties of the left of the French Overseas Departments, including the PPDG (the list was headed by Moutoussamy), won the greatest share of the votes cast (37.2%) in Guadeloupe.

Meanwhile, local political affairs were dominated by scandals involving prominent public figures. Twice during 1993 the Antilles-Guyane Chambre régionale des comptes—the body responsible for overseeing public finances in the region—rejected budget figures submitted by Guadeloupe's Conseil régional, deeming that the Conseil's deficit projections were severely underestimated. In January 1994 an administrative tribunal in Basse-Terre ruled that Michaux-Chevry had been unjustified in dismissing (following the first rejection of the budget) the Conseil régional's director of finances, who had submitted departmental accounts, as required by law, to the Chambre régionale des comptes; this judgment was upheld at an appeal in Paris in April 1995. In January 1993 Chammougon, the Mayor of Baie-Mahault, was sentenced to three years' imprisonment, fined and deprived of his civic and civil rights for 10 years, following his conviction on corruption charges dating as far back as 1980. He remained at liberty pending an appeal and the prison sentence was suspended in November and the deprivation of rights reduced to five years in 1994. In September 1993 Chammougon was further implicated in charges of 'passive corruption' and the abuse and misappropriation of public funds. In November 1994 the French Constitutional Council revoked Chammougon's membership of the Assemblée nationale.

At the 1995 national presidential election the PS candidate, Lionel Jospin, who enjoyed the expressed support of all the parties of the left, won 55.1% of the votes cast in the department in the second round on 7 May, defeating Jacques Chirac of the RPR. At municipal elections in June, Michaux-Chevry became mayor of Basse-Terre, defeating the incumbent PPDG candidate. Michaux-Chevry and Larifla were elected to the Sénat in September; Philippe Chaulet of the RPR was subsequently elected to take Michaux-Chevry's seat in the Assemblée nationale.

At elections to the Assemblée nationale in late May and early June 1997, Moutoussamy, Andy and Chaulet all retained their seats, while Daniel Marsin, a candidate of the independent left, was elected in the constituency of Les Abymes, Pointe-à-Pitre. The RPR performed strongly in elections to the Conseil régional in March 1998; Michaux-Chevry was re-elected as President of the Conseil. The composition of the Conseil général remained largely unchanged following concurrent cantonal elections, although the RPR doubled its representation; Marcellin Lubeth, of the PPDG, was elected to the presidency, defeating Larifla.

Social and industrial unrest intensified in Guadeloupe in October 1999, prior to a two-day visit by Prime Minister Lionel Jospin. Demonstrations escalated into rioting in Pointe-à-Pitre, following the sentencing of Armand Toto, a leading member of

the Union Générale des Travailleurs de la Guadeloupe (UGTG), to four months' imprisonment for assaulting two policemen and threatening to kill another while occupying the premises of a motor vehicle company in support of a dismissed worker. Further protests ensued a few days later when an appeal against Toto's sentence failed. Moreover, banana producers demonstrated around the port of Basse-Terre, demanding the disbursement of 100m. French francs, and additional assistance for the restructuring of their businesses, as compensation for a significant decline in banana prices on the European market. Meanwhile, an indefinite strike by hospital workers, organized by the UGTG, affected Guadeloupe's 16 private clinics. However, calls issued by several trade union and political organizations for a 48-hour general strike during Jospin's visit were largely ignored, and the Prime Minister announced an emergency plan for the banana sector.

The institutional future of the Overseas Departments provoked much discussion in 1999 and 2000. Following a series of meetings, in December 1999 the Presidents of the Conseils Régionaux of French Guiana, Guadeloupe and Martinique signed a joint declaration in Basse-Terre, affirming their intention to propose, to the President and the Government, a legislative amendment, possibly constitutional, aimed at creating a new status of overseas region. The declaration, however, was dismissed by the Secretary of State for Overseas Departments and Territories, Jean-Jack Queyranne, in February 2000 as unconstitutional and exceeding the mandate of politicians responsible. Proposals regarding the institutional evolution of Guadeloupe were provisionally accepted by the Assemblée nationale in May, and were subsequently adopted, by a narrow margin, by the Sénat, following a number of modifications. In November the Assemblée nationale approved the amended proposals, and in December they were ratified by the Constitutional Council. At a referendum held in September, Guadeloupe voted overwhelmingly in favour of reducing the presidential mandate from seven years to five.

In municipal elections held in March 2001 Michaux-Chevry was re-elected mayor of Basse-Terre, despite corruption charges against her. Following her election, Michaux-Chevry relinquished the post to Pierre Martin, in order to comply with regulations that no official may hold more than two elected posts simultaneously (she already held the positions of Senator and President of the Conseil régional). Henri Bangou of the PPDG was also re-elected to the mayoralty of Pointe-à-Pitre. In the concurrently held election to the presidency of the Conseil général, Jacques Gillot of Guadeloupe Unie, Socialisme et Réalité (GUSR) defeated Marcellin Lubeth of the PPDG.

In early June 2001 riots occurred in Pointe-à-Pitre in which a number of people were injured. The riots were in protest at the arrest of the leader of the UGTG, Michel Madassamy, who had been charged in late May with vandalizing a number of shops that had remained open on the day of the anniversary of the abolition of slavery in Guadeloupe, in defiance of the UGTG's recommendations. The General Secretary of the UGTG subsequently called for a general strike to be held for the duration of Madassamy's incarceration. A period of severe drought, necessitating the rationing of water supplies, served to exacerbate the deteriorating social situation on the island in 2001.

Following a meeting of members of the Conseil régional and the Conseil général in late June 2001, a series of administrative restructuring proposals, to be presented to the French Government, was agreed upon. These included: the division of the territory into four districts; the creation of a 'collectivité territoriale' (territorial community), governed by a 41-member Assembly elected for a five-year term; and the establishment of an independent executive council. Furthermore, the proposals included a request that the territory be given control over legislative and administrative affairs, as well as legislative authority on matters concerning Guadeloupe alone. In November the French Government of Jean-Pierre Raffarin announced itself to be in favour of the proposals, and in March 2003 the French parliament approved constitutional changes that, *inter alia*, allowed for local referendums to be held on proposals for greater decentralization in overseas possessions. In the referendum, held on 7 December, some 73% of participating voters rejected legislative reforms that envisaged the replacement of the Conseil général and the Conseil régional with a single assembly. The proposals had received the support of both councils; however, it was widely feared that restructuring would lead to autonomy for the department and the consequent loss of central government funding. At the same time, voters in Saint-Barthélemy and the northern half of Saint-Martin rejected the continuation of their status as dependencies of Guadeloupe, after having received assurances from the administration in Paris that their special tax privileges would remain unchanged. Instead, the dependencies were to adopt the status of 'collectivités territoriales d'outre-mer', although it remained unclear in early 2005 when this would occur.

In mid-2001 the French President, Jacques Chirac, rejected a joint request by French Guiana, Guadeloupe and Martinique that they be permitted to join, as associate members, the Association of Caribbean States. In the first round of the presidential election, held on 21 April 2002, Christine Taubira won 37.2% of the vote in the Department (although she was eliminated nationally), ahead of Chirac, who obtained 28.9%. In the second round, held on 5 May, Chirac overwhelmingly defeated Jean-Marie Le Pen of the extreme right-wing Front National, receiving 91.3% of the vote. In June all four incumbent deputies were defeated in elections to the Assemblée nationale; they were replaced by Gabrielle Louis-Carabin and Joël Beaugendre, both representing the Union pour la Majorité Présidentielle (UMP), a right-wing alliance that included the Objectif Guadeloupe, Eric Jalton, also of a right-wing coalition, and Victorin Lurel of the PS. The RPR subsequently merged into the successor party to the UMP, the Union pour un Mouvement Populaire (also known as the UMP). In August Dominique Vian replaced Jean-François Carenco as Prefect. At elections to the Conseil régional in March 2004 the UMP alliance, led by Michaux-Chevry, was resoundingly defeated, obtaining only 12 of the 41 seats, compared with the 29 seats won by the Guadeloupe pour Tous, a coalition comprising the PS, the PPDG, the GUSR and other left-wing candidates. Victorin Lurel of the PS subsequently became President of the Conseil.

Government
France is represented in Guadeloupe by an appointed prefect. There are two councils with local powers: the 42-member Conseil général (General Council) and the 41-member Conseil régional (Regional Council). Both are elected by universal adult suffrage for a period of up to six years. Guadeloupe elects four deputies to the Assemblée nationale in Paris, and sends three indirectly-elected representatives to the Sénat. The Department is also represented at the European Parliament.

Defence
At 1 August 2004 France maintained a military force of 4,100 and a gendarmerie in the Antilles, with headquarters in Fort-de-France (Martinique).

Economic Affairs
In 2001, according to UN estimates, Guadeloupe's gross domestic product (GDP), measured at current prices, was US $4,460m., equivalent to $10,323 per head. During 1990–2001 GDP increased, in real terms, at an average annual rate of 2.2%; growth in 2001 was 4.6%. Between the censuses of 1990 and 1999, according to provisional figures, the population increased at an average annual rate of 1.0%.

Agriculture, hunting, forestry and fishing contributed an estimated 4.1% of GDP in 1999 and, according to FAO estimates, engaged 2.4% of the economically active population in mid-2003. In that year agricultural produce accounted for some 30% of exports. The principal cash crops are bananas and sugar cane; exports of the former provided 21.9% of total export earnings in 1997, while exports of raw sugar accounted for 23.7% of the total in that year. Yams, sweet potatoes and plantains are the chief subsistence crops. Fishing, mostly at an artisanal level, fulfilled about two-thirds of domestic requirements in the 1990s; shrimp-farming was developed during the 1980s. According to UN estimates, agricultural GDP decreased at an average annual rate of 0.3% in 1990–98; the sector increased by 4.1% in 1998.

The industrial sector (including mining, manufacturing, construction and power) contributed an estimated 15.9% of GDP in 1999 and engaged 12.8% of the active labour force in 2001. Manufacturing, mining and power provided some 6.8% of GDP in 1998, while construction contributed 9.1%. The main manufacturing activity is food processing, particularly sugar production, rum distillation, and flour-milling. The sugar industry was in decline in the 1990s, owing to deteriorating equipment and a reduction in the area planted with sugar cane (from 20,000 ha in 1980 to 9,600 ha in 1999), although there was some recovery in the early 2000s (to 14,300 ha by 2003). In 2003 sugar accounted for some 60% of processed agricultural products for consumption and rum some 20%. Industrial GDP (excluding

construction) increased at an average annual rate of 5.2% in 1990–98. Construction expanded at an average rate of 2.2% per year in the same period.

Of some 700,000 tons of petroleum imported annually, about one-third is used for the production of electricity. Efforts are currently being concentrated on the use of renewable energy resources—notably solar, geothermal and wind power—for energy production; there is also thought to be considerable potential for the use of sugar cane as a means of generating energy in Guadeloupe. Imports of mineral fuels accounted for 11.2% of total expenditure on imports in 2002.

The services sector engaged 84.4% of the active labour force in 2001 and provided an estimated 80% of GDP in 1999. Tourism superseded sugar production in 1988 as the Department's principal source of income, and there is significant potential for the further development of the sector, particularly 'eco-tourism'. In 2003 tourist arrivals totalled some 650,000, and in 2001 receipts from tourism amounted to €238m. In that year some 89% of arrivals came from metropolitan France or dependent territories.

In 2003 Guadeloupe recorded a trade deficit of some €1,800m. The value of exports in that year was €171m., less than one-10th of the total value of imports, which were worth €1,878m. In 2002 the principal source of imports (62.1%) was metropolitan France, which was also the principal market for exports (63.0%). Martinique, the USA and Germany are also important trading partners. The principal exports in 1997 were sugar, bananas, boats and rum. The principal imports in 2002 were machinery and transport equipment (mainly road vehicles), food and live animals, miscellaneous manufactured articles, basic manufactures and chemicals.

Guadeloupe's budget deficit was estimated by the metropolitan authorities to amount to some 800m. French francs (including arrears) in 1993. Under the 1998 departmental budget it was estimated that expenditure would total €318m. The annual rate of inflation averaged 1.8% in 1990–2003; consumer prices increased by 2.3% in 2002 and by 2.0% in 2003. Some 26.9% of the labour force were unemployed in 2003.

As an integral part of France, Guadeloupe belongs to the European Union (EU, see p. 217).

Economic growth in Guadeloupe has been restricted by certain inherent problems: its location; the fact that the domestic market is too narrow to stimulate the expansion of the manufacturing base; the lack of primary materials; and the inflated labour and service costs compared with those of neighbouring countries. Following the destruction caused by 'Hurricane Hugo' in 1989 the French Government undertook to provide more than 2,000m. French francs for reconstruction, and additional aid for the modernization of the sugar industry. The banana-growing sector and the tourist industry, both of which were particularly adversely affected, recovered well. However, Hurricanes Luis and Marilyn, which struck in September 1995, caused severe infrastructural damage. In the late 1990s Guadeloupe's banana sector was adversely affected by declining prices on the European market, while a dispute between the USA and four major Latin American producers and the EU over the latter's banana import regime also threatened the sector. A quota system employed by the EU was to be replaced by a universal tariff system from 2006. Concern was expressed that tourism in the Guadeloupean dependency of Saint-Martin (an island shared with the Dutch territory of St Maarten) would be adversely affected by the decision of AOM Compagnie Aérienne Française (subsequently Air Lib) to cease flights to St Maarten in March 2001. Moreover, it was thought that a renewed monopoly on flights by Air France would further affect the tourism sector (the deregulation of air transport in 1986, ending Air France's monopoly on flights to Guadeloupe, was a major factor in attracting more visitors to the main island). In November 2002 the French hotel group Accor announced that it would close its five hotels in Martinque and Guadeloupe, citing high operating costs, poor industrial relations and decreasing tourist arrivals. In early 2003 the French Minister of the Overseas Possessions announced plans to stimulate the economies of Guadeloupe, Martinique and French Guiana that included the introduction of tax incentives for the hotel sector. Furthermore, in late 2003 it was announced that a subsidiary of Air Caraïbe was to begin an additional air service between Paris and Pointe-à-Pitre.

Education
The education system is similar to that of metropolitan France (see chapter on French Guiana). In 1996 secondary education was provided at 40 junior comprehensives, or collèges, 10 voca-

tional lycées, 10 general and technological lycées and one agricultural lycée. In 2002/03 there were 63,553 students in pre-primary and primary education, while in secondary education there were 52,916 students (including 8,280 students in vocational education), of whom some 90% attended state schools. There were also two teacher-training institutes, and colleges of agriculture, fisheries, hotel management, nursing, midwifery and child care. A branch of the Université Antilles-Guyane, at Pointe-à-Pitre, has faculties of law, economics, sciences, medicine and Caribbean studies. The university in Guadeloupe had 5,800 enrolled students in 1997. An Academy for Guadeloupe was established in January 1997. Total government expenditure on education amounted to 2,842m. French francs in 1993.

Public Holidays

2005: 1 January (New Year's Day), 7–8 February (Lenten Carnival), 25–28 March (Easter), 1 May (Labour Day), 5 May (Ascension Day), 8 May (Victory Day), 16 May (Whit Monday), 14 July (National Day), 21 July (Victor Schoëlcher Day), 15 August (Assumption), 1 November (All Saints' Day), 11 November (Armistice Day), 25 December (Christmas Day).

2006: 1 January (New Year's Day), 27–28 February (Lenten Carnival), 14–17 April (Easter), 1 May (Labour Day), 8 May (Victory Day), 20 May (Ascension Day), 5 June (Whit Monday), 14 July (National Day), 21 July (Victor Schoëlcher Day), 15 August (Assumption), 1 November (All Saints' Day), 11 November (Armistice Day), 25 December (Christmas Day).

Weights and Measures

The metric system is in use.

Statistical Survey

Sources (unless otherwise stated): Institut National de la Statistique et des Etudes Economiques (INSEE), ave Paul Lacavé, BP 96, 97102 Basse-Terre; tel. 99-0250; internet www.insee.fr/fr/insee_regions/guadeloupe; Service de Presse et d'Information, Ministère des départements et territoires d'outre-mer, 27 rue Oudinot, 75700 Paris 07 SP, France; tel. 1-53-69-20-00; fax 1-43-06-60-30; internet www.outre-mer.gouv.fr.

AREA AND POPULATION

Area: 1,705 sq km (658.3 sq miles), incl. dependencies (La Désirade, Les Saintes, Marie-Galante, Saint-Barthélemy, Saint-Martin).

Population: 327,002 (males 160,112, females 166,890) at census of 9 March 1982; 387,034 (males 189,187, females 197,847) at census of 15 March 1990; 422,496 at census of 8 March 1999. *2004* (official estimate at 1 January, rounded figure): 442,500.

Density (at 1 January 2004): 259.5 per sq km.

Principal Towns (population at 1999 census): Les Abymes 63,054; Saint-Martin 29,078; Le Gosier 25,360; Baie-Mahault 23,389; Pointe-à-Pitre 20,948; Le Moule 20,827; Petit Bourg 20,528; Sainte Anne 20,410; Basse-Terre (capital) 12,410.

Births, Marriages and Deaths (1997, provisional figures): Registered live births 7,554 (birth rate 17.4 per 1,000); Registered marriages 1,936 (marriage rate 4.7 per 1,000); Registered deaths 2,441 (death rate 5.6 per 1,000). *2002:* Registered live births 7,032; Registered marriages 1,824; Registered deaths 2,614 (preliminary).

Expectation of Life (UN estimates, years at birth): 77.3 (males 73.6; females 80.9) in 1995–2000. Source: UN, *World Population Prospects: The 2002 Revision.*

Economically Active Population (persons aged 15 years and over, 1990 census): Agriculture, hunting, forestry and fishing 8,391; Industry and energy 9,630; Construction and public works 13,967; Trade 15,020; Transport and telecommunications 6,950; Financial services 2,802; Other marketable services 26,533; Non-marketable services 34,223; *Total employed* 117,516 (males 68,258, females 49,258); Unemployed 54,926 (males 25,691, females 29,235); *Total labour force* 172,442 (males 93,949, females 78,493). *2001* (estimates, salaried employees at 31 December): Agriculture 3,075; Industry (excl. construction) 7,798; Construction 6,521; Services 94,144; Total 111,538. *2001* (estimates, non-salaried employees at 31 December): Total 22,856. *Mid-2003* (estimates): Agriculture, etc. 5,000; Total labour force 205,000 (males 110,000, females 95,000) (Source: FAO). *December 2003:* Unemployed 44,298.

HEALTH AND WELFARE

Key Indicators

Physicians (per 1,000 head, 1996): 1.6.

Hospital Beds (per 1,000 head, 1996): 29.1.
For sources and definitions, see explanatory note on p. vi.

AGRICULTURE, ETC.

Principal Crops (FAO estimates, '000 metric tons, 2003): Sweet potatoes 4.3; Yams 10; Other roots and tubers 4.2; Sugar cane 820.0; Cabbages 2.3; Lettuce 3.2; Tomatoes 3.1; Cucumbers and gherkins 3.9; Other fresh vegetables 15.1; Cantaloupes and other melons 4.1; Bananas 115.5; Plantains 9.2; Pineapples 7.0; Other fruits 6.7. Source: FAO.

Livestock (FAO estimates, '000 head, year ending September 2003): Cattle 85; Goats 28; Pigs 19; Sheep 3.2. Source: FAO.

Livestock Products (FAO estimates, '000 metric tons, 2003): Beef and veal 3.3; Pig meat 1.0; Hen eggs 1.7. Source: FAO.

Forestry ('000 cubic metres, 2003): *Roundwood Removals* (excl. bark): Sawlogs, veneer logs and logs for sleepers 0.3; Fuel wood 15.0; Total 15.3. *Sawnwood Production* (incl. railway sleepers): Total 1.0. Source: FAO.

Fishing (metric tons, live weight, 2002): Capture 10,100 (Common dolphinfish 700—FAO estimate; Blackfin tuna 500; Other mackerel-like fishes 1,600—FAO estimate; Marine fishes 6,600—FAO estimate; Stromboid conchs 550); Aquaculture 14; *Total catch* 10,114. Source: FAO.

MINING

Production ('000 metric tons, 2001, estimates): Pozzolan 210.0. Source: US Geological Survey.

INDUSTRY

Production: Raw sugar 65,200 metric tons in 2001; Rum 62,679 hl in 1998; Cement 230,000 metric tons in 2001 (estimate); Electric energy (million kWh) 1,220 in 2000 (estimate). Source: mainly UN, *Industrial Commodity Statistics Yearbook.*

FINANCE

Currency and Exchange Rates: The French franc was used until the end of February 2002. Euro notes and coins were introduced on 1 January 2002, and the euro became the sole legal tender from 18 February. Some of the figures in this Survey are still in terms of francs. For details of exchange rates, see French Guiana.

Budget: *State Budget* (million French francs, 1990): Revenue 2,494; Expenditure 4,776. *Regional Budget* (preliminary, excl. debt rescheduling, € million, 2002): Total revenue 287 (Direct taxes 13, Indirect taxes 126, Transfers 109, Loans 38, Other 1); Total expenditure 287. *Departmental Budget* (€ million, 1998): Revenue 332; Expenditure 318.

Money Supply (million French francs at 31 December 1996): Currency outside banks 1,148; Demand deposits at banks 6,187; Total money 7,335.

Cost of Living (Consumer Price Index for urban areas; base: 1990 = 100): 120.6 in 2001; 123.4 in 2002; 125.9 in 2003. Source: UN, *Monthly Bulletin of Statistics.*

Expenditure on the Gross Domestic Product (million French francs at current prices, 1994): Government final consumption expenditure 5,721; Private final consumption expenditure 16,779; Increase in stocks 161; Gross fixed capital formation 5,218; *Total domestic expenditure* 27,879; Exports of goods and services 912; *Less* Imports of goods and services 9,040; *GDP in purchasers' values* 19,751.

Gross Domestic Product by Economic Activity (million French francs at current prices, 1992): Agriculture, hunting, forestry and fishing 1,206.9; Mining, quarrying and manufacturing 1,237.5; Electricity, gas and water 307.5; Construction 1,164.4; Trade, restaurants and hotels 2,907.9; Transport, storage and communications 1,415.4; Finance, insurance, real estate and business services 2,023.0; Government services 4,769.7; Other community, social and personal services 2,587.7; Other services 348.0; *Sub-total* 17,968.0; Import duties 699.4; Value-added tax 615.7; *Less* Imputed bank service charge 1,311.2; *GDP in purchasers' values* 17,972.0 (Source: UN, *National Accounts Statistics). 2000* (€ million): GDP in purchasers' values 5,593.

EXTERNAL TRADE

Principal Commodities: *Imports c.i.f.* (US $ million, 1995): Food and live animals 302.8 (Meat and meat preparations 74.7, Dairy products and birds' eggs 51.9, Cereals and cereal preparations 55.6, Vegetables and fruit 51.4; Beverages and tobacco 88.1 (Beverages 78.8); Mineral fuels, lubricants, etc. 110.7 (Petroleum, petroleum products, etc. 52.5, Gas, natural and manufactured 58.0); Chemicals and related products 172.8 (Medicinal and pharmaceutical products 78.1); Basic manufactures 259.5 (Paper, paperboard and manufactures 39.3); Machinery and transport equipment 607.0 (Office machines and automatic data-processing equipment 40.7, Telecommunications and sound equipment 43.0, Road vehicles and parts 217.7, Other transport equipment 100.0); Miscellaneous manufactured articles 282.6 (Furniture and parts 47.2, Clothing and accessories, excl. footwear, 52.6, Printed matter 39.5); Total (incl. others) 1,901.3 (Source: UN, *International Trade Statistics Yearbook*). *Exports f.o.b.* (million French francs, 1997): Bananas 179.7; Melons and fresh papayas 33.8; Sugar 193.9; Rum 40.2; Wheaten or rye flour 35.3; Yachts and sports boats 50.7; Total (incl. others) 819.4. *2000* (€ million): *Imports:* 2,010; *Exports:* 210.

Principal Trading Partners (million French francs, 1997): *Imports c.i.f.:* Belgium-Luxembourg 161.8; Curaçao (Netherlands Antilles) 212.6; France (metropolitan) 6,435.7; Germany 445.5; Italy 395.0; Japan 247.6; Martinique 114.0; Spain 190.2; Trinidad and Tobago 189.3; United Kingdom 151.7; USA 315.4; Total (incl. others) 10,236.6. *Exports f.o.b.:* Belgium-Luxembourg 23.0; France (metropolitan) 497.2; French Guiana 20.6; Italy 21.7; Martinique 152.2; United Kingdom 18.7; USA 36.6; Total (incl. others) 819.4.

TRANSPORT

Road Traffic ('000 motor vehicles in use, 2001): Passenger cars 117.7; Commercial vehicles 31.4. Source: UN, *Statistical Yearbook*.

Shipping: *Merchant Fleet* (vessels registered, '000 grt at 31 December 1992): Total displacement 6. (Source: Lloyd's Register-Fairplay, *World Fleet Statistics*). *International Sea-borne Traffic* (1999): Vessels entered 2,988; Goods loaded 428,000 metric tons; Goods unloaded 2,747,000 metric tons; Passengers carried 1,296,000.

Civil Aviation (2003): Passengers carried 1,761,500; Freight carried 15,000 metric tons.

TOURISM

Tourist Arrivals: 650,000 in 2003.

Tourist Arrivals by Country (2000): Canada 10,431; France 440,779; Italy 15,670; Switzerland 9,766; USA 92,474; Total (incl. others) 623,134. Source: World Tourism Organization, *Yearbook of Tourism Statistics*.

Receipts from Tourism (US $ million): 466 in 1998; 375 in 1999; 418 in 2000. Source: World Tourism Organization.

COMMUNICATIONS MEDIA

Radio Receivers ('000 in use): 113 in 1997.

Television Receivers ('000 in use): 118 in 1997.

Telephones ('000 main lines in use): 210.0 in 2001.

Facsimile Machines (number in use): 3,400 in 1996.

Mobile Cellular Telephones ('000 subscribers): 323.5 in 2002.

Personal Computers ('000 in use): 100 in 2001.

Internet Users ('000): 20.0 in 2001.

Daily Newspaper: 1 (estimate) in 1996 (estimated average circulation 35,000 copies).
Sources: UNESCO, *Statistical Yearbook*; UN, *Statistical Yearbook*; International Telecommunication Union.

EDUCATION

Pre-primary (2002/03): 136 institutions; 23,461 students (Source: Ministère de l'Education Nationale, de l'Enseignement Supérieur et de la Recherche, *Repères et références statistiques sur les enseignements, la formation et la recherche 2003*).

Primary (2002/03): 220 institutions; 3,241 teachers (3,011 state, 230 private); 40,092 students (Source: Ministère de l'Education Nationale, de l'Enseignement Supérieur et de la Recherche, *Repères et références statistiques sur les enseignements, la formation et la recherche 2003*).

Secondary (2002/03): 4,700 teachers (4,282 state, 418 private); 52,916 students (Source: Ministère de l'Education Nationale, de l'Enseignement Supérieur et de la Recherche, *Repères et références statistiques sur les enseignements, la formation et la recherche 2003*).

Higher (1997): 5,800 students (Université Antilles-Guyane).
Adult Literacy Rate: 90.1% (males 89.7%; females 90.5%) in 1992.

Directory

The Government
(April 2005)

Prefect: PAUL GIROT DE LANGLADE, Préfecture, Palais d'Orléans, rue Lardenoy, 97109 Basse-Terre Cédex; tel. 5-90-99-39-00; fax 5-90-81-58-32; internet www.guadeloupe.pref.gouv.fr.

President of the General Council: Dr JACQUES GILLOT (GUSR), Hôtel du Département, blvd Félix Eboué, 97109 Basse-Terre; tel. 5-90-99-77-77; fax 5-90-99-76-00; e-mail info@cg971.com; internet www.cg971.com.

President of the Economic and Social Committee: GUY FRÉDÉRIC.

Deputies to the French National Assembly: ÉRIC JALTON (PCG), GABRIELLE LOUIS-CARABIN (UMP), JOËL BEAUGENDRE (UMP), VICTORIN LUREL (PS).

Representatives to the French Senate: JACQUES GILLOT (Rassemblement démocratique et social européen), DANIEL MARSIN (Groupe Socialiste), LUCETTE MICHAUX-CHEVRY (UMP).

Conseil Régional
Ave Paul Lacavé, Petit-Paris, 97109 Basse-Terre; tel. 5-90-80-40-40; fax 5-90-81-34-19; internet www.cr-guadeloupe.fr.

President: VICTORIN LUREL (PS).

Elections, 21 and 28 March 2004

	Seats
Guadeloupe pour Tous*	29
Action Guadeloupe pour l'Initiative et le Rassemblement (AGIR)†	12
Total	**41**

Seven other lists contested the elections: NOFWAP; Combat Ouvrier; Alternative Citoyenne; Union pour une Guadeloupe Responsable; Lé Verts Sé Nou Tout; Le Renouveau Guadeloupéen; and Priorité à l'Education et à l'Environnement.
* Comprising the PS, PPDG, GUSR and other left-wing candidates.
† Comprising the UMP, other right-wing candidates and socialist dissidents.

Political Organizations

Combat Ouvrier: BP 213, 97156 Point-à-Pitre Cédex; Leaders JEAN-MARIE NOMERTIN, GÉRARD SÉNÉ; Trotskyist; sister organization of Lutte Ouvrière; mem of the Internationalist Communist Union.

Guadeloupe Respect: Goyave; Leader JEAN EMMANUEL LAGUERRE; formed by dissidents from the right-wing Objectif Guadeloupe coalition.

Guadeloupe Unie, Socialisme et Réalité (GUSR): Pointe-à-Pitre; e-mail d.larifla@senat.fr; 'dissident' faction of the Parti Socialiste; Pres. DOMINIQUE LARIFLA.

Konvwa pou Liberasyon Nasyon Gwadloup (KLNG): Pointe-à-Pitre; f. 1997; pro-independence; Leader LUC REINETTE.

Lutte Ouvrière: Pointe-à-Pitre; internet www.lutte-ouvriere.org; extreme left-wing; sister organization of Combat Ouvrier; mem of the Internationalist Communist Union.

Parti Communiste Guadeloupéen (PCG): 119 rue Vatable, 97110 Pointe-à-Pitre; tel. 5-90-88-23-07; f. 1944; Sec.-Gen. MONA CADOCE.

Parti Radical de Gauche: Bergette, 97150 Petit Bourg; tel. 5-90-95-72-83; f. 1902; Pres. FLAVIEN FERRANT; Gen. Sec. LUCIEN ANAÏS.

Parti Socialiste (PS): 8 Résidence Légitimus, blvd Légitimus, 97110 Pointe-à-Pitre; tel. and fax 5-90-21-65-72; fax 5-90-83-65-20-51; e-mail fede971@parti-socialiste.fr; internet www.parti-socialiste.fr; divided into two factions to contest the March 1992 and March 1993 elections; Jt First Secs MARLÈNE MELISSE, FAVROT DAVRAIN.

Renouveau Socialiste: ZAC de Boisrepeaux, Abymes, Pointe-à-Pitre; e-mail d.marsin@senat.fr; f. 2003; Leader DANIEL MARSIN.

Union pour un Mouvement Populaire (UMP): Lotissement SIG, Sainte-Anne; tel. 5-90-99-52-99; fax 5-90-99-52-99; f. 2002; centre-right; local br. of the metropolitan party; Departmental Sec. ALDO BLAISE.

Les Verts: 32 rue Alsace-Lorraine, 97110 Pointe-à-Pitre; tel. 5-90-35-41-90; fax 5-90-25-02-62; internet www.les-verts.org; green party; Gen. Sec. MICHÈLE MAXO; Regional Dirs HARRY DURIMEL, MARIE LINE PIRBAKAS.

Other political organizations participating in the 2004 elections included Mouvement pour la Démocratie et le Développement (MDDP), Union Populaire pour la Libération de la Guadeloupe (UPLG), Mouvman Gwadloupéyen (MG), Parti Progressiste Démocratique Guadeloupéen (PPDG), Renouveau Socialiste; and the coalitions Priorité à l'Education et à l'Environnement and Union pour une Guadeloupe Responsable.

Judicial System

Cour d'Appel: Palais de Justice, 4 blvd Félix Eboué, 97100 Basse-Terre; tel. 5-90-80-63-36; fax 5-90-80-63-39; First Pres. JEAN-PIERRE ATTHENONT; Procurator-Gen. MICHEL MAROTTE; two Tribunaux de Grande Instance, four Tribunaux d'Instance.

Religion

The majority of the population belong to the Roman Catholic Church.

CHRISTIANITY

The Roman Catholic Church

Guadeloupe comprises the single diocese of Basse-Terre, suffragan to the archdiocese of Fort-de-France, Martinique. At 31 December 2002 there were an estimated 373,000 adherents, representing some 85% of the total population. The Bishop participates in the Antilles Episcopal Conference, currently based in Port of Spain, Trinidad and Tobago.

Bishop of Basse-Terre: Rt Rev. ERNEST MESMIN LUCIEN CABO, Evêché, pl. Saint-François, BP 369, 97100 Basse-Terre Cédex; tel. 5-90-81-36-69; fax 5-90-81-98-23; e-mail eveche@catholique-guadeloupe.info.

The Press

L'Etincelle: 119 rue Vatable, 97110 Pointe-à-Pitre; tel. 5-90-91-12-77; fax 5-90-83-69-90; f. 1944; weekly; organ of the PCG; Dir RAYMOND BARON; circ. 5,000.

France-Antilles: 1 rue Hincelin, BP 658, 97159 Pointe-à-Pitre; tel. 5-90-90-25-25; fax 5-90-91-78-31; daily; Dir FRANÇOIS MERCADER; circ. 50,000.

Match: 33 rue Peyrier, 97110 Pointe-à-Pitre; tel. and fax 5-90-82-01-87; fortnightly; Dir MARIE ANTONIA JABBOUR; circ. 6,000.

Newsmagazine Guadeloupéen: Résidence Vatable, Bâtiment B, BP 1286, 97178 Pointe-à-Pitre; tel. 5-90-91-16-94; fax 5-90-82-22-38; f. 1994; fmrly *Magwa*; fortnightly; independent; Editor DANNICK ZANDRONIS; circ. 4,000.

Le Progrès Social: rue Toussaint L'Ouverture, 97100 Basse-Terre; tel. 5-90-81-10-41; weekly; Dir JEAN-CLAUDE RODES; circ. 5,000.

Sept Mag Communication: Immeuble Curaçao, Voie Verte, 97122 Baie-Mahault; tel. 26-60-50; fax 26-61-87; e-mail jcannval@outremer.com; weekly; Dir JACQUES CANNEVAL; circ. 30,000.

TV Magazine Guadeloupe: 1 rue Paul Lacavé, BP 658, 97169 Pointe-à-Pitre; tel. 5-90-90-25-25; weekly.

Broadcasting and Communications

BROADCASTING

Réseau France Outre-mer (RFO): BP 180, 97122 Baie Mahault Cédex; tel. 5-90-60-96-96; fax 5-90-60-96-82; internet www.rfo.fr; fmrly Société Nationale de Radio-Télévision Française d'Outre-mer, renamed as above 1998; radio and television broadcast 24 hours daily; Pres. ANDRÉ-MICHEL BESSE; Regional Dir JEAN PHILLIPPE PASCAL; Gen. Man. FRANÇOIS GUILBEAU.

Radio

More than 30 private FM radio stations are in operation.

Radio Actif: rue Ferdinand Forest, 97122 Baie-Mahault; tel. 5-90-26-68-93; commercial; satellite link to Radio Monte-Carlo (Monaco and France).

Radio Caraïbes International (RCI): BP 1309, 97187 Point-à-Pitre Cédex; tel. 5-90-83-96-96; fax 5-90-83-96-97; two commercial

stations broadcasting 24 hours daily; Dir JEAN-FRANÇOIS FERANDIER-SICARD.

Radio Saint-Martin: Port de Marigot, 97150 Saint-Martin; commercial station broadcasting 94 hours weekly; Man. H. COOKS.

Radio Voix Chrétiennes de Saint-Martin: BP 103, Marigot, 97150 Saint-Martin; tel. 5-90-87-13-59; religious; Man. Fr CORNELIUS CHARLES.

Television

Canal Antilles: 2 Lotissement les Jardins de Houelbourg, 97122 Baie-Mahault; tel. 5-90-26-81-79; private 'coded' station.

TCI Guadeloupe: Montauban, 97190 Grosier; commercial station.

Finance

(cap. = capital; res = reserves; dep. = deposits; m. = million; brs = branches; amounts in euros unless otherwise indicated)

BANKING

Central Bank

Institut d'Emission des Départements d'Outre-mer (IEDOM): blvd Légitimus, BP 196, 97155 Pointe-à-Pitre Cédex; tel. 5-90-93-74-00; fax 5-90-93-74-25; e-mail iedom.gpe@wanadoo.fr; internet www.iedom.com; Dir F. ROCHE TOUSSAINT.

Commercial Banks

Banque des Antilles Françaises: pl. de la Victoire, BP 696, 97110 Pointe-à-Pitre Cédex; tel. 5-90-26-80-07; fax 5-90-26-74-48; internet www.bdaf.gp; f. 1853; cap. 7.5m., res 8.4m., dep. 506.1m. (Dec. 2002); Chair. SERGE J. ROBERT; Gen. Man. MICHEL SPRECHT; 19 brs; 350 employees.

Banque Française Commerciale Antilles-Guyane (BFC Antilles-Guyane): Immeuble BFC AG, Grand Camp-La Rocade, BP 13, 97151 Pointe-à-Pitre Cédex; tel. 5-90-21-56-70; fax 5-90-21-56-80; e-mail f.aujoulat@bfc-ag.com; internet www.bfc-ag.com; f. 1976 as branch of Banque Française Commerciale SA, separated 1984; total assets 3,609.1m. French francs (1998); Chair. JEAN-YVES BOUTADOU; Gen. Man. FRANCIS DUBUS.

BNP Paribas Guadeloupe: pl. de la Rénovation, BP 161, 97155 Pointe-à-Pitre; tel. 5-90-90-58-58; fax 5-90-90-04-07; internet www.bnpparibas.com; f. 1941; subsidiary of BNP Paribas; CEO GÉRARD D'HÈRE; Gen. Sec. FRANÇOIS PASETTI; 12 brs.

BRED Banque Populaire (BRED-BP): 10 rue Achille René Boisneuf, BP 35, 97110 Pointe-à-Pitre; tel. 5-90-89-67-00.

Caisse d'Epargne de la Guadeloupe: 20 Lotissement Plazza II, Grand Camp-La Rocade, 97142 Abymes, BP 22, 97151 Pointe-à-Pitre Cédex; tel. 5-90-93-12-12; fax 5-90-93-12-13; Pres. DANIEL NUCCIO.

Crédit Agricole de la Guadeloupe: Petit Pérou-Abymes, 97139 Pointe-à-Pitre; 97176 Abymes Cédex; tel. 5-90-90-65-65; fax 5-90-90-65-89; e-mail catelnet@cr900.credit-agricole.fr; internet www.ca-guadeloupe.fr; Pres. CHRISTIAN FLÉREAU; Gen. Man. ROGER WUNSCHEL.

Crédit Maritime de la Guadeloupe: 36 rue Achille René-Boisneuf, BP 292, 97175 Pointe-à-Pitre; tel. 5-90-21-08-40; fax 5-90-83-46-37; e-mail pointe-a-pitre-agence-cmm@creditmaritime.com; internet www.creditmaritime-outremer.com; 4 agencies; Pres. YVES JOLIMAN; Gen. Man. PHILIPPE BEAUVOIR.

Société Générale de Banque aux Antilles (SGBA): 30 rue Frébault, BP 55, 97152 Pointe-à-Pitre; tel. 5-90-25-49-77; fax 5-90-25-49-78; e-mail sgba@wanadoo.fr; internet www.sgba.fr; f. 1979; cap. 18.6m., res 0.6m., dep. 246m. (Dec. 2002); Chair. JEAN-LOUIS MATTEI; Gen. Man. PATRICK LE BUFFE; 5 brs.

Development Banks

Banque de Développement de Petites et Moyennes Entreprises (BDPME): c/o AFD, blvd Légitimus, BP 160, 97159 Pointe-à-Pitre Cédex ; tel. 5-90-89-65-58; fax 5-90-21-04-55; Representative MUGUETTE DAIJARDIN.

Société de Crédit pour le Développement de Guadeloupe (SODEGA): Carrefour Raizet Baimbridge, BP 54, 97152 Pointe-à-Pitre; tel. 5-90-82-65-00; fax 5-90-90-17-91; e-mail informatique@sodega.fr; internet www.sodega.fr; f. 1970; bought from the Agence Française de Développement (AFD—q.v.) by BRED-BP in 2003.

Foreign Companies

Some 30 of the principal European insurance companies are represented in Pointe-à-Pitre, and another six companies have offices in Basse-Terre.

Trade and Industry

GOVERNMENT AGENCIES

Conseil Economique et Social: rue Peynier, 97100 Basse-Terre; tel. 5-90-41-05-15; fax 5-90-41-05-23; internet www.cr-guadeloupe.fr; Pres. JEAN-MICHEL PENCHARD.

Direction de l'Agriculture et de la Forêt (DAF): Jardin Botanique, 97100 Basse-Terre; tel. 5-90-99-09-09; fax 5-90-99-09-10; e-mail daf.guadeloupe@wanadoo.fr; Man. GÉRARD CHUITON.

Direction Régionale de l'Industrie, de la Recherche et de l'Environnement (DRIRE): 20 rue de la Chapelle, Z. I. Jarry, BP 448, 97122 Baie-Mahault; tel. 5-90-38-03-47; fax 5-90-38-03-50; e-mail henri.kaltembacher@industrie.gouv.fr; active in industry, business services, transport, public works, tourism and distribution; Departmental Co-ordinator HENRI KALTEMBACHER.

Direction Régionale des Affaires Maritimes (DRAM): 1 quai Layrle, BP 473, 97164 Pointe-à-Pitre; tel. 5-90-82-03-13; fax 5-90-90-07-33; responsible for shipping, fishing and other maritime issues at a national and Community level.

Direction Régionale du Commerce Extérieur (DRCE): see chapter on Martinique.

DEVELOPMENT ORGANIZATIONS

Agence de l'Environnement et de la Maîtrise de l'Energie (ADEME): Immeuble Café Center, rue Ferdinand Forest, Z. I. Jarry, 97122 Baie-Mahault; tel. 5-90-26-78-05; fax 5-90-26-87-15; e-mail ademegua@wanadoo.fr; internet www.ademe.fr; developing energy and waste management; Man. GUY SIMONNOT.

Agence Française de Développement (AFD): blvd Légitimus, BP 160, 97159 Pointe-à-Pitre Cédex; tel. 5-90-89-65-65; fax 5-90-83-03-73; e-mail afdpointeapitre@gp.groupe-afd.org ; internet www.afd.fr; fmrly Caisse Française de Développement; Man. YVES MALPEL.

Agence pour la Promotion des Investissements en Guadeloupe (APRIGA): 12 Convenance's Center, Lieu-dit Convenance, 97122 Baie-Mahault; tel. 5-90-94-45-40; fax 5-90-95-86-47; e-mail apriga@apriga.com; internet www.apriga.com; f. 1979 as Agence pour la Promotion de l'Industrie de la Guadeloupe; Pres. LYLIANE PIQUION SALOME.

CHAMBERS OF COMMERCE

Chambre d'Agriculture de la Guadeloupe: Rond-Point Destrelland, 97122 Baie-Mahault; tel. 5-90-25-17-17; fax 5-90-26-07-22; e-mail direction@guadeloupe.chambagri.fr; Pres. MAURICE RAMASSAMY.

Chambre de Commerce et d'Industrie de Basse-Terre: 6 rue Victor Hugues, 97100 Basse-Terre; tel. 5-90-99-44-44; fax 5-90-81-21-17; e-mail cci-basse-terre@wanadoo.fr; internet www.basse-terre.cci.fr; f. 1832; 24 mems; Pres. GÉRARD THÉOBALD.

Chambre de Commerce et d'Industrie de Pointe-à-Pitre: Hôtel Consulaire, rue Félix Eboué, 97159 Pointe-à-Pitre Cédex; tel. 5-90-93-76-00; fax 5-90-90-21-87; e-mail contacts@cci-pap.org; internet www.cci-pap.org; Pres. COLETTE KOURY; Dir-Gen. JACQUES GARRETA.

Chambre de Métiers de la Guadeloupe: route Choisy, BP 61, 97120 Saint-Claude; tel. 5-90-80-23-33; fax 5-90-80-08-93; e-mail sgr@cmguadeloupe.org; Pres. MAURICE SONGEONS; Sec.-Gen. SERGE NIRLEP.

Jeune Chambre Economique de Basse-Terre: BP 316, 97100 Basse-Terre; tel. 5-90–81-13-73; e-mail jce.bt@laposte.net; Pres. BERNARD SAULCHOIR.

Jeune Chambre Economique de Pointe-à-Pitre: BP 505, 97168 Pointe-à-Pitre Cédex; tel. 5-90-89-01-30; fax 5-90-91-72-98; e-mail jcepap2006@wanadoo.fr; Pres. JEAN-CHRISTOPHE HODEBAR.

EMPLOYERS' ORGANIZATIONS

Association des Moyennes et Petites Industries (AMPI): CWTC—Zone de Commerce International, Pointe Jarry, BP 2325, 97187 Jarry Cédex; tel. 5-90-25-06-28; fax 5-90-25-06-29; e-mail mpi.guadeloupe@wanadoo.fr; internet www.mpi-guadeloupe.com; f. 1974; Pres. PATRICK DOQUIN; Gen. Sec JEAN JOACHIM; 116 mem cos.

Ordre des pharmaciens du département Guadeloupe: Rocade Forum de Grand Camp, Bâtiment A, No 1, 97142 Pointe-à-Pitre; tel. 5-90-21-66-05; fax 5-90-21-66-07; Pres. CLAUDIE ESPIAND.

Syndicat des Producteurs-Exportateurs de Sucre et de Rhum de la Guadeloupe et Dépendances: Z. I. de la Pointe Jarry, 97122 Baie-Mahault; BP 2015, 97191 Pointe-à-Pitre; tel. 5-90-26-62-12; fax 5-90-26-86-76; f. 1937; Pres. AMÉDÉE HUYGHUES-DESPOINTES; 4 mems.

Union des Entreprises–Mouvement des Entreprises de France (UDE–MEDEF): Immeuble SCI BTB, voie Principale, Z.I. Jarry, 97122 Baie Mahault; tel. 5-90-26-83-58; fax 5-90-26-83-67; e-mail ude.medef@medef-guadeloupe.com; Pres. CHRISTIAN VIVIES; Gen. Sec. BERTRAND JOYAU.

UTILITIES

EDF Guadeloupe: BP 85, 97153 Pointe-à-Pitre; tel. 5-90-82-40-13; fax 5-90-83-30-02; e-mail emma.dahomay@edfgdf.fr; internet guadeloupe.edf.fr; electricity producer; Man. JEAN-MICHEL LEBEAU; electricity producer.

Veolia Water-Générale des Eaux Guadeloupe: Centre de la Guadeloupe, 7 Morne Vergain, BP 17, 91139 Abymes, Pointe-à-Pitre; tel. 5-90-89-76-76; fax 5-90-91-39-10; fmrly SOGEA.

TRADE UNIONS

Centrale des Travailleurs Unis (CTU): Logement Test 14, BP 676, Bergevin, 97169 Pointe-à-Pitre; tel. 5-90-83-16-50; fax 5-90-91-78-02; affiliated to the Confédération Française Démocratique du Travail; Sec.-Gen. HENRI BERTHELOT.

Confédération Générale du Travail de la Guadeloupe (CGTG): 4 Cité Artisanale de Bergevin, BP 779, 97110 Pointe-à-Pitre Cédex; tel. 5-90-82-34-61; fax 5-90-91-04-00; f. 1961; Sec.-Gen. JEAN-MARIE NOMERTIN; 5,000 mems.

Fédération Départementale des Syndicats d'Exploitants de la Guadeloupe (FDSEA): Chambre d'Agriculture, Rond-Point de Destrellan, 97122 Baie-Mahault; tel. 5-90-26-06-47; fax 5-90-26-48-82; e-mail fdsea5@wanadoo.fr; affiliated to the Fédération Nationale des Syndicats d'Exploitants; Pres. ERIC NELSON.

Union Départementale de la Confédération Française des Travailleurs Chrétiens: 29 rue Victor Hugo, BP 245, 97159 Pointe-à-Pitre; tel. 5-90-82-04-01; f. 1937; Sec.-Gen. ALBERT SARKIS; 3,500 mems.

Union Départementale des Syndicats CGT-FO: 59 rue Lamartine, BP 687, 97110 Pointe-à-Pitre; tel. 5-90-82-86-83; fax 5-90-82-16-12; e-mail udfoguadeloupe@force-ouvriere.fr; Gen. Sec. MAX EVARISTE; 1,500 mems.

Union des Moyennes et Petites Entreprises de Guadeloupe (UMPEG): 17 Immeuble Patio, Grand Camp, 97142 Abymes, Pointe-à-Pitre; tel. 5-90-91-79-31; fax 5-90-93-09-18.

Union Générale des Travailleurs de la Guadeloupe (UGTG): rue Paul Lacavé, 97110 Pointe-à-Pitre; tel. 5-90-83-10-07; fax 5-90-89-08-70; e-mail ugtg@ugtg.org; f. 1973; confederation of pro-independence trade unions including l'Union des Employés du Commerce (UEC), l'Union des Travailleurs des Communes (UTC), l'Union des Travailleurs de l'Hôtellerie, du Tourisme et de la Restauration (UTHTR), l'Union des Travailleurs des Produits Pétroliers (UTPP), and l'Union des Travailleurs des Télécommunications (UTT); Leader MICHEL MADASSAMY; Gen. Sec. RAYMOND GAUTHIEROT; 4,000 mems.

Union Régionale Guadeloupe: Immeuble Jabol, 5ème, rue de l'Assainissement, 97110 Pointe-à-Pitre; tel. 5-90-91-01-15; fax 5-90-83-08-64; e-mail unsa@unsa.org; internet www.unsa.org; member union of l'Union Nationale des Syndicats Autonomes (UNSA).

UNSA Education Guadeloupe: Immeuble Jabol, 5ème, rue de l'Assainissement, 97110 Point-à-Pitre; tel. 5-90-91-01-15; fax 5-90-83-08-64; e-mail pelage.girard@wanadoo.fr; internet ; f. ; Sec.-Gen. GIRARD PELAGE.

Transport

RAILWAYS

There are no railways in Guadeloupe.

ROADS

In 1990 there were 2,069 km (1,286 miles) of roads in Guadeloupe, of which 323 km were Routes Nationales.

SHIPPING

The major port is at Pointe-à-Pitre, and a new port for the export of bananas has been built at Basse-Terre.

Compagnie Générale Portuaire: Marina Bas-du-Fort, 97110 Pointe-à-Pitre; tel. 5-90-93-66-20; fax 5-90-90-81-53; e-mail marina@marina-pap.com; internet www.marina-pap.com; port authority; Man. PHILIPPE CHEVALLIER; Harbour Master TONY BRESLAU; 1,000 berths for non-commercial traffic.

Compagnie Générale Maritime Antilles-Guyane: Z. I. de la Pointe Jarry, BP 92, 97100 Baie-Mahault; tel. 5-90-26-72-39; fax 5-90-26-74-62.

Port Autonome de la Guadeloupe: Gare Maritime, BP 485, 97165 Pointe-à-Pitre Cédex; tel. 5-90-21-39-00; fax 5-90-21-39-69;

e-mail v-tarer@port-guadeloupe.com; internet www
.port-guadeloupe.com; port authority; Pres. AMÉDÉE ADELAIDE; Gen.
Man. CHRISTIAN BROUTIN.

**Société Guadeloupéenne de Consignation et Manutention
(SGCM):** 8 rue de la Chapelle, BP 2360, 97001 Jarry Cédex; tel. 5-
90-38-05-55; fax 5-90-26-95-39; e-mail gerard.petrelluzzi@sgcm.fr;
internet www.sgcm.gp; f. 1994; shipping agents, stevedoring; Chair.
BERNARD AUBERY; Gen. Man. GERARD PETRELLUZZI; 17 berths.

Société de Transport Maritimes Brudey Frères: 78 centre St
John Perse, 97110 Pointe-à-Pitre; tel. 5-90-91-60-87; fax 5-90-93-00-
79; e-mail brudey.freres@wanadoo.fr; internet www.brudey-freres
.fr; f. 1983; inter-island ferry service; Dir DENIS BRUDEY; 5 vessels; c.
400,000 passengers per year.

CIVIL AVIATION

Raizet International Airport is situated 3 km (2 miles) from Pointe-
à-Pitre and is equipped to handle jet-engined aircraft. There are
smaller airports on the islands of Marie-Galante, La Désirade and
Saint-Barthélémy.

Air Caraïbes (CAT): Immeuble le Caducée, Morne Vergain, 97139
Abymes, Pointe-à-Pitre; tel. 5-90-82-47-47; fax 5-90-82-47-49; e-mail
info@aircaraibes.com; internet www.aircaraibes.com; f. 2000 following merger of Air St Martin, Air St Barts, Air Guadeloupe and
Air Martinique; owned by Groupe Dubreuil; operates inter-island
and regional services within the Eastern Caribbean and flights to

Miami (USA); CEO PHILIPPE CHEVALLIER; 14 aircraft; 452,000 passengers (2003); 375 employees.

Air Caraïbes Atlantique: Aéroport, 97232 Le Lamentin; f. 2003;
subsidiary of Air Caraïbes; services between Pointe-à-Pitre and
Fort-de-France (Martinique) and Paris; Pres. FRANÇOIS HERSEN.

Tourism

Guadeloupe is a popular tourist destination, especially for visitors
from metropolitan France (who account for some 89% of tourists)
and the USA. The main attractions are the beaches, the mountainous scenery and the unspoilt beauty of the island dependencies. In
2003 some 650,000 tourists visited Guadeloupe. Receipts from
tourism totalled €238m. in 2002. In that year there were 162 hotels,
with some 8,000 rooms.

Comité du Tourisme: 5 sq. de la Banque, BP 422, 97110 Pointe-à-
Pitre Cédex; tel. 5-90-82-09-30; fax 5-90-83-89-22; e-mail info@
lesilesdeguadeloupe.com ; internet www.lesilesdeguadeloupe.com;
Pres. PATRICK VIAL-COLLET.

Delégation Régionale au Tourisme: 5 rue Victor Hugues, 97100
Basse-Terre; tel. 5-90-81-10-44; fax 5-90-81-94-82; e-mail
dntourisme@wanadoo.fr; Dir JEAN FRANÇOIS DESBROCHES.

Syndicat d'Initiative de Pointe-à-Pitre-: Centre Commercial de
la Marina, 97110 Pointe-à-Pitre; tel. 5-90-90-70-02; fax 5-90-90-74-
70; internet www.sivap.gp; Pres. M. FORTUNE.

MARTINIQUE

Introductory Survey

Location, Climate, Language, Religion, Capital

Martinique is one of the Windward Islands in the West Indies,
with Dominica to the north and Saint Lucia to the south. The
island is dominated by the volcanic peak of Mont Pelée. The
climate is tropical, but tempered by easterly and north-easterly
breezes. The more humid and wet season runs from July to
November, and the average temperature is 26°C (79°F). French
is the official language, but a Creole patois is widely spoken. The
majority of the population profess Christianity and belong to the
Roman Catholic Church. The capital is Fort-de-France.

Recent History

Martinique has been a French possession since 1635. The prosperity of the island was based on the sugar industry, which was
devastated by the volcanic eruption of Mont Pelée in 1902.
Martinique became a Department of France in 1946, when the
Governor was replaced by a Prefect, and an elected Conseil
général (General Council) was created.

During the 1950s there was a growth of nationalist feeling, as
expressed by Aimé Césaire's Parti Progressiste Martiniquais
(PPM) and the Parti Communiste Martiniquais (PCM). However, economic power remained concentrated in the hands of the
békés (descendants of white colonial settlers), who owned most of
the agricultural land and controlled the lucrative import-export
market. This provided little incentive for innovation or self-
sufficiency, and fostered resentment against lingering colonial
attitudes.

In 1974 Martinique, together with Guadeloupe and French
Guiana, was given regional status as part of France's governmental reorganization. An indirectly elected Regional
Council (Conseil régional) was created, with some control over
the local economy. In 1982 and 1983 the socialist Government of
President François Mitterrand, which had pledged itself to
decentralizing power in favour of the Overseas Departments,
made further concessions towards autonomy by giving the local
councils greater control over taxation, local police and the
economy. At the first direct elections to the new Conseil
régional, held in February 1983, left-wing parties (the PPM, the
PCM and the Fédération Socialiste de la Martinique—FSM)
won 21 of the 41 seats. This success, and the election of Aimé
Césaire as the Conseil's President, strengthened his influence

against the pro-independence elements in his own party. (Full
independence for Martinique attracted support from only a
small minority of the population; the majority sought reforms
that would bring greater autonomy, while retaining French
control.) The Mouvement Indépendantiste Martiniquais (MIM),
the most vocal of the separatist parties, fared badly in the
elections, obtaining less than 3% of the total vote. At elections to
the enlarged Conseil général, held in March 1985, the left-wing
parties increased their representation, but the centre-right coalition of the Union pour la Démocratie Française (UDF) and the
Rassemblement pour la République (RPR) maintained their
control of the administration.

For the general election to the Assemblée nationale in March
1986, Martinique's representation was increased from three to
four deputies. Césaire and a member of the FSM were elected
from a unified list of left-wing candidates, while the RPR and the
UDF (which had also presented a joint list) each won one seat.
In concurrent elections to the Conseil régional the left-wing
parties (including the PPM, the FSM and the PCM) won 21 of
the 41 seats, and the RPR and the UDF together won the
remaining seats. Césaire retained the presidency of the Council
until 1988, when he relinquished the post to Camille Darsières
(the Secretary-General of the PPM). In September 1986 indirect
elections were held for Martinique's two seats in the Sénat. As in
the March elections, the left-wing parties united, and, as a
consequence, Martinique acquired a left-wing senator for the
first time since 1958, a PPM member, while the other successful
candidate belonged to the UDF.

Following the recent trend in Martinique, the incumbent,
François Mitterrand of the Parti Socialiste (PS), won a decisive
majority of the island's votes at the 1988 French presidential
election. Left-wing candidates secured all four seats at elections
to the Assemblée nationale in June. Furthermore, in September–October, for the first time in 40 years, the parties of the
left achieved a majority at elections to the Conseil général.
Emile Maurice of the RPR was, none the less, elected President
of the Conseil général for a seventh term.

In June 1990 the results of the 1986 election to the Conseil
régional were annulled because of a technicality, and another
election was held in October. Pro-independence candidates won
nearly 22% of the votes, and secured nine seats (of which seven
were won by the MIM). The PPM, the FSM and the PCM again
formed a joint electoral list, but won only 14 seats, and consequently lost their absolute majority on the Conseil; Camille
Darsières was, however, re-elected to the presidency of the

Conseil. The success of the pro-independence candidates was attributed to local apprehension concerning the implications of plans within the European Community (EC, known as the European Union, EU (see p. 217), from November 1993) for a single market, which would, it was feared, expose Martinique's economy to excessive competition.

At elections to the Conseil général in March 1992, left-wing parties secured 26 seats and right-wing organizations 19. Claude Lise, a PPM deputy to the Assemblée nationale, was elected President of the Conseil général. In concurrent elections to the Conseil régional the RPR and the UDF, contesting the election as the Union pour la France (UPF), won 16 seats, the MIM (which contested the election under the title Patriotes Martiniquais) and the PPM secured nine seats each, and the PCM (under the title Pour une Martinique au Travail) and the FSM (as the Nouvelle Génération Socialiste) won four and three seats, respectively. Following three rounds of voting, Emile Capgras of the PCM was finally elected President of the Conseil régional.

In September 1992 72.3% of voters in Martinique approved ratification of the Treaty on European Union (see p. 217), although the abstention rate was high. In November of that year banana-growers in Guadeloupe and Martinique suspended economic activity in their respective Departments by obstructing access to ports and airports and blocking roads, in protest at the threatened loss of special advantages under the Single European Act. Order was restored after four days, however, following assurances that subsidies would be maintained and that certain products, such as bananas (one of Martinique's principal exports), would be protected under EC proposals.

At the March 1993 elections to the Assemblée nationale there was a marked swing in favour of the parties of the right: André Lesueur and Pierre Petit were elected to represent the RPR, while a third right-wing candidate, Anicet Turinay, campaigned successfully on behalf of the UPF. Césaire did not seek re-election, and was replaced at the Assemblée nationale by Camille Darsières.

The composition of the Conseil général remained largely unchanged at cantonal elections in March 1994, at which the PPM retained 10 seats, the RPR seven and the UDF three; Lise was subsequently re-elected President of the Council. At elections to the European Parliament in June, the government list secured the greatest proportion (36.6%) of the votes cast. A combined list of parties of the left of the four Overseas Departments (which included the PPM and the Parti Martiniquais Socialiste) took 20.2% of the votes.

At the first round of voting in the 1995 presidential election, on 23 April, Martinique was the only French overseas possession in which the candidate of the PS, Lionel Jospin, received the greatest proportion of the valid votes cast (34.4%). Jospin, supported by all the parties of the left, took 58.9% of the votes cast at the second round on 7 May. At municipal elections in June the PPM retained control of Martinique's principal towns. In September Lise was elected to the Sénat, while the incumbent PPM representative, Rodolphe Désiré, was returned to office.

At elections to the Assemblée nationale in May and June 1997, Turinay and Petit, representing the RPR, were re-elected, together with Darsières of the PPM. Alfred Marie-Jeanne, the First Secretary and a founding member of the MIM, was elected in a constituency hitherto held by the RPR. At elections to the Conseil régional in March 1998, the left retained its majority. The pro-independence MIM performed well, increasing its representation by four seats, to 13, while the PPM secured seven seats, the RPR six and the UDF five. Marie-Jeanne was elected President of the Conseil régional. In concurrent elections to the Conseil général the left again increased its majority. Lise was re-elected to the presidency of the Conseil.

A two-month strike by workers in the banana sector, which had severely disrupted economic activity around the port of Fort-de-France, was ended in January 1999, when a pay agreement was reached. The social climate deteriorated further in May, as two companies were affected by strike action. Workers at the Toyota motor company were demanding substantial pay increases and a reduction in working hours, while employees of the Roger Albert distribution group were protesting against the dismissal of two colleagues. In early October tension escalated as trade unions took sympathetic action, blocking access to the main industrial and commercial zones around the capital for two days. Subsequent negotiations between the local authorities and

a trade union delegation resulted in the removal of the blockades and an agreement to hold talks on the resolution of the two conflicts. The dispute at Roger Albert was concluded shortly afterwards, following the intervention of Marie-Jeanne, but, despite mediation efforts, industrial action at Toyota continued. In mid-October trade unions organized a week-long blockade of the port of Fort-de-France in protest against proposed redundancies at Toyota. Later that month, prior to a two-day visit to Martinique by Jospin, the Prime Minister, banana producers occupied the headquarters of the French naval forces for several days, demanding the disbursement of exceptional aid to compensate for the adverse effect on their industry of a dramatic decline in prices on the European market. Marie-Jeanne, who was opposed to the limited nature of the Government's plans for institutional reform, refused to participate in the events organized for Jospin's stay. The Prime Minister announced an emergency plan for the banana sector and, while attending a conference on regional co-operation, agreed, in principle, to a proposal for greater autonomy for the local authorities in conducting relations with neighbouring countries and territories. In November, following two weeks of direct negotiations between trade union representatives and the management of Toyota, a protocol was signed, marking the end of the five-month dispute; a pay increase was awarded and dismissal proceedings against 12 employees were annulled.

Following a series of meetings, in December 1999 the Presidents of the Conseils régionaux of French Guiana, Guadeloupe and Martinique signed a joint declaration in Basse-Terre, Guadeloupe, affirming their intention to propose, to the President and the Government, a legislative amendment aimed at creating a new status of overseas region, despite an earlier statement by Jospin indicating that the Government did not envisage a change in status for the Departments. Further meetings of the three regional Presidents were held in January and February 2000. Proposals regarding the institutional future and socio-economic development of the Departments were provisionally accepted by the French Assemblée nationale in May 2000, and a modified version of the proposals was subsequently adopted, by a narrow margin, by the Sénat. In November the Assemblée nationale approved the proposals and in December they were ratified by the Constitutional Council. Following a meeting of members of the Conseil régional and the Conseil général in late June 2001, a series of proposals on greater autonomy, to be presented to the French Government, was agreed upon. These included: the division of the territory into four districts; the creation of a 'collectivité territoriale' (territorial community), governed by a 41-member Assembly elected for a five-year term; and the establishment of an independent executive council. Furthermore, the proposals included a request that the territory be given control over legislative and administrative affairs, as well as legislative authority on matters concerning Martinique alone. In November the French Government announced itself to be in favour of the suggested constitutional developments, and in March 2003 the two houses of the French parliament approved constitutional changes that, *inter alia*, allowed for local referendums to be held on proposals for greater decentralization in overseas possessions. In the referendum, held on 7 December, some 51% of participating voters rejected legislative reforms that envisaged the replacement of the Conseil général and the Conseil régional with a single assembly.

At a referendum held in September 2000, Martinique voted overwhelmingly in favour (91% of those voting) of reducing the presidential mandate from seven years to five. In municipal elections held in March 2001 the PPM retained control of the majority of municipalities (including Fort-de-France, where Césaire, retiring as mayor after 55 years, was succeeded by a fellow PPM member, Sérge Letchimy, who defeated Marie-Jeanne, President of the Conseil régional). In the concurrently held election to the Conseil général, Lise was re-elected President. In mid-2001 the French President, Jacques Chirac, rejected a joint request by French Guiana, Guadeloupe and Martinique that they be permitted to join, as associate members, the Association of Caribbean States. In the first round of the presidential election, held on 21 April 2002, Chirac obtained 33.0% of the votes cast in the Department, followed by Jospin with 29.2%, who was, however, eliminated nationally. In the second round, held on 5 May, Chirac overwhelmingly defeated Jean-Marie Le Pen of the extreme right-wing Front National, securing 96.1% of the votes cast. At elections to the Assemblée nationale in June, Marie-Jeanne was re-elected, while Turinay lost his seat to Louis-Joseph Mansour of the PS, and Darsière lost his to Pierre-Jean Samot of the left-wing Bâtir le Pays Martinique; Alfred Almont, representing the right-wing alliance of the Union pour la Majorité Présidentielle (UMP) and the RPR, secured the remaining seat. The RPR subsequently merged into the successor party to the UMP, the Union pour un Mouvement Populaire (also known as the UMP). In March 2003 the Conseil constitutionnel ordered Samot to resign for having received campaign funds for the 2002 election from his party, which was not officially registered at the time. As a result, a by-election was held in May 2003, which was won by Philippe Edmond-Mariette, also of Bâtir le Pays Martinique.

At an election to the Conseil régional in March 2004 the Patriotes Martiniquais, a pro-independence alliance comprising the MIM and the Conseil National des Comités Populaires and the Alliance pour le Pays Martinique (which was absorbed by the two larger groupings after the first round of voting), won an overwhelming majority, obtaining 28 of the 41 council seats. A joint list comprising the PPM and other left-wing candidates obtained nine seats, while the right-wing Forces Martiniquaises de Progrès secured the remaining four seats.

Government

France is represented in Martinique by an appointed prefect. There are two councils with local powers: the 45-member Conseil général (General Council) and the 41-member Conseil régional (Regional Council). Both are elected by universal adult suffrage for a period of up to six years. Martinique elects four deputies to the Assemblée nationale in Paris, and sends two indirectly-elected representatives to the Sénat. The Department is also represented at the European Parliament.

Defence

At 1 August 2004 France maintained a military force of 4,100 and a gendarmerie in the Antilles, with headquarters in Fort-de-France.

Economic Affairs

In 2001 Martinique's gross domestic product (GDP), measured at current prices, was estimated at US $4,161m., equivalent to $10,723 per head. During 1990–2001, according to UN estimates, GDP increased, in real terms, at an average rate of 1.5% per year; growth in 2001 was 2.1%. Between the censuses of 1990 and 1999, according to provisional figures, the population increased at an average annual rate of 0.7%.

Agriculture, hunting, forestry and fishing contributed an estimated 4% of GDP in 2000, and according to FAO figures engaged an estimated 3.2% of the labour force in 2003; the sector accounted for one-third of total exports in that year. The principal cash crops are bananas (which accounted for some 40% of export earnings in 2002), sugar cane (primarily for the production of rum), limes, melons and pineapples. The cultivation of cut flowers is also of some significance. Roots and tubers and vegetables are grown for local consumption. Agricultural production increased at an average rate of 1.3% per year during 1990–98; the sector declined by 0.2% in 1999.

The industrial sector (including construction and public works) engaged 10.6% of the total labour force in 1998 and contributed an estimated 14% of GDP in 2002. Mining, manufacturing and power provided some 10% of GDP in 1998. The most important manufacturing activities are petroleum refining (exports of refined petroleum products accounted for some 26% of the value of total exports in 2003) and the processing of agricultural products (11% of exports in 2003), the production of rum being of particular significance. Martiniquais rum was accorded the designation of Appellation d'origine contrôlée (AOC) in 1996 (the first AOC to be designated outside metropolitan France). Other areas of activity include metals, cement, chemicals, plastics, wood, printing and textiles. Energy is derived principally from mineral fuels. Imports of mineral fuels (including crude petroleum destined for the island's refinery) accounted for some 10% of the value of total imports in 2002.

The services sector engaged 55.2% of the total labour force in 1998 and provided an estimated 82% of GDP in 2000. Tourism is a major activity on the island and one of the most important sources of foreign exchange: in 2001 earnings from the tourism industry totalled an estimated €226.6m; some 83.5% of visitors were from metropolitan France in that year. In 2003 some 453,160 tourists visited the island.

In 2002 Martinique recorded a trade deficit of €1,499m. In 2000 the principal source of imports was metropolitan France (64%); Venezuela, Germany and Italy were also significant trading partners. France was also the principal market for exports, accounting for 57.8% of the total in 2000. In 2003 Guadeloupe and French Guiana together accounted for some 20% of Martinique's exports. The principal exports were bananas, refined petroleum products and rum. The principal imports included machinery and transport equipment (especially road vehicles), food and live animals, miscellaneous manufactured goods, chemicals and mineral fuels.

In 2001 the departmental budget was expected to balance. The annual rate of inflation averaged 2.0% in 1990–2003; consumer prices increased by 2.1% in 2002 and by 2.1% in 2003. Some 23.5% of the labour force were unemployed in 2003.

As an integral part of France, Martinique belongs to the European Union (EU, see p. 217).

Martinique's economic development has created a society that combines a relatively high standard of living with a weak economic base in agricultural and industrial production, as well as a chronic trade deficit. Levels of unemployment and emigration are high, although the rate of growth of both these factors has slowed since the mid-1980s. The linking of wage levels to those of metropolitan France, despite the island's lower level of productivity, has increased labour costs and restricted development. In the late 1990s the value of banana exports declined owing to a significant fall in prices on the European market, while the end of the EU's preferential banana import regime from 2006 also threatened Martinique's banana-growing sector. In November 2002 the French hotel group Accor announced that it would close its five hotels in Martinique and Guadeloupe, citing high operating costs, poor industrial relations and decreasing tourist arrivals. The liquidation of the French airline Air Lib in February 2003 had a further negative impact on the sector. In early 2003 the French Minister of Overseas Departments announced plans to stimulate the economies of Martinique, Guadeloupe and French Guiana that included the introduction of tax incentives for the hotel sector. Furthermore, in late 2003 it was announced that a subsidiary of Air Caraïbe was to begin an additional air service between Paris and Fort-de-France.

Education

The educational system is similar to that of metropolitan France (see chapter on French Guiana). In 2002/03 there were 50,137 pupils in pre-primary and primary education, while in secondary education there were 49,426 students (including 7,891 students in vocational education), of whom some 92% attended state schools. Higher education in law, French language and literature, human sciences, economics, medicine and Creole studies is provided in Martinique by a branch of the Université Antilles-Guyane. The university as a whole had 12,000 enrolled students in 2004. There are also two teacher-training institutes, and colleges of agriculture, fisheries, hotel management, nursing, midwifery and child care. Separate Academies for Martinique, French Guiana and Guadeloupe were established in January 1997, replacing the single Academy for the Antilles-Guyane (which was based in Fort-de-France). Departmental expenditure on education and culture was estimated at 111.5m. French francs in 2001.

Public Holidays

2005: 1 January (New Year's Day), 7–8 February (Carnival), 9 February (Ash Wednesday), 25–28 March (Easter), 1 May (Labour Day), 5 May (Ascension Day), 8 May (Victory Day), 16 May (Whit Monday), 14 July (National Day), 15 August (Assumption), 1 November (All Saints' Day), 11 November (Armistice Day), 25 December (Christmas Day).

2006: 1 January (New Year's Day), 27–28 February (Carnival), 1 March (Ash Wednesday), 14–17 April (Easter), 1 May (Labour Day), 8 May (Victory Day), 25 May (Ascension Day), 5 June (Whit Monday), 14 July (National Day), 15 August (Assumption), 1 November (All Saints' Day), 11 November (Armistice Day), 25 December (Christmas Day).

Weights and Measures

The metric system is in use.

Statistical Survey

Sources (unless otherwise stated): Institut national de la statistique et des études économiques (INSEE), Service Régional de Martinique, Centre Delgrès, blvd de la Pointe des Sables, Les Hauts de Dillon, BP 641, 97262 Fort-de-France Cédex; tel. 60-73-60; fax 60-73-50; internet www.insee.fr/fr/insee_regions/martinique; Ministère des départements et territoires d'outre-mer, 27 rue Oudinot, 75700 Paris 07 SP; tel. 1-53-69-20-00; fax 1-43-06-60-30; internet www.outre-mer.gouv.fr.

AREA AND POPULATION

Area: 1,100 sq km (424.7 sq miles).

Population: 359,579 (males 173,878, females 185,701) at census of 15 March 1990; 381,427 at census of 8 March 1999. *2004* (official estimate at 1 January, rounded figure): 392,500.

Density (at 1 January 2004): 356.8 per sq km.

Principal Towns (at 1999 census): Fort-de-France (capital) 94,049; Le Lamentin 35,460; Le Robert 21,240; Schoelcher 20,845; Sainte-Marie 20,098; Le François 18,559; Saint-Joseph 15,785; Ducos 15,240. *Mid-2003* (UN estimate, incl. suburbs): Fort-de-France 93,138 (Source: UN, *World Urbanization Prospects: The 2003 Revision*).

Births, Marriages and Deaths (2001): Registered births 5,774 (birth rate 14.9 per 1,000); Registered marriages 1,571; Registered deaths 2,734 (death rate 7.1 per 1,000). *2002:* Registered births 5,391; Registered marriages 1,511; Registered deaths 2,659 (preliminary).

Expectation of Life (years at birth, 1997): Males 75.2; Females 81.7.

Economically Active Population (persons aged 15 years and over, 1998): Agriculture and fishing 7,650; Industry 7,103; Construction and public works 10,405; Trade 16,196; Transport 4,383; Financial services and real estate 3,354; Business services 8,376; Public services 14,179; Education 14,991; Health and social security 10,676; Administrative services 18,742; *Total employed* 116,055 (males 62,198, females 53,857); Unemployed 48,537 (males 22,628, females 25,909); *Total labour force* 164,592 (males 84,826, females 79,766). *Mid-2003*: Agriculture, etc. 6,000; Total labour force 187,000 (Source: FAO). *December 2003:* Unemployed 37,751.

HEALTH AND WELFARE

Key Indicators

Number of Physicians (1995): 680.

Number of Hospital Beds (1995): 2,100.
For definitions, see explanatory note on p. vi.

AGRICULTURE, ETC.

Principal Crops (FAO estimates, '000 metric tons, 2003): Yams 7.5; Other roots and tubers 13.3; Sugar cane 207; Lettuce 7.8; Tomatoes 6.1; Cucumbers and gherkins 4; Other fresh vegetables 8.7; Bananas 310; Plantains 16; Pineapples 20.8. Source: FAO.

Livestock (FAO estimates, '000 head, year ending September 2003): Cattle 25; Sheep 34; Pigs 35; Goats 17. Source: FAO.

Livestock Products (FAO estimates, '000 metric tons, 2003): Beef and veal 2.3; Pig meat 1.7; Poultry meat 1.0; Cows' milk 2.2; Hen eggs 1.5. Source: FAO.

Forestry: Roundwood removals ('000 cu m, excluding bark, 1999): Sawlogs, veneer logs and logs for sleepers 2; Fuel wood 10; Total 12. *2001–3:* Production as in 1999 (FAO estimates). Source: FAO.

Fishing (estimates, metric tons, live weight, 2002): Capture 6,200 (Clupeoids 4,000; Common dolphinfish 220—FAO estimate; Atlantic bonito 530—FAO estimate; Blackfin tuna 470—FAO estimate; Caribbean spiny lobster 190; Clams, etc. 700); Aquaculture 51; *Total catch* 6,251. Source: FAO, *Yearbook of Fishery Statistics*.

MINING

Production (estimates, '000 metric tons, unless otherwise indicated, 2001): Pumice 130.0; Petroleum ('000 barrels) 4,800; Salt 200. Source: US Geological Survey.

INDUSTRY

Production ('000 metric tons, 2000, unless otherwise indicated): Pineapple juice 3.2 (1994); Canned or bottled pineapples 18.4 (1994); Raw sugar 5.3 (2002); Rum (hl) 91,629 (2002); Motor spirit (petrol) 155 (estimate); Kerosene 134 (estimate); Gas-diesel (distillate fuel) oils 162 (estimate); Residual fuel oils 278 (estimate); Liquefied petroleum gas 22 (estimate); Cement 220 (estimate, 2001); Electric energy (million kWh) 1,085 (estimate). Source: partly UN, *Industrial Commodity Statistics Yearbook*.

FINANCE

Currency and Exchange Rates: The French franc was used until the end of 2001. Euro notes and coins were introduced on 1 January 2002, and the euro became the sole legal tender from 18 February. Some of the figures in this Survey are still in terms of francs. For details of exchange rates, see French Guiana.

Budget (forecasts, million French francs, 2001): *Revenue*: Tax revenue 836.9 (Departmental taxes 332.0, Fuel tax 295.0, Transfer taxes, etc. 58.0, Motor vehicle tax 68.0, Fiscal subsidy 53.0); Other current revenue 886.6 (Refunds of social assistance 65.0, Operational allowance 315.0, Decentralization allowance 477.0); Capital revenue 499.5 (EU development funds 71.0, Capital allowances 59.0, Other receipts 101.4, Borrowing 270.0); Total 2,223.0. *Expenditure*: Current expenditure 1,482.2 (Finance service 57.1, Permanent staff 394.7, General administration 65.1, Other indirect services 69.0, Administrative services 108.4, Public health 49.9, Social assistance 503.6, Support costs of minimum wage 99.8, Economic services 114.7); Capital expenditure 740.8 (Road system 139.5, Networks 47.9, Education and culture 111.5, Other departmental programmes 101.6, Other public bodies 83.7, Other programmes 96.3, Non-programme expenditure 162.3); Total 2,223.0. Note: Figures refer only to the departmental budget.

State Budget (million francs, 1998): Revenue 4,757, Expenditure 8,309.

Regional Budget (€ million, 2002, excl. debt rescheduling): Total revenue 247 (Direct taxes 22, Indirect taxes 107, Transfers 79, Loans 38, Other 1); Total expenditure 247.

Money Supply (million French francs at 31 December 1998): Currency outside banks 924; Demand deposits at banks 6,330; Total money 7,254.

Cost of Living (Consumer Price Index; base: 2000 = 100): 102.1 in 2001; 104.2 in 2002; 106.4 in 2003. Source: ILO.

Expenditure on the Gross Domestic Product (million French francs at current prices, 1994): Government final consumption expenditure 6,962; Private final consumption expenditure 20,133; Increase in stocks 20; Gross fixed capital formation 5,102; *Total domestic expenditure* 32,217; Exports of goods and services 1,439; *Less* Imports of goods and services 9,150; *GDP in purchasers' values* 24,506. *2000* (€ million): GDP in purchasers' values 5,496.

Gross Domestic Product by Economic Activity (million French francs at current prices, 1992): Agriculture, hunting, forestry and fishing 1,106.3; Mining, quarrying and manufacturing 1,770.6; Electricity, gas and water 483.6; Construction 1,145.3; Trade, restaurants and hotels 4,022.1; Transport, storage and communications 1,427.6; Finance, insurance, real estate and business services 2,590.1; Government services 5,416.0; Other community, social and personal services 3,576.4; Other services 330.5; *Sub-total* 21,868.5; Import duties 791.0; Value-added tax 640.9; *Less* Imputed bank service charge 1,207.1; *GDP in purchasers' values* 22,093.4. Source: UN, *National Accounts Statistics*.

EXTERNAL TRADE

Principal Commodities: *Imports c.i.f.* US $ million, 1995): Food and live animals 319.6 (Meat and meat preparations 82.8, Dairy products and birds' eggs 53.6, Fish and fish preparations 38.6, Cereals and cereal preparations 45.6, Vegetables and fruit 49.1); Beverages and tobacco 52.0 (Beverages 45.0); Mineral fuels, lubricants, etc. 148.0 (Petroleum and petroleum products 146.2); Chemicals and related products 189.5 (Medicinal and pharmaceutical products 83.9); Basic manufactures 260.1 (Paper, paperboard and manufactures 45.1); Machinery and transport equipment 637.6 (Power-generating machinery and equipment 62.8, General industrial machinery, equipment and parts 83.2, Telecommunications and sound equipment 41.1, Road vehicles and parts 240.7, Ships and boats 50.3); Miscellaneous manufactured articles 288.5 (Furniture and parts 46.2, Clothing and accessories, excl. footwear 62.6); Total (incl. others) 1,969.8 (Source: UN, *International Trade Statistics Yearbook*). *Exports f.o.b.* (million French francs, 1997): Bananas 462.2; Rum 126.7; Flavoured or sweetened water 78.8; Refined petroleum products 201.9; Yachts and sports boats 74.4; Total (incl. others) 1,263.3. *1997* (million French francs): *Imports:* 9,947.0; *Exports:* 1,239.0. *1998* (million French francs): *Imports:* 10,046.8;

Exports: 1,701.4. *1999* (million French francs): *Imports:* 10,605.6; *Exports:* 1,715.1. *2000* (million French francs): *Imports:* 1,759; *Exports:* 294. *2001* (€ million): *Imports:* 1,885.5; *Exports:* 308.9. *2002* (€ million): *Imports:* 1,824.2; *Exports:* 324.8. Sources: Direction Générale des Douanes, Chambre de Commerce et d'Industrie de la Martinique.

Principal Trading Partners (€ million, 2000): *Imports c.i.f.*: France (metropolitan) 1,117; Germany 69; Italy 55; Japan 36; Netherland Antilles 41; USA 36; Venezuela 102; Total (incl. others) 1,759; *Exports f.o.b.*: Belgium-Luxembourg 8; France (metropolitan) 170; French Guiana 11; Guadeloupe 63; United Kingdom 10; Total (incl. others) 294.

TRANSPORT

Road Traffic ('000 motor vehicles in use, 1995): Passenger cars 95.0; Commercial vehicles 21.5. Source: UN, *Statistical Yearbook*.

Shipping: *Merchant Fleet* (vessels registered '000 grt at 31 December, 1992): 1 (Source: Lloyd's Register of Shipping). *International Sea-borne Traffic* (2002): Goods loaded 848,000 metric tons; Goods unloaded 1,943,000 metric tons (Source: Direction Départementale de l'Equipement).

Civil Aviation (203): Passengers carried 1,519,000; Freight carried 13,354 metric tons. Source: Chambre de Commerce et d'Industrie de la Martinique.

TOURISM

Tourist Arrivals (excl. same-day visitors and cruise-ship arrivals): 460,383 in 2001; 446,689 in 2002; 453,160 in 2003. Source: Comité martiniquais du tourisme.

Tourist Arrivals by Country (excl. same-day visitors and cruise-ship arrivals, 2001): France 384,355, Guadeloupe 27,476, French Guiana 14,171; Total (incl. others) 460,383.

Receipts from Tourism (US $ million): 384 in 1995; 382 in 1996; 400 in 1997. *2001* (€ million): Total receipts 226.6. Source: mainly World Tourism Organization, *Yearbook of Tourism Statistics*.

COMMUNICATIONS MEDIA

Radio Receivers ('000 in use): 82 in 1997.

Television Receivers ('000 in use): 62 in 1999.

Telephones ('000 main lines in use): 172.0 in 2001.

Facsimile Machines (number in use): 5,200 in 1997.

Mobile Cellular Telephones ('000 subscribers): 319.9 in 2002.

Personal Computers ('000 in use): 52 in 2001.

Internet Users ('000): 40 in 2001.

Daily Newspaper: 1 (estimate) in 1996 (estimated average circulation 30,000 copies).
Sources: UNESCO, *Statistical Yearbook*; UN, *Statistical Yearbook*; International Telecommunication Union.

EDUCATION

Pre-primary (2002/03): 85 institutions; 19,041 students (Source: Ministère de l'Education Nationale, de l'Enseignement Supérieur et de la Recherche, *Repères et références statistiques sur les enseignements, la formation et la recherche 2003*).

Primary (2002/03): 188 institutions; 1,971 teachers (1,863 state, 108 private); 31,096 students (Source: Ministère de l'Education Nationale, de l'Enseignement Supérieur et de la Recherche, *Repères et références statistiques sur les enseignements, la formation et la recherche 2003*).

Secondary (2002/03, unless otherwise indicated): 78 institutions (2001/02); 2,024 teachers (1,887 state, 137 private); 49,426 students (Source: Ministère de l'Education Nationale, de l'Enseignement Supérieur et de la Recherche, *Repères et références statistiques sur les enseignements, la formation et la recherche 2003*).

Vocational (1998/99): 15 institutions (9 state, 6 private); 7,661 students (7,101 state, 560 private) (Source: Ministère de l'Education Nationale, de l'Enseignement Supérieur et de la Recherche, *Repères et références statistiques sur les enseignements, la formation et la recherche 2003*).

Higher (2004): 12,000 students (Université Antilles-Guyane).

Directory

The Government

(April 2005)

Prefect: Yves Dassonville, Préfecture, 82 rue Victor Sévère, BP 647–648, 97262 Fort-de-France Cédex; tel. 5-96-63-18-61; fax 5-96-71-40-29.

President of the General Council: Claude Lise (PPM), Conseil Général de la Martinique, blvd Chevalier Sainte-Marthe, 97200 Fort-de-France Cédex; tel. 5-96-55-26-00; fax 5-96-73-59-32; internet www.cg972.fr.

Deputies to the French National Assembly: Louis-Joseph Manscour (PS), Alfred Almont (UMP), Philippe Edmond-Mariette (Bâtir le Pays Martinique), Alfred Marie-Jeanne (MIM).

Representatives to the French Senate: Serge Larcher (Groupe Socialiste), Claude Lise (Groupe Socialiste).

Conseil Régional

Hôtel de Région, rue Gaston Deferre, BP 601, 97200 Fort-de-France Cédex; tel. 5-96-59-63-00; fax 5-96-72-68-10; e-mail cr972.com-ext@wanadoo.fr; internet www.cr-martinique.fr.

President: Alfred Marie-Jeanne (MIM).

Elections, 21 and 28 March 2004

	Seats
Patriotes Martiniquais*	28
Convergences Martiniquaises†	9
Forces Martiniquaises de Progrès	4
Total	41

* A joint list comprising the Mouvement Indépendantiste Martiniquais, the Conseil National des Comités Populaires and the Alliance pour le Pays Martinique.
† A joint list comprising the Parti Progressiste Martiniquais and other left-wing candidates.

Political Organizations

Bâtir le Pays Martinique: Fort-de-France; f. 1998; left-wing; split from the Parti Communiste Martiniquais; Leader Pierre-Jean Samot.

Combat Ouvrier: BP 821, 97258 Fort-de-France Cédex; Trostskyist; mem. of the Communist Internationalist Union; Leader Ghislaine Joachim-Arnaud.

Conseil National des Comités Populaires: Fort-de-France; pro-independence party; contested the 2004 regional elections in alliance with the MIM (q.v.).

Fédération Socialiste de la Martinique (FSM): 52 rue du Capitaine Pierre-Rose, 97200 Fort-de-France; tel. 5-96-60-14-88; e-mail fede972@parti-socialiste.fr; internet www.parti-socialiste.fr; local br. of the **Parti Socialiste (PS)**; Sec.-Gen. Jean Crusol.

Forces Martiniquaises de Progrès: 12 rue Ernest Deproge, 97200 Fort-de-France; tel. 5-96-71-83-26; e-mail contacts@fmp-regionales.org; internet www.fmp-regionales.org; f. 1998 to replace the local branch of the Union pour la Démocratie Française; Pres. Miguel Laventure.

Mouvement des Démocrates et Écologistes pour une Martinique Souveraine (MODEMAS): Fort-de-France; Pres. Garcin Malsa.

Mouvement Indépendantiste Martiniquais (MIM): Fort-de-France; f. 1978; pro-independence party; First Sec. Alfred Marie-Jeanne.

Mouvement Populaire Franciscain: Fort-de-France; Leader Maurice Antiste; left-wing.

Osons Oser: Fort-de-France; f. 1998; right-wing; affiliated with the national Union pour un Mouvement Populaire (UMP); Pres. Pierre Petit.

Parti Progressiste Martiniquais (PPM): Fort-de-France; tel. 5-96-71-86-83; f. 1957; left-wing; Leader Madeleine de Grandmaison; Sec.-Gen. Pierre Suédile.

Parti Radical de Gauche: 27 ancienne route de Schoelcher, 97233 Schoelcher; tel. 5-96-47-54-97; e-mail didier.saint-louis@wanadoo.fr; f. 1902; Pres. Didier Saint-Louis; Gen. Sec. Roland Rosillette.

Les Verts Martinique: Lot D, 54 rue Madinina, Cluny, 97200 Fort-de-France; tel. 5-96-73-07-45; fax 5-96-71-58-21; Leader Louis Lecurieux-Lafferonnay.

Judicial System

Cour d'Appel de Fort-de-France: Palais de Justice, pl. Légitimée Défense, BP 634, 97262 Fort-de-France Cédex; tel. 5-96-70-62-62; fax 5-96-63-52-13; e-mail ca-fort-de-france@justice.fr; highest court of appeal for Martinique and French Guiana; First Pres. RENÉ SALOMON; Procurator-Gen. GÉRARD LOUBENS; Chief Clerk MARIETTE BELHUMEUR.

There are two Tribunaux de Grande Instance, at Fort-de-France and Cayenne (French Guiana), and three Tribunaux d'Instance (two in Fort-de-France and one in Cayenne).

Religion

The majority of the population belong to the Roman Catholic Church.

CHRISTIANITY

The Roman Catholic Church

Martinique comprises the single archdiocese of Fort-de-France, with an estimated 297,515 adherents (some 78% of the total population) at 31 December 2002. The Archbishop participates in the Antilles Episcopal Conference, currently based in Port of Spain, Trinidad and Tobago.

Archbishop of Fort-de-France and Saint-Pierre: Rev. MAURICE MARIE-SAINTE (designate), Archevêché, 5–7 rue du Révérend Père Pinchon, BP 586, 97207 Fort-de-France Cédex; tel. 5-96-63-70-70; fax 5-96-63-75-21; e-mail archeveche-martinique@wanadoo.fr.

Other Churches

Among the denominations active in Martinique are the Assembly of God, the Evangelical Church of the Nazarene and the Seventh-day Adventist Church.

The Press

Antilla: BP 46, Lamentin; tel. 5-96-75-48-68; fax 5-96-75-58-46; e-mail antilla@wanadoo.fr; weekly; Dir ALFRED FORTUNE.

Aujourd'hui Dimanche: Presbytère de Bellevue, Fort-de-France; tel. 5-96-71-48-97; weekly; Dir Père GAUTHIER; circ. 12,000.

Carib Hebdo: 97200 Fort-de-France; f. 1989; Dir GISÈLE DE LA FARGUE.

Combat Ouvrier: BP 213, 97156 Pointe-à-Pitre Cédex; e-mail combatouvrier@fr.fm; internet www.chez.com/combatouvrier; weekly; communist; Dir M. G. BEAUJOUR.

France-Antilles: pl. Stalingrad, 97200 Fort-de-France; tel. 5-96-59-08-83; fax 5-96-60-29-96; f. 1964; daily; Dir HENRI MERLE; circ. 30,000 (Martinique edition).

Justice: rue Andrè Aliker, 97200 Fort-de-France; tel. 5-96-71-86-83; fax 5-96-63-13-20; e-mail ed.justice@wanadoo.fr; weekly; organ of the PCM; Dir FERNAND PAPAYA; circ. 8,000.

Le Naif: Fort-de-France; weekly; Dir R. LAOUCHEZ.

Le Progressiste: Fort-de-France; weekly; organ of the PPM; Dir PAUL GABOURG; circ. 13,000.

TV Magazine: Immeuble Gouya, Z. I. Californie, BP 1064, 97200 Fort-de-France; tel. 5-96-42-51-28; fax 5-96-42-98-94; e-mail tv.mag@media-antilles.fr; f. 1989; weekly.

Broadcasting and Communications

BROADCASTING

Réseau France Outre-mer (RFO): La Clairière, BP 662, 97263 Fort-de-France; tel. 5-96-59-52-00; fax 5-96-63-29-88; internet www.rfo.fr; fmrly Société Nationale de Radio-Télévision Française d'Outre-mer, renamed as above 1998; broadcasts 24 hours of radio programmes daily and 37 hours of television programmes weekly; Pres. ANDRÉ-MICHEL BESSE; Regional Dir MARIJOSÉ ALIE-MONTHIEUX; Editor-in-Chief GÉRARD LE MOAL.

Radio

There are some 40 licensed private FM radio stations.

Radio Caraïbe International (RCI): 2 blvd de la Marne, 97200 Fort-de-France; tel. 5-96-63-98-70; fax 5-96-63-26-59; internet www.fwinet.com/rci.htm; commercial station broadcasting 24 hours daily; Dir YANN DUVAL.

Television

ATV Antilles Télévision: 28 rue Arawaks, 97200 Fort de France; tel. 5-96-75-44-44; fax 5-96-75-55-65; commercial station; Dir DANIEL ROBIN.

Canal Antilles: Centre Commerciale la Galléria, 97232 Le Lamentin; tel. 5-96-50-57-87; private commercial station.

Finance

(cap. = capital; res = reserves; dep. = deposits; m. = million; brs = branches; amounts in French francs)

BANKING

Central Bank

Institut d'Emission des Départements d'Outre-mer (IEDOM): 1 blvd du Général de Gaulle, BP 512, 97206 Fort-de-France Cédex; tel. 5-96-59-44-00; fax 5-96-59-44-04; e-mail agence@iedom-martinique.fr; internet www.iedom.com; Dir C. APANON.

Major Commercial Banks

Banque des Antilles Françaises: 28–34 rue Lamartine, BP 582, 97207 Fort-de-France Cédex; tel. 5-96-60-72-72; fax 5-96-60-72-54; internet www.bdaf.gp; f. 1853; Dir ALBERT CLERMONT.

BNP Paribas Martinique: 72 ave des Caraïbes, BP 588, 97200 Fort-de-France; tel. 5-96-59-46-00; fax 5-96-63-71-42; e-mail bnpm@bnp.mq; internet www.bnpparibas.com; f. 1941; subsidiary of BNP Paribas; 12 brs.

BRED Banque Populaire: 5 pl. Monseigneur Romero, 97200 Fort-de-France; tel. 5-96-63-77-63; internet www.bred.fr; Chair. STEVE GENTILI.

Crédit Agricole: rue Case Nègre–pl. d'Armes, 97232 Le Lamentin Cédex 2; tel. 5-96-66-59-39; fax 5-96-66-59-67; internet www.ca-martinique.fr; f. 1950; Pres. GUY RANLIN; Dir-Gen. PASCAL DURIEUX.

Crédit Martiniquais: 17 rue de la Liberté, 97200 Fort-de-France; tel. 5-96-59-93-00; fax 5-96-60-29-30; f. 1922; associated since 1987 with Chase Manhattan Bank (USA) and, since 1990, with Mutuelles du Mans Vie (France); cap. 185.4m. (1998); Administrator ALAIN DENNHARDT; 10 brs.

Société Générale de Banque aux Antilles: 19–21 rue de la Liberté, BP 408, 97200 Fort-de-France; tel. 5-96-72-82-82; internet www.sgba.fr; f. 1979; cap. 15m.; Dir ODETTE MAZARIN; 4 brs.

Development Bank

Société de crédit pour le développement de Martinique (SODEMA): 12 blvd du Général de Gaulle, BP 575, 97242 Fort-de-France Cédex; tel. 5-96-72-87-72; fax 5-96-72-87-70; e-mail sodema@compuserve.com; f. 1970; part of the Agence Française de Développement (AFD—q.v.); cap. 25m.; medium- and long-term finance; Dir-Gen. JACKIE BATHANY.

INSURANCE

Caraïbe Assurances: 11 rue Victor Hugo, BP 210, 97202 Fort-de-France; tel. 5-96-63-92-29; fax 5-96-63-19-79.

Groupement Français d'Assurances Caraïbes (GFA Caraïbes): 46–48 rue Ernest Desproges, 97205 Fort-de-France; tel. 5-96-59-04-04; fax 5-96-73-19-72.

La Nationale (GAN): 30 blvd Général de Gaulle, BP 185, Fort-de-France; tel. 5-96-71-30-07; Reps MARCEL BOULLANGER, ROGER BOULLANGER.

Le Secours: 74 ave Duparquet, 97200 Fort-de-France; tel. 5-96-70-03-79; Dir Y. ANGANI.

Trade and Industry

GOVERNMENT AGENCIES

Conseil Economique et Social: Hôtel de la Région, ave Gaston Deferre, Plateau Roy Cluny, BP 601, 97200 Fort-de-France; tel. 5-96-59-63-00; fax 5-96-59-64-43; Pres. RENÉ FABIEN.

Direction Régionale du Commerce Extérieur Antilles-Guyane (DRCE): c/o Préfecture SGAR, BP 647, 97262 Fort-de-France Cédex; tel. 5-96-39-49-90; fax 5-96-60-08-14; e-mail drceantilles@missioneco.org; internet www.missioneco.org/antilles-guyane; Regional Man. MARTIN LAMMERT.

Direction Régionale de l'Industrie, de la Recherche et de l'Environnement (DRIRE): see chapter on French Guiana.

DEVELOPMENT ORGANIZATIONS

Agence Française de Développement (AFD): Immeuble AFD/IEDOM, 12 blvd du Général de Gaulle, BP 804, 97244 Fort-de-France Cédex; tel. 5-96-59-44-73; fax 5-96-59-44-88; e-mail afdfdf@wanadoo.fr; internet www.afd.fr; fmrly Caisse Française de Développoppement; Man. JEAN-YVES CLAVEL.

Secrétariat Général pour les Affaires Régionales (SGAR)— Bureau de la Coopération Régionale: Préfecture, 97262 Fort-de-France; e-mail jean-charles.barrus@martinique.pref.gouv.fr; tel. 5-96-39-49-78; fax 5-96-39-49-59; successor to the Direction de l'Action Economique Régionale (DAER); research, documentation and technical and administrative advice on investment in industry and commerce; Chief JEAN-CHARLES BARRUS.

CHAMBERS OF COMMERCE

Chambre d'Agriculture: pl. d'Armes, BP 312, 97286 Le Lamentin; tel. 5-96-51-75-75; fax 5-96-51-93-42; e-mail chambagri@ais.mq; internet paris.apca.chambagri.fr; Pres. GUY OVIDE-ETIENNE; Dir NICAIRE MONROSE.

Chambre de Commerce et d'Industrie de la Martinique: 50 rue Ernest Desproge, BP 478, 97241 Fort-de-France Cédex; tel. 5-96-55-28-00; fax 5-96-60-66-68; e-mail ccim.doi@martinique.cci.fr; internet www.martinique.cci.fr; f. 1907; Pres. CLAUDE POMPIÈRE; Sec. JOSEPH DE JAHAM.

Chambre des Métiers de la Martinique: 2 rue du Temple, Morne Tartenson, BP 1194, 97200 Fort-de-France; tel. 5-96-71-32-22; fax 5-96-70-47-30; f. 1970; Pres. CHRISTIAN CAYOL; 8,000 mems.

EMPLOYERS' ORGANIZATIONS

Banalliance: Centre d'Affaires le Baobab, rue Léon Gontran Damas, 97232 Le Lamentin; tel. 5-96-57-42-42; fax 5-96-57-35-18; f. 1996; Pres. DANIEL DISIER; 220 mems.

Banamart: Quartier Bois Rouge, 97224 Ducos; tel. 5-96-42-43-44; fax 5-96-51-47-70; f. 2005; formed by merger of SICABAM and GIPAM; represents banana producers.

Compagnie Bananière de la Martinique (COBAMAR): Immeuble les Palétuviers Z. I. Lézarde, 97232 Le Lamentin; tel. 5-96-30-00-50; fax 5-96-57-14-03; internet www.cobamar.fr; f. 1993; Pres. MARCEL FABRE; 200 mems.

Ordre des Médecins de la Martinique: 80 rue de la République, 97200 Fort-de-France; tel. 5-96-63-27-01; fax 5-96-60-58-00; Pres. Dr RENÉ LEGENDRI.

Ordre des Pharmaciens de la Martinique: BP 587, 97207 Fort-de-France Cédex; tel. 5-96-52-23-67; fax 5-96-52-20-92; e-mail ordrepharmacienmartinik@wanadoo.fr; Pres. JEAN BIGNON.

UTILITIES

EDF Martinique: Pointe des Carrières, BP 573, 97242 Fort-de-France Cédex 01; tel. 5-96-59-20-00; fax 5-96-60-29-76; e-mail edf-services-martinique@edfgdf.fr; internet www.edf.fr/martinique; f. 1975; electricity supplier; electricity supplier; successor to Société de Production et de Distribution d'Electricité de la Martinique (SPDEM); Dir GÉRARD BELLANGER; 160,000 customers.

Société Martiniquaise des Eaux (SME): pl. d'Armes, BP 213, 97284 Le Lamentin Cédex 02; tel. 5-96-51-80-51; fax 5-96-51-80-55; internet www.martiniquaisedeseaux.com.

TRADE UNIONS

Centrale Démocratique Martiniquaise du Travail (CDMT): Maison des Syndicats, Jardin Desclieux, 97200 Fort-de-France; tel. 5-96-70-19-86; fax 5-96-71-32-25; Sec.-Gen. NICOLE ELANA.

Confédération Générale du Travail de la Martinique (CGTM): Maison des Syndicats, Jardin Desclieux, 97200 Fort-de-France; tel. 5-96-60-45-21; f. 1961; affiliated to World Federation of Trade Unions; Sec.-Gen. GHISLAINE JOACHIM-ARNAUD.

Fédération Départementale des Syndicats d'Exploitants Agricoles de la Martinique (FDSEA): Immeuble Chambre d'Agriculture, pl. d'Armes, 97232 Le Lamentin; tel. 5-96-51-61-46; fax 5-96-57-05-43; e-mail fdsea.martinique@wanadoo.fr; affiliated to the Fédération Nationale des Syndicats d'Exploitants Agricoles; Pres. LOUIS-DANIEL BERTOME.

Union Départementale CFTC Martinique (UD-CFTC): Maison des Syndicats, Jardin Desclieux, 97200 Fort-de-France; tel. 5-96-60-95-10; fax 5-96-60-39-10.

Union Départementale Force Ouvrière Martinique (UD-FO): rue Bouillé, BP 1114, 97248 Fort-de-France Cédex; tel. 5-96-70-07-04; fax 5-96-70-18-20; e-mail udfomartinique@force-ouvriere.fr; affiliated to International Confederation of Free Trade Unions; Sec.-Gen. MARIE-ALICE MEDEUF-ANDRIEUX.

Union Régionale Martinique: Maison de Syndicats, Jardin Desclieux, Salles 5–7, 97200 Fort-de-France; tel. 5-96-70-16-80.

UNSA Education Martinique (SE-UNSA): Maison des Syndicats, Salles 6–7, Jardin Desclieux, 97200 Fort-de-France; tel. 5-96-72-64-74; fax 5-96-70-16-80; e-mail unsa972@wanadoo.fr ; Sec.-Gen MICHEL CRISPIN.

Transport

RAILWAYS

There are no railways in Martinique.

ROADS

There were 2,077 km of roads in 1998, of which 261 km were motorways and first-class roads.

SHIPPING

Direction des Concessions Services Portuaires: quai de l'Hydro Base, BP 782, 97244 Fort-de-France Cédex; tel. 5-96-59-00-00; fax 5-96-71-35-73; e-mail port@martinique.cci.fr; port services management; Dir FRANTZ THODIARD; Operations Man. VICTOR EUSTACHE.

Direction Départementale des Affaires Maritimes: blvd Chevalier de Sainte-Marthe, BP 620, 97261 Fort-de-France Cédex; tel. 5-96-71-90-05; fax 5-96-63-67-30; Dir FRANÇOIS NIHOUL.

Alcoa Steamship Co, Alpine Line, Agdwa Line, Delta Line, Raymond Witcomb Co, Moore MacCormack, Eastern Steamship Co: c/o Etablissements Ren, Cottrell, Fort-de-France.

American President Lines: c/o Compagnie d'Agence Multiples Antillaise (CAMA), 44 rue Garnier Pages, 97205 Fort-de-France Cédex; tel. 5-96-71-31-00; fax 5-96-63-54-40.

CMA-CGM CGM Antilles-Guyane: 8 ave Maurice Bishop, BP 574, 97242 Fort-de-France Cédex; tel. 5-96-55-32-05; fax 5-96-60-47-84; e-mail fdf.jdurand@cma-cgm.com; internet www.cma-cgm.com; also represents other passenger and freight lines; Dir JEAN-LUC DURAND.

Compagnie de Navigation Mixte: Immeuble Rocade, La Dillon, BP 1023, 97209 Fort-de-France; Rep. R. M. MICHAUX.

CIVIL AVIATION

Martinique's international airport is at Le Lamentin, 6 km from Fort-de-France.

Direction des Services Aéroportuaires: BP 279, 97285 Le Lamentin; tel. 5-96-42-16-00; fax 5-96-42-18-77.

Air Caraïbe: see chapter on Guadeloupe (Civil Aviation).

Tourism

Martinique's tourist attractions are its beaches and coastal scenery, its mountainous interior, and the historic towns of Fort-de-France and Saint-Pierre. In 2002 there were 122 hotels, with some 5,115 rooms. Tourism receipts in 2001 totalled €226.6m. In 2003 some 453,160 tourists visited the island.

Comité Martiniquais du Tourisme: Immeuble Beaupré, Pointe de Jaham, 97233 Schoelcher; tel. 5-96-61-61-77; fax 5-96-61-22-72; internet www.touristmartinique.com; Sec.-Gen. ROBERT CONRAD.

Délégation Régionale au Tourisme: 41 rue Gabriel Périé 97200 Fort-de-France; tel. 5-96-63-18-61; Dir GILBERT LECURIEUK.

Fédération Martiniquaise des Offices de Tourisme et Syndicats d'Initiative (FMOTSI): Maison du Tourisme Vert, 9 blvd du Général de Gaulle, BP 491, 97207 Fort-de-France Cédex; tel. 5-96-63-18-54; fax 5-96-70-17-61; f. 1984; Pres. VICTOR GRANDIN.

Office Départemental du Tourisme de la Martinique: 2 rue Ernest Desproges, BP 520, 97206 Fort-de-France; tel. 5-96-63-79-60; fax 5-96-73-66-93.

RÉUNION

Introductory Survey

Location, Climate, Language, Religion, Capital

Réunion is an island in the Indian Ocean, lying about 800 km (500 miles) east of Madagascar. The climate varies greatly according to altitude: at sea-level it is tropical, with average temperatures between 20°C (68°F) and 28°C (82°F), but in the uplands it is much cooler, with average temperatures between 8°C (46°F) and 19°C (66°F). Rainfall is abundant, averaging 4,714 mm annually in the uplands, and 686 mm at sea-level. The population is of mixed origin, including people of European, African, Indian and Chinese descent. The official language is French. A large majority of the population are Christians belonging to the Roman Catholic Church. The capital is Saint-Denis.

Recent History

Réunion was first occupied by France in 1642, and was ruled as a colony until 1946, when it received full departmental status. In 1974 it became an Overseas Department with the status of a region.

In 1978 the Organization of African Unity (OAU, now the African Union, see p. 144) adopted a report recommending measures to hasten the independence of the island, and condemned its occupation by a 'colonial power'. However, this view seemed to have little popular support in Réunion. Although the left-wing political parties on the island advocated increased autonomy (amounting to virtual self-government), few people were in favour of complete independence.

In 1982 the French Government proposed a decentralization scheme, envisaging the dissolution of the General and Regional Councils in the Overseas Departments and the creation in each department of a single assembly, to be elected on the basis of proportional representation. As a result of considerable opposition in Réunion and the other Overseas Departments, the Government was eventually forced to abandon the project. Revised legislation on decentralization in the Overseas Departments, however, was approved by the French National Assembly (Assemblée nationale) in December 1982. Elections to the Regional Council (Conseil régional) took place in Réunion in February 1983, when left-wing candidates won 50.8% of the votes cast.

In elections to the Assemblée nationale in March 1986, Réunion's representation was increased from three to five deputies. The Parti Communiste Réunionnais (PCR) won two seats, while the Union pour la Démocratie Française (UDF), the Rassemblement pour la République (RPR) and a newly formed right-wing party, France-Réunion-Avenir (FRA), each secured one seat. In concurrent elections to the Conseil régional, an alliance between the RPR and the UDF obtained 18 of the 45 seats, while the PCR secured 13 and the FRA eight. The leader of the FRA, Pierre Lagourgue, was elected as President of the Conseil régional.

In the second round of the French presidential election in May 1988, François Mitterrand, the incumbent President and a candidate of the Parti Socialiste (PS), received 60.3% of the votes cast in Réunion, while Jacques Chirac, the RPR Prime Minister, obtained 39.7%. At elections to the Assemblée nationale in June, the PCR won two of the seats allocated to Réunion, while the UDF and the RPR (which contested the elections jointly as the Union du Rassemblement du Centre—URC), and the FRA each won one seat. (The RPR and FRA deputies later became independents, although they maintained strong links with the island's right-wing groups.) Relations between the PCR and the PS subsequently deteriorated, following mutual recriminations concerning their failure to co-operate in the general election.

In the elections for the newly enlarged 44-member General Council (Conseil général) in September and October 1988, the PCR and the PS won nine and four seats respectively, while left-wing independent candidates obtained two seats. The UDF secured six seats and right-wing independent candidates 19, but the RPR, which had previously held 11 seats, won only four. Later in October, Eric Boyer, a right-wing independent candidate, was elected as President of the Conseil général. The results of the municipal elections in March 1989 represented a slight decline in support for the left-wing parties; for the first time since the 1940s, however, a PS candidate, Gilbert Annette, became mayor of Saint-Denis.

In September 1990, following the restructuring of the RPR under the new local leadership of Alain Defaud, several right-wing and centrist movements, including the UDF and the RPR, established an informal alliance, known as the Union pour la France (UPF), to contest the regional elections in 1992. During a visit to Réunion in November 1990 the French Minister for Overseas Departments and Territories, Louis Le Pensec, announced a series of proposed economic and social measures, in accordance with the pledges made by Mitterrand in 1988 regarding the promotion of economic development and social equality between the Overseas Departments and metropolitan France. However, the proposals were criticized as insufficient by right-wing groups and by the PCR. Following a meeting in Paris between Le Pensec and a delegation from Réunion, the adoption of a programme of social and economic measures was announced in April 1991.

In March 1990 violent protests took place in support of an unauthorized television service, Télé Free-DOM, following a decision by the French national broadcasting commission, the Conseil supérieur de l'audiovisuel (CSA), to award a broadcasting permit to a rival company. In February 1991 the seizure by the CSA of Télé Free-DOM's broadcasting transmitters prompted renewed demonstrations in Saint-Denis. Some 11 people were killed in ensuing riots, and the French Government dispatched police reinforcements to restore order. Le Pensec, who subsequently visited Réunion, ascribed the violence to widespread discontent with the island's social and economic conditions. In March a commission of enquiry attributed the riots in February to the inflammatory nature of television programmes that had been broadcast by Télé Free-DOM in the weeks preceding the disturbances, and cited the station's director, Dr Camille Sudre, as responsible. However, the commission refuted allegations by right-wing and centrist politicians that the PCR had orchestrated the violence.

In March 1992 Annette expelled Sudre, who was one of the deputy mayors of Saint-Denis, from the majority coalition in the municipal council, after Sudre presented a list of independent candidates to contest the forthcoming regional elections. In the elections to the Conseil régional, which took place on 22 March, Sudre's list of candidates (known as Free-DOM) secured 17 seats, while the UPF obtained 14 seats, the PCR nine seats and the PS five seats. In concurrent elections to the Conseil général (newly enlarged to 47 seats), right-wing independent candidates won 20 seats, although the number of PCR deputies increased to 12, and the number of PS deputies to six; Boyer retained the presidency of the Conseil. Following the elections, the Free-DOM list of candidates formed an alliance with the PCR, thereby obtaining a narrow majority of 26 of the 45 seats in the Conseil régional. Under the terms of the agreement, Sudre was to assume the presidency of the Conseil régional. Sudre was accordingly elected as President of the Conseil régional by a majority of 27 votes, with the support of members of the PCR. The PS subsequently appealed against the results of the regional elections on the grounds of media bias; Sudre's privately owned radio station, Radio Free-DOM, had campaigned on his behalf prior to the elections. Following his election to the presidency of the Conseil régional, Sudre announced that Télé Free-DOM was shortly to resume broadcasting. The CSA indicated, however, that it would continue to regard transmissions by Télé Free-DOM as illegal, and liable to judicial proceedings. Jean-Paul Virapoullé, a deputy to the Assemblée nationale, subsequently proposed the adoption of legislation that would legalize Télé Free-DOM and would provide for the establishment of an independent media sector on Réunion. In April Télé Free-DOM's transmitters were returned, and at the end of May a full broadcasting service was resumed (without the permission of the CSA).

In June 1992 a delegation from the Conseil régional met President Mitterrand to submit proposals for economic reforms, in accordance with the aim of establishing parity between Réunion and metropolitan France. In early July, however, the French Government announced increases in social security benefits that were substantially less than had been expected, resulting in widespread discontent on the island. In September the PCR demanded that the electorate refuse to participate in the forthcoming French referendum on ratification of the Treaty on European Union (see p. 217), in protest at the alleged failure of the French Government to recognize the requirements of the Overseas Departments. At the referendum, which took place later that month, the ratification of the Treaty was approved by the voters of Réunion, although only 26.3% of the registered electorate voted.

At the end of September 1992 Boyer and the former President of the Conseil régional, Pierre Lagourgue, were elected as representatives to the French Senate (Sénat). (The RPR candidate, Paul Moreau, retained his seat.) In October the investigation of allegations that members of the Conseil général had misappropriated funds and obtained contracts by fraudulent means commenced. In December increasing discontent with deteriorating economic conditions on Réunion prompted violent rioting in Saint-Denis and in the town of Le Port.

In March 1993 Sudre announced that he was to contest Virapoullé's seat on behalf of the Free-DOM–PCR alliance in the forthcoming elections to the Assemblée nationale. However, at the elections, which took place later that month, Sudre was defeated by Virapoullé in the second round of voting, while another incumbent right-wing deputy, André Thien Ah Koon (who contested the elections on behalf of the UPF), also retained his seat. The PCR, the PS and the RPR each secured one of the remaining seats.

In May 1993 the French Conseil d'état declared the results of the regional elections in March 1992 to be invalid, and prohibited Sudre from engaging in political activity for a year, on the grounds that programmes broadcast by Radio Free-DOM prior to the elections constituted political propaganda. Sudre subsequently nominated his wife, Margie, to assume his candidacy in further elections to the Conseil régional. In the elections, which took place in June 1993, the Free-DOM list of candidates, headed by Margie Sudre, secured 12 seats, while the UDF obtained 10 seats, the RPR eight seats, the PCR nine seats and the PS six seats. Margie Sudre was subsequently elected as President of the Conseil régional, with the support of the nine PCR deputies and three dissident members of the PS, obtaining a total of 24 votes.

In April 1993 a number of prominent business executives were arrested in connection with the acquisition of contracts by fraudulent means; several senior politicians, including Boyer and Pierre Vergès (the mayor of Le Port and son of Paul Vergès), were also implicated in malpractice, following the investigation into their activities. Both Boyer and Pierre Vergès subsequently fled in order to evade arrest. In August Boyer, who had surrendered to the security forces, was formally charged with corruption and placed in detention. (Joseph Sinimalé, a member of the RPR, temporarily assumed the office of President of the Conseil général.)

In January 1994 Jules Raux, a deputy mayor of Saint-Denis who was also the local treasurer of the PS, was arrested on charges of corruption: it was alleged that both local and French enterprises had obtained contracts from the Saint-Denis municipality in exchange for a share in profits (which was apparently used, in part, to finance PS activities on the island). In February two municipal councillors from Saint-Denis were arrested on suspicion of involvement in the affair. In the same month a French citizen was arrested on Réunion on charges of having transferred the funds that had been illegally obtained by the Saint-Denis municipality to enterprises in Djibouti. In March Annette, who was implicated in the affair, resigned as mayor of Saint-Denis, and was subsequently charged with corruption. Later that month Boyer and Moussa were convicted and sentenced to terms of imprisonment.

At elections to the Conseil général, which took place in March 1994, the PCR retained 12 seats, while the number of PS deputies increased to 12. The number of seats held by the RPR and UDF declined to five and 11 respectively. The RPR and UDF subsequently attempted to negotiate an alliance with the PCR; however, the PCR and PS established a coalition (despite the long-standing differences between the two parties), thereby securing the support of 24 of the 47 seats in the Conseil général. In April a member of the PS, Christophe Payet, was elected President of the Conseil général (obtaining 26 votes), defeating Sinimalé; the right-wing parties (which had held the presidency of the Conseil général for more than 40 years) boycotted the poll. The PS and PCR signed an agreement whereby the two parties were to control the administration of the Conseil général jointly,

and indicated that centrist deputies might be allowed to join the alliance. In July, following a judicial appeal, Boyer's custodial sentence was reduced to a term of one year.

In the second round of the French presidential election, which took place in May 1995, the socialist candidate, Lionel Jospin, secured 56% of votes cast on Réunion, while Jacques Chirac, the official candidate of the RPR, won 44% of the votes (although Chirac obtained the highest number of votes overall); the PCR and Free-DOM had urged their supporters not to vote for Balladur in the first round, owing to his opposition to the principle of social equality between the Overseas Departments and metropolitan France. Following Chirac's election to the French presidency, Margie Sudre was nominated Minister of State with responsibility for Francophone Affairs, prompting concern among right-wing organizations on Réunion.

In August 1995 Pierre Vergès was sentenced *in absentia* to a custodial term of 18 months; an appeal was rejected in July 1996. In September the mayor of Salazie, who was a member of the RPR, was also charged with corruption. In November 1995 Boyer lost an appeal against his 1994 conviction and was expelled from the Sénat.

With effect from the beginning of 1996 the social security systems of the Overseas Departments were aligned with those of metropolitan France. In February Alain Juppé, the French Prime Minister, invited representatives from the Overseas Departments to Paris to participate in discussions on social equality and development. The main issue uniting the political representatives from Réunion was the need to align the salaries of civil servants on the island with those in metropolitan France. Several trade unionists declared themselves willing to enter into negotiations, on condition that only new recruits would be affected. Paul Vergès, joint candidate of the PCR and the PS, was elected to the Sénat in April, securing 51.9% of the votes cast. Fred K/Bidy won 40.0% of the votes, failing to retain Eric Boyer's seat for the RPR. In the by-election to replace Paul Vergès, which took place in September, Claude Hoarau, the PCR candidate, was elected as a deputy to the Assemblée nationale with 56.0% of the votes cast, while Margie Sudre obtained 44.0%. A new majority alliance between Free-DOM, the RPR and the UDF was subsequently formed in the Conseil régional, with the re-election of its 19-member permanent commission in October.

In October 1996 the trial of a number of politicians and business executives, who had been arrested in 1993–94 on charges of corruption, took place, after three years of investigations. Gilbert Annette and Jules Raux were convicted and, in December 1996, received custodial sentences, although Annette's sentence was reduced on appeal in December 1997. Jacques de Châteauvieux, the Chairman of Groupe Sucreries de Bourbon, was found guilty of bribery, and was also imprisoned. Two senior executives from the French enterprise, Compagnie Générale des Eaux, were given suspended sentences, although the public prosecutor subsequently appealed for part of the sentences to be made custodial. Some 20 others were also found guilty of corruption. Pierre Vergès surrendered to the authorities in December and appeared before a magistrate in Saint-Pierre, where he was subsequently detained; in February 1997 he was released by the Court of Appeal. Also in December 1996 voting on the regional budget for 1997 was postponed three times, as a result of the abstention of eight Free-DOM councillors, led by the first Vice-President of the Conseil régional, Jasmin Moutoussamy, who demanded the dismissal of Gilbert Payet, a Sub-Prefect and special adviser to Sudre, and greater delegation of power to the Vice-Presidents. They also objected to Sudre's alliance with the RPR-UDF majority. In late March 1997 the regional budget was eventually adopted, although Sudre and many right-wing councillors abstained from voting because of the opposition's insistence on a number of amendments, most significantly to the composition of the Conseil's permanent commission, in which it had no representation. Following the vote, Sudre suspended the session to allow for discussion between the political organizations.

Meanwhile, civil servants and students protested violently against a French government proposal, made earlier in March 1997, to undertake reform of the civil service, including a reduction in the incomes of new recruits to bring them closer to those in metropolitan France. Senator Pierre Lagourgue was designated to mediate between the French Government and the civil servants' trade unions, but strike action and demonstrations continued into April, leading to violent clashes with the security forces.

Four left-wing candidates were successful in elections to the Assemblée nationale held in May and June 1997. Claude Hoarau (PCR) retained his seat and was joined by Huguette Bello and Elie Hoarau, also both from the PCR, and Michel Tamaya (PS), while Thien Ah Koon, representing the RPR-UDF coalition, was re-elected.

In February 1998 the PCR (led by Paul Vergès), the PS and several right-wing mayors presented a joint list of candidates, known as the Rassemblement, to contest forthcoming elections. In the elections to the Conseil régional, which took place on 15 March, the Rassemblement secured 19 seats, while the UDF obtained nine seats and the RPR eight, with various left-wing candidates representing Free-DOM winning five. Vergès was elected President of the Conseil régional on 23 March, with the support of the deputies belonging to the Rassemblement and Free-DOM groups. In concurrent elections to an expanded 49-member Conseil général, right-wing candidates (including those on the Rassemblement's list) secured 27 seats, while left-wing candidates obtained 22 seats, with the PCR and the PS each winning 10 seats. At the end of the month Jean-Luc Poudroux, of the UDF, was elected President of the Conseil général, owing to the support of two left-wing deputies.

In October 1998 Réunion's three PCR deputies to the Assemblée nationale proposed legislation providing for the division of the island into two departments, with Saint-Pierre to join Saint-Denis as a departmental town. In December 1999, whilst attending the heads of state summit of the Indian Ocean Commission (IOC, see p. 374) on the island, President Chirac announced that he supported the creation of a second department on Réunion, as part of a number of proposed changes to the institutional future and socio-economic development of the French Overseas Departments. In March 2000 the French Secretary of State for Overseas Departments, Jean-Jack Queyranne, declared that Réunion was to be divided into two departments, Réunion South and Réunion North, as of 1 January 2001. However, both the proposed date and the geographical division of the island were rejected by the PS, although it stated that it remained in favour of the creation of a second department. The leader of the UDF, Virapoullé, expressed his opposition to the proposals. Demonstrations both for and against the division of the island took place in March 2000. It was subsequently agreed that the proposals would not be effected until 1 January 2002, and changes were made to the initial plans regarding the division of the island. However, on 15 June 2000 the creation of a second department was rejected by the Sénat by 203 votes to 111. In November the Assemblée nationale definitively rejected the creation of a second department, but approved the changes to the institutional future of the Overseas Departments, which were finally ratified by the Constitutional Council in December. Also in that month Paul Vergès was arrested on charges of forgery and fraud in connection with his election to the Sénat in 1996.

At municipal elections, held in March 2001, the left-wing parties experienced significant losses. Notably, the PS mayor of Saint-Denis, Michel Tamaya, was defeated by the RPR candidate, René-Paul Victoria. The losses were widely interpreted as a general rejection of Jospin's proposals to create a second department on the island. At elections to the Conseil général, held concurrently, the right-wing parties also made substantial gains, obtaining 38 of the 49 seats; the UDF retained its majority, and Poudroux was re-elected as President. In July Elie Hoarau was obliged to resign from the Assemblée nationale, following his conviction on charges of electoral fraud, as a result of which he received a one-year prison sentence and was banned from holding public office for a period of three years.

In January 2002 Réunion's infrastructure was severely damaged by Cyclone Dina, which also destroyed a large proportion of the crops on the island. The French Government later pledged some €32.5m. in aid to assist in the island's rehabilitation. In the first round of the presidential election, which was held on 21 April, Jospin secured 39.0% of the valid votes cast in the department (although he was eliminated nationally), followed by Chirac, who received 37.1%. In the second round, on 5 May, Chirac overwhelmingly defeated the candidate of the extreme right-wing Front National, Jean-Marie Le Pen, with 91.9% of the vote. At elections to the Assemblée nationale in June, Thien Ah Koon, allied to the new Union pour la Majorité Présidentielle (UMP, which had recently been formed by the merger of the RPR, the Démocratie Libérale and elements of the UDF), and

Bello were re-elected. Tamaya lost his seat to Victoria of the UMP, Claude Hourau lost to Bertho Audifax of the UMP, while Elie Hourau, who was declared ineligible to stand for re-election, was replaced by Christophe Payet of the PS. In November the UMP was renamed the Union pour un Mouvement Populaire.

In elections to the Conseil régional, which took place on 21 and 28 March 2004, the Alliance, a joint list of candidates led by the PCR, secured 27 seats. The UMP won 11 seats, and an alliance of the PS and Les Verts Réunion obtained seven seats. Following concurrent elections to the Conseil général, to renew 25 of the 49 seats, right-wing candidates held 30 seats, while left-wing candidates held 19. On 1 April Nassimah Dindar of the UMP was elected to succeed Poudroux as President of the Conseil général. Paul Vergès was re-elected as President of the Conseil régional on the following day.

In January 1986 France was admitted to the IOC, owing to its sovereignty over Réunion. Réunion was given the right to host ministerial meetings of the IOC, but would not be allowed to occupy the presidency, owing to its status as a non-sovereign state.

Government

France is represented in Réunion by an appointed Prefect. There are two councils with local powers: the 49-member Conseil général and the 45-member Conseil régional. Both are elected for up to six years by direct universal suffrage. Réunion sends five directly elected deputies to the Assemblée nationale in Paris and three indirectly elected representatives to the Sénat. The Department is also represented at the European Parliament.

Defence

Réunion is the headquarters of French military forces in the Indian Ocean. At 1 August 2004 there were 3,600 French troops stationed on Réunion and Mayotte, as well as a gendarmerie.

Economic Affairs

Réunion's gross national income (GNI) in 1995 was estimated at 29,200m. French francs, equivalent to about 44,300 francs per head. During 1990–97, according to World Bank estimates, Réunion's population increased at an average annual rate of 1.7%. In 2001, according to the UN, Réunion's gross domestic product (GDP), measured at current prices, was US $6,744m., equivalent to $9,188 per head. GDP increased, in real terms, at an average annual rate of 2.9% in 1990–2001; growth in 2001 was 2.4%.

Agriculture (including hunting, forestry and fishing) contributed 2.9% of GDP in 1999, and engaged 2.5% of the economically active population in mid-2003. The principal cash crops are sugar cane (sugar accounted for 40.3% of export earnings in 2002), maize, tobacco, vanilla, and geraniums and vetiver root, which are cultivated for the production of essential oils. Fishing and livestock production are also important to the economy. According to the UN, agricultural GDP increased at an average annual rate of 3.9% during 1990–2000; growth in 2001 was 3.1%.

Industry (including mining, manufacturing, construction and power) contributed 14.3% of GDP in 1999, and employed 14.1% of the working population in 1999. The principal branch of manufacturing is food-processing, particularly the production of sugar and rum. Other significant sectors include the fabrication of construction materials, mechanics, printing, metalwork, textiles and garments, and electronics. According to the UN, industrial GDP (excluding construction) increased at an average annual rate of 4.3% during 1990–99; growth in 2001 was 3.7%.

There are no mineral resources on the island. Energy is derived principally from thermal and hydroelectric power. Imports of products of cokeries, petroleum refineries and nuclear industries comprised 6.9% of the value of total imports in 2002.

Services (including transport, communications, trade and finance) contributed 82.8% of GDP in 1999, and employed 80.4% of the working population in 1999. The public sector accounts for about one-half of employment in the services sector. Tourism is also significant; in 2003 432,000 tourists visited Réunion, and tourism revenue totalled €311.3m.

In 2002 Réunion recorded a trade deficit of €2,711m. The principal source of imports in 2002 was metropolitan France, providing 64.0% of the total; other major suppliers in that year were Saudi Arabia and Germany. Metropolitan France was also the principal market for exports in 2002, taking 58.2% of the total; other significant purchasers were Japan, Mayotte and the USA. The principal exports in 2002 were sugar and capital equipment. The principal imports in that year were prepared foodstuffs, road motor vehicles and parts, and chemical products.

In 1998 there was an estimated state budgetary deficit of 8,048.9m. French francs. The annual rate of inflation averaged 2.2% in 1990–2002; consumer prices increased by 2.7% in 2002. An estimated 32.9% of the labour force were unemployed in December 2003.

Réunion is represented by France in the Indian Ocean Commission (IOC, see p. 374). As an integral part of France, Réunion belongs to the European Union (EU, see p. 217).

Réunion has a relatively developed economy, but is dependent on financial aid from France. The economy has traditionally been based on agriculture, and is therefore vulnerable to poor climatic conditions. From the 1990s the production of sugar cane (which dominates this sector) was adversely affected by increasing urbanization, which resulted in a decline in agricultural land. In 1994 the Government indicated that it intended to give priority to the reduction of unemployment and announced a programme of economic and social development. However, Réunion's rate of unemployment remained the highest of all the French Departments in 2003, with youth unemployment of particular concern. Although favourable economic progress was reported in 1998, sustained largely by tourism, economists have identified Réunion's need to expand external trade, particularly with fellow IOC members, if the island's economy is to continue to prosper. In May 2000 the French Government announced that it had agreed to equalize the minimum taxable wage in the Overseas Departments with that of metropolitan France within a period of three years; the current minimum taxable wage in Réunion was 20% lower than that of metropolitan France. This measure was approved by the French Senate in June. In early 2001 the French Government announced that it was to spend €84m. on improving educational facilities on Réunion, as part of a major programme of investment in the Overseas Territories and Departments. In 2002 two cyclones and heavy rains adversely affected agricultural production, with prices rising substantially as a result. It was hoped that a decision to allow Réunion to negotiate co-operation agreements with regional states from 2004 would enhance its trading position. In December 2004 the airline Air Bourbon, which had been established in June 2003, went into liquidation with operating losses of €3m.; the company was placed in receivership for an eight-month period.

Education

Education is modelled on the French system, and is compulsory for 10 years between the ages of six and 16 years. Primary education begins at six years of age and lasts for five years. Secondary education, which begins at 11 years of age, lasts for up to seven years, comprising a first cycle of four years and a second of three years. For the academic year 2003/04 there were 45,663 pupils enrolled at 174 pre-primary schools, 76,126 at 358 primary schools, and 101,522 at 120 secondary schools. There is a university, with several faculties, providing higher education in law, economics, politics, and French language and literature, and a teacher-training college.

Public Holidays

2005: 1 January (New Year's Day), 28 March (Easter Monday), 1 May (Labour Day), 5 May (Ascension Day), 8 May (Liberation Day), 16 May (Whit Monday), 14 July (National Day, Fall of the Bastille), 15 August (Assumption), 1 November (All Saints' Day), 11 November (Armistice Day), 20 December (Abolition of Slavery Day), 25 December (Christmas Day).

2006: 1 January (New Year's Day), 17 April (Easter Monday), 1 May (Labour Day), 8 May (Liberation Day), 25 May (Ascension Day), 5 June (Whit Monday), 14 July (National Day, Fall of the Bastille), 15 August (Assumption), 1 November (All Saints' Day), 11 November (Armistice Day), 20 December (Abolition of Slavery Day), 25 December (Christmas Day).

Weights and Measures

The metric system is in use.

Statistical Survey

Source (unless otherwise indicated): Institut National de la Statistique et des Etudes Economiques, Service Régional de la Réunion, 15 rue de l'Ecole, 97490 Sainte-Clotilde; tel. 48-81-00; fax 41-09-81; internet www.insee.fr/fr/insee_regions/reunion.

AREA AND POPULATION

Area: 2,507 sq km (968 sq miles).

Population: 597,828 (males 294,256, females 303,572) at census of 15 March 1990; 706,180 (males 347,076, females 359,104) at census of 8 March 1999; 763,204 (official estimate) at 1 January 2004.

Density (1 January 2004): 304.4 per sq km.

Principal Towns (population at census of March 1999): Saint-Denis (capital) 131,557; Saint-Paul 87,712; Saint-Pierre 68,915; Le Tampon 60,323; Saint-Louis 43,519; Saint-André 43,174. *Mid-2003* (UN estimate, incl. suburbs): Saint-Denis 177,648 (Source: UN, *World Urbanization Prospects: The 2003 Revision*).

Births, Marriages and Deaths (2001): Registered live births 14,541 (birth rate 19.8 per 1,000); Registered marriages 3,508 (marriage rate 4.8 per 1,000); Registered deaths 3,829 (death rate 5.2 per 1,000). *2002* (provisional): Registered live births 14,815 (birth rate 19.8 per 1,000); Registered marriages 3,161 (marriage rate 4.2 per 1,000); Registered deaths 4,012 (death rate 5.4 per 1,000). *2003:* Registered live births 14,389.

Expectation of Life (years at birth, 2004): Males 71.3; Females 79.8.

Economically Active Population (persons aged 15 years and over, 1999 census): Agriculture, hunting, forestry and fishing 9,562; Mining, manufacturing, electricity, gas and water 13,424; Construction 11,003; Wholesale and retail trade 24,658; Transport, storage and communications 5,494; Financing, insurance and real estate 4,851; Business services 11,225; Public administration 39,052; Education 23,325; Health and social work 17,376; Other services 13,707; *Total employed* 173,677 (males 100,634, females 73,043); Unemployed 124,203 (males 63,519, females 60,684); *Total labour force* 297,880 (males 164,153, females 133,727). Figures exclude 967 persons on compulsory military service (males 945, females 22). *2000* (estimates, '000 persons aged 15 years and over): Total employed 179.5; Unemployed 130.4; Total labour force 309.9. *Mid-2003* (estimates): Agriculture, etc. 8,000; Total labour force 318,000 (Source: FAO).

HEALTH AND WELFARE

Key Indicators

Total Fertility Rate (children per woman, 2002): 2.5.

Physicians (per 1,000 head, 2001): 2.2.

Hospital Beds (per 1,000 head, 2000): 3.7.
For definitions, see explanatory note on p. vi.

AGRICULTURE, ETC.

Principal Crops (FAO estimates, '000 metric tons, 2003): Maize 17; Potatoes 4; Sugar cane 2,000; Cabbages 5; Lettuce 2; Tomatoes 4; Cauliflower 5; Onions and shallots (green) 5; Bananas 2; Tangerines, mandarins, clementines and satsumas 4; Pineapples 10. Source: FAO.

Livestock (FAO estimates, '000 head, 2003): Cattle 30; Pigs 79; Sheep 2; Goats 37; Chickens 13,000. Source: FAO.

Livestock Products (FAO estimates, '000 metric tons, 2003): Beef and veal 2; Pig meat 12; Poultry meat 19; Cow's milk 23; Hen eggs 6. Source: FAO.

Forestry ('000 cubic metres, 1991): *Roundwood Removals:* Sawlogs, veneer logs and logs for sleepers 4.2; Other industrial wood 0.9 (FAO estimate); Fuel wood 31.0 (FAO estimate); Total 36.1. *Sawnwood Production:* 2.2. *1992–2003:* Annual production as in 1991 (FAO estimates). Source: FAO.

Fishing (FAO estimates, metric tons, live weight, 2002): Capture 3,700 (Albacore 521; Yellowfin tuna 591; Bigeye tuna 151; Swordfish 1,572; Common dolphinfish 141; Striped marlin 117; Carangids 131); Aquaculture 110; *Total catch* 3,810. Source: FAO.

INDUSTRY

Selected Products (metric tons, 2003 unless otherwise indicated): Sugar 209,651; Oil of geranium 3.2 (2002); Oil of vetiver root 0.4 (2002); Rum (hl) 112,568; Electric energy (million kWh) 2,078 (net production).

FINANCE

Currency and Exchange Rates: The French franc was used until the end of February 2002. Euro notes and coins were introduced on 1 January 2002, and the euro became the sole legal tender from 18 February. Some of the figures in this Survey are still in terms of francs. For details of exchange rates, see Mayotte.

Budget (forecasts, € million, 2003): *Regional Budget:* Revenue 492 (Direct taxes 32, Indirect taxes 157, Transfers received 202, Loans 100, Other receipts 1); Expenditure 492 (Current expenditure 185, Capital 307). *Departmental Budget:* Revenue 743 (Direct taxes 66, Indirect taxes 150, State endowments 349, Subsidies, etc. 73, Loans 77, Other receipts 28); Expenditure 743 (Current 504, Capital 239).

Money Supply (million francs at 31 December 1996): Currency outside banks 4,050; Demand deposits at banks 7,469; Total money 11,519.

Cost of Living (Consumer Price Index for urban areas, average of monthly figures; base: 1990 = 100): All items 127.1 in 2001; 130.5 in 2002; 132.0 in 2003. Source: UN, *Monthly Bulletin of Statistics.*

Expenditure on the Gross Domestic Product (€ million at current prices, 1999): Collective final consumption expenditure 666; Individual final consumption expenditure 8,108; Increase in stocks −75; Gross fixed capital formation 1,523; *Total domestic expenditure* 10,222; Exports of goods and services 520; *Less* Imports of goods and services 2,537; *GDP in purchasers' values* 8,205.

Gross Domestic Product by Economic Activity (€ million at current prices, 1996): Agriculture, forestry and fishing 222; Mining, manufacturing, electricity, gas and water 594; Construction 512; Wholesale and retail trade 816; Hotels and restaurants 152; Transport and communications 463; Finance and insurance 358; Public administration 1,053; Education, health and social work 1,856; Other marketable services 1,024; Other non-market services 698; *Sub-total* 7,750; *Less* Imputed bank service charge 284; *GDP at basic prices* 7,466; Taxes on products, *less* subsidies on products 739; *GDP in purchasers' values* 8,205.

EXTERNAL TRADE

Principal Commodities (€ million, 2002): *Imports c.i.f.:* Prepared foodstuffs 458.6; Articles of clothing and furs 121.6; Road motor vehicles and parts 354.6; Machinery and mechanical appliances 211.2; Radio, television and communications equipment 107.5; Chemical products 342.3; Products of cokeries, petroleum refineries and nuclear industries 203.5; Total (incl. others) 2,931.0. *Exports f.o.b.:* Crops and livestock products (unprocessed) 6.3; Prepared foodstuffs 153.1 (Sugar 88.6); Other consumer goods 7.4; Road motor vehicles and parts 11.8; Other capital goods 28.3; Intermediate goods 12.5; Total (incl. others) 220.0.

Principal Trading Partners (€ million, 2002): *Imports c.i.f.:* Belgium 60.7; France (metropolitan) 1,876 (approximate figure); Germany 105.8; Italy 84.3; Saudi Arabia 123.2; South Africa 65.5; Total (incl. others) 2,931.0. *Exports f.o.b.:* Belgium 7.0; France (metropolitan) 128 (approximate figure); Japan 22.9; Madagascar 6.9; Mauritius 5.2; Mayotte 12.2; USA 11.3; Total (incl. others) 220.0.

TRANSPORT

Road Traffic (1 Jan. 2003): Motor vehicles in use 280,771.

Shipping: *Merchant Fleet* (total displacement at 31 December 1992): 21,000 grt (Source: UN, *Statistical Yearbook*); *Traffic* (2003): Vessels entered 748; Freight unloaded 2,911,400 metric tons; Freight loaded 523,300 metric tons; Passenger arrivals 15,201; Passenger departures 15,508.

Civil Aviation (commercial flights, 2003): Passenger arrivals 772,257; Passenger departures 771,686; Freight unloaded 18,124 metric tons; Freight loaded 7,423 metric tons.

TOURISM

Tourist Arrivals ('000): 424 in 2001; 426 in 2002; 432 in 2003.

Arrivals by Country of Residence (2002): France (metropolitan) 334,300; EU 17,200; Mauritius 30,600; Total (incl. others) 426,000.

Tourism Receipts (€ million, excl. advance payments): 271.5 in 2001; 302.0 in 2002; 311.3 in 2003.

COMMUNICATIONS MEDIA

Radio Receivers (1997): 173,000 in use. Source: UNESCO, *Statistical Yearbook.*

Television Receivers (1998): 130,000 in use. Source: UNESCO, *Statistical Yearbook.*

Telephones (main lines, 1999): 268,496. Source: International Telecommunication Union.

Facsimile Machines (1996): 9,164 in use. Source: UN, *Statistical Yearbook.*

Mobile Cellular Telephones (2000): 276,100 subscribers. Source: International Telecommunication Union.

Personal Computers ('000 in use, 1999): 32. Source: International Telecommunication Union.

Internet Users ('000, 2000): 130.0. Source: International Telecommunication Union.

Book Production (1992): 69 titles (50 books; 19 pamphlets). Source: UNESCO, *Statistical Yearbook.*

Daily Newspapers (1996): 3 (estimated average circulation 55,000 copies). Source: UNESCO, *Statistical Yearbook.*

Non-daily Newspapers (1988, estimates): 4 (average circulation 20,000 copies). Source: UNESCO, *Statistical Yearbook.*

EDUCATION

Pre-primary and Primary (2003/04): Schools 532 (pre-primary 174, primary 358); teachers 6,148; pupils 121,789 (pre-primary 45,663, primary 76,126).

Secondary (2003/04): Schools 120; teachers 8,051; pupils 101,522.

University (2003/04): Institution 1; teaching staff 343 (2001/02); students 10,759.

Teacher-Training (2003/04): Institution 1; teaching staff 82 (2001/02); students 1,355.

Other Higher (2003/04): Students 4,736.

Directory

The Government

(March 2005)

Prefect: DOMINIQUE VIAN, Préfecture, place du Barachois, 97405 Saint-Denis Cédex; tel. 40-77-77; fax 41-73-74; e-mail prefet974@ guetali.fr.

President of the General Council: NASSIMAH DINDAR (UMP), Hôtel du Département, 2 rue de la Source, 97400 Saint-Denis; tel. 90-30-30; fax 90-39-99; internet www.cg974.fr.

Deputies to the French National Assembly: BERTHO AUDIFAX (UMP), HUGUETTE BELLO (PCR), CHRISTOPHE PAYET (PS), ANDRÉ THIEN AH KOON (independent right-wing, allied to the UMP), RENÉ-PAUL VICTORIA (UMP).

Representatives to the French Senate: ANNE-MARIE PAYET (Union Centriste), PAUL VERGÈS (PCR), JEAN-PAUL VIRAPOULLÉ (UMP).

GOVERNMENT OFFICES

Direction de l'Agriculture et de la Forêt: Blvd de la Providence, 97489 Saint-Denis Cédex; tel. 48-61-00; fax 48-61-99.

Direction du Développement Économique et de l'Économie Solidaire: Ave de la Victoire, 97488 Saint-Denis Cédex; tel. 90-31-90; fax 90-39-89.

Direction du Développement Local, des Actions Sociales, de Santé: 2 rue de la Source, 97488 Saint-Denis Cédex; tel. 90-33-33; fax 90-39-96.

Direction de l'Environnement: 60 rue Fénélon, 97488 Saint-Denis Cédex; tel. 90-24-00; fax 90-24-19.

Direction des Finances: Ave de la Victoire, 97488 Saint-Denis Cédex; tel. 90-39-39; fax 90-39-92.

Direction Générale des Services: 2 rue de la Source, 97488 Saint-Denis Cédex; tel. 90-30-30; fax 90-39-99.

Direction de l'Informatique: 19 route de la Digue, 97488 Saint-Denis Cédex; tel. 90-32-00; fax 90-32-99; e-mail fneyra@cg974.fr.

Direction des Infrastructures Départementales: 1A rue Charles Gounod, 97488 Saint-Denis Cédex; tel. 41-56-52; fax 21-73-19; e-mail jcdumay.did@cg974.fr.

Direction de la Logistique: 2 rue de la Source, 97488 Saint-Denis Cédex; tel. 90-31-38; fax 90-39-91.

Direction du Patrimoine: 6B rue Rontaunay, 97488 Saint-Denis Cédex; tel. 90-86-86; fax 90-86-90.

Direction de la Presse et de la Communication: 42 rue du Général de Gaulle, 97488 Saint-Denis Cédex; tel. 21-86-30; fax 21-39-45.

Direction de la Promotion Culturelle et Sportive: 18 rue de Paris, 97488 Saint-Denis Cédex; tel. 90-35-35; fax 20-26-03.

Direction de la Promotion de l'Enfance, de la Famille et de la Santé: 2 rue de la Source, 97488 Saint-Denis Cédex; tel. 90-33-33; fax 90-39-96.

Direction des Resources Humaines: 2 rue de la Source, 97488 Saint-Denis Cédex; tel. 90-37-37; fax 90-34-90.

Direction des Transports: 34 rue de la Source, 97488 Saint-Denis Cédex; tel. 20-38-08; fax 41-72-88.

Direction de la Vie Éducative: Ave de la Victoire, 97488 Saint-Denis Cédex; tel. 90-31-31; fax 90-39-98.

Conseil Régional

Hôtel de la Région Pierre Lagourgue, ave René Cassin, Le Moufia BP 402, 97494 Sainte-Clotilde Cédex; tel. 48-70-00; fax 48-70-71; e-mail emmanuelle.ganne@guetali.fr; internet www.region-reunion.com.

President: PAUL VERGÈS (PCR).

Election, 21 and 28 March 2004

Party	Seats
Alliance*	27
UMP	11
PS-Les Verts Réunion	7
Total	45

* An alliance of seven political parties and movements, dominated by the PCR, and also including Free-DOM.

Political Organizations

Front National (FN)—Fédération de la Réunion: Saint-Denis; tel. 51-38-97; e-mail fatna@frontnational.com; internet www.frontnational.com; f. 1972; extreme right-wing; Sec. RICHARD ALAVIN.

Mouvement pour l'Indépendance de la Réunion (MIR): f. 1981 to succeed the fmr Mouvement pour la Libération de la Réunion; grouping of parties favouring autonomy.

Mouvement National Républicain (MNR)—Fédération de la Réunion: tel. 22-34-69; Sec. RÉMI BERTIN.

Parti Communiste Réunionnais (PCR): Saint-Denis; f. 1959; Pres. PAUL VERGÈS; Sec.-Gen. ELIE HOARAU.

> **Mouvement pour l'Egalité, la Démocratie, le Développement et la Nature:** affiliated to the PCR; advocates political unity; Leader RENÉ PAYET.

Parti Radical de Gauche (PRG)—Fédération de la Réunion: 18 rue des Demoiselles, Hermitage les Bains, 97434 Saint-Gilles-les-Bains; tel. 33-94-73; internet www.radical-gauche.org; f. 1977; fmrly Mouvement des Radicaux de Gauche; advocates full independence and an economy separate from, but assisted by, France; Pres. RÉMY MASSAIN.

Parti Socialiste (PS)—Fédération de la Réunion: 18 ave Stanislas Gimard, 97490 Saint-Denis; tel. 97-46-42; fax 28-53-03; e-mail fede974@parti-socialiste.fr; internet www.parti-socialiste.fr; left-wing; Sec. MICHEL VERGOZ.

Rassemblement des Démocrates pour l'Avenir de la Réunion (RADAR): Saint-Denis; f. 1981; centrist.

Rassemblement des Socialistes et des Démocrates (RSD): Saint-Denis; Sec.-Gen. DANIEL CADET.

Union pour la Démocratie Française (UDF): Saint-Denis; internet www.udf.org; f. 1978; centrist.

Union pour un Mouvement Populaire (UMP)—Fédération de la Réunion: 6 bis blvd Vauban, BP 11, 97461 Saint-Denis Cédex; tel. 20-21-18; fax 41-73-55; f. 2002; centre-right; local branch of the metropolitan party; Departmental Sec. JEAN-LUC POUDROUX.

Les Verts Réunion: BP 31, 97429 Petite Ile; tel. and fax 31-61-74; e-mail verts.reunion@voila.fr; internet www.chez.com/rayonvert; ecologist; Sec. V. DENES.

Judicial System

Cour d'Appel: Palais de Justice, 166 rue Juliette Dodu, 97488 Saint-Denis; tel. 40-58-58; fax 21-95-32; Pres. JEAN-CLAUDE CARRIÉ.

There are two Tribunaux de Grande Instance, one Tribunal d'Instance, two Tribunaux pour Enfants and two Conseils de Prud'hommes.

Religion

A substantial majority of the population are adherents of the Roman Catholic Church. There is a small Muslim community.

CHRISTIANITY

The Roman Catholic Church

Réunion comprises a single diocese, directly responsible to the Holy See. At 31 December 2002 there were an estimated 595,000 adherents, equivalent to some 92.2% of the population.

Bishop of Saint-Denis de la Réunion: Mgr GILBERT AUBRY, Evêché, 36 rue de Paris, BP 55, 97461 Saint-Denis Cédex; tel. 94-85-70; fax 94-85-71; e-mail evechediocesereunion@wanadoo.fr; internet www.diocese_reunion.com.

The Press

DAILIES

Journal de l'Ile de la Réunion: 357 rue du Maréchal Leclerc, BP 166, 97463 Saint-Denis Cédex; tel. 90-46-00; fax 90-46-01; f. 1956; Dir JACQUES TILLIER; circ. 35,000.

Quotidien de la Réunion et de l'Océan Indien: BP 303, 97712 Saint-Denis Cédex 9; tel. 92-15-15; fax 28-43-60; f. 1976; Dir MAXIMIN CHANE KI CHUNE; circ. 38,900.

PERIODICALS

AGRI-MAG Réunion: Chambre d'Agriculture, 24 rue de la Source, BP 134, 97463 Saint-Denis Cédex; tel. 94-25-94; fax 21-06-17; e-mail chambagri.cda-97@wanadoo.fr; f. 2001; monthly; Dir Guy Derand; Chief Editor HERVÉ CAILLEAUX; circ. 8,000.

Al-Islam: Centre Islamique de la Réunion, BP 437, 97459 Saint-Pierre Cédex; tel. 25-45-43; fax 35-58-23; e-mail centre-islamique .reunion@wanadoo.fr; internet www.centre-islamique.com; f. 1975; 4 a year; Dir SAÏD INGAR.

Cahiers de la Réunion et de l'Océan Indien: 24 blvd des Cocotiers, 97434 Saint-Gilles-les-Bains; monthly; Man. Dir CLAUDETTE SAINT-MARC.

L'Economie de la Réunion: c/o INSEE, Parc Technologique, 10 rue Demarne, BP 13, 97408 Saint-Denis Messag Cédex 9; tel. 48-89-21; fax 48-89-89; e-mail insee-contact@insee.fr; internet www.insee .fr/reunion; 4 a year; Dir JEAN GAILLARD; Editor-in-Chief COLLETTE BERTHIER.

L'Eglise à la Réunion: 18 rue Montreuil, 97469 Saint-Denis; tel. 41-56-90; fax 40-92-17; e-mail eglise-reunion@wanadoo.fr; monthly; Dir ELIE CADET.

L'Enjeu: Saint-Denis; tel. 21-75-76; fax 41-60-62; Dir BLANDINE ETRAYEN; Editor-in-Chief JEAN-CLAUDE VALLÉE; circ. 4,000.

Le Journal de la Nature: Saint-Denis; tel. 29-45-45; fax 29-00-90; Dir J. Y. CONAN.

Le Mémento Industriel et Commercial Réunionnais: 80 rue Pasteur, 97400 Saint-Denis; tel. 21-94-12; fax 41-10-85; e-mail memento@oceanes.fr; internet www.memento.fr; f. 1970; monthly; Dir CATHERINE LOUAPRE POTTIER; Editor GEORGES-GUILLAUME LOUAPRE POTTIER; circ. 10,000.

974 Ouest: Montgaillard, 97400 Saint-Denis; monthly; Dir DENISE ELMA.

Télé 7 Jours Réunion: 6 rue Montyon, BP 405, 93200 Saint-Denis; weekly; Dir MICHEL MEKDOUD; circ. 25,000.

Témoignage Chrétien de la Réunion: 21 bis rue de l'Est, BP 192, 97465 Saint-Denis; weekly; Dir RENÉ PAYET; circ. 2,000.

Témoignages: 6 rue du général Emile Rolland, BP 1016, 97828 Le Port Cédex; tel. 55-21-21; e-mail temoignages@wanadoo.fr; internet www.temoignages.re; f. 1944; publ. of the PCR; weekly; Dir ELIE HOARAU; circ. 6,000.

Visu: 97712 Saint-Denis Cédex 9; tel. 90-20-60; fax 90-20-61; weekly; Editor-in-Chief GUY LEBLOND; circ. 53,000.

NEWS AGENCY

Imaz Press Réunion: Saint-Denis; tel. 20-05-65; fax 20-05-49; e-mail ipr@iprenunion.com; internet www.ipreunion.com.

Broadcasting and Communications

TELECOMMUNICATIONS

Cegetel: Saint-Denis; sole cellular telephone operator on Réunion; 93,000 subscribers.

BROADCASTING

Réseau France Outre-mer (RFO): 1 rue Jean Chatel, 97716 Saint-Denis Cédex; tel. 40-67-67; fax 21-64-84; internet www.rfo.fr;

fmrly Société Nationale de Radio-Télévision Française d'Outre-mer; home radio and television relay services in French; operates two television channels and two radio frequencies; Pres. ANDRÉ-MICHEL BESSE; Regional Dir DOMINIQUE RICHARD; Dir of Television GÉRARD CHRISTIAN HOARAU; Dir of Radio JEAN-PAUL MELADE.

Radio

Radio Free-DOM: BP 666, 97473 Saint-Denis Cédex; tel. 41-51-51; fax 21-68-64; e-mail freedom@guetali.fr; internet www.freedom.fr; f. 1981; privately owned radio station; Dir Dr CAMILLE SUDRE.

Television

Antenne Réunion: BP 80001, 97801 Saint-Denis Cédex 9; tel. 48-28-28; fax 48-28-26; f. 1991; broadcasts 10 hours daily; Dir CHRISTOPHE DUCASSE.

Canal Réunion: 35 chemin Vavangues, 97490 Sainte-Clotilde; tel. 29-02-02; fax 29-17-09; subscription television channel; broadcasts a minimum of 19 hours daily; Chair. DOMINIQUE FAGOT; Dir JEAN-BERNARD MOURIER.

TV-4: 8 chemin Fontbrune, 97400 Saint-Denis; tel. 52-73-73; broadcasts 19 hours daily.

TV Sud: 10 rue Aristide Briand, 97430 Le Tampon; tel. 57-42-42; commenced broadcasting in 1993; broadcasts 4 hours daily.

Other privately owned television services include TVB, TVE, RTV, Télé-Réunion and TV-Run.

Finance

(cap. = capital; res = reserves; dep. = deposits; m. = million; brs = branches)

BANKING

Central Bank

Institut d'Emission des Départements d'Outre-mer: 4 rue de la Compagnie, 97487 Saint-Denis Cédex; tel. 90-71-00; fax 21-41-32; Dir GUY DEBUYS.

Commercial Banks

Banque Française Commerciale Océan Indien (BFCOI): 60 rue Alexis de Villeneuve, BP 323, 97468 Saint-Denis Cédex; tel. 40-55-55; fax 20-09-07; Chair. PHILIPPE BRAULT; Dir PHILIPPE LAVIT D'HAUTEFORT; 8 brs.

Banque Nationale de Paris Intercontinentale: 67 rue Juliette Dodu, BP 113, 97463 Saint-Denis; tel. 40-30-30; fax 41-39-09; e-mail bnpipmv@guetali.fr; internet www.bnpgroup.com; f. 1927; 100% owned by BNP Paribas; Chair. MICHEL PEBEREAU; Man. Dir JEAN TABARIES; 11 brs.

Banque de la Réunion (BR), SA: 27 rue Jean Chatel, 97711 Saint-Denis Cédex; tel. 40-01-23; fax 40-00-61; e-mail br@banquedelareunion.fr; internet www.banquedelareunion.fr; f. 1849; cap. €50.0m., res €52.0m., dep. €1,120.7m. (Dec. 2001); Pres. JEAN-CLAUDE CLARAC; Gen. Man. JEAN-LOUIS FILIPPI; 12 brs.

BRED-Banque Populaire: 33 rue Victor MacAuliffe, 97461 Saint-Denis; tel. 90-15-60; fax 90-15-99.

Crédit Agricole de la Réunion: Les Camélias, Cité des Lauriers, BP 84, 97462 Saint-Denis Cédex; tel. 40-81-81; fax 40-81-40; internet www.credit-agricole.fr; f. 1949; Chair. CHRISTIAN DE LA GIRODAY; Dir ERIC PRADEL.

Development Bank

Banque Populaire Fédérale de Développement: 33 rue Victor MacAuliffe, 97400 Saint-Denis; tel. 21-18-11; Dir OLIVIER DEVISME; 3 brs.

Société Financière pour le Développement Economique de la Réunion (SOFIDER): 3 rue Labourdonnais, BP 867, 97477 Saint-Denis Cédex; tel. 40-32-32; fax 40-32-00; part of the Agence Française de Développment; Dir-Gen. CLAUDE PÉRIOU.

INSURANCE

More than 20 major European insurance companies are represented in Saint-Denis.

Trade and Industry

GOVERNMENT AGENCIES

Conseil Economique et Social de la Réunion (CESR): 10 rue du Béarn, BP 7191, 97719, Saint-Denis Messag Cédex; tel. 97-96-30; fax 97-96-31; e-mail webmaster@cesr-reunion.fr; internet www

.cesr-reunion.fr; f. 1984; Pres. JEAN-RAYMOND MONDON; Dir DIDIER LAMOTTE.

Direction Régionale du Commerce Extérieur (DRCE): MRST, 100 route de la Rivière des Pluies, BP 17, 97491 Sainte Clotilde Cédex; tel. 92-24-70; fax 92-24-70; e-mail reunion@dree.org; internet www.missioneco.org/reunion; Dir OLIVIER PARQUET.

Direction Régionale de l'Industrie, de la Recherche et de l'Environnement: 130 rue Léopold Rambaud, 97491 Sainte Clotilde Cédex; tel. 92-41-10; fax 29-37-31; e-mail drire-reunion@industrie.gouv.fr ; internet www.reunion.drire.gouv.fr; Reg. Dir JEAN-CHARLES ARDIN; Sec.-Gen. JACQUELINE LECHEVIN.

DEVELOPMENT ORGANIZATIONS

Agence Française de Développement (AFD): 44 rue Jean Cocteau, BP 2013, 97488 Saint-Denis Cédex; tel. 90-00-90; fax 21-74-58; e-mail afdstdenis@re.groupe-afd.org; Dir PATRICK PEAUCELLIER.

Association pour le Développement Industriel de la Réunion: 8 rue Philibert, BP 327, 97466 Saint-Denis Cédex; tel. 94-43-00; fax 94-43-09; e-mail adir@adir.info; internet www.adir.info; f. 1975; 190 mems; Pres. MAURICE CERISOLA.

Chambre d'Agriculture de la Réunion: 24 rue de la Source, BP 134, 97463 Saint-Denis Cédex; tel. 21-25-88; fax 21-06-17; e-mail chambagri.cda-97@wanadoo.fr; Pres. JEAN-YVES MINATCHY; Dir-Gen. FATMA BADAT.

Direction de l'Action Economique: Secrétariat Général pour les Affaires Economiques, ave de la Victoire, 97405 Saint-Denis; tel. 40-77-10; fax 40-77-01.

Jeune Chambre Economique de Saint-Denis de la Réunion: 25 rue de Paris, BP 1151, 97483 Saint-Denis; f. 1963; 30 mems; Chair. JEAN-CHRISTOPHE DUVAL.

Société de Développement Economique de la Réunion (SODERE): 26 rue Labourdonnais, 97469 Saint-Denis; tel. 20-01-68; fax 20-05-07; f. 1964; Chair. RAYMOND VIVET; Man. Dir ALBERT TRIMAILLE.

CHAMBERS OF COMMERCE

Chambre de Commerce et d'Industrie de la Réunion (CCIR): 15 route de la Balance, 97410 Saint Pierre; tel. 96-96-96; fax 94-22-90; internet www.reunion.cci.fr; f. 1830; Pres. ERIC MAGAMOOTOO; Sec. DANIEL MOREAU.

Chambre de Métiers et de l'Artisanat: 42 rue Jean Cocteau, Champ–Fleuri, 97490 Sainte-Clotilde; tel. 21-04-35; fax 21-68-33; e-mail scom.cdm@wanadoo.fr; internet www.cm-reunion.fr; f. 1968; Pres. JOCELYN DE LAVERGNE; Sec. CHANTAL TANGUY; 12 mem orgs.

EMPLOYERS' ASSOCIATIONS

Fedération Réunionnaise du Bâtiment et des Travaux Publics: BP 108, 97462 Saint-Denis Cédex; tel. 41-70-87; fax 21-55-07; Pres. J. M. LE BOURVELLEC.

Ordre National de Médecins: 2 Résidence Halley, Bât. A4, rue Camille-Vergoz, 97400 Saint-Denis; tel. 20-11-58; fax 21-08-02.

Conseil de l'Ordre des Pharmaciens: 1 bis rue Sainte Anne, Immeuble le Concorde, Appt. 26, 1er étage, 97400 Saint-Denis; tel. 41-85-51; fax 21-94-86; internet ; Pres. CHRISTIANE VAN DE WALLE.

Mouvement des Entreprises de France Réunion (MEDEF): 14 rampes Ozoux, BP 354, 97467 Saint-Denis; tel. 20-01-30; fax 41-68-56; e-mail colier@guetali.fr; Pres. PAUL MARTINEL.

Syndicat des Fabricants de Sucre de la Réunion: La Mare, BP 53, 97438 Sainte Marie de la Réunion; tel. 72-18-00; fax 72-18-01; e-mail info@sfsrun.com; Chair. XAVIER THIEBLIN.

Syndicat des Producteurs de Rhum de la Réunion: 46 rue Labourdonnais, BP 284, 97466 Saint-Denis Cédex; tel. 90-45-00; fax 41-24-13; e-mail prestsuc@groupemace.com; Chair. XAVIER THIEBLIN.

TRADE UNIONS

Confédération Française des Travailleurs Chrétiens (CFTC): Résidence Pointe des Jardins, 1 rue de l'Atillerie, 97400 Saint-Denis; tel. 41-22-85; fax 41-26-85; e-mail usctr@wanadoo.fr.

Confédération Générale du Travail de la Réunion (CGTR): 144 rue du Général de Gaulle, BP 1132, 97482 Saint-Denis Cédex; Sec.-Gen. GEORGES MARIE LEPINAY.

Fédération Départementale des Syndicats d'Exploitants Agricoles de la Réunion (FDSEA): 7 bis allée du Petit Paris, Z.I. No. 1, 97410 Saint-Denis; tel. 96-33-53; fax 96-33-90; e-mail fdsea-reunion@wanadoo.fr; affiliated to the Fédération Nationale des Syndicats d'Exploitants; Sec.-Gen. JEAN-BERNARD HOARAU.

Force Ouvrière (FO): 81 rue Labourdonnais, BP 853, 97477 Saint-Denis Cédex; tel. 21-31-35; fax 41-57-45; e-mail emarguerite@force-ouvriere.fr; Sec.-Gen. Eric Marguerite.

Union Interprofessionnelle de la Réunion (UI CFDT): 58 rue Fénelon, 97400 Saint-Denis; tel. 90-27-67; fax 21-03-22; e-mail uir .cfdt@wanadoo.fr; affiliated to the Confédération Française Démocratique du Travail.

Union Régionale la Réunion: BP 220, 97466 Saint-Denis Cedex; tel. 26-64-65; fax 26-68-78 .

Transport

ROADS

A route nationale circles the island, generally following the coast and linking the main towns. Another route nationale crosses the island from south-west to north-east linking Saint-Pierre and Saint-Benoît. In 1994 there were 370 km of routes nationales, 754 km of departmental roads and 1,630 km of other roads; 1,300 km of the roads were bituminized.

SHIPPING

In 1986 work was completed on the expansion of the Port de la Pointe des Galets, which was divided into the former port in the west and a new port in the east (the port Ouest and the port Est), known together as Port Réunion. In 2003 some 2.9m. metric tons of freight were unloaded and 523,300 tons loaded at the two ports. The Chambre de Commerce et d'Industrie de la Réunion also manages three yachting marinas.

Port Authority (Concession Portuaire): Rue Evariste de Parny, BP 18, 97821, Le Port Cédex; tel. 42-90-00; fax 42-47-90; e-mail pr.com@reunion.cci.fr; internet www.reunion.port.fr; Dir Gilles Ham-Chou-Chong.

CMACGM Réunion: 1 rue Jesse Owens, Z.I. no 2, BP 2007, 97822 Le Port Cédex; tel. 55-10-10; fax 42-16-73; e-mail par.vseveno@cma-cgm.com; internet www.gmc-cgm.com; f. 1996 by merger of Compagnie Générale Maritime and Compagnie Maritime d'Affrètement; shipping agents; Dir Valérie Seveno.

Coopérative Ouvrière Réunionaise (COR): 1 voie de Liaison Portuaire, BP 119, 97823 Le Port Cédex; tel. 43-05-14; fax 43-09-44; e-mail la.cor@wanadoo.fr; stevedoring; Pres. Jaques Virin.

Mediterranean Shipping Co France, S.A. (MSC).

Réunion Ships Agency (RSA): 7 rue Ambroise Croizat, BP 1869, 97825 Le Port Cedex; tel. 43-85-85; fax 42-03-10; e-mail isles@indoceanic.com; internet www.indoceanic.com; subsidiary of Indoceanic Services; Man. Dir Harold José Thomson.

Société d'Acconage et de Manutention de la Réunionnaise (SAMR): 3 ave Théodore Drouhet, Z.A.C. 2000, BP 2006, 97822 Le Port Cédex; tel. 55-17-11; fax 55-17-12; e-mail dti.reunion@oceanes .fr ; stevedoring; Pres. Dominique Lafont; Man. Michel Antonelli.

Société de Manutention et de Consignation Maritime (SOMACOM): 1 rue Evariste de Parny, BP 2007, 97420 Le Port; tel. 42-60-00; fax 42-60-10; e-mail somacom@oceanes.fr; stevedoring and shipping agents; Gen. Man. Daniel Rigat.

Société Réunionnaise de Services Maritimes (SRSM): 3 ave Théodore Drouhet, Z.A.C. 2000, BP 2006, 97822 Le Port Cédex; tel. 55-17-57; fax 55-17-58; e-mail dti-reunion@oceanes.fr; freight only; Man. Michel Antonelli.

CIVIL AVIATION

Réunion's international airport, Roland Garros-Gillot, is situated 8 km from Saint-Denis, and offers daily flights to metropolitan France. A programme to develop the airport was completed in 1994, and in 1997 work commenced on the extension of its terminal, at a cost of some 175m. French francs. The Pierrefonds airfield, 5 km from Saint-Pierre, commenced operating as an international airport in December 1998, offering daily flights to Mauritius, following its development at an estimated cost of nearly 50m. French francs.

Air Austral: Zone Aéroportuaire, Aéroport de la Réunion Roland Garros, 97438 Sainte-Marie, BP 611, 97472 Saint-Denis; tel. 93-10-10; fax 29-28-95; e-mail info@air-austral.com; internet www .airaustral.com; f. 1975; subsidiary of Air France; scheduled regional services; Dir-Gen. Gérard Etheve.

Air Bourbon: Aéroport de la Réunion Roland Garros, 97438 Sainte Marie; tel. 31-20-00; fax 48-18-82; e-mail contactez.nous@air-bourbon.com ; internet www.air-bourbon.com; f. 2003; placed in receivership Dec. 2004; Pres. Erick Lazarus; Dir-Gen. Frédéric Pralus.

Tourism

Tourism is being extensively promoted. Réunion's attractions include spectacular scenery and a pleasant climate. In January 2003 the island had some 2,910 hotel rooms. In 2003 432,000 tourists visited Réunion, and revenue from tourism totalled €311.3m.

Comité du Tourisme de la Réunion (CTR): Pl. du 20 décembre 1848, BP 615, 97472 Saint-Denis Cédex; tel. 21-00-41; fax 21-00-21; e-mail ctr@la-reunion-tourisme.com; internet www .la-reunion-tourisme.com; Pres. Jocelyne Lauret.

Délégation Régionale au Commerce, à l'Artisanat et au Tourisme: Préfecture de la Réunion, 97400 Saint-Denis; tel. 40-77-58; fax 50-77-15; e-mail drcat974@wanadoo.fr; Dir Philippe Jean Leglise.

Office du Tourisme Intercommunal du Nord: 53 rue Pasteur, 97400 Saint-Denis; tel. 41-83-00; fax 21-37-76; e-mail otinord@wanadoo.fr; Pres. Jean-Marie Dupuis.

French Overseas Collectivité Territoriale

The overseas Collectivité territoriale is Saint Pierre and Miquelon. It is an integral part of the French Republic and is administered by a Prefect (Préfet), who is appointed by the French Government. The Prefect is assisted by an elected General Council (Conseil général). The Collectivité territoriale is represented in the French Assemblée nationale and Sénat in Paris, and also in the European Parliament.

SAINT PIERRE AND MIQUELON

Introductory Survey

Location, Climate, Language, Religion, Capital

The territory of Saint Pierre and Miquelon (Iles Saint-Pierre-et-Miquelon) consists of a number of small islands which lie about 25 km (16 miles) from the southern coast of Newfoundland and Labrador, Canada, in the North Atlantic Ocean. The principal islands are Saint Pierre, Miquelon (Grande Miquelon) and Langlade (Petite Miquelon)—the last two being linked by an isthmus of sand. Winters are cold, with temperatures falling to −20°C (−4°F), and summers are mild, with temperatures averaging between 10° and 20°C (50° and 68°F). The islands are particularly affected by fog in June and July. The language is French, and the majority of the population profess Christianity and belong to the Roman Catholic Church. The capital is Saint-Pierre, on the island of Saint Pierre.

Recent History

The islands of Saint Pierre and Miquelon are the remnants of the once extensive French possessions in North America. They were confirmed as French territory in 1815, and gained departmental status in July 1976. The departmentalization proved unpopular with many of the islanders, since it incorporated the territory's economy into that of the European Community (EC, now European Union, see p. 217), and was regarded as failing to take into account the islands' isolation and dependence on Canada for supplies and transport links. In March 1982 socialist and other left-wing candidates, campaigning for a change in the islands' status, were elected unopposed to all seats in the Conseil général (General Council). Saint Pierre and Miquelon was excluded from the Mitterrand administration's decentralization reforms, undertaken in 1982.

In 1976 Canada imposed an economic interest zone extending to 200 nautical miles (370 km) around its shores. Fearing the loss of traditional fishing areas and thus the loss of the livelihood of the fishermen of Saint Pierre, the French Government claimed a similar zone around the islands. Hopes of discovering valuable reserves of petroleum and natural gas in the area heightened the tension between France and Canada.

In December 1984 legislation was approved giving the islands the status of a Collectivité territoriale with effect from 11 June 1985. This was intended to allow Saint Pierre and Miquelon to receive the investment and development aid suitable for its position, while allaying Canada's fears of EC exploitation of its offshore waters. Local representatives, however, remained apprehensive about the outcome of negotiations between the French and Canadian Governments to settle the dispute over coastal limits. (France continued to claim a 200-mile fishing and economic zone around Saint Pierre and Miquelon, while Canada wanted the islands to have only a 12-mile zone.) The dispute was submitted to international arbitration. Discussions began in March 1987, and negotiations to determine quotas for France's catch of Atlantic cod over the period 1988–91 were to take place simultaneously. In the mean time, Canada and France agreed on an interim fishing accord, which would allow France to increase its cod quota. The discussions collapsed in October, however, and French trawlers were prohibited from fishing in Canadian waters. In February 1988 Albert Pen and Gérard Grignon, Saint Pierre's elected representatives to the French legislature, together with two members of the Saint Pierre administration and 17 sailors, were arrested for fishing in Canadian waters. This episode, and the arrest of a Canadian trawler captain in May for fishing in Saint Pierre's waters, led to an unsuccessful resumption of negotiations in September. An agreement was reached on fishing rights in March 1989, whereby France's annual quotas for Atlantic cod and other species were determined for the period until the end of 1991. (Further quotas were subsequently stipulated for the first nine months of 1992.) At the same time the Governments agreed upon the composition of an international arbitration tribunal which would delineate the disputed maritime boundaries and exclusive economic zones.

In July 1991 the international arbitration tribunal began its deliberations in New York, USA. The tribunal's ruling, issued in June 1992, was generally deemed to be favourable to Canada. France was allocated an exclusive economic zone around the territory totalling 2,537 square nautical miles (8,700 sq km), compared with its demand for more than 13,000 square nautical miles. The French authorities claimed that the sea area granted would be insufficient to sustain the islands' fishing community. Talks on new fishing quotas for the area off Newfoundland (known as Newfoundland and Labrador from December 2001) failed, and, in the absence of a new agreement, industrial fishing in the area was effectively halted until November 1994, when the Governments of the two countries signed an accord specifying new quotas for a period of 10 years. In the following month deputies in the Assemblée nationale expressed concern that the terms of the agreement would be detrimental to Saint Pierre and Miquelon's interests, although the Government asserted that the accord recognized the islanders' historic fishing rights in Canadian waters. Meanwhile, in January of that year Saint Pierre and Miquelon protested at what it alleged was an unauthorized entry into the islands' waters by Canadian coastguards (who had been attempting to intercept goods being smuggled from Saint-Pierre to Newfoundland).

At the March 1986 election to the Assemblée nationale the islands' incumbent deputy, Pen of the Parti Socialiste (PS), was re-elected. Pen was also the sole candidate at the indirect election to choose the islands' representative in the Sénat in September. A fresh election for a deputy to the Assemblée nationale was held in November, when Gérard Grignon, representing the centre-right Union pour la Démocratie Française (UDF), was elected. At the 1988 French presidential election Jacques Chirac of the right-wing Rassemblement pour la République (RPR) received 56% of the votes cast by the islanders in the second round, in May, against the successful PS incumbent, François Mitterrand. In June Grignon was re-elected to the Assemblée nationale, taking 90.3% of the valid votes. In September–October, however, the parties of the left won a majority at elections to the Conseil général, securing 13 of the 19 seats.

In September 1992 64.2% of voters approved ratification of the Treaty on European Union (see p. 217), although only a small percentage of the electorate participated in the referendum. Grignon was re-elected to the Assemblée nationale in March 1993; some 83% of the electorate participated in the poll. At the 1995 presidential election Chirac was the winning candidate at the second round on 7 May, taking 66.9% of the votes cast. At elections to the Sénat in September, Pen was narrowly defeated at a second round of voting by Victor Reux of the RPR, since 1994 the Secretary of the islands' Economic and Social Council. Grignon was re-elected to the Assemblée nationale at a second round of voting on 1 June 1997, with 52.34% of the votes cast.

A number of government proposals regarding the socio-economic and institutional development of the Overseas Departments, certain provisions of which were also to be applied to Saint Pierre and Miquelon, were provisionally accepted by the Assemblée nationale in May 2000, and subsequently adopted by the Sénat (following a number of modifications). The proposals were definitively approved by the Assemblée nationale in November and were ratified by the Constitutional Council in

December. Measures included provisions for improving and supporting the economic development of the islands, as well the introduction of proportional representation in elections to the Conseil général. In the first round of the presidential election, held on 5 May 2002, Chirac won 30.8% of the vote on the islands, followed by Jospin, with 13.7%, who was, however, eliminated nationally. In the second round, held on 5 May, Chirac overwhelmingly defeated Jean-Marie Le Pen of the Front National, with 90.0% of the vote. Grignon, representing an alliance of the Union pour la Majorité Présidentielle and the UDF, was re-elected to the Assemblée nationale in June, with 69% of the valid votes cast on the islands in the second round. In October Claude Valleix replaced Jean-François Tallec as Prefect. At elections to the Sénat in September 2004 the mayor of Miquelon, Denis Detcheverry, narrowly defeated the mayor of Saint-Pierre, Karine Claireaux, attracting 51.35% of the votes cast. In December Claude Valleix was replaced as Prefect by Albert Dupuy.

Government

The French Government is represented in Saint Pierre by an appointed Prefect. There is a Conseil général (General Council), with 19 members (15 for Saint Pierre and four for Miquelon), elected by adult universal suffrage for a period of six years. Saint Pierre and Miquelon elects one deputy to the Assemblée nationale and one representative to the Sénat in Paris.

Defence

France is responsible for the islands' defence.

Economic Affairs

The soil and climatic conditions of Saint Pierre and Miquelon do not favour agricultural production, which is mainly confined to smallholdings, except for market-gardening and the production of eggs and chickens.

The principal economic activity of the islands is traditionally fishing and related industries, which employed some 18.5% of the working population in 1996. However, the sector has been severely affected by disputes with Canada regarding territorial waters and fishing quotas; the absence of quotas in 1992–94 effectively halted industrial fishing. New arrangements have been to the detriment of Saint Pierre and Miquelon, although there is some optimism regarding potential for the exploitation of shellfish, notably mussels and scallops, in the islands' waters. The first comercially farmed scallops were due to be sold in 2004. The total fish catch increased from 747 metric tons in 1996 to 6,485 tons in 2000, before falling to 3,802 tons in 2001 and to 3,654 tons in 2002.

Processing of fish provides the basis for industrial activity, which engages about 41% of the labour force. It is dominated by one major company, which produces frozen and salted fish, and fish meal for fodder. Following a sharp decrease in production in the late 1980s, much of the fish processed is now imported. Electricity is generated by two thermal power-stations, with a combined capacity of 23 MW. In 2000 plans were well advanced for the construction of a wind power-station, which, it was hoped, would generate some 40% of the islands' electricity requirements. The resolution of a boundary dispute between the Canadian provinces of Nova Scotia and Newfoundland and Labrador in 2002 accorded the islands about 500 sq miles of waters over the Gulf of Saint Lawrence basin, believed to contain substantial reserves of petroleum and gas.

The replenishment of ships' (mainly trawlers') supplies was formerly an important economic activity, but has now also been adversely affected by the downturn in the industrial fishing sector. Efforts were made to promote tourism, and the opening of the Saint Pierre–Montréal air route in 1987 led to an increase in air traffic in the 1990s. In 1999 the completion of a new airport capable of accommodating larger aircraft further improved transport links. Tourist arrivals in 2001 were estimated at 14,293.

In 1997 Saint Pierre and Miquelon recorded a trade deficit of 356m. French francs In 2003 the total value of exports was €4,626m.; the total value of imports in that year was €66,065m. Most trade is with Canada and France and other countries of the European Union (EU, see p. 217). The only significant exports are fish and fish meal. The principal imports in 2004 were motor vehicles, building supplies and food from Canada. Items such as clothing and other consumer goods are generally imported from France.

The annual rate of inflation averaged 2.5% in 1997–2001; consumer prices increased by 1.2% in 2002 and by 2.1% in 2003.

Some 12.8% of the labour force were unemployed at the 1999 census.

Given the decline of the fishing sector, the development of the port of Saint-Pierre and the expansion of tourism (particularly from Canada and the USA) are regarded by Saint Pierre and Miquelon as the principal means of maintaining economic progress. The islands will, none the less, remain highly dependent on budgetary assistance from the French central Government.

Education

The education system is modelled on the French system, and education is compulsory for children between the ages of six and 16 years. In 2002 there were eight primary schools, two secondary schools (one of which is private and has a technical school annex) and one technical school.

Public Holidays

2005: 1 January (New Year's Day), 25–28 March (Easter), 1 May (Labour Day), 5 May (Ascension Day), 16 May (Whit Monday), 14 July (National Day), 11 November (Armistice Day), 25 December (Christmas Day).

2006: 1 January (New Year's Day), 14–17 April (Easter), 1 May (Labour Day), 25 May (Ascension Day), 5 June (Whit Monday), 14 July (National Day), 11 November (Armistice Day), 25 December (Christmas Day).

Weights and Measures

The metric system is in use.

Statistical Survey

Source: Préfecture, pl. du Lieutenant-Colonel Pigeaud, BP 4200, 97500 Saint-Pierre; tel. 41-10-10; fax 41-47-38.

AREA AND POPULATION

Area: 242 sq km (93.4 sq miles): Saint Pierre 26 sq km, Miquelon-Langlade 216 sq km.

Population: 6,392 at census of 15 March 1990: Saint-Pierre 5,683, Miquelon-Langlade 709; 6,316 (males 3,147, females 3,169) at census of 8 March 1999.

Density (1999): 26.1 per sq km.

Births, Marriages and Deaths (1997): Live births 92; Marriages 36; Deaths 51.

Economically Active Population (1992): Fish and fish-processing 540; Construction 333; Transport 192; Dockers 44; Trade 409; Restaurants and hotels 154; Business services 417; Government employees 727; Activities not adequately defined 106; *Total labour force* 2,922. *1999:* Total economically active population 3,198 (of which government employees 825).

FISHING

Total Catch (metric tons, live weight, 2002): Capture 3,654 (Atlantic cod 2,219; American plaice (Long rough dab) 115; Yellowtail flounder 137; Haddock 222; Saithe (Pollock) 135; Atlantic redfishes 319; Rays 238; Queen crab 150). Source: FAO.

FINANCE

Currency and Exchange Rates: French currency was used until the end of 2001. Euro notes and coins were introduced on 1 January 2002, and the euro became the sole legal tender from 18 February. Some of the figures in this Survey are still in terms of French francs. For details of exchange rates, see French Guiana.

Expenditure by Metropolitan France (1997): 280 million francs.

Budget (estimates, million francs, 1997): Expenditure 244 (current 128; capital 116).

Money Supply (million francs at 31 December 1997): Currency outside banks 281; Demand deposits at banks 897; Total money 1,178.

Cost of Living (Consumer price index; base: 2000 = 100): 91.3 in 1998; 92.2 in 1999; 102.3 in 2001. Source: ILO.

EXTERNAL TRADE

Total (million francs, 1997): *Imports:* 385; *Exports:* 29. Most trade is with Canada, France (imports), other countries of the European Union (exports) and the USA.

TRANSPORT

Road Traffic (1997): 3,876 motor vehicles in use.

Shipping (1995): Ships entered 884; Freight entered 20,400 metric tons. *1997:* Ships entered 918.

Civil Aviation (2004): Passengers carried 32,313; Freight carried 102.5 metric tons (Source: Service de l'Aviation Civile de Saint Pierre et Miquelon).

TOURISM

Tourist Arrivals (2001): 14,293. Source: Institut d'Emission des Départements d'Outre-Mer.

Tourist Arrivals by Country of Residence (2000): Canada 7,092; France 919; USA 3,185; Total (incl. others) 12,156 Source: Service Loisirs Accueil.

COMMUNICATIONS MEDIA

Radio Receivers (estimate, '000 in use): 5.0 in 1997.

Television Receivers (estimate, '000 in use): 3.5 in 1997.

EDUCATION

Primary (2002): 8 institutions; 73 teachers ; 736 students.

Secondary (2002): 2 institutions; 56 teachers ; 329 students.

Technical (2002): 1 institution; 25 teachers; 134 students.
Source: Service de l'Education Nationale de Saint Pierre et Miquelon.

Directory

The Government

(February 2005)

Prefect: ALBERT DUPUY, pl. du Lieutenant-Colonel Pigeaud, BP 4200, 97500 Saint-Pierre; tel. 41-10-10; fax 41-47-38.

Deputy to the French National Assembly: GÉRARD GRIGNON (UMP).

Representative to the French Senate: DENIS DETCHEVERRY (UMP).

Conseil Régional

pl. de l'Eglise, BP 4208, 97500 Saint-Pierre; tel. 41-01-02; fax 41-22-97; e-mail cgspm@wanadoo.fr.
The General Council has 19 members (St Pierre 15, Miquelon four).
President: MARC PLANTEGENEST.

Political Organizations

Archipel Demain: 1 rue Amiral Muselier, BP 1179, 97500 Saint-Pierre; f. 1985; right-wing; Pres. YANNICK ABRAHAM.

Cap sur l'Avenir/Parti Radical de Gauche SPM (PRG-SPM): 1 rue des Basques, BP 4254, 97500 Saint-Pierre; tel. 41-40-08; fax 41-47-81; internet www.capsurlavenir.com; f. 2000; left-wing and green coalition; Pres. YANNICK CAMBRAY; Nat. Sec. ANNICK GIRARDIN.

Union pour un Mouvement Populaire (UMP): 15 rue Ange Gautier, BP 113, 97500 Saint-Pierre; e-mail ggrignon@assemblee-nationale.fr; tel. 41-35-73; fax 41-29-97; centre-right; local br. of the metropolitan party; Sec. GÉRARD GRIGNON.

Judicial System

Tribunal Supérieur d'Appel: 14 rue Emile Sasco, BP 4215, 97500 Saint-Pierre; tel. 41-03-20; fax 41-03-23; e-mail francoisbillon@justice.fr; Presiding Magistrate FRANÇOIS BILLON.

Tribunal de Première Instance: 14 rue Emile Sasco, BP 4215, 97500 Saint-Pierre; tel. 41-03-20; fax 41-41-03-23; e-mail francois.goulard-de-curraize@justice.fr; Presiding Magistrate FRANÇOISE GOULARD DE CURRAIZE.

Religion

Almost all of the inhabitants are adherents of the Roman Catholic Church.

CHRISTIANITY

The Roman Catholic Church

The islands form the Apostolic Vicariate of the Iles Saint-Pierre et Miquelon. At 31 December 2002 there were an estimated 6,314 adherents.

Vicar Apostolic: LUCIEN FISCHER (Titular Bishop of Avioccala), Vicariat Apostolique, BP 4245, 97500 Saint-Pierre; tel. 41-02-40; fax 41-47-09; e-mail mission-catho.spm@wanadoo.fr.

Other Churches

Eglise Evangélique de Saint-Pierre et Miquelon : 5 bis rue Paul Lebailly, BP 4325, 97500 Saint Pierre; tel. 41-92-39; fax 41-59-75; e-mail pasteurspm@cheznoo.net; f. 1995; affiliated to the Fédération Nationale des Assemblées de Dieu de France and Commission des Eglises Evangéliques d'Expression Française à l'Extérieure; Pastor LOUIS FOUCHÉ.

The Press

L'Echo des Caps Hebdo: rue Georges Daguerre, BP 4213, 97500 Saint-Pierre; tel. 41-10-90; fax 41-49-33; e-mail echohebd@cheznoo.net; f. 1982; weekly; Editor-in-Chief DIDIER GIL; circ. 2,500.

Recueil des Actes Administratifs: 4 rue du Général Leclerc, BP 4233, 97500 Saint-Pierre; tel. 41-24-50; fax 41-20-85; e-mail imprimeriepref@cheznoo.net; f. 1866; monthly; Dir JOSEPH DIBARRAT.

Trait d'Union: BP 113, 97500 Saint-Pierre; tel. 41-35-73; fax 41-29-97; e-mail vicreuz@cheznoo.net; 10 a year.

Le Vent de la Liberté: 1 rue Amiral Muselier, BP 1179, 97500 Saint-Pierre; tel. 41-42-19; fax 41-48-06; e-mail archipel@cheznoo.net; f. 1986; monthly; circ. 550; Dir GÉRARD GRIGNON.

Broadcasting and Communications

TELECOMMUNICATIONS

SPM Telecom: 6 pl. du Général de Gaulle, BP 4253, 97500 Saint Pierre; tel. 41-00-39; fax 41-00-39; e-mail accueil@spmtelecom.com; internet www.spmtelecom.com.

RADIO AND TELEVISION

Réseau France Outre-mer (RFO): BP 4227, 97500 Saint-Pierre; tel. 41-11-11; fax 41-22-19; internet www.rfo.fr; fmrly Société Nationale de Radio-Télévision Française d'Outre-mer, renamed as above 1998; broadcasts 24 hours of radio programmes daily and 195 hours of television programmes weekly on two channels; Pres. ANDRÉ-MICHEL BESSE; Dir JEAN-FRANÇOIS MOENNAN.

Radio Atlantique: BP 1282, 97500 Saint-Pierre; tel. 41-24-93; fax 41-56-33; e-mail adlian@cheznoo.net; f. 1982; private; broadcasts 24 hours of radio programmes daily; Pres. and Dir MARGARITA BRAEM; Sec ANDRÉ PARDOËN.

Finance

(cap. = capital, res = reserves, dep. = deposits; m. = million; amounts in euros)

BANKING

Central Bank

Institut d'Emission des Départements d'Outre-mer (IEDOM): 4 rue de la Roncière, BP 4202, 97500 Saint-Pierre; tel. 41-43-57; fax 41-58-55; e-mail iedomspm@cancom.net; internet www.iedom.fr; Dir BERNARD RATAFIKA.

Major Banks

Banque des Iles Saint-Pierre-et-Miquelon: 2 rue Jacques Cartier, BP 4223, 97500 Saint-Pierre; tel. 41-01-40; fax 41-01-50; e-mail informatique@bdispm.com; f. 1889; cap. €5.5m., res 1.7m., dep. 95.9m. (Dec. 2002); Pres. JEAN-MARC VARGEL; Gen. Man. PIERRE BALSAN.

Crédit Saint Pierrais: 20 pl. du Général de Gaulle, BP 4218, 97500 Saint-Pierre; tel. 41-21-95; fax 41-25-96; e-mail crespi2@wanadoo.fr; f. 1962; cap. €5.7m., res 1.3m., dep. 48.8m. (Dec. 2002); Pres. GEORGES HARAN-RIO; Gen. Man. HERVÉ LOMBARD.

INSURANCE

Cabinet Paturel Assurances, Agent Général AGF: 31 rue Maréchal Foch, BP 4288, 97500 Saint-Pierre; tel. 41-04-40; fax 41-51-65;

internet www.agfspm.com; Gen. Agent GUY PATUREL; Man. NATHALIE PATUREL.

Mutuelle des Iles: 5 rue Maréchal Foch, BP 1112, 97500 Saint-Pierre; tel. 41-28-69; fax 41-51-13.

Trade and Industry

GOVERNMENT AGENCY

Comité Economique et Social de l'Archipel de Saint-Pierre-et-Miquelon: 4 rue Borda, 97500 Saint-Pierre; tel. 41-45-50; fax 41-42-45; Pres. RÉMY L. BRIAND.

DEVELOPMENT AGENCIES

Agence Française de Développement (AFD): 4 rue de la Roncière, BP 4202, 97500 Saint-Pierre; tel. 41-43-57; fax 41-25-98; e-mail iedomspm@cancom.net; internet www.afd.fr; fmrly Caisse Française de Développement; Man. BERNARD RATAFIKA.

SODEPAR: Palais Royal, rue Borda, BP 4365, 97500 Saint-Pierre; tel. 41-15-15; fax 41-15-16; e-mail sodepar@cheznoo.net; internet www.sodepar.com; f. 1989; economic development agency; Chair. MARC PLANTEGENEST; Dir THIERRY BASLE.

CHAMBER OF COMMERCE

Chambre d'Agriculture, de Commerce, d'Industrie et de Métiers (CACIM): 4 rue Constant-Colmay, BP 4207, 97500 Saint-Pierre; tel. 41-45-12; fax 41-32-09; e-mail cacim975@cheznoo.net; Pres. MONIQUE WALSH.

TRADE UNIONS

Syndicat des Armateurs à la Pêche Côtière: BP 937, 97500 Saint-Pierre ; tel. 41-30-13; fax 41-73-89; e-mail kenavo@cheznoo.net; Pres. JEAN BEAUPERTUIS.

Syndicat CFDT (Union Interprofessionnelle SPM): 15 rue du Docteur Dunan, BP 4352, 97500 Saint-Pierre; tel. 41-23-20; fax 41-27-99; affiliated to the Confédération Française Démocratique du Travail; Sec.-Gen. PHILIPPE GUILLAUME.

Syndicat CFTC (UD CFTC Saint Pierre et Miquelon): 15 rue du Docteur Dunan, BP 1117, 97500 Saint-Pierre; tel. 41-37-19; fax 41-44-71; affiliated to the Confédération Française des Travailleurs Chrétiens.

Union Départementale Force Ouvrière: 15 rue Dr Dunan, BP 4241, 97500 Saint-Pierre; tel. 41-25-22; fax 41-46-55; e-mail max.claude.olaisola@wanadoo.fr; affiliated to the Confédération Générale du Travail-Force Ouvrière; Sec.-Gen. MAX OLAISOLA.

Union Intersyndicale CGT de Saint-Pierre et Miquelon: 97500 Saint-Pierre; tel. 41-41-86; affiliated to the Confédération Générale du Travail; Sec.-Gen. RONALD MANET.

Transport

SHIPPING

Packet boats and container services operate between Saint-Pierre, Halifax, Nova Scotia, Boston, MA, and France. The seaport at Saint-Pierre has three jetties and 1,200 metres of quays.

Alliance, S.A.: 1 rue Abbé Pierre Gervain, BP4257, 97500 Saint-Pierre; tel. 41-07-00; fax 41-07-01; e-mail contact@alliancesa.com; weekly freight service from Saint-Pierre to Halifax and Fortune; Pres. JEAN-CLAUDE BRIAND.

Compagnie Maritime des Transports Frigorifiques (COMAT): 14 rue Maître Georges Lefèvre, 97500 Saint-Pierre; tel. 41-22-77.

SPM Shipping: 16 rue Soeur Césarine, BP 4222, 97500 Saint-Pierre; tel. 41-16-61; fax 41-16-62; daily service between St-Pierre and Newfoundland and Labrador.

CIVIL AVIATION

There is an airport on St Pierre, served by airlines linking the territory with France and Canada. Construction of a new airport, able to accommodate larger aircraft and thus improve air links, was completed in 1999.

Air Saint-Pierre: 18 rue Albert Briand, Saint-Pierre, BP 4225, 97500 Saint-Pierre; tel. 41-00-00; fax 41-00-02; e-mail asp@cancom.net; internet www.airsaintpierre.com; f. 1964; connects the territory directly with Newfoundland and Labrador, Nova Scotia and Québec; Pres. RÉMY L. BRIAND; Man. THIERRY BRIAND.

Tourism

There were 14,293 tourist arrivals in 2001. In that year there were 173 hotel rooms.

Service Loisirs Accueil: pl. du Général de Gaulle, BP 4274, 97500 Saint-Pierre; tel. 41-02-22; fax 41-33-55; e-mail tourispm@cheznoo.net; internet www.st-pierre-et-miquelon.com; f. 1989; Pres. FRANÇOISE DUPONT.

French Overseas Collectivité Départementale

The overseas Collectivité départementale is Mayotte. It is an integral part of the French Republic and is administered by a Prefect, who is appointed by the French Government. Under the terms of its status, which was approved by the French Parliament in July 2001, executive power in Mayotte was transferred from the Prefect to the

President of the locally elected General Council (Conseil général) in April 2004, and the position of Prefect was to be dissolved by 2007. The Collectivité départementale is represented in the French Assemblée nationale and in the Sénat in Paris, and also in the European Parliament.

MAYOTTE

Introductory Survey

Location, Climate, Language, Religion, Capital

Mayotte forms part of the Comoros archipelago, which lies between the island of Madagascar and the east coast of the African mainland. The territory comprises a main island, Mayotte (Mahoré), and a number of smaller islands. The climate is tropical, with temperatures averaging between 24°C and 27°C (75°F to 81°F) throughout the year. The official language is French but Shimaore (Maorese) and Shibushi are also spoken. Islam is the main religion. The capital is Dzaoudzi, which is connected to the island of Pamandzi by a causeway.

Recent History

Since the Comoros unilaterally declared independence in July 1975, Mayotte has been administered separately by France. The independent Comoran state claims sovereignty of Mayotte, and officially represents it in international organizations, including the UN. In December 1976 France introduced the special status of Collectivité territoriale for the island. Following a coup in the Comoros in May 1978, Mayotte rejected the new Government's proposal that it should rejoin the other islands under a federal system, and reaffirmed its intention of remaining linked to France. In December 1979 the Assemblée nationale approved legislation that extended Mayotte's special status for another five years, during which the islanders were to be consulted. In October 1984, however, the Assemblée nationale further prolonged Mayotte's status, and the referendum on the island's future was postponed indefinitely. The UN General Assembly has adopted a number of resolutions in support of the sovereignty of the Comoros over the island. Until 1999 the main political party on Mayotte, the Mouvement Populaire Mahorais (MPM), demanded full departmental status for the island (as held by Réunion), but France was reluctant to grant this in view of Mayotte's lack of development.

At the general election to the Assemblée nationale in March 1986, Henry Jean-Baptiste, a member of the Centre des Démocrates Sociaux (CDS), which was affiliated to the Union pour la Démocratie Française (UDF), was elected as deputy for Mayotte. During a visit to Mayotte in October the French Prime Minister, Jacques Chirac, assured the islanders that they would remain French citizens for as long as they wished. Relations between the MPM and the French Government rapidly deteriorated after the Franco-African summit in November 1987, when Chirac expressed reservations concerning the elevation of Mayotte to the status of an Overseas Department (despite his announcement, in early 1986, that he shared the MPM's aim to upgrade Mayotte's status).

In the second round of the French presidential election, which took place in May 1988, François Mitterrand, the incumbent President and the candidate of the Parti Socialiste (PS), received 50.3% of the votes cast on Mayotte, defeating Chirac, the candidate of the Rassemblement pour la République (RPR). At elections to the Assemblée nationale, which took place in June, Jean-Baptiste retained his seat. (Later that month, he joined the newly formed centrist group in the Assemblée nationale, the Union du Centre—UDC.) In elections to the Conseil général in September and October, the MPM retained the majority of seats. In November the Conseil général demanded that the French Government introduce measures to restrict immigration to Mayotte from neighbouring islands, particularly from the Comoros.

In 1989–90 concern about the number of Comoran immigrants seeking employment on the island resulted in an increase in racial tension. In 1989 more than 150 Comoran refugees were prevented from landing on Mayotte by security forces. In January 1990 demonstrators in the town of Mamoudzou protested against illegal immigration to the island. A paramilitary organization, known as Caiman, was subsequently formed in support of the expulsion of illegal immigrants, but was refused legal recognition by the authorities.

In June 1992 increasing resentment resulted in further attacks against Comoran immigrants resident in Mayotte. In early September representatives of the MPM met the French Prime Minister, Pierre Bérégovoy, to request the reintroduction of entry visas to restrict immigration from the Comoros. Later that month the MPM organized a boycott of Mayotte's participation in the French referendum on the Treaty on European Union (see p. 217), in support of the provision of entry visas. In December the Prefect, Jean-Paul Costes, and a number of other prominent officials were charged in connection with the deaths of six people in domestic fires, which had been caused by dangerous fuel imported from Bahrain. In February 1993 a general strike, which was staged in support of claims for wage increases, culminated in protracted violent rioting. Security forces were subsequently dispatched from Réunion to restore order, while trade unions agreed to end the strike. Later that month Costes was replaced as Prefect.

At elections to the Assemblée nationale, which took place in March 1993, Jean-Baptiste was returned, securing 53.4% of votes cast, while the Secretary-General of the RPR, Mansour Kamardine, received 44.3% of the votes. Kamardine (who contested the elections as an independent candidate) subsequently accused Jean-Baptiste of illegally claiming the support of an electoral alliance of the RPR and the UDF, known as the Union pour la France, by forging the signatures of party officials on a document. Jean-Baptiste, however, denied the allegations, and began legal proceedings against Kamardine for calumny.

Elections to the Conseil général (which was enlarged from 17 to 19 members) took place in March 1994: the MPM retained 12 seats, while the RPR secured four seats, and independent candidates three seats. During an official visit to Mayotte in November, the French Prime Minister, Edouard Balladur, announced the reintroduction of entry visas as a requirement for Comoran nationals, and the adoption of a number of security measures, in an effort to reduce illegal immigration to the island. In January 1995 the reimposition of visa requirements prompted widespread protests on the Comoros; the Comoran Government suspended transport links between Mayotte and the Comoros in response to the measure. In the first round of the French presidential election in April, Balladur received the highest number of votes on Mayotte (although Chirac subsequently won the election).

In elections to the Sénat in September, the incumbent MPM representative, Marcel Henry, was returned by a large majority. During a visit to Mayotte in October, the French Secretary of State for Overseas Departments and Territories pledged that a referendum on the future status of the island would be conducted by 1999. In October 1996 he confirmed that two commissions, based in Paris and Mayotte, were preparing a consultation document, which would be presented in late 1997, and announced that the resulting referendum would take place before the end of the decade.

Partial elections to fill nine seats in the Conseil général were held in March 1997; the MPM secured three seats (losing two that it had previously held), the RPR won three seats, the local

PS one seat, and independent right-wing candidates two seats. In elections to the Assemblée nationale Jean-Baptiste, representing the alliance of the UDF and the Force Démocrate (FD, formerly the CDS), defeated Kamardine, securing 51.7% of votes cast in the second round of voting, which took place in June.

In July 1997 the relative prosperity of Mayotte was believed to have prompted separatist movements on the Comoran islands of Nzwani and Mwali to demand the restoration of French rule, and subsequently to declare their independence in August. Illegal immigration from the Comoros continued to prove a major concern for the authorities on Mayotte; during January–February 1997 some 6,000 Comorans were expelled from the island, with many more agreeing to leave voluntarily.

Meanwhile, uncertainty remained over the future status of Mayotte. In April 1998 one of the commissions charged with examining the issue submitted its report, which concluded that the present status of Collectivité territoriale was no longer appropriate, but did not advocate an alternative. In May the MPM declared its support for an adapted form of departmental administration, and urged the French authorities to decide on a date for a referendum. In July Pierre Bayle succeeded Philippe Boisadam as Prefect. In December two rounds of preparatory talks on the island's future constitutional status took place between local political organizations and senior French government officials. However, further negotiations, which were to be held in February 1999, were suspended, owing to France's concerns over the political instability in the Comoros. In May Bamana made an appeal that the inhabitants of Mayotte be allowed to organize their own vote on their future, and later that month Jean-Baptiste introduced draft legislation to the Assemblée nationale, which proposed the holding of a referendum regarding the island's future before the end of 1999. In August, following negotiations between the French Secretary of State for Overseas Departments and Territories, Jean-Jack Queyranne, and island representatives, Mayotte members of the RPR and the PS and Bamana (the leader of the MPM) signed a draft document providing for the transformation of Mayotte into a Collectivité départementale, if approved at a referendum. However, both Henry and Jean-Baptiste rejected the document. The two politicians subsequently announced their departure from the MPM and formed a new political party entitled the Mouvement Départementaliste Mahorais (MDM), while reiterating their demands that Mayotte be granted full overseas departmental status.

Following the approval of Mayotte's proposed new status by the Conseil général (by 14 votes to five) and the municipal councils, an accord to this effect was signed by Queyranne and political representatives of Mayotte on 27 January 2000. On 2 July a referendum was held, in which the population of Mayotte voted overwhelmingly in favour of the January accord, granting Mayotte the status of Collectivité départementale for a period of 10 years. In November the commission established to define the terms of Mayotte's new status published a report, which envisaged the transfer of executive power from the Prefect to the Conseil général by 2004, the dissolution of the position of Prefect by 2007 and the concession of greater powers to the local Government, notably in the area of regional co-operation.

At elections to the Conseil général, held in March 2001, no party established a majority. The MPM experienced significant losses, with only four of its candidates being elected, while the RPR won five seats, the Mouvement des Citoyens (MDC) two, the MDM one, the PS one, and various right-wing independent candidates six seats. Bamana was re-elected as President of the Conseil général. The French Parliament approved Mayotte's status as a Collectivité départementale in July 2001. In September Philippe de Mester succeeded Bayle as Prefect.

In the first round of the French presidential election, which was held on 21 April 2002, Chirac received the highest number of votes on Mayotte, winning 43.0% of the valid votes cast; the second round, held on 5 May, was also won resoundingly by Chirac, who secured 88.3% of votes cast on the island, defeating the candidate of the extreme right-wing Front National, Jean-Marie Le Pen. At elections to the Assemblée nationale, held in June, Jean-Baptiste did not stand. Kamardine, representing the recently formed Union pour la Majorité Présidentielle (UMP, which incorporated the RPR, the Démocratie Libérale and significant elements of the UDF), defeated the MDM-UDF candidate, Siadi Vita. Jean-Jacques Brot replaced de Mester as Prefect in July. In November the UMP was renamed the Union pour un Mouvement Populaire.

At elections to the Conseil général in March 2004, the UMP won eight seats in alliance with the MPM, which secured one seat, while the MDM and the MDC, also in alliance, obtained five and two seats, respectively; independent candidates were elected to the remaining three seats. With the election of Saïd Omar Oili, an independent, as President of the Conseil général on 2 April, executive power was transferred from the Prefect to the Conseil. In January 2005 Jean-Paul Kihl replaced Jean-Jacques Brot as Prefect.

(For further details of the recent history of the island, see the chapter on the Comoros.)

Government

The French Government is represented in Mayotte by an appointed Prefect. There is a Conseil général, with 19 members, elected by universal adult suffrage. Mayotte elects one deputy to the Assemblée nationale, and one representative to the Sénat. Mayotte is also represented at the European Parliament. Under the terms of its status as a Collectivité départementale, which was approved by the French Parliament in July 2001, executive power in Mayotte was transferred from the Prefect to the Conseil général in April 2004, and the position of Prefect was to be dissolved by 2007.

Defence

At 1 August 2004 there were 3,600 French troops stationed in Mayotte and Réunion.

Economic Affairs

Mayotte's gross domestic product (GDP) per head in 1991 was estimated at 4,050 French francs. Between the censuses of 1991 and 2002 the population of Mayotte increased at an average annual rate of 10.1%.

The economy is based mainly on agriculture. In 2002 10.2% of the employed labour force were engaged in this sector. The principal export crops are ylang ylang and vanilla. Rice, cassava and maize are cultivated for domestic consumption. Livestock-rearing and fishing are also important activities. However, Mayotte imports large quantities of foodstuffs, which comprised 26.8% of the value of total imports in 2003.

Industry (which is dominated by the construction sector) engaged 23.0% of the employed population in 2002. There are no mineral resources on the island. Imports of mineral products comprised 3.5% of the value of total imports in 2003 and base metals and metal products comprised 7.8%.

Services engaged 66.8% of the employed population in 2002. The annual total of tourist arrivals (excluding cruise-ship passengers) increased from 6,700 in 1995 to 21,000 in 1999, and was estimated at 35,000 in 2002. The number fell to 23,000 in 2003; of these some 40% were from France. Receipts from tourism in 1999 totalled 50m. French francs and €12.3m. in 2003.

In 2003 Mayotte recorded a trade deficit of €180.4m. The principal source of imports in 2003 was France (55.1%). France was also the principal market for exports (taking 61.4% of exports in that year); the other significant purchaser was the Comoros (24.7%). The principal exports in 2003 were fish products, ylang ylang and vanilla. The principal imports in that year were foodstuffs, machinery and appliances, chemicals and related products, base metals and metal products and transport equipment.

In 1997 Mayotte's total budgetary revenue was estimated at 1,022.4m. French francs, while total expenditure was estimated at 964.2m. French francs. Official debt was 435.7m. French francs at 31 December 1995. Mayotte recorded deflation of 2.0% in the year to December 2003. Some 30% of the labour force was unemployed in 2003.

Mayotte suffers from a persistently high trade deficit, owing to its reliance on imports, and is largely dependent on French aid. From the late 1980s the French Government granted substantial aid to finance a number of construction projects, in an attempt to encourage the development of tourism on the island. Mayotte's remote location, however, continued to prove an impediment to the development of the tourist sector. A five-year Development Plan (1986–91) included measures to improve infrastructure and to increase investment in public works; the Plan was subsequently extended to the end of 1993. In 1995 Mayotte received credit from France to finance further investment in infrastructure, particularly in the road network. As Mayotte's labour force has continued to increase (mostly owing to a high birth rate and the continued arrival of immigrants—estimated at 55,000 in 2004, of whom some 10,000 were believed to have arrived illegally), youth unemployment has caused particular concern. In 1997 37.8% of the unemployed population were under 25 years of age. In December 2002 a development agreement was signed with the French Government for the period 2003–07; of the €115m. required for its implementation, the French State was to provide €104m. Transfers from the French State to Mayotte increased from €243m. in 2001 to €337m. in 2004.

Education

Education is compulsory for children aged six to 15 years, and comprises five years' primary and five years' secondary schooling. In 2002/03 there were 111 primary schools on the island. In the same year there were 15 secondary schools, comprising 13 collèges (junior comprehensives) and two lycées. There were also two vocational and technical institutions. A further four collèges were due to be opened by 2010. Some 9,606 pre-primary school pupils, 28,591 primary school pupils and 15,626 secondary school pupils were enrolled in 2002/03. A further 1,733 students were enrolled at vocational and technical institutions.

Public Holidays

The principal holidays of metropolitan France are observed.

Statistical Survey

Source (unless otherwise indicated): Institut National de la Statistique et des Etudes Economiques; 51 hauts des Jardins du Collège, BP 1369, 97600 Mamoudzou; tel. 61-36-65; fax 61-39-56; internet www.insee.fr/mayotte.

AREA AND POPULATION

Area: 374 sq km (144 sq miles).

Population: 94,410 (census of August 1991); 131,368 (males 66,600, females 64,768) at census of 5 August 1997; 160,265 at census of 30 July 2002.

Principal Towns (population of communes at 2002 census): Mamoudzou 45,485, Koungou 15,383, Dzaoudzi (capital) 12,308.

Density (30 July 2002): 428.5 per sq km.

Births and Deaths (2001): Registered live births 6,678 (birth rate 43.4 per 1,000); Death rate 5.6 per 1,000 (1997).

Economically Active Population (persons aged 15 years and over, census of 30 July 2002): Agriculture and fishing 3,229; Electricity, gas and water 519; Industry 1,105; Construction 5,614; Wholesale and retail trade 5,435; Transport and telecommunications 2,007; Other marketable services 852; Finance and insurance 145; Other non-marketable services 12,608; _Total employed_ 31,514 (males 22,182, females 9,332); Unemployed 13,044 (males 5,179, females 7,865); _Total labour force_ 44,558 (males 27,361, females 17,197). _December 2003:_ Unemployed 13,348.

HEALTH AND WELFARE

Key Indicators

Total Fertility Rate (children per woman, 1997): 5.0.

Physicians (per 1,000 head, 1997): 0.4.

Hospital Beds (per 1,000 head, 1997): 1.4.
For definitions see explanatory note on p. vi.

AGRICULTURE, ETC.

Livestock (1995): Cattle 15,000; Sheep 2,700; Goats 23,000.

Fishing (metric tons, live weight, 2002): Skipjack tuna 188; Yellowfin tuna 1,313; Tuna-like fishes 520; _Total catch_ 4,299 (all capture). Source: FAO.

FINANCE

Currency and Exchange Rates: 100 cent = 1 euro. _Sterling and Dollar Equivalents_ (31 December 2004): £1 sterling = €1.418; US $1 = €0.7341; €100 = £70.52 = US $136.21. _Average Exchange Rate_ (euros per US dollar): 1.0626 in 2002; 0.8860 in 2003; 0.8054. The French franc was used until the end of February 2002. Euro notes and coins were introduced on 1 January 2002, and the euro became the sole legal tender from 18 February. Some of the figures in this Survey are still in terms of French francs.

Budget (million French francs, 1997): Total revenue 1,022.4 (current 783.7, capital 238.7); Total expenditure 964.2 (current 725.4, capital 238.7).

Money Supply (million French francs at 31 December 1997): Currency outside banks 789; Demand deposits 266; Total money 1,055.

Cost of Living (Consumer Price Index; base: December 1996 = 100): 103.5 in December 2001; 109.1 in December 2002; 106.9 in December 2003.

EXTERNAL TRADE

Principal Commodities (€ million, 2003): _Imports:_ Foodstuffs 49.5; Mineral products 6.5; Chemical products 15.9; Plastics and rubber 7.3; Wood and wood products 5.0; Textiles and clothing 6.7; Base metals and metal products 14.4; Machinery and appliances 17.2; Transport equipment 12.8; Total (incl. others) 184.8. _Exports:_ Vanilla 0.2; Ylang ylang 0.5; Fish products 0.8; Total (incl. others) 4.4. Source: Service des Douanes.

Principal Trading Partners (€ million, 2003): _Imports:_ France 101.8; South Africa 8.9; Thailand 6.5; China 5.9; Germany 5.2; Spain 5.0; Mauritius 4.6; Italy 4.3; Total (incl. others) 184.8. _Exports:_ France 2.7; Comoros 1.1; Réunion 0.3; Total (incl. others) 4.4. Source: Service des Douanes.

TRANSPORT

Road Traffic (1998): Motor vehicles in use 8,213.

Shipping: _Traffic_ (metric tons, 2002): Goods unloaded 229,715; Goods loaded 112,074; 54,123 passengers.

Civil Aviation (2002): _Passengers Carried:_ 133,686; _Freight Carried:_ 1,048 metric tons; _Post Carried_ 493 metric tons.

TOURISM

Visitor Arrivals (excluding cruise-ship passengers): 9,500 in 1997; 11,400 in 1998; 21,000 in 1999. _2003:_ 23,000 arrivals.

Tourism Receipts (€ million): 12.3 in 2003.

COMMUNICATIONS MEDIA

Telephones ('000 main lines in use, 2001): 10.0.

Mobile Cellular Telephones (subscribers, 2002): 21,700. Source: International Telecommunication Union.

EDUCATION

Pre-primary (2002/03): 68 schools; 9,606 pupils.

Primary (2002/03): 111 schools; 28,591 pupils.

Primary (pre-vocational) (2002/03): 12 schools; 798 pupils.

General Secondary (2002/03): 15 schools; 15,626 pupils.

Vocational and Technical (2002/03): 2 institutions (1997); 1,733 students.

Directory

The Constitution

Mayotte has an elected General Council (Conseil général), comprising 19 members, which assists the Prefect in the administration of the island. Under the status of Collectivité départementale, which was adopted by the French Parliament in July 2001, executive power was transferred from the Prefect to the President of the Conseil général in April 2004, and the position of Prefect was to be dissolved by 2007.

The Government

(March 2005)

Prefect: JEAN-PAUL KIHL.

Secretary-General: GUY MASCRES.

Deputy to the French National Assembly: MANSOUR KAMARDINE (UMP).

Representative to the French Senate: ADRIEN GIRAUD (MDM, Union Centriste), SOIBAHADDINE IBRAHIM (UMP).

Economic and Social Adviser: ANZIZA MOUSTOIFA.

GOVERNMENT DEPARTMENTS

Department of Agriculture and Forestry: BP 103, 15 rue Mariazé, 97600 Mamoudzou; tel. 61-12-13; fax 61-10-31; e-mail daf .mayotte@wanadoo.fr.

Department of Education: BP 76, 97600 Mamoudzou; tel. 61-10-24; fax 61-09-87; e-mail vice-rectorat@ac-mayotte.fr; internet www.ac-mayotte.fr.

Department of Health and Social Security: BP 104, rue de l'Hôpital, 97600 Mamoudzou; tel. 61-12-25; fax 60-19-56.

Department of Public Works: BP 109, rue Mariazé, 97600 Mamoudzou; tel. 61-12-54; fax 60-92-85; e-mail de-mayotte@equipement.gouv.fr.

Department of Work, Employment and Training: BP 174, pl. Mariazé, 97600 Mamoudzou; tel. 61-16-57; fax 61-03-37; e-mail dtefp@wanadoo.fr.

Department of Youth and Sports: BP 94, rue Mariazé, 97600 Mamoudzou; tel. 61-10-87; fax 61-01-26; e-mail mayotte.djs@wanadoo.fr.

Conseil Général

Conseil Général, BP 101, 108 rue de l'Hôpital, 97600 Mamoudzou; tel. 61-12-33; fax 61-10-18; e-mail conseil-general-de-mayotte@wanadoo.fr.

The Conseil général comprises 19 members. At elections held on 21 and 28 March 2004, the Union pour un mouvement populaire (UMP) won eight seats in alliance with the Mouvement populaire mahorais (MPM), which secured one seat, while the Mouvement départementaliste mahorais (MDM) and the Mouvement des citoyens (MDC), also in alliance, obtained five and two seats, respectively; independent candidates were elected to the remaining three seats.

President: Saïd Omar Ali (Independent).

Political Organizations

Fédération de Mayotte de l'Union pour un Mouvement Populaire (UMP): Route nationale, Immeuble "Jardin Créole", 97600 Mamoudzou; tel. 61-64-64; fax 60-87-89; e-mail ahamed.attoumani@wanadoo.fr ; centre-right; local branch of the metropolitan party; Sec.-Gen. Mansour Kamardine; Departmental Sec. Ahamed Attoumani.

Fédération du Front National: Route Nationale 1, M'tsahara, 97630 M'tzamboro; BP 1331, 97600 Mamoudzou Cédex; tel. and fax 60-50-24; e-mail fatna@frontnational.com; Regional Sec. Huguette Fatna.

Fédération du mouvement national républicain (MNR) de Mayotte: 15 rue des Réfugiers, 97615 Pamandzi; tel. 60-33-21; fax 60-33-21; Departmental Sec. Abdou Mihidjay.

Mouvement de la Gauche Ecologiste de Mayotte: 33 ave des Jardins, Localité de Pamandzi, 97600 Pamandzi, Mayo; tel. 61-09-70; fax 61-09-70; internet www.lesverts.fr; fmrly Les verts Mayotte; affiliated to Mouvement de la gauche réunionnaise; Gen. Sec. Ahamada Salime.

Mouvement Départementaliste Mahorais (MDM): 97610 Dzaoudzi; f. 1999 by former members of the MPM; seeks full overseas departmental status for Mayotte; Leader Younoussa Ben Ali.

Mouvement des Citoyens (MDC): Chirongui; Leader Ali Halifa.

Mouvement Populaire Mahorais (MPM): 97610 Dzaoudzi; seeks departmental status for Mayotte; Leader Younoussa Bamana.

Parti Socialiste (PS): Dzaoudzi; local branch of the French party of the same name; Leader Ibrahim Aboubacar.

Judicial System

Palais de Justice: BP 106 (Kawéni), 12 rue de l'Hôpital, 97600 Mamoudzou; tel. 61-11-15; fax 61-19-63.

Tribunal Supérieur d'Appel

16 rue de l'Hôpital, BP 106, 97600 Mamoudzou; tel. 61-11-15; fax 61-19-63.

Pres. Jean-Baptiste Flori; Prosecutor Jean-Louis Bec.

Procureur de la République: Jean-Louis Bec.

Tribunal de Première Instance: Pres. Alain Chateauneuf.

Religion

Muslims comprise about 98% of the population. Most of the remainder are Christians, mainly Roman Catholics.

CHRISTIANITY

The Roman Catholic Church

Mayotte is within the jurisdiction of the Apostolic Administrator of the Comoros.

Office of the Apostolic Administrator: BP 1012, 97600 Mamoudzou; tel. and fax 61-11-53.

The Press

Flash-Infos: BP 60, 97600 Mamoudzou; tel. 61-54-45; fax 61-54-47; e-mail flash-infos@wanadoo.fr; daily e-mail bulletin; Dir Laurent Canavate.

Mayotte Hebdo: BP 60, 97600 Mamoudzou; tel. 61-20-04; fax 60-35-90; e-mail mayotte.hebdo@wanadoo.fr; weekly; Dir Laurent Canavate; circ. 2,000.

Tounda: BP 60, 97600 Mamoudzou; tel. 61-20-04; fax 60-35-90; e-mail tounda@mayottehebdo.com; weekly; culture and leisure; Dir Laurent Canavate; circ. 5,000.

Broadcasting and Communications

TELECOMMUNICATIONS

France Télécom Mayotte: Résidence Allamanda, rue de la Grande Traversée, 97600 Mamoudzou; tel. 61-00-14; fax 61-19-02; e-mail richard.roques@francetelecom.com.

RADIO AND TELEVISION

Réseau France Outre-mer (RFO): BP 103, 1 rue du Jardin, 97615 Pamandzi; tel. 60-10-17; fax 60–16–06; e-mail annick.henry@rfo.fr; internet www.rfo.fr; fmrly Société Nationale de Radio-Télévision Française d'Outre-mer; f. 1977; govt-owned; radio broadcasts in French and more than 70% in Mahorian; television transmissions began in 1986; a satellite service was launched in 2000; Regional Dir Laurence Mayerfeld.

Finance

BANKS

Issuing Authority

Institut d'Emission d'Outre-mer: BP 500, ave de la Préfecture, 97600 Mamoudzou; tel. 61-05-05; fax 61-05-02; e-mail iedom.mayotte@wanadoo.fr; Dir Max Remblin.

Commercial Banks

Banque Française Commerciale Océan Indien: Pl. du Marché, BP 222, 97600 Mamoudzou; tel. 61-10-91; fax 61-17-40; e-mail mayotte@bfcoi.com; internet www.bfcoi.com; f. 1976; jtly owned by Société Générale and Mauritius Commercial Bank Ltd; Pres. Gérald Lacaze; Dir Gen Jean-Marie d'Espagnac; br. at Dzaoudzi.

Banque de la Réunion: 30 pl. Mariage, 97600 Mamoudzou; tel. 61-20-30; fax 61-20-28; 3 brs.

BRED Banque Populaire: Centre d'Affaires Mayotte, pl. Mariage, Z.I. 3, 97600 Mamoudzou; tel. 90-71-60; fax 90-29-57.

INSURANCE

AGF: BP 184, pl. Mariage, 97600 Mamoudzou; tel. 61-44-33; fax 61-14-89; e-mail jl.henry@wanadoo.fr; Gen. Man. Jean-Luc Henry.

Groupama: BP 665, Z.I. Nel, Lot 7, 97600 Mamoudzou; tel. 62-59-92; fax 60-76-08; e-mail groupama.assurance.mayotte@wanadoo.fr.

Prudence Créole: BP 480, Immeuble Sana, rue du Commerce, 97600 Mamoudzou; tel. 61-11-10; fax 61-11-21; e-mail prudencecreolemayotte@wanadoo.fr; 87% owned by Groupe Générali; 2 brs.

Vectra Paic Océan Indien: BP 65, 55 champs des Ylangs, 97680 Combani; tel. 62-44-54; fax 62-46-97; e-mail cfonteneau@wanadoo.fr.

Trade and Industry

DEVELOPMENT ORGANIZATION

Agence Française de Développement (AFD): Ave de la Préfecture, BP 500, 97600 Mamoudzou; tel. 61-05-05; fax 61-05-02; e-mail afd.mayotte@wanadoo.fr; internet www.afd.fr; Dir Jean-François Hoarau.

EMPLOYERS' ORGANIZATIONS

Mouvement des Entreprises de France Mayotte (MEDEF): Z.I. de Kaouéni, Immeuble GMOI, BP 570, 97600 Mamoudzou; tel. 61-44-22; fax 61-46-10; e-mail contact@medef-mayotte.com; internet www.medef-mayotte.com; Pres. SERGE CASTEL.

Ordre National des Médecins: BP 675 Kaweni, 97600 Mamoudzou; tel. 61-02-47; fax 61-36-61.

UTILITIES

Electricity

Electricité de Mayotte (EDM): BP 333, Z.I. Kawéni, 97600 Kawéni; tel. 61-44-44; fax 60-10-92; e-mail edm.mayotte@wanadoo.fr; f. 1997; subsidiary of SAUR.

Water

Syndicat des Eaux: BP 289, 97600 Mamoudzou; tel. 62-11-11; fax 62-10-31.

TRADE UNIONS

Confédération Inter-Syndicale de Mayotte (CISMA—CFDT): 18 rue Mahabou, BP 1038, 97600 Mamoudzou; tel. 61-12-38; fax 61-36-16; f. 1993; affiliated to the Confédération Française Démocratique du Travail; Gen. Sec. SAÏD BOINALI.

Fédération Départementale des Syndicats d'Exploitants Agricoles de Mayotte (FDSEA): 150 rue Mbalamanga-Mtsapéré, 97600 Mamoudzou; tel. 61-34-83; fax 61-34-83; e-mail fdsea.mayotte@wanadoo.fr; affiliated to the Fédération Nationale des Syndicats d'Exploitants; Pres. AMBODY ALI; Dir. MOUHTAR RACHIDE.

Transport

ROADS

In 1998 the road network totalled approximately 230 km, of which 90 km were main roads.

SHIPPING

Coastal shipping is provided by locally owned small craft. There is a deep-water port at Longoni.

Service des Affaires Maritimes Mayotte: BP 37, 97615 Pamandzi; tel. 60-31-38; fax 60-31-39; e-mail sam-mayotte@equipement.gouv.fr; Head of Service MATTHIEU LE GUERN.

Service des Transports Maritimes (STM): BP 186, 97610 Dzaoudzi; tel. 60-10-69; fax 60-80-25; e-mail info@mayotte-stm.com; internet www.mayotte-stm.com; Dir MICHEL KERAMBRUN; 8 vessels; 218 employees.

CIVIL AVIATION

There is an airport at Dzaoudzi, serving four-times weekly commercial flights to Réunion, twice-weekly services to Madagascar, Njazidja, Nzwani and Mwali, and weekly services to Kenya and Mozambique. The proposed establishment of Air Mayotte International in early 2002 was expected to improve transport links to Réunion, Mauritius, the Seychelles and the Comoros; however, the project was abandoned in September 2004. In January 2004 plans were approved for the construction a new runway to allow the commencement of direct flights to Paris.

Air Austral: Pl. Mariage, BP 1429, 97600 Mamoudzou; tel. 60-90-90; fax 61-61-94; e-mail mayotte@air-austral.com; internet www.air-austral.com; Pres. GÉRARD ETHÈVE.

Tourism

Tropical scenery provides the main tourist attraction. Excluding cruise-ship passengers, Mayotte received 23,000 visitors in 2003, and tourism receipts totalled €12.3m. in that year. In 2002 there were nine hotels with some 350 rooms.

Comité du Tourisme de Mayotte: rue de la Pompe, BP 1169, 97600 Mamoudzou; tel. 61-09-09; fax 61-03-46; e-mail info@mayotte-tourisme.com; internet www.mayotte-tourisme.com; Dir GEORGE MECS.

French Overseas Territories

The two Overseas Territories (Territoires d'outre-mer) are the French Southern and Antarctic Territories and the Wallis and Futuna Islands. They are integral parts of the French Republic. Each Territory is administered by a High Commissioner or Chief Administrator, who is appointed by the French Government. Each permanently inhabited Territory also has a Territorial Assembly or Congress, elected by universal adult suffrage. Certain members of

the Territorial Assembly or Congress sit in the French Assemblée nationale and in the Sénat in Paris. The Territories have varying degrees of internal autonomy. French Polynesia was formerly an Overseas Territory, but, following the promulgation, in February 2004, of legislation providing for autonomy, it formally assumed the status of an Overseas Country (Pays d'outre-mer) within the French Republic.

FRENCH SOUTHERN AND ANTARCTIC TERRITORIES

Introduction

The French Southern and Antarctic Territories (Terres australes et antarctiques françaises) form an Overseas Territory but are administered under a special statute. The territory comprises Adélie Land, a narrow segment of the mainland of Antarctica together with a number of offshore islets, and three groups of sub-Antarctic islands (the Kerguelen and Crozet Archipelagos and Saint-Paul and Amsterdam Islands) in the southern Indian Ocean.

Under the terms of legislation approved by the French Government on 6 August 1955, the French Southern and Antarctic Territories were placed under the authority of a chief administrator, responsible to the government member responsible for Overseas Departments and Territories. The Chief Administrator is assisted by a Consultative Council, which meets at least twice annually. The Council is composed of seven members who are appointed for five years by the Minister of Defence and the government member responsible for Overseas Departments and Territories (from among members of the Office of Scientific Research and from those who have participated in scientific missions in the sub-Antarctic islands and Adélie Land) and by other designated ministers. Under the terms of a decree promulgated in February 1997, administration of the French Southern and Antarctic Territories was formally transferred from Paris to Saint-Pierre, Réunion, in April 2000.

From 1987 certain categories of vessels were allowed to register under the flag of the Kerguelen Archipelago, provided that 25% of their crew (including the captain and at least two officers) were French. These specifications were amended to 35% of the crew and at least four officers in April 1990. Following an initial proposal in April 2003, negotiations were ongoing in early 2005 to replace the so-called 'Kerguelen Register' with a new French International Register whereby, *inter alia*, the stipulated quota of French crew members would be reduced. At 31 December 2003 there were 116 registered vessels.

In 1992 the French Government created a Public Interest Group, the Institut Français pour la Recherche et la Technologie Polaires (IFRTP), to assume responsibility for the organization of scientific and research programmes in the French Southern and Antarctic Territories. The IFRTP was renamed the Institut Polaire Français Paul Emile Victor (IPEV) in January 2002. France is a signatory to the Antarctic Treaty (see p. 529).

Fishing for crayfish and Patagonian toothfish in the territories' 200-nautical mile Exclusive Economic Zone is strictly regulated by quotas (see Statistical Survey). During 2004/05 eight vessels were licensed to fish in the EEZ; of these seven were included on the Kerguelen Register. Limited numbers of tourists have since 1994 been permitted to visit Crozet, Kerguelen and Amsterdam: about 60 tourists travel to the territories each year aboard the supply and oceanographic vessel *Marion Dufresne II*.

Statistical Survey

Area (sq km): Kerguelen Archipelago 7,215, Crozet Archipelago 515, Amsterdam Island 58, Saint-Paul Island 8, Adélie Land (Antarctica) 432,000.

Population (the population, comprising members of scientific missions, fluctuates according to season, being higher in the summer; the figures given are approximate): Kerguelen Archipelago, Port-aux-Français 80; Amsterdam Island at Martin de Viviès 30; Adélie Land at Base Dumont-d'Urville 27; the Crozet Archipelago at Alfred Faure (on Ile de la Possession) 35; Saint-Paul Island is uninhabited. Total population (April 2000): 172.

Fishing (catch quotas in metric tons, 2004/05): Crayfish (spiny lobsters) in Amsterdam and St Paul: 380; Patagonian toothfish (caught by French and foreign fleets) in the Kerguelen and Crozet Archipelagos: 6,050.

Currency: French currency was used until the end of 2001. Euro notes and coins were introduced on 1 January 2002, and the euro became the sole legal tender from 18 February. For details of exchange rates, see French Guiana.

Budget: Projected at €163.2m. in 2002, of which official subventions comprised €45.2m.

External Trade: Exports consist mainly of crayfish and other fish to France and Réunion. The Territories also derive revenue from the sale of postage stamps and other philatelic items.

Directory

Government: e-mail taaf.com@wanadoo.fr; internet www.taaf.fr. the central administration is in Saint-Pierre, Réunion.
Prefect, Chief Administrator Michel Champon.

Consultative Council: Pres. JEAN-PIERRE CHARPENTIER.

Institut Polaire Français Paul Emile Victor (IPEV): Technopôle de Brest-Iroise, BP 75, 29280 Plouzané, France; tel. 2-98-05-65-00; fax 2-98-05-65-55; e-mail infoipev@ipev.fr; internet www.ipev/fr; f. 1992 as Institut Français pour la Recherche et la Technologie Polaires, name changed 2002; Dir GÉRARD JUGIE.

Transport:
An oceanographic and supply vessel, the *Marion Dufresne II*, operated by the French Government, provides regular links between Réunion and the sub-Antarctic islands. Another specialized vessel, the *Astrolabe*, owned by the Groupe Bourbon and operating from Hobart, Tasmania, calls five times a year at the Antarctic mainland.

Research Stations:
There are meteorological stations and geophysical research stations on Kerguelen, Amsterdam, Adélie Land and Crozet. Research in marine microbiology is conducted from the Crozet and Kerguelen Archipelagos, and studies of atmospheric pollution are carried out on Amsterdam Island. The French atomic energy authority, the Commissariat à l'énergie atomique, also maintains a presence on Crozet, Kerguelen and Adélie Land.

WALLIS AND FUTUNA ISLANDS

Introductory Survey

Location, Climate, Language, Religion, Capital

The Territory of Wallis and Futuna comprises two groups of islands: the Wallis Islands, including Wallis Island (also known as Uvea) and 10 islets *(motu)* on the surrounding reef, and Futuna (or Hooru) to the south-west, comprising the two small islands of Futuna and Alofi. The islands are located north-east of Fiji and west of Samoa. Temperatures are generally between about 23°C (73°F) and 30°C (86°F), and there is a cyclone season between December and March. French and the indigenous Polynesian languages Wallisian (Uvean) and Futunian are spoken in the Territory. Nearly all of the population is nominally Roman Catholic. The capital is Mata'Utu, on Wallis Island.

Recent History

The Wallis and Futuna Islands were settled first by Polynesian peoples, Wallis from Tonga and Futuna from Samoa. Futuna was subsequently discovered by the Dutch navigators, Schouten and Le Maire, in 1616, and Uvea was discovered by Samuel Wallis in 1767. Three kingdoms later emerged, and in 1837 the first Marist missionaries arrived. By 1842 the majority of the population had been converted to Christianity. In April 1842 the authorities requested French protection, coinciding with a similar proclamation in Tahiti (now French Polynesia). In 1851 a *fakauvea* war between the Catholic majority and the Methodist minority assisted by Tonga (which had commenced in 1843) came to an end when 500 Wallisians left for Tonga. Protectorate status was formalized in 1887 for Wallis and in 1888 for the two kingdoms of Futuna, but domestic law remained in force. The islands were never formally annexed, and nor were French law or representative institutions introduced, although Wallis and Futuna were treated as a dependency of New Caledonia. During the Second World War, Wallis was used as an airforce base by the USA. In 1959 the traditional Kings and chiefs requested integration into the French Republic. The islands formally became an Overseas Territory in July 1961, following a referendum in December 1959, in which 94.4% of the electorate requested this status (almost all the opposition was in Futuna, which itself recorded dissent from only 22.2% of the voters; Wallis was unanimous in its acceptance).

Although there was no movement in Wallis and Futuna seeking secession of the Territory from France (in contrast with the situation in the other French Pacific Territories, French Polynesia and New Caledonia), the two Kings whose kingdoms share the island of Futuna requested in November 1983, through the Territorial Assembly, that the island groups of Wallis and Futuna become separate Overseas Territories of France, arguing that the administration and affairs of the Territory had become excessively concentrated on Uvea (Wallis Island).

At elections to the 20-member Territorial Assembly in March 1982, the Rassemblement pour la République (RPR) and its allies won 11 seats, while the remaining nine were secured by candidates belonging to, or associated with, the Union pour la Démocratie Française (UDF). Later that year one member of the Lua Kae Tahi, a group affiliated to the metropolitan UDF, defected to the RPR group. In November 1983, however, three of the 12 RPR members joined the Lua Kae Tahi, forming a new majority. In the subsequent election for President of the Territorial Assembly, this 11-strong bloc of UDF-associated members supported the ultimately successful candidate, Falakiko Gata, even though he had been elected to the Territorial Assembly in 1982 as a member of the RPR.

In April 1985 Falakiko Gata formed a new political party, the Union Populaire Locale (UPL), which was committed to giving priority to local, rather than metropolitan, issues.

In 1987 a dispute broke out between two families both laying claim to the throne of Sigave, the northern kingdom on the island of Futuna. The conflict arose following the deposition of the former King, Sagato Keletaona, and his succession by Sosefo Vanaï. The intervention of the island's administrative authorities, who attempted to ratify Vanaï's accession to the throne, was condemned by the Keletaona family as an interference in the normal course of local custom, according to which such disputes are traditionally settled by a fight between the protagonists.

At elections to the Territorial Assembly held in March 1987, the UDF (together with affiliated parties) and the RPR each won seven seats. However, by forming an alliance with the UPL, the RPR maintained its majority, and Falakiko Gata was subsequently re-elected President. At elections to the French National Assembly in June 1988, Benjamin Brial was re-elected Deputy. However, when the result was challenged by an unsuccessful candidate, Kamilo Gata, the election was investigated by the French Constitutional Council and the result declared invalid, owing to electoral irregularities. When the election was held again in January 1989, Kamilo Gata was elected Deputy, obtaining 57.4% of total votes.

Statistical information, gathered in 1990, showed that the emigration rate of Wallis and Futuna islanders had risen to over 50%. In October of that year 13,705 people (of whom 97% were Wallisians and Futunians) lived in the Territory, while 14,186 were resident in New Caledonia. At the 1996 census the number of Wallisians and Futunians resident in New Caledonia had increased to 17,563. According to the results, a proportion of the islanders had chosen to emigrate to other French Overseas Possessions or to metropolitan France. The principal reason for the increase was thought to be the lack of employment opportunities in the islands.

At elections to the Territorial Assembly in March 1992 the newly founded Taumu'a Lelei secured 11 seats, while the RPR won nine. The new Assembly was remarkable for being the first since 1964 in which the RPR did not hold a majority. At elections to the French National Assembly in March 1993, Kamilo Gata was re-elected Deputy, obtaining 52.4% of total votes cast to defeat Clovis Logologofolau. In June 1994 the Union Locale Force Ouvrière organized a general strike in protest at the increasing cost of living in the Territory and the allegedly inadequate education system. It was reported that demonstrations continued for several days, during which the Territorial Assembly building was damaged in an arson attack.

In October 1994 it was reported that the King of Sigave, Lafaele Malau, had been deposed by a unanimous decision of the kingdom's chiefs. The action followed the appointment of two customary leaders to represent the Futunian community in New Caledonia, which had led to unrest among the inhabitants of Sigave. He was succeeded by Esipio Takasi.

At elections to the Territorial Assembly in December 1994 the RPR secured 10 seats, while a coalition group, Union Populaire pour Wallis et Futuna (UPWF), won seven, and independent candidates three. Mikaele Tauhavili was subsequently elected President of the Assembly.

The refusal by 10 of the 20 members of the Territorial Assembly to adopt budgetary proposals in January 1996, led to appeals for the dissolution of the Government by France and the organization of new elections. The budget (which, at US $20m., was some $4.5m. smaller than the previous year) aroused opposition for its apparent lack of provision for development funds, particularly for the islands' nascent tourist industry.

Elections to the Territorial Assembly took place on 16 March 1997. A participation rate of 87.2% was recorded at the poll, in which RPR candidates secured 14 seats and left-wing candidates (including independents and members of various political groupings) won six seats. Victor Brial, a representative of the RPR, was elected President of the Territorial Assembly. At the second round of elections to the French National Assembly, on 1 June, Brial defeated Kamilo Gata, obtaining 3,241 votes (51.3% of the total).

Allegations that electoral irregularities had occurred in the elections to the Territorial Assembly of March 1997 were investigated and upheld for 11 of the seats. As a result, new elections were organized for the 11 seats on 6 September 1998, at which the RPR's representation in the Assembly was reduced to 11 seats overall, while left-wing and independent members increased their share of seats to nine. Also in September 1998, in a second round of voting, Fr Robert Laufoaulu was elected to the French Senate, defeating Kamilo Gata in a vote by the Territorial Assembly. Laufoaulu, a priest and director of Catholic education in the islands, stood as a left-wing candidate, nominated by RPR candidates, but was elected with the support of right-wing politicians.

In late March 1999 festivities were held to commemorate the 40th anniversary of the accession of the King of Wallis Island, Lavelua Tomasi Kulimoetoke. From March 2000 delegations from Wallis and Futuna visited New Caledonia to discuss mutual arrangements concerning free trade and employment rights between the two Territories.

In January 2001 two candidates of the RPR contested the presidency of the Territorial Assembly. Patalione Kanimoa was elected by the majority of the RPR (eight votes) and of the UPWF (four votes). Soane Muni Uhila, the previous President of the Territorial Assembly, then formed a new party, La Voix des Peuples Wallisiens et Futuniens, along with five other RPR dissidents. The new majority RPR-UPWF grouping elected Albert Likuvalu (of the UPWF) president of the permanent commission.

In June 2001 senior officials from Wallis and Futuna and from New Caledonia agreed on a project to redefine their bilateral relationship under the Nouméa Accord on greater autonomy, signed in 1998. The Accord gave the New Caledonian authorities the power to control immigration from Wallis and Futuna; following decades of migration, the population of Wallis and Futuna was 15,000, while the number of migrants and descendants from the islands in New Caledonia had risen to 20,000. In exchange for controlling immigration, New Caledonia stated that it would make a financial contribution to economic development in Wallis and Futuna. The Nouméa Accord also called for a separate arrangement allowing for open access to New Caledonia for residents of Wallis and Futuna. The French State was to address the issue of financial aid before the two territories' assemblies approved the arrangement.

In January 2002 a delegation from Wallis and Futuna met President Jacques Chirac in Paris to discuss the situation of members of their community living in New Caledonia. Under the Nouméa Accord, New Caledonia was to have signed a separate agreement with Wallis and Futuna better to define the islanders' status, with particular regard to the job market.

A general election was held on 10 March 2002 for the 20 seats of the Territorial Assembly. The RPR won 12 of the seats, whilst socialist candidates, or affiliated independents, won eight. An unprecedented 82.7% of some 9,500 registered voters cast their vote. The election campaign was the first to give parties coverage on television and radio, provided by the national broadcasting company. The territory's only newspaper, Te-Fenua Fo'ou, ceased publication in April 2002, following a dispute over the King of Wallis's alleged support for an electoral candidate, Make Pilioko. The paper contested that Pilioko, a former member of the Territorial Assembly, was unfit for office, having been convicted in 1999 of misuse of public funds. The publisher and editor of the newspaper, respectively Michel Boudineau and Laurent Gourlez (both of whom were French), were summoned before the King and ordered not to publish any further articles on the matter. However, the paper asserted its right to freedom of expression and, in defiance of the King, printed and distributed its next edition from New Caledonia. The police subsequently removed computers and other equipment from the newspaper's office in Mata'Utu. Boudineau filed a complaint with the French authorities for theft and obstruction of press freedom but was forced to close the paper and to dismiss its staff.

At elections to the National Assembly in June 2002, Victor Brial, representing a coalition of the Union pour la Majorité Présidentielle (subsequently Union pour un Mouvement Populaire—UMP) and the RPR, was re-elected as the Territory's deputy to the French legislature, winning 50.4% of the votes cast in the first round. However, in December the Constitutional Council ruled that the result was invalid as certain ballot papers had been improperly marked; Brial subsequently won the by-election in March 2003. Meanwhile, Christian Job replaced Alain Waquet as Chief Administrator of the islands in August 2002. In late November 2002 Soane Patita Maituka was enthroned as King of Alo following the deposition of Sagato Alofi in the previous month. In December the French Senate approved a bill providing for a constitutional amendment that would allow Wallis and Futuna (along with French Polynesia) to become an Overseas Country; both houses of the National Assembly in Paris ratified the amendments to the Constitution in March 2003. In July of that year, during an official visit to the neighbouring Overseas Country of New Caledonia, President Chirac received a delegation from Wallis and Futuna.

In October 2003 Pasilio Keletaona was deposed as King of Sigave by members of his own clan. He was succeeded in mid-March 2004 by Visesio Moeliku. In December 2003 the President of New Caledonia signed a special accord governing relations between France, New Caledonia and Wallis and Futuna. The signing of the accord, which had been agreed two years previously in an attempt to address the situation of the 20,000 Wallis and Futuna islanders permanently resident in New Caledonia, had been delayed by the continuing ethnic tensions there. Under the agreement, Wallis and Futuna and New Caledonia were henceforth to deliver separate public services. Concerns had been raised by the former's increasing debt (estimated to total 2,500m. francs CFP) to the Government of New Caledonia, a major creditor being the New Caledonian hospital. It was therefore hoped that Wallis and Futuna would become more self-sufficient in the areas of health and secondary education and that the islanders would be encouraged to remain on Wallis and Futuna, while those already settled in New Caledonia would become more integrated.

Between February and April 2003 the postal service was affected by strike action, which was resolved in favour of the striking workers. During May–June 2004 a strike prevented television and radio transmissions from the territory's main broadcasting company, and again the dispute was resolved in favour of the striking employees, whose demands included the resignation of the station manager.

In January 2005 Xavier de Furst replaced Christian Job as Chief Administrator of the islands. In February Albert Likuvalu, representing the newly formed Alliance grouping, a coalition of UDF members and left-wing independents, was elected President of the Territorial Assembly by 11 votes to nine, replacing Patalione Kanimoa of the Union pour un Mouvement Populaire (UMP) grouping. The Alliance comprised three members of the UDF and two left-wing ministers, including Likuvalu himself; they were supported by the UPWF grouping.

Government

The Territory of Wallis and Futuna is administered by a representative of the French Government, the Chief Administrator, who is assisted by the Territorial Assembly. The Assembly has 20 members and is elected for a five-year term. The three traditional kingdoms, from which the Territory was formed, one on Wallis and two sharing Futuna, have equal rights, although the kings' powers are limited. In addition, the Territory elects one Deputy to the French National Assembly in Paris and one representative to the French Senate. The islands may also be represented at the European Parliament.

Economic Affairs

In 1995 it was estimated that Wallis and Futuna's gross domestic product (GDP) was US $28.7m., equivalent to some $2,000 per head. Most monetary income in the islands is derived from government employment (accounting for three out of every four employees at September 2003) and remittances sent home by islanders employed in New Caledonia and Metropolitan France.

Agricultural activity is of a subsistence nature. Yams, taro, bananas, cassava and other food crops are also cultivated. Tobacco is grown for local consumption. In 1998 almost all the cultivated vegetation on the island of Wallis, notably the banana plantations, was destroyed by a cyclone. In response to the cyclone damage, the French Government provided exceptional aid of 80m. francs CFP to alleviate the situation. An estimated 25,000 pigs a year are reared on the islands. Three units rear 800, 500 and 450 hens a year respectively, which are used principally for eggs, and meet an estimated 80% of the territory's commercial needs. Apiculture was revived in 1996, and in 2000 honey production was sufficient to meet the demands of the local market. Fishing activity in the Territory's exclusive economic zone increased during the 1990s; the total catch was estimated at 300 metric tons in 2001, compared with 70 tons in 1991. The Territorial Assembly accorded Japan deep-water fishing rights to catch 3,000 tons of fish a year in the islands' exclusive economic zone, a broad area of 200 miles (370 km) around Wallis and Futuna over which France exerts sovereignty.

Mineral fuels are the main source of electrical energy, although it is hoped that hydroelectric power can be developed, especially on Futuna. There is a 4,000-kW thermal power station on Wallis, and a 2,600-kW thermal power station was completed on Futuna in 2000. The hydroelectric power station on Futuna (Vainifao) provided 10% of the production needed. Total electricity output in 2003 reached almost 4.8m. kWh.

There were 291 businesses in the Territory in 2000, of which 24 were in the industrial and artisanal sector, 68 in construction and 199 in the service and commercial sectors; 47 of those businesses were located on Futuna. A new commercial centre opened in Wallis in 2002. In August 1989 a new earth station for satellite communications was inaugurated. The islands also benefited from an increase in building activity and public works in the early 1990s. The tourism sector, however, is very limited. In 2002 Wallis had four hotels and Futuna two. In September 2004 the Territory established its own airline, Air Wallis, as a joint venture between government and local private investors. Previously the country had been served only by Aircalin, and it was hoped that competition would lead to a reduction in the price of air fares. The inaugural flight—to New Caledonia—was scheduled to take place in January 2005; other destinations were to include Vanuatu, Fiji and French Polynesia.

In 2000 the cost of the islands' imports reached 4,735.7m. francs CFP. Road vehicles, parts and accessories accounted for 10.0% of the total value of imports, followed by mineral fuels and products (9.8%), electrical machinery and sound and television apparatus (7.4%) and meat products (6.4%). Exports totalled only 22.4m. francs CFP. Traditional food products, mother of pearl (from the Trochus shell) and handicrafts are the only significant export commodities. Exports of copra from Wallis ceased in 1950, and from Futuna in the early 1970s. The principal sources of imports in 2000 were France, which supplied 28.7% of the total, and Australia (22.6%). Most of the islands' exports were purchased by Italy. In August 2001 the frequency of supplies to Wallis and Futuna was significantly improved when the Sofrana shipping company, based in Auckland, began operating a new route linking New Zealand, Tonga and the Samoas to Wallis and Futuna.

French aid to Wallis and Futuna totalled 7,048m. francs CFP in 1999, increasing to 10,329m. francs CFP in 2002. The islands' budgetary expenditure in 2001 totalled an estimated US $25.0m. Budgetary aid from France was to rise from €83,178m. in 2001 to €86,610m. in 2002. The territorial budget in 2003 totalled 3,087.3m. francs CFP.

The annual rate of inflation in 1989–2002 averaged 1.5%. The rate of inflation in 2003 reached 1.8%. In July 2001 the islands' Chief Administrator acknowledged that the minimum wage (of 58,178 francs CFP per month) had not been revised since July 1998. He therefore announced that the monthly minimum wage was to be raised to 70,000 francs CFP by July 2002; the increase was to be implemented in three stages. A rise in the cost of living was expected to follow.

The Territory of Wallis and Futuna forms part of the Franc Zone (see p. 266). Although France is also a member of the organization, Wallis and Futuna has membership in its own right of the Pacific Community (see p. 337), which is based in New Caledonia and provides technical advice, training and assistance in economic, cultural and social development to the region.

In November 1999 the Territory signed a co-operation agreement with the European Union (EU). Under the agreement Wallis and Futuna was to receive francs CFP 768m. from the European Development Fund over the following six years; of this, 382m. was allocated for improving port infrastructure and 346m. for environmental protection. In mid-2003 the National Assembly approved the Overseas Territories Development Bill, which would provide support for economic and social development in Wallis and Futuna (together with French Polynesia and New Caledonia) by attracting foreign investment, and among other benefits allow for overseas French residents to travel to mainland France to take advantage of free education. Discussions began in December 2004 regarding the replacement of the franc CFP with the euro. If consensus could be reached by Wallis and Futuna, New Caledonia and French Polynesia, the introduction of the new currency was anticipated by January 2007.

Education

The Catholic Mission is responsible for state primary education; secondary education is entirely within the state system. In 2002/03 there were 19 state-financed primary schools (including three pre-primary, 14 primary and two homecraft centres), with an enrolment of 2,938 pupils at the 14 primary schools, and seven secondary schools (including two vocational schools) in Wallis and Futuna, with a total of 2,293 pupils. In 1999/2000 361 students attended various universities overseas.

Public Holidays

2005: 1 January (New Year's Day), 5 March (Missionary Day), 28 March (Easter Monday), 1 May (Labour Day), 5 May (Ascension Day), 8 May (Liberation Day), 15 May (Whit Monday), 14 July (Fall of the Bastille), 8 September (Internal Autonomy Day), 24 September (anniversary of possession by France), 1 November (All Saints' Day), 11 November (Armistice Day), 25 December (Christmas Day).

2006: 1 January (New Year's Day), 5 March (Missionary Day), 17 April (Easter Monday), 1 May (Labour Day), 8 May (Liberation Day), 25 May (Ascension Day), 5 June (Whit Monday), 14 July (Fall of the Bastille), 8 September (Internal Autonomy Day), 24 September (anniversary of possession by France), 1 November (All Saints' Day), 11 November (Armistice Day), 25 December (Christmas Day).

Weights and Measures

The metric system is in force.

Statistical Survey

Source (unless otherwise indicated): Service Territorial de la Statistique et des Etudes Economiques, Centre de Havelu, Mata'Utu, 98600 Uvea, Wallis Islands, Wallis and Futuna, via Nouméa, New Caledonia; tel. and fax 722403; e-mail stats@wallis .co.nc; internet www.wallis.co.nc/stats.

AREA AND POPULATION

Area (sq km): 160.5. *By Island:* Uvea (Wallis Island) 77.5; Other Wallis Islands 18.5; Futuna Island 45; Alofi Island 19.5.

Population: Total population 14,166 (males 6,984, females 7,182) at census of 1996; 17,563 Wallisians and Futunians resided in New Caledonia. *July 2003* (provisional census figures): Wallis Islands 10,071; Futuna Island 4,873 (Alo 2,993, Sigave 1,880); Total 14,944.

Density (provisional, census of July 2003): 93.1 per sq km.

Principal Town (provisional, census of July 2003): Mata'Utu (capital), population 1,191.

Births and Deaths (estimates, 2000): Birth rate 21.7 per 1,000; Death rate 5.6 per 1,000.

Expectation of Life (estimates, years at birth): 73.8 (males 73.2; females 74.4) in 1998.

Economically Active Population (salaried workers, 1996): 2,465 (males 1,397, females 1,068). *Unemployment* (persons actively seeking work, 2002): 456 (males 259, females 197). In addition, 46 persons were enrolled as trainees at the national employment training agency.

AGRICULTURE, ETC.

Principal Crops (FAO estimates, '000 metric tons, 2003): Cassava 2.4; Taro (coco yam) 1.6; Yams 0.5; Other roots and tubers 1.0; Coconuts 2.3; Vegetables 0.5; Bananas 4.1; Other fruits (excl. melons) 4.6. Source: FAO.

Livestock (FAO estimates, '000 head, year ending September 2003): Pigs 25; Goats 7; Chickens 63. Source: FAO.

Livestock Products (FAO estimates, metric tons, 2003): Pig meat 315; Goat meat 15; Poultry meat 46; Cows' milk 30; Hen eggs 33; Honey 11. Source: FAO.

Fishing (FAO estimates, metric tons, live weight, 2002): Total catch 300 (Marine fishes 294). Note: Figures exclude trochus shells (FAO estimate, metric tons): 25. Source: FAO.

INDUSTRY

Electricity Production ('000 kWh, net production, 2003): 4,778.

FINANCE

Currency and Exchange Rates: 100 centimes = 1 franc de la Communauté française du Pacifique (franc CFP or Pacific franc). *Sterling, Dollar and Euro Equivalents* (31 December 2004): £1 sterling = 169.21 francs CFP; US $1 = 87.61 francs CFP; €1 = 119.33 francs CFP; 1,000 francs CFP = £5.591 = $11.414 = €8.380. *Average Exchange Rate* (francs CFP per US $): 126.80 in 2002; 105.73 in 2003; 96.11 in 2004. Note: Until 31 December 1998 the value of the franc CFP was fixed at 5.5 French centimes (1 French franc = 18.1818 francs CFP). Since the introduction of the euro, on 1 January 1999, an official exchange rate of 1,000 francs CFP = €8.38 (€1 = 119.332 francs CFP) has been in operation. Accordingly, the value of the franc CFP has been adjusted to 5.4969 French centimes (1 French franc = 18.1920 francs CFP), representing a 'devaluation' of 0.056%.

Territorial Budget (million francs CFP): 3,271.1 in 2001; 3,388.6 in 2002; 3,087.7 in 2003 (provisional).

Public Expenditure (million francs CFP, 2003): Operational expenditure 6,616.0 (Agriculture and fisheries department 95.5, Education 4,629.3, Economy, finance and industry department 265.7, Interior and decentralization department 99.2, Justice 39.5, Overseas affairs 864.1, Transport and communications 10.9, Maritime department 0.8, Youth and sports department 49.1, Health and welfare 501.6, Labour 58.6, Environment 1.7); Investment expenditure 603.4; Special Treasury accounts 24.0; Extra-budgetary expenditure 16.1; Total expenditure 7,259.6.

Aid from France (million francs CFP, 2002): 10,329. Source: Institut d'Emission d'Outre-Mer.

Money Supply (million francs CFP at 30 Sept. 2001): Currency in circulation 759; Demand deposits 1,595; Total money 2,355. Source: Institut d'Emission d'Outre-Mer.

Cost of Living (Consumer Price Index; base: July–Sept. 1989 = 100): All items 120.7 in 2001; 123.6 in 2002; 125.8 in 2003.

EXTERNAL TRADE

Principal Commodities (million francs CFP): *Imports c.i.f.* (2000): Meat and edible meat offal 302.1; Preparations of meat, of fish or of crustaceans, molluscs or other aquatic invertebrates 178.2; Beverages, spirits and vinegar 199.0; Mineral fuels, mineral oils and products of their distillation; bituminous substances; mineral waxes 462.5; Articles of iron or steel 153.9; Boilers, machinery, mechanical appliances and parts 281.2; Electrical machinery, equipment and parts; sound and television apparatus 350.4; Road vehicles, parts and accessories 474.2; Total (incl. others) 4,735.7. *Exports f.o.b.* (2001): Preparations of molluscs and other aquatic invertebrates 0.3; Coral and shells 5.5; Braids and mats of vegetable material 0.9; Total 5.6.

Principal Trading Partners (million francs CFP): *Imports c.i.f.* (2003): Australia 1,051.7; Fiji 215.5; France (incl. Monaco) 1,371.4; Japan 161.3; New Caledonia 325.1; New Zealand 433.8; Spain 130.7; USA 103.6; Total (incl. others) 4,377.8. *Exports f.o.b.* (2001): Samoa 5.5; Japan 0.3; New Caledonia 0.9; Total 5.6.

TRANSPORT

Shipping: *Merchant Fleet* (31 December 2003): Vessels registered 4; displacement ('000 grt): 113.7. Source: Lloyd's Register-Fairplay, *World Fleet Statistics*.

Civil Aviation (2001): aircraft arrivals and departures 1,310; freight handled 131.1 metric tons; passenger arrivals and departures 32,445; mail loaded and unloaded 58.3 metric tons.

TOURISM

Visitors (1985): 400.

COMMUNICATIONS MEDIA

Telephones (2003): 1,683 main lines in use.

Facsimile Machines (1993): 90 in use (Source: UN, *Statistical Yearbook*).

Internet Users (2003): 384.

EDUCATION

Pre-primary (2002/03): 3 institutions.

Primary (2002/03): 14 institutions; 2,938 students (incl. pre-primary); 271 teachers.

Secondary (2002/03): 7 institutions (2 vocational); 2,293 students; 191 teachers.

Source: Vice-Rectorat de Wallis et Futuna.

Directory

The Constitution

The Territory of the Wallis and Futuna Islands is administered according to a statute of 1961, and subsidiary legislation, under the Constitution of the Fifth Republic. The Statute declares the Wallis and Futuna Islands to be an Overseas Territory of the French Republic, of which it remains an integral part. The Statute established an administration, a Council of the Territory, a Territorial Assembly and national representation. The administrative, political

and social evolution envisaged by, and enacted under, the Statute is intended to effect a smooth integration of the three customary kingdoms with the new institutions of the Territory. The Kings are assisted by ministers and the traditional chiefs. The Chief Administrator, appointed by the French Government, is the representative of the State in the Territory and is responsible for external affairs, defence, law and order, financial and educational affairs. The Chief Administrator is required to consult with the Council of the Territory, which has six members: three by right (the Kings of Wallis, Sigave and Alo) and three appointed by the Chief Administrator upon the advice of the Territorial Assembly. This Assembly assists in the administration of the Territory; there are 20 members elected on a common roll, on the basis of universal adult suffrage, for a term of up to five years. The Territorial Assembly elects, from among its own membership, a President to lead it. The Territory elects national representatives (one Deputy to the National Assembly, one Senator and one Economic and Social Councillor) and votes for representatives to the European Parliament in Strasbourg. In 2003 both the National Assembly and Senate in Paris ratified amendments to the Constitution providing for Wallis and Futuna (along with French Polynesia) to become an Overseas Country.

The Government

(April 2005)

Chief Administrator (Administrateur Supérieur): Xavier de Furst (appointed 15 December 2004).

CONSEIL DU TERRITOIRE

Chair: Chief Administrator.

Members by Right: King of Wallis, King of Sigave, King of Alo.

Appointed Members: Mikaele Halagahu (Faipule), Atoloto Uhila (Kulitea), Keleto Lakalaka (Sous réserves).

GOVERNMENT OFFICE

Government Headquarters: Bureau de l'Administrateur Supérieur, Havelu, BP 16, Mata'Utu, 98600 Uvea, Wallis Islands, Wallis and Futuna; tel. 722727; fax 722324; all departments.

Legislature

ASSEMBLÉE TERRITORIALE

The Territorial Assembly has 20 members and is elected for a five-year term. Within the Assembly, ministers may form political groupings of five members or more. These groupings are not necessarily formed along party lines, and alliances may be made in support of a common cause. The most recent general election took place on 10 March 2002, at which RPR candidates secured a total of 12 seats and various left-wing candidates (including independents) won eight seats.

President: Apeleto 'Albert' Likuvalu (Alliance).

Territorial Assembly: Assemblée Territoriale, Havelu, BP 31, Mata'Utu, 98600 Uvea, Wallis Islands, Wallis and Futuna; tel. 722504; fax 722054.

PARLEMENT

Deputy to the French National Assembly: Victor Brial (UMP).

Representative to the French Senate: Fr Robert Laufoaulu (UMP).

Social and Economic Adviser: (vacant).

The Kingdoms

WALLIS
(Capital: Mata'Utu on Uvea)

Lavelua, King of Wallis: Tomasi Kulimoetoke.

Council of Ministers: Prime Minister (Kivalu) and five other ministers; Kivalu Kamaliele Muliloto.

The Kingdom of Wallis is divided into three districts (Hihifo, Hahake, Mua), and its traditional hierarchy includes three district chiefs (Faipule) and 20 village chiefs (Pule).

SIGAVE
(Capital: Leava on Futuna)

Keletaona, King of Sigave: Visesio Moeliku.

Council of Ministers: six ministers, chaired by the King.

The Kingdom of Sigave is located in the north of the island of Futuna; there are five village chiefs.

ALO
(Capital: Ono on Futuna)

Tu'i Agaifo, King of Alo: SOANE PATITA MAITUKU.

Council of Ministers: five ministers, chaired by the King.

The Kingdom of Alo comprises the southern part of the island of Futuna and the entire island of Alofi. There are nine village chiefs.

Political Organizations

Alliance: c/o Assemblée Territoriale; f. 2005; coalition of UDF mems and left-wing independents; Pres. APITONE MUNIKIHAAFATA.

Taumu'a Lelei (Bright Future): c/o Assemblée Territoriale; f. 1992; Leader SOANE MUNI UHILA.

Union pour la Démocratie Française (UDF): c/o Assemblée Territoriale; centrist; based on Uvean (Wallis) support.

Union Populaire pour Wallis et Futuna (UPWF): c/o Assemblée Territoriale; affiliated to the Parti Socialiste of France in 1998; f. 1994; Leader KAMILO GATA.

Union pour un Mouvement Populaire (UMP): c/o Assemblée Territoriale; f. 2002; centre-right; local branch of the metropolitan party; includes fmr mems of the NI party; Territorial Leader CLOVIS LOGOLOGOFOLAU.

La Voix des Peuples Wallisiens et Futuniens: c/o Assemblée Territoriale; f. 2001 by dissident RPR mems.

Religion

Almost all of the inhabitants profess Christianity and are adherents of the Roman Catholic Church.

CHRISTIANITY

The Roman Catholic Church

The Territory comprises a single diocese, suffragan to the archdiocese of Nouméa (New Caledonia). The diocese estimated that there were 14,700 adherents (98% of the population) at 31 December 2002. The Bishop participates in the Catholic Bishops' Conference of the Pacific, currently based in Fiji.

Bishop of Wallis and Futuna: Mgr LOLESIO FUAHEA, Evêché Lano, BP G6, 98600 Mata'Utu, Uvea, Wallis Islands, Wallis and Futuna; tel. 722932; fax 722783; e-mail eveche.wallis@wallis.co.nc.

The Press

'Uvea Mo Futuna: Tuku'atu Ha'afuasia, Uvea, Wallis Islands, Wallis and Futuna; e-mail filihau@uvea-mo-futuna.com; internet www.uvea-mo-futuna.com; f. 2002; monthly; electronic; Editor FILIHAU ASI TAIATINI.

The territory's only newspaper, Te-Fenua Fo'ou, was forced to close in April 2002, following a dispute with the King of Wallis.

Broadcasting and Communications

TELECOMMUNICATIONS

France Telecom (FCR): Télécommunications extérieures de Wallis et Futuna, BP 54, 98600 Mata'Utu, Uvea, Wallis Islands, Wallis and Futuna; tel. 722436; fax 722255; e-mail admin@wallis.co .nc.

Service des Postes et Télécommunications: Administration Supérieure des Iles Wallis et Futuna, BP 00, 98600 Mata'Utu, Uvea, Wallis Islands, Wallis and Futuna; tel. 722121; fax 722500; e-mail ft .tui@wallis.co.nc.

BROADCASTING

Radio and Television

RFO Wallis et Futuna: BP 102, 97911 Mata'Utu, Uvea, Wallis Islands, Wallis and Futuna; tel. 722020; fax 722346; e-mail rfo .wallis@wallis.co.nc; internet www.rfo.fr; part of Réseau France Outre-mer; fmrly Radiodiffusion Française d'Outre-mer (RFO); transmitters at Mata'Utu (Uvea) and Alo (Futuna); programmes broadcast 24 hours daily in Uvean (Wallisian), Futunian and French; a television service on Uvea, transmitting for 12 hours daily in French, began operation in 1986; a television service on Futuna was inaugurated in December 1994; satellite television began operation in March 2000; Regional Dir JOSEPH CAIHÉ; Chief Editor LUSIA KAVAKAVA.

Finance

BANKING

Bank of Issue

Institut d'Emission d'Outre-Mer: Havelu–Hahake, BP G5, 98600 Mata'Utu, Uvea, Wallis Islands, Wallis and Futuna; tel. 722505; fax 722003; e-mail ieomwf.co.nc; internet www.ieom.fr; f. 1998; Dir RICHARD LAMBERT.

Other Banks

Agence Française de Développement: 98600 Mata'Utu, Uvea, Wallis Islands, Wallis and Futuna; tel. 722505; fmrly Caisse Française de Développement; development bank.

Banque de Wallis et Futuna: BP 59, 98600 Mata'Utu, Uvea, Wallis Islands, Wallis and Futuna; tel. 722124; fax 722156; e-mail bnp.nc@bnpparibas.com; internet www.bnp.nc/bwf/identite.htm; f. 1991; 51% owned by BNP Paribas (New Caledonia).

Paierie de Wallis et Futuna: 98600 Mata'Utu, Uvea, Wallis Islands, Wallis and Futuna, via Nouméa, New Caledonia.

Trade and Industry

GOVERNMENT AGENCY

Economie Rurale et Pêche: BP 05, 98600 Mata'Utu, Uvea, Wallis Islands, Wallis and Futuna; Antenne de Futuna, BP 05, 98620 Sigave, Futuna, Wallis and Futuna; tel. 720400; fax 720404; e-mail ecoru@wallis.co.nc; tel. 723214; fax 723402.

UTILITIES

Electricité et Eau de Wallis et Futuna (EEWF): BP 28, 98600 Mata'Utu, Uvea, Wallis Islands, Wallis and Futuna; tel. 721500; fax 721196; e-mail eewf@wallis.co.nc; 32.3% owned by the territory and 66.64% owned by EEC of New Caledonia; Dir FRANK HULTSCH.

TRADE UNIONS

Union Interprofessionnelle CFDT Wallis et Futuna (UI CFDT): BP 178, 98600 Mata'Utu, Uvea, Wallis Islands, Wallis and Futuna; tel. 721880; Sec. Gen. KALOLO HANISI.

Union Territoriale Force Ouvrière: BP 325, Mata-Utu, 98600 Wallis and Futuna; tel. 721732; fax 721732; Sec.-Gen. CHRISTIAN VAAMEI.

Transport

ROADS

Uvea has a few kilometres of road, one route circling the island, and there is also a partially surfaced road circling the island of Futuna; the only fully surfaced roads are in Mata'Utu.

SHIPPING

Mata'Utu serves as the seaport of Uvea and the Wallis Islands, while Sigave is the only port on Futuna. A total of 45 general freight ships and 17 gas and petroleum tankers docked in Wallis in 1999.

Services des Douanes et Affaires Maritimes: Aka'aka, 98600 Mata'Utu, Uvea, Wallis Islands, Wallis and Futuna; tel. 722571; fax 722986.

AMACAL (General Agent): POB 1080, Nouméa, New Caledonia; tel. 232910; fax 287388; e-mail amb@amb.nc.

CIVIL AVIATION

There is an international airport in Hihifo district on Uvea, about 5 km from Mata'Utu. Air Calédonie International (Aircalin—New Caledonia) operates five flights a week from Wallis to Futuna, one flight a week from Wallis to Tahiti (French Polynesia) and two flights a week from Wallis to Nouméa (New Caledonia). The airport on Futuna is at Vele, in the south-east, in the Kingdom of Alo. The Compagnie Aérienne de Wallis et Futuna (Air Wallis) was established in 2004, as a joint venture between the Government and local business interests, and was scheduled to commence operations in January 2005.

Tourism

Tourism remains undeveloped. There are four small hotels on Uvea, Wallis Islands. In 1985 there were some 400 tourist visitors, in total, to the islands. There are two small guest-houses for visitors on Futuna.

French Overseas Countries

New Caledonia and French Polynesia were formerly Overseas Territories (Territoires d'outre-mer) of France. The Nouméa Accord, concluded in 1998, and a number of constitutional amendments, approved in July of that year, provide for a gradual transfer of powers to New Caledonia, which became an Overseas Country (Pays d'outre-mer) within the French Republic in 1999. Legislation promulgated in February 2004 granted autonomy to French Polynesia, which was henceforth to have the status of an Overseas Country within the French Republic.

FRENCH POLYNESIA

Introductory Survey

Location, Climate, Language, Religion, Flag, Capital

French Polynesia comprises several scattered groups of islands in the South Pacific Ocean, lying about two-thirds of the way between the Panama Canal and New Zealand. Its nearest neighbours are the Cook Islands, to the west, and the Line Islands (part of Kiribati), to the north-west. French Polynesia consists of the following island groups: the Windward Islands (Iles du Vent—including the islands of Tahiti and Moorea) and the Leeward Islands (Iles Sous le Vent—located about 160 km north-west of Tahiti) which, together, constitute the Society Archipelago; the Tuamotu Archipelago, which comprises some 80 atolls scattered east of the Society Archipelago in a line stretching north-west to south-east for about 1,500 km; the Gambier Islands, located 1,600 km south-east of Tahiti; the Austral Islands, lying 640 km south of Tahiti; and the Marquesas Archipelago, which lies 1,450 km north-east of Tahiti. There are 35 islands and 83 atolls in all, of which 76 are populated. The average monthly temperature throughout the year varies between 20°C (68°F) and 29°C (84°F), and most rainfall occurs between November and April, the average annual precipitation being 1,625 mm (64 ins). The official languages are French and Tahitian. Seven Polynesian languages and their dialects are spoken by the indigenous population. The principal religion is Christianity; about 55% of the population is Protestant and some 34% Roman Catholic. The official flag is the French tricolour. Subordinate to this, the French Polynesian flag (proportions 2 by 3), comprises three horizontal stripes, of red, white (half the depth) and red, with, in the centre, the arms of French Polynesia, consisting of a representation in red of a native canoe, bearing a platform supporting five stylized persons, on a circular background (five wavy horizontal dark blue bands, surmounted by 10 golden sunrays). The capital is Papeete, on the island of Tahiti.

Recent History

Tahiti, the largest of the Society Islands, was declared a French protectorate in 1842, and became a colony in 1880. The other island groups were annexed during the last 20 years of the 19th century. The islands were governed from France under a decree of 1885 until 1946, when French Polynesia became an Overseas Territory, administered by a Governor in Papeete. A Territorial Assembly and a Council of Government were established to advise the Governor.

Between May 1975 and May 1982 a majority in the Territorial Assembly sought independence for French Polynesia. Following pressure by Francis Sanford, leader of the largest autonomist party in the Assembly, a new Constitution for the Territory was negotiated with the French Government and approved by a newly elected Assembly in 1977. Under the provisions of the new statute, France retained responsibility for foreign affairs, defence, monetary matters and justice, but the powers of the territorial Council of Government were increased, especially in the field of commerce. The French Governor was replaced by a High Commissioner, who was to preside over the Council of Government and was head of the administration, but had no vote. The Council's elected Vice-President, responsible for domestic affairs, was granted greater powers. An Economic, Social and Cultural Council, responsible for all development matters, was also created, and French Polynesia's economic zone was extended to 200 nautical miles (370 km) from the islands' coastline.

Following elections to the Territorial Assembly in May 1982, the Gaullist Tahoera'a Huiraatira, led by Gaston Flosse, which secured 13 of the 30 seats, formed successive ruling coalitions, first with the Ai'a Api party and in September with the Pupu Here Ai'a Te Nunaa Ia Ora party. Seeking self-government, especially in economic matters, elected representatives of the Assembly held discussions with the French Government in Paris in 1983, and in September 1984 a new statute was approved by the French National Assembly. This allowed the territorial Government greater powers, mainly in the sphere of commerce and development; the Council of Government was replaced by a Council of Ministers, whose President was to be elected from among the members of the Territorial Assembly. Flosse became the first President of the Council of Ministers.

At elections held in March 1986 the Tahoera'a Huiraatira gained the first outright majority to be achieved in the Territory, winning 24 of the 41 seats in the Territorial Assembly. Leaders of opposition parties subsequently expressed dissatisfaction with the election result, claiming that the Tahoera'a Huiraatira victory had been secured only as a result of the allocation of a disproportionately large number of seats in the Territorial Assembly to one of the five constituencies. The constituency at the centre of the dispute comprised the Mangareva and Tuamotu islands, where the two French army bases at Hao and Mururoa constituted a powerful body of support for Flosse and the Tahoera'a Huiraatira, which, in spite of winning a majority of seats, had obtained a minority of individual votes in the election. At concurrent elections for French Polynesia's two seats in the National Assembly in Paris, Flosse and Alexandre Léontieff, the candidates of the Rassemblement pour la République (RPR—to which the Tahoera'a Huiraatira was affiliated, latterly the Union pour un Mouvement Populaire), were elected, Flosse subsequently ceding his seat to Edouard Fritch. Later in March the French Prime Minister, Jacques Chirac, appointed Flosse to a post in the French Council of Ministers, assigning him the portfolio of Secretary of State for South Pacific Affairs.

In April 1986 Flosse was re-elected President of the Council of Ministers. However, he faced severe criticism from leaders of the opposition for his allegedly inefficient and extravagant use of public funds, and was accused, in particular, of corrupt electoral practice. Flosse resigned as President in February 1987, and was replaced by Jacques Teuira.

In December 1987, amid growing discontent over his policies, Teuira and the entire Council of Ministers resigned and were replaced by a coalition of opposition parties and the Te Tiaraama party (a breakaway faction of the Tahoera'a Huiraatira) under the presidency of Alexandre Léontieff. The Léontieff Government survived several challenges in the Territorial Assembly to its continuation in office during 1988–89. Amendments to the Polynesian Constitution, which were approved by the French Parliament and enacted by July 1990, augmented the powers of the President of the Council of Ministers and increased competence of the Territorial Assembly. The major purpose of these amendments was to clarify the areas of responsibility of the State, the Territory and the judiciary, which was considered particularly necessary following various disputes about the impending single market of the European Community (EC—now European Union—EU, see p. 217). In June 1989, in protest, 90% of the electorate refused to vote in the elections to the European Parliament.

At territorial elections in March 1991 the Tahoera'a Huiraatira won 18 of the 41 seats. Flosse then formed a coalition with the Ai'a Api, thereby securing a majority of 23 seats in the Territorial Assembly. Emile Vernaudon, leader of the Ai'a Api, was elected President of the Assembly and Flosse was elected President of the Council of Ministers. In September Flosse announced the end of the coalition between his party and the Ai'a Api, accusing Vernaudon of disloyalty, and signed a new alliance with the Pupu Here Ai'a Te Nunaa Ia Ora led by Jean Juventin.

In April 1992 Flosse was found guilty of fraud (relating to an illegal sale of government land to a member of his family) and there were widespread demands for his resignation. In November Juventin and Léontieff were charged with 'passive' corruption, relating to the construction of a golf course by a Japanese company. In the following month the French Court of Appeal upheld the judgment against Flosse, who received a six-month, suspended prison sentence. The case provoked a demonstration by more than 3,000 people in January 1993, demanding the resignation of Flosse and Juventin. In September 1994 Flosse succeeded in having the conviction overturned, on a procedural issue, in a second court of appeal. In October 1997, however, Léontieff was found guilty of accepting substantial bribes in order to facilitate a business venture and was sentenced to three years in prison (half of which was to be suspended). In May 1998 Léontieff was sentenced to a further three years' imprisonment (two of which were to be suspended) for corruption. (In August 2004 Emile Vernaudon, then Minister for Outer Islands Development, was convicted of using public property for personal benefit while serving as Mayor of Mahina between 1992 and 1999; he received a one-year suspended prison sentence and was fined US $30,000.)

French presidential elections took place in April–May 1995. During the second round of voting in the Territory, the socialist candidate, Lionel Jospin, received 39% of the total votes, while the RPR candidate, Jacques Chirac, won 61%. (Chirac was elected to the presidency with 52.6% of votes cast throughout the republic.)

In November 1995 the Territorial Assembly adopted a draft statute of autonomy, which proposed the extension of the Territory's powers to areas such as fishing, mining and shipping rights, international transport and communications, broadcasting and the offshore economic zone. France, however, would retain full responsibility for defence, justice and security in the islands. Advocates of independence for French Polynesia criticized the statute for promising only relatively cosmetic changes, while failing to increase the democratic rights of the islanders. The statute was approved by the French National Assembly in December and came into force in April 1996.

At territorial elections held on 13 May 1996 the Tahoera'a Huiraatira achieved an outright majority, although the principal pro-independence party, Tavini Huiraatira/Front de Libération de la Polynésie (FLP), made considerable gains throughout the Territory (largely owing to increased popular hostility towards France since the resumption of nuclear-weapons tests at Mururoa Atoll—see below). The Tahoera'a Huiraatira secured 22 of the 41 seats in the Territorial Assembly, with 38.7% of total votes cast, while Tavini Huiraatira won 10 seats, with 24.8% of votes. Other anti-independence parties won a total of eight seats and an additional pro-independence grouping secured one seat. Flosse defeated the pro-independence leader, Oscar Temaru, by 28 votes to 11 to remain as President of the Council of Ministers later in the month, and Justin Arapari was elected President of the Territorial Assembly. Allegations of voting irregularities led to legal challenges, which overturned the results in 11 constituencies. Following by-elections in May 1998 for the 11 seats, the Tahoera'a Huiraatira increased its representation by one seat. Tavini Huiraatira again claimed that the elections had not been fairly conducted.

At elections for French Polynesia's two seats in the French National Assembly in May 1997 Michel Buillard and Emile Vernaudon, both supporters of the RPR, were elected with 52% and 59% of total votes cast, respectively. However, Oscar Temaru was a strong contender for the western constituency seat, securing 42% of the votes. Flosse was re-elected as the Territory's representative to the French Senate in September 1998.

In March 1999 proposals to increase French Polynesia's autonomy, as part of constitutional reforms, were announced in Paris. These proposals followed an initial agreement between the Territory and the French Government in late 1998, on the future of French Polynesia. In October 1999 the French Senate adopted a constitutional amendment granting French Polynesia a greater degree of autonomy. According to the bill (which had

also been approved by the National Assembly in June), the status of the islands was to be changed from that of overseas territory to overseas country, and a new Polynesian citizenship was to be created. Although France was to retain control over areas such as foreign affairs, defence, justice and electoral laws, French Polynesia would have the power to negotiate with other Pacific countries and sign its own international treaties. The constitutional amendment was presented to a joint session of the French Senate and National Assembly for final ratification in late January 2000, although no decision on the matter was taken.

In November 1999 Flosse was found guilty of corruption, on charges of accepting more than 2.7m. French francs in bribes from the owner of an illegal casino, allegedly to help fund his party. Flosse was sentenced to a two-year suspended prison term, a large fine, and a one-year ban on seeking office. Demonstrations, organized by the pro-independence FLP, took place in Tahiti, in protest at Flosse's refusal to resign from his post as President of the Council of Ministers. In October 2000 Flosse lodged an appeal with the High Court, which reversed the ruling in May 2001. In November 2002 the Court of Appeal in Paris announced that Flosse should be pardoned.

In December 2000 some 2,000 workers went on strike in Papeete, protesting against low wages, and demanding that their pay be raised to a level commensurate with the prosperous state of the Territory's economy. In that month provision was made for the number of seats in the Territorial Assembly to be increased from 41 to 49, in an attempt to reflect demographic changes in the Territory more accurately. At the elections, held on 6 May 2001, the Tahoera'a Huiraatira won 28 seats, securing a fifth successive term in office. The pro-independence Tavini Huiraatira took 13 seats. Flosse was subsequently re-elected President of the Council of Ministers, and a government reorganization ensued.

In January 2002 representatives of state and local government met to review the first five years of the Restructuring Fund, an agreement implemented in 1996 to further the economic autonomy of Polynesia and to regulate financial subsidies to the Territory following the cessation of nuclear testing (see Economic Affairs, below). The President and Prime Minister of France took part in further such meetings in June and July. It was agreed that funding would be extended for 10 years after 2006. The French delegation supported the proposal for a new autonomy statute to grant more powers of self-government to French Polynesia. In June 2002 elections for the Territory's two seats in the National Assembly were won by the Tahoera'a Huiraatira candidates Michel Buillard and Béatrice Vernaudon.

In December 2002 the French Senate approved a bill providing for a constitutional amendment that would allow French Polynesia (along with Wallis and Futuna) to become an Overseas Country; in Paris both houses of the National Assembly ratified the amendments to the Constitution in March 2003. In July the Territorial Assembly and the Government ratified the amendments. Meanwhile, in May 2003 it was announced that French Polynesia (together with New Caledonia) would be allocated one additional seat in the French Senate, probably effective from 2007. Also in May, a strike by 400 doctors, protesting against changes in the social security system, had lasted for several weeks. The union of medical professionals hoped to draw renewed attention to these concerns during President Chirac's visit to French Polynesia in July (see below).

The final text of the autonomy statute was approved by the National Assembly in January 2004, and, with minor amendments, by the Constitutional Council in mid-February. In March, when President Chirac signed the requisite decree, French Polynesia formally became an Overseas Country of France, henceforth being permitted to 'govern itself freely and democratically'. French Polynesia was thus granted greater authority over matters such as labour law, civil aviation and regional relations, with France retaining control of law and order, defence and money supply. In April 2004 the local legislature was dissolved, in preparation for the holding of an election to a new 57-member Assembly in May.

At elections for the newly expanded French Polynesia Assembly held on 23 May 2004, the Tahoera'a Huiraatira, led by Gaston Flosse, won 28 of the 57 seats. An opposition coalition, the Union pour la démocratie (UPD), comprising the pro-independence Tavini Huiraatira and various minor parties, secured 27 seats and the remaining two seats were taken by opposition parties favouring autonomy. The Tahoera'a Huiraatira thus lost its overall majority in the Assembly for the first time in 20 years. Flosse disputed the results, claiming that there had been irregularities in the electoral process, in particular in the Windward Islands, the largest of the constituencies. In June the new legislature elected Antony Géros of the pro-independence Tavini Huiraatira party as President of the Assembly. Oscar Temaru, leader of Tavini Huiraatira, was elected President of the Council of Ministers and announced the composition of a streamlined 10-member cabinet two days later.

In early September divisions over the 2004 appropriation bill brought the legislative process to a standstill. Three members of the Assembly resigned from the UPD coalition, two of them to sit as independents, with the third joining the opposition Tahoera'a Huiraatira. In early October separate motions of no confidence were filed against the Government by the Tahoera'a Huiraatira and the newly formed Te' Avei'a (Te Ara) party, made up of six former members of the ruling UPD coalition and the Tahoera'a Huiraatira. In early October Oscar Temaru twice appealed to the French Government to dissolve the Assembly and to hold new elections. On 16 October some 22,000 people took part in the largest demonstration ever witnessed in French Polynesia, demanding the dissolution of the Assembly. However, the French Minister for Overseas Territories, Brigitte Girardin, refused to accept that such demands were justified because French Polynesia's institutions were continuing to function normally. The motions of no confidence were endorsed by 29 of the 57 legislators—the members of the UPD refusing to vote—thus requiring the Assembly to choose a new President of the Council of Ministers. The 23 Tahoera'a Huiraatira and six Te' Avei'a members elected Gaston Flosse as President on 20 October. However, the UPD members boycotted the vote and refused to recognize Flosse's authority. Temaru and his ministers refused to vacate the presidential building (several hundred pro-Temaru supporters were reported to be continuing their occupation of government buildings in early 2005) and Flosse's newly appointed 17-member Council of Ministers—largely drawn from his previous administration, including former Vice-President Edouard Fritch—were forced to work at the adjacent Economic, Social and Cultural Council buildings.

The validity of Oscar Temaru's removal and the subsequent vote to elect Gaston Flosse as President of the Council of Ministers were both upheld by the French State Council. Under the new autonomy statute (see above) the Assembly could vote to dissolve itself if it received a petition from 10% of the electorate, then roughly equivalent to 15,000 people; by 19 November the UPD claimed to have collected 42,890 signatures, representing some 28% of the electorate. Both Temaru and Flosse sent delegations to Paris, to make representations to the French Government, led respectively by Nicole Bouteau (leader of the No Oe e Te Nunaa party) and Edouard Fritch. Temaru claimed that an audit into the accounts of the previous Flosse administration (1999–2004), begun in September, had been stopped. The French State Council began investigations into the conduct of the May legislative election and in mid-November declared the results in the Windward Islands null and void, thus requiring the holding of by-elections within three months. The decision also meant that the 37 legislators affected automatically lost their seats, among them Flosse, Temaru and the President of the Assembly, Antony Géros, who was replaced by Hiro Tefaarere. At the end of November leading representatives from all parties were summoned to Paris for discussions, which included Flosse, Temaru, Nicole Bouteau, Philip Schyle (of the Fetia Api party) and Jacky Briant (of the Heuira-Greens party). Despite an initial agreement in principle to hold a fresh legislative election, the talks broke down in early December. In mid-December the French State Council validated Gaston Flosse's appointment as President.

In early January 2005 it was announced that by-elections would be held in the Windward Islands constituency on 13 February. Nicole Bouteau and Philip Schyle announced that their parties would be standing on a joint platform (the Alliance pour une Démocratie Nouvelle—ADN) offering a 'third way'. Gaston Flosse's Tahoera'a Huiraatira won 10 of the 37 seats, having secured 40.0% of the votes. The seven-party UPD coalition, led by Oscar Temaru, won 25 seats, receiving 46.9% of the votes. The newly formed ADN took the constituency's remaining two seats. Overall, therefore, the Tahoera'a Huiraatira and the UPD now held 27 seats each in the Assembly. The ADN held three seats but refused to co-operate with either the Tahoera'a Huiraatira or the UPD, as a result of which neither of the two groupings was able to form a majority. Temaru brought a motion of no confidence against President Flosse, which was endorsed

by 30 of the 57 members. The Assembly had 14 days within which to elect a new President of the Council of Ministers, while Flosse and his Government remained in office in an interim capacity. Temaru announced that he would be standing again for the presidency, while the Tahoera'a Huiraatira put forward Gaston Tong Sang, the serving Minister for Small- and Medium-sized Enterprises, Industry, Trade and Energy. The first attempt to elect a President was abandoned, following a boycott by the members of the Tahoera'a Huiraatira, with the result that the required quorum of three-fifths could not be reached. At a second attempt, on 4 March, Temaru was returned as President by 29 votes to 26. There were two blank ballots cast, believed to have been those of Nicole Bouteau and Philip Schyle. Within four days Temaru announced the composition of his new 17-member Council of Ministers, which included Louis Frébault as Minister for Outer Islands Development, the portfolio he had held under the recent Flosse administration. Jacqui Drollet was reappointed as Vice-President.

In July 1962 the French Government transferred its nuclear testing facilities to Mururoa and Fangataufa atolls, in the Tuamotu Archipelago, establishing the Centre d'Expérimentation du Pacifique (CEP). The first nuclear device was tested at Fangataufa four years later in July 1966. In July 1985 the *Rainbow Warrior*, the flagship of the anti-nuclear environmentalist group, Greenpeace, which was to have led a protest flotilla to Mururoa, was sunk in Auckland Harbour, New Zealand, in an explosion that killed one crew member. Two agents of the French secret service, the Direction Générale de Sécurité Extérieure (DGSE), were subsequently convicted of manslaughter and imprisoned in New Zealand, and relations between France and New Zealand were seriously affected by the resultant dispute, especially regarding the treatment of the two agents (see the chapter on New Zealand for further details). In May 1991, during a visit to New Zealand, the French Prime Minister, Michel Rocard, formally apologized for the bombing of the *Rainbow Warrior*; however, in July tension between France and the region was exacerbated by the French Government's decision to award a medal for 'distinguished service' to one of the agents convicted for his role in the bombing. Between 1966 and 1974 France conducted at least 41 atmospheric tests in the Territory, and 134 underground tests between 1975 and 1991.

In April 1992 the French Government announced that nuclear tests would be suspended until the end of the year. Although the decision was welcomed throughout the South Pacific, concern was expressed in French Polynesia over the economic implications of the move, because of the Territory's dependence on income received from hosting the nuclear-test programme. Similarly, it was feared that unemployment resulting from the ban would have a serious impact on the economy. A delegation of political leaders subsequently travelled to Paris to express its concerns, and in January 1993 accepted assistance worth 7,000m. francs CFP in compensation for lost revenue and in aid for development projects.

Shortly after his election in May 1995, President Jacques Chirac announced that France would resume nuclear testing, with a programme of eight tests between September 1995 and May 1996. The decision provoked almost universal outrage in the international community, and was condemned for its apparent disregard for regional opinion, as well as for undermining the considerable progress made by Western nations towards a worldwide ban on nuclear testing. Scientists also expressed concern at the announcement; some believed that further explosions at Mururoa could lead to the collapse of the atoll, which had been weakened considerably. Large-scale demonstrations and protest marches throughout the region were accompanied by boycotts of French products and the suspension of several trade and defence co-operation agreements. Opposition to the French Government intensified in July 1995, when French commandos violently seized *Rainbow Warrior II*, the flagship of Greenpeace, and its crew, which had been protesting peacefully near the test site. Chirac continued to defy mounting pressure from within the EU, from Japan and Russia, as well as from Australia, New Zealand and the South Pacific region, to reverse the decision to carry out the tests.

French Polynesia became the focus of world attention when the first test took place in September 1995. The action attracted further statements of condemnation from Governments around the world, and provoked major demonstrations in many countries. In Tahiti hitherto peaceful protests soon developed into full-scale riots, as several thousand demonstrators rampaged through the capital, demanding an end to French rule. Meanwhile, violent clashes with police, and the burning of dozens of buildings in Papeete during the riots, left much of the capital in ruins. In defiance of world opinion, a further five tests were carried out, the sixth and final one being conducted in January 1996. In early 1996 the French Government confirmed reports by a team of independent scientists that radioactive isotopes had leaked into the waters surrounding the atoll, but denied that they represented a threat to the environment. However, following the election of a new socialist administration in France in mid-1997, the French Minister of the Environment demanded in August 1998 that the matter be investigated further, stating that she had not been reassured by the initial reports. Work to dismantle facilities at the test site began in 1997 and was completed in July 1998. Some 1,800 French military personnel were still based at the CEP site in 1998; these numbers were expected to be reduced.

In September 1998 the trial of more than 60 people charged with offences relating to the riots and protests of September 1995 began in Papeete. Hiro Tefaare, a pro-independence member of the Territorial Assembly and former police officer, was found guilty of instigating the riots and was sentenced to three years' imprisonment (of which 18 months were to be suspended). Furthermore, in September 1999 the French Government was ordered by the Administrative Tribunal to pay 204m. francs CFP in compensation for failing to maintain law and order.

In early 1999 a study by the French Independent Research and Information Commission reported that there was serious radioactive leakage into underground water, lagoons and the ocean at Mururoa and Fangataufa atolls. These claims were dismissed by a New Zealand scientist who had taken part in an earlier study by the International Atomic Energy Agency, which had claimed that radiation levels were nearly undetectable. In May a French government official admitted that fractures had been found in the coral cone at the Mururoa and Fangataufa nuclear testing sites. The reports, by Greenpeace, that the atoll was in danger of collapsing had always been previously denied by France. However, France's claim that no serious long-term damage had been done was contested by Greenpeace, which also suggested the need for an urgent independent study of the test sites. In January 2000, in what was considered to be a significant development, the commander of the French armed forces in French Polynesia admitted that there were significant cracks in the coral reef surrounding Mururoa, and that these might lead to the occurrence of a tsunami. In October 2002 a new agreement was reached for France to provide the Territory with €150m. a year in compensation for lost revenue from the CEP.

In July 2003 some 2,000 islanders, led by Oscar Temaru, demonstrated in favour of self-determination during an official visit by President Chirac to Papeete. Chirac attempted to assure islanders that the nuclear tests had created no danger to health and pledged that France would assume responsibility should any evidence to the contrary emerge. At the beginning of Chirac's visit, some 200 members of an association of those formerly employed at Mururoa and Fangataufa staged a demonstration to demand that France recognize the existence of a connection between nuclear testing and the subsequent health of those involved, as Australia and the USA had done. Following his election as President of the Council of Ministers, in May 2004 (see above), Temaru agreed to establish a body to investigate the impact of the French nuclear programme on the health of the population and on the environment. He also expressed his support for the Nuclear Veterans' Association, which was seeking compensation from the French Government: according to the group around 30% of some 15,000 former nuclear workers were either suffering—or had died—from cancers or related diseases; the French military estimated the number to be only 4,700. In late September a pre-trial investigation began in France in relation to a case filed in November 2003 by the French Nuclear Veterans' Association and Moruroa Tatou, the French Polynesian association of former test workers, against an unidentified defendant.

Government

The French Government is represented in French Polynesia by its High Commissioner, and controls various important spheres of government, including defence, foreign diplomacy and justice. A local Assembly, with 57 members (increased from 49 at the May 2004 election), is elected for a five-year term by universal adult suffrage. The Assembly may elect a President of an executive body, the Council of Ministers, who in turn submits a list of between six and 12 members of the Assembly to serve as ministers, for approval by the Assembly.

In addition, French Polynesia elects two deputies to the French National Assembly in Paris and one representative to the French Senate, all chosen on the basis of universal adult suffrage. (In 2003 it was announced that French Polynesia would be allocated one additional seat in the Senate, probably effective from 2007.) French Polynesia is also represented at the European Parliament.

Defence

France tested nuclear weapons at Mururoa and Fangataufa atolls, in the Tuamotu Archipelago, between 1966 and 1996. In August 2004 France maintained a force of 2,400 military personnel in the Territory.

Economic Affairs

In 2000, according to World Bank estimates, French Polynesia's gross national income (GNI), measured at average 1998–2000 prices, was US $3,447.5m., equivalent to $16,150 per head (or $24,820m. per head on an international purchasing-power parity basis). During 1990–2003, it was estimated, the population increased at an average annual rate of 1.6%, while GDP per head increased at an average annual rate of 0.5% during 1990–2000. Overall gross domestic product (GDP) increased, in real terms, at an average annual rate of 2.3% in 1990–2000. Real GDP increased by 4.0% in both 1999 and 2000.

Agriculture, forestry and fishing contributed only 4.7% of GDP in 2000, but provided most of French Polynesia's exports. The sector engaged 3.7% of the employed labour force at December 2003. Coconuts are the principal cash crop, and in 2003 the estimated harvest was 88,000 metric tons. Vegetables, fruit (especially pineapples and citrus fruit), vanilla and coffee are also cultivated. Most commercial fishing, principally for tuna, is conducted, under licence, by Japanese and Korean fleets. The total fish catch in 2002 was 15,600 tons; production by the aquaculture sector included 45 tons of shrimps. In 2003 the Government aimed to raise production of tuna to some 30,000 metric tons by 2008, of which 22,000 tons would be for export. Another important activity is the production of cultured black pearls, of which the quantity exported increased from 112 kg in 1984 to 11,541 kg in 2000, declining to 7,273 kg in 2004. In 2004 export earnings from cultured pearls totalled CFP 8,907.1m, compared with CFP 20,173.2m. in 2000. In 2001 development of the black pearl industry appeared to be decelerating. Auctions early in the year raised less revenue than expected, with a marked reduction in the number of buyers from Japan in particular, largely owing to the downturn in that country's economy, as well as from Europe and the USA. In December 2001 the pearl industry lowered prices to maintain the level of sales, while at the same time forming a centralized buying syndicate, ensuring minimum prices. In early 2003 the Government allocated some francs CFP 150m. for the promotion of the black pearl industry overseas.

Industry (comprising mining, manufacturing, construction and utilities) engaged 16.9% of the employed labour force at December 2003, and provided 15.5% of GDP in 1997. There is a small manufacturing sector, which is heavily dependent on agriculture. Coconut oil and copra are produced, as are beer, dairy products and vanilla essence. Important deposits of phosphates and cobalt were discovered during the 1980s.

Mining and manufacturing engaged 7.2% of the employed labour force at December 2003, and provided 7.0% of GDP in 1997. Construction is an important industrial activity, contributing 5.3% of GDP in 1997, and engaging 9.0% of the employed labour force at December 2003.

Hydrocarbon fuels are the main source of energy in the Territory, with the Papeete thermal power station providing about three-quarters of the electricity produced. Hydroelectric and solar energy also make a significant contribution to French Polynesia's domestic requirements. Hydroelectric power dams, with the capacity to generate the electricity requirements of 36% of Tahiti's population, have been constructed. Solar energy is also increasingly important, especially on the less-populated islands.

Tourism is the Territory's major industry. In 1990 the trade, restaurants and hotels sector contributed 22.7% of GDP. In 2004 some 210,000 tourists visited French Polynesia, compared with about 212,767 in the previous year. Receipts from tourism in 2004 totalled an estimated US $420m. accounting for some 76% of the Territory's earnings. French Polynesia's hotel capacity amounted to 4,418 rooms in 2001; the sector aimed to increase this number to 6,000 rooms by 2005. The services sector engaged 79.5% of the employed labour force at December 2003, and provided 80.4% of GDP in 1997.

In 2000, according to the Institut d'Émission d'Outre-Mer (IEOM—the French overseas reserve bank), French Polynesia recorded a visible trade deficit of 81,052m. francs CFP. On the current account of the balance of payments there was a surplus of 45,660m. francs CFP, equivalent to 11% of GDP and an increase of 75.8% compared with the previous year. In 2003 the value of imports reached 126,061.7m. francs CFP, while that of exports amounted to 15,140.2m. francs CFP. In 2004 the principal sources of imports were France (which provided 34.1% of total imports), Australia (9.7%) and the USA (9.4%). The principal markets for exports in that year were Japan (accounting for 29.3% of the total), Hong Kong (19.4%) and the USA (17.1%). The principal imports in 2004 included road vehicles (10.9%), and nuclear reactors, boilers, machinery and their parts (10.8%). In that year the principal commodity exports were cultured black pearls (providing some 64.1% of total export revenue).

A budgetary deficit of 38,314m. francs CFP was projected in 2001. In 2002 expenditure by the French State in the Territory totalled 131,626m. francs CFP, 25.8% of which was on the military budget. The budget for 2005 envisaged expenditure of 173,600m. francs CFP. In May 2004 the incoming Government of Oscar Temaru inherited a deficit from the previous administration of around US $140m. The total external debt was estimated at US $390m. in 1992. The annual rate of inflation averaged 1.3% during 1990–2002, rising to 2.9% in 2002. However, in 2003 the inflation rate declined to 0.4%. A high unemployment rate (recorded at 13.2% of the labour force in 1996) is exacerbated by the predominance of young people in the population (in 1996 some 43% of the population were under the age of 20 years).

French Polynesia forms part of the Franc Zone (see p. 266), and is an associate member of the UN Economic and Social Commission for Asia and the Pacific (ESCAP, see p. 31). Although France is also a member of the organization, French Polynesia has membership in its own right of the Pacific Community (see p. 337), which is based in New Caledonia and provides technical advice, training and assistance in economic, cultural and social development to the region.

French Polynesia's traditional agriculture-based economy was distorted by the presence of large numbers of French military and civilian personnel (in connection with the presence of the CEP—see above), stimulating employment in the construction industry and services at the expense of agriculture, and encouraging migration from the outer islands to Tahiti. These dramatic changes effectively transformed French Polynesia from a state of self-sufficiency to one of import dependency in less than a generation. The development of tourism had a similar effect. The Contract for Development, an agreement for metropolitan France to provide the Territory with 28,300m. francs CFP annually between 1996 and 2006, was concluded in 1995 and took effect upon completion of the last series of nuclear tests in early 1996. It was hoped that the arrangement would enable French Polynesia to establish an economy that was more reliant upon local resources and would consequently create greater employment. During a visit to French Polynesia in mid-2003, President Chirac of France confirmed that the annual grant of €151m. would be continued indefinitely. However, in July 2004 Oscar Temaru expressed concern at the French Government's decision to finish grant payments at the end of that year. In May 2004 the incoming Temaru administration revealed that the French Government owed French Polynesia payments in arrears, in a variety of fields, amounting to some US $250m.

French Polynesia's steady economic growth has partly been as a result of the development of the services sector, notably in hotel construction and other tourism-related services, which has led to significant employment creation. Other sectors of the economy, such as pearl farming, however, have not expanded as rapidly, principally because of regional economic conditions (notably the recession in Japan, one of the largest importers of black pearls). The continued expansion of GDP throughout the late 1990s was principally due to the financial support provided by France, but also to a significant rise in the number of tourists visiting the Territory (a 16.8% increase between 1997 and 1999). It was hoped that revenue from tourism would eventually replace the grants provided by the French State. In 2001 customs duties were decreased, while VAT rates were maintained at similar levels, as the Government continued the anti-infla-

tionary policy that it had instigated in 1996. The principal aim of the 2002 budget, however, was to avoid recession and to counter the repercussions of the deteriorating global economic situation. VAT rates were increased by an average of 3.3%, and total VAT receipts for the year were expected to reach 36,600m. francs CFP. The 2002 budget also introduced new taxes on alcohol, soft drinks, sugar and new road vehicles. The Government defended the introduction of these new taxes by citing the 'economic uncertainties' faced by French Polynesia. The 2003 budget allocated more than 5% of expenditure to social housing programmes. The tourism sector proved vulnerable in the wake of the terrorist attacks on the USA on 11 September 2001. The number of visitor arrivals declined sharply in late 2001, and by early 2002 many of French Polynesia's hotels were reporting occupancy rates as low as 35%. In 2002 the total number of visitors declined by 17.0% compared with the previous year, but by 2004 the number had increased by some 12%. In mid-2003 the National Assembly approved the Overseas Territories Development Bill, which would provide support for economic and social development in French Polynesia (together with New Caledonia and Wallis and Futuna) by attracting foreign investment, and among other benefits allow for overseas French residents to travel to mainland France to take advantage of free education. Discussions began in December 2004 over replacing the franc CFP with the euro. If French Polynesia, New Caledonia and Wallis and Futuna could reach a consensus, the introduction of the new currency was anticipated by January 2007.

Education

Education is compulsory for eight years between six and 14 years of age. It is free of charge for day pupils in government schools. Primary education, lasting six years, is financed by the French Polynesian budget, while secondary and technical education are supported by state funds. In 2001/02 there were 54 kindergartens, with 15,136 children enrolled, and 173 primary schools, with 28,988 pupils. Secondary education is provided by both church and government schools. In 2001/02 there were 29,466 pupils at general secondary schools, including some 3,032 pupils enrolled at vocational institutions. The French University of the Pacific was established in French Polynesia in 1987. In 1999 it was divided into two separate branches, of which the University of French Polynesia is now based in Papeete. In 1995 the Papeete branch had 50 teachers and, in 2003/04, some 2,343 students. Total government expenditure on education in the Territory was 40,300m. francs CFP in 1999.

Public Holidays

2005: 1 January (New Year's Day), 5 March (Arrival of the Gospel), 25–28 March (Easter), 1 May (Labour Day), 5 May (Ascension Day), 8 May (Liberation Day), 16 May (Whit Monday), 14 July (Fall of the Bastille), 15 August (Assumption), 8 September (Internal Autonomy Day), 1 November (All Saints' Day), 11 November (Armistice Day), 25 December (Christmas Day).

2006: 1 January (New Year's Day), 5 March (Arrival of the Gospel), 14–17 April (Easter), 1 May (Labour Day), 8 May (Liberation Day), 25 May (Ascension Day), 5 June (Whit Monday), 14 July (Fall of the Bastille), 15 August (Assumption), 8 September (Internal Autonomy Day), 1 November (All Saints' Day), 11 November (Armistice Day), 25 December (Christmas Day).

Weights and Measures

The metric system is in force.

Statistical Survey

Source (unless otherwise indicated): Institut Statistique de la Polynésie Française, Immeuble UUPA, rue Edouard Ahne, BP 395, 98713 Papeete; tel. 473434; fax 427252; e-mail ispf@ispf.pf; internet www.ispf.pf.

AREA AND POPULATION

Area: Total 4,167 sq km (1,609 sq miles); Land area 3,521 sq km (1,359 sq miles).

Population: 188,814 at census of 6 September 1988; 219,521 (males 113,934, females 105,587) at census of 3 September 1996; 245,516 at census of 7 November 2002. *2004* (official estimate): 249,200 at 1 January.

Population by Island Group (2002 census): Society Archipelago 214,445 (Windward Islands 184,224, Leeward Islands 30,221); Marquesas Archipelago 8,712; Austral Islands 6,386; Tuamotu-Gambier Islands 15,973.

Density (land area only, official estimate at 1 January 2004): 70.8 per sq km.

Ethnic Groups (census of 15 October 1983): Polynesian 114,280; 'Demis' 23,625 (Polynesian-European 15,851, Polynesian-Chinese 6,356, Polynesian-Other races 1,418); European 19,320; Chinese 7,424; European-Chinese 494; Others 1,610; Total 166,753. *1988 Census* ('000 persons): Polynesians and 'Demis' 156.3; Others 32.5.

Principal Towns (population at 2002 census): Faaa 28,339; Papeete (capital) 26,181; Punaauía 23,706; Pirae 14,499; Moorea-Maiao 14,550; Mahina 13,334; Paea 12,276. *Mid-2003* (UN estimate, incl. suburbs): Papeete 126,193 (Source: UN, *World Urbanization Prospects: The 2003 Revision*).

Births, Marriages and Deaths (provisional figures, 2003 unless otherwise indicated): Registered live births 4,503 (birth rate 18.3 per 1,000); Marriages (1997) 1,176 (marriage rate 5.3 per 1,000); Registered deaths 1,121 (death rate 4.5 per 1,000).

Expectation of Life (years at birth, 2000): Males 72.5; Females 77.2. Source: UN, *Statistical Yearbook for Asia and the Pacific*.

Economically Active Population (persons aged 14 years and over, 1996 census): Agriculture, hunting, forestry and fishing 10,888; Mining and manufacturing 6,424; Electricity, gas and water 459; Construction 4,777; Trade, restaurants and hotels 9,357; Transport, storage and communications 3,788; Financial services 1,482; Real estate 383; Business services 3,710; Private services 9,033; Education, health and social welfare 10,771; Public administration 13,475; *Total employed* 74,547 (males 46,141, females 28,406); Persons on compulsory military service 1,049 (all males); Unemployed 11,525 (males 6,255, females 5,270); *Total labour force* 87,121 (males 53,445, females 33,676). *December 2003*: Agriculture, hunting, forestry and fishing 2,305; Mining and manufacturing 4,533; Electricity, gas and water 488; Construction 5,632; Trade and repairs 9,725; Hotels and restaurants 6,432; Transport, storage and communications 5,675; Financial services 1,488; Real estate, renting and business services 4,482; Domestic services 1,433; Education, health, collective services and social welfare 6,638; Public administration 14,273; Total employed 63,104.

HEALTH AND WELFARE

Key Indicators

Physicians (per 1,000 head, 2001): 1.8.
For definitions, see explanatory note on p. vi.

AGRICULTURE, ETC.

Principal Crops (FAO estimates, metric tons, 2003): Roots and tubers 12,400; Vegetables and melons 7,210; Pineapples 3,500; Other fruit 4,120; Coconuts 88,000; Vanilla 35; Coffee (green) 18. Source: FAO.

Livestock (FAO estimates, year ending September 2003): Cattle 11,000; Horses 2,200; Pigs 29,000; Goats 16,500; Sheep 440; Chickens 240,000; Ducks 33,000. Source: FAO.

Livestock Products (FAO estimates, metric tons, 2003): Beef and veal 200; Pig meat 1,000; Goat meat 75; Poultry meat 693; Cows' milk 1,200; Hen eggs 1,600; Other poultry eggs 85; Honey 32. Source: FAO.

Fishing ('000 metric tons, live weight, 2002): Capture 15.5 (Common dolphinfish 0.6; Skipjack tuna 1.5; Albacore 4.7; Yellowfin tuna 1.2; Bigeye tuna 0.7; Marlins and sailfishes 0.5; Sharks, rays, skates, etc. 1.1); Aquaculture 0.1; *Total catch* 15.6. Note: Figures exclude pearl oyster shells (kilograms): 1,289,490. Source: FAO.

INDUSTRY

Production: Copra 4,143.1 metric tons (sales, 2004); Coconut oil 5,000 metric tons (2001)*; Oilcake 2,500 metric tons (2001)*; Beer 129,000 hectolitres (1992); Printed cloth 200,000 m (1979); Japanese sandals 600,000 pairs (1979); Electric energy 533.5m. kWh (2004).
*FAO estimate.

FINANCE

Currency and Exchange Rates: see Wallis and Futuna Islands.

Territorial Budget (million francs CFP, 2002): *Revenue*: Current 111,351 (Indirect taxation 64,346). *Expenditure*: Current 107,103, Capital 42,562; Total 149,665.

French State Expenditure (million francs CFP, 1996): Civil budget 61,706 (Current 56,564, Capital 5,142); Military budget 46,119 (Current 37,160, Capital 8,959); Pensions 10,458; Total (incl. others) 123,774 (Current 109,060, Capital 14,714). *1998* (million francs CFP): 121,788 (incl. military budget 37,982). *1999* (million francs CFP): 120,631 (incl. military budget 34,343). *2000* (million francs CFP): 124,800 (incl. military budget 35,400). *2001* (million francs CFP): 128,586 (incl. military budget 36,774). *2002* (million francs CFP): 131,626 (incl. military budget 33,926).

Money Supply (million francs CFP at 31 December 2001): Currency in circulation 9,366; Demand deposits 100,617; Total money 109,983. Source: Institut d'Emission d'Outre-Mer.

Cost of Living (Consumer Price Index; base: 1990 = 100): All items 114.0 in 2001; 117.3 in 2002; 117.8 in 2003. Source: UN, *Monthly Bulletin of Statistics*.

Gross Domestic Product (million francs CFP at current prices): 378,501 in 1997; 404,886 in 1998; 412,100 in 1999; 453,460 in 2000.

Expenditure on the Gross Domestic Product (million francs CFP at current prices, 1993): Government final consumption expenditure 126,127; Private final consumption expenditure 202,563; Increase in stocks −536; Gross fixed capital formation 53,494; *Total domestic expenditure* 381,648; Exports of goods and services 34,523; *Less* Imports of goods and services 86,905; *GDP in purchasers' values* 329,266. Source: UN, *National Accounts Statistics*.

Gross Domestic Product by Economic Activity (million francs CFP at current prices, 1997): Agriculture, forestry and fishing 15,534; Manufacturing 26,360*; Electricity, gas and water 12,221*; Construction 20,104; Trade 81,854; Transport and telecommunications 27,832. Other private services 96,714; Government services 97,238; Domestic services 646; *GDP in purchasers' values* 378,503. *Manufacturing of energy-generating products is included in electricity, gas and water. Source: UN, *National Accounts Statistics*.

Balance of Payments (million francs CFP, 2003): Goods (net) − 145,995; Services (net) 33,898; *Balance on goods and services* − 112,097; Other income (net) 50,735; *Balance on goods, services and income* −61,632; Current transfers (net) 44,206; *Current balance* − 17,156; Capital account (net) 101; Direct investment (net) 5,556; Portfolio investment (net) −7,969; Other capital (incl. charges in reserves) 15,871; Net errors and omissions 3,800. Source: Institut d'Emission d'Outre-Mer.

EXTERNAL TRADE

Principal Commodities (million francs CFP, 2004): *Imports c.i.f.*: Live animals and animal products 9,537.0 (Meat and edible meat offal 6,110.9); Prepared foodstuffs; beverages, spirits and vinegar; tobacco and manufactured substitutes 24,539.2; Mineral products 11,331.0 (Mineral fuels, mineral oils and products of their distillation; bituminous substances; mineral waxes 9,887.7); Products of chemical or allied industries 10,002.3 (Pharmaceutical products 4,685.7); Plastics, rubber and articles thereof 4,929.9; Paper-making materials; paper and paperboard and articles thereof 3,912.4; Textiles and textile articles 4,031.5; Base metals and articles thereof 8,448.9; Machinery and mechanical appliances; electrical equipment; sound and television apparatus 25,898.0 (Nuclear reactors, boilers, machinery, mechanical appliances and parts 13,553.6, Electrical machinery, equipment, etc. 8,583.6); Vehicles, aircraft, vessels and associated transport equipment 18,836.9 (Aircraft and aeronautical craft 1,776.9; Road vehicles, parts and accessories 13,800.3); Miscellaneous manufactured articles 5,433.4; Total (incl. others) 126,061.7. *Exports f.o.b.*: Animal products 568.7 (Fish and crustaceans, molluscs and other aquatic invertebrates 354.4); Prepared foodstuffs; beverages, spirits and vinegar; tobacco and manufactured substitutes 2,304.9 (Preparations of vegetables, fruit, nuts or other parts of plants 1,349.5); Natural or cultured pearls, precious or semi-precious stones, precious metals and articles thereof; imitation jewellery; coin 9,707.1; Vehicles, aircraft, vessels and associated transport equipment 1,757.6 (Aircraft, spacecraft and parts 1,498.6); Total (incl. others) 15,140.2.

Principal Trading Partners (million francs CFP, 2004): *Imports*: Australia 12,220.2; Belgium 2,782.3; China, People's Republic 6,088.0; France 42,978.3; Germany 4,562.8; Italy 4,238.4; Japan 4,899.0; New Zealand 9,778.3; Singapore 3,777.1; Thailand 4,000.2; USA 11,845.8; Total (incl. others) 126,061.7. *Exports*: Belgium 200.8; Canada 246.4; France 2,385.1; Hong Kong 2,943.2; Japan 4,428.9; New Caledonia 325.2; New Zealand 198.9; Thailand 853.6; USA 2,589.2; Total (incl. others) 15,140.2.

TRANSPORT

Road Traffic (1987): Total vehicles registered 54,979; *1996 Census*: Private cars 47,300.

Shipping (2003): *International Traffic*: Passengers carried 27,852; Freight handled 1,019,090 metric tons (Goods unloaded 994,880 metric tons; Goods loaded 24,210 metric tons). *Domestic Traffic*: Passengers carried 1,407,092; Freight handled 688,940 metric tons.

Civil Aviation (2003): *International Traffic*: Passengers carried 620,523; Freight handled 9,736 metric tons. *Domestic Traffic*: Passengers carried 803,842; Freight handled 3,231.6 metric tons (Source: Service d'État de l'Aviation Civile en Polynésie Française).

TOURISM

Visitors (excluding cruise passengers and excursionists): 189,030 in 2002; 212,767 in 2003; 211,893 in 2004.

Tourist Arrivals by Country of Residence (2004): Australia 7,687; France 45,069; Germany 4,412; Italy 10,278; Japan 23,630; New Zealand 7,721; North America 79,264; United Kingdom 8,050; Total (incl. others) 211,893 (Source: Ministère du Tourisme).

Tourism Receipts (US $ million): 359 in 1997; 354 in 1998; 394 in 1999 (Source: World Tourism Organization). *2004:* Receipts from tourism US $420m.

COMMUNICATIONS MEDIA

Radio Receivers (1997): 128,000 in use*.

Television Receivers (2000): 44,000 in use†.

Telephones (2002): 52,500 main lines in use†.

Facsimile Machines (1998): 3,000 in use†.

Mobile Cellular Telephones (subscribers, 2002): 90,000†.

Internet Users (2002): 35,000†.

Personal Computers (number in use, 2002): 70,000.

Daily Newspapers (2000): 2.

* Source: UNESCO, *Statistical Yearbook*.
† Source: International Telecommunication Union.

EDUCATION

Pre-primary (2001/02 unless otherwise indicated): 54 schools; 408 teachers (1996/97); 15,136 pupils.

Primary (2001/02 unless otherwise indicated): 173 schools; 2,811 teachers (1996/97); 28,988 pupils.

General Secondary (2001/02 unless otherwise indicated): 2,035 teachers (1998/99); 29,466 pupils.

Vocational (2001/02 unless otherwise indicated): 316 teachers (1992) ; 3,032 students.

Tertiary (2003/04 unless otherwise indicated): 50 teachers (1999); 2,343 students.
Source: partly UNESCO, *Statistical Yearbook*.

Directory

The Constitution

The constitutional system in French Polynesia was established under the aegis of the Constitution of the Fifth French Republic and specific laws of 1977, 1984 and 1990. The French Polynesia Statute 1984, the so-called 'internal autonomy statute', underwent amendment in a law of July 1990. A further extension of the Territory's powers under the statute was approved by the French National Assembly in Paris in December 1995. In January 2000 a constitutional amendment granting French Polynesia a greater degree of autonomy was presented to a joint session of the French Senate and National Assembly for final ratification (see History). In March 2003 both the National Assembly and Senate ratified amendments to the Constitution providing for French Polynesia (along with Wallis and Futuna) to become an Overseas Country. In July the Territorial Assembly and the Government of French Polynesia ratified the amendments. The approval of the French State Council, the French Government and the Constitutional Council duly followed, and in March 2004 French Polynesia became an Overseas Country.

French Polynesia is declared to be an Overseas Country of the French Republic, of which it remains an integral part. The High Commissioner, appointed by the French Government, exercises the prerogatives of the State in matters relating to defence, foreign relations, the maintenance of law and order, communications and citizenship. The head of the local executive and the official who represents the Overseas Country is the President of the Government, who is elected by the French Polynesian Assembly from among its own members. The President appoints and dismisses the Council of Ministers and has competence in international relations

as they affect French Polynesia and its exclusive economic zone, and is in control of foreign investments and immigration. The Assembly, which has financial autonomy in budgetary affairs and legislative authority within French Polynesia, is elected for a term of up to five years on the basis of universal adult suffrage. Following the elections of May 2004, it comprised 57 members: 37 elected by the people of the Windward Islands (Iles du Vent—Society Islands), eight by the Leeward Islands (Iles Sous le Vent—Society Islands), three by the Gambier Islands-East Tuamotu Archipelago, three by the West Tuamotu Archipelago, three by the Austral Islands and three by the Marquesas Islands. The Assembly elects a Permanent Commission from among its members, and itself meets for two ordinary sessions each year and upon the demand of the majority party, the President or the High Commissioner. Local government is conducted by the municipalities. There is an Economic, Social and Cultural Council (composed of representatives of professional groups, trade unions and other organizations and agencies which participate in the economic, social and cultural activities of French Polynesia), an Audit Office and a judicial system which includes a Court of the First Instance, a Court of Appeal and an Administrative Court. The Overseas Country, as a part of the French Republic, also elects two deputies to the National Assembly and one member of the Senate, and may be represented in the European Parliament.

The Government

(April 2005)

High Commissioner: MICHEL MATHIEU (appointed October 2001).
Secretary-General: JACQUES MICHAUT.

COUNCIL OF MINISTERS

President and Minister for International Relations, Statutory Reform, Decentralization, Rural Development and Management Reform for Pacific Islanders: OSCAR TEMARU.

Vice-President, Minister for Tourism, Civil Aviation, Communication and Government Unity, Government Spokesman: JACQUI DROLLET.

Minister for Economy, Finance, Industry, Small and Medium Businesses, Budget and Tax: EMILE VANFASSE.

Minister for Maritime Affairs and the Black Pearl Industry: KEITAPU MAAMAATUAIAHUTAPU.

Minister for Agriculture, Livestock and Forestry: AHITI ROOMAATAROA.

Minister for Education, responsible for Multilingualism and the Advancement of Polynesian Languages: JEAN-MARIUS RAAPOTO.

Minister for Health, Food Security and Traditional Medicine: PIA FAATOMO.

Minister for Outer Islands Development: LOUIS FRÉBAULT.

Minister for Public Utilities, Land and Sea Transport, Ports and Airports, Advancement of Renewable Energies and Mining: JAMES SALMON.

Minister for Labour, Employment, Vocational Training, Public Service, Relations with the Assembly of French Polynesia and the Social and Economic Council: PIERRE FRÉBAULT.

Minister for Post and Telecommunications, Sports, Information and Communication Technologies: EMILE VERNAUDON.

Minister for Urban Affairs, Housing and Land Issues: GILLES TEFAATAU.

Minister for Sustainable Development, Planning Environment, Quality of Life and Natural-disaster Prevention: GEORGES HANDERSON.

Minister for Social and Senior Citizens' Affairs: PATRICIA JENNINGS.

Minister for Family and Women's Issues: TINA CROSS.

Minister for Youth, Culture and Heritage: TAUHITI NENA.

Minister for Traditional Arts and Crafts: NATACHA TAURUA.

GOVERNMENT OFFICES

Office of the High Commissioner of the Republic: Bureau du Haut Commissaire, ave Bruat, BP 115, 98713, Papeete; tel. 468597; fax 468556; e-mail bcom@haut-commissariat.pf; internet www .polynesie-francaise.gouv.fr.

Office of the President of the Government: BP 2551, 98713 Papeete; tel. 472000; fax 419781; e-mail presid@mail.pf; internet www.presidence.pf.

Government of French Polynesia: BP 2551, Papeete; 28 blvd Saint-Germain, 75005 Paris, France; tel. 472000; fax 419781; e-mail presid@mail.pf; tel. 426510; fax 426409.

Economic, Social and Cultural Council (CESC): Ave Bruat, BP 1657, 98716 Papeete; tel. 416500; fax 419242; e-mail cesc@cesc.gov .pf; internet www.cesc.pf; f. 1977 as the Economic and Social Council; name changed as above in 1984; Pres. PIERRE FRÉBAULT; Sec.-Gen KATIA TESTARD.

Ministry of Agriculture: Fare Ute, BP 100, 2444-001 Papeete; tel. 428144; fax 420831; e-mail secretariat@ressources.gov.pf; internet www.agriculture.gov.pf.

Ministry of Craft Industry: BP 4451, 98713 Papeete; tel. 423225; fax 436478; e-mail maraea.teissier@broche.pf; internet www .artisanat.gov.pf.

Ministry of Culture: BP 543, 98713 Papeete; tel. 432695; fax 425251; e-mail sce@culture.gov.pf; internet www.culture.gov.pf.

Ministry of the Economy and Finance: BP 2551, 98713 Papeete; tel. 468250; fax 450050; e-mail nicole.levesques@finances.min.gov .pf; internet www.finances.gov.pf.

Ministry of Education: BP 2551, 98713 Papeete; tel. 501501; fax 424285; e-mail titaua.peu@education.gov.pf; internet www .education.gov.pf.

Ministry of Environment: Quartier Broche, rue Dumont d'Urville, BP 2551, 98713 Papeete; tel. 472000; fax 472005; e-mail dircab-cab@presidence.pf; internet www.environnement.gov.pf.

Ministry of Fisheries: BP 20, 98713 Papeete; tel. 502550; fax 434979; e-mail accueil@peche.gov.pf; internet www.mer.gov.pf.

Ministry of Health: BP 611, 98713 Papeete; tel. 460002; fax 433974; e-mail dircab.msa@sante.gov.pf; internet www.sante.gov .pf.

Ministry of Housing: Ave Bruat—Gouvernement, Rez de chaussée, BP 2551, 98713 Papeete; tel. 549575; fax 454343; e-mail dircab.mla@logement.gov.pf; internet www.logement.gov.pf.

Ministry of Land Affairs: BP 114, 98713 Papeete; tel. 549575; fax 454343; e-mail dircab.maa@foncier.gov.pf; internet www.foncier.gov .pf.

Ministry of the Pearl Industry: BP 2551, 98713 Papeete; tel. 472295; fax 472287; e-mail secretariat@ressources.gov.pf; internet www.perle.gov.pf.

Ministry of Public Works and Harbours: Bâtiment A1, rue du Commandant Destremeau, BP 85, 98713 Papeete; tel. 468019; fax 483792; e-mail contact.met@equipement.gov.pf; internet www .equipement.gov.pf.

Ministry of Solidarity and Family Affairs: Service des Affaires Sociales, BP 1707, 98713 Papeete; tel. 465846; fax 438920; e-mail dir .das@mail.pf; internet www.solidarite.gov.pf.

Ministry of Tourism and Transportation: BP 2551, 98713 Papeete; tel. 472152; fax 472005; e-mail maraea.teissier@broche.pf; internet www.tourisme.gov.pf.

Ministry of Youth: BP 2551, 98713 Papeete; tel. 501501; fax 424285; e-mail titaua.peu@education.gov.pf; internet www.jeunesse .gov.pf.

Legislature

ASSEMBLÉE

President: ANTONY GÉROS.

Assembly: Assemblée de la Polynésie Française, BP 28, 98713 Papeete; tel. 416100; fax 416149; internet www.assemblee.pf.

Election, 23 May 2004*

Party	Seats
Tahoera'a Huiraatira	28
Tavini Huiraatira†	27
Fe'tia Api†	1
No Oe E Te Nunaa†	1
Total	**57**

* Following the nullification in November 2004 of the election results of the Windward Islands constituency, 37 legislators were removed from office. A by-election for these 37 seats was held on 13 February 2005, following which the Tahoera'a Huiraatira held 27 seats and the Union pour la Démocratie (UPD—see below) also 27 seats; the Alliance pour une Démocratie Nouvelle (ADN), a newly formed coalition between Fe'tia Api and No Oe E Te Nunaa, held three seats.

† Campaigned as part of the original UPD coalition, which also

included candidates from Ai'a Api, Here Ai'a and Heiura-Les Verts Polynésiens.

PARLEMENT

Deputies to the French National Assembly: MICHEL BUILLARD (Tahoera'a Huiraatira/UMP), BÉATRICE VERNAUDON (Tahoera'a Huiraatira/UMP).

Representative to the French Senate: GASTON FLOSSE (Tahoera'a Huiraatira/UMP).

Political Organizations

Ai'a Api (New Land): BP 11055, Mahina, Tahiti; tel. 481135; f. 1982; after split in Te E'a Api; Leader EMILE VERNAUDON.

Fe'tia Api (New Star): c/o Assemblée de la Polynésie Française, BP 140 512, Arue; part of the Alliance pour une Démocratie Nouvelle coalition; Leader PHILIP SCHYLE.

Heiura-Les Verts Polynésiens: BP 44, Borabora; tel. and fax 677174; e-mail heiura@mail.pf; Pres. JACKY BRYANT.

Ia Mana Te Nunaa (Power to the People): rue du Commandant Destrémau, BP 1223, Papeete; tel. 426699; f. 1976; advocates 'socialist independence'; Sec.-Gen. JACQUI DROLLET.

No Oe E Te Nunaa (This Country is Yours): c/o Assemblée de la Polynésie Française, BP 28, Papeete; favours autonomy; part of the Alliance pour une Démocratie Nouvelle coalition; Leader NICOLE BOUTEAU.

Pupu Here Ai'a Te Nunaa Ia Ora: BP 3195, Papeete; tel. 420766; f. 1965; advocates autonomy; 8,000 mems.

Taatiraa No Te Hau: BP 2916, Papeete; tel. 437494; fax 422546; f. 1977; Pres. ROBERT TANSEAU.

Tahoera'a Huiraatira (People's Rally): rue du Commandant Destrémeau, BP 471, Papeete; tel. 429898; fax 450004; e-mail courrier@ tahoeraahuiraatira.pf; internet tahoeraahuiraatira.pf; f. 1977; fmrly l'Union Tahitienne; supports links with France, with internal autonomy; Pres. GASTON FLOSSE; Hon. Pres. JACQUES TEUIRA.

Tapura Amui No Te Faatereraa Manahune-Tuhaa Pae: c/o Assemblée de la Polynésie Française, BP 140 512, Arue; represents the Austral Islands; Leader CHANTAL FLORES.

Tavini Huiraatira no te ao Ma'ohi /Front de Libération de la Polynésie (Polynesian People's Servant): c/o Assemblée de la Polynésie Française, BP 140 512, Arue; f. 1977; independence movement; anti-nuclear; Leader OSCAR TEMARU.

Te' Avei'a (Te Ara): c/o Assemblée de la Polynésie Française, BP 140 512, Arue; f. 2004 by fmr mems of Fe'tia Api and Tavini Huiraatira; Pres. ANTONIO PEREZ.

Te Henua Enana Kotoa: Papeete; Leader LOUIS TAATA.

Te Hono e Tau I te Honaui (Link Between Generations): Papeete; f. 2002; Leader STANLEY CROSS.

Judicial System

Court of Appeal: Cour d'Appel de Papeete, ave Bruat, BP 101, 98713 Papeete; tel. 415546; fax 453767; e-mail sec.pp.ca-papeete@ justice.fr; Pres. OLIVIER AIMOT; Attorney-General FRANÇOIS DEBY; Clerk of the Court DENISE BIANCONI.

Court of the First Instance: Tribunal de Première Instance de Papeete, ave Bruat BP 101, Papeete; tel. 415500; fax 454012; internet www.polynesie-francaise.gouv.fr; e-mail tapapeete@mail .pf; Pres. GUY RIPOLL; Procurator JEAN BIANCONI; Clerk of the Court DENISE DANGLADE.

Court of Administrative Law: Tribunal Administratif, ave Bruat, BP 4522, Papeete; tel. 509025; fax 451724; e-mail tadelapolynesiefrancaise@mail.pf; Pres. ALFRED POUPET; Cllrs MARIE-CHRISTINE LUBRANO, ALAIN LEVASSEUR, HÉLÈNE ROULAND, DONA GERMAIN.

Religion

About 54% of the population are Protestants and 38% are Roman Catholics.

CHRISTIANITY

Protestant Church

At mid-2000 there were an estimated 110,000 Protestants.

Maohi Protestant Church: BP 113, Papeete; tel. 460600; fax 419357; e-mail eepf@mail.pf; f. 1884; autonomous since 1963; fmrly L'Eglise évangélique en Polynésie française (Etaretia Evaneria i Porinetia Farani); c. 95,000 mems; Pres. of Council Rev. TAAROANUI MARAEA.

The Roman Catholic Church

French Polynesia comprises the archdiocese of Papeete and the suffragan diocese of Taiohae o Tefenuaenata (based in Nuku Hiva, Marquesas Is). At 31 December 2002 there were an estimated 89,000 adherents in the Territory. The Archbishop and the Bishop participate in the Episcopal Conference of the Pacific, based in Fiji.

Archbishop of Papeete: Most Rev. HUBERT COPPENRATH, Archevêché, BP 94, Vallée de la Mission, 98713 Papeete; tel. 502351; fax 424032; e-mail catholic@mail.pf.

Other Churches

There are small Sanito, Church of Jesus Christ of Latter-day Saints (Mormon), and Seventh-day Adventist missions. At mid-2000 there were an estimated 30,000 adherents to other forms of Christianity.

The Press

La Dépêche de Tahiti: Société Océanienne de Communication, BP 50, Papeete; tel. 464343; fax 464350; e-mail journalistes@france-antilles.pf; internet www.ladepechedetahiti.com; f. 1964; daily; French; Editor-in-Chief THIERRY DURIGNEUX; Dir-Gen. CHRISTOPHE RUET; circ. 15,000.

Les Nouvelles de Tahiti: place de la Cathédrale, BP 629, Papeete; tel. 508100; fax 508109; f. 1956; daily; French; Editor MURIEL PONTAROLLO; Publr PHILIPPE HERSANT; circ. 6,500.

Le Semeur Tahitien: BP 94, 98713 Papeete; tel. 502350; e-mail catholic@mail.pf; f. 1909; bi-monthly; French; publ. by the Roman Catholic Church.

Tahiti Beach Press: BP 887, 98713 Papeete; tel. 426850; fax 423356; e-mail tahitibeachpres@mail.pf; f. 1980; monthly; English; Publr G. WARTI; circ. 10,000.

Tahiti Pacifique Magazine: BP 368, Maharepa, Moorea; tel. 562894; fax 563007; e-mail tahitipm@mail.pf; internet www.tahiti-pacifique.com; monthly; French; Dir and Editor ALEX DU PREL; circ. 5,000.

Tahiti Rama: Papeete; weekly.

La Tribune Polynésienne: place du Marché, BP 392, Papeete; tel. 481048; fax 481220; weekly; Dir LOUIS BRESSON.

Ve'a Katorika: BP 94, 98713 Papeete; f. 1909; monthly; publ. by the Roman Catholic Church.

Ve'a Porotetani: BP 113, Papeete; tel. 460623; fax 419357; e-mail eepf@mail.pf; f. 1921; monthly; French and Tahitian; publ. by the Evangelical Church; Dir IHORAI JACQUES; circ. 5,000.

NEWS AGENCIES

Tahitian Press Agency (ATP): Papeete; f. 2001; bilingual French and English news service providing pictures and radio reports.

Foreign Bureaux

Agence France-Presse (AFP): BP 629, Papeete; tel. 508100; fax 508109; e-mail international@france-antilles.pf; Correspondent CHRISTIAN BRETAULT.

Associated Press (AP) (USA): BP 912, Papeete; tel. 437562; Correspondent AL PRINCE.

Reuters (UK): BP 50, Papeete; tel. 475298; fax 475297; e-mail danielpardon@mail.pf; Correspondent DANIEL PARDON.

Publishers

Haere Po No Tahiti: BP 1958, Papeete; fax 582333; f. 1981; travel, history, botany, linguistics and local interest.

Au Vent des Iles: BP 5670, 98716 Pirae; tel. 509595; fax 509597; e-mail mail@auventdesiles.pf; internet www.auventdesiles.pf; f. 1992; Gen. Man. CHRISTIAN ROBERT.

GOVERNMENT PRINTER

Imprimerie Officielle: 43 rue des Poilus-Tahitiens, BP 117, 98713 Papeete; tel. 500580; fax 425261; e-mail compta.clients@imprimerie.gov.pf; f. 1843; printers, publrs; Dir CLAUDINO LAURENT (acting).

Broadcasting and Communications

TELECOMMUNICATIONS

France Câbles et Radio (FCR): Télécommunications extérieures de la Polynésie française, BP 99, Papeete; tel. 415400; fax 437553.

Office des Postes et Télécommunications: 8 rue de la Reine Pomare IV, Papeete; tel. 414242; fax 436767; internet www.opt.pf; Chair. ALPHONSE TERIIEROOITERAI; Dir-Gen. MATAHI BROTHERS.

BROADCASTING

Radio

RFO Polynésie: 410 rue Dumont d'Urville, POB 60, Pamatai; tel. 861616; fax 861611; e-mail jrbodin@mail.pf; internet www.rfo.fr.html; public service radio and television station operated by Réseau France Outre-Mer (RFO), Paris; daily programmes in French and Tahitian; Regional Man. MICHEL KOPS; Communications Man. JEAN-RAYMOND BODIN.

Private Stations

NRJ Radio: Papeete; tel. and fax 464346; e-mail nrj@mail.pf; French.

Radio Bleue: Papeete; tel. 483436; fax 480825; e-mail redaction@radiobleue.pf; French; affiliated to the political party Ai'a Api.

Radio Maohi: Maison des Jeunes, Pirae; tel. 819797; fax 825493; e-mail tereo@mail.pf; French and Tahitian; owned by the political party Tahoera'a Huiraatira.

Radio One: Fare Ute, BP 3601, Papeete; tel. 434100; fax 423406; e-mail infos@radio1.pf; Editor-in-chief YVES FORTUNET.

Radio Tefana: Papeete; tel. 819797; fax 825493; e-mail tereo@mail.pf; French and Tahitian; affiliated to the political party Tavini Huiraatira.

Radio Tiare: Fare Ute, Papeete; tel. 434100; fax 423406; e-mail contact@tiarefm.pf.

Television

Radio-Télé-Tahiti: see Radio.

Canal Plus Polynésie: Immeuble Pomare, blvd Paofai, BP 20051, 98713 Papeete; tel. 540754; fax 540755; e-mail serge.lamagnere@canal-caledonie.com; privately owned; CEO SERGE LAMAGNÈRE.

TNTV (Tahiti Nui Television): BP 348 98713, Papeete; tel. 473636; fax 532721; e-mail tntv@tntv.pf; internet www.tntv.pf; broadcasts in French and Tahitian; Pres. NICK TOOMARU; Gen. Man. LOÏC BRIGATO (acting).

TNS (Tahiti Nui Satellite): see TNTV; French.

Finance

(cap. = capital; res = reserves; dep. = deposits; m. = million; brs = branches; amounts in CFP francs)

BANKING

Commercial Banks

Banque de Polynésie SA: 355 blvd Pomare, BP 530, 98713 Papeete; tel. 466666; fax 466664; e-mail bdp@sg-bdp.pf; internet www.socgen.com/sgcb; f. 1973; 80% owned by Société Générale (France); cap. 1,380.0m.,res 3,509.0m., dep. 94,102.9m. (Dec. 2002); Pres. and Chair. RONALD GEORGES; Gen. Man. ROGER MUNOZ; 14 brs.

Banque de Tahiti SA: 38 rue François Cardella, BP 1602, 98713 Papeete; tel. 417000; fax 423376; e-mail contact@bt.pf; internet www.banque-tahiti.pf; f. 1969; owned by Financière Océor (95.4%); merged with Banque Paribas de Polynésie, Aug. 1998; cap. 1,336.5m., res 4,787.8m., dep. 85,986.8m. (Dec. 2002); Chair. and Pres. GILLES THERRY; Gen. Man. JEAN-CHRISTOPHE IRRMANN; 17 brs.

Banque SOCREDO—Société pour le Crédit et le Développement en Océanie: 115 rue Dumont d'Urville, BP 130, 98713 Papeete; tel. 415123; fax 433661; internet www.socredo.com; e-mail dirgen@bank-socredo.pf; f. 1959; public body; affiliated to Banque Nationale de Paris (France); total assets 182.9m. (Dec. 2003); Pres. JEAN VERNAUDON; Dir ERIC POMMIER; 24 brs.

Trade and Industry

DEVELOPMENT ORGANIZATIONS

Agence pour l'Emploi et la Formation Professionnelle: BP 540, Papeete; tel. 426375; fax 426281.

Agence Française de Développement (ACFD): Immeuble Hoku-le'a, 2 rue Cook–Paofai, BP 578, Papeete; tel. 544600; fax 544601; e-mail afdpapeete@pf.groupe-afd.org; internet www.afd.fr; public body; development finance institute; Dir FRANÇOIS DALLIER.

Service de l'Artisanat Traditionnel: BP 4451, Papeete 98713; tel. 423225; fax 436478; Dir TEURA IRITI.

Service du Développement de l'Industrie et des Métiers (SDIM): Bâtiment des Affaires Economiques à Fare Ute, 1er étage, BP 9055, 98713 Papeete; tel. 502880; fax 412645; e-mail secretariat

.sdim@industrie.gov.pf; internet www.creation-entreprises.pf; f. 1988; industry and small business development administration.

Société pour le Développement de l'Agriculture et de la Pêche: BP 1247, Papeete; tel. 836798; fax 856886; agriculture and marine industries.

SODEP (Société pour le Développement et l'Expansion du Pacifique): BP 4441, Papeete; tel. 429449; f. 1961 by consortium of banks and private interests; regional development and finance co.

CHAMBERS OF COMMERCE

Chambre de Commerce, d'Industrie, des Services et des Métiers de Polynésie Française (CCISM): 41 rue du Docteur Cassiau, BP 118, Papeete 98713; tel. 472700; fax 540701; e-mail info@cci .pf; internet www.ccism.pf; f. 1880; 36 mems; Pres. JULES CHANGUES; Sec. ADRIEN BEAUMONT.

Chambre d'Agriculture et de la Pêche Lagonaire: route de l'Hippodrome, BP 5383, Pirae; tel. 425393; fax 438754; f. 1886; 10 mems; Pres. CLAUDE HAUATA.

Jeune Chambre Economique de Tahiti: BP 2576, Papeete; tel. 454542; fax 466070; internet www.jce.pf; Pres. CATHY GOURBAULT.

EMPLOYERS' ORGANIZATIONS

Association Française des Banques/Comité en Polynésie Française (AFB/CPF): BP 530, 98713 Papeete.

Association des Transporteurs Locaux de Polynésie Française (ATAL): BP 314, 98713 Papeete.

Chambre Syndicale des Entrepreneurs du Bâtiment et des Travaux Publics (CSEBTP): BP 2218, 98713 Papeete; tel. 541040; fax 423237; Pres. GEORGES TRAMINI.

Chambre Syndicale des Métiers du Génie Civil (CSMGCTP): BP 51120, 98716 Pirae.

Confédération Générale des Petites et Moyennes Entreprises de Polynésie Française (CGPME): BP 1733, 98713 Papeete; tel. 426333; fax 835608; e-mail courrier@cgpme.pf; internet www.cpme .pf; Pres. CHRISTOPHE PLÉE.

Conseil des Employeurs: Immeuble Farnham, rue Clappier, BP 972, Papeete; tel. 541040; fax 423237; internet cepf@cepf.pf; f. 1983; Pres. JACQUES BILLON-TYRARDE; Sec.-Gen. CÉDRIC VIDAL.

Conseil des Professionnels de l'Hotellerie (CPH): BP 972, 98713 Papeete.

Fédération Générale du Commerce (FGC): angle rue Albert Leboucher et rue Clappier, BP 1607, 98713 Papeete; e-mail fgc@ mail.pf ; internet www.fgc.pf; tel. 541042; fax 422359; Pres. GILLES YAU; Sec. PATRICIA LO MONACO.

Syndicat des Industriels de Polynésie Française (SIPOF): f. 1974; represents workers in industry, engineering, manufacturing and printing; 2,000 mems in 53 cos; Pres. ALAIN SIU; Sec. BRUNO BELLANGER.

Syndicat Professionnel des Producteurs de Perles: BP 850, 98713 Papeete.

Union Polynésienne de l'Hôtellerie (UPHO): 76 rue Wallis, BP 9179 Motu Uta, Papeete; tel. 429553.

Union Patronale de Polynésie Française (UPPF): BP 317, 98713 Papeete; tel. 541040; fax 423237; f. 1948; 63 mems; Pres. DIDIER CHOMER.

UTILITIES

Electricity

Electricité de Tahiti (EDT): route de Puurai, BP 8021, Faaa-Puurai; tel. 867777; internet www.edt.pf; subsidiary of Suez; c. 61,000 customers (2000); Pres. JOËL ALLAIN; Dir-Gen. CHRISTIAN LEK-KIEFRE.

Water

Société Polynésienne des Eaux et Assainissements: BP 25795, 98713 Papeete, Tahiti; fax 421548; e-mail spea@spea.pf.

Syndicat Central de l'Hydraulique: Tahiti.

TRADE UNIONS

Confédération A Tia I Mua: Immeuble Ia Ora, 1er étage, ave Georges Clemenceau, BP 4523, Papeete; tel. 544010; fax 450245; e-mail atiaimua@ifrance.com; affiliated to CFDT (France); Gen. Sec. TU YAN.

Confédération des Syndicats des Travailleurs de Polynésie/Force Ouvrière (CSTP/FO): Immeuble Farnham, 1er

étage, BP 1201, 98713 Papeete; tel. 426049; fax 450635; Pres. COCO TERAIEFA CHANG; Sec.-Gen. PATRICK GALENON.

Confédération des Syndicats Independants de la Polynésie Française (CSIP): Immeuble Allegret, 1er étage, ave du Prince Hinoi, BP 468, 98713 Papeete.

Confédération O Oe To Oe Rima: Immeuble Brown, 1er étage, Papeete, BP 52866, 98716; tel. 483445; fax 483445; Gen. Sec. RONALD TERORUTUA.

Confédération Otahi: Immeuble Allegret, 1er étage, ave du Prince Hinoi BP148, 98713 Papeete; tel. 450654; fax 451327.

Transport

ROADS

French Polynesia has 792 km of roads, of which about one-third are bitumen-surfaced and two-thirds stone-surfaced.

SHIPPING

The principal port is Papeete, on Tahiti.

Port Authority: Port Autonome de Papeete, Motu Uta, BP 9164, 98715 Papeete; tel. 505454; fax 421950; e-mail portppt@portppt.pf; internet www.portdepapeete.pf; Harbour Master MARCEL PELLETIER; Port Man. BÉATRICE CHANSIN.

Agence Maritime Internationale de Tahiti: BP 274, Papeete, Tahiti; tel. 428972; fax 432184; e-mail amitahiti@mail.pf; services from Asia, the USA, Australia, New Zealand, American Samoa and Europe.

CGM Tour du Monde SA: 80 rue du Général de Gaulle, BP 96, Papeete; tel. 420890; fax 436806; shipowners and agents; freight services between Europe and many international ports; Dir HENRI C. FERRAND.

Compagnie Française Maritime de Tahiti: Immeuble Importex No. 45 Fare Ute, POB 368, 98713 Papeete; tel. 426393; fax 420617; e-mail taporo@mail.pf; Man. MORTON GARBUTT.

Compagnie Polynésienne de Transport Maritime: BP 220, Papeete; tel. 426240; fax 434889; e-mail aranui@mail.pf; internet www.aranui.com; Dir JEAN WONG.

EURL Transport Maritime des Tuamotu Ouest: BP 1816, 98713 Papeete; tel. 422553; fax 422557; Dir SIMÉON RICHMOND.

Leprado Valere SARL: POB 3917, Papeete; tel. 450030; fax 421049.

SARL Société de Transport Insulaire Maritime (STIM): BP 635, 98713 Papeete; tel. 452324; fax 452444; Dir ROLAND PAQUIER.

Société de Navigation des Australes: BP 1890, Papeete; tel. 509609; fax 420609.

CIVIL AVIATION

There is one international airport, Faaa airport, 6 km from Papeete, on Tahiti, and there are about 40 smaller airstrips. In October 2004 the Government commissioned a study into the building of a new international airport on Tupai in the Austral Islands. International services are operated by Air France, Air New Zealand, LAN-Chile, Air Outre Mer, Air Calédonie International, Corsair and Hawaiian Airlines (USA).

Service d'État de l'Aviation Civile: BP 6404, 98702, Faaa, Papeete; tel. 861000; fax 861009; e-mail buchwalter_axelle@seac.pf; internet www.seac.pf; Dir GUY YEUNG.

Air Moorea: BP 6019, Faaa; tel. 864100; fax 864269; e-mail freddy .chanseau@airmoorea.pf; internet www.airmoorea.com; f. 1968; operates internal services between Tahiti and Moorea Island and charter flights throughout the Territory; Pres. MARCEL GALENON; Dir-Gen. FREDDY CHANSEAU.

Air Tahiti: BP 314, 98713 Papeete; tel. 864000; fax 864009; e-mail direction.generale@airtahiti.pf; internet www.airtahiti.pf; f. 1953; Air Polynésie 1970–87; operates domestic services to 41 islands; 732,000 passengers (2004); Chair. and CEO CHRISTIAN VERNAUDON; Gen. Man. MARCEL GALENON.

Air Tahiti Nui: Rue Paul Gauguin, BP 1673, 98713 Papeete; tel. 460202; fax 460290; e-mail fly@airtahitinui.pf; internet www .airtahitinui.com; f. 1996; commenced operations 1998; scheduled services to the USA, France, Japan and New Zealand; Chair. and CEO GEFFRY SALMON.

Tourism

Tourism is an important and developed industry in French Polynesia, particularly on Tahiti. Some 210,000 people visited the Territory in 2004, when the tourism industry earned an estimated US $420m. In 2004 some 37% of arrivals were from North America,

21% from France and 11% from Japan. There were 44 hotels with 4,418 rooms in 2001.

GIE Tahiti Tourisme: Immeuble Paofai, bâtiment D, blvd Pomare, BP 65, 98713 Papeete; tel. 505700; fax 436619; e-mail tahiti-tourisme@mail.pf; internet www.tahiti-tourisme.pf; f. 1966 as autonomous public body, transformed into private corpn in 1993; tourist promotion; CEO DANY PANERO.

Service du Tourisme: Bâtiment Administratif de Putiaro, 4ème étage, Quartier de la Mission, BP 4527, Papeete; tel. 476200; fax 476202; e-mail sto@tourisme.gov.pf; govt dept; manages Special Fund for Tourist Development; Dir CLARISSE GODEFROY.

Syndicat d'Initiative de la Polynésie Française: BP 326, Papeete; Pres. PIU BAMBRIDGE.

NEW CALEDONIA

Introductory Survey

Location, Climate, Language, Religion, Capital

New Caledonia comprises one large island and several smaller ones, lying in the South Pacific Ocean, about 1,500 km (930 miles) east of Queensland, Australia. The main island, New Caledonia (la Grande-Terre), is long and narrow, and has a total area of 16,372 sq km. Rugged mountains divide the west of the island from the east, and there is little flat land. The nearby Loyalty Islands, which are administratively part of New Caledonia, are 1,981 sq km in area, and a third group of islands, the uninhabited Chesterfield Islands, lies about 400 km north-west of the main island. The islands are surrounded by the world's largest continuous coral barrier reef, encompassing some 40,000 sq km. The climate is generally mild, with an average temperature of about 24°C (75°F) and a rainy season between December and March. The average rainfall in the east of the main island is about 2,000 mm (80 ins) per year, and in the west about 1,000 mm (40 ins). French is the official language and the mother tongue of the Caldoches (French settlers). The indigenous Kanaks (Melanesians) also speak Melanesian languages: 29 languages were taken into account at the census of 1996, when it was recorded that 38% of the total indigenous Kanak population spoke a Melanesian language. Other immigrants speak Polynesian and Asian languages. New Caledonians almost all profess Christianity; about 59% are Roman Catholics, and there is a substantial Protestant minority. The capital is Nouméa, on the main island.

Recent History

New Caledonia became a French possession in 1853, when the island was annexed as a dependency of Tahiti. In 1860 a separate administration was established, and in 1885 a Conseil général was elected to defend the local interests before metropolitan France. France took possession of Melanesian land and began mining nickel and copper in 1864, displacing the indigenous Kanak population. This provoked a number of rebellions, including the Kanak revolt of 1878. From 1887 two separate administrations existed, for Melanesian Kanaks and expatriates, until New Caledonia became an Overseas Territory of the French Republic in 1946. In 1956 the first Territorial Assembly, with 30 members, was elected by universal adult suffrage, although the French Governor effectively retained control of the functions of government. New Caledonian demands for a measure of self-government were answered in 1976 by a new statute, which gave the Council of Government, elected from the Territorial Assembly, responsibility for certain internal affairs. The post of Governor was replaced by that of French High Commissioner to the Territory. In 1978 the Kanak-supported, pro-independence parties obtained a majority of the posts in the Council of Government. In early 1979, however, the French Government dismissed the Council, following its failure to support a proposal for a 10-year 'contract' between France and New Caledonia, because the plan did not acknowledge the possibility of New Caledonian independence. The Territory was then placed under the direct authority of the High Commissioner. A general election was held in July, but a new electoral law, which affected mainly the pro-independence parties, ensured that minor parties were not represented in the Assembly. Two parties loyal to France (Rassemblement pour la Calédonie dans la République—RPCR, and Fédération pour une Nouvelle Société Calédonienne—FNSC) together won 22 of the 36 seats.

Following the election of François Mitterrand as President of France, tension increased in September 1981 after the assassination of Pierre Declercq, the Secretary-General of the pro-independence party, Union Calédonienne (UC). In December of that year the French Government made proposals for change that included equal access for all New Caledonians to positions of authority, land reforms and the fostering of Kanak cultural institutions. To assist in effecting these reforms, the French Government simultaneously announced that it would rule by decree for a period of at least one year. In 1982 the FNSC joined with the opposition grouping, Front Indépendantiste (FI), to form a government that was more favourable to the proposed reforms.

In November 1983 the French Government proposed a five-year period of increased autonomy from July 1984 and a referendum in 1989 to determine New Caledonia's future. The statute was opposed in New Caledonia, both by parties in favour of earlier independence and by those against, and it was rejected by the Territorial Assembly in April 1984. However, the proposals were approved by the French National Assembly in September 1984. Under the provisions of the statute, the Territorial Council of Ministers was given responsibility for many internal matters of government, its President henceforth being an elected member instead of the French High Commissioner; a second legislative chamber, with the right to be consulted on development planning and budgetary issues, was created at the same time. All of the main parties seeking independence (except the Libération Kanak Socialiste—LKS—party, which left the FI) boycotted elections for the new Territorial Assembly in November 1984 and, following the dissolution of the FI, formed a new movement called the Front de Libération Nationale Kanak Socialiste (FLNKS). On 1 December, the FLNKS Congress established a 'provisional government', headed by Jean-Marie Tjibaou. The elections to the Territorial Assembly attracted only 50.1% of the electorate, and the anti-independence party Rassemblement pour la Calédonie dans la République (RPCR) won 34 of the 42 seats. An escalation of violence began in November, and in the following month three settlers were murdered by pro-independence activists and 10 Kanaks were killed by *métis* settlers.

In January 1985 Edgard Pisani, the new High Commissioner, announced a plan by which the Territory might become independent 'in association with' France on 1 January 1986, subject to the result of a referendum in July 1985. Kanak groups opposed the plan, insisting that the indigenous population be allowed to determine its own fate. At the same time, the majority of the population, which supported the RPCR, demonstrated against the plan and in favour of remaining within the French Republic. A resurgence of violence followed the announcement of Pisani's plan, and a state of emergency was declared after two incidents in which a leading member of the FLNKS was killed by security forces and the son of a French settler was killed by Kanak activists.

In April 1985 the French Prime Minister, Laurent Fabius, put forward new proposals for the future of New Caledonia, whereby the referendum on independence was deferred until an unspecified date not later than the end of 1987. Meanwhile, the Territory was to be divided into four regions, each to be governed by its own elected autonomous council, which would have extensive powers in the spheres of planning and development, education, health and social services, land rights, transport and housing. The elected members of all four councils together would serve as regional representatives in a Territorial Congress (to replace the Territorial Assembly).

The 'Fabius plan' was well received by the FLNKS, although the organization reaffirmed the ultimate goal of independence. It was also decided to maintain the 'provisional Government' under Jean-Marie Tjibaou at least until the end of 1985. The RPCR, however, condemned the plan, and the proposals were rejected by the predominantly anti-independence Territorial Assembly in May. However, the necessary legislation was approved by the French National Assembly in July, and the Fabius plan came into force. Elections were held in September, and as expected only in the region around Nouméa, where the bulk of the population is non-Kanak, was an anti-independence majority recorded. However, the pro-independence Melanesians, in spite of their majorities in the three non-urban regions, would be in a minority in the Territorial Congress.

The FLNKS boycotted the general election to the French National Assembly in March 1986, in which only about 50% of the eligible voters in New Caledonia participated. In May the French Council of Ministers approved a draft law providing for a referendum to be held in New Caledonia within 12 months, whereby voters would choose between independence and a further extension of regional autonomy. In December, in spite of strong French diplomatic opposition, the UN General Assembly voted to reinscribe New Caledonia on the UN list of non-self-governing territories, thereby affirming the population's right to self-determination.

The FLNKS decided to boycott the referendum on 13 September 1987, at which 98.3% of the votes cast were in favour of New Caledonia's continuation as part of the French Republic and only 1.7% of those cast favoured independence. Of the registered electorate, almost 59% voted, a higher level of participation than was expected, although 90% of the electorate abstained in constituencies inhabited by a majority of Kanaks.

In October 1987 seven pro-French loyalists were acquitted on a charge of murdering 10 Kanak separatists in 1984. Jean-Marie Tjibaou, who reacted to the ruling by declaring that his followers would have to abandon their stance of pacifism, and his deputy, Yeiwéné Yeiwéné, were indicted for 'incitement to violence'. In April 1988 four gendarmes were killed, and 27 held hostage in a cave on the island of Ouvéa, by supporters of the FLNKS. Two days later, Kanak separatists prevented about one-quarter of the Territory's polling stations from opening when local elections were held. The FLNKS boycotted the elections. Although 12 of the gendarmes taken hostage were subsequently released, six members of a French anti-terrorist squad were captured. French security forces immediately laid siege to the cave, and in the following month made an assault upon it, leaving 19 Kanaks and two gendarmes dead. Following the siege, allegations that three Kanaks had been executed or left to die, after being arrested, led to an announcement by the new French Socialist Government that a judicial inquiry into the incident was to be opened.

At the elections to the French National Assembly in June 1988, both New Caledonian seats were retained by the RPCR. Michel Rocard, the new French Prime Minister, chaired negotiations in Paris, between Jacques Lafleur (leader of the RPCR) and Jean-Marie Tjibaou, who agreed to transfer the administration of the Territory to Paris for 12 months. Under the provisions of the agreement (known as the Matignon Accord), the Territory was to be divided into three administrative Provinces prior to a territorial plebiscite on independence to be held in 1998. Only people resident in the Territory in 1988, and their direct descendants, would be allowed to vote in the plebiscite. The agreement also provided for a programme of economic development, training in public administration for Kanaks, and institutional reforms. The Matignon Accord was presented to the French electorate in a referendum, held on 6 November 1988, and approved by 80% of those voting (although an abstention rate of 63% of the electorate was recorded). The programme was approved by a 57% majority in New Caledonia, where the rate of abstention was 37%. In November, under the terms of the agreement, 51 separatists were released from prison, including 26 Kanaks implicated in the incident on Ouvéa.

In May 1989 the leaders of the FLNKS, Jean-Marie Tjibaou and Yeiwéné Yeiwéné, were murdered by separatist extremists, alleged to be associated with the Front Uni de Libération Kanak (FULK), a grouping which had until then formed part of the FLNKS, but which opposed the Matignon Accord on the grounds that it conceded too much to the European settlers. The assassinations were regarded as an attempt to disrupt the implementation of the Accord. Elections to the three Provincial Assemblies were nevertheless held, as scheduled, in June: the

FLNKS won a majority of seats in the North Province and the Loyalty Islands Province, while the RPCR obtained a majority in the South Province, and also emerged as the dominant party in the Territorial Congress, with 27 of the 54 seats; the FLNKS secured 19 seats.

The year of direct rule by France ended, as agreed, on 14 July 1989, when the Territorial Congress and Provincial Assemblies assumed the administrative functions allocated to them in the Matignon Accord (see Government, below). In November the French National Assembly approved an amnesty (as stipulated in the Matignon Accord) for all who had been involved in politically-motivated violence in New Caledonia before August 1988, despite strong opposition from the right-wing French parties.

In April 1991 the LKS announced its intention to withdraw from the Matignon Accord, accusing the French Government, as well as several Kanak political leaders, of seeking to undermine Kanak culture and tradition. The RPCR's policy of encouraging the immigration of skilled workers from mainland France and other European countries continued to be a source of conflict between the conservative coalition and the FLNKS.

At elections for the Representative to the French Senate in September 1992, the RPCR's candidate, Simon Loueckhote, narrowly defeated Roch Wamytan, the Vice-President of the FLNKS.

Debate concerning the political future of the Territory continued in 1994. In October Jacques Lafleur proposed that New Caledonia abandon the planned 1998 referendum on self-determination, in favour of a 30-year agreement with France, similar to the Matignon Accord, but with provision for greater autonomy in judicial matters. The UC, however, rejected the proposal and reiterated its demand for a gradual transfer of power from France to New Caledonia, culminating in a return to sovereignty in 1998.

French presidential elections took place in April–May 1995. During the second round of voting in the Territory, the socialist candidate, Lionel Jospin, received 25.9% of the total votes, while the candidate of the Gaullist Rassemblement pour la République (RPR), Jacques Chirac, won 74.1%. (Chirac was elected to the presidency with 52.6% of votes cast throughout the republic.)

At provincial elections in July 1995 the RPCR remained the most successful party, although its dominance was reduced considerably. The FLNKS remained in control of the North Province and the Loyalty Islands, while the RPCR retained a large majority in the the South Province. The RPCR retained an overall majority in the Territorial Congress, while the FLNKS remained the second largest party. Considerable gains were made by a newly-formed party led by Nouméa businessman Didier Leroux, Une Nouvelle-Calédonie pour Tous (UNCT), which secured seven seats in the Territorial Congress and seven seats in the Provincial Government of the South. An estimated 67% of the electorate participated in the elections. However, a political crisis subsequently arose as a result of the UNCT's decision to align itself with the FLNKS, leaving the RPCR with a minority of official positions in the congressional committees. Jacques Lafleur would not accept a situation in which the UNCT appeared to be the dominant party in the chamber, and Pierre Frogier, the RPCR's President of Congress, refused to convene a congressional sitting under such circumstances. The deadlock was broken only when the FLNKS released a statement in October, reiterating the importance of the relationship between the FLNKS and the RPCR as signatories of the Matignon Accord, and proposing the allocation of congressional positions on a proportional basis.

Negotiations between the French Government and delegations from the FLNKS and the RPCR were held in Paris in late 1995. It was agreed that further discussions would take place in early 1996, involving representatives from numerous interest groups in the Territory, to examine the possibility of achieving a consensus solution on the future of the islands. Thus, the major political groups in New Caledonia sought to achieve a consensus solution on the Territory's future, which could be presented to the electorate for approval in the 1998 referendum. It was widely believed that this was preferable to a simple 'for' or 'against' vote on independence, which would necessarily polarize the electorate and create a confrontational political climate.

Elections to the French National Assembly in May–June 1997 were boycotted by the pro-independence FLNKS and LKS, resulting in a relatively low participation rate among the electorate. Jacques Lafleur and Pierre Frogier, both RPCR candi-

dates, were elected to represent New Caledonia. Intensive negotiations involving the RPCR, the FLNKS and the French Government took place throughout early 1996. The process, however, was disrupted by a dispute over the disclosure of confidential information regarding the talks to the French press
(responsibility for which was later admitted by Lafleur) and the
belief by pro-independence leaders that France had apparently
reneged on its promise to consider all available options for the
Territory's political future by discounting the possibility of outright independence. France's refusal to grant final approval for
a large-scale nickel smelter project in the North Province (see
Economic Affairs, below) until the achievement of consensus in
the discussions on autonomy prompted accusations of blackmail
from several sources within the Territory and fuelled suspicions
that metropolitan France would seek to retain control of the
islands' valuable mineral resources in any settlement on New
Caledonia's future status. The issue proved to be a serious
obstacle in the negotiations and resulted in the virtual cessation
of discussions between the two sides during the remainder of
1996. The FLNKS argued that the smelter project should be
administered by local interests, consistent with the process of
reallocating responsibility for the economy from metropolitan
France to the Territory as advocated in the Matignon Accord.
Their demands were supported by widespread industrial action
in the mining sector during late 1996.

In February 1997 the French Minister for Overseas Territories, Jean-Jacques de Peretti, travelled to the Territory in an
attempt to achieve an exchange agreement on nickel between
the Société Minière du Sud-Pacifique (SMSP), controlled by the
North Province, and a subsidiary of the French mining conglomerate Eramet, Société Le Nickel (SLN). The minister failed
to resolve the dispute during his visit; however, at the end of the
month, in a complete reversal of its previous position, the
French Government announced its decision not to compensate
SLN for any losses incurred. The decision provoked strong
criticism from SLN and Eramet, and attracted protests from
shareholders and employees of the company. During March
large-scale demonstrations were held by the UC and the pro-
independence trade union, USTKE, in support of the SMSP's
acquisition of the smelter. Meanwhile, another trade union,
USOENC (which represented a high proportion of SLN
employees), organized a protest rally against the unequal
exchange of mining sites. Frustrated at SLN's seemingly intransigent position during the negotiations, the FLNKS organized
protests and blockades at all the company's major mining installations. Supporters of the pro-independence organization also
restricted shipments of ore around the Territory. Consequently,
four mines were forced to close, while a 25% reduction in
working hours was imposed on 1,500 mine workers, prompting
protests by SLN employees and demands from USOENC that
the blockades be removed. In January 1998 Roch Wamytan
urged the French Prime Minister, Lionel Jospin, to settle the
dispute by the end of the month in order that official negotiations on the political future of the Territory, in preparation for
the referendum, might begin. The position of the FLNKS had
been somewhat undermined by the decision, in the previous
month, of a breakaway group of pro-independence politicians—
including prominent members of the UC, Parti de Libération
Kanak (PALIKA), the UMP and the LKS—to begin negotiations
with the RPCR concerning the dispute. These moderate supporters of independence formed the Fédération des Comités de
Coordination des Indépendantistes (FCCI) in 1998. A draft
agreement on the exchange of deposits was signed by SLN and
the SMSP on 1 February, and in April the SMSP concluded a
deal with a Canadian company, Falconbridge, to build a nickel
smelter (see Economic Affairs, below). If construction of the
smelter had not begun by the end of 2005, control of the nickel
deposits transferred to the SMSP was to revert to SLN. Meanwhile, the French Government agreed to pay compensation of
some 1,000m. French francs to Eramet for the reduction in the
company's reserves. In mid-August 2004 a public inquiry raised
concerns about the environmental impact of a proposed Inco
nickel-cobalt plant at Goro in the South Province (see Economic
Affairs, below). The inquiry recommended that the development
proceed and an operating licence was granted in October. However, in February 2005 environmental protesters from a Kanak
non-governmental organization, Rheebu Nuu, blockaded the
Goro site to highlight its concerns about the disposal of industrial waste into the sea. In that month an agreement was
reached between Inco and the newly formed Société de Participation Minière du Sud Calédonien (a shareholding company

representing the three New Caledonia provinces) to acquire a
10% share in the Goro development.

Tripartite talks on the constitutional future of New Caledonia
resumed in Paris in late February 1998. Discussions between
representatives of the French Government, the FLNKS and the
RPCR continued in March, despite a temporary boycott of the
talks by the RPCR delegation, which requested the inclusion of
various other minor political groups in the negotiations,
including the FCCI. On 21 April, following a final round of talks
in Nouméa, an agreement was concluded by the three sides. The
agreement, which became known as the Nouméa Accord, postponed the referendum on independence for a period of between
15 and 20 years but provided for a gradual transfer of powers to
local institutions. The document also acknowledged the negative
impact of many aspects of French colonization on the Territory
and emphasized the need for greater recognition of the importance of the Kanak cultural identity in the political development
of the islands. The Nouméa Accord was signed on 5 May.

On 6 July 1998 the French Parliament (the National
Assembly and the Senate) voted in favour of adopting the
proposed changes regarding the administration of New Cale-
donia, which were to be incorporated in an annex to the French
Constitution. The following month the French Minister for
Overseas Territories, Jean-Jack Queyranne, returned to New
Caledonia for discussion on draft legislation for the devolution
process. In September a new political group, the Comité Provisoire pour la Défense des Principes Républicains de la Nouvelle-
Calédonie Française, was formed in opposition to the Nouméa
Accord, with support from members of the Front National and
other right-wing parties. The UNCT, which was dissatisfied
with several aspects of the accord, also urged its supporters to
vote against the agreement.

The Nouméa Accord was presented to the electorate of New
Caledonia in a referendum on 8 November 1998, when it was
decisively approved, with 71.9% of votes cast in favour of the
agreement. The North Province registered the strongest vote in
favour of the agreement (95.5%), while the South Province
recorded the most moderate level of approval (62.9%). In late
December the French National Assembly unanimously
approved draft legislation regarding the definitive adoption of
the accord. The Senate similarly approved the legislation in
February 1999. In March of that year, however, the French
Constitutional Council declared its intention to allow any
French person who had resided in New Caledonia for 10 years or
more to vote in provincial elections. This decision was criticized
by Roch Wamytan, leader of the FLNKS, as well as by politicians
in the French National Assembly and Senate, who claimed that
this was in breach of the Nouméa Accord, whereby only those
residing in New Caledonia in 1998 would be permitted to vote in
provincial elections. Pro-independence groups threatened to
boycott the elections (to be held in May). In response to this, the
French Government announced that the Accord would be honoured, claiming that the Constitutional Council had breached
the Nouméa Accord, and stating that this contravention would
be rectified. In June the French Council of Ministers announced
that it had drafted legislation restricting eligibility for voting in
provincial elections and in any future referendums on sovereignty, to those who had been eligible to vote in the November
1998 referendum on the Nouméa Accord, and to their children
upon reaching the age of majority. This decision was condemned
by the right-wing Front National, and by Jacques Lafleur,
leader of the RPCR. In January 2005 the European Court of
Human Rights upheld the ruling, but the matter was expected to
be discussed at talks in Paris later that month as part of the
follow-up process to the Nouméa Accord; Lafleur, who had since
been replaced as leader of the RPCR by Pierre Frogier, had
already proposed reducing to three years the period of residence
required before one would be allowed to vote and was threatening to boycott the talks.

At the general election held on 9 May 1999, no party gained an
absolute majority. However, Jacques Lafleur's anti-independence RPCR won 24 of the 54 seats in the Congress and formed a
coalition with the recently-established FCCI and, on an informal
level, with the Front National, thus creating an anti-independence block of 31 seats in the chamber. The pro-independence
FLNKS won 18 seats. Simon Loueckhote was re-elected as
President of the Congress in late May. Results of the elections in
the Loyalty Islands were officially challenged by the moderate
independence parties, LKS and FCCI, as well as by the RPCR,
following the issue by the electoral commissioner for the Province of a report claiming that a large number of irregularities

had occurred. A new election was held in June 2000, at which a coalition of the RPCR, FCCI, LKS and FULK obtained 44.8% of votes and six seats. The FLNKS obtained 37.3% of votes and six seats, and PALIKA 17.8% of votes and two seats. The composition of the Congress therefore remained unchanged. Robert Xowie was re-elected as President of the Province.

On 28 May 1999 the Congress elected Jean Lèques as the first President of the Government of New Caledonia, under the increased autonomy terms of the Nouméa Accord. The new Government was elected on the basis of proportional representation and replaced the French High Commissioner as New Caledonia's executive authority. The election of Léopold Jorédié, leader of the FCCI, as Vice-President was denounced by the FLNKS, which argued that, as the second largest party in Congress and as joint negotiators in the Nouméa Accord, the post should have gone to its leader, Roch Wamytan. In the formation of the Government the RPCR-FCCI was awarded seven positions and the FLNKS four.

In October 1999 Wamytan threatened to withdraw from the Government, in protest at the lack of co-operation among parties. He claimed that sections of the Nouméa Accord requiring power to be distributed among the various political parties had not been observed (see above). In December Vice-President Léopold Jorédié received a one-year suspended prison sentence following accusations of misuse of public funds. Jorédié was charged with illegally obtaining grants totalling an estimated 5.5m. francs CFP, for the benefit of his son.

In July 2000 concern was expressed by the French Government over the implementation of the 'collegiality' clause in the Nouméa Accord, which provides for greater political co-operation among parties. Repeated threats by the FLNKS to withdraw from the Government because of its discontent with the RPCR's lack of power-sharing led to the establishment of an agreement between New Caledonia and the French State detailing the role of the two Governments in areas such as education and foreign policy; the role of the traditional chiefs in legal matters was also specified. In August Jacques Lafleur threatened to resign from his seat in the French National Assembly, following the decision to uphold a ruling that convicted him of slander against Bruno Van Peteghem, an activist opposing construction plans for a complex near Nouméa. However, in early September Lafleur retracted his threat, following pleas by RPCR members.

In August 2000 the Government introduced a 'social pact', aimed at addressing social issues and ongoing industrial conflicts. It proposed an increase in the minimum wage and suggested local employment priorities, subject to ratification by employers' unions in September.

At the FLNKS's annual conference, held in November 2000, Roch Wamytan was re-elected President of the party (Wamytan was also narrowly re-elected leader of the UC); at the same time a new pro-independence party, the Groupe UC du Congrès, formed by a breakaway faction of the UC, was officially recognized by both the UC and the FLNKS.

Municipal elections held in March 2001 confirmed the predominance of the RPCR in the south, when it won 39 of the 49 seats in Nouméa. However, in the country as a whole the RPCR controlled only 14 of the 33 municipalities in New Caledonia, while pro-independence parties, principally the UC, PALIKA, LKS and FLNKS, held 19. The FLNKS won a majority in the north and took all three communes in the Loyalty Islands. Jean Lèques resigned as President and was replaced by fellow RPCR politician, Pierre Frogier, in April. Déwé Gorodey of the FLNKS was elected Vice-President. The election to the two most senior posts took place after the Congress had elected an 11-member Government consisting of seven RPCR-FCCI coalition members, three from the FLNKS and one from the UC.

In October 2001 the French Council of State ruled that the 11th seat in the New Caledonian Government had been incorrectly allocated to the FLNKS following the local elections of April 2001. As a result, FCCI leader Raphaël Mapou replaced Aukusitino Manuohalalo of the FLNKS as Minister for Social Security and Health. Roch Wamytan, threatened to resign from the Government in protest. In the same month, however, Wamytan was replaced as President of the UC by his deputy, Pascal Naouna; many members believed that Wamytan's dual role as President of both the UC and the FLNKS was weakening the party. Then, in November, Wamytan lost the presidency of the FLNKS following a leadership struggle between its two main factions, the UC and PALIKA. The political bureau of the FLNKS was to lead the party until its internal disputes were

settled. Wamytan was subsequently replaced as Minister for Customary Affairs and Relations with the Senate by Mapou, who was in turn replaced as Minister for Social Security and Health by Manuohalalo.

In June 2001, as a result of the failure to resolve industrial action over the dismissal of 12 employees from public works company Lefèbvre Pacifique, the Union Syndicale des Travailleurs Kanak et des Exploités (USTKE) extended its strike to 24-hour blockades of supermarkets, petrol stations, state radio and television companies, schools, the port and airport. In July 2001 a 100,000 francs CFP monthly minimum wage (as provided for in the 'social pact' brokered by Jacques Lafleur in September 2000) was implemented. Further strike action affected the tourist industry when, in December, USTKE launched a strike and occupation of the Château Royal complex, following Club Med's announcement of the Nouméa holiday resort's closure.

Meanwhile, a long-standing dispute over the ownership of a Wallisian settlement—Ave Maria, near Nouméa—had led to intense fighting between Wallisian and Kanak communities from December 2001. The Kanak community in neighbouring Saint Louis demanded the departure of all Wallisians from Ave Maria by March 2002. The French High Commissioner mediated at several meetings in January 2002 in an attempt to resolve the issue, leading to the Wallisian spokesman's suggestion that his community might be prepared to leave Ave Maria, provided it was offered an alternative 25 ha of land on which to resettle. Four working groups were established in April to rehouse Wallisians, to improve the area's public facilities, and to reintegrate youths who had abandoned the education system. In November the Kanak and Wallisian communities signed an agreement, mediated by the High Commissioner, to end the violence, which had claimed three lives in total. About half of the 140 Wallisian families present in Saint Louis had left by the end of 2002; under the terms of the agreement, the remainder were to be resettled in 2003. In June of that year some 100 Wallisians were forced to flee Ave Maria and take up residence in temporary housing, following another outbreak of racial violence with the Kanak community. By mid-September the remaining 30 Wallisian families had left the area to be resettled in and around Nouméa. The leader of the opposition Alliance pour la Calédonie, Didier Leroux, condemned the failure of the French Government to intervene as tantamount to 'ethnic cleansing'.

In the first round of the presidential election, held on 21 April 2002, Jacques Chirac obtained 48.4% of the vote on the islands, followed by Lionel Jospin, who won 22.4%, and was eliminated nationally. In the second round, held on 5 May, Chirac overwhelmingly defeated Jean-Marie Le Pen of the extreme right-wing Front National, with 80.4% of the vote. Elections to the French National Assembly were held in June 2002. The UC and PALIKA could not agree upon their choice of President for the FLNKS. The UC therefore refused to take part in the elections and urged its supporters to abstain from the poll, thereby depriving the President of PALIKA, Paul Néaoutyine, of any chance of re-election to the National Assembly. Jacques Lafleur was thus re-elected as a deputy in the French legislature, winning 55.7% of the votes cast in the second round of polling; Pierre Frogier was also re-elected, with 55.7% of the vote; the rate of abstention was almost 60%. In December Lafleur announced his 'progressive retirement' from politics, although he gave no precise date.

Following two resignations in July 2002, a series of ministerial reorganizations took place. The Minister for Employment and Public Services resigned and was replaced by a fellow RPCR member, Georges Naturel. In late July Raphaël Mapou resigned, following his criticism of the tendering of mining and prospecting rights in the South Province to a Canadian mining company. He was replaced by Corinne Fuluhea of the RPCR. Shortly afterwards, her portfolio was altered to that of Professional Training. In November the sole UC member of the Government, Gerald Cortot, resigned, prompting the immediate dissolution of the Government, as stipulated in the Nouméa Accord. Later that month the size of the Council of Ministers was reduced to 10 members, and the Congress appointed a new administration, with Pierre Frogier reappointed as President; the incoming Government contained seven members of the RPCR-FCCI coalition, two from the FLNKS and one from the UC. In May 2003 it was announced that New Caledonia (together with French Polynesia) would be granted one additional seat in the French Senate, probably effective from the next senatorial elections in 2007. Also in May 2003, at a congress of the FLNKS, officials of the party reportedly claimed that the terms of the Nouméa Accord were not being fully observed by the French Government. In July the USTKE called a general strike to coincide with a visit to New Caledonia by President Chirac. A rally organized by the mainly Kanak trade union was attended by 2,000 protesters. Chirac's four-day visit also provoked demonstrations by several hundred members of the UC. Police used tear gas in an attempt to disperse the pro-independence protesters, who had gathered near an official ceremony in honour of the visiting head of state. Kanak representatives, meanwhile, expressed dismay at their exclusion from meetings with the French President. During his visit Chirac refrained from making any direct comment on the status of New Caledonia.

Legislative elections took place on 9 May 2004. The RPCR lost its majority in both the Congress of New Caledonia and in the South Province. The results demonstrated an increase in support for the pro-independence movements, notably the recently formed Avenir Ensemble. Each Provincial Assembly in turn elected its President: Philippe Gomès of the Avenir Ensemble became President of the South Province, replacing Jacques Lafleur; Paul Néaoutyine of the UNI-FLNKS was re-elected in the North Province; and Néko Hnépeune, also of the UNI-FLNKS, was elected President in the Loyalty Islands. At its inaugural meeting in late May the incoming Congress elected Harold Martin of the Avenir Ensemble as its President and began the process of appointing a new Government. In early June Marie-Noëlle Thémereau of the Avenir Ensemble and Déwé Gorodey of the UNI-FLNKS were respectively nominated President and Vice-President. However, the Government collapsed within hours following the resignation of three UMP cabinet ministers, who claimed that they were entitled to four seats under power-sharing terms set out in the Nouméa Accord. Congress granted the UMP the seats but with the result that the decision of the Council of Ministers on its leadership reached a stalemate. In late June, following negotiations that also involved the French High Commissioner in New Caledonia and discussions in Paris between Harold Martin and the French Government, a new vote returned Thémereau and Gorodey to their elected posts. The incoming Government endorsed a code of conduct that emphasized the importance of consensus-building among the parties and 'collegiality' in the decision-making process. In late January 2005 representatives of the Avenir Ensemble for the first time took part in talks with the French Government in Paris as part of the follow-up process to the Nouméa Accord (see above).

In late July 2004 USTKE members blockaded the harbour wharf in protest at moves by stevedoring companies to consolidate cargo-handling activities, which it was believed would lead to redundancies. Police intervention provoked a 'roving' general strike by some 5,000 workers which disrupted freight services at the wharf and airport, and refuse collections. Nickel-mining companies were affected by the action, as was the principal flour mill, leading to a shortage of bread. Blockades of fuel depots forced the closure of service stations and brought school bus services to a standstill. The RFO radio and television network was unable to broadcast. After three days the cargo-handling agreement was reversed and the USTKE withdrew its pickets in early August. However, in an unrelated strike over contractual terms, the USTKE forced RFO off the air again in mid-August; the strike action spread in September, halting production for two weeks at the newspaper *Les Nouvelles Calédoniennes*. The strike at RFO was finally resolved in December and led to the replacement of the station manager.

In September 2004 politicians from across the political spectrum urged a boycott of the population census on the grounds that it would not record individuals' ethnic identity. During his visit to New Caledonia in July 2003 President Chirac had declared his opposition to the inclusion of such details, taking the position that France recognized French citizens without regard to specific ethnicity. However, some 10% of the population were believed to have abstained from the census. An additional survey of ethnicity was scheduled to take place in April 2005 at a cost of some US $1.5m.

Government

The French Government is represented in New Caledonia by its High Commissioner, and controls a number of important spheres of government, including external relations, defence, justice, finance, external trade and secondary education. In July 1989 administrative reforms were introduced, as stipulated in the Matignon Accord (which had been approved by national referendum in November 1988). New Caledonia was divided into three Provinces (North, South and Loyalty Islands), each governed by an assembly, which is elected on a proportional basis. The members of the three Provincial Assemblies together form the Congress. Members are subject to re-election every five years. The responsibilities of the Congress include New Caledonia's budget and fiscal affairs, infrastructure and primary education, while the responsibilities of the Provincial Assemblies include local economic development, land reform and cultural affairs. The Government of New Caledonia is elected by the Congress, and comprises between seven and 11 members. Under the terms of the Nouméa Accord (which was approved by a referendum in November 1998), it replaces the French High Commissioner as New Caledonia's executive authority. A gradual transfer of power from metropolitan France to local institutions was to be effected over a period of between 15 and 20 years under the terms of the Nouméa Accord.

In addition, New Caledonia elects two deputies to the French National Assembly in Paris and one representative to the French Senate on the basis of universal adult suffrage; one Economic and Social Councillor is also nominated. (In 2003 it was announced that New Caledonia would be granted one additional seat in the French Senate, probably effective from 2007.) New Caledonia may also be represented at the European Parliament.

Defence

In August 2004 France was maintaining a force of 2,700 military personnel in New Caledonia, including a gendarmerie.

Economic Affairs

In 2000, according to World Bank estimates, New Caledonia's gross national income (GNI) at average 1998–2000 prices totalled US $2,682m., equivalent to $14,030 per head (or $22,300m. per head on an international purchasing-power parity basis). During 1990–2003, it was estimated, the population rose at an average annual rate of 2.3%, while gross domestic product (GDP) per head decreased, in real terms, by an average of 0.7% during 1990–2000. Overall GDP increased in real terms, at an average annual rate of 1.6% in 1990–2000, rising by 0.9% in 1999 and by 2.1% in 2000.

Agriculture and fishing contributed only 1.9% of GDP in 1999, and 4.8% of the employed labour force were engaged in the sector in 2001. Maize, yams, sweet potatoes and coconuts have traditionally been the principal crops. However, pumpkins (squash) became an important export crop for the Japanese market during the 1990s, with 2,200 metric tons exported in 2000 (compared with 500 tons in 1993). Livestock consists mainly of cattle and pigs. The main fisheries products are tuna and shrimps (most of which are exported to Japan). An estimated total of 1,815 metric tons of farmed shrimps and prawns was produced in 2002 (compared with 632 tons in 1993). The value of prawn exports increased from 1,797m. francs CFP in 2000 to 1,958m. in 2001. In that year, overall, exports of fisheries and aquaculture products were worth 2,973m. francs CFP, accounting for some 5.0% of total exports.

Industry (comprising mining, manufacturing, construction and utilities) provided 19.6% of GDP in 1997, and employed 28.0% of the working population in 2001. Although mining employed only 3.4% of New Caledonia's working population in 2001, it constitutes the most important industrial sector. In 1999 mining and quarrying contributed an estimated 10% of GDP. New Caledonia possesses among the world's largest known nickel deposits and is a major producer of ferro-nickel. Sales of nickel ores and concentrates and nickel mattes accounted for 43.9% of export revenues in 2004. Compared with the previous year, metallurgical production increased by 3.9% in 2001. The introduction of the single European currency in January 2002 provided a boost to the nickel industry (both the one and two-euro coins used New Caledonian nickel). In November 2001, however, in response to a decline in world nickel prices, the Société Minière du Sud Pacifique (SMSP) announced plans to reduce its mining activity by 50%, entailing the redundancy of 600 workers. In that year the Canadian company Inco announced that it would proceed with the construction of a fully integrated nickel-cobalt mining and processing facility at Goro, in the South Province, but work was suspended in December 2002 as the projected cost had escalated from US $1,460m. to $2,000m. In October 2004 Inco announced that work would resume in early 2005, having reduced the projected cost of the plant to $1,880m., some $500m. of which was to be provided by the French Government. The plant was expected to be operational by 2007, reaching 75% of its annual capacity of 60,000 metric tons of nickel within 12 months and 90% within two years; cobalt production was projected at 4,300–5,000 tons. In January 2005 discussions were ongoing between SMSP and the Canadian company Falconbridge over the proposed construction of a nickel-smelting plant at Koniambo in the North Province (see Recent History, above); annual production was estimated at 30,000 metric tons over a 60-year period. The projected cost of developing the site rose from US $1,600m. to in excess of US $2,000m. and a final decision was postponed from the end of 2004 to December 2005. In December 2004 Société Le Nickel (SLN) commissioned a second smelter at its Tiébaghi site, with the aim of boosting the company's nickel output to 75,000 tons by 2006. Overall, New Caledonia's annual nickel production capacity was expected to rise to 200,000 tons by 2007.

The manufacturing sector, which provided 4.0% of GDP in 1997 and (together with electricity, gas and water) engaged 11.0% of the employed labour force in 2001, consists mainly of small and medium-sized enterprises, most of which are situated around the capital, Nouméa, producing building materials, furniture, salted fish, fruit juices and perishable foods.

Electrical energy is provided mainly by thermal power stations (some 80% in 2004), by hydroelectric plants, and more recently by wind power. Mineral fuels accounted for 14.8% of total imports in 2000. As part of the Government's plans to reduce expensive imports of diesel fuel investment a target was set to provide 60,000 kWh of wind-generated electricity by 2010, equivalent to some 15% of New Caledonia's energy requirements. In 2001 Vergnet installed three windmills on l'Ile des Pins, south of Nouméa, and nine on Lifou. In 2003 the company installed a further 31 windmills at Prony in the South Province; the project was financed by the energy operator Enercal at a cost of some francs CFP 1,900m. and was eventually expected to produce some 6,800 kWh. In February 2005 a new project was scheduled for commission at Kafeate in the North Province; initially 22 windmills were to be installed out of a total of 42 units which, it was expected, would produce some 11,000 kWh. In July 2004 Prony Energies announced that it would begin construction of a 50-MW coal-fired power station at Goro, in a joint venture with Enercal and Elyo of France; a decision on a second 50-MW station, to supply the Inco nickel plant, was expected at the end of September. Plans for the Falconbridge nickel plant at Koniambo also envisaged the construction of a 390-MW power station.

Service industries together contributed 73.7% of GDP in 1999 and engaged 67.1% of the employed labour force in 2001. The tourism sector in New Caledonia, however, has failed to witness an expansion similar to that experienced in many other Pacific islands, and tourist arrivals have been intermittently affected by political unrest. The number of tourist arrivals declined to 101,933 in 2003 from 103,933 in the previous year and continued to decline in 2004, to 99,515. Receipts from tourism decreased from US $110m. in 2000 to $93m. in 2001.

In 2003 New Caledonia recorded a visible trade deficit of some 72,058m. francs CFP, and there was a deficit of 9,391m. francs CFP on the current account of the balance of payments (a surplus of 25,242m. francs CFP was registered in 1999). The principal imports in 1999 were mineral fuels, foodstuffs and machinery and transport equipment. France is the main trading partner, providing some 40.3% of imports and purchasing 26.1% of exports in 2001; other major trading partners in that year were Japan (which purchased 23.1% of exports), Taiwan (17.6% of exports), Australia and Singapore.

The budget for 2001 envisaged revenue and expenditure balancing at 81,337m. francs CFP. Budgetary expenditure for 2002 was set at 86,400m. francs CFP. Budgetary aid from France totalled the equivalent of €755,317m. in 2001, increasing to €777,965 in 2002. The annual rate of inflation in Nouméa averaged 1.9% in 1990–2003. The rate of inflation rose by an average of 1.9% in 2002 and by 1.2% in 2003. Some 16.0% of the labour force were unemployed in 2001. A total of 10,187 were registered as unemployed at the end of 2003.

New Caledonia forms part of the Franc Zone (see p. 266), is an associate member of the UN Economic and Social Commission for Asia and the Pacific (ESCAP, see p. 31) and is a member, in its own right, of the Pacific Community (see p. 337). Following the adoption of the Nouméa Accord in 1998 (see Recent History, above), New Caledonia obtained observer status at the Pacific Islands Forum (see p. 339) in September 1999. In January 2005 the Government was considering joining the Forum's Pacific Islands Free Trade Agreement (PICTA).

New Caledonia's economy is vulnerable to factors affecting the islands' important nickel industry, which included political unrest during the 1980s and fluctuations in international prices for the commodity. The Nouméa Accord, approved by referendum in November 1998 (see Recent History), aimed to improve the economic conditions of the Kanak population and to increase their participation in the market economy and in public administration. Despite previous attempts to redress the balance of New Caledonian society (most importantly with the Matignon Accord of 1988), the indigenous population remained largely excluded from New Caledonia's economic and political administration, and a considerable proportion continued to experience economic hardship. In mid-1999 the RPCR leader, Jacques Lafleur, revealed proposals for the creation of an interprovincial committee for economic development, which would allow the comparatively wealthy South Province to assist the economic development of the other Provinces. Moreover, it was hoped that the development of those sectors generally considered not to have reached their full potential (notably tourism, aquaculture, fishing and farm agriculture) would alleviate the economic uncertainty created by the need to reduce dependency on France. In an effort to encourage investment in New Caledonia, legislation to replace the system of tax deductions with one of tax credits was expected to be adopted in 2002. In the tourism sector, visitor arrivals declined by 8.3% in 2001 compared with the previous year, but rose by 3.3% in 2002, before decreasing again during 2003–04. In March 2003, furthermore, Air France ceased its operations in New Caledonia. The route to Tokyo, where Air France would provide connections to Paris, was taken over by Air Calédonie International (AirCalin), which was given a tax concession by the French Government on the cost of two new aircraft. In August 2004 the Australian airline Virgin Blue was granted landing rights in New Caledonia, which it was hoped would raise tourist numbers. However, owing to a disagreement over airport service charges the company postponed its inaugural flight indefinitely. Between October 2004 and February 2005 strike action by firemen disrupted international flights at the Nouméa-LaTontouta airport; AirCalin claimed that the strike action had cost the company some francs CFP 26m. In late 1999 a joint French and Australian research mission made an offshore discovery of what was believed to be the world's largest gas deposit, measuring an estimated 18,000 sq km. It was hoped that this indicated the presence of considerable petroleum reserves. The effect of the decline in world nickel prices during 2001 was compounded by the downturn in the aviation industry that followed the terrorist attacks on the USA in September (aeronautical companies normally being significant consumers of special nickel alloys). Nickel prices, however, recovered in mid-2002 and rose strongly during 2003–04, principally owing to the demand in China. In mid-2003 the National Assembly approved the Overseas Territories Development Bill, which would provide support for economic and social development in New Caledonia (together with French Polynesia and Wallis and Futuna) by attracting foreign investment, and among other benefits allow for overseas French nationals to travel to mainland France to take advantage of free education. Discussions began in December 2004 on the replacement of the franc CFP with the euro. If consensus could be reached by New Caledonia, French Polynesia and Wallis and Futuna, the introduction of the new currency was anticipated by January 2007. However, pro-independence parties were opposing the move, which they warned would continue to make currency matters dependent on decisions made in Europe, whereas under the terms of the Nouméa Accord currency was to become an issue of local competence.

Education

Education is compulsory for 10 years between six and 16 years of age. Schools are operated by both the State and churches, under the supervision of three Departments of Education: the Provincial department responsible for primary level education, the New Caledonian department responsible for primary level inspection, and the State department responsible for secondary level education. The French Government finances the state secondary system. Primary education begins at six years of age, and lasts for five years; secondary education, beginning at 11 years of age, comprises a first cycle of four years and a second, three-year cycle. Overall, in 2004 some 71% of pupils were enrolled at state institutions. In that year 13,527 pupils attended 83 pre-primary schools and 23,522 pupils attended 202 primary schools; there were some 1,885 teachers employed in pre-primary and primary education. A total of 31,230 pupils attended 64 secondary schools and there were 2,677 teachers employed in secondary education. There were 21 technical and higher institutions and their annexes (of which 8 were private). In 1999 some 400 students attend universities in France. In 1987 the French University of the Pacific (based in French Polynesia) was established, with a centre in Nouméa, and divided into two universities in 1999. In 2005 the University of New Caledonia had 70 teachers and researchers and some 2,200 students. Several other vocational tertiary education centres exist in New Caledonia, including a teacher training college and two agricultural colleges. In 1989 the rate of adult illiteracy averaged 6.9% (males 6.0%, females 7.9%). According to UNESCO, total public expenditure on education in 1993 was 1,652m. French francs. According to UNESCO, total public expenditure on education in 1993 was 1,652m. French francs.

Public Holidays

2005: 1 January (New Year's Day), 5 March (Missionary Day), 28 March (Easter Monday), 1 May (Labour Day), 5 May (Ascension Day), 8 May (Liberation Day), 16 May (Whit Monday), 14 July (Fall of the Bastille), 8 September (Internal Autonomy Day), 24 September (anniversary of possession by France), 1 November (All Saints' Day), 11 November (Armistice Day), 25 December (Christmas Day).

2006: 1 January (New Year's Day), 5 March (Missionary Day), 17 April (Easter Monday), 1 May (Labour Day), 8 May (Liberation Day), 25 May (Ascension Day), 5 June (Whit Monday), 14 July (Fall of the Bastille), 8 September (Internal Autonomy Day), 24 September (anniversary of possession by France), 1 November (All Saints' Day), 11 November (Armistice Day), 25 December (Christmas Day).

Weights and Measures

The metric system is in force.

Statistical Survey

Source (unless otherwise stated): Institut Territorial de la Statistique et des Etudes Economiques, BP 823, 98845 Nouméa; tel. 275481; fax 288148; internet www.itsee.nc.

AREA AND POPULATION

Area (sq km): New Caledonia island (Grande-Terre) 16,372; Loyalty Islands 1,981 (Lifou 1,207, Maré 642, Ouvéa 132); Isle of Pines 152; Belep Archipelago 70; Total 18,575 (7,172 sq miles).

Population: 164,173 (males 83,862, females 80,311) at census of 4 April 1989; 196,836 (males 100,762, females 96,074) at census of 16 April 1996; 220,467 (official estimate) at 1 July 2003. *Population By Province* (1996 census): Loyalty Islands 20,877; North Province 41,413; South Province 134,546.

Density (1 July 2003): 11.9 per sq km.

Ethnic Groups (census of 1996): Indigenous Kanaks (Melanesians) 86,788; French and other Europeans 67,151; Wallisians and Futunians (Polynesian) 17,763; Indonesians 5,003; Tahitians (Polynesian) 5,171; Others 14,960.

Principal Town (1 January 2003): Nouméa (capital), population 83,266. *Mid-2003* (UN estimate, incl. suburbs) Nouméa 139,798 (Source: UN, *World Urbanization Prospects: The 2003 Revision*).

Births, Marriages and Deaths (2001): Registered live births 4,326 (birth rate 20.2 per 1,000); Registered marriages 925 (marriage rate 4.3 per 1,000); Registered deaths 1,131 (death rate 5.3 per 1,000). *2003:* Birth rate 18.6 per 1,000; Marriage rate 4.0 per 1,000; Death rate 5.1 per 1,000.

Expectation of Life (years at birth, 2001): Males 70.5; Females 76.1.

Employment (2001): Agriculture, hunting, forestry and fishing 2,490; Mining and quarrying 1,772; Manufacturing and Electricity, gas and water 5,720; Construction 7,031; Trade, restaurants and hotels 9,799; Transport, storage and communications 2,861; Financing, insurance, real estate and business services 5,461; Community, social and personal services 11,165; Activities not adequately defined 5,488; *Total employed* 51,787; Unemployed 9,860; *Total labour force* 61,647. Source: UN, *Statistical Yearbook for Asia and the Pacific. 2003* Unemployed 10,187.

AGRICULTURE, ETC.

Principal Crops (FAO estimates, '000 metric tons, 2003): Maize 3.8; Potatoes 2.0; Sweet potatoes 3.0; Cassava 2.8; Taro (Coco yam) 2.3; Yams 11.0; Coconuts 16.0; Vegetables 4.0; Bananas 1.0; Other fruits 3.2. Source: FAO.

Livestock (FAO estimates, '000 head, year ending September 2003): Horses 11.5; Cattle 111.0; Pigs 25.5; Sheep 2.3; Goats 8.1; Poultry 510. Source: FAO.

Livestock Products (FAO estimates, '000 metric tons, 2003): Beef and veal 4.0; Pig meat 1.4; Poultry meat 0.8; Cows' milk 3.6; Hen eggs 1.6; Cattle hides (fresh) 0.5. Source: FAO.

Forestry ('000 cubic metres, 1994): *Roundwood Removals*: Sawlogs and veneer logs 2.8; Other industrial wood 2.0 (FAO estimate); Total 4.8. *Sawnwood Production*: 3.3 (all broadleaved). *1995–2003*: Annual output as in 1994 (FAO estimates). Source: FAO.

Fishing (metric tons, live weight, 2002): Capture 3,417 (Albacore 1,165; Yellowfin tuna 572; Bigeye tuna 189; Other tuna-like fishes 265; Sea cucumbers 450 (FAO estimate)); Aquaculture 1,882 (Shrimps and prawns 1,815); Total catch 5,299. Source: FAO.

MINING

Production ('000 metric tons): Nickel ore (metal content) 123.5 in 2000; 60.0 in 2001; 59.9 in 2002 (provisional figure). Source: US Geological Survey.

INDUSTRY

Production (2004): Ferro-nickel and nickel matte 55,180 metric tons (nickel content); Electric energy 1,677 million kWh.

Cement: 100,080 metric tons in 2002 (provisional figure). Source: US Geological Survey.

FINANCE

Currency and Exchange Rates: see Wallis and Futuna Islands.

Territorial Budget (million francs CFP, 2001): *Revenue*: 81,337; *Expenditure*: 81,337. French government transfers 86,344.

Aid from France (US $ million): 336.6 in 1997; 336.3 in 1998; 314.9 in 1999. Source: UN, *Statistical Yearbook for Asia and the Pacific*.

Money Supply (million francs CFP at 31 December 2001): Currency in circulation 10,473; Demand deposits 94,525; Total money 104,998. Source: Institut d'Emission d'Outre-Mer.

Cost of Living (Consumer Price Index for Nouméa; base: December 1992 = 100): 111.4 in 1999; 113.1 in 2000; 115.7 in 2001.

Gross Domestic Product (million francs CFP at current prices): 347,303 in 2000. Source: *Bank of Hawaii, An Update on New Caledonia*.

Expenditure on the Gross Domestic Product (million francs CFP at current prices, 1992): Government final consumption expenditure 94,770; Private final consumption expenditure 159,514; Increase in stocks 416; Gross fixed capital formation 66,818; *Total domestic expenditure* 321,518; Exports of goods and services 47,246; *Less* Imports of goods and services 88,403; *Sub-total* 280,361; Statistical discrepancy 1,066; *GDP in purchasers' values* 281,427. Source: UN, *National Accounts Statistics*.

Gross Domestic Product by Economic Activity (million francs CFP at current prices, 1997): Agriculture and food processing 12,835; Energy, mining and metallurgy 37,232; Other manufactures 13,815; Construction and public works 17,447; Transport and communication 23,415; Services and commerce 152,659; Salaries 91,857; *Total* 349,260. Source: Bank of Hawaii, *An Update on New Caledonia*.

Balance of Payments (million francs CFP, 2003): Goods (net) – 72,058; Services (net) –6,888; *Balance on goods and services* –78,946; Other income (net) 35,761; *Balance on goods, services and income* –43,185; Current transfers (net) 33,794; *Current balance* –9,391; Capital account (net) 135; Direct investment (net) –10,786; Portfolio investment (net) –1,439; Other capital (incl. charges in reserves) –5,712; Net errors and omissions –8,094. Source: Institut d'Emission d'Outre-Mer.

EXTERNAL TRADE

Principal Commodities (million francs CFP, 1999): *Imports:* Prepared foodstuffs, beverages, spirits and vinegar, tobacco and manufactured substitutes 18,233; Mineral products 10,579; Products of chemical or allied industries 8,860; Plastics, rubber and articles thereof 4,526; Paper-making material, paper and paperboard and articles thereof 3,115; Textiles and textile articles 3,967; Base metals and articles thereof 8,048; Machinery and mechanical appliances, electrical equipment, sound and television apparatus 22,617; Vehicles, aircraft, vessels and associated transport equipment 17,613; Total (incl. others) 112,808. *Exports:* Ferro-nickel 29,445; Nickel matte 8,764; Nickel ore 8,583; Prawns 1,868; Total (incl. others) 52,388. *2003* (million francs CFP): Total imports 163,869; Total exports 82,152 (Ferro-nickel and matte 65,604; Nickel ore 9,288; Fish products 2,532). *2004* (million francs CFP): Total imports 156,767; Total exports 93,527 (Ferro-nickel and matte 68,791; Nickel ore 15,826; Fish products 2,897).

Principal Trading Partners (million francs CFP, 2001): *Imports:* Australia 20,666.6; Belgium 1,659.9; China, People's Republic 2,977.9; France (metropolitan) 50,046.6; Germany 3,996.6; Italy 3,619.7; Japan 3,868.5; Korea, Republic 1,445.0; New Zealand 6,131.5; Singapore 7,551.4; Spain 2,485.9; United Kingdom 2,812.1; USA 4,910.6; Total (incl. others) 124,037.8. *Exports:* Australia 4,492.4; Belgium 1,236.2; Finland 1,422.2; France (metropolitan) 15,523.2; Italy 1,370.8; Japan 13,733.0; Korea, Republic 2,612.7; Spain 4,355.3; Taiwan 10,455.8; USA 1,446.4; Total (incl. others) 59,511.9. Source: Direction Régionale des Douanes.

TRANSPORT

Road Traffic (motor vehicles in use, 2001): Total 85,499.

Shipping (2001): Vessels entered 478; Goods unloaded 1,298,829 metric tons, Goods loaded 210,197 metric tons. *Merchant Fleet* (vessels registered, '000 grt, at 31 December 1992): 14.

Civil Aviation (La Tontouta airport, Nouméa, 2001): Passengers arriving 173,913, Passengers departing 172,854; Freight unloaded 3,661 metric tons, Freight loaded 1,401 metric tons.

TOURISM

Foreign Tourist Arrivals (arrivals by air): 103,933 in 2002; 101,983 in 2003; 99,515 in 2004.

Tourist Arrivals by Country of Residence (2004): Australia 16,212; France 27,358; Japan 29,229; New Zealand 6,368; Total (incl. others) 99,515.

Receipts (US $ million): 112 in 1999; 110 in 2000; 93 in 2001. Source: UN, *Statistical Yearbook for Asia and the Pacific*.

COMMUNICATIONS MEDIA

Radio Receivers (1997): 107,000 in use*.

Television Receivers (2000): 106,000 in use†.

Telephones (2001): 50,700 main lines in use†.

Facsimile Machines (1994): 2,200 in use‡.

Mobile Cellular Telephones (2002): 80,000 subscribers†.

Internet Users (estimate, 2002): 25,000†.

Daily Newspapers (1999): 1.
* Source: UNESCO, *Statistical Yearbook*.
† Source: International Telecommunication Union.
‡ Source: UN, *Statistical Yearbook*.

EDUCATION

Pre-primary (2004): 83 schools; 13,527 pupils.

Primary (2004): 202 schools; 1,885 teachers (incl. pre-primary); 23,522 pupils.

Secondary (2004): 64 schools; 2,677 teachers; 31,230 pupils.

Higher (2005): 70 teachers/researchers ; 2,200 students.
Source: mainly Vice-Rectorat de Nouvelle-Calédonie.

Adult Literacy Rate (1989): Males 94.0%; Females 92.1%.

Directory

The Constitution

The constitutional system in New Caledonia is established under the Constitution of the Fifth French Republic and specific laws, including those enacted in July 1989 in accordance with the terms agreed by the Matignon Accord and the Transitional Provisions appended by legislation on 20 July 1998. A referendum on the future of New Caledonia (originally expected to be conducted in 1998) was postponed for a period of between 15 and 20 years while a gradual transfer of power from metropolitan France to local institutions is effected under the terms of the Nouméa Accord, concluded in 1998. Under the Nouméa Accord, the islands are declared to be an Overseas Country of the French Republic, of which they remain an integral part. The High Commissioner is the representative of the State in New Caledonia and is appointed by the French Government. The High Commissioner is responsible for external relations, defence, law and order, finance and secondary education. New Caledonia is divided into three Provinces, of the South, the North and the Loyalty Islands. Each is governed by a Provincial Assembly, which is elected on a proportional basis and is responsible for local economic development, land reform and cultural affairs. Members of the Assemblies (40 for the South, 22 for the North and 14 for the Loyalty Islands) are subject to re-election every five years. A proportion of the members of the three Provincial Assemblies together form the Congress of New Caledonia (32 for the South, 15 for the North and seven for the Loyalty Islands), which is responsible for the New Caledonian budget and fiscal affairs, infrastructure and primary education. The Assemblies and the Congress each elect a President as leader. The Government of New Caledonia is elected by the Congress, and comprises between seven and 11 members. Under the terms of the Nouméa Accord, it replaces the French High Commissioner as New Caledonia's executive authority. Provision is also made for the maintenance of Kanak tradition: there are eight custom regions, each with a Regional Consultative Custom Council. These eight Councils, with other appropriate authorities, are represented on the Customary Senate, which is composed of 16 members (two elected from each regional council for a six-year period); the Senate is consulted by the Congress and the Government. Local government is conducted by 33 communes. New Caledonia also elects two deputies to the National Assembly in Paris and one Senator, on the basis of universal adult suffrage. One Economic and Social Councillor is also nominated. New Caledonia may be represented in the European Parliament.

The Government

(April 2005)

STATE GOVERNMENT

High Commissioner: DANIEL CONSTANTIN (took office August 2002).
Secretary-General: ALAIN TRIOLLE.
Deputy Secretary-General: LOUIS LE FRANC.

LOCAL GOVERNMENT

Secretary-General: ALAIN SWETSCHKIN.
Deputy Secretary-General: MARTINE MICHEL.
Deputy Secretary-General: LÉON WAMYTAN.

COUNCIL OF MINISTERS

President, responsible for Social Affairs and Solidarity: MARIE-NOËLLE THÉMEREAU (AE).

Vice-President and Minister for Culture, Women's Affairs and Citizenship: EPÉRI 'DÉWÉ' GORODEY (UNI-FLNKS).

Minister for Agriculture, Fisheries and Livestock: ERIC BABIN (AE).

Minister for Education and Research: CHARLES WASHETINE (UNI-FLNKS).

Minister for Vocational Training, Employment and Public Services: ALAIN SONG (AE).

Minister for Transport, Road Safety, Infrastructure and Energy: GÉRALD CORTOT (UC).

Minister for Foreign Trade, External Affairs and Relations with the European Union: PIERRE FROGIER (UMP).

Minister for Finance and the Budget: JEAN-CLAUDE BRIAULT (UMP).

Minister for the Economy, Taxes, Sustainable Development, Mines, Aviation and Communication: DIDIER LEROUX (AE).

Minister for Health and the Disabled: MARIANNE DEVAUX (UMP).

Minister for Youth and Sports: MAURICE PONGA (UMP).

GOVERNMENT OFFICES

Office of the High Commissioner: Haut-commissariat de la République en Nouvelle-Calédonie, 1 ave Maréchal Foch, BP C5, 98844 Nouméa Cédex; tel. 266300; fax 272828; e-mail haussariat@

nouvelle-caledonie.gouv.fr; internet www.nouvelle-caledonie.gouv.fr.

New Caledonian Government: *Présidence du Gouvernement:* 8 route des Artifices, BP M2, 98849 Nouméa Cédex; *Congrès de la Nouvelle-Calédonie:* 1 blvd Vauban, BP 31, 98845 Nouméa Cédex; tel. 246565; fax 246550; tel. 273129; fax 277020; e-mail cellule .communication@gouv.nc; e-mail courrier@congres.nc.

Office of the Secretary-General of the Government of New Caledonia: Immeuble administratif Jacques Iekawe, 18 ave Paul Doumer, BP M2, 98844 Nouméa Cédex; tel. 256000; fax 286848; e-mail lmoprini@gouv.nc; internet www.gouv.nc.

Government of the the Loyalty Islands Province: Gouvernement Provincial des Iles Loyauté, BP 50, 98820 Wé, Lifou, Loyalty Islands; tel. 455100; fax 455100; e-mail loyalty@loyalty.nc; internet www.loyalty.nc.

Government of the North Province: Gouvernement Provincial du Nord, Hôtel de la Province Nord, BP 41, 98860 Koné, Grande-Terre; tel. 477100; fax 472475; e-mail presidence@province-nord.nc; internet www.province-nord.nc.

Government of the South Province: Hôtel de la Province Sud, 9 Route des Artifices Artilleries, Port Moselle, BP 4142, 98846 Nouméa Cédex; tel. 258000; fax 274900; e-mail presidence@province-sud.nc; internet www.province-sud.nc.

GOVERNMENT DEPARTMENTS

Department of Administrative Services and Computer Technology (SMAI): 3 rue Gustave Flaubert, Baie de l'Orphelinat, BP 8231, 98807 Nouméa Cédex; tel. 275888; fax 281919; e-mail smai@gouv.nc; internet www.gouv.nc.

Department of Civil Aviation: 179 rue Gervolino, BP H01, 98849 Nouméa Cédex; tel. 265200; fax 265202; e-mail dac-nc@aviation-civile.gouv.fr; internet www.dgac.fr; Dir M. HAMY.

Department of the Budget and Financial Affairs (DBAF): 18 ave Paul Doumer, BP M2, 98849 Nouméa Cédex; tel. 256082; fax 283133; e-mail dbaf@gouv.nc.

Department of Culture: Mission aux Affaires Culturelles, Haut-Commisariat de la Republique en Nouvelle Calédonie, 56 Rue Bataille, BP C5, Nouméa; tel. 242181; fax 242180; e-mail jj.garnier@nouvelle-caledonie.gouv.fr; Dir JEAN-JACQUES GARNIER.

Department of Education (DENC): Immeuble Foch, 19 ave du Maréchal Foch, BP 8244, 98807 Nouméa Cédex; tel. 239600; fax 272921; e-mail denc@gouv.nc; internet www.prim.edu.gouv.nc.

Department of Employment (DT): 12 rue de Verdun, BP 141, 98845 Nouméa Cédex; tel. 275572; fax 270494; e-mail dt@gouv.nc; internet www.dtnc.gouv.nc.

Department of Economic Affairs (DAE): 7 rue du Général Gallieni, BP 2672, 98846 Nouméa Cédex; tel. 279200; fax 272675; e-mail dae@gouv.nc; internet www.gouv.nc.

Department of Fiscal Affairs (DSF): Fiscaux Hôtel des Impôts, 13 rue de la Somme, BP D2, 98848 Nouméa Cédex ; tel. 257500; fax 251166; e-mail dsf@gouv.nc; internet www.dsf.gouv.nc.

Department of Human Resources and Civil Service (DRHFPT): 18 ave Paul Doumer, BP M2, 98849 Nouméa Cédex; tel. 256000; fax 274700; e-mail drhfpt@gouv.nc; internet www.drhfpt.gouv.nc.

Department of Infrastructure, Topography and Transport (DITTT): 1 bis rue Edouard Unger, 1ère, Vallée du Tir, BP A2, 98848 Nouméa Cédex; tel. 280300; fax 281760; e-mail dittt@gouv.nc; internet www.gouv.nc.

Department of Maritime Affairs: 2 bis rue Félix Russeil, BP 36, Nouméa Cédex; tel. 272626; fax 287286; e-mail affmar@gouv.nc; internet www.gouv.nc.

Department of Health and Social Services (DASS): 5 rue Galliéni, BP N4, 98851 Nouméa Cédex; tel. 243704; fax 243702; e-mail dass@gouv.nc; internet www.dass.gouv.nc.

Department of Industry, Mines and Energy (DIMENC): 1 ter rue Edouard Unger, 1ère, Vallée du Tir, BP 465, 98845 Nouméa Cédex; tel. 273944; fax 272345; internet www.gouv.nc.

Department of Veterinary, Food and Rural Affairs (DAVAR): 209 rue Auguste Bénébig, BP 256, 98845 Nouméa Cédex; tel. 255100; fax 255129; e-mail davar@gouv.nc; internet www.davar.gouv.nc.

Department of Vocational Training (DFPC): 19 ave du Maréchal Foch, BP 110, 98845 Nouméa Cédex; tel. 246622; fax 281661; e-mail dfpc@gouv.nc.

Department of Youth and Sports (DJS): 23 rue Jean Jaurès, BP810, 98845 Nouméa Cédex; tel. 252384; fax 254585; e-mail djsnc@gouv.nc; internet www.djs.gouv.nc.

Legislature

ASSEMBLÉES PROVINCIALES

Members of the Provincial Assemblies are elected on a proportional basis for a five-year term. Each Provincial Assembly elects its President. A number of the members of the Provincial Assemblies sit together to make up the Congress of New Caledonia. The Assembly of the North Province has 22 members (including 15 sitting for the Congress), the Loyalty Islands 14 members (including seven for the Congress) and the South Province has 40 members (including 32 for the Congress).

Election, 9 May 2004 (results by province)

Party	North	South	Loyalty Islands
Le Rassemblement-Union pour un Mouvement Populaire (UMP)	3	16	2
L'Avenir Ensemble	1	19	—
Union Nationale pour l'Indépendance-Front de Libération Nationale Kanak Socialiste (UNI-FLNKS)	11	—	2
Union Calédonienne (UC)	7	—	4
Front National (FN)	—	5	—
Fédération des Comités de Coordination des Indépendantistes (FCCI)	—	—	2
Libération Kanak Socialiste (LKS)-KAP Identité	—	—	2
Unir et Construire dans le Renouveau (UCR)	—	—	2
Total	**22**	**40**	**14**

North Province: President PAUL NÉAOUTYINE (UNI-FLNKS).

South Province: President PHILIPPE GOMÈS (Avenir Ensemble).

Loyalty Islands Province: President NÉKO HNÉPEUNE (UNI-FLNKS).

CONGRÈS

A proportion of the members of the three Provincial Assemblies sit together, in Nouméa, as the Congress of New Caledonia. There are 54 members (out of a total of 76 sitting in the Provincial Assemblies).

President: HAROLD MARTIN.

Election, 9 May 2004 (results for the Territory as a whole)

Party	Votes	%	Seats
Le Rassemblement-UMP	21,880	24.43	16
L'Avenir Ensemble	20,338	22.71	16
UNI-FLNKS	12,556	14.02	8
UC	10,624	11.86	7
FN	6,684	7.46	4
FCCI-FULK	2,864	3.20	1
LKS-KAP Identité	2,572	2.87	1
UC Renouveau	1,587	1.77	1
Others	10,467	11.69	—
Total	**89,572**	**100.00**	**54**

PARLEMENT

Deputies to the French National Assembly: JACQUES LAFLEUR (RPCR), PIERRE FROGIER (RPCR).

Representative to the French Senate: SIMON LOUECKHOTE (RPCR).

Political Organizations

L'Avenir Ensemble (AE): 19 blvd Extérieur, Faubourg Blanchot, Nouméa; tel. 870371; fax 870379; e-mail courier@avenirensemble.nc; internet www.avenirensemble.nc; f. 2004; combined list including fmr mems of Rassemblement pour la Calédonie dans la République and Alliance pour la Calédonie; Pres. HAROLD MARTIN.

Fédération des Comités de Coordination des Indépendantistes (FCCI): f. 1998 by breakaway group from FLNKS; includes Front du Développement des Iles Loyauté and Front Uni de Libération Kanak; Leaders LÉOPOLD JORÉDIÉ, RAPHAËL MAPOU, FRANÇOIS BURCK.

Front Calédonien (FC): extreme right-wing; Leader M. SARRAN.

Front de Libération Nationale Kanak Socialiste (FLNKS): Nouméa; tel. 272599; f. 1984 following dissolution of Front Indépendantiste; pro-independence; Pres. (vacant); a grouping of the following parties:

Groupe UC du Congrès: Nouméa; f. 2000 by breakaway faction of the UC.

Parti de Libération Kanak (PALIKA): f. 1975; 5,000 mems; Leader PAUL NÉAOUTYINE.

Rassemblement Démocratique Océanien (RDO): Nouméa; f. 1994 by breakaway faction of UO; supports Kanak sovereignty; Pres. ALOISIO SAKO.

Union Nationale pour l'Indépendance (UNI): Leader PAUL NÉAOUTYINE.

Union Progressiste Mélanésienne (UPM): f. 1974 as Union Progressiste Multiraciale; 2,300 mems; Pres. VICTOR TUTUGORO; Sec.-Gen. RENÉ POROU.

Front National (FN): BP 4198, 98846 Nouméa; tel. 258068; fax 258064; e-mail george@province-sud.nc; right-wing; Leader GUY GEORGE.

Génération Calédonienne: f. 1995; youth-based; aims to combat corruption in public life; Pres. JEAN-RAYMOND POSTIC.

Libération Kanak Socialiste (LKS): Maré, Loyalty Islands; moderate, pro-independence; Leader NIDOÏSH NAISSELINE.

Le Rassemblement-UMP: 13 rue de Sebastopol, BP 306, 98845 Nouméa; tel. 282620; fax 284033; e-mail rassemblement@bluepack .nc; f. 1977; affiliated to the metropolitan Union pour un Mouvement Populaire (UMP); includes fmr mems of Rassemblement pour la Calédonie dans la République (RPCR); in favour of retaining the status quo in New Caledonia; Leader PIERRE FROGIER; a coalition of the following parties:

Centre des Démocrates Sociaux (CDS): f. 1971; Leader JEAN LÈQUES.

Parti Républicain (PR): Leader PIERRE MARESCA.

Union Calédonienne (UC): f. 1952; left FLNKS coalition prior to elections of 2004; 11,000 mems; Pres. PASCAL NAOUNA; Sec.-Gen. DANIEL YEIWÉNÉ.

Union Océanienne (UO): Nouméa; f. 1989 by breakaway faction of RPCR; represents people whose origin is in the French Overseas Territory of Wallis and Futuna; conservative; Leader MICHEL HEMA.

Other political organizations participating in the elections of May 2004 included: Avance, Calédonie Mon Pays, Construire Ensemble l'Avenir, Le FLNKS pour l'Indépendance, Mouvement Chiraquien des Démocrates Chrétiens UMP, Mouvement des Citoyens Calédoniens, Patrimoine et Environnement avec les Verts, Rassemblement Océanien dans la Calédonie (ROC) and Union Calédonienne Renouveau.

Judicial System

Court of Appeal: Palais de Justice, BP F4, 98848 Nouméa; tel. 279350; fax 269185; e-mail pp.ca-noumea@justice.fr; First Pres. GÉRARD FEY; Procurator-Gen. GÉRARD NÉDELLEC.

Court of the First Instance: 2 blvd Extérieur, BP F4, 98848 Nouméa; fax 276531; e-mail p.tpi-noumea@justice.fr; Pres. JEAN PRADAL; Procurator of the Republic ROBERT BLASER; There are two subsidiary courts, with resident magistrates, at Koné (North Province) and Wé (Loyalty Islands Province).

Customary Senate of New Caledonia: Conseil Consultatif Coutumier, 68 ave J. Cook, POB 1059, Nouville; tel. 242000; fax 249320; f. 1990; consulted by Local Assembly and French Govt on matters affecting land, Kanak tradition and identity; 40 mem. authorities from eight custom areas; Pres. Chief PAUL JEWINE; Sec.-Gen. SARIMIN BOUENGHI.

Religion

The majority of the population is Christian, with Roman Catholics comprising about 55% of the total in 2002. About 3% of the inhabitants, mainly Indonesians, are Muslims.

CHRISTIANITY

The Roman Catholic Church

The Territory comprises a single archdiocese, with an estimated 110,000 adherents in 2002. The Archbishop participates in the Catholic Bishops' Conference of the Pacific, based in Fiji.

Archbishop of Nouméa: Most Rev. MICHEL-MARIE-BERNARD CALVET, Archevêché, 4 rue Mgr-Fraysse, BP 3, 98845 Nouméa; tel. 265353; fax 265352; e-mail archeveche@ddec.nc.

The Anglican Communion

Within the Church of the Province of Melanesia, New Caledonia forms part of the diocese of Vanuatu (q.v.). The Archbishop of the Province is the Bishop of Central Melanesia (resident in Honiara, Solomon Islands). At mid-2000 there were an estimated 160 adherents.

Protestant Churches

At mid-2000 there were an estimated 30,000 adherents.

Eglise évangélique en Nouvelle-Calédonie et aux Iles Loyauté: BP 277, Nouméa; f. 1960; Pres. Rev. SAILALI PASSA; Gen. Sec. Rev. TELL KASARHEROU.

Other churches active in the Territory include the Assembly of God, the Free Evangelical Church, the Presbyterian Church, the New Apostolic Church, the Pentecostal Evangelical Church and the Tahitian Evangelical Church. At mid-2000 there were an estimated 15,500 adherents professing other forms of Christianity.

The Press

L'Avenir Calédonien: 10 rue Gambetta, Nouméa; organ of the Union Calédonienne; Dir PAÏTA GABRIEL.

La Calédonie Agricole: BP 111, 98845 Nouméa Cédex; tel. 243160; fax 284587; every 2 months; official publ. of the Chambre d'Agriculture; Pres. ANDRÉ MAZURIER; Man. PATRICK LAUBREAUX; circ. 3,000.

Eglise de Nouvelle-Calédonie: BP 3, 98845 Nouméa; fax 265352; f. 1976; monthly; official publ. of the Roman Catholic Church; circ. 450.

Les Nouvelles Calédoniennes: 41–43 rue de Sébastopol, BP G5, 98848 Nouméa; tel. 272584; fax 281627; e-mail lnc@canl.nc; internet www.info.lnc.nc; f. 1971; daily; Publr ROBERT HERSANT; Gen. Man. THIERRY MASSÉ; Editor-in-Chief PHILIPPE MINARD; circ. 18,500.

Télé 7 Jours: Route de Vélodrome, BP 2080, 98846 Nouméa Cédex; tel. 284598; weekly.

NEWS AGENCY

Agence France-Presse (AFP): 15 rue Docteur Guégan, 98800 Nouméa; tel. 263033; fax 278699; Correspondent FRANCK MADOEUF.

Publishers

Editions d'Art Calédoniennes: 3 rue Guynemer, BP 1626, Nouméa; tel. 277633; fax 281526; art, reprints, travel.

Editions du Santal: 5 bis rue Emile-Trianon, 98846 Nouméa; tel. and fax 262533; history, art, travel, birth and wedding cards; Dir PAUL-JEAN STAHL.

Grain de Sable: BP 577, 98845 Nouméa; tel. and fax 273057; e-mail lokisa@canl.nc; internet www.pacific-bookin.com; literature, travel.

Ile de Lumière: BP 8401, Nouméa Sud; tel. 289858; history, politics.

Savannah Editions SARL: BP 3086, 98846 Nouméa; e-mail savannahmarc@hotmail.com; f. 1994; sports, travel, leisure.

Société d'Etudes Historiques de la Nouvelle-Calédonie: BP 63, 98845 Nouméa; tel. 767155.

Broadcasting and Communications

TELECOMMUNICATIONS

France Câbles et Radio (FCR): Télécommunications extérieures de la Nouvelle-Calédonie, BP A1, 98848 Nouméa Cédex; tel. 266600; fax 266666; Dir CLAUDE BONNEAU.

Offices des Postes et Télécommunications: Le Waruna, 2 rue Monchovet, Port Plaisance, 98841 Nouméa Cédex; tel. 268217; fax 262927; e-mail direction@opt.nc; internet www.opt.nc; Dir JEAN-YVES OLLIVAUD.

BROADCASTING

Radio

NRJ Nouvelle-Calédonie: 41–43 rue Sébastopol, BP G5, 98848 Nouméa; tel. 279446; fax 279447.

Radio Djiido: 29 rue du Maréchal Juin, BP 1671, 98803 Nouméa Cédex; tel. 253515; fax 272187; f. 1985; community station; broadcasts in French; pro-independence.

Radio Nouvelle-Calédonie: Radio Télévision Française d'Outre Mer (RFO), 1 rue Maréchal Leclerc, Mont Coffyn, BP G3, 98848 Nouméa Cédex; tel. 239999; fax 239975; e-mail internet.nc@rfo.fr; f.

1942; fmrly Radiodiffusion Française d'Outre-mer (RFO); 24 hours of daily programmes in French; Gen. Man. FRANÇOIS GUILEBEAU; Editor-in-Chief FRANCIS ORNY.

Radio Rythme Bleu: BP 578, Nouméa; tel. 254646; fax 284928; e-mail RRB@lagoon.nc; Dir CHRISTIAN PROST.

Television

RFO-Télé Nouvelle-Calédonie: Radio Télévision Française d'Outre Mer (RFO), 1 rue Maréchal Leclerc, Mont Coffyn, BP G3, 98848 Nouméa Cédex; tel. 239999; fax 239975; e-mail internet.nc@rfo.fr; internet www.rfo.fr; f. 1965; transmits 10 hours daily; Gen. Man. BENOÎT SAUDEAU.

Canal Calédonie: 30 rue de la Somme, BP 1797, 98845 Nouméa; CEO SERGE LAMAGNÈRE; subscription service.

Canal Outre-mer (Canal+): Nouméa; f. 1995; cable service.

Finance

(cap. = capital; res = reserves; dep. = deposits; m. = million; brs = branches; amounts in CFP francs unless otherwise stated)

BANKING

Agence Française de Développement: 5 rue Barleux, BP JI, 98849 Nouméa Cédex; tel. 282088; fax 282413.

Banque de Nouvelle-Calédonie: 25 ave de la Victoire, BP L3, 98849 Nouméa Cédex; tel. 257400; fax 274147; internet www.bnc.nc; f. 1974; adopted present name Jan. 2002; 95.8% owned by Financière Océor; cap. 3,711.1m., res 1,252.6m., dep. 44,640.4m. (Dec. 2002); Pres. JEAN-CLAUDE CLARAC; Gen. Man. JEAN-PIERRE FLOTAT; 7 brs.

Banque Calédonienne d'Investissement (BCI): 54 ave de la Victoire, BP K5, 98846 Nouméa; tel. 256565; fax 274035; e-mail dg@bci.nc; internet www.bci.nc; cap. 7,500m. (Dec. 2003); Pres. DIDIER LEROUX; Gen. Man. ALAIN CELESTE.

BNP Paribas Nouvelle-Calédonie (France): 37 ave Henri Lafleur, BP K3, 98849 Nouméa Cédex; tel. 258400; fax 258459; e-mail bnp.nc@bnpparibas.com; f. 1969 as Banque Nationale de Paris; present name adopted in 2001; cap. €28.0m., res €315.6m. (Dec. 2001); Pres. GÉRARD HAYAUD; Gen. Man. JEAN-CLAUDE DANG; 10 brs.

Société Générale Calédonienne de Banque: 44 rue de l'Alma, Siège et Agence Principale, BP G2, 98848 Nouméa Cédex; tel. 256300; fax 276245; e-mail svp.sgcb@canl.nc; f. 1981; cap. 1,068.4m., res 5,053.5m., dep. 81,547.6m. (Dec. 2001); Gen. Man. DOMINIQUE POIGNON; Chair. JEAN-LOUIS MATTEI; 12 brs.

Trade and Industry

DEVELOPMENT ORGANIZATIONS

New Caledonia Economic Development Agency (ADECAL): 15 rue Guynemer, BP 2384, 98846 Nouméa Cédex; tel. 249077; fax 249087; e-mail adecal@offratel.nc; internet www.adecal.nc; f. 1995; promotes investment within New Caledonia; Dir JEAN-MICHEL ARLIE.

Agence de Développement de la Culture Kanak (ADCK): Centre Tjibaou, rue des Accords de Matignon BP 378, 98845 Nouméa Cédex; tel. 414545; fax 414546; e-mail adck@adck.nc; internet www.adck.nc; Pres. MARIE-CLAUDE TJIBAOU; Dir-Gen. OCTAVE TOGNA; Dir of Culture EMMANUEL KASARHEROU.

Agence de Développement Rural et d'Aménagement Foncier (ADRAF): 1 rue de la Somme, BP 4228, 98847 Nouméa Cédex; tel. 258600; fax 258604; e-mail dgadraf@offratel.nc; f. 1986, reorganized 1989; acquisition and redistribution of land; Chair. DANIEL CONSTANTIN; Dir-Gen. LOUIS MAPOU.

Agence pour l'Emploi de Nouvelle Calédonie: 3 rue de la Somme, BP 497, 98845 Nouméa Cédex; tel. 281082; fax 272079; internet www.apenc.nc.

Conseil Economique et Social: 14 ave Georges Clemenceau, BP 4766, 98847 Nouméa Cédex; tel. 278517; fax 278509; e-mail ces@gouv.nc; represents trade unions and other organizations that are involved in economic, social and cultural life; Pres. BERNARD PAUL; Gen. Sec. YOLAINE ELMOUR.

Institut Calédonien de Participation: Nouméa; f. 1989 to finance development projects and encourage the Kanak population to participate in the market economy.

CHAMBERS OF COMMERCE

Chambre d'Agriculture: 3 rue A. Desmazures, BP 111, 98845 Nouméa Cédex; tel. 243160; fax 284587; e-mail canc-js@canl.nc; f. 1909; 33 mems; Pres. ANDRÉ MAZURIER.

Chambre de Commerce et d'Industrie: 15 rue de Verdun, BP M3, 98849 Nouméa Cédex; tel. 243100; fax 243131; e-mail cci@cci.nc; internet www.cci.nc; f. 1879; 29 mems; Pres. MICHEL QUINTARD; Dir-Gen. MICHEL MERZEAU.

Chambre des Métiers: 10 ave James Cook, BP 4186, 98846 Nouméa Cédex; tel. 282337; fax 282729.

STATE-OWNED INDUSTRIES

Société de Participation Minière du Sud Calédonien SAS (SPMSC): f. 2005; holding co managing 10% share in the Goro nickel development for financial wings of the three Provinces: PROMOSUD (South Province); Société Financière du Nord—SOFINOR (North Province); and SODIL (Loyalty Islands); Pres. PHILIPPE GOMÈS.

Société Minière du Sud Pacifique (SMSP): Nouméa; dirgen@smsp.nc; 87% owned by SOFINOR, 5% owned by SODIL; nickel-mining co; subsidiaries: Nouméa Nickel, Nickel Mining Corporation (NMC), Bienvenue, Sam 3; Man. Dir ANDRÉ DANG VAN NHA.

Société Le Nickel (SLN): Doniambo, Nouméa; tel. 245300; fax 275989; privatized 1999; 60% owned by the Eramet group; nickel mining, processing and sales co; Chair. and CEO JACQUES BACARDATS; Man. Dir PHILIPPE VECTEN.

EMPLOYERS' ORGANIZATION

MEDEF de Nouvelle-Calédonie/Fédération Patronale: Immeuble Jules Ferry, 1 rue de la Somme, BP 466, 98845 Nouméa Cédex; tel. 273525; fax 274037; e-mail medefnc@medef.nc; f. 1936; represents the leading cos of New Caledonia in the defence of professional interests, co-ordination, documentation and research in socio-economic fields; affiliated to the Mouvement des Entreprises de France; Pres. JEAN-YVES BOUVIER; Sec.-Gen. FRANÇOIS PERONNET.

TRADE UNIONS

Confédération des Travailleurs Calédoniens: Nouméa; Sec.-Gen. R. JOYEUX; grouped with:

Fédération des Fonctionnaires: Nouméa; Sec.-Gen. GILBERT NOUVEAU.

Syndicat Général des Collaborateurs des Industries de Nouvelle-Calédonie: Sec.-Gen. H. CHAMPIN.

Union Syndicale des Travailleurs Kanak et des Exploités (USTKE): BP 4372, Nouméa; tel. 277210; fax 277687; Pres. GÉRARD JODARD; Sec.-Gen CLAUDE WEMA.

Union des Syndicats des Ouvriers et Employés de Nouvelle-Calédonie (USOENC): BP 2534, Vallée du Tir, 98846 Nouméa; tel. 259640; fax 250164; e-mail usoenc@canl.nc; Sec.-Gen. DIDIER GUÉNANT-JEANSON.

Union Territoriale de Force Ouvrière: 13 rue Jules Ferry, BP 4733, 98847 Nouméa Cédex; tel. 274950; fax 278202; internet www.ifrance.com/fo98000; e-mail utfonc98@ifrance.com; f. 1982; Sec.-Gen. JEAN-CLAUDE NÈGRE.

Transport

ROADS

In 1983 there was a total of 5,980 km of roads on New Caledonia island; 766 km were bitumen-surfaced, 589 km unsealed, 1,618 km stone-surfaced and 2,523 km tracks in 1980. The outer islands had a total of 470 km of roads and tracks in 1980.

SHIPPING

Most traffic is through the port of Nouméa. Passenger and cargo services, linking Nouméa to other towns and islands, are regular and frequent. There are plans to develop Nepoui, in the North Province, as a deep-water port and industrial centre.

Port Autonome de la Nouvelle-Calédonie: BP 14, 98845 Nouméa Cédex; tel. 255000; fax 275490; e-mail noumeaportnc@canl.nc; Port Man. PHILIPPE LAFLEUR; Harbour Master EDMUND MARTIN.

Compagnie Wallisienne de Navigation: BP 1080, Nouméa; tel. 232910; fax 287388; e-mail jyboileau@amb.nc; Chair. ARMAND BALLANDE; Man. Dir JEAN-YVES BOILEAU.

Moana Services: BP 2099, 98846 Nouméa; tel. 273898; fax 259315; e-mail moana@canl.nc; fmrly Somacal.

CIVIL AVIATION

There is an international airport, Tontouta, 47 km from Nouméa, and an internal network, centred on Magenta airport, which provides air services linking Nouméa to other towns and islands. Air France, which formerly operated a service between Nouméa and

Paris via Tokyo, Japan, ceased operations in New Caledonia in early 2003. The route to Tokyo was taken over by Air Calédonie International (Aircalin). AOM operates flights from Paris to Nouméa via Sydney. Other airlines providing services to the island include Air New Zealand, Air Vanuatu and Qantas.

Air Calédonie: BP 212, Nouméa; tel. 250300; fax 254869; e-mail directoire@air-caledonie.nc; internet www.air-caledonie.nc; f. 1955; services throughout New Caledonia; 301,000 passengers carried in 2000/01; Pres. and CEO OLIVIER RAZAVET.

Air Calédonie International (Aircalin): 8 rue Frédéric Surleau, BP 3736, 98846 Nouméa Cédex; tel. 265546; fax 272772; e-mail aircalin@aircalin.nc; internet www.aircalin.nc/aci.htm; f. 1983; 27% owned by Agence pour la Desserte Aérienne de la Nouvelle-Calédonie (NC Air Transport Agency); 72% by Caisse Nationale des Caisses d'Epargne et de Prevoyance; 1% by others; services to Sydney and Brisbane (Australia), Auckland (New Zealand), Nadi (Fiji), Papeete (French Polynesia), Wallis and Futuna Islands, Port Vila (Vanuatu) and Osaka and Tokyo (Japan); Chair. CHARLES LAVOIX; CEO JEAN-MICHEL MASSON.

Tourism

An investment programme was begun in 1985 with the aim of developing and promoting tourism. A total of 2,388 hotel rooms were available in 1999. In 2004 there were 99,515 visitors to New Caledonia, of whom 29.4% came from Japan, 27.5% from France, and 16.3% from Australia. The industry earned US $93m. in 2001.

New Caledonia Tourism South: Galerie Nouméa Centre, 20 rue Anatole France; BP 688, 98845 Nouméa Cédex; tel. 242080; fax 242070; e-mail info@nctps.com; internet www.nctps.com; f. 2001; international promotion of tourism in the South Province of New Caledonia; Chair. CHRISTINE GAMBEY; Gen. Man. JEAN-MICHEL FOUTREIN.

GABON

Introductory Survey

Location, Climate, Language, Religion, Flag, Capital

The Gabonese Republic is an equatorial country on the west coast of Africa, with Equatorial Guinea and Cameroon to the north and the Congo to the south and east. The climate is tropical, with an average annual temperature of 26°C (79°F) and an average annual rainfall of 2,490 mm (98 ins). The official language is French, but Fang (in the north) and Bantu dialects (in the south) are also widely spoken. About 60% of the population are Christians, mainly Roman Catholics. Most of the remainder follow animist beliefs. The national flag (proportions 3 by 4) has three equal horizontal stripes, of green, yellow and blue. The capital is Libreville.

Recent History

Formerly a province of French Equatorial Africa, Gabon was granted internal autonomy in November 1958, and proceeded to full independence on 17 August 1960. Léon M'Ba, the new Republic's President, established Gabon as a one-party state. Following his death in November 1967, M'Ba was succeeded by the Vice-President, Albert-Bernard (later Omar) Bongo, who organized a new ruling party, the Parti démocratique gabonais (PDG). Gabon enjoyed political stability and rapid economic growth in the 1970s, underpinned by substantial foreign investment in the development and exploitation of its petroleum reserves. However, the social and economic problems that accompanied the subsequent decline in world petroleum prices led to the emergence in 1981 of a moderate opposition group, the Mouvement de redressement national (MORENA), which demanded the restoration of a multi-party system. Bongo maintained his commitment to a single-party framework, in which he undertook to allow democratic debate. MORENA responded by forming a government-in-exile in Paris, France, from which it unsuccessfully sought to put forward a candidate to challenge Bongo in the presidential election held in November 1986.

Following a period of preoccupation with internal divisions, MORENA resumed its campaign against the Government in early 1989. In May the Chairman of MORENA, Fr Paul M'Ba Abessole, visited Gabon and, after a meeting with Bongo, announced that he and many of his supporters would return to Gabon. In January 1990 representatives of MORENA announced that M'Ba Abessole had been dismissed from the leadership of the movement, following his declaration of support for the Government. M'Ba Abessole subsequently formed a breakaway faction, known as MORENA des bûcherons (renamed Rassemblement national des bûcherons in 1991 to avoid confusion with the rival MORENA—originels).

A number of arrests took place in October 1989, following an alleged conspiracy to overthrow the Government. It was claimed that the plot had been initiated by Pierre Mamboundou, the leader of the Union du peuple gabonais (UPG, an opposition movement based in Paris). In early 1990 a series of strikes and demonstrations reflected increasing public discontent with economic austerity measures. In February a 'special commission for democracy' (which had been established by the PDG) submitted a report condemning Gabon's single-party political system. Bongo subsequently announced that extensive political reforms were to be introduced and that the ruling party was to be replaced by a new organization, the Rassemblement social-démocrate gabonais (RSDG). However, strike action continued in a number of sectors, resulting in severe disruption.

In March 1990 the PDG announced that a multi-party system was to be introduced, under the supervision of the RSDG, at the end of a five-year transitional period. Later that month a national conference, attended by representatives of more than 70 political organizations, rejected Bongo's proposals for a transitional period of political reform under the aegis of the RSDG, and demanded the immediate establishment of a multi-party system and the formation of a new government, which would hold office only until legislative elections could take place. Bongo acceded to the decisions of the conference, and in late April Casimir Oye Mba, the Governor of the Banque des états de l'Afrique centrale, was appointed Prime Minister of a transitional administration, which included several opposition members.

In May 1990 the Central Committee of the PDG and the legislature, the Assemblée nationale, approved constitutional changes that would facilitate the transition to a multi-party political system. The existing presidential mandate (effective until January 1994) was to be respected; thereafter, elections to the presidency would be contested by more than one candidate, and the tenure of office would be reduced to five years, renewable only once. At the same time, Bongo resigned as Secretary-General of the PDG. In the same month the death, in suspicious circumstances, of Joseph Rendjambe, the Secretary-General of the opposition Parti gabonais du progrès (PGP), provoked violent demonstrations in protest at Bongo's alleged complicity in the death. A national curfew was imposed in response to the increasing unrest, while French troops were briefly deployed in Gabon, to protect the interests of the 20,000 resident French nationals, and several hundred Europeans were evacuated. It was announced in early June that the French military reinforcements were to be withdrawn, and the national curfew was lifted in the following month.

Legislative elections were scheduled for 16 and 23 September 1990. The first round of the elections was disrupted by violent protests by voters who claimed that the PDG was engaging in electoral fraud. Following further allegations of widespread electoral malpractices, results in 32 constituencies were declared invalid, although the election of 58 candidates (of whom 36 were members of the PDG) was confirmed. The interim Government subsequently conceded that electoral irregularities had taken place, and further voting was postponed until 21 and 28 October. At the elections the PDG won an overall majority in the 120-member Assemblée nationale, with 62 seats, while opposition candidates secured 55 seats.

On 27 November 1990 a Government of National Unity, under Casimir Oye Mba, was formed. Sixteen posts were allocated to members of the PDG, while the remaining eight portfolios were distributed among members of five opposition parties. A new draft Constitution, which was promulgated on 22 December, endorsed reforms that had been included in the transitional Constitution, introduced in May. Further measures included the proposed establishment of an upper house, to be known as the Sénat, which was to control the balance and regulation of power. A Constitutional Council was to replace the administrative chamber of the Supreme Court, and a National Communications Council was to be formed to ensure the impartial treatment of information by the state media.

The final composition of the Assemblée nationale was determined in March 1991, when elections took place in five constituencies, where the results had been annulled, owing to alleged malpractice. Following the completion of the elections, the PDG held a total of 66 seats in the Assemblée nationale, while various opposition groups held 54 seats. The two most prominent opposition movements, the PGP and the Rassemblement national des bûcherons (RNB), held 19 and 17 seats, respectively.

In May 1991 six opposition parties formed an alliance, known as the Co-ordination de l'opposition démocratique (COD), in protest at the delay in the implementation of the new Constitution. The COD also demanded the appointment of a new Prime Minister, the abolition of certain institutions under the terms of the Constitution, and the liberalization of the state-controlled media. Following a general strike, organized by the COD, Bongo announced the resignation of the Council of Ministers, and declared that he was prepared to implement fully the new Constitution. He also claimed that, in accordance with the Constitution, several institutions, including the High Court of Justice, had been dissolved, and that a Constitutional Court and a National Communications Council had been established. However, opposition parties within the COD refused to be represented in a new Government of National Unity, of which Oye Mba was appointed as Prime Minister. Later that month opposition deputies who had taken part in the boycott of the Assemblée nationale resumed parliamentary duties. On 22 June Oye

Mba appointed a new coalition Government, in which 14 members of the previous Council of Ministers retained their portfolios. Members of MORENA–originels, the Union socialiste gabonaise (USG) and the Association pour le socialisme au Gabon (APSG) were also represented in the Government.

In February 1992 MORENA–originels, the USG and the Parti socialiste gabonais formed an alliance within the COD, known as the Forum africain pour la reconstruction (FAR). Later in February the Government announced that a multi-party presidential election would take place in December 1993.

In mid-February 1992 a meeting of supporters of the RNB was violently suppressed by security forces. In the same month the university in Libreville was closed, and a ban on political gatherings and demonstrations was imposed, following protests by students against inadequate financing. Later in February the COD organized a one-day general strike in Port-Gentil (which was only partially observed), followed by a one-day campaign of civil disobedience, which suspended economic activity in Port-Gentil and Libreville. At the end of February the Government reopened the university, and ended the ban on political gatherings and demonstrations. In March, however, the COD instigated a further one-day campaign of civil disobedience in Libreville, following the violent suppression of a demonstration by teachers who were demanding improvements in salaries and working conditions. In April the PDG organized a pro-Government demonstration, in an attempt to gain public support.

In early July 1992 the Assemblée nationale adopted a new electoral code, despite protests by the FAR that the Government had failed to comply with the demands presented by the COD in October 1991. Later in July a motion of censure against the Government, proposed by opposition deputies in the Assemblée nationale in response to the postponement of local government elections, was defeated. The Council of Ministers was reshuffled in August, and in December three members of the PDG, including a former minister, were expelled from the party, after establishing a faction, known as the Cercle des libéraux réformateurs (CLR).

In November 1993 five political associations, the PDG, the USG, the APSG, the CLR and the Parti de l'unité du peuple gabonais, agreed to support Bongo's candidacy in the forthcoming presidential election, while eight opposition candidates established an informal alliance, known as the Convention des forces du changement. Later in the same month a number of demonstrations were staged by members of the opposition, in support of demands for the revision of the electoral register. Clashes between opposition and government supporters ensued, following opposition allegations that irregularities in the electoral register indicated deliberate malpractice on the part of the Government. In early December the Government agreed to revise the register in part, but rejected opposition demands that the election be postponed.

At the presidential election, which took place on 5 December 1993, Bongo was re-elected, winning 51.18% of votes cast, while M'Ba Abessole (the leader of the RNB) secured 26.51% of the votes. The official announcement of the results prompted rioting by opposition supporters. Five deaths were reported after security forces suppressed the unrest, and a national curfew and state of alert were subsequently imposed. M'Ba Abessole, however, claimed that he had won the election, and formed a Haut conseil de la République, later redesignated as the Haut conseil de la résistance (HCR), which included the majority of opposition presidential candidates, and a parallel government. Despite the reports by international observers that the elections had been conducted fairly, the opposition appealed to the Constitutional Court to annul the results, on the grounds that the Government had perpetrated electoral malpractice. In December Bongo condemned M'Ba Abessole's formation of a parallel administration, and invited the other candidates who had contested the election to participate in a government of national consensus. As a result of the administrative confusion, local government elections, which were due to take place in late December, were postponed until March 1994. (In February 1994 they were further postponed, to August.)

In early January 1994 the USA criticized Bongo's administration for alleged infringement of human rights, after three opposition leaders, including two presidential candidates, were prevented from leaving the country. Later that month the Constitutional Court ruled against the appeal by the opposition and endorsed the election results. On 22 January Bongo was officially inaugurated as President. In mid-February the national curfew and the state of alert, which had been in force

since December 1993, were repealed, but later that month were reimposed, after a general strike, in support of demands for an increase in salaries to compensate for a devaluation of the CFA franc in January, degenerated into violence. Strike action was suspended after four days, following negotiations between the Government and trade unions; nine people had been killed during that period, according to official figures (although the opposition claimed that a total of 38 had died).

In March 1994 Oye Mba resigned and dissolved the Council of Ministers. Later that month he was reappointed as Prime Minister, and, following the opposition's refusal to participate in a government of national unity, formed a 38-member administration, solely comprising representatives of the presidential majority (apart from one member of the PGP, who was expected to be expelled from that party). In the same month the Assemblée nationale approved a constitutional amendment that provided for the establishment of a Sénat (which the opposition had resisted) and repealed legislation prohibiting unsuccessful presidential candidates from participating in the Government within a period of 18 months. In June opposition parties agreed to a further postponement of the local government elections, to early 1995. In August opposition parties announced that they were prepared to participate in a coalition government, on condition that it was installed as a transitional organ pending legislative elections. In September negotiations between the Government and opposition took place in Paris, under the auspices of the Organization of African Unity (OAU, now the African Union, see p. 144), in order to resolve remaining differences concerning the results of the presidential election and the proposed formation of a government of national unity.

At the end of September 1994 an agreement was reached, as a result of the Paris meetings, whereby a transitional coalition government was to be installed, with local government elections scheduled to take place after a period of one year, followed by legislative elections six months later; the electoral code was to be revised and an independent electoral commission established, in an effort to ensure that the elections be conducted fairly. In early October Oye Mba resigned from office and dissolved the Council of Ministers. Shortly afterwards Bongo appointed Dr Paulin Obame-Nguema, a member of the PDG who had served in former administrations, as Prime Minister. Obame-Nguema subsequently formed a 27-member Council of Ministers, which included six opposition members. The composition of the new Government was, however, immediately criticized by the opposition, on the grounds that it was entitled to one-third of ministerial portfolios in proportion to the number of opposition deputies in the Assemblée nationale; the HCR announced that the opposition would boycott the new administration, which, it claimed, was in violation of the Paris accord. Four opposition members consequently refused to accept the portfolios allocated to them, although two of these finally agreed to join the Government. (The portfolios that remained vacant were later assigned to a further two opposition members.)

In January 1995 controversy emerged over the extent of the authority vested in the Assemblée nationale, after members of the HCR refused to participate in the drafting of the new electoral code until the Paris agreement was ratified. The Constitutional Court subsequently ruled that the Assemblée nationale was not empowered, under the terms of the Constitution, to ratify the agreement. In February, however, opposition deputies ended a boycott of the Assemblée nationale, following a further ruling by the Constitutional Court that the Assemblée nationale was entitled to act as a parliamentary body, pending the installation of a Sénat after the legislative elections in 1996, but that the constitutional provisions adopted under the terms of the Paris accord would require endorsement by referendum. In April Bongo announced that a referendum to endorse the constitutional amendments would take place in June. In the same month, in accordance with the Paris accord, the Cabinet approved legislation providing for the release of prisoners detained on charges involving state security. Later in April Gabon withdrew its ambassador in Paris, in protest at reports by the French media regarding Bongo's alleged involvement with prostitutes; a number of demonstrations in support of Bongo took place in Libreville. Government efforts to prohibit two pro-opposition newspapers, which had published French press reports considered to be critical of Bongo, were rejected by the National Communications Council. At the national referendum (which had been postponed until 24 July), the constitutional amendments were approved by 96.5% of votes cast, with 63% of the electorate participating. In September 1995, following dissent within the UPG, Sébastien Mamboundou Mouyama, the Minister of Social Affairs and National Solidarity, was elected party Chairman, replacing Pierre Mamboundou. However, the latter subsequently regained the leadership of the UPG.

During early 1996 opposition parties criticized the Government for delaying the implementation of the electoral timetable contained in the Paris accord. At the beginning of May, following a meeting attended by all the officially recognized political parties, Bongo agreed to establish a National Electoral Commission to formulate a timetable for local, legislative and senatorial elections, in consultation with all the official parties. It was also decided that access to state-controlled media and election funding should be equitably divided. On 20 May 1996 the Assemblée nationale's mandate expired, and Obame-Nguema's Government resigned at the beginning of June, in accordance with the Paris accord. Bongo, however, rejected the resignation on the grounds that the Government should, before leaving office, organize the elections and finalize pending agreements with the IMF and the World Bank. At the beginning of October the National Electoral Commission adopted a timetable for legislative elections: the first round was to take place on 17 November, with a second round scheduled for 1 December. HCR representatives denounced the timetable, withdrew from the commission and demanded the postponement of the local and legislative elections.

Organizational problems disrupted the local elections, which were held on 20 October 1996, having been postponed twice previously; according to reports, only 15% of the electorate participated. The PDG gained control of the majority of the municipalities, although the PGP secured victory in Port-Gentil, while the RNB was successful in the north of the country. Elections in Fougamou (where voting had not taken place) and Libreville (where the results had been invalidated) were eventually rescheduled for 24 November, although the RNB demanded the validation of the original results. On 24 November the RNB secured 62 of the 98 seats available in Libreville; M'Ba Abessole was subsequently elected mayor.

Legislative elections were rescheduled on several occasions, owing to the delay in the release of the local election results and the failure to revise electoral registers in time. The first round of the elections took place on 15 December 1996, without major incidents. Later that month it was reported that the PDG had obtained 47 of the 55 seats that were decided in the first round of voting. The opposition disputed the results, and there were demands for a boycott of the second round of voting. The PDG secured a substantial majority of the seats decided in the second round, which was held on 29 December, winning 84 seats, while the RNB obtained seven, the PGP six and independent candidates four, with the remaining 14 seats shared by the CLR, the UPG, the USG and others. Polling was unable to proceed for the five remaining seats, and results in a number of other constituencies were later annulled, owing to irregularities. (Following by-elections held in August 1997, during which five people were reportedly killed in violent incidents in north-east Gabon, the PDG held 88 seats, the PGP nine and the RNB five.) Guy Ndzouba Ndama was elected President of the new Assemblée nationale. Obame-Nguema was reappointed Prime Minister on 27 January, and a new Council of Ministers, dominated by members of the PDG, was announced on the following day. The PGP, the main opposition party represented in the Assemblée nationale, had refused to participate in the new Government.

Elections to the new Sénat took place on 26 January and 9 February 1997, with senators to be elected by members of municipal councils and departmental assemblies. The PDG won 53 of the Sénat's 91 seats, while the RNB secured 20 seats, the PGP four, the Alliance démocratique et républicaine (ADERE) three, the CLR one, and the RDP one, with independent candidates obtaining nine seats. The results for a number of seats were annulled, however, and in subsequent by-elections, held later that year, the PDG increased its representation to 58 seats, while the RNB held 20 seats and the PGP four.

In mid-April 1997 a congress of deputies and senators adopted constitutional amendments which extended the presidential term to seven years, provided for the creation of the post of Vice-President and formally designated the Sénat as an upper chamber of a bicameral legislature. Opposition demands that a referendum be held were ignored. The Vice-President was to deputize for the President as required, but was not to have any power of succession. In late May Didjob Divungui-di-N'Dingue,

a senior member of the ADERE and a candidate in the 1993 presidential election, was appointed to the new post.

In September 1998 opposition parties withdrew their members from the National Electoral Commission in protest at alleged irregularities in the voter registration process for the forthcoming presidential election. In October President Bongo confirmed that he was to seek re-election; his candidature was formally accepted later that month, together with those of Kombila, M'Ba Abessole and Alain Egouang Nze for the RNB, Pierre Mamboundou for the HCR, Maganga Moussavou for the PSD, and two independents.

At the presidential election, which was held on 6 December 1998, Bongo was re-elected by 66.55% of votes cast, while Mamboundou received 16.54% of the votes and M'Ba Abessole secured 13.41%. The reported rate of participation was 53.8%. Opposition parties rejected the results, again alleging electoral malpractice, and called for fresh elections to be held. None the less, Bongo was inaugurated as President on 21 January 1999, and a new 42-member Council of Ministers, headed by Jean-François Ntoutoume Emane, was subsequently appointed.

In early 1999 student demonstrations and strike action by civil servants severely disrupted health and education services, with some schools closed for up to three months. Industrial action by university teachers occurred in April and June 2000. In January 2001 post and telecommunications workers began a nation-wide strike in support of their demands for improved working conditions. The industrial action ended in early February when the Government agreed to the financial demands of the workers.

In December 1999 it was announced that Bongo had reduced the Council of Ministers in size from 42 to 31 members. In August 2000 four opposition parties, including the RNB (which subsequently changed its name to the Rassemblement pour le Gabon—RPG), formed a coalition, the Front des parties du changement, in preparation for legislative and local elections scheduled to be held in 2001. In August the Government requested a postponement of the local elections owing to financial difficulties; the Constitutional Court concurred, and they were delayed until April 2002. Despite a ruling by the Constitutional Court that they should take place no later than 30 September, local elections were subsequently postponed further, until 29 December.

Meanwhile, elections to the Assemblée nationale took place on 9 and 23 December 2001. Three opposition parties accused the Government of falsely inflating voter registration lists and boycotted the elections, while others called for the first round to be annulled, as a result of reputed irregularities and high abstention rates, reported to have reached some 80% in urban areas. In the event, the elections were postponed in three districts until 6 January 2002, owing to violent incidents, and voting was repeated on 20 January in a further two constituencies where candidates had received the same number of votes and in a third district where violence had marred the initial ballot. An outbreak of the Ebola virus (see below) resulted in the indefinite postponement of voting in the north-eastern district of Zadie. The PDG won 86 seats in the Assemblée, which were supplemented by 19 seats secured by independents with links to the PDG and other parties affiliated to the ruling party. Opposition parties obtained a total of 14 seats (the RPG eight, the PSD two and the UPG one).

A new, enlarged 39-member Council of Ministers, which included four opposition representatives, was appointed in late January 2002. Ntoutoume Emane was reappointed as Prime Minister, while M'Ba Abessole was named Minister of State for Human Rights and Missions. The new Government's priorities were stated to be poverty alleviation, social reintegration and the eradication of corruption. In the same month two universities were closed by the Government in an attempt to end industrial action by lecturers, who had been on strike since November 2001, in support of demands for salary increases and the payment of arrears.

During March and April 2002 the Constitutional Court annulled the results of voting in the December 2001 elections to the Assemblée nationale in 12 constituencies, including eight in which the PDG had been successful, owing to irregularities. On 26 May and 9 June by-elections took place in these 12 constituencies and in Zadie (where voting had been postponed); the PDG won 10 of the 13 seats contested, increasing its representation to 88 seats. Notably, two government ministers, the Minister of National Education, Daniel Ona Ondo, and the Minister-delegate for the Budget, Senturel Ngoma Madoungou, had their election to the Assemblée confirmed at the by-elections held in their constituencies.

Throughout late 2002 the ruling PDG formed a number of alliances with minor opposition parties. In November the Parti de l'unité du peuple gabonais and the Mouvement commun de développement agreed formally to join the PDG, and in the same month the Parti gabonais du centre indépendant resolved to support the 'presidential majority' in the local elections scheduled for December.

In the local elections of 29 December 2002 the PDG again achieved an overwhelming victory, although success was marred by the apparent apathy of the electorate, with voter participation estimated at less than 20% in some areas. The opposition called for the results to be annulled, citing allegedly fraudulent adjustments carried out to the register of voters prior to the elections (some 73,000 persons were officially removed from the register in November 2002, bringing the total removed since the 2001 legislative elections to some 243,000). In late January 2003 Vice-President Divungui-di-N'Dingue was the target of an assassination attempt, perpetrated, his office claimed, by members of the PSD. Although Maganga Moussavou denied the accusations, Bongo dismissed him from the Council of Ministers in a reshuffle on the following day, promoting M'Ba Abessole to the post of Vice-Prime Minister, Minister of Agriculture, Livestock and Rural Development, in charge of Human Rights. Elections to the Senate took place on 9 February 2003; the PDG won more than 60 of the upper chamber's 91 seats, followed by the RPG, which secured eight seats. In early April a further, minor reshuffle was effected.

In July 2003 the Assemblée nationale voted to revoke the Constitution's limit on the number of terms of office for which the President is eligible to seek re-election. Opposition politicians claimed that Bongo thus intended to become 'President for Life' by means of continuous fraud in future presidential elections. In September, in response to a series of strikes and protests, the Government and representatives of labour groups announced the signing of a so-called 'social truce', which included commitments to lower the prices of essential items and reduce the extent of political patronage over the following three years. However, renewed protests over reductions in state expenditure in early 2004 appeared to threaten the viability of the agreement.

In early September 2004 President Bongo carried out a minor cabinet reshuffle, in which several leading opposition figures were awarded ministerial portfolios in the newly enlarged 44-member Council of Ministers. Emane retained the post of Prime Minister and the key ministerial portfolios remained unchanged. It was widely believed that the inclusion of opposition leaders in the Government was intended to reduce the number of candidates opposing Bongo and the PDG in the presidential and legislative elections scheduled for 2005 and 2006, respectively.

President Bongo has pursued a policy of close co-operation with France in the fields of economic and foreign affairs. Relations became strained in March 1997, however, when allegations that Bongo had been a beneficiary in an international fraud emerged, during a French judicial investigation into the affairs of the petroleum company Elf Aquitaine (now part of Total). The Chairman of Elf-Gabon, André Tarallo, was temporarily detained, and overseas bank accounts, said to contain Gabonese government funds, were blocked. In response, Bongo cancelled a visit to France and reportedly threatened to impose economic sanctions on French oil interests in Gabon. In October 1999 a further judicial investigation into the affairs of Elf Aquitaine, carried out by Swiss authorities, revealed that Tarallo had used bank accounts in that country secretly to transfer large sums of money to several African heads of state, among them Bongo. Bongo denied personally receiving direct payments from Elf and maintained that such 'bonus' payments were made only to the Gabonese Government. However, a report released in November, following a separate investigation by the US Congress into money-laundering and corruption among political figures, alleged further improper financial dealing between Bongo and Elf. In March 2003 the trial commenced in Paris of 37 defendants accused of permitting the embezzlement of the equivalent of some €300m. of funds from Elf Aquitaine. Furthermore, it was claimed that an apartment in Paris had been illicitly procured for Bongo's private use. In November Tarallo was sentenced to four years' imprisonment and fined €2m., while 29 others also received terms of imprisonment. In January 2004, however, Tarallo was released from prison on the grounds of ill-

health, although he was forced to surrender his passport. The prosecution subsequently appealed for harsher sentences to be imposed upon Tarallo and 14 others convicted in November 2003. In March 2005 Tarallo's sentence was increased to seven years' imprisonment.

Bongo has often acted as an intermediary in regional disputes, chairing the OAU *ad hoc* committee seeking to resolve the border dispute between Chad and Libya, and encouraging dialogue between Angola and the USA. In 1997 he mediated in civil conflicts in Zaire (now the Democratic Republic of the Congo—DRC), the Central African Republic (CAR) and the Republic of the Congo. In July of that year the Government expressed concern at the large numbers of refugees arriving in Gabon and subsequently announced plans for repatriation. Throughout late 1998 Bongo participated in discussions with other central African leaders in an attempt to find a solution to the political and military crisis in the DRC, which had been invaded by Rwandan and Ugandan troops in August of that year. At a summit meeting held in Libreville in September, it was decided that Bongo would chair a monitoring and consultations committee on the conflict.

In July 1999 a summit meeting of central African heads of government took place in Libreville to discuss the problem of displaced people in the region. Bongo appealed for regional solidarity in addressing this issue, and proposed the formation of a new organization to assist the region's refugees. Later that month the Gabonese Government appealed for international assistance following a further influx of refugees from renewed fighting in the DRC. At the Gulf of Guinea summit held in Libreville in November the seven countries represented agreed to form the Commission du Golfe de Guinée, a consultation framework designed to promote co-operation and development among the member countries as well as to take measures towards the prevention and resolution of conflicts affecting those countries. In the same month Gabon established diplomatic relations with Libya. In December Bongo was designated as the official mediator in negotiations between the Government and militia groups in the Republic of the Congo, which subsequently led to the conclusion of a peace agreement. Nevertheless, 11,945 Congolese refugees remained in Gabon at the end of 2002.

At a meeting of the Communauté économique et monétaire de l'Afrique centrale (CEMAC) in Libreville in early December 2001, Bongo was appointed to chair a commission, also comprising Presidents Idriss Deby and Denis Sassou-Nguesso of Chad and the Republic of the Congo, respectively, to find a lasting solution to instability in the CAR (q.v.). In October 2002 a CEMAC summit in Libreville sought to defuse tensions between the CAR and Chad, following outbreaks of violence on their common border. In November Gabonese soldiers arrived in the CAR as part of a CEMAC peace-keeping force; the Gabonese contingent totalled some 139 troops in January 2004. In January 2005 Bongo was influential in resolving a dispute over candidacies to the forthcoming presidential election in the CAR.

Following a visit to Gabon in February 2004 by the Chinese President, Hu Jintao, agreements were signed providing for greater economic co-operation between the two countries; most notably, the French oil corporation Total concluded an agreement to export Gabonese oil to the People's Republic of China. Relations were further strengthened following Bongo's visit to China in September, during which he secured some US $5m. in aid from the Jintao administration. In that month a Chinese company signed an agreement to exploit about 1,000m. metric tons of Gabonese iron ore. In February 2005 it was announced that in 2004 Chinese exports to Gabon had increased by some 60%, compared with the previous year.

In February 1996 the northern part of Gabon was quarantined in response to an outbreak of Ebola haemorrhagic fever, in which at least 13 people died, according to WHO. In April it was reported that the World Bank and the World Wide Fund for Nature were seeking to identify areas of equatorial forest for conservation, amid fears that increasing exploitation by logging companies would imperil the survival of indigenous plant and animal species. (In January 2003 the European Union—EU—and the USA donated US $6.5m. and $53m., respectively, towards forest conservation initiatives.) It was also feared that opening up the forest could lead to another outbreak of the Ebola virus, of which forest-dwelling fauna are believed to be carriers. In October 1996 a second outbreak claimed 14 lives in the north-east of the country, and by January 1997 a further 40 deaths had been reported. The Ebola virus re-emerged in the north-east of

GABON

Introductory Survey

Gabon in December 2001, resulting in 11 deaths. The whole region was quarantined, but by early April 2002 WHO had confirmed 65 cases. The EU donated $260,370 to Gabon to combat the Ebola virus. In early May it was announced that the outbreak had been contained, although the disease had claimed an estimated 53 lives. In January 2005 Gabon secured a US $500,000 loan from the African Development Bank to construct a surveillance centre to monitor the spread of the virus.

In March 2003 relations with Equatorial Guinea became tense, following Gabon's occupation of the uninhabited island of Mbagne, which lies in potentially oil-rich waters in Corisco Bay, north of Libreville. Both countries claimed sovereignty over the island. Equatorial Guinea rejected Bongo's proposal for joint exploitation of any petroleum reserves found in the vicinity of the island, despite an official visit to Libreville in early May by the Equato-Guinean President, Gen. Obiang Nguema Mbasogo. Attempts to reach a negotiated settlement failed in December, although the two countries agreed to the appointment of a UN mediator in the dispute in January 2004. In July a provisional agreement was reached to explore jointly for petroleum in the disputed territories and at a meeting in Libreville in January 2005 Bongo and Obiang Nguema expressed optimism that an amicable agreement would soon be finalized.

Government

The Constitution of March 1991 provides for a multi-party system, and vests executive power in the President, who is directly elected by universal suffrage for a period of seven years. The President appoints the Prime Minister, who is Head of Government and who (in consultation with the President) appoints the Council of Ministers. Legislative power is vested in the Assemblée nationale, comprising 120 members, who are elected by direct universal suffrage for a term of five years, and the 91-member Sénat, which is elected by members of municipal councils and departmental assemblies for a term of six years. The independence of the judiciary is guaranteed by the Constitution. Gabon is divided into nine provinces, each under an appointed governor, and 37 prefectures.

Defence

At 1 August 2004 the army consisted of 3,200 men, the air force of 1,000 men, and the navy of an estimated 500 men. Paramilitary forces numbered 2,000. Military service is voluntary. France maintains a military detachment of 800 in Gabon. The defence budget for 2004 was estimated at 9,000m. francs CFA.

Economic Affairs

In 2003, according to estimates by the World Bank, Gabon's gross national product (GNI), measured at average 2001–03 prices, was US $5,205m., equivalent to $3,580 per head (or $5,700 per head on an international purchasing-power parity basis). During 1990–2003, it was estimated, the population increased at an average annual rate of 2.7%, while gross domestic product (GDP) per head declined, in real terms, by an average of 0.2% per year. Overall GDP increased, in real terms, at an average annual rate of 2.5% in 1990–2003; growth in 2003 was 3.4%.

Agriculture (including forestry and fishing) contributed an estimated 8.7% of GDP in 2003. About 34.0% of the labour force were employed in the agricultural sector in 2003. Cocoa, coffee, oil palm and rubber are cultivated for export. Gabon has yet to achieve self-sufficiency in staple crops: imports of food and live animals accounted for 15.1% of the value of total imports in 2000. The principal subsistence crops are plantains, cassava and maize. The exploitation of Gabon's forests (which cover about 75% of the land area) is a principal economic activity. In 2003 okoumé timber accounted for an estimated 39% of all timber exports. Although Gabon's territorial waters contain important fishing resources, their commercial exploitation is minimal. Agricultural GDP increased at an average annual rate of 0.5% in 1990–2003; growth in 2003 was 5.4%.

Industry (including mining, manufacturing, construction and power) contributed an estimated 67.1% of GDP in 2003. About 14.1% of the working population were employed in the sector in 1991. Industrial GDP increased at an average annual rate of 1.7% in 1990–2003; growth in 2003 was 2.9%.

Mining accounted for an estimated 44.7% of GDP in 2002 (with 43.1% contributed by the petroleum sector alone). In 2002 sales of petroleum and petroleum products provided an estimated 79.0% of export revenue. Production of crude petroleum was estimated at 289,700 barrels per day in 2003 and at the end of that year Gabon had proven petroleum reserves of 2,500m.

barrels and proven natural gas reserves of 1,200,000m. cu ft, according to the US Energy Information Administration. Gabon is among the world's foremost producers and exporters of manganese (which contributed an estimated 4.6% of export earnings in 2002). In 2004 some 2.7m. metric tons of manganese were exported. Major reserves of iron ore remain undeveloped, although in September 2004 a Chinese company signed an agreement to exploit some 1,000m. tons of Gabonese iron ore (see above), and there are also substantial niobium (columbium) reserves at Mabounie. Small amounts of gold are extracted, and the existence of many mineral deposits, including talc, barytes, phosphates, rare earths, titanium and cadmium, has also been confirmed. In 1996–2002, according to the IMF, mining GDP declined at an estimated average annual rate of 6.5%. The IMF estimated a decline of 2.1% in mining GDP in 2002.

The manufacturing sector contributed an estimated 5.3% of GDP in 2003. The principal activities are the refining of petroleum and the processing of other minerals, the preparation of timber and other agro-industrial processes. The chemicals industry is also significant. According to IMF estimates, manufacturing GDP increased at an average annual rate of 6.8% in 1996–2002; growth in 2002 was an estimated 3.9%.

In 2000 71.3% of electrical energy was provided by hydro-electric power, 18.1% by petroleum and 10.7% by natural gas. Imports of fuel and energy comprised an estimated 4.2% of the total value of merchandise imports in 2000.

Services engaged 18.8% of the economically active population in 1991 and provided an estimated 24.1% of GDP in 2002. The GDP of the services sector increased at an average annual rate of 3.7% in 1990–2003; growth in 2003 was 3.6%.

According to preliminary estimates, in 2003 Gabon recorded a trade surplus of 1,252,600m. francs CFA, and there was a surplus of 336.9m. francs CFA on the current account of the balance of payments. In 2000 the principal source of imports (44.1%) was France; other major sources were the USA and the Netherlands. The principal market for exports in that year was the USA (62.6%); Australia and the People's Republic of China were also important purchasers. The principal exports in 2002 were petroleum and petroleum products, timber and manganese. The principal imports in 2000 were machinery and transport equipment, food and live animals, and chemicals and related products.

In 2002 there was an estimated budgetary surplus of 121,900m. francs CFA (equivalent to 3.5% of GDP). Gabon's external debt totalled US $3,533m. at the end of 2002, of which $3,231m. was long-term public debt. In that year the cost of debt-servicing was equivalent to 11.7% of the value of exports of goods and services. In 1996–2002 the average annual rate of inflation was 1.2%. Consumer prices increased by 0.5% in 2002. The Government estimated about 20% of the labour force to be unemployed in 1996.

Gabon is a member of the Central African organs of the Franc Zone (see p. 267), and of the Communauté économique des états de l'Afrique centrale (CEEAC, see p. 373). In 1996 Gabon, which had been a member of the Organization of the Petroleum Exporting Countries (OPEC, see p. 331) since 1973, withdrew from the organization.

Gabon's potential for economic growth is based on its considerable mineral and forestry resources. Petroleum provides the country's principal source of income, but production is estimated to be in long-term decline. Gabon's adherence to the African Uniform Business Law Act in 1998 considerably improved investor confidence in the country and in October 2000 the IMF approved a new 18-month stand-by agreement, worth some US $119m. However, the Government largely failed to implement a sufficiently strict austerity policy in accordance with the IMF's recommendations. As petroleum prices declined in 2001, arrears of foreign debt continued to accumulate, despite the rescheduling of some $532m. owed to the 'Paris Club' of international creditors. A further $717m. of debt held by the 'Paris Club' was rescheduled in June 2004. In mid-2002 the Government concurred with predictions by the World Bank that petroleum production in Gabon would decline by some 50%, in relation to 1996 levels, during the following five years. Nonetheless, revenue from petroleum exports was estimated to have increased in 2003, following improvements in extractive technologies and a rise in international prices. Efforts to increase revenue from non-petroleum sectors remained a key priority and it was envisaged that measures to diversify the economy, and thus reduce reliance on mineral exports, could be achieved through further development of the forestry, agriculture, fisheries and services sectors, notably with the promotion of Gabon as a tourist destination. It was also hoped that the ratio of external debt to GDP, which stood at 56% at the end of 2003, would decrease to 45% by the end of 2005. In May 2004 the IMF approved a $102m. stand-by agreement and in December the Fund approved a disbursement of $21.4m., following a broadly positive review of government fiscal management. In response to IMF recommendations, government spending decreased by some 16.8% in 2003. However, levels of government corruption were reported to be increasing in the early 2000s, and allegations of nepotism and misappropriation continued to threaten Gabon's financial credibility. Accordingly, the Government's objectives for 2005 included improvements in tax collection and the regulation of public-sector salaries. Revenues from the hydrocarbon sector were also to be subjected to closer scrutiny. GDP growth in 2004 was estimated at 1.9% and was predicted to decrease to 0.9% in 2005.

Education

Education is officially compulsory for 10 years between six and 16 years of age. Primary and secondary education is provided by state and mission schools. Primary education begins at the age of six and lasts for six years. Secondary education, beginning at 12 years of age, lasts for up to seven years, comprising a first cycle of four years and a second of three years. In 2000/01 88% of children in the relevant age-group (89% of boys; 87% of girls) attended primary schools, according to UNESCO estimates. In that year enrolment at secondary schools was equivalent to 60% of children in the relevant age-group (61% of boys; 58% of girls),

according to UNESCO estimates. The Université Omar Bongo Ondimba is based at Libreville and the Université des Sciences et des Techniques de Masuku at Franceville. In 1998 7,473 students were enrolled at institutions providing tertiary education. The 1994 budget allocated 78,850m. francs CFA (19% of total administrative spending) to expenditure on education.

Public Holidays

2005: 1 January (New Year's Day), 21 January* (Id al-Adha, feast of the Sacrifice), 12 March (Anniversary of Renovation, foundation of the Parti démocratique gabonais), 28 March (Easter Monday), 21 April* (Mouloud, birth of Muhammad), 1 May (Labour Day), 16 May (Whit Monday), 17 August (Anniversary of Independence), 1 November (All Saints' Day), 4 November* (Id al-Fitr, end of Ramadan), 25 December (Christmas).

2006: 1 January (New Year's Day), 11 January* (Id al-Adha, feast of the Sacrifice), 12 March (Anniversary of Renovation, foundation of the Parti démocratique gabonais), 11 April* (Mouloud, birth of Muhammad), 17 April* (Easter Monday), 1 May (Labour Day), 5 June (Whit Monday), 17 August (Anniversary of Independence), 24 October* (Id al-Fitr, end of Ramadan), 1 November (All Saints' Day), 25 December (Christmas).

*These holidays are dependent on the Islamic lunar calendar and may vary by one or two days from the dates given.

Weights and Measures

The metric system is in official use.

Statistical Survey

Source (unless otherwise stated): Direction Générale de l'Economie, Ministère de la Planification, de l'Economie et de l'Administration Territoriale, Libreville.

Area and Population

AREA, POPULATION AND DENSITY

Area (sq km)	267,667*
Population (census results)	
8 October 1960–May 1961	448,564
31 July 1993	
Males	501,784
Females	513,192
Total	1,014,976
Population (UN estimates at mid-year)†	
2001	1,283,000
2002	1,306,000
2003	1,329,000
Density (per sq km) at mid-2003	5.0

* 103,347 sq miles.
† Source: UN, *World Population Prospects: The 2002 Revision*.

REGIONS
(1993 census)

Region	Area (sq km)	Population	Density (per sq km)	Chief town
Estuaire . .	20,740	463,187	22.3	Libreville
Haut-Ogooué .	36,547	104,301	2.9	Franceville
Moyen-Ogooué .	18,535	42,316	2.3	Lambaréné
N'Gounié . .	37,750	77,781	2.1	Mouila
Nyanga . . .	21,285	39,430	1.9	Tchibanga
Ogooué-Ivindo .	46,075	48,862	1.1	Makokou
Ogooué-Lolo .	25,380	43,915	1.7	Koula-Moutou
Ogooué-Maritime .	22,890	97,913	4.3	Port-Gentil
Woleu-N'Tem .	38,465	97,271	2.5	Oyem
Total . . .	267,667	1,014,976	3.8	

PRINCIPAL TOWNS
(population at 1993 census)

Libreville (capital) .	419,596	Mouila		16,307
Port-Gentil . . .	79,225	Lambaréné . . .		15,033
Franceville . . .	31,183	Tchibanga . . .		14,054
Oyem	22,404	Koulamoutou . .		11,773
Moanda	21,882	Makokou		9,849

Mid-2003 (UN estimate, incl. suburbs): Libreville (capital) 611,033 (Source: UN, *World Urbanization Prospects: The 2003 Revision*).

BIRTHS AND DEATHS
(UN estimates, annual averages)

	1985–90	1990–95	1995–2000
Birth rate (per 1,000)	39.9	38.5	34.5
Death rate (per 1,000)	12.5	12.0	11.9

Source: UN, *World Population Prospects: The 2002 Revision*.

Expectation of life (WHO estimates, years at birth): 59.4 (males 57.3; females 61.4) in 2002 (Source: WHO, *World Health Report*).

ECONOMICALLY ACTIVE POPULATION
(estimates, '000 persons, 1991)

	Males	Females	Total
Agriculture, etc.	187	151	338
Industry	62	9	71
Services	69	26	95
Total labour force	318	186	504

Source: UN Economic Commission for Africa, *African Statistical Yearbook*.

Mid-2003 (estimates, '000 persons): Agriculture, etc. 203; Total 597 (Source: FAO).

Health and Welfare

KEY INDICATORS

Total fertility rate (children per woman, 2002)	4.0
Under-5 mortality rate (per 1,000 live births, 2003)	91
HIV/AIDS (% of persons aged 15–49, 2003)	8.1
Hospital beds (per 1,000 head, 1990)	3.19
Health expenditure (2001): US $ per head (PPP)	197
Health expenditure (2001): % of GDP	3.6
Health expenditure (2001): public (% of total)	47.9
Access to water (% of persons, 2002)	87
Access to sanitation (% of persons, 2002)	36
Human Development Index (2002): ranking	122
Human Development Index (2002): value	0.648

For sources and definitions, see explanatory note on p. vi.

Agriculture

PRINCIPAL CROPS
(FAO estimates unless otherwise indicated, '000 metric tons)

	2001	2002	2003
Maize*	33	31	31
Cassava (Manioc)	230	230	230
Taro (Coco yam)	59	59	59
Yams	155	155	155
Sugar cane	235	235	235
Groundnuts (in shell)	20	20	20
Oil palm fruit	32	32	32
Vegetables	35	35	35
Bananas	12	12	12
Plantains	270	270	270
Other fruits	10	10	10
Natural rubber	11	11	11

* Unofficial figures.

Source: FAO.

LIVESTOCK
(FAO estimates, '000 head, year ending September)

	2001	2002	2003
Cattle	36	36	35
Pigs	213	212	212
Sheep	198	195	195
Goats	90	90	90
Chickens	3,200	3,100	3,100
Rabbits	300	300	300

Source: FAO.

LIVESTOCK PRODUCTS
(FAO estimates, '000 metric tons)

	2001	2002	2003
Beef and veal	1.0	1.0	0.7
Pig meat	3.1	3.1	3.1
Poultry meat	3.9	3.9	4.0
Rabbit meat	1.8	1.8	1.8
Game meat	21.0	21.0	21.0
Cows' milk	1.6	1.6	1.6
Hen eggs	2.0	2.0	2.0

Source: FAO.

Forestry

ROUNDWOOD REMOVALS
('000 cubic metres)

	2001	2002	2003
Sawlogs, veneer logs and logs for sleepers	2,584*	1,688	3,563
Fuel wood*	518	520	523
Total	3,102	2,208	4,086

* FAO estimate(s).

Source: FAO.

SAWNWOOD PRODUCTION
('000 cubic metres, incl. railway sleepers)

	2001	2002	2003
Total	112	176	231

Source: FAO.

Fishing

('000 metric tons, live weight)

	2000	2001	2002
Capture	47.5	42.9	40.9
Tilapias	4.2	3.4	3.7
Other freshwater fishes	5.7	5.9	5.1
Barracudas	1.0	1.6	1.4
West African croakers	2.3	2.2	2.6
Lesser African threadfin	2.5	3.1	2.1
Bonga shad	14.8	12.7	11.4
Sardinellas	1.4	1.1	1.3
Penaeus shrimp	0.1	1.9	1.7
Aquaculture	0.5	0.1	0.1
Total catch	48.0	43.0	41.0

Source: FAO .

Mining

	2000	2001	2002
Crude petroleum ('000 barrels)*	118,625	110,000	108,000
Natural gas (million cu metres)*	99	99	99
Diamonds (carats)*	500	500	500
Hydraulic cement ('000 metric tons)	210	210	210
Manganese ore ('000 metric tons): gross weight†	1,706	1,758	1,816
Manganese ore ('000 metric tons): metal content‡	37	33	40
Gold (kilograms)*†§	70	70	70

* Estimated production.
† Figures refer to the metal content of ore.
‡ Figures refer to the weight of chemical-grade pellets.
§ Excluding production smuggled out of the country (estimated at more than 400 kg annually in recent years).

Source: US Geological Survey.

Industry

PETROLEUM PRODUCTS
('000 metric tons)

	1998	1999	2000
Liquefied petroleum gas . . .	10	17	11
Motor spirit (petrol)	60	65	63
Kerosene	85	87	23
Jet fuel	56*	58	58
Distillate fuel oils	213	225	185
Residual fuel oils	242	287	283
Bitumen (asphalt)	17	16	19

* Provisional or estimated figure.

Source: UN, *Industrial Commodity Statistics Yearbook.*

SELECTED OTHER PRODUCTS
('000 metric tons, unless otherwise indicated)

	2000	2001	2002
Palm oil (crude)*†	6	6	6
Plywood ('000 cu metres)† . .	104	76	141
Veneer sheets ('000 cu metres)† .	91	110	110
Cement*‡	210	210	210
Beer ('000 hectolitres)	812	867	n.a.
Soft drinks ('000 hectolitres) . .	516	578	n.a.
Electric energy (million kWh) . .	1,354	n.a.	n.a.

* Estimated production.
† Data from FAO.
‡ Data from the US Geological Survey.
Source: UN, *Industrial Commodity Statistics Yearbook.*

Finance

CURRENCY AND EXCHANGE RATES

Monetary Units
 100 centimes = 1 franc de la Coopération financière en Afrique centrale (CFA).

Sterling, Dollar and Euro Equivalents (31 December 2004)
 £1 sterling = 930.119 francs CFA;
 US $1 = 481.577 francs CFA;
 €1 = 655.957 francs CFA;
 10,000 francs CFA = £10.75 = $20.77 = €15.24.

Average Exchange Rate (francs CFA per US $)
 2002   696.988
 2003   581.200
 2004   528.285

Note: An exchange rate of 1 French franc = 50 francs CFA, established in 1948, remained in force until January 1994, when the CFA franc was devalued by 50%, with the exchange rate adjusted to 1 French franc = 100 francs CFA. This relationship to French currency remained in effect with the introduction of the euro on 1 January 1999. From that date, accordingly, a fixed exchange rate of €1 = 655.957 francs CFA has been in operation.

BUDGET
('000 million francs CFA)

Revenue*	2002	2003	2004†
Petroleum revenue	609.0	570.2	640.0
Non-petroleum revenue . . .	479.0	478.9	513.4
Direct taxes	134.2	122.6	147.2
Indirect taxes	83.5	109.6	110.2
Taxes on international trade and			
transactions	210.0	200.3	205.6
Import duties	180.9	171.2	176.1
Value-added tax	88.6	83.9	86.3
Export duties	29.1	29.1	29.5
Other revenue	51.3	46.4	50.4
Total	**1,088.0**	**1,049.1**	**1,153.4**

Expenditure‡	2002	2003	2004†
Current expenditure . . .	687.4	613.5	617.7
Wages and salaries . .	220.6	229.0	226.0
Other goods and services . .	156.7	124.8	125.5
Transfers and subsidies . . .	158.8	118.3	121.0
Interest payments	151.3	141.5	145.3
Domestic	33.7	30.4	28.7
External	117.6	111.1	116.6
Capital expenditure	136.6	155.0	162.5
Domestically financed			
investment	117.0	122.0	142.5
Externally financed investment	19.6	8.7	20.0
Total	**824.0**	**768.5**	**780.2**

* Excluding grants received ('000 million francs CFA): 1.9 in 2002; 1.2 in 2003; 7.9 in 2004 (projection).
† Projections.
‡ Excluding net lending, restructuring cost of public enterprises, and road maintenance and other special funds ('000 million francs CFA): 145.1 in 2002; 44.5 in 2003 (funds only); 48.0 in 2004 (funds only).

Source: IMF, *Gabon: Second Review Under the Stand-By Arrangement, Request for Waiver of Performance Criterion, and Review of Financing Assurances--Staff Report; Press Release on the Executive Board Discussion; and Statement by the Executive Director for Gabon* (January 2005).

INTERNATIONAL RESERVES
(US $ million at 31 December)

	2001	2002	2003
Gold*	3.57	4.40	5.36
IMF special drawing rights . .	0.06	—	—
Reserve position in IMF . . .	0.23	0.24	0.27
Foreign exchange	9.57	139.40	196.30
Total	**13.42**	**144.05**	**201.93**

* Valued at market-related prices.
Source: IMF, *International Financial Statistics.*

MONEY SUPPLY
('000 million francs CFA at 31 December)

	2001	2002	2003
Currency outside banks . . .	128.19	132.02	124.22
Demand deposits at commercial			
and development banks . . .	203.74	214.27	220.52
Total money (incl. others) . .	**332.22**	**346.69**	**345.10**

Source: IMF, *International Financial Statistics.*

COST OF LIVING
(Consumer price index, Libreville; base: 1975 = 100)

	2000	2001	2002
Food	449.2	467.8	465.0
Clothing	377.1	365.7	377.7
Housing	393.7	401.1	416.4
All items (incl. others)	**470.7**	**475.1**	**477.3**

Source: IMF, *Gabon: Statistical Annex* (February 2004).

NATIONAL ACCOUNTS
('000 million francs CFA at current prices)

Expenditure on the Gross Domestic Product

	2000	2001	2002*
Government final consumption			
expenditure	344.9	396.6	377.3
Private final consumption			
expenditure	1,241.6	1,359.1	1,426.6
Gross fixed capital formation . .	790.3	888.2	842.5
Total domestic expenditure .	**2,376.8**	**2,643.8**	**2,646.4**
Exports of goods and services . .	2,422.7	2,036.3	1,998.8
Less Imports of goods and services	1,181.3	1,231.6	1,196.3
GDP at market prices . . .	**3,618.3**	**3,448.5**	**3,448.9**

* Estimates.

Source: IMF, *Gabon: Statistical Annex* (February 2004).

Gross Domestic Product by Economic Activity

	2000	2001	2002*
Agriculture, livestock, hunting and fishing	138.4	143.9	148.2
Forestry	85.9	76.2	60.0
Petroleum exploitation and research	1,702.0	1,390.6	1,380.4
Other mining	46.8	49.4	51.7
Manufacturing†	193.5	216.9	228.5
Electricity and water	33.6	37.0	45.2
Construction and public works	53.9	79.8	83.1
Trade	238.7	256.9	241.1
Transport	165.8	185.7	191.7
Financial services	18.6	19.1	20.4
Government services	290.7	293.1	293.4
Other services	391.7	450.4	459.9
GDP at factor cost	3,359.6	3,199.0	3,203.6
Indirect taxes	258.7	249.5	245.3
GDP in purchasers' values	3,618.3	3,448.5	3,448.9

* Estimates.
† Includes processing of primary products and research and oil services.
Source: IMF, *Gabon: Statistical Annex* (February 2004).

BALANCE OF PAYMENTS
(francs CFA '000 million)

	2002	2003*	2004†
Exports of goods f.o.b.	1,806.5	1,881.7	2,316.5
Imports of goods f.o.b.	−665.1	−629.1	−724.1
Trade balance	1,141.4	1,252.6	1,592.4
Services (net)	−905.8	−862.3	−1,105.1
Balance on goods and services	235.6	390.3	487.3
Transfers (net)	−57.3	−53.4	−46.6
Current balance	178.3	336.9	440.7
Capital account (net)	−316.8	−373.7	−400.9
Overall balance	−138.5	−36.9	39.9

* Preliminary.
† Projections.
Source: IMF, *Gabon: Second Review Under the Stand-By Arrangement, Request for Waiver of Performance Criterion, and Review of Financing Assurances--Staff Report; Press Release on the Executive Board Discussion; and Statement by the Executive Director for Gabon* (January 2005).

External Trade

PRINCIPAL COMMODITIES

Imports c.i.f. (US $ million)*	1999	2000
Food and live animals	140.9	144.5
Meat and meat preparations	34.9	44.1
Fresh, chilled or frozen meat	30.8	40.1
Cereals and cereal preparations	45.3	44.2
Mineral fuels, lubricants, etc.	19.3	39.8
Refined petroleum products	16.9	36.2
Chemicals and related products	80.4	78.8
Medicinal and pharmaceutical products	30.0	30.5
Medicaments (incl. veterinary)	28.5	28.2
Basic manufactures	131.5	124.0
Iron and steel	22.6	25.4
Tubes, pipes and fittings	14.5	16.2
Machinery and transport equipment	417.2	456.7
Power-generating machinery and equipment	31.8	27.6
Machinery specialized for particular industries	37.5	49.6
Civil engineering and contractors' plant and equipment	20.7	28.1
General industrial machinery, equipment and parts	69.9	76.9
Pumps, centrifuges, etc.	16.9	23.6
Electrical machinery, apparatus, etc.	32.2	41.0
Road vehicles and parts	64.1	76.1
Passenger motor cars (excl. buses)	23.3	24.2
Other transport equipment	148.6	120.6
Ships, boats and floating structures	92.3	70.0

Imports c.i.f. (US $ million)— *continued**	1999	2000
Miscellaneous manufactured articles	69.4	68.5
Professional, scientific and controlling instruments, etc.	14.4	14.4
Total (incl. others)	901.4	956.1

* Figures for 1998 are not available.
Source: UN, *International Trade Statistics Yearbook*.

Exports (million francs CFA)	2000	2001	2002*
Petroleum and petroleum products	1,828	1,509	1,484
Manganese	86	72	86
Timber	281	258	227
Total (incl. others)	2,288	1,919	1,878

* Estimates.
Source: IMF, *Gabon: Statistical Annex* (February 2004).

PRINCIPAL TRADING PARTNERS
(US $ million)

Imports c.i.f.*	1999	2000
Cameroon	17.5	23.6
China, People's Republic	9.6	7.1
Côte d'Ivoire	12.7	17.9
France (incl. Monaco)	419.5	421.4
Germany	35.8	32.7
Italy	39.6	29.6
Netherlands	31.2	44.1
South Africa	n.a.	10.1
Spain	29.5	29.7
Thailand	13.5	14.2
USA	106.3	106.4
Total (incl. others)	901.4	956.1

Exports f.o.b.*	1999	2000
Australia	74.1	143.8
Austria	37.8	13.7
China, People's Republic	160.4	175.3
France (incl. Monaco)	177.3	116.6
Hong Kong	14.5	27.4
Italy	25.5	25.8
Korea, Republic	50.2	96.7
Netherlands	21.8	20.0
Singapore	38.7	1.3
Spain	4.4	27.8
USA	1,223.1	1,628.0
Total (incl. others)	2,071.4	2,600.2

* Figures for 1998 are not available.
Source: UN, *International Trade Statistics Yearbook*.

Transport

RAILWAYS
(traffic)

	1999	2000	2001*
Passengers carried ('000)	201	237	276
Freight carried ('000 metric tons)	2,821	3,168	2,953

* Preliminary figures.
Source: IMF, *Gabon: Statistical Annex* (February 2004).

ROAD TRAFFIC
(estimates, motor vehicles in use)

	1994	1995	1996
Passenger cars	22,310	24,000	24,750
Lorries and vans	14,850	15,840	16,490

Source: IRF, *World Road Statistics*.

SHIPPING

Merchant Fleet
(registered at 31 December)

	2001	2002	2003
Number of vessels	44	44	45
Total displacement ('000 grt) . .	12.5	12.5	12.7

Source: Lloyd's Register-Fairplay, *World Fleet Statistics.*

International Sea-borne Freight Traffic
('000 metric tons, Port-Gentil and Owendo)

	1999	2000	2001
Goods loaded	17,717	16,485	15,993
Goods unloaded	852	924	778

Source: IMF, *Gabon: Statistical Annex* (February 2004).

CIVIL AVIATION
(traffic on scheduled services)

	1999	2000	2001
Kilometres flown (million) . . .	8	8	7
Passengers carried ('000) . . .	423	447	374
Passenger-kilometres (million) .	782	847	637
Total ton-kilometres (million) . .	124	135	107

Source: UN, *Statistical Yearbook.*

Tourism

	2000	2001	2002
Tourist arrivals	155,432	169,191	208,348

Tourism receipts (US $ million): 11 in 1999; 7 in 2000; 7 in 2001.

Source: World Tourism Organization.

Communications Media

	2001	2002	2003
Telephones ('000 main lines in use)	37.2	32.1	38.4
Mobile cellular telephones ('000 subscribers)	258.1	279.3	300.0
Personal computers ('000 in use) .	15	25	30
Internet users ('000)	15	25	35

1996: 2 daily newspapers (average circulation 33,000 copies).

1997: 501 facsimile machines in use

1999: 600,000 radio receivers in use.

2002: 400,000 television receivers in use.

Sources: UNESCO, *Statistical Yearbook*; UN, *Statistical Yearbook*; International Telecommunication Union.

Education

(1998/99)

	Institu-tions	Tea-chers	Pupils		
			Males	Females	Total
Pre-primary* . . .	9	37	465	485	950
Primary	1,175	6,022	133,524	131,720	265,244
Secondary:					
General	88†	3,078	42,308	37,974	80,282
Technical and vocational . .	11†		4,038	2,123	6,161
Tertiary	2*	585	4,806	2,667	7,473

* 1991/92 figure(s).

† 1996 figure.

Source: UNESCO Institute for Statistics.

Adult literacy rate (UNESCO estimates): 63.3% (males 73.7%; females 53.4%) in 1995 (Source: UNESCO, *Statistical Yearbook*).

Directory

The Constitution

The Constitution of the Gabonese Republic was adopted on 14 March 1991. The main provisions are summarized below.

PREAMBLE

Upholds the rights of the individual, liberty of conscience and of the person, religious freedom and freedom of education. Sovereignty is vested in the people, who exercise it through their representatives or by means of referendums. There is direct, universal and secret suffrage.

HEAD OF STATE*

The President is elected by direct universal suffrage for a five-year term, renewable only once. The President is Head of State and of the Armed Forces. The President may, after consultation with his ministers and leaders of the Assemblée nationale, order a referendum to be held. The President appoints the Prime Minister, who is Head of Government and who is accountable to the President. The President is the guarantor of national independence and territorial sovereignty.

EXECUTIVE POWER

Executive power is vested in the President and the Council of Ministers, who are appointed by the Prime Minister, in consultation with the President.

LEGISLATIVE POWER

The Assemblée nationale is elected by direct universal suffrage for a five-year term. It may be dissolved or prorogued for up to 18 months by the President, after consultation with the Council of Ministers and President of the Assemblée. The President may return a bill to the Assemblée for a second reading, when it must be passed by a majority of two-thirds of the members. If the President dissolves the Assemblée, elections must take place within 40 days.

The Constitution also provides for the establishment of an upper chamber (the Sénat), to control the balance and regulation of power.

POLITICAL ORGANIZATIONS

Article 2 of the Constitution states that 'Political parties and associations contribute to the expression of universal suffrage. They are formed and exercise their activities freely, within the limits delineated by the laws and regulations. They must respect the principles of democracy, national sovereignty, public order and national unity'.

JUDICIAL POWER

The President guarantees the independence of the judiciary and presides over the Conseil Supérieur de la Magistrature. Supreme judicial power is vested in the Supreme Court.

* A constitutional amendment, adopted by the legislature on 18 April 1997, extended the presidential term to seven years and provided for the creation of the post of Vice-President. On 29 July 2003 the Constitution was further amended to remove the restriction on the number of terms of office the President may serve.

The Government

HEAD OF STATE

President: El Hadj OMAR (ALBERT-BERNARD) BONGO ONDIMBA (took office 2 December 1967, elected 25 February 1973, re-elected December 1979, November 1986, December 1993 and December 1998).

Vice-President: DIDJOB DIVUNGUI-DI-N'DINGUE.

COUNCIL OF MINISTERS
(April 2005)

The Government comprises members of the Parti démocratique gabonais (PDG), the Rassemblement pour le Gabon (RPG) and the Parti social-démocrate (PSD).

Prime Minister and Head of Government: JEAN-FRANÇOIS NTOU-TOUME EMANE (PDG).

Vice-Prime Minister, Minister of Territorial Administration: EMMANUEL ONDO-METHOGO (PDG).

Vice-Prime Minister, Minister of Towns: ANTOINE DE PADOUE MBOUMBOU MIYAKOU (PDG).

Vice-Prime Minister, Minister of Transport and Civil Aviation, in charge of Human Rights: Fr PAUL M'BA ABESSOLE (RPG).

Minister of State for Planning and Development: CASIMIR OYÉ MBA (PDG).

Minister of State for Foreign Affairs, Co-operation and Francophone Affairs: JEAN PING (PDG).

Minister of State for Economic Affairs, Finance, the Budget and Privatization: PAUL TOUNGUI (PDG).

Minister of State for Public Health: PAULETTE MISSAMBO (PDG).

Minister of State for Small and Medium-sized Enterprises, in charge of Regional Integration: JEAN-RÉMY PENDY-BOUYIKI (PDG).

Minister of State for Housing, Urbanization and Cadastral Services: JACQUES ADIAHÉNOT (PDG).

Minister of State, in charge of Missions and Reform: PIERRE CLAVER MAGANGA MOUSSAVOU (PSD).

Minister of Agriculture, Livestock and Rural Development: FAUSTIN BOUKOUBI (PDG).

Minister of the Interior and Decentralization: CLOTAIRE CHRISTIAN IVALA (PDG).

Minister of Justice, Guardian of the Seals: HONORINE DOSSOU NAKI (PDG).

Minister of National Defence: ALI BONGO ONDIMBA (PDG).

Minister of Mining, Energy, Petroleum and Water Resources: RICHARD ONOUVIET (PDG).

Minister of the Public Affairs, Administrative Reform and Modernization of the State: EGIDE BOUNDONO SIMANGOYE (PDG).

Minister of Public Security, in charge of Immigration: PASCAL DÉSIRÉ MISSONGO (PDG).

Minister of Communications and Information Technology: MEHDI TEALE (PDG).

Minister of Post and Telecommunications: Prof. DANIEL ONA ONDO.

Minister of National Solidarity and Social Affairs and Welfare: ANDRÉ MBA OBAME (PDG).

Minister of National Education: FRANÇOIS ENGONGA OWONO (PDG).

Minister of Water, Forestry, Fishing, Reafforestation and the Environment: EMILE DOUMBA (PDG).

Minister of Family Affairs, the Protection of Children and Women: ANGÉLIQUE NGOMA (PDG).

Ministry of Tourism and Crafts: JEAN MASSIMA (PDG).

Minister of Public Works, Equipment and Construction: Gen. IDRISS NGARI (PDG).

Minister of Higher Education, Research and Technology: VINCENT MOULENGUI BOUKOSS (RPG).

Minister in charge of Relations with Parliament, Government Spokesperson: RENÉ NDEMEZO OBIANG (PDG).

Minister of Commerce and Industrial Development, in charge of NEPAD: PAUL BIYOGHÉ-MBA (PDG).

Minister of Youth and Sports: ALFRED MABICKA (PDG).

Minister of the Merchant Navy and Ports: ALICE LAMOU.

Minister of Professional Training and Social Reintegration: BARNABÉ NDAKI (PDG).

Minister of Culture, the Arts and Popular Education: PIERRE AMOUGHE MBA (RPG).

Minister of Labour and Employment: JEAN BONIFACE ASSELE.

Minister of State Control Inspection, in charge of the Fight against Poverty and the Illegal Acquisition of Wealth: MARTIN MABALA (PDG).

There were also eight Ministers-delegate.

MINISTRIES

Office of the Prime Minister: BP 546, Libreville; tel. 77-89-81.

Ministry of Agriculture, Livestock and Rural Development: BP 551, Libreville; tel. 77-59-22; fax 76-38-34.

Ministry of Commerce and Industrial Development: Libreville.

Ministry of Communications and Information Technology: Libreville; tel. 76-11-15.

Ministry of Culture, the Arts and Popular Education: BP 1007, Libreville; tel. 76-32-33; tel. 72-36-88.

Ministry of Economic Affairs, Finance, the Budget and Privatization: BP 165, Libreville; tel. 76-12-10; fax 76-59-74.

Ministry of Family Affairs, the Protection of Children and Women: BP 5684, Libreville; tel. 77-50-32; fax 76-69-29.

Ministry of Foreign Affairs, Co-operation and Francophone Affairs: BP 2245, Libreville; tel. 72-95-21; fax 72-91-73.

Ministry of Higher Education, Research and Technology: BP 2217, Libreville; tel. 76-39-09; fax 76-39-09.

Ministry of Housing, Urbanization and Cadastral Services: BP 512, Libreville; tel. 77-31-04; fax 74-04-62.

Ministry of the Interior and Decentralization: BP 2110, Libreville; tel. 74-35-06; fax 72-13-89.

Ministry of Justice: BP 547, Libreville; tel. 74-66-28; fax 72-33-84.

Ministry of Labour and Employment: BP 4577, Libreville; tel. 74-32-18.

Ministry of the Merchant Navy and Ports: Libreville.

Ministry of Mining, Energy, Petroleum and Water Resources: BP 576, Libreville; tel. 77-22-39.

Ministry of National Defence: BP 13493, Libreville; tel. 77-86-96; fax 77-86-96.

Ministry of National Education: BP 6, Libreville; tel. 72-44-61; fax 72-19-74.

Ministry of National Solidarity and Social Affairs and Welfare: Libreville.

Ministry of Planning and Development: Libreville.

Ministry of Post and Telecommunications: Libreville.

Ministry of Professional Training and Social Reintegration: Libreville; tel. 73-37-35; fax 73-37-39.

Ministry of Public Affairs, Administrative Reform and Modernization of the State: BP 496, Libreville; tel. 76-38-86.

Ministry of Public Health: BP 50, Libreville; tel. 76-36-11.

Ministry of Public Security: Libreville.

Ministry of Public Works, Equipment and Construction: BP 49, Libreville; tel. 76-38-56; fax 74-80-92.

Ministry of Small and Medium-sized Enterprises: BP 3096, Libreville; tel. 74-59-21.

Ministry of Territorial Administration: Libreville; tel. 72-29-83; fax 77-29-62.

Ministry of Tourism and Crafts: BP 178, Libreville; tel. 76-34-62.

Ministry of Towns: Libreville; tel. 31-68-98.

Ministry of Transport, Civil Aviation, in charge of Human Rights: BP 803, Libreville; tel. 74-71-96; fax 77-33-31.

Ministry of Water, Forestry, Fishing, Reafforestation and the Environment: BP 3974, Libreville; tel. 76-01-09; fax 76-61-83.

Ministry of Youth and Sports: BP 2150, Libreville; tel. 74-00-19; fax 74-65-89.

President and Legislature

PRESIDENT

Presidential Election, 6 December 1998

Candidate	% of votes
El Hadj Omar (Albert-Bernard) Bongo	66.55
Pierre Mamboundou	16.54
Fr Paul M'Ba Abessole	13.41
Pierre-André Kombila	1.54
Pierre-Claver Maganga Moussavou	0.99
Others	0.97
Total	**100.00**

ASSEMBLÉE NATIONALE

President: Guy Ndzouba Ndama.

Secretary-General: Jean-Baptiste Yama-Legnongo.

General Election, 9 and 23 December 2001

Party	Seats
Parti démocratique gabonais (PDG)	86
Independents	12
Rassemblement pour le Gabon (RPG)	8
Parti gabonais du progrès (PGP)	3
Parti social-démocrate (PSD)	2
Union du peuple gabonais (UPG)	1
Others	7
Total	**119***

* Including results of elections that were postponed until 6 and 20 January 2002, owing to violent incidents, and of elections that were repeated in two constituencies where candidates received the same number of votes. Voting was postponed indefinitely in the district of Zadie following an outbreak of Ebola fever. During March and April the Constitutional Court annulled the results of voting in a further 12 constituencies, owing to irregularities. On 26 May and 9 June by-elections took place in these 12 constituencies and in Zadie; the PDG won 10 of the 13 seats contested, increasing its overall representation to 88 seats.

SÉNAT

President: Georges Rawiri.

Secretary-General: Félix Owansango Deackeu.

Indirect elections to the 91-member Sénat were held on 9 February 2003. The PDG won more than 60 seats, and the RPG secured eight seats.

Political Organizations

Alliance démocratique et républicaine (ADERE): Pres. Mboumbou Ngoma; Sec.-Gen. Didjob Divungui-di-N'Dingue.

Alliance des républicains pour le développement (ARD): f. 2001; Pres. Marie-Augustine Houangni Ambouroue.

Association pour le socialisme au Gabon (APSG): Pres. V. Mapangou Moucani Mouetsa.

Cercle des libéraux réformateurs (CLR): f. 1993 by breakaway faction of the PDG; Leader Jean-Boniface Assele.

Cercle OMEGA: Leader Marcel Ntchoreret.

Cercle pour le renouveau et le progrès (CRP).

Congrès pour la démocratie et la justice (CDJ): Pres. Jules Bourdes Ogouliguende.

Convention des forces du changement: f. 1993 as an informal alliance of eight opposition presidential candidates.

Coordination de l'opposition démocratique (COD): f. 1991 as an alliance of eight principal opposition parties; Chair. Sébastien Mamboundou Mouyama.

Forum africain pour la reconstruction (FAR): f. 1992; a factional alliance within the COD; Leader Prof. Léon Mbou-Yembi; comprises three political parties.

> **Mouvement de redressement national (MORENA—originels):** f. 1981 in Paris, France; Leader Pierre-André Kombila Koumba.
>
> **Parti socialiste gabonais (PSG):** f. 1991; Leader Prof. Max Obame Ondo.
>
> **Union socialiste gabonais (USG):** Leader Dr Serge Mba Bekale.

Forum centriste de socialisme africain: f. 2000; Leader André Eyeghe.

Front démocratique et culturel: Leader Jean-Claude Quentin.

Front national (FN): f. 1991; Leader Martin Efayong.

Front des parties du changement (FPC): f. 2000 as an alliance of four opposition parties to contest the 2001 legislative elections.

Front pour l'unité nationale et le développement utilitaire (FUNDU): Leader Noël Borobo Epembia.

Gabon Avenir: f. 1999; Leader Sylvestre Oyouomi.

Mouvement africain de développement (MAD): Leader Pierre Claver Nzeng Ebome.

Mouvement africain pour le renouveau social (MARS): Alain Engouang Nze.

Mouvement alternatif: f. 1996; Leader Sébastien Mamboundou Mouyama.

Mouvement pour la démocratie, le développement et la réconciliation nationale (Modern): Libreville; f. 1996; Leader Gaston Mozogo Ovono.

Mouvement d'emancipation socialiste du peuple: Leader Mouanga Mbadinga.

Parti démocratique gabonais (PDG): BP 268, Libreville; tel. 70-31-21; fax 70-31-46; f. 1968; sole legal party 1968–90; Leader Omar Bongo; Sec.-Gen. Simplice Guedet Manzela.

Parti pour le développement national (PDN): Leader Pierre Mapiga.

Parti gabonais du centre indépendant (PGCI): allied to the PDG; Leader Jérôme Okinda.

Parti gabonais du progrès (PGP): f. 1990; Pres. Pierre-Louis Agondjo-Okawé; Sec.-Gen. Anselme Nzoghe.

Parti des libéraux démocrates (PLD).

Parti radical des républicains indépendants (PARI): Leader Anaclé Bissielo.

Parti social-démocrate (PSD): f. 1991; Leader Pierre-Claver Maganga Moussavou.

Rassemblement des démocrates (RDD): f. 1993; Leader Serge Christian Maroga.

Rassemblement des démocrates républicains (RDR): Leader Max Mebale m'Obame.

Rassemblement pour la démocratie et le progrès (RDP): Pres. Pierre Emboni.

Rassemblement pour le Gabon (RPG): f. 1990 as MORENA des bûcherons, renamed Rassemblement national des bûcherons in 1991, name changed as above in 2000; allied to the PDG; Leader Fr Paul M'Ba Abessole; Vice-Pres. Prof. Vincent Moulengui Boukosso.

Rassemblement des Gaullois: Libreville; f. 1994; registered 1998; 5,000 mems; Pres. Max Anicet Koumba-Mbadinga.

Rassemblement national des républicains (RNR): Libreville; f. 2002; Pres. Gérard Ella Nguema; Sec-Gen. Christian Abiaghe Ngomo.

Union pour la démocratie et le développement Mayumba (UDD).

Union démocratique et sociale (UDS): f. 1996; Leader Hervé Assamanet.

Union nationale pour la démocratie et le développement (UNDD): f. 1993; supports President Bongo.

Union pour le développement et la liberté (UDL): Leader Jean-François Ekouaghé Mba.

Union du peuple gabonais (UPG): f. 1989 in Paris, France; Leader Pierre Mamboundou; Sec.-Gen. David Badinga.

Union pour le progrès national (UPN): Leader Daniel Tengue Nzoundo.

Union républicaine pour la démocratie et le progrès (URDP): Leader Jean Marcel Malolas.

Diplomatic Representation

EMBASSIES IN GABON

Algeria: BP 4008, Libreville; tel. 73-23-18; fax 73-14-03; e-mail ambalgabon@tiggabon.com; Ambassador Abdelhamid Chebchoub.

Angola: BP 4884, Libreville; tel. 73-04-26; fax 73-76-24; Ambassador Bernardo Dombele M'Bala.

Belgium: Quartier Bas de Gué-Gué, Bord de Mer à côté de la Délégation de la Commission Européenne, BP 4079, Libreville; tel. 73-29-92; fax 73-96-94; e-mail Libreville@diplobel.org; Ambassador Ivo Goemans.

Benin: BP 3851, Akebe, Libreville; tel. 73-76-82; fax 73-77-75; Ambassador El Hadj Lassissi Adébo.

Brazil: BP 3899, Libreville; tel. 76-05-35; fax 74-03-43; e-mail emblibreville@inet.ga; internet www.ambassadedubresil-gabon.org; Ambassador Sergio Seabra de Noronha.

Cameroon: BP 14001, Libreville; tel. 73-28-00; Ambassador Jean Koé Ntonga.

Canada: blvd Pasteur, Quartier Batterie IV, BP 4037, Libreville; tel. 73-73-54; fax 73-73-88; e-mail lbvre@dfait-maeci.gc.ca; Ambassador Louis Guay.

Central African Republic: Libreville; tel. 72-12-28; Ambassador (vacant).

China, People's Republic: BP 3914, Libreville; tel. 74-32-07; fax 74-75-96; e-mail gzy@internetgabon.com; Ambassador FAN ZHEN-SHUI.

Congo, Democratic Republic: BP 2257, Libreville; tel. 74-32-53; Ambassador KABANGI KAUMBU BULA.

Congo, Republic: BP 269, Libreville; tel. 73-29-06; Ambassador PIERRE OBOU.

Côte d'Ivoire: Charbonnages, BP 3861, Libreville; tel. 73-82-70; fax 73-82-87; Ambassador CLAUDINE YAPOBI RICCI.

Egypt: Immeuble Pavillon, Quartier Batterie IV, BP 4240, Libreville; tel. 73-25-38; fax 73-25-19; Ambassador AHMED KHATTAB.

Equatorial Guinea: BP 1462, Libreville; tel. 75-10-56; Ambassador JOSÉ ESONO BACALE.

France: blvd de l'Indépendance, BP 2125, Libreville; tel. 76-10-56; fax 74-48-78; e-mail ambafran@inet.ga; internet www.chez.com/ambafrangabon; Ambassador PHILIPPE SELZ.

Germany: blvd de l'Indépendance, Immeuble les Frangipaniers, BP 299, Libreville; tel. 76-01-88; fax 72-40-12; e-mail amb-allegmagne@inet.ga; Ambassador ILSE LINDEMANN-MACHA.

Guinea: BP 4046, Libreville; tel. 73-85-09; Ambassador MOHAMED SAMPIL.

Holy See: blvd Monseigneur Bessieux, BP 1322, Libreville (Apostolic Nunciature); tel. 74-45-41; e-mail nonapcg@yahoo.com; Apostolic Nuncio Mgr ANDRÉS CARRASCOSA COSO (Titular Archbishop of Elo).

Italy: Immeuble Personnaz et Gardin, rue de la Mairie, BP 2251, Libreville; tel. 74-28-92; fax 74-80-35; Ambassador LUDOVICO TASSONI ESTENSE DE CASTELVECCHIO.

Japan: blvd du Bord de Mer, BP 2259, Libreville; tel. 73-22-97; fax 73-60-60; Ambassador SADAMU FUJIWARA.

Korea, Democratic People's Republic: Ambassador KIM RYONG YONG.

Korea, Republic: BP 2620, Libreville; tel. 73-40-00; fax 73-99-05; e-mail gabon-ambcoree@mofat.go.kr; internet www.mofat.go.kr/mission/emb/embassy_en.mof?si_dcode=GA-GA; Ambassador CHO WON-HO.

Lebanon: BP 3341, Libreville; tel. 73-14-77; e-mail amb.lib.gab@inet.ga; Ambassador GHARAMY HABIB AYOUB.

Mali: BP 4007, Quartier Batterie IV, Libreville; tel. 73-77-58; fax 73-82-80; Ambassador TRAORÉ ROKIATOU GUIKINE.

Mauritania: BP 3917, Libreville; tel. 74-31-65; Ambassador El Hadj THIAM.

Morocco: blvd de l'indépendance, Immeuble CK 2, BP 3983, Libreville; tel. 77-41-51; fax 77-41-50; e-mail sifamalbv@inet.ga; Ambassador LARBI REFFOUH.

Nigeria: ave du Président Léon-Mba, Quartier blvd. Léon-M'Ba, BP 1191, Libreville; tel. 73-29-14; fax 73-10-17; Ambassador Chief IGNATIUS H. AJURU.

Russia: BP 3963, Libreville; tel. 72-48-69; fax 72-48-70; e-mail ambrusga@inet.ga; Ambassador VSEVOLOD SOUKHOV.

São Tomé and Príncipe: BP 489, Libreville; tel. 72-09-94; Ambassador URBINO JOSÉ GONHALVES BOTELÇO.

Senegal: BP 3856, Libreville; tel. 77-42-67; Ambassador IBRAHIM KABA.

Serbia and Montenegro: Libreville; tel. 73-30-05; Ambassador ČEDOMIR STRBAC.

South Africa: Immeuble les Arcades, 142 rue des Chavannes, BP 4063, Libreville; tel. 77-45-30; fax 77-45-36; e-mail saegabon@internetgabon.com; Ambassador MAHLOMOLA JOMO KHASU.

Spain: Immeuble Diamant, 2ème étage, blvd de l'Indépendance, BP 1157, Libreville; tel. 72-12-64; fax 74-88-73; e-mail ambespga@mail.mae.es; Ambassador JAVIER SANGRO LINIERS.

Togo: BP 14160, Libreville; tel. 73-29-04; fax 73-32-61; Ambassador AHLONKO KOFFI AQUEREBURU.

Tunisia: BP 3844, Libreville; tel. 73-28-41; Ambassador EZZEDINE KERKENI.

USA: blvd de la Mer, BP 4000, Libreville; tel. 76-20-03; fax 74-55-07; e-mail clolibreville@state.gov; internet usembassy.state.gov/libreville; Ambassador REUBEN BARRIE WALKLEY.

Judicial System

Supreme Court: BP 1043, Libreville; tel. 72-17-00; three chambers: judicial, administrative and accounts; Pres. BENJAMIN PAMBOU-KOMBILA.

Constitutional Court: Libreville; tel. 72-57-17; fax 72-55-96; Pres. MARIE MADELEINE MBORANTSUO.

Courts of Appeal: Libreville and Franceville.

Court of State Security: Libreville; 13 mems; Pres. FLORENTIN ANGO.

Conseil Supérieur de la Magistrature: Libreville; Pres. El Hadj OMAR BONGO ONDIMBA; Vice-Pres. BENJAMIN PAMBOU-KOMBILA (*ex officio*).

There are also Tribunaux de Première Instance (County Courts) at Libreville, Franceville, Port-Gentil, Lambaréné, Mouila, Oyem, Koula-Moutou, Makokou and Tchibanga.

Religion

About 60% of Gabon's population are Christians, mainly adherents of the Roman Catholic Church. About 40% are animists, and fewer than 1% are Muslims.

CHRISTIANITY

The Roman Catholic Church

Gabon comprises one archdiocese, four dioceses and one Apostolic Vicariate. At 31 December 2003 the estimated number of adherents in the country was equivalent to 46.7% of the total population.

Bishops' Conference

Conférence Episcopale du Gabon, BP 2146, Libreville; tel. 72-20-73. f. 1989; Pres. Most Rev. BASILE MVÉ ENGONE (Archbishop of Libreville).

Archbishop of Libreville: Most Rev. BASILE MVÉ ENGONE, Archevêché, Sainte-Marie, BP 2146, Libreville; tel. 72-20-73.

Protestant Churches

Christian and Missionary Alliance: Gabon Field, BP 13021, Libreville; e-mail gabonfd@inet.ga; active in the south of the country; Field-Dir Rev. ALBERT STOMBAUGH; 16,000 mems.

Eglise Evangélique du Gabon: BP 10080, Libreville; tel. 72-41-92; f. 1842; independent since 1961; 120,000 mems; Pres. Pastor SAMUEL NANG ESSONO; Sec. Rev. EMILE NTETOME.

The Evangelical Church of South Gabon and the Evangelical Pentecostal Church are also active in Gabon.

The Press

Afric'Sports: BP 3950, Libreville; tel. 76-24-74; monthly; sport; CEO SERGE ALFRED MPOUHO; Man. YVON PATRICE AUBIAN; circ. 5,000.

L'Autre Journal: Libreville; f. 2003; independent; bi-monthly; publ. suspended Dec. 2003; Editor ANACLET SEGALT.

Le Bûcheron: BP 6424, Libreville; tel. 72-50-20; f. 1990; weekly; official publ. of the Rassemblement pour le Gabon; Editor DÉSIRÉ ENAME.

Bulletin Evangélique d'Information et de Presse: BP 80, Libreville; monthly; religious.

Bulletin Mensuel de Statistique de la République Gabonaise: BP 179, Libreville; monthly; publ. by Direction Générale de l'Economie.

L'Economiste Gabonais: BP 3906, Libreville; quarterly; publ. by the Centre gabonais du commerce extérieur.

Gabon d'Aujourd'hui: BP 750, Libreville; weekly; publ. of the Ministry of Culture, the Arts and Popular Education.

Gabon Libre: BP 6439, Libreville; tel. 72-42-22; weekly; Dir DZIME EKANG; Editor RENÉ NZOVI.

Gabon-Matin: BP 168, Libreville; daily; publ. by Agence Gabonaise de Presse; Man. HILARION VENDANY; circ. 18,000.

Gabon Show: Libreville; f. 2004; independent; satirical; printed in Cameroon; Man. Editor FULBERT WORA; weekly; circ. 3,000.

Gris-Gris International: Paris; f. 1990; weekly; independent; satirical; distribution forbidden in 2001; Editor-in-Chief RAPHAEL NTOUTOUME NKOGHE; Editor MICHEL ONGOUNDOU.

Journal Officiel de la République Gabonaise: BP 563, Libreville; f. 1959; fortnightly; Man. EMMANUEL OBAMÉ.

Le Misamu: BP 887, Libreville; tel. 74-74-59; fortnightly; Founder NOËL NGWA NGUEMA.

Ngondo: BP 168, Libreville; monthly; publ. by Agence Gabonaise de Presse.

Le Progressiste: blvd Léon-M'Ba, BP 7000, Libreville; tel. 74-54-01; f. 1990; Dir BENOÎT MOUITY NZAMBA; Editor JACQUES MOURENDE-TSIOBA.

La Relance: BP 268, Libreville; tel. 72-93-08; weekly; publ. of the Parti démocratique gabonais; Pres. JACQUES ADIAHÉNOT; Dir RENÉ NDEMEZO'O OBIANG.

Le Réveil: BP 20386, Libreville; tel. and fax 73-17-21; weekly; Man. ALBERT YANGARI; Editor RENÉ NZOVI; circ. 8,000.

La Sagaie: fortnightly; satirical; distribution suspended September 2003.

Sept Jours: BP 213, Libreville; weekly.

Sub-Version: Libreville; fortnightly; f. 2003; independent; satirical; printed in Douala, Cameroon; publ. suspended in 2003.

La Tribune des Affaires: BP 2234, Libreville; tel. 72-20-64; fax 74-12-20; monthly; publ. of the Chambre de Commerce, d'Agriculture, d'Industrie et des Mines du Gabon.

L'Union: Sonapresse, BP 3849, Libreville; tel. 73-58-61; fax 73-58-62; f. 1974; 75% state-owned; daily; official govt publ.; Man. Dir and Editor VINCENT MAVOUNGOU; circ. 20,000.

La Voix du Peuple: BP 4049, Libreville; tel. 76-20-45; f. 1991; weekly; Editor-in-Chief JEAN KOUMBA; Editor MAURIC-BLAISE NDZA-DIENGA MAYILA; circ. 4,000.

Zoom Hebdo: Carrefour London, BP 352, Libreville; tel. 76-44-54; fax 74-67-50; e-mail actismedia; Friday; f. 1991; Dir-Gen. HANS RAYMOND KWAAITAAL; circ. 12,000–20,000.

NEWS AGENCIES

Agence Gabonaise de Presse (AGP): BP 168, Libreville.

Association Professionnelle de la Presse Ecrite Gabonaise (APPEG): BP 3849, Libreville; internet www.gabon-presse.org.

BERP International: BP 8483, Libreville; tel. 33-80-16; fax 77-58-81; e-mail berp8483@hotmail.com; f. 1995; Dir ANTOINE LAWSON.

Foreign Bureau

Agence France-Presse (AFP): ave du Colonel Parent, Immeuble Sogapal, Les Filaos, BP 788, Libreville; tel. 76-14-36; fax 72-45-31; e-mail afp-libreville@tiggabon.com; Dir JEAN-PIERRE REJETE.

Publishers

Gabonaise d'Imprimerie (GABIMP): BP 154, Libreville; tel. 70-22-55; fax 70-31-85; e-mail gabimp@inet.ga; f. 1973; Dir BÉATRICE CAILLOT.

Multipress Gabon: blvd Léon-M'Ba, BP 3875, Libreville; tel. 73-22-33; fax 73-63-72; e-mail mpg@inet.ga; monopoly distributors of magazines and newspapers; f. 1973; Chair. PAUL BORY.

Société Imprimerie de Gabon: BP 9626, Libreville; f. 1977; Man. Dir AKWANG REX.

Société Nationale de Presse et d'Edition (SONAPRESSE): BP 3849, Libreville; tel. 73-21-84; f. 1975; Pres. and Man. Dir JOSEPH RENDJAMBE.

Broadcasting and Communications

TELECOMMUNICATIONS

Gabon Télécom: Immeuble du Delta Postal, BP 20000, Libreville; tel. 78-76-05; fax 78-67-70; f. 2001; provider of telecommunications, including satellite, internet and cellular systems; partial privatization (51%) pending in 2005; Dir-Gen. HERVÉ FULGENCE OSSAMY.

Société des Télécommunications Internationales Gabonaises (TIG): BP 2261, Libreville; tel. 78-77-56; fax 74-19-09; f. 1971; cap. 3,000m. francs CFA; 61% state-owned; privatization pending; planning and devt of international telecommunications systems; Man. Dir A. N'GOUMA MWYUMALA.

Celtel Gabon, Libertis and Telecel Gabon operate mobile telecommunication services covering 85% of Gabon's territory.

BROADCASTING

Radio

The national network, 'La Voix de la Rénovation', and a provincial network broadcast for 24 hours each day in French and local languages.

Africa No. 1: BP 1, Libreville; tel. 76-00-01; fax 74-21-33; e-mail africa@africa1.com; internet www.africa1.com; f. 1980; 35% state-controlled; international commercial radio station; daily programmes in French and English; Pres. LOUIS BARTHÉLEMY MAPANGOU; Sec.-Gen. MICHEL KOUMBANGOYE.

Radiodiffusion-Télévision Gabonaise (RTG): BP 150, Libreville; tel. 73-20-25; f. 1959; state-controlled; Dir-Gen. JOHN JOSEPH MBOUROU; Dir of Radio GILLES TERENCE NZOGHE.

Radio Fréquence 3: f. 1996.

Radio Génération Nouvelle: f. 1996; Dir JEAN-BONIFACE ASSELE.

Radio Mandarine: f. 1995.

Radio Soleil: f. 1995; affiliated to Rassemblement pour le Gabon.

Radio Unité: f. 1996.

Television

Radiodiffusion-Télévision Gabonaise (RTG): BP 150, Libreville; tel. 73-21-52; fax 73-21-53; f. 1959; state-controlled; Dir-Gen. JOHN JOSEPH MBOUROU; Dir of Television JULES CÉSAR LEKOGHO.

Télé-Africa: Libreville; tel. 76-10-42; f. 1985; private channel; daily broadcasts in French.

Télédiffusion du Gabon: f. 1995.

TV Sat (Société de Télécommunications Audio-Visuelles): Immeuble TV SAT BP 184, Libreville; tel. 72-49-22; fax 76-16-83; f. 1994.

Finance

(cap. = capital; res = reserves; dep. = deposits; m. = million; brs = branches; amounts in francs CFA)

BANKING

Central Bank

Banque des Etats de l'Afrique Centrale (BEAC): BP 112, Libreville; tel. 76-13-52; fax 74-45-63; e-mail beaclbv@beac.int; HQ in Yaoundé, Cameroon; f. 1973; bank of issue for mem. states of the Communauté économique et monétaire de l'Afrique centrale (CEMAC, fmrly Union douanière et économique de l'Afrique centrale), comprising Cameroon, the Central African Repub., Chad, the Repub. of the Congo, Equatorial Guinea and Gabon; cap. 45,000m., res 176,661m., total assets 2,144,626m. (Nov. 2003); Gov. JEAN-FÉLIX MAMALEPOT; Dir in Gabon PHILIBERT ANDZEMBE; 4 brs in Gabon.

Commercial Banks

Banque Internationale pour le Commerce et l'Industrie du Gabon, SA (BICIG): ave du Colonel Parant, BP 2241, Libreville; tel. 77-76-80; fax 74-64-10; e-mail bicigdoi@inet.ga; internet www.bicig-gabon.com; f. 1973; 26.30% state-owned, 46.67% BNP Paribas SA; cap. 12,000.0m., res 18,134.0m., dep. 255,008.3m., total 311,379.0m. (Dec. 2002); Pres. ETIENNE GUY MOUVAGHA TCHIOBA; Dir-Gen. CLAUDE AYO-IGEDHA; 9 brs.

Banque Internationale pour le Gabon: Immeuble Concorde, blvd de l'Indépendance, BP 106, Libreville; tel. 76-26-26; fax 76-20-53.

BGFIBANK: blvd du Bord de Mer, BP 2253, Libreville; tel. 76-40-35; fax 74-08-94; e-mail bgfi@internetgabon.com; internet www.bgfi.com; f. 1972 as Banque Gabonaise et Française Internationale (BGFI); name changed as above in March 2000; 8% state-owned; cap. 25,065.4m., res 12,595.0m., total assets 341,296.0m. (Dec. 2002); Chair. PATRICE OTHA; Dir-Gen. HENRI-CLAUDE OYIMA; 3 brs.

Citibank: 810 blvd Quaben, rue Kringer, BP 3940, Libreville; tel. 73-19-16; fax 73-37-86; total assets 1,000m. (Dec. 2004); Dir-Gen. FUNMI ADE AJAYI; Dep. Dir-Gen. JULIETTE WEISFLOG.

Financial Bank Gabon: Immeuble des Frangipaniers, blvd de l'Indépendance, BP 20333, Libreville; tel. 77-50-78; fax 72-41-97; cap. and res 758.9m., total assets 1,863.7m. (Dec. 2001); 69,78% owned by Financial BC, SA (Togo), 9.52% state-owned; Pres. RENÉ-HILAIRE ADIAHENO; Dir-Gen. YANNICK CHAUVIN.

Union Gabonaise de Banque, SA (UGB): ave du Colonel Parant, BP 315, Libreville; tel. 77-70-00; fax 76-46-16; e-mail ugbdio@internetgabon.com; f. 1962; 25% state-owned, 56.25% owned by Crédit Lyonnais (France); cap. 5,000m., res 5,993.4m., dep.

98,668.5m. (Dec. 2001); Chair. MARCEL DOUPAMBY-MATOKA; Dir-Gen. CHRISTIAN LEVRARD; 6 brs.

Development Banks

Banque Gabonaise de Développement (BGD): rue Alfred Marche, BP 5, Libreville; tel. 76-24-29; fax 74-26-99; e-mail bdg@internetgabon.com; internet www.bgd-gabon.com; f. 1960; 69.01% state-owned; cap. 25,200.0m., res 8,524.2m., dep. 7,799.8m. (Dec. 2001); Pres. GASTON NOËL MBOUMBOU-NGOMA; Dir-Gen. CHRISTIAN BONGO.

Banque Gabonaise et Française Internationale Participations: blvd de l'Indépendance, BP 2253, Libreville; tel. 76-23-26; fax 76-08-94; e-mail bgfi@internetgabon.com; internet www.bgfi.com; f. 1997; cap. 294,119m., dep 193,096m. (Dec. 2003); Dir-Gen. HENRI-CLAUDE OYIMA; Chair. PATRICE OTHA.

Banque Nationale de Crédit Rural (BNCR): ave Bouet, BP 1120, Libreville; tel. 72-47-42; fax 74-05-07; f. 1986; 74% state-owned; under enforced administration since March 2002; total assets 5,601m. (Dec. 2000); Pres. GÉRARD MEYO M'EMANE; Man. JOSEPH KOYAGBELE.

Banque Populaire du Gabon: 413 blvd de l'Indépendance, BP 6663, Libreville; tel. 72-86-89; fax 72-86-91.

BICI-Bail Gabon: Immeuble BICIG, 5ème étage, ave du Colonel Parant, BP 2241, Libreville; tel. 77-75-52; fax 77-48-15; internet www.bicig.ga/bicibail.htm; BNP Paribas-owned.

Société Gabonaise de Crédit Bail (SOGABAIL): Imm. Sogaca, BP 63, Libreville; tel. 76-08-46; fax 74-56-83.

Société Nationale d'Investissement du Gabon (SONADIG): BP 479, Libreville; tel. 72-09-22; fax 74-81-70; f. 1968; state-owned; cap. 500m.; Pres. ANTOINE OYIEYE; Dir-Gen. NARCISSE MASSALA TSAMBA.

Financial Institution

Caisse Autonome d'Amortissement du Gabon: BP 912, Libreville; tel. 74-41-43; management of state funds; Dir-Gen. MAURICE EYAMBA TSIMAT.

INSURANCE

Agence Gabonaise d'Assurance et de Réassurance (AGAR): BP 1699, Libreville; tel. 74-02-22; fax 76-59-25; f. 1987; Dir-Gen. ANGE GOULOUMES.

Assurances Générales Gabonaises (AGG): ave du Colonel Parant, BP 2148, Libreville; tel. 76-09-73; fax 76-57-41; f. 1974; Dir-Gen. ALAIN WELLER.

Assurances Nouvelles du Gabon: ave du Colonel Parant, BP 2225, Libreville; tel. 72-13-90; fax 74-17-02; fmrly Mutuelle Gabonaise d'Assurances; Dir-Gen. EKOMIE CÉSARE AFENE.

Assureurs Conseils Franco-Africains du Gabon (ACFRA-GABON): BP 1116, Libreville; tel. 72-32-83; Chair. FRÉDÉRIC MARRON; Dir M. GARNIER.

Assureurs Conseils Gabonais-Faugère et Jutheau & Cie (ACG): Immeuble Shell-Gabon, rue de la Mairie, BP 2138, Libreville; tel. 74-32-90; fax 76-04-39; e-mail acgberson@inet.ga; represents foreign insurance cos; Dir GÉRARD MILAN.

Fédération gabonaise des assureurs (FEGASA): BP 4005, Libreville; tel. 74-45-29; fax 77-58-23; Pres. JACQUES AMVAMÉ.

Gras Savoye Gabon: Avenue Colonel Parant, BP 2148, Libreville; tel. 76-09-73; fax 76-57-41; e-mail gsgabon@internetgabon.com; internet www.grassavoye.com/fr/index.html.

Groupement Gabonais d'Assurances et de Réassurances (GGAR): Libreville; tel. 74-28-72; f. 1985; Chair. RASSAGUIZA AKEREY; Dir-Gen. DENISE OMBAGHO.

Omnium Gabonais d'Assurances et de Réassurances (OGAR): 546 blvd Triomphal Omar Bongo, BP 201, Libreville; tel. 76-15-96; fax 76-58-16; e-mail ogan@inet.ga; f. 1976; owned by Assurances Générales de France; general; Pres. MARCEL DOUPAMBY-MATOKA; Man. Dir EDOUARD VALENTIN.

Société Nationale Gabonaise d'Assurances et de Réassurances (SONAGAR): ave du Colonel Parant, BP 3082, Libreville; tel. 76-28-97; f. 1974; owned by l'Union des Assurances de Paris (France); Dir-Gen. JEAN-LOUIS MESSAN.

SOGERCO-Gabon: BP 2102, Libreville; tel. 76-09-34; f. 1975; general; Dir M. RABEAU.

L'Union des Assurances du Gabon (UAG): ave du Colonel Parant, BP 2141, Libreville; tel. 74-34-34; fax 74-14-53; f. 1976; Chair. ALBERT ALEWINA CHAVIOT; Dir EKOMIE AFENE.

Trade and Industry

GOVERNMENT AGENCY

Conseil Economique et Social de la République Gabonaise: BP 1075, Libreville; tel. 73-19-46; fax 73-19-44; comprises representatives from salaried workers, employers and Govt; commissions on economic, financial and social affairs and forestry and agriculture; Pres. LOUIS GASTON MAYILA.

DEVELOPMENT ORGANIZATIONS

Agence Française de Développement (AFD): BP 64, Libreville; tel. 74-33-74; fax 74-51-25; e-mail afdlbv@inet.ga; internet www.afd.fr/; fmrly Caisse Française de Développement; Dir YVES BOUDOT.

Agence Nationale de Promotion de la Petite et Moyenne Entreprise (PROMOGABON): BP 2111, Libreville; tel. 26-79-19; fax 74-89-59; e-mail promogabon@inet.ga; f. 1964; state-controlled; promotes and assists small- and medium-sized industries; Pres. SIMON BOULAMATARI; Man. Dir JEAN-FIDÈLE OTANDO.

Centre Gabonais de Commerce Extérieur (CGCE): Imm. Rénovation, 3ème étage, BP 3906, Libreville; tel. 72-11-67; fax 74-71-53; promotes foreign trade and investment in Gabon; Gen. Dir PIERRE SOCKAT.

Commerce et Développement (CODEV): BP 2142, Libreville; tel. 76-06-73; f. 1976; 95% state-owned; proposed transfer to private ownership announced 1986; import and distribution of capital goods and food products; Chair. and Man. Dir JÉRÔME NGOUA-BEKALE.

Conservation et Utilisation Rationelle des Ecosystèmes Forestiers en Afrique Centrale (ECOFAC): BP 15115, Libreville; tel. 73-23-43; fax 73-23-45; e-mail coordination@ecofac.org; internet www.ecofac.org/.

Groupes d'Etudes et de Recherches sur la Démocratie et le Développement Economique et Social (GERDDES): BP 13114, Libreville; tel. 76-56-65; Pres. MARYVONNE NTSAME.

Mission Française de Coopération: BP 2105, Libreville; tel. 76-10-56; fax 74-55-33; administers bilateral aid from France; Dir JEAN-CLAUDE QUIRIN.

Office Gabonais d'Amélioration et de Production de Viande (OGAPROV): BP 245, Moanda; tel. 66-12-67; f. 1971; development of private cattle farming; manages ranch at Lekedi-Sud; Pres. PAUL KOUNDA KIKI; Dir-Gen. VINCENT EYI-NGUI.

Palmiers et Hévéas du Gabon (PALMEVEAS): BP 75, Libreville; f. 1956; state-owned; palm-oil development.

Programme des Nations Unies pour le Développement (PNUD): BP 2183, Libreville; tel. 74-34-37; fax 74-34-99; e-mail fo.gab@undp.org; internet www.primature.gouv.ga/ORGINTER/cyberpole/agonu/pnud/pnudindex.htm.

Programme Régionale de Gestion de l'Information Environnementale en Afrique Centrale (PRGIE): BP 4080, Libreville; tel. 76-30-19; fax 77-42-61; e-mail urge@adie-prgie.org; internet www.adie-prgie.org.

Société de Développement de l'Agriculture au Gabon (AGRO-GABON): BP 2248, Libreville; tel. 76-40-82; fax 76-44-72; f. 1976; 93% state-owned; acquired by the Société Industrielle Agricole du Tabac Tropical in April 2004; Man. Dir ANDRÉ PAUL-APANDINA.

Société de Développement de l'Hévéaculture (HEVEGAB): BP 316, Libreville; tel. 72-08-29; fax 72-08-30; f. 1981; acquired by the Société Industrielle Agricole du Tabac Tropical in April 2004; development of rubber plantations in the Mitzic, Bitam and Kango regions; Chair. FRANÇOIS OWONO-NGUEMA; Man. Dir JANVIER ESSONO-ASSOUMOU.

Société Gabonaise de Recherches et d'Exploitations Minières (SOGAREM): Libreville; state-owned; research and development of gold mining; Chair. ARSÈNE BOUNGUENZA; Man. Dir SERGE GASSITA.

Société Gabonaise de Recherches Pétrolières (GABOREP): BP 564, Libreville; tel. 75-06-40; fax 75-06-47; exploration and exploitation of hydrocarbons; Chair. HUBERT PERRODO; Man. Dir P. F. LECA.

Société Nationale de Développement des Cultures Industrielles (SONADECI): Libreville; tel. 76-33-97; f. 1978; state-owned; agricultural development; Chair. PAUL KOUNDA KIKI; Man. Dir GEORGES BEKALÉ.

CHAMBER OF COMMERCE

Chambre de Commerce, d'Agriculture, d'Industrie et des Mines du Gabon: BP 2234, Libreville; tel. 72-20-64; fax 74-64-77; f. 1935; regional offices at Port-Gentil and Franceville; Pres. JOACHIM BOUSSAMBA-MAPAGA; Sec.-Gen. DOMINIQUE MANDZA.

EMPLOYERS' ORGANIZATIONS

Confédération Patronale Gabonaise: BP 410, Libreville; tel. 76-02-43; fax 74-86-52; e-mail patronat.gabon@assala.net; internet www.africannuaire.com/htm/fr/partners/cpg/; f. 1959; represents industrial, mining, petroleum, public works, forestry, banking, insurance, commercial and shipping interests; Pres. J. C. BALOCHE; Sec.-Gen. ERIC MESSERSCHMITT.

Conseil National du Patronat Gabonais (CNPG): Libreville; Pres. RAHANDI CHAMBRIER; Sec.-Gen. THOMAS FRANCK EYA'A.

Syndicat des Entreprises Minières du Gabon (SYNDI-MINES): BP 260, Libreville; Pres. ANDRÉ BERRE; Sec.-Gen. SERGE GREGOIRE.

Syndicat des Importateurs Exportateurs du Gabon (SIMPEX): Libreville; Pres. ALBERT JEAN; Sec.-Gen. R. TYBERGHEIN.

Syndicat des Producteurs et Industriels du Bois du Gabon: BP 84, Libreville; tel. 72-26-11; fax 77-44-43; e-mail synfoga@inet.ga.

Syndicat Professionnel des Usines de Sciages et Placages du Gabon: Port-Gentil; f. 1956; Pres. PIERRE BERRY.

Union des Représentations Automobiles et Industrielles (URAI): BP 1743, Libreville; Pres. M. MARTINENT; Sec. R. TYBERGHEIN.

Union Nationale du Patronat Syndical des Transports Urbains, Routiers et Fluviaux du Gabon (UNAPASY-TRUFGA): BP 1025, Libreville; f. 1977; represents manufacturers of vehicle and construction parts; Pres. LAURENT BELLAL BIBANG-BI-EDZO; Sec.-Gen. AUGUSTIN KASSA-NZIGOU.

UTILITIES

Société d'Energie et d'Eau du Gabon (SEEG): BP 2187, Libreville; tel. 76-78-07; fax 76-11-34; e-mail laroche.lbv@inet.ga; internet www.seeg-gabon.com; f. 1950; 51% owned by Vivendi (France); controls 35 electricity generation and distribution centres and 32 water production and distribution centres; Pres. FRANÇOIS LAROCHE.

TRADE UNIONS

Confédération Gabonaise des Syndicats Libres (CGSL): BP 8067, Libreville; tel. 77-37-82; fax 74-45-25; f. 1991; Sec.-Gen. FRANCIS MAYOMBO; 16,000 mems.

Confédération Syndicale Gabonaise (COSYGA): BP 14017, Libreville; f. 1969 by the Govt, as a specialized organ of the PDG, to organize and educate workers, to contribute to social peace and economic development, and to protect the rights of trade unions; Gen. Sec. MARTIN ALLINI.

Transport

RAILWAYS

The construction of the Transgabonais railway, which comprises a section running from Owendo (the port of Libreville) to Booué (340 km) and a second section from Booué to Franceville (357 km), was completed in 1986. By 1989 regular services were operating between Libreville and Franceville. Some 2.9m. metric tons of freight and 215,000 passengers were carried on the network in 1999. In 1998 the railways were transferred to private management.

Office du Chemin de Fer Transgabonais (OCTRA): BP 2198, Libreville; tel. 70-24-78; fax 70-20-38; operates Transgabonais railway; 51% owned by SNBG; Chair. CHRISTIAN BONGO.

ROADS

In 2000 there were an estimated 8,464 km of roads, including 2,093 km of main roads and 6,371 km of secondary roads; about 9.9% of the road network was paved.

A.R.T.: BP 9391, Libreville; tel. 70-57-26; fax 70-57-28; e-mail bergon@inet.ga; freight; Dir-Gen. PHILIPPE BERGON.

Transitex: BP 20323, Libreville; tel. 77-84-26; fax 77-84-35; e-mail helenepedemonte@transitex.ga; freight; Man. FRÉDÉRIC GONZALEZ.

INLAND WATERWAYS

The principal river is the Ogooué, navigable from Port-Gentil to Ndjolé (310 km) and serving the towns of Lambaréné, Ndjolé and Sindara.

Compagnie de Navigation Intérieure (CNI): BP 3982, Libreville; tel. 72-39-28; fax 74-04-11; f. 1978; scheduled to be privatized; responsible for inland waterway transport; agencies at Port-Gentil, Mayumba and Lambaréné; Chair. JEAN-PIERRE MENGWANG ME NGYEMA; Dir-Gen. JEAN LOUIS POUNAH-NDJIMBI.

SHIPPING

The principal deep-water ports are Port-Gentil, which handles mainly petroleum exports, and Owendo, 15 km from Libreville, which services mainly barge traffic. The main ports for timber are at Owendo, Mayumba and Nyanga, and there is a fishing port at Libreville. The construction of a deep-water port at Mayumba is planned. A new terminal for the export of minerals, at Owendo, was opened in 1988. In 2003 the merchant shipping fleet numbered 45 and had a total displacement of 12,697 grt. In 1997 the Islamic Development Bank granted a loan of 11,000m. francs CFA for the rehabilitation of Gabon's ports.

Compagnie de Manutention et de Chalandage d'Owendo (COMACO): BP 2131, Libreville; tel. 70-26-35; f. 1974; Pres. GEORGES RAWIRI; Dir in Libreville M. RAYMOND.

Office des Ports et Rades du Gabon (OPRAG): BP 1051, Libreville; tel. 70-00-48; fax 70-37-37; f. 1974; 25-year management concession acquired in April 2004 by the Spanish PIP group; national port authority; Pres. ALI BONGO; Dir-Gen. JEAN PIERRE OYIBA.

SAGA Gabon: BP 518, Port-Gentil; tel. 55-54-00; fax 55-21-71; e-mail sagalbv@internetgabon.com; Chair. G. COGNON; Man. Dir DANIEL FERNÁNDEZ.

SDV Gabon: Zone Portuaire d'Owendo, BP 77, Libreville; tel. 70-26-36; fax 70-23-34; e-mail sdvg10@calva.com; internet www.sdv.com; freight by land, sea and air.

Société Nationale d'Acconage et de Transit (SNAT): BP 3897, Libreville; tel. 70-04-04; fax 70-13-11; e-mail jean-claude.simon@smtp.saga.fr; internet www.saga.fr/fiche_agence.asp?strPays=GABON; f. 1976; 51% state-owned; scheduled to be privatized; freight transport; Dir-Gen. GUSTAVE BONGO.

Société Nationale de Transports Maritimes (SONATRAM): BP 3841, Libreville; tel. 74-44-04; fax 74-59-87; f. 1976; relaunched 1995; 51% state-owned; river and ocean cargo transport; Man. Dir RAPHAEL MOARA WALLA.

Société du Port Minéralier d'Owendo: f. 1987; majority holding by Cie Minière de l'Ogooué; management of a terminal for minerals at Owendo.

SOCOPAO–Gabon: Imm. Socapao, Zone Portuaire d'Owendo, BP 4, Libreville; tel. 56-09-13; fax 55-45-43; e-mail socopaolibreville@vpila.fr; f. 1983; freight transport and storage; Dir DANIEL BECQUERELLE.

CIVIL AVIATION

There are international airports at Libreville, Port-Gentil and Franceville, 65 other public and 50 private airfields linked mostly with the forestry and petroleum industries.

Air Affaires Gabon: BP 3962, Libreville; tel. 73-25-13; fax 73-49-98; f. 1975; domestic passenger chartered and scheduled flights; Chair. RAYMOND BELLANGER.

Air Service Gabon (ASG): BP 2232, Libreville; tel. 73-24-08; fax 73-60-69; f. 1965; charter flights; Chair. JEAN-LUC CHEVRIER; Gen. Man. FRANÇOIS LASCOMBES.

Compagnie Nationale Air Gabon: BP 2206, Libreville; tel. 77-90-51; fax 72-61-95; f. 1951 as Cie Aérienne Gabonaise; began operating international services in 1977, following Gabon's withdrawal from Air Afrique (see under Côte d'Ivoire); 80% state-owned; scheduled to be privatized; internal and international cargo and passenger services; Chair. MARTIN BONGO; Man. Dir RENÉ MORVAN.

Société de Gestion de l'Aéroport de Libreville (ADL): BP 363, Libreville; tel. 73-62-44; fax 73-61-28; e-mail adl@inet.ga; f. 1988; 26.5% state-owned; management of airport at Libreville; Pres. CHANTAL LIDJI BADINGA; Dir-Gen. PIERRE ANDRÉ COLLET.

Tourism

Tourist arrivals were estimated at 208,348 in 2002, and receipts from tourism totalled US $7m. in 2001. The tourism sector is being extensively developed, with new hotels and associated projects and the promotion of national parks. In 1996 there were 74 hotels, with a total of 4,000 rooms.

Centre Gabonais de Promotion Touristique (GABONTOUR): ave du Colonel Parant, BP 2085, Libreville; tel. 72-85-04; fax 72-85-03; e-mail gabontour@internetgabon.com; internet www.internetgabon.com/tourisme; f. 1988; Dir-Gen. JOSEPH ADJEMBI-MANDE.

Office National Gabonais du Tourisme: BP 161, Libreville; tel. 72-21-82.

THE GAMBIA

Introductory Survey

Location, Climate, Language, Religion, Flag, Capital

The Republic of The Gambia is a narrow territory around the River Gambia on the west coast of Africa. Apart from a short coastline on the Atlantic Ocean, the country is a semi-enclave in Senegal. The climate is tropical, with a rainy season from July to September. Away from the river swamps most of the terrain is covered by savannah bush. Average temperatures in Banjul range from 23°C (73°F) in January to 27°C (81°F) in July, while temperatures inland can exceed 40°C (104°F). English is the official language, while the principal vernacular languages are Mandinka, Fula and Wolof. About 85% of the inhabitants are Muslims; most of the remainder are Christians, and there are a small number of animists. The national flag (proportions 2 by 3) has red, blue and green horizontal stripes, with two narrow white stripes bordering the central blue band. The capital is Banjul.

Recent History

Formerly administered with Sierra Leone, The Gambia became a separate British colony in 1888. Party politics rapidly gained momentum following the establishment of a universal adult franchise in 1960. Following legislative elections in May 1962, the leader of the People's Progressive Party (PPP), Dr (later Sir) Dawda Kairaba Jawara, became Premier. Full internal self-government followed in October 1963. On 18 February 1965 The Gambia became an independent country within the Commonwealth, with Jawara as Prime Minister. The country became a republic on 24 April 1970, whereupon Jawara took office as President. He was re-elected in 1972 and again in 1977, as a result of overwhelming PPP victories in legislative elections.

In July 1981 a coup was attempted while Jawara was visiting the United Kingdom. Left-wing rebels formed a National Revolutionary Council and proclaimed their civilian leader, Kukoi Samba Sanyang, as Head of State. Under the terms of a mutual defence pact, Senegalese troops assisted in suppressing the rebellion although a state of emergency remained in force until February 1985. All those convicted of involvement in the insurrection were released by early 1991.

The first presidential election by direct popular vote was held in May 1982. Jawara was re-elected, with 72% of the votes cast; he was opposed by the leader of the National Convention Party (NCP), Sheriff Mustapha Dibba (who remained in detention until June for his alleged involvement in the abortive coup). In the concurrent legislative elections the PPP won 27 of the 35 elective seats in the House of Representatives. At legislative elections in March 1987 the PPP took 31 of the 36 directly elected seats in the House of Representatives. In the presidential election Jawara was re-elected with 59% of the votes cast; Dibba received 27% of the votes, and Assan Musa Camara, a former Vice-President who had recently formed the Gambian People's Party (GPP), won 14%. Rumours of financial impropriety, corruption and the abuse of power at ministerial level persisted throughout the decade, with at least four government members dismissed between 1984 and 1990.

Plans were announced in August 1981 for a confederation of The Gambia and Senegal, to be called Senegambia. The confederal agreement came into effect in February 1982; a Confederal Council of Ministers, headed by President Abdou Diouf of Senegal (with President Jawara as his deputy), held its inaugural meeting in January 1983, as did a 60-member Confederal Assembly. Agreements followed on co-ordination of foreign policy, communications, defence and security, but Jawara was reluctant to proceed towards full economic and political integration. In August 1989 Diouf announced that Senegalese troops were to leave The Gambia, apparently in protest at a request by Jawara that The Gambia be accorded more power within the confederal structures. The confederation was dissolved in September, and a period of tension between the two countries followed: The Gambia alleged that the Senegalese authorities had introduced trade and travel restrictions, while Senegal accused The Gambia of harbouring rebels of the Mouvement des forces démocratiques de la Casamance (MFDC), an organization seeking independence for the Casamance region—

which is virtually separated from the northern segment of Senegal by the enclave of The Gambia. In January 1991 the two countries signed an agreement of friendship and co-operation.

Jawara was elected for a sixth time in April 1992, receiving 58% of the votes cast, while Dibba took 22%. In elections to the House of Representatives the PPP retained a clear majority, with 25 elected members. The NCP secured six seats, the GPP two and independent candidates the remaining three.

On 22 July 1994 Jawara was deposed by a self-styled Armed Forces Provisional Ruling Council (AFPRC), a group of five young army officers led by Lt (later Col) Yahya Jammeh, in a bloodless coup. Jawara left The Gambia aboard a US navy vessel and later took up residence in the United Kingdom. The AFPRC suspended the Constitution and banned all political activity. The new regime undertook to eliminate corruption, pledging a return to civilian rule once this had been accomplished. Jammeh pronounced himself Head of State and appointed a mixed civilian and military Government. Purges of the armed forces and public institutions were implemented, and in November it was announced that 10 of Jawara's former ministers would be tried on charges of corruption.

The AFPRC's timetable for a transition to civilian rule, published in October 1994, envisaged a programme of reform culminating in the inauguration of new elected institutions in December 1998. The length of the transition period prompted criticism both internationally and domestically. In November 1994 the AFPRC announced that a coup attempt, involving military officers who reputedly wished to install an entirely military regime, had been foiled. Some 50 soldiers were reported to have been killed during the attempt and its suppression, and several arrests were made.

In November 1994 Jammeh commissioned a National Consultative Committee (NCC) to make recommendations regarding a possible shortening of the period of transition to civilian rule. In January 1995 two members of the AFPRC (the Vice-President, Sana Sabally, and Sadibou Hydara, the Minister of the Interior), both of whom were said to be opposed to a curtailment of the transition period (the NCC proposed a return to civilian government in July 1996), were arrested, following an alleged attempt to seize power. In December Sabally was sentenced to nine years' imprisonment for plotting to overthrow Jammeh; Hydara was reported to have died of natural causes while in detention.

The death penalty, which had been abolished in April 1993, was restored by governmental decree in August 1995, reportedly in response to a recent increase in the murder rate. In November 1995 a government decree conferring wide powers of arrest and detention on the Minister of the Interior was issued. In January 1996 Jawara was charged *in absentia* with embezzlement, following investigations into the alleged diversion of proceeds from the sale of petroleum donated by Nigeria. In subsequent months the confiscation was ordered of the assets in The Gambia of Jawara and 11 former government members.

Although the AFPRC stated its commitment to freedom of expression, a ban on the publication of journals by political organizations was introduced shortly after the July 1994 coup. Subsequent periodic incidents of the arrest of, or fines against, journalists provoked considerable international concern, while several non-Gambian journalists were deported.

The draft of a report by a Constitutional Review Commission (established in April 1995) was published in March 1996. Despite demands by the European Union (EU) and the Commonwealth, as well as by individual countries that had previously been major donors to The Gambia, for an expedited return to civilian rule, the AFPRC continued to assert that it would adhere to its revised timetable. In April, however, it was announced that it would be impossible to complete the return to elected civilian government by July, and in May new dates were set for the constitutional referendum, and for presidential and legislative elections, which would now take place in August, September and December, respectively. Opponents of the AFPRC criticized provisions of the Constitution that, they alleged, had been formulated with the specific intention of facilitating Jammeh's election to the presidency (although the Head of State had frequently asserted that he would not seek election).

The constitutional referendum took place on 8 August 1996. The rate of participation was high (85.9%), and 70.4% of voters endorsed the new document. A presidential decree was issued in the following week reauthorizing party political activity. Shortly afterwards, however, a further decree (Decree 89) was promulgated, according to which all holders of executive office in the 30 years prior to July 1994 were to be prohibited from seeking public office, with the PPP, the NCP and the GPP barred from contesting the forthcoming presidential and parliamentary elections. Thus, the only parties from the Jawara era authorized to contest the elections were the People's Democratic Organization for Independence and Socialism (PDOIS) and the People's Democratic Party. The effective ban on the participation of all those associated with political life prior to the military take-over in the restoration of elected institutions was strongly criticized by the Commonwealth Ministerial Action Group on the Harare Declaration (CMAG, see p. 182), which had hitherto made a significant contribution to the transition process. At the same time the AFPRC announced that the presidential poll was to be postponed until 26 September 1996.

Jammeh formally announced his intention to contest the presidency in mid-August 1996. At the end of the month the establishment of a political party supporting Jammeh, the Alliance for Patriotic Reorientation and Construction (APRC), was reported. In early September Jammeh resigned from the army, in order to contest the presidency as a civilian, as required by the Constitution. The presidential election proceeded on 26 September. According to official results, Jammeh secured the presidency with 55.77% of the votes cast, ahead of Ousainou Darboe, the leader of the United Democratic Party (UDP), who received 35.84%. The rate of participation by voters was again high, especially in rural areas, although observers, including CMAG, expressed doubts as to the credibility of the election results. The dissolution of the AFPRC was announced the same day. Jammeh was inaugurated as President on 18 October. In November an unconditional amnesty was extended to more than 40 political detainees.

Legislative elections took place on 2 January 1997, after a postponement of three weeks. All the registered parties presented candidates for the 45 elective seats in the new National Assembly. The Gambian authorities, opposition groups and most international observers expressed broad satisfaction at the conduct of the poll. (The Commonwealth did not send observers, owing to the continued ban on former members of Jawara's administration from seeking public office.) As expected, the APRC won an overwhelming majority of seats, securing 33 elective seats (including five in which the party was unopposed). The UDP obtained seven elective seats, the National Reconciliation Party (NRP) two, the PDOIS one and independent candidates two. The overall rate of participation by voters was 73.2%. As Head of State, Jammeh was empowered by the Constitution to nominate four additional members of parliament, from whom the Speaker and Deputy Speaker would be chosen. The opening session of the National Assembly, on 16 January, accordingly elected Mustapha Wadda, previously Secretary-General of the APRC and Secretary at the Presidency, as Speaker. This session denoted the full entry into force of the Constitution and thus the inauguration of the Second Republic.

Under the new Constitution, ministers of cabinet rank were designated Secretaries of State, and the Government was reorganized to this effect in March 1997. Isatou Njie-Saidy, Secretary of State for Health, Social Welfare and Women's Affairs, was appointed Vice-President. However, most of the responsibilities hitherto associated with this post were transferred to the Secretary of State for the Office of the President, a position now held by Edward Singhateh: although Singhateh had succeeded Sabally as AFPRC Vice-President in early 1995, he was, under the terms of the new Constitution, too young (at 27 years of age) to assume the office of Vice-President. In April 1997 civilian appointees, including Jawara's former head of police, replaced the remaining four military regional governors.

Supporters of the new regime attributed the electoral success of Jammeh and the APRC to the popularity within The Gambia of the ambitious infrastructure projects undertaken since July 1994, citing in particular the construction of more new schools and hospitals than had been built in 30 years by the Jawara administration, as well as a new airport terminal and modernized port facilities, a television station, and plans for a national

university. However, Jammeh's critics condemned what they regarded as excessive expenditure on 'prestige' projects.

In April 1997 the trial began (in camera) of five alleged mercenaries suspected of involvement in an attack on the Farafenni barracks, which took place in November 1996 and resulted in the deaths of six people. The accused apparently confirmed reports that they had formed part of a 40-strong commando group, trained in Libya and led by Kukoi Samba Sanyang, which had fought for Charles Taylor's National Patriotic Front of Liberia during the early 1990s. Four of the accused were subsequently sentenced to death on charges of treason; the fifth defendant died in detention in May 1997. In October the Supreme Court ruled that the convictions were unsustainable and ordered that the four be retried on conspiracy charges, however they remained in prison, serving life sentences.

Concern arose in the late 1990s over press freedom, following the closure in February 1998 of a private radio station, *Citizen FM* (and an associated newspaper), and the detention of two of its staff. (In July 2000 the Supreme Court finally upheld the appeal by the director, Baboucar Gaye, against the closure of the station and ordered that Gaye's confiscated broadcasting equipment be returned to him; *Citizen FM* was reopened later in the year.) In May 1999 the *Daily Observer*, the only remaining newspaper that openly criticized the Government, was purchased by a businessman closely associated with Jammeh. Despite assurances of non-interference in editorial matters, staff who had criticized the Government were subsequently removed from their posts. In July *The Independent*, a recently launched newspaper, was ordered to suspend publication because of alleged irregularities in its registration. It was, however, claimed that the Government had ordered the suspension following the publication of an article that repeated accusations, made by the UDP, of widespread corruption in the Jammeh regime. Meanwhile, opposition activists continued to allege harassment by the Government. In May 1998 nine people, including Lamine Wa Juwara of the UDP, were arrested. Juwara was involved in a lawsuit seeking compensation for alleged wrongful imprisonment for 20 months without charge following the 1994 coup. Darboe was also briefly imprisoned. In July Juwara's claim for damages was rejected by the Supreme Court.

In January 1999 four cabinet members were dismissed, as was the Managing Director of the National Water and Electricity Company, amid allegations that financial mismanagement had occurred in certain government departments. In January 2000 further allegations of government corruption emerged after the disclosure in legal proceedings in the United Kingdom that significant sums of money generated by the sale of crude petroleum had been paid into an anonymous Swiss bank account. The crude petroleum had been granted to The Gambia for trading purposes by the Nigerian Government between August 1996 and June 1998, reportedly in recognition of Jammeh's opposition in 1995 to the imposition of sanctions by the Commonwealth against Nigeria. Jammeh vigorously denied any involvement in the matter.

In January 2000 the security forces announced that they had forestalled an attempted military coup. It was reported that during efforts to arrest the conspirators a lieutenant in the State Guard had been killed and the Commander of the State Guard, Lt Landing Sanneh, the officer in charge of security at the presidential palace, had been wounded. Another member of the State Guard was killed on the following day, while attempting to evade arrest. In February 2001 Sanneh was acquitted of charges of treason, but was immediately rearrested; in September he was convicted by court martial of plotting to overthrow the Government and sentenced to 16 years' imprisonment with hard labour.

Meanwhile, in April 2000 the death of a student in firemen's barracks, reputedly following torture, and the alleged rape of a schoolgirl by a member of the security forces precipitated serious student unrest in Banjul, Brikama and Serrekunda. Some 14 people were killed and 30 injured during the disturbances and despite initial official denials, it became apparent that the security forces had used live ammunition to quell the protests. In May Jammeh assured the UN Secretary-General that those responsible for the deaths would be brought to justice and announced that a commission of inquiry had been established. In May 2000 five men were detained by the National Intelligence Agency in connection with an alleged plot to assassinate Jammeh and overthrow the APRC Government. After their arrest without trial was declared unconstitutional by the High

Court, a total of seven men were subsequently charged with treason. The trial, which opened in December 2000, was adjourned several times, recommencing in February 2003. By October four of the seven men had been acquitted. In July 2004 the remaining three were acquitted, although two were immediately rearrested on charges which appeared to be unconnected. Lawyers for the Government subsequently appealed against the ruling.

In August 2000 the APRC suggested that it would not be possible to hold local government elections in November, as scheduled, as the National Assembly had yet to approve the local government act. A major cabinet reshuffle took place that month. In December Jammeh dismissed Anglican Bishop Solomon Tilewa Johnson from his position as Chairman of the Independent Electoral Commission (IEC). Johnson's predecessor, Gabriel Roberts, was reappointed, despite allegations that he had been involved in fraudulent behaviour to benefit the APRC at the elections of 1996 and 1997. The dismissal of Johnson, which the opposition described as unconstitutional, followed his instigation of a court case in response to the Government's failure to enact the local government act.

In January 2001 the commission of inquiry into the student unrest of April 2000 published its report. The Government rejected the commission's recommendation that the Secretary of State for the Interior, Ousman Badjie, and senior police officials should accept responsibility for the disturbances. Shortly afterwards Pap Cheyassin Secka was dismissed as Secretary of State for Justice and Attorney-General and replaced by Joseph Henry Joof. Secka's dismissal was widely welcomed by opposition members, who claimed that he had increased political interference in the judiciary.

In May 2001 the National Assembly and the President approved a number of constitutional amendments, which were to be submitted to a referendum. The opposition protested that the proposed changes, including the extension of the presidential term from five to seven years, the introduction of a presidential prerogative to appoint local chiefs, and the replacement of the permanent IEC with an *ad hoc* body, would further increase the powers of the President and precipitate acts of electoral fraud at the forthcoming parliamentary and presidential elections.

In July 2001 Jammeh announced the abrogation of Decree 89, although several prominent individuals who had participated in pre-1994 administrations, including Jawara and Sabally, remained prohibited from seeking public office. None the less, the PPP, the NCP and the GPP were subsequently re-established. In August the UDP, the PPP and the GPP formed a coalition and announced that Darboe would be its presidential candidate in the forthcoming election. Opposition supporters and other observers claimed that the compilation of voters' lists had been accompanied by widespread fraud. In particular, concern was expressed that foreign citizens (notably Senegalese nationals of the Diola ethnic group) resident in The Gambia had been registered as eligible to vote. In the same month the Secretary of State for Foreign Affairs, Sedate Jobe, resigned, reportedly in connection with the recent expulsion from The Gambia of a British diplomat (see below). Blaise Baboucar Jagne, Secretary of State for Foreign Affairs in 1995–96, was reappointed to the post.

By September 2001 five candidates had announced their intention to contest the presidential election, which was to be held in October. In addition to Darboe, the candidate of the opposition UDP-PPP-GPP coalition, Jammeh would be challenged by Dibba for the NCP, Hamat Bah for the NRP and Sidia Jatta for the PDOIS. A number of violent incidents were reported during the week before the presidential election. In Serrekunda, a suburb of Banjul, members of the security forces fired shots in order to disperse a rally by supporters of Darboe, and one person was killed during clashes between opposition supporters and soldiers. The dead man was reportedly an unarmed opposition activist who had been shot by a police-officer, and an inquiry into the incident was launched by the Department of State for the Interior.

The presidential election was held, as scheduled, on 18 October 2001. Controversy was provoked by a reported relaxation in identification requirements for voters, and a turn-out of some 90% was recorded. Jammeh was re-elected to the presidency, with 52.84% of the votes cast, according to official results, ahead of Darboe, who won 32.59% of the votes. Bah secured 7.78%, followed by Dibba and Jatta, with 3.77% and 3.02% respectively. Although Darboe conceded defeat, members of the

opposition subsequently disputed the legitimacy of the results, reiterating claims of incorrect practice in the distribution of voting credentials and in the counting of ballots. None the less, international observers described the poll as being largely free and fair.

Following the election, a number of eminent opposition figures were arrested. In October 2001 a leading Gambian human rights activist, Lamin Sillah, was detained after he alleged that members of the opposition had been subject to harassment and sustained detention. Subsequent reports suggested that up to 60 opposition supporters had been arrested in the week after the election, and that the homes of prominent members of the UDP had been attacked, allegedly by members of the youth wing of the APRC. Following pressure from international human rights campaigners, Sillah was released. Baboucar Gaye was also arrested, and *Citizen FM* again closed. In early November Darboe announced his party's intention to take legal action to secure the release of UDP activists who remained in prison. Additionally, it was reported that several senior civil servants who were believed to be sympathetic to opposition parties, including the director of the national radio and television stations and a number of military officers, had been dismissed after the election. Meanwhile, the IEC announced the postponement of the referendum on proposed constitutional changes. In late December, at his inauguration, President Jammeh granted an unconditional amnesty to Jawara, guaranteeing the former President's security should he decide to return to The Gambia.

In December 2001 the UDP-PPP-GPP coalition announced that it would boycott legislative elections scheduled for January 2002, as a result of the alleged addition of some 50,000 foreign citizens to electoral lists and the reputed transfer of voters between the electoral lists of different constituencies. Having denied these accusations, the IEC announced that the APRC had secured 33 of the 48 elective seats in the enlarged National Assembly, in constituencies where the party was unopposed owing to the boycott. At the elections, which took place on 17 January, the APRC won 12 of the 15 contested seats, giving the party an overall total of 45 elective seats; the PDOIS obtained two seats, and the NRP one. Electoral turn-out was reportedly low. An additional five members of parliament were appointed by President Jammeh, in accordance with the Constitution. Dibba, whose NCP had formed an alliance with the APRC prior to the elections, was appointed Speaker of the new National Assembly.

The long-delayed municipal elections, which were finally held in April 2002, were boycotted by the UDP and the PDOIS; consequently, the APRC was unopposed in some 85 of the 113 local seats, and won a total of 99 seats, securing control of all seven regional authorities. The NRP was the only other political organization to gain representation in local government in the elections, winning five seats; the remaining nine seats were secured by independent candidates. In early May the National Assembly approved legislation that imposed stricter regulations over the print media, in accordance with which all journalists not working for the state-controlled media would be required to register with a National Media Commission. The law was condemned by the Gambia Press Union, which announced that it would not co-operate with the Commission. In early June Jawara returned to The Gambia from exile; at the end of the month he was officially received by Jammeh, and later tendered his resignation as leader of the PPP. In July legislation was adopted that allowed Jammeh to appoint up to 20 secretaries of state to his Cabinet, instead of 15.

In August 2002 Juwara alleged that the UDP's campaign funds had been diverted prior to the April elections to pay for Darboe's outstanding income-tax debts. The UDP expelled Juwara, accusing him of trying to challenge Darboe for the leadership, and in mid-October Juwara formed a new party, the National Democratic Action Movement (NDAM). In November the leader of the youth wing of the UDP, Shyngle Nyassi, was arrested in connection with information from the NIA that allegedly implicated him in the sale of forged documents to Gambians seeking asylum abroad. Nyassi, however, claimed that his arrest was a response to his criticism of the Government's economic policies. Nyassi was arrested again later that month, along with Darboe and two other members of the UDP, in connection with the murder of an APRC supporter, Alieu Njie, in June 2000; their trial commenced in April 2003, but was adjourned in July. Also in November 2002, the opposition UDP-PPP-GPP coalition split, following the resignation of its Chairman, Assan Musa Camara, while President Jammeh dismissed a number of members of his Cabinet, accusing them of lacking seriousness.

In September 2003 Joof resigned as Secretary of State for Justice and Attorney-General, and President Jammeh dismissed Badjie and Famara Jatta, the Secretary of State for Finance and Economic Affairs. Bakary Njie, the Secretary of State for Communication, Information and Technology, was removed from his post in October. In the same month the President launched an anti-corruption drive, named 'Operation No Compromise', which led to a number of high-profile arrests. In November Baba Jobe, the leader of the APRC in the National Assembly, was charged with fraud. (In April 2004 he was sentenced to nine years in prison.) In December 2003 Yankuba Touray, appointed to replace Njie as Secretary of State for Communication, Information and Technology, was dismissed from the Government.

In June 2003 the National Media Commission was created, despite continuing opposition from journalists, and was given far-reaching powers, including the authority to imprison journalists for terms of up to six months. It was originally envisaged that media organizations would have to register with the Commission by 14 May 2004; however, following a self-imposed week-long media blackout, the deadline was extended by three months. Reports continued throughout 2003 and 2004 of journalists being arrested or subjected to harassment. In September 2003 the editor-in-chief of *The Independent*, Abdoulaye Sey, was reportedly detained for four days, shortly after the newspaper published an article criticizing Jammeh. In October the newspaper's offices in Banjul were set on fire and in April 2004 the printing press was destroyed. In early December legislation providing for terms of imprisonment of up to three years for journalists found guilty of libel or sedition, and obliging members of the media to re-register with the state, was approved by the National Assembly, despite protests by members of the Gambian and international media. In mid-December Deyda Hydara, the editor of the independent newspaper *The Point*, who had been severely critical of the new legislation, was murdered in Banjul. The incident precipitated a demonstration in the capital, reportedly attended by several hundred journalists, and later that month a one-week media strike was observed. In January 2005 Reporters sans frontières called for an independent commission to be established to investigate the murder of Hydara and maintained that it had been carried out by a contract killer. In March it was claimed that the new legislation had been signed into law by Jammeh on 28 December 2004, although not published until March 2005, thus contravening the Constitution, which stated that legislation must be published within 30 days of promulgation.

Meanwhile, in October 2003 Juwara was arrested on a charge of sedition, after urging Gambians to demonstrate in protest at price rises. Although his arrest was later ruled to be illegal, in mid-December his bail was revoked, and he was once again taken into custody. In mid-February 2004 Juwara was sentenced to six months' imprisonment; an appeal against the ruling was filed later that month and he was eventually released in June.

In May 2004 Samba Bah became Secretary of State for the Interior and Religious Affairs and in the following month Amadou Scattred Janneh and Sulayman Mboob were appointed Secretaries of State for Communication, Information and Technology, and Agriculture, respectively. In July a commission into official corruption, chaired by the Nigerian judge Madubochi Azubuike Paul, began hearings, however, it was criticized as neither members of Parliament nor the President were to appear before it. In mid-September Fatou Faye was appointed Secretary of State for Education, and Bai Mass Taal became Secretary of State for Fisheries, Natural Resources and the Environment. Sidi Moro was appointed Secretary of State for Foreign Affairs in October, bringing to 87 the total number of cabinet changes since Jammeh came to power in 1994. In January 2005 the National Alliance for Democracy and Development, a coalition of five opposition parties comprising the UDP, NRP, NDAM, PDOIS and PPP, was formed to participate in the presidential elections due in late 2006. In March 2005 Jammeh effected a reorganization of the Cabinet, most notably dismissing Mboob and assuming personal responsibility for the agriculture portfolio and appointing Raymond Sock as Secretary of State for Justice and Attorney-General.

After the 1994 coup The Gambia's traditional aid donors and trading partners suspended much co-operation, although vital aid projects generally continued. The Jammeh administration

therefore sought new links: diplomatic relations with Libya, severed in 1980, were restored in November 1994, and numerous co-operation agreements ensued. Links with the Republic of China (Taiwan), ended in 1974, were re-established in July 1995, whereupon Taiwan became one of the Gambia's major sources of funding.

Despite the presence in Senegal of prominent opponents of his Government, Jammeh also sought to improve relations with that country, and in January 1996 the two countries signed an agreement aimed at increasing bilateral trade and at minimizing cross-border smuggling; a further trade agreement was concluded in April 1997. In June the two countries agreed to take joint measures to combat insecurity, illegal immigration, arms-trafficking and drugs-smuggling. In January 1998 the Government of Senegal welcomed an offer by Jammeh to mediate in the conflict in the southern province of Casamance: the separatist MFDC is chiefly composed of the Diola ethnic group, of which Jammeh is a member. In December 2000 the Gambian Government sent a delegation to participate in talks between the MFDC and the Senegalese Government. At the end of 2002 there were some 4,230 refugees from Casamance resident in The Gambia, although by late 2004 only 500 were registered with the United Nations High Commissioner for Refugees. Conflict between the transport unions of Senegal and The Gambia over border duties led to the temporary closure of border-crossings with Senegal on several occasions during 2002. In June 2003 relations were strained by the deportation of some 750 Senegalese nationals illegally resident in The Gambia.

In June 1998 Jammeh offered to mediate in the conflict between the Government and rebel forces in Guinea-Bissau (q.v.); the rebel leader, Brig. Ansumane Mané, was a Diola of Gambian extraction. In January 1999 The Gambia agreed to provide troops for an ECOMOG peace-keeping mission of the Economic Community of West African States (see p. 205) in Guinea-Bissau. After the defeat of government forces in Guinea-Bissau in May 1999, the Gambian authorities secured the safe passage of former President Vieira to The Gambia, from where he departed for Portugal. The killing of Mané in December 2000 was widely regarded as a serious set-back for Gambian foreign policy. In June 2002 relations with Guinea-Bissau were strained after President Kumba Yalá of Guinea-Bissau threatened to invade The Gambia, accusing Jammeh of involvement in a failed coup attempt in May and of support for the Casamance rebels. An exchange of visits by the foreign ministers of the two countries, followed by UN intervention in July, relieved the tension, however; relations had improved further by September, when Yalá visited Banjul.

In January 2001 the Gambian Government denied that it was implicated, as stated in a UN report, in the illicit trafficking of diamonds to benefit dissident groups in Angola and Sierra Leone.

Relations with the United Kingdom were strained in 2001, following the expulsion of the British Deputy High Commissioner, Bharat Joshi, from The Gambia in late August. The Gambian authorities alleged that the diplomat had interfered in the country's internal affairs, following his attendance at an opposition meeting, but emphasized the action had been taken against Joshi, and not the United Kingdom. However, in late September the Gambian Deputy High Commissioner in London was expelled from the United Kingdom, and further retaliatory measures were implemented against The Gambia. Relations were restored during 2002, although in January of that year the EU representative, George Marc-André, was declared *persona non grata* by the Gambian authorities and requested to leave the country.

In September 2003 The Gambia contributed 150 troops to the Economic Community of West African States' Mission in Liberia (ECOMIL). In October the Gambian troops were transferred to a longer-term UN stabilization force, the UN Mission in Liberia (UNMIL, see p 73), which replaced ECOMIL, with a mandate to support the implementation of a comprehensive peace agreement in that country. In December 2004 The Gambia contributed 196 military personnel to the African Union Mission in Sudan.

The Gambia is a member of the Community of Sahel-Saharan States—CEN-SAD (see p. 373).

Government

The Constitution of the Second Republic of The Gambia, which was approved in a national referendum on 8 August 1996, entered into full effect on 16 January 1997. Under its terms, the Head of State is the President of the Republic, who is directly elected by universal adult suffrage. No restriction is placed on the number of times a President may seek re-election. Legislative authority is vested in the National Assembly, comprising 48 members elected by direct suffrage and five members nominated by the President of the Republic. The President appoints government members, who are responsible both to the Head of State and to the National Assembly. The Gambia is divided into eight local government areas.

Defence

In August 2004 the Gambian National Army comprised 800 men (including a marine unit of about 70 and a presidential guard) in active service. Military service has been mainly voluntary; however, the Constitution of the Second Republic, which entered into full effect in January 1997, makes provision for compulsory service. The defence budget for 2004 was estimated at D65m.

Economic Affairs

In 2003, according to estimates by the World Bank, The Gambia's gross national income (GNI), measured at average 2001–03 prices, was US $411m., equivalent to $310 per head (or $1,820 on an international purchasing-power parity basis). During 1990–2003, it was estimated, the population increased at an average annual rate of 3.3%, while gross domestic product (GDP) per head increased by 0.2%. Overall GDP increased, in real terms, at an average annual rate of 3.5% in 1990–2003; GDP declined by 3.1% in 2002, but increased by 8.8% in 2003.

Agriculture (including forestry and fishing) contributed an estimated 32.8% of GDP in 2003. About 78.1% of the labour force were employed in the sector in that year. The dominant agricultural activity is the cultivation of groundnuts. Exports of groundnuts and related products accounted for an estimated 68.2% of domestic export earnings in 1999, however, according to the IMF, that figure declined to an estimated 10.4% of total exports (including re-exports) in 2003, following a drought which destroyed over 50% of the 2001/02 harvest. A significant proportion of the groundnut crop is frequently smuggled for sale in Senegal. Cotton, citrus fruits, mangoes, avocados and sesame seed are also cultivated for export. The principal staple crops are millet, rice, sorghum and maize, although The Gambia remains heavily dependent on imports of rice and other basic foodstuffs. Fishing makes an important contribution both to the domestic food supply and to export earnings: exports of fish and fish products contributed an estimated 14.4% of the value of domestic exports in 2003. In 2001 the Government announced the construction of a major new fishing port in Banjul, at a cost of US $10m. In July a loan of US $7.1m. was agreed with the International Fund for Agricultural Development for watershed-management. Agricultural GDP increased at an average annual rate of 3.0% in 1990–2003; it declined by 28.2% in 2002 but growth of 16.0% was recorded in 2003.

Industry (including manufacturing, construction, mining and power) contributed an estimated 13.7% of GDP in 2003. About 9.7% of the labour force were employed in the sector at the time of the 1993 census. Industrial GDP increased at an average annual rate of 3.6% in 1990–2003; growth in 2003 was 7.2%.

The Gambia has no economically viable mineral resources, although seismic surveys have indicated the existence of petroleum deposits off shore. Deposits of kaolin and salt are currently unexploited.

Manufacturing contributed an estimated 5.2% of GDP in 2003, and employed about 6.3% of the labour force in 1993. The sector is dominated by agro-industrial activities, most importantly the processing of groundnuts and fish. Beverages and construction materials are also produced for the domestic market. Manufacturing GDP increased at an average annual rate of 2.3% in 1990–2003; growth in 2003 was 4.5%.

The Gambia is highly reliant on imported energy. Imports of fuel and energy comprised an estimated 11.9% of the value of total merchandise imports in 2000.

The services sector contributed an estimated 53.5% of GDP in 2003. The tourism industry is of particular significance as a generator of foreign exchange. Tourism contributed about 10% of annual GDP in the early 1990s, and employed about one-third of workers in the formal sector at that time. The international response to the 1994 coup and its aftermath had a severe impact on tourism, although the industry recovered strongly from 1996 onwards. The Jammeh administration has expressed its intention further to exploit the country's potential as a transit point for regional trade and also as a centre for regional finance and telecommunications. The GDP of the services sector increased at

an average annual rate of 4.2% in 1990–2003; growth in 2003 was 3.2%.

In 2003 The Gambia recorded an estimated visible trade deficit of US $51.8m., while there was a deficit of $18.9m. on the current account of the balance of payments. In 1999 the principal source of imports was Germany, which supplied an estimated 13.8% of total imports; other major sources were the United Kingdom, France, the People's Republic of China and Belgium. The two largest markets for exports in that year were Belgium (an estimated 7.7% of total exports) and the United Kingdom. The Gambia's principal domestic exports in 2003 were groundnuts and related products, fruit and vegetables, and fish and fish products. The principal imports in 2002 were food and live animals, machinery and transport equipment, mineral fuels and lubricants, chemicals and beverages and tobacco.

In 2003, according to preliminary figures, there was an overall budget deficit of D520.0m. The Gambia's total external debt was US $572.6m. at the end of 2002, of which $503.6m. was long-term public debt. In 2002 the cost of debt-servicing was equivalent to 6.4% of the value of exports of goods and services. The average annual rate of inflation was 4.6% in 1990–2002; consumer prices increased by an average of 17.0% in 2003. The rate of unemployment was estimated at some 26% of the labour force in mid-1994.

The Gambia is a member of the Economic Community of West African States (ECOWAS, see p. 205), of the Gambia River Basin Development Organization (OMVG, see p. 374), of the African Groundnut Council (see p. 369), of the West Africa Rice Development Association (WARDA, see p. 372), and of the Permanent Inter-State Committee on Drought Control in the Sahel (CILSS, see p. 375).

The military coup of July 1994 caused considerable economic disruption to The Gambia. A return to growth from 1995 was, in large part, underpinned by the recovery in the tourism sector. The installation of elected civilian institutions in early 1997 prompted the international economic community to recommence full support, which had been partially suspended following the coup, and in mid-1998 the IMF approved an Enhanced Structural Adjustment Facility (subsequently renamed the Poverty Reduction and Growth Facility, PRGF) in support of the Government's economic programme for 1998–2001. In December 2000 it was announced that The Gambia was to receive US $91m. in debt-service relief over 15 years under the IMF/World Bank initiative for heavily indebted poor countries. The Gambia's overriding dependence on the largely unmodernized groundnut sector remains an obstacle to sustained growth, although the gradual introduction of reforms, which sought to improve relations between public- and private-sector interests, and between production and marketing interests, in the sector, commenced in 2000. Concern has also been expressed at the level of borrowing incurred by the Jammeh Government to finance its extensive infrastructural programme; the level of The Gambia's international indebtedness has risen sharply since 1995. In March 2002 the USA finally lifted economic sanctions imposed on the Gambia following the 1994 coup, and on 1 January 2003 The Gambia became eligible for funding under the US African Growth and Opportunity Act. In July the IMF approved a further PRGF, in support of the economic programme for 2002–05, equivalent to some $27m., however, in December 2003 the Fund suspended PRGF assistance to The Gambia and issued a statement expressing concern at the deteriorating economic situation and alleged inaccuracies in economic data provided by the Gambian authorities. In early 2004 the IMF requested that The Gambia repay two non-complying disbursements (equivalent to a total of some $10.1m.) that had been made following PRGF reviews in 2001—the Central Bank reported in December 2004 that the sums had been repaid ahead of schedule—and again criticized the Government for failing to meet PRGF goals and providing misleading financial information. Nevertheless, it was expected that disbursements under the PRGF would recommence in 2005. GDP growth for that year was forecast at 7.1% and it was anticipated that President Jammeh's anti-corruption initiative (see above) would lead to an improvement in the Government's fiscal discipline, while the establishment of the Revenue Authority would increase the efficiency of tax collection.

Education

Primary (or basic) education, beginning at seven years of age, is free but not compulsory and lasts for nine years. Secondary education, from 16 years of age, lasts for three years. In 2000/01 total enrolment at primary schools included 69% of children in the relevant age-group (boys 71%; girls 66%), according to UNESCO estimates, while secondary enrolment included only 29% of the appropriate age-group (boys 34%; girls 23%). The Jammeh administration has, since 1994, embarked on an ambitious project to improve educational facilities and levels of attendance and attainment. A particular aim has been to ameliorate access to schools for pupils in rural areas. Post-secondary education is available in teacher training, agriculture, health and technical subjects. Some 1,591 students were enrolled at tertiary establishments in 1994/95. The University of The Gambia, at Banjul, was officially opened in 2000. In 1977 The Gambia introduced Koranic studies at all stages of education, and many children attend Koranic schools (daara). In 1999 current expenditure by the central Government on education was an estimated D146.0m., equivalent to 22.9% of non-interest current spending.

Public Holidays

2005: 1 January (New Year's Day), 21 January* (Eid al-Kebir, Feast of the Sacrifice), 18 February (Independence Day), 25 March (Good Friday), 21 April* (Eid al-Moulid, Birth of the Prophet), 1 May (Workers' Day), 22 July (Anniversary of the Second Republic), 15 August (Assumption/St Mary's Day), 4 November* (Eid al-Fitr, end of Ramadan), 25 December (Christmas).

2006: 1 January (New Year's Day), 11 January* (Eid al-Kebir, Feast of the Sacrifice), 18 February (Independence Day), 11 April* (Eid al-Moulid, Birth of the Prophet), 14 April (Good Friday), 1 May (Workers' Day), 22 July (Anniversary of the Second Republic), 15 August (Assumption/St Mary's Day), 24 October* (Eid al-Fitr, end of Ramadan), 25 December (Christmas).

*These holidays are dependent on the Islamic lunar calendar and may vary by one or two days from the dates given.

Weights and Measures

Imperial weights and measures are used. Importers and traders also use the metric system.

Statistical Survey

Sources (unless otherwise stated): Department of Information Services, 14 Daniel Goddard St, Banjul; tel. 4225060; fax 4227230; Central Statistics Department, Central Bank Building, 1/2 Ecowas Ave, Banjul; tel. 4228364; fax 4228903; e-mail director@csd.gm.

Area and Population

AREA, POPULATION AND DENSITY

Area (sq km)	11,295*
Population (census results)	
15 April 1993	1,038,145
15 April 2003†	
Males	687,781
Females	676,726
Total	1,364,507
Density (per sq km) at 15 April 2003	120.8†

* 4,361 sq miles.
† Provisional.

ETHNIC GROUPS

1993 census (percentages): Mandinka 39.60; Fula 18.83; Wolof 14.61; Jola 10.66; Serahule 8.92; Serere 2.77; Manjago 1.85; Bambara 0.84; Creole/Aku 0.69; Others 1.23.

ADMINISTRATIVE DIVISIONS
(population at 2003 census, provisional results)

Banjul . . .	34,828	Kanifing . . .		322,410
Basse	183,033	Kerewan . . .		172,806
Brikama . . .	392,987	Kuntaur . . .		79,098
Georgetown . .	106,799	Mansakonko . .		72,546

PRINCIPAL TOWNS
(population at 1993 census)

Serrekunda . .	151,450	Lamin . . .		10,668
Brikama . . .	42,480	Gunjur . . .		9,983
Banjul (capital) . .	42,407	Basse . . .		9,265
Bakau . . .	38,062	Soma . . .		7,925
Farafenni . .	21,142	Bansang . . .		5,405
Sukuta . . .	16,667			

Mid-2003 (UN estimate, incl. suburbs): Banjul 372,366 (Source: UN, *World Urbanization Prospects: The 2003 Revision*).

BIRTHS AND DEATHS
(UN estimates, annual averages)

	1985–90	1990–95	1995–2000
Birth rate (per 1,000) . . .	45.0	41.0	38.8
Death rate (per 1,000) . . .	17.4	14.9	13.6

Source: UN, *World Population Prospects: The 2002 Revision*.

Expectation of life (WHO estimates, years at birth): 57.1 (males 55.4; females 58.9) in 2002 (Source: WHO, *World Health Report*).

ECONOMICALLY ACTIVE POPULATION*
(persons aged 10 years and over, 1993 census)

	Males	Females	Total
Agriculture, hunting and forestry .	82,886	92,806	175,692
Fishing	5,610	450	6,060
Mining and quarrying	354	44	398
Manufacturing	18,729	2,953	21,682
Electricity, gas and water supply .	1,774	84	1,858
Construction	9,530	149	9,679
Wholesale and retail trade; repair of motor vehicles, motorcycles and personal and household goods	33,281	15,460	48,741
Hotels and restaurants . . .	3,814	2,173	5,987
Transport, storage and communications	13,421	782	14,203
Financial intermediation . . .	1,843	572	2,415
Other community, social and personal service activities . .	25,647	15,607	41,254
Activities not adequately defined .	10,421	6,991	17,412
Total labour force	207,310	138,071	345,381

* Figures exclude persons seeking work for the first time, but include other unemployed persons.

Mid-2003 (estimates in '000): Agriculture, etc. 564; Total labour force 722 (Source: FAO).

Health and Welfare

KEY INDICATORS

Total fertility rate (children per woman, 2002)	4.8
Under-5 mortality rate (per 1,000 live births, 2003) . . .	123
HIV/AIDS (% of persons aged 15–49, 2003)	1.2
Physicians (per 1,000 head, 2001)	0.14
Hospital beds (per 1,000 head, 2000)	1.00
Health expenditure (2001): US $ per head (PPP)	78
Health expenditure (2001): % of GDP	6.4
Health expenditure (2001): public (% of total)	49.4
Access to water (% of persons, 2002)	82
Access to sanitation (% of persons, 2002)	53
Human Development Index (2002): ranking	155
Human Development Index (2002): value	0.452

For sources and definitions, see explanatory note on p. vi.

Agriculture

PRINCIPAL CROPS
('000 metric tons)

	2001	2002	2003
Rice (paddy)	32.6	20.5	20.5*
Maize	29.0	18.6	25.0†
Millet	105.0	84.6	100.0†
Sorghum	33.4	15.2	25.0*
Cassava (Manioc)*	7.5	7.5	7.5
Pulses*	3.2	3.2	3.2
Groundnuts (in shell) . . .	151.1	71.5	76.4†
Oil palm fruit*	35.0	35.0	35.0
Other vegetables*	9.0	9.0	9.0
Mangoes*	0.5	0.6	0.6
Other fruits*	3.6	3.6	3.6

* FAO estimate(s).
† Official estimate(s).
Source: FAO.

LIVESTOCK
('000 head, year ending September)

	2001	2002	2003
Cattle	323.2	326.6	327.0*
Goats	228.4	262.0	262.0*
Sheep	129.2	145.6	146.0*
Pigs	8.0	17.2	17.5*
Asses*	35.0	35.0	35.0
Horses*	17.0	17.0	27.0
Chickens	586	591	600*

* FAO estimate(s).
Source: FAO.

LIVESTOCK PRODUCTS
(FAO estimates, '000 metric tons)

	2001	2002	2003
Beef and veal	3.1	3.1	3.2
Goat meat	0.6	0.7	0.7
Mutton and lamb	0.4	0.4	0.4
Poultry meat	0.9	0.9	1.1
Game meat	1.0	1.0	1.0
Cows' milk	7.6	7.6	7.6
Poultry eggs	0.7	0.7	0.7

Source: FAO.

Forestry

ROUNDWOOD REMOVALS
(FAO estimates, '000 cubic metres, excluding bark)

	2001	2002	2003
Sawlogs, veneer logs and logs for sleepers*	106	106	106
Other industrial wood†	7	7	7
Fuel wood	611	620	629
Total	724	733	742

* Assumed to be unchanged since 1994.
† Assumed to be unchanged since 1993.
Source: FAO.

Fishing

('000 metric tons, live weight)

	2000	2001	2002
Capture*	29.0	34.5	45.8
Tilapias	1.1	1.1	1.1
Sea catfishes	0.7	0.9	2.2
Bonga shad	20.5	18.5	22.8
Croakers and drums . . .	1.3	1.9	2.0
Sharks, rays, skates . . .	0.7	4.0	6.1
Aquaculture*	0.0	0.0	0.0
Total catch*	29.0	34.5	45.8

* FAO estimates.
Source: FAO.

Mining

	2000	2001*	2002*
Clay (metric tons)	1,960	2,000	2,000
Silica sand ('000 metric tons) . .	170	170	170

* Estimates.
Source: US Geological Survey.

Industry

SELECTED PRODUCTS
('000 metric tons, unless otherwise stated)

	2001	2002	2003
Cured fish	0.1	n.a.	n.a.
Palm oil—unrefined*	2.5	2.5	2.5
Groundnut oil*	33.0	5.9	19.0
Beer of millet	43.9	35.1	41.8
Electric energy (million kWh)† .	134.0	144.1*	n.a.

* Estimate(s) or provisional figure(s).
† Data from the National Water and Electricity Company Ltd.
Source: mainly FAO.

Finance

CURRENCY AND EXCHANGE RATES

Monetary Units
100 butut = 1 dalasi (D)

Sterling, Dollar and Euro Equivalents (30 June 2003)
£1 sterling = 46.002 dalasi
US $1 = 27.878 dalasi
€1 = 31.857 dalasi
1,000 dalasi = £21.74 = $35.87 = €31.39

Average Exchange Rate (dalasi per US $)
2000   12.788
2001   15.687
2002   19.918

BUDGET
(million dalasi)

Revenue*	2001	2002†	2003‡
Tax revenue	853.8	1,040.2	1,371.4
Direct taxes	251.0	318.0	414.8
Taxes on personal incomes .	102.6	122.4	149.3
Taxes on corporate profits .	132.7	176.8	244.9
Indirect taxes	602.8	722.2	956.6
Domestic taxes on goods and services	73.9	124.9	233.6
Domestic sales tax . . .	59.8	108.0	203.0
Excise duties	11.5	10.8	25.6
Taxes on international trade .	528.9	597.3	722.9
Customs duties	327.4	367.7	420.4
Sales tax on imports . .	201.5	229.6	302.6
Non-tax revenue	136.0	161.5	197.8
Government services and charges	97.6	134.8	152.2
Interest and dividends . . .	34.2	24.1	42.1
Total	**989.9**	**1,201.8**	**1,569.1**

Expenditure§	2001	2002†	2003‡
Current expenditure . . .	1,237.1	1,318.2	1,703.3
Wages and salaries . . .	342.0	395.2	450.4
Other goods and services . .	533.4	512.2	561.5
Interest payments	293.8	370.5	620.8
Internal	225.0	286.6	434.6
External	68.7	84.0	186.2
Heavily Indebted Poor Countries (HIPC) programme expenditure	68.0	39.9	70.7
Capital expenditure	732.5‖	585.3	656.2
Total	**2,037.4**	**1,870.7**	**2,327.9**

* Excluding grants received (million dalasi): 135.9 in 2001; 326.9 in 2002; 207.2 in 2003.
† Estimates.
‡ Preliminary figures.
§ Excluding lending minus repayments (million dalasi): 67.8 in 2001; −32.8 in 2002; −31.6 in 2003.
‖ Including retroactive loan of US $28.5m. from the Central Bank of The Gambia.

Source: IMF, *The Gambia: Selected Issues and Statistical Appendix* (May 2004).

INTERNATIONAL RESERVES
(US $ million at 31 December)

	2000	2001	2002
IMF special drawing rights . .	0.23	0.02	0.02
Reserve position in IMF . .	1.93	1.87	2.02
Foreign exchange	107.27	104.13	104.84
Total	**109.43**	**106.01**	**106.88**

Source: IMF, *International Financial Statistics*.

2003 (US $ million at 31 December): IMF special drawing rights 0.03; Reserve position in IMF 2.21 (Source: IMF, *International Financial Statistics*).

MONEY SUPPLY
(million dalasi at 31 December)

	2000	2001	2002
Currency outside banks . .	540.26	600.75	797.37
Demand deposits at commercial banks	443.27	524.66	959.40
Total money	**983.53**	**1,125.41**	**1,756.77**

Source: IMF, *International Financial Statistics*.

COST OF LIVING
(Consumer Price Index for Banjul and Kombo St Mary's; base: 1974 = 100)

	1997	1998	1999
Food	1,511.8	1,565.8	1,628.8
Fuel and light	2,145.8	1,854.9	2,076.0
Clothing*	937.5	981.8	999.9
Rent	1,409.6	1,431.3	1,428.6
All items (incl. others)	**1,441.5**	**1,457.3**	**1,512.8**

* Including household linen.

All items: 1,525.7 in 2000; 1,594.2 in 2001; 1,731.5 in 2002; 2,026.4 in 2003 (Source: IMF, *The Gambia: Selected Issues and Statistical Appendix* (May 2004)).

NATIONAL ACCOUNTS
(million dalasi at current prices)

Expenditure on the Gross Domestic Product

	2001*	2002†	2003†
Government final consumption expenditure	1,615.4	1,234.2	1,517.1
Private final consumption expenditure	4,199.2	5,050.6	7,567.5
Increase in stocks . . . . . } Gross fixed capital formation . }	1,137.7	1,561.8	2,016.6
Total domestic expenditure .	**6,952.3**	**7,846.6**	**11,101.2**
Exports of goods and services .	2,483.4	3,323.9	4,559.7
Less Imports of goods and services	2,879.8	3,806.2	5,385.7
GDP in purchasers' values .	**6,555.9**	**7,364.3**	**10,275.2**
GDP at constant 1976/77 prices	**782.5**	**757.1**	**823.5**

Gross Domestic Product by Economic Activity

	2001*	2002†	2003†
Agriculture, hunting, forestry and fishing	2,042.3	1,832.7	3,054.8
Manufacturing	301.6	378.2	485.4
Electricity and water . . .	84.7	102.5	123.7
Construction and mining . .	350.5	483.7	665.1
Trade	650.5	778.6	1,012.7
Restaurants and hotels . . .	305.7	408.9	611.4
Transport and communications .	1,040.4	1,279.8	1,740.8
Real estate and business services .	400.3	478.8	567.1
Government services . . .	525.8	607.7	712.9
Other services	251.2	291.1	344.8
GDP at factor cost	**5,953.1**	**6,642.1**	**9,318.7**
Indirect taxes, *less* subsidies . .	602.8	722.2	956.6
GDP in purchasers' values . .	**6,555.9**	**7,364.3**	**10,275.2**

* Estimates.
† Preliminary figures.

Source: IMF, *The Gambia: Selected Issues and Statistical Appendix* (May 2004).

BALANCE OF PAYMENTS
(US $ million, year ending 30 June)

	1995	1996	1997
Exports of goods f.o.b.	122.96	118.75	119.61
Imports of goods f.o.b.	−162.53	−217.10	−207.09
Trade balance	**−39.57**	**−98.35**	**−87.48**
Exports of services	53.71	101.21	109.35
Imports of services	−69.25	−77.03	−74.67
Balance on goods and services	**−55.11**	**−74.17**	**−52.81**
Other income received	4.37	6.01	3.73
Other income paid	−9.58	−9.28	−11.30
Balance on goods, services and income	**−60.32**	**−77.44**	**−60.38**
Current transfers received	55.81	35.10	45.04
Current transfers paid	−3.68	−5.35	−8.22
Current balance	**−8.19**	**−47.70**	**−23.56**
Capital account (net)	—	8.52	5.74
Direct investment from abroad	7.78	10.80	11.98
Other investment assets	−3.66	5.62	10.28
Investment liabilities	20.65	42.18	17.19
Net errors and omissions	−15.63	−4.94	−14.22
Overall balance	**0.94**	**14.47**	**7.40**

Source: IMF, *International Financial Statistics*.

2003 (preliminary, US $ million): Exports 102.0; Imports −153.8; Trade balance −51.8; Services and factor income (net) −2.4; Current transfers (net) 35.3; Current-account balance −18.9; Capital account 4.3; Errors and omissions 3.2; Overall balance −11.4 (Source: IMF, *The Gambia: Selected Issues and Statistical Appendix* (May 2004)).

External Trade

PRINCIPAL COMMODITIES
(US $ '000)

Imports c.i.f.	2000	2001	2002
Food and live animals	59,000	29,642	37,581
Beverages and tobacco	4,527	13,782	8,231
Mineral fuels, lubricants, etc.	22,627	9,160	17,008
Animal and vegetable oils	6,023	7,252	6,078
Chemicals	13,154	8,701	16,201
Machinery and transport equipment	35,820	36,755	27,262
Miscellaneous manufactured articles	21,561	12,557	15,563
Total (incl. others)	**189,858**	**144,659**	**160,105**

Exports f.o.b.	2000	2001	2002
Groundnut products	13,738	17,553	23,920
Fish and fish products	2,562	2,199	2,857
Fruit and vegetables	3,561	4,467	4,089
Cotton products	171	421	319
Total (incl. others*)	**126,579**	**101,607**	**110,989**

* Of which, re-exports: 105,442 in 2000; 75,849 in 2001; 78,190 in 2002.

2003 (exports f.o.b., preliminary figures, US $ '000): Groundnut products 10,622; Fish and fish products 3,124; Fruit and vegetables 4,868; Cotton products 467; Total (incl. others, of which re-exports 80,253) 101,968.

Source: IMF, *The Gambia: Selected Issues and Statistical Appendix* (May 2004).

PRINCIPAL TRADING PARTNERS
(million dalasi)

Imports c.i.f.	1997	1998	1999
Belgium	86.8	163.1	126.8
China, People's Repub.	68.9	140.5	140.8
Côte d'Ivoire	104.3	145.2	89.8
France (incl. Monaco)	167.3	220.6	148.3
Germany	148.0	179.6	305.3
Hong Kong	50.5	82.8	96.7
Italy	47.9	30.6	31.8
Japan	55.3	77.2	71.5
Netherlands	84.5	163.8	105.3
Senegal	42.8	38.1	50.0
Spain	67.8	87.1	38.1
Thailand	6.2	125.6	27.3
United Kingdom	261.2	338.5	235.1
USA	171.2	168.9	109.2
Total (incl. others)	**1,773.8**	**2,426.4**	**2,206.9**

Exports f.o.b.	1997	1998	1999
Belgium	7.3	16.8	24.2
China, People's Repub.	2.6	6.9	1.4
France (incl. Monaco)	27.5	153.9	2.3
Germany	3.5	20.6	10.1
Hong Kong	2.6	1.4	0.8
Japan	3.2	5.3	2.1
Netherlands	7.4	9.0	3.3
Senegal	5.3	7.3	5.9
Spain	29.2	8.9	7.7
United Kingdom	22.0	34.8	15.7
USA	6.5	1.4	3.0
Total (incl. others)	**150.4**	**279.6**	**313.0**

Transport

ROAD TRAFFIC
(estimates, motor vehicles in use)

	1995	1996	1997
Passenger cars	6,972	6,925	7,267
Lorries and vans	3,778	4,045	4,147

SHIPPING

Merchant Fleet
(registered at 31 December)

	2001	2002	2003
Number of vessels	8	9	9
Total displacement (grt)	1,884	2,183	2,183

Source: Lloyd's Register-Fairplay, *World Fleet Statistics*.

International Sea-borne Freight Traffic
('000 metric tons)

	1996	1997	1998
Goods loaded	55.9	38.1	47.0
Goods unloaded	482.7	503.7	493.2

CIVIL AVIATION
(traffic on scheduled services)

	1992	1993	1994
Kilometres flown (million) . . .	1	1	1
Passengers carried ('000) . . .	19	19	19
Passenger-km (million)	50	50	50
Total ton-km (million)	5	5	5

Source: UN, *Statistical Yearbook*.

Tourism

FOREIGN VISITORS BY COUNTRY OF ORIGIN*

	1999	2000	2001
Austria	1,356	506	166
Belgium	3,984	4,392	3,264
Denmark	2,956	3,597	1,605
Germany	25,393	12,156	3,065
Netherlands	9,625	9,668	6,592
Sweden	5,556	4,997	4,043
United Kingdom	40,588	37,594	34,399
Total (incl. others)	96,122	78,710	57,231

* Air charter tourist arrivals.

Source: World Tourism Organization, *Yearbook of Tourism Statistics*.

Air charter tourist arrivals (preliminary figures): 75,212 in 2001; 78,893 in 2002.

Receipts from tourism (million dalasi): 734.4 in 1998; 726.9 in 1999; 608.2 in 2000 (preliminary figure) (Source: IMF, *The Gambia: Selected Issues and Statistical Appendix* (May 2004)).

Communications Media

	2000	2001	2002
Television receivers ('000 in use) .	4	n.a.	n.a.
Telephones ('000 main lines in use)	33.3	35.0	38.4
Mobile cellular telephones ('000 subscribers)	5.6	55.1	100.0
Personal computers ('000 in use) .	15	17	19
Internet users ('000)	4	18	25

Source: International Telecommunication Union.

Radio receivers ('000 in use): 196 in 1997.

Facsimile machines (number in use, year ending 31 March): 1,149 in 1997/98.

Daily newspapers: 1 in 1996 (average circulation 2,000 copies).

Non-daily newspapers: 4 in 1996 (estimated average circulation 6,000 copies).

Book production: 10 titles in 1998 (10,000 copies).

Sources: UNESCO, *Statistical Yearbook*; UN, *Statistical Yearbook*.

Education

(1998/99, unless otherwise indicated)

	Institu- tions	Teachers	Students		
			Males	Females	Total
Pre-primary . .	264	408*	15,205	13,618	28,823
Primary . . .	332	4,578	81,360	69,043	150,403
Junior Secondary	75	1,338	20,142	14,018	34,160
Senior Secondary	27	598	8,102	4,507	12,609
Tertiary . . .	5	155	1,018*	573*	1,591*

* 1994/95 figure.

Source: Department of State for Education, Banjul.

Adult literacy rate (UNESCO estimates): 37.8% (males 45.0%; females 30.9%) in 2001 (Source: UN Development Programme, *Human Development Report*).

Directory

The Constitution

Following the *coup d'état* of July 1994, the 1970 Constitution was suspended and the presidency and legislature, as defined therein, dissolved. A Constitutional Review Commission was inaugurated in April 1995; the amended document was approved in a national referendum on 8 August. The Constitution of the Second Republic of The Gambia entered into full effect on 16 January 1997.

Decrees issued during the transition period (1994–96) are deemed to have been approved by the National Assembly and remain in force so long as they do not contravene the provisions of the Constitution of the Second Republic.

The Constitution provides for the separation of the powers of the executive, legislative and judicial organs of state. The Head of State is the President of the Republic, who is directly elected by universal adult suffrage. No restriction is placed on the number of times a President may seek re-election. Legislative authority is vested in the National Assembly, comprising 48 members elected by direct universal suffrage and five members nominated by the President of the Republic. The Speaker and Deputy Speaker of the Assembly are elected, by the members of the legislature, from among the President's nominees. The Constitution upholds the principle of executive accountability to parliament. Thus, the Head of State appoints government members, but these are responsible both to the President and to the National Assembly. Ministers of cabinet rank take the title of Secretary of State. Committees of the Assembly have powers to inquire into the activities of ministers and of government departments, and into all matters of public importance.

In judicial affairs, the final court of appeal is the Supreme Court. Provision is made for a special criminal court to hear and determine all cases relating to the theft and misappropriation of public funds.

The Constitution provides for an Independent Electoral Commission, an Independent National Audit Office, an Office of the Ombudsman, a Lands Commission and a Public Service Commission, all of which are intended to ensure transparency, accountability and probity in public affairs.

The Constitution guarantees the rights of women, of children and of the disabled. Tribalism and other forms of sectarianism in politics are forbidden. Political activity may be suspended in the event of a state of national insecurity.

The Government

HEAD OF STATE

President: Col (retd) Alhaji YAHYA A. J. J. JAMMEH (proclaimed Head of State 26 July 1994; elected President 26 September 1996, re-elected 18 October 2001).

Vice-President: ISATOU NJIE-SAIDY.

THE CABINET
(April 2005)

President and Secretary of State for Agriculture, Energy and Defence: Col (retd) Alhaji YAHYA A. J. J. JAMMEH.

Vice-President and Secretary of State for Women's Affairs: ISATOU NJIE-SAIDY.

Secretary of State for Finance and Economic Affairs: MARGARET KEITA.

Secretary of State for Foreign Affairs: Mousa Gibril Bala Gaye.

Secretary of State for the Interior: Col. (retd) Baboucar Jatta.

Secretary of State for Justice and Attorney-General: Raymond Sock.

Secretary of State for Works, Construction, Infrastructure and National Assembly Matters: Bala Garba Jahumpa.

Secretary of State for Fisheries and Water Resources: Bai-Mass M. Taal.

Secretary of State for Forestry and the Environment: Capt. (retd) Edward David Singhateh.

Secretary of State for Health and Social Welfare: Dr Alhaji Tamsir Mbowe.

Secretary of State for Local Government and Lands: Ismaila Sambou.

Secretary of State for Education: Fatou Faye.

Secretary of State for Tourism and Culture: Susan Waffa-Ogoo.

Secretary of State for Communication, Information and Technology: Amadou Scattred Janneh.

Secretary of State for Trade, Industry and Employment: Neneh Macdouall-Gaye.

Secretary of State for Youth, Sports and Religious Affairs: Samba Faal.

Secretary-General, Head of the Civil Service: Alieu Ngum.

DEPARTMENTS OF STATE

Office of the President: PMB, State House, Banjul; tel. 4223811; fax 4227034; e-mail info@statehouse.gm; internet www.statehouse.gm.

Office of the Vice-President: State House, Banjul; tel. 4227605; fax 4224012; e-mail vicepresident@statehouse.gm.

Department of State for Agriculture: The Quadrangle, Banjul; tel. 228291; fax 223578.

Department of State for Communication, Information and Technology: Half-Die, Banjul; tel. 4227668; e-mail amjanneh@aol.com.

Department of State for Education: Willy Thorpe Bldg, Banjul; tel. 4227236; fax 4224180; internet www.edugambia.gm.

Department of State for Finance and Economic Affairs: The Quadrangle, POB 9686, Banjul; tel. 4228291; fax 4227954.

Department of State for Fisheries, Natural Resources and the Environment: 5 Marina Parade, Banjul; tel. 4228702; fax 4228628.

Department of State for Foreign Affairs: 4 Col. Muammar Ghadaffi Ave, Banjul; tel. 4225654; fax 4223578.

Department of State for Health and Social Welfare: The Quadrangle, Banjul; tel. 4227881; fax 4223178; e-mail dpi@dosh.gm; internet www.dosh.gm.

Department of State for the Interior and Religious Affairs: ECOWAS Ave, Banjul; tel. 4228511; fax 4223063.

Department of State for Justice and Attorney General's Chambers: Marina Parade, Banjul; tel. 4228181; fax 4225352; e-mail sthydara@hotmail.com.

Department of State for Local Government and Lands: The Quadrangle, Banjul; tel. 4228291.

Department of State for Tourism and Culture: New Administrative Bldg, The Quadrangle, Banjul; tel. 4227593; fax 4227753; e-mail masterplan@gamtel.gm; internet www.linktogambia.gm.

Department of State for Trade, Industry and Employment: Central Bank Bldg, Independence Dr., Banjul; tel. 4228868; fax 4227756; e-mail tiewebmaster@qanet.gm; internet www.gambia.gm.

Department of State for Works, Construction, Infrastructure and National Assembly Matters: MID Rd, Kanifing, Banjul; tel. 4227449; fax 4226655.

Department of State for Youth and Sports: The Quadrangle, Banjul; tel. 4225264; fax 4225267; e-mail dosy-s@qanet.gm.

President and Legislature

PRESIDENT

Presidential Election, 18 October 2001

Candidate	Votes	% of votes
Yahya A. J. J. Jammeh (APRC) . . .	242,302	52.84
Ousainou N. Darboe (UDP-PPP-GPP Coalition)	149,448	32.59
Hamat N. K. Bah (NRP)	35,671	7.78
Sheriff Mustapha Dibba (NCP) . . .	17,271	3.77
Sidia Jatta (PDOIS)	13,841	3.02
Total	458,533	100.00

NATIONAL ASSEMBLY

Speaker: Sheriff Mustapha Dibba.

National Assembly: Parliament Buildings, Independence Drive, Banjul; tel. 4228305; fax 4225123; e-mail assemblyclerk@yahoo.com.

General Election, 17 January 2002

Party	Seats
Alliance for Patriotic Reorientation and Construction (APRC)	45*
People's Democratic Organization for Independence and Socialism (PDOIS)	2
National Reconciliation Party (NRP)	1
Total	48†

* Including 33 seats taken in constituencies in which the party was unopposed.
† The President of the Republic is empowered by the Constitution to nominate five additional members of parliament. The total number of members of parliament is thus 53.

Political Organizations

Alliance for Patriotic Reorientation and Construction (APRC): 72 Tafsir Demba Ndow St, Banjul; tel. 4222020; fax 4222021; f. 1996; Chair. President Yahya A. J. J. Jammeh.

Gambia People's Party (GPP): Banjul; f. 1986; socialist; banned from contesting the 1996 presidential election and 1997 legislative elections; contested 2001 presidential election in coalition with the PPP and the UDP; boycotted 2002 legislative elections; Leader Assan Musa Camara.

The Gambia Party for Democracy and Progress (GPDP): Banjul; f. 2004; Sec.-Gen. Henry Gomez.

National Convention Party (NCP): 47 Antouman Faal St, Banjul; f. 1977; banned from contesting the 1996 presidential election and 1997 legislative elections; supported the APRC in 2002 legislative elections; Leader Sheriff Mustapha Dibba.

Diplomatic Representation

EMBASSIES AND HIGH COMMISSIONS IN THE GAMBIA

China (Taiwan): 26 Radio Gambia St, Kanifing South, POB 916, Banjul; tel. 4374046; fax 4374055; e-mail rocemb@qanet.gm ; Ambassador Patrick Pei-Chi Chang.

Cuba: C/ 801, POB 1487, Banjul; tel. and fax 460789; e-mail embacuba@ganet.gm; Ambassador Mariano Lores Betancourt.

Libya: Independence Dr., Banjul; tel. 4223213; fax 4223214; Chargé d'affaires a.i. Abdussalam Abuzaid.

Nigeria: Garba Jahumpa Rd, Bakau Newtown, POB 630, Banjul; tel. 4495803; fax 4496456; High Commissioner Mariam Muhammed.

Senegal: Kairaba Ave, POB 385, Banjul; tel. 4373752; fax 4373750; Ambassador N'Diouga Ndiaye.

Sierra Leone: 67 Daniel Goddard St, POB 448, Banjul; tel. 4228206; fax 4229814; High Commissioner Foday Saisay.

United Kingdom: 48 Atlantic Rd, Fajara, POB 507, Banjul; tel. 4495133; fax 4496134; e-mail bhcbanjul@gamtel.gm; internet www.britishhighcommission.gov.uk/thegambia; High Commissioner Eric Jenkinson.

USA: The White House, Kairaba Ave, Fajara, PMB 19, Banjul; tel. 4392856; fax 4392475; e-mail consularbanjul@state.gov; Ambassador JOSEPH D. STAFFORD.

Judicial System

The judicial system of The Gambia is based on English Common Law and legislative enactments of the Republic's Parliament which include an Islamic Law Recognition Ordinance whereby an Islamic Court exercises jurisdiction in certain cases between, or exclusively affecting, Muslims.

The Constitution of the Second Republic guarantees the independence of the judiciary. The Supreme Court is defined as the final court of appeal. Provision is made for a special criminal court to hear and determine all cases relating to theft and misappropriation of public funds.

Supreme Court of The Gambia

Law Courts, Independence Dr., Banjul; tel. 4227383; fax 4228380. Consists of the Chief Justice and up to six other judges.

Chief Justice: STEPHEN BROBBEY.

The **Banjul Magistrates Court**, the **Kanifing Magistrates Court** and the **Divisional Courts** are courts of summary jurisdiction presided over by a magistrate or in his absence by two or more lay justices of the peace. There are resident magistrates in all divisions. The magistrates have limited civil and criminal jurisdiction, and appeal from these courts lies with the Supreme Court. **Islamic Courts** have jurisdiction in matters between, or exclusively affecting, Muslim Gambians and relating to civil status, marriage, succession, donations, testaments and guardianship. The Courts administer Islamic *Shari'a* law. A cadi, or a cadi and two assessors, preside over and constitute an Islamic Court. Assessors of the Islamic Courts are Justices of the Peace of Islamic faith. **District Tribunals** have appellate jurisdiction in cases involving customs and traditions. Each court consists of three district tribunal members, one of whom is selected as president, and other court members from the area over which it has jurisdiction.

Attorney-General: RAYMOND SOCK.

Solicitor-General: ROUGIE BAH THOMASI.

Religion

About 85% of the population are Muslims. The remainder are mainly Christians, and there are a few animists, mostly of the Diola and Karoninka ethnic groups.

ISLAM

Banjul Central Mosque: King Fahd Bun Abdul Aziz Mosque, Box Bar Rd, POB 562, Banjul; tel. 4228094; Imam Ratib Alhaji ABDOULIE M. JOBE; Dep. Imam Ratib Alhaji TAFSIR GAYE.

Supreme Islamic Council: Banjul; Chair. Alhaji BANDING DRAMMEH; Vice-Chair. Alhaji OUSMAN JAH.

CHRISTIANITY

Christian Council of The Gambia: MDI Rd, Kanifing, POB 27, Banjul; tel. 4392092; e-mail gchristianc@hotmail.com; f. 1966; seven mems (churches and other Christian bodies); Chair. Rt Rev. MICHAEL J. CLEARY (Roman Catholic Bishop of Banjul); Sec.-Gen. DANIEL ABLE-THOMAS.

The Anglican Communion

The diocese of The Gambia, which includes Senegal and Cape Verde, forms part of the Church of the Province of West Africa. The Archbishop of the Province is the Bishop of Koforidua, Ghana. There are about 1,500 adherents in The Gambia.

Bishop of The Gambia: Rt Rev. SOLOMON TILEWA JOHNSON, Bishopscourt, POB 51, Banjul; tel. 4227405; fax 4229495; e-mail anglican@qanet.gm.

The Roman Catholic Church

The Gambia comprises a single diocese (Banjul), directly responsible to the Holy See. At 31 December 2002 there were an estimated 34,400 adherents of the Roman Catholic Church in the country, equivalent to 2.1% of the population. The diocese administers a development organization (Caritas, The Gambia), and runs 63 schools and training centres. The Bishop of Banjul is the President of the Inter-territorial Catholic Bishops' Conference of The Gambia and Sierra Leone (based in Freetown, Sierra Leone).

Bishop of Banjul: Rt Rev. MICHAEL J. CLEARY, Bishop's House, POB 165, Banjul; tel. 4393437; fax 4390998; e-mail mcleary@gamtel.gm.

Protestant Churches

Abiding Word Ministries: POB 207, Serrekunda; tel. and fax 4394035; e-mail ncwc.awm@commit.gm; f. 1988; Senior Pastor Rev. FRANCIS FORBES.

Methodist Church: 1 Macoumba Jallow St, POB 288, Banjul; tel. 4227506; fax 4228510; e-mail methodist@qanet.gm; f. 1821; Chair. and Gen. Supt Rev. NORMAN A. GRIGG.

BAHÁ'Í FAITH

National Spiritual Assembly: POB 583, Banjul; tel. 4229015; e-mail alsalihi@commit.gm.

The Press

All independent publications are required to register annually with the Government and to pay a registration fee.

The Daily Observer: POB 131, Banjul; tel. 4496608; fax 4496878; e-mail info@observer.gm; internet www.observer.gm; f. 1992; daily; independent; Man. Dir BUBACARR BALOEH; Editor-in-Chief MOMODOU SANYANG.

Foroyaa (Freedom): 1 Sambou St, Churchill's Town, POB 2306, Serrekunda; tel. 4393177; fax 4393177; e-mail foroyaa@qanet.gm; 2 a week; publ. by the PDOIS; Editors HALIFA SALLAH, SAM SARR, SIDIA JATTA.

The Gambia Daily: Dept of Information, 14 Daniel Goddard St, Banjul; tel. 4225060; fax 4227230; e-mail gamna@gamtel.gm; f. 1994; govt organ; Dir of Information EBRUMA COLE; circ. 500.

The Gambia News and Report: Banjul; weekly; magazine.

The Gambian: Banjul; 3 a week; Editor NGAING THOMAS.

The Independent: next to A–Z Supermarket, Kairaba Ave, Banjul; e-mail independent@qanet.gm; f. 1999; 2 a week; independent; Dir Alhaji YORRO JALLOW; Editor-in-Chief ABDOULAYE SEY.

The Point: 2 Garba Jahumpa Rd, Fajara, Banjul; tel. 4497441; fax 4497442; e-mail point@qanet.gm; f. 1991; 3 a week; Editor-in-Chief PAP SAINE; circ. 3,000.

The Toiler: 31 OAU Blvd, POB 698, Banjul; Editor PA MODOU FALL.

The Worker: 6 Albion Place, POB 508, Banjul; publ. by the Gambia Labour Union; Editor M. M. CEESAY.

NEWS AGENCY

The Gambia News Agency (GAMNA): Dept of Information, 14 Daniel Goddard St, Banjul; tel. 4225060; fax 4227230; e-mail gamna@gamtel.gm; Dir EBRIMA COLE.

PRESS ASSOCIATION

The Gambia Press Union (GPU): 78 Mosque Rd, Serrekunda, POB 1440, Banjul; tel. and fax 4377020; fax 4497946; e-mail gpu@qanet.gm; affiliated to West African Journalists' Association; Pres. DEMBA ALI JAWO.

Publishers

National Printing and Stationery Corpn: Sankung Sillah St, Kanifing; tel. 4374403; fax 4395759; f. 1998; state-owned.

Baroueli: 73 Mosque Rd, Serrekunda, POB 976, Banjul; tel. 4392480; e-mail baroueli@qanet.gm; internet ; f. 1986; educational.

Observer Company: Bakau New Town Rd, Kanifing, PMB 131, Banjul; tel. 4496087; fax 4496878; f. 1995; indigenous languages and non-fiction.

Sunrise Publishers: POB 955, Banjul; tel. 4393538; e-mail sunrise@qanet.gm; regional history, politics and culture.

WEC International: 2351 Serrekunda, Somita Village, Western Division; tel. 4373104; fax 4373104; f. 1992.

Broadcasting and Communications

TELECOMMUNICATIONS

Africell (Gambia): Banjul; tel. 4750111; internet www.africell.gm; f. 2001; provider of mobile cellular telecommunications.

The Gambia Telecommunications Co Ltd (GAMTEL): Gamtel House, 3 Nelson Mandela St, POB 387, Banjul; tel. 4229999; fax 4228004; e-mail gen-info@gamtel.gm; internet www.gamtel.gm; f.

1984; state-owned; also operates mobile cellular telecommunications network, Gamcel; Man. Dir OMAR P. NDOW.

BROADCASTING

Radio

The Gambia Radio and Television Services (GRTS): Serrekunga Exchange Complex, Karaiba Ave, POB 307 Serrekunda; tel. 4495101; fax 4495102; e-mail bora@gamtel.gm; internet www.grts .gm; f. 1962; state-funded, non-commercial broadcaster; radio broadcasts in English, Mandinka, Wolof, Fula, Diola, Serer and Serahuli; Dir-Gen. BORA MBOGE.

Citizen FM: Banjul; independent commercial broadcaster; broadcasts news and information in English, Wolof and Mandinka; rebroadcasts selected programmes from the British Broadcasting Corpn; operations suspended in Oct. 2001; Propr BABOUCAR GAYE; News Editor EBRIMA SILLAH.

Farafenni Community Radio: Farafenni; tel. 5735527.

FM B Community Radio Station: Brikama; tel. 4483000; FM broadcaster.

Radio 1 FM: 44 Kairaba Ave, POB 2700, Serrekunda; tel. 4396076; fax 4394911; e-mail george.radio1@qanet.gm; f. 1990; private station broadcasting FM music programmes to the Greater Banjul area; Dir GEORGE CHRISTENSEN.

Radio Gambia: Mile 7, Banjul; tel. 4495101; fax 4495923; e-mail semafye@hotmail.com.

Radio Syd: POB 279, Banjul; tel. 4228170; fax 4226490; e-mail radiosyd@gamtel.gm; f. 1970; commercial station broadcasting mainly music; programmes in English, French, Wolof, Mandinka and Fula; also tourist information in Swedish; not broadcasting at present, due to antenna problems; Dir CONSTANCE WADNER ENHÖRNING; Man. BENNY HOLGERSON.

Sud FM: Buckle St, POB 64, Banjul; tel. 4222359; fax 4222394; e-mail sudfm@gamtel.gm; Man. MAMADOU HOUSSABA BA.

West Coast Radio: Manjai Kunda, POB 2687, Serrekunda; tel. 4460911; fax 4461193; e-mail info@westcoast.gm; internet www .westcoast.gm; FM broadcaster.

The Gambia also receives broadcasts from Radio Democracy for Africa (f. 1998), a division of the Voice of America, and the British Broadcasting Corpn.

Television

The Gambia Radio and Television Services (GRTS): see Radio; television broadcasts commenced 1995.

There is also a private satellite channel, Premium TV.

Finance

(cap. = capital; res = reserves; dep. = deposits; m. = million; brs = branches; amounts in dalasi)

BANKING

Central Bank

Central Bank of The Gambia: 1–2 ECOWAS Ave, Banjul; tel. 4228103; fax 4226969; e-mail centralbank.gambia@gamtel.gm; f. 1971; bank of issue; monetary authority; cap. 1.0m., res 3.0m., dep. 993.6m. (Dec. 1998); Gov. FAMARA JATTA; Gen. Man. HADDY A. SALLA.

Other Banks

Arab-Gambian Islamic Bank: 7 ECOWAS Ave, POB 1415, Banjul; tel. 4222222; fax 4223770; e-mail agib@qanet.gm; internet www.agib.gm; f. 1996; 21.1% owned by The Gambia National Insurance Co Ltd, 20.0% owned by Islamic Development Bank (Saudi Arabia); cap. and res 9.0m., total assets 116.9m. (Dec. 2001); Chair. Alhaji MARIE TAMBADOU; Man. Dir MAMOUR MALICK JAGNE; 1 br.

Continent Bank Ltd: 61 ECOWAS Ave, POB 142, Banjul; tel. 4229961; fax 4229711; e-mail continent.bank@gamtel.gm; internet www.gambianews.com/clientwebs/continentbank; f. 1990; cap. 3.6m., dep. 66.6m. (Dec. 1999); Chair. KARIM BAYZID; Man. Dir ANTHONY G. CARVALHO; 2 brs.

First International Bank Ltd: 6 OAU Blvd, POB 1997, Banjul; tel. and fax 4202000; e-mail fib@gamtel.gm; internet www.fibgm .com; f. 1999; 61.9% owned by Slok Ltd (Nigeria); cap. 27.5m., dep. 46.3m. (Dec. 2003); Chair. Dr J. O. IRUKWU; Man. Dir and CEO MODOU S. MUSA.

International Bank for Commerce (Gambia) Ltd: 11A Liberation Ave, POB 211, Banjul; tel. 4228144; fax 4229312; e-mail ibc@

qanet.gm; f. 1968; owned by Banque Mauritanienne pour le Commerce International; cap. and res 58,170m., dep. 307.0m. (Dec. 2003); Chair. MOULAY ABBASS; Man. Dir MORY GUEBA CISSÉ; 2 brs.

Standard Chartered Bank (Gambia) Ltd: 8 ECOWAS Ave, POB 259, Banjul; tel. 4228681; fax 4227714; e-mail stsik@scbgamb.mhs .compuserve.com; internet www.standardchartered.com/gm/index .html; f. 1978; 75% owned by Standard Chartered Holdings BV, Amsterdam; cap. 8.9m., res 62.8m., dep. 1,839.3m. (Dec. 2003); Chair. MOMODOU B. A. SENGHORE; 5 brs.

Trust Bank Ltd (TBL): 3–4 ECOWAS Ave, POB 1018, Banjul; tel. 4225777; fax 4225781; e-mail trust@gamtel.com; internet www .trustbank.gm; f. 1992; fmrly Meridien BIAO Bank Gambia Ltd; 30% owned by Data Bank, 25% by Social Security and Housing Finance Corpn, 10% by Boule & Co Ltd; cap. 30m., res 35m., dep. 785.7m. (Dec. 2002); Chair. KEN OFORI ATTA; Man. Dir PA MACOUMBA NJIE; 4 brs.

INSURANCE

Capital Insurance Co Ltd: 22 Anglesea St, POB 268, Banjul; tel. 4227480; fax 4229219; e-mail capinsur@gamtel.gm; f. 1985; CEO DODOU TAAL.

The Gambia National Insurance Co Ltd (GNIC): 19 Karaiba Ave, Fajara, KSMD, POB 750, Banjul; tel. 4395725; fax 4395716; e-mail info@gnic.gm; internet www.gnic.gm; f. 1974; privately owned; Chair. M. O. DRAMMEH; 3 brs.

Gamstar Insurance Co Ltd: 79 Daniel Goddard St, POB 1276, Banjul; tel. 4226021; fax 4229755; internet www.gamstarinsurance .net; f. 1991; Man. Dir BAI NDONGO FAAL.

Global Security Insurance Co. Ltd: 73A Independence Dr., POB 1400, Banjul; tel. 4223716; fax 4223715; e-mail global@gamtel.gm; f. 1996; Man. Dir KWASU DARBOE.

Great Alliance Insurance Co: 10 Nelson Mandela St, POB 1160, Banjul; tel. 4227839; fax 4229444; e-mail gaichq@qanet.gm; internet www.gaic.gm; f. 1989; Man. Dir YABOR W. FORSTER.

Londongate (Gambia) Insurance Co: 1–3 Liberation Ave, POB 602, Banjul; tel. 4201740; fax 4201742; e-mail izadi@londongate.gm; internet www.londongate.co.uk/gambia_profile.htm; f. 1999; owned by Boule & Co Ltd; Marketing Man. T. OGOH.

New Vision Insurance Co. Ltd: 3–4 Ecowas Ave, POB 239, Banjul; tel. 4223045; fax 4223040; Dir A. F. PROM.

Prime Insurance Co Ltd: 10C Nelson Mandela St, POB 277, Banjul; tel. 4222476; e-mail prime@qanet.gm; f. 1997; Exec. Dir JARREH F. M. TOURAY; Man. Dir PA ALASSAN JAGNE.

Insurance Association

Insurance Association of The Gambia (IAG): Banjul.

Trade and Industry

GOVERNMENT AGENCIES

The Gambia Divestiture Agency (GDA): 80 OAU Blvd, POB 391, Banjul; tel. 4202530; fax 4202533; e-mail gda@gda.gm; internet www.gda.gm; f. 2001; Man. Dir (vacant).

The Gambia Investment Promotion and Free Zones Agency (GIPFZA): 48 Kairaba Ave, Serrekunda, KMC, POB 757, Banjul; tel. 4377377; fax 4377379; e-mail info.gipfza@qanet.gm; internet www.gipfza.gm.

Indigenous Business Advisory Services (IBAS): POB 2502, Bakau; tel. 4496098; e-mail payibas@gamtel.gm.

National Investment Promotion Authority (NIPA): Independence Drive, Banjul; tel. 4228332; fax 4229220; f. 1994 to replace the National Investment Bd; CEO S. M. MBOGE.

DEVELOPMENT AGENCY

The Gambia Rural Development Agency (GARDA): Soma Village, Jarra West, PMB 452, Serrekunda; tel. 4496676; fax 4390095.

CHAMBER OF COMMERCE

The Gambia Chamber of Commerce and Industry (GCCI): 55 Kairaba Ave, KSMD, Serrekunda, POB 3382, Serrekunda; tel. 4378929; fax 4378936; e-mail gcci@qanet.gm; internet www .gambiachamber.gm; f. 1967 by merger; Acting CEO MAM CHERNO JALLOW.

INDUSTRIAL AND TRADE ASSOCIATIONS

Association of Gambian Entrepreneurs (AGE): POB 200, Banjul; tel. 4393494.

Gambia Produce Marketing Board (GPMB): Marina Foreshore, POB 284 Banjul; tel. 4227278; fax 4228037.

UTILITIES

A programme of rural electrification was commenced in 2004.

National Water and Electricity Co Ltd (NAWEC): POB 609, Banjul; tel. 4496430; fax 4496751; f. 1996; in 1999 control was transferred to the Bassau Development Corpn, Côte d'Ivoire, under a 15-year contract; electricity and water supply, sewerage services; Chair. Momodou A. Jeng; Man. Dir Baboucar M. Jobe.

CO-OPERATIVES

Federation of Agricultural Co-operatives: Banjul.

The Gambia Co-operative Union (GCU): Dept of Co-operatives, 14 Marina Parade, Banjul; tel. 4227507; fax 4392582; Chief Officer Bakary Sonko.

TRADE UNIONS

Agricultural Workers' Association (AWA): Banjul; Pres. Sheikh Tijan Sosseh; 247 mems.

Association of Gambian Sailors: c/o 31 OAU Blvd, POB 698, Banjul; tel. 4223080; fax 4227214.

Dock Workers' Union: Albert Market, POB 852, Banjul; tel. 4229448; fax 4225049.

The Gambia Labour Union: 6 Albion Place, POB 508, Banjul; f. 1935; Pres. B. B. Kebbeh; Gen. Sec. Mohamed Ceesay; 25,000 mems.

The Gambia National Trades Union Congress (GNTUC): Trade Union House, 31 OAU Blvd, POB 698, Banjul; Sec.-Gen. Ebrima Garba Cham.

Gambia Teachers' Union (GTU): POB 133, Banjul; tel. 4392075; fax 4392075; e-mail gtu@gamtel.gm; Pres. Omar J. Ndure.

The Gambia Workers' Confederation: Trade Union House, 72 OAU Blvd, POB 698, Banjul; tel. and fax 4222754; e-mail gambiawc@hotmail.com; f. 1958 as The Gambia Workers' Union, present name adopted in 1985; Sec.-Gen. Pa Momodou Faal; 30,000 mems (2001).

Transport

The Gambia Public Transport Corpn: Factory St, Kanifing Housing Estate, POB 801, Kanifing; tel. 4392230; fax 4392454; f. 1975; operates road transport and ferry services; Man. Dir Bakary Huma.

RAILWAYS

There are no railways in The Gambia.

ROADS

In 1999 there were an estimated 2,700 km of roads in The Gambia, of which 850 km were main roads, and 520 km were secondary roads. In that year only about 35% of the road network was paved. Some roads are impassable in the rainy season. The expansion and upgrading of the road network is planned, as part of the Jammeh administration's programme to improve The Gambia's transport infrastructure. Among intended schemes is the construction of a motorway along the coast, with the aid of a loan of US $8.5m. from Kuwait. In early 1999 Taiwan agreed to provide $6m. for road construction programmes, and in early 2000 work began on the construction of a dual carriageway between Serrekunda, Mandina and Ba, supported by funds from the Islamic Development Fund and the Organization of the Petroleum Exporting Counties. In 2004 construction was under way, or about to commence, on a number of road projects.

SHIPPING

The River Gambia is well suited to navigation. A weekly river service is maintained between Banjul and Basse, 390 km above Banjul, and a ferry connects Banjul with Barra. Small ocean-going vessels can reach Kaur, 190 km above Banjul, throughout the year. Facilities at the port of Banjul were modernized and expanded during the mid-1990s, with the aim of enhancing The Gambia's potential as a transit point for regional trade. In 1999 three advanced storage warehouses were commissioned with total storage space of 8,550 sq m. The Gambia's merchant fleet consisted of nine vessels, totalling 2,183 grt, at 31 December 2003.

The Gambia Ports Authority: 34 Liberation Ave, POB 617, Banjul; tel. 4229940; fax 4227268; e-mail info@gamport.gm; internet www.gamport.gm; f. 1972; Man. Dir Adama M. Deen.

Gambia River Transport Co Ltd: 61 Wellington St, POB 215, Banjul; tel. 4227664; river transport of groundnuts and general cargo; Man. Dir Lamin Juwara; 200 employees.

The Gambia Shipping Agency Ltd: 1A Cotton St, POB 257, Banjul; tel. and fax 4227518; e-mail gamship@qanet.gm; f. 1984; shipping agents and forwarders; Man. Dir N. Langgaard-Sorensen; 30 employees.

Interstate Shipping Co (Gambia) Ltd: 34 Liberation Ave, POB 437, Banjul; tel. 4229388; fax 4229347; e-mail interstate@gamtel.gm; transport and storage; Man. Dir B. F. Sagnia.

Maersk Gambia Ltd: POB 1399, Bedford Place, Banjul; tel. 4224450; fax 4224025; e-mail gamtop@maersk.com; internet www2.maersksealand/thegambia; f. 1993; owned by Maersk Sealand.

CIVIL AVIATION

Banjul International Airport, at Yundum, 27 km from the capital, handled some 275,000 passengers and 3,000 metric tons of cargo in 1992. Construction of a new terminal, at a cost of some US $10m., was completed in late 1996. Facilities at Yundum have been upgraded by the US National Aeronautics and Space Administration (NASA), to enable the airport to serve as an emergency landing site for space shuttle vehicles. Upgrades were ongoing at Banjul International Airport in 2005.

Atlantic Express Airlines: Banjul; f. 2004; flights within West Africa.

The Gambia Civil Aviation Authority (GCAA): Banjul International Airport, Yundum; tel. 4472831; fax 4472190; internet www.gambia.gm/gcaa.

The Gambia International Airlines: PMB 353, Banjul; tel. 4472770; fax 4223700; e-mail info@gia.gm; internet www.gia.com; f. 1996; state-owned; sole handling agent at Banjul, sales agent; Chair. Bai Ndong Faal; Man. Dir Lamin Jabang.

Slok Air International (Gambia) Ltd: Banjul International Airport, Yundum; commenced operations in The Gambia in 2004; Man. Dir Capt. E. I. Bell-gam.

Tourism

Tourists are attracted by The Gambia's beaches and also by its abundant birdlife. A major expansion of tourism facilities was carried out in the early 1990s. Although there was a dramatic decline in tourist arrivals in the mid-1990s (owing to the political instability), the tourism sector recovered well. In 2001 some 75,212 air charter tourists visited The Gambia. This figure increased to 78,893 in 2002. In 2000 estimated earnings from tourism were D608.2m. An annual 'Roots Festival' was inaugurated in 1996, with the aim of attracting African-American visitors to The Gambia.

The Gambia Hotels' Association: c/o The Bungalow Beach Hotel, POB 2637, Serrekunda; tel. 4465288; fax 4466180; e-mail info@bbhotel.gm; Chair. Ardy Sarge.

The Gambia Tourist Authority: Kololi, POB 4085, Bakau; tel. 4462491; fax 4462487; e-mail info@gta.gm; internet www.visitthegambia.gm; f. 2001; Chair. Ardy Sarge.

GEORGIA

Introductory Survey

Location, Climate, Language, Religion, Flag, Capital

Georgia is situated in west and central Transcaucasia, on the southern foothills of the Greater Caucasus mountain range. There is a frontier with Turkey to the south-west and a western coastline on the Black Sea. The northern frontier with Russia follows the axis of the Greater Caucasus, and includes borders with the following territories of the Russian Federation, arranged from west to east: Krasnodar Krai; the Karachai-Cherkess Republic; the Kabardino-Balkar Republic; the Republic of North Osetiya (Ossetia)—Alaniya; the Republic of Ingushetiya; the Chechen (Nokchi) Republic; and the Republic of Dagestan. To the south lies Armenia, and to the south-east is Azerbaijan. Georgia includes two autonomous republics (Abkhazia and Ajaria), of which the former remained outside of central government control in early 2005; additionally, the territories of the former autonomous oblast (region) of South Ossetia (abolished in 1990) were only under partial control of the central Government at that time. The Black Sea coast and the Rion plains have a warm, humid, subtropical climate, with annual rainfall of more than 2,000 mm and average temperatures of 6°C (42°F) in January and 23°C (73° F) in July. Eastern Georgia has a more continental climate, with cold winters and hot, dry summers. The official language is Georgian, a member of the South Caucasian (Kartavelian) language group, which is written in the Georgian script. Most of the population are adherents of Christianity; the principal denomination is the Georgian Orthodox Church. Islam is professed by Ajarians, Azerbaijanis, Kurds and some others. Most Ossetians are Eastern Orthodox Christians. There are also other Christian groups, and a small number of adherents of the Jewish faith (both European and Georgian Jews). In January 2004 Parliament adopted a new national flag (proportions 100 by 147), consisting of a white field, with a centred red cross and a smaller red cross in each quarter. The capital is Tbilisi.

Recent History

A powerful kingdom in medieval times, Georgia subsequently came under periods of foreign domination, and was annexed by the Russian Empire from the 19th century, until its collapse in 1917. An independent Georgian state was established on 26 May 1918; ruled by a Menshevik Socialist Government. Although it received recognition from the Bolshevik Government of Soviet Russia in May 1920, Bolshevik troops invaded Georgia and proclaimed a Georgian Soviet Socialist Republic (SSR) on 25 February 1921. In December 1922 it was absorbed into the Transcaucasian Soviet Federative Socialist Republic (TSFSR), which, on 22 December, became a founder member of the USSR. The Georgian SSR became a full union republic in 1936, when the TSFSR was disbanded.

During the 1930s Georgians suffered persecution under the Soviet leader, Stalin (Iosif V. Dzhugashvili), himself an ethnic Georgian. The first victims had been opponents of Stalin during his time as a revolutionary leader in Georgia, but later the persecution became more indiscriminate. Most members of the Georgian leadership were dismissed after Stalin's death in 1953. There was a further purge in 1972, when Eduard Shevardnadze became First Secretary of the Communist Party of Georgia (CPG) and attempted to remove officials who had been accused of corruption. Shevardnadze remained leader of the CPG until July 1985, when he became Minister of Foreign Affairs in the Government of the USSR.

The increased freedom of expression that followed the election of Mikhail Gorbachev as the Soviet leader in 1985 allowed the formation of unofficial groups, which campaigned on linguistic, environmental and ethnic issues. Such groups were prominent in organizing demonstrations in November 1988 against russification in Georgia. In February 1989 Abkhazians renewed a campaign, begun in the 1970s, for secession of their autonomous republic (in north-western Georgia) from the Georgian SSR (see below). Counter-demonstrations were staged in the Georgian capital, Tbilisi, to demand that Georgia's territorial integrity be preserved. On the night of 8–9 April 1989 Soviet security forces attacked demonstrators in Tbilisi, who were advocating Geor-

gian independence (with Abkhazia as an integral part of the republic), killing 16 people and injuring many more. Despite the subsequent resignation of state and party officials (including the First Secretary of the CPG, Jumber Patiashvili) and the announcement of an official investigation into the deaths, anti-Soviet sentiment increased sharply in Georgia. In November the Georgian Supreme Soviet (legislature), which was dominated by CPG members, declared the supremacy of Georgian laws over all-Union (USSR) laws. In February 1990 the same body declared Georgia 'an annexed and occupied country', and in the following month the republican Constitution was amended, removing the CPG's monopoly on power. Pressure from newly established opposition parties forced the elections to the Georgian Supreme Soviet (Supreme Council—legislature), which were scheduled for 25 March, to be postponed to allow a more liberal election law to be drafted. Legislation permitting full multi-party elections was adopted in August.

Attempts to create a united front for the independence movement were unsuccessful. In early 1990, however, many of the principal political parties formed the Round Table–Free Georgia coalition, which aimed to achieve independence by parliamentary means. More radical parties, however, united in the National Forum, headed by Giorgi Chanturia, announced their intention to boycott the elections to the Supreme Soviet and, instead, elect a rival parliament, the 'National Congress'. The announcement of elections to the Congress, to be held on 30 September (thus pre-empting the elections to the Supreme Soviet, scheduled for late October), caused increased tension. However, although the elections to the National Congress took place as scheduled, only 51% of the electorate participated, and many parties did not present candidates.

In the elections to the Supreme Soviet, held on 28 October and 11 November 1990, the Round Table–Free Georgia coalition, led by Zviad Gamsakhurdia, won 155 seats in the 250-seat chamber, and 64% of the votes cast. All 14 of the political parties and coalitions involved in the election campaign, including the CPG, declared their support for Georgia's independence. The CPG won 64 seats, while the remainder were won by the Georgian Popular Front (GPF), smaller coalitions and independents. The elections were boycotted by many non-ethnic Georgians, since parties limited to one area of the country were prevented from participating.

The new Supreme Soviet convened for the first time on 14 November 1990 and elected Gamsakhurdia as its Chairman. Two symbolic gestures of independence were adopted: the territory was, henceforth, to be called the Republic of Georgia and the white, black and cornelian red-coloured flag of independent Georgia (and of the Menshevik Party of that period) was officially adopted. Tengiz Sigua, also a member of the Round Table–Free Georgia coalition, was appointed Chairman of the Council of Ministers. The new Supreme Soviet adopted several controversial laws at its first session, declaring illegal the conscription of Georgians into the Soviet armed forces. Many young men were reported to have joined nationalist paramilitary groups or were ready to join the National Guard (a de facto republican army), which the Supreme Soviet established in January 1991.

The Georgian authorities officially boycotted the all-Union referendum on the future of the USSR, held in nine other Soviet republics in March 1991, but polling stations were opened in the autonomous republic of Abkhazia, in local military barracks and in the territories of the former autonomous oblast of South Ossetia (which had been abolished in December 1990). (It was reported that in Abkhazia almost the entire non-Georgian population voted to preserve the Union, and that in the territories formerly included in South Ossetia only nine people voted against the preservation of the USSR.) On 31 March the Government conducted a referendum asking whether 'independence should be restored on the basis of the act of independence of 26 May 1918'. Of those eligible to vote, 95% participated in the referendum, 93% of whom voted for independence, according to official figures. On 9 April 1991 the Georgian Supreme Council approved a decree formally restoring Georgia's independence.

Georgia thus became the first republic to secede from the USSR. Direct elections to the newly established post of executive President, held in May, were won by Gamsakhurdia, who received 86.5% of the votes cast. Voting did not take place in Abkhazia or the South Ossetian territories.

Although Gamsakhurdia received a high level of popular support, there was considerable opposition from other politicians to what was perceived as an authoritarian style of rule. His actions during the failed Soviet coup of August 1991 were also strongly criticized, and he initially refrained from publicly condemning the conservative communist coup leaders (although the CPG was subsequently disbanded). After the coup had collapsed, Gamsakhurdia's position became tenuous. Tengiz Kitovani, the leader of the National Guard (who had been dismissed by Gamsakhurdia on 19 August, when the Soviet coup attempt began), announced that 15,000 of his men had remained loyal to him and were no longer subordinate to the President. Kitovani was joined in opposition to Gamsakhurdia by Sigua, who had resigned as Chairman of the Council of Ministers in mid-August. In September 30 opposition parties united to demand the resignation of Gamsakhurdia and organized a series of anti-Government demonstrations. When opposition supporters occupied the television station in Tbilisi, several people were killed in clashes between Kitovani's troops and those forces loyal to Gamsakhurdia.

Throughout October 1991 demonstrations continued, but the strength of Gamsakhurdia's support among the rural and working-class population, his arrests of prominent opposition leaders and imposition of a state of emergency in Tbilisi, and his effective monopoly of the republican media all weakened the position of the opposition. In December armed conflict broke out in Tbilisi, as the opposition resorted to force to oust the President, who was besieged in the parliamentary buildings. Kitovani and Jaba Ioseliani, the leader of the paramilitary *Mkhedrioni* (Horsemen) group, were joined by other opposition figures and increasing numbers of former Gamsakhurdia supporters. More than 100 people were believed to have been killed. Gamsakhurdia and some of his supporters (or 'Zviadists') fled Georgia on 6 January 1992. A few days previously the opposition had declared Gamsakhurdia deposed and formed a Military Council, led by Kitovani and Ioseliani, which appointed Tengiz Sigua as acting Chairman of the Council of Ministers. The office of President was abolished, and the functions of Head of State were to be exercised by the Chairman of the Supreme Council.

In mid-January 1992 Sigua began the formation of a new Government. An Interim Consultative Council, comprising representatives of all the major political groups, was established, in an attempt to create stability. In early March 1992 Shevardnadze returned to Georgia, and a State Council was created to replace the Military Council in legislative and executive matters. The State Council, of which Shevardnadze was designated Chairman, comprised 50 members, drawn from all the major political organizations, and included Sigua, Ioseliani and Kitovani. Shevardnadze succeeded in reconciling the various factions of the State Council, as well as the leaders of the National Guard and the *Mkhedrioni*. The loyalty of these forces was essential to Shevardnadze in suppressing repeated attempts by Gamsakhurdia and his supporters to re-establish control in early 1992. By April government troops had re-established control in the rebellious areas. In July, however, one of Georgia's deputy premiers was taken hostage by Zviadists in western Georgia. This was followed by the kidnapping of the Minister of Internal Affairs, and several other officials. In response, the State Council dispatched more than 3,000 National Guardsmen to Abkhazia, where the hostages were believed to be held, prompting armed resistance by Abkhazian militia. By August several of the hostages had been released.

Elections to the Supreme Council were held on 11 October 1992, amid intensified hostilities in Abkhazia and the threat of disruptive actions by Zviadists. In the event, however, the elections were conducted peacefully, although they were boycotted in South Ossetia, Mingrelia (south-east of Abkhazia) and parts of Abkhazia. An estimated 75% of the total electorate participated. Of the more than 30 parties and alliances contesting the elections, none succeeded in obtaining a significant representation in the 235-seat legislature. The largest number of seats (29) was won by the centrist Peace bloc, which mainly comprised former communists and intellectuals. Of greater consequence, however, was the direct election of the legislature's Chairman—effectively a presidential role—which was held simultaneously. Shevardnadze was the sole candidate for the

post, winning more than 95% of the total votes cast, thus obtaining the legitimate popular mandate that he had hitherto lacked. The Supreme Council convened for the first time in early November 1992 and adopted a decree on state power, whereby supreme executive authority was vested in Shevardnadze, in conjunction with the Council of Ministers, while the Supreme Council remained the highest legislative body. Shevardnadze was also elected Commander-in-Chief of the Georgian armed forces and Sigua was re-elected Chairman of the Council of Ministers. One of the principal aims of the new Government was to create a unified army; a National Security and Defence Council was established for this purpose in early 1993. A comprehensive programme of economic reform was also initiated.

Almost immediately, Shevardnadze was confronted by opposition from within his own administration. In response to allegations that Kitovani was plotting to overthrow him, Shevardnadze suspended the National Security and Defence Council in May 1993, also dismissing Kitovani from his post as Minister of Defence. In August the Council of Ministers tendered its resignation, following the legislature's rejection of the proposed budget. In September Shevardnadze appointed a new Council of Ministers, which was headed by Otar Patsatsia, a former CPG official. Shevardnadze himself tendered his resignation as Head of State in mid-September, in response to accusations of dictatorial methods. However, crowds blockaded the parliament building, demanding his reinstatement, and the Supreme Council rejected Shevardnadze's resignation. By late September 1993 Georgia appeared ungovernable: confronted by the growing political and economic crisis and military defeat in Abkhazia (see below), Shevardnadze's position was made more precarious by the reappearance of Gamsakhurdia and Zviadists in western Georgia. In early October the former President's forces captured the Black Sea port of Poti as well as the strategic town of Samtredia, blocking all rail traffic to Tbilisi. As the rebel forces advanced eastwards, Shevardnadze persuaded the Supreme Council to agree to Georgia's immediate membership of the Commonwealth of Independent States (CIS, see p. 189), established in December 1991 by 11 former Soviet republics. In late October 1993 Russian troops were dispatched to Georgia, and by early November the Zviadists had been entirely routed from the republic. In early January 1994 it was reported that Gamsakhurdia had committed suicide, apparently after having been surrounded by government troops in western Georgia.

Georgia's formal admittance to the CIS was delayed until early December 1993, when all of the member states finally granted their approval. Meanwhile, following the restoration of some measure of stability in the republic, Shevardnadze created his own party, the Citizens' Union of Georgia (CUG), from several existing parties.

Throughout 1994 Shevardnadze sought to curb the increasing level of organized crime in the republic; however, assassinations and other acts of political violence remained widespread, as rival paramilitary groups competed for influence. Shevardnadze's own administration was undermined by clan-based rivalries and by increasing popular opposition to the regime. New opposition parties emerged: a National Liberation Front (NLF) was established by Sigua and Kitovani with the declared aim of restoring Georgia's territorial integrity (i.e. regaining Abkhazia). In December Chanturia was assassinated. In January 1995 Kitovani led an armed convoy of some 350 NLF supporters towards Abkhazia in an apparent attempt to 'liberate' the region. The convoy was halted and disarmed by government security forces; Kitovani was arrested and the NLF was banned. Attempts to curtail the criminal activities of the numerous politico-military groups operating in Georgia culminated in May, when the leading such group, the Rescue Corps (formed on the basis of the *Mkhedrioni* in early 1994), was ordered to surrender its arms.

In August 1995 the Supreme Council adopted Georgia's new Constitution. The document provided for a strong executive presidency and a 235-member unicameral Sakartvelos Parlamenti (Parlamenti—Georgian Parliament). The Government was to be directly subordinate to the President, to whom it would act as an advisory body. The post of Prime Minister was abolished; the most senior position in the Government was henceforth to be that of the Minister of State, who was to co-ordinate the ministers' work and liaise with the President. The country (the official title of which was changed from the Republic of Georgia to Georgia) was described as 'united and undivided'; however, the territorial status of Abkhazia and Ajaria was not defined, while the incorporation of the former South Ossetian territories into various other, non-ethnically based regions, was confirmed. It was stated that, following the eventual resumption of central government control across the entire territory of Georgia, Parlamenti would be transformed into a bicameral body.

The Constitution was due to be signed at an official ceremony on 29 August 1995, but the signing was postponed until 17 October, following an assassination attempt on Shevardnadze. Igor Giorgadze, the Minister of State Security, was subsequently named by state prosecutors as the chief instigator of the plot, along with his deputy and a leading member of the Rescue Corps. The three men consequently fled abroad, and Shevardnadze announced the complete disbandment of the Rescue Corps.

A direct election to the restored post of President was held on 5 November 1995, in which Shevardnadze won almost 75% of the votes cast. His closest rival (with only 19%) was Patiashvili. The election of Parlamenti was held simultaneously with the presidential election. A mixed system of voting was employed: 150 seats were to be filled by proportional representation, while the remaining 85 deputies were to be elected by majority vote in single-member constituencies. The elections were boycotted in Abkhazia and in parts of the South Ossetian territories. Only three parties contesting the 150 proportional seats succeeded in obtaining the requisite 5% of the votes to obtain representation on this basis. Of these, Shevardnadze's CUG won the largest number of seats (90), followed by the National Democratic Party of Georgia (which had been led by Chanturia prior to his death— 31) and the All-Georgian Union of Revival, chaired by Aslan Abashidze, the regional leader of Ajaria (25 seats). Only about one-half of the single-mandate seats were filled; however, following a further two rounds of voting, all 85 deputies were elected. The CUG held a total of 107 seats, but it was supported by many of the other parties that obtained representation. Approximately 64% of the registered electorate was reported to have participated in the legislative elections.

Parlamenti convened for the first time in late November 1995 and elected as its Chairman (Speaker) Zurab Zhvania, the General Secretary of the CUG. In December Shevardnadze appointed Nikoloz Lekishvili, formerly Mayor of Tbilisi, as Minister of State. The remaining members of the Government were appointed later in the month. In January 1996, in accordance with the Constitution, a National Security Council was established as a consultative body.

Meanwhile, in late 1995 criminal proceedings commenced in Tbilisi against Kitovani, in connection with the NLF's attempted raid on Abkhazia in early 1995 (see above). In May 1996 Ioseliani was convicted of complicity in the assassination attempt against Shevardnadze in August 1995 (he was released in April 2000 and died in March 2003). In June 1996 supporters of Gamsakhurdia received lengthy prison sentences for their roles in the civil conflict of 1993. In September 1996 Kitovani was convicted on charges of establishing an illegal armed formation and was sentenced to eight years' imprisonment. (He was released in May 1999.)

In early February 1998 Shevardnadze survived a second attempt on his life. Investigations into the assassination attempt, which reportedly involved 20 Zviadists, were completed in December, although the results were not made public. In March Guram Absandze, Minister of Finance under Gamsakhurdia, was arrested in the Russian capital, Moscow, and returned to Georgia for trial. Absandze escaped from a maximum security prison in Tbilisi in October 1999, but he was recaptured, and sentenced to 17 years' imprisonment in August 2001 (although he was later pardoned). Further arrests were made in May 1999, following the discovery of a new plot to overthrow Shevardnadze. All those arrested (who included both existing and former state officials) were reported to have links with Giorgadze; one of the accused died in detention, and 10 others were sentenced to terms of imprisonment in November 2001. In July 1998 most of the Government, including the Minister of State, Lekishvili, resigned, to permit the President to carry out a major ministerial reorganization. In August the former ambassador to Russia, Vazha Lortkipanidze, was appointed the new Minister of State. In October a two-day armed insurrection by rebel troops in western Georgia ended when the Zviadist mutineers surrendered to government forces at Kutaisi. Following this incident and the subsequent escape of the rebel leaders, the Minister of State Security, Jemal Gakhokidze, resigned in late October.

In July 1999 Parlamenti approved a constitutional amendment, which increased the minimum requirement for parliamentary representation from 5% to 7% of the votes cast under the system of proportional representation. A number of blocs and alliances were formed following the announcement in August of legislative elections, to be held on 31 October. The most significant bloc, the Union for the Revival of Georgia, was chaired by Aslan Abashidze, the Chairman of the Supreme Council of the Autonomous Republic of Ajaria. The elections, held in two rounds, on 31 October and 14 November, were contested by 32 parties and blocs, with the participation of 68% of the electorate. Final results showed a resounding victory for the CUG, which obtained 130 seats (85 proportional and 45 constituency). The Union for the Revival of Georgia bloc and the Industry Will Save Georgia bloc secured 58 seats (51 proportional) and 15 seats (14 proportional), respectively. The mandate of the 12 Abkhazian deputies was extended. Despite opposition allegations of irregularities, observers from the Organization for Security and Co-operation in Europe (OSCE, see p. 314) declared the elections lawful. The new Parlamenti re-elected Zhvania as Chairman. In late November Lortkipanidze was awarded presidential powers for the settlement of conflicts in Georgia, and in the following month the President expanded the responsibilities of the Minister of State.

In the presidential election of 9 April 2000, Shevardnadze demonstrated the strength of his position against the fragmented opposition, securing 79.8% of the votes cast. Patiashvili was again second placed, with 16.7%. Electoral violations were noted by the OSCE, but the Parliamentary Assembly of the Council of Europe (see p. 199) and the Central Election Committee (CEC) reported no major infringements of voting procedure. On 11 May Parlamenti endorsed the appointment of Giorgi (Gia) Arsenishvili as Minister of State, and the council of ministers was approved three days later.

In September 2001 the Minister of Justice, Mikheil Saakashvili, resigned, apparently in response to a perceived lack of support for his anti-corruption campaign; he subsequently founded a new political party, the National Movement. In that month Shevardnadze announced his resignation from the chairmanship of the CUG. At the end of October public discontent culminated in large-scale protests in Tbilisi, after Rustavi 2, an independent television station that had been critical of the Government, was raided by security officials during a live broadcast. Suspicions of state interference in the actions of the media had already been roused, following the murder, in July, of a journalist for the station, who had been carrying out an investigation into official corruption. Zhvania, as parliamentary Chairman, urged both the Minister of State Security and the Minister of Internal Affairs to resign in order to avert further protests. However, the latter refused to comply with this request, and the popular protests intensified, with demands for further resignations, including that of Shevardnadze. Consequently, on 1 November Shevardnadze announced the dismissal of the entire Government. The Prosecutor-General, subsequently resigned, as did Zhvania, who stated that Shevardnadze no longer understood the needs of the public; he was replaced by Nino Burjanadze. On 21 December Avtandil Jorbenadze, hitherto Minister of Labour, Health and Social Welfare, was appointed as Minister of State, and the new Government was approved by Parlamenti six days later.

Following divisions within the CUG, in late May 2002 the Supreme Court ruled that the faction of the CUG that continued to support President Shevardnadze was the legitimate grouping, rather than an opposing 'reformist' faction, which had been established by Zhvania; in June Zhvania founded a new political party, the United Democrats. At municipal elections, held in early June, the CUG suffered a serious reverse, failing to win any seats on Tbilisi City Council, while the New Conservative Party, another party composed of former CUG members, won the largest number of seats nation-wide. In late June Jorbenadze was elected as the new Chairman of the CUG, which was to be restructured in advance of parliamentary elections, due to be held in late 2003.

Preparations for the parliamentary elections took place throughout 2003. From April a student-based protest organization, *Kmara* (Enough), co-ordinated anti-Government rallies to demand free and fair elections and the resignation of President Shevardnadze. In early June the country's principal opposition parties also organized demonstrations outside Parlamenti to demand the appointment of a new CEC and the replacement of the Georgian leadership. In August Zhvania and Burjanadze (the parliamentary Chairman, who had been increasingly forth-right in her criticism of Shevardnadze in recent months) announced the formation of an electoral alliance in advance of the legislative elections, the Burjanadze-Democrats bloc.

On 2 November 2003 elections were held to Parlamenti. Preliminary results indicated that the pro-presidential For a New Georgia bloc had obtained the majority of the votes cast. However, international monitors from the Council of Europe and the OSCE noted electoral irregularities, and there were widespread allegations of electoral malpractice and the falsifica-tion of results. On 4 November thousands of people assembled in Tbilisi to protest against the conduct of the elections, and Saakashvili (who claimed that his National Movement had attracted the most support in the elections) led demands for Shevardnadze's resignation. Further large-scale protest demon-strations subsequently took place in Tbilisi and elsewhere in the country. Shevardnadze warned against an escalation into civil conflict, and held talks with opposition leaders in an attempt to stabilize the situation. On 20 November the CEC announced the final results of the elections (although five members of the Committee refused to endorse the results). According to the official results, the For a New Georgia bloc had received a total of 57 seats in Parlamenti (including 38 of the 150 seats allocated by proportional representation), followed by Abishidze's Demo-cratic Union of Revival, with 39 seats (33 of a proportional basis), and the National Movement, with 36 seats (32 on a proportional basis). The Georgian Labour Party obtained 21 seats, the Burjanadze-Democrats bloc 16, the New Right bloc 15 and the Industry Will Save Georgia bloc two; 16 seats were won by independents, and repeat elections were scheduled to be held in other constituencies. The leaders of the National Movement and the Burjanadze-Democrats bloc reiterated their claims that the results were invalid, while international criticism of the conduct of the election notably obtained the support of the USA. A referendum, held concurrently with the parliamentary elec-tions, approved an eventual reduction in the number of parlia-mentary deputies to a maximum of 150. Saakashvili announced his intention to organize a peaceful protest march for 22 November, in an attempt to prevent the new legislature from convening for its opening session. On 21 November the Secre-tary of the National Security Council, Tedo Japaridze, acknow-ledged the legitimacy of criticism levelled at the conduct of the elections and proposed that new polls be scheduled once Parla-menti had convened. However, the next day some 30,000 dem-onstrators proceeded to the parliament building, precipitating what became known as the 'rose revolution'. Troops attached to the Ministry of Internal Affairs failed to prevent protesters from besieging the main parliamentary chamber, and Shevardnadze was evacuated from the building. He subsequently declared a nation-wide state of emergency. The Russian Minister of For-eign Affairs, Igor Ivanov, was dispatched to Tbilisi, and on 23 November Shevardnadze and Saakashvili attended a meeting, mediated by Ivanov, at which Shevardnadze agreed to tender his resignation, in return for guarantees of immunity from prosecution. Nino Burjanadze immediately assumed the presi-dency in an interim capacity, pending a presidential election, and the state of emergency was lifted the following day.

The Minister of State, Avtandil Jorbenadze, resigned on 25 November 2003, together with several other senior ministers. On the same day the Supreme Court annulled the results of the legislative elections for the 150 mandates allocated by propor-tional representation. (The single-member constituency man-dates, were, however, to remain valid.) On 27 November 2003 Zhvania was approved as the new Minister of State, and new appointments were made as Minister of Internal Affairs, Min-ister of Foreign Affairs, Minister of Finance and Chairman of the CEC. Although Shevardnadze's removal from power had taken place peacefully, some civil unrest followed. On 3 December a bomb exploded at the state television centre in Tbilisi, but there were no casualties. Five days later Guram Absandze was appointed as a Deputy Minister of State, with responsibility for national reconciliation.

In the presidential election, held on 4 January 2004, Mikheil Saakashvili obtained 96.3% of the votes cast, and the rate of participation by the electorate was 88.0%. On 14 January the legislature adopted a new national flag, hitherto the party flag of the National Movement. A new Prosecutor-General was appointed. On 25 January Saakashvili was inaugurated as President. Following the new President's confirmation in office, the interim Government submitted its resignation, as stipulated

by the Constitution. Saakashvili immediately announced his intention of pursuing those suspected of large-scale corruption.

In early February 2004 Parlamenti adopted several constitu-tional amendments, proposed by President Saakashvili, which provided for, *inter alia*, the reintroduction of the post of prime minister and the removal of the government by means of two consecutive legislative votes of 'no confidence'. On 17 February Parlamenti approved the composition of the new Government, headed by Zhvania as Prime Minister. The members of the Government, none of whom had served in the Shevardnadze administration, were predominantly young and western-edu-cated. In mid-March 2004 Saakashvili announced the appoint-ment of Salomé Zurabishvili, hitherto the French ambassador to Georgia, as Minister of Foreign Affairs.

Elections to fill the 150 proportional seats in Parlamenti were held on 28 March 2004. A coalition of the National Movement and the United Democrats won 67.3% of the votes cast and 135 seats (giving them a total of 152 seats of the 235 in Parlamenti, taking into account their single-member constituency man-dates). Although international observers commended the overall conduct of the elections, some violations were reported and the Government attracted criticism from the Council of Europe for its refusal to reduce the threshold for representation in Parla-menti under the proportional system from 7% of the votes to 5%. The Rightist Opposition (an alliance of Industry Will Save Georgia and the New Conservative Party) was the only other party or grouping to secure seats in the legislature on a party-list basis (with 7.5% of the votes and 15 seats—meaning that they held 23 seats overall). Abashidze, whose Democratic Union of Revival obtained 6.0% of the proportional votes, subsequently claimed that the results had been falsified. On 22 April Burja-nadze was re-elected as Chairman of Parlamenti. In May Koba Davitashvili and Zviad Dzidziguri resigned from the majority parliamentary faction to establishing a new faction, which formed the basis for the foundation of the Conservative Party of Georgia. On 10 June Zhvania's proposals for a ministerial reorganization were approved by Parlamenti. The hitherto Minister of Internal Affairs, Giorgi Baramidze, became Minister of Defence, being replaced in his former capacity by Irakli Okruashvili, the hitherto Prosecutor-General. Vano (Ivane) Merabishvili was appointed Deputy Prime Minister and Min-ister of State Security, succeeding Zurab Adeishvili, who became Prosecutor-General. Among other changes, Kakha Bendu-khidze, a prominent Georgian industrialist with major business interests in Russia was appointed as Minister of the Economy. In the same month the Republican Party of Georgia announced that it would no longer co-operate with the National Movement–United Democrats bloc, becoming an opposition party; however, this depleted the pro-presidential parliamentary majority by only four, with two of the party's deputies continuing to support the Government.

On 27 December 2004 Parlamenti approved a further reor-ganization of the cabinet of ministers: in which Okruashvili was appointed as Minister of Defence, while Baramidze became Deputy Prime Minister with responsibility for European Inte-gration; the Ministry of State Security, headed by Merabishvili, was merged with the Ministry of Internal Affairs, while Bend-ukhidze was appointed to the more senior position of State Minister, responsible for Economic Reform. Zinaida Bestaeva, an ethnic Ossetian, was approved as State Minister, responsible for Civil Integration.

On 3 February 2005 PrimeMinister Zhvania and a junior government official were discovered dead, apparently from poi-soning attributed to an accidental gas leak; President Saa-kashvili assumed the duties of the premier in an interim capacity. The hitherto Minister of Finance, Zurab Noghaideli, an associate of Zhvania, was nominated to succeed him; Nog-haideli was expected to continue the implementation of a sus-tained programme of reform. On 17 February Parlamenti approved a reshuffled cabinet of ministers. Among the principal appointments were Valeri Chechelashvili, hitherto Ambassador to Russia, as Minister of Finance, and Konstantine Kemularia, hitherto Chairman of the Supreme Court, as Deputy Prime Minister and Minister of Justice. On 23 February Parlamenti endorsed the constitutional amendments, providing for a reduc-tion in the number of parliamentary deputies, that had been approved by referendum in November 2003; the measure was to take effect from the legislative elections scheduled for 2008.

Following his return to Georgia in March 1992, Eduard Shev-ardnadze struggled to resolve the inter-ethnic tensions in sev-eral regions of Georgia that had enjoyed a nominally autonomous status during the Soviet period, which had intensified following the election of Gamsakhurdia's nationalist Government in 1990, and which led to serious armed conflict in South Ossetia and Abkhazia. Ossetia, the original inhabitants of which are an East Iranian people, was divided into two parts under Stalin, North Osetiya (Ossetia)—Alaniya falling under Russian jurisdiction as a nominally autonomous republic and South Ossetia assuming the lesser status of an autonomous oblast (region) within Georgia. At the census of 1979 ethnic Ossetians comprised 66% of the oblast's population. The long-standing Georgian animosity towards the Ossetians was exacerbated by the Ossetians' traditional pro-Russian stance. The current dispute began in 1989, when Ossetian demands for greater autonomy and eventual reunification with North Osetiya (which would entail secession from Georgia and integration into Russia) led to violent clashes between local Georgians and Ossetians. Troops of the Soviet Ministry of Internal Affairs were dispatched to South Ossetia in January 1990, but in September the South Ossetian Supreme Soviet (legislature) proclaimed South Ossetia's independence from Georgia (as the 'South Ossetian Soviet Democratic Republic') and state sovereignty within the USSR. This decision was declared unconstitutional by the Georgian Supreme Soviet, which in December revoked the region's nominally autonomous status. Following renewed violence, the Georgian legislature declared a state of emergency in Tskhinvali, the principal city in South Ossetia (by which name the Georgian authorities now referred to the entire region).

In January 1991 Soviet President Gorbachev annulled both South Ossetia's declaration of independence and the Georgian Supreme Soviet's decision of December 1990. However, violence continued throughout 1991, with the resulting displacement of many thousands of refugees, both prior and subsequent to Georgia's declaration of independence, despite a series of short-lived cease-fires. In December the South Ossetian Supreme Soviet declared a state of emergency and a general mobilization, in response to the Georgian Government's dispatch of troops to the region. In the same month the South Ossetian legislature adopted a second declaration of the region's independence, as well as a resolution in favour of its integration into Russia. The resolutions were endorsed by South Ossetians at a referendum held in January 1992. While denouncing these developments, the new administration in Tbilisi (the Military Council) none the less declared its willingness to discuss the issue. However, hostilities continued between the rival factions, compounded by the intervention of Georgian government troops. The situation was further complicated by the arrival of volunteer fighters from North Osetiya, in support of their South Ossetian neighbours.

In June 1992 negotiations between Shevardnadze and President Boris Yeltsin of Russia led to an agreement to secure a lasting cease-fire and a peaceful solution to the conflict (in which more than 400 Georgians and 1,000 Ossetians had been killed since 1989). Peace-keeping monitors (comprising Georgians, Ossetians and Russians) were deployed in South Ossetia during July, with the simultaneous withdrawal of all armed forces from the region. The return of refugees began in that month. However, no political settlement to the conflict was reached, and South Ossetia remained effectively a seceded territory; on 23 December 1993 it introduced a new Constitution, which referred to the territory as the 'Republic of South Ossetia'. (However, reports suggested that separatists had at no stage gained control over the full territorial extent of the former Autonomous Oblast, but that political control over the territory was characterised by the existence of discrete areas controlled either by supporters of the central Government in Tbilisi, or of the separatist 'Republic', a situation that continued to prevail in early 2005.) The lack of a formal settlement delayed the repatriation of refugees: in early 1994 some 11,000 South Ossetians remained in North Osetiya, while some 7,000 ethnic Georgians had yet to return to their homes. In July 1995 representatives from Georgia, Russia, North Osetiya and South Ossetia reopened talks on a political settlement, under the aegis of the OSCE. Significant progress was achieved in April 1996, when a memorandum 'on strengthening mutual trust and security measures' was initialled in Tskhinvali; it was signed in Moscow in the following month. Meetings were subsequently held between President Shevardnadze and Ludvig Chibirov, the Chairman of the South Ossetian legislature, to negotiate South Ossetia's political status. In September, however, the separatist legislature approved an amendment to its Constitution to allow the introduction of a presidential system of government. Despite the Georgian leadership's declaration that the results of any

election would be considered illegitimate, an election to the post of 'President' of South Ossetia was held on 10 November, and was won by Chibirov.

Quadripartite negotiations were held throughout 1997, and it was agreed that the policing role of peace-keeping forces deployed in South Ossetia was to be transferred to regional law-enforcement bodies. Talks held in Moscow in March confirmed the principle of Georgia's territorial integrity, while allowing a measure of self-determination for South Ossetia. In September, at a meeting between Shevardnadze and Chibirov, an agreement was signed on the return of refugees to South Ossetia, described as the main concern of the two sides. Legislative elections took place in the regions of South Ossetia controlled by separatists in May 1999; the Communist Party secured about 39% of the votes cast. The elections were not recognized by the OSCE or by the Georgian authorities. In April 2001 a referendum was held in South Ossetia, at which 69% of those who participated voted in favour of adopting amendments to the 1993 Constitution, which included the designation of both Georgian and Russian as official languages, in addition to Ossetian. The plebiscite was not recognized as legal by the Georgian Government, and it was boycotted by South Ossetia's ethnic Georgian population. In a presidential election held in November–December 2001 a Russian-based businessman, Eduard Kokoyev (Kokoiti), emerged as the victor, after a second round of voting, in which he secured 55% of the votes cast. Although Kokoyev declared himself to be willing to resume talks with the Georgian Government, he also expressed an interest in developing closer ties with Russia, particularly with North Osetiya. Kokoyev was inaugurated on 18 December; in subsequent months he oversaw a policy of granting Russian citizenship to many residents of the regions of South Ossetia under separatist control. (Some commentators suggested this might provide a pretext for an eventual augmentation of Russian involvement in the territory.) In July 2003 Kokoyev purged his Government, allegedly pre-empting an attempted coup, thus undermining both the political power and business connections of several high-ranking figures, and strengthening his own position, which had previously been regarded as tenuous. In September he appointed Igor Sanakoyev, a Russian citizen, as Prime Minister, having dismissed the incumbent Government. Kokoyev's Unity Party won a majority of seats in legislative elections held on 23 May 2004.

Both Russian and South Ossetian authorities regarded the deployment of some 300 servicemen to a key checkpoint between Russia and South Ossetia by the new Georgian regime in May 2004, as part of its efforts to curb smuggling and illegal trade, as threatening. Intermittent skirmishes ensued and on 19 August Georgian forces stormed and occupied three strategic hills near Tskhinvali, apparently in response to the activities of rebels whom it was claimed had been sabotaging a cease-fire agreement. Georgia ceded the area to peace-keeping forces, whilst seeking the greater involvement of international forces in the region. Georgia was slow to meet its obligations in demilitarizing the conflict zone (most recently agreed in November), consistently failing to meet planned deadlines, while repeated instances of kidnapping, attributed to supporters of both the South Ossetian and Georgian authorities, were reported. In late January 2005 President Saakashvili presented a peace plan to the Council of Europe that would grant South Ossetia advanced autonomy, including the right to directly-elected local self-governance; however, the separatist leadership rejected the proposals, as it had another plan presented by Saakashvili to the UN in September 2004. On 1 February 2005 a bomb was detonated near the police station in Gori, the capital of Shida Kartli Mkhare (region—which incorporated most of the former autonomous oblast); three police officers were killed by the explosion. The separatist South Ossetian authorities disclaimed all responsibility for the act, while the Georgian authorities announced that they could not rule out the involvement of foreign parties in the attack.

The cease-fire that was declared in South Ossetia in mid-1992 coincided with a resurgence of violence in the Autonomous Republic of Abkhazia. As in South Ossetia, a movement for Abkhazian secession from Georgia had been revived in 1989. Abkhazians are a predominantly Muslim (although secularized) people and their region had enjoyed virtual sovereignty within Georgia during the 1920s. In 1930 Abkhazia was made an autonomous republic and, on Stalin's orders, large numbers of western Georgians were resettled in the region. By 1989 ethnic Abkhazians comprised only 18% of the area's population, and

Georgians constituted the largest ethnic group (46%). The Georgian Government repeatedly rejected Abkhazian secessionist demands on these demographic grounds. The movement for Abkhazian independence was also fiercely resisted by the local Georgian population. In July 1989 there were violent clashes between ethnic Georgians and Abkhazians in Sukhumi (Sukhum), the republic's capital, resulting in 14 deaths. A state of emergency was imposed throughout Abkhazia, but troops did not succeed in preventing further inter-ethnic violence.

In August 1990 the Abkhazian Supreme Soviet voted to declare independence from Georgia. This declaration was pronounced invalid by the Georgian Supreme Soviet, and ethnic Georgians in Abkhazia staged protests and began a rail blockade of Sukhumi. In late August Georgian deputies in the Abkhazian legislature succeeded in reversing the declaration of independence. Inter-ethnic unrest continued during late 1990 and in 1991. Following the overthrow of Zviad Gamsakhurdia in January 1992, there was renewed unrest in Abkhazia, as large numbers of ethnic Georgians demonstrated in support of the former President. In July the Abkhazian legislature declared Abkhazia's sovereignty as the 'Republic of Abkhazia'.

A period of violent armed conflict began in August 1992, when the Georgian Government dispatched some 3,000 members of the National Guard to the republic, allegedly in order to release senior officials who had been taken hostage by Zviadists and who were apparently being held in Abkhazia (see above). The Chairman of the Abkhazian legislature and leader of the independence campaign, Vladislav Ardzinba, retreated north with his forces. The situation was complicated by the dispatch of Russian paratroopers to the region to protect former Russian (former Soviet) military bases, and relations between Georgia and Russia became strained, amid reports of Russian complicity in supplying military assistance to the separatists. In October 1992 an Abkhazian counter-offensive resulted in separatist forces regaining control of northern Abkhazia; hostilities intensified further in the first half of 1993. None the less, a provisional peace agreement was signed in July by Georgian and Abkhazian leaders. The cease-fire held (albeit with minor violations) until mid-September, when a series of attacks by Abkhazian forces resulted in the recapture of Sukhumi after 11 days of intense fighting. Shevardnadze, who had arrived in Sukhumi at the beginning of the offensive, was forced to flee by air, under heavy bombardment. By late September almost all Georgian forces had been expelled from Abkhazia, and the region was declared 'liberated'.

Several hundred people were believed to have been killed during the fighting, and more than 200,000 people fled Abkhazia. Many thousands of the refugees were subsequently stranded, in freezing conditions, near the mountainous southeastern border region of Abkhazia, where large numbers perished. The situation in Abkhazia following the rout of the Georgian forces was reported to be close to anarchy, with atrocities allegedly being perpetrated against remaining ethnic Georgians by Abkhazians. Nevertheless, in early December 1993 Georgian and Abkhazian officials signed an eight-point 'memorandum of understanding' at UN-sponsored talks in Geneva, Switzerland. A small number of UN military personnel, part of the UN Observer Mission in Georgia (UNOMIG, see p. 76) were subsequently dispatched to Sukhumi in a peace-keeping capacity.

Outbreaks of violence continued in Abkhazia throughout 1994, despite the holding of peace talks at regular intervals. The fundamental disagreement between the Georgian and Abkhazian delegations concerned the future status of Abkhazia: Ardzinba demanded full independence (or confederal ties at the least) for Abkhazia, while the Georgian Government insisted on the preservation of Georgia's territorial integrity. However, hope for a peaceful solution was raised in May, by the declaration of a full cease-fire (only statements or memorandums had been issued up to this point). Under the accord, a contingent of some 2,500 CIS (mainly Russian) peace-keepers were deployed in June, joining the (augmented) UN observer force in Abkhazia. Nevertheless, the peace-keeping presence was unable to prevent renewed hostilities.

In November 1994 the Abkhazian legislature adopted a new Constitution, which declared the 'Republic of Abkhazia' to be a sovereign state. Ardzinba was elected to the new post of 'President'. The declaration of sovereignty was condemned by the Georgian Government, and the peace negotiations were suspended. Protests were also expressed by the USA, Russia and the UN Security Council, all of which reaffirmed their recognition of Georgia's territorial integrity. Peace talks were resumed in 1995, despite periodic outbreaks of violence in Abkhazia. In January 1996, at a summit meeting of CIS leaders in Moscow, it was agreed to implement Shevardnadze's request for economic sanctions to be imposed against Abkhazia until it consented to rejoin Georgia.

On 23 November 1996 elections to the secessionist Abkhazian legislature, the People's Assembly, were held. The UN and the OSCE severely criticized the holding of the elections, and the Georgian authorities declared the election results to be invalid. The mandate of the CIS peace-keeping forces in Abkhazia was the focus of much controversy in 1997, and members of the Abkhazian faction in Parlamenti staged a hunger strike in March, demanding their withdrawal. The peace-keepers' mandate was extended at a CIS summit meeting held later that month, and again in October, although ethnic Georgian refugees and the Tbilisi-based 'government in exile' of Abkhazia continued to demand the withdrawal of the forces. Meanwhile, violent clashes had taken place in the Kodori Gorge region of Abkhazia in July. Peace talks sponsored by the UN were subsequently held in Geneva, but no formal conclusion was reached. The UN observers' mandate, which expired on 31 July, was renewed for a further six months, and was subsequently granted successive six-monthly extensions. Russian proposals for a settlement of the conflict, which provided for substantial autonomy for Abkhazia, while retaining Georgia's territorial integrity, were welcomed by Shevardnadze, but rejected by Ardzinba, who continued to demand equal status for Abkhazia within a confederation. In August 1997, for the first time since 1992, Ardzinba visited Tbilisi, together with the Russian Minister of Foreign Affairs, Yevgenii Primakov. Talks were held with Shevardnadze and a reaffirmation of both sides' commitment to a peaceful resolution of the conflict was made. Further talks were held in the following month. In mid-November 1997 UN-sponsored talks were convened, at which it was agreed to establish a joint Co-ordinating Council, with the task of incorporating working groups to resolve the three main issues: a cessation of armed hostilities, the repatriation of refugees and the settlement of economic and social issues. Representatives of the parties to the conflict, as well as Russian, UN and European Union (EU, see p. 217) delegates, were to participate in the council.

In May 1998 there was a renewal of hostilities, following an attempt by Abkhazian troops to enter the neutral zone between Abkhazia and the remainder of Georgia in order to force ethnic Georgians out of the district of Gali. Georgian forces were put on full combat alert, and tens of thousands of ethnic Georgian refugees fled the region. Following emergency peace talks, a cease-fire was agreed and came into force on 26 May. Ardzinba subsequently imposed a state of emergency. Peace negotiations were resumed in June; Georgia's principal demand was the prompt and unconditional repatriation to Gali, in south-eastern Abkhazia, of some 35,000 ethnic Georgians who had been forced to flee. In January 1999 Ardzinba finally agreed to permit ethnic Georgian refugees to return to Gali from 1 March. However, their return was hindered by a one-month blockade of the road bridge permitting access to Abkhazia by refugees demanding, *inter alia*, that Georgia leave the CIS and that persecution of ethnic Georgian guerrillas be stopped. The Russian peacekeeping forces and UNOMIG were not permitted to pass, thus thwarting scheduled quadripartite talks due to be held in Gali. In August the Georgian National Security Council voted to extend the mandate of the CIS peace-keepers.

On 3 October 1999 Ardzinba, the sole candidate, was reelected 'President', reportedly with 99% of the votes cast; the rate of participation was 87.7%. The election was declared illegal by international observers. In a referendum held concurrently, 97% of the votes cast upheld the 1994 Constitution, proclaiming the region as an independent, democratic republic. Shortly afterwards the Abkhazian legislature unanimously passed the State Independence Act. None the less, Georgia remained determined to pursue peace talks, and in July 2000 a UN-sponsored protocol on stabilization measures was signed by Abkhazia and Georgia. However, violent incidents continued.

In mid-March 2001, at a summit meeting held in Yalta, Crimea, Ukraine, under UN auspices, Abkhazia and Georgia signed an accord renouncing the use of force. However, hostilities resumed in Abkhazia in early October, when a UN helicopter was shot down over the Kodori Gorge, killing all nine of its passengers, including a senior UNOMIG official. The UN mission was subsequently suspended, and violence in the region intensified. Abkhazian officials blamed the attack on pro-Georgian guerrillas and on dissidents from the separatist Chechen Republic within Russia; they also claimed that Georgian forces had launched earlier attacks on both Abkhazian villages and the Russian-led peace-keeping forces, in an attempt to regain control of the Kodori region, although these allegations were strongly denied by the Georgian Government. The Abkhazian authorities blamed Georgia for subsequent aerial attacks on villages in the Gorge; Georgia, in turn, attributed responsibility for the attacks to Russia, and made repeated allegations of violations of Georgian airspace by Russian aircraft in October–November. The Georgian Government dispatched troops to the region in mid-October, ostensibly to protect the ethnic Georgian population there, in what was deemed by the UN to be a violation of the cease-fire agreement of 1994. The Abkhazian authorities also interpreted the deployment of Georgian troops in the region as an act of aggression, and were reported to have appealed to Russia to help prevent full-scale civil conflict. Russia, which pledged a policy of non-interference in Georgia's internal affairs, was subsequently reported to have implemented strengthened security measures along the Georgian–Russian border.

In mid-October 2001 Parlamenti voted to request the immediate withdrawal of the CIS peace-keeping forces from Abkhazia; however, Shevardnadze argued against their removal, as no substitute force was forthcoming. In January 2002 the Georgian and Abkhazian authorities signed a protocol, according to which Georgia agreed to withdraw the troops deployed in the Kodori Gorge; the two sides signed a further protocol in early April, and later that month the Georgian Ministry of Defence announced that the withdrawal of its military forces had taken place as agreed. However, in the same month the Abkhazian authorities suspended their participation in the UN-sponsored Co-ordinating Council. Meanwhile, UNOMIG resumed its activities in February 2002, recommencing patrols of the Kodori Gorge, together with the Russian-led peace-keeping forces, in late March, following the extension of their mandate. At a CIS summit meeting, held in Almaty, Kazakhstan, at the beginning of March, Shevardnadze and the Russian President, Vladimir Putin, agreed to amend the mandate of the CIS peace-keeping forces, to satisfy Georgian demands that they withdraw to a more northerly position, undertake policing duties and include forces from countries other than Russia. Legislative elections, postponed from November 2001, which were held in Abkhazia on 2 March 2002, were deemed to be illegal by the Georgian Government, and were not recognized as valid by international organizations, including the UN and the OSCE.

On 29 July 2002 the UN Security Council adopted Resolution 1427, which called for the resumption of negotiations on Abkhazia's status within Georgia; however, no progress was made during the remainder of 2002. In late January 2003 the National Security Council ruled that Georgia would not approve a renewal of the CIS peace-keepers' mandate (which had expired at the end of December 2002) until, *inter alia*, the definition of the conflict zone was extended and a recently resumed railway service from the Russian Black Sea port of Sochi to Tbilisi, via Sukhumi, was halted; the Government objected to the operation of the railway link prior to the repatriation of refugees. In late January 2003, at a summit meeting of the CIS, Shevardnadze and Putin held talks on the CIS peace-keeping forces, and it was subsequently reported that Putin had capitulated to demands for the temporary suspension of the train service. On 30 January the UN Security Council adopted Resolution 1462, which, while welcoming the reduction in tension in the Kodori region, expressed regret at the lack of progress in reaching a political settlement on the status of Abkhazia, and warned that should an agreement on the extension of the CIS peace-keepers' mandate not be reached, the mandate of the unarmed UN monitors in Abkhazia would be reviewed. In mid-February the US Department of State issued a statement recommending the extension of the peace-keepers' mandate. Finally, on 17 February the National Security Council agreed to remove all objections to its renewal. In early March Shevardnadze and Putin held talks in Sochi. On 7 March the Presidents issued a joint statement, according to which they agreed to expedite the repatriation of displaced persons to Abkhazia, prior to the resumption of the Sochi–Sukhumi–Tbilisi railway service. In addition, they agreed to extend indefinitely the mandate of the CIS peace-keeping forces, until either Georgia or Abkhazia explicitly demanded their withdrawal.

In early June 2003 four UN observers were taken hostage for several days in the Kodori Gorge, and there were fears that unrest in the region might increase following the 'rose revolution' in November (see above). After Shevardnadze's removal from power, there were demands for the resignation of Gen. Tamaz Nadareishvili, the Chairman of the Tbilisi-based Abkhazian parliament-in-exile (comprising deputies elected to the Abkhazian parliament in 1991), who was accused of corruption. Nadareishvili eventually resigned in mid-January 2004, and was replaced by Temur Mzhavia, a member of President Mikheil Saakashvili's National Movement, in mid-March. (Nadareishvili died in August.)

An internationally unrecognized presidential election took place on 3 October in which former Prime Minister Raul Khadzhimba, the candidate endorsed by Ardzinba and supported by Russia, was initially declared the winner. However, following the processing of disputed results from the Gali region, Khadzhimba's rival Sergei Bagapsh (the head of the Chernomorenergo energy company) was ultimately judged to have received the most votes, by a narrow margin. Khadzhimba disputed this result, demanding the annulment of the ballot. (On 13 November the Georgian Ministry of Foreign Affairs issued a formal statement demanding that Russia 'refrain from interfering in the internal affairs of an autonomous republic within a foreign state'. In early December Russia suspended the rail link with the region, which had only been resumed from September, on the basis of security concerns.) Following protest demonstrations by supporters of both candidates, an agreement was reached on 6 December, under the mediation of Russian officials, whereby the two candidates would participate jointly in a new election, with Bagapsh to contest the presidency, with Khadzhimba as his vice president, and with the powers of the latter role to be augmented by constitutional amendment. In the repeat election held on 12 January 2005 Sergei Bagapsh was elected as President with some 90% of the votes cast; following his inauguration in February one month later, he nominated Aleksandr Ankvab, a close ally of Bagapsh, as Prime Minister. Ankvab survived an assassination attempt in late February, which was officially attributed to unknown criminal groups. In spite of Russia's apparent preference for Khadzhimba's presidential candidacy, Bagapsh also demonstrated continuity on the territory's policy of seeking a strategic union with Russia. In February 2005 Saakashvili appointed Irakli Alasania, the head of the Tbilisi-based Abkhazian parliament-in-exile, as special envoy for negotiations with the Abkhaz authorities; however, the authorities refused to conduct talks with him on the basis that they did not recognize his official title as legitimate. Meanwhile, in late January the UN Security Council voted to extend the mandate of its observer force in Abkhazia for a further six months.

The Autonomous Republic of Ajaria initially proved to be the least troubled of Georgia's three autonomous territories. Despite being of ethnic Georgian origin, the Ajars, whose autonomous status was the result of a Soviet-Turkish Treaty of Friendship (1921), retained a sense of separate identity, owing to their adherence to Islam (although in a highly secularized form). Tensions between Muslims and Christians increased in 1991, after the Georgian Supreme Soviet ruled as unconstitutional a law relating to elections to the Ajar Supreme Soviet, which restricted nominations for the forthcoming elections to permanent residents of Ajaria. In April there were prolonged demonstrations in protest against proposals to abolish Ajar autonomy and against the perceived 'Christianization' of the Muslim population. Ajaria remained calm from the latter half of 1991. In February 1993, however, there were reports of provocations against Russian troops in Ajaria by armed Ajar groups.

Elections to the Supreme Council (legislature) of Ajaria were held in September 1996, and Aslan Abashidze was re-elected Chairman of the Ajarian Supreme Council (regional leader). In December the deployment of armoured vehicles, allegedly from Russian military units, on the streets of Batumi, the republic's capital, led to tension between the Georgian authorities and the leadership of Ajaria; Abashidze denied reports that a state of emergency had been declared, and announced that the military units were carrying out deployment exercises.

In November 2001 Abashidze stood as the only candidate in a direct election to the new post of Head of the Republic, which replaced that of Chairman of the Ajarian Supreme Council. In the same month he was appointed as President Shevardnadze's personal representative for conflict resolution in Abkhazia. In early December Ajaria's new bicameral legislature (composed of the Council of the Republic and the Senate), held its inaugural session, following the implementation of amendments to the region's Constitution, which had been agreed in July.

Following the disputed Georgian legislative elections of early November 2003 (see above), Abashidze announced the dispatch of hundreds of supporters to Tbilisi, in an attempt to prevent the overthrow of Shevardnadze's regime. (According to the official results of the national elections, which were declared invalid on 25 November, Abashidze's Democratic Union of Revival had been the second-placed party.) On 8 November the regional legislature, meeting in emergency session, designated Abashidze President of the Republic (in the English version of its Constitution), as well as supreme commander of the republic's armed forces, and awarded him the rank of brigadier-general. In response to Shevardnadze's resignation on 23 November, Abashidze declared an immediate state of emergency in Ajaria. He subsequently pledged to boycott the national presidential election due to be held in early January 2004, condemning it as unconstitutional, and announcing that polling stations in Ajaria would not open. In the event, following US pressure, the region did participate in the election, but the state of emergency, which had been lifted the day before the election took place, was swiftly reimposed, prompting criticism from the Georgian Government. Meanwhile, a number of opposition movements (in particular, Our Ajaria and a regional branch of the student organization *Kmara*) had became active in the region, with the clear aim of replicating the peaceful transfer of power that had taken place within the central Government, amid reports of their repression by the local authorities.

Further tensions between the Ajarian leader and the central Government emerged in mid-March 2004. On 13 March the Georgian Minister of Finance, Zurab Noghaideli, was briefly detained by the Ajarian security services while visiting Batumi, and the following day the recently elected Georgian President, Mikheil Saakashvili, was prevented from entering the region. He subsequently issued an ultimatum, demanding that Ajaria: allow members of the central Government freedom of movement within Ajaria; ensure that the national parliamentary elections, due to take place on 28 March, were conducted freely and fairly in the region; disarm all illegal armed formations; and cede to the central Government supervision of finance and communications (including borders and customs controls). Wide-ranging economic sanctions were subsequently imposed on the region. As the situation threatened to escalate into armed conflict, Russia warned the Georgian Government against the use of force. Following Russian mediation, talks between Saakashvili and Abashidze took place in Batumi on 18 March, at which Abashidze agreed to permit free campaigning for the national legislative elections, in return for a pledge by the Georgian President to remove the economic blockade. Abashidze gave assurances that a state of emergency, imposed at the beginning of the crisis, would be lifted once Georgian troops, deployed along the border between Ajaria and the rest of the country, had been withdrawn.

However, tensions subsequently escalated on 2 May 2004, when Abashidze ordered the destruction of bridges linking Ajaria with neighbouring regions of Georgia, following military manoeuvres by government troops close to the border, despite assurances by Saakashvili that the Government did not intend to take military action against the region. Saakashvili immediately threatened to dismiss Abashidze and schedule new elections in the region, unless the Ajarian leader disarmed his security forces and agreed to comply with the 'framework of the Georgian Constitution' within a period of 10 days. Large-scale public demonstrations against Abashidze ensued, with security forces refusing to suppress them. Following discussions with the Chairman of the Security Council of the Russian Federation (and former Minister of Foreign Affairs), Igor Ivanov, on 5 May Abashidze resigned from office and departed for Russia, under a guarantee of immunity from prosecution. Saakashvili immediately imposed presidential rule on the region and on 6 May Parlamenti voted to approve the President's authority to dismiss the Parliament and the Government of the Autonomous Republic of Ajaria and to schedule new elections. The Ajarian Supreme Council also voted to abolish the post of Head of the Republic, scheduled new parliamentary elections and dissolved itself. Immunity from prosecution was extended to armed groups which surrendered their weapons within seven days. Levan Varshalomidze was appointed as the head of an interim council to rule the region. On 20 June elections to the new republican unicameral legislature, the Supreme Council, took place, although they were regarded as having fallen short of democratic standards. The Saakashvili—Victorious Ajaria party received some 75% of the votes cast and 28 of the 30 seats in the council; the Republican Party won the remaining two seats. On 1 July Parlamenti approved legislation on the status of the Ajarian Autonomous Republic, whereby the President of Georgia would be empowered to dismiss the Ajarian Government, dissolve the parliament and annul legislation; the legislation also prescribed which ministries the Ajarian Government should comprise, specifically excluding those of security and defence. Mikheil Makharadze was elected Chairman of the newly elected Supreme Council; Levan Varshalomidze was the sole candidate for Chairman of the Government. Abashidze's personal fortune and estate was confiscated by the authorities on the basis of having been illegally acquired. In January 2005 the Parliamentary Assembly of the Council of Europe issued a resolution which commended the peaceful reintegration of Ajaria but declared the region to be an inadequate model of autonomy, on the basis that the leader of the republic should be directly elected (rather than selected by the President of Georgia for the approval of the Ajarian parliament). Varshalomidze was subsequently accused of nepotism and failing to remove from office several officials remaining from the Abashidze regime.

Georgia was one of only four republics of those that had constituted the USSR not to join the CIS at its formation in December 1991. However, as civil and separatist conflicts threatened to destroy the country, Shevardnadze was forced to reverse official policy on the CIS, and in late 1993 the republic was admitted to that body, including its collective security system. In May 1999, however, Georgia failed to renew its adherence to the Collective Security Treaty. Georgia's relations with Russia were strained by developments in secessionist Abkhazia in 1992–93 and by Georgian accusations of Russian support for the separatists. However, in February 1994 Georgia and Russia signed a 10-year treaty of friendship and co-operation, which provided, *inter alia*, for the establishment of Russian military bases in Georgia. In 1996 President Shevardnadze and the Georgian legislature threatened to close the military bases, unless Russia adopted a firmer stance against the separatists in South Ossetia and Abkhazia. In July 1998 Georgia assumed control of its maritime borders, following the withdrawal of Russian maritime patrols. A 150-km section of the state land border with Turkey was transferred from Russian to Georgian military control in December. In May 2000 representatives of Bulgaria, Georgia, Romania, Russia, Turkey and Ukraine agreed to establish an international naval unit, Blackseafor.

The lifting of customs and travel restrictions on the Russian–Abkhazian border in September 1999 angered Georgia, and further tension occurred later in the year, owing to the renewed conflict in the Chechen Republic. Georgia denied allegations that it was harbouring Chechen soldiers and selling arms to the breakaway republic. Shevardnadze consistently declined Russian requests for Russian and Georgian troops to patrol jointly the Georgian border with Dagestan and confirmed his opposition to the use of existing Russian bases in Georgia to initiate attacks on Chechnya. In August 2000, following an accidental bomb attack by Russia on the border with Chechnya, it was agreed that all Russian border guards deployed in Abkhazia and Ajaria would be withdrawn by the beginning of November. Furthermore, in November it was agreed that two of the four Russian military bases on Georgian territory would be closed by mid-2001 (the bases were eventually closed in November of that year). Negotiations on the closure of the two remaining bases were ongoing.

In 2000 there were violent disturbances in the Pankisi Gorge, close to the Chechen border, which was inhabited by both ethnic Chechens and Chechen refugees. There were repeated kidnappings. Despite this, in December Shevardnadze reiterated Georgia's refusal to carry out joint operations in the area with Russian troops. Russia's decision to implement a full visa regime for Georgian citizens entering its territory from January 2001 caused further antagonism between the two countries, particularly since citizens of the separatist republics in Abkhazia and South Ossetia were to be exempt from the requirement. In January 2002 Georgian security forces launched a campaign to reassert government authority and restore order to the Pankisi region, prompting speculation that the operation had been undertaken in an attempt to forestall direct military intervention by Russia. At the end of January Georgia's Deputy Minister of State Security was shot and killed in the Pankisi

Gorge, and four police-officers were taken hostage in the Gorge in February, prompting élite government security forces to be dispatched to the region; the hostages were released after three days. In the same month the US Chargé d'affaires in Georgia announced that international Islamist militants were believed to have established bases in the Pankisi Gorge, a claim that the Georgian authorities appeared unable to refute. At the end of February 2002 the USA announced that it was to implement a military-training programme in Georgia, in order to equip the armed forces for operations in the Pankisi Gorge; the Georgia Train and Equip programme was officially inaugurated in late May.

Relations between Georgia and Russia deteriorated later in 2002. In late August Georgia accused Russia of perpetrating an act of aggression, and announced its preparedness to make use of 'all possible means' to repel subsequent attacks, when the aerial bombardment of the Pankisi Gorge by unmarked aircraft led to at least one death; Russia denied responsibility for the attack. Some 1,000 Georgian troops consequently attempted to impose control over the region. In September Russian President Vladimir Putin wrote to the UN Secretary-General, warning that unless the Georgian Government was prepared to take direct action to eliminate the Chechen rebels alleged to be operating from its territory, Russia would take unilateral action to counteract the perceived terrorist threat. In early October Georgia extradited five suspected Chechen militants to Russia, although this prompted demonstrations by Chechen refugees living in the Pankisi region. Relations with Russia subsequently improved when, on 6 October, at a CIS summit meeting held in Chişinău, Moldova, Presidents Shevardnadze and Putin reached an agreement, according to which the two countries were to resume joint patrols of their common border, and seek to resolve border issues by diplomatic means.

In February 2004 the recently inaugurated President of Georgia, Mikheil Saakashvili, attended talks with President Putin in Moscow, where progress was made towards the planned signature of a framework agreement on issues of significance for the two countries, including energy, the Abkhazian conflict and co-operation in efforts to combat terrorism. However, consultations on such a treaty proved difficult and protracted, especially with regard to the closure of the two remaining Russian military bases on Georgian territory. In December Russia vetoed the renewal of the mandate for OSCE observer mission on the Russian–Georgian border, on the basis that the mandate was fulfilled. However, Georgia continued to insist upon the importance of international representation on the border, requesting in March 2005 that the EU consider such a mission. Following the repeated failure of Russia to agree to a deadline for the closure of the military bases, on 10 March Parlamenti adopted a resolution instructing the Government to take measures against the Russian military bases stationed in Georgia if an agreement over a reasonable time-frame for their withdrawal was not reached by 15 May. The date stipulated by Parlamenti for the complete withdrawal of the Russian bases was 1 January 2006. (The Russian authorities subsequently stated that the bases could be closed over a period of four years, rather than 14 years, as they had initially proposed). Another obstacle to improved relations between the two countries was the Russian demand that Georgia formally commit not to host military bases from any third country on its territory.

Relations with the USA had been increasing in significance even before Shevardnadze's removal from power in late 2003. The USA openly condemned the conduct of the parliamentary elections of November 2003, and the US Secretary of State subsequently attended US-educated Mikheil Saakashvili's inauguration as President in January 2004. In February Saakashvili visited Washington, DC, where he attended talks with US President George W. Bush. (In December 2004 the US allocated US $40m. for a Sustainment and Stability Operation Programme with the Georgian armed forces, to consolidate the previous US-funded Train and Equip Programme, which ended in 2004.)

In January 2005 President Saakashvili visited the newly inaugurated President Viktor Yushchenko in Ukraine (see chapter on Ukraine), signing an agreement known as the 'Carpathian Declaration', which referred to the events that had led to both leaders coming to power as marking a 'new wave of the liberation of Europe, that would lead to the final victory of freedom and democracy on the European continent'. In March Saakashvili signed two declarations on democratic values and secessionist conflicts with President Vladimir Voronin in Mol-

dova, immediately prior to the holding of legislative elections; the two heads of state emphasized that their co-operation was not directed against Russia. International observers queried whether the resurgence of co-operation between these countries heralded the revival of the GUUAM grouping of countries (Georgia, Ukraine, Uzbekistan, Azerbaijan and Moldova), which had been largely inactive for some years.

In April 1996 Georgia (together with Armenia and Azerbaijan), signed an agreement on partnership and co-operation with the EU, and in January 1999 it joined the Council of Europe. Concerns expressed within a resolution passed in January 2005 by the Parliamentary Assembly of the Council of Europe reiterated that the country did not yet have 'an effective system of checks and balances' to limit the strong presidential powers. In March 2005 the European Commission recommended a significant intensification of relations with Georgia under its European Neighbourhood Policy, in which Georgia was included in June 2004. In November 2002 Georgia formally applied for membership of the North Atlantic Treaty Organization (NATO, see p. 301). In October 2004 NATO approved a two-year Individual Partnership Action Plan with Georgia, the intention of which was to enhance dialogue and consultation between the parties. In March 2005 the Georgian authorities signed a transit agreement with NATO whereby NATO troops, equipment and hardware were authorized to transit the country; this agreement was related to the International Security Assistance Force in Afghanistan.

Government

Under the Constitution of August 1995, the President of Georgia is Head of State and the head of the executive, and also Commander-in-Chief of the Armed Forces. The President is directly elected for a five-year term (and may not hold office for more than two consecutive terms). The Government is accountable to the President, to whom it acts as an advisory body. Following the adoption of constitutional amendments in February 2004, the Government is headed by the Prime Minister (rather than the Minister of State). The supreme legislative body is the unicameral, 235-member Sakartvelos Parlamenti (Georgian Parliament), which is directly elected for four years. (The Constitution provides for a future bicameral Parliament, comprising a Council of the Republic and a Senate, following the eventual restoration of Georgia's territorial integrity.) Georgia contains two nominally autonomous territories: the Autonomous Republic of Ajaria; and Abkhazia. The status of Abkhazia and the former autonomous oblast (region) of South Ossetia were both disputed. Those parts of the country under central government control are divided into nine mkharebi (regions—singular mkhare) headed by trustees (governors) appointed by the President, and the city of Tbilisi, headed by a mayor, also appointed by the President. (Most of the disputed territory of South Ossetia, or Tskhinvali, is officially included in Shida Kartli Mkhare, although some parts of the former autonomous oblast are incorporated into other mkharebi.) A second tier of local government comprises seven cities of special status and 60 districts (raions), and a third tier comprises a total of 966 villages and settlements.

Defence

One of the principal objectives of the Government following independence in 1991 was to create a unified army from the various existing paramilitary and other groups. A National Security Council (headed by the President of Georgia) was established in early 1996 as a consultative body co-ordinating issues related to defence and security. In August 2004 the country's total armed forces numbered some 17,700: an army of 8,620, a navy of 2,000, an air force of 1,350, and some 5,800 in centrally controlled units. The militia of 6,300 troops controlled by the Ministry of Internal Affairs was incorporated into the armed forces and restructured from January 2005, and 1,400 officers were dismissed from the armed forces, as part of a drastic restructuring process. There was also a border guard of 5,400. There were an estimated 3,000 Russian troops based in Georgia. Military service was extended from 12 months to 18 months from April 2005 until January 2008. In March 1994 Georgia joined NATO's 'Partnership for Peace' (see p. 303) programme of military co-operation. The new Government under Mikheil Saakashvili planned to implement far-reaching military reform, according to which the armed forces would be reduced in size and expenditure would increase, in conformity with NATO guide-lines. However, several instances of mutiny and desertion occurred in 2004 as a result of poor conditions.

There was strong criticism of fraud and corruption within the forces and the internal misuse of defence funds, and the leadership of the General Staff of the armed forces was also dismissed in February 2005. In 2002 spending on defence amounted to 47.9m. lari (equivalent to 0.6% of GDP). The 2004 budget allocated some 75m. lari to defence. In March 2005 some 550 Georgian troops were deployed to Iraq, in addition to 300 troops already serving in the country, guarding UN facilities.

Economic Affairs

In 2003, according to estimates by the World Bank, Georgia's gross national income (GNI), measured at average 2001–03 prices, was US $3,887m., equivalent to $830 per head (or $2,540 per head on an international purchasing-power parity basis). During 1990–2003, it was estimated, the population decreased by an average of 0.5% per year, while gross domestic product (GDP) per head decreased, in real terms, by an annual average of 6.0%. Overall GDP decreased, in real terms, by an average of 4.7% annually during 1990–2003. Real GDP increased by 5.5% in 2002 and by 8.6% in 2003.

Agriculture contributed an estimated 20.3% of GDP in 2003, and the sector (including hunting, forestry and fishing) provided 54.9% of employment in that year. Georgia's exceedingly favourable climate allows the cultivation of subtropical crops, such as tea and oranges. Other fruit (including wine grapes), flowers, tobacco and grain are also cultivated. The mountain pastures are used for sheep- and goat-farming. In 2002 private farms accounted for 94% of agricultural crop harvest. Although the GDP of the agricultural sector declined dramatically from 1990, growth was recorded from 1995. During 1995–2000, according to the World Bank, agricultural GDP increased, in real terms, by an average of 1.4% per year. According to IMF figures, agricultural GDP increased by 8.2% in 2001, but declined by 1.4% in 2002. The World Bank estimated that the sector decreased by 1.4% in 2002, but average annual growth was 10.5% in 2003.

Industry contributed 20.6% of GDP in 2003, and the sector (comprising mining, manufacturing, utilities and construction) provided 8.3% of employment in the same year. The most significant parts of the sector are the agro-processing and energy industries. According to the World Bank, industrial GDP decreased, in real terms, by an annual average of 5.4% in 1995–2000. According to IMF figures, industrial GDP declined by 4.5% in 2001, but increased by 7.8% in 2002. Construction work on two international pipelines (see below) contributed to significant expansion in the construction, industrial and services sectors in the early 2000s. The World Bank estimated that the average annual growth of the sector in 2002 was 14.4% and 15.1% in 2003.

Mining and quarrying accounted for just 0.2% of employment in 2003. The principal minerals extracted are coal, petroleum and manganese ore, but reserves of high-grade manganese ore are largely depleted. There are also deposits of coal, copper, gold and silver. Substantial natural gas deposits were discovered in 1994–96.

The manufacturing sector contributed 9.2% of GDP in 2003, and it provided 4.9% of employment in that year. Although the machinery and metal-working industries, traditionally the most important parts of the sector, were in decline in the late 1990s, manufacturing GDP increased, in real terms, by an average of 7.6% per year in 1991–2000. Real manufacturing GDP increased by 3.0% each year in 1999 and 2000. According to World Bank estimates, the sector increased by average annual growth of 8.3% in 2002 and of 6.9% in 2003.

From 1993, when the prices of imported energy were raised to international market prices, there was a significant reduction in the amount of fuel imported, leading to widespread energy shortages. In 2001 hydroelectric power accounted for 79.9% of total electricity production and natural gas for 19.7% of production. However, the country's largest hydroelectric power station was located in the secessionist region of Abkhazia, and the IMF estimated that more than one-third of the power it produced was consumed without payment. Imports of fuel and energy comprised an estimated 14.4% of total imports in 2004. In April 1999 a pipeline transporting petroleum to Supsa, on Georgia's Black Sea coast, from Baku, Azerbaijan, officially entered into service. Construction work on a pipeline to carry petroleum from Baku to Ceyhan, Turkey, via Tbilisi (the BTC pipeline) commenced in April 2003, and was expected to conclude by early 2005; some 248 km of the 1,767-km pipeline were to traverse Georgia. A natural gas pipeline from Baku to Erzurum, Turkey, via Georgia (the South Caucasus Gas Pipeline Project), was also under construction, running in parallel

with much of the BTC pipeline, and scheduled for completion in 2006; Georgia was to receive 5% of the gas transported by the pipeline, as a transit fee, according to an agreement signed in October 2003. In the mean time, Georgia obtained natural gas from Russia, via Armenia. However, Georgia hoped to become less dependent on Russia for its energy requirements, by developing its own energy resources. Construction of a gas-turbine electricity generator was scheduled to commence in 2005, as was the reconstruction of several hydro-electric power plants, as part of measures intended to make the country self-sufficient in electricity.

The services sector contributed an estimated 59.1% of GDP in 2003, and engaged 36.8% of the employed labour force. Trade and transport and communications are the sector's most significant areas of activity, with telecommunications and hotels and restaurants demonstrating the greatest growth in 2000–03. According to the World Bank, the GDP of the services sector decreased, in real terms, by an annual average of 8.6% in 1995–2000. However, real sectoral GDP increased by 1.7% in 1999 and by 5.5% in 2000. According to World Bank estimates, the sector increased by an annual average of 4.9% in 2002 and of 11.5% in 2003.

In 2003 Georgia recorded a visible trade deficit of US $636.0m., and there was a deficit of $378.7m. on the current account of the balance of payments. In 2002 Russia was the principal source of imports (accounting for 16.6% of the total), followed by Turkey (12.0%); other major sources were Azerbaijan (11.0%), Ukraine and Germany. The principal market for exports in that year was Russia (accounting for 17.6% of the total), while Turkey purchased 15.5% of exports; other important purchasers were Turkmenistan, the United Kingdom and Azerbaijan. The principal exports in 2004 were iron and steel scrap, aircraft, wine and related products and ferrous metals. The principal imports in that year were crude petroleum and petroleum products, automobiles, natural gas, tubes and pipes, medicines and wheat.

In 2003 there was a budgetary deficit of 341.6m. lari (equivalent to 4.0% of GDP). At the end of 2002 Georgia's total external debt was US $1,838m., of which $1,444m. was long-term public debt. The cost of debt-servicing in that year was equivalent to 11.0% of the value of exports of goods and services. The annual rate of inflation averaged 23.9% during 1994–2002. Consumer prices increased by 5.6% in 2002 and by 4.8% in 2003. In 2003 the rate of unemployment was 11.6%, according to the IMF.

In 1992 Georgia became a member of the IMF and the World Bank, as well as joining the European Bank for Reconstruction and Development (EBRD, see p. 212). Georgia is also a member of the Organization of the Black Sea Economic Co-operation (see p. 325). In June 2000 Georgia became a full member of the World Trade Organization (WTO, see p. 357).

The collapse of the USSR in 1991 and the *de facto* secession of Abkhazia and South Ossetia adversely affected Georgia's economy, while declining tax revenues weakened the Government's ability to provide basic services and resulted in accumulating wages and pensions arrears. Economic progress was severely disrupted by the Russian financial crisis of 1998, but growth had recovered by 2001, when the IMF resumed lending to Georgia, which had been suspended since July 1999. However, the release of funds was disrupted in 2002–03, as the Government failed to comply with the IMF's recommendations. None the less, a new tax code was adopted in 2003, and Georgia was estimated to have recorded average annual GDP growth of at least 7%. Agreement was also reached on the construction of the planned Baku–Tbilisi–Erzurum natural gas pipeline, and construction work commenced on the BTC pipeline (see above). However, although the economy was likely to be stimulated in the short term by increased activity in the construction sector and transit fees, in the longer term the country would benefit from greater access to regional markets and, in particular, improved relations with Russia, which in recent years had imposed a visa regime and strict border controls. The administration of President Mikheil Saakashvili that assumed office in early 2004 announced its intention of implementing wide-ranging institutional reforms and undertaking measures to eliminate pervasive corruption. To this end, the Government negotiated international assistance of some US $1,100m. in aid pledges at a donors' meeting held in June 2004; the lending programmes of the IMF and the World Bank resumed in the same month and the 'Paris Club' of creditors restructured $161m. of the country's debt. The reform process was regarded by the IMF as having made sustained progress in 2004, in conjunction with strong economic performance. As part of the reforms, some 30,000 civil service positions were eliminated in 2004, while payment terms in the sector were reformed in an attempt to reduce corruption. The Government also implemented a financial amnesty programme for illegally acquired property and assets of former state officials; the scheme had generated some $500m. by October 2004. In 2004 revenue collection increased substantially (although difficulties remained in relation to the regulation and collection of customs duties in the separatist regions), as did state expenditure on the restructuring of the law-and-order and defence bodies. In December 2004 Parlamenti approved a new tax code, which, *inter alia*, decreased the rate of value-added tax from 20% to 18% (with effect from July 2005), and introduced a flat-rate system of personal income tax (of 12%). A one-off amnesty on undeclared tax obligations was also announced in order to promote the reduction of the informal sector. A wide-ranging privatization programme, expected to cover some 400 state enterprises and properties, was announced in mid-2004. Declared budgetary priorities for 2005 included the payment of pension arrears, the reduction of poverty and the strengthening of the armed forces. In February 2005 a two-year programme to tackle the energy crisis in the country was launched, focusing on security and diversification of supplies and improving the profitability of the sector. It was anticipated that transit revenue from the initiation of activity in the BTC pipeline would mitigate the deficit on the current account of the balance of payments in 2005 and 2006.

Education

Education is officially compulsory for nine years, between the ages of six and 14. Primary education begins at six years of age and lasts for four years. Secondary education, beginning at the age of 10, lasts for a maximum of seven years, comprising a first cycle of five years and a second cycle of two years. Free secondary education is available for the highest-achieving 30% of primary-school pupils. In 2003 25% of children of the relevant age-group were enrolled at pre-primary schools and 87.5% of those were instructed solely in Georgian. In 2000/01 primary enrolment was equivalent to 95% of the relevant age group, and in 1998/99 the comparable ratio for secondary enrolment was 73%. In 2003/04 there were 1,737 secondary day schools, with a total enrolment of 565,400 pupils. In 2003/04 86.4% of primary- and secondary-school pupils were taught in Georgian-language schools, while 5.3% were taught in Azerbaijani-language schools, 4.9% in Russian-language schools and 3.3% in Armenian-language schools. In 2003/04 153,254 students were enrolled at institutions of higher education (including universities); enrolment was equivalent to 42% of the relevant age-group in 1996/97. Government expenditure on education amounted to a total of 37.0m. lari (equivalent to 0.5% of GDP) in 2002.

Public Holidays

2005: 1 January (New Year), 7 January (Christmas), 19 January (Epiphany), 13 March (Mother's Day), 30 April–2 May (Easter), 26 May (Independence Day), 28 August (St Mary's Day, Mariamoba), 14 October (Svetitskhovloba), 23 November (St Giorgi's Day, Giorgoba).

2006: 1 January (New Year), 7 January (Christmas), 19 January (Epiphany), 13 March (Mother's Day), 22–24 April (Easter), 26 May (Independence Day), 28 August (St Mary's Day, Mariamoba), 14 October (Svetitskhovloba), 23 November (St Giorgi's Day, Giorgoba).

Weights and Measures

The metric system is in force.

Statistical Survey

Source (unless otherwise indicated): State Department for Statistics, 380085 Tbilisi, K. Gamsakhurdia 4; tel. (32) 33-14-50; fax (32) 93-89-36; e-mail info@statistics.gov.ge; internet www.statistics.ge.

Area and Population

AREA, POPULATION AND DENSITY

Area (sq km)	69,700*
Population (census results)†	
12 January 1989	5,400,841
17 January 2002‡	
Males	2,061,753
Females	2,309,782
Total	4,371,535
Population (official estimates at 1 January)§	
2001	4,634,800
2002	4,601,500
2003	4,571,100
Density (per sq km) at 1 January 2003	65.6

* 26,911 sq miles.

† Population is *de jure*. The *de facto* total at the 2002 census was 4,355,700.

‡ The former autonomous oblast (district) of South Ossetia was not included in the census of 2002, and its exclusion from official Georgian territory reduced the total land area of the country by some 200 sq km. It was estimated that there were 230,000 people living in the Autonomous Republic of Abkhazia and in South Ossetia, the regions not controlled by the central Georgian Government.

§ Including the territories not under the control of the central Government.

POPULATION BY ETHNIC ORIGIN
('000, 2002 census result)

		%
Georgian	3,661.2	83.8
Azeri	284.8	6.5
Armenian	248.9	5.7
Russian	67.7	1.5
Ossetian	38.0	0.9
Kurdish	20.8	0.5
Greek	15.2	0.3
Ukrainian	7.0	0.2
Jewish	3.6	0.1
Abkhazian	3.5	0.1
Total (incl. others)	4,371.5	100.0

PRINCIPAL TOWNS
(census of 17 January 2002, preliminary figures)

Tbilisi (capital) . .	1,081,700	Rustavi	116,400
Kutaisi	186,000	Sukhumi (Sukhum) .	112,000*
Batumi	121,800	Zugdidi	68,900

* 1 January 1994.

BIRTHS, MARRIAGES AND DEATHS
(rounded totals)

	Registered live births Number	Rate (per 1,000)	Registered marriages Number	Rate (per 1,000)	Registered deaths Number	Rate (per 1,000)
1997 . .	54,000	11.9	17,100	3.8	47,600	10.5
1998 . .	51,500	11.5	15,300	3.4	47,300	10.5
1999 . .	48,700	10.9	13,800	3.1	47,200	10.6
2000 . .	48,800	11.0	12,900	2.9	47,400	10.7
2001 . .	47,600	10.8	13,300	3.0	46,200	10.5
2002 . .	46,600	10.7	12,500	2.9	46,400	10.7

Expectation of life (WHO estimates, years at birth): 71.7 (males 68.4; females 75.0) in 2002 (Source: WHO, *World Health Report*).

EMPLOYMENT
(annual averages, '000 persons)*

	2001	2002	2003
Agriculture, hunting and forestry	989.9	988.4	994.9
Fishing	0.5	0.6	0.7
Mining and quarrying	7.3	5.2	2.8
Manufacturing	102.4	85.3	88.8
Electricity, gas and water supply	29.2	26.6	19.8
Construction	35.3	34.1	40.1
Wholesale and retail trade; repair of motor vehicles and personal and household goods	181.5	215.4	198.5
Hotels and restaurants . . .	16.0	15.1	16.6
Transport, storage and communications	83.1	78.3	76.9
Financial intermediation . . .	10.2	7.7	9.8
Real estate, renting and business activities	38.7	20.4	32.3
Public administration and defence; compulsory social security . .	105.6	108.5	91.4
Education	138.7	129.7	135.6
Health and social work . . .	85.3	63.4	49.0
Other community, social and personal service activities . .	46.5	52.0	45.2
Private households with employed persons	4.2	8.2	7.8
Extra-territorial organizations and bodies	2.0	0.3	3.5
Activities not adequately defined	1.3	—	—
Total employed	1,877.6	1,839.2	1,813.7
Unemployed	235.6	265.0	235.9
Total labour force	2,113.2	2,104.2	2,049.6
Males	1,093.5	1,109.6	1,081.5
Females	1,019.7	994.6	968.1

* Figures exclude employment in the informal sector, estimated to total about 750,000 persons at the end of 1997.

Health and Welfare

KEY INDICATORS

Total fertility rate (children per woman, 2002)	1.4
Under-5 mortality rate (per 1,000 live births, 2003) . . .	45
HIV/AIDS (% of persons aged 15–49, 2003)	<0.10
Physicians (per 1,000 head, 2002)	3.88
Hospital beds (per 1,000 head, 2001)	4.30
Health expenditure (2001): US $ per head (PPP) . . .	108
Health expenditure (2001): % of GDP	3.6
Health expenditure (2001): public (% of total)	37.8
Human Development Index (2002): ranking	97
Human Development Index (2002): value	0.739

For sources and definitions, see explanatory note on p. vi.

Agriculture

PRINCIPAL CROPS
('000 metric tons)

	2001	2002	2003
Wheat	306.5	199.7	225.4
Barley	98.9	57.5	48.3
Maize	288.6	400.1	461.9
Potatoes	422.2	415.3	425.2
Nuts	24.6	28.4	27.6
Sunflower seed	41.8	21.3	25.5
Cabbages	99.0	123.7	117.0
Tomatoes	146.5	126.7	147.8
Cucumbers and gherkins* . . .	80.0	83.0	90.0
Dry onions	31.7	30.1	29.2
Other vegetables*	44.1	42.1	46.0
Watermelons	83.9	125.1	125.2*
Oranges	60.0	33.1	55.0
Apples	66.4	64.8	86.3
Pears	27.4	19.1	35.6
Sour cherries	16.4	14.0*	15.0*
Peaches and nectarines	10.2	4.8	13.3
Plums	15.3	9.8	19.8
Grapes	150.0	90.0	200.0
Other fruit†	36.4	27.0	35.0
Tea (made)	23.0	24.0	24.5
Tobacco (leaves)	1.6	2.1	1.5

* Unofficial figure(s).
† FAO estimate(s).

Source: FAO.

LIVESTOCK
('000 head at 1 January)

	2001	2002	2003
Horses	38.6	38.6	39.0†
Cattle	1,177	1,180	1,216
Buffaloes	33	36	37
Pigs	443	445	446
Sheep	547	567	611
Goats	81	92	88
Chickens	8,495	8,899	9,201
Turkeys†	390	400	400

† FAO estimate(s).

Source: FAO.

LIVESTOCK PRODUCTS
('000 metric tons)

	2001	2002	2003
Beef and veal	47.0	49.2	50.1
Mutton and lamb	7.6	8.2	8.4
Pig meat	34.7	36.1	36.7
Poultry meat	12.8	13.2	13.4
Cows' milk	690.4	720.7	743.3
Hen eggs*	21.9	22.7	25.4

* Unofficial figures.

Source: FAO.

Fishing

(metric tons, live weight)

	2000	2001	2002
Capture	2,200	1,830	2,537
European anchovy	2,080	1,652	2,096
Aquaculture	86	80	52
Total catch	2,286	1,910	2,589

Source: FAO.

Mining

('000 metric tons, unless otherwise indicated)

	2000	2001	2002
Coal	7.3	5.0	6.0
Crude petroleum	109.5	98.8	73.9
Natural gas (million cu m) . . .	79.5	40.2	16.7
Manganese ore	63	98	103

Industry*

SELECTED PRODUCTS

('000 metric tons, unless otherwise indicated)

	2000	2001	2002
Refined sugar	35.3	n.a.	47.9
Wine ('000 hectolitres) . . .	167	198	190
Beer ('000 hectolitres) . . .	234	257	270
Vodka and liqueurs ('000 hectolitres) . . .	51	58	n.a.
Soft drinks ('000 hectolitres) . .	286	350	380
Mineral water ('000 hectolitres)	362	398	n.a.
Cigarettes (million)	296	1,615	1,800
Mineral fertilizers	100.2	39.2	83.2
Synthetic ammonia	136.2	57.9	111.3
Motor spirit (petrol)	40	n.a.	n.a.
Distillate fuel oil (diesel fuel) . .	8.8	8.6	0.9
Building bricks (million) . . .	4.7	5.7	5.9
Electric energy (million kWh) . .	7,146	n.a.	n.a.

Source: partly UN, *Industrial Commodity Statistics Yearbook*.
* Data for South Ossetia and Abkhazia are not included.

Finance

CURRENCY AND EXCHANGE RATES

Monetary Units
100 tetri = 1 lari.

Sterling, Dollar and Euro Equivalents (31 December 2004)
£1 sterling = 3.525 lari;
US $1 = 1.825 lari;
€1 = 2.486 lari;
100 lari = £28.37 = $54.79 = €40.23.

Average Exchange Rate (lari per US $)
2002   2.1957
2003   2.1457
2004   1.9166

Note: On 25 September 1995 Georgia introduced the lari, replacing interim currency coupons at the rate of 1 lari = 1,000,000 coupons. From April 1993 the National Bank of Georgia had issued coupons in various denominations, to circulate alongside (and initially at par with) the Russian (formerly Soviet) rouble. From August 1993 coupons became Georgia's sole legal tender, but their value rapidly depreciated. The transfer from coupons to the lari lasted one week, and from 2 October 1995 the lari became the only permitted currency in Georgia.

BUDGET

(million lari)*

Revenue†	2001	2002	2003
Tax revenue	782	889	1,245
Taxes on income	136	143	179
Taxes on profits	65	82	111
Value-added tax	348	405	386
Excise	87	87	110
Customs duties	55	59	84
Other taxes	91	114	123
Other current revenue	79	81	98
Total‡	862	970	1,343

Expenditure§	2000	2001	2002
General state services	100.8	172.7	218.0
Defence	28.9	36.2	48.0
Civil order and security . . .	63.9	77.7	80.4
Education	26.9	31.5	37.0
Health	20.4	33.0	39.9
Social insurance and social care	240.4	233.2	267.0
Public services	4.2	3.8	4.3
Recreation, culture, sports and religion	21.2	20.0	24.7
Fuel-energy services	25.3	9.0	16.9
Agriculture, forestry, fisheries and hunting	12.3	14.8	9.0
Mining and mineral-processing industries, construction . .	0.3	0.6	0.8
Transport and communications .	31.1	34.2	36.9
Other services related to economic activities	1.7	2.2	2.8
Other expenditures	256.5	237.7	264.0
Total	833.9	906.4	1,049.4

* Figures represent a consolidation of the State Budget (covering the central Government and local administrations) and extrabudgetary funds.
† Excluding grants received (million lari): 48 in 2001; 23 in 2002; 48 in 2003.
‡ Excluding extra-budgetary revenue (comprising the revenues of the Social Protection Fund, the Single State Employment Fund and the State Road Fund) (million lari): 173 in 2001; 165 in 2002; 254 in 2003.
§ Excluding net lending.

2003 (million lari): Current expenditure 1,453 (Wages and salaries 269, Goods and services 173, Transfers and subsidies 138, Interest 178; Extra-budgetary expenditures 341, Local government expenditures 354); Capital expenditure 70; Net lending 78; Total expenditure and net lending 1,601.

Sources: Ministry of Finance; IMF, *Georgia: First Review Under the Three-Year Arrangement Under the Poverty Reduction and Growth Facility and Request for Waiver of Performance Criterion—Staff Report* (January 2005).

INTERNATIONAL RESERVES

(US $ million at 31 December)

	2001	2002	2003
IMF special drawing rights . .	3.96	2.89	4.91
Reserve position in the IMF . .	0.01	0.01	0.01
Foreign exchange	155.40	194.64	185.79
Total	159.37	197.55	190.71

Source: IMF, *International Financial Statistics*.

MONEY SUPPLY

(million lari at 31 December)

	2001	2002	2003
Currency outside banks . . .	348.85	390.79	441.54
Demand deposits	45.33	62.01	75.32
Total money (incl. others) . .	394.23	452.84	516.92

Source: IMF, *International Financial Statistics*.

COST OF LIVING

(Consumer price index for five cities; base: 1995 = 100)

	1999	2000	2001
Food, beverages and tobacco . .	171.4	173.7	185.2
Fuel and light	305.6	373.5	394.8
Clothing (incl. footwear) . . .	168.4	168.0	169.4
Rent	129.3	136.0	140.1
All items (incl. others) . . .	184.3	191.7	200.7

2002: Food, beverages and tobacco 199.1; All items (incl. others) 211.9.
Source: ILO.

NATIONAL ACCOUNTS
(million lari at current prices)

Expenditure on the Gross Domestic Product

	2001	2002	2003
Final consumption expenditure .	6,205.1	6,921.0	7,477.8
Households	5,500.9	6,132.2	6,640.6
Non-profit institutions serving households	60.5	58.8	76.0
General government . . .	643.6	729.9	761.2
Gross capital formation	1,457.7	1,644.5	2,088.1
Gross fixed capital formation .	1,388.6	1,574.2	2,003.8
Changes in inventories . . .	69.1	70.2	84.4
Total domestic expenditure .	7,662.8	8,565.5	9,565.9
Exports of goods and services . .	1,632.6	2,137.7	2,700.4
Less Imports of goods and services	2,594.1	3,066.5	3,939.8
Statistical discrepancy	−53.4	−181.1	238.4
GDP in market prices . . .	6,647.9	7,455.6	8,564.9

Gross Domestic Product by Economic Activity

	2001	2002	2003
Agriculture, forestry and fishing	1,372.8	1,435.2	1,647.5
Mining and quarrying	37.9	49.5	79.0
Manufacturing	515.3	624.0	744.8
Electricity, gas and water supply .	256.8	311.6	314.5
Construction	259.6	379.5	538.3
Wholesale and retail trade; repair of motor vehicles, motorcycles and personal and household goods	871.0	956.2	1,138.8
Hotels and restaurants	192.1	218.6	222.9
Transport, storage and communications	911.1	1,057.4	1,193.6
Financial intermediation . . .	93.7	108.5	126.0
Real estate, renting and business activities	456.4	445.6	507.0
Public administration and defence; compulsory social security . .	245.2	295.4	307.6
Education	238.4	273.4	278.5
Health and social work	320.4	347.9	366.6
Other community, social and personal services	192.1	191.6	276.6
Private households with employed persons	11.0	9.0	8.5
Activities not adequately defined .	301.0	329.5	370.2
Sub-total	6,274.8	7,032.9	8,120.4
Less Financial intermediation services indirectly measured .	63.0	72.7	77.8
Gross value added in basic prices	6,211.8	6,960.2	8,042.6
Taxes on products	490.1	550.4	578.3
Less Subsidies on products . . .	54.1	55.0	56.1
GDP in market prices . . .	6,647.9	7,455.6	8,564.9

BALANCE OF PAYMENTS
(US $ million)

	2001	2002	2003
Exports of goods f.o.b.	496.1	601.7	830.6
Imports of goods f.o.b.	−1,045.6	−1,084.7	−1,466.6
Trade balance	−549.5	−483.0	−636.0
Exports of services	314.1	392.2	442.8
Imports of services	−236.9	−356.7	−388.6
Balance on goods and services	−472.3	−447.5	−581.8
Other income received	97.7	166.1	179.3
Other income paid	−65.4	−127.4	−145.0
Balance on goods, services and income	−440.0	−408.8	−547.5
Current transfers received . . .	246.4	222.0	210.1
Current transfers paid	−18.1	−34.6	−41.3
Current balance	−211.7	−221.3	−378.7
Capital account (net)	−5.2	18.4	19.9
Direct investment abroad . . .	0.1	−4.1	−3.8
Direct investment from abroad .	109.8	167.4	337.9
Portfolio investment assets . .	−0.1	—	—
Portfolio investment liabilities .	n.a.	n.a.	n.a.
Other investment assets . . .	−24.6	−72.8	−15.3
Other investment liabilities . .	124.5	−71.3	3.0
Net errors and omissions . . .	34.9	−6.0	−12.0
Overall balance	27.7	−189.7	−49.0

Source: IMF, *International Financial Statistics*.

External Trade

PRINCIPAL COMMODITIES
(US $ million)

Imports f.o.b.	2002	2003	2004
Crude petroleum and petroleum products . . .	88.9	104.9	186.4
Petroleum gases and other gaseous hydrocarbons . .	52.4	66.0	80.1
Tubes and pipes	n.a.	93.7	80.0
Sugar	34.5	53.0	50.8
Wheat	15.5	28.0	75.0
Medicines	46.0	62.9	78.0
Automobiles	21.6	47.0	116.6
Total (incl. others)	731.4	1,141.1	1,847.0

Exports f.o.b.	2002	2003	2004
Iron and steel scrap . . .	36.6	60.1	95.9
Ferro-alloys	15.5	26.1	42.5
Gold (unwrought or semi-manufactured)	28.6	n.a.	n.a.
Aircraft	44.5	20.3	83.7
Sugar	n.a.	34.0	34.3
Fertilizers	12.0	18.4	28.8
Copper ore	13.2	23.4	31.8
Wine and related products .	33.1	42.6	48.7
Wheat	n.a.	10.7	22.8
Mineral water	17.4	19.7	19.3
Total (incl. others)	347.8	465.3	648.8

Source: National Bank of Georgia.

PRINCIPAL TRADING PARTNERS
(US $ million)

Imports c.i.f.	2000	2001	2002
Armenia	13.5	10.4	8.5
Azerbaijan	55.4	73.2	80.1
Brazil	5.4	4.0	18.4
Bulgaria	15.5	10.6	14.3
France	10.9	18.7	15.0
Germany	50.2	63.7	57.2
Italy	17.3	25.5	34.0
Netherlands	8.0	8.9	15.0
Russia	93.6	97.6	121.3
Switzerland	22.7	14.0	18.2
Turkey	104.0	105.0	87.6
Turkmenistan	13.3	17.6	14.6
Ukraine	35.4	49.5	59.0
United Arab Emirates	10.0	8.2	6.1
United Kingdom	23.0	25.1	26.5
USA	35.7	27.8	24.8
Total (incl. others)	652.5	685.0	731.4

Exports f.o.b.	2000	2001	2002
Armenia	13.7	12.3	20.5
Azerbaijan	21.3	10.6	29.8
Germany	34.3	7.9	5.5
Iran	6.8	4.3	3.3
Italy	12.4	8.6	7.6
Kazakhstan	4.5	4.3	3.0
Russia	69.6	73.5	61.1
Switzerland	13.4	15.6	24.4
Turkey	74.8	68.7	53.9
Turkmenistan	10.6	28.9	36.7
Ukraine	11.0	11.7	12.7
United Kingdom	10.3	22.9	32.8
USA	7.3	9.5	13.5
Total (incl. others)	329.9	320.0	347.8

2004 (US $ million): *Imports:* Armenia 25.4; Azerbaijan 157.7; Germany 151.1; Italy 61.5; Russia 257.8; Turkey 202.3; Turkmenistan 32.7; Ukraine 142.4; United Kingdom 171.4; USA 111.0; Total 1,847.0. *Exports:* Armenia 54.5; Azerbaijan 25.3; Germany 15.9; Italy 11.6; Russia 104.6; Turkey 118.7; Turkmenistan 115.1; Ukraine 15.3; United Kingdom 31.6; USA 21.3; Total 648.8.

Source: National Bank of Georgia.

Transport

RAILWAYS
(traffic)

	2001	2002	2003
Passengers carried (million)	2.1	2.1	2.2
Passenger-km (million)	400.9	400.6	395.5
Freight ('000 tons)	13,209.6	14,951.5	16,280.0
Freight net ton-km (million)	4,480.6	5,074.5	5,447.8

ROAD TRAFFIC
('000 motor vehicles in use)

	2001	2002	2003
Passenger cars	247.8	252.0	255.2
Buses	22.7	24.1	25.7
Lorries and vans	47.0	45.5	42.9
Total (incl. others)	319.6	323.6	325.0

SHIPPING
Merchant Fleet
(registered at 31 December)

	2001	2002	2003
Number of vessels	201	261	303
Total displacement ('000 grt)	276.6	569.3	814.9

Source: Lloyd's Register-Fairplay, *World Fleet Statistics*.

CIVIL AVIATION
(traffic on scheduled services)

	2001	2002	2003
Passengers carried ('000)*	100	100	200
Passenger-km (million)	240.5	297.3	400.3
Total ton-km (million)	27	29	43

* Figures are rounded.

Tourism

FOREIGN TOURIST ARRIVALS

Country of residence	2000	2001	2002
CIS countries*	220,327	184,057	176,419
Germany	7,275	5,510	6,423
Turkey	84,170	57,005	56,460
USA	9,308	6,536	7,132
Total (incl. others)	387,258	302,215	298,469

* Comprising Armenia, Azerbaijan, Belarus, Kazakhstan, Kyrgyzstan, Moldova, Russia, Tajikistan, Turkmenistan, Ukraine and Uzbekistan.

Tourism receipts (US $ million): 413 in 2000; 442 in 2001; 472 in 2002.

Source: World Tourism Organization.

Communications Media

	2001	2002	2003
Telephones ('000 main lines in use)	569.0	648.5	650.5
Mobile cellular telephones ('000 subscribers)	301.3	503.6	522.3
Internet users ('000)	46.5	73.5	150.5
Personal computers (in use, '000)	143	156	n.a.
Newspapers: titles	200	175	n.a.
Newspapers: circulation	600,000	900,000	n.a.

Radio receivers ('000 in use): 3,020 in 1997.

Television receivers ('000 in use): 2,590 in 2000.

Facsimile machines: 500 in 1996.

Book production (including pamphlets): 581 titles in 1996 (834,000 copies); 697 titles in 1999.

Sources: UN, *Statistical Yearbook*; UNESCO, *Statistical Yearbook*; and International Telecommunication Union.

Education

(2002/03)

	Institutions	Students†
Pre-primary schools	1,213	73,300
General education: Day schools (primary)*	1,436	89,300
General education: Day schools (secondary)	1,694	574,700
General education: Day schools (special)	17	2,100
General education: Evening schools	27	4,700
State secondary specialized schools	85	22,618
Private secondary specialized schools	63	5,555
Vocational/technical schools	78	10,400
State higher schools (incl. universities)	26	122,223
Private higher schools (incl. universities)	154	31,465

* Including primary schools covering part of the secondary syllabus.
† Figures are rounded.

Teachers (2002/03): Total in general day schools 69,700 (excl. teachers in special schools); Total in institutes of higher education 27,357 (15,393 in public institutions, 11,964 in non-state institutions).

Adult literacy rate (UNESCO estimates): 99.5% (males 99.7%; females 99.4%) in 1995 (Source: UNESCO, *Statistical Yearbook*).

Directory

The Constitution

A new Constitution was approved by the Georgian legislature on 24 August 1995; it entered into force on 17 October. The Constitution replaced the Decree on State Power of November 1992 (which had functioned as an interim basic law). The following is a summary of the Constitution's main provisions, as subsequently amended:

GENERAL PROVISIONS

Georgia is an independent, united and undivided state, as confirmed by the referendum conducted throughout the entire territory of the country (including the Autonomous Republic of Abkhazia and the territories of the former autonomous oblast of South Ossetia) on 31 March 1991, and in accordance with the Act on the Restoration of the State Independence of Georgia of 9 April. The Georgian state is a democratic republic. Its territorial integrity and the inviolability of its state borders are confirmed by the republic's Constitution and laws.

All state power belongs to the people, who exercise this power through referendums, other forms of direct democracy, and through their elected representatives. The State recognizes and defends universally recognized human rights and freedoms. The official state language is Georgian; in Abkhazia both Georgian and Abkhazian are recognized as state languages. While the State recognizes the exceptional role played by the Georgian Orthodox Church in Georgian history, it declares the complete freedom of faith and religion as well as the independence of the Church from the State. The capital is Tbilisi.

FUNDAMENTAL HUMAN RIGHTS AND FREEDOMS

Georgian citizenship is acquired by birth and naturalization. A Georgian citizen may not concurrently be a citizen of another state. Every person is free by birth and equal before the law, irrespective of race, colour, language, sex, religion, political and other views, national, ethnic and social affiliation, origin and place of residence. Every person has the inviolable right to life, which is protected by law. No one may be subjected to torture or inhuman, cruel or humiliating treatment or punishment.

Freedom of speech, thought, conscience and faith are guaranteed. The mass media are free. Censorship is prohibited. The right to assemble publicly is guaranteed, as is the right to form public associations, including trade unions and political parties. Every citizen who has attained the age of 18 years has the right to participate in referendums and elections of state and local administrative bodies.

PARLAMENTI

Parlamenti (Sakartvelos Parlamenti, or the Georgian Parliament) is the supreme representative body, implementing legislation and determining the basis of the country's domestic and foreign policies. It controls the activities of the Government, within the limits prescribed by the Constitution, and has other powers of implementation.

Parlamenti is elected on the basis of universal, equal and direct suffrage by secret ballot, for a term of four years. It is composed of 235 members: 150 elected by proportional representation (with a minimum requirement of 7% of the votes cast to secure parliamentary representation) and 85 by majority vote in single-member constituencies. (A referendum held in November 2003, and approved by Parlamenti in February 2005, provided for a reduction in the number of deputies to a maximum of 150, of whom 100 were to be elected by proportional representation, to take effect from the legislative elections scheduled to be held in 2008.) Any citizen who has attained the age of 25 years and has the right to vote may be elected to Parlamenti. The instigation of criminal proceedings against a member of the legislature, and his/her detention or arrest, are only permitted upon approval by Parlamenti. A member of Parlamenti may not hold any position in state service or engage in entrepreneurial activities.

Parlamenti elects a Chairman and Deputy Chairmen (including one Deputy Chairman each from deputies elected in Abkhazia and Ajaria), for the length of its term of office. Members of Parlamenti may unite to form parliamentary factions. A faction must have no fewer than 10 members.

Following the creation of the appropriate conditions throughout the territory of Georgia and the formation of bodies of local self-government, Parlamenti will be composed of two chambers: the Council of the Republic and the Senate. The Council of the Republic will be composed of deputies elected according to the proportional system. The Senate will be composed of deputies elected in Abkhazia, Ajaria and other territorial units of Georgia, and five members appointed by the President of Georgia.

THE PRESIDENT OF GEORGIA AND THE GOVERNMENT

The President of Georgia is Head of State and the head of executive power. The President directs and implements domestic and foreign policy, ensures the unity and territorial integrity of the country, and supervises the activities of state bodies in accordance with the Constitution. The President is the supreme representative of Georgia in foreign relations. He/she is elected on the basis of universal, equal and direct suffrage by secret ballot, for a period of five years. The President may not be elected for more than two consecutive terms. Any citizen of Georgia who has the right to vote and who has attained the age of 35 years and lived in Georgia for no less than 15 years, is eligible to be elected President.

The President of Georgia concludes international treaties and agreements and conducts negotiations with foreign states; with the consent of Parlamenti, appoints and dismisses Georgian ambassadors and other diplomatic representatives; receives the credentials of ambassadors and other diplomatic representatives of foreign states and international organizations; with the consent of Parlamenti, appoints members of the Government and Ministers; is empowered to remove Ministers from their posts; submits to Parlamenti the draft state budget, after agreeing upon its basic content with parliamentary committees; in the event of an armed attack on Georgia, declares a state of war, and concludes peace; during war or mass disorders, when the country's territorial integrity is threatened, or in the event of a *coup d'état* or an armed uprising, an ecological catastrophe or epidemic, or in other instances when the bodies of state power cannot implement their constitutional powers normally, declares a state of emergency; with the consent of Parlamenti, has the right to halt the activities of representative bodies of self-government or territorial units (if their activities create a threat to the sovereignty and territorial integrity of the country) as well as to halt state bodies in the exercise of their constitutional powers; signs and promulgates laws; decides questions of citizenship and the granting of political asylum; grants pardons; schedules elections to Parlamenti and other representative bodies; has the right to revoke acts of subordinate executive bodies; is the Commander-in-Chief of the Armed Forces; and appoints members of the National Security Council, chairs its meetings, and appoints and dismisses military commanders.

The President enjoys immunity. During his/her period in office, he/she may not be arrested, and no criminal proceedings may be instigated against him/her. In the event that the President violates the Constitution, betrays the State or commits other crimes, Parlamenti may remove him/her from office (with the approval of the Constitutional Court or the Supreme Court).

Parlamenti appoints and dismisses a Prime Minister. Members of the Government are accountable to the President. They do not have the right to hold other posts (except party posts), to engage in entrepreneurial activities or to receive a wage or any other permanent remuneration for any other activities. Members of the Government may be removed from their posts by an edict of the President or by Parlamenti, or by two successive legislative votes expressing 'no confidence' (adopted by a two-thirds' majority in Parlamenti). Ministries perform state management in specific spheres of state and public life. Each Ministry is headed by a Minister, who independently adopts decisions on questions within his/her sphere of jurisdiction.

JUDICIAL POWER

Judicial power is independent and is implemented only by the courts. Judges are independent in their activities and are subordinate only to the Constitution and the law. Court proceedings are held in public (except for certain specified instances). The decision of the court is delivered in public. Judges enjoy immunity. It is prohibited to instigate criminal proceedings against a judge or to detain or arrest him/her, without the consent of the Chairman of the Supreme Court.

The Constitutional Court is the legal body of constitutional control. It is composed of nine judges, three of whom are appointed by the President, three elected by Parlamenti, and three appointed by the Supreme Court. The term of office of members of the Constitutional Court is 10 years.

The Supreme Court supervises legal proceedings in general courts according to the established judicial procedure and, as the court of first instance, examines cases determined by law. On the recommendation of the President of Georgia, the Chairman and judges of the Supreme Court are elected by Parlamenti for a period of at least 10 years.

The Procurator's Office is an institution of judicial power, which carries out criminal prosecution, supervises the preliminary investigation and the execution of a punishment, and supports the state prosecution. On the recommendation of the President of Georgia, the Procurator-General is appointed by Parlamenti for a term of five years. Lower-ranking procurators are appointed by the Procurator-General.

DEFENCE OF THE STATE

Georgia has armed forces to protect the independence, sovereignty and territorial integrity of the country, and also to fulfil international obligations. The President of Georgia approves the structure of the armed forces and Parlamenti ratifies their numerical strength, on the recommendation of the National Security Council. The National Security Council, which is headed by the President of Georgia, carries out military organizational development and the defence of the country.

The Government

HEAD OF STATE

President: MIKHEIL SAAKASHVILI (elected 4 January 2004; inaugurated 25 January 2004).

GOVERNMENT
(April 2005)

Prime Minister: ZURAB NOGHAIDELI.

Deputy Prime Minister and Minister of Justice: KONSTANTINE KEMULARIA.

State Minister, responsible for Relations with the European Union: GIORGI BARAMIDZE.

State Minister, responsible for Conflict Resolution: GIORGI KHAINDRAVA.

State Minister, responsible for Economic Reform: KAKHA BENDUKHIDZE.

State Minister, responsible for Civil Integration: ZINAIDA BESTAEVA.

Minister of Agriculture and Produce: MIKHEIL SVIMONISHVILI.

Minister of Culture, Protection of Monuments and Sport: GIORGI GABASHVILI.

Minister of Defence: IRAKLI OKRUASHVILI.

Minister of Economic Development: LEXO ALEKSISHVILI.

Minister of Education and Science: ALEXANDER LOMAIA.

Minister of Environmental Protection and Natural Resources: GIORGI PAPUASHVILI.

Minister of Finance: VALERI CHECHELASHVILI.

Minister of Foreign Affairs: SALOMÉ ZURABISHVILI.

Minister of Internal Affairs: IVANE MERABISHVILI.

Minister of Power Engineering: NIKOLOZ GILAURI.

Minister of Labour, Health and Social Affairs: VLADIMIR CHIPASHVILI.

Minister of Refugee Affairs: ETER ASTEMIROVA.

MINISTRIES

Office of the President: 0134 Tbilisi, Ingorovka 7; tel. (32) 99-00-70; fax (32) 99-88-87; e-mail secretariat@admin.gov.ge; internet www.president.gov.ge.

Office of the Government: 0134 Tbilisi, Ingorovka 7; tel. (32) 93-59-07; fax (32) 98-23-54.

Ministry of Agriculture and Produce: 0123 Tbilisi, Kostava 41; tel. (32) 99-62-61; fax (32) 99-94-44; e-mail ministry@maf.ge; internet www.maf.ge.

Ministry of Culture, Protection of Monuments and Sport: 0108 Tbilisi, Rustaveli 37; tel. (32) 93-22-55; fax (32) 99-90-37; e-mail info@mc.gov.ge.

Ministry of Defence: 0107 Tbilisi, Universitetis 2A; tel. (32) 98-39-30; fax (32) 98-39-29.

Ministry of Economic Development: 0108 Tbilisi, Chanturia 12; tel. (32) 92-22-55; fax (32) 93-35-75; e-mail info@privatization.ge; internet privatization.ge.

Ministry of Education and Science: 0102 Tbilisi, Uznadze 52; tel. and fax (32) 95-88-86; e-mail alomaia@wanex.net; internet www.mes.gov.ge.

Ministry of Environmental Protection and Natural Resources: 0115 Tbilisi, Kostava 68A; tel. (32) 23-06-64; fax (32) 33-39-52; e-mail gmep@access.sanet.ge.

Ministry of Finance: 0168 Tbilisi, Abashidze 70; tel. (32) 22-68-05; fax (32) 93-19-22; e-mail minister@mof.ge; internet www.mof.ge.

Ministry of Foreign Affairs: 0118 Tbilisi, 9 April 4; tel. (32) 28-47-47; fax (32) 28-47-61; e-mail inform@mfa.gov.ge; internet www.mfa.gov.ge.

Ministry of Internal Affairs: 0114 Tbilisi, Didi Kheivani 10; tel. (32) 99-62-96; fax (32) 98-65-32; internet www.police.ge.

Ministry of Justice: 0114 Tbilisi, Didi Kheivani 10; tel. (32) 75-82-29; fax (32) 75-82-22; e-mail justice@justice.gov.ge; internet www.justice.gov.ge.

Ministry of Labour, Health and Social Affairs: 0160 Tbilisi, K. Gamsakhurdia 30; tel. (32) 38-70-71; fax (32) 77-00-86; internet www.health.net.ge.

Ministry of Power Engineering: 0107 Tbilisi, Lermontov 10; tel. (32) 99-60-98; fax (32) 93-35-42.

Ministry of Refugee Affairs: 0180 Tbilisi, Dadiani 30; tel. (32) 92-13-05; fax (32) 92-14-27.

President and Legislature

PRESIDENT

Presidential Election, 4 January 2004

Candidates	Votes	%
Mikheil Saakashvili	1,890,256	96.27
Teimuraz Shashiashvili	36,398	1.85
Others	16,029	0.82
Total*	**1,963,556**	**100.00**

* Including invalid votes and votes cast against all candidates (1.07% of the total).

LEGISLATURE

Sakartvelos Parlamenti
(Georgian Parliament)
0108 Tbilisi, Rustaveli 8; tel. (32) 93-61-70; fax (32) 99-93-86; e-mail hdstaff@parliament.ge; internet www.parliament.ge.

Chairman: NINO BURDJANADZE.

General Election, 2 November 2003 and 28 March 2004*

Parties and blocs	% of votes†	Seats	Single-member constituency seats	Total seats
National Movement-United Democrats	67.32	135	17	152
Rightist Opposition	7.51	15	8	23
Democratic Union of Revival	6.03	—	6	6
Georgian Labour Party	5.97	—	4	4
Freedom (Tavisupleba)	4.31	—	—	—
Citizens' Union of Georgia	—	—	19	19
Independents	—	—	20	20
Vacant‡	—	—	11	11
Total (incl. others)	**100.00**	**150**	**85**	**235**

* Final preliminary results. Seventy-four of the single-member constituency seats were filled on 2 November 2003. New elections for deputies elected on the basis of party lists were held on 28 March 2004, following the annulment of the earlier results.
† Each party was required to obtain at least 7% of the total votes cast in order to win seats on the basis of party lists.
‡ One single-member constituency seat remained vacant, while the remaining ten mandates (representing the secessionist region of Abkhazia), to which the terms of those members elected in 1992 had been renewed, were revoked on 30 April 2004.

Political Organizations

In early 2004 47 political parties and alliances were registered with the Central Electoral Commission. The following were among the most prominent parties in Georgia in early 2005:

Christian Democratic Union of Georgia: 0108 Tbilisi, Kazbegi 37; tel. (32) 48-20-01; fax (32) 48-20-04; e-mail cdu@cdu.ge; internet www.cdu.ge; f. 1990; centre-right; contested (subsequently annulled) 2003 legislative elections as mem. of the For a New Georgia bloc; Leader Vazha Lortkipanidze.

Citizens' Union of Georgia (CUG) (SMK): Tbilisi, Chavchavadze 55; tel. (32) 99-94-79; fax (32) 93-15-84; e-mail cug@access.sanet.ge; f. 1993; contested (subsequently annulled) 2003 legislative elections as mem. of the For a New Georgia bloc; Chair. Avtandil Jorbenadze.

Communist Party of Georgia: Tbilisi; tel. (32) 53-25-17; f. 1992; Chair. Ivane Tsiklauri.

Conservative Party (Sakartvelos konservatorebi): 0008 Tbilisi, Lagidze 3; tel. (32) 99-74-97; e-mail conservators@access.sanet.ge; internet www.conservators.ge; f. 2003 on the basis of the Union of National Forces and the Union for Georgia's Unity; in 2004 left the National Movement to become a member of the political opposition; Leaders Zviad Dzidziguri, Koba Davitashvili.

Democratic Truth Party: Tbilisi.

Freedom (Tavisupleba): Tbilisi; f. 2004 by a son of former President Zviad Gamsakhurdia; nationalist; Leader Konstantine Gamsakhurdia.

Georgian Labour Party: Tbilisi, Javakhishvili 48; tel. (32) 94-39-22; fax (32) 96-60-46; f. 1997; Chair. Shalva Natelashvili; 64,000 mems.

Georgian Social Democratic Party: 380018 Tbilisi, 9 April 2; tel. (32) 99-95-50; fax (32) 98-73-89; f. 1990; contested (subsequently annulled) 2003 legislative elections as mem. of the Jumber Patiashvili-Unity bloc; Chair. Prof. Jemal Kakhniashvili.

Green Party (Mtsvanta Partia): 0112 Tbilisi, D. Aghmashenebeli 182; tel. (32) 95-20-33; fax (32) 35-16-74; e-mail info@greensparty.ge; f. 1990; contested (subsequently annulled) 2003 legislative elections as mem. of the For a New Georgia bloc; Chair. Giorgi Gachechiladze.

Industry Will Save Georgia: Tbilisi, Marjvena Sanapiro 7; tel. (32) 94-09-81; f. 1999; contested (subsequently annulled) 2003 legislative elections in alliance with Sporting Georgia; contested 2004 legislative elections as mem. of Rightist Opposition bloc; Chair. Giorgi Topadze.

Motherland Political Alliance (Samshoblo): Tbilisi; left-wing alliance, which included the Georgian Conservative-Monarchist Party to contest the 2003 general election; renamed in 2003 (fmrly the All-Georgian Patriotic Alliance, which included the People's Patriotic Union); Co-Chair. Igor Giorgadze, Temur Zhorzholiani.

National Democratic Party of Georgia: 380008 Tbilisi, Rustaveli 21; tel. (32) 98-35-36; fax (32) 93-19-78; e-mail ndpfc@parliament.ge; f. 1981; centre-right; formed part of the For a New Georgia bloc in 2003; announced alliance with the Union of Georgian Traditionalists in Dec. 2003; both parties were to be penalized by the Central Electoral Commission for failing to submit their expenditures for the March 2004 legislative election; Gen. Sec. Bachuki Kardava.

National Ideology Party of Georgia: Tbilisi, Chavchavadze 82; f. 1991; Chair. Zurab Gagnidze.

National Independence Party: 380007 Tbilisi, Machabeli 8; tel. (32) 98-27-70; f. 1988; Chair. Irakli Tsereteli.

Nationalist Party: Tbilisi; tel. (32) 95-14-85; f. 1993; Chair. Gia Mamaladze.

New Conservative Party (Axali Memarjveneebi—Axlebi): 0114 Tbilisi, Bevreti 3; tel. (32) 92-03-13; fax (32) 92-38-58; e-mail ncp@ncp.ge; internet www.ncp.ge; f. 2001; contested (subsequently annulled) 2003 legislative elections as mem. of the New Right bloc, and the 2004 legislative election as mem. of the Rightist Opposition bloc; Chair. Dr David Gamkrelidze; Gen. Sec. David Saganelidze.

Party for Liberation of Abkhazia: Tbilisi; advocates the restoration of the jurisdiction of Georgia and constitutional order in Abkhazia; f. 1998; formed part of the For a New Georgia bloc in 2003.

People's Front of Georgia: Tbilisi, Pushkin 5; tel. (32) 93-17-10; f. 1989; Chair. Nodar Natadze.

People's Party (Didgori): Tbilisi, Uznadze 56; tel. (32) 96-03-69; fax (32) 93-57-98; f. 1996; Chair. Mamuka Giorgadze.

Republican Party of Georgia: Tbilisi, Antoneli 31/2; tel. and fax (32) 95-25-36; e-mail cdc@access.sanet.ge; internet www.republic.org.ge; f. 1995; absorbed Georgian Popular Front (f. 1989); Chair. David Berdzenishvili.

Round Table—Free Georgia: Tbilisi, Dgebuadze 4; tel. (32) 95-48-20; f. 1990; party uniting supporters of former President Zviad Gamsakhurdia; Chair. Soso Jajanidze.

Socialist Party of Georgia: Tbilisi, Leselidze 41; tel. (32) 93-10-21; fax (32) 93-27-09; e-mail spg@geo-plus.net; f. 1995; formed part of the For a New Georgia bloc for the 2003 general election; Chair. Irakli Mindeli.

Union of Georgian Traditionalists: Tbilisi, Arsena 10; f. 1990; contested (subsequently annulled) 2003 legislative elections as mem. of the Burjanadze-Democrats bloc; alliance with the National Democratic Party of Georgia announced in Dec. 2003; both parties were to be penalized by the Central Electoral Commission for failing to submit their expenditures for the March 2004 legislative election; Chair. Akaki Asatiani.

United Communist Party of Georgia: Tbilisi; tel. (32) 38-41-65; f. 1994; First Sec. Panteleimon Giorgadze; 87,000 mems (2000).

United National Movement: 0118 Tbilisi, Vukol Beridze 9; tel. (32) 93-89-69; fax (32) 92-12-31; e-mail i_kavtaradze@hotmail.com; f. Nov. 2004 by merger of National Movement and United Democrats; Chair. Mikheil Saakashvili.

Unity Alliance (Ertoba): Tbilisi, Svobodi pl.; tel. (32) 92-30-65; fax (32) 93-46-94; e-mail ertoba@post.com; f. 2001; contested (subsequently annulled) 2003 legislative elections as mem. of the Jumber Patiashvili-Unity bloc; Co-Chair. Jumber Patiashvili, Aleksander Chachia.

Diplomatic Representation

EMBASSIES IN GEORGIA

Armenia: 380002 Tbilisi, Tetelashvili 4; tel. (32) 95-17-23; fax (32) 99-01-26; e-mail armemb@caucasus.net; Ambassador George Khosroev.

Azerbaijan: 380079 Tbilisi, Vacke-Saburtalo Distr., Nutsubidze St 47; tel. (32) 25-26-39; fax (32) 25-00-13; e-mail azembassy@internet.ge; Ambassador Ramiz Ayvaz oğlu Hasanov.

China, People's Republic: 380008 Tbilisi, Barnov 52; POB 224; tel. (32) 99-80-11; fax (32) 93-12-76; e-mail gzj@access.sanet.ge; Ambassador Xu Jianguo.

Czech Republic: 0154 Tbilisi, Tsereteli 57; tel. (32) 35-64-27; fax (32) 35-66-92; e-mail tbilisi@embassy.mzv.cz; Ambassador Jozef Vrabec.

France: 380008 Tbilisi, Gogebashvili 15; tel. (32) 99-99-76; fax (32) 95-33-75; Ambassador Philippe Lefort.

Germany: 380012 Tbilisi, Davit Aghmashenebeli 166; tel. (32) 95-09-36; fax (32) 95-89-10; e-mail deut.bot.tbilissi@access.sanet.ge; internet www.tiflis.diplo.de; Ambassador Uwe Schramm.

Greece: 380079 Tbilisi, Arakishvili 5; tel. and fax (32) 93-89-81; fax (32) 00-10-39; e-mail grembgeo@access.sanet.ge; Ambassador Constantina Mavroskelidou.

Holy See: 380086 Tbilisi, Jenti 40, Nutsubidze Plateau II; tel. (32) 94-13-05; fax (32) 29-39-44; e-mail nuntius@access.sanet.ge; Apostolic Nuncio Most Rev. Claudio Gugerotti (Titular Archbishop of Ravello).

Iran: 380060 Tbilisi, Zovreti 16; tel. (32) 98-69-90; fax (32) 98-69-93; Ambassador Hossein Amian Tusimi.

Israel: 0102 Tbilisi, Davit Aghmashenebeli 61; tel. (32) 94-27-05; fax (32) 95-52-09; e-mail info@tbilisi.mfa.gov.il; Ambassador Shabtai Tsur.

Italy: 380008 Tbilisi, Chitadze 3a; tel. (32) 99-64-18; fax (32) 99-64-15; e-mail ambita.tbilisi@access.sanet.ge; Ambassador Fabrizio Romano.

Korea, Republic: Tbilisi; Ambassador Yi Chong-Pin.

Lithuania: 0162 Tbilisi, Tengiz Abuladze 27; tel. (32) 91-29-33; fax (32) 22-17-93; e-mail amb.ge@urm.lt; Ricardas Degutis (designate).

Poland: Tbilisi, Zubalashvili 19; tel. (32) 92-03-98; fax (32) 92-03-97; e-mail ambpolgruzja@access.sanet.ge; Chargé d'affaires Jacek Multanowski.

Romania: Tbilisi, Lvov 7; tel. (32) 38-53-10; fax (32) 38-52-10; e-mail ambasada@caucasus.net; Ambassador Constantin Girbea.

Russia: 380062 Tbilisi, Chavchavadze 51; tel. (32) 91-24-06; fax (32) 91-27-38; e-mail russianembassy@caucasus.net; internet www.georgia.mid.ru; Ambassador Vladimir I. Chkhikvishvili.

Turkey: 380002 Tbilisi, Davit Aghmashenebeli 61; tel. (32) 95-20-14; fax (32) 95-18-10; e-mail tiblisbe@mfa.gov.tr; Ambassador Ertan Tezgor.

Ukraine: 380060 Tbilisi, Oniashvili 75; tel. (32) 98-93-62; fax (32) 23-71-45; e-mail emb_ge@mfa.gov.ua; Ambassador MYKOLA SPYS.

United Kingdom: 380003 Tbilisi, Sheraton Palace Hotel; tel. (32) 95-54-97; fax (32) 00-10-65; e-mail british.embassy@caucasus.net; internet www.britishembassy.gov.uk/georgia; Ambassador DONALD MacLAREN OF MacLAREN.

USA: 0105 Tbilisi, Atoneli 25; tel. (32) 98-99-67; fax (32) 93-37-59; internet georgia.usembassy.gov; Ambassador RICHARD MILES.

Judicial System

Constitutional Court: Tbilisi, Rustaveli 29; e-mail court@const .gov.ge; internet www.constcourt.gov.ge; Chair. JONI KHETSURIANI.

Supreme Court
0110 Tbilisi, Zubalashvili 32; tel. (32) 93-12-62; fax (32) 92-08-76; e-mail reception@supremecourt.ge; internet www.supremecourt.ge. Chair. KOTE KUBLASHVILI.

Prosecutor-General: ZURAB ADEISHVILI.

High Council of Justice: Tbilisi, Bochorma 12; tel. and fax (32) 27-31-02; fax (32)27-31-16; e-mail justice@caucasus.net; internet www .coj.gov.ge; f. 1997; 9-member council that co-ordinates the appointment of judges and their activities; three mems nominated by the President, three by Parlamenti and three from the judiciary; Exec. Sec. VALERI TSERTSVADZE; Chair. President of the Republic MIKHEIL SAAKASHVILI.

Religion

CHRISTIANITY

The Georgian Orthodox Church
The Georgian Orthodox Church is divided into 27 dioceses, and includes not only Georgian parishes, but also several Russian, Greek and Armenian Orthodox communities, which are under the jurisdiction of the Primate of the Georgian Orthodox Church. There are 40 monasteries and convents, two theological academies and four seminaries.

Georgian Patriarchate: 380005 Tbilisi, King Erekle II Sq. 1; tel. (32) 99-03-78; fax (32) 98-71-14; e-mail orthodox@patriarchate.ge; internet www.patriarchate.ge; Catholicos-Patriarch of All Georgia ILIA II.

The Roman Catholic Church
The Apostolic Administrator of the Caucasus is the Apostolic Nuncio to Georgia, Armenia and Azerbaijan, who is resident in Tbilisi (see Diplomatic Representation).

ISLAM
The principal Islamic communities in Georgia are those among the Ajarians, Abkhazians, Azerbaijanis and Kurds.

The Press

PRINCIPAL NEWSPAPERS

In 2002 175 newspaper titles were printed. Those listed below appear in Georgian, except where otherwise stated.

Axali Taoba (New Generation): Tbilisi, Davit Aghmashenebeli 89/24; tel. (32) 95-25-89; fax (32) 94-06-91; e-mail akhtao@geo.net.ge; internet www.opentext.org.ge/akhalitaoba; f. 1993; Editor SOSO GONIASHVILI.

Axali Versia (New Possibility): Tbilisi, Agladze 39; tel. (32) 95-69-38; internet versia-online.com; Editor-in-Chief ALEKO TSKITISHVILI.

Dilis Gazeti (Morning Newspaper): Tbilisi, Marjanishvili 5; tel. (32) 96-91-88; fax (32) 96-91-81; e-mail dilgazet@access.sanet.ge; Editor MANANA KARTOZIA.

Droni (The Times): Tbilisi, Kostava 14; tel. (32) 99-56-54; e-mail newspdroni@usa.net; 2 a week; Editor-in-Chief GIORGI CHOCHISHVILI.

Georgian Messenger: Tbilisi, Chavchavadze 55; tel. and fax (32) 22-76-21; e-mail gtze@messenger.com.ge; internet www.messenger .com.ge; daily; in English; Editor-in-Chief ZAZA GACHECHILADZE.

Georgian Times: Tbilisi, Lermontov 10; tel. and fax (32) 93-44-05; e-mail geotimes@geotimes.ge; internet www.geo.ge; f. 1993; weekly; Mondays; in English, Georgian and Russian; Editor-in-Chief ZVIAD POCHKHUA.

Iberia Spektri (Iberian Spectrum): Tbilisi, Machabeli 11; tel. (32) 98-73-87; fax (32) 98-73-88; Editor IRAKLI GOTSIRIDZE.

Literaturuli Sakartvelo (Literary Georgia): Tbilisi, Gudiashvili Sq. 2; tel. (32) 99-84-04; internet www.opentext.org.ge/ literaturulisakartvelo; weekly; organ of the Union of Writers of Georgia; Editor TAMAZ TSIVTSIVADZE.

Respublika (Republic): 380060 Tbilisi, Kostava 14; tel. and fax (32) 93-43-91; f. 1990; weekly; independent; Editor J. NINUA; circ. 40,000.

Rezonansi (Resonance): 0102 Tbilisi, Davit Aghmashenebeli Ave 89–24; tel. (32) 35-61-47; fax (32) 95-06-42; e-mail n1001@geo.net.ge; internet www.resonance.ge; f. 1992; daily; Group Editor-in-Chief ZURAB MATCHARADZE; circ. 7,000.

Sakartvelo (Georgia): 380096 Tbilisi, Kostava 14; tel. (32) 99-92-26; 5 a week; organ of the Georgian Parliament; Editor SERGO JANASHIA.

Shvidi Dghe (Seven Days): Tbilisi, Krilov 5; tel. (32) 94-35-52; fax (32) 95-40-76; e-mail dge7@caucasus.net; f. 1991; weekly; Editor KOBA AKHALBEDASHVILI; circ. 3,000.

Svobodnaya Gruziya (Free Georgia): Tbilisi, Rustaveli 42; tel. (32) 93-13-54; fax (32) 93-17-06; e-mail new@caucasus.net; internet www .svobodnaya-gruzia.com; f. 1922 as *Zarya Vostoka (Dawn of the East)*; present name adopted 1991; in Russian; Editor-in-Chief TATO LASCHISHVILI; circ. 5,000.

Tbilisi Times: 380007 Tbilisi, Kostava 20; tel. (32) 98-76-13; fax (32) 99-63-24; e-mail david@tbilisitimes.com; internet www .tbilisitimes.com; in English and Georgian; independent, non-profit; Dirs DAVID DZIDZIKASHVILI, SHAVLEG SHAVERDASHVILI.

PRINCIPAL PERIODICALS

Dila (Morning): 380096 Tbilisi, Kostava 14; tel. (32) 93-41-30; internet www.dila.ge; f. 1904; fortnightly; illustrated; for 5–12 year-olds; Editor-in-Chief DODO TSIVTSIVADZE; circ. 4,500.

Literaturnaya Gruziya (Literary Georgia): 0108 Tbilisi, Kostava 5; tel. (32) 99-06-59; fax (32) 22-47-37; e-mail abzianidze@hotmail .com; f. 1957; quarterly journal; politics, art and fiction; in Russian; Editor Prof. ZAZA ABZIANIDZE.

Metsniereba da Tekhnika (Science and Technology): 380060 Tbilisi; f. 1949; monthly; journal of the Georgian Academy of Sciences; popular; Editor Z. TSILOSANI.

Nakaduli (Stream): Tbilisi, Kostava 14; tel. (32) 93-31-81; f. 1926; fmrly *Pioneri*; monthly; journal of the Ministry of Education; illustrated; for 10–15-year-olds; Editor MANANA GELASHVILI; circ. 5,000.

Sakartvelos Metsnierebata Akedemiis Matsne (Proceedings of the Georgian Academy of Sciences, Biological Series): 0108 Tbilisi, Rustaveli 52, Georgian Academy of Sciences, Dept of Biology; tel. and fax (32) 93-58-92; e-mail bio@gw.acnet.ge; internet www.acnet .ge/matsne/biology; f. 1975; in 2003 the Biological Series publication was divided into Series A: physiological and medical articles, and Series B: other fields of biology; 4 a year; in English; Editor-in-Chief, Series A VAZHA OKUJAVA; Editor-in-Chief, Series B MALKHAZ ZAA-LISHVILI.

Sakartvelos Metsnierebata Akedemiis Matsne (Herald of the Georgian Academy of Sciences, Chemical Series): Tbilisi; f. 1975; quarterly; in Georgian, English and Russian; Editor-in-Chief TEIMURAZ ANDRONIKASHVILI.

Sakartvelos Metsnierebata Akademiis Moambe (Bulletin of Georgian Academy of Sciences): 0108 Tbilisi, Rustaveli 52; tel. (32) 99-75-93; fax (32) 99-88-23; e-mail bulletin@presid.achet.ge; f. 1940; 6 a year; in Georgian and English; Editor-in-Chief ALBERT TAVKHE-LIDZE.

Sarke: Tbilisi, Chubinashvili 50; tel. (32) 96-75-43; Editor MEDEA SANAIA.

Saunje (Treasure): 380007 Tbilisi, Dadiani 2; tel. (32) 72-47-31; f. 1974; 6 a year; organ of the Union of Writers of Georgia; foreign literature in translation; Editor S. NISHNIANIDZE.

Tsiskari (Dawn): 380007 Tbilisi, Khidis 1/29; tel. (32) 99-85-81; f. 1957; monthly; organ of the Union of Writers of Georgia; fiction; Editor ZAUR KALANDIA.

NEWS AGENCIES

Black Sea Press: Tbilisi, Rustaveli 42; tel. (32) 98-94-69; fax (32) 93-17-49; e-mail bspress@caucasus.net; internet www.bspress.org; f. 1994; Dir DAVIT IMEDASHVILI.

Iprinda: Tbilisi, Rustaveli 19; tel. (32) 99-03-77; fax (32) 98-73-65; first independent news agency in Georgia; Dir KETEVAN BOKHUA.

Inter-Press: 0193 Tbilisi, M. Aleksidze 3; tel. (32) 99-67-72; fax (32) 93-56-39; e-mail ipcommerce@interpress.ge; internet www .interpress.ge; f. 2000; international news agency; in Georgian, Russian and English.

Kavkasia-Press (Caucasus Press): 0108 Tbilisi, Rustaveli 42; tel. (32) 99-82-69; fax (32) 99-01-39.

Prime News Agency (PNA): 380005 Tbilisi, Ingorovka 6; tel. (32) 92-32-02; fax (32) 92-32-14; e-mail pna@pna.com.ge; internet www.primenewsonline.com; f. 1997 after dissolution of BGI news agency.

Sarke Information Agency: 0102 Tbilisi, Davit Aghmashenebeli 71; tel. (32) 95-06-59; fax (32) 95-08-37; e-mail info@sarke.com; internet www.sarke.com; f. 1992; economic and business news from Georgia and the Caucasus; Dir VALERIAN KHUKHUNASHVILI; Editor-in-Chief VICTORIA GUJELASHVILI.

JOURNALISTS' ASSOCIATIONS

Independent Association of Georgian Journalists: 380002 Tbilisi, Marjanishvili 5, Rm 230; tel. and fax (32) 95-68-50; e-mail iagj@gol.ge; internet www.iagj.gol.ge; f. 2000; Pres. ZVIAD POCHKHUA.

Journalists' Federation of Georgia: 380005 Tbilisi, Erekles 6; tel. (32) 98-24-47; e-mail foraf@geotvr.ge; Chair. AKAKI SIKHARULIDZE.

Publishers

Bakur Sulakauri Publishing: 0012 Tbilisi, D. Agmashenebeli 150; tel. and fax (32) 91-09-54; e-mail book@access.sanet.ge; internet www.sulakauri.com.ge; f. 1998; reference, fiction and children's literature.

Ganatleba (Education): 380064 Tbilisi, Chubinashvili 50; tel. (32) 95-50-97; f. 1957; educational, literature; Dir L. KHUNDADZE.

Georgian National Universal Encyclopaedia: Tbilisi, Tsereteli 1; Editor-in-Chief A. SAKVARELIDZE.

Khelovneba (Art): 380002 Tbilisi, Davit Aghmashenebeli 179; f. 1947; Dir N. JASHI.

Merani (Writer): 0108 Tbilisi, Rustaveli 42; tel. (32) 99-64-92; fax (32) 93-46-75; e-mail hmerani@iberiapac.ge; f. 1921; fiction; Dir G. GVERDTSITELI.

Meridian Publishing Co: 0192 Tbilisi, Grmagele 22/10A; tel. (32) 61-27-98; fax (32) 95-56-35; e-mail info@meridianpub.com; internet www.meridianpub.com; f. 1994; academic and schools; Editor-in-Chief GIORGI GIGINEISHVILI.

Metsniereba (Sciences): 380060 Tbilisi, Gamrekeli 19; tel. and fax (32) 37-22-97; e-mail publicat@gw.acnet.ge; f. 1941; Industrial-Publishing Corpn of the Georgian Academy of Sciences; Dir DAVID KOLOTAURI; Editor CISANA KARTOZIA.

Nakaduli (Stream): 380094 Tbilisi, Gamsakhurdia 28; tel. (32) 38-69-12; f. 1938; books for children and youth; Dir BAKUR SULAKAURI.

Sakartvelo (Georgia): 380002 Tbilisi, Marjanishvili 5; tel. (32) 95-42-01; f. 1921; fmrly *Sabchota Sakartvelo* (Soviet Georgia); political, scientific and fiction; Dir JANSUL GVINJILIA.

Tbilisi State University Publishing House: 0128 Tbilisi, Chavchavadze 14; f. 1933; scientific and educational literature; Editor V. GAMKRELIDZE.

Broadcasting and Communications

TELECOMMUNICATIONS

Georgian National Communications Commission: 0177 Tbilisi, al. Kazbegi 42; tel. (32) 92-16-67; fax (32) 92-16-25; e-mail post@gncc.ge; internet www.gncc.ge; Chair. VAKHTANG ABASHIDZE.

Geocell: 380102 Tbilisi, POB 48; tel. (32) 77-01-00; fax (32) 77-01-01; e-mail cc@geocell.com.ge; internet www.geocell.com.ge; f. 1996; mobile cellular communications.

Magti GSM: 380186 Tbilisi, Jikia 5; tel. (32) 32-23-31; fax (32) 32-28-83; e-mail office@magtigsm.ge; internet www.magticom.ge; f. 1997; mobile cellular communications; Dir DAVIT LAWRENSE.

Telecom Georgia (Sakartvelos Telekomi): 380058 Tbilisi, Rustaveli 31; tel. (32) 99-91-97; fax (32) 00-11-11; e-mail isonishvili@telecom.ge; internet www.telecom.ge; f. 1994; provides telecommunications services; 82% owned by Metromedia International Telecommunications Inc (USA); Pres. G. KHMALADZE; Dir N. KAKHELI.

BROADCASTING

Television

Ajaria TV: 384500 Batumi, Memed Abashidze 41; tel. (222) 74-370; fax (222) 74-371; e-mail ajaratv@ajaratv.com; internet www.ajaratv.com; Chief Exec. EVGENI TAVDGIRIDZE.

Georgian Television and Radio Broadcasting: 380071 Tbilisi, Kostava 68; tel. and fax (32) 29-42-54; e-mail office@geotvr.ge; internet www.geotvr.ge; f. 1956; Chair. ZAZA SHENGELIA.

Imedi TV (Hope): 0159 Tbilisi, Ljubljana 5; tel. (32) 91-93-12; fax (32) 91-90-41; e-mail info@imedi.ge; internet www.imedi.ge; Chair. BADRI PATARKATSISHVILI; Gen. Dir BIDZINA BARATASHVILI.

Rustavi 2: 380077 Tbilisi, Vazha-Pshavela 45; tel. (32) 20-11-11; fax (32) 20-00-12; e-mail tv@rustavi2.com; internet www.rustavi2.com; f. 1994; independent; Gen. Dir NIKA TABATADZE.

Radio

Georgian Radio: 380071 Tbilisi, Kostava 68; tel. (32) 36-83-62; fax (32) 36-86-65; f. 1956; govt-controlled; Dir VAKHTANG NANITASHVILI.

Radio Imedi: 0159 Tbilisi, Ljubljana 5; e-mail info@radio-imedi.ge; internet www.radio-imedi.ge; f. 2001; national broadcasting, 24 hours; news; Dir IRAKLI KHETERELI.

Radio Sakartvelo: 380059 Tbilisi, Marshal Gelovani 2; tel. (32) 33-10-10; fax (32) 33-03-14; e-mail tamara@fortuna.ge; internet www.fortuna.ge; owns and runs Radio Fortuna and Radio Fortuna Plus; popular and classical music; Gen. Dir GURAM CHIGOGIDZE.

Finance

(cap. = capital; res = reserves; dep. = deposits; m. = million; brs = branches; amounts in lari, unless otherwise indicated)

BANKING

In August 1991 the Georgian Supreme Soviet adopted legislation which nationalized all branches of all-Union (USSR) banks in Georgia. Georgian branches of the USSR State Bank (Gosbank) were transferred to the National Bank of Georgia. At the end of 2004 there were 21 commercial banks operating in Georgia (of which 12 were owned by foreign organizations).

Central Bank

National Bank of Georgia: 0105 Tbilisi, Leonidze 3–5; tel. (32) 99-65-05; fax (32) 99-93-46; e-mail nbg@access.sunet.ge; internet www.nbg.gov.ge; f. 1991; cap. 6.8m., res 46.2m., dep. 122.1m. (Dec. 2002); Pres. and Chair. of Bd IRAKLI MANAGADZE; 9 brs.

Other Banks

Agro-Business Bank: Tbilisi, Budapeshti 10; tel. (32) 25-08-20; fax (32) 93-28-80; e-mail abg@caucasus.net; internet www.abg.com.ge; f. 2000; cap. 6.9m., dep. 0.4m. (Dec. 2002); wholly owned by the European Commission; Gen.Dir GEORGE KALANDARISHVILI; 61 brs.

Bank of Georgia (Sakartvelos Banki): 0105 Tbilisi, Pushkin 3; tel. (32) 44-41-05; fax (32) 44-42-47; e-mail welcome@bog.ge; internet www.bog.ge; f. 1991; present name adopted 1994; universal joint-stock commercial bank; cap. 9.9m., res 19.9m., dep. 173.8m. (Dec. 2003); Pres. VLADIMER PATEISHVILI; Gen. Dir DAVID PANJAKIDZE; 25 brs.

Bank Republic: 0179 Tbilisi, Ateni 2; tel. (32) 29-45-98; fax (32) 22-75-66; e-mail info@republic.com.ge; internet www.republic.ge; f. 1991; cap. 5.8m., res 1.7m., dep. 50.0m. (Dec. 2003); Pres. LASHA PAPASHVILI.

Basisbank: 0103 Tbilisi, K. Tsamebuli 1; tel. (32) 92-29-22; fax (32) 98-65-48; e-mail info@basisbank.ge; internet www.basisbank.ge; f. 1993; cap. 5.0m., dep. 11.6m. (Dec. 2003); Gen. Dir ZURAB TSIKHISTAUI.

Cartu Bank: 0162 Tbilisi, Chavchavadze 39A; tel. (32) 23-00-21; fax (32) 23-03-83; e-mail cartubank@cartubank.ge; internet www.cartubank.ge; f. 1996 name changed as above Sept. 1998; merged with Absolute Bank in 2001; 25% owned by Cartu Group, 25% owned by Iagundi Ltd, 25% owned by Interservice Ltd, 25% owned by Transinvest Ltd; cap. 30.1m., res 15.2m., dep. 62.8m. (Dec. 2003); Pres. GEORGE LOMAIA; Chair. of Bd G. CHRDILELI; 5 brs.

Cavcasioni: 380062 Tbilisi, Chubinishvili 41; tel. (32) 95-14-44; fax (32) 95-93-93; e-mail caucasioni@iberiapac.ge; f. 1992; cap. 3.0m., res 0.1m., dep. 0.4m. (Dec. 1999); Pres. BESO MAGRADZE; Chair. ZAZIA PANKVELASHVILI.

Emporiki Bank — Georgia: 0108 Tbilisi, Chanturia 14; tel. (32) 92-23-76; fax (32) 92-24-33; e-mail bank@emporiki.ge; f. 1996 as International Commercial Black Sea Bank; name changed to Commercial Bank of Greece (Georgia) in 2001; present name adopted 2003; 86.1% owned by Emporiki Bank of Greece; cap. 8.1m., res 0.9m., dep. 12.3m. (Dec. 2002); Man. Dir IOANNIS PILINIS.

Georgian Post Bank: 380064 Tbilisi, Rustaveli 12; tel. (32) 99-01-10; fax (32) 956-82-69; e-mail info@postbank.ge; internet www.postbank.ge; f. 1995; jt-stock co; 35 brs.

Intellectbank: 380064 Tbilisi, Davit Aghmashenebeli 127; tel. (32) 98-97-91; fax (32) 98-97-92; e-mail info@intellect.ge; internet www

.intellectbank.com; f. 1993; cap. 5.0m., res 1.3m., dep. 27.4m. (Dec. 2003); Pres. DEVI VEPKHAVADZE; Gen. Dir VALERIAN SHARIKADZE; 13 brs.

ProCredit Bank, Georgia: 0112 Tbilisi, Tamar Mephe 18; tel. (32) 20-22-22; fax (32) 25-05-80; e-mail info@procreditbank.ge; internet www.procreditbank.ge; f. 1999 as Microfinance Bank of Georgia JSC; renamed as above in Sept. 2003; 39% owned by Internationale Micro Investitionen AG (Germany); cap. 20.0m., res 4.1m., dep. 102.6m. (Dec. 2003); Chief Exec. PHILIP SIGWART.

TBC Bank: 0179 Tbilisi, Chavchavadze 11; tel. (32) 22-06-61; fax (32) 22-04-06; e-mail info@tbcbank.com.ge; internet www.tbcbank .com.ge; f. 1992; cap. 5.4m., res 4.7m., dep. 211.4m. (Dec. 2003); Pres. VAKHTANG BUTSKHRIKIDZE; 9 brs.

Tbiluniversalbank: 0171 Tbilisi, Kostava 70; tel. and fax (32) 36-50-50; e-mail info@tub.ge; internet www.tbiluniversalbank.com; f. 1994; present name adopted 1995; cap. 5.0m., dep. 22.3m. (Dec. 2003); Chair. of Bd of Dirs VASIL DZOTSENIDZE; 3 brs.

United Georgian Bank (UGB): 0102 Tbilisi, Uznadze 37; tel. (32) 95-60-85; fax (32) 99-91-39; e-mail admin@ugb.com.ge; internet www.ugb.com.ge; f. 1995; 51% owned by Vneshtorgbank (Russia); cap. 21.0m., res 0.4m., dep. 98.4m. (Dec. 2003); Chair. of Supervisory Bd ZAZA SIORIDZE; Man. Dir IRAKLI MEKVABISHVILI; 19 brs.

STOCK EXCHANGE

Georgian Stock Exchange: 380062 Tbilisi, Chavchavadze 74A; tel. (32) 22-07-18; fax (32) 25-18-76; e-mail info@gse.ge; internet www .gse.ge; f. 1999; Chair. of Supervisory Bd GEORGE LOLADZE; Gen. Dir VAKHTANG SVANADZE.

CURRENCY EXCHANGE

Tbilisi Interbank Currency Exchange (TICEX): 380005 Tbilisi, Galaktion Tabidze 4; tel. (32) 92-34-43; fax (32) 92-23-01; Gen. Dir DAVIT KLDIASHVILI.

INSURANCE

At the end of 2004 there were 14 insurance companies in Georgia.

State Insurance Supervision Service: 380064 Tbilisi, G. Chitaia 21; tel. (32) 95-64-89; fax (32) 95-71-42; e-mail isssg@caucasus.net; internet www.insurance.caucasus.net; f. 1997; provides state regulation of insurance activity; Dir ARCHIL TSERTSVADZE.

Aldagi Insurance Co: 0179 Tbilisi, Melikishvili 16; tel. (32) 92-44-11; fax (32) 29-49-05; e-mail aldagi@aldagi.com.ge; internet www .aldagi.com; f. 1990; Chair. GURAM ASSATHIANY; Gen. Dir EVA IASHVILI.

Anglo-Georgian Insurance Co (AGIC): 380030 Tbilisi, I. Abashidze 29; tel. (32) 25-03-51; fax (32) 25-03-50; e-mail post@ agic.com.ge; internet www.agic.com.ge; f. 1998 as a joint-stock co; all types of insurance; Gen. Dir FRANCIS MATHEW.

British-Caucasian Insurance Co: 380008 Tbilisi, Rustaveli 27; tel. (32) 98-59-55; fax (32) 25-28-08; e-mail bci@caucasus.net; internet www.bci.ge; Dir RAMAZ KUKULADZE.

ENIC Co: Tbilisi, Kipshidze 2; tel. (32) 25-35-27; Exec. Dir GOCHA GORDEZIANI.

Europace: 0112 Tbilisi, Aghmashenebeli 150; tel. (32) 91-06-04; fax (32) 91-06-08; e-mail nabatinsu@geo.net.ge; internet www.europace .ge; f. 1998; formerly Nabati Ltd; Dir VASIL AKHRAKHADZE.

Georgian Pension and Insurance Holding Co: Tbilisi, Chavchavadze 1, Bldg 5; tel. (32) 92-01-20; internet www.gpih.ge; Gen. Dir PAATA GADZADZE.

Imedi L International Co: Tbilisi, Chavchavadze 20; tel. (32) 22-35-20; fax (32) 29-30-75; e-mail info@imedi.ge; internet www.imedi .ge; Dir ALEXANDER LORTKIPANIDZE.

Trade and Industry

GOVERNMENT AGENCIES

Georgian Investment Centre: 380077 Tbilisi, Kazbegi 42; tel. (32) 23-41-34; fax (32) 92-18-40; e-mail gic@access.sanet.ge; internet www.gic.ge; f. 1996 to promote foreign and domestic investment; Dir SABA SARISHVILI.

State Property Management Agency: 0108 Tbilisi, Chanturia 12; tel. (32) 99-74-16; internet www.privatization.ge; responsible for divestment of state-owned enterprises.

CHAMBER OF COMMERCE

Georgian Chamber of Commerce and Industry: 380079 Tbilisi, Chavchavadze 11; tel. (32) 23-00-45; fax (32) 23-57-60; e-mail gcci@ access.sanet.ge; internet www.gcci.ge; f. 1963; brs in Sukhumi and Batumi; Chair. JEMAL INAISHVILI.

TRADE ASSOCIATION

Georgian Import Export Asscn (Geoimpex): 380008 Tbilisi, Giorgiashvili 12; tel. (32) 99-70-90; fax (32) 98-25-41; Gen. Dir T. A. GOGOBERIDZE.

UTILITIES

Regulatory Authorities

Georgian National Energy Regulation Committee: Tbilisi, Kazbegi Ave 45; tel. (32) 24-10-40; fax (32) 24-10-42; e-mail mail@ gnerc.org; internet www.gnerc.org; f. 1997; Dir GIA TAVADZE.

State Agency for the Regulation of Oil and Gas Resources: Tbilisi, Kazbegi Ave 45; tel. (32) 25-33-11; e-mail sarogr@access .sanet.ge; f. 1999; Dir G. ITONISHVILI.

Electricity

Georgian State Electrosystem (GSE): Tbilisi, Baratashvili 2; tel. and fax (32) 92-31-42; internet www.gse.com.ge; f. 2002 from the merger of Electrodispetcherizatsia 2000 and Elektrogadatsema, formerly part of Sakenergo; operator of electricity transmission grid; state-owned; managed from March 2003 by ESBI Georgia, a subsidiary of ESBI International (Ireland); Gen. Dir JOE CORBETT.

Georgian United Energy Distribution Co (GUDC): 380007 Tbilisi, Lermontov 10; tel. (32) 93-13-84; internet www.uedc.ge; f. 2002 by amalgamation of the majority of regional electricity cos, excluding the regions of Tbilisi, Ajaria and Kakheti; managed on an interim basis by PA Consulting (USA) from May 2003; Dir DEAN WHITE, GIVI VARDIASHVILI; 5,000 employees.

Sakenergo: 380005 Tbilisi, V. Vekua 1; tel. (32) 98-98-14; fax (32) 98-31-97; formerly state-owned energy supplier; in 1996 restructured into three cos (generation, transmission and distribution); further restructured in 1998, see Georgian United Energy Distribution Co and Sakenergogeneratsia; Gen. Dir VAZHA METREVELI.

Sakenergogeneratsia: 38005 Tbilisi, V. Vekua 1; tel. and fax (32) 98-98-13; f. 1996; state power-generating co; Gen. Dir G. BADURASHVILI.

Telasi: 380054 Tbilisi, Vani 3; tel. (32) 25-52-11; fax (32) 77-99-78; internet www.telasi.ge; privatized in 1999; 75% owned by Unified Energy Systems (Russia); Tbilisi distribution grid; Dir DANGIRAS MIKALAJUNAS.

Gas

Georgian Gas International (GIC): 380044 Tbilisi, 300 Aragveli 24; tel. (32) 92-29-55; fax (32) 92-32-29; e-mail public@ggic.ge; internet www.ggic.ge; f. 1997; state-owned; exclusive operator, owner, user, disposer, and manager of natural and liquid gas import and transit in Georgia; Chair. Dr ALEKSANDR GOTSIRIDZE.

Sakgazi (Geogas): 380082 Tbilisi, Kiziki 13; tel. (32) 70-10-25; fax (32) 70-10-23; e-mail office@georgiangas.com.ge; internet www .georgiangas.com.ge; f. 1998; jt-stock co; gas distribution; six distribution centres; majority-owned by Itera (Russia).

Saktransgasmretsvi: 0077 Tbilisi, Delisi III 22; tel. (32) 93-29-81; fax (32) 53-78-02; e-mail transgas@access.sanet.ge; f. 1962; state-owned; operates main gas pipelines; Chair. of Bd IVANE ZAZASHVILI.

Tbilgazi: 380007 Tbilisi, Mitskevichi 18; tel. (32) 38-76-25; fax (32) 37-56-51; gas-distribution co for the Tbilisi region; Chair. DAVIT MORCHILADZE.

Water

Tbilisi Water Utility (Tbiltskalkanali): 380119 Tbilisi, Khizabavri 1; tel. (32)67-96-45; scheduled for privatization; water supply and sewerage system.

TRADE UNION CONFEDERATION

Amalgamation of Trade Unions of Georgia (GTUA): 380122 Tbilisi, Shartava 7; tel. (32) 38-29-95; fax (32) 22-46-63; e-mail gtua@ geo.net.ge; f. 1995 as Confederation of Trade Unions of Georgia, name changed as above in 2000; comprises branch unions with a total membership of approx. 800,000; in February 2005 the association ceded 90% of its property to the state; following legislative amendments all members were required to re-register; Chair. IRAKLI TUGUSHI.

Transport

RAILWAYS

In 2003 Georgia's rail network (including the sections within the secessionist republic of Abkhazia) totalled approximately 1,655 km.

However, some 500 km of track was reported to be in a poor state of repair, as a result of which the capacity of some sections of the network had decreased by more than 75% since 1990. The main rail links are with Russia, along the Black Sea coast, with Azerbaijan, with Armenia and with Iran. In December 2004 an agreement was signed on the construction of a rail link between Kars in Turkey and Akhalkalaki in Georgia, continuing to Azerbaijan, and the rehabilitation of the section between Akhalkalaki and Tbilisi. In January 2005 an agreement was reached on opening a direct rail-ferry link between the Kavkaz terminal at Novorossiisk in Russia and Poti in Georgia; this would reduce costs aand facilitate the transport of freight with Armenia as well.

The first section of the Tbilisi Metro was opened in 1966; by 2005 the system comprised two lines with 21 stations, totalling 28.5 km in length in 2003, and three extensions, totalling 15 km, were under construction.

Georgian Railways Co: 0112 Tbilisi, Tamar Mepe 15; tel. (32) 95-14-95; fax (32) 95-02-25; e-mail onoprishvili@railway.ge; internet www.railway.ge; Chair. DAVID ONOPRISHVILI.

Tbilisi Metro (Tbilisi Metropolitena): 380012 Tbilisi, Pl. Vokzalnaya 2; tel. (32) 95-15-78; fax (32) 93-41-86; e-mail almer@iberiapac .ge; f. 1966; Gen. Man. GURAM GABUNIA.

ROADS

In 2003 the total length of roads in use was an estimated 20,247 km (including 1,474 km of main roads, 3,326 km of secondary roads). In that year 93.8% of the road network was paved.

SHIPPING

There are international shipping services with Black Sea and Mediterranean ports. The main ports are at Batumi, Poti and Sukhumi. Of these, Sukhumi is located in the separatist 'Republic of Abkhazia', while Batumi is in the Autonomous Republic of Ajaria.

Shipowning Companies

Georgian Ocean Shipping Co (OSCO): 380060 Tbilisi, Al. Kazbegi Ave 12A; tel. (32) 25-18-95; fax (32) 25-18-97; e-mail osco.os@ wanex.net; internet www.osco.ge; f. 1999; privatized in 2005; owns 15 petroleum-product and chemical-carrier tankers; Chair. GURAM DOLBAIA.

Georgian Shipping Co: 384517 Batumi, Gogebashvili 60; tel. (222) 14-02-312; fax (222) 73-91-114; Pres. Capt. B. VARSHANIDZE.

Port Authorities

Port of Batumi: 384500 Batumi, Gogebashvili 20; tel. (222) 76-261; fax (222) 76-830; e-mail bsport@batumi.net; internet www.batport .batumi.net; operates cargo port; Gen. Dir TEMUR USTIASHVILI; 1,413 employees.

Port of Poti: 4401 Poti, D. Agmashenebeli 52; tel. (393) 20-660; fax (393) 20-688; e-mail mail@potiport.com; internet www.potiport.com; operation of cargo port; Gen. Dir JEMAL INAISHVILI.

Port of Sukhumi: 384900 Sukhumi, nab. Mahajirov 66; tel. (393) 23–400.

CIVIL AVIATION

Georgia's primary airport is Tbilisi International Airport, Lochini. There are three other airports in operation in Batumi, Kutaisi and Senaki.

Civil Aviation Authority: 380060 Tbilisi, Al. Kazbegi 12; tel. (32) 93-30-92; fax (32) 99-74-80; e-mail inspect@access.sanet.ge; f. 2002; Dir GIORGI MZHAVANADZE.

Caucasus Airlines (CA): 380060 Tbilisi, Saburtalo 32; tel. (32) 25-30-58; fax (32) 25-30-59; e-mail sra@access.sanet.ge; internet www .caucasusairlines.ge; f. 2002; regional airline flying between Tbilisi and: Batumi, Yerevan (Armenia), Baku (Azerbaijan) and Sochi (Russia).

Georgian Airlines: 0160 Tbilisi, J. Shartava 40; tel. (32) 25-26-68; fax (32) 94-07-82; e-mail international@georgian-airways.com; internet www.georgian-airways.com; f. 1999 as Airzena Georgian Airlines by merger of Airzena, Air Georgia and World International; present name adopted 2004; privately owned national airline; flies to Greece, Israel, Russia, Ukraine and various other destinations in Europe; Pres. TAMAZ GAIASHVILI.

Tourism

Prior to the disintegration of the USSR, Georgia attracted some 1.5m. tourists annually (mainly from other parts of the USSR), owing to its location on the Black Sea and its favourable climate. However, following the outbreak of civil conflict in the early 1990s in South Ossetia and Abkhazia, there was an almost complete cessation in tourism. Efforts to regenerate the sector were made in the late 1990s, with the historic buildings of Tbilisi and the surrounding area one of the primary attractions. The ski resort at Gudauri also remained popular with foreign tourists in the winter months. Other attractions included the mineral spas in the Borzhomi Gorge, and Mount Kazbek. According to the World Tourism Organization, there were 302,215 tourist arrivals in 2001, compared with 387,258 in 2000, and receipts from tourism totalled US $472m. in 2002.

Department of Tourism and Resorts of Georgia: 0162 Tbilisi, Chavchavadze 80; tel. (32) 22-61-25; fax (32) 29-40-52; e-mail georgia@tourism.gov.ge; internet www.tourism.gov.ge; forms part of the Ministry of Economic Development; Chair. SABA KIKNADZE.

GERMANY

Introductory Survey

Location, Climate, Language, Religion, Flag, Capital

The Federal Republic of Germany, which was formally established in October 1990 upon the unification of the Federal Republic of Germany (FRG, West Germany) and the German Democratic Republic (GDR, East Germany), lies in the heart of Europe. Its neighbours to the west are the Netherlands, Belgium, Luxembourg and France, to the south Switzerland and Austria, to the east the Czech Republic and Poland, and to the north Denmark. The climate is temperate, with an annual average temperature of 9°C (48°F), although there are considerable variations between the North German lowlands and the Bavarian Alps. The language is German. There is a small Sorbian-speaking minority (numbering about 100,000 people). About 33% of the population are Protestants and a further 32% are Roman Catholics. The national flag (proportions 3 by 5) consists of three equal horizontal stripes, of black, red and gold. The capital is Berlin.

Recent History

Following the defeat of the Nazi regime and the ending of the Second World War in 1945, Germany was divided, according to the Berlin Agreement, into US, Soviet, British and French occupation zones. Berlin was similarly divided. The former German territories east of the Oder and Neisse rivers, with the city of Danzig (now Gdańsk), became part of Poland, while the northern part of East Prussia, around Königsberg (now Kaliningrad), was transferred to the USSR. After the failure of negotiations to establish a unified German administration, the US, French and British zones were integrated economically in 1948. In May 1949 a provisional Constitution, the Grundgesetz (Basic Law), came into effect in the three zones (except in Saarland—see below), and federal elections were held in August. On 21 September 1949 a new German state, the Federal Republic of Germany (FRG), was established in the three Western zones. The FRG was governed from Bonn in Nordrhein-Westfalen. (Saarland was not incorporated into the FRG until 1957.) In October 1949 Soviet-occupied Eastern Germany declared itself the German Democratic Republic (GDR), with the Soviet zone of Berlin as its capital. This left the remainder of Berlin (West Berlin) as an enclave of the FRG within the territory of the GDR.

The FRG and GDR developed sharply divergent political and economic systems. The leaders of the GDR created a socialist state, based on the Soviet model. As early as 1945 large agricultural estates in eastern Germany were nationalized, followed in 1946 by major industrial concerns. Exclusive political control was exercised by the Sozialistische Einheitspartei Deutschlands (SED, Socialist Unity Party of Germany), which had been formed in April 1946 by the merger of the Communist Party of Germany and the branch of the Sozialdemokratische Partei Deutschlands (SPD, Social Democratic Party of Germany) in the Soviet zone. Other political parties in eastern Germany were under the strict control of the SED, and no political activity independent of the ruling party was permitted. In 1950 Walter Ulbricht was appointed Secretary-General (later restyled First Secretary) of the SED.

The transfer, as war reparations, of foodstuffs, livestock and industrial equipment to the USSR from eastern Germany had a devastating effect on the area's economy in the immediate post-war period. In June 1953 increasing political repression and severe food shortages led to uprisings and strikes, which were suppressed by Soviet troops. The continued failure of the GDR to match the remarkable economic recovery of the FRG prompted a growing number of refugees to cross from the GDR to the FRG (between 1949 and 1961 an estimated 2.5m. GDR citizens moved permanently to the FRG). Emigration was accelerated by the enforced collectivization of many farms in 1960, and in August 1961 the GDR authorities hastily constructed a guarded wall between East and West Berlin (the Berlin Wall).

In May 1971 Ulbricht was succeeded as First Secretary of the SED by Erich Honecker. Ulbricht remained Chairman of the Council of State (Head of State), a post that he had held since 1960, until his death in August 1973. He was initially succeeded in this office by Willi Stoph, but in October 1976 Stoph returned to his previous post as Chairman of the Council of Ministers, and Honecker became Chairman of the Council of State. Under Honecker, despite some liberalization of relations with the FRG, there was little relaxation of repressive domestic policies. Honecker strongly opposed the political and economic reforms that began in the USSR and some other Eastern European countries in the mid-1980s.

The 1949 elections in the FRG resulted in victory for the conservative Christlich-Demokratische Union Deutschlands (CDU, Christian Democratic Union of Germany), together with its sister party in Bavaria, the Christlich-Soziale Union (CSU, Christian Social Union). The SPD was the largest opposition party. Dr Konrad Adenauer, the leader of the CDU, was elected Federal Chancellor by the Bundestag (Federal Assembly); Theodor Heuss became the first President of the Republic. Under Adenauer's chancellorship (which lasted until 1963) and the direction of Dr Ludwig Erhard, his Minister of Economics (and successor as Chancellor), the FRG rebuilt itself rapidly to become one of the most affluent and economically dynamic states in Europe, as well as an important strategic ally of other Western European states and the USA. The Paris Agreement of 1954 gave full sovereign status to the FRG from 5 May 1955, and also granted it membership of NATO (see p. 301).

The CDU/CSU held power in coalition with the SPD from 1966 to 1969, under the chancellorship of Dr Kurt Kiesinger, but lost support at the 1969 general election, allowing the SPD to form a coalition Government with the Freie Demokratische Partei (FDP, Free Democratic Party), under the chancellorship of Willy Brandt, the SPD leader. Following elections in November 1972, the SPD became, for the first time, the largest party in the Bundestag. In May 1974, however, Brandt resigned as Chancellor, after the discovery that his personal assistant had been a clandestine agent of the GDR. He was succeeded by Helmut Schmidt of the SPD, hitherto the Minister of Finance. A deteriorating economic situation was accompanied by a decline in the popularity of the Government and increasing tension between the coalition partners. In the general election of October 1976 the SPD lost its position as largest party in the Bundestag, but the SPD-FDP coalition retained a slender majority.

At the general election of October 1980 the SPD-FDP coalition secured a 45-seat majority in the Bundestag. However, over the next two years the coalition became increasingly unstable, with the partners divided on issues of nuclear power, defence and economic policy. In September 1982 the coalition finally collapsed when the two parties failed to agree on budgetary measures. In October the FDP formed a Government with the CDU/CSU, under the chancellorship of Dr Helmut Kohl, the leader of the CDU. This new partnership was consolidated by the results of the general election of March 1983, when the CDU/CSU substantially increased its share of the votes cast, obtaining 48.8% of the total, compared with 38.8% for the SPD, now led by Hans-Jochen Vogel. An environmentalist party, Die Grünen (The Greens), gained representation in the Bundestag for the first time. In July 1984 Prof. Karl Carstens, who had held the post of Federal President since 1979, was succeeded by Dr Richard von Weizsäcker, also of the CDU. The CDU/CSU-FDP coalition retained power after the general election of January 1987, although with a reduced majority; Kohl was reappointed Chancellor by the Bundestag.

During the period 1949–69 the FRG, under the CDU/CSU, remained largely isolated from Eastern Europe, owing to the FRG Government's refusal to recognize the GDR as an independent state or to maintain diplomatic relations with any other states that recognized the GDR. When Willy Brandt of the SPD became Chancellor in 1969, he adopted a more conciliatory approach to relations with Eastern Europe and, in particular, towards the GDR, a policy which came to be known as Ostpolitik. In 1970 formal discussions were conducted between representatives of the GDR and the FRG for the first time, and there was a significant increase in diplomatic contacts between the FRG and the other countries of Eastern Europe. In 1970 treaties were signed with the USSR and Poland, in which the FRG formally renounced claims to the eastern territories of the Third

Reich and recognized the 'Oder–Neisse Line' as the border between Germany (actually the GDR) and Poland. Further negotiations between the GDR and the FRG, following a quadripartite agreement on West Berlin in September 1971, clarified access rights to West Berlin and also allowed West Berliners to visit the GDR. In December 1972 the two German states signed a 'Basic Treaty', agreeing to develop normal, neighbourly relations with each other, to settle all differences without resort to force, and to respect each other's independence. The Treaty permitted both the FRG and the GDR to join the UN in September 1973, and allowed many Western countries to establish diplomatic relations with the GDR, although both German states continued to deny formal diplomatic recognition to each other.

In December 1981 the first official meeting took place between the two countries' leaders for 11 years, when Chancellor Schmidt of the FRG travelled to the GDR for discussions with Honecker. Inter-German relations deteriorated following the deployment, in late 1983, of US nuclear missiles in the FRG, and the subsequent siting of additional Soviet missiles in the GDR. Nevertheless, official contacts were maintained, and Honecker made his first visit to the FRG in September 1987.

Relations between the two German states were dramatically affected by political upheavals that occurred in the GDR in late 1989 and 1990. In the latter half of 1989 many thousands of disaffected GDR citizens emigrated illegally to the FRG, via Czechoslovakia, Poland and Hungary. The exodus was accelerated by the Hungarian Government's decision, in September 1989, to permit citizens of the GDR to leave Hungary without exit visas. Meanwhile, there was a growth in popular dissent within the GDR, led by Neues Forum (New Forum), an independent citizens' action group which had been established to encourage discussion of democratic reforms, justice and environmental issues.

In early October 1989, following official celebrations to commemorate the 40th anniversary of the foundation of the GDR, anti-Government demonstrations erupted in East Berlin and other large towns. Eventually, as the demonstrations attracted increasing popular support, intervention by the police ceased. (It was later reported that the SED Politburo had voted narrowly against the use of the armed forces to suppress the civil unrest.) In mid-October, as the political situation became more unsettled, Honecker resigned as General Secretary of the SED, Chairman of the Council of State and Chairman of the National Defence Council, ostensibly for reasons of ill health. He was replaced in all these posts by Egon Krenz, a senior member of the SED Politburo. Krenz immediately offered concessions to the opposition, initiating a dialogue with the members of Neues Forum (which was legalized in early November) and with church leaders. There was also a noticeable liberalization of the media, and an amnesty was announced for all persons who had been detained during the recent demonstrations and for those imprisoned for attempting to leave the country illegally. However, large demonstrations, to demand further reforms, continued in many towns throughout the GDR.

On 7 November 1989, in a further attempt to placate the demonstrators, the entire membership of the GDR Council of Ministers (including the Chairman, Willi Stoph) resigned. On the following day the SED Politburo also resigned. On 9 November restrictions on foreign travel for GDR citizens were ended, and all border crossings to the FRG were opened. During the weekend of 10–11 November an estimated 2m. GDR citizens crossed into West Berlin, and the GDR authorities began to dismantle sections of the wall dividing the city. Dr Hans Modrow, a leading member of the SED who was regarded as an advocate of greater reforms, was appointed Chairman of a new Council of Ministers. The new Government pledged to introduce comprehensive political and economic reforms and to hold free elections in 1990.

In early December 1989 the Volkskammer (the GDR's legislature) voted to remove provisions in the Constitution that protected the SED's status as the single ruling party. However, the mass demonstrations continued, prompted by revelations of corruption and personal enrichment by the former leadership and of abuses of power by the state security service (Staatssicherheitsdienst, known colloquially as the Stasi, which was subsequently disbanded). A special commission was established to investigate such charges, and former senior officials, including Honecker and Stoph, were expelled from the SED and placed under house arrest, pending legal proceedings. As the political situation became increasingly unstable, the entire

membership of the SED Politburo and Central Committee, including Krenz, resigned, and both bodies, together with the post of General Secretary, were abolished. Shortly afterwards, Krenz also resigned as Chairman of the Council of State; he was replaced by Dr Manfred Gerlach, the Chairman of the Liberal-Demokratische Partei Deutschlands (LDPD, Liberal Democratic Party of Germany). Dr Gregor Gysi, a prominent defence lawyer who was sympathetic to the opposition, was elected to the new post of Chairman of the SED (restyled the Partei des Demokratischen Sozialismus—PDS, Party of Democratic Socialism, in February 1990).

In December 1989 and January 1990 all-party talks took place in the GDR, resulting in the formation, in early February, of a new administration, designated the Government of National Responsibility (still led by Modrow), to remain in office until elections were held. The GDR's first free legislative elections took place on 18 March 1990, with the participation of 93% of those eligible to vote. The East German CDU obtained 40.8% of the total votes cast, while the newly re-established East German SPD and the PDS secured 21.8% and 16.4% respectively. In April a coalition Government was formed, headed by Lothar de Maizière, leader of the Eastern CDU. Five parties were represented in the new Government: the CDU, the SPD, the Liga der Freien Demokraten (League of Free Democrats) and two smaller parties—the Deutsche Soziale Union (German Social Union) and Demokratische Aufschwung (Democratic Departure). The PDS was not invited to join the coalition.

As a result of the changes within the GDR and the subsequent free contact between Germans of east and west, the issue of possible unification of the two German states inevitably emerged. In November 1989 Chancellor Kohl proposed a plan for the eventual unification of the two countries by means of an interim confederal arrangement. In December Kohl made his first visit to the GDR, where he held discussions with the East German leadership. The two sides agreed to develop contacts at all levels and to establish joint economic, cultural and environmental commissions. However the GDR Government initially insisted that the GDR remain a sovereign, independent state. Nevertheless, in February 1990, in response to growing popular support among GDR citizens for unification, Modrow publicly advocated the establishment of a united Germany. Shortly afterwards, Kohl and Modrow met in Bonn, where they agreed to establish a joint commission to achieve full economic and monetary union between the GDR and the FRG. The new coalition Government of the GDR, formed in April 1990, pledged its determination to achieve German unification in the near future. In mid-May the legislatures of the GDR and the FRG approved the Treaty Between the FRG and the GDR Establishing a Monetary, Economic and Social Union; the Treaty came into effect on 1 July. Later in July the Volkskammer approved the re-establishment on GDR territory of the five Länder (states)—Brandenburg, Mecklenburg-Vorpommern (Mecklenburg-Western Pomerania), Sachsen (Saxony), Sachsen-Anhalt (Saxony-Anhalt) and Thüringen (Thuringia)—which had been abolished by the GDR Government in 1952 in favour of 14 Berzirke (districts). On 31 August 1990 the Treaty Between the FRG and the GDR on the Establishment of German Unity was signed in East Berlin by representatives of the two Governments. The treaty stipulated, *inter alia*, that the newly restored Länder would accede to the FRG on 3 October 1990, and that the 23 boroughs of East and West Berlin would jointly form the Land (state) of Berlin.

Owing to the complex international status of the FRG and the GDR and the two countries' membership of opposing military alliances (respectively, NATO and the now-defunct Warsaw Pact), the process of German unification also included negotiations with other countries. In February 1990 representatives of 23 NATO and Warsaw Pact countries agreed to establish the so-called 'two-plus-four' talks (the FRG and the GDR, plus the four countries that had occupied Germany after the Second World War—France, the USSR, the United Kingdom and the USA) to discuss the external aspects of German unification. In June both German legislatures approved a resolution recognizing the inviolability of Poland's post-1945 borders, stressing that the eastern border of a future united Germany would remain along the Oder–Neisse line. In July, at bilateral talks in the USSR with Chancellor Kohl, the Soviet leader, Mikhail Gorbachev, agreed that a united Germany would be free to join whichever military alliance it wished, thus permitting Germany to remain a full member of NATO. The USSR also pledged to withdraw its armed forces (estimated at 370,000 in 1990) from GDR territory within four years, and it was agreed that a united Germany would reduce the strength of its armed forces to 370,000 within the same period. This agreement ensured a successful result to the 'two-plus-four' talks, which were concluded in September in Moscow, where the Treaty on the Final Settlement with Respect to Germany was signed. In late September the GDR withdrew from the Warsaw Pact.

On 1 October 1990 representatives of the four countries that had occupied Germany after the Second World War met in New York to sign a document in which Germany's full sovereignty was recognized. Finally, on 3 October, the two German states were formally unified. On the following day, at a session of the Bundestag (which had been expanded to permit the representation of former deputies of the GDR Volkskammer), five prominent politicians from the former GDR were sworn in as Ministers without Portfolio in the Federal Government.

Prior to unification, the CDU, the SPD and the FDP of the GDR had merged with their respective counterparts in the FRG to form three single parties. At state elections in the newly acceded Länder, held in mid-October 1990, the CDU obtained an average of 41% of the total votes cast and won control of four Land legislatures, while the SPD received an average of 27% of the total votes cast and gained a majority only in Brandenburg. This surge of support for Chancellor Kohl and the CDU was confirmed by the results of elections to the Bundestag in early December (the first all-German elections since 1933). The CDU (together with the CSU) won 43.8% of the total votes cast, and thus secured a total of 319 seats in the 662-member Bundestag. The SPD achieved its poorest result in a general election since 1957, receiving 33.5% of the votes cast and winning 239 seats in the legislature (a result attributed, in large part, to the party's cautious stance on unification). The FDP won 11% of the total votes cast, and consequently 79 seats in the Bundestag, its most successful result in legislative elections since 1961. Unexpectedly, the West German Grünen lost the 42 seats that they had previously held in the legislature, having failed to obtain the necessary 5% of the votes cast in the area formerly constituting the FRG. However, as a result of a special clause in the electoral law (adopted in October 1990, and valid only for the legislative elections of December 1990), which permitted representation in the Bundestag for parties of the former GDR that received at least 5% of the total votes cast in former GDR territory, the party's eastern German counterpart, in coalition with Bündnis 90 (Alliance 90), secured eight seats in the legislature. Under the same ruling, the PDS won 17 seats in the Bundestag (having received almost 10% of the total votes cast in the area formerly constituting the GDR).

Dr Kohl was formally re-elected to the post of Federal Chancellor in mid-January 1991, immediately after the formation of the new Federal Government. This comprised 20 members, but included only three politicians from the former GDR. The FDP's representation was increased from four to five ministers, reflecting the party's success in the recent legislative elections.

Investigations into the abuse of power by the administration of the former GDR, conducted during the early 1990s, prompted the dismissal or resignation from government posts of several former SED politicians. In January 1991 the German authorities temporarily suspended efforts to arrest Honecker on charges of manslaughter (for complicity in the deaths of people who had been killed while attempting to escape from the GDR), owing to the severe ill health of the former GDR leader. In March it was announced that Honecker had been transferred, without the permission of the German authorities, to the USSR, and in December he took refuge in the Chilean embassy in Moscow.

One of the most serious problems confronting the Government immediately following unification was that of escalating unemployment in eastern Germany, as a result of the introduction of market-orientated reforms which were intended to integrate the economic system of the former GDR with that of the rest of the country. A substantial increase in the crime rate in eastern Germany was also recorded. A further disturbing social issue, particularly in the eastern Länder, was the resurgence of extreme right-wing and neo-Nazi groups. Moreover, there were also fears of a resurgence of political violence, following a series of terrorist acts culminating in the assassination, in April 1991, of Detlev Rohwedder, the executive head of the Treuhandanstalt (the trustee agency that had been established in March 1990 to supervise the privatization of state-owned enterprises in the former GDR). Responsibility for this and other attacks was claimed by the Rote Armee Fraktion (RAF, Red Army Faction),

a terrorist organization that had been active in the FRG during the 1970s. (The RAF eventually disbanded in 1998.)

Increasing popular discontent with the Government's post-unification policies was reflected in successive victories for the SPD in Land elections in the first half of 1991, causing the SPD to regain its majority in the Bundesrat, which it lost to the CDU/CSU-FDP coalition in October 1990. In June 1991 the Bundestag voted in favour of Berlin as the future seat of the legislature and of government; it was envisaged that the transfer of organs of government from Bonn to Berlin would be completed by 2000.

At the beginning of January 1992 some 2m. Stasi files were opened to public scrutiny. In February Erich Mielke, the former head of the Stasi, was brought to trial on charges of murder, and in September Markus Wolf, the former head of East Germany's intelligence service, was charged with espionage, treason and corruption; both were subsequently found guilty and each was sentenced to six years' imprisonment. Meanwhile, Honecker returned to Germany from Russia in July 1992. He was brought to trial in November, together with five other defendants (among them Mielke and Stoph), on charges of manslaughter and embezzlement. In April 1993, however, the charges against Honecker were suspended. (The former East German leader, who was terminally ill, had been allowed to leave for Chile in January of that year; he died in May 1994.) Stoph was also released on grounds of ill health. In May 1993 Hans Modrow was found guilty of electoral fraud at communal elections that had taken place in the former GDR in 1989; Modrow was subsequently sentenced to nine months' imprisonment (suspended).

The issue of asylum-seekers dominated domestic politics during the early 1990s. At Land elections in April 1992, both the CDU and the SPD lost considerable support to right-wing extremist parties. In June the Bundestag approved controversial legislation which aimed to accelerate the processing of applications by refugees and introduced stricter rules for the granting of asylum. A six-week limit was imposed on the time that could be devoted to the consideration of each case, during which period applicants would be required to stay in special camps. Extreme nationalistic sentiment in some quarters led to an escalation in brutal attacks against asylum-seekers and foreign workers during the early 1990s. In August 1992 neo-Nazi youths attacked refugee centres in more than 15 towns and bombed a memorial to the Holocaust (the Nazis' extermination of an estimated 6m. Jews) in Berlin. Sporadic attacks continued throughout Germany (though mainly in the east) in September and October. Several neo-Nazi vandals were arrested, but there was criticism of the lenient sentences imposed on those convicted. The murder in November of three Turkish immigrants in an arson attack in Mölln, Schleswig-Holstein, prompted the Government to ban several right-wing groups that were believed to have been responsible for co-ordinating attacks on foreigners. In December the main political parties reached agreement on the terms of a constitutional amendment to the law of asylum, and the new provisions, empowering immigration officials to refuse entry to economic migrants while still facilitating the granting of asylum to persons who were deemed to be political refugees, were approved by the Bundestag and the Bundesrat in May 1993. The Ministry of the Interior estimated that a record total of 438,191 people had sought asylum in Germany during 1992. By 1998, however, mainly as a result of the 1993 legislation, the number of applications had fallen to 98,644. During May 1993 the deaths of five Turkish women in an arson attack near Köln precipitated protest demonstrations throughout Germany and widespread condemnation in the international media. In May 1994 the Bundesrat approved measures to impose stricter penalties on perpetrators of right-wing violence and on those who denied the existence of the Holocaust; further strong measures against nationalist extremists were adopted in September.

The CDU/CSU-FDP coalition was re-elected at a general election held in October 1994; its majority in the Bundestag (enlarged to 672 seats) was, however, sharply reduced, from 134 to 10 seats. The CDU (with the CSU) won 41.4% of the votes cast and 294 seats, the SPD 36.4% of the votes cast and 252 seats, Bündnis 90/Die Grünen 7.3% of the votes cast and 50 seats, the FDP (which had lost representation at several Land parliament elections during 1994) 6.9% of the votes cast and 47 seats, and the PDS 4.4% of the votes cast and 30 seats. (The PDS secured 17.7% of the votes cast in the eastern Länder.) The right-wing extremist organizations did not attract strong support. In early November the ruling coalition negotiated a new political programme, with the creation of jobs a priority. Shortly afterwards Dr Kohl was formally re-elected as the Federal Chancellor, by a narrow margin of five votes.

In May 1995 the Federal Constitutional Court ruled that alleged former East German spies should not be prosecuted by Federal courts regarding crimes that were committed against the Federal Republic on behalf of the former GDR prior to unification; consequently in October the 1992 conviction of Markus Wolf on espionage charges was overturned. In November 1996 the Federal Constitutional Court ruled that the legal principles of the FRG regarding human rights could be retroactively applied to actions carried out within the former GDR. Thus, in January 1997 Wolf was charged with abduction, coercion and assault. In August Egon Krenz and two other former senior SED members, Günther Schabowski and Günther Kleiber, were found guilty of the manslaughter and attempted manslaughter of people who had sought to flee the former GDR; all three were sentenced to terms of imprisonment. The convictions were upheld in November 1999, following unsuccessful appeals. Krenz's conviction was again upheld in 2001, following an unsuccessful appeal to the European Court of Human Rights. Schabowski and Kleiber were pardoned in September 2000 and were released on the eve of the 10th anniversary of German reunification in early October.

The activities of extreme right-wing organizations increased significantly in 1997, and during the latter half of the year a series of incidents was reported that suggested the infiltration of some sections of the armed forces by neo-Nazi interests. In late April 1998 the extreme right-wing and openly xenophobic Deutsche Volksunion (DVU, German People's Union) won unprecedented support at an election to the Land parliament for the economically depressed Sachsen-Anhalt region of eastern Germany, securing 12.9% of the votes cast.

Tensions within the CDU/CSU-FDP coalition became apparent in 1997, mainly concerning the desirability and means of meeting the so-called 'convergence criteria' for participation in European Economic and Monetary Union (EMU) by 1999. Record levels of unemployment continued to cause concern, as well as an unexpectedly large deficit on the 1997 budget. In January 1998 three economists and a professor of law initiated a challenge at the Federal Constitutional Court to Germany's proposed participation in EMU, on the grounds that it would contravene the Government's constitutional duty to pursue sound monetary policy. However, in early April the Court ruled that the issue of a common European currency was outside its jurisdiction and was, rather, the responsibility of the Government. In late April, despite evidence of widespread opposition to the new currency, the Bundestag voted strongly in favour of Germany's participation in EMU.

At the general election held in late September 1998 the CDU/CSU-FDP coalition was decisively defeated by the SPD, which won 298 of the total seats in the Bundestag (reduced to 669). The CDU took 198 seats, both the CSU and Bündnis 90/Die Grünen secured 47, the FDP 43 and the PDS 36. Neither the right-wing Republikaner nor the DVU gained representation in the federal legislature. Following the election, Kohl resigned as Chairman of the CDU; he was replaced by the party's parliamentary leader, Dr Wolfgang Schäuble. Meanwhile, the SPD and Bündnis 90/Die Grünen swiftly negotiated a coalition pact, which was formally approved by both parties at conferences in late October. Shortly afterwards Gerhard Schröder of the SPD (formerly the Minister President of Niedersachsen) was elected Federal Chancellor by a large majority of Bundestag members; the following day a new Federal Government was announced, which included three ministers representing Bündnis 90/Die Grünen. The most prominent of these was the new Federal Vice-Chancellor and Minister of Foreign Affairs, Joseph (Joschka) Fischer, who was formerly the parliamentary leader of the ecological parties. Oskar Lafontaine, the Chairman of the SPD, was appointed Minister of Finance, charged with the responsibility for guiding Germany into EMU. The SPD-Bündnis 90/Die Grünen coalition held a 21-seat majority in the Bundestag.

In early November 1998 Schröder delivered his first major policy statement, placing high priority on reducing the rising level of unemployment; measures were also planned to expedite the economic reconstruction of the eastern Länder, to reform the pension system, to impose an 'ecological' tax on energy consumption and gradually to curtail the country's nuclear energy programme. It soon became apparent, however, that the two coalition partners envisaged very different time-scales for the abandonment of atomic power. While the SPD favoured the

phased closure of the 19 national nuclear power plants over a minimum period of 25 years, the ecological parties aimed to act far more swiftly. In mid-December Schröder overruled his Bündnis 90/Die Grünen Minister of the Environment, Nature Conservation and Nuclear Safety, Jürgen Trittin, when Trittin unilaterally attempted both to cancel contracts with British and French companies for the reprocessing of German nuclear waste and to dismiss the chiefs of the national atomic power safety commissions.

In early March 1999 Lafontaine resigned as Minister of Finance, apparently in protest at an evident lack of support for his economic policies and management from within both the business community and the Government; he also vacated his seat in the Bundestag and the chairmanship of the SPD. Hans Eichel of the SPD, hitherto the Minister-President of Hesse, was appointed as the new Minister of Finance. In the following month Schröder was elected to the post of Chairman of the SPD. In early May the Government approved legislation which enabled people born in Germany of resident foreign parents to hold both German citizenship (hitherto denied them) and the nationality of one parent until adulthood, whereupon they would be required to relinquish one. This represented a significant departure from previous ethnically-orientated citizenship legislation, and was intended to encourage the social assimilation of Germany's foreign population (numbering some 7m. in 1999). The opposition CDU had strongly opposed an initial proposal to grant a full right of dual nationality.

At the beginning of June 1999 Dr Roman Herzog of the CDU was replaced as Federal President by Prof. Dr Johannes Rau of the SPD, formerly Minister-President of Nordrhein-Westfalen. During mid-1999 most organs of government moved from Bonn to Berlin (the capital and henceforth permanent seat of government). Both the Bündnis 90/Die Grünen alliance (which was becoming increasingly polarized between idealist and more pragmatic elements) and the SPD (which was popularly regarded as having betrayed its avowed commitment to social justice following the announcement in June of a package of economic austerity measures designed to redress the decelerating economic growth rate and to appease the alienated business sector) performed poorly at elections to several Land legislatures during the second half of 1999; by late 1999 the ruling coalition had control of less than two-fifths of votes in the Bundesrat (Federal Council). Nevertheless, in early December Schröder was re-elected to the post of Chairman of the SPD, by a higher margin of support than that achieved at the April party election.

During November 1999 the opposition CDU became embroiled in a scandal concerning the discovery of a system of secret bank accounts, which had been used to deposit undisclosed donations to the party throughout the 1990s. (In accordance with the Grundgesetz, all substantial funding of political parties must be declared.) Allegations subsequently emerged that the CDU leadership had covertly (and possibly with the knowledge of former French President François Mitterrand) accepted a large bribe from the then state-owned French oil company Elf Aquitaine, in connection with its purchase in 1992 of an eastern German oil refinery. It was also alleged that, in 1998, the CDU had granted an export licence to an arms exporting interest in return for an undeclared party donation. The former Chancellor, Kohl, admitted knowledge of some secret party funding, but repeatedly refused to name any sources; in late December 1999 he became the subject of a criminal investigation. Kohl resigned his honorary chairmanship of the CDU following an ultimatum from party members to clarify his role in the scandal or risk suspension from his honorary position. The incumbent CDU leadership was also implicated in the scandal, including the party Chairman, Dr Schäuble, who had been a close ally of Kohl under the previous administration. Schäuble was, however, confirmed by the party as its Chairman in January 2000, despite his offer of resignation, following his belated confession earlier in the month that in 1994 he had accepted a cash donation from an arms dealer, Karlheinz Schreiber, who was implicated in the funding scandal. (In August 2000 a court ruled that Schreiber should stand trial on charges of tax evasion, bribery and conspiracy to defraud in connection with the German Government's sale of tanks to Saudi Arabia during the Gulf War.) Schäuble established a CDU independent inquiry into the funding scandal in January 2000, which subsequently revealed that funding irregularities had persisted for decades in German politics. The inquiry established that during the 1970s between US $15m. and $20m. was paid in cash to the main political parties by the German intelligence agency to support developing democracies in Spain and Portugal. Throughout January 2000 further revelations emerged, including the secretion of more than DM 13m. in illegal foreign accounts by the Hesse regional branch of the CDU. The Minister-President of Hesse, Roland Koch, however, retained the support of both his party and its regional coalition partner, the FDP. In September Koch also won a vote of confidence in the state legislature following fresh media accusations that he had benefited from large corporate donations in the late 1990s. In February 2000 the CDU was fined DM 41m. for irregularities in the Hesse accounts for 1998. The following day Schäuble resigned as Chairman of the CDU, accepting responsibility for mishandling the funding scandal. In March a formal investigation was launched into suspected illegal party financing by the former head of the Chancellery under Schröder, Bodo Hombach; the SPD had not previously been implicated in the party funding scandals. In November 2001 federal prosecutors abandoned their investigation of Schäuble, thus enabling him to contend the forthcoming national elections. By January 2002, however, another funding scandal had emerged when the Bundestag and state prosecutors launched preliminary investigations into allegations that the CSU had improperly obtained funds from federal authorities by incorrectly classifying its income.

Meanwhile, following the withdrawal from contention in March 2000 of the former Minister of Defence, Volke Rühe (owing to the party's poor performance under his leadership in the state legislative election in Schleswig-Holstein in late February), the CDU's Secretary-General, Angela Merkel, was elected Chairman at the party congress in April. Merkel, who had secured significant support as a result of her determination to expose the CDU's financial irregularities, was considered more liberal than her predecessors. In March excerpts from transcripts of telephone conversations of the CDU treasurer under Kohl, Uwe Lüthje, and other CDU officials, which had been illegally recorded by the Stasi, appeared to indicate that Kohl had been aware of the irregular party funding earlier than he had previously admitted. Following a campaign by Kohl, the leaders of the principal parties agreed in May to forbid the use of the transcripts by the parliamentary committee investigating financial irregularities in the CDU, and, in July 2001, Kohl secured a court ruling banning the publication of the transcripts. However, in May 2000 the state prosecutor concluded that there were sufficient grounds for the criminal prosecution of Kohl on charges of fraud and bribery (although as an incumbent member of the legislature Kohl was immune from prosecution). In his testimony in June to the parliamentary committee Kohl continued to admit accepting illegal secret contributions to party funds, but refuted allegations that such donations had influenced government policy decisions (including the sale of an East German oil refinery to Elf Aquitaine). Kohl's credibility was diminished still further that month when a report was published revealing that two-thirds of chancellery records relating to the period in question had been destroyed following Kohl's defeat in the 1998 general election. The files were however, discovered in July in the archives of the Konrad Adenauer Foundation, a right-wing policy unit. A criminal investigation into the missing files was closed in October 2003 when prosecutors failed to find any evidence of wrongdoing.

In September 2000 Kohl resumed his seat in the legislature for the first time since December 1999. He declined an invitation to the 10th anniversary celebration of unification in October 2000 on the grounds that, despite his central role in achieving German unification, he had not been invited to speak. In December another fine, of DM 7.7m., was imposed on the CDU by the Speaker of the Bundestag, Wolfgang Thierce, as a consequence of illegal fund-raising. Kohl had transferred DM 8m. (largely raised through donations) to the CDU in June to contribute to the payment of fines. The CDU's appeal against the previous fine, of DM 41m., was upheld by a court in January 2001, although Thierce announced his intention to appeal against the ruling. In February Kohl accepted the proposal of the state prosecutor that he should pay a fine of DM 300,000 in exchange for the abandonment of the criminal investigation into his acceptance of illegal contributions to the CDU in the 1990s; this arrangement subsequently gained judicial approval. The parliamentary inquiry continued, however, as did Kohl's refusal to name the illegal contributors to his party.

In December 1999 the German Government agreed to pay a substantial sum in compensation to people who had worked as forced labourers for German companies or been deprived of their assets under the Nazi regime; it was hoped that this would forestall a growing number of lawsuits taken out against German industrial interests and banks by survivors of the Holocaust. Chancellor Schröder announced that the Government would raise DM 5,000m. towards the proposed DM 10,000m. fund; the other DM 5,000m. was to be raised by Germany's largest banks and companies. The Government's share was to be financed by state privatizations and contributions from the Länder. The USA agreed to contribute US $10m. as a gesture of solidarity. In March 2000 Schröder announced an improved agreement, which resolved differences between categories of victims and added a further DM 200m. to the compensation fund. The extra money was to derive from interest income and from a separate settlement between Swiss banks and Holocaust victims. The larger German insurers declined to contribute to the fund being raised by industry because of potentially overlapping claims from separate negotiations involving many leading European insurers. The compensation agreement was eventually signed in July, and, following the resolution of legal difficulties, payments began in May 2001.

In June 2000, following months of negotiations between the Government and the nuclear industry, Schröder announced that an agreement had been concluded to decommission the country's 19 nuclear power plants (which accounted for almost one-third of power requirements) without compensation by 2021. Under the accord, the reprocessing of nuclear fuel would end by 2005 (although the transportation of spent fuel for reprocessing elsewhere could continue under certain conditions). Despite some reservations on the part of a significant number of members of Bündnis 90/Die Grünen who had favoured an immediate cessation of nuclear power generation, the agreement was endorsed at a party conference later that month. Rioting erupted over three days in March 2001 as thousands of anti-nuclear protesters attempted to halt a consignment of nuclear waste being transported by train and lorry from France to a storage site at a disused salt-mine in Gorleben in Lower Saxony. Around 20,000 riot police and other security units were deployed to remove the activists, some of whom had chained and cemented themselves to the rail track; about 600 protesters were arrested. The police action constituted the largest police deployment in Germany's post-war history. In September the Federal Government approved a bill regulating the phasing out of nuclear power, which was subsequently approved by the Bundestag. The first closure took place in mid-November 2003, when Germany's second oldest nuclear reactor, in Stade near Hamburg, was shut down. The reactor at Obrigheim in Baden-Württemberg, Germany's oldest, was the next scheduled for closure; it was to be shut down by November 2005.

In August 2000, in response to growing fears concerning the escalation of neo-Nazi violence against immigrants, the Government announced a series of measures to combat racist attacks, including the establishment of a panel to investigate a potential ban on the extremist right-wing party, the Nationaldemokratische Partei Deutschlands (NPD, National Democratic Party). Despite some opposition to the plan, on the grounds that it was unconstitutional and would afford neo-Nazis an undesirably high level of publicity, in early October the Federal Minister of the Interior formally proposed the ban, which subsequently received the support of 14 of the 16 Länder. The application to the Constitutional Court to ban the NPD on the grounds that it was anti-Semitic, racist and supported violence was approved by the Bundesrat in November and by the Bundestag in December. In January 2002, however, the Court postponed hearing the case when it emerged that one of the senior NPD activists whose statements were to be used in evidence against the party was an informant for the Bundesamt für Verfassungsschutz (BfV, Office for the Protection of the Constitution); the Court dismissed the case in March 2003. Meanwhile, in the latter half of 2000 Schröder demanded stricter application of existing legislation and tougher sentencing from the courts when dealing with right-wing extremists. In August the Government approved the expenditure of DM 75m. over three years to support local youth initiatives committed to fighting racism, anti-Semitism and xenophobia, and in January 2001 the Minister of Justice, Herta Däubler-Gmelin, announced that her Ministry would provide DM 10m. to compensate the victims of far-right violence, threats or insults.

In the latter half of 2003 the police engaged in a campaign to prevent the staging of violence by far-right extremists to mark the anniversary of *Kristallnacht*—the Nazi pogrom of 1938 in which dozens of Jews were murdered and hundreds of synagogues burnt down throughout Germany. In mid-September 10 members of the neo-Nazi group Southern Brotherhood were arrested on suspicion of plotting to detonate a bomb during the inauguration of a synagogue in Munich that President Rau and Paul Spiegel, the head of the German Jewish community, were due to attend. The following month police-officers carried out raids on more than 50 premises in Kiel and Flensburg; they confiscated weapons and illegal Nazi insignia, and arrested 10 members of the neo-Nazi group Combat 18.

In January 2001 a series of photographs emerged which appeared to show the Minister of Foreign Affairs assaulting a police-officer during a demonstration in Frankfurt in 1973. Fischer had never hidden his leftist militant past, but claimed he was a firm advocate of peaceful protest. He admitted to having fought unarmed against the police, but only after intense provocation, and flatly denied ever having used weapons. Fischer gave evidence later that month as a character witness in the trial of a former international militant activist, Hans Joachim Klein, when he again asserted that he had never favoured armed struggle.

In January 2001 the Minister of Health, Andrea Fischer, and the Minister of Food, Agriculture and Forestry, Karl-Heinz Funke, resigned amid growing national alarm at the spread of bovine spongiform encephalopathy (BSE) in cattle and accusations that they had ignored the risks posed by infected beef, which was linked to a new strain of Creutzfeldt-Jakob disease, a fatal degenerative illness affecting humans. Despite the crisis that had afflicted the agricultural sector in the United Kingdom, Funke had initially insisted that special anti-BSE measures were inappropriate in Germany. Such measures were, however, introduced in November 2000 following the confirmation of the first two cases of BSE in German cattle. By the end of January 2001 confirmed cases of BSE in German cattle had increased to 20. In response to public fears about BSE, Schröder created a new Ministry of Consumer Protection, Food and Agriculture. In February the Government introduced new legislation intended to combat the spread of BSE.

In late September 2001, following the attacks in the USA by suspected Islamist extremists, the Federal Government abolished the so-called 'religious privilege', thus removing legal protection for and allowing the banning of any religious organizations suspected of promoting terrorism. In early December police raided the premises of 20 militant Islamist groups throughout Germany, some of which were suspected of having links with the al-Qa'ida (Base) organization (an Islamist extremist group led by the Saudi-born militant Osama bin Laden, which was widely believed to have organized the attacks in the USA in September). Public concern was heightened by the fact that there was evidence that at least three of the presumed perpetrators of the US atrocities had recently lived in Hamburg and other German cities. Plans to introduce more liberal immigration laws were abandoned, and further new legislation was introduced to increase national security, including the extension of existing anti-terrorism legislation, which had hitherto only covered terrorist acts in Germany, to apply, in addition, to such acts committed in other countries. Measures to block funding channels for militant activists allowed the police access to bank account details of alleged terrorists. Further steps to control money-laundering were introduced, including the foundation of a centralized Financial Intelligence Unit, and the burden of proof regarding the authenticity of suspicious funds was moved from the banks and police to the client. Controls on employees with access to high-security areas of airports were made more stringent. All of these measures were to be funded by an immediate increase in tax on cigarettes and insurance policies.

In August 2002 a Moroccan national, Mounir El Motassadeq, was charged with offences under anti-terrorism legislation relating to the suicide attacks of 11 September 2001 in the USA; prosecutors claimed that El Motassadeq had been involved in financing the attacks. He stood trial in Hamburg, was convicted as an accessory to 3,066 murders, and was sentenced to 15 years' imprisonment. In August 2003 the trial began of a second Moroccan national, Abdelghani Mzoudi, who was also accused of helping to plan the attacks. However, Mzoudi was freed from custody in early December after the Bundeskriminalamt (BKA—the Federal Office of Criminal Investigation) submitted testimony from an unnamed source—believed to be the suspected al-Qa'ida activist Ramzi bin al-Shibh, who was in US custody—that the Hamburg cell had comprised only four members: three suicide pilots and one other man, an alleged senior

al-Qa'ida operative who was already in US custody. The prosecutors appealed against the decision to free the defendant, citing the alleged unreliability of the evidence. Within minutes of the collapse of the case against Mzoudi, lawyers acting on behalf of the imprisoned El Motassadeq stated that they would appeal against their client's conviction; they sought access to the testimony, but their application was rejected. Despite his release from custody, Mzoudi's prosecutors continued the trial against him; he was finally acquitted, however, in early February 2004 owing to lack of incriminating evidence. The following month the Federal Criminal Court in Karlsruhe overturned El Motassadeq's conviction on the grounds that he had not received a fair trial, principally because the Hamburg court had not had access to transcripts of al-Shibh's interrogation by the US authorities. El Motassadeq's retrial began in Hamburg in August. The US authorities again refused defence requests for access to certain al-Qa'ida suspects in US custody, although partial transcripts of the interrogations of three detainees (including al-Shibh) were provided.

In August 2002 the German authorities banned 16 Islamist groups linked to the Cologne-based 'Kalifatsstaat' ('Caliphate State'), an extremist Islamist group dedicated to the overthrow of Turkey's secular Government which had been banned, together with 20 related associations, in December 2001. Police raids against the Kalifatsstaat and other Islamist groups continued throughout 2002 and 2003. Several men were arrested on suspicion of recruiting 'suicide bombers' for operations in Iraq, following the deposal of the regime of the Iraqi President, Saddam Hussain, by US-led military action in March/April 2003. Following the release from German prison in March 2003 of the leader of the Kalifatsstaat, Metin Kaplan, Turkey requested his extradition to face treason charges. Germany had previously refused such requests as Kaplan would have thus faced the death sentence in Turkey. Following Turkey's abolition of the death sentence, however, and promises that Kaplan would receive a fair trial, a court in Cologne ruled in May 2004 that Kaplan's extradition to Turkey should proceed. Despite his temporary disappearance and attempts to appeal against the decision, Kaplan was deported to Turkey in October.

At the general election held on 22 September 2002 the SPD received 38.5% of the votes cast, winning 251 seats in the Bundestag. The CDU obtained 29.5% of the votes cast and secured 190 seats, the CSU 9.0% (58 seats), Die Grünen 8.6% (55 seats), the FDP 7.4% (47 seats) and the PDS 4.0% (two seats). The SPD-Bündnis 90/Die Grünen coalition remained in government. The SPD's position was, however, severely weakened and the Government's popularity suffered as a result of financial austerity measures adopted in an attempt to ward off economic recession. Legislative elections were held in two Länder, Niedersachsen and Hesse, in February 2003, at which the SPD suffered emphatic defeats at the hands of the CDU, which strengthened its majority in the Bundesrat to such an extent that it was able to block government legislation.

On 27 January 2003 (the 58th anniversary of the liberation of the Nazi concentration camp Auschwitz) the Government signed an agreement establishing a formal partnership with the Jewish population in Germany, according the Jewish faith the same legal status as the Protestant and Roman Catholic churches in Germany.

In August 2003 the Federal Government approved the 12 bills that comprised Schröder's so-called 'Agenda 2010' package of economic reforms. The proposed reforms, the main aims of which were to reduce the rate of unemployment and to revive Germany's stagnant economy, constituted the most extensive overhaul of the country's welfare state since the founding of the Federal Republic almost 60 years previously. The proposals were, however, deeply unpopular among the general public, trade unions and many members of the SPD, and the passage of the legislation through both chambers of the legislature was expected to prove difficult. With a negligible majority in the Bundestag (of just four), and no majority at all in the Bundesrat, it was widely forecast that Schröder would ultimately be forced to rely on the CDU-controlled Bundesrat to pass the legislation.

The first bill to be voted on by the Bundestag, in late September 2003, was a health reform bill, which had been drawn up jointly with CDU/CSU members and which was intended to reduce annual health-care costs by €23,000m. by 2007. In order to instil discipline for future 'Agenda 2010' votes, which were expected to be more divisive, Schröder insisted on passing the bill without having to rely on votes from the CDU. Several SPD members had threatened to vote against the bill, but, following

Schröder's threats to resign unless the bill were passed by votes from the governing coalition alone, only six coalition members carried out their threat and the bill was passed. On the same day legislation to amend labour regulations (and consequently reduce the level of unemployment) was also passed by the Bundestag, by 305 votes to 250. The reforms contained in the bill were, however, particularly unpopular with the trade unions, which had long been traditional allies of the SPD, and their introduction was widely viewed as an act of betrayal on the part of the Government.

In mid-October 2003 the Bundestag voted on welfare and tax reforms. Most notably, the welfare legislation proposed the merging of unemployment benefit and social welfare payments (which, in effect, amounted to a reduction in the level of benefits paid). As part of the tax reforms, tax reductions of some €22,000m. were proposed, which, it was hoped, would stimulate consumption and thereby reduce public indebtedness (which was at its highest level in Germany's post-war history). For the majority, however, most of the benefits accrued from these reductions were likely to be swiftly cancelled out by a lowering of tax concessions and subsidies; additionally, there was to be an increase in tax on tobacco. Despite a backbench revolt, the bills were passed by 306 votes to 291, although, to achieve this, Schröder was forced to summon a number of seriously ill SPD members to vote and he himself left an EU summit meeting in Brussels early in order to attend the vote (leaving President Jacques Chirac of France to represent Germany on his behalf). Furthermore, Schröder had once again threatened to resign if the bills were not passed. Polls revealed that the SPD was losing support throughout Germany, largely owing to the unpopularity of the reforms.

A few days after the passage of the welfare and tax legislation through the Bundestag, Schröder announced a 'freeze' on pensions. This was one of five emergency measures approved by the Government to cover the €8,000m. shortfall in government 'pay-as-you-go' pension schemes expected in 2004 without raising contributions, and to reduce Germany's prohibitively high non-wage labour costs. The move alienated many within the SPD and was thought likely to complicate subsequent 'Agenda 2010' votes. The Government endorsed longer-term pension reform measures, which were to be presented to the legislature before the end of 2003, under which workers were to be encouraged to take out more private pension cover, greater benefits were to be paid to those who retired later, and the age of retirement was to be raised to 67 years.

Such was the unpopularity of the various reforms within the SPD, that in late October 2003 Rudolf Scharping, the party's Deputy Chairman, resigned in protest at Schröder's policies; on 1 November some 100,000 people demonstrated against the reforms. Their unpopularity was also reflected in the SPD's poor performance in local elections in Bavaria. Nevertheless, Schröder vowed to pursue the reforms. On 7 November the CDU used its majority in the Bundesrat to block the legislation on debt-financed tax reductions (passed by the Bundestag in mid-October), fearing the debt burden would overwhelm the economy rather than revive it; the chamber voted to assemble a cross-party mediation committee in an attempt to reach a compromise on 'Agenda 2010'. The tax legislation was eventually passed (with amendments) in mid-December; the tax reductions were to be implemented in two stages, with only one-quarter of them to be financed by debt—the remainder were to be financed by the sale of government holdings in Deutsche Telekom and Deutsche Post. The tax cuts were also to be reduced from an original total of some €22,000m. to approximately €15,000m.

At the SPD conference held in mid-November 2003, Schröder was re-elected Chairman of the party, with 80.8% of votes cast (some 8% less than two years previously); this result was widely attributed, however, to a reluctance on the part of the SPD delegates to undermine their Chancellor. The party's General Secretary, Olaf Scholz, was also re-elected at the conference, but with just 53% of the votes cast, compared with 91% in 2001. Many SPD members felt that the 'Agenda 2010' reforms were a betrayal of the party's core values, and during 2003 the party lost some 5% of its membership (about 26,400 people—most of them long-time members). Conversely, some members of more right-wing parties believed that the reforms did not go far enough.

On 19 December 2003 the various bills comprising 'Agenda 2010', including the amended tax reductions (see above), were finally passed by both houses of the legislature, despite some dissent among the members of the governing coalition. Schröder

had repeated his threat to resign in the event of the reforms not being approved. Bitterness and divisions remained within the SPD, however, following the approval of 'Agenda 2010', with the party leadership increasingly being seen as isolated from the rest of the membership. Consequently, on 6 February 2004, Schröder announced his resignation as Chairman of the SPD; he was, however, to remain in his post as Chancellor. The SPD elected Franz Müntefering as its new leader at a special party conference in March.

On 23 May 2004 the Bundesversammlung—a specially convened Federal Convention consisting of the members of the Bundestag and an equal number of delegates from the legislatures of the 16 Länder—elected Dr Horst Köhler, the joint candidate of the CDU and the FDP, as the new Federal President; he was inaugurated on 1 July.

In May 2004 the governing SPD-Bündnis 90/Die Grünen coalition reached a compromise agreement with the CDU on the content of a bill to regulate immigration, the previous version of which had been rejected by the CDU-dominated Bundesrat in June 2003. The bill provided for the admission of a controlled number of skilled workers, self-employed persons and students who had completed their studies in Germany; government proposals for a general points system for would-be immigrants were abandoned at the CDU's insistence. The bill also strengthened the Government's powers to combat illegal immigration and to deport failed political asylum seekers as well as foreign religious leaders who engaged in extremist preaching in Germany. It was adopted by the Bundesrat on 9 July. The CDU announced that it intended to propose an additional piece of legislation to allow the detention of terrorist suspects without trial for up to two years.

In June 2004, following a four-year legal process, the Bundesverwaltungsgericht (Federal Administrative Court) ruled that files compiled by the Stasi on former Chancellor Kohl (see above) could be released with the consent of those affected where the information was not already public and where the files related to Kohl's public life only. Files containing personal information were to be released for research purposes alone, on the condition that they did not fall into the wrong hands or be published. Consequently the majority of the Stasi files on Kohl were expected to remain sealed for the foreseeable future.

In August 2004 two former members of the GDR Politburo, Hans-Joachim Böhme and Siegfried Lorenz, were convicted of abetting the killing of three persons attempting to escape over the Berlin Wall in 1986–89. They received suspended sentences of 15 months. This was the final 'Berlin Wall' trial; a total of 126 former GDR officials had been convicted of such charges since reunification.

In mid-2004 the 'Agenda 2010' reforms again dominated the political arena in Germany. In July the Bundesrat passed the 'Hartz IV' bill, which legislated for reform (and ultimately a reduction) of unemployment and social welfare benefits; the law was to take effect on 1 January 2005. Opposition to Hartz IV was strong throughout Germany, but particularly so in the Länder of the former GDR, where long-term unemployment was endemic. Many thousands regularly took to the streets in *Montagsdemos* (Monday protests), which were intended to mirror the demonstrations that led to the fall of the Berlin Wall. For six weeks the weekly protests were held in Berlin, Dresden, Leipzig, Magdeburg, and other, smaller cities throughout Germany. The *Montagsdemos* were small compared with protests staged against other 'Agenda 2010' reforms earlier that year, but they were increasingly physical: Schröder had eggs and stones thrown at him. At their height it appeared that they might precipitate a political crisis—Oskar Lafontaine, the former Minister of Finance known as 'Red Oskar' for his left-wing views—demanded Schröder's resignation, openly incited revolt within the SPD and threatened to support a left-wing political movement composed of disaffected SPD members and trade unionists. Support for the SPD fell dramatically in mid-2004, reflecting not only the widespread anger at the reforms, but also the long-standing frustration of many east Germans at the failed economic integration of the east since reunification.

At local elections held on 19 September 2004 in Brandenburg and Sachsen (Saxony) support for extreme right-wing parties increased sharply, largely at the expense of the SPD. The DVU won 6 seats in Brandenburg, and the NPD won 12 seats in Sachsen. This surge in support was largely attributed to protest votes against the Hartz IV reforms, but the two parties' co-operation agreement and the more mainstream image adopted by their candidates were also believed to be contributory factors to their success. Following the elections the DVU and the NPD announced their intention to merge in order to contest the federal legislative election in 2006.

By late September 2004 the *Montagsdemos* had virtually ceased as resignation set in amongst the protestors. The Government offered some concessions, but the basic structure of the benefit reforms remained unchanged. Over a short period of time Schröder's support in opinion polls recovered from a nadir of 23% to 33%, helped perhaps by his adoption of a three-year-old Russian orphan. Moreover, the opposition parties were unable to agree on a viable alternative to the reforms or on other important issues such as the restructuring of Germany's health system and Turkey's possible accession to the EU. However, when the reforms to the benefits system came into force in January 2005 the rate of unemployment rose, partly owing to new methods of calculation, to the psychologically critical level of 5m., which once again jeopardized the SPD's popular support. This was reflected in local elections in Schleswig-Holstein, held on 20 February 2005, where the SPD performed poorly.

In December 2004 it was announced that a 32-member, all-party commission established a year earlier to propose reforms to the 1949 Grundgesetz had failed to reach an agreement. Its main aims had been to redress the balance of power between the Bundestag and the Bundesrat and to simplify relations between the Federal Government and the 16 Länder.

The orientation of Germany's foreign policy after unification broadly followed that of the pre-1990 FRG. The united Germany remained committed to a leading role in the European Community (EC—now European Union—EU, see p. 217), of which the FRG was a founding member, and NATO, while placing greater emphasis on defence co-operation with France. The country was also strongly committed to close relations with Eastern Europe, in particular with the USSR and, subsequently, its successor states. Relations between the FRG and the USSR had improved significantly during the 1980s, culminating in the signing, in September 1990, of a Treaty on Good-Neighbourliness, Partnership and Co-operation. In April 1992 Germany and Russia agreed to a mutual cancellation of debts, and in December of the same year the two countries concluded an agreement whereby the Russian Government would grant autonomy to the 2.5m. ethnic Germans in the Volga region of Russia. In September 1996 the Land interior ministers agreed that the Länder could begin deporting some of the 320,000 refugees from Bosnia and Herzegovina who had been given temporary refuge in Germany. In October the German Government signed an agreement with the Federal Republic of Yugoslavia (FRY—now Serbia and Montenegro), providing for the return of about 135,000 Yugoslav refugees to the FRY over a three-year period (from the beginning of December). In January 1997, following more than a year of complex diplomatic negotiations, Dr Kohl and the Prime Minister of the Czech Republic, Václav Klaus, signed a joint declaration regretting past wrongs committed on both sides before, during and after the Second World War.

Following the Iraqi invasion and annexation of Kuwait in August 1990, the German Government expressed support for the deployment of US-led allied forces in the region of the Persian (Arabian) Gulf, and contributed substantial amounts of financial and technical aid to the effort to liberate Kuwait, although there were mass demonstrations against the allied action in many parts of Germany. Despite criticism from certain countries participating in the alliance, Germany did not contribute troops to the allied force, in accordance with a provision in the Grundgesetz that was widely interpreted as prohibiting intervention outside the area of NATO operations. In July 1992, however, the Government announced that it was to send a naval destroyer and reconnaissance aircraft to the Adriatic Sea to participate in the UN force monitoring the observance of UN sanctions on the FRY. This deployment was subsequently approved by the Bundestag. In April 1993 the Constitutional Court ruled that German forces could join the UN operation to enforce an air exclusion zone over Bosnia and Herzegovina. Germany dispatched troops to assist the UN relief effort in Somalia in mid-1993. In May 1994 the Constitutional Court declared the participation of German military units in collective international defence and security operations, with the approval of the Bundestag in each instance, to be compatible with the Grundgesetz. In March 1997, while supervising the evacuation from Albania of citizens of western European states, German troops opened fire on hostile forces for the first time since 1945. From March to early June 1999 Germany participated in the

ongoing NATO military offensive against the FRY, despite misgivings from left-wing elements within the ruling SPD-Bündnis 90/Die Grünen coalition.

In May 1992 Germany and France reached agreement on the establishment of a combined defence corps, which, they envisaged, would provide the basis for a pan-European military force under the aegis of Western European Union (WEU, see p. 352). The so-called Eurocorps became operational in November 1995. In December 2000 the heads of government of the EU (except Denmark) endorsed the plan for a 60,000-strong European Rapid Reaction Force (ERRF), which had been adopted by EU ministers in November (although NATO was to remain central to European defence). The logistics involved in creating such a body proved extremely difficult, and little progress had been made in achieving the EU's original plan with regard to the establishment of the ERRF by early 2004. In November 2004, however, the EU defence ministers agreed to create 13 'battle groups' (each numbering 1,000–1,500 men) by 2007, which could be deployed at short notice (within 10 days) to carry out peace-keeping activities at crisis points around the world.

In early September 2001 German troops were dispatched to participate in a NATO peace-keeping mission in the former Yugoslav republic of Macedonia, despite opposition to the deployment by members of Bündnis 90/Die Grünen. In the aftermath of the terrorist attacks in the USA on 11 September, Schröder pledged 'unlimited solidarity' to the US Administration, and announced plans to send 3,900 troops to take part in the US-led military action in Afghanistan. These plans were strongly opposed by the majority of members of Bündnis 90/Die Grünen, although Schröder enjoyed the support of the Green Minister of Foreign Affairs, Joseph Fischer. Opposition to the proposed deployment of German troops in Afghanistan increased to such an extent that by early November the governing coalition appeared close to collapse. Schröder embarked on the high-risk strategy of linking the parliamentary vote on the troop deployment to a vote of confidence in his Government; the Chancellor won the confidence vote, which was held on 16 November, albeit by a narrow majority. In November 2002 the Bundestag voted to extend the deployment of troops in Afghanistan by a further year. In June 2003 Germany announced that its troops would remain in Afghanistan for at least another year; in October Germany extended its peace-keeping mission beyond the capital, Kabul, by dispatching troops to form part of a 'provincial reconstruction team' in the northern city of Kunduz. In September 2004 the Bundestag overwhelmingly approved a motion authorizing the deployment of 2,250 German peace-keeping troops in Afghanistan for a further 12 months.

In late 2002 and early 2003 the Franco-German *entente* was renewed, largely owing to the two countries' shared opposition to the US-led military action in Iraq. In February Germany and France, together with Belgium, vetoed proposals to deploy NATO troops in Turkey; they later ended their vetoes on the condition that the troops be deployed only to defend Turkey, and not to attack Iraq. Relations between Germany and the USA were strained during most of 2003, although in May of that year Germany did support the USA in calling for the UN to lift sanctions against Iraq. Germany opposed US plans for the reconstruction of Iraq following the deposal of Saddam Hussain's regime in March/April and advocated instead greater UN involvement and the swifter transfer of governing powers to Iraqis. Relations with the USA improved in September, however, when Schröder, in the course of a meeting with the US President, George W. Bush, in New York, offered to provide resources for the training of Iraqi police, security staff and military personnel (whilst continuing to refuse to send German peace-keeping troops to Iraq). Bush held talks with Schröder during the US President's official visit to various European destinations in February 2005; in the course of these negotiations the German Chancellor reiterated his Government's opposition to dispatching German peace-keepers to Iraq.

In December 1992 the Bundestag ratified the Treaty on European Union, which had been approved by EC Heads of Government at Maastricht in December 1991. At the same time the lower house approved an amendment to the Grundgesetz (negotiated in May 1992 with the Länder), whereby the state assemblies would be accorded greater involvement in the determination of German policy within the EC. The Bundesrat ratified the Maastricht Treaty later in December 1992. In April 1998 the Bundestag approved Germany's participation in EMU, which took effect in January 1999. Following the eventual approval of the draft EU constitutional treaty on 18 June 2004 by the Heads of State and of Government of the member states of the EU, the German Government expressed its desire that Germany ratify it the document as soon as possible. Germany's Grundgesetz, however, prevented the holding of a national referendum on the issue, and in February 2005 the Bundesrat began debating the treaty with a view to legislative ratification, which would require a two-thirds' majority in both houses.

From late 2002 Germany and France began a phase of markedly good bilateral relations, partly owing, as mentioned above, to both countries' opposition to the US-led military action in Iraq. The two countries were also united in their attitude towards the proposed EU constitution, and in the defence of their budgetary deficits, which were in breach of the EU's Stability and Growth Pact (see Economic Affairs). Relations improved to such a point that, in mid-October 2003, Schröder allowed President Chirac of France to represent Germany at an EU summit meeting in Brussels (see above).

Germany's relations with Poland were for a long time influenced by the Second World War. In the course of the negotiations on EU enlargement during the 1990s, Germany strongly supported Poland's accession, citing the need for an historic conciliation with its eastern neighbour. Following Poland's accession to the EU in May 2004, German diplomacy shifted to the position that its past debts had thus been repaid, and began to work towards closer relations within the EU. In early 2004 Chancellor Schröder visited the Polish Prime Minister, Leszek Miller, to put the case against Poland's opposition to the proposed EU constitution. In August Schröder attended a ceremony in Warsaw to mark the 60th anniversary of the failed uprising there, during which he acknowledged the 'immeasurable suffering' inflicted by Nazi troops on Poland. This *rapprochement* was threatened, however, by the right-wing Preussische Treuhand (Prussian Trust), which launched a series of lawsuits claiming compensation and the restitution of property on behalf of the families of Germans expelled from Poland following the Second World War. In September Schröder and the new Polish Prime Minister, Marek Belka, jointly announced the creation of a commission to ensure that such claims would be stripped of any legal basis. In February 2005 President Köhler attended a ceremony in Poland to mark the 60th anniversary of the liberation of the Nazi concentration camp at Auschwitz.

Government

Germany is composed of 16 Länder (states), each Land having its own constitution, legislature and government.

The country has a parliamentary regime, with a bicameral legislature. The Upper House is the Bundesrat (Federal Council), with 69 seats. Each Land has between three and six seats, depending on the size of its population. The term of office of Bundesrat members varies in accordance with Land election dates. The Lower House, and the country's main legislative organ, is the Bundestag (Federal Assembly), with 669 deputies, who are elected for four years by universal adult suffrage (using a mixed system of proportional representation and direct voting).

Executive authority rests with the Federal Government, led by the Federal Chancellor, who is elected by an absolute majority of the Bundestag and appoints the other Ministers. The Federal President is elected by a Federal Convention (Bundesversammlung), which meets only for this purpose and consists of the Bundestag and an equal number of members elected by Land parliaments. The President is a constitutional Head of State with little influence on government.

Each Land has its own legislative assembly, with the right to enact laws except on matters that are the exclusive right of the Federal Government, such as defence, foreign affairs and finance. Education, police, culture and environmental protection are in the control of the Länder. Local responsibility for the execution of Federal and Land laws is undertaken by the Gemeinden (communities).

Defence

Germany is a member of the North Atlantic Treaty Organization (NATO, see p. 301). In January 2001 the Government announced that the Bundeswehr (armed forces) was to be reduced from 310,000 to 280,000, with the number of conscripts being lowered from 130,000 to 80,000 through the reduction of military service from 10 months to nine months. In January 2004 it was announced that the size of the armed forces was to be reduced further, and that by around 2010 the Bundeswehr was to be reorganized into a rapid reaction force of 35,000 troops, a second force of 70,000 troops for low- and medium-intensity

conflict and a third force of 137,500 civilians providing medical and logistical support; more than 100 army bases were also to be closed as part of the streamlining process and the number of conscripts was to be decreased to 55,000. Germany's special forces, the Kommando Spezial Kräfte (KSK) were to be increased from 450 to 1,000. In August 2004 Germany's armed forces totalled some 284,500, including 94,500 conscripts. The strength of the army stood at 191,350, including 73,450 conscripts. The navy numbered 25,650 (including 4,950 conscripts), and there were 67,500 in the air force (16,100 conscripts). The defence budget for 2004 totalled €24,100m.

At German unification, the National People's Army of the former GDR was dissolved, and 50,000 of its members were incorporated into the German Bundeswehr. In accordance with a Soviet-German agreement, concluded in September 1990, the USSR withdrew its 370,000 troops from the territory of the former GDR during 1990–94, while Germany significantly reduced the total strength of its armed forces during the 1990s and first half of the 2000s. In August 2003 the USA and the United Kingdom had approximately 95,500 troops stationed in Germany, while France and the Netherlands maintained, respectively, forces of 3,200 and 2,600 men. Belgium withdrew its troops from Germany during 2002–03. In 2004 the USA announced that it was to withdraw some 30,000 troops from Germany as part of a wider redeployment of its troops abroad. The US military was, however, to retain its European command in Germany. Key bases were to be expanded and three new, smaller brigades (of 3,000–5,000 men each) were to be stationed in Germany. US air force bases in Germany were to be unaffected by the withdrawals.

Economic Affairs

In 2003, according to estimates by the World Bank, Germany's gross national income (GNI), measured at average 2001–2003 prices, was US $2,388,140m., equivalent to $25,250 per head (or $27,460 per head on an international purchasing-power parity basis). During 1990–2003, it was estimated, the population increased by an average of 0.3% per year, while Germany's gross domestic product (GDP) per head grew, in real terms, by an average of 1.2% annually. Overall GDP expanded, in real terms, at an average annual rate of 1.5% in 1990–2003; growth was 0.2% in 2002 and 0.0% in 2003.

Agriculture (including hunting, forestry and fishing) engaged 2.5% of the employed labour force in 2003, and provided 1.1% of Germany's GDP in that year. The principal crops are sugar beet, wheat, potatoes and barley. Wine production is also important in western Germany. Agricultural GDP increased, in real terms, at an average annual rate of 0.9% in 1990–2002; it expanded by 1.1% in 2001 and declined by 1.3% in 2002.

Industry (including mining, power, manufacturing and construction) engaged 31.1% of the employed labour force and contributed 28.6% of GDP in 2003. Industrial GDP increased at an average annual rate of just 0.1% in 1990–2001; it expanded by 3.8% in 2000 and declined by 1.3% in 2001.

The mining sector engaged 0.4% of the employed labour force and, with energy, gas and water supply, contributed 2.2% of GDP in 2003. The principal mining activities are the extraction of lignite (low-grade brown coal), hard coal and salts.

The manufacturing sector employed 22.8% of the employed labour force and provided 22.2% of GDP in 2003. Measured by value of output, the principal branches of manufacturing in 1999 were transport equipment (accounting for 18.3% of the total), non-electric machinery (11.8%), chemical products (10.0%) and food products (9.7%). Passenger motor cars remain an important export. During the 1990s companies specializing in microelectronics and biotechnology performed well in both eastern and western Germany. Real manufacturing GDP declined at an average annual rate of 0.1% in 1990–2002; it declined by 0.9% in 2001 and by 1.2% in 2002.

Of the total energy produced in 2001, coal accounted for 51.5% (24.3% was hard coal and 27.2% was lignite, or brown coal, which is primarily used in the eastern Länder), nuclear power accounted for 30.1%, natural gas for 11.7% and petroleum for 0.8%. In 2000 the Government announced plans to abandon the use of nuclear power by 2021; the closure of nuclear reactors began in 2003 (see Recent History). In 2003 imports of mineral fuels accounted for 8.9% of Germany's total imports.

Services engaged 66.4% of the employed labour force and contributed 70.2% of GDP in 2003. The GDP of the services sector increased, in real terms, at an average annual rate of 2.8% in 1990–2002: it grew by 1.7% in 2001 and by 1.2% in 2002.

In 2003 Germany recorded a visible trade surplus of US $151,660m., and there was a surplus of $54,870m. on the current account of the balance of payments. More than one-half of Germany's total trade in 2003 was conducted with other countries of the European Union (EU, see p. 217). France is the most significant individual trading partner, supplying 9.1% of imports and purchasing 10.4% of exports in 2003. Other principal sources of imports in that year were the Netherlands (7.9%), the USA (7.3%) and Italy (6.4%); the other major purchasers of exports were the USA (9.3%), the United Kingdom (8.4%) and Italy (7.3%). The principal imports in 2003 were machinery and transport equipment (accounting for 39.5% of the total, with road vehicles and parts comprising 10.5%), basic manufactures (13.2%), miscellaneous manufactured articles (12.7%), and chemicals and related products (11.0%). The principal exports were machinery and transport equipment (accounting for 52.7% of the total, with road vehicles and parts comprising 19.2%), basic manufactures (13.7%), chemicals and related products (13.5%), and miscellaneous manufactured articles (10.0%).

The budgetary deficit for 2003 totalled €74,649m. (equivalent to 3.5% of GDP—a breach of the 3.0% ceiling permitted under the EU's Stability and Growth Pact). Annual inflation averaged 1.6% during 1992–2003. Consumer prices rose by an annual average of 1.4% in 2002 and 1.1% in 2003. Some 10.0% of the labour force were unemployed in April 2003.

Germany is a member of the EU (see p. 217) and of the Organisation for Economic Co-operation and Development (OECD, see p. 307).

In the opening years of the 21st century Germany's economy first stagnated and then declined. GDP per head, which had been around 20% higher than the EU average during the 1980s, declined to 1% below average by 2003 (measured on an international purchasing-power parity basis), with only four other EU member states having a lower level. That Germany's GDP per head was above the EU average in 2004 was due only to a lowering of the average itself, brought about by the enlargement of the EU in that year. Germany's budgetary deficit, which had persisted since unification more than a decade earlier, continued to cause problems. In both 2002 and 2003 Germany's annual budgetary deficit was greater than the ceiling of 3% of GDP permitted under the terms of the EU's Stability and Growth Pact (SGP). Together with France, which had also exceeded the limit, Germany persuaded other EU member states to permit a suspension of the SGP to allow for economic recovery. The German Government forecast that it would exceed the 3% limit yet again in 2004 and 2005, largely owing to a fall in tax revenue; measures to reduce the deficit were introduced in late 2004, including a pay 'freeze' for civil servants and the sale of securities worth €5,500m. to investors. (A proposal to scrap Unity Day, which, it was thought, would add as much as 0.1% to GDP, was swiftly dropped as a result of public opposition.) Given such persistent breaches of the SGP, the European Commission conceded in December 2004 that it would not impose sanctions against the transgressors. In January 2005 Chancellor Schröder advocated reform of the SGP to allow countries meeting certain criteria (those adopting costly structural reforms, suffering economic stagnation or shouldering 'special economic burdens') to breach the 3% limit. In 2004 Germany's economy, driven by strong exports, grew at its fastest rate since 2000. However, major companies, including Volkswagen, DaimlerChrysler and Siemens, had spent much of 2004 in negotiations with trade unions over reducing jobs and costs, and increasing working hours without extra pay. Moreover, rising unemployment and the Agenda 2010 reforms had dampened domestic demand. Towards the end of the year these factors began to outweigh the benefits of Germany's rising exports: GDP growth was zero in the third quarter of 2004 and declined by 0.2% in the fourth quarter, thwarting hopes of a sustained recovery. GDP growth for the whole year was revised downwards from 1.7% to 1.6%. The euro's strength against the US dollar was also a cause for concern, as it threatened to have an adverse effect on exports. Fears of rising interest rates to counter inflationary pressure also threatened economic recovery. In January 2005 a combina-tion of the enactment of the Hartz IV law (see History), the adoption of new statistical methods and seasonal factors together resulted in the rate of unemployment exceeding 5m.; in addition, a further 1.5m.–2m. people on subsidized employment schemes were, at that time, looking for 'real' jobs—consequently a further increase in unemployment was expected. Most importantly, however, the Agenda 2010 reforms had failed to address the main challenges to the economy: namely, that EMU had deprived Germany of the means to adjust interest and exchange rates to optimize its own economic recovery; that reunification had been hugely expensive, costing €1,250,000m. since 1990, and was still consuming 4% of GDP in transfers each year, with the added burden of high levels of long-term unemployment in the Länder of the former GDR; that the federal structure was deliberately designed to weaken the ability of a central government to impose radical reform, and was proving all too effective; and that Germany's cumbersome and expensive labour laws were becoming a crippling anachronism in the modern, globalized economy. However, Germany's net investment flow in 2004 was positive. Non-German equity firms were still keen to buy and restructure German companies, seeing value in them despite the country's economic problems. Indeed it could be said that many German firms were in fact undervalued. While further reform was undeniably necessary, the potential for economic success remained strong.

Education

The Basic Law assigns the control of important sectors of the education system to the governments of the Länder. These do, however, co-operate quite closely to ensure a large degree of conformity in the system. Compulsory schooling begins at six years of age and continues for nine years (in some Länder for 10). Until the age of 18, all young people who do not continue to attend a full-time school must attend a part-time vocational school (Berufsschule). Primary education lasts four years (six years in some Länder) and is provided free of charge. Attendance at the Grundschule (elementary school) is obligatory for all children, after which their education continues at one of four types of secondary school. Approximately one-third of this age-group attend the Hauptschule (general school) for five or six years, after which they may enter employment, but continue their education part-time for three years at a vocational school. Alternatively, pupils may attend the Realschule (intermediate school) for up to nine years, the Gymnasium (grammar school) for nine years (for eight years in some Länder), or the Gesamtschule (comprehensive school, not available in all parts of the country) for up to nine years. The Abitur (grammar school leaving certificate) is a necessary prerequisite for university education.

In 2000 total expenditure on education by the Federal Government, the Länder Governments and the municipalities amounted to €575,490m.

Public Holidays

2005: 1 January (New Year's Day), 6 January (Epiphany)*, 25 March (Good Friday), 28 March (Easter Monday), 1 May (Labour Day), 5 May (Ascension Day), 16 May (Whit Monday), 25 May (Corpus Christi)*, 15 August (Assumption)*, 3 October (Day of Unity), 31 October (Reformation Day)*, 1 November (All Saints' Day)*, 25–26 December (Christmas), 31 December (New Year's Eve).

2006: 1 January (New Year's Day), 6 January (Epiphany)*, 14 April (Good Friday), 17 April (Easter Monday), 1 May (Labour Day), 25 May (Ascension Day), 5 June (Whit Monday), 15 June (Corpus Christi)*, 15 August (Assumption)*, 3 October (Day of Unity), 31 October (Reformation Day)*, 1 November (All Saints' Day)*, 25–26 December (Christmas), 31 December (New Year's Eve).

*Religious holidays observed in certain Länder only.

In Sachsen (Saxony) only, *Buss und Bettag* (Repentence Day) is celebrated on the first Wednesday on or after 16 November each year: 16 November in 2005; 22 November in 2006.

Weights and Measures

The metric system is in force.

Statistical Survey

Source (unless otherwise indicated): Statistisches Bundesamt, 65180 Wiesbaden; tel. (611) 752405; fax (611) 753330; e-mail info@statistik-bund.de; internet www.statistik-bund.de.

Area and Population

AREA, POPULATION AND DENSITY

Area (sq km)*	357,027
Population (official estimates at 31 December)	
2001	82,440,309
2002	82,536,680
2003†	82,531,700
Males	40,349,000
Females	42,172,600
Density (per sq km) at 31 December 2003	231.2

* 137,849 sq miles.

† Figures are rounded, and therefore sum of components may not be equal to total.

LÄNDER

	Area (sq km)	Population ('000) at 31 Dec. 2003	Density (per sq km)	Capital
Baden-Württemberg	35,751.6	10,692.6	299.1	Stuttgart
Bayern (Bavaria)	70,549.3	12,423.4	176.1	München
Berlin	891.8	3,388.5	3,799.6	Berlin
Brandenburg	29,476.7	2,574.5	87.3	Potsdam
Bremen	404.3	663.1	1,640.2	Bremen
Hamburg	755.3	1,734.1	2,295.9	Hamburg
Hessen (Hesse)	21,114.9	6,089.4	288.4	Wiesbaden
Mecklenburg-Vorpommern (Mecklenburg-Western Pomerania)	23,173.5	1,732.2	74.8	Schwerin
Niedersachsen (Lower Saxony)	47,618.0	7,993.4	167.9	Hannover
Nordrhein-Westfalen (North Rhine-Westphalia)	34,082.8	18,079.7	530.5	Düsseldorf
Rheinland-Pfalz (Rhineland-Palatinate)	19,846.9	4,058.9	204.5	Mainz
Saarland	2,568.5	1,061.4	413.2	Saarbrücken
Sachsen (Saxony)	18,413.3	4,321.4	234.7	Dresden
Sachsen-Anhalt (Saxony-Anhalt)	20,444.7	2,522.9	123.4	Magdeburg
Schleswig-Holstein	15,762.9	2,823.2	179.1	Kiel
Thüringen (Thuringia)	16,172.2	2,373.2	146.7	Erfurt
Total	357,026.6	82,531.7	231.2	—

PRINCIPAL TOWNS
(estimated population at 31 December 2003)

Berlin (capital)	3,388,477	Karlsruhe	282,595
Hamburg	1,734,083	Gelsenkirchen	272,445
München (Munich)	1,247,873	Wiesbaden	271,995
Köln (Cologne)	965,954	Münster	269,579
Frankfurt am Main	643,432	Mönchengladbach	262,391
Dortmund	589,661	Augsburg	259,217
Essen	589,499	Aachen (Aix-la-Chapelle)	256,045
Stuttgart	589,161	Chemnitz	249,922
Düsseldorf	572,511	Braunschweig (Brunswick)	245,076
Bremen	544,853	Halle an der Saale*	240,119
Hannover (Hanover)	516,160	Krefeld	238,565
Duisburg	506,496	Kiel	233,039
Leipzig	497,531	Magdeburg	227,535
Nürnberg (Nuremberg)	493,553	Oberhausen	220,033
Dresden	483,632	Lübeck	212,754
Bochum	387,283	Freiburg im Breisgau	212,459
Wuppertal	362,137	Erfurt	201,645
Bielefeld	328,452	Hagen	200,039
Bonn	311,052	Rostock	198,303
Mannheim	308,353	Kassel	194,322

* Including Halle-Neustadt.

BIRTHS, MARRIAGES AND DEATHS

	Registered live births Number	Rate (per 1,000)	Registered marriages Number	Rate (per 1,000)	Registered deaths Number	Rate (per 1,000)
1996	796,013	9.7	427,297	5.2	882,843	10.8
1997	812,173	9.9	422,776	5.2	860,389	10.5
1998	785,034	9.6	417,420	5.1	852,382	10.4
1999	770,744	9.4	430,674	5.2	846,330	10.3
2000	766,999	9.3	418,550	5.1	838,797	10.2
2001	734,475	8.9	389,591	4.7	828,541	10.1
2002	719,250	8.7	391,963	4.7	841,686	10.2
2003	706,721	n.a.	382,911	n.a.	853,946	n.a.

Expectation of life (WHO estimates, years at birth): 78.7 (males 75.6; females 81.6) in 2002 (Source: WHO, *World Health Report*).

IMMIGRATION AND EMIGRATION
('000 persons)

	2001	2002	2003
Immigrant arrivals	879.2	842.5	769.0
Emigrant departures	606.5	623.3	626.3

ECONOMICALLY ACTIVE POPULATION

(sample surveys, '000 persons aged 15 years and over, at April unless otherwise indicated)

	2001	2002	2003*
Agriculture, hunting and forestry	937	917	890
Fishing	5	6	5
Mining and quarrying	139	136	128
Manufacturing	8,609	8,483	8,243
Electricity, gas and water	282	287	287
Construction	2,904	2,750	2,607
Wholesale and retail trade; repair of motor vehicles, motorcycles and personal and household goods	5,248	5,085	5,069
Hotels and restaurants	1,228	1,240	1,227
Transport, storage and communications	2,055	2,030	2,001
Financial intermediation	1,346	1,343	1,351
Real estate, renting and business activities	3,005	3,120	3,221
Public administration and defence; compulsory social security	3,065	2,986	2,973
Education	1,996	2,021	2,033
Health and social work	3,797	3,926	4,030
Other community, social and personal service activities	2,028	2,038	1,943
Private households with employed persons	142	137	138
Extra-territorial organizations and bodies	30	31	28
Total employed	36,816	36,536	36,172
Unemployed	3,150	3,486	4,023
Total labour force	39,966	40,022	40,195
Males	22,383	22,315	22,312
Females	17,583	17,707	17,883

* At May.

Source: ILO.

Health and Welfare

KEY INDICATORS

Total fertility rate (children per woman, 2002)	1.3
Under-five mortality rate (per 1,000 live births, 2003)	5
HIV/AIDS (% of persons aged 15–49, 2003)	0.1
Physicians (per 1,000 head, 2001)	3.30
Hospital beds (per 1,000 head, 2000)	9.10
Health expenditure (2001): US $ per head (PPP)	2,820
Health expenditure (2001): % of GDP	10.8
Health expenditure (2001): public (% of total)	74.9
Human Development Index (2002): ranking	19
Human Development Index (2002): value	0.925

For sources and definitions, see explanatory note on p. vi.

Agriculture

PRINCIPAL CROPS

('000 metric tons)

	2001	2002	2003
Wheat	22,838	20,818	19,260
Barley	13,495	10,928	10,596
Maize	3,505	3,738	3,422
Rye	5,132	3,666	2,277
Oats	1,151	1,016	1,202
Triticale (wheat-rye hybrid)	3,419	3,068	2,480
Potatoes	11,503	11,114	9,916
Sugar beet*	24,730	26,794	23,716
Dry broad beans	81	65	61
Sunflower seed	54	52	73
Rapeseed	4,160	3,849	3,634
Cabbages	692	599	n.a.
Cauliflowers	131	128	137
Cucumbers and gherkins	163	191	180
Dry onions	287	293	272
Green beans	48	50	38
Carrots	444	415	426

— continued	2001	2002	2003
Grapes†	1,226‡	1,425‡	1,170
Apples§	922	763	818
Pears§	47	76	53
Cherries (sweet and sour)§	69	50	67
Plums§	41	46	52
Strawberries§	110	105	95
Currants†	148	148‖	148‖

* Deliveries to sugar factories.
† Source: FAO.
‡ Unofficial figure.
§ Marketed production only.
‖ FAO estimate.

LIVESTOCK

('000 head at December)

	2001	2002	2003
Horses	506.2	506.2*	524.8
Cattle†	14,226.6	13,732.0	13,385.8
Pigs†	25,957.8	26,251.5	26,495.3
Sheep	2,771	2,722	2,679
Goats	160	160	n.a.
Chickens	109,993	109,993*	109,793
Geese	408	408*	384
Ducks	2,185	2,185*	2,626
Turkeys	9,471	9,471*	10,604

* At May.
† At November.

LIVESTOCK PRODUCTS

('000 metric tons)

	2001	2002	2003
Beef and veal	1,361.5	1,316.4	1,226.2
Mutton and lamb	46.1	43.9	45.6
Pig meat	4,074.3	4,110.2	4,239.3
Poultry meat	860.0	892.0	963.0
Cows' milk	28,191.0	27,874.4	28,350.0
Goats' milk	22.0	25.0	30.0
Butter	420.2	434.5	452.0*
Cheese	1,742.7	1,745.9	1,795.2
Hen eggs	887.0	868.0	814.0
Honey	26.0	14.6	23.7
Wool: greasy†	15.0	15.0	15.0
Wool: scoured†	7.0	7.0	7.0
Cattle hides†	153.3	151.3	151.3

* Unofficial figure.
† FAO estimates.

Source: FAO.

Forestry

ROUNDWOOD REMOVALS

('000 cubic metres, excluding bark)

	2001	2002	2003
Sawlogs, veneer logs and logs for sleepers	22,456	24,446	30,590
Pulpwood	10,653	10,398	11,127
Other industrial wood	3,393	2,911	3,698
Fuel wood	2,981	4,625	5,767
Total	39,483	42,380	51,182

Source: FAO.

SAWNWOOD PRODUCTION

('000 cubic metres, including railway sleepers)

	2001	2002	2003
Coniferous (softwood)	14,889.0	15,869.0	16,525.0
Broadleaved (hardwood)	1,242.0	1,140.4*	1,070.9*
Total	16,131.0	17,009.4	17,595.9

* Unofficial figure.

Source: FAO.

Fishing

('000 metric tons, live weight)

	2000	2001	2002
Capture	205.7	211.3	224.5
Freshwater fishes	20.4	20.4	20.3
Atlantic cod	18.4	19.2	15.4
Saithe (Pollock)	12.4	13.3	14.5
Blue whiting (Poutassou)	12.7	19.1	17.1
Atlantic redfishes	14.3	12.8	15.6
Atlantic horse mackerel	16.8	12.5	15.9
Atlantic herring	47.0	50.7	56.7
Atlantic mackerel	23.0	25.3	26.5
Common shrimp	17.4	12.6	16.0
Aquaculture	65.9	53.4	49.9
Common carp	10.5	10.5	11.4
Rainbow trout	25.0	25.0	24.2
Blue mussel	24.1	11.6	8.0
Total catch	271.6	264.7	274.3

Note: Figures exclude aquatic mammals, recorded by number rather than by weight. The number of harbour porpoises caught was: 5 in 2000; 8 in 2001; 8 in 2002.

Source: FAO.

Mining

('000 metric tons, unless otherwise indicated)

	2001	2002	2003
Hard coal	27,361	26,363	25,869
Brown coal	175,301	181,714	179,058
Crude petroleum	3,365	3,703	3,802
Salt (unrefined)	6,537	7,382	7,300

Natural gas (petajoules) (2001): 604.6 (Source: UN, *Monthly Bulletin of Statistics*).

Industry

SELECTED PRODUCTS

('000 metric tons, unless otherwise indicated)

	2001	2002	2003
Margarine	508	515	505
Flour	4,383	4,490	4,602
Refined sugar	3,783	3,937	3,913
Beer ('000 hl)	106,372	102,136	98,933
Cigarettes (million)	213,793	212,500	205,237
Cotton yarn (pure and mixed)	89	73	59
Woven cotton fabrics ('000 sq metres)	411,344	361,647	362,292
Newsprint	2,090	2,082	2,143
Brown-coal briquettes	1,740	1,494	1,465
Pig-iron	29,184*	29,427	29,481
Crude steel	44,803*	45,015	44,809
Motor spirit (petrol)	24,779	24,978	24,660
Diesel oil†	24,816	27,704	29,442
Cement	n.a.	30,458	32,243
Sulphuric acid	1,594	1,732	n.a.
Nitrogenous fertilizers (N)	1,079	1,205	1,292
Artificial resins and plastics	13,531	15,202	14,868
Synthetic rubber	583	768	810
Soap	148	143	n.a.
Aluminium (unwrought):			
primary	458	422	487
secondary	542	625	646
Refined lead (unwrought)	268	278	266
Refined zinc (unwrought)	313	344	304
Refined copper	544	547	502
Passenger cars and minibuses ('000)	5,487	5,513	5,605
Bicycles ('000)	2,673	2,561	2,752
Clocks, watches and non-electronic time-measuring instruments ('000)	10,236	10,240	9,861

— *continued*	2001	2002	2003
Footwear ('000 pairs)‡	26,911	19,625	16,175
Electricity (million kWh)	569,325	n.a.	n.a.

* Source: US Geological Survey.
† Including light heating oil.
‡ Excluding rubber and plastic footwear.

Finance

CURRENCY AND EXCHANGE RATES

Monetary Units
100 cent = 1 euro (€).

Sterling and Dollar Equivalents (31 December 2004)
£1 sterling = 1.4180 euros;
US $1 = 0.7342 euros;
100 euros = £70.52 = $136.21.

Average Exchange Rate (euros per US $)
2002   1.0626
2003   0.8860
2004   0.8054

Note: The national currency was formerly the Deutsche Mark (DM). From the introduction of the euro, with German participation, on 1 January 1999, a fixed exchange rate of €1 = 1.95583 DM was in operation. Euro notes and coins were introduced on 1 January 2002. The euro and local currency circulated alongside each other until 28 February, after which the euro became the sole legal tender.

BUDGET
(€ million)*

Revenue	2001	2002	2003
Current receipts	888,412	892,433	895,380
Taxes and similar revenue	810,930	810,790	817,307
Income from economic activity	21,287	25,934	19,924
Interest	7,860	6,255	6,259
Allocations and grants for current purposes	238,112	254,701	257,046
Other receipts	30,094	30,095	31,393
Less Deductible payments on the same level	219,870	235,341	236,549
Capital receipts	34,060	28,694	31,713
Sale of property	17,526	14,079	14,438
Loans and grants for investment	24,823	21,651	21,893
Repayment of loans	12,101	11,029	13,287
Public sector borrowing	575	523	673
Less Deductible payments on the same level	20,965	18,588	18,578
Total	922,472	921,127	927,093

Expenditure	2001	2002	2003
Current expenditure	886,120	910,631	922,744
Personnel expenses	181,033	184,969	186,107
Goods and services	215,481	219,305	222,324
Interest	66,870	n.a.	66,194
Allocations and grants for current purposes	642,605	675,208	684,668
Less Deductible payments on the same level	219,870	235,341	236,549
Capital expenditure	85,964	77,273	78,998
Construction	30,415	28,747	27,843
Purchase of property	10,666	10,483	8,946
Allocations and grants for investment	48,247	44,766	49,472
Loans	9,960	8,672	7,601
Sale of shares	6,919	2,365	2,881
Repayment expenses in the public sector	724	827	833
Less Deductible payments on the same level	20,965	18,588	18,578
Total	972,084	987,904	1,001,742

* Figures represent a consolidation of the accounts of all public authorities, including the Federal Government and Land administrations.

INTERNATIONAL RESERVES
(US $ million at 31 December)

	2001	2002	2003
Gold*	30,728	37,972	46,141
IMF special drawing rights . .	1,793	1,980	1,942
Reserve position in IMF . . .	5,901	6,695	7,656
Foreign exchange	43,710	42,495	41,095
Total	82,132	89,142	96,834

* National valuation.

Source: IMF, *International Financial Statistics*.

MONEY SUPPLY
(€ '000 million at 31 December)

	2001	2002	2003
Currency issued	82.8	112.2*	125.9*
Demand deposits at banking institutions	532.7	582.9	631.4

* Currency put into circulation by the Deutsche Bundesbank was €141,300m. in 2002 and €170,500m. in 2003.

Source: IMF, *International Financial Statistics*.

COST OF LIVING
(Consumer Price Index for all private households; base: 2000 = 100)

	2002	2003	2004
Food	105.3	105.2	104.8
Alcohol and tobacco	105.8	111.4	119.1
Clothes and shoes	101.5	100.7	100.0
Housing, energy and fuel . .	103.4	104.9	106.5
All items (incl. others) . . .	103.4	104.5	106.2

NATIONAL ACCOUNTS
(provisional, € million at current prices, rounded to nearest €10m.)

National Income and Product

	2001	2002	2003
Compensation of employees . .	1,126,660	1,132,740	1,132,190
Operating surplus	419,980	438,390	437,070
Domestic factor incomes . .	1,546,640	1,571,130	1,569,260
Consumption of fixed capital . .	312,070	318,480	318,270
Gross domestic product at factor cost*	1,858,710	1,889,610	1,914,470
Indirect taxes	246,330	249,510	225,400
Less Subsidies	33,840	30,920	11,670
GDP in purchasers' values . .	2,071,200	2,108,200	2,128,200
Factor income from abroad . .	125,990	115,470	104,610
Less Factor income paid abroad .	141,400	124,560	118,630
Gross national product . . .	2,055,790	2,099,110	2,114,180
Less Consumption of fixed capital	312,070	318,480	318,270
National income in market prices	1,743,720	1,780,630	1,795,910
Other current transfers from abroad	9,790	9,800	9,790
Less Other current transfers paid abroad	29,820	33,110	34,660
National disposable income .	1,723,690	1,757,320	1,771,040

* Including adjustment.

Expenditure on the Gross Domestic Product

	2001	2002	2003
Government final consumption expenditure	393,520	402,790	408,540
Private final consumption expenditure	1,232,150	1,241,880	1,255,300
Increase in stocks	−9,370	−7,280	−7,620
Gross fixed capital formation . .	416,310	387,780	379,800
Total domestic expenditure	2,032,610	2,025,170	2,036,020
Exports of goods and services . .	726,900	748,270	769,290
Less Imports of goods and services	688,310	665,240	677,110
GDP in purchasers' values . .	2,071,200	2,108,200	2,128,200
GDP at constant 1995 prices .	1,980,800	1,984,300	1,985,200

Gross Domestic Product by Economic Activity

	2001	2002	2003
Agriculture, hunting and forestry Fishing	23,510	21,950	22,040
Mining and quarrying . . . Electricity, gas and water supply	41,700	42,370	44,290
Manufacturing	428,380	432,930	438,410
Construction	91,630	87,210	84,010
Wholesale and retail trade; repair of motor vehicles, motorcycles and personal and household goods	219,130	220,700	211,670
Hotels and restaurants . . .	25,080	24,990	22,680
Transport, storage and communications	115,610	119,310	122,160
Financial intermediation . . . Real estate, renting and business activities*	572,320	589,970	603,530
Public administration and defence; compulsory social security . . . . Education . . . . Health and social work . . . Other community, social and personal service activities . Private households with employed persons	411,770	424,150	429,980
Sub-total	1,929,130	1,963,580	1,978,770
Less Imputed bank service charges	65,300	65,000	64,300
GDP at basic prices . . .	1,863,830	1,898,580	1,914,470
Taxes on products	219,400	221,130	225,400
Less subsidies on products . .	12,030	11,510	11,670
GDP in purchasers' values .	2,071,200	2,108,200	2,128,200

* Including imputed rents of owner-occupied dwellings.

BALANCE OF PAYMENTS
(US $ million*)

	2001	2002	2003
Exports of goods f.o.b.	570,540	617,500	753,100
Imports of goods f.o.b.	-481,280	-489,300	-601,440
Trade balance	89,250	128,210	151,660
Exports of services	88,360	104,640	123,000
Imports of services	-141,930	-147,330	-173,420
Balance on goods and services	35,680	85,510	101,240
Other income received	93,430	90,390	110,550
Other income paid	-102,910	-106,090	-124,400
Balance on goods, services and income	26,200	69,820	87,390
Current transfers received	14,830	15,370	18,430
Current transfers paid	-39,320	-41,740	-50,960
Current balance	1,710	43,440	54,870
Capital account (net)	-330	-230	360
Direct investment abroad	-36,500	-9,280	-1,520
Direct investment from abroad	20,830	35,550	11,270
Portfolio investment assets	-111,500	-60,360	-37,590
Portfolio investment liabilities	133,140	101,760	103,520
Financial derivatives liabilities	6,050	-1,080	-700
Other investment assets	-102,400	-164,470	-170,320
Other investment liabilities	66,640	27,690	15,680
Net errors and omissions	16,950	25,010	23,770
Overall balance	-5,470	-1,980	-680

* Figures are rounded to the nearest US $10m.

Source: IMF, *International Financial Statistics*.

DEVELOPMENT AID
(public and private development aid to developing countries and multilateral agencies, € million)

	1999	2000	2001
Public development co-operation	5,177	5,458	5,571
Bilateral	3,076	2,915	3,186
Multilateral	864	1,201	1,110
Other public transactions	-168	-495	-740
Bilateral	-40	-495	-740
Multilateral	-128	—	—
Private development aid	931	918	903
Other private transactions	12,838	7,499	823
Bilateral	13,070	9,310	1,787
Multilateral	-232	-1,811	-964
Total	18,777	13,380	6,557

External Trade

(Note: Figures include trade in second-hand ships, and stores and bunkers for foreign ships and aircraft. Imports exclude military supplies under the offshore procurement programme and exports exclude war reparations and restitutions, except exports resulting from the Israel Reparations Agreement)

PRINCIPAL COMMODITIES
(distribution by SITC, € million)

Imports c.i.f.	2001	2002	2003
Food and live animals	32,354	32,522	33,494
Crude materials (inedible) except fuels	17,922	17,095	16,453
Mineral fuels, lubricants, etc.	47,607	43,596	47,522
Petroleum, petroleum products, etc.	31,876	28,073	29,460
Chemicals and related products	57,688	57,725	58,793
Organic chemicals	17,852	11,592	12,197
Medicinal and pharmaceutical products	11,927	19,156	19,102
Basic manufactures	73,547	69,918	70,672
Machinery and transport equipment	216,320	206,251	211,094
Power-generating machinery and equipment	18,752	18,723	19,276
General industrial machinery, equipment and parts	19,387	18,985	19,620
Office machines and automatic data-processing equipment	31,524	29,410	28,378
Telecommunications and sound equipment	20,571	19,567	19,295
Other electrical machinery, apparatus and appliances	43,290	39,479	40,520
Road vehicles (incl. air-cushion vehicles) and parts*	49,726	52,043	56,064
Other transport equipment	19,270	15,706	16,007
Miscellaneous manufactured articles	70,647	68,092	67,844
Articles of apparel and clothing accessories (excl. footwear)	21,582	20,781	20,198
Total (incl. others)†	542,774	518,532	534,534

Exports f.o.b.	2001	2002	2003
Food and live animals	23,154	23,342	24,470
Chemicals and related products	84,300	84,169	89,562
Medical and pharmaceutical products	20,165	18,494	23,199
Basic manufactures	89,242	91,236	90,938
Machinery and transport equipment	339,841	349,171	349,986
Power-generating machinery and equipment	22,830	23,429	23,950
Machinery specialized for particular industries	32,007	32,258	31,603
General industrial machinery and equipment	41,956	43,154	43,621
Office machines and automatic data-processing equipment	17,653	17,473	19,205
Telecommunications and sound equipment	20,238	20,111	19,432
Electrical machinery, apparatus and appliances	52,049	52,014	53,339
Road vehicles (incl. air-cushion vehicles) and parts*	117,229	125,734	128,391
Other transport equipment	25,292	24,304	20,283
Miscellaneous manufactured articles	62,393	65,882	66,151
Total (incl. others)†	638,268	651,320	664,455

* Excluding tyres, engines and electrical parts.

† Including monetary gold. Also included are returns and replacements, not allocated to their appropriate headings.

PRINCIPAL TRADING PARTNERS
(€ million, including gold)*

Imports c.i.f.	2001	2002	2003†
Austria	20,663.6	21,046.6	21,452.6
Belgium	26,735.1	24,665.8	24,148.9
China, People's Republic	19,941.7	21,388.5	25,681.4
Czech Republic	14,549.6	16,239.6	17,537.6
Denmark	9,096.4	9,263.6	9,485.9
Finland	6,465.1	6,136.9	6,366.5
France	49,742.7	48,200.1	48,544.6
Hungary	12,029.6	12,154.3	12,297.4
Ireland	15,721.5	13,496.8	13,627.0
Italy	35,279.8	33,482.1	24,258.7
Japan	22,910.2	19,896.4	19,683.8
Korea, Republic	4,897.1	4,713.2	5,724.0
Netherlands	43,233.3	40,751.1	42,301.5
Norway	11,554.4	11,878.5	13,445.0
Poland	13,489.8	14,193.4	15,888.1
Portugal	5,125.0	4,905.7	4,923.8
Russia	14,558.2	13,178.0	14,230.7
Spain	15,225.6	15,532.4	16,517.8
Sweden	8,998.6	8,868.0	9,501.3
Switzerland	19,752.6	19,461.4	19,092.6
Taiwan	6,567.0	5,839.0	5,534.4
Turkey	6,575.8	6,928.1	7,248.8
United Kingdom	37,259.1	33,075.5	31,711.5
USA	45,981.7	40,375.8	39,231.0
Total (incl. others)	542,773.7	518,531.8	534,534.0

Exports f.o.b.	2001	2002	2003†
Austria	33,486.1	33,862.6	35,857.0
Belgium	32,269.6	31,096.4	35,310.1
China, People's Republic	12,118.1	14,570.7	18,264.5
Czech Republic	14,939.8	16,009.6	16,784.8
Denmark	10,485.0	11,287.1	11,271.6
Finland	6,682.1	6,618.6	6,686.0
France	69,600.5	68,720.8	69,024.8
Hungary	10,519.7	11,184.8	11,860.4
Italy	47,119.0	47,334.9	48,414.3
Japan	13,103.1	12,576.3	11,889.0
Netherlands	40,011.1	40,462.9	42,219.0
Poland	15,206.1	16,102.7	16,361.8
Portugal	6,368.2	6,764.6	6,343.9
Russia	10,267.6	11,373.7	12,119.9
Spain	27,840.9	29,435.9	32,364.0
Sweden	12,978.0	13,495.6	14,239.7
Switzerland	27,489.3	26,702.3	26,009.0
Turkey	5,950.4	7,503.0	8,850.0
United Kingdom	52,763.8	53,760.9	55,596.9
USA	67,823.9	68,263.1	61,653.6
Total (incl. others)	638,268.4	651,320.0	664,454.6

* Imports by country of production; exports by country of consumption.
† Provisional figures.

Transport

FEDERAL RAILWAYS
(traffic)

	2001	2002	2003
Passengers (million)	2,001	1,971	2,024
Passenger-km (million)	75,314	70,814	71,292
Freight net ton-km (million)	74,260	72,014	79,841

ROAD TRAFFIC
('000 licensed vehicles at 1 January)

	2002	2003	2004
Passenger cars	44,383.3	44,657.3	45,022.9
Lorries	2,649.1	2,619.3	2,856.3
Buses	86.5	85.9	86.5
Motorcycles	3,557.4	3,656.9	3,745.0
Trailers	5,105.3	5,210.8	5,317.4

SHIPPING
Inland Waterways

	2001	2002	2003
Freight ton-km (million)	64,818	64,166	58,154

Merchant Fleet
(registered at 31 December)

	2001	2002	2003
Number of vessels	906	857	782
Displacement ('000 grt)	6,300.2	6,545.8	6,111.8

Source: Lloyd's Register-Fairplay, *World Fleet Statistics*.

Sea-borne Traffic

	1997	1998	1999
Vessels entered ('000 net registered tons):*			
domestic (coastwise)	19,785	43,667	21,213
international	260,553	263,470	269,637
Vessels cleared ('000 net registered tons):*			
domestic	19,664	67,036	20,529
international	235,110	237,071	246,887
Freight unloaded ('000 metric tons):†			
international	136,249	140,846	137,759
Freight loaded ('000 metric tons):†			
international	69,058	69,098	73,858
Total domestic freight ('000 metric tons)	8,011	7,444	10,005

* Loaded vessels only.
† Including transhipments.

CIVIL AVIATION
(traffic on scheduled services)

	1999	2000	2001
Kilometres flown (million)	788	850	861
Passengers carried ('000)	54,247	58,679	56,389
Passenger-km (million)	104,602	114,124	111,303
Total ton-km (million)	16,950	18,495	18,004

Source: UN, *Statistical Yearbook*.

Tourism

FOREIGN TOURIST ARRIVALS
('000)*

Country of residence	2001	2002	2003
Austria	790.8	799.6	836.8
Belgium and Luxembourg	743.9	765.6	814.2
Denmark	640.6	644.7	659.1
France	818.4	822.8	866.2
Italy	988.6	1,009.6	1,073.7
Japan	778.8	762.1	646.3
Netherlands	2,053.5	2,108.7	2,167.1
Poland	334.7	315.2	323.3
Spain	411.9	435.4	454.6
Sweden	711.1	723.3	738.7
Switzerland	1,057.1	1,123.9	1,218.2
United Kingdom	1,664.8	1,596.0	1,588.9
USA	1,916.8	1,762.1	1,672.3
Total (incl. others)	16,886.6	16,976.8	17,229.2

* Figures refer to arrivals at registered accommodation establishments.

Tourism receipts (€ million): 20,569 in 2001; 20,261 in 2002; n.a. in 2003.

Communications Media

	2001	2002	2003
Telephones ('000 main lines in use)	52,280	53,720	54,350
Mobile cellular telephones ('000 subscribers)	56,245	59,200	64,800
Personal computers ('000 in use)	31,317	35,600	n.a.
Internet users ('000)	31,000	36,000	39,000

Source: International Telecommunication Union.

Television receivers ('000 in use, 2000): 48,170.

Facsimile machines ('000 in use, 1998): 6,000.

Radio receivers ('000 in use, 1997): 77,800.

Book production (titles*, 1996): 71,515.

Daily newspapers (1996): 375, average circulation ('000 copies) 25,500.

Non-daily newspapers (1996): 36, average circulation ('000 copies) 6,600.
* Including pamphlets.

Sources: UNESCO, *Statistical Yearbook*; UN, *Statistical Yearbook*.

Education

(2002/03)

	Teachers	Students
Pre-primary	120,203	2,316,687
Primary	235,179	3,303,737
Secondary:		
lower secondary	420,402	5,664,594
upper secondary:		
general	95,194	1,052,126
vocational	79,792	1,729,839
Post-secondary non-tertiary:		
general	6,020	68,328
vocational	13,355	395,013
Higher:		
non-university institutions	56,591	339,989
universities and equivalent institutions	227,525	1,902,408
Level unknown	17,629	69,333
Total	1,271,890	16,842,054

Directory

The Constitution

The Basic Law (Grundgesetz), which came into force in the British, French and US Zones of Occupation in Germany (excluding Saarland) on 23 May 1949, was intended as a provisional Constitution to serve until a permanent one for Germany as a whole could be adopted. (Saarland was incorporated into the Federal Republic of Germany in 1957.) The Parliamentary Council which framed the Basic Law intended to continue the tradition of the Constitution of 1848–49, and to preserve some continuity with subsequent German constitutions (with Bismarck's Constitution of 1871, and with the Weimar Constitution of 1919), while avoiding the mistakes of the past.

With the accession of the five newly re-established eastern Länder and East Berlin to the Federal Republic on 3 October 1990, the Basic Law became the Constitution of the entire German nation.

The Basic Law has 182 articles, divided into 14 sections, and is introduced by a short preamble.

I. BASIC RIGHTS

The opening articles of the Constitution guarantee the dignity of man, the free development of his personality, the equality of all persons before the law, and freedom of faith and conscience. Men and women shall have equal rights, and no one shall suffer discrimination because of sex, descent, race, language, homeland and origin, faith or religion or political opinion.

No one may be compelled against his conscience to perform war service as a combatant (Article 4). All Germans have the right to assemble peacefully and unarmed and to form associations and societies. Everyone has the right freely to express and to disseminate his opinion through speech, writing or pictures. Freedom of the press and freedom of reporting by radio and motion pictures are guaranteed (Article 5). Censorship is not permitted.

The State shall protect marriage and the family, property and the right of inheritance. The care and upbringing of children is the natural right of parents. Illegitimate children shall be given the same conditions for their development and their position in society as legitimate children. Schools are under the supervision of the State. Religion forms part of the curriculum in the State schools, but parents have the right to decide whether the child shall receive religious instruction (Article 7).

A citizen's dwelling is inviolable; house searches may be made only by Court Order. No German may be deprived of his citizenship if he would thereby become stateless. The politically persecuted enjoy the right of asylum (Article 16).

II. THE FEDERATION AND THE LÄNDER

Article 20 describes the Federal Republic (Bundesrepublik Deutschland) as a democratic and social federal state. The colours of the Federal Republic are black-red-gold, the same as those of the Weimar Republic. Each Land within the Federal Republic has its own Constitution, which must, however, conform to the principles laid down in the Basic Law. All Länder, districts and parishes must have a representative assembly resulting from universal, direct, free, equal and secret elections (Article 28). The exercise of governmental powers is the concern of the Länder, in so far as the Basic Law does not otherwise prescribe. Where there is incompatibility, Federal Law overrides Land Law (Article 31). Every German has in each Land the same civil rights and duties.

Political parties may be freely formed in all the states of the Federal Republic, but their internal organization must conform to democratic principles, and they must publicly account for the sources of their funds. Parties that seek to impair or abolish the free and democratic basic order or to jeopardize the existence of the Federal Republic of Germany are unconstitutional (Article 21). So are activities tending to disturb the peaceful relations between nations, and, especially, preparations for aggressive war, but the Federation may join a system of mutual collective security in order to preserve peace (Articles 26 and 24). The rules of International Law shall form part of Federal Law and take precedence over it and create rights and duties directly for the inhabitants of the Federal territory (Article 25).

The territorial organization of the Federation may be restructured by Federal Law, subject to regional plebiscites and with due regard to regional, historical and cultural ties, economic expediency and the requirements of regional policy and planning.

III. THE BUNDESTAG

The Federal Assembly (Bundestag) is the Lower House. Its members are elected by the people in universal, free, equal, direct and secret elections, for a term of four years*. Any person who has reached the age of 18 is eligible to vote and any person who has reached the age of 18 is eligible for election (Article 38). A deputy may be arrested for a punishable offence only with the permission of the Bundestag, unless he be apprehended in the act or during the following day.

The Bundestag elects its President and draws up its Standing Orders. Most decisions of the House require a majority vote. Its meetings are public, but the public may be excluded by the decision of a two-thirds' majority. Upon the motion of one-quarter of its members the Bundestag is obliged to set up an investigation committee.

* The elections of 1949 were conducted on the basis of direct election, with some elements of proportional representation. In January 1953 the draft of a new electoral law was completed by the Federal Government and was approved shortly before the dissolution. The new law represents a compromise between direct election and proportional representation, and is designed to prevent the excessive proliferation of parties in the Bundestag.

IV. THE BUNDESRAT

The Federal Council (Bundesrat) is the Upper House, through which the Länder participate in the legislation and the administration of the Federation, and in matters relating to the European Union (EU). The Bundesrat consists of members of the Land governments, which appoint and recall them (Article 51). Each Land has at least three votes; Länder with more than two million inhabitants have four, and those with more than six million inhabitants have five. Länder with more than seven million inhabitants have six votes. The votes of each Land may only be given as a block vote. The Bundesrat elects its President for one year. Its decisions are taken by simple majority vote. Meetings are public, but the public may be excluded. The members of the Federal Government have the right, and, on demand, the obligation, to participate in the debates of the Bundesrat.

V. THE FEDERAL PRESIDENT

The Federal President (Bundespräsident) is elected by the Federal Convention (Bundesversammlung), consisting of the members of the Bundestag and an equal number of members elected by the Land Parliaments (Article 54). Every German eligible to vote in elections for the Bundestag and over 40 years of age is eligible for election. The candidate who obtains an absolute majority of votes is elected, but if such majority is not achieved by any candidate in two ballots, whoever receives most votes in a further ballot becomes President. The President's term of office is five years. Immediate re-election is permitted only once. The Federal President must not be a member of the Government or of any legislative body or hold any salaried office. Orders and instructions of the President require the counter-signature of the Federal Chancellor or competent Minister, except for the appointment or dismissal of the Chancellor or the dissolution of the Bundestag.

The President represents the Federation in its international relations and accredits and receives envoys. The Bundestag or the Bundesrat may impeach the President before the Federal Constitutional Court on account of wilful violation of the Basic Law or of any other Federal Law (Article 61).

VI. THE FEDERAL GOVERNMENT

The Federal Government (Bundesregierung) consists of the Federal Chancellor (Bundeskanzler) and the Federal Ministers (Bundesminister). The Chancellor is elected by an absolute majority of the Bundestag on the proposal of the Federal President (Article 63). Ministers are appointed and dismissed by the President upon the proposal of the Chancellor. Neither he nor his Ministers may hold any other salaried office. The Chancellor determines general policy and assumes responsibility for it, but within these limits each Minister directs his department individually and on his own responsibility. The Bundestag may express its lack of confidence in the Chancellor only by electing a successor with the majority of its members; the President must then appoint the person elected (Article 67). If a motion of the Chancellor for a vote of confidence does not obtain the support of the majority of the Bundestag, the President may, upon the proposal of the Chancellor, dissolve the House within 21 days, unless it elects another Chancellor within this time (Article 68).

VII. THE LEGISLATION OF THE FEDERATION

The right of legislation lies with the Länder in so far as the Basic Law does not specifically accord legislative powers to the Federation. Distinction is made between fields within the exclusive legislative powers of the Federation and fields within concurrent legislative powers. In the field of concurrent legislation the Länder may legislate so long and so far as the Federation makes no use of its legislative right. The Federation has this right only in matters relating to the creation of equal living conditions throughout the country and in cases where the preservation of legal and economic unity is perceived to be in the national interest. Exclusive legislation of the Federation is strictly limited to such matters as foreign affairs, Federal finance, citizenship, migration, currency, copyrights, customs, railways, waterways, shipping and post and telecommunications. In most other fields, as enumerated (Article 74), concurrent legislation exists.

The legislative organ of the Federation is the Bundestag, to which Bills are introduced by the Government, by members of the Bundestag or by the Bundesrat (Article 76). After their adoption they must be submitted to the Bundesrat, which may demand, within three weeks, that a committee of members of both houses be convened to consider the Bill (Article 77). In so far as its express approval is not needed, the Bundesrat may veto a law within two weeks. This veto can be overruled by the Bundestag, with the approval of a majority of its members. When the Bill requires the consent of the Bundesrat, such an overruling may not take place.

An amendment of the Basic Law requires a majority of two-thirds in both houses, but an amendment affecting the division of the Federation into Länder and the basic principles contained in Articles 1 and 20 is inadmissible (Article 79).

VIII. THE EXECUTION OF FEDERAL LAWS AND THE FEDERAL ADMINISTRATION

The Länder execute Federal Laws as matters of their own concern in so far as the Basic Law does not otherwise determine. In doing so, they regulate the establishment of the authorities and the administrative procedure, but the Federal Government exercises supervision in order to ensure that the Länder execute Federal Laws in an appropriate manner.

In order to avert imminent danger to the existence of the democratic order, a Land may call in the police forces of other Länder; and if the Land in which the danger is imminent is itself not willing or able to fight the danger, the Federal Government may place the police in the Land, or the police forces in other Länder, under its instructions (Article 91).

IX. THE ADMINISTRATION OF JUSTICE

Judicial authority is vested in independent judges, who are subject only to the law and who may not be dismissed or transferred against their will (Article 97).

Justice is exercised by the Federal Constitutional Court, by the Superior Federal Courts and by the Courts of the Länder. The Federal Constitutional Court decides on the interpretation of the Basic Law in cases of doubt, on the compatibility of Federal Law or Land Law with the Basic Law, and on disputes between the Federation and the Länder or between different Länder. Superior Federal Courts are responsible for the spheres of ordinary, administrative, fiscal, labour and social jurisdiction. If a Superior Federal Court intends to judge a point of law in contradiction to a previous decision of another Superior Federal Court, it must refer the matter to a special senate of the Superior Courts. Extraordinary courts are inadmissible.

The freedom of the individual may be restricted only on the basis of a law. No one may be prevented from appearing before his lawful judge (Article 101). Detained persons may be subjected neither to physical nor to mental ill-treatment. The police may hold no one in custody longer than the end of the day following the arrest without the decision of a court. Any person temporarily detained must be brought before a judge who must either issue a warrant of arrest or set him free, at the latest on the following day. A person enjoying the confidence of the detainee must be notified forthwith of any continued duration of a deprivation of liberty. An act may be punished only if it was punishable by law before the act was committed, and no one may be punished more than once for the same criminal act. A criminal act may not be punished by sentence of death.

X. FINANCE

The Federation has the exclusive power to legislate only on customs and fiscal monopolies; on most other taxes, especially on income, property and inheritance, it has concurrent power to legislate with the Länder (see VII, above).

Customs, fiscal monopolies, excise taxes (with the exception of the beer tax) and levies within the framework of the EU are administered by Federal finance authorities, and the revenues thereof accrue to the Federation. The remaining taxes are administered, as a rule, by the Länder and the Gemeinden (communities) to which they accrue. Income tax, corporation tax and value-added tax are shared taxes, accruing jointly to the Federation and the Länder (after deduction of a proportion of income tax for the municipalities; Article 106). The Federation and the Länder shall be self-supporting and independent of each other in their fiscal administration (Article 109). In order to ensure the working efficiency of the Länder with low revenues and to equalize their differing burdens of expenditure, there exists a system of revenue-sharing among the Länder; in addition, the Federation may make grants, out of its own funds, to the poorer Länder. All revenues and expenditures of the Federation must be estimated for each fiscal year and included in the budget, which must be established by law before the beginning of the fiscal year. Decisions of the Bundestag or the Bundesrat that increase the budget expenditure proposed by the Federal Government require its approval (Article 113).

XI. TRANSITIONAL AND CONCLUDING PROVISIONS

Articles 116–146 regulate a number of unrelated matters of detail, such as the relationship between the old Reich and the Federation. Article 143 contains divergences from the Basic Law, with regard to the newly acceded Länder, as stipulated in the Unification Treaty.

The Government

HEAD OF STATE

Federal President: Prof. Dr HORST KÖHLER (inaugurated 1 July 2004).

THE FEDERAL GOVERNMENT
(April 2005)

A coalition of the Sozialdemokratische Partei Deutschlands (Social Democratic Party—SPD) and Bündnis 90/Die Grünen (Alliance 90/Greens).

Federal Chancellor: GERHARD SCHRÖDER (SPD).

Federal Vice-Chancellor and Minister of Foreign Affairs: JOSEPH (JOSCHKA) FISCHER (Bündnis 90/Die Grünen).

Minister of the Interior: OTTO SCHILY (SPD).

Minister of Justice: BRIGITTE ZYPRIES (SPD).

Minister of Finance: HANS EICHEL (SPD).

Minister of Economics and Labour: WOLFGANG CLEMENT (Independent).

Minister of Consumer Protection, Food and Agriculture: RENATE KÜNAST (Bündnis 90/Die Grünen).

Minister of Defence: PETER STRUCK (SPD).

Minister of Family Affairs, Senior Citizens, Women and Youth: RENATE SCHMIDT (SPD).

Minister of Health and Social Security: ULLA SCHMIDT (SPD).

Minister of Transport, Building and Housing: MANFRED STOLPE (SPD).

Minister of the Environment, Nature Conservation and Nuclear Safety: JÜRGEN TRITTIN (Bündnis 90/Die Grünen).

Minister of Education and Research: EDELGARD BULMAHN (SPD).

Minister of Economic Co-operation and Development: HEIDEMARIE WIECZOREK-ZEUL (SPD).

MINISTRIES

Office of the Federal President: Schloss Bellevue, 11010 Berlin; tel. (30) 20000; fax (30) 20001999; e-mail posteingang@bundespraesident.de; internet www.bundespraesident.de.

Federal Chancellery: Willy-Brandt Str. 1, 10557 Berlin; tel. (30) 40000; fax (30) 40002357; e-mail bundeskanzler@bundeskanzler.de; internet www.bundeskanzler.de.

Press and Information Office of the Federal Government: Dorotheenstr. 84, 10117 Berlin; tel. (0) 1802720000; fax (0) 18882722555; e-mail internetpost@bundesregierung.de; internet www.bundesregierung.de.

Ministry of Consumer Protection, Food and Agriculture: Postfach 42, 10177 Berlin; Wilhelmstr. 54, 10121 Berlin; tel. (30) 20060; fax (30) 20064262; e-mail internet@bml.bund.de; internet www.bml.de.

Ministry of Defence: Stauffenbergstr. 18, 10785 Berlin; tel. (0) 1888240; fax (0) 1888242129; e-mail poststelle@bmvg.bund400.de; internet www.bundeswehr.de.

Ministry of Economic Co-operation and Development: Stresemannstr. 94, Europahaus, 10963 Berlin; tel. (0) 18885350; fax (0) 18885353500; e-mail poststelle@bmz.bund.de; internet www.bmz.de.

Ministry of Economics and Labour: Scharnhorststr. 34–37, 10115 Berlin; tel. (0) 18886150; fax (0) 18886157010; e-mail info@bmwi.bund.de; internet www.bmwi.de.

Ministry of Education and Research: Hannoversche Str. 28–30, 10115 Berlin; tel. (0) 1888570; fax (0) 18885783601; e-mail bmbf@bmbf.bund.de; internet www.bmbf.de.

Ministry of the Environment, Nature Conservation and Nuclear Safety: Alexanderpl. 6, 10178 Berlin; tel. (0) 18883050; fax (0) 18883054375; e-mail maileingang@bmu.bund.de; internet www.bmu.de.

Ministry of Family Affairs, Senior Citizens, Women and Youth: Taubenstr. 42/43, 10117 Berlin; tel. (0) 18885550; fax (30) 206551145; e-mail info@bmfsfj.bund.de; internet www.bmfsfj.de.

Ministry of Finance: Wilhelmstr. 97, 10117 Berlin; tel. (30) 22420; fax (30) 22423260; e-mail poststelle@bmf.bund.de; internet www.bundesfinanzministerium.de.

Ministry of Foreign Affairs: Werderscher Markt 1, 10117 Berlin; tel. (30) 50000; fax (30) 50003402; e-mail poststelle@auswaertiges-amt.de; internet www.auswaertiges-amt.de.

Ministry of Health and Social Security: Postfach 080163, 10117 Berlin; Mohrenstr. 62, 10001 Berlin; tel. (30) 206400; fax (30) 206404974; e-mail info@bmg.bund.de; internet www.bmgesundheit.de.

Ministry of the Interior: Alt-Moabit 101D, 10559 Berlin; tel. (0) 18886810; fax (0) 18886812926; e-mail poststelle@bmi.bund.de; internet www.bmi.bund.de.

Ministry of Justice: Mohrenstr. 37, 10117 Berlin; tel. (30) 202570; fax (30) 20259525; e-mail poststelle@bmj.bund.de; internet www.bmj.bund.de.

Ministry of Transport, Building and Housing: Invalidenstr. 44, 10115 Berlin; tel. (30) 20080; fax (30) 20081920; e-mail buergerinfo@bmvbw.bund.de; internet www.bmvbw.de.

Legislature

BUNDESTAG
(Federal Assembly)

Pl. der Republik 1, 11011 Berlin; tel. (30) 2270; fax (30) 22736878; e-mail mail@bundestag.de; internet www.bundestag.de.

President: WOLFGANG THIERSE (SPD).

Vice-Presidents: Dr SUSANNE KASTNER (SPD), Dr NORBERT LAMMERT (CDU/CSU), Dr ANTJE VOLLMER (Bündnis 90/Die Grünen), Dr HERMANN OTTO SOLMS (FDP).

General Election, 22 September 2002

Parties and Groups	Votes*	% of votes	Seats
Sozialdemokratische Partei Deutschlands (SPD)	18,488,668	38.52	251
Christlich-Demokratische Union Deutschlands (CDU)	14,167,561	29.52	190
Christlich-Soziale Union Deutschlands (CSU)	4,315,080	8.99	58
Bündnis 90/Die Grünen	4,110,355	8.56	55
Freie Demokratische Partei (FDP)	3,538,815	7.37	47
Partei des Demokratischen Sozialismus (PDS)	1,916,702	3.99	2
Others	1,459,299	3.04	—
Total	**47,996,480**	**100.00**	**603**

*Figures refer to valid second votes (i.e. for state party lists). The total number of valid first votes (for individual candidates) was 47,841,724.

BUNDESRAT
(Federal Council)

President: Prof. Dr WOLFGANG BÖHMER (CDU).

The Bundesrat has 69 members. Each Land (state) has three, four, five or six votes, depending on the size of its population, and may send as many members to the sessions as it has votes. The head of government of each Land is automatically a member of the Bundesrat. Members of the Federal Government attend the sessions, which are held every two to three weeks.

Länder	Seats
Nordrhein-Westfalen (North Rhine-Westphalia)	6
Bayern (Bavaria)	6
Baden-Württemberg	6
Niedersachsen (Lower Saxony)	6
Sachsen (Saxony)	5
Hessen (Hesse)	4
Rheinland-Pfalz (Rhineland-Palatinate)	4
Berlin	4
Sachsen-Anhalt (Saxony-Anhalt)	4
Thüringen (Thuringia)	4
Brandenburg	4
Schleswig-Holstein	4
Mecklenburg-Vorpommern (Mecklenburg-Western Pomerania)	3
Hamburg	3
Saarland	3
Bremen	3
Total	**69**

The Land Governments

The 16 Länder of Germany are autonomous but not sovereign states, enjoying a high degree of self-government and extensive legislative powers. Thirteen of the Länder have a Landesregierung (Government) and a Landtag (Assembly). The equivalent of the Landesregierung in Berlin, Bremen and Hamburg is the Senate. The equivalent of the Landtag is the House of Representatives in Berlin and the City Council in Bremen and Hamburg.

BADEN-WÜRTTEMBERG

The Constitution was adopted by the Assembly in Stuttgart on 11 November 1953 and came into force on 19 November. The Minister-President, who is elected by the Assembly, appoints and dismisses Ministers. The Government, which is responsible to the Assembly, is currently formed by a coalition of the CDU and the FDP/DVP.

Minister-President: ERWIN TEUFEL (CDU).

Landtag von Baden-Württemberg: Haus des Landtags, Konrad-Adenauer-Str. 3, 70173 Stuttgart; tel. (711) 20630; fax (711) 2063299; e-mail post@landtag-bw.de; internet www.landtag-bw.de.

The composition of the Assembly, as the result of elections held on 25 March 2001, is as follows:

President of Assembly: PETER STRAUB (CDU).

Party	Seats
Christlich-Demokratische Union Deutschlands (CDU)	63
Sozialdemokratische Partei Deutschlands (SPD) . .	45
Bündnis 90/Die Grünen	10
Freie Demokratische Partei/Demokratische Volkspartei (FDP/DVP)	10

The Land is divided into four administrative districts: Stuttgart, Karlsruhe, Tübingen and Freiburg.

BAYERN (BAVARIA)

The Constitution of Bavaria provides for a bicameral Assembly and a Constitutional Court. Provision is also made for referendums. The Minister-President, who is elected by the Assembly for four years, appoints the Ministers and Secretaries of State with the consent of the Assembly.

Minister-President: Dr EDMUND STOIBER (CSU).

Bayerischer Landtag: Landtagsamt, Maximilaneum, 81627 München; tel. (89) 41260; fax (89) 41261392; e-mail poststelle@bayern.landtag.de; internet www.bayern.landtag.de.

The composition of the Assembly, as a result of elections held on 21 September 2003, is as follows:

President of Assembly: ALOIS GLÜCK (CSU).

Party	Seats
Christlich-Soziale Union Deutschlands (CSU) . . .	124
Sozialdemocratische Partei Deutschlands (SPD) . .	41
Bündnis 90/Die Grünen	15

The Senate, or second chamber, consists of 60 members, divided into 10 groups representing professional interests, e.g. agriculture, industry, trade, the professions and religious communities. Every two years one-third of the Senate is newly elected. In February 1998 a majority of voters who participated in a Land referendum on the future of the Senate favoured its abolition.

President of the Senate: HERIBERT THALLMAIR (CSU).

Bayern is divided into seven districts: Mittelfranken, Oberfranken, Unterfranken, Schwaben, Niederbayern, Oberpfalz and Oberbayern.

BERLIN

The House of Representatives (Abgeordnetenhaus) is the legislative body. The executive agency is the Senate, which is composed of the Governing Mayor (Regierender Bürgermeister) and up to 10 Senators, from among whom the deputy mayor is elected. The Governing Mayor and the senators are elected by a majority of the House of Representatives. The Senate is responsible to the House of Representatives and dependent on its confidence. The Senate is currently composed of a coalition of the SPD and Bündnis 90/Die Grünen.

Regierender Bürgermeister: KLAUS WOWEREIT (SPD).

Abgeordnetenhaus von Berlin: Niederkirchnerstr. 5, 10117 Berlin; tel. (30) 23251060; e-mail verwaltung@parlament-berlin.de; internet www.parlament-berlin.de.

The composition of the House of Representatives, as the result of elections held on 21 October 2001, is as follows:

President of House of Representatives: WALTER MOMPER (SPD).

Party	Seats
Sozialdemokratische Partei Deutschlands (SPD) . .	44
Christlich-Demokratische Union Deutschlands (CDU)	35
Partie des Demokratischen Sozialismus (PDS) . .	33
Freie Demokratische Partei (FDP)	15
Bündnis 90/Die Grünen	14

BRANDENBURG

The Constitution of Brandenburg was adopted on 14 June 1992 and came into force on 20 August. It was amended on 7 April 1999. The Government is currently formed from a coalition of the SPD and the CDU.

Minister-President: MATTHIAS PLATZECK (SPD).

Landtag Brandenburg: Postfach 601064, 14410 Potsdam; Am Havelblick 8, 14473 Potsdam; tel. (331) 9660; fax (331) 9661210; e-mail poststelle@landtag.brandenburg.de; internet www.landtag.brandenburg.de.

The composition of the Assembly, as a result of elections held on 19 September 2004, is as follows:

President of Assembly: Dr HERBERT KNOBLICH (SPD).

Party	Seats
Sozialdemokratische Partei Deutschlands (SPD) . .	33
Partei des Demokratischen Sozialismus (PDS) . .	29
Christlich-Demokratische Union Deutschlands (CDU)	20
Deutsche Volksunion (DVU)	6

BREMEN

The Constitution of the Free Hanseatic City of Bremen was sanctioned by referendum of the people on 12 October 1947. The main constitutional organs are the City Council (legislature), the Senate (government) and the Constitutional Court. The Senate is the executive organ elected by the Council for the duration of its own tenure of office. The Senate elects from its own ranks two Mayors (Bürgermeister), one of whom becomes President of the Senate. Decisions of the Council are subject to the delaying veto of the Senate. The Senate is currently formed from a coalition of the SPD and the CDU.

First Bürgermeister and President of the Senate: Dr HENNING SCHERF (SPD).

Bremische Bürgerschaft: Am Markt 20, 28195 Bremen; tel. (421) 3614555; fax (421) 36112492; e-mail geschaeftsstelle@buergerschaft.bremen.de; internet www.bremische-buergerschaft.de.

The election of 25 May 2003 resulted in the following composition:

President of the City Council: CHRISTIAN WEBER (SPD).

Party	Seats
Sozialdemokratische Partei Deutschlands (SPD) . .	40
Christlich-Demokratische Union Deutschlands (CDU)	29
Bündnis 90/Die Grünen	13
Deutsche Volksunion (DVU)	1
Freie Demokratische Partei (FDP)	1

HAMBURG

The Constitution of the Free and Hanseatic City of Hamburg was adopted in June 1952. The City Council (legislature) elects the members of the Senate (government), which in turn elects the President and the President's deputy from its own ranks. The President remains in office for one year, but may stand for re-election. The Senate is currently formed by a coalition of the CDU, the FDP and the Partei Rechtsstaatlicher Offensive.

President of Senate and First Bürgermeister: OLE VON BEUST (CDU).

Bürgerschaft der Freien und Hansestadt Hamburg: Rathaus, Rathausmarkt 1, 20095 Hamburg; tel. (40) 428312408; fax (40) 428312558; e-mail oeffentlichkeitsservice@blc.hamburg.de; internet www.hamburg.de/buergerschaft.

The City Council was elected on 29 February 2004, and is composed as follows:

President: Dr DOROTHEE STAPELFELDT (SPD).

Party	Seats
Christlich-Demokratische Union Deutschlands (CDU)	63
Sozialdemokratische Partei Deutschlands (SPD) . .	41
Die Grünen/Grüne Alternative Liste (GAL) . . .	17

HESSEN (HESSE)

The Constitution of this Land dates from 1 December 1946. The Minister-President is elected by the Assembly, and appoints and dismisses Ministers with its consent. The Assembly can force the resignation of the Government by a vote of no confidence. The Government is currently formed from a coalition of the CDU and FDP.

Minister-President: ROLAND KOCH (CDU).

Hessischer Landtag: Schlosspl. 1–3, 65183 Wiesbaden; tel. (611) 3500; fax (611) 350434; e-mail poststelle@ltg.hessen.de; internet www.hessischer-landtag.de.

The Assembly, elected on 2 February 2003, is composed as follows:

President of Assembly: KLAUS PETER MÖLLER (CDU).

Party	Seats
Christlich-Demokratische Union Deutschlands (CDU)	56
Sozialdemokratische Partei Deutschlands (SPD) . .	33
Bündnis 90/Die Grünen	12
Freie Demokratische Partei (FDP)	9

Hessen is divided into three governmental districts: Kassel, Giessen and Darmstadt.

MECKLENBURG-VORPOMMERN (MECKLENBURG-WESTERN POMERANIA)

The Constitution was adopted by the Assembly on 14 May 1993. The Government is currently formed from a coalition of the SPD and the PDS.

Minister-President: HARALD RINGSTORFF (SPD).

Landtag Mecklenburg-Vorpommern: Schloss, Lennéstr. 1, 19053 Schwerin; tel. (385) 5250; fax (385) 5252121; e-mail poststelle@landtag-mv.de; internet www.landtag-mv.de.

The composition of the Assembly, as a result of elections held on 22 September 2002, is as follows:

President of Assembly: SYLVIA BRETSCHNEIDER (SPD).

Party	Seats
Sozialdemokratische Partei Deutschlands (SPD) . .	33
Christlich-Demokratische Union Deutschlands (CDU)	25
Partei des Demokratischen Sozialismus (PDS) . . .	13

NIEDERSACHSEN (LOWER SAXONY)

The Constitution was adopted by the Assembly on 19 May 1993 and came into force on 1 June. The Government is currently formed from a coalition of the CDU and the FDP.

Minister-President: CHRISTIAN WULFF.

Landtag Niedersachsen: Hinrich-Wilhelm-Kopf-Pl. 1, 30159 Hannover; tel. (511) 30300; fax (511) 30302806; e-mail pressestelle@lt.niedersachsen.de; internet www.landtag-niedersachsen.de.

As a result of elections held on 2 February 2003, the Assembly is composed as follows:

President of Assembly: JÜRGEN GANSÄUER (CDU).

Party	Seats
Christlich-Demokratische Union Deutschlands (CDU)	91
Sozialdemokratische Partei Deutschlands (SPD) . .	63
Freie Demokratische Partei (FDP)	15
Bündnis 90/Die Grünen	14

Niedersachsen is divided into four governmental districts: Braunschweig, Hannover, Lüneburg and Weser-Ems.

NORDRHEIN-WESTFALEN (NORTH RHINE-WESTPHALIA)

The present Constitution was adopted by the Assembly on 6 June 1950, and was endorsed by the electorate in the elections held on 18 June. The Government is presided over by the Minister-President, who appoints Ministers. It is currently formed from a coalition of the SPD and Bündnis 90/Die Grünen.

Minister-President: PEER STEINBRÜCK (SPD).

Landtag von Nordrhein-Westfalen: Postfach 101143, 40002 Düsseldorf; Pl. des Landtags 1, 40221 Düsseldorf; tel. (211) 8840; fax (211) 8842258; e-mail email@landtag.nrw.de; internet www.landtag.nrw.de.

The Assembly, elected on 14 May 2000, is composed as follows:

President of Assembly: ULRICH SCHMIDT (SPD).

Party	Seats
Sozialdemokratische Partei Deutschlands (SPD) . .	102
Christlich-Demokratische Union Deutschlands (CDU)	88
Freie Demokratische Partei (FDP)	24
Bündnis 90/Die Grünen	15

The Land is divided into five governmental districts: Düsseldorf, Münster, Arnsberg, Detmold and Köln.

RHEINLAND-PFALZ (RHINELAND-PALATINATE)

The three chief agencies of the Constitution of this Land are the Assembly, the Government and the Constitutional Court. The Minister-President is elected by the Assembly, with whose consent he/she appoints and dismisses Ministers. The Government, which is dependent on the confidence of the Assembly, is currently composed of a coalition of the SPD and the FDP.

Minister-President: KURT BECK (SPD).

Landtag Rheinland-Pfalz: Postfach 3040, 55020 Mainz; Deutschhauspl. 12, 55116 Mainz; tel. (6131) 2080; fax (6131) 2082447; e-mail poststelle@landtag.rlp.de; internet www.landtag.rheinland-pfalz.de.

The members of the Assembly are elected according to a system of proportional representation. Its composition, as the result of elections held on 25 March 2001, is as follows:

President of Assembly: CHRISTOPH GRIMM (SPD).

Party	Seats
Sozialdemokratische Partei Deutschlands (SPD) . .	49
Christlich-Demokratische Union Deutschlands (CDU)	38
Freie Demokratische Partei (FDP)	8
Bündnis 90/Die Grünen	6

Rheinland-Pfalz is divided into three districts: Koblenz, Rheinhessen-Pfalz (Rheinhessen-Palatinate) and Trier.

SAARLAND

Under the Constitution, which came into force on 1 January 1957, Saarland was politically integrated into the FRG as a Land. It was economically integrated into the FRG in July 1959. The Minister-President is elected by the Assembly. The Government is currently formed by the majority party (CDU).

Minister-President: PETER MÜLLER (CDU).

Landtag des Saarlandes: Postfach 101833, 66018 Saarbrücken; e-mail postmaster@landtag-saar.de; internet www.landtag-saar.de.

The composition of the Assembly, as a result of elections held on 5 September 2004, is as follows:

President of the Assembly: HANS LEY (CDU).

Party	Seats
Christlich-Demokratische Union Deutschlands (CDU)	27
Sozialdemokratische Partei Deutschlands (SPD) . .	18
Freie Demokratische Partei (FDP)	3
Bündnis 90/Die Grünen	3

SACHSEN (SAXONY)

The Constitution of Sachsen was adopted on 26 May 1992 and came into force on 6 June. The Government is formed by the majority party (CDU).

Minister-President: Prof. Dr GEORG MILBRADT (CDU).

Sächsischer Landtag: Postfach 120705, 01008 Dresden; Bernhard-von-Lindenau Pl. 1, 01067 Dresden; tel. (351) 49350; fax (351) 4935900; e-mail post@slt.sachsen.de; internet www.landtag.sachsen.de.

The composition of the Assembly, as a result of elections held on 19 September 2004, is as below:

President of Assembly: ERICH ILTGEN (CDU).

Party	Seats
Christlich-Demokratische Union Deutschlands (CDU)	55
Partei des Demokratischen Sozialismus (PDS) . . .	31
Sozialdemokratische Partei Deutschlands (SPD) . .	13
Nationaldemokratische Partei Deutschlands (NPD) .	12
Freie Demokratische Partei (FDP)	7
Bündnis 90/Die Grünen	6

SACHSEN-ANHALT (SAXONY-ANHALT)

The Constitution of Sachsen-Anhalt was adopted on 16 July 1992. The Government is currently formed by the majority party (CDU).

Minister-President: Prof. Dr WOLFGANG BÖHMER (CDU).

Landtag von Sachsen-Anhalt: Dompl. 6–9, 39104 Magdeburg; tel. (391) 5600; fax (391) 5601123; e-mail landtag@lt.lsa-net.de; internet www.landtag.sachsen-anhalt.de.

The composition of the Assembly, as a result of elections held on 21 April 2002, is as follows:

President of Assembly: Prof. Dr ADOLF SPOTKA (CDU).

Party	Seats
Christlich-Demokratische Union Deutschlands (CDU)	48
Sozialdemokratische Partei Deutschlands (SPD) . .	25
Partei des Demokratischen Sozialismus (PDS) . .	25
Deutsche Volksunion (DVU)	17

Sachsen-Anhalt is divided into three governmental districts: Magdeburg, Halle and Dessau.

SCHLESWIG-HOLSTEIN

The Provisional Constitution was adopted by the Assembly on 13 December 1949. The Government consists of the Minister-President and the Ministers appointed by the Minister-President. The Government is formed by a coalition of the SPD and the CDU.

Minister-President: PETER HARRY CARSTENSEN (CDU).

Landtag Schleswig-Holstein: Düsternbrooker Weg 70, 24105 Kiel; tel. (431) 9881120; fax (431) 9881119; e-mail joachim.koehler@landtag.ltsh.de; internet www.sh-landtag.de.

The composition of the Assembly, as the result of elections held on 20 February 2005, is as follows:

President of Assembly: MARTIN KAYENBURG (CDU).

Party	Seats
Christlich-Demokratische Union Deutschlands (CDU)	30
Sozialdemokratische Partei Deutschlands (SPD) . .	29
Freie Demokratische Partei (FDP)	4
Bündnis 90/Die Grünen	4
Südschleswigscher Wählerverband*	2

* Represents the Danish minority in Schleswig-Holstein.

THÜRINGEN (THURINGIA)

The Constitution of Thüringen was adopted on 25 October 1993. The Assembly Government is currently led by the CDU.

Minister-President: DIETER ALTHAUS (CDU).

Thüringer Landtag: Postschliessfach 101951, 99019 Erfurt; tel. (361) 37700; fax (361) 3772016; e-mail pressestelle@landtag.thueringen.de; internet www.landtag.thueringen.de.

The composition of the Assembly, as a result of elections held on 13 June 2004, is as follows:

President of Assembly: CHRISTINE LIEBERKNECHT (CDU).

Party	Seats
Christlich-Demokratische Union Deutschlands (CDU)	45
Partei des Demokratischen Sozialismus (PDS) . .	28
Sozialdemokratische Partei Deutschlands (SPD) . .	15

Political Organizations

Bündnis 90/Die Grünen (Alliance 90/Greens): Pl. vor dem Neuen Tor 1, 10115 Berlin; tel. (30) 284420; fax (30) 28442210; e-mail info@gruene.de; internet www.gruene.de; f. 1993 by merger of Bündnis 90 (f. 1990, as an electoral political asscn of citizens' movements of the former GDR) and Die Grünen (f. 1980, largely composed of the membership of the Grüne Aktion Zukunft, the Grüne Liste, Umweltschutz and the Aktionsgemeinschaft Unabhängiger Deutscher, also including groups of widely varying political views); essentially left-wing party programme includes ecological issues, democratization of society at all levels, social justice, comprehensive disarmament; Chair. ANGELIKA BEER, REINHARD BÜTIKOFER; Parliamentary Leaders KATRIN GÖRING-ECKARDT, KRISTA SAGER; Sec.-Gen. STEFFI LEMKE.

Christlich-Demokratische Union Deutschlands (in Bavaria: Christlich-Soziale Union Deutschlands) (CDU/CSU) (Christian Democratic and Christian Social Union):

CDU: Konrad-Adenauer-Haus, Klingelhöferstr. 8, 10785 Berlin; tel. (30) 220700; fax (30) 22070111; e-mail post@cdu.de; internet www.cdu.de; f. 1945; became a federal party in 1950; advocates united action between Catholics and Protestants for rebuilding German life on a Christian-Democratic basis, while guaranteeing private property and the freedom of the individual, and for a 'free and equal Germany in a free, politically united and socially just Europe'; other objectives are to guarantee close ties with allies within NATO and the EU; in Oct. 1990 incorporated the CDU of the former GDR; c. 590,000 mems (Feb. 2004); Chair. and Parliamentary Leader Dr ANGELA MERKEL; Sec.-Gen. VOLKER KAUDER.

CSU: Nymphenburger Str. 64, 80335 München; tel. (89) 12430; fax (89) 1243220; e-mail landesleitung@csu-bayern.de; internet

www.csu.de; f. 1946; Christian Social party, aiming for a free-market economy 'in the service of man's economic and intellectual freedom'; also combines national consciousness with support for a united Europe; 181,000 mems; Chair. Dr EDMUND STOIBER; Sec.-Gen. MARKUS SÖDER.

Deutsche Kommunistische Partei (DKP) (German Communist Party): Hoffnungstr. 18, 45127 Essen; tel. (201) 225148; fax (201) 202467; e-mail dkp.pv@t-online.de; internet www.dkp.de; 7,000 mems (1998); Chair. HEINZ STEHR.

Deutsche Volksunion (DVU) (German People's Union): Postfach 600464, 81204 München; tel. (89) 896085; fax (89) 8341534; internet www.dvu.net; f. 1987; extreme right-wing.

Freie Demokratische Partei (FDP) (Free Democratic Party): Reinhardtstr. 14, 10117 Berlin; tel. (30) 2849580; fax (30) 28495822; e-mail tdh@fdp.de; internet www.fdp.de; f. 1948; represents democratic and social liberalism and makes the individual the focal point of the State and its laws and economy; in Aug. 1990 incorporated the three liberal parties of the former GDR—the Association of Free Democrats, the German Forum Party and the FDP; publishes *Elde*; c. 65,192 mems (Dec. 2003); Chair. Dr GUIDO WESTERWELLE; Dep. Chair. RAINER BRÜDERLE, Prof. Dr ANDREAS PINKWART; Chair. in Bundestag Dr WOLFGANG GERHARDT; Sec.-Gen. CORNELIA PIEPER.

Freie Demokratische Partei/Demokratische Volkspartei (FDP/DVP): Konrad Adenauer-Str. 12, 70173 Stuttgart; tel. (711) 2063627; fax (711) 2063610; e-mail post@fdp.landtag-bw.de; internet www.fdp-dvp-fraktion.de; f. 1948; Chair. ERNST PFISTER.

Nationaldemokratische Partei Deutschlands (NPD) (National Democratic Party of Germany): Postfach 840157, 12531 Berlin; tel. (30) 650110; fax (30) 65011142; e-mail bgst@npd.de; internet www.npd.de; f. 1964; right-wing; 15,000 mems; youth organization Junge Nationaldemokraten (JN), 6,000 mems; Chair. UDO VOIGT.

Neues Forum (New Forum): Rosa-Luxemburg-Str. 19, 10178 Berlin; tel. (30) 2479404; fax (30) 2477261; e-mail info@neuesforum.de; internet www.neuesforum.de; f. 1989 as a citizens' action group; played prominent role in democratic movement in former GDR; Leaders KAROLIN SCHUBERT, MATTHIAS BÜCHNER, MICHAEL BONEHR.

Partei des Demokratischen Sozialismus (PDS) (Party of Democratic Socialism): Kleine Alexanderstr. 28, 10178 Berlin; tel. (30) 240090; fax (30) 24009425; e-mail redaktion@pds-online.de; internet www.pds-online.de; successor to the Sozialistische Einheitspartei Deutschlands (SED—Socialist Unity Party, f. 1946 as a result of the unification of the Social Democratic Party and the Communist Party in Eastern Germany), which had been the dominant political force in the GDR until late 1989; adopted present name Feb. 1990; has renounced Stalinism, opposes fascism, right-wing extremism and xenophobia, advocates a socially- and ecologically-orientated market economy with public, collective and private ownership of the means of production, supports international disarmament and peaceful solutions to international conflicts; 65,000 mems (Dec. 2004); Chair. Prof. LOTHAR BISKY; Hon. Chair. Dr HANS MODROW.

Die Republikaner (REP) (Republican Party): Postfach 870210, 13162 Berlin; tel. (30) 79098310; fax (30) 79098315; e-mail republikaner-bgs@t-online.de; internet www.rep.de; f. 1983; conservative right wing; c. 15,000 mems; Chair. Dr ROLF SCHLIERER.

Sozialdemokratische Partei Deutschlands (SPD) (Social Democratic Party of Germany): Wilhelmstr. 141, 10963 Berlin; tel. (30) 259910; fax (30) 410; e-mail parteivorstand@spd.de; internet www.spd.de; f. 1863; maintains that a vital democracy can be built only on the basis of social justice; advocates for the economy as much competition as possible, as much planning as necessary to protect the individual from uncontrolled economic interests; favours a positive attitude to national defence, while supporting controlled disarmament; rejects any political ties with Communism; in September 1990 incorporated the SPD of the former GDR; 650,798 mems (Dec. 2003); Chair. FRANZ MÜNTEFERING; Sec.-Gen. KLAUS-UWE BENNETER.

There are also numerous other small parties, none of them represented in the Bundestag, covering all shades of the political spectrum and various regional interests.

Diplomatic Representation

EMBASSIES IN GERMANY

Afghanistan: Wilhemlstr. 65, 10117 Berlin; tel. (30) 2067550; fax (30) 2291510; e-mail info@afghan-embassy-berlin.gov.af; internet www.afghan-embassy-berlin.gov.af; Ambassador HAMIDULLAH NASSER ZIA.

Albania: Friedrichstr. 231, 10363 Berlin; tel. (30) 2593040; fax (30) 25931890; e-mail kanzlei@botschaft-albanien.de; Ambassador GAZMEND TURDIU.

Algeria: Görschstr. 45–46, 13187 Berlin; tel. (30) 437370; fax (30) 48098716; e-mail info@algerische-botschaft.de; internet www .algerische-botschaft.de; Ambassador MOURAD BENCHEIKH.

Angola: Wallstr. 58, 10179 Berlin; tel. (30) 2408970; fax (30) 24089712; e-mail botschaft@botschaftangola.de; internet www .botschaftangola.de; Ambassador ALBERTO DO CARMO BENTO RIBEIRO.

Argentina: Kleiststr. 23–26, 10787 Berlin; tel. (30) 2266890; fax (30) 2291400; e-mail info@argentinische-botschaft.de; internet www .argentinische-botschaft.de; Ambassador ENRIQUE J. A. CANDIOTI.

Armenia: Hillmannstr. 5, 13467 Berlin; tel. (30) 4050910; fax (30) 40509125; e-mail armemb@t-online.de; Ambassador KARINE KAZI-NIAN.

Australia: Wallstr. 76–79, 10179 Berlin; tel. (30) 8800880; fax (30) 880088310; e-mail info@australian-embassy.de; internet www .australian-embassy.de; Ambassador PAMELA JEAN FAYLE.

Austria: Stauffenbergstr. 1, 10785 Berlin; tel. (30) 202870; fax (30) 2290569; e-mail berlin-ob@bmaa.gv.at; internet www .oesterreichische-botschaft.de; Ambassador Dr CHRISTIAN PROSL.

Azerbaijan: Axel-Springer-Str. 54A, 10117 Berlin; tel. (30) 2191613; fax (30) 21916152; e-mail azerbembgermany@aol.com; internet www.botschaft-aserbaidschan.de; Ambassador HUSEINAGA SADIQOV.

Bahrain: Klingelhöfer Str. 7, 10785 Berlin; tel. (30) 86877777; fax (30) 86877788; Ambassador ADEL YOUSIF H. SATER.

Bangladesh: Dovestr. 1, 5th Floor, 10587 Berlin; tel. (30) 3989750; fax (30) 39897510; e-mail bdootbn@aol.com; internet www .bangladeshembassy.de; Ambassador ALIMUL HAQUE.

Belarus: Am Treptower Park, 12345 Berlin; tel. (30) 5363590; fax (30) 53635923; e-mail info@belarus-botschaft.de; Ambassador VLA-DIMIR SKVORTSOV.

Belgium: Jägerstr. 52–53, 10117 Berlin; tel. (30) 206420; fax (30) 20642200; e-mail berlin@diplobel.org; internet www.diplomatie.be/ berlin; Ambassador LODEWIJK WILLEMS.

Benin: Postfach 200254, 53179 Bonn; Rüdigerstr. 10, 53132 Bonn; tel. (228) 943870; fax (228) 857192; Ambassador ISSA KPARA.

Bolivia: Wichmannstr. 6, 10787 Berlin; tel. (30) 2639150; fax (30) 26391515; e-mail embajada.bolivia@berlin.de; internet www.bolivia .de; Ambassador JORGE ALBERTO BALCÁZAR ARANIBAR.

Bosnia and Herzegovina: Ibsenstr. 14, 10439 Berlin; tel. (30) 81471210; fax (30) 81471211; Ambassador NEDELJKO DESPOTOVIĆ.

Brazil: Wallstr. 57, 10179 Berlin; tel. (30) 726280; fax (30) 72628320; e-mail brasil@brasemberlin.de; internet www .brasilianische-botschaft.de; Ambassador JOSÉ ARTUR DENOT MEDEIROS.

Brunei: Kronenstr. 55–58, 10117 Berlin; tel. (30) 2060760; Ambassador Dato' Paduka Haji MOHD ADNAN BUNTAR.

Bulgaria: Mauerstr. 11, 10117 Berlin; tel. (30) 2010922; fax (30) 2086838; e-mail info@botschaft-bulgarien.de; internet www .botschaft-bulgarien.de; Ambassador NIKOLAI APOSTOLOFF.

Burkina Faso: Karolingerpl. 10–11, 14052 Berlin; tel. (30) 30105990; fax (30) 301059920; e-mail embassy_burkina_faso@ t-online.de; Ambassador XAVIER NIODOGO.

Burundi: Berliner Str. 36, 10715 Berlin; tel. (30) 2345670; fax (30) 23456720; e-mail info@burundi-embassy-berlin.com; internet www .burundi-embassy-berlin.com; Chargé d'affaires PIERRE SINARINZI.

Cambodia: Benjamin-Vogelsdorf-Str., 13187 Berlin; tel. (30) 48637901; fax (30) 48637973; e-mail rec-berlin@t-online.de; Ambassador PHANDARAVONG SISOWATH.

Cameroon: Rheinallee 76, 53173 Bonn; tel. (228) 356038; fax (228) 359058; e-mail botschaftkamerun@yahoo.fr; Ambassador JEAN MELAGA.

Canada: Friedrichstr. 95, 10117 Berlin; tel. (30) 203120; fax (30) 20312590; e-mail brlin@international.gc.ca; internet www .kanada-info.de; Ambassador MARIE BERNARD-MEUNIER.

Cape Verde: Dorotheenstr. 43, 10117 Berlin; tel. (30) 20450955; fax (30) 20450966; e-mail info@embassy-capeverde.de; internet www .embassy-capeverde.de; Ambassador OLIVIO MELÍCIO PIRES.

Central African Republic: Rheinaustr. 120, 53225 Bonn; tel. (228) 233564; Ambassador MARTIN-GÉRARD TEBITO.

Chad: Basteistr. 80, 53173 Bonn; tel. (228) 356026; fax (228) 355887; e-mail ambatchad-rfa@t-onlinc.dc; Ambassador MAHAMAT ABDELRASSOUL.

Chile: Mohrenstr. 42, 10117 Berlin; tel. (30) 7262035; fax (30) 7262203; e-mail embachilealemania@echileberlin.de; internet www .embajadaconsuladoschile.de; Ambassador Dr MARIO ADOLFO FERN-ÁNDEZ BAEZA.

China, People's Republic: Märkisches Ufer 54, 10179 Berlin; tel. (30) 27582922; fax (30) 27588221; e-mail chinesischebotschaft@ debital.net; internet www.china-botschaft.de; Ambassador MA CHAN-RONG.

Colombia: Kurfürstenstr. 84, 10787 Berlin; tel. (30) 2639610; fax (30) 26396125; e-mail info@botschaft-kolumbien.de; Ambassador MARIA DORA VICTORIANA MEJIA MARULANDA.

Congo, Democratic Republic: Im Meisengarten 133; 53179 Bonn; tel. (228) 858160; fax (228) 9349237; Ambassador LHELO BOLOTO.

Congo, Republic: Rheinallee 45, 53173 Bonn; tel. and fax (228) 358355; e-mail botschaft.kongobrz@t-online.de; Chargé d'affaires a.i. SERGE MICHEL ODZOCKI.

Costa Rica: Dessauer Str. 28–29, 10963 Berlin; tel. (30) 26398990; fax (30) 26557210; e-mail emb-costa-rica@t-online.de; Ambassador BERND NIEHAUS QUESADA.

Côte d'Ivoire: Königstr. 93, 53115 Bonn; tel. (228) 212098; fax (228) 217313; e-mail ambic@t-online.de; Ambassador FLORENT AMIN ATSE.

Croatia: Ahornstr. 4, 10787 Berlin; tel. (30) 21915514; fax (30) 23628965; e-mail info@kroatische-botschaft.de; Ambassador VESNA CVJETKOVIĆ KURELEC.

Cuba: Stavanger Str. 20, 10439 Berlin; tel. (30) 91611810; fax (30) 9164553; e-mail embacuba-berlin@t-online.de; internet www .botschaft-kuba.de; Ambassador MARCELINO MEDINA GONZÁLEZ.

Cyprus: Wallstr. 27, 10179 Berlin; tel. (30) 3086830; fax (30) 27591454; e-mail cyprusembassy@t-online.de; Ambassador LEONIDAS MARKIDES.

Czech Republic: Wilhelmstr. 44, 10117 Berlin; tel. (30) 226380; fax (30) 2294033; e-mail berlin@embassy.mzv.cz; internet www.mfa.cz/ berlin; Ambassador BORIS LAZAR.

Denmark: Rauchstr. 1, 10785 Berlin; tel. (30) 50502000; fax (30) 50502050; e-mail beramb@um.dk; internet www.daenemark.org; Ambassador GUNNAR ORTMANN.

Dominican Republic: Dessauer Str. 28–29, 10963 Berlin; tel. (30) 25757760; fax (30) 25757761; e-mail embajadomal@t-online.de; Ambassador PEDRO JERGES.

Ecuador: Kaiser-Friedrich-Str. 90, 10585 Berlin; tel. (30) 2386217; fax (30) 34787126; e-mail kanzlei@botschaft-ecuador.org; internet www.botschaft-ecuador.org; Chargé d'affaires a.i. Dr DIEGO MOREJÓN PAZMIÑO.

Egypt: Stauffenbergstr. 6–7, 10785 Berlin; tel. (30) 47901880; fax (30) 4774000; internet www.egyptian-embassy.de; Ambassador MOHAMED ABDELHAY M. ELORABI.

El Salvador: Joachim-Karnatz-Allee 47, 10557 Berlin; tel. (30) 2064660; fax (30) 22488244; e-mail info@botschaft-elsalvador.de; internet www.botschaft-elsalvador.de; Ambassador EDGARDO SUÁREZ MALLAGRAY.

Eritrea: Stavanger Str. 18, 10439 Berlin; tel. (30) 4467460; fax (30) 44674621; e-mail er.embassy@freenet.de; Ambassador ZEMEDE TEKLE WOLDETATIOS.

Estonia: Hildebrandstr. 5, 10785 Berlin; tel. (30) 25460600; fax (30) 25460601; e-mail embassy.berlin@mfa.ee; internet www.estemb.de; Ambassador Dr RIINA KIONKA.

Ethiopia: Boothstr. 20A, 12207 Berlin; tel. (30) 772060; fax (30) 7720626; e-mail emb.ethiopia@t-online.de; internet www .aethiopien-botschaft.de; Ambassador HIRUY AMANUEL.

Finland: Rauchstr. 1, 10787 Berlin; tel. (30) 505030; fax (30) 5050333; e-mail ber.sanomat@formin.fi; internet www.finland.de; Ambassador LEIF RICHARD FAGERNÄS.

France: Pariser Pl. 5, 10117 Berlin; tel. (30) 590035000; fax (30) 590039110; e-mail info@botschaft-frankreich.de; Ambassador CLAUDE PIERRE MARCEL MARTIN.

Gabon: Hohensteinerstr. 16, 14197 Berlin; tel. (30) 89733440; fax (30) 89733444; e-mail botschaft@web-gabun.de; internet www .africaweb.de/gabun; Ambassador PAUL BUNDUKU LATHA.

Georgia: Heinrich-Mann-Str. 32, 13156 Berlin; tel. (30) 4849070; fax (30) 48490720; e-mail info@botschaftgeorgien.de; Ambassador Dr MAJA PANSHIKIDSE.

Ghana: Stavangerstr. 17–19, 10439 Berlin; tel. (30) 5471490; fax (30) 44674063; e-mail chancery@ghanaemberlin.de; internet www .ghanaemberlin.de; Ambassador ROWLAND ISSIFU ALHASSAN.

Greece: Jägerstr. 54/55, 10117 Berlin; tel. (30) 206260; fax (30) 20626444; e-mail greekembassyberlin@t-online.de; internet www .griechenland-botschaft.de; Ambassador DIMITRIOS KYPREOS.

Guatemala: Joachim-Karnatz-Allee 47, 10557 Berlin; tel. (30) 2064363; fax (30) 20643659; e-mail embaguate.alemania@t-online .de; internet www.guatemala.travel.com.gt; Ambassador JULIO ROBERTO PALOMO SILVA.

Guinea: Rochusweg 50, 53129 Bonn; tel. (228) 231098; fax (228) 231097; Ambassador ABRAHAM DOUKOURE.

Haiti: Meinekestr. 5, 10719 Berlin; tel. (30) 88554134; fax (30) 88554135; e-mail haibot@aol.com; Ambassador Dr ALRICH NICOLAS.

Holy See: Postfach 610218, 10923 Berlin; Lilienthalstr. 3A, 10965 Berlin; tel. (30) 616240; fax (30) 61624300; e-mail apostoliche@ nuntiatur.de; internet www.nuntiatur.de; Apostolic Nuncio Most Rev. ERWIN JOSEF ENDER.

Honduras: Cuxhavenerstr. 14, 10555 Berlin; tel. (30) 39743710; fax (30) 39749712; e-mail informacion@embahonduras.de; Ambassador ROBERT FLORES BERMUDEZ.

Hungary: Unter den Linden 76, 10117 Berlin; tel. (30) 203100; fax (30) 2291314; e-mail nktitkarsag@ungarische-botschaft.de; internet www.ungarische-botschaft.de; Ambassador Dr SÁNDOR PEISCH.

Iceland: Rauchstr. 1, 10787 Berlin; tel. (30) 50504000; fax (30) 50504300; e-mail icemb.berlin@utn.stjr.is; internet www .botschaft-island.de; Ambassador ÓLAFUR DAVIDSSON.

India: Tiergartenstr. 17, 10785 Berlin; tel. (30) 257950; fax (30) 25795102; e-mail info@indianembassy.de; internet www .indianembassy.de; Ambassador T. C. A. RANGACHARI.

Indonesia: Lehrter Str. 16–17, 10557 Berlin; tel. (30) 478070; fax (30) 44737142; internet www.kbri-berlin.org; Ambassador RAHARDJO JAMOTO.

Iran: Podbielskiallee 65–67, 14195 Berlin; tel. (30) 843530; fax (30) 54353535; e-mail iran.botschaft@t-online.de; internet www .iranbotschaft.de; Ambassador SEYED SHAMSEDDIN KHAREGHANI.

Iraq: Riemeisterstr. 20, 14169 Berlin; tel. (30) 814880; fax (30) 81488222; e-mail info@iraqiembassy-berlin.de; internet iraqiembassy-berlin.de; Ambassador ALAA A. HUSSAIN AL-HASHIMY.

Ireland: Friedrichstr. 200, 10117 Berlin; tel. (30) 220720; fax (30) 22072299; e-mail info@irish-embassy.de; internet www .botschaft-irland.de; Ambassador SEAN O'HUIGINN.

Israel: Auguste-Victoria-Str. 74–76, 14193 Berlin; tel. (30) 89045500; fax (30) 89045309; e-mail botschaft@israel.de; internet www.israel.de; Ambassador SHIMON STEIN LESHEM.

Italy: Hiroshimatr. 1, 10785 Berlin; tel. (30) 254400; fax (30) 25440166; e-mail botschaftler@botschaft-italien.de; Ambassador SILVIO FAGIOLO.

Jamaica: Schmargendorfer Str. 32, 12159 Berlin; tel. (30) 8599450; fax (30) 85994540; e-mail info@jamador.de; internet www.jamador .de; Ambassador MARCIA YVETTE GILBERT-ROBERTS.

Japan: Hiroshimastr. 6, 10785 Berlin; tel. (30) 210940; fax (30) 21094222; e-mail info@embjapan.de; internet www.embjapan.de; Ambassador YUSHU TAKASHIMA.

Jordan: Heerstr. 201, 13595 Berlin; tel. (30) 3699600; fax (30) 36996011; e-mail jordan@jordanembassy.de; internet www .jordanembassy.de; Ambassador Dr SALEH S. RUSHEIDAT.

Kazakhstan: Nordendstr. 14–17, 13156 Berlin; tel. (30) 470070; fax (30) 47007125; e-mail kasger@ndh.net; Ambassador KAIRAT SARYBAY.

Kenya: Markgrafenstr. 63, 10969 Berlin; tel. (30) 2592660; fax (30) 25926650; e-mail office@embassy-of-kenya.de; Ambassador FROST EDWIN OTIENO JOSIAH.

Korea, Democratic People's Republic: Glinkastr. 5–7, 10117 Berlin; tel. (30) 2293189; fax (30) 2293191; Ambassador HYON BO PAK.

Korea, Republic: Schöneberger Ufer 89/91, 10785 Berlin; tel. (30) 260650; fax (30) 2606551; e-mail koremb-ge@mofat.go.kr; internet www.korea-botschaft.de; Ambassador YOUNGMIN KWON.

Kuwait: Griegstr. 5–7, 14193 Berlin; tel. (30) 8973000; fax (30) 89730010; e-mail info@kuwait-botschaft.de; Ambassador ABDUL-HAMID AL-AWADHI.

Kyrgyzstan: Otto-Suhr-Allee 146, 10585 Berlin; tel. (30) 34781338; fax (30) 34781362; internet www.botschaft-kirgisien.de; Ambassador Dr ASKAR SARYGULOV.

Laos: Bismarckallee 2A, 14193 Berlin; tel. (30) 89060647; fax (30) 89060648; Chargé d'affaires a.i. KHOUANTA PHALIVONG.

Latvia: Reinerzstr. 40–41, 14193 Berlin; tel. (30) 8260020; fax (30) 82600233; e-mail latembger@mfa.gov.lv; internet www .botschaft-lettland.de; Ambassador Dr MĀRTIŅŠ VIRJIS.

Lebanon: Berliner Str. 127, 13187 Berlin; tel. (30) 4749860; fax (30) 47487858; e-mail lubnan@t-online.de; Ambassador HICHAM DIMANCH-KIEH.

Lesotho: Dessauer Str. 28–29, 10963 Berlin; tel. (30) 2575720; fax (30) 25757222; e-mail embleso@yahoo.com; Ambassador SEYMOUR REHAUHELE KIKINE.

Liberia: Mainzstr. 259, 53179 Bonn; tel. (228) 340822; Ambassador RUFUS WEBSTER SIMPSON.

Libya: Schützenstr. (Mosse-Zentrum) 15–17, 10117 Berlin; tel. (30) 2005960; fax (30) 20059699; e-mail libysch-arab.volksbuero@ t-online.de; Sec. of the People's Bureau Dr SAID ABDULAATI MOHAMED.

Liechtenstein: Mohrenstr. 42, 10117 Berlin; tel. (30) 52000630; fax (30) 52000631; e-mail vertretung@ber.rep.llv.li; Ambassador JOSEF THEODOR WOLF.

Lithuania: Charitestr. 9, 10117 Berlin; tel. (30) 8906810; fax (30) 89068115; e-mail info@botschaft-litauen.de; internet www.de.urm .lt; Ambassador EVALDAS IGNATAVIČIUS.

Luxembourg: Klingelhöfer Str. 7, 10785 Berlin; tel. (30) 2639570; fax (30) 26395727; e-mail berlin.amb@mae.etat.lu; Ambassador Dr JULIEN ALEX.

Macedonia, former Yugoslav republic: Koenigsallee 2–4, 14193 Berlin; tel. (30) 8906950; fax (30) 89541194; e-mail amba.berlin@ t-online.de; Ambassador Dr GORAN RAFAJLOVSKI.

Madagascar: Seepromenade 92, 14612 Falkensee; tel. (3322) 23140; fax (3322) 231429; e-mail info@botschaft-madagaskar.de; internet www.botschaft-madagaskar.de; Ambassador Dr DENIS ANDRIAMANDROSO.

Malawi: Westfälische Str. 86, 10709 Berlin; tel. (30) 86313450; fax (30) 86313451; e-mail malawibonn@aol.com; Ambassador GILTON BAZILIO CHIWAULA.

Malaysia: Klingelhöferstr. 6, 10785 Berlin; tel. (30) 8857490; fax (30) 88574950; e-mail mwberlin@compuserve.com; Ambassador KAMAL ISMAUN.

Mali: Kufürstendamm 72, 10709 Berlin; tel. (30) 3199883; fax (30) 31998848; Ambassador AMINATA SIDIBÉ SOUMARÉ.

Malta: Klingelhöfer Str. 7, 10785 Berlin; tel. (30) 2639110; fax (30) 26391123; e-mail maltaembassy.berlin@gov.mt; Ambassador WILLIAM C. SPITERI.

Mauritania: Kommandantenstr. 80, 10117 Berlin; Ambassador MELAININE OULD MOCTAR NECHE.

Mauritius: Kurfürstenstr. 82, 10787 Berlin; tel. (30) 2639360; fax (30) 26558323; e-mail mu.embln.3@t-online.de; internet www .mauritius-embassy.de; Ambassador MOHURRLALL HATON.

Mexico: Klingelhöfer Str. 3, 10785 Berlin; tel. (30) 2693230; fax (30) 269323700; e-mail mail@embamexale.de; internet www.embamex .de; Ambassador JORGE CASTRO-VALLE K.

Moldova: Gotlandstr. 16, 10439 Berlin; tel. (30) 44652970; fax (30) 44652972; e-mail office@botschaft-moldau.de; internet www .botschaft-moldau.de; Ambassador IGOR CORMAN.

Monaco: Klingelhöfer Str. 7, 10785 Berlin; tel. (30) 2639033; fax (30) 2690344; e-mail ambassademonaco@aol.com; Ambassador RAI-NIER IMPERTI.

Mongolia: Dietzgen-Str. 31, 13156 Berlin; tel. (30) 4748060; fax (30) 47480616; e-mail mongolbot@aol.com; Ambassador DENDEV TERBISH-DAGVA.

Morocco: Niederwallstr. 39, 10117 Berlin; tel. (30) 2061240; fax (30) 20612420; e-mail marokko-botschaft@t-online.de; internet www .marokko-botschaft.de; Ambassador MOHAMED RACHAD BOUHLAL.

Mozambique: Stromstr. 47, 10551 Berlin; tel. (30) 39876506; fax (30) 39876503; e-mail emoza@aol.com; Ambassador ANTONIO CORRELA FERNANDES SUMBANA.

Myanmar: Zimmerstr. 56, 10117 Berlin; tel. (30) 2061570; fax (30) 20649757; e-mail emb.my.berlin@t-online.de; Ambassador U NYUNT MAUNG SHEIN.

Namibia: Wichmannstr. 5, 10787 Berlin; tel. (30) 2540950; fax (30) 25409555; e-mail namibiaberlin@aol.com; Ambassador HANNO BURK-HARD RUMPF.

Nepal: Guerickestr. 27, 10587 Berlin; tel. (30) 34359920; fax (30) 34359906; e-mail rneberlin@t-online.de; internet www.nepal-forum .de/botschaft.htm; Ambassador Dr MADAN KUMAR BHATTARAI.

Netherlands: Klosterstr. 50, 10179 Berlin; tel. (30) 209560; fax (30) 20956441; e-mail nlgovbln@bln.nlamb.de; internet www .niederlandeweb.de; Ambassador Dr NIKOLAOS VAN DAM.

New Zealand: Friedrichstr. 60, 10117 Berlin; tel. (30) 206210; fax (30) 20621114; e-mail nzemb@t-online.de; internet www.nzembassy .com; Ambassador PETER WILLIAM HAMILTON.

Nicaragua: Joachim-Karnatz-Allee 45, 10557 Berlin; tel. (30) 2064380; fax (30) 22487891; e-mail embanic-berlin@t-online.de; Ambassador SUYAPA INDIANA PADILLA TERCERO.

Niger: Dürenstr. 9, 53173 Bonn; tel. (228) 3502782; fax (228) 3502768; Ambassador AMADOU TOURÉ.

Nigeria: Neue Jakobstr. 4, 10179 Berlin; tel. (30) 212300; fax (30) 21230212; e-mail nigeriaembassy@yahoo.com; internet www .nigeriaembassygermany.org; Ambassador TUNDE ADENIRAN.

Norway: Rauchstr. 1, 10787 Berlin; tel. (30) 505050; fax (30) 505055; e-mail emb.berlin@mfa.no; internet www.norwegen.org; Ambassador BJØRN TORE GODAL.

Oman: Lindenallee 11, 53173 Bonn; tel. (228) 357031; fax (228) 357045; Ambassador AHMED MOHAMED ZAHIR AL-HINAI.

Pakistan: Schaperstr. 29, 10719 Berlin; tel. (30) 212440; fax (30) 21244210; e-mail pakemb.berlin@t-online.de; Ambassador SAEED KHALID.

Panama: Joachim-Karnatz-Allee 45, 10557 Berlin; tel. (30) 22605811; fax (30) 22605812; Ambassador HÉCTOR ROLANDO CRESPO BARRIA.

Paraguay: Hardenbergstr. 12, 10623 Berlin; tel. (30) 3199860; fax (30) 31998617; e-mail embapyde@t-online.de; Ambassador JOSÉ MILCIADES MARTÍNEZ LEZCANO.

Peru: Mohrenstr. 42, 10117 Berlin; tel. (30) 2064103; fax (30) 20641077; e-mail gabinete@embaperu.de; internet www.botschaft-peru.de; Ambassador CARLOS A. HIGUERAS.

Philippines: Uhlandstr. 97, 10715 Berlin; tel. (30) 8649500; fax (30) 8732551; e-mail berlinpe@t-online.de; internet www.philippine-embassy.com; Ambassador MINERVA JEAN A. FALCON.

Poland: Lassenstr. 19–21, 14193 Berlin; tel. (30) 223130; fax (30) 2213155; e-mail info@botschaft-polen.de; internet www.botschaft-polen.de; Ambassador ANDRZEJ BYRT.

Portugal: Zimmerstr. 56, 10117 Berlin; tel. (30) 590063500; fax (30) 590063600; e-mail mail@botschaftportugal.de; Ambassador Dr JOÃO DE VALLERA.

Qatar: Postfach 48, 53132 Bonn; Brunnenallee 6, 53117 Bonn; tel. (228) 957520; fax (228) 9575255; e-mail qatarbonn@compuserve.com; Ambassador SALEH MOHAMED SALEH AL-NESEF.

Romania: Dorotheenstr. 62–66, 10117 Berlin; tel. (30) 21239202; fax (30) 21239399; e-mail office@rumaenische-botschaft.de; internet www.rumaenische-botschaft.de; Ambassador ADRIAN COSMIN VIERIȚA.

Russia: Unter den Linden 63–65, 10117 Berlin; tel. (30) 2291110; fax (30) 2299397; e-mail posolstvo@russische-botschaft.de; internet www.russische-botschaft.de; Ambassador VLADIMIR V. KOTENEV.

Rwanda: Beethovenallee 72, 53173 Bonn; tel. (228) 3670236; fax (228) 351922; e-mail ambrwabonn@aol.com; internet www.rwanda-botschaft.de; Ambassador LAUREN NGIRABANZI.

Saudi Arabia: Kurfürstendamm 63, 10787 Berlin; Chargé d'affaires a.i. JUDIYA ALHATHAL.

Senegal: Dessauerstr. 28–29, 10963 Berlin; tel. (30) 8562190; Ambassador Gen. BABACAR GAYE.

Serbia and Montenegro: Taubertstr. 18, 14193 Berlin; tel. (30) 8957700; fax (30) 8252206; e-mail info@botschaft-smg.de; Ambassador MILOVAN BOZINOVIĆ.

Sierra Leone: Rheinallee 20, 53173 Bonn; tel. (228) 352001; fax (228) 364269; e-mail slembassybonn@hotmail.com; Ambassador FODAY, Seisay.

Singapore: Friedrichstr. 200, 10117 Berlin; tel. (30) 2263430; fax (30) 22634355; e-mail info@singapore-embassy.de; internet www.mfa.gov.sg/berlin-german; Ambassador A. SELVERAJAH.

Slovakia: Pariser Str. 44, 10707 Berlin; tel. (30) 8892620; fax (30) 88926222; e-mail presse@botschaft-slowakei.de; internet www.berlin.mfa.sk; Ambassador IVAN KORČOK.

Slovenia: Hausvogteipl. 3–4, 10117 Berlin; tel. (30) 2061450; fax (30) 20614570; e-mail vbn@mzz-dkp.gov.si; Ambassador DRAGOLJUBA BENCINA.

South Africa: Tiergartenstr. 18, 10785 Berlin; tel. (30) 220730; fax (30) 22073190; e-mail botschaft@suedafrika.de; internet www.suedafrika.de; Ambassador MOSES M. CHIKANE.

Spain: Liechtensteinallee 1, 10787 Berlin; tel. (30) 2540070; fax (30) 25799557; e-mail embespde@mail.mae.es; internet www.spanischebotschaft.de; Ambassador GABRIEL BUSQUETS APARICIO.

Sri Lanka: Niklasstr. 19, 14163 Berlin; tel. (30) 80909761; fax (30) 80909757; e-mail info@srilanka-botschaft.de; internet www.srilanka-botschaft.de; Ambassador C. D. CASIECHETTY.

Sudan: Kurfürstendamm 151, 10709 Berlin; tel. (30) 8906980; fax (30) 89409693; e-mail post@sudan-embassy.de; internet www.sudan-embassy.de; Ambassador AHMED GAAFAR ABDELKARIM.

Sweden: Rauchstr. 1, 10787 Berlin; tel. (30) 505060; fax (30) 50506789; e-mail ambassaden.berlin@foreign.ministry.se; internet www.schweden.org; Ambassador CARL GUSTAV WILHELM THAM.

Switzerland: Otto-von-Bismarck-Allee 4A, 10557 Berlin; tel. (30) 3904000; fax (30) 3911030; e-mail info@botschaft-schweiz.de; internet www.botschaft-schweiz.de; Ambassador Dr WERNER BAUMANN.

Syria: Rauchstr. 25, 10787 Berlin; tel. (30) 501770; fax (30) 50177311; Ambassador HUSSEIN OMRAN.

Tajikistan: Otto-Suhr-Allee 84, 10585 Berlin; tel. (30) 3479300; fax (30) 34793029; Ambassador NURALI SAIDOV.

Tanzania: Theaterpl. 26, 53177 Bonn; tel. (228) 358051; fax (228) 358226; e-mail tzbonn.habari@t-online.de; internet www.tanzania-gov.de; Ambassador ALI ABEID AMANI KARUME.

Thailand: Lepsiusstr. 64–66, 12163 Berlin; tel. (30) 794810; fax (30) 79481511; Ambassador CHOLCHINEEPAN CHIRANOND.

Togo: Grabbeallee 43, 13156 Berlin; tel. (30) 48476471; fax (30) 49908968; e-mail info@togo.de; internet www.botschaft-togo.de; Ambassador ESSOHANAM COMLA PAKA.

Tunisia: Lindenallee 16, 14050 Berlin; tel. (30) 30820673; fax (30) 30820683; Ambassador FETHI MERDASSI.

Turkey: Rungestr. 9, 10179 Berlin; tel. (30) 275850; fax (30) 27590915; e-mail turk.em.berlin@t-online.de; internet www.turkischebotschaft.de; Ambassador MEHMET ALI IRTEMÇELIK.

Turkmenistan: Langobardenallee 14, 14052 Berlin; tel. (30) 30102452; fax (30) 30102453; e-mail botschaft-turkmenistan@t-online.de; Chargé d'affaires a.i. MURATDURDY HASHAYEV.

Ukraine: Albrechtstr. 26, 10117 Berlin; tel. (30) 288870; fax (30) 28887163; e-mail ukremb@t-online.de; internet www.botschaft-ukraine.de; Ambassador SERHIY FARENYK.

United Arab Emirates: Katharine-Heinrith-Ufer 1, 10787 Berlin; tel. (228) 267070; fax (228) 2670714; Ambassador ALI MOHAMMAD AL-ZAROUNI.

United Kingdom: Wilhelmstr. 70, 10117 Berlin; tel. (30) 204570; fax (30) 20457594; e-mail info@britischebotschaft.de; internet www.britischebotschaft.de; Ambassador Sir PETER JAMES TORRY.

USA: Neustädtische Kirche 4/5, 10117 Berlin; tel. (30) 83052805; fax (30) 20453644; internet www.usembassy.de; Ambassador DANIEL R. COATS.

Uruguay: Budapester Str. 39, 10787 Berlin; tel. (30) 2639016; fax (30) 26390170; e-mail urubrande@t-online.de; Ambassador Dr ZULMA DELIA GUELMAN GUIGOU.

Uzbekistan: Perleberger Str. 62, 10559 Berlin; tel. (30) 3940980; fax (30) 39409862; e-mail botschaft@uzbekistan.de; internet www.uzbekistan.de; Ambassador ISON MUSTAFOEV.

Venezuela: Wichmannstr. 9–10, 10785 Berlin; tel. (30) 8322400; fax (30) 83224020; e-mail info@botschaft-venezuela.de; Ambassador BLANCA NIEVES PORTOCARRERO.

Viet Nam: Elsenstr. 3, 12435 Berlin; tel. (30) 53630108; fax (30) 53630200; e-mail sqvnberlin@t-online.de; internet www.vietnambotschaft.org; Ambassador Dr NGUYEN BA SON.

Yemen: Budapester Str. 37, 10787 Berlin; tel. (30) 8973050; fax (30) 89730562; e-mail info@botschaft-jemen.de; internet www.botschaft-jemen.de; Ambassador YAHYA AL-ABIADH.

Zambia: Axel-Springer Str. 54A; tel. (30) 2062940; fax (30) 20629419; e-mail botschaftvonsambia@t-online.de; Ambassador Gen. (retd) GODWIN KINGSLEY CHINKULI.

Zimbabwe: Kommandantenstr. 80, 10117 Berlin; tel. (30) 2062263; fax (30) 20455062; e-mail zimberlin@t-online.de; Ambassador LUCIA MUVINGI.

Judicial System

Justice is administered in accordance with the federal structure through the courts of the Federation and the Länder, as well as the Federal Constitutional Court and the Constitutional Courts of the Länder. Judges are independent and responsible to the law. They are not removable except by the decision of a court. One-half of the judges of the Federal Constitutional Court are elected by the Bundestag and the other half by the Bundesrat. A committee for the selection of judges participates in the appointment of judges of the Superior Federal Courts.

FEDERAL CONSTITUTIONAL COURT

Bundesverfassungsgericht
(Federal Constitutional Court)

Postfach 1771, 76006 Karlsruhe; Schlossbezirk 3, 76131 Karlsruhe; tel. (721) 91010; fax (721) 9101382; e-mail bverfg@bundesverfassungsgericht.de; internet www.bundesverfassungsgericht.de.

President: Prof. Dr HANS-JÜRGEN PAPIER.

Vice-President: Prof. Dr WINFRIED HASSEMER.

Director: Dr ELKE LUISE BARNSTEDT.

Judges of the First Senate: R<small>ENATE</small> J<small>AEGER</small>, Prof. Dr E<small>VELYN</small> H<small>AAS</small>, Dr D<small>IETER</small> H<small>ÖMIG</small>, Prof. Dr U<small>DO</small> S<small>TEINER</small>, Dr C<small>HRISTINE</small> H<small>OHMANN</small>-D<small>ENNHARDT</small>, Dr H<small>OFFMANN</small>-R<small>IEM</small>, Prof. Dr B<small>RUN</small>-O<small>TTO</small> B<small>RYDE</small>.

Judges of the Second Senate: Dr H<small>ANS</small>-J<small>OACHIM</small> J<small>ENTSCH</small>, Prof. Dr S<small>IEGFRIED</small> B<small>ROSS</small>, Prof. Dr L<small>ERKE</small> O<small>STERLOH</small>, Prof. Dr U<small>DO</small> D<small>IE</small> F<small>ABIO</small>, R<small>UDOLF</small> M<small>ELLINGHOFF</small>, Prof. Dr G<small>ERTRUDE</small> L<small>ÜBBE</small>-W<small>OLFF</small>, Dr M<small>ICHAEL</small> G<small>ERHARDT</small>.

SUPERIOR FEDERAL COURTS

Bundesarbeitsgericht
(Federal Labour Court)

Hugo-Preuss-Pl. 1, 99084 Erfurt; tel. (361) 26360; fax (361) 26362000; internet www.bundesarbeitsgericht.de.

President: Prof. Dr H<small>ELLMUT</small> W<small>ISSMANN</small>.

Vice-President: H<small>ANS</small>-J<small>ÜRGEN</small> D<small>ÖRMER</small>.

Bundesgerichtshof
(Federal Court of Justice)

Herrenstr. 45A, 76133 Karlsruhe; tel. (721) 1590; fax (721) 1591609; e-mail eingangsstelle@bgh.bund.de; internet www.bundesgerichtshof.de.

President: Prof. Dr H<small>IRSCH</small>.

Vice-President: Dr J<small>OACHIM</small> W<small>ENZEL</small>.

Presidents of the Senate: Prof. Dr E<small>IKE</small> U<small>LLMANN</small>, V<small>OLKER</small> R<small>ÖHRICHT</small>, W<small>OLFGANG</small> S<small>CHLICK</small>, W<small>ILFRIED</small> T<small>ERNO</small>, Dr G<small>ERDA</small> M<small>ÜLLER</small>, Dr W<small>OLF</small>-D<small>IETER</small> D<small>RESSLER</small>, Dr K<small>ATHARINA</small> D<small>EPPERT</small>, Dr G<small>ERHART</small> K<small>REFT</small>, G<small>ERD</small> N<small>OBBE</small>, Dr M<small>EO</small>-M<small>ICAELA</small> H<small>AHNE</small>, A<small>RMIN</small> N<small>ACK</small>, Prof. Dr K<small>LAUS</small> T<small>OLKSDORF</small>, Dr I<small>NGEBORG</small> T<small>EPPERWIEN</small>, M<small>ONIKA</small> H<small>ARMS</small>, Dr R<small>UTH</small> R<small>ISSING</small>-<small>VAN</small> S<small>AAN</small>.

Federal Solicitor-General: K<small>AY</small> N<small>EHM</small>.

Federal Prosecutors: Dr K<small>ARL</small> H<small>EINZ</small> S<small>CHNARR</small>, V<small>OLKHARD</small> W<small>ACHE</small>, Dr H<small>ANS</small>-J<small>OACHIM</small> K<small>URTH</small>.

Bundessozialgericht
(Federal Social Court)

Graf-Bernadotte-Pl. 5, 34119 Kassel; tel. (561) 31071; fax (561) 3107475; e-mail bundessozialgericht@bsg.bund.de; internet www.bundessozialgericht.de.

President: M<small>ATTHIAS</small> <small>VON</small> W<small>ULFFEN</small>.

Vice-President: Dr R<small>UTH</small> W<small>ETZEL</small>-S<small>TEINWEDEL</small>.

Bundesverwaltungsgericht
(Federal Administrative Court)

Postfach 100854, 04008 Leipzig; Simsonpl. 1, 04107 Leipzig; tel. (341) 20070; fax (341) 20071000; e-mail pressestelle@bverwg.bund.de; internet www.bverwg.de.

President: E<small>CKART</small> H<small>IEN</small>.

Vice-President: M<small>ARION</small> E<small>CKERTZ</small>-H<small>ÖFER</small>.

Presidents of the Senate: Dr H<small>ORST</small> S<small>ÄCKER</small>, Prof. Dr H<small>ANS</small>-J<small>OACHIM</small> D<small>RIEHAUS</small>, Dr S<small>TEFAN</small> P<small>AETOW</small>, H<small>ARTMAT</small> A<small>LBERS</small>, Dr F<small>RANZ</small> B<small>ARDENHEWER</small>, Prof. Dr R<small>AINER</small> P<small>IETZNER</small>, W<small>OLFGANG</small> S<small>AILER</small>, C<small>HRISTOPH</small> G<small>ÖDEL</small>, Dr U<small>LRICH</small> S<small>TOROST</small>.

Bundesfinanzhof
(Federal Financial Court)

Postfach 860240, 81629 München; Ismaninger Str. 109, 81675 München; tel. (89) 92310; fax (89) 9231201; e-mail bundesfinanzhof@bfh.bund.de; internet www.bundesfinanzhof.de.

President: Dr I<small>RIS</small> E<small>BLING</small>.

Vice-President: W<small>OLFGANG</small> S<small>PINDLER</small>.

Presidents of the Senate: Prof. Dr F<small>RANZ</small> W<small>ASSERMEYER</small>, Dr G<small>ERHARD</small> M<small>ÖSSLANG</small>, H<small>EIDE</small> B<small>OEKER</small>, C<small>HRISTIAN</small> H<small>ERDEN</small>, Dr W<small>ILFRIED</small> W<small>AGNER</small>, Prof. Dr W<small>ALTER</small> D<small>RENSECK</small>, Dr W<small>ERNER</small> H<small>EIN</small>, Dr H<small>ANS</small> J<small>OACHIM</small> H<small>ERRMANN</small>, Dr G<small>EORG</small> G<small>RUBE</small>.

Religion

CHRISTIANITY

Arbeitsgemeinschaft Christlicher Kirchen in Deutschland (Council of Christian Churches in Germany): Postfach 900617, 60446 Frankfurt a.M.; Ludolfusstr. 2–4, 60487 Frankfurt a.M.; tel. (69) 2470270; fax (69) 24702730; e-mail info@ack-oec.de; internet www.oekumene-ack.de; 23 affiliated Churches, including the Roman Catholic Church and the Orthodox Church in Germany.

The Roman Catholic Church

Germany comprises seven archdioceses and 20 dioceses. At 31 December 2003 there were an estimated 26,228,737 adherents (about 32% of the population).

Bishops' Conference

Deutsche Bischofskonferenz, Postfach 2962, 53019 Bonn; Bonner Talweg 177, 53129 Bonn; tel. (228) 103290; fax (228) 103299; e-mail sekretariat@dbk.de.

Pres. Cardinal Dr K<small>ARL</small> L<small>EHMANN</small> (Bishop of Mainz); Sec. Pater Dr H<small>ANS</small> L<small>ANGENDÖRFER</small>.

Archbishop of Bamberg: Prof. Dr L<small>UDWIG</small> S<small>CHICK</small>, Dompl. 3, 96054 Bamberg; tel. (951) 5020; fax (951) 502250.

Archbishop of Berlin: Cardinal G<small>EORG</small> S<small>TERZINSKY</small>, Postfach 040856, 10064 Berlin; tel. (30) 326840; fax (30) 32684276.

Archbishop of Freiburg im Breisgau: Dr R<small>OBERT</small> Z<small>OLLITSCH</small>, Herrenstr. 35, 79098 Freiburg i. Br.; tel. (761) 21881; fax (761) 2188599; e-mail erzbischof@ordinariat-freiburg.de; internet www.erzbistum-freiburg.de.

Archbishop of Hamburg: Dr W<small>ERNER</small> T<small>HISSEN</small>, Postfach 101925, 20013 Hamburg; Danzigerstr. 52A, 20099 Hamburg; tel. (40) 248770; fax (40) 24877233; e-mail egv@erzbistum-hamburg.de; internet www.erzbistum-hamburg.de.

Archbishop of Köln: Cardinal Dr J<small>OACHIM</small> M<small>EISNER</small>, Generalvikariat, Marzellenstr. 32, 50668 Köln; tel. (221) 16420; fax (221) 16421700.

Archbishop of München and Freising: Cardinal Dr F<small>RIEDRICH</small> W<small>ETTER</small>, Postfach 330360, 80063 München; Rochsusstr. 5–7, 80303 München; tel. (89) 21370; fax (89) 21371478.

Archbishop of Paderborn: H<small>ANS</small>-J<small>OSEF</small> B<small>ECKER</small>, Erzbischöfliches Generalvikariat, Dompl. 3, 33098 Paderborn; tel. (5251) 1250; fax (5251) 125470.

Commissariat of German Bishops—Catholic Office: Postfach 040660, 10063 Berlin; Hannoversche Str. 5, 10115 Berlin; tel. (30) 288780; fax (30) 28878108; e-mail post@kath-buero.de; represents the German Conference of Bishops before the Federal Govt and international institutions on political issues; Leader Prälat Dr K<small>ARL</small> J<small>ÜSTEN</small>.

Central Committee of German Catholics: Hochkreuzallee 246, 53175 Bonn; tel. (228) 382970; fax (228) 3829744; e-mail info@zdk.de; internet www.zdk.de; f. 1868; summarizes the activities of Catholic laymen and lay-organizations in Germany; Pres. Prof. Dr H<small>ANS</small> J<small>OACHIM</small> M<small>EYER</small>; Gen. Sec. Dr S<small>TEFAN</small> V<small>ESPER</small>.

Evangelical (Protestant) Churches

About 33% of the population are members of the Evangelical Churches.

Evangelische Kirche in Deutschland (EKD) (Evangelical Church in Germany): Herrenhäuser Str. 12, 30419 Hannover; tel. (511) 27960; fax (511) 2796707; e-mail presse@ekd.de; internet www.ekd.de; the governing bodies of the EKD are its Synod of 120 clergy and lay members, which meets at regular intervals, the Conference of member churches, and the Council, composed of 15 elected members; the EKD has an ecclesiastical secretariat of its own (the Evangelical Church Office), including a special office for foreign relations; Chair. of the Council Right Rev. Prof. Dr W<small>OLFGANG</small> H<small>UBER</small>; Pres. of the Office V<small>ALENTIN</small> S<small>CHMIDT</small>.

Synod of the EKD: Herrenhäuser Str. 12, 30419 Hannover; tel. (511) 2796114; fax (511) 2796707; e-mail synode@ekd.de; Pres. B<small>ARBARA</small> R<small>INKE</small>.

Deutscher Evangelischer Kirchentag (German Evangelical Church Convention): Postfach 1555, 36005 Fulda; Magdeburger Str. 59, 36037 Fulda; tel. (661) 969500; fax (661) 9695090; e-mail fulda@kirchentag.de; internet www.kirchentag.de; Pres. Prof. Dr E<small>CKHARD</small> N<small>AGEL</small>; Gen. Sec. F<small>RIEDERIKE</small> <small>VON</small> K<small>IRCHBACH</small>.

Churches and Federations within the EKD:

Union Evangelischer Kirchen in der EKD (UEK): Jebensstr. 3, 10623 Berlin; tel. (30) 310010; fax (30) 31001200; e-mail postfach@kirchenkanzlei.de; internet www.uek-online.de; f. 2003 by merger of Arnoldshainer Konferenz and Evangelische Kirche der Union; union of 14 regional churches (11 United, two Reformed and one Lutheran) with approx. 13.4m. mems; promotes unity among churches in the EKD; Chair. Vollkonferenz and Presidium Bishop Dr U<small>LRICH</small> F<small>ISCHER</small> (Evangelical Church of Baden); Vice-Chairs C<small>HRISTIAN</small> D<small>RÄGERT</small> (Evangelical Church in the Rhineland), Dr H<small>ANS</small>-W<small>ILHELM</small> P<small>IETZ</small> (Evangelical Church in the Silesian Oberlausitz); Pres. of Administration Dr W<small>ILHELM</small> H<small>ÜFFMEIER</small>.

Bremen Evangelical Church: Postfach 106929, Franziuseck 2–4, 28199 Bremen; tel. (421) 55970; Pres. B<small>RIGITTE</small> B<small>OEHME</small>.

Church of Lippe: Leopoldstr. 27, 32756 Detmold; tel. (5231) 97660; fax (5231) 976850; e-mail oeff@lippische-landeskirche.de; internet www.lippische-landeskirche.de; Landessuperintendent GERRIT NOLTENSMEIER.

Evangelical Church in Baden: Postfach 2269, 76010 Karlsruhe; Blumenstr. 1, 76133 Karlsruhe; tel. (721) 91750; fax (721) 9175550; e-mail info@ekiba.de; internet www.ekiba.de; Landesbischof Dr ULRICH FISCHER.

Evangelical Church in Berlin-Brandenburg schlesiche Oberlausitz: Georgenkirchstr. 69/70, 10249 Berlin; tel. (30) 2434400; fax (30) 24344500; e-mail info@ekbo.de; internet www.ekbo.de; Bischof Prof. Dr WOLFGANG HUBER.

Evangelical Church in Hessen and Nassau: Pauluspl. 1, 64285 Darmstadt; tel. (6151) 405290; fax (6151) 405444; Pres. Prof. Dr PETER STEINACKER.

Evangelical Church in the Rhineland: Postfach 300339, 40403 Düsseldorf; Hans-Böckler-Str. 7, 40476 Düsseldorf; tel. (211) 45620; fax (211) 4562490; e-mail pressestelle@ekir.de; internet www.ekir.de; Pres. NIKOLAUS SCHNEIDER.

Evangelical Church of Kurhessen-Waldeck: Postfach 410260, 34117 Kassel-Wilhelmshöhe; Wilhelmshöher Allee 330, 34131 Kassel; tel. (561) 93780; fax (561) 9378400; e-mail landeskirchenamt@ekkw.de; internet www.ekkw.de; Bischof Dr MARTIN HEIN.

Evangelical Church of the Palatinate: Dompl. 5, 67346 Speyer; tel. (6232) 6670; fax (6232) 667228; e-mail kirchenpraesident@evkirchepfalz.de; internet www.evpfalz.de; Pres. EBERHARD CHERDRON.

Evangelical Church of Westfalen: Altstädter Kirchpl. 5, 33602 Bielefeld; tel. (521) 5940; fax (521) 594129; e-mail landeskirchenamt@lka.ekvw.de; internet www.ekvw.de; Präses ALFRED BUSS.

Evangelical-Lutheran Church in Württemberg: Postfach 101342, 70012 Stuttgart; tel. (711) 21490; fax (711) 2149236; e-mail okr@elk.wue.de; internet www.elk-wue.de; Landesbischof Dr GERHARD MAIER.

Reformierter Bund (Reformed Alliance): Vogelsangstr. 20, 42109 Wuppertal; tel. (202) 755111; fax (202) 754202; e-mail info@reformierter-bund.de; f. 1884; unites the Reformed Territorial Churches and Congregations of Germany (with an estimated 2m. mems). The central body of the Reformed League is the 'Moderamen', the elected representation of the various Reformed Churches and Congregations; Moderator Rev. PETER BUKOWSKI; Gen. Sec. Rev. HERMANN SCHAEFER.

Vereinigte Evangelisch-Lutherische Kirche Deutschlands (VELKD) (The United Evangelical-Lutheran Church of Germany): Postfach 510409, 30634 Hannover; Richard-Wagner-Str. 26, 30177 Hannover; tel. (511) 62611; fax (511) 6261511; e-mail zentrale@velkd.de; internet www.velkd.de; f. 1948; 10.4m. mems; unites all but three of the Lutheran territorial Churches within the Evangelical Church in Germany; Presiding Bishop Bischof Dr HANS CHRISTIAN KNUTH (Schleswig).

Evangelical-Lutheran Church in Bayern: Meiserstr. 11–13, 80333 München; tel. (89) 55950; fax (89) 5595444; e-mail poep@elkb.de; internet www.bayern-evangelisch.de; Landesbischof Dr JOHANNES FRIEDRICH.

Evangelical-Lutheran Church of Hannover: Haarstr. 6, 30169 Hannover; tel. (511) 5635830; fax (511) 56358311; e-mail landesbischoefin@evlka.de; internet www.evlka.de; Landesbischöfin Dr MARGOT KÄSSMANN.

Evangelical-Lutheran Church of North Elbe: Bischof Dr HANS CHRISTIAN KNUTH (Plessenstr. 5a, 24837 Schleswig; tel. (4621) 22056; fax (4621) 22194); Bischof BÖRBEL VON WARLENBERG-POFLER (Bädenstr. 3–5, 23564 Lübeck; tel. (451) 790201); Bishop MARIA JEPSEN (20457 Hamburg, Neue Burg 1; tel. (40) 373050); Pres. of North Elbian Church Administration Bischöfin BÄRBEL WARTENBERG-POTTER.

Evangelical-Lutheran Church of Schaumburg-Lippe: Herderstr. 27, 31675 Bückeburg; tel. (5722) 9600; e-mail lka-bueckeburg@t-online.de; Landesbischof JÜRGEN JOHANNESDOTTER.

Also affiliated to the EKD:

Bund Evangelisch-Reformierter Kirchen (Association of Evangelical Reformed Churches): Wieblingenweg 6, 38112 Braunschweig; tel. (531) 312640; e-mail dresler-krommingen@reformierte.de; Chair. Präses SABINE DRESSLER-KROMMINGA.

Evangelical-Lutheran Church in Braunschweig: Dietrich-Bonhoeffer-Str. 1, 38300 Wolfenbüttel; tel. (5331) 8020; fax (5331) 802707; e-mail info@luth-braunschweig.de; internet www.landeskirche-braunschweig.de; Landesbischof Dr FRIEDRICH WEBER.

Evangelical-Lutheran Church in Oldenburg: Philosophenweg 1, 26121 Oldenburg; tel. (441) 77010; fax (441) 7701299; e-mail presse@ev-kirche-ol.de; internet www.ev-kirche-oldenburg.de; Bischof PETER KRUG.

Evangelical-Lutheran Church in Thuringia: Dr-Moritz-Mitzenheim Str. 2A, 99817 Eisenach; tel. (3691) 67899; fax (3691) 678355; e-mail landeslandeskirchenamt@elkth.de; internet www.elkth-online.de; Landesbischof Prof. Dr CRISTOPH KÄHLER.

Evangelical-Lutheran Church of Mecklenburg: Münzstr. 8, Postfach 111063, 19010 Schwerin; tel. (385) 51850; fax (385) 5185170; e-mail okr@ellm.de; internet www.kirche-mv.de; Landesbischof HERMANN BESTE.

Evangelical-Lutheran Church of Saxony: Postfach 120552, 01006 Dresden; Lukasstr. 6, 01069 Dresden; tel. (351) 46920; fax (351) 4692109; e-mail kirche@evlks.de; internet www.evlks.de; Landesbischof JOCHEN BOHL.

Evangelical-Reformed Church: Saarstr. 6, 26789 Leer; tel. (491) 91980; fax (491) 9198251; e-mail info@reformiert.de; internet www.reformiert.de; Moderator Rev. JANN SCHMIDT; Synod Clerk Dr JOHANN WEUSMANN.

Herrnhuter Brüdergemeine or Europäisch-Festländische Brüder-Unität (European Continental Province of the Moravian Church): Badwasen 6, 73087 Bad Boll; tel. (7164) 94210; fax (7164) 942199; f. 1457; there are 25 congregations in Germany, Switzerland, Denmark, Sweden, Estonia and the Netherlands, with approx. 30,000 mems; Chair. ANNEGRET SCHOLZ.

Other Evangelical (Protestant) Churches

Arbeitsgemeinschaft Mennonitischer Gemeinden in Deutschland (Asscn of Mennonite Congregations in Germany): Ringstr. 3, 67677 Enkenbach-Alsenborn; tel. (6303) 3883; fax (6303) 983739; e-mail amg-funck@mennoniten.de; internet www.mennoniten.de; f. 1886; re-organized 1990; Chair. WERNER FUNCK.

Bund Evangelisch-Freikirchlicher Gemeinden in Deutschland K.d.ö.R. (Union of Evangelical Free Churches (Baptists) in Germany): Johann-Gerhard-Oncken-Str. 7, 14641 Wustermark; tel. (33) 234740; fax (33) 23474199; e-mail befg@baptisten.org; internet www.baptisten.org; f. 1849; Pres. SIEGFRIED GROSSMANN; Vice-Pres. Dr RAIMUND UTSCH; Gen. Sec. REGINA CLAAS.

Bund Freier evangelischer Gemeinden (Covenant of Free Evangelical Churches in Germany): Postfach 4005, 58426 Witten; Goltenkamp 4, 58452 Witten; tel. (2302) 9370; fax (2302) 93799; e-mail bund@feg.de; internet www.feg.de; f. 1854; Pres. PETER STRAUCH; Administrator KLAUS KANWISCHER; 35,000 mems.

Evangelisch-altreformierte Kirche von Niedersachsen (Evangelical Reformed Church of Lower Saxony): Boenster Str. 20, 26831 Bunde; tel. (4953) 922599; e-mail gerdschrader@compuserve.de; Sec. Rev. GERHARD SCHRADER.

Evangelisch-methodistische Kirche (United Methodist Church): Wilhelm-Leuschner-Str. 8, 60329 Frankfurt a.M.; tel. (69) 2425210; fax (69) 24252129; e-mail kirchenkanzlei@emk.de; f. 1968; Bishop Dr WALTER KLAIBER.

Gemeinschaft der Siebenten-Tags-Adventisten (Seventh-Day Adventist Church): Postfach 4260, 73745 Ostfildern; Senefelderstr. 15, 73760 Ostfildern; tel. (711) 448190; fax (711) 4481960; e-mail sdv.zentrale@adventisten.de.

Heilsarmee in Deutschland (Salvation Army in Germany): Salierring 23–27, 50677 Köln; tel. (221) 208190; fax (221) 2081951; e-mail nhq@ger.salvationarmy.org; internet www.heilsarmee.de; f. 1886; Leader Commdr WERNER FREI.

Mülheimer Verband Freikirchlich-Evangelischer Gemeinden (Pentecostal Church): Habenhauser Dorfstr. 27, 28279 Bremen; tel. (421) 8399130; fax (421) 8399136; e-mail mv-bremen@t-online.de; f. 1913.

Selbständige Evangelisch-Lutherische Kirche (Independent Evangelical-Lutheran Church): Schopenhauerstr. 7, 30625 Hannover; tel. (511) 557808; fax (511) 551588; e-mail selk@selk.de; internet www.selk.de; f. 1972; Bishop Dr DIETHARDT ROTH; Exec. Sec. Rev. MICHAEL SCHÄTZEL.

Other Christian Churches

Alt-Katholische Kirche (Old Catholic Church): Gregor-Mendel-Str. 28, 53115 Bonn; tel. (228) 232285; fax (228) 238314; e-mail info@alt-katholisch.de; internet www.alt-katholisch.de; seceded from the Roman Catholic Church as a protest against the declaration of Papal infallibility in 1870; belongs to the Utrecht Union of Old Catholic Churches; in full communion with the Anglican Communion; Pres. Bischof JOACHIM VOBBE (Bonn); 28,000 mems.

Apostelamt Jesu Christi: Madlower Hauptstr. 38, 03050 Cottbus; tel. (355) 541227; Pres. WALDEMAR ROHDE.

Armenisch-Apostolische Orthodoxe Kirche in Deutschland: Allensteiner Str. 5, 50735 Köln; tel. (221) 7126223; fax (221) 7126267; e-mail armenische_diozese@hotmail.com; Archbishop KAREKIN BEKDJIAN.

Griechisch-Orthodoxe Metropolie von Deutschland (Greek Orthodox Metropoly of Germany): Postfach 300555, 53185 Bonn; Dietrich-Bonhoeffer-Str. 2, 53227 Bonn; tel. (228) 462041; fax (228) 464989; e-mail webmaster@orthodoxie.net; internet www .orthodoxie.net; Geistliches Oberhaupt Metropolit AUGOUSTINOS LABARDAKIS von Deutschland und Exarch von Zentraleuropa.

Religiöse Gesellschaft der Freunde (Quäker) (Society of Friends): Planckstr. 20, 10117 Berlin; tel. (30) 2082284; fax (30) 20458142; f. 1925; 290 mems.

Russische Orthodoxe Kirche—Berliner Diözese (Russian Orthodox Church): Postfach 17, 10267 Berlin; Wildensteiner Str. 10, 10318 Berlin; tel. (30) 50379488; fax (30) 5098153; e-mail red .stimme@snafu.de; Archbishop FEOFAN.

ISLAM

According to government figures, there were an estimated 3.2m. Muslims in Germany in late 2000.

Zentralrat der Muslime in Deutschland eV (Central Council of Muslims in Germany): Postfach 1224, 52232 Eschweiler; Indestr. 93, 52249 Eschweiler; tel. (2403) 702075; fax (2403) 702076; e-mail sekretariat@zentralrat.de; internet www.zentralrat.de; f. 1994; 19 mem. asscns; Chair. Dr NADEEM ELYAS.

JUDAISM

The membership of Jewish synagogues in Germany numbered some 74,289 in 1998.

Zentralrat der Juden in Deutschland (Central Council of Jews in Germany): Tucholskystr. 9, Leo-Baeck-Haus, 10117 Berlin; tel. (30) 2844560; fax (30) 28445613; e-mail info@zentralratdjuden.de; internet www.zentralratdjuden.de; Pres. Bd of Dirs PAUL SPIEGEL; Exec. Dir and Sec.-Gen. STEPHAN J. KRAMER.

Jüdische Gemeinde zu Berlin (Jewish Community in Berlin): Fasanenstr. 79–80, 10623 Berlin; e-mail vorstand@jg-berlin.org; Pres. Dr ALEXANDER BRENNER.

The Press

The German Press Council was founded in 1956 as a self-regulatory body, and is composed of publishers and journalists. It formulates guide-lines and investigates complaints against the press.

In 1968 a government commission stipulated various limits on the proportions of circulation that any one publishing group should be allowed to control: (1) 40% of the total circulation of newspapers or 40% of the total circulation of magazines; (2) 20% of the total circulation of newspapers and magazines together; (3) 15% of the circulation in one field if the proportion owned in the other field is 40%.

Deutscher Presserat (German Press Council): Postfach 7160, 53071 Bonn; tel. (228) 985720; fax (228) 9857299; e-mail info@ presserat.de; internet www.presserat.de; Dir LUTZ TILLMANNS.

The principal newspaper publishing groups are:

Axel Springer Verlag AG: Axel-Springer-Str. 65, 10888 Berlin; and Axel-Springer-Pl. 1, 20355 Hamburg; tel. (30) 25910; fax (30) 251606; tel. (40) 34700; fax (40) 345811; internet www.asv.de; f. 1946; the largest newspaper publishing group in continental Europe; includes five major dailies *Die Welt*, *Hamburger Abendblatt*, *Bild*, *Berliner Morgenpost*, *BZ*, three Sunday papers *Welt am Sonntag*, *Bild am Sonntag*, *BZ am Sonntag*, and radio, television, women's and family magazines; Chair. AUGUST A. FISCHER.

Gruner + Jahr AG & Co Druck- und Verlagshaus: Am Vossbarg, 25524 Itzehoe; and Am Baumwall 11, 20459 Hamburg; tel. (4821) 7771; fax (4821) 777449; tel. (40) 37030; fax (40) 3703600; internet www.co.guj.de; owns, amongst others, *Stern*, *Brigitte*, *Capital*, *Eltern*, *Schöner Wohnen*, *Hamburger Morgenpost*; *Financial Times Deutschland*, a jt venture with *Financial Times* (UK) was launched in Feb. 2000.

Süddeutscher-Verlag GmbH: Sendlingerstr. 80, 80331 München; tel. (89) 21830; fax (89) 2183787; internet www.sueddeutsche.de; f. 1945; owns *Süddeutsche Zeitung*, special interest periodicals.

JahreszeitenVerlag GmbH: Possmoorweg 5, 22301 Hamburg; tel. (40) 27170; fax (40) 27172056; f. 1948; owns, amongst others, the periodicals *Für Sie* and *Petra*; Pres. THOMAS GANSKE.

Heinrich-Bauer-Verlag: Postfach 4660, 20077 Hamburg; Burchardstr. 11, 20095 Hamburg; and Charles-de-Gaulle-Str. 8, 81737 München; tel. (40) 30190; fax (40) 30191043; tel. (89) 678600; fax (89) 6702033; internet www.bauerverlag.de; owns 108 popular illustrated magazines, including *Bravo* (München), *Neue Revue* (Hamburg), *Maxi*, *Neue Post*, *TV Horen + Sehen* and *TV Movie*; Pres. HEINRICH BAUER.

Verlag Aenne Burda GmbH & Co KG: Am Kesterdamm 1, 77652 Offenburg; tel. (781) 840; fax (781) 843291; internet www.burda.de; f. 1908; publs incl. *Burda Modemagazin*, *Bild + Funk*, *Focus*, *Freundin*, *Meine Familie & ich* and *Schweriner Volkszeitung*; 10 Mans.

PRINCIPAL DAILIES

Aachen

Aachener Nachrichten: Postfach 110, 52002 Aachen; Dresdner Str. 3, 52068 Aachen; tel. (241) 51010; fax (241) 5101399; internet www.an-online.de; f. 1872; circ. 67,000.

Aachener Zeitung: Postfach 500110, 52085 Aachen; Dresdner Str. 3, 52068 Aachen; tel. (241) 51010; fax (241) 5101399; internet www .aachener-zeitung.de; f. 1946; Editor-in-Chief BERND MATHIEU; circ. 106,000.

Ansbach

Fränkische Landeszeitung: Postfach 1362, 91504 Ansbach; Nürnberger Str. 9–17, 91522 Ansbach; tel. (981) 95000; fax (981) 13961; Editor-in-Chief PETER M. SZYMANOWSKI; circ. 50,000.

Aschaffenburg

Main-Echo: Postfach 548, 63736 Aschaffenburg; Weichertstr. 20, 63739 Aschaffenburg a.M.; tel. (6021) 3960; fax (6021) 396499; e-mail redaktionssekretariat@main-echo.de; internet www .main-echo.de; Editors HELMUT WEISS, Dr HELMUT TEUFEL; circ. 93,000.

Augsburg

Augsburger Allgemeine: Curt-Frenzel-Str. 2, 86167 Augsburg; tel. (821) 7770; fax (821) 7772039; e-mail chefredaktion@ augsburger-allgemeiner.de; internet www.augsburger-allgemeine .de; daily (Mon. to Sat.); Editor-in-Chief RAINER BONHORST; circ. 370,000.

Baden-Baden

Badisches Tagblatt: Postfach 120, 76481 Baden-Baden; Stefanienstr. 1–3, 76530 Baden-Baden; tel. (7221) 215241; fax (7221) 215240; Editors-in-Chief HARALD BESINGER, VOLKER-BODO ZANGER; circ. 41,000.

Bamberg

Fränkischer Tag: Gutenbergstr. 1, 96050 Bamberg; tel. (951) 1880; fax (951) 188118; internet www.fraenkischer-tag.de; Publr Dr HELMUTH JUNGBAUER; circ. 75,800.

Bautzen

Serbske Nowiny: Tuchmacher Str. 27, 02625 Bautzen; tel. (3591) 577232; e-mail serbske-nowiny@t-online.de; evening; Sorbian language paper; Editor BENEDIKT DYRLICH; circ. 1,500.

Berlin

Berliner Kurier: Karl-Liebknecht-Str. 29, 10178 Berlin; tel. (30) 23279; fax (30) 23275606; e-mail berliner-kurier@berlinonline.de; internet www.Berliner-kurier.de; f. 1990; evening; publ. by Gruner + Jahr AG; Editor CAROLINE METHNER; circ. 149,795.

Berliner Morgenpost: Axel-Springer-Str. 65, 10888 Berlin; tel. (30) 25910; fax (30) 2516071; e-mail redaktion@morgenpost.de; internet www.morgenpost.de; f. 1898; publ. by Ullstein GmbH; Editor-in-Chief CARSTEN ERDMANN; circ. 153,135.

Berliner Zeitung: Karl-Liebknecht-Str. 29, 10178 Berlin; tel. (2) 23279; fax (30) 23275581; e-mail berliner-zeitung@berlinonline.de; internet www.berliner-zeitung.de; f. 1945; morning (except Sun.); publ. by Gruner + Jahr AG; Editor Dr UWE VORKÖTTER; circ. 193,493.

BZ (Berliner Zeitung): Axel-Springer-Str. 65, 10888 Berlin; tel. (30) 25910; fax (30) 2510928; internet www.bz-berlin.de; f. 1877; publ. by Axel Springer Verlag AG; Editor WOLFGANG KRYSZOHN; circ. 313,500.

Junge Welt: Berlin; tel. (30) 22330; fax (30) 1302865; internet www .jungewelt.de; f. 1947; morning; Editor JENS KÖNIG; circ. 158,000.

Neues Deutschland: Alt-Stralau 1–2, 10245 Berlin; tel. (30) 293905; fax (30) 29390600; e-mail redaktion@nd-online.de; internet www.nd-online.de; f. 1946; morning; independent; Editor DIETMAR BARTSCH; circ. 52,000.

Der Tagesspiegel: Verlag der Tagesspiegel GmbH, 10876 Berlin; tel. (30) 260090; fax (30) 26009332; e-mail infotsp@tagesspiegel.de; internet www.tagesspiegel.de; f. 1945; circ. 151,000.

Die Welt: Axel-Springer-Str. 65, 10888 Berlin; tel. (30) 25910; fax (30) 251606; internet www.welt.de; f. 1946; publ. by Axel Springer Verlag AG; Editor Dr THOMAS LÖFFELHOLZ; circ. 216,800.

Bielefeld

Neue Westfälische: Postfach 100225, 33502 Bielefeld; Niedernstr. 21–27, 33602 Bielefeld; tel. (521) 5550; fax (521) 555520; internet www.nw-news.de; f. 1967; circ. 254,753.

Westfalen-Blatt: Postfach 8740, 33531 Bielefeld; Südbrackstr. 14–18, 33611 Bielefeld; tel. (521) 5850; fax (521) 585370; internet www .westfalen-blatt.de; f. 1946; Editor CARL-W. BUSSE; circ. 147,400.

Bonn

General-Anzeiger: Justus-von-Liebig-Str. 15, 53121 Bonn; tel. (228) 66880; fax (228) 6688170; internet www .general-anzeiger-bonn.de; f. 1725; independent; Publrs HERMANN NEUSSER, HERMANN NEUSSER, Jr, MARTIN NEUSSER; Editor Dr HELMUT HERLES; circ. 90,000.

Braunschweig

Braunschweiger Zeitung: Postfach 3263, 38022 Braunschweig; Hamburger Str. 277, 38114 Braunschweig; tel. (531) 39000; fax (531) 3900610; internet www.newsclick.de; circ. 170,400.

Bremen

Bremer Nachrichten: Postfach 107801, 28078 Bremen; Martinistr. 43, 28195 Bremen; tel. (421) 36710; fax (421) 3379233; f. 1743; Publr HERBERT C. ORDEMANN; Editor DIETRICH IDE; circ. 30,000.

Weser-Kurier: Postfach 107801, 28078 Bremen; Martinistr. 43, 28195 Bremen; tel. (421) 36710; fax (421) 3379233; internet www .weser-kurier.de; f. 1945; Publr HERBERT C. ORDEMANN; Editor VOLKER WEISE; circ. 160,000.

Bremerhaven

Nordsee-Zeitung: Postfach 27512, 27512 Bremerhaven; Hafenstr. 140, 27576 Bremerhaven 1; tel. (471) 5970; fax (471) 597567; internet www.nordsee-zeitung.de; Chief Editor JÖRG JUNG; circ. 77,500.

Chemnitz

Freie Presse: Postfach 261, Brückenstr. 15, 09111 Chemnitz; tel. (371) 6560; fax (371) 643042; internet www.freiepresse.de; f. 1963; morning; Editor DIETER SOIKA; circ. 461,900.

Cottbus

Lausitzer Rundschau: Postfach 100279, 03002 Cottbus; Str. der Jugend 54, 03050 Cottbus; tel. (355) 4810; fax (355) 481245; internet www.lr-online.de; independent; morning; Chief Officers FRANK LÜDECKE, B. LISKE; circ. 160,000.

Darmstadt

Darmstädter Echo: Postfach 100155, 64276 Darmstadt; Holzhofallee 25–31, 64295 Darmstadt; tel. (6151) 3871; fax (6151) 387448; internet www.echo-online.de; f. 1945; Publrs Dr HANS-PETER BACH, HORST BACH; Editor-in-Chief ROLAND HOF; circ. 87,300.

Dortmund

Ruhr-Nachrichten: Postfach 105051, Westenhellweg 86–88, 44047 Dortmund; internet www.westline.de; f. 1949; Editor FLORIAN LENSING-WOLFF; circ. 215,400.

Westfälische Rundschau: Postfach 105067, 44047 Dortmund; Brüderweg 9; Dortmund 44135; tel. (201) 8040; fax (201) 8042841; e-mail zentralredaktion@westfaelische-rundschau.de; internet www.westfaelische-rundschau.de; Editor FRANK BÜNTE; circ. 250,000.

Dresden

Dresdner Morgenpost: Ostra-Allee, 01067 Dresden; tel. (51) 4864; fax (51) 4951116; circ. 126,700.

Dresdner Neueste Nachrichten/Union: Hauptstr. 21, 01097 Dresden; tel. (351) 8075210; fax (351) 8075212; internet www .dnn-online.de; morning; Editor-in-Chief DIRK BIRGEL; circ. 35,000.

Sächsische Zeitung: Haus der Presse, Ostra-Allee 20, 01067 Dresden; tel. (351) 48640; fax (351) 48642354; e-mail redaktion@ sz-online.de; internet www.sz-online.de; f. 1946; morning; publ. by Gruner + Jahr AG; Editor-in-Chief PETER CHRIST; circ. 397,700.

Düsseldorf

Düsseldorf Express: Postfach 1132, 40002 Düsseldorf; Königsallee 27, 40212 Düsseldorf; tel. (211) 13930; fax (211) 324835.

Handelsblatt: Postfach 102741, 40018 Düsseldorf; Kasernenstr. 67, 40213 Düsseldorf; tel. (211) 8870; fax (211) 329954; e-mail handelsblatt@vhb.de; internet www.handelsblatt.de; 5 a week; Publr DIETER VON HOLTZBRINCK; circ. 156,473.

Rheinische Post: Zülpicherstr. 10, 40549 Düsseldorf; tel. (211) 5050; fax (211) 5052575; internet www.rp-online.de; f. 1946; Editor ULRICH REITZ; circ. 349,200.

Westdeutsche Zeitung: Postfach 101132, 40002 Düsseldorf; Königsallee 27, 40212 Düsseldorf; tel. (211) 83820; fax (211) 83822392; e-mail wzn@wz-newsline.de; internet www.wz-newsline .de; Editor-in-Chief FRIEDRICH ROEINGH; Publr Dr M. GIRARDET; circ. 176,800.

Erfurt

Thüringer Allgemeine: Gottstedter Landstr. 6, 99092 Erfurt; tel. (361) 2274; fax (361) 2275144; e-mail redaktion@ thueringer-allgemeine.de; internet www.thueringer-allgemeine.de; f. 1946; morning; Editor-in-Chief SERGEJ LOCHTHOFEN; circ. 330,000.

Essen

Neue Ruhr Zeitung: Friedrichstr. 34–38, 45128 Essen; tel. (201) 8042605; fax (201) 8042121; Editor-in-Chief Dr RICHARD KIESSLER; circ. 215,000.

Westdeutsche Allgemeine Zeitung: Friedrichstr. 34–38, 45128 Essen; tel. (201) 8040; fax (201) 8042841; Editor RALF LEHMANN; circ. 650,000.

Flensburg

Flensburger Tageblatt: Postfach 1553, 25804 Flensburg; Nikolaistr. 7, 24937 Flensburg; tel. (461) 8080; fax (461) 8082121.

Frankfurt am Main

Frankfurter Allgemeine Zeitung: Hellerhofstr. 2–4, 60327 Frankfurt a.M.; tel. (69) 75910; fax (69) 75911743; internet www.faz .net; f. 1949; Editors DIETER ECKART, BERTHOLD KOHLER, Dr GÜNTHER NONNENMACHER, Dr FRANK SCHIRRMACHER, HOLGER STELTZNER; circ. 400,000.

Frankfurter Neue Presse: Postfach 100801, 60008 Frankfurt a.M.; Frankenallee 71–81, 60327 Frankfurt a.M.; tel. (69) 75010; fax (69) 75014330; internet www.fnp.de; independent; Editor GERHARD MUMME; circ. 110,440.

Frankfurter Rundschau: Grosse Eschenheimer Str. 16–18; 60313 Frankfurt a.M.; tel. (69) 21991; fax (69) 21993521; e-mail redaktion@ fr-aktuell.de; internet www.fr-aktuell.de; Editors Dr WOLFGANG STORZ, STEPHAN HEBEL, JUERGEN METKEMEYER; circ. 183,000.

Frankfurt an der Oder

Märkische Oderzeitung: Postfach 178, 15201 Frankfurt a.d. Oder; Kellenspring 6, 15230 Frankfurt a.d. Oder; tel. (335) 55300; fax (335) 23214; morning; Editor HEINZ KURTZBACH; circ. 150,633.

Freiburg im Breisgau

Badische Zeitung: Pressehaus, Basler Str. 88, 79115 Freiburg i. Br.; tel. (761) 4960; fax (761) 4965008; e-mail redaktion@ badische-zeitung.de; internet www.badische-zeitung.de; f. 1946; Editor THOMAS HAUSER; circ. 171,990.

Gera

Ostthüringer Zeitung: De-Smit-Str. 18, 6500 Gera; tel. (70) 6120; fax (70) 51233; morning; Editor-in-Chief ULLRICH ERZIGKEIT; circ. 237,537.

Göttingen

Göttinger Tageblatt: Postfach 1953, 37009 Göttingen; Dransfelder Str. 1, 37079 Göttingen; tel. (551) 9011; fax (551) 901229; e-mail info@goettinger.tageblatt.de; internet www .goettinger-tageblatt.de; f. 1889; Man. Dirs HERBERT FLECKEN, GÜNTER GRIFFELS; Editor-in-Chief BERNO HILDER; circ. 50,200.

Hagen

Westfalenpost: Schürmannstr. 4, 58097 Hagen; tel. (2331) 9170; fax (2331) 9174263; e-mail westfalenpost@cityweb.de; f. 1946; Chief Editor BODO ZAPP; circ. 160,000.

Halle

Haller Kreisblatt: Postfach 1452, 33779 Halle; Gutenbergstr. 2, 33790 Halle.

Hamburg

Bild: Axel-Springer-Pl. 1, 20355 Hamburg; tel. (40) 34700; fax (40) 345811; internet www.bild.de; f. 1952; publ. by Axel Springer Verlag AG; Chief Editor KAI DIEKMANN; circ. 4,412,200.

Hamburger Abendblatt: Axel-Springer-Pl. 1, 20355 Hamburg; tel. (40) 34700; fax (40) 345811; internet www.abendblatt.de; publ. by Axel Springer Verlag AG; Editor-in-Chief KLAUS KRUSE; circ. 315,600.

Hamburger Morgenpost: Griegstr. 75, 22763 Hamburg; tel. (40) 8830303; fax (40) 88303237; e-mail verlag@mopo.de; internet www .mopo.de; publ. by Gruner + Jahr AG; circ. 110,000.

Hannover

Hannoversche Allgemeine Zeitung: Bemeroder Str. 58, 30148 Hannover, 30559 Hannover; tel. (511) 5180; fax (511) 527328; internet www.niedersachsen.com; circ. 269,600.

Neue Presse: Postfach 149, 30001 Hannover; Bemeroder Str. 58, 30559 Hannover; tel. (511) 51010; fax (511) 524554.

Heidelberg

Rhein-Neckar-Zeitung: Postfach 104560, 69035 Heidelberg; Hauptstr. 23, 69117 Heidelberg; tel. (6221) 5191; fax (6221) 519217; e-mail rnz-kontakt@rnz.de; internet www.rnz.de; f. 1945; morning; Publrs Dr LUDWIG KNORR, WINFRIED KNORR, Dr RUPRECHT SCHULZE; circ. 102,500.

Heilbronn

Heilbronner Stimme: Allee 2, 74072 Heilbronn; tel. (7131) 6150; fax (7131) 615200; e-mail gl@stimme.de; internet www.stimme.de; f. 1946; Editor-in-Chief Dr WOLFGANG BOK; circ. 102,500.

Hof-Saale

Frankenpost: Postfach 1320, 95012 Hof-Saale; Poststr. 9–11, 95028 Hof-Saale; tel. (9281) 8160; fax (9281) 816283; e-mail fp-redaktion@frankenpost.de; internet www.frankenpost.de; publ. by Frankenpost Verlag GmbH; Editor-in-Chief MALTE BUSCHBECK; circ. 85,000.

Ingolstadt

Donaukurier: Postfach 100259, 85002 Ingolstadt; Stauffenbergstr. 2A, 85051 Ingolstadt; tel. (841) 96660; fax (841) 9666255; e-mail redaktion@donaukurier.de; internet www.donaukurier.de; f. 1872; Publr ELIN REISSMÜLLER; circ. 84,700.

Kassel

Hessische/Niedersächsische Allgemeine: Postfach 101009, 34010 Kassel; Frankfurter Str. 168, 34121 Kassel; tel. (561) 20300; fax (561) 2032116; internet www.hna.de; f. 1959; independent; circ. 189,200.

Kempten

Allgäuer Zeitung: Postfach 3155, 87440 Kempten; Heisinger Str. 14, 87437 Kempten; tel. (831) 2060; fax (831) 206379; internet www .all-in.de; f. 1968; Publrs GEORG FÜRST VON WALDBURG-ZEIL, GÜNTER HOLLAND; circ. 117,900.

Kiel

Kieler Nachrichten: Postfach 1111, 24100 Kiel; Fleethörn 1–7, 24103 Kiel; tel. (431) 9030; fax (431) 903935; internet www.kn.online .de; publ. by Axel Springer Verlag; Chief Editor JÜRGEN HEINEMANN; circ. 113,400.

Koblenz

Rhein-Zeitung: Postfach 1540, August-Horch-Str. 28, 56070 Koblenz; tel. (261) 89200; fax (261) 892476; internet www .rhein-zeitung.de; Editor MARTIN LOHMANN; circ. 246,100.

Köln

Express: Postfach 100410, 50450 Köln; Breite Str. 70, 50667 Köln; tel. (221) 2240; fax (211) 2242524; internet www.express.de; f. 1964; Publr ALFRED NEVEN DUMONT; circ. 370,000.

Kölner Stadt-Anzeiger: Amsterdamer Str. 192, 50735 Köln; tel. (221) 2240; fax (221) 2242524; internet www.ksta.de; f. 1876; Publr ALFRED NEVEN DUMONT; Editor FRANZ SOMMERFELD; circ. 294,400.

Kölnische Rundschau: Postfach 102145, 50461 Köln; Stolkgasse 25–45, 50667 Köln; tel. (221) 16320; fax (221) 1632491; e-mail jost .springensguth@kr-redaktion.de; internet www.rundschau-online .de; f. 1946; Publr HELMUT HEINEN; Editor-in-Chief JOST SPRINGENS-GUTH; circ. 155,100.

Konstanz

Südkurier: Postfach 102001, Presse- und Druckzentrum, 78420 Konstanz; Max-Stromeyer-Str. 178, 78467 Konstanz; tel. (7531) 9990; fax (7531) 991485; e-mail redaktion@suedkurier.de; internet www.skol.de; f. 1945; circ. 148,990.

Leipzig

Leipziger Volkszeitung: Petersteinweg 19, 04107 Leipzig; tel. (341) 21810; fax (341) 310992; internet www.lvz-online.de; f. 1894; morning; publ. by Verlagsgesellschaft Madsach and Axel Springer Verlag AG; circ. 264,000.

Leutkirch im Allgäu

Schwäbische Zeitung: Postfach 1145, 88291 Leutkirch im Allgäu; Rudolf-Roth-Str. 18, 88299 Leutkirch im Allgäu; tel. (7561) 800; fax (7561) 80134; e-mail redaktion@schwaebische-zeitung.de; internet www.schwaebische-zeitung.de; f. 1945; Editor JOACHIM UMBACH; circ. 196,000.

Lübeck

Lübecker Nachrichten: Herrenholz 10–12, 23556 Lübeck; tel. (451) 1440; fax (451) 1441022; internet www.ln-online.de; f. 1945; publ. by Axel Springer Verlag AG; Chief Editor MANFRED VON THIEN; circ. 115,900.

Ludwigshafen

Die Rheinpfalz: Postfach 211147, 67011 Ludwigshafen; Amtsstr. 5–11, 67059 Ludwigshafen; tel. (621) 590201; fax (621) 5902336; Dir Dr THOMAS SCHAUB; circ. 249,410.

Magdeburg

Magdeburger Volksstimme: Bahnhofstr. 17, 39104 Magdeburg; tel. (391) 59990; fax (391) 388400; f. 1890; morning; publ. by Magdeburger Verlags- und Druckhaus GmbH; Editor-in-Chief Dr HEINZ-GEORG OETTE; circ. 316,900.

Mainz

Allgemeine Zeitung: Postfach 3120, 55021 Mainz; Erich-Dombrowski-Str. 2, 55127 Mainz; tel. (6131) 1440; fax (6131) 144504; internet www.main-rheiner.de; publ. by Rhein-Main-Presse; circ. 134,000.

Mannheim

Mannheimer Morgen: Postfach 102164, 68021 Mannheim; Dudenstr. 12–26, 68167 Mannheim; tel. (621) 39201; fax (621) 3921376; e-mail redaktion@mamo.de; internet www.morgenweb.de; f. 1946; Publr R. VON SCHILLING; Chief Editor HORST ROTH; circ. 166,438.

München

Abendzeitung: Sendlingerstr. 10, 80331 München; tel. (89) 23770; fax (89) 2377478; internet www.abendzeitung.de; f. 1948; Dir CHRISTOPH MATTES; Editor-in-Chief KURT RÖTTGEN; circ. 165,836.

Münchner Merkur: Paul-Heyse-Str. 2–4, 80336 München; tel. (89) 53060; fax (89) 53068651; internet www.merkur-online.de; Publr Dr DIRK IPPEN; Editor ERNST HEBEKER; circ. 283,000.

Süddeutsche Zeitung: Sendlingerstr. 8, 80331 München; tel. (89) 21830; fax (89) 2183787; internet www.sueddeutsche.de; f. 1945; publ. by Süddeutscher-Verlag GmbH; Editors-in-Chief HANS-WERNER KILZ, Dr GERNOT SITTNER; circ. 427,644.

TZ: Paul-Heyse-Str. 2–4, 80336 München; tel. (89) 53060; fax (89) 5306552; e-mail sekretariat@tz-online.de; f. 1968; Editor KARL SCHERMANN; circ. 154,695.

Münster

Münstersche Zeitung: Postfach 5560, 48030 Münster; Neubrückenstr. 8–11, 48143 Münster; tel. (251) 5920; fax (251) 592212; e-mail mz-redaktion@westline.de; internet www.westline.de; f. 1871; independent; Editor Dr GREGOR BOTHE; circ. 46,860.

Westfälische Nachrichten: Soester Str. 13, 48155 Münster; tel. (251) 690700; fax (251) 690705; internet www.westline.de; Chief Editor Dr NORBERT TIEMANN; circ. 121,211.

Neubrandenburg

Nordkurier: Flurstr. 2, 17034 Neubrandenburg; tel. (395) 45750; fax (395) 4575694; internet www.nordkurier.de; Editor-in-Chief Dr ANDRÉ UZULIS; circ. 250,000.

Nürnberg

Nürnberger Nachrichten: Marienstr. 9–11, 90402 Nürnberg; tel. (911) 2160; fax (911) 2162326; internet www.nn-online.de; f. 1945; Editor FELIX HARTLIEB; circ. 344,000.

Oberndorf-Neckar

Schwarzwälder Bote: Postfach 1380, 78722 Oberndorf-Neckar; Kirchtorstr. 14, 78727 Oberndorf-Neckar; tel. (7423) 780; fax (7423) 7873; internet www.swol.de; circ. 104,300.

Oelde

Die Glocke: Engelbert-Holterdorf-Str. 4–6, 59302 Oelde; tel. (2522) 730; fax (2522) 73216; f. 1880; Editors FRIED GEHRING, ENGELBERT HOLTERDORF; circ. 65,500.

Offenbach

Offenbach Post: Postfach 100263, 63002 Offenbach; Waldstr. 226, 63071 Offenbach; tel. (69) 850080; fax (69) 85008198; internet www.op-online.de; f. 1947; Publr UDO BINTZ; circ. 53,200.

Oldenburg

Nordwest-Zeitung: Postfach 2527, 26015 Oldenburg; Peterstr. 28–34, 26121 Oldenburg; tel. (441) 998801; fax (441) 99882029; internet www.nwz-online.de; publ. by Nordwest-Zeitung Verlagsgesellschaft mbH & Co KG; Editor ROLF SEELHEIM; circ. 130,000.

Osnabrück

Neue Osnabrücker Zeitung: Postfach 4260, 49032 Osnabrück; Breiter Gang 10–16 and Grosse Str. 17–19, 49074 Osnabrück; tel. (541) 3250; fax (541) 325275; e-mail redaktion@neue-oz.de; internet www.neue-oz.de; f. 1967; Editors-in-Chief EWALD GELDING, Dr JÜRGEN WERMSER; circ. 179,700.

Passau

Passauer Neue Presse: Medienstr. 5, 94036 Passau; tel. (851) 8020; fax (851) 802256; internet www.pnp.de; f. 1946; circ. 177,282.

Potsdam

Märkische Allgemeine: Postfach 601153, 14411 Potsdam; Friedrich-Engels-Str. 24, 14473 Potsdam; tel. (331) 28400; fax (331) 2840310; e-mail chefredaktion@mazonline.de; internet www.maerkischeallgemeine.de; f. 1990; morning; independent; Chief Editor Dr KLAUS ROST; circ. 180,000.

Regensburg

Mittelbayerische Zeitung: Margaretenstr. 4, 93047 Regensburg; tel. (941) 207270; fax (941) 207307; e-mail gf@mz.donau.de; internet www.donau.de; f. 1945; Editors PETER ESSER, THOMAS ESSER; circ. 133,803.

Rostock

Ostsee-Zeitung: Richard-Wagner-Str. 1A, 18055 Rostock; tel. (81) 3650; fax (81) 365244; internet www.ostsee-zeitung.de; f. 1952; publ. by Axel Springer Verlag AG; Editor GERD SPILKER; circ. 214,300.

Saarbrücken

Saarbrücker Zeitung: Gutenbergstr. 11–23, 66117 Saarbrücken; tel. (681) 5020; fax (681) 5022500; internet www.sol.de; f. 1761; Editor PETER STEGAN HERBST; circ. 167,184.

Schwerin

Schweriner Volkszeitung: Gutenbergstr. 1, 19061 Schwerin; tel. (385) 63780; fax (385) 3975140; internet www.svz.de; f. 1946; Editor CHRISTOPH HAMM; circ. 144,800.

Straubing

Straubinger Tagblatt: Ludwigspl. 30, 94315 Straubing; tel. (9421) 940115; fax (9421) 940155; e-mail service@idowa.de; internet www.idowa.de; f. 1860; morning; Chief Editor Dr HERMANN BALLE; circ. 140,000.

Stuttgart

Stuttgarter Nachrichten: Postfach 104452, 70039 Stuttgart; Plieninger Str. 150, 70567 Stuttgart; tel. (711) 72050; fax (711) 7205747; internet www.stuttgarter-nachrichten.de; f. 1946; Editor-in-Chief JÜRGEN OFFENBACH; circ. 270,000.

Stuttgarter Zeitung: Postfach 106032, 70049 Stuttgart; Plieninger Str. 150, 70567 Stuttgart; tel. (711) 72050; fax (711) 72051234; e-mail redaktion@stz.zgs.de; internet www.stuttgarter-zeitung.de; f. 1945; Chief Editor PETER CHRIST; circ. 151,600.

Trier

Trierischer Volksfreund: Postfach 3770, 54227 Trier; Hanns-Martin-Schleyer-Str. 8, 54294 Trier; tel. (651) 71990; fax (651) 7199990; e-mail redaktion@intrinet.de; internet www.intrinet.de; Chief Editor WALTER W. WEBER; circ. 100,000.

Ulm

Südwest Presse: Frauenstr. 77, 89073 Ulm; tel. (731) 1560; fax (731) 156308; internet www.suedwest-presse.de; circ. 107,800.

Weiden

Der Neue Tag: Postfach 1340, 92603 Weiden; Weigelstr. 16, 92637 Weiden; tel. (961) 850; fax (961) 44499; Editor-in-Chief HANS KLEMM; circ. 87,400.

Weimar

Thüringische Landeszeitung: Marienstr. 14, 99423 Weimar; tel. (3643) 206411; fax (3643) 206413; f. 1945; morning; Editor HANS HOFFMEISTER; circ. 62,000.

Wetzlar

Wetzlarer Neue Zeitung: Elsa-Brandström-Str. 18, 35578 Wetzlar; tel. (6441) 9590; fax (6441) 71684; f. 1945; Editor WULF EIGENDORF; circ. 75,000.

Wiesbaden

Wiesbadener Kurier: Postfach 6029, 65050 Wiesbaden; Langgasse 21, 65183 Wiesbaden; tel. (611) 3550; fax (611) 355377; internet www.main-rheiner-de; Chief Editors MATTHIAS FRIEDRICH, FRIEDRICH ROEINGH; circ. 86,700.

Würzburg

Main-Post: Berner Str. 2, 97084 Würzburg; tel. (931) 60010; fax (931) 6001242; internet www.mainpost.de; f. 1883; independent; Publrs MANFRED WINTERBACH, DAVID BRANDSTÄTTER, KNUT MÜLLER; Editor-in-Chief MICHAEL REINHARD; circ. 153,300.

SUNDAY AND WEEKLY PAPERS

Bayernkurier: Nymphenburger Str. 64, 80636 München; tel. (89) 120041; e-mail redaktion@bayernkurier.de; internet www.bayernkurier.de; weekly; organ of the CSU; Chief Editor PETER SCHMALZ; circ. 71,610.

Bild am Sonntag: Axel-Springer-Pl. 1, 20350 Hamburg; tel. (40) 34700; fax (40) 34724514; f. 1956; Sunday; publ. by Axel Springer Verlag AG; Chief Editor CLAUS STRUNZ; circ. 2,202,005.

BZ am Sonntag: Axel-Springer-Str. 65, 10888 Berlin; tel. (30) 25910; fax (30) 259173131; e-mail redaktion@bz-berlin.de; internet www.bz-berlin.de; f. 1992; publ. by Ullstein GmbH; Editor-in-Chief FLORIAN V. HEINTZE; circ. 129,636.

Frankfurter Allgemeine Sonntagszeitung: Hellerhofstr. 2–4, 60327 Frankfurt a.M.; tel. (69) 75910; fax (69) 75911773; e-mail sonntagszeitung@faz.de; internet www.faz.de; Sunday; Publrs DIETER ECKART, BERTHOLD KOHLER, GÜNTHER NONNENMACHER, FRANK SCHIRRMACHER, HOLGER STELTZNER; circ. 267,700 (2002).

Rheinischer Merkur: Postfach 201164, 53141 Bonn; Godesberger Allee 91, 53175 Bonn; tel. (228) 8840; fax (228) 884299; e-mail anzeigen@merkur.de; internet www.merkur.de; f. 1946; weekly; circ. 106,000.

Sonntag Aktuell: Plieninger Str. 150, 70567 Stuttgart; tel. (711) 72050; fax (711) 72053509; e-mail redaktion@soak.zgs.de; Sunday; circ. 869,500.

Welt am Sonntag: Axel-Springer-Str. 65, 10888 Berlin; tel. (30) 259100; e-mail leserbriefe@wams.de; internet www.weltamsonntag.de; Sunday; publ. by Axel Springer Verlag AG; Editor CHRISTOPHE KEESE; circ. 412,000.

Die Zeit: Speersort 1, Pressehaus, 20095 Hamburg; tel. (40) 32800; fax (40) 327111; internet www.zeit.de; f. 1946; weekly; Editors-in-Chief Dr JOSEF JOFFE, Dr MICHAEL NAUMANN; circ. 455,000.

SELECTED PERIODICALS

Agriculture

Agrar Praxis: Ernst-Mey-Str. 8, 7022 Leinfelden-Echterdingen; tel. (711) 7594423; f. 1882; monthly; Editor-in-Chief KLAUS NIEHÖRSTER; circ. 60,250.

Bauernzeitung: Postfach 310448, 10634 Berlin; Wilhelmsaue 37, 10713 Berlin; e-mail bauernzeitung@bauernverlag.de; internet www.bauernzeitung.de; f. 1960; agricultural weekly; Editor RALF STEPHAN; circ. 32,000.

Bayerisches Landwirtschaftliches Wochenblatt: Postfach 200523, 80005 München; Bayerstr. 57, 80335 München; tel. (89) 53098901; fax (89) 5328537; e-mail blw@dlv.de; internet www .wochenblatt-dlv.de; f. 1810; weekly; organ of the Bayerischer Bauernverband; Editor-in-Chief JOHANNES URBAN; circ. 108,000.

Eisenbahn-Landwirt: Postfach 2026, 76008 Karlsruhe; Ostring 6, 76131 Karlsruhe; tel. (721) 62830; fax (721) 628310; internet www .druck-verlag-sw.de/verlag-ebl-1.htm; f. 1918; monthly; publ. by Druckhaus Karlsruhe, Druck + Verlagsgesellschaft Südwest mbH; Dir HANS HÜSKEN; circ. 120,000.

Das Landvolk: Warmbüchenstr. 3, 30159 Hannover; fax (511) 3670468; fortnightly; issued by Landbuch-Verlag GmbH; Chief Editor GÜNTHER MARTIN BEINE; circ. 98,000.

Landpost: Wollgrasweg 31, 70599 Stuttgart; tel. (711) 451275; fax (711) 456603; e-mail raiser@vdaw.de; internet www.vdaw.de; f. 1945; weekly; agriculture and gardening; Editor ERICH REICH; circ. 31,000.

Art, Drama, Architecture and Music

Art. Das Kunstmagazin: Am Baumwall 11, 20459 Hamburg; tel. (40) 37030; fax (40) 37035618; e-mail kunst@art-magazin.de; internet www.art-magazin.de; monthly; publ. by Gruner + Jahr AG; circ. 70,000.

Intelligente Architektur: Fasanenweg 18, 70771 Leinfelden-Echterdingen; tel. (711) 7591286; fax (711) 7591410; e-mail ait-red@ ait-online.de; internet www.xia-online.de; f. 1890; monthly; Editor Dr D. DANNER; circ. 17,500.

Theater der Zeit: Klosterstr. 68–70, 10179 Berlin; tel. (30) 24722414; fax (30) 24722415; e-mail redaktion@theaterderzeit.de; internet www.theaterderzeit.de; f. 1946; monthly; theatre, drama, opera, children's theatre, puppet theatre, dance; Editors ANJA DÜRRSCHMIDT, NINA PETERS, DIRK PILZ; circ. 8,000.

Theater heute: Reinhardtstr. 29, 10117 Berlin; tel. (30) 25449510; fax (30) 25449512; e-mail redaktion@theaterheute.de; internet www .theaterheute.de; f. 1960; monthly; Editors BARBARA BURCKHARDT, EVA BEHRENDT, Dr MICHAEL MERSCHMEIER, Dr FRANZ WILLE.

Economics, Finance and Industry

Absatzwirtschaft: Postfach 101102, 40002 Düsseldorf; Kasernenstr. 67, 40213 Düsseldorf; tel. (211) 8871422; fax (211) 8871420; e-mail absatzwirtschaft@vhb.de; internet www.absatzwirtschaft.de; f. 1958; monthly; marketing; Dir UWE HOCH; Editor CRISTOPH BERDI; circ. 23,000.

Atw—Internationale Zeitschrift für Kernenergie: Postfach 101102, 40002 Düsseldorf; tel. (211) 8871442; fax (211) 8871440; e-mail w.liebholz@vhb.de; f. 1956; monthly; technical, scientific and economic aspects of nuclear engineering and technology; Editors Dr W.-M. LIEBHOLZ, E. PASCHE; circ. 4,500.

Der Betrieb: Postfach 101102, 40002 Düsseldorf; Kasernenstr. 67, 40123 Düsseldorf; tel. (211) 8871451; fax (211) 8871450; e-mail der-betrieb@vhb.de; weekly; business administration, revenue law, corporate law, labour and social legislation; circ. 36,000.

Capital: Gruner + Jahr AG, 50927 Köln; tel. (221) 490800; fax (221) 4908285; e-mail capital@capital.de; internet www.capital.de; f. 1962; six a year; business magazine; circ. 219,000.

Creditreform: Postfach 1102, Kasernenstr. 67, 40002 Düsseldorf; tel. (211) 8871461; fax (211) 8871463; f. 1879; Editor KLAUS-WERNER ERNST; circ. 124,870.

Finanzwirtschaft: Am Friedrichshain 22, 10400 Berlin; tel. (30) 42151237; fax (30) 42151300; 12 a year; public-sector finance and economics; circ. 4,818.

Getränketechnik, Zeitschrift für das technische Management: Nürnberg; tel. (911) 23830; fax (911) 204956; six a year; trade journal for the brewing and beverage industries; circ. 8,518.

H&V Journal Handelsvermittlung und Vertrieb: Mainzer-Land-Str. 238, 60326 Frankfurt a.M.; Siegel-Verlag Otto Müller GmbH; tel. (69) 75890950; fax (69) 75890960; e-mail hv-journal@ svffm.de; internet www.svffm.de; f. 1949; monthly; Editor Dr ANDREAS PAFFHAUSEN; circ. 16,027.

Industrie-Anzeiger: Postfach 100252, 70746 Leinfelden-Echterdingen; tel. (711) 7594452; internet www.industrie-anzeiger.de; f. 1879; weekly; Editor-in-Chief Dr R. LANGBEIN; circ. 45,000.

Management International Review: Abraham-Lincoln-Str. 46, 65189 Wiesbaden; tel. (611) 7878230; fax (611) 7878411; quarterly; English; publ. by Gabler Verlag; Editor Prof. Dr K. MACHARZINA (Stuttgart-Hohenheim).

VDI Nachrichten: Postfach 101054, Heinrichstr. 24, 40001 Düsseldorf; tel. (211) 61880; fax (211) 6188112; e-mail redaktion@ vdi-nachrichten.com; internet www.vdi-nachrichten.com; f. 1946; weekly; technology and economics; circ. 165,000.

Versicherungswirtschaft: Klosestr. 20–24, 76137 Karlsruhe; tel. (721) 35090; fax (721) 3502-201; e-mail knippenberg@vvw.de; internet www.vvw.de; f. 1946; fortnightly; Editor HUBERT CLEMENS; circ. 10,000.

Wirtschaftswoche: Kasernenstr. 67, 40213 Düsseldorf; tel. (211) 8870; fax (211) 887972114; e-mail wiwo@vhb.de; internet www.wiwo .de; weekly; business; Editor STEFAN BARON; circ. 183,000.

Education and Youth

Bravo: Charles-de-Gaulle-Str. 8, 81737 München; tel. (89) 6786700; fax (89) 6702033; e-mail post@bravo.de; internet www.bravo.de; weekly; for young people; circ. 500,000.

Computer Bild: Axel-Springer-Pl. 1, 20350 Hamburg; tel. (40) 34724300; fax (40) 34724683; e-mail redaktion@computerbild.de; internet www.computerbild.de; f. 1996; publ. by Axel Springer Verlag AG; circ. 947,807.

Deutsche Lehrerzeitung: Berlin; tel. (2) 23809414; fax (2) 20183645; f. 1954; weekly for teachers; Editor RAINER WINKEL; circ. 22,000.

Erziehung und Wissenschaft: Goldammerweg 16, 45134 Essen; tel. (201) 843000; fax (201) 472590; e-mail info@stamm.de; internet www.stamm.de; f. 1948; monthly; Editor-in-Chief ULF RÖDDE; circ. 255,775.

PÄDAGOGIK: Werderstr. 10, 69469 Weinheim; tel. (6201) 6007349; fax (6201) 6007354; f. 1949; monthly; Editor Prof. Dr J. BASTIAN; circ. 13,000.

Praxis Deutsch: Postfach 100150, 30917 Seelze; tel. (511) 40004139; fax (511) 40004219; e-mail redaktion.pd@friedrich-verlag .de; six a year; German language and literature; circ. 25,000.

Law

Deutsche Richterzeitung: Seufertstr. 27, 53173 Bonn; fax (228) 334723; f. 1909; monthly; circ. 11,000.

Juristenzeitung: Postfach 2040, 72010 Tübingen; Wilhelmstr. 18, 72074 Tübingen; tel. (7071) 92352; fax (7071) 92367; e-mail jz@mohr .de; f. 1944; fortnightly; Editor HEIDE SCHAPKA; circ. 6,000.

Juristische Rundschau: Postfach 303421, 10728 Berlin; Lützowstr. 33, 10785 Berlin; tel. (30) 26005123; fax (30) 26005329; e-mail jr@degruyter.de; internet www.degruyter.de; f. 1922; monthly; publ. by De Gruyter Rechtswissenschaften Verlags GmbH; Editors-in-Chief Prof. Dr DIRK OLZEN, Dr GERHARD SCHÄFER.

Neue Juristische Wochenschrift: Bretsozenstr. 7B, 60325 Frankfurt a.M.; tel. (69) 7560910; fax (69) 75609149; f. 1947; weekly; Editor-in-Chief R. A. MARTIN W. KEEFF; circ. 55,000.

Rabels Zeitschrift für ausländisches und internationales Privatrecht: Mittelweg 187, 20148 Hamburg; tel. (40) 41900263; fax (40) 41900288; e-mail heinrich@mpipriv-hh.mpg.de; internet www.mpipriv-hh.mpg.de; f. 1927; quarterly; Editors JÜGEN BASEDOW, KLAUS J. HOPT, REINHARD ZIMMERMANN.

Versicherungsrecht: Klosestr. 20–24, 76137 Karlsruhe; tel. (721) 35090; fax (721) 3509206; e-mail redaktion-versr@vvw.de; internet www.vvw.de; f. 1950; insurance law; three a month; Editor Prof. Dr EGON LORENZ; circ. 6,600.

Zeitschrift für die gesamte Strafrechtswissenschaft: Postfach 303421, 10728 Berlin; Lützowstr. 33, 10785 Berlin; tel. (30) 26005123; fax (30) 26005329; e-mail recht@degruyter.com; internet www.degruyter.de; f. 1881; quarterly; publ. by De Gruyter Rachtswissenschaften Verlags GmbH; Editors-in-Chief Prof. Dr KRISTIAN KÜHL, Prof. Dr JOACHIM VOGEL.

Politics, Literature, Current Affairs

Akzente: Vilshofener Str. 10, 81679 München; tel. (89) 998300; fax (89) 99830460; e-mail zeller@hanser.de; internet www.hanser.de; f. 1954; Editor MICHAEL KRÜGER.

Eulenspiegel: Gubener Str. 47, 10243 Berlin; tel. (30) 29346311; fax (30) 29346322; e-mail redaktion@eulenspiegel-zeitschrift.de; internet www.eulenspiegel-zeitschrift.de; f. 1946; political, satirical and humorous monthly; Editors JÜRGEN NOWAK, HARTMUT BERLIN; circ. 120,000.

Focus: Arabellastr. 23, 81925 München; tel. (89) 92500; fax (89) 92502026; e-mail anzeigen@focus.de; internet www.focus.de; f. 1993; weekly; political, general; publ. by Burda GmbH & Co KG; circ. 764,000.

Gesellschaft-Wirtschaft-Politik (GWP): Postfach 300551, 51334 Leverkusen (Opladen); tel. (2171) 49070; fax (2171) 490711; e-mail lesbudpubl@aol.com; internet www.leske-budrich.de; quarterly; economics, politics, education; publ. by Leske Verlag + Budrich GmbH; Editors S. REINHARDT, H.-H. HARTWICH, B. SCHÄFERS, R. STURM.

Internationale Politik: Rauchstr. 17/18, 10787 Berlin; tel. (30) 25423146; fax (30) 25423167; e-mail ip@dgap.org; internet www .internationalepolitik.de; f. 1946; monthly; journal of the German Council on Foreign Relations; edns in English (*IP International Edition*, quarterly) and Russian (bimonthly); publ. by Frankfurts Societäts-Druckerei GmbH, Frankfurt a.M.; Exec. Editor SABINE ROSENBLADT; circ. 5,000.

Literarische Welt: Axel-Springer-Str. 65, 10888 Berlin; tel. (30) 259172916; fax (30) 259172939; e-mail literaturwelt@welt.de; f. 1971; weekly; literary supplement of *Die Welt*.

Merian Jahreszeiten Verlag: Harvestehuder Weg 42, 20149 Hamburg; tel. (40) 44188240; fax (40) 44188310; e-mail redaktion@ merian.de; internet www.merian.de; f. 1948; monthly; every issue deals with a country or a city; Chief Editor ANDREAS HALLASCHKA; circ. 150,000.

Merkur (Deutsche Zeitschrift für europäisches Denken): München; tel. (89) 29163111; fax (89) 29163114; internet www .merkur.de; f. 1947; monthly; literary, political; Editors KARL HEINZ BOHRER, KURT SCHEEL; circ. 6,000.

Neue Deutsche Literatur: Neue Promenade 6, 10178 Berlin; tel. (30) 28394238; fax (30) 28394100; e-mail ndl@aufbau-verlag.de; f. 1953; six a year; review of literature; Editor JÜRGEN ENGLER.

Neue Gesellschaft—Frankfurter Hefte: Hiroshimastr. 17, 10785 Berlin; tel. (30) 2693581920; fax (30) 26935855; e-mail norbert .seitz@fes.de; internet www.ngfh.de; f. 1946; monthly; cultural, political; Editors ANKE FUCHS, SIGMAR GABRIEL, KLAUS HARPPRECHT, JÜRGEN KOCKA, THOMAS MEYER; circ. 6,000.

Neue Rundschau: Hedderichstr. 114, 60596 Frankfurt a.M.; tel. (69) 60620; fax (69) 6062319; e-mail neuerundschau@fischerverlage .de; f. 1890; quarterly; literature and essays; Editors HANS-JÜRGEN BALMES, JÖRG BONG, HELMUT MAYER; circ. 3,000.

Sozialdemokrat Magazin: Am Michaelshof 8, 5300 Bonn 2; tel. (228) 361011; publ. by Vorwärts Verlag GmbH; circ. 834,599.

Der Spiegel: Brandstwiete 19/Ost-West-Str. 23, 20457 Hamburg; tel. (40) 30070; fax (40) 30072247; e-mail spiegel@spiegel.de; internet www.spiegel.de; f. 1947; weekly; political, general; Publr RUDOLF AUGSTEIN; Editor-in-Chief STEFAN AUST; circ. 1,050,000.

Universitas: Postfach 101061, 70009 Stuttgart; Birkenwaldstr. 44, 70191 Stuttgart; tel. (711) 25820; fax (711) 2582290; e-mail universitas@hirzel.de; internet www.hirzel.de/universitas; f. 1946; monthly; scientific, literary and philosophical; Editors Dr CHRISTIAN ROTTA, DIRK KATZSCHMANN; circ. 4,500.

VdK-Zeitung: Wurzerstr. 4A, 53175 Bonn; tel. (228) 820930; fax (228) 8209343; e-mail info@vdk.de; internet www.vdk.de; f. 1950; monthly; publ. by Sozialverband VdK Deutschland eV; Editors ULRICH LASCHET, SABINE KOHLS, MICHAEL PAUSDER, TANJA SCHÄFER, THOMAS A. SEEHUBER; circ. 1,300,000.

VdK-Zeitung, Bayern: Schellingstr. 31, 80799 München; tel. (89) 2117217; fax (89) 2117280; e-mail info@vdk.de; internet www .vdk-bayern.de; f. 1948; monthly; publ. by Sozialverband VdK Deutschland eV; Editor ALBRECHT ENGEL; circ. 1,100,000.

Popular

Anna: Arabellastr. 23, 81925 München; tel. (89) 92502772; fax (89) 92502745; f. 1974; publ. by Burda GmbH & Co KG; knitting and needlecrafts; Editor AENNE BURDA.

AUTO BILD: Brieffach 3910, 20350 Hamburg; tel. (40) 34700; fax (40) 345660; e-mail redaktion@autobild.de; internet www.autobild .de; f. 1986; weekly; publ. by Axel Springer Verlag AG; circ. 735,000.

Das Beste Readers Digest: Postfach 106020, 70049 Stuttgart; Augustenstr. 1, 70178 Stuttgart; tel. (711) 66020; fax (711) 6602547; e-mail verlag@dasbeste.de; internet www.dasbeste.de; magazines, general, serialized and condensed books, music and video programmes; Man. Dir WERNER NEUNZIG; circ. 1,100,000.

Bild der Frau: Axel-Springer-Pl. 1, 20355 Hamburg; tel. (40) 34700; f. 1983; publ. by Axel Springer Verlag AG; circ. 1,858,711.

Bild + Funk: München; tel. (89) 92502772; fax (89) 92502745; internet www.burda.de; publ. by Burda GmbH & Co KG; radio and television weekly; Editor GÜNTER VAN WAASEN; circ. 1,040,829.

Brigitte: Am Baumwell 11, 20459 Hamburg; tel. (40) 37030; fax (40) 37035679; internet www.brigitte.de; fortnightly; women's magazine; publ. by Gruner + Jahr AG; circ. 1,000,000.

Bunte: Arabellastr. 23, 81925 München; tel. (89) 92500; fax (89) 92503427; internet www.bunte.de; f. 1948; weekly family illustrated; publ. by Bunte Entertainment Verlag GmbH; circ. 780,238.

Burda Modemagazin: Am Destendamm 1, 77652 Offenburg; tel. (781) 840; fax (781) 843291; e-mail burdamoden@vab.burda.com; internet www.burdamode.de; f. 1949; monthly; fashion, beauty; publ. by Verlag Aenne Burda GmbH & Co KG; circ. 1,000,000.

Deutschland: Postfach 10081, 60008 Frankfurt a.M.; Frankenallee 71–81, 60628 Frankfurt a.M.; tel. (69) 75014272; fax (69) 75014502; e-mail vertrieb.deutschland@fsd.de; internet www .magazine-deutschland.de; six a year; edns in German, Arabic, Chinese, English, French, Hebrew, Hungarian, Japanese, Portuguese, Russian, Spanish, Turkish; Editor-in-Chief PETER HINTEREDER; circ. 400,000.

Elle: Arabellastr. 23, 81925 München; tel. (89) 92500; fax (89) 92503332; e-mail elle@elle.burda.com; internet www.elle.de; monthly; publ. by ELLE Verlag GmbH.

Eltern: Weihenstephanerstr. 7, 81673 München; tel. (89) 41520; fax (89) 4152666; e-mail lewicki.marie-luise@muc.guj.de; internet www .eltern.de; f. 1966; monthly; for parents; publ. by Gruner + Jahr AG & Co KG; Editor MARIE-LUISE LEWICKI; circ. 400,000.

Familie & Co: Kaiser-Joseph-Str. 263, 79098 Freiburg i.Br.; tel. (761) 705780; fax (761) 70578656; e-mail redaktion@familie.de; internet www.familie.de; f. 1996; monthly; publ. by Family Media GmbH & Co; circ. 215,785.

FF: Mauerstr. 86–88, 10117 Berlin; tel. (30) 231010; fax (30) 23101265; weekly; Editor ALFRED WAGNER; circ. 610,000.

Frau aktuell: Adlerstr. 22, Düsseldorf; tel. (211) 36660; fax (211) 3666231; e-mail frauaktuell@waso.de; f. 1965; Editor INGRID THEIS; circ. 450,000.

Frau im Spiegel: Griegstr. 75, 22763 Hamburg; tel. (40) 8830305; fax (40) 88303486; women's magazine; circ. 690,861.

Freundin: Arabellastr. 23, 81925 München; tel. (89) 92500; fax (89) 92503991; e-mail freundin@burda.com; internet www.freundin.com; f. 1948; fortnightly; for young women; publ. by Burda GmbH & Co KG; Chief Editor RENATE ROSENTHAL; circ. 517,280.

Funk Uhr: Axel-Springer-Pl. 1, 20355 Hamburg; tel. (40) 34726315; fax (40) 34722601; f. 1952; television weekly; publ. by Axel Springer Verlag AG; Editor JAN VON FRENDELL; circ. 1,000,000.

Für Dich: Karl-Liebknecht-Str. 29, 10178 Berlin; tel. (2) 2440; fax (2) 2443327; f. 1962; women's weekly; Editors Dr HANS EGGERT, PETER PANKAU; circ. 350,000.

Für Sie: Possmoorweg 5, 22301 Hamburg; tel. (40) 27172300; fax (40) 27172048; e-mail anzeigen@fuer-sie.de; internet www.fuer-sie .de; fortnightly; women's magazine; circ. 572,159.

Gong: Postfach 400748, 80707 München; GONG Verlag GmbH & Co KG, Münchner Str. 101/09, 85737 Ismaning; tel. (89) 272700; fax (89) 272707490; e-mail kontakt@gongverlag.de; internet www.gong .de; f. 1948; radio and TV weekly; Editor CARSTEN PFEFFERKORN.

Guter Rat: Superillu Verlag GmbH & Co KG, Zimmerstr. 28, 10969 Berlin; tel. (30) 23876600; fax (30) 23876395; e-mail redaktion@ guter-rat.de; f. 1945; monthly; consumer magazine; Editor-in-Chief WERNER ZEDLER; circ. 260,000.

Hörzu: Postfach 4110, Axel-Springer-Pl. 1, 20355 Hamburg; tel. (40) 34700; fax (40) 34722628; f. 1946; radio and television; publ. by Axel Springer Verlag AG; Editor MICHAEL HOHMANN; circ. 2,300,000.

Journal für die Frau: Axel-Springer-Pl. 1, 20350 Hamburg; tel. (40) 34700; fax (40) 34724201; e-mail chefredaktion@journal.de; f. 1978; fortnightly; women's magazine; publ. by Axel Springer Verlag AG; circ. 270,000.

Kicker-Sportmagazin: Badstr. 4–6, 90402 Nürnberg; tel. (911) 2160; e-mail info@kicker.de; internet www.kicker.de; f. 1920; two a week; illustrated sports magazine; publ. by Olympia Verlag; Man. Dir DIETRICH PUSCHMANN; circ. 238,986 (Mon.), 214,336 (Thurs.) (2004).

Marie Claire: Weihenstephaner Str. 7, 81673 München; tel. (89) 415200; fax (89) 4152636; e-mail marie.claire@muc.guj.de; publ. by Gruner + Jahr AG; Editor-in-Chief HANS-HERMANN SPRADO; circ. 163,388.

Meine Familie & ich: Arabellastr. 23, 81925 München; tel. (89) 92500; fax (89) 92503030; publ. by Burda GmbH & Co KG; circ. 620,000.

Neue Post: Postfach 2427, Burchardstr. 11, 20095 Hamburg; weekly; circ. 1,728,750.

Neue Revue: Postfach 2411, Ost-West-Str. 20, 20077 Hamburg; tel. (40) 30190; fax (40) 30194401; e-mail neue-revue@hbv.de; f. 1946; illustrated weekly; Editor-in-Chief PETER BARTEL; circ. 1,121,184.

Petra: Jahreszeiten Verlag, Possmoorweg 5, 22301 Hamburg; tel. (40) 27173009; fax (40) 27173020; e-mail redaktion@petra.de; internet www.petra.de; monthly; circ. 253,744.

Praline: Hammerbrookstr. 5, 20097 Hamburg; fax (40) 24870190; weekly; women's magazine; circ. 569,300.

Schöner Wohnen: Am Baumwall 11, 20459 Hamburg; tel. (40) 37032701; monthly; homes and gardens; publ. by Gruner + Jahr AG; Editor ANGELIKA JAHR; circ. 327,000.

7 Tage: Postfach 2071, 76490 Baden-Baden; Rotweg 8, 76532 Baden-Baden; tel. (7221) 3501501; fax (7221) 3501599; e-mail 7tage@klambt.de; internet www.klambt.de; f. 1843; weekly; Chief Editor PETER VIKTOR KULIG; circ. 480,000.

Sport Bild: Axel-Springer-Pl. 1, 20350 Hamburg; tel. (40) 34700; fax (40) 34722085; e-mail sportbild@asv.de; internet www.sportbild .de; f. 1988; weekly; publ. by Axel Springer Verlag AG; circ. 522,717.

Stern: 20444 Hamburg; tel. (40) 37030; fax (40) 37035631; e-mail stern@stern.de; internet www.stern.de; illustrated weekly; publ. by Gruner + Jahr AG & Co KG; Editors-in-Chief THOMAS OSTERKORN, ANDREAS PETZOLD; circ. 1,102,075.

TV Hören + Sehen: Burchardstr. 11, 20095 Hamburg; tel. (40) 30194001; fax (40) 30194081; f. 1962; weekly; Chief Editor MARION HORN; circ. 2,936,670.

TVneu: Axel-Springer-Pl. 1, 20355 Hamburg; tel. (40) 34700; fax (40) 345811; publ. by Axel Springer Verlag AG; circ. 917,293.

Wochenend: Burchardstr. 11, 20095 Hamburg; tel. (40) 30190; fax (40) 30194081; f. 1948; weekly; Editor GERD ROHLOF; circ. 668,278.

Religion and Philosophy

Christ in der Gegenwart: Hermann-Herder-Str. 4, 79104 Freiburg i. Br.; tel. (761) 2717276; fax (761) 2717243; e-mail cig@herder .de; internet www.christ-in-der-gegenwart.de; f. 1948; weekly; Editor JOHANNES RÖSER; circ. 36,000.

Der Dom: Karl-Schurz-Str. 26, 33100 Paderborn; tel. (5251) 1530; fax (5251) 153104; e-mail karl.wegner@bonifatius.de; internet www .derdom.org; f. 1946; weekly; Catholic; publ. by Bonifatius GmbH, Druck-Buch-Verlag; circ. 65,000.

Europa Magazin: Postfach 104864, Landhausstr. 82, 70190 Stuttgart; tel. (711) 285500; fax (711) 2855083; e-mail verlag@ europamagazin.de; f. 1949; six a year; publ. by Verlag Axel B. Trunkel.

Evangelischer Digest: Postfach 104864, Landhausstr. 82, 70190 Stuttgart; tel. (711) 285500; fax (711) 2855083; e-mail verlag@ trunkel.de; internet www.trunkel.de; f. 1958; monthly; publ. by Verlag Axel B. Trunkel; circ. 9,300.

Katholischer Digest: Postfach 104864, Landhausstr. 82, 70190 Stuttgart; tel. (711) 285500; fax (711) 2855083; e-mail verlag@ trunkel.de; internet www.trunkel.de; f. 1949; monthly; publ. by Verlag Axel B. Trunkel; circ. 28,900.

Katholisches Sonntagsblatt: Senefelderstr. 12, 73760 Ostfildern; tel. (711) 44060; fax (711) 4406101; e-mail ks@schwabenverlag.de; internet www.schwabenverlag.de; f. 1848; weekly; publ. by Schwabenverlag AG; circ. 71,500.

Katholische Sonntagszeitung für Deutschland: Verlag Christliche Familie GmbH, Komödienstr. 48, 50667 Köln; tel. (821) 502420; fax (821) 5024241; e-mail voss@suv.de; internet www .katolische-sonntagszeitung.de; f. 1885; weekly; Publr Dr DIRK HERMANN VOSS; Chief Editor Dr GERDA RÖDER.

Die Kirche: Berlin; tel. (30) 28303922; fax (30) 2829321; f. 1945; Protestant weekly; Editors-in-Chief GERHARD THOMAS, LUTZ BORGMANN; circ. 35,000.

Kirche und Leben: Postfach 4320, 48024 Münster; Breul 27, 48143 Münster; tel. (251) 48390; fax (251) 4839122; e-mail k-und-l@ muenster.de; internet www.kirche-und-leben.muenster.de; f. 1945; weekly; Catholic; Chief Editor Dr HANS-JOSEF JOEST; circ. 160,000.

Kirchenzeitung für das Erzbistum Köln: Postfach 102041, 50460 Köln; Ursulapl. 1, 50668 Köln; tel. (221) 1619131; fax (221) 1619216; weekly; Chief Editor Mgr ERICH LÄUFER; circ. 120,000.

Philosophisches Jahrbuch: Ludwig-Maximilians-Universität, Geschwister-Scholl-Pl. 1, 80539 München; f. 1893; two a year.

Der Sonntagsbrief: Postfach 104864, Landhausstr. 82, 70190 Stuttgart; tel. (711) 285500; fax (711) 2855083; e-mail verlag@ trunkel.de; internet www.trunkel.de; f. 1974; monthly; publ. by Verlag Axel B. Trunkel; circ. 36,000.

Standpunkt: Berlin; tel. (2) 6350915; f. 1973; Protestant monthly; circ. 3,000.

Der Weg: Postfach 102253, 40013 Düsseldorf; tel. (211) 915110; e-mail wegredaktion@wegredaktion.de; weekly; Protestant; Editor ANDREAS KRZOK; circ. 50,000.

Weltbild: 86131 Augsburg; tel. (821) 70048350; fax (821) 70048349; f. 2001; fortnightly; Catholic; Editor ALBERT HERCHENBACH; circ. 270,000.

Science and Medicine

Angewandte Chemie: Postfach 101161, 69451 Weinheim; tel. (6201) 606315; fax (6201) 602328; e-mail angewandte@wiley-vch.de; internet www.angewandte.de; f. 1888; applied chemistry; weekly, 48 a year; circ. 3,800; international edition in English, f. 1962; circ. 3,900.

Ärztliche Praxis: Gabrielenstr. 9, 80636 München; tel. (89) 89817404; fax (89) 89817400; e-mail khp@rbi.de; internet www .aerztlichepraxis.de; two a week; publ. by Reed Business Information GmbH; Editor-in-Chief KARL-HEINZ PATZER; circ. 60,000.

Berichte der Bunsen-Gesellschaft für physikalische Chemie: VCH Verlagsgesellschaft mbH, Postfach 101161, Pappelallee 3, 69451 Weinheim/Bergstr.; tel. (6201) 6060; f. 1894; monthly; Editors R. AHLRICHS, W. FREYLAND, M. KAPPES, P. C. SCHMIDT; circ. 2,300.

Chemie-Ingenieur-Technik: Postfach 101161, 69451 Weinheim; tel. (6201) 606520; fax (6201) 606500; e-mail cit@wiley-vch.de; f. 1928; monthly; Editor B. BOECK; circ. 7,807.

Der Chirurg: Kirschnerstr. 1 (INF 110), 69120 Heidelberg; tel. (6221) 402813; fax (6221) 402014; f. 1928; surgery; monthly; Editor Prof. Dr Ch. HERFARTH; circ. 7,650.

Deutsche Apotheker Zeitung: Postfach 101061, 70009 Stuttgart; Birkenwaldstr. 44, 70191 Stuttgart; tel. (711) 2582238; fax (711) 2582291; e-mail daz@deutscher-apotheker-verlag.de; internet www .deutscher-apotheker-verlag.de; f. 1861; weekly; Editor PETER DITZEL; circ. 34,000.

Deutsche Medizinische Wochenschrift: Rüdigerstr. 14, 70469 Stuttgart; tel. (711) 8931232; fax (711) 8931235; e-mail dmw@ thieme.de; internet www.thieme.de/dmw; f. 1875; weekly; Editor-in-Chief M. MIDDEKE; circ. 30,000.

Deutsche Zahnärztliche Zeitschrift: Deutscher Ärzte-Verlag, Dieselstr. 2, 50859 Köln; tel. (2234) 7011242; fax (2234) 7011515; e-mail dey@aerzteverlag.de; internet www.zahnheilkunde.de; f. 1945; monthly; dental medicine; Editors Prof. Dr GEURTSEN, Prof. Dr TH. KERSCHBAUM, Dr G. MASCHINSKI; circ. 15,000.

Elektro Automation: Ernst-Mey-Str. 8, 70771 Leinfelden-Echterdingen; tel. (711) 7594279; fax (711) 7594221; e-mail ea.redaktion@ konradin.de; internet www.ea-online.de; f. 1948; monthly; Editor-in-Chief STEFAN ZIEGLER; circ. 21,100.

Europa Chemie: Frankfurt a.M.; tel. (69) 25561516; fax (69) 239564; e-mail europa-chemie@metronet.de; f. 1949; three a month; industrial chemistry, the environment and economics; Editor-in-Chief Dr G. SCHRIMPF; circ. 2,800.

Geographische Rundschau: Georg-Westermann-Allee 66, 38104 Braunschweig; tel. (531) 708385; fax (531) 708329; e-mail gr@ westermann.de; internet www.geographischerunschau.de; f. 1949; monthly; Man. Editor REINER JUENGST; circ. 12,000.

Geologische Rundschau: Geologische Vereinigung e.V., Vulkanstr. 23, 56743 Mendig; tel. (2652) 989360; fax (2652) 989361; e-mail geol.ver@t-online.de; internet www.g-v.de; f. 1910; six a year; general, geological; Pres. Prof. Dr GEROLD WEFER; circ. 1,800.

Handchirurgie, Mikrochirurgie, Plastische Chirurgie: Postfach 300504, 70445 Stuttgart; Rüdigerstr. 14, 70469 Stuttgart; tel. (711) 89310; fax (711) 8931453; six a year; Editors Prof. Dr D. BUCK-GRAMCKO, Prof. Dr W. SCHNEIDER.

Journal of Neurology: Steinkopff Verlag, Poststr. 9, 64293 Darmstadt; tel. (6151) 828990; fax (6151) 8289940; e-mail tschech .steinkopff@springer.de; internet www.steinkopff.springer.de; f. 1891; official journal of the European Neurological Society; Editors-in-Chief T. BRANDT, D. H. MILLER.

Mund-, Kiefer- und Gesichtschirurgie: Glückstr. 11, 91054 Erlangen; tel. (9131) 8533601; fax (9131) 8536228; e-mail friedrich .neukam@mkg.imed.uni-erlangen.de; internet www.mkg .uni-erlangen.de; seven a year; oral and maxillofacial surgery and oral pathology; Editor Prof. Dr FRIEDRICH W. NEUKAM.

Medizinische Klinik: Neumarkter Str. 43, 81673 München; tel. (89) 532920; fax (89) 53292100; e-mail verlag@urban-vogel.de; internet www.urban-vogel.de; f. 1904; monthly; Editor ANNA-MARIA WORSCH; circ. 14,000.

Nachrichten aus der Chemie: Postfach 900440, 60444 Frankfurt a.M.; tel. (69) 7917462; fax (69) 7917463; e-mail nachrichten@gdch .de; internet www.gdch.de/nch; f. 1953; monthly; journal of the German Chemical Society; Editor-in-Chief Dr ERNST GUGGOLZ; circ. 27,000.

Natur + Kosmos: Ernst-May-Str. 8, 70771 Leinfelden-Echterdingen; tel. (711) 21910; fax (711) 2191199; f. 1904; monthly; popular nature journal; Editor Dr RAINER KÖTHE; circ. 80,000.

Naturwissenschaftliche Rundschau: Postfach 101061, 70009 Stuttgart; Birkenwaldstr. 44, 70191 Stuttgart; tel. (711) 2582295; fax (711) 2582283; e-mail nr@wissenschaftliche-verlagsgesellschaft .de; internet www.naturwissenschaftliche-rundschau.de; f. 1948; monthly; scientific; Editor KLAUS REHFELD; circ. 5,000.

Planta Medica: Postfach 301120, 70451 Stuttgart; Georg Thieme Verlag, Rüdigerstr. 14, 70469 Stuttgart; tel. (711) 89310; fax (711)

8931298; e-mail leser.service@thieme.de; f. 1952; 12 a year; journal of the Society of Medicinal Plant Research; Editor Prof. Dr ADOLF NAHRSTEDT.

rfe: Am Friedrichshain 22, 10407 Berlin; tel. (30) 42151313; fax (30) 42151208; e-mail rfe.redaktion@hussberlin.de; internet www .rfe-online.de; f. 1952; monthly; technology and marketing of consumer goods electronics, digital imaging, multimedia, audio, video, broadcasting, TV; circ. 30,000.

Zahnärztliche Praxis: München-Gräfelfing; tel. (89) 898170; fax (89) 853799; dental medicine; monthly; circ. 16,500.

Zeitschrift für Allgemeinmedizin: Postfach 301120, 70451 Stuttgart; Rüdigerstr. 14, 70469 Stuttgart; tel. (711) 89310; fax (711) 8931706; e-mail volker.niem@thieme.de; internet www.thieme.de/zfa; f. 1924; monthly; general and family medicine; publ. by Georg Thieme Verlag KG, Stuttgart; Editors Prof. Dr M. KOCHEN, Prof. Dr H.-H. ABHOLZ, Prof. Dr W. NIEBLING; circ. 4,000.

Zeitschrift für Klinische Psychologie, Psychiatrie u. Psychotherapie: Postfach 2540, Jühenpl. am Rathaus, 33055 Paderborn; f. 1952; quarterly; Editor Prof. Dr F. PETERMANN.

Zeitschrift für Metallkunde: Heisenbergstr. 3, 70569 Stuttgart; tel. (711) 6893525; fax (711) 6893653; e-mail ruehle@mf.mpg.de; f. 1911; monthly; materials research; Editors M. RÜHLE, G. PETZOW, P. P. SCHEPP.

Zeitschrift für Zahnärztliche Implantologie: Deutscher Zahnärzte-Verlag, Dieselstr. 2, 50859 Köln; tel. (2234) 7011242; fax (2234) 7011515; e-mail dey@aerzteverlag.de; internet www .zahnheilkunde.de; f. 1984; quarterly; dental medicine; Editors Prof. Dr W. WAGNER, Dr S. SCHMIDINGER; circ. 6,000.

Zentralblatt für Neurochirurgie: Friedrich-Wilhelms Universität, Sigmund-Freud-Str. 25, 53127 Bonn; tel. (228) 2876501; fax (228) 2876573; e-mail zblatt.nch@ukb.uni-bonn.de; f. 1936; four a year; neuro-surgery, spine surgery, traumatology; Editor Prof. Dr J. SCHRAMM; circ. 1,200.

NEWS AGENCIES

DDP Nachrichtenagentur GmbH: Friedrichstr. 108, 10117 Berlin; tel. (30) 2312210; fax (30) 23122170; e-mail redaktion@ddp .de; internet www.ddp.de; f. 1946; fmrly official news agency of the GDR; maintains 32 branch offices in Germany; provides a daily news service and features in German; Man. Dirs LUTZ SCHUMACHER, ALEXANDER ROP.

Deutsche Presse-Agentur GmbH (dpa): Mittelweg 38, 20148 Hamburg; tel. (40) 41130; fax (40) 41132219; e-mail info@dpa.com; internet www.dpa.de; f. 1949; supplies all the daily newspapers, broadcasting stations and more than 1,000 further subscribers throughout Germany with its international, national and regional text, photo, audio, graphics and online services; English, Spanish, Arabic and German language news is also transmitted via direct satellite and the internet to press agencies, newspapers, radio and television stations, online services and non-media clients in more than 100 countries; Dir-Gen. Dr WALTER RICHTBERG; Editor-in-Chief Dr WILM HERLYN.

VWD: Niederurseler Allee 8–10, 65760 Eschborn; tel. (6196) 4050; fax (6196) 405303; e-mail feedback@vwd.de; internet www.vwd.de; f. 1949; economic and financial news; Man. Dirs EDMUND J. KEFERSTEIN, SPENCER BOSSE.

Foreign Bureaux

Agence France-Presse (AFP): Friedrichstr. 108–109, 10117 Berlin; tel. (30) 30876110; fax (30) 30876270; e-mail post@afp.de; internet www.afp.de; Mans N. C. WORTMANN, P. FEUILLY.

Agencia EFE (Spain): Berlin; Bureau Chief GUILLERMO DÍAZ.

Agenzia Nazionale Stampa Associata (ANSA) (Italy): Berlin; tel. (30) 726262500; fax (30) 726262525; Bureau Chief FLAMINIA BUSSOTTI.

Anadolu Ajansi (Turkey): Presshouse 5217, Schbauerdamm 40, 10117 Berlin; tel. (30) 22620547; fax (30) 22620546; e-mail berlin@ anadoluajansi.com.tr.

Associated Press GmbH (AP) (USA): Moselstr. 27, Frankfurt a.M.; tel. (69) 272300; fax (69) 251289; also in Hamburg, Stuttgart, Berlin, München; Man. STEPHEN H. MILLER.

Česká tisková kancelář (ČTK) (Czech Republic): Lesser-Ury-Weg 3, 10557 Berlin; f. 1918.

Informatsionnoye Telegrafnoye Agentstvo Rossii-Telegrafnoye Agentstvo Suverennykh Stran (ITAR-TASS) (Russia): Berlin.

Inter Press Service (IPS) (Italy): Potsdamer Platz 11 10785 Berlin; tel. (30) 25894597; fax (30) 25894100; e-mail rjaura@ips.org; internet www.ips.org; Bureau Chief RAMESH JAURA.

Jiji Tsushin (Japan): Mittelweg 38, 20148 Hamburg; tel. (40) 445553; fax (40) 456849.

Kyodo Tsushin (Japan): Bonn; tel. (228) 225543; fax (228) 222198; Chief Correspondent KAKUYA OGATA.

Magyar Távirati Iroda (MTI) (Hungary): Georg Schroeder Str. 9C, 13591 Berlin; tel. (30) 36704844; fax (30) 36704845; Correspondent FERENC KOVÁCS.

Reuters (UK): Friedrich-Ebert-Anlage 49, 60327 Frankfurt a.M.; tel. (69) 75651000; fax (69) 75651515; internet www.reuters.de.

United Press International (UPI) (USA): Bonn; tel. (228) 263787; Bureau Man. and Chief Correspondent PETER G. BILD.

Xinhua (New China) News Agency (People's Republic of China): Lyngsbergstr. 33, 5300 Bonn 2; tel. (228) 331845; fax (228) 331247; Chief Correspondent HU XUDONG.

RIA—Novosti (Russia) is also represented.

PRESS AND JOURNALISTS' ASSOCIATIONS

Bundesverband Deutscher Zeitungsverleger eV (German Newspaper Publishers' Association): Markgrafenstr. 15, 10969 Berlin; tel. (30) 7262980; fax (30) 726298299; e-mail bdzv@bdzv.de; internet www.bdzv.de; 11 affiliated Land Asscns; Pres. HELMUT HEINEN; Chief Sec. Dr VOLKER SCHULZE.

Deutscher Journalisten-Verband (German Journalists' Association): Bennauerstr. 60, 53115 Bonn; tel. (228) 201720; fax (228) 2017233; e-mail djv@djv.de; internet www.djv.de; Chair. Prof. Dr SIGFRIED WEISCHENBERG; Man. Dir HUBERT ENGEROFF; 16 Land Asscns.

Verband Deutscher Zeitschriftenverleger eV (VDZ) (Association of German Magazine Publishers): Markgrafenstr. 15, 10969 Berlin; tel. (30) 726298101; fax (30) 7262898103; e-mail info@vdz.de; internet www.vdz.de; seven affiliated Land Asscns; Pres. Dr HUBERT BURDA; Man. Dir WOLFGANG FÜRSTNER.

Verein der Ausländischen Presse eV (VAP) (Foreign Press Association): Pressehaus/1306, Schiffbauerdamm 40, 10117 Berlin; tel. (30) 22489547; fax (30) 22489548; e-mail info@vap-berlin.de; internet www.vap-berlin.de; f. 1951; Chair. Dr ALEXANDRA FÖDERL-SCHMID.

Publishers

The following is a selection of the most prominent German publishing firms:

ADAC Verlag GmbH: Am Westpark 8, 81373 München; tel. (89) 76760; fax (89) 76764621; e-mail bettina.volk@adac.de; internet www.adac.de; f. 1958; guidebooks, legal brochures, maps, magazines ADAC-Motorwelt, Deutsches Autorecht; Man. Dir Dr RALF UEDING.

Ariston Verlag GmbH & Co KG: München; tel. (89) 7241034; fax (89) 7241718; f. 1964; medicine, psychology; Man. Dir FRANK AUERBACH.

Aufbau Verlagsgruppe GmbH: Neue Promenade 6, 10178 Berlin; tel. (30) 283940; fax (30) 28394100; e-mail info@aufbau-verlag.de; f. 1945; fiction, non-fiction, classical literature; Dirs RENÉ STRIEN, JENS MARQUARDT.

J. P. Bachem Verlag GmbH: Ursulapl. 1, 50668 Köln; tel. (221) 16190; fax (221) 1619159; e-mail info@bachem-verlag.de; internet www.bachem-verlag.de; f. 1818; history, dialect, art history, architecture, sociology and walking/cycling tours of the Cologne and Rhine area; church and society; Dirs LAMBERT BACHEM, CLAUS BACHEM.

Bauverlag BV GmbH: Avenwedderstr. 55, 33311 Gütersloh; tel. (5241) 802119; fax (5241) 809582; e-mail ulrike.mattern@ springer-sbm.com; internet www.bauverlag.de; f. 1929; civil engineering, architecture, environment, energy, etc.; Dir STEFAN RÜHLING.

Verlag C. H. Beck oHg: Postfach 400340, 80703 München, Wilhelmstr. 9, 80801 München; tel. (89) 381890; fax (89) 38189398; e-mail info@beck.de; internet www.beck.de; f. 1763; law, science, theology, archaeology, philosophy, philology, history, politics, art, literature; Dirs Dr HANS DIETER BECK, WOLFGANG BECK.

Bibliographisches Institut und F. A. Brockhaus GmbH: Postfach 100311, 68167 Dudenstr. 6, 68003 Mannheim; tel. (621) 390101; fax (621) 3901391; f. 1805; encyclopaedias, dictionaries, travel, natural sciences, memoirs, archaeology; Dirs HUBERTUS BROCKHAUS, CLAUS GREUNER, Dr MICHAEL WEGNER.

BLV Buchverlag GmbH & Co KG: Lothstr. 29, 80797 München; tel. (89) 127050; fax (89) 12705545; e-mail blv-verlag@blv.de; internet www.blv.de; f. 1946; gardening, nature, sports, fitness, equestrian, hunting, fishing, travel, food and drink, agriculture; Man. Dirs HARTWIG SCHNEIDER, HANS MÜLLER.

Breitkopf & Härtel: Postfach 1707, Walkmühlstr. 52, 65195 Wiesbaden; tel. (611) 450080; fax (611) 4500859; e-mail info@breitkopf

.com; internet www.breitkopf.com; f. 1719; music and music books; Dirs LIESELOTTE SIEVERS, GOTTFRIED MÖCKEL.

Verlag Bruckmann München: Innsbrucker Ring 15, 81673 München; tel. (89) 1306990; fax (89) 13069930; f. 1858; travel guides, illustrated travel books, video cassettes; Man. Dir Dr JÖRG D. STIEBNER.

Bund-Verlag GmbH: Postfach, 60424 Frankfurt; Heddernheimer Landstr. 144, 60439 Frankfurt; tel. (69) 7950100; fax (69) 79501010; e-mail kontakt@bund-verlag.de; internet www.bund-verlag.de; f. 1947; labour and social law; Man. Dirs CHRISTIAN POULSEN, NORBERT SCHAEPE.

Verlag Georg D. W. Callwey GmbH & Co: Streitfeldstr. 35, 81673 München; tel. (89) 4360050; fax (89) 436005113; e-mail buch@callwey.de; internet www.callwey.de; f. 1884; architecture, gardens, crafts; Man. Dir AMOS KOTTE.

Carlsen Verlag GmbH: Postfach 500380, 22703 Hamburg; Völckersstr. 14–20, 22765 Hamburg; tel. (40) 398040; fax (40) 39804390; e-mail info@carlsen.de; internet www.carlsen.de; f. 1953; children's and comic books; Dirs KLAUS HUMANN, KLAUS KÄMPFE-BURGHARDT.

Cornelsen Verlag GmbH & Co: Mecklenburgische Str. 53, 14197 Berlin; tel. (30) 897850; fax (30) 89786299; e-mail c-mail@cornelsen.com; internet www.cornelsen.com; f. 1946; school textbooks, educational software; Man. Dirs HANS-JÖRG DÜLLEMANN, ALFRED GRÜNER, WOLF-RÜDGER FELDMANN, MARTIN HÜPPE, WALTER FUNKEN.

Delius Klasing Verlag: Siekerwall 21, 33602 Bielefeld; tel. (521) 5590; fax (521) 559113; e-mail info@delius-klasing.de; internet www.delius-klasing.de; f. 1911; yachting, motor boats, surfing, mountain biking, race biking, basketball, motor cars; Dir KONRAD DELIUS.

Deutsche Verlags-Anstalt GmbH: Postfach 106012, 70049 Stuttgart; Neckarstr. 121, 70190 Stuttgart; tel. (711) 26310; fax (711) 2631292; e-mail info@dva.de; f. 1831; general; CEO JÜRGEN HORBACH.

Deutscher Taschenbuch Verlag GmbH & Co KG (DTV): Postfach 400422, 80704 München; Friedrichstr. 1A, 80801 München; tel. (89) 381670; fax (89) 346428; e-mail verlag@dtv.de; internet www.dtv.de; f. 1961; general fiction, history, music, reference, children, natural and social science, medicine, textbooks; Man. Dirs WOLFGANG BALK, MARKUS ANGST.

Verlag Moritz Diesterweg: Hedderichstr. 108–110, 60596 Frankfurt a.M.; tel. (69) 420810; fax (69) 42081200; internet www.diesterweg.de; f. 1860; text books, languages, social sciences, sciences, pedagogics; Dirs RALF MEIER, ULRICH POKERN.

DuMont Monte GmbH & Co KG: Amsterdamer Str. 192, 50735 Köln; tel. (221) 2241831; fax (221) 2241878; e-mail montevertrieb@dumontverlag.de; internet www.dumontverlag.de; f. 1956; art, garden, cookery, calendars; Publr HELENA BOMMETSHEIM.

Egmont Pestalozzi Verlag GmbH: Schleissheimer Str. 267, 80809 München; tel. (89) 358116; fax (89) 35811869; internet www.pestalozzi-verlag.de; f. 1844; children's books; Man. Dirs REHNÉ HERZIG, FRANK KNAU.

Egmont vgs Verlagsgesellschaft mbH: Gertrudenstr. 30–36, 50667 Köln; tel. (221) 208110; fax (221) 2081166; e-mail info@vgs.de; internet www.vgs.de; f. 1970; fiction, hobbies, natural sciences, culture, popular culture, TV, history; Dirs Dr MICHAEL SCHWEINS, BERNWARD MALAKA.

Eichborn Verlag: Kaiserstr. 66, 60329 Frankfurt a.M. 1; tel. (69) 2560030; fax (69) 25600330; f. 1980; literature, non-fiction, historical science, humour, cartoons; Man. Dir Dr MATTHIAS KIERZEK.

Elsevier GmbH: Postfach 100537, 07705 Jena; Löbdergraben 14A, 07745 Jena; tel. (3641) 6263; fax (3641) 626500; e-mail journals@elsevier.com; internet www.elsevier.de/journals; f. 1878; biological science, medical science; Dir BERND ROLLE.

Europaverlag: Neuer Wall 10, 20354 München; tel. (40) 3554340; fax (40) 35543466; e-mail info@europaverlag.de; internet www.europaverlag.de; fiction, non-fiction, poetry, biography and current events; Dirs GISELA ANNA STÜMPEL, WOLFGANG WEIDMANN.

Albania: Friedrichstr. 231, 10363 Berlin; tel. (30) 2593040; fax (30) 25931890; e-mail kanzlei@botschaft-albanien.de; Ambassador GAZMEND TURDIU.

Falken-Verlag GmbH: Schöne Aussicht 21, 65527 Niedernhausen; tel. (6127) 7020; fax (6127) 702133; internet www.falken.de; f. 1923; health, cooking, management, business; Man. Dir Dr HANS-ULRICH VON FREYBERG.

S. Fischer Verlag GmbH: Postfach 700355, 60553 Frankfurt a.M.; Hedderichstr. 114, 60596 Frankfurt a.M.; tel. (69) 60620; fax (69) 6062319; e-mail info@fischerverlage.de; internet www.fischerverlage.de; f. 1886; general, paperbacks; Publrs PETER LOHMANN, Dr JÖRG BORG; Man. Dirs LOTHAR KLEINER, JOERG BONG, PETER LOHMANN.

Franzis' Verlag GmbH: Gruber Str. 46, 85586 Poing; tel. (8121) 950; fax (8121) 951696; internet www.franzis.de; f. 1924; Gen. Man. Dr RÜDIGER HENNIGS.

Gräfe und Unzer Verlag GmbH: Grillparzerstr. 12, 81675 München; tel. (89) 41981140; fax (89) 41981406; internet www.graefe-und-unzer.de; f. 1722; cookery and wine, fitness, health and wellbeing, living and learning, gardening, nature, pets; Man. Dirs URBAN MEISTER, GEORG KESSLER, GÜNTER KOPIETZ.

Walter de Gruyter GmbH & Co KG Verlag: Postfach 303421, 10728 Berlin; Genthiner Str. 13, 10785 Berlin; tel. (30) 260050; fax (30) 26005251; internet www.degruyter.de; f. 1919; humanities and theology, law, science, medicine, mathematics, economics, general; Man. Dirs REINHOLD TOKAR, Dr HANS-ROBERT CRAM.

Hallwag Verlag GmbH: Grillparzerstr. 12, 81675 München; tel. (89) 419810; fax (89) 41981492; internet www.hallwag.de; maps, travel guides, wine, other reference.

Carl Hanser Verlag: Kolbergerstr. 22, 81679 München; tel. (89) 998300; fax (89) 984809; e-mail info@hanser.de; internet www.hanser.de; f. 1928; modern literature, plastics, technology, chemistry, science, economics, computers, children's books; Man. Dirs WOLFGANG BEISLER, STEPHAN D. JOSS, MICHAEL KRÜGER.

Harenberg Kommunikation Verlags- und Mediengesellschaft mbH & Co KG: Postfach 101852, 44018 Dortmund; Königswall 21, 44137 Dortmund; tel. (231) 90560; fax (231) 9056110; e-mail post@harenberg.de; internet www.harenberg.de; f. 1973; almanacs, encyclopaedias, calendars, periodicals; Man. Dir BODO HARENBERG.

Rudolf Haufe Verlag GmbH & Co KG: Hindenburgstr. 64, 79102 Freiburg i. Br.; tel. (761) 36830; fax (761) 3683195; e-mail online@haufe.de; internet haufe.de; f. 1934; business, law, taxation, information management, finance, social science; Man. Dirs UWE RENALD MÜLLER, MARTIN LAQUA, HELMUTH HOPFNER.

Verlag Herder GmbH: Hermann-Herder-Str. 4; 79104 Freiburg i. Br.; tel. (761) 27170; fax (761) 2717520; e-mail info@herder.de; internet www.herder.de; f. 1801; religion, philosophy, psychology, history, education, art, encyclopaedias, children's books, gift books, periodicals; Proprs Dr HERMANN HERDER, MANUEL GREGOR HERDER.

Wilhelm Heyne Verlag: Paul-Heyse-Str. 28, 80336 München; tel. (89) 51480; fax (89) 51482229; e-mail verlag@heyne.de; internet www.heyne.de; f. 1934; fiction, biography, history, cinema, etc.; Publr ULRICH GENZLER.

Hoffmann und Campe Verlag: Postfach 1304445, 20139 Hamburg; Harvestehuder Weg 42, 20149 Hamburg; tel. (40) 441880; fax (40) 44188202; e-mail presse@hoca.de; internet www.hoffmann-und-campe.de; f. 1781; biography, fiction, history, economics, science; Man. Dirs GÜNTER BEG, MARKUS GLOSE.

Dr Alfred Hüthig Verlag GmbH: Im Weiher 10, 6900 Heidelberg; tel. (6221) 4890; fax (6221) 489279; f. 1925; chemistry, chemical engineering, metallurgy, dentistry, etc.

Axel Juncker Verlag GmbH: Postfach 401120, 80711 München; Mies-van-der-Rohe-Str. 1, 80807 München; tel. (89) 360960; fax (89) 36096222; e-mail redaktion@axel-juncker.de; internet www.langenscheidt.de; f. 1902; dictionaries, language courses, reference; Man. Dirs KARL ERNST TIELEBIER-LANGENSCHEIDT, ANDREAS LANGENSCHEIDT.

S. Karger GmbH: Lörracherstr. 16A, 79115 Freiburg i. Br.; tel. (761) 452070; fax (761) 4520714; f. 1890; medicine, psychology, natural science; Man. Dir S. KARGER.

Verlag Kiepenheuer & Witsch & Co: Rondorferstr. 5, 50968 Köln 51; tel. (221) 376850; fax (221) 388595; e-mail umolitor@kiwi-koeln.de; internet www.kiwi-koeln.de; f. 1948; general fiction, biography, history, sociology, politics; Man. Dir Dr REINHOLD NEVEN DU MONT.

Ernst Klett Verlag GmbH: Postfach 106016, 70049 Stuttgart; Rotebühlstr. 77, 70178 Stuttgart; tel. (711) 66720; fax (711) 6672800; internet www.klett.de; f. 1844; secondary school and university textbooks (especially German as a foreign language), dictionaries, atlases, teaching aids; Dirs MICHAEL KLETT, ROLAND KLETT, Dr THOMAS KLETT.

Verlag W. Kohlhammer GmbH: Hessbrühlstr. 69, 70565 Stuttgart; tel. (711) 78630; fax (711) 78638263; e-mail info@kohlhammer.de; internet www.kohlhammer.de; f. 1866; periodicals, general textbooks; Man. Dirs Dr JÜRGEN GUTBROD, LEOPOLD FREIHERR VON UND ZU WEILER.

Kösel-Verlag GmbH & Co: Flüggenstr. 2, 80639 München; tel. (89) 178010; fax (89) 17801111; e-mail info@koesel.de; internet www.koesel.de; f. 1593; philosophy, religion, psychology, spirituality, family and education; Dir JUERGEN HORBACH.

Kreuz Verlag GmbH: Postfach 800669; Breitwiesenstr. 30, 70565 Stuttgart; tel. (711) 788030; fax (711) 7880310; f. 1983; theology, psychology, pedagogics; Man. Dir Dr SABINE SCHUBERT.

Verlag der Kunst GmbH: Rosa-Menzer-Str. 12, 01309 Dresden; tel. (351) 3100052; fax (351) 3105245; e-mail verlag-der-kunst.dd@t-online.de; internet www.txt.de/vdk; f. 1952; art books and reproductions; Dir ROGER N. GREENE.

Peter Lang GmbH—Europäischer Verlag der Wissenschaften: Postfach 940225, 60460 Frankfurt a.M.; Eschborner Landstr. 42–50, 60489 Frankfurt a.M.; tel. (69) 7807050; fax (69) 78070550; e-mail zentrale.frankfurt@peterlang.com; internet www.peterlang.de; sociology, politics, communications, linguistics, science of law, literature, theology, economics.

Langenscheidt-Verlag: Postfach 401120, 80711 München; Mies-van-der-Rohe Str. 1, 80807 München; tel. (89) 360960; fax (89) 36096222; e-mail mail@langenscheidt.de; internet www.langenscheidt.de; f. 1856; foreign languages, German for foreigners, dictionaries, textbooks, language guides, CDs, CD-ROMs, cassettes, software, electronic dictionaries; Man. Dirs KARL ERNST TIELEBIER-LANGENSCHEIDT, ANDREAS LANGENSCHEIDT.

Verlagsgruppe Lübbe GmbH & Co KG: Scheidtbachstr. 23–31, 51469 Bergisch Gladbach; tel. (2202) 1210; internet www.luebbe.de; f. 1964; general fiction and non-fiction, biography, history, etc.; Man. Dirs Dr PETER LIEGER, Dr UWE SERTEL, KARLHEINZ JUNGBECK.

Hermann Luchterhand Verlag GmbH: Postfach 2352, 56513 Neuwied; Heddesdorfer Str. 31, 56564 Neuwied; tel. (2631) 8010; fax (2631) 801204; e-mail info@luchterhand.de; internet www.luchterhand.de; f. 1924; insurance, law, taxation, labour; Man. Dir J. LUCZAK.

Mairs Geographischer Verlag: Marco-Polo-Zentrum, 73760 Ostfildern; tel. (711) 45020; fax (711) 4502310; internet www.mair-gruppe.de; f. 1848; road maps, atlases, tourist guides; Man. Dir Dr VOLKMAR MAIR.

J. B. Metzler Verlag: Postfach 103241, 70028 Stuttgart; Werastr. 21–23, 70182 Stuttgart; tel. (711) 21940; fax (711) 2194249; e-mail info@metzlerverlag.de; internet www.metzlerverlag.de; f. 1682; literature, music, pedagogics, linguistics, history, economics, commerce, textbooks; Dir Dr BERND LUTZ.

Verlag Moderne Industrie AG & Co KG: Justus-von-Liebig-Str. 1, 86895 Landsberg; tel. (8191) 1250; fax (8191) 125211; f. 1952; management, investment, technical; Man. Dir JOHANNES SEVKET GÖZALAN.

Morgenbuch Verlag GmbH: Berlin; tel. (2) 6504151; f. 1958; belles-lettres, politics; Dir Dr WOLFGANG TENZLER.

Verlagsgesellschaft Rudolf Müller GmbH & Co KG: Stolberger Str. 84, 50933 Köln; tel. (221) 54970; fax (221) 5497326; e-mail gf@rudolf-mueller.de; internet www.rudolf-mueller.de; f. 1840; architecture, construction, engineering, education; Publrs Dr CHRISTOPH MÜLLER, RUDOLF M. BLESER.

MVS Medizinverlage Stuttgart GmbH & Co KG: Oswald-Hesse-Str. 50, 70469 Stuttgart; tel. (711) 89310; fax (711) 8931706; e-mail kunden.service@thieme.de; internet www.medizinverlage.de; imprints are Karl F. Haug, Hippokrates, Sonntag, Enke, Parey and TRIAS und Haug Sachbuch; CEO Dr THOMAS SCHERB.

Verlag Friedrich Oetinger: Poppenbütteler Chaussee 53, 22397 Hamburg; tel. (40) 60790902; fax (40) 6072326; e-mail oetinger@verlagsgrupper-oetinger.de; internet www.oetinger.de; juvenile, illustrated books; Man. Dirs SILKE WEITENDORF, THOMAS HUGGLE, JAN WEITENDORF.

Oldenbourg Verlage: Rosenheimerstr. 145, 81671 München; tel. (89) 450510; fax (89) 45051333; internet www.oldenbourg.de; f. 1858; technology, science, history, textbooks, mathematics, economics, dictionaries, periodicals; Dirs Dr D. HOHM, WOLFGANG DICK, JOHANNES OLDENBOURG.

Omnis Verlag GmbH: Berlin; tel. (30) 85962838; fax (30) 85962840; e-mail info@omnis-verlag.de; art, children's, belles-lettres, history.

Pabel-Moewig Verlag KG: Karlsruher Str. 31, 76437 Rastatt; tel. (7222) 130; fax (7222) 13301; Gen. Man. GERHARD STEDTFELD.

Manfred Pawlak Grossantiquariat und Verlagsgesellschaft mbH: Mielkprülerstr. 31, 82211 Herrsching; tel. (8152) 37070; fax (8152) 370748; f. 1949; history, art, general interest; Dir ULRIKE PAWLAK.

Piper Verlag GmbH: Postfach 430861, Georgenstr. 4, 80799 München; tel. (89) 3818010; fax (89) 338704; e-mail info@piper.de; internet www.piper.de; f. 1904; literature, philosophy, theology, psychology, natural sciences, political and social sciences, history, biographies, music; Dir VIKTOR NIEMANN.

Verlagsgruppe Random House GmbH: Neumarkter Str. 28, 81673 München; tel. (89) 41360; fax (89) 43722938; e-mail verlagsgrupper@randomhouse.de; internet www.randomhouse.de; f. 1994; general, reference; Chair. Dr JOERG PFUHR.

Ravensburger Buchverlag Otto Maier GmbH: Postfach 1860, Marktstr. 22–26, 88188 Ravensburg, 88212 Ravensburg; tel. (751) 860; fax (751) 861289; e-mail info@ravensburger.de; internet www.ravensburger.de; f. 1883; Man. Dirs RENATE HERRE, JOHANNES HAUENSTEIN.

Philipp Reclam jun. Verlag GmbH: Siemensstr. 32, 71254 Ditzingen bei Stuttgart; tel. (7156) 1630; fax (7156) 163197; e-mail werbung@reclam.de; internet www.reclam.de; f. 1828; literature, literary criticism, fiction, history of culture and literature, philosophy and religion, biography, fine arts, music; Partner FRANK RAINER MAX.

Rowohlt Verlag GmbH: Hamburgerstr. 17, 21465 Reinbek bei Hamburg; tel. (40) 72720; fax (40) 7272319; internet www.rowohlt.de; f. 1908/1953; politics, science, fiction, translations of international literature; Dirs Dr HELMUT DÄHNE, ALEXANDER FEST, LUTZ KETTMANN.

K. G. Saur Verlag GmbH: Postfach 70 16 20, 81316 München; Ortlerstr. 8, 81373 München; tel. (89) 769020; fax (89) 76902150; e-mail saur.info@thomson.com; internet www.saur.de; f. 1949; library science, reference, dictionaries, encyclopedias, books, journals, microfiches, CD-ROMs, DVDs, online databases; 2 brs in Leipzig and Osnabrück; part of Thomson Corpn.

Schattauer GmbH: Postfach 104543, 70040 Stuttgart; Hoelderlinstr. 3, 70174 Stuttgart; tel. (711) 229870; fax (711) 2298750; e-mail info@schattauer.de; internet www.schattauer.de; f. 1949; medicine and related sciences; Publr DIETER BERGEMANN.

Verlag Dr Otto Schmidt KG: Unter den Ulmen 96–98, 50968 Köln; tel. (221) 9373801; fax (221) 93738943; f. 1905; university textbooks, jurisprudence, tax law; Man. Dir K. P. WINTERS.

Egmont Franz Schneider Verlag GmbH: Schleissheimer Str. 267, 80809 München; tel. (89) 358116; fax (89) 35811755; e-mail postmaster@schneiderbuch.de; internet www.schneiderbuch.de; f. 1913; children's books; Editor-in-Chief (vacant).

Schroedel Schulbuchverlag GmbH: Hildesheimer Str. 202–206, 30519 Hannover; tel. (511) 83880; fax (511) 8388343; f. 1982; school textbooks and educational software; Man. Dirs THOMAS BAUMANN, Dr WERNER KUGEL.

Springer-Verlag GmbH: Heidelberger Pl. 3, 14197 Berlin; tel. (30) 827870; fax (30) 8214091; f. 1842; medicine, biology, mathematics, physics, chemistry, psychology, engineering, geosciences, management, law, economics, humanities and social sciences; wholly-owned subsidiary of Springer Science+Business Media GmbH & Co KG; CEO DERK HAANK.

Stamm Verlag: Fuggerstr. 7, 51149 Köln; e-mail info@stam.de; internet www.stam.de; reference.

Stollfuss Verlag Bonn GmbH & Co KG: Dechenstr. 7, 53115 Bonn; tel. (228) 7240; fax (228) 659723; reference, fiscal law, economics, investment, etc.; Man. Dir WOLFGANG STOLLFUSS.

Suhrkamp Verlag GmbH & Co: Postfach 101945, 60019 Frankfurt a.M.; Suhrkamp Haus, Lindenstr. 29–35, 60325 Frankfurt a.M.; tel. (69) 756010; fax (69) 75601522; e-mail geschaeftsleitung@suhrkamp.de; internet www.suhrkamp.de; f. 1950; modern German and foreign literature, philosophy, poetry; Chair. ULLA UNSELD-BERKÉVICZ.

Sybex Verlag GmbH: Emil-Hoffmann-Str. 1, 50996 Köln; tel. (2236) 3999700; fax (2236) 3999229; e-mail sybex@sybex.de; internet www.sybex.de; f. 1981; computer books and software; Man. Dirs HANS NOLDEN, GERHARD PROLLIUS, ANJA SCHRIEVER.

Georg Thieme Verlag: Postfach 301120; 70451 Stuttgart; Rüdigerstr. 14, 70469 Stuttgart; tel. (711) 89310; fax (711) 8931298; e-mail info@thieme.com; internet www.thieme.com; f. 1886; medicine and natural science; Man. Dirs Dr GÜNTHER HAUFF, ALBRECHT HAUFF.

Thienemann Verlag GmbH: Blumenstr. 36, 70182 Stuttgart; tel. (711) 210550; fax (711) 2105539; e-mail info@thienemann.de; internet www.thienemann.de; f. 1849; picture books, children's books, juveniles; Dir KLAUS WILLBERG.

Transpress Verlagsgesellschaft mbH: Borkumstr. 2, 13181 Berlin; tel. (30) 47805151; fax (30) 47805160; f. 1990; specialized literature on transport and marketing; Man. Dr HARALD BÖTTCHER.

Verlag Eugen Ulmer GmbH & Co: Postfach 700561, 70574 Stuttgart; tel. (711) 45070; fax (711) 4507120; e-mail info@ulmer.de; f. 1868; agriculture, horticulture, science, periodicals; Dir ROLAND ULMER.

Verlag Ullstein GmbH: Charlottenstr. 13, 10969 Berlin; tel. (30) 25913570; fax (30) 25913523; f. 1894; literature, art, music, theatre, contemporary history, biography; Pres. Dr JÜRGEN RICHTER.

Ullstein Heyne List GmbH & Co KG: Paul-Heyse-Str. 28, 80336 München; tel. (89) 51480; fax (89) 51482229; f. 1894; general fiction, history, music, art, philosophy, religion, psychology; Editorial Dir CHRISTIAN STRASSER.

Verlagsgruppe Weltbild GmbH: Steinerne Furt 67–72, 86167 Augsburg; tel. (821) 70040; fax (821) 70042790; internet www .weltbild.com; f. 1949; religion, philosophy, fashion, heraldry, nature and environment, culture, history, photography, literature, health, travel.

Georg Westermann Verlag GmbH: Postfach 3320, Georg-Westermann-Allee 66, 38023 Braunschweig; tel. (531) 7080; fax (531) 708248; f. 1838; non-fiction, paperbacks, periodicals; Dir Dr HANS-DIETER MÖLLER.

Wiley-VCH Verlag GmbH & Co KGaA: Boschstr. 12, 69469 Weinheim; tel. (6201) 6060; fax (6201) 606328; e-mail service@ wiley-vch.de; internet www.wiley-vch.de; f. 1921; natural sciences, especially chemistry, chemical engineering, civil engineering, architecture, biotechnology, materials science, life sciences, information technology and physics, scientific software, business, management, computer science, finance and accounting; Man. Dir Dr MANFRED ANTONI.

Verlag Klaus Wingefeld: Lindenstr. 12, 71686 Remseck; fax (7146) 871881; e-mail kinderbuchverlag@t-online.de.

PRINCIPAL ASSOCIATION OF BOOK PUBLISHERS AND BOOKSELLERS

Börsenverein des Deutschen Buchhandels eV (German Publishers and Booksellers Association): Postfach 100442, 60004 Frankfurt a.M.; Grosser Hirschgraben 17–21, 60311 Frankfurt a.M.; tel. (69) 13060; fax (69) 1306201; e-mail info@boev.de; internet www .boersenverein.de; f. 1825; Chair. DIETER SCHORMANN; Man. Dir Dr HARALD HEKER.

Broadcasting and Communications

TELECOMMUNICATIONS

Debitel AG: 70545 Stuttgart; e-mail presse@de.debitel.com; internet www.debitel.com; owned by Swisscom AG.

Deutsche Telekom AG: Postfach 2000, 53105 Bonn; tel. (228) 1810; fax (228) 18171915; internet www.telekom.de; f. 1989; partially privatized 1995 with further privatization pending; 25% state-owned, 12% owned by Kreditanstalt für Wiederaufbau, 63% owned by private shareholders; fmr monopoly over national telecommunications network removed Jan. 1998; Chair. Supervisory Bd Dr HANS-DIETRICH WINKHAUS; Chair. Bd of Management Prof. Dr HELMUT SIHLER; CEO KAI-UWE RICKE.

E-plus Mobilfunk GmbH: Postfach 300307, 40403 Düsseldorf; E-Plus-Pl. 1, 40468 Düsseldorf; tel. (211) 4480; fax (211) 4482222; internet www.eplus.de; f. 1995; Chair. Supervisory Bd ALAIN D. BANDLE.

Mannesmann Mobilfunk GmbH: Am Seestern 1, 40547 Düsseldorf; tel. (211) 5330; fax (211) 5332200; internet www .d2mannesmann.de; operates D2 mobile telephone network; subsidiary of Mannesmann AG, Telecommunications Division (takeover by Vodafone-AirTouch PLC, UK, pending); Chair. JÜRGEN VON KUCZ-KOWSKI.

Mannesmann o-tel-o GmbH: Deutz-Mulheimer-Str. 111, 51063 Köln; tel. (221) 8080; fax (221) 8087566; internet www.o-tel-o.com; operates fixed line telephone network; subsidiary of Mannesmann AG, Telecommunications Division (takeover by Vodafone-AirTouch PLC, UK, pending).

Mannesmann Arcor AG: Kölnerstr. 5, 65760 Eschborn; fax (69) 21694444; e-mail arcor@arcor.net; internet www.arcor.de; operates fixed line telephone network; subsidiary of Mannesmann AG, Telecommunications Division (takeover by Vodafone-AirTouch PLC, UK, pending).

MobilCom AG: Postfach 520, 24753 Rendsburg; Hollerstr. 126, 24782 Rendsburg; internet www.mobilcom.de; f. 1991; Chair. GERHARD SCHMID.

T-Mobil: internet www.t-mobil.de; f. 1992; subsidiary of Deutsche Telekom AG; f. 1992; operates T-D1 mobile telephone network.

Viag Interkom: internet www.viaginterkom.de; f. 1995; Chair. MAXIMILIAN ARDELT.

Associations

Bundesverband Digitale Wirtschaft eV: Kaistr. 14, 40221 Düsseldorf; tel. (211) 6004560; fax (211) 60045633; e-mail kehlen@dmmv .de; internet www.bvdw.org; fmrly Deutscher Multimedia Verband (dmmv); 900 mems (Aug. 2004).

Verband Privater Rundfunk und Telekommunikation eV (VPRT) (Asscn of Commercial Broadcasting and Telecommunications Cos): Stromstr. 1, 10555 Berlin; tel. (30) 398800; fax (30) 39880148; e-mail vprt@vprt.de; internet www.vprt.de; 150 mems (March 2004).

Regulatory Authority

Regulierungsbehörde für Telekommunikation und Post (RegTP): Tulpenfeld 4, 53113 Bonn; tel. (228) 140; fax (228) 148872; e-mail poststelle@regtp.de; internet www.regtp.de; f. 1997 as a regulatory body responsible for supervising the liberalization (commencing in Jan. 1998) of the post and telecommunications sector; Pres. MATTHIAS KURTH.

BROADCASTING

Radio

Regional public radio stations are co-ordinated by the ARD (see below). There are also numerous regional commercial radio stations.

In 2005 Digital Audio Broadcast (DAB) services were available to approximately 80% of the population. In that year there were around 80 stations on the air. DAB was first introduced in Germany in Sachsen-Anhalt in 1999. Since then DAB has been implemented in all Länder, although coverage in Schleswig-Holstein and Mecklenburg-Vorpommern is still considerably less extensive than in other Länder.

Public Stations

Arbeitsgemeinschaft der öffentlich-rechtlichen Rundfunkanstalten der Bundesrepublik Deutschland (ARD) (Association of Public Law Broadcasting Organizations): Bertramstr. 8, 60320 Frankfurt a.M.; tel. (69) 590607; fax (69) 1552075; e-mail info@ard.de; internet www.ard.de; f. 1950; Chair. Prof. JOBST PLOG; the co-ordinating body of Germany's public service radio and television organizations; each of the following radio stations broadcasts 3–5 channels:

Bayerischer Rundfunk: Rundfunkpl. 1, 80300 München; tel. (89) 590001; fax (89) 59002375; internet www.bronline.de; Dir-Gen. Prof. ALBERT SCHARF; Chair. Broadcasting Council Prof. Dr WILHELM WIMMER; Chair. Admin. Bd JOHANN BÖHM.

Deutsche Welle: Kurt-Schumacher-Str. 3, 53113 Bonn; tel. (228) 4290; fax (228) 4293000; e-mail info@dw-world.de; internet www .dw-world.de; f. 1953; German short-wave radio and satellite television service; broadcasts daily in 30 languages for Europe and overseas; Dir-Gen. ERIK BETTERMANN.

DeutschlandRadio: Hans Rosenthal Pl., 10825 Berlin; tel. (30) 85030; internet www.deutschlandradio.de; Dir-Gen. ERNST ELLITZ.

Hessischer Rundfunk: Bertramstr. 8, 60320 Frankfurt a.M.; tel. (69) 1551; fax (69) 1552900; internet www.hr-online.de; Dir-Gen. Dr HELMUT REITZE.

Mitteldeutscher Rundfunk: Kanstr. 71–73, 04275 Leipzig; tel. (341) 3000; fax (341) 3005544; internet www.mdr.de; f. 1992; Dir-Gen. Prof. Dr UDO REITER.

Norddeutscher Rundfunk: Rothenbaumchaussee 132, 20149 Hamburg; tel. (40) 41560; fax (40) 447602; internet www.ndr.de; f. 1956; Dir-Gen. JOBST PLOG.

Radio Bremen: Bürgermeister-Spitta-Allee 45, 28329 Bremen; tel. (421) 2460; fax (421) 2461010; internet www.radiobremen.de; f. 1945; radio and television; Dir-Gen. Dr HEINZ GLÄSSGEN.

Rundfunk Berlin-Brandenburg (RRB): Masurenallee 8–14, 14057 Berlin; tel. (30) 30310; fax (30) 3015062; e-mail presse@ rrb-online.de; internet www.rrb-online.de; fmrly Ostdeutscher Rundfunk Brandenburg; Dir-Gen. DAGMAR REIM.

Saarländischer Rundfunk: Funkhaus Halberg, 66100 Saarbrücken; tel. (681) 6020; fax (681) 6023874; internet www .sr-online.de; f. 1952; Dir-Gen. FRITZ RAFF.

Südwestrundfunk: Neckarstr. 230, 70150 Stuttgart; tel. (49) 9290; fax (49) 9292600; internet www.swr.de; Dir-Gen. PETER VOSS.

WDR (Westdeutscher Rundfunk): Appellhofpl. 1, 50667 Köln; tel. (221) 2200; fax (221) 2204800; internet www.wdr.de; Dir-Gen. FRITZ PLEITGEN.

Commercial Radio

Verband Privater Rundfunk und Telekommunikation eV (VPRT): see under Telecommunications; represents privately-owned radio stations.

Television

There are three public-service television channels. The autonomous regional broadcasting organizations combine to provide material for the First Programme, which is produced by ARD. The Second Programme (Zweites Deutsches Fernsehen/ZDF) is completely separate and is controlled by a public corporation of all the Länder. It is partly financed by advertising. The Third Programme (also produced by ARD) provides a cultural and educational service in the evenings only with contributions from several of the regional bodies. Commercial television channels also operate.

Digital Video Broadcasting (DVB) was introduced in Germany in 2002. By the end of 2003 it was estimated that 2.5m. households were able to receive DVB services. Analogue broadcasting was due to be abandoned by 2010. By 2005 Berlin and Brandenburg had already switched off analogue broadcasting.

Public Stations

ARD: Programmdirektion Deutsches Fernsehen: Arnulfstr. 42, 80335 München; tel. (89) 590001; fax (89) 59003249; e-mail info@ daserste.de; internet www.daserste.de; Chair. and Dir of Programmes Prof. JOBST PLOG; co-ordinates the following regional public-service television organizations: Bayerischer Rundfunk, Hessischer Rundfunk, MDR, NDR, Radio Bremen, Saarländischer Rundfunk, Rundfunk Berlin-Brandenberg, Südwestrundfunk, WDR.

Zweites Deutsches Fernsehen (ZDF): 55100 Mainz; tel. (6131) 702050; fax (6131) 702052; e-mail international@zdf.de; internet www.zdf.de; f. 1961 by the Länder Govts as a second television channel; 104 main transmitters; Dir-Gen. MARKUS SCHÄCHTER.

Commercial Television

Verband Privater Rundfunk und Telekommunication eV (VPRT): see under Telecommunications; represents privately-owned satellite, cable and digital television cos.

Premiere Fernsehen GmbH & Co KG: Medienallee 4, 85774 Unterföhring; tel. (89) 995802; fax (89) 99586239; e-mail info@ premiere.de; internet www.premiere.de; f. 1988; subscriber service offering 26 television and 21 audio channels; CEO Dr GEORG KOFLER.

ProSiebenSat.1 Media AG: Medienallee 7, 85774 Unterföhring; tel. (89) 95071180; fax (89) 95071184; e-mail info@prosiebensat1 .com; internet www.prosiebensat1.com; f. 2000 by merger of Pro-Sieben Media AG and Sat.1; operates Sat. 1, ProSieben, Kabel 1 and N24; Chair., Exec. Bd GUILLAUME DE POSCH; Chair., Supervisory Bd HAIM SABAN.

Finance

(cap. = capital; res = reserves; dep. = deposits; m. = million; brs = branches; amounts in Deutsche Marks (DM) or euros (€))

The Deutsche Bundesbank, the central bank of Germany, consists of the central administration in Frankfurt am Main (considered to be the financial capital of the country) and 9 main offices (Hauptverwaltungen) with 140 branches. In carrying out its functions as determined by law the Bundesbank is independent of the Federal Government, but is required to support the Government's general economic policy. As a member of the European System of Central Banks (ESCB), the Bundesbank implements the single monetary policy determined by the Governing Council of the European Central Bank (ECB).

All credit institutions other than the Bundesbank are subject to governmental supervision through the Federal Banking Supervisory Office (Bundesaufsichtsamt für das Kreditwesen) in Berlin. Banks outside the central banking system are divided into three groups: private commercial banks, credit institutions incorporated under public law and co-operative credit institutions. All these commercial banks are 'universal banks', conducting all kinds of customary banking business. There is no division of activities. As well as the commercial banks there are a number of specialist banks, such as private or public mortgage banks.

The group of private commercial banks includes all banks incorporated as a company limited by shares (Aktiengesellschaft—AG, Kommanditgesellschaft auf Aktien—KGaA) or as a private limited company (Gesellschaft mit beschränkter Haftung—GmbH) and those which are known as 'regional banks' because they do not usually function throughout Germany; and those banks which are established as sole proprietorships or partnerships and mostly have no branches outside their home town. The main business of all private commercial banks is short-term lending. The private bankers fulfil the most varied tasks within the banking system.

The public law credit institutions are the savings banks (Sparkassen) and the Landesbank-Girozentralen. The latter act as central banks and clearing houses on a national level for the savings banks. Laws governing the savings banks limit them to certain sectors—credits, investments and money transfers—and they concentrate on the areas of home financing, municipal investments and the trades.

In 2002 there were 534 savings banks and 13 Landesbank-Girozentralen in Germany.

The head institution of the co-operative system is the DZ BANK Deutsche Zentrale-Genossenschaftsbank AG. In 2002 there were 1,621 credit co-operatives, including central institutions.

In 1990 there was a total of 4,700 banks in Germany; by 2002 this number had decreased to 2,522.

BANKS

The Central Banking System

Germany participates in the ESCB, which, in April 2004, consisted of the ECB and the national central banks of all 15 European Union (EU) member states. Stage III of European Monetary Union (EMU), the launch of the euro, commenced (with 11 initial participants) on 1 January 1999. Euro banknotes and coins were issued on 1 January 2002; the Deutsche Mark remained legal tender until 28 February 2002.

Deutsche Bundesbank: Postfach 100602, 60006 Frankfurt a.M.; Wilhelm-Epstein-Str. 14, 60431 Frankfurt a.M.; tel. (69) 95661; fax (69) 5601071; e-mail presse-information@bundesbank.de; internet www.bundesbank.de; f. 1957; aims, in conjunction with the other members of the ESCB, to maintain price stability in the euro area. The Bundesbank, *inter alia*, holds and maintains foreign reserves of the Federal Republic of Germany, arranges for the execution of domestic and cross-border payments, contributes to the stability of payment and clearing systems and is involved in surveillance of credit and financial services institutions. The Bundesbank (which has nine regional offices—Hauptverwaltungen) is the principal bank of the Federal Länder Govts, carrying accounts for public authorities, executing payments and assisting with borrowing on the capital market. The Bundesbank has reserve positions in, and claims on, the IMF and the ECB. The Executive Board determines the Bundesbank's business policy; members of the Federal Govt may take part in the deliberations of the Board but may not vote; Pres. Dr AXEL WEBER; Vice-Pres. Dr JÜRGEN STARK.

Hauptverwaltung Berlin: Steinpl. 2, 10623 Berlin; tel. (30) 34750; fax (30) 34751990; e-mail volkswirtschaft.hv-berlin@bundesbank .de; internet www.bundesbank.de/hv/hv_berlin.php; Pres. Bd of Management ULRICH PREUSS.

Hauptverwaltung Düsseldorf: Berliner Allee 14, 40212 Düsseldorf; tel. (211) 8740; e-mail stab.hv-duesseldorf@bundesbank.de; internet www.bundesbank.de/hv/hv_duesseldorf.php; Pres. FRIEDEL FLECK.

Hauptverwaltung Frankfurt: Taunusanlage 5, 60329 Frankfurt a.M.; tel. (69) 23880; fax (69) 23882130; e-mail presse-information@ lzb-hessen.bundesbank.de; internet www.bundesbank.de/hv/ hv_frankfurt.php; Pres. Dr HANS RECKERS; Vice-Pres. JÖRGEN HETTINGER.

Hauptverwaltung Hamburg: Ost-West-Str. 73, 20459 Hamburg; tel. (40) 37070; fax (40) 37072205; e-mail lzb-hms-pressestelle@ t-online.de; internet www.bundesbank.de/hv/hv_hamburg.php; Pres. Bd of Management Prof. Dr ROLF EGGERT.

Hauptverwaltung Hannover: Postfach 245, 30002 Hannover; tel. (511) 30330; fax (511) 30332500; e-mail pressestelle.hv-hannover@ bundesbank.de; internet www.bundesbank.de/hv/hv_hannover.php; Pres. Bd of Management GEORG KUTTER.

Hauptverwaltung Leipzig: Postfach 901121, 04358 Leipzig; tel. (341) 8600; fax (341) 8602389; e-mail hv-leipzig@bundesbank.de; internet www.bundesbank.de/hv/hv_leipzig.php.

Hauptverwaltung Mainz: Hegelstr. 65, 52122 Mainz; tel. (6131) 3770; fax (6131) 377750; e-mail volkswirtschaft.hv-mainz@ bundesbank.de; internet www.bundesbank.de/hv/hv_mainz.php; Pres. HELMUT RITTGEN.

Hauptverwaltung München: Ludwigstr. 13, 80539 München; tel. (89) 28895; fax (89) 28893598; e-mail post.hv-muenchen@ bundesbank.de; internet www.bundesbank.de/hv/hv_muenchen .php; Pres. Bd of Management GÜNTHER BÄUMER.

Hauptverwaltung Stuttgart: Marstallstr. 3, 70173 Stuttgart; tel. (711) 9440; fax (711) 9441903; e-mail hv-stuttgart@bundesbank.de; internet www.bundesbank.de/hv/hv_stuttgart.php; Pres. Bd of Management WILHELM ERGENZINGER.

Private Commercial Banks

In December 2002 354 private commercial banks were operating in Germany. The most prominent of these are listed below:

Baden-Württembergische Bank AG: Postfach 106014, 70049 Stuttgart; Kleiner Schlosspl. 11, 70173 Stuttgart; tel. (711) 1800; fax (711) 1801712; e-mail info@bw-bank.de; internet www.bw-bank.de; f. 1977 by merger of Badische Bank, Handelsbank Heilbronn and Württembergische Bank; cap. €92m., res €607m., dep. €22,536m. (Dec. 2000); Chair. GERHARD STRATTHAUS; 53 brs.

Bankgesellschaft Berlin AG: Alexanderpl. 2, 10178 Berlin; tel. (30) 245500; fax (30) 245509; e-mail ir@bankgesellschaft.de; internet www.bankgesellschaft.de; f. 1994; cap. €558m., res €3,524m., dep. €189,503m. (Dec. 2000); majority stake held by Berlin Land Govt; Chair. Supervisory Bd Dr CLAUS G. ADAM; Chair. Bd of Management HANS-JÖRG VETTER.

Bayerische Hypo- und Vereinsbank AG (HypoVereinsbank): Postfach 100101, 80333 München; Am Tucherpark 16, 80538 München; tel. (89) 3780; fax (89) 378113422; e-mail info@hypovereinsbank.de; internet www.hypovereinsbank.de; f. 1998 by merger of Bayerische Hypotheken- und Wechsel Bank AG (f. 1835) and Bayerische Vereinsbank AG (f. 1869); cap. €1,607m., res €17,532m., dep. €616,509m. (Dec. 2000); Chair. Supervisory Bd Dr KURT VIERMETZ; Chair. Bd of Management Dr ALBRECHT SCHMIDT; 1,426 brs.

Berliner Volksbank eG: Budapester Str. 35, 10787 Berlin; tel. (30) 30630; fax (30) 30631550; e-mail international.division@berliner-volksbank.de; internet www.berliner-volksbank.de; f. 1860; cap. DM 572m., res DM 477m., dep. DM 18,072m. (Dec. 2000); Chair. Prof. Dr DIETMAR WINJE.

Citibank Privatkunden AG & Co KGaA: Postfach 101818, 40009 Düsseldorf; Kasernenstr. 10, 40213 Düsseldorf; tel. (211) 89840; fax (211) 8984222; internet www.citibank.de; f. 1926 as KKB Bank KGaA; present name adopted 1991; cap. €139m., res €588m., dep. €8,845m. (Dec. 2002); Man. CHRISTINE LICCI; 286 brs.

Citigroup Global Markets Deutschland AG & Co KGaA: Postfach 110333, 60038 Frankfurt a.M.; Frankfurter Welle Reuterweg 16, 60323 Frankfurt a.M.; tel. (69) 13660; fax (69) 13661113; internet www.citigroup.com; f. 1976 as Citibank AG, current name adopted 2003; cap. €180m., res €115m., dep. €4,774m. (Dec. 2001); Chair. Supervisory Bd Prof. K. PETER MAILÄNDER; Chair. Bd of Management Dr MICHAEL ZITZMANN; 2 brs.

Commerzbank AG: Kaiserpl., 60311 Frankfurt a.M.; tel. (69) 13620; fax (69) 285389; e-mail info@commerzbank.de; internet www.commerzbank.de; f. 1870; cap. €1,378m., res €7,376m., dep. €303,416m. (Dec. 2002); Chair. Supervisory Bd Dr MARTIN KOHLHAUSSEN; Chair. Bd of Management KLAUS-PETER MÜLLER; 964 brs.

Deutsche Bank AG: Taunusanlage 12, 60325 Frankfurt a.M.; tel. (69) 91000; fax (69) 91033422; e-mail db.presse@db.com; internet www.deutsche-bank.de; f. 1870; cap. €1,490m., res €6,226m., dep. €598,928m. (Dec. 2003); Chair. Supervisory Bd ROLF E. BREUER; Chair. Bd of Management JOSEF ACKERMANN; 133 brs.

Dresdner Bank AG: Jürgen-Ponto-Pl. 1, 60329 Frankfurt a.M.; tel. (69) 2630; fax (69) 634004; e-mail investor.relations@dresdner-bank.com; internet www.dresdner-bank.de; f. 1872; cap. €1,503m., res €10,013m., dep. €441,170m. (Dec. 2003); Chair. Supervisory Bd MICHAEL DIEKMANN; Chair. Bd of Management Dr HERBERT WALTER; more than 1,400 brs.

Dresdner Bank Lateinamerika AG: Postfach 301246, 20305 Hamburg; Neuer Jungfernstieg 16, 20354 Hamburg; tel. (40) 35950; fax (40) 35953314; e-mail public-relations@dbla.com; internet www.dbla.com; f. 1906; fmrly Deutsch-Südamerikanische Bank AG; cap. €125m., res €179m., dep. €3,408m. (Dec. 2003); Chair. Supervisory Bd JAN ERIC KVARNSTRÖM; Chair. Bd of Management WOLFGANG DAMBMANN.

HSBC Trinkaus & Burkhardt KGaA: Postfach 101108, 40002 Düsseldorf; Königsallee 21–23, 40212 Düsseldorf; tel. (211) 9100; fax (211) 910616; f. 1785; current name adopted 1999; cap. €70m., res €626m., dep. €6,740m. (Dec. 2003); Chair. and Man. Dir Dr SIEGHARDT ROMETSCH; 6 brs.

ING BHF-Bank AG: Bockenheimer Landstr. 10, 60323 Frankfurt a.M.; tel. (69) 7180; fax (69) 7182296; e-mail kontakt@bhf.ing.com; internet www.ing-bhf-bank.com; f. 1856; cap. €215m., res €2,463m., dep. €46,976m. (Sept. 2002); Man. Dir SYTSE ADRIAAN ANDRINGA.

J. P. Morgan AG: Grüneburgweg 2, 60322 Frankfurt a.M.; tel. (69) 71581; fax (69) 71582209; f. 1947; cap. €59m., res €83m., dep. €4,711m. (Dec. 1999); Chair. RAINER GEBBE.

Merck Finck & Co: Pacellistr. 16, 80333 München; tel. (89) 21040; fax (89) 299814; e-mail info@merckfinck.de; internet www.merckfinck.de; f. 1870; cap. €155m., res €9m., dep. €1,398m. (Dec. 2002); Partners ALEXANDER METTENHEIMER, UTZ-DIETER BOLSTORFF, ANDREW LAWSON.

Oldenburgische Landesbank AG: Postfach 2605, 26016 Oldenburg; Stau 15–17, 26122 Oldenburg; tel. (441) 2210; fax (441) 210310; e-mail olb@olb.de; internet www.olb.de; f. 1868; cap. €60m., res €324m., dep. €7,278m. (Dec. 2003); Chair. Bd of Management Dr JÖRG BLECKMANN.

Oppenheim (Sal) Jr & Cie KGaA: Postfach 102743, 50467 Köln; Unter Sachsenhausen 4; 50667 Köln; tel. (221) 14501; fax (221) 1451512; e-mail info@oppenheim.de; internet www.oppenheim.de; f.

1789; cap. €200m., res €856m., dep. €6,704m. (Dec. 2003); Chair. MATTHIAS GRAF VON KROCKOW; 16 brs.

SchmidtBank AG: Postfach 1629, 95015 Hof; Ernst-Reuter-Str. 119, 95030 Hof; tel. (9281) 6010; fax (9281) 601427; e-mail bankrelations@schmidtbank.de; internet www.schmidtbank.de; f. 1828; cap. €75m., res €70m., dep. €1,541m. (Dec. 2002); Chair. Dr PAUL WIEANDT; 125 brs.

SEB AG: Ulmenstr. 30, 60283 Frankfurt a.M.; tel. (69) 2580; fax (69) 2587578; e-mail info@seb.de; internet www.seb.de; f. 1958 as BfG—Bank AG, adopted current name 2000; cap. €775m., res €476m., dep. €23,691m. (Dec. 2003); Chair. FREDRIK BOHEMAN; 175 brs.

> **Skandinaviska Enskilda Banken AG:** Postfach 101957, 60019 Frankfurt a.M.; Rahmhofstr. 2–4, 60313 Frankfurt a.M.; tel. (69) 290210; fax (69) 284191; f. 1975; 100% owned by SEB AG; cap. DM 81m., res DM 69m., dep. DM 2,027m. (Dec. 1999); Chair. ZAID PEDERSEN; Man. Dirs WOLFGANG AZGELANDER, LARS TÖRNQUIST; 2 brs.

UBS Investment Bank AG: Stephanstr. 14–16, 60313 Frankfurt a.M.; tel. (69) 13690; fax (69) 13691366; internet www.ubs.com; f. 1998 as Warburg Dillon Read AG by merger of Schweizerischer Bankverein (Deutschland) and Union Bank of Switzerland (Deutschland) AG; present name adopted 2003; cap. €125m., res €166m., dep. €21,795m. (Dec. 2002); CEO STEFAN WINTER; Dirs HERMANN PREECE, WOLFGANG STOLZ.

Vereins- und Westbank AG: Alter Wall 22, 20457 Hamburg; tel. (40) 369201; fax (40) 36922870; internet www.vuw.de; f. 1974 by merger; cap. €175m., res €752m., dep. €21,793m. (Dec. 2003); Man. Dirs JENS-PETER NEUMANN, ROLF KIRCHFELD, MICHAEL PAPENFUSS, Dr STEFAN SCHMITTMANN; 190 brs.

Weberbank Privatbankiers KGaA: Postfach 110580, 10835 Berlin; Hohenzollerndamm 134, 14199 Berlin; tel. (30) 897980; fax (30) 89798900; internet www.weberbank.de; f. 1949 as Weberbank Berliner Industriebank, current name adopted 2001; cap. €52m., res €126m., dep. €4,946m. (Dec. 2001); Partners Dr ANDREAS BÖDECKER, Dr CHRISTIAN GRÜN, MICHAEL GRAF STRASOLDO; 3 brs.

Westfalenbank AG: Postfach 102710, 44727 Bochum; Huestr. 21–25, 44787 Bochum; tel. (234) 6160; fax (234) 6164400; e-mail info@westfalenbank.de; internet www.westfalenbank.de; f. 1921; cap. €51m., res €89m., dep. €1,698m. (Dec. 2002); Man. Dirs Dr HEINZ J. HOCKMANN, Dr JOHANNES-JÖRG RIEGLER.

Public-Law Credit Institutions

Together with the private banks, the banks incorporated under public law (savings banks—Sparkassen—and their central clearing houses—Landesbank-Girozentralen) play a major role within the German banking system. In 2002 there were 534 savings banks and 13 central clearing houses. In July 2001 the Government signed an agreement with the EU to end state guarantees for the Landesbanken over four years.

Bayerische Landesbank: Brienner Str. 18, 80333 München; tel. (89) 217101; fax (89) 217123579; e-mail info@bayernlb.de; internet www.bayernlb.de; f. 1972; cap. €4,714m., res €4,397m., dep. €280,830m. (Dec. 2003); Chair. Bd of Management WERNER SCHMIDT.

Bremer Landesbank Kreditanstalt Oldenburg: Domshof 26, 28195 Bremen; tel. (421) 3320; fax (421) 3322625; e-mail kontakt@bremerlandesbank.de; internet www.bremerlandesbank.de; f. 1983; cap. €748m., res €311m., dep. €31,968m. (Dec. 2001); Chair. Dr PETER HASSKAMP.

DekaBank Deutsche Girozentrale: Mainzer Landstr. 16 60325 Frankfurt am Main; tel. (89) 7147652; fax (89) 71471376; e-mail service@deka.de; internet www.deka.de; f. 1999; a merger of Deutsche Girozentrale-Deutsche Kommunalbank and Dekabank GmbH; issues Pfandbriefe (bonds); cap. €587m., res €549m., dep. €73,348m. (Dec. 2000); Chair. Bd of Management Dr DIETRICH H. HOPPENSTEDT.

HSH Nordbank AG: Gerhart-Hauptmann-Pl. 50, 20095 Hamburg; tel. (40) 33330; fax (40) 333334001; e-mail info@hsh-nordbank.com; internet www.hsh-nordbank.com; f. 2003 by merger of Hamburgische Landesbank-Girozentrale and Landesbank Schleswig-Holstein Girozentrale; cap. and res €5,770m., dep. €163,440m. (Dec. 2002); CEO ALEXANDER STUHLMANN.

Landesbank Baden-Württemberg: Postfach 106049, 70049 Stuttgart; tel. (711) 1270; fax (711) 1273278; e-mail kontakt@lbbw.de; internet www.lbbw.de; f. 1999 by merger of Landesgirokasse, L-Bank Landeskreditbank Baden-Württemberg and Südwestdeutsche Landesbank Girozentrale; cap. €4,684m., res €4,635m., dep. €298,749m. (Dec. 2002); Chair. Bd of Management HANS DIETMAR SAUER.

Landesbank Berlin Girozentrale: Bundesallee 171, 10889 Berlin-Wilmersdorf; tel. (30) 869801; fax (30) 86983074; e-mail information@lbb.de; internet www.lbb.de; f. 1818; cap. €844m., res €1,426m., dep. €79,885m. (Dec. 2002); Chair. Bd of Management HANS-JÖRG VETTER; 178 brs.

Landesbank Hessen-Thüringen Girozentrale: Main Tower, Neue Mainzer Str. 52–58, 60297 Frankfurt a.M.; tel. (69) 913201; fax (69) 291517; e-mail presse@helaba.de; internet www.helaba.de; cap. €2,345m., res €1,174m., dep. €127,330m. (Dec. 2004); Chair. Dr GÜNTHER MERL.

Landesbank Saar: Ursulinenstr. 2, 66111 Saarbrücken; tel. (681) 38301; fax (681) 3831295; e-mail saarlb@aol.com; internet www .saarlb.de; f. 1941; cap. €239m., res €116m., dep. €15,138m. (Dec. 2002); Pres. Dr MAX HÄRING; Chair. KARL HEINZ TRAUTMANN.

LRP Landesbank Rheinland-Pfalz Girozentrale: Grosse Bleiche 54–56, 55098 Mainz; tel. (6131) 1301; fax (6131) 132724; e-mail lrp@lrp.de; internet www.lrp.de; f. 1958; cap. €718m., res €726m., dep. €62,377m. (Dec. 2002); Chair. and CEO Dr KLAUS G. ADAM.

Norddeutsche Landesbank Girozentrale (NORD/LB): Friedrichswall 10, 30159 Hannover; tel. (511) 3610; fax (511) 3612502; e-mail info@nordlb.de; internet www.nordlb.de; f. 1970 by merger of several north German banks; cap. €1,883m., res €2,344m., dep. €128,703m. (Dec. 2002); Chair. Dr MANFRED BODIN; 172 brs.

WestLB AG: Herzogstr. 15, 40217 Düsseldorf; tel. (211) 82601; fax (211) 8266119; e-mail presse@westlb.de; internet www.westlb.de; f. 1969; cap. €951m., res €4,046m., dep. €240,742m. (Dec. 2002); Chair. Dr THOMAS R. FISCHER.

Central Bank of Co-operative Banking System

DZ BANK (Deutsche Zentral-Genossenschaftsbank AG): Pl. der Republik, 60265 Frankfurt a.M.; tel. (69) 744701; fax (69) 74471685; e-mail mail@dzbank.de; internet www.dzbank.de; f. 1949; cap. €2,879m., res €3,061m., dep. €278,606m. (Dec. 2002); Chair. Supervisory Bd CHRISTOPHER PLEISTER; Chair. Bd of Management Dr ULRICH BRIXNER; 46 brs.

DZ BANK is a specialist wholesale bank and is the central institution in the German co-operative banking sector, which comprises local co-operative banks, three regional central banks and a number of specialist financial institutions. In 2002 there were 1,621 credit co-operatives, including central institutions.

Specialist Banks

Although Germany is considered the model country for universal banking, banks that specialize in certain types of business are also extremely important. In December 1998 there were 51 specialist banks. A selection of the most prominent among these is given below:

Aareal Bank AG: Postfach 2169, 65011 Wiesbaden; Paulinenstr. 15, 65189 Wiesbaden; tel. (611) 3480; fax (611) 3482549; e-mail aareal@aareal-bank.com; internet www.aareal-bank.com; f. 1922; fmrly DePfa Deutsche Pfandbriefbank AG; cap. €107m., res €1,430m., dep. €165,931m. (Dec. 2001); Chair. Supervisory Bd Dr JÜRGEN WESTPHAL.

Allgemeine HypothekenBank Rheinboden AG: Postfach 170162, 60075 Frankfurt a.M.; Bockenheimer Landstr. 25, 60325 Frankfurt a.M.; tel. (69) 71790; fax (69) 7179100; e-mail info@ahbr .com; internet www.ahbr.com; f. 1962 as Allgemeine Hypotheken Bank AG, present name adopted 2001; cap. €101m., res €876m., dep. €87,521m. (Dec. 2001); Chair. HORST ALEXANDER SPITZKOPF; 8 brs.

Berlin-Hannoversche Hypothekenbank AG: Budapester Str. 1, 10787 Berlin; tel. (30) 259990; fax (30) 25999131; e-mail kommunikation@berlinhyp.de; internet www.berlinhyp.de; f. 1996 by merger; cap. €74m., res €594m., dep. €43,597m. (Dec. 2000); Chair. Supervisory Bd Dr WOLFGANG RUPF; Chair. Bd of Management KLAUS LANDOWSKY.

Deutsche Hypothekenbank AG: Georgspl. 8, 30159 Hannover; tel. (511) 30450; fax (511) 3045459; e-mail mail@deutsche-hypo.de; internet www.deutsche-hypo.de; f. 1872; cap. €81m., res €323m., dep. €25,183m. (Dec. 2002); Chair. Supervisory Bd LOUIS GRAF VON ZECH; Man Dirs JÜRGEN GEIGER, JÜRGEN MORR, THOMAS FUHR VON TUCHEV; 7 brs.

Deutsche Postbank AG: Friedrich-Ebert-Allee 114–126, 53113 Bonn; tel. (228) 9200; fax (228) 9202818; internet www.postbank.de; f. 1990; cap. €410m., res €3,887m., dep. €129,762m. (Dec. 2002); 100% owned by Deutsche Post AG; Chair. Prof. Dr WULF VON SCHIMMELMANN.

Eurohypo AG: Taunusanlage 9, 60329 Frankfurt a.M.; tel. (180) 3497600; fax (180) 3497688888; e-mail info@deutschehyp.de; internet www.eurohypo.com; f. 2002 by merger of Deutsche Hyp (f. 1862), Europhypo (f. 1862) and Rheinhyp (f.1871); cap. €842m., res €3,777m., dep. €217,748m. (Dec. 2002); Chair. Management Bd Dr KARSTEN VON KÖLLER; Chair. Supervisory Bd Dr JOACHIM VON HARBOU; 16 brs.

Hypo Real Estate Bank AG: Von-der-Tann-Str. 2, 80539 München; tel. (89) 28800; fax (89) 288010226; internet www .hyporealestate.de; f. 2001 by merger of Bayerische Handelsbank

AG, Süddeutsche Bodencreditbank AG and Nürnberger Hypothekenbank AG; cap. €133m., res €995m., dep. €75,032m. (Dec. 2002); Chair. Supervisory Bd GEORG FUNKE; Chair. Management Bd JOHANN BERGER.

IKB Deutsche Industriebank AG: Postfach 101118, 40002 Düsseldorf; Willhelm-Bötzkes-Str. 1, 40474 Düsseldorf; tel. (211) 82210; fax (211) 82212559; internet www.ikb.de; f. 1949; cap. €226m., res €1,115m., dep. €32,964m. (March 2003); Gen. Mans JOACHIM NEUPEL, STEFAN ORTSEIFEN, Dr A. V. TIPPELSKIRCH, G.-J. V. PUTTKAMER.

KfW Bankengruppe (Kreditanstalt für Wiederaufbau): Postfach 111141, 60046 Frankfurt a.M.; Palmengartenstr. 5–9, 60325 Frankfurt a.M.; tel. (69) 74310; fax (69) 74312944; e-mail info@kfw.de; internet www.kfw.de; f. 1948; cap. €3,300m., res €2,680m., dep. €233,783m. (Dec. 2002); Chair. Bd of Management HANS W. REICH.

Münchener Hypothekenbank eG: Karl-Scharnagl-Ring 10, 80539 München; tel. (89) 5387800; fax (89) 5387900; e-mail serviceteam800@muenchenerhyp.de; internet www .muenchenerhyp.de; f. 1896; cap. €209m., res €209m., dep. €28,599m. (Dec. 2001); Chair. Prof. Dr WILLIBALD J. FOLZ.

Bankers' Organizations

Bundesverband deutscher Banken (Association of German Banks): Postfach 040307, 10062 Berlin; Burgstr. 28, 10178 Berlin; e-mail bdb@bdb.de; internet www.bdb.de; f. 1951; Gen. Man. MANFRED WEBER.

Bundesverband der Deutschen Volksbanken und Raiffeisenbanken eV (BVR) (Association of German Co-operative Banks and Agricultural Credit Co-operatives): Schellingstr. 4, 10785 Berlin; e-mail poststelle@bvr.de; internet www.bvr.de; f. 1972; Pres. Dr CHRISTOPHER PLEISTER; 1,500 mems.

Bundesverband Öffentlicher Banken Deutschlands eV (Association of German Public-Sector Banks): Lennéstr. 11, 10785 Berlin; tel. (30) 81920; fax (30) 8192222; e-mail postmaster@voeb.de; internet www.voeb.de.

Deutscher Sparkassen- und Giroverband eV (German Savings Banks Association): Postfach 110180, 10831 Berlin; Charlottenstr. 47, 10117 Berlin; tel. (30) 202250; fax (30) 20225250; e-mail postmaster@dsgv.de; internet www.dsgv.de; Pres. Dr DIETRICH H. HOPPENSTEDT.

STOCK EXCHANGES

Frankfurt am Main: Deutsche Börse AG, Börsenplatz 4, 60313 Frankfurt a.M.; tel. (69) 21010; fax (69) 29977580; internet www .exchange.de; f. 1585 as Frankfurter Wertpapierbörse; 269 mems; Chair. Supervisory Bd ROLF-ERNST BREUER; Chair. of Bd of Management Dr WERNER G. SEIFERT.

Berlin: Börse Berlin-Bremen, Fasanenstr. 85, 10623 Berlin; tel. (30) 3110910; fax (30) 31109178; internet www.boerse-berlin-bremen.de; f. 1685; 109 mems; Pres. Dr JÖRG FRANKE.

Bremen: Bremer Wertpapierbörse, Postfach 100726, 28007 Bremen; Kohlhökerstr. 29, 28203 Bremen; tel. (421) 277440; fax (421) 2774490; e-mail info@boerse-bremer.de; internet www .boerser-bremer.de; 67 mems; Pres. HORST-GÜNTER LUCKE; Man. AXEL H. SCHUBERT.

Düsseldorf: Börse Düsseldorf AG, Ernst-Schneider-Pl. 1, 40212 Düsseldorf; e-mail kontakt@boerse-duesseldorf.de; internet www .boerse-duesseldorf.de; tel. (211) 13890; fax (211) 133287; f. 1935; 125 mem. firms; Pres. HAROLD HORAUF; Gen. Mans Dr DETLEF IRMEN, DIRK ELBERSKIRCH.

München: Bayerische Börse AG, Lenbachpl. 2A, 80333 München; tel. (89) 5490450; fax (89) 54904531; e-mail info@bayerische-boerse .de; internet www.bayerische-boerse.de; 145 mems; Chair. Supervisory Bd Dr ALBRECHT SCHMIDT; Chair. Bd of Management Dr NORBERT JUCHEM.

North Germany (Hamburg and Hannover): BOAG Börsen AG, Rathenaustr. 2, 30159 Hannover; tel. (40) 3613020; fax (40) 36130223; internet www.boersenag.de; f. 1999 by merger of Hanseatische Wertpapierbörse Hamburg and Niedersächsische Börse zu Hannover; 109 and 81 mems, respectively; Pres. (Hamburg) UDO BANDOW; Chair. and Pres. FRIEDRICH KERSTING.

Stuttgart: Baden-Württembergische Wertpapierbörse, Königstr. 28, 70173 Stuttgart; tel. (711) 2229850; fax (711) 2268119; f. 1861; 141 mems; Pres. ROLF LIMBACH; Man. Dir Dr PETER LUDWIG.

INSURANCE

German law specifies that property and accident insurance may not be jointly underwritten with life, sickness, legal protection or credit insurance by the same company. Insurers are therefore obliged to establish separate companies to cover the different classes of insurance.

Aachener und Münchener Lebensversicherung AG: Robert-Schuman-Str. 51, 52066 Aachen; tel. (241) 600101; fax (241) 60015138; internet www.aachenerundmuenchener.de; f. 1868; Chair. Dr WOLFGANG KASKE; Gen. Man. Dr MICHAEL KALKA.

Albingia Versicherungs-AG: Ballindamm 39, 20095 Hamburg; tel. (40) 30220; fax (40) 30222585; e-mail infoa@albingia.de; internet www.albingia.de; f. 1901; Chair. Dr K. ASCHER; Gen. Man. V. BREMKAMP.

Allianz AG: Königinstr. 28, 80802 München; tel. (89) 38000; fax (89) 349941; internet www.allianz.com; f. 1890; Chair. Supervisory Bd Dr KLAUS LIESEN; Chair. Bd of Management Dr HENNING SCHULTE-NOELLE.

Allianz Lebensversicherungs-AG: Reinsburgstr. 19, 70178 Stuttgart; tel. (711) 6630; fax (711) 6632654; internet www.allianzgroup.com; f. 1922; Chair. Supervisory Bd MICHAEL DIEKMANN; Chair. Bd of Management Dr G. RUPPRECHT.

Allianz Private Krankenversicherungs AG: Fritz-Schäffer-Str. 9, 81737 München; tel. (89) 67850; fax (89) 67856523; internet www.gesundheit.allianz.de; f. 1925; Chair. Dr ULRICH RUMM.

Allianz Versicherungs AG: Elsa-Brandström-Str. 10–12, 80802 München; tel. (89) 38000; fax (89) 349941; e-mail medienzentrale@allianz.de; f. 1985; Chair. Dr H. SCHULTE-NOELLE; Gen. Man. Dr R. HAGEMANN.

AXA Colonia Krankenversicherung AG: 50592 Köln; tel. (221) 148125; fax (221) 14832602; f. 1962; Chair. CLAAS KLEYBOLDT; Gen. Man. Dr CARL HERMANN SCHLEIFFER.

AXA Lebensversicherung AG: Colonia-Allee 10–20, 51067 Köln; tel. (1803) 556622; fax (221) 14822750; e-mail service@axa.de; internet www.axa.de; f. 1853; Chair.Supervisory Bd CLAAS KLEYBOLDT; Chair. Bd of Management Dr CLAUS-MICHAEL DILL.

AXA Versicherung AG: Colonia-Allee 10–20, 50670 Köln; tel. (1803) 556622; fax (221) 14822740; e-mail service@axa.de; internet www.axa.de; f. 1839 as Colonia Kölnischer Freuer Versicherung AG, present name adopted 2001; property and casualty insurance; Chair. Supervisory Bd CLAAS KLEYBOLDT; Chair. Bd of Management Dr CLAUS-MICHAEL DILL.

Continentale Krankenversicherung AG: Postfach 105032, 44047 Dortmund; tel. (231) 9190; fax (231) 9191799; f. 1926; Chair. F. LENSING-WOLFF; Gen. Man. Dr H. HOFFMANN.

DBV-Winterthur Lebensversicherung AG: Frankfurter Str. 50, 65178 Wiesbaden; tel. (611) 3630; fax (611) 3636565; e-mail info@dbv-winterthur.de; f. 1872; Chair. T. SCHULTE; Man. Dir H. FALK.

Debeka Krankenversicherungsverein AG: Ferdinand-Sauerbruch-Str. 18, 56058 Koblenz; tel. (261) 4980; fax (261) 41402; f. 1905; Chair. P. GREISLER; Gen. Man. UWE LAUE.

Deutsche Krankenversicherung AG: Postfach 100865, 50448 Köln; Aachener Str. 300, 50933 Köln; tel. (221) 5780; fax (221) 5783694; internet www.dkv.com; f. 1927; Chair. Dr HANS-JÜRGEN SCHINZLER; Gen. Man. Dr J. BOETIUS.

Deutscher Herold Lebensversicherungs-AG: Postfach 1448, 53004 Bonn; tel. (228) 26801; fax (228) 2683692; internet www.herold.de; f. 1921; part of the Zürich Group; CEO EDUARD THOMETZECK.

Frankfurter Versicherungs-AG: Theodor-Stern-Kai 1, 60596 Frankfurt a.M.; tel. (69) 71260; fax (69) 712684455; internet www.frankfurter-alliance.de; f. 1929; Chair. Dr R. HAGEMANN; Gen. Man. Dr KARL LUDWIG FRHR VON FREYBERG.

Gerling-Konzern Allgemeine Versicherungs-AG: Postfach 100808, 50448 Köln; tel. (221) 1441; fax (221) 1443319; internet www.gerling.com; f. 1918; Chair. Supervisory Bd Dr J. ZECH; Chair. Bd of Management B. JANSKI.

Gothaer Versicherungsbank Versicherungsverein AG: Arnoldipl. 1, 50598 Köln; tel. (221) 30800; fax (221) 308103; internet www.gothaer.de; f. 1820; Chair. Supervisory Bd Dr KLAUS MURMANN; Chair. Bd of Management Dr WOLFGANG PEINER.

Haftpflicht-Unterstützungs-Kasse kraftfahrender Beamter Deutschlands AG in Coburg (HUK-COBURG): Bahnhofspl., 96444 Coburg; tel. (9561) 960; fax (9561) 963636; e-mail info@huk-coburg.de; internet www.huk.de; f. 1933; CEO ROLF-PETER HOENEN.

HDI Industrie Versicherungs AG: Postfach 510369, 30633 Hannover; tel. (511) 6450; fax (511) 6454545; internet www.hdi.de; f. 1903; Chair. W.-D. BAUMGARTL; CEO Dr C. HINSCH.

HDI Privat Versicherung AG: Postfach 210369, 30633 Hannover; tel. (511) 6450; fax (511) 6454545; internet www.hdi.de; Chair. W.-D. BAUMGARTL; CEO Dr C. HINSCH.

Hamburg-Mannheimer Versicherungs-AG: Überseering 45, 22297 Hamburg; tel. (40) 63760; fax (40) 63762885; e-mail prr@hamburg-mannheimer.de; internet www.hamburg-mannheimer.de;

merger with Victoria Versicherung AG pending; f. 1899; Chair. Dr EDGAR JAMMOTT; Gen. Man. Dr GÖTZ WRICKE.

IDUNA Vereinigte Lebensversicherung AG für Handwerk, Handel und Gewerbe: Neue Rabenstr. 15–19, 20354 Hamburg; tel. (40) 41240; e-mail info@signal-iduna.de; internet www.signal-iduna.de; f. 1914; Chair. Supervisory Bd G. KURTZ; Gen. Man. REINHOLD SCHULTE.

LVM Versicherungen: Kolde-Ring 21, 48126 Münster; tel. (251) 7020; fax (251) 7021099; e-mail info@lvm.de; internet www.lvm.de; f. 1896; Chair. JOCHEN BORCHERT; Gen. Man. G. KETTLER.

SIGNAL Krankenversicherung AG: Joseph-Scherer-Str. 3, 44139 Dortmund; tel. (231) 1350; fax (231) 1354638; e-mail info@signal-iduna.de; internet www.signal-iduna.de; f. 1907; Chair. Supervisory Bd G. KUTZ; Gen. Man. REINHOLD SCHULTE.

Talanx AG: Riethorst 2, 30659 Hannover; tel. (511) 37470; fax (511) 37472525; e-mail info@talanx.com; internet www.talanx.com; f. 1996; CEO D. BAUMGARTL.

Victoria Versicherung AG: Victoriapl. 1–2, 40198 Düsseldorf; tel. (221) 4770; fax (211) 4772222; e-mail info@victoria.de; internet www.victoria.de; merger with Hamburg-Mannheimer Versicherungs-AG pending; f. 1904; Chair. Dr E. JANNOTT; Gen. Man. HORST DÖRING.

Victoria Lebensversicherung AG: Victoriapl. 1–2, 40198 Düsseldorf; tel. (211) 4770; fax (211) 4772222; e-mail info@victoria.de; internet www.victoria.de; merger with Hamburg-Mannheimer Versicherungs-AG pending; f. 1929; Chair. Dr E. JANNOTT; Gen. Man. MICHAEL ROSENBERG.

Volksfürsorge Deutsche Lebensversicherung AG: Postfach 106420, 20043 Hamburg; tel. (40) 28650; fax (40) 28653369; f. 1913; Chair. Dr WOLFGANG KASKE; Gen. Man. Dr H. JÄGER.

Württembergische AG Versicherungs-Beteiligungsgesellschaft: Gutenbergstr. 30, 70176 Stuttgart; tel. (711) 6620; fax (711) 6622520; e-mail keu@wuerttembergische.de; internet www.wuerttembergische.de; f. 1828; Chair. Supervisory Bd Dr G. BÜCHNER; Chair. Bd of Management G. MEHL.

Reinsurance

Deutsche Rückversicherung AG: Düsseldorf; tel. (211) 455401; fax (211) 4554199; f. 1951; Chair. Dr HEIKO WINKLER; Gen. Man. JÜRGEN REHMANN.

DARAG Deutsche Versicherungs- und Rückversicherungs-AG: Postfach 10, 13062 Berlin; Gustav-Adolf-Str. 130, 13086 Berlin; tel. (30) 477080; fax (30) 47708100; e-mail info@darag.de; internet www.darag.de; f. 1958; re-formed 1990; fire and non-life, technical, cargo transport, marine hull, liability, aviation insurance and reinsurance; Chair. Supervisory Bd Dr WERNER SCHIMMING; Chair. Bd of Management VOLKER REIFENSCHEID; Gen. Man. Dr INGO WELTHER.

ERC-Aachener Rückversicherungs-Gesellschaft AG: Postfach 25, 52001 Aachen; tel. (241) 93690; fax (241) 9369205; f. 1853; Chair. Supervisory Bd KAJ AHLMANN; Chair. Bd of Management BERNHARD C. FINK.

GE Frankona Rückversicherungs-AG: Postfach 860380, 81630 München; Maria-Theresia-Str. 35, 81675 München; tel. (89) 92280; fax (89) 92287395; internet www.geercgroup.com/gpc; f. 1886; Chair. RICHARD F. SMITH; Gen. Man. KENNETH BRANDT.

Globale Rückversicherungs-AG: Hohenzollernring 72, 50672 Köln; tel. (221) 1441; fax (221) 1443718; e-mail info@globalre.com; internet www.globalre.com; f. 1954; Chair. Dr ACHIM KANN.

Hamburger Internationale Rückversicherung AG: Postfach 1161, 25452 Rellingen; Halstenbekerweg 96A, 25462 Rellingen; tel. (4101) 4710; fax (4101) 471298; f. 1965; Chair. IVOR KIVERSTEIN; Gen. Man. R. SOLL.

Hannover Rückversicherung AG: Postfach 610369, 30603 Hannover; Karl-Wiechert-Allee 50, 30625 Hannover; tel. (511) 56040; fax (511) 56041188; e-mail info@hannover-re.com; internet www.hannover-re.com; f. 1966; Chair. Supervisory Bd W. BAUMGARTL; Chair. Bd of Management W. ZELLER.

Kölnische Rückversicherungs-Gesellschaft AG: Postfach 102244, 50668 Köln; Theodor-Heuss-Ring 11, 50462 Köln; tel. (221) 97380; fax (221) 9738494; e-mail contact@genre.com; internet www.genre.com; f. 1846; Chair. Dr PETER LÜTKE-BORNEFELD.

Münchener Rückversicherungs-Gesellschaft AG: Königinstr. 107, 80802 München; tel. (89) 38910; fax (89) 399056; e-mail info@munichre.com; internet www.munichre.com; f. 1880; all classes of reinsurance; Chair. ULRICH HARTMANN; Gen. Man. NICKOLAUS VON BOMHARD.

R + V Versicherung-AG Reinsurance: Sonnenberger Str. 44, 65193 Wiesbaden; tel. (611) 533940; fax (611) 529610; f. 1935; all classes of reinsurance; Chair. W. GRÜGER; Gen. Man. Dr J. FÖRTERER.

Swiss Re Germany AG: Dieselstr. 11, 85774 Unterföhring bei München; tel. (89) 38440; fax (89) 38442279; e-mail info.srmuc@ swissre.com; internet www.swissre.com; Chair. Dr B. GAS; Gen. Man. M. LIÈS.

Principal Insurance Association

Gesamtverband der Deutschen Versicherungswirtschaft eV: Friedrichstr. 191, 10117 Berlin; tel. (30) 20205000; fax (30) 20206000; e-mail berlin@gdv.org; internet www.gdv.de; f. 1948; affiliating three mem. asscns and 457 mem. cos; Pres. Dr BERNHARD SCHARECK (Karlsruhe); CEO Dr FRANK VON FÜRSTENWERTH.

Trade and Industry

GOVERNMENT AGENCIES

Bundesagentur für Aussenwirtschaft (German Office for Foreign Trade): Postfach 100522, 50445 Köln; Agrippastr. 87–93, 50676 Köln; tel. (221) 20570; fax (221) 2057212; e-mail info@bfai.de; internet www.bfai.de.

Bundesverband des Deutschen Gross- und Aussenhandels eV: Bonn; tel. (228) 260040; fax (228) 2600455; f. 1949; Dir-Gen. Dr PETER SPARY; 77 mem. asscns.

Hauptverband des Deutschen Einzelhandels eV: Berlin; tel. (30) 7262500; fax (30) 72625099; e-mail hde@einzelhandel.de; internet www.einzelhandel.de; f. 1947; Chair. HERMANN FRANZEN; Exec. Dir HOLGER WENZEL.

Industrial Investment Council (IIC): Friedrichstr. 60, 10117 Berlin; tel. (30) 20945660; fax (30) 20945666; e-mail info@iic.de; internet www.iic.de; promotes investment in eastern Germany; Chair. Dr HORST DIETZ.

Zentralverband Gewerblicher Verbundgruppen: Vorgebirgsstr. 43, 53119 Bonn; tel. (228) 985840; fax (228) 9858410; f. 1992; six dirs; c. 400 mems.

CHAMBERS OF COMMERCE

Deutscher Industrie- und Handelstag (Association of German Chambers of Industry and Commerce): Adenauerallee 148, 53113 Bonn; tel. (228) 1040; fax (228) 104158; Pres. HANS PETER STIHL; Sec.-Gen. Dr FRANZ SCHOSER; affiliates 83 Chambers of Industry and Commerce.

There are Chambers of Industry and Commerce in all the principal towns and also 14 regional associations including:

Arbeitsgemeinschaft Hessischer Industrie- und Handelskammern: Börsenpl. 4, 60313 Frankfurt a.M.; tel. (69) 21971384; fax (69) 21971497; internet www .arbeitsgemeinschaft-hessischer-ihks.de; Chair. Dr JOACHIM VON HARBOM; Sec.-Gen. Dr WOLFGANG LINDSTAEDT; 11 mems.

Arbeitsgemeinschaft der Industrie- und Handelskammern in Mecklenburg-Vorpommern: Schlossstr. 17, 19053 Schwerin; tel. (385) 51030; fax (385) 5103136; e-mail info@schwerin.ihk.de; internet www.ihkzuschwerin.de; Pres. JOERGEN THIELE; Man. Dir KLAUS-MICHAEL ROTHE.

Arbeitsgemeinschaft der Industrie- und Handelskammern in Sachsen: Str. der Nationen 25, 0911 Chemnitz; tel. (371) 69000; fax (371) 643018.

Arbeitsgemeinschaft Norddeutscher Industrie- und Handelskammern: Adolphspl. 1, 20457 Hamburg; tel. (40) 366382; Vice-Pres. Dr MARTIN WILLICH; Sec. Dr UWE CHRISTIANSEN.

Arbeitsgemeinschaft der Thuringer Industrie- und Handelskammern: Weimarische Str. 45, 99099 Erfurt; tel. (361) 34840; fax (361) 3485972; f. 1991; Pres. NIELS LUND CHRESTENSEN.

Baden-Württembergischer Industrie- und Handelskammertag: Jägerstr. 40, 70174 Stuttgart; tel. (711) 22550060; fax (711) 22550077; e-mail info@bw.ihk.de; internet www.bw.ihk.de; Chair. TILL CASPER.

Bayerischer Industrie- und Handelskammertag: Max-Joseph-Str. 2, 80333 München; tel. (89) 51160; fax (89) 5116306; e-mail iszihkmail@muenchn-ihk.de; Pres. Prof. Dr ERICH GREIPL; Sec.-Gen. Dr REINHARD DÖRFLER; 260,000 mems.

IHK-Arbeitsgemeinschaft Rheinland-Pfalz: Herzogenbuscher Str. 12, 54292 Trier; tel. (651) 9777101; fax (651) 9777105; e-mail lamberty@trier.ihk.de; Sec. WOLFGANG NATUS; four mems.

IHK-Vereinigung Schleswig-Holstein: Bergstr. 2, 24103 Kiel; tel. (431) 5194215; fax (431) 5194515; e-mail ihk@kiel.ihk.de; internet www.kiel-ihk.de; Chair. Prof. Dr HANS HEINRICH DRILLMANN; Sec.-Gen. WOLF-RÜDIGER JANZEN.

Industrie- und Handelskammer Magdeburg: Postfach 1840, Alter Markt 8, 39104 Magdeburg; tel. (391) 56930; fax (391) 5693193; e-mail internet@magdeburg.ihk.de; internet www .magdeburg.ihk.de; f. 1825; Pres. Dr KLAUS HIECKMANN.

Industrie- und Handelskammern Potsdam: Breite Str. 2A–C, 14467 Potsdam; tel. (331) 2786251; fax (331) 2786190; e-mail ullmann@potsdam.ihk.de; internet www.potsdam.ihk24.de; f. 1990; Pres. Dr VICTOR STIMMING; CEO PETER EGENTER.

Niedersächsischer Industrie- und Handelskammertag (NIHK): Postfach 3029, 30030 Hannover; Schiffgraben 49, 30175 Hannover; tel. (511) 3107289; fax (511) 3107383; e-mail nihk@ hannover.ihk.de; f. 1899; Pres. Prof. Dr KLAUS E. GOEHRMANN; Man. Dir Dr WILFRIED PREWO; 7 mems.

Vereinigung der Industrie- und Handelskammern in Nordrhein-Westfalen: Postfach 240120, 40090 Düsseldorf; tel. (211) 367020; fax (211) 3670221; CEO HANS GEORG CRONE-ERDMANN; Pres. Dr JÖRG MITTELSTEN SCHEID; 16 mems.

INDUSTRIAL AND TRADE ASSOCIATIONS

Bundesverband der Deutschen Industrie eV (Federation of German Industry): Breite Str. 29, 10178 Berlin; tel. (30) 20281566; fax (30) 20282566; e-mail presse@bdi-online.de; Pres. Dr MICHAEL ROGOWSKI; Dir-Gen. Dr LUDOLF VON WARTENBERG; mems include some of the following asscns:

Arbeitsgemeinschaft Keramische Industrie eV (Ceramics): Postfach 1624, 95090 Selb; Schillerstr. 17, 95100 Selb; tel. (9287) 8080; fax (9287) 70492; e-mail info@keramverbaende.de; internet www.keramverbaende.de; Pres. WENDELIN VON BOCH; Man. PETER FRISCHHOLZ.

Bundesverband Baustoffe—Steine und Erden eV (Building Materials): Postfach 610486, 10928 Berlin; Kochstr. 6–7, 10969 Berlin; tel. (30) 72619990; fax (30) 726199912; e-mail info@ bvbaustoffe.de; internet www.baustoffindustrie.de; f. 1948; Pres. Dr GERNOT SCHAEFER; Chief Dir Dr MICHAEL WEIßENHORN.

Bundesverband Bekleidungsindustrie eV (Clothing): Postfach 100955, 50449 Köln; Mevissenstr. 15, 50668 Köln; tel. (221) 7744110; fax (221) 7744118; e-mail bbi@bbi-online.de; internet www .bbi-online.de; Pres. PAUL DANKBAR; Dirs-Gen. BERND KEMPER, FRIED-HELM N. SARTORIS.

Bundesverband der Deutschen Entsorgungswirtschaft (BDE) (Waste Disposal and Recycling): Tempelhofer Ufer 37, 10963 Berlin; tel. (30) 59003350; fax (30) 590033599; e-mail info@ bde-berlin.de; internet www.bde-berlin.de; Pres. BERNARD KEMPER; Dir-Gen. FRANK-RAINER BILLIGMANN.

Bundesverband der Deutschen Luft- und Raumfahrtindustrie eV (BDLI) (German Aerospace Industries Asscn): Friedrichstr. 60, 10117 Berlin; tel. (30) 2061400; fax (30) 20614090; e-mail info@bdli.de; internet www.bdli.de; f. 1952; Pres. RAINER HERTRICH; Man. Dir HANS-JOACHIM GANTE.

Bundesverband Druck und Medien eV (Printing and Media): Postfach 1869, 65008 Wiesbaden; Biebricher Allee 79, 65187 Wiesbaden; tel. (611) 8030; fax (611) 803113; e-mail info@bvdm-online.de; f. 1947; Pres. MANFRED ADRIAN; Man. Dir THOMAS MAYER; 12 mem. asscns.

Bundesverband Glasindustrie eV (Glass): Postfach 101753, 40008 Düsseldorf; Am Bonneshof 5, 40474 Düsseldorf; tel. (211) 4796134; fax (211) 9513751; e-mail info@bvglas.de; internet www .bvglas.de; Chair. PAUL NEETESON; 4 mem. asscns.

Bundesverband Schmuck, Uhren, Silberwaren und Verwandte Industrien eV: Zerrenstr. 32, 75172 Pforzheim; tel. (7231) 33041; fax (7231) 355887; e-mail info@bv-schmuck-uhren.de; internet www.bv-schmuck-uhren.de; Pres. LOTHAR KELLER; Man. Dir Dr ALFRED SCHNEIDER.

Bundesvereinigung der Deutschen Ernährungsindustrie eV (BVE) (Food): Postfach 200212, 53132 Bonn; Godesberger Allee 142–148, 53175 Bonn; tel. (228) 308290; fax (228) 3082999; e-mail bve@bve-online.de; internet www.bve-online.de; f. 1949; Chair. JÜRGEN ABRAHAM; Chief Gen. Man. Prof. Dr MATTHIAS HORST.

Deutscher Giessereiverband (Foundries): Postfach 10 19 61, 40010 Düsseldorf; Sohnstr. 70, 40237 Düsseldorf; tel. (211) 6871215; fax (211) 6871205; e-mail info@dgv.de; internet www.dgv.de; f. 1865; Pres. Dr ARNOLD KAWLATH; Man. Dir Dr KLAUS URBAT.

Deutscher Hotel- und Gaststättenverband eV (DEHOGA): Am Weidendamm 1A, 10117 Berlin; tel. (30) 7262520; fax (30) 72625242; f. 1949; Pres. ERNST FISCHER; Gen. Sec. CHRISTIAN EHLERS; over 85,000 mems.

Gemeinschaftsausschuss der Deutschen gewerblichen Wirtschaft (Joint Committee for German Industry and Commerce): Köln; tel. (221) 370800; fax (221) 3708730; f. 1950; a discussion

forum for the principal industrial and commercial orgs; Pres. Dr
TYLL NECKER; 16 mem. orgs.

Gesamtverband kunststoffverarbeitende Industrie eV (GKV)
(Plastics): Am Hauptbahnhof 12, 60329 Frankfurt a.M.; tel. (69)
271050; fax (69) 232799; e-mail tenhagen-gkv@t-online.de; internet
www.gkv.de; f. 1950; Chair. GÜNTER SCHWANK; Sec.-Gen. JOACHIM DEN
HAGEN; 750 mems.

Gesamtverband der deutschen Textil und Modeindustrie eV
(Textiles and Clothing): Postfach 5340, 65728 Eschborn; Frankfurter Str. 10–14, 65760 Eschborn; tel. (6196) 9660; fax (6196)
42170; e-mail info@textil-mode.de; internet www.textil-online.de; f.
1948; Dir-Gen. Dr WOLF R. BAUMANN.

Hauptverband der Deutschen Bauindustrie eV (Building):
Kurfürstenstr. 129, 10785 Berlin; tel. (30) 212860; fax (30)
21286240; e-mail bauind@bauindustrie.de; internet www
.bauindustrie.de; f. 1948; Pres. Dr OTHMAR FRANZ; Dir-Gen. MICHAEL
KNIPPER; 23 mem. asscns.

**Hauptverband der Deutschen Holz und Kunststoffe
verarbeitenden Industrie und verwandter Industriezweige
eV (HDH)** (Woodwork): Flutgraben 2, 53604 Bad-Honnef; tel. (2224)
93770; fax (2224) 937777; e-mail info@hdh-ev.de; internet www
.hdh-ev.de; f. 1948; Pres. HELMUT LÜBKE; Man. Dir DIRK-UWE KLAAS;
24 mem. asscns.

**Hauptverband der Papier, Pappe und Kunststoffe verarbei-
tenden Industrie eV (HPV)** (Paper, Board and Plastic): Strub-
bergstr. 70, 60489 Frankfurt a.M.; tel. (69) 9782810; fax (69)
97828130; e-mail info@hpv-ev.org; internet www.hpv-ev.org; f. 1948;
10 regional groups, 20 production groups; Pres. LUTZ BOEDER; Dir-
Gen. THOMAS BECK; 1,300 mems.

Kaliverein eV (Potash): Postfach 410554, 34067 Kassel; Wilhelmshöher Allee 239, 34121 Kassel; tel. (561) 318270; fax (561) 3182716;
e-mail kaliverein@k-plus-s.com; internet www.kaliverein.de; f.
1905; Pres. Dr RALF BETHKE; Man. Dir Dr ARNE BROCKHOFF.

Mineralölwirtschaftsverband eV (Petroleum): Steindamm 55,
20099 Hamburg; tel. (40) 248490; fax (40) 24849-253; e-mail mwv@
mwv.de; internet www.mwv.de; f. 1946; Chair. THIERRY PFLIMLIN;
Man. Dir Dr KLAUS PICARD.

**SPECTARIS—Deutscher Industrieverband für optische,
medizinische und mechatronische Technologien eV** (German
Industrial Asscn for Optical, Medical and Mechatronical Technologies): Kirchweg 2, 50858 Köln; tel. (221) 9486280; fax (221)
94862880; e-mail info@spectaris.de; internet www.spectaris.de; f.
1949; Chair. Prof. Dr UTZ CLAASSEN; Dir SVEN BEHRENS.

Verband der Automobilindustrie eV (Motor Cars): Postfach
170563, 60079 Frankfurt a.M.; Westendstr. 61, 60325 Frankfurt
a.M.; tel. (69) 975070; fax (69) 97507261; e-mail info@vda.de;
internet www.vda.de; Dir BERND GOTTSCHALK.

Verband der Chemischen Industrie eV (Chemical Industry):
Karlstr. 21, 60329 Frankfurt a.M.; tel. (69) 25560; fax (69) 2556-
1471; e-mail vci@vci.de; internet www.chemische-industrie.de; f.
1877; Pres. Dr JÜRGEN HAMBRECHT; Dir-Gen. Dr WILFRIED SAHM; 1,600
mems.

Verband der Cigarettenindustrie (Cigarettes): Neustädtische
Kirchstr. 8, 10117 Berlin; tel. (30) 206050; fax (30) 20605250; e-mail
vdc@vdc.berlin.de; internet www.vdc-berlin.de; Chair. WOLFGANG
HAINER.

Verband Deutscher Maschinen- und Anlagenbau eV (VDMA)
(German Engineering Federation): Postfach 710864, 60498 Frankfurt a.M.; Lyoner Str. 18, 60528 Frankfurt a.M.; tel. (69) 66030; fax
(69) 66031511; e-mail puoe@vdma.org; internet www.vdma.org; f.
1892; Pres. EBERHARD REUTHER; Gen. Man. Dr HANNES HESSE.

Verband Deutscher Papierfabriken eV (Paper): Adenauerallee
55, 53113 Bonn; tel. (228) 267050; fax (228) 2670562; Pres. HANS-
MICHAEL GELLENKAMP; Dir-Gen. KLAUS WINDHAGEN.

Verband für Schiffbau und Meerestechnik eV (Shipbuilding):
An der Alster 1, 20099 Hamburg; tel. (40) 2801520; fax (40)
28015230; e-mail info@vsm.de; internet www.vsm.de; Gen. Dir Dr
WERNER LUNDT; Man. Dirs VOLKHARD MEIER, Dr MATHIAS MÜNCHAU.

Verein der Zuckerindustrie (Sugar): Am Hofgarten 8, 53113
Bonn; tel. (228) 22850; fax (228) 2285100; e-mail wvz-vdz@
zuckerverbaende.de; internet www.zuckerverbaende.de; f. 1850;
Chair. HORST W. MEWIS; Dir-Gen. Dr DIETER LANGENDORF.

**Wirtschaftsverband der Deutschen Kautschukindustrie eV
(WDK)** (Rubber): Zeppelinallee 69, 60487 Frankfurt a.M.; tel. (69)
79360; fax (69) 7936165; e-mail info@wdk.de; internet www.wdk.de;
f. 1894; Pres. PAUL EBERHARD-KRUG; Gen. Man. FRITZ KATZENSTEINER;
87 mems.

Wirtschaftsverband Erdöl- und Erdgasgewinnung eV
(Association of Crude Oil and Gas Producers): Brühlstr. 9, 30169
Hannover; tel. (511) 121720; fax (511) 1217210; e-mail info@

erdoel-erdgas.de; internet www.erdoel-erdgas.de; f. 1945; Pres. Dr
CERNOT KALKOFFEN; Gen. Man. JOSEF SCHMID.

Wirtschaftsverband Stahlbau und Energietechnik (SET)
(Steel and Energy): Postfach 320420, 40419 Düsseldorf; Sternstr. 36,
40479 Düsseldorf; tel. (211) 4987092; fax (211) 4987036; e-mail info@
set-online.de; internet www.set-online.de; Chair. KLAUS DIETER REN-
NERT; Dir-Gen. R. MAASS.

**WSM—Wirtschaftsverband Stahl- und Metallverarbeitung
eV** (Steel and Metal-Processing Industry): Postfach 30 10 42, 40410
Düsseldorf; Kaiserswerther Str. 135, 40474 Düsseldorf; tel. (211)
4564108; fax (211) 4564169; e-mail hwolff@wsm-net.de; internet
www.wsm-net.de; Pres. JÜRGEN R. THUMANN; Dir-Gen. Dr ANDREAS
MOEHLENKAMP.

**Centralvereinigung Deutscher Wirtschaftsverbände für
Handelsvermittlung und Vertrieb:** Am Weidendamm 1A, 10117
Berlin; tel. (30) 72625600; fax (30) 72625699; e-mail
centralvereinigung@cdh.de; internet www.cdh.de; f. 1902; Pres.
HORST PLATZ; Gen. Sec. Dr ANDREAS PAFFHAUSEN; 18,000 mems.

Wirtschaftsvereinigung Bergbau eV (Mining): Postfach 120736,
10597 Berlin; Am Schillertheater 4, 10625 Berlin; tel. (30) 31518242;
e-mail info@wv-bergbau.de; internet www.wv-bergbau.de; Pres.
Prof. Dr KARL-FRIEDRICH JAKOB; Gen. Man. Dr HEINZ-NORBERT
SCHÄCHTER; 14 mem. asscns.

WirtschaftsVereinigung Metalle (Metal): Postfach 105463,
40045 Düsseldorf; Am Bonneshof 5, 40474 Düsseldorf; tel. (211)
47960; fax (211) 4796400; e-mail info@wvmetalle.de; internet www
.wvmetalle.de; Pres. Dr KARL-HEINZ DÖRNER; Dir-Gen. MARTIN KNEER.

Wirtschaftsvereinigung Stahl (Steel): Postfach 105464, 40045
Düsseldorf; Sohnstr. 65, 40237 Düsseldorf; tel. (211) 67070; fax (211)
6707310; e-mail wvstahl@wvstahl.de; internet www.stahl-online.de;
Pres. Prof. Dr DIETER AMELING; Dir ALBRECHT KORMANN.

Wirtschaftsvereinigung Ziehereien und Kaltwalzwerke eV
(Metal): Drahthaus, Kaiserswerther Str. 137, 40474 Düsseldorf; tel.
(211) 4564246; fax (211) 432154; Chair. JÜRGEN R. THUMANN; Gen.
Man. GÜNTER MÜLLER.

Zentralverband des Deutschen Handwerks: Mohrenstr. 20/21,
10117 Berlin; tel. (30) 206190; fax (30) 20619460; e-mail info@zdh
.de; internet www.zdh.de; f. 1949; Pres. OTTO KENTZLER; Gen. Sec.
HANNS-EBERHARD SCHLEYER; 54 mem. chambers, 38 asscns.

**Zentralverband Elektrotechnik- und Elektronikindustrie eV
(ZVEI)** (Electrical and Electronic Equipment): Postfach 701261,
60591 Frankfurt a.M.; Stresemannallee 19, 60596 Frankfurt a.M.;
tel. (69) 63020; fax (69) 6302317; e-mail zvei@zvei.org; internet www
.zvei.org; f. 1918; Chair. Prof. Dr EDWARD G. KRUBASIK; Dirs GOTTHARD
GRASS, Dr OLIVER BLANK, Dr HORST GERLACH; 1,400 mems.

EMPLOYERS' ORGANIZATIONS

**Bundesvereinigung der Deutschen Arbeitgeberverbände
(BDA)** (Confederation of German Employers' Associations): im
Haus der Deutschen Wirtschaft, 11054 Berlin; tel. (30) 20330; fax
(30) 20331055; e-mail info@bda-online.de; internet www.bda-online
.de; f. 1904; represents the professional and regional interests of
German employers in the social policy field, affiliates 14 regional
asscns and 53 branch asscns, of which some are listed under industrial asscns; Pres. Dr DIETER HUNDT; Dirs Dr REINHARD GÖHNER,
ALEXANDER GUNKEL, PETER CLEVER.

Affiliated associations:

Arbeitgeberverband der Cigarettenindustrie (Employers'
Association of Cigarette Manufacturers): Harvestehuder Weg 88,
20149 Hamburg; tel. (40) 445739; fax (40) 443039; f. 1949; Pres.
SIEGFRIED HANKE; Dir LUTZ SANNIG.

Arbeitgeberverband der Deutschen Binnenschiffahrt eV
(Employers' Association of German Inland Waterway Transport):
Dammstr. 15–17, 47119 Duisburg; tel. (203) 8000631; fax (203)
8000628; e-mail info@adb-ev.de; internet www
.schulschiffrhein-adb.de; f. 1974; Pres. Dr WOLFGANG HÖNEMANN;
Dir G. DÜTEMEYER.

Arbeitgeberverband der Deutschen Glasindustrie eV
(German Glass Industry Employers' Association): Postfach
200219, 80002 München; Max-Joseph-Str. 5, 80333 München; tel.
(89) 55178400; fax (89) 55178444; e-mail info@avglas.de; internet
www.avglas.de; Pres. PETER WEINMANN; Gen. Man. GERNOT STEIN-
BACHER.

**Arbeitgeberverband der Deutschen Kautschukindustrie
(ADK) eV** (German Rubber Industry Employers' Association):
Schiffgraben 36, 30175 Hannover; tel. (511) 85050; fax (511)
8505201; e-mail agv-hannover@vmn.de; internet www.adk-ev.de;
Pres. JÜRGEN KREBAUM; Gen. Man. DIETRICH KRÖNCKE.

Arbeitgeberverband Deutscher Eisenbahnen eV (German
Railway Employers' Association): Volksgartenstr. 54A, 50677

Köln; tel. (221) 9318450; fax (221) 93184588; Pres. Dr HANS-PETER SCHIFF; Dir Dr HANS-PETER ACKMANN.

Arbeitgeberverband des Gesamtverbandes der deutschen Textil- und Modeindustrie eV (General Textile Employers' Organization): Frankfurter Str. 10–14, 65760 Eschborn; tel. (6196) 9660; fax (6196) 42170; internet www.textil-online.de; Chair. WOLFGANG BRINKMANN; Gen. Man. HELGE MARTIN KROLLMANN; 13 mem. asscns.

Arbeitgeberverband des Privaten Bankgewerbes eV (Private Banking Employers' Association): Burgstr. 28, 10178 Berlin; tel. (30) 590011270; e-mail service@agvbanken.de; f. 1954; 120 mems; Pres. DIETER RAMPL; Dir GERD BENRATH.

Arbeitgeberverband der Versicherungsunternehmen in Deutschland (Employers' Association of Insurance Companies): Postfach 860120, 81628 München; Arabellastr. 29, 81925 München; tel. (89) 9220010; fax (89) 92200150; e-mail agvvers@agv-vers.de; internet www.agv-vers.de; f. 1950; Pres. Dr JOACHIM LEMPPENAU; Dir-Gen. Dr JÖRG MÜLLER-STEIN.

Bundesarbeitgeberverband Chemie eV (Federation of Employers' Associations in the Chemical Industry): Postfach 1280, 65002 Wiesbaden; Abraham-Lincoln-Str. 24, 65189 Wiesbaden; tel. (611) 778810; fax (611) 7788123; e-mail info@bavc.de; internet www.bavc.de; Pres. Dr RÜDIGER ERCKEL; Dir HANS PAUL FREY; 11 mem. asscns.

Bundesvereinigung der Arbeitgeber im Bundesverband Bekleidungsindustrie eV (Confederation of Employers of the Clothing Industry): Postfach 100955, 50449 Köln; Mevissenstr. 15, 50668 Köln; tel. (221) 7744110; fax (221) 7744118; e-mail bbi@bbi-online.de; internet www.bbi-online.de; Pres. WILFRIED BRANDES; Dir BERND KEMPER; 18 mem. asscns.

Gesamtverband der Deutschen Land- und Forstwirtschaftlichen Arbeitgeberverbände eV (Federation of Agricultural and Forestry Employers' Associations): Godesberger Allee 142–148, 53175 Bonn; tel. (228) 8198249; fax (228) 8198204; e-mail glfa@bauernverband.net; Pres. LOTHAR LAMPE; Sec. BURKHARD MÖLLER.

Gesamtverband der Metallindustriellen Arbeitgeberverbände eV (Federation of the Metal Trades Employers' Associations): Postfach 060249, 10052 Berlin; Voßstr. 16, 10117 Berlin; tel. (30) 551500; e-mail info@gesamtmetall.de; internet www.gesamtmetall.de; Pres. MARTIN KANNEGIESSER; 15 mem. asscns.

Vereinigung der Arbeitgeberverbände der Deutschen Papierindustrie eV (Federation of Employers' Associations of the German Paper Industry): Adenauerallee 55, 53113 Bonn; tel. (228) 2672810; fax (228) 215270; e-mail info@vap-papier.de; internet www.vap-papier.de; Pres. EBERHARD POTEMPA; Dir HANS-JOACHIM BLÖMEKE; 8 mem. asscns.

Vereinigung der Arbeitgeberverbände energie- und versorgungswirtschaftlicher Unternehmungen (Employers' Federation of Energy and Power Supply Enterprises): Kurt Schumacher-Str. 24, 30159 Hannover; tel. (511) 911090; fax (511) 9110940; f. 1962; Pres. Dr ACHIM MIDDELSCHULTE; Dir HERMANN D. STRÖHMBERG; 6 mem. asscns.

Regional employers' associations:

Landesvereinigung Baden-Württembergischer Arbeitgeberverbände eV: Postfach 700501, 70574 Stuttgart; Löffelstr. 22–24, 70597 Stuttgart; tel. (711) 76820; fax (711) 7651675; e-mail info@suedwestmetall.de; internet www.agv-bw.de; Pres. Dr DIETER HUNDT; Dir Dr ULRICH BROCKER; 42 mem. asscns.

Vereinigung der Bayerischen Wirtschaft (Federation of Employers' Associations in Bavaria): Postfach 202061, 80020 München; Max-Joseph-Str. 5, 80333 München; tel. (89) 55178100; fax (89) 55178111; e-mail info@vbw-bayern.de; internet www.vbw-bayern.de; Pres. RANDOLF RODENSTOCK; Gen. Man STEPHAN GÖTZL; 76 mem. asscns.

Vereinigung der Unternehmensverbände in Berlin und Brandenburg eV (Federation of Employers' Associations in Berlin and Brandenburg): Am Schillertheater 2, 10625 Berlin; tel. (30) 310050; fax (30) 31005166; e-mail uvb@uvb-online.de; internet www.uvb-online.de; Pres. GERD VON BRANDENSTEIN; Dir Dr HARTMANN KLEINER; 62 mem. asscns.

Die Unternehmensverbände im Lande Bremen eV (Federation of Employers' Associations in the Land of Bremen): Postfach 100727, 28007 Bremen; Schillerstr. 10, 28195 Bremen; tel. (421) 368020; fax (421) 3680249; Pres. INGO KRAMER; Dir EBERHARD SCHODDE; 15 mem. asscns.

UVNord—Vereinigung der Unternehmensverbände in Hamburg und Schleswig-Holstein eV (Federation of Employers' Associations in Hamburg and Schleswig-Holstein): Postfach 601969, 22219 Hamburg; Kapstadtring 10, 22297 Hamburg; tel. (40) 63785100; fax (40) 63785075; e-mail kemmet@uvnord.de; internet www.uvnord.de; Pres. Prof. Dr HANS HEINRICH DRIFTMANN; Dir Dr KLAUS KEMMET; 53 mem. asscns.

Vereinigung der Hessischen Unternehmerverbände eV (Hessian Federation of Enterprise Associations): Postfach 500561, 60394 Frankfurt a.M.; Emil-von-Behring-Str. 4, 60439 Frankfurt a.M.; tel. (69) 958080; fax (69) 95808126; e-mail info@vhu.de; internet www.vhu.de; f. 1947; Pres. Prof. DIETER WEIDEMANN; Dir and Sec. VOLKER FASBENDER; 50 mem. asscns.

Vereinigung der Unternehmensverbände für Mecklenburg-Vorpommern eV (Federation of Employers' Associations of Mecklenburg-West Pomerania): Eckdrift 93, 19061 Schwerin; tel. (385) 6356100; fax (385) 6356151; e-mail info@vumv.de; internet www.vumv.de; Pres. KLAUS HERING; Dir Dr THOMAS KLISCHAN; 29 mem. asscns.

Unternehmensverbände Niedersachsen eV (Federation of Employers' Associations in Lower Saxony): Schiffgraben 36, 30175 Hannover; tel. (511) 8505243; fax (511) 8505268; e-mail uvn@uvn-online.de; internet www.uvn-online.de; f. 1951; Pres. GOETZ VON ENGELBRECHTEN; Dir Dr VOLKER MÜLLER; 67 mem. asscns.

Landesvereinigung der Arbeitgeberverbände Nordrhein-Westfalen eV (North Rhine-Westphalia Federation of Employers' Associations): Postfach 300643, 40406 Düsseldorf; Uerdingerstr. 58–62, 40474 Düsseldorf; tel. (211) 45730; fax (211) 4573206; e-mail arbeitgebernrw@arbeitgebernrw.de; internet www.arbeitgebernrw.de; Pres. Dr JOCHEN F. KIRCHHOFF; Dir Dr HANSJÖRG DÖPP; 92 mem. asscns.

Landesvereinigung Unternehmerverbände Rheinland-Pfalz eV (LVU) (Federation of Employers' Associations in the Rhineland Palatinate): Postfach 2966, 55019 Mainz; Hindenburgstr. 32, 55118 Mainz; tel. (6131) 55750; fax (6131) 557539; e-mail contact@lvu.de; internet www.lvu.de; f. 1963; Pres. Dr GERHARD F. BRAUN; Gen. Man. WERNER SIMON; 25 mem. asscns.

Vereinigung der Saarländischen Unternehmensverbände (Federation of Employers' Associations in Saarland): Postfach 650433, 66143 Saarbrücken; Harthweg 15, 66119 Saarbrücken; tel. (681) 954340; fax (681) 9543474; e-mail kontakt@vsu.de; internet www.vsu.de; Pres. Dr WALTER KOCH; Dir Dr HEIKO JÜTTE; 16 mem. asscns.

Vereinigung der Sächsischen Wirtschaft eV (VSW) (Federation of Employers' Associations in Saxony): Postfach 300200, 01131 Dresden; Washingtonstr. 16/16A, 01139 Dresden; tel. (351) 255930; fax (351) 2559378; e-mail info@wirtschaftsverbaende-sachsen.de; internet www.wirtschaftsverbaende-sachsen.de; Pres. WOLFGANG HEINZE; Gen. Man. Dr ANDREAS WINKLER; 40 mem. asscns.

Landesvereinigung der Arbeitgeber-und-Wirtschaftsverbände Sachsen-Anhalt eV (Provincial Federation of Employers' and Managers' Associations of Saxony-Anhalt): Hegelstr. 39, 39104 Magdeburg; tel. (391) 5982250; fax (391) 5982259; e-mail info@lvsa.org; internet www.lvsa.org; Pres. Dr HELGE FÄNGER; Gen. Man. KLAUS LIEDKE; 31 mem. asscns.

Verband der Wirtschaft Thüringens eV (Association of Thuringian Management): Postfach 100753, 99007 Erfurt; Lossiusstr. 1, 99094 Erfurt; tel. (361) 67590; fax (361) 6759222; e-mail info@vwt.de; internet www.vet.de; Pres. WALTER BOTSCHATZKI; Dir LOTAR SCHMIDT; 37 mem. asscns.

UTILITIES

Electricity

Bewag AG: 12432 Berlin; tel. (30) 26711077; fax (30) 26714667; e-mail bewag@bewag.com; internet www.bewag.de; f. 1884; supplies Berlin; promotes development of urban utilization of renewable energy resources.

E.ON Energie AG: Brienner Str. 40, 80333 München; tel. (89) 125401; fax (89) 12541401; e-mail info@eon-energie.de; internet www.eon-energie.de; f. 2000 by merger of Bayernwerk AG and Preussenelektra AG; Chair. Dr JOHANNES TEYSSEN.

Energie Baden-Württemberg (EnBW): Durlacher Allee 93; tel. (800) 999; e-mail info@enbw.de; internet www.enbw.com.

Hamburgische Electricitäts-Werke AG (HEW): Überseering 12, 22297 Hamburg; tel. (40) 63960; fax (40) 63962770; e-mail hew@hew.de; internet www.hew.de; 73% owned by regional Govt; supplies Hamburg region.

RWE Energie AG: Postfach 103165, 45031 Essen; Kruppstr. 5, 45128 Essen; tel. (201) 1851; fax (201) 1854313; internet www.rweenergie.de; acquired Thames Water Utilities Ltd (UK) in 2000 and American Water Works Asscn (USA) in 2001; Pres. DIETMAR KUHNT; CEO HARRY ROELS.

VDEW—Verband der Elektrizitätswirtschaft eV: Stresemann-allee 23, 60596 Frankfurt a.M.; tel. (69) 63041; fax (69) 6304289; e-mail vdew-info@vdew.net; internet www.strom.de; asscn of electricity supply cos; Dir-Gen. Dr Eberhard Meller.

Vereinigte Energiewerke AG (VEAG): Chaussestr. 23, 10115 Berlin; tel. (30) 51512521; fax (30) 51502220; e-mail info@veag.de; internet www.veag.de; serves eastern Germany.

Gas

Bundesverband der Deutschen Gas- und Wasserwirtschaft eV (BGW): Reinhardstr. 14, 10117 Berlin; tel. (30) 280410; fax (30) 28041520; e-mail info@bgw.de; internet www.bgw.de; asscn of gas and water cos; Pres. Dr Wolf Pluge.

E.ON Ruhrgas AG: Huttropstr. 60, 45138 Essen; tel. (201) 18400; fax (201) 1843766; e-mail info@eon-ruhrgas.com; internet www.eon-ruhrgas.de; f. 1926; Chair. Dr Burckhard Bergmann.

GASAG Berliner Gaswerke AG: 10703 Berlin; tel. (30) 78720; fax (30) 78723044; e-mail service@gasag.de; internet www.gasag.de; Chair. Supervisory Bd Dr Karl Kauermann.

Gasversorgung Süddeutschland GmbH (GVS): Stuttgart; internet www.gvs-erdgas.de; f. 1961; Chair. Supervisory Bd Gerhard Widder.

TRADE UNIONS

Following German unification in October 1990, the trade unions of the former GDR were absorbed into the member unions of the DGB (see below).

Deutscher Gewerkschaftsbund (DGB): Henriette-Herz-Pl. 2, 10178 Berlin; tel. (30) 240600; fax (30) 24060471; e-mail int@bvv.dgb .de; internet www.dgb.de; f. 1949; Pres. Michael Sommer; Vice-Pres. Ursula Engelen-Kefer.

The following unions, with a total of 8,310,783 members (December 1998), are affiliated to the DGB:

Industriegewerkschaft Bauen-Agrar-Umwelt (Building and Construction Trade): Olof-Palme-Str. 19, 60439 Frankfurt a.M.; tel. (69) 957370; fax (69) 95737800; e-mail presse@igbau.de; internet www.igbau.de; Pres. Klaus Wiesehügel; 539,744 mems (Dec. 2000).

Industriegewerkschaft Bergbau, Chemie, Energie (IG BCE) (Mining, Chemical and Energy): Postfach 3047, 30030 Hannover; Königsworther Pl. 6, 30167 Hannover; tel. (511) 76310; fax (511) 7631715; e-mail abt.internationales.europa@igbce.de; internet www .igbce.de; Pres. Hubertus Schmoldt; 770,000 mems (Jan. 2005).

Gewerkschaft der Eisenbahner Deutschlands (Railwaymen): Weilburger Str. 24; 60326 Frankfurt a.M.; tel. (69) 7536204; fax (69) 7536223; e-mail gdad.hansen@t-online.de; Pres. Norbert Hansen; 352,161 mems (Dec. 1998).

Gewerkschaft Erziehung und Wissenschaft (Education and Sciences): Reifenberger Str. 21, 60489 Frankfurt a.M.; tel. (69) 789730; fax (69) 78973201; e-mail info@gew.de; internet www.gew .de; Pres. Dr Eva-Maria Stange; 260,842 mems (Dec. 2003).

Gewerkschaft Leder (Leather): Willi-Bleicher-Str. 20, 70174 Stuttgart; tel. (711) 295555; fax (711) 293345; Pres. Werner Dick; 25,000 mems (Dec. 1994).

IG Metall—die Gewerkschaft in Produktion und Dienstleistung der Bereiche Metall-Elektro, Textil-Bekleidung, Holz-Kunststoff (Metal Workers' Union): Lyoner Str. 32, 60528 Frankfurt a.M.; tel. (69) 66930; fax (69) 66932843; e-mail presse.igm@igmetall.de; internet www.igmetall.de; Chair. Jürgen Peters; 2.7m. mems (1999).

Gewerkschaft Nahrung-Genuss-Gaststätten (Food, Delicacies and Catering): Haubachstr. 76, 22765 Hamburg; tel. (40) 380130; fax (40) 3892637; e-mail hauptverwaltung@ngg.net; internet www.ngg .net; f. 1949; Pres. Franz-Josef Möllenberg; 226,000 mems (Dec. 2004).

Gewerkschaft der Polizei (Police Union): Stromstr. 4, 10555 Berlin; tel. (30) 399921111; fax (30) 39921211; e-mail buero-vorstand@gdp-online.de; f. 1950; Chair. Konrad Freiberg; Sec. W. Dicke; 181,793 mems (Dec. 2004).

Vereinte Dienstleistungsgewerkschaft—Ver.di (United Services Union): Paula-Thiede-Ufer 10, 10179 Berlin; tel. (30) 69560; e-mail info@verdi.de; internet www.verdi.de; f. 2001 by a merger of Gewerkschaft Handel, Banken und Versicherungen, Industriegewerkschaft Medien, Gewerkschaft Öffentliche Dienste, Transport und Verkehr, Deutsche Postgewerkschaft and Deutsche Angestellten-Gewerkschaft; Chair. Frank Bsirske; 3m. mems (2001).

The following is the largest union outside the DGB:

DBB—Beamtenbund und Tarifunion (Civil Servants' Federation and Tariff Union): Friedrichstr. 169–170, 10117 Berlin; tel. (30) 408140; fax (30) 40814999; e-mail post@dbb.de; internet www .dbb.de; f. 1918; Pres. Peter Heesem; 1.3m. mems (2001).

Transport

RAILWAYS

In 1999 the total length of track in Germany was 80,447 km, of which 46,373 km was electrified. In June 2001 new inter-city express rail links were opened on the Berlin–Hamburg, München–Zürich and Nürnberg–Dresden routes.

Deutsche Bahn AG (German Railways): Potsdamer Pl. 2, 10785 Berlin; tel. (30) 29761131; fax (30) 29761919; e-mail medienbetreuung@bku.db.de; internet www.bahn.de; f. 1994; following merger of Deutsche Bundesbahn and Deutsche Reichsbahn; state-owned (transfer to private-sector ownership pending); Chair. Hartmut Mehdorn.

Metropolitan Railways

Berliner Verkehrsbetriebe (BVG) (Berlin Transport Authority): Anstalt des öffentlichen Rechts, 10783 Berlin; Potsdamer Str. 188, 10729 Berlin; Postfach 303131, 10773 Berlin; tel. (30) 2560; fax (30) 25649256; e-mail info@bvg.de; internet www.bvg.de; f. 1929; operates approx. 143.3 km of underground railway; also runs tram and bus services; Chair. Andreas Graf von Arnim.

Münchner Verkehrsgesellschaft mbH (MVG): Emmy-Noether-Str. 2, 80287 München; tel. (89) 21910; fax (89) 21912405; e-mail info@swm.de; internet www.mvg-mobil.de; underground (85 km), tramway (71 km), omnibus (412 km); Man. Herbert König.

Association

Verband Deutscher Verkehrsunternehmen (VDV) (Association of German Transport Undertakings): Kamekestr. 37–39, 50672 Köln; tel. (221) 579790; fax (221) 514272; e-mail info@vdv.de; internet www.vdv.de; f. 1895; public transport, freight transport by rail; publishes *Der Nahverkehr* (10 a year), *Bus + Bahn* (monthly) and *Güterbahnen* (4 a year); Pres. Günter Elste; Exec. Dir Prof Dr Adolf Müller-Hellmann.

ROADS

In 1999 there were 11,515 km of motorway, 41,321 km of other main roads and 177,899 km of secondary roads. A new 200-km motorway connecting Lübeck, via Rostock, to Stettin (in Poland) was due to be completed in 2005, at an expected cost of DM 3,700m.

INLAND WATERWAYS

There are 7,467 km of navigable inland waterways, including the Main–Danube Canal, linking the North Sea and the Black Sea, which was opened in 1992. Inland shipping accounts for about 20% of total freight traffic.

Associations

Bundesverband der Deutschen Binnenschiffahrt eV (BDB): Dammstr. 15–17, 47119 Duisburg; tel. (203) 8000650; fax (203) 8000621; e-mail infobdb@binnenschiff.de; internet www .binnenschiff.de; f. 1978; central Inland Waterway Association to further the interests of operating firms; Pres. Heinz Hofmann.

Bundesverband Öffentlicher Binnenhäfen eV: Str. des 17. Juni 114, 10623 Berlin; tel. (30) 39802870; fax (30) 39802880; e-mail info-boeb@binnenhafen.de; internet www.binnenhafen.de; Chair. Erich Staake.

Bundesverband der Selbstständigen Abteilung Binnenschiffahrt eV (BDS): August-Bier-Str. 18, 53129 Bonn; tel. (228) 746337; fax (228) 746569; e-mail infobds@binnenschiff.de; Man. Dir Andrea Beckschäfer.

Deutsche Binnenreederei Binnenschiffahrt Spedition Logistik GmbH: Revaler Str. 100, 10243 Berlin; tel. (30) 293760; fax (30) 29376201; e-mail dbr@binnenreederei.de; internet www .binnenreederei.de; f. 1949; Dir-Gen. Hans-Wilhelm Dünner.

Hafenschiffahrtsverband Hamburg eV: Mattentwiete 2, 20457 Hamburg; tel. (40) 3789090; fax (40) 37890970.

Verein für europäische Binnenschiffahrt und Wasserstrassen eV (VBW): Dammstr. 15–17, 47119 Duisburg; tel. (203) 8000627; fax (203) 8000628; e-mail info@vbw-ev.de; internet www .vbw-ev.de; f. 1877; represents all brs of the inland waterways; Pres. Prof. D. Schröder; Dir G. Dütemeyer.

SHIPPING

The principal seaports for freight are Bremen, Hamburg, Rostock-Überseehafen and Wilhelmshaven. Some important shipping companies are:

Argo Reederei Richard Adler & Söhne: Postfach 107529, 28075 Bremen; Am Wall 187–189, 28195 Bremen; tel. (421) 363070; fax (421) 321575; e-mail argo@argo-adler.de; internet www.argo-adler .de; f. 1896; shipowners; Propr MAX ADLER.

Aug. Bolten, Wm. Miller's Nachfolger GmbH & Co: Mattentwiete 8, 20457 Hamburg; tel. (40) 36010; fax (40) 3601423; e-mail info@aug-bolten.de; internet www.aug-bolten.de; tramp; Man. Dirs GERHARD BINDERS, MICHAEL SAY.

Bugsier- Reederei- und Bergungs-Gesellschaft mbH & Co: Postfach 112273, 20422 Hamburg; Johannisbollwerk 10, 20459 Hamburg; tel. (40) 311110; fax (40) 313693; e-mail info@bugsier.de; internet www.bugsier.de; salvage, towage, tugs, ocean-going heavy lift cranes, submersible pontoons, harbour tugs; Man. Dirs B. J. SCHUCHMANN, J. W. SCHUCHMANN, A. HUETTMANN.

Christian F. Ahrenkiel GmbH & Co KG: Postfach 10 02 20, 20001 Hamburg; An der Alster 45, 20099 Hamburg; tel. (40) 248380; fax (40) 24838346; e-mail info@ahrenkiel.net; internet www .ahrenkiel.net; f. 1950; shipowners, operators and managers.

DAL Deutsche Afrika-Linien GmbH & Co KG: Palmaille 45, 22767 Hamburg; tel. (40) 380160; fax (40) 38016663; Europe and South Africa; Man. Dirs Dr E. VON RANTZAU, H. VON RANTZAU.

Deutsche Seereederei GmbH: Silo4plus5, Business-Center am Stadthafen, Am Strande 3E, 18055 Rostock; tel. (381) 4584043; fax (381) 4584001; e-mail info@deutsche-seereederei.de; internet www .deutsche-seereederei.de; container ships, general cargo ships, bulk carriers, cargo trailer ships, railway ferries, special tankers.

Döhle, Peter, Schiffahrts–KG: Postfach 500440, 22704 Hamburg; Palmaille 33, 22767 Hamburg; tel. (40) 381080; fax (40) 38108255; internet www.doehle.de; Man. Dir JOCHEN DÖHLE; shipbrokers, chartering agent, shipowners.

Ernst Russ GmbH: Alsterufer 10, 20354 Hamburg; tel. (40) 414070; fax (40) 41407111; f. 1893; world-wide.

F. Laeisz Schiffahrtsgesellschaft mbH & Co KG: Postfach 111111, 20411 Hamburg; Trostbrücke 1, 20457 Hamburg; tel. (40) 368080; fax (40) 364876; e-mail info@laeisz.de; internet www.laeisz .de; f. 1983; Dirs NIKOLAUSW. SCHÜES, NIKOLAUS H. SCHÜES, HERBERT JUNIEL.

Fisser & v. Doornum GmbH & Co: Postfach 130365, Feldbrunnenstr. 43, 20148 Hamburg; tel. (40) 441860; fax (40) 4108050; f. 1879; tramp; Man. Dirs CHRISTIAN FISSER, Dr MICHAEL FISSER.

Hamburg Südamerikanische Dampfschiffahrts-Gesellschaft KG: Ost-West-Str. 59–61, 20457 Hamburg; tel. (40) 37050; fax (40) 37052400; e-mail central@ham.hamburg-sued.com; internet www .hamburg-sued.com; f. 1871; world-wide services.

Hapag-Lloyd AG: Ballindamm 25, 20095 Hamburg; tel. (40) 30010; fax (40) 336432; e-mail info@hapag-lloyd.de; internet www .hapag-lloyd.com; f. 1970; North, Central and South America, Middle East, Asia, Australasia; Chair. MICHAEL BEHRENDT.

John T. Essberger GmbH & Co KG: Postfach 500429, Palmaille 45, 22767 Hamburg; tel. (40) 380160; fax (40) 38016579; f. 1924; Man. Dirs Dr E. VON RANTZAU, H. VON RANTZAU.

Oldenburg-Portugiesische Dampfschiffs-Rhederei GmbH & Co KG: Postfach 110869, 20408 Hamburg; Kajen 10, 20459 Hamburg; tel. (40) 361580; fax (40) 364131; e-mail info@opdr.de; internet www.opdr.de; f. 1882; Gibraltar, Spain, Portugal, Madeira, North Africa, Canary Islands; Man. Dirs G. KEMPF, J. BERGMANN.

Oldendorff Carriers GmbH & Co KG: Willy-Brandt-Allee 6, 235544 Lübeck; tel. (451) 15000; fax (451) 73522; internet www .oldendorff.com; formerly Egon Oldendorff; Chair. HENNING OLDENDORFF; CEO PETER TWISS.

Rhein-, Maas und See-Schiffahrtskontor GmbH: Krausstr. 1A, 47119 Duisburg; tel. (203) 8040; fax (203) 804-330; e-mail rms-team@rheinmaas.de; internet www.rheinmaas.de; f. 1948.

Sloman Neptun Schiffahrts-AG: Postfach 101469, 28014 Bremen; Langenstr. 44, 28195 Bremen; tel. (421) 17630; fax (421) 1763321; e-mail info@sloman-neptun.com; internet www .sloman-neptun.com; f. 1873; liner services from Northern Europe

and Mediterranean to North Africa; gas carriers; agencies; Mans SVEN-MICHAEL EDYE, DIRK LOHMANN.

Walther Möller & Co: Thedestr. 2, 22767 Hamburg; tel. (40) 3803910; fax (40) 38039199; e-mail chartering@wmco.de; internet www.wmco.de.

Shipping Organizations

Verband Deutscher Reeder eV (German Shipowners' Association): Postfach 305580, 20317 Hamburg; Esplanade 6, 20354 Hamburg; tel. (40) 350970; fax (40) 35097211; e-mail vdr@reederverband .de; internet www.reederverband.de; Pres. FRANK LEONHARDT; Man. Dirs Dr HANS-HEINRICH NOELL, Dr DIERK LINDEMANN.

Zentralverband der Deutschen Seehafenbetriebe eV (Federal Association of German Seaport Operators): Am Sandtorkai 2, 20457 Hamburg; tel. (40) 366203; fax (40) 366377; e-mail info@ zds-seehaefen.de; internet www.zds-seehaefen.de; f. 1934; Chair. DETTHOLD ADEN; 201 mems.

CIVIL AVIATION

There are two international airports in the Berlin region (a third, Tempelhof airport, closed in late 2004) and further international airports at Köln-Bonn, Dresden, Düsseldorf, Frankfurt, Hamburg, Hannover, Leipzig, München and Stuttgart. Construction of a major new international airport to serve Berlin was expected to commence in 2006.

Aero Lloyd Flugreisen Luftverkehrs-KG: Postfach 2029, Lessingstr. 7–9, 61440 Oberursel; tel. (6171) 62501; fax (6171) 625109; f. 1981; charter services; Gen. Mans Dr W. SCHNEIDER, WOLFGANG JOHN.

Deutsche Lufthansa AG: Von-Gablenz-Str. 2–6, 50679 Köln; tel. (221) 8260; fax (221) 8263818; f. 1953; extensive world-wide network; Chair. Supervisory Bd Dr KLAUS SCHELDE; Chair. Exec. Bd JÜRGEN WEBER.

Germania Fluggesellschaft mbH: Flughafen Berlin Tegel, Gebäude Z3, 13405 Berlin; tel. (30) 41012836; fax (30) 41013500; e-mail info@germaniaairline.de; internet www.germania-flug.de; f. 1978; charter and scheduled flights; Man. Dr HINRICH BISCHOFF.

Hapag-Lloyd Flug-GmbH: Postfach 420240, Flughafenstr. 10, 30855 Langenhagen; tel. (511) 97270; fax (511) 9727739; e-mail info@hlag.de; internet www.hapag-lloyd.de; f. 1972; charter and scheduled passenger services; Exec. Chair. MICHAEL BEHRENDT.

LTU Lufttransport-Unternehmen GmbH: Flughafen, Halle 8, 40474 Düsseldorf; tel. (211) 9418888; fax (211) 9418881; e-mail service@ltu.de; internet www.ltu.de; f. 1955; charter and scheduled services; Man. Dir JÜRGEN MARBACH.

Lufthansa Cargo AG: Langer Kornweg 34, 65441 Kelsterbach; tel. (6107) 777615; fax (6107) 777888; f. 1993; wholly-owned subsidiary of Lufthansa; freight-charter world-wide; Man. Dirs WALTER GEHL, JEAN-PETER JANSEN, STEFAN LAUER.

Lufthansa CityLine GmbH: Flughafen Köln/Bonn, Heinrich-Steinmann-Str., 51147 Köln; tel. (2203) 5960; fax (2203) 596801; e-mail unternehmenskommunikation@dlh.de; internet www .lufthansacityline.com; scheduled services; Man. Dirs KARL-HEINZ KÖPFLE, Dr THOMAS DRÄGER.

Thomas Cook: Am Grunen Weg 3, 65440 Kelsterbach; tel. (6107) 9390; fax (6107) 939440; internet www.condor.com; f. 1955 as Condor Flugdienst GmbH, current name adopted 2003; 90% owned by Thomas Cook AG, 10% owned by Lufthansa; charter airline; Man. Dirs MANFRED SCHWABENBAUER, CLAUS DIETER WEHR.

Tourism

Germany's tourist attractions include spas, summer and winter resorts, mountains, medieval towns and castles, and above all a variety of fascinating cities. The North and Baltic Sea coasts, the Rhine Valley, the Black Forest, the mountains of Thuringia, the Erzgebirge and Bavaria are the most popular areas. The total number of foreign visitors was 17.2m. in 2003; in 2002 receipts from tourism totalled €20,261m.

Deutsche Zentrale für Tourismus eV (DZT) (German National Tourist Board): Beethovenstr. 69, 60325 Frankfurt a.M.; tel. (69) 974640; fax (69) 751903; e-mail info@d-z-t.com; internet www .germany-tourism.de; f. 1948; CEO PETRA HEDORFER.

GHANA

Introductory Survey

Location, Climate, Language, Religion, Flag, Capital

The Republic of Ghana lies on the west coast of Africa, with Côte d'Ivoire to the west and Togo to the east. It is bordered by Burkina Faso to the north. The climate is tropical, with temperatures generally between 21°C and 32°C (70°–90°F) and average annual rainfall of 2,000 mm (80 ins) on the coast, decreasing inland. English is the official language, but there are 10 major national languages (each with more than 250,000 speakers), the most widely spoken being Akan, Ewe, Mole-Dagomba and Ga. Many of the inhabitants follow traditional beliefs and customs. Christians comprise an estimated 69% of the population. The national flag (proportions 2 by 3) has three equal horizontal stripes, of red, yellow and green, with a five-pointed black star in the centre of the yellow stripe. The capital is Accra.

Recent History

Ghana was formed as the result of a UN-supervised plebiscite in May 1956, when the British-administered section of Togoland, a UN Trust Territory, voted to join the Gold Coast, a British colony, in an independent state. Ghana was duly granted independence, within the Commonwealth, on 6 March 1957, becoming the first British dependency in sub-Saharan Africa to achieve independence under majority rule. Dr Kwame Nkrumah, the Prime Minister of the former Gold Coast since 1952, became Prime Minister of the new state. Ghana became a republic on 1 July 1960, with Nkrumah as President. In 1964 the Convention People's Party, led by Nkrumah, was declared the sole authorized party.

In February 1966 Nkrumah was deposed in a military coup, the leaders of which established a governing National Liberation Council, led by Gen. Joseph Ankrah. In April 1969 Ankrah was replaced by Brig. (later Lt-Gen.) Akwasi Afrifa, and a new Constitution was introduced. Power was returned in October to an elected civilian Government, led by Dr Kofi Busia. However, in reaction to increasing economic and political difficulties, the army again seized power in January 1972, under the leadership of Lt-Col (later Gen.) Ignatius Acheampong. Some improvement in Ghana's economic situation was achieved by the military, which announced in 1977 that it intended to relinquish power following a general election to be held in 1979. These plans, however, were forestalled in July 1978 by Acheampong's deputy, Lt-Gen. Frederick Akuffo, who assumed power in a bloodless coup. Tensions within the army became evident in May 1979, when junior military officers staged an unsuccessful coup attempt. The alleged leader of the conspirators, Flight-Lt Jerry Rawlings, was imprisoned, but was subsequently released by other officers. On 4 June he and his associates successfully seized power, amid popular acclaim, established the Armed Forces Revolutionary Council, led by Rawlings, and introduced measures to eradicate corruption. Acheampong and Akuffo were among nine senior officers who were convicted on charges of corruption and executed.

At elections held in June 1979 the People's National Party, led by Dr Hilla Limann, emerged with the largest number of parliamentary seats and formed a coalition Government with support from the smaller United National Convention. Civilian rule was restored in September when Dr Limann took office as President. However, dissatisfaction with measures taken by the Government to improve the economy provoked widespread civil unrest.

On 31 December 1981 Rawlings seized power for a second time, and established a governing Provisional National Defence Council (PNDC), with himself as Chairman. In 1982 city and district councils were replaced by People's Defence Committees (PDC), which were designed to allow popular participation in local government. In 1984 the PDC were redesignated as Committees for the Defence of the Revolution.

The PNDC's policies initially received strong support, but discontent with the regime and with the apparent ineffectiveness of its economic policies was reflected by a series of coup attempts; between 1984 and 1987 some 34 people were executed for their alleged involvement in plots to overthrow the Government. In July 1987 the PNDC announced that elections for district assemblies, scheduled for mid-1987, were to be postponed until late 1988, and that the ban on political parties was to remain. In April 1988 there was an extensive government reshuffle. Elections for the district assemblies were held between December 1988 and February 1989. Although one-third of the 7,278 members of the district assemblies were appointed by the PNDC, the establishment of the assemblies was envisaged as the first stage in the development of a new political system of national democratic administration.

On 24 September 1989 a coup attempt was staged, led by a close associate of Rawlings, Maj. Courage Quashigah. Shortly afterwards the Commander of the Armed Forces was dismissed, and Rawlings assumed personal control of the armed forces until June 1990. In October 1989 five senior members of the security forces, including Quashigah, were arrested on charges of conspiring to assassinate Rawlings. The predominance of the Ewe ethnic group in government positions and other important posts was initially considered to be the cause of the revolt, although a board of inquiry into the allegations of treason concluded that most of the conspirators were motivated by personal grievances and ambition. In January 1990 five more arrests were made in connection with the coup attempt. In August the human rights organization Amnesty International criticized the continued detention of Quashigah and six other members of the security forces, claiming that they were imprisoned for political dissension.

In July 1990, in response to pressure from Western aid donors to introduce further democratic reforms, the PNDC announced that a National Commission for Democracy (NCD) would organize a series of regional debates to consider Ghana's political and economic future. (Ten such debates took place between July and October 1992.) In August the newly formed Movement for Freedom and Justice (MFJ) criticized the NCD, claiming that it was too closely associated with the PNDC, and also demanded the abolition of legislation prohibiting political associations, the release of all political prisoners, the cessation of press censorship and the holding of a national referendum on the restoration of a multi-party system. In September the MFJ accused the PNDC of intimidation, after its inaugural meeting was suppressed by security forces. In October the PNDC pledged to accept the conclusions of any national consensus on future democracy in the country.

In December 1990 Rawlings announced proposals for the introduction of a constitution by the end of 1991; the PNDC was to consider recommendations presented by the NCD, and subsequently to convene a consultative body to determine constitutional reform. However, the MFJ, the Christian Council of Ghana and the Ghana Bar Association objected to the proposals, on the grounds that no definite schedule for political reform had been presented, and that no criteria had been established for the composition of the consultative body.

In March 1991 the NCD presented a report on the democratic process, which recommended the election of an executive President for a fixed term, the establishment of a legislature and the creation of the post of Prime Minister. In May the PNDC endorsed the restoration of a multi-party system and approved the NCD's recommendations, although it was emphasized that the formation of political associations remained prohibited. Later in May the Government announced the establishment of a 260-member Consultative Assembly, which was to present a draft constitution to the PNDC by the end of 1991. The Government appointed a nine-member committee of constitutional experts, who were to submit recommendations for a draft constitution to the Consultative Assembly by the end of July.

In June 1991 the Government reiterated denials that a number of political prisoners were detained in Ghana. In the same month the PNDC announced an amnesty for political exiles, which did not, however, include persons who were implicated in acts of subversion against the Government. In August the committee of constitutional experts submitted a series of recommendations for reform, which included the establishment of a parliament and a council of state. It was proposed that the President, who would also be Commander-in-Chief of the Armed Forces, would be elected by universal suffrage for a four-year term of office, while the leader of the party that commanded a majority in the legislature would be appointed as Prime Minister. However, the subsequent review of the draft Constitution by the Consultative Assembly was impeded by opposition demands for a boycott, on the grounds that the number of government representatives in the Assembly was too high. Later in August Rawlings announced that presidential and legislative elections were to take place in late 1992.

In December 1991 the Government established an Interim National Electoral Commission (INEC), which was to be responsible for the demarcation of electoral regions and the supervision of elections and referendums. In January 1992 the Government extended the allocated period for the review of the draft Constitution to the end of March. In March Rawlings announced a programme for transition to a multi-party system, which was to be completed on 7 January 1993. Later in March 1992 the Government granted an amnesty to 17 prisoners who had been convicted of subversion, including Quashigah.

At the end of March 1992 the Consultative Assembly approved the majority of the constitutional recommendations that had been submitted to the PNDC. However, the proposed creation of the post of Prime Minister was rejected by the Assembly; executive power was to be vested in the President, who would appoint a Vice-President. Opposition groups subsequently objected to a provision in the draft Constitution that members of the Government be exempt from prosecution for human rights violations allegedly committed during the PNDC's rule. At a national referendum on 28 April, however, the draft Constitution was approved by 92% of votes cast, with 43.7% of the electorate voting.

On 18 May 1992 the Government introduced legislation permitting the formation of political associations; political parties were henceforth required to apply to the INEC for legal recognition, although emergent parties were not permitted to use names or slogans associated with 21 former political organizations that remained proscribed, and individual monetary contributions to political parties were restricted. Later in May the High Court rejected an application for an injunction against the legislation by opposition leaders, who claimed that it was biased in favour of the PNDC.

In June 1992 a number of political associations were established, many of which were identified with supporters of former President Nkrumah; six opposition movements, including the People's National Convention (PNC), led by ex-President Limann, were subsequently granted legal recognition. In the same month a coalition of pro-Government organizations, the National Democratic Congress (NDC), was formed to contest the forthcoming elections on behalf of the PNDC. However, an existing alliance of Rawlings' supporters, the Eagle Club, refused to join the NDC, and created its own political organization, the Eagle Party (later known as the EGLE—Every Ghanaian Living Everywhere—Party). In July Rawlings rejected the EGLE Party's nomination as its candidate for the presidential election. In August the Government promulgated a new electoral code, which included a provision that in the event that no presidential candidate received more than 50% of votes cast the two candidates with the highest number of votes would contest a second round within 21 days. In September Rawlings officially retired from the air force (although he retained the post of Commander-in-Chief of the Armed Forces in his capacity as Head of State), in accordance with the new Constitution, and accepted a nomination to contest the presidential election as a candidate of the NDC. The NDC, the EGLE Party and the National Convention Party (NCP) subsequently formed a pro-Government electoral coalition, known as the Progressive Alliance.

Rawlings was elected President on 3 November 1992, securing 58.3% of the votes cast. The four opposition parties that had presented candidates, the PNC, the New Patriotic Party (NPP), the National Independence Party (NIP) and the People's Heritage Party (PHP), claimed that there had been widespread electoral malpractice, although international observers maintained that, despite isolated irregularities, the election had been conducted fairly. Later in November these four parties withdrew from the forthcoming legislative elections (scheduled for 8 December), in protest at the Government's refusal to comply with their demands for the compilation of a new electoral register and the investigation of alleged misconduct during the presidential election. As a result, the legislative elections were postponed until 22 December, and subsequently by a further week, and the nomination of new candidates permitted. In

December the opposition claimed that many of its members had left Ghana, as a result of widespread intimidation by the Government. In the legislative elections, which took place on 29 December, the NDC secured 189 of the 200 seats in the Parliament, while the NCP obtained eight seats, the EGLE Party one seat and independent candidates the remaining two. According to official figures, however, only 29% of the electorate voted in the elections.

On 7 January 1993 Rawlings was sworn in as President of what was designated the Fourth Republic, the PNDC was dissolved and the new Parliament was inaugurated. Later that month Rawlings began to submit nominations for members of the Council of Ministers and the Council of State for approval by the Parliament. However, he announced that members of the existing Government were to remain in office in an interim capacity, pending the appointment of a Council of Ministers and other officials. The opposition subsequently criticized the delay in the formation of a new government and protested that the new Constitution did not permit members of the former PNDC to remain in office. In March the nomination of a number of ministers was approved by the Parliament. Later that month legislation was promulgated to exempt from prosecution perpetrators of offences that had been committed under the auspices of the former PNDC Government.

In April 1993 elections took place for the regional seats in the Council of State. In May a 17-member Council of Ministers, which included several ministers who had served in the former PNDC administration, was inaugurated. In July the Supreme Court upheld a motion by the NPP that certain existing legislation was in contravention of the Constitution. In August the NPP announced that it was prepared to recognize the legitimacy of the Government. In November a 20-member National Security Council, chaired by the Vice-President, Kow Nkensen Arkaah, was inaugurated. In December the PHP, the NIP and a faction of the PNC, all of which comprised supporters of ex-President Nkrumah, merged to form a new organization, known as the People's Convention Party (PCP).

In February 1994 long-standing hostility between the Konkomba ethnic group and the land-owning Nanumba intensified into clashes in the Northern Region in which some 500 people were killed, following demands by the Konkomba for traditional status that would entitle them to own land. The Government subsequently dispatched troops and imposed a state of emergency in seven districts. None the less, skirmishes continued in the region, and subsequently involved several other ethnic groups. Some 6,000 Konkomba were reported to have fled to Togo. In April the Government instigated negotiations between representatives of the various groups involved in the conflict in the Northern Region. In the same month the authorities claimed that reported threats to kill Quashigah (the instigator of the coup attempt in 1989) and editors of two privately owned newspapers were part of a conspiracy to destabilize the Government. Meanwhile, the state of emergency in the Northern Region (where a total of 1,000 people had been killed, and a further 150,000 displaced) was extended for one month. In early June, however, the factions involved in the hostilities signed a peace agreement that provided for the imposition of an immediate cease-fire. The Government subsequently announced that troops were to be permanently stationed in the Northern Region in order to prevent further conflict, and established a negotiating team that was to attempt to resolve the inter-ethnic differences. In early August the Government announced that order had been restored in the Northern Region and repealed the state of emergency.

In March 1995 the Government imposed a curfew in the Northern Region following renewed ethnic violence, in which about 100 people were killed. In April a joint commission, comprising prominent members of the Konkomba and Nanumba, was established, in an effort to resolve the conflict. Meanwhile, the imposition, in February, of value-added tax (VAT) prompted widespread protests; a series of demonstrations culminated in May, when five people were killed in clashes between government supporters and protesters. (The Government subsequently agreed to suspend VAT, although it was reintroduced, at a lower rate, in 1999.) Later in May the National Executive Committee of the NCP decided to withdraw the party from the government coalition, claiming that the NDC had dominated the alliance. However, Arkaah, a member of the NCP, announced that he was to retain the office of Vice-President, as his mandate remained valid. In July the long-serving Minister of Finance, Kwesi Botchwey, resigned, apparently in response to the failure to introduce VAT. In October the Chairman of the NCP resigned, following dissent within the party. In November the Commission on Human Rights and Administrative Justice commenced investigations into allegations of corruption on the part of government ministers and civil servants.

In early 1996 opposition parties demanded the resignation of Rawlings, following an incident in which the President allegedly assaulted Arkaah. In April presidential and parliamentary elections were scheduled for December. A consolidation of the opposition parties took place prior to the deadline for the nomination of candidates in September. In May the Popular Party for Democracy and Development merged with the PCP and declared its support for unity with the NPP. In July the NCP announced that it had removed Arkaah as its leader, following his selection as presidential candidate by the PCP. In August the NPP and the PCP formed an electoral coalition, the Great Alliance; it was subsequently announced that John Kufuor, of the NPP, was to be the Great Alliance's presidential candidate, with Arkaah as the candidate for the vice-presidency. The NCP stated that it would support the NDC in the forthcoming elections, while the PNC announced its intention to contest the elections alone, with Edward Mahama as its presidential candidate. In September the NDC nominated Rawlings as its presidential candidate. By 18 September, the official deadline for the nomination of candidates, only the Great Alliance, the Progressive Alliance (the NDC, the EGLE party and the Democratic People's Party—DPP) and the PNC had succeeded in having their nomination papers accepted. In October the NCP, which, according to the Electoral Commission (EC), had not presented the appropriate papers, declared its intention to take legal action against the Commission. In November a network of independent Domestic Election Observers was created to oversee the December elections. The resignation of the Minister of the Interior in October was followed, in November, by the resignations of the Minister of Trade and Industry and a presidential aide, following corruption allegations.

In the presidential election, which took place on 7 December 1996, Rawlings was re-elected, with 57.2% of the votes cast, while Kufuor secured 39.8%. In the parliamentary elections the NDC's representation was reduced to 133 seats, while the NPP won 60 seats, the PCP five and the PNC one seat. Voting was postponed in one constituency, owing to a legal dispute concerning the eligibility of candidates. (The seat was subsequently won by the NPP in a by-election in June 1997.) Despite opposition claims of malpractice, international observers declared that the elections had been conducted fairly, and an electoral turnout of 76.8% was reported. At the end of December the PCP announced that the Great Alliance had broken down. On 7 January 1997 Rawlings was sworn in as President.

The appointment of a new Council of Ministers led to a protracted dispute between the NDC and the opposition, prompting a series of parliamentary boycotts by the NPP, which insisted that all ministerial appointees be approved by the parliamentary appointments committee prior to assuming their duties. Owing to the NDC's parliamentary majority, however, procedures were approved to allow those ministers who had been retained from the previous Government to avoid the vetting process. The majority of ministerial appointments had been made by April, although a number of posts were not filled until June. In early June the Supreme Court ruled that all presidential nominees for ministerial positions had to be approved by Parliament, even if they had served in the previous Government and the Government subsequently announced that it was prepared to submit all ministers to vetting procedures.

Following further accusations of government corruption, Rawlings dismissed a Minister of State in February 1998, after a committee of inquiry discovered lapses of propriety regarding a sea defence project. In August the NCP and the PCP merged to form the Convention Party. An earlier attempt by the party to register as the Convention People's Party (CPP) had been rejected on the grounds that the use of the name of a proscribed party was unconstitutional. (This decision was reversed in 2000, however, when the Convention Party was permitted to adopt the name and logo of Nkrumah's former party.) In October 1998 the NPP nominated Kufuor to stand as its presidential candidate, in elections due to be held in 2000. At an NDC congress in December 1998 the position of 'Life Chairman' of the party was created for Rawlings, who confirmed that he would comply with the terms of the Constitution and not stand for a third term as President. In April 1999 Rawlings announced that the incum-

bent Vice-President, Prof. John Evans Atta Mills, was to contest the election on behalf of the NDC. In June, owing to dissatisfaction within the NDC at the changes carried out at the party congress and at Rawlings' pronouncement regarding his successor, a group of party members broke away to form a new political organization, the National Reform Party (NRP). At the end of April Mills was elected unopposed as the NDC presidential candidate. Seven parties had submitted presidential candidates by the closure of nominations in September. In addition to Mills and Kufuor, the candidates included Mahama, for the PNC, and George Hagan, for the CPP. The EGLE Party and the DPP announced their support for Mills.

Isolated outbreaks of violence occurred between supporters of the NPP and the NDC in November 2000, prompting traditional chiefs to organize a 'peace conference'. The conference, which was attended by representatives of all the political parties contesting the elections, accused politicians of making inflammatory statements, but was criticized by opposition groups for failing to apportion sufficient blame on the President. The INEC, meanwhile, admitted that the electoral register included some 1.5m. non-existent voters.

An estimated 62% of the electorate voted in the elections, which took place on 7 December 2000 (although, as a result of the inaccurate voters' register, it was claimed that the real rate of participation could have been as high as 80%). Observers from the Organization of African Unity (now the African Union, see p. 144) declared the elections to have been held in an orderly and fair manner. In the elections to the 200-seat Parliament the NPP won 100 seats, while the NDC obtained 92 seats, the PNC three, the CPP one, and independent candidates four. The NPP thus became the largest parliamentary party for the first time, gaining an unprecedented degree of support in rural areas. In the presidential election Kufuor won 48.2% of the valid votes cast, and Mills 44.5%.

In late December 2000 there were reports of isolated violent incidents of a politically motivated nature across Ghana. Although the second round of the presidential election proceeded largely without incident on 28 December, minor disruptions to voting were reported; it was also reported that an NPP deputy had been stabbed in Accra by uniformed men, who had also fired on two of his supporters. Kufuor was elected to the presidency, with 56.9% of the valid votes cast. The NPP attributed its victory to discontent with corruption in the former administration and its reluctance to implement economic and structural reforms.

On 7 January 2001 Kufuor was inaugurated as President; on the following day it was announced that Rawlings had accepted a goodwill ambassadorial post at the UN for one year. President Kufuor subsequently appointed 23 ministers and four ministers of state, including his brother, Kwame Addo Kufuor as Minister of Defence. The Government notably included one member from each of the CPP, the NRP and the PNC. The stated priority of the new Government was the creation of wealth, which was to be encouraged by greater promotion of the private sector and through the eradication of corruption within government and in the parastatal sector. To this effect, Vice-President Alhaji Aliu Mahama announced that a code of conduct for ministers and government appointees would be implemented. In February it was announced that members of the military were to be forbidden from celebrating the anniversaries of the coups staged by Rawlings in 1979 and 1981, and that their participation in quasi-political organizations was also to be prohibited. In addition, Kufuor ordered the suspension of the heads of six public-sector financial institutions, to facilitate an investigation into allegations of embezzlement.

Also in February 2001 Kufuor announced that a National Reconciliation Commission (NRC) was to be established to investigate allegations of human rights abuses and other violations committed by state representatives. According to proposed legislation, the NRC, which would operate for a period of one year (with a provision permitting its operation to be extended by a further six months), would be charged with investigating three periods of military rule and unconstitutional government since independence: 24 February 1966–21 August 1969, 13 January 1972–23 September 1979 and 31 December 1981–6 January 1983, although the NRC would also be permitted to investigate complaints relating to events outside these periods. Despite protests by the NDC, which had sought to ensure that the mandate of the proposed NRC would incorporate the entire period from independence in 1957 until January 1993, in January 2002 Kufuor endorsed the creation of the Commission. The

NRC was officially launched in May, although it did not commence work until September.

The new Government's attempts to improve the financial situation of the country proved controversial. In February 2001 the Government announced that the price of petroleum was to be gradually doubled in order to reduce the state debt, although wages were also to be increased, to reduce the impact of the rise. Further disquiet was provoked by the announcement that Ghana was to seek assistance under the initiative for heavily indebted poor countries of the IMF and the World Bank. The Minister of Youth and Sports, Mallam Ali Yussif Issah, the sole ministerial representative of the PNC in the Government, resigned in March after allegedly losing a suitcase containing US $46,000 intended as a bonus for the national football team; in July Issah was sentenced to four years' imprisonment for theft and fraudulently causing the loss of state resources. In December a former Deputy Minister of Finance in the Rawlings Government, Victor Selormey, was sentenced to eight years' imprisonment and fined 20m. cedis, after being convicted of defrauding the Ghanaian Government.

In December 2001 violent clashes between members of the Mamprusi and Kusasi ethnic groups in Bawku reportedly resulted in some 50 deaths. A curfew was imposed in the town, and a delegation of ministers and military officials visited the region and announced the establishment of a commission of inquiry into the dispute. In March 2002 the Minister of the Interior and the Minister for the Northern Region both resigned, following the deaths of some 40 people during inter-ethnic clashes in the north of Ghana, which had been prompted by the abduction and murder of Ya-na Yakuba Andani, king of the Dagomba, in Yendi. A commission of inquiry was established, headed by traditional leaders, and a state of emergency was declared. (The state of emergency ended in the majority of districts in October 2003, but remained in place in Tamale municipality and Yendi district until August 2004.) In May 2002 Lt-Gen. Joshua Hamidu, the National Security Adviser, resigned after allegations of his involvement in the murder were investigated by the commission. In April, meanwhile, the election of Dr Obed Asamoah as the new Chairman of the NDC created divisions within the party between supporters of Asamoah and Rawlings.

During August 2002 Rawlings accused the Kufuor Government of incompetence, urging 'positive defiance' from the Ghanaian people; he was subsequently summoned for questioning by the Bureau of National Investigations. In September a number of accusations of financial impropriety were made against Rawlings and former associates. In November, following the arrest of three NDC parliamentarians on charges of fraud and the reckless loss of state revenues, the NDC boycotted the Parliament in protest; this followed an earlier boycott over a controversial US $1,000m. development loan.

In December 2002 Mills was nominated as the NDC's candidate for the presidential election due in December 2004, and in January 2003 the NPP endorsed Kufuor as its candidate. The NRC commenced public hearings in January, by which time some 2,800 complaints had been received, mostly relating to events that took place under military regimes. In late March Kufuor effected a major government reshuffle. In April a 'fast-track' court, such as those that had convicted Issah and Selormey in 2001, found three former NDC officials guilty of soliciting a US $20m. loan for a non-existent project. In August 2003, in response to reports regarding a foiled coup plot, the Government confirmed that three military officers had been detained and interrogated in relation to an alleged attempt to destabilize the country. The NDC, however, dismissed rumours of a coup.

In February 2004 Rawlings appeared briefly before the NRC to answer questions about the murders of three high court judges and a retired military officer in 1982 and about extra-judicial military killings in 1984. In July 2004 the NRC ended its hearings, prior to the submission of its report in October, which recommended that victims of state brutality receive compensation and that state institutions, including the security services, be reformed. In early November police claimed to have arrested seven ex-army officers who were alleged to have been plotting to overthrow the state. All but one were subsequently released.

On 31 October 2004 the four presidential candidates submitted their nominations to the Chairman of the EC. As expected, Kufuor represented the NPP, while Mills was selected as the candidate for the NDC. Also contesting the election were George Aggudey of the CPP and Edward Mahama of the PNC for the Grand Coalition, which comprised the PNC and EGLE (the Great Consolidated People's Party, led by Dan Lartey, had withdrawn from the coalition in late September over the election of the coalition's presidential candidate). Prior to the election it had been widely predicted that Kufuor would win another four-year term, due in part to his successful economic policies, although opinion polls indicated that there was much support, especially in rural areas, for the NDC.

The parliamentary and presidential elections were held as scheduled on 7 December 2004 and were conducted in a largely peaceful atmosphere, although three people were reported to have died in pre-election violence. Kufuor was declared the winner of the presidential election on 9 December, after votes in 225 of the 230 constituencies had been counted. Final results, released by the EC on 1 January 2005, indicated that Kufuor had secured 52.4% of the valid votes cast, while Mills won 44.6%. Mahama and Aggudey took 1.9% and 1.0%, respectively. In the parliamentary election the NPP won 128 seats, with 55.6% of the vote, while the NDC won 94 seats, the PNC four and the CPP three. The remaining seat was taken by an independent candidate. Voter turnout at the elections was recorded at 85.1%. International and independent internal observers praised the elections as being free, fair and peaceful.

The new Parliament was inaugurated on 7 January 2005; Ebenezer Begyina Seki Hughes was elected to the post of Speaker. On the same day Kufuor and Aliu Mahama were sworn in as President and Vice-President, respectively, following which Kufuor reorganized the Government. After being approved by the Parliament, 29 ministers were inaugurated on 1 February; the remaining nine were inaugurated later that month. The most notable changes included the appointments of Kwadwo Baah-Wiredu as Minister of Finance and Economic Planning (Yaw Osafu-Maafo, his predecessor, became the Minister of Education and Sports), Nii Ayikoi Otoo as Minister of Justice and Attorney-General and Papa Owusu Ankomah as Minister of the Interior.

Following a military coup in Burkina Faso in October 1987, which was condemned by the Ghanaian Government, links between the two countries were temporarily strained, but improved following meetings between Rawlings and Capt. Blaise Compaoré, the Burkinabè leader, in early 1988. In December 1989, however, Ghana was accused by Burkina Faso of involvement in an attempt to overthrow the Burkinabè Government. In March 1998 Ghana and Burkina Faso agreed to establish a joint commission to manage water resources. Tensions had previously arisen over Burkinabè plans to build hydro-electric dams on a major tributary of the Volta river. Further agreements on co-operation were signed in August during a visit to Ghana by Compaoré.

In 1986 relations between Ghana and Togo became strained and the border was temporarily closed, following subversive activity by Ghanaian dissidents based in Togo, and an attempted coup in Togo, which was allegedly initiated from Ghanaian territory. In October 1991 the Governments of Ghana and Togo signed a bilateral agreement on the free movement of goods and persons. In October 1992, however, Ghana denied claims that it was implicated in subversive activity by Togolese dissidents based in Ghana. In March 1993 the Rawlings administration denied allegations, made by the Togolese Government, of Ghanaian complicity in an armed attack on the residence of Togo's President, Gen. Gnassingbé Eyadéma. In January 1994 relations with Togo deteriorated further, following an attempt to overthrow the Togolese Government, which the Togolese authorities claimed had been staged by armed dissidents based in Ghana. The Ghanaian chargé d'affaires in Togo was arrested, and Togolese forces killed 12 Ghanaians and attacked a customs post and several villages near the border. Ghana, however, denied any involvement in the coup attempt, and threatened to retaliate against further acts of aggression. In May allegations by the Togolese Government that Ghana was responsible for bomb attacks in Togo, owing to a lack of border security, led to further tension between the two nations. Later that year, however, relations improved, and in November full diplomatic links were formally restored. In December Togo's border with Ghana (which had been closed in January 1994) was reopened. In August 1995 the Togolese Government denied involvement in the assassination of a political opponent who had taken refuge in Ghana. In February 1996 the Parliaments of Ghana and Togo established friendship groups. By the end of 1996 some 48,000 Togolese refugees were estimated to have received payment for voluntary repatriation. Eyadéma and Rawlings met in May

1998, and in August a joint operation was mounted to arrest a group of armed men from Ghana who had attacked military posts in Togo. In August 1999, following recent Togolese incursions into Ghanaian territory and airspace, delegations from the two countries met for negotiations. In September the Ghanaian Government proposed that the Ghana–Togo border demarcation commission resume its work. In January 2001 President Kufuor's first state visit was to Togo, provoking criticism from pro-democracy protesters.

Ghana enjoys a reputation as a peace-keeper in the region, and in 2002 was the fifth largest contributor to UN peace-keeping missions world-wide. During the conflict in Liberia (q.v.), which commenced in December 1989, Ghana contributed troops to the Monitoring Group (ECOMOG) of the Economic Community of West African States (ECOWAS, see p. 205). As Chairman of the ECOWAS Conference of Heads of State and Government, Rawlings mediated negotiations between the warring Liberian factions in the mid-1990s, and by mid-1997 some 17,000 Liberian refugees had arrived in Ghana. In August Rawlings was the first foreign leader to visit Liberia following its return to civilian rule.

In June 1997 Ghana, Côte d'Ivoire, Guinea and Nigeria formed the 'committee of four', which was established by ECOWAS to monitor the situation in Sierra Leone, following the staging of a military coup; troops were dispatched to participate in a peace-keeping force. It was reported in February 1998 that Ghana had opposed the use of force by the Nigerian contingent of this peace-keeping unit to overthrow the military government in Sierra Leone. Following the reinstatement of the democratically elected Government in March, ECOMOG units remained in the country and continued to launch attacks against rebel forces, which still retained control of a number of areas. In August 2004 it was estimated that 793 Ghanaian troops were stationed in Sierra Leone as part of the UN Mission in Sierra Leone (UNAMSIL, see p. 74).

The Kufuor administration has sought to increase Ghanaian involvement in conflict resolution within west and central Africa. In November 2001 some 401 Ghanaian troops were dispatched to participate in peace-keeping duties in the Democratic Republic of the Congo, under the auspices of the UN Mission in the Democratic Republic of the Congo (MONUC, see p. 75). After the outbreak of an armed rebellion in Côte d'Ivoire (q.v.) in September 2002, Ghana denied accusations by the Ivorian rebels that it had intervened in support of President Laurent Gbagbo. At the end of September an emergency ECOWAS summit on the conflict was convened in Accra. In late October Ghana pledged to provide troops to an ECOWAS military mission in Côte d'Ivoire (ECOMICI), and the first contingent of the 266 Ghanaian soldiers to be contributed was deployed in February 2003. Further ECOWAS summit meetings on Côte d'Ivoire took place in Accra in March and November 2003. Ghanaian troops in Côte d'Ivoire were to be transferred to a UN Operation in Côte d'Ivoire (UNOCI, see p. 77), which was deployed from April 2004. In August 2004 there were 354 Ghanaian troops stationed in Côte d'Ivoire as part of UNOCI. A conference held in Accra in that month led to the signing of a peace accord between rival Ivorian factions, known as Accra III.

In 2003 Ghana also hosted peace negotiations concerning Liberia, and from September contributed troops to the ECOWAS Mission in Liberia (ECOMIL). In October the Ghanaian troops were transferred to a longer-term UN stabilization force, the UN Mission in Liberia (UNMIL, see p. 73), which replaced ECOMIL, with a mandate to support the implementation of a comprehensive peace agreement in that country. By late 2004 there were 42,000 Liberian refugees registered in Ghana, some of whom were in the process of repatriation.

In January 2004 a peace-keeping training centre, which was primarily to be used by ECOWAS, was established in Accra. In May 2004 Ghana became a full member of the Community of Sahel-Saharan States (see p. 373).

Government

Under the terms of the Constitution, which was approved by national referendum on 28 April 1992, Ghana has a multi-party political system. Executive power is vested in the President, who is the Head of State and Commander-in-Chief of the Armed Forces. The President is elected by direct universal suffrage for a maximum of two four-year terms of office. Legislative power is vested in a 230-member unicameral Parliament, which is elected by direct universal suffrage for a four-year term. The President appoints a Vice-President, and nominates a Council of Ministers, subject to approval by the Parliament. The Con-

stitution also provides for a 25-member Council of State, principally comprising regional representatives and presidential nominees, and a 20-member National Security Council, chaired by the Vice-President, which act as advisory bodies to the President.

Ghana has 10 regions, each headed by a Regional Minister, who is assisted by a regional co-ordinating council. The regions constitute 110 administrative districts, each with a District Assembly, which is headed by a District Chief Executive. Regional colleges, which comprise representatives selected by the District Assemblies and by regional Houses of Chiefs, elect a number of representatives to the Council of State.

Defence

In August 2004 Ghana had total armed forces of 7,000 (army 5,000, navy 1,000 and air force 1,000). At that time Ghanaian troops were deployed in six overseas peace-keeping missions. The defence budget for 2004 was estimated at 200,000m. cedis.

Economic Affairs

In 2003, according to estimates by the World Bank, Ghana's gross national income (GNI), measured at average 2001–03 prices, was US $7,501m., equivalent to $320 per head (or $2,190 on an international purchasing-power parity basis). During 1990–2003, it was estimated, the population increased at an average annual rate of 2.3%, while gross domestic product (GDP) per head increased, in real terms, by an average of 2.1% per year. Overall GDP increased at an average annual rate of 4.4% in 1990–2003; growth in 2003 was 5.2%.

Agriculture (including forestry and fishing) contributed 35.2% of GDP in 2003. An estimated 56.1% of the labour force were employed in the sector in 2003. The principal cash crops are cocoa beans (in 2002 Ghana was the world's second largest producer—after a poor harvest in 2001/2, the 2002/3 harvest showed an increase of 16.4% to a value of US $890m., and the 2003/4 harvest was valued at $1,100m.), coffee, bananas, cassava, oil palm, coconuts, limes, kola nuts and shea-nuts (karité nuts). In 2004 development of the palm oil and cassava sectors was underway. Timber production is also important, with the forestry sector accounting for 4.4% of GDP in 2002, and cork and wood, and manufactures thereof, contributing 9.0% of total export earnings in 2000. Fishing satisfies more than three-quarters of domestic requirements, and contributed 4.9% of GDP in 2002. During 1990–2003, according to the World Bank, agricultural GDP increased at an average annual rate of 3.5%; growth in 2003 was 4.6%.

Industry (including mining, manufacturing, construction and power) contributed 24.8% of GDP in 2003 , and employed 12.8% of the working population in 1984. According to the World Bank, industrial GDP increased at an average annual rate of 3.0% in 1990–2003; growth in 2003 was 0.7%.

Mining contributed 5.3% of GDP in 2002, and employed 0.5% of the working population in 1984. Gold and diamonds are the major minerals exported (in 2003 gold production was an estimated 71 metric tons), although Ghana also exploits large reserves of bauxite and manganese ore. The Government is attempting to increase exploitation of salt, bauxite and clay. According to central bank figures, the GDP of the mining sector increased by an average of 5.3% per year in 1991–2003; growth in 2003 was 4.7%, according to provisional figures.

Manufacturing contributed 8.4 of GDP in 2003, and employed 10.9% of the working population in 1984. The most important sectors are food processing, textiles, vehicles, cement, paper, chemicals and petroleum. According to the World Bank, manufacturing GDP declined at an average annual rate of 1.7% in 1990–2003; the GDP of the sector decreased by 1.4% in 2003.

According to figures published by the World Bank, some 84.1% of Ghana's production of electricity was from hydro-electric power in 2001, with the Akosombo and Kpong plants being the major sources, and 15.9% from petroleum (an increase from 8.5% in 2000). Low rainfall resulted in a severe energy crisis in 1998, prompting the Government to accelerate plans for the further development of thermal power, and in mid-2004 it was announced that the World Bank was providing a loan of US $60m. to increase the production of the thermal power generator, Takoradi II. In November 2004 the World Bank agreed to finance the construction of the West African Gas Pipeline, which was to supply natural gas from Nigeria to Ghana, Benin and Togo. Imports of fuel and energy comprised 6.6% of the total value of merchandise imports in 2003. Electricity is exported to Benin and Togo. Ghana was expected to become a net exporter of power in 2004.

The services sector contributed 40.1% of GDP in 2003, and engaged 26.1% of the working population in 1984. According to the World Bank, the GDP of the services sector increased at an average annual rate of 5.6% in 1990–2003; growth in 2003 was 6.9%.

In 2003 Ghana recorded a visible trade deficit of US $713.7m., however, there was a surplus of $254.9m. on the current account of the balance of payments. In 2000 the principal source of imports was Nigeria (10.9%); other major sources were the United Kingdom, the USA and Germany. Switzerland was the principal market for exports (taking 23.5% of the total) in that year; other important purchasers were the United Kingdom, the Netherlands and the USA. The principal exports in 2000 were gold (which accounted for 36.7% of total export earnings), cocoa beans and timber and timber products. The principal imports in 2000 were machinery and transport equipment, petroleum products, basic manufactures, and food and live animals.

Ghana's overall budget deficit for 2003 was 5,856,000m. cedis (equivalent to 3.3% of GDP). Ghana's external debt totalled US $7,338m. at the end of 2002, of which $6,382m. was long-term public debt. In that year the cost of debt-servicing was equivalent to 8.0% of exports of goods and services. According to government figures, total external debt was $6,200m. at the end of 2004. In 1990–2002 the average annual rate of inflation was 25.3%. Consumer prices increased by 26.7% in 2003. The 2004 budget aimed to reduce inflation to under 10%. In 1995 some 41,000 people were registered as unemployed in Ghana.

Ghana is a member of the Economic Community of West African States (ECOWAS, see p. 205), of the International Cocoa Organization (ICCO, see p. 370), and of the International Coffee Organization (ICO, see p. 370).

Although Ghana's economy has made steady progress since the transfer to civilian rule in 1992, it remains vulnerable to unfavourable weather conditions and to fluctuations in international commodity prices. In May 1999 the IMF approved a three-year Enhanced Structural Adjustment Facility (subsequently renamed the Poverty Reduction and Growth Facility—PRGF), equivalent to US $209.4m., in support of the Government's economic reform programme. In February 2002 it was announced that Ghana was to receive a total of some $3,700m. in debt-service relief from its creditors over a period of 20 years, under the initiative of the IMF and the World Bank for heavily indebted poor countries (HIPCs). It was forecast that this would allow Ghana to reduce debt-servicing payments from an annual average of $350m. in 1997–2000 to an annual average of $230m. in 2002–2004. In May 2003 the IMF approved a new three-year arrangement under the PRGF, amounting to some $258m., and also agreed to provide Ghana with additional assistance of some $22m. under the enhanced HIPC initiative. Following the first review of economic performance under the PRGF in December, the IMF commended Ghana's progress. In 2003 the Government adopted a policy of price adjustment for petroleum, electricity and water in an attempt to halt losses in the public enterprises responsible for these sectors, and the removal of the subsidy on petroleum products was expected in 2005. The value of exports of gold and cocoa increased significantly in 2003, to an estimated $770m. and $772m. (compared with $380m. in 2001), respectively, as a result of a strong recovery in international prices for these commodities in 2002–03. In January 2004 it was announced that Ghana had achieved three of the four convergence criteria required for participation in a proposed West African Monetary Zone, which was scheduled to be inaugurated in July 2005 with the launch of a common currency, to be known as the 'eco'. In July the Minister of Finance and Economic Planning announced that Ghana had complied with the criteria set for the HIPC initiative, and following a meeting of the Ghana's 'Paris Club' creditors, it was agreed to reduce the country's debt to those countries from $1,940,000m. to $300m. In the same month the IMF completed the second review under the PRGF facility, and praised the Government's economic policies. A further $39m. was therefore made available. In mid-2004 the European Union announced a grant of €62m. to support the 2004–06 budgets. According to official figures, GDP growth of 5.8% was recorded in 2004, while inflation fell to 11.8% (from 23% in 2003). Growth of 5.8% and inflation of 17.3% was forecast for 2005, while the budget deficit was predicted to decline to 2.7% of GDP, compared with 3.2% the previous year.

Education

Education is officially compulsory for eight years between the ages of six and 14. Primary education begins at the age of six and lasts for six years. Secondary education, beginning at the age of 12, lasts for a further seven years, comprising a first cycle lasting four years and a second cycle of three years. Following four years of junior secondary education, pupils are examined to determine admission to senior secondary school courses, or to technical and vocational courses. In 2000/01 primary enrolment included 58% of children in the relevant age-group (boys 60%; girls 57%), while UNESCO estimated that the comparable ratio for secondary enrolment in that year was 31% (boys 33%; girls 28%). Some 82,346 students were enrolled in higher education in 1996/97, with 23,126 students attending the country's five universities. By 1998/99 there were seven universities in Ghana, and other tertiary institutions included 38 teacher-training colleges, eight polytechnics and 61 technical colleges. Expenditure on education by the central Government in 1998 was 608,000m. cedis (18.2% of total spending). In late 2003 the Government was granted US $27m. by donor agencies for the improvement of the education system and in early 2004 the World Bank granted credit of $78m. for educational development.

Public Holidays

2005: 1 January (New Year's Day), 21 January* (Eid-al-Adha, Feast of the Sacrifice), 7 March (for Independence Day), 25–28 March (Easter), 1 May (Labour Day), 25 May (African Union Day), 1 July (Republic Day), 4 November* (Eid-al-Fitr, end of Ramadan), 2 December (National Farmers' Day), 25–26 December (Christmas).

2006: 1 January (New Year's Day), 11 January* (Eid-al-Adha, Feast of the Sacrifice), 6 March (Independence Day), 14–17 April (Easter), 1 May (Labour Day), 25 May (African Union Day), 1 July (Republic Day), 24 October* (Eid-al-Fitr, end of Ramadan), 3 December (National Farmers' Day), 25–26 December (Christmas).

*These holidays are dependent on the Islamic lunar calendar and may vary by one or two days from the dates given.

Weights and Measures

The metric system is in force.

Statistical Survey

Source (except where otherwise stated): Ghana Statistical Service, POB GP1350, Accra; e-mail csps@ncs.gom.gh.

Area and Population

AREA, POPULATION AND DENSITY

Area (sq km)	238,537*
Population (census results)	
11 March 1984	12,296,081
26 March 2000	
Males	9,320,794
Females	9,524,471
Total	18,845,265
Population (UN estimates at mid-year)†	
2001	20,028,000
2002	20,471,000
2003	20,922,000
Density (per sq km) at mid-2003	87.7

* 92,100 sq miles.
† Source: UN, *World Population Prospects: The 2002 Revision.*

POPULATION BY REGION
(2000 census)

Region	Population	Capital
Ashanti	3,600,358	Kumasi
Brong-Ahafo	1,798,058	Sunyani
Central	1,593,888	Cape Coast
Eastern	2,101,650	Koforidua
Greater Accra	2,903,753	Accra
Northern	1,805,428	Tamale
Upper East	919,549	Bolgatanga
Upper West	575,579	Wa
Volta	1,630,254	Ho
Western	1,916,748	Takoradi
Total	**18,845,265**	

PRINCIPAL TOWNS
(population at 1984 census)

Accra (capital) . .	867,459	Takoradi	61,484
Kumasi	376,249	Cape Coast . . .	57,224
Tamale	135,952	Sekondi	31,916
Tema	131,528		

Mid-2003 (UN estimate, incl. suburbs): Accra 1,847,432 (Source: UN, *World Urbanization Prospects: The 2003 Revision*).

BIRTHS AND DEATHS
(UN estimates, annual averages)

	1985–90	1990–95	1995–2000
Birth rate (per 1,000)	41.3	37.5	34.0
Death rate (per 1,000)	12.0	10.7	10.3

Source: UN, *World Population Prospects: The 2002 Revision.*

Expectation of life (WHO estimates, years at birth): 57.6 (males 56.3; females 58.8) in 2002 (Source: WHO, *World Health Report*).

ECONOMICALLY ACTIVE POPULATION
(1984 census)

	Males	Females	Total
Agriculture, hunting, forestry and fishing	1,750,024	1,560,943	3,310,967
Mining and quarrying	24,906	1,922	26,828
Manufacturing	198,430	389,988	588,418
Electricity, gas and water . . .	14,033	1,404	15,437
Construction	60,692	3,994	64,686
Trade, restaurants and hotels . .	111,540	680,607	792,147
Transport, storage and communications	117,806	5,000	122,806
Financing, insurance, real estate and business services . . .	19,933	7,542	27,475
Community, social and personal services	339,665	134,051	473,716
Total employed	**2,637,029**	**2,785,451**	**5,422,480**
Unemployed	87,452	70,172	157,624
Total labour force	**2,724,481**	**2,855,623**	**5,580,104**

Source: ILO, *Yearbook of Labour Statistics.*

Mid-2003 (estimates in '000): Agriculture, etc. 5,881; Total 10,476 (Source: FAO).

Health and Welfare

KEY INDICATORS

Total fertility rate (children per woman, 2002)	4.2
Under-5 mortality rate (per 1,000 live births, 2003) . . .	95
HIV/AIDS (% of persons aged 15–49, 2003)	3.1
Physicians (per 1,000 head, 1996)	0.06
Hospital beds (per 1,000 head, 1997)	1.46
Health expenditure (2001): US $ per head (PPP)	60
Health expenditure (2001): % of GDP	4.7
Health expenditure (2001): public (% of total)	59.6
Access to water (% of persons, 2002)	79
Access to sanitation (% of persons, 2002)	58
Human Development Index (2002): ranking	131
Human Development Index (2002): value	0.568

For sources and definitions, see explanatory note on p. vi.

Agriculture

PRINCIPAL CROPS
('000 metric tons)

	2001	2002	2003
Rice (paddy)	274.6	280.0	238.8
Maize	938.0	1,400.0	1,288.6
Millet	134.4	159.1	175.7
Sorghum	279.7	316.1	337.7
Sweet potatoes* . . .	90.0	90.0	90.0
Cassava (Manioc)	8,965.8	9,731.0	10,239.3
Taro (Coco yam) . . .	1,687.5	1,860.0	1,804.7
Yams	3,546.7	3,900.0	3,812.8
Sugar cane*	140.0	140.0	140.0
Groundnuts (in shell)	258.0	520.0	439.2
Coconuts*	315.0	315.0	315.0
Copra*	10.8	10.8	11.7
Oil palm fruit	1,102.1	1,100.0*	1,100.0*
Karité nuts (Shea nuts)* . .	65.0	60.0	65.0
Tomatoes*	200.0	200.0	200.0
Chillies and green peppers* . . .	270.0	270.0	270.0
Dry onions*	38.5	38.5	38.5
Green beans*	20.0	20.0	20.0
Okra*	100.0	100.0	100.0
Bananas*	10.0	10.0	10.0
Plantains	2,073.8	2,278.8	2,328.6
Oranges	300.0	300.0*	300.0*
Lemons and limes*	30.0	30.0	30.0
Pineapples*	60.0	60.0	60.0
Other fruit*	41.0	41.0	41.0
Cottonseed	7.9*	8.3*	5.4†
Pimento and allspice* . . .	22.0	22.0	22.0
Cocoa beans	389.6	340.6	497.0†
Natural rubber	12.0†	12.0†	12.0*

* FAO estimate(s).
† Unofficial figure.

Source: FAO.

LIVESTOCK
('000 head, year ending September)

	2001	2002	2003
Horses	2.7*	2.7	3.0*
Asses	13.5*	13.1	13.5*
Cattle	1,315.0	1,330.0	1,344.0
Pigs	312.0	310.0	303.0
Sheep	2,771.0	2,922.0	3,015.0
Goats	3,199.0	3,230.0	3,560.0
Chickens	22,032	24,251	26,395

* FAO estimate.

Source: FAO.

LIVESTOCK PRODUCTS
(FAO estimates, '000 metric tons)

	2001	2002	2003
Beef and veal	24.0	24.1	24.4
Mutton and lamb . . .	9.6	10.1	10.4
Goat meat	10.6	10.7	11.7
Pig meat	10.6	10.4	10.2
Poultry meat	21.0	23.4	25.5
Game meat	57.0	57.0	57.0
Other meat	33.0	33.0	33.0
Cows' milk	34.2	34.6	35.1
Hen eggs	22.3	23.3	24.4
Cattle hides	2.8	2.8	2.8

Source: FAO.

Forestry

ROUNDWOOD REMOVALS
('000 cubic metres, excl. bark)

	2001	2002	2003
Sawlogs, veneer logs and logs for sleepers	1,212	1,104	1,400
Fuel wood*	20,678	20,678	20,678
Total	21,890	21,782	22,078

* FAO estimates (output assumed to be unchanged since 1994).

Source: FAO.

SAWNWOOD PRODUCTION
('000 cubic metres, incl. railway sleepers)

	2001	2002	2003
Total (all broadleaved)	480	461	496

Source: FAO.

Fishing

('000 metric tons, live weight)

	2000	2001	2002
Capture	452.1	447.7	371.2
Freshwater fishes	74.5	74.5	74.5
Bigeye grunt	10.0	13.8	9.3
Jack and horse mackerels . .	2.2	2.1	0.5
Round sardinella . . .	102.0	67.3	64.3
Madeiran sardinella . . .	15.0	15.9	13.7
Other sardinellas	18.4	8.3	1.5
European anchovy	83.5	68.2	57.6
Skipjack tuna	30.0	43.3	31.9
Yellowfin tuna	17.0	30.6	23.5
Chub mackerel	29.6	15.2	7.0
Sharks, rays, skates . . .	22.2	41.0	26.3
Aquaculture	5.0	6.0	6.0*
Total catch	457.1	453.7	377.2

* FAO estimate.

Source: FAO.

Mining

('000 metric tons, unless otherwise indicated)

	2000	2001	2002
Crude petroleum ('000 barrels) .	2,555	3,825	3,300*
Bauxite	504	678	684
Manganese ore: gross weight . .	896	1,077	1,136
Manganese ore: metal content* .	287	344	363
Silver (kilograms)†	6,101	1,945	2,129
Gold (kilograms)‡	72,080	68,699	69,707
Salt (unrefined)*	150	68	99
Diamonds ('000 carats)§ . . .	878	1,170	963

* Estimated production.
† Estimated silver content of exported doré.
‡ Gold content of ores and concentrates, excluding smuggled or undocumented output.
§ Of the total, the estimated production of gemstones (in '000 carats) was: 700 in 2000; 936 in 2001; 770 in 2002.

Source: US Geological Survey.

Industry

SELECTED PRODUCTS
('000 metric tons, unless otherwise indicated)

	2001	2002	2003
Groundnut oil*	32.3	98.9	75.6
Coconut oil	6.5*	6.5*	7.0†
Palm oil†	108.0	108.0	108.4
Palm kernel oil*	10.5	10.8	13.3
Butter of karité nuts (shea butter)*	3.7	8.4	10.0
Beer of barley*	80.0	100.0	100.0
Beer of millet*	56.1	666	73.8
Beer of sorghum*	237.5	234.6	288.4
Gasoline (petrol)	2,190	5,850	n.a.
Jet fuel	730	625	n.a.
Kerosene	365	1,950	n.a.
Distillate fuel oil	2,555	4,450	n.a.
Residual fuel oil	1,825	1,250	n.a.
Cement	1,490	n.a.	n.a.
Aluminium (unwrought)‡	144	117	n.a.
Electric energy (million kWh)	7,180.0	6,891.0	5,882.0

* FAO estimates.
† Provisional or estimated figure(s).
‡ Primary metal only.

Sources: FAO; UN, *Industrial Commodity Statistics Yearbook*; US Geological Survey; Energy Commission of Ghana.

Finance

CURRENCY AND EXCHANGE RATES

Monetary Units
100 pesewas = 1 new cedi.

Sterling, Dollar and Euro Equivalents (31 December 2004)
£1 sterling = 17,487.40 cedis;
US $1 = 9,054.26 cedis;
€1 = 12,332.82 cedis;
100,000 cedis = £5.72= $11.04 = €8.11.

Average Exchange Rate (cedis per US $)
2002   7,932.70
2003   8,677.37
2004   9,004.63

GENERAL BUDGET
('000 million new cedis)

Revenue*	2001	2002	2003
Tax revenue	6,545.5	8,547.5	12,762.1
Income and property	2,123.7	2,795.4	4,091.5
Personal (PAYE)	677.4	928.8	1,534.8
Company tax	966.6	1,161.5	1,632.5
Domestic goods and services	900.5	1,448.4	2,179.9
Petroleum tax	646.6	1,080.0	1,705.9
International trade	1,557.1	1,994.9	3,159.6
Import duties	1,257.1	1,626.1	2,367.2
Cocoa export duty	299.6	326.4	768.9
Non-tax revenue	347.7	252.4	363.3
Total	6,893.2	8,799.9	13,125.3

Expenditure†	2001	2002	2003
Recurrent expenditure	6,971.3	9,786.6	12,643.2
Wages and salaries	2,277.9	4,197.1	5,661.0
Goods and services	589.7	1,452.4	1,762.9
Subventions	788.0	0.0	0.0
Transfers to households	528.4	1,138.0	1,585.8
Interest payments	2,787.2	2,999.0	3,633.4
Domestic (accrual)	2,309.5	2,210.0	2,786.9
External (accrual)	477.7	789.0	846.6
Capital expenditure	2,856.0	2,814.1	5,471.8
Domestic	1,211.3	1,162.5	2,396.1
External	1,644.8	1,651.5	3,075.7
Statistical discrepancy	—	175.1	866.3
Total	9,827.3	12,775.8	18,981.3

* Excluding grants received ('000 million new cedis): 1,570.0 in 2001; 1,524.6 in 2002; 3,118.8 in 2003. Also excluded are the proceeds from the divestiture of state-owned enterprises ('000 million new cedis): 154.4 in 2001; 10.9 in 2002; 421.4 in 2003.
† Including net lending ('000 million new cedis): –1.2 in 2001; –2.0 in 2002; 35.0 in 2003.

Source: Bank of Ghana.

INTERNATIONAL RESERVES
(US $ million at 31 December)

	2001	2002	2003
Gold*	78.9	96.5	116.1
IMF special drawing rights	4.0	3.7	46.8
Foreign exchange	294.2	536.1	1,306.0
Total	377.1	639.9	1,468.9

* National valuation.

Source: IMF, *International Financial Statistics*.

MONEY SUPPLY
('000 million new cedis at 31 December)

	2001	2002	2003
Currency outside banks	3,089.0	4,671.6	6,337.8
Deposits of non-financial public enterprises	4.4	283.4	3.4
Demand deposits at deposit money banks	1,930.3	3,339.5	4,342.8
Total money (incl. others)	5,035.0	8,048.6	10,723.4

Source: IMF, *International Financial Statistics*.

COST OF LIVING
(Consumer Price Index; base: 2000 = 100)

	2001	2002	2003
All items	132.9	152.6	193.3

Source: IMF, *International Financial Statistics*.

NATIONAL ACCOUNTS
('000 million new cedis at current prices)

National Income and Product

	1999	2000	2001
GDP at market prices	20,580	27,153	38,071
Net factor income from abroad	–434	–797	–774
National income	20,146	26,355	37,297
Net transfers from abroad	1,655	3,528	6,197
National disposable income	21,801	29,883	43,494

Source: IMF, *Ghana: Statistical Appendix* (May 2003).

Expenditure on the Gross Domestic Product
(preliminary figures)

	1999	2000	2001
Government final consumption expenditure	3,084	4,602	6,793
Private final consumption expenditure	16,684	21,049	28,605
Gross fixed capital formation . .	4,314	6,591	10,089
Inventories	110	−81	38
Total domestic expenditure .	24,192	32,161	45,525
Exports of goods and services . .	6,602	13,251	17,221
Less Imports of goods and services	10,213	18,259	24,675
GDP in purchasers' values . .	20,580	27,153	38,071
GDP at constant 1993 prices .	4,957	5,142	5,357

Source: IMF, *Ghana: Statistical Appendix* (May 2003).

2002: GDP in purchasers' values 47,012; GDP at constant 1993 prices 5,600,800m. (Source: Bank of Ghana).

2003: GDP in purchasers' values at constant 1993 prices 6,203,600m. (Source: Bank of Ghana).

Gross Domestic Product by Economic Activity

	2000	2001	2002
Agriculture and livestock . . .	5,976	8,471	10,533
Cocoa	1,305	1,744	2,051
Forestry and logging	1,055	1,493	1,852
Fishing	1,241	1,709	2,077
Mining and quarrying	1,352	1,796	2,219
Manufacturing	2,448	3,428	4,246
Electricity, water and gas . . .	732	1,029	1,266
Construction	2,366	3,347	4,154
Transport, storage and communications	1,165	1,660	2,074
Wholesale and retail trade, restaurants and hotels . .	1,824	2,588	3,230
Finance, insurance, real estate and business services	1,155	1,630	2,033
Government services	2,731	3,871	4,740
Community, social and personal services	694	998	1,233
Private non-profit services . . .	254	355	432
GDP at factor cost	24,299	34,119	42,139
Indirect taxes, *less* subsidies . .	2,854	3,953	4,873
GDP at market prices . . .	27,153	38,071	47,012

Sources: IMF, *Ghana: Statistical Appendix* (May 2003); Bank of Ghana.

BALANCE OF PAYMENTS
(US $ million)

	2001	2002	2003
Exports of goods f.o.b.	1,867.1	2,015.2	2,562.4
Imports of goods f.o.b.	−2,968.5	−2,707.0	−3,276.1
Trade balance	−1,101.4	−691.8	−713.7
Exports of services	531.7	554.9	630.0
Imports of services	−606.1	−620.9	−903.7
Balance on goods and services	−1,175.8	−757.8	−987.4
Other income received	16.3	14.7	21.4
Other income paid	−124.1	−188.9	−178.3
Balance on goods, services and income	−1,283.6	−932.0	−1,144.3
Current transfers received . .	978.4	912.2	1,408.4
Current transfers paid	−19.4	−12.2	−9.2
Current balance	−324.6	−31.8	254.9
Direct investment from abroad .	89.3	58.9	136.7
Other investment assets . . .	65.0	94.7	68.0
Other investment liabilities . .	237.9	−192.3	142.6
Net errors and omissions . . .	−189.1	195.1	−46.9
Overall balance	−121.5	124.6	555.3

Source: IMF, *International Financial Statistics*.

External Trade

PRINCIPAL COMMODITIES
(distribution by SITC, US $ million)

Imports c.i.f.	1998	1999	2000
Food and live animals . . .	282.6	328.3	319.9
Fish, crustaceans and molluscs, and preparations thereof . .	103.5	105.2	80.1
Fish, fresh, chilled or frozen	96.4	97.3	75.7
Fish, frozen, excluding fillets	86.7	94.3	70.1
Cereals and cereal preparations .	92.9	101.6	115.3
Crude materials (inedible), except fuels	97.2	96.7	140.7
Mineral fuels, lubricants, etc. .	535.0	532.6	629.2
Petroleum, petroleum products, etc.	490.7	466.1	579.4
Crude petroleum and oils obtained from bituminous materials	171.7	252.1	315.1
Petroleum products, refined . .	303.2	187.0	238.0
Chemicals and related products	279.4	309.1	282.0
Basic manufactures	382.3	388.5	433.4
Non-metallic mineral manufactures	81.3	85.9	94.1
Iron and steel	87.9	91.5	73.9
Machinery and transport equipment	1,134.1	1,131.9	890.1
Power-generating machinery and equipment	137.7	67.4	65.3
Machinery specialized for particular industries	193.8	147.5	107.2
General industrial machinery and equipment, and parts thereof .	150.7	161.3	141.7
Telecommunications, sound recording and reproducing equipment	47.5	99.0	62.2
Other electric machinery, apparatus and appliances, and parts thereof	118.9	118.9	124.8
Road vehicles and parts* . . .	448.7	493.3	340.1
Passenger motor vehicles (excluding buses)	122.3	268.8	179.0
Motor vehicles for the transport of goods or materials . . .	218.4	144.7	106.5
Miscellaneous manufactured articles	140.8	168.4	153.9
Total (incl. others)	2,911.3	3,003.8	2933.2

* Data on parts exclude tyres, engines and electrical parts.

Exports f.o.b.	1998	1999	2000
Food and live animals . . .	628.5	636.4	483.3
Fish, crustaceans and molluscs, and preparations thereof . .	69.2	72.2	75.7
Fish, prepared or preserved . .	51.2	54.3	57.1
Vegetables and fruit	25.8	98.0	87.3
Fruit and nuts, fresh, dried . .	17.4	90.5	32.6
Fruit, fresh or dried . .	10.5	81.6	12.4
Pineapples, fresh or dried . .	9.3	80.5	11.1
Coffee, tea, cocoa, spices and manufactures thereof . . .	521.7	458.2	313.3
Cocoa	512.5	450.5	305.4
Cocoa beans, raw, roasted .	447.5	400.6	258.6
Cocoa butter and paste . .	64.9	49.4	45.3
Cocoa butter (fat or oil) . .	50.1	39.7	29.9
Crude materials (inedible) except fuels	162.2	165.9	165.1
Cork and wood	100.1	110.8	94.2
Wood, non-coniferous species, sawn, planed, tongued, grooved, etc.	97.9	107.1	82.3
Wood, non-coniferous species, sawn lengthwise, sliced or peeled	95.2	104.5	61.3

Exports f.o.b.— *continued*	1998	1999	2000
Mineral fuels, lubricants, etc. .	37.8	56.1	81.8
Basic manufactures	154.9	226.4	239.1
Cork and wood manufactures (excl. furniture)	105.1	93.8	56.6
Veneers, plywood, 'improved' wood and other wood, worked . . .	101.2	57.5	51.3
Wood sawn lengthwise, veneer sheets, etc., up to 5 mm in thickness	96.5	40.9	38.1
Aluminium and aluminium alloys, unwrought	23.8	54.6	146.9
Machinery and transport equipment	8.4	38.1	19.3
Gold, non-monetary, unwrought or semi-manufactured	120.4	100.6	612.7
Total (incl. others)	1,158.0	1,269.7	1670.9

Source: UN, *International Trade Statistics Yearbook.*

2002 (US $ million): *Imports:* Fuel and energy 275; Total imports c.i.f. 4,099. *Exports:* Cocoa 463; Timber 182; Total exports f.o.b. 2,681 (Source: World Bank).

2003 (US $ million): *Imports:* Fuel and energy 295; Total imports c.i.f. 4,469. *Exports:* Cocoa 772; Timber 176; Total exports f.o.b. 3,015 (Source: World Bank).

Source: World Bank.

PRINCIPAL TRADING PARTNERS
(US $ million)

Imports c.i.f.	1998	1999	2000
Australia	42.0	40.3	38.0
Belgium	124.7*	202.6	144.0
Brazil	36.7	40.9	53.2
Canada	54.4	55.8	57.8
China, People's Republic . . .	65.6	96.8	93.3
Côte d'Ivoire	69.4	77.2	68.6
France (incl. Monaco) . . .	93.5	87.9	93.5
Germany	237.9	222.7	207.5
Hong Kong	21.6	35.2	23.5
India	43.2	52.3	49.5
Israel	47.3	5.6	3.3
Italy (incl. San Marino) . . .	127.4	112.8	147.4
Japan	123.0	84.4	53.1
Korea, Democratic People's Republic	4.1	5.3	68.0
Korea, Republic	97.3	136.3	0.0
Malaysia	10.7	30.4	n.a.
Nigeria	115.7	240.5	320.6
Netherlands	150.0	209.8	186.2
SACU†	104.4	104.1	n.a.
South Africa	—	—	98.2
Spain	123.2	84.0	141.2
Sweden	45.5	35.3	34.1
Switzerland-Liechtenstein . . .	45.7	24.4	30.2
Thailand	22.3	31.4	36.5
Togo	29.2	36.0	50.3
United Kingdom	348.8	307.8	268.4
USA	313.5	261.3	219.3
Total (incl. others)	2,911.3	3,003.8	2,933.2

Exports f.o.b.	1998	1999	2000
Bahamas	0.1	0.9	19.5
Belgium	60.1*	46.7	31.8
Benin	1.7	13.5	11.0
Burkina Faso	7.3	62.3	6.3
China, People's Republic . . .	2.0	3.3	27.7
Cyprus	0.7	2.7	25.1
France (incl. Monaco)	66.6	50.1	41.8
The Gambia	0.2	18.3	0.5
Germany	87.4	57.3	89.7
Ireland	26.9	9.6	14.1
Italy (incl. San Marino)	59.5	81.2	49.0
Japan	49.5	50.4	24.0
Netherlands	184.3	179.2	186.9
Niger	7.4	18.1	10.8
Nigeria	8.5	6.8	27.0
Russia	19.0	4.4	7.8
SACU†	40.2	41.2	—
South Africa	—	—	29.8
Spain	87.3	35.7	22.3
Switzerland-Liechtenstein . . .	43.2	37.7	392.6
Togo	27.0	44.9	63.8
Trinidad and Tobago	0.0	33.4	0.0
Turkey	11.7	11.3	18.5
United Kingdom	219.5	288.0	315.0
USA	54.4	69.2	98.1
Total (incl. others)	1,158.0	1,269.7	1,670.9

* Including Luxembourg.
† Southern African Customs Union, comprising Botswana, Lesotho, Namibia, South Africa and Swaziland.

Source: UN, *International Trade Statistics Yearbook.*

Transport

RAILWAYS
(traffic)

	2001	2002
Passengers carried ('000)	600	n.a.
Freight carried ('000 metric tons)	1,500	n.a.
Passenger-km (million)	62	238
Net ton-km (million)	220	168

Source: Railway Gazette, *Railway Directory* and UN, *Statistical Yearbook.*

ROAD TRAFFIC
('000 motor vehicles in use at 31 December)

	1998	2000*	2002*
Passenger cars	301	397	463
Lorries and vans	44	53	56

* Figures for 1999 and 2001 not available.

Source: Ghana Highway Authority.

SHIPPING

Merchant Fleet
(registered at 31 December)

	2001	2002	2003
Number of vessels	212	213	207
Total displacement ('000 grt) . .	123.1	126.2	121.3

Source: Lloyd's Register-Fairplay, *World Fleet Statistics.*

International Sea-borne Freight Traffic
(estimates, '000 metric tons)

	1991	1992	1993
Goods loaded	2,083	2,279	2,424
Goods unloaded	2,866	2,876	2,904

Source: UN Economic Commission for Africa, *African Statistical Yearbook.*

CIVIL AVIATION
(traffic on scheduled services)

	1999	2000	2001
Kilometres flown (million) . . .	9	9	18
Passengers carried ('000) . . .	304	314	301
Passenger-km (million)	1,097	1,204	1,233
Total ton-km (million) . . .	151	162	157

Source: UN, *Statistical Yearbook.*

Tourism

ARRIVALS BY NATIONALITY

	2000	2001	2002
Côte d'Ivoire	19,183	21,098	23,204
France	14,418	15,857	17,440
Germany	19,251	21,173	23,286
Liberia	10,463	11,508	12,656
Netherlands	9,659	10,623	11,684
Nigeria	54,764	60,231	66,244
Togo	11,941	13,133	14,444
United Kingdom	34,546	37,994	41,787
USA	26,317	28,945	31,834
Total (incl. others)*	398,998	438,828	482,637

* Includes Ghanaian nationals resident abroad: 108,609 in 2000; 119,451 in 2001; 131,376 in 2002.

Source: World Tourism Organization, *Yearbook of Tourism Statistics.*

Receipts from tourism (US $ million): 335 in 2000; 351 in 2001; 358 in 2002.

Communications Media

	2001	2002	2003
Telephones ('000 main lines in use)	242.1	274.0	302.3
Mobile cellular telephones ('000 subscribers)	193.8	449.4	799.9
Personal computers ('000 in use) .	70	82	n.a.
Internet users ('000)	40.5	170	n.a.

Source: International Telecommunication Union.

Radio receivers ('000 in use): 4,400 in 1997.

Television receivers ('000 in use): 2,390 in 2000.

Facsimile machines (number in use, estimate): 5,000 in 1995.

Daily newspapers: 4 titles in 1996 (average circulation 250,000).

Book production (titles, 1998): 7.

Sources: UNESCO, *Statistical Yearbook*; UN, *Statistical Yearbook.*

Education

(1996/97, unless otherwise indicated)

	Institutions	Teachers	Students		
			Males	Females	Total
Primary . . .	13,014	71,330	1,245,036	1,088,311	2,333,347
Junior secondary	5,880	40,417	413,686	324,362	738,048
Senior secondary .	504	11,458	118,948	75,837	194,785
Technical institutes . .	61	n.a.	n.a.	n.a.	23,642
Teacher training .	38	1,001*	n.a.	n.a.	20,399
Polytechnics . .	8	n.a.	n.a.	n.a.	15,179
Universities . .	5	700*†	n.a.	n.a.	23,126

* 1989/90 figure.
† Excluding the University of Ghana.

1998/99: *Primary* 13,115 institutions; *Junior secondary* 6,394 institutions; *Senior secondary* 512 institutions; *Teacher training* 38 institutions; *Technical institutes* 61 institutions; *Polytechnics* 8 institutions; *Universities* 7 institutions.

Source: mainly former Ministry of Education, Accra.

Adult literacy rate (UNESCO estimates): 73.8% (males 81.9%; females 65.9%) in 2002 (Source: UN Development Programme, *Human Development Report*).

Directory

The Constitution

Under the terms of the Constitution of the Fourth Republic, which was approved by national referendum on 28 April 1992, Ghana has a multi-party political system. Executive power is vested in the President, who is Head of State and Commander-in-Chief of the Armed Forces. The President is elected by universal adult suffrage for a term of four years, and designates a Vice-President (prior to election). The duration of the President's tenure of office is limited to two four-year terms. It is also stipulated that, in the event that no presidential candidate receives more than 50% of votes cast, a new election between the two candidates with the highest number of votes is to take place within 21 days. Legislative power is vested in a 230-member unicameral Parliament, which is elected by direct adult suffrage for a four-year term. (This number was increased from 200 at the general election of December 2004.) The Council of Ministers is appointed by the President, subject to approval by the Parliament. The Constitution also provides for a 25-member Council of State, principally comprising presidential nominees and regional representatives, and a 20-member National Security Council (chaired by the Vice-President), both of which act as advisory bodies to the President.

The Government

HEAD OF STATE

President and Commander-in-Chief of the Armed Forces: JOHN AGYEKUM KUFUOR (inaugurated 7 January 2001; re-elected 7 December 2004 and inaugurated 7 January 2005).

Vice-President: Alhaji ALIU MAHAMA.

CABINET MINISTERS
(April 2005)

The Cabinet comprises members of the New Patriotic Party (NPP) and independents (Ind.).

Senior Minister, responsible for Public-Sector Reform and the National Institutional Renewal Programme: JOSEPH HENRY MENSAH (NPP).

Minister of Finance and Economic Planning: KWADWO BAAH-WIREDU (NPP).

Minister of Defence: Dr KWAME ADDO KUFUOR (NPP).

Minister of Foreign Affairs: NANA ADDO DANKWA AKUFUO-ADDO (NPP).

Attorney-General, Minister of Justice: NII AYIKOI OTOO (Ind.).

Minister of Trade and Industry: ALAN KYEREMANTENG (Ind.).

Minister of the Interior: PAPA OWUSU ANKOMAH (NPP).

Minister of Local Government and Rural Development: CHARLES BINIPONG BINTIM (NPP).

Minister of Education and Sports: YAW OSAFO-MAAFO (NPP).

Minister of Food and Agriculture: ERNEST AKUBOUR DEBRAH (NPP).

Minister of Health: Maj. (retd) COURAGE QUASHIGAH (NPP).

Minister of Lands, Forestry and Mines: Prof. DOMINIC K. FOBIH (NPP).

Minister of Works and Housing: HACKMAN OWUSU AGYEMANG (NPP).

Minister of Energy: Prof. MIKE OQUAYE (NPP).

Minister of Tourism and the Modernization of the Capital City: JAKE OTANKA OBETSEBI-LAMPTEY (NPP).

Minister of Women's and Children's Affairs: Hajia ALIMA MAHAMA (NPP).

Minister of Fisheries: GLADYS ASMAH (NPP).

Minister of Parliamentary Affairs: FELIX OWUSU-ADJAPONG (NPP).

Minister of Information: DANIEL KWAKU BOTWE (NPP).

MINISTERS NOT IN THE CABINET
(April 2005)

Minister of Communications: ALBERT KAN-DAPAAH (NPP).

Minister of Presidential Affairs: KWADWO MPIANI (NPP).

Minister of Ports, Harbours and Railways: Prof. CHRISTIAN AKUMFI-AMEYAW (NPP).

Minister of Manpower, Youth and Employment: JOSEPH KOFI ADDA (NPP).

Minister of Road Transport: Dr RICHARD WINFRED ANANE (NPP).

Minister of Private-Sector Development and Special Presidential Initiatives: KWAMENA BARTELS (NPP).

Minister of Regional Co-operation and NEPAD: Dr KOFI KONADU APRAKU.

Minister of Science and the Environment: CHRISTINE CHURCHER (NPP).

Minister of State in charge of Public Sector Reform: Dr PAA KWESI NDUOM.

REGIONAL MINISTERS
(April 2005)

Ashanti: SAMPSON KWEKU BOAFO.

Brong Ahafo: NANA KWADWO SEINTI.

Central: ISAAC E. EDUMADZE.

Eastern: YAW BARIMAH.

Greater Accra: Sheikh IBRAHIM CUDJOE QUAYE.

Northern: BONIFACE ABUBAKAR SADDIQUE.

Upper East: BONIFACE GAMBILA.

Upper West: AMBROSE DERY.

Volta: KOFI DZAMESI.

Western: JOSEPH BOAHEN AIDOO.

MINISTRIES

Office of the President: POB 1627, Osu, Accra; tel. (21) 665415; internet www.ghanacastle.gov.gh.

Ministry of Communications: POB M42, Accra; tel. (21) 685606; fax (21) 667114; e-mail moct@ghana.gov.gh.

Ministry of Defence: Burma Camp, Accra; tel. and fax (21) 777611.

Ministry of Education and Sports: POB M45, Accra; tel. (21) 666070; fax (21) 664067; internet www.ghana.edu.gh.

Ministry of Energy: FREMA House, Spintex Rd, POB MB40, Stadium, Accra; tel. (21) 667151; fax (21) 668262; e-mail energy1@ncs.com.gh; internet www.energycom.gov.gh.

Ministry of Finance and Economic Planning: POB M40, Accra; tel. (21) 686204; fax (21) 668879; internet www.finance.gov.gh.

Ministry of Fisheries: Accra.

Ministry of Food and Agriculture: POB M37, Accra; tel. (21) 663036; fax (21) 668245; e-mail info@mofa.gov.gh; internet www.mofa.gov.gh.

Ministry of Foreign Affairs: Treasury Rd, POB M53, Accra; tel. (21) 664951; fax (21) 680017; e-mail ghmafoo@ghana.com; internet www.mfa.gov.gh.

Ministry of Health: POB M44, Accra; tel. (21) 666151; fax (21) 666810.

Ministry of Information: POB 745, Accra; tel. (21) 228059; fax (21) 235800; e-mail webmaster@moi.gov.gh.

Ministry of the Interior: POB M42, Accra; tel. (21) 662688; fax (21) 667450.

Ministry of Justice: POB M60, Accra; tel. (21) 665051; fax (21) 667609; e-mail attorneygeneral@ghana.com.

Ministry of Lands, Forestry and Mines: POB M212, Accra; tel. (21) 665949; fax (21) 666896; e-mail motgov@hotmail.com.

Ministry of Local Government and Rural Development: POB M50, Accra; tel. (21) 664763; fax (21) 661015.

Ministry of Manpower, Youth and Employment: State House, POB M1627, Accra; tel. (21) 665349; fax (21) 667251; e-mail manpower@idngh.com.

Ministry of Parliamentary Affairs: State House, POB 1627, Accra; tel. (21) 665349; fax (21) 667251.

Ministry of Ports, Harbours and Railways: Accra.

Ministry of Private-Sector Development and Special Presidential Initiatives: State House, POB 1627, Accra; tel. (21) 665349; fax (21) 665251.

Ministry of Public-Sector Reform and the National Institutional Renewal Programme: Accra.

Ministry of Regional Co-operation and the New Partnership for Africa's Development: POB CT633, Accra; tel. (21) 771777; fax (21) 771778; e-mail www.planning.gov.gh.

Ministry of Road Transport: POB M57, Accra; tel. (21) 668314; fax (21) 672676; e-mail info@mrt.gov.gh; internet www.mrt.gov.gh.

Ministry of Science and the Environment: POB 232, Accra; tel. (21) 666049; fax (21) 666828; e-mail mest@ghana.com.

Ministry of Tourism and the Modernization of the Capital City: POB 4386, Accra; tel. (21) 666701; fax (21) 666182; e-mail motgov@hotmail.com; internet www.ghanatourism.gov.gh.

Ministry of Trade and Industry: POB M47, Accra; tel. (21) 663327; fax (21) 662428; e-mail mis-moti@africaonline.com.gh; internet www.moti-ghana.com.

Ministry of Women's and Children's Affairs: POB M186, Accra; tel. (21) 255411; fax (21) 688182; e-mail barnes@africaonline.com.gh.

Ministry of Works and Housing: POB M43, Accra; tel. (21) 665940; fax (21) 667689; e-mail mwh@ighmail.com.

President and Legislature

PRESIDENT

Presidential Election, 7 December 2004

Candidate	Valid votes	% of valid votes
John Agyekum Kufuor (NPP)	4,524,074	52.45
John Evans Atta Mills (NDC)	3,850,368	44.64
Edward Nasigre Mahama (PNC)	165,375	1.92
George Aggudey (CPP)	85,968	1.00
Total	8,625,785*	100.00

* Excluding 188,213 spoilt papers.

PARLIAMENT

Parliament: Parliament House, Accra; tel. and fax (21) 665957; e-mail clerk@parliament.gh; internet www.parliament.gh.

Speaker: EBENEZER BEGYINA SEKI HUGHES.

Legislative Elections, 7 December 2004

Party	% of votes	Seats
New Patriotic Party (NPP) . . .	55.6	128
National Democratic Congress (NDC) . .	40.9	94
People's National Convention (PNC) . .	1.7	4
Convention People's Party (CPP)	1.3	3
Independents	0.4	1
Total	**100.0**	**230**

COUNCIL OF STATE

Chairman: Prof. DANIEL ADZEI BEKOE.

Political Organizations

Convention People's Party (CPP): 825/3 Mango Tree Ave, Asylum Down, POB 10939, Accra-North; tel. (21) 221773; f. 1998 as Convention Party by merger of the National Convention Party (f. 1992) and the People's Convention Party (f. 1993); present name adopted in 2000; Nkrumahist; Chair. Dr EDMUND DELLE; Sec.-Gen. Dr NII NOI DOWUONA.

Democratic People's Party (DPP): 698/4 Star Ave, Kokomlemle, Accra; tel. (21) 221671; f. 1992; Chair. THOMAS WARD-BREW; Gen. Sec. G. M. TETTEY.

Grand Coalition: Accra; f. 2004 to contest general election; Chair. DAN LARTEY.

EGLE (Every Ghanaian Living Everywhere) Party: Kokomlemle, POB 1859, Accra; tel. (21) 231873; f. 1992 as the Eagle Party; Chair. DANIEL OFFORI-ATTA.

Great Consolidated People's Party (GCPP): Citadel House, POB 3077, Accra; tel. (21) 311498; f. 1996; Nkrumahist; Chair. DAN LARTEY; Sec.-Gen. NICHOLAS MENSAH.

People's National Convention (PNC): Kokomlemle, near Sadisco, POB 7795, Accra; tel. (21) 236389; f. 1992; Nkrumahist; Leader Dr EDWARD MAHAMA; Chair. Dr MIKE MENSAH.

National Democratic Congress (NDC): 641/4 Ringway Close, Kokomlemle, POB 5825, Accra-North; tel. and fax (21) 230761; e-mail ndc2004@hotmail.com; internet www.ndc.org.gh; f. 1992; party of fmr Pres. Jerry Rawlings; Chair. Dr OBED ASAMOAH; Sec.-Gen. Dr JOSIAH ARYEH.

National Reform Party (NRP): 31 Mango Tree Ave, Asylum Down, POB 19403, Accra-North; tel. (21) 228578; f. 1999 by a breakaway group from the NDC; Sec.-Gen. OPOKU KYERETWIE.

New Patriotic Party (NPP): C912/2 Duade St, Kokomlemle, POB 3456, Accra-North; tel. (21) 227951; fax (21) 224418; e-mail npp@africaonline.com.gh; internet www.nppghana.org; f. 1992 by supporters of the fmr Prime Minister, Kofi Busia, and J. B. Danquah; Chair. HARONA ESSEKU; Interim Sec.-Gen. EDDIE ANNAN.

United Ghana Movement (UGM): 1 North Ridge Cres., POB C2611, Cantonments, Accra; tel. (21) 225581; fax (21) 231390; e-mail info@ugmghana.org; f. 1996 by a breakaway group from the NPP; Chair. WEREKO BROBBY.

Diplomatic Representation

EMBASSIES AND HIGH COMMISSIONS IN GHANA

Algeria: 22 Josif Broz Tito Ave, POB 2747, Cantonments, Accra; tel. (21) 776719; fax (21) 776828; e-mail embdzacc@africaonline.com.gh; Ambassador LAKHAL BENKELAI.

Benin: 19 Volta St, Second Close, Airport Residential Area, POB 7871, Accra; tel. (21) 774860; fax (21) 774889; Ambassador PIERRE SADELER.

Brazil: Millennium Heights Bldg 2A, 14 Liberation Link, Airport Commercial Area, POB CT3859, Accra; tel. (21) 774908; fax (21) 778566; e-mail brasemb@brasilghana.org; Ambassador PAULO AMÉRICO VEIGA WOLOWSKI.

Bulgaria: 3 Kakramadu Rd, East Cantonments, POB 3193, Accra; tel. (21) 772404; fax (21) 774231; e-mail bulembgh@ghana.com; Chargé d'affaires GEORGE MITEV.

Burkina Faso: 772 Asylum Down, off Farrar Ave, POB 65, Accra; tel. (21) 221988; fax (21) 217774; e-mail ambafaso@ghana.com; Ambassador SINI PIERRE SANOU.

Canada: 42 Independence Ave, POB 1639, Accra; tel. (21) 228555; fax (21) 773792; e-mail accra@international.gc.ca; internet www.accra.gc.ca; High Commissioner DONALD J. BOBIASH.

China, People's Republic: 6 Agostino Neto Rd, Airport Residential Area, POB 3356, Accra; tel. (21) 777073; fax (21) 774527; e-mail chinaemb@ghana.com; Ambassador ZHANG KEYUAN.

Côte d'Ivoire: 9 18th Lane, off Cantonments Rd, POB 3445, Christiansborg, Accra; tel. (21) 774611; fax (21) 773516; e-mail aci@ambaci-ghana.org; Ambassador AMON TANOE EMMANUEL.

Cuba: 20 Amilcar Cabral Rd, Airport Residential Area, POB 9163 Airport, Accra; tel. (21) 775868; fax 774998; e-mail embghana@africaonline.com.gh; Ambassador LUCAS DOMINGO HERNÁNDEZ POLLEDO.

Czech Republic: C260/5, Kanda High Rd No. 2, POB 5226, Accra-North; tel. (21) 223540; fax (21) 225337; e-mail accra@embassy.mzv.cz; Ambassador JINDŘICH JUNEK.

Denmark: 67 Dr Isert Road, North Ridge, POB 596, Accra; tel. (21) 253473; fax (21) 228061; e-mail accamb@um.dk; internet www.ambaccra.um.dk; Ambassador FLEMMING BJØRK PEDERSEN.

Egypt: 20 Josif Broz Tito Ave, Cantonments, POB 2508, Accra; tel. and fax (21) 776795; e-mail boustaneaccra@hotmail.com; Ambassador EKRAM MOHAMED ZAAFARANI.

Ethiopia: 2 Milne Close, Airport Residential Area, POB 1646, Accra; tel. (21) 775928; fax (21) 776807; e-mail ethioemb@ghana.com; Ambassador REDA BELETE.

France: 12th Rd, off Liberation Ave, POB 187, Accra; tel. (21) 774480; fax (21) 778321; e-mail ambaccra@africaonline.com.gh; internet www.ambafrance-gh.org; Ambassador PIERRE JACQUEMONT.

Germany: 6 Ridge St, North Ridge, POB 1757, Accra; tel. (21) 221311; fax (21) 221347; e-mail geremb@wwwplus.com; internet www.accra.diplo.de; Ambassador PETER LINDER.

Guinea: 11 Osu Badu St, Dzorwulu, POB 5497, Accra-North; tel. (21) 777921; fax (21) 760961; Ambassador DORE DIALE DRUS.

Holy See: 8 Drake Ave, Airport Residential Area, POB 9675, Accra; tel. (21) 777759; fax (21) 774019; e-mail nuncio@ghana.com; Apostolic Nuncio Most Rev. GEORGE KOCHERRY (Titular Archbishop of Othona).

India: 9 Ridge Rd, Roman Ridge, POB 5708, Cantonments, Accra; tel. (21) 775601; fax (21) 772176; e-mail indiahc@ncs.com.gh; internet www.india-ghana.com; High Commissioner KAIKHOSROU K. FRAMJI.

Iran: 3 Nme Lane, Airport Residential Area, POB 12673, Accra-North; tel. (21) 774474; fax (21) 777043; Ambassador VALIOLLAH MOHAMMADI NASRABADI.

Italy: Jawaharlal Nehru Rd, POB 140, Accra; tel. (21) 775621; fax (21) 777301; e-mail ambital@africaonline.com.gh; Ambassador GIANCARLO IZZO.

Japan: Fifth Ave, West Cantonments, POB 1637, Accra; tel. (21) 765060; fax (21) 762553; Ambassador KAZUKO ASAI.

Korea, Democratic People's Republic: 139 Nortei Ababio Loop, Ambassadorial Estate, Roman Ridge, POB 13874, Accra; tel. (21) 777825; Ambassador KIM PYONG GI.

Korea, Republic: 3 Abokobi Rd, East Cantonments, POB GP13700, Accra-North; tel. (21) 776157; fax (21) 772313; e-mail koreaadm@africaonline.com.gh; Ambassador LEE SANG-PAL.

Lebanon: F864/1 off Cantonments Rd, Osu, POB 562, Accra; tel. (21) 776727; fax (21) 764290; e-mail lebanon@its.com.gh; Ambassador JAB EL-HASSAN.

Liberia: 10 West Cantonments, off Jawaharlal Nehru Rd, POB 895, Accra; tel. (21) 775641; Ambassador W. ELWOOD GREAVES.

Libya: 14 Sixth St, Airport Residential Area, POB 9665, Accra; tel. (21) 774820; Secretary of People's Bureau MUHAMMAD AL-GAMUDI.

Malaysia: 18 Templesi Lane, Airport Residential Area, POB 16033, Accra; tel. (21) 763691; fax (21) 764910; e-mail mwaccra@ghana.com; High Commissioner MUHAMMAD BIN ALIAS.

Mali: 1st Bungalow, Liberia Rd, Airport Residential Area, POB 1121, Accra; tel. and fax (21) 666942; Ambassador MUPHTAH AG HAIRY.

Netherlands: 89 Liberation Rd, Ako Adjei Interchange, POB CT1647, Accra; tel. (21) 785487; fax (21) 773655; e-mail acc@minbuza.nl; internet www.ambaccra.nl; Ambassador ARIE VAN DER WIEL.

Niger: E104/3 Independence Ave, POB 2685, Accra; tel. and fax (21) 229011; Ambassador ABDOULKARIMOU SEINI.

Nigeria: 5 Tito Ave, POB 1548, Accra; tel. (21) 776158; fax (21) 774395; e-mail nighicom@africaonline.com.gh; High Commissioner OLATUNJI KOLAPO.

Russia: 856/1 Ring Road East, 13 Lane, POB 1634, Accra; tel. (21) 775611; fax (21) 772699; e-mail russia@ghana.com; internet www.ghana.mid.ru; Ambassador VALERY ORLOV.

Saudi Arabia: 10 Noi Fetreke St, Roman Ridge, Airport Residential Area, POB 670, Accra; tel. (21) 774311; fax (21) 773424; e-mail ghemb@mofa.gov.sa; Chargé d'affaires a.i. ANWAR ABDUL FATTAH ABDRABBUH.

Sierra Leone: 83A Senchi St, Airport Residential Area, POB 55, Cantonments, Accra; tel. (21) 769189; fax (21) 769478; e-mail slhc@ighmail.com; High Commissioner ALIE BANGURA.

South Africa: 10 Klotey Cres., Labone North, POB 298, Accra; tel. (21) 762380; fax (21) 762381; e-mail sahcgh@africaonline.com.gh; High Commissioner Dr R. S. MOLEKANE.

Spain: Drake Ave Extension, Airport Residential Area, PMB KA44, Accra; tel. (21) 774004; fax (21) 776217; e-mail embespgh@mail.mae .es; Ambassador JORGE MONTEALEGRE BUIRE.

Switzerland: Kanda Highway, North Ridge, POB 359, Accra; tel. (21) 228125; fax (21) 223583; e-mail vertretung@acc.rep.admin.ch; internet www.eda.admin.ch/accra; Ambassador GEORG ZUBLER.

Togo: Togo House, near Cantonments Circle, POB C120, Accra; tel. (21) 777950; fax (21) 777961; Ambassador ASSIONGBOR FOLIVI.

United Kingdom: Osu Link, off Gamel Abdul Nasser Ave, POB 296, Accra; tel. (21) 7010650; fax (21) 7010655; e-mail high .commission.accra@fco.gov.uk; internet www .britishhighcommission.gov.uk/ghana; High Commissioner GORDON WETHERELL.

USA: Ring Road East, POB 194, Accra; tel. (21) 775348; fax (21) 776008; e-mail prsaccra@pd.state.gov; internet usembassy.state .gov/accra; Ambassador MARY CARLIN YATES.

Judicial System

The civil law in force in Ghana is based on the Common Law, doctrines of equity and general statutes which were in force in England in 1874, as modified by subsequent Ordinances. Ghanaian customary law is, however, the basis of most personal, domestic and contractual relationships. Criminal Law is based on the Criminal Procedure Code, 1960, derived from English Criminal Law, and since amended. The Superior Court of Judicature comprises a Supreme Court, a Court of Appeal, a High Court and a Regional Tribunal; Inferior Courts include Circuit Courts, Circuit Tribunals, Community Tribunals and such other Courts as may be designated by law. In 2001 'fast-track' court procedures were established to accelerate the delivery of justice.

Supreme Court
Consists of the Chief Justice and not fewer than nine other Justices. It is the final court of appeal in Ghana and has jurisdiction in matters relating to the enforcement or interpretation of the Constitution.

Chief Justice: KINGSLEY ACQUAH.

Court of Appeal: Consists of the Chief Justice and not fewer than five Judges of the Court of Appeal. It has jurisdiction to hear and determine appeals from any judgment, decree or order of the High Court.

High Court: Comprises the Chief Justice and not fewer than 12 Justices of the High Court. It exercises original jurisdiction in all matters, civil and criminal, other than those for offences involving treason. Trial by jury is practised in criminal cases in Ghana and the Criminal Procedure Code, 1960, provides that all trials on indictment shall be by a jury or with the aid of Assessors.

Circuit Courts: Exercise original jurisdiction in civil matters where the amount involved does not exceed C100,000. They also have jurisdiction with regard to the guardianship and custody of infants, and original jurisdiction in all criminal cases, except offences where the maximum punishment is death or the offence of treason. They have appellate jurisdiction from decisions of any District Court situated within their respective circuits.

District Courts: To each magisterial district is assigned at least one District Magistrate who has original jurisdiction to try civil suits in which the amount involved does not exceed C50,000. District Magistrates also have jurisdiction to deal with all criminal cases, except first-degree felonies, and commit cases of a more serious nature to either the Circuit Court or the High Court. A Grade I District Court can impose a fine not exceeding C1,000 and sentences of imprisonment of up to two years and a Grade II District Court may impose a fine not exceeding C500 and a sentence of imprisonment of up to 12 months. A District Court has no appellate jurisdiction, except in rent matters under the Rent Act.

Juvenile Courts: Jurisdiction in cases involving persons under 17 years of age, except where the juvenile is charged jointly with an adult. The Courts comprise a Chairman, who must be either the District Magistrate or a lawyer, and not fewer than two other

members appointed by the Chief Justice in consultation with the Judicial Council. The Juvenile Courts can make orders as to the protection and supervision of a neglected child and can negotiate with parents to secure the good behaviour of a child.

National Public Tribunal: Considers appeals from the Regional Public Tribunals. Its decisions are final and are not subject to any further appeal. The Tribunal consists of at least three members and not more than five, one of whom acts as Chairman.

Regional Public Tribunals: Hears criminal cases relating to prices, rent or exchange control, theft, fraud, forgery, corruption or any offence which may be referred to them by the Provisional National Defence Council.

Special Military Tribunal: Hears criminal cases involving members of the armed forces. It consists of between five and seven members.

Attorney-General: NII AYIKOI OTOO.

Religion

According to the 2000 census, 69% of the population were Christians and 15.6% Muslims, while 6.9% followed indigenious beliefs.

CHRISTIANITY

Christian Council of Ghana: POB 919, Accra; tel. (21) 776678; fax (21) 776725; f. 1929; advisory body comprising 14 mem. churches (2001); Gen. Sec. Rev. ROBERT ABOAGYE-MENSAH.

The Anglican Communion
Anglicans in Ghana are adherents of the Church of the Province of West Africa, comprising 13 dioceses and a missionary region, of which nine are in Ghana.

Archbishop of the Province of West Africa and Bishop of Koforidua and Ho: Most Rev. ROBERT GARSHONG ALLOTEY OKINE, POB 980, Koforidua; tel. (81) 2329; fax (21) 669125; e-mail archbishopwa@yahoo.com; internet netministries.org/see/churches/ch00609.

Bishop of Accra: Rt Rev. JUSTICE OFEI AKROFI, Bishopscourt, POB 8, Accra; tel. (21) 662292; fax (21) 669125; e-mail cpwa@ghana.com.

Bishop of Cape Coast: Rt Rev. KOBINA ADDUAH QUASHIE, Bishopscourt, POB A233, Adisadel Estates, Cape Coast; tel. (42) 32502; fax (42) 32637.

Bishop of Kumasi: Rt Rev. DANIEL YINKAH SAFO, Bishop's Office, St Cyprian's Ave, POB 144, Kumasi; tel. and fax (51) 24117; e-mail kumangli@africaonline.com.gh.

Bishop of Sekondi: Rt Rev. ANDREW KWAKU FUACHIE OKOH, POB 85, Sekondi; tel. (21) 669125.

Bishop of Sunyani: Rt Rev. THOMAS AMPAH BRIENT, Bishop's House, POB 23, Sunyani; tel. (61) 213; fax (61) 7203; e-mail deegyab@ighmail.com.

Bishop of Tamale: Rt Rev. EMMANUEL ARONGO, POB 110, Tamale NR; tel. (71) 22906; fax (71) 22849.

The Roman Catholic Church
Ghana comprises four archdioceses and 14 dioceses. At 31 December 2002 there were 2,355,663 adherents in the country, equivalent to 11.1.% of the total population.

Ghana Bishops' Conference
National Catholic Secretariat, POB 9712, Airport, Accra; tel. (21) 500491; fax (21) 500493; e-mail dscncs@africaonline.com.gh.

f. 1960; Pres. Cardinal PETER KODWO APPIAH-TURKSON (Archbishop of Cape Coast).

Archbishop of Accra: Most Rev. GABRIEL CHARLES PALMER-BUCKLE, Chancery Office, POB 247, Accra; tel. (21) 222728; fax (21) 231619.

Archbishop of Cape Coast: Cardinal PETER KODWO APPIAH-TURKSON, Archbishop's House, POB 112, Cape Coast; tel. (42) 33471; fax (42) 33473; e-mail archcape@ghana.com.

Archbishop of Kumasi: Most Rev. PETER KWASI SARPONG, POB 99, Kumasi; tel. (51) 24012; fax (51) 28476; e-mail cadiokum@ghana .com.

Archbishop of Tamale: Most Rev. GREGORY EBO KPIEBAYA, Gumbehini Rd, POB 42, Tamale; tel. and fax (71) 22425; e-mail tamdio2@yahoo.co.uk.

Other Christian Churches

African Methodist Episcopal Zion Church: POB MP522, Mamprobi, Accra; tel. (21) 669200; e-mail amezion@africaonline.com.gh; f. 1898; Pres. Rt Rev. WARREN M. BROWN.

Christian Methodist Episcopal Church: POB 3906, Accra; Pres. Rev. YENN BATA.

Church of Pentecost: POB 2194 Accra; tel. and fax (21) 772193; e-mail cophq@ghana.com; internet www1.thechurchofpentecost .com; Chair. Apostle M. K. NTUMY; Gen.-Sec. Apostle ALFRED KODUAH; 1,021,856 mems (July 2002).

Evangelical-Lutheran Church of Ghana: POB KN197, Kaneshie; tel. (21) 223487; fax (21) 220947; e-mail elcga@africaonline.com .gh; Pres. Rt Rev. Dr PAUL KOFI FYNN; 26,000 mems.

Evangelical-Presbyterian Church of Ghana: 19 Main St, Tesano, PMB, Accra-North; tel. (21) 220381; fax (21) 233173; f. 1847; Moderator Rev. JAPHET YAO LEDO; 295,000 mems.

Ghana Baptist Convention: PMB, Kumasi; tel. (51) 25215; fax (51) 28592; e-mail gbconv@africaonline.com; internet www .gbconvention.com.gh; f. 1963; Pres. Rev. Dr KOJO OSEI-WUSUH; Sec. Rev. KOJO AMO; 65,000 mems.

Ghana Mennonite Church: POB 5485, Accra; fax (21) 220589; f. 1957; Moderator Rev. MICHAEL BADASU; Sec. ISAAC K. QUARTEY; 4,800 mems.

Ghana Union Conference of Seventh-day Adventists: POB GP1016, Accra; tel. (21) 223720; fax (21) 227024; e-mail salarmie@ compuserve.com; f. 1943; Pres. Pastor P. O. MENSAH; Sec. Pastor SAMUEL A. LARMIE; 23,700 mems.

Methodist Church of Ghana: E252/2, Liberia Rd, POB 403, Accra; tel. (21) 228120; fax (21) 227008; e-mail mcghqs@africaonline.com .gh; Pres. Rt Rev. Dr SAMUEL ASANTE ANTWI; Sec. Rev. MACLEAN AGYIRI KUMI; 341,000 mems.

Presbyterian Church of Ghana: POB 106, Accra; tel. (21) 662511; fax (21) 665594; f. 1828; Moderator Rt Rev. SAM PREMPEH; Sec. Rev. Dr D. N. A. KPOBI; 422,500 mems.

The African Methodist Episcopal Church, the F'Eden Church and the Religious Society of Friends (Quakers) are also active in Ghana.

ISLAM

In 2000 some 15.6% of the population of Ghana were Muslims, with a particularly large concentration in the Northern Region. The majority are Malikees.

Coalition of Muslim Organizations: Accra.

Ghana Muslim Representative Council: Accra.

Chief Imam: Sheikh USMAN NUHU SHARABUTU.

BAHÁ'Í FAITH

National Spiritual Assembly: BP 7098, Accra-North; tel. (21) 222127; e-mail bahaigh@africaonline.com; Sec. ROSEMARY MILLS-TETTEY.

The Press

DAILY NEWSPAPERS

Accra Daily Mail: POB CT4910, Cantonments, Accra; e-mail accmail@africaonline.com.gh; internet www.accra-mail.com; Man. Editor A.R. HARUNA ATTAH.

The Daily Dispatch: 1 Dade Walk, North Labone, POB C1945, Cantonments, Accra; tel. (21) 763339; e-mail ephson@usa.net; Editor BEN EPHSON.

Daily Graphic: Graphic Communications Group Ltd, POB 742, Accra; tel. (21) 228911; fax (21) 234754; e-mail info@graphicghana .com; internet www.graphicghana.com; f. 1950; state-owned; Editor YAW BOADU AYEBOAFO; circ. 100,000.

Daily Guide: Accra; internet www.dailyguidenews.com; privately owned; Editor GINA BLAY.

The Evening News: POB 2638, Accra.

The Ghanaian Times: New Times Corpn, Ring Rd West, POB 2638, Accra; tel. (21) 228282; fax (21) 229398; e-mail newtimes@ ghana.com; f. 1958; state-owned; Editor AJOA YEBOAH-AFARI (acting); circ. 45,000.

PERIODICALS

Thrice Weekly

Ghanaian Chronicle: General Portfolio Ltd, PMB, Accra-North; tel. (21) 227789; fax (21) 2326208; e-mail chronicle@africaonline.com .gh; internet www.ghanaian-chronicle.com; Editor EBO QUANSAH; circ. 60,000.

Network Herald: NBS Multimedia, PMB, OSU, Accra; tel. (21) 701184; fax (21) 762173; e-mail support@ghana.com; internet www .networkherald.gh; f. 2001; Editor ELVIS QUARSHIE.

Bi-Weekly

The Ghanaian Voice: Newstop Publications, POB 514, Mamprobi, Accra; tel. (21) 324644; fax (21) 314939; e-mail managingeditor@ ghanaianvoice.com ; internet www.ghanaianvoice.com; Editor CHRISTIANA ANSAH; circ. 100,000.

Weekly

Business and Financial Times: POB CT16, Cantonments, Accra; tel. and fax (21) 223334; e-mail editor@financialtimesghana.com; internet www.financialtimesghana.com; f. 1989; Editor JOHN HANSON; circ. 20,000.

Champion: POB 6828, Accra-North; tel. (21) 229079; Man. Dir MARK D. N. ADDY; Editor FRANK CAXTON WILLIAMS; circ. 300,000.

The Crusading Guide: POB 8523, Accra-North; tel. (21) 763339; fax (21) 761541; Editor KWEKU BAAKO, Jr.

Echo: POB 5288, Accra; f. 1968; Sun.; Man. Editor M. K. FRIMPONG; circ. 40,000.

Entertaining Eye: Kad Publications, POB 125, Darkuman-Accra; Editor NANA KWAKYE YIADOM; circ. 40,000.

Evening Digest: News Media Ltd, POB 7082, Accra; tel. (21) 221071; Editor P. K. ANANTITETTEH.

Experience: POB 5084, Accra-North; Editor ALFRED YAW POKU; circ. 50,000.

Free Press: Tommy Thompson Books Ltd, POB 6492, Accra; tel. (21) 225994; independent; Editor EBEN QUARCOO.

Ghana Life: Ghana Life Publications, POB 11337, Accra; tel. (21) 229835; Editor NIKKI BOA-AMPONSEM.

Ghana Palaver: Palaver Publications, POB WJ317, Wejia-Accra; tel. (21) 850495; e-mail palaver@www.ghana-palaver.com; internet www.ghana-palaver.com; f. 1994; Editor JOJO BRUCE QUANSAH.

Graphic Showbiz: Graphic Communications Group Ltd, POB 742, Accra; tel. (21) 228911; fax (21) 234754; e-mail info@graphicghana .com ; internet www.graphicghana.info; state-owned; Editor NANABANYIN DADSON.

Graphic Sports: Graphic Communications Group Ltd, POB 742, Accra; tel. (21) 228911; fax (21) 234754; e-mail info@graphicghana .com; state-owned; Editor FELIX ABAYATEYE; circ. 60,000.

The Guide: Western Publications Ltd, POB 8253, Accra-North; tel. (21) 232760; Editor KWEKU BAAKO, Jr.

The Heritage: POB AC503, Arts Center, Accra; tel. (21) 258820; fax (21) 258823; e-mail heritage@africaonline.gh; internet www .theheritagenews.com; Chair. STEPHEN OWUSU; Editor NII NOI VANDERPUYE.

High Street Journal: POB 7974, Accra-North; tel. (12) 239835; fax (12) 239837; e-mail hsjaccra@ghana.com; Editor SHEIKH ABUTIATE.

The Independent: Clear Type Press Bldg Complex, off Graphic Rd, POB 4031, Accra; tel. and fax (12) 661091; internet www .independent-gh.com; f. 1989; Editor EDGAR FABILE.

The Mirror: Graphic Communications Group Ltd, POB 742, Accra; tel. (21) 228911; fax (21) 234754; e-mail info@graphicghana.com; internet www.graphicghana.info; f. 1953; state-owned; Sat.; Editor E. N. O. PROVENCAL; circ. 90,000.

The National Democrat: Democrat Publications, POB 13605, Accra; tel. (21) 76804; Acting Editor KOFI TWUMASI.

The New Ghanaian: Tudu Publishing House, POB 751, Tamale; tel. (71) 22579; Editor RAZAK EL-ALAWA.

New Nation: POB 6828, Accra-North; Editor S. N. SASRAKU; circ. 300,000.

Public Agenda: P. A. Communications, POB 5564, Accra-North; tel. (21) 238821; fax (21) 231687; e-mail isodec@ghana.com; f. 1994; Editor YAO GRAHAM; circ. 12,000.

Sporting News: POB 5481, Accra-North; f. 1967; Man. Editor J. OPPONG-AGYARE.

The Standard: Standard Newspapers & Magazines Ltd, POB 765, Accra; tel. (21) 220165; Roman Catholic; Editor ISAAC FRITZ ANDOH; circ. 10,000.

Statesman: Kinesic Communications, POB 846, Accra; tel. and fax (21) 233242; official publ. of the New Patriotic Party; Editor GABBY OKYERE DARKO.

The Weekend: Newstop Publications, POB 514, Mamprobi, Accra; tel. (21) 324644; fax (21) 314939; internet www.ghanaianvoice.com; Editor EMMANUEL YARTEY; circ. 40,000.

Weekly Events: Clear Type Image Ltd, 29 Olympic Street (Enterprise House), Kokomlemle, POB 7634, Accra-North; tel. (21) 223085; Editor JORIS JORDAN DODOO.

Weekly Insight: Militant Publications Ltd, POB K272, Accra New Town, Accra; tel. (21) 660148; fax (21) 774338; e-mail insight93@yahoo.com; f. 1993; independent; English; Editor KWESI PRATT, Jr.

Weekly Spectator: New Times Corpn, Ring Road West, POB 2638, Accra; tel. (21) 228282; fax (21) 229398; state-owned; f. 1963; Sun.; Editor WILLIE DONKOR; circ. 165,000.

Other

African Observer: POB 1171, Kaneshie, Accra; tel. (21) 231459; bi-monthly; Editor STEVE MALLORY.

African Woman: Ring Rd West, POB 1496, Accra; monthly.

AGI Newsletter: c/o Asscn of Ghana Industries, POB 8624, Accra-North; tel. (21) 779023; e-mail agi@agighana.org; internet www.agighana.org; f. 1974; monthly; Editor SOLACE ASAFO; circ. 1,500.

AGOO: Newstop Publications, POB 514, Mamprobi, Accra, Accra; tel. (21) 324644; fax (21) 314939; internet www.ghanaianvoice.com; monthly; lifestyle magazine; Publr KOJO BONSU.

Akwansosem: Ghana Information Services, POB 745, Accra; tel. (21) 228011; quarterly; in Akuapim Twi, Asanti Twi and Fante; Editor KATHLEEN OFOSU-APPIAH.

Armed Forces News: General Headquarters, Directorate of Public Relations, Burma Camp, Accra; tel. (21) 776111; f. 1966; quarterly; Editor ADOTEY ANKRAH-HOFFMAN; circ. 4,000.

Boxing and Football Illustrated: POB 8392, Accra; f. 1976; monthly; Editor NANA O. AMPOMAH; circ. 10,000.

Business and Financial Concord: Sammy Tech Consult Enterprise, POB 5677, Accra-North; tel. (21) 232446; fortnightly; Editor KWABENA RICHARDSON.

Business Watch: Sulton Bridge Co. Ltd, POB C3447, Cantonments, Accra; tel. (21) 233293; monthly.

Chit Chat: POB 7043, Accra; monthly; Editor ROSEMOND ADU.

Christian Messenger: Presbyterian Book Depot Bldg, POB 3075, Accra; tel. and fax (21) 663124; e-mail danbentil@yahoo.com; f. 1883; English-language; every two weeks; quarterly; Editor GEORGE MARTINSON; circ. 40,000.

Drum: POB 1197, Accra; monthly; general interest.

Ghana Journal of Science: Ghana Science Asscn, POB 7, Legon; tel. (21) 500253; monthly; Editor Dr A. K. AHAFIA.

Ghana Official News Bulletin: Information Services Dept, POB 745, Accra; English; political, economic, investment and cultural affairs.

Ghana Review International: POB 14307, Accra; tel. (21) 234056; fax (21) 237970; e-mail accra@ghanareview.com; internet www.ghanareview.com; monthly; general interest; Publr NANA OTUO ACHEAMPONG; Man. Editor (Ghana Office) EFAM AWO DOVI; circ. 100,000 (internationally).

Ideal Woman (Obaa Sima): POB 5737, Accra; tel. (21) 221399; f. 1971; fortnightly; Editor KATE ABBAM.

Insight and Opinion: POB 5446, Accra; quarterly; Editorial Sec. W. B. OHENE.

Legon Observer: POB 11, Legon; fax (21) 774338; f. 1966; publ. by Legon Society on National Affairs; fortnightly; Chair. J. A. DADSON; Editor EBOW DANIEL.

Police News: Police HQ, Accra; monthly; Editor S. S. APPIAH; circ. 20,000.

The Post: Ghana Information Services, POB 745, Accra; tel. (21) 228011; f. 1980; monthly; current affairs and analysis; circ. 25,000.

Radio and TV Times: Ghana Broadcasting Corpn, Broadcasting House, POB 18167, Accra; tel. (21) 508927; fax (21) 773612; f. 1960; quarterly; Editor SAM THOMPSON; circ. 5,000.

The Scope: POB 8162, Tema; monthly; Editor EMMANUEL DOE ZIORKLUI; circ. 10,000.

Students World: POB M18, Accra; tel. (21) 774248; fax (21) 778715; e-mail afram@wwwplus.co.za; f. 1974; monthly; educational; Man. Editor ERIC OFEI; circ. 10,000.

The Teacher: Ghana National Asscn of Teachers, POB 209, Accra; tel. (21) 221515; fax (21) 226286; f. 1931; quarterly; circ. 30,000.

Truth and Life: Gift Publications, POB 11337, Accra-North; monthly; Editor Pastor KOBENA CHARM.

Uneek: POB 230, Achimota, Accra; tel. (21) 543853; fax (21) 231355; e-mail info@uneekmagazine.com; internet www.uneekmagazine.com; f. 1998; monthly; leisure, culture; CEO and Editor FRANCIS ADAMS.

The Watchman: Watchman Gospel Ministry, POB GP 4521, Accra; tel. and fax (21) 500631; e-mail sonlife@africaonline.com.gh; fortnightly; Pres. and CEO DIVINE P. KUMAH; Chair. Dr E. K. OPUNI; circ. 5,000.

NEWS AGENCY

Ghana News Agency: POB 2118, Accra; tel. (21) 215135; fax (21) 669841; e-mail ghnews@ncs.com.gh; f. 1957; Gen. Man. SAM B. QUAICOE; 10 regional offices and 110 district offices.

PRESS ASSOCIATION

Ghana Journalists Association: POB 4636, Accra; tel. (21) 234692; fax (21) 234694; e-mail info@ghanamedia.com; internet www.ghanamedia.com/gja; Pres. AJOA YEBOAH-AFARI.

Publishers

Advent Press: POB 0102, Osu, Accra; tel. (21) 777861; fax (21) 775327; e-mail eaokpoti@ghana.com; f. 1937; publishing arm of the Ghana Union Conference of Seventh-day Adventists; Gen. Man. EMMANUEL C. TETTEH.

Adwinsa Publications (Ghana) Ltd: Advance Press Bldg, 3rd Floor, School Rd, POB 92, Legoh Accra; tel. (21) 221654; f. 1977; general, educational; Man. Dir KWABENA AMPONSAH.

Afram Publications: C 184/22 Midway Lane, Abofu-Achimota, POB M18, Accra; tel. (21) 412561; e-mail afram@wwwplus.co.za; internet www.aframpublications.com.gh; f. 1973; textbooks and general; Man. Dir ERIC OFEI.

Africa Christian Press: POB 30, Achimota; tel. (21) 244147; fax (21) 220271; e-mail acpbooks@ghana.com; f. 1964; religious, fiction, theology, children's, leadership; Gen. Man. RICHARD A. B. CRABBE.

Allgoodbooks Ltd: POB AN10416, Accra-North; tel. (21) 664294; fax (21) 665629; e-mail allgoodbooks@hotmail.com; f. 1968; children's; Man. Dir MARY ASIRIFI.

Asempa Publishers: POB GP919, Accra; tel. (21) 233084; fax (21) 235140; e-mail asempa@ghana.com; f. 1970; religion, social issues, African music, fiction, children's; Gen. Man. Rev. EMMANUEL B. BORTEY.

Assembly Press Ltd-Ghana Publishing Corpn: POB 124, Accra; tel. (21) 664338; fax (21) 664330; e-mail asspcom@africaonline.com.gh; internet www.africaonline.com.gh/Assembly; f. 1965; state-owned; textbooks and general fiction and non-fiction; Man. Dir F. K. NYARKO.

Baafour and Co: POB K189, Accra New Town; f. 1978; general; Man. B. KESE-AMANKWAA.

Benibengor Book Agency: POB 40, Aboso; fiction, biography, children's and paperbacks; Man. Dir J. BENIBENGOR BLAY.

Black Mask Ltd: POB CT770, Cantonments, Accra; tel. (21) 234577; f. 1979; textbooks, plays, novels, handicrafts; Man. Dir YAW OWUSU ASANTE.

Editorial and Publishing Services: POB 5743, Accra; general, reference; Man. Dir M. DANQUAH.

Educational Press and Manufacturers Ltd: POB 9184, Airport-Accra; tel. (21) 220395; f. 1975; textbooks, children's; Man. G. K. KODUA.

Encyclopaedia Africana Project: POB 2797, Accra; tel. (21) 776939; fax (21) 779228; e-mail eap@africaonline.com.gh; internet encyclopaediaafricana.org; f. 1962; reference; Dir GRACE BANSA.

Frank Publishing Ltd: POB MB414, Accra; tel. (21) 240711; f. 1976; secondary school textbooks; Man. Dir FRANCIS K. DZOKOTO.

Ghana Universities Press: POB GP4219, Accra; tel. (21) 513401; fax (21) 513402; f. 1962; scholarly, academic and general and textbooks; CEO Dr K. M. GANU.

Golden Wings Publications: 26 Mantse Kwao St, POB 1337, Accra; educational and children's; Man. Editor GREGORY ANKRAH.

Miracle Bookhouse: POB 7487, Accra-North; tel. (21) 226684; f. 1977; general; Man. J. APPIAH-BERKO.

Moxon Paperbacks: POB M160, Accra; tel. (21) 761175; fax (21) 777971; f. 1967; travel and guide books, fiction and poetry, Africana, telephone directory; Man. Dir JAMES MOXON.

Sam-Woode Ltd: A.979/15 Dansoman High Street, POB 12719, Accra-North; tel. (21) 305287; fax (21) 310482; e-mail samwoode@ ghana.com; f. 1984; educational and children's; Chair. KWESI SAM-WOODE.

Sedco Publishing Ltd: Sedco House, 5 Tabon St, North Ridge, POB 2051, Accra; tel. (21) 221332; fax (21) 220107; e-mail sedco@ africaonline.com.gh; f. 1975; educational; Chair. COURAGE K. SEG-BAWU; Man. Dir FRANK SEGBAWU.

Sheffield Publishing Co: Accra; tel. (21) 667480; fax (21) 665960; f. 1970; religion, politics, economics, science, fiction; Publr RONALD MENSAH.

Unimax Macmillan Ltd: 42 Ring Rd South Industrial Area, POB 10722, Accra-North; tel. (21) 227443; fax (21) 225215; e-mail info@ unimacmillan.com; internet www.unimacmillan.com; representative of Macmillan UK; atlases, educational and children's; Man. Dir EDWARD ADDO.

Waterville Publishing House: POB 195, Accra; tel. (21) 663124; f. 1963; general fiction and non-fiction, textbooks, paperbacks, Africana; Man. Dir E. ANIM-ANSAH.

Woeli Publishing Services: POB NT601, Accra New Town; tel. and fax (21) 229294; e-mail woeli@libr.ug.edu.gh; f. 1984; children's, fiction, academic; Dir W. A. DEKUTSEY.

PUBLISHERS' ASSOCIATIONS

Ghana Book Development Council: POB M430, Accra; tel. (21) 229178; f. 1975; govt-financed agency; promotes and co-ordinates writing, production and distribution of books; Exec. Dir D. A. NIMAKO.

Ghana Book Publishers' Association (GBPA): POB LT471, Laterbiokorshie, Accra; tel. (21) 229178; fax (21) 220271; e-mail acpbooks@ghana.com; Exec. Sec. STEPHEN BROBBEY.

Private Newspaper Publishers' Association of Ghana (PRINPAG): POB 125, Darkuman, Accra; Chair. NANA KOFI KOOMSON; Gen. Sec. K. AGYEMANG DUAH.

Broadcasting and Communications

TELECOMMUNICATIONS

National Communication Authority (NCA): Accra; e-mail nca@ ghana.com; f. 1996; regulatory body; Interim Dir-Gen. Maj. (retd) J. R. K. TANDOH.

ACG Telesystems (Westel) Ghana Ltd: Dr Isert Rd, 7th Ave Ext., Ridge PMB, Accra-North; tel. (21) 232308; fax (21) 232309; e-mail btaylor@acg.com.gh; f. 1997; owned jointly by Ghana National Petroleum Corpn and Western Wireless Corpn USA; Man. Dir WILLIAM TAYLOR.

Ghana Telecom: Telecom House, nr Kwame Nkrumah Circle, Accra-North; tel. (21) 221001; fax (21) 227965; e-mail ghanatel@ncs .com.gh; internet www.ghanatel.com; f. 1995; 30% transferred to private ownership in 1997; Dir-Gen. Brig. HENRY KWAME ANYIDOHO; Man. Dir ADNAN ROFIEE.

Millicom Ghana Ltd: Millicom Place, Barnes Rd, PMB 100, Accra; tel. (21) 7010888; fax (27) 7503999; e-mail info@mobitelghana.com; internet www.mobitelnet.com; f. 1990; mobile cellular telephone services through the network Mobitel; Man. Dir SOBAN PASHA.

Scancom Ltd: Auto Parts Bldg, 41A Graphic Rd, South Industrial Area, POB 281, International Trade Fair Lane, Accra; tel. (21) 300000; fax (21) 231974; internet www.spacefon.com; f. 1994; Ghana's largest mobile cellular telephone provider, through the network Spacefon.

BROADCASTING

There are internal radio broadcasts in English, Akan, Dagbani, Ewe, Ga, Hausa and Nzema, and an external service in English and French. There are three transmitting stations, with a number of relay stations. The Ghana Broadcasting Corporation operates two national networks, Radio 1 and Radio 2, which broadcast from Accra, and four regional FM stations. In 2002 there were also 15 independent commercial and community FM stations. There are eight main colour television transmitters.

Ghana Broadcasting Corpn: Broadcasting House, POB 1633, Accra; tel. (21) 221161; fax (21) 221157; e-mail gbc@ghana.com; internet www.gbc.com.gh; f. 1935; Dir-Gen. Dr EVA LOKKO; Dir of TV Prof. MARK DUODU; Dir of Radio YAW OWUSU-ADDO.

CitiFM: 11 Tettey Loop, Adabraka, Accra; tel. (21) 226171; fax (21) 224043; e-mail info@citifmonline.com; internet www.citifmonline .com; Man. Dir SAMUEL ATTA MENSAH.

Joy FM: 355 Faanofa St, Kokomlemle, POB 17202, Accra; tel. (21) 7011998; fax (21) 224405; e-mail info@myjoyonline.com; internet www.myjoyonline.com; f. 1995; news, information and music broadcasts; Dir KWESI TWUM.

Metro TV: POB C1609, Cantonments, Accra; tel. (21) 765701; fax (21) 765702; e-mail webdesign@metrotv.com.gh; internet www .metrotv.com.gh.

Radio Ada: POB KA9482, Accra; tel. (968) 3713; fax (21) 500032; e-mail radioada@ghana.com; f. 1998; community broadcasts in Dangme; Dirs ALEX QUARMYNE, WILMA QUARMYNE.

Radio Gold FM: POB 17298, Accra; tel. (22) 779404; fax (22) 300284; Man. Dir BAFFOE BONNIE.

Vibe FM: 4 Norla St, Labone, PMB 183 Accra; tel. (21) 7011405; internet www.vibefm.com.gh; educational.

Sky Broadcasting Co., Ltd: 45 Water Rd, Kanda Overpass, North Ridge, POB CT 3850, Cantonments, Accra; tel. (21) 225716; fax (21) 221983; e-mail vayiku@yahoo.com; internet www.spirit.fm; f. 2000; Chief Operations Officer VERONICA AYIKU; Gen. Man. ANDY GLOVER.

TV3: 12th Road, Kanda, opposite French embassy, Accra; tel. (21) 228679; fax (21) 763450; e-mail cbo@tv3.com.gh; internet www.tv3 .com.gh; f. 1997; private television station; progamming in English and local languages; Man. Dir MUSNI BINMOHAMAD.

Finance

(cap. = capital; res = reserves; dep. = deposits; m. = million;
brs = branches; amounts in cedis)

BANKING

The commercial banking sector comprised 10 commercial banks, three development banks, five merchant banks and five foreign banks in 2004. There were also 115 rural banks and several non-banking financial institutions.

Central Bank

Bank of Ghana: Cedi House, High St, POB 2674, Accra; tel. (21) 666902; fax (21) 662996; e-mail secretary@bog.gov.gh; internet www .bog.gov.gh; f. 1957; bank of issue; cap. 100,000m., res 489,304m., dep. 2,328,924m. (Dec. 2002); Gov. PAUL ACQUAH.

Commercial and Development Banks

Amalgamated Bank Ltd: POB CT 1541, 131–3 Farrar Ave, Cantonments, Accra; tel. (21) 249690; fax (21) 249697; e-mail amalbank@amalbank.com.gh; f. 1999; Chair WELBECK ABRA-APPIAH.

Ghana Commercial Bank Ltd: Thorpe Road, POB 134, Accra; tel. (21) 664914; fax (21) 662168; e-mail prelatioms@gcb.com.gh; internet www.gcb.gh; f. 1953; 46.8% state-owned; cap. 20,000m., res 5,607,047m., dep. 4,265,733m. (Dec. 2004); Chair. K. G. OSEI-BONSU; Man. Dir LAWRENCE NEWTON ADU-MANTE; 131 brs.

NTHC Ltd: Martco House, Okai Mensah Link, off Kwame Nkrumah Ave, POB 9563, Adabraka, Accra; tel. (21) 238492; fax (21) 229975; e-mail nthc@ghana.com; internet www.nthcghana.com; fmrly National Trust Holding Co Ltd; f. 1976 to provide stockbrokerage services, asset management and financial advisory services; cap. 9,000m. (2001); Chair. BENJAMIN ADU-AMANKWA; Man. Dir Dr A. W. Q. BARNOR.

Prudential Bank Ltd: Kingsway Stores Building, 2nd Floor, PMB GPO, Accra; tel. (21) 226322; fax (21) 226803; e-mail prudential@ ghana.com; f. 1996; cap. and res 9,739.7m., total assets 212,371.5m. (Dec. 2001); Chair. JOHN SACKAH ADDO; Man. Dir STEPHEN SEKYERE-ABANKWA.

The Trust Bank Ltd: Re-insurance House, 68 Kwame Nkrumah Ave, POB 1862, Accra; tel. (21) 240049; fax (21) 240059; e-mail trust@ghana.com; internet www.ttbgh.net; f. 1996; 35% owned by Banque Belgolaise (Belgium), 33% owned by the Social Security and National Insurance Trust; cap. 10,000m., res 37,332m., dep. 494,866m. (Dec. 2003); Chair. KAJO OKAI ANDAH; Man. Dir PAUL CARDOEN; 6 brs.

Development Banks

Agricultural Development Bank: Cedi House, Liberia Rd, POB 4191, Accra; tel. (21) 662758; fax (21) 662846; e-mail adbweb@ agribank.com; internet www.adbghana.com; f. 1965; 51.8% state-owned, 48.2% owned by Bank of Ghana; credit facilities for farmers and commercial banking; cap. and res 390,064.5m., dep. 968,713.0m. (Dec. 2002); Chair. PAUL S. M. KORANTENG; Man. Dir SAMMY A. WELBECK; 32 brs.

National Investment Bank Ltd (NIB): 37 Kwame Nkrumah Ave, POB 3726, Accra; tel. (21) 661701; fax (21) 661730; e-mail sec@

nib-ghana.com; internet www.nib-ghana.com; f. 1963; 86.4% state-owned; provides long-term investment capital, jt venture promotion, consortium finance man. and commercial banking services; cap. 3,260m., surplus & res 128,436m., dep. 345,108m. (Dec. 2003); Chair. Dr CHARLES DANYAGRI JUBUNI; Man. Dir DANIEL CHARLES GYIMAH; 11 brs.

Merchant Banks

CAL Merchant Bank Ltd: 23 Independence Ave, POB 14596, Accra; tel. (21) 680068; fax (21) 680081; e-mail calbank@calbank-gh .com; internet www.calbank-gh.com; f. 1990; cap. 6,578m., res 64,482m., dep. 385,704m. (Dec. 2003); Chair. GEORGE VICTOR OKOH; Man. Dir FRANK BRAKO ADU, Jr.

Ecobank Ghana Ltd (EBG): 19 Seventh Ave, Ridge West, PMB-GPO, Accra; tel. (21) 681148; fax (21) 680428; e-mail ecobankgh@ ecobank.com; internet www.ecobank.com; f. 1989; 92.2% owned by Ecobank Transnational Inc (Togo, operating under the auspices of the Economic Community of West African States); cap. 18,200m., res 84,289m., dep. 1,125,859m. (Dec. 2001); Chair. EDWARD PATRICK LARBI GYAMPOH; Man. Dir ALBERT K. EISEN; 7 brs.

First Atlantic Merchant Bank Ltd: Atlantic Place, 1 Seventh Ave, Ridge West, POB C1620, Cantonments, Accra; tel. (21) 682203; fax (21) 679250; e-mail info@firstatlanticbank.com.gh; internet www .firstatlanticbank.com.gh; f. 1994; cap. 3,385m., res 22,798m., dep. 244,128m. (Dec. 2002); Chair. PHILIP OWUSU; Man. Dir JUDE ARTHUR.

Merchant Bank (Ghana) Ltd: Merban House, 44 Kwame Nkrumah Ave, POB 401, Accra; tel. (21) 666331; fax (21) 667305; e-mail merban_services@merbangh.com; internet www.merbankgh .com; f. 1972; cap. 5,000m., res 59,077m., dep. 625,211m. (Dec. 2002); Chair. and Man. Dir B. O. MANKWA; 8 brs.

Foreign Banks

Barclays Bank of Ghana Ltd (UK): Barclays House, High St, POB 2949, Accra; tel. (21) 664901; fax (21) 667420; e-mail barclays .ghana@barclays.com; internet www.africa.barclays.com/ghana .htm; f. 1971; 90% owned by Barclays Bank Plc; 10% owned by Government of Ghana; res 389,484m., dep. 9,810m. (Dec. 2003); Chair. NANA WEREKO AMPEM II; Man. Dir K. QUANSAH; 26 brs.

International Commerical Bank (Ghana) Ltd (Taiwan): Independence Ave, Makola Shopping Mall, POB 20057, Accra; tel. (21) 666190; fax (21) 668221; e-mail icb@icbank-gh.com; cap. and res 19,134m., total assets 78,401m. (Dec. 2001); Chair. JOSEPHINE SIVARETNAM; CEO GEORGE KOSHY.

SG-SSB Bank Ltd: I Cola Ave, Kokomlemle, POB 13119, Accra; tel. (21) 228334; fax (21) 220713; e-mail enquiries@ssb.com.gh; internet www.ssb.com.gh; f. 1976 as Social Security Bank; 51.0% owned by Société Générale, France; cap. 6,735m., surplus and res 319,667m., dep. 1,491,561m. (Dec. 2003); Chair. GÉRALD LACAZE; Man. Dir PIERRE ANDRÉ TAULET; 38 brs.

Stanbic Bank Ghana: Valco Trust House, Castle Rd Ridge, POB CT2344, Cantonments, Accra; tel. (21) 234683; fax (21) 234685; e-mail stanbic@ghana.com; internet www.stanbic.com.gh; f. 1999; subsidiary of the Standard Bank of South Africa Ltd; cap. and res 14,981m., total assets 97,253m. (Dec. 2001); Chair. DENNIS W. KENNEDY; Man. Dir W. A. THOMAS; 1 br.

Standard Chartered Bank Ghana Ltd (UK): High St, POB 768, Accra; tel. (21) 664591; fax (21) 667751; e-mail dzaney@scb.ghana .nhs.compuserve.com; internet www.standardchartered.com/gh/ index.html; f. 1896 as Bank of British West Africa; cap. 40,405m., res 367,034m., dep. 2,905,945m. (Dec. 2003); Chair. PETER SULLIVAN; CEO VISHNU MOHAN; 18 brs.

STOCK EXCHANGE

Ghana Stock Exchange (GSE): Cedi House, 5th Floor, Liberia Rd, POB 1849, Accra; tel. (21) 669908; fax (21) 669913; e-mail info@ gsedata.com; internet www.gse.com.gh; f. 1990; 27 listed cos in mid-2004; Chair. NORBERT KUDJAWU; Man. Dir KOFI YAMOAH.

INSURANCE

In 2004 there were 19 insurance companies.

Donewell Insurance Co Ltd: POB 2136, Accra; tel. (21) 760483; fax (21) 760484; e-mail donewell@africaonline.com.gh; internet www .ghanaclassifieds.com/donewell; f. 1992; Chair. JOHN S. ADDO.

Enterprise Insurance Co Ltd: POB GP 50, Accra; tel. (21) 666848; fax (21) 666186; e-mail mails@eicghana.com; f. 1972; Chair. TREVOR TREFGARNE; Man. Dir GEORGE OTOO.

Ghana Union Assurance Co Ltd: POB 1322, Accra; tel. (21) 780625; fax (21) 780647; e-mail gua@ghanaunioninsurancecompany .com; f. 1973; insurance underwriting; Man. Dir NANA AGYEI DUKU.

Great African Insurance Co Ltd: POB 12349, Accra North; tel. (21) 227459; fax (21) 228905; f. 1980; Man. Dir KWASI AKOTO.

Metropolitan Insurance Co Ltd: POB GP20084, Accra; tel. (21) 225296; fax (21) 237872; e-mail met@africaonline.com.gh; internet www.met-insurance.com; f. 1994; Chair. P. K. THOMPSON; CEO MARTIN WRIGHT.

State Insurance Corpn of Ghana Ltd: POB 2363, Accra; tel. (21) 666961; fax (21) 662205; e-mail sic.info@ighmail.com; f. 1962; state-owned; privatization pending; all classes of insurance; Chair. LARRY ADJETEY; Man. Dir EBENEZER ALLOTEY.

Social Security and National Insurance Trust: Pension House, POB M149, Accra; tel. (21) 667742; fax (21) 662226; f. 1972; covers over 650,000 contributors; Dir-Gen. ERIC ADJEI.

Vanguard Assurance Co Ltd: POB 1868, Accra; tel. (21) 666485; fax (21) 668610; e-mail vanguard@ghana.com; internet www .vanguard.com; f. 1974; general accident, marine, motor and life insurance; Chair. NANA AWUAH-DARKO APEM; 7 brs.

Trade and Industry

GOVERNMENT AGENCIES

Divestiture Implementation Committee: F35/5 Ring Road East, Labone, POB CT102, Cantonments, Accra; tel. (21) 772049; fax (21) 773126; e-mail dic@ncs.com.gh; internet www.ghana.com.gh/dic; f. 1988; Chair. C. O. NYANOR; Exec. Sec. BENSON POKU-ADJEI.

Environmental Protection Agency (EPA): 91 Starlets Rd, POB M326, Accra; tel. (21) 664697; fax (21) 662690; e-mail epaed@ africaonline.com.gh; internet www.epa.gov.gh; f. 1974; Exec. Dir JONATHAN A. ALLOTEY.

Ghana Export Promotion Council (GEPC): Republic House, POB M146, Accra; tel. (21) 228813; fax (21) 668263; e-mail gepc@ ghana.com; internet www.exportghana.org; f. 1974; Exec. Sec. EDWARD BOATENG.

Ghana Food Distribution Corpn: POB 4245, Accra; tel. (21) 228428; fax (21) 225352; f. 1970; buys, stores, preserves, distributes and retails foodstuffs through 10 regional centres; Man. Dir JIMMY EDWARD.

Ghana Free Zones Board: POB M626, Accra; tel. (21) 780532; fax (21) 780534; e-mail freezone@africaonline.com.gh; internet www .ghanaclassifieds.com/gfzb; f. 1996; approves establishment of cos in export-processing zones; Dir ANDY APPIAH-KUBI (acting); Exec.-Sec. GEORGE ABOAGYE.

Ghana Heavy Equipment Ltd: Accra; fmrly subsidiary of Ghana National Trading Corpn; organizes exports, imports and production of heavy equipment; Chair. KOFI ASARE DARKWA POKU.

Ghana Investment Promotion Centre (GIPC): POB M193, Accra; tel. (21) 665125; fax (21) 663801; e-mail info@gipc.org.gh; internet www.gipc.org.gh; f. 1994; negotiates new investments, approves projects, registers foreign capital and decides extent of govt participation; Chair. P. V. OBENG.

Ghana Minerals Commission: 9 Switchback Rd Residential Area, Cantonments, POB M248, Accra; tel. (21) 772783; fax (21) 773324; e-mail mincom@mincomgh.org; internet www.mincomgh.org; f. 1986 to regulate and promote Ghana's mineral industry; CEO BENJAMIN NII AYI ARYEE.

Ghana Standards Board: POB MB245, Accra; tel. (21) 500065; fax (21) 500092; e-mail gsbdir@ghanastandards.org; f. 1967; establishes and promulgates standards; promotes standardization, industrial efficiency and development and industrial welfare, health and safety; operates certification mark scheme; 402 mems; Chair. Prof. EMMANUEL KENNETH AGYEI; Exec. Dir LAWRENCE E. YANKEY.

Ghana Trade and Investment Gateway Project (GHATIG): POB M47, Accra; tel. 663439; fax 773134; e-mail gateway1@ghana .com; promotes private investment and trade, infrastructural development of free-trade zones and export-processing zones.

National Board for Small-scale Industries: Ministry of Trade, Industry and Special Presidential Initiatives, POB M85, Accra; tel. (21) 668641; fax (21) 661394; e-mail nbssided@ghana.com; f. 1985; promotes small and medium-scale industrial and commercial enterprises by providing credit, advisory services and training; Exec. Dir Dr NANA BAAH BOAKYE.

In late 2004 the Ghana Trade Centre and the Ghana ECOWAS Trading Co were launched to facilitate trade by small and medium-sized enterprises.

DEVELOPMENT ORGANIZATION

Agence Française de Développement (AFD): 8th Rangoon Close, POB 9592, Airport, Accra; tel. (21) 778757; fax (21) 778755; e-mail afdacera@gh.groupe-afd.org; internet www.afd.fr; f. 1985;

fmrly Caisse Française de Développement; Resident Man. JEAN-FRANÇOIS ARNAL.

CHAMBER OF COMMERCE

Ghana National Chamber of Commerce: 65 Kojo Thompson Rd, POB 2325, Accra; tel. (21) 662427; fax (21) 662210; e-mail gncc@ncs.com.gh; f. 1961; promotes and protects industry and commerce, organizes trade fairs; 2,500 individual mems and 10 mem. chambers; Pres. ATO AMPIAH; CEO SAL D. AMEGAVIE.

INDUSTRIAL AND TRADE ORGANIZATIONS

Federation of Associations of Ghanaian Exporters (FAGE): POB M124, Accra; tel. (21) 232554; fax (21) 232726; e-mail fage@ighmail.com; internet www.ghana-exporter.org; non-governmental, not-for-profit organization for exporters of non-traditional exports; over 2,500 mems.

Foresty Commission of Ghana, Timber Industry Development Division (TIDD): 4 Third Ave, Ridge, POB MB434, Accra; tel. (31) 22921; fax (31) 23339; e-mail info@hq.fcghana.com; internet www.ghanatimber.org; f. 1985; promotes the development of the timber industry and the sale and export of timber.

Ghana Cocoa Board (COCOBOD): Cocoa House, Kwame Nkrumah Ave, POB 933, Accra; tel. (21) 221212; fax (21) 667104; e-mail cocobod@africaonline.com.gh; f. 1985; monopoly purchaser of cocoa until 1993; responsible for purchase, grading and export of cocoa, coffee and shea nuts; also encourages production and scientific research aimed at improving quality and yield of these crops; controls all exports of cocoa; CEO KWAME SARPONG.

Grains and Legumes Development Board: POB 4000, Kumasi; tel. (51) 4231; e-mail gldb@africaonline.com.gh; f. 1970; state-controlled; produces, processes and stores seeds and seedlings, and manages national seed security stocks.

EMPLOYERS' ORGANIZATION

Ghana Employers' Association: State Enterprises Commission Bldg, POB 2616, Accra; tel. (21) 678455; fax (21) 678405; e-mail geadmin@ghanaemployers.org; internet www.ghanaemployers.org; f. 1959; 500 mems (2005); Pres. ATO AMPIAH; Vice-Pres. Dr CHARLES MENSA; Vice-Pres. JOYCE R. ARYEE.

Affiliated Bodies

Association of Ghana Industries: Trade Fair Centre, POB AN8624, Accra-North; tel. (21) 779023; fax (21) 773143; e-mail agi@agi.org.gh; internet www.agi.org.gh; f. 1957; Pres. Prince KOFI KLUDJESON; Exec. Dir ANDREW LAWSON; 500 mems.

Ghana Booksellers' Association: POB 10367, Accra-North; tel. (21) 773002; fax (21) 773242; e-mail minerva@ghana.com; Pres. FERD J. REIMMER; Gen. Sec. ADAMS AHIMAH.

Ghana Chamber of Mines: Minerals House 10, Sixth St, Airport Residential Area, POB 991, Accra; tel. (21) 760652; fax (21) 760653; e-mail chamber@ghanachamines.com; internet www.ghanachamines.com; f. 1928; Pres. JAMES K. ANAMAN; CEO JOYCE WEREKO-BROBBY.

Ghana Electrical Contractors' Association: POB 1858, Accra.

Ghana National Contractors' Association: c/o J. T. Osei and Co, POB M11, Accra.

Ghana Timber Association (GTA): POB 1020, Kumasi; tel. and fax (51) 25153; f. 1952; promotes, protects and develops timber industry; Chair. TETTEH NANOR.

UTILITIES

Regulatory Body

Public Utilities Regulatory Commission (PURC): 51 Liberation Rd, African Liberation Circle, POB CT3095, Cantonments, Accra; tel. (21) 244181; fax (21) 224188; e-mail purc@purcghana.com; internet www.purc.com.gh; f. 1997.

Electricity

Electricity Co of Ghana (ECG): Electro-Volta House, POB 521, Accra; tel. (21) 664941; fax (21) 666262; e-mail ecgho@gh.com; Chair. KWAME SAARAH MENSAH; Man. Dir Chief MUSA B. ADAM.

Volta River Authority: Electro-Volta House, POB M77, Accra; tel. (21) 664941; fax (21) 662610; e-mail paffaiu@vra.com; f. 1961; controls the generation and distribution of electricity; CEO JOSHUA OFEDIE.

Water

Ghana Water Co Ltd (GWCL): POB M194, Accra; tel. (21) 666781; fax (21) 663552; e-mail gwsc@africaonline.com.gh; f. 1965 to provide, distribute and conserve water supplies for public, domestic and industrial use, and to establish, operate and control sewerage systems; undergoing privatization in 2005; Chair. C. W. SACKEYFIO; Man. Dir JONATHAN NII AHELE NUNOO (acting).

CO-OPERATIVES

In 1998 there were 11,154 registered co-operative societies, grouped into four sectors: industrial, financial, agricultural and service.

Department of Co-operatives: POB M150, Accra; tel. (21) 666212; fax (21) 772789; f. 1944; govt-supervised body, responsible for registration, auditing and supervision of co-operative socs; Registrar R. BUACHIE-APHRAM.

Ghana Co-operatives Council Ltd (GACOCO): POB 4034, Accra; tel. (21) 232195; f. 1951; co-ordinates activities of all co-operative socs and plays advocacy role for co-operative movement; comprises 11 active nat. asscns and two central organizations; Sec.-Gen. ALBERT AGYEMAN PREMPEH.

The five national associations and two central organizations include the Ghana Co-operative Marketing Asscn Ltd, the Ghana Co-operative Credit Unions Asscn Ltd, the Ghana Co-operative Distillers and Retailers Asscn Ltd, and the Ghana Co-operative Poultry Farmers Asscn Ltd.

TRADE UNIONS

Ghana Federation of Labour: POB 209, Accra; tel. (27) 552433; Sec.-Gen. ABRAHAM KOOMSON; 10,540 mems.

Trades Union Congress (Ghana) (TUC): Hall of Trade Unions, POB 701, Accra; tel. (21) 662568; fax (21) 667161; e-mail tuc@ighmail.com; f. 1945; 17 affiliated unions; Chair. ALEX K. BONNEY; Sec.-Gen. KWASI ADU-AMANKWAH.

Transport

RAILWAYS

Ghana has a railway network of 1,300 km, which connects Accra, Kumasi and Takoradi. In late 2004 OPEC provided a loan of US $5m. to upgrade the Accra–Tema railway.

Ghana Railways Corpn (GRC): POB 251, Takoradi; tel. (31) 22181; fax (31) 23797; f. 1901; responsible for the operation and maintenance of all railways; to be run under private concession from April 2004; 947 km of track in use in 2003; Man. Dir SAMUEL BARNES.

ROADS

In 1996 Ghana had an estimated total road network of 37,800 km, including 30 km of motorways, 5,230 km of main roads, and 9,620 km of secondary roads; some 24.1% of the road network was paved. A five-year Road Sector Expenditure Programme, costing US $259m., commenced in 1995. Construction work on 36 bridges nation-wide, funded by the Japanese Government, commenced in 2003. In 2003 work began on the Mallam–Kasoa and Kasoa–Winneba roads.

Ghana Highway Authority: POB 1641, Accra; tel. (21) 666591; fax (21) 665571; e-mail eokonadu@highways.mrt.gov.gh; f. 1974 to plan, develop, administer and maintain trunk roads and related facilities; CEO E. ODURO-KONADI.

Vanef STC: POB 7384, 1 Adjuma Cres., Ring Rd West Industrial Area, Accra; tel. (21) 221912; fax (21) 221945; e-mail stc@ghana.com; internet www.vanef-stc.com; f. 1965; fmrly State Transport Company, transferred to private-sector ownership in 2000; regional and international coach services; CEO JAMES OWUSU BONSU.

SHIPPING

The two main ports are Tema (near Accra) and Takoradi, both of which are linked with Kumasi by rail. A project to upgrade facilities at both ports, at a cost of US $365m., was to commence in 1998. In 1996 some 6.7m. metric tons of goods were handled at the two ports. At 31 December 2003 the merchant fleet comprised 207 vesels, totalling 121,300 grt.

Ghana Ports and Harbour Authority: POB 150, Tema; tel. (22) 202631; fax (22) 202812; e-mail ghpa@ghana.com; holding co for the ports of Tema and Takoradi; Dir-Gen. BEN OWUSU MENSAH.

Alpha (West Africa) Line Ltd: POB 451, Tema; operates regular cargo services to West Africa, the United Kingom, the USA, the Far East and northern Europe; shipping agents; Man. Dir AHMED EDGAR COLLINGWOOD WILLIAMS.

Black Star Line Ltd: 4th Lane, Kuku Hill Osu, POB 248, Accra; tel. (21) 2888; fax (21) 2889; f. 1957; state-owned; transfer to private sector pending; operates passenger and cargo services to Europe, the United Kingdom, Canada, the USA, the Mediterranean and West

Africa; shipping agents; Chair. MAGNUS ADDICO; Man. Dir Capt. V. N. ATTUQUAYEFIO.

Liner Agencies and Trading (Ghana) Ltd: POB 214, Tema; tel. (22) 202987; fax (22) 202989; e-mail enquiries@liner-agencies.com; international freight services; shipping agents; Dir J. OSSEI-YAW.

Maersk Sealand Ghana: Obourwe Bldg, Torman Rd, Fishing Harbour Area, POB 8800, Community 7, Tema; tel. (22) 206740; fax (22) 202048; e-mail tmamkt@maersk.com; internet www .maersksealand.com/Ghana; f. 2001; owned by Maersk (Denmark); offices in Tema, Takoradi and Kumasi; Man. Dir PETER SMIDT-NIELSEN.

Scanship (Ghana) Ltd: CFAO Bldg, High St, POB 1705, Accra; tel. (21) 664314; shipping agents.

Association

Ghana Shippers' Council: Enterprise House, 5th Floor, High St, POB 1321, Accra; tel. (21) 666915; fax (21) 668768; e-mail scouncil@ shippers-gh.com; internet www.ghanashipperscouncil.org; f. 1974; represents interests of 28,000 registered Ghanaian shippers; also provides cargo-handling and allied services; Chief Exec. KOFI MBIAH.

CIVIL AVIATION

The main international airport is at Kotoka (Accra). There are also airports at Kumasi, Takoradi, Sunyani, Tamale and Wa. The construction of a dedicated freight terminal at Kotoka Airport was completed in 1994. In 2001 622,525 passengers and 44,779 metric tons of freight passed through Kotoka Airport.

Ghana Civil Aviation Authority (GCAA): PMB, Kotoka International Airport, Accra; tel. (21) 776171; fax (21) 773293; e-mail info@ gcaagh.com; internet www.gcaa.com.gh; f. 1986; Chair. S. AKUFFO; Dir-Gen. Capt. JOE A. BOACHIE.

Gemini Airlines Ltd (Aero Gem Cargo): America House, POB 7238, Accra-North; tel. (21) 771921; fax (21) 761939; e-mail aerogemcargo@hotmail.com; f. 1974; operates weekly cargo flight between Accra and London; Gen. Man. ENOCH ANAN-TABURY.

Ghana Airways Ltd.: Ghana Airways House, Ghana Airways Avenue, POB 1636, Accra; tel. (21) 773321; fax (21) 772738; e-mail ghanaairways@ighmail.com; f. 1958; state-owned; officially ceased operations mid-February 2005; due to be replaced by Ghana International Airlines; operates regional services and international routes to West African, Asian and European destinations, and to the USA and South Africa; CEO (vacant); Man. Dir (vacant).

Ghana International Airlines (GIA): Accra; f. 2005 to replace Ghana Airways; due to commence flights in 2005; new national carrier; owned by Government of Ghana and Sky West Airlines (US); CEO J. RALPH ATKIN.

Tourism

Ghana's attractions include fine beaches, game reserves, traditional festivals, and old trading forts and castles. In 1996 a 15-year Integrated National Tourism Development Plan was initiated, under which annual tourist arrivals were targeted to exceed 1m. by 2020. In 2002 some 483,000 tourists visited Ghana, with revenue from tourism totalling US $358m.

Ghana Tourist Board: POB GP3106, Accra-North; tel. (21) 222153; fax (21) 244611; e-mail gtb@africaonline.com.gh; internet www.ghanatourism.gov.gh; f. 1968; Exec. Dir MARTIN MIREKU (acting).

Ghana Association of Tourist and Travel Agencies: Ramia House, Kojo Thompson Rd, POB 7140, Accra; tel. (21) 228933; Pres. JOSEPH K. ANKUMAH; Sec. JOHNNIE MOREAUX.

Ghana Tourist Development Co Ltd: POB 8710, Accra; tel. (21) 776109; fax (21) 772093; f. 1974; develops tourist infrastructure, incl. hotels, restaurants and casinos; operates duty-free shops; Man. Dir ALFRED KOMLADZEI.

GREECE

Introductory Survey

Location, Climate, Language, Religion, Flag, Capital

The Hellenic Republic lies in south-eastern Europe. The country consists mainly of a mountainous peninsula between the Mediterranean Sea and the Aegean Sea, bounded to the north by Albania, the former Yugoslav republic of Macedonia and Bulgaria, and to the east by Turkey. To the south, east and west of the mainland lie numerous Greek islands, of which the largest is Crete. The climate is Mediterranean, with mild winters and hot summers. The average temperature in the capital is 28°C (82°F) in July and 9°C (48°C) in January. The language is Greek, of which there are two forms—the formal language (katharevoussa) and the language commonly spoken and taught in schools (demotiki). Almost all of the inhabitants profess Christianity, and the Greek Orthodox Church, to which about 97% of the population adhere, is the established religion. The national flag (proportions 2 by 3) displays nine equal horizontal stripes of blue and white, with a white cross throughout a square canton of blue at the upper hoist. The capital is Athens (Athenai).

Recent History

The liberation of Greece from the German occupation (1941–44) was followed by a civil war, which lasted until 1949. The communist forces were defeated, and the constitutional monarchy re-established. King Konstantinos (Constantine) II acceded to the throne on the death of his father, King Pavlos (Paul), in 1964. A succession of weak governments and conflicts between the King and his ministers, and an alleged conspiracy involving military personnel, culminated in a coup, led by right-wing army officers, in April 1967. An attempted counter-coup, led by the King, failed, and he went into exile. Col Georgios Papadopoulos emerged as the dominant personality in the new regime, becoming Prime Minister in December 1967 and Regent in March 1972. The regime produced nominally democratic constitutional proposals, but all political activity was banned and its opponents were expelled from all positions of power or influence.

Following an abortive naval mutiny, Greece was declared a republic in June 1973, and Papadopoulos was appointed President. Martial law was ended, and a civilian Cabinet was appointed in preparation for a general election. However, a student uprising in Athens in November was violently suppressed by the army, and Papadopoulos was overthrown by another military coup. Lt-Gen. Phaidon Ghizikis was appointed President, and a mainly civilian Cabinet, led by Adamantios Androutsopoulos, was installed, but effective power lay with a small group of officers and the military police under Brig.-Gen. Demetrios Ioannides. As a result of the failure of the military junta's attempt to overthrow President Makarios of Cyprus, and its inability to prevent the Turkish invasion of the island (see the chapter on Cyprus), the Androutsopoulos Cabinet collapsed in July 1974. President Ghizikis summoned from exile a former Prime Minister, Konstantinos Karamanlis, who was invited to form a civilian Government of National Salvation. Martial law was ended, the press was released from state control and political parties, including the communists, were allowed to operate freely. A general election in November resulted in a decisive victory for Karamanlis's New Democracy Party (ND), which won 220 of the 300 parliamentary seats. A referendum in December rejected proposals for a return to constitutional monarchy, and in June 1975 a new republican Constitution, providing for a parliamentary democracy, was promulgated. In the same month Prof. Konstantinos Tsatsos, a former cabinet minister, was elected President by the Vouli (Parliament).

In the general election of November 1977 ND was re-elected with a reduced majority. In May 1980 Karamanlis was elected President, Georgios Rallis subsequently assumed the leadership of ND and was appointed Prime Minister. Rallis encountered considerable opposition from the increasingly popular Panhellenic Socialist Movement (PASOK). On 1 January 1981 Greece acceded to the European Community (EC, now the European Union—EU, see p. 217). In the general election of October 1981 PASOK secured an absolute majority in the Vouli. The PASOK leader, Andreas Papandreou, became Prime Minister of the first ever socialist Government, which was initially committed to withdrawal from the EC, to the removal of US military bases from Greek territory and to the implementation of an extensive programme of domestic reform.

In March 1985 Papandreou unexpectedly withdrew support for President Karamanlis's candidature for a further five-year term in office. The Prime Minister planned to amend the 1975 Constitution to relieve the President of all executive power and render the Head of State's functions largely ceremonial. Karamanlis resigned in protest, and the Vouli elected Christos Sartzetakis, a judge, as President, in a vote that was widely considered to be unconstitutional. A general election was held in June 1985 to enable the Government to secure support for the proposed constitutional changes. PASOK was returned to power, winning 161 seats in the 300-member Vouli; ND secured 126 seats. In October the Government introduced a stringent programme of economic austerity, provoking widespread industrial unrest, which continued throughout 1986. In March 1986, despite considerable opposition from ND, the Vouli approved a series of constitutional amendments limiting the influence of the President, whose executive powers were transferred to the legislature.

In May 1987, in response to numerous accusations made by ND of mismanagement and corruption on the part of the Government, Papandreou sought and won a parliamentary vote of confidence in his Government. The Government suffered a serious reverse in November 1988, when several leading members of the Cabinet were implicated in a major financial scandal involving alleged embezzlement from the Bank of Crete, and were forced to resign.

In January 1989 the Greek Left Party, led by Leonidas Kyrkos, formed an electoral alliance with the 'Exterior' faction of the Communist Party of Greece (KKE), under the leadership of Charilaos Florakis, to create the Coalition of the Left and Progress (the Left Coalition). At a general election in June, ND won the largest proportion of the votes cast, but failed to attain an overall majority in the Vouli. Following the failure of both ND and PASOK to reach an agreement with the Left Coalition to form a coalition government, President Sartzetakis empowered the Left Coalition to seek a coalition agreement. The Left Coalition unexpectedly agreed to form an interim administration with ND, on the condition that the ND leader, Konstantinos Mitsotakis, renounced his claim to the premiership. Accordingly, Tzannis Tzannetakis, an ND deputy, was appointed Prime Minister in a new Cabinet, which included two communist ministers. The unprecedented conservative-communist coalition announced its intention to govern for only three months, during which time it would aim to implement a *katharsis* (campaign of purification) of Greek politics. Accordingly, the administration resigned in early October, having initiated investigations into the involvement of officials of the former socialist Government, including Papandreou, in a number of scandals involving banking, armaments and financial transactions. (In March 1991 Papandreou and three of his former ministers were tried on charges of complicity in large-scale embezzlement from the Bank of Crete during their terms of office. Papandreou, who asserted that his indictment had been politically motivated, was tried *in absentia*; in January 1992 he was acquitted of all charges, while two of the former ministers received minor sentences; the third had died during the trial.) The President of the Supreme Court, Ioannis Grivas, was subsequently appointed Prime Minister in an interim Cabinet comprising non-political figures, which was to oversee the second general election of the year. However, the results of the election, conducted in November, were again inconclusive (ND won 46% of the total votes cast, PASOK 41% and the Left Coalition 11%). The political crisis was temporarily resolved in mid-November, when the three parties agreed to form a coalition that would administer the country, pending the results of a further poll, to be conducted in April 1990. Xenofon Zolotas, a former Governor of the Bank of Greece, was appointed Prime Minister to lead the interim Cabinet. However, following a dispute over military promotions in February 1990, the Government collapsed, and the same non-political individuals who had overseen the November 1989 election were reinstated to govern until the new general election. Attempts by the Vouli in February and March 1990 to elect a head of state by the required majority were unsuccessful, owing largely to a decision taken by ND representatives to abstain from voting, following the refusal of their candidate, Karamanlis, to contest the election. A general election, conducted in April, finally resolved the parliamentary impasse; ND secured 150 seats in the Vouli. Following the announcement of the results, Mitsotakis secured the support of Konstantinos Stefanopoulos, the leader (and the one elected parliamentary representative) of the Party of Democratic Renewal, thereby enabling him to form the first single-party Government since 1981. In May 1990 Karamanlis took office as President for a five-year term, following his election by 153 of the 300 members of the Vouli. Stefanopoulos formally rejoined ND in June.

The failure of the interim administrations to reach a consensus on comprehensive economic programmes, and the unpopularity of austerity measures introduced by the new Government, led to widespread industrial unrest. Throughout 1990 appeals by trade unions for general strikes were regularly supported by more than 1m. workers, seriously disrupting public services and industry. In November reforms to the electoral law, providing for a modified form of proportional representation, in which political parties wishing to appoint representatives to the Vouli would require a minimum of 3% of the national vote in a general election, were finally ratified. Left-wing parties vehemently criticized the new electoral system, which also incorporated procedural disincentives to the formation of political alliances to contest elections, as unconstitutional.

In August 1991 Mitsotakis effected a comprehensive reorganization of the Cabinet (including the removal of his daughter from the post of Under-Secretary to the Prime Minister), in response to public criticism of family involvement in politics. In April 1992 the Prime Minister successfully sought a vote of confidence from the Vouli, following the dismissal of the Minister of Foreign Affairs, Antonis Samaras, and Mitsotakis's assumption of the portfolio, in order to co-ordinate personally the Greek response to attempts by the former Yugoslav republic of Macedonia (FYRM) to achieve international recognition as the independent Republic of Macedonia (see below). As part of a cabinet reorganization effected in August (which included the controversial reappointment of the Prime Minister's daughter to her previous post), Michalis Papakonstantinou, a staunch defender of national territorial integrity, was allocated the foreign affairs portfolio. Ministerial disaffection with what was perceived as Mitsotakis's moderate stance regarding the FYRM, and with the Government's policy of economic austerity, increased in late 1992, but was curtailed somewhat, following the Prime Minister's dismissal and reorganization of the entire Cabinet in early December. Industrial unrest continued throughout 1992 and 1993, in response to privatization plans and further austerity measures.

In September 1993 two ND deputies resigned, following an appeal for support by Political Spring (POLAN), a centre-right party that had been established in July by Samaras. The consequent loss of Mitsotakis's one-seat majority in the Vouli obliged him to offer the Government's resignation and schedule an early general election. At the election, conducted in October, PASOK obtained 46.9% of the total votes cast and 170 of the 300 parliamentary seats, while ND received 39.3% of the votes and 111 seats, and POLAN secured 4.9% of the votes and 10 seats. At the end of October Mitsotakis resigned as leader of ND. Papandreou's victory in the general election provoked immediate concern among members of the EU, owing to the anti-European attitude the PASOK leader had adopted during his previous tenure of office; however, he gave assurances of his commitment to European integration. Following a reduction in electoral support for PASOK in elections to the European Parliament in June 1994, Papandreou undertook a reorganization of the Cabinet.

In March 1995 Stefanopoulos was elected President by 181 of the 300 members of the Vouli, having failed to secure the required two-thirds' majority in two earlier rounds of voting; jointly favoured by PASOK and POLAN, he took office on 10 March. From mid-1995 tensions within the governing PASOK became increasingly evident. In August a deputy was expelled from the party, following his public criticism of the political influence of Papandreou's wife, Dimitra Liani-Papandreou (who

had been appointed Chief of Staff in October 1993). In September 1995 the Minister of Industry, Energy and Technology and of Commerce, Konstantinos Simitis, resigned, citing interference in his policies by senior PASOK officials. Simitis, together with: Theodhoros Pangalos, who had resigned from the party's executive committee earlier in the month; Vasiliki (Vasso) Papandreou, a former EU Commissioner; and Paraskevas Avgerinos, a former Minister of EU Affairs, constituted a group of 'dissident' PASOK deputies (referred to as the Group of Four) who urged the resignation of Papandreou, in view of his failing health, and the implementation of further reforms within the party. In November Papandreou was admitted to hospital suffering from pneumonia; Apostolos-Athanassios (Akis) Tsohatzopoulos, a close associate of Papandreou, who had joined the Cabinet in September, assumed the prime ministerial duties, in an acting capacity. Papandreou's condition remained critical throughout December, and in January 1996 the opposition parties expressed their concern at his continued absence, although a parliamentary motion of 'no confidence' in the Government was defeated. On 15 January Papandreou submitted his resignation as Prime Minister, although he remained leader of PASOK. Three days later Simitis was elected to the premiership, having won the support of 86 of the 167 members of the PASOK parliamentary party (compared with 75 votes for his nearest opponent, Tsohatzopoulos) in a second round of voting. Simitis awarded Pangalos the foreign affairs portfolio, but retained Tsohatzopoulos and Gerasimos Arsenis (another supporter of Papandreou, who had also contested the leadership election) in the Cabinet in an attempt to unite the party. However, pro-European ministers who supported Simitis's desire for economic reform replaced the majority of Papandreou's former associates.

Almost immediately, Simitis was confronted by a sharp escalation in hostilities with Turkey (see below). Following his acceptance of a US-brokered compromise to defuse the situation, Simitis was vigorously condemned by all opposition parties. In February 1996 the Prime Minister dismissed the Chief of the General Staff of the armed forces, Adm. Christos Lyberis, owing to the latter's disclosure of government deliberations concerning the use of military force against Turkey during the crisis over sovereignty in the Aegean Sea.

Following the death of Papandreou in June 1996, Simitis was elected leader of PASOK, with 53.5% of the votes cast, defeating his closest rival, Tsohatzopoulos, who represented the 'populist' wing of the party. None the less, in August Simitis announced that an early general election was to be held, in order to obtain a firm mandate for his Government to pursue the reforms needed to achieve the EU's economic and monetary union (EMU) targets, and for the Government's implementation of its proposed foreign affairs policies. In the poll, which was held on 22 September 1996, PASOK won 162 of the 300 parliamentary seats, with 41.5% of the votes cast, securing victory over ND, with 108 seats (38.2%). Support for POLAN declined substantially, and the party lost all 10 of the seats obtained at the previous election. Key ministers in the new PASOK administration were retained from the outgoing Cabinet. In March 1997 Konstantinos Karamanlis (a nephew of his namesake, the former President and ND party leader) was elected leader of ND, despite his lack of experience in government.

Labour unrest was reported in late 1996 and early 1997, and a widely observed general strike was staged in November 1996, in protest against new austerity measures. Despite increasing criticism from former supporters, who accused him of abandoning PASOK's commitment to protecting low-income workers, Simitis continued to implement austerity policies in accordance with his commitment to meeting the 'convergence' criteria of EMU. In December Simitis expelled three deputies from PASOK's parliamentary group for voting against budget proposals for 1998, which were subsequently adopted by a considerable margin in the Vouli. Industrial action continued to cause disruption in 1998. In May a widely observed general strike was organized in protest at privatization plans and the implementation of further austerity measures. The response to the strikes, in particular the use of riot police, caused divisions within the Government; however, at the end of June, after six weeks, the strike ended and the privatization programme was approved. Following a defeat sustained by PASOK at the local elections, held in October, a minor cabinet reorganization was effected. In late November, in response to criticism of its austerity programme, the Government sought and won a parliamentary vote of confidence; Simitis had threatened to expel PASOK deputies from the party if they failed to support the motion.

In February 1999 it emerged that Abdullah Öcalan, the leader of the proscribed Kurdistan Workers' Party (Partiya Karkeren Kurdistan—PKK), accused by Turkey of a number of terrorist charges, had been given refuge at the Greek embassy in Kenya before being captured by the Turkish authorities. Kenya officially denounced Greece for allowing Öcalan to enter the country without informing the Kenyan authorities. Kurdish groups demonstrated at Greek embassies across Europe, and the Ministers of the Interior, Public Administration and Decentralization, of Foreign Affairs and of Public Order resigned, prompting a cabinet reorganization. Vasiliki (Vasso) Papandreou, formerly Minister of Development, was appointed Minister of the Interior, Public Administration and Decentralization, and Georgios Papandreou (the son of the late Andreas Papandreou) replaced Pangalos as Minister of Foreign Affairs.

Industrial action continued in 1999, and was accompanied by student demonstrations, in protest at an educational reform law. At the beginning of February 2000 Prime Minister Simitis announced that an early general election was to be held on 9 April. On 9 February Stefanopoulos was re-elected President by 269 of the 300 members of the Vouli, defeating his sole opponent, Leonidas Kyrkos of the Left Coalition. In the April general election PASOK was returned to office, winning 43.8% of the votes cast and 158 parliamentary seats, narrowly defeating ND, with 42.7% of the votes and 125 seats. On 12 April Simitis formed a new Government, in which the principal portfolios remained unchanged. In November Simitis dismissed Pangalos, who had returned to the Cabinet as Minister of Culture, after Pangalos expressed criticism of government policies, including draft legislation on labour-market reform.

In April 2001 government plans to raise the retirement age and reform the pension system precipitated widely supported public protests, including a general strike. In May the first papal visit to Greece in over 1,000 years took place; in the course of his visit Pope John Paul II attempted to assuage Orthodox sensitivities, apologizing for past Roman Catholic transgressions. Also in October Simitis reorganized the Cabinet, following his re-election as party leader at a PASOK congress held earlier in the month. The Prime Minister's main party rival, Tsohatzopoulos, was transferred to the post of Minister of Development.

In January 2002 a daily newspaper published a report linking some 124 PASOK parliamentary deputies to terrorist groups operating in the 1970s and 1980s. The report, based on a Greek intelligence document produced in 1988, also accused Andreas Papandreou and three former ministers of having undergone training in Palestinian-run camps in Lebanon in the late 1970s. PASOK officials denied the accusations.

Meanwhile, in late January 2002 farmers began to blockade the main highway linking Athens and Thessaloníki, demanding higher cotton subsidies and compensation for massive crop damage, caused by severe weather conditions. In early April farmers staged renewed blockades, after having failed to reach agreement with the Government. A series of one-day strikes by public-sector workers, in continuing protests against government plans to reform the largest state pension fund, resulted at the end of May in the closure of airports, ports and public offices. In September consumer groups organized a widely observed, one-day boycott of shops and retailers, in protest against the price increases that had followed the adoption of the euro as the national currency at the beginning of the year. Another one-day strike was organized by airport and public-sector workers in early December, bringing further disruption to the country.

In late October 2002 Dora Bakoyanni, a former Minister of Culture and the daughter of former Prime Minister Mitsotakis, was elected Mayor of Athens, with almost 60% of the votes cast; Bakoyanni, a member of ND, had been supported by the conservative opposition. At the same time conservative forces registered strong gains in local and regional elections. In December Bakoyanni narrowly escaped assassination when a gunman opened fire on her car; although Bakoyanni's husband had been assassinated in 1989 by a member of the November 17 Revolutionary Organization (see below), there was no apparent link to that organization.

In early July 2003 PASOK elected a new executive bureau, following a decision by Simitis that its members should not simultaneously hold a position in the Cabinet. Michalis Chrisochoidhis, hitherto Minister of Public Order, replaced Costas Laliotis as Secretary-General. A minor government reorganization was subsequently implemented. In October public-sector workers staged further widespread strikes to demand pay increases. In early January 2004 Simitis announced his resignation from the leadership of PASOK, and declared that early legislative elections would take place on 7 March, declaring that an administration with a new mandate was necessary to address developments on the issue of Cyprus (see below). On 8 February, following amendments to the party charter (whereby the leader would be selected by members nationally), Georgios Papandreou was elected unopposed as the President of PASOK. (Anastassios Giannitsis subsequently took over the post of Minister of Foreign Affairs, pending the elections.) In February a large anti-terrorist exercise, involving some 2,000 members of the Greek military and security services, was conducted in Athens as part of security preparations for the summer Olympic Games, which Greece was to host in August. At the legislative elections of 7 March, ND secured 45.4% of the votes cast, thereby removing PASOK, which won 40.6% of the votes, from government. On 9 March Karamanlis formed a new administration, under his leadership, which was officially installed on the following day. The new Prime Minister, who also held the culture portfolio, pledged to expedite the preparations for the Olympic Games (which at that time were substantially behind the schedule for completion). On 5 May three bombs exploded in Athens, increasing concerns that security arrangements for the Olympic Games were inadequate. In July a further bomb attack was launched against the offices of the Ministry of Culture; however, no serious injuries resulted from these explosions. Although there were reports that many of the Olympic construction projects were behind schedule and greatly exceeded cost projections, the staging of the Olympiad on 13–29 August, with 202 nations participating, was widely viewed as a success for the Greek Government. Anti-US demonstrations, staged in Athens to coincide with the Games, were suppressed by security forces.

In September 2004 the Chief of Staff of the Air Force, Lt-Gen. Panagotias Papanikolau, tendered his resignation, after the Greek Orthodox Patriarch of Alexandria and All Africa, and 16 other passengers, were killed in a helicopter crash; media reports had focused attention on the failure of the aerial surveillance system. In November the Government publicly conceded that the PASOK administration had significantly understated public-debt and budgetary-deficit figures for several years in order for Greece to qualify for membership of EMU in January 2001, after evidence to that effect emerged; it appeared that continued misrepresentation of defence expenditure had partially caused the discrepancies. The statement provoked a clash between the ruling ND and PASOK, which criticized the revision of past official figures. The Government was expected to avoid legal proceedings for the contravention of EU critieria if it fulfilled its subsequent pledge to restrain the budgetary deficit to within the stipulated limit (of 3% of GDP) by 2006.

On 8 February 2005 Karolos Papoulias, a member of PASOK and a former Minister of Foreign Affairs, was elected unopposed as the new President by an overwhelming majority of 279 votes in the 300-member Vouli (thereby ending speculation that early legislative elections would be organized in 2005). He had been nominated by Karamanlis, who had viewed him as the candidate most likely to secure political consensus. Papoulias was inaugurated as President on 12 March, following the expiry of the second five-year term of Stefanopoulos.

Throughout the 1990s numerous attacks against military and commercial targets (particularly those associated with the US administration or US commercial interests) in Greece were carried out by dissident groups, in particular the extremist left-wing November 17 Revolutionary Organization (active since 1975) and the Revolutionary People's Struggle (ELA). In July 1992 November 17 claimed responsibility for an attempt to assassinate the Minister of Finance, in which a member of the public died, and in December an ND deputy was shot and injured by the same group. In 1994 further attacks targeted foreign companies, and in July the November 17 group claimed responsibility for the assassination of a Turkish diplomat. A series of measures to combat terrorism was announced by the Government in September, following a bomb attack on a police vehicle. In February 1996 an attempted attack on the US embassy in Athens was believed by police to have been co-ordinated by November 17 activists. In January 1998 the police arrested more than 15 suspected members of the Fighting Guerrilla Faction, a left-wing group believed to be responsible for a number of bombings, including an attack on the offices of Alitalia, the Italian airline, in 1997. In January and February

1998 there were several explosions at the offices of US companies in Greece; these were thought to be related to US military action in Iraq (see the chapter on Iraq), although an anti-tank rocket attack on a US bank was attributed to November 17. During May an incendiary attack was carried out at the office of the Minister of Press and Mass Media and an explosive device was found at the office of the Minister of Transport and Communications; there were also explosions at the Ionian and Popular Bank of Greece and Olympic Airways. Dissident activities continued into the early 2000s. In June 2000 the British defence attaché, Brig. Stephen Saunders, was assassinated by the November 17 group, which claimed that Saunders had helped to co-ordinate the bombing offensive by the North Atlantic Treaty Organization (NATO, see p. 301) of Serbia and Montenegro in 1999 (which had been strongly opposed in Greece—see below). Saunders' murder led to international concern that Greece was failing to co-operate fully with international anti-terrorist efforts, although in July 2000 a series of anti-terrorist initiatives was agreed between Greece and the United Kingdom. In November, however, the ELA claimed responsibility for four further bomb attacks and in January 2001 a member of the Vouli was injured in a further attack that was attributed to November 17. In June the Vouli approved widespread changes to criminal legislation in an attempt to improve Greece's record on combating dissident activity. The amendments, which introduced non-jury criminal trials, a limited right to appeal and broader police powers of surveillance, and which permitted the non-consensual DNA testing of suspects, provoked strong objections from legal associations and civil liberties groups.

In 2002 the Government made significant progress in combating terrorist activity. Notably, in July the authorities apprehended 14 suspected members of November 17. The first to be arrested was Savvas Xiros (representing the first arrest of an alleged member of the organization), who had been injured in a bomb explosion, and the police were subsequently able to arrest the suspected leader of November 17, Alexandros Giotopoulos, and two of Xiros's brothers, one of whom had reportedly confessed to the assassination in 2000 of Brig. Stephen Saunders. Shortly afterwards the Government announced that November 17 had been dismantled. In September 2002 Dimitris Koufodinas, believed to be the second highest-ranking member of November 17, surrendered to police in Athens. By January 2003 a total of 19 suspected members of November 17 had been apprehended, and in February the police arrested four suspected members of ELA. Meanwhile, in January it had been reported that a number of Greece's wealthiest individuals had paid large sums of money to November 17, in order not to be targeted by the organization. The trial of Giotopoulos, Koufodinas and the 17 other alleged members of November 17 commenced in March. The two principal defendants were accused of over 1,000 criminal acts, including some 23 killings and numerous bomb attacks, although, by law, they were unable to be charged with acts perpetrated more than 20 years previously. The trial was concluded in December. Of the 19 defendants, four were acquitted owing to lack of evidence. Giotopoulos, Koufodinas and four others were sentenced to life imprisonment, while eight defendants received less severe custodial sentences. The remaining defendant, who had testified against the others, received a suspended sentence. In October, following an eight-month trial, five members of the ELA, including the movement's reputed leader, were each sentenced to 25 years' imprisonment on charges relating to more than 100 bomb attacks.

Greece became a full member of the EC (now EU) in January 1981, having signed the treaty of accession in 1979. Although originally critical of Greece's membership, the PASOK Government confined itself to seeking modification of the terms of accession, in order to take into account the underdeveloped Greek economy, and gave qualified assent to concessions proposed by the EC in 1983. In July 1992 the Vouli voted to ratify the Treaty on European Union.

Relations with Turkey have been characterized by long-standing disputes concerning Cyprus (q.v.) and sovereignty over the continental shelf beneath the Aegean Sea. The difficulties in relations with Turkey were exacerbated by the unilateral declaration of an 'independent' Turkish Cypriot state in Cyprus in November 1983 (the 'Turkish Republic of Northern Cyprus'—'TRNC'), together with various minor sovereignty disputes over islands in the Aegean Sea, which led to Greece's withdrawal from NATO military exercises in August 1984 and to a boycott of manoeuvres in subsequent years. In March 1987 a disagreement between Greece and Turkey over petroleum-prospecting rights

in disputed areas of the Aegean Sea almost resulted in military conflict. In January 1988, however, the Greek and Turkish Prime Ministers, meeting in Davos, Switzerland, agreed that the two countries' premiers should meet annually in order to improve bilateral relations (the Davos meeting was the first formal contact between Greek and Turkish Heads of Government for 10 years), and that joint committees should be established to negotiate peaceful solutions to disputes.

In 1994 the issue of the demarcation of territorial waters in the Aegean Sea re-emerged as a major source of tension. Greece's right to extend its territorial waters from six to 12 nautical miles, as enshrined in the international Convention on the Law of the Sea (see the International Seabed Authority, see p. 283), was strongly condemned by Turkey, which feared the loss of shipping access, via the Aegean Sea, to international waters. The dispute intensified prior to the scheduled entry into force of the Convention, in mid-November, with both countries conducting concurrent military exercises in the Aegean. In early 1995 the Greek Government obstructed an agreement to establish a customs union between Turkey and the EU until, in March, it secured a defined agreement from the EU regarding a timetable for accession negotiations with Cyprus. The concern surrounding the international Convention on the Law of the Sea re-emerged in June, when the Vouli ratified the treaty; Turkey conducted further military exercises in the region. In early 1996 tensions were exacerbated by conflicting claims of sovereignty over Imia (Kardak), a group of uninhabited islands in the Aegean Sea. By late January Greek and Turkish military vessels were patrolling the islands and attempts were made to raise the respective national flags on the territory. The situation was defused when the new PASOK administration complied with a petition by the US Administration to withdraw all military vessels and troops from the area and to remove the national flags.

In February 1996 Greek opposition delayed the implementation of a financial protocol of the EU-Turkey customs union; Greece claimed that Turkey's aggressive action in the Aegean violated the terms of the customs union agreement. Although the Greek Prime Minister, Konstantinos Simitis, resolved to pursue a more constructive foreign policy stance towards Turkey, a series of incidents throughout 1996 involving alleged violations of Greek airspace by Turkish aircraft and confrontations between Greek and Turkish patrol vessels in the Aegean precluded any improvement in relations. In July Greece finally withdrew its opposition to Turkey's participation in an EU-Mediterranean assistance programme, in response to a joint statement by EU Heads of Government urging an end to Turkey's 'hostile policy' towards Greece; however, the block on funds from the customs-union agreement remained in effect.

In April 1997 the Greek Deputy Minister of Foreign Affairs met his Turkish counterpart in Malta, under EU auspices, and it was agreed to establish two committees of independent experts who would communicate through the EU to explore ways of improving relations between the two countries. At a NATO summit meeting in Madrid, Spain, in July Simitis and the Turkish President, Süleyman Demirel, held direct talks (the first such meeting for three years), which led to an agreement, known as the Madrid Declaration, in which they pledged not to use violence or the threat of violence in resolving the countries' bilateral disputes. However, relations remained strained, particularly concerning Greek support for Cyprus's application for membership of the EU; Turkey threatened annexation of the 'TRNC' should Cyprus be admitted to the organization. Further tension was caused by frequent alleged violations of Greek airspace by Turkish military aircraft. In November, however, Simitis held a meeting with the Turkish Prime Minister, Mesut Yılmaz, at which it was agreed to explore confidence-building measures. None the less, also in November Greece threatened to oppose Turkey's participation in a planned EU enlargement conference in London, United Kingdom, unless Turkey abandoned its attempts to prevent EU accession talks with Cyprus, which were due to begin in 1998, and threatened to veto the admission to the EU of other applicant countries if Cyprus were rejected. At a NATO summit in early December 1997 an agreement was signed, under which Greece and Turkey would share control of military flights in the Aegean under NATO's new military command structure (although this agreement had yet to be endorsed by the political leaders of each country). Later that month, however, further Turkish violations of Greek airspace over the Aegean by Turkish planes were reported.

As Cyprus began accession talks with the EU in March 1998, Greece reiterated its intention to veto the admission of other countries if Cyprus were not included, and maintained its refusal to lift its veto on EU financial aid to Turkey. In June the NATO Secretary-General, Javier Solana, announced that Greece and Turkey had agreed to continue talks regarding confidence-building measures and to activate a 1988 agreement providing for a flight moratorium over the Aegean in July and August. In an attempt to improve relations with Turkey, in August Greece attempted to persuade Cyprus to cancel its proposed purchase of an anti-aircraft missile system. Turkey later welcomed the decision, taken at the end of December, not to deploy the missile system in Cyprus, although, in Greece, missiles were deployed on Crete in March 1999.

In July 1999 Greece alleged that two Turkish military aircraft had intercepted a Greek aircraft carrying the Minister of Transport to Cyprus and had forced it briefly to alter course. Relations between the two countries improved in late August, however, when Greece offered both financial and material assistance to Turkey, following a severe earthquake in the north-west of that country; Greece also announced its intention to lift its veto on EU financial aid to Turkey. Turkey reciprocated Greece's provision of emergency assistance when an earthquake struck Athens in early September. At an EU summit, held in Helsinki, Finland, in December, a diplomatic impasse was finally ended when Greece formally lifted its objections to Turkey's membership of the EU, although the conditions for its accession depended on the resolution of both the Cyprus issue and of its dispute with Greece in the Aegean. The notable improvement in relations between Greece and Turkey was evident in late January 2000 when the Greek Minister of Foreign Affairs, Georgios Papandreou, visited Ankara for talks with his Turkish counterpart, İsmail Cem, and the Turkish Prime Minister, in the first official visit by a Greek Minister of Foreign Affairs to Turkey since 1962. During negotiations a number of agreements on matters such as investment, crime and tourism were signed by the two sides. In early February 2000 the *rapprochement* between Greece and Turkey continued with an official visit to Athens by the Turkish Minister of Foreign Affairs, during which further co-operation agreements (primarily relating to economic affairs) were signed. In October, however, Greece withdrew from a joint NATO military exercise in the Aegean Sea, after it accused Turkey of preventing Greek airplanes from flying over the disputed islands of Limnos and Ikaria.

Despite this reverse, in April 2001 both Greece and Turkey announced significant reductions in their weapons-procurement programmes. In November Greece and Turkey signed an agreement that allowed the former country to repatriate illegal Turkish immigrants. (The Greek Government believed that as many as 750,000 illegal immigrants had entered the country from Turkey since 1998.) None the less, the issue of Cyprus continued to overshadow bilateral relations and in May Cem announced there would be 'no limits' to Turkey's response were Cyprus to be admitted to full membership of the EU before a political settlement had been reached. In February 2002, however, the Greek and Turkish Ministers of Foreign Affairs recommenced talks, following the resumption of negotiations between the Greek and Turkish Cypriot sides over the issue of Cyprus.

In late March 2002 Greece and Turkey signed an agreement to build a 285-km natural gas pipeline, which would eventually allow Turkey to supply Greece with 500,000 cu m of gas per day. During late 2002 and early 2003 the Greek- and Turkish Cypriot leaders made significant progress towards reaching a final peace agreement on Cyprus, although this peace plan collapsed in March 2003. However, following UN-mediated discussions in New York, in mid-February 2004 agreement was reached on a plan for the resolution of the reunification issue, which would provide for Cyprus's accession to the EU as a single state in May. The Greek Cypriot President, Tassos Papadopoulos, and the Turkish Cypriot leader, Rauf Denktaş, resumed UN-sponsored negotiations in the Cypriot capital, Nicosia, on 19 February. The final plan for reunification, submitted for approval by the Greek and Turkish Cypriot communities at referendums on 24 April, was endorsed by the Turkish Cypriots by 64.9% of the votes cast, but rejected by the Greek Cypriots by a decisive majority of 75.8% of the votes (with the result that only the Greek part of Cyprus joined the EU on 1 May). In early May the Turkish Prime Minister, Reçep Tayyip Erdoğan, made an official visit to Greece (the first by a Turkish premier in 16 years), in a demonstration of the improvement in bilateral relations. In July the Greek Minister of Public Order and his Turkish counterpart

signed a security co-operation agreement in the Turkish capital, İstanbul.

In August 1985 Greece and Albania reopened their borders, which had remained closed since 1940, and Greece formally annulled claims to North Epirus (southern Albania), where there is a sizeable Greek minority. In August 1987 the Greek Government put a formal end to a legal vestige of the Second World War by proclaiming that it no longer considered Greece to be at war with Albania. In April 1988 the two countries signed an agreement to promote trade between their border provinces. During the early 1990s, however, bilateral relations were severely strained by persisting concerns relating to the treatment of ethnic Greeks residing in Albania (numbering an estimated 300,000), the illegal immigration of several thousand Albanians seeking work opportunities or political asylum in Greece and the efforts of the Greek Government to secure their return. In March 1996 President Stefanopoulos signed a treaty of friendship and co-operation with Albania's President, Sali Berisha. Several issues appeared to have been resolved, with Albania agreeing to provide Greek-language education in schools serving the ethnic Greek population and Greece declaring its willingness to issue temporary work permits for at least 150,000 seasonal workers from Albania.

Following a revolt in southern Albania in March 1997, the Greek Government mediated in negotiations with rebel leaders, in an effort to restore stability. Greece contributed 700 men to a multinational force led by Italy, which was established with a mandate to facilitate the distribution of humanitarian aid. In August Greece agreed to legitimize the status of tens of thousands of illegal Albanian immigrants by granting them temporary work permits in exchange for assistance from Albania in combating cross-border crime. During April 1998 the two countries signed a military-training accord; plans were later announced for joint military exercises and Greece pledged to provide military reconstruction aid to Albania. In August the establishment was announced of a free border zone between the two countries to take effect in 2000; citizens of either country living in this area were to be given special entry documents for both Greece and Albania. A new border crossing was opened between Greece and Albania in May 1999. By 2002 there were an estimated 600,000 Albanians living in Greece. However, the stabilization of the political situation in Albania meant that the influx of Albanians into Greece had decreased considerably in recent years.

During the conflicts in the former Yugoslavia, Greece maintained close relations with the authorities of the Federal Republic of Yugoslavia (reconstituted as the State Union of Serbia and Montenegro from 2003) and advocated the removal of the UN-imposed trade embargo against the FRY. Greece's stance, which was shared notably by Bulgaria and Russia, contributed to a strengthening of relations between these countries. Greece advocated a diplomatic solution to the conflict in the Serbian province of Kosovo and Metohija (Kosovo—see the chapter on Serbia and Montenegro), and refused to participate in the March–June 1999 NATO air offensive against Serbian targets. Insurgent activity, in protest at the NATO bombardment, increased in Greece during 1999; in April a bomb in an Athens hotel resulted in one person being killed and another seriously injured. In May rocket attacks, attributed to the November 17 Revolutionary Organization, were launched on the residences of the Dutch and German ambassadors to Greece and on three foreign banks in Athens. The murder of the British defence attaché, Brig. Stephen Saunders, in June 2000 was also attributed to November 17, which cited his alleged involvement in the co-ordination of the NATO action (see above). Public opinion in Greece was, in general, strongly opposed to the NATO bombardment and a planned three-day visit by US President Bill Clinton in November was reduced to a 24-hour visit, following a series of protests (including two bombing incidents). In 2001 the Greek Central Bank had increased measures to counter money 'laundering', amid international concern about the role of Greek banks in handling funds of the former President of Serbia and the FRY, Slobodan Milošević (who had been indicted by the International Criminal Tribunal for the former Yugoslavia—ICTY), and his associates. In early 2002 the Greek authorities agreed to provide ICTY war crimes investigators with records of transactions from bank accounts suspected of being connected with former members of Milošević's regime.

Attempts after 1991 by the FYRM to achieve international recognition as an independent state were strenuously opposed by the Greek Government, which insisted that 'Macedonia' was a purely geographical term (delineating an area that included a large part of northern Greece) and expressed fears that the adoption of such a name could imply ambitions on the Greek province of Macedonia and might foster a false claim to future territorial expansion. In early 1993 the Greek administration withdrew its former objection to the use of the word 'Macedonia', and its derivatives, as part of a fuller name for the new republic. At the end of March the Greek Government accepted a UN proposal that the title 'the former Yugoslav republic of Macedonia' should be used temporarily and agreed to hold direct talks with the FYRM to consider confidence-building measures. In late 1993 the newly elected PASOK Government strongly criticized recognition of the FYRM by several EU members and, despite assurances that it would adopt a more conciliatory attitude, in February 1994 the Government condemned a decision by the USA (the final permanent member of the UN Security Council to do so) to recognize the FYRM. At an emergency meeting in mid-February, the Cabinet agreed to prevent any movement of goods, other than humanitarian aid, into the FYRM via the Greek port of Thessaloníki. The initiative was widely criticized by the international community as effectively constituting an illegal trade embargo, and the EU ministers responsible for foreign affairs urged Greece to revoke the measures, which, it was determined, violated EU law. Intensive negotiations with the Greek authorities failed to resolve the issue and in mid-April the European Commission commenced legal proceedings against Greece at the Court of Justice of the European Communities. In April 1995 a preliminary opinion of the Court determined that the embargo was not in breach of Greece's obligations under the Treaty of Rome. In September the ministers responsible for foreign affairs of Greece and the FYRM, meeting in New York, under UN auspices, signed an interim accord to normalize relations between the two countries, which included recognition of the existing international border. Under the terms of the agreement, Greece was to grant access to the port facilities at Thessaloníki and to remove all obstructions to the cross-border movement of people and goods, while the FYRM was to approve a new state flag (removing the symbolic Vergina sun). The measures were successfully implemented by mid-October; a few days later agreement was concluded on the establishment of liaison offices in the two countries' capitals. Negotiations were to be pursued regarding the issue of a permanent name for the FYRM, which would be acceptable to both sides. In March 1997 the Greek Minister of Foreign Affairs visited the FYRM for the first time since its independence from Yugoslavia. In the first half of 2001 armed insurrection by ethnic Albanian militants of the self-styled National Liberation Army in the FYRM (q.v.) caused alarm in Greece, and there was international concern that Greek armed forces would intervene in any full-scale civil conflict in the FYRM. However, following the deployment of a NATO force in June (which was replaced by an EU-led mission in March 2003) and the signature of a peace agreement in August 2001, stability was gradually restored to the republic. Meanwhile, in 1999 work had commenced on the construction of a pipeline to carry petroleum from the FYRM's capital, Skopje, to Thessaloníki; the 214-km pipeline was inaugurated in early July 2002. Greece strongly objected to the decision by the US Administration, announced in November 2004, that it would henceforth recognize the FYRM by its constitutional name of 'the Republic of Macedonia', and UN-mediated negotiations on the issue continued in early 2005.

Government

Under the Constitution of June 1975, the President is Head of State and is elected by the Vouli (Parliament) for a five-year term. The President appoints the Prime Minister and, upon his recommendation, the other members of the Cabinet. In March 1986 the Vouli approved a series of constitutional amendments, divesting the President of his executive powers and transferring them to the legislature (see The Constitution). The unicameral Vouli has 300 members, directly elected by universal adult suffrage for four years. Greece comprises 13 regions, which are sub-divided into 54 administrative divisions (nomoi).

Defence

Greece returned to the military structure of the North Atlantic Treaty Organization (NATO, see p. 301) in 1980, after an absence of six years. Military service is compulsory for all men between 18 and 40 years of age, and lasts for up to 19 months. Women have the right to volunteer for military service of 30–50 days' basic training and for specialized training. In 1998 a law was passed providing for the conscription of women (for four days a year) to assist in the defence of the border regions. At 1 August 2004 the armed forces numbered 170,800, of whom 98,321 were conscripts, and included an army of 110,000 (with a national guard of 34,000), a navy of 19,000 and an air force of 30,200; in addition, there was a coast guard and customs force of 4,000. The USA occupied two military bases in Greece, with a total of 538 troops stationed there in August 2004. In 2003 reforms were introduced, with the aim of reducing the size of the armed forces to 90,000 by 2005. The duration of compulsory military service was to be reduced to 12 months, and many units were to be disbanded. Defence expenditure for 2003 was estimated at US $7,169m.

Economic Affairs

In 2003, according to estimates by the World Bank, Greece's gross national income (GNI), measured at average 2001–03 prices, was US $172,594m., equivalent to $13,720 per head (or $19,920 per head on an international purchasing-power parity basis). During 1990–2003, it was estimated, the population increased at an average annual rate of 0.4%, while gross domestic product (GDP) per head increased, in real terms, at an average annual rate of 2.4%. Overall GDP increased, in real terms, at an average annual rate of 2.8% in 1990–2003. Real GDP rose by 4.7% in 2003.

Agriculture (including hunting, forestry and fishing) contributed some 7.4% of GDP and engaged 15.8% of the employed labour force in 2002. The principal cash crops are fruit and vegetables (which, together, accounted for 10.4% of total export earnings in 2001), cereals, sugar beet and tobacco. Real agricultural GDP increased at an average annual rate of 0.9% in 1990–2002; however, the GDP of the agricultural sector declined by 0.2% in 2002.

Industry (including mining, manufacturing, utilities and construction) provided 22.4% of GDP and engaged 22.5% of the employed labour force in 2002. During 1990–2002 real industrial GDP increased at an average annual rate of 1.9%; the GDP of the industrial sector rose by 5.7% in 2002. Construction accounted for 7.8% of GDP in 2001.

Mining and quarrying contributed 0.7% of GDP in 2001, and engaged 0.5% of the employed labour force in 2002. Mineral fuels and lubricants, iron and steel, and aluminium and aluminium alloys are the major mineral and metal exports. Lignite, magnesite, silver ore and marble are also mined. In addition, Greece has small reserves of uranium and natural gas.

Manufacturing provided 13.4% of GDP in 2001, and engaged 13.7% of the employed labour force in 2002. The GDP of the manufacturing sector increased, in real terms, by an annual average of 0.6% in 1990–98; manufacturing production increased by an annual average of 1.6% in 1998–2002.

Energy is derived principally from lignite, which accounted for 66.8% of production in 2001, followed by petroleum (16.0%) and natural gas (11.6%). Greece is exploiting an offshore petroleum deposit in the north-eastern Aegean Sea. Solar power resources are also being developed. Mineral fuels represented 15.2% of the total value of imports in 2001.

The services sector contributed 70.3% of GDP and engaged 61.7% of the employed labour force in 2002. Tourism is an important source of foreign exchange. In 2002 visitor arrivals totalled 14.2m., while receipts from the tourist sector reached US $9,741m. (an increase of 5.6%, compared with the previous year). During 1990–2002 the GDP of the services sector increased, in real terms, at an average annual rate of 3.0%; sectoral GDP increased by 3.7% in 2002.

In 2003 Greece recorded a visible trade deficit of US $25,606m., and there was a deficit of $11,225m. on the current account of the balance of payments. In 2001 the principal source of imports was Germany (13.9%), closely followed by Italy (12.2%); other major sources were France (including Monaco), the Netherlands and the United Kingdom. The principal market for exports in that year was also Germany (11.3%); other major purchasers were Italy, the United Kingdom, the USA, Bulgaria and Cyprus. The principal exports in 2001 were basic manufactures (in particular, non-ferrous metals), miscellaneous manufactured articles (especially clothing and accessories), food and live animals, machinery and transport equipment, mineral fuels and lubricants, chemicals and crude materials. The principal imports were machinery and transport equipment (most notably road vehicles and parts), mineral fuels and lubricants (mainly petroleum and petroleum products), basic manufactures, chemicals, miscellaneous manufactured articles, and food and live animals.

According to revised government figures, the budgetary deficit was €5,276m. (equivalent to 3.7% of GDP) at September 2002 and €6,997m. (4.6% of GDP) at September 2003. Greece's total public external debt was estimated at €148,023m. at the end of 2002. In 1999 the cost of debt-servicing was equivalent to 9% of GDP. According to revised figures, total public debt was equivalent to 110% of GDP in 2003. In 1990–2003 the average annual rate of inflation was 6.0%; consumer prices increased by 3.6% in 2002 and by 3.5% in 2003. The official rate of unemployment was 10.1% at September 2004.

Greece is a member of the European Union (EU, see p. 217), the Organisation for Economic Co-operation and Development (OECD, see p. 307) and the Organization of the Black Sea Economic Co-operation (see p. 325).

From the second half of the 1990s the Government's priority was to ensure the admittance of Greece to EU economic and monetary union (EMU) by 2001. The budgetary deficit announced for 1999 met the target for EMU entry and in early 2000 an inflation rate of 2% was recorded, thereby qualifying Greece for full EMU membership from 1 January 2001. Greece thus became the 12th member country in the 'euro zone', and the common European currency, the euro, duly replaced the drachma as the country's legal tender from 1 January 2002. Although Greece failed to satisfy the further stipulated requirement that the ratio of government debt to GDP be less than 60%, the Government planned to achieve this objective by the end of the decade, and introduced a privatization programme to generate revenue. Improved relations with Turkey resulted in a project for the construction of an Ankara (Turkey)–Kotomini (Greece) pipeline (agreed in March 2002). The stabilization of the countries of the former Yugoslavia and the Balkans also provided Greece with an opportunity to expand its commercial influence in the region. However, the admission to the EU of several central and eastern European countries in May 2004 resulted in a reduction in EU transfers to Greece, as funds were to be diverted to new members. Higher than projected growth in 2003 was stimulated by construction activity relating to Greece's hosting of the Olympic Games in August 2004 and by EU structural aid. At legislative elections in March 2004 the socialist Government was removed from office by the centre-right New Democracy Party of Konstantinos Karamanlis. With the staging of the summer Olympic Games in August, investment growth and declining unemployment continued in that year, while the tourism industry also benefited (although security concerns were reported to have acted as a deterrent). Later that year evidence emerged that the previous administration had significantly understated budgetary deficit and public debt figures since 1999 in order to qualify for EMU membership. Substantial revisions of data indicated that the fiscal levels were considerably higher than presented, contravening the EU criteria since Greece's admission in 2001 and the Government undertook to conduct an immediate audit. The average rate of inflation remained among the highest in the 'euro zone'. Expenditure on the Olympic Games (which was estimated at some €9,000m., nearly twice the original budget) contributed to the poor fiscal situation. The Government pledged to reduce the budgetary deficit, principally through contained pension and public salary levels, to below the 'euro zone' maximum level of 3% by 2006 (which would enable Greece to avoid legal proceedings for the contraventions). The fiscal consolidation measures to be introduced were expected, however, to inhibit growth in subsequent years, while the increasing proportion of pensioners in the general population, with concomitant rising pension and health care costs, was a further source of long-term concern.

Education

Education is available free of charge at all levels, and is officially compulsory for all children between the ages of six and 15 years. Primary education begins at the age of six and lasts for six years. Secondary education, beginning at the age of 12, is generally for six years, divided into two equal cycles. The vernacular language (demotiki) has replaced the formal version (katharevoussa) in secondary education. Primary enrolment in 2001 included 97% of children in the relevant age-group (males 97%; females 97%), and the comparable ratio at secondary schools was 87% (males 86%; females 89%). In 2001 the equivalent of 63% of the relevant age-group were enrolled in tertiary education (males 60%; females 66%). There are 18 universities. In 2000, according to provisional data, budgetary expenditure on education was 1,440,000m. drachmae (representing 9.3% of total expenditure). In late 2004 it was announced that the Government planned to introduce reforms of the educational system, including extension of the period of compulsory education from nine to 12 years.

Public Holidays

2005: 1 January (New Year's Day), 6 January (Epiphany), 14 March (Clean Monday), 25 March (Independence Day), 29 April–2 May (Greek Orthodox Easter), 1 May (Labour Day), 20 June (Whit Monday), 15 August (Assumption of the Virgin Mary), 28 October ('Ochi' Day, anniversary of Greek defiance of Italy's 1940 ultimatum), 25–26 December (Christmas).

2006: 1 January (New Year's Day), 6 January (Epiphany), 6 March (Clean Monday), 25 March (Independence Day), 21–24 April (Greek Orthodox Easter), 1 May (Labour Day), 12 June (Whit Monday), 15 August (Assumption of the Virgin Mary), 28 October ('Ochi' Day, anniversary of Greek defiance of Italy's 1940 ultimatum), 25–26 December (Christmas).

Weights and Measures

The metric system is in force.

Statistical Survey

Source (unless otherwise stated): National Statistical Service of Greece, Odos Lykourgou 14–16, 101 66 Athens; tel. (1) 03289530; fax (1) 03241102; e-mail info@statistics.gr; internet www.statistics.gr.

Area and Population

AREA, POPULATION AND DENSITY

Area (sq km)	131,957*
Population (census results)†	
17 March 1991	10,259,900
March 2001	
Males	5,413,426
Females	5,520,671
Total	10,934,097
Population (official estimates at 1 January)	
2002	10,988,000
2003	11,018,400
Density (per sq km) at 1 January 2003	83.5

* 50,949 sq miles.
† Including armed forces stationed abroad, but excluding foreign forces stationed in Greece.

PRINCIPAL TOWNS
(population at 2001 census)

Athinai (Athens, the capital)	745,514	Larissa	126,076
Thessaloníki (Salonika) . . .	363,987	Volos	82,439
Piraeus	175,697	Kavala	63,293
Patras	163,446	Serres	56,145
Iráklion	137,711	Canea	53,373

Source: Thomas Brinkhoff, *City Population* (internet www.citypopulation.de).

BIRTHS, MARRIAGES AND DEATHS

	Registered live births Number	Rate (per 1,000)	Registered marriages Number	Rate (per 1,000)	Registered deaths Number	Rate (per 1,000)
1994 . .	103,763	9.9	56,813	5.4	97,807	9.4
1995 . .	101,495	9.7	63,987	6.1	100,158	9.6
1996 . .	100,718	9.6	45,408	4.3	100,740	9.6
1997 . .	102,038	9.7	60,535	5.8	99,738	9.5
1998 . .	100,894	9.6	55,489	5.3	102,668	9.8
1999 . .	116,038	11.0	61,848	5.9	104,190*	9.9*
2000 . .	117,140	11.7	63,585	6.4	105,219	10.5
2001 . .	102,282	10.2	57,000*	5.7	102,559*	10.2*

* Provisional figure.

Source: UN, *Demographic Yearbook*.

Expectation of life (WHO estimates, years at birth): 78.4 (males 75.8; females 81.1) in 2002 (Source: WHO, *World Health Report*).

ECONOMICALLY ACTIVE POPULATION
(sample surveys, '000 persons aged 15 years and over, April–June)*

	2000	2001	2002
Agriculture, hunting and forestry .	659.5	615.7	610.3
Fishing	11.2	11.3	13.6
Mining and quarrying . . .	16.5	17.8	18.9
Manufacturing	557.0	557.4	540.8
Electricity, gas and water supply .	38.1	34.3	33.7
Construction	276.6	284.8	293.9
Wholesale and retail trade; repair of motor vehicles, motorcycles and personal and household goods	677.9	673.2	674.6
Hotels and restaurants . . .	252.7	255.0	272.7
Transport, storage and communications	251.4	250.0	243.5
Financial intermediation . .	107.7	108.0	92.9
Real estate, renting and business activities	195.5	213.0	231.4
Public administration and defence; compulsory social security . .	293.1	290.3	294.0
Education	242.1	251.1	248.5
Health and social work . . .	183.7	177.8	179.6
Other community, social and personal service activities . .	128.4	126.8	147.6
Private households with employed persons	54.7	51.1	52.4
Extra-territorial organizations and bodies	0.2	n.a.	0.7
Total employed	3,946.3	3,917.5	3,948.9
Unemployed	491.1	444.7	420.1
Total labour force	4,437.4	4,362.2	4,369.0
Males	2,650.7	2,606.6	2,604.2
Females	1,786.7	1,755.7	1,764.8

* Including members of the regular armed forces, but excluding persons on compulsory military service.

Source: ILO.

Health and Welfare

KEY INDICATORS

Total fertility rate (children per woman, 2002)	1.3
Under-5 mortality rate (per 1,000 live births, 2003) . . .	5
HIV/AIDS (% of persons aged 15–49, 2003)	0.2
Physicians (per 1,000 head, 2001)	4.4
Hospital beds (per 1,000 head, 1999)	4.9
Health expenditure (2001): US $ per head (PPP)	1,522
Health expenditure (2001): % of GDP	9.4
Health expenditure (2001): public (% of total)	56.0
Human Development Index (2002): ranking	24
Human Development Index (2002): value	0.902

For sources and definitions, see explanatory note on p. vi.

Agriculture

PRINCIPAL CROPS
('000 metric tons)

	2001	2002	2003
Wheat	2,187.7	2,075.9	1,631.7
Rice (paddy)	150.2	168.7	175.0*
Barley	276.1	273.1	185.5
Maize	2,192.1	2,162.6	2,205.7
Rye	37.9	32.4	26.3
Oats	83.5	82.3	59.1
Potatoes	959.8	881.9	850.0*
Sugar beet	2,890.4	2,712.6	2,200.0
Dry beans	22.1	22.0	23.0*
Other pulses	12.3	12.0	12.0*
Almonds	55.3	37.3	33.9
Olives	2,249.4	2,573.8	2,050.3
Sunflower seed	22.8	23.0	14.0†
Cabbages	200.0	200.0†	200.0*
Tomatoes	1,819.9	1,882.5	1,800.0*
Cucumbers and gherkins . .	163.0	165.0	165.0*
Aubergines	79.0	80.0*	80.0*
Chillies and green peppers . .	98.4	95.5	95.0*
Dry onions	208.0	209.0	200.0*
Watermelons	644.2	633.0†	650.0*
Cantaloupes and other melons .	176.7	169.0	170.0*
Grapes	1,288.0	1,000.0*	1,200.0*
Apples	243.2	269.0	199.0
Pears	85.3	60.4	58.0
Peaches and nectarines . . .	927.1	739.6	1,300.0
Oranges	1,022.3	1,164.5	967.7
Tangerines, mandarins, clementines and satsumas . .	107.5	119.3	103.6
Lemons and limes	174.3	151.5	110.6
Apricots	68.5	74.7	66.8
Tobacco (leaves)	136.5	127.0	121.0†
Cotton (lint)†	374.0	333.1	359.0

* FAO estimate.
† Unofficial figure(s).

Source: FAO.

LIVESTOCK
('000 head, year ending 30 September)

	2001	2002	2003
Horses*	29	29	29
Mules*	30	29	28
Asses*	68	68	68
Cattle	568	559	573
Pigs	936	861	1,027
Sheep	9,269	9,205	8,932
Goats	5,180	5,450	5,468
Chickens*	28,000	28,000	28,000

* FAO estimates.

Source: FAO.

LIVESTOCK PRODUCTS
('000 metric tons)

	2001	2002	2003
Beef and veal	59.9	62.0	75.0*
Mutton and lamb	79.4	81.5	82.0*
Goat meat	42.8	44.6	44.5*
Pig meat	136.6	139.4	134.0†
Horse meat*	2.7	2.7	2.7
Poultry meat*	154.4	155.4	134.4
Other meat*	7.0	7.0	7.0
Cows' milk	757.8	795.0†	830.0†
Sheep's milk	753.3	735.5†	700.0†
Goats' milk	521.1	465.0†	456.5†
Cheese	243.6	250.6	244.1
Butter	3.7	4.2	3.7
Poultry eggs	110.2	107.1	105.6
Honey	17.6	14.9	15.1
Wool: greasy	9.5	9.6*	9.6*
Wool: scoured	5.8	5.8*	5.8*
Cattle hides*	11.6	12.1	14.7
Sheepskins*	16.3	16.3	16.3
Goatskins*	9.4	9.9	9.9

* FAO estimate(s).
† Unofficial figure.
Source: FAO.

Forestry

ROUNDWOOD REMOVALS
('000 cubic metres, excl. bark)

	2001	2002	2003
Sawlogs, veneer logs and logs for sleepers	410	409	528
Other industrial wood	105	89	71
Fuel wood	1,401	1,093	1,074
Total	1,916	1,591	1,673

Source: FAO.

SAWNWOOD PRODUCTION
('000 cubic metres, incl. railway sleepers)

	2001*	2002	2003
Coniferous (softwood)	71*	81	81
Broadleaved (hardwood)	52*	115	115
Total	123	196	196

Source: FAO.
* FAO estimates.

Fishing

('000 metric tons, live weight)

	2000	2001	2002
Capture	99.3	94.4	89.0
Freshwater fishes	2.9	2.7	2.5
Mediterranean horse mackerel	3.9	3.4	3.3
European pilchard (sardine)	16.0	14.4	14.0
European anchovy	9.9	10.8	10.5
Mediterranean mussel	0.5	0.3	0.3
Aquaculture	95.4	97.5	87.9
European seabass	26.7	25.3	23.9
Gilthead seabream	38.6	40.7	37.9
Mediterranean mussel	24.3	25.9	21.8
Total catch	194.7	191.9	176.9

Note: Figures exclude aquatic plants and aquatic mammals.
Source: FAO, *Yearbook of Fishery Statistics*.

Mining

('000 metric tons, unless otherwise indicated)

	2000	2001	2002*
Lignite	64,026	66,987	65,000
Crude petroleum ('000 barrels)	2,093	1,435	1,500
Iron ore*†	575	575	575
Bauxite	1,966	1,931	2,052
Zinc concentrates	20.3	20.5	30.0
Lead concentrates	18.2	28.6	29.3
Silver ore (metric tons)†	37.1	61.5	74.8
Magnesite	443	483	500
Salt (unrefined)	245	250	250
Bentonite	1,149	1,150	1,150
Kaolin	54	55	55
Gypsum	801	820	800
Marble ('000 cu m)	191	200	200
Natural gas ('000 barrels)*	350	350	350

* Estimate(s).
† Figures refer to the metal content of ores and concentrates.
Source: US Geological Survey.

Industry

SELECTED PRODUCTS
('000 metric tons, unless otherwise indicated)

	1999	2000	2001
Edible fats	38.9	39.6	n.a.
Olive oil (crude)	432	463	481
Raw sugar	252	400	342
Wine ('000 hectolitres)	1,485	1,475	1,470
Beer ('000 hectolitres)	4,129	4,223	4,502
Cigarettes (million)	34,322	34,381	33,256
Cotton yarn (metric tons)	107,800	106,900	109,600
Woven cotton fabrics—pure and mixed (metric tons)	3,000	3,000	3,000
Wool yarn (metric tons)	4,700	4,600	4,800
Yarn of artificial material (metric tons)	2,500	2,600	3,400
Leather footwear ('000 pairs)	2,636	2,585	3,867
Wrapping and packaging paper and paperboard	394	235	235
Sulphuric acid	911	966	515
Polyvinyl chloride	112.2	117.7	74.0
Liquefied petroleum gas	553	766	n.a.
Naphthas	885	1,036	n.a.
Motor spirit (petrol)	3,205	3,758	n.a.
Jet fuels	1,900	2,087	n.a.
Distillate fuel oils	4,866	5,647	n.a.
Residual fuel oils	6,326	7,510	6,959
Cement	13,624	14,147	15,563
Crude steel (incl. alloys)	960	1,056*	1,000*
Aluminium (unwrought)	160.8	168.0*	163.0*
Electric energy (million kWh)	49,855	49,296	n.a.

* Source: US Geological Survey.
Source: UN, *Industrial Commodity Statistics Yearbook*.

Finance

CURRENCY AND EXCHANGE RATES

Monetary Units
100 cent = 1 euro (€)

Sterling, Dollar and Euro Equivalents (31 December 2004)
£1 sterling = 1.4180 euros;
US $1 = 0.7342 euros;
100 euros = £70.52 = $136.21.

Average Exchange Rate (euros per US $)
2001	1.1175
2002	1.0626
2003	0.8860

Note: The national currency was formerly the drachma. Greece became a member of the euro area on 1 January 2001, after which a fixed exchange rate of €1 = 340.75 drachmae was in operation. Euro notes and coins were introduced on 1 January 2002. The euro and local currency circulated alongside each other until 28 February, after which the euro became the sole legal tender. Some of the figures in this Survey are still in terms of drachmae.

BUDGET
('000 million drachmae)*

Revenue	1998	1999	2000†
Ordinary budget	9,498.4	10,592.9	11,650.0
Tax revenue	8,839.7	9,897.3	10,890.2
Direct taxes	3,591.3	4,043.5	4,527.0
Personal income tax . . .	1,587.0	1,825.3	1,780.0
Corporate income tax . .	1,018.3	1,136.7	1,550.0
Indirect taxes	5,248.2	5,853.8	6,363.2
Consumption taxes . . .	1,856.1	1,909.0	1,895.0
Transaction taxes . . .	3,251.0	3,778.6	4,276.0
Value-added tax . . .	2,723.3	2,987.5	3,380.0
Stamp duty	292.5	288.9	301.0
Non-tax revenue	658.7	695.6	759.8
Capital receipts	378.2	400.9	442.0
Investment budget	914.0	1,010.0	1,200.0
Receipts from European Union .	891.0	977.0	1,130.0
SAGAP‡	793.0	806.0	895.0
Total	11,205.4	12,408.9	13,745.0

Expenditure	1998	1999†	2000†
Defence	1,018	1,053	1,186
Education	1,217	1,402	1,440
Health, social welfare and			
insurance	2,229	2,194	2,424
Agriculture	1,242	1,256	1,416
Interest payments§	3,024	3,123	3,165
Other purposes	4,602	5,304	5,779
Total§	13,331	14,332	15,410
Ordinary budget	10,661	11,276	11,995
Investment budget	1,877	2,250	2,520
SAGAP‡	793	806	895

* Figures refer to the budgetary transactions of the central Government, excluding the operations of social security funds and public entities (such as hospitals, educational institutions and government agencies) with individual budgets.
† Provisional.
‡ Special Account for Guarantees of Agricultural Products.
§ Excluding capitalized interest ('000 million drachmae): 27 in 1998.

Source: IMF, *Greece: Selected Issues and Statistical Appendix* (April 2001).

INTERNATIONAL RESERVES
(US $ million at 31 December)*

	2001	2002	2003
Gold†	1,090.0	1,348.7	1,439.9
IMF special drawing rights . .	9.7	15.1	21.4
Reserve position in IMF . . .	357.3	438.4	496.7
Foreign exchange	4,787.2	7,629.3	3,843.3
Total	6,244.2	9,431.5	5,801.3

* Figures exclude deposits made with the European Monetary Institute.
† Gold reserves are valued at market-related prices.

Source: IMF, *International Financial Statistics*.

MONEY SUPPLY
(€ '000 million at 31 December)

	2001	2002	2003
Currency in circulation* . . .	8.71	9.21	10.65
Demand deposits	70.81	71.71	79.45
Total money	79.52	80.92	90.10

* Currency put into circulation by the Bank of Greece (€ '000 million): 8.71 in 2001; 9.21 in 2002; 10.65 in 2003.

Source: IMF, *International Financial Statistics*.

COST OF LIVING
(Consumer Price Index; base: 1990 = 100)

	2000	2001	2002
Food	215.6	226.6	238.8
Fuel and light	173.8	174.1	177.2
Clothing	233.4	241.2	249.8
Rent	330.8	343.9	360.9
All items (incl. others)	242.4	250.7	259.6

Source: ILO.

NATIONAL ACCOUNTS
(€ '000 million at current prices)*

Expenditure on the Gross Domestic Product

	2001	2002	2003
Government final consumption			
expenditure	22.0	24.2	23.6
Private final consumption			
expenditure	89.2	94.8	102.2
Increase in stocks	−0.1	0.2	0.1
Gross fixed capital formation . .	31.3	33.8	40.0
Total domestic expenditure .	142.4	153.0	165.9
Exports of goods and services . .	31.2	29.5	30.5
Less Imports of goods and services	42.4	41.5	42.7
GDP in purchasers' values . .	131.3	141.5	153.0
GDP at constant 1995 prices .	98.7	102.3	106.9

Source: IMF, *International Financial Statistics*.

Gross Domestic Product by Economic Activity

	1999	2000	2001
Agriculture, hunting, forestry and			
fishing	8.1	8.0	8.4
Mining and quarrying	0.6	0.7	0.7
Manufacturing	11.6	12.4	13.4
Electricity, gas and water . . .	2.1	2.1	2.3
Construction	7.4	7.9	9.3
Wholesale and retail trade . . .	13.8	15.6	17.1
Hotels and restaurants	7.8	7.9	8.7
Transport, storage and			
communication	7.3	8.7	9.7
Financial intermediation† . . .	5.3	5.6	5.9
Real estate, renting and business			
activities	17.5	19.2	20.4
Public administration and defence	7.2	7.7	8.2
Education	5.0	5.4	5.7
Health and social work	5.5	5.7	6.2
Other services	2.7	2.7	3.3
Private households with employed			
persons	0.4	0.4	0.4
Sub-total	102.3	110.2	119.1
Less Financial intermediation			
services indirectly measured	3.4	3.9	4.5
Gross value added in basic			
prices	98.8	106.3	114.6
Indirect taxes, *less* subsidies . .	14.0	15.4	16.4
GDP in market prices . . .	112.9	121.6	130.9

* Totals may not be equal to the sum of components, owing to rounding.
† Including imputed rents of owner-occupied dwellings.
Source: UN, *National Accounts Statistics*.

GDP at constant 1995 prices (€ '000 million): 98.7 in 2001; 102.3 in 2002; 106.9 in 2003 (Source: IMF, *International Financial Statistics*).

BALANCE OF PAYMENTS
(US $ million)

	2001	2002	2003
Exports of goods f.o.b.	10,615	9,868	12,578
Imports of goods f.o.b.	−29,702	−31,320	−38,184
Trade balance	**−19,087**	**−21,452**	**−25,606**
Exports of services	19,456	20,223	24,286
Imports of services	−11,589	−10,677	−11,253
Balance on goods and services	**−11,220**	**−11,906**	**−12,573**
Other income received	1,885	1,530	1,769
Other income paid	−3,652	−3,487	−4,693
Balance on goods, services and income	**−12,987**	**−13,863**	**−15,497**
Current transfers received	4,592	4,901	7,202
Current transfers paid	−1,005	−1,443	−2,930
Current balance	**−9,400**	**−10,405**	**−11,225**
Capital account (net)	2,153	1,522	1,411
Direct investment abroad	−611	−669	−9
Direct investment from abroad	1,585	53	717
Portfolio investment assets	−474	−1,893	−9,807
Portfolio investment liabilities	9,012	12,315	23,456
Financial derivatives liabilities	74	−176	111
Other investment assets	−1,539	−6,953	−4,413
Other investment liabilities	−7,511	8,896	−3,887
Net errors and omissions	1,011	−828	−1,076
Overall balance	**−5,699**	**1,863**	**−4,722**

Sources: IMF, *International Financial Statistics*.

External Trade

PRINCIPAL COMMODITIES
(US $ million)

Imports c.i.f.	1999	2000	2001
Food and live animals	3,197.3	2,727.4	2,642.9
Meat and meat preparations	765.3	685.0	623.7
Crude materials (inedible) except fuels	732.5	707.0	719.3
Mineral fuels, lubricants, etc.	1,694.5	4,013.2	4,294.7
Petroleum, petroleum products, etc.	1,540.3	3,739.9	3,930.6
Crude petroleum oils, etc.	1,006.2	3,015.0	3,323.4
Chemicals and related products	3,602.7	3,414.9	3,416.0
Medicinal and pharmaceutical products	1,193.3	1,133.2	1,160.6
Medicaments (incl. veterinary medicaments)	1,016.4	974.7	1,003.4
Basic manufactures	4,675.5	4,566.0	4,227.4
Textile yarn, fabrics, etc.	1,040.4	859.2	811.2
Iron and steel	729.1	838.9	777.4
Machinery and transport equipment	11,787.7	10,195.6	8,882.6
Machinery specialized for particular industries	1,076.2	676.4	559.5
General industrial machinery equipment and parts	1,325.1	1,177.8	1,049.2
Telecommunications and sound equipment	1,406.1	1,293.4	1,087.4
Other electrical machinery apparatus, etc.	1,179.3	1,101.4	1,096.1
Road vehicles and parts*	3,414.4	2,841.6	2,163.3
Passenger motor cars (excl. buses)	2,121.4	1,886.1	1,297.4
Other transport equipment*	1,969.5	1,820.8	1,869.1
Ships, boats and floating structures	1,047.3	1,568.3	1,133.2
Miscellaneous manufactured articles	3,780.1	3,386.4	3,283.7
Clothing and accessories (excl. footwear)	1,070.3	1,005.3	990.1
Total (incl. others)	30,434.5	29,816.0	28,184.0

* Excluding tyres, engines and electrical parts.

Exports f.o.b.	1999	2000	2001
Food and live animals	1,838.1	1,596.3	1,712.1
Vegetables and fruit	1,117.6	999.2	1,070.0
Fresh or dried fruit and nuts (excl. oil nuts)	477.9	417.5	476.4
Preserved fruit and fruit preparations	268.1	292.7	283.0
Beverages and tobacco	640.8	513.5	462.2
Tobacco and manufactures	502.6	393.6	347.5
Unmanufactured tobacco (incl. refuse)	360.1	264.0	224.7
Crude materials (inedible) except fuels	637.3	594.8	555.5
Textile fibres and waste	358.3	313.1	280.5
Cotton	350.8	305.0	271.0
Raw cotton (excl. linters)	333.2	289.4	253.2
Mineral fuels, lubricants, etc.	1,004.9	1,611.8	1,147.9
Petroleum, petroleum products, etc.	974.9	1,527.7	1,089.9
Refined petroleum products	830.4	1,373.6	983.2
Animal and vegetable oils, fats and waxes	563.0	247.0	242.0
Fixed vegetable oils and fats	556.6	243.4	239.0
Soft fixed vegetable oils	555.8	241.8	237.8
Olive oil	535.9	226.5	225.8
Chemicals and related products	753.0	837.9	888.2
Basic manufactures	2,069.8	1,965.7	2,087.0
Textile yarn, fabrics, etc.	471.4	406.7	384.7
Non-metallic mineral manufactures	358.0	328.4	319.6
Lime, cement, etc.	259.9	246.3	253.8
Non-ferrous metals	594.1	640.0	724.3
Aluminium	441.1	455.3	537.6
Worked aluminium and aluminium alloys	337.1	367.9	520.1
Machinery and transport equipment	1,166.8	1,314.9	1,178.8
Electrical machinery, apparatus etc.	312.1	328.6	334.5
Miscellaneous manufactured articles	2,175.4	1,937.1	1,834.9
Clothing and accessories (excl. footwear)	1,682.7	1,405.3	1,323.8
Total (incl. others)	11,035.1	10,964.5	10,302.9

Source: UN, *International Trade Statistics Yearbook*.

PRINCIPAL TRADING PARTNERS
(US $ million)*

Imports c.i.f.	1999	2000	2001
Austria	314.0	249.4	227.2
Belgium	1,090.5	817.9	820.6
Bulgaria	357.2	398.8	418.9
China, People's Republic	556.5	699.4	834.2
Denmark	388.5	305.1	343.2
Egypt	189.7	142.9	100.5
Finland	405.1	452.3	281.6
France (incl. Monaco)	2,696.6	2,153.4	1,782.6
Germany	4,710.3	3,812.9	3,916.6
Iran	455.8	1,166.1	958.5
Italy	4,781.9	3,855.6	3,446.9
Japan	1,297.5	1,179.0	855.2
Korea, Republic	955.8	1,110.8	847.9
Netherlands	1,961.6	1,734.8	1,578.9
Russia	523.1	1,094.5	1,568.7
Saudi Arabia	290.4	949.1	1,039.6
Spain	1,065.5	1,018.0	942.3
Sweden	573.4	550.0	412.0
Switzerland	523.4	413.3	437.7
Turkey	374.2	396.1	488.7
United Kingdom	1,963.0	1,482.5	1,261.9
USA	1,493.4	1,022.5	982.2
Total (incl. others)	30,434.5	29,816.0	28,184.0

Exports f.o.b.	1999	2000	2001
Albania	223.8	248.8	347.4
Austria	122.6	91.6	68.2
Belgium	191.4	154.2	104.1
Bulgaria	415.7	450.5	564.2
Cyprus	412.9	509.4	531.7
Egypt	88.8	109.7	81.3
France (incl. Monaco)	476.1	374.1	379.4
Germany	1,823.2	1,345.7	1,163.9
Israel	119.1	185.6	123.3
Italy	1,527.1	1,011.1	870.0
Lebanon	105.7	145.3	76.0
Macedonia, former Yugoslav republic	426.9	470.8	407.8
Malta	112.1	136.4	151.8
Netherlands	333.3	316.8	253.4
Romania	213.4	384.3	353.5
Russia	245.1	249.2	287.3
Spain	353.7	334.7	331.7
Sweden	136.1	136.1	98.0
Turkey	336.1	550.3	349.9
Ukraine	46.0	42.1	45.2
United Kingdom	740.6	691.8	817.0
USA	597.4	638.2	567.0
Yugoslavia	110.9	131.4	183.1
Total (incl. others)	11,035.1	10,964.5	10,302.9

* Imports by country of first consignment; exports by country of consumption.

Source: UN, *International Trade Statistics Yearbook*.

Transport

RAILWAYS
(estimated traffic)

	1998	1999	2000
Passenger-kilometres (million)	1,552	1,453	1,629
Net ton-kilometres (million)	322	347	427

ROAD TRAFFIC
(motor vehicles in use at 31 December)

	1999	2000	2001*
Passenger cars	2,928,881	3,195,065	3,423,704
Buses and coaches	26,769	27,037	27,115
Lorries and vans	1,023,987	1,057,422	1,085,811
Motorcycles	710,755	781,361	853,366

* Estimates.

SHIPPING

Merchant Fleet
(registered at 31 December)

	2001	2002	2003
Number of vessels	1,529	1,548	1,558
Total displacement ('000 grt)	28,678.2	28,782.8	32,203.1

Source: Lloyd's Register-Fairplay, *World Fleet Statistics*.

International Sea-borne Freight Traffic
('000 metric tons)

	1998	1999	2000
Goods loaded	19,356	20,748	21,384
Goods unloaded	38,700	40,332	40,164

Source: UN, *Monthly Bulletin of Statistics*.

CIVIL AVIATION
(traffic on scheduled services)

	1999	2000	2001
Kilometres flown (million)	75	90	95
Passengers carried ('000)	6,267	7,937	8,430
Passenger-kilometres (million)	8,306	9,841	9,801
Total ton-kilometres (million)	899	1,067	1,029

Source: UN, *Statistical Yearbook*.

Tourism

TOURISTS BY COUNTRY OF ORIGIN
(foreign citizens, excl. cruise passengers)

Country	2000	2001	2002
Austria	474,996	495,928	461,672
Belgium-Luxembourg	331,942	393,062	358,010
Denmark	338,603	365,847	342,966
France	602,353	726,816	735,568
Germany	2,395,185	2,345,440	2,510,849
Italy	823,245	889,925	805,008
Netherlands	655,285	715,926	721,413
Norway	314,224	190,934	181,383
Sweden	485,749	516,857	465,772
Switzerland	322,575	299,384	220,476
United Kingdom	2,772,256	2,932,342	2,858,360
USA	218,731	164,689	146,754
Yugoslavia	158,670	160,471	190,814
Total (incl. others)	13,095,545	14,057,035	14,179,999

Receipts (US $ million): 8,783 in 1999; 9,221 in 2000; 9,741 in 2002.

Source: World Tourism Organization, *Yearbook of Tourism Statistics*.

Communications Media

	2001	2002	2003
Television receivers ('000 in use)	5,500	n.a.	n.a.
Telephones ('000 main lines in use)	5,607.7	5,412.8	5,205.1
Mobile cellular telephones ('000 subscribers)	7,962.0	9,314.3	8,936.2
Personal computers ('000 in use)	860	900	n.a.
Internet users ('000)	1,400.0	1,704.9	1,718.4

Radio receivers ('000 in use): 5,020 in 1997.

Facsimile machines ('000 in use, estimate): 40,000 in 1996.

Daily newspapers (1997): Number 207; Average circulation ('000 copies) 1,389.

Books (titles published): 4,225 in 1996.

Sources: UN, *Statistical Yearbook*, UNESCO, *Statistical Yearbook*, and International Telecommunication Union.

Education

(2001/02, unless otherwise indicated)

	Institutions	Teachers	Students
Pre-primary	5,694*	n.a.	144,055
Primary	6,074	49,842	647,041
Secondary: General	3,244	54,123	589,669
Secondary: Technical, vocational and ecclesiastical†	669	15,270	157,217
Higher: Universities†	18	10,149	148,772
Higher: Technical, vocational and ecclesiastical†	74	8,902	91,564

* In addition there were 10,211 kindergartens.
† Figures for 2000/01.

Adult literacy rate (UNESCO estimates): 97.3% (males 98.6%; females 96.1%) in 2002 (Source: UN Development Programme, *Human Development Report*).

Directory

The Constitution

A new Constitution for the Hellenic Republic came into force on 11 June 1975. The main provisions of this Constitution, as subsequently amended, are summarized below.

Greece shall be a parliamentary democracy with a President as Head of State. All powers are derived from the people and exist for the benefit of the people. The established religion is that of The Eastern Orthodox Church of Christ.

EXECUTIVE AND LEGISLATIVE

The President

In March 1986 a series of amendments to the Constitution was approved by a majority vote of Parliament, which relieved the President of his executive power and transferred such power to the legislature, thus confining the Head of State to a largely ceremonial role.

The President is elected by Parliament for a period of five years. The re-election of the same person shall be permitted only once. The President represents the State in relations with other nations, is Supreme Commander of the armed forces and may declare war and conclude treaties. The President shall appoint the Prime Minister and, on the Prime Minister's recommendation, the other members of the Government. The President shall convoke the Vouli (Parliament) once every year and in extraordinary session whenever he deems it reasonable. In exceptional circumstances the President may preside over the Cabinet, convene the Council of the Republic, and suspend the Vouli for a period not exceeding 30 days. The President can dissolve the Vouli only if the resignation of two Governments in quick succession demonstrates the absence of political stability. If no party has a majority in the Vouli, the President must offer an opportunity to form a government to the leader of each of the four biggest parties in turn, strictly following the order of their parliamentary strengths. If no party leader is able to form a government, the President may try to assemble an all-party government; failing that, the President must appoint a caretaker cabinet, led by a senior judge, to hold office until a fresh election takes place. The Constitution continues to reserve a substantial moderating role for the President, however, in that he retains the right to object to legislation and may request the Vouli to reconsider it or to approve it with an enlarged majority.

The Government

The Government consists of the Cabinet which comprises the Prime Minister and Ministers. The Government determines and directs the general policy of the State in accordance with the Constitution and the laws. The Cabinet must enjoy the confidence of the Vouli and may be removed by a vote of no confidence. The Prime Minister is to be the leader of the party with an absolute majority in the Vouli, or, if no such party exists, the leader of the party with a relative majority.

The Council of the Republic

The Council of the Republic shall be composed of all former democratic Presidents, the Prime Minister, the leader of the Opposition and the parliamentary Prime Ministers of governments which have enjoyed the confidence of the Vouli, presided over by the President. It shall meet when the largest parties are unable to form a government with the confidence of the Vouli and may empower the President to appoint a Prime Minister who may or may not be a member of the Vouli. The Council may also authorize the President to dissolve the Vouli.

Vouli

The Vouli (Parliament) is to be unicameral and composed of not fewer than 200 and not more than 300 deputies elected by direct, universal and secret ballot for a term of four years. the Vouli shall elect its own President, or Speaker. It must meet once a year for a regular session of at least five months. Bills passed by the Vouli must be ratified by the President and the President's veto can be nullified by an absolute majority of the total number of deputies. The Vouli may impeach the President by a motion signed by one-third and passed by two-thirds of the total number of deputies. The Vouli is also empowered to impeach present or former members of the Government. In these cases the defendant shall be brought before an *ad hoc* tribunal presided over by the President of the Supreme Court and composed of 12 judges. Certain legislative work, as specified in the Constitution, must be passed by the Vouli in plenum, and the Vouli cannot make a decision without an absolute majority of the members present, which under no circumstances shall be less than one-quarter of the total number of deputies. The Constitution provides for certain legislative powers to be exercised by not more than two Parliamentary Departments. The Vouli may revise the Constitution in accordance with the procedure laid down in the Constitution.

THE JUDICIAL AUTHORITY

Justice is to be administered by courts of regular judges, who enjoy personal and functional independence. The President, after consultations with a judicial council, shall appoint the judges for life. The judges are subject only to the Constitution and the laws. Courts are divided into administrative, civil and penal and shall be organized by virtue of special laws. They must not apply laws which are contrary to the Constitution. The final jurisdiction in matters of judicial review rests with a Special Supreme Tribunal.

Certain laws, passed before the implementation of this Constitution and deemed not contrary to it, are to remain in force. Other specified laws, even if contrary to the Constitution, are to remain in force until repealed by further legislation.

INDIVIDUAL AND SPECIAL RIGHTS

All citizens are equal under the Constitution and before the law, having the same rights and obligations. No titles of nobility or distinction are to be conferred or recognized. All persons are to enjoy full protection of life, honour and freedom, irrespective of nationality, race, creed or political allegiance. Retrospective legislation is prohibited and no citizen may be punished without due process of law. Freedom of speech, of the Press, of association and of religion are guaranteed under the Constitution. All persons have the right to a free education, which the state has the duty to provide. Work is a right and all workers, irrespective of sex or other distinction, are entitled to equal remuneration for rendering services of equal value. The right of peaceful assembly, the right of a person to property and the freedom to form political parties are guaranteed under the Constitution. The exercise of the right to vote by all citizens over 18 years of age is obligatory. No person may exercise his rights and liberties contrary to the Constitution.

MOUNT ATHOS

The district of Mount Athos shall, in accordance with its ancient privileged status, be a self-governing part of the Greek State and its sovereignty shall remain unaffected.

The Government

HEAD OF STATE

President: Karolos Papoulias (inaugurated 12 March 2005).

THE CABINET
(April 2005)

Prime Minister: Dr Konstantinos (Costas) Karamanlis.

Minister of State: Theodoros Roussopoulos.

Minister of the Economy and Finance: Georgios Alogoskoufis.

Minister of Foreign Affairs: Petros Molyviatis.

Minister of National Defence: Spilios Spiliotopoulos.

Minister of the Interior, Public Administration and Decentralization: Prokopis Pavlopoulos.

Minister of Development: Dimitris Sioufas.

Minister of the Environment, Physical Planning and Public Works: Georgios Souflias.

Minister of Education and Religious Affairs: Marietta Giannakou.

Minister of Labour and Social Security: Panos Panagiotopoulos.

Minister of Health and Welfare: Nikitas Kaklamanis.

Minister of Agricultural Development and Food: Savas Tsitouridis.

Minister of Justice: Anastasios Papaligouras.

Minister of Culture: Dr Konstantinos (Costas) Karamanlis.

Minister of Transport and Communications: Michalis Liapis.

Minister of Public Order: GEORGIOS VOULGARAKIS.

Minister of Merchant Marine: MANOLIS KEFALOGIANNIS.

Minister of Macedonia and Thrace: NIKOS TSIARTSIONIS.

Minister of the Aegean: ARISTOTELIS PAVLIDIS.

Minister of Tourism: DIMITRIOS AVRAMOPOULOS.

MINISTRIES

Office of the President: Odos Vas. Georgiou 7, 106 74 Athens; tel. (21) 07283111; fax (21) 07248938.

Office of the Prime Minister: Maximos Mansion, Herodou Atticou 19, 106 74 Athens; tel. (21) 03385282; fax (21) 07240762; e-mail mail@primeminister.gr; internet www.primeminister.gr.

Ministry of the Aegean: Filellinon 9, 105 57 Athens; tel. (21) 03311714; fax (21) 03227544; e-mail athens1@ypai.gr; internet www.ypai.gr.

Ministry of Agricultural Development and Food: Odos Acharnon 5, 104 32 Athens; tel. (21) 02124000; fax (21) 05240475; e-mail webmaster@minagric.gr; internet www.minagric.gr.

Ministry of Culture: Odos Bouboulinas 20–22, 106 82 Athens; tel. (21) 08201648; fax (21) 08201435; e-mail minister@culture.gr; internet www.culture.gr.

Ministry of Development: Odos Mihalakopoulou 80, 101 92 Athens; tel. (21) 07482770; fax (21) 07788279; internet www.ypan.gr.

Ministry of the Economy and Finance: Odos Nikis 5–7, 101 80 Athens; tel. (21) 03332000; e-mail ypetho@mnec.gr; internet www.ypetho.gr.

Ministry of Education and Religious Affairs: Odos Metropoleos 15, 101 85 Athens; tel. (21) 03230461; fax (21) 03248264; e-mail webmaster@ypepth.gr; internet www.ypepth.gr.

Ministry of the Environment, Physical Planning and Public Works: Odos Amaliados 17, 115 23 Athens; tel. (21) 06415700; fax (21) 06432589; e-mail minister@minenv.gr; internet www.minenv.gr.

Ministry of Foreign Affairs: Odos Akadimias 1, 106 71 Athens; tel. (21) 03681000; fax (21) 03624195; e-mail mfa@mfa.gr; internet www.mfa.gr.

Ministry of Health and Welfare: Odos Aristotelous 17, 104 33 Athens; tel. (21) 05232820; fax (21) 05231707; e-mail info@ypyp.gr; internet www.ypyp.gr.

Ministry of the Interior, Public Administration and Decentralization: Odos Stadiou 27, 101 83 Athens; tel. (21) 03223521; fax (21) 03240631; e-mail info@ypes.gr; internet www.ypes.gr.

Ministry of Justice: Odos Mesogeion 96, 115 27 Athens; tel. (21) 07711019; fax (21) 07759879; e-mail minjust@otenet.gr; internet www.ministryofjustice.gr.

Ministry of Labour and Social Security: Odos Pireos 40, 104 37 Athens; tel. (21) 05295000; fax (21) 05249805; e-mail postmaster@www.labor-ministry.gr; internet www.ypergka.gr.

Ministry of Macedonia and Thrace: Administration Bldg, 541 23 Thessaloníki; tel. (231) 0264321; fax (231) 0263332; e-mail webmaster@mathra.gr; internet www.mathra.gr.

Ministry of Merchant Marine: Odos Gregoriou Lambraki 150, Piraeus; tel. (21) 04121211; fax (21) 04134286; e-mail dopy_g@mail.yen.gr; internet www.yen.gr.

Ministry of National Defence: Odos Mesogeion 227–231, 154 51 Athens; tel. (21) 06598607; fax (21) 06443832; e-mail minister@mod.mil.gr; internet www.mod.gr.

Ministry of Public Order: P. Khanellopoulou 4, 101 77 Athens; tel. (21) 06977000; fax (21) 06921675; e-mail ydt@otenet.gr; internet www.ydt.gr.

Ministry of Transport and Communications: Odos Xenofontos 13, 101 91 Athens; tel. (21) 03251211; fax (21) 03239039; e-mail comm@yme.gr; internet www.yme.gr.

Legislature

Vouli
(Parliament)

Parliament Bldg, Syntagma Sq., 101 80 Athens; tel. (21) 03288434; fax (21) 03310013; e-mail infopar@parliament.gr; internet www.parliament.gr.

President: ANNA PSAROUDA-BENAKI.

General Election, 7 March 2004

Parties	Votes	% of votes	Seats
New Democracy Party	3,347,645	45.4	165
Panhellenic Socialist Movement	2,992,069	40.6	117
Communist Party	434,643	5.9	12
Coalition of the Left of Movements and Ecology	240,240	3.3	6
Others	363,661	4.9	—
Total	7,378,258	100.0	300

Political Organizations

Coalition of the Left of Movements and Ecology (Synaspismos Tis Aristeras Ton Kinimaton Kai Tis Oikologias): Pl. Elefthrias 1, 105 53 Athens; tel. (21) 03378400; fax (21) 03217003; e-mail intrelations@syn.gr; internet www.syn.gr; f. 1992 on the basis of an alliance (f. 1989) of the nine political groups comprising the Greek Left Party and the Communist Party of Greece ('of the Exterior'); present name adopted 2003; Pres. ALEXANDROS ALANANOS.

Communist Party of Greece (KKE) (Kommunistiko Komma Ellados): Leoforos Irakliou 145, Perissos, 142 31 Athens; tel. (21) 02592111; fax (21) 02592286; e-mail cpg@kke.gr; internet www.kke.gr; f. 1918; banned 1947, reappeared 1974; Gen. Sec. ALEKA PAPARIGA.

Democratic Social Movement (DIKKI): Odos Halkokondili 9, 106 77 Athens; tel. (21) 03829051; fax (21) 03839047; e-mail dikki@otenet.gr; internet www.dikki.gr; f. 1995; leftist; opposes further integration with the EU; Leader DIMITRIS TSOVOLAS.

Democratic Socialist Party (KODISO): Odos Mavromichali 9, 106 79 Athens; tel. (21) 03602716; fax (21) 03625901; f. 1979 by former EDIK deputies; favours membership of the EU and political wing of NATO, decentralization and a mixed economy; Pres. CH. PROTOPAPAS.

Greek National Political Union (EPEN): Athens; tel. (21) 03643760; fax (21) 08943100; f. 1984; right-wing; Leader CHRYSSANTHOS DIMITRIADIS.

Hellenic Liberal Party: Athens; tel. (21) 03606111; f. 1910; aims to revive political heritage of fmr Prime Minister Eleftherios Venizelos; 6,500 mems; Pres. NIKITAS VENIZELOS.

Liberal Party—The Bulls: Athens; e-mail admin@bulls.gr; internet www.liberals.gr; f. 1999; Founder STEFANOS MANOS.

New Democracy Party (ND) (Nea Demokratia): Odos Rhigillis 18, 106 74 Athens; tel. (21) 07290071; fax (21) 07214327; e-mail ir@nd.gr; internet www.nd.gr; f. 1974; broadly-based centre-right party advocating social reform in the framework of a liberal economy; supports European integration and enlargement; Pres. Dr KONSTANTINOS (COSTAS) KARAMANLIS; Sec. of the Central Committee VANGELIS MEIMARAKIS.

Panhellenic Socialist Movement (PASOK) (Panellinion Socialistikon Kinima): Odos Charilaou Trikoupi 50, Athens; tel. (21) 03232049; e-mail pasok@pasok.gr; internet www.pasok.gr; f. 1974; incorporates Democratic Defence and Panhellenic Liberation Movement resistance organizations; supports social welfare, decentralization and self-management, aims at a Mediterranean socialist development through international co-operation; 500 local organizations, 30,000 mems; Pres. GEORGIOS PAPANDREOU; Sec.-Gen. MICHALIS CHRISOCHOIDHIS.

Political Spring (POLAN) (Politiki Anixi): Patision 67, 104 34 Athens; tel. (21) 08228301; fax (21) 08210531; e-mail anixi@otenet.gr; f. 1993; centre-right; Leader ANTONIS C. SAMARAS.

Union of Democratic Centre Party (EDIK) (Enossi Dimokratikou Kentrou): Odos Charilaou Trikoupi 18, 106 79 Athens; tel. (21) 03609711; fax (21) 03612792; e-mail karabelas@edik.gr; internet www.edik.gr; f. 1974; democratic socialist party, merging Centre Union (f. 1961 by Georgios Papandreou) and New Political Forces (f. 1974 by Prof. Ioannis Pesmazoglou and Prof. G. A. Mangakis); favours a united Europe; Chair. Prof. NEOKLIS SARRIS; Sec.-Gen. KARABELAS STAVROS.

Diplomatic Representation

EMBASSIES IN GREECE

Albania: Odos Vekiareli 7, Filothei, 152 37 Athens; tel. (21) 06876200; fax (21) 06876223; e-mail albem@ath.forthnet.gr; Ambassador BASHKIM ZENELI.

Algeria: Leoforos Vassileos Konstantinou 14, 116 35 Athens; tel. (21) 07264191; fax (21) 07018681; e-mail ambdzath@otenet.gr; Ambassador AHMED BENYAMINA.

Argentina: Leoforos Vassilissis Sofias 59, 115 21 Athens; tel. (21) 07224753; fax (21) 07227568; e-mail egrecmrs@compulink.gr; Ambassador RAUL ALBERTO RICARDES.

Armenia: Leoforos Sygrou 159, 171 21 Athens; tel. (21) 09345727; fax (21) 09352187; e-mail armenia@hol.gr; Ambassador VAHRAN KAZ-GOIAN.

Australia: Thon Bldg, Odos Kifisias/Odos Alexandras, Ambelokipi, POB 14070, 115 10 Athens; tel. (21) 08704000; fax (21) 08704111; e-mail ae.athens@dfat.gov.au; internet www.ausemb.gr; Ambassador PAUL TIGHE.

Austria: Leoforos Alexandras 26, 106 83 Athens; tel. (21) 08257230; fax (21) 08219823; e-mail austria@ath.forthnet.gr; Ambassador Dr RENÉ POLLITZER.

Belgium: Odos Sekeri 3, 106 71 Athens; tel. (21) 03617886; fax (21) 03604289; e-mail athens@diplobel.org; internet www.diplomatie.be/athens; Ambassador PETER MOORS.

Bosnia and Herzegovina: Hatzikosta 3, 115 21 Athens; tel. (21) 06410788; fax (21) 06411978; Ambassador SRDJAN LJUBOJEVIĆ.

Brazil: Plateia Philikis Etairias 14, 106 73 Athens; tel. (21) 07213039; fax (21) 07244731; Ambassador ALCIDES DA COSTA GUI-MARĀES FILHO.

Bulgaria: Odos Stratigou Kallari 33A, Palaio Psychiko, 154 52 Athens; tel. (21) 06478105; fax (21) 06478130; Ambassador STEFAN STOYANOV.

Canada: Odos Ioannou Ghennadiou 4, 115 21 Athens; tel. (21) 07273400; fax (21) 07273480; e-mail athns@dfait-maeci.gc.ca; internet www.dfait-maeci.gc.ca/canadaeuropa/greece; Ambassador PHILIP SOMERVILLE.

Chile: Leoforos Vasilissis Sofias 25, 106 74 Athens; tel. (21) 07252574; fax (21) 07252536; e-mail embachilegr@ath.forthnet.gr; Ambassador MARCIA COVARRUBIAS.

China, People's Republic: Odos Krinon 2A, Palaio Psychiko, 154 52 Athens; tel. (21) 06723282; fax (21) 06723819; e-mail embchina@otenet.gr; Ambassador TANG ZHENQI.

Colombia: Vrasida 3, 115 28 Athens; tel. (21) 07236848; fax (21) 07246270; Ambassador ENRIQUE GAVIRIA-LIEVANO.

Congo, Democratic Republic: Athens; tel. (21) 06847013; Ambassador BOMOLO LOKOKA.

Croatia: Tzavela 4, Neo Psychiko, 154 51 Athens; tel. (21) 06777059; fax (21) 06711208; e-mail croatemb@hol.gr; Ambassador NEVEN MADEY.

Cuba: Odos Sofokleos 5, Filothei, 152 37 Athens; tel. (21) 06855550; fax (21) 06842907; e-mail embacuba@eexi.gr; Ambassador JORGE QUESADA CONCEPCIÓN.

Cyprus: Odos Herodotou 16, 106 75 Athens; tel. (21) 07232727; fax (21) 04536373; e-mail cyempkl@hol.gr; Ambassador LEONIDAS PAN-TELIDIS.

Czech Republic: Odos Georgiou Seferis 6, Palaio Psychiko, 154 52 Athens; tel. (21) 06713755; fax (21) 06710675; e-mail athens@embassy.mzv.cz; internet www.mzv.cz/athens; Ambassador JANA BULENOVÁ.

Denmark: Mourouzilo 10, 106 74 Athens; tel. (21) 07256440; fax (21) 07256473; e-mail athamb@athamb.um.dk; internet www.denmark.gr; Ambassador HANS GRUNNET.

Egypt: Leoforos Vassilissis Sofias 3, 106 71 Athens; tel. (21) 03618612; fax (21) 03603538; e-mail emthens@hol.gr; Ambassador Dr MAGDA SHAHIN.

Estonia: Patriarchou Ioakeim 48, 106 76 Athens; tel. (21) 07229803; fax (21) 07229804; e-mail estemb@otenet.gr; Ambassador ANDRES UNGA.

Finland: Odos Eratosthenous 1, 116 35 Athens; tel. (21) 07010444; fax (21) 07515064; e-mail sanomat.ate@formin.fi; internet www.finland.gr; Ambassador OLE NORRBACK.

France: Leoforos Vassilissis Sofias 7, 106 71 Athens; tel. (21) 03391000; fax (21) 03391009; e-mail ambafran@hol.gr; internet www.ambafrance-gr.org; Ambassador BRUNO DELAYE.

Georgia: Odos Agiou Dimitriou 24, 154 52 Palaio Psychiko, Athens; tel. (21) 06716737; fax (21) 06716722; e-mail embassygeo@hol.gr; Ambassador ZVIAD CHUMBURIDZE.

Germany: Odos Karaoli and Dimitriou 3, 106 75 Athens; tel. (21) 07285111; fax (21) 07251205; e-mail boathens@internet.gr; internet www.athen.diplo.de; Ambassador Dr ALBERT SPIEGEL.

Holy See: POB 65075, Odos Mavili 2, Palaio Psychiko, 154 52 Athens; tel. (21) 06722728; fax (21) 06742849; e-mail nunate@mail

.otenet.gr; Apostolic Nuncio Most Rev. PATRICK COVENEY (Titular Archbishop of Satriano).

Honduras: Leoforos Kifissias 74, 115 26 Athens; tel. (21) 06982021; fax (21) 06982080; e-mail hondugre@otenet.gr; Chargé d'affaires a.i. TEODOLINDA BANEGAS DE MAKRIS.

Hungary: Odos Kalvou 16, Palaio Psychiko, 154 52 Athens; tel. (21) 06725337; fax (21) 06740890; e-mail huembath@otenet.gr; Ambassador CSABA KOROSI.

India: Odos Kleanthous 3, 106 74 Athens; tel. (21) 07216227; fax (21) 07211252; e-mail indembassy@ath.forthnet.gr; Ambassador A. K. BANERJEE.

Indonesia: Odos Papanastasidu 55, Palaio Psychiko, 154 52 Athens; tel. (21) 06712737; fax (21) 06756955; Ambassador FRAN-CISCO LOPEZ DA CRUZ.

Iran: Odos Kalari 16, Palaio Psychiko, 154 52 Athens; tel. (21) 06471436; fax (21) 06477945; e-mail irembatn@compulik.gr; Ambassador MEHDI MOHTASHAMI.

Iraq: Odos Mazaraki 4, Palaio Psychiko, Athens; tel. (21) 0672330; fax (21) 06717185; e-mail atnemb@iraqmofamail.net; Ambassador AHMED ISMAEL IBRAHIM.

Ireland: Leoforos Vassileos 7, Konstantinou, Athens; tel. (21) 07232771; fax (21) 07240217; Ambassador MARGARET HENNESSY.

Israel: Odos Marathonodromou 1, Palaio Psychiko, 154 52 Athens; tel. (21) 06719530; fax (21) 06479510; e-mail info@athens.mfa.gov.il; Ambassador RAM IVIRAM.

Italy: Odos Sekeri 2, 106 74 Athens; tel. (21) 03617260; fax (21) 03617330; e-mail ambasciata.atene@esteri.it; Ambassador GIAN PAOLO CAVARAI.

Japan: 21st Floor, Athens A Tower, Leoforos Messoghion 2–4, Pirgas Athinon, 115 27 Athens; tel. (21) 07758101; fax (21) 07758206; internet www.gr.emb-japan.go.jp; Ambassador TOSHIO MOCHIZUKI.

Jordan: Odos Papadiamnti 21, Palaio Psychiko, 154 52 Athens; tel. (21) 06744161; fax (21) 06740578; e-mail jor_embl@otenet.gr; Ambassador AMJAD MAJALI.

Korea, Republic: Odos Eratosthenous 1, 116 35 Athens; tel. (21) 07012122; Ambassador TAE KYU HAN.

Kuwait: Odos Marathonodromou 27, Palaio Psychiko, 154 52 Athens; tel. (21) 06473593; fax (21) 06875875; Ambassador ALI FAHED AZ-ZAID.

Latvia: Odos Irodotou 9, Kolonaki, 106 74 Athens; tel. (21) 07294483; fax (21) 07294479; e-mail latvia@otenet.gr; Ambassador JĀNIS EICHMANIS.

Lebanon: 6, Odos Maritou 25, Palaio Psychiko, 154 52 Athens; tel. (21) 06755873; fax (21) 06755612; e-mail grlibemb@otenet.gr; Ambassador WILLIAM HABIB.

Libya: Odos Vironos 13, Palaio Psychiko, 154 52 Athens; tel. (21) 06472120; Secretary of the People's Bureau (Ambassador) AYAD M. TAYARI.

Malta: Leoforos Vassilissis Sofias 63, 115 21 Athens; tel. (21) 07258153; fax (21) 07258152; Ambassador EVARIST SALIBA.

Mexico: Plateia Philikis Etairias 14, 106 73 Athens; tel. (21) 07294780; fax (21) 07294783; e-mail embgrecia@sre.gob.mx; Ambassador ALEJANDRO DÍAZ Y PÉREZ DUARTE.

Morocco: Odos Marathonodromou 5, Palaio Psychiko, 154 52 Athens; tel. (21) 06744209; fax (21) 06749480; Ambassador MUHAMMAD LOFTI AOUAD.

Netherlands: Leoforos Vassileos Konstantinou 5–7, 106 74 Athens; tel. (21) 07239701; fax (21) 07248900; e-mail ath@minbuza.gr; internet www.dutchembassy.gr; Ambassador P. R. BROUWER.

New Zealand: Leoforos Kifissias 268, 152 32 Halandri, Athens; tel. (21) 06874700; fax (21) 06874444; e-mail costas.cotsilinis@gr.pwcglobal.com; Ambassador PETER BENNETT.

Nigeria: Odos Iakinthon 50, Palaio Psychiko, Athens; tel. (21) 06718007; fax (21) 06718008; Ambassador FRANKLIN NCHITA OGBUEWU.

Norway: Leoforos Vassilissis Sofias 23, 106 74 Athens; tel. (21) 07246173; fax (21) 07244989; e-mail norwemba@netplan.gr; Ambassador FINN FOSTERVELL.

Pakistan: Odos Loukianou 6, Kolonaki, 106 75 Athens; tel. (21) 07290122; fax (21) 07257641; e-mail info@pak-embassy.gr; internet www.pak-embassy.gr; Ambassador JAVED HAFIZ.

Panama: Akti Miaoyli 23, Athens; tel. (21) 04133180.

Peru: Semitelou 2, 115 28, Athens; tel. (21) 07792761; fax (21) 07792905; e-mail lepruate@compulink.gr; Ambassador BERTHA VEGA PÉREZ.

Philippines: Xenophodos 9, Athens; tel. (21) 03241615; Ambassador Lourdes G. Morales.

Poland: Odos Chryssanthemon 22, Palaio Psychiko, 154 52 Athens; tel. (21) 06797700; fax (21) 06797711; e-mail info@poland-embassy .gr; internet www.poland-embassy.gr; Ambassador Grzegorz Dziemidowicz.

Portugal: Leoforos Vassilissis Sofias 23, 106 74 Athens; tel. (21) 07290096; fax (21) 07245122; e-mail embportg@otenet.gr; Ambassador Carlos Neves Ferreira.

Romania: Odos Emmanuel Benaki 7, Palaio Psychiko, Athens; tel. (21) 06728875; fax (21) 06728883; e-mail bartha@ath.forthnet.gr; Ambassador Caius Träian Dragomir.

Russia: Odos Nikiforou Litra 28, Palaio Psychiko, 154 52 Athens; tel. (21) 06725235; fax (21) 06479708; Ambassador Andrei Vdovin.

Saudi Arabia: Odos Marathonodromou 71, Palaio Psychiko, 154 52 Athens; tel. (21) 06716911; Ambassador Sheikh Abdullah Abd ar-Rahman al-Malhooq.

Serbia and Montenegro: Leoforos Vassilissis Sofias 106, Athens 115 27; tel. (21) 07774344; e-mail beograd@hol.gr; internet www .embassyscg.gr; Ambassador Dusan Bataković.

Slovakia: Odos Georgiou Seferis 4, Palaio Psychiko, 154 52 Athens; tel. (21) 06771980; fax (21) 06771878; e-mail embassy@athens.mfa .sk.

South Africa: Leoforos Kifissias 60, 151 25 Athens; tel. (21) 06106645; fax (21) 06106640; e-mail embassy@southafrica.gr; internet www.southafrica.gr; Ambassador Jannie Momberg.

Spain: Odos D. Areapagitou 21, 117 42 Athens; tel. (21) 09213123; fax (21) 09214264; e-mail emb-esp@otenet.gr; Ambassador Javier Jiménez-Ugarte.

Sweden: Leoforos Vassileos Konstantinou 7, 106 74 Athens; tel. (21) 07266100; fax (21) 07266150; e-mail ambassaden.athens@foreign .ministry.se; internet www.swedenabroad.com/athen; Ambassador Mårten Grunditz.

Switzerland: Odos Iassiou 2, 115 21 Athens; tel. (21) 07230364; fax (21) 07249209; e-mail vertretung@ath.rep.admin.ch; internet www .eda.admin.ch/athens; Ambassador Pierre Monod.

Syria: Diamandidou 61, Palaio Psychiko, 154 52 Athens; tel. (21) 06725577; fax (21) 06716402; e-mail syrembas@otenet.gr; Ambassador Souad M. Al-Ayoubi.

Thailand: Odos Taigetou 23, Palaio Psychiko, 154 52 Athens; tel. (21) 06717969; fax (21) 06479508; Ambassador Precha Pitisant.

Tunisia: Odos Anthéon 2, Palaio Psychiko, 154 52 Athens; tel. (21) 06717590; fax (21) 06713432; e-mail tunisie@otenet.gr; Ambassador Muhammad Bachrouch.

Turkey: Odos Vassileos Gheorghiou B 8, 106 74 Athens; tel. (21) 07263000; fax (21) 07229597; e-mail turemgr@hotmail.com; Ambassador Tahsin Burcuoğlu.

Ukraine: Odos Stefanou Delta 2–4, 152 37 Athens; tel. (21) 06800230; fax (21) 06854154; e-mail ukrembas@otenet.gr; internet www.ukrembas.gr; Ambassador Viktor Kalnyk.

United Kingdom: Odos Ploutarchou 1, 106 75 Athens; tel. (21) 07272600; fax (21) 07272734; e-mail britania@hol.gr; internet www .british-embassy.gr; Ambassador Simon Gass.

USA: Leoforos Vassilissis Sofias 91, 106 60 Athens; tel. (21) 07212951; fax (21) 07226724; e-mail usembassy@usembassy.gr; internet www.usembassy.gr; Ambassador Charles P. Reis.

Uruguay: Odos Likavitou I G, 106 72 Athens; tel. (21) 03613549; Ambassador Ulysses Pereira Reverbel.

Venezuela: Leoforos Vassilissis, Sophias 112, Athens; tel. (21) 07708769; Ambassador Lisan Stredel Balliache.

Judicial System

The Constitution of 1975 provided for the establishment of a Special Supreme Tribunal. Other provisions in the Constitution provided for a reorganization of parts of the judicial system to be accomplished through legislation.

SUPREME ADMINISTRATIVE COURTS

Special Supreme Tribunal: Odos Patision 30, Athens; has final jurisdiction in matters of constitutionality.

Council of State
Odos Panepistimiou 47, 105 64 Athens; tel. (21) 03710098; fax (21) 03710097; e-mail s-epikr@otenet.gr.

Has appellate powers over acts of the administration and final rulings of administrative courts; has power to rule upon matters of judicial review of laws.

President: Christos G. Yeraris.

Supreme Civil and Penal Court
Leoforos Alexandros 121, 115 22 Athens; tel. (21) 06411506; fax (21) 06433799; e-mail areios@otenet.gr.

Supreme court in the State, having also appellate powers; consists of six sections, four Civil and two Penal, and adjudicates in quorum.

President: Stephanos Mathias.

COURTS OF APPEAL

There are 12 Courts of Appeal with jurisdiction in cases of Civil and Penal Law of second degree, and, in exceptional penal cases, of first degree.

COURTS OF FIRST INSTANCE

There are 59 Courts of First Instance with jurisdiction in cases of first degree, and in exceptional cases, of second degree. They function both as Courts of First Instance and as Criminal Courts. For serious crimes the Criminal Courts function with a jury.

In towns where Courts of First Instance sit there are also Juvenile Courts. Commercial Tribunals do not function in Greece, and all commercial cases are tried by ordinary courts of law. There are, however, Tax Courts in some towns.

OTHER COURTS

There are 360 Courts of the Justice of Peace throughout the country. There are 48 Magistrates' Courts (or simple Police Courts).

In all the above courts, except those of the Justice of Peace, there are District Attorneys. In Courts of the Justice of Peace the duties of District Attorney are performed by the Public Prosecutor.

Religion

CHRISTIANITY

The Eastern Orthodox Church

The Orthodox Church of Greece
Odos Ioannou Gennadiou 14, 115 21 Athens; tel. (21) 07218381; e-mail contact@ecclesia.gr; internet www.ecclesia.gr.

f. 1850; 78 dioceses, 8,335 priests, 84 bishops, 9,025,000 adherents (1985).

The Greek branch of the Holy Eastern Orthodox Church is the officially established religion of the country, to which nearly 97% of the population profess adherence. The administrative body of the Church is the Holy Synod of 12 members, elected by the bishops of the Hierarchy.

Primate of Greece: Archbishop of Athens and All Greece Christodoulos Paraskevaides.

Within the Greek State there is also the semi-autonomous Church of Crete, composed of seven Metropolitans and the Holy Archbishopric of Crete. The Church is administered by a Synod consisting of the seven Metropolitans under the Presidency of the Archbishop; it is under the spiritual jurisdiction of the Ecumenical Patriarchate of Constantinople (based in Istanbul, Turkey), which also maintains a degree of administrative control.

Archbishop of Crete: Archbishop Timotheos (whose See is in Heraklion).

There are also four Metropolitan Sees of the Dodecanese, which are spiritually and administratively dependent on the Ecumenical Patriarchate and, finally, the peninsula of Athos, which constitutes the region of the Holy Mountain (Mount Athos) and comprises 20 monasteries. These are dependent on the Ecumenical Patriarchate of Constantinople, but are autonomous and are safeguarded constitutionally.

The Roman Catholic Church

Latin Rite
Greece comprises four archdioceses (including two, Athens and Rhodes, directly responsible to the Holy See), four dioceses and one Apostolic Vicariate. At 31 December 2002 there were an estimated 51,000 adherents in the country.

Bishops' Conference
Odos Homirou 9, 106 72 Athens; tel. (21) 03624311; fax (21) 03618632.

f. 1967; Pres. Most Rev. NIKOLAOS FÓSKOLOS (Archbishop of Athens).

Archbishop of Athens: Archbishop Most Rev. NIKOLAOS FÓSKOLOS.

Archbishop of Corfu, Zante and Cefalonia: Most Rev. IOANNIS SPITERIS.

Archbishop of Naxos, Andros, Tinos and Mykonos: Most Rev. NIKOLAOS PRINTESIS.

Archbishop of Rhodes: (vacant).

Apostolic Vicariate of Thessaloníki: Kolokotroni 19B, 546 45 Thessaloníki; tel. (231) 0539550; fax (2661) 031675; e-mail cathepco@otenet.gr; Apostolic Administrator Archbishop of Corfu, Zante and Cefalonia Most Rev. IOANNES SPITERIS.

Byzantine Rite

Apostolic Exarchate for the Byzantine Rite in Greece: Odos Akarnon 246, 112 53 Athens; tel. (21) 08670170; fax (21) 08677039; e-mail grcathex@hol.gr; 3 parishes; 2,300 adherents (31 Dec. 2002); Exarch Apostolic Rt Rev. ANARGHYROS PRINTESIS (Titular Bishop of Gratianopolis).

Armenian Rite

Exarchate for the Armenian Catholics in Greece: Odos René Piot 2, 117 44 Athens; tel. (21) 09014089; fax (21) 09012109; 550 adherents (31 Dec. 2002); Exarch Archpriest NICHAN KARAKEHEYAN.

Protestant Church

Greek Evangelical Church (Reformed): Odos Markon Botsari 24, 117 41 Athens; tel. (21) 09222684; e-mail info@gec.gr; internet www.gec.gr; f. 1858; comprises 32 organized churches; 5,000 adherents (1996); Moderator Rev. MELETIS MELETIADIS.

ISLAM

The law provides as religious head of the Muslims a Chief Mufti; the Muslims in Greece possess a number of mosques and schools.

JUDAISM

The Jewish population of Greece, estimated in 1943 at 75,000 people, was severely reduced as a result of the Nazi German occupation. In 1994 there were about 5,000 Jews in Greece.

Central Board of the Jewish Communities of Greece: Odos Voulis 36, 105 57 Athens; tel. (21) 03244315; fax (21) 03313852; e-mail info@kis.gr; internet www.kis.gr; f. 1945; officially recognized representative body of the communities of Greece; Pres. MOSES KONSTANTINIS.

The Press

PRINCIPAL DAILY NEWSPAPERS

Morning papers are not published on Mondays, nor afternoon papers on Sundays. Afternoon papers are more popular than morning ones. In 1997 there were 122 daily newspaper titles.

Athens

Apogevmatini (The Afternoon): Odos Phidiou 12, 106 78 Athens; tel. (21) 06430011; fax (21) 03609876; e-mail info@apogevmatini.gr; internet www.apogevmatini.gr; f. 1956; independent; Editor P. KARAYANNIS; circ. 30,000.

Athens Daily Post: Odos Stadiou 57, Athens; tel. (21) 03249504; f. 1952; morning; English; Owner G. SKOURAS.

Athens News: Odos Christou Lada 3, 102 37 Athens; tel. (21) 03333555; fax (21) 03231384; e-mail athnews@dolnet.gr; internet www.athensnews.gr; f. 1952; morning; in English; Editor JOHN PSAROPOULOS; circ. 10,000.

Athlitiki Icho (Athletics Echo): Konstantinoupelos 161, 104 41 Athens; tel. (21) 05232201; fax (21) 05232433; e-mail text@athlitiki-iho.gr; f. 1945; morning; Editor DEMOSTHENES CHRISTOU; circ. 40,000.

Avgi (Dawn): Odos Ag. Konstantiou 12, 104 31 Athens; tel. (21) 05231831; fax (21) 05231830; e-mail editors@avgi.gr; internet www.avgi.gr; f. 1952; morning; independent newspaper of the left; Editor NIKOS PHILES; circ. 5,400.

Avriani (Tomorrow): Odos Dimitros 11, 177 78 Athens; tel. (21) 03424090; fax (21) 03452190; f. 1980; evening; Publr GEORGE KOURIS; circ. 51,317.

Dimokratikos Logos (Democratic Speech): Odos Dimitros 11, 177 78 Athens; tel. (21) 03424023; fax (21) 03452190; f. 1986; morning; Dir and Editor KOSTAS GERONIKOLOS; circ. 7,183.

Eleftherotypia (Press Freedom): Odos Minou 10–16, 117 43 Athens; tel. (21) 09296001; fax (21) 09028311; internet www.enet.gr; f. 1974; evening; Publr CHR. TEGOPOULOS; circ. 115,000.

Estia (Vesta): Odos Anthimou Gazi 7, 105 61 Athens; tel. (21) 03230650; fax (21) 03243071; e-mail estianews@otenet.gr; f. 1894; afternoon; Editor E. PETROU; circ. 60,000.

Ethnos (Nation): Odos Benaki 152, Metamorfosi Chalandriou, 152 35 Athens; tel. (21) 06580640; fax (21) 06396515; internet www.ethnos.gr; f. 1981; evening; Dir TH. KALOUDIS; circ. 84,735.

Express: Odos Halandriou 39, Paradissos Amaroussiou, 151 25 Athens; tel. (21) 06850200; fax (21) 06852202; internet express.gr; f. 1963; morning; financial; publ. by Hellenews Publications; Editor D. G. KALOFOLIAS; circ. 28,000.

Filathlos: Odos Dimitros 31, 177 78 Athens; tel. (21) 03486000; fax (21) 03486450; e-mail info@filathlos.gr; internet www.filathlos.gr; f. 1982; morning; sports; Editor G. KOLOKOTRONIS; circ. 40,000.

Imerissia (Daily): Odos Benaki & Ag. Nektariou, Metamorfosi Chalandriou, 152 35 Athens; tel. (21) 06061729; fax (21) 06016563; e-mail imerissia@pegasus.gr; f. 1947; morning; financial; Editor ANTONIS DALIPIS; circ. 26,000.

Kathimerini (Every Day): Ethnarchou Makariou 185–47 & Odos Falireos 2, Athens; tel. (21) 04808000; fax (21) 04808000; e-mail kathi-editor@ekathimerini.com; internet www.kathimerini.gr; f. 1919; morning; conservative; Editor CH. PANAGOPOULOS; circ. 34,085.

Kerdos (Profit): Leoforos Kifissias 178, Halandri, 152 31 Athens; tel. (21) 06747881; fax (21) 06747893; e-mail mail@kerdos.gr; internet www.kerdos.gr; f. 1985; morning; financial; Editor VASILIS STEFANAKADIS; circ. 18,000.

Naftemporiki (Daily Journal): Odos Lenorman 205, 104 42 Athens; tel. (21) 05198000; fax (21) 05146013; e-mail info@naftemporiki.gr; internet www.naftemporiki.gr; f. 1924; morning; non-political journal of finance, commerce and shipping; Editor D. KEFALAKOS; circ. 35,000.

Ora Gia Spor (Time for Sport): Ioannou Metaxa 8, 173 43 Athens; tel. (21) 09251200; fax (21) 09761211; f. 1991; sport; Editor D. AVOURIS.

Rizospastis (Radical): Lefkis 134, Perissos, 145 65 Athens; tel. (21) 06297000; fax (21) 06297999; e-mail mailbox@rizospastis.gr; internet www.rizospastis.gr; f. 1974; morning; Editor T. TSIGGAS; circ. 28,740.

Ta Nea (News): Odos Christou Lada 3, 102 37 Athens; tel. (21) 03333555; fax (21) 03228797; e-mail tanea@dolnet.gr; internet ta-nea.dolnet.gr; f. 1944; liberal; evening; Editor HLIAS MATSIKAS; circ. 135,000.

Vradyni (Evening Press): L. Ionias 166, 111 44 Athens; tel. (21) 02113600; fax (21) 02113648; e-mail vradyni@otenet.gr; f. 1923; evening; right-wing; Editor PANOS TSIROS; circ. 71,914.

Patras

Peloponnesos: Maizonos 206, 262 22 Patras; tel. (261) 0312530; fax (261) 0312535; internet www.peloponnisos.com.gr; f. 1886; independent conservative; Publr and Editor S. DOUKAS; circ. 7,000.

Thessaloníki

Ellinikos Vorras (The Greek North): Odos Grammou-Vitsi 19, 551 34 Thessaloníki; tel. (231) 0416621; f. 1935; morning; Dir N. MERGIOS; circ. 14,467.

Thessaloníki: Odos Monastiriou 85, 546 27 Thessaloníki; tel. (231) 0521621; f. 1963; evening; Editor KATERINA VELLIDI; circ. 36,040.

SELECTED PERIODICALS

Agora (Market): Leoforos Kifissias 178, Halandri, 151 31 Athens; tel. (21) 06473384; fax (21) 06477893; e-mail agora@kerdos.gr; internet www.kerdos.gr/agora; f. 1987; fortnightly; politics, finance; Dir ANT. KEFALAS; circ. 20,000.

Aktines: Odos Karytsi 14, 105 61 Athens; tel. (21) 03235023; f. 1938; monthly; Christian publication on current affairs, science, philosophy, arts; circ. 10,000.

Athèmes: Athens; monthly; in French; cultural; Editor-in-Chief EMMANUEL ADELY; circ. 5,000.

The Athenian: Athens; tel. (21) 03222802; fax (21) 03223052; e-mail the-athenian@hol.gr; f. 1974; monthly; English; Editor JOANNA STAVROPOULOS; circ. 14,000.

Auto Express: Odos Halandriou 39, Halandri, 152 32 Athens; tel. (21) 06816906; fax (21) 06825858; Dir D. KALOFOLIAS; circ. 19,000.

Computer Gia Olous (Computers for All): Leoforos Syngrou 44, 117 42 Kallithea, Athens; tel. (21) 09238672; fax (21) 09216847; internet www.cgomag.gr; monthly; Editor GEORGE CHRISTOPOULOS.

Deltion Diikiseos Epichiriseon Euro-Unial (Business Administration Bulletin Euro-Unial): Odos Rhigillis 26, 106 74 Athens; tel. (21) 07235736; fax (21) 07240000; e-mail busadmibul@otenet.gr; monthly; Editor I. PAPAMICHALAKIS; circ. 26,000.

Ekonomicos Tachydromos (Financial Courier): Odos Christou Lada 3, 102 37 Athens; tel. (21) 03333630; fax (21) 03238740; e-mail oikonomikos@dolnet.gr; internet oikonomikos.dolnet.gr; f. 1926; weekly; Man. Dir DENNIS ANTYPAS; circ. 23,000.

Elle: Odos Kleisthenous 213, 153 44 Athens; tel. (21) 06062531; fax (21) 06062648; e-mail magelle@compulink.gr; f. 1988; monthly; women's magazine; Editor FLORA TZIMAKA; circ. 57,120 (1997).

Epiloghi: Odos Stadiou 4, 105 64 Athens; tel. (21) 03238427; fax (21) 03235160; e-mail epilogi@mail.hol.gr; f. 1962; weekly; economics; Editor GEORGE MALOUHOS.

Greece's Weekly for Business and Finance: Odos Fokiodos 10, 115 26 Athens; tel. (21) 07707280; weekly; English; finance; Dir V. KORONAKIS.

Gynaika (Women): Odos Fragoklissias 7, Marousi, 151 25 Athens; tel. (21) 06199149; fax (21) 06104707; f. 1950; monthly; Publr CHRISTOS TERZOPOULOS; circ. 45,000.

Hellenews: Odos Halandriou 39, Marousi, 151 25 Athens; tel. (21) 06199400; fax (21) 06199421; e-mail alexm@express.kapatel.gr; weekly; English; finance and business; Editor J. M. GERMANOS.

Idaniko Spiti (Ideal Home): Odos St Nectarios, 152 35 Athens; tel. (1) 06061777; fax (1) 06011044; e-mail pa@pegasus.gr; internet www .idanikospiti.gr; f. 1990; monthly; interior decoration; Editor PETROS ANTONIADIS; circ. 60,000 (2002).

Klik: Odos Fragoklisias 7, 151 25 Athens; tel. (21) 06897945; fax (21) 06899153; internet www.klik.gr; f. 1987; monthly; popular music, media and fashion; Editor PETROS COSTOPOULOS.

Marie Claire: Odos Stadiou 24, 105 64 Athens; tel. (21) 03333654; fax (21) 03227770; e-mail marieclaire@dolnet.gr; monthly; women's magazine.

Men: Odos Fragoklisias 7, 151 25 Athens; tel. (21) 06826680; fax (21) 06824730; e-mail mensynt@dolnet.gr; internet www.men.gr; six a year; men's fashion and general interest.

Oikonomiki Viomichaniki Epitheorissis (Industrial Review): Odos Zalokosta 4, 106 71 Athens; tel. (21) 03626360; fax (21) 03626388; e-mail editor@oikonomiki.gr; internet www.oikonomiki .gr; f. 1934; monthly; industrial and economic review; Editor D. KARAMANOS; circ. 25,000.

48 Ores (48 Hours): Leoforos Alexandras 19, 114 73 Athens; tel. (21) 06430313; fax (21) 06461361; weekly; Dir and Editor SP. KARATZAFERIS; circ. 9,127.

Pantheon: Odos Christou Lada 3, 102 37 Athens; tel. (21) 03230221; fax (21) 03228797; every two weeks; Publr and Dir N. THEOFANIDES; circ. 23,041.

Politika Themata: Odos Ypsilantou 25, 106 75 Athens; tel. (21) 07218421; weekly; Dir C. KYRKOS.

Pontiki (Mouse): Odos Massalias 10, 106 81 Athens; tel. (21) 03609531; weekly; humour; Dir and Editor K. PAPAIOANNOU.

Ptisi & Diastima (Flight & Space): Odos Helioupoleos 2–4, 172 37 Athens; tel. (21) 09792500; fax (21) 09792528; e-mail ptisi@techlink .gr; internet www.ptisi.gr; f. 1975; monthly; Editor FAITHON KARAIOSSIFIOIS; circ. 12,000 (2003).

Radiotileorassi (Radio-TV): Odos Rhigillis 4, 106 74 Athens; tel. (21) 07407032; fax (21) 07224812; e-mail radiotileorasi@ert.gr; weekly; circ. 55,000.

Technika Chronika (Technical Times): Odos Karageorgi Servias 4, 105 62 Athens; tel. (21) 03291200; fax (21) 03221772; e-mail intrel@central.tee.gr; internet www.tee.gr; f. 1932; every 2 months; general edition on technical and economic subjects; Editor YANNIS ALAVANOS; circ. 12,000.

Tilerama: Odos Voukourestiou 18, 106 71 Athens; tel. (21) 03607160; fax (21) 03607032; f. 1977; weekly; radio and television; circ. 189,406.

To Vima (Tribune): Odos Christou Lada 3, 102 37 Athens; tel. (21) 03333103; fax (21) 03239097; e-mail tovima@dolnet.gr; internet tovima.dolnet.gr; f. 1922; weekly; liberal; Dir and Editor STAVROS R. PSYCHARIS; circ. 250,000.

La Tribune héllenique: Athens; weekly; French; politics, economics; Dir THEODORE BENAKIS; circ. 3,000.

NEWS AGENCIES

Athens News Agency (ANA): Odos Tsoha 36, 115 21 Athens; tel. (21) 06400560; fax (21) 06400581; e-mail ape@ana.gr; internet www .ana.gr; f. 1895; correspondents in leading capitals of the world and towns throughout Greece; Man. Dir NIKOLAS VOULELIS; Gen. Dir ANDREAS CHRISTODOULIDES.

Foreign Bureaux

Agence France-Presse (AFP): Odos Millioni 5, 106 73 Athens; tel. (21) 03633646; fax (21) 03614457; e-mail athensbureau@afp.com; Bureau Chief JEAN-PIERRE ALTIER.

Agencia EFE (Spain): Athens; tel. (21) 03635826; Bureau Chief D. MARÍA-LUISA RUBIO.

Agenzia Nazionale Stampa Associata (ANSA) (Italy): Odos Kanari 9, 106 71 Athens; tel. (21) 03605285; fax (21) 03635367; Correspondent FRANCESCO INDRACCOLO.

Associated Press (AP) (USA): Leoforos Amalias 52, 105 52 Athens; tel. (21) 03310802; fax (21) 03310804.

Deutsche Presse-Agentur (dpa) (Germany): Miniati 1, 116 36 Athens; tel. (21) 09247774; fax (21) 09222185; Correspondent HILDEGARD HÜLSENBECK.

Dow Jones Newswire (USA): Odos Philellinon 34, 105 58 Athens; tel. (21) 03312881; fax (21) 03313180.

ITAR—TASS (Information Telegraph Agency of Russia-Telegraphic Agency of the Sovereign Countries) (Russia): Odos Gizi 39, Palaio Psychiko, 15 452 Athens; tel. and fax (21) 06713069; Bureau Chief VLADIMIR V. MALYSHEV.

Reuters (United Kingdom): 1 Kolokotroni & Stadiou, 105 62 Athens; tel. (21) 03311800; fax (21) 03311830; e-mail athens .newsroom@reuters.com; Man. Dir WILLIAM CAIRLEY.

RIA—Novosti (Russian Information Agency—News) (Russia): Odos Irodotou 9, 138 Athens; tel. (21) 07291016; Bureau Chief BORIS KOROLYOV.

Xinhua (New China) News Agency (China): Odos Amarilidos 19, Palaio Psychiko, Athens; tel. (21) 06724997; Bureau Chief XIE CHENGHAO.

PRESS ASSOCIATIONS

Enosis Antapokriton Xenou Tipou (Foreign Press Association of Greece): Odos Akademias 23, 106 71 Athens; tel. (21) 03637318; fax (21) 03605035.

Enosis Syntakton Imerission Ephimeridon Athinon (Journalists' Union of Athens Daily Newspapers): Odos Akademias 20, 106 71 Athens; tel. (21) 03632601; fax (21) 03632608; e-mail info@esiea .gr; internet www.esiea.gr; f. 1914; Pres. FANI PETRALIA; Gen. Sec. ANASTASIA DAOUDAKI; 1,400 mems.

Enosis Syntakton Periodikou Tipou (Journalists' Union of the Periodical Press): Odos Valaoritou 9, 106 71 Athens; tel. (21) 03633427; fax (21) 03638627; e-mail espt@otenet.gr; internet www .espit.org; Pres. GIANNIS PLACHOURIS; 835 mems.

Publishers

Agkyra Publications: Leoforos Kifisou 85, Egaleo, 122 41 Athens; tel. (21) 03455276; fax (21) 03474732; f. 1890; general; Man. Dir DIMITRIOS PAPADIMITRIOU.

Akritas: Odos Efessou 24, 171 21 Athens; tel. (21) 09334554; fax (21) 09311436; e-mail akritaspublications@ath.forthnet.gr; f. 1979; history, spirituality, children's books.

D. I. Arsenidis & Co: Odos Akademias 57, 106 79 Athens; tel. (21) 03629538; fax (21) 03618707; f. 1952; biography, literature, children's books, history, philosophy, social sciences; Man. Dir JOHN ARSENIDIS.

Boukoumanis Editions: Odos Mavromichali 1, 106 79 Athens; tel. (21) 03618502; fax (21) 03630669; f. 1967; history, politics, sociology, psychology, belles-lettres, educational, arts, children's books, ecology; Man. ELIAS BOUKOUMANIS.

Dorikos Publishing House: Odos Charalabou Sotiriou 9–11, 114 72 Athens; tel. (21) 06454726; fax (21) 03301866; f. 1958; literature, fiction, history, politics; Editor ROUSSOS VRANAS.

Ekdotike Athenon: Odos Akademias 34, 106 72 Athens; tel. (21) 03608911; fax (21) 03606157; e-mail ekdath@aias.gr; internet www .add.gr/comp/ekdotiki; f. 1961; history, archaeology, art; Pres. GEORGE A. CHRISTOPOULOS.

G. C. Eleftheroudakis: Odos Panepistimiou 17, 105 64 Athens; tel. (21) 03314180; fax (21) 03239821; e-mail elebooks@netor.gr; internet www.books.gr; f. 1915; general, technical and scientific; Man. Dir VIRGINIA ELEFTHEROUDAKIS-GREGOU.

Exandas Publications: Odos Didotou 57, 106 81 Athens; tel. (21) 03804885; fax (21) 03813065; e-mail info@exandasbooks.gr; internet www.exandasbooks.gr; f. 1974; fiction, literature, social sciences; Pres. MAGDA N. KOTZIA.

Govostis Publishing: Zoodohou Pigis 21, 106 81 Athens; tel. (21) 03815433; fax (21) 03816661; e-mail cotsos@compulink.gr; f. 1926; arts, fiction, politics; Pres. COSTAS GOVOSTIS.

Denise Harvey: Katounia, 340 05 Limni, Evia; tel. and fax (2227) 031154; e-mail denise@teledomenet.gr; f. 1972; modern Greek literature and poetry, belles-lettres, theology, translations, selected general list (English and Greek); Man. Dir DENISE HARVEY.

Hestia-I.D. Kollaros & Co: Odos Solonos 60, 106 72 Athens; tel. (21) 03615077; fax (21) 03606759; f. 1885; literature, history, politics, architecture, philosophy, travel, religion, psychology, textbooks, general; Gen. Dir MARINA KARAITIDIS.

Kastaniotis Editions: Odos Zalogou 11, 106 78 Athens; tel. (21) 03301208; fax (21) 03822530; e-mail info@kastaniotis.com; internet www.kastaniotis.com; f. 1969; fiction and non-fiction, including arts, social sciences and psychology, children's books; Man. Dir ATHANA-SIOS KASTANIOTIS.

Kritiki Publishing: Odos Koletti 25, 106 77 Athens; tel. (21) 03803730; fax (21) 03803740; e-mail biblia@kritiki.gr; internet www .kritiki.gr; f. 1987; economics, politics, literature, philosophy, business/management, popular science; Pres. THEMIS MINOGLOU.

Kronos: Odos Egnatia 33, 546 26 Thessaloníki; tel. (231) 0532077; fax (231) 0538158; Dir TH. GIOTAS.

Livani Publishing Organization: Odos Solonos 98, 106 80 Athens; tel. (21) 03661200; fax (21) 03617791; e-mail rights@livani .gr; internet www.livanis.gr; f. 1972; general; Publr A. A. LIVANI.

Minoas SA: Odos Posseidonos 1, 141 21 N. Iraklio, Athens; tel. (21) 02711222; fax (21) 02711056; e-mail info@minoas.gr; internet www .minoas.gr; f. 1952; fiction, art, history; Man. Dir IOANNIS KONSTANTAR-OPOULOS.

Odos Panos: Odos Didotou 39, 106 08 Athens; tel. and fax (21) 03616782; internet www.odospanos-cigaret.gr; poetry, drama, biography.

Papazissis Publishers: Nikitara 2, 106 78 Athens; tel. (21) 03822496; fax (21) 03809150; e-mail papazisi@otenet.gr; internet www.papzisi.gr; f. 1929; economics, politics, law, history, school books; Man. Dir VICTOR PAPAZISSIS.

Patakis Publications: Odos Valtetsiou 14, 106 80 Athens; tel. (21) 03638362; fax (21) 03628950; internet www.patakis.gr; f. 1974; art, reference, fiction, educational, philosophy, psychology, sociology, religion, music, children's books, audiobooks; Pres. STEFANOS PATAKIS.

Pontiki Publications: Odos Massalias 10, 106 80 Athens; tel. (21) 03609531; fax (21) 03645406; f. 1979; govt, history, political science; Man. Dir KOSTAS TABANIS.

John Sideris: Odos Stadiou 44, 105 64 Athens; tel. (21) 03229638; fax (21) 03245052; f. 1898; school textbooks, general; Man. J. SIDERIS.

J. G. Vassiliou: Odos Hippokratous 15, 106 79 Athens; tel. (21) 03623382; fax (21) 03623580; f. 1913; fiction, history, philosophy, dictionaries and children's books; Pres. J. VASSILIOU.

GOVERNMENT PUBLISHING HOUSE

Ethnikon Tupographeion (National Printing House): Odos Kapo-distriou 34, 104 32 Athens; tel. (21) 05248320.

PUBLISHERS' ASSOCIATIONS

Hellenic Federation of Publishers and Booksellers: Odos Themistokleus 73, 106 83 Athens; tel. (21) 03300924; fax (21) 03301617; e-mail poev@otenet.gr; f. 1961; Pres. GEORGE DARDANOS; Gen. Sec. TITOS MYLONOPOULOS.

Publishers' and Booksellers' Association of Athens: Odos Themistokleus 73, 106 83 Athens; tel. (21) 03303268; fax (21) 03823222; e-mail seva@otenet.gr; Pres. STELIOS ELLINIADIS; Sec. LOUCAS RINO-POULOS.

Broadcasting and Communications

TELECOMMUNICATIONS

National Telecommunications Commission (NTC): Leoforos Kifissias 60, 151 25 Athens; tel. (21) 06151000; fax (21) 06805049; e-mail info@eet.gr; internet www.eet.gr; regulatory body; Chair. EMMANOUIL GIACOUMAKIS.

Organismos Telepikoinonion tis Elladas (OTE) (Hellenic Telecommunications Organization): Leoforos Kifissias 99, 151 24 Maroussi, Athens; tel. (21) 08827015; fax (21) 06115825; internet www .ote.gr; f. 1949; 38% owned by the Government, 62% by public

shareholders; 6m. lines in service; Chief Exec. and Chair. PANAGIS VOURLOUMIS.

COSMOTE: Leoforos Kifissias 44, 151 25 Athens; tel. (21) 06177700; fax (21) 06177594; e-mail customercare@cosmote.gr; internet www.cosmote.gr; f. 1998; 59% owned by OTE; mobile cellular telecommunications; Man. Dir EVANGELOS MARTIGOPOULOS.

Maritel: Odos Egaleo 8, 185 45 Piraeus; tel. (21) 04599500; fax (21) 04599600; e-mail maritel@maritel.gr; internet www.maritel .gr; OTE subsidiary; marine telecommunications; Chair. THEO-DOROS VENIAMIS; Man. Dir MICHALIS MICHAELIDES.

Telestet Hellas: Leoforos Alex. Papagoy 8, 157 71 Athens; tel. (21) 07772033; e-mail po@telestet.gr; internet www.telestet.gr; 75%-owned by STET International; mobile cellular telecommunications; Man. Dir GIACINTO CICCHESE.

Vodafone Panafon: Leoforos Messoghion 2, 115 27 Athens; tel. (21) 07483601; e-mail webmaster@panafon.gr; internet www.vodafone .gr; 55%-owned by Vodafone Europe Holdings (United Kingdom); mobile cellular telecommunications; Chief Exec. GEORGE KORONIAS.

RADIO

Elliniki Radiophonia Tileorassi (ERT) (Greek Radio-Television): Leoforos Messoghion 432, 153 42 Athens; tel. (21) 06066835; fax (21) 06009325; e-mail president@ert.gr; internet www.ert.gr; state-controlled; Chair. and Man. Dir A. STAGKOS.

Elliniki Radiophonia (ERA) (Greek Radio): POB 60019, Leoforos Messoghion 432, 153 42 Aghia Paraskevi, Athens; tel. (1) 06066815; fax (1) 06009425; e-mail ijanetakos@ert.gr; internet www.ert.gr/radio; Dir IOANNIS TZANNETAKOS.

Macedonia Radio Station: Odos Angelaki 2, 546 21 Thessaloníki; tel. (231) 0299400; fax (231) 0299451; e-mail info@ert3.gr; internet www.ert3.gr.

TELEVISION

A television network of 17 transmitters is in operation. The State's monopoly of television broadcasting ended in 1990, and by 1998 there were 17 private broadcasters.

State stations

Elliniki Radiophonia Tileorassi (ERT, SA) (Greek Radio-Television): see Radio.

Elliniki Tileorassi 1 (ET1) (Greek Television 1): Leoforos Messoghion 136, 115 27 Athens; tel. (21) 07758824; fax (21) 07797776; e-mail kalavanos@ert.gr; internet www.ert.gr/et1; Dir-Gen. KONSTANTINOS ALAVANOS.

ET2: Leoforos Messoghion 136, 115 25 Athens; tel. (21) 07701911; fax (21) 07797776; Dir-Gen. PANAYOTIS PANAYOTOU.

ET3: Aggelaki 2, 546 21 Thessaloníki; tel. (231) 0299610; fax (231) 0299655; e-mail pr@ert3.gr; internet www.ert.gr/et3; Dir-Gen. DEMETRIS KATSANTONIS.

Private stations

Antenna TV: Leoforos Kifissias 10–12, 151 25 Maroussi, Athens; tel. (21) 0688600; fax (21) 06834349; e-mail webmaster@antenna.gr; internet www.antenna.gr; Chair. M. X. KYRIAKOU.

Channel Seven-X: Leoforos Kifissias 64, 151 25 Maroussi, Athens; tel. (21) 06897600; fax (21) 06897608.

City Channel: Leoforos Kastoni 14, 41223 Larissa; tel. (241) 232839; fax (241) 232013.

Mega Channel: Leoforos Messoghion 117, 115 26 Athens; tel. (21) 06903000; fax (21) 06983600; e-mail ngeorgiou@megatv.com; internet www.megatv.com; f. 1989; Man. Dir ELIAS TSIGAS.

Neo Kanali: Pireos 9–11, 105 52 Athens; tel. (21) 05238230; fax (21) 05247325.

Serres TV: Nigritis 27, 62124 Serres.

Skai TV: Phalereos & Ethnarchou 2, Macaroiu, N. Phaliro.

Star Channel: Odos Thermopylon 87, 351 00 Lamia; tel. (2231) 046725; fax (2231) 038903; e-mail starch@lam.forthnet.gr; f. 1988; Pres. VASILEIOS CHEIMONIDIS.

Tele City: Praxitelous 58, 17674 Athens; tel. (21) 09429222; fax (21) 09413589.

Teletora: Lycabetous 17, 10672 Athens; tel. (21) 03617285; fax (21) 03638712.

Traki TV: Central Square, 67100 Xanthi; tel. (2541) 020670; fax (2541) 027368.

TRT: Odos Zachou 5, 38333 Volos; tel. (2421) 0288013; fax (2421) 036888.

TV Macedonia: Nea Egnatia 222, 54642 Thessaloníki; tel. (231) 0850512; fax (231) 0850513.

TV Plus: Athens; tel. (21) 09028707; fax (21) 09028310.

TV-100: Odos Aggelaki 16, 54621 Thessaloníki; tel. (231) 0265828; fax (231) 0267532.

Finance

(cap. = capital; res = reserves; dep. = deposits; m. = million; br. = branch; amounts in Euros, unless otherwise stated; dre = drachmae; SDR = Special Drawing Rights)

BANKING

In 2003 there were 174 banks in Greece, of which 91 were state owned.

Central Bank

Bank of Greece: Leoforos E. Venizelos 21, 102 50 Athens; tel. (21) 03201111; fax (21) 03232239; e-mail secretariat@bankofgreece.gr; internet www.bankofgreece.gr; f. 1927; state bank of issue; cap. 66.7m., res 624.9m., dep. 4,135.1m. (Dec. 2001); Gov. NIKOS GARGANOS; 27 brs.

Commercial Banks

Agricultural Bank of Greece: Odos Panepistimiou 23, 105 64 Athens; tel. (21) 03298364; fax (21) 03255079; e-mail ategt@ate.gr; internet www.ate.gr; f. 1929; state-owned; cap. 1,649.5m., res −681.0m., dep. 16,081.7m. (Dec. 2003); Pres. and Gov. DIMITRIOS MILIAKOS; 443 brs.

Alpha Bank: Stadiou 40, 102 52 Athens; tel. (21) 03260000; fax (21) 03265438; e-mail secretariat@alpha.gr; internet www.alpha.gr; f. 1879; present name adopted 2000; cap. 953.7m., res 1,110.6m., dep. 25,292.1m. (Dec. 2003); Chair. and Gen. Man. IOANNIS S. COSTOPOULOS; 402 brs.

Aspis Bank: Odos Othonos 4, Syntagma, 105 57 Athens; tel. (21) 03364000; fax (21) 03243473; e-mail aspis@aspisbank.gr; internet www.aspisbank.gr; f. 1992; cap. 107.3m., res 27.4m., dep. 1,522.4m (Dec. 2003); Chair. and Man. Dir KONSTANTINOS KARATZAS.

Bank of Attica: Odos Omirou 23, 106 72 Athens; tel. (21) 03646910; fax (21) 03634067; e-mail attiki3@netor.gr; internet www.bankofattica.gr; f. 1925; cap. 14.6m., res 117.6m., dep. 1,5457.2m. (Dec. 2002); Chair. and Man. Dir KONSTANTINOS STAMOULIS; 50 brs.

Black Sea Trade and Development Bank: Odos Komninon 1, 546 24 Thessaloníki; tel. (231) 0290400; fax (231) 0221796; e-mail info@bstdb.org; internet www.bstdb.org; f. 1997; owned by 11 member states: Greece, Russian Federation, Turkey (16.5% each); Bulgaria, Romania, Ukraine (13.5% each); Albania, Armenia, Azerbaijan, Georgia, Moldova (2% each); cap. SDR 250.1m., res SDR 3.7m. (Dec. 2003); Pres. MUSTAFA GÜRTIN.

EFG Eurobank Ergasias: Odos Othonos 8, 105 57 Athens; tel. (21) 03337000; fax (21) 03337256; internet www.eurobank.gr; f. 1990; present name adopted 2000; cap. 930.7m., res 739.5m., dep. 25,048.0m. (Dec. 2003); Pres. X. NIKITAS; Man. Dir NIKOLAS NANOPOULOS; 330 brs.

Egnatia Bank: Odos Danaidon 4, 546 26 Thessaloníki; tel. (231) 0598600; fax (231) 0598675; e-mail becker@egnatiabank.gr; internet www.egnatiabank.gr; f. 1991; cap. 111.6m., res 180.8m., dep. 2,215.3m. (Dec. 2003); Pres. and Chair. VASSILLIS THEOCHARAKIS; Man. Dir VASSILLIS KELTSOPOULOS; 64 brs.

Emporiki Bank of Greece: Odos Sophokleous 11, 102 35 Athens; tel. (21) 03284000; fax (21) 03253746; e-mail pubrel@emporiki.gr; internet www.emporiki.gr; f. 1907; present name adopted 2003; cap. 429.7m., res 838.9m., dep. 15,067.2m. (Dec. 2003); Chair. and Chief Exec. GEORGE A. PROVOPOULOS; 375 brs.

FBB First Business Bank: Odos Michalakopoulou, 115 28 Athens; tel. (21) 07499700; fax (21) 07499766; e-mail info@fbb.gr; internet www.fbb.gr; f. 2001; 44.0% owned by Agricultural Bank of Greece; cap. 88.2m., res 0.7m., dep. 603.4m. (Dec. 2003); Chair. DIMITRIOS MILIAKOS.

Geniki Bank—General Bank of Greece: Odos Messoghion 109–111, 115 26 Athens; tel. (21) 06975457; fax (21) 06975910; e-mail intdiv@geniki.gr; internet www.geniki.gr; f. 1937; present name adopted 1998; cap. 141.0m., res 73.8m., dep. 3,010.3m. (Dec. 2003); Chair. and Man. Dir ANTONIS HASIOTIS; Gen. Man. JACQUES TUOURNEBIZE; 108 brs.

Investment Bank of Greece: Leoforus Kifissias 24B, 151 25 Athens; tel. (21) 08171810; fax (21) 09281800; internet www.ibog.gr; f. 2000; cap. 89.6m., res −0.6m., dep. 26.7m. (Dec. 2003); Man. Dir PANAGIOTIS DOUMANOGLOU.

Laiki Bank (Hellas): Odos Panepistimiou 16, 106 72 Athens; tel. (21) 03550000; fax (21) 03243141; e-mail cm_lbh@otenet.gr; internet www.laiki.gr; f. 1992; present name adopted 2000; 72.0% owned by Cyprus Popular Bank (Cyprus); cap. 55.0m., res 52.3m., dep. 1,787.7m. (Dec. 2003); Chair. and Pres. KIKIS LAZARIDES; Man. Dir RENA ROUVITHA-PANOU; 42 brs.

Marfin Bank: Leoforos Kifissias 24, 151 25 Athens; tel. (21) 0817000; fax (21) 08170101; e-mail mail@marfinbank.gr; internet www.marfinbank.gr; f. 1981; present name adopted 2002; cap. 47.4m., res 10.2m., dep. 553.6m. (Dec. 2004); Pres. and Chair. ANDREAS VGENOPOULOS; Man. Dir NIKI PLAKOMICHELAKI; 8 brs.

National Bank of Greece (NBG): Odos Aeolou 86, 102 32 Athens; tel. (21) 03441000; fax (21) 03346550; internet www.nbg.gr; f. 1841; state-controlled, but operates independently of the Government; cap. 1,147.8m., res 1,165.5m., dep. 44,363.7m. (Dec. 2003); Gov. TAKIS ARAPOGLOU; 594 brs.

Omega Bank: Odos Amaliados and Eslin 20, Attiki, 115 23 Athens; tel. (21) 06970000; fax (21) 06970111; e-mail operation@omegabank.gr; internet www.omegabank.gr; f. 2001; cap. 33.0m., res 57.1m., dep. 719.3m. (Dec. 2003); Pres. and Chair. PANAGIOTIS GENNIMATAS.

Piraeus Bank: Leoforos Amalias 20 & Odos Souri 5, 105 57 Athens; tel. (21) 03335000; fax (21) 03335080; e-mail investor-relations@piraeusbank.gr; internet www.piraeusbank.gr; f. 1916; cap. 819.9m., res 404.1m., dep. 11,847.3m. (Dec. 2003); Chair. MICHALIS G. SALLAS; 6 brs.

Development Banks

Hellenic Industrial Development Bank: Leoforos Syngrou 87, 117 45 Kallithea, Athens; tel. (21) 09242900; fax (21) 09241513; e-mail news@etba.gr; internet www.etba.gr/etba/etbag.html; f. 1964; limited liability banking company; major Greek institution in the field of industrial investment; cap. dre 245,890.0m., res dre 44,424.3m., dep. dre 502,897.6m. (Dec. 1996); Chair. and Gov. GEORGE KASMAS; 11 brs.

National Investment Bank for Industrial Development: Leoforos Amalias 12–14, 105 57 Athens; tel. (21) 03242651; fax (21) 03296211; e-mail public@eteba.gr; internet www.eteba.gr; f. 1963; cap. dre 8,971.8m., res dre 51,740.9m., dep. dre 354,932.3m. (Dec. 2000); long-term loans, equity participation, promotion of co-operation between Greek and foreign enterprises; Chair. THEODORE KARATZAS; Man. Dir DIMITRIOS GOUMAS; 1 br.

STOCK EXCHANGE

Athens Stock Exchange: Odos Sophokleous 10, 105 59 Athens; tel. (21) 03211301; fax (21) 03213938; e-mail webmaster@ase.gr; internet www.ase.gr; f. 1876; Pres. PANAYOTIS ALEXAKIS; Vice-Pres. THEODOROS PANTOLAKIS.

PRINCIPAL INSURANCE COMPANIES

Agrotiki Hellenic Insurance Co: Leoforos Syngrou 163, 171 21 Kallithea, Athens; tel. (21) 9379100; fax (21) 09358924; e-mail info@agroins.com; internet www.agroins.com; Gen. Man. TR. LISIMACHOU.

Alpha Insurance: Odos Michalakopoulou 48, 115 28 Athens; tel. (21) 07268000; fax (21) 07268810; e-mail info@alpha-insurance.gr; internet www.alpha-insurance.gr; f. 1999; by merger; Chair. PHOTIS P. COSTOPOULOS; Man. Dir D. PALEOLOGOS; Gen. Man. NIKOLAOS GIANNOULAS.

Aspis Pronia General Insurance SA: Leoforos Kifissias 62, 151 25 Maroussi, Athens; tel. (21) 06198960; fax (21) 06198974; e-mail info@aspis.gr; internet www.aspis.gr; f. 1941; Pres. and Chief Exec. PAUL PSOMIADES.

Atlantiki Enosis: Odos Messoghion 71 & Ilidos 36, 115 26 Athens; tel. (21) 07799211; fax (21) 07794446; e-mail atlantiki@atlantiki.gr; internet www.atlanticunion.gr; f. 1970; Pres. SARANDOS STASINOPOULOS; Man. Dir NOTIS LAPATAS.

Commercial Value: D. Aeropagitou and Makri 1, 11742 Athens; tel. (21) 09290808; fax (21) 09231952; e-mail admin@nch.gz; internet www.commercialvalue.gr; f. 2002; Pres. D. DASKALOPOULOS; Man. Dir P. ATHENEOS.

Dynamis: Leoforos Syngrou 106, 117 41 Kallithea, Athens; tel. (21) 09227255; fax (21) 09237768; e-mail genka@asfgenka.gr; f. 1977; Man. Dir NIKOLAS STAMATOPOULOS.

Egnatia Co: Odos Fragon 1, 546 26 Thessaloníki; tel. (231) 0523325; fax (231) 0523555; Rep. P. MIGAS.

Emporiki Life: Odos Korai 6, 105 64 Athens; tel. (21) 03282346; fax (21) 03282441; e-mail mzanatta@emporikilife.gr; f. 1940; Chair. DIMITRIS FRANGETIS; Exec. Dir MICHAEL ZANATTA.

Ethniki Hellenic General Insurance Co SA: Odos Karageorgi Servias 8, 102 10 Athens; tel. (21) 03299000; fax (21) 03236101;

e-mail ethniki@ethniki-asfalistiki.gr; internet www
.ethniki-asfalistiki.gr; f. 1891; Gen. Man. C. PHILIPOU.

Galaxias Insurance Co: Leoforos Syngrou 40–42, 117 42 Kallithea, Athens; tel. (21) 09241082; fax (21) 09241698; f. 1967; Gen. Man. K. ANAGNOSTAKIS.

Gothaer Hellas: Odos Michalakopoulou 174, 115 27 Athens; tel. (21) 07750801; fax (21) 07757094; Gen. Man. S. GALANIS.

Hellas Insurance Co: Leoforos Kifissias 119, 151 24 Marousi, Athens; tel. (21) 08127600; fax (21) 08027189; e-mail nick.nardis@aig.com; internet www.aig-greece.gr; f. 1973; Gen. Man. N. NARDIS.

Hellenic Reliance General Insurances: Leoforos Kifissias 304, 152 32 Halandri, Athens; tel. (21) 06843733; fax (21) 06843734; f. 1990; Man. Dir S. F. TRIANTAFYLLAKIS.

Hellenobretanniki General Insurances: Leoforos Messoghion 2–4, 115 27 Athens; tel. (21) 07755301; fax (21) 07714768; f. 1988.

Helvetia General Insurance Co: Leoforos Kifissias 124, 115 26 Athens; tel. (21) 06980840; fax (21) 06923446; f. 1943; Gen. Man. J. DELENDAS.

Horizon General Insurance Co: Leoforos Amalias 26A, 105 57 Athens; tel. (21) 03227932; fax (21) 03225540; e-mail horizon@hol.gr; f. 1965; Gen. Mans THEODORE ACHIS, CHR. ACHIS.

Hydrogios: Odos Solonos 137, 176 75 Athens; tel. (21) 09401300; fax (21) 09407072; Gen. Man. A. KASKARELIS.

Ikonomiki: Odos Kapodistriou 38, 104 32 Athens; tel. (21) 05243374; fax (21) 05234962; f. 1968; Gen. Man. D. NIKOLAIDIS.

Imperial Hellas: Leoforos Syngrou 253, 171 22 N. Smirni, Athens; tel. (21) 09426352; fax (21) 09426202; e-mail imperiasf@hol.gr; internet www.imperial.gr; f. 1971; Gen. Man. G. TZANIS.

Interamerican Hellenic Life Insurance Co: Interamerican Plaza, Leoforos Kifissias 117, 151 80 Maroussi, Athens; tel. (21) 06191111; fax (21) 06191877; e-mail moissism@interamerican.gr; internet www.interamerican.gr; f. 1971; 79.4% owned by Eureko (Netherlands); subsidiary cos provide medical, property and casualty, and automobile insurance; Pres. and Man. Dir DIMITRI KONTOMINAS.

Kykladiki Insurance Co: Leoforos Syngrou 80–88, 117 41 Kallithea, Athens; tel. (21) 09247664; fax (21) 09247344; f. 1919; Gen. Man. PAN. KATSIKOSTAS.

Phoenix General Insurance Co of Greece: Odos Omirou 2, 105 64 Athens; tel. (21) 03295111; fax (21) 03239135; e-mail phoenix@phoenix.gr; f. 1928; general insurance.

Poseidon: Odos Karaiskou 163, 185 35 Piraeus; tel. (21) 04522685; fax (21) 04184337; e-mail poseidon@otenet.gr; f. 1972; Gen. Man. THANOS J. MELAKOPIDES.

Sideris Insurance Co: Odos Lekka 3–5, 105 63 Athens; tel. (21) 03224484; e-mail siderisa@acci.gr; fax (21) 03231066; Dir G. SIDERIS.

Syneteristiki General Insurance Co: Leoforos Syngrou 367, 175 64 Kallithea, Athens; tel. (21) 09491280; fax (21) 09403148; e-mail syne-ins@hol.gr; Gen. Man. D. ZORBAS.

Victoria General Insurance Co SA: Odos Tsimiski 21, 546 22 Thessaloníki; tel. (231) 0371100; fax (231) 0371392; e-mail victoria@victoria.gr; internet www.victoria.gr; f. 1972; Man. Dir G. ANDONIADIS.

A large number of foreign insurance companies also operate in Greece.

Insurance Association

Association of Insurance Companies: Odos Xenophontos 10, 105 57 Athens; tel. (21) 03334100; fax (21) 03334149; e-mail info@eaee.gr; internet www.eaee.gr; 114 mems, of which 32 are foreign insurance companies operating in Greece; Gen. Man. MARGARITA ANTONAKI.

Trade and Industry

GOVERNMENT AGENCY

Organismos Anasinkrotiseos Epicheiriseon (Industrial Reconstruction Organization): Athens; f. 1982; reconstruction and sale of Greek businesses under state receivership.

CHAMBERS OF COMMERCE

Athens Chamber of Commerce and Industry: Odos Akademias 7, 106 71 Athens; tel. (21) 03625342; fax (21) 03618810; e-mail info@acci.gr; internet www.acci.gr; f. 1919; Pres. DRACOULIS FOUNDOUKAKOS; Sec.-Gen. PANAGIOTIS KOUTSIKOS; 70,000 mems.

Athens Chamber of Small and Medium-sized Industries: Odos Akademias 18, 106 71 Athens; tel. (21) 03680700; fax (21) 03614726;

e-mail info@acsmi.gr; internet www.acsmi.gr; f. 1940; Pres. D. CHARISIS; Sec.-Gen. ATH. PAVLOU; c. 60,000 mems.

Crafts Chamber of Piraeus: Odos Karaiscou 111, 185 32 Piraeus; tel. (21) 04110443; fax (21) 04179495; e-mail info@bep.gr; internet www.bep.gr; f. 1925; Pres. KONSTANTINOS MOSCHOLIOS; Sec.-Gen. PANTELIS ANTONIADIS; 18,500 mems.

Piraeus Chamber of Commerce and Industry: Odos Loudovikou 1, 185 31 Piraeus; tel. (21) 4177241; fax (21) 4178680; f. 1919; Pres. GEORGE KASSIMATIS; Sec.-Gen. KONSTANTINOS SARANTOPOULOS.

Thessaloníki Chamber of Commerce and Industry: Odos Tsimiski 29, 546 24 Thessaloníki; tel. (231) 0224438; fax (231) 0230237; f. 1919; Pres. PANTELIS KONSTANTINIDIS; Sec.-Gen. EMMANUEL VLACHOYANNIS; 14,500 mems.

INDUSTRIAL AND TRADE ASSOCIATIONS

Federation of Greek Industries (SEV): Odos Xenophontos 5, 105 57 Athens; tel. (21) 03237325; fax (21) 03222929; e-mail main@fgi.org.gr; internet www.fgi.org.gr; f. 1907; Chair. ELEFTHERIOS ANTONAKOPOULOS; 950 mems.

Federation of Industries of Northern Greece: Morihovou 1, 7th Floor, 546 35 Thessaloníki; tel. (231) 0539817; fax (231) 0546244; e-mail secretariat@sbbe.gr; internet www.sbbe.gr; f. 1915; Pres. SIMEONIDIS DIMITRIOS.

Hellenic Cotton Board: Leoforos Syngrou 150, 176 71 Kallithea, Athens; tel. (21) 09225011; fax (21) 09249656; f. 1931; state organization; Pres. P. K. MYLONAS.

Hellenic Organization of Small and Medium-sized Enterprises and Handicrafts (EOMMEX): Odos Xenias 16, 115 28 Athens; tel. (21) 07491100; fax (21) 07491146; e-mail interel@eommex.gr; internet www.eommex.gr; Pres. NICKOLAOS I. KAKOURIS.

UTILITIES

Electricity

Public Power Corpn (DEI): Odos Xalkokondyli 30, 104 32 Athens; tel. (21) 05230301; fax (21) 05238445; e-mail info@dei.gr; internet www.dei.gr; f. 1950; 84% state-owned; generating capacity 12,069 MW (2003); generation, transmission and distribution of electricity; Chief Exec. and Man. Dir S. NEZIS.

Gas

Public Gas Corpn (DEPA): Leoforos Messoghion 207, 115 25 Athens; tel. (21) 06793500; fax (21) 06749504; e-mail info@depa.gr; internet www.depa.gr; f. 1988; 35% owned by Hellenic Petroleum SA, 65% state-owned; undergoing privatization; began gas imports 1997, initially for industrial use; Man. Dir ARISTEIDIS VAKIRLIS.

Water

In 1980 a law was passed under which Municipal Enterprises for Water Supply and Sewerage (DEYA) were created to manage drinking water and sewerage throughout Greece. Since then some 90 DEYA have been established.

The Hellenic Union of Municipal Enterprises for Water Supply and Sewerage (EDEYA): Odos Anthimou Gaza 3, 4122 22 Larissa; internet www.edeya.gr; f. 1989; 67 mems.

TRADE UNIONS

There are about 5,000 registered trade unions, grouped together in 82 federations and 86 workers' centres, which are affiliated to the Greek General Confederation of Labour.

Greek General Confederation of Labour (GSEE): Odos Patission 69, Athens; tel. (21) 08834611; fax (21) 08229802; e-mail info@gsee.gr; internet www.gsee.gr; f. 1918; Pres. CHRISTOS PROTOPAPAS; Gen. Sec. IOANNIS THEONAS; 700,000 mems.

Pan-Hellenic Federation of Seamen's Unions (PNO): Livanos Bldg, Akti Miaouli 47–49, 185 36 Piraeus; tel. (21) 04292960; fax (21) 04293040; f. 1920; confederation of 14 marine unions; Pres. IOANNIS CHELAS; Gen. Sec. JOHN HALAS.

Transport

RAILWAYS

A five-year programme to upgrade the Greek rail network was initiated in 1996, supported by 350m. drachmae from EU structural funds. The major undertaking was to electrify the 500-km Athens–Thessaloníki line and to extend services to the Bulgarian border. Construction of a 26.3 km electrified extension to the Athens–Piraeus line, in order to provide a three-line urban railway system for Athens, designated Metro Line 1, was completed in 2000. Metro

Lines 2 and 3, each measuring some 9 km, opened prior to the holding of the Olympic Games in 2004.

Attiko Metro: Leoforos Messoghion 191–93, 115 25 Athens; tel. (21) 06792399; fax (21) 06726126; e-mail info@ametro.gr; internet www .ametro.gr; f. 1999; operate underground railway in Athens; Chair. IOANNIS CHRISSIKOPOULOS.

Ilektriki Sidirodromi Athinon–Pireos (ISAP) (Athens–Piraeus Electric Railways): Odos Athinas 67, 105 52 Athens; tel. (21) 03248311; fax (21) 03223935; internet www.isap.gr; state-owned; 25.6 km of electrified track; Chair. GEORGE PAPAVASSILIOU; Man. Dir DIONISSIOS RAPPOS.

Organismos Sidirodromon Ellados (OSE) (Hellenic Railways Organization Ltd): Odos Karolou 1–3, 104 37 Athens; tel. (21) 05248395; fax (21) 05243290; internet www.ose.gr; f. 1971; state railways; total length of track: 2,474 km; Chair. NIKOLAOS BALTAS; Dir-Gen. A. LAZARIS.

ROADS

In 1999 there were an estimated 117,000 km of roads in Greece. Of this total, an estimated 9,100 km were main roads, and 470 km were motorways. Construction of the 680 km Egnatia highway, extending from the Adriatic coast to the Turkish border, was one of the largest road projects in Europe and, having commenced in the early 1990s, was scheduled for completion in 2008; some 350 km of the planned road had been opened to traffic by 2003.

INLAND WATERWAYS

There are no navigable rivers in Greece.

Corinth Canal: built 1893; over six km long, links the Corinthian and Saronic Gulfs; shortens the journey from the Adriatic to the Piraeus by 325 km; spanned by three single-span bridges, two for road and one for rail; can be used by ships of a maximum draught of 22 ft and width of 60 ft; managed since June 2001 by Sea Containers Group (United Kingdom).

SHIPPING

In 2003 the Greek merchant fleet totalled 1,558 vessels, with a combined aggregate displacement of 32.2m. grt. Greece controls one of the largest merchant fleets in the world. The principal ports are Piraeus, Patras and Thessaloníki.

Union of Greek Shipowners: Akti Miaouli 85, 185 38 Piraeus; f. 1916; Pres. NICOS EFTHYMIOU.

Port Authorities

Port of Patras: Patras Port Authority, Central Port Office, Patras; tel. (261) 0316400; fax (261) 0327136; internet www.patrasport.gr; Pres. GEORGE LAZARIS; Harbour Master Capt. NIKOLAS RAFAILOVITS.

Piraeus Port Authority: Piraeus Port Authority, Akti Miaouli 10, 185 35 Piraeus; tel. (21) 04520911; fax (21) 04286843; e-mail olpdsx@ otenet.gr; internet www.olp.gr; 25% privatized; Man. Dir HARILAOS PSARAFTIS.

Port of Thessaloníki: Thessaloníki Port Authority, POB 10467, 541 10 Thessaloníki; tel. (231) 0593129; fax (231) 0510500; e-mail secretariat@thpa.gr; internet www.thpa.gr; Man. Dir SOTIRIS I. GENITSARIS.

Shipping Companies

The following are among the largest or most important shipping companies.

Anangel Shipping Enterprises: Akti Miaouli, POB 80004, 185 10 Piraeus; tel. (21) 04224500; fax (21) 04224819; Man. Dir J. PLATSIDAKIS.

Attika Shipping Co: Odos Voucourestion 16, 10671 Athens; tel. (21) 03609631; fax (21) 03601439; Dir G. PRIOVOLOS.

Bilinder Marine Corpn: Odos Igias 1–3 and Akti Themistokleos, 185 36 Piraeus; tel. (21) 04287300; fax (21) 04287355; Gen. Man. V. ARMOGENI.

Blue Star Ferries: C. Karamanli 157, 16673 Voula, Athens; tel. (21) 08919800; fax (21) 08919829; e-mail bluestarferries@ bluestarferries.com; internet www.bluestarferries.com; Man. Dir G. STRINTZIS.

Ceres Hellenic Shipping Enterprises Co: Akti Miaouli 69, 185 37 Piraeus; tel. (21) 04591000; fax (21) 04283552; e-mail chse@ceres .gr; internet www.ceres.gr; Chief Exec. NIKOLAOS G. FISTES.

Chandris (Hellas) Co: POB 80067, Akti Miaouli 95, 185 38 Piraeus; tel. (21) 04290300; fax (21) 04290256; e-mail chandris@

19080845.multimessage.com; Man. Dirs A. C. PIPERAS, M. G. SKORDIAS.

Costamare Shipping Co: Odos Zephyrou 60, 175 64 Kallithea, Athens; tel. (21) 09390000; fax (21) 09409051; Pres. Capt. V. C. KONSTANTAKOPOULOS.

European Navigation Co: Odos Artemissiou 2, 166 75 Athens; tel. (21) 08981581; fax (21) 08946777; Dir P. KARNESSIS.

Glafki (Hellas) Maritime Co: Odos Mitropoleos 3, 105 57 Athens; tel. (21) 03244991; fax (21) 03228944; Dirs M. FRAGOULIS, G. PANAGIOTOU.

Golden Union Shipping Co: Odos Aegales 8, 185 45 Piraeus; tel. (21) 04061000; fax (21) 04061199; e-mail infgusc@goldenunion.gr; internet www.goldenunion.gr; f. 1977; Chair. THEODORE VENIAMIS.

M. Koutlakis & Co: Makras Stoas 5, 185 31 Piraeus; tel. (21) 04129428; fax (21) 04178755; Dir M. KOUTLAKIS.

Laskaridis Shipping Co: Odos Chimaras 5, 151 25 Maroussi, Athens; tel. (21) 06899090; fax (21) 06806762; e-mail athens@ laskship.cc.cwmail.com; Man. Dirs P. C. LASKARIDIS, A. C. LASKARIDIS.

Marmaras Navigation Co: Odos Filellinon 4–6, Okeanion Bldg, 185 36 Piraeus; tel. (21) 04294226; fax (21) 04294304; Dir D. DIAMANTIDES.

Minoan Lines Shipping Co: Odos 25 August 17, 712 02 Iraklion; tel. (281) 0399800; fax (281) 0330308; e-mail info@minoan.gr; internet www.minoan.gr; Pres. KONSTANTINOS KLIRONOMAS.

Naftomar Shipping and Trading Co: Leoforos Alkyonidon 243, 166 73 Voula; tel. (21) 08914200; fax (21) 08914235; e-mail naftomar@naftomar.gr; internet www.naftomar.gr; Man. Dir RIAD ZEIN.

Thenamaris (Ships Management) Co: Odos Athinas 16, Kavouri, 166 71 Athens; tel. (21) 08969111; fax (21) 08969653; e-mail thena@ thenamaris.gr; internet www.thenamaris.gr; Dir K. MARTINOS.

Tsakos Shipping and Trading Co: Macedonia House, Leoforos Syngrou 367, POB 79141, 175 02 Athens; tel. (21) 09380700; fax (21) 09480710; e-mail mail@tsakoshellas.gr; Dirs P. N. TSAKOS, E. SAROGLOU.

United Shipping and Trading Co of Greece Co: Odos Iassonos 6, 185 37 Piraeus; tel. (21) 04283660; fax (21) 04283630; Dir CH. TSAKOS.

Varnima Corpn International Co: Odos Irodou Attikou 12A, 151 24 Maroussi, Athens; tel. (21) 08093000; fax (21) 08093222; e-mail john_k@attglobal.net; Gen. Man. S. V. SPANOUDAKIS.

CIVIL AVIATION

There are international airports at Athens, Thessaloníki, Alexandroupolis, Corfu, Lesbos, Andravida, Rhodes, Kos and Heraklion/Crete, and 24 domestic airports (of which 13 are authorized to receive international flights). A new international airport, Eleftherios Venizelos, at Spata, some 25 km east of Athens, was opened in March 2001. The airport was expected to have a handling capacity of 16m. passengers per year.

Aegean Airlines: Leoforos Vouliagmenis 572, 164 51 Athens; tel. (21) 09988350; fax (21) 09957598; internet www.aegeanair.com; f. 1987; domestic and international services; Pres. and Chief Exec. THEODOROS VASSILAKIS.

Olympic Airlines: Leoforos Syngrou 96–100, 117 41 Kallithea, Athens; tel. (21) 09269111; fax (21) 09267154; e-mail ebusms@ olympicairlines.com; internet www.olympicairlines.com; f. 1957; state-owned; restructured Dec. 2003, pending privatization; domestic services linking principal cities and islands in Greece, and international services to Singapore, Thailand, South Africa and the USA, and throughout Europe and the Middle East; Chair. and Chief Exec. DIONYSIOS KALOFONOS.

Tourism

The sunny climate, the natural beauty of the country and its great history and traditions attract tourists to Greece. There are numerous islands and many sites of archaeological interest. The number of tourists visiting Greece increased from 1m. in 1968 to 14.2m. in 2002. Receipts from tourism, which totalled US $120m. in 1968, reached $9,741m. in 2002. Many visitors were attracted to Greece in 2004, when the country hosted the Olympic Games.

Ellinikos Organismos Tourismou (EOT) (Greek National Tourist Organization): Odos Tsoha 7, 115 21 Athens; tel. (21) 08707000; e-mail info@gnto.gr; internet www.gnto.gr; Pres. Dr ARISTIDIS S. CALOGEROPOULOS-STRATIS.

GRENADA

Introductory Survey

Location, Climate, Language, Religion, Flag, Capital

Grenada, a mountainous, heavily-forested island, is the most southerly of the Windward Islands, in the West Indies. The country also includes some of the small islands known as the Grenadines, which lie to the north-east of Grenada. The most important of these are the low-lying island of Carriacou and its neighbour, Petit Martinique. The climate is semi-tropical, with an average annual temperature of 28°C (82°F) in the lowlands. Annual rainfall averages about 1,500 mm (60 ins) in the coastal area and 3,800 mm to 5,100 mm (150–200 ins) in mountain areas. Most of the rainfall occurs between June and December. The majority of the population speak English, although a French patois is sometimes spoken. According to the census of 1991, 82% of Grenada's population were of African descent, while 13% were of mixed ethnic origins. Most of the population profess Christianity, and the main denominations are Roman Catholicism (to which some 55% of the population adhered in 2002) and Anglicanism (about 14% of the population). The national flag (proportions 1 by 2) consists of a diagonally-quartered rectangle (yellow in the upper and lower segments, green in the right and left ones) surrounded by a red border bearing six five-pointed yellow stars (three at the upper edge of the flag, and three at the lower edge). There is a red disc, containing a large five-pointed yellow star, in the centre, and a representation of a nutmeg (in yellow and red) on the green segment near the hoist. The capital is St George's.

Recent History

Grenada was initially colonized by the French but was captured by the British in 1762. The Treaty of Versailles recognized British control in 1783. Grenada continued as a British colony until 1958, when it joined the Federation of the West Indies, remaining a member until the dissolution of the Federation in 1962. Full internal self-government and statehood in association with the United Kingdom were achieved in March 1967. During this period, the political life of Grenada was dominated by Herbert Blaize, the leader of the Grenada National Party (GNP), and Eric Gairy, a local trade union leader, who in 1950 founded the Grenada United Labour Party (GULP), with the support of an associated trade union. Gairy became Premier after the elections of 1967 and again after those of 1972, which he contested chiefly on the issue of total independence. Grenada became independent, within the Commonwealth, on 7 February 1974, with Gairy as Prime Minister. Domestic opposition to Gairy was expressed in public unrest, and the formation by the three opposition parties—the GNP, the United People's Party and the New Jewel Movement (NJM)—of the People's Alliance, which contested the 1976 general elections and reduced GULP's majority in the Lower House.

The opposition regarded the rule of Sir Eric Gairy, as he became in June 1977, as increasingly autocratic and corrupt, and on 13 March 1979 he was replaced in a bloodless coup by the leader of the left-wing NJM, Maurice Bishop. The new People's Revolutionary Government (PRG) suspended the 1974 Constitution and announced the imminent formation of a People's Consultative Assembly to draft a new constitution. Meanwhile, Grenada remained a monarchy, with the British Queen as Head of State, represented in Grenada by a Governor-General. During 1980–81 there was an increase in repression, against a background of mounting anti-Government violence and the PRG's fears of an invasion by US forces.

By mid-1982 relations with the USA, the United Kingdom and the more conservative members of the Caribbean Community and Common Market (CARICOM, see p. 172) were becoming increasingly strained: elections had not been arranged, restrictions against the privately-owned press had been imposed, many detainees were still awaiting trial, and Grenada was aligning more closely with Cuba and the USSR. Cuba was contributing funds and construction workers for the airport at Point Salines, a project which further strengthened the US Government's conviction that Grenada was to become a centre for Soviet manoeuvres in the area.

In March 1983 the armed forces were put on alert, in response to renewed fears that the USA was planning to invade. (The USA strenuously denied any such plans.) In June Bishop sought to improve relations with the USA, and announced the appointment of a commission to draft a new constitution. The more left-wing members of the PRG denounced this attempt at conciliation as an ideological betrayal. A power struggle developed between Bishop and his deputy, Bernard Coard, the Minister of Finance and Planning. In October Bishop was placed under house arrest, allegedly for his refusal to share power with Coard. The commander of the People's Revolutionary Army (PRA), Gen. Austin Hudson, subsequently announced that Bishop had been expelled from the NJM. On 19 October thousands of Bishop's supporters stormed the house, freed Bishop, and demonstrated outside the PRA headquarters. PRA forces responded by firing into the crowd. Later in the day, Bishop, three of his ministers and two trade unionists were executed by the PRA. The Government was replaced by a 16-member Revolutionary Military Council (RMC), led by Gen. Austin and supported by Coard and one other minister. The remaining NJM ministers were arrested and imprisoned, and a total curfew was imposed.

Regional and international outrage at the assassination of Bishop, in addition to fears of a US military intervention, were so intense that after four days the RMC relaxed the curfew, reopened the airport and promised a swift return to civilian rule. However, the Organisation of Eastern Caribbean States (OECS, see p. 384) resolved to intervene in an attempt to restore democratic order, and asked for assistance from the USA, which readily complied. (It is unclear whether the decision to intervene preceded or followed a request for help to the OECS by the Grenadian Governor-General, Sir Paul Scoon.) On 25 October 1983 some 1,900 US military personnel invaded the island, accompanied by 300 troops from Jamaica, Barbados and member countries of the OECS. Fighting continued for some days, and the USA gradually increased its troop strength, with further reinforcements waiting off shore with a US naval task force. The RMC's forces were defeated, while Coard, Austin and others who had been involved in the coup were detained.

On 9 November 1983 Scoon appointed a non-political interim Council to assume responsibility for the government of the country until elections could be held. Nicholas Brathwaite, a former Commonwealth official, was appointed Chairman of this Council in December. The 1974 Constitution was reinstated (although the country did not rejoin the East Caribbean Supreme Court), and an electoral commission was created. By mid-December the USA had withdrawn all its forces except 300 support troops who were to assist the 430 members of Caribbean forces remaining on the island. A 550-member police force, trained by the USA and the United Kingdom, was established, including a paramilitary body that was to be the new defence contingent.

Several political parties that had operated clandestinely or from exile during the rule of the PRG re-emerged and announced their intention of contesting the elections for a new House of Representatives. Sir Eric Gairy returned to Grenada in January 1984 to lead GULP, but stated that he would not stand as a candidate himself. In May three former NJM ministers formed the Maurice Bishop Patriotic Movement (MBPM) to contest the elections. A number of centrist parties emerged or re-emerged, including Blaize's GNP. Fears that a divided opposition would allow GULP to win a majority of seats in the new House resulted in an agreement by several of these organizations, in August 1984, to form the New National Party (NNP), led by Blaize.

At the general election held in December 1984 the NNP achieved a convincing victory by winning 14 of the 15 seats in the House of Representatives, with 59% of the popular votes. Both GULP (which won 36% of the votes cast) and the MBPM claimed that the poll had been fraudulent, and the one successful GULP candidate, Marcel Peters, initially refused to take his seat in protest. He subsequently accepted the seat, but was expelled from the party and formed the Grenada Democratic Labour Party (GDLP). Blaize became Prime Minister. US and

Caribbean troops remained in Grenada, at Blaize's request, until September 1985.

The trial of 19 detainees (including Coard, his wife, Phyllis, and Gen. Austin), accused of murder and conspiracy against Bishop and six of his associates, opened in November 1984. However, repeated adjournments postponed the trial of 18 of the detainees until April 1986. One of the detainees agreed to give evidence for the State in return for a pardon. Eventually, the jury returned verdicts on 196 charges of murder and conspiracy to murder in December. Fourteen of the defendants were sentenced to death, three received prison sentences of between 30 and 45 years, and one was acquitted. In July 1991 the Court of Appeal upheld the original verdicts that had been imposed in 1986 on the defendants in the Bishop murder trial, and further pleas for clemency were rejected. Preparations for the imminent hanging of the 14, however, provoked international outrage, and in August Brathwaite announced that the death sentences were to be commuted to terms of life imprisonment.

Internal differences gradually led to the disintegration of the NNP. In 1986 its parliamentary strength was reduced to 12 seats, following the resignation of two members who subsequently formed the Democratic Labour Congress (DLC). Three more government members resigned in April 1987, and joined forces with the DLC and the GDLP in July to form a united opposition, with six seats in the House of Representatives. In October they formally launched a new party, the National Democratic Congress (NDC), led by George Brizan, who had earlier been appointed parliamentary opposition leader. In January 1989 Brizan resigned as leader of the NDC in order to allow the election of Nicholas Brathwaite (head of the interim Government of 1983–84) to that post.

During 1988–89 the actions of the Blaize Government, under provisions of the controversial Emergency Powers Act of 1987, gave rise to concerns both within the opposition and among regional neighbours. Deportation orders and bans were enforced by the administration against prominent left-wing politicians and journalists from the region, and a variety of books and journals were proscribed.

In January 1989 Blaize was replaced as party leader by his cabinet colleague, Dr Keith Mitchell, although he remained Prime Minister. In July, however, following allegations of corruption by the NDC, Blaize announced the dismissal of Mitchell and the Chairman of the NNP, accusing them of violating the principles of cabinet government. Amid uncertainty as to whether the Blaize faction had formed a separate party, two more members of the Government resigned, thus reducing support for the Blaize Government to only five of the 15 members of the House of Representatives. Blaize did not officially announce the formation of a new party, the National Party (TNP), until late August, by which time he had advised the acting Governor-General to prorogue Parliament. (The Government thereby avoided being defeated in a motion of 'no confidence', the immediate dissolution of Parliament and the prospect of an early general election.) The term of the Parliament was due to expire at the end of December, and a general election had to be held within three months. However, Blaize died in mid-December, and the Governor-General appointed Ben Jones, Blaize's former deputy and the new leader of TNP, as Prime Minister. At the general election, held in March 1990, no party achieved an absolute majority in the House of Representatives. The NDC, with seven of the 15 legislative seats, achieved a working majority in Parliament when one of GULP's successful candidates announced his defection to the NDC. Brathwaite subsequently became Prime Minister and appointed a new Cabinet.

Brathwaite resigned as leader of the NDC in September 1994 and was succeeded by George Brizan. In February 1995 Brathwaite resigned as Prime Minister, and was succeeded by Brizan. At the general election held in June, the NNP secured eight of the 15 seats in the House of Representatives, while the NDC's representation was reduced to five seats. The remaining two seats were secured by GULP. Dr Keith Mitchell, leader of the NNP, became Prime Minister and appointed a Cabinet. The NNP subsequently undertook negotiations with GULP in an attempt to strengthen its single-seat majority and to secure the two-thirds' majority required to amend the Constitution. In July Francis Alexis resigned as deputy leader of the NDC; in November he and three other former NDC members announced the formation of a new opposition group, the Democratic Labour Party (DLP).

The appointment in August 1996 of Daniel (later Sir Daniel) Williams to the post of Governor-General provoked considerable controversy because of Williams' connections with the NNP (he had been deputy leader of the party during the 1980s) and his previous role as a cabinet minister in the Government of Herbert Blaize. Opposition members staged a walk-out at his inauguration ceremony, a protest that led to Brizan, the Leader of the Opposition, being suspended from the House of Representatives for one month.

In March 1997 the Government's Mercy Committee rejected a request made by the Conference of Churches of Grenada for the release, on the grounds of their deteriorating physical and mental health, of Phyllis Coard and another of those serving terms of life imprisonment for the murder of Maurice Bishop. None the less, the Committee gave assurances that the detainees' medical requirements would receive attention, and that conditions at the prison where they were being held would be improved.

In late November 1998 the resignation of the Minister of Foreign Affairs, Raphael Fletcher, from the Government and NNP in order to join GULP, resulted in an early general election being called. At the general election, held on 18 January 1999 (in which 56.5% of the electorate voted), the NNP achieved a comprehensive victory, obtaining all of the 15 seats in the House of Representatives. The NNP's return to power constituted the first time in the country's history that a political party had been given two successive terms in government. In its electoral campaign the party had highlighted its recent successes in maintaining strong economic growth and reducing unemployment.

In late September and early October 1999 two leading journalists were arrested on separate charges of alleged criminal libel. One of the detainees was the editor of *Grenada Today*, George Worme, who had published a letter accusing Mitchell of having bribed voters during the last election campaign. Opposition parties, human rights organizations and media associations claimed that the Government was seeking to intimidate independent journalists. In November 2000 the Grenada High Court ruled that the charge brought against Worme was unconstitutional, since it violated his right to free expression.

Also in early October 1999 Bernard Coard, the former Deputy Prime Minister serving a term of life imprisonment with 16 others for the 1983 murder of Prime Minister Maurice Bishop and a number of his associates (see above), issued a statement in which he accepted full responsibility for the crimes; it was, however, unclear as to whether he was speaking on behalf of all 17 prisoners. In February 2002 it was announced that three former soldiers jailed in 1986 for Bishop's murder and that of seven others during the 1983 coup attempt were to be released. A High Court judge deemed it unconstitutional that their multiple sentences for manslaughter should be served consecutively. Furthermore, in March 2004 the Court of Appeal ruled that the life sentences imposed on the 17 prisoners were unconstitutional; the prisoners were to receive new sentences, possibly resulting in their release from jail. However, on 26 April, the day before the prisoners were to be resentenced, the Court of Appeal of the OECS, based in Saint Lucia, overturned the ruling. This decision was confirmed after a further hearing in February 2005; lawyers for the men stated that they would appeal against the judgment to the Privy Council, based in the United Kingdom.

In June 2000 Mitchell dismissed Michael Baptiste from the Government after he was reported to have openly criticized Mitchell's running of the country. (Baptiste had been dismissed as Minister of Agriculture, Lands, Forestry and Fisheries in 1999 and demoted to Secretary of State.) Baptiste subsequently left the NNP and became the sole opposition member in the House of Representatives. In January 2001 Baptiste formed a new opposition party, the United Labour Congress (ULC). Later in the year the ULC merged with GULP and at the party's convention in December Baptiste was elected opposition leader.

In February 2003 Gloria Payne-Banfield succeeded Baptiste as GULP leader, in preparation for legislative elections, scheduled to be held by April 2004, but widely expected to be held earlier. At the general election, which was duly held on 27 November, the NNP secured a third successive term in office, although its parliamentary majority was reduced to just one seat. The NDC won the seven remaining seats in the 15-seat House of Representatives. Keith Mitchell was sworn in again as Prime Minister on 29 November. The electoral campaign was dominated by opposition claims that the Mitchell Government had allowed national debt and unemployment to increase to critical levels; the NNP, however, successfully argued that the party had guided the economy back to real growth.

Mitchell appointed a new Cabinet in early December 2003; the most significant change was the transferral of the agriculture portfolio to Gregory Bowen, the erstwhile Minister of Communications, Works and Public Utilities, as part of a wider plan to transform the ailing agricultural sector, in particular the nutmeg industry. Bowen was also appointed Deputy Prime Minister. On 16 December a defeated NDC candidate, George Prime, issued a legal challenge to the election result in the Carriacou/Petit Martinique seat, claiming that a number of irregularities had surrounded the voting there. In January 2004 the NNP responded by filing a petition challenging the results in two other seats, also citing voting irregularities. In August the Prime Minister commenced legal proceedings against George Prime, as well as against a local company and a US-based publication after corruption allegations were made relating to the appointment of Eric Resteiner, a former Grenadian diplomat. Later in the same month an official inquiry into the allegations was established; Richard Cheltenham, a prominent Barbadian lawyer, was appointed to lead the investigation.

Grenada was severely devastated by 'Hurricane Ivan', which struck the island in early September 2004. Some 39 Grenadians were killed and around 90% of the housing stock was destroyed; as a result of the infrastructural damage caused by the hurricane, the country's economy was expected to enter a recession lasting several years. According to the OECS, full rehabilitation would cost at least US $814m. Opposition MPs, who urged the NNP to establish an interim coalition Government, strenuously criticized the Government's relief efforts and the country's perceived slow recovery progress. In October Grenada established the Agency for Reconstruction and Development to implement and monitor reconstruction projects and to manage the receipt of grants from the numerous international donors. Widespread looting and violent crime was brought under relative control after intervention from regional (primarily Trinidadian) security forces.

Meanwhile, in February 2005 the Government was embroiled in an argument with the Grenada Bar Association (GBA) over the former's nomination of Hugh Wildman, the Director of the Financial Intelligence Unit of the Grenada International Financial Services Authority, for the post of Attorney-General. Wildman attracted intense criticism from the GBA in his previous role as Director of Public Prosecutions and it was finally agreed that the Cabinet would review the nomination. The decision was passed to the Judicial and Legal Services Commission of the OECS, which has the power to adjudicate on senior judicial appointments, and in late February Wildman's appointment was rejected. The Government accepted the ruling and in March the position of Attorney-General was added to the responsibilities of Elvin Nimrod—who, in addition to holding several other portfolios, was also the Minister of Legal Affairs. Wildman, meanwhile, was given the apparently newly created role of legal adviser to the Cabinet; an appointment that opposition MPs regarded as a crude attempt by Mitchell to circumvent the Constitution and as a waste of resources.

As a member of the OECS, Grenada has been involved in discussions concerning the possible formation of a political union. In 1988 Grenada, Dominica, Saint Lucia and Saint Vincent and the Grenadines decided to proceed with their own plans for a political union. In 1990 it was agreed that a Windward Islands Regional Constituent Assembly (RCA) would be convened to discuss the economic and political feasibility of creating a federation. Successive Governments participated in negotiations towards the establishment of the Caribbean Court of Justice (CCJ), which would replace the Privy Council as the final court of appeal. By early 2005, however, legislation giving ultimate judicial power to the CCJ had still to be approved by the Grenadian Parliament.

In May 1996 Grenada signed two treaties with the USA, relating to mutual legal assistance and extradition, as part of a regional campaign to combat drugs-trafficking. Improved relations with Cuba, which had been severely strained since 1983 when diplomatic ties were suspended, resulted in offers of assistance with education, health and agriculture in Grenada in 1997. Diplomatic relations between the two countries were restored in December 1999, and in January 2003 a new hospital was opened in St George's, partly financed by the Cuban Government. In 2000 Grenada also restored diplomatic relations with Libya, also suspended in 1983. In the following year Libya granted Grenada, along with other eastern Caribbean islands,

access to a US $2,000m. development fund. It was also reported, in September, that Libya had agreed to purchase the entire output of Grenada's bananas and would provide the island with a set of grants and loans worth $4m., as well as cancelling a $6m. loan for the construction of Grenada's international airport in 1981.

Following the terrorist attacks in the USA in September 2001, Grenada came under increased international pressure to abandon its Economic Citizenship Programme, under which passports were sold to non-citizens. The Government initially refused to bow to international pressure, but, in December 2002, it announced the closure of the Programme.

In September 2000 three diplomats from the People's Republic of China, including the ambassador to Trinidad and Tobago, were deported after they were accused of making statements that 'constituted interference in the internal affairs of Grenada'. The delegation were staying on the island for three days as guests of the Grenada-China Friendship Society, a recently formed non-political organization that aimed to promote closer links between the two countries. From 1983 Grenada had maintained diplomatic relations with the Taiwan instead of the People's Republic of China; however, in December 2004 Taiwan recalled its ambassador to Grenada after Mitchell visited mainland China. It was reported in the same month that the Chinese Government had promised Mitchell substantial funds for development projects in Grenada. Mitchell emphasized that the destruction caused by 'Hurricane Ivan' had forced the Government to reconsider its international relationships and on 20 January 2005 Grenada duly established official ties with the People's Republic of China. One week later Taiwan severed its relations with Grenada.

Government

Grenada has dominion status within the Commonwealth. The British monarch is Head of State and is represented locally by a Governor-General. The Cabinet, led by the Prime Minister, holds executive power. Parliament comprises the Senate, made up of 13 Senators appointed by the Governor-General on the advice of the Prime Minister and the Leader of the Opposition, and the 15-member House of Representatives, elected by universal adult suffrage. The Cabinet is responsible to Parliament.

Defence

A regional security unit was formed in 1983, modelled on the British police force and trained by British officers. A paramilitary element, known as the Special Service Unit and trained by US advisers, acts as the defence contingent and participates in the Regional Security System, a defence pact with other East Caribbean states.

Economic Affairs

In 2003, according to estimates by the World Bank, Grenada's gross national income (GNI), measured at average 2001–03 prices, was US $401.9m., equivalent to US $3,790 per head (or US $6,710 per head on an international purchasing-power parity basis). In 1990–2003 Grenada's population increased at an average rate of 0.8% per year, while gross domestic product (GDP) per head increased, in real terms, by an average of 1.8% per year. Overall GDP increased, in real terms, at an average annual rate of 2.7% in 1990–2003. Real GDP decreased by 4.4% in 2001 and by a further 0.4% in 2002, before increasing by an estimated 5.7% in 2003.

According to preliminary figures, agriculture (including hunting, forestry and fishing) contributed 9.1% of GDP in 2003. The sector engaged 13.8% of the employed labour force in 1998. Grenada, known as the Spice Island of the Caribbean, is one of the world's largest producers of nutmeg (although Indonesia produces some 75% of the world's total). In 2002 sales of nutmeg and mace (the pungent red membrane around the nut) accounted for 21.5% of Grenada's domestic export earnings. The other principal cash crops are cocoa and bananas. Exports of bananas were suspended in early 1997 by the Windward Islands Banana Development and Exporting Company (WIBDECO) because of poor quality, but were permitted to resume in late 1998, following a rehabilitation programme. Nevertheless, exports of bananas were still greatly reduced in 1999–2003. Livestock production, for domestic consumption, is important on Carriacou. There are extensive timber reserves on the island of Grenada; forestry development is strictly controlled and involves a programme of reafforestation. Exports of fish contributed an estimated 7.4% of domestic export earnings in 2002. Agricultural GDP increased at an average annual rate of 0.2% in

1990–2003. The sector expanded by 19.0% in 2002, but decreased by 2.4% in 2003.

Industry (mining, manufacturing, construction and utilities) provided 22.1% of GDP in 2003 and engaged 23.9% of the employed labour force in 1998. The mining sector accounted for only 0.2% of employment in 1998 and 0.5% of GDP in 2003. Manufacturing, which contributed 5.8% of GDP in 2003 and employed 7.4% of the working population in 1998, consists mainly of the processing of agricultural products and of cottage industries producing garments and spice-based items. From the late 1990s the electronic component sector gained in significance. Exports from this sector accounted for nearly two-fifths (39.2%) of domestic merchandise exports in 2002. Rum, soft drinks, paints and varnishes, household paper products and the tyre-retreading industries are also important. Manufacturing GDP increased by an average of 4.1% per year in 1990–2003; however, the sector's GDP decreased by 3.8% in 2002 and by a further 2.8% in 2003. Overall, industrial GDP increased by an annual average of 5.4% in 1990–2003. The GDP of the industrial sector decreased by 1.0% in 2002, but, led by an expanding construction sector, increased by 11.4% in 2003.

Grenada is dependent upon imports for its energy requirements, and in 2002 fuel accounted for an estimated 9.9% of the total cost of imports.

The services sector contributed 68.8% of GDP in 2003, when hotels and restaurants accounted for some 7.8% of GDP. Tourism receipts totalled around US $169.5m. in 2003. From the mid-1980s until the late 1990s Grenada's tourist industry experienced a rapid expansion. However, total visitor arrivals declined dramatically in the early 21st century. The decrease was mainly owing to a massive fall in cruise-ship arrivals (26.6% in 2000, 18.2% in 2001 and 8.3% in 2002). Stop-over arrivals, however, remained relatively stable in all three years. In 2003 the industry recovered slightly; the number of stop-over arrivals increased by some 7.5%, while the depressed cruise-ship sector improved by 8.7%, in terms of the number of passengers carried to the island. Of total stop-over visitors (excluding non-resident Grenadians) in 2001, 29.7% were from the USA, 26.3% were from the United Kingdom and 25.4% were from Caribbean countries. The GDP of the services sector increased at an average annual rate of 3.2% in 1990–2003; the sector contracted by 1.5% in 2002, but increased by an estimated 4.5% in 2003.

In 2003 Grenada recorded a visible trade deficit of EC $494.71m. and there was a deficit of $407.54m. on the current account of the balance of payments. In 2002 the principal source of imports was the USA, accounting for 45.8% of the total, according to preliminary figures. The USA is also the principal market for exports, taking 38.9% of the total in the same year. The principal exports are electronic components and nutmeg. The principal imports in 2002 were machinery and transport equipment, basic manufactures and foodstuffs. The trade deficit is partly offset by earnings from tourism, capital receipts and remittances from the large numbers of Grenadians working abroad.

In 2002 there was an overall budgetary deficit of EC $210.2m. (equivalent to 19.4% of GDP). Grenada's total external debt was US $339.3m. at the end of 2002, of which US $268.7m. was long-term public debt. In that year the cost of debt-servicing was equivalent to 13.6% of the value of exports of goods and services. The average annual rate of inflation was 2.2% in 1990–2002; consumer prices increased by 3.1% in 2001 and by 1.6% in 2002. According to estimates, 10.9% of the labour force were unemployed at the end of 2003, although the rate was presumed to have increased to over 25% in early 2005 after 'Hurricane Ivan' destroyed much of the island's economic infrastructure.

Grenada is a member of CARICOM (see p. 172). It is also a member of the Economic Commission for Latin America and the Caribbean (ECLAC, see p. 33), the Organization of American States (OAS, see p. 319), the Organisation of Eastern Caribbean States (OECS, see p. 384) and is a signatory of the Cotonou Agreement (see p. 262), the successor arrangement to the Lomé Conventions between the African, Caribbean and Pacific (ACP) countries and the European Union. Grenada is a member of the Eastern Caribbean Securities Exchange (based in Saint Christopher and Nevis).

Grenada's economy remains fairly dependent upon agriculture, which is vulnerable to adverse weather conditions and infestation by pests. From 1997 a decline in production of nutmeg in Indonesia resulted in higher prices on the external market, stimulating a significant increase in Grenada's output.

In 1999 export earnings from nutmeg increased to US $16.8m. (compared with $8.7m. in 1998). However, this figure had decreased to $13.8m. by 2002. The need for further economic diversification has recently been underscored by the loss, from 2006, of preferential access to European markets for banana producers of the ACP countries. In September 2004 'Hurricane Ivan' destroyed that season's nutmeg, banana and cocoa crops.

In the late 1990s the Government attempted to diversify the economy partly through the expansion of the 'offshore' financial sector. Since the introduction of legislation in 1997, some 900 'offshore' financial companies (including 21 banks) have been registered in Grenada; in September 1999 the creation of a regulatory body, the International Business and Finance Corporation, was announced. In January 2000, moreover, the Government established the Grenada International Financial Services Authority (GIFSA) to regulate the international financial services sector. In the same year, following Grenada's inclusion on international money-laundering and tax 'havens' blacklists and the collapse (and subsequent government takeover) of an 'offshore' bank, the Government introduced measures to strengthen the GIFSA. These included: redoubling efforts to combat money-laundering and drugs-trafficking; the establishment of a bank supervision department to ensure that all financial institutions operated within the norms of the sector; and a review of all existing legislation governing the financial services sector to comply with the requirements of the Organisation for Economic Co-operation and Development (OECD) by March 2001. As part of this effort, the Government has revoked the licences of over 40 'offshore' banks and trusts, and, after making a commitment to move towards the exchange of information in tax investigations by 2005, in March 2002 Grenada was removed from the OECD list. By the end of 2003 there were just two 'offshore' banks operating in Grenada; the 'offshore' sector also included 2,293 international business companies at that time.

The most promising sector of the economy was tourism, from which revenue more than doubled between 1990 and 2000. However, revenue from the sector fell in 2001 as a result of repercussions of the terrorist attacks in the USA in September of that year. Revenues and tourist arrivals recovered in 2002 and 2003, and, until 'Hurricane Ivan' devastated the island in September, further growth was expected in 2004. After the successful reconstruction of most of the country's major hotels, Grenada was 'relaunched' as an international tourist destination in early 2005. Growth in tourism during the 1990s, in turn, stimulated the construction sector, the GDP of which expanded by an annual average of 56.4% in 1990–2003. In 2003 the IMF urged the Grenadian Government to tighten fiscal policy in order to improve the unsustainable state of public finances (which continued to suffer from sizeable internal and external debts). However, reduced government revenue and increased salary costs resulted in an increase of the fiscal deficit from 3.2% in 2000 to 19.4% of GDP in 2002, financed mainly through local commercial borrowing and an accumulation of arrears. Preliminary figures suggested a deficit equivalent to 5.2% of GDP for 2003, with budgetary estimates projecting a similar result for 2004. A contraction in GDP of 0.4% was recorded in 2002, although a return to positive growth (of 5.7%), boosted by a recovering tourism industry and a buoyant construction sector, was estimated in 2003. A similar growth rate had been predicted for 2004 until the magnitude of the hurricane damage sustained in September became apparent. As a consequence, negative growth rates were certain to be recorded in that year and in 2005. Numerous international donors provided funds and raw materials for the reconstruction effort and it was hoped that, after the initial recovery process, the rebuilding work would stimulate the economy. Some observers, however, believed the damage was so acute that the economy would not return to positive growth for 15 years. In December 2004 the Government, which was unable to meet its interest payment obligations, announced the country's external debt commitments were to be restructured.

Education

Education is free and compulsory for children between the ages of five and 16 years. Primary education begins at five years of age and lasts for seven years. Secondary education, beginning at the age of 12, lasts for a further five years. In 2001 a total of 19,134 children received public primary education; there were 57 primary schools in 1995. There were 20 public secondary schools in 2002, with 9,891 pupils registered, in 2001. Technical Centres have been established in St Patrick's, St David's and St John's, and the Grenada National College, the Mirabeau Agricultural School and the Teachers' Training College have been incorporated into the Technical and Vocational Institute in St George's. The Extra-Mural Department of the University of the West Indies has a branch in St George's. A School of Medicine has been established at St George's University (SGU), where a School of Arts and Sciences was also founded in 1997, while there is a School of Fishing at Victoria. In May 2003 Grenada successfully completed negotiations with the World Bank and the Organisation of Eastern Caribbean States for an EC $11.3m. loan and credit agreement for educational development. Total budgetary expenditure on education was $52.5m. in 2001 (equivalent to 12.5% of total expenditure).

Public Holidays

2005: 1 January (New Year's Day), 7 February (Independence Day), 25 March (Good Friday), 28 March (Easter Monday), 5 May (Labour Day), 16 May (Whit Monday), 26 May (Corpus Christi), 1–2 August (Emancipation Holidays), 8–9 August (Carnival), 25 October (Thanksgiving Day), 25–26 December (Christmas).

2006: 1 January (New Year's Day), 7 February (Independence Day), 14 April (Good Friday), 17 April (Easter Monday), 1 May (Labour Day), 5 June (Whit Monday), 15 June (Corpus Christi), 7–8 August (Emancipation Holidays), 14–15 August (Carnival), 25 October (Thanksgiving Day), 25–26 December (Christmas).

Weights and Measures

The metric system is in use.

Statistical Survey

Source (unless otherwise stated): Central Statistical Office, Ministry of Finance, Financial Complex, The Carenage, St George's; tel. 440-2731; fax 440-4115; e-mail director@economicaffairs.grenada.gd; internet economicaffairs.grenada.gd.

AREA AND POPULATION

Area: 344.5 sq km (133.0 sq miles).

Population: 94,806 (males 46,637, females 48,169) at census of 12 May 1991 (excluding 537 persons in institutions and 33 persons in the foreign service); 100,895 at census of 25 May 2001 (preliminary). *2003* (mid-year estimate): 104,614 (Source: World Bank, *World Development Indicators*).

Density (mid-2003): 303.7 per sq km.

Principal Town (population at 2001 census, preliminary): St George's (capital) 3,908. *Mid-2003* (UN estimate, incl. suburbs): St George's 32,707 (Source: UN, *World Urbanization Prospects: The 2003 Revision*).

Births and Deaths (registrations, 2001, provisional): Live births 1,899 (birth rate 18.8 per 1,000); Deaths 727 (death rate 7.2 per 1,000).

Expectation of Life (WHO estimates, years at birth): 67.4 (males 65.9; females 68.8) in 2002. Source: WHO, *World Health Report*.

Employment (employees only, 1998): Agriculture, hunting, forestry and fishing 4,794; Mining and quarrying 58; Manufacturing 2,579; Electricity, gas and water 505; Construction 5,163; Wholesale and retail trade 6,324; Restaurants and hotels 1,974; Transport, storage and communications 2,043; Financing, insurance and real estate 1,312; Public administration, defence and social security 1,879; Community services 3,904; Other services 2,933; Activities not adequately defined 1,321; *Total employed* 34,789 (males 20,733, females 14,056). *Mid-2003* (estimates): Agriculture, etc. 8,000; Total labour force 37,000 (Source: FAO).

HEALTH AND WELFARE

Key Indicators

Total Fertility Rate (children per woman, 2002): 3.5.

Under-5 Mortality Rate (per 1,000 live births, 2003): 23.

Physicians (per 1,000 head, 1997): 0.50.

Hospital Beds (per 1,000 head, 1996): 5.27.

Health Expenditure (2001): US $ per head (PPP): 445.

Health Expenditure (2001): % of GDP: 5.3.

Health Expenditure (2001): public (% of total): 71.9.

Access to Water (% of persons, 2002): 95.

Access to Sanitation (% of persons, 2002): 97.

Human Development Index (2002): ranking: 93.

Human Development Index (2002): value: 0.745.

For sources and definitions, see explanatory note on p. vi.

AGRICULTURE, ETC.

Principal Crops (FAO estimates, '000 metric tons, 2003): Roots and tubers 3.2; Sugar cane 7.2; Pigeon peas 0.5; Coconuts 6.5; Vegetables 2.6; Bananas 4.1; Plantains 0.7; Oranges 0.9; Grapefruit and pomelos 2.0; Apples 0.5; Plums 0.7; Mangoes 1.9; Avocados 1.5; Other fruits 4.5; Cocoa beans 0.7; Nutmeg, mace and cardamons 2.7. Source: FAO.

Livestock (FAO estimates, '000 head, year ending September 2003): Cattle 4.5; Pigs 5.9; Sheep 13.2; Goats 7.2; Asses 0.7; Poultry 268. Source: FAO.

Livestock Products (FAO estimates, '000 metric tons, 2003): Poultry meat 0.6; Cows' milk 0.5; Hen eggs 0.9. Source: FAO.

Fishing (metric tons, live weight, 2002): Blackfin tuna 255; Yellowfish tuna 593; Atlantic sailfish 151; Atlantic blue marlin 69; Bigeye scad 67; Common dolphinfish 178; *Total catch* (incl. others) 2,171. Source: FAO.

INDUSTRY

Production (1994): Rum 300,000 litres; Beer 2,400,000 litres; Wheat flour 4,000 metric tons (1996); Cigarettes 15m.; Electricity 118 million kWh (2000). Source: mainly UN, *Industrial Commodity Statistics Yearbook*.

FINANCE

Currency and Exchange Rates: 100 cents = 1 Eastern Caribbean dollar (EC $). *Sterling, US Dollar and Euro Equivalents* (31 December 2004): £1 sterling = EC $5.215; US $1 = EC $2.700; €1 = EC $3.678; EC $100 = £19.18 = US $37.04 = €27.19. *Exchange Rate:* Fixed at US $1 = EC $2.70 since July 1976.

Budget (preliminary, EC $ million 2002): *Revenue:* Tax revenue 262.4 (Taxes on income and profits 43.5, Taxes on property 18.0, Taxes on domestic goods and services 49.6, Taxes on international trade and transactions 151.3); Other current revenue 30.1; Capital revenue 2.7; Total 295.2, excluding grants received (23.5). *Expenditure:* Current expenditure 291.4 (Personal emoluments 124.6, Goods and services 57.6, Interest payments 49.7, Transfers and subsidies 59.3); Capital expenditure 237.5; Total 528.9. Source: Eastern Caribbean Central Bank.

International Reserves (US $ million at 31 December 2003): IMF special drawing rights 0.00; Foreign exchange 83.22; Total 83.22. Source: IMF, *International Financial Statistics*.

Money Supply (EC $ million at 31 December 2003): Currency outside banks 84.68; Demand deposits at deposit money banks 197.21; Total money (incl. others) 281.93. Source: IMF, *International Financial Statistics*.

Cost of Living (Consumer Price Index; base: 2000 = 100): 103.2 in 2001; 104.3 in 2002; 106.6 in 2003. Source: ILO.

Expenditure on the Gross Domestic Product (preliminary, EC $ million at current prices, 2003): Government final consumption expenditure 179.38; Private final consumption expenditure 830.15; Gross fixed capital formation 505.08; *Total domestic expenditure* 1,514.61; Exports of goods and services 504.10; *Less* Imports of goods and services 837.80; *GDP in purchasers' values* 1,180.91. Source: Eastern Caribbean Central Bank.

Gross Domestic Product by Economic Activity (EC $ million at current prices, 2003): Agriculture, hunting, forestry and fishing 94.25; Mining and quarrying 5.71; Manufacturing 60.58; Electricity and water 59.01; Construction 104.33; Wholesale and retail trade 108.04; Restaurants and hotels 81.49; Transport and communications 189.59; Finance and insurance 115.18; Real estate 33.83; Government services 157.89; Other services 29.56; *Sub-total* 1,039.46; *Less* Imputed bank service charge 92.39; *GDP at factor cost* 947.07. Source: Eastern Caribbean Central Bank.

Balance of Payments (EC $ million, 2003): Exports of goods f.o.b. 112.98; Imports of goods f.o.b. –607.69; *Trade balance* –494.71; Exports of services 391.12; Imports of services –230.11; *Balance on goods and services* –333.70; Other income received 12.40; Other income paid –150.34; *Balance on goods, services and income* –471.64; Current transfers received 88.77; Current transfers paid –24.67; *Current balance* –407.54; Capital account (net) 117.16; Direct investment from abroad 217.06; Portfolio investment assets –1.20; Portfolio investment liabilities 38.18; Other investment (net) –37.95; Net errors and omissions 42.93; *Overall balance* –31.36. Source: Eastern Caribbean Central Bank.

EXTERNAL TRADE

Principal Commodities (preliminary, US $ million, 2002): *Imports:* Food 38.7; Fuel 23.0; Chemicals 25.9; Basic manufactures 39.1; Machinery and transport equipment 63.9; Miscellaneous manufactured articles 30.1; Total (incl. others) 233.2 (excl. unrecorded imports). *Exports:* Nutmeg 12.8; Fish 4.4; Flour 5.0; Electronic components 23.4; Total (incl. others) 59.7 (excl. re-exports 4.7). Source: IMF, *Grenada: Statistical Appendix* (February 2003).

Principal Trading Partners (US $ million, 2001): *Imports c.i.f.:* Barbados 5.3; Canada 6.0; Germany 2.1; Guyana 2.2; Japan 8.8; Netherlands 2.4; Trinidad and Tobago 41.1; United Kingdom 15.0; USA 99.5; Venezuela 2.8; Total (incl. others) 212.2. *Exports f.o.b.:* Antigua and Barbuda 1.1; Argentina 0.8; Barbados 1.7; Belgium 1.0; Canada 0.7; Dominica 1.9; France 0.8; Germany 4.0; Ireland 7.0; Jamaica 0.7; Netherlands 7.1; Saint Christopher and Nevis 1.4; Saint Lucia 2.6; Trinidad and Tobago 2.6; United Kingdom 0.6; USA 22.6; Total (incl. others) 58.6. Source: UN, *International Trade Statistics Yearbook. 2002* (preliminary, EC $ million): Imports c.i.f. 572.1 (CARICOM 146.1; EU 71.5; USA 262.1); Exports f.o.b. 161.1 (CARICOM 35.8; EU 55.6; USA 62.7). Source: IMF, *Grenada: Statistical Appendix* (February 2003).

TRANSPORT

Road Traffic ('000 motor vehicles in use, 2001): Passenger cars 15.8; Commercial vehicles 4.2. Source: UN, *Statistical Yearbook*.

Shipping: *Merchant Fleet* (registered at 31 December 2003) 11 vessels (total displacement 2,821 grt) (Source: Lloyd's Register-Fairplay, *World Fleet Statistics*). *International Sea-borne Freight Traffic* (estimates, '000 metric tons, 1995): Goods loaded 21.3; Goods unloaded 193.0. *Ship Arrivals* (1991): 1,254. *Fishing Vessels* (registered, 1987): 635.

Civil Aviation (aircraft arrivals, 1995): 11,310.

TOURISM

Visitor Arrivals ('000): *Stop-overs:* 123.4 in 2001; 132.4 in 2002; 142.3 in 2003. *Cruise-ship Passengers:* 147.4 in 2001; 135.1 in 2002; 146.9 in 2003.

Receipts from Tourism (estimates, US $ million): 163.0 in 2001; 169.5 in 2002; 169.5 in 2003.
Source: Caribbean Development Bank, *Social and Economic Indicators*.

COMMUNICATIONS MEDIA

Radio Receivers (1997): 57,000 in use*.

Television Receivers (1999): 35,000 in use*.

Telephones (2002): 33,500 main lines in use‡.

Facsimile Machines (1996): 270 in use†.

Mobile Cellular Telephones (2002): 7,600 subscribers‡.

Personal Computers (2001): 13,000 in use‡.

Internet Users (2002): 6,500‡.

Non-daily Newspapers (1996): 4; circulation 14,000*.

* Source: UNESCO, *Statistical Yearbook*.
† Source: UN, *Statistical Yearbook*.
‡ Source: International Telecommunication Union.

EDUCATION

Pre-primary (1994): 74 schools; 158 teachers; 3,499 pupils.

Primary (1995): 57 schools; 849 teachers; 19,134 pupils (2001).

Secondary: 20 schools (2002); 381 teachers (1995); 9,891 pupils (2001).

Higher (excluding figures for the Grenada Teachers' Training College, 1993): 66 teachers; 651 students.
Source: partly Caribbean Development Bank, *Social and Economic Indicators*.

Adult Literacy Rate: 94.4% in 2001. Source: Secretariat of the Organisation of Eastern Caribbean States.

Directory

The Constitution

The 1974 independence Constitution was suspended in March 1979, following the coup, and almost entirely restored between November 1983, after the overthrow of the Revolutionary Military Council, and the elections of December 1984. The main provisions of this Constitution are summarized below:

The Head of State is the British monarch, represented in Grenada by an appointed Governor-General. Legislative power is vested in the bicameral Parliament, comprising a Senate and a House of Representatives. The Senate consists of 13 Senators, seven of whom are appointed on the advice of the Prime Minister, three on the advice of the Leader of the Opposition and three on the advice of the Prime Minister after he has consulted interests which he considers Senators should be selected to represent. The Constitution does not specify the number of members of the House of Representatives, but the country consists of 15 single-member constituencies, for which representatives are elected for up to five years, on the basis of universal adult suffrage.

The Cabinet consists of a Prime Minister, who must be a member of the House of Representatives, and such other ministers as the Governor-General may appoint on the advice of the Prime Minister.

There is a Supreme Court and, in certain cases, a further appeal lies to Her Majesty in Council.

The Government

HEAD OF STATE

Monarch: HM Queen ELIZABETH II (succeeded to the throne 6 February 1952).

Governor-General: Sir DANIEL WILLIAMS (appointed 8 August 1996).

THE CABINET
(April 2005)

Prime Minister and Minister of National Security, Information, Business and Private-Sector Development, Youth Development and Information Communications Technology: Dr KEITH CLAUDIUS MITCHELL.

Deputy Prime Minister and Minister of Agriculture, Lands, Forestry and Fisheries, Public Utilities, Energy and the Marketing and National Importing Board: Sen. GREGORY BOWEN.

Minister of Finance and Planning: ANTHONY BOATSWAIN.

Minister of Foreign Affairs and International Trade, of Carriacou and Petit Martinique Affairs, and of Legal Affairs, and Attorney-General: Sen. ELVIN NIMROD.

Minister of Communications, Works and Transport: CLARICE MODESTE-CURWEN.

Minister of Education and Labour: CLARIS CHARLES.

Minister of Sports, Community Development and Co-operatives, with responsibility for Community Development and Co-operatives, and Minister in the Ministry of Finance with responsibility for Revenue Administration: ROLAND BHOLA.

Minister of Health, Social Security and the Environment: ANN DAVID ANTOINE.

Minister of Tourism, Civil Aviation, Culture and the Performing Arts: Sen. BRENDA HOOD.

Minister of Housing, Social Services and Gender and Family Affairs: YOLANDE BAIN JOSEPH.

Minister of State in the Ministry of Sports, Community Development and Co-operatives, with responsibility for Sports: ADRIAN MITCHELL.

Minister of State in the Prime Minister's Office with responsibility for Information, Business and Private-Sector Development and Information Communications Technology: EINSTEIN LOUISON.

Minister of State in the Prime Minister's Office with responsibility for Youth Development: EMMALIN PIERCE.

MINISTRIES

Office of the Governor-General: Government House, St George's; tel. 440-6639; fax 440-6688; e-mail patogg@caribsurf.com.

Office of the Prime Minister: Ministerial Complex, 6th Floor, Botanical Gardens, St George's; tel. 440-2255; fax 440-4116; e-mail pmoffice@gov.gd.

Ministry of Agriculture, Lands, Forestry and Fisheries: Ministerial Complex, 2nd and 3rd Floors, Botanical Gardens, St George's; tel. 440-2708; fax 440-4191; e-mail agriculture@gov.gd.

Ministry of Carriacou and Petit Martinique Affairs: Beauséjour, Carriacou; tel. 443-6026; fax 443-6040; e-mail minccoupm@caribsurf.com.

Ministry of Communications, Works and Transport: Ministerial Complex, 4th Floor, Botanical Gardens, St George's; tel. 440-2181; fax 440-4122; e-mail ministerworks@caribsurf.com.

Ministry of Education and Labour: Ministerial Complex, Botanical Gardens, Tanteen, St George's; tel. 440-2166; fax 440-6650; e-mail psmined@yahoo.com.

Ministry of Finance and Planning: Financial Complex, The Carenage, St George's; tel. 440-2731; fax 440-4115; e-mail director@economicaffairs.grenada.gd; internet economicaffairs.grenada.gd.

Ministry of Foreign Affairs and International Trade: Ministerial Complex, 4th Floor, Botanical Gardens, St George's; tel. 440-2640; fax 440-4184; e-mail foreignaffairs@gov.gd.

Ministry of Health, Social Security and the Environment: Ministerial Complex, 1st and 2nd Floors, Botanical Gardens, St George's; tel. 440-2649; fax 440-4127; e-mail min-healthgrenada@caribsurf.com.

Ministry of Housing, Social Services and Gender and Family Affairs: Ministerial Complex, 1st and 2nd Floors, Botanical Gardens, St George's; tel. 440-7994; fax 440-7990; e-mail mhousing@hotmail.com.

Ministry of Information: Ministerial Complex, 6th Floor, Botanical Gardens, St George's; tel. 440-2255; fax 440-4116.

Ministry of Legal Affairs: Church St, St George's; tel. 440-2050; fax 440-6630; e-mail legalaffairs@caribsurf.com.

Ministry of National Security: Ministerial Complex, Botanical Gardens, St George's; tel. 440-2255.

Ministry of Public Utilities and Energy: Ministerial Complex, 4th Floor, Botanical Gardens, St George's; tel. and fax 440-2181.

Ministry of Tourism, Civil Aviation, Culture and the Performing Arts: Ministerial Complex, 4th Floor, Botanical Gardens, St George's; tel. 440-0366; fax 440-0443; e-mail mot@caribsurf.com; internet www.spiceisle.com.users.mot.

Ministry of Sports, Community Development and Co-operatives: Ministerial Complex, 2nd Floor, Botanical Gardens, St George's; tel. 440-6917; fax 440-6924; e-mail yscm@caribsurf.com.

GOVERNMENT AGENCY

Agency for Reconstruction and Development (ARD): Ministerial Complex, Botanical Gardens, St George's; f. Oct. 2004 to oversee Grenada's recovery from the effects of 'Hurricane Ivan', which struck the island in Sept., and to handle donations for reconstruction projects; Chair. MARIUS ST ROSE (acting); CEO RICHARDSON ANDREW.

Legislature

PARLIAMENT

Houses of Parliament: Church St, St George's; tel. 440-2090; fax 440-4138.

Senate

President: Sen. Dr JOHN WATTS.
There are 13 appointed members.

House of Representatives

Speaker: LAWRENCE JOSEPH.

General Election, 27 November 2003

	Votes	%	Seats
New National Party (NNP)	22,566	47.8	8
National Democratic Congress (NDC)	21,445	45.4	7
Grenada United Labour Party (GULP)	2,243	4.7	—
People's Labour Movement (PLM)	933	2.0	—
Others	52	0.0	—
Total	47,239	100.0	15

Political Organizations

Grenada United Labour Party (GULP): St George's; f. 1950; merged with United Labour Congress in 2001; right-wing; Pres. WILFRED HAYES; Leader GLORIA PAYNE-BANFIELD.

National Democratic Congress (NDC): St George's; f. 1987 by former members of the NNP and merger of Democratic Labour Congress and Grenada Democratic Labour Party; centrist; Leader TILLMAN THOMAS; Dep. Leader GEORGE PRIME.

New National Party (NNP): St George's; f. 1984 following merger of Grenada Democratic Movement, Grenada National Party and National Democratic Party; centrist; Chair. LAWRENCE JOSEPH; Leader Dr KEITH MITCHELL; Dep. Leader GREGORY BOWEN.

People's Labour Movement (PLM): St George's; f. 1995 by former members of the NDC; fmrly known as the Democratic Labour Party; Leader Dr FRANCIS ALEXIS; Pres. Dr TERRANCE MARRYSHOW.

Diplomatic Representation

EMBASSIES AND HIGH COMMISSION IN GRENADA

Belgium: St George's; Ambassador BOUDOIUM VANDERHULST.

China, People's Republic: St George's; Ambassador SHEN HONGSHUN.

Cuba: L'Anse aux Epines, St George's; tel. 444-1884; fax 444-1877; e-mail embacubagranada@caribsurf.com; Ambassador HUMBERTO RIVERO ROSARIO.

United Kingdom: British High Commission, Netherlands Bldg, Grand Anse, St George's; tel. 440-3536; fax 440-4939; e-mail bhcgrenada@caribsurf.com; High Commissioner resident in Barbados.

USA: POB 54, St George's; tel. 444-1173; fax 444-4820; e-mail usemb_gd@caribsurf.com; internet www.spiceisle.com/homepages/usemb_gd; Ambassador resident in Barbados.

Venezuela: Upper Lucas St, POB 201, St George's; tel. 440-1721; fax 440-6657; e-mail embavengda@caribsurf.com; Ambassador EDNA FIGUERA CEDEÑO.

Judicial System

Justice is administered by the West Indies Associated States Supreme Court, composed of a High Court of Justice and a Court of Appeal. The Itinerant Court of Appeal consists of three judges and sits three times a year; it hears appeals from the High Court and the Magistrates' Court. The Magistrates' Court administers summary jurisdiction.

In 1988 the OECS excluded the possibility of Grenada's readmittance to the East Caribbean court system until after the conclusion of appeals by the defendants in the Maurice Bishop murder trial (see Recent History). Following the conclusion of the case in 1991, Parliament voted to rejoin the system, thus also restoring the right of appeal to the Privy Council in the United Kingdom.

Attorney-General: ELVIN NIMROD.

Puisne Judges: DENYS BARROW, KENNETH BENJAMIN, LYLE K. ST PAUL.

Registrar of the Supreme Court: ROBERT BRANCH.

President of the Court of Appeal: C. M. DENNIS BYRON.

Office of the Attorney-General: Church St, St George's; tel. 440-2050; fax 440-6630; e-mail legalaffairs@caribsurf.com.

Religion

CHRISTIANITY

The Roman Catholic Church

Grenada comprises a single diocese, suffragan to the archdiocese of Castries (Saint Lucia). The Bishop participates in the Antilles Episcopal Conference (based in Port of Spain, Trinidad and Tobago). At 31 December 2002 there were an estimated 55,888 adherents in the diocese.

Bishop of St George's in Grenada: Rev. VINCENT DARIUS, Bishop's House, Morne Jaloux, POB 375, St George's; tel. 443-5299; fax 443-5758; e-mail bishopgrenada@caribsurf.com.

The Anglican Communion

Anglicans in Grenada are adherents of the Church in the Province of the West Indies, and represented 14% of the population at the time of the 1991 census. The country forms part of the diocese of the Windward Islands (the Bishop, the Rt Rev. SEHON GOODRIDGE, resides in Kingstown, Saint Vincent).

Other Christian Churches

The Presbyterian, Methodist, Plymouth Brethren, Baptist, Salvation Army, Jehovah's Witness, Pentecostal (7.2% of the population in 1991) and Seventh-day Adventist (8.5%) faiths are also represented.

The Press

NEWSPAPERS

Barnacle: Frequente Industrial Park, St George's; tel. 440-5151; monthly; Editor IAN GEORGE.

The Grenada Informer: Market Hill, POB 622, St George's; tel. 440-1530; fax 440-4119; e-mail movanget@caribsurf.com; f. 1985; weekly; Editor CARLA BRIGGS; circ. 6,000.

Grenada Today: St John's St, POB 142, St George's; tel. 440-4401; internet www.belgrafix.com/gtoday98.htm; weekly; Editor GEORGE WORME.

The Grenadian Voice: Frequente Industrial Park, Bldg 1B, Maurice Bishop Highway, POB 633, St George's; tel. 440-1498; fax 440-4117; e-mail gvoice@caribsurf.com; internet www.grenadianvoice.com; weekly; Editor LESLIE PIERRE; circ. 3,000.

Government Gazette: St George's; weekly; official.

PRESS ASSOCIATION

Press Association of Grenada: St George's; f. 1986; Pres. LESLIE PIERRE.

Inter Press Service (IPS) (Italy) is also represented.

Publisher

Anansi Publications: Hillsborough St, St George's; tel. 440-0800; e-mail aclouden@caribsurf.com.

Broadcasting and Communications

TELECOMMUNICATIONS

Regulatory Authority

Eastern Caribbean Telecommunications Authority: Castries, Saint Lucia; f. 2000 to regulate telecommunications in Grenada, Dominica, Saint Christopher and Nevis, Saint Lucia and Saint Vincent and the Grenadines.

National Telecommunications Regulatory Commission: Suite 8, Grand Anse Shopping Centre, POB 854, St George's; tel. 435-6872; fax 435-2132; e-mail gntrc@caribsurf.com; internet www.spiceisle.com/gntrc; Chair. LINUS SPENCER THOMAS; Dir of Telecommunications ROBERT OLIVER FINLAY.

Major Service Providers

AT & T Wireless Services: St George's; f. 2004; awarded licence to operate cellular telephone services in September 2003; US ownership.

Cable & Wireless Grenada Ltd: POB 119, The Carenage, St George's; tel. 440-1000; fax 440-4134; e-mail gndinfo@caribsurf.com; internet www.candw.gd; f. 1989; until 1998 known as Grenada Telecommunications Ltd (Grentel); 30% govt-owned; Chief Exec. IAN BLANCHARD.

Digicel Grenada Ltd: St George's; f. 2003; began operating cellular telephone services in Oct. 2003; owned by an Irish consortium.

Grenada Postal Corporation: Burns Point, St George's; tel. 440-2526; fax 440-4271; e-mail gpc@caribsurf.com; internet gndonline.com; Chair. GORDON ROBERTSON; Man. LEO ROBERTS.

BROADCASTING

Grenada Broadcasting Network (GBN): Observatory Rd, POB 535, St George's; tel. 440-2446; fax 440-4180; e-mail gbn@caribsurf.com; internet www2.spiceisle.com; f. 1972; 60% privately-owned, 40% govt-owned; Chair. KEN GORDON; Man. Dir RICHARD PURCELL.

Radio

Grenada Broadcasting Network (Radio): see Broadcasting.

The Harbour Light of the Windwards: Carriacou; tel. and fax 443-7628; e-mail harbourlight@caribsurf.com; internet www.harbourlightradio.org; Station Man. RANDY CORNELIUS; Chief Engineer JOHN MCPHERSON.

Spice Capitol Radio FM 90: Springs, St George's; tel. 440-0162.

Television

Television programmes from Trinidad and from Barbados can be received on the island.

Grenada Broadcasting Network (Television): see Broadcasting.

Finance

(cap. = capital; res = reserves; dep. = deposits; amounts in Eastern Caribbean dollars)

The Eastern Caribbean Central Bank, based in Saint Christopher, is the central issuing and monetary authority for Grenada.

Eastern Caribbean Central Bank—Grenada Office: Monckton St, St George's; tel. 440-3016; fax 440-6721; e-mail eccbgnd@caribsurf.com.

BANKING

Regulatory Authority

Grenada International Financial Services Authority: Bldg 5, Financial Complex, The Carenage, St George's; tel. 440-6575; fax 440-4780; e-mail gifsa@caribsurf.com; internet gifsa-grenada.com; f. 1999; revenues 4.2m. (2002); Chair. TIMOTHY ANTOINE; Exec. Dir SHARON GRIFFITH.

Commercial Banks

Diak Bank Ltd: POB 1354, Mon Tout, Grand Anse, St George's; tel. 439-3232; fax 439-3233; e-mail diak@caribsurf.com; internet www.diakbank.com; f. 1999; Chair., Gen. Man. and Pres. CLIFFORD S. PITT.

Grenada Co-operative Bank Ltd: 8 Church St, POB 135, St George's; tel. 440-2111; fax 440-6600; e-mail co-opbank@caribsurf.com; f. 1932; Man. Dir and Sec. G. V. STEELE; brs in St Andrew's, St George's and St Patrick's.

Grenada Development Bank: Melville St, POB 734, St George's; tel. 440-2382; fax 440-6610; e-mail gdbbank@caribsurf.com; f. 1976 following merger; Chair. ARNOLD CRUICKSHANK; Man. CAMPBELL BLENMAN.

National Commercial Bank of Grenada Ltd: NCB House, POB 857, Grand Anse, St George's; tel. 444-2265; fax 444-5500; e-mail ncbgnd@caribsurf.com; internet www.ncbgrenada.com; f. 1979; 51% owned by Republic Bank Ltd, Port of Spain, Trinidad and Tobago; cap. 15.0m., res 29.4m., dep. 487.6m. (Sept. 2003); Chair. RONALD HARFORD; Man. Dir DANIEL ROBERTS; 9 brs.

Foreign Banks

Bank of Nova Scotia (Canada): Granby and Halifax Sts, POB 194, St George's; tel. 440-3274; fax 440-4173; Man. B. ROBINSON; 3 brs.

Caribbean Commercial Bank (Trinidad and Tobago): St George's; 1 br.

FirstCaribbean International Bank Ltd: Church St, St George's; tel. 440-3232; internet www.firstcaribbeanbank.com; f. 2003; 87.5% owned by Barclays Bank PLC (United Kingdom) and Canadian Imperial Bank of Commerce; CEO CHARLES PINK; Exec. Dir SHARON BROWN; 4 brs.

RBTT Bank Grenada Ltd: Corner of Cross and Halifax Sts, POB 4, St George's; tel. 440-3521; fax 440-4153; e-mail gbcltd@caribsurf

.com; f. 1983; 10% govt-owned; cap. 7.4m., res 8.8m., dep. 256.6m. (Dec. 2000); Chair. PETER JULY; Man. Dir MAXIM PAZOS.

STOCK EXCHANGE

Eastern Caribbean Securities Exchange: based in Basseterre, Saint Christopher and Nevis; e-mail info@ecseonline.com; internet www.ecseonline.com; f. 2001; regional securities market designed to facilitate the buying and selling of financial products for the eight member territories—Anguilla, Antigua and Barbuda, Dominica, Grenada, Montserrat, Saint Christopher and Nevis, Saint Lucia and Saint Vincent and the Grenadines; Gen. Man. TREVOR BLAKE.

INSURANCE

Several foreign insurance companies operate in Grenada and the other islands of the group. Principal locally-owned companies include the following:

Grenada Insurance and Finance Co Ltd: Young St, POB 139, St George's; tel. 440-3004.

Grenada Motor and General Insurance Co Ltd: Scott St, St George's; tel. 440-3379.

Grenadian General Insurance Co Ltd: Corner of Young and Scott Sts, POB 47, St George's; tel. 440-2434; fax 440-6618.

Trade and Industry

CHAMBERS OF COMMERCE

Grenada Chamber of Industry and Commerce, Inc: DeCaul Bldg, Mt Gay, POB 129, St George's; tel. 440-2937; fax 440-6627; e-mail gcic@caribsurf.com; internet www.spiceisle.com/homepages/gcic; f. 1921; incorporated 1947; 170 mems; Pres. CHRISTOPHER DEALLIE; Exec. Dir CHRISTOPHER DERIGGS.

Grenada Manufacturing Council: POB 129, St George's; tel. 440-2937; fax 440-6627; e-mail gcic@caribsurf.com; f. 1991 to replace Grenada Manufacturers' Asscn; Chair. CHRISTOPHER DEALLIE.

INDUSTRIAL AND TRADE ASSOCIATIONS

Grenada Cocoa Association: Scott St, St George's; tel. 440-2234; fax 440-1470; e-mail gca@caribsurf.com; f. 1987 following merger; changed from co-operative to shareholding structure in late 1996; Chair. REGINALD BUCKMIRE; Man. ANDREW HASTICK.

Grenada Co-operative Banana Society: Scott St, St George's; tel. 440-2486; fax 440-4199; e-mail gbcs@caribsurf.com; f. 1955; a statutory body to control production and marketing of bananas; Exec. Chair. DANIEL LEWIS; Gen. Man. JOHN MARK (acting).

Grenada Co-operative Nutmeg Association: Lagoon Rd, POB 160, St George's; tel. 440-2117; fax 440-6602; e-mail gcna.nutmeg@caribsurf.com; internet www.grenadanutmeg.com; f. 1947; processes and markets all the nutmeg and mace grown on the island; to include the production of nutmeg oil; Chair. RAMSEY RUSH; Gen. Man. TERENCE MOORE.

Grenada Industrial Development Corporation: Frequente Industrial Park, Frequente, St George's; tel. 444-1035; fax 444-4828; e-mail gidc@caribsurf.com; internet www.grenadaworld.com; f. 1985; Chair. R. ANTHONY JOSEPH; Man. SONIA RODEN.

Marketing and National Importing Board: Young St, St George's; tel. 440-1791; fax 440-4152; e-mail mnib.com@caribsurf.com; f. 1974; govt-owned; imports basic food items, incl. sugar, rice and milk; Chair. RICHARDSON ANDREWS; Gen. Man. FITZROY JAMES.

EMPLOYERS' ORGANIZATION

Grenada Employers' Federation: Mt Gay, POB 129, St George's; tel. 440-1832; e-mail gef@caribsurf.com; 60 mems.

There are several marketing and trading co-operatives, mainly in the agricultural sector.

UTILITIES

Public Utilities Commission: St George's.

Electricity

Grenada Electricity Services Ltd (Grenlec): Halifax St, POB 381, St George's; tel. 440-2097; fax 440-4106; e-mail grenlec@caribsurf.com; internet www.carilec.org/grenlec; generation and distribution; 90% privately-owned, 10% govt-owned; Chair. G. ROBERT BLANCHARD, Jr; Gen. Man. VERNON LAWRENCE.

Water

National Water and Sewerage Authority: The Carenage, POB 392, St George's; tel. 440-2155; fax 440-4107; f. 1969; Chair. MICHAEL PIERRE; Man. ALLEN McQUIRE.

TRADE UNIONS

Grenada Trade Union Council (GTUC): Green St, POB 411, St George's; tel. 440-3733; fax 440-3733; e-mail gtuc@caribsurf.com; Pres. DEREK ALLARD; Gen. Sec. RAY ROBERTS.

Bank and General Workers' Union (BGWU): Bain's Alley, St George's; tel. 440-3563; fax 440-0778; e-mail bgwu@caribsurf.com; Pres. DEREK ALLARD; Gen. Sec. JUSTIN CAMPBELL.

Commercial and Industrial Workers' Union: Bain's Alley, POB 191, St George's; tel. 440-3423; fax 440-3423; Pres. ELLIOT BISHOP; Gen. Sec. BARBARA FRASER; 492 mems.

Grenada Manual, Maritime and Intellectual Workers' Union (GMMIWU): c/o Birchgrove, St Andrew's; tel. 442-7724; fax 442-7724; Pres. BERT LATOUCHE; Gen. Sec. OSCAR WILLIAMS.

Grenada Union of Teachers (GUT): Marine Villa, POB 452, St George's; tel. 440-2992; fax 440-9019; f. 1913; Pres. MARVIN ANDALL; Gen. Sec. ELAINE McQUEEN; 1,300 mems.

Media Workers' Association of Grenada (MWAG): St George's; f. 1999; Gen. Sec. RAE ROBERTS.

Public Workers' Union (PWU): Tanteen, POB 420, St George's; tel. 440-2203; fax 440-6615; e-mail pwu-cpsa@caribsurf.com; f. 1931; Pres. LAURETTE CLARKSON; Gen. Sec. SHIRLEY MODESTE.

Seamen and Waterfront Workers' Union: Ottway House, POB 154, St George's; tel. 440-2573; fax 440-7199; e-mail swwu@caribsurf.com; f. 1952; Pres. ALBERT JULIEN; Gen. Sec. LYLE SAMUEL; 350 mems.

Technical and Allied Workers' Union (TAWU): Green St, POB 405, St George's; tel. 440-2231; fax 440-5878; f. 1958; Pres.-Gen. Sen. CHESTER HUMPHREY; Gen. Sec. ANDRÉ LEWIS.

Transport

RAILWAYS

There are no railways in Grenada.

ROADS

In 1999 there were approximately 1,040 km (646 miles) of roads, of which 61.3% were paved. Public transport is provided by small private operators, with a system covering the entire country.

SHIPPING

The main port is St George's, with accommodation for two ocean-going vessels of up to 500 ft. A number of shipping lines call at St George's. Grenville, on Grenada, and Hillsborough, on Carriacou, are used mostly by small craft. The first phase of a project to expand the port at St George's and enable the harbour to accommodate modern super-sized cruise ships was completed in July 2003.

Grenada Ports Authority: POB 494, The Carenage, St George's; tel. 440-7678; fax 440-3418; e-mail grenport@caribsurf.com; internet www.grenadaports.com; Chair. WALTER ST JOHN; Gen. Man. AMBROSE PHILLIP.

CIVIL AVIATION

The Point Salines International Airport, 10 km (6 miles) from St George's, was opened in October 1984, and has scheduled flights to most East Caribbean destinations, including Venezuela, and to the United Kingdom and North America. There is an airfield at Pearls, 30 km (18 miles) from St George's, and Lauriston Airport, on the island of Carriacou, offers regular scheduled services to Grenada, Saint Vincent and Palm Island (Grenadines of Saint Vincent).

Grenada is a shareholder in the regional airline, LIAT (Antigua and Barbuda).

Grenada Airports Authority: Point Salines Int. Airport, POB 385, St George's; tel. 444-4101; fax 444-4838; e-mail gaa@caribsurf.com; f. 1985; Chair. RICHARD MENEZES; CEO PHILIPPE BARIL; Gen. Man. DONALD McPHAIL.

Airlines of Carriacou: Point Salines International Airport, POB 805, St Georges; tel. 444-1475; fax 444-2898; e-mail cayar@caribsurf.com; internet www.travelgrenada.com/aircarriacou.htm; f. 1992; national airline, operates in association with LIAT; Man. Dir ARTHUR W. BAIN.

Tourism

Grenada has the attractions of both white sandy beaches and a scenic, mountainous interior with an extensive rainforest. There are also sites of historical interest, and the capital, St George's, is a noted beauty spot. In 2003 there were an estimated 142,300 stop-over arrivals and 146,900 cruise-ship passengers; in that year tourism earned some US $169.5m. There were approximately 1,670 hotel rooms in 1996. In 1997 a joint venture between the Government of Grenada and the Caribbean Development Bank to upgrade and market some 50 unprofitable hotels was implemented. In addition, the Ministry of Tourism, in conjunction with the Board of Tourism and the Hotel Association, announced a 10-year development plan to increase hotel capacity to 2,500 rooms.

Grenada Board of Tourism: Burns Point, POB 293, St George's; tel. 440-2279; fax 440-6637; e-mail gbt@caribsurf.com; internet www .grenada.org; f. 1991; Chair. RICHARD STRACHAN; Dir WILLIAM JOSEPH.

Grenada Hotel and Tourism Association Ltd: POB 440, St George's; tel. 444-1353; fax 444-4847; e-mail grenhota@caribsurf .com; internet www.grenadahotelsinfo.com; f. 1961; Pres. IAN DA BREO; Dirs SHEREE ANN ADAMS, LAWRENCE LAMBERT, ROYSTON HOPKIN, RUSS FIELDEN, CLIVE BARNES, COLEMAN REDHEAD, MIRIAM BEDEAU, ANN BAYNE GRIFFITH, VALENTINE FRASER, CHRISTOPHER MILLS.

GUATEMALA

Introductory Survey

Location, Climate, Language, Religion, Flag, Capital

The Republic of Guatemala lies in the Central American isthmus, bounded to the north and west by Mexico, with Honduras and Belize to the east and El Salvador to the south. It has a long coastline on the Pacific Ocean and a narrow outlet to the Caribbean Sea. The climate is tropical in the lowlands, with an average temperature of 28°C (83°F), and more temperate in the central highland area, with an average temperature of 20°C (68°F). The official language is Spanish, but more than 20 indigenous languages are also spoken. Almost all of the inhabitants profess Christianity: the majority are Roman Catholics, while about 10% are Protestants. The national flag (proportions 5 by 8) has three equal vertical stripes, of blue, white and blue, with the national coat of arms (depicting a quetzal, the 'bird of freedom', and a scroll, superimposed on crossed rifles and sabres, encircled by a wreath) in the centre of the white stripe. The capital is Guatemala City.

Recent History

Under Spanish colonial rule, Guatemala was part of the Viceroyalty of New Spain. Independence was obtained from Spain in 1821, from Mexico in 1824 and from the Federation of Central American States in 1838. Subsequent attempts to revive the Federation failed and, under a series of dictators, there was relative stability, tempered by periods of disruption. A programme of social reform was begun by Juan José Arévalo (President in 1944–50) and his successor, Col Jacobo Arbenz Guzmán, whose policy of land reform evoked strong opposition from landowners. In 1954 President Arbenz was overthrown in a coup led by Col Carlos Castillo Armas, who invaded the country with US assistance. Castillo became President but was assassinated in July 1957. The next elected President, Gen. Miguel Ydigoras Fuentes, took office in March 1958 and ruled until he was deposed in March 1963 by a military coup, led by Col Enrique Peralta Azurdia. He assumed full powers as Chief of Government, suspended the Constitution and dissolved the legislature. A Constituent Assembly, elected in 1964, introduced a new Constitution in 1965. Dr Julio César Méndez Montenegro was elected President in 1966, and in 1970 the candidate of the Movimiento de Liberación Nacional (MLN), Col (later Gen.) Carlos Araña Osorio, was elected President. Despite charges of fraud in the elections of March 1974, Gen. Kjell Laugerud García of the MLN took office as President in July.

President Laugerud sought to discourage extreme right-wing violence and claimed some success, although it was estimated that 50,000–60,000 people were killed in political violence between 1970 and 1979. In March 1978 Gen. Fernando Romeo Lucas García was elected President. The guerrilla movement increased in strength in 1980–1981, while the Government was accused of the murder and torture of civilians and, particularly, persecution of the country's indigenous Indian inhabitants, who comprise 60% of the population.

In the presidential elections of March 1982, from which the left-wing parties were absent, the Government's candidate, Gen. Angel Aníbal Guevara, was declared the winner; however, the elections were denounced as fraudulent by the other presidential candidates. Guevara was prevented from taking office in July by a coup on 23 March, in which a group of young right-wing military officers installed Gen. José Efraín Ríos Montt (a candidate in the 1974 presidential elections) as leader of a three-man junta. The Congreso Nacional (National Congress) was closed, and the Constitution and political parties suspended. In June Gen. Ríos Montt dissolved the junta and assumed the presidency. He attempted to fight corruption, reorganized the judicial system and disbanded the secret police. The number of violent deaths diminished. However, after initially gaining the support of the national university, the Roman Catholic Church and the labour unions and hoping to enter into dialogue with the guerrillas, who refused to respond to an amnesty declaration in June, Ríos Montt declared a state of siege, and imposed censorship of the press, in July. In addition, the war against the guerrillas intensified, and a civil defence force of Indians was established. The efficiency and ruthlessness of the army

increased. Whole villages were burnt, and many inhabitants killed, in order to deter the Indians from supporting the guerrillas. Ríos Montt's increasingly corporatist policies alienated all groups, and his fragile hold on power was threatened in 1982 by several attempted coups, which he managed to forestall.

The US Administration was eager to renew sales of armaments and the provision of economic and military aid to Guatemala, which had been suspended in 1977 as a result of serious violations of human rights. In January 1983 the US Government, satisfied that there had been a significant decrease in such violations during Ríos Montt's presidency, announced the resumption of arms sales to Guatemala. However, independent reports claimed that the situation had deteriorated, and revealed that 2,600 people had been killed during the first six months of Ríos Montt's rule. In March the army was implicated in the massacre of 300 Indian peasants at Nahulá, and there was a resurgence in the activity of both left- and right-wing 'death squads'. The President declared a 30-day amnesty for guerrillas and political exiles, and lifted the state of siege. Furthermore, he announced the creation of an electoral tribunal to oversee a proposed transfer from military rule to civilian government. The Government's pacification programme comprised three phases of aid programmes, combined with the saturation of the countryside by anti-guerrilla units. The 'guns and beans' policy provided food and medicine in exchange for recruitment to the Patrullas de Autodefensa Civil (PAC), a pro-Government peasant militia. The 'roofs, bread and work' phase involved the development of 'model villages', and the 'Aid Programme for Areas in Conflict' was an ambitious rural development scheme.

By mid-1983 opposition to the President was widespread. On 8 August Gen. Oscar Humberto Mejía Victores, the Minister of Defence, led a successful coup against President Ríos Montt. The new President ended press censorship. A 90-day amnesty for guerrillas was announced in October and subsequently extended throughout 1984. Urban and rural terrorism continued to escalate, however, and in November 1983 the Government was accused of directing a campaign of kidnappings against the Roman Catholic Church. Following the murder in northern Guatemala of six US aid workers, the USA suspended US $50m. in aid to Guatemala in 1984. Israel continued to supply weapons to Guatemala, and Israeli military advisers were reported to be active in the country. In accordance with the President's assurance of electoral reform, elections for a Constituent Assembly were held in July 1984, at which the centre groups, including the newly formed Unión del Centro Nacional (UCN), obtained the greatest number of votes. Under the system of proportional representation, however, the right-wing coalition of the MLN and the Central Auténtica Nacionalista (CAN) together obtained a majority of seats in the Assembly.

Guatemala's new Constitution was promulgated in May 1985. Elections for the presidency, the Congreso Nacional and 331 mayoralties were scheduled to be held in November. Prior to the elections, there was a substantial increase in rebel activity and political assassinations by 'death squads'. Furthermore, in September violent protests, led by students and trade unionists, erupted in reaction to a series of price increases.

Eight candidates participated in the presidential election in November 1985, but the main contest was between Jorge Carpio Nicolle, the candidate of the UCN, and Mario Vinicio Cerezo Arévalo, the candidate of the Partido Democracia Cristiana Guatemalteca (PDCG). As neither of the leading candidates obtained the requisite majority, a second round of voting was held in December, when Cerezo secured 68% of the votes cast. The PDCG formed the majority party in the new Congreso Nacional and won the largest proportion of mayoralties. Cerezo was believed to enjoy the support of the US Administration, which increased its allocation of economic aid and resumed military aid to Guatemala, in support of the new civilian Government.

Immediately prior to the transfer of power in January 1986, the outgoing military Government decreed a general amnesty to encompass those suspected of involvement in abuses of human rights since March 1982. In the following month, however, in an attempt to curb the continuing violence and to improve the country's poor record for the observance of human rights, the notorious Department of Technical Investigations was dissolved and replaced by a new criminal investigations unit. Violence continued unabated, however, with 700 killings reported in the first six months of 1986. Cerezo claimed that not all murders were politically motivated, while his relations with the armed forces remained precarious. Meanwhile, a grouping of relatives of victims of repression, the Grupo de Apoyo Mutuo (GAM) attracted increasing support, and in August about 3,000 demonstrators took part in a protest to demand information on the fate of the thousands of *desaparecidos* ('disappeared'). In April 1987 the creation of a government commission to investigate disappearances was announced. Nevertheless, by mid-1988 there were frequent reports of torture and killings by right-wing 'death squads' as discontent with the Government's liberal policies increased. In September 1989 the Consejo Nacional de Desplazados de Guatemala (CONDEG) was created to represent the 1m. refugees who had fled their homes since 1980. According to the UN Commission for Human Rights almost 3,000 complaints of human rights abuses were lodged in 1989.

In August 1987 a peace plan for the region was signed in Guatemala City by the Presidents of Costa Rica, El Salvador, Guatemala, Honduras and Nicaragua. Subsequently, a Commission of National Reconciliation (CNR) was formed in compliance with the terms of the accord. In October representatives of the Guatemalan Government and the main guerrilla grouping, the Unidad Revolucionaria Nacional Guatemalteca (URNG), met in Spain, but the peace negotiations ended without agreement. Right-wing pressure on the Government, and an attempted coup in May 1988, forced Cerezo to postpone further negotiations with the URNG. After another coup plot was discovered in July, Cerezo rejected the URNG's proposal for a truce.

During 1989 guerrilla activity by groups from both the right and the left intensified. Many political figures and labour leaders fled the country after receiving death threats from paramilitary groups. Meanwhile, Cerezo refused to negotiate with the URNG for as long as its members remained armed. In September the URNG made further proposals for negotiations, following the signing of the Tela Agreement (the Central American peace plan accord), but these were rejected. A major counter-insurgency operation was launched by the Government in December. In the same month, Cerezo accused the ruling party in El Salvador of supplying weapons to the right-wing death squads of Guatemala.

In May 1989 another coup attempt was foiled without bloodshed. During August and September a secret right-wing military organization perpetrated a series of terrorist attacks in an attempt to destabilize the Government. At the same time, the ruling party was undergoing a political crisis, following its internal presidential primary elections in August. One of the candidates, Danilo Barillas, had been assassinated a short while before the selection procedure, allegedly by the extreme right, which, by provoking disunity within the PDCG, hoped to give an advantage to its own candidates. The former military ruler, Gen. José Efraín Ríos Montt, also presented his candidacy for the presidential election that was to take place one year later. However, in October 1990 his candidacy was declared invalid on constitutional grounds (under the Constitution, anyone taking part in, or benefiting from, a military coup was disqualified from participating in elections).

Despite Cerezo's promise to restrict the unlawful activities of the armed forces and right-wing death squads, the number of politically-motivated assassinations and 'disappearances' escalated in 1990. In March the US ambassador was recalled, in protest at the President's continued failure to curb the growing incidence of human rights violations. In the same month the URNG and the CNR began discussions in Norway with a view to resolving the problem of reincorporating the armed movements into the country's political process. In June representatives of the CNR and of nine political parties, including the ruling PDCG, met for further talks with the URNG in Spain. As a result of these negotiations, the URNG pledged not to disrupt the presidential and legislative elections scheduled for November, and agreed to participate in a constituent assembly to reform the Constitution.

In the presidential election of November 1990 none of the presidential candidates obtained an absolute majority in the first round, leading to a second ballot on 6 January 1991 between the two leading candidates, which was won by Jorge

Serrano Elías of the Movimiento de Acción Solidaria (MAS). The MAS failed to secure a majority in the legislative elections, however, and in an effort to offset the imbalance in the Congreso, Serrano invited members of the Plan por el Adelantamiento Nacional (PAN) and the Partido Socialista Democrático (PSD) to participate in the formation of a coalition Government.

In April 1991 a fresh round of direct talks between the URNG and the Government began in Mexico City. However, in an attempt to destabilize the Government's efforts at national reconciliation, members of the state security forces, believed to be acting independently of their superiors, launched a campaign of violence, directing death threats against leaders of trade unions and human rights organizations, and murdering a PSD politician. These actions indicated a clear division within the military between those favouring a negotiated settlement and those regarding the talks merely as a political platform for the rebels. In late 1991 the ombudsman, Ramiro de León Carpio, secured the resignation of the Director of the National Police, Col. Mario Enrique Paíz Bolanos, who was alleged to be responsible for the use of torture. Further peace talks at the end of the year failed to produce any agreement.

Negotiations between the Government and the URNG, which took place in Mexico City in August 1992, led to concessions by the Government, which agreed to curb the expansion of the PAC. These self-defence patrols played a major role in the army's counter-insurgency campaign and were widely accused of human rights violations. The URNG, which maintained that *campesinos* (peasants) were forcibly enlisted into the PAC, included in its conditions for a peace agreement the immediate dissolution of the patrols. In November the Government accepted renewed proposals by the URNG for the establishment of a commission on past human rights violations, but only on the pre-condition that the rebels sign a definitive peace accord. In January 1993 Serrano announced his commitment to the negotiation and signing of a peace agreement with the URNG within 90 days. In response, the URNG called for a 50% reduction in the size of the armed forces, and repeated demands for the immediate dissolution of the PAC and the dismissal of military officials implicated in human rights violations. The Government rejected these proposals. Talks stalled in March, owing principally to government demands that the URNG disarm as a precondition to the implementation of procedures for the international verification of human rights in Guatemala. Negotiations were suspended in May, owing to the prevailing constitutional crisis (see below).

In June 1993 the URNG announced a unilateral cease-fire as a gesture of goodwill to the incoming President Ramiro de León Carpio (see below). Government proposals announced in July, which aimed to involve all sectors of society in a Permanent Forum for Peace addressing social, economic and human rights problems independently of simultaneous cease-fire negotiations with the URNG, were rejected by the rebels. In August, in a concession to the URNG, de León announced the reform of the Estado Mayor Presidencial, a military body widely accused of human rights offences. However, in the following month the army announced that it would be resuming military operations against the rebels, which had been suspended in June. In October the Government presented a revised peace plan to the UN, providing for the creation of a Permanent Forum for Peace and renewed cease-fire negotiations with a view to an eventual amnesty for the URNG; the plan was, however, rejected by the rebels. Preliminary talks were finally resumed in Mexico in January 1994.

In May 1993 unrest at economic austerity measures escalated as public confidence in the Government declined. A rally attended by some 10,000 people was staged in the capital to demand Serrano's resignation. With the MAS no longer able to effect a constructive alliance in the Congreso and the country's stability in jeopardy, on 25 May Serrano, with the support of the military, suspended parts of the Constitution and dissolved the Congreso and the Supreme Court. A ban was imposed on the media and Serrano announced that he would rule by decree pending the drafting of a new constitution by a constituent assembly, which was to be elected within 60 days. The constitutional coup provoked almost unanimous international condemnation, with the USA immediately suspending in excess of US $30m. in aid. Such pressure, in addition to overwhelming domestic opposition, led the military to reappraise its position and, opting to effect a return to constitutional rule, it forced the resignation of Serrano, who relinquished his post on 1 June and subsequently fled to El Salvador. He was later granted political asylum in Panama. The Minister of National Defence, Gen. José Domingo García Samayoa, assumed control of the country, pending the election of a new president.

On 3 June 1993 the entire Cabinet, excluding García and the Minister of the Interior, Francisco Perdomo Sandoval, resigned. On the same day the Attorney-General presented charges, including those of violation of the Constitution, abuse of authority and embezzlement, against Serrano, Espina and Perdomo. Two days later, following an order by the Constitutional Court, the Congreso reconvened and conducted elections for a new president. The Instancia Nacional de Consenso (INC), a broad coalition of political parties, business leaders and trade unions which had been instrumental in removing Serrano from office, proposed three candidates, of whom Ramiro de León Carpio, the former human rights ombudsman, was elected President in an uncontested second round of voting. The USA subsequently restored its aid programme to Guatemala.

In August 1993, as an initial measure in a campaign to eradicate corruption from state institutions and restore dwindling public confidence in his Government, de León requested the voluntary resignation of the Congreso and the Supreme Court. The request caused a serious division in the legislature, which separated into two main factions, the Gran Grupo Parlamentario (GGP), which included some 70 members of the MAS, UCN, PAN and the Frente Republicano Guatemalteco (FRG) and supported the dismissal of 16 deputies identified by the INC as corrupt, and a group of 38 deputies, including members of the PDCG and independents, who supported the voluntary resignation of all 116 deputies. In September, following the suspension of a congressional session by the President of the Congreso, Fernando Lobo Dubón (a member of the PDCG), the GGP defied the decision and elected a new congressional President. Although Lobo was temporarily reinstated by the Constitutional Court, the GGP threatened to boycott any further sessions convened by him. In order to resolve the impasse, de León requested the Supreme Electoral Tribunal to put the issue to a referendum. However, in early November the Constitutional Court upheld a Supreme Court injunction of the previous month, suspending the referendum.

In mid-November 1993 a compromise was reached between the Government and the legislature, involving a series of constitutional reforms that were summarily approved by the Congreso and subsequently by a referendum. Fewer than 20% of the electorate participated in the voting, reflecting popular concern that more extensive reforms were necessary. The reforms took effect in early April, and fresh legislative elections were to be held in August. The new Congreso, which was to serve until 14 January 1996, was to appoint the members of a new, enlarged Supreme Court. Other reforms included a reduction in the terms of office of the President, legislature and municipal authorities (from five to four years), and of the Supreme Court justices (from six to five years), and a reduction in the number of seats in the Congreso.

In March 1994 the Government and the URNG agreed a timetable of formal peace negotiations aimed at achieving a definitive peace agreement by the end of the year. In addition, a general human rights agreement was signed, providing guarantees, including a government commitment to eliminate illegal security corps, strengthen national human rights institutions and cease obligatory military recruitment. Agreement was also reached on the establishment of a UN deputation to verify the implementation of the accord. The Human Rights Verification Mission in Guatemala (MINUGUA) was to comprise 220 human rights observers, 60 police and 10 military officers. Further talks in Oslo, Norway, resulted in the signing, in June, of agreements on the resettlement of people displaced by the civil war (estimated to number some 1m.), and on the establishment of a Comisión para el Esclarecimiento Histórico (CEH—Commission for Historical Clarification) to investigate human rights violations committed during the 33-year conflict.

In August 1994 the URNG withdrew from the peace negotiations and accused the Government of failing to observe the human rights provisions agreed in March. Talks resumed in November, but remained deadlocked until February 1995, when a new timetable for negotiations, achieved with UN mediation, was announced. The new agenda, which was formally agreed by the Government and the URNG in March, provided for a cease-fire agreement by June and the signing of a definitive peace accord in August. In March the issue of the identity and rights of indigenous peoples was finally resolved. The principal remaining issues to be discussed included agrarian and other

socio-economic reform, the role of the armed forces, the resettlement of displaced people and the incorporation of URNG guerrillas into civilian life. However, talks continued beyond the agreed deadline, and throughout 1995, without agreement on the substantive issues.

At the legislative election held in August 1994 only some 20% of the electorate exercised their vote, again reflecting widespread scepticism at the extent to which the reforms instigated by de León would serve to rid Guatemalan institutions of corruption. Despite winning the greatest number of seats in the 80-seat legislature, the FRG, led by Gen. (retd) José Efraín Ríos Montt, was excluded from the 12-member congressional directorate by an alliance of the PAN, PDCG, MLN and UD. However, in December the PDCG transferred its allegiance to the FRG and Ríos Montt was subsequently elected President of the Congreso. His inauguration in January 1995 provoked demonstrations by human rights organizations, which considered him responsible for the deaths of as many as 15,000 civilians as a result of counter-insurgency operations conducted during his period as *de facto* ruler in 1982–83.

In March 1995 Guatemala's record on human rights came under particular scrutiny. At the beginning of the month the USA announced that it had suspended all remaining military aid to the country, in protest at the Government's failure to investigate cases involving the murder or disappearance of US citizens in Guatemala. In the same month MINUGUA issued its first report. The document drew attention to human rights abuses perpetrated by the security forces and the PAC, and the Government's failure to investigate such incidents was once again condemned.

In June 1995 Ríos Montt formally requested registration as a candidate in the forthcoming presidential election, despite the constitutional provision precluding the candidacy of anyone who had previously come to power by means of a coup, as Ríos Montt had done in 1982. In August the Supreme Electoral Tribunal confirmed that he was not eligible to stand for election and in the same month the Supreme Court ruled that he should be temporarily suspended from his position as President of the Congreso to answer charges of abuse of authority and violation of the Constitution. The charges concerned an attempt by Ríos Montt and several other FRG deputies to impeach the magistrates of the Supreme Electoral Tribunal without first securing congressional approval.

The presidential and legislative elections on 12 November 1995 were notable for the return to the electoral process, for the first time for more than 40 years, of the left wing, which was represented by the Frente Democrático Nueva Guatemala (FDNG). In addition, the URNG, which had boycotted all previous elections, declared a unilateral cease-fire to coincide with the electoral campaign and urged people to exercise their vote. As no candidate received the necessary 50% of the votes to win the presidential election outright, the two leading candidates, Alvaro Enrique Arzú Irigoyen of the PAN and Alfonso Portillo of the FRG, contested a second round of voting on 7 January 1996, at which Arzú secured a narrow victory. At the legislative election the PAN secured 43 seats in the Congreso, while the FRG won 21.

Shortly after assuming office in January 1996, Arzú implemented a comprehensive reorganization of the military high command, replacing those officers who were not in favour of a negotiated peace settlement. In late February Arzú met the high command of the URNG in Mexico City, the first direct meeting between a Guatemalan President and the rebels since the early 1970s. In March Congress ratified the International Labour Organization's Convention on the rights of indigenous peoples. However, the document, which had been before the Congreso since 1992 and had encountered strong opposition from landed interests, had been amended by the Congreso, prompting protests by Indian organizations. On 20 March the URNG announced an indefinite unilateral cease-fire. Arzú responded immediately by ordering the armed forces to suspend counter-insurgency operations.

On 6 May 1996 the Government and the URNG signed an agreement on agrarian and socio-economic issues. The accord provided for the introduction of a new agrarian bank that would supply funds for *campesinos* to purchase property, the establishment of a land registry to define ownership and the introduction of a land tax. The Government also undertook to double expenditure on health and education over the next four years. In response, the URNG suspended its 'war-tax' (protection money extorted from landowners and businesses). In that month the

Congreso approved legislation limiting the right of public-sector employees to strike. In the following month the Congreso adopted legislation that made members of the armed forces accountable to civilian courts for all but strictly military crimes.

In September 1996 the Government and the URNG signed an agreement in Mexico City on the strengthening of civilian power and the role of the armed forces. Under the terms of the accord, all military and intelligence services were to be placed under the authority of the Government. The police force was to be reorganized, with the creation of a new National Civilian Police force (Policía Nacional Civil—PNC), which would replace the existing units from mid-1997. The armed forces were to be reduced in size by one-third and were to relinquish responsibility for internal security. Also confirmed in the accord was the abolition of the PAC. By early December the demobilization of the PAC, estimated to number some 202,000 members, was officially concluded. Later that month a general amnesty law was approved by the Congreso. Whilst the law did not exonerate former combatants for human rights violations, the rebels expressed concern that the amnesty was too extensive and that atrocities committed by the armed forces would go unpunished.

On 29 December 1996 the Government and the URNG signed the definitive peace treaty in Guatemala City, bringing to an end some 36 years of civil war, during which an estimated 140,000 people had died. The demobilization of URNG guerrillas, estimated to number some 3,250, was to be supervised by MINUGUA. Earlier in the year the URNG had established a 44-member political council to prepare for the reconstitution of the organization as a broad-based political party. Demobilization was completed in May 1997. In the following month the URNG registered as a political party in formation and, in December 1998, formally engaged as a political party.

In February 1998, in an effort to curb rising violent crime, the Government began the deployment of an additional 10,000 troops and police throughout the country. In April the UN Human Rights Commission removed Guatemala from the list of countries under its observation. The decision did not affect the operations of MINUGUA, whose mandate had been renewed for a further year in order to monitor the implementation of the peace treaty. In June MINUGUA released a report detailing the rising incidence of crime in Guatemala and criticizing the Government's failure to control the activities of paramilitary vigilante groups and the apparent inability of the justice system to deal with cases of serious crime.

In April 1998 the auxiliary bishop of the metropolitan diocese of Guatemala City, Juan José Gerardi Conedera, was murdered. Gerardi had been a founder of the Roman Catholic Church's Oficina de Derechos Humanos del Arzobispado (ODHA—Archbishopric's Human Rights Office), and a prominent critic of the armed forces. Days before his death Gerardi had presented a report by the ODHA documenting human rights abuses committed during the civil conflict, of which army personnel were found responsible for some 80%. Although two civilian suspects were subsequently detained in connection with Gerardi's murder, the Church and human rights groups expressed the widely-held belief that the real perpetrators had been members of the armed forces. In July, in what the Church and human rights groups interpreted as a further attempt to conceal the truth, a priest, Mario Orantes Nájera, was arrested. He was formally charged with Gerardi's murder in October. In November, in a report commissioned by the Church, former chief prosecutor Acisclo Valladares Molina asserted that the murder revealed all the signs of an extra-judicial execution. In February 1999 the presiding judge in the case, Henry Monroy, ordered the release of Orantes on grounds of insufficient evidence. However, in March Monroy withdrew from the case after allegedly receiving threats against his life. In October the state prosecutor investigating the murder, Celvin Galindo, also resigned after receiving death threats. The case finally went to trial in 2001 and on 8 June former intelligence chief Col (retd) Disrael Lima Estrada, his son, Capt. Byron Lima Oliva, and a former member of the presidential guard, José Obdulio Villanueva, were convicted of Bishop Gerardi's murder; Orantes was convicted of conspiring in his death. In early August the Chief Public Prosecutor, Leopoldo Zeissig, was forced to flee the country after also receiving death threats. However, in October 2002 a Court of Appeal overturned the convictions and ordered a retrial, after accepting the defence's argument that there had been irregularities in the testimony of a key witness.

In August 1999, in what was widely regarded as a test case for the judicial system, 25 members of the armed forces convicted of

the massacre in 1995 of 11 civilians in Xamán, Alta Verapaz, received minimum sentences of five years' imprisonment. The case was the first in which military personnel accused of killing civilians had been tried by a civilian court and the decision, which provoked public outrage, served greatly to undermine confidence in the courts' ability to administer justice in the remaining 625 cases of massacres attributed to the security forces. By contrast, in late 1998 death sentences had been passed on three members of the PAC found guilty of participating in massacres of civilians. In December 1999 MINUGUA issued a report stating that commitments made by the Arzú administration under the 1996 peace treaty to reduce the influence of the military remained unfulfilled. In late 2000 the UN Secretary-General, Kofi Annan, recommended that MINUGUA's mandate be renewed for a further year. According to MINUGUA, the number of extra-judicial executions doubled between 1996 and 2000 and in the latter year the incidence of death threats increased significantly.

In February 1999 the CEH published its final report, in which it attributed more than 93% of human rights violations committed during the civil conflict to the armed forces and state paramilitaries. It announced that 200,000 people had been killed or had 'disappeared' between 1962 and 1996, the majority of them Mayan Indians. It described counter-insurgency operations during the period 1981–83 as 'genocide' against the Mayan people. It also concluded that the USA had financed and trained Guatemalan forces responsible for atrocities. The report recommended that compensation be provided for the families of victims, that prosecutions be brought against those suspected of crimes against humanity and that a purge of the armed forces be implemented. It proposed that a special commission be established to study the conduct of the army and security forces during the armed conflict. In response, the Government described the Commission's findings as 'controversial', and did not express any intention of pursuing its recommendations.

In late 1999 the Guatemalan Nobel Peace Prize winner, Rigoberta Menchú, filed a case in Spain against former generals Ríos Montt, Lucas García and Mejía Victores, and other military officers, for the crimes of genocide, state terrorism and torture. However, in December 2000 the Spanish National High Court ruled that it was not competent to investigate the case. In August 2000 the Government accepted responsibility for 44 cases of human rights violations being investigated by the Inter-American Commission on Human Rights and, in early 2001, paid compensation for those deaths involving street children. Also in December, the Commission also ruled that the military was responsible for the torture and murder of guerrilla leader Efraín Bamaca Velásquez. In March 2002 the Government was ordered to make indemnity payments amounting to US $500,000 to Bamaca's family. At the end of 2000 the ODHA filed a case against Ríos Montt for human rights violations during his regime. On 6 June 2001 11 indigenous communities filed genocide charges against Ríos Montt and other senior officers in his command, for his role in a series of massacres by the army during his rule.

In October 1998 the Congreso approved constitutional reforms provided for in the 1996 peace accords. The reforms, which concerned the rights of indigenous peoples, the role of the armed forces and the police, and the strengthening of the courts, were subject to ratification in a referendum. However, at the referendum, on 16 May 1999, 55.6% of participating voters rejected the constitutional amendments. The turn-out was extremely low, with only 18.6% of the 4m. registered voters taking part, and observers attributed the result to a lack of information and to mistrust of the political establishment by the electorate rather than to the rejection of the peace accords themselves. The Government, for its part, pledged that the peace process would not be affected by the outcome. At presidential and legislative elections, conducted on 7 November, the voter turn-out, at some 40%, was greatly improved. As no candidate received the necessary 50% of the votes to win the presidential election outright, the two leading candidates, Alfonso Antonio Portillo Cabrera of the FRG and Oscar Berger Perdomo of the PAN, contested a second round of voting on 26 December, in which Portillo secured victory with 68.3% of the votes cast. Of the 113 seats in the legislature (enlarged from 80 seats) the FRG secured an outright majority with 63 seats.

The new Government of President Portillo, which took office on 14 January 2000, immediately undertook the promised demilitarization of the upper echelons of government, and announced that one of its priorities was the narrowing of the fiscal deficit. A Governability Pact was unveiled, intended to build consensus between the representatives of the state and the country's political and social leaderships. Local levels of government were to promote debate among civil society organizations on six issues: citizen security, justice, demilitarization and human rights; decentralization, rural development and the environment; education; political reform and civil-society participation; integral human development; and the Fiscal Pact, a long-term public-expenditure strategy.

However, disputes between the Government and the Congreso Nacional resulted in virtual paralysis in policy-making throughout 2001. In mid-March two deputies defected from the FRG to join the Unidad Nacional de la Esperanza (UNE), a coalition established by the former presidential candidate Alvaro Colom Caballero. Furthermore, throughout the year the Government was beset by allegations of corruption; the Ministers of Public Finance and of Communications, Transport and Public Works both left the Cabinet in 2001 after irregular practices were uncovered in their ministries, while in November Brig.-Gen. (retd) Eduardo Arévalo Lacs, hitherto the Minister of National Defence, was appointed Minister of the Interior, replacing Byron Barrientes, who was subsequently charged with the embezzlement of government funds. Civil society and human rights groups claimed that Lacs' appointment to the interior ministry contravened the peace agreements. There were further protests in January 2002 when Gen. Lacs dismissed the director of the police force, Ennio Rivera Cardona, and replaced him with a former head of the disbanded national police, Luis Arturo Paniagua, who had been accused of human rights abuses. President Portillo's announcement in the same month of the establishment of a human rights team to monitor the security forces did little to allay the objections. At a meeting of international donors in Washington, DC, USA, in February the Government was criticized for its lack of progress in implementing the terms of the peace accords.

In March 2002 a congressional commission was formed to investigate claims made by a Panamanian newspaper that President Portillo, Vice-President Francisco Reyes López and other prominent government officials had established bank accounts in Panama for the purpose of money-laundering. The Attorney-General and the Auditor-General's Office also began separate investigations. The allegations provoked mass protests in Guatemala City by trade-union members and socialist and religious groups, who demanded the President's resignation. The former President and human rights ombudsman, Ramiro León de Carpio, resigned his seat in the Congreso in protest at government corruption and 10 other FRG deputies threatened to do the same. At the end of the month the Auditor-General's Office closed its investigation into the allegations, declaring that evidence used to support the claims had been fabricated. None the less, the congressional commission instigated a full inquiry, although in June this investigation also collapsed, owing to a lack of evidence. President Portillo claimed that he had been the victim of powerful business interests who objected to his reformist policies.

Meanwhile, violent attacks against public figures continued in 2002. In mid-March, days after he had given a speech at the anti-Portillo demonstrations, the leader of the opposition group Partido Patriótico, Jorge Rosal Zea, was shot and killed. In September, following an increase in extra-judicial executions, MINUGUA warned that the rule of law was jeopardized in several regions of the country. Furthermore, in the following month, the US Assistant Secretary of State for the Western Hemisphere, Otto Reich, expressed his concern at levels of corruption, drugs-trafficking and continuing human rights abuses in Guatemala. The Government reacted angrily to what it perceived to be unwarranted intervention into domestic affairs by the USA and recalled its ambassador to the USA in protest. Nevertheless, President Portillo subsequently announced a number of reforms to the security forces, including the dissolution of the Departmento de Operaciones Antinarcoticos (DNOA—Department of Anti-Narcotics Operations) and the creation of a new unit, Unidades Moviles Operativas, to combat drugs-trafficking and terrorism. In February 2003, nevertheless, the USA added Guatemala to the list of nations it considered unco-operative in combating drugs-trafficking.

In August 2002 some 30,000 *campesinos* occupied farms and blocked major roads across the country, preventing access to ports and border crossings to Mexico, Honduras and El Salvador. The protest was organized by the Coordinadora Nacional de Organizaciones Campesinas (CNOC—National Co-ordi-

nating Committee of Peasant Organizations) in support of land reform.

In early October 2002 Col (retd) Juan Valencia Osorio was convicted of ordering the murder of anthropologist Myrna Mack in 1990. The prosecution maintained that the killing had been carried out in reaction to a report produced by Mack implicating the Government in violent anti-insurgency campaigns against Mayan Indians during the civil war. Osorio was sentenced to 30 years' imprisonment. His two co-defendants were cleared of charges of complicity. The trial was only the second in which former members of the military élite had been tried for war crimes and was interpreted as an encouraging sign that the state was increasingly willing to act in curbing the power of the military.

In November 2002 the opposition PAN once again selected the former mayor of Guatemala City, Oscar Berger Perdomo, as its candidate in the forthcoming presidential election. However, in May 2003, following internal divisions, Berger announced he had left the party and would stand as the candidate of the Gran Alianza Nacional (GANA), a small, centre-right alliance supported by the private sector and comprising the Partido Progresista, the Partido Reformador Guatemalteco and the Partido Solidaridad Nacional. Nine PAN deputies followed suit. The PAN subsequently nominated the defeated candidate in the November primary, Leonel López Rodas, to be its presidential nominee, while the centre-left UNE selected Alvaro Colom Caballeros. President Portillo supported the nomination of Ríos Montt as the FRG's nominee. However, constitutionally, Ríos Montt was barred from standing for presidential office, having come to power through unconstitutional means in 1982. In June 2003 the Supreme Electoral Tribunal rejected his candidature on these grounds, a decision supported by a supreme court ruling in early July. However, on 15 July the Constitutional Court overturned the ban, ruling that the former military leader could stand for re-election on the grounds that the pertinent legislation had been introduced in 1987, four years after Ríos Montt had left office. The decision was criticized by human rights organizations. The Supreme Court subsequently barred the candidacy of Ríos Montt, prompting violent protests outside the court buildings by his supporters, resulting in the death of a journalist, Hector Ramírez. However, at the end of the month the Consitutional Court again overruled the supreme court decision and instructed the Electoral Tribunal to register Ríos Montt as a candidate.

Presidential and legislative elections took place on 9 November 2003. Berger won 34.3% of the votes cast, followed by Colom with 26.4%. Ríos Montt secured 19.3% of the ballot and López Rodas 8.4%. As no candidate secured more than 50% of the ballot, the two leading candidates contested a second round of voting on 28 December, in which Berger narrowly secured the presidency with 54.1% of the votes cast. In the concurrently held legislative elections, GANA secured the largest number of seats in the expanded assembly, although it failed to secure a congressional majority, winning 49 of the 158 seats. The FRG won 42 seats, followed by the UNE with 33 seats and the PAN with 16 seats. The Partido Unionista obtained seven seats and the Alianza Nueva Nación secured six, while the URNG and the Unión Democrática each secured two seats. The remaining seat was won by the Democracia Social Participativa. Some 54.5% of the electorate voted in the legislative elections. A similarly high proportion (55.9%) voted in the first round presidential ballot, although this fell to 46.8% in the second round. Fears that the FRG or the PAC would interfere with the electoral process were not realized, although in the weeks preceding the elections some 20 party activists and regional leaders were murdered.

Having failed to secure a congressional majority, GANA was forced to enter into negotiations with other parties in order to establish a legislative alliance. Eventually, in mid-January 2004 the party agreed a two-year governability pact with the UNE and the PAN. The pact set out key legislative priorities, which included a programme of austere but transparent public expenditure, compliance with the peace accords, and political and electoral reform. Berger took office on 14 January. His new Cabinet was criticized for not being inclusive; it was predominantly composed of businessmen and contained one woman and one indigenous minister. In his inauguration speech Berger undertook to address the problems of crime and corruption, to improve governance and national security, and to create jobs, by stimulating domestic and foreign investment and by implementing public-works programmes. The new President also promised US $9m. in compensation to civilians who had lost relatives and property during the civil war. Furthermore, he pledged his support for the UN-appointed Commission for the Investigation of Illegal Groups and Clandestine Security Operations (CICIACS), established in March 2003 to investigate paramilitary organizations in Guatemala. However, on 6 August the Constitutional Court declared the creation of CICIACS to be unconstitutional because the Commission could exercise powers that were by law, exclusive to the judiciary. None the less, Berger assured the UN that his Government would attempt to resolve the objections raised by the Court and establish CICIACS.

In late February 2004 the Constitutional Court lifted the parliamentary immunity Ríos Montt had hitherto enjoyed. Early in the following month Ríos Montt was charged with premeditated murder, coercion, and threats in connection to the violence outside the Supreme Court in July 2003, and placed under house arrest. Also in February, former President Portillo and former Vice-President Reyes also lost their parliamentary immunity from prosecution. Shortly after, Portillo left the country for Mexico. An injunction for his arrest on charges of money-laundering and misuse of public funds was subsequently issued and the US embassy revoked his visa. In addition, a private action was brought against Portillo for allegedly orchestrating the outbreaks of violence by his supporters in July 2003. Reyes was arrested on 28 July 2004 and charged with fraud, embezzlement and abuse of authority. He was released on bail in December pending further investigations.

Government attempts to implement a programme of fiscal reform met with some opposition in 2004, both from the Congreso, where GANA lacked an overall majority, and the private sector, which was hostile to tax increases. In an attempt to secure opposition support for the proposed legislation, in May President Berger met with Ríos Montt. However, the meeting was heavily criticized by Berger's allies: the UNE and the PAN withdrew from the governability pact and the Partido Patriota (PP) left GANA in protest, leaving the Government even more reliant on securing FRG support.

The Government faced further challenges in June 2004, when protests took place in 20 of the country's 22 departmental capitals. The demonstrations were initiated by the rural indigenous organization, Frente Maya Campesino, in protest at the forceful eviction of peasants from unused private and state-owned land. However, it was joined by teachers and members of trade unions and non-governmental organizations protesting against the proposed Central American Free Trade Agreement (CAFTA) and proposed increases in taxes and electricity prices. In response, President Berger agreed to end the compulsory eviction of peasants and to establish an agency to settle land disputes. He made no concessions with regard to CAFTA, beyond undertaking to have reports on the agreement published in indigenous languages. However, the Government did assent to some changes to the fiscal reform legislation. These included maintaining the current rate of value-added tax (VAT) and current income-tax threshold, and the withdrawal of plans to tax redundancy and annual bonus payments. Further protests were held in March 2005 after the Congreso ratified CAFTA.

Upon taking office President Berger had pledged to address the problems of the high rates of violent crime and corruption in the public sector. In the first six months of 2004 the number of violent crimes increased by 13% on the previous year. Following the exposure of several senior police officers with links to criminal groups, in June 2004 Berger dismissed the head of the PNC. In the following month, the Government launched two initiatives to improve public security: the first encouraged members of the public to surrender weapons in return for money or material goods, such as sewing machines, while the second entailed the deployment of police and military officers on public transport in an attempt to reduce the increasing incidences of bus hijackings. The rise in violent crime led to the resignation of the Minister of the Interior, Arturo Soto, on 19 July. He was succeeded by prominent businessman Carlos Vielman Montes. In late July, in a campaign named 'Crusade against Violence', some 4,000 police and military officers were deployed in areas with particularly high crime rates. In spite of these initiatives, the murder rate increased by 25% in 2004 to 4,346. In mid-August more than 12,000 demonstrators representing some 560 civic associations participated in a anti-crime march through the capital, led by Sergio Morales, the ombudsman for human rights. Domestic security and the eradication of corruption within the PNC were likely to remain priorities in 2005 and

President Berger was expected to continue the controversial deployment of the armed forces to support the police.

On 11 August 2004 former members of the PAC held a protest outside the Congreso in an attempt to prevent legislators leaving the building until they had approved payment to the militias of the remainder of the compensation agreed during President Portillo's term in office. Portillo had decreed the payment of US $640 to former members of the PAC, but only $215 had been disbursed. During 2004 the Congreso approved legislation to compensate PAC members on three separate occasions, but each time human rights organizations successfully appealed to the Constitutional Court that the laws were unconstitutional. In December the Government announced it was to establish a social fund for the former militias; however, protests by PAC members continued in 2005, and in March President Berger agreed to resubmit compensation legislation to the Congreso.

During 2004 internal political conflicts and the consequent defection of congressional deputies destabilized the major political organizations and impeded the Government's efforts to introduce legislative reforms. By February 2005, although remaining the largest party in the Congreso, GANA's representation was reduced to 31 seats (from 49 in January 2004), while the FRG retained 30 deputies (from 42) and the UNE 28 deputies (from 33). Despite some success in addressing the corruption of the previous administration, Berger's popularity waned significantly in the first year of his presidency. In late 2004 a MINUGUA report noted that efforts to reform the criminal justice system had been largely ineffective and that the state remained unable to ensure that laws were observed. Upon its withdrawal from Guatemala in December, a MINUGUA report stated that the Government still had to overcome three major challenges: public security, judicial reform and discrimination against indigenous peoples.

Under the Portillo administration, bilateral relations with the USA had deteriorated. However, the incoming Government of Oscar Berger pledged a commitment to fighting drugs-trafficking. In January 2004 members of the new Government met US officials to discuss the joint maritime agreement that allowed counter-narcotics teams to board and search vessels in Guatemalan waters. However, in September President Berger requested more US assistance if his Government was to meet US demands for narcotics-interception targets. The Berger Government also indicated its support for the establishment of CAFTA with the USA, negotiations towards which were concluded in late 2003. Relations between the two countries were expected to be further consolidated after CAFTA was ratified in March 2005 (see Economic Affairs).

Until the return to civilian government in 1986, Guatemala remained steadfast in its claims to the neighbouring territory of Belize, a former British dependency. However, Guatemala's new Constitution, which took effect in January 1986, did not include Belize in its delineation of Guatemalan territory. In May 1988 representatives of Guatemala, Belize and the United Kingdom agreed to establish a permanent Joint Commission to formulate a draft treaty to resolve Guatemala's claims to Belize. In October the Commission announced the establishment of three subcommissions, to be responsible for drafting the treaty; the delimitation of the border; and the creation of a joint development zone, with the co-operation of the United Kingdom and the European Community (EC, now European Union—EU). Approval of the treaty was to be decided by referendums, to be held in both Guatemala and Belize.

In September 1991 Guatemala and Belize signed an accord under the terms of which Belize pledged to legislate to reduce its maritime boundaries and to allow Guatemala access to the Caribbean Sea and use of its port facilities. In return, President Serrano officially announced his country's recognition of Belize as an independent state and established diplomatic relations. Serrano's decision to recognize Belize, made without consulting the Congreso and without holding a referendum, provoked protests from the opposition, who claimed that it was unconstitutional; however, in November the Congreso voted to ratify Serrano's decision to recognize Belize.

In April 1993 Guatemala and Belize signed a non-aggression pact, affirming their intent to refrain from the threat or use of force against each other. In March 1994 Guatemala formally reaffirmed its territorial claim to Belize. Concern was expressed by the Standing Committee of Ministers of Foreign Affairs of the Caribbean Community and Common Market (CARICOM, see p. 172), which reaffirmed its support for Belizean sovereignty. In

September 1996 the Ministers of Foreign Affairs of Guatemala and Belize conducted preliminary talks in New York, USA, concerning a resumption of negotiations on the territorial dispute. In November 1998 a joint Guatemalan–Belizean commission was established to deal with immigration and cross-border traffic. In August 2000 a panel of negotiators was established at the headquarters of the Organization of American States (OAS, see p. 319) in Washington, DC, to supervise the process of bilateral negotiations. Negotiations in 2001 focused on the issue of Guatemalans living in the disputed border area, who, according to Belize, were being used by Guatemala to assert sovereignty over the territory; an agreement was later reached to relocate the families. In May 2002 the Belizean Government formally compensated the families of three Guatemalans killed in the disputed area in the previous year.

In 2002 relations with Belize appeared to improve following further OAS-mediated discussions on the border issue in June. Further negotiations in August yielded some success; in early September proposals were outlined for a solution to the dispute. These included the provision that Guatemala would recognize Belize's land boundary as set out in the Treaty of 1859, and the creation of a model settlement for peasants and landless farmers in the area. Guatemalan farmers occupying land within the Belize border were to have priority rights of residency to this settlement. These was also provision for a free trade agreement between the two countries and a Development Trust Fund, managed by the Inter-American Development Bank, to fund poverty-alleviation schemes in the border region. In addition, Guatemala would receive an Exclusive Economic Zone in the Gulf of Honduras, amounting to 2,000 sq miles of marine territory, contributed by both Belize and Honduras, although those countries were to retain fishing rights and 50% of any mineral resources discovered in the sea-bed. A commission, comprising representatives from Belize, Guatemala and Honduras, would oversee the establishment and management of an Ecological Marine Park in the coastal areas and a separate Tripartite Regional Fisheries Management Commission would manage fishing in the Gulf of Honduras. The two countries were to hold simultaneous public referendums on the agreement by the end of November. However, the fatal shooting of a Guatemalan on the Belizean side of the border in early October delayed the referendums. Following further conciliatory discussions, in February 2003 the foreign ministers of both countries signed a co-operation agreement pending a final settlement of the dispute. In May 2004 delegations from the two countries participated in OAS-sponsored negotiations to establish a series of initiatives designed to promote mutual confidence, including a free trade agreement. Earlier, in March, representatives of Guatemala and El Salvador signed a customs union that was expected to facilitate the cross-border movement of goods and people, thus promoting trade and tourism. Negotiations to secure a free trade agreement with Taiwan were scheduled to be concluded in June 2005.

Government

Guatemala is a republic comprising 22 departments. Under the 1986 Constitution (revised in 1994), legislative power is vested in the unicameral Congreso Nacional (National Congress), with 158 members elected for four years by universal adult suffrage. Of the total seats, 127 are filled by departmental representation and 31 according to national listing. Executive power is held by the President (also directly elected for four years), assisted by a Vice-President and an appointed Cabinet.

Defence

In August 2004 the armed forces totalled an estimated 29,200, of whom 27,000 were in the army (including 23,000 conscripts), 1,500 in the navy (including 650 marines) and 700 in the air force. In addition, there were paramilitary forces of 19,000. Military service is by selective conscription for 30 months. In September 1996, as part of the ongoing peace process, the Government signed an agreement with the rebel URNG whereby the armed forces were to be placed under the control of the Government. Under the terms of the accord, the armed forces were reduced in number by one-third. This reduction included the disbanding of the Policía Militar Ambulante (Mobile Military Police), which was completed in late 1997. The accord also provided for the abolition of the Patrullas de Autodefensa Civil (PAC), which were demobilized in late 1996. In March 2004 President Berger announced that the military was to be reduced by almost 45%, to 17,500 personnel, in accordance

with the peace accords. Defence expenditure in 2003 was estimated at US $102m.

Economic Affairs

In 2003, according to estimates by the World Bank, Guatemala's gross national income (GNI), measured at average 2001–03 prices, was US $24,380.3m., equivalent to $1,910 per head (or $4,060 per head on an international purchasing-power parity basis). During 1990–2003, it was estimated, the population increased by an average of 2.7% per year, while gross domestic product (GDP) per head increased, in real terms, by an average of 1.0% per year. Overall GDP increased, in real terms, at an average annual rate of 3.7% in 1990–2003; GDP grew by an estimated 2.2% in 2002 and by a further estimated 2.1% in 2003.

Agriculture, including hunting, forestry and fishing, contributed an estimated 22.7% of GDP, measured in constant prices, in 2003. In 2002 42.0% of the active labour force were employed in this sector. The principal cash crops are coffee (which accounted for 11.7% of export earnings in 2002), sugar cane and bananas. Exports of shrimps are also significant. In recent years the country has successfully expanded production of less traditional crops, such as mangoes, berries and green beans. Following the drought in 2001, in September of that year the Government announced an aid programme of 'soft' loans and refinancing credits for the coffee sector. None the less, owing to a regional crisis in the coffee industry, coffee exports fell by 14.7% in 2002, compared with the harvest of 2001. During 1990–2003 agricultural GDP increased, in real terms, by an estimated average of 2.5% per year. Growth in agricultural GDP was 1.8% in 2002 and an estimated 3.1% in 2003.

Industry, including mining, manufacturing, construction and power, contributed an estimated 19.2% of GDP, measured in constant prices, in 2003. This sector employed 20.6% of the working population in 2002. Industrial GDP increased by an estimated average of 3.5% per year in 1990–2003. Growth in industrial GDP was 1.0% in 2001 and an estimated 1.3% in 2003.

Mining contributed an estimated 0.6% of GDP, measured in constant prices, in 2003 and employed 0.2% of the working population in 2002. The most important mineral export is petroleum, which accounted for 6.7% of total export earnings in 2002. In addition, copper, antimony, lead, zinc and tungsten are mined on a small scale. There are also deposits of nickel, gold and silver. Mining GDP increased by 9.8% in 2002 and by estimated 2.7% in 2003.

Guatemala's industrial sector is the largest in Central America. Manufacturing contributed an estimated 12.6% of GDP, measured in constant prices, in 2003 and employed 13.4% of the working population in 2002. The main branches of manufacturing, measured by gross value of output, are food-processing, textiles, plastic products, paper and paper products, pharmaceuticals and industrial chemicals. Manufacturing GDP increased by an average of 2.4% per year in 1990–2003. Growth in manufacturing GDP was 0.8% in 2002 and an estimated 0.6% in 2003. Guatemala's clothing assembly, or *maquila*, manufacturing sector expanded in the late 1990s and employed some 80,000 workers in 1998. However, in 2001, owing to the introduction of a business tax and the economic slowdown in the USA towards the end of the year, the sector contracted; 38 *maquila* factories closed, while a further 229 were threatened with closure.

Energy is derived principally from mineral fuels and hydroelectric power. Petroleum provided 44.1% of electric energy in 2001 while hydroelectric power was responsible for 32.9% of total electricity production in the same year. Guatemala is a marginal producer of petroleum and, in 2002, produced an estimated 9.0m. barrels. Petroleum reserves were estimated at 526m. barrels in January 2000. Reserves of natural gas were put at some 109,000m. cu ft in the same year. Imports of petroleum and petroleum products comprised 11.4% of the value of total imports in 2002. In late 1998 80% of the capital of the state-owned Empresa Eléctrica de Guatemala was sold to foreign investors for US $520m. At the same time, the Instituto Nacional de Electrificación was sold for $100m. In late 2001 Guatemala and Mexico reached agreement, under the 'Plan Puebla–Panamá' (see below), on a project to link their electricity grids. It was hoped that the project would improve regional power infrastructure and attract investment in the sector.

In 2003 the services sector contributed an estimated 58.1% of GDP, measured in constant prices, and in 2002 the sector employed 36.5% of the working population. The GDP of the services sector increased by an average of 4.3% per year in 1990–

2003; growth in the sector was 2.9% in 2002 and an estimated 2.0% in 2003.

In 2003 Guatemala recorded a visible trade deficit of US $3,126.7m., and there was a deficit of $1,050.9m. on the current account of the balance of payments. In 2002 the principal source of imports (36.1%) was the USA; other major suppliers were Mexico, Japan and El Salvador. The USA was also the principal market for exports (taking 30.2% of exports in that year); other significant purchasers were El Salvador, Honduras, Costa Rica and Nicaragua. The main exports in 2002 were chemical products, vegetables and fruits and coffee. The principal imports were petroleum and related products, road vehicles and parts, and paper, paperboards and manufactures. Remittances from citizens working abroad represented the second largest hard currency inflow into the country after non-traditional exports. In 2004 remittances from the USA totalled US $2,550m.

In 2001 there was a budgetary deficit of 638.8m. quetzales, equivalent to some 0.3% of GDP. At the end of 2002 Guatemala's total external debt stood at US $4,676m. of which US $3,744m. was long-term public debt. In that year the cost of debt-servicing was equivalent to 7.5% of the value of exports of goods and services. In 1990–2003 the average annual rate of inflation was 10.4%. Consumer prices increased by an average of 8.1% in 2002 and by 5.6% in 2003. An estimated 1.8% of the labour force were unemployed in 2002.

Guatemala is a member of the Central American Common Market (CACM, see p. 176). In 2000 Guatemala, El Salvador and Honduras signed a free trade agreement with Mexico, which promised greater market access and increased bilateral trade. As a consequence of the implementation of the agreement, trade with Mexico increased by 22% in 2002, in spite of a fall in the overall value of exports in that year. In May 2001 the Central American countries, including Guatemala, reached an agreement with Mexico to establish a series of joint transport, industry and tourism projects intended to integrate the region, called the 'Plan Puebla–Panamá'. Negotiations towards a free trade agreement, to be known as the Central American Free Trade Agreement (CAFTA), between Guatemala, Costa Rica, El Salvador, Honduras, Nicaragua and the USA were concluded in December 2003. The agreement, which was ratified by the Congreso in March 2005, entailed the gradual elimination of tariffs on most industrial and agricultural products over the next 10 and 20 years, respectively, and was expected to lead to an increase in exports. In May 2004 the Presidents of Guatemala, El Salvador, Honduras and Nicaragua signed an agreement creating a Central American customs union.

The signing of the peace accord in December 1996, which signalled the end of the civil conflict, improved Guatemala's economic prospects significantly. In January 1997 international donors pledged US $1,900m. in loans and donations towards the Government's reconstruction programme. However, the funding was contingent upon the Government significantly increasing tax revenues. In 2000 the Government of Alfonso Portillo introduced a Fiscal Pact, which aimed, *inter alia*, to increase tax revenue. In February 2002, at a meeting in Washington, DC, international donors pledged a further US $1,300m. in loans and grants to aid Guatemala's post-war reconstruction programmes, less than the Government had been hoping for. The Portillo administration's lack of progress in implementing the peace accords was considered the main reason for the shortfall

in funding. Furthermore, in June of that year the country had also been placed on the Financial Action Task Force on Money Laundering's (FATF) 'blacklist' of countries targeted for international scrutiny regarding potential money-laundering activities within the banking sector. In 2003 Guatemala's 11 'offshore' banks were inspected and a licensing system was introduced. The country was finally removed from the list in July 2004.

The incoming administration of President Oscar Berger Perdomo pledged to foster economic growth and create jobs through austere economic policies and the encouragement of domestic and foreign investment. In 2004 Berger presented a series of economic reforms to the Congreso that aimed to narrow the fiscal deficit by increasing tax revenue and decreasing budgetary expenditure. However, his party lacked an overall majority in the Congreso and struggled to achieve consensus on the proposed measures. The political manoeuvring necessary to gain legislative approval highlighted the challenges faced by the Berger Government in implementing policies intended to improve Guatemala's economic position. The economy was estimated to have grown by 2.3% in 2004 and was forecast to expand by 2.8% in 2005.

Education

Elementary education is free and, in urban areas, compulsory between seven and 14 years of age. Primary education begins at the age of seven and lasts for six years. Secondary education, beginning at 13 years of age, lasts for up to six years, comprising two cycles of three years each. In 2000 there were 10,424 pre-primary schools, and in 2001 there were 16,931 primary schools and 3,422 secondary schools. In 2001/02 enrolment at primary schools was equivalent to 85.0% of children in the relevant age-group (males 86.9%; females 82.9%). The comparable figure for secondary education in that year was 29.3% (males 29.9%; females 28.7%). There are currently 12 universities. The inauguration of Guatemala's first indigenous university, the Universidad Maya de Guatemala, was expected to take place in early 2005. Open to both indigenous and non-indigenous students, the institution would offer courses in medicine, education, Mayan Law, art, architecture, community development and agriculture. In 2000/01 enrolment in primary, secondary and tertiary education was equivalent to 57% of the relevant age groups. In 2003 budgetary expenditure on education was an estimated 3,255m. quetzales.

Public Holidays

2005: 1 January (New Year's Day), 6 January (Epiphany), 25–28 March (Easter), 1 May (Labour Day), 30 June (Anniversary of the Revolution), 15 August (Assumption, Guatemala City only), 15 September (Independence Day), 12 October (Columbus Day), 20 October (Revolution Day), 1 November (All Saints' Day), 24–25 December (Christmas), 31 December (New Year's Eve).

2006: 1 January (New Year's Day), 6 January (Epiphany), 14–17 April (Easter), 1 May (Labour Day), 30 June (Anniversary of the Revolution), 14 August (Assumption, Guatemala City only), 15 September (Independence Day), 12 October (Columbus Day), 20 October (Revolution Day), 1 November (All Saints' Day), 24–25 December (Christmas), 31 December (New Year's Eve).

Weights and Measures

The metric system is in official use.

Statistical Survey

Sources (unless otherwise stated): Banco de Guatemala, 7a Avda 22-01, Zona 1, Apdo 365, Guatemala City; tel. 230-6222; fax 253-4035; internet www .banguat.gob.gt ; Instituto Nacional de Estadística, Edif. América 4°, 8a Calle 9-55, Zona 1, Guatemala City; tel. 232-6136; fax 232-4790; e-mail info-ine@ ine.gob.gt; internet www.segeplan.gob.gt/ine.

Area and Population

AREA, POPULATION AND DENSITY

Area (sq km)	
Land	108,429
Inland water	460
Total	108,889*
Population (census results)†	
17 April 1994	8,322,051
24 November 2002	11,237,196
Density (per sq km) at November 2002	103.2

* 42,042 sq miles.
† Excluding adjustments for underenumeration, estimated to have been 13.7% in 1981.

DEPARTMENTS
(population at census of November 2002)

Alta Verapaz	776,246	Quetzaltenango	624,716
Baja Verapaz	215,915	Quiché	655,510
Chimaltenango	446,133	Retalhuleu	241,411
Chiquimula	302,485	Sacatepéquez	248,019
El Progreso	139,490	San Marcos	794,951
Escuintla	538,746	Santa Rosa	301,370
Guatemala	2,541,581	Sololá	307,661
Huehuetenango	846,544	Suchitepéquez	403,945
Izabal	314,306	Totonicapán	339,254
Jalapa	242,926	Zacapa	200,167
Jutiapa	389,085		
Petén	366,735	**Total**	11,237,196

PRINCIPAL TOWNS
(population at census of November 2002)

Guatemala City	942,348	Cobán	144,461
Mixco	403,689	Quetzaltenango	127,569
Villa Nueva	355,901	Escuintla	119,897
San Juan Sacatepéquez	152,583	Jalapa	105,796
San Pedro Carcha	148,344	Totonicapán	96,392

BIRTHS, MARRIAGES AND DEATHS

	Registered live births		Registered marriages		Registered deaths	
	Number	Rate (per 1,000)	Number	Rate (per 1,000)	Number	Rate (per 1,000)
1995	371,091	34.9	49,701	4.7	65,159	6.1
1996	377,723	34.6	47,428	4.3	60,618	5.5
1997	387,862	36.9	51,908	4.9	67,691	6.4
1998	378,438	35.0	52,499	4.9	69,633	6.4
1999	409,034	36.9	62,034	5.6	65,139	5.9
2000	425,410	37.4	58,311	5.1	67,284	5.9
2001	415,410	35.6	54,722	4.7	68,041	5.8
2002	387,287	34.5	51,857	4.6	66,089	5.9

Expectation of life (WHO estimates, years at birth): 65.9 (males 66.1; females 69.0) in 2002 (Source: WHO, *World Health Report*).

ECONOMICALLY ACTIVE POPULATION
(at census of November 2002)

	Males	Females	Total
Agriculture, forestry, hunting and fishing	1,278,739	178,364	1,457,103
Mining and quarrying	5,313	756	6,069
Manufacturing	301,222	164,725	465,947
Construction	186,611	21,266	207,877
Electricity, gas, water and sanitary services	23,518	10,135	33,653
Commerce	343,586	228,114	571,700
Transport, storage and communications	96,410	16,913	113,323
Financial and property services	82,644	42,839	125,483
Public administration and defence	60,853	25,137	85,990
Education	42,366	59,796	102,162
Community and personal services	68,165	197,794	265,959
Activities not adequately described	18,256	9,875	28,131
Total	2,525,683	937,714	3,463,397

Health and Welfare

KEY INDICATORS

Total fertility rate (children per woman, 2002)	4.5
Under-5 mortality rate (per 1,000 live births, 2003)	47
HIV/AIDS (% of persons aged 15–49, 2003)	1.1
Physicians (per 1,000 head, 1997)	0.93
Hospital beds (per 1,000 head, 1996)	0.98
Health expenditure (2001): US $ per head (PPP)	199
Health expenditure (2001): % of GDP	4.8
Health expenditure (2001): public (% of total)	48.3
Access to water (% of persons, 2002)	95
Access to sanitation (% of persons, 2002)	61
Human Development Index (2002): ranking	121
Human Development Index (2002): value	0.649

For sources and definitions, see explanatory note on p. vi.

Agriculture

PRINCIPAL CROPS
('000 metric tons)

	2001	2002	2003
Maize	1,091.5	1,050.1	1,053.6*
Sugar cane	16,934.9	17,489.9	17,500.0†
Pulses†	129.4	129.4	129.7†
Oil palm fruit†	466.6	540.0	540.0†
Tomatoes	175.0	187.2	187.2†
Other fresh vegetables†	487.2	475.2	475.2
Watermelons†	126.2	126.2	126.2
Cantaloupes and other melons	188.2	188.2†	188.2†
Bananas	898.0	1,000.0†	1,000.0†
Plantains	266.5	268.0†	268.0†
Lemons and limes	130.8	142.9	142.9†
Mangoes†	183.0	187.0	187.0
Other fresh fruit†	396.8	397.6	397.6
Coffee (green)*	275.7	221.8	210.0

* Unofficial figure(s).
† FAO estimate(s).

Source: FAO.

LIVESTOCK
('000 head, year ending September)

	2001	2002	2003
Horses*	120	122	124
Asses*	10	10	10
Mules*	38	39	39
Cattle*	2,500	2,540	2,540
Sheep	245	250*	260
Pigs*	763	800	780
Goats	112*	112*	112
Chickens*	24,000	25,500	27

* FAO estimate(s).

Source: FAO.

LIVESTOCK PRODUCTS
('000 metric tons)

	2001	2002	2003
Beef and veal*	62.0	63.0	63.0
Pig meat*	25.0	25.5	26.0
Chicken meat	144.0†	155.0†	155.0*
Other meat*	3.9	3.9	4.0
Cows' milk*	270.0	270.0	270.0
Cheese*	11.3	11.3	11.3
Butter*	0.6	0.6	0.6
Hen eggs†	82.5	85.0	85.0
Honey	1.5*	1.5*	1.5
Cattle hides*	8.8	8.9	8.9

* FAO estimate(s).
† Unofficial figure(s).

Source: FAO.

Forestry

ROUNDWOOD REMOVALS
('000 cubic metres, excl. bark)

	2001	2002	2003*
Sawlogs, veneer logs and logs for sleepers	425	492	492
Other industrial wood	19	26	26
Fuel wood*	14,870	15,207	15,552
Total	15,313	15,725	16,070

* FAO estimates.

Source: FAO.

SAWNWOOD PRODUCTION
('000 cubic metres, incl. railway sleepers)

	1998	1999	2000
Coniferous (softwood)	263*	195	180
Broadleaved (hardwood) . . .	45	40	160
Total	308	235	340

* FAO estimate.

2001–2003: Figures unchanged from 2000.

Fishing
('000 metric tons, live weight)

	2000	2001*	2002
Capture	39.2	22.4	24.2
Freshwater fishes	7.3	7.3	7.3*
Skipjack tuna	12.3	6.5	10.1
Yellowfin tuna	4.8	4.0	2.4
Bigeye tuna	12.4	2.5	2.6
Other marine fishes	0.7	0.9	1.0
Penaeus shrimps	1.2	0.9	0.6†
Aquaculture	4.0	5.1	8.0
Tilapias	1.8	1.9	1.9
Penaeus shrimps	1.5	2.5	5.4
Total catch	43.2	27.5	32.1

* FAO estimate(s).
† Preliminary figure.

Source: FAO.

Mining
('000 metric tons, unless otherwise indicated)

	2000	2001*	2002*
Crude petroleum ('000 42-gallon barrels)	7,571	21,000	19,000
Limestone	4,532	2,775	3,040
Sand and gravel	4,158	4,000	4,000
Silica sand	173	170	170
Crushed stone	50,000	50,000	50,000

* Estimates.

Source: US Geological Survey.

Industry

SELECTED PRODUCTS
('000 metric tons, unless otherwise indicated)

	1999	2000	2001
Sugar	752	883	1,670
Motor spirit (petrol)	139	150	—
Cigarettes (million)	4,376	4,262	—
Cement	2,120	2,039	1,600
Electric energy (million kWh) . .	5,236	6,048	—

Finance

CURRENCY AND EXCHANGE RATES

Monetary Units
100 centavos = 1 quetzal.

Sterling, Dollar and Euro Equivalents (30 November 2004)
£1 sterling = 14.779 quetzales;
US $1 = 7.748 quetzales;
€1 = 10.302 quetzales;
1,000 quetzales = £67.67= $129.06 = €97.07.

Average Exchange Rate (quetzales per US dollar)
2001   7.8586
2002   7.8216
2003   7.9409

Note: In December 2000 legislation was approved to allow the circulation of the US dollar and other convertible currencies, for use in a wide range of transactions, from 1 May 2001.

BUDGET
(million quetzales)

Revenue*	1999	2000	2001
Current revenue	14,683.2	16,039.4	17,639.6
Taxation	13,863.1	15,071.6	15,966.2
Taxes on income, profits and capital gains	2,896.5	3,688.7	4,139.8
Corporate	1,495.8	2,004.3	2,059.7
Domestic taxes on goods and services	8,885.6	9,376.1	9,679.2
Sales, turnover or value-added taxes	6,241.0	7,037.9	6,983.1
Excises	1,829.6	1,797.0	2,177.3
Taxes on international trade and transactions	1,817.5	1,807.3	1,979.9
Customs duties	1,814.1	1,805.8	1,979.0
Other current revenue	820.2	967.8	1,673.4
Entrepreneurial and property income	179.9	314.3	897.4
Administrative fees, non-industrial and incidental sales	300.8	264.2	295.0
Contributions to government employee pension and welfare funds within government	302.6	356.7	414.2
Capital revenue	0.3	0.2	2.5
Total	13,967.1	15,205.8	17,656.2

Expenditure†	1999	2000	2001
Current expenditure	12,631.4	14,680.7	17,226.0
Expenditure on goods and services	9,511.5	10,822.7	12,802.5
Interest payments	1,528.6	1,672.7	2,111.2
Subsidies and other current transfers	1,591.2	2,185.3	2,312.3
Transfers to non profit-making institutions and households	1,243.0	1,900.2	2,063.5
Capital expenditure	3,546.5	3,336.8	3,601.8
Acquisition of fixed capital assets	2,143.9	1,838.9	1,654.7
Capital transfers	1,402.5	1,497.9	1,947.0
Domestic transfers	1,305.4	1,222.2	1,711.0
To other levels of national government	1,297.3	1,217.9	1,705.8
Adjustment	195.9	203.2	207.4
Total	16,373.7	18,220.8	21,035.2

* Excluding grants received (million quetzales): 188.2 in 1999; 348.5 in 2000; 565.7 in 2001.
† Excluding lending minus repayments (million quetzales): 1,585.5 in 1999; −974.6 in 2000; −2,174.5 in 2001.
Source: IMF, *Government Finance Statistics Yearbook*.

2002 (million quetzales): Total revenue 20,503.5; Total expenditure 22,233.1 (Source: IMF, *International Financial Statistics*).

2003 (million quetzales): Total revenue 21,811.6; Total expenditure 25,630.2 (Source: IMF, *International Financial Statistics*).

INTERNATIONAL RESERVES
(US $ million at 31 December)

	2001	2002	2003
Gold*	9.2	9.1	9.3
IMF special drawing rights	8.5	8.2	8.2
Foreign exchange	2,283.7	2,290.9	2,825.0
Total	2,292.2	2,299.1	2,842.5

* Valued at US $42.22 per troy ounce.

Source: IMF, *International Financial Statistics*.

MONEY SUPPLY
(million quetzales at 31 December)

	2001	2002	2003
Currency outside banks	8,360.7	8,729.4	10,608.8
Demand deposits at deposit money banks	12,512.2	13,930.4	16,188.0
Total money (incl. others)	21,059.0	22,835.7	26,937.7

Source: IMF, *International Financial Statistics*.

COST OF LIVING
(Consumer Price Index; base: 1990 = 100)

	1998	1999	2000
Food	255.7	261.3	272.6
Clothing	200.1	207.0	213.6
Rent	255.0	278.0	292.9
All items (incl. others)	266.4	280.2	297.0

2001 (base: 2000 = 100): Food 110.0; All items 107.3.
2002 (base: 2000 = 100): Food 121.5; All items 116.0.
2003 (base: 2000 = 100): Food 128.5; All items 122.5.
Source: ILO.

NATIONAL ACCOUNTS
Expenditure on the Gross Domestic Product
(million quetzales at current prices)

	2001	2002	2003
Government final consumption expenditure	12,420	13,005	14,105
Private final consumption expenditure	139,919	156,809	171,424
Increase in stocks	3,567	5,612	4,567
Gross fixed capital formation	25,504	28,486	28,894
Total domestic expenditure	181,410	203,912	218,990
Exports of goods and services	30,926	29,379	31,902
Less Imports of goods and services	47,541	51,345	54,495
GDP in purchasers' values	164,795	181,945	196,396

Source: IMF, *International Financial Statistics*.

Gross Domestic Product by Economic Activity
(million quetzales at constant 1958 prices)

	2001	2002*	2003†
Agriculture, hunting, forestry and fishing	1,171.3	1,192.5	1,229.9
Mining and quarrying	26.6	29.2	30.0
Manufacturing	675.6	681.0	685.0
Electricity, gas and water	204.6	223.2	93.8
Construction	110.6	93.7	232.1
Trade, restaurants and hotels	1,282.9	1,319.2	582.4
Transport, storage and communications	522.7	552.3	1,346.3
Finance, insurance and real estate	260.6	265.3	269.2
Ownership of dwellings	239.0	245.4	252.5
General government services	398.1	395.8	377.6
Other community, social and personal services	300.2	311.2	322.3
Total	5,191.9	5,308.7	5,420.9

* Preliminary figures.
† Estimates.

BALANCE OF PAYMENTS
(US $ million)

	2001	2002	2003
Exports of goods f.o.b. . . .	2,864.6	2,818.9	3,048.3
Imports of goods f.o.b. . . .	−5,142.1	−5,791.0	−6,175.0
Trade balance	−2,277.5	−2,972.1	−3,126.7
Exports of services	1,031	1,145.4	1,058.8
Imports of services	−898.0	−1,066.1	−1,126.8
Balance on goods and services	−2,144.5	−2,892.8	−3,194.7
Other income received . . .	317.5	161.1	178.7
Other income paid	−407.6	−479.5	−496.8
Balance on goods, services and income	−2,234.6	−3,211.1	−3,512.9
Current transfers received . .	1,031.8	2,077.7	2,558.9
Current transfers paid . . .	−35.1	−101.5	−97.0
Current balance	−1,237.9	−1,234.9	−1,050.9
Capital account (net) . . .	93.3	124.2	133.8
Direct investment from abroad .	455.5	110.6	115.8
Portfolio investment assets .	−44.9	−38.3	21.7
Portfolio investment liabilities . .	−175.4	−107.8	−11.0
Other investment assets . .	156.7	196.4	116.0
Other investment liabilities . .	778.1	1,035.6	913.4
Net errors and omissions . .	98.1	−64.7	311.4
Overall balance	474.3	21.2	550.1

Source: IMF, *International Financial Statistics.*

External Trade

PRINCIPAL COMMODITIES
(US $ million)

Imports c.i.f.	2000	2001	2002
Food and live animals . .	494.7	663.5	681.5
Cereals and cereal preparations	150.4	220.9	260.5
Mineral fuels, lubricants, etc. .	622.1	764.6	773.6
Petroleum, petroleum products etc.	535.8	673.3	693.0
Crude petroleum oils, etc. . .	169.8	158.2	114.0
Refined petroleum products .	356.3	506.3	562.9
Other fuel oils	174.4	246.7	n.a.
Chemicals and related products	780.0	947.2	1,008.4
Medicinal and pharmaceutical products	185.2	244.1	258.2
Medicaments (incl. veterinary medicaments)	152.4	200.8	207.6
Artificial resins, plastic materials etc.	169.8	186.0	200.2
Products of polymerizations, etc.	146.5	156.6	168.3
Basic manufactures	826.7	912.2	935.5
Paper, paperboards and manufactures	230.9	253.3	268.0
Paper and paperboard . . .	150.7	157.3	172.1
Iron and steel	174.4	182.4	177.1
Machinery and transport equipment	1,583.7	1,578.7	1,823.5
Power-generating machinery and equipment	157.4	67.9	150.0
Machinery specialized for particular industries	150.0	139.9	161.4
Telecommunications and sound equipment	282.6	263.4	304.2
Road vehicles and parts . . .	499.6	573.5	636.2
Passenger motor cars (excl. buses)	213.5	259.5	295.0
Motor vehicles for the transport of goods	158.3	175.6	189.7
Miscellaneous manufactured articles	376.2	507.3	321.6
Total (incl. others)	4,882.4	5,597.6	6,074.5

Exports f.o.b.	2000	2001	2002
Food and live animals . . .	1,406.3	1,127.9	1,079.4
Cereals and cereal preparations	74.7	90.9	82.1
Vegetables and fruit . . .	353.5	300.6	318.9
Fresh or dried fruit and nuts (excl. oil nuts)	243.3	223.3	253.2
Bananas and plantains . . .	178.1	201.2	240.4
Sugar, sugar preparations and honey	203.7	231.7	252.3
Sugar and honey	197.6	224.1	244.9
Raw beet and cane sugars .	190.8	212.6	227.1
Coffee, tea, cocoa and spices .	657.5	407.1	359.1
Coffee (incl. husks and skins) and substitutes containing coffee .	575.4	306.9	261.7
Crude materials (inedible) except fuels	162.3	135.0	115.1
Mineral fuels, lubricants, etc.	162.4	130.1	154.9
Crude petroleum oils, etc. . . .	159.3	100.8	149.4
Chemicals and related products	308.8	350.7	314.6
Medicinal and pharmaceutical products	85.2	73.2	73.1
Medicaments (incl. veterinary)	82.0	69.7	70.5
Essential oils, perfume materials and cleansing preparations . .	110.4	138.1	126.4
Basic manufactures	301.4	321.8	251.0
Miscellaneous manufactured articles	204.5	178.0	144.1
Total (incl. others)	2,699.4	2,412.6	2,227.5

PRINCIPAL TRADING PARTNERS
(US $ million)

Imports c.i.f.	2000	2001	2002
Brazil	67.3	84.3	122.5
Canada	124.7	140.6	125.5
Costa Rica	200.9	232.2	216.3
El Salvador	313.8	385.0	333.1
Germany	126.2	158.9	171.8
Honduras	84.1	129.3	84.0
Italy	55.7	56.9	71.7
Japan	166.6	289.7	340.1
Korea, Republic	69.2	77.1	77.6
Mexico	576.0	595.0	587.4
Panama	162.0	69.5	81.9
Spain	69.3	83.6	104.6
USA	2,071.2	1,964.6	2,195.4
Venezuela	275.8	271.8	224.5
Total (incl. others)	5,171.4	5,606.6	6,077.7

Exports f.o.b.	2000	2001	2002
Belgium*	34.8	11.9	11.8
Canada	63.1	42.7	34.9
Costa Rica	126.8	156.3	119.1
El Salvador	341.1	477.3	403.6
Germany	107.8	58.3	46.1
Honduras	233.1	295.3	236.6
Japan	62.5	42.3	29.3
Korea, Republic	28.6	94.0	85.5
Mexico	120.2	79.0	76.4
Netherlands	30.7	15.8	14.2
Nicaragua	114.3	130.6	114.5
Panama	54.7	43.4	48.2
Russian Federation	20.7	31.3	n.a.
Saudi Arabia	47.6	55.9	46.3
USA	971.2	643.1	672.1
Total (incl. others)	2,699.0	2,412.6	2,227.7

* Includes figures for Luxembourg.

Transport

RAILWAYS
(traffic)

	1994	1995	1996
Passenger-km (million) . . .	991	0	0
Freight ton-km (million) . . .	25,295	14,242	836

Source: UN, *Statistical Yearbook*.

ROAD TRAFFIC
(motor vehicles in use at 31 December)

	1997	1998	1999
Passenger cars	470,016	508,868	578,733
Buses and coaches	9,843	10,250	11,017
Lorries and vans	34,220	37,057	42,219
Motorcycles and mopeds . . .	111,358	117,536	129,664

Source: IRF, *World Road Statistics*.

SHIPPING

Merchant Fleet
(registered at 31 December)

	2001	2002	2003
Number of vessels	8	11	9
Total displacement ('000 grt) . .	4.6	8.9	5.3

Source: Lloyd's Register-Fairplay, *World Fleet Statistics*.

International Sea-borne Freight Traffic
('000 metric tons)

	1992	1993	1994
Goods loaded	2,176	1,818	2,096
Goods unloaded	3,201	3,025	3,822

CIVIL AVIATION
(traffic on scheduled services)

	1997	1998	1999
Kilometres flown (million) . . .	5	7	5
Passengers carried ('000) . . .	508	794	506
Passenger-km (million) . . .	368	480	342
Total ton-km (million) . . .	77	50	33

Source: UN, *Statistical Yearbook*.

Tourism

TOURIST ARRIVALS BY COUNTRY OF ORIGIN

	2000	2001	2002
Canada	15,915	17,277	23,945
Costa Rica	21,851	28,974	28,918
El Salvador	289,970	214,114	228,018
France	13,965	15,312	16,119
Germany	20,045	20,985	23,559
Honduras	51,545	59,224	75,355
Italy	16,241	18,358	17,310
Mexico	53,576	61,326	65,331
Nicaragua	16,207	15,882	24,607
Spain	18,144	24,190	24,125
USA	186,784	193,285	199,614
Total (incl. others)	826,240	835,492	884,190

Tourism receipts (US $ million): 535 in 2000; 493 in 2001; 612 in 2002.

Communications Media

	2000	2001	2002
Telephones ('000 main lines in use)	650	756	846
Mobile cellular telephones ('000 subscribers)	857	1,146	1,577
Personal computers ('000 in use)	n.a.	150	173
Internet users ('000)	80	200	400

Source: International Telecommunication Union.

Radio receivers ('000 in use): 835 in 1997.

Television receivers ('000 in use): 680 in 1999 (Source: UN, *Statistical Yearbook*).

Daily newspapers (number): 7 in 1996.

Facsimile machines (number in use): 10,000 in 1996.

Education

(2003, unless otherwise indicated)

	Institu-tions	Teachers	Students
Pre-primary	10,424*	15,708	399,842
Primary	16,609	69,954	2,163,760
Secondary	3,585	26,372	444,345
Tertiary	1,946	16,188	210,225

* 2000 data.

Adult literacy rate (UNESCO estimates): 69.9% (males 77.3%; females 62.5%) in 2002 (Source: UN Development Programme, *Human Development Report*).

Directory

The Constitution

In December 1984 the Constituent Assembly drafted a new Constitution (based on that of 1965), which was approved in May 1985 and came into effect in January 1986. A series of amendments to the Constitution were approved by referendum in January 1994 and came into effect in April 1994. The Constitution's main provisions are summarized below:

Guatemala has a republican representative democratic system of government and power is exercised equally by the legislative, executive and judicial bodies. The official language is Spanish. Suffrage is universal and secret, obligatory for those who can read and write and optional for those who are illiterate. The free formation and growth of political parties whose aims are democratic is guaranteed. There is no discrimination on grounds of race, colour, sex, religion, birth, economic or social position or political opinions.

The State will give protection to capital and private enterprise in order to develop sources of labour and stimulate creative activity.

Monopolies are forbidden and the State will limit any enterprise which might prejudice the development of the community. The right to social security is recognized and it shall be on a national, unitary, obligatory basis.

Constitutional guarantees may be suspended in certain circumstances for up to 30 days (unlimited in the case of war).

CONGRESS

Legislative power rests with Congress, which is made up of 158 deputies, elected according to a combination of departmental and proportional representation. Congress meets on 15 January each year and ordinary sessions last four months; extraordinary sessions can be called by the Permanent Commission or the Executive. All Congressional decisions must be taken by absolute majority of the members, except in special cases laid down by law. Deputies are elected for four years; they may be re-elected after a lapse of one session, but only once. Congress is responsible for all matters concerning the President and Vice-President and their execution of their offices; for all electoral matters; for all matters concerning the laws of the Republic; for approving the budget and decreeing taxes; for declaring war; for conferring honours, both civil and military; for fixing the coinage and the system of weights and measures; for approving, by two-thirds' majority, any international treaty or agreement affecting the law, sovereignty, financial status or security of the country.

PRESIDENT

The President is elected by universal suffrage, by absolute majority for a non-extendable period of four years. Re-election or prolongation of the presidential term of office are punishable by law. The President is responsible for national defence and security, fulfilling the Constitution, leading the armed forces, taking any necessary steps in time of national emergency, passing and executing laws, international policy, nominating and removing Ministers, officials and diplomats, co-ordinating the actions of Ministers of State. The Vice-President's duties include presiding over Congress and taking part in the discussions of the Council of Ministers.

ARMY

The Guatemalan Army is intended to maintain national independence, sovereignty and honour and territorial integrity. It is an indivisible, apolitical, non-deliberating body and is made up of land, sea and air forces.

LOCAL ADMINISTRATIVE DIVISIONS

For the purposes of administration the territory of the Republic is divided into 22 Departments and these into 330 Municipalities, but this division can be modified by Congress to suit interests and general development of the Nation without loss of municipal autonomy. Municipal authorities are elected every four years.

JUDICIARY

Justice is exercised exclusively by the Supreme Court of Justice and other tribunals. Administration of Justice is obligatory, free and independent of the other functions of State. The President of the Judiciary, judges and other officials are elected by Congress for five years. The Supreme Court of Justice is made up of 13 judges. The President of the Judiciary is also President of the Supreme Court. The Supreme Court nominates all other judges. Under the Supreme Court come the Court of Appeal, the Administrative Disputes Tribunal, the Tribunal of Second Instance of Accounts, Jurisdiction Conflicts, First Instance and Military, the Extraordinary Tribunal of Protection. There is a Court of Constitutionality presided over by the President of the Supreme Court.

The Government

HEAD OF STATE

President: OSCAR JOSÉ RAFAEL BERGER PERDOMO (took office 14 January 2004).

Vice-President: EDUARDO STEIN BARILLAS.

CABINET
(April 2005)

Minister of Foreign Affairs: JORGE BRIZ ABULARACH.

Minister of the Interior: CARLOS VIELMAN MONTES.

Minister of National Defence: Gen. CARLOS HUMBERTO ALDANA VILLANUEVA.

Minister of Public Finance: MARIA ANTONIETA DEL CID DE BONILLA.

Minister of Economy: MARCIO RONALDO CUEVAS POSADAS.

Minister of Public Health and Social Welfare: MARCO TULIO SOSA RAMÍREZ.

Minister of Communications, Infrastructure and Housing: MANUEL EDUARDO CASTILLO ARROYO.

Minister of Agriculture, Livestock and Food: ALVARO AGUILAR PRADO.

Minister of Education: MARÍA DEL CARMEN ACEÑA.

Minister of Employment and Social Security: JORGE FRANCISCO GALLARDO FLORES.

Minister of Energy and Mines: LUIS ROMEO ORTIZ PELÁEZ.

Minister of Culture and Sport: MANUEL DE JESÚS SALAZAR TETZAHUIC.

Minister of the Environment and Natural Resources: JUAN MARIO DARY FUENTES.

MINISTRIES

Ministry of Agriculture, Livestock and Food: Edif. Monja Blanca, 7 Avda 12-90, Zona 13, Guatemala City; tel. 2362-4764; fax 2332-8302; e-mail magadest@intelnet.net.gt; internet www.maga.gob.gt.

Ministry of Communications, Infrastructure and Housing: Edif. Antiguo Cocesna, 8a Avda y 15 Calle, Zona 13, Finca Nacional La Aurora, Guatemala City; tel. 2361-0827; fax 2362-6051; e-mail relpublicas@micivi.gob.gt; internet www.civ.gob.gt.

Ministry of Culture and Sport: 12 Avda 11-65, Zona 1, Guatemala City; tel. 2253-0543; fax 2253-0540; internet www.minculturadeportes.gob.gt.

Ministry of Economy: 8a Avda 10-43, Zona 1, Guatemala City; tel. 2238-3330; fax 2238-2413; e-mail nhernandez@mail.mineco.gob.gt; internet www.mineco.gob.gt.

Ministry of Education: Palacio Nacional, 6a Calle 1-87, Zona 10, Guatemala City; tel. 2360-0911; fax 2361-0350; e-mail informatica@mineduc.gob.gt; internet www.mineduc.gob.gt.

Ministry of Employment and Social Security: Edif. NASA, 14 Calle 5-49, Zona 1, Guatemala City; tel. 2230-1361; fax 2251-3559; e-mail info@mintrabajo.gob.gt; internet www.mintrabajo.gob.gt.

Ministry of Energy and Mines: Diagonal 17, 29-78, Zona 11, Guatemala City; tel. 2477-0743; fax 2476-8506; e-mail informatica@mem.gob.gt; internet www.mem.gob.gt.

Ministry of the Environment and Natural Resources: Edif. MARN, 20 Calle 28-58, Zona 10, Guatemala City; tel. 512-2914; e-mail marnguatemala@marn.gob.gt; internet www.marn.gob.gt.

Ministry of Foreign Affairs: 2a Avda La Reforma 4-47, Zona 10, Guatemala City; tel. 2331-8410; fax 2331-8510; e-mail webmaster@minex.gob.gt; internet www.minex.gob.gt.

Ministry of the Interior: 6a Avda 4-64, Zona 4, 3°, Guatemala City; tel. 2367-5402; fax 2362-0239; internet www.mingob.gob.gt.

Ministry of National Defence: Antigua Escuela Politécnica, Avda La Reforma 1-45, Zona 10, Guatemala City; tel. 2360-9890; fax 2360-9909; internet www.mindef.mil.gt.

Ministry of Public Finance: Centro Cívico, 8a Avda y 21 Calle, Zona 1, Guatemala City; tel. 2248-5053; fax 2248-5054; e-mail info@minfin.gob.gt; internet www.minfin.gob.gt.

Ministry of Public Health and Social Welfare: Escuela de Enfermería, 3°, 6a Avda 3-45, Zona 1, Guatemala City; tel. 2475-2121; fax 2475-2168; e-mail info@mspas.gob.gt; internet www.mspas.gob.gt.

President and Legislature

PRESIDENT

Presidential Election, 9 November and 28 December 2003

Candidate	First round % of votes	Second round % of votes
Oscar Berger Perdomo (GANA)*	34.3	54.1
Alvaro Colom Caballeros (UNE)	26.4	45.9
Gen. (retd) José Efraín Ríos Montt (FRG)	19.3	—
Leonel López Rodas (PAN)	8.4	—
Fritz García-Gallont (PU)	3.0	—
Rodrigo Asturias (URNG)	2.6	—
Jacobo Arbenz (DCG)	1.6	—
José Angel Lee (DSP)	1.4	—
Total (incl. others)	100.0	100.0

*The Gran Alianza Nacional, an electoral alliance comprising the Partido Patriota, the Movimiento Reformador and the Partido Solidaridad Nacional.

CONGRESO DE LA REPÚBLICA

President: JORGE MÉNDEZ HERBRUGER.

Vice-Presidents: ALEJANDRO BALTAZAR MALDONADO AGUIRRE, EDGAR LEONEL RODRÍGUEZ LARA, INGRID ROXANA BALDETTI ELIAS.

Legislative Elections, 9 November 2003

	Seats
Gran Alianza Nacional (GANA)*	49
Frente Republicano Guatemalteco (FRG)	42
Unidad Nacional de la Esperanza (UNE)	33
Partido de Avanzada Nacional (PAN)	16
Partido Unionista (PU)	7
Alianza Nueva Nación (ANN)	6
Unidad Revolucionaria Nacional Guatemalteca (URNG)	2
Others	3
Total	**158**

*An electoral alliance comprising the Partido Patriota, the Movimiento Reformador and the Partido Solidaridad Nacional.

Political Organizations

Alianza Nueva Nación (ANN): 15 Avda 5-60, Zona 1, Guatemala City; tel. 2251-2514; Sec.-Gen. ALFONSO BAUER PAZ.

Bienestar Nacional (BIEN): 8a Avda 6-30, Zona 2, Guatemala City; tel. 524-1448; Sec.-Gen. RUBEN GARCÍA LÓPEZ.

Centro de Acción Social (CASA): Guatemala City; f. 2003; represents indigenous peoples; Leader RIGOBERTO QUEMÉ CHAY.

Democracia Cristiana Guatemalteca (DCG): Avda Elena 20-66, Zona 3, Guatemala City; tel. 2238-4988; fax 2337-0966; e-mail vcerezo@congreso.go.gt; f. 1955; 130,000 mems; Sec.-Gen. MARCO VINICIO CEREZO AREVALO.

Desarrollo Integral Auténtico (DIA): 12a Calle 'A' 2-18, Zona 1, Guatemala City; tel. and fax 2232-8044; e-mail morlain@guate.net; f. 1998; left-wing party; Sec.-Gen. JORGE LUIS ORTEGA TORRES.

Frente Democrático Nueva Guatemala (FDNG): left-wing faction of Partido Revolucionario; Pres. JORGE GONZÁLEZ DEL VALLE; Sec.-Gen. RAFAEL ARRIAGA.

Frente Republicano Guatemalteco (FRG): 3a Calle 5-50, Zona 1, Guatemala City; tel. 2238-0826; internet www.frg.org.gt; f. 1988; right-wing group; Leader Gen. (retd) JOSÉ EFRAÍN RÍOS MONTT.

Gran Alianza Nacional (GANA): 7a Avda, 10-40, Zona 9, Guatemala City; tel. 2331-0121; fax 2331-0144; internet www.ganaconoscarberger2003.org; f. 2003, following split with the PAN; Leader OSCAR JOSÉ RAFAEL BERGER PERDOMO; centre-right alliance comprising:

> **Movimiento Reformador:** Vía 6, 4-09, Zona 4, Guatemala City; tel. 2360-0745; e-mail ruben@itelgua.com; f. 1995 as the Partido Laborista Guatemalteco; adopted present name in 2002; Sec.-Gen. ALFREDO SKINNER KLEE ARENALES.

> **Partido Solidaridad Nacional (PSN):** 3a Avda 15-14, Zona 1, Guatemala City; e-mail cqa_74@hotmail.com; Sec.-Gen. JORGE FRANCISCO GALLARDO FLORES.

Movimiento de Liberación Nacional (MLN): Of. 10A, Condiminio Reforma, Avda Reforma 10-00, Zona 9, Guatemala City; tel. 2331-1093; fax 2331-6865; e-mail mln@wepa.com.gt; internet www.wepa.com.gt/mln; f. 1960; extreme right-wing; 95,000 mems; Sec.-Gen. ULYSSES CHARLES DENT WEISSENBERG; Public Relations Sec. JOSÉ GARAVITO GORDILLO.

Movimiento Principios y Valores: Guatemala City; f. 2003; Sec.-Gen. FRANCISCO BIANCHI; Sec. MANOLO BENDFELDT.

Partido de Avanzada Nacional (PAN): 7a Avda 10-38, Zona 9, Guatemala City; tel. 2334-1702; fax 2331-9906; internet www.pan.org.gt; Leader ALVARO ENRIQUE ARZÚ YRIGOYEN; Sec.-Gen. LEONEL ELISEO LÓPEZ RODAS.

Partido Libertador Progresista (PLP): 5a Calle 5-44, Zona 1, Guatemala City; tel. 2232-5548; e-mail plp@intelnet.net.gt; f. 1990; Sec.-Gen. ACISCLO VALLADARES.

Partido Patriota (PP): 11 Calle 11-54, Zona 1, Guatemala City; tel. 2230-6227; e-mail comunicacion@partidopatriota.org; internet www.partidopatriota.org; f. 2002; contested 2003 elections as part of GANA (q.v.); withdrew from GANA in May 2004; Sec.-Gen. OTTO PÉREZ MOLINA.

Partido Petenero: Guatemala City; f. 1983; defends regional interests of El Petén.

Partido Unionista (PU): 3a Avda A 14-23, Zona 9, Guatemala City; tel. 2331-7468; fax 2331-6141; e-mail info@unionista.org; internet www.unionistas.org; f. 1917; Sec.-Gen. FRITZ GARCÍA-GALLONT.

Transparencia: 11 Avda 15-61, Zona 10, Guatemala City; tel. 2333-7330; contested the 2003 elections; Sec.-Gen. PEDRO CHITAY RODRÍGUES.

Unidad Nacional Autentica (UNA): Calzado San Juan, Col. Monserrat 1, 2°, Zona 4, Mixco; tel. 437-6816; Sec.-Gen. GERARDO VILLEDA GUERRA.

Unidad Nacional de la Esperanza (UNE): 2a Avda 5-11, Zona 9, Guatemala City; tel. 2232-4685; e-mail ideas@une.org.gt; internet www.une.org.gt; f. 2001 following a split within the PAN; Founder and Pres. ALVARO COLOM CABALLEROS.

Unidad Revolucionaria Nacional Guatemalteca (URNG): Avda Simeón Cañas 8-01, Zona 2, Guatemala City; tel. 2288-4440; fax 2254-0572; e-mail prensaurng@guate.net; internet www.urng.org.gt; f. 1982 following unification of principal guerrilla groups engaged in the civil war; formally registered as a political party in 1998, following the end of the civil war in December 1996; Sec.-Gen. ALBA ESTELA MALDONADO GUEVARA.

Unión Democrática (UD): Of. E, 3°, Vista Hermosa II, 1a Calle 18-83, Zona 15, 01015 Guatemala City; tel. 2369-7074; fax 2369-3062; e-mail fito.paiz@ud.org.gt; internet www.ud.org.gt; f. 1983; Sec.-Gen. RODOLFO ERNESTO (FITO) PAIZ ANDRADE.

Los Verdes (LV): Vista Hermosa II, 1a Calle 22-08, Zona 15, Guatemala City; Sec.-Gen. RODOLFO ROSALES GARCÍA SALAS.

Diplomatic Representation

EMBASSIES IN GUATEMALA

Argentina: Edif. Europlaza 1703, 5 Avda 5-55, Zona 14, Apdo 120, Guatemala City; tel. and fax 2385-3786; e-mail embajadadeargentina@hotmail.com; internet www.embajadadeargentina.com; Ambassador CARLOS MARIO FORADORI.

Austria: Edif. Plaza Marítima, 4°, 6a Avda 20-25, Zona 10, Guatemala City; tel. 2368-1134; fax 2333-6180; e-mail austriabot@intelnet.net.gt; Ambassador MONIKA GRUBER-LANG.

Belize: Edif. El Reformador, Suite 803, 8°, Avda de la Reforma 1-50, Zona 9, Guatemala City; tel. 2334-5531; fax 2334-5536; e-mail embelguat@guate.net; internet www.embajadadebelize.org; Ambassador ALFREDO MARTINEZ.

Brazil: 18a Calle 2-22, Zona 14, Apdo 196-A, Guatemala City; tel. 2337-0949; fax 2337-3475; e-mail braembx@intelnet.net.gt; Ambassador RENAN PAES BARRETO.

Canada: Edif. Edyma Plaza, 8°, 13a Calle 8-44, Zona 10, Apdo 400, Guatemala City; tel. 2333-6102; fax 2333-6189; e-mail gtmla@dfait-maeci.gc.ca; internet www.dfait-maeci.gc.ca/guatemala; Ambassador JAMES LAMBERT.

Chile: 14 Calle 15-21, Zona 13, Guatemala City; tel. 2334-8273; fax 2334-8276; e-mail chilegu@intelnet.net.gt; Ambassador JORGE MOLINA VALDIVIESO.

China (Taiwan): 4a Avda 'A' 13-25, Zona 9, Apdo 1646, Guatemala City; tel. 2339-0711; fax 2332-2668; e-mail echina@intelnet.net.gt; Ambassador HONG-LIEN OU.

Colombia: Edif. Europlaza 1603, 5a Avda 5-56, Zona 14, Guatemala City; tel. 2385-3432; fax 2335-3603; e-mail embaguate@inter.net.co; Ambassador HERNANDEZ RÁMIREZ JARAMILLO.

Costa Rica: 1a Avda 15-52, Zona 10, Guatemala City; tel. 2363-1345; fax 2368-0506; e-mail embarica@intelnet.net.gt; Ambassador HORACIO ALVARADO BOGANTES.

Cuba: Avda las Americas 20-72, Zona 13, Guatemala City; tel. 2332-4066; fax 2332-5525; e-mail embagua@intelnet.net.gt; Ambassador ANGEL LORENZO ABASCAL IGLESIAS.

Dominican Republic: Edif. Géminis 10, Suite 804, Torre Sur, 12 Calle 1-25, Zona 10, Guatemala City; tel. 2338-2170; fax 2338-2171; e-mail embardom@intelnet.net.gt; Ambassador MIGDALIA TORRES GARCÍA.

Ecuador: 4 Avda 12-04, Zona 14, Guatemala City; tel. 2337-2994; fax 2368-1831; e-mail embecuad@guate.net; Ambassador MAURICIO PÉREZ MARTÍNEZ.

Egypt: Edif. Cobella, 5°, 5 Avda 10-84, Zona 14, Apdo 502, Guatemala City; tel. 2333-6296; fax 2368-2808; e-mail egyptemb@quetzal.net; Ambassador MOHAMED HADI MOUSTAFA EL TONSI.

El Salvador: 5a Avda 8-15, Zona 9, Guatemala City; tel. 2360-7660; fax 2334-2069; e-mail emsalva@pronet.net.gt; Ambassador RAFAEL ANTONIO CARBALLO ARÉVALO.

France: Edif. Marbella, 11°, 16a Calle 4-53, Zona 10, Apdo 971-A, Guatemala City; tel. 2337-4080; fax 2337-3180; e-mail ambfrguate@intelnet.net.gt; internet www.ambafrance.org.gt; Ambassador GILLES VIDAL.

Germany: Edif. Plaza Marítima, 2°, 20 Calle 6-20, Zona 10, Guatemala City; tel. 2364-6700; fax 2333-6906; e-mail embalemana@intelnet.net.gt; internet www.guatemala.diplo.de; Ambassador CLAUDE-ROBERT ELLNER.

Holy See: 10a Calle 4-47, Zona 9, Apdo 22, Guatemala City (Apostolic Nunciature); tel. 2332-4274; fax 2334-1918; e-mail nuntius@gua.net; Apostolic Nuncio Most Rev. BRUNO MUSARÒ (Titular Archbishop of Abari).

Honduras: Edif. Géminis 10, 12°, Torre Sur, 12 Calle 1-25, Of. 1211-1206B, Zona 10, Guatemala City; tel. 2335-3281; fax 2335-2851; e-mail embhond@intelnet.net.gt; Ambassador EDGUARDO PAZ.

Israel: 13a Avda 14-07, Zona 10, Guatemala City; tel. 2333-4624; fax 2333-6950; e-mail isrembgu@guaweb.net; Ambassador YAACOV PARAN.

Italy: 5a Avda 8-59, Zona 14, Guatemala City; tel. 2337-4557; fax 2337-0795; e-mail ambaguat@intelnet.net.gt; Ambassador PIETRO PORCARELLI.

Japan: Edif. Torre Internacional, 10°, Avda de la Reforma 16-85, Zona 10, Guatemala City; tel. 2367-2244; fax 2367-2245; e-mail embjpninfo@micro.com.gt; Ambassador KAGEFUMI UENO.

Korea, Republic: Edif. El Reformador, 7°, Avda de la Reforma 1-50, Zona 9, Apdo 1649, Guatemala City; tel. 2334-5480; fax 2334-5481; e-mail korembsy@mofat.go.kr; Ambassador KIM HONG-RAK.

Mexico: 2a Avda 7-57, Zona 10, Apdo 1455, Guatemala City; tel. 2420-3400; fax 2420-3410; e-mail embamexguat@itelgua.com; internet www.sre.gob.mx/guatemala; Ambassador ROSALBA OJEDA Y CARDENAS.

Nicaragua: 10a Avda 14-72, Zona 10, Guatemala City; tel. 2368-0785; fax 2337-4264; e-mail embaguat@terra.com.gt; Ambassador Dr JOSÉ RENÉ GUTIÉRREZ HUETE.

Norway: Edif. Murano Center 15°, Of. 1501, 14 Calle 3-51, Zona 10, Apdo 1764, Guatemala City; tel. 2366-5908; fax 2366-5928; e-mail ambgua@norad.no; Ambassador ROLF O. BERG.

Panama: 10 Avda 18-53, La Cañada, Apdo 929A, Zona 14, Guatemala City; tel. 2368-2805; fax 2333-3835; Ambassador JOSÉ ORLANDO CALVO VELÁZQUEZ.

Peru: 2a Avda 9-67, Zona 9, Guatemala City; tel. 2331-8558; fax 2334-3744; e-mail leprugua@concyt.gob.gt; Ambassador ALFREDO ARECCO SABLICH.

Spain: 6a Calle 6-48, Zona 9, Guatemala City; tel. 2379-3530; fax 2379-3533; e-mail embaespa@terra.com.gt; Ambassador JUAN LÓPEZ-DORIGA PÉREZ.

Sweden: 8a Avda 15-07, Zona 10, Guatemala City; tel. 2384-7300; fax 2384-7350; e-mail ambassaden.guatemala@foreign.ministry.se; internet www.swedenabroad.com/pages/general_23845.asp; Ambassador EIVOR HALKJAER.

Switzerland: Edif. Torre Internacional, 14°, 16 Calle 0-55, Zona 10, Apdo 1426, Guatemala City; tel. 2367-5520; fax 2367-5811; e-mail vertretung@gua.rep.admin.ch; Ambassador URS STEMMLER.

United Kingdom: Edif. Torre Internacional, 11°, Avda de la Reforma, 16 Calle, Zona 10, Guatemala City; tel. 2367-5425; fax 2367-5430; e-mail embassy@intelnett.com; Ambassador RICHARD LAVERS.

USA: Avda de la Reforma 7-01, Zona 10, Guatemala City; tel. 2331-1541; fax 2331-8885; internet guatemala.usembassy.gov; Ambassador JOHN R. HAMILTON.

Uruguay: Edif. Plaza Marítima, 3°, Of. 341, 6a Avda 20-25, Zona 10, Guatemala City; tel. 2368-0810; fax 2333-7553; e-mail uruguate@guate.net; Ambassador ESTELLA RUBY ARMAND UGON SEPULVEDA.

Venezuela: 13 Calle 3-40, Zona 10, Edif. Atlantis, Of. 601, Apdo 152, Guatemala City; tel. 2366-9832; fax 2366-9838; e-mail embavene@concyt.gob.gt; Chargé d'affaires a.i. FELIX MÉNDEZ CORREA.

Judicial System

Corte Suprema

Centro Cívico, 21 Calle 7-70, Zona 1, Guatemala City; internet www.organismojudicial.gob.gt.

The members of the Supreme Court are appointed by the Congress.

President of the Supreme Court: RODOLFO DE LEÓN MOLINA.

Members: A. E. LÓPEZ RODRÍGUEZ, R. E. HIGUEROS GIRÓN, L. S. SECAIRA PINTO, J. F. DE MATA VELA, Dr V. M. RIVERA WÖLTKE, O. H. VÁSQUEZ OLIVA, E. R. PACAY YALIBAT, C. E. DE LEÓN CÓRDOVA, B. O. DE LEÓN REYES, L. FERNÁNDEZ MOLINA, J. G. CABRERA HURTARTE, C. G. CHACÓN TORREBIARTE.

Civil Courts of Appeal

10 courts, five in Guatemala City, two in Quetzaltenango, one each in Jalapa, Zacapa and Antigua. The two Labour Courts of Appeal are in Guatemala City.

Judges of the First Instance: Seven civil and 10 penal in Guatemala City, two civil each in Quetzaltenango, Escuintla, Jutiapa and San Marcos, one civil in each of the 18 remaining Departments of the Republic.

Religion

Almost all of the inhabitants profess Christianity, with a majority belonging to the Roman Catholic Church. In recent years the Protestant Churches have attracted a growing number of converts.

CHRISTIANITY

The Roman Catholic Church

For ecclesiastical purposes, Guatemala comprises two archdioceses, 10 dioceses and the Apostolic Vicariates of El Petén and Izabal. At 31 December 2002 adherents represented about 74% of the total population.

Bishops' Conference

Conferencia Episcopal de Guatemala, Secretariado General del Episcopado, Km 15, Calzada Roosevelt 4-54, Zona 7, Mixco, Apdo 1698, Guatemala City; tel. 543-1827; fax 593-1834; e-mail ceg@quetzal.net; internet www.iglesiacatolica.org.gt.

f. 1973; Pres. Cardinal RODOLFO QUEZADA TORUÑO (Archbishop of Guatemala City).

Archbishop of Guatemala City: Cardinal RODOLFO QUEZADA TORUÑO, Arzobispado, 7a Avda 6-21, Zona 1, Apdo 723, Guatemala City; tel. 232-9707; fax 238-0004; e-mail curiaarzobispal@intelnet.net.gt.

Archbishop of Los Altos, Quetzaltenango-Totonicapán: VÍCTOR HUGO MARTÍNEZ CONTRERAS, Arzobispado, 11a Avda 6-27, Zona 1, Apdo 11, 09001 Quetzaltenango; tel. 761-2840; fax 761-6049.

The Anglican Communion

Guatemala comprises one of the five dioceses of the Iglesia Anglicana de la Región Central de América.

Bishop of Guatemala: Rt Rev. ARMANDO GUERRA SORIA, Avda Castellana 40-06, Zona 8, Apdo 58-A, Guatemala City; tel. 2272-0852; fax 2472-0764; e-mail diocesis@infovia.com.gt; diocese founded 1967.

Protestant Churches

The largest Protestant denomination in Guatemala is the Full Gospel Church, followed by the Assembly of God, the Central American Church, and the Prince of Peace Church. The Baptist, Presbyterian, Lutheran and Episcopalian churches are also represented.

The Baptist Church: Convention of Baptist Churches of Guatemala, 12a Calle 9-54, Zona 1, Apdo 322, 01901 Guatemala City; tel. and fax 2232-4227; e-mail cibg@intelnet.net.gt; f. 1946; Pres. Lic. JOSÉ MARROQUÍN R.; 43,876 mems.

Church of Jesus Christ of Latter-day Saints: 12a Calle 3-37, Zona 9, Guatemala City; e-mail contactos@mormones.org.gt; internet www.mormones.org.gt; 17 bishoprics, nine chapels; Pres. GORDON B. HINCKLEY.

Congregación Luterana La Epifanía (Evangelical Lutheran Congregation La Epifanía): 2a Avda 15-31, Zona 10, Apdo 651, 01010 Guatemala City; tel. 2368-0301; fax 2366-4968; e-mail schweikle@web.de; Pres. MÓNICA HEGEL; 200 mems.

Iglesia Nacional Evangélica Menonita Guatemalteca: Guatemala City; tel. 2339-0606; e-mail AlvaradoJE@ldschurch.org; Contact JULIO ALVARADO; members 5,000.

Divine Saviour Lutheran Church: Zacapa; tel. 7941-0254; e-mail hogarluterano@hotmail.com; Pastor GERARDO VENANCIO VÁSQUEZ SALGUERO.

Presbyterian Church: Iglesia Evangélica Presbiteriana Central, 6a Avda 'A' 4-68, Zona 1, Apdo 655, Guatemala City; tel. 2232-0791; fax 2232-2832; internet www.presbiterianacentral.org; f. 1882; 36,000 mems; Pastor Rev. JOSÉ RAMIRO BOLAÑOS RIVERA.

Union Church: 12 calle 7-37, Zona 9, 01009 Guatemala City; tel. 2361-2037; fax 2362-3961; e-mail unionchurch@guate.net; f. 1943; Pastor W. KARL SMITH.

The Press

PRINCIPAL DAILIES

Al Día: Avda de la Reforma 6-64, Zona 9, Guatemala City; tel. 2339-0870; fax 2339-1276; f. 1996; Pres. LIONEL TORIELLO NÁJERA; Dir GERARDO JIMÉNEZ ARDÓN.

Diario de Centroamérica: 18a Calle 6-72, Zona 1, Guatemala City; tel. 2222-4418; internet www.diariodecentroamerica.gob.gt; f. 1880; morning; official; Dir LUIS MENDIZÁBAL; circ. 15,000.

La Hora: 9a Calle 'A' 1-56, Zona 1, Apdo 1593, Guatemala City; tel. 2250-0447; fax 2251-7084; e-mail lahora@lahora.com.gt; internet www.lahora.com.gt; f. 1920; evening; independent; Dir OSCAR MARROQUÍN ROJAS; circ. 18,000.

Impacto: 9a Calle 'A' 1-56, Apdo 1593, Guatemala City; tel. 2222-6864; fax 2251-7084; daily.

La Nación: 1a Avda 11-12, Guatemala City.

El Periódico: 15a Avda 24-51, Zona 13, Guatemala City; tel. 2362-0242; fax 2332-9761; e-mail redaccion@elperiodico.com.gt; internet www.elperiodico.com.gt; f. 1996; morning; independent; Pres. JOSÉ RUBÉN ZAMORA; Editors JUAN LUIS FONT, SYLVIA GEREDA; circ. 50,000.

Guía Interamericana: Guía Interamericana, 20 Calle 5-35, Zona 10, Edif. Plaza los Arcos, 3°, Guatemala City; Editor ALFREDO MAYORGA; circ. 5,000.

Prensa Libre: 13a Calle 9-31, Zona 1, Apdo 2063, Guatemala City; tel. 2230-5096; fax 2251-8768; e-mail webmaster@prensalibre.com.gt; internet www.prensalibre.com; f. 1951; morning; independent; Gen. Man. EDGAR CONTRERAS MOLINA; Editor GONZALO MARROQUÍN GODOY; circ. 120,000.

Siglo Veintiuno: 7a Avda 11-63, Zona 9, Guatemala City; tel. 2360-6704; fax 2331-9145; e-mail buzon21@sigloxxi.com; internet www.sigloxxi.com; f. 1990; morning; Pres. LIONEL TORIELLO NÁJERA; circ. 65,000.

La Tarde: 14a Avda 4-33, Guatemala City.

PERIODICALS

AGA: 9a Calle 3-43, Zona 1, Guatemala City; monthly; agricultural.

Amiga: 13 Calle 9-31, Zona 1, Guatemala City; e-mail revistas@prensalibre.com.gt; health; Dir CAROLINA VÁSQUEZ.

Control TV: 13 Calle 9-31, Zona 1, Guatemala City; e-mail revistas@prensalibre.com.gt; Dir CAROLINA VÁSQUEZ.

Crónica Semanal: Guatemala City; tel. 2235-2155; fax 2235-2360; f. 1988; weekly; politics, economics, culture; Publr FRANCISCO PÉREZ.

Especiales: Edif. El Gráfico, 14 Avda 4-33, Zona 1, Guatemala City; e-mail moneda@guate.net; international news magazine; Dir KATIA DE CARPIO.

Gerencia: La Asociación de Gerentes de Guatemala, 6 Avda 1-36, Zona 14, 01014 Guatemala City; tel. 2231-1644; fax 2231-1646; e-mail agg@guate.net; internet www.nortropic.com/gerencia; f. 1967; monthly; official organ of the Association of Guatemalan Managers; Editor MARGARITA DE TARANO.

Guatemala Business News: 10a Calle 3-80, Zona 1, Guatemala City; monthly; Editor RODOLFO GARCÍA; circ. 5,000.

El Industrial: 6a Ruta 9-21, Zona 4, Guatemala City; monthly; official organ of the Chamber of Industry.

Inforpress Centroamericana: Guatemala City; fax 2232-9034; e-mail inforpre@inforpressca.com; internet www.inforpressca.com; f. 1972; weekly; Spanish and English; regional political and economic news and analysis; Dir ARIEL DE LEÓN.

Magazine Business Guatemala: 6a Avda 14-77, Zona 10, Guatemala City; consumer magazine.

Panorama Internacional: 13a Calle 8-44, Zona 9, Apdo 611-A, Guatemala City; tel. 2233-6367; fax 2233-6203; weekly; politics, economics, culture.

Mundo Motor: 13 Calle 9-31, Zona 1, Guatemala City; e-mail evasquez@prensalibre.com.gt; Dir CAROLINA VÁSQUEZ.

Revista Data Export: Edif. Camara de Industria, 5°, Ruta 6, 9-21, Zona 4, Guatemala; monthly; Editor REGINA CEREZO, circ. 1,500.

Revista Mundo Comercial: 10a Calle 3-80, Zona 1, 01001 Guatemala City; monthly; business; circ. 11,000.

Usurarios: 13 Calle 9-31, Zona 1, Guatemala City; e-mail revistas@prensalibre.com.gt; computing; Dir CAROLINA VÁSQUEZ.

Viajes: 13 Calle 9-31, Zona 1, Guatemala City; e-mail revistas@prensalibre.com.gt; tourism; Dir CAROLINA VÁSQUEZ.

PRESS ASSOCIATIONS

Asociación de Periodistas de Guatemala (APG): 14a Calle 3-29, Zona 1, Guatemala City; tel. 2232-1813; fax 2238-2781; e-mail apege@intelnet.net.gt; internet www.freewebs.com/apg; f. 1947; Pres. JULIO SANTOS; Sec. WALTER HERMOSILLA.

Cámara Guatemalteca de Periodismo (CGP): Guatemala City; Pres. EDUARDO DÍAZ REINA.

Círculo Nacional de Prensa (CNP): Guatemala City; Pres. ISRAEL TOBAR ALVARADO.

NEWS AGENCIES

Inforpress Centroamericana: Calle Mariscal 6-58, Zona 11, 0100 Guatemala City; tel. and fax 2473-1704; e-mail inforpre@guate.net; internet www.inforpressca.com/CAR; f. 1972; independent news agency; publishes two weekly news bulletins, in English and Spanish.

Foreign Bureaux

ACAN-EFE (Central America): Edif. El Centro, 8°, Of. 8-21, 9a Calle y 7a Avda, Zona 1, Guatemala City; tel. 2251-9454; fax 2251-9484; Man. ANA CAROLINA ALPÍREZ A.

Agenzia Nazionale Stampa Associata (ANSA) (Italy): Torre Norte, Edif. Géminis 10, Of. 805, 12a Calle 1-25, Zona 10, Guatemala City; tel. 2335-3039; e-mail ansagua@guate.net; Chief ALFONSO ANZUETO LÓPEZ.

Deutsche Presse-Agentur (dpa) (Germany): 5a Calle 4-30, Zona 1, Apdo 2333, Guatemala City; tel. 2251-7505; fax 2251-7505; Correspondent JULIO CÉSAR ANZUETO.

Inter Press Service (IPS) (Italy): Edif. El Centro, 3°, Of. 13, 7a Avda 8-56, Zona 1, Guatemala City; tel. 2253-8837; fax 2251-4736; internet www.ipslatam.net; Correspondent GEORGE RODRÍGUEZ-OTEIZA.

United Press International (UPI) (USA): Guatemala City; tel. and fax 2251-4258; Correspondent AMAFREDO CASTELLANOS.

Publishers

Ediciones Gama: 5a Avda 14-46, Zone 1, Guatemala City; tel. 2234-2331; Man. Dir SARA MONZÓN DE ECHEVERRÍA.

Ediciones Legales Comercio e Industria: 12a Avda 14-78, Zone 1, Guatemala City; tel. 2253-5725; fax 2220-7592; Man. Dir LUIS EMILIO BARRIOS.

Editorial del Ministerio de Educación: 15a Avda 3-22, Zona 1, Guatemala City.

Editorial Nueva Narrativa: Edif. El Patrio, Of. 108, 7a Avda 7-07, Zona 4, Guatemala City; tel. 2360-0732; fax 5704-7895; e-mail maxaraujo@intelnet.gt; Man. Dir MAX ARAÚJO A.

Editorial Oscar de León Palacios: 6a Calle 'A' 10-12, Zone 11, Guatemala City; tel. 2272-1636; educational texts; Man. Dir OSCAR DE LEÓN CASTILLO.

Editorial Palo de Hormigo: 0 Calle 16-40, Zone 15, Col. El Maestro, Guatemala City; tel. 2369-2080; fax 2369-8858; e-mail juanfercif@hotmail.com; f. 1990; Man. Dir JUAN FERNANDO CIFUENTES.

Editorial Universitaria: Edif. de la Editorial Universitaria, Universidad de San Carlos de Guatemala, Ciudad Universitaria, Zona 12, Guatemala City; tel. and fax 2476-9628; literature, social sciences, health, pure and technical sciences, humanities, secondary and university educational textbooks; Editor RAÚL FIGUEROA SARTI.

F & G Editores: 31 Avda 'C' 5-54, Zona 7, Guatemala City; tel. 2433-2361; fax 2433-2361; e-mail fgeditor@guate.net; internet www.fygeditores.com; f. 1990 as Figueroa y Gallardo, changed name in 1993; law, literature and social sciences; Editor RAÚL FIGUEROA SARTI.

Piedra Santa: 5a Calle 7-55, Zona 1, Guatemala City; tel. 2220-1524; fax 2232-9053; f. 1947; children's literature, text books; Man. Dir IRENE PIEDRA SANTA.

Broadcasting and Communications

TELECOMMUNICATIONS

Regulatory Authority

Superintendencia de Telecomunicaciones de Guatemala: Edif. Murano Center, 16°, 14a Calle 3-51, Zona 10, 01010 Guatemala City; tel. 2366-5880; fax 2366-5890; e-mail supertel@sit.gob.gt; internet www.sit.gob.gt; f. 1996; Supt OSCAR STUARDO CHINCHILLA.

Major Service Providers

BellSouth Guatemala: Edif. Torre Empresarial 10°, 7a Avda 3-33, Zona 9, Guatemala City; tel. 2385-6000; fax 2385-6162; e-mail info@bellsouth.com.gt; internet www.bellsouth.com.gt; f. 2000; bought by Telefónica Móviles, SA, in 2004, still operates under former name; provides mobile telecommunications services in Guatemala; 329,000 customers.

Empresa Guatemalteca de Telecomunicaciones (Guatel): Guatemala City; internet www.guatel.com.gt; 95% share transferred to private ownership in 1998; Dir ALFREDO GUZMÁN.

Telefónica MoviStar Guatemala, SA: Blvd Los Próceres, 20-09 Torre Telefónica, 9°, Zona 10, Guatemala City; tel. 2379-7979; e-mail servicioalcliente@telefonica.com.gt; internet www.telefonica.com.gt/MoviStar; owned by Telefónica Móviles, SA; 298,000 customers.

Other service providers include: FT & T (Telered), Cablenet, Universal de Telecomunicaciones, Comunicaciones Celulares, Telefónica Centroamérica Guatemala, Servicios de Comunicaciones Personales Inalámbricas, A-tel Communications, Telecomunicaciones de Guatemala, Cybernet de Centroamérica, Teléfonos del Norte, Americatel Guatemala, Desarrollo Integral, BNA, TTI, Optel, Concert Global Networks.

BROADCASTING

Dirección General de Radiodifusión y Televisión Nacional: Edif. Tipografía Nacional, 3°, 18 de Septiembre 6-72, Zona 1, Guatemala City; tel. 2253-2539; f. 1931; government supervisory body; Dir-Gen. ENRIQUE ALBERTO HERNÁNDEZ ESCOBAR.

Radio

There are currently five government and six educational stations, including:

La Voz de Guatemala: 18a Calle 6-72, Zona 1, Guatemala City; tel. 2253-2539; government station; Dir ARTURO SOTO ECHEVERRÍA.

Radio Cultural TGN: 4a Avda y 30 Calle, Zona 3, Apdo 601, Guatemala City; tel. 2471-4378; fax 2440-0260; e-mail tgna@guate.net; internet www.pacogarcia.com/radiocultural.htm; f. 1950; religious and cultural station; programmes in Spanish and English, Cakchiquel and Kekchí; Dir ESTEBAN SYWULKA; Man. ANTHONY WAYNE BERGER.

There are some 80 commercial stations, of which the most important are:

Emisoras Unidas de Guatemala: 4a Calle 6-84, Zona 13, Guatemala City; tel. 2440-5133; fax 2440-5159; e-mail rboileau@tikal.net.gt; internet www.emisorasunidas.com; f. 1964; 5 stations: Yo Sí Sideral, Supercadena, Atmósfera, Fabustereo and La Grande; Pres. JORGE EDGARDO ARCHILA MARROQUÍN; Vice-Pres. ROLANDO ARCHILA MARROQUÍN.

Radio Continental: Guatemala City; Dir ROBERTO VIZCAÍNO R.

Radio Nuevo Mundo: 6a Avda 10-45, Zona 1, Apdo 281, Guatemala City; fax 2232-2036; f. 1947; Man. ALFREDO GONZÁLEZ GAMARRA.

Radio Panamericana: 1a Avda 35-48, Zona 7, Guatemala City; Dir JAIME J. PANIAGUA.

La Voz de las Américas: Guatemala City; Dir AUGUSTO LÓPEZ S.

Television

Canal 5—Televisión Cultural y Educativa, SA: 4a Calle 18-38, Zona 1, Guatemala City; tel. 2253-1913; fax 2232-7003; f. 1980; cultural and educational programmes; Dir ALFREDO HERRERA CABRERA.

Radio-Televisión Guatemala, SA: 30a Avda 3-40, Zona 11, Apdo 1367, Guatemala City; tel. 2434-6320; fax 2294-7492; e-mail canal3@canal3.co.gt; internet www.canal3.com.gt; f. 1956; commercial station; operates channels 3 and 10; Pres. Lic. MAX KESTLER FARNÉS; Vice-Pres. J. F. VILLANUEVA.

Teleonce: 20a Calle 5-02, Zona 10, Guatemala City; tel. 2368-2532; fax 2368-2221; e-mail jcof@infovia.com.gt; internet canal11y13.homestead.com/20CALLE.html; f. 1968; commercial; channel 11; Gen. Dir JUAN CARLOS ORTIZ.

Telesiete, SA: 30a Avda 3-40, Zona 11, Apdo 1242, Guatemala City; tel. 594-5320; fax 2369-1393; internet www.canal7.com.gt; f. 1988; commercial station channel 7; Dir ABDÓN RODRÍGUEZ ZEA.

Trecevisión, SA: 20a Calle 5-02, Zona 10, Guatemala City; tel. 2368-2532; e-mail jcof@infovia.com.gt; internet canal11y13.homestead.com/20CALLE.html; commercial; channel 13; Dir Ing. PEDRO MELGAR R.; Gen. Man. GILDA VALLADARES ORTIZ.

Finance

(cap. = capital; p.u. = paid up; res = reserves; dep. = deposits; m. = million; brs = branches; amounts in quetzales)

BANKING

Superintendencia de Bancos: 9a Avda 22-00, Zona 1, Apdo 2306, Guatemala City; tel. 2232-0001; fax 2232-0002; e-mail info@sib.gob.gt; internet www.sib.gob.gt; f. 1946; Supt DOUGLAS O. BORJA VIELMAN.

Central Bank

Banco de Guatemala: 7a Avda 22-01, Zona 1, Apdo 365, Guatemala City; tel. 2230-6222; fax 2253-4035; e-mail webmaster@banguat.gob.gt; internet www.banguat.gob.gt; f. 1946; state-owned; cap. 41,049.4, res 94.8m., dep. 23,941.5m. (Dec. 2001); Pres. LIZARDO ARTURO SOSA LÓPEZ; Man. EDWIN HAROLDO MATUL RUANO; emps 751.

State Commercial Bank

Crédito Hipotecario Nacional de Guatemala (CHN): 7a Avda 22-77, Zona 1, Apdo 242, Guatemala City; tel. 2384-5222; fax 2238-0744; e-mail mercadeo@chn.com.gt; internet www.chn.com.gt; f. 1930; govt-owned; Pres. FREDDY ARNOLDO MUÑOZ MORÁN; Gen. Man. HUGO LEONEL CRUZ MONTERROSO; 4 brs, 72 agencies.

Private Commercial Banks

Banco Agromercantil de Guatemala, SA: 7a Avda 7-30, Zona 9, 01009 Guatemala City; tel. 2338-6565; fax 2232-5406; e-mail agromercantil@bam.com.gt; internet www.agromercantil.com.gt; f. 2000 as Banco Central de Guatemala; changed name to Banco Agrícola Mercantil in 1948; name changed as above in 2000, following merger with Banco del Agro; Man. ALFONSO E. VILLA DEVOTO; 78 agencies.

Banco de América Central, SA: Local 6-12, 1°, 7a Avda 6-26, Zona 9, Guatemala City; tel. 2360-9440; fax 2331-8720.

Banco Americano, SA: 11 Calle 7-44, Zona 9, 01009 Guatemala City; tel. 2386-1700; fax 2386-1753; e-mail grufin@infovia.com.gt; internet www.bancoamericano.com.gt.

Banco de Antigua, SA: 5a Avda 12-35, Zona 9, Guatemala City; tel. 2420-5555; fax 2336-8205.

Banco del Café, SA: Avda de la Reforma 9-30, Zona 9, Apdo 831, Guatemala City; tel. 2361-3645; fax 2331-1418; e-mail bancafeonline@bancafe.com.gt; internet www.bancafe.com.gt; f. 1978; merged with Multibanco in 2000; cap. 286.6m., res 57.2m., dep. 6,143.2m. (2002); Pres. EDUARDO MANUEL GONZÁLEZ RIVERA.

Banco de Comercio: Edif. Centro Operativo, 6a Avda 8-00, Zona 9, Guatemala City; tel. 2339-0504; fax 2339-0555; internet www.bancomercio.com.gt; f. 1991; 33 brs.

Banco Corporativo, SA: 6a Avda 4-38, Zona 9, 01009 Guatemala City; tel. 2279-9999; fax 2279-9990; e-mail mercadeo@corpobanco.com.gt.

Banco Cuscatlán de Guatemala, SA: Edif. Céntrica Plaza, 15 Calle 1-04, Zona 10, 01010 Guatemala City; tel. 2250-2000; fax 2250-2001; internet www.bancocuscatlan.com; acquired Guatemalan assets of Lloyds TSB in Dec. 2003.

Banco de Desarrollo Rural, SA: Avda La Reforma 2-56, Zona 9, Guatemala City; tel. 2334-1383; fax 2360-9740; e-mail internacional4@banrural.com.gt; internet www.banrural.com.gt; f. 1971 as Banco de Desarrollo Agrícola, name changed as above 1998; Pres. JOSE ANGEL LÓPEZ CAMPOSECO; Gen. Man. ADOLFO FERNANDO PEÑA PEREZ; 235 agencies.

Banco de Exportación, SA (BANEX): Avda de la Reforma 11-49, Zona 10, Guatemala City; tel. 2331-9861; fax 2332-2879; e-mail infbanex@banex.net.gt; internet www.banex.net.gt; f. 1985; cap. 322.5m., res 66.4m., dep. 1,560.6m. (Dec. 2004); Pres. ALEJANDRO BOTRÁN; Man. ROBERTO ORTEGA HERRERA; 15 brs.

Banco Industrial, SA (BAINSA): Edif. Centro Financiero, Torre 1, 7a Avda 5-10, Zona 4, Apdo 744, Guatemala City; tel. 2334-5111; fax 2331-9437; e-mail webmaster@bi.com.gt; internet www.bi.com.gt; f. 1964 to promote industrial development; total assets 7.91m. (1999); Pres. JUAN MIGUEL TORREBIARTE LANTZENDORFFER; Gen. Man. Lic. DIEGO PULIDO ARAGÓN.

Banco Inmobilario, SA: 7a Avda 11-59, Zona 9, Apdo 1181, Guatemala City; tel. 2339-3777; fax 2332-1418; e-mail bcoinmob.com.gt; internet www.bcoinmob.com.gt; f. 1958; cap. 77.6m., res 0.4m., dep. 738.6m. (Dec. 2002); Pres. EMILIO ANTONIO PERALTA PORTILLO; 38 brs.

Banco Internacional, SA: Torre Internacional, Avda Reforma 15-85, Zona 10, Apdo 2588, Guatemala City; tel. 2366-6666; fax 2366-6743; e-mail info@bco.inter.com; internet www.bancointernacional.com.gt; f. 1976; cap. 50.0m., res 15.4m., dep. 822.6m. (Dec. 1997);

Pres. Juan Ruiz Skinner-Klée; Gen. Man. Juan Manuel Ventas Benitez; 35 brs.

Banco Privado para el Desarrollo, SA: 7a Avda 8-46, Zona 9, Guatemala City; tel. 2361-7777; fax 2361-7217; e-mail info@bancosol .com.gt.

Banco del Quetzal, SA: Edif. Plaza El Roble, 7a Avda 6-26, Zona 9, Apdo 1001-A, 01009 Guatemala City; tel. 2331-8333; fax 2334-0613; e-mail negocios@banquetzal.com.gt; internet banquetzal.com.gt; f. 1984; Pres. Lic. Mario Roberto Leal Pivaral; Gen. Man. Alfonso Villa Devoto.

Banco Reformador, SA: 7a Avda 7-24, Zona 9, 01009 Guatemala City; tel. 2362-0888; fax 2362-0847; internet www.bancoreformador .com; cap. 129.1m., res 141.5m., dep 2,128.4m. (Dec. 2001); merged with Banco de la Construcción in 2000; Pres. Miguel Aguirre; 47 brs.

Banco SCI: Edif. SCI Centre, Avda La Reforma 9-76, Zona 9, 01009 Guatemala City; tel. 2331-7515; fax 2339-0755; e-mail atencion@sci .net.gt; internet www.sci.com.gt; f. 1967.

Banco de los Trabajadores: Avda Reforma 6-20, Zona 9, 01001 Guatemala City; tel. 2339-8600; fax 2339-4750; e-mail bantrab@ terra.com.gt; f. 1966; deals with loans for establishing and improving small industries as well as normal banking business; Pres. Lic. César Amilcar Bárcenas; Gen. Man. Lic. Oscar H. Andrade Elizondo.

Banco Uno: Edif. Unicentro, 1°, Blvd Los Próceres, 18 Calle 5-56, Zona 10, 01010 Guatemala City; tel. 2366-1777; fax 2366-1553; e-mail bancouno@gua.pibnet.com; internet www.bancouno.com.gt.

G & T Continental: 7a Avda 1-86, Zona 4, Guatemala City; and Plaza Continental, 6a Avda 9-08, Zona 9, Guatemala City; tel. 2331-2337; fax 2332-2682; e-mail consultas@gytcontinental.com.gt; internet www.gytcontinental.com.gt; f. 2000 following merger of Banco Continental and Banco Granai y Townson; total assets 11.4m. (2000); 130 brs.

Vivibanco, SA: 6a Avda 12-98, Zona 9, 01009 Guatemala City; tel. 2277-7878; fax 2277-7805; e-mail mestrada@vivibanco.com; internet www.vivibanco.com.

Finance Corporations

Corporación Financiera Nacional (CORFINA): 11a Avda 3-14, Zona 1, Guatemala City; tel. 2253-4550; fax 2232-5805; e-mail corfina@guate.net; internet www.guate.net/corfina; f. 1973; provides assistance for the development of industry, mining and tourism.

Financiera Guatemalteca, SA (FIGSA): 1a Avda 11-50, Zona 10, Apdo 2460, Guatemala City; tel. 2338-8000; fax 2331-0873; e-mail figsa@figsa.com; internet www.figsa.com; f. 1962; investment agency; Pres. Carlos González Barrios; Gen. Man. Ing. Roberto Fernández Botrán.

Financiera Industrial, SA (FISA): Centro Financiero, Torre 1, 7a Avda 5-10, Zona 4, Apdo 744, Guatemala City; tel. 2334-5111; fax 2331-9437; internet www.bi.com.gt; f. 1981; subsidiary of Banco Industrial (q.v.); cap. 3m., res 6.2m. (Aug. 1991); Pres. Carlos Arías Masselli; Gen. Man. Lic. Elder F. Calderón Reyes.

Financiera de Inversión, SA: 11a Calle 7-44, Zona 9, Guatemala City; tel. 2332-4020; fax 2332-4320; f. 1981; investment agency; cap. 15.0m. (June 1997); Pres. Lic. Mario Augusto Porras González; Gen. Man. Lic. José Rolando Porras González.

Banking Association

Asociación Bancaria de Guatemala: Edif. Margarita 2, Of. 502, Diagonal 6, Zona 10, Guatemala City; tel. 2336-6060; fax 2336-6094; internet www.abg.org.gt; f. 1961; represents all state and private banks; Pres. Lic. Luis Lara Grojec.

STOCK EXCHANGE

Bolsa de Valores Nacional, SA: 7 Avda 5-10, Zona 4, Centro Financiero, Torre II, 2°, Guatemala City; tel. 2338-4400; fax 2332-1721; e-mail bvn@bvnsa.com.gt; internet www.bvnsa.com; f. 1987; the exchange is commonly owned (one share per associate) and trades stocks from private companies, government bonds, letters of credit and other securities; Pres. Juan Carlos Castillo; Gen. Man. Rolando San Román.

INSURANCE

National Companies

Aseguradora La Ceiba, SA: 20 Calle 15-20, Zona 13, Guatemala City; tel. 2379-1800; fax 2334-8167; e-mail aceiba@aceiba.com.gt; internet www.aceiba.com.gt; f. 1978; Man. Alejandro Beltranena.

Aseguradora General, SA: 10a Calle 3-71, Zona 10, Guatemala City; tel. 2332-5933; fax 2334-2093; e-mail generaliguate@generali .com.gt; f. 1968; Pres. Juan O. Niemann; Man. Enrique Neutze A.

Cía de Seguros El Roble, SA: Torre 2, 7a Avda 5-10, Zona 4, Guatemala City; tel. 2332-1702; fax 2332-1629; e-mail rerales@ elroble.com; f. 1973; Gen. Man. Hermann Giron.

Comercial Aseguradora Suizo-Americana, SA: 7a Avda 7-07, Zona 9, Apdo 132, Guatemala City; tel. 2334-1661; fax 2331-5495; e-mail seguros@grupocasa.com.gt; internet www.grupocasa.com.gt; f. 1946; Pres. William Bickford B.; Gen. Man. David H. Lemus Pivaral.

Departamento de Seguros y Previsión del Crédito Hipotecario Nacional: 7a Avda 22-77, Zona 1, Centro Cívico, Guatemala City; tel. 2250-0271; fax 2253-8584; e-mail vjsc@chn.com.gt; internet www.chn.com.gt; f. 1942; Pres. Freddy A. Muñoz Moran; Man. Hugo Cruz Monterroso.

Empresa Guatemalteca Cigna de Seguros, SA: 5a Avda 5-55, Zona 14, Guatemala City; tel. 2384-5454; fax 2384-5400; e-mail cigna@starnet.com.gt; f. 1951; Gen. Man. Lic. Ricardo Estrada Dardón.

La Seguridad de Centroamérica, SA: 7a Avda 12-23, Edif. Etísa, Plazuela España, Zona 9, Guatemala City; tel. 2285-5900; fax 2361-3026; e-mail servicios.cmg@aig.com; internet www.aig.com; f. 1967; Gen. Man. Juan Manuel Friederich; Legal Rep. Marta de Toriello.

Seguros Alianza, SA: 7a Avda 12-23, Edif. Etísa, 6°, Plazuela España, Zona 9, Guatemala City; tel. 2331-5475; fax 2331-0023; e-mail segualia@terra.com.gt; f. 1968; Pres. Luis Fernando Samayoa.

Seguros Generales G & T, SA: 7a Avda 1-84, Zona 4, Guatemala City; tel. 2334-1361; fax 2332-8970; e-mail seguros@gyt.co.gt; f. 1947; Pres. Ernesto Townson R.; Exec. Man. Mario Granai Fernández; Gen. Man. Enrique Rodríguez.

Seguros de Occidente, SA: 7a Calle 'A' 7-14, Zona 9, Guatemala City; tel. 2331-1222; fax 2334-2787; e-mail occidente@occidente.com .gt; internet www.occidente.com.gt; f. 1979; Pres. Lic. Pedro Aguirre; Gen. Man. Carlos Lainfiesta.

Seguros Panamericana, SA: Avda de la Reforma 9-00, Edif. Plaza Panamericana, Zona 9, Guatemala City; tel. 2332-5922; fax 2331-5026; e-mail sortega@exchange.palic.com; f. 1968; Pres. Frank Purvis; Gen. Man. Lic. Salvador Ortega.

Seguros Universales, SA: 4a Calle 7-73, Zona 9, Apdo 1479, Guatemala City; tel. 2334-0733; fax 2332-3372; e-mail seguros@ universales.net; f. 1962; Man. Pedro Nolasco Sicilia.

Insurance Association

Asociación Guatemalteca de Instituciones de Seguros (AGIS): Edif. Torre Profesional I, Of. 703, 4°, 6a Avda 0-60, Zona 4, Guatemala City; tel. 2335-2140; fax 2335-2357; e-mail agis@intelnet .net.gt; internet www.agis.centroamerica.com; f. 1953; 12 mems; Pres. Alejandro Beltranena; Vice-Pres. Lic. Hermann Girón.

Trade and Industry

DEVELOPMENT ORGANIZATIONS

Comisión Nacional Petrolera: Diagonal 17, 29-78, Zona 11, Guatemala City; tel. 2276-0680; fax 2276-3175; f. 1983; awards petroleum exploration licences.

Corporación Financiera Nacional (CORFINA): see under Finance (Finance Corporations).

Fondo de Inversión Social (FIS): 2a Avda 10-13, Edif. Los Arcos, Zona 10, Guatemala City; tel. 2367-2891; fax 2367-2890; e-mail comunicacion@fis.gob.gt; internet www.fis.gob.gt; f. 1993; supports community efforts to improve social and economic conditions in the country; mandate due to expire in 2006; Pres. Dr Luis A. Flores Asturias; Gen. Man. Ing. Luis A. Bolaños Zabarburú.

Instituto de Fomento de Hipotecas Aseguradas (FHA): Edif. Aristos Reforma, 2°, Avda Reforma 7-62, Zona 9, Guatemala City; tel. 2362-9434; fax 2362-9492; e-mail promocion@fha.com.gt; internet www.fha.com.gt; f. 1961; insured mortgage institution for the promotion of house construction; Pres. Lic. Homero Augusto González Barillas; Man. Lic. José Salvador Samayoa Aguilar.

Instituto Nacional de Administración Pública (INAP): 5a Avda 12-65, Zona 10, Apto 2753, Guatemala City; tel. 2366-3021; fax 2366-2655; e-mail inap@inap-gt.org; internet www.inap-gt.org; f. 1964; provides technical experts to assist the Government in administrative reform programmes; provides in-service training for local and central government staff; has research programmes in administration, sociology, politics and economics; provides postgraduate education in public administration; Man. Héctor Toussaint Cabrera Gaillard.

Instituto Nacional de Transformación Agraria (INTA): 14a Calle 7-14, Zona 1, Guatemala City; tel. 2228-0975; f. 1962 to carry out agrarian reform; current programme includes development of the 'Faja Transversal del Norte'; Pres. Ing. NERY ORLANDO SAMAYOA; Vice-Pres Ing. SERGIO FRANCISCO MORALES-JUÁREZ, ROBERTO EDMUNDO QUIÑÓNEZ LÓPEZ.

Secretaría de Planificación y Programación (SEGEPLAN): 9a Calle 10-44, Zona 1, Guatemala City; tel. 2251-4549; fax 2253-3127; e-mail segeplan@segeplan.gob.gt; internet www.segeplan.gob.gt; f. 1954; prepares and supervises the implementation of the national economic development plan.

CHAMBERS OF COMMERCE AND INDUSTRY

Comité Coordinador de Asociaciones Agrícolas, Comerciales, Industriales y Financieras (CACIF): Edif. Cámara de Industria de Guatemala, 6a Ruta 9-21, Zona 4, Guatemala City; tel. 2231-0651; e-mail info@cacif.org.gt; internet www.cacif.org.gt; co-ordinates work on problems and organization of free enterprise; mems: 6 chambers; Pres. JORGE BRIZ; Sec.-Gen. RAFAEL POLA.

Cámara de Comercio de Guatemala: 10a Calle 3-80, Zona 1, Guatemala City; tel. 2253-5353; fax 2220-9393; e-mail info@camaradecomercio.org.gt; internet www.negociosenguatemala.com; f. 1894; Pres. EDGARDO WAGNER DURÁN.

Cámara de Industria de Guatemala: 6a Ruta 9-21, 12°, Zona 4, Apdo 214, Guatemala City; tel. 2334-0850; fax 2334-1090; e-mail cig@industriaguate.com; internet www.industriaguate.com; f. 1959; Exec. Dir OSCAR VILLAGRÁN.

Cámara Oficial Española de Comercio de Guatemala: Edif. Géminis, 10°, Torre Sur, Of. 1513, 12 Calle 1-25, Zona 10, Apdo 2480, Guatemala City; tel. 2335-2735; fax 2335-3380; e-mail camacoes@terra.com.gt; internet www.camacoes-guate.com; Pres. ANDRES SICILIA; Gen. Man. BEATRIZ SÁNCHEZ.

INDUSTRIAL AND TRADE ASSOCIATIONS

Asociación de Azucareros de Guatemala (ASAZGUA): Edif. Europlaza, 17°, 5a Avda 5-55, Zona 14, Guatemala City; tel. 2386-2000; fax 2386-2020; e-mail asazgua@azucar.com.gt; internet www.asazgua.com.gt; f. 1957; sugar producers' asscn; 15 mems; Pres. FRATERNO VILA; Gen. Man. ARMANDO BOESCHE.

Asociación General de Agricultores: 9a Calle 3-43, Zona 1, Guatemala City; f. 1920; general farmers' assc; 350 mems; Pres. DAVID ORDÓÑEZ; Man. PEDRO ARRIVILLAGA RADA.

Asociación de Gremiales de Exportadores de Productos No Tradicionales (AGEXPRONT): 15 Avda 14-72, Zona 13, Guatemala City; tel. 2362-2002; fax 2362-1950; internet www.export.com.gt; f. 1982; devt of export of non-traditional products.

Asociación Nacional de Avicultores (ANAVI): Edif. Galerías Reforma, Torre 2, 9°, Of. 904, Avda de la Reforma 8-60, Zona 9, Guatemala City; tel. 2231-1381; fax 2234-7576; f. 1964; national assc of poultry farmers; 60 mems; Pres. Lic. FERNANDO ROJAS; Dir Dr MARIO A. MOTTA GONZÁLEZ.

Asociación Nacional de Fabricantes de Alcoholes y Licores (ANFAL): Guatemala City; tel. 2292-0430; f. 1947; distillers' assc; Pres. FELIPE BOTRÁN MERINO.

Asociación Nacional del Café—Anacafé: Edif. Etisa, Plazuela España, Zona 9, Guatemala City; tel. 2236-7180; fax 2234-7023; e-mail sellodepureza@anacafe.org; internet www.anacafe.org; f. 1960; national coffee assc; Pres. WILLIAM STIXRUD.

Cámara del Agro: 15a Calle 'A' 7-65, Zona 9, Guatemala City; tel. 2226-1473; e-mail camagro@intelnet.net.gt; f. 1973; Pres. ROBERTO CASTAÑEDA.

Gremial de Huleros de Guatemala: Edif. Galerias España, 7 Avda 11-63, 3°, Guatemala City; tel. 2331-8269; fax 2332-1553; e-mail gremulgt@pronet.net.gt; f. 1970; rubber producers' guild; 125 mems; Man. ALEJANDRO SOSA BROL.

UTILITIES

Electricity

Empresa Eléctrica de Guatemala, SA: 6a Avda 8-14, Zona 1, Guatemala City; tel. 230-4040; fax 253-1746; e-mail consultas@eegsa.net; internet www.eegsa.com; f. 1972; state electricity producer; 80% share transferred to private ownership in 1998; Pres. RICARDO CASTILLO SINIBALDI.

Instituto Nacional de Electrificación (INDE): Edif. La Torre, 7a Avda 2-29, Zona 9, Guatemala City; tel. (2) 34-5711; fax (2) 34-5811; e-mail gerencia.general@inde.gob.gt; internet www.inde.gob.gt; f. 1959; former state agency for the generation and distribution of hydroelectric power; principal electricity producer; privatized in 1998; CEO CARLOS COLOM; Gen. Man JORGE JUÁREZ.

CO-OPERATIVES

Instituto Nacional de Cooperativas (INACOP): 13 Calle 5-16, Zona 1, Guatemala City; tel. 2234-1097; fax 2234-7536; technical and financial assistance in planning and devt of co-operatives; Pres. LUIS ANTONIO SALAZAR.

TRADE UNIONS

Frente Nacional Sindical (FNS) (National Trade Union Front): Guatemala City; f. 1968 to achieve united action in labour matters; affiliated are two confederations and 11 federations, which represent 97% of the country's trade unions and whose General Secretaries form the governing council of the FNS. The affiliated organizations include:

Comité Nacional de Unidad Sindical Guatemalteca (CONUS): Guatemala City; Leader MIGUEL ANGEL SOLÍS; Sec.-Gen. GERÓNIMO LÓPEZ DÍAZ.

Confederación General de Sindicatos (General Trade Union Confederation): 18a Calle 5-50, Zona 1, Apdo 959, Guatemala City.

Confederación Nacional de Trabajadores (National Workers' Confederation): Guatemala City; Sec.-Gen. MIGUEL ANGEL ALBIZÚREZ.

Federación Autónoma Sindical Guatemalteca (Guatemalan Autonomous Trade Union Federation): Guatemala City; Gen. Sec. MIGUEL ANGEL SOLÍS.

Federación de Obreros Textiles (Textile Workers' Federation): Edif. Briz, Of. 503, 6a Avda 14-33, Zona 1, Guatemala City; f. 1957; Sec.-Gen. FACUNDO PINEDA.

Federación de Trabajadores de Guatemala (FTG) (Guatemalan Workers' Federation): 5a Calle 4-33, Zona 1, Guatemala City; tel. 2222-6515; Promoter ADRIAN RAMÍREZ.

A number of unions exist without a national centre, including the Union of Chicle and Wood Workers, the Union of Coca-Cola Workers and the Union of Workers of the Enterprise of the United Fruit Company.

Central General de Trabajadores de Guatemala (CGTG): 3a Avda 12-22, Zona 1, Guatemala City; tel. 2232-1010; fax 2251-3212; e-mail cgtg@guate.net.gt; f. 1987; Sec.-Gen. JOSÉ E. PINZÓN SALAZAR.

Central Nacional de Trabajadores (CNT): Guatemala City; f. 1972; cover all sections of commerce, industry and agriculture including the public sector; clandestine since June 1980; Sec.-Gen. JULIO CELSO DE LEÓN; 23,735 mems.

Federación Sindical de Trabajadores de la Alimentación Agro-Industrias y Similares de Guatemala (FESTRAS): 6a Avda 15-41, Zona 1, 4°, Of. 6, Guatemala City; tel. and fax 2338-3075; affiliated to International Union of Food, Agricultural, Hotel, Restaurants, Catering, Tobacco and Allied Workers' Associations; Sec.-Gen. JOSÉ DAVID MORALES C.

Unidad de Acción Sindical y Popular (UASP): 10 Avda 'A' 5-40, Zona 1, Guatemala City; f. 1988; broad coalition of leading labour and peasant organizations; includes:

Comité de la Unidad Campesina (CUC) (Committee of Peasants' Unity): 31 Avda 'A' 14-46, Zona 7, Ciudad de Plata, Apdo 1002, Guatemala City; tel. and fax 594-9754; e-mail cuc@guate.net; internet cuc.mundoweb.org.

Confederación de Unidad Sindical de Guatemala (CUSG): 12 Calle 'A', Zona 1, Guatemala City; tel. and fax 2232-8154; e-mail cusg@itelgua.com; f. 1983; member of ICFTU; Sec.-Gen. FRANCISCO ALFARO MIJANGOS.

Federación Nacional de Sindicatos de Trabajadores del Estado de Guatemala (FENASTEG): 10 Avda 5-40, Zona 1, Guatemala City; tel. and fax 2232-2772; Sec. ARMANDO SÁNCHEZ.

Sindicato de Trabajadores del Instituto Guatemalteco de Seguridad Social (STIGSS): 11 Calle 11-15, Zona 1, Guatemala City; f. 1953.

Unidad Sindical de Trabajadores de Guatemala (UNSITRAGUA): 9 Avda 1-43, Zona 1, Guatemala City; tel. and fax 2238-2272; e-mail unsitragua@pronet.net.gt; f. 1985; member unions are mostly from the private industrial sector and include STECSA, SITRALU and SCTM; Co-ordinator DANIEL VÁSQUEZ.

Transport

RAILWAYS

In 1998 there were 1,390 km of railway track in Guatemala, of which some 102 km were plantation lines.

Ferrocarriles de Guatemala (FEGUA): 18 Calle 9-03, Zona 1, Guatemala City; tel. 2232-7720; fax 2238-3039; e-mail fegua@

GUATEMALA

quetzalnet.com; internet www.quetzalnet.com/quetzalnet/fegua; f. 1968; 50-year concession to rehabilitate and operate railway awarded in 1997 to the US Railroad Devt Corpn; 782 km from Puerto Barrios and Santo Tomás de Castilla on the Atlantic coast to Tecún Umán on the Mexican border, via Zacapa, Guatemala City and Santa María. Branch lines: Santa María–San José; Las Cruces–Champerico. From Zacapa another line branches southward to Anguiatú, on the border with El Salvador; owns the ports of Barrios (Atlantic) and San José (Pacific); first 65-km section, Guatemala City–El Chile, and a further 300-km section, extending to Barrios, reopened in 1999; Interventor ANDRÉS PORRAS.

ROADS

In 1999 there were an estimated 14,021 km of roads, of which 3,081 km were paved. The Guatemalan section of the Pan-American highway is 518.7 km long and totally asphalted. In 2002 plans were discussed for the construction of a highway between Huehuetenango and Izabal under the 'Plan Puebla–Panamá' at an estimated cost of US $292m. The highway would take five years to complete. In May 2003 the World Bank approved a loan of US $46.7m. to repair existing roads and construct new networks in rural areas.

SHIPPING

Guatemala's major ports are Puerto Barrios and Santo Tomás de Castilla, on the Gulf of Mexico, San José and Champerico on the Pacific Ocean, and Puerto Quetzal, which was redeveloped in the late 1990s. In June 2002 the Government announced plans for the expansion of shipping facilities at Puerto Quetzal and Santo Tomás de Castilla in the near future.

Armadora Marítima Guatemalteca, SA: 14a Calle 8-14, Edif. Armagua, 5°, Zona 1, Apdo 1008, Guatemala City; tel. 2230-4686; fax 2253-7464; cargo services; Pres. and Gen. Man. L. R. CORONADO CONDE.

Empresa Portuaria 'Quetzal': Edif. Torre Azul, 1°, 4a Calle 7-53, Zona 9, Guatemala City; tel. 2334-7101; fax 2334-8172; e-mail pquetzal@terra.com.gt; internet www.puerto-quetzal.com; port and shipping co; Man. LEONEL MONTEJO.

Empresa Portuaria Nacional Santo Tomás de Castilla: Calle Real de la Villa, 17 Calle 16-43, Zona 10, Guatemala City; tel. 2366-9413; fax 2366-9445; internet www.empornac.gob.gt; Man. ENRIQUE SALAZAR.

Flota Mercante Gran Centroamericana, SA: Guatemala City; tel. 2231-6666; f. 1959; services from Europe (in association with WITASS), Gulf of Mexico, US Atlantic and East Coast Central American ports; Pres. R. S. HERRERÍAS; Gen. Man. J. E. A. MORALES.

Líneas Marítimas de Guatemala, SA: Edif. Plaza Marítima, 8°, 6a Avda 20-25, Zona 10, Guatemala City; tel. 2237-0166; cargo services; Pres. J. R. MATHEAU ESCOBAR; Gen. Man. F. HERRERÍAS.

Several foreign lines link Guatemala with Europe, the Far East and North America.

CIVIL AVIATION

There are two international airports, 'La Aurora' in Guatemala City and Santa Elena Petén. In June 2002 the Government announced plans for the potential construction of a new international airport outside Guatemala City and for the renovation and modernization of the airport at Santa Elena Petén.

Aerolíneas de Guatemala (AVIATECA): Avda Hincapié 12-22, Aeropuerto 'La Aurora', Zona 12, Guatemala City; tel. 2331-0375; fax 2334-7846; internet www.grupotaca.com; f. 1945; internal services and external services to the USA, Mexico, and within Central America; transferred to private ownership in 1989; CEO ROBERTO KRIETE; Pres. ALFREDO SCHILDKNECHT.

Aeroquetzal: Avda Hincapié, Hangar EH-05, Zona 13, Guatemala City; tel. 2334-7689; fax 2232-1491; scheduled domestic passenger and cargo services, and external services to Mexico.

Aviones Comerciales de Guatemala (Avcom): Avda Hincapié 18, Aeropuerto La Aurora, Zona 13, Guatemala City; tel. 2331-5821; fax 2332-4946; domestic charter passenger services.

Tikal Jets: Avda Hincapié 18, Aeropuerto La Aurora, Zona 13, Guatemala City; tel. 2334-5631.

Tourism

Following the end of the civil war in 1996 the number of tourist arrivals increased steadily and were recorded at some 884,190 in 2002. In that year receipts were an estimated $612m.

Instituto Guatemalteco de Turismo (INGUAT) (Guatemala Tourist Commission): Centro Cívico, 7a Avda 1-17, Zona 4, Guatemala City; tel. 2331-1333; fax 2331-4416; e-mail informacion@inguat.gob.gt; internet www.inguat.gob.gt; f. 1967; policy and planning council: 11 mems representing the public and private sectors; Pres. DANIEL MOONEY; Dir ALEJANDRO SINIBALDI APARICIO.

Asociación Guatemalteca de Agentes de Viajes (AGAV) (Guatemalan Association of Travel Agents): Edif. El Reformador, Avda La Reforma 1-50, Zona 9, Apdo 2735, Guatemala City; tel. 2332-0782; fax 2334-5217; e-mail agav@intelnet.net.gt; Pres. LAURA MAYORGA DE ESTRADA.

GUINEA

Introductory Survey

Location, Climate, Language, Religion, Flag, Capital

The Republic of Guinea lies on the west coast of Africa, with Sierra Leone and Liberia to the south, Senegal and Guinea-Bissau to the north, and Mali and Côte d'Ivoire inland to the east. The climate on the coastal strip is hot and moist, with temperatures ranging from about 32°C (90°F) in the dry season to about 23°C (73°F) in the wet season (May–October). The interior is higher and cooler. The official language is French, but Soussou, Manika and six other national languages are widely spoken. Most of the inhabitants are Muslims, but some follow traditional animist beliefs. Around 2% are Roman Catholics. The national flag (proportions 2 by 3) consists of three equal vertical stripes, of red, yellow and green. The capital is Conakry.

Recent History

The Republic of Guinea (formerly French Guinea, part of French West Africa) became independent on 2 October 1958, after 95% of voters rejected the Constitution of the Fifth Republic under which the French colonies became self-governing within the French Community. The new state was the object of punitive reprisals by the outgoing French authorities: all aid was withdrawn, and the administrative infrastructure destroyed. The Parti démocratique de Guinée—Rassemblement démocratique africain (PDG—RDA) became the basis for the construction of new institutions. Its leader, Ahmed Sekou Touré, became President, and the PDG—RDA the sole political party.

Sekou Touré, formerly a prominent trade unionist, pursued vigorous policies of socialist revolution. Opposition was ruthlessly crushed, and Sekou Touré perpetuated rumours of a 'permanent conspiracy' by foreign powers to overthrow his regime. Notably, an abortive invasion by Portuguese troops and Guinean exiles in 1970 prompted the execution of many of those convicted of involvement. By 1983 almost 2m. Guineans were estimated to have fled the country.

All private trade was forbidden in 1975, and an 'economic police' established. In August 1977 demonstrations in Conakry, in protest against the abolition of the traditional market and the abuse of power by the 'economic police', provoked rioting in other towns, as a result of which three state governors were killed. Sekou Touré subsequently disbanded the 'economic police', and allowed limited private trading to recommence in July 1979. In November 1978 it was announced that the functions of the PDG—RDA and the State were to be merged, and the country was renamed the People's Revolutionary Republic of Guinea. There was, none the less, a general move away from rigid Marxism and a decline in relations with the USSR, as Guinea sought a political and economic *rapprochement* with its African neighbours, with France and with other Western powers.

In January 1984 a plot to overthrow the Government was disclosed; thousands of Guineans were reportedly detained, accused of complicity in the affair. In March Sekou Touré died while undergoing surgery in the USA. On 3 April, before a successor had been chosen by the ruling party, the armed forces seized power in a bloodless coup. A Comité militaire de redressement national (CMRN) was appointed, headed by Col (later Gen.) Lansana Conté, and Col Diarra Traoré became Prime Minister. The PDG—RDA and the legislature were dissolved, and the Constitution was suspended. The CMRN released some 250 political prisoners, and a relaxation of press restrictions was announced. In May the 'Second Republic of Guinea' was proclaimed. By mid-1984 an estimated 200,000 Guinean exiles had returned to the country.

Trials of former associates of Sekou Touré began in November 1984. In December President Conté assumed the posts of Head of Government and Minister of Defence; the post of Prime Minister was abolished, and Traoré was demoted to a lesser post. In July 1985 Traoré attempted to seize power while Conté was out of the country. Troops loyal to Conté suppressed the revolt, and Traoré was arrested, along with more than 200 suspected sympathizers. In May 1987 it was announced that 58 people, including nine former government ministers, had been sentenced to death in secret trials for crimes committed under Sekou Touré or following the 1985 coup attempt. The an-nouncement did little to allay international suspicions that many detainees had been executed in the aftermath of the abortive coup, and in December 1987 Conté admitted that Traoré had died in the hours following his arrest.

In late 1989 Conté announced that, following a referendum on a proposed new constitution, a joint civilian and military Comité transitoire de redressement national (CTRN) would replace the CMRN. After a transitional period of not more than five years, civilian rule would be established, with an executive and legislature directly elected within a two-party system. The draft Constitution of what was designated the Third Republic was reportedly endorsed by 98.7% of the 97.4% of the electorate who voted in a referendum on 23 December 1990; the CTRN was inaugurated in February 1991 under Conté's chairmanship.

In November 1990, meanwhile, Conté appealed to political exiles to return to Guinea. Alpha Condé, the leader of the Rassemblement populaire guinéen (RPG—an unofficial political organization whose activities the authorities had suppressed), returned to Guinea in May 1991, after a long period of exile. Three arrests were made when security forces dispersed a meeting of Condé's supporters, and a ban was subsequently imposed on unauthorized meetings and demonstrations. Condé was subsequently granted political asylum in Senegal.

In October 1991 Conté announced that a law authorizing the registration of an unlimited number of political parties would come into effect in April 1992, and that legislative elections would be held before the end of 1992. The Constitution was promulgated on 23 December 1991, and in January 1992 Conté ceded the presidency of the CTRN, in conformity with the constitutional separation of powers. In February most military officers and all those who had returned from exile after the 1984 coup (known as *Guinéens de l'extérieur*) were removed from the Council of Ministers.

In April 1992 17 political parties, including the RPG, were legalized; Condé returned to Guinea in June. It was subsequently rumoured that the pro-Conté Parti pour l'unité et le progrès (PUP), established by prominent *Guinéens de l'extérieur*, was benefiting from state funds. In December the Government postponed indefinitely the legislative elections, which had been scheduled for later that month. Subsequent indications that the parliamentary elections would not take place until after a presidential election caused resentment among the opposition, which had hoped to present a single candidate (from the party that had performed best in the legislative elections) for the presidency.

In October 1993 the Supreme Court approved eight candidates for the presidential election, scheduled for December. Among Conté's main rivals were Condé, Mamadou Boye Bâ of the Union pour la nouvelle République (UNR) and Siradiou Diallo of the Parti pour le renouveau et le progrès (PRP). At least 10 deaths were recorded in violence before and during the election, which took place on 19 December. The official rate of participation by voters was 78.5%. Preliminary results indicated that Conté had secured an absolute majority of the votes cast, obviating the need for a second round of voting. Opposition claims that the result had been manipulated in favour of Conté intensified when the Supreme Court annulled the outcome of voting in the Kankan and Siguiri prefectures (in both of which Condé had won more than 95% of the votes). According to official results, Conté was elected with 51.7% of the votes cast; Condé took 19.6% of the votes, Bâ 13.4% and Diallo 11.9%. Conté, who had resigned from the army in order to contest the election as a civilian, was inaugurated as President on 29 January 1994. A major restructuring of the Council of Ministers was implemented in August. In February 1995 Conté readopted his military title.

Some 846 candidates, from 21 parties, contested the 114 seats in the Assemblée nationale at the delayed legislative elections, held on 11 June 1995. As preliminary results indicated that the PUP had won an overwhelming majority in the legislature, the so-called 'radical' opposition (the RPG, the PRP and the UNR) announced their intention to boycott the assembly, protesting that voting had been conducted fraudulently. According to the final results, which were verified by the Supreme Court in July (whereupon the Assemblée nationale officially superseded the CTRN), the PUP won 71 seats—having taken 30 of the 38 single-member constituencies and 41 of the 76 seats elected on the basis of national lists. Of the eight other parties to win representation, the RPG secured 19 seats, while the PRP and the UNR each won nine seats. The rate of participation was reported to be 63%. In July the RPG, the PRP and the UNR joined with nine other organizations in a Coordination de l'opposition démocratique (Codem), which indicated its willingness to enter into a dialogue with the authorities. El Hadj Boubacar Biro Diallo, of the PUP, was elected as the Speaker of the Assemblée nationale, which was officially inaugurated on 30 August.

In February 1996 Conté was reportedly seized as he attempted to flee the presidential palace during a mutiny by disaffected elements of the military, and was held by rebels for some 15 hours until he made concessions including a doubling of salaries and immunity from prosecution for those involved in the uprising. The Minister of Defence, Col Abdourahmane Diallo, was dismissed, and Conté assumed personal responsibility for defence. It was estimated that about 50 people were killed and at least 100 injured, as up to 2,000 rebels clashed with forces loyal to Conté.

In February 1996 Codem withdrew from a parliamentary commission investigating the circumstances surrounding the coup attempt, in protest at Conté's allusions to opposition links with anti-Government elements within the military. In March it was announced that eight members of the military, including four senior officers, had been charged with undermining state security in connection with the coup attempt. The armed forces Chief of Staff and the military Governor of Conakry, both of whom had been regarded as close associates of the President, were replaced in April. In July Conté announced the appointment of a non-partisan economist, Sidya Touré, as Prime Minister, the first time that position had existed under the Third Republic. (The Constitution made no explicit provision for such a post.) A comprehensive reorganization of the Government included the division of the Ministry of the Interior into two separate departments (one responsible for territorial administration and decentralization, the other for security).

In June 1997 it was announced that a State Security Court was to be established to deal with matters of exceptional jurisdiction, and that its first task would be to try the alleged leaders of the 1996 mutiny, including Cmmdr Joseph Gbago Zoumanigui, a former member of the CMRN. The establishment of the court provoked strong criticism both by the opposition parties and the Guinean lawyers' association, which expressed particular concern that there was no constitutional provision for such a court, that its members were to be personally appointed by Conté, and that the mutiny trial was to be held in camera. A ministerial reorganization was effected in October 1997. Notably, Dorank Assifat Diasseny, hitherto Minister of Territorial Administration and Decentralization, was transferred to the higher education and scientific research portfolio, but shortly afterwards was appointed Minister of National Defence (thereby becoming the first civilian to hold this post since the 1984 *coup d'état*). In March 1998 Bâ and two other UNR deputies were arrested, following the deaths of nine people as a result of violence in Conakry. Bâ was released in June, and in September his two UNR colleagues resumed their seats in the legislature, having been released from custody. Also in September the State Security Court sentenced 38 of those charged with offences related to the attempted coup of 1996 to custodial sentences of up to 15 years, some with hard labour (Zoumanigui was sentenced *in absentia*), while 51 defendants were acquitted.

Meanwhile, Codem denounced proposals for the establishment of an Haut conseil aux affaires électorales (HCE), which was to act in conjunction with the Ministry of the Interior and Decentralization in preparing and supervising the forthcoming presidential election. The 68-member HCE was to comprise representatives of the parliamentary majority, as well as opposition delegates, ministerial representatives and members of civil society. The opposition also protested that a ban on public demonstrations would disadvantage candidates other than Conté. At the polling, held on 14 December 1998, Conté was challenged by four candidates, including Bâ, representing the Union pour le progrès et le renouveau (UPR, formed in 1998 by a merger of the UNR and the PRP), and Alpha Condé (who had been outside Guinea since April 1997, owing to fears for his safety), for the RPG. The arrest of Condé two days after the poll, near the border with Côte d'Ivoire, on the grounds that he was

seeking to leave the country illegally and was plotting against the state, provoked an upsurge of violence, in which at least 12 people were reported to have been killed. In late December Condé was formally charged with having recruited mercenaries with the aim of overthrowing the Conté regime. Meanwhile, opposition representatives denounced the conduct of the election as fraudulent and withdrew from the HCE. The official results confirmed a decisive victory for Conté, with 56.1% of the valid votes cast; Bâ won 24.6% and Condé 16.6%. The rate of participation by registered voters was 71.4%. Conté was reinaugurated as President on 30 January 1999.

In March 1999 Lamine Sidimé, hitherto Chief Justice of the Supreme Court, was appointed Prime Minister of a new Government. An apparent purge of the military high command, in mid-March, included the removal from office of former Chief of Staff Col Oumar Sanko; 18 officers were dismissed, accused of high treason, and 13 retired early, on the grounds of what were termed 'serious faults' arising from the 1996 mutiny. Local government elections were postponed in June.

Opposition groups and human rights organizations campaigned throughout 1999 and 2000 for the release of Alpha Condé and other activists detained at the time of the 1998 presidential election. Condé's trial by the State Security Court finally commenced in April 2000 and in September Condé was found guilty of sedition and sentenced to five years' imprisonment, while seven other defendants were given custodial sentences of between 18 months and three years; 40 other defendants were acquitted. Two days prior to the conclusion of the trial, President Conté had accused Condé of having instigated fighting on Guinea's borders with Sierra Leone and Liberia.

In January 2000 a major government reshuffle was announced. Conté effected a further ministerial reshuffle in June, in which the Ministry of Security was abolished and incorporated into the Ministry of Territorial Administration and Decentralization. Legislative elections, scheduled for 25 June, were postponed, although local elections, scheduled for the same date, were held, contested by eight parties. Prior to the announcement of the results (in which the PUP and its allies secured control of 33 of the 38 constituencies), a series of clashes between the security forces and UPR members resulted in at least five deaths.

In early September 2000 an armed rebellion in the forest region of south-east Guinea reportedly resulted in at least 40 deaths. Instability subsequently intensified in regions near the borders with Sierra Leone and Liberia. Fighting between armed groups and Guinean soldiers was reported to have led to some 360 deaths between early September and mid-October. The Government attributed the upsurge in violence to forces supported by the Governments of Liberia and Burkina Faso, and to members of the Sierra Leonean rebel group, the Revolutionary United Front (RUF, see the chapter on Sierra Leone), in alliance with Guinean dissidents. In October 2000 a previously unknown organization, the Rassemblement des forces démocratiques de Guinée, claimed responsibility for the armed attacks, which, it stated, were an attempt to overthrow President Conté. Following an attack on the town of Forécariah, the local Governor expelled some 32,000 refugees from the region, many of whom were subject to further attacks, particularly following a speech made by Conté, in which he accused refugees from Sierra Leone and Liberia of forming alliances with rebel groups seeking to destabilize Guinea.

Meanwhile, the Assemblée nationale failed to reconvene, as planned, on 25 September 2000. The Government announced that the delayed legislative elections would be held on 26 November. However, Codem declared that it would not participate in elections until national security had been re-established, and in November Conté issued a decree postponing the legislative elections indefinitely. In late November a series of cross-border attacks were reportedly conducted by former members of a faction of a dissolved Liberian dissident group, the United Liberation Movement of Liberia for Democracy (ULIMO), ULIMO—K (see the chapter on Liberia), which President Conté had previously supported. In December rebel attacks on the southern towns of Guéckédou and Kissidougou led to more than 230 deaths, and the almost complete destruction of Guéckédou. The Government estimated that some 94,000 people had been displaced as a result of fighting in the region, and aid agencies withdrew from south-east Guinea later in the month, as a result of the heightened instability.

In early January 2001 Conté assumed personal control of defence; Diasseny, hitherto Minister at the Presidency, in charge of National Defence, was, however, retained as a cabinet member, receiving the title of Minister, Special Adviser at the Presidency. As rebel attacks continued, reports that Guinean planes had launched minor air offensives on rebel-held border areas of Sierra Leone emerged in mid-January 2001. In late January and early February more than 130 deaths were reported in a series of attacks around Macenta. Allegations persisted that an unofficial alliance between former ULIMO—K rebels and Guinean government forces had broken down, with the result that ULIMO—K forces were now attacking Guinean military and civilian targets. Renewed clashes around Guéckédou delayed, and ultimately prevented, the proposed deployment by the Economic Community of West African States (ECOWAS, see p. 205) of an ECOMOG force, which had been intended to monitor stability and border security in the region from mid-February. Meanwhile, in February the death penalty, which had been suspended in 1984, was officially restored, and four of five defendants sentenced to death in 1995 were executed by firing squad (the fifth had died in detention).

Alpha Condé and two of his co-defendants were unexpectedly released from prison in mid-May 2001, following the granting of a presidential pardon. Condé, none the less, was prohibited from participating in political activities for a period of unspecified duration. In mid-June President Conté announced his intention to hold a referendum on proposed constitutional amendments that would remove the restriction on the number of terms of office the President could serve and allow candidates aged over 70 years to contest the presidency. (These changes would enable Conté to contest a third term of office.) Additionally, Conté sought to increase the presidential mandate from five years to seven, to take effect from the presidential election of 2003. It remained unclear whether the referendum would itself meet constitutional requirements, as it sought to validate a presidential decree without any reference to the legislature; international donors to Guinea, including the USA and the European Union (EU), urged Guinea to abide by democratic standards and to uphold the provisions of its Constitution.

In June 2001 N'Faly Kaba, the leader of a hitherto unknown rebel group, the Union des forces pour une Guinée nouvelle, announced that his organization was leading the continuing rebellion in the south of Guinea. Kaba stated that the group comprised close associates of former Prime Minister Diarra Traoré and those involved in the failed coup of July 1985, and that Zoumanigui was co-ordinating the rebellion. In late September 2001, however, Kaba was arrested in Côte d'Ivoire, as he attempted to enter that country illegally from Guinea, and denied any involvement in armed insurgency. (Kaba announced his reconciliation with the Guinean authorities in October 2003, although he remained outside the country.)

Meanwhile, in late June 2001, in response to a court ruling, gendarmes enforced the closure of the headquarters of the Union des forces républicaines (UFR), the party led by former Prime Minister Sidya Touré, who had recently formed a group to oppose Conté's proposed constitutional amendments, the Mouvement contre le référendum et pour l'alternance démocratique (Morad). At the end of September Condé resumed his functions as a parliamentary deputy. Morad also announced its intention to prevent the conduct of the overdue legislative elections, which were scheduled to take place on 27 December. Condé's status remained a subject of controversy: the Speaker of the Assemblée nationale, Boubacar Biro Diallo, refuted allegations, made in October by the Minister of Justice, Abou Camara, that Condé's return to parliament was illegal, on the grounds that his conviction had not been quashed, while opposition deputies contended that, as Condé had never officially been deprived of his parliamentary immunity, his arrest and detention had been unlawful.

The constitutional referendum took place on 11 November 2001, following violent clashes between security forces and those opposed to the referendum. According to official results, 98.4% of those who voted approved the amendments, and 87.2% of the registered electorate participated. Opposition members disputed the results, alleging that less than 20% of the electorate had voted. The presidential term of office was thus extended from five years to seven, with effect from the presidential election due in 2003, and the constitutional provision restricting the President to two terms of office was rescinded. Moreover, the President was to be permitted to appoint local government officials, who were hitherto elected. At the end of November the legislative elections were again postponed indefinitely; Codem had announced that it was to boycott the elections earlier in the

month. Despite the overwhelming official result in favour of the amendments, opposition to the referendum was expressed very strongly, in particular by Boubacar Biro Diallo (who remained Speaker of the reconvened Assemblée nationale, whose mandate had, officially, expired in July 2000) and by Jean-Marie Doré, the leader of the Union pour le progrès de la Guinée (UPG), both of whom deplored the lack of involvement of the legislature in deciding such a major constitutional change.

In mid-April 2002 President Conté issued a decree, scheduling the repeatedly postponed elections to the Assemblée nationale for 30 June; a further presidential decree, issued later in April, established a Conseil national electoral, to be responsible for the supervision of the electoral process. However, concern was expressed that the short period between the establishment of the Conseil and the holding of elections would be insufficient to ensure transparency in the conduct of the polls, and the EU subsequently withheld funding towards the elections. In late May four opposition parties, which had announced their intention to boycott the legislative elections, including the RPG and the UFR, announced the formation of a political alliance, the Front de l'alternance démocratique (FRAD). Notably, Boubacar Biro Diallo, who was not affiliated to any party, and Bâ, the honorary President of the UPR, pledged allegiance to the FRAD, and a split in the UPR became increasingly apparent between those, led by Siradiou Diallo, the President of the party, who sought to engage with the electoral process, and those, led by Bâ, who rejected any such engagement. In early June Conté appointed François Lonceny Fall, previously the representative of Guinea to the UN, as Minister at the Presidency, responsible for Foreign Affairs.

The elections to the Assemblée nationale were held on 30 June 2002, as scheduled. A turn-out of 71.6% was recorded, according to official figures. The PUP increased its majority in the legislature, winning all 38 single-member constituency seats (in all of which the party was unopposed) and 47 of the 76 seats allocated by proportional representation, giving it a total of 85 seats. Other pro-presidential parties secured five seats, while the UPR became the second largest party in the Assemblée, with 20 seats, and the UPG won three seats. Opposition parties, both those of the FRAD and those that contested the elections, alleged that fraudulent practice had been widespread in the conduct of the elections, and the US ambassador to Guinea expressed concern at apparent irregularities in the poll. During July several opposition parties, including the UPG and the UPR, demanded that fresh elections be held; the UPG also announced that its three deputies were to boycott parliament, although the results of the elections were confirmed by the Supreme Court at the end of that month. In late September the Secretary-General of the PUP, Aboubacar Somparé, was elected as Speaker of the Assemblée nationale.

In mid-October 2002 Bâ was elected as President of a new party, the Union des forces démocratiques de Guinée (UFDG), which largely comprised the faction of the UPR that had boycotted the elections to the Assemblée nationale. The UFDG was affiliated to the FRAD, which announced its intention of nominating a common opposition candidate at the presidential election scheduled to be held in December 2003. At the end of December 2002 the FRAD issued a statement in which it denounced both the constitutional referendum held in November 2001 and the recent elections to the Assemblée nationale as illegitimate.

Meanwhile, following a period of several weeks during which President Conté seldom appeared in public (with his premature return from a state visit to Saudi Arabia and the cancellation of a state visit to Japan particularly notable), rumours circulated regarding the President's health. In mid-December 2002 Conté made an unexpected public appearance, having reportedly returned from abroad, and announced what was termed a minor government reshuffle; a Secretary of State for Security was appointed, and other reforms were made to the security apparatus. At the end of December it was confirmed that Conté was receiving medical treatment in Morocco. None the less, it was announced in mid-January 2003 that Conté was to contest the forthcoming presidential election. Meanwhile, internal political tensions continued to be evident. Bâ publicly stated that a temporary take-over by the armed forces, prior to the preparation of free elections, would be a 'lesser evil' than allowing the PUP to produce its own successor to Conté; similar views were subsequently expressed by a number of principal opposition leaders. In April the Minister of Justice, Keeper of the Seals, Abou Camara, was dismissed, reportedly after he had attempted to arrest the Minister of the Economy and Finance, Cheick Amadou Camara, for alleged misappropriation of funds. The former head of the State Security Court, Mamadou Sylla Sima, was appointed in his place.

In mid-September 2003 a technical commission, established by an inter-ministerial committee, that was intended to facilitate inter-party dialogue in advance of the presidential election, issued a memorandum specifying preconditions for the involvement of political parties in the electoral process. Foremost among these demands were an amnesty for all political prisoners and guarantees to ensure the fair, free and permanent access of opposition parties to the state-owned media. However, in late September, several days after the formal nomination of Conté as the presidential candidate of the PUP, the FRAD announced that negotiations between the Government and opposition parties had broken down. In mid-October a rally in Conakry, organized by the FRAD in support of demands for Conté to withdraw his candidacy, attracted between 5,000 and 10,000 people.

Although Doré and Sidya Touré, the leader of the UFR, had previously announced their intention to contest the presidential election, in early November 2003 the FRAD announced that it was to boycott the polls. (Later in the month the UPR also announced that it would boycott the election.) Meanwhile, in an apparent effort to encourage opposition candidates to contest the election, the Assemblée nationale hastily approved legislation providing for an amnesty for those convicted of political crimes, including, most notably, Condé, who would thereby be permitted to contest the presidential election. However, in the event, the sole candidate approved to contest the election, apart from Conté, was Mamadou Bhoye Barry, the leader of a small political party, the Union pour le progrès national—Parti pour l'unité et le développement, which had won one seat, and less than 1% of the votes cast, in the legislative elections of 2002. It was reported that the Supreme Court had rejected on technical grounds the nominations of six other candidates. At the end of November 2003 it was reported that several army officers and soldiers, including a senior member of the presidential guard, had been arrested in Conakry and three provincial towns on suspicion of plotting a *coup d'état*. (The authorities did not admit to holding the men in custody until their trial began in October 2004.) Meanwhile, persistent reports that Conté was suffering from ill-health appeared to be confirmed by his infrequent public appearances; it was reported that the President attended only one rally during the campaign for his re-election.

Voting in the presidential election proceeded, as scheduled, on 21 December 2003. In the absence of any significant opposition, Conté was re-elected to a further seven-year term of office, receiving 95.25% of the votes cast, according to official figures. Although the opposition claimed that turn-out had been as low as 15% of the electorate, official figures indicated a rate of participation of approximately 82%. Barry, meanwhile, alleged that the official results were fraudulent, and that he had, in fact, received a majority of the votes cast. On 23 February 2004 Conté dismissed Sidimé and appointed a substantially reshuffled Government, headed by Fall as Prime Minister. Further changes were made to the Government on 1 March, when a new Minister of the Economy and Finance, Mady Kaba Camara, was appointed; the Governor of the central bank, Ibrahim Chérif Bah, was also dismissed, amid increasing concern at the country's economic performance. In mid-March Siradiou Diallo died; he was replaced as President of the UPR by Ousmane Bah. In late March three senior members of the UFR were detained on suspicion of involvement in an alleged plot to assassinate President Conté; although all three were provisionally released in mid-April, it was reported that they were to be charged with breaching national security, and were to remain under judicial control. Later in the month, following his arrest on charges of complicity in a plot to undermine the authority of the state, Sidya Touré was conditionally released, but was prohibited from engaging in political activity and forbidden to leave Guinea. In July, however, Touré was acquitted of the charges by an appeal court judge, and the restrictions were lifted.

In late April 2004 it was announced that Fall had resigned as Prime Minister and had fled Guinea; the former premier subsequently claimed that his Government had been obstructed in its attempts to implement economic and judicial reforms. The post of Prime Minister remained vacant for eight months until the appointment in December of Cellou Dalein Diallo, previously Minister of Fishing and Aquaculture and a government minister since 1996. Diallo pledged to reopen dialogue with

opposition parties and suggested that private ownership of radio stations, hitherto prohibited, could be legalized.

In January 2005 Antoine Gbokolo Soromou, leader of the opposition Alliance nationale pour le developpement (who had been among those imprisoned with Alpha Condé between 1998 and 2001) was arrested, allegedly in connection with the forgery of national identity cards. He was released and placed under judicial control, but subsequently disappeared. Also in January it was announced that President Conté had survived an assassination attempt during an attack on his convoy in Conakry. There was speculation that Sierra Leonean and Ivorian elements had been involved in the incident, while opposition commentators denounced the attack as staged. A number of people were arrested following the attack, including a Muslim Imam, who later died in custody. Also among those detained by the authorities were Paul Yomba Korouma, a lawyer who had been representing Soromou, and Benn Pepito, news editor of the weekly *La Lance*, who had published several articles on the subject of Soromou's arrest and disappearance. Both men were subsequently released. In March Conté removed three senior members from the Council of Ministers. The Minister of Security, Moussa Sampil, was replaced by Ousmane Camara; also dismissed were the Minister of Foreign Affairs and Co-operation, Mamady Condé, whose portfolio was assumed by the former Guinean ambassador to Nigeria, Sidibé Fatoumata Kaba, and the Minister of Mines and Geology, Dr Alpha Mady Soumah, who was replaced by Ahmed Tidiane Souaré, hitherto Inspector-General at the Ministry of the Economy and Finance. It was rumoured that Sampil's dismissal was related to his handling of the investigation into the assassination attempt on Conté.

In August 1990 Guinean armed forces were deployed along the border with Liberia, following a series of violent incursions by deserters from the Liberian army. Guinean army units also participated in the ECOMOG cease-fire monitoring group, deployed in Liberia in that month (see ECOWAS). In April 1991 it was announced that a Guinean contingent was to be dispatched to Sierra Leone to assist that country in repelling violations of its territory by Charles Taylor's National Patriotic Front of Liberia. In October 1992 the Guinean Government admitted that Liberian forces were being trained in Guinea; it was stated that those receiving instruction were to constitute the first Liberian government forces following an eventual restoration of peace in that country.

Following the *coup d'état* in Sierra Leone in April 1992, ex-President Maj.-Gen. Joseph Momoh was granted asylum in Guinea. His successor, Capt. Valentine Strasser, also took refuge in Guinea after he was deposed in January 1996. President Ahmed Tejan Kabbah, in turn, fled to Guinea in May 1997, following the seizure of power in Sierra Leone by forces led by Maj. Johnny Paul Koroma. Some 1,500 Guinean troops were dispatched in support of the Nigerian-led ECOMOG force in Sierra Leone (occupying in the process the Sierra Leonean border village of Yenga, see below). Guinea joined other members of the international community in condemning the subversion of constitutional order in Sierra Leone, prior to Kabbah's reinstatement, in March 1998, as President of Sierra Leone.

The Liberian Government formally protested to Guinea in April 1999, in response to what it termed an invasion from Guinea of the border town of Voinjama, although the Guinean Government denied the accusations. In August the Liberian Government declared a state of emergency, again claiming that an invasion force had entered Liberia from Guinea, and the border between the two countries was closed. In August ECOWAS ministers responsible for foreign affairs agreed to establish a commission in an effort to resolve the issue of border insecurity in this region. In September Guinea protested to the Organization of African Unity (now the African Union, see p. 144), the UN and ECOWAS, after 28 people were allegedly killed in attacks by Liberian troops on villages in the Macenta region. None the less, at an extraordinary summit meeting of ECOWAS leaders in mid-September, Presidents Conté and Taylor made pledges of good neighbourliness and non-aggression. The summit condemned the attacks, without apportioning blame. The functions of the Mano River Union (MRU, see p. 375), comprising Guinea, Liberia and Sierra Leone, were to be reactivated, and a joint committee on border security was to be established.

Liberia reopened the border with Guinea in February 2000, and in April the ministers responsible for security of the MRU states agreed to allow reciprocal inspections of border areas; a meeting between military officials from the three countries took place in May. None the less, in July the Liberian Government reported renewed fighting, apparently following an attack by rebel groups allegedly based in Guinea. The Liberian Government, which dispatched reinforcements to the border with Guinea, threatened to attack the bases of the rebel groups in Guinea and accused the Guinean authorities of complicity with the rebels. Relations between Guinea and Liberia deteriorated as tensions in the border region intensified from early September (see above). In that month the Liberian consul-general was declared *persona non grata* by the Guinean Government. In early October tripartite discussions were held between Guinea, Liberia and Sierra Leone. In January 2001 Liberia accused the Guinean Government of having supported the recent shelling of towns in its Foya district and recalled its ambassador from Conakry. The Liberian Government accused Guinea of launching further air and artillery attacks on Voinjama in late February, while the US-based Human Rights Watch claimed that Guinean shellfire had killed at least 41 civilians in Sierra Leone since September 2000. Conté boycotted an ECOWAS conference in Abuja, Nigeria, in April 2001, which had been organized to discuss the conflict in the countries of the MRU, in protest at Taylor's attendance: Liberia had recently expelled the ambassadors of Guinea and Sierra Leone and also sealed its borders with the two countries. In mid-May Guinean forces fired artillery shells at RUF-held positions in northern Sierra Leone, as a UN-supported disarmament process commenced in that country. As the peace process in Sierra Leone advanced in mid-2001, violent unrest in Guinea also abated. In June Kabbah and Conté met in Kambia, in northern Sierra Leone, to discuss regional tensions; following the discussions it was announced that the commercial highway between Conakry and Freetown, closed since 1998, was to reopen. In August 2001 the Liberian authorities withdrew all restrictions imposed on the Guinean and Sierra Leonean diplomatic presences in the Liberian capital, Monrovia, and the ambassadors of the two countries resumed their duties. At the end of September Taylor announced that Liberia was to reopen its borders with Guinea and Sierra Leone.

In February 2002, as violence by rebel groups in Liberia escalated and extended to the outskirts of Monrovia, the Guinean authorities denied allegations, made by Taylor (and subsequently reiterated by Guinean opposition leader Jean-Marie Doré), that Guinea supported rebels of the Liberians United for Reconciliation and Democracy (LURD—see the chapter on Liberia). In late February Taylor, Conté and Kabbah participated in a summit in Rabat, Morocco, to discuss the cross-border insurgencies affecting the three countries. Following further meetings of ministers from the three countries, agreement was reached on the deployment of joint defence and security troops along the common borders to facilitate the return of refugees and to monitor the movement of small arms in the region. In mid-April it was reported that Guinea had begun to deploy troops along its border with Liberia in compliance with this initiative. Relations with Liberia improved markedly from August 2003, when Taylor was forced into exile and the incumbent Government, rebel factions, political opposition and civil organizations in Liberia reached a peace agreement providing for the formation of a transitional power-sharing government and legislature. Sekou Damate Conneh, the Chairman of LURD, who was reported to be an associate of President Conté, returned to Liberia from Guinea in September.

Relations between Guinea and Sierra Leone were complicated in the early 2000s by the ongoing dispute over ownership of the border town of Yenga, in a reportedly diamond-rich region of Sierra Leone, which Guinean troops had occupied in 1998. In a joint statement in September 2004, signed by Presidents Conté and Tabbah, it was announced that both countries recognised Yenga as belonging to Sierra Leone, on the basis of a border agreement of 1912 between the British and French colonial powers. However, it was reported in early 2005 that Guinean troops continued to occupy the area.

The protracted conflicts in Liberia and Sierra Leone, and the civil conflict in Côte d'Ivoire from 2002, have resulted in the presence in Guinea of large numbers of refugees, variously estimated to number 5%–15% of the total population. The office of the UN High Commissioner for Refugees (UNHCR) assessed the total number of refugees in Guinea at 501,544 at the beginning of 2000, of which 129,096 were Liberian and 370,631 Sierra Leonean. By the beginning of 2003, however, the total number of refugees had decreased to 182,163. In 2003 the

UNHCR assisted 27,713 Sierra Leonean refugees to return home, but 39,586 new arrivals were registered in that year. By the end of 2003 the UNHCR estimated the total population of refugees in Guinea at 184,341, including 149,639 from Liberia and some 25,000 from Sierra Leone. The number of refugees from Côte d'Ivoire totalled 2,188 in 2002 and rose to 9,552 in 2003, following the outbreak of conflict in that country.

Relations with both the Government of France and with private French interests strengthened considerably in the 1990s: official assistance from, and trade with, France is of great importance to the Guinean economy, as is French participation in the mining sector and in newly privatized organizations. However, in the early 2000s military assistance from France to Guinea was reduced and, to some extent, supplanted by support from other sources: Guinea signed a pact of military co-operation with Russia in 2001, and received military aid from the People's Republic of China in 2002, while in mid-2002 the US military participated in the training of Guinean troops.

Government

Under the terms of the Constitution promulgated on 23 December 1991, and amended in April 1992 and November 2001, the President of the Republic, who is Head of State, is elected for seven years by universal adult suffrage, in the context of a multi-party political system. The 114-member Assemblée nationale, which holds legislative power, is elected by universal suffrage for a five-year term. The President of the Republic is also Head of Government, and in this capacity appoints the other members of the Council of Ministers.

Local administration is based on eight administrative entities (the city of Conakry and seven administrative regions) each under the authority of an appointed Governor; the country is sub-divided into 33 prefectures. Conakry, which comprises a separate administrative unit, is divided into five communes.

Defence

In August 2004 Guinea's active armed forces totalled 9,700, comprising an army of 8,500, a navy of 400 and an air force of 800. Paramilitary forces comprised a Republican Guard of 1,600 and a 1,000-strong gendarmerie, as well as a reserve 'people's militia' of 7,000. Military service is compulsory (conscripts were estimated at some 7,500 in 2001) and lasts for two years. The defence budget for 2003 was estimated at 142,000m. FG.

Economic Affairs

In 2003, according to estimates by the World Bank, Guinea's gross national income (GNI), measured at average 2001–03 prices, was US $3,559m., equivalent to $430 per head (or $2,100 on an international purchasing-power parity basis). During 1990–2003, it was estimated, the population increased at an average annual rate of 2.5%, while gross domestic product (GDP) per head increased, in real terms, by an average of 1.3% per year. Overall GDP increased, in real terms, at an average annual rate of 3.8% in 1990–2003, with GDP growth of 2.1% recorded in 2003.

Measured at constant 1996 prices, agriculture (including hunting, forestry and fishing) contributed an estimated 19.4% of GDP in 2003. About 82.7% of the labour force were employed in the agricultural sector in 2003. The principal cash crops are fruits, oil palm, groundnuts and coffee. Important staple crops include cassava, rice and other cereals and vegetables. The attainment of self-sufficiency in rice and other basic foodstuffs remains a priority. The food supply is supplemented by the rearing of cattle and other livestock. The Government has made efforts towards the commercial exploitation of Guinea's forest resources (forests cover about two-thirds of the country's land area) and substantial fishing stocks. According to the World Bank, during 1990–2003 agricultural GDP increased at an average annual rate of 4.5%; growth in agricultural GDP in 2003 was 4.5%.

Industry (including mining, manufacturing, construction and power) contributed an estimated 32.2% of GDP (at 1996 prices) in 2003. An estimated 1.9% of the employed labour force were engaged in the industrial sector in 1990. According to the World Bank, industrial GDP increased at an average annual rate of 4.0% in 1990–2003; growth in 2003 was 0.5%.

Mining contributed an estimated 17.2% of GDP (at 1996 prices) in 2003. Only 0.7% of the employed labour force were engaged in the sector at the time of the 1983 census. Guinea is the world's foremost exporter of bauxite and the second largest producer of bauxite ore, possessing between one-quarter and one-third of known reserves of the mineral. In 2001 exports of aluminium ore and concentrates and aluminium hydroxide together provided 71.0% of export earnings. Despite the importance to the national economy of the extraction of bauxite, only a small proportion of output is processed into alumina in Guinea; various plans to increase the production of alumina have been proposed. Production of alumina increased by an average of 7.6% per year in 1998–2002, according to the US Geological Survey, although the mining of bauxite declined slightly during the same period. Gold and diamonds are also mined: in 2001 gold contributed 20.6% of export earnings; in 2002 diamonds contributed some 4.9% of export revenue. Exploitation of valuable reserves of high-grade iron ore at Mt Nimba, near the border with Liberia, has been impeded by political instability in the region. Of Guinea's other known mineral deposits, only granite is exploitable on a commercial scale. The GDP of the mining sector increased at an average annual rate of 2.8% in 1997–2002, according to the IMF; growth in 2003 was estimated at 2.6%.

The manufacturing sector remains largely undeveloped, contributing only an estimated 4.0% of GDP (at 1996 prices) in 2003. In 1983 only 0.6% of the employed labour force were engaged in the manufacturing sector. Other than the country's one alumina smelter, most industrial companies are involved in import-substitution, including the processing of agricultural products and the manufacture of construction materials. According to the World Bank, manufacturing GDP increased at an average annual rate of 4.3% in 1990–2003. It increased by 6.0% in 2002 but declined by 1.5% in 2003.

Electricity generation is, at present, insufficient to meet demand, and power failures outside the mining and industrial sectors (in which the largest operators generate their own power supplies) have been frequent. However, Guinea possesses considerable hydroelectric potential. The 75-MW Garafiri dam project was inaugurated in 1999, and a further major scheme, at Kaléta, was scheduled for completion in the mid-2000s. In the mean time, some 600,000 metric tons of hydrocarbons are imported annually, and in 2001 imports of fuel accounted for 18.6% of the value of total merchandise imports. In October 2001 it was announced that the Nigerian National Petroleum Corpn was to begin supplying petroleum products to Guinea

The services sector contributed an estimated 48.4% of GDP (at 1996 prices) in 2003. During 1990–2003, according to the World Bank, the sector's GDP increased at an average annual rate of 2.8%; growth in 2003 was 1.9%.

In 2003 Guinea recorded a visible trade deficit of US $35.0m., while there was a deficit of $187.5m. on the current account of the balance of payments. The principal suppliers of imports in 2001 were France (which supplied 17.4% of the total), Belgium, Côte d'Ivoire and the USA. The principal markets for exports in that year were France (which took 26.0% of exports), the USA, Ireland and Spain. Ukraine and Russia are notable markets for Guinean bauxite. The principal exports in 2001 were aluminium ore and concentrate, gold and aluminium hydroxide. The principal imports included machinery and transport equipment, refined petroleum products, food and live animals, and basic manufactures.

In 2003 Guinea's overall budget deficit was estimated by the IMF at 369,800m. FG, equivalent to 7.7% of GDP. The country's total external debt was US $3,401m. at the end of 2002, of which $2,972m. was long-term public debt. In that year the cost of debt-servicing was equivalent to 13.6% of the value of exports of goods and services. Annual inflation averaged 5.23% in 1991–2003; consumer prices increased by an average of 12.9% in 2003.

Guinea is a member of the Economic Community of West African States (ECOWAS, see p. 205), of the Gambia River Basin Development Organization (OMVG, see p. 374), of the International Coffee Organization (see p. 370), of the West Africa Rice Development Association (WARDA, see p. 372) and of the Mano River Union (see p. 375).

Guinea's potential for the attainment of wealth is substantial, owing to its valuable mineral deposits, water resources and generally favourable climate; however, the economy remains over-dependent on revenue from bauxite reserves and on external assistance, the country's infrastructure is inadequate and its manufacturing base narrow. Since 1985 economic liberalization measures have been undertaken, and by the late 1990s success had been achieved in reducing the rate of inflation, foreign-exchange reserves had increased, as had private investment in the economy, while considerable GDP growth had been achieved. However, insecurity in neighbouring Liberia and Sierra Leone during the 1990s had a detrimental effect on Guinea's economy, and instability in the southern regions of Guinea in 2000–01 adversely affected agricultural output. Conversely, the rebellion that commenced in Côte d'Ivoire in September 2002 resulted in a marked increase in international trade routed through the port of Conakry, as access to the larger Ivorian port at Abidjan became increasingly uncertain. In December 2000 the IMF and the World Bank announced that Guinea would be a recipient of some $880m. in debt relief as part of their initiative for heavily indebted poor countries. In May 2001 the IMF approved a three-year arrangement under its Poverty Reduction and Growth Facility for Guinea, worth US $82m. over three years. Measures adopted as part of a Poverty Reduction Strategy Paper in 2001 sought to reduce poverty, and to improve levels of health care and education. In 2003 political instability, both within Guinea and in neighbouring countries, and frequent interruptions to water and electricity supplies contributed to much lower GDP growth than anticipated, at an estimated 1.2%. The continued deterioration in the economic situation in 2004, characterized in particular by a sharp rise in the price of rice, high electricity costs, and unpaid public sector wages, provoked a series of strikes and disturbances across the country. In January 2005 it was announced that a proposed joint visit to Guinea by the World Bank and the IMF had been cancelled, following the publication of the latter's 2004 Article IV Consultation Report the previous October, in which the Guinean Government's economic policy was severely criticized. GDP growth of 2.6% was forecast for 2004, however, in the longer term sustained growth remains dependent on the maintenance of political stability, continued economic reform and a diversification and expansion of the manufacturing sector.

Education

Education is provided free of charge at every level in state institutions. Primary education, which begins at seven years of age and lasts for six years, is officially compulsory. In 2000/01, however, enrolment at primary schools included only 47% of children in the relevant age-group (males 52%; females 41%). Secondary education, from the age of 13, lasts for seven years, comprising a first cycle (collège) of four years and a second (lycée) of three years. According to UNESCO estimates, enrolment at secondary schools in 1998/99 included only 12% of children in the appropriate age-group (boys 17%; girls 6%). There are universities at Conakry and Kankan, and other tertiary institutions at Manéyah, Boké and Faranah. Independent schools, which had been banned for 23 years under the Sekou Touré regime, were legalized in 1984. Budget estimates for 1999 allocated 62,300m. FG to education (equivalent to 8.1% of total budgetary expenditure).

Public Holidays

2005: 1 January (New Year's Day), 28 March (Easter Monday), 21 April* (Mouloud, birth of Muhammad), 1 May (Labour Day), 27 August (Anniversary of Women's Revolt), 28 September (Referendum Day), 2 October (Republic Day), 1 November (All Saints' Day), 4 November* (Id al-Fitr, end of Ramadan), 22 November (Day of 1970 Invasion), 25 December (Christmas).

2006: 1 January (New Year's Day), 11 April* (Mouloud, birth of Muhammad), 17 April (Easter Monday), 1 May (Labour Day), 27 August (Anniversary of Women's Revolt), 28 September (Referendum Day), 2 October (Republic Day), 24 October* (Id al-Fitr, end of Ramadan), 1 November (All Saints' Day), 22 November (Day of 1970 Invasion), 25 December (Christmas).

* These holidays are determined by the Islamic lunar calendar and may vary by one or two days from the dates given.

Weights and Measures

The metric system is in force.

Statistical Survey

Source (unless otherwise stated): Direction Nationale de la Statistique, BP 221, Conakry; tel. 44-21-48.

Area and Population

AREA, POPULATION AND DENSITY

Area (sq km)	245,857*
Population (census results)	
4–17 February 1983	4,533,240†
31 December 1996‡	
Males	3,497,551
Females	3,658,855
Total	7,156,406
Population (UN estimates at mid-year)§	
2001	8,242,000
2002	8,359,000
2003	8,480,000
Density (per sq km) at mid-2003	34.5

* 94,926 sq miles.
† Excluding adjustment for underenumeration.
‡ Including refugees from Liberia and Sierra Leone (estimated at 640,000).
§ Source: UN, *World Population Prospects: The 2002 Revision*.

ETHNIC GROUPS

1995 (percentages): Peul 38.7; Malinké 23.3; Soussou 11.1; Kissi 5.9; Kpellé 4.5; Others 16.5 (Source: La Francophonie).

PRINCIPAL TOWNS
(population at 1996 census)

Conakry (capital)	1,092,936	Kankan	100,192
N'Zérékoré	107,329		

Mid-2003 (UN estimate, incl. suburbs): Conakry 1,365,778 (Source: UN, *World Urbanization Prospects: The 2003 Revision*).

BIRTHS AND DEATHS
(UN estimates, annual averages)

	1985–90	1990–95	1995–2000
Birth rate (per 1,000)	46.8	44.0	45.6
Death rate (per 1,000)	21.6	18.7	17.8

Source: UN, *World Population Prospects: The 2002 Revision*.

Expectation of life (WHO estimates, years at birth): 52.3 (males 50.9; females 53.7) in 2002 (Source: WHO, *World Health Report*).

ECONOMICALLY ACTIVE POPULATION
(ILO estimates, '000 persons at mid-1990)

	Males	Females	Total
Agriculture, hunting, forestry and fishing	1,338	1,336	2,674
Industry	40	18	58
Manufacturing	13	6	18
Services	234	101	335
Total labour force	1,612	1,455	3,067

Source: ILO.

1996 census: Total employed labour force 3,278,834.

Mid-2003 ('000 persons): Agriculture, etc. 3,459; Total labour force 4,183 (Source: FAO).

Health and Welfare

KEY INDICATORS

Total fertility rate (children per woman, 2002)	5.9
Under-5 mortality rate (per 1,000 live births, 2003)	160
HIV/AIDS (% of persons aged 15–49, 2003)	3.2
Physicians (per 1,000 head, 1995)	0.13
Hospital beds (per 1,000 head, 1990)	0.55
Health expenditure (2001): US $ per head (PPP)	61
Health expenditure (2001): % of GDP	3.5
Health expenditure (2001): public (% of total)	54.1
Access to water (% of persons, 2002)	51
Access to sanitation (% of persons, 2002)	13
Human Development Index (2002): ranking	160
Human Development Index (2002): value	0.425

For sources and definitions, see explanatory note on p. vi.

Agriculture

PRINCIPAL CROPS
('000 metric tons)

	2001	2002	2003
Rice (paddy)	789.2	842.5	845.0*
Maize	99.1	103.0	90.0†
Fonio	128.1	132.9	135.0*
Sweet potatoes	135.0*	86.5	90.0*
Cassava (Manioc)	1,026.1	1,137.8	1,150.0*
Taro (Coco Yam)*	30	30	30
Yams	90.0*	44.5	45.0*
Sugar cane*	270	270	270
Pulses*	60	60	60
Groundnuts (in shell)	226.1	248.3	252.0*
Coconuts*	22.5	22.5	22.5
Oil palm fruit*	830	830	830
Vegetables*	216	220	220
Bananas*	150	150	150
Plantains*	430	430	430
Citrus fruit*	210	210	210
Mangoes	120.0*	155.8	160.0*
Pineapples	85.0*	102.0	105.0*
Other fruit*	45	45	45
Cotton (lint)*	30	15	15
Cottonseed*	20	15	15
Coffee (green)*	20.5	20.5	20.5

* FAO estimate(s).
† Unofficial figure.

Source: FAO.

LIVESTOCK
('000 head, year ending September)

	2001	2002	2003*
Cattle	2,973	3,139	3,285
Sheep	885	945	1,005
Goats	1,052	1,128	1,201
Pigs	58	60*	65
Horses*	3	3	3
Asses*	2	2	2
Poultry*	12,560	13,300	13,500

* FAO estimate(s).

Source: FAO.

GUINEA

LIVESTOCK PRODUCTS
(FAO estimates, '000 metric tons)

	2001	2002	2003
Beef and veal	33.4	33.9	35.5
Poultry meat	4.2	4.4	4.5
Mutton and lamb	3.6	3.8	4.0
Goat meat	4.7	5.0	5.3
Other meat	5.7	5.8	5.9
Cows' milk	75.0	77.0	79.0
Goats' milk	6.0	6.3	6.7
Poultry eggs	12.9	16.7	16.7
Cattle hides	5.9	6.0	6.3

Source: FAO.

Forestry

ROUNDWOOD REMOVALS
(FAO estimates, '000 cubic metres, excl. bark)

	2001	2002	2003
Sawlogs, veneer logs and logs for sleepers	138	138	138
Other industrial wood	513	513	513
Fuel wood	11,490	11,537	11,585
Total	12,141	12,188	12,236

Source: FAO.

SAWNWOOD PRODUCTION
('000 cubic metres, incl. railway sleepers)

	1998	1999	2000
Total (all broadleaved)	26	26*	26*

* FAO estimate.
Figures for 2001–03 assumed to be unchanged from 2000 (FAO estimates).
Source: FAO.

Fishing
('000 metric tons, live weight)

	2000	2001	2002*
Freshwater fishes	4.0	4.0	4.0
Sea catfishes	4.6	6.2	6.2
Bobo croaker	4.0	5.2	5.1
West African croakers	3.4	3.6	3.6
Porgies and seabreams	1.8	4.6	4.5
Sardinellas	13.3	8.0	8.0
Bonga shad	29.0	38.4	38.0
Jack and horse mackerels	6.1	5.2	5.1
Total catch (incl. others)	91.5	105.2	104.0

* FAO estimates.
Source: FAO.

Mining
('000 metric tons, unless otherwise indicated)

	2000	2001	2002
Bauxite*	15,700	15,100†	15,300†
Gold (kilograms)‡	13,104	16,264	16,666
Salt (unrefined)†	15	15	15
Diamonds ('000 carats)‡	369	364	491

* Dried equivalent of crude ore.
† Estimate(s).
‡ Including artisanal production.
Source: US Geological Survey.

Industry

SELECTED PRODUCTS
('000 metric tons, unless otherwise indicated)

	2000	2001	2002
Salted, dried or smoked fish*	11.0	11.0	n.a.
Palm oil (unrefined)*†	50	50	50
Beer of barley*†	11.5	7.8	7.8
Raw sugar*	25‡	25†	25†
Alumina (calcined equivalent)§	541	674	670
Electric energy (million kWh)†	569	n.a.	n.a.

* Data from FAO.
† Estimate(s).
‡ Unofficial figure.
§ Data from the US Geological Survey.
Source: mainly FAO; UN, *Industrial Commodity Statistics Yearbook*.

Finance

CURRENCY AND EXCHANGE RATES

Monetary Units
100 centimes = 1 franc guinéen (FG or Guinean franc).

Sterling, Dollar and Euro Equivalents (30 June 2004)
£1 sterling = 3,623.4 Guinean francs;
US $1 = 2,000.0 Guinean francs;
€1 = 2,431.0 Guinean francs;
10,000 Guinean francs = £2.76 = $5.00 = €4.11.

Average Exchange Rate (Guinean francs per US $)
2001 1,950.6
2002 1,975.8
2003 1,984.9

BUDGET
('000 million Guinean francs)

Revenue*	2001	2002	2003†
Mining-sector revenue	166.6	145.4	105.9
Special tax on mining products	154.1	131.2	94.9
Other revenue	503.6	618.5	648.2
Tax revenue	440.6	547.2	599.3
Taxes on income and profits	78.1	94.9	102.4
Taxes on domestic production and trade	248.5	313.2	347.9
Value-added tax (VAT)‡	156.2	184.8	217.1
Excise surcharge	10.8	10.6	15.1
Petroleum excise tax	72.8	77.4	84.3
Taxes on international trade	114.0	139.1	149.1
Import duties	88.0	108.4	112.7
Total	670.3	763.9	754.1

Expenditure§	2001	2002	2003†
Current expenditure	684.7	776.1	929.0
Wages and salaries	215.1	236.9	258.6
Other goods and services	133.9	209.9	254.5
Subsidies and transfers	246.1	224.0	263.2
Interest due on external debt	62.1	74.1	83.4
Interest due on domestic debt	27.5	31.2	69.2
Capital expenditure	423.4	368.9	390.6
Domestically financed	34.7	78.4	93.1
Externally financed	388.7	290.5	297.5
Restructuring of banking system	4.5	7.9	1.5
Total	1,112.5	1,153.0	1,321.1

* Excluding grants received ('000 million Guinean francs): 202.8 in 2001; 113.0 in 2002; 198.6 in 2003 (estimate).
† Estimates.
‡ Includes value-added tax on imports.
§ Excluding lending minus repayments ('000 million Guinean francs): 1.3 in 2001; 4.4 in 2002; 1.4 in 2003 (estimate).
Sources: IMF, *Guinea: Statistical Appendix* (August 2004).

INTERNATIONAL RESERVES
(excluding gold, US $ million at 31 December)

	2000	2001	2002
IMF special drawing rights . .	0.25	0.80	1.66
Reserve position in IMF . . .	0.10	0.09	0.10
Foreign exchange	147.56	199.34	169.64
Total	147.91	200.23	171.40

Source: IMF, *International Financial Statistics*.

2003 (US $ million at 31 December): IMF special drawing rights 0.22; Reserve position in IMF 0.11 (Source: IMF, *International Financial Statistics*).

MONEY SUPPLY
(million Guinean francs at 31 December)

	2001	2002	2003
Currency outside banks . . .	310,063	349,781	478,133
Demand deposits at commercial banks	226,047	300,520	386,359
Total (incl. others)	559,993	681,228	893,055

Source: IMF, *International Financial Statistics*.

COST OF LIVING
(Consumer Price Index for Conakry; base: 1991 = 100)

	2001	2002	2003
Food	177.2	188.1	223.6
Clothing	136.2	139.3	145.5
Housing	146.1	147.4	155.9
Electricity and water	149.2	153.0	165.0
All items (incl. others)	169.2	174.2	196.6

Source: IMF, *Guinea: Statistical Appendix* (August 2004).

NATIONAL ACCOUNTS

Expenditure on the Gross Domestic Product
('000 million Guinean francs at current prices)

	2001	2002	2003*
Government final consumption expenditure	405.6	477.5	539.2
Private final consumption expenditure	4,686.2	5,282.9	6,139.8
Gross fixed capital formation . .	852.8	817.6	710.9
Change in stocks	54.0	13.7	3.7
Total domestic expenditure .	5,998.6	6,591.7	7,393.6
Exports of goods and services . .	1,575.4	1,550.9	1,587.4
Less Imports of goods and services	1,654.4	1,802.3	1,771.2
GDP at market prices . . .	5,919.7	6,340.3	7,209.8

* Estimates.

Gross Domestic Product by Economic Activity
('000 million Guinean francs at constant 1996 prices)

	2001	2002	2003*
Agriculture, livestock, forestry and fishing	857.1	900.6	926.3
Mining	778.5	801.2	822.0
Manufacturing	189.6	200.9	192.8
Electricity and water	28.3	29.1	27.5
Construction	468.4	502.7	497.7
Trade	1,225.8	1,248.3	1,267.0
Transport	275.3	281.1	283.9
Administration	250.8	257.0	260.9
Other services	485.7	495.1	504.6
GDP at factor cost	4,559.4	4,716.0	4,782.6
Indirect taxes	166.0	207.3	201.8
GDP at constant prices . . .	4,725.4	4,923.3	4,984.3

* Estimates.

Source: IMF, *Guinea: Statistical Appendix* (August 2004).

BALANCE OF PAYMENTS
(US $ million)

	2001	2002	2003
Exports of goods f.o.b.	731.1	708.6	609.3
Imports of goods f.o.b.	−561.9	−668.5	−644.3
Trade balance	169.2	40.1	−35.0
Exports of services	102.8	90.5	133.7
Imports of services	−319.0	−330.6	−307.3
Balance on goods and services	−47.0	−200.1	−208.6
Other income received	11.3	6.1	12.6
Other income paid	−113.6	−51.6	−124.3
Balance on goods, services and income	−149.3	−245.6	−320.3
Current transfers received . . .	91.6	70.5	194.6
Current transfers paid	−44.5	−24.8	−61.7
Current balance	−102.2	−199.8	−187.5
Capital account	—	91.9	57.6
Direct investment from abroad .	1.7	30.0	79.0
Portfolio investment assets . .	4.6	5.1	−4.6
Other investment assets . . .	11.7	−71.0	−4.4
Other investment liabilities . .	−30.1	−79.2	−11.4
Net errors and omissions . . .	−2.2	143.1	−157.1
Overall balance	−116.5	−79.8	−228.5

Source: IMF, *International Financial Statistics*.

External Trade

PRINCIPAL COMMODITIES
(US $ million)

Imports c.i.f.	1999	2000	2001
Food and live animals	125.6	110.0	110.9
Cereals and cereal preparations	64.0	55.9	61.2
Rice	40.5	28.8	33.2
Rice, semi-milled or wholly milled	40.4	28.5	32.7
Rice, semi-milled or milled (unbroken)	24.4	17.0	20.3
Sugar, sugar preparations and honey	21.0	15.5	18.1
Sugar and honey	18.3	13.8	17.1
Refined sugar, etc.	17.7	13.5	16.8
Beverages and tobacco	35.4	26.3	22.1
Tobacco and tobacco manufactures	31.4	23.6	19.2
Tobacco, manufactured	30.3	23.1	18.8
Cigarettes	29.8	23.0	18.7
Mineral fuels, lubricants, etc.	44.5	152.8	112.0
Petroleum products, refined	43.9	151.6	111.1
Chemicals and related products	53.1	51.6	65.7
Inorganic chemicals	13.3	6.2	25.5
Inorganic chemical elements, oxides and halogen salts	8.2	4.1	17.2
Medicinal and pharmaceutical products	18.3	23.3	15.7
Medicaments (incl. veterinary medicaments)	17.3	21.6	14.2
Medicaments (incl. veterinary medicaments) containing other substances	17.1	21.5	14.0
Basic manufactures	81.0	81.5	83.4
Non-metallic mineral manufactures	20.3	19.0	28.4
Lime, cement and fabricated construction materials	14.8	13.7	22.4
Cement	14.5	12.7	19.2
Iron and steel	15.2	19.3	16.1
Machinery and transport equipment	147.1	116.2	149.7
Power-generating machinery and equipment	19.2	6.3	7.5
General industrial machinery, equipment and parts	27.4	22.8	37.1
Electrical machinery, apparatus and parts	33.1	13.7	11.8
Household type equipment	17.9	2.5	2.4
Domestic refrigerators and freezers	17.3	1.5	1.4
Domestic refrigerators	16.8	1.2	1.0
Road vehicles	41.0	53.1	61.8
Passenger motor vehicles (excl. buses)	15.3	26.3	36.6
Miscellaneous manufactured articles	48.2	51.0	39.2
Total (incl. others)	555.9	612.4	600.8

Exports f.o.b.	1999	2000	2001
Crude materials (inedible) except fuels	294.6	283.5	310.8
Aluminium ore and concentrate	291.9	269.9	309.8
Chemicals and related products	84.6	56.9	98.6
Aluminium hydroxide	84.6	56.9	98.4
Miscellaneous manufactured articles	0.3	61.9	15.5
Unused postage; stamp-impressed papers; stock; cheque books, etc.	—	61.3	14.7
Gold, non-monetary, unwrought or semi-manufactured	80.0	96.3	118.6
Total (incl. others)	473.9	522.4	574.9

Source: UN, *International Trade Statistics Yearbook*.

PRINCIPAL TRADING PARTNERS
(US $ million)

Imports c.i.f.	1999	2000	2001
Australia	12.6	7.2	11.9
Belgium	42.3	47.4	78.9
Canada	6.1	1.4	2.8
China, People's Republic	33.2	28.4	32.4
Côte d'Ivoire	42.0	130.9	76.4
Cyprus	4.4	9.6	0.3
Denmark	5.5	4.1	9.5
France (incl. Monaco)	118.7	121.2	104.8
Gabon	4.1	7.3	3.6
Germany	20.4	19.2	13.6
Hong Kong	7.3	6.1	6.0
India	16.6	11.4	9.3
Indonesia	5.4	5.6	6.5
Italy	27.0	21.0	20.6
Japan	46.0	34.2	23.2
Netherlands	25.2	14.3	28.7
Senegal	4.0	4.0	6.8
Spain	10.3	11.5	17.8
Switzerland-Liechtenstein	3.5	4.5	9.6
Thailand	5.8	5.8	11.4
United Arab Emirates	3.8	4.2	6.1
United Kingdom	10.9	9.2	15.8
USA	33.2	48.4	42.8
Viet Nam	6.6	3.2	2.7
Total (incl. others)	555.9	612.4	600.8

Exports f.o.b.	1999	2000	2001
Belgium	2.8	2.7	16.0
Cameroon	18.8	9.6	15.5
Canada	5.2	17.2	15.8
France (incl. Monaco)	99.1	172.6	149.7
Germany	11.2	32.1	37.6
Hungary	—	5.8	—
Ireland	161.9	47.5	65.1
Malta	—	6.3	—
Morocco	5.6	7.3	5.6
Netherlands	—	0.3	7.3
Russia	20.2	21.6	44.6
Seychelles	8.1	5.8	0.3
Spain	87.8	50.1	54.6
Sudan	0.1	6.5	—
Switzerland-Liechtenstein	1.0	26.5	5.5
Ukraine	0.1	15.5	1.6
United Kingdom	14.6	17.4	32.3
USA	26.5	66.7	96.9
Total (incl. others)	473.9	522.4	574.9

Source: UN, *International Trade Statistics Yearbook*.

Transport

RAILWAYS
(estimated traffic)

	1991	1992	1993
Freight ton-km (million)	660	680	710

Source: UN Economic Commission for Africa, *African Statistical Yearbook*.

ROAD TRAFFIC
(estimates, '000, motor vehicles in use)

	1994	1995	1996
Passenger cars	13.2	13.7	14.1
Lorries and vans	18.0	19.4	21.0

Source: IRF, *World Road Statistics*.

SHIPPING

Merchant Fleet
(registered at 31 December)

	2001	2002	2003
Number of vessels	33	35	37
Total displacement ('000 grt) . .	11.4	11.8	14.5

Source: Lloyd's Register-Fairplay, *World Fleet Statistics*.

International Sea-borne Freight Traffic
(Port of Conakry, '000 metric tons)

	1997	1998	1999
Goods loaded	2,130	2,194	2,089
Goods unloaded	1,610	1,680	1,850

CIVIL AVIATION
(traffic on scheduled services)

	1997	1998	1999
Kilometres flown (million) . . .	1	1	1
Passengers carried ('000) . . .	36	36	59
Passenger-km (million)	55	55	94
Total ton-km (million)	6	6	10

Source: UN, *Statistical Yearbook*.

Tourism

FOREIGN VISITOR ARRIVALS*

Country of origin	1999	2000	2001
Belgium	1,651	1,438	1,077
Canada	849	1,006	814
Côte d'Ivoire	1,327	2,081	1,315
France	4,982	7,333	6,201
Germany	716	949	1,047
Italy	686	811	525
Liberia	708	254	254
Mali	612	1,118	964
Nigeria	455	379	792
Senegal	1,265	2,651	2,558
Sierra Leone	1,693	2,948	5,144
United Kingdom	960	1,316	764
USA	1,423	2,532	2,490
Total (incl. others)	27,345	32,598	37,677

* Arrivals of non-resident tourists at national borders.

2002: 42,507 arrivals.

Receipts from tourism (US $ million): 1 in 1998; 7 in 1999; 12 in 2000; 14 in 2001; 31 in 2002.

Source: World Tourism Organization.

Communications Media

	2001	2002	2003
Telephones ('000 main lines in use) .	25.5	26.0	26.2
Mobile cellular telephones ('000 subscribers)	55.7	90.8	111.5
Personal computers ('000 in use) . .	32	42	43
Internet users ('000)	15	35	40

Source: International Telecommunication Union.

Television receivers ('000 in use): 351 in 2000 (Source: UNESCO, *Statistical Yearbook*).

Radio receivers ('000 in use): 380 in 1999 (Source: UNESCO, *Statistical Yearbook*).

Facsimile machines (estimated number in use): 3,186 in 1999 (Source: UNESCO, *Statistical Yearbook*).

Non-daily newspapers: 1 title in 1996 (average circulation 20,000) (Source: UNESCO, *Statistical Yearbook*).

Education

(1997/98, unless otherwise indicated)

	Institutions	Teachers	Students Males	Females	Total
Pre-primary .	202*	594	n.a.	n.a.	30,857
Primary . . .	3,723	17,340†	425,644	249,088	790,497†
Secondary‡ . .	358	5,356	122,598	43,336	165,934
Tertiary* . .	n.a.	307	780	1,098	1,878

* 1996/97 figure(s).
† 1999/2000 figure.
‡ 1998/99 figures.

Adult literacy rate (UNESCO estimates): 35.9% (males 50.0%; females 22.0%) in 1995.

Sources: International Development Association; IMF, *Guinea: Poverty Reduction Strategy Paper—Joint Staff Assessment* (July 2001); UNESCO, *Statistical Yearbook*.

Directory

The Constitution

The Constitution (*Loi fondamentale*) of the Third Republic of Guinea was adopted in a national referendum on 23 December 1990 and promulgated on 23 December 1991. An 'organic law' of 3 April 1992, providing for the immediate establishment of an unlimited number of political parties, countermanded the Constitution's provision for the eventual establishment of a two-party political system. There was to be a five-year period of transition, overseen by a Comité transitoire de redressement national (CTRN), to civilian rule, at the end of which executive and legislative authority would be vested in organs of state elected by universal adult suffrage in the context of a multi-party political system. The CTRN was dissolved following the legislative elections of June 1995. Amendments to provisions concerning the President were approved by referendum in November 2001.

The Constitution defines the clear separation of the powers of the executive, the legislature and the judiciary. The President of the Republic, who is Head of State, must be elected by an absolute majority of the votes cast, and a second round of voting is held should no candidate obtain such a majority at a first round. The duration of the presidential mandate is seven years, and elections are by universal adult suffrage. Any candidate for the presidency must be more than 40 years old, must not be a serving member of the armed forces, and must be proposed by a political party. There are no restrictions on the number of terms of office the President may serve. The President is Head of Government, and is empowered to appoint ministers and to delegate certain functions. The legislature is the 114-member Assemblée nationale. One-third of the Assemblée's members are elected as representatives of single-member constituencies, the remainder being appointed from national lists, according to a system of proportional representation. The legislature is elected, by universal suffrage, with a five-year mandate.

The Government

HEAD OF STATE

President: Gen. LANSANA CONTÉ (took office 4 April 1984; elected 19 December 1993; re-elected 14 December 1998 and 21 December 2003).

COUNCIL OF MINISTERS
(April 2005)

President of the Republic and President of the Council of Ministers: Gen. LANSANA CONTÉ.

Prime Minister: CELLOU DALEIN DIALLO.

Minister, Secretary-General of the Government: El Hadj FODÉ BANGOURA.

Minister of Foreign Affairs and Co-operation: SIDIBÉ FATOUMATA KABA.

Minister of Co-operation: El Hadj THIERNO HABIB DIALLO.

Minister of the Economy and Finance: MADY KABA CAMARA.

Minister of Planning: EUGÈNE CAMARA.

Minister of Territorial Administration and Decentralization: KIRIDI BANGOURA.

Minister of Security: OUSMANE CAMARA.

Minister of Justice, Keeper of the Seals: MAMADOU SYLLA SIMA.

Minister of Posts and Telecommunications: JEAN-CLAUDE SULTAN.

Minister of Trade, Industry and Small and Medium-sized Enterprises: DJÈNÈ SARAN CAMARA.

Minister of Mines and Geology: AHMED TIDIANE SOUARÉ.

Minister of the Environment: ABDEL KADER SANGARÉ.

Minister of Agriculture and Livestock: JEAN-PAUL SARR.

Minister of Fishing and Aquaculture: IBRAHIMA SORY TOURÉ.

Minister of Energy and Water: Hadja DIOUBATÉ FATOUMATA BINTA.

Minister of Transport: ALIOU CONDÉ.

Minister of Town Planning and Housing: BLAISE OUO FOROMOU.

Minister of Information: Hadja AÏSSATOU BELLA DIALLO.

Minister of Higher Education and Scientific Research: SÉKOU DÉCASY CAMARA.

Minister of Technical Education and Professional Training: IBRAHIMA SOUMAH.

Minister of Pre-university and Civil Education: GALÉMA GILAVOGUI.

Minister of Public Health: Dr AMARA CISSÉ.

Minister of Employment and the Civil Service: ALPHA IBRAHIMA KÉIRA.

Minister of Social Affairs, the Promotion of Women and Children's Affairs: Hadja MARIAMA ARIBOT.

Minister of Youth, Sports and Culture: FODÉ SOUMAH.

Minister of Tourism, Hotels and Handicrafts: Hadja SYLLA KOUMBA DIAKITÉ.

MINISTRIES

Ministry of Agriculture and Livestock: face à la Cité du Port, BP 576, Conakry; tel. 41-11-81; fax 41-11-69.

Ministry of the Economy and Finance: face au collège Boulbinet, BP 221, Conakry; tel. 45-17-95; fax 41-30-59.

Ministry of Employment and the Civil Service: près de la Cathédrale Sainte-Marie, Conakry; tel. 41-16-09.

Ministry of Energy and Water: Conakry.

Ministry of the Environment: Conakry.

Ministry of Fishing and Aquaculture: face à la Cité du Port, BP 307, Conakry; tel. 41-35-23; fax 41-35-28.

Ministry of Foreign Affairs and Co-operation: face au Port, ex-Primature, BP 2519, Conakry; tel. 41-33-42; fax 41-16-21.

Ministry of Higher Education and Scientific Research: face à la Cathédrale Sainte-Marie, BP 964, Conakry; tel. 41-19-01; fax 41-20-12.

Ministry of Information: Conakry.

Ministry of Justice: face à l'Immeuble 'La Paternelle', Conakry; tel. 45-29-06.

Ministry of Mines and Geology: BP 295, Conakry; tel. 41-38-33; fax 41-49-13.

Ministry of Planning: BP 221, Conakry; tel. 44-37-15; fax 41-43-50.

Ministry of Posts and Telecommunications: Boulbinet près de l'ORTG, BP 617, Conakry; tel. 41-50-01; fax 41-47-97; e-mail com@sotelgui.net.gn.

Ministry of Pre-university and Civil Education: BP 2201, Conakry; tel. 41-19-05.

Ministry of Public Health: BP 585, Conakry; tel. 41-20-32; fax 41-41-38.

Ministry of Security: Conakry.

Ministry of Social Affairs, the Promotion of Women and Children's Affairs: Corniche-Ouest, face au Terminal Conteneurs du Port de Conakry, BP 527, Conakry; tel. 41-20-15; fax 41-46-60.

Ministry of Technical Education and Professional Training: face aux Jardins du 2 Octobre, BP 2201, Conakry; tel. 41-44-84; fax 41-33-54.

Ministry of Territorial Administration and Decentralization: près de la Gendarmerie Nationale, BP 3495, Conakry; tel. 41-44-15; fax 45-45-07.

Ministry of Tourism, Hotels and Handicrafts: Conakry; tel. 41-49-94.

Ministry of Town Planning and Housing: blvd du Commerce, BP 846, Conakry; tel. 41-32-00; fax 41-46-88.

Ministry of Trade, Industry and Small and Medium-sized Enterprises: BP 468, Conakry; tel. 44-26-06; fax 44-49-90.

Ministry of Transport: BP 715, Conakry; tel. 41-36-39; fax 41-35-77.

Ministry of Youth, Sports and Culture: ave du Port Secrétariat, BP 262, Conakry; tel. 41-10-88; fax 41-19-26.

President and Legislature

PRESIDENT

Election, 21 December 2003

Candidate	Votes	% of votes
Lansana Conté (PUP)	3,884,594	95.25
Mamadou Bhoye Barry (UPN—PUD)	193,579	4.75
Total	**4,078,173**	**100.00**

ASSEMBLÉE NATIONALE

Assemblée nationale: Palais du Peuple, BP 414, Conakry; tel. 45-21-56; fax 45-17-00; e-mail s.general@assemblee.gov.gn; internet www.assemblee.gov.gn.

Speaker: ABOUBACAR SOMPARÉ.

General election, 30 June 2002

Party	% of votes	Seats
Parti de l'unité et du progrès (PUP)	61.57	85
Union pour le progrès et le renouveau (UPR)	26.63	20
Union pour le progrès de la Guinée (UPG)	4.11	3
Parti démocratique de Guinée—Rassemblement démocratique africain (PDG—RDA)	3.40	3
Alliance nationale pour le progrès (ANP)	1.98	2
Union pour le progrès national—Parti pour l'unité et le développement (UPN—PUD)	0.69	1
Others	1.61	—
Total	**100.00**	**114***

*Comprising 76 seats allocated by proportional representation from national party lists and 38 seats filled by voting in single-member constituencies, all of which were won by the PUP.

Advisory Council

Economic and Social Council: Immeuble FAWAZ, Corniche Sud, Coléaah, Matam, BP 2947, Conakry; tel. 45-21-35; fax 45-31-24; e-mail ces@sotelgui.net.gn; f. 1997; 45 mems; Pres. MICHEL KAMANO; Sec.-Gen. MAMADOU BOBO CAMARA.

Political Organizations

There were 46 officially registered parties in mid-2003, of which the following are the most important:

Alliance nationale pour le progrès (ANP): Conakry; opposes Govt of Pres. Conté; Leader Dr SAGNO MOUSSA.

Front de l'alternance démocratique (FRAD): Conakry; f. 2002; opposes Govt of Pres. Conté; boycotted legislative elections in 2002 and presidential election in 2003; Pres. MAMADOU BOYE BÀ; affiliated parties include:

> **Alliance nationale pour le developpement:** Conakry; Sec.-Gen. ANTOINE GBOKOLO SOROMOU.

> **Parti démocratique africain (PDA):** Conakry; Pres. MARCEL CROS.

> **Parti Dyama:** Conakry; moderate Islamist party; Leader MOHAMED MANSOUR KABA.

> **Rassemblement du peuple de Guinée (RPG):** Conakry; e-mail admin@rpgguinee.org; internet www.rpgguinee.org; socialist; Pres. ALPHA CONDÉ.

> **Union des forces démocratiques (UFD):** Conakry; Pres. (vacant).

> **Union des forces démocratiques de Guinée (UFDG):** Conakry; f. 2002 by faction of UPR (q.v.) in protest at that party's participation in elections to Assemblée nationale; Pres. MAMADOU BOYE BÀ; Sec.-Gen. AMADOU OURY BAH.

> **Union des forces républicaines (UFR):** Immeuble 'Le Golfe', 4e étage, BP 6080, Conakry; tel. 45-42-38; fax 45-42-31; e-mail ufrguinee@yahoo.fr; internet www.ufrguinee.net; f. 1992; liberal-conservative; Pres. SIDYA TOURÉ; Sec.-Gen. BAKARY G. ZOUMANIGUI.

> **Union pour le progrès de la Guinée (UPG):** Conakry; opposes Govt of Pres. Conté; Leader JEAN-MARIE DORÉ.

Parti démocratique de Guinée—Rassemblement démocratique africain (PDG—RDA): Conakry; f. 1946; revived 1992; supports Govt of Pres. Conté; Sec.-Gen. El Hadj ISMAËL MOHAMED GASSIM GHUSSEIN.

Parti écologiste de Guinée (PEG—Les Verts): BP 3018, Quartier Boulbinet, 5e blvd, angle 2e ave, Commune de Kaloum, Conakry; tel. 44-37-01; supports Govt of Pres. Conté; Leader OUMAR SYLLA.

Parti du peuple de Guinée (PPG): BP 1147, Conakry; socialist; opposes Govt of Pres. Conté; boycotted presidential election in 2003, following the Supreme Court's rejection of its nominated candidate; Leader CHARLES-PASCAL TOLNO.

Parti de l'unité et du progrès (PUP): Camayenne, Conakry; Pres. Gen. LANSANA CONTÉ; Sec.-Gen. El Hadj Dr SÉKOU KONATÉ.

Union pour le progrès et le renouveau (UPR): Conakry; f. 1998 by merger of the Parti pour le renouveau et le progrès and the Union pour la nouvelle République; opposes Govt of Pres. Conté; boycotted presidential election in 2003; Pres. OUSMANE BAH.

Union pour le progrès national—Parti pour l'unité et le développement (UPN—PUD): Conakry; Leader MAMADOU BHOYE BARRY.

Diplomatic Representation

EMBASSIES IN GUINEA

Algeria: Commune de Kaloum, face Etat Major de la Gendarmerie Nationale, BP 1004, Conakry; tel. 44-15-05; fax 41-15-35.

Canada: BP 99, South Cornish, Coléah, Conakry; tel. 46-23-95; fax 46-42-35; e-mail cnaky@dfait-maeci.gc.ca; Ambassador PHILIPPE BEAULNE.

China, People's Republic: Quartier Donka, Cité Ministérielle, Commune de Dixinn, BP 714, Conakry; tel. 41-48-35; fax 45-15-26; e-mail chinaemb_gn@mfa.gov.cn; Ambassador LIU YUKUN.

Congo, Democratic Republic: Quartier Almamya, ave de la Gare, Commune du Kaloum, BP 880, Conakry; tel. 45-15-01.

Côte d'Ivoire: blvd du Commerce, BP 5228, Conakry; tel. 45-10-82; fax 45-10-79; Ambassador JEANNOT ZORO BI BAH.

Cuba: Corniche-Nord 1162, Coronthie, Commune du Kaloum, BP 71, Conakry; tel. 41-42-68; fax 41-50-76; e-mail embagcon@sotelgui.net.gn; Ambassador MARCELLO CABALLERO TORRES.

Egypt: Corniche-Sud, BP 389, Conakry; tel. and fax 41-23-94; e-mail ambconakry@hotmail.com; Ambassador MOHAMED ABD ELHAY HASSOUNA.

France: Immeuble Chavanel, blvd du Commerce, BP 570, Conakry; tel. 41-16-05; fax 43-12-15; e-mail amb.fr.conakry@biasy.net; internet www.ambafrance-gn.org; Ambassador BERNADETTE LEFORT.

Germany: 2e blvd, Kaloum, BP 540, Conakry; tel. 41-15-06; fax 45-22-17; e-mail amball@sotelgui.net.gn; internet www.conakry.diplo.de; Ambassador Dr DIRK BAUMGARTNER.

Ghana: Immeuble Ex-Urbaine et la Seine, BP 732, Conakry; tel. 44-15-10; Ambassador Alhaji SHAIBU MUSAH SHARIF.

Guinea-Bissau: Quartier Bellevue, Commune de Dixinn, BP 298, Conakry; Ambassador MALAM CAMARA.

Holy See: La Minière, BP 2016, Conakry; tel. 42-26-76; fax 46-36-71; e-mail nonce@biasy.net; Apostolic Nuncio Most Rev. ALBERTO BOTTARI DE CASTELLO (Titular Archbishop of Foraziana).

Iran: Commune de Dixinn, BP 310, Conakry; tel. 22-01-97; fax 46-56-38; Ambassador JAVAD ROWSHAN ZAMIR.

Japan: Lanseboundji, Corniche Sud, Commune de Matam, BP 895, Conakry; tel. 46-85-10; fax 46-85-09; Ambassador KEIICHI KITABAN.

Korea, Democratic People's Republic: BP 723, Conakry; Ambassador KIM KYONG SIN.

Liberia: Cité Ministérielle, Donka, Commune de Dixinn, BP 18, Conakry; tel. 42-26-71; Chargé d'affaires a. i. SIAKA FAHNBULLEH.

Libya: Commune de Kaloum, BP 1183, Conakry; tel. 41-41-72; Ambassador B. AHMED.

Malaysia: quartier Mafanco, Coleah Corniche Sud, BP 5460, Conakry; tel. 46-76-54; fax 45-14-03; e-mail mwcnakry@sotelgui.net.gn; Ambassador OTHMAN SAMIN.

Mali: rue D1–15, Camayenne, Corniche Nord, BP 299, Conakry; tel. 46-14-18; fax 46-37-03; Ambassador HAMADOUN IBRAHIMA ISSABRÉ.

Morocco: Cité des Nations, Villa 12, Commune du Kaloum, BP 193, Conakry; tel. 41-36-86; fax 41-38-16; e-mail sifamgui@biasy.net; Ambassador MOHAMED LASFAR.

Nigeria: Corniche Sud, Quartier de Matam, BP 54, Conakry; tel. 41-43-75; Ambassador ABDULKADIR SANI.

Russia: Matam-Port, km 9, BP 329, Conakry; tel. 46-37-25; fax 41-27-77; e-mail ambrus@biasy.net; Ambassador DMITRII V. MALEV.

Saudi Arabia: Quartier Camayenne, Commune de Dixinn, BP 611, Conakry; tel. 46-24-87; fax 46-58-84; e-mail gnemb@mofa.gov.sa; Chargé d'affaires a. i. ABDULLAH NASSER AL-CHARIF.

Senegal: BP 842, Conakry; tel. and fax 44-44-13; Ambassador MAKHILY GASSAMA.

Sierra Leone: Quartier Bellevue, face aux cases présidentielles, Commune de Dixinn, BP 625, Conakry; tel. 44-50-08; Ambassador Commdr MOHAMED DIABY.

Ukraine: Commune de Calum, Corniche Nord, Quartier Camayenne, BP 1350, Conakry; tel. 45-37-56; fax 45-37-95; e-mail ambgv@sotelgui.net.gn; Chargé d'affaires OLEKSANDR O. SHULGA.

United Kingdom: BP 6729, Conakry; tel. 45-58-07; fax 45-60-20; e-mail britcon.oury@biasy.net; Ambassador JOHN McMANUS.

USA: rue KA 038, BP 603, Conakry; tel. 41-15-20; fax 41-15-22; e-mail amemconakry.adm@eti-bull.net; internet usembassy.state.gov/conakry; Ambassador JACKSON CHESTER McDONALD.

Judicial System

The Constitution of the Third Republic embodies the principle of the independence of the judiciary, and delineates the competences of each component of the judicial system, including the Higher Magistrates' Council, the Supreme Court, the High Court of Justice and the Magistrature.

Supreme Court
Corniche-Sud, Camayenne, Conakry; tel. 41-11-67.

Director of Public Prosecutions: ANTOINE IBRAHIM DIALLO.

Note: A State Security Court was established in June 1997, with exceptional jurisdiction to try, 'in times of peace and war', crimes against the internal and external security of the State. Members of the court are appointed by the President of the Republic. There is no constitutional provision for the existence of such a tribunal.

President of the State Security Court: Commdr SAMA PANNIVAL BANGOURA.

Religion

It is estimated that 85% of the population are Muslims and 8% Christians, while 7% follow animist beliefs.

ISLAM

Ligue Islamique Nationale: BP 386, Conakry; tel. 41-23-33; f. 1988; Sec.-Gen. El Hadj AHMED TIDIANE TRAORÉ.

CHRISTIANITY

The Roman Catholic Church

Guinea comprises one archdiocese and two dioceses. At 31 December 2002 there were an estimated 170,199 Roman Catholics in Guinea, comprising about 2.6% of the total population.

Bishops' Conference

Conférence Episcopale de la Guinée, BP 1006 bis, Conakry; tel. and fax 41-32-70; e-mail dhewara@eti.met.gn.

Pres. Most Rev. PHILIPPE KOUROUMA (Bishop of N'Zérékoré).

Archbishop of Conakry: Most Rev. VINCENT COULIBALY, Archevêché, BP 2016, Conakry; tel. and fax 41-32-70; e-mail dhewara@eti.met.gn.

The Anglican Communion

Anglicans in Guinea are adherents of the Church of the Province of West Africa, comprising 12 dioceses. The diocese of Guinea was established in 1985 as the first French-speaking diocese in the Province. The Archbishop and Primate of the Province is the Bishop of Koforidua, Ghana.

Bishop of Guinea: Rt Rev. ALBERT D. GÓMEZ, Cathédrale Toussaint, BP 105, Conakry; tel. 45-13-23.

BAHÁ'Í FAITH

Assemblée spirituelle nationale: BP 2010, Conakry 1; e-mail kouchek@sotelgui.net.gn.

The Press

REGULATORY AUTHORITY

Conseil National de la Communication (CNC): en face Primature, BP 2955, Conakry; tel. 46-15-05; fax 41-23-85; f. 1991; regulates the operations of the press, and of radio and television; regulates political access to the media; nine mems; two meetings each week; Pres. (vacant).

NEWSPAPERS AND PERIODICALS

In early 2004 there were more than 200 periodicals and newspapers officially registered with the Conseil National de la Communication, although only around 60 were believed to be in operation at that time.

Le Démocrate: Quartier Manquepas, 4e ave, axe Soguidip-Ministère des finances, près du restaurant 'Relaxe', Commune de Kaloum, BP 2427, Conakry; tel. 45-54-34; fax 41-43-19; e-mail mamadoudianb@yahoo.fr; internet www.mirinet.com/lindependant/ledemocrate/index.htm; weekly; Editor-in-Chief THIERNO DAYEDIO BARRY.

Le Diplomate: BP 2427, Conakry; tel. and fax 41-23-85; f. 2002; weekly; Dir SANOU KERFALLAH CISSÉ.

L'Enquêteur: Conakry; e-mail yacine@boubah.com; internet www.boubah.com/hosting/enqueteur; f. 2001; two a month; Editor BOUABACAR YACINE DIALLO.

L'Evénement de Guinée: BP 796, Conakry; tel. 44-33-91; monthly; independent; f. 1993; Dir BOUBACAR SANKARELA DIALLO.

Fonike: BP 341, Conakry; sport and general; Dir IBRAHIMA KALIL DIARE.

La Guinée Actuelle: Sans Fils, près Le Makity, BP 3618, Conakry; tel. 69-36-20.

Le Guinéen: Conakry; f. 2002; Dir JEAN-MARIE MORGAN.

Horoya (Liberty): Coléah, BP 191, Conakry; tel. 41-34-75; fax 45-10-16; e-mail horoya@leland-gn.org; govt daily; Dir OUSMANE CAMARA.

L'Indépendant: Quartier Manquepas, 4e ave, axe Soguidip-Ministère des finances, près du restaurant 'Relaxe', Commune de Kaloum, BP 2427, Conakry; tel. 54-20-24; fax 41-43-19; e-mail lindependant@afribone.net.gn; internet www.mirinet.com/lindependant; weekly; also *L'Indépendant Plus*; Publr ABOUBACAR SYLLA; Editor-in-Chief HASSANE KABA; Editor-in-Chief, *L'Indépendant Plus* ALADJI CELLOU.

Journal Officiel de Guinée: BP 156, Conakry; fortnightly; organ of the Govt.

La Lance: route du Palais du Peuple, BP 2427, Conakry; tel. and fax 41-23-85; internet www.mirinet.com/lynx/lce; weekly; general information; Dir SOULEYMANE E. DIALLO.

Le Lynx: Immeuble Baldé Zaïre Sandervalia, BP 4968, Conakry; tel. 41-23-85; fax 45-36-96; e-mail le-lynx@afribone.net.gn; internet www.mirinet.net.gn/lynx; f. 1992; weekly; satirical; Editor SOULEYMANE DIALLO.

La Nouvelle Tribune: blvd Diallo Tally entre 5e et 6e avenue, BP 6698, Conakry; tel. 54-69-79; e-mail abdcond@yahoo.fr; weekly, Tuesdays; independent; general information and analysis; Dir of Publication and Editing ABDOULAYE CONDÉ.

L'Observateur: Immeuble Baldé, Conakry; tel. 40-05-24; independent; Dir EL-BÉCHIR DIALLO.

L'Oeil du Peuple: Conakry; weekly; independent; Dir of Publishing ISMAËL BANGOURA.

Sanakou: Labé, Foutah Djallon, Moyenne-Guinée; tel. 51-13-19; e-mail sanakoulabe@yahoo.fr; f. 2000; monthly; general news; Publr IDRISSA SAMPIRING DIALLO; Editor-in-Chief YAMOUSSA SOUMAH; circ. 1,000.

Le Scribe: 124 rue MO-268, BP 1305, Conakry; tel. 22-75-87; internet www.mirinet.net.gn/lescribe/; f. 1997; evangelical Christian magazine; Dir JOSEPH SOURO CAMARA; Editor-in-Chief PIERRE CAMARA.

Le Soleil: BP 3576, Conakry; tel. 67-17-73; e-mail soleil2000gn@yahoo.fr.

3-P Plus (Parole-Plume-Papier) Magazine: 7e ave Bis Almamyah, BP 5122, Conakry; tel. 45-22-32; fax 45-29-31; e-mail 3p-plus@mirinet.net.gn; internet www.mirinet.net.gn/3p_plus; journal of arts and letters; supplements *Le Cahier de l'Economie, Mag-Plus: Le Magazine de la Culture*; monthly; Pres. MOHAMED SALIFOU KEÏTA; Editor-in-Chief NAMAN CAMARA.

NEWS AGENCY

Agence Guinéenne de Presse: BP 1535, Conakry; tel. 46-54-14; f. 1960; Man. Dir MOHAMED CONDÉ.

PRESS ASSOCIATION

Association Guinéenne des Editeurs de la Presse Indépendante (AGEPI): Conakry; f. 1991; an asscn of independent newspaper publishers; Chair. BOUBACAR SANKARELA DIALLO.

Publishers

Les Classiques Guinéens (SEDIS sarl): 545 rue KA020, Mauquepas, BP 3697, Conakry; tel. 11-21-18-57 ; fax 13-40-92-62; e-mail cheick.sedis@mirinet.net.gn; f. 1999; art, history, youth litertaure; Dir CHEICK ABDOUL KABA.

Editions du Ministère de l'Education Nationale: Direction nationale de la recherche scientifique, BP 561, Conakry; tel. 44-19-50; f. 1959; general and educational; Dir Prof. KANTÉ KABINÉ.

Editions Ganndal (Knowledge): BP 542, Conakry; tel. and fax 46-35-07; e-mail ganndal@mirinet.net.gn; internet www.editionsganndal.com; f. 1992; educational, youth and children, general literature and books in Pular; Dir MAMADOU ALIOU SOW.

Société Africaine d'Edition et de Communication (SEAC): Belle-Vue, Commune de Dixinn, BP 6826, Conakry; tel. 29-71-41; e-mail dtniane@yahoo.fr; social sciences, reference, literary fiction; Editorial Assistant OUMAR TALL.

Broadcasting and Communications

TELECOMMUNICATIONS

Regulatory Bodies

Comité National de Coordination des Télécommunications (CNCT): BP 5000, Conakry; tel. 41-40-79; fax 45-31-16; Exec. Sec. SEKOU BANGOURA.

Direction Nationale des Postes et Télécommunications (DNPT): BP 5000, Conakry; tel. 41-13-31; fax 45-31-16; e-mail dnpt.dnr@biasy.net; f. 1997; regulates transport, postal and telecommunications services; Dir KOLY CAMARA.

Service Providers

Intercel: Quartier Coleah Larseboundji, près du pont du 8 Novembre, Immeuble le Golfe, BP 965, Conakry; tel. 45-57-44; fax 40-92-92; e-mail info@gn.intercel.net; mobile cellular telephone operator; fmrly Telecel Guinée; Dir FRANÇOIS DICK.

Société des Télécommunications de Guinée (SOTELGUI): 4e blvd, BP 2066, Conakry; tel. 41-12-12; fax 45-02-01; e-mail marzuki@sotelgui.net.gn; internet www.sotelgui.net.gn; f. 1993; privatized 1995; 60% owned by Telkom Malaysia; 40% state-owned; also provides mobile cellular services (as Lagui); 51,020 subscribers (1998); Dir El Hadj MARZUKI ABDULLAH.

Spacetel Guinée SA (Mobilis Guinée): BP 835, Conakry; tel. and fax 12-66-00-11; e-mail info@spacetelguinee.com; f. 1994; mobile cellular telephone operator; operates with a range of 70km around Conakry; 35,000 subscribers (2002); also operates GSM satellite telephone network; Chair. K. ABOU KHALIL.

BROADCASTING

Regulatory Authority

Conseil National de la Communication (CNC): see The Press.

Radio

Radiodiffusion-Télévision Guinéenne (RTG): BP 391, Conakry; tel. 44-22-01; fax 41-50-01; broadcasts in French, English, Créole-English, Portuguese, Arabic and local languages; Dir-Gen. AISSATOU BELLA DIALLO; Dir of Radio ISSA CONDÉ.

Radio Rurale de Guinée: BP 391, Conakry; tel. 2-11-09; fax 41-47-97; e-mail ruralgui@mirinet.net.gn; network of rural radio stations.

Television

Radiodiffusion-Télévision Guinéenne (RTG): see Radio; transmissions in French and local languages; one channel; f. 1977.

Finance

(cap. = capital; res = reserves; m. = million; brs = branches; amounts in Guinean francs)

BANKING

Central Bank

Banque Centrale de la République de Guinée (BCRG): 12 blvd du Commerce, BP 692, Kaloum, Conakry; tel. 41-26-51; fax 41-48-98; e-mail gouv.bcrg@eti-bull.net; internet www.bcrg.gov.gn; f. 1960; bank of issue; Gov. ALKALY MOHAMED DAFFE; Dep. Gov. DAOUDA BANGOURA.

Commercial Banks

Banque Internationale pour le Commerce et l'Industrie de la Guinée (BICI—GUI): ave de la République, BP 1484, Conakry; tel. 41-45-15; fax 41-39-62; e-mail dg.bicigui@biasy.net; f. 1985; 51% state-owned, affiliated to BNP Paribas (France); cap. and res 25,299.7m., total assets 230,278.8m. (Dec. 2001); Pres. IBRAHIMA SOUMAH; Dir-Gen. BERNARD DELEUZE; 11 brs.

Banque Populaire Maroco-Guinéenne (BPMG): Immeuble BPMG, blvd du Commerce, Kaloum, BP 4400, Conakry 01; tel. 41-36-93; fax 41-32-61; e-mail bpmg@sotelgui.net.gn; internet www.bpmg.net.gn; f. 1991; 55% owned by Crédit Populaire du Maroc, 42% state-owned; cap. 24.7m., res 5.2m., dep. 20.5m. (Dec. 2002); Pres. EMMANUEL GNAN; Dir-Gen. AHMED HOUSSAINI IRAQUI; 3 brs.

Ecobank Guinée: Immeuble Al Iman, ave de la République, BP 5687, Conakry; tel. 45-58-77; fax 45-42-41; e-mail ecobankgn@ecobank.com; internet www.ecobank.com; f. 1999; wholly owned by Ecobank Transnational Inc. (Togo—operating under the auspices of the Economic Community of West African States); cap. and res 6,474.2m., total assets 70,602.9m. (Dec. 2001); Pres. SANGARE N'FALY; Man. Dir KUMLAN ADJARHO OWEH; 2 brs.

First American Bank of Guinea: blvd du Commerce, angle 9e ave, BP 4540, Conakry; tel. 41-34-32; fax 41-35-29; f. 1994; jt-owned by Mitan Capital Ltd, Grand Cayman and El Hadj Haidara Abdourahmane Chérif, Mali.

International Commercial Bank: 4e ave Boulbinet, Bâtiment 346, BP 3547, Conakry; tel. 41-25-89; fax 41-25-92; f. 1997; total assets 19.6m. (Dec. 1999); Pres. JOSÉPHINE PREMLA; Man. Dir HAMZA BIN ALIAS.

Société Générale de Banques en Guinée (SGBG): Immeuble Boffa, Cité du Chemin de Fer, BP 1514, Conakry; tel. 41-17-41; fax 41-25-65; e-mail contact@sgbg.net.gn; internet www.sgbg.net.gn; f. 1985; 42% owned by Société Générale (France); cap. and res 10,988m., total assets 130,514m. (Dec. 2001); Pres., Dir-Gen. and Administrator DANIEL TERUIN; 5 brs.

Union Internationale de Banques en Guinée (UIBG): 6e ave de la République, angle 5e blvd, BP 324, Conakry; tel. 41-43-09; fax 97-26-30; e-mail uibg@financial-bank.com; f. 1988; 68.3% owned by FINANCIAL; cap. and res 5,700m., total assets 104,000m. (Dec. 2004); Pres. ALPHA AMADOU DIALLO; Dir-Gen. JACQUES DE VIGNAUD.

Islamic Bank

Banque Islamique de Guinée: Immeuble Nafaya, 6 ave de la République, BP 1247, Conakry; tel. 41-50-86; fax 41-50-71; e-mail bigmiconakry@eti-bull.net; f. 1983; 68.5% owned by Dar al-Maal al-Islami Trust (Switzerland); cap. and res 8,500.0m., total assets 24,983.3m. (Dec. 2001); Pres. ADERRAOUF BENESSAIAH; Dir-Gen. AZHAR SALEEM KHAN.

INSURANCE

Gras Savoye Guinée: 4e ave, angle 4e blvd, Quartier Boulbinet, Commune de Kaloum, Conakry; tel. 45-58-43; fax 45-58-42; e-mail grasavoye@biasy.net; internet www.grassavoye.com; affiliated to Gras Savoye (France); Man. CHÉRIF BAH.

Société Guinéenne d'Assurance Mutuelle (SOGAM): BP 4340, Conakry; tel. 44-50-58; fax 41-25-57; f. 1990; Chair. Dr M. K. BAH; Man. Dir P. I. NDAO.

Société Nouvelle d'Assurance de Guinée (SONAG): BP 3363, Conakry; tel. 41-49-77; fax 41-43-03.

Union Guinéenne d'Assurances et de Réassurances (UGAR): Place des Martyrs, BP 179, Conakry; tel. 41-48-41; fax 41-17-11; e-mail ugar@ugar.com.gn; f. 1989; 40% owned by AXA (France), 35% state-owned; cap. 2,000m.; Man. Dir RAPHAËL Y. TOURÉ.

Trade and Industry

GOVERNMENT AGENCIES

Centre de Promotion et de Développement Miniers (CPDM): BP 295, Conakry; tel. 41-15-44; fax 41-49-13; e-mail cpdm@mirinet.net.gn; f. 1995; promotes investment and co-ordinates devt strategy in mining sector; Dir MOCIRÉ SYLLA.

Entreprise Nationale Import-Export (IMPORTEX): BP 152, Conakry; tel. 44-28-13; state-owned import and export agency; Dir MAMADOU BOBO DIENG.

Office de Promotion des Investissements Privés-Guichet Unique (OPIP): Conakry; tel. 41-49-85; fax 41-39-90; e-mail dg@opip.org.gn; f. 1992; promotes private investment; Dir-Gen. DIANKA KOEVOGUI.

DEVELOPMENT ORGANIZATIONS

Agence Française de Développement (AFD): 5e ave, BP 283, Conakry; tel. 41-25-69; fax 41-28-74; e-mail afd@mirinet.net.gn; internet www.afd.fr; Dir in Guinea YVES BOUDOT.

Association Française des Volontaires du Progrès (AFVP): BP 570, Conakry; tel. 46-14-78; fax 46-20-71; e-mail afvp-gui@biasy.net; internet www.afvp.org; f. 1987; development and research projects; Nat. Delegate EMMANUEL POILANE.

Mission Française de Coopération et d'Action Culturelle: BP 373, Conakry; tel. 41-23-45; fax 41-43-56; administers bilateral aid; Dir in Guinea ANDRÉ BAILLEUL.

CHAMBERS OF COMMERCE

Chambre de Commerce, d'Industrie et de l'Artisanat (CCIA): BP 545, Conakry; tel. 45-45-16; fax 45-45-17; f. 1985; Pres. El Hadj MAMADOU SYLLA.

Chambre Economique de Guinée: BP 609, Conakry.

TRADE AND EMPLOYERS' ASSOCIATIONS

Association des Commerçants de Guinée: BP 2468, Conakry; tel. 41-30-37; fax 45-31-66; Sec.-Gen. OUMAR CAMARA.

Association des Femmes Entrepreneurs de Guinée (AFEG): BP 104, Conakry; tel. 28-02-95; fax 41-32-06; e-mail afeguine@yahoo.fr.

Conseil National du Patronat Guinéen (CNPG): Dixinn Bora, BP 6403, Conakry; tel. and fax 41-24-70; e-mail msylla@leland-gn.org; f. 1992; Pres. El Hadj MAMADOU SYLLA.

Fédération Patronale de l'Agriculture et de l'Elevage (FEPAE): BP 5684, Conakry; tel. 22-95-56; fax 41-54-36; Pres. El Hadj MAMDOU SYLLA; Sec.-Gen. MAMADY CAMARA.

Groupement des Importateurs Guinéens (GIG): BP 970, Conakry; tel. 42-18-18; fax 42-19-19; Pres. FERNAND BANGOURA.

UTILITIES

Electricity

Barrage Hydroélectrique de Garafiri: BP 1770, Conakry; tel. 41-50-91; inaugurated 1999.

Electricité de Guinée (EDG): BP 1463, Conakry; tel. 45-18-56; fax 45-18-53; e-mail di.sogel@biasy.net; f. 2001 to replace Société Guinéenne d'Electricité; majority state-owned; production, transport and distribution of electricity; Dir-Gen. NOUCTAR BARRY.

Entreprise Nationale d'Electricité de Guinée (ENELGUI): BP 322, Conakry; tel. 41-42-43; fax 44-17-51; production of electricity; Man. Dir BOKARY SYLLA.

Water

Service National d'Aménagement des Points d'Eau (SNAPE): BP 2064, Conakry; tel. 41-18-93; fax 41-50-58; e-mail snape@mirinet .net.gn; supplies water in rural areas.

Société Nationale des Eaux de Guinée (SONEG): BP 150, Conakry; tel. 45-44-77; e-mail oaubot@seg.org.gn; f. 1988; national water co; Dir-Gen. Dr OUSMANE ARIBOT; Sec.-Gen. MAMADOU DIOP.

TRADE UNIONS

Confédération Nationale des Travailleurs de Guinée (CNTG): Bourse du Travail, Corniche Sud 004, BP 237, Conakry; tel. and fax 41-50-44; f. 1984; Sec.-Gen. MOHAMED SAMBA KÉBÉ.

Organisation Nationale des Syndicats Libres de Guinée (ONSLG): BP 559, Conakry; tel. 41-52-17; fax 43-02-83; 27,000 mems (1996).

Union Syndicale des Travailleurs de Guinée (USTG): BP 1514, Conakry; tel. 41-25-65; fax 41-25-58; 26,000 mems (1996).

Transport

RAILWAYS

There are 1,086 km of railways in Guinea, including 662 km of 1-m gauge track from Conakry to Kankan in the east of the country, crossing the Niger at Kouroussa. The contract for the first phase of the upgrading of this line was awarded to a Slovak company in early 1997. Three lines for the transport of bauxite link Sangaredi with the port of Kamsar in the west, via Boké, and Conakry with Kindia and Fria, a total of 383 km.

Office National des Chemins de Fer de Guinée (ONCFG): BP 589, Conakry; tel. 44-46-13; fax 41-35-77; f. 1905; Man. Dir MOREL MARGUERITE CAMARA.

Chemin de Fer de Boké: BP 523, Boké; operations commenced 1973.

Chemin de Fer Conakry–Fria: BP 334, Conakry; operations commenced 1960; Gen. Man. A. CAMARA.

Chemin de Fer de la Société des Bauxites de Kindia: BP 613, Conakry; tel. 41-38-28; operations commenced 1974; Gen. Man. K. KEITA.

ROADS

The road network comprised 21,215 km of roads (of which 1,959 km were paved) in 1999. An 895-km cross-country road links Conakry to Bamako, in Mali, and the main highway connecting Dakar (Senegal) to Abidjan (Côte d'Ivoire) also crosses Guinea. The road linking Conakry to Freetown (Sierra Leone) forms part of the Trans West African Highway, extending from Morocco to Nigeria.

La Guinéenne-Marocaine des Transports (GUIMAT): Conakry; f. 1989; owned jtly by Govt of Guinea and Hakkam (Morocco); operates national and regional transport services.

Société Générale des Transports de Guinée (SOGETRAG): Conakry; f. 1985; 63% state-owned; bus operator.

SHIPPING

Conakry and Kamsar are the international seaports. Conakry handled 3.9m. metric tons of foreign trade in 1999, while in 1994 some 12m. tons of bauxite were transported to Kamsar for shipment.

Getma Guinea SA: Cité du Chemin de Fer, BP 1648, Conakry; tel. 41-32-05; fax 41-42-73; e-mail contact@getma.com; internet www .getma.com; f. 1978; fmrly Société Guinéenne d'Entreprises de Transports Maritimes et Aeriens; marine transportation; Chair. JEAN-JACQUES GRENIER.

Port Autonome de Conakry (PAC): BP 805, Conakry; tel. 41-27-28; fax 41-26-04; e-mail pac@eti-bull.net; haulage, porterage; Gen. Man. ALIOU DIALLO.

Société Navale Guinéenne (SNG): BP 522, Conakry; tel. 44-29-55; fax 41-39-70; f. 1968; state-owned; shipping agents; Dir-Gen. NOUNKÉ KEITA.

SOAEM: BP 3177, Conakry; tel. 41-25-90; fax 41-20-25; e-mail soaem.gn@mirinet.net.gn.

SOTRAMAR: Kamsar; e-mail sotramar@sotramar.com; f. 1971; exports bauxite from mines at Boké through port of Kamsar.

Transmar: 33 blvd du Commerce, Kaloum, BP 3917, Conakry; tel. 43-05-41; fax 43-05-42; e-mail transmar@eti.net.gn; shipping, stevedoring, inland transport.

CIVIL AVIATION

There is an international airport at Conakry-Gbessia, and smaller airfields at Labé, Kankan and Faranah. Facilities at Conakry have been upgraded, at a cost of US $42.6m.; the airport handled some 300,000 passengers in 1999.

Air Guinée Express: 6 ave de la République, BP 12, Conakry; tel. 44-46-02; fax 41-29-07; e-mail air-guinee@mirinet.net.gn; f. 2002 to replace Air Guinée (f. 1960); regional and internal services; Dir-Gen. ANTOINE CROS.

Guinée Air Service: Aéroport Conakry-Gbessia; tel. 41-27-61.

Guinée Inter Air: Aéroport Conakry-Gbessia; tel. 41-37-08.

Société de Gestion et d'Exploitation de l'Aéroport de Conakry (SOGEAC): BP 3126, Conakry; tel. 46-48-03; f. 1987; manages Conakry-Gbessia international airport; 51% state-owned.

Union des Transports Aériens de Guinée (UTA): scheduled and charter flights to regional and international destinations.

Tourism

Some 42,507 tourists visited Guinea in 2002; receipts from tourism in that year totalled an estimated US $31m., an increase from $14m. in 2001.

Office National du Tourisme: Immeuble al-Iman, 6e ave de la République, BP 1275, Conakry; tel. 45-51-63; fax 45-51-64; e-mail ontour@leland-gn.org; internet www.mirinet.net.gn/ont; f. 1997; Dir-Gen. IBRAHIM A. DIALLO.

GUINEA-BISSAU

Introductory Survey

Location, Climate, Language, Religion, Flag, Capital

The Republic of Guinea-Bissau lies on the west coast of Africa, with Senegal to the north and Guinea to the east and south. The climate is tropical, although maritime and Sahelian influences are felt. The average temperature is 20°C (68°F). The official language is Portuguese, of which the locally spoken form is Creole (Crioulo). There are 19 local languages, of which the most widely spoken are Balanta-Kentohe, Pulaar (Fula), Mandjak, Mandinka and Papel. The principal religious beliefs are animism and Islam. There is a small minority of Roman Catholics and other Christian groups. The national flag (proportions 1 by 2) has two equal horizontal stripes, of yellow over light green, and a red vertical stripe, with a five-pointed black star at its centre, at the hoist. The capital is Bissau.

Recent History

Portuguese Guinea (Guiné) was colonized by Portugal in the 15th century. Nationalist activism began to emerge in the 1950s. Armed insurgency commenced in the early 1960s, and by 1972 the Partido Africano da Independência da Guiné e Cabo Verde (PAIGC) was in control of two-thirds of the country. The independence of the Republic of Guinea-Bissau was unilaterally proclaimed in September 1973, with Luís Cabral (the brother of the founder of the PAIGC, Amílcar Cabral) as President of the State Council. Hostilities ceased following the military coup in Portugal in April 1974, and on 10 September Portugal recognized the independence of Guinea-Bissau under the leadership of Luís Cabral.

The PAIGC regime introduced measures to establish a single-party socialist state. At elections in December 1976 and January 1977 voters chose regional councils from which a new National People's Assembly (Assembléia Nacional Popular—ANP) was later selected. In 1978 the Chief State Commissioner, Francisco Mendes, died; he was succeeded by Commander João Vieira, hitherto State Commissioner for the Armed Forces and President of the ANP.

The PAIGC initially supervised both Cape Verde and Guinea-Bissau, the Constitutions of each remaining separate but with a view to eventual unification. These arrangements were terminated in November 1980, when President Cabral was deposed in a coup organized by Vieira, who was installed as Chairman of the Council of the Revolution. Diplomatic relations between Guinea-Bissau and Cape Verde were restored after the release of Cabral from detention in 1982. In May 1982 President Vieira removed several left-wing ministers from the Government and appointed Vítor Saúde Maria, Vice-Chairman of the Council of the Revolution and former Minister of Foreign Affairs, as Prime Minister.

In 1983 Vieira established a commission to examine plans for the revision of the Constitution and the electoral code. In March 1984 Vieira dismissed Saúde Maria from the premiership. Although his removal from office was attributed to his alleged involvement in a coup plot, it appeared that the principal reason for Saúde Maria's dismissal was his opposition to the proposed constitutional changes, which would accord more power to the President. In late March Vieira formally assumed the role of Head of Government, and elections to regional councils took place. In May the ANP, which had been dissolved following the 1980 coup, was re-established, and the Council of the Revolution was replaced by a 15-member Council of State (Conselho de Estado), selected from among the members of the ANP. Vieira was subsequently elected as President of the Conselho de Estado and Head of State. The ANP immediately ratified the new Constitution, and formally abolished the position of Prime Minister.

A campaign against corruption, initiated by Vieira in August 1985, apparently provoked a military coup attempt in November, led by Col Paulo Correia, the First Vice-President of the Conselho de Estado, and other senior army officers. Correia was subsequently executed. In November 1986 the PAIGC endorsed proposals for the liberalization of the economy and re-elected Vieira as party Secretary-General for a further four years. In February 1987 Vieira appointed Dr Vasco Cabral, hitherto Minister of Justice, as Permanent Secretary of the Central Committee of the PAIGC, in an attempt to reinforce party support for the programme of economic liberalization.

In early 1989 it was announced that the PAIGC had established a six-member national commission to revise the Constitution. Regional elections took place in early June, at which 95.8% of those who voted endorsed the single PAIGC list. In mid-June the Regional Councils, in turn, elected the ANP, which subsequently elected the Conselho de Estado, of which Vieira was re-elected President.

In December 1990 the Central Committee of the PAIGC agreed to the adoption of a multi-party system, following a period of transition, and the holding of a presidential election in 1993. In May 1991 a series of constitutional amendments ending one-party rule were approved by the ANP, terminating the political monopoly of the PAIGC. In addition, all links between the PAIGC and the armed forces were severed, and the introduction of a free-market economy was guaranteed. New legislation in October accorded greater freedom to the press and permitted the formation of new trade unions. In November the Frente Democrática (FD) became the first opposition party to obtain official registration.

In December 1991 a major government reshuffle took place, in which the office of Prime Minister was restored. Carlos Correia was appointed to the post. In late 1991 and early 1992 three further opposition parties obtained legal status: the Resistência da Guiné-Bissau—Movimento Bah-Fatah (RGB—MB), led by Domingos Fernandes Gomes; the Frente Democrática Social (FDS), led by Rafael Barbosa; and the Partido Unido Social Democrático (PUSD), led by Vítor Saúde Maria. Following a split in the FDS, a further party, the Partido para a Renovação Social (PRS), was established in January 1992 by the former Vice-Chairman of the FDS, Kumba Yalá. In the same month four opposition parties—the PUSD, FDS, RGB—MB and the Partido da Convergência Democrática (PCD), led by Victor Mandinga—agreed on the establishment of a 'democratic forum', whose demands included the dissolution of the political police, the creation of an electoral commission and an all-party consultation on the setting of election dates.

In May 1992 a dissident group, known as the 'Group of 121', broke away from the PAIGC to form the Partido de Renovação e Desenvolvimento (PRD). In mid-May the leader of the RGB—MB, Domingos Fernandes Gomes, returned from exile in Portugal and, with the leaders of the FD, PCD, FDS and the PUSD, met Vieira to discuss further democratic reform. In July 1992, following threats by the 'democratic forum' that it would form a parallel government and boycott elections if the PAIGC did not seek consensus with the opposition on electoral issues, the Government agreed to establish a multi-party national transition commission to organize and oversee the democratic process. In late July the leader of the Frente da Luta para a Libertação da Guiné, François Kankoila Mendy, returned from The Gambia after a 40-year exile. Two further opposition parties were legalized in August. In November 1992 the Government announced the postponement of presidential and legislative elections until March 1993.

Legislation preparing for the transition to a multi-party democracy was approved by the ANP in February 1993, and in the following month a commission was appointed to supervise the forthcoming elections. However, reports in March of an attempted coup threatened to disrupt the transition to democracy. Initial reports indicated that Maj. Robalo de Pina, commander of the Forças de Intervenção Rápida (an élite guard responsible for presidential security), had been assassinated in what appeared to be an army rebellion, provoked by disaffection at poor standards of pay and living conditions. Some 50 people were arrested, including the leader of the PRD, João da Costa. Opposition politicians claimed that the incident had been contrived by the Government in an effort to discredit the opposition. Da Costa and nine other PRD detainees were released in June pending trial, but were forbidden to engage in political activity. In May, following a further split in the FDS, a new political party, the Partido da Convenção Nacional , was formed. In July

Vieira announced that multi-party presidential and legislative elections would be held in March 1994. In August 1993 da Costa was rearrested for allegedly violating the conditions of his parole, prompting renewed accusations by opposition politicians that the Government's actions were politically motivated. Following a threatened boycott of the National Electoral Commission by the opposition, da Costa was conditionally released. He was subsequently tried, but was acquitted in February 1994.

One week before the designated date of the elections, Vieira announced their postponement, owing to financial and technical difficulties. In May 1994 it was announced that the elections would be held in July. In early May six opposition parties, the FD, the FDS, the Movimento para a Unidade e a Democracia, the Partido Democrático do Progresso, the PRD and the Liga Guineense de Protecção Ecológica (LIPE), formed a coalition, the União para a Mudança (UM). The elections took place on 3 July, although voting was extended for two days, owing to logistical problems. The PAIGC secured a clear majority in the ANP, winning 62 of the 100 seats, while in the presidential election Vieira obtained 46.3% of the votes, and his nearest rival, Kumba Yalá of the PRS, secured 21.9% of the votes. As no candidate had obtained an absolute majority, the two leading candidates contested a second round of polling on 7 August. Despite receiving the combined support of all the opposition parties, Yalá was narrowly defeated, securing 48.0% of the votes, compared with Vieira's 52.0%. International observers later declared the elections to have been free and fair. Vieira was inaugurated as President on 29 September and appointed Manuel Saturnino da Costa (the Secretary-General of the PAIGC) as Prime Minister in late October. The Council of Ministers was appointed in November, comprising solely members of the PAIGC.

In April 1995 the UM coalition was reconstituted; João da Costa was elected President and Amine Saad Secretary-General. The LIPE, which had two representatives in the legislature and was a member of the original UM coalition, did not join the new organization, which was granted legal status in November. In August legal status was granted to a new party, the Partido Social Democrático (PSD), formed by dissidents from the RGB—MB.

Guinea-Bissau attained membership of the Union économique et monétaire ouest-africaine (see p. 267) in March 1997 and entered the Franc Zone in April. The national currency was replaced by the franc CFA, and the Banque centrale des états de l'Afrique de l'ouest assumed central banking functions.

In May 1997, in order to address what Vieira described as a serious political crisis that was undermining the functioning of the State, da Costa was dismissed. Carlos Correia was subsequently appointed Prime Minister, and a new 14-member Council of Ministers was inaugurated in June. In October Correia was dismissed, bringing to an end an institutional crisis that had lasted since his appointment. The legislative process had been obstructed by opposition deputies who claimed that, by omitting to consult those parties represented in the legislature on Correia's appointment, Vieira had acted unconstitutionally. In October the Supreme Court ruled that Vieira had indeed contravened the Constitution. Following consultations with party leaders, Vieira reappointed Correia, with the full support of the main opposition parties.

In March 1998, following protest by opposition parties at delays in the organization of legislative elections, an independent national elections commission was established. The elections were due to be held in July. In April a new political party, the União Nacional para a Democracia e o Progresso (UNDP) was established. In the same month Brig. (later Gen.) Ansumane Mané, who had recently been dismissed as Chief of Staff of the Armed Forces, publicly accused the Minister of Defence and a group of officers of the armed forces of involvement in arms-trafficking to separatists from the Senegalese region of Casamance, a practice which, he maintained, continued with the acquiescence of Vieira.

In June 1998 rebel troops, led by Mané, seized control of the Bra military barracks in the capital, as well as other strategic locations in the city, including the international airport. Mané subsequently formed a 'military junta for the consolidation of democracy, peace and justice' and demanded the resignation of Vieira and his administration. With the support of Senegalese and Guinean soldiers, troops loyal to the Government attempted unsuccessfully to regain control of rebel-held areas of the city, and heavy fighting ensued. Over the following days more than 3,000 foreign nationals were evacuated from the capital to Senegal. An estimated further 200,000 residents of Bissau fled

the city. Fighting continued into July, with many members of the Guinea-Bissau armed forces reportedly defecting to the side of the rebels.

On 26 July 1998, following mediation by a delegation from the lusophone commonwealth body, the Comunidade dos Países de Língua Portuguesa (CPLP, see below), the Government and the rebels agreed to implement a truce. In August representatives of the Government and the rebels met, under the auspices of the CPLP and the Economic Community of West African States (ECOWAS, see p. 205), and an agreement was reached to transform the existing truce into a cease-fire. The accord provided for the deployment of international forces to maintain and supervise the cease-fire. In September talks between the Government and the rebels resumed. However, the rebels' demand that all Senegalese and Guinean forces be withdrawn from the country as a prerequisite to a definitive peace agreement was rejected by the Government. The rebels, in turn, rejected a proposal for the establishment by Senegal of a buffer zone within Guinea-Bissau territory along the border with Casamance. In October the rebels agreed to a government proposal for the creation of a demilitarized zone separating the opposing forces in the capital. However, before the proposal could be formally endorsed, the cease-fire collapsed. On 20 October the Government imposed a nation-wide curfew, and on the following day Vieira declared a unilateral cease-fire. By that time almost all of the government troops had joined forces with the rebels, who were thought to control some 99% of the country. On 23 October Mané agreed to conform to a 48-hour truce to allow Vieira to clarify his proposals for a negotiated peace settlement, and agreement was subsequently reached for direct talks to be held. At the talks the rebels confirmed that they would not seek Vieira's resignation. Further talks, held under the aegis of ECOWAS, resulted in the signing of a peace accord on 1 November. Under the terms of the accord, the two sides reaffirmed the cease-fire of 25 August, and resolved that the withdrawal of Senegalese and Guinean troops from Guinea-Bissau be conducted simultaneously with the deployment of an ECOMOG (ECOWAS Cease-fire Monitoring Group) interposition force, which would guarantee security on the border with Senegal. It was also agreed that a government of national unity would be established, to include representatives of the rebel junta, and that presidential and legislative elections would be held no later than March 1999. In November 1998 agreement was reached on the composition of a Joint Executive Commission to implement the peace accord. In December Francisco José Fadul was appointed Prime Minister, and Vieira and Mané reached agreement on the allocation of portfolios to the two sides.

In January 1999 Fadul announced that presidential and legislative elections would not take place until the end of the year. Also in January agreement was reached between the Government, the rebel military junta and ECOWAS on the strength of the ECOMOG interposition force, which was to comprise some 710 troops. Agreement was also reached on a timetable for the withdrawal of Senegalese and Guinean troops from the country. However, at the end of January hostilities resumed in the capital. In February talks between the Government and the rebels produced agreement on a cease-fire and provided for the immediate withdrawal of Senegalese and Guinean troops. On 20 February the new Government of National Unity was announced. The disarmament of rebel troops and those loyal to the President began in March and the withdrawal of Senegalese and Guinean troops was completed that month. In April a report was released by the ANP exonerating Mané of charges of trafficking arms to the Casamance rebels. While the report called for the reinstatement of Mané as Chief of Staff of the Armed Forces, it revealed that Vieira's presidential guard had been heavily implicated in the arms-trafficking. On 30 April the UN Secretary-General established the UN Peace-building Support Office in Guinea-Bissau (UNOGBIS), with a mandate to aid peace-building efforts, support the consolidation of democracy and the rule of law, encourage friendly relations with the country's neighbours and assist in the electoral process; its mandate was regularly extended in subsequent years.

In early May 1999 Vieira announced that the elections would take place on 28 December. However, on 7 May, to widespread condemnation by the international community, Vieira was overthrown by the rebel military junta. Fighting had erupted in Bissau on the previous day when rebel troops seized stockpiles of weapons that had been at Bissau airport since the disarmament of the rival forces in March. The rebels, who claimed that their actions had been prompted by Vieira's refusal to allow his presidential guard to be disarmed, surrounded the presidential palace and forced its surrender. On 10 May Vieira signed an unconditional surrender. The President of the ANP, Malam Bacai Sanhá, was appointed acting President of the Republic pending a presidential election, and the Government of National Unity remained in office. Vieira was replaced as President of the PAIGC in an interim capacity by Manuel Saturnino da Costa. At a meeting in late May of representatives of the Government, the military junta and the political parties, agreement was reached that Vieira should stand trial for his involvement in arms-trafficking to the Casamance separatists and for political and economic crimes relating to his terms in office. Vieira agreed to stand trial, but only after receiving medical treatment abroad, after which, he pledged, he would return to Guinea-Bissau. ECOMOG forces were withdrawn from the country in June. That month Vieira went into exile in Portugal where he was offered political asylum. In July constitutional amendments were introduced limiting the tenure of presidential office to two terms and abolishing the death penalty. It was also stipulated that the country's principal offices of state could only be held by Guinea-Bissau nationals born of Guinea-Bissau parents.

In September 1999 an extraordinary congress of the PAIGC voted to expel Vieira from the party. Also expelled were former Prime Minister Carlos Correia and five ministers from his administration, while the incumbent Minister of Defence and Freedom Fighters, Francisco Benante, was appointed President of the party. In September and October mass graves were discovered containing the bodies of 36 people thought to have been executed during the Vieira regime. Later in October the Attorney-General, Amine Michel Saad, announced that he had sufficient evidence to prosecute Vieira for crimes against humanity and expressed his intention to seek Vieira's extradition from Portugal.

Presidential and legislative elections took place on 28 November 1999. Of the 102 seats in the enlarged legislature, the PRS secured 38, the RGB—MB 28, the PAIGC 24, the Aliança Democrática (AD, an alliance of the FD and the PCD) four, the UM three, the PSD three, and the FDS and the UNDP one each. As no candidate received the necessary 50% of the votes to win the presidential election outright, the leading candidates, Kumba Yalá of the PRS and Malam Bacai Sanhá of the PAIGC, contested a second round of voting on 16 January 2000, at which Yalá secured victory with 72% of the votes cast. Yalá was inaugurated on the following day and installed a new Council of Ministers, which included members of several former opposition parties, later that month. Caetano N'Tchama of the PRS was appointed Prime Minister. The election was subsequently judged by international observers to have been 'free and fair'. In May tensions were reported between Yalá and certain elements in the army who viewed Mané as the rightful leader of the country, on the grounds that it was he who had ousted Vieira from power. Also in that month a new political party, the Aliança Socialista da Guiné-Bissau (ASG) was formed. In October Yalá appointed a State Council, comprising members of all parliamentary political parties, which was to have an advisory role.

Demonstrations organized by the PAIGC, in support of demands for the resignation of the coalition Government, took place in Bissau in November 2000. In late November Mané declared himself Commander-in-Chief of the armed forces, following renewed violence in Bissau, instigated by soldiers loyal to Mané. However, government troops quickly suppressed the insurgency, and a number of opposition leaders were arrested. Mané fled the capital, and was subsequently killed by the security forces. In August 2002 the Commander of the Navy, Capt. Mohamed Lamine Sanhá, was sentenced to 10 years in prison. Others allegedly involved in the attempted coup also received gaol sentences.

In early 2000 the RGB—MB withdrew from the coalition Government (formed with the PRS). In March Yalá dismissed N'Tchama in an attempt to increase stability in the minority Government; the former Deputy Prime Minister and Minister of Foreign Affairs, Faustino Fudut Imbali, was appointed in his place and subsequently formed a new broad-based Government, which included a number of members of opposition parties (despite the appointments not being endorsed by the respective political parties). None the less, despite opposition from many of its members, the PAIGC agreed to support the new minority Government. Opposition parties established the United Opposi-

tion Platform and proposed a motion of 'no confidence' in the Government in April; however, the vote was suspended for two weeks, in order to allow Imbali to form a new Government more agreeable to the opposition. In May the Government's programme was accepted by the Assembléia Nacional Popular, with the support of the PAIGC. Nevertheless, in August renewed calls for the Government's resignation were prompted by revelations that an estimated US $15m. in state funds had inexplicably disappeared (see Economic Affairs). Later that month the Minister of Internal Administration, António Artur Sanhá, was dismissed following his involvement in a personal scandal.

In October 2001 a motion of 'no confidence' in Yalá was approved by the ANP; the vote had been instigated by opposition parties in response to what they considered to be increasingly unconstitutional actions by the President. Yalá then threatened to suspend the ANP. A demonstration against Yalá in Bissau, attended by some 10,000 people, followed further demands for the President's resignation by a coalition of opposition parties.

In December 2001 the Government stated that it had prevented a military *coup d'état*, and arrested the Deputy Chief of Staff of the Armed Forces and a former navy head. Prime Minister Imbali was dismissed later that month, and was replaced by Almara Nhassé, a member of the PRS and hitherto Minister of Internal Administration. Nhassé immediately formed a new Government, composed solely of members of the ruling coalition. Nhassé was subsequently elected President of the PRS, in place of Yalá.

In February 2002 Carlos Gomes Júnior was elected as President of the PAIGC. Also in that month the leader of the ASG, Fernando Gomes, was arrested on suspicion of misappropriating donations during his time as President of the national Human Rights League. The current Vice-President of the League was also apprehended. The arrests were criticized by the ASG, as well as by the human rights organization Amnesty International, on the grounds that they were politically motivated. Gomes was released later that month, while the Human Rights League dismissed its current President and Vice-President in late March for their alleged involvement in the scandal. Meanwhile, in early March Yalá replaced the late Mario Lopes with António Man as President of the Supreme Court in an action deemed unconstitutional by opposition parties.

In May 2002 Yalá announced that some 24 people had been arrested following an attempted coup. The President threatened to invade The Gambia, which he accused of having supported the leaders of the unsuccessful coup, prompting a diplomatic crisis (see below). An amnesty was later declared for those involved in the alleged coups of December 2001 and May 2002. At the RGB—MB conference in July, Helder Vaz was elected President of the party, despite internal splits and the conference being declared illegal by the Ministry of Internal Administration. After filing a case against Nhassé for abuse of power, the Attorney-General, Caetano N'Tchama, was dismissed in August; the President and Deputy President of the Supreme Court were also arrested, in connection with the misappropriation of funds. Artur Sanhá, then Minister of Fisheries and the Sea, rejected the post of Supreme Court President and was dismissed from his ministerial position. Yalá's actions were subsequently deemed unconstitutional.

In September 2002 Yalá dismissed Rui Sanhá as Minister of Internal Administration; he was replaced in October by António Man, erstwhile President of the Supreme Court. Also in September, Mandinga, the leader of the PCD, reported an assassination attempt, following his criticism of the Government; the Government denied such an attempt had occurred. The developing political uncertainty in the country intensified in November, when Yalá dissolved the ANP and dismissed the Government, citing its incompetence in coping with the economic crisis. Legislative elections were scheduled initially for February 2003, although later delayed. Mario Pires was appointed as Prime Minister, to head a transitional Government, which was dominated by the PRS.

Further government changes were effected in December 2002 and January 2003. During February five members of the PAIGC, including former Prime Minister Carlos Correia, were arrested without charge; they were subsequently released at Yalá's request. Several political coalitions opposing the PRS were formed in late 2002 and early 2003 in preparation for the legislative elections, which had been postponed until 20 April. In December 2002 the PSD, the LIPE, the Partido da Renovação e Progresso and the Partido Socialista Guineense created the União Eleitoral. In February 2003 the Plataforma Unida—

Mufunessa Larga Guiné (PU—MLG) was formed by the AD (comprising the FD and the PCD), the FDS, the Frente para a Libertação e Independência da Guiné and the Grupo de Democratas Independentes, which had been established by Vaz and other former members of the RGB—MB, following a court decision to award the leadership of that party to Salvador Tchongo.

In March 2003 Yalá announced that the elections were to be further delayed, until 6 July. Man was dismissed as Minister of Internal Administration in April. This was followed in early May by the dismissal and unexplained arrest of the Minister of Defence, Marcelino Cabral, and the Minister of the Presidency of the Council of Ministers, José de Piña; they were released in June. Meanwhile, Cabral was replaced by Filomena Tipote, although tension arose when military chiefs failed to attend her inauguration. In May the army demanded the resignation of Prime Minister Pires, on the grounds that they had not been paid for six months. In April and May President Yalá held a series of meetings with ministers and opposition leaders in an attempt to broaden support for his increasingly isolated presidency. In June five new ministers, all with connections to opposition parties, were appointed to the Government. In the same month the elections were postponed until 12 October. In July the Minister of Foreign Affairs and the Secretary of State for Information were dismissed; the latter's replacement was himself dismissed in early September. The elections were again postponed in early September.

On 14 September 2003 President Yalá was detained by the armed forces in a bloodless coup d'état, which was widely welcomed within Guinea-Bissau. The Chief of Staff of the Armed Forces, Gen. Veríssimo Correia Seabra, who led the coup, stated that the seizure of power had been a response to increasing unrest in the army and the worsening political and economic situation. Seabra proclaimed himself interim President of Guinea-Bissau, and President of a Comité Militar para a Recuperação da Ordem Constitucional e Democrática (Military Committee for the Restoration of Constitutional and Democratic Order). On 17 September Yalá officially resigned the presidency, and on 28 September Henrique Pereira Rosa, a business executive, and Artur Sanhá were sworn in as interim President and Prime Minister, respectively. On 2 October a transitional civilian Government, comprising a further 11 ministers and five secretaries of state, was appointed, in accordance with an agreement signed by political organizations and the military authorities. Ministers were not permitted to hold posts in political organizations. It was envisaged that elections to the ANP (which had been dissolved in November 2002) would be held within six months, and a presidential election within 18 months. A 56-member National Transition Council (NTC), composed of representatives of political and civil groups and the army, was to monitor government policy.

In mid-October 2003 President Rosa dismissed ex-President Yalá's close aides and appointed five new advisers, with the rank of minister. At the beginning of November the Government began paying civil servants' salaries, but warned that the 11 months of arrears owed to them would only be paid when funds became available. In the same month schools were reopened, having been closed for much of the previous two years owing to a series of strikes by unpaid teachers, after the World Bank provided a loan of US $2.5m. to pay salaries. In early December the NTC announced that legislative elections would be held on 28 March 2004, with the presidential election expected to be held a year later.

In January 2004 eight regional governors were sworn in and a new President of the Supreme Court was elected; during the previous two years the latter had been appointed by presidential decree, in contravention of the Constitution. In March Yalá, who had been under house-arrest since the coup, was released.

Elections to the ANP took place on 28 and 30 March 2004; the second day of voting was required in Bissau, where many polling stations had failed to open as a result of logistical problems. International observers declared themselves generally satisfied with the conduct of the elections, despite poor organization in the capital, and voter turn-out was estimated at 74.6%. The PAIGC won 45 of the 100 seats, leaving it short of an absolute majority, while the PRS secured 35 and the PUSD 17. The President of the PAIGC, Carlos Gomes Júnior announced his intention to form a broad-based coalition government. Negotiations between the PAIGC and the PUSD were unsuccessful, however, and the PAIGC reached an agreement with the PRS, whereby the latter undertook to support the Government. In return for this commitment, members of the PRS were appointed to senior positions in the ANP, in governmental departments and other state institutions. The ANP was inaugurated on 7 May; Francisco Benante was subsequently elected speaker. Gomes Júnior took office as Prime Minister on 10 May, and pledged to rehabilitate the country's infrastructure and improve conditions in the military. The new Council of Ministers, which comprised 16 ministers and seven secretaries of state, was sworn in on 12 May. Joaquim Mumini Embalo and Martinho N'Dafa Cabi became Deputy Prime Ministers, Soares Sambu was appointed Minister of Foreign Affairs, International Co-operation and Communities, while Daniel Gomes and João Mamadu Fadiah became Minister of Defence and of the Economy and Finance, respectively.

In June 2004 a UN mission to Guinea-Bissau declared that, although some progress had been made, stability in the country remained fragile. In September President Rosa announced that a presidential election would be held in April or May 2005 (according to the Transitional Charter drafted in October 2003, the election was to take place no later than 12 months after the legislative elections); Rosa, however, stated that he would not stand. In September the PUSD expelled eight of its 17 parliamentarians, after they had supported the Government's legislative agenda in June. In October a new party, the Partido da Reconciliação Nacional, was founded by Almara Nhassé. In December a group of traditional leaders urged Kumba Yalá to consider running for president. By that month a total of eight candidates had expressed their intention to contest the presidential election.

On 6 October 2004 Seabra and a senior military official, Lt Col Domingos de Barros were taken hostage and murdered by a group of disaffected soldiers, led by Maj. Buate Yanta Namam, in protest at their non-payment for a peace-keeping operation undertaken in Liberia. On 6 and 7 October the soldiers, who emphasized that they were not seeking to overthrow the Government, presented their demands, which included an improvement in army conditions, a salary increase and the payment of salary arrears, and on 7 October President Rosa announced that the soldiers had agreed to refrain from further acts of violence. Meanwhile, Gomes Júnior attributed the unrest to political forces dissatisfied with the outcome of the April elections (widely assumed as referring to members of the PRS). On 10 October a Memorandum of Understanding was signed by Gomes Júnior, Yanta Naman and Maj.-Gen. Baptista Tagmé Na Wai, representing the armed forces, according to which the soldiers would return to their barracks and salary arrears would be paid. An amnesty was to be granted to the mutineers and later in October Gomes Júnior announced that nearly all salary arrears had been settled. A new military high command, reportedly chosen by the mutineers, was also installed. Na Wai became Chief of Staff of the Armed Forces, while José Americo Bubo Na Tchuto was appointed Navy Chief of Staff.

In December 2004 a parliamentary commission, formed in November to investigate the condition of the Government and the PAIGC, recommended that a new, broad-based, coalition government be formed to deal with the ongoing political and economic crisis. In the same month, in view of continuing instability in Guinea-Bissau, the UN announced the extension of the mandate of UNOGBIS until December 2005. Also in December 2004 health care and education workers commenced industrial action in protest at the non-payment of salaries. Meanwhile, in late 2004 Almara Nhassé, Bothie Candé, a former Minister of Trade, and António Man, the former Minister of Internal Administration, were reported to be the subjects of investigations into corruption during their periods in office.

In mid-January 2005 Gomes Júnior, in his capacity as leader of the PAIGC, dismissed the parliamentary leader of the PAIGC, Cipriano Cassamá, who was alleged to have retained close links to former President Vieira. A new register of voters was scheduled for compilation in February, although, following negotiations between the Government and opposition parties, it was announced in early March that the presidential election would be postponed until mid-July, thus contravening the conditions stipulated in the Transitional Charter. In mid-March, however, it was announced that the presidential election would take place on 19 June and the registration of voters proceeded later in March. Malam Bacai Sanhá, who served as acting President in 1999, was chosen as the candidate for the PAIGC, while both Vieira (who was standing as an independent) and Kumba Yalá, representing the PRS, announced their candidacies. By mid-April a total of 21 potential candidates had registered with the

Supreme Court and were awaiting approval to contest the election.

In mid-April 2005 Gomes Júnior effected a major reorganization of the Council of Ministers. Most notably, Daniel Gomes, previously Minister of Defence, became Minister of the Presidency of the Council of Ministers, Social Communication and Parliamentary Affairs, while Martinho N'Dafa Cabi, hitherto Deputy Prime Minister and Minister of Energy and Natural Resources, assumed the the national defence portfolio. Furthermore, the Ministry of the Economy and Finance was separated; Issufo Sanhá was appointed Minister of the Economy, while El Hadj João Mamadu Fadiah remained in charge of the finance portfolio.

In late 1987 the head of security at the embassy of Guinea-Bissau in Lisbon, Portugal, requested political asylum and disclosed the presence of explosive devices in the embassy, allegedly intended for use against members of the RGB—MB (see above). These allegations were vehemently denied by the Government of Guinea-Bissau. A visit by the Portuguese Prime Minister, Aníbal Cavaco Silva, in 1989 signified an improvement in relations between the two countries. In July 1996 Vieira made an official visit to Portugal, during which agreement was reached on improved bilateral relations. In the same month Guinea-Bissau was among the five lusophone African nations which, along with Brazil and Portugal, officially established the CPLP, a lusophone grouping intended to benefit each member state by means of joint co-operation in technical, cultural and social matters.

In 1989 a dispute arose between Guinea-Bissau and Senegal over the demarcation of maritime borders. Guinea-Bissau began proceedings against Senegal in the International Court of Justice (ICJ) after rejecting an international arbitration tribunal's ruling in favour of Senegal. Guinea-Bissau requested direct negotiations with Senegal, and enlisted the aid of President Mubarak of Egypt, then the President of the Organization of African Unity (now the African Union—AU), and President Soares of Portugal as mediators. In November 1991 the ICJ ruled that a 1960 agreement regarding the demarcation of maritime borders between Guinea-Bissau and Senegal remained valid. In December 1992, in retaliation for the deaths of two Senegalese soldiers, the Senegalese air force and infantry bombarded alleged Casamance separatist bases in the São Domingos area of Guinea-Bissau. In response, the Government of Guinea-Bissau protested to the Senegalese authorities against the violation of Guinea-Bissau's borders and air space and denied Senegalese claims that it was providing support for the rebels. The Senegalese Government offered assurances that there would be no repetition of the incident. In March, in an apparent attempt to convince Senegal that it did not support the rebels, the Government handed over Abbé Augustin Diamacouné Senghor, one of the exiled leaders of the Casamance separatists, to the Senegalese authorities. In October 1993 the Presidents of Guinea-Bissau and Senegal signed an agreement providing for the joint management and exploitation of the countries' maritime zones. Petroleum resources were to be divided, with Senegal receiving an 85% share and Guinea-Bissau the remaining 15%. Fishing resources were to be divided according to the determination of a joint management agency. The agreement was renewable after a period of 20 years. In December 1995 the legislature authorized the ratification of the October 1993 accord. In the previous month the ICJ announced that Guinea-Bissau had halted all proceedings regarding the border dispute with Senegal.

In February 1995 the Senegalese air force bombarded a village in Guinea-Bissau, close to the border with Senegal. Despite an acknowledgement by the Senegalese authorities that the bombing had occurred as a result of an error, the Senegalese armed forces conducted a similar attack later that month. In March President Abdou Diouf of Senegal visited Guinea-Bissau to provide a personal apology for the two recent incidents and to offer a commitment that Senegal would respect Guinea-Bissau's sovereignty. In September agreement was reached on strengthening co-operation and establishing dialogue concerning security on the countries' joint border. However, a further attack by the Senegalese air force in October prompted the Guinea-Bissau legislature to form a commission of inquiry to investigate such border incidents.

In April 2000 there were renewed reports of incidents on the border between Senegal and Guinea-Bissau, in which five people were alleged to have been killed; however, the Senegalese Government denied accusations that its troops had entered Guinea-Bissau, and in May requested assistance from Guinea-Bissau to resolve the Casamance conflict. Also in that month, calls by the Senegalese President, Abdoulaye Wade, for the presence of UN military observers along the border between the two countries, were rejected by Yalá. However, in July Yalá agreed to provide assistance to Senegal, in the hope of finding a rapid solution to the separatist conflict in that country. In August an agreement was signed by Yalá and Wade ordering the immediate reopening of the border between the two countries; moreover, the agreement provided for the establishment of a joint military force to patrol the border area. It was also agreed that a joint commission would be set up to 'identify and return' goods allegedly stolen by Guinea-Bissau citizens in the area. In July 2001 Senegal and Guinea-Bissau issued a joint statement reaffirming their commitment to the agreement reached in August of the previous year. In March 2002 Alexandre Djibas, the leader of a Casamance rebel faction, was arrested and deported to Senegal, following assurances that he would be released. Also during March, 124 Senegalese fishermen were arrested for fishing in Guinea-Bissau's territorial waters. Improved security arrangements along the Casamance border were confirmed at a meeting in July, following a decline in border incidents.

Relations between Guinea-Bissau and The Gambia were severely strained in June 2002, when President Yalá accused the Government of The Gambia of harbouring and training Casamance rebels and former associates of Gen. Mané, the leader of the coup of 1998 and attempted coup of 2000. With specific reference to the alleged attempted coup of May 2002, Yalá threatened invasion of The Gambia if support for the rebels continued; President Jammeh of The Gambia denied any such support was being provided. A visit to The Gambia by Guinea-Bissau's Minister of Foreign Affairs in mid-June eased tensions somewhat, and was followed by UN intervention in July, which recommended the reactivation of a joint commission of the two countries. An improvement in relations was signalled by a visit by Yalá to The Gambia in September.

Despite being generally welcomed in Guinea-Bissau, the coup of September 2003 was officially condemned by the international community, and sanctions imposed by the USA were not lifted until August 2004, following the legislative elections. However, President Rosa visited Portugal and a number of West African countries in late 2003 in an effort to gain support and financial aid for the transitional Government, as well as the US headquarters of the UN, the IMF and the World Bank. Representatives from ECOWAS, the AU and the CPLP mediated in talks between the Government and soldiers during the mutiny of October 2004. In November a delegation from the CPLP visited Guinea-Bissau to conduct talks with political and military leaders with the aim of strengthening the country's fragile political structure.

In 2004 Guinea-Bissau became a member of the Community of Sahel-Saharan States. (see p. 373)

Government

Under the terms of the 1984 Constitution (revised in 1991, 1996 and 1999), Guinea-Bissau is a multi-party state, although the formation of parties on a tribal or geographical basis is prohibited. Legislative power is vested in the Assembléia Nacional Popular, which comprises 100 members, elected by universal adult suffrage for a term of four years. Executive power is vested in the President of the Republic, who is Head of State and who governs with the assistance of an appointed Council of Ministers, led by the Prime Minister. The President is elected by universal adult suffrage for a term of five years. However, on 14 September 2003 the elected President, Kumba Yalá, was deposed in a military coup led by the Chief of Staff of the Armed Forces, Gen. Veríssimo Correia Seabra. Yalá formally announced his resignation on 17 September. Transitional civilian institutions were inaugurated on 28 September, in accordance with an agreement signed by political organizations and the military authorities; Henrique Pereira Rosa became interim President. Elections to the Assembléia Nacional Popular (which had been dissolved by Yalá in November 2002) took place on 28 and 30 March 2004. A presidential election was to be held 12 months later, however, in March 2005 it was announced that the election would not take place until July.

Defence

In August 2004 the armed forces officially totalled an estimated 9,250 men (army 6,800, navy 350, air force 100 and paramilitary gendarmerie 2,000). Expenditure on defence in 2005 was forecast at €9.74m, or 4% of total expenditure.

Economic Affairs

In 2003, according to estimates by the World Bank, Guinea-Bissau's gross national income (GNI), measured at average 2001–03 prices, was US $228.6m., equivalent to $140 per head (or $660 on an international purchasing-power parity basis). During 1990–2003, it was estimated, the population increased at an average annual rate of 3.0%, while gross domestic product (GDP) per head decreased, in real terms, by an average of 3.0% per year. Overall GDP decreased, in real terms, at an average annual rate of 0.5% in 1990–2003; real GDP declined by 7.2% in 2002 and by 1.2% in 2003.

Agriculture (including forestry and fishing) contributed 59.6% of GDP in 2003, and employed an estimated 82.0% of the labour force in 2003. The main cash crops are cashew nuts (exports of which amounted to 93,000 metric tons and earned US $61m. in 2004) and cotton. Other crops produced include rice, roots and tubers, groundnuts, maize, millet and sorghum. Livestock and timber production are also important. A locust invasion in December 2004 and January 2005 put the cashew harvest at risk prompting Prime Minister Gomes Júnior to appeal for international assistance. The fishing industry developed rapidly during the 1990s, and earnings from fishing exports and the sale of fishing licences are a significant source of government revenue (revenue from fishing licences was 7,430m. francs CFA in 2001, equivalent to 26.0% of total revenue). A study conducted in 2004 revealed that the potential annual fishing catch was 96,000 tons. According to the World Bank, agricultural GDP increased, in real terms, by an average of 3.0% per year in 1990–2003; it declined by 4.2% in 2002 but increased by 6.9% in 2003.

Industry (including mining, manufacturing, construction and power) employed an estimated 4.1% of the economically active population at mid-1994 and provided 11.3% of GDP in 2003. According to the World Bank, industrial GDP increased, in real terms, by an average of 1.2% per year in 1990–2003; growth of 25.6% was recorded in 2003.

The mining sector is underdeveloped, although Guinea-Bissau possesses reserves of bauxite, phosphates, diamonds and gold. A Canadian company was attempting to develop phosphate mining at Farim, in the north of the country, in the early 2000s. In late 2003 recoverable petroleum reserves were estimated at 2,000m. barrels per day.

The sole branches of the manufacturing sector are food-processing, brewing and timber- and cotton-processing, while there are plans to develop fish-processing. Manufacturing, mining and power contributed 9.7% of GDP in 2003. According to the World Bank, manufacturing GDP increased, in real terms, by an average of 1.6% per year in 1990–2003; growth of 27.3% was recorded in 2003.

Energy is derived principally from thermal and hydroelectric power. Imports of petroleum and petroleum products comprised 6.2% of the value of total imports in 2001. Energy production since 1999 has been insufficient to supply demand in Bissau, mainly owing to fuel shortages caused by government-set low prices, and to equipment failures caused by poor maintenance. As a result, most energy is currently supplied by private generators. A hydroelectric plant due to commence operations in Guinea in 2009 was expected to improve Guinea-Bissau's power supply.

Services employed an estimated 19.4% of the economically active population at mid-1994, and provided 29.0% of GDP in 2003. According to the World Bank, the combined GDP of the service sectors increased, in real terms, at an average rate of 1.3% per year in 1990–2003; growth in 2003 was 0.2%.

In 2002 Guinea-Bissau recorded a trade deficit of US $4.1m., and there was a deficit of $8.7m. on the current account of the balance of payments. In 2003 the principal source of imports was Portugal (20.2%); other major suppliers were the People's Republic of China, Senegal, France and the Netherlands. In that year India was the principal market for exports (85.2%); according to official figures, exports of cashew nuts to India were worth US $60m. in that year, while Singapore was also a major purchaser. In 2001 the principal export was cashew nuts. The principal imports in that year were food and live animals, transport equipment, electrical equipment and machinery, and passenger vehicles.

In 2003 there was an estimated budgetary deficit of 12,500m. francs CFA , equivalent to 9.2% of GDP. Guinea-Bissau's total external debt was US $699.2m. at the end of 2002, of which $662.1m. was long-term public debt. In 2001 the cost of debt-servicing was equivalent to 41.1% of the total value of exports of goods and services. In 1990–2002 the average annual rate of inflation was 27.0%. Consumer prices decreased by 3.5% in 2003.

Guinea-Bissau is a member of the Economic Community of West African States (ECOWAS, see p. 205) and of the West African organs of the Franc Zone (see p. 267).

Guinea-Bissau is one of the world's poorest, and most indebted, countries. Its economy is largely dependent on the traditional rural sector, which employs the vast majority of the labour force and produces primarily for subsistence. The economy remains very dependent on foreign financing, which accounts for a significant part of budget revenue, and on exports of cashew nuts. In December 2000 the IMF and the World Bank awarded some US $790m. in debt-service relief as part of their enhanced initiative for heavily indebted poor countries. Moreover, a three-year Poverty Reduction and Growth Facility, worth some $18m., was awarded by the IMF in support of the Government's 2000–03 programme of economic reform. However, in May 2001, as the Government appeared to be struggling to achieve its objectives, the IMF and the World Bank suspended the aid programme, pending an investigation into the disappearance of $15m. in donor assistance. Although Guinea-Bissau was still able to resort to bilateral aid, the suspension represented a significant set-back, as 80% of the 2001 budget was to be financed by foreign aid. The results of the investigation, published in November, indicated the presence of non-justifiable government expenditure, valued at some 10,500m. francs CFA. Meanwhile, a programme of privatization, which had been interrupted by the military conflict, resumed in May. The economy continued to deteriorate during 2002–03, and army and public-sector workers were unpaid for several months, leading to social tension and a series of strikes that paralysed public services. Following the coup in September, interim President Rosa appealed to the international community for $35m. in immediate aid, notably for the payment of salary arrears. In December the UN Development Programme agreed to oversee an emergency aid fund, and in January 2004 the World Bank donated $13m. to be used primarily to settle internal debts, demobilize former combatants and organize the legislative elections. In July 2004 Prime Minister Gomes Júnior unveiled his Government's economic programme for 2004–08, which would place strict controls on public spending, reduce poverty and corruption, and encourage economic development. In July 2004 the budget for the remainder of that year, which predicted GDP growth of 1.7%, and that inflation would remain stable at 2.6%, was approved, however, by late 2004 it was estimated that the budget deficit would reach the equivalent of €14.5m. In November 2004 the IMF commended the Government's economic programme and in the same month the Government repaid some €4.6m., which had been embezzled from the European Union in 2001, thus enabling the Government to access assistance to the value of €17.2m. The 2005 budget, which anticipated expenditure of 71,535m. francs CFA, and revenue of 37,000m. francs CFA, was approved by the ANP in early February of that year. Aid granted in 2004 included a pledge of €44.4m. over three years from the Portuguese Government, and $19m. for a HIV/AIDS programme. At a conference, held in Lisbon in February 2005, international donors favoured waiting for the results of the presidential election, before committing funds to cover the anticipated budget deficit. The 2005 budget predicted GDP growth of 2.0% and inflation of 2.0%.

Education

Education is officially compulsory only for the period of primary schooling, which begins at seven years of age and lasts for six years. Secondary education, beginning at the age of 13, lasts for up to five years (a first cycle of three years and a second of two years). In 1999/2000 enrolment at primary schools included 53.6% of children in the relevant age-group (males 62.6%; females 44.5%), while enrolment at secondary schools was equivalent to 20.4% of children in the relevant age-group (males 26.4%; females 14.4%). In that year 463 students were enrolled in tertiary education. Some 200 students completed their studies in Havana, Cuba, in 2002, while a further 186 had scholarships to study in Paris, France, and Dakar, Senegal. In November 2003 President Rosa opened the country's first university, the Amílcar Cabral University; a private university, Colinas de Boe, had also opened in September. According to the 2005 budget, expenditure on education was forecast at 15.0% of total spending.

Public Holidays

2005: 1 January (New Year), 20 January (Death of Amílcar Cabral), 21 January* (Tabaski, Feast of the Sacrifice), 8 March (International Women's Day), 2 May (for Labour Day), 3 August (Anniversary of the Killing of Pidjiguiti), 24 September (National Day), 4 November* (Korité, end of Ramadan), 14 November (Anniversary of the Movement of Readjustment), 25 December (Christmas Day).

2006: 1 January (New Year), 11 January* (Tabaski, Feast of the Sacrifice), 20 January (Death of Amílcar Cabral), 8 March (International Women's Day), 1 May (Labour Day), 3 August (Anniversary of the Killing of Pidjiguiti), 24 September (National Day), 24 October* (Korité, end of Ramadan), 14 November (Anniversary of the Movement of Readjustment), 25 December (Christmas Day).

*These holidays are dependent on the Islamic lunar calendar and may vary by one or two days from the dates given.

Weights and Measures

The metric system is used.

Statistical Survey

Area and Population

AREA, POPULATION AND DENSITY

Area (sq km)	36,125*
Population (census results)	
16–30 April 1979	753,313
1 December 1991	
Males	476,210
Females	507,157
Total	983,367
Population (UN estimates at mid-year)†	
2001	1,407,000
2002	1,449,000
2003	1,493,000
Density (per sq km) at mid-2003	41.3

* 13,948 sq miles.
† Source: UN, *World Population Prospects: The 2002 Revision.*

ETHNIC GROUPS

1996 (percentages): Balante 30; Fulani 20; Mandjak 14; Mandinka 12; Papel 7; Other 16 (Source: Comunidade dos Países de Língua Portuguesa).

POPULATION BY REGION
(1991 census)

Bafatá	143,377	Gabú	134,971
Biombo	60,420	Oio	156,084
Bissau	197,610	Quinara . . .	44,793
Bolama/Bijagos . .	26,691	Tombali . . .	72,441
Cacheu	146,980	**Total**	983,367

PRINCIPAL TOWNS
(population at 1979 census)

Bissau (capital) . .	109,214	Catió	5,170
Bafatá	13,429	Cantchungo† . . .	4,965
Gabú*	7,803	Farim	4,468
Mansôa	5,390		

* Formerly Nova Lamego.
† Formerly Teixeira Pinto.

Mid-2003 (UN estimate, including suburbs): Bissau 335,876 (Source: UN, *World Urbanization Prospects: The 2003 Revision*).

BIRTHS AND DEATHS

	2000	2001	2002
Birth rate (per 1,000)	50.0	49.9	49.9
Death rate (per 1,000)	20.0	19.8	19.6

Source: African Development Bank.

Expectation of life (WHO estimates, years at birth, 2002): 47.2 (males 45.7; females 48.7) in 2002 (Source: WHO, *World Health Report*).

ECONOMICALLY ACTIVE POPULATION
('000 persons at mid-1994)

	Males	Females	Total
Agriculture, etc.	195	175	370
Industry	15	5	20
Services	80	14	94
Total	290	194	484

Source: UN Economic Commission for Africa, *African Statistical Yearbook*.

Mid-2003 (estimates in '000): Agriculture, etc. 527; Total labour force 643 (Source: FAO).

Health and Welfare

KEY INDICATORS

Total fertility rate (children per woman, 2002)	7.1
Under-5 mortality rate (per 1,000 live births, 2003) . . .	204
HIV/AIDS (% of persons aged 15–49, 2001)	2.81
Physicians (per 1,000 head, 1996)	0.17
Hospital beds (per 1,000 head, 1990)	1.48
Health expenditure (2001): US $ per head (PPP)	37
Health expenditure (2001): % of GDP	5.9
Health expenditure (2001): public (% of total)	53.8
Access to water (% of persons, 2002)	459
Access to sanitation (% of persons, 2002)	34
Human Development Index (2002): ranking	172
Human Development Index (2002): value	0.350

For sources and definitions, see explanatory note on p. vi.

Agriculture

PRINCIPAL CROPS
('000 metric tons)

	2001	2002	2003
Rice (paddy)	85.1	87.9	97.0*
Maize	28.1	22.1	20.0*
Millet	28.6	24.2	22.0*
Sorghum	15.1	14.7	15.0*
Cassava†	34.0	34.0	34.0
Other roots and tubers† . . .	65.0	65.0	65.0
Sugar cane†	5.5	5.5	5.5
Cashew nuts†	85.0	80.0	85.0
Groundnuts (in shell)†	19.0	19.0	19.0
Coconuts†	45.5	45.5	45.5
Oil palm fruit†	80.0	80.0	80.0
Vegetables†	25.0	25.0	25.0
Plantains†	38.0	38.0	38.0
Oranges†	5.0	5.0	5.0
Other fruits†	17.0	17.0	17.0

* Unofficial estimate.
† FAO estimates.

Source: FAO.

LIVESTOCK
(FAO estimates, '000 head, year ending September)

	2001	2002	2003
Cattle	515	515	520
Pigs	350	350	360
Sheep	285	285	290
Goats	325	325	330
Chickens	1,400	1,500	1,500

Source: FAO.

LIVESTOCK PRODUCTS
(FAO estimates, '000 metric tons)

	2001	2002	2003
Beef and veal	4.5	4.5	4.6
Pig meat	10.8	10.8	11.1
Other meat	2.9	3.0	3.0
Cows' milk	13.3	13.3	13.3
Goats' milk	2.9	2.9	2.9

Source: FAO.

Forestry

ROUNDWOOD REMOVALS
('000 cubic metres, excluding bark)

	1997	1998	1999
Sawlogs, veneer logs and logs for sleepers*	40	40	40
Other industrial wood	124	127	130
Fuel wood†	422	422	422
Total	586	589	592

* Assumed to be unchanged since 1971.
† Assumed to be unchanged since 1979.

2000–03: Production as in 1999 (FAO estimates).
Source: FAO.

SAWNWOOD PRODUCTION
('000 cubic metres, including railway sleepers)

	1997	1998	1999
Total*	16	16	16

* Assumed to be unchanged since 1971.

2000–03: Production as in 1999 (FAO estimates).
Source: FAO.

Fishing
(FAO estimates, metric tons, live weight)

	1997	1998	1999
Freshwater fishes	250	200	200
Meagre	500	430	350
Croakers and drums	1,040	850	650
Mullets	3,200	2,650	2,200
Natantian decapods	1,100	900	800
Total catch (incl. others)	7,250	6,000	5,000

2000–02: Figures assumed to be unchanged from 1999.
Source: FAO.

Industry

SELECTED PRODUCTS
('000 metric tons, unless otherwise indicated)

	1999	2000	2001*
Hulled rice	62.7	65.8	69.1
Groundnuts (processed)	6.2	6.5	6.8
Bakery products	6.3	6.9	7.6
Frozen fish	1.5	1.6	1.7
Dry and smoked fish	3.3	3.5	3.6
Vegetable oils (million litres)	3.2	3.4	3.6
Beverages (million litres)	3.1	3.3	3.5
Distilled liquor (million litres)	1.0	1.1	1.1
Dairy products (million litres)	1.0	1.1	1.1
Wood products	4.2	4.4	4.7
Soap	2.4	2.5	2.6
Electric energy (million kWh)	15.5	20.8	20.0

* Preliminary.
Source: IMF, *Guinea-Bissau: Statistical Appendix* (July 2002).

Finance

CURRENCY AND EXCHANGE RATES

Monetary Units
100 centimes = 1 franc de la Communauté financière africaine (CFA).

Sterling, Dollar and Euro Equivalents (31 December 2004)
£1 sterling = 9380.12 francs CFA;
US $1 = 481.58 francs CFA;
€1 = 655.957 francs CFA;
10,000 francs CFA = £10.75 = $20.76 = €15.25.

Average Exchange Rate (francs CFA per US $)
2002   696.99
2003   581.20
2004   528.28

Note: An exchange rate of 1 French franc = 50 francs CFA, established in 1948, remained in force until January 1994, when the CFA franc was devalued by 50%, with the exchange rate adjusted to 1 French franc = 100 francs CFA. This relationship to French currency remained in effect with the introduction of the euro on 1 January 1999. From that date, accordingly, a fixed exchange rate of €1 = 655.957 francs CFA has been in operation. Following Guinea-Bissau's admission in March 1997 to the Union économique et monétaire ouest-africaine, the country entered the Franc Zone on 17 April. As a result, the Guinea peso was replaced by the CFA franc, although the peso remained legal tender until 31 July. The new currency was introduced at an exchange rate of 1 franc CFA = 65 Guinea pesos. At 31 March 1997 the exchange rate in relation to US currency was $1 = 36,793.3 Guinea pesos.

BUDGET
(million francs CFA)

Revenue*	1999	2000	2001
Tax revenue	12,820	17,543	14,724
Income taxes	1,796	3,132	2,731
Business profits	687	1,739	1,325
Individuals	1,102	1,383	1,379
Consumption taxes	1,292	1,439	1,453
General sales tax	2,367	3,959	3,487
Taxes on international trade and transactions	7,018	8,304	6,467
Import duties	2,444	3,702	2,409
Export duties	3,248	4,166	3,807
Port service charges	1,326	436	251
Non-tax revenue	11,070	11,976	13,806
Entrepreneurial and property income	336	395	1,949
Fees and duties	8,661	8,336	7,885
Fishing licences	8,404	7,625	7,430
Total	23,890	29,519	28,530

Expenditure	1999	2000	2001
Current expenditure	28,488	51,800	41,513
Wages and salaries	6,918	10,499	11,270
Goods, services and transfers .	12,769	10,865	6,675
Scheduled external interest			
payments	8,800	8,800	12,226
Capital expenditure	14,900	15,807	21,648
Total	43,388	67,607	63,162

* Excluding grants received ('000 million francs CFA): 6.0 in 1999; 21.7 in 2000; 19.0 in 2001.

Source: IMF, *Guinea-Bissau: Statistical Appendix* (July 2002).

2002 ('000 million francs CFA): *Revenue:* Tax revenue 11.9; Non-tax revenue 9.8; Total 21.7 (excl. grants of 8.7; *Expenditure:* Current expenditure 33.8 (Wages and salaries 10.5, Interest payments 6.9, Other 16.4); Capital expenditure 13.7; Total 47.5 (Source: Banque central des états de l'Afrique de l'ouest).

2003 ('000 million francs CFA): *Revenue:* Tax revenue 11.4; Non-tax revenue 10.5; Total 21.9 (excl. grants of 7.8; *Expenditure:* Current expenditure 30.9 (Wages and salaries 9.2, Interest payments 4.7, Other 17.0); Capital expenditure 11.3; Total 42.2 (Source: Banque central des états de l'Afrique de l'ouest).

CENTRAL BANK RESERVES
(US $ million at 31 December)

	2001	2002	2003
IMF special drawing rights . .	0.20	0.40	1.18
Foreign exchange	69.28	102.31	163.20
Total	69.47	102.71	164.38

Source: IMF, *International Financial Statistics.*

MONEY SUPPLY
(million francs CFA at 31 December)

	2001	2002	2003
Currency outside banks . . .	53,054	70,223	89,569
Demand deposits at deposit money			
banks	16,261	14,623	8,319
Total money (incl. others) . .	69,535	85,074	98,209

Source: IMF, *International Financial Statistics.*

COST OF LIVING
(Consumer Price Index; base: 2000 = 100)

	2001	2002	2003
All items	103.2	106.6	102.9

Source: IMF, *International Financial Statistics.*

NATIONAL ACCOUNTS
(million francs CFA at current prices)*

Expenditure on the Gross Domestic Product

	2001	2002	2003
Government final consumption			
expenditure	24,500	25,900	30,800
Private final consumption			
expenditure	114,800	116,100	124,300
Increase in stocks . . . . . ⎤			
Gross fixed capital formation . ⎦	23,100	31,900	20,200
Total domestic expenditure .	162,400	173,900	175,300
Exports of goods and services .	51,400	40,100	38,500
Less Imports of goods and			
services	68,000	72,000	75,700
GDP in purchasers' values .	145,900	141,900	138,200

Gross Domestic Product by Economic Activity

	2001	2002	2003
Agriculture, hunting, forestry			
and fishing	80,400	80,000	80,900
Mining and quarrying . . . ⎤			
Manufacturing . . . . . . ⎬	14,800	14,800	13,200
Electricity, gas and water . . ⎦			
Construction	3,400	3,500	2,200
Trade, restaurants and hotels .	24,300	23,600	22,200
Transport, storage and			
communications	5,800	5,700	5,700
Finance, insurance, real estate, ⎤			
etc. . . . . ⎬	500	500	500
Community, social and personal			
services (excl. government) . ⎦			
Government services	14,200	11,500	11,000
GDP at factor cost	143,500	139,700	135,800
Indirect taxes	2,400	2,200	2,400
GDP at market prices . . .	145,900	141,900	138,200

* Figures are rounded to nearest 100 million, and totals may not be equivalent to the sum of component parts as a result.

Source: Banque centrale des états de l'Afrique de l'ouest.

BALANCE OF PAYMENTS
(US $ million)

	2001	2002
Exports of goods f.o.b.	62.9	54.4
Imports of goods f.o.b.	−61.7	−58.5
Trade balance	1.2	−4.1
Exports of services	4.5	6.5
Imports of services	−30.3	−27.5
Balance on goods and services . . .	−24.6	−25.1
Other income paid	−12.0	−8.8
Balance on goods, services and income .	−36.6	−33.9
Current transfers (net)	9.7	25.2
Current balance	−26.9	−8.7
Capital account (net)	25.3	38.9
Financial account (net)	−17.3	−21.4
Net errors and omissions	5.9	−2.9
Overall balance	−13.0	5.9

Source: IMF, *International Financial Statistics.*

External Trade

PRINCIPAL COMMODITIES
(US $ million)

Imports c.i.f.	1999	2000	2001
Food and live animals	24.0	21.5	18.1
Rice	17.7	7.0	6.4
Beverages and tobacco	2.0	6.0	5.3
Other consumer goods	3.5	4.7	4.2
Petroleum and petroleum products	7.9	4.7	6.0
Diesel fuel and gasoline . . .	7.1	4.4	4.7
Construction materials	0.4	6.5	5.0
Transport equipment	5.9	9.4	12.8
Passenger vehicles	1.6	5.2	6.9
Freight vehicles	1.9	3.4	4.5
Vehicle parts	2.6	0.9	1.2
Electrical equipment and			
machinery	2.9	5.4	7.4
Total (incl. others)	82.0	103.8	96.7

Exports f.o.b.	1999	2000	2001
Cashew nuts	48.6	59.8	45.1
Total (incl. others)	51.2	62.1	47.2

Source: IMF, *Guinea-Bissau: Statistical Appendix* (July 2002).

PRINCIPAL TRADING PARTNERS
(percentage of trade)

Imports	2001	2002	2003
China, People's Repub.	10.9	6.2	18.3
Côte d'Ivoire	0.2	0.2	0.0
France	4.7	5.7	8.6
Germany	2.4	2.4	1.5
Italy	1.1	1.1	3.3
Netherlands	7.7	5.2	8.3
Portugal	29.9	30.0	20.2
Senegal	27.4	25.8	15.3
USA	0.2	0.0	0.2

Exports	2001	2002	2003
France	1.7	0.0	0.5
India	41.7	94.3	85.2
Portugal	3.8	3.9	2.2
Senegal	2.5	0.0	0.5
Singapore	43.8	0.0	7.2
Spain	0.1	1.5	0.2

Source: Banco de Portugal.

Transport

ROAD TRAFFIC
(motor vehicles in use, estimates)

	1994	1995	1996
Passenger cars	5,940	6,300	7,120
Commercial vehicles	4,650	4,900	5,640

Source: International Road Federation, *World Road Statistics*.

SHIPPING

Merchant Fleet
(registered at 31 December)

	2001	2002	2003
Number of vessels	24	24	23
Total displacement (grt)	6,459	6,459	5,943

Source: Lloyd's Register-Fairplay, *World Fleet Statistics*.

International Sea-Borne Freight Traffic
(UN estimates, '000 metric tons)

	1991	1992	1993
Goods loaded	40	45	46
Goods unloaded	272	277	283

Source: UN Economic Commission for Africa, *African Statistical Yearbook*.

CIVIL AVIATION
(traffic on scheduled services)

	1996	1997	1998
Kilometres flown (million)	1	0	0
Passengers carried ('000)	21	21	20
Passenger-km (million)	10	10	10
Total ton-km (million)	1	1	1

Source: UN, *Statistical Yearbook*.

Tourism

TOURIST ARRIVALS BY NATIONALITY

	2001
Cape Verde	278
France	710
Italy	354
Libya	169
Portugal	2,130
Senegal	881
Spain	174
USA	172
Total (incl. others)	7,754

Source: World Tourism Organization, *Yearbook of Tourism Statistics*.

Communications Media

	2001	2002	2003
Telephones ('000 main lines in use)	9.9	11.2	10.6
Internet users ('000)	4	14	19

Mobile cellular telephones ('000 subscribers): 1,300 in 2003.

Facsimile machines (number in use): 550 in 2000.

Radio receivers ('000 in use): 49 in 1997.

Daily newspapers: 1 (average circulation 6,000 copies) in 1996.

Sources: UNESCO, *Statistical Yearbook*; UN, *Statistical Yearbook*; International Telecommunication Union.

Education

(1999)

	Institu- tions	Teachers	Students Males	Students Females	Students Total
Pre-primary	54	194	2,027	2,132	4,159
Primary	759	4,306	89,401	60,129	149,530
Secondary: general	n.a.	1,913*	16,109	8,925	25,034
Secondary: technical and vocational	n.a.		208	72	280
Tertiary	n.a.	n.a.	n.a.	n.a.	463

* UNESCO estimate.

Source: UNESCO Institute for Statistics.

Adult literacy rate (UNESCO estimates): 39.6% (males 55.2%; females 24.7%) in 2001 (Source: UN Development Programme, *Human Development Report*).

Directory

The Constitution

A new Constitution for the Republic of Guinea-Bissau was approved by the Assembléia Nacional Popular on 16 May 1984 and amended in May 1991, November 1996 and July 1999 (see below). The main provisions of the 1984 Constitution were:

Guinea-Bissau is an anti-colonialist and anti-imperialist Republic and a State of revolutionary national democracy, based on the people's participation in undertaking, controlling and directing public activities. The Partido Africano da Independência da Guiné e Cabo Verde (PAIGC) shall be the leading political force in society and in the State. The PAIGC shall define the general bases for policy in all fields.

The economy of Guinea-Bissau shall be organized on the principles of state direction and planning. The State shall control the country's foreign trade.

The representative bodies in the country are the Assembléia Nacional Popular and the regional councils. Other state bodies draw their powers from these. The members of the regional councils shall be directly elected. Members of the councils must be more than 18 years of age. The Assembléia Nacional Popular shall have 150 members, who are to be elected by the regional councils from among their own members. All members of the Assembléia Nacional Popular must be over 21 years of age.

The Assembléia Nacional Popular shall elect a 15-member Council of State (Conselho de Estado), to which its powers are delegated between sessions of the Assembléia. The Assembléia also elects the President of the Conselho de Estado, who is also automatically Head of the Government and Commander-in-Chief of the Armed Forces. The Conselho de Estado will later elect two Vice-Presidents and a Secretary. The President and Vice-Presidents of the Conselho de Estado form part of the Government, as do Ministers, Secretaries of State and the Governor of the National Bank.

The Constitution can be revised at any time by the Assembléia Nacional Popular on the initiative of the deputies themselves, or of the Conselho de Estado or the Government.

Note: Constitutional amendments providing for the operation of a multi-party political system were approved unanimously by the Assembléia Nacional Popular in May 1991. The amendments stipulated that new parties seeking registration must obtain a minimum of 2,000 signatures, with at least 100 signatures from each of the nine provinces. (These provisions were adjusted in August to 1,000 and 50 signatures, respectively.) In addition, the amendments provided for the Assembléia Nacional Popular (reduced to 100 members) to be elected by universal adult suffrage, for the termination of official links between the PAIGC and the armed forces, and for the operation of a free-market economy. Multi-party elections took place in July 1994.

In November 1996 the legislature approved a constitutional amendment providing for Guinea-Bissau to seek membership of the Union économique et monétaire ouest-africaine and of the Franc Zone.

In July 1999 constitutional amendments were introduced limiting the tenure of presidential office to two terms and abolishing the death penalty. It was also stipulated that the country's principal offices of state could only be held by Guinea-Bissau nationals born of Guinea-Bissau parents.

The Government

HEAD OF STATE

Interim President: HENRIQUE PEREIRA ROSA (took office 28 September 2003).

COUNCIL OF MINISTERS
(April 2005)

Prime Minister: CARLOS DOMINGOS GOMES JÚNIOR.

Minister of the Presidency of the Council of Ministers, Social Communication and Parliamentary Affairs: DANIEL GOMES.

Minister of National Defence: MARTINHO N'DAFA CABI.

Minister of Internal Administration: El Hadj JOAQUIM MUMINI EMBALO.

Minister of Foreign Affairs, International Co-operation and Communities: SOARES SAMBU.

Minister of the Economy: ISSUFO SANHÁ.

Minister of Finance: El Hadj JOÃO MAMADU FADIAH.

Minister of Justice: FILOMENO LOBO DE PINA.

Minister of Combatants for the Independence of the Homeland: ISABEL BUSCARDINY.

Minister of Administrative Reform, Public Functions and Labour: PEDRO GODINHO GOMES.

Minister of Transport and Telecommunications: RAIMUNDO PEREIRA.

Minister of Energy and Natural Resources: RUI GOMES ARAÚJO.

Minister of Trade, Industry and Handicrafts: ADIATU DJALÓ NANDIGNA.

Minister of Social Solidarity, the Family and the Fight against Poverty: EUGÉNIA SALDANHA ARAÚJO.

Minister of Health: ODETE SEMEDO.

Minister of National Education: MARCIANO SILVA BARBEIRO.

Minister of Agriculture and Rural Development: JOÃO DE CARVALHO.

Minister of Fisheries: HELENA MARIA NOSOLINY EMBALÓ.

Minister of Public Works, Construction and Urbanization: DOMINGOS SIMÕES PEREIRA.

There are, in addition, six Secretaries of State.

MINISTRIES

Office of the Prime Minister: Avda Unidade Africana, CP 137, Bissau; tel. 211308; fax 201671.

Ministry of Administrative Reform, Public Functions and Labour: Bissau.

Ministry of Agriculture and Rural Development: Avda Amílcar Cabral, CP 102, Bissau; tel. 221200; fax 201157.

Ministry of Combatants for the Independence of the Homeland: Bissau.

Ministry of the Economy: CP 67, Avda 3 de Agosto, Bissau; tel. 215193; fax 203670.

Ministry of Energy and Natural Resources: CP 255/399 Bissau; tel. 221925; fax 223149.

Ministry of Finance: CP 67, Avda 3 de Agosto, Bissau; tel. 215193; fax 203670.

Ministry of Fisheries: Avda Amilcar Cabral, CP 102 Bissau; tel. 201699; fax 202580.

Ministry of Foreign Affairs, International Co-operation and Communities: Rua Gen. Omar Torrijo, Bissau; tel. 204301; fax 202378.

Ministry of Health: CP 50, Bissau; tel. 204438; fax 201701.

Ministry of Internal Administration: Avda Unidade Africana, Bissau; tel. 203781.

Ministry of Justice: Avda Amílcar Cabral, CP 17, Bissau; tel. 202185.

Ministry of National Defence: Amura, Bissau; tel. 223646.

Ministry of National Education: Rua Areolino Cruz, Bissau; tel. 202244.

Ministry of the Presidency of the Council of Ministers, Social Communication and Parliamentary Affairs: Bissau.

Ministry of Public Works, Construction and Urbanization: Bissau.

Ministry of Social Solidarity, the Family and the Fight against Poverty: Bissau.

Ministry of Trade, Industry and Handicrafts: Avda 3 de Agosto, CP 67, Bissau; tel. 202172; fax 202171.

Ministry of Transport and Telecommunications: Bissau; fax 201137.

President and Legislature

On 14 September 2003 the elected President, Kumba Yalá, was deposed in a military coup led by the Chief of Staff of the Armed Forces, Gen. Veríssimo Correia Seabra. Yalá formally announced his resignation on 17 September. Transitional civilian institutions were inaugurated on 28 September, in accordance with an agreement signed by political organizations and the military authorities; Henrique Pereira Rosa became interim President. Elections to the Assembléia Nacional Popular were held on 28 and 30 March 2004 (see below), and a presidential election was to take place 12 months later. However, in March 2005 it was announced that the election would not take place until 19 July.

ASSEMBLÉIA NACIONAL POPULAR

President: FRANCISCO BENANTE.

General Election, 28 and 30 March 2004

Party	Votes	% of votes	Seats
Partido Africano da Independência da Guiné e Cabo Verde (PAIGC)	141,455	31.45	45
Partido para a Renovação Social (PRS)	111,354	24.76	35
Partido Unido Social Democrático (PUSD)	72,362	16.09	17
União Eleitoral (UE)	18,253	4.06	2
Aliança Popular Unida (APU)	5,776	1.28	1
Total (incl. others)	449,755	100.00	100

Political Organizations

The legislative elections of March 2004 were contested by 12 parties and three coalitions or alliances. Prior to the legislative elections in 2004, more than 20 parties were registered.

Aliança Popular Unida (APU): Bissau; f. 2003 as coalition to contest the legislative elections of March 2004; Leader FERNANDO GOMES.

Aliança Socialista da Guiné-Bissau (ASG): Bissau; f. 2000; Leader FERNANDO GOMES.

Partido Popular Guineense (PPG): Bissau; Leader JOÃO TÁTIS SÁ.

Foro Cívico da Guiné/Social Democracia (FCG/SD): Bissau; Leader ANTONIETA ROSA GOMES.

Manifesto do Povo: Bissau; f. 2003 to contest legislative elections; Leader FAUSTINO FUTUT IMBALI.

Movimento Democrático da Guiné-Bissau: Bissau; f. 2002; Leader SILVESTRE ALVES.

Partido Africano da Independência da Guiné e Cabo Verde (PAIGC): CP 106, Bissau; f. 1956; fmrly the ruling party in both Guinea-Bissau and Cape Verde; although Cape Verde withdrew from the PAIGC following the coup in Guinea-Bissau in Nov. 1980, Guinea-Bissau has retained the party name and initials; Pres. CARLOS DOMINGOS GOMES JÚNIOR.

Partido Democrático Guineense (PDG): Lisbon, Portugal; f. 2002; Leader MANUEL CÁ.

Partido para o Desenvolvimento e a Cidadania (PDC): Lisbon, Portugal; f. 2001; banned from contesting 2003 legislative elections; Leader FRANCISCO JOSÉ FADUL.

Partido da Reconciliação Nacional (PRN): Bissau; f. 2004; Leader ALMARA NHASSÉ; Sec.-Gen. OLUNDO MENDES.

Partido para a Renovação Social (PRS): c/o Assembléia Nacional Popular, Bissau; f. 1992; Pres. (acting) ALBERTO NAMBEIA; Vice-Pres. IAIA DJALO.

Partido de Solidariedade e Trabalho (PST): Bissau; f. 2002; Leader IANCUBA INDJAI.

Partido da Unidade Nacional (PUN): Bissau; f. 2002; Leader IDRISSA DJALO.

Partido Unido Social Democrático (PUSD): Bissau; f. 1991; officially registered in Jan. 1992; Leader FRANCISCO JOSÉ FADUL.

Plataforma Unida—Mufunessa Larga Guiné: f. 2003 as coalition to contest legislative elections; comprises the following parties:

Aliança Democrática (AD): c/o Assembléia Nacional Popular, Bissau; Leader VICTOR MANDINGA.

Frente Democrática (FD): Bissau; f. 1991; officially registered in Nov. 1991; Pres. CANJURA INJAI; Sec.-Gen. MARCELINO BATISTA.

Partido da Convergência Democrática (PCD): Bissau; Leader VICTOR MANDINGA.

Frente Democrática Social (FDS): c/o Assembléia Nacional Popular, Bissau; f. 1991; legalized in Dec. 1991; Leader RAFAEL BARBOSA.

Frente para a Libertação e Independência da Guiné (FLING): Bissau; f. 1962 as an external opposition movement; legally registered in May 1992; Leader KATENGUL MENDY.

Grupo de Democratas Independentes (GDI): Bissau; f. 2003 by fmr mems of the RGB—MB; Leader HELDER VAZ.

Resistência da Guiné-Bissau—Movimento Bah-Fatah (RGB—MB): Bissau; internet www.rgb-guinebissau.org; f. 1986 in Lisbon, Portugal, as Resistência da Guiné-Bissau—Movimento Bafatá; adopted present name prior to official registration in Dec. 1991; maintains offices in Paris (France), Dakar (Senegal) and Praia (Cape Verde); President Lic. SALVADOR TCHONGO; Sec.-Gen. MÁRIO USSUMANE BALDÉ.

União Eleitoral (UE): f. 2002 as coalition to contest legislative elections; Leader JOAQUIM BALDÉ; comprises the following parties:

Liga Guineense de Protecção Ecológica (LIPE): Bairro Missirá 102, CP 1290, Bissau; tel. and fax 252309; f. 1991; ecology party; Pres. Alhaji BUBACAR DJALÓ.

Partido da Renovação e Progresso (PRP): Bissau; Leader MAMADÚ URI DJALÓ.

Partido Social Democrático (PSD): c/o Assembléia Nacional Popular, Bissau; f. 1995 by breakaway faction of RGB—MB; Leader JOAQUIM BALDÉ; Sec.-Gen. GASPAR FERNANDES.

Partido Socialista Guineense (PSG): Bissau; Leader CIRÍLO VIEIRA.

União para a Mudança (UM): Bissau; f. 1994 as coalition to contest presidential and legislative elections, re-formed April 1995; comprises the following parties:

Movimento para a Unidade e a Democracia (MUDE): Bissau; officially registered in Aug. 1992; Leader FILINTO VAZ MARTINS.

Partido Democrático do Progresso (PDP): Bissau; f. 1991; officially registered in Aug. 1992; Pres. of Nat. Council AMINE MICHEL SAAD.

Partido de Renovação e Desenvolvimento (PRD): Bissau; f. 1992 as the 'Group of 121' by PAIGC dissidents; officially registered in Oct. 1992; Leaders MANUEL RAMBOUT BARCELOS, AGNELO REGALA.

União Nacional para a Democracia e o Progresso (UNDP): c/o Assembléia Nacional Popular, Bissau; f. 1998; Leader ABUBACAR BALDÉ.

Diplomatic Representation

EMBASSIES IN GUINEA-BISSAU

Brazil: Rua São Tomé, Esquina Rua Moçambique, CP 29, Bissau; tel. 212551; fax 201317; e-mail emb_brasil_bxo@hotmail.com; Ambassador ARTHUR MEYER.

China, People's Republic: Avda Francisco João Mendes, Bissau; tel. 203637; fax 203590; e-mail chinaemb_gw@mail.mfa.gov.cn; Ambassador TIAN GUANGFENG.

Cuba: Rua Joaquim N'Com 1, y Victorino Costa, POB 258, Bissau; tel. 213579; fax 201301; e-mail embcuba@sol.gtelecom.gw; Chargé d'affaires a.i. JOÃO ESTEVES DIAZ.

France: Avda 14 de Novembro, Bairro de Penha, CP 195, 1011 Bissau; tel. 201312; fax 201285; Ambassador SIMONE POUDADE.

The Gambia: 146 Avda 14 Novembro 146, POB 529, 1037 Bissau; tel. 203928; fax 251099; Ambassador (vacant).

Guinea: Rua 14, no. 9, CP 396, Bissau; tel. 212681; Ambassador SALIFOU SYLLA.

Libya: Rua 16, CP 362, Bissau; tel. 212006; Representative DOKALI ALI MUSTAFA.

Portugal: Avda Cidade de Lisboa, CP 76, 1021 Bissau; tel. 201261; fax 201269; e-mail emb.port.bissau@mail.sol.gtelecom.gw; Ambassador JOSÉ MANUEL SOARES B. PAIS MOREIRA.

Russia: Avda 14 de Novembro, CP 308, Bissau; tel. 251036; fax 251028; Chargé d'affaires a.i. VIACHELAV ROZHNOV.

Senegal: Avda Omar Torrijos 43A, Bissau; tel. 211561; Ambassador ABDOULAYE DIENG.

Judicial System

The Supreme Court is the final court of appeal in criminal and civil cases and consists of nine judges. Nine Regional Courts serve as the final court of appeal for the 24 Sectoral Courts, and deal with felony cases and major civil cases. The Sectoral Courts hear minor civil cases.

President of the Supreme Court: MARIA DO CEU SILVA MONTEIRO.

Religion

According to the 1991 census, 45.9% of the population are Muslims, 39.7% are animists and 14.4% are Christians, mainly Roman Catholics.

CHRISTIANITY

The Roman Catholic Church

Guinea-Bissau comprises two dioceses, directly responsible to the Holy See. The Bishops participates in the Episcopal Conference of Senegal, Mauritania, Cape Verde and Guinea-Bissau, currently based in Senegal. At 31 December 2002 there were an estimated 151,000 adherents in the country.

Bishop of Bafatá: Rev. CARLOS PEDRO ZILLI, CP 17 Bafatá; tel. 411507; e-mail diocesebafata@mail.bissau.net.

Bishop of Bissau: JOSÉ CÂMNATE NA BISSIGN, Avda 14 de Novembro, CP 20, 1001 Bissau; tel. 251057; fax 251058; e-mail diocesebissau@hotmail.com.

ISLAM

Associação Islâmica Nacional: Bissau; Sec.-Gen. El-Hadj ABDÚ BAIO.

The Press

REGULATORY AUTHORITY

Conselho Nacional de Comunicação Social (CNCS): Bissau; f. 1994; dissolved in 2003, recreated in November 2004; regulates media; Pres. AUGUSTO MENDES.

NEWSPAPERS AND PERIODICALS

Baguerra: Bissau; owned by the Partido da Convergência Democrática.

Banobero: Rua José Carlos Schwarz, CP 760, Bissau; tel. 230702; fax 230705; e-mail banobero@netscape.net; weekly; Dir FERNANDO JORGE PEREIRA.

Correio-Bissau: Bissau; weekly; f. 1992; Editor-in-Chief JOÃO DE BARROS; circ. 9,000.

Diário de Bissau: Rua Vitorino Costa 29, Bissau; tel. 203049; daily.

Fraskera: Bairro da Ajuda, 1ª fase, CP 698, Bissau; tel. 253060; fax 253070.

Gazeta de Notícias: Avda dos Combatentes da Liberdade, Bissau; tel. 222881; weekly; Dir HUMBERTO MONTEIRO.

Journal Nô Pintcha: Avda do Brasil, CP 154, Bissau; tel. 213713; Dir Sra CABRAL; circ. 6,000.

Voz de Bissau: Rua Eduardo Mondlane, Apdo 155, Bissau; tel. 202546; twice weekly.

Wandan: Rua António M'Bana, 6, CP 760, Bissau; tel. 201789.

NEWS AGENCIES

Agência Bissau Media e Publicações: Rua Eduardo Mondlane 52, CP 1069, Bissau; tel. 206147; e-mail agenciabissau@agenciabissau.com; internet www.agenciabissau.com.

Agência Noticiosa da Guiné-Bissau (ANG): Avda Domingos Ramos, CP 248, Bissau; tel. 212151; fax 202155.

Foreign Bureau

Agência Lusa de Informação (Portugal): Bissau; Bureau Chief RICARDO BORDALO.

Broadcasting and Communications

TELECOMMUNICATIONS

In June 2004 a 10-year agreement was signed by Guiné Telecom and Portugal Telecom to develop the telecommunications sector.

Instituto das Comunicações da Guiné-Bissau (ICGB): Avda Domingos Ramos 53, CP 1372, Bissau; tel. 204873; fax 204876; e-mail icgb@mail.bissau.net; internet www.icgb.org; regulatory authority; Pres. MUSSA DJASSY.

Guiné Telecom (GT): Bissau; tel. 202427; f. 2003 to replace the Companhia de Telecomunicações da Guiné-Bissau (Guiné Telecom—f. 1989); 40% owned by Portugal Telecom; 90% state-owned.

Guinétel: Bissau; f. 2003; 55% owned by Portugal Telecom; mobile operator.

RADIO AND TELEVISION

An experimental television service began transmissions in 1989. Regional radio stations were to be established at Bafatá, Cantchungo and Catió in 1990. In 1990 Radio Freedom, which broadcast on behalf of the PAIGC during Portuguese rule and had ceased operations in 1974, resumed transmissions. Other radio stations included Radio Televisão Portuguesa Africa (RTP/Africa), which broadcasts from Bissau, and Rádio Sintchã Oco.

Radiodifusão Nacional da República da Guiné-Bissau: Avda Domingos Ramos, Praça dos Martires de Pindjiguiti, CP 191, Bissau; tel. 212426; fax 253070; e-mail rdn@eguitel.com; internet www.guine-bissau.net/guine_net/rdn; f. 1974; govt-owned; broadcasts in Portuguese on short-wave, MW and FM; Dir-Gen. ALFREDO ANTÓNIO SAMI.

Rádio Bafatá: CP 57, Bafatá; tel. 411185.

Rádio Bombolom: Bairro Cupelon, CP 877, Bissau; tel. 201095; f. 1996; independent; Dir AGNELO REGALA.

Rádio Mavegro: Rua Eduardo Mondlane, CP 100, Bissau; tel. 201216; fax 201265.

Rádio Pindjiguiti: Bairro da Ajuda, 1ª fase, CP 698; tel. 253070; f. 1995; independent.

Televisão da Guiné-Bissau (TGB): Bairro de Luanda, CP 178, Bissau; tel. 221920; fax 221941; Dir-Gen. FRANCISCO BARRETO.

Finance

(cap. = capital; res = reserves; m. = million; brs = branches; amounts in francs CFA unless otherwise indicated)

BANKING

Central Bank

Banque Centrale des Etats de l'Afrique de l'Ouest (BCEAO): Avda Amílcar Cabral 124, CP 38, Bissau; tel. 215548; fax 201305; internet www.bceao.int; HQ in Dakar, Senegal; f. 1955; bank of issue for the mem. states of the Union économique et monétaire ouest-africaine (UEMOA, comprising Benin, Burkina Faso, Côte d'Ivoire, Guinea-Bissau, Mali, Niger, Senegal and Togo); cap. and res 859,313m., total assets 5,671,675m. (Dec. 2002); Gov. CHARLES KONAN BANNY; Dir in Guinea-Bissau LUÍS CÂNDIDO LOPES RIBEIRO.

Other Banks

Banco da África Ocidental, SARL: Rua Guerra Mendes 18A, CP 1360, 1360 Bissau; tel. 203418; fax 203412; e-mail bao@sol.gtelecom.gw; f. 2000; 15% owned by Banco Efisa (Portugal), 15% owned by Montepio Geral (Portugal); Chair. Dr GONÇALO SEQUEIRA BRAGA; Dir VITOR GUILHERME DE MATOS FILIPE.

Caixa de Crédito da Guiné: Bissau; govt savings and loan institution.

Caixa Económica Postal: Avda Amílcar Cabral, Bissau; tel. 212999; postal savings institution.

STOCK EXCHANGE

In 1998 a regional stock exchange, the Bourse Régionale des Valeurs Mobilières, was established in Abidjan, Côte d'Ivoire, to serve the member states of the UEMOA.

INSURANCE

Instituto Nacional de Seguros e Previdência Social: CP 62, Bissau; tel. and fax 201665; state-owned; Gen. Man. A. MONDES.

Trade and Industry

CHAMBER OF COMMERCE

Câmara de Comércio, Industria e Agricultura da Guiné-Bissau: Sede Provisória, Rua Guerra Mendes 20, CP 88, Bissau; tel. and fax 201602; f. 1987; Pres. Mamadou Baba Jaité; Sec.-Gen. Saliu Ba.

INDUSTRIAL AND TRADE ASSOCIATIONS

Associação Industrial da Guiné-Bissau: Rua Vitorino Costa 46, 1° andar, CP 48, Bissau; tel. and fax 204025.

Direcção de Promoção do Investimento Privado (DPIP): Rua 12 de Setembro, Bissau Velho, CP 1276, Bissau; tel. 205156; fax 203181; e-mail dpip@mail.bissau.net.

Procajú: Bissau; internet www.steelecom/cashew; private-sector association of cashew producers.

UTILITIES

Electricity and Water

Empresa de Electricidade e Águas da Guiné-Bissau (EAGB): CP 6, EAGB E.P., Bissau; tel. 215191; fax 202716; operated under contract by private management co; Dir-Gen. Wasna Papai Dafna.

Gas

Empresa Nacional de Importação e Distribuição de Gás Butano: CP 269, Bissau; state gas distributor.

TRADE UNIONS

Sindicato Nacional dos Marinheiros (SINAMAR): Bissau.

União Nacional dos Trabalhadores da Guiné (UNTG): 13 Avda Ovai di Vievra, CP 98, Bissau; tel. 212094; Pres. Desejado Lima da Costa; Sec.-Gen. Mário Mendes Correia.

Legislation permitting the formation of other trade unions was approved by the Assembléia Nacional Popular in 1991.

Transport

RAILWAYS

There are no railways in Guinea-Bissau. In March 1998 Guinea-Bissau and Portugal signed an agreement providing for the construction of a railway linking Guinea-Bissau with Guinea.

ROADS

In 1999, according to International Road Federation estimates, there were about 4,400 km of roads, of which 453 km were paved. A major road rehabilitation scheme is proceeding, and an international road, linking Guinea-Bissau with The Gambia and Senegal, is planned.

SHIPPING

Under a major port modernization project, the main port at Bissau was to be renovated and expanded, and four river ports were to be upgraded to enable barges to load and unload at low tide. The total cost of the project was estimated at US $47.4m., and finance was provided by the World Bank and Arab funds. At 31 December 2003 the merchant fleet comprised 23 vessels, totalling 5,943 grt. In mid-2004 plans were announced to improve links with the Bijagós islands, by providing a regular ferry service.

Empresa Nacional de Agências e Transportes Marítimos: Rua Guerva Mendes 4–4A, CP 244, Bissau; tel. 212675; fax 213023; state shipping agency; Dir-Gen. M. Lopes.

CIVIL AVIATION

There is an international airport at Bissau, which there are plans to expand, and 10 smaller airports serving the interior.

Air Bissau: CP 111, Bissau; tel. 251063; fax 251008.

Guinea-Bissau Airlines: Bissau; f. 2001.

Air Luxor (Guiné-Bissau): Aeropeurto Osvaldo Vieira; tel. 206423; 49% owned by Air Luxor (Portugal); weekly scheduled flight to Lisbon commenced 2003.

Tourism

There were 7,754 tourist arrivals in 2001.

Central de Informação e Turismo: CP 294, Bissau; tel. 213905; state tourism and information service.

Direcção Geral do Turismo: CP 1024, Bissau; tel. 202195; fax 204441.

GUYANA

Introductory Survey

Location, Climate, Language, Religion, Flag, Capital

The Republic of Guyana lies on the north coast of South America, between Venezuela to the west and Suriname to the east, with Brazil to the south. The narrow coastal belt has a moderate climate with two wet seasons, from April to August and from November to January, alternating with two dry seasons. Inland, there are tropical forests and savannah, and the dry season lasts from September to May. The average annual temperature is 27°C (80°F), with average rainfall of 1,520 mm (60 ins) per year inland, rising to between 2,030 mm (80 ins) and 2,540 mm (100 ins) on the coast. English is the official language but Hindi, Urdu and Amerindian dialects are also spoken. The principal religions are Christianity (which is professed by about 50% of the population), Hinduism (about 33%) and Islam (less than 10%). The national flag (proportions 3 by 5 when flown on land, but 1 by 2 at sea) is green, with a white-bordered yellow triangle (apex at the edge of the fly) on which is superimposed a black-bordered red triangle (apex in the centre). The capital is Georgetown.

Recent History

Guyana was formerly British Guiana, a colony of the United Kingdom, formed in 1831 from territories finally ceded to Britain by the Dutch in 1814. A new Constitution, providing for universal adult suffrage, was introduced in 1953. The elections of April 1953 were won by the left-wing People's Progressive Party (PPP), led by Dr Cheddi Bharat Jagan. In October, however, the British Government, claiming that a communist dictatorship was threatened, suspended the Constitution. An interim administration was appointed. The PPP split in 1955, and, in 1957 some former members founded a new party, the People's National Congress (PNC), under the leadership of Forbes Burnham. The PNC drew its support mainly from the African-descended population, while PPP support came largely from the (Asian-descended) 'East' Indian community.

A revised Constitution was introduced in December 1956 and fresh elections were held in August 1957. The PPP won and Dr Jagan became Chief Minister. Another Constitution, providing for internal self-government, was adopted in July 1961. The PPP won the elections in August and Dr Jagan was appointed premier in September. In the elections of December 1964, held under the system of proportional representation that had been introduced in the previous year, the PPP won the largest number of seats in the Legislative Assembly, but not a majority. A coalition Government was formed by the PNC and The United Force (TUF), with Burnham as Prime Minister. This coalition led the colony to independence, as Guyana, on 26 May 1966.

The PNC won elections in 1968 and in 1973, although the results of the latter, and every poll thenceforth until the defeat of the PNC in 1992, were disputed by the opposition parties. Guyana became a co-operative republic on 23 February 1970, and Arthur Chung was elected non-executive President in March. In 1976 the PPP, which had boycotted the National Assembly since 1973, offered the Government its 'critical support'. Following a referendum in July 1978 that gave the Assembly power to amend the Constitution, elections to the Assembly were postponed for 15 months. The legislature assumed the role of a constituent assembly, established in November 1978, to draft a new constitution. In October 1979 elections were postponed for a further year. In October 1980 Forbes Burnham declared himself executive President of Guyana, and a new Constitution was promulgated.

Internal opposition to the PNC Government had increased after the assassination in June 1980 of Dr Walter Rodney, leader of the Working People's Alliance (WPA). The Government was widely believed to have been involved in the incident; an official inquest in 1988 produced a verdict, rejected by the opposition, of death by misadventure. All opposition parties except the PPP and TUF boycotted the December 1980 elections to the National Assembly. The PNC, under Burnham, received 77.7% of the votes, according to official results, and won 41 of the 53 elective seats, although allegations of substantial electoral malpractice were made, both within the country and by international observers. None the less, Burnham was formally inaugurated as President in January 1981.

In 1981 arrests and trials of opposition leaders continued, and in 1982 the Government's relations with human rights groups, and especially the Christian churches, deteriorated further. Editors of opposition newspapers were threatened, political violence increased, and the Government was accused of interference in the legal process. Industrial unrest and public discontent continued in 1983, as Guyana's worsening economic situation increased opposition to the Government, and led to growing disaffection within the trade union movement and the PNC. There were more strikes in 1984, and in December Burnham announced some concessions, including a rise in the daily minimum wage (virtually the only increase since 1979).

Burnham died in August 1985 and was succeeded as President by Desmond Hoyte, hitherto the First Vice-President and Prime Minister. President Hoyte's former posts were assumed by Hamilton Green, previously the First Deputy Prime Minister. At a general election in December the PNC won 78% of the votes and 42 of the elective seats in the National Assembly. Opposition groups, including the PPP and WPA, denounced the poll as fraudulent and in January 1986 five of the six opposition parties formed the Patriotic Coalition for Democracy (PCD).

During 1988 the opposition expressed fears about the independence of the judiciary and claimed that the Government's continued recourse to the laws of libel against its critics was an abuse of the legal system. Social unrest and industrial disruption in 1988 continued to impede government efforts to reform the economy, while the Government's hold on power was further compromised, following a division within the trade union movement. Seven unions withdrew from the Trades Union Congress (TUC) in September, alleging that elections for TUC officials were weighted in favour of PNC-approved candidates. The seven independent unions formed a separate congress, the Federation of Independent Trade Unions in Guyana (FITUG), in October. However, the Government refused to negotiate with the FITUG, accusing it of being politically motivated. Furthermore, the severity of austerity measures contained in the budget of March 1989, which included a devaluation of the currency, prompted a six-week strike in the sugar and bauxite industries.

Outside the formal opposition of the political parties, the Government also experienced pressure from members of the Guyana Human Rights Association, business leaders and prominent religious figures. This culminated, in January 1990, in the formation of a movement for legal and constitutional change, Guyanese Action for Reform and Democracy (Guard), which initiated a series of mass protests, urging the Government to accelerate the process of democratic reform. To counter this civic movement, the PNC began mobilizing its own newly-established Committees to Re-elect the President (Creeps). Guard accused the Creeps of orchestrating violent clashes at Guard's rallies, and of fomenting racial unrest in the country in an attempt to regain support from the Afro-Guyanese population.

In October 1990 the former US President Jimmy Carter visited President Hoyte to discuss matters related to electoral reform. It was agreed that a new electoral register would be compiled. However, the date of the forthcoming general election was postponed, following the approval of legislation by the PNC in January 1991 extending the term of office of the National Assembly by two months after its official dissolution date of 2 February 1991. In March a further two-month extension of the legislative term provoked the resignation of TUF and PPP members from the National Assembly (in addition to the WPA members, who had resigned a month earlier). Similar extensions followed in May and July, owing to alleged continuing problems relating to electoral reforms. The National Assembly was finally dissolved in late September. The publication of the revised electoral register in that month, however, revealed widespread inaccuracies, including the omission of an estimated 100,000 eligible voters. In November several opposition parties announced a boycott of the general election, which had been rescheduled for mid-December. However, on 28 November

Hoyte declared a state of emergency (subesequently extended until June 1992) in order to legitimize a further postponement of the election. Legislation restoring the opposition seats in the National Assembly followed, and the Assembly was reconvened. A further revised electoral register was finally approved by the Elections Commission in August 1992. The election took place on 5 October and resulted in a narrow victory for the PPP in alliance with the CIVIC movement (a social and political movement of businessmen and professionals), which secured 32 of the 65 elective seats in the National Assembly, while the PNC secured 31 elective seats. The result, which signified an end to the PNC's 28-year period in government, provoked riots by the mainly Afro-Guyanese PNC supporters in Georgetown, in which two people were killed. International observers were, however, satisfied that the elections had been fairly conducted, and on 9 October Dr Cheddi Bharat Jagan took office as President. On the following day Jagan appointed Samuel Hinds, an industrialist who was not a member of the PPP, as Prime Minister.

In August 1995 a serious environmental incident resulted in the temporary closure of Omai Gold Mines Ltd (OGML). The company, which began production in the Omai District of Essequibo province in 1993, was responsible for an increase of some 400% in Guyana's gold production in subsequent years and was Guyana's largest foreign investor. However, in August 1995 a breach in a tailings pond (a reservoir where residue from the gold extraction process is stored) resulted in the spillage of some 3.5m. cu m of cyanide-tainted water, of which a large volume flowed into the Omai river, a tributary of the Essequibo river. The National Assembly approved a resolution to close the mine for an indefinite period pending an inquiry into the incident. OGML resumed operations in February 1996 following the implementation of government-approved environmental safeguards.

In February 1996, amid growing public concern at an increase in criminal violence, Guyana resumed judicial executions with the hanging of a convicted murderer. The execution, the first for more than five years, provoked protest from human rights organizations.

In March 1997, following the death of Dr Cheddi Bharat Jagan, Prime Minister Hinds succeeded to the presidency, in accordance with the provisions of the Constitution. Hinds subsequently appointed Janet Jagan, the widow of the former President, to the post of Prime Minister. In September the PPP/CIVIC alliance formally adopted Jagan as its presidential candidate for the forthcoming general election.

At the general election of 15 December 1997 delays in the verification of votes prompted protest by PNC supporters who accused the Government of electoral fraud; 11 protesters were injured during clashes with the security forces. With some 90% of the votes counted, the Chairman of the Elections Commission, Doudnauth Singh, declared that Jagan had established an unassailable lead, and on 19 December she was inaugurated as President. Singh's actions were strongly criticized as being premature by opposition parties, and the PNC expressed its intention to appeal to the High Court to have Jagan's appointment annulled. In the following days PNC supporters began a series of public demonstrations in protest at the alleged electoral fraud and at Jagan's appointment. On 31 December the final election results were declared. With two legislative seats remaining to be decided by the National Congress of Local Democratic Organs, the PPP/CIVIC alliance secured 34 seats, the PNC won 26, and TUF, the Alliance for Guyana and the Guyana Democratic Party each obtained one seat. (In February 1998 the remaining two seats were declared to have been won by the PPP/CIVIC alliance.)

In January 1998, in the light of continued unrest being fomented by opposition supporters, the Government accepted a proposal by private-sector leaders for an international audit of the election to be conducted. The PNC, however, rejected the proposal and demanded instead the holding of fresh elections. In mid-January, in rejection of an appeal by the PNC, the Chief Justice ruled that it was beyond the jurisdiction of the High Court to prohibit Jagan from exercising her presidential functions pending a judicial review of the election. The ruling provoked serious disturbances in Georgetown, which, in turn, prompted the Government to introduce a one-month ban on public assemblies and demonstrations in the capital. Nevertheless, public protests by PNC supporters continued in defiance of the ban, resulting in confrontation with the security forces. However, in mid-January, following mediation by a three-member Caribbean Community and Common Market (CAR-

ICOM, see p. 172) commission, headed by a former Minister of Foreign Affairs of Barbados, Sir Henry Forde, it was announced that an agreement (the Herdmanston Agreement) had been signed by Jagan and PNC leader Desmond Hoyte, which provided for the organization of fresh elections within 36 months and the creation of a constitutional commission to make recommendations on constitutional reform, subsequently to be submitted to a national referendum and a National Assembly vote. The agreement also made provision for an independent audit of the December election, and in February the PPP/CIVIC alliance and the PNC agreed on the legal procedures necessary for the audit, which was to be conducted by a CARICOM electoral team, to be authorized. Meanwhile, although the PNC had submitted the names of 22 deputies who would represent the party in an emergency, the PNC continued to boycott the National Assembly. In early June the CARICOM commission upheld the published results of the December poll, declaring that there had been only minor procedural irregularities. While both the PPP and the PNC were bound to abide by the findings of the commission (under the terms of the Herdmanston Agreement), Hoyte continued publicly to question the legitimacy of the Jagan administration. Later in the month, mounting political frustration, arising from the National Assembly's informing the PNC that its deputies had effectively forfeited their legislative seats (having failed to attend six consecutive sittings), erupted onto the streets of Georgetown. PNC supporters congregated in the capital, where violent demonstrations against the Government escalated into riots that were dispersed by the security forces with rubber bullets and tear gas. However, renewed CARICOM mediation between the PPP and the PNC, at the CARICOM annual summit in Saint Lucia in early July, produced fresh commitments from both sides to restore peaceful political dialogue, renew discussions on constitutional reform and reinstate full legislative participation. Legislation designed to enable the PNC deputies to recover their seats in the legislature was subsequently formulated by both sides, and the PNC (with the exception of Hoyte—who continued to deny the legitimacy of Jagan's authority) rejoined the National Assembly on 14 July.

In January 1999 a select parliamentary committee on constitutional reform announced the creation of a 20-member Constitutional Reform Commission, comprising representatives of the country's principal political parties and community groups. In July the Commission published its report. It included proposals (submitted by the PPP/CIVIC alliance) that the country should be renamed the Republic of Guyana, that the President should be limited to two consecutive terms of office, and that the President should no longer be empowered to dissolve the National Assembly should he/she be censured by the Assembly. The Commission further proposed that the President should no longer have the power to dismiss a public officer in the public interest, and the President and Cabinet should be collectively responsible to the National Assembly and should resign if defeated in a vote of 'no confidence'.

In late April 1999 the Guyana Public Service Union (GPSU) called a general strike over salary increases. Other public-sector unions later joined the GPSU in taking industrial action, and much of the country was paralysed. Tension was exacerbated following the serving of legal summonses to three prominent union leaders for having organized protest marches in defiance of a government ban, while in mid-May the police opened fire (with pellet guns) on an allegedly violent crowd of strikers, injuring 17 people. After 56 days of industrial action, an agreement was finally reached between the unions and the authorities in late June, which granted public-sector workers an interim pay rise of 4.6% prior to the full settlement of their claim by an arbitration tribunal. Many members of the GPSU were reported to be dissatisfied with the agreement, and the headquarters of the union were subsequently attacked, while the Minister for Public Service, George Fung-On, was assaulted in his car. In September the arbitration tribunal awarded public-sector workers an increase of 31.6% in 1999 and 26.7% in 2000. The Government, however, announced that it would only be bound by the tribunal's findings if it could be proved that the tribunal had followed the correct procedures, and it also warned the unions that the cost of the pay rises might necessitate redundancies.

In early August 1999 President Jagan announced her retirement on the grounds of ill health. She was replaced as President by the erstwhile Minister of Finance, Bharrat Jagdeo. The appointment of Jagdeo, whose relative youth (he was 35 years of age), reported willingness to reach across the political divide, and strong background in economics all contributed to his popularity, was widely welcomed in Guyana and by the international community. Jagdeo, who announced that he was to continue the largely market-orientated policies of the Jagan administration, reappointed Samuel Hinds as Prime Minister (Hinds had earlier resigned in accordance with the requirements of the Constitution), and announced that there was to be no cabinet reorganization in the immediate future. There was, however, controversy at the absence of Hoyte and other PNC representatives from the President's inauguration ceremony; Hoyte, who had refused to recognize Jagan as President, was reported to have declined to recognize any successor nominated by her.

In December 1999 the National Assembly approved the establishment of a committee to supervise the revision of the Constitution prior to the legislative elections scheduled for mid-January 2001. Two 'task forces' were also established by the National Assembly; one was to deal with electoral reform and the other was to establish an Ethnic Relations Commission. In July 2000 the National Assembly approved legislation making the electoral reform task force a permanent institution (to be known as the Guyana Elections Commission—GECOM). In August legislation allowing for the creation of the Ethnic Relations Commission was passed (although it was not officially established until December). In October the legislature unanimously approved a constitutional amendment establishing a mixed system of proportional representation combining regional constituencies and national candidate lists. Also approved was the abolition of the Supreme Congress of the People of Guyana and the National Congress of Local Democratic Organs.

However, on 17 November 2000 GECOM announced that the elections that, according to the Herdmanston Agreement, were to be held on 17 January 2001, were to be postponed, owing to delays in the enactment of the proposed reform. A dispute had arisen between the Government and the PNC over the number of parliamentary seats that were to be allocated by region. In December an all-party committee decided that the PPP/CIVIC was to remain in office until the revised election date of March 2001, but was to limit its powers. In the same month the National Assembly approved a constitutional amendment removing the President's immunity from prosecution and limiting his power to appoint only four ministers from outside the National Assembly.

The general and regional elections of 19 March 2001 were preceded by demonstrations over the late distribution of voter identification cards (despite the announcement, in mid-February, that voters would be allowed to use other forms of identification). The elections, which were contested by 11 political parties, were overseen by an international delegation led by former US President Jimmy Carter. The PPP/CIVIC secured 53.0% of the votes cast. The party also obtained a majority in the National Assembly, with 34 seats; while the PNC (which contested the elections as the PNC/Reform) won 27 seats, the Guyana Action Party, in alliance with the WPA, won two seats, while Rise, Organize and Rebuild Guyana Movement and TUF each secured one seat. Some 89.9% of the registered electorate participated. International observers declared the elections to be generally free and fair, and on 23 March Jagdeo was officially declared President-elect. However, the PNC/Reform alleged that there had been a number of breaches of electoral procedure and successfully obtained a High Court injunction postponing the presidential inauguration. Three people were injured in the subsequent violent demonstrations. In late March the Chief Justice refused a further request to stay the proceedings, and ordered an immediate declaration of the official results. On 31 March Bharrat Jagdeo was sworn in as President. A new Cabinet was announced in early April, with additional ministers announced over the next few months. Further protests greeted the reappointment of PPP member Roger Luncheon as head of the civil service.

In an attempt to reduce the intensity of the continuing violence, on 25 April 2001 Jagdeo and Hoyte announced confidence-building measures and the establishment of joint committees to examine and report on critical issues, including land distribution and housing, and the bauxite industry. In May the Government announced the depoliticization of the social service: a Ministry of Public Service Management was to be created, separate from the Office of the President.

In June 2001 the National Assembly approved legislation making the appointment of the Chancellor of Justice and Chief of Justice the joint responsibility of the President and the Leader of the Opposition. In September Dr Steve Surujbally was appointed Chairman of the Elections Commission; the Commission was preparing for local elections, which had been last held in 1994 and had been due in 1997. However, in December 2003 the local elections were postponed for a further year, owing to a lack of progress on electoral reform.

On 15 March 2002 opposition parties walked out of a debate on the 2002 budget, in protest at the delay in the implementation of the recommendations of the various joint committees. The PNC/Reform and the PPP announced that they would pursue a policy of active non-co-operation with the Government. A period of social unrest ensued, accompanied by a high incidence of violent crime. The disorder culminated on 3 July in an attack by opposition protesters on the presidential offices during a meeting of CARICOM heads of government. The security forces opened fire on the protesters, killing two and wounding 15. The protesters had been participating in a demonstration organized by the recently formed People's Solidarity Movement. While condemning the violence, the PNC/Reform leadership announced their support for the demonstrators' grievances of racial discrimination and police brutality. Later in the month the leaders of the opposing parties began a series of consultations with representatives from the Church, trade unions, private sector companies and the judiciary, in an effort to ascertain their ideas of how shared governance could function in Guyana.

In August 2002 President Jagdeo announced plans for the creation of an additional special police force to combat the rising crime rate. Nevertheless, the social unrest continued, prompting businesses in Georgetown to close for two days in early October. In late September the National Assembly approved stricter laws for prosecuting crime; however, further anti-terrorism legislation, proposed by the Minister of Legal Affairs, Doodnauth Singh, was criticized by senior members of the judiciary as well as by human rights groups, who feared a contravention of basic civil liberties guaranteed by the Constitution.

In February 2003 Robert Corbin was elected as the new leader of the PNC/Reform following the unexpected death of Hoyte in December 2002. Corbin pledged a policy of 'constructive engagement' with the PPP and, following negotiations between party leaders, in early May Jagdeo and Corbin signed an agreement on a number of issues, including local government reform, opposition representation on state bodies, particularly the government-owned media. It was also agreed that an inquiry into the conduct of the police force would be held. In the same month the PNC/Reform ended its boycott of the National Assembly. A 'stakeholder group' was established to monitor the implementation of the accord. Progress was slow and acrimonious throughout the year; in August Corbin accused the Government of delaying unnecessarily the implementation of the agreement. None the less, in December agreement was reached by the two parties on the establishment of four constitutional commissions to oversee reform of the judiciary, the police, the civil service and the teaching sector. Furthermore, in January 2004 President Jagdeo announced his intention to establish a constitutional commission to promote the rights of Guyana's indigenous people.

Crime, in particular violent crime, continued to increase in 2003 and 2004. Following an increase in the number of abductions in the first months of 2003, in June the National Assembly approved legislation to increase the terms of imprisonment for those convicted of kidnap. In December a parliamentary report by the Disciplined Forces Commission referred to the possible existence of a clandestine, government-run paramilitary group. It was claimed that the group targeted suspected criminals and persons linked to known criminals. The allegations were supported in the following month by George Bacchus, who claimed he had been an informant for the so-called 'death squad', which had been allegedly responsible for more than 40 extra-judicial killings in 2003. Bacchus alleged that the Minister of Home Affairs, Ronald Gajraj, had orchestrated the group's operations. As a result, in late January 2004 the Canadian and US Governments revoked Gajraj's visa. Gajraj subsequently took a leave of absence from his ministerial post pending a government inquiry into the allegations. The Minister of Culture, Youth and Sports, Gail Teixeira, was appointed acting Minister of Home Affairs. In March the US Embassy also revoked the visa of former Commissioner of Police Floyd McDonald on the grounds of possible involvement in the covert organization. In May a three-member commission was finally appointed to investigate the allegations. However, on 24 June, the day that he was scheduled to testify before the commission, George Bacchus was shot and killed. The murder of Bacchus, the chief witness in the case, led to increased calls by the opposition for an independent inquiry to investigate the matter. In April 2005 a Presidential Commission of Inquiry cleared Gajraj of involvement in the activities of the 'death squads', He was immediately reinstated to his cabinet post, but, following opposition and international pressure, at the end of the month Gajraj stepped down from office.

Guyana has border disputes with its neighbours, Venezuela and Suriname, although relations with Brazil have continued to improve through trade and military agreements. Suriname restored diplomatic representation in Guyana in 1979 and bilateral meetings were resumed at the end of the year. In 1983 relations improved further as a result of increased trade links between the countries. In late 1998 it was announced that a joint border commission, created to negotiate the settlement of a territorial dispute between Suriname and Guyana, was to be revived, after a two-year suspension. The two countries were also expected to conclude an agreement on fishing rights. However, in May 2000 Suriname formally claimed that Guyana had violated its territorial integrity by granting a concession to the Canadian-based company, CGX Energy Inc, to explore for petroleum and gas. Negotiations to settle the dispute opened in Kingston, Jamaica, in July 2001, but ended inconclusively. In January 2002 the Presidents of the two countries met to discuss the possibility of a production-sharing agreement. However, relations deteriorated when, in June, the Surinamese navy forcibly ejected a rig that had been authorized by Guyana to drill in waters disputed by the two countries. In late October a further meeting of the joint border commission was held in Suriname. On 24 February 2004 Guyana referred the dispute to arbitration under the Convention on the Law of the Sea. In May representatives of the two countries participated in talks presided over by Judge Dolliver Nelson, the President of the International Tribunal for the Law of the Sea, in Hamburg, Germany. Guyana requested that gas and oil exploration be allowed to continue during the negotiations. It was anticipated that a provisional ruling would be followed by a substantive hearing within three years.

In 1962 Venezuela renewed its claim to 130,000 sq km (50,000 sq miles) of land west of the Essequibo river (nearly two-thirds of Guyanese territory). The area was accorded to Guyana in 1899, on the decision of an international tribunal, but Venezuela based its claim on a papal bull of 1493, referring to Spanish colonial possessions. The Port of Spain Protocol of 1970 put the issue in abeyance until 1982. Guyana and Venezuela referred the dispute to the UN in 1983, and, after a series of UN efforts and a visit to Venezuela by President Hoyte, the two countries agreed to a mutually acceptable intermediary, suggested by the UN Secretary-General, in August 1989. In March 1999 Guyana and Venezuela established a joint commission, the High Level Binational Commission, which was intended to expedite the resolution of the territorial dispute and to promote mutual co-operation. However, in September the Venezuelan Government alleged that the Guyanese authorities had granted concessions to petroleum companies within the disputed areas, and in October President Chávez of Venezuela, speaking on the 100th anniversary of the international tribunal's decision, announced his Government's intention to reopen its claim to the territory. Reports of Venezuelan troop movements near the border area caused alarm in Guyana, but were described by the Venezuelan authorities as part of a campaign against drugs-traffickers. In December an agreement was reached between the two countries on co-operation in the fisheries sector. Early in 2000 Guyana signed an agreement with the US-based Beal Aerospace Corpn to build the world's first private satellite-launching facility in the disputed territory of Essequibo. However, following objections by Venezuela and financial difficulties, the company abandoned the project. Nevertheless, in January 2001 Venezuela announced an oil exploration project in the same disputed zone. Later in the year the Venezuelan Government allegedly refused to grant Guyana entry to the Caracas energy accord for special oil concessions, as it had other Caribbean nations, owing to the border dispute. However, Guyana was later invited to join the accord.

Throughout the 1990s Guyana became more closely integrated with CARICOM (see p. 172), and CARICOM played an active role in attempts to achieve a peace agreement between the PPP and PNC in the late 1990s. In 2000 President Jagdeo led negotiations on entry into the World Trade Organization (see p. 357). In September 2001 construction began in Georgetown on the new CARICOM headquarters. At the third Summit of the Americas, held in Québec City, Canada, in April 2001, President Jagdeo reiterated the need for a fund to assist Caribbean nations in the transition to free trade.

Government

Under the 1980 Constitution, legislative power is held by the unicameral National Assembly, with 65 members: 53 elected for five years by universal adult suffrage, on the basis of proportional representation; 40 members are elected from national lists, and a further 25 members are elected from regional constituency lists. Executive power is held by the President, who leads the majority party in the Assembly and holds office for its duration. The President appoints and heads a Cabinet, which includes the Prime Minister, and may include up to four Ministers who are not elected members of the Assembly. The Cabinet is collectively responsible to the National Assembly. Guyana comprises 10 regions.

Defence

In August 2004 the Combined Guyana Defence Force consisted of some 1,600 men (of whom 1,400 were in the army, 100 were in the air force and some 100 in the navy). One-third of the combined forces are civilian personnel. A paramilitary force, the People's Militia, totalled 1,500. Defence expenditure totalled at an estimated US $5m. for 2003.

Economic Affairs

In 2003, according to estimates by the World Bank, Guyana's gross national income (GNI), measured at average 2001–03 prices, was US $698.2m., equivalent to US $900 per head (or US $3,950 per head on an international purchasing-power parity basis). During 1990–2003, it was estimated, the population increased at an average annual rate of 0.4%, while gross domestic product (GDP) per head increased, in real terms, by an average of 3.5% per year. Overall GDP increased, in real terms, at an average annual rate of 3.9% in 1990–2003; GDP increased by 1.1% in 2002, but declined by 0.6% in 2003.

Agriculture (including forestry and fishing) provided an estimated 37.5% of GDP in 2003 and employed an estimated 16.9% of the total labour force in mid-2002. The principal cash crops are sugar cane (sugar providing an estimated 25.6% of the value of total domestic exports in 2003) and rice (9.0% in 2003). The sugar industry alone accounted for an estimated 15.0% of GDP in 2003, and, it was estimated, employed about 24,000 people at peak season in 2000. At the beginning of the 21st century the sugar industry was threatened by the disappearing preferential markets and the increasing cost of employment. Despite this, sugar exports increased by 9.4% in 2002. In July 2004 the European Commission announced long-anticipated plans to reform comprehensively the European Union's (EU) sugar regime, ending the preferential prices paid to Guyanese producers. The proposed measures would reduce the EU price paid for sugar by 20% in 2005/06 and by a further 16% in 2006/07. According to Michael Boast, the head of the state sugar company Guysuco (Guyana Sugar Corpn Inc), this would represent an annual loss to Guyana of some US $37m. Guyana and the other sugar-producing members of the African Caribbean Pacific (ACP) group of countries issued a statement condemning the proposals, noting that they would adversely impact on rural development, employment and investment. In late 2004 the Government announced that funding had been secured to upgrade the Skeldon sugar refinery in Berbice and to construct a 30 MW co-generation facility, of which 15 MW would be supplied to Guysuco. The US $135m. project would be jointly financed by the Government, Guysuco and international lending instituions. Vegetables and fruit are cultivated for the local market, and livestock-rearing is being developed. Fishing is also important (particularly shrimp fishing), which accounted for an estimated 6.8% of GDP in 2003. Agricultural production increased at an average annual rate of 3.2% during 1993–2003. Agricultural GDP increased by 3.4% in 2001 and by a further 5.2% in 2002.

Timber resources in Guyana are extensive and underdeveloped. In 2003 the forestry sector contributed 2.0% of GDP. About three-quarters of the country's total land area consists of forest and woodland. In 2003 timber shipments provided an estimated 6.1% of total domestic exports, compared with 7.3% in the previous year. Although foreign investment in Guyana's largely undeveloped interior continues to be encouraged by the Government, there is much popular concern at the extent of the exploitation of the rainforest. The forestry sector increased at an average annual rate of 4.6% in 1993–2003. In 2002 the sector declined by 7.7%, but in 2003 it increased by 1.7%.

Industry (including mining, manufacturing and construction) provided an estimated 21.1% of GDP in 2003 and engaged 20.4% of the employed labour force in 1992. Industrial GDP increased at an average annual rate of 2.7% in 1993–2003. Industrial GDP was stagnant in 2002 and declined by 1.8% in 2003.

Mining contributed an estimated 12.9% of GDP in 2003, and employed 4.8% of the total working population in 1980. Bauxite, which is used for the manufacture of aluminium, is one of Guyana's most valuable exports, and accounted for an estimated 8.8% of total domestic exports in 2003. The value of bauxite exports decreased significantly in 2002 following the withdrawal, in January of that year, of the US-based aluminium company Alcoa from the Aroaima bauxite and aluminium mine, owing to high production costs and unfavourable investment conditions. Alcoa sold its share to the Guyanese Government. Figures for 2002 indicated that bauxite production subsequently decreased by 18.5% and exports by 42.1%, compared with 2001. In September 2002 the Government merged the Bermine and Aroaima bauxite companies in an effort to improve the performance of the sector. Bauxite exports increased from US $35.3m. in 2002 to US $44.5 in 2003. The registered production of gold (which accounted for 25.9% of domestic exports in 2003) increased considerably during the 1990s. After reaching a peak in 1998, productivity declined in 1999, owing to high production costs and poor ore quality. Production recovered in 2000 and in 2001, before declining by 4.2% in 2002 and by a further 10.4% in 2003. Although the value of gold exports increased by 7.3% in 2002, they decreased the following year (by some 4.0%). In 2000 the gold industry was estimated to directly employ some 32,000 people. There are also significant diamond resources and some petroleum reserves. In 2000 Mazaruni Granite Products Ltd initiated a US $34m. development and modernization programme of granite production. The GDP of the mining sector was estimated to have increased by an average of 1.0% per year in 1993–2003. The sector's GDP decreased, in real terms, by 6.9% in 2002 and by a further 8.7% in the following year. The sector was expected further to contract substantially in 2005, as a result of the scheduled closure of the Omai gold mine in late 2005. Operating machinery was to be removed and the buildings dismantled, to allow for reafforestation.

Manufacturing (including power) accounted for an estimated 3.1% of GDP in 2003 and, according to the 1980 census, employed 14.4% of the total working population. The main activities are the processing of bauxite, sugar, rice and timber. Manufacturing GDP increased at an average annual rate of 2.3% in 1993–2003. The sector increased by 10.9% in 2002, but remained stagnant in 2003.

Energy requirements are almost entirely met by imported hydrocarbon fuels. In 2003 fuels and lubricants constituted 25.7%of the total value of imports (mainly from Venezuela and Trinidad and Tobago). Despite the border dispute, in early 2001 Venezuela granted Guyana, along with a number of other Caribbean nations, entry to the Caracas energy accord for special petroleum concessions. In November 2002 Venezuela agreed to supply oil at a discount of 25%, providing that the price on world markets remained above US $30 per barrel. In June 2002 the Inter-American Development Bank (IDB) approved a loan for US $27.4m. to fund the extension of electricity lines to the coastal regions. The Government of the People's Republic of China granted US $3.8m. in October 2004 for the renovation of the Moco Moco hydroelectric station. Construction began in mid-2002 on the 100 MW Amaila Falls hydroelectric power project. However, the project failed to gain the support of the state power company, Guyana Power and Light Inc (GPL), and construction was halted in early 2003. In April 2003 the Government assumed control of GPL for the nominal sum of US $1 from its partner A C Power and, one year later, 50% of GPL was offered for sale on the local market for US $30m. In November 2004 the Government announced the deregulation of the sale of aviation fuel; thus ending the monopoly of Texaco Guyana. The decision was prompted by a fuel shortage in July and August that grounded Guyana's fleet of light aircraft, and was expected to lead to lower fuel prices in the long-term.

The services sector contributed an estimated 41.4% of GDP in 2003 and engaged 43.2% of the employed labour force in 1980. The GDP of the services sector increased by an average of 3.0% per year in 1993–2003. Services GDP increased, in real terms, by 0.4% in 2002 and by 1.4% in 2003. A plan to promote the tourism sector was announced by the Government in early 2004.

In 2003 Guyana recorded a visible trade deficit of US $92.7m. and a deficit of US $118.9m. on the current account of the balance of payments. In 2001 the principal source of imports was the USA (38.1%). Trinidad and Tobago (7.6%), the United Kingdom (6.2%) and Japan (5.1%) were other important suppliers. In the same year Canada was the principal market for exports (42.9% of total exports), followed by the USA (25.3%), the United Kingdom (9.4%) and Jamaica (3.3%). The principal exports are gold, sugar, rice and bauxite, and the principal imports are consumer goods and fuel and lubricants.

In 2004 the overall budget deficit was an estimated G $25,970.8m. (equivalent to 20.4% of GDP). According to World Bank estimates, by the end of 2002 Guyana's external debt totalled US $1,459m. of which US $1,218m. was long-term public debt. The cost of debt-servicing in 2002 was US $78m., equivalent to 10.7% of exports of goods and services. The annual rate of inflation averaged 8.4% in 1994–2003. Consumer prices increased by 7.1% in 2002 and by 4.9% in 2003. An estimated 11.7% of the labour force were unemployed in 1992.

Guyana is a founder member of CARICOM (see p. 172). It is also a member of the UN Economic Commission for Latin America and the Caribbean (ECLAC, see p. 33) and of the International Sugar Organization (see p. 371).

In 1988, in response to serious economic decline, the Government introduced an extensive recovery programme of adjustment measures and structural reforms. Funds were made available under two Enhanced Structural Adjustment Facilities (ESAF), approved by the IMF in 1990 and in 1994. In 1996 negotiations with the 'Paris Club' of creditor nations and Trinidad and Tobago resulted in the cancellation of 67% of Guyana's bilateral debt with five creditor nations (a total reduction of US $395m.). In 1998, following a substantial period of drought that adversely affected economic growth, the Government secured a new three-year ESAF with the IMF, and in May 1999 the IMF and the World Bank declared that Guyana had become eligible for some US $410m. in nominal debt-service relief under the Heavily Indebted Poor Countries (HIPC) initiative. In November 2000 Guyana became eligible for additional debt relief totalling US $590m. under the Enhanced HIPC initiative, subject to certain conditions. To this end, in November 2002 the IMF approved a US $64m. debt relief programme for Guyana. In January 2004 the IMF, the World Bank's International Development Association and the Paris Club announced that Guyana had met the criteria for the additional debt relief and would receive the remaining US $334.5m. in credit. This was in addition to US $20m. in loans that had been cancelled by the People's Republic of China in August 2003 (a further US $16.5m. of bilateral debt was cancelled by the German Government in December 2004). The HIPC funding was expected to reduce Guyana's external debt by nearly 50%. In June 2004 the IDB approved a 40-year loan of US $28m. to finance reform of the fiscal sector, and a further US $23m. to improve the national health care system.

According to the IMF in mid-2004 economic growth in Guyana was inhibited by the difficult political situation between the Government and the PNC/Reform. However, it noted that some structural reforms, nevertheless, had been undertaken in the areas of financial management, governance and public enterprise. The IMF recommended that in 2004–05 Jagdeo's administration further improve transparency in the banking sector and reform the state-owned sugar and bauxite companies. In October 2004 the World Trade Organization criticized Guyana's continued economic dependence on gold, sugar, bauxite and rice. The economy contracted by 0.6% in 2003. This was primarily owing to a decline in agricultural production, caused by adverse weather conditions. However, preliminary estimates indicated a strong recovery in the sugar industry would contribute to GDP growth of 2.5% in 2004. However, the economy was projected to contract by 0.2% in 2005, owing to the expected closure of Omai Gold Mine Ltd in the third quarter of 2005 and to the extensive floods that affected the country in January of that year.

Education

Education is officially compulsory, and is provided free of charge, for eight years between six and 14 years of age. Primary education begins at six years of age and lasts for at least six years. Secondary education, beginning at 12 years of age, lasts for up to five years, comprising a first cycle of three years and a second cycle of two years. Gross primary enrolment in 1998/1999 was equivalent to an estimated 97.5% of children in the relevant age-group (boys 100.0%; girls 94.3%). Gross secondary enrolment in 1997 was equivalent to an estimated 74.9% of children in the relevant age-group (boys 73.4%; girls 76.4%). There are also 14 technical, vocational, special and higher educational institutions. These include the University of Guyana in George-town and a teacher training college. Expenditure on education by the central Government in 2004 was estimated at G $14,500m., and represented 14.5% of total government expenditure in that year. In 2002 the IDB approved a loan of US $30m. to assist with the modernization of basic education in Guyana. In 2004 the Government announced the construction of 25 new schools.

Public Holidays

2005: 1 January (New Year's Day), 21 January (Id al-Adha, feast of the Sacrifice*), 23 February (Mashramani, Republic Day), 25 March (Good Friday), 28 March (Easter Monday), 21 April (Yum an-Nabi, birth of the Prophet*), 1 May (Labour Day), 5 May (Indian Heritage Day), 4 July (Caribbean Day), 1 August (Freedom Day), 4 November (Id al-Fitr, end of Ramadan*), 25–26 December (Christmas).

2006: 1 January (New Year's Day), 11 January (Id al-Adha, feast of the Sacrifice*), 23 February (Mashramani, Republic Day), 11 April (Yum an-Nabi, birth of the Prophet*), 14 April (Good Friday), 17 April (Easter Monday), 1 May (Labour Day), 5 May (Indian Heritage Day), 3 July (Caribbean Day), 1 August (Freedom Day), 24 October (Id al-Fitr, end of Ramadan*), 25–26 December (Christmas).

* These holidays are dependent on the Islamic lunar calendar and may vary by one or two days from the dates given.
In addition, the Hindu festivals of Holi Phagwah (usually in March) and Divali (October or November) are celebrated. These festivals are dependent on sightings of the moon and their precise date is not known until two months before they take place.

Weights and Measures

The metric system has been introduced.

Statistical Survey

Sources (unless otherwise stated): Bank of Guyana, 1 Church St and Ave of the Republic, POB 1003, Georgetown; tel. 226-3261; fax 227-2965; e-mail communications@solutions2000.net; internet www.bankofguyana.org.gy; Bureau of Statistics, Ministry of Finance, Main and Urquhart Sts, Georgetown; tel. 227-1114; fax 226-1284.

AREA AND POPULATION

Area: 214,969 sq km (83,000 sq miles).

Population: 758,619 (males 375,481, females 382,778) at census of 12 May 1980; 701,704 (males 344,928, females 356,776) at census of 12 May 1991; 751,000 in 2003 (official estimate at mid-year).

Density (2003): 3.5 per sq km.

Ethnic Groups (official estimates, 1999): 'East' Indians 51%, Africans 41%, Amerindians 6%, Portuguese and Chinese 2%, Others less than 1%.

Regions (estimated population, 1986): Barima–Waini 18,500; Pomeroon–Supenaam 42,000; Essequibo Islands–West Demerara 102,800; Demerara–Mahaica 310,800; Mahaica–Berbice 55,600; East Berbice–Corentyne 149,000; Cuyuni–Mazaruni 17,900; Potaro–Siparuni 5,700; Upper Takutu–Upper Essequibo 15,300; Upper Demerara–Berbice 38,600.

Principal Towns (official estimates, 1991): Georgetown (capital) 151,679; Linden 28,560; New Amsterdam 18,460; Corriverton 13,429 (Source: Government Information Agency). *Mid-2003* (UN estimate, incl. suburbs): Georgetown 231,007 (Source: UN, *World Urbanization Prospects: The 2003 Revision*).

Births, Marriages and Deaths (official estimates): Birth rate 21.8 per 1,000 in 1995–2000, 23.6 per 1,000 in 2001; Marriage rate 7.3 per 1,000 in 2001; Crude death rate 7.4 per 1,000 in 1995–2000, 6.6 per 1,000 in 2000.

Expectation of Life (WHO estimates, years at birth): 64.3 (males 61.9; females 66.5) in 2002. Source: WHO, *World Health Report*.

Economically Active Population (persons between 15 and 65 years of age, 1980 census): Agriculture, forestry and fishing 48,603; Mining and quarrying 9,389; Manufacturing 27,939; Electricity, gas and water 2,772; Construction 6,574; Trade, restaurants and hotels 14,690; Transport, storage and communications 9,160; Financing, insurance, real estate and business services 2,878; Community, social and personal services 57,416; Activities not adequately defined 15,260; *Total employed* 194,681 (males 153,645, females 41,036); Unemployed 44,650 (males 26,439, females 18,211); *Total labour force* 239,331 (males 180,084, females 59,247). *Mid-2003* (estimates): Agriculture, etc. 55,000; Total labour force 329,000 (Source: FAO).

HEALTH AND WELFARE

Key Indicators

Total Fertility Rate (children per woman, 2002): 2.3.

Under-5 Mortality Rate (per 1,000 live births, 2003): 69.

HIV/AIDS (% of persons aged 15–49, 2003): 2.5.

Physicians (per 1,000 head, 1997): 0.18.

Hospital Beds (per 1,000 head, 1996): 3.87.

Health Expenditure (2001): US $ per head (PPP): 215.

Health Expenditure (2001): % of GDP: 5.3.

Health Expenditure (2001): public (% of total): 79.9.

Access to Water (% of persons, 2002): 83.

Access to Sanitation (% of persons, 2002): 70.

Human Development Index (2002): ranking: 104.

Human Development Index (2002): value: 0.719.

For sources and definitions, see explanatory note on p. vi.

AGRICULTURE, ETC.

Principal Crops (FAO estimates unless otherwise indicated, '000 metric tons, 2003): Rice (paddy) 501.5 (unofficial estimate); Cassava (Manioc) 29; Roots and tubers 11; Sugar cane 3,000; Coconuts 45; Vegetables 45; Bananas 17; Plantains 17; Other fruit 34. Source: FAO.

Livestock (FAO estimates, '000 head, year ending September 2003): Horses 2.4; Asses 1; Cattle 110; Sheep 130; Pigs 20; Goats 79; Chickens 21,300. Source: FAO.

Livestock Products (FAO estimates, '000 metric tons, 2003): Beef and veal 1.8; Sheep and goat meat 0.8; Pig meat 0.5; Chicken meat 23.7; Cows' milk 30; Hen eggs 1.5. Source: FAO.

Forestry (FAO estimates, '000 cubic metres, 2003): *Roundwood Removals:* Sawlogs, veneer logs and logs for sleepers 142, Pulpwood 112, Other industrial wood 15, Fuel wood 870; Total 1,139; *Sawnwood Production:* Total (all broadleaved) 35. Source: FAO.

Fishing ('000 metric tons, live weight, 2002): Capture 48.0 (Marine fishes 26.7; Atlantic seabob 17.7); Aquaculture 0.6; *Total catch* 48.6. Source: FAO.

MINING

Production (2003): Bauxite 1,715,705 metric tons; Gold 12,172 kilograms.

INDUSTRY

Selected Products (2003, unless otherwise indicated): Raw sugar 302,378 metric tons; Rice 355,019 metric tons; Bauxite 1,715,705 metric tons; Raw gold 102,662 oz; Rum 145,586 hectolitres (2002); Beer 108,550 hectolitres (2002); Electric energy 549.3m. kWh.

FINANCE

Currency and Exchange Rates: 100 cents = 1 Guyana dollar ($ G). Sterling, *US Dollar and Euro Equivalents* (29 October 2004): £1 sterling = $ G366.380; US $1 = $ G200.000; €1 = $ G254.740; $ G1,000 = £2.73 = US $5.00 = €3.93. *Average Exchange Rate:* ($ G per US $): 187.3 in 2001; 190.7 in 2002; 193.9 in 2003.

Budget (estimates, $ G million, 2004): *Revenue:* Tax revenue 44,460.3 (Income tax 20,657.3, Consumption tax 16,968.2, Trade taxes 4,631.3, Other tax 2,203.5); Other current revenue 3,439.8; Total 47,900.1. *Expenditure:* Current expenditure 50,032.3 (Personnel emoluments 17,716.4, Other goods and services 12,971.6, Interest 7,237.6, Transfers 12,106.7); Capital expenditure 23,838.6; Total (excl. lending minus repayments) 73,870.9.

International Reserves (US $ million at 31 December 2003): IMF special drawing rights 4.84; Foreign exchange 271.55; *Total* 276.39. Source: IMF, *International Financial Statistics*.

Money Supply ($ G million at 31 December 2003): Currency outside banks 17,888; Demand deposits at commercial banks 14,223; Total money (including also private-sector deposits at the Bank of Guyana) 32,117. Source: IMF, *International Financial Statistics*.

Cost of Living (Consumer Price Index; base: 1994 = 100): 183.3 in 2001; 196.4 in 2002; 206.0 in 2003.

Expenditure on the Gross Domestic Product ($ G million at current prices, 2003): Government final consumption expenditure 37,928; Private final consumption expenditure 71,615; Gross fixed capital formation (incl. changes in stocks) 50,473; *Total domestic expenditure* 160,016; Net exports of goods and services −15,952; *GDP in purchasers' values* 144,064.

Gross Domestic Product by Economic Activity ($ G million at current prices, 2003): Agriculture 35,463 (Sugar 18,448, Rice 8,621, Livestock 2,979); Forestry 2,411; Fishing 8,389; Mining and quarrying 15,930; Manufacturing (incl. utilities) 3,874; Engineering and construction 6,199; Distribution 4,996; Transport and communication 11,502; Rented dwellings 5,087; Financial services 4,400; Other services 2,201; Government 22,809; *GDP at factor cost* 123,261; Indirect taxes, *Less* Subsidies, 20,803; *GDP in purchasers' values* 144,064.

Balance of Payments (budget estimates, US $ million, 2003): Exports of goods f.o.b. 512.8; Imports of goods f.o.b. −571.7; *Trade balance* −58.8; Exports of services (net) −69.8; *Balance on goods and services* −128.6; Current transfers received (net) 40.3; *Current balance* −88.3; Capital transfer 43.8; Medium and long-term capital (net) 38.5; Short-term capital (net) −27.3; Net errors and omissions 24.5 *Overall balance* −8.9.

EXTERNAL TRADE

Principal Commodities (US $ million, 2003): *Imports c.i.f.:* Capital goods 116.1; Consumer goods 149.4; Fuel and lubricants 147.2; Other intermediate goods 158.3; Total (incl. others) 571.7 *Exports f.o.b.:* Bauxite 44.6; Sugar 129.2; Rice 45.3; Gold 130.9; Shrimps 53.9; Timber 30.7; Total (incl. others, excl. re-exports) 505.6.

Principal Trading Partners ($ G million, 2001, rounded figures): *Imports:* USA 45,200; Trinidad and Tobago 9,000; United Kingdom 7,400; Japan 6,100; Venezuela 4,500; Netherlands 3,900; China 3,200; Canada 1,600; Total (incl. others) 118,700. *Exports:* Canada 56,300; USA 33,200; United Kingdom 12,300; Jamaica 4,300; Netherlands 2,600; Trinidad and Tobago 2,400; Barbados 2,300; Total (incl. others) 131,300.

TRANSPORT

Road Traffic ('000 vehicles in use, 2001): Passenger cars 61.3; Commercial vehicles 15.5. Source: UN, *Statistical Yearbook*.

Shipping: *International Sea-borne Freight Traffic* ('000 metric tons, estimates, 1990): Goods loaded 1,730; Goods unloaded 673 (Source: UN, *Monthly Bulletin of Statistics*). *Merchant Fleet* (at 31 December 2003): Vessels 104; Displacement 31,633 grt (Source: Lloyd's Register-Fairplay, *World Fleet Statistics*).

Civil Aviation (traffic on scheduled services, 2001): Kilometres flown (million) 1; passengers carried ('000) 48; passenger-km (million) 475; total ton-km (million) 17. Source: UN, *Statistical Yearbook*.

TOURISM

Tourist Arrivals ('000): 74.9 in 1999; 105.0 in 2000; 95.1 in 2001.

Tourism Receipts (US $ million): 75 in 2000; 61 in 2001; 49 in 2002.
Sources: Caribbean Development Bank, *Social and Economic Indicators 2002*; World Tourism Organization.

COMMUNICATIONS MEDIA

Radio Receivers (1999): 400,000 in use.

Television Receivers (2000): 70,000 in use.

Telephones (2003): 80,400 main lines in use.

Facsimile Machines (1990): 195 in use.

Mobile Cellular Telephones (2002): 87,300 subscribers.

Personal Computers (2002): 24,000 in use.

Internet Users (2002): 125,000.

Daily Newspapers (1998): 2; estimated circulation 56,750.

Non-daily Newspapers (2000): 4; estimated circulation 47,700.

Book Production (1997): 25.
Sources: mainly UNESCO, *Statistical Yearbook*; UN, *Statistical Yearbook*; International Telecommunication Union.

EDUCATION

Pre-primary (1999/2000): Institutions 320; Teachers 2,218; Students 36,995.

Primary (1999/2000): Institutions 423; Teachers 3,951; Students 105,800.

General Secondary (1999/2000): Institutions 70; Teachers 1,972; Students 36,055.

Special Education (1999/2000): Institutions 6; Teachers 64; Students 617.

Technical and Vocational (1999/2000): Institutions 6; Teachers 215; Students 4,662.

Teacher Training (1999/2000): Institutions 1; Teachers 297; Students 1,604.

University (1999/2000): Institutions 1; Teachers 371; Students 7,496.

Private Education (1999/2000): Institutions 7; Teachers 120; Students 1,692.
Source: Ministry of Education.

Adult Literacy Rate (UNESCO estimates): 98.6% (males 99.0%; females 98.2%) in 2001. Source: UN Development Programme, *Human Development Report*.

Directory

The Constitution

Guyana became a republic, within the Commonwealth, on 23 February 1970. A new Constitution was promulgated on 6 October 1980, and amended in 1998, 2000 and 2001. Its main provisions are summarized below:

The Constitution declares the Co-operative Republic of Guyana to be an indivisible, secular, democratic sovereign state in the course of transition from capitalism to socialism. The bases of the political, economic and social system are political and economic independence, involvement of citizens and socio-economic groups, such as co-operatives and trade unions, in the decision-making processes of the State and in management, social ownership of the means of production, national economic planning and co-operativism as the principle of socialist transformation. Personal property, inheritance, the right to work, with equal pay for men and women engaged in equal work, free medical attention, free education and social benefits for old age and disability are guaranteed. Additional rights include equality before the law, the right to strike and to demonstrate peacefully, the right of indigenous peoples to the protection and preservation of their culture, and a variety of gender and work-related rights. Individual political rights are subject to the principles of national sovereignty and democracy, and freedom of expression to

the State's duty to ensure fairness and balance in the dissemination of information to the public. Relations with other countries are guided by respect for human rights, territorial integrity and non-intervention.

THE PRESIDENT

The President is the supreme executive authority, Head of State and Commander-in-Chief of the armed forces, elected for a five-year term of office, with no limit on re-election. The successful presidential candidate is the nominee of the party with the largest number of votes in the legislative elections. The President may prorogue or dissolve the National Assembly (in the case of dissolution, fresh elections must be held immediately) and has discretionary powers to postpone elections for up to one year at a time for up to five years. The President may be removed from office on medical grounds, or for violation of the Constitution (with a two-thirds' majority vote of the Assembly), or for gross misconduct (with a three-quarters' majority vote of the Assembly if allegations are upheld by a tribunal).

The President appoints a First Vice-President and Prime Minister who must be an elected member of the National Assembly, and a Cabinet of Ministers, which may include four non-elected members and is collectively responsible to the legislature. The President also appoints a Leader of the Opposition, who is the elected member of the Assembly deemed by the President most able to command the support of the opposition.

THE LEGISLATURE

The legislative body is a unicameral National Assembly of 65 members (66 in special circumstances), elected by universal adult suffrage in a system of proportional representation; 40 members are elected at national level, and a further 25 are elected from regional constituency lists. The Assembly passes bills, which are then presented to the President, and may pass constitutional amendments.

LOCAL GOVERNMENT

Guyana is divided into 10 Regions, each having a Regional Democratic Council elected for a term of up to five years and four months, although it may be prematurely dissolved by the President.

OTHER PROVISIONS

Impartial commissions exist for the judiciary, the public service and the police service. An Ombudsman is appointed, after consultation between the President and the Leader of the Opposition, to hold office for four years.

The Government

HEAD OF STATE

President: Bharrat Jagdeo (sworn in 11 August 1999; re-elected 19 March 2001).

CABINET
(April 2005)

Prime Minister and Minister of Public Works and Communication: Samuel A. Hinds.

Minister of Parliamentary Affairs in the Office of the President: Pandit Reepu Daman Persaud.

Minister of Home Affairs: (vacant).

Minister of Foreign Affairs: Dr Rudy Insanally.

Minister of Foreign Trade in the Ministry of Foreign Affairs: Clement Rohee.

Minister of Finance: Saisnarine Kowlessar.

Minister of Agriculture and of Fisheries, Crops and Livestock: Satyadeow Sawh.

Minister of Legal Affairs and Attorney-General: Doodnauth Singh.

Minister of Information: Prem Misir.

Minister of Education: Dr Henry Benfield Jeffrey.

Minister of Health: Dr Leslie Ramsammy.

Minister of Housing and Water: Shaik Baksh.

Minister of Labour, Human Services and Social Security: Dr Dale Bisnauth.

Minister of Tourism, Industry and Commerce: Manzoor Nadir.

Minister of Amerindian Affairs: Carolyn Rodrigues.

Minister of Local Government and Regional Development: Harripersaud Nokta.

Minister of Public Service Management: Jennifer Westford.

Minister of Transport and Hydraulics: Carl Anthony Xavier.

Minister of Culture, Youth and Sports: Gail Teixeira.

Secretary to the Cabinet: Dr Roger Luncheon.

MINISTRIES

Office of the President: New Garden St, Bourda, Georgetown; tel. 225-1330; fax 227-3050; e-mail opmed@sdnp.org.gy; internet www.op.gov.org.gy.

Office of the Prime Minister: Wight's Lane, Georgetown; tel. 227-3101; fax 226-7573; e-mail pmoffice@sdnp.org.gov.gy; internet www.pm.gov.org.gy.

Office of Amerindian Affairs: New Garden St, Bourda, Georgetown; tel. 227-5067; e-mail ministryofamerindian@networksgy.com.

Ministry of Agriculture: Regent and Vlissengen Rds, POB 1001, Georgetown; tel. 227-5527; fax 227-3638; e-mail moa@sdnp.org.gov.gy; internet www.sdnp.org.gy/minagri.

Ministry of Culture, Youth and Sports: 71 Main St, North Cummingsburg, Georgetown; tel. 226-8542; fax 226-8549; e-mail psmincys@guyana.net.gy.

Ministry of Education: 26 Brickdam, Stabroek, POB 1014, Georgetown; tel. 226-3094; fax 225-5570; e-mail moegyweb@yahoo.com; internet www.sdnp.org.gy/minedu.

Ministry of Finance: Main St, Kingston, Georgetown; tel. 227-1114; fax 226-1284; e-mail guyanadmd@solutions2000.net.

Ministry of Fisheries, Crops and Livestock: Regent Rd, Bourda, Georgetown; tel. 226-1565; fax 227-2978; e-mail minfcl@sdnp.org.gy; internet www.sdnp.org.gy/minagri.

Ministry of Foreign Affairs: Takuba Lodge, 254 South Rd, Bourda, Georgetown; tel. 226-1607; fax 225-9192; e-mail minfor@sdnp.org.gy; internet www.sdnp.org.gy/minfor.

Ministry of Health: Brickdam, Stabroek, Georgetown; tel. 226-1560; fax 225-4505; e-mail moh@sdnp.org.gy; internet www.sdnp.org.gy/moh.

Ministry of Home Affairs: 6 Brickdam, Stabroek, Georgetown; tel. 225-7270; fax 226-2740.

Ministry of Housing and Water: 41 Brickdam, Stabroek, Georgetown; tel. 225-7192; fax 227-3455; e-mail mhwps@sdnp.org.gy.

Ministry of Information: Area B, Homestretch Ave, Durban Park, Georgetown; tel. 227-1101; fax 226-4003; internet www.sdnp.org.gy/mininfo.

Ministry of Labour, Human Services and Social Security: 1 Water St, Stabroek, Georgetown; tel. 225-0566; fax 226-6076; e-mail khadoo@networksgy.com; internet www.sdnp.org.gy/mohss.

Ministry of Legal Affairs and Office of the Attorney-General: 95 Carmichael St, Georgetown; tel. 225-3663; fax 226-9721.

Ministry of Local Government and Regional Development: De Winkle Bldg, Fort St, Kingston, Georgetown; tel. 225-8621; fax 226-5070; e-mail mlgrdps@telsnetgy.net.

Ministry of Public Service Management: 164 Waterloo St, North Cummingsburg, Georgetown; tel. 227-1193; fax 227-2700; e-mail psm@sdnp.org.gy.

Ministry of Public Works and Communication: Georgetown.

Ministry of Tourism, Industry and Commerce: 229 South Rd, Lacytown, Georgetown; tel. 226-2505; fax 225-4370; e-mail ministry@mintic.gov.gy; internet www.sdnp.org.gy/mtti.

Ministry of Transport and Hydraulics: Wights Lane, Kingston, Georgetown; tel. 226-1875; fax 225-8395; e-mail minoth@networksgy.com.

President and Legislature

NATIONAL ASSEMBLY

Speaker: Ralph Ramkarran.
Deputy Speaker: Clarissa Riehl.
Election, 19 March 2001

Party	No. of seats		
	Regional	National	Total
People's Progressive Party/CIVIC (PPP/CIVIC)	11	23	34
People's National Congress/Reform (PNC/Reform)	13	14	27
Guyana Action Party/Working People's Alliance (GAP/WPA)	1	1	2
Rise, Organize and Rebuild Guyana Movement (ROAR)	—	1	1
The United Force (TUF)	—	1	1
Total	25	40	65

Under Guyana's system of proportional representation, the nominated candidate of the party receiving the most number of votes was elected to the presidency. Thus, on 23 March 2001 the candidate of the PPP/CIVIC alliance, Bharrat Jagdeo, was declared President-elect, defeating Hugh Desmond Hoyte of the PNC/Reform alliance. Jagdeo was inaugurated as President on 31 March.

Political Organizations

CIVIC: New Garden St, Georgetown; social/political movement of businessmen and professionals; allied to PPP; Leader Samuel Archibald Anthony Hinds.

Guyana Action Party (GAP): Georgetown; allied to WPA; Leader PAUL HARDY.

Guyana Democratic Party (GDP): Georgetown; f. 1996; Leaders ASGAR ALLY, NANDA K. GOPAUL.

Guyana National Congress (GNC): Georgetown.

Guyana People's Party (GPP): Georgetown; f. 1996; Leader MAX MOHAMED.

Guyana Republican Party (GRP): Paprika East Bank, Essequibo; f. 1985; right-wing; Leader LESLIE PRINCE (resident in the USA).

Horizon and Star (HAS): Georgetown.

Justice For All Party (JFAP): 73 Robb and Wellington Sts, Lacytown, Georgetown; tel. 226-5462; fax 227-3050; e-mail sharma@guyana.net.gy; internet www.jfa-gy.com; Leader CHANDRANARINE SHARMA.

National Democratic Front (NDF): Georgetown; Leader JOSEPH BACCHUS.

National Front Alliance: Georgetown.

Democratic Labour Movement (DLM): 34 Robb and King Sts, 4th Floor, Lacytown, POB 10930, Georgetown; f. 1983; democratic-nationalist; Pres. PAUL NEHRU TENNASSEE.

People's Democratic Movement (PDM): Stabroek House, 10 Croal St, Georgetown; tel. 226-4707; fax 226-3002; f. 1973; centrist; Leader LLEWELLYN JOHN.

People's Progressive Party (PPP): Freedom House, 41 Robb St, Lacytown, Georgetown; tel. 227-2095; fax 227-2096; e-mail ppp@guyana.net.gy; internet www.ppp-civic.org; f. 1950; Marxist-Leninist; allied to CIVIC; Gen. Sec. DONALD RAMOTAR.

National Independence Party: Georgetown; Leader SAPHIER HUSSIEN.

People's National Congress Reform (PNC Reform): Congress Place, Sophia, POB 10330, Georgetown; tel. 225-7852; fax 225-6055; e-mail pnc@guyana-pnc.org; internet www.guyanapnc.org; f. 1955 after a split with the PPP; Reform wing established in 2000; PNC Leader ROBERT H. O. CORBIN; Chair. VINCENT ALEXANDER.

Rise, Organize and Rebuild Guyana Movement (ROAR): 186 Parafield, Leonora, West Coast Demerara, POB 101409, Georgetown; tel. 068-2452; e-mail guyroar@hotmail.com; f. 1999.

The United Force (TUF): 95 Robb and New Garden Sts, Bourda, Georgetown; tel. 226-2596; fax 225-2973; e-mail manzoornadir@yahoo.com; f. 1960; right-wing; advocates rapid industrialization through govt partnership and private capital; Leader MANZOOR NADIR.

United People's Party: 77 Winter Pl., Brickdam, Georgetown; tel. 227-5217; fax 227-5166; e-mail unitedguyana@yahoo.com.

Unity Party: 77 Hadfield St, Georgetown; tel. 227-6744; fax 227-6745; e-mail unityp@networksgy.com; f. 2005; promotes private enterprise and coalition politics; Pres. CHEDDI (JOEY) JAGAN, Jr.

Working People's Alliance (WPA): Walter Rodney House, 80, Croal St, Stabroek, Georgetown; tel. and fax 225-3679; internet www.guyanacaribbeanpolitics.com/wpa/wpa.html; originally popular pressure group, became political party 1979; independent Marxist; allied to GAP; Collective Leadership Dr CLIVE THOMAS, Dr RUPERT ROOPNARINE.

Diplomatic Representation

EMBASSIES AND HIGH COMMISSIONS IN GUYANA

Brazil: 308 Church St, Queenstown, POB 10489, Georgetown; tel. 225-7970; fax 226-9063; e-mail guibrem@solutions2000.net; Ambassador NEY DO PRADO DIEGUEZ.

Canada: High and Young Sts, POB 10880, Georgetown; tel. 227-2081; fax 225-8380; e-mail grgtn@international.gc.ca; internet www.dfait-maeci.gc.ca/guyana; High Commissioner BRUNO PICARD.

China, People's Republic: Botanic Gardens, Mandella Ave, Georgetown; tel. 227-1651; fax 231-6602; e-mail chinaemb_gy@mfa.gov.cn; Ambassador SHEN QING.

Cuba: 46 High St, Georgetown; tel. 225-1881; fax 226-1824; e-mail emguyana@networksgy.com; Ambassador JOSÉ MANUEL INCLAN EMBADE.

India: Bank of Baroda Bldg, 10 Ave of the Republic, POB 101148, Georgetown; tel. 226-3996; fax 225-7012; High Commissioner AVINASH C. GUPTA.

Russia: 3 Public Rd, Kitty, Georgetown; tel. 227-1738; fax 227-2975; e-mail reing@networks.gy.com; Ambassador VLSDIMIR STEPANOVICH STARIKOV.

Suriname: 304 Church St, POB 10508, Georgetown; tel. 226-7844; fax 225-0759; e-mail surnemb@gol.net.gy; Ambassador MANORMA SOEKNANDAN.

United Kingdom: 44 Main St, POB 10849, Georgetown; tel. 226-5881; fax 225-3555; e-mail enquiries@britain-in-guyana.org; internet britain-in-guyana.org; High Commissioner STEPHEN HISCOCK.

USA: 100 Young and Duke Sts, POB 10507, Kingston, Georgetown; tel. 225-4900; fax 225-8497; Ambassador ROLAND W. BULLEN.

Venezuela: 296 Thomas St, South Cummingsburg, Georgetown; tel. 226-1543; fax 225-3241; e-mail embveguy@gol.net.gy; Ambassador FRANÇOIS PULVENIS.

Judicial System

The Judicature of Guyana comprises the Supreme Court of Judicature, which consists of the Court of Appeal and the High Court (both of which are superior courts of record), and a number of Courts of Summary Jurisdiction.

The Court of Appeal, which came into operation in 1966, consists of the Chancellor as President, the Chief Justice, and such number of Justices of Appeal as may be prescribed by the National Assembly.

The High Court of the Supreme Court consists of the Chief Justice as President of the Court and Puisne Judges. Its jurisdiction is both original and appellate. It has criminal jurisdiction in matters brought before it on indictment. A person convicted by the Court has a right of appeal to the Guyana Court of Appeal. The High Court of the Supreme Court has unlimited jurisdiction in civil matters and exclusive jurisdiction in probate, divorce and admiralty and certain other matters. Under certain circumstances, appeal in civil matters lies either to the Full Court of the High Court of the Supreme Court, which is composed of no fewer than two judges, or to the Guyana Court of Appeal. On 4 November 2004 the National Assembly approved legislation recognizing the Caribbean Court of Justice (CCJ) as Guyana's highest court of appeal. The CCJ was inaugurated in Port of Spain, Trinidad and Tobago, on 16 April 2005.

A magistrate has jurisdiction to determine claims where the amount involved does not exceed a certain sum of money, specified by law. Appeal lies to the Full Court.

Chancellor of Justice: DESIRÉE BERNARD.

Chief Justice: CARL SINGH.

High Court Justices: NANDRAM KISSOON, CLAUDETTE SINGH.

Attorney-General: DOODNAUTH SINGH.

Religion

CHRISTIANITY

Guyana Council of Churches: 26 Durban St, Lodge, Georgetown; tel. 225-3020; e-mail bishopedghill@hotmail.com; f. 1967 by merger of the Christian Social Council (f. 1937) and the Evangelical Council (f. 1960); 15 mem. churches, 1 assoc. mem.; Chair. Bishop JUAN A. EDGHILL; Sec. Rev. NIGEL HAZEL.

The Anglican Communion

Anglicans in Guyana are adherents of the Church in the Province of the West Indies, comprising eight dioceses. The Archbishop of the Province is the Bishop of the North Eastern Caribbean and Aruba, resident in St John's, Antigua. The diocese of Guyana also includes French Guiana and Suriname. In 1996 the estimated membership in the country was 118,000.

Bishop of Guyana: Rt Rev. RANDOLPH OSWALD GEORGE, The Church House, 49 Barrack St, POB 10949, Georgetown 1; tel. and fax 226-4183; e-mail dioofguy@networksgy.com; internet www.anglican.bm/G/01.html.

The Baptist Church

The Baptist Convention of Guyana: POB 10149, Georgetown; tel. 226-0428; 1,823 mems.

The Lutheran Church

The Evangelical Lutheran Church in Guyana: Lutheran Courts, Berbice, POB 88, New Amsterdam; tel. and fax 333-6479; e-mail lcg@guyana.net.gy; f. 1947; 11,000 mems; Pres. Rev. ROY K. THAKURDYAL.

The Roman Catholic Church

Guyana comprises the single diocese of Georgetown, suffragan to the archdiocese of Port of Spain, Trinidad and Tobago. At 31 December 2002 adherents of the Roman Catholic Church comprised about 11% of the total population. The Bishop participates in the Antilles Episcopal Conference Secretariat, currently based in Port of Spain, Trinidad.

Bishop of Georgetown: FRANCIS DEAN ALLEYNE, Bishop's House, 27 Brickdam, POB 10720, Stabroek, Georgetown; tel. 226-4469; fax 225-8519; e-mail rcbishop@networksgy.com.

Other Christian Churches

Other denominations active in Guyana include the African Methodist Episcopal Church, the African Methodist Episcopal Zion Church, the Church of God, the Church of the Nazarene, the Ethiopian Orthodox Church, the Guyana Baptist Mission, the Guyana Congregational Union, the Guyana Presbyterian Church, the Hallelujah Church, the Methodist Church in the Caribbean and the Americas, the Moravian Church and the Presbytery of Guyana.

BAHÁ'Í FAITH

National Spiritual Assembly: 220 Charlotte St, Bourda, Georgetown; tel. and fax 226-5952; e-mail nsaguy@sdnp.org.gy; internet www.sdnp.org.gy/bahai; incorporated in 1976.

HINDUISM

Hindus constituted an estimated 35% of the population.

Hindu Religious Centre: 162 Lamaha St, POB 10576, Georgetown; tel. 225-7443; f. 1934; Hindus account for about one-third of the population; Gen. Sec. CHRISHNA PERSAUD.

ISLAM

Muslims in Guyana comprised approximately 10% of the population.

The Central Islamic Organization of Guyana (CIOG): M.Y.O. Bldg, Woolford Ave, Thomas Lands, POB 10245, Georgetown; tel. 225-8654; fax 227-2475; e-mail ciog@sdnp.org.gy; internet www .sdnp.org.gy/ciog; Pres. Alhaji FAZEEL M. FEROUZ; Gen. Sec. MUJTABA NASIR.

Guyana United Sad'r Islamic Anjuman: 157 Alexander St, Kitty, POB 10715, Georgetown; tel. 226-9620; f. 1936; 120,000 mems; Pres. Haji A. HAFIZ RAHAMAN.

The Press

DAILIES

Guyana Chronicle: 2A Lama Ave, Bel Air Park, POB 11, Georgetown; tel. 226-3243; fax 227-5208; e-mail gm@guyanachronicle.com; internet www.guyanachronicle.com; f. 1881; govt-owned; also produces weekly *Sunday Chronicle* (tel. 226-3243); Editor-in-Chief SHARIEF KHAN; circ. 23,000 (weekdays), 43,000 (Sundays).

Stabroek News: 46–47 Robb St, Lacytown, Georgetown; tel. 227-4080; fax 225-4637; e-mail stabroeknews@stabroeknews.com; internet www.stabroeknews.com; f. 1986; also produces weekly *Sunday Stabroek*; liberal independent; Editor-in-Chief DAVID DE CAIRES; Editor ANAND PERSAUD; circ. 13,500 (weekdays), 26,000 (Sundays).

WEEKLIES AND PERIODICALS

The Catholic Standard: 293 Oronoque St, Queenstown, POB 10720, Georgetown; tel. 226-1540; f. 1905; weekly; Editor COLIN SMITH; circ. 10,000.

Diocesan Magazine: 144 Almond and Oronoque Sts, Queenstown, Georgetown; quarterly.

Guyana Business: 156 Waterloo St, POB 10110, Georgetown; tel. 225-6451; f. 1889; organ of the Georgetown Chamber of Commerce and Industry; quarterly; Editor C. D. KIRTON.

Guyana Review: 143 Oronoque St, POB 10386, Georgetown; tel. 226-3139; fax 227-3465; e-mail guyrev@networksgy.com; internet www.guyanareview.com; f. 1993; monthly.

Guynews: Georgetown; monthly.

Kaieteur News: 24 Saffon St, Charlestown; tel. 225-8452; fax 225-8473; e-mail kaieteur@guyana.net.gy; internet www.kaieteurnews .com; f. 1994; independent weekly; Editor W. HENRY SKERRETT; circ. 30,000.

Mirror: Lot 8, Industrial Estate, Ruimveldt, Greater Georgetown; tel. 226-2471; fax 226-2472; e-mail ngmirror@guyana.net.gy; internet www.mirrornewsonline.com; owned by the New Guyana Co Ltd; Sundays; Editor ROBERT PERSAUD; circ. 25,000.

New Nation: Congress Pl., Sophia, Georgetown; tel. 226-7891; f. 1955; organ of the People's National Congress; weekly; Editor FRANCIS WILLIAMS; circ. 26,000.

The Official Gazette of Guyana: Guyana National Printers Ltd, Lot 1, Public Rd, La Penitence; weekly; circ. 450.

Thunder: Georgetown; f. 1950; organ of the People's Progressive Party; quarterly; Editor RALPH RAMKARRAN; circ. 5,000.

PRESS ASSOCIATION

Guyana Press Association (GPA): Georgetown; Pres. DENIS CHABROL; Vice-Pres. JULIA JOHNSON.

NEWS AGENCIES

Guyana Information Services: Office of the President, New Garden St and South Rd, Georgetown; tel. 226-3389; fax 226-4003; f. 1993; Dir MILTON DREPAUL.

Foreign Bureaux

Xinhua (New China) News Agency (People's Republic of China): 52 Brickdam, Stabroek, Georgetown; tel. 226-9965.

Associated Press (USA) and Informatsionnoye Telegrafnoye Agentstvo Rossii—Telegrafnoye Agentstvo Suverennykh Stran (ITAR—TASS) (Russia) are also represented.

Publishers

Guyana Free Press: POB 10386, Georgetown; tel. 226-3139; fax 227-3465; e-mail guyrev@networksgy.com; books and learned journals.

Guyana National Printers Ltd: 1 Public Rd, La Penitence, POB 10256, Greater Georgetown; tel. 225-3623; e-mail gnpl@guyana.net .gy; f. 1939; govt-owned printers and publishers; privatization pending.

Guyana Publications Inc: 46/47 Robb St, Lacytown, Georgetown; tel. 225-7473; fax 225-4637; e-mail stabroeknews.com; internet www .stabroeknews.com; Man. Dir DOREEN DeCAIRES.

Broadcasting and Communications

TELECOMMUNICATIONS

The telecommunications sector was restructured and opened up to competition in 2002.

Guyana Telephones and Telegraph Company (GT & T): 79 Brickdam, POB 10628, Georgetown; tel. 226-7840; fax 226-2457; internet www.gtt.co.gy; f. 1991; fmrly state-owned Guyana Telecommunications Corpn; 80% ownership by Atlantic Tele-Network (USA); CEO SONITA JAGAN; Chair. CORNELIUS PRIOR.

Trans-World Telecom Guyana (TWT Guyana): 56 High St, POB 101845, Georgetown; tel. 223-6531; fax 223-6532; e-mail info@ celstarguyana.net; internet www.twtcaribbean.com/guyana; f. 1999; acquired Cel Star Guyana in 2003; GSM cellular telecommunications network; mem. of Trans-World Telecom Caribbean group; COO PIERRE STRASSER.

BROADCASTING

In May 2001 the Government implemented the regulation of all broadcast frequencies. All television broadcast operations were required to be fully licensed by 31 July. By December 15 of the 18 television stations in Guyana had acquired licences. Two private stations relay US satellite television programmes.

National Communications Network (NCN): Homestretch Ave, D'Urban Park, Georgetown; tel. 225-166; fax 225-2253; e-mail gm@ guyana.net.gy; f. 2004 following merger of Guyana Broadcasting Corpn (f. 1979) and Guyana Television and Broadcasting Co (f. 1993); govt-owned; operates three radio channels and six TV channels; CEO DESMOND MOHAMED; Editor-in-Chief WILFRED CAMERON.

Radio

National Communications Network (NCN): see Broadcasting; operates three channels:

Hot FM.

Radio Roraima.

Voice of Guyana.

Television

National Communications Network: see Broadcasting; TV network covers channels 8, 11, 13, 15, 21 and 26.

Finance

(cap. = capital; res = reserves; dep. = deposits; m. = million; brs = branches; amounts in Guyana dollars)

BANKING

Central Bank

Bank of Guyana: 1 Church St and Ave of the Republic, POB 1003, Georgetown; tel. 226-3250; fax 227-2965; e-mail communications@ bankofguyana.org.gy; internet www.bankofguyana.org.gy; f. 1965; cap. 1,000m., res 4,062.7m., dep. 86,482.3m. (Dec. 2003); central bank of issue; acts as regulatory authority for the banking sector; Gov. LAWRENCE T. WILLIAMS (acting).

Commercial Banks

Citizens' Bank Guyana Inc: 201 Camp and Charlotte Sts, Lacy-town, Georgetown; tel. 226-1705; fax 227-1719; f. 1994; 51% owned by Banks DIH; Chair. CLIFFORD REIS; Man. Dir ALAN PARRIS.

Demerara Bank Ltd: 230 Camp and South Sts, Georgetown; tel. and fax 225-0610; e-mail banking@demerarabank.com; internet www.demerarabank.com; f. 1994; cap. 450m., res 139m., dep. 11,719m. (Sept. 2002); Chair. YESU PERSAUD; Man. Dir AHMAD M. KHAN.

Guyana Americas Merchant Bank (GBTI): GTBI Bldg, 138 Regent St, Lacytown, Georgetown; tel. 223-5193; fax 223-5195; e-mail gambi@networksgy.com; f. 2001; merchant bank.

Guyana Bank for Trade and Industry Ltd: 47–48 Water St, POB 10280, Georgetown; tel. 226-8430; fax 227-1612; e-mail banking@ gbtibank.com; internet www.gbtibank.com; f. 1987 to absorb the operations of Barclays Bank; cap. 800m., res 601.5m., dep. 21,724.6m. (Dec. 2003); CEO RADHA KRISHNA SHARMA; Dir JOHN TRACEY; 6 brs.

National Bank of Industry and Commerce (NBIC): Promenade Court, 155–156 New Market St, Georgetown; tel. 223-7938; fax 227-4506; e-mail main@nbicgy.com; internet www.nbicgy.com; f. 1984; 51% owned by Republic Bank Ltd, Port of Spain, Trinidad and Tobago; acquired Guyana National Co-operative Bank in 2003; cap. 300m., res 2,899.3m., dep. 48,589.7m. (Sept. 2003); Man. Dir MICHAEL ARCHIBALD; 5 brs.

Foreign Banks

Bank of Baroda (India): 10 Ave of the Republic, POB 10768, Georgetown; tel. 226-4005; fax 225-1691; e-mail bobinc@networksgy .com; f. 1908; Chief Man. P. SAVID.

Bank of Nova Scotia (Canada): 104 Carmichael St, POB 10631; Georgetown; tel. 225-9222; fax 225-9309; e-mail ian.cooper@ scotiabank.com; internet www.scotiabank.com; Man. IAN COOPER; 5 brs.

STOCK EXCHANGE

Guyana Association of Securities Companies and Intermediaries (GASCI): Hand-in-Hand Bldg, 1–4 Ave of the Republic, Georgetown; tel. 223-6175; e-mail info@gasci.com; internet www .gasci.com; f. 2003; Chair. CHANDRA GAJRAJ.

INSURANCE

Demerara Mutual Life Assurance Society Ltd: Demerara Life Bldg, 63 Robb St and Ave of the Republic, POB 10409, Georgetown; tel. 231-3636; fax 225-8995; e-mail demlife@demeraramutual.com; internet www.demeraramutual.com; f. 1891; Chair. RICHARD B. FIELDS; CEO KEITH N. CHOLMONDELEY.

Diamond Fire and General Insurance Inc: High St, Kingston, Georgetown; tel. 223-9771; fax 223-9770; e-mail diamondins@ solutions2000.net; f. 2000; privately-owned; Man. TARA CHANDRA; cap. $G 100m.

Guyana Co-operative Insurance Service: 47 Main St, Georgetown; tel. 225-9153; f. 1976; 67% sowned by the Hand-in-Hand Group; Area Man. SAMMY RAMPERSAUD.

Guyana and Trinidad Mutual Life Insurance Co Ltd: 27–29, Robb and Hinck St, Georgetown; tel. 225-7910; fax 225-9397; e-mail gtmgroup@gtm-gy.com; f. 1925; Chair. HAROLD B. DAVIS; Man. Dir R. E. CHEONG; affiliated company: Guyana and Trinidad Mutual Fire Insurance Co Ltd.

Hand-in-Hand Mutual Fire and Life Group: Hand-in-Hand Bldg, 1–4 Ave of the Republic, POB 10188, Georgetown; tel. 225-0462; fax 225-7519; f. 1865; fire and life insurance; Chair. J. A. CHIN; Gen. Man. K. A. EVELYN.

Insurance Association

Insurance Association of Guyana: 54 Robb St, Bourda, POB 10741, Georgetown; tel. 226-3514; f. 1968.

Trade and Industry

GOVERNMENT AGENCIES

Environmental Protection Agency, Guyana: University of Guyana Campus, Turkeyen, Georgetown; tel. 022-5783; fax 022-2442; e-mail epa@epaguyana.org; internet www.epaguyana.org; f. 1988 as Guyana Agency for the Environment, renamed 1996; formulates, implements and monitors policies on the environment; Exec. Dir DOORGA PERSAUD.

Guyana Energy Agency (GEA): 295 Quamina St, POB 903, Georgetown; tel. 226-0394; fax 226-5227; e-mail ecgea@sdnp.org.gy; internet www.sdnp.org.gy/gea; f. 1998 as successor to Guyana National Energy Authority.

Guyana Office for Investment (Go-Invest): 190 Camp and Church Sts, Georgetown; tel. 225-0653; fax 225-0655; e-mail goinvest@goinvest.gov.gy; internet www.goinvest.gov.gy; f. 1994; Chair. BHARRAT JAGDEO; CEO GEOFFREY DA SILVA.

Guyana Public Communications Agency: Georgetown; tel. 227-2025; f. 1989; Exec. Chair. KESTER ALVES.

'New' Guyana Marketing Corporation: 87 Robb and Alexander Sts, POB 10810, Georgetown; tel. 226-8255; fax 227-4114; e-mail newgmc@networksgy.com; internet www.agrinetguyana.org.gy/ ngmc; Chair. GEOFREY DA SILVA; Gen. Man. NIZAM HASSAN.

DEVELOPMENT ORGANIZATION

Institute of Private Enterprise Development (IPED): 254 South Rd, Bourda, Georgetown; tel. 225-3067; fax 226-4675; internet www.ipedgy.com; f. 1986 to help establish small businesses; total loans provided $ G771m. and total jobs created 9,021 (1999); Chair. YESU PERSAUD.

CHAMBER OF COMMERCE

Georgetown Chamber of Commerce and Industry: 156 Waterloo St, Cummingsburg, POB 10110, Georgetown; tel. 225-5846; fax 226-3519; internet www.georgetownchamberofcommerce .org; f. 1889; 122 mems; Pres. EDWARD BOYER.

INDUSTRIAL AND TRADE ASSOCIATIONS

Guyana Rice Development Board: 117 Cowan St, Georgetown; tel. 225-8717; fax 225-6486; e-mail grdb@gol.net.gy; f. 1994 to assume operations of Guyana Rice Export Board and Guyana Rice Grading Centre; CEO KEITH WARD (acting).

National Dairy and Development Programme (NDDP): REPAHA Compound, Agriculture Rd, Mon Repos, East Coast Demerara; tel. 220-6556; e-mail nichanw@yahoo.com; f. 1984; aims to increase domestic milk and beef production; Dir Dr NICHOLAS WALDRON.

EMPLOYERS' ASSOCIATIONS

Consultative Association of Guyanese Industry Ltd: 157 Waterloo St, POB 10730, Georgetown; tel. 226-4603; fax 227-0725; e-mail cagi@guyana.net.gy; f. 1962; 193 mems, 3 mem. asscns, 159 assoc. mems; Exec. Dir DAVID YANKANA.

Forest Products Association of Guyana: 157 Waterloo St, Georgetown; tel. 226-9848; f. 1944; 47 mems; Pres. L. J. P. WILLEMS; Exec. Officer WARREN PHOENIX.

Guyana Manufacturers' Association Ltd: 157 Waterloo St, North Cummingsburg, Georgetown; tel. 227-4295; fax 227-5615; internet www.gy-gma.org; f. 1967; 190 mems; Pres. NORMAN MCLEAN.

Guyana Rice Producers' Association (GRPA): 126 Parade & Barrack St, Georgetown; tel. 226-4411; fax 223-7249; e-mail grpa .riceproducers@networksgy.com; f. 1946; NGO; 18,500 mems; Gen. Sec. DHARAMKUMAR SEERAJ.

UTILITIES

Electricity

Guyana Power and Light Inc (GPL): 40 Main St, POB 10390, Georgetown; tel. 225-4618; fax 227-1978; e-mail gplit@solutions2000 .net; internet www.gplinc.com; f. 1999; fmrly Guyana Electricity Corpn; state-owned; Chair. ADAM HEDAYAT; CEO JOHN LYNN.

Water

Guyana Water Inc (GWI): 10 Fort St, Georgetown; tel. 225-0471; fax 225-0478; e-mail gwi@networks.gy.com; f. 2002, following merger of Guyana Water Authority (GUYWA) and Georgetown Sewerage and Water Comm.; Chair. WILLIAM WILSON; Man. Dir DERRICK HUDSON.

CO-OPERATIVE SOCIETIES

Chief Co-operatives Development Officer: Ministry of Labour, Human Services and Social Security, 1 Water and Cornhill Sts, Stabroek, Georgetown; tel. 225-8644; fax 227-1308; e-mail coopdept@telsnet.gy.net; f. 1948; Dir CLIVE NURSE.

In October 1996 there were 1,324 registered co-operative societies, mainly savings clubs and agricultural credit societies, with a total membership of 95,950.

TRADE UNIONS

Trades Union Congress (TUC): Critchlow Labour College, Woolford Ave, Non-pareil Park, Georgetown; tel. 226-1493; fax 227-0254; e-mail gtuc@guyana.net.gy; f. 1940; national trade union body; 22 affiliated unions; 70,000 mems; merged with the Federation of Independent Trade Unions in Guyana in 1993; Pres. NORRIS WITTER; Gen. Sec. LINCOLN LEWIS.

Amalgamated Transport and General Workers' Union: 46 Urquhart St, Georgetown; tel. 226-6243; fax 225-6602; Pres. RICHARD SAMUELS; Gen. Sec. VICTOR JOHNSON.

Association of Masters and Mistresses: c/o Critchlow Labour College, Georgetown; tel. 226-8968; Pres. GANESH SINGH; Gen. Sec. T. ANSON SANCHO.

Clerical and Commercial Workers' Union (CCWU): Clerico House, 140 Quamina St, South Cummingsburg, POB 101045, Georgetown; tel. 225-2827; fax 227-2618; e-mail ccwu@guyana.net .gy; Pres. ROY HUGHES; Gen. Sec. GRANTLEY L. CULBARD.

Guyana Bauxite and General Workers' Union: 180 Charlotte St, Georgetown; tel. 225-4654; Pres. CHARLES SAMPSON; Gen. Sec. LEROY ALLEN.

Guyana Labour Union: 198 Camp St, Cummingsburg, Georgetown; tel. 227-1196; fax 225-0820; e-mail glu@solutions2000.net; Pres. SAMUEL WALKER; Gen. Sec. CARVILLE DUNCAN; 6,000 mems.

Guyana Local Government Officers' Union: Woolford Ave, Georgetown; tel. 227-2131; fax 227-6905; e-mail daleantford@ yahoo.com; Pres. ANDREW GARNETT; Gen. Sec. DALE BERESFORD.

Guyana Mining, Metal and General Workers' Union: 56 Wismar St, Linden, Demerara River; tel. 204-6822; Pres. VERNON SEMPLE; Gen. Sec. LESLIE GONSALVES; 5,800 mems.

Guyana Postal and Telecommunication Workers' Union: 310 East St, Georgetown; tel. 226-5255; fax 225-1633; e-mail dawnc_edwards@hotmail.com; Pres. BENJAMIN NEDD; Gen. Sec. DAWN EDWARDS.

Guyana Teachers' Union: Woolford Ave, POB 738, Georgetown; tel. 226-3183; fax 227-0403; Pres. LANCELOT BAPTISTE; Gen. Sec. SHIRLEY HOOPER.

National Mining and General Workers Union: 10 Church St, New Amsterdam, Berbice; tel. 203-3496; Pres. CYRIL CONWAY; Gen. Sec. MARILYN GRIFFITH.

National Union of Public Service Employees: 4 Fort St, Kingston, Georgetown; tel. 227-1491; Pres. ROBERT JOHNSON; Gen. Sec. PATRICK QUINTYNE.

Printing Industry and Allied Workers' Union: c/o Guyana TUC, Georgetown; tel. 226-8968; Gen. Sec. LESLIE REECE.

Public Employees' Union: Regent St, Georgetown; Pres. REUBEN KHAN.

Union of Agricultural and Allied Workers (UAAW): 10 Hadfield St, Werk-en-Rust, Georgetown; tel. 226-7434; Pres. JEAN SMITH; Gen. Sec. SEELO BAICHAN.

University of Guyana Workers' Union: POB 841, Turkeyen, Georgetown; tel. 222-3586; e-mail adeolaplus@yahoo.com; supports Working People's Alliance; Pres. Dr ADELOA JAMES; Sec. AUDREY IRVING.

Guyana Agricultural and General Workers' Union (GAWU): 59 High St and Wight's Lane, Kingston, Georgetown; tel. 227-2091; fax 227-2093; e-mail gawu@networksgy.com; Pres. KOMAL CHAND; Gen. Sec. SEEPAUL NARINE; 20,000 mems.

Guyana Public Service Union (GPSU): 160 Regent and New Garden Sts, Georgetown; tel. 225-0518; fax 226-5322; e-mail gpsu@ guyana.net.gy; Pres. PATRICK YARDE; Gen. Sec. LAWRENCE MENTIS; 11,600 mems.

National Association of Agricultural, Commercial and Industrial Employees (NAACIE): 64 High St, Kingston, Georgetown; tel. 227-2301; f. 1946; Pres. KENNETH JOSEPH; Gen. Sec. KAISREE TAKECHANDRA; c. 2,000 mems.

Transport

RAILWAY

There are no public railways in Guyana.

Linmine Railway: Mackenzie, Linden; tel. 444-2279; fax 444-6699; e-mail orin_barnwell@cambior.com; bauxite transport; 15 km of track, Coomaka to Linden; Dept Head ORIN BARNWELL.

ROADS

The coastal strip has a well-developed road system. In 1999 there were an estimated 7,970 km (4,859 miles) of paved and good-weather roads and trails. In September 2001 a European Union-funded road improvement programme between Crabwood Creek and the Guyana–Suriname Ferry Terminal was completed; the project was intended to help integrate the region. In the same year construction began on a bridge across the Takutu river, linking Guyana to Brazil; construction was suspended in 2002, owing to difficulties with planning regulations and financing, but was expected to resume in 2004. The US $40m. rehabilitation of the Mahaica–Rosignol road partly funded by the Inter-American Development Bank, began in 2003. In the same year work began on a complementary project to remove and relocate both the Mahaica and Mahaicony bridges. Construction of a bridge over the Berbice river was to begin in early 2004.

SHIPPING

Guyana's principal ports are at Georgetown and New Amsterdam. The port at Linden serves for the transportation of bauxite products. A ferry service is operated between Guyana and Suriname. Communications with the interior are chiefly by river, although access is hindered by rapids and falls. There are 1,077 km (607 miles) of navigable rivers. The main rivers are the Mazaruni, the Potaro, the Essequibo, the Demerara and the Berbice. In 2000 the Brazilian Government announced that it was to finance the construction of both a deep-water port and a river bridge.

Transport and Harbours Department: Battery Rd, Kingston, Georgetown; tel. 225-9350; fax 227-8545; e-mail t&hd@ solutions2000.net; Gen. Man. WILLIAM JOSEPH.

Shipping Association of Guyana Inc: 5–9 Lombard St, Georgetown; tel. 226-1448; fax 225-0849; e-mail gnsc@futurenetgynet.com; f. 1952; non-governmental forum; Pres. CLINTON WILLIAMS; Vice Pres. TARACHANDRA KHELAWAN; members:

Guyana National Industrial Company Inc (GNIC): 2–9 Lombard St, Charlestown, POB 10520, Georgetown; tel. 225-8428; fax 225-8526; e-mail gnicadmin@futurenetgy.com; internet gnicgy .tripod.com/home.htm; metal foundry, ship building and repair, agents for a number of international transport cos; privatized 1995; CEO CLINTON WILLIAMS; Gen. Man. MICHAEL FORDE.

Guyana National Shipping Corporation Ltd: 5–9 Lombard St, La Penitence, POB 10988, Georgetown; tel. 225-0849; fax 225-3815; e-mail gnsc@guyana.net.gy; internet www.gnsc.com; govt-owned; Man. Dir M. F. BASCOM.

John Fernandes Ltd: 24 Water St, POB 10211, Georgetown; tel. 227-3344; fax 226-1881; e-mail chris@jf-ltd.com; internet www .jf-ltd.com; ship agents, pier operators and stevedore contractors; Chair and CEO CHRIS FERNANDES.

CIVIL AVIATION

The main airport, Cheddi Jaggan International Airport, is at Timehri, 42 km (26 miles) from Georgetown. In 1998 there were some 94 airstrips.

Roraima Airways: 101 Cummings St, Bourda, Georgetown; tel. 225-9648; fax 225-9646; e-mail ral@roraimaairways.com; internet www.roraimaairways.com; f. 1992; flights to Venezuela and 4 domestic destinations; Owner GERALD GOUVEIA.

Trans Guyana Airways: Ogle Aerodrome, Ogle, East Coast Demerara; tel. 222-2525; fax ; e-mail commercial@transguyana.com; internet www.transguyana.com; f. 1956; internal flights to 22 destinations.

Universal Airlines: 65 Main St, Georgetown; tel. 226-9262; fax 226-9264; e-mail RES@Universal-Airlines.com; internet www.universal-airlines.com; f. 2001; Owners CHANDRAMATTIE HARPAUL, RAMASHREE SINGH.

Tourism

Despite the beautiful scenery in the interior of the country, Guyana has limited tourist facilities, and began encouraging tourism only in the late 1980s. During the 1990s Guyana began to develop its considerable potential as an eco-tourism destination. However, tourist arrivals declined towards the end of the decade. The total number of visitors to Guyana in 2001 was 95,100. In the following year, tourism receipts totalled US $49m.

Tourism and Hospitality Association of Guyana: 157 Waterloo Street, Georgetown; tel. 225-0807; fax 225-0817; e-mail thag@networksgy.com; internet www.exploreguyana.com; f. 1992; Pres. Capt. GERALD GOUVEIA; Exec. Dir MAUREEN PAUL.

HAITI

Introductory Survey

Location, Climate, Language, Religion, Flag, Capital

The Republic of Haiti occupies the western part of the Caribbean island of Hispaniola (the Dominican Republic occupies the remaining two-thirds) and some smaller offshore islands. Cuba, to the west, is less than 80 km away. The climate is tropical but the mountains and fresh sea winds mitigate the heat. Temperatures vary little with the seasons, and the annual average in Port-au-Prince is about 27°C (80°F). The rainy season is from May to November. The official languages are French and Creole. About 70% of the population belong to the Roman Catholic Church, the country's official religion, and other Christian churches are also represented. The folk religion is voodoo, a fusion of beliefs originating in West Africa involving communication with the spirit-world through the medium of trance. In April 2003 the Government announced that, henceforth, voodoo was to be given the status of an official religion. The national flag (proportions variable) has two equal vertical stripes, of dark blue and red. The state flag (proportions 3 by 5) has, in addition, a white rectangular panel, containing the national coat of arms (a palm tree, surmounted by a Cap of Liberty and flanked by flags and cannons), in the centre. The capital is Port-au-Prince.

Recent History

Haiti was first colonized in 1659 by the French, who named the territory Saint-Domingue. French sovereignty was formally recognized by Spain in 1697. Following a period of internal unrest, a successful uprising, begun in 1794 by African-descended slaves, culminated in 1804 with the establishment of Haiti as an independent state, ruled by Jean-Jacques Dessalines, who proclaimed himself Emperor. Hostility between the negro population and the mulattos continued throughout the 19th century until, after increasing economic instability, the USA intervened militarily and supervised the government of the country from 1915 to 1934. Mulatto interests retained political ascendancy until 1946, when a negro President, Dumarsais Estimé, was installed following a military coup. Following the overthrow of two further administrations, Dr François Duvalier, a country physician, was elected President in 1957.

The Duvalier administration soon became a dictatorship, maintaining its authority by means of a notorious private army, popularly called the Tontons Macoutes (Creole for 'Bogeymen'), who used extortion and intimidation to crush all possible opposition to the President's rule. In 1964 Duvalier became President-for-Life, and at his death in April 1971 he was succeeded by his 19-year-old son and designated successor, Jean-Claude Duvalier.

At elections held in February 1979 for the 58-seat National Assembly, 57 seats were won by the official government party, the Parti de l'Unité Nationale. The first municipal elections for 25 years, which took place in 1983, were overshadowed by allegations of electoral fraud and Duvalier's obstruction of opposition parties. No opposition candidates were permitted to contest the elections for the National Assembly held in February 1984.

In April 1985 Duvalier announced a programme of constitutional reforms, including the eventual appointment of a Prime Minister and the formation of political parties, subject to certain limiting conditions. In September Roger Lafontant, the minister most closely identified with the Government's acts of repression, was dismissed. However, protests organized by the Roman Catholic Church and other religious groups gained momentum, and further measures to curb continued disorder were adopted in January 1986. The university and schools were closed indefinitely, and radio stations were forbidden to report on current events. Duvalier imposed a state of siege and declared martial law.

In February 1986, following intensified public protests, Duvalier and his family fled from Haiti to exile in France, leaving a five-member National Council of Government (Conseil National Gouvernemental—CNG), led by the Chief of Staff of the army, Gen. Henri Namphy, to succeed him. The interim military-civilian Council appointed a new Cabinet. The National Assembly was dissolved, and the Constitution was suspended.

Later in the month, the Tontons Macoutes were disbanded. Prisoners from Haiti's largest gaol were freed under a general amnesty. However, renewed rioting occurred to protest against the inclusion in the new Government of known supporters of the former dictatorship. In March 1986 there was a cabinet reshuffle. The new, three-member, CNG comprised Gen. Namphy, Col (later Brig.-Gen.) Williams Régala and Jacques François.

In April 1986 Gen. Namphy announced a proposed timetable for elections to restore constitutional government by February 1988. The first of these elections, to select 41 people (from 101 candidates) who would form part of the 61-member Constituent Assembly that was to revise the Constitution, took place in October 1986. However, the level of participation at the election was only about 5%.

The new Constitution was approved by 99.8% of voters in a referendum held on 29 March 1987. An estimated 50% of the electorate voted. An independent Provisional Electoral Council (Conseil Electoral Provisoire—CEP) was appointed to supervise the presidential and legislative elections, which were scheduled for 29 November.

On 29 November 1987 the elections were cancelled three hours after voting had begun, owing to renewed violence and killings, for which former members of the Tontons Macoutes were believed to be responsible. The Government dissolved the CEP and took control of the electoral process. In December a new CEP was appointed by the Government, and elections were rescheduled for 17 January 1988. Leslie Manigat of the Rassemblement des Démocrates Nationalistes et Progressistes (RDNP), with 50.3% of the total votes cast, was declared the winner of the presidential election. Legislative and municipal elections were held concurrently. Opposition leaders alleged that there had been extensive fraud and malpractice.

The Manigat Government took office in February 1988, but was overthrown by disaffected members of the army in June. Gen. Namphy, whom Manigat had attempted to replace as army Chief of Staff, assumed the presidency and appointed a Cabinet comprising members of the armed forces. The Constitution of 1987 was abrogated, and Duvalier's supporters returned to prominence, as did the Tontons Macoutes.

On 18 September 1988 Gen. Namphy was ousted in a coup, led by Brig.-Gen. Prosper Avril (who became President), who advocated the introduction of radical reforms. In November an independent electoral body, the Collège Electoral d'Haïti (CEDA), was established to supervise future elections, to draft an electoral law and to ensure proper registration of voters.

In March 1989 President Avril partially restored the Constitution of 1987 and restated his intention to hold democratic elections. In the following month the Government survived two coup attempts by the Leopard Corps, the country's élite anti-subversion squadron, and the Dessalines battalion, based in Port-au-Prince. Both battalions were subsequently disbanded.

Avril resigned as President in March 1990, in response to sustained popular and political opposition, together with diplomatic pressure from the USA. Before entering temporary exile in the USA, Avril ceded power to the Chief of the General Staff, Gen. Hérard Abraham, who subsequently transferred authority to Ertha Pascal-Trouillot, a member of the Supreme Court. As President of a civilian interim Government, Pascal-Trouillot shared power with a 19-member Council of State, whose principal function was to assist in preparations for the elections that were to be held later in the year. In May a new CEP was established. In September the CEP announced the postponement, until mid-December, of the elections, owing to a delay in the arrival of necessary funds and materials from donor countries.

The presidential and legislative elections took place on 16 December 1990. Fr Jean-Bertrand Aristide, a left-wing Roman Catholic priest representing the Front National pour le Changement et la Démocratie (FNCD), won an overwhelming victory in the presidential election, securing some 67% of the votes cast. His closest rival was Marc Bazin, the candidate of the centre-right Mouvement pour l'Instauration de la Démocratie en Haïti

(MIDH), who obtained about 14% of the poll. However, the results of the concurrent first round of legislative voting were less decisive. Aristide's FNCD won five of the 27 seats in the Senate, and 18 (of 83) seats in the Chamber of Deputies, while the Alliance Nationale pour la Démocratie et le Progrès (ANDP) secured 16 seats in the lower house. Seven other seats in the Chamber of Deputies were distributed among other political parties.

In January 1991, one month before Aristide was due to be sworn in as President, a group of army officers, led by Roger Lafontant, seized control of the presidential palace, and forced Pascal-Trouillot to announce her resignation. However, the army remained loyal to the Government and arrested Lafontant and his associates. A low turn-out in the second round of legislative voting, on 20 January 1991, was attributed to popular unease as a result of the recent coup attempt. The most successful party, the FNCD, won a further nine seats in the Chamber of Deputies, and an additional eight in the Senate, thereby failing to secure an overall majority in the two legislative chambers.

Aristide was inaugurated as President on 7 February 1991. The new Head of State subsequently initiated proceedings to secure the extradition from France of ex-President Duvalier to face charges that included embezzlement, abuse of power and murder. Aristide also undertook the reform of the armed forces (in July Gen. (later Lt-Gen.) Raoul Cédras replaced Gen. Hérard Abraham as Commander-in-Chief). In February the new President nominated one of his close associates, René García Préval, as Prime Minister.

In April 1991 Ertha Pascal-Trouillot was arrested on charges of complicity in the attempted coup three months previously. She was initially released, pending the completion of investigations, and in September left the country. In July Roger Lafontant was found guilty of organizing the attempted coup and sentenced to life imprisonment.

On 30 September 1991 a military junta, led by Gen. Cédras, overthrew the Government. Following diplomatic intervention by the USA, France and Venezuela, Aristide was allowed to go into exile. The coup received international condemnation, and an almost immediate economic embargo was imposed on Haiti by the Organization of American States (OAS, see p. 319). Many hundreds of people were reported to have been killed during the coup, including the imprisoned Lafontant. On 7 October military units assembled 29 members of the legislature and coerced them into approving the appointment of Joseph Nerette as interim President, and several days later a new Cabinet was announced. The OAS, however, continued to recognize Aristide as the legitimate President.

During the following months the OAS attempted to negotiate a settlement. However, the two sides remained deadlocked over the conditions for Aristide's return, the main obstacles being Aristide's insistence that Cédras be imprisoned or exiled, and the legislature's demands for an immediate repeal of the OAS embargo and a general amnesty. In February 1992, following OAS-supervised talks in Washington, DC, USA, between Aristide and members of a Haitian legislative delegation, an agreement was signed providing for the installation of René Théodore, leader of the Mouvement pour la Reconstruction Nationale, as Prime Minister. He was to govern in close consultation with the exiled Aristide and facilitate his return. Aristide undertook to respect all decisions taken by the legislature since the coup of September 1991, and agreed to a general amnesty for the police and armed forces. The economic embargo imposed by the OAS was to be revoked on ratification of the agreement by the legislature. However, in mid-March 1992 politicians opposed to the accord were reportedly coerced into withdrawing from a joint session of the Senate and the Chamber of Deputies, leaving it inquorate. In late March, following an appeal by interim President Nerette, the Supreme Court declared the agreement null and void, on the grounds that it violated the Constitution by endangering the country's sovereignty. In response, the OAS increased economic sanctions against Haiti.

In May 1992, following a tripartite summit meeting involving the legislature, the Government and the armed forces, an agreement providing for a 'consensus government' was ratified by the Senate. The agreement envisaged the appointment of a new Prime Minister and a multi-party government of national consensus to seek a solution to the political crisis and negotiate an end to the economic embargo. In June the legislature, in the absence of the FNCD (which boycotted the sessions), approved the nomination of Marc Bazin, of the MIDH, to be Prime Minister. Under the terms of the tripartite agreement, the presidency was left vacant, ostensibly to allow for Aristide's return, although commentators suggested that this was purely a political manoeuvre by the military-backed Government and that such an eventuality was unlikely. A Cabinet, comprising members of most major parties (with the exception of the FNCD), was installed, with the army retaining control of the interior and defence. The appointment of the new Government provoked world-wide condemnation.

In July 1992 a 10-member 'presidential commission' was appointed by Aristide to hold negotiations with what he termed the 'real forces' in Haiti, referring to the armed forces and the wealthy élite. In September the Government agreed to allow the presence of an 18-member OAS commission in Haiti to help to guarantee human rights, reduce violence and assess progress towards a resolution of the prevailing political crisis. In February 1993 a further agreement was reached with the OAS and the UN on sending another international civil commission comprising some 200 representatives.

In April 1993 the joint envoy of the UN and the OAS, Dante Caputo, visited Haiti to present a series of proposals for the restoration of democratic rule in Haiti. These provided for the resignation of the military high command in return for a full amnesty for those involved in the coup of 1991, and for the establishment of a government of consensus and the eventual reinstatement of Aristide. A sum of US $1,000m. in economic aid was to become available once democracy was restored. However, the proposals were rejected by Cédras.

In early June 1993 the USA imposed sanctions against Haiti. Shortly afterwards Bazin resigned as Prime Minister. His position was believed to have become untenable following the refusal of several cabinet ministers to respect his demand for their resignation, and the withdrawal of the support in the legislature of the Parti National Progressiste Révolutionnaire (PANPRA)—which deprived the Government of a parliamentary majority. In late June, following the imposition of a world-wide petroleum and arms embargo by the UN Security Council, Cédras agreed to attend talks with Aristide on Governor's Island, New York, USA, under the auspices of the UN and the OAS. On 3 July the so-called Governor's Island peace accord was signed, delineating a 10-point agenda for Aristide's reinstatement. Under the terms of the accord the embargo was to be revoked following the installation of a new Prime Minister (to be appointed by Aristide), Cédras would retire and a new Commander-in-Chief of the armed forces would be appointed by Aristide, who would return to Haiti by 30 October. The accord was approved by Haiti's main political parties, and a six-month political 'truce' was agreed to facilitate the transition. Legislation providing for a series of political and institutional reforms, as required under the terms of the accord, was to be enacted, including provision for the transfer of the police force to civilian control.

In August 1993 the legislature ratified the appointment by Aristide of Robert Malval as Prime Minister. The UN Security Council subsequently suspended its petroleum and arms embargo. In September a concerted campaign of political violence and intimidation by police auxiliaries, known as 'attachés', threatened to undermine the Governor's Island accord. Demands made by Malval that the attachés be disbanded were ignored by the chief of police, Col Joseph Michel François. With the upsurge of a Duvalierist tendency, largely embodied by the attachés, a new political party, the Front Revolutionnaire pour l'Avancement et le Progrès d'Haïti (FRAPH), was founded in opposition to any attempt to reinstate Aristide. In late September the UN Security Council approved a resolution providing for the immediate deployment of a lightly-armed UN Mission In Haiti (UNMIH, renamed UN Support Mission in Haiti in June 1996, UN Transition Mission in Haiti in July 1997, and UN Civilian Police Mission in Haiti (MIPONUH) in November 1997). A new unarmed mission, the International Civilian Support Mission in Haiti, superseded MIPONUH in March 2000, comprising 150 members, to advise in the creation of a new police force and the modernization of the army. The new mission's mandate ended on 6 February 2001.

In October 1993, in violation of the Governor's Island accord, Cédras and François refused to resign their posts, asserting that the terms of the amnesty offered by Aristide were not sufficiently broad. In that month the campaign of political violence by the attachés escalated. A US vessel transporting members of the UNMIH was prevented from docking at Port-au-Prince, and its arrival prompted violent demonstrations of defiance by the attachés. Several days later the Minister of Justice, Guy Malary, was assassinated. In response, the US Government ordered six warships into Haitian territorial waters to enforce the reimposed UN embargo. As a result of the instability, the UN/OAS international civil commission and other foreign government personnel were evacuated to the Dominican Republic.

In December 1993 Malval officially resigned as Prime Minister. In discussions with the US Government held earlier in the month, Malval announced a new initiative for a National Salvation Conference, involving multi-sector negotiations (to include the military) on a return to democratic rule. However, Aristide rejected the proposals, proposing instead a National Reconciliation Conference, excluding the military, which took place in Miami, USA, in mid-January 1994. Following the military regime's failure to meet the revised UN deadline of 15 January to comply with the terms of the Governor's Island accord, in late January the USA unilaterally imposed further sanctions denying officers of the military regime access to assets held in the USA and cancelling their travel visas. In that month members of the UN/OAS international civil commission began to return to Haiti.

In February 1994 a 13-member faction of the Senate—including eight members elected in January 1993 in partial legislative elections condemned as illegal by the USA and UN and widely regarded as an attempt by the military regime to legitimize its rule—appointed Bernard Sansaricq as President of the Senate. However, the incumbent President of the Senate, Firmin Jean-Louis, did not relinquish his position and continued to be recognized by the international community. In the same month Aristide twice rejected peace plans drafted by the USA, demanding instead the implementation of the Governor's Island accord.

In April 1994 the US Government abandoned its attempts to effect a compromise solution to the crisis in Haiti in favour of the implementation of more rigorous economic sanctions with a view to forcing the military regime to relinquish power. In May the UN Security Council approved a resolution introducing sanctions banning all international trade with Haiti, excluding food and medicine, reducing air links with the country and preventing members of the regime from gaining access to assets held outside Haiti.

In early 1994 the 13-member faction of the Senate led by Bernard Sansaricq declared the presidency of the Republic vacant, invoking Article 149 of the Constitution, which provides that, in case of prolonged absence by the Head of State, the position may be assumed by the President of the Court of Cassation. In May, with the support of the armed forces, the 13 Senators and 30 members of the Chamber of Deputies—not a sufficient number to form a quorum—appointed the President of the Court of Cassation, Emile Jonassaint, provisional President of the Republic. He subsequently appointed a new Cabinet. The appointment of the Jonassaint administration was denounced as illegal by the international community and by the outgoing acting Prime Minister, Robert Malval. In the following month, the USA increased sanctions against Haiti. Jonassaint's appointment also revealed a division within the three-man junta at the head of the military regime—namely Cédras, François and the Chief of Staff of the army, Brig.-Gen. Philippe Biamby. François reportedly opposed the move and did not attend the inauguration ceremony.

In July 1994 the Haitian junta issued an order providing for the expulsion of the UN/OAS international civil commission. The order was immediately condemned by the UN Security Council. On 31 July the UN Security Council passed a resolution authorizing 'all necessary means' to remove the military regime from power. The terms of the resolution also provided for a UN peace-keeping force to be deployed once stability had been achieved, to remain in Haiti until February 1996, when Aristide's presidential term expired. In August the UN officially abandoned efforts to effect a peaceful solution to the crisis in Haiti. In the same month leaders of the Caribbean Community and Common Market (CARICOM, see p. 172) agreed to support a US-led military invasion.

On 19 September 1994 a nominally multinational force composed almost entirely of US troops began a peaceful occupation of Haiti. The occupation followed the diplomatic efforts of a mission led by former US President Jimmy Carter, which resulted in a compromise agreement, thus narrowly avoiding a full-scale invasion. Under the terms of the agreement, the Haitian security forces were to co-operate with the multilateral force in effecting a transition to civilian rule. All sanctions were to be lifted and the military junta granted 'early and honourable

retirement' following legislative approval of a general amnesty law, or by 15 October at the latest (the date when Aristide was to return from exile to resume his presidency). The agreement did not, however, require the junta's departure from Haiti, nor did it address the reform of the security forces. Those legislators elected illegally in January 1993 were replaced by legislators returning from exile in the USA. Following the occupation, acts of violence by the Haitian police against supporters of Aristide led to a modification of the rules of operation of the multinational force, allowing for intervention to curb the violence. In late September the USA announced the suspension of its unilateral sanctions, although the Haitian military's assets in the USA remained frozen. A few days later the UN Security Council approved a resolution ending all sanctions against Haiti with effect from the day after the return of Aristide.

In early October 1994 Aristide signed a decree authorizing legislation, approved by the legislature that month, for the amnesty of those involved in the coup of September 1991. Cédras and Biamby promptly went into exile in Panama, whilst François was reported to have already fled to the Dominican Republic, where he was granted asylum. Later that month the USA formally ended its freeze on the assets of the Haitian military regime, estimated to be worth some US $79m. On 12 October Robert Malval resumed office as interim Prime Minister following the resignation of the Jonassaint administration. Aristide returned to Haiti on 15 October to resume his presidency and on 25 October appointed Smarck Michel as premier. He also appointed Gen. Jean-Claude Duperval provisional Commander-in-Chief of the armed forces and Gen. Bernardin Poisson Chief of Staff of the army.

A new Cabinet, comprising mainly members of the pro-Aristide Organisation Politique Lavalas (OPL), was inaugurated on 8 November 1994. In mid-November Gen. Poisson succeeded Gen. Duperval as Commander-in-Chief of the armed forces. Later that month the legislature approved the separation of the police from the army.

In December 1994 the formation of a new CEP, responsible for organizing and supervising the forthcoming legislative, local and municipal elections, was completed. However, owing to procedural delays the elections were thought unlikely to be held until mid-1995, leaving a period of legislative inactivity between the end of the current legislative term, ending in January 1995, and the inauguration of a new legislature, at a time when reform would be vital to the successful transition to peaceful civilian rule. In mid-December 1994 Aristide authorized the creation of a national commission of truth and justice to investigate past human rights violations, and ordered the reduction of the armed forces to 1,500 (from an estimated combined army and police force of 7,000–7,500). In the following month two commissions were established for the restructuring of the armed forces and the new civilian police force.

In January 1995 US military commanders certified that the situation in Haiti was sufficiently stable to enable the transfer of authority to the UN. On 30 January the UN Security Council adopted a resolution authorizing the deployment of a UN force of 6,000 troops and 900 civil police to succeed the incumbent multinational force. The UN force, entitled (like that deployed in 1993) the UN Mission in Haiti (UNMIH), was to be led by a US commander and include some 2,400 US troops. It was to be responsible for reducing the strength of the army and training both the army and the 4,000-strong (subsequently increased to 6,000) civilian police force, as well as maintaining the 'secure and stable' environment.

On 31 March 1995, against a background of increasing violence and criticism at the inadequacy of the interim police force, authority was officially transferred from the multinational force to the UNMIH. The security situation deteriorated further in April, revealing widespread discontent at high prices, unemployment and the planned privatization of state enterprises. In late April Aristide announced that, following the election of the new legislature, he would seek a constitutional amendment providing for the abolition of the armed forces. (The armed forces were subsequently disbanded, although the constitutional amendment providing for their official abolition could not be approved until the end of the new legislative term.)

The first round of legislative, local and municipal elections (including elections to 18 of the 27 seats in the Senate, all 83 seats in the Chamber of Deputies, 125 mayorships and 555 local councils) were held on 25 June 1995. Owing to administrative failures and isolated incidents of violence and intimidation, voting continued into the following day. Despite the extension, thousands of intending voters were unable to participate, and a further, complementary poll was to be scheduled. The widespread irregularities prompted several opposition parties to demand the annulment of the elections and the dissolution of the CEP, which many perceived as too closely associated with the OPL, the party with majority representation in the Government. The official election results, which were released in mid-July, indicated that all of the 21 seats so far decided had been won by the Plateforme Politique Lavalas (PPL), a three-party electoral alliance comprising the OPL, the Mouvement pour l'Organisation du Pays and the Pati Louvri Baryè. The results were rejected by the majority of opposition parties, which announced a boycott of the electoral process. Continued criticism of the CEP by the opposition led to the resignation of the President of the CEP, Anselme Rémy, in late July.

In early August 1995 the FNCD, MIDH and PANPRA withdrew their respective representatives from the Government, in protest at the absence of a resolution to the electoral dispute. The Minister of Culture, Jean-Claude Bajeux, of the Congrès National des Movements Démocratiques (KONAKOM) resisted his party's demand that he resign, and remained the sole opposition member in the Cabinet. On 13 August, following successive postponements, the complementary elections, for voters who had been denied the opportunity to vote on 25 June, were conducted in 21 districts. A further 17 seats were decided, all of which were won by the PPL. In late August the US Government presented a plan aimed at resolving the electoral dispute. However, its proposals, which included the annulment of the first-round elections in many areas, were rejected by the CEP. The second round of voting was held on 17 September, despite the boycott that was maintained by the main opposition parties, and resulted in further large gains for the PPL, which won 17 of the 18 contested seats in the 27-member Senate and 68 seats in the 83-member Chamber of Deputies. The remaining contested seats were won mainly by independent candidates.

In October 1995 Michel resigned as Prime Minister, and was succeeded by the Minister of Foreign Affairs, Claudette Werleigh. She indicated that the new administration intended to retain control of strategic state enterprises, which Michel had planned to sell, and would seek a national debate on the issue of privatization.

In November 1995, despite extensive popular support for Aristide to continue in office for a further three years (to compensate for those years spent in exile), the President confirmed that he would leave office in February 1996. At a presidential election held on 17 December 1995, which was boycotted by all the main opposition parties except KONAKOM, the candidate endorsed by Aristide, René Préval (Prime Minister between February and September 1991), was elected with some 87.9% of the votes cast. He was inaugurated as President on 7 February 1996, and later that month the legislature approved the appointment of Rosny Smarth as Prime Minister. A new Cabinet was sworn in on 6 March.

The months following the inauguration of the Smarth administration were marked by a high incidence of violence in the capital. In mid-August 1996, against a background of unrest and general hostility towards government economic policy, in particular plans for the privatization of state enterprises, a series of armed attacks were conducted against public buildings. The attacks followed the arrest that month, at the headquarters of the right-wing Mobilisation pour le Développement National (MDN), of some 20 former officers of the armed forces who were accused of plotting against the Government. In August two leading members of the MDN were murdered by unidentified gunmen. Opposition politicians accused the Government of responsibility for the killings, and evidence emerged implicating members of the presidential guard in the murders. In mid-September, on the advice of the US Government, Préval dismissed the head of the presidential guard and initiated a reorganization of the unit.

In November 1996, as a result of diverging interests within the PPL, Aristide officially established a new political party, La Fanmi Lavalas (FL), which, it was anticipated, would promote his candidacy for the next presidential election. Aristide had openly expressed his opposition to Préval's adoption of economic policies proposed by the IMF, notably the privatization of state enterprises. Unrest continued, and in mid-January 1997 a general strike, in support of demands for the resignation of the Smarth administration and the reversal of the planned divestment of state enterprises, received considerable support.

On 6 April 1997 partial legislative elections were held for nine of the 27 seats in the Senate and two seats in the Chamber of Deputies, as well as elections to local councils. The elections were boycotted by many opposition parties, and less than 5% of the electorate participated in the poll. Of the legislative seats contested only two, in the Senate, were decided, both of which were secured by candidates of the FL. The OPL, the majority party in the governing coalition, alleged that members of the CEP had manipulated the election results in favour of Aristide's party, and demanded the resignation of the CEP and the conduct of a fresh ballot. OAS observers of the poll supported the claims of electoral irregularities, and, following strong international pressure, the CEP postponed the second round of the elections, scheduled for 25 May, until mid-June (they were subsequently postponed indefinitely). The OPL had announced that it would boycott the second-round elections.

In the light of mounting popular opposition, on 9 June 1997 Smarth resigned from office, although he remained Prime Minister in a caretaker capacity pending the appointment of a replacement. Smarth criticized the CEP for failing to annul the results of the April elections and thus perpetuating the electoral impasse. In the following month Préval nominated Ericq Pierre as Smarth's replacement, but his nomination was rejected by the Chamber of Deputies. In September supporters of Aristide announced the formation of a new 25-member Anti-Neoliberal Bloc in the lower house. In the light of Préval's failure to nominate a candidate for Prime Minister who was acceptable to the legislature, on 20 October Smarth announced that he was to cease his role as caretaker Prime Minister and recommended that his Cabinet resign. Several ministers complied with this request and in late October Préval redesignated their portfolios to remaining cabinet members.

In November 1997, in an effort to resolve the political crisis, Préval nominated Hervé Y. Denis, an economist and former Minister of Information, Culture and Co-ordination in the Government of Robert Malval, as Prime Minister. In addition, Préval announced the establishment of an electoral commission, comprising three independent legal experts, to resolve the electoral deadlock, and the resignation of six of the nine members of the CEP. The OPL, however, continued to demand the annulment of the April elections and the replacement of the entire CEP. In January 1998 the legislature formally announced its decision to reject the nomination of Denis. The FL subsequently rejected a proposal by the OPL for the creation of a body to mediate in the legislature and thus facilitate the appointment of a new Prime Minister.

In March 1998, following negotiations with the Anti-Neoliberal Bloc, the OPL (renamed the Organisation du Peuple en Lutte in February) withdrew its demands for the annulment of the April 1997 elections as a precondition for the approval of a new Prime Minister, and proposed three candidates. However, Préval subsequently renominated Denis: his candidacy was rejected by the legislature for a second time in April. In July Préval finally agreed to replace the CEP. Préval subsequently received the support of the OPL for the nomination of the incumbent Minister of National Education, Jacques Edouard Alexis, for Prime Minister. Conversely, the Anti-Neoliberal Bloc opposed the nomination of Alexis, who, it maintained, favoured the structural adjustment policies advocated by the IMF. In August the FL announced that it had formally gone into opposition to the Préval administration.

In November 1998 the Senate voted to extend the legislature's current term to October 1999; under electoral legislation adopted in 1995, the term of office of legislators elected in that year's delayed vote had been shortened by one year in order to restore the constitutional timetable of elections, and was thus due to end in January 1999. In December 1998 Alexis was finally declared eligible to assume the office of Prime Minister, subject to his nomination being approved by the legislature (which did not occur until November 2000). The decision had been delayed by a report by the state auditing board, subsequently declared inaccurate, which found irregularities in Alexis' tenure as Minister of National Education. On 11 January 1999 Préval announced that he would no longer recognize the legislature, rejecting the Senate's earlier decision to extend its mandate, and declared that he would install a new government by presidential decree. In mid-January Préval withdrew parliamentary funding, prompting the legislature to seek a Supreme Court ruling on the constitutionality of the 1995 electoral law. Préval also entered into consultations with opposition parties in an effort to reach agreement on the composition of a new CEP. In

February the Supreme Court postponed indefinitely a decision concerning the electoral law.

On 25 March 1999 Préval appointed by decree a new Cabinet headed by Alexis and including representatives of five small opposition parties that had negotiated an agreement with the President to end the political impasse. The OPL, which had ceased negotiations following the murder, in early March, of one of its leaders, was not included in the new administration. The party, which alleged that the killing had been perpetrated by supporters of Aristide, also stated that it would boycott any elections organized by the new CEP, which was appointed in that month. In May the Supreme Court refused to rule on the legality of Préval's decision to end the funding of the outgoing parliament. The OPL subsequently announced that it had accepted that the parliamentary term had ended and that it would participate in the forthcoming elections. In June the CEP announced that it would disregard the results of the flawed partial legislative elections of April 1997, and presented draft electoral legislation that envisaged the holding of legislative elections in November and December 1999. Préval criticized the CEP's decision concerning the 1997 elections, but in July 1999 he signed a decree annulling them. A new electoral law set 28 November as a provisional date for the first round of legislative and local elections; however, the elections were subsequently postponed, for logistical and financial reasons, on several occasions, prompting violent protests in the capital.

On 21 May 2000 the first round of legislative and municipal elections was held; an estimated 60% of the electorate participated. Opposition parties alleged that the results had been manipulated in favour of the FL, claims supported by OAS observers, and demanded the annulment of the election and the conduct of a fresh ballot. The CEP rejected these claims, but in mid-June the CEP President, Léon Manus, fled to the Dominican Republic, claiming that he had received death threats following his refusal to validate the first-round results. His flight prompted demonstrations by Aristide supporters, demanding the publication of the results. According to official first-round results, the FL won 16 of the 19 contested seats in the Senate, and 26 of the 83 seats in the lower house. The results were criticized as inaccurate by the UN, the OAS and numerous foreign governments. Nevertheless, a second round of voting went ahead on 9 July (postponed from 25 June). Opposition protests and a boycott by the 15-party opposition coalition, the Convergence Démocratique (CD), resulted in a low voter turnout (an estimated 10%) and a high incidence of violence, with 10 separate bombs killing two people. According to official results, the FL won 72 seats in the Chamber of Deputies and 18 of the 19 seats contested in the 27-seat upper house (the Pati Louvri Baryè won one seat). The party also secured control of some 80% of the local councils. In September Préval announced that elections to the presidency and to renew the remaining eight senate seats would be held in November. The CD immediately announced its intention to boycott the elections.

In mid-October 2000 it was revealed that an attempt by members of the police force to overthrow the Government had been uncovered. The seven police officers accused of planning the coup fled to the Dominican Republic, and were subsequently granted asylum in Ecuador. The Government reacted by dismissing several senior police officers. In November a court sentenced Gen. Cédras and 36 other senior army officers to life imprisonment with hard labour, *in absentia*, for their role in the murders of 15 people in the shanty town of Raboteau in May 1994.

At the presidential election of 26 November 2000, Aristide was elected with some 91.7% of the votes cast; the remaining six candidates all won less than 2.0% of the ballot. According to official estimates some 60.5% of the electorate voted, although opposition leaders claimed a far lower participation. The only official observer mission, from CARICOM, estimated a 30% voter turn-out. In concurrently-held partial legislative elections, the FL also won the remaining eight seats in the Senate, and the one remaining seat in the Chamber of Deputies.

An eight-member Transition Committee was established in December 2000 to oversee the smooth transfer of power to Aristide, who was to take office on 7 February 2001. However, on 7 December the CD announced the formation of an alternative, provisional Government, known as the Front Alternatif, with the intention of holding fresh elections within two years. The announcement provoked widespread violent demonstrations by Aristide supporters. In early February 2001 the CD further announced that this Front Alternatif was to be headed by Gérard Gourgue. Discussions between the President-elect and opposition leaders ended without agreement. On 15 February seven of the Senators controversially awarded seats in the May 2000 election resigned. Two days after his inauguration, President Aristide named Jean-Marie Chérestal, a former Minister of Finance, as Prime Minister, and in early March a new Cabinet was appointed. The CD responded by calling for a month of anti-Government protests. In the same month, in an attempt to end the political impasse, Aristide appointed a new nine-member CEP to investigate the results of the disputed May 2000 elections. The CD was not represented on the Council. In March it was announced that legislative elections would be held one year early, in November 2002, in order to satisfy international and opposition criticism and to restore the flow of foreign aid, suspended since May 2000. (As well as an end to the political crisis and a strengthening of the democratic process, the resumption of aid was also dependent on Haiti implementing anti-drugs-trafficking measures and improving its human rights record.) Three days later violent protests broke out in Port-au-Prince, in which three people died and dozens were injured. Violence continued over the following months and a number of opposition party members were arrested on treason and terrorism charges. In July, following further OAS mediation, the Government stated that legislative and local elections would be held in 2002, although a timetable remained to be agreed; an accord was also reached on the composition of the new CEP. The CEP would additionally organize an election to the seven Senate seats vacated in February.

Political violence continued throughout 2001. In late July an attempted *coup d'état*, responsibility for which was attributed to former members of the armed forces, resulted in the deaths of six policemen. In October the FL announced the resumption of OAS-mediated talks with the opposition, but these again ended unsuccessfully. In early November three people were killed during violent demonstrations in the La Saline district of Port-au-Prince and one week later the CD organized a widely-observed national strike in protest at the deteriorating economic situation. Then, on 18 December, an armed group, allegedly composed of former members of the armed forces, attacked the presidential palace. At least four people were killed in the coup attempt, which prompted further outbreaks of violence as hundreds of government supporters attacked the homes and offices of opposition leaders in retaliation. The Government announced that former police chief Guy Philippe was wanted in connection with the palace attack; he subsequently fled the country. The opposition claimed that the coup attempt had been staged by the Government in order to justify further repression, and demanded that a UN mission be deployed to monitor the situation. In July 2002 an OAS Commission of Inquiry reported that no attempted coup had taken place and chastised the Government for its reluctance to punish those of its supporters who engaged in violence against the opposition.

In 2001 the investigation into the death of radio journalist Jean Léopold Dominique, who had been murdered in April 2000, was obstructed by death threats and pressure from supporters of the principal suspect in the case, FL Senator and former police chief Dany Toussaint. In June Claudy Gassant, the judge supervising the investigation, resigned, complaining of insufficient protection against death threats. He subsequently left the country. The investigation was stalled until July 2002, when a new investigating magistrate, Bernard Saint Vil, was appointed. In August 2003 three of the six individuals charged in connection with Dominique's murder were released by the Court of Appeal, which called for the case to be reopened.

On 23 January 2002, against a background of continuing political and economic turmoil, Prime Minister Chérestal resigned his post, following allegations of corruption, and criticism over his inability to resolve the crisis. On 15 March Aristide appointed Senate speaker and prominent FL member, Yvon Neptune, as Prime Minister. Neptune subsequently reshuffled his Cabinet, removing several ministers who had attracted controversy; he signalled his commitment to encouraging dialogue to end the political stalemate by appointing Marc Bazin as Minister without Portfolio with specific responsibility for negotiations with the opposition. (Bazin resigned in September of that year, claiming that his job had become impossible.) In June Aristide met with opposition leaders for the first time in two years, but the talks achieved little progress. Further OAS-mediated dialogue in the following month also failed to make any significant headway. Meanwhile, Haiti's accession to full membership of CARICOM in July increased international pressure on Aristide to bring about an end to political instability in the country and allow new elections to take place. In August violent demonstrations occurred in the northern city of Gonaïves when the political activist Amiot Métayer escaped from prison, together with over 100 other inmates. Métayer was one of several Government supporters imprisoned for damaging the homes of opposition members following the attack on the presidential palace in December 2001.

In late 2002 the ongoing political unrest in the country intensified as the November deadline for the creation of a new CEP passed unfulfilled. On 17 November some 15,000 people in Cap-Haïtien participated in the largest anti-Government rally held in the country since the re-election of President Aristide in 2000. Meanwhile, shortly afterwards supporters of Aristide rioted in Port-au-Prince to protest against the anti-Government rallies. President Aristide refused to resign, stating that he believed the crisis could best be resolved through the formation of a CEP and the holding of new elections. While the opposition continued to refuse to nominate representatives to the CEP, five of the nation's civil groups chose representatives in November, having initially refused to do so until the Government demonstrated its commitment to guaranteeing public safety. In early December a general strike led by the opposition was joined by members of Haiti's private sector. During an address to his supporters in Les Cayes, President Aristide accused the opposition of attempting to orchestrate a coup. Meanwhile, opposition parties united in calling for the resignation of Aristide as the demonstrations continued. In December 2002, frustrated by the continued political instability, a total of 184 business and civil society organizations, led by a local businessman, André Apaid, agreed to form the 'Group of 184'. The grouping subsequently emerged as a major element of the opposition to Aristide.

In 2003 the political stalemate between the Government and the opposition remained unresolved, despite further efforts by the OAS to mediate in the dispute. Most nominees to the nine-member CEP refused to assume their posts, claiming that they were unconvinced that the Government would not resort to fraudulent practices in future legislative elections, as it had done in 2000. The CD and other opposition groups continued to insist that their participation in any elections would be conditional upon the resignation of President Aristide. In June the newly-appointed chief of police, Jean-Robert Faveur, resigned after only two weeks in the post, complaining of widespread corruption. He subsequently claimed that his life was in danger and fled to the USA. He was replaced by Jocelyne Pierre, the head of the Port-au-Prince civil court. In October clashes occurred between police and demonstrators in Gonaïves, following the murder of Amiot Métayer in the previous month; at least four people died as a result of the violence. In December three members of the Cabinet—Minister of Tourism Martine Deverson, Minister of National Education Marie-Carmelle Austin and Minister of the Environment Webster Pierre—resigned in protest at the Government's increasing use of violence to suppress the continuing demonstrations.

In November 2003, in an attempt to end the ongoing political crisis, the Roman Catholic Bishops' Conference of Haiti called for the legislature to appoint a broadly-representative council to advise President Aristide and thus to enable new elections to be held. In January 2004 the USA declared its support for the proposal, which was, however, later withdrawn by the Bishops' Conference, owing to the deterioration of the political situation. Early in the same month the opposition organized a 48-hour general strike as violent anti-Government protests continued. Meanwhile, Haiti commemorated the bicentenary of its independence from French colonial rule. President Thabo Mbeki of South Africa was the only foreign dignitary to attend the celebrations, during which President Aristide announced that the country was to begin legal action in order to claim reparations totalling approximately US $21,700m. from France, in compensation for the 90m. francs that it had paid in order to secure recognition of its independence in 1804. Critics claimed that the announcement was merely an attempt by the President to divert attention from the country's worsening political situation.

On 12 January 2004 the mandates of all the members of the Chamber of Deputies and 12 of the 27 members of the Senate expired, leaving Haiti effectively without a legislature and entitling President Aristide to rule by decree. The President subsequently pledged to hold legislative elections within six months, an offer quickly rejected by the Haitian opposition. Meanwhile, another general strike was held as public demonstrations demanding the President's resignation continued.

Later in the same month, in an attempt to resolve the escalating political crisis, members of CARICOM met with leading members of the Haitian opposition in the Bahamas. CARICOM threatened to impose economic sanctions on Haiti unless President Aristide satisfied a number of conditions, including the formation of a new electoral council and the holding of legislative elections. Aristide appeared to accept the conditions, stating that he was prepared to enter into constructive dialogue with the opposition, and agreed to meet with opposition members and CARICOM leaders later that month. Following the meeting, which was held in Kingston, Jamaica, Aristide agreed to implement a number of reforms within the following two months, including: nominating an independent prime minister; reforming the police force; creating a neutral electoral council; releasing illegally-imprisoned members of the opposition; and disarming his supporters. However, it was feared that Aristide's continued refusal to bow to demands for his resignation would undermine any hope of ending the impasse.

In February 2004 Prime Minister Yvon Neptune accused the opposition of attempting to orchestrate a coup and demanded that opposition parties actively discourage the ongoing demonstrations. However, as violent protests escalated across the country, anti-Government forces, led by Buter Métayer, the brother of Amiot Métayer, took control of Gonaïves and, subsequently, several other cities in the north of the country. Shortly afterwards, former members of the Haitian armed forces, led by ex-police chief Guy Philippe and the former deputy commander of the FRAPH, Louis-Jodel Chamblain, returned from exile in the Dominican Republic to participate in the insurrection, joining with the rebels to form the Front pour la Libération et la Reconstruction Nationales (FLRN). President Aristide appealed to the international community for assistance in suppressing the rebellion. A plan to end the violence, proposed by France, CARICOM and the OAS, was subsequently accepted by Aristide but rejected by the opposition as it failed to provide for the President's departure. Meanwhile, the uprising continued to gather momentum as the insurgents advanced towards the capital, Port-au-Prince, insisting that they would attack unless Aristide tendered his resignation. Cap-Haïtien had been brought under rebel control on 22 February. At a meeting of the UN Security Council in late February, Caribbean nations called for a multilateral force to be sent to the country in an attempt to bring an end to the violence. However, the USA and France insisted that a political settlement would have to be reached before any forces were deployed to Haiti.

On 29 February 2004 President Aristide finally resigned, largely owing to increasing international pressure, and fled to the Central African Republic, where he claimed he had been unconstitutionally removed from office by the USA. The USA maintained that Aristide had requested assistance to leave Haiti. In line with the provisions made by the Constitution, the President of the Supreme Court, Boniface Alexandre, was sworn in as interim President. On the same day the UN Security Council, acting in response to a request from Alexandre, authorized the establishment of a Multinational Interim Force (MIF) to help to secure law and order prior to the deployment of a larger peace-keeping mission. The MIF eventually comprised around 3,600 troops from the USA, France, Canada and Chile. On 9 March Alexandre and the recently established Council of Elders appointed Gérard Latortue, an economist who had briefly served as Minister of Foreign Affairs under Leslie Manigat in 1988, as Prime Minister. One week later Latortue appointed a new Government, which was composed of independents and technocrats and which excluded any members from the main political parties. The installation of the new Cabinet was generally welcomed by the international community, although CARICOM refused to recognize the Latortue Government, and subsequently suspended Haiti's participation in the councils of the Community. In mid-March Aristide arrived in Jamaica at the invitation of the Government of P. J. Patterson; his arrival prompted Latortue to suspend diplomatic relations with Jamaica in protest.

In early April 2004 Latortue, the seven members of the Council of Elders, representatives of the main political organizations (with the exception of the FL) and leaders of civil society organizations signed an agreement on political transition, which provided for the organization of presidential, legislative and municipal elections in 2005, leading to the inauguration of a new administration by 7 February 2006. A new CEP was to be formed, while the establishment of a truth, justice and reconciliation commission and an anti-corruption agency was also envisaged. The FL refused to designate a representative to the CEP, demanding that alleged persecution and repression of its supporters cease. In the same month Jocelerme Privert, the former Minister of the Interior, was arrested on suspicion of having ordered the killing of a number of anti-Aristide protesters in February.

Louis-Jodel Chamblain surrendered to the authorities in late April 2004 to be retried for crimes of which he had been convicted *in absentia* in 1995 and 2000, respectively: the murder of Antoine Izmery, an associate of Aristide, in 1993 and involvement in the killings of several people in Raboteau in 1994. In August 2004 Chamblain and his co-defendant, Jackson Joanis, a former police chief in Port-au-Prince, were acquitted of the murder of Izmery. However, the US Department of State and human rights organizations were severely critical of the conduct of the retrial and the haste with which it was organized.

In a report to the UN Security Council presented in April 2004, the Secretary-General of the organization, Kofi Annan, accused Aristide of having formed an alliance with armed groups, known as *chimères*, in order to reinforce his position in power and of having condoned their engagement in organized crime, including drugs-smuggling. In mid-May Guy Philippe announced the formation of a new political party, the Front de Reconstruction Nationale (FRN). Aristide went into exile in South Africa at the end of May, having been offered temporary political asylum by President Thabo Mbeki.

A UN peace-keeping force, the UN Stabilization Mission in Haiti (MINUSTAH), was officially established on 1 June 2004 and replaced the MIF later that month, following a transitional period. MINUSTAH, which had an authorized strength of 6,700 military personnel and 1,622 civilian police, was to assist the interim administration with preparations for elections and the disarmament and demobilization of armed militias. Meanwhile, the OAS General Assembly approved a resolution declaring Aristide's removal from power to be unconstitutional, although it continued to recognize Latortue's Government. In mid-June Latortue announced the Government's intention to hold local and legislative elections in September 2005, followed by a presidential election in November of that year.

Former Prime Minister Neptune was arrested in late June 2004 in connection with the deaths of demonstrators in the uprising against Aristide's administration in February. In July the Latortue Government issued a deadline of 15 September for armed groups to surrender their weapons. The disarmament of the rebels was one of CARICOM's principal demands, and a five-member ministerial delegation from the Community arrived in Port-au-Prince the day after the deadline was announced to discuss developments in Haiti. International donors at a conference sponsored by the World Bank in Washington, DC, in mid-July pledged US $1,080m. in development aid for Haiti over the period 2004–06. In August 2004 former President Manigat declared his intention to contest the forthcoming presidential election as the candidate of the RDNP. The 15 September deadline for the surrender of weapons passed unfulfilled. A few days earlier the UN Security Council had urged the Government to accelerate the establishment and implementation of a national disarmament, demobilization and reintegration programme. Latortue responded by accusing MINUSTAH of failing adequately to counter insecurity in the country. More than 2,000 people were killed in extensive flooding in September. Rescue efforts were reportedly hindered by the fact that many of the worst affected areas in the north of the country remained effectively under the control of armed groups.

At the end of September 2004 violence broke out between the police and supporters of Aristide at a rally in Port-au-Prince in support of the former President's return from exile. On the following day the decapitated bodies of three police officers were discovered in the La Saline district of the capital. Clashes continued, and by early November at least 80 people had been killed. Tensions were exacerbated by the arrival in Port-au-Prince of more than 200 former soldiers, who demanded to be allowed to confront the so-called *chimères*. Three members of the FL, including the former President of the Senate, Yvon Feuillé, were arrested in early October on suspicion of inciting the violence and possessing illegal firearms, and 75 suspected members of the *chimères* were also detained by the national police and MINUSTAH troops in a joint operation. Latortue accused Aristide of co-ordinating the uprising from exile. By mid-October only around 2,100 troops of the 6,700-strong authorized MINUSTAH force had actually been deployed. The deteriorating security situation prompted the IMF to withdraw its country representative from Haiti and to postpone a planned mission to discuss the interim Government's request for emergency post-conflict assistance.

In late October 2004 Prime Minister Latortue effected a minor government reshuffle and announced the creation of two new cabinet portfolios. Alix Baptiste was appointed Minister of Haitians Living Abroad, while Yves-André Wainright was named as Minister of the Environment. The President of the CEP, Roselaure Julien, resigned in early November, claiming that considerable pressure had been exerted on her, particularly by the 'Group of 184', to allow manipulation of the electoral process. In mid-November a five-member Anti-Corruption Commission was established to investigate alleged corruption between 7 February 2001 and 29 February 2004. At the Rio Group summit in Brazil in early November, the President of the Dominican Republic, Leonel Fernández Reyna, was one of several heads of state to propose Aristide's inclusion in talks on Haiti's political future, a suggestion that was strongly opposed by Latortue's administration, the USA and France. A few days later, following a meeting in Trinidad and Tobago, CARICOM issued a 'consensus statement' reaffirming its decision not to recognize Latortue's Government. In late November the UN Security Council approved the extension of MINUSTAH's mandate until 1 June 2005. In December 2004, amid continuing political violence and civil unrest, MINUSTAH troops entered the Cité Soleil area of Port-au-Prince, a stronghold of the pro-Aristide gangs, and successfully seized control of two police stations and other official buildings that had been occupied by the *chimères* for several months; it was reported that six people were killed during the operation. By the end of January 2005 the MINUSTAH force had increased to 5,994 troops and 1,398 civilian police. Meanwhile, following pressure from the UN Secretary-General to free politicians detained without formal charge, the authorities provisionally released the three FL members arrested in early October.

In late December 2004 the interim Government began paying compensation to former soldiers who had been serving in the army at the time of its dissolution in 1995; it was believed that some 6,000 people were entitled to receive payment. Earlier that month a group of ex-soldiers had temporarily occupied the former residence of Aristide in support of a number of demands. The Government offered to provide employment or pensions for former members of the military, as well as the compensation for lost earnings, but resolutely refused to reinstate the armed forces.

In early January 2005 CARICOM announced that Haiti's participation in the Community's councils would not resume until elections had been held and democracy restored. In late January the CEP, under its newly appointed President, Pierre-Richard Duchemin, announced a timetable for the forthcoming elections: the municipal elections were to take place on 9 October, followed by legislative and presidential elections in two rounds, on 13 November and 18 December. A permanent register of voters was to be compiled prior to the elections, and national identity cards were to be issued. It was hoped that proposed mediation by the African Union (see p. 144) would result in the participation of the FL, which continued to demand the release of former officials of the Aristide administration, such as Yvon Neptune and Jocelerme Privert, and other 'political' prisoners. Latortue had earlier announced that he and his cabinet ministers would not contest the presidency. In early February 2005 the Government created a National Disarmament Commission to facilitate and monitor the recovery of illegal weapons. (According to a report released by the National Coalition for Human Rights, 403 people—384 civilians and 19 police officers—had been shot dead in Port-au-Prince since the end of September 2004.) On the same day Latortue effected a minor cabinet reshuffle, notably appointing Georges Moïse as Minister of the Interior and National Security, to replace Gen. (retd) Hérard Abraham, who became Minister of Foreign Affairs and Religion.

International relations, although improved after 1971, continued to be strained because of Haiti's unpopular political regimes and government corruption. Relations between Haiti and its neighbour on the island of Hispaniola, the Dominican Republic, have traditionally been tense because of the use of the border area by anti-Government guerrillas, smugglers and illegal emigrants, resulting in the periodic closure of the border. In March 1996, following an official visit to the Dominican Republic by Préval, the first by a Haitian President since 1935, a joint communiqué was issued establishing a bilateral commission to promote improved co-operation between the two countries. In June 1998, following an official visit to Haiti by the President of the Dominican Republic, Leonel Fernández Reyna, agreement was reached to establish joint border patrols to combat the traffic of drugs and other contraband between the two countries. In November 1999 Préval submitted a formal protest to the Dominican Republic following a spate of summary deportations of Haitians from the neighbouring country; according to human rights observers, some 8,000 Haitians were forcibly repatriated in the first three weeks of that month. Following a direct meeting between representatives of the two Governments, a protocol was signed in early December limiting the repatriations. Relations between the two countries were strained in November 2000 following the Dominican Republic's refusal to extradite the police officers accused of planning a coup against the Préval Government in the previous month (see above). The number of Haitians entering the Dominican Republic increased in 2001, owing to the deteriorating economic situation in the country as a result of the continuing suspension of foreign aid. At the end of the year bilateral relations were strained further when the Dominican Republic refused to extradite former Haitian police chief Guy Philippe, who was suspected of plotting the December attack on the presidential palace (see above). In January 2002 President Aristide paid his first official visit to the Dominican Republic and held talks with President Rafael Mejía, during which agreements were signed on economic co-operation and border and immigration issues. In November 2004 the Senate of the Dominican Republic adopted a resolution requesting that its Government deport illegal Haitian immigrants, who were estimated to number more than 500,000. Meanwhile, in response to increasing instability in Haiti, the Dominican army increased its presence in the border area.

Following the coup of 30 September 1991, the USA came under international criticism for its forced repatriation of Haitian refugees fleeing the repressive military regime. In November, following an appeal by the Haitian Refugee Center in Miami, USA, a US federal judge in Florida ordered a temporary halt to the repatriation. However, at the end of January 1992 the US Supreme Court annulled the federal judge's ruling, and repatriation resumed. While a small percentage of refugees were considered for political asylum, the US Government insisted that the majority were economic refugees and therefore not eligible for asylum. In May President George Bush issued an executive order providing for refugees who were intercepted at sea by the US coastguard to be repatriated immediately without any evaluation being made of their right to asylum. The decision, which was condemned by human rights groups, was overturned in July by an appeals court in New York. However, in August the US Supreme Court suspended the appeals court decision, and the executive order stood pending a definitive ruling by the Supreme Court itself. In June 1993 the US Supreme Court ruled to uphold the executive order of May 1992, continued under the Clinton Administration. In May 1994, following concerted pressure by US groups, including a 40-strong black caucus in the US Congress, the US Government reversed its policy regarding Haitian refugees, agreeing to resume hearings for all asylum applications—to be conducted at screening centres established later on the British dependent territory of the island of Grand Turk and off the shore of Jamaica. The new policy prompted a renewed exodus of thousands of refugees, forcing a further change of US policy in July under which refugees granted asylum were henceforth to be held indefinitely in 'safe havens' outside the USA. In early 2002 Haiti was 'decertified' by the USA for its failure to combat drugs-trafficking. In October of that year around 200 Haitian illegal immigrants arrived in Florida, prompting the launch of a campaign by Haitian-American leaders to encourage US businesses to invest in Haiti in an attempt to halt the flow of those emigrating for economic reasons. The USA contributed some 1,900 troops to the MIF deployed in Haiti following the resignation of Aristide in February 2004. US Secretary of State Colin Powell visited Haiti in April and December to hold talks with the interim Government. In early February 2005 the USA despatched the first 50 marines of an intended 200-strong mission to Gonaïves in the north of Haiti to undertake humanitarian projects, largely related to damage caused by severe flooding in September 2004.

Government

The Constitution, approved by referendum in March 1987, provided for a bicameral legislature, comprising a 77-member Chamber of Deputies (later enlarged to 83 members) and a 27-member Senate. The Chamber of Deputies was elected for a term of four years, while the Senate was elected for a term of six years with one-third renewed every two years. Both houses were elected by universal adult suffrage. Executive power was held by the President, who was elected by universal adult suffrage for a five-year term and could not stand for immediate re-election. The President selected a Prime Minister from the political party commanding a majority in the legislature. The Prime Minister chose a Cabinet in consultation with the President. However, the Constitution was interrupted by successive coups, in June and September 1988 and September 1991. A return to constitutional rule was finally effected in October 1994, following the intervention of a US-led multinational force and the reinstatement of the exiled President Aristide. In January 2004, owing to the country's failure to hold legislative elections, the mandates of all 83 members of the Chamber of Deputies and 12 members of the Senate expired, entitling the President to rule by decree.

There are nine Départements, subdivided into arrondissements and communes.

Defence

Following the return to civilian rule in 1994, measures providing for the separation of the armed forces from the police force were approved by the legislature. In December of that year two commissions were established for the restructuring of the armed forces and the formation of a new 4,000-strong civilian police force (later enlarged to 6,000). In 1995 the armed forces were effectively dissolved, although officially they remained in existence pending an amendment to the Constitution providing for their abolition. In August 2004 the civilian police force numbered an estimated 2,000. There was also a coast guard of 30. In June 2004 the UN Stabilization Mission in Haiti (MINUSTAH) commenced operations in Haiti. MINUSTAH, which had an authorized strength of 6,700 military personnel and 1,622 civilian police, was to assist the interim administration with preparations for elections in 2005 and the disarmament and demobilization of armed militias. The security budget for 2003 was an estimated US $23m.

Economic Affairs

In 2003, according to estimates by the World Bank, Haiti's gross national income (GNI), measured at average 2001–03 prices, was US $2,731m., equivalent to $380 per head (or $1,630 per head on an international purchasing-power parity basis). In 1990–2003 the population increased at an average annual rate of 2.1%, while gross domestic product (GDP) per head decreased, in real terms, by an average of 3.1% per year. Haiti's overall GDP decreased, in real terms, at an average annual rate of 1.1% in 1990–2003; real GDP increased by 0.4% in 2002/03.

Agriculture (including hunting, forestry and fishing) contributed an estimated 27.1% of GDP in 2002. About 60.7% of the total labour force were engaged in agricultural activities in mid-2003. The principal cash crop is coffee (which accounted for 4.1% of export earnings in 1999/2000). From 1998 coffee production decreased significantly, prompting the Government to announce plans for its revival in 2003. The export of oils for cosmetics and pharmaceuticals was also important. However, the deteriorating security situation in the country meant that by 2005 all exports virtually had ceased. The main food crops are sugar, bananas, maize, sweet potatoes and rice. Falling quality and cheaper imports of sugar cane forced closure of all the country's major sugar factories in recent years, although one of them, at Darbonne, near Léogane, reopened in January 2001. During 1990–2000, according to the World Bank, the real GDP of the agricultural sector decreased at an average annual rate of 1.8%; agricultural GDP decreased by an estimated 3.6% in 1999/2000, but increased by an estimated 0.6% in 2000/01.

Industry (including mining, manufacturing, construction and power) contributed 16.3% of GDP at constant prices in 2002. About 8.8% of the employed labour force were engaged in the sector in 1990. According to the World Bank, industrial GDP declined at an average annual rate of 0.9% in 1990–2000; it increased by 3.3% in 1999/2000, but decreased by an estimated 1.3% in 2000/01.

Mining contributed 0.1% of GDP at constant prices in 2000/01. About 1% of the employed labour force were engaged in extractive activities in 1990. Marble, limestone and calcareous clay are mined. There are also unexploited copper, silver and gold deposits.

Manufacturing contributed 7.9% of GDP at constant prices in 2000/01. Some 35,000 people were engaged in the sector in mid-2000. The most important branches of manufacturing were food products, textiles (including apparel, leather and fur products and footwear), chemicals (including rubber and plastic products) and tobacco. Manufacturing GDP decreased by an average of 11.8% per year in 1989–99; manufacturing GDP decreased by 0.1% in 1999/2000, but increased by an estimated 0.2% in 2000/01.

Energy is derived principally from local timber and charcoal. In 2001 51.7% of the country's public electricity came from hydroelectric power, while 48.3% of electricity came from petroleum. Severe shortfalls of electricity in 2000–01 led the Government to contract a Dominican and a US-Haitian company to add 70 MW to the national supply, increasing it by one-third. Imports of fuel products accounted for 17.1% of the value of imports in 1999/2000.

The services sector contributed 56.5% of GDP at constant prices in 2002 and engaged 22.8% of the employed labour force in 1990. According to the World Bank, the GDP of the services sector increased by an average of 0.1% per year in 1990–2000. It increased by 3.9% in 1999/2000, but decreased by an estimated 0.2% in 2000/01.

In 2002/03 Haiti recorded a visible trade deficit of US $782.7m., and there was a deficit of $13.1m. on the current account of the balance of payments. In 1998 the principal source of imports (60%) was the USA; the USA was also the principal market for exports (87%) in that year. Other significant trading partners were France, Canada, Japan and the Dominican Republic. The principal exports in 1999/2000 were manufactured articles (30.7%) and coffee (4.1%). The principal imports in that year were food and live animals (22.7%), manufactured goods and mineral fuels. In 2000 smuggling was estimated to have accounted for two-thirds of Haiti's imports.

In the financial year ending 30 September 2003 there was a budgetary deficit of 4,338m. gourdes (equivalent to 3.7% of GDP). At the end of 2002 Haiti's total external debt was US $1,248m., of which $1,063m. was long-term public debt. In 2001 the cost of debt-servicing was equivalent to 5.2% of the total value of exports of goods and services. The annual rate of inflation averaged 20.8% in 1992–2003. Consumer prices increased by an average of 9.8% in 2002 and by 39.3% in 2003. Some 60% of the labour force were estimated to be unemployed in 2001. Remittances from Haitians living abroad were equivalent to 17% of GDP in 2000.

Haiti is a member of the International Coffee Organization (see p. 370) and the Latin American Economic System (SELA, see p. 374). In July 2002 Haiti became a full member of the Caribbean Community and Common Market (CARICOM, see p. 172). Haiti is also a signatory of the European Union's (EU) Cotonou Agreement (see p. 262), which replaced the Lomé Convention from June 2000, although from 2000 the disbursement of funds under this accord were suspended while the political crisis continued (see Recent History).

In terms of average income, Haiti is the poorest country in the Western hemisphere, and there is extreme inequality of wealth. The suspension of all non-humanitarian aid and the imposition of successive, and increasingly severe, economic sanctions by the international community, following the military coup of September 1991 exacerbated the extreme poverty endured by the majority of the population. Following the return to civilian rule in late 1994, sanctions were ended and measures were agreed by donor nations for the implementation of an Emergency Economic Recovery Programme, subject to the conclusion of a stand-by agreement with the IMF. However, structural adjustment measures stipulated by the IMF were not approved by the legislature until late 1996. The IMF subsequently authorized a three-year credit of US $131m. under an Enhanced Structural Adjustment Facility (ESAF), which, in turn, facilitated access to further multilateral development aid totalling in excess of $1,000m. However, owing to a parliamentary crisis (see Recent History) the majority of the reforms were not implemented, thus obstructing the disbursement of development aid. By the time of the expiry of the ESAF in October 1999 the bulk of the IMF financing had not been drawn. Furthermore, in November the Government revealed that international agencies had almost entirely failed to honour promises to finance its $311m. short-term economic action plan, initiated in May. Economic growth slowed further from 2000 onwards, exacerbated by the ongoing political impasse, which continued to impede investment and private-sector confidence, as well as the implementation of the necessary structural adjustments that would allow economic development. The main source of growth was the continued

expansion of exports, principally from the textile sector. However, it was the continuing suspension of international aid to Haiti that was the main reason for the deteriorating economy. Although humanitarian funds continued to be disbursed, the international community made it clear that confidence in Haiti's democratic process had to be restored before financial aid could be resumed. In an attempt to encourage foreign investment the Government approved a new law offering several incentives, including a 15-year 'tax holiday', to foreign businesses prepared to invest in the country. In early 2003 the Government attempted to stabilize the country's fiscal situation by introducing a series of austerity measures and in mid-2003 an agreement was reached with the IMF. Shortly afterwards, in an attempt to secure further aid, the Government paid $32m. in arrears to the Inter-American Development Bank (IDB), enabling the release of $146m. of 'frozen' loans from the IDB. GDP increased only slightly in 2003 (by 0.4%), while inflation increased dramatically (to 39.3%). Furthermore, the ongoing political instability in 2004, coupled with the widespread flooding in the country in September, led to forecasts of an economic contraction of 4.5% in that year and a further 5.0% decline in 2005. Following the overthrow of the Aristide Government in February 2004, in July the interim administration of Gérard Latortue secured some US $1,500m. in international aid, intended to fund reconstruction of the economy. However, disbursement of the funding was slow and the crisis precipitated by the September floods meant that much of the aid received was redirected towards humanitarian causes. Furthermore, a planned IMF visit to dicuss emergency funding in October was cancelled owing to the deteriorating security situation in the country. Although the international community reiterated its commitment to providing financial aid to Haiti, the ongoing political instability ensured that such a pledge remained unrealized in early 2005.

Education

Education is provided by the State, by the Roman Catholic Church and by other religious organizations, but many schools charge for tuition, books or uniforms. Teaching is based on the French model, and French is used as the language of instruction. Primary education, which normally begins at six years of age and lasts for six years, is officially compulsory. Secondary education usually begins at 12 years of age and lasts for a further six years, comprising two cycles of three years each. In 1997 primary enrolment included only 19.4% of children in the relevant age-group (18.9% of boys; 19.9% of girls). Enrolment at secondary schools in 1997 was equivalent to only 34.2% of children in the relevant age-group (35.2% of boys; 33.2% of girls). In 1999 combined enrolment in primary, secondary and tertiary education was 52%. Higher education is provided by 18 vocational training centres and 42 domestic science schools, and by the Université d'Etat d'Haïti, which has faculties of law, medicine, dentistry, science, agronomy, pharmacy, economic science, veterinary medicine and ethnology. Government expenditure on education in 1990 was 216m. gourdes, equivalent to 20.0% of total government expenditure.

Public Holidays

2005: 1 January (Independence Day), 2 January (Heroes of Independence), 7 February (Shrove Monday, half-day), 8 February (Shrove Tuesday), 25 March (Good Friday), 14 April (Pan-American Day), 2 May (for Labour Day), 18 May (Flag Day), 23 May (for National Sovereignty), 15 August (Assumption), 24 October (United Nations Day), 2 November (All Souls' Day, half-day), 18 November (Army Day and Commemoration of the Battle of Vertières), 5 December (Discovery Day), 25 December (Christmas Day).

2006: 1 January (Independence Day), 2 January (Heroes of Independence), 27 February (Shrove Monday, half-day), 28 February (Shrove Tuesday), 14 April (Good Friday and Pan-American Day), 1 May (Labour Day), 18 May (Flag Day), 22 May (National Sovereignty), 15 August (Assumption), 24 October (United Nations Day), 2 November (All Souls' Day, half-day), 18 November (Army Day and Commemoration of the Battle of Vertières), 5 December (Discovery Day), 25 December (Christmas Day).

Weights and Measures

Officially the metric system is in force but many US measures are also used.

Statistical Survey

Sources (unless otherwise stated): Banque de la République d'Haïti, angle rue du Magasin d'État et rue des Miracles, BP 1570, Port-au-Prince; tel. 299-1200; fax 299-1045; e-mail webmaster@brh.net; internet www.brh.net; Ministère des Finances, Port-au-Prince; Institut Haitien de Statistique et d'Informatique.

Area and Population

AREA, POPULATION AND DENSITY

Area (sq km)	27,750*
Population (census results)†	
30 August 1982	5,053,792
7 July 2003‡	
Males	3,832,980
Females	4,096,068
Total	7,929,048
Density (per sq km) at January 2003	285.7

* 10,714 sq miles.
† Excluding adjustment for underenumeration.
‡ Preliminary results.

DEPARTMENTS
(preliminary figures, 2003 census)

	Population	Capital
Ouest	3,093,699	Port-au-Prince
Sud-Est	449,585	Jacmel
Nord	773,546	Cap-Haitien
Grand'Anse	603,894	Jérémie
Nord-Est	300,493	Fort Liberté
L'Artibonit (Artibonite)	1,070,397	Gonaïves
Centre	565,043	Hinche
Sud	627,311	Les Cayes
Nord-Ouest	445,080	Port-de-Paix
Total	7,929,048	—

PRINCIPAL TOWNS
(estimated population at mid-1999)

Port-au-Prince			
(capital) . .	990,558	Delmas	284,079
Carrefour	336,222		

Source: UN Statistics Division.

Mid-2003 (UN estimate, incl. suburbs): Port-au-Prince 1,961,455 (Source: UN, *World Urbanization Prospects: The 2003 Revision*).

BIRTHS AND DEATHS
(World Bank estimates)

	2000	2002*
Crude birth rate (per 1,000)	32.6	32.3
Crude death rate (per 1,000)	13.1	13.5

* Figures for 2001 not available.

Source: World Bank, *World Development Indicators*.

Expectation of life (WHO estimates, years at birth): 50.1 (males 49.1; females 51.1) in 2002 (Source: WHO, *World Health Report*).

ECONOMICALLY ACTIVE POPULATION
(official estimates, persons aged 10 years and over, mid-1990)

	Males	Females	Total
Agriculture, hunting, forestry and fishing	1,077,191	458,253	1,535,444
Mining and quarrying	11,959	12,053	24,012
Manufacturing	83,180	68,207	151,387
Electricity, gas and water . . .	1,643	934	2,577
Construction	23,584	4,417	28,001
Trade, restaurants and hotels . .	81,632	271,338	352,970
Transport, storage and communications	17,856	2,835	20,691
Financing, insurance, real estate and business services . .	3,468	1,589	5,057
Community, social and personal services	81,897	73,450	155,347
Activities not adequately defined .	33,695	30,280	63,975
Total employed	1,416,105	923,356	2,339,461
Unemployed	191,333	148,346	339,679
Total labour force	1,607,438	1,071,702	2,679,140

Source: ILO, *Yearbook of Labour Statistics*.

Mid-2003 (estimates in '000): Agriculture, etc. 2,213; Total labour force 3,645 (Source: FAO).

Health and Welfare

KEY INDICATORS

Total fertility rate (children per woman, 2002)	4.0
Under-5 mortality rate (per 1,000 live births, 2003) . . .	118
HIV/AIDS (% of persons aged 15–49, 2003)	5.6
Physicians (per 1,000 head, 1992)	0.08
Hospital beds (per 1,000 head, 1996)	0.71
Health expenditure (2001): US $ per head (PPP) . . .	56
Health expenditure (2001): % of GDP	5.0
Health expenditure (2001): public (% of total)	53.4
Access to water (% of persons, 2002)	71
Access to sanitation (% of persons, 2002)	34
Human Development Index (2002): ranking	153
Human Development Index (2002): value	0.463

For sources and definitions, see explanatory note on p. vi.

Agriculture

PRINCIPAL CROPS
('000 metric tons)

	2001	2002*	2003*
Rice (paddy)	103	104	105
Maize	180	185	198
Sorghum	80	85	95
Sweet potatoes	174	175	175
Cassava (Manioc)	332	335	340
Yams	197	198	199
Other roots and tubers* . . .	52	52	53
Sugar cane	1,008	1,010	1,050
Fresh vegetables (incl. melons)* .	199	200	204
Bananas	290	295	300
Plaintains*	280	285	283
Mangoes	250	260	261
Other fruit*	149	162	170

* FAO estimates.

Source: FAO.

LIVESTOCK
(FAO estimates, '000 head, year ending September)

	2001	2002	2003
Horses	501	501	501
Mules	82	82	83
Asses	215	215	220
Cattle	1,440	1,450	1,455
Pigs	1,001	1,001	1,002
Sheep	152	153	154
Goats	1,942	1,943	1,944
Poultry	5,905	6,005	6,075

Source: FAO.

LIVESTOCK PRODUCTS
(FAO estimates, '000 metric tons)

	2001	2002	2003
Beef and veal	40.5	42.0	42.5
Goat meat	6.5	6.5	6.5
Pig meat	31.2	29.1	29.1
Horse meat	5.6	5.6	5.7
Poultry meat	8.3	8.6	9.1
Cows' milk	42.0	42.5	44.0
Goats' milk	24.4	24.8	25.2
Hen eggs	4.2	4.3	4.4
Cattle hides	5.8	6.2	6.3

Source: FAO.

Forestry

ROUNDWOOD REMOVALS
(FAO estimates, '000 cubic metres, excl. bark)

	2001	2002	2003
Sawlogs, veneer logs and logs for sleepers*	224	224	224
Other industrial wood*	15	15	15
Fuel wood	1,971	1,978	1,985
Total	2,210	2,217	2,224

* Output assumed to be unchanged since 1971.

Source: FAO.

SAWNWOOD PRODUCTION
('000 cubic metres, incl. railway sleepers)

	1969	1970	1971
Coniferous (softwood)	5	8	8
Broadleaved (hardwood)	10	5	6
Total	14	13	14

1972–2003: Annual production as in 1971 (FAO estimates).

Source: FAO.

Fishing

(metric tons, live weight)

	1997	1998	1999*
Freshwater fishes*	500	500	500
Marine fishes*	4,000	4,000	3,800
Marine crabs	71	59	50
Caribbean spiny lobster*	200	200	200
Natantian decapods*	150	150	150
Stromboid conchs*	380	350	300
Total catch	5,301	5,259	5,000

* FAO estimates.
Note: Figures exclude corals and madrepores (FAO estimates, metric tons):
13 in 1997, 10 in 1998, 10 in 1999.

2000–2: Annual catch as in 1999 (FAO estimates).

Source: FAO.

Industry

SELECTED PRODUCTS
(metric tons, unless otherwise indicated, year ending 30 September)

	1999/2000
Edible oils	38,839.6
Butter	2,972.2
Margarine	2,387.4
Cornflour	104,542.6
Soap	30,069.9
Detergent	4,506.1
Beer ('000 cases of 24 bottles)	784.5
Beverages ('000 cases of 24 bottles)	1,807.7
Rum ('000 750ml bottles)	2,009.5
Electric energy (million kWh)	697.6

Finance

CURRENCY AND EXCHANGE RATES

Monetary Units
100 centimes = 1 gourde.

Sterling, Dollar and Euro Equivalents (29 October 2004)
£1 sterling = 68.067 gourdes;
US $1 = 37.156 gourdes;
€1 = 47.329 gourdes;
1,000 gourdes = £14.69 = $26.91 = €21.13.

Average Exchange Rate (gourdes per US $)
2001   24.429
2002   29.250
2003   42.367

Note: The official rate of exchange was maintained at US $1 = 5 gourdes until September 1991, when the central bank ceased all operations at the official rate, thereby unifying the exchange system at the 'floating' free market rate.

BUDGET
(million gourdes, year ending 30 September)

Revenue	2001	2002	2003*
Current receipts	6,509	7,826	10,746
Internal receipts	4,504	5,587	7,462
Customs	1,772	2,069	2,762
Transfers from public enterprises	—	2	—
Total	6,509	7,828	10,746

Expenditure	2001	2002	2003*
Current expenditure	7,150	8,864	11,156
Wages and salaries	3,387	3,480	3,862
Operations	2,627	3,888	4,845
Interest on public debt	767	729	1,050
External debt	436	353	561
Internal debt	331	376	489
Transfers and subsidies	369	767	1,399
Capital expenditure	1,578	1,908	3,928
Total	8,728	10,772	15,084

* Preliminary figures.

Source: IMF, *Haiti: Staff-Monitored Program* (August 2003 and July 2004).

INTERNATIONAL RESERVES
(US $ million at 31 December)*

	2001	2002	2003
IMF special drawing rights	0.5	0.5	0.3
Reserve position in IMF	0.1	0.1	0.1
Foreign exchange	140.8	81.1	61.6
Total	141.4	81.7	62.0

* Excluding gold (valued at market-related prices, US $ million): 6.6 in 1989.

Source: IMF, *International Financial Statistics*.

MONEY SUPPLY
(million gourdes at 31 December)

	2001	2002	2003
Currency outside banks . . .	6,584.3	8,687.5	9,843.2
Demand deposits at commercial banks	3,749.2	4,394.7	6,142.5
Total money (incl. others) . .	10,610.2	13,501.5	16,222.1

Source: IMF, *International Financial Statistics.*

COST OF LIVING
(Consumer Price Index, year ending 30 September; base: 2000 = 100, metropolitan areas)

	2001	2002	2003
Food	115.5	127.4	174.2
Clothing and footwear	112.6	123.4	155.1
Rent	111.3	121.9	170.1
All items (incl. others)	114.0	125.3	174.5

Source: ILO.

NATIONAL ACCOUNTS
(million gourdes, year ending 30 September)

Expenditure on the Gross Domestic Product
(at current prices)

	2000/01	2001/02	2002/03
Final consumption expenditure .	83,921	92,375	117,891
Gross capital formation	22,158	23,425	36,704
Total domestic expenditure .	106,079	115,800	154,595
Exports of goods and services . .	10,594	11,403	19,389
Less Imports of goods and services	30,973	33,363	55,815
GDP in purchasers' values . .	85,700	93,840	118,169
GDP at constant 1987 prices .	13,001	12,929	12,976

Source: IMF, *International Financial Statistics.*

Gross Domestic Product by Economic Activity
(at constant 1987/88 prices)

	1998/99	1999/2000	2000/01
Agriculture, hunting, forestry and fishing	3,553.1	3,423.8	3,445.6
Mining and quarrying	13.6	14.4	13.7
Manufacturing	987.4	985.6	987.7
Electricity, gas and water . . .	90.4	87.0	48.7
Construction	869.6	939.3	947.9
Trade, restaurants and hotels . .	3,250.8	3,402.9	3,423.6
Transport, storage and communication	665.3	725.3	750.8
Business services	1,500.7	1,566.4	1,552.2
Other services	1,444.4	1,433.4	1,385.4
Sub-total	12,377.3	12,578.1	12,555.6
Less Imputed bank service charge	343.0	459.3	494.4
Total	12,034.3	12,118.8	12,061.2
Import duties	992.4	1,019.7	920.0
GDP in purchasers' values .	13,026.7	13,138.5	12,981.2

BALANCE OF PAYMENTS
(US $ million, year ending 30 September)

	2001	2002	2003
Exports of goods f.o.b.	305.2	274.4	333.2
Imports of goods f.o.b.	−1,055.4	−980.4	−1,115.8
Trade balance	−750.2	−706.0	−782.7
Exports of services	139.0	148.0	136.0
Imports of services	−242.5	−251.6	−259.0
Balance on goods and services	−853.7	−809.6	−905.7
Other income paid	−9.5	−13.7	−14.3
Balance on goods, services and income	−863.1	−823.3	−919.9
Current transfers received . . .	768.6	775.7	906.8
Current balance	−94.6	−47.6	−13.1
Direct investment from abroad .	4.4	5.7	7.8
Other investment assets . . .	−3.0	27.3	−98.0
Other investment liabilities . .	81.1	−50.3	13.7
Net errors and omissions . . .	6.9	−3.1	85.0
Overall balance	−5.2	−67.9	−4.6

Source: IMF, *International Financial Statistics.*

External Trade

PRINCIPAL COMMODITIES
(US $ million, year ending 30 September)

Imports c.i.f.	1998	1999	2000
Food and others*	307.9	361.6	308.9
Mineral fuels, lubricants, etc. . .	80.8	83.2	186.6
Machinery and transport equipment	142.1	164.9	171.5
Manufactured goods	223.2	257.2	289.1
Total (incl. others)	883.9	1,010.6	1,090.7

* Including beverages, oils and fats, and pharmaceutical products.

Exports f.o.b.	1998	1999	2000
Agricultural exports	40.7	37.7	32.4
Coffee	21.8	18.0	13.5
Light manufactures*	244.9	295.5	281.3
Domestic inputs	33.7	30.4	23.6
Imported inputs	211.2	265.1	257.7
Total (incl. others)	299.4	348.7	327.1

* Includes valuation and classification adjustments made by Banque de la République d'Haiti.

Source: IMF, *Haiti: Selected Issues* (February 2002).

PRINCIPAL TRADING PARTNERS
(US $ million, year ending 30 September)*

Imports c.i.f.	1989/90	1990/91	1991/92
Belgium	3.4	3.7	2.9
Canada	22.0	31.9	15.2
France	24.5	32.4	17.2
Germany, Federal Republic . .	14.6	19.2	10.0
Japan	23.6	31.2	17.7
Netherlands	11.2	13.9	8.7
United Kingdom	5.6	6.7	4.2
USA	153.1	203.2	126.7
Total (incl. others)	332.2	400.5	277.2

Exports f.o.b.†	1989/90	1990/91	1991/92
Belgium	15.9	19.5	6.0
Canada	4.5	4.7	2.3
France	17.4	21.6	6.1
Germany, Federal Republic	5.4	6.6	2.4
Italy	16.5	20.7	8.7
Japan	2.4	2.9	0.9
Netherlands	3.4	4.3	1.4
United Kingdom	2.3	2.3	0.7
USA	78.3	96.3	39.7
Total (incl. others)	163.7	198.7	74.7

* Provisional.
† Excluding re-exports.

Source: Administration Générale des Douanes.

Transport

ROAD TRAFFIC
('000 motor vehicles in use)

	1994	1995	1996
Passenger cars	30.0	49.0	59.0
Commercial vehicles	30.0	29.0	35.0

1999 ('000 motor vehicles in use): Passenger cars 93.0; Commercial vehicles 61.6.

Source: UN, *Statistical Yearbook*.

SHIPPING

Merchant Fleet
(registered at 31 December)

	2001	2002	2003
Number of vessels	4	5	5
Total displacement ('000 grt)	1.2	1.3	1.3

Source: Lloyd's Register-Fairplay, *World Fleet Statistics*.

International Sea-borne Freight Traffic
('000 metric tons)

	1988	1989	1990
Goods loaded	164	165	170
Goods unloaded	684	659	704

Source: UN, *Monthly Bulletin of Statistics*.

CIVIL AVIATION (international flights, 1995): Passengers arriving 367,900; Passengers departing 368,330.

Tourism

TOURIST ARRIVALS BY COUNTRY OF ORIGIN

	1999	2000	2001
Canada	15,955	14,752	14,953
Dominican Republic	6,769	7,034	7,401
France	6,318	6,420	6,473
Jamaica	3,069	3,531	3,351
USA	92,543	92,921	93,065
Total (incl. others)	143,362	140,492	141,632

Source: World Tourism Organization, *Yearbook of Tourism Statistics*.

Receipts from tourism (US $ million): 55 in 1999; 54 in 2000; 54 in 2001 (Source: World Tourism Organization).

Communications Media

	2000	2001	2002
Telephones ('000 main lines in use)	72.5	80.0	130.0
Mobile cellular telephones ('000 subscribers)	55.0	91.5	140.0
Internet users ('000)	20.0	30.0	80.0

Personal computers ('000 in use): 2.0 in 1999.

Source: International Telecommunication Union.

Radio receivers ('000 in use): 415 in 1997.

Television receivers ('000 in use): 42 in 1999.

Daily newspapers: 4 in 1996 (total circulation 20,000 copies).

Book production: 340 titles published in 1995.

Sources (unless otherwise indicated): UNESCO, *Statistical Yearbook*; UN, *Statistical Yearbook*.

Education

(1994/95)

	Institutions	Teachers	Students
Pre-primary	n.a.	n.a.	230,391*
Primary	10,071	30,205	1,110,398
Secondary	1,038	15,275	195,418
Tertiary	n.a.	654*	6,288*

* 1990/91 figure.

Adult literacy rate (UNESCO estimates): 51.9% (males 53.8%; females 50.0%) in 2002 (Source: UN Development Programme, *Human Development Report*).

Directory

The Constitution

The Constitution of the Republic of Haiti, which was approved by the electorate in a referendum held in March 1987, provided for a system of power-sharing between a President (who may not serve two consecutive five-year terms), a Prime Minister, a bicameral legislature (comprising a chamber of deputies elected for four years and a senate whose members serve six-year terms, one-third of whom are elected every two years) and regional assemblies. The army and the police were no longer to be a combined force. The death penalty was abolished. Official status was given to the Creole language spoken by Haitians and to the folk religion, voodoo (vaudou). The Constitution was suspended after a military *coup d'état* in June 1988. It was restored when the military ruler, Brig.-Gen. Prosper Avril, fled in March 1990 and an interim President was appointed, pending a presidential election in December 1990. Fr Jean-Bertrand Aristide was elected President, but was deposed in September 1991 by a military coup. In October a new President and Government were installed by the army. In June 1992 the presidency was declared to be vacant, but in May 1994 a pro-military faction of the Senate declared the head of the Supreme Court, Émile Jonassaint, provisional President. Following US mediation, US forces (officially an international peace-keeping force) arrived on the island in September. In October Jonassaint and Lt-Gen. Raoul Cédras, the Commander-in-Chief of the armed forces, resigned. In the same month President Aristide returned to Haiti, to begin the restoration of constitutional government. He declared the army dissolved in April 1995. The constitutional amendment formally abolishing it was due to be passed by the legislature elected in May and July 2000. However, the amendment was never presented to the legislature and, after the fall of Aristide in February 2004, there were calls for the revival of the army. The head of the Supreme Court, Boniface Alexandre, succeeded Aristide, and a Council of Elders appointed Gérard Latortue as Prime Minister. The Council was to expand into an informal consultative body until new legislative elections were held. The Government and Haiti's political parties agreed in April to suspend the constitutional requirement that new elections be held within 90 days of a presidential resignation. The Government later announced that elections would be held in November 2005.

The Government

HEAD OF STATE

Acting President: BONIFACE ALEXANDRE (assumed office on 29 February 2004 following the resignation of Jean-Bertrand Aristide).

CABINET
(April 2005)

Prime Minister: GÉRARD LATORTUE.

Minister of Agriculture, Natural Resources and Rural Development: PHILIPPE MATHIEU.

Minister of Culture and Communications: MAGALIE COMEAU DENIS.

Minister of Economy and Finance: HENRI BAZIN.

Minister of the Environment: YVES-ANDRÉ WAINRIGHT.

Minister of Foreign Affairs and Religion: Gen. (retd) HÉRARD ABRAHAM.

Minister of Haitians Residing Abroad: ALIX BAPTISTE.

Minister of Health: JOSETTE BIJOUX.

Minister of the Interior and National Security: GEORGES MOÏSE.

Minister of Justice and Public Security: BERNARD GOUSSE.

Minister of National Education, Youth and Sport: PIERRE BUTEAU.

Minister of Planning and External Co-operation: ROLAND PIERRE.

Minister of Public Works, Transport and Communications: FRITZ ADRIEN.

Minister of Social Affairs: PIERRE CLAUDE CALIXTE.

Minister of Trade and Industry: FRITZ KÉNOL.

Minister of Women's Affairs and Rights: ADELINE MAGLOIRE CHANCY.

MINISTRIES

Office of the President: Palais National, rue de la République, Port-au-Prince; tel. 222-3024; e-mail webmestre@palaisnational .info; internet www.palaisnational.info/pnh/accueil.php.

Office of the Prime Minister: Villa d'Accueil, Delmas 60, Musseau, Port-au-Prince; tel. 245-0007; fax 245-1624.

Ministry of Agriculture, Natural Resources and Rural Development: BP 1441, Damien, Port-au-Prince; tel. 250-7558.

Ministry of Culture and Communications: 4 rue Nagny, Port-au-Prince; tel. 221-1716; e-mail dg1@haiticulture.org; internet www .haiticulture.org.

Ministry of Economy and Finance: Palais des Ministères, rue Monseigneur Guilloux, Port-au-Prince; tel. 222-7113; fax 223-1247.

Ministry of the Environment: Haut Turgeau 181, Port-au-Prince; tel. 245-7572; fax 245-7360; e-mail dgmde@rehred-haiti.net; internet www.rehred-haiti.net.

Ministry of Foreign Affairs and Religion: blvd Harry S Truman, Cité de l'Exposition, Port-au-Prince; tel. 222-8482; fax 223-1668; e-mail webmaster@maehaitiinfo.org; internet www.maehaitiinfo .org.

Ministry of Haitians Residing Abroad: 87 ave Jean-Paul II, Turgeau, Port-au-Prince; tel. 244-4321; fax 245-3400; internet haiti2004lakay.com; f. 1995.

Ministry of Health: Palais de Ministères, Port-au-Prince; tel. 222-1583; fax 222-4066.

Ministry of the Interior and Social Security: Palais des Ministères, Port-au-Prince; tel. 222-6490; fax 223-5742.

Ministry of Justice: ave Charles Sumner 19, Port-au-Prince; tel. 245-1626.

Ministry of National Education, Youth and Sport: rue Dr Audain, Port-au-Prince; tel. 222-1036; fax 223-7887.

Ministry of Planning and External Co-operation: Palais des Ministères, Port-au-Prince; tel. 222-4148; fax 223-4193.

Ministry of Public Works: Palais des Ministères, rue Mgr Guilloux, Port-au-Prince; tel. 222-2528; fax 222-3240; e-mail bmministre@haititptc.org; internet www.haititptc.org.

Ministry of Social Affairs: 16 rue de la Révolution, Port-au-Prince; tel. 222-1244; fax 223-8084.

Ministry of Trade and Industry: rue Légitime, Champ-de-Mars, BP 200, Port-au-Prince; tel. 222-1628; fax 223-8402.

Ministry of Women's Affairs and Rights: Delmas 31, rue Louverture et Biassou 2, Port-au-Prince; tel. 249-5913.

President and Legislature

PRESIDENT

Presidential Election, 26 November 2000

Candidates	% of votes
Jean-Bertrand Aristide (FL)	91.7
Jean-Arnold Dumas	2.0
Evan Nicolas	1.6
Serge Sylvain	1.3
Calixte Dorisca	1.3
Jacques Philippe Dorce	1.1
Paul Arthur Fleurival	1.0
Total (incl. others)	100.0

LEGISLATURE

In January 2004, owing to the country's failure to hold legislative elections, the mandates of all 83 members of the Chamber of Deputies and 12 members of the Senate expired, leaving Haiti effectively without a legislature and entitling the President to rule by decree.

Sénat
(Senate)

President: (vacant).

Elections, 21 May, 9 July and 26 November 2000

	Seats
La Fanmi Lavalas (FL)	26*
Pati Louvri Baryè (PLB)	1
Total	27

* In June 2001 seven FL senators resigned their seats.

Chambre des Députés
(Chamber of Deputies)

President: (vacant).

Elections, 21 May, 9 July and 26 November 2000

	Seats
La Fanmi Lavalas (FL)	73
Mouvement Chrétien pour Batir une Nouvelle Haïti (MOCHRENA)	3
Espace de Concertation	2
Pati Louvri Baryè (PLB)	2
Koordinasyon Resistans Grandans (KOREGA-ESCANP)	1
Organisation du Peuple en Lutte (OPL)	1
Independent	1
Total	83

Political Organizations

Alliance pour la Libération et l'Avancement d'Haïti (ALLAH): Haut Turgeau 95, BP 13350, Port-au-Prince; tel. 245-0446; fax 257-4804; e-mail reynoldgeorges@yahoo.com; f. 1975; Leader REYNOLD GEORGES.

L'Alternative pour le Changement (AC): 88 Chemin des Dalles, Port-au-Prince; tel. 557-7388; f. 2000; Leader GÉRARD BLOT.

Coalitions des Forces Démocratiques: f. 2000; coalition of 2 opposition parties.

Congrès National des Mouvements Démocratiques (KONAKOM): 101 Bois Verna, Port-au-Prince; tel. 245-6228; f. 1987; social democratic; Leader VICTOR BENOÎT.

Convergence Démocratique (CD): 101 Bois Verna, Port–au–Prince; tel. 257-5359; f. 2000; coalition of 13 anti-Lavalas parties; Leaders HUBERT DE RONCERAY, SERGE GILLES, EVANS PAUL, MICHA GAILLARD.

Espace de Concertation: f. 1999; centre-left coalition; Leaders EVANS PAUL, MICHA GAILLARD.

La Fanmi Lavalas: blvd 15 Octobre, Tabarre, Port-au-Prince; tel. 256-7208; f. 1996 by Jean-Bertrand Aristide; formed a coalition with the MOP, the OPL and the PLB; Leader YVON FEUILLÉ.

Front de Reconstruction Nationale (FRN): Gonaïves; f. 2004; Pres. BUTEUR MÉTAYER; Sec.-Gen. GUY PHILIPPE.

Front National pour le Changement et la Démocratie (FNCD): f. 1990; social-democratic; Leader EVANS PAUL.

Grand Front de Centre Droit (GFCD): 21 blvd Harry Truman, Cité de l'Exposition, Port-au-Prince; tel. 245-6251; e-mail hdr@mdnhaiti.org; internet www.gcfd.org; centre-right alliance; Pres. HUBERT DE RONCERAY.

Jeunesse Pouvoir Populaire (JPP): 410 rue Tiremasse, Port-au-Prince; tel. 558-1647; f. 1997; Leader RENÉ CIVIL.

Konvansyon Inite Demokratik (KID): 14 rue Camille Leon, Port-au-Prince; tel. 245-0185; f. 1986; fmrly Konfederasyon Inite Demokratik; Leader EVANS PAUL.

Koordinasyon Resistans Grandans (KOREGA-ESCANP): e-mail crb@maf.org; regionally based; radical left; Leader Fr JOACHIM SAMEDI.

Mobilisation pour le Développement National (MDN): c/o CHISS, 33 rue Bonne Foi, BP 2497, Port-au-Prince; tel. 222-3829; e-mail info@mdnhaiti.org; internet www.mdnhaiti.org; f. 1986; Pres. HUBERT DE RONCERAY; Sec.-Gen. MAX CARRE.

Mouvement Chrétien pour une Nouvelle Haïti (MOCHRENA): 7 angle rue Jacob et Mon Repos 36, Carrefour; tel. 401-3120; f. 1991; Leaders LUC MÉSADIEU, GILBERT N. LÉGER.

Mouvement Démocratique pour la Libération d'Haïti (MODELH): FRANÇOIS LATORTUE.

Mouvement pour l'Instauration de la Démocratie en Haïti (MIDH): 114 ave Jean Paul II, Port-au-Prince; tel. 245-8377; f. 1986; centre-right; Pres. MARC BAZIN.

Mouvement National et Patriotique du 28 Novembre (MNP-28): Leader DÉJEAN BÉLIZAIRE.

Mouvement pour l'Organisation du Pays (MOP): 9 rue Stella, Delmas 31, Port-au-Prince; tel. 249-3408; f. 1946; centre party; Leader JEAN MOLIÈRE.

Mouvement Patriotique pour le Sauvetage National (MPSN): f. 1998; right-wing coalition; Leader HUBERT DE RONCERAY.

Mouvement pour la Reconstruction Nationale (MRN): f. 1991; Leader JEAN-ENOL BUTEAU.

Mouvman Konbit Nasyonal (MKN): Leader VOLVICK RÉMY JOSEPH.

Organisation du Peuple en Lutte (OPL): 105 rue Lamartinière, Bois Verna, Port-au-Prince; tel. 245-4214; e-mail info@oplpeople.com; internet www.oplpeople.com/home.html; f. 1991 as Organisation Politique Lavalas; name changed as above 1998; Leaders GÉRARD PIERRE-CHARLES, SAUVEUR PIERRE-ÉTIENNE.

Parti Agricole et Industrie National (PAIN): f. 1956; Spokesman TOUSSAINT DESROSIERS.

Parti des Démocrates Haïtiens (PADEMH): Leader JEAN-JACQUES CLARK PARENT.

Parti Démocratique et Chrétien d'Haïti (PDCH): 127 rue du Magasin de l'Etat, Port-au-Prince; tel. 550-7282; f. 1979; Christian Democrat party; Leaders OSNER FÉVRY, JOACHIN PIERRE.

Parti pour un Développement Alternatif (PADH): Leader GÉRARD DALVIUS.

Parti Nationale Démocratique Progressiste d'Haïti (PNDPH): Port-au-Prince; Pres. TURNEB DELPÉ.

Parti National Progressiste Révolutionnaire (PANPRA): 5 rue Marcelin, Port-au-Prince; tel. 257-5359; f. 1989; social-democratic; Leader SERGE GILLES.

Parti National des Travailleurs (PNT): Port-au-Prince.

Parti Populaire National: 11 rue Capois, Port-au-Prince; tel. 222-6513; f. 1999; Sec. Gen. BEN DUPUY.

Parti Revolutionnaire Démocratique d'Haïti (PRDH): fmrly Mouvement Démocratique pour la Libération d'Haïti (MODELH); Leader FRANÇOIS LATORTUE.

Parti Social Chrétien d'Haïti (PSCH): BP 84, Port-au-Prince; f. 1979; Leader GRÉGOIRE EUGÈNE.

Pati Louvri Baryè (PLB): f. 1992 by Renaud Bernardin; Sec.-Gen. FRANÇOIS PIERRE-LOUIS.

Rassemblement des Démocrates Chrétiens (RDC): 177 rue du Centre, Port-au-Prince; tel. 234-4214; Leader EDDY VOLEL.

Rassemblement des Démocrates Nationalistes et Progressistes (RDNP): 234 route de Delmas, Delmas, Port-au-Prince; tel. 246-3313; f. 1979; centre party; Sec.-Gen. LESLIE FRANÇOIS MANIGAT.

Union Démocrates Patriotiques (UDP): 30 rue Geffrard, Port-au-Prince; tel. 256-1953; Leader ROCKFELLER GUERRE.

Union Patriotique: f. 2002; coalition of four opposition parties; Sec.-Gen. LESLIE FRANÇOIS MANIGAT.

Diplomatic Representation

EMBASSIES IN HAITI

Argentina: 4 impasse Dumain, Montana Pétionville, BP 1755, Port-au-Prince; tel. 257-1635; fax 256-6414; e-mail embarghaiti@hainet.net; Chargé d'affaires a.i. MARIO JOSÉ PINO.

Bahamas: 12 rue Goulard, Place Boyer, Pétionville; tel. 257-8782; fax 256-5729; e-mail bahamasemb@hainet.net; Ambassador Dr EUGENE NEWRY.

Brazil: 34 rue Lamarre, Pétionville, BP 6140, Port-au-Prince; tel. 256-9662; fax 510-6111; e-mail brasemb1@transnethaiti.com; Ambassador WALTER MOREIRA.

Canada: 18 route de Delmas, Edif. Scotiabank, BP 826, Port-au-Prince; tel. 298-3050; fax 298-3801; e-mail prnce@dfait-maeci.gc.ca; internet www.dfait-maeci.gc.ca/haiti; Ambassador CLAUDE BOUCHER.

Chile: 2 rue Coutilien, Musseau, Port-au-Prince; tel. 256-7960; fax 257-0623; e-mail myoung@minrel.gov.cl; Ambassador ALAIN MARCEL YOUNG DEBEUF.

China (Taiwan): 16 rue Léon Nau, Pétionville, BP 655, Port-au-Prince; tel. 257-2899; fax 256-8067; e-mail hti@ms90.url.com.tw; Ambassador HSIN-PING HSIEH.

Cuba: 18 rue Marion, Peguy Ville, POB 15702, Port-au-Prince; tel. 256-3812; fax 257-8566; e-mail ecuhaiti@hainet.net; Ambassador ROLANDO GÓMEZ GONZÁLEZ.

Dominican Republic: rue Panaméricaine 121, BP 56, Pétionville, Port-au-Prince; tel. 257-0568; fax 221-8718; e-mail embrepdomhai@yahoo.com; Ambassador JOSÉ SERULLE RAMIA.

France: 51 pl. des Héros de l'Indépendance, BP 1312, Port-au-Prince; tel. 222-0951; fax 223-9858; e-mail ambafrance@hainet.net; internet www.ambafrance-ht.org; Ambassador THIERRY BURKARD.

Germany: 2 impasse Claudinette, Bois Moquette, Pétionville, BP 1147, Port-au-Prince; tel. 257-7280; fax 257-4131; e-mail germanem@haitelonline.com; Ambassador Dr GORDON KRICKE.

Holy See: rue Louis Pouget, Morne Calvaire, BP 326, Port-au-Prince; tel. 257-6308; fax 257-3411; e-mail nonciature@haitiworld.com; Apostolic Nuncio Most Rev. MARIO GIORDANA (Titular Archbishop of Minora).

Jamaica: 141 rue Pavée, Edif. Firestone, BP 1065, Port-au-Prince; tel. 248-0589; fax 226-0613; Ambassador PETER BLACK.

Japan: Villa Bella Vista, 2 impasse Tulipe, Desprez, BP 2512, Port-au-Prince; tel. 245-3333; fax 245-8834; Ambassador HARUO OKOMOTO.

Mexico: Delmas 60, 2, BP 327, Port-au-Prince; tel. 257-8100; fax 256-6528; e-mail embmxhai@yahoo.com; Ambassador ANACELIA PÉREZ CHARLES.

Spain: 54 rue Pacot, State Liles, BP 386, Port-au-Prince; tel. 245-4410; fax 245-3901; e-mail ampespht@mail.mae.es; Ambassador PAULINO GONZÁLEZ FERNÁNDEZ-CORUGEDO.

USA: 5 blvd Harry S Truman, BP 1761, Port-au-Prince; tel. 222-0200; fax 223-9038; internet usembassy.state.gov/haiti; Ambassador JAMES FOLEY.

Venezuela: blvd Harry S Truman, Cité de l'Exposition, BP 2158, Port-au-Prince; tel. 222-0973; e-mail venhtamb@compa.net; Ambassador MARCO REQUENA.

Judicial System

Law is based on the French Napoleonic Code, substantially modified during the presidency of François Duvalier.

Courts of Appeal and Civil Courts sit at Port-au-Prince and the three provincial capitals: Gonaïves, Cap Haïtien and Port de Paix. In principle each commune has a Magistrates' Court. Judges of the Supreme Court and Courts of Appeal are appointed by the President.

Supreme Court
Port-au-Prince; tel. 222-3212.
Pres. (vacant); Vice-Pres. PRADEL PÉAN.

Citizens' Rights Defender: NECKER DESSABLES.

Religion

Roman Catholicism and the folk religion voodoo (vaudou) are the official religions. There are various Protestant and other denominations.

CHRISTIANITY

The Roman Catholic Church

For ecclesiastical purposes, Haiti comprises two archdioceses and seven dioceses. At 31 December 2002 adherents represented some 65.8% of the population.

Bishops' Conference

Conférence Episcopale de Haïti, angle rues Piquant et Lamarre, BP 1572, Port-au-Prince; tel. 222-5194; fax 223-5318; e-mail ceh56@hotmail.com.
f. 1977; Pres. Rt Rev. HUBERT CONSTANT (Archbishop of Cap-Haïtien).

Archbishop of Cap-Haïtien: Most Rev. HUBERT CONSTANT, Archevêché, rue 19–20 H, BP 22, Cap-Haïtien; tel. 262-1278; fax 262-0593.

Archbishop of Port-au-Prince: Most Rev. FRANÇOIS-WOLFF LIGONDÉ, Archevêché, rue Dr Aubry, BP 538, Port-au-Prince; tel. 222-2043; e-mail archeveche.pap@globalsud.com.

The Anglican Communion

Anglicans in Haiti fall under the jurisdiction of a missionary diocese of Province II of the Episcopal Church in the USA.

Bishop of Haiti: Rt Rev. JEAN ZACHE DURACIN, Eglise Episcopale d'Haïti, BP 1309, Port-au-Prince; fax 257-3412; e-mail epihaiti@globalsud.net.

Protestant Churches

Baptist Convention: BP 20, Cap-Haïtien; tel. 262-0567; e-mail conventionbaptiste@yahoo.com; f. 1964; Pres. Rev. GÉDÉON EUGÈNE.

Evangelical Lutheran Church of Haiti: 144 rue Capitale, BP 15, Les Cayes; tel. 286-3398; e-mail israelsonisidor37@hotmail.com; internet www.haitimissions.org; f. 1975; Pres. Rev. ISRAEL IZIDOR.

Other denominations active in Haiti include Methodists and the Church of God 'Eben-Ezer'.

The Press

DAILIES

Le Matin: 6 rue du Quai, BP 367, Port-au-Prince; tel. 222-2040; fax 223-2551; f. 1908; French; independent; Editor DUMAYRIC CHARLIER; circ. 5,000.

Le Nouvelliste: 198 rue du Centre, BP 1013, Port-au-Prince; tel. 223-2114; fax 223-2313; f. 1898; evening; French; independent; Editor CARLO DÉSINOR; circ. 6,000.

PERIODICALS

Ayiti Fanm: 3 bis, rue Sapotille, Port-au-Prince; tel. 245-1930; Creole; Dir CLORINDE ZÉPHYR.

Bon Nouvèl: 103 rue Pavée, Étage Imprimerie La Phalange, BP 1594, Port-au-Prince; tel. 223-9186; fax 222-8105; e-mail bonnouvel@rehred-haiti.net; internet www.rehred-haiti.net/membres/bonouvel/; f. 1967; monthly; Creole; Dir JEAN HOET.

Bulletin de Liaison: Centre Pedro-Arrupe, BP 1710, Port-au-Prince; tel. 245-2360; e-mail dcm3@georgetown.edu; internet liaison.lemoyne.edu; f. 1996; 4 a year; Editors ANDRÉ CHARBONNEAU, ALFRED DORVIL, DONALD MALDARI.

Haïti en Marche: 74 bis, rue Capois, Port-au-Prince; tel. and fax 221–8596; e-mail pub@haitienmarche.com; internet www.haitienmarche.com; f. 1987; weekly; Editor MARCUS GARCIA.

Haïti Observateur: 98 ave John Brown, Port-au-Prince; tel. 228-0782; f. 1971; weekly; Editor LÉO JOSEPH.

Haïti Progrès: 11 rue Capois, Port-au-Prince; tel. 222-6513; fax 222-7022; e-mail editor@haiti-progres.com; internet www.haiti-progres.com; f. 1983; weekly; Dir BEN DUPUY.

Jounal Libète: BP 13441, Delmas, Port-au-Prince; tel. 254-7766; fax 245-7760; e-mail jyurfie@acn.com; f. 1990; weekly; Creole; Dir JEAN-YVES URFIÉ; Editor GARY BÉLIZAIRE.

Liaison: 9 rue Chochotte, Babiole, BP 2481, Port-au-Prince; tel. 245-1186; fax 245-3629; e-mail havainfo@acn.com; French; available in Creole as *Aksyon*; Dir IVES-MARIE CHANEL.

Le Messager du Nord-Ouest: Port de Paix; weekly.

Le Moniteur: rue du Centre, BP 214 bis, Port-au-Prince; tel. 222-1744; f. 1845; 2 a week; French; the official gazette; circ. 2,000.

Optique: Institut Français d'Haiti, BP 1316, Port-au-Prince; tel. 245-7766; monthly; arts.

Le Septentrion: Cap-Haïtien; weekly; independent; Editor NELSON BELL; circ. 2,000.

Superstar Détente: 3 ruelle Chériez, Port-au-Prince; tel. 245-3450; fax 222-6329; cultural magazine; Dir CLAUDEL VICTOR.

NEWS AGENCIES

Agence Haïtienne de Presse (AHP): 6 rue Fernand, Port-au-Prince; tel. 245-7222; fax 245-5836; e-mail ahp@yahoo.com; internet www.ahphaiti.org; f. 1989; Dir-Gen. GEORGES VENEL REMARAIS.

AlterPresse: 14A Delmas 43, Port-au-Prince; tel. 554-1882; e-mail alterpresse@medialternatif.org; internet www.medialternatif.org/alterpresse; f. 2001; independent; Dir GOTSON PIERRE.

Foreign Bureaux

Agence France-Presse (AFP): 177 rue du Centre, Cour Buromatic, Port-au-Prince; tel. 222-3469; fax 222-3759; Bureau Chief DOMINIQUE LEVANTI.

Agencia EFE (Spain): Port-au-Prince; tel. 255-9517; Correspondent HEROLD JEAN-FRANÇOIS.

Associated Press (AP) (USA): Port-au-Prince; e-mail hib@igc.apc.com; Correspondent AMY BRACKEN.

Inter Press Service (Italy): 16 rue Malval, Turgeau, Port-au-Prince; tel. 260-5512; fax 260-5513; e-mail ipshaiti@mediacom-ht.com; Correspondent IVES-MARIE CHANEL.

Prensa Latina (Cuba): Port-au-Prince; tel. 246-5149; internet www.prensa-latina.org; Correspondent JACQUELÍN TELEMAQUE.

Reuters (United Kingdom): Port-au-Prince; Correspondent GUYLER C. DELVA.

Publishers

Editions des Antilles: route de l'Aéroport, Port-au-Prince.

Editions Caraïbes S.A.: 57 rue Pavée, BP 2013, Port-au-Prince; tel. 222-0032; Man. PIERRE J. ELIE.

Editions du Soleil: BP 2471, rue du Centre, Port-au-Prince; tel. 222-3147; education.

L'Imprimeur Deux: Le Nouvelliste, 198 rue du Centre, Port-au-Prince.

Maison Henri Deschamps—Les Entreprises Deschamps Frisch, SA: 25 rue Dr Martelly Seïde, BP 164, Port-au-Prince; tel. 223-2215; fax 223-4976; e-mail entreprisesdeschamps@globelsud.net; f. 1898; education and literature; Man. Dir JACQUES DESCHAMPS, Jr; CEO PETER J. FRISCH.

Natal Imprimerie: rue Barbancourt, Port-au-Prince; Dir ROBERT MALVAL.

Théodore Imprimerie: rue Dantes Destouches, Port-au-Prince.

Broadcasting and Communications

TELECOMMUNICATIONS

Conseil National des Télécommunications (CONATEL): 16 ave Marie Jeanne, Cité de l'Exposition, BP 2002, Port-au-Prince; tel. 222-0300; fax 223-9229; e-mail conatel@haiticonatel.org; internet www.haiticonatel.org; f. 1969; govt communications licensing authority; Dir-Gen. JEAN MICHEL BOISROND.

Télécommunications d'Haïti (Téléco): blvd Jean-Jacques Dessalines, BP 814, Port-au-Prince; tel. 245-2200; fax 223-0002; e-mail info@haititeleco.com; internet www.haititeleco.com; Dir-Gen. RENÉ MÉRONEY.

BROADCASTING

Radio

Radio Antilles International: 175 rue du Centre, BP 2335, Port-au-Prince; tel. 223-0696; fax 222-0260; f. 1984; independent; Dir-Gen. JACQUES SAMPEUR.

Radio Cacique: 5 Bellevue, BP 1480, Port-au-Prince; tel. 245-2326; f. 1961; independent; Dir JEAN-CLAUDE CARRIÉ.

Radio Caraïbes: 19 ruelle Chavannes, Port-au-Prince; tel. 223-0644; fax 223-4955; f. 1949; independent; Dir PATRICK MOUSSIGNAC.

Radio Céleste: 106 rue de la Réunion, Port-au-Prince; tel. 222-4714; fax 222-6636; f. 1991; Dir JEAN-EDDY CHARLEUS.

Radio Galaxie: 17 rue Pavée, Port-au-Prince; tel. 223-9942; f. 1990; independent; Dir YVES JEAN-BART.

Radio Ginen: 9 bis, Delmas 31, Port-au-Prince; tel. 249-1738; e-mail feedback@radyoginen.com; internet www.radyoginen.com; f. 1994; Dir LUCIEN BORGES.

Radio Haïti Inter: Delmas 66A, 522, en face de Delmas 91, BP 737, Port-au-Prince; tel. 257-3111; f. 1935; independent; ceased broadcasting indefinitely in Feb. 2003; Dir MICHÈLE MONTAS.

Radio Kadans FM: 3 rue Neptune, Delmas 65, Port-au-Prince; tel. 249-4040; fax 245-2672; f. 1991; Dir LIONEL BENJAMIN.

Radio Kiskeya: 7 rue Pavée, Port-au-Prince; tel. 222-6002; fax 223-6204; f. 1994; Dir SONY BASTIEN.

Radio Lakansyèl: 285 route de Delmas, Port-au-Prince; tel. 246-2020; independent; Dir ALEX SAINT-SURIN.

Radio Lumière: Côte-Plage 16, BP 1050, Port-au-Prince; f. 1959; tel. 234-0330; internet www.radiolumiere.org; f. 1959; Protestant; independent; Dir VARNEL JEUNE.

Radio Magic Stéreo: 346 route de Delmas, Port-au-Prince; tel. 245-5404; f. 1991; independent; Dir FRITZ JOASSIN.

Radio Mélodie: 74 bis, rue Capois, Port-au-Prince; tel. 221-8567; fax 221-1323; e-mail melodiefm@hotmail.com; f. 1998; Dir MARCUS GARCIA.

Radio Metropole: 18 Delmas 52, BP 62, Port-au-Prince; tel. 246-2626; fax 249-2020; internet www.metropolehaiti.com; f. 1970; independent; Dir-Gen. RICHARD WIDMAIER.

Radio Nationale d'Haïti: 174 rue du Magasin de l'Etat, BP 1143, Port-au-Prince; tel. 223-5712; fax 223-5911; f. 1977; govt-operated; Dir-Gen. MICHEL FAVARD.

Radio Plus: 85 rue Pavée, BP 1174, Port-au-Prince; tel. 222-1588; fax 223-2288; f. 1988; independent; Dir GUY CÉSAR.

Radio Port-au-Prince: Stade Sylvio Cator, BP 863, Port-au-Prince; f. 1979; independent; Dir GEORGE L. HÉRARD.

Radio Sans Souci: 16 rue Malval, Turgeau, Port-au-Prince; tel. 262-5445; fax 262-5444; e-mail info@radiosanssouci.com; internet www.radiosanssouci.com; f. 1998; Dir IVES-MARIE CHANEL.

Radio Signal FM: 127 rue Louverture, Pétionville, BP 391, Port-au-Prince; tel. 298-4370; fax 298-4372; e-mail signalfm@netcourrier.com; internet www.signalfmhaiti.com; f. 1991; independent; Dir-Gen. MARIO VIAU.

Radio Soleil: BP 1362, Archevêché de Port-au-Prince; tel. 222-3062; fax 222-3516; e-mail contact@radiosoleil.com; internet www.radiosoleil.com; f. 1978; Catholic; independent; educational; broadcasts in Creole and French; Dir Fr ARNOUX CHÉRY.

Radio Solidarité: 6 rue Fernand, Port-au-Prince; tel. 244-0469; fax 244-6698; e-mail solidarite@haitiwebs.com; internet www.haitiwebs.com/radiosolidarite/; Dir VENEL REMARAIS.

Radio Superstar: 38 rue Safran, Delmas 68, Port-au-Prince; tel. 257-7219; fax 257-3015; e-mail superstar1029fmfr@yahoo.fr; f. 1987; independent; Dir-Gen. ALBERT CHANCY.

Radio Timoun: 27 bis, rue Camille Léon, Port-au-Prince; tel. 245-1099; f. 1996; Dir MARIE KEMLY PERCY.

Radio Tropic FM: 6 ave John Brown, Port-au-Prince; tel. 223-6565; f. 1991; independent; Dir GUY JEAN.

Radio Tropicale Internationale: Delmas 27–29, Dubois Shopping Center, Port-au-Prince; tel. 249-1646; f. 1994; Dir JOEL BORGELLA.

Radio Vision 2000: 184 ave John Brown, Port-au-Prince; tel. 245-4914; internet www.radiovision2000.com; f. 1991; Dir LÉOPOLD BERLANGER.

Television

Galaxy 2: 6 rue Henri Christophe, Jacmel; tel. 288-2324; f. 1989; independent; Dir MILOT BERQUIN.

PVS Antenne 16: 137 rue Monseigneur Guilloux, Port-au-Prince; tel. and fax 222-1277; f. 1988; independent; Dir-Gen. RAYNALD DELERME.

Télé Eclair: 526 route de Delmas, Port-au-Prince; tel. 256-4505; fax 256-3828; f. 1996; independent; Dir PATRICK ANDRÉ JOSEPH.

Télé Express Continentale: rue de l'Eglise, Jacmel; tel. 288-2246; fax 288-2191; f. 1985; independent; Dirs JEAN-FRANÇOIS VERDIER, JACQUES JEAN-PIERRE.

Télé Haïti: blvd Harry S Truman, BP 1126, Port-au-Prince; tel. 222-3887; fax 222-9140; f. 1959; independent; pay-cable station with 33 channels; in French, Spanish and English; Dir MARIE CHRISTINE MOURRAL BLANC.

Télé Smart: Hinche; tel. 277-0347; f. 1998; independent; Dir MOZART SIMON.

Télé Timoun: blvd 15 Octobre, Tabarre; tel. 250-1924; fax 250-9972; f. 1996; independent.

Télémax: 3 Delmas 19, Port-au-Prince; tel. 246-2002; fax 246-1155; f. 1994; independent; Dir ROBERT DENIS.

Télévision Nationale d'Haïti: Delmas 33, BP 13400, Port-au-Prince; tel. 246-2952; fax 246-0693; e-mail tnh@tnhaiti.org; internet www.tnhaiti.org; f. 1979; govt-owned; cultural; 4 channels in Creole, French and Spanish; administered by four-mem. board; Dir JEAN RAYNALD LOUIS.

Trans-America: ruelle Roger, Gonaïves; tel. 274-0113; f. 1990; independent; Dir-Gen. HÉBERT PELISSIER.

TV Magik: 16 rue Conty, Jacmel; tel. 288-2456; f. 1992; independent; Dirs LOUIS ANTONIN BLAISE, RICHARD CYPRIEN.

TVA: rue Liberté, Gonaïves; independent; cable station with three channels; Dir-Gen. GÉRARD LUC JEAN-BAPTISTE.

Finance

(cap. = capital; m. = million; res = reserves; dep. = deposits; brs = branches; amounts in gourdes)

BANKING

Central Bank

Banque de la République d'Haïti: angle rues du Quai et Pavée, BP 1570, Port-au-Prince; tel. 299-1200; fax 299-1045; e-mail brh_adm@brh.net; internet www.brh.net; f. 1911 as Banque Nationale de la République d'Haïti; name changed as above in 1979; bank of issue; cap. 50m., res 4,084.0m., dep. 9,986.4m. (Sept. 2001); Gov. RAYMOND MAGLOIRE; Dir-Gen. CHARLES CASTEL.

Commercial Banks

Banque Industrielle et Commerciale d'Haïti: 158 rue Dr Aubry, Port-au-Prince; tel. 299-6800; fax 299-6804; f. 1974.

Banque Nationale de Crédit: angle rues du Quai et des Miracles, BP 1320, Port-au-Prince; tel. 299-4081; fax 299-4045; f. 1979; cap. 25m., dep. 729.9m. (Sept. 1989); Pres. GUITEAU TOUSSAINT; Dir-Gen. LEVÊQUE VALBRUN.

Banque Populaire Haïtienne: angle rues des Miracles et du Centre, Port-au-Prince; tel. 299-6000; fax 222-4389; e-mail bphinfo@brh.net; f. 1973; state-owned; cap. and res 22m., dep. 614m. (31 Dec. 2001); 3 brs; Dir-Gen. ERNST GILLES; Pres. RODNÉE DESCHINEAUX.

Banque de l'Union Haïtienne: angle rues du Quai et Bonne Foi, BP 275, Port-au-Prince; tel. 299-8500; fax 223-2852; e-mail buh@buhsa.com; internet www.buhsa.com; f. 1973; cap. 30.1m., res 6.2m., dep. 1,296.7m. (Sept. 1997); Pres. OSWALD J. BRANDT II; 9 brs.

Capital Bank: 149–151 rue des Miracles, BP 2464, Port-au-Prince; tel. 299-6500; fax 299-6519; e-mail capitalbank@brh.net; f. 1985; fmrly Banque de Crédit Immobilier, SA; Pres. BERNARD ROY; Gen. Man. LILIANE C. DOMINIQUE.

PROMOBANK (Banque de Promotion Commerciale et Industrielle, SA): angle des rues Faubert et Rigaud, Pétionville, Port-au-Prince; tel. 299-8000; fax 299-8125; e-mail info@promointer.net; internet www.promointer.net; f. 1974 as B.N.P. Haïti, name changed as above in 1994; cap. 60.4m., res 16.4m., dep. 1,183.4m. (Dec. 1998); Pres. and Chair. MICHAEL GAY; Gen. Man. JOSSELINE COLIMON-FÉTHIÈRE.

Société Caraïbéenne de Banque, SA (SOCABANK): 37 rue Pavée, BP 80, Port-au-Prince; tel. 299-7000; fax 299-7036; e-mail socabankcard@usa.net; internet www.socabank.net; f. 1994; Pres. JEAN-CLAUDE NADAL; Dir-Gen. CHARLES CLERMONT.

Sogebank, SA (Société Générale Haïtienne de Banque, SA): route de Delmas BP 1315, Delmas; tel. 229-5000; fax 229-5022; internet www.sogebank.com; f. 1986; cap. 79.5m.; Pres. GERARD MOSCOSO; 7 brs.

Sogebel (Société Générale Haïtienne de Banque d'Espargne et de Logement): route de l'Aéroport, BP 2409, Delmas; tel. 229-5353; fax 229-5352; f. 1988; cap. 15.1m., dep. 249.9m.; Gen. Man. CLAUDE PIERRE-LOUIS; 2 brs.

Unibank: 94 place Geffard, BP 46, Port-au-Prince; tel. 299-2300; fax 229-2332; e-mail info@unibankhaiti.com; internet www.unibankhaiti.com; f. 1993; cap. 100m., res 17.5m., dep. 3,366m. (Sept. 1999); Pres. F. CARL BRAUN; Dir-Gen. FRANCK HELMCKE; 20 brs.

Foreign Banks

Bank of Nova Scotia (Canada): 360 blvd J. J. Dessalines, BP 686, Port-au-Prince; tel. 299-3000; fax 229-3204; Man. Chester A. S. Hinkson; 3 brs.

Citibank, NA (USA): 242 route de Delmas, BP 1688, Port-au-Prince; tel. 299-3200; fax 299-3227; internet www.citibank.com/haiti; Dir Gladys M. Coupet.

Development Bank

Banque Haïtienne de Développement: 20 ave Lamartiniére, Port-au-Prince; tel. 245-4422; fax 244-3737; f. 1998; Dir-Gen. Yves Lerebours.

INSURANCE

National Companies

L'Atout Assurance, SA: 77 rue Lamarre, Port-au-Prince; tel. 223-9378; Dir Jean Eveillard.

Compagnie d'Assurances d'Haïti, SA (CAH): étage Dynamic Entreprise, route de l'Aéroport, BP 1489, Port-au-Prince; tel. 246-0700; fax 246-0236; f. 1978; Pres. Philippe R. Armand.

Excelsior Assurance, SA: rue 6, no 24, Port-au-Prince; tel. 245-8881; fax 245-8598; Dir-Gen. Emmanuel Sanon.

Générale d'Assurance, SA: Champ de Mars, Port-au-Prince; tel. 222-5465; fax 222-6502; f. 1985; Dir-Gen. Roland Acra.

Haïti Sécurité Assurance, SA: 16 rue des Miracles, BP 1754, Port-au-Prince; tel. 223-2118; Dir-Gen. William Phipps.

International Assurance, SA (INASSA): angle rues des Miracles et Pétion, Port-au-Prince; tel. 222-1058; Dir-Gen. Raoul Mérové-Pierre.

Multi Assurances, SA: route de l'Aéroport, Port-au-Prince; tel. 246-0700; fax 246-0236; Dir-Gen. Philippe Armand.

National Assurance, SA (NASSA): 25 rue Ferdinand Canapé-Vert, Port-au-Prince, HT6115; tel. 245-9800; fax 245-9701; e-mail nassa@nassagroup.com; Dir-Gen. Fritz Dupuy.

Office National d'Assurance Vieillesse (ONA): Champ de Mars, Port-au-Prince; tel. 222-1655; Dir-Gen. Margareth Lamur.

Société de Commercialisation d'Assurance, SA (SOCOMAS): autoroute de Delmas, BP 636, Port-au-Prince; tel. 249-3090; Dir-Gen. Jean Didier Gardère.

Foreign Companies

Les Assurances Léger, SA (France): 40 rue Lamarre, BP 2120, Port-au-Prince; tel. 222-3451; fax 223-8634; Pres. Gérard N. Léger.

Cabinet d'Assurances Fritz de Catalogne (USA): angle rues du Peuple et des Miracles, BP 1644, Port-au-Prince; tel. 222-6695; fax 223-0827; Dir Fritz de Catalogne.

Capital Life Insurance Company Ltd (Bahamas): angle rues du Peuple et des Miracles, BP 1644, Port-au-Prince; tel. 222-6695; fax 223-0827; Agent Fritz de Catalogne.

Groupement Français d'Assurances (France): Port-au-Prince; Agent Albert A. Dufort.

National Western Life Insurance (USA): 13 rue Pie XII, Cité de l'Exposition, Port-au-Prince; tel. 223-0734; Agent Vorbe Barrau Dupuy.

Insurance Association

Association des Assureurs d'Haïti: 153 rue des Miracles, Port-au-Prince; tel. 223-0796; fax 223-8634; Dir Fritz de Catalogne.

Trade and Industry

GOVERNMENT AGENCY

Conseil de Modernisation des Enterprises Publiques (CMEP): Palais National, Port-au-Prince; tel. 222-4111; fax 222-7761; f. 1996; oversees modernization and privatization of state enterprises.

DEVELOPMENT ORGANIZATIONS

Fonds de Développement Industriel (FDI): Immeuble PROMO-BANK, 4 étage, ave John Brown et rue Lamarre, BP 2597, Port-au-Prince; tel. 222-7852; fax 222-8301; e-mail FDI-Finance@globelsud.net; f. 1981; Dir Roosevelt Saint-Dic.

Société Financière Haïtienne de Développement, SA (SOFIHDES): 11 blvd Harry S Truman, BP 1399, Port-au-Prince; tel. 222-8904; fax 222-8997; f. 1983; industrial and agro-industrial project financing, accounting, data processing, management consultancy; cap. 7.5m. (1989); Dir-Gen. Faubert Gustave; 1 br.

CHAMBERS OF COMMERCE

Chambre de Commerce et d'Industrie d'Haïti (CCIH): blvd Harry S Truman, Cité de l'Exposition, BP 982, Port-au-Prince; tel. 223-0786; fax 222-0281; e-mail ccih@compa.net; internet www.intervision2000.com/iv2-trop/index.html; f. 1895; Pres. Reginald Boulos.

Chambre de Commerce et d'Industrie Haïtiano-Américaine (HAMCHAM): 6 rue Oge, Pétionville, Port-au-Prince; tel. 511-3024; e-mail csjean@hamcham.org; f. 1979; Exec. Dir Chantal Salomon-Jean.

Chambre de Commerce et d'Industrie des Professions du Nord: BP 244, Cap-Haïtien; tel. 262-2360; fax 262-2895.

Chambre Franco-Haïtienne de Commerce et d'Industrie (CFHCI): Le Plaza Holiday Inn, 10 rue Capois, Champ de Mars, Port-au-Prince; tel. 223-8424; fax 223-8131; e-mail cfhci@haitiworld.com; internet www.inhaiti.com/forms/cfhci-home.html; f. 1987; Pres. Philippe Lahens; Dir Josette Nazon.

INDUSTRIAL AND TRADE ORGANIZATIONS

Association des Exportateurs de Café (ASDEC): rue Barbancourt, BP 134, Port-au-Prince; tel. 249-2919; fax 249-2142; Pres. Hubert Duport.

Association des Industries d'Haïti (ADIH): 199 route de Delmas, entre Delmas 31 et 33, étage Galerie 128, BP 2568, Port-au-Prince; tel. 246-4509; fax 246-2211; e-mail adih@acn2.net; f. 1980; Pres. (vacant).

Association Nationale des Distributeurs de Produits Pétroliers (ANADIPP): Centre Commercial Dubois, route de Delmas, Bureau 401, Port-au-Prince; tel. 246-1414; fax 245-0698; f. 1979; Pres. Max Romain.

Association Nationale des Importateurs et Distributeurs de Produits Pharmaceutiques (ANIDPP): blvd Harry S Truman, Port-au-Prince; tel. 222-0268; fax 222-7887; e-mail mdweil@direcway.com; Pres. Ralph Edmond.

Association des Producteurs Agricoles (APA): BP 1318, Port-au-Prince; tel. 246-1848; fax 246-0356; f. 1985; Pres. Reynold Bonnefil.

Association des Producteurs Nationaux (APRONA): c/o Mosaïques Gardère, ave Hailé Sélassié, Port-au-Prince; tel. and fax 511-8611; e-mail frantzgardere@hotmail.com; Pres. Frantz Gardère.

UTILITIES

Electricity

Electricité d'Haïti: rue Dante Destouches, Port-au-Prince; tel. 222-4600; state energy utility company; Dir-Gen. Charles Albert Jacques.

Péligre Hydroelectric Plant: Artibonite Valley.

Saut-Mathurine Hydroelectric Plant: Les Cayes.

Water

Service Nationale d'Eau Potable (SNEP): 48 route de Delmas, Port-au-Prince; Dir-Gen. Pétion Roy.

TRADE UNIONS

Association des Journalistes Haïtiens (AJH): f. 1954; Sec.-Gen. Guyler C. Delva.

Centrale Autonome des Travailleurs Haïtiens (CATH): 93 rue des Casernes, Port-au-Prince; tel. 222-4506; f. 1980; Sec.-Gen. Fignole Saint-Cyr.

Confédération Ouvriers Travailleurs Haïtiens (KOTA): 155 rue des Césars, Port-au-Prince.

Confédération Nationale des Educateurs Haïtiens (CNEH): rue Berne 21, Port-au-Prince; tel. 245-1552; fax 245-9536; e-mail lana14@caramail.com; f. 1986.

Confédération des Travailleurs Haïtiens (CTH): f. 1989; Sec.-Gen. Jacques Belzin.

Fédération Haïtienne de Syndicats Chrétiens (FHSC): BP 416, Port-au-Prince; Pres. Léonvil Leblanc.

Fédération des Ouvriers Syndiques (FOS): angle rues Dr Aubry et des Miracles 115, BP 371, Port-au-Prince; tel. 222-0035; f. 1984; Pres. Joseph J. Sénat.

Organisation Générale Indépendante des Travailleurs et Travailleuses d'Haïti (OGITH): 121, 2–3 étage, angle route Delmas et Delmas 11, Port-au-Prince; tel. 249-0575; e-mail pnumas@yahoo.fr; f. 1988; Gen. Sec. Patrick Numas.

Syndicat des Employés de l'EDH (SEEH): c/o EDH, rue Joseph Janvier, Port-au-Prince; tel. 222-3367.

Union Nationale des Ouvriers d'Haïti (UNOH): Delmas 11, 121 bis, Cité de l'Exposition, BP 3337, Port-au-Prince; f. 1951; Pres. Marcel Vincent; Sec.-Gen. Fritzner St Vil; 3,000 mems from 8 affiliated unions.

A number of unions are non-affiliated and without a national centre, including those organized on a company basis.

Transport

RAILWAYS

The railway service, for the transportation of sugar cane, closed during the early 1990s.

ROADS

In 1999, according to International Road Federation estimates, there were 4,160 km (2,585 miles) of roads, of which 24.3% was paved.

SHIPPING

Many European and American shipping lines call at Haiti. The two principal ports are Port-au-Prince and Cap-Haïtien. There are also 12 minor ports.

Autorité Portuaire Nationale: blvd La Saline, BP 616, Port-au-Prince; tel. 222-1942; fax 223-2440; e-mail jjulio@mail.com; f. 1978; Dir-Gen. Jean Evens Charles.

CIVIL AVIATION

The international airport, situated 8 km (5 miles) outside Port-au-Prince, is the country's principal airport, and is served by many international airlines linking Haiti with the USA and other Caribbean islands. There is an airport at Cap-Haïtien, and smaller airfields at Jacmel, Jérémie, Les Cayes and Port-de-Paix.

Office National de l'Aviation Civile (OFNAC): Aéroport International Mais Gate, BP 1346, Port-au-Prince; tel. 246-2701; fax 246-0998; Dir-Gen. Jean-Lemerque Pierre.

Air Haïti: Aéroport International, Port-au-Prince; tel. 246-3311; f. 1969; began cargo charter operations 1970; scheduled cargo and mail services from Port-au-Prince to Cap-Haïtien, San Juan (Puerto Rico), Santo Domingo (Dominican Republic), Miami and New York (USA).

Caribintair: Aéroport International, Port-au-Prince; tel. 246-0778; scheduled domestic service and charter flights to Santo Domingo (Dominican Republic) and other Caribbean destinations.

Haiti Air Freight, SA: Aéroport International, BP 170, Port-au-Prince; tel. 246-2572; fax 246-0848; cargo carrier operating scheduled and charter services from Port-au-Prince and Cap-Haïtien to Miami (USA) and Puerto Rico.

Haiti International Airlines: Delmas 65, Rue Zamor 2, Port-au-Prince; tel. 434-7201; f. 1996; scheduled passenger and cargo services from Port-au Prince to Miami and New York (USA); Pres. and Chair. Khan Rahman.

Tropical Airways d'Haïti, SA: 76 rue Panaméricaine, Pétionville, Port-au-Prince; tel. 250-3420; fax 250-3422; internet www.tropical-haiti.com; f. 1998; domestic and regional services; Pres. Philip Gornail.

Tourism

Tourism was formerly Haiti's second largest source of foreign exchange. However, as a result of political instability, the number of cruise ships visiting Haiti declined considerably, causing a sharp decline in the number of tourist arrivals. With the restoration of democracy in late 1994, the development of the tourism industry was identified as a priority by the Government. In 2001 stop-over tourists totalled 141,632, while cruise-ship excursionists numbered 246,221 in 1998. Receipts from tourism in 2001 totalled US $54m.

Secrétariat d'Etat au Tourisme: 8 rue Légitime, Champ de Mars, Port-au-Prince; tel. 221-5960; fax 222-8659; e-mail info@haititourisme.org; internet www.haititourisme.org; Sec. of State for Tourism Harold Florentino Latortue.

Association Haïtienne des Agences de Voyages: 17 rue des Miracles, Port-au-Prince; tel. 222-8855; fax 222-2054.

Association Touristique d'Haïti: rue Lamarre, BP 2562, Port-au-Prince; tel. 257-4647; fax 257-4134; Pres. Dominique Carvonis; Dir Elizabeth Silvera Ducasse.

HONDURAS

Introductory Survey

Location, Climate, Language, Religion, Flag, Capital

The Republic of Honduras lies in the middle of the Central American isthmus. It has a long northern coastline on the Caribbean Sea and a narrow southern outlet to the Pacific Ocean. Its neighbours are Guatemala to the west, El Salvador to the south-west and Nicaragua to the south-east. The climate ranges from temperate in the mountainous regions to tropical in the coastal plains: temperatures in the interior range from 15°C (59°F) to 24°C (75°F), while temperatures in the coastal plains average about 30°C (86°F). There are two rainy seasons in upland areas, May–July and September–October. The national language is Spanish. Almost all of the inhabitants profess Christianity, and in 2002 about 83% of the population were adherents of the Roman Catholic Church. The national flag (proportions 1 by 2) has three horizontal stripes, of blue, white and blue, with five blue five-pointed stars, arranged in a diagonal cross, in the centre of the white stripe. The capital is Tegucigalpa.

Recent History

Honduras was ruled by Spain from the 16th century until 1821 and became a sovereign state in 1838. From 1939 the country was ruled as a dictatorship by Gen. Tiburcio Carías Andino, leader of the Partido Nacional (PN), who had been President since 1933. In 1949 Carías was succeeded as President by Juan Manuel Gálvez, also of the PN. In 1954 the leader of the Partido Liberal (PL), Dr José Ramón Villeda Morales, was elected President, but was immediately deposed by Julio Lozano Díaz, himself overthrown by a military Junta in 1956. The Junta organized elections in 1957, when the PL secured a majority in Congress and Villeda was re-elected President. He was overthrown in 1963 by Col (later Gen.) Oswaldo López Arellano, the Minister of Defence, who, following elections held on the basis of a new Constitution, was appointed President in June 1965.

A presidential election in March 1971 was won by Dr Ramón Ernesto Cruz Uclés, the PN candidate. In December 1972, however, Cruz was deposed in a bloodless coup, led by former President López. In March 1974, at the instigation of the Consejo Superior de las Fuerzas Armadas (Supreme Council of the Armed Forces), President López was replaced as Commander-in-Chief of the Armed Forces by Col (later Gen.) Juan Melgar Castro, who was appointed President in April 1975. President Melgar was forced to resign by the Consejo Superior de las Fuerzas Armadas in August 1978, and was replaced by a military Junta. The Commander-in-Chief of the Armed Forces, Gen. Policarpo Paz García, assumed the role of Head of State, and the Junta promised that elections would take place.

Military rule was ended officially when, in April 1980, elections to a Constituent Assembly were held. The PL won 52% of the votes but was unable to assume power. Gen. Paz was appointed interim President for one year. At a general election in November 1981 the PL, led by Dr Roberto Suazo Córdova, secured an absolute majority in the Asamblea Nacional (National Assembly). Suazo was sworn in as President in January 1982. However, real power lay in the hands of Col (later Gen.) Gustavo Alvarez Martínez, who was appointed Head of the Armed Forces in the same month. In November Gen. Alvarez became Commander-in-Chief of the Armed Forces, having brought about a constitutional amendment separating the posts of President and Commander-in-Chief of the Armed Forces. During 1982 and 1983 Gen. Alvarez suppressed increasing political unrest by authorizing the arrests of trade union activists and left-wing sympathizers; 'death squads' were allegedly also used to eliminate 'subversive' elements of the population. In March 1984 Gen. Alvarez was deposed as Commander-in-Chief by a group of army officers.

At the November 1985 presidential election the leading candidate of the PN, Rafael Leonardo Callejas Romero, obtained 42% of the individual votes cast, but the leading candidate of the PL, José Simeón Azcona del Hoyo (who had obtained only 27% of the individual votes cast), was declared the winner because, in accordance with a new electoral law, the combined votes of the

PL's candidates secured the requisite majority of 51% of the total votes cast.

In February 1988 a report by the human rights organization Amnesty International gave evidence of an increase in violations of human rights by the armed forces and by right-wing 'death squads'. In August of that year, and again in 1989, the Inter-American Court of Human Rights (an organ of the Organization of American States—OAS, see p. 319) found the Honduran Government guilty of the 'disappearances' of Honduran citizens between 1981 and 1984, and ordered that compensation be paid to the families involved. In 1991 Amnesty International published a further report alleging the mistreatment, torture and killing of detainees by members of the Honduran security forces. In January 1989 Gen. Alvarez was killed by left-wing guerrillas in Tegucigalpa. The PL secured a majority of seats in the Asamblea Nacional at legislative elections held in November, while Callejas of the PN won the concurrent presidential election, receiving 51% of the votes cast. Callejas assumed office in January 1990. The new administration promptly adopted economic austerity measures, which provoked widespread social unrest.

In March 1993, in response to increasing pressure by human rights organizations and criticism by the State Department of the USA, the Government established a special commission to investigate allegations of human rights violations by the armed forces. The commission recommended, *inter alia*, the replacement of the armed forces' much-criticized secret counter-intelligence organization, the División Nacional de Investigaciones (DNI), with a body under civilian control.

At presidential and legislative elections in November 1993 Carlos Roberto Reina Idiaquez, the candidate of the PL, was elected President, winning 52% of the votes cast. The PL also obtained a clear majority in the Asamblea Nacional, with 71 seats, while the PN secured 55 seats and the Partido Innovación y Unidad—Social Democracia (PINU) won the remaining two seats. Legislation replacing the DNI with a new ministry, the Dirección de Investigación Criminal (DIC), was approved in December 1993. On taking office in January 1994 Reina, a former President of the Inter-American Court of Human Rights, expressed his commitment to the reform of the judicial system and the armed forces, reducing the latter's size and sphere of influence. In that month, following the release by the National Commission for the Protection of Human Rights of a report incriminating the armed forces in the disappearance of 184 people in the previous decade, the head of the Commission, Leo Valladares Lanza, demanded the resignation of the Commander-in-Chief of the Armed Forces, Gen. Luis Alonso Discua Elvir. At the time of the disappearances Discua had been the Commander of Battalion 3-16, the army intelligence unit widely regarded as responsible for the murder of left-wing political activists.

In May 1994 the Asamblea Nacional approved a constitutional reform abolishing compulsory military service (the amendment was ratified in April 1995). Also approved was the transfer of the police from military to civilian control. In that month measures initiated by the Callejas administration for the establishment of a Public Ministry were officially completed. The new ministry was to be supervised by the DIC, which was inaugurated in January 1995.

In July 1994, following protracted demonstrations in the capital, 4,000 members of indigenous organizations occupied the Asamblea Nacional building and succeeded in securing an agreement with the Government granting rights and social assistance to the country's indigenous community, including the creation of the first indigenous municipality in Yamaranguila, Intibucá. The following months were characterized by growing social and political tension, including several bomb attacks. Concern was raised by human rights organizations that the climate of instability was being fomented by the armed forces in an attempt to stem the rapid diminution of its powers. In mid-August an increase in the incidence of crime and violent demonstrations resulting from the accumulating effect of austerity measures, a worsening energy crisis and food shortages, forced the Government to declare a state of national emergency and to deploy the armed forces to maintain order.

In July 1995 sustained protests by members of indigenous organizations, in support of demands that the Government honour its commitments of July 1994 to the indigenous community, culminated in a 2,000-strong demonstration in the capital. The protests resulted in renewed pledges by the Government to provide social assistance and grant land titles to the indigenous population. In September the PL, PN, PINU and Partido Demócrata Cristiano de Honduras (PDCH) established the Consejo Nacional de Convergencia (National Convergence Council) in order to seek a consensus on political, social and economic issues.

In July 1995, in an unprecedented development in the Government's efforts to investigate past human rights violations, a civilian court issued indictments against 10 senior officers of the security services who had been involved in the activities of Battalion 3-16 during the 1980s. The charges concerned the kidnapping, torture and attempted murder in 1982 of six left-wing students. However, the officers refused to appear in court, invoking an amnesty granted in 1991 which, they claimed, afforded them immunity from prosecution. In October a warrant was issued for the arrest of several of the officers, who promptly went into hiding. In January 1996 the Supreme Court ruled that the officers were not entitled to protection under the 1991 amnesty law, overturning an earlier decision by the Court of Appeal. Information concerning the activities of Battalion 3-16, which had been financed and trained by the US Central Intelligence Agency, was sought from the US Government by Valladares to support the prosecution of this and other human rights cases. Also in January 1996, Col. Mario Raúl Hung Pacheco succeeded Gen. Discua as Commander-in-Chief of the Armed Forces.

In July 1996 the Human Rights Defence Committee (Codeh) claimed that the extra-judicial execution of five former military intelligence agents had occurred in recent months, and alleged that the killings were the responsibility of military officers who were attempting to prevent evidence of human rights violations from coming to light. Later that month four officers of the armed forces were arrested for allegedly conspiring to overthrow the Commander-in-Chief of the Armed Forces. Gen. Hung, however, dismissed the incident, claiming that it merely reflected the discontent within the ranks at low pay and reductions in the defence budget.

In October 1996 a bomb exploded, without causing injury, at the parliament building in the capital. A further device was defused outside the headquarters of the PL. Responsibility for the attacks was claimed later that month by a previously unknown organization describing itself as 'Hambre' (Hunger), which claimed to be acting in response to recent rises in fuel prices. However, the President of Codeh, Ramón Custodio, expressed the popular suspicion that the attacks had been perpetrated by the armed forces in an attempt to pressurize the civilian authorities into reversing the decline in military influence in the country. Subsequent grenade attacks on Custodio's home and on a court building in Tegucigalpa prompted the Government to deploy some 3,000 troops to patrol the capital and San Pedro Sula.

In February 1997 demonstrations by thousands of public-sector employees, who were protesting in support of demands for salary increases, culminated in violent clashes between demonstrators and the security forces. The Government subsequently signed a social pact with labour leaders, which included commitments to increased social spending and price controls on basic goods. In May, following the killing of two ethnic minority leaders in the previous month, more than 3,000 members of the indigenous community conducted a march from the western departments of Copán and Ocotepeque to the capital to protest outside the presidential palace. As a result, Reina signed an agreement to conduct a full investigation into the killings and to accelerate the distribution of some 7,000 ha of land to the indigenous community. However, the killing of a further two ethnic minority leaders later that month led to accusations by human rights groups that attempts were being made to eliminate minority autonomous organizations.

At the general election held on 30 November 1997 Carlos Roberto Flores Facussé, the candidate of the ruling PL, was elected President. The PL also obtained a majority in the Asamblea Nacional. Flores was inaugurated on 27 January 1998.

In May 1998 control of the police force was transferred from the military to the civilian authorities. The Fuerza de Seguridad

Pública, which had been under military control since 1963 and was widely suspected of perpetrating human rights abuses, was replaced by a new force, the Policía Nacional. Nevertheless, reports of human rights abuses continued.

In November 1998, in the wake of the devastation caused by 'Hurricane Mitch', which struck the country in late October, causing losses estimated at US $5,000m., Flores declared a state of emergency and imposed a curfew in order to combat widespread looting. At least 6,600 people were estimated to have died, with a further 8,052 people reported missing, as a result of the storms, which left some 2.13m. homeless and caused widespread damage to the country's infrastructure, as well as destroying principal export crops.

In January 1999 the Asamblea Nacional ratified a constitutional amendment abolishing the post of Commander-in-Chief of the Armed Forces and transferring its responsibilities to the Minister of National Defence and Public Security. The military's ruling body, the Consejo Superior de las Fuerzas Armadas, was also disbanded. In July, acting on intelligence reports of a plot by senior-ranking military officers to overthrow the Government, Flores implemented a number of changes to the military high command. Notably, the Head of the Joint Chiefs of Staff, Col Eugenio Romero Eucedo, who was suspected of being one of the principal instigators of the coup plot, was replaced by the head of the presidential guard, Col Daniel López Carballo, who was considered to be loyal to the presidency. The plot itself was believed to have been prompted by resentment in the officer corps at the determination of the Minister of National Defence, Edgardo Dumas Rodríguez, to exert civilian control over the armed forces, and in particular at his plans to investigate military expenditure and supervise the armed forces' extensive business activities.

In August 2001 the Government engaged a UN Special Rapporteur on extra-judicial, summary and arbitrary executions, Asama Jahangir, to investigate the alleged organized murder of street children in recent years. Jahangir concluded that since 1998, some 800 children had been killed by youth gangs and members of the police and private security forces. The Minister of Public Security, Gautama Fonseca Zuniga, subsequently announced an inquiry into police involvement in the killings. In the same month, in response to increasing conflict between the youth gangs, President Flores ordered the deployment of 3,000 army troops and armed police on to the streets of Tegucigalpa, San Pedro Sula and El Progreso. In response to pressure from human rights organizations, in March 2003 the Government announced that a special commission would be established to investigate the murders of street children. The Permanent Commission on Physical and Moral Integrity of Children would comprise of church leaders and government officials.

Legislative and presidential elections were held on 25 November 2001.Five candidates contested the presidential election; the PN candidate, Ricardo Maduro Joest, emerged victorious, with 52.21% of valid votes cast, compared to 44.26% secured by the PL nominee, Rafael Piñeda Ponce. The PN also gained a majority in the Asamblea Nacional, winning 61 seats. The number of PL deputies was reduced to 55, while the remaining 12 seats were distributed among the PUD (five seats), the PINU (four seats) and the PDCH (three seats). Observers from the OAS reported no serious irregularities, although a PN legislative candidate was assassinated in Tegucigalpa the day before the election; three PL party workers were later arrested.

Maduro assumed the presidency on 27 January 2002 and a new Government was installed, which included Guillermo Pérez-Cadalso Arias as Minister of Foreign Affairs and Jorge Ramón Hernández Alcerro as Minister of the Interior and Justice. The new President immediately began an offensive against crime, sending 10,000 troops to patrol the streets of Tegucigalpa, San Pedro Sula, La Ceiba and Choluteca. Maduro announced that the armed forces would play a greater role in the anti-crime effort, a declaration that was met with opposition domestically and internationally. He affirmed his intention to reorganize the police force and to reform the criminal justice system, in order to reduce corruption. The number of supreme court judges was subsequently increased to 15 and the panel appointed to select the judges was depoliticized by the incorporation of lawyers and civilians. Another stated priority of Maduro upon taking office was tax reform and a reduction in government expenditure, in an attempt to secure debt relief from the IMF. This aim was met with hostility by opposition parties, who argued that proposals to levy taxes on a broader range of basic goods and services would exacerbate poverty levels in the country. They suggested that public money should instead be invested in measures to alleviate deprivation. Nevertheless, in May the fiscal reform bill was approved in the Asamblea Nacional.

Also in May 2002 teachers began a strike in protest at their wages and working conditions. The Minister of Public Education, Carlos Avila Molina, reacted by reducing the striking teachers' wages. A pay deal offered in August was rejected. Later in the same month coffee growers demonstrated in Tegucigalpa against the Government's alleged failure to make available a US $20m. loan granted by Taiwan to help stimulate the coffee sector. The demonstration escalated into violence and some 500 protesters were arrested. In November the Government announced a new housing initiative, which controversially involved borrowing funds from public-sector pensions. The programme placed further strain on relations between the Government and public-sector workers. Teachers, together with employees of the state water company, who objected to plans to transfer responsibility for water services from the state to the municipalities, held a two-day demonstration in Tegucigalpa. The protest resulted in violent clashes between protesters and the police, which left 20 injured.

Industrial unrest persisted in 2003; in March medical staff at public hospitals began intermittent strikes to demand higher salaries. Public dissatisfaction with reductions in public expenditure culminated in August with a 'Marcha por la Dignidad' (March for Dignity), organized by the Coordinadora Nacional de Resistencia Popular, an alliance of trade unions and opposition groups. On 26 August some 10,000 protesters converged on Tegucigalpa in protest at, *inter alia*, the decentralization of water services and at government plans for civil service reform. The protesters accused the Government of introducing IMF-proposed reforms at the expense of the welfare of the population and called for President Maduro's resignation. The demonstration escalated into violent clashes between protesters and the police; some 21 people were injured. President Maduro's woes were compounded in that month by the resignation of two of his Cabinet; the Minister of Public Security, Juan Angel Arias, and the Minister of Foreign Affairs, Guillermo Pérez-Cadalso Arias (who was succeeded by Leonidas Rosa Bautista). In October some 30,000 doctors, nurses, teachers and other public-sector employees held a one-day strike in protest at the Government's economic austerity measures. Demonstrations were held outside government buildings to demand that the Government abandon its attempts to meet the IMF's debt-reduction criteria (see Economic Affairs). Further protests were held later in the month to coincide with the arrival of an IMF delegation in Tegucigalpa.

In August 2003 Maduro was also accused of failing to address the question of land reform. The indigenous pressure group, the Cívico de Organizaciones Populares e Indígenas de Honduras, demonstrated outside the Supreme Court following the deaths of two farmers who had occupied land that they alleged had belonged to their ancestors. In September, in an attempt to mitigate domestic and international criticism, the Government instigated the 'National Dialogue', a discussion forum designed to reach policy consensus with opposition groups. The initiative brought together a cross-section of society, including businessmen, farmers and members of the Roman Catholic Church, and was expected to address topics such as agriculture and drugs-related crime.

In May 2004 President Maduro announced the withdrawal of Honduras from the Central American Court of Justice, declaring that the funding dedicated to the regional court would be more usefully invested in social, health and educational programmes. In September the Government announced the withdrawal of funding for the Central American parliament, known as Parlacen, for similar reasons.

Despite the implementation of increased security measures by the administration of President Maduro, Honduras experienced rising levels of violent crime in recent years. Controversial legislation approved by the Asamblea Nacional in August 2003 introduced prison sentences of between nine and 12 years and fines of between US $570 and $11,430 for members of street gangs (*maras*). These gangs were held to be responsible for much of the crime in Honduras. However, the continued high incidence of kidnappings of businessmen and foreigners in 2004–05 prompted many to flee the country, it was also feared that the high crime rate would deter foreign investment, particularly in the *maquila* sector. In December 2004 the Government introduced further legislation, increasing the maximum prison sentence for 'illicit association' from 20 to 30 years and extending

the period of detention without charge to 72 hours. However, President Maduro's strict policies towards criminals, particularly gang members, also raised fears of human rights abuses regarding the conditions in which the prisoners were kept. In May 2004 more than 100 inmates died in a fire at a prison in San Pedro Sula. The victims were predominantly members of the *Mara Salvatrucha* youth gang. Representatives of the gang claimed that police and prison guards started the fire and subsequently refused to free the prisoners. The incident echoed another in April 2003 when 69 people, principally members of the *Mara 18* gang, died in a riot and subsequent fire at prison in La Ceiba. The riot had been in protest at overcrowding and poor conditions in the gaol. A government inquiry into the deaths at La Ceiba later concluded that 51 of the victims had been summarily executed by prison officials who then set the fire to conceal their actions. On 23 December 2004 the massacre of 28 people on a bus near San Pedro Sula was attributed to an organized street gang.

In October 2004 the Prosecutor-General, Ovidio Navarro, was accused of abusing his position to protect former President Callejas after he dismissed 10 public prosecutors and transferred a further six to different duties. The dismissed prosecutors had criticized an earlier decision by Navarro to abandon a number of corruption cases, including seven against the former PN President. The controversial decision prompted industrial action in the prosecution service and demonstrations. Protesters called on the Supreme Court to overturn the dismissal of the corruption cases, and for the resignation of Navarro. In November the Supreme Court ordered the investigations to be resumed.

Throughout 2004 the Government faced intermittent civil unrest. At the end of June a six-day march across the country culminated on 30 June in a demonstration in Tegucigalpa against deforestation and unregulated mining. This so-called 'Second March for Life' was led by the priest Andrés Tomayo and co-ordinated by the environmental organization Movimiento Ambientalista de Olancho (MAO) and the Comité de Detenidos Desaparecidos de Honduras (Cofadeh). Following a breakdown in negotiations on salary increases in the same month, some 50,000 teachers also joined the demonstration. Further anti-Government protests took place on 1 and 2 July, arranged by the Coordinadora Nacional de Resistencia Popular, against high fuel prices, the devaluation of the lempira and the privatization of the health and education sectors. The industrial dispute between teachers and the Government was successfully resolved on 10 July, without contravening the IMF stipulations laid down in February (see Economic Affairs). Nevertheless, Maduro's popularity continued to decline in 2004, mainly owing to the austere economic policies of his Government and to the high crime rates.

Two ministers tendered their resignations in 2004. José Arturo Alvarado was succeeded as Minister of Finance by his former deputy, William Chong Wong at the end of August, while Carlos Avila Molina was replaced as Minister of Education by Roberto Martínez Lozano, former general manager of the Empresa Nacional de Acueductos y Alcantarillados, on 1 October. Both ministers cited personal reasons for their departure from government.

Presidential and legislative elections were scheduled to be held on 27 November 2005. To this end, in February both the PN and the PL held primary elections. The PN's candidate was Porfirio Lobo Sosa, President of the Asamblea Nacional, who attracted 58% of the party's votes. The PL nominated Manuel Zelaya Rosales, a minister in the Government of President Flores.

From the early 1980s former members of the Nicaraguan National Guard, regarded by the left-wing Sandinista Government of Nicaragua as counter-revolutionaries ('Contras'), established bases in Honduras, from which they conducted raids across the border between the two countries, allegedly with support from the Honduran armed forces. In 1983, when Honduran foreign policy was controlled by the pro-US Gen. Alvarez (the Commander-in-Chief of the Armed Forces), US involvement in Honduras increased substantially. In February 1983 the USA and Honduras initiated 'Big Pine', a series of joint military manoeuvres on Honduran territory which enabled the USA to construct permanent military installations in Honduras. In return for considerable military assistance from the USA, the Honduran Government permitted US military aid to be supplied to the Contras based in Honduras.

Following the overthrow of Gen. Alvarez in 1984, public opposition to the US military presence in Honduras increased, causing a temporary deterioration in relations between Honduras and the USA. Relations with Nicaragua deteriorated sharply in 1986, when Honduran troops were mobilized in an attempt to curb alleged border incursions by Nicaraguan government forces. In December, however, following revelations that the USA had secretly sold weapons to the Government of Iran and that the proceeds had been used to finance the activities of the Contra rebels, President Azcona requested the departure of the Contras from Honduras.

In August 1987 Honduras, Costa Rica, El Salvador, Guatemala and Nicaragua signed a Central American peace plan, known as the 'Esquipulas agreement', the crucial provisions of which were the implementation of simultaneous cease-fires in Nicaragua and El Salvador, a halt to foreign assistance to rebel groups, democratic reform in Nicaragua, a ban on the use of foreign territory as a base for attack, and the establishment of national reconciliation commissions in each of the Central American nations. However, the Honduran Government opposed a clause in the agreement providing for the establishment of a committee to monitor the dismantling of Contra bases in Honduras. In December 1988 the International Court of Justice (ICJ) announced it would consider an application by the Nicaraguan Government, which contended that Honduras had breached international law by allowing the Contras to operate from its territory. In response, the Honduran Government threatened to withdraw support from the Esquipulas agreement.

In February 1989, at summit meeting of the five Central American Presidents in El Salvador, an agreement was reached whereby the Contra forces encamped in Honduras would demobilize, while President Ortega of Nicaragua guaranteed that free and fair elections would take place in his country by February 1990. At a further summit meeting, held in August at Tela, Honduras, the conditions for the demobilization of the Contras were expanded. The Honduran Government agreed to the establishment by the UN and the OAS of an international commission to oversee the voluntary repatriation or removal to a third country of the rebel forces by December 1989; in return, the Nicaraguan Government agreed to abandon the action that it had initiated against Honduras at the ICJ. The rebel units officially disbanded and left Honduras in June 1990.

In June 1995 Honduras and Nicaragua signed an accord providing for the visible demarcation of each country's territorial waters in the Gulf of Fonseca, and the establishment of a joint naval patrol to police the area. The agreement followed frequent disputes concerning fishing rights in the Gulf, which occurred as a consequence of inefficient demarcation. Despite the agreement, however, conflict continued, and the demarcation process did not begin until May 1998.

In December 1999 a further dispute arose with Nicaragua, prompting it to sever commercial ties with, and impose import taxes on, Honduras, in direct contravention of Central American free trade undertakings. The dispute stemmed from the Caribbean Sea Maritime Limits Treaty, which Honduras had signed with Colombia in 1986 and had finally ratified in November 1999, thereby formally recognizing a frontier with Colombia, the demarcation of which granted Colombia territorial rights to areas of the Caribbean historically claimed by Nicaragua. In February 2000, following OAS mediation, the two countries agreed to establish a maritime exclusion zone in the disputed area. In the following month, representatives of Honduras and Nicaragua met in Washington, DC, where they signed an accord on joint patrols in the Caribbean, pending a ruling by the ICJ, and on combined operations in the Gulf of Fonseca. Agreement was also reached on the withdrawal of forces from the land border area. However, in February 2001 the Nicaraguan defence minister accused Honduras of violating the accords by carrying out military exercises in the area. Following further talks under OAS auspices, in June the foreign ministers of the two countries agreed to allow monitors into the disputed area to verify troop deployment. In August 2001, however, the Nicaraguan authorities again accused Honduras of moving troops and military equipment into the area, with the intention of launching an attack on their country. The Government denied the accusations. In July 2002 the situation further deteriorated when the Nicaraguan Government announced plans to sell oil-drilling rights in the disputed area. The ICJ had not issued a ruling on the dispute in early 2005.

A long-standing dispute between Honduras and El Salvador, regarding the demarcation of the two countries' common border and rival claims to three islands in the Gulf of Fonseca, caused hostilities to break out between the two countries in 1969. Although armed conflict soon subsided, the Honduran and Salvadorean Governments did not sign a peace treaty until 1980. IIn September 1992 the ICJ awarded Honduras sovereignty over some two-thirds of the disputed mainland territory and over one of the disputed islands in the Gulf of Fonseca. However, in subsequent years disputes continued to arise concerning the legal rights of those people resident in the reallocated territory, particularly with regard to land ownership. Following protracted negotiation, a convention governing the acquired rights and nationality of those people was finally signed by the Presidents of both countries in January 1998. An agreement was also signed providing for the demarcation of the countries' common border to be undertaken within one year. In August 2001 the Government unexpectedly expelled two members of the El Salvadorean military from the country, accusing them of obtaining highly sensitive documents relating to national security matters. In September 2003 the El Salvadorean Government requested that the ICJ review its 1992 decision, claiming that evidence had come to light that potentially undermined the ruling; however, the application was rejected by the ICJ.

In November 1991 the Presidents of Honduras and El Salvador signed an agreement to establish a free trade zone on their common border, and subsequently to seek economic union. In May 1992 the Governments of Honduras, El Salvador and Guatemala agreed to promote trade and investment between the three countries. A further agreement, concluded by Honduras, El Salvador and Guatemala in October of that year, provided for the eventual establishment of a Central American political federation.

In January 2002 Honduras restored diplomatic relations with Cuba, suspended since the 1959 revolution that brought Fidel Castro Rúz to power. Relations between the two countries had gradually improved thereafter, and Cuba supplied doctors and medical aid to Honduras following the devastation caused by 'Hurricane Mitch' in 1998. Increased economic activity between the two countries prompted the Honduran Government to open an interests section in the Cuban capital in late 2001. In December 2001 the Government also concluded an agreement with the United Kingdom defining the maritime border between Honduras and the Cayman Islands. In March 2004 President Maduro announced that the 360-strong contingent of Honduran troops serving in Iraq would be withdrawn in June.

Government

Under the provisions of the Constitution approved by the Asamblea Nacional in 1982, the President is elected by a simple majority of the voters. The President holds executive power and has a single four-year mandate. Legislative power is vested in the Asamblea Nacional (National Assembly), with 128 members elected by universal adult suffrage for a term of four years. The country is divided into 18 local Departments.

Defence

Military service is voluntary. Active service lasts eight months, with subsequent reserve training. In August 2004 the armed forces totalled 12,000 men, of whom 8,300 were in the army, 1,400 in the navy and 2,300 in the air force. Paramilitary forces numbered 8,000 men. In 2004 the defence budget was put at 950m. lempiras. In 2003 annual assistance from the USA was US $0.6m. (compared with $20.2m. in 1990). In that same year some 390 US troops were based in Honduras.

Economic Affairs

In 2003, according to estimates by the World Bank, Honduras' gross national income (GNI), measured at average 2001–03 prices, was US $6,782.9m., equivalent to $970 per head (or $2,580 per head on an international purchasing-power parity basis). During 1990–2003, it was estimated, the population increased at an average annual rate of 2.8%, while gross domestic product (GDP) per head increased, in real terms, by an average of 0.3% per year. Overall GDP increased, in real terms, at an average annual rate of 3.1% in 1990–2003; growth was 2.5% in 2002 and 3.0% in 2003.

Agriculture (including hunting, forestry and fishing) contributed an estimated 12.9% of GDP and employed 37.4% of the economically active population in 2003. The principal cash crop is traditionally coffee, although owing to high production costs and low prices on the world markets, coffee exports contributed only 13.8% of all export earnings in 2003, compared with 24.8% in 2000. Banana production decreased during the 1990s and in 1998 more than 70% of the total crop was destroyed as a result of 'Hurricane Mitch'. Furthermore, in June 2000 one of the principal banana corporations, Chiquita Brands, announced a substantial reduction in its operations in the country following hurricane damage and a downturn in the market. In spite of these set-backs, by 2001 earnings from banana exports had risen to 15.4% of total export earnings, compared with just 3.0% in 1999. However, banana prices declined substantially from US \$8 per box in 2001 to \$5.44 in 2003. As a result, banana export earnings declined over the same period, totalling 9.9% of total export earnings in 2003. The main subsistence crops include maize, plantains, beans, rice, sugar cane and citrus fruit. Exports of shellfish make a significant contribution to foreign earnings (supplying 14.4% of total export earnings in 2003). Agricultural GDP increased at an average annual rate of 3.0% during 1990–2003; the sector increased by 4.8% in 2002 and by 9.0% in 2003.

Industry (including mining, manufacturing, construction and power) contributed an estimated 31.9% of GDP and employed 21.4% of the economically active population in 2003. Industrial GDP increased at an average annual rate of 3.6% during 1990–2003; it increased by 0.7% in 2002 and by a further 4.4% in 2003.

Mining contributed an estimated 1.9% of GDP and employed 0.2% of the economically active population in 2003. In that year gold was the major mineral export, contributing an estimated 5.0% of total export earnings. Lead, zinc, silver, copper and low-grade iron ore are also mined. In addition, small quantities of petroleum derivatives are exported. Until the end of the 1990s, when new funding was announced, the gold, silver and other mineral deposits had remained unexplored. The GDP of the mining sector increased by an average of 4.9% per year in 1994–2003; it increased by an estimated 4.2% in 2002 and by a further estimated 3.2% in 2003.

Manufacturing contributed an estimated 20.6% of GDP and employed 15.7% of the economically active population in 2003. The most important branches, measured by gross value of output, were food products, beverages (including beer), cigarettes, apparel and wood products. In 2000 the successful *maquiladora* (assembly plant) sector employed some 100,000 local workers. Manufacturing GDP increased at an average annual rate of 4.0% during 1990–2003; the sector increased by 2.8% in 2002 and by 3.8% in 2003.

Energy is derived principally from hydroelectric power, which accounted for some 59.5% of electricity production in 2001. Petroleum accounted for 38.6% of electrical energy output. Imports of mineral fuels and lubricants accounted for an estimated 15.9% of the value of total imports in 2003. Fuel wood remains a prime source of domestic energy. In 2001 the US company, AES Corporation, announced plans to construct a US \$650m. natural gas plant that would supply some 800 MW of electricity to Honduras and other countries in the region. In May 2002 a cable connecting the electricity distribution networks of Honduras and El Salvador was activated; the connection process was completed in September. Nevertheless, in 2003 there were frequent power shortages throughout the country. The state-run energy company, ENEE (Empresa Nacional de Energía Eléctrica), began cutting power to certain parts of the country, in an attempt to ensure that large cities were not without electricity. Furthermore, in June it reached an agreement to import electricity from Costa Rica.

The services sector contributed an estimated 55.2% of GDP and engaged 41.2% of the working population in 2003. The GDP of the services sector increased by an average of 3.5% per year in 1990–2003; the sector increased by 2.9% in 2002, before contracting by 0.6% in the following year.

In 2003 Honduras recorded a visible trade deficit of US \$987.2m., while there was a deficit of \$279.2m. on the current account of the balance of payments. Workers' remittances from abroad were a vital source of income; according to the Central Bank, remittances totalled more than \$1,200m. in 2004. The majority of remittances came from the USA, home to an estimated 500,000 Hondurans. In 2003 the principal source of imports (37.5%) was the USA; other major suppliers were Guatemala, El Salvador, Costa Rica and Mexico. The USA was also the principal market for exports (44.7%) in that year; other significant purchasers were El Salvador, Guatemala and Germany. The principal exports in 2003 were shellfish and coffee. The principal imports in 2003 were machinery and electrical

equipment, mineral fuels and lubricants, and chemicals and related products.

In 2003 there was a budgetary deficit of 6,526.7m. lempiras (equivalent to 5.4% of GDP in that year). Honduras' external debt totalled US \$5,395m. at the end of 2002, of which \$4,675m. was long-term public debt. In that year the cost of debt-servicing represented 12.3% of the value of exports of goods and services. The annual rate of inflation averaged 15.5% in 1990–2003. Consumer prices increased by an annual average of 8.1% in 2002 and 6.8% in 2003. Some 3.8% of the labour force were unemployed in 2002; however, it was estimated that some 26.6% of the work-force were underemployed.

Honduras is a member of the Central American Common Market (CACM, see p. 176). Negotiations towards a Central American Free Trade Agreement (CAFTA) between Honduras, El Salvador, Guatemala, Nicaragua and the USA were concluded in December 2003. The Agreement, which was ratified by the Asamblea Nacional in March 2005, entailed the gradual elimination of tariffs on most industrial and agricultural products over the next 10 and 20 years, respectively. It was hoped that the advent of CAFTA would encourage export-oriented growth in Honduras and in the region. In May 2004 the Presidents of Honduras, El Salvador, Guatemala and Nicaragua signed an agreement creating a Central American customs union.

In terms of average income, Honduras is among the poorest nations in the Western hemisphere, with some 79% of the population living below the poverty line. In October 1998 the Honduran economy was devastated by the effects of 'Hurricane Mitch'. Much of the country's infrastructure was destroyed, and as many as 2.13m. people left homeless. The total cost to the economy of the hurricane damage was estimated at \$5,000m. In 1999 international financial agencies and donor countries agreed to provide \$2,800m. for the reconstruction process. In March of that year the IMF approved a three-year Enhanced Structural Adjustment Facility (ESAF) totalling \$215m., and in the following month the 'Paris Club' of creditor governments agreed to suspend Honduras' bilateral debt-service payments for a period of three years, and offered a 67% reduction in its debt of \$1,170m. on the condition that it complied with the terms of the ESAF. These included commitments by the Government to reduce public expenditure, rationalize state bureaucracy, and sustain its privatization programme. The successful implementation of these measures also facilitated further debt relief under the 'heavily indebted poor countries' (HIPC) initiative of the World Bank, to which Honduras was admitted in December.

The Government of Ricardo Maduro Joest, which took office in January 2002, pledged to maintain an austere economic policy and to reduce violent crime in an attempt to attract foreign investment and qualify for further IMF funding. To this end, President Maduro declared his intention to proceed with the much-delayed privatization of the state telecommunications company, Hondutel, and of ENEE. The first stage of the privatization of ENEE was completed by the end of 2002; and in November the Government announced plans to sell a 25% stake in Hondutel by 2005. The first private telecommunications contract, to supply 50,000 fixed telephone lines, was awarded in late 2003. Under pressure to reduce the high fiscal deficit sufficiently to satisfy the IMF, in 2003 Maduro announced that the rate of taxation on high incomes would be increased and that public-sector salaries would be 'frozen'. He also proposed linking public-sector wages to GDP growth. All the measures were met with worker opposition. Finally, in February 2004, the IMF announced that Honduras had met the criteria to qualify for debt relief. Some US \$15.4m. was immediately released under the HIPC initiative, with a further \$110m. available under a three-year Poverty Reduction and Growth Facility (PRGF) programme. However, the Fund stipulated continuing stringent legislative reforms and set the ambitious fiscal targets of a reduction in the budget deficit to 1.8% of GDP by 2006 (it was equivalent to 4.5% of GDP in 2003) and a fall in the annual inflation rate to 5% by 2007. In June 2004 the Government secured \$1,000m. in credit and a donation of \$800m. from international donors and credit organizations. In September the Paris Club of creditors suspended debt-service payments for a further year and two months later, under a Paris Club agreement, the USA cancelled \$98m.-worth of debt. In early 2005 the IMF announced that Maduro's Government had achieved the PRGF targets agreed a year earlier, and was expected to reach the completion point for entry into the HIPC initiative by March 2005. GDP increased by an estimated 4.3% in 2004. Nevertheless, the Government continued to face a formidable task in fulfilling economic targets, particularly in an election year, not only owing to the rising crime rate and social unrest, but also because it lacked the necessary political consensus to implement reform.

Education

Primary education, beginning at six years of age and comprising three cycles of three years, is officially compulsory and is provided free of charge. Secondary education, which is not compulsory, begins at the age of 15 and lasts for three years. In 2002 the enrolment at primary schools included 99.0% of children in the relevant age-group, while enrolment at secondary schools in that year was equivalent to only 42.0% of children in the appropriate age-group. There are eight universities, including the Autonomous National University in Tegucigalpa. The education budget in 2003 was 8,783m. lempiras, representing 26.7%

of total government expenditure. In December 2002 the World Bank announced a grant of US $90m. to fund schemes to enable more children to attend secondary school.

Public Holidays

2005: 1 January (New Year's Day), 25–28 March (Easter), 14 April (Pan-American Day/Bastilla's Day), 1 May (Labour Day), 15 September (Independence Day), 3 October (Morazán Day), 21 October (Army Day), 25 December (Christmas).

2006: 1 January (New Year's Day), 14 April (Pan-American Day/Bastilla's Day), 14–17 April (Easter), 1 May (Labour Day), 15 September (Independence Day), 3 October (Morazán Day), 21 October (Army Day), 25 December (Christmas).

Weights and Measures

The metric system is in force, although some old Spanish measures are used, including: 25 libras = 1 arroba; 4 arrobas = 1 quintal (46 kg).

Statistical Survey

Sources (unless otherwise stated): Department of Economic Studies, Banco Central de Honduras, Avda Juan Ramón Molina, 1a Calle, 7a Avda, Apdo 3165, Tegucigalpa; tel. 237-2270; fax 238-0376; e-mail jreyes@bch.hn; internet www.bch.hn; Instituto Nacional de Estadística, Edif. Gómez, Blvd Suyapa, Col. Florencia Sur, Apdo 9412, Tegucipgalpa; e-mail info@ine.online.hn; internet www.ine-hn.org.

Area and Population

AREA, POPULATION AND DENSITY

Area (sq km)	112,492*
Population (census results)†	
29 May 1988	4,614,377
1 August 2001	
Males	3,230,958
Females	3,304,386
Total	6,535,344
Population (official estimates at mid-year)	
2001	6,530,300
2002	6,694,800
2003	6,860,800
Density (per sq km) at mid-2003	61.0

* 43,433 sq miles.

† Excluding adjustments for underenumeration, estimated to have been 10% at the 1974 census.

PRINCIPAL TOWNS

(estimated population, '000 at mid-2001)

Tegucigalpa (captial) .	1,089.2	Siguatepeque . . .	53.7
San Pedro Sula . .	490.6	Puerto Cortés . . .	36.0
El Progreso	115.0	Juticalpa	34.8
La Ceiba	111.2	Santa Rosa de Copán .	28.6
Choluteca	101.6	Tela	26.6
Comayagua . . .	77.4	Olanchito	23.9
Danlí	68.8		

Mid-2003 (UN estimate, incl. suburbs): Tegucigalpa 1,006,592 (Source: UN, *World Urbanization Prospects: The 2003 revision*).

BIRTHS AND DEATHS

(World Bank estimates, annual averages)

	2000	2002*
Birth rate (per 1,000)	31.2	29.7
Death rate (per 1,000)	6.4	6.3

* Data for 2001 not available.

Source: World Bank, *World Development Indicators*.

Expectation of life (WHO estimates, years at birth): 67.2 (males 64.2; females 70.4) in 2002 (Source: WHO, *World Health Report*).

ECONOMICALLY ACTIVE POPULATION

('000 persons)

	2001	2002	2003
Agriculture, hunting, forestry and fishing	844.8	931.2	906.3
Mining and quarrying	5.1	4.6	5.8
Manufacturing	367.0	337.3	381.2
Electricity, gas and water . . .	11.5	8.8	9.6
Construction	123.6	120.8	122.8
Trade, restaurants and hotels .	462.7	507.0	495.9
Transport, storage and communications	71.7	71.6	79.1
Financing, insurance, real estate and business services . . .	66.5	57.4	73.3
Community, social and personal services	335.8	312.4	352.1
Total	**2,288.7**	**2,351.1**	**2,426.1**

Health and Welfare

KEY INDICATORS

Total fertility rate (children per woman, 2002)	3.8
Under-5 mortality rate (per 1,000 live births, 2003) . . .	41
HIV/AIDS (% of persons aged 15–49, 2003)	1.8
Physicians (per 1,000 head, 1997)	0.83
Hospital beds (per 1,000 head, 1996)	1.06
Health expenditure (2001): US $ per head (PPP)	153
Health expenditure (2001): % of GDP	6.1
Health expenditure (2001): public (% of total)	53.1
Access to water (% of persons, 2002)	90
Access to sanitation (% of persons, 2002)	68
Human Development Index (2002): ranking	115
Human Development Index (2002): value	0.672

For sources and definitions, see explanatory note on p. vi.

Agriculture

PRINCIPAL CROPS
('000 metric tons)

	2001	2002	2003
Maize	516	392	502
Sorghum	75	43	52
Sugar cane	3,451	3,451†	5,363
Dry beans	59	50	69
Oil palm fruit	669	736	740†
Tomatoes	50	53*	53†
Other vegetables*	140	142	142
Melons*	114	182	145
Bananas	516	965	965*
Plantains*	260	260	260
Oranges	142*	167	167*
Pineapples	67*	62	62*
Other fruit*	71	77	77
Coffee (green)	206	182†	150

* FAO estimate(s).
† Unofficial estimate.

Source: FAO.

LIVESTOCK
('000 head, year ending September)

	2001	2002	2003
Cattle	1,875*	1,860	2,403*
Sheep†	14	14	13
Goats†	32	32	32
Pigs	538*	538	478*
Horses†	180	180	181
Mules†	70	70	70
Asses†	23	23	23
Poultry	18,000†	18,648	18,700†

* Unofficial figure.
† FAO estimate(s).

Source: FAO.

LIVESTOCK PRODUCTS
('000 metric tons)

	2001	2002	2003
Beef and veal	55.3	62.0*	57.0
Pig meat	9.7	10.5†	9.6†
Poultry meat	66.3	66.3†	74.0†
Cows' milk	593.8	595.5†	597.0†
Cheese†	9.0	9.2	9.0
Butter†	4.4	4.5	4.5
Hen eggs†	44.4	44.4	40.0
Cattle hides†	9.5	9.5	9.5

* Unofficial estimate.
† FAO estimate(s).

Source: FAO.

Forestry

ROUNDWOOD REMOVALS
('000 cubic metres, excl. bark)

	2001	2002	2003
Sawlogs, veneer logs and logs for sleepers	832	971	801
Fuel wood*	8,720	8,710	8,703
Total *	9,552	9,681	9,504

* FAO estimates.

Source: FAO.

SAWNWOOD PRODUCTION
('000 cubic metres, incl. railway sleepers)

	2001	2002	2003
Coniferous (softwood) . . .	412	470	421
Broadleaved (hardwood) . . .	7	—	—
Total	419	470	421

Source: FAO.

Fishing

('000 metric tons, live weight)

	2000	2001	2002
Capture	14.5	12.6	11.4
Marine fishes	6.2	5.5	4.9
Caribbean spiny lobster . . .	0.8	0.9	0.8
Penaeus shrimps	5.2	5.2	4.7
Stromboid conches	0.7	0.7	0.8
Aquaculture	9.1	12.8	15.4
Nile tilapia	0.9	1.9*	2.9
Penaeus shrimps	8.2	10.9	12.6
Total catch	23.6	25.3	26.8

* FAO estimate.

Source: FAO.

Mining

(metal content)

	2000	2001	2002
Lead (metric tons)	4,805	6,750	8,128
Zinc (metric tons)	31,226	48,485	46,339
Silver (kilograms)	31,958	46,831	52,877
Gold (kilograms)	878	4,574	4,984

Source: US Geological Survey.

Industry

SELECTED PRODUCTS

	2001	2002	2003
Raw sugar ('000 quintales) . .	7,610	7,220	6,385
Cement ('000 bags of 42.5 kg) . .	31,000	28,803	30,531
Cigarettes ('000 packets of 20) . .	299,220	300,491	308,042
Beer ('000 12 oz bottles) . .	244,968	260,007	255,173
Soft drinks ('000 12 oz bottles) .	1,357,492	1,453,703	1,457,876
Wheat flour ('000 quintales) . .	2,484	2,566	2,498
Fabric ('000 yards)	119,010	135,290	187,750
Liquor and spirits ('000 litres) . .	8,162	9,576	11,008
Vegetable oil and butter ('000 libras)	157,932	169,664	177,148
Electric energy (million kWh) . .	4,183.5	4,494.9	4,845.2

Finance

CURRENCY AND EXCHANGE RATES

Monetary Units
  100 centavos = 1 lempira.

Sterling, Dollar and Euro Equivalents (31 December 2004)
  £1 sterling = 35.987 lempiras;
  US $1 = 18.633 lempiras;
  €1 = 25.380 lempiras;
  1,000 lempiras = £27.79 = $53.67 = €39.40.

Average Exchange Rate (lempiras per US $)
  2002   16.4334
  2003   17.3453
  2004   18.2062

BUDGET
(million lempiras)

Revenue			2001	2002	2003*
Current revenue			17,848.9	19,776.0	22,175.1
Taxes			16,083.1	17,229.0	19,632.4
Non-tax revenue			1,765.8	2,547.0	2,542.7
Capital revenue			31.4	—	—
Transfers			1,657.8	1,302.3	1,328.1
Other revenue			188.4	62.8	58.8
Total			19,726.5	21,141.1	23,562.1

Expenditure			2001	2002	2003*
Current expenditure			17,400.7	19,593.3	22,823.0
Consumption expenditure . .			12,680.9	14,223.1	15,441.1
Interest and other charges . .			1,186.4	1,296.8	1,469.9
Internal debt			300.7	314.4	406.2
External debt†			885.6	982.4	1,063.7
Transfers			3,533.5	4,073.3	5,912.0
Capital expenditure			6,744.7	5,433.7	6,594.2
Real investment			2,824.6	2,448.9	2,795.0
Transfers			3,920.1	2,984.8	3,799.2
Total‡			24,145.4	25,027.0	29,417.2

* Preliminary figures.
† Excludes debt-servicing relief.
‡ Excluding net lending (million lempiras): 821.0 in 2001; 1,262.0 in 2002; 671.6 in 2003 (preliminary).

Source: Ministry of Finance, *Memoria Secretaria de Finanzas*.

CENTRAL BANK RESERVES
(US $ million at 31 December)

	2001	2002	2003
Gold*	6.05	7.11	9.26
IMF special drawing rights . .	0.32	0.47	0.11
Foreign exchange	1,404.40	1,511.80	1,417.10
Reserve position in IMF . . .	10.84	11.73	12.82
Total	1,453.29	1,531.11	1,439.29

* National valuation.

Source: IMF, *International Financial Statistics*.

MONEY SUPPLY
(million lempiras at 31 December)

	2001	2002	2003
Currency outside banks . .	5,166	5,549	6,448
Demand deposits at commercial banks	6,344	7,658	9,315
Total money (incl. others) . .	12,388	14,224	17,251

Source: IMF, *International Financial Statistics*.

COST OF LIVING
(Consumer Price Index, December; base: 1999 = 100)

	2001	2002	2003
Food	117.4	120.1	126.1
Alcohol and tobacco . . .	123.2	135.7	151.5
Rent, water, fuel and power . .	120.5	141.3	153.2
Clothing and footwear . . .	120.3	131.3	140.7
Health	145.6	154.9	165.0
Transport	121.2	135.5	146.3
Communications	103.4	93.5	94.5
Culture and recreation . . .	117.5	121.8	127.8
Education	136.0	158.2	180.9
Restaurants and hotels . .	118.8	128.7	136.8
All items (incl. others) . . .	119.8	129.5	138.3

NATIONAL ACCOUNTS
(million lempiras at current prices)

Expenditure on the Gross Domestic Product

	2001*	2002*	2003†
Government final consumption expenditure	13,792	14,925	16,209
Private final consumption expenditure	72,198	82,063	91,627
Increase in stocks	5,756	3,710	4,261
Gross fixed capital formation . .	23,525	23,992	28,124
Total domestic expenditure	115,271	124,691	140,221
Exports of goods and services . .	37,481	41,203	46,684
Less Imports of goods and services	53,720	57,770	66,440
GDP in purchasers' values	99,032	108,124	120,465
GDP at constant 1978 prices .	7,324	7,523	7,785

* Preliminary figures.
† Estimates.

Gross Domestic Product by Economic Activity

	2001*	2002*	2003†
Agriculture, hunting, forestry and fishing	12,122	12,895	13,701
Mining and quarrying	1,591	1,794	1,998
Manufacturing	17,540	19,640	21,980
Electricity, gas and water . . .	3,728	4,263	5,052
Construction	4,269	3,966	4,922
Wholesale and retail trade, restaurants and hotels . . .	10,870	12,050	13,412
Transport, storage and communications	5,096	5,643	6,354
Finance, insurance and real estate	9,441	10,406	11,458
Owner-occupied dwellings . . .	5,201	5,840	6,552
Public administration and defence	6,139	7,095	7,478
Other services	10,561	12,177	13,577
GDP at factor cost	86,558	95,769	106,484
Indirect taxes, *less* subsidies . .	12,474	12,355	13,981
GDP in purchasers' values .	99,032	108,124	120,465

* Preliminary figures.
† Estimates.

BALANCE OF PAYMENTS
(US $ million)

	2001	2002	2003
Exports of goods f.o.b.	1,935.5	1,973.6	2,078.2
Imports of goods f.o.b.	−2,768.1	−2,809.2	−3,065.4
Trade balance	−832.6	−835.6	−987.2
Exports of services	487.2	530.3	576.2
Imports of services	−626.6	−601.9	−653.2
Balance on goods and services	−972.0	−907.2	−1,064.2
Other income received . . .	88.0	66.8	56.7
Other income paid	−259.2	−249.7	−240.0
Balance on goods, services and income	−1,143.2	−1,090.0	−1,247.5
Current transfers received . .	894.0	946.6	1,072.2
Current transfers paid	−89.9	−98.9	−104.0
Current balance	−339.1	−242.3	−279.2
Capital account (net)	36.7	23.6	21.0
Direct investment from abroad .	189.5	175.5	198.0
Portfolio investment assets . .	−3.6	−3.8	−4.1
Other investment assets . . .	−102.3	24.2	−77.6
Other investment liabilities . .	76.5	−56.6	−136.3
Net errors and omissions . .	68.3	60.5	76.1
Overall balance	−74.0	−18.8	−202.1

Source: IMF, *International Financial Statistics*.

External Trade

PRINCIPAL COMMODITIES
(US $ million, preliminary figures)

Imports c.i.f.	2001	2002	2003
Vegetables and fruit	141.7	151.5	155.4
Mineral fuels and lubricants . .	395.1	413.5	519.2
Chemicals and related products .	397.3	445.1	457.0
Plastic and manufactures . . .	169.6	184.3	196.9
Paper, paperboard and manufactures	158.7	166.9	176.6
Textile yarn, fabrics and manufactures	87.7	96.7	99.3
Metal and manufactures . . .	291.3	201.3	246.3
Food products	282.8	285.9	302.2
Machinery and electrical appliances	463.8	481.2	559.4
Transport equipment	276.8	275.7	241.8
Total (incl. others)	2,941.8	2,981.1	3,275.6

Exports f.o.b.	2001	2002	2003
Bananas	204.2	172.4	132.4
Coffee	160.7	182.5	183.3
Gold	63.8	80.5	66.6
Lead and zinc	41.8	31.8	30.0
Shellfish	190.7	172.4	191.8
Soaps and detergents	50.6	26.1	33.7
Total (incl. others)	1,324.4	1,321.2	1,332.3

PRINCIPAL TRADING PARTNERS
(US $ million, preliminary figures)

Imports c.i.f.	2001	2002	2003
Brazil	29.9	43.6	66.0
Colombia	30.2	34.3	36.9
Costa Rica	115.2	148.4	164.0
El Salvador	183.5	165.3	182.0
Germany	43.7	34.3	40.7
Guatemala	244.9	249.4	268.1
Japan	140.9	97.6	114.0
Mexico	149.9	169.3	162.1
Nicaragua	31.4	45.9	48.7
Spain	51.3	33.1	48.0
Trinidad and Tobago	33.5	79.6	26.5
USA	1,097.9	1,104.6	1,227.3
Venezuela	23.9	57.4	48.6
Total (incl. others)	2,941.8	2,981.1	3,275.6

Exports f.o.b.	2001	2002	2003
Belgium	70.5	41.0	41.1
Canada	43.9	31.2	29.5
Costa Rica	35.8	30.6	32.8
El Salvador	135.0	157.0	150.5
France	14.0	9.8	13.0
Germany	57.4	83.9	64.1
Guatemala	129.3	83.9	78.0
Italy	14.6	19.6	8.5
Japan	30.0	20.2	15.1
Mexico	7.4	11.2	36.4
Netherlands	19.2	23.9	50.4
Nicaragua	26.5	19.1	43.0
Spain	32.8	39.3	42.9
United Kingdom	21.6	31.8	39.3
USA	571.4	616.5	595.3
Total (incl. others)	1,324.4	1,321.2	1,332.3

Transport

ROAD TRAFFIC
(licensed vehicles in use)

	2001	2002	2003
Passenger cars	345,931	369,303	386,468
Buses and coaches	20,380	21,814	22,514
Lorries and vans	81,192	86,893	91,230
Motorcycles and bicycles . . .	36,828	39,245	41,852

SHIPPING

Merchant Fleet
(registered at 31 December)

	2001	2002	2003
Number of vessels	1,183	1,155	1,143
Total displacement ('000 grt) . .	966.5	933.2	812.5

Source: Lloyd's Register-Fairplay, *World Fleet Statistics*.

International Sea-borne Freight Traffic
('000 metric tons)

	1988	1989	1990
Goods loaded	1,328	1,333	1,316
Goods unloaded	1,151	1,222	1,002

Source: UN, *Monthly Bulletin of Statistics*.

CIVIL AVIATION
(traffic on scheduled services)

	1993	1994	1995
Kilometres flown (million) . . .	4	5	5
Passengers carried ('000) . . .	409	449	474
Passenger-km (million) . . .	362	323	341
Total ton-km (million)	50	42	33

Source: UN, *Statistical Yearbook*.

Tourism

TOURIST ARRIVALS BY COUNTRY OF ORIGIN

	2000	2001	2002
Canada	8,732	9,000	8,844
Costa Rica	15,755	16,854	17,845
El Salvador	79,365	95,338	110,931
Guatemala	66,924	78,717	86,068
Italy	7,245	10,210	11,684
Mexico	10,902	10,579	10,948
Nicaragua	64,350	77,774	96,532
Spain	6,975	7,939	7,028
USA	150,531	148,554	137,953
Total (incl. others)	470,727	517,914	549,500

Receipts from tourism (US $ million): 260 in 2000; 275 in 2001; 342 in 2002.

Source: World Tourism Organization.

Communications Media

	2001	2002	2003
Television receivers ('000 in use)* . .	640	n.a.	n.a.
Telephones ('000 main lines in use) .	310.6	322.5	334.4
Mobile cellular telephones ('000 subscribers)	237.6	326.5	351.3
Personal computers ('000 in use)* . .	80	91	n.a.
Internet users ('000)	90.0	168.6	185.4
Daily newspapers	4	4	4
Weekly newspapers	3	3	3

* Source: International Telecommunication Union.

Radio receivers ('000 in use): 2,450 in 1997 (Source: UN, *Statistical Yearbook*).

Education

(2003)

	Institutions	Teachers	Students
Pre-primary	5,357	15,232	197,408
Primary (grades 1 to 6) . .}	11,115	42,788 {	1,255,859
Secondary (grades 7 to 9) . .}			290,100
High school	871	16,435	454,489
University level	8	3,707	75,643

Adult literacy rate (UNESCO estimates): 80.0% (males 80.2%; females 79.8%) in 2002 (Source: UN Development Programme, *Human Development Report*).

Directory

The Constitution

Following the elections of April 1980, the 1965 Constitution was revised. The new Constitution was approved by the National Assembly in November 1982, and amended in 1995. The following are some of its main provisions:

Honduras is constituted as a democratic Republic. All Hondurans over 18 years of age are citizens.

THE SUFFRAGE AND POLITICAL PARTIES

The vote is direct and secret. Any political party that proclaims or practises doctrines contrary to the democratic spirit is forbidden. A National Electoral Council will be set up at the end of each presidential term. Its general function will be to supervise all elections and to register political parties. A proportional system of voting will be adopted for the election of Municipal Corporations.

INDIVIDUAL RIGHTS AND GUARANTEES

The right to life is declared inviolable; the death penalty is abolished. The Constitution recognizes the right of habeas corpus and arrests may be made only by judicial order. Remand for interrogation may not last more than six days, and no-one may be held incommunicado for more than 24 hours. The Constitution recognizes the rights of free expression of thought and opinion, the free circulation of information, of peaceful, unarmed association, of free movement within and out of the country, of political asylum and of religious and educational freedom. Civil marriage and divorce are recognized.

WORKERS' WELFARE

All have a right to work. Day work shall not exceed eight hours per day or 44 hours per week; night work shall not exceed six hours per night or 36 hours per week. Equal pay shall be given for equal work. The legality of trade unions and the right to strike are recognized.

EDUCATION

The State is responsible for education, which shall be free, lay, and, in the primary stage, compulsory. Private education is liable to inspection and regulation by the State.

LEGISLATIVE POWER

Deputies are obliged to vote, for or against, on any measure at the discussion of which they are present. The National Assembly has power to grant amnesties to political prisoners; approve or disapprove of the actions of the Executive; declare part or the whole of the Republic subject to a state of siege; declare war; approve or withhold approval of treaties; withhold approval of the accounts of public expenditure when these exceed the sums fixed in the budget; decree, interpret, repeal and amend laws, and pass legislation fixing the rate of exchange or stabilizing the national currency. The National Assembly may suspend certain guarantees in all or part of the Republic for 60 days in the case of grave danger from civil or foreign war, epidemics or any other calamity. Deputies are elected in the proportion of one deputy and one substitute for every 35,000 inhabitants, or fraction over 15,000. Congress may amend the basis in the light of increasing population.

EXECUTIVE POWER

Executive power is exercised by the President of the Republic, who is elected for four years by a simple majority of the people. No President may serve more than one term.

JUDICIAL POWER

The Judiciary consists of the Supreme Court, the Courts of Appeal and various lesser tribunals. The nine judges and seven substitute judges of the Supreme Court are elected by the National Assembly for a period of four years. The Supreme Court is empowered to declare laws unconstitutional.

THE ARMED FORCES

The Armed Forces are declared by the Constitution to be essentially professional and non-political. The President exercises direct authority over the military.

LOCAL ADMINISTRATION

The country is divided into 18 Departments for purposes of local administration, and these are subdivided into 290 autonomous Municipalities; the functions of local offices shall be only economic and administrative.

The Government

HEAD OF STATE

President: RICARDO MADURO JOEST (assumed office 27 January 2002).

Vice-President: VICENTE WILLIAMS AGASSE.

CABINET
(April 2005)

Minister of the Interior and Justice: JORGE RAMÓN HERNÁNDEZ ALCERRO.

Minister in the Office of the President: LUIS COSENZA JIMÉNEZ.

Minister of Foreign Affairs: LEONIDAS ROSA BAUTISTA.

Minister of Industry and Commerce: NORMAN GARCÍA.

Minister of Finance: WILLIAM CHONG WONG.

Minister of National Defence: FEDERICO BREVÉ TRAVIESO.

Minister of Public Security: OSCAR ALVAREZ GUERRERO.

Minister of Labour and Social Welfare: GERMÁN LEITZELAR VIDAURRETA.

Minister of Health: ELÍAS LIZARDO ZELAYA.

Minister of Public Education: ROBERTO MARTÍNEZ LOZANO.

Minister of Public Works, Transport and Housing: JORGE CARRANZA DÍAZ.

Minister of Culture, Art and Sports: ARNOLDO AVILÉS.

Minister of Agriculture and Livestock: MARIANO JIMÉNEZ TALAVERA.

Minister of Natural Resources and Environment: PATRICIA PANTING GALO.

Minister of Tourism: THIERRY DE PIERREFEU.

Minister of Strategy and Communication: RAMÓN MEDINA LUNA.

Minister of International Co-operation: BRENIE LILIANA MATUTE.

MINISTRIES

Office of the President: Palacio José Cecilio del Valle, Blvd Juan Pablo II, Tegucigalpa; tel. 232-6282; fax 231-0097; internet www .casapresidencial.hn.

Ministry of Agriculture and Livestock: Tegucigalpa; tel. 235-7388; e-mail infoagro@sag.gob.hn; internet www.sag.gob.hn.

Ministry of Culture, Art and Sports: Avda La Paz, Apdo 3287, Tegucigalpa; tel. 236-9643; fax 236-9532; e-mail editc@sdnhon.org .hn; internet www.secad.gob.hn.

Ministry of Finance: 5a Avda, 3a Calle, Tegucigalpa; tel. 222-1278; fax 238-2309; e-mail despacho@sefin.gob.hn; internet www .sefin.gob.hn.

Ministry of Foreign Affairs: Centro Cívico Gubernamental, Antigua Casa Presidencial, Blvd Kuwait, Contiguo a la Corte Suprema de Justicia, Tegucigalpa; tel. 234-1962; fax 234-1484; internet www.sre.hn.

Ministry of Health: 4a Avda, 3a Calle, Tegucigalpa; tel. 222-8518; fax 238-4141; internet www.secsalud.hn.

Ministry of Industry and Commerce: Edif. Salame, 5a Avda, 4a Calle, Tegucigalpa; tel. 238-2025; fax 237-2836; internet www.sic .gob.hn.

Ministry of the Interior and Justice: Residencia La Hacienda, Calle La Estancia, Tegucigalpa; tel. 232-1892; fax 232-0226; e-mail atencionalpublico@gobernacion.gob.hn; internet www.gobernacion .gob.hn.

Ministry of International Co-operation: Edif. El Sol, Col. Puerta del Sol, 1 c. atrás del Blvd La Hacienda, Tegucigalpa; tel. 239-5545; fax 239-5277; e-mail webmaster@setco.gob.hn; internet www.setco .gob.hn.

Ministry of Labour and Social Welfare: Edif. Olympus (STSS), Col. Puerta del Sol, Contiguo a SETCO, Intersección Bulevares Villa Olímpica, La Hacienda, Tegucigalpa; tel. 235-3455; fax 235-3456.

Ministry of National Defence: 5a Avda, 4a Calle, Tegucigalpa; tel. 238-3427; fax 238-0238.

Ministry of Natural Resources and Environment: 100 m al sur del Estadio Nacional, Apdo 1389, Tegucigalpa; tel. 235-7833; fax 232-6250; e-mail sdespacho@serna.gob.hn; internet www.serna.gob .hn.

Ministry of Public Education: 1a Avda, 2a y 3a Calle 201, Comayagüela, Tegucigalpa; tel. 222-8571; fax 237-4312; e-mail info@ se.gob.hn; internet www.se.gob.hn.

Ministry of Public Security: 5a Avda, 4a Calle, Tegucigalpa.

Ministry of Public Works, Transport and Housing: Barrio La Bolsa, Comayagüela, Tegucigalpa; tel. 225-0489; fax 225-2227; internet www.soptravi.gob.hn.

Ministry of Strategy and Communication: Tegucigalpa.

Ministry of Tourism: Edif. Salame, 5a Avda, 4a Calle, Tegucigalpa; tel. 238-2025; fax 237-2836; internet www.letsgohonduras .com.

President and Legislature

PRESIDENT

Election, 25 November 2001

Candidate						Votes cast	% of votes
Ricardo Maduro Joest (PN)	.	.	.	.	.	1,137,734	52.21
Rafael Piñeda Ponce (PL)	.	.	.	.	.	964,590	44.26
Olban F. Valladares (PINU)	.	.	.	.	.	31,666	1.45
Matías Funes (PUD)	.	.	.	.	.	24,102	1.11
Marco Orlando Iriarte (PDCH)	.	.	.	.		21,089	0.97
Total*	.	.	.	.	.	2,179,181	100.00

* Excluding 23,927 blank ballots, 81,959 spoilt votes and 1,163,213 abstentions.

ASAMBLEA NACIONAL

President: PORFIRIO LOBO SOSA.

General Election, 25 November 2001

	Seats
Partido Nacional (PN)	61
Partido Liberal (PL)	55
Partido de Unificación Democrática (PUD)	5
Partido Innovación y Unidad— Social Democracia (PINU)	4
Partido Demócrata Cristiano de Honduras (PDCH) . . .	3
Total	128

Political Organizations

Partido Demócrata Cristiano de Honduras (PDCH): Col. San Carlos, Tegucigalpa; tel. 236-5969; fax 236-9941; e-mail pdch@ hondutel.hn; internet www.pdch.hn; legally recognized in 1980; Pres. Dr HERNÁN CORRALES PADILLA; Vice-Pres. VICENTE WILLIAMS.

Partido Innovación y Unidad—Social Democracia (PINU): Calle Real, entre 9 y 10 calles, Comaygüela; tel. 237-1357; fax 237-4245; f. 1970; legally recognized in 1978; Leader OLBAN F. VALLADARES.

Partido Liberal (PL): Col. Miramonte, Tegucigalpa; tel. 232-0520; fax 232-0797; f. 1891; factions within the party include the Movimiento Pinedista (Leader Dr RAFAEL PINDA PONCE), the Movimiento LIBRE (Leader JAIME ROSENTHAL OLIVA, and the Movimiento Esperanza Liberal (Leader MANUEL ZELAYA); has a youth organization called the Frente Central de Juventud Liberal de Honduras (Pres. EDUARDO RAINA GARCÍA); Pres. Dr RAFAEL PIÑEDA PONCE; Sec.-Gen. JAIME ROSENTHAL OLIVA.

Partido Nacional (PN): Paseo el Obelisco, Comayagüela, Tegucigalpa; tel. 237-7310; fax 237-7365; f. 1902; traditional right-wing party; internal opposition tendencies include Movimiento Democratizador Nacionalista (MODENA), Movimiento de Unidad y Cambio (MUC), Movimiento Nacional de Reivindicación Callejista (MONARCA) and Tendencia Nacionalista de Trabajo; Pres. RAFAEL LEONARDO CALLEJAS ROMERO.

Partido de Unificación Democrática (PUD): Barrio La Plazuela, Avda Cervantes, Tegucigalpa; tel. and fax 238-2498; f. 1993; left-wing coalition comprising Partido Revolucionario Hondureño, Partido Renovación Patriótica, Partido para la Transformación de Honduras and Partido Morazanista.

Diplomatic Representation

EMBASSIES IN HONDURAS

Argentina: Calle Palermo 302, Col. Rubén Darío, Apdo 3208, Tegucigalpa; tel. 232-3376; fax 231-0376; e-mail ehond@mrecic.gov.ar; Ambassador ALFREDO WALDO FORTI.

Brazil: Col. Palmira, Calle República del Brasil, Apdo 341, Tegucigalpa; tel. 221-4432; fax 236-5873; e-mail brastegu@sigmanet.hn; Ambassador SERGIO LUIZ BEZERRA CAVALCANTI.

Chile: Calle Oslo C-4242, Col. Lomas del Guijarro, Tegucigalpa; tel. 232-2114; fax 239-7925; e-mail echilehn@123.hn; Ambassador MARIA CORREA MARIN.

China (Taiwan): Col. Lomas del Guijarro, Calle Eucaliptos 3750, Apdo 3433, Tegucigalpa; tel. 239-5837; fax 232-5103; e-mail hnd@ mofa.gov.tw; Ambassador TIEN-DER YOU.

Colombia: Edif. Palmira, 4°, Col. Palmira, Apdo 468, Tegucigalpa; tel. 232-9709; fax 232-8133; e-mail ehonduras@minrelext.gov.co; Ambassador JUAN ANTONIO RANGEL.

Costa Rica: Residencial El Triángulo, 1 Calle, Lomas del Guijarro, Apdo 512, Tegucigalpa; tel. 232-1768; fax 232-1876; e-mail embacori@multivisionhn.net; Ambassador EDGAR GARCÍA MIRANDA.

Cuba: Col. Florencia Sur, Avda Principal 4313, Tegucigalpa; tel. 239-0610; fax 235-7624; e-mail oficuba@cybertelh.hn; Ambassador ELIS ALBERTO GONZÁLEZ POLANCO.

Dominican Republic: Calle Principal frente al Banco Continental, Col. Miramontes, Tegucigalpa; tel. 239-0130; fax 239-1594; e-mail embadom@compunet.hn; Ambassador ELADIO KNIPPING VICTORIA.

Ecuador: Casa 2968, Sendero Senecio, Col. Castaños Sur, Apdo 358, Tegucigalpa; tel. 221-1049; fax 235-4074; e-mail mecuahon@ multivisionhn.ne; Ambassador FRANCISCO MARTINEZ SALAZAR.

El Salvador: Col. Rubén Darío, 2a Avda y 5a Calle No 620, Apdo 1936, Tegucigalpa; tel. 239-0901; fax 239-7009; e-mail embasalva@ cablecolor.hn; Ambassador SIGIFREDO OCHOA PÉREZ.

France: Col. Palmira, Avda Juan Lindo, Callejón Batres 337, Apdo 3441, Tegucigalpa; tel. 236-6800; fax 236-8051; e-mail ambafrance@cablecolor.hn; Ambassador Frédéric Basaguren.

Germany: Edif. Paysen, 3°, Blvd Morazán, Apdo 3145, Tegucigalpa; tel. 232-3161; fax 239-9018; e-mail embalema@multivisionhn.net; internet www.tegucigalpa.diplo.de; Ambassador Dr Thomas Bruns.

Guatemala: Col. Las Minitas, Calle Arturo López Rodezno 2421, Tegucigalpa; tel. 232-5018; fax 232-1580; e-mail embhonduras@minex.gob.gt; Ambassador Erwin Fernando Guzmán Ovalle.

Holy See: Palacio de la Nunciatura Apostólica, Col. Palmira, Avda Santa Sede 412, Apdo 324, Tegucigalpa; tel. 232-6613; fax 239-8869; e-mail nunciatureateg@multivisionhn.net; Apostolic Nuncio Most Rev. Antonio Arcari (Titular Archbishop of Ceciti).

Italy: Col. Montecarlo, Avda Enrique Tierno Galván, Apdo U-9093, Tegucigalpa; tel. 236-6391; fax 236-5659; e-mail conibah@multivisionhn.net; internet www.ambitaliahn.org; Ambassador Estefano María Cacciaguerra Ranghieri.

Japan: Col. San Carlos, Calzada Rep. Paraguay, Apdo 3232, Tegucigalpa; tel. 236-2628; fax 236-6100; internet www.hn.emb-japan.go.jp; Ambassador Masami Takemoto.

Mexico: Col. Lomas de Guijarro, Col. Eucalipto 1001, Tegucigalpa; tel. 232-4039; fax 232-4719; e-mail embamexhon@newcom.hn; Ambassador Walterio Astié Burgos.

Nicaragua: Col. Tepeyac, Bloque M-1, Avda Choluteca 1130, Apdo 392, Tegucigalpa; tel. 231-1977; fax 231-1412; e-mail embanic@multivisionhn.net; Ambassador Julio Delgado Mendoza.

Panama: Edif. Palmira, 2°, Col. Palmira, Apdo 397, Tegucigalpa; tel. 239-5508; fax 232-8147; e-mail ephon@hondudata.com; Ambassador Iris Oneida Vega Ramos.

Peru: Col. La Reforma, Calle Principal 2618, Tegucigalpa; tel. 221-0596; fax 236-6070; e-mail embajdadelperu@cablecolor.hn; Ambassador Gustavo Otero Zapata.

Spain: Col. Matamoros, Calle Santander 801, Apdo 3221, Tegucigalpa; tel. 236-6875; fax 236-8682; e-mail embesphn@correo.mae.es; Ambassador Augustin Núñez Martínez.

USA: Avda La Paz, Apdo 3453, Tegucigalpa; tel. 236-9320; fax 236-9037; internet honduras.usembassy.gov; Ambassador Larry Palmer.

Venezuela: Col. Rubén Darío, 2116 Circuito Choluteca, Apdo 775, Tegucigalpa; tel. 232-1879; fax 232-1016; e-mail emvenezue@hondutel.hn; Ambassador María Salazar Sanabria.

Judicial System

Justice is administered by the Supreme Court (which has 15 judges), five Courts of Appeal and departmental courts (which have their own local jurisdiction).

Tegucigalpa has two Courts of Appeal which have jurisdiction (1) in the department of Francisco Morazán, and (2) in the departments of Choluteca Valle, El Paraíso and Olancho.

The Appeal Court of San Pedro Sula has jurisdiction in the department of Cortés; that of Comayagua has jurisdiction in the departments of Comayagua, La Paz and Intibucá; and that of Santa Bárbara in the departments of Santa Bárbara, Lempira and Copán.

Supreme Court: Edif. Palacio de Justicia, contiguo Col. Miraflores, Centro Cívico Gubernamental, Tegucigalpa; tel. 233-9208; fax 233-6784.

President of the Supreme Court of Justice: Vilma Cecilia Morales Montalván.

Attorney-General: Sergio Zavala Leiva.

Religion

The majority of the population are Roman Catholics; the Constitution guarantees toleration to all forms of religious belief.

CHRISTIANITY

The Roman Catholic Church

Honduras comprises one archdiocese and six dioceses. At 31 December 2002 some 83% of the population were adherents.

Bishops' Conference

Conferencia Episcopal de Honduras, Blvd Estadio Suyapa, Apdo 847, Tegucigalpa; tel. 324-043; fax 327-838; e-mail ceh-ceh@sdnhon.org.hn.

f. 1929; Pres. Cardinal Oscar Andrés Rodríguez Maradiaga (Archbishop of Tegucigalpa).

Archbishop of Tegucigalpa: Cardinal Oscar Andrés Rodríguez Maradiaga, Arzobispado, 3a y 2a Avda 1113, Apdo 106, Tegucigalpa; tel. 237-0353; fax 222-2337; e-mail orodriguez@unicah.edu.

The Anglican Communion

Honduras comprises a single missionary diocese, in Province IX of the Episcopal Church in the USA.

Bishop of Honduras: Rt Rev. Lloyd Allen, Apdo 586, San Pedro Sula; tel. 556-6155; fax 556-6467; e-mail emmanuel@anglicano.hn.

The Baptist Church

Baptist Convention of Honduras: Apdo 2176, Tegucigalpa; tel. and fax 236-6717; e-mail conibah@sigmanet.hn; Pres. Pastor Alexis Salvador Vides; mems 21,355.

Other Churches

Iglesia Cristiana Luterana de Honduras (Christian Lutheran Church of Honduras): Apdo 2861, Tegucigalpa; tel. and fax 225-4464; fax 225-4893; e-mail iclh@123.hn; Pres. Rev. J. Guillermo Flores V.; 1,000 mems.

BAHÁ'Í FAITH

National Spiritual Assembly: Sendero de los Naranjos 2801, Col. Castaños, Apdo 273, Tegucigalpa; tel. 232-6124; fax 231-1343; e-mail bahaihon@bahaihon.org; internet www.bahaihon.org; 40,000 mems resident in more than 500 localities.

The Press

DAILIES

La Gaceta: Tegucigalpa; f. 1830; morning; official govt paper; Dir Marcial Lagos; circ. 3,000.

El Heraldo: Avda los Próceres, Frente Instituto del Tórax, Barrio San Felipe, Apdo 1938, Tegucigalpa; tel. 236-6000; internet www.elheraldo.hn; f. 1979; morning; independent; Dir José Francisco Morales Cálix; circ. 45,000.

El Nuevo Día: 3a Avda, 11–12 Calles, San Pedro Sula; tel. 52-4298; fax 57-9457; e-mail nuevodia@el-nuevodia.com; internet ea.el-nuevodia.com; f. 1994; morning; independent; Pres. Abraham Andonie; Editor Armando Cerrato; circ. 20,000.

El Periódico: Carretera al Batallón, Tegucigalpa; tel. 234-3086; fax 234-3090; f. 1993; morning; Pres. Emin Abufele; Editor Oscar Armando Martínez.

La Prensa: 3a Avda, 6a–7a Calles No 34, Apdo 143, San Pedro Sula; tel. 53-3101; fax 53-0778; e-mail correos@laprensa.com; internet www.laprensahn.com; f. 1964; morning; independent; Pres. Jorge Canahuati Larach; Exec. Dir Nelson Edgardo Fernández; circ. 50,000.

El Tiempo: 1a Calle, 5a Avda 102, Santa Anita, Apdo 450, San Pedro Sula; tel. 53-3388; fax 53-4590; e-mail tiempo@continental.hn; internet www.tiempo.hn; f. 1960; morning; left-of-centre; Pres. Jaime Rosenthal Oliva; Editor Manuel Gamero; circ. 35,000.

La Tribuna: Col. Santa Bárbara, Comayagüela, Apdo 1501, Tegucigalpa; tel. 233-1138; fax 233-1188; e-mail tribuna@david.intertel.hn; internet tribuna.icomstec.com; f. 1977; morning; independent; Dir Adán Elvir Flores; Pres. José Daniel Villeda; circ. 45,000.

PERIODICALS

Cambio Empresarial: Apdo 1111, Tegucigalpa; tel. 237-2853; fax 237-0480; monthly; economic, political, social; Editor Joaquín Medina Oviedo.

El Comercio: Cámara de Comercio e Industrias de Tegucigalpa, Blvd Centroamérica, Apdo 3444, Tegucigalpa; tel. 232-4200; fax 232-0759; f. 1970; monthly; commercial and industrial news; Dir-Gen. Lic. Héctor Manuel Ordóñez.

Extra: Tegucigalpa; tel. 237-2533; f. 1965; monthly; independent; current affairs; Editor Vicente Machado Valle.

Hablemos Claro: Edif. Torre Libertad, Blvd Suyapa, Tegucigalpa; tel. 232-8058; fax 239-7008; e-mail abrecha@hondutel.hn; internet www.hablemosclaro.com; f. 1990; weekly; Editor Rodrigo Wong Arévalo; circ. 9,000.

Hibueras: Apdo 955, Tegucigalpa; Dir Raúl Lanza Valeriano.

Honduras This Week: Centro Comercial Via Mare, Blvd Morazan, Apdo 1323, Tegucigalpa; tel. 232-8818; internet www.marrder.com;

f. 1988; weekly; English language; tourism, culture and the environment; Man. Editor ALEJANDRA PAREDES.

Pregonero Evangélico: Tegucigalpa; e-mail mcm@sdnhon.org.hn; internet www.mcmhn.org/pregonero; f. 2000; quarterly; Christian magazine.

PRESS ASSOCIATION

Asociación de Prensa Hondureña: Apdo 893, Tegucigalpa; tel. 378-107; fax 378-102; f. 1930; Pres. GUILLERMO PAGÁN SOLORZANO.

FOREIGN NEWS AGENCIES

Agencia EFE (Spain): Edif. Jiménez Castro, 5°, Of. 505, Tegucigalpa; tel. 22-0493; Bureau Chief ARMANDO ENRIQUE CERRATO CORTÉS.

Agenzia Nazionale Stampa Associata (ANSA) (Italy): Edif. JS, Cubículo 202, Blvd Tegucigalpa, Tegucigalpa; tel. 239-3943; Correspondent RAÚL MONCADA.

Deutsche Presse-Agentur (dpa) (Germany): Edif. Jiménez Castro, Of. 203, 4a Calle y 5a Avda, No 405, Apdo 3522, Tegucigalpa; tel. 237-8570; Correspondent WILFREDO GARCÍA CASTRO.

Inter Press Service (IPS) (Italy): Apdo 228, Tegucigalpa; tel. 232-5342; Correspondent JUAN RAMÓN DURÁN.

Publishers

Centro Editorial: San Pedro Sula; tel. and fax 558-1282; e-mail escoto@globalnet.hn; Dir JULIO ESCOTO.

Ediciones Ramses: Edif. Torres Fiallos, Avda Jerez, Apdo 5600, Tegucigalpa; tel. 220-4248; fax 220-0833; e-mail servicioalcliente@edicionesramses.hn; internet edicionesramses.galeon.com; educational material.

Editora Fuego Nuevo: Col. Florencia Sur, Blvd Suyapa, Tegucigalpa; tel. 232-4638; fax 232-4964; e-mail mirna_detorres@yahoo.com; Dir MYRNA LANZA GONZÁLEZ.

Editorial Pez Dulce: 143 Paseo La Leona, Barrio La Leona, Tegucigalpa; tel. and fax 222-1220; e-mail pezdulce@yahoo.com.

Guaymuras: Apdo 1843, Tegucigalpa; tel. 237-5433; fax 237-4931; e-mail ediguay@123.hn; f. 1980; Dir ISOLDA ARITA MELZER.

Universidad Nacional Autónoma de Honduras: Blvd Suyapa, Tegucigalpa; tel. 231-4601; fax 231-4601; f. 1847.

Broadcasting and Communications

TELECOMMUNICATIONS

Regulatory Authority

Comisión Nacional de Telecomunicaciones (Conatel): Col. Modelo, 6a Avda Suroeste, Apdo 15012, Tegucigalpa; tel. 234-8600; fax 234-8611; e-mail conatel@conatel.hn; internet www.conatel.hn; Pres. MARLON RAMSSÉS TÁBORA.

Major Service Providers

Empresa Hondureña de Telecomunicaciones (Hondutel): Apdo 1794, Tegucigalpa; tel. 221-6555; fax 236-7795; e-mail miguel.velez@hondutelnet.hn; internet www.hondutel.hn; scheduled for partial privatization by 2005; Gen. Man. ALONSO VALENZUELA.

Multifon: Tegucigalpa; f. 2003; subsidiary of MultiData; awarded govt contract with UT Starcom (q.v.) for fixed telephone lines in 2003; Pres. JOSÉ RAFAEL FERRARI.

UT Starcom (USA): Tegucigalpa; awarded govt contract with Multifon (q.v.) for fixed telephone lines in 2003; Pres. and CEO HONG LIANG LU; Vice-Pres. (Latin America) RENÉ MÉNDEZ.

BROADCASTING

Radio

Estereo McIntosh: La Ceiba, Atlantida; tel. 440-0326; fax 440-0325; e-mail McIntosh@psinet.hn; internet www.psinet.hn/mcintosh; commercial channel.

HRN, La Voz de Honduras: Blvd Suyapa, Apdo 642, Tegucigalpa; internet www.radiohrn.hn; commercial station; f. 1933; broadcasts 12 channels; 23 relay stations; Gen. Man. NOEMI VALLADARES.

Power FM: Tegucigalpa; tel. 552-4898; fax ; e-mail xavier@powerfm.hn; internet www.powerfm.hn; Gen. Man. XAVIER SIERRA.

Radio América: Col. Alameda, frente a la Droguería Mandofer, Apdo 259, Tegucigalpa; tel. 232-8338; fax 232-1009; internet www.hondutel.hn; commercial station; broadcasts Radio San Pedro, Radio Continental, Radio Monderna, Radio Universal, Cadena Radial Sonora, Super Cien Stereo, Momentos FM Stereo and 3 regional channels; f. 1948; 13 relay stations; Gen. Man. ARTURO VARELA.

Radio Club Honduras: Salida Chamelecon, Apdo 273, San Pedro Sula; tel. 556-6173; e-mail hr2rch@mayanet.hn; internet www.qsl.net/hr2rch; amateur radio club; Pres. NORMA LEIVA.

Radio Esperanza: La Esperanza, Intibucá; tel. 783-0025; fax 783-0644; e-mail radioesperanza1@hotmail.com; internet www.honducontact.com/Radio%20Esperanza.htm; Dir J. M. DEL CID.

Radio la Voz del Atlántico: 12 Calle, 2-3 Avda, Barrio Copen, Puerto Cortés; tel. 665-5166; fax 665-2401; e-mail atlantico@sescomnet.com; internet radioatlantico.8m.com.

Radio Nacional de Honduras: Avda La Paz, contiguo a la Secretaría de Cultura, Artes y Deportes, Tegucigalpa; tel. 236-7551; fax 236-7400; f. 1976; official station, operated by the Govt; Gen. Man. ROLANDO SARMIENTO.

La Voz de Centroamérica: 9a Calle, 10a Avda 64, Apdo 120, San Pedro Sula; tel. 52-7660; fax 57-3257; f. 1955; commercial station; Gen. Man. NOEMI SIKAFFY.

Television

Televicentro: Edif. Televicentro, Blvd Suyapa, Apdo 734, Tegucigalpa; e-mail mercadeoventas@televicentro.hn; internet www.televicentro.hn; f. 1987; 11 relay stations.

    Canal 5: tel. 232-7835; fax 232-0097; f. 1959; Gen. Man. JOSÉ RAFAEL FERRARI.

    Telecadena 7 y 4: tel. 239-2081; fax 232-0097; f. 1959; Pres. JOSÉ RAFAEL FERRARI; Gen. Man. RAFAEL ENRIQUE VILLEDA.

    Telesistema Hondureño, Canal 3 y 7: tel. 232-7064; fax 232-5019; f. 1967; Gen. Man. RAFAEL ENRIQUE VILLEDA.

VICA Television: 9a Calle, 10a Avda 64, Barrio Guamilito, Apdo 120, San Pedro Sula; tel. 552-4478; fax 557-3257; e-mail info@mayanet.hn; internet www.vicatv.hn; f. 1986; operates regional channels 2, 9 and 13; Pres. BLANCA SIKAFFY.

Finance

(cap. = capital; res = reserves; dep. = deposits; m. = million;
brs = branches; amounts in lempiras unless otherwise stated)

BANKING

Central Bank

Banco Central de Honduras (BANTRAL): Avda Juan Ramón Molina, 7a Avda y 1a Calle, Apdo 3165, Tegucigalpa; tel. 237-2270; fax 237-1876; e-mail eanariba@mail.bch.hn; internet www.bch.hn; f. 1950; bank of issue; cap. 218.9m., res 477.8m., dep. 22,679.5m. (Dec. 2002); Pres. MARÍA ELENA MONDRAGÓN; 4 brs.

Commercial Banks

Banco Atlántida, SA (BANCATLAN): Plaza Bancatlán, Blvd Centroamérica, Apdo 3164, Tegucigalpa; tel. 232-1050; fax 232-6120; e-mail webmaster@bancatlan.hn; internet www.bancatlan.hn; f. 1913; cap. 1,000m., res 344.6m., dep. 10,825.3m. (Dec. 2004); Exec. Pres. GUILLERMO BUESO; Exec. Vice-Pres GUSTAVO OVIEDO, ILDOIRA G. DE BONILLA; 17 brs.

Banco Continental, SA (BANCON): Edif. Continental, 3a Avda 7, entre 2a y 3a Calle, Apdo 390, San Pedro Sula; tel. 550-0880; fax 550-8580; e-mail pattyr@continental.hn; internet www.bancon.hn; f. 1974; cap. 250m., res 134.7m., dep. 1,081.0m. (Dec. 2002); Pres. JAIME ROSENTHAL OLIVA; 41 brs.

Banco de las Fuerzas Armadas, SA (BANFFAA): Centro Comercial Los Castaños, Blvd Morazán, Apdo 877, Tegucigalpa; tel. 232-4208; fax 239-4252; e-mail webmaster@banffaa.hn; internet www.banffaa.hn; f. 1979; cap. 10m., res 33.2m., dep. 428.1m. (Dec. 1992); Pres. LUIS ALFONSO DISCUA ELVIR; Gen. Man. CARLOS RIVERA XATRUCH; 38 brs.

Banco Grupo El Ahorro Hondureño (BGA): Intersección Blvd Suyapa y Blvd Juan Pablo Segundo, Apdo 344, Tegucigalpa; tel. 232-0909; fax 232-0743; e-mail bga@bancobga.com; internet www.bancobga.com; f. 2000; following a merger of Banco del Ahorro Hondureño and Banco La Capitalizadora Hondureña; cap. 704.1m., res 82.7m., dep. 8,077.8m. (Dec. 2003); 125 brs; Pres. ALBERTO VALLARINO CLÉMENT.

Banco de Honduras, SA: Blvd Suyapa, Col. Loma Linda Sur, Tegucigalpa; tel. 232-6122; fax 232-6167; e-mail patricia.ferro@citicorp.com; internet www.bancodehonduras.citibank.com; f. 1889; total assets 15,106m. (1999); Gen. Man. MAXIMO R. VIDAL; 2 brs.

Banco Mercantil, SA: Blvd Suyapa, frente a Emisoras Unidas, Apdo 116, Tegucigalpa; tel. 232-0006; fax 239-4509; internet www.bamernet.hn; Pres. JOSÉ LAMAS; Vice-Pres. MANUEL VILLEDA TOLEDO.

Banco de Occidente, SA (BANCOCCI): 6a Avda, Calle 2–3, Apdo 3284, Tegucigalpa; tel. 237-0310; fax 237-0486; e-mail bancocci@cybertelh.hn; f. 1951; cap. and res 69m., dep. 606m. (June 1994); Pres. and Gen. Man. JORGE BUESO ARIAS; Vice-Pres. EMILIO MEDINA R.; 146 brs.

Banco de los Trabajadores, SA (BANCOTRAB): 3a Avda, 13a Calle, Paseo El Obelisco, Comayagüela, Apdo 3246, Tegucigalpa; tel. 238-0136; fax 238-0077; e-mail marcio@btrab.com; f. 1967; cap. and res US $6.6m., dep. $43.1m. (Dec. 1992); Pres. ROLANDO DEL CID VELÁSQUEZ; 13 brs.

Development Banks

Banco Centroamericano de Integración Económica: Edif. Sede BCIE, Blvd Suyapa, Apdo 772, Tegucigalpa; tel. 228-2182; fax 228-2183; e-mail cmartine@bcie.hn; internet www.bcie.org; f. 1960 to finance the economic development of the Central American Common Market and its mem. countries; mems Costa Rica, El Salvador, Guatemala, Honduras, Nicaragua; cap. and res US $1,020.0m. (June 2003); Exec. Pres. HARRY BRAUTIGAN.

Banco Financiera Centroamericana, SA (FICENSA): Edif. La Interamericana, Blvd Morazán, Apdo 1432, Tegucigalpa; tel. 238-1661; fax 238-1630; e-mail rrivera@ficensa.com; internet www.ficensa.com; f. 1974; private org. providing finance for industry, commerce and transport; Pres. OSWALDO LÓPEZ ARELLANO; Gen. Man. ROQUE RIVERA RIBAS.

Banco Hondureño del Café, SA (BANHCAFE): Calle República de Costa Rica, Blvd Juan Pablo II, Col. Lomas del Mayab, Apdo 583, Tegucigalpa; tel. 232-8370; fax 232-8782; e-mail bcaferhu@hondutel.hn; f. 1981 to help finance coffee production; owned principally by private coffee producers; cap. 119.2m., res 77.6m., dep. 1,379.9m. (Dec. 2002); Pres. MIGUEL ALFONSO FERNÁNDEZ RÁPALO; Gen. Man. RENÉ ARDÓN MATUTE; 50 brs.

Banco Municipal Autónomo (BANMA): 6a Avda, 6a Calle, Tegucigalpa; tel. 237-8503; fax 237-6946; e-mail bancomunicipal@tutopia.com; f. 1963; Pres. JUSTO PASTOR CALDERÓN; 2 brs.

Banco Nacional de Desarrollo Agrícola (BANADESA): 4a Avda y 5a Avda, 13a y 14a Calles, Barrio Concepción, Apdo 212, Tegucigalpa; tel. 237-2201; fax 237-5187; e-mail info@banadesa.hn; f. 1980; govt development bank (transfer to private ownership pending); loans to agricultural sector; cap. 34.5m., res 42.7m., dep. 126.9m. (March 1993); Gen. Man. ENRIQUE ALBERTO CASTELLON; 35 brs.

Financiera Nacional de la Vivienda (FINAVI): Apdo 1194, Tegucigalpa; f. 1975; housing development bank; Exec. Pres. Lic. ELMAR LIZARDO.

Banking Associations

Asociación Hondureña de Instituciones Bancarias (AHIBA): Edif. AHIBA, Blvd Suyapa, Apdo 1344, Tegucigalpa; tel. 235-6770; fax 239-0191; e-mail ahiba@ahiba.hn; f. 1957; 21 mem. banks; Exec. Dir. MARÍA LYDIA SOLANO.

Comisión Nacional de Bancos y Seguros (CNBS): Calle 6 y 7, Avda Juan Ramón Molina, Tegucigalpa; tel. 238-0580; fax 237-6232; internet www.cnbs.gov.hn; Pres. ANA CRISTINA MEJÍA DE PEREIRA.

STOCK EXCHANGE

Bolsa Hondureña de Valores: Edif. Martínez Valenzuela, 1°, 2a Calle, 3a Avda, Apdo 161, San Pedro Sula; tel. 553-4410; fax 553-4480; e-mail bhvsps@bhv.hn; internet www.bhv.hn; Pres. JOSÉ RUBÉN MENDOZA.

INSURANCE

American Home Assurance Co: Edif. Los Castaños, 4°, Blvd Morazán, Apdo 3220, Tegucigalpa; tel. 232-3938; fax 232-8169; f. 1958; Mans LEONARDO MOREIRA, EDGAR WAGNER.

Aseguradora Hondureña, SA: Edif. El Planetario, 4°, Col. Lomas de Guijarro Sur, Calle Madrid, Avda Paris, Apdo 312, Tegucigalpa; tel. 232-2729; fax 231-0982; e-mail gerencia@asegurahon.hn; internet www.laaseguradora.com.hn; f. 1954; Pres. GERARDO CORRALES.

Compañía de Seguros El Ahorro Hondureño, SA: Edif. Trinidad, Avda Colón, Apdo 3643, Tegucigalpa; tel. 237-8219; fax 237-4780; e-mail pbetanco@eahsa.hn; internet www.seguroselahorro.hn; f. 1917; Pres. DORIS PATRICIA HERNÁNDEZ VALERIANO.

Interamericana de Seguros, SA: Col. Los Castaños, Apdo 593, Tegucigalpa; tel. 232-7614; fax 232-7762; internet www.ficohsa.hn; f. 1957; Part of Grupo Financiero Ficohsa; Pres. LEONEL GIANNINI.

Pan American Life Insurance Co (PALIC): Edif. PALIC, Avda República de Chile 804, Tegucigalpa; tel. 220-5757; fax 232-3907; e-mail palic@david.intertel.hn; f. 1944; Gen. Man. ALBERTO AGURCIA.

Previsión y Seguros, SA: Edif.Grupo Financiero IPM, 4°, Blvd Centroamérica, Apdo 770, Tegucigalpa; tel. 232-4119; fax 232-4113; internet www.previsahn.com; f. 1982; Gen. Man. GERARDO A. RIVERA.

Seguros Atlántida: Edif. Sonisa, Costado Este Plaza Bancatlán, Tegucigalpa; tel. 232-4014; fax 232-3688; e-mail info@seatlan.comn; internet www.seatlan.com; f. 1986; Pres. GUILLERMO BUESO; Gen. Man. JUAN MIGUEL ORELLANA.

Seguros Continental, SA: Edif. Continental, 4°, 3a Avda SO, 2a y 3a Calle, Apdo 320, San Pedro Sula; tel. 550-0880; fax 550-2750; e-mail seguros@continental.hn; f. 1968; Pres. JAIME ROSENTHAL OLIVA; Gen. Man. MARIO R. SOLÍS.

Seguros Crefisa: Edif. Ficensa, 1°, Blvd Morazán, Apdo 3774, Tegucigalpa; tel. 238-1750; fax 238-1714; e-mail gerencia@crefisa.hn; internet www.crefisa.hn; f. 1993; Pres. OSWALDO LÓPEZ ARELLANO; Gen. Man. MARIO BATRES PIÑEDA.

Insurance Association

Cámara Hondureña de Aseguradores (CAHDA): Edif. Casa Real, 3°, Col. San Carlos, Tegucigalpa; tel. 221-5354; fax 221-5356; e-mail cahda@gbm.hn; internet www.cahda.org; f. 1974; Man. JOSÉ LUIS MONCADA RODRÍGUEZ.

Trade and Industry

GOVERNMENT AGENCIES

Fondo Hondureño de Inversión Social (FHIS): Antiguo Edif. I.P.M., Col. Godoy, Comayagüela, Apdo 3581, Tegucigalpa; e-mail dir.ejectutiva@fhis.hn; internet www.fhis.hn; tel. 234-5231; fax 534-5255; social investment fund; Dir LEONI YUWAI.

Fondo Social de la Vivienda (FOSOVI): Col. Florencia, Tegucigalpa; tel. 239-1605; social fund for housing, urbanization and devt; Gen. Man. MARIO MARTÍ.

Secretaria Técnica del Consejo Superior de Planificación Económica (CONSUPLANE): Edif. Bancatlán, 3°, Apdo 1327, Comayagüela, Tegucigalpa; tel. 22-8738; f. 1965; national planning office; Exec. Sec. FRANCISCO FIGUEROA ZÚNIGA.

DEVELOPMENT ORGANIZATIONS

Consejo Hondureño de la Empresa Privada (COHEP): Edif. 8, Calle Yoro, Col. Tepeyac, Apdo 3240, Tegucigalpa; tel. 235-3336; fax 235-3345; e-mail consejo@cohep.com; internet www.cohep.com; f. 1968; represents 52 private sector trade associations; Pres. JOSÉ MARÍA AGURCIA.

Corporación Financiera de Olancho: f. 1977 to co-ordinate and manage all financial aspects of the Olancho forests project; Pres. RAFAEL CALDERÓN LÓPEZ.

Corporación Hondureña de Desarrollo Forestal (COHDEFOR): Salida Carretera del Norte, Zona El Carrizal, Comayagüela, Apdo 1378, Tegucigalpa; tel. 22-8810; fax 22-2653; f. 1974; control and man. of the forestry industry; Gen. Man. PORFIRIO LOBO S.

Dirección General de Minas e Hidrocarburos (General Directorate of Mines and Hydrocarbons): Blvd Miraflores, Apdo 981, Tegucigalpa; tel. 232-7848; fax 232-7848; Dir-Gen. MIGUEL VILLEDA VILLELA.

Instituto Hondureño del Café (IHCAFE): Apdo 40-C, Tegucigalpa; tel. 237-3131; f. 1970; coffee devt programme; Gen. Man. FERNANDO D. MONTES M.

Instituto Hondureño de Mercadeo Agrícola (IHMA): Apdo 727, Tegucigalpa; tel. 235-3193; fax 235-5719; f. 1978; agricultural devt agency; Gen. Man. TULIO ROLANDO GIRÓN ROMERO.

Instituto Nacional Agrario (INA): Col. La Almeda, 4a Avda, entre 10a y 11a Calles, No 1009, Apdo 3391, Tegucigalpa; tel. 232-8400; fax 232-8398; agricultural devt programmes; Exec. Dir ERASMO PORTILLO FERNÁNDEZ.

CHAMBERS OF COMMERCE

Cámara de Comercio e Industrias de Copán: Edif. Comercial Romero, 2°, Barrio Mercedes, Santa Rosa de Copán; tel. 662-0843;

fax 662-1783; e-mail info@camaracopan.com; internet www .camaracopan.com; f. 1940; Pres. EUDOCIO LEIVA AMAYA.

Cámara de Comercio e Industrias de Cortés (CCIC): Col. Trejo, 17a Avda, 10a Calle, Apdo 14, San Pedro Sula; tel. 53-0761; fax 553-3777; e-mail ccic@ccichonduras.org; internet www.ccichonduras.org; f. 1931; 812 mems; Pres. OSCAR GALEANO; Dir RAÚL REINA.

Cámara de Comercio e Industrias de Tegucigalpa: Blvd Centroamérica, Apdo 3444, Tegucigalpa; tel. 232-4200; fax 232-0159; e-mail ccit@ccit.hn; internet www.ccit.hn; Pres. AMÍLCAR BULNES.

Federación de Cámaras de Comercio e Industrias de Honduras (FEDECAMARA): Edif. Castañito, 2°, 6a Avda, Col. los Castaños, Apdo 3393, Tegucigalpa; tel. 232-1870; fax 232-6083; e-mail fedecamara@sigmanet.hn; f. 1948; 1,200 mems; Pres. JOSÉ NOLASCO; Exec. Dir JUAN MANUEL MOYA.

Fundación para la Inversión y Desarrollo de Exportaciones (FIDE) (Foundation for Investment and Export Development): Col. La Estancia, Plaza Marte, final del Blvd. Morazán, POB 2029, Tegucigalpa; tel. 221-6303; fax 221-6318; internet www .hondurasinfo.hn/eng/fide/fide.asp; f. 1984; private, non-profit agency; Pres. VILMA SIERRA DE FONSECA.

Honduran American Chamber of Commerce (Amcham Honduras): Commercial Area Hotel Honduras Maya, POB 1838, Tegucigalpa; tel. 232-6035; fax 232-2031; e-mail amcham1@ quikhonduras.com; internet www.amchamhonduras.org; f. 1981; Pres. OSCAR CACERES.

INDUSTRIAL AND TRADE ASSOCIATIONS

Consejo Hondureño de la Empresa Privada (COHEP): Edif. 8, Col. Tepeyac, Calle Yoro, Apdo 3240, Tegucigalpa; tel. 235-3336; fax 235-3345; e-mail consejo@cohep.com; internet www.cohep.com; f. 1968; umbrella org. representing 54 industrial and trade asscns; Pres. JOSÉ MARÍA AGURCIA.

Asociación Hondureña de Productores de Café (AHPROCAFE) (Coffee Producers' Association): Edif. AHPROCAFE, Avda La Paz, Apdo 959, Tegucigalpa; tel. 236-8286; fax 236-8310; e-mail ahprocafe@multivision.hn; Pres. FREDY ESPINOZA MONDRADON; Gen. Man. PEDRO MENDOZA FLORES.

Asociación Nacional de Acuicultores de Honduras (National Fish Farmers' Association of Honduras): Pasaje Sarita Rubinstein 11, 2°, Apdo 229, Choluteca; tel. 882-0986; fax 882-3848; e-mail andahn@hondutel.hn; f. 1986; 136 mems; Pres. ISMAEL WONG; Exec. Dir FRANCISCO AVALOS.

Asociación Nacional de Exportadores de Honduras (ANEXHON) (National Association of Exporters): Local de la C.C.I.C, Tegucigalpa; tel. 553-3029; fax 557-0203; e-mail Roberto@ itsa.com; comprises 104 private enterprises; Pres. ROBERTO PANAYOTTI.

Asociación Nacional de Industriales (ANDI) (National Association of Manufacturers): Edif. Fundación Covelo, 3°, Col. Castaño Sur, Blvd Morazán, Apdo 3447, Tegucigalpa; tel. 232-2221; fax 221-5199; e-mail andi@andi.hn; internet www.andi.hn; Pres. ADOLFO FACUSSÉ; Exec. Sec. GRACO PAREDES HERRERA.

Federación Nacional de Agricultores y Ganaderos de Honduras (FENAGH) (Farmers and Livestock Breeders' Association): Apdo 3209, Tegucigalpa; tel. 239-1303; fax 231-1392; Pres. ROBERTO GALLARDO LARDIZÁBAL.

UTILITIES

Electricity

AES Honduras: Tegucigalpa; subsidiary of AES Corpn (USA); CEO CARLOS LARACH.

Empresa Nacional de Energía Eléctrica (ENEE) (National Electrical Energy Co): Edif. Autobanco Atlántida, 5°, Calle Real Comayagüela, Apdo 99, Tegucigalpa; tel. 238-5977; fax 237-9881; e-mail dirplan@enee.hn; internet www.enee.hn; f. 1957; state-owned electricity co; scheduled for privatization; Pres. GILBERTO RAMOS DUBÓN; Man. ANGELO BOTAZZI.

Luz y Fuerza de San Lorenzo, SA (LUFUSA).

TRADE UNIONS

Central General de Trabajadores de Honduras (CGTH) (General Confederation of Labour of Honduras): Barrio La Granja, antiguo Local CONADI, Comayagüela, Apdo 1236, Tegucigalpa; tel. 225-2509; fax 225-2525; e-mail cgt@david.intertel.hn; f. 1970; legally recognized from 1982; attached to Partido Demócrata Cristiano; Sec.-Gen. DANIEL A. DURÓN.

Federación Auténtica Sindical de Honduras (FASH): Barrio La Granja, antiguo Local CONADI, Comayagüela,

Tegucigalpa; tel. 225-2509; affiliated to CGTH, CCT, CLAT, CMT; Sec.-Gen. JOSÉ HUMBERTO LARA ENAMORANDO.

Federación Sindical del Sur (FESISUR): Barrio La Ceiba, 1 c. al norte del Instituto Santa María Goretti, Apdo 256, Choluteca; tel. 882-0328; affiliated to CGT, CLAT, CMT; Pres. REINA DE ORDÓÑEZ.

Unión Nacional de Campesinos (UNC) (National Union of Farmworkers): antiguo Local CONADI, Barrio La Granja, Comayagüela, Tegucigalpa; tel. 225-1005; linked to CLAT; Sec.-Gen. VÍCTOR MANUEL CAMPO.

Confederación Hondureña de Cooperativas (CHC): 3001 Blvd Morazán, Edif. I.F.C., Apdo 3265, Tegucigalpa; tel. 232-2890; fax 231-1024; Pres. JOSÉ R. MORENO PAZ.

Confederación de Trabajadores de Honduras (CTH) (Workers' Confederation of Honduras): Edif. Beige, 2°, Avda Juan Ramón Molina, Barrio El Olvido, Apdo 720, Tegucigalpa; tel. 238-7859; fax 237-8575; e-mail dinoraaceituno@yahoo.com; f. 1964; affiliated to CTCA, ORIT, CIOSL, FIAET and ICFTU; Pres. WILFREDO GALEAS ANGEL MEZA; Sec.-Gen. REINA DINORA ACEITUNO; 200,000 mems; comprises the following federations:

Asociación Nacional de Campesinos Hondureños (ANACH) (National Association of Honduran Farmworkers): Edif. Chávez Mejía, 2°, Calle Juan Ramón Molina, Barrio El Olvido Tegucigalpa; tel. 238-0558; f. 1962; affiliated to CTH, ORIT, CIOSL; Pres. BENEDICTO CÁRCAMO MEJÍA; 80,000 mems.

Federación Central de Sindicatos de Trabajadores Libres de Honduras (FECESITLIH) (Honduran Federation of Free Trade Unions): antiguo Edif. EUKZKADI, 3a Avda 3 y 4, Calles 336, Comayagüela, Tegucigalpa; tel. 237-3955; affiliated to CTH, ORIT, CIOSL; Pres. ROSA ALTAGRACIA FUENTES.

Federación Sindical de Trabajadores Nacionales de Honduras (FESITRANH) (Honduran Federation of Farmworkers): 10a Avda, 11a Calle, Barrio Los Andes, San Pedro Sula, Apdo 245, Cortés; tel. 57-2539; f. 1957; affiliated to CTH; Pres. MAURO FRANCISCO GONZÁLES.

Sindicato Nacional de Motoristas de Equipo Pesado de Honduras (SINAMEQUIPH) (National Union of HGV Drivers): Avda Juan Ramón Molina, Barrio El Olvido, Tegucigalpa; tel. 237-4415; affiliated to CTH, IFF; Pres. ERASMO FLORES.

Confederación Unitaria de Trabajadores de Honduras (CUTH): Barrio Bella Vista, 10 Calle, 8 y 9 Avda, Casa 829, Tegucigalpa; tel. and fax 220-4732; f. 1992; Dir JOSÉ LUIS BAQUEDANO.

Asociación Nacional de Empleados Públicos de Honduras (ANDEPH) (National Association of Public Employees of Honduras): Barrio Los Dolores, Avda Paulino Valladares, frente Panadería Italiana, atrás Iglesia Los Dolores, Tegucigalpa; tel. 237-4393; Pres. FAUSTO MOLINA CASTRO.

Federación Unitaria de Trabajadores de Honduras (FUTH): Barrio La Granja, contiguo Banco Atlántida, Casa 3047, frente a mercadito la granja, Apdo 1663, Comayagüela, Tegucigalpa; tel. 225-1010; f. 1981; linked to left-wing electoral alliance Frente Patriótico Hondureño; Pres. JUAN ALBERTO BARAHONA MEJÍA; 45,000 mems.

Federación de Cooperativas de la Reforma Agraria de Honduras (FECORAH): Casa 2223, antiguo Local de COAPALMA, Col. Rubén Darío, Tegucigalpa; tel. 232-0547; fax 225-2525; f. 1970; legally recognized from 1974; Pres. Ing. WILTON SALINAS.

Transport

RAILWAYS

The railway network is confined to the north of the country and most lines are used for fruit cargo. There are 595 km of railway track in Honduras, of which 349 km are narrow guage.

Ferrocarril Nacional de Honduras (National Railway of Honduras): 1a Avda entre 1a y 2a Calle, Apdo 496, San Pedro Sula; tel. and fax 552-8001; f. 1870; govt-owned; Gen. Man. M. A. QUINTANILLA.

Tela Railroad Co: La Lima; tel. 56-2037; Pres. RONALD F. WALKER; Gen. Man. FREDDY KOCH.

Vaccaro Railway: La Ceiba; tel. 43-0511; fax 43-0091; fmrly operated by Standard Fruit Co.

ROADS

In 2002 there were an estimated 13,686 km of roads in Honduras, of which 2,8454 km were paved. A further 3,156 km of roads have been constructed by the Fondo Cafetero Nacional and some routes have been built by COHDEFOR in order to facilitate access to coffee plantations and forestry development areas. In November 2000 the

World Bank approved a US $66.5m. loan to repair roads and bridges damaged or destroyed by 'Hurricane Mitch' in 1998. In March 2003 the Central American Bank for Economic Integration approved funding, worth $22.5m., for the construction of a highway from Puerto Cortés to the Guatemalan border.

Dirección General de Caminos: Barrio La Bolsa, Comayagüela, Tegucigalpa; tel. 225-1703; fax 225-0194; e-mail miayapew@mailcity .com; f. 1915; highways board; Dir MARCIO ALVARADO ENAMORADO.

SHIPPING

The principal port is Puerto Cortés on the Caribbean coast, which is the largest and best-equipped port in Central America. Other ports include Tela, La Ceiba, Trujillo/Castilla, Roatán, Amapala and San Lorenzo; all are operated by the Empresa Nacional Portuaria. There are several minor shipping companies. A number of foreign shipping lines call at Honduran ports.

Empresa Nacional Portuaria (National Port Authority): Apdo 18, Puerto Cortés; tel. 55-0192; fax 55-0968; e-mail gerencia@enp.hn; internet www.enp.hn; f. 1965; has jurisdiction over all ports in Honduras; a network of paved roads connects Puerto Cortés and San Lorenzo with the main cities of Honduras, and with the principal cities of Central America; Gen. Man. ROBERTO VALENZUELA SIMÓN.

CIVIL AVIATION

Local airlines in Honduras compensate for the deficiencies of road and rail transport, linking together small towns and inaccessible districts. There are four international airports: Golosón airport in La Ceiba, Ramón Villeda Morales airport in San Pedro Sula, Toncontín airport in Tegucigalpa and Juan Manuel Gálvaz airport in Roatán. In 2001 it was announced that San Francisco Airport, USA, was to invest some US $150m. in the four airports over two years. In 2000 plans for a new airport inside the Copán Ruinas archaeological park, 400 km west of Tegucigalpa, were announced.

Isleña Airlines: Avda San Isidro, frente al Parque Central, Barrio El Iman, Apdo 402, La Ceiba; tel. 440-0505; fax 43-2632; e-mail islena@caribe.hn; internet www.caribe.hn; domestic service and service to Guatemala, Nicaragua and the Cayman Islands; Pres. and CEO ARTURO ALVARADO WOOD.

Líneas Aéreas Nacionales, SA (LANSA): La Ceiba; f. 2001; scheduled international services and flights within Central America.

Sol Air: Edif. Corporativo, Hotel Real Clarion, Col. Alameda, 1521 Avda Juan Manuel Gálvez, Apdo 1861, Tegucigalpa; tel. 235-3737; fax 232-5005; internet www.solair.net; f. 2002; alliance between Aero Honduras, Falcon Air Express and Pegasus; flights to Managua, Nicaragua, Dallas, TX, and Miami, FL, USA.

Tourism

Tourists are attracted by the Mayan ruins, the fishing and boating facilities in Trujillo Bay and Lake Yojoa, near San Pedro Sula, and the beaches on the northern coast. There is an increasing eco-tourism industry. In May 2001 the tomb of a Mayan king was discovered near to the Copán Ruinas archaeological park; it was expected to become an important tourist attraction. Honduras received around 549,500 tourists in 2002, when tourism receipts totalled US $342m.

Instituto Hondureño de Turismo: Edif. Europa, 5°, Col. San Carlos, Apdo 3261, Tegucigalpa; tel. and fax 222-2124; e-mail tourisminfo@iht.hn; internet www.letsgohonduras.com; f. 1972; dept of the Secretaría de Cultura y Turismo; Dir-Gen. THIERRY DE PIERREFEU.

Asociación Hotelera y Afines de Honduras (AHAH): Hotel Escuela Madrid, Suite 402, Col. 21 de Octubre-Los Girasoles, Tegucigalpa; tel. 221-5805; fax 221-4789; e-mail ahah@123.hn.

Asociación Nacional de Agencias de Viajes y Turismo de Honduras: Blvd Morazán, frente a McDonald's, Tegucigalpa; tel. 236-9455; e-mail travelex@multivisiohn.net.

Asociación de Tour Operadores de Honduras: Barrio Río El Centro, Copán Ruinas, Copán; tel. 651-4453; fax 651-4297; e-mail mctours@mctours-honduras.com; Pres. JUAN ANGEL WELCHEZ.

HUNGARY

Introductory Survey

Location, Climate, Language, Religion, Flag, Capital

The Republic of Hungary lies in central-eastern Europe, bounded to the north by Slovakia, to the east by Ukraine and Romania, to the south by the Serbian province of Vojvodina (Serbia and Montenegro) and Croatia, and to the west by Slovenia and Austria. Its climate is continental, with long, dry summers and severe winters. Temperatures in Budapest are generally between –3°C (27°F) and 28°C (82°F). The language is Hungarian (Magyar). There is a large Romany community (numbering between 500,000 and 700,000 people), and also Croat, German, Romanian, Serb, Slovak, Slovene and Jewish minorities. Most of the inhabitants profess Christianity, and the largest single religious denomination is the Roman Catholic Church, representing about 62% of the population. Other Christian groups are the Calvinists (20%), the Lutheran Church (5%) and the Hungarian Orthodox Church. The national flag (proportions 2 by 3) consists of three equal horizontal stripes, of red, white and green. The capital is Budapest.

Recent History

Although Hungary co-operated with Nazi Germany before the Second World War and obtained additional territory when Czechoslovakia was partitioned in 1938 and 1939, when it sought to break the alliance in 1944 the country was occupied by German forces. In January 1945 Hungary was liberated by Soviet troops and signed an armistice, restoring the pre-1938 frontiers. It became a republic in February 1946. Nationalization measures began in December, despite opposition from the Roman Catholic Church. In the 1947 elections the communists became the largest single party, with 22.7% of the votes. The communists merged with the Social Democrats to form the Hungarian Workers' Party in June 1948. A People's Republic was established in August 1949.

As First Secretary of the Workers' Party, Mátyás Rákosi became the leading political figure, and opposition was removed by means of purges and political trials. Rákosi became Prime Minister in 1952, but after the death of the Soviet leader Stalin (Iosif V. Dzhugashvili) one year later, he was replaced by the more moderate Imre Nagy, and a short period of liberalization followed. Rákosi, however, remained as First Secretary, and in 1955 forced Nagy's resignation. András Hegedüs, sponsored by Rákosi, was appointed Prime Minister. Dissension between the Rákosi and Nagy factions increased in 1956; in July Rákosi was forced to resign but was replaced by a close associate, Ernő Gerő. The consequent discontent provoked demonstrations against communist domination, and in October fighting broke out. Nagy was reinstated as Prime Minister, renounced membership of the Warsaw Pact (the defence grouping of the Soviet bloc) and promised other controversial reforms. In November Soviet troops, stationed in Hungary under the 1947 peace treaty, intervened, and the uprising was suppressed. A new Soviet-supported Government, led by János Kádár, was installed. Some 20,000 participants in the uprising were arrested, of whom 2,000 were subsequently executed, including Nagy and four associates. Many opponents of the regime were deported to the USSR. Kádár, who was appointed the leader of the renamed Hungarian Socialist Workers' Party (HSWP), held the premiership until January 1958, and from September 1961 to July 1965.

In March 1985 Kádár was re-elected as leader of the party, with the new title of General Secretary of the Central Committee. The legislative elections in June 1985 were the first to give voters a wider choice of candidates under the system of mandatory multiple nominations. In May 1988 Kádár was replaced as General Secretary of the Central Committee by Károly Grósz (Chairman of the Council of Ministers since June 1987), and promoted to the new and purely ceremonial post of HSWP President; he lost his membership of the Politburo (Political Bureau). About one-third of the members of the Central Committee were replaced by younger politicians. The new Politburo included Rezső Nyers, who had been largely responsible for economic reforms, initiated in 1968 (and ongoing in the 1980s), but who had been demoted in 1975. Grósz declared his commitment to radical economic and political change, although he excluded the immediate possibility of a multi-party political system. In June 1988 Dr Brunó Ferenc Straub, who was not a member of the HSWP, was elected to the post of largely ceremonial post of President of the Presidential Council. In November Miklós Németh, a prominent member of the HSWP, replaced Grósz as Chairman of the Council of Ministers.

Following Grósz's appointment as leader of the HSWP, there was a relaxation of censorship laws and independent political groups were formally established. In January 1989 the right to strike was fully legalized. In the same month Az ország háza (The National Assembly—legislature) enacted legislation guaranteeing the right to demonstrate and to form associations and political parties independent of the HSWP. In February the HSWP agreed to abandon the constitutional clause upholding the party's leading role in society. In March an estimated 100,000 people took part in a peaceful anti-Government demonstration in Budapest, in support of demands for democracy, free elections, the withdrawal of Soviet troops and an official commemoration of the 1956 uprising and of the execution of Imre Nagy in 1958.

During 1989 there was increasing evidence of dissension within the HSWP between conservative and reformist members. (At least 100,000 members had tendered their resignations between late 1987 and early 1989.) In April the Politburo was replaced by a smaller body. In May the Council of Ministers declared its independence from the HSWP; Kádár was removed from the presidency and the Central Committee of the party, officially for health reasons. In June a radical restructuring of the HSWP was effected, following increasing dissatisfaction among members with Grósz's leadership: although Grósz remained as General Secretary of the party, the newly elected Chairman, Nyers, effectively emerged as the party's leading figure. Evidence of the opposition's increasing strength was provided at a provincial by-election in July 1989, when a joint candidate of the centre-right Hungarian Democratic Forum (HDF), the liberal Alliance of Free Democrats (AFD) and the Federation of Young Democrats (FYD) became the first opposition deputy since 1947 to win representation in the legislature. Four of five further by-elections were won by opposition candidates in July–September. At an HSWP Congress in October, delegates voted to reconstitute the party as the Hungarian Socialist Party (HSP), with Nyers as Chairman. The HSP initially failed to attract a large membership, however, and in December HSWP activists declared that their party had not been dissolved, and elected a new leader.

On 23 October 1989 (the anniversary of the 1956 uprising) the Republic of Hungary was proclaimed. In preparation, Az ország háza approved fundamental amendments to the Constitution, including the removal of the clause guaranteeing one-party rule. A new electoral law was approved, and the Presidential Council was replaced by the post of President of the Republic. Mátyás Szűrös, the President (Speaker) of Az ország háza, was named President of the Republic, on an interim basis.

Hungary's first free multi-party elections since 1945 were held, in two rounds, on 25 March and 8 April 1990. The elections were held under a mixed system of proportional and direct representation and were contested by a total of 28 parties and groups. The HDF received the largest proportion of the total votes cast (42.7%) and 165 of the 386 seats in Az ország háza. The AFD obtained the second largest proportion of the votes (23.8%), winning 92 legislative seats. The Independent Smallholders' Party (ISP, which advocated the restoration to its original owners of land collectivized after 1947) and the Christian Democratic People's Party (CDPP), both of which contested the second round of polling in alliance with the HDF, secured 43 and 21 seats, respectively. The HSP secured 33 seats, while the FYD (which was closely aligned with the AFD) obtained 21 seats. The HSWP failed to secure the 4% of the votes required for representation.

A coalition Government was formed in May 1990, comprising members of the HDF (which held the majority of posts), the ISP, the CDPP and three independents. József Antall, the Chairman of the HDF, had earlier been elected to chair the new Council of

Ministers. Among the declared aims of the new Government was membership of the European Community (now European Union—EU, see p. 217) and a full transition to a Western-style market economy. In the same month Gyula Horn, the Minister of Foreign Affairs in the outgoing Government, replaced Nyers as leader of the HSP. In August Árpád Göncz, a writer and member of the AFD, was elected President of the Republic by the legislature. At municipal and local elections in September and October a coalition of the AFD and the FYD won control of Budapest and many other cities, while in rural areas independent candidates obtained a majority of the votes. The governing coalition's poor result was attributed, in large part, to its failure to redress the recent sharp increase in the rates of inflation and unemployment.

In May 1991 Az ország háza approved legislation to provide compensation for persons killed, imprisoned or deported, or whose property had been expropriated for political reasons during 1939–89. Further legislation was approved in early 1993 allowing for prosecutions in connection with crimes committed under the communist regime.

In February 1992 the Chairman of the ISP, József Torgyán, announced that his party was to withdraw from the Government, in protest at what he claimed to be a lack of political influence. However, most of the ISP's legislative deputies refused to withdraw their support for the Government, thus causing a rift in the party. In April as many as 20,000 people were reported to have attended an anti-Government demonstration organized by Torgyán in Budapest. The split in the party was formalized in June, when members who remained loyal to the Government formed what subsequently became the United Historic Smallholders' Party; the ISP subsequently renamed itself the Independent Smallholders' and Peasants' Party (ISPP).

In September 1992 some 50,000 people demonstrated in Budapest against extreme right-wing figures within the HDF, including the Vice-Chairman of the party, István Csurka. At an HDF congress in January 1993 Antall avoided a threatened revolt by accepting the election of six right-wing extremists to the party's presidium. In May Lajos Für resigned as Secretary-General of the HDF, claiming that he had not been able to maintain the unity of the party, which was divided between supporters of Csurka and centrists led by Antall. In July, however, Csurka was expelled from the HDF for his increasingly unacceptable views. (He subsequently founded the Hungarian Justice and Life Party—HJLP.) Antall died in December. He was succeeded as Prime Minister by Dr Péter Boross, an independent and hitherto the Minister of the Interior, who had acted as premier while Antall was receiving medical treatment. In February 1994 Für was elected Chairman of the HDF.

Elections to Az ország háza, held on 8 and 29 May 1994, resulted in a clear parliamentary majority for the HSP, which received 33.0% of the votes cast for regional party lists and won 209 of the 386 legislative seats. The AFD won 19.8% of the votes and 70 seats, while the HDF won only 11.7% of the votes and 37 seats. The ISPP, the CDPP and the FYD won, respectively, 26, 22 and 20 seats. Csurka's HJLP attracted only 1.6% of the votes in the first round and did not proceed to the second. Horn announced that the HSP would be willing to form a government with the AFD, and the two parties signed a coalition agreement in late June. With 279 legislative seats, the coalition held the two-thirds' majority necessary to institute constitutional reforms. Horn was invested as Prime Minister in July.

Meanwhile, controversy over alleged government interference in branches of the mass media had arisen in mid-1992. During 1992–93 many senior media figures had resigned or been dismissed, and in October 1993 some 10,000 people had demonstrated in Budapest to demand press freedom. In June 1994 129 Hungarian Radio employees, who had been dismissed in March, were reinstated; their dismissal had prompted further mass demonstrations and widespread accusations that the Government sought to use the state radio service for propaganda purposes, since many of those dismissed were known for their anti-Government views. In July the directors of Hungarian Radio and Hungarian Television were dismissed, having been accused of favouring the former HDF administration. In October the Constitutional Court declared government interference in the media to be unlawful.

In January 1995 László Bekesi, the Minister of Finance, resigned, following disagreements with Horn regarding economic reform; he was replaced in the following month by Lajos Bokros. A new president of the central bank was also appointed.

Economic austerity measures, adopted in March, prompted strong domestic criticism, and the ministers responsible for public health and for national security resigned shortly afterwards. In May Az ország háza approved legislation that was designed to accelerate the privatization process. On 19 June Göncz was re-elected President of the Republic by Az ország háza. At the end of the month the Constitutional Court ruled that elements of the austerity programme (specifically those relating to welfare provisions) were unconstitutional. Accordingly, in late July Az ország háza approved adjustments, including increases in fuel prices and reductions in government expenditure, in an attempt to mitigate losses arising from the judgment. The economic programme continued to cause dissent within the Government, and the Minister of Labour tendered her resignation in October. Bokros resigned in mid-February 1996, and a banker, Péter Medgyessy, was appointed as the new Minister of Finance. (Notably, all those ministers that had resigned from the Government during the previous year had been members of the HSP.) Divisions within the HDF were reported in early March 1996, following the election of Sándor Lezsák to the party leadership. Denouncing what it regarded as an increasingly nationalistic tendency in the party, a faction led by the former Minister of Finance in the HDF Government formed a new organization, the Hungarian Democratic People's Party.

In September 1997 Horn rejected demands for his resignation, after a committee established to investigate the past careers of senior politicians claimed that he had served with a paramilitary force that had restored communist power following the 1956 rebellion, and that he had used the security services to suppress political opposition. In December 1997 the HDF established an electoral alliance with the Federation of Young Democrats—Hungarian Civic Party (FYD—HCP, which had been reconstituted from the FYD) and the Hungarian Christian Democratic Federation, a newly formed association of breakaway members of the CDPP.

The first round of the legislative elections, which was contested by 26 parties, took place on 10 May 1998: the HSP secured 32.3% of the votes cast, the FYD—HCP won 28.2% of the votes, and the ISPP 13.8%. Following a second round of voting on 24 May, however, the FYD—HCP, with 147 seats, obtained the largest representation in Az ország háza; the HSP received 134 seats, the ISPP 48, the AFD 24, the HDF 18 and the HJLP 14. In June János Áder of the FYD—HCP, was elected President of Az ország háza. In the same month, following inter-party negotiations, the FYD—HCP signed an agreement with the HDF and the ISPP, providing for the formation of a new coalition government. In July Az ország háza elected Viktor Orbán, the Chairman of the FYD—HCP, as Prime Minister; his Government comprised 11 representatives of the FYD—HCP, four of the ISPP (later renamed the Independent Smallholders' and Civic Party—ISCP), one of the HDF and one of the Hungarian Christian Democratic Federation. The new Government presented a programme for the reduction of crime and the improvement of social and economic conditions.

In September 1998, following the resignation of Horn from the leadership of the HSP (in response to the party's electoral defeat), a former minister, László Kovács, was elected Chairman. In January 2000, László Kövér replaced Orbán as leader of the FYD—HCP.

In the presidential election, held on 5 June 2000, Ferenc Mádl, the sole candidate, obtained 251 votes of the possible 386 in the first round of voting in Az ország háza. Two further rounds were held on 6 June in order to secure the requisite two-thirds' majority. Mádl took office on 4 August. In February József Torgyán, the leader of the ISCP, resigned as Minister of Agriculture and Regional Development, owing to his implication in a corruption scandal. (He was expelled from the parliamentary faction of the party later in the year, and from the membership of the party in late 2002.)

In June 2001 Az ország háza approved legislation that, with effect from January 2002, granted ethnic Hungarians living in adjacent countries education, employment and medical rights in Hungary (although not permanent residence—a referendum on citizenship was held in December 2004). This legislation, widely referred to as the 'status' or 'benefit' law prompted protests from Romania and Slovakia (see below) that the law discriminated against their non-ethnic Hungarian populations and constituted a violation of sovereignty. The law was regarded by the opposition parties as a populist measure in advance of the parliamentary elections, which were scheduled to be held in April 2002.

In September 2001 the governing FYD—HCP and HDF signed a co-operation agreement for the forthcoming legislative elections; in December a number of ISCP deputies agreed to participate in the elections in co-operation with the FYD—HCP and the HDF. The legislative elections were held, as scheduled, on 7 and 21 April 2002. Although the FYD—HCP-HDF alliance won 48.7% of the total votes cast (188 seats), a left-wing coalition of the HSP (46.1% of the votes and 178 seats) and the AFD (5.2% of the votes and 20 seats) secured an overall majority in Az ország háza. Medgyessy of the HSP was sworn in as Prime Minister on 27 May; the Council of Ministers comprised eight further members of the HSP, four members of the AFD and three independents.

In June 2002 media allegations prompted the new Prime Minister to reveal that he had served as a counter-intelligence agent at the Ministry of Finance in 1977–82. Medgyessy insisted that he had worked to protect sensitive economic information from the KGB (the Soviet secret service), in order to negotiate Hungarian membership of the IMF (which it joined in 1982), and the Government announced plans for legislation that would grant improved access to secret service records; the AFD subsequently retracted a threat to withdraw from the governing coalition. In July two parliamentary commissions were established to investigate both the past role of Medgyessy and the alleged links of other post-communist government officials with the Soviet-era security service. Meanwhile, in early July the leader of the FYD—HCP, Zoltán Pokorni, who had led demands for Medgyessy's resignation, had relinquished his own party and parliamentary posts, after his father's role as a communist informer was revealed. It subsequently emerged that several members of the FYD—HCP (which had emphasized its anti-communist past during campaigning for the legislative elections) had counter-intelligence associations, thereby severely damaging the party's reputation. Controversy increased in August, when two senior figures, President Mádl and the Governor of the National Bank, Zsigmond Járai, reportedly refused to allow information pertaining to their own counter-intelligence histories to be made public. Local elections took place on 20 October, in which the governing coalition consolidated its position; the results of the elections confirmed the FYD—HCP's diminishing popularity.

In mid-December 2002 Az ország háza voted to adopt a number of constitutional amendments, which were required to enable the country to become a full member of the EU (see below). In mid-February 2003 the Minister without Portfolio attached to the Prime Minister's office, Elemér Kiss, had become the first minister to resign from the HSP-AFD Government, owing to allegations of corruption. He was replaced by Péter Kiss, hitherto the Minister of Labour and Employment; Sándor Burány took the labour and employment portfolio. However, Medgyessy's failure to consult the minority AFD before reorganizing the Council of Ministers temporarily led to tensions within the governing coalition. In May 2003 Medgyessy implemented a further governmental reshuffle, replacing three ministers and creating two new posts of minister without portfolio (with responsibility for equal opportunities and EU integration, respectively). In the same month, at a convention of the FYD—HCP, the party was transformed into a new right-wing alliance, known henceforth as the FYD—Hungarian Civic Alliance (HCA), with former premier Orbán as its leader. In early September Judit Csehák resigned as Minister of Health, Social and Family Affairs, amid speculation that her resignation had been prompted by stringent budgetary reductions, agreed upon by the Government one day previously. Mihály Kökény was named as her successor.

In January 2004 the Minister of Finance, Csaba László, left office in response to the fiscal results for 2003, which had exceeded government targets and eroded international confidence in the economy, thus jeopardizing the country's schedule for the adoption of the common European currency (see Economic Affairs). Tibor Draskovics replaced László in mid-February, and implemented a financial austerity plan shortly afterwards. Draskovics also indicated that the country should be prepared for a reduction in expenditure on the state sector, in particular hospitals, schools, government ministries and public-sector agencies. On 1 May 2004 Hungary acceded to full membership of the EU. On 13 June, in elections to the European Parliament the opposition FYD—HCA won 12 of the 24 seats allocated to Hungary, the ruling HSP secured nine seats, its coalition partner the AFD won two seats and the HDF obtained one seat. The results reflected public disaffection with the ruling coalition. Medgyessy had sought to submit a 'joint list' of candidates for the elections; this idea was firmly rejected by opposition parties, who preferred to run on individual party lists.

On 18 August 2004 Medgyessy resigned as Prime Minister following a decline in support for his party and a severe dispute with the AFD over changes he wished to make to the Council of Ministers, in particular the proposed dismissal of the AFD politician and Minister of the Economy and Transport, István Csillag. On 24 August the HSP elected one of the country's wealthiest business executives, Ferenc Gyurcsány, hitherto the Minister of Children, Youth and Sports, as Prime Minister-designate to replace Medgyessy, subject to his approval by the legislature. Gyurcsány, who secured 73% of the votes at a party congress, was chosen in preference to Péter Kiss, who had been widely regarded as the favourite to succeed Medgyessy. Gyurcsány was duly sworn in as Prime Minister on 4 October, following the overwhelming approval of his appointment by the legislature; in his inaugural speech he promised to improve living standards and to apply 'truly social democratic' values to Hungary. The Prime Minister appointed seven new ministers in October; the main structural change was the addition of a Minister without Portfolio, Etele Baráth, with responsibility for EU issues. Elsewhere, Kiss retained his position as Minister in charge of the Prime Minister's Office, while Csillag resigned from his post in order to spare the new regime 'unnecessary conflicts' and was succeeded by another notably wealthy business executive, János Kóka. The Council of Ministers now comprised 12 members of the HSP, four AFD politicians and two independents.

In February 2005 Gyurcsány appointed Andras Bozoki as Minister of Cultural Heritage. Bozoki's predecessor, István Hiller, had in October 2004 been appointed Chairman of the HSP; he resigned from his ministerial duties in order to prepare the party for the next legislative elections, due by April 2006. In February 2005 Col-Gen. Andras Havril replaced Lt-Gen. Zoltan Szenes as Chief of the Defence Staff; Szenes, who retired from the military, had objected to recent defence reforms and reductions in expenditure. Gyurcsány made two further adjustments to the Council of Ministers in April 2005: János Veres, a member of the executive committee of the HSP, replaced the non-partisan Tibor Draskovics as Minister of Finance, and József Graf was appointed as Minister of Agriculture and Rural Development, replacing Imre Nemeth.

Meanwhile, in December 2004 a national referendum (supported by the FYD—HCA and held following the submission of a petition of some 200,000 signatures) to grant citizenship to ethnic Hungarians resident in adjacent countries was not successful. (The proposal was intended as an extension of the provisions of the status law in force since 2002.) At least 25% of registered voters would have had to vote in favour of the proposal for it to have been approved; in the event, the total rate of participation in the plebiscite was just 37%, of which 52% voted for the change—a total of 19% of the electorate. There are some 1.4m. ethnic Hungarians in Romania and other large groups in Slovakia, Serbia and Montenegro (particularly in the Serbian province of Vojvodina) and Ukraine; Gyurcsány, who campaigned against the proposal, stated that the granting of citizenship on such a scale could cause potential damage to the economy, should a significant proportion of the diaspora eventually migrate to Hungary.

There has been considerable activism within Hungary by the country's ethnic minorities for the protection of their rights. In July 1993 Az ország háza adopted legislation guaranteeing the cultural, civil and political rights of 12 minority groups and prohibiting all forms of ethnic discrimination. Following the approval of this legislation, minority-rights activists launched a new campaign to change Hungary's electoral law, with the aim of securing the direct representation of ethnic groups in the legislature. In the 1994 municipal elections, ethnic minorities were able to elect their own local ethnic authorities, with consultative roles on cultural and educational issues affecting the community. In February 1995 Hungary signed the Council of Europe (see p. 199) Convention on the Protection of National Minorities. In April the Roma of Hungary elected their own governing body, the National Autonomous Authority of the Romany Minority (the first such body in the former Eastern bloc), which was empowered to administer funds and deliberate issues affecting the Roma. In the elections held in April 1995 and in January 1999 all of the Authority's 53 seats were won by the Lungo Drom Alliance, led by Florian Farkas. Further elections to the National Autonomous Authority, which took place in January 2003, were declared invalid, and new elections were held on 1 March. The left-wing Democratic Roma Coalition secured 49 of the 53 seats available, defeating the Lungo Drom Alliance.

In September 1996 Hungary and Romania signed a bilateral treaty, guaranteeing the inviolability of the joint border between the two countries and the rights of ethnic minorities. In February 1997 a defence co-operation between the two countries was signed, providing, *inter alia*, for the establishment of a joint military unit, to be deployed in peace-keeping operations. In May President Árpád Göncz made an official visit to Romania (the first by a Hungarian Head of State).

In early August 2001 a meeting between Viktor Orbán and Prime Minister Adrian Năstase of Romania failed to resolve the tensions arising from Hungary's status law that took effect from January 2002 and applying to the ethnic Hungarian diaspora (see above—There were some 1,434,000 ethnic Hungarians in Romania in 2002.) However, a memorandum of understanding was signed by the two Prime Ministers in late December 2001, which extended the short-term employment rights offered to ethnic Hungarians under the terms of the law to all Romanian citizens. President Ferenc Mádl made a state visit to Romania in October 2002. Finally, in late September 2003 a bilateral agreement on the implementation of the status law in Romania was signed in the Romanian capital, Bucharest, by Péter Medgyessy and Năstase.

Apart from issues arising from the presence of a large ethnic Hungarian minority in Slovakia (numbering some 520,500 in 2001), relations between Hungary and Slovakia were strained by a dispute over the Gabčíkovo-Nagymaros hydroelectric project (a joint Hungarian-Czechoslovak scheme initiated in 1977), involving the diversion of a 222-km stretch of the River Danube and the construction of a twin-dam system. In November 1989 the Hungarian Government announced that it was to abandon the scheme, following pressure from environmentalists. In July 1991 Czechoslovakia decided to proceed unilaterally with the project; the resumption of work, in February 1992, prompted the Hungarian Government to abrogate the 1977 treaty. In April 1993 it was agreed to refer the case to the International Court of Justice (ICJ) and to operate a temporary water-management scheme in the mean time.

In March 1995 Prime Minister Horn and his Slovak counterpart, Vladimír Mečiar, signed a Treaty of Friendship and Co-operation, according to which the two countries undertook to guarantee the rights of ethnic minorities and recognized the inviolability of their joint border. The Treaty came into effect in May 1996, following its ratification by the Slovak President. In August 1997 discussions between Horn and Mečiar resulted in an agreement that a joint committee be established to monitor the standard of human rights of ethnic Hungarians resident in Slovakia and the Slovak community in Hungary; however, there was subsequent dissent over the composition of the proposed committee. In September relations between Hungary and Slovakia became strained, after Horn rejected a suggestion by Mečiar that a voluntary repatriation programme for the respective ethnic communities in the two countries be initiated. Later in September the ICJ concluded proceedings regarding the dispute over the Gabčíkovo-Nagymaros hydroelectric project, ruling that both countries had contravened international law: Hungary had breached the terms of the agreement by withdrawing from the project, and the former Czechoslovakia had continued work without the permission of the Hungarian Government. Both Hungary and Slovakia were required to pay compensation for damages incurred, and to resume negotiations regarding the further implementation of the agreement. In December 1999 Hungary submitted a document to the Slovak Government, in which it renounced any claim to a share of the hydroelectric energy produced by the dam project, but requested an increase in the flow of common water along the Danube, in order to maintain the ecological balance. In February 2001 Slovakia accepted that it had no legal means to compel Hungary to proceed with the project, but stated that it would seek compensation. In December 2003 an inter-governmental commission was established to co-ordinate further negotiations on the issue.

The entry into force of the Hungarian status law (see above) in January 2002 threatened to damage relations with Slovakia, although that country had in place a similar law, which granted privileges to the Slovakian diaspora. In February the Slovak

parliament voted to reject the Hungarian law, claiming that it abrogated the treaty of May 1996. In early March 2003 the Council of Europe drafted a resolution urging the Hungarian Government to amend the status law. Also in early March, however, Hungary agreed to suspend the application of the law in Slovakia, pending the approval by Az ország háza of a draft amendment stipulating that the legislation was not to apply in EU member countries (Slovakia was due to accede to the EU in May 2004, along with Hungary—see below). Finally, in December 2003 the Ministers of Foreign Affairs of Hungary and Slovakia signed a bilateral agreement on the implementation of the status law in Slovakia.

In November 1990 Hungary was the first former eastern-bloc European country to become a member of the Council of Europe. In March 1996 Hungary was admitted to the Organisation for Economic Co-operation and Development (OECD, see p. 307). Meanwhile, Hungary's associate membership of the EU came into effect on 1 February 1994, and in April Hungary became the first post-communist state to apply for full EU membership. In December 2002 Hungary was one of 10 countries formally invited to join the EU on 1 May 2004. In a national referendum, held on 12 April 2003, 83.8% of participants voted in support of Hungarian membership of the EU. (The rate of participation was 45.6%.) In December 2004 Az ország háza approved the ratification of the proposed EU constitutional treaty, becoming the second member state (after Lithuania) to do so.

Following a North Atlantic Treaty Organization (NATO, see p. 301) summit meeting in Madrid, Spain, in July 1997, Hungary was invited to enter into discussions regarding its application for membership of the Alliance. A national referendum on the country's entry into NATO was conducted on 16 November, at which its accession was approved by 85.3% of the votes cast, with the participation of 49% of the electorate. Hungary was formally admitted to NATO in March 1999 (although it was subsequently subject to some criticism for failing to fulfil its financial commitments). During the NATO bombardment of Yugoslavia (Serbia and Montenegro—which commenced in late March 1999—see the chapter on Serbia and Montenegro) the Hungarian Government allowed NATO forces to use its military bases and airspace. In early 2003 an airbase at Taszar, in south-western Hungary, was used by the USA for the training of Iraqi opposition forces, in relation to the US-led military campaign in Iraq (see the chapters on the USA and Iraq). Hungary subsequently contributed 300 soldiers to the international peace-keeping force in Iraq. In November 2004 at a ceremony marking the end of compulsory military service, Prime Minister Ferenc Gyurcsány, following significant public and political opposition to the US-led operation in Iraq, announced that Hungarian troops would be withdrawn from the region by the end of March 2005. However, in December 2004 it was agreed to provide the NATO mission in Iraq with a further 150 soldiers for training and peace-keeping work, with effect from June 2005.

Government

Legislative power is held by the unicameral Az ország háza (The National Assembly), comprising 386 members, who are elected for four years by universal adult suffrage under a mixed system of proportional and direct representation. The President of the Republic (Head of State) is elected by Az ország háza for a term of five years. The President, who is also Commander-in-Chief of the Armed Forces, may be re-elected for a second term. The Council of Ministers, the highest organ of state administration, is elected by the Assembly on the recommendation of the President. For local administrative purposes Hungary is divided into 19 counties (*megyei*) and the capital city (with 23 districts). A 53-member National Autonomous Authority of the Romany Minority, first elected in April 1995, is empowered to administer funds disbursed by the central Government.

Defence

Military service begins at the age of 18 years. The period of military service was reduced from one year to nine months in November 1997, and further reduced to six months with effect from March 2002. Compulsory military service was abolished in November 2004. The total regular forces in August 2004 numbered 32,300 (including 2,000 conscripts): army 23,950, air force 7,500 and centrally controlled personnel 850. Paramilitary forces comprised 12,000 border guards, as well as 2,000 members of the internal security forces. In March 1999 Hungary became a member of the North Atlantic Treaty Organization (NATO, see p. 301). Defence expenditure amounted to some 355,000m. forint in 2003, in conformity with NATO recommendations that Hungary increase its spending on defence to the equivalent of 2% of GDP by 2006. The budget for 2004 allocated 351,000m. forint to defence.

Economic Affairs

In 2003, according to estimates by the World Bank, Hungary's gross national income (GNI), measured at average 2001–03 prices, was US $78,293.4m., equivalent to $6,330 per head (or $13,780 per head on an international purchasing-power parity basis). During 1990–2003, it was estimated, the population decreased at an average annual rate of 0.2%, while gross domestic product (GDP) per head increased, in real terms, by an average of 1.6% per year. Hungary's overall GDP increased, in real terms, at an average annual rate of 1.4% during 1990–2003; real GDP increased by 3.5% in 2002 and by 2.9% in 2003.

Agriculture (including hunting, forestry and fishing) contributed 3.3% of GDP in 2003, and 5.5% of the employed labour force were engaged in the sector in the same year. The principal crops are wheat, maize, sugar beet, barley and potatoes. Viticulture is also important. During 1990–2002, according to the World Bank, real agricultural GDP declined at an average annual rate of 1.2%. The GDP of the sector increased by 23.4% in 2001 and by 2.4% in 2002.

Industry (including mining, manufacturing, construction and power) contributed 30.6% of GDP in 2003, and engaged 33.3% of the employed labour force in the same year. 53.2% of total industrial production was exported in 2003; industrial exports increased by 5.6% in 2002 and by 10.9% in 2003. In 2002 the output of the construction sector increased by 20% compared with the previous year, owing to state-financed infrastructural investment; activity in the sector increased by a further 27.1% in 2003. The World Bank estimated that real industrial GDP increased at an average annual rate of 2.1% in 1990–2002. Industrial GDP increased by 1.4% in 2001 and by 2.4% in 2002.

Mining and quarrying accounted for just 0.2% of GDP in 2001, and engaged 0.3% of the employed labour force in 2003. Hungary's most important mineral resources are lignite (brown coal) and natural gas. Petroleum, bauxite and hard coal are also exploited. During 1990–98 the output of the mining sector declined at an average annual rate of 11.1%. Production fell by 8.4% in 1997 and by 20.4% in 1998.

The manufacturing sector contributed 22.7% of GDP in 2001, and engaged 23.6% of the employed labour force in 2003. In 1999 the principal branches of the sector, in terms of their contribution to gross production, were food products (accounting for 16.6% of the total), motor vehicles (14.4%), office, accounting and computing machinery (8.9%) and chemicals (7.5%). Manufacturing GDP increased, in real terms, at an average annual rate of 6.7% in 1991–2002. Manufacturing GDP increased by 2.5% in 2001 and by 2.4% in 2002.

In 2001 38.8% of Hungary's electricity production was generated by nuclear power, 24.5% was generated by coal, 24.3% by natural gas and 11.5% by petroleum. Fuel imports represented 7.4% of the value of total merchandise imports in 2002.

The services sector has a significant role in the Hungarian economy, contributing 66.1% of GDP in 2003, and engaging 61.2% of the employed labour force in the same year. According to the World Bank, the GDP of the services sector increased, in real terms, at an average rate of 1.6% per year in 1990–2002. The GDP of the services sector increased by 5.7% in 2001 and by 2.4% in 2002.

In 2003 Hungary recorded a visible trade deficit of US $3,365m., and there was a deficit of $7,364m. on the current account of the balance of payments. In 2002 the principal source of imports was Germany (accounting for 24.3% of the total); other major sources were Italy, Austria and Russia. Germany was also the principal market for exports in that year (35.4%); other important purchasers were Austria, Italy and France. The principal exports in 2002 were machinery and transport equipment, miscellaneous manufactured articles (most notably clothing and accessories), basic manufactures, food and live animals and chemical products. The main imports in that year were machinery and transport equipment (most notably electrical machinery and apparatus), basic manufactures, miscellaneous manufactured articles, chemical products and mineral fuels.

Hungary's overall budgetary deficit in 2003 was an estimated 1,094,549m. forint (equivalent to 5.9% of GDP). The country's total external debt at the end of 2002 was estimated to be US $34,958m., of which $13,551m. was long-term public debt. In

that year the cost of debt-servicing was equivalent to 33.9% of the value of exports of goods and services. The annual rate of inflation averaged 8.8% in 1997–2003; consumer prices increased by 5.3% in 2002, by 4.6% in 2003 and by 6.8% in 2004. The average rate of unemployment was 6.1% in 2004.

Hungary is a member of the European Bank for Reconstruction and Development (EBRD, see p. 212), and was admitted to the Organisation for Economic Co-operation and Development (OECD, see p. 307) in March 1996. Hungary became an associate member of the European Union (EU, see p. 217) in February 1994, and acceded as a full member, with effect from 1 May 2004.

In 1990 the Hungarian Government pledged to effect a full transition to a Western-style market economy, and by the late 1990s the Government's fiscal policy had resulted in a decline in both the public-sector deficit and the annual rate of inflation. In December 1999 it was announced that, as a result of the country's success in achieving economic stabilization, Hungary would be one of the first applicant nations to be admitted to the EU; in December 2002 it was invited to become a full member from May 2004. However, although GDP growth remained positive in 2004 (reportedly at around 4%), the rate of inflation increased, the deficit on the current account of the balance of payments widened significantly. Most problematically, the budgetary deficit had not been reduced to a level consistent with Hungary adopting the common European currency, the euro, by 2010. In 2004, despite the Government's intention to reduce the fiscal deficit to 4.6% of GDP, the rate was estimated at around 5.3%. The EU stipulated that countries intending to adopt the euro should record a budgetary deficit of no more than 3% of GDP in the two preceding years, Hungary's targeted date for entry into the 'euro zone', originally envisaged for 2008 and later delayed to 2010, appeared optimistic. In early 2004 a new Minister of Finance, Tibor Draskovics, implemented an economic austerity plan. Prime Minister Gyurcsány insisted in late 2004 that Hungary could adopt the euro by 2010 provided annual economic growth remained in excess of 4%.

Education

Children under the age of three years attend crèches (bölcsődék), and those between the ages of three and six years attend kindergartens (óvodák). Education is compulsory between the ages of six and 16 years. Children attend basic or primary school (általános iskola) until the age of 14. In 2000 primary enrolment included 98% of children in the relevant age-group, while the comparable ratio for secondary education was 97%. In southern Hungary bilingual schools have been established to promote the languages of the national minorities. The majority of children continue with their education after 16 years of age. The most popular types of secondary school are the grammar school (gimnázium) and the vocational school (szakközépiskola). The gimnázium provides a four-year course of mainly academic studies, although some vocational training does feature on the curriculum. The szakközépiskola offers full vocational training together with a general education, emphasis being laid on practical work. Apprentice training schools (szakmunkásképző intézetek) are attached to factories, agricultural co-operatives, etc., and lead to full trade qualifications. In 1999–2000 the system of higher education underwent a major reorganization, as a result of which from 1 January 2000 there were 30 state-run universities and colleges, 26 church universities and colleges and six colleges run by various foundations. In 2000 an estimated 25% of the relevant age-group continued into tertiary education. Expenditure on education in 2003 was some 1,070,400m. forint (equivalent to 12.2% of total government expenditure). In 2003 the Government allocated more than 1,000m. forint in grants to support Romany students pursuing higher education.

Public Holidays

2005: 1 January (New Year's Day), 15 March (Anniversary of 1848 uprising against Austrian rule), 28 March (Easter Monday), 1 May (Labour Day), 16 May (Whit Monday), 15 August (Assumption), 20 August (Constitution Day), 23 October (Day of the Proclamation of the Republic), 1 November (All Saints' Day), 25–26 December (Christmas).

2006: 1 January (New Year's Day), 15 March (Anniversary of 1848 uprising against Austrian rule), 17 April (Easter Monday), 1 May (Labour Day), 5 June (Whit Monday), 15 August (Assumption), 20 August (Constitution Day), 23 October (Day of the Proclamation of the Republic), 1 November (All Saints' Day), 25–26 December (Christmas).

Weights and Measures

The metric system is in force.

Statistical Survey

Source (unless otherwise stated): Központi Statisztikai Hivatal (Hungarian Central Statistical Office), 1525 Budapest, Keleti Károly u. 5–7; tel. (1) 345-6136; fax (1) 345-6378; e-mail erzsebet.veto@office.ksh.hu; internet www.ksh.hu.

Area and Population

AREA, POPULATION AND DENSITY

Area (sq km)	93,030*
Population (census results)	
1 January 1990	10,374,823
1 February 2001	
Males	4,863,610
Females	5,333,509
Total	10,197,119
Population (official estimates at 30 December)†	
2001	10,175,000
2002	10,142,000
2003	10,117,000
Density (per sq km) at 30 December 2003	108.7

* 35,919 sq miles.
† Figures are rounded.

Languages (2001 census): Magyar (Hungarian) 98.6%; Romany 0.5%; German 0.3%; Slovak 0.1%; Croatian 0.1%; Ukrainian 0.1%; Others 0.2%.

ADMINISTRATIVE DIVISIONS
(2001 census)

	Area (sq km)	Population	Density (per sq km)	County town (with population)*
Counties:				
Bács-Kiskun . .	8,445	546,753	64.7	Kecskemét (105,464)
Baranya . . .	4,430	408,019	92.1	Pécs (158,607)
Békés . . .	5,631	397,074	70.5	Békéscsaba (63,958)
Borsod-Abaúj-Zemplén . .	7,247	745,154	102.8	Miskolc (173,629)
Csongrád . .	4,263	433,388	101.7	Szeged (159,133)
Fejér . . .	4,359	434,547	99.7	Székesfehérvár (105,293)
Győr-Moson-Sopron . .	4,089	434,956	106.4	Győr (127,275)
Hajdú-Bihar .	6,211	553,043	89.0	Debrecen (205,032)
Heves . . .	3,637	325,673	89.5	Eger (57,891)
Jász-Nagykun-Szolnok . .	5,582	415,819	74.5	Szolnok (76,875)
Komárom-Esztergom . .	2,265	316,780	139.9	Tatabánya (72,054)
Nógrád . .	2,544	220,576	86.7	Salgótarján (44,404)
Pest . . .	6,393	1,080,759	169.1	Budapest† (1,838,753)
Somogy . .	6,036	335,463	55.6	Kaposvár (66,826)
Szabolcs-Szatmár-Bereg	5,937	582,795	98.2	Nyíregyháza (112,882)
Tolna . . .	3,703	250,062	67.5	Szekszárd (35,358)
Vas . . .	3,337	268,653	80.5	Szombathely (82,074)
Veszprém . .	4,613	374,346	81.2	Veszprém (62,631)
Zala . . .	3,784	298,056	78.8	Zalaegerszeg (61,033)
Capital city				
Budapest† . .	525	1,775,203	3,381.3	—
Total	93,030	10,197,119	109.6	—

* At 1 January 1999.
† Budapest has separate County status. The area and population of the city are not included in the larger County (Pest) which it administers.

PRINCIPAL TOWNS
(population at 1 January 2002)

Budapest (capital) .	1,739,569	Nyíregyháza . . .	117,002
Debrecen . . .	206,564	Kecskemét . .	107,267
Miskolc	182,408	Székesfehérvár . .	104,059
Szeged	163,699	Szombathely . .	81,228*
Pécs	159,794	Szolnok	75,962*
Győr	129,287	Tatabánya . . .	71,701*

* 1 January 2000.

Source: Statistics Finland.

BIRTHS, MARRIAGES AND DEATHS

	Registered live births		Registered marriages		Registered deaths	
	Number	Rate (per 1,000)	Number	Rate (per 1,000)	Number	Rate (per 1,000)
1995 . .	112,054	11.0	53,463	5.2	145,431	14.2
1996 . .	105,272	10.3	48,930	4.8	143,130	14.0
1997 . .	100,350	9.9	46,905	4.6	139,434	13.7
1998 . .	97,301	9.6	44,915	4.4	140,870	13.9
1999 . .	94,645	9.4	45,465	4.5	143,210	14.2
2000 . .	97,597	9.6	48,110	4.7	135,601	13.3
2001 . .	97,047	9.5	43,583	4.3	132,183	13.0
2002 . .	96,804	9.5	46,008	4.5	132,833	13.1
2003 . .	94,650	9.3	45,400	4.5	135,850	13.4

Expectation of Life (years at birth, 2003): Males 68.2; Females 76.5.

ECONOMICALLY ACTIVE POPULATION
(labour force surveys, '000 persons aged 15 years to 74 years)

	2001	2002	2003
Agriculture, hunting, forestry and fishing	239.4	240.9	215.2
Mining and quarrying	13.0	14.8	12.8
Manufacturing	955.8	959.9	925.5
Electricity, gas and water supply .	79.5	74.2	68.2
Construction	272.7	271.0	299.4
Wholesale and retail trade; repair of motor vehicles, motorcycles and personal and household goods	548.4	552.1	553.1
Hotels and restaurants	143.0	137.3	139.4
Transport, storage and communications	310.9	309.7	303.2
Financial intermediation . . .	78.9	75.3	72.8
Real estate, renting and business activities	219.6	232.8	265.9
Public administration and defence; compulsory social security . .	289.6	282.1	295.4
Education	309.8	318.0	329.0
Health and social work	234.9	240.7	267.2
Other community, social and personal service activities . .	164.0	161.8	174.8
Total employed	3,859.5	3,870.6	3,921.9
Unemployed	232.9	238.8	244.5
Total labour force	4,092.4	4,109.4	4,166.4
Males	2,273.3	2,250.5	n.a.
Females	1,819.1	1,858.9	n.a.

Health and Welfare

KEY INDICATORS

Total fertility rate (children per woman, 2002)	1.2
Under-5 mortality rate (per 1,000 live births, 2003) . . .	8
HIV/AIDS (% of persons aged 15–49, 2003)	0.1
Physicians (per 1,000 head, 2001)	2.9
Hospital beds (per 1,000 head, 2000)	8.2
Health expenditure (2001): US $ per head (PPP)	914
Health expenditure (2001): % of GDP	6.8
Health expenditure (2001): public (% of total)	75.0
Access to water (% of persons, 2002)	99
Access to sanitation (% of persons, 2002)	95
Human Development Index (2002): ranking	38
Human Development Index (2002): value	0.848

For sources and definitions, see explanatory note on p. vi.

Agriculture

PRINCIPAL CROPS
('000 metric tons)

	2001	2002	2003
Wheat	5,196.8	3,910.2	2,941.0
Barley	1,299.1	1,045.9	810.0
Maize	7,857.7	6,120.9	4,532.0
Rye	121.1	95.4	67.0
Oats	149.7	137.6	102.0
Triticale (wheat-rye hybrid) . .	393.9	358.9	278.0
Potatoes	908.4	752.2	582.0
Sugar beet	2,903.0	2,273.8	1,812.0
Dry peas	64.1	49.4	30.0
Soybeans (Soya beans)	41.5	56.2	30.8*
Sunflower seed	632.3	776.9	992.0
Rapeseed	205.1	207.5	104.0
Cabbages	165.9	172.6	157.3
Tomatoes	235.8	247.2	281.2
Cucumbers and gherkins . . .	98.6	96.4	94.3
Chillies and green peppers . . .	134.8	116.9	107.8
Dry onions	174.3	122.3	93.7
Green peas	113.3	101.7	68.7
Carrots	99.3	104.0	80.7
Green corn	415.6	467.8	565.9
Other vegetables	311.3*	287.5*	297.5†
Apples	605.4	526.9	508.0
Sour cherries	56.0	38.2	49.0
Peaches and nectarines	56.7	22.2	32.0
Plums	89.8	49.3	45.0
Grapes	811.4	501.0	581.5
Watermelons	130.2	165.6	228.3
Other fruit	117.7*	79.2†	114.0†
Pimento	59.7	55.1	57.0†
Tobacco (leaves)	8.9	11.0	10.5

* Unofficial figure.
† FAO estimate.
Source: FAO.

LIVESTOCK
('000 head, year ending September)

	2001	2002	2003
Cattle	805	783	770
Pigs	4,834	4,822	5,335
Sheep	1,129	1,136	1,103
Goats	103	90	140*
Horses	74	65	67
Chickens	30,716	34,343	32,206
Ducks	1,480	2,837	3,443
Geese	1,470	2,175	2,009
Turkeys	3,350	3,924	3,251

* FAO estimate.
Source: FAO.

LIVESTOCK PRODUCTS
('000 metric tons)

	2001	2002	2003
Beef and veal	51.6	49.9	64.0*
Mutton and lamb	2.6	2.5†	2.6†
Pig meat	556.1	639.7	665.0*
Poultry meat	472.3	479.6	438.6
Rabbit meat†	10.8	10.8	10.8
Cows' milk	2,142.2	2,129.8	2,038.3
Sheep's milk	41.5	33.4	30.0†
Goats' milk	11.2	10.1	10.0†
Butter	13.6	13.9*	14.2*
Cheese	108.4	120.6	110.9†
Hen eggs	180.8	188.7	188.8
Other poultry eggs	3.4	4.0	4.1*
Honey	15.3	15.2	21.0
Wool: greasy	3.9	4.0	4.1
Wool: scoured*	2.4	2.4	2.5
Cattle hides (fresh)†	3.2	3.5	3.5

* Unofficial figure(s).
† FAO estimate(s).
Source: FAO.

Forestry

ROUNDWOOD REMOVALS
('000 cu metres, excl. bark)

	2001	2002	2003
Sawlogs, veneer logs and logs for sleepers	1,430	1,860	1,571
Pulpwood	594	623	583
Other industrial wood	1,468	956	850
Fuel wood	2,319	2,398	2,781
Total	**5,811**	**5,836**	**5,785**

Source: FAO.

SAWNWOOD PRODUCTION
('000 cu metres, incl. railway sleepers)

	2001	2002	2003
Coniferous (softwood)	79	79	92
Broadleaved (hardwood) . . .	185	194	207
Total	**264**	**293**	**299**

Source: FAO.

Fishing

(metric tons, live weight)

	2000	2001	2002
Capture	7,101	6,638	6,750
Common carp	3,212	2,470	2,787
Silver carp	365	997	525
Other cyprinids	1,710	2,155	2,418
Aquaculture	12,886	13,056	11,574
Common carp	8,656	8,226	7,735
Grass carp	526	655	470
Silver carp	1,640	2,126	1,516
North African catfish	n.a.	889	878
Freshwater fishes	1,393	653	470
Total catch	**19,987**	**19,694**	**18,324**

Source: FAO.

Mining

('000 metric tons, unless otherwise indicated)

	1999	2000	2001*
Hard coal	738	744	573
Brown coal	5,207	5,670	5,384
Lignite	7,696	7,862	8,043
Crude petroleum	1,243	1,128	1,059
Bauxite	935	1,046	1,000
Natural gas (million cu metres)†	3,100	3,350	3,280

* Reported figures.
† Marketed production.
Source: US Geological Survey.

Industry

SELECTED PRODUCTS
('000 metric tons, unless otherwise indicated)

	1999	2000	2001
Crude steel	1,920	1,970	2,065
Cement	2,980	3,326	3,452
Nitrogenous fertilizers*	188	269	269
Refined sugar	438	280	444
Buses (number)	706	809	870
Non-rubber footwear ('000 pairs)	14,386	15,045	15,536
Electric energy (million kWh)	37,831	34,991	n.a.
Radio receivers ('000)	2,412	2,320	3,459

* Production in terms of nitrogen.
Source: UN, *Industrial Commodity Statistics Yearbook*.

Finance

CURRENCY AND EXCHANGE RATES

Monetary Units
100 fillér = 1 forint.

Sterling, Dollar and Euro Equivalents (31 December 2004)
£1 sterling = 348.21 forint;
US $1 = 180.29 forint;
€1 = 245.57 forint;
1,000 forint = £2.87 = $5.55 = €4.07.

Average Exchange Rate (forint per US dollar)
2002 257.887
2003 224.307
2004 202.746

BUDGET
('000 million forint)*

Revenue†	1998	1999	2000
Tax revenue	3,221.8	3,857.1	4,227.3
Taxes on income, profits and capital gains	694.8	840.6	988.4
Individual	477.5	578.1	695.7
Corporate	217.3	262.5	292.7
Social security contributions	1,069.0	1,323.9	1,288.0
Domestic taxes on goods and services	1,241.2	1,460.9	1,710.6
General sales, turnover or value-added taxes	796.9	941.8	1,153.7
Excises	320.6	463.7	505.9
Import duties	131.6	141.1	137.7
Other current revenue	438.1	522.1	508.8
Entrepreneurial and property income	150.4	174.6	164.2
Administrative fees and charges, non-industrial and incidental sales	168.5	154.7	207.7
Capital revenue	26.3	23.3	26.5
Total	3,686.2	4,402.5	4,762.6

Expenditure‡	1998	1999	2000
General public services	237.6	240.3	387.3
Defence	102.1	102.1	142.6
Public order and safety	169.6	169.6	198.2
Education	381.2	381.2	256.2
Health	265.4	265.3	321.6
Social security and welfare	1,331.1	1,331.4	1,703.3
Housing and community amenities	68.9	68.9	81.8
Recreational, cultural and religious affairs and services	79.5	79.5	99.5
Economic affairs and services	558.3	449.4	717.5
Agriculture, forestry, fishing and hunting	157.0	157.0	178.5
Transport and communications	184.6	112.0	242.0
Other purposes	1,329.7	1,802.3	1,375.6
Interest payments	779.0	843.9	788.0
Total	4,523.2	4,890.1	5,283.6
Current	4,111.2	4,476.2	4,631.3
Capital	412.0	413.9	652.3

* Figures refer to the consolidated operations of the central Government, comprising the State Budget, the Pension Fund, the Health Insurance Fund and six extrabudgetary funds.
† Excluding grants received ('000 million forint): 78.6 in 1998; –33.9 in 1999; 19.4 in 2000.
‡ Excluding lending minus repayments ('000 million forint): –106.2 in 1998; –98.0 in 1999; –36.9 in 2000.
Source: partly IMF, *Government Finance Statistics Yearbook*.
2002 (million forint): Total revenue 6,829,907; Total expenditure 8,503,894.
2003 (million forint): Total revenue 7,595,963; Total expenditure 8,690,512.

INTERNATIONAL RESERVES
(US $ million at 31 December)

	2001	2002	2003
Gold*	28	35	42
IMF special drawing rights	21	33	46
Reserve position in IMF	405	595	676
Foreign exchange	10,302	9,721	12,015
Total	10,755	10,384	12,779

* National valuation.
Source: IMF, *International Financial Statistics*.

MONEY SUPPLY
('000 million forint at 31 December)

	2001	2002	2003
Currency outside banks	1,037.6	1,181.8	1,346.4
Demand deposits at commercial and savings banks	1,738.3	2,113.5	2,288.3
Total money (incl. others)	2,779.0	3,298.1	3,639.6

Source: IMF, *International Financial Statistics*.

COST OF LIVING
(Consumer Price Index; base: 2000 = 100)

	2001	2002	2003
Food	113.8	119.9	123.1
Fuel and power	110.3	116.4	124.9
Clothing and footwear	105.3	109.6	112.9
Services	109.8	116.8	123.7
All items (incl. others)	109.2	115.0	120.4

NATIONAL ACCOUNTS
('000 million forint at current prices)

Expenditure on the Gross Domestic Product

	2001	2002	2003
Government final consumption expenditure	1,513.7	1,813.1	2,034.0
Private final consumption expenditure*	9,583.8	11,088.7	12,673.7
Increase in stocks*	487.9	309.2	577.6
Gross fixed capital formation	3,493.0	3,916.9	4,086.1
Total domestic expenditure	15,078.4	17,127.9	19,371.4
Exports of goods and services	10,803.4	10,709.3	11,472.0
Less Imports of goods and services	11,032.0	11,096.8	12,269.5
GDP in purchasers' values	14,849.8	16,740.4	18,574.0
GDP at constant 2000 prices	13,679.4	14,157.9	14,573.9

* Includes non-profit institutions serving households.

Source: IMF, *International Financial Statistics*.

Gross Domestic Product by Economic Activity

	1999	2000	2001
Agriculture, hunting, forestry and fishing	483.5	490.9	562.7
Mining and quarrying	28.4	29.9	30.1
Manufacturing	2,340.2	2,754.4	2,974.6
Electricity, gas and water supply	389.2	412.4	421.9
Construction	463.8	595.7	666.4
Wholesale and retail trade; repair of motor vehicles, motorcycles and personal and household goods	1,097.5	1,226.3	1,496.0
Hotels and restaurants	178.1	204.0	231.1
Transport, storage and communications	1,018.4	981.5	1,103.7
Financial intermediation	394.5	408.1	462.1
Real estate, renting and business activities	1,603.9	1,991.0	2,322.1
Public administration and defence; compulsory social security	723.4	948.3	1,130.4
Education	478.0	544.1	644.1
Health and social work	446.1	526.6	597.0
Other community, social and personal service activities	328.0	369.7	448.5
Sub-total	9,973.0	11,482.7	13,090.6
Less Financial intermediation services indirectly measured	283.8	273.1	310.7
Gross value added in basic prices	9,689.2	11,209.6	12,779.9
Taxes *less* subsidies on products	1,704.3	1,962.7	2,069.7
GDP in market prices	11,393.5	13,172.3	14,849.6

Source: UN, *National Accounts Statistics*.

BALANCE OF PAYMENTS
(US $ million)

	2001	2002	2003
Exports of goods f.o.b.	31,080	34,792	43,229
Imports of goods f.o.b.	−33,318	−36,911	−46,594
Trade balance	−2,237	−2,119	−3,365
Exports of services	6,645	6,893	7,974
Imports of services	−5,199	−6,322	−8,171
Balance on goods and services	−791	−1,548	−3,562
Other income received	1,302	1,234	1,330
Other income paid	−4,152	−4,866	−5,785
Balance on goods, services and income	−3,640	−5,180	−8,017
Current transfers received	781	1,067	1,278
Current transfers paid	−377	−553	−625
Current balance	−3,236	−4,666	−7,364
Capital account (net)	317	192	−77
Direct investment abroad	−364	−279	−1,598
Direct investment from abroad	3,944	2,863	2,506
Portfolio investment assets	−149	−45	35
Portfolio investment liabilities	1,523	1,844	2,900
Financial derivatives assets	582	1,901	2,929
Financial derivatives liabilities	−471	−2,113	−2,893
Other investment assets	−2,754	−1,369	−2,606
Other investment liabilities	465	−447	6,039
Net errors and omissions	61	327	466
Overall balance	−84	−1,792	336

Source: IMF, *International Financial Statistics*.

External Trade

Note: Beginning in 1997, Hungary's customs territory includes the country's industrial free zones.

PRINCIPAL COMMODITIES
(distribution by SITC, US $ million)

Imports c.i.f.	2000	2001	2002
Mineral fuels, lubricants, etc.	1,531.4	1,832.8	2,800.0
Petroleum, petroleum products, etc.	329.5	364.7	1,334.9
Petroleum gases	1,008.1	1,250.9	1,199.8
Chemicals and related products	2,693.4	2,844.6	3,240.4
Basic manufactures	5,429.6	5,617.0	6,267.4
Textile yarn, fabrics, etc.	1,084.9	1,072.1	1,124.9
Metal manufactures	1,026.4	1,070.6	1,293.7
Machinery and transport equipment	16,341.4	17,278.9	19,384.5
Power-generating machinery and equipment	1,716.4	1,838.4	1,965.3
General industrial machinery equipment and parts	1,701.5	1,843.3	2,088.1
Office machines and automatic data-processing machines	2,245.9	1,998.9	2,125.9
Telecommunications and sound equipment	2,067.0	1,996.0	2,337.7
Other electrical machinery apparatus, etc.	5,096.8	5,873.7	6,364.7
Road vehicles and parts (excl. tyres, engines and electrical parts)	2,362.0	2,459.8	3,039.2
Miscellaneous manufactured articles	3,173.9	3,221.2	3,584.3
Total (incl. others)	32,079.5	33,681.7	37,611.6

Exports f.o.b.	2000	2001	2002
Food and live animals	1,798.0	2,140.1	2,197.4
Chemicals and related products	1,681.9	1,832.1	2,083.6
Basic manufactures	3,088.9	3,270.2	3,611.3
Machinery and transport equipment	16,756.0	17,505.5	20,124.6
Power-generating machinery and equipment	2,806.3	3,246.2	3,723.2
Office machines and automatic data-processing machines	3,886.8	2,542.6	2,454.3
General industrial machinery equipment and parts	770.0	932.8	1,097.3
Telecommunications and sound equipment	2,998.1	3,838.6	5,351.7
Other electrical machinery apparatus, etc.	3,335.1	3,616.5	3,825.4
Road vehicles and parts (excl. tyres, engines and electrical parts)	2,459.6	2,712.7	2,979.3
Miscellaneous manufactured articles	3,132.9	3,798.6	4,319.1
Clothing and accessories (excl. footwear)	1,232.5	1,335.9	1,284.6
Total (incl. others)	28,091.8	30,497.7	34,336.6

PRINCIPAL TRADING PARTNERS
(US $ million)*

Imports c.i.f.	2000	2001	2002
Austria	2,366.0	2,487.8	2,594.9
Belgium	720.8	767.0	720.2
China, People's Republic	938.3	1,333.6	2,084.9
Czech Republic	646.2	714.8	871.5
Finland	372.7	353.6	402.9
France	1,401.0	1,579.1	1,808.1
Germany	8,213.0	8,393.1	9,145.1
Italy	2,407.2	2,647.5	2,838.3
Japan	1,701.1	1,555.4	1,571.0
Korea, Republic	525.7	413.2	588.5
Malaysia	299.8	477.6	612.9
Netherlands	708.4	699.4	783.3
Philippines	196.5	188.7	431.9
Poland	605.9	777.0	950.5
Romania	328.6	362.0	432.1
Russia	2,588.6	2,369.3	2,284.0
Singapore	509.0	518.4	438.7
Slovakia	574.9	602.6	679.7
Spain	572.8	616.6	686.5
Sweden	368.8	348.3	440.1
Switzerland and Liechtenstein	424.4	468.4	492.4
United Kingdom	1,017.1	992.7	1,069.0
USA	1,223.6	1,424.2	1,379.1
Total (incl. others)	32,079.5	33,681.9	37,611.6

Exports f.o.b.	2000	2001	2002
Austria	2,442.5	2,416.8	2,434.1
Belgium	878.3	996.9	922.4
Czech Republic	465.3	553.4	649.3
France	1,470.5	1,818.8	1,945.1
Germany	10,471.2	10,859.4	12,162.6
Ireland	250.7	329.5	144.3
Italy	1,654.4	1,905.3	1,984.1
Netherlands	1,522.4	1,402.2	1,457.4
Poland	605.2	609.4	727.1
Romania	574.2	764.2	784.3
Russia	455.4	472.3	454.8
Slovakia	288.5	411.5	496.8
Slovenia	279.7	308.4	301.6
Spain	522.5	629.4	819.2
Sweden	254.4	301.2	1,403.8
Switzerland and Liechtenstein	349.0	382.4	385.5
United Kingdom	1,156.3	1,314.4	1,615.1
USA	1,475.0	1,525.3	1,199.4
Total (incl. others)	28,091.8	30,497.7	34,336.6

* Imports by country of origin; exports by country of destination.
Source: UN, *International Trade Statistics Yearbook*.

Transport

RAILWAYS
(traffic)

	1998	1999	2000
Passengers carried (million)	157.0	156.8	156.4
Passenger-kilometres (million)	8,884	9,514	9,789
Transportation of goods (million net ton-kilometres)	8,150	7,734	7,842

Transportation of goods (million net ton-kilometres): 7,731 in 2001; 7,752 in 2002; 8,109 in 2003.

ROAD TRAFFIC
(motor vehicles in use at 31 December)

	2001	2002	2003
Passenger cars	2,611,770	2,629,526	2,777,219
Buses and coaches	17,817	17,873	17,877
Lorries and vans	355,221	369,295	377,111
Motor cycles and mopeds	93,088	97,593	108,538
Road tractors	25,220	26,786	29,752

SHIPPING

Merchant Fleet
(registered at 31 December)

	2001	2002	2003
Number of vessels	1	1	2
Total displacement (grt)	1,901	3,784	7,568

Source: Lloyd's Register-Fairplay, *World Fleet Statistics*.

INLAND WATERWAYS
(traffic)

	2001	2002	2003
Freight carried ('000 metric tons)	2,903	3,006	2,105
Freight ton-km (million)	1,055	1,120	1,117

CIVIL AVIATION
(traffic)

	1998	1999	2000
Passengers carried	2,188,000	2,352,000	2,476,000
Passenger-km ('000)	3,038,000	3,513,000	3,539,000
Cargo carried: metric tons	15,000	16,000	31,000
Cargo ton-km	42,100,000	55,500,000	68,000,000

Tourism

TOURISTS BY COUNTRY OF ORIGIN
('000 arrivals, including visitors in transit)

	2002	2003	2004
Austria	4,790	4,870	5,237
Croatia	2,115	1,540	1,280
Germany	2,739	2,875	3,136
Poland	906	768	1,007
Romania	5,660	5,976	7,435
Serbia and Montenegro	3,912	3,347	3,618
Slovakia	4,051	4,425	5,548
Ukraine	2,642	2,450	2,564
Total (incl. others)	31,739	31,412	36,635

Tourist receipts ('000 million forint): 1,078.6 in 2001; 838.7 in 2002; 722.7 in 2003 (Jan.–Nov.).

Communications Media

	1998	1999	2000
Radio receivers ('000 in use) . .	7,245	7,231	n.a.
Television receivers ('000 in use) .	4,377	4,519	4,451
Telephones ('000 main lines in use)	3,423.0	3,725.8	3,479.6
Facsimile machines ('000 in use)	180	n.a.	n.a.
Mobile cellular telephones ('000 subscribers)	1,070.2	1,628.2	3,076.2
Personal computers ('000 in use) .	400	750	870
Internet users ('000)	660	600	715
Book production: titles	10,626	9,731	8,986
Book production: copies	47,046	44,652	35,246
Daily newspapers	33	n.a.	n.a.
Average daily circulation . .	1,846,000	n.a.	n.a.

2001: Telephones ('000 main lines in use) 3,258.5; Mobile cellular telephones ('000 subscribers) 4,967.4; Personal computers ('000 in use) 1,000; Internet users ('000) 1,480; Book production (titles) 8,837, (copies) 32,615.

2002: Telephones ('000 main lines in use) 3,095.2; Mobile cellular telephones ('000 subscribers) 6,886.1; Personal computers ('000 in use) 1,100; Internet users ('000) 1,600; Book production (titles) 9,990, (copies) 45,502.

2003: Telephones ('000 main lines in use) 3,012.8; Mobile cellular telephones ('000 subscribers) 7,944.6; Internet users ('000) 2,400; Book production (titles) 9,204, (copies) 32,627.

Sources: partly UNESCO, *Statistical Yearbook*, and International Telecommunication Union.

Education

(1999/2000, estimates, unless otherwise indicated)

	Institu-tions	Teachers	Students		
			Males	Females	Total
Pre-primary . .	4,643	31,409	188,565	177,139	365,704
Primary . . .	3,696	82,829	491,101	469,500	960,601
Secondary: general . .	1,533	14,155	57,641	87,569	145,210
Secondary: teacher training* . .	n.a.	n.a.	159	1,045	1,104
Secondary: vocational . .	990	26,512	195,268	162,035	357,303
Higher: universities etc.	30	12,804	53,520†	52,761†	88,479
Higher: other .	59	8,338	23,167†	33,716†	83,037

* Estimated figures for full-time teacher training.
† 1998/99 figure.

Adult literacy rate (UNESCO estimates): 99.3% (males 99.5%; females 99.2%) in 2002 (Source: UN Development Programme, *Human Development Report*).

Directory

The Constitution

A new Constitution was introduced on 18 August 1949, and the Hungarian People's Republic was established two days later. The Constitution was amended in April 1972 and December 1983. Further, radical amendments were made in October 1989. Shortly afterwards, the Republic of Hungary was proclaimed.

The following is a summary of the main provisions of the Constitution, as amended in October 1989.

GENERAL PROVISIONS

The Republic of Hungary is an independent, democratic constitutional state in which the values of civil democracy and democratic socialism prevail in equal measures. All power belongs to the people, which they exercise directly and through the elected representatives of popular sovereignty.

Political parties may, under observance of the Constitution, be freely formed and may freely operate in Hungary. Parties may not directly exercise public power. No party has the right to guide any state body. Trade unions and other organizations for the representation of interests safeguard and represent the interests of employees, members of co-operatives and entrepreneurs.

The State safeguards the people's freedom, the independence and territorial integrity of the country as well as the frontiers thereof, as established by international treaties. The Republic of Hungary rejects war as a means of settling disputes between nations and refrains from applying force against the independence or territorial integrity of other states, and from threats of violence.

The Hungarian legal system adopts the universally accepted rules of international law. The order of legislation is regulated by an Act of constitutional force.

The economy of Hungary is a market economy, availing itself also of the advantages of planning, with public and private ownership enjoying equal right and protection. Hungary recognizes and supports the right of undertaking and free competition, limitable only by an Act of constitutional force. State-owned enterprises and organs pursuing economic activities manage their affairs independently, in accordance with the mode and responsibility as provided by law.

The Republic of Hungary protects the institutions of marriage and the family. It provides for the indigent through extensive social measures, and recognizes and enforces the right of each citizen to a healthy environment.

GOVERNMENT

Legislature

The highest organ of state authority in the Republic of Hungary is Az ország háza (The National Assembly), which exercises all the rights deriving from the sovereignty of the people and determines the organization, direction and conditions of government. Az ország háza enacts the Constitution and laws, determines the state budget, decides the socio-economic plan, elects the President of the Republic and the Council of Ministers, directs the activities of ministries, decides upon declaring war and concluding peace and exercises the prerogative of amnesty.

Az ország háza is elected for a term of four years and members enjoy immunity from arrest and prosecution without parliamentary consent. It meets at least twice a year and is convened by the President of the Republic or by a written demand of the Council of Ministers or of one-fifth of the Assembly's members. It elects a President, Deputy Presidents and Recorders from among its own members, and it lays down its own rules of procedure and agenda. As a general rule, the sessions of the Az ország háza are held in public.

Az ország háza has the right of legislation which can be initiated by the President of the Republic, the Council of Ministers or any committee or member of Az ország háza. Decisions are valid only if at least half of the members are present, and they require a simple majority. Constitutional changes require a two-thirds' majority. Acts of Az ország háza are signed by the President of the Republic.

Az ország háza may pronounce its dissolution before the expiry of its term, and in the event of an emergency may prolong its mandate or may be reconvened after dissolution. A new Az ország háza must be elected within three months of dissolution and convened within one month of polling day.

Members of Az ország háza are elected on the basis of universal, equal and direct suffrage by secret ballot, and they are accountable to their constituents, who may recall them. All citizens of 18 years and over have the right to vote, with the exception of those who are unsound of mind, and those who are deprived of their civil rights by a court of law.

President of the Republic

The President of the Republic is the Head of State of Hungary. He/she embodies the unity of the nation and supervises the democratic operation of the mechanism of State. The President is also the Commander-in-Chief of the Armed Forces. The President is elected by Az ország háza for a period of five years, and may be re-elected for a second term. Any citizen of Hungary qualified to vote, who has reached 35 years of age before the day of election, may be elected President.

The President may issue the writ for general or local elections, convene Az ország háza, initiate legislation, hold plebiscites, direct local government, conclude international treaties, appoint diplomatic representatives, ratify international treaties, appoint higher civil servants and officers of the armed forces, award orders and titles, and exercise the prerogative of mercy.

Council of Ministers

The highest organ of state administration is the Council of Ministers, responsible to Az ország háza and consisting of the Prime Minister and other Ministers who are elected by Az ország háza on the recommendation of the President of the Republic. The Council of Ministers directs the work of the ministries (listed in a special enactment) and ensures the enforcement of laws and the fulfilment of economic plans; it may issue decrees and annul or modify measures taken by any central or local organ of government.

Local Administration

The local organs of state power are the county, town, borough and town precinct councils, whose members are elected for a term of four years by the voters in each area. Local councils direct economic, social and cultural activities in their area, prepare local economic plans and budgets and supervise their fulfilment, enforce laws, supervise subordinate organs, maintain public order, protect public property and individual rights, and direct local economic enterprises. They may issue regulations and annul or modify those of subordinate councils. Local Councils are administered by an Executive Committee elected by and responsible to them.

JUDICATURE

Justice is administered by the Supreme Court of the Republic of Hungary, county and district courts. The Supreme Court exercises the right of supervising in principle the judicial activities and practice of all other courts.

All judicial offices are filled by election; Supreme Court, county and district court judges are all elected for an indefinite period; the President of the Supreme Court is elected by Az ország háza. All court hearings are public unless otherwise prescribed by law, and those accused are guaranteed the right of defence. An accused person must be considered innocent until proved guilty.

Public Prosecutor

The function of the Chief Public Prosecutor is to supervise the observance of the law. He is elected by Az ország háza, to whom he is responsible. The organization of public prosecution is under the control of the Chief Public Prosecutor, who appoints the public prosecutors.

RIGHTS AND DUTIES OF CITIZENS

The Republic of Hungary guarantees for its citizens the right to work and to remuneration, the right of rest and recreation, the right to care in old age, sickness or disability, the right to education, and equality before the law; women enjoy equal rights with men. Discrimination on grounds of sex, religion or nationality is a punishable offence. The State also ensures freedom of conscience, religious worship, speech, the press and assembly. The right of workers to organize themselves is stressed. The freedom of the individual, and the privacy of the home and of correspondence are inviolable. Freedom for creative work in the sciences and the arts is guaranteed.

The basic freedoms of all workers are guaranteed and foreign citizens enjoy the right of asylum.

Military service (with or without arms) and the defence of their country are the duties of all citizens.

The Government

HEAD OF STATE

President of the Republic: FERENC MÁDL (elected 6 June 2000; took office 4 August 2000).

COUNCIL OF MINISTERS
(April 2005)

A coalition of the Hungarian Socialist Party (HSP) and the Alliance of Free Democrats (AFD).

Prime Minister: FERENC GYURCSÁNY (HSP).

Minister of Foreign Affairs: FERENC SOMOGYI (HSP).

Minister of Defence: FERENC JUHÁSZ (HSP).

Minister of Finance: JÁNOS VERES (HSP).

Minister of Economy and Transport: JÁNOS KÓKA (AFD).

Minister of Home Affairs: MÓNIKA LAMPERTH (HSP).

Minister of Agriculture and Rural Development: JÓZSEF GRAF (HSP).

Minister of Health: JENŐ RÁCZ (HSP).

Minister of Justice: JÓZSEF PETRÉTEI (Independent).

Minister of Labour and Employment: GÁBOR CSIZMÁR (HSP).

Minister of Environmental Protection and Water Management: MIKLÓS PERSÁNYI (AFD).

Minister of Information Technology and Telecommunications: KÁLMÁN KOVÁCS (AFD).

Minister of Cultural Heritage: ANDRAS BOZOKI (HSP).

Minister of Education: BÁLINT MAGYAR (AFD).

Minister of Children, Youth and Equal Opportunities: KINGA GÖNCZ (HSP).

Minister in charge of the Prime Minister's Office: PÉTER KISS (HSP).

Minister without Portfolio, responsible for Housing and Construction, Tourism and Regional Issues: ISTVÁN KOLBER (HSP).

Minister without Portfolio, responsible for European Union Issues: ETELE BARÁTH (HSP).

MINISTRIES

Office of the President: 1014 Budapest, Szent György tér 1–2; tel. (1) 224-5009.

Office of the Prime Minister: 1055 Budapest, Kossuth Lajos tér 1–3; tel. (1) 441-4000; fax (1) 268-3050; internet www.kancellaria.gov.hu.

Ministry of Agriculture and Rural Development: 1055 Budapest, Kossuth Lajos tér 11; tel. (1) 301-4000; fax (1) 301-0408; internet www.fvm.hu.

Ministry of Children, Youth and Equal Opportunities: 1054 Budapest, Hold u. 1; tel. (1) 311-9080; fax (1) 269-0188; internet www.ism.hu/start.htm.

Ministry of Cultural Heritage: 1077 Budapest, Wesselényi u. 20–22; tel. (1) 484-7100; fax (1) 484-7172; internet www.nkom.hu.

Ministry of Defence: 1055 Budapest, Balaton u. 7–11; tel. (1) 236-5111; fax (1) 311-0182; internet www.honvedelem.hu.

Ministry of Economy and Transport: 1055 Budapest, Honvéd u. 13–15; tel. (1) 374-1700; fax (1) 374-2700; e-mail press@gkm.hu; internet www.gkm.hu.

Ministry of Education: 1055 Budapest, Szalay u. 10–14; tel. (1) 302-0600; fax (1) 302-2002; internet www.om.hu.

Ministry of Environmental Protection and Water Management: 1011 Budapest, POB 351, Fő u. 44–50; tel. (1) 457-3300; fax (1) 201-2846; e-mail kozonsir@mail.ktm.hu; internet www.ktm.hu.

Ministry of Finance: 1051 Budapest, József Nádor tér 2–4; tel. (1) 318-2066; fax (1) 318-2570; internet www.p-m.hu.

Ministry of Foreign Affairs: 1027 Budapest, Bem rkp. 47; tel. (1) 458-1000; fax (1) 212-5981; internet www.mfa.gov.hu.

Ministry of Health: 1051 Budapest, Arany János u. 6–8; tel. (1) 301-7800; internet www.eszcsm.hu.

Ministry of Home Affairs: 1051 Budapest, József Attila u. 2–4; tel. (1) 331-3700; fax (1) 118-2870; internet www.b-m.hu.

Ministry of Information Technology and Telecommunications: 1400 Budapest, POB 87; tel. (1) 322-0220; e-mail info@ihm.hu; internet www.ihm.hu.

Ministry of Justice: 1055 Budapest, Kossuth Lajos tér 4; tel. (1) 441-3003; internet www.im.hu.

Ministry of Labour and Employment: 1054 Budapest, Alkotmány u. 3; tel. (1) 473-8100; fax (1) 473-8101; e-mail info@fmm.gov.hu; internet www.fmm.gov.hu/.

Legislature

Az ország háza
(The National Assembly)

1055 Budapest, Kossuth Lajos tér 1–3; 1357 Budapest, POB 2; tel. (1) 441-4000; fax (1) 441-5000; internet www.mkogy.hu.

President: KATALIN SZILI.

General Election, 7 and 21 April 2002

Parties	% of votes	Seats
Federation of Young Democrats—Hungarian Civic Party-Hungarian Democratic Forum (FYD—HCP-HDF) coalition	48.70	188
Hungarian Socialist Party (HSP)	46.11	178
Alliance of Free Democrats (AFD)	5.18	20
Total	100.00	386

Political Organizations

Agrarian Association—National Agrarian Party (Agrárszövetsége—Nemzeti Agrárpárt—ASz): 1013 Budapest, Krisztina tér 1; tel. (1) 201-2627; e-mail agrarszov@elender.hu; Chair. TAMÁS NAGY.

Alliance of Free Democrats (AFD) (Szabad Demokraták Szövetsége—SzDSz): 1143 Budapest, Gizella u. 36; tel. and fax (1) 223-2045; e-mail dora.veress@szdsz.hu; internet www.szdsz.hu; f. 1988; 19,000 mems (2000); Chair. GÁBOR KUNCZE.

Alliance of Green Democrats: 1054 Budapest, Vadász u. 29; tel. (1) 353-0100; fax (1) 354-1902; e-mail zd@zd.hu; internet www.zd .hu; f. 2003; from the merger of the Alliance of Greens, the Hungarian Women's Party, the New Left and others; Chair. GYÖRGY DROPPA.

Centrum Party: 1243 Budapest, POB 715; tel. (1) 301-5040; fax (1) 301-5048; e-mail centruminfo@axelero.hu; internet www .centrum-part.hu; f. 2001; electoral coalition of the Hungarian Democratic People's Party, the Christian Democratic People's Party, the Third Side for Hungary Association (HOME) and the Green Democrats Party; Chair. MIHÁLY KUPA.

Christian Democratic People's Party (CDPP) (Kereszténydemokrata Néppárt—KDNP): 1126 Budapest, Nagy Jenő u. 5; tel. (1) 175-0333; fax (1) 155-5772; e-mail kulugy@kdnp.hu; internet www .kdnp.hu; re-formed 1989; formed an electoral alliance, the Centrum Party (q.v.), to contest the 2002 legislative election; Chair. TIDAVAR BARTÓK.

Democratic Roma Coalition: ethnic Roma party; left-wing.

Entrepreneurs' Party (Vállalkozók Pártja): 6000 Kecskemét, Csány János körút 12; tel. (76) 509-527; f. 1989; formed an alliance with the Hungarian Democratic Forum, the Hungarian Democratic People's Party and the Independent Smallholders' Party for elections to the European Parliament in 2004; Chair. JÓSZEF TACAKS.

Federation of Young Democrats—Hungarian Civic Alliance (FYD—HCA) (Magyar Polgári Szöevetség—FIDESZ—MPSZ): 1062 Budapest, Lendvay u. 28; tel. (1) 269-5353; fax (1) 269-5343; e-mail fidesz@fidesz.hu; internet www.fidesz.hu; f. 1988 as the Federation of Young Democrats; renamed April 1995; re-formed as an alliance in 2003, with a new charter; 10,000 mems; Chair. VIKTOR ORBÁN.

Hungarian Christian Democratic Federation (MKDSZ): f. 1997 by breakaway members of the Christian Democratic People's Party; allied to the Federation of Young Democrats—Hungarian Civic Alliance; Chair. LÁSZLÓ SURJAN.

Hungarian Democratic Forum (HDF) (Magyar Demokrata Fórum—MDF): 1026 Budapest, Szilágyi Erszébet fasor 73; 1539 Budapest, POB 579; tel. (1) 212-2828; fax (1) 225-2290; internet www.mdf.hu; f. 1987; centre-right; formed an alliance with the Entrepreneurs Party, the Hungarian Democratic People's Party and the Independent Smallholders' Party for elections to the European Parliament in 2004; 25,000 mems (2001); Chair. Dr IBOLYA DÁVID.

Hungarian Democratic People's Party (HDPP) (Magyar Demokrata Néppárt—MDN): Budapest; f. 1996 by former mems of the Hungarian Democratic Forum; moderate; formed an alliance with the Entrepreneurs Party, the Hungarian Democratic Forum and the Independent Smallholders' Party for elections to the European Parliament in 2004; Chair. ERZSÉBET PUSZTAI.

Hungarian Justice and Life Party (HJLP) (Magyar Igazság és Élet Pártja—MIEP): 1085 Budapest, Rökk Szilárd u. 19; tel. and fax (1) 3171-2692; internet www.miep.hu; f. 1993; extreme right-wing, nationalist party; Chair. ISTVÁN CSURKA.

Hungarian National Front (Magyar Nemzeti Front): Budapest; internet www.nemzetifront.hu; f. 2003 by fmr mems of the Hungarian Justice and Life Party; Chair. ERNO ROZGONYI (acting).

Hungarian Social Democratic Party (HSDP) (Magyarországi Szociáldemokrata Párt—MSzDP): Budapest; tel. and fax (1) 342-3547; f. 1890; absorbed by Communist Party in 1948; revived 1988; affiliated with the Social Democratic Youth Movement; Chair. LASZLO KAPOLYI.

Hungarian Socialist Party (HSP) (Magyar Szocialista Párt—MSzP): 1081 Budapest, Köztársaság tér 26; tel. (1) 210-0046; fax (1) 210-0081; internet www.mszp.hu; f. 1989 to replace the Hungarian Socialist Workers' Party; 40,000 mems (Dec. 1999); Chair. ISTVÁN HILLER.

Hungarian Workers' Party (HWP) (Magyar Munkáspárt—MMP): 1082 Budapest, Baross u. 61; tel. (1) 334-2721; fax (1) 313-5423; e-mail mpzoo@matavnet.hu; internet www.munkaspart.hu; f. 1956 as Hungarian Socialist Workers' Party; dissolved and replaced by Hungarian Socialist Party (see above) in 1989; re-formed in 1989 as Hungarian Socialist Workers' Party, name changed as above 1992; approx. 30,000 mems (Oct. 1992); Pres. Dr GYULA THÜRMER.

Independent Smallholders' and Civic Party (ISCP) (Független Kisgazda-, Földmunkás- és Polgári Párt—FKgP): Budapest; tel. and fax (1) 318-1824; internet www.fkgp.hu; f. 1988 as the Independent Smallholders' Party, name subsequently changed to the Independent Smallholders' and Peasants' Party; 60,000 mems; Chair. Dr MIKLOS RETI.

Lungo Drom Alliance: 5000 Szolnok, Szapáry u. 19; tel. (56) 420-110; ethnic Roma party; right-wing; Leader FLORIAN FARKAS.

Smallholder Alliance—Party of the Smallholder Federation: Budapest; f. 2002 by former mems of the ISCP; conservative; Chair. SANDOR CSEH.

United Historic Smallholders' Party (UHSP) (Egyesült Kisgazdapárt—Történelmi Tagozat—EKgP-TT): Budapest; f. 1992 as the 'Historical Section' of the Independent Smallholders' Party (now the ISCP); renamed 1993; Gen. Sec. ANTAL BELAFI.

Diplomatic Representation

EMBASSIES IN HUNGARY

Albania: 1026 Budapest, Gábor Áron u. 55; tel. (1) 326-8905; fax (1) 326-8904; e-mail albemb@enternet.hu; Ambassador EDUARD SULO.

Algeria: 1121 Budapest, Zugligeti út 27; tel. (1) 200-6860; fax (1) 200-6781; e-mail ambalbud@axelero.hu; Ambassador BACHIR ROUIS.

Argentina: 1023 Budapest, Vérhalom u. 12–16, II, 3A; tel. (1) 325-0492; fax (1) 326-0494; e-mail eungr@mrecic.gov.ar; Ambassador HORACIO EMILIO SOLARI.

Australia: 1126 Budapest, Királyhágó tér 8–9; tel. (1) 457-9777; fax (1) 201-9792; e-mail ausembbp@mail.datanet.hu; internet www .australia.hu; Ambassador CLARE BIRGIN.

Austria: 1068 Budapest, Benczúr u. 16; tel. (1) 479-7010; fax (1) 352-8795; e-mail austroamb-budapest@pronet.hu; internet www .austrian-embassy.hu; Ambassador Dr GÜNTER BIRBAUM.

Azerbaijan: Budapest, Szabadság tér 7, Bank Center, Platina Tower, 5th floor; tel. and fax (1) 302-3535; f. 2004; Ambassador HASAN HASANOV.

Belgium: 1027 Budapest, Kapàs u. 11–15; tel. (1) 457-9960; fax (1) 375-1566; e-mail bdapest@diplobel.org; internet www.diplomatie.be/ budapest; Ambassador MARC TRENTESEAU.

Belarus: 1126 Budapest, Agárdi u. 3B; tel. (1) 214-0553; fax (1) 214-0554; e-mail hungary@belembassy.org; internet belembassy.org/ hungary; Chargé d'affaires a.i. VASILIY KURLOVICH.

Bosnia and Herzegovina: 1026 Budapest, Pasaréti út 48; tel. (1) 212-0106; fax (1) 212-0109; Ambassador MIRSA MUHAREMAGIĆ.

Brazil: 1062 Budapest, Délibáb u. 30; tel. (1) 351-0060; fax (1) 351-0066; e-mail embassy@brazil.hu; internet www.brazil.hu; Ambassador ROBERTO SOARES DE OLIVEIRA.

Bulgaria: 1062 Budapest, Andrássy u. 115; tel. (1) 322-0824; fax (1) 322-5215; e-mail bgembhu@attglobal.net; Ambassador GIRNO GYAVROV.

Canada: 1121 Budapest, Zugligeti u. 51–53; tel. (1) 392-3360; fax (1) 392-3390; internet www.kanada.hu; Ambassador ROBERT HAGE.

Chile: 1023 Budapest, Vérhalom. u. 12–16, III, 35; tel. (1) 212-0061; fax (1) 212-0059; e-mail echilehu@pronet.hu; internet www.chile.hu; Ambassador CELSO ENRIQUE MORENO LAVAL.

China, People's Republic: 1068 Budapest, Benczúr u. 15; tel. (1) 413-2400; fax (1) 413-2451; e-mail chinaemb_hu@mfa.gov.cn; internet www.chinaembassy.hu; Ambassador ZHU ZUSHOU.

Colombia: 1025 Budapest, Józsefhegyi u. 28-30 G-6; tel. (1) 325-7617; fax (1) 325-7618; e-mail embajada.budapest@colombia.hu; Ambassador BELARMINO PINILLA.

Croatia: 1065 Budapest, Munkácsy Mihály u. 15; tel. (1) 354-1315; fax (1) 354-1319; e-mail croemb.bp@mvp.hu; Ambassador Dr STANKO NICK.

Cuba: 1025 Budapest, Józsefhegyi u. 28–30, II, 6u.; tel. (1) 325-7290; fax (1) 438-5956; e-mail segundosec@embacuba.hu; internet www.embacuba.hu; Ambassador SONIA DÍAZ.

Cyprus: 1051 Budapest, Dorottya u. 3, III, 2–3u.; tel. (1) 266-1330; fax (1) 266-0538; Ambassador GEORGE SHIAKALLIS.

Czech Republic: 1064 Budapest, Rózsa u. 61; tel. (1) 351-0539; fax (1) 351-9189; e-mail budapest@embassy.mzv.cz; internet www.mfa .cz/budapest; Ambassador HANA HUBÁČKOVÁ.

Denmark: 1122 Budapest, Határőr út 37; tel. (1) 487-9000; fax (1) 487-9045; e-mail budamb@um.dk; internet www.ambbudapest.um .dk; Ambassador HANS MICHAEL KOFOED-HANSEN.

Ecuador: 1023 Budapest, Levél u. 4; tel. (1) 315-2114; fax (1) 315-2104; e-mail embajada@ecuador.hu; internet www.ecuador.hu; Ambassador Dr Dr. ALFONSO LÓPEZ ARAUJO.

Egypt: 1016 Budapest, Bérc u. 16; tel. (1) 381-0475; fax (1) 381-0571; e-mail ambegbp@pronet.hu; Ambassador MUHAMMAD ES-SAYED ABBAS.

Estonia: 1062 Budapest, Lendvay u. 12, Fsz. 3; tel. (1) 354-2570; fax (1) 354-2571; e-mail embassy.budapest@mfa.ee; Ambassador TOIVO TASA.

Finland: 1118 Budapest, Kelenhegyi út 16A; tel. (1) 279-2500; fax (1) 385-0843; e-mail sanomat.bud@formin.fi; internet www.finland.hu; Ambassador PEKKA KUJASALO.

France: 1062 Budapest, Lendvay u. 27; tel. (1) 332-4980; fax (1) 311-8291; e-mail ambasfn-presse@matavnet.hu; internet www.ambafrance.hu; Ambassador PHILIPPE ZELLER.

Germany: 1014 Budapest, Úri u. 64–66; tel. and fax (1) 488-3500; e-mail info@deutschebotschaft-budapest.hu; internet www.deutschebotschaft-budapest.hu; Ambassador URSULA SEILER-ALBRING.

Greece: 1063 Budapest, Szegfű u. 3; tel. (1) 413-2600; fax (1) 342-1934; e-mail greekemb@axelero.hu; Ambassador DIMITRIS CONTUMAS.

Holy See: 1126 Budapest, Gyimes u. 1–3; tel. (1) 355-8979; fax (1) 355-6987; e-mail nuntbud@communio.hcbc.hu; Apostolic Nuncio Most Rev. KARL-JOSEF RAUBER (Titular Archbishop of Iubaltiana).

India: 1025 Budapest, Búzavirág u. 14; tel. (1) 325-7742; fax (1) 325-7745; e-mail chancery@indianembassy.hu; internet www.indianembassy.hu; Ambassador MANBIR SINGH.

Indonesia: 1068 Budapest, Városligeti fasor 26; tel. (1) 413-3800; fax (1) 322-8669; e-mail kbribud@indonesia.hu; internet www.indonesia.hu; Ambassador SAPARTINI SINGGIH KUNTJORO JAKTI.

Iran: 1143 Budapest, Stefánia út 97; tel. (1) 460-9260; fax (1) 460-9430; e-mail embiran@iranembassy.hu; internet www.iranembassy.hu; Ambassador ABULFAZ RAHNAMA HEZAVEI.

Ireland: 1944 Budapest, Bank Center Gránit Torony, VII; tel. (1) 302-9600; fax (1) 302-9599; e-mail iremb@hu.inter.net; Ambassador BRENDAN MCMAHON.

Israel: 1026 Budapest, Fullánk u. 8; tel. (1) 392-6200; fax (1) 200-0783; e-mail info@budapest.mfa.gov.il; internet budapest.mfa.gov.il; Ambassador DAVID ADMON.

Italy: 1143 Budapest, Stefánia út 95; tel. (1) 460-6200; fax (1) 460-6260; e-mail ambasciata.budapest@esteri.it; internet www.ambitalia.hu; Ambassador PAOLO GUIDO SPINELLI.

Japan: 1125 Budapest, Zalai út 7; tel. (1) 398-3100; fax (1) 275-1281; e-mail japan.embassy@mail.datanet.hu; internet www.hu.emb-japan.go.jp; Ambassador TERUYOSHI INAGAWA.

Kazakhstan: 1025 Budapest, II ker., Kapy u. 59; tel. (1) 275-1300; fax (1) 275-2092; e-mail kazak@euroweb.hu; Ambassador SAGYNBEK TURSUNOV.

Korea, Republic: 1062 Budapest, Andrássy út 109; tel. (1) 351-1179; fax (1) 351-1182; e-mail hungary@mofat.go.kr; internet www.mofat.go.kr/hungary; Ambassador LEE HO-JIN.

Lebanon: 1112 Budapest, Sasadi u. 160; tel. (1) 249-0900; fax (1) 249-0901.

Libya: 1143 Budapest, Stefánia u. 111; tel. (1) 343-6076; fax (1) 343-1583; Head of People's Bureau (Ambassador) OMAR MUFTAH DALLAL.

Macedonia, former Yugoslav republic: 1024 Budapest, Margit Körut út 43–45; tel. and fax (1) 336-0510; fax 315-1921; e-mail macedonia.embassy@axelero.hu; Chargé d'affaires a.i. SAŠO VELJANOVSKI.

Malaysia: 1026 Budapest, Pasaréti út 29; tel. (1) 488-0810; fax (1) 488-0824; e-mail mwbdpest@axelero.hu; Ambasssador WAN YUSOF EMBONG.

Mexico: 1024 Budapest, Rómer Flóris u. 58; tel. (1) 326-0447; fax (1) 326-0485; e-mail embamexhu@axelero.hu; Ambassador JOSÉ LUIS MARTÍNEZ Y HERNÁNDEZ.

Moldova: 1111 Budapest, Budafoki u. 9–11; tel. (1) 209-1191; fax (1) 209-1195; Ambassador (vacant).

Mongolia: 1022 Budapest II, K. Bogár u. 14/C; tel. (1) 212-4579; fax (1) 212-5731; e-mail mnk@mail.matavnet.hu; Ambassador DERGELDALIYN DZAMBADZANCAN.

Morocco: 1026 Budapest, Törökvész Lejtő u. 12A; tel. (1) 200-7855; fax (1) 275-1437; e-mail sifamabudap@axelero.hu; Ambassador LEMHOUER AL-HASSANE.

Netherlands: 1022 Budapest, Füge u. 5–7; tel. (1) 336-6300; fax (1) 326-5978; e-mail bdp@minbuza.nl; internet www.netherlandsembassy.hu; Ambassador F. P. R. VAN NOUHUYS.

Nigeria: 1022 Budapest, Árvácska u. 6; tel. (1) 212-2021; fax (1) 212-2025; e-mail embassy@nigerianembassy.hu; internet www.nigerianembassy.hu; Ambassador: Chief ABAYOMI AKINTOLA.

Norway: 1015 Budapest, Ostrom u. 13, POB 32; tel. (1) 212-9400; fax (1) 212-9410; e-mail emb.budapest@mfa.no; internet www.norvegia.hu; Ambassador JAN G. JØLLE.

Pakistan: 1125 Budapest, Adonis u. 3A; tel. (1) 355-8017; fax (1) 375-1402; e-mail parepbudapest@hotmail.com.

Panama: 1118 Budapest, Iglói u. 6/B2; tel. and fax (1) 466-9817; e-mail embpanbu@freemail.c3.hu.

Peru: 1023 Budapest, Vérhalom u. 12–16; tel. (1) 326-0984; fax (1) 326-1087; e-mail peru1@axelero.hu; internet www.peru.hu; Ambassador GUILLERMO RUSSO CHECA.

Philippines: 1026 Budapest, Gábor Áron u. 58; tel. (1) 200-5523; fax (1) 200-5528; e-mail phbuda@mail.datanet.hu; Ambassador ALEJANDRO DEL ROSARIO.

Poland: 1068 Budapest, Városligeti fasor 16; tel. (1) 413-8200; fax (1) 351-1722; e-mail info@polishemb.hu; internet www.lengyelorszag.hu; Ambassador RAFAŁ WIŚNIEWSKI.

Portugal: 1126 Budapest, Edifício C. Alkotás u. 53; tel. (1) 201-7617; fax (1) 201-7619; e-mail embport@axelero.hu; Ambassador LUÍS FILIPE CASTRO MENDES.

Romania: 1146 Budapest, Thököly u. 72; tel. (1) 384-0271; fax (1) 384-5535; e-mail postmaster@roembbud.axelero.net; Ambassador CALIN FABIAN.

Russia: 1062 Budapest, Bajza u. 35; tel. (1) 302-5230; fax (1) 353-4164; Ambassador VALERII MUSATOV.

Serbia and Montenegro: 1068 Budapest, Dózsa György u. 92B; tel. (1) 322-9838; fax (1) 322-1438; e-mail ambjubp@mail.datanet.hu; Ambassador Dr DEJAN JANČA.

Slovakia: 1143 Budapest, Stefánia u. 22-24; tel. (1) 460-9010; fax (1) 460-9020; e-mail slovakem@matavnet.hu; Ambassador JURAJ MIGAŠ.

Slovenia: 1025 Budapest, Cseppkö u. 68; tel. (1) 438-5600; fax (1) 325-9187; e-mail vbp@mzz-dkp.gov.si; Ambassador ANDREJ GERENČER.

South Africa: 1026 Budapest, Gárdonyi Géza út 17; tel. (1) 392-0999; fax (1) 200-7277; e-mail saemb@sa-embassy.hu; internet www.sa-embassy.hu; Ambassador Dr DUDUZILE M. KHOZA.

Spain: 1067 Budapest, Eötvös u. 11B; tel. (1) 342-9992; fax (1) 351-0572; Ambassador ANTONIO ORTIZ GARCIA.

Sweden: 1146 Budapest, Ajtósi Dürer sor 27A; tel. (1) 460-6020; fax (1) 460-6021; e-mail ambassaden.budapest@foreign.ministry.se; internet www.swedenabroad.com/budapest; Ambassador BENGT LUNDBORG.

Switzerland: 1143 Budapest, Stefánia út 107; tel. (1) 460-7040; fax (1) 343-9492; e-mail vertretung@bud.rep.admin.ch; internet www.swissembassy.hu; Ambassador MARC-ANDRÉ SALAMIN.

Syria: 1026 Budapest, Harangvirág u. 3; tel. (1) 200-8046; fax (1) 200-8048; Ambassador (vacant).

Thailand: 1025 Budapest, Verecke u. 79; tel. (1) 438-4020; fax (1) 438-4023; e-mail thaiemba@mail.datanet.hu; Ambassador H. TAWATCHAI PIYARATA.

Tunisia: 1021 Budapest, Budakeszi u. 55D; tel. (1) 200-8929; fax (1) 200-8931; e-mail ambtunb@mail.matav.hu; Chargé d'affaires ABDELWAHEB BOUZOUITA.

Turkey: 1062 Budapest, Andrássy u. 123; tel. (1) 344-5025; fax (1) 344-5143; e-mail budapest@turkisembassy.hu; Ambassador UMUR APAYDIN.

Ukraine: 1143 Budapest, Stefania u. 77; tel. (1) 422-4122; fax (1) 220-9873; e-mail ukran.kovetseg@mail.datanet.hu; Ambassador Dr YURIY MUSHKA.

United Kingdom: 1051 Budapest, Harmincad u. 6; tel. (1) 266-2888; fax (1) 266-0907; e-mail info@britemb.hu; internet www.britishembassy.hu; Ambassador JOHN NICHOLS.

USA: 1054 Budapest, Szabadság tér 12; tel. (1) 475-4400; fax (1) 475-4764; e-mail postmaster@usembassy.hu; internet budapest.usembassy.gov; Ambassador GEORGE H. WALKER.

Uruguay: 1023 Budapest 2, Vérhalom u. 12–16, I, 3; tel. and fax (1) 326-0459; e-mail urupest@euroweb.hu; Ambassador HOMERO DIEGO MARTÍNEZ LAWLOR.

Venezuela: 1023 Budapest, Vérhalom u. 12–16, I, 14; tel. (1) 326-0460; fax (1) 326-0450; e-mail venhu@ibm.net; Ambassador JORGE A. GONZÁLEZ.

Viet Nam: 1068 Budapest 2, Benczúr u. 18; tel. (1) 342-5583; fax (1) 325-8798; Ambassador DAO THI TAM.

Yemen: 1025 Budapest, Józsefhegyi u. 28-30, D/6; tel. (1) 212-3991; fax (1) 212-3883; e-mail al-yemen.al-saida@matavnet.hu; Ambassador (vacant).

Judicial System

The system of court procedure in Hungary is based on an Act that came into effect in 1953 and has since been updated frequently. The system of jurisdiction is based on the local courts (district courts in Budapest, city courts in other cities), labour courts, county courts (or the Metropolitan Court) and the Supreme Court. In the legal remedy system of two instances, appeals against the decisions of city and district courts can be lodged with the competent county court and the Metropolitan Court of Budapest respectively. Against the judgment of first instance of the latter, appeal is to be lodged with the Supreme Court. The Chief Public Prosecutor and the President of the Supreme Court have the right to submit a protest on legal grounds against the final judgment of any court.

By virtue of the 1973 Act, effective from 1974 and modified in 1979, the procedure in criminal cases is differentiated for criminal offences and for criminal acts. In the first instance, criminal cases are tried, depending on their character, by a professional judge; where justified by the magnitude of the criminal act, by a council composed of three members, a professional judge and two lay assessors, while in major cases the court consists of five members, two professional judges and three lay assessors. In the Supreme Court, second instance cases are tried only by professional judges. The President of the Supreme Court is elected by the Országgyülés. Judges are appointed by the President of the Republic for an indefinite period. Assessors are elected by the local municipal councils.

In the interest of ensuring legality and a uniform application of the law, the Supreme Court exercises a principled guidance over the jurisdiction of courts. In the Republic of Hungary judges are independent and subject only to the Law and other legal regulations.

The Minister of Justice supervises the general activities of courts. the Chief Public Prosecutor is elected by the Országgyülés. The Chief Public Prosecutor and the Prosecutor's Office provide for the consistent prosecution of all acts violating or endangering the legal order of society, the safety and independence of the state, and for the protection of citizens.

The Prosecutors of the independent prosecuting organization exert supervision over the legality of investigations and the implementation of punishments, and assist with specific means in ensuring that legal regulations should be observed by state, economic and other organs and citizens, and they support the legality of court procedures and decisions.

Supreme Court (Legfelsőbb Bíróság): 1055 Budapest, Markó u. 16; tel. (1) 268-4500; fax (1) 268-4740; e-mail fotitkar@legfelsobb.birosag.hu; internet www.lb.hu; Pres. Zoltán Lomnici; Chief Public Prosecutor Péter Polt.

Constitutional Court (Alkotmánybíróság): 1015 Budapest, Donáti u. 35-45; tel. (1) 488-3100; fax (1) 212-1170; internet www.mkab.hu; Pres. Andras Hollo.

Religion

CHRISTIANITY

Ecumenical Council of Churches in Hungary (Magyarországi Egyházak Ökumenikus Tanácsa): 1026 Budapest, Bimbó u. 127; tel. (1) 394-4847; fax (1) 394-1210; e-mail oikoumene@lutheran.hu; internet oikoumene.lutheran.hu; f. 1943; member churches: Baptist, Bulgarian Orthodox, Evangelical Lutheran, Hungarian Orthodox, Methodist, Reformed Church, Romanian Orthodox and Serbian Orthodox; Pres. Bishop Dr Mihály Márkus; Gen. Sec. Dr Tibor Görög.

The Roman Catholic Church

Hungary comprises four archdioceses, nine dioceses (including one for Catholics of the Byzantine rite) and one territorial abbacy (directly responsible to the Holy See). At 31 December 2002 the Church had an estimated 6,264,000 adherents in Hungary.

Bishops' Conference

1046 Budapest, POB 79; tel. (1) 342-6959; fax (1) 342-6957; e-mail pkt@katolikus.hu; internet www.katolikus.hu.

f. 1969; Pres. Most Rev. Dr István Seregély (Archbishop of Eger) Latin Rite:

Archbishop of Eger: Most Rev. Dr István Seregély.

Archbishop of Esztergom-Budapest: Cardinal Dr Péter Erdő (Primate of Hungary).

Archbishop of Kalocsa-Kecskemét: Most Rev. Dr Balázs Bábel.

Archbishop of Veszprém: Most Rev. Dr Gyula Márfi.

Apostolic Administrator of Miskolc for Catholics of the Byzantine Rite in the Hungarian Territories, Bishop of Hajdúdorog: Szilárd Keresztes, 4401 Nyiregyháza, Bethlen u. 5, POB 60; tel. (42) 317-397; fax (42) 314-734.

253,000 adherents in diocese of Hajdúdorog (Dec. 1999); an estimated 25,000 adherents in the Apostolic Exarchate of Miskolc (Dec. 1999).

Protestant Churches

Baptist Union of Hungary (Magyarországi Baptista Egyház): 1068 Budapest, Benczur u. 31; tel. (1) 343-0618; fax (1) 352-9707; e-mail baptist.convention@mail.datanet.hu; f. 1846; 11,310 mems (2004); Pres. Rev. Dr Kálmán Mészáros; Gen.-Sec. Rev. Kornél Mészáros.

Evangelical Lutheran Church in Hungary (Magyarországi Evangélikus Egyház): 1085 Budapest, Üllöi u. 24; tel. (1) 483-2260; fax (1) 486-3554; e-mail orszagos@lutheran.hu; internet www.lutheran.hu; 430,000 mems (1992); Presiding Bishop Imre Szebik.

United Methodist Church in Hungary (Magyarországi Metodista Egyház): 1032 Budapest, Kiscelli u. 73; tel. (1) 250-1536; fax (1) 250-1849; e-mail office@metodista.hu; internet www.metodista.hu; f. 1898; Superintendent István Csernák.

Reformed Church in Hungary—Presbyterian (Magyarországi Református Egyház): 1146 Budapest, Abonyi u. 21; tel. (1) 343-7870; e-mail rch@mail.elender.hu; Pres. of Gen. Synod Bishop Dr Gusztáv Bölcskei.

Unitarian Church in Hungary (Magyarországi Unitárius Egyház): 1055 Budapest V, Nagy Ignác u. 4; tel. (1) 111-2801; Bishop Rev. Martin Bencze.

The Eastern Orthodox Church

Hungarian Orthodox Church (Magyar Ortodox Egyház): 1052 Budapest, Petőfi tér 2/1/2.; tel. (1) 318-4813; Archbishop Pavel (Ponomarjov).

The Bulgarian, Romanian, Russian and Serbian Orthodox Churches are also represented.

ISLAM

There are about 3,000 Muslims in Hungary.

Hungarian Islamic Community (Magyar Iszlám Közösség): Budapest; tel. (1) 177-7602; Leader Dr Balázs Mihálffy.

JUDAISM

The Jewish community in Hungary is estimated to number between 100,000 and 120,000 people. Some 80% of Hungary's Jewish community resides in Budapest.

Federation of Jewish Communities in Hungary (Magyarországi Zsidó Hitközségek Szövetsége): 1075 Budapest, Sip u. 12, Budapesti Zsidó Hitközség (Jewish Community of Budapest); tel. (1) 413-5575; fax (1) 342-1790; e-mail bzstitk@hotmail.com; internet www.zsido.hu; 80,000 mems; 40 active synagogues; Orthodox and Conservative; Pres. András Heisler; Chief Rabbi of Hungary Dr Péter Kardos.

The Press

Budapest dailies circulate nationally. The most popular are: *Népszabadság*, *Nemzeti Sport* and *Népszava*. *Népszabadság*, the most important daily, was formerly the central organ of the Hungarian Socialist Workers' Party, but is now independent. Most daily newspapers were partially foreign-owned.

PRINCIPAL DAILIES

Békéscsaba

Békés Megyei Hírlap (Békés County News): 5601 Békéscsaba, Munkácsy u. 4; tel. (66) 446-242; fax (66) 441-020; internet www.bmhirlap.hu; f. 1945; Editor-in-Chief Zoltán Árpási; circ. 49,000.

Budapest

Blikk: 1062 Budapest, Aradi u. 22. Iv/1; internet www.blikk.hu; f. 1994; colour tabloid.

Magyar Hírlap (Hungarian Journal): 1087 Budapest, Kerepesi u. 29B; tel. (1) 210-0050; fax (1) 210-3737; f. 1968; 100% foreign-owned; Editor-in-Chief Mátyás Vince; circ. 75,000.

Magyar Nemzet (Hungarian Nation): Budapest; tel. (1) 141-4320; internet www.magyarnemzet.com; 45% foreign-owned; Editor-in-Chief GÁBOR LISZKAY; circ. 100,000.

Mai Nap (Today): 1145 Budapest, Szugló u. 14; tel. (1) 470-1382; fax (1) 470-1351; e-mail info@mainap.hu; internet www.ringier.hu; f. 1988; Editor-in-Chief FERENC KÖSZEGI; circ.100,000.

Metro: 1106 Budapest, Fehér u. 10, 21-es épület; tel. (1) 431-6464; fax (1) 431-6465; e-mail szerk@metro.hu; internet www.metro.hu; Editor IZBÉKI GÁBOR.

Napi Gazdaság (World Economy): 1135 Budapest, Csata u. 32; tel. (1) 350-4349; fax (1) 350-1117; e-mail napi@mail.eleuder.hu; internet www.napi.hu; Editor-in-Chief ADÁM DANKÓ; circ. 16,000.

Nemzeti Sport (National Sport): 1141 Budapest, Szugló u. 83-85; tel. (1) 460-2600; fax (1) 460-2612; e-mail szerkesztoseg@ nemzetisport.hu; internet www.nemzetisport.hu; Editor-in-Chief TAMÁS SZEKERES; circ. 140,000.

Népszabadság (People's Freedom): 1960 Budapest, Bécsi u. 122-124; tel. (1) 436-4500; fax (1) 387-8699; e-mail eotvosp@ nepszabadsag.hu; internet www.nepszabadsag.hu; f. 1942; independent; Editor-in-Chief (vacant); circ. 200,000.

Népszava (Voice of the People): 1022 Budapest, Törökvész u. 30A; tel. (1) 202-7788; fax (1) 202-7798; e-mail online@nepszava.hu; internet www.nepszava.hu; f. 1873; Editor ANDRÁS KERESZTY; circ. 120,000.

Üzlet (Business): Budapest; tel. (1) 111-8260; Editor-in-Chief IVÁN ÉRSEK.

Debrecen

Hajdú-Bihari Napló (Hajdú-Bihar Diary): 4024 Debrecen, Dósa nádor tér 10; tel. (52) 413-395; fax (52) 412-326; e-mail naplo@iscomp .hu; internet www.naplo.hu; f. 1944; Editor-in-Chief ZSOLT PORCSIN; circ. 60,000.

Dunaújváros

A Hírlap (The Journal): 2400 Dunaújváros, Városháza tér 1; tel. (25) 16-010; Editor-in-Chief CSABA D. KISS.

Eger

Heves Megyei Hírlap (Heves County Journal): 3301 Eger, Barkóczy u. 7; tel. (36) 13-644; e-mail hmhirlap@axels.hu; internet www .agria.hu/hmhirlap; Editor-in-Chief LEVENTE KAPOSI; circ. 33,000.

Győr

Kisalföld: 9021 Győr, Újlak u. 4/a; tel. (96) 504-444; fax (96) 504-414; e-mail kisalfoldmail@matav.hu; internet www.kisalfold.hu; Editor-in-Chief NYERGES CSABA.

Kaposvár

Somogyi Hírlap (Somogy Journal): 7401 Kaposvár, Latinca Sándor u. 2A; tel. (82) 11-644; internet www.somogyihirlap.hu; Editor-in-Chief Dr IMRE KERCZA; circ. 59,000.

Kecskemét

Petőfi Népe: 6000 Kecskemét, Szabadság tér 1A; tel. (76) 481-391; internet www.petofinepe.hu; Editor-in-Chief Dr DÁNIEL LOVAS; circ. 60,000.

Miskolc

Déli Hírlap (Midday Journal): 3527 Miskolc, Bajcsy-Zsilinszky u. 15; tel. (46) 42-694; Editor-in-Chief DEZSŐ BEKES; circ. 20,000.

Észak-Magyarország (Northern Hungary): 3527 Miskolc, Bajcsy-Zsilinszky u. 15; tel. (46) 341-888; internet www.eszak.hu; Editor-in-Chief LÁSZLÓ GÖRÖMBÖLYI; circ. 45,000.

Nyíregyháza

Kelet-Magyarország (Eastern Hungary): 4401 Nyíregyháza, Zrínyi u. 3–5; tel. (42) 11-277; Editor-in-Chief Dr SÁNDOR ANGYAL; circ. 80,000.

Pécs

Új Dunántúli Napló: 7601 Pécs, Hunyadi u. 11; tel. (72) 15-000; internet www.dunantulinaplo.hu; Editor-in-Chief JENŐ LOMBOSI; circ. 84,000.

Salgótarján

Új Nógrád (New Nógrád): 3100 Salgótarján, Palócz Imre tér 4; tel. (32) 10-589; Editor-in-Chief LÁSZLÓ SULYOK; circ. 23,000.

Szeged

Délvilág (Southern World): 6740 Szeged, Tanácsköztársaság u. 10; tel. (62) 14-911; internet www.delvilag.hu; Editor-in-Chief ISTVÁN NIKOLÉNYI; circ. 20,000.

Délmagyarország (Southern Hungary): 6740 Szeged, Stefánia 10; tel. (62) 481-281; internet www.delmagyar.szeged.hu; Editor-in-Chief IMRE DLUSZTUS; circ. 70,000.

Székesfehérvár

Fejér Megyei Hírlap (Fejér County Journal): 8003 Székesfehérvár, Honvéd u. 8; tel. (22) 12-450; internet www.fmh.hu; Editor-in-Chief JÁNOS Á. SZABÓ; circ. 52,000.

Szekszárd

Tolnai Népújság (Tolna News): 7100 Szekszárd, Liszt Ferenc tér 3; tel. (74) 16-211; Editor-in-Chief GYÖRGYNÉ KAMARÁS; circ. 32,000.

Szolnok

Új Néplap (New People's Paper): 5001 Szolnok, Kossuth tér 1, I. Irodaház; tel. (56) 42-211; internet www.ujneplap.hu; Editor-in-Chief JÓZSEF HAJNAL; circ. 46,000.

Szombathely

Vas Népe (Vas People): 9700 Szombathely, Fő tér 3–5; tel. (94) 528-288; fax (94) 528-290; e-mail hirdetes.szhely@plt.hu; internet www .vasnepe.hu; Editor-in-Chief SÁNDOR LENGYEL; circ. 65,000.

Tatabánya

24 Óra (24 Hours): 2800 Tatabánya, Fö tér 4; tel. (34) 514-012; fax (34) 514-011; e-mail szerk.kom@axels.hu; internet www.24ora.hu; Editor-in-Chief FERENC SZTRAPÁK; circ. 23,000.

Veszprém

Napló (Diary): 8201 Veszprém, Szabadság tér 15; tel. (80) 27-444; Editor-in-Chief ELEMÉR BALOGH; circ. 58,000.

Zalaegerszeg

Zalai Hírlap (Zala Journal): 8901 Zalaegerszeg, Ady Endre u. 62; tel. (92) 12-575; Editor-in-Chief JÓZSEF TARSOLY; circ. 71,000.

WEEKLIES

The Budapest Sun: 1122 Budapest, Maros u. 12; tel. (1) 489-4343; fax (1) 489-4344; e-mail editor@bpsun.hu; internet www .budapestsun.com; f. 1993; majority-share owned by Associated Newspapers (United Kingdom); in English; Editor-in-Chief ROBIN MARSHALL.

The Budapest Times/Budapester Zeitung: 1036 Budapest, Pacsirtamezö u. 41; tel. (1) 453-0752; fax (1) 240-7583; e-mail editor@ budapesttimes.hu ; internet www.budapesttimes.hu; internet www .budapester.hu; f. 1999 (Budapester Zeitung); f. 2003 (The Budapest Times); English and German edns; Editor FRASER ALLEN (The Budapest Times), JAN MAINKA (Budapester Zeitung).

Élet és Irodalom (Life and Literature): 1089 Budapest, Rezsö tér 15; tel. (1) 210-2157; fax (1) 303-9211; e-mail es@es.hu; internet www.es.hu; f. 1957; literary and political; Editor ZOLTÁN KOVÁCS; circ. 22,000.

Élet és Tudomány (Life and Science): 1088 Budapest, Bródy Sándor u. 16; tel. and fax (1) 138-2472; f. 1946; popular science; Editor-in-Chief Dr HERCZEG JÁNOS; circ. 20,000.

Evangélikus Élet (Evangelical Life): 1085 Budapest, Üllői u. 24; tel. and fax (1) 117-1108; f. 1933; Evangelical Lutheran Church newspaper; Editor MIHÁLY TÓTH-SZÖLLŐS; circ. 12,000.

Heti Világgazdaság (World Economy Weekly): 1124 Budapest, Németvölgy u. 62-64; tel. (1) 3555-411; fax (1) 3555-693; internet www.hvg.hu; f. 1979; Editor-in-Chief IVÁN LIPOVECZ; circ. 141,000.

Képes Újság (Illustrated News): 1085 Budapest, Gyulai Pál u. 14; tel. (1) 113-7660; f. 1960; Editor MIHÁLY KOVÁCS; circ. 400,000.

Ludas Matyi: Budapest; tel. (1) 133-5718; satirical; Editor JÓZSEF ÁRKUS; circ. 352,000.

L'udové Noviny (People's News): 1065 Budapest, Nagymező u. 49; tel. (1) 331-9184; fax (1) 332-3158; e-mail ludove@axelero.hu; internet www.luno.hu; in Slovak, for Slovaks in Hungary; Editor IMRICH FUL; circ. 1,700.

Magyar Mezőgazdaság (Hungarian Agriculture): 1355 Budapest, Kossuth Lajos tér 11; tel. (1) 112-2433; f. 1946; Editor-in-Chief Dr KÁROLY FEHÉR; circ. 24,000.

Magyar Nők Lapja (Hungarian Women's Journal): 1022 Budapest, Törökvész u. 30A; tel. (1) 212-4020; fax (1) 326-8264; e-mail noklapja@noklapja.ekh.hu; f. 1949; Editor-in-Chief LILI ZÉTÉNYI; circ. 550,000.

Magyarország (Hungary): Budapest; tel. (1) 138-4644; f. 1964; news magazine; Editor DÉNES GYAPAY; circ. 200,000.

Narodne Novine (People's News): 1396 Budapest, POB 495; tel. (1) 112-4869; f. 1945 for Yugoslavs in Hungary; in Serbo-Croat and Slovene; Chief Editor MARKO MARKOVIĆ; circ. 2,800.

Neue Zeitung (New Paper): 1062 Budapest, Lendvay u. 22; tel. (1) 302-6877; e-mail neueztg@hu.inter.net; internet www.neue-zeitung.hu; f. 1957 for Germans in Hungary; Editor JOHANN SCHUTH; circ. 4,500.

Reform: Budapest; tel. and fax (1) 122-4240; f. 1988; popular tabloid; 50% foreign-owned; Editor PÉTER TŐKE; circ. 300,000.

Reformátusok Lapja: 1395 Budapest, POB 424; tel. (1) 117-6809; fax (1) 117-8386; f. 1957; Reformed Church paper for the laity; Editor-in-Chief and Publr ATTILA P. KOMLÓS; circ. 30,000.

RTV Részletes (Radio and TV News): 1801 Budapest; tel. (1) 328-8114; fax (1) 328-7349; e-mail rturszer@axelero.hu; internet www.rtvreszletes.hu; f. 1924; Editor KATALIN MOLDOVAN; circ. 100,000.

Szabad Föld (Free Earth): 1087 Budapest, Könyves Kálmán krt 76; tel. and fax (1) 133-6794; f. 1945; Editor GYULA ECK; circ. 720,000.

Szövetkezet (Co-operative): 1054 Budapest, Szabadság tér 14; tel. (1) 131-3132; National Council of Hungarian Consumer Co-operative Societies; Editor-in-Chief ATTILA KOVÁCS; circ. 85,000.

Tallózó: 1133 Budapest, Visegrádi u. 110–112; tel. and fax (1) 149-8707; f. 1989; news digest; Editor-in-Chief GYÖRGY ANDAI; circ. 35,000.

Tőzsde Kurir (Hungarian Stock Market Courier): Budapest; tel. (1) 122-3273; fax (1) 142-8356; business; Editor-in-Chief ISTVÁN GÁBOR BENEDEK.

Új Ember (New Man): 1053 Budapest, Kossuth Lajos u. 1; tel. (1) 317-3933; fax (1) 317-3471; e-mail ujember@katolikus.hu; internet ujember.katolikus.hu; f. 1945; weekly; Roman Catholic; Editor TAMÁS PAPP; circ. 40,000.

OTHER PERIODICALS
(Published monthly unless otherwise indicated)

Beszélő (The Speaker): 1054 Budapest, Akadémia u. 1/48–50; tel. and fax (1) 302-1271; e-mail mailto:beszelo@enternet.hu; internet beszelo.c3.hu; f. 1991; cultural; Editor-in-Chief MINK ANDRÁS.

Business Partner Hungary: 1081 Budapest, Csokonai u. 3; tel. (1) 303-9586; fax (1) 303-9582; e-mail nemeth@kopdat.hu; internet www.kopdat.hu; f. 1986; every two months; English and German; economic journal; Head of Dept ILONA NÉMETH.

Egyházi Krónika (Church Chronicle): 1052 Budapest, Petőfi tér 2.1.2; tel. and fax (1) 318-4813; f. 1952; every two months; Eastern Orthodox Church journal; Editor Archpriest Dr FERIZ BERKI.

Elektrotechnika (Electrical Engineering): 1055 Budapest, Kossuth Lajos tér 6–8; tel. (1) 353-0117; fax (1) 353-4069; e-mail lernyei@mee.hu; f. 1908; organ of Electrotechnical Association; Editor Dr JÁNOS BENCZE; circ. 6,500.

Élelmezési Ipar (Food Industry): 1372 Budapest, POB 433; tel. (1) 214-6691; fax (1) 214-6692; e-mail mail.mete@mtesz.hu; internet www.mtesz.hu; f. 1947; publ. by Scientific Society for Food Industry; Editor Dr ISTVÁN TÓTH-ZSIGA.

Energia és Atomtechnika (Energy and Nuclear Technology): 1055 Budapest, Kossuth Lajos tér 6–8; tel. (1) 153-2751; fax (1) 156-1215; f. 1947; every two months; publ. by Scientific Society for Energy Economy; Editor-in-Chief Dr G. BŐKI.

Energiagazdálkodás (Energy Economy): 1055 Budapest, Kossuth Lajos tér 6; tel. (1) 153-2751; fax (1) 153-3894; publ. by Scientific Society for Energetics; Editor Dr ANDOR ANESINI.

Ezermester 2000 (Handyman 2000): 1145 Budapest, Mexikói u. 35A; tel. (1) 222-6392; fax (1) 220-9065; e-mail ezermester2000@axelero.hu; internet www.ezermester2000.hu; f. 1957; do-it-yourself magazine; Editor JÓZSEF PERÉNYI; circ. 50,000.

Gép (Machinery): 1027 Budapest, Fő u. 68; tel. (1) 135-4175; fax (1) 153-0818; f. 1949; Scientific Society of Mechanical Engineering; Editor Dr KORNÉL LEHOFER.

Ipar-Gazdaság (Industrial Economy): 1371 Budapest, POB 433; tel. (1) 202-1083; f. 1948; Editor Dr TAMÁS MÉSZÁROS; circ. 4,000.

Jogtudományi Közlöny (Law Gazette): 1525 Budapest, POB 773; 1015 Budapest, Donáti u. 35-45; tel. (1) 355-0330; fax (1) 355-0441; e-mail jogtud@mkab.hu; f. 1866; legal and administrative sciences; Editor-in-Chief Dr IMRE VÖRÖS; circ. 1,000.

Kortárs (Contemporary): 1426 Budapest, POB 108; tel. (1) 342-1168; e-mail kortars@elender.hu; f. 1957; literary; Editor-in-Chief IMRE KIS PINTÉR; circ. 5,000.

Közgazdasági Szemle (Economic Review): 1112 Budapest, Budaörsi u. 43–45; tel. (1) 315-3165; fax (1) 315-3166; internet www.kozgazdasagiszemle.hu; f. 1954; publ. by Cttee for Economic Sciences of Hungarian Academy of Sciences; Editor KATALIN SZABÓ; circ. 3,000.

Magyar Hírek (Hungarian News): Budapest; tel. (1) 122-5616; fax (1) 122-2421; every two weeks; illustrated magazine primarily for Hungarians living abroad; Editor GYÖRGY HALÁSZ; circ. 70,000.

Magyar Jog (Hungarian Law): 1054 Budapest, Szemere u. 10; tel. (1) 311-4880; fax (1) 311-4013; f. 1953; Editor-in-Chief Dr JÁNOS NÉMETH; circ. 2,200.

Magyar Közlöny (Official Gazette): Budapest; tel. (1) 112-1236; Editor Dr ELEMÉR KISS; circ. 90,000.

Magyar Tudomány (Hungarian Science): Hungarian Academy of Sciences, 1051 Budapest, Nádor u. 7; tel. and fax (1) 317-9524; e-mail matud@hefka.iif.hu; internet www.matud.hu; f. 1846; multidisciplinary science review; Editors VILMOS CSÁNYI, ZSUZSA SZENT-GYÖRGYI.

Pedagógusok Lapja (Teachers' Review): 1068 Budapest, Városligeti fasor 10; tel. (1) 322-8464; e-mail psz-seh@mail.matav.hu; internet www.deltasoft.hu/pszseh; f. 1945; published by the Hungarian Union of Teachers; Editor-in-Chief ÁROK ANTAL; circ. 10,000.

Református Egyház (Reformed Church): 1146 Budapest, Abonyi u. 21; tel. (1) 343-7870; f. 1949; official journal of the Hungarian Reformed Church; Editor-in-Chief LAJOS TÓTH; circ. 1,300.

Statisztikai Szemle (Statistical Review): 1525 Budapest, POB 51; tel. (1) 487-4343; fax (1) 487-4344; e-mail statszemle@ksh.gov.hu; internet www.ksh.hu/statszml; f. 1923; Editor-in-Chief Dr LÁSZLÓ HUNYADI; circ. 800.

Technika (Technology): 1027 Budapest, Fö u. 68; tel. (1) 225-3105; fax (1) 201-6457; e-mail tcinfo@eqnet.hu; internet www.e-technika.hu; f. 1957; official journal of the Hungarian Academy of Engineering; monthly in Hungarian, annually in English, German and Russian; Editor-in-Chief MARGIT WELLEK.

Turizmus (Tourism): 1088 Budapest, Múzeum u. 11; tel. (1) 266-5853; fax (1) 338-4293; e-mail turizmus@mail.matav.hu; Editor ZSOLT SZEBENI; circ. 8,000.

Új Élet (New Life): 1075 Budapest, Síp u. 12; tel. (1) 322-2829; every two weeks; Jewish interest; Editor Dr PÉTER KARDOS; circ. 5,000.

Új Technika (New Technology): Budapest; tel. (1) 155-7122; f. 1967; popular industrial quarterly; circ. 35,000.

Vigilia: 1364 Budapest, POB 48; tel. (1) 517-7246; fax (1) 486-4445; e-mail vigilia@vigilia.hu; internet www.vigilia.hu; f. 1935; Catholic; Editor LÁSZLÓ LUKÁCS; circ. 3,500.

NEWS AGENCIES

HT Press News Agency: 1149 Budapest, Angol u. 22; tel. and fax (1) 363-1472.

Hungarian News Agency Co (Magyar Távirati Iroda Rt—MTI): 1016 Budapest, Naphegy tér 8; tel. (1) 375-6722; fax (1) 375-3973; internet www.mti.hu; f. 1880; 20 brs in Hungary; 10 bureaux abroad; Pres. MATYAS VINCE.

Foreign Bureaux

Agence France-Presse (AFP) (France): 1016 Budapest, Naphegy u. 29 II/2; tel. (1) 356-8416; fax (1) 201-9161; e-mail afpbud@elender.hu; Correspondent ESZTER SZÁMADÓ.

Agenzia Nazionale Stampa Associata (ANSA) (Italy): 1054 Budapest, Vadász u. 31; tel. (1) 332-3555; fax (1) 332-3556; Bureau Chief GAETANO ALIMENTI.

Associated Press (AP) (USA): Budapest; tel. (1) 156-9129; Correspondent ALEX BANDY.

Dow-Jones News Service (USA): 1051 Budapest, Bajcsy-Zsilinszky út 12, VI/602; tel. (1) 267-0622; fax (1) 267-0624; Gen. Dir MARGIT FEHER.

ITAR—TASS (Information Telegraph Agency of Russia—Telegraphic Agency of the Sovereign Countries) (Russia): 1023 Budapest, Vérhalom u. 12–16; Correspondent YEVGENII POPOV.

Reuters (United Kingdom): 1088 Budapest, Rákóczi u. 1–3, East-West Business Centre; tel. (1) 266-2410; fax (1) 266-2030; internet www.reuters.hu; Chief Correspondent MITYA NEW.

RIA—Novosti (Russian Information Agency—News) (Russia): Budapest; tel. (1) 132-0594; fax (1) 142-3325.

Tlačová agentúra Slovenskej republiky (TASR) (Slovakia): Budapest; tel. and fax (1) 135-1843; Bureau Chief PETER KLENKO.

Xinhua (New China) News Agency (People's Republic of China): Budapest; tel. (1) 176-7548; fax (1) 176-2571; Chief Correspondent ZHOU DONGYAO.

PRESS ASSOCIATIONS

Hungarian Newspaper Publishers' Association: 1034 Budapest, Bécsi út 122-124; tel. (1) 368-8674; fax (1) 388-6707; e-mail mle .peto@mail.matav.hu; f. 1990; Gen. Sec. János Pető; 40 mems.

National Association of Hungarian Journalists (Magyar Újságírók Országos Szövetsége—MUOSZ): 1062 Budapest, Andrássy u. 101; tel. (1) 322-1699; fax (1) 322-1881; f. 1896; Gen. Sec. Gábor Bencsik; 7,000 mems.

Publishers

PRINCIPAL PUBLISHING HOUSES

Akadémiai Kiadó: 1117 Budapest, Prielle Kornélia u. 4; tel. (1) 464-8200; fax (1) 464-8201; e-mail custservice@akkrt.hu; internet www.akkrt.hu; f. 1828; humanities, social, natural and technical sciences, dictionaries, textbooks and periodicals; Hungarian and English; Man. Dir Bucsi Szabó Zsolt.

Corvina Kiadó: 1072 Budapest, Rákóczi út 16; tel. (1) 318-4148; fax (1) 318-4410; e-mail corvina@exelero.hu; f. 1955; art and educational books, fiction and non-fiction, tourist guides, cookery books and musicology; Man. Dir László Kunos.

EMB Music Publisher: 1132 Budapest, Victor Hugo u. 11–15; tel. (1) 236-1100; fax (1) 236-1101; e-mail emb@emb.hu; internet www .emb.hu; f. 1950; music publishing and books on musical subjects; Dir Antal Boronkay.

Európa Könyvkiadó: 1055 Budapest, Kossuth Lajos tér 13–15; tel. (1) 131-2700; fax (1) 131-4162; f. 1945; world literature translated into Hungarian; Man. Levente Osztovits.

Gondolat Könyvkiadó Vállalat: Budapest; tel. (1) 138-3358; fax (1) 138-4540; f. 1957; popular scientific publications on natural and social sciences, art, encyclopaedic handbooks; Dir György Fehér.

Helikon Kiadó: 1053 Budapest, Papnövelde u. 8; tel. (1) 117-4865; fax (1) 117-4865; bibliophile books; Dir Katalin Berger.

Képzőművészeti Kiadó: Budapest; tel. (1) 251-1527; fax (1) 251-1527; fine arts; Man. Dr Zoltán Kemenczei.

Kossuth Kiadó: 1043 Budapest, Csányi László u. 36; tel. (1) 370-0607; fax (1) 370-0602; e-mail rt@kossuted.hu; f. 1944; social sciences, educational and philosophy publications, information technology books; Man. András Sándor Kocsis.

Közgazdasági és Jogi Könyvkiadó: Budapest; tel. (1) 112-6430; fax (1) 111-3210; f. 1955; business, economics, law, sociology, psychology, tax, politics, education, dictionaries; Man. Dir David G. Young.

Magvető Könyvkiadó: 1806 Budapest, POB 123; tel. (1) 235-5032; e-mail magveto@lira.hu; f. 1955; literature; Dir Géza Morcsányi.

Medicina Könyvkiadó: 1054 Budapest, Zoltan u. 8; tel. (1) 112-2650; fax (1) 112-2450; f. 1957; books on medicine, sport, tourism; Dir Borbála Farkasvölgyi.

Mezőgazda Kiadó: 1165 Budapest, Koronafürt u. 44; tel. (1) 407-1018; fax (1) 407-1012; e-mail mezoig@mezogazdakiado.hu; internet www.mezogazdakiado.hu; ecology, natural sciences, environmental protection, food industry; Man. Dr Lajos Lelkes.

Móra Ferenc Ifjúsági Kiadó: 1134 Budapest, Váci u. 19; tel. (1) 320-4740; fax (1) 320-5382; e-mail mora_kiado@elender.hu; f. 1950; youth and children's books; Man. Dr János Cs. Tóth.

Műszaki Könyvkiadó: 1033 Budapest, Szentendre u. 89–93; tel. (1) 437-2405; fax (1) 437-2404; e-mail lakatosz@muszakikiado.hu; internet www.muszakikiado.hu; f. 1955; scientific and technical, vocational and general text books; Man. Sándor Bérczi.

Nemzeti Tankönyvkiadó (National Textbook Publishing House): 1143 Budapest, Szobránc u. 6–8; tel. (1) 460-1800; fax (1) 460-1869; e-mail public@ntk.hu; internet www.ntk.hu; f. 1949; school and university textbooks, pedagogical literature and language books; Gen. Man. József Pálfi.

Népszava Lapés Könyvkiadó Vállalat: Budapest; tel. (1) 122-4810; publishing house of National Confederation of Hungarian Trade Unions; Man. Dr Jenő Kiss.

Statiqum Kiadó és Nyomda: 1033 Budapest, Kaszásdülő u. 2; tel. (1) 250-0311; fax (1) 168-8635; f. 1991; publications on statistics, system-management and computer science; Dir Benedek Belecz.

Szépirodalmi Könyvkiadó: Budapest; tel. (1) 122-1285; f. 1950; modern and classical Magyar literature; Man. Sándor Z. Szalai.

Zrinyi Kiadó: 1087 Budapest, Kerepesi u. 29B; tel. (1) 133-9165; military literature; Man. Máté Eszes.

PUBLISHERS' ASSOCIATION

Hungarian Publishers' and Booksellers' Association (Magyar Könyvkiadók és Könyvterjesztők Egyesülése): Budapest; tel. (1) 343-2540; fax (1) 343-2541; e-mail mkke@mkke.hu; f. 1795; most leading Hungarian publishers are members of the Association; Pres. István Bart; Sec.-Gen. Péter Zentai.

Broadcasting and Communications

TELECOMMUNICATIONS

Regulatory Authority

National Communications Authority (Nemzeti Hírközlési Hatóság): 1525 Budapest, POB 75; tel. (1) 457-7100; fax (1) 356-5520; e-mail info@hif.hu; internet www.nhh.hu; Chair. Dániel Pataki.

Service Providers

Matáv Hungarian Telecommunications Co: 1541 Budapest, Krisztina krt 6–8; tel. (1) 458-0000; fax (1) 458-7176; e-mail investor .relations@ln.matav.hu; internet www.matav.hu; f. 1991; 60% owned by Deutsche Telekom AG (Germany); telecommunications service provider; Chief Exec. Elek Straub; 16,034 employees.

Pannon GSM Telecommunications: 2040 Budaörs, Baross u. 165; tel. (1) 930-4000; fax (1) 930-4100; internet www.pgsm.hu; f. 1993; 100% owned by Telenor (Norway); mobile telecommunications; CEO Ove Fredheim.

Vodafone Hungary: Budapest; internet www.vodafone.hu; f. 1999; mobile cellular telecommunications; owned by Vodafone (United Kingdom); Gen. Man. Attila Vitai; 1m. subscribers (May 2003).

T-Mobile Magyarország: 1117 Budapest, Kaposvár u. 5–7; tel. (1) 265-9210; fax (1) 204-4128; e-mail ugyfelszolgalat@t-mobile.hu; internet www.t-mobile.hu; f. 1994 as Westel; owned by Deutsche Telekom AG (Germany); present name adopted 2004; mobile cellular telecommunications services; Chief Exec. András Sugár; 3.8m. subscribers (2004).

BROADCASTING

Hungarian National Radio and Television Board (Országos Rádió és Televízió Testület—ORTT): 1088 Budapest, Reviczky u. 5; tel. (1) 429-8600; fax (1) 267-2612; e-mail ehorvath@ortt.hu; internet www.ortt.hu; Dir Gyorgy Kovacs.

Radio

Hungarian Radio (Magyar Rádió): 1800 Budapest, Bródy Sándor u. 5–7; tel. (1) 328-8388; fax (1) 328-7004; internet www.radio.hu; f. 1924; stations: Radio Kossuth, Radio Petőfi, Radio Bartók (mainly classical music); eight regional studios; external broadcasts in English, German, Hungarian, Romanian, Russian, Serbian and Slovak; Pres. Katalin Kondor.

Antenna Hungária Magyar Műsorszóró és, Rádióhírközlési Rt: 1119 Budapest, Petzvál József u. 31–33; tel. (1) 203-6060; fax (1) 203-6093; internet www.ahrt.hu; f. 1989; radio and television broadcasting; Chief Exec. István Máté; 1,290 employees.

Radio C: 1086 Budapest, Teleki tér. 7; tel. (1) 459-0095; fax (1) 459-0094; internet www.radioc.hu; f. 2001; Roma radio station; news and cultural programming suspended in April 2003 owing to lack of funds; Man. György Kerenyi.

Radio Danubius: f. 1986; privatized 1998; broadcasts news, music and information in Hungarian 24 hours a day; transmitting stations in Budapest, Lake Balaton region, Sopron, Szeged and Debrecen; Dir József László.

Television

Hungarian Television (Magyar Televízió): 1810 Budapest, Szabadság tér 17; tel. (1) 353-3200; fax (1) 373-4133; e-mail martinak@ mtv.hu; internet www.mtv.hu; f. 1957; first channel, MTV 1, terrestrial, broadcasts 19 hours a day and the second channel, MTV 2, satellite, 24 hours a day, colour transmissions; 100 high-capacity relay stations; Pres. Zoltán Rudi.

Antenna Hungária Magyar Műsorszóró és, Rádióhírközlési Rt: 1119 Budapest, Petzvál József u. 31–33; tel. (1) 203-6060; fax (1) 464-2525; internet www.ahrt.hu; f. 1989; radio and television broadcasting; Chief Exec. Dr Géza László; 912 employees.

Finance

(cap. = capital; res = reserves; dep. = deposits; m. = million; amounts in forint unless otherwise stated)

By 2005 there was a total of 30 commercial banks in operation in Hungary. Responsibility for bank supervision is divided between the National Bank of Hungary and the Hungarian Financial Supervisory Authority. Under legislation introduced in January 1997, the supervisory responsibilities of the National Bank were restricted to areas relating to the operation of monetary policy and the foreign-exchange system.

BANKING

Central Bank

National Bank of Hungary (Magyar Nemzeti Bank): 1850 Budapest, Szabadság tér 8–9; tel. (1) 428-2600; fax (1) 428-2500; e-mail info@mnb.hu; internet www.mnb.hu; f. 1924; bank of issue; conducts international transactions; supervises banking system; cap. 10,000m., res 206,097m., dep. 1,029,267m. (Dec. 2003); Pres. ZSIGMOND JÁRAI; 23 brs.

Commercial Banks

Bank of Hungarian Savings Co-operatives (Magyar Takarékszövetkezeti Bank): 1122 Budapest, Pethényi köz 10; 1525 Budapest, POB 775; tel. (1) 202-3777; fax (1) 355-9082; e-mail info@tbank.hu; internet www.takarekbank.hu; f. 1989; 71.9% owned by DZ Bank AG (Germany); cap. 2,041m., res 3,487m., dep. 146,974m. (Dec. 2003); Pres. ANTAL VARGA; CEO PÉTER CSICSÁKY.

BNP Paribas (Hungaria) Bank: 1055 Budapest, Honvéd u. 20; tel. (1) 374-6300; fax (1) 269-3967; e-mail info.hu@bnpparibas.com; f. 1991; wholly owned by BNP Paribas (France); cap. 3,500.0m., res 5,217.8m., dep. 83,587.6m. (Dec. 2003); Chair. JACQUES DE LAROSIÈRE; Gen. Man. LÁSZLÓ HAÁS.

Budapest Credit and Development Bank: 1138 Budapest, POB 1852, Váci út 202; tel. (1) 450-6000; fax (1) 450-6001; e-mail info@bbrt.hu; internet www.budapestbank.hu; f. 1987; cap. 19,346m., res 19,316m., dep. 319,594m. (Dec. 2003); 99.25% owned by GE Capital International Financing Corpn (USA); Chief Exec. MARK ARNOLD; 55 brs.

Central-European International Bank (CIB): 1537 Budapest, Medve u. 4–14, POB 394; tel. (1) 212-1330; fax (1) 212-4200; e-mail cib@cib.hu; internet www.cib.hu; f. 1979; 100% owned by Intesa Holding International SA (Luxembourg); cap. 23,500m., res 21,159m., dep. 937,869m. (Dec. 2003); Chair. Dr GYÖRGY SURÁNYI; Dir-Gen. and Chief Exec. ADÁM FARKAS.

Citibank: 1367 Budapest, POB 123; tel. (1) 374-5000; fax (1) 374-5100; internet www.citibank.hu; f. 1986; wholly owned by Citibank Overseas Investment Corpn (USA); cap. 13,005m., res 6,015m., dep. 279,771m. (Dec. 2002); Chair. ZDENEK TUREK.

Commerzbank (Budapest): 1254 Budapest, POB 1070; tel. (1) 374-1000; fax (1) 269-4530; e-mail commerzbank@commerzbank.hu; internet www.commerzbank.hu; f. 1993; cap. 4,010.3m., res 9,671.1m., dep. 115,545.3m. (Dec. 2002); Pres. and Chair. of Supervisory Bd WOJCIECH KOSTRZEWA; Chair. and Chief Exec. TAMÁS HÁKKOVÁCS.

Deutsche Bank RT: 1054 Budapest, Hold u. 27; tel. (1) 301-3700; fax (1) 269-3239; e-mail db.rt@db.com; wholly owned by Deutsche Bank AG (Germany); cap. 8,110m., res 3,196.5m., dep. 57,645.5m. (Dec. 2002); Chief Exec. FARBOD LOTFI.

Erste Bank Hungary: 1054 Budapest, Hold u. 16; tel. (1) 373-2400; fax (1) 373-2499; internet www.erstebank.hu; f. 1987; present name adopted 1998; absorbed Postbank and Savings Bank Corpn—Postabank in 2004; 99.3% owned by Erste Bank der öesterreichischen Sparkassen AG (Austria); cap. 15,210m., res 2,506m., dep. 462,736m. (Dec. 2003); Chair. REINHARD ORTNER; Chief Exec. PÉTER KISBENEDEK; 160 brs.

General Banking and Trust Co (Általános Értékforgalmi Bank): 1055 Budapest, Markó u. 9; 1991 Budapest, POB 150; tel. (1) 462-7600; fax (1) 462-7606; e-mail info@gbt.hu; internet www.gbt.hu; f. 1922; 25.5% owned by Gazprombank (Russia); cap. US $76.9m., res $3.0m., dep. $907.6m. (Dec. 2003); Chair. and Chief Exec. MEGDET RAKHIMKULOV; 16 brs.

Hungarian Development Bank (Magyar Fejlesztési Bank—MFT): 1051 Budapest, Nádor u. 31; tel. (1) 428-1400; fax (1) 428-1490; e-mail bank@mfb.hu; internet www.mfb.hu; f. 1991 as an investment company; authorized as a bank 1993; state-owned; cap. 87,570m., res 158,725m., dep. 388,099m. (Dec. 2003); Chair. of Bd GYÖRGY ZDEBORSKY.

Hungarian Foreign Trade Bank (Magyar Külkereskedelmi Bank): 1056 Budapest, V. Váci u. 38; tel. (1) 269-0922; fax (1) 269-

0959; e-mail exterbank@mkb.hu; internet www.mkb.hu; f. 1950; commercial banking; 89.3% owned by Bayerische Landesbank (Germany); absorbed Konzumbank in 2003; cap. 11,520m., res 88,494m., dep. 886,991m. (Dec. 2003); Chair. and Chief Exec. TAMÁS ERDEI; 29 brs.

HVB Bank Hungary: 1054 Budapest, Akadémia u. 17; 1242 Budapest, POB 386; tel. (1) 269-0812; fax (1) 353-4959; e-mail info@hu.hvb-cee.com; internet www.hvb.hu; f. 2001 by merger of Bank Austria Creditanstalt Hungary RT and Hypovereinsbank Hungary RT; 100% owned by Bank Austria Creditanstalt AG; cap. 24,118m., res 16,294m., dep. 626,698m. (Dec. 2003); CEO Dr MATTHIAS KUNSCH.

ING Bank RT: 1461 Budapest, POB 320; tel. (1) 235-8700; fax (1) 322-2288; internet www.ing.hu; f. 1992 as NMB Bank; present name adopted 1996; 100% owned by ING Bank NV (Netherlands); cap. 15,758m., res 5,281m., dep. 134,648m. (Dec. 1999); Man. Dir RANDOLPH S. KOPPA.

Inter-Európa Bank: 1054 Budapest, Szabadság tér 15; 1364 Budapest, POB 65; tel. (1) 373-6000; fax (1) 269-2526; e-mail ieb@ieb.hu; internet www.ieb.hu; f. 1981 as Interinvest; name changed as above in 1989; cap. 7,019m., res 3,954m., dep. 171,399m. (Dec. 2003); Chair. FERENC BARTHA; 20 brs.

Kereskedelmi és Hitelbank (K&H Bank): 1051 Budapest, Vigadó tér 1; tel. (1) 328-9000; fax (1) 328-9696; e-mail khbinfo@khb.hu; internet www.khb.hu; f. 1987; 59.1% owned by KBC Bank NV (Belgium), 40.2% owned by ABN Amro Bank NV (Netherlands); dep. 1,248,381m., total assets 1,435,490m. (Dec. 2003); Chair. Dr ISTVÁN SZALKAI; CEO TIBOR E. REJTÖ; 176 brs.

National Savings and Commercial Bank (Országos Takarékpénztár és Kereskedelmi Bank—OTP Bank): 1051 Budapest, Nádor u. 16; tel. (1) 353-1444; fax (1) 312-6858; e-mail otpbank@otpbank.hu; internet www.otpbank.hu; f. 1949; savings deposits, credits, foreign transactions; privatized in 1996; cap. 28,000m., res 248,176m., dep. 2,357,648m. (Dec. 2003); Chair. and CEO Dr SÁNDOR CSÁNYI; 427 brs.

Raiffeisen Bank RT: 1364 Budapest, POB 173; tel. (1) 484-4400; fax (1) 484-4444; e-mail info@raiffeisen.hu; internet www.raiffeisen.hu; f. 1986; present name adopted 1999; 98.26% owned by Raiffeisen Banking Group (Austria); cap. 26,904m., res 15,427m., dep. 569,442m. (Dec. 2002); Pres. Dr HERBERT STEPIC; Man. Dir Dr PÉTER FELCSUTI; 63 brs.

WestLB Hungaria Bank: 1075 Budapest, Madách Imre út 13–14; tel. (1) 268-1680; fax (1) 268-1933; e-mail public@westlb.hu; internet www.westlb.de; f. 1985; owned by WestLB AG (Germany); cap. 4,485.8m., res 7,240.1m., dep. 78,474.9m. (Dec. 2003); Chair. and Man. Dir JÜRGEN PHILIPPER.

Specialized Financial Institutions

Hungarian Export-Import Bank (EXIMBANK): 1065 Budapest, Nagymezö u. 46-48; tel. (1) 374-9100; fax (1) 269-4476; e-mail eximh@eximbank.hu; internet www.eximbank.hu; f. 1994; state-owned; cap. 10,100m., res 2,168m., dep. 151,978m. (Dec. 2003); CEO Dr FRIGYES BÁNKI.

Merkantil Bank: 1051 Budapest, József Attila u. 24; tel. (1) 429-7600; fax (1) 429-7601; e-mail molnar.andrasne@mail.merkantil.hu; internet www.merkantil.hu; f. 1988; affiliated to National Savings and Commercial Bank Ltd—OTP Bank; automobile financing transactions; cap. 1,100m.; Chair. and Chief Exec. ADÁM KOLOSSVÁRY.

Opel Bank Hungary RT: 1027 Budapest, Kapás u. 11–15; tel. (1) 457-9110; Gen. Man. JARI ARJAVALTA.

Porsche Bank Hungaria: 1139 Budapest, Váci út 85; tel. (1) 465-4700; fax (1) 465-4775; e-mail info@porschebank.hu; internet www.porschebank.hu; Pres. PÁL ANTALL.

Rákóczi Regional Development Bank (Rákóczi Regionális Fejlesztési Bank RT): 3530 Miskolc, Mindszent tér 1; tel. (46) 510-300; fax (46) 510-396; e-mail central@rakoczibank.hu; f. 1992; Gen. Man. KORNÉL KOSZTICZA.

Other Financial Institution

Central Corporation of Banking Companies (Pénzintézeti Központ): 1093 Budapest, Lónyay u. 38; tel. (1) 117-1255; fax (1) 215-9963; f. 1916; banking, property, rights and interests, deposits, securities, and foreign exchange management; cap. 11,127m., res 3,548m., dep. 12,289m.; Chair. and Chief Exec. PÉTER KIRÁLY; 3 brs.

Supervisory Authority

Hungarian Financial Supervisory Authority (HFSA) (Pénzügyi Szervezetek Állami Felügyelete—PSZAF): 1535 Budapest, 114, POB 777; tel. (1) 489-9100; fax (1) 489-9102; e-mail pszaf@pszaf.hu; internet www.pszaf.hu; Chair. of Supervisory Bd ISTVÁN FARKAS; Dir Gen. ERIKA MARSI.

STOCK EXCHANGE

Budapest Stock Exchange (Budapesti Értéktőzsde—BET): 1052 Budapest, Deák Ferenc u. 5; tel. (1) 429-6700; fax (1) 429-6800; e-mail info@bse.hu; internet www.bse.hu; 68.8% owned by a consortium comprising HVB Bank Hungary (25.2%), the Vienna Stock Exchange AG (Austria—14%), Erste Bank AG (Austria—12.2%) and Osterreichische Kontrollbank AG (Austria—11%); allied with the Vienna (Austria) and Warsaw (Poland) Stock Exchanges from May 2004; Pres. ATTILA SZALAU-BERZEVICZY.

COMMODITY EXCHANGE

Budapest Commodity Exchange (Budapesti Árutőzsde—BAT): 1134 Budapest, Róbert Károly krt 61–65; tel. (1) 465-6979; fax (1) 465-6981; e-mail bce@bce-bat.com; internet www.bce-bat.com; Chair. ATTILA KOVÁCS.

INSURANCE

In early 2005 there were 29 insurance companies.

AB-AEGON Általános Biztosító: 1091 Budapest, u. Üllői 1; tel. (1) 218-1866; fax (1) 217-7065; internet www.aegon.hu; f. 1949; present name adopted 1992; pensions, life and property insurance, insurance of agricultural plants, co-operatives, foreign insurance, etc.; Gen. Man. Dr GÁBOR KEPECS.

Garancia Insurance Co (Garancia Biztosító): 1054 Budapest, Vadász u. 12; tel. (1) 269-2533; fax (1) 269-2549; f. 1988; cap. 4,050m.; Gen. Man. and Chief Exec. Dr ZOLTÁN NAGY; 25 brs.

Hungária Insurance Co (Hungária Biztosító): 1054 Budapest, Bajcsy u. 52; tel. (1) 301-6565; fax (1) 301-6100; f. 1986; handles international insurance, industrial and commercial insurance and motor-car, marine, life, household, accident and liability insurance; cap. 4,266m.; Chair. and Chief Exec. Dr MIHÁLY PATAI.

QBE Atlasz Insurance Co (QBE Atlasz Biztosító): 1143 Budapest, Stefánia út 51; tel. (1) 460-1400; fax (1) 460-1499; e-mail qbe-atlasz@qbeatlasz.hu; internet www.qbeatlasz.hu; f. 1988; cap. 1,000m.; Gen. Man. DORON GROSSMAN.

Trade and Industry

GOVERNMENT AGENCY

Hungarian Privatization and State Holding Co (Állami Privatizációs és Vagyonkezelő—ÁPV): 1133 Budapest, Pozsonyi u. 56; tel. (1) 237-4400; fax (1) 237-4100; e-mail apvrt@apvrt.hu; internet www.apvrt.hu; f. 1995; Chair. CSABA FARAGÓ.

NATIONAL CHAMBERS OF COMMERCE AND OF AGRICULTURE

Hungarian Chamber of Agriculture (Magyar Agrárkamara): 1119 Budapest, Etele út 57; tel. (1) 371-5517; fax (1) 371-5510; e-mail agota@kozpont.agrarkamara.hu; internet www.agrarkamara.hu; Pres. MIKLÓS CSIKAI.

Hungarian Chamber of Commerce and Industry (Magyar Kereskedelmi és Iparkamara): 1372 Budapest V, POB 452; tel. (1) 474-5141; fax (1) 250-5138; e-mail mkik@mkik.hu; f. 1850; central organization of the 23 Hungarian county chambers of commerce and industry; based on a system of voluntary membership; over 46,000 mems.; Pres. Dr LÁSZLÓ PARRAGH; Sec.-Gen. PÉTER DUNAI.

REGIONAL CHAMBERS OF COMMERCE

There are regional chambers of commerce in each of the 20 principal administrative divisions of Hungary (comprising the 19 counties and the City of Budapest). The following are among the most important:

Borsod-Abaúj-Zemplén County Chamber of Commerce and Industry (Borsod-Abaúj-Zemplén Kereskedelmi és Iparkamara): 3525 Miskolc, Szentpáli u. 1; tel. (46) 328-539; fax (46) 328-722; e-mail bokik@mail.bokik.hu; internet www.bokik.hu; f. 1990; membership of 1,100 cos; Pres. TAMÁS BIHALL; Sec. ANNA BAÁN-SZILÁGYI.

Budapest Chamber of Industry and Commerce (Budapesti Kereskedelmi és Iparkamara): 1016 Budapest, Krisztina krt 99; tel. (1) 488-2173; fax (1) 488-2180; e-mail nemzetkozi@bkik.hu; internet www.bkik.hu; f. 1850; Chair. LÁSZLÓ KOJI; Sec.-Gen. CSABA BAZSC.

Csongrád County Chamber of Commerce and Industry: 6721 Szeged, Tisza L. krt 2–4; tel. (62) 423-451; fax (62) 426-149; e-mail info@csmkik.hu; internet www.csmkik.hu; Chair. ISTVÁN SZERI; Sec. LAJOS HORVÁTH.

Hajdú-Bihar County Chamber of Commerce and Industry: 4025 Debrecen, Petőfi tér 10; tel. (52) 500-721; fax (52) 500-720; internet www.hbkik.hu; Chair. FERENC MIKLÓSSY; Sec. Dr EVA SKULTÉTI.

Pécs-Baranya Chamber of Commerce and Industry: 7625 Pécs, Dr Majorossy I. u. 36; tel. (72) 507-149; fax (72) 507-152; e-mail pbkik@pbkik.hu; internet www.pbkik.hu; Chair. GYULA HIGI; Sec. TAMÁS SÍKFŐI.

Pest County Chamber of Commerce and Industry (Pest Megyei Kereskedelmi és Iparkamara): 1056 Budapest, Vàci u. 40; tel. (1) 317-7666; fax (1) 317-7755; e-mail titkarsag@pmkik.hu; internet www.pmkik.hu; Chair. Dr ZOLTÁN VERECZKEY; Sec.-Gen. Dr LAJOS KUPCSOK.

Szabolcs-Szatmár-Bereg County Chamber of Commerce and Industry: 4400 Nyíregyháza, Széchenyi u. 2; tel. (42) 416-074; fax (42) 311-750; Chair. Dr JÁNOS VERES; Sec. NAGY KATALIN VARGA.

EMPLOYERS' ASSOCIATIONS

Confederation of Hungarian Employers and Industrialists (Munkaadók és Gyáriparosok Országos Szövetsége—MGYOSZ): 1055 Budapest, Kossuth L. tér. 6–8; fax (1) 474-2065; e-mail mgyosz@mgyosz.hu; internet www.mgyosz.hu; f. 1902; re-estd 1990; 64 member organizations; Sec. Gen. ISTVÁN WIMMER.

National Asscn of Entrepreneurs and Employers (Vállalkozók és Munkáltatók Országos Szövetsége—VOSZ): 1107 Budapest, Mázsa tér 2-6, Porta Office Bldg, 2nd floor; tel. (1) 414-2181; fax (1) 414-2180; e-mail center@vosz.hu; internet www.vosz.hu; Sec. Gen. MIKLÓS KÁROLYI.

INDUSTRIAL AND TRADE ASSOCIATIONS

HUNICOOP Foreign Trade Co for Industrial Co-operation: 1036 Budapest, Lajos u. 80; 1367 Budapest 5, POB 111; tel. (1) 250-8117; fax (1) 250-8121; e-mail hunicoop@matavnet.hu; agency for foreign companies in Hungary, export and import; Dir GÁBOR TOMBÁCZ.

Hungarian Industrial Asscn (Magyar Iparszövetség—OKISZ): 1146 Budapest, Thököly u. 58–60; tel. (1) 343-5570; fax (1) 343-5521; e-mail okisz@okiszinfo.hu; safeguards interests of over 1,100 member enterprises (all private); Pres. LÁSZLÓ HÖRÖMPÖLY.

National Asscn of Industrial Corporations (Ipartestületek Országos Szövetsége—IPOSZ): 1054 Budapest, Kálmán Imre út 20; tel. (1) 354-3140; e-mail titkarsag@iposz.hu; internet www.iposz.hu; Chair. GYÖRGY SZŰCS.

National Co-operative Council (Országos Szövetkezeti Tanács—OSZT): 1054 Budapest, Szabadság tér 14; tel. (1) 312-7467; fax (1) 311-3647; f. 1968; Pres. TAMÁS FARKAS; Sec. Dr JÓZSEF PÁL.

National Federation of Agricultural Co-operators and Producers (Mezőgazdasági Szövetkezők és Termelők Országos Szövetsége—MOSZ): 1054 Budapest, Akadémia u. 1–3; tel. and fax (1) 353-2552; e-mail mosztit@mosz.tvnet.hu; internet www.mosz.net; f. 1990; Pres. TAMÁS NAGY; Sec.-Gen. GÁBOR HORVÁTH; est. 1,300 mem. orgs.

National Federation of Consumer Co-operatives (Általános Fogyasztási Szövetkezetek Országos Szövetsége—ÁFEOSz): 1054 Budapest, Szabadság tér 14; tel. (1) 353-4222; fax (1) 311-3647; e-mail afeosz@afeosz.hu; internet www.afeosz.hy; safeguards interests of Hungarian consumer co-operative societies; organizes co-operative wholesale activities; Pres. Dr PÁL BARTUS; 800,000 mems.

UTILITIES

Supervisory Organization

Hungarian Energy Office: 1081 Budapest, Köztársaság tér 7; tel. (1) 317-4089; fax (1) 317-1330; e-mail hivatal.energia@eh.ikm.x400gw.itb.hu; f. 1994; regulation and supervision of activities performed by gas and electricity companies, price regulation and protection of consumer interest; Pres. GYÖRGY HATVANI.

Electricity

AES-Tisza Erőmű (AES-Tisza Power Plant Co): 3581 Tiszaújváros Pf 53; tel. (49) 547-333; fax (49) 341-756; internet www.aes.hu; f. 1992; owned by AES Corpn (USA); electricity generation and merchandising; Chair. ALLAN B. DWYER; Man. Dir PETER LITHGOW; 182 employees.

Budapest Electricity Co (Budapesti Elektromos Művek) (ELMŰ): 1132 Budapest, Váci u. 72–74; tel. (1) 238-1000; fax (1) 238-2822; e-mail elmu@elmu.hu; internet www.elmu.hu; f. 1949; transmission and distribution of electricity; Chair. of Supervisory Bd Dr KLAUS BUSSFELD; 3,371 employees.

Démász (South Hungarian Power Supply Co): 6720 Szeged, Klauzál tér 9; tel. (62) 476-576; fax (62) 482-500; internet www.demasz.hu; f. 1951; distributes electricity to South-Eastern Hungary; Chair. of Bd Dr DANIEL DUMONT.

Dunamenti Hőerőmű (Power Plant) Co: 2440 Százhalombatta, Erőmű u. 2; tel. (23) 354-161; fax (23) 354-381; electricity generation; Chair. TIBOR KUHL.

Émász (North Hungarian Electricity Supply Co): 3525 Miskolc, Dózsa Gy, u. 13; tel. (46) 411-875; fax (46) 411-871; e-mail emasz@ emasz.hu; internet www.emasz.hu.

E.ON Del-dunántúli Áramszolgáltató: 7626 Pécs, Rákóczi, u. 73B; tel. (72) 501-000; fax (72) 501-208; internet www .eon-deldunantul.com; fmrly Dédász (South-West Hungarian Electricity Supply Co); present name adopted 2004; 100% owned by E.ON Hungária Rt; Chair. ZOLTÁN PALUSKA.

E.ON Észak-dunántúli Áramszolgáltató: 9027 Győr, Kandó Kálmán u. 11–13; tel. (96) 521-000; fax (96) 521-888; e-mail webmaster@edasz.hu; internet www.eon-eszakdunantul.com; f. 1951; fmrly Édász (North-West Hungarian Electricity Co); present name adopted 2004; generates and supplies electricity; 98.57% owned by E.ON Hungária Rt; Chair. BÉLA KÜNSZLER; 2,272 employees.

E.ON Hungária Rt: 1054 Budapest, Széchenyi rkp. 8; tel. (1) 472-2300; e-mail info@eon-hungaria.com; internet www.eon-hungaria .com; f. 2000; 85.98% owned by E.ON Energie AG (Germany); owns shares in Édász, Dédász, Titász, DDGáz Rt (South Transdanubian Gas Supply Corpn) and Kögáz RT (Central Transdanubian Gas Supply Corpn) ; Chair. of Bd of Dirs KONRAD KRAUSER.

E.ON Tiszántúli Áramszolgáltató: 4024 Debrecen, Kossuth Lajos u. 4; tel. (52) 410-011; fax (52) 414-031; internet www.eon-tiszantul .com; 97.2% owned by E.ON Hungária; fmrly Titász (North-East Hungarian Electricity Co); present name adopted 2004; Chair. FRANZ ERÉNYI.

Hungarian Power Companies Co (Magyar Villamos Művek R—MVM): 1255 Budapest, POB 77; 1011 Budapest, Vám u. 5–7; tel. (1) 224-6200; fax (1) 202-1246; e-mail mvm@mvm.hu; internet www .mvm.hu; Hungarian national electricity wholesaler and power-system controller; Chair. GYULA LENGYEL.

Mátrai Power Plant (Erőmű Részvénytársaság) Co: 3272 Visonta, Erőmű u. 11; tel. (37) 328-001; fax (37) 328-036; internet www.mert.hu; electricity generation; Chair. JÓSZEF VALASKA; 3,645 employees.

Paks Nuclear Plant Co (Paksi Atomerőmű): 7031 Paks, POB 71; tel. (75) 508-833; fax (75) 506-662; internet www.npp.hu; f. 1992; electrical energy production; Plant Man. SÁNDOR NAGY; 2,800 employees.

Vértesi Power Plant (Erőmű) Co: 2840 Oroszlány, POB 23; tel. (34) 360-255; fax (34) 360-882; e-mail vert@vert.hu; internet www .vert.hu; electricity and heat generation; Chair. KÁROLY TAKÁCS; 5,438 employees.

Gas

Dégáz—Delalfoldi Gázszolgáltató (South-Western Gas) Co: 6724 Szeged, Pulcz u. 44; tel. (62) 569-600; fax (63) 473-943; e-mail ugyfel@degas.hu; internet www.degaz.hu; gas supply and services in Bács-Kiskun, Békés and Csongrád counties; 99.8% owned by Gaz de France (France).

(Főgáz—Fővárosi Gázművek (Budapest Gas) Co: 1081 Budapest, Köztársaság tér 20; tel. (1) 477-1111; fax (1) 477-1277; internet www.fogaz.hu; f. 1856; gas distribution; Chair. DEZSŐ VASANITS.

MOL—Magyar Olaj és Gázipari (Hungarian Oil and Gas Co): 1117 Budapest, Október huszonharmadika u. 18; tel. (1) 209-0000; fax (1) 209-0005; e-mail webmaster@mol.hu; internet www.mol.hu; f. 1991; privatized in 1995; the state retains a 12.2% share; petroleum and gas exploration, processing, transportation and distribution; 12,000 employees; Chair. and Chief Exec. ZSOLT HERNÁDI; Chief Exec. GYÖRGI MOSONYI.

Tigáz—Tiszántúli Gázszolgáltató (Tiszá Gas) Co: 4200 Hajdúszoboszló, Rákóczi u. 184; tel. (52) 558-100; fax (52) 361-149; e-mail titkarsaga@tigaz.hu; internet www.tigas.hu; f. 1950; 40% owned by Italgas Gruppo (Italy); gas distribution in north-eastern regions of Hungary; Chair. MARINO BIAGIO.

TRADE UNIONS

From 1988, and particularly after the restructuring of the former Central Council of Hungarian Trade Unions (SzOT) as the National Confederation of Hungarian Trade Unions (MSzOSz) in 1990, several new union federations were created. Several unions are affiliated to more than one federation, and others are completely independent. In May 2000 a trade-unions co-operation council was established.

Trade Union Federations

Association of Hungarian Free Trade Unions (Magyar Szabad Szakszervezetek Szövetsége): Budapest; f. 1994; 200,000 mems.

Autonomous Trade Union Confederation (Autonóm Szakszervezetek Svövetsége): 1068 Budapest, Benczúr u. 45; tel. (1) 342-1776; Pres. LAJOS FÓCZE.

Democratic Confederation of Free Trade Unions (Független Szakszervezetek Demokratikus Ligája—FSzDL): 1068 Budapest, Benczúr u. 41; tel. (1) 321-5262; fax (1) 321-5405; e-mail info@liganet .hu; f. 1988; Pres. ISTVÁN GASKÓ; 98,000 mems.

Principal affiliated unions include:

Democratic Trade Union of Scientific Workers (Tudományos Dolgozók Demokratikus Szakszervezete—TDDSz): 1068 Budapest, Városligeti fasor 38; tel. (1) 142-8438; f. 1988; Chair. PÁL FORGACS.

Federation of Unions of Intellectual Workers (Értelmiségi Szakszervezeti Tömörülés—ÉSzT): 1068 Budapest, Városligeti fasor 10; tel. (1) 122-8456; Pres. Dr LÁSZLÓ KIS; Gen. Sec. Dr GÁBOR BÁNK.

Forum for the Co-operation of Trade Unions (Szakszervezetek Együttműködési Fóruma—SzEF): 1068 Budapest VIII, Puskin u. 4; tel. (1) 138-2651; fax (1) 118-7360; f. 1990; Pres. Dr ENDRE SZABÓ.

Principal affiliated unions include:

Federation of Hungarian Public Service Employees' Unions (Közszolgálati Szakszervezetek Szövetsége): 1081 Budapest, Kiss u. 8; tel. (1) 313-5436; fax (1) 133-7223; f. 1945; Pres. PÉTER MICHALKO.

National Confederation of Hungarian Trade Unions (Magyar Szakszervezetek Országos Szövetsége—MSzOSz): 1086 Budapest, Magdolna u. 5–7; tel. (1) 323-2660; fax (1) 323-2662; e-mail gykiss@ mszosz.hu; internet www.mszosz.hu; f. 1898; reorganized 1990; Pres. Dr LÁSZLO SÁNDOR; 405,000 mems in 41 mem. orgs.

Principal affiliated unions include:

Commercial Employees' Trade Union (Kereskedelmi Alkalmazottak Szakszervezete): 1066 Budapest, Jókai u. 6; tel. (1) 331-8970; fax (1) 332-3382; e-mail saling@axelero.hu; f. 1900; Pres. Dr JÓZSEF SÁLING; 80,000 mems.

Federation of Agricultural, Forestry and Water Supply Workers' Unions (Mezőgazdasági, Erdészeti es Vizügyi Dolgozók Szakszervezeti Szövetsége—MEDOSZ): 1066 Budapest, Jókai u. 2; tel. (1) 301-9050; fax (1) 331-4568; e-mail medosz.net@ mail.datanet.hu; f. 1906; Gen. Sec. Dr ANDRÁS BERECZKY; 9,277 mems.

Federation of Chemical Workers' Unions of Hungary, Confederation Founding Section (Magyar Vegyipari Dolgozók Szakszervezeti Szövetsége, össz-szövetségi alapító tagozata): Budapest; tel. (1) 342-1778; fax (1) 342-9975; Gen. Sec. GYÖRGY PASZTERNÁK; 12,000 mems.

Federation of Communal Service Workers' Unions (Kommunális Dalgozók Szakszervezete): 1068 Budapest, Benczur u. 43; tel. (1) 111-6950; Gen. Sec. ZSOLT PÉK; 28,000 mems.

Federation of Hungarian Artworkers' Unions (Müvészeti Szakszervezetek Szövetsége): 1068 Budapest, Városligeti fasor 38; tel. (1) 342-8927; fax (1) 342-8372; e-mail eji@mail.datanet.hu; f. 1957; Pres. LÁSZLÓ GYIMESI; 32,000 mems.

Federation of Hungarian Metalworkers' Unions (Vasas Szakszervezeti Szövetség): 1086 Budapest, Magdolna u. 5–7; tel. (1) 210-9610; fax (1) 210-0116; e-mail lasurgo.s@ vasasszakszervezet.hu; internet www.vasasszakszervezet.hu; f. 1877; Pres. BÉLA BALOGH; 53,000 mems.

Federation of Local Industry and Municipal Workers' Unions (Helyiipari és Városgazdasági Dolgozók Szövetségének): 1068 Budapest, Benczúr u. 43; tel. (1) 311-6950; f. 1952; Pres. JÓZSEFNÉ SVEVER; Gen. Sec. PÁL BAKÁNYI; 281,073 mems.

Federation of Municipal Industries and Service Workers' Unions (Települési Ipari és Szolgáltatási Dolgozók Szakszervezete): 1068 Budapest, Benczur u. 43; tel. (1) 111-6950; Gen. Sec. ZOLTÁN SZIKSZAI; 20,000 mems.

Federation of Postal and Telecommunications Workers' Unions (Postai és Hirközlési Dolgozók Szakszervezeti Szövetsége): 1146 Budapest, Cházár András u. 13; tel. (1) 142-8777; fax (1) 121-4018; f. 1945; Pres. ENIKÓ HESZKY-GRICSER; 69,900 mems.

Hungarian Federation of Food Industry Workers' Unions (Magyar Élelmezésipari Dolgozók Szakszervezeteinek Szövetsége): 1068 Budapest, Városligeti fasor 44; tel. (1) 122-5880; fax (1) 142-8568; f. 1905; Pres. GYULA SÖKI; Gen. Sec. BÉLA VANEK; 226,243 mems.

Hungarian Union of Teachers (Magyar Pedagógusok Szakszervezete): 1068 Budapest, Városligeti fasor 10; tel. (1) 122-8456; fax (1) 142-8122; f. 1945; Gen. Sec. ISTVÁNNÉ SZÖLLŐSI; 200,000 mems.

Hungarian Union of Textile Workers (Magyar Textilipari Dolgozók Szakszervezete): 1068 Budapest, Rippl-Rónai u. 2; tel. (1) 428-196; fax (1) 122-5414; f. 1905; Gen. Sec. Tamás Keleti; 70,241 mems.

Union of Health Service Workers (Egészségügyben Dolgozók Szakszervezeteinek Szövetsége): 1051 Budapest, Nádor u. 32, POB 36; tel. (1) 110-645; f. 1945; Pres. Dr Zoltán Szabó; Gen. Sec. Dr Pálné Kállay; 280,536 mems.

Union of Clothing Workers (Ruházatipari Dolgozók Szakszervezete): 1077 Budapest, Almássy tér 2; tel. (1) 342-3702; fax (1) 122-6717; f. 1892; Gen. Sec. Tamás Wittich; 22,000 mems.

Workers Unions of Mining and Energy (Bánya—és Energiaipari Dolgozók Szakszervezete): 1068 Budapest, Városligeti fasor 46–48; tel. (1) 322-1226; fax (1) 342-1942; e-mail bdsz@ banyasz.hu; f. 1913; Pres. Ferenc Rabi; 80,000 mems.

Transport

RAILWAYS

In 2003 the rail network in Hungary amounted to a length of 8,137 km. Some 156.4m. passengers were carried in 2000. There is an underground railway in Budapest, which had a network of three lines, totalling 33 km in 2002; a fourth line was also planned. The European Union (EU) provided funding for several railway-modernization projects from the late 1990s.

Budapest Transport Company (BKV): 1072 Budapest, Akácfa u. 15; tel. (1) 461-6500; fax (1) 461-6557; internet www.bkv.hu; operates metro system, suburban railway network, trams, trolley buses, and conventional buses; Chair. Botond Aba.

Hungarian State Railways Co (Magyar Államvasutak—MÁV): 1940 Budapest, Andrássy u. 73–75; tel. (1) 322-0660; fax (1) 342-8596; internet www.mav.hu; f. 1868; total network 7,785 km, including 2,628 km of electrified lines (2000); Chief Exec. Zoltán Mándoki; Gen. Dir Márton Kukely.

Railway of Győr–Sopron–Ebenfurth (Győr–Sopron–Ebenfurti-Vasút—GySEV/ROeEE): 1011 Budapest, Szilágyi Dezső tér 1; internet www.gysev.hu; Hungarian-Austrian-owned railway; 162 km in Hungary, 65 km in Austria, all electrified; transport of passengers and goods; Dir-Gen. Dr László Fehérvári.

ROADS

In 2003 there were 542 km of motorways and 30,536 km of national public roads. There are extensive long-distance bus services. In 2003 a road development programme was approved, for the construction of 420 km of roads, including 326 km of motorways by the beginning of 2007, at a cost of 1,100m. forint. This programme was to be partly funded by loans from the European Bank for Reconstruction and Development and the European Investment Bank. The central budget for 2003 allocated 79,400m. forint for road development.

Hungarocamion: 1442 Budapest, POB 108; tel. (1) 257-3600; fax (1) 256-6755; international road freight transport company; 17 offices in Europe and the Middle East; fleet of 1,100 units for general and specialized cargo; Gen. Man. Gabriella Szakál; 3,800 employees.

Volánbusz: 1091 Budapest, Üllői út 131; tel. (1) 219-8000; e-mail info@volanbusz.hu; internet www.volanbusz.hu; 100% state-owned; operates local, national and international passenger coach services.

SHIPPING AND INLAND WATERWAYS

MAFRACHT International Shipping, Forwarding and Agency Ltd Co: 1364 Budapest 4, POB 105; tel. (1) 266-1208; fax (1) 266-1329; shipping agency.

MAHART—Magyar Hajózás (Hungarian Shipping) Co: 1366 Budapest, POB 58; 1052 Budapest, Apáozai Cs. J, u. 11; tel. (1) 484-6421; fax (1) 484-6422; e-mail freeport@mahart.hu; internet www .freeport.hu; f. 1895; transportation of goods on the Rhine–Main–Danube waterway; carries passenger traffic on the Danube; operates port activities at Budapest Csepel National and Free Port (port agency service, loading, storage, handling goods); management of multi-modal and combined transport (cargo booking, oversized goods, chartering); ship-building and ship-repair services; Dir-Gen. Capt. László Somlóvári.

CIVIL AVIATION

The Ferihegy international airport is 16 km from the centre of Budapest. In 1999 a new passenger terminal opened. Balatonkiliti airport, near Siófok in western Hungary, also serves international traffic. Public internal air services resumed in 1993, after an interval of 20 years, between Budapest and Nyíregyháza, Debrecen, Szeged, Pécs, Szombathely and Győr.

Civil Aviation Authority (Polgári Légiközlekedésigyi Hatóság): Budapest; tel. (1) 296-9502; fax (1) 296-8808; e-mail info@caa.hu; internet www.caa.hu; controls civil aviation; Dir-Gen. Zoltán Antal.

Hungarocontrol (Hungarian Air Navigation Services): 1185 Budapest, POB 80, Igló u. 33–35; tel. (1) 296-9098; fax (1) 296-9026; e-mail info@hungarocontrol.hu; internet www.hungarocontrol.hu; f. 2002; state-owned; operation of air traffic control in Hungary; Dir István Mudra; 700 employees.

LinAir Hungarian Regional Airlines: 1675 Budapest, POB 53; tel. (1) 296-7092; fax (1) 296-7891; e-mail info@linair.hu; internet www.linair.hu; f. 1994; regional carrier; Man. Dir Tamás Kovács.

Malév Hungarian Airlines: 1051 Budapest, Roosevelt tér 2, POB 122; tel. (1) 235-3535; fax (1) 266-2685; internet www.malev.hu; f. 1946; regular services from Budapest to Europe, North Africa, North America, Asia and the Middle East; Pres. Ferenc Szarvas; Chief Exec. Ferenc Kovács.

Wizz Air Hungary: 2220 Vescés, Lorinci út 59; tel. (22) 351-9499; e-mail info@wizzair.com; internet www.wizzair.com; f. 2004; wholly-owned subsidiary of Wizz Air (United Kingdom); mem. of European Low Fares Airline Asscn; Chair. and Chief Exec. József Váradi.

Tourism

Tourism has developed rapidly and is an important source of foreign exchange. Lake Balaton is the main holiday centre for boating, bathing and fishing. Hungary's cities have great historical and recreational attractions, and the annual Budapest Spring Festival is held in March. Budapest has numerous swimming pools watered by thermal springs, which are equipped with modern physiotherapy facilities. Revenue from tourism totalled 722,700m. forint in the first 11 months of 2003 (compared with 838,700m. forint in the whole of 2003), and there were 36.6m. foreign visitors in 2004.

Association of Hungarian Travel Agencies (Magyar Utazásszervezők és Utazásközvetítők Szövetsége—MUISZ): 1051 Budapest, Erzsébet tér Park; tel. (1) 327-9020; fax (1) 317-8657; e-mail muisz@ mail.selectrade.hu; internet www.muisz.com; f. 1974; Pres. Gabriella Molnár.

Hungarian Tourism Office: 1052 Budapest, Sütő u. 2; tel. (1) 317-9800; fax (1) 317-9656; e-mail tourinform@mail.hungarytourism.hu; internet www.hungarytourism.hu.

Tourism Office of Budapest: 1364 Budapest, POB 215; tel. (1) 266-0479; fax (1) 266-7477; e-mail info@budapestinfo.hu; internet www.budapestinfo.hu; Dir László Fekete.

ICELAND

Introductory Survey

Location, Climate, Language, Religion, Flag, Capital

The Republic of Iceland comprises one large island and numerous smaller ones, situated near the Arctic Circle in the North Atlantic Ocean. The main island lies about 300 km (190 miles) south-east of Greenland, about 1,000 km (620 miles) west of Norway and about 800 km (500 miles) north of Scotland. The Gulf Stream keeps Iceland warmer than might be expected, with average temperatures ranging from 10°C (50°F) in the summer to 1°C (34°F) in winter. Icelandic is the official language. Almost all of the inhabitants profess Christianity: the Evangelical Lutheran Church is the established church and embraces about 86% of the population. The civil flag (proportions 18 by 25) displays a red cross, bordered with white, on a blue background, the upright of the cross being towards the hoist; the state flag (proportions 9 by 16) bears the same design, but has a truncated triangular area cut from the fly. The capital is Reykjavík.

Recent History

Iceland became independent on 17 June 1944, when the Convention that linked it with Denmark, under the Danish crown, was terminated. Iceland became a founder member of the Nordic Council (see p. 296) in 1952, and has belonged to both the North Atlantic Treaty Organization (NATO, see p. 301) and the Council of Europe (see p. 199) since 1949. Membership of the European Free Trade Association (EFTA, see p. 214) was formalized in 1970.

From 1959 to 1971 Iceland was governed by a coalition of the Independence Party (IP) and the Social Democratic Party (SDP). Following the general election of June 1971, Ólafur Jóhannesson, the leader of the Progressive Party (PP), formed a coalition Government with the left-wing People's Alliance (PA) and the Union of Liberals and Leftists. At the general election held in June 1974 voters favoured right-wing parties, and in August the IP and the PP formed a coalition Government, led by the leader of the IP, Geir Hallgrímsson. Failure adequately to address economic difficulties resulted in a decline in the coalition's popularity, however, and prompted the Government's resignation in June 1978, following extensive electoral gains by the PA and the SDP. Disagreements over economic measures, and over the PA's advocacy of Icelandic withdrawal from NATO, led to two months of negotiations before a new government could be formed. In September Jóhannesson formed a coalition of the PP with the PA and the SDP, but this Government, after addressing immediate economic necessities, resigned in October 1979, when the SDP withdrew from the coalition. An interim administration was formed by Benedikt Gröndal, the leader of the SDP. The results of a general election, held in December, were inconclusive, and in February 1980 Gunnar Thoroddsen of the IP formed a coalition Government with the PA and the PP.

In June 1980 Vigdís Finnbogadóttir, a non-political candidate who was favoured by left-wing groups because of her opposition to the US military airbase at Keflavík, achieved a narrow victory in the election for the mainly ceremonial office of President. She took office on 1 August 1980, becoming the world's first popularly-elected female Head of State. The coalition Government lost its majority in the Lower House of the Althingi/Alþingi (parliament) in September 1982, and a general election took place in April 1983. The IP received the largest share (38.7%) of the votes cast, but two new parties, the Social Democratic Alliance (SDA) and the Women's List (WL), together won almost 13% of the votes cast. A centre-right coalition was formed by the IP and the PP, with Steingrímur Hermannsson (the leader of the PP and former Minister of Fisheries and Communications) as Prime Minister. In May 1985 the Althingi unanimously approved a resolution declaring the country a 'nuclear-free zone', i.e. banning the entry of nuclear weapons.

A general election for an enlarged, 63-seat Althingi was held in April 1987. Both parties of the outgoing coalition suffered losses: the IP's representation decreased from 24 to 18 seats, and the PP lost one of its 14 seats. The right-wing Citizens' Party (CP, which had been formed only one month earlier by Albert Guðmundsson, following his resignation from the Ministry of Energy and Industry and from the IP) won seven seats. Ten seats were won by the SDP, which included former members of the SDA (disbanded in 1986). A coalition of the IP, the PP and the SDP was formally constituted in July 1987. Thorsteinn Pálsson, the leader of the IP since November 1983 and the Minister of Finance in the outgoing Cabinet, was appointed Prime Minister.

In June 1988 President Finnbogadóttir (who had begun a second term in office, unopposed, in August 1984) was elected for a third term, receiving more than 90% of the votes cast. This was the first occasion on which an incumbent Icelandic President seeking re-election had been challenged. In August 1992 the President began a fourth term of office, her candidacy being unopposed.

In September 1988 the SDP and the PP withdrew from the Pálsson Government, following disagreements over economic policy. Later that month, the leader of the PP, Steingrímur Hermannsson, became Prime Minister in a centre-left coalition with the SDP and the PA. The new Government committed itself to a series of devaluations of the króna, and introduced austerity measures, with the aim of lowering the rate of inflation and stimulating the fishing industry.

Following the resignation of Guðmundsson from the leadership of the CP in January 1989, relations between this party and the left improved, and in September a new Government, based on a coalition agreement between the PP, the SDP, the PA, the CP and the Association for Equality and Social Justice, was formed. Hermannsson, who remained as Prime Minister, affirmed that the new Government would not change its policies, emphasizing the need to reduce inflation and to stimulate economic growth, as well as reiterating an earlier declaration of the Althingi that no nuclear weapons would be located in Iceland.

In March 1991 Davîð Oddsson, the mayor of Reykjavík, successfully challenged Pálsson for the leadership of the IP. At a general election in April the IP emerged as the largest single party, securing 26 seats (with 38.6% of the votes cast), mostly at the expense of the CP. Although the incumbent coalition would have retained an overall majority of seats, the SDP decided to withdraw from the coalition, chiefly as a result of the failure to reach agreement on Iceland's position in the discussions between EFTA and the European Community (EC—now European Union—EU, see p. 217), with regard to the creation of a European Economic Area (EEA, see p. 214). A new coalition Government was formed in late April by the IP and the SDP, with Oddsson as Prime Minister; the new administration promised economic liberalization and a strengthening of links with the USA and Europe (although no application for membership of the EC was envisaged), but was faced with a deteriorating economic situation.

In 1991 Iceland's Constitution was amended, ending the system whereby the Althingi was divided into an Upper House (one-third of the members) and a Lower House.

Although the IP secured the largest number of seats (25, with 37% of the votes cast) at a general election in April 1995, the SDP obtained only seven seats, three fewer than in the previous election. Later in the month a new coalition Government was formed, comprising the IP and the PP, with Oddsson continuing as Prime Minister, and Halldór Ásgrímsson, the leader of the PP, being named Minister of Foreign Affairs. Since both parties in the coalition opposed the Common Fisheries Policy of the EU, it was considered unlikely that Iceland would apply for full membership of the EU in the near future.

Following the decision by Finnbogadóttir not to seek re-election as President in 1996, the principal candidates were Ólafur Ragnar Grímsson, a former leader of the PA (who had previously opposed Iceland's membership of NATO), Pétur Hafstein, a justice in the Supreme Court, and Guðrún Agnarsdóttir of the WL. In the election, held in June 1996, Grímsson secured 41% of the votes cast, while Hafstein won 29% and Agnarsdóttir gained 26%. Grímsson duly took office as President in August. He began a second term of office in August 2000, his candidacy being unopposed.

At a general election held in May 1999 the IP obtained the largest share of the votes cast (40.7%) and won 26 seats, thereby remaining the party with the largest representation in the Althingi. An left-wing electoral grouping entitled The Alliance, which was composed of the PA, the SDP, the People's Movement and the WL, received 26.8% of the votes and won 17 seats, while the PP won 18.4% (12 seats). Two new parties also secured seats in the Althingi: the Left-Green Movement, established by three former PA deputies, obtained 9.1% of the votes cast (six seats), while the Liberal Party, founded by the former IP minister Sverrir Hermannsson, won 4.2% (two seats). A new coalition Government, which, once again, comprised the IP and the PP, and which continued to be led by Oddsson, took office at the end of the month.

At the general election held on 10 May 2003, the IP remained the party with the largest representation in the Althingi, winning 33.7% of the votes cast and securing 22 seats. The IP renewed its coalition with the PP, which had won 17.7% of the votes cast and 12 seats, with Oddsson remaining as Prime Minister. The two parties agreed that Oddsson would relinquish the premiership in September 2004 in favour of the Chairman of the PP, Halldór Ásgrímsson, who had been reappointed as Minister of Foreign Affairs. The Alliance won 31.0% of the votes cast and 20 seats, the Left-Green Movement 8.8% and five seats, and the Liberal Party 7.4% and four seats.

On 25 May 2004 the Althingi narrowly passed a bill to limit media ownership. Although the legislation was drafted following the publication of a report by a government-appointed committee that expressed concerns regarding the increased consolidation of media corporations, it provoked uncharacteristic public protests as many perceived the bill to be directed against a particular company, the Baugur Group, which dominated Iceland's retail, financial and media sectors, and whose media outlets had been openly critical of Oddson. A petition urging President Grímsson to veto the bill attracted 30,000 signatures, an amount roughly equivalent to 10% of the population. Grímsson, who favoured a more active role for the presidency, refused to sign the bill, stating that it lacked the necessary consensus. It was the first time the presidential power of veto had been used in the 60-year history of the Republic. Grímsson was re-elected President for a third four-year term on 26 June, with 85.6% of the votes cast. However, discontent at his deployment of the veto was perhaps manifested in the low participation rate at the election of only 62.5% (compared with a turnout of 85.9% at the previous presidential election in 1996) and the significantly high proportion of blank ballots (20.7%). Under the terms of the Constitution, the media bill was to be subject to a referendum in August 2004, but Oddsson instead withdrew the legislation and presented a lightly amended version to the Althingi. The Althingi, however, rejected this new version of the bill in July.

Oddsson's defeat, the only one during his 13 years as Prime Minister, was followed by a period of ill health. On 15 September, in accordance with an agreement between the IP and PP following the elections of May 2003, Oddsson stood down as Prime Minister in favour of the former Minister of Foreign Affairs, Halldór Ásgrímsson, whose post Oddsson assumed.

In December 2004 opposition parties attacked Ásgrímsson's claim, in a televised interview, that the Althingi had been consulted prior to Iceland's endorsement of the US-led invasion of Iraq in March 2003. Opposition leaders accused Ásgrímsson and Oddsson, an outspoken supporter of the war in Iraq, of making the decision for Iceland to join the 'coalition of the willing' unilaterally. Ásgrímsson and Oddsson stated the decision was supported by a vote of the Foreign Affairs Committee, however other committee members claimed they were unable to recall any deliberations on the issue. Ásgrímsson's popularity declined, but he was re-elected as Chairman of the PP at a party conference in March 2005 (albeit with a 10% decline in support).

In May 2003 it emerged that the USA was planning to withdraw the four remaining F-15/F-16 fighter jet aircraft stationed at Keflavík airbase, near Reykjavík, following a review of its international military commitments. The Iceland Defence Force (IDF), which, in mid-2003, was composed of 1,658 US troops and which had been stationed in Iceland since 1951 when an agreement had been drawn up between Iceland and the USA, was traditionally viewed as providing protection for Iceland, which had no military of its own; moreover, many Icelanders in the nearby town of Reykjanesbær depended on the Keflavík airbase for their livelihood. Oddsson suggested that if the USA withdrew the aircraft it would have to end its military presence in Iceland altogether—an unpalatable proposition for the USA, which still regarded its reconnaissance of the North Atlantic as a high priority. The possibility of Iceland forming its own national guard was the topic of much debate amongst Icelandic government officials. Concern among Icelanders was such that the Government requested that the Secretary-General of NATO, Lord Robertson of Port Ellen, intervene on their behalf. Following Lord Robertson's subsequent non-partisan representations in July 2003, the US authorities announced that they had delayed their decision with regard to the aircraft at Keflavík, which would instead be taken as part of a later general review of its military presence in Europe. The USA had previously withdrawn eight fighter aircraft from Iceland in 1994, but had agreed to retain four aircraft on a permanent basis at the Keflavík airbase; this agreement had originally been due to be renegotiated in 2001, but this had been postponed following the terrorist attacks in the USA of 11 September of that year.

The importance of fishing to Iceland's economy, and fears of excessive exploitation of the fishing grounds near Iceland by foreign fleets, caused the Icelandic Government to extend its territorial waters to 12 nautical miles (22 km) in 1964 and to 50 nautical miles (93 km) in 1972. British opposition to these extensions resulted in two 'cod wars'. In October 1975 Iceland unilaterally introduced a fishing limit of 200 nautical miles (370 km), both as a conservation measure and to protect Icelandic interests. The 1973 agreement on fishing limits between Iceland and the United Kingdom expired in November 1975, and failure to reach a new agreement led to the third and most serious 'cod war'. Casualties occurred, and in February 1976 Iceland temporarily severed diplomatic relations with the United Kingdom, the first diplomatic break between two NATO countries. In June the two countries reached an agreement, and in December the British trawler fleet withdrew from Icelandic waters. In June 1979 Iceland declared its exclusive rights to the 200-mile fishing zone. Following negotiations between the EC and EFTA on the creation of the EEA, an agreement was reached (in October 1991) allowing tariff-free access to the EC for 97% of Iceland's fisheries products by 1997, while Iceland was to allow EC vessels to catch 3,000 metric tons of fish per year in its waters, in return for some access to EC waters. The EEA agreement was ratified by the Althingi in January 1993 and entered into force in January 1994.

In August 1993 a dispute developed between Iceland and Norway over fishing rights in an area of the Barents Sea fished by Iceland, over which Norway claimed jurisdiction. The dispute continued throughout 1994, and in June the Norwegian coastguards cut the nets of Icelandic trawlers fishing for cod in the disputed region. Iceland's case was weakened in January 1995, when Canada officially recognized Norway's sovereign rights over the disputed area (a fisheries protection zone extending 200 km around the Svalbard archipelago). A similar dispute arose in August 1996 between Iceland and Denmark over fishing rights in an area of the Atlantic Ocean between Iceland and Greenland (a self-governing province of Denmark). The Danish Government claimed that an agreement had been concluded in 1988 to allow fishing boats that were in possession of a licence issued in Greenland to operate in the area. Iceland, however, denied the existence of such an agreement, and announced that Danish boats would not be permitted to fish in the disputed area.

Iceland strongly criticized the moratorium on commercial whaling, imposed (for conservation purposes) by the International Whaling Commission (IWC, see p. 366) in 1986, and continued to catch limited numbers of whales for scientific purposes until 1989, when it halted whaling, following appeals by environmental organizations for an international boycott of Icelandic products. In 1991 Iceland announced its withdrawal from the IWC (with effect from June 1992), claiming that certain species of whales were not only too plentiful to be in danger of extinction, but were also threatening Iceland's stocks of cod and other fish. In 1994 a report, commissioned by the Government, recommended that limited hunting be resumed in the future. In March 1999 the Althingi voted to end the self-imposed 10-year ban on whaling and requested the Government to implement the ruling, urging a resumption of hunting as soon as possible. Iceland's application to rejoin the IWC, with an unprecedented exemption that would allow it to disregard the moratorium on commercial whaling, was rejected in July 2001. It was, however, granted permission to attend discussions as an observer without voting rights. Its bid for full membership was rejected again in May 2002, but in October of that year Iceland was readmitted, when the Government undertook not to allow the resumption of commercial whaling until at least 2006 and after that not to resume commercial whaling while negotiations on a revised management plan were in progress. In August 2003, however, Iceland resumed whaling, provoking widespread international criticism and renewed calls for a boycott of Icelandic products. The Government authorized the capture of 38 minke whales by the end of September, ostensibly for the purpose of scientific research into the impact on fish stocks. From the 1990s whale watching emerged as a tourist attraction; it attracted some 59,000 tourists in 2001.

In April 2002 President Ólafur Ragnar Grímsson became the first Icelandic Head of State to visit Russia. Grímsson met with President Vladimir Putin, amongst other high-ranking Russian officials, to discuss political, economic, and cultural co-operation between the two countries; bilateral trade was expected to increase as a result of the meeting.

Government

According to the Constitution, executive power is vested in the President (elected for four years by universal adult suffrage) and the Cabinet, consisting of the Prime Minister and other ministers appointed by the President. In practice, however, the President performs only nominally the functions ascribed in the Constitution to this office, and it is the Cabinet alone that holds real executive power. Legislative power is held jointly by the President and the unicameral Althingi (parliament), with 63 members elected by universal suffrage for four years (subject to dissolution by the President), using a system of proportional representation in eight multi-member constituencies. The Cabinet is responsible to the Althingi. For the purposes of local government Iceland was composed of 101 municipalities at 1 December 2004; the municipalities were undergoing a process of amalgamation.

Defence

Apart from a 130-strong coastguard, Iceland has no defence forces of its own, but it is a member of NATO (see p. 301). There are units of US forces at Keflavík airbase, which is used for observation of the North Atlantic Ocean, under a bilateral agreement made in 1951 between Iceland and the USA. In 2004 the US Government announced that it intended to conduct a review with regard to the continuing presence (or otherwise) of US forces in Iceland (see above). The airfield at Keflavík is a base for the US airborne early warning system. In August 2004 a total of 1,658 US military personnel (navy 960, air force 650, marines 48) were stationed in Iceland, together with a 16-strong naval contingent from the Netherlands.

Economic Affairs

In 2003, according to estimates by the World Bank, Iceland's gross national income (GNI), measured at 2001–03 prices, was US $10,320.8m., equivalent to $30,810 per head (or $30,140 per head on an international purchasing-power parity basis). During 1990–2003, it was estimated, the population increased at an average annual rate of 0.9%, while gross domestic product (GDP) per head increased, in real terms, by an average of 1.5% per year. Iceland's overall GDP increased, in real terms, at an average annual rate of 2.4% during 1990–2003; GDP decreased by 0.5% in 2002 and increased by 1.9% in 2003.

Agriculture (including fishing and fish processing) contributed some 9.6% of GDP in 2004 (agriculture alone accounted for only 1.5% in 2002); 6.9% of the employed labour force were engaged in the agricultural and fishing sectors in 2003, with a further 3.4% employed in fish processing. The principal agricultural products are dairy produce and lamb, although these provided less than 0.5% of export earnings in 2003. Marine products accounted for 53.6% of total export earnings in 2003. A cod quota system is in place to avoid the depletion of fish stocks through over-fishing as happened in previous years. During 1990–2001 agricultural GDP (including fishing) declined at an average annual rate of 1.7%; agricultural GDP (excluding fishing) increased at an average annual rate of 1.1% during 1990–99, while the GDP of the fishing sector declined by 2.3% per year. Agricultural GDP (excluding fishing) decreased, in real terms, by 3.0% in 2000 and by 0.8% in 2001; the GDP of the fishing sector declined by 8.0% in 1998 and by 1.6% in 1999.

Industry (including mining, manufacturing, construction and power) contributed 21.9% of GDP in 2004 and engaged 21.7% of the employed labour force (including the 3.4% employed in fish processing) in 2003. Mining activity is negligible. During 1990–2001 industrial GDP increased at an average annual rate of

3.4%; industrial GDP increased by 8.0% in 2000 and by 6.9% in 2001.

Manufacturing (excluding fish processing) contributed 9.3% of GDP in 2004, and employed 10.4% of the labour force in 2003. The most important sectors, measured by gross value of output (excluding fish processing, which dominates the sector), are the production of aluminium, diatomite, fertilizer, cement and ferrosilicon. Aluminium and ferro-silicon processing contributed 1.3% of GDP in 2004. In March 2003 the Althingi approved proposals to construct a new aluminium smelter in the Eastern Highlands, despite considerable popular opposition on environmental grounds. The proposals included the damming of two rivers to create a reservoir of 22 sq km above Vatnajökull (Europe's biggest glacier), in order to produce hydroelectric power for the smelter. Fish processing contributed 4.9% of GDP in 1997; however, the GDP of the fish-processing sector declined by 5.3% in 1998 and by 1.1% in 1999. Manufacturing GDP (including fish processing) increased, in real terms, at an average annual rate of 2.4% in 1990–99; it grew by 4.1% in 1998 and by 4.9% in 1999.

Iceland is potentially rich in hydroelectric and geothermal power, but both energy sources are significantly underexploited. Hydroelectric power has promoted the development of the aluminium industry, while geothermal energy provides nearly all the country's heating and hot water. In 2001 hydroelectric power provided 81.9% of the country's electricity. Fuel imports comprised 7.8% of the value of merchandise imports in 2003. In 2001 Iceland announced its intention to develop the world's first economy free of carbon dioxide emissions by using hydrogen or methanol-powered fuel cells. Hydrogen-fuelled buses began operating in Reykjavík in 2003. The construction of two new hydroelectric power plants in Kárahnjúkar, in the east of the country, began in 2003.

Services contributed 68.7% of GDP in 2004 and employed 71.4% of the labour force in 2003. GDP from services increased, in real terms, at an average annual rate of 3.5% during 1990–2001; it grew by 6.3% in 2000 and by 2.0% in 2001. The tourism sector is becoming an increasingly significant source of revenue; the number of overnight stays by foreign visitors in hotels and guest houses totalled 1,376,788 in 2003; receipts from tourism totalled 37,148m. krónur in 2002.

In 2003 Iceland recorded a visible trade deficit of US $210m., while there was a deficit of $539m. on the current account of the balance of payments. In 2003 the principal sources of imports were Germany (providing 11.8% of total imports), Denmark (8.0%) the United Kingdom and the USA (7.4% each); the principal market for exports was the United Kingdom (accounting for 17.5% of total exports), followed by Germany (17.4%), the Netherlands (11.2%) and the USA (9.3%). In 2003 member countries of the European Economic Area—EEA (see p. 214) provided 63.8% of Iceland's merchandise imports and took 76.5% of its exports. The principal imports in 2003 were machinery and transport equipment (which accounted for 35.3% of the total value of imports), miscellaneous manufactured articles (15.7%), basic manufactures (14.6%) and chemicals and related products (10.4%). The principal exports in the same year were food and live animals (accounting for 61.0% of the total value of exports—fish, crustaceans, molluscs and fish preparations provided 53.6% of the total), and basic manufactures (23.6%—nonferrous metals, mostly aluminium, provided 18.8% of the total).

In 2003 there was a budgetary surplus of 11,843m. krónur, equivalent to 1.5% of GDP. Iceland's net external debt was equivalent to 20.6% of GDP in 2003; the cost of debt-servicing was equivalent to an estimated 21.0% of export earnings in 1998. The annual rate of inflation averaged 3.5% in 1990–2003; consumer prices increased by 4.8% in 2002 and by 2.1% in 2003. The unemployment rate averaged 3.3% in 2003.

Iceland is a member of the Nordic Council (see p. 296), the Nordic Council of Ministers (see p. 297), the European Free Trade Association (EFTA, see p. 214) and the Organisation for Economic Co-operation and Development (OECD, see p. 307). Although Iceland is not a member of the European Union (EU, see p. 217), it joined the EU's Schengen Agreement along with Denmark, Finland and Sweden (all EU members) by virtue of its membership in the Nordic passport union. (Norway also joined.)

During the late 1990s the Icelandic economy expanded rapidly, partly as a result of the recovery of the fishing industry but largely owing to the diversification of the economy through extensive deregulation and restructuring (begun in the early 1990s). The tourism sector expanded rapidly, while significant biotechnology and information technology industries were also developed. The financial sector benefited from the liberalization of capital flows and a series of privatizations, although the energy sector remained in public ownership. The Icelandic economy remained volatile with overheating in the economy leading to a mild recession in 2002. The structural reforms had given the economy greater resilience, however, and the recovery in 2003 was swifter than expected, owing to an increase in domestic demand and the stimulatory impact of a large aluminium-related investment project. The construction of a large aluminium smelting plant and associated hydroelectric power plants (including a controversial dam) in Kárahnjúkar in the Eastern Highlands, commenced in 2003, and was scheduled for completion in 2007. The smelting plant was expected to double Iceland's annual exports of aluminium and the projects, including the power plants, were equivalent to 30% of one year's GDP over 2003–2008. The short-term objectives of the Government were to maintain economic stability as the projects, which were led by foreign investment, contributed to rising current-account deficits, increased inflationary pressures and raised levels of foreign debt. A framework of inflation targeting and a floating exchange rate had been introduced in 2001 and the Central Bank had successfully reduced inflation to the official objective of 2.5%. However, the inflationary pressures caused by the construction work in Kárahnjúkar and high domestic demand led to a sharp increase in inflation in 2004 and the rate stood at 4.5% in February 2005, above the Bank's upper limit of 4.0%. Pressures on the labour market, which would also fuel inflation, were being successfully avoided during construction of the projects by flexibility in the immigration system, as labour demand was significant. Fiscal policy, which had been relaxed in 2003 to counter the effects of the recession, was tightened again in 2004, broadly balancing the budget. Budget surpluses were planned for 2005 and 2006 (when construction in Kárahnjúkar was expected to peak) although tax reductions scheduled for 2005–07 were likely to have a negative impact on revenues. In terms of long-term development Iceland needed to continue reforms to competition and regulatory policies and improve the educational attainment of Icelanders to sustain the improvements in Iceland's productivity. Iceland has benefited greatly from its membership of the EEA, but remained reluctant to join the EU, owing to the potentially adverse effects of the Common Fisheries Policy on the Icelandic fishing industry. However, the Government was likely to come under increased pressure in the future to establish some form of link with the European single currency, the euro, to protect certain industries, notably tourism, from the effects of currency fluctuations.

Education

Education is compulsory and free for 10 years between six and 16 years of age (primary and lower secondary levels). Upper secondary education begins at 16 years of age and usually lasts for four years. In 2000 90% of 16-year-olds were continuing their education at a secondary school. In 2002 Iceland had 14 institutions providing tertiary-level education. Budgetary expenditure by the Ministry of Education, Science and Culture was forecast at 32,250m. krónur in 2004, representing 11.8% of total estimated public expenditure. Local communities finance compulsory education.

Public Holidays

2005: 1 January (New Year's Day), 24 March (Maundy Thursday), 25 March (Good Friday), 28 March (Easter Monday), 21 April (First Day of Summer), 1 May (Labour Day), 5 May (Ascension Day), 17 June (National Day), 20 June (Whit Monday), 1 August (Bank Holiday), 24 (Christmas Eve)*, 25 December (Christmas Day), 26 December (Boxing Day), 31 December (New Year's Eve)*.

2006: 1 January (New Year's Day), 13 April (Maundy Thursday), 14 April (Good Friday), 17 April (Easter Monday), 20 April (First Day of Summer), 1 May (Labour Day), 25 May (Ascension Day), 5 June (Whit Monday), 17 June (National Day), 7 August (Bank Holiday), 24 (Christmas Eve)*, 25 December (Christmas Day), 26 December (Boxing Day), 31 December (New Year's Eve)*.

Holidays falling on a Saturday or Sunday will not be taken on the following Monday.

*Afternoon only.

Weights and Measures

The metric system is in force.

Statistical Survey

Sources (unless otherwise stated): Statistics Iceland, Borgartúni 21A, 150 Reykjavík; tel. 5281000; fax 5281099; e-mail statice@statice.is; internet www.statice.is; Seðlabanki Íslands (Central Bank of Iceland), Kalkofnsvegur 1, 150 Reykjavík; tel. 5699600; fax 5699605; e-mail sedlabanki@sedlabanki.is; internet www.sedlabanki.is.

AREA AND POPULATION

Area: 103,000 sq km (39,769 sq miles).

Population: 293,577 (males 147,170, females 146,407) at 31 December 2004 (national population register).

Density (per sq km): 2.9 (2004).

Principal Towns (population at 31 December 2004): Reykjavík (capital) 113,022; Kópavogur 25,803; Hafnarfjörður 22,000; Akureyri 16,308; Garðabær 9,053.

Births, Marriages and Deaths (2003): Live births 4,143 (birth rate 14.3 per 1,000); Marriages 1,473 (marriage rate 5.1 per 1,000); Deaths 1,827 (death rate 6.3 per 1,000).

Expectation of Life (years at birth, WHO estimates): 80.1 (males 78.4; females 81.8) in 2002. Source: WHO, *World Health Report*.

Economically Active Population (2003, figures rounded to nearest 100 persons): Agriculture 5,700; Fishing 5,100; Manufacturing (excl. fish-processing) 16,300; Fish-processing 5,400; Electricity and water supply 1,600; Construction 10,800; Wholesale and retail trade, repairs 20,500; Restaurants and hotels 5,500; Transport, storage and communications 9,700; Financial intermediation 6,200; Real estate and business services 14,300; Public administration 8,200; Education 12,200; Health services and social work 24,800; Other services not specified 10,600; *Total* 156,900; Unemployed 5,400; *Total labour force* 162,400 (males 85,500, females 76,900).

HEALTH AND WELFARE

Key Indicators

Total Fertility Rate (children per woman, 2002): 1.9.

Under-5 Mortality Rate (per 1,000 live births, 2003): 4.

HIV/AIDS (% of persons aged 15–49, 2003): 0.2.

Physicians (per 1,000 head, 2002): 3.57.

Hospital Beds (per 1,000 head, 2001): 7.8.

Health Expenditure (2001): US $ per head (PPP): 2,612.

Health Expenditure (2001): % of GDP: 9.1.

Health Expenditure (2001): public (% of total): 83.3.

Human Development Index (2002): ranking: 7.

Human Development Index (2002): value: 0.941.

For sources and definitions, see explanatory note on p. vi.

AGRICULTURE, ETC.

Principal Crops (metric tons, 2003): Cereals 4,337; Potatoes 7,090; Cabbages 555; Tomatoes 1,074; Cucumbers 896; Turnips 959.

Livestock (2003): Cattle 66,035; Sheep 463,006; Horses 71,412; Pigs 3,852; Hens 165,242; Other poultry 48,953; Mink 26,434; Foxes 2,388.

Livestock Products (metric tons, unless otherwise indicated, 2003): Mutton and lamb 8,792; Beef and veal 3,624; Pig meat 6,205; Poultry meat 5,706; Milk ('000 litres, processed) 108,384; Cheese 4,190; Wool (unwashed) 697; Sheepskins 1,920 (FAO estimate); Eggs 2,650. Source: partly FAO.

Fishing (metric tons, live weight, 2003): Atlantic cod 206,405; Saithe 51,935; Haddock 60,330; Atlantic redfishes 111,143; Capelin 675,625; Atlantic herring 250,097; Shrimp 28,595; Total (incl. others) 1,979,545.

INDUSTRY

Selected Products ('000 metric tons, 2002, unless otherwise indicated): Frozen fish 292.6 (demersal catch); Salted, dried or smoked fish 110.7; Cement 125.2 (2001); Ferro-silicon 111.9 (2001); Aluminium (unwrought) 245.1 (2001); Electric energy 8,409 million kWh.

FINANCE

Currency and Exchange Rates: 100 aurar (singular: eyrir) = 1 new Icelandic króna (plural: krónur). *Sterling, Dollar and Euro Equivalents* (31 December 2004): £1 sterling = 117.89 krónur; US $1 = 61.04 krónur; €1 = 83.14 krónur; 1,000 krónur = £8.482 = $16.383 = €12.028. *Average Exchange Rate* (krónur per US $): 91.662 in 2002; 76.709 in 2003; 70.192 in 2004.

Budget (budget forecasts, million krónur, 2004): *Revenue:* Tax revenue 252,273 (Personal income tax 73,900, Corporate income tax 7,900, Social security tax 29,007, New wealth taxes 8,260, Value-added tax 86,021, Other taxes on goods and services 44,944, Other taxes 2,241); Other current revenue 25,470 (Dividends income 3,726, Interest income 15,121, Other income 6,623); Revenue from sales of assets 540; Revenue and cost sharing transfers 1,143; Total 279,425. *Expenditure:* The Presidency, Althingi and Supreme Court 2,390; Office of the Prime Minister 1,130; Ministry of Education, Science and Culture 32,250; Ministry of Foreign Affairs 5,457; Ministry of Agriculture 11,743; Ministry of Fisheries 3,071; Ministry of Justice and Ecclesiastical Affairs 15,176; Ministry of Social Affairs 22,944; Ministry of Health and Social Security 110,181; Ministry of Finance 26,000; Ministry of Communications 17,982; Ministry of Industry 3,442; Ministry of Commerce 1,467; Statistics Iceland 514; Ministry of the Environment 4,149; Interest expenditure 15,140; Total 273,035.

International Reserves (US $ million at 31 December 2003): Gold 26.4; Reserve position in IMF 27.6; Foreign exchange 764.6; Total 818.6. Source: IMF, *International Financial Statistics*.

Money Supply (million krónur at 31 December 2002): Currency outside banks 7,666; Demand deposits at commercial and savings banks 76,624; Total money 84,290. Source: IMF, *International Financial Statistics*.

Cost of Living (consumer price index for Reykjavík; average of monthly figures; base: May 1988 = 100): 212.4 in 2001; 222.6 in 2002; 227.3 in 2003.

National Income and Product (million krónur at current prices, 2004, estimates): Compensation of employees 509,023; Gross operating surplus 236,591; *Gross domestic product at factor cost* 745,614; Taxes on production and imports 150,564; *Less* Subsidies 11,681; Statistical discrepancy –25,578; *Gross domestic product in market prices* 858,921; Net primary incomes received from abroad –17,717; *Gross national income* 841,204; *Less* Consumption of fixed capital 106,046; *Net national income* 735,158; Net current transfers from abroad –1,201; *Net national disposable income* 733,957.

Expenditure on the Gross Domestic Product (million krónur at current prices, 2004, estimates): Government final consumption expenditure 228,244; Private final consumption expenditure 496,292; Increase in stocks –3,383; Gross fixed capital formation 188,742; *Total domestic expenditure* 909,895; Exports of goods and services 316,139; *Less* Imports of goods and services 367,113; *Gross domestic product in market prices* 858,921.

GDP by Economic Activity (million krónur at current prices, 2003, estimates): Agriculture, hunting and forestry 11,322; Fishing and fish-processing 63,594; Mining, quarrying and manufacturing 67,189; Electricity, gas and water supply 26,420; Construction 61,905; Wholesale and retail trade, restaurants and hotels 93,801; Transport, storage and communications 57,567; Other private services 187,374; Government services 156,852; *Sub-total* 726,025; *Less* Financial intermediation services indirectly measured 49,577; Statistical discrepancy –7,193; *Gross value added at basic prices* 669,255; Taxes on production and imports 140,273; *Less* Subsidies 12,041; *GDP in market prices* 797,487.

Balance of Payments (US $ million, 2003): Exports of goods f.o.b. 2,386, Imports of goods f.o.b. –2,596, *Trade balance* –210; Exports of services 1,372, Imports of services –1,477, *Balance on goods and services* –315; Other income received 377, Other income paid –585, *Balance on goods, services and income* –523; Current transfers received 12, Current transfers paid –28, *Current balance* –539; Capi-

tal account (net) –5, Direct investment abroad –352, Direct investment from abroad 345, Portfolio investment assets –593, Portfolio investment liabilities 3,696, Other investment assets –2,069, Other investment liabilities –477, Net errors and omissions 168, *Overall balance* 175. Source: IMF, *International Financial Statistics*.

EXTERNAL TRADE

Principal Commodities (distribution by SITC, million krónur, 2003): *Imports c.i.f.:* Food and live animals 18,495.8; Crude materials, inedible 12,521.6 (Metalliferous ores and metal scrap 7,305.2); Mineral fuels and lubricants 16,795.2 (Petroleum and petroleum products 15,604.6); Chemicals and related products 22,523.2 (Medicinal and pharmaceutical products 7,313.8); Basic manufactures 31,548.3 (Metal products 14,656.4); Machinery and transport equipment 76,512.9 (Machinery specialized for particular industries 10,344.5; General industrial machinery and equipment 8,525.7; Office machines and computers 7,668.8; Telecommunications equipment, etc. 7,252.6; Other electrical machinery, apparatus and appliances 14,197.3; Road vehicles 20,959.2); Miscellaneous manufactured articles 33,950.9 (Apparel and clothing accessories 7,949.0); Total (incl. others) 216,525.2. *Exports f.o.b.:* Food and live animals 111,324.8 (Fish, crustaceans, molluscs and preparations thereof 97,950.5); Animal feeds (excl. unmilled cereals) 11,937.9); Animal and vegetable oils, fats and waxes 5,695.658 (Animal oils and fats 5,695.538); Chemicals and related products 6,563.8; Basic manufactures 43,131.7 (Non-ferrous metals 34,279.9); Machinery and transport equipment 7,228.5; Total (incl. others) 182,580.0.

Principal Trading Partners (million krónur, country of consignment, 2003): *Imports c.i.f.:* Australia 2,583.3; Belgium 4,828.2; China, People's Republic 7,719.2; Denmark (incl. Faroe Islands and Greenland) 18,681.1; Estonia 6,420.4; Finland 3,188.9; France 6,919.1; Germany 25,578.8; Ireland 5,112.3; Italy 10,100.7; Japan 8,266.6; Latvia 2,149.8; Netherlands 13,355.2; Norway 15,009.0; Russia 6,054.0; Spain 3,936.3; Suriname 2,217.9; Sweden 13,955.0; Switzerland 2,610.3; United Kingdom 16,096.6; USA 16,122.9; Total (incl. others) 216,525.2. *Exports f.o.b.:* Belgium 3,215.8; Denmark (incl. Greenland but excl. Faroe Islands) 9,561.2; Faroe Islands 2,307.5; France 7,381.5; Germany 31,829.3; Italy 2,464.7; Japan 5,914.8; Netherlands 20,459.9; Nigeria 2,993.4; Norway 8,157.4; Portugal 6,916.4; Spain 11,546.5; Sweden 2,348.9; Switzerland 3,555.9; United Kingdom 31,990.1; USA 16,927.3; Total (incl. others) 182,580.0.

TRANSPORT

Road Traffic (registered motor vehicles at 1 January 2003): Passenger cars 163,420; Buses and coaches 1,699; Goods vehicles 20,278; Motorcycles 2,557.

Shipping: *Merchant Fleet* (registered vessels, 1 January 2003): Fishing vessels 951 (displacement 188,970 grt); Passenger ships, tankers and other vessels 176 (displacement 44,156 grt). *International Freight Traffic* ('000 metric tons, excl. transport by ferries and dredged materials, 2002): Goods loaded 1,751.8; Goods unloaded 3,019.5.

Civil Aviation (scheduled external Icelandic traffic, million unless otherwise stated, 2001): Kilometres flown 32; Passengers ('000) 1,358; Passenger-kilometres 3,714; Total ton-kilometres 475 (Source: UN, *Statistical Yearbook*).

TOURISM

Overnight Stays by Foreign Visitors in Hotels and Guesthouses, by Country of Origin (2003): Denmark 81,102; France 127,889; Germany 262,218; Italy 63,007; Netherlands 70,568; Norway 73,613; Spain 31,809; Sweden 78,549; Switzerland 46,114; United Kingdom 195,077; USA 127,686; Total (incl. others) 1,376,788.

Receipts from Tourism (million krónur): 30,459 in 2000; 37,720 in 2001; 37,148 in 2002.

COMMUNICATIONS MEDIA

Radio Receivers (2002): 94,840 licensed.

Television Receivers (2002): 91,952 licensed.

Telephones (2003): 190,700 main lines in use*.

Facsimile Machines (1993): 4,100 in use (Source: UN, *Statistical Yearbook*).

Mobile Cellular Telephones ('000 subscribers, 2003): 279.1*.

Personal Computers ('000 in use, 2002): 130*.

Internet Users ('000, 2003): 195*.

Books (production, 2000): 1,967 titles (incl. new editions).

Daily Newspapers (2002): 3 (combined circulation 100,000 copies per issue).

*Source: International Telecommunication Union.

EDUCATION

Institutions (2002, unless otherwise indicated): Pre-primary 267 (2003); Primary and secondary (lower level) 192; Secondary (higher level) 36; Tertiary (universities and colleges) 14.

Teachers (incl. part-time, 2003): Pre-primary 4,052; Primary and secondary (lower level) 4,743; Secondary (higher level) 2,341; Tertiary 2,587.

Students (2003): Pre-primary 16,685; Primary and Secondary (lower level) 44,809; Secondary (higher level) 21,904; Tertiary 15,466.

Directory

The Constitution

The Constitution came into force on 17 June 1944, when Iceland became an independent Republic. The main provisions of the Constitution, including subsequent amendments, are summarized below:

GOVERNMENT

Legislative power is vested jointly in the President of the Republic and the Althingi (Alþingi). Executive power is vested in the President. The authority vested in the President shall be exercised through the Cabinet. The President appoints the Ministers to the Cabinet under the auspices of the Prime Minister, or the Prime Minister-elect when a new Cabinet is being assembled. The President may be dismissed only if a resolution supported by three-quarters of the Alþingi is approved by a plebiscite.

The President is elected for four years by universal suffrage. All those qualified to vote who have reached the age of 35 years are eligible for the Presidency.

The Alþingi is composed of 63 Members, elected by the people by secret ballot on the basis of proportional representation, for four years, in six multi-member constituencies. The franchise for general elections to the Alþingi is universal above the age of 18. Every national having the right to vote and an unblemished reputation is eligible to be elected to the Alþingi, except for the Justices of the Supreme Court. Seats that fall vacant between legislative elections are filled by substitutes elected at the same time as titular Members.

The Alþingi is convened by the President for a regular session every year on 1 October and continues in session until the same date next year, unless the election period of its Members has elapsed earlier or it has been dissolved. The President may adjourn meetings of the Alþingi, but not for more than two weeks not more than once a year. The President may dissolve the Alþingi. Elections must then be held within two months and the Alþingi must reassemble within eight months. Sessions are held in one chamber and its meetings are public. The Alþingi elects a Speaker, who presides over its proceedings.

Legislative bills are either submitted to the Alþingi by the President through his/her Ministers or by individual Members of the Alþingi. Bills must be given three readings in the Alþingi and be approved by a simple majority before they are submitted to the President. If the President disapproves a bill it nevertheless becomes valid, but must be submitted to a plebiscite.

Each Member of the Alþingi has the right to request, subject to the permission of the Alþingi, information from a Minister or an answer, orally or in writing, regarding a public matter, by tabling a question or requesting a report. Ministers are responsible to the Alþingi and may be impeached by that body, in which case they are tried by the Court of Impeachment.

LOCAL GOVERNMENT

Iceland is divided into 101 municipalities (at 1 December 2004), which have definite geographical boundaries and cover the entire island. These municipalities are currently undergoing a process of amalgamation, which is expected to continue over the next few years. In each municipality there is a municipal council, elected every four years. All citizens over the age of 18 years are eligible to vote. In larger municipalities councillors are elected by proportional representation and frequently on party political lines. In the smallest rural areas councillors are usually elected on an individual basis. Municipal councils are enacted to set their own property rates and local income taxes, within certain limits determined by law. A municipal executive council (elected every year) is in charge of the chief administration, including municipal finances, budgeting, personnel and legal matters. Executive councils may also take charge of infrastructural investments and public works.

The Government

HEAD OF STATE

President: ÓLAFUR RAGNAR GRÍMSSON (took office 1 August 1996; began a second term in August 2000; re-elected 26 June 2004).

THE CABINET
(April 2005)

A coalition of the Independence Party (IP) and the Progressive Party (PP).

Prime Minister and Minister of the Statistical Bureau of Iceland: HALLDÓR ÁSGRÍMSSON (PP).

Minister of Foreign Affairs: DAVÍÐ ODDSSON (IP).

Minister of Justice and Ecclesiastical Affairs: BJÖRN BJARNASON (IP).

Minister of Finance: GEIR H. HAARDE (IP).

Minister of Agriculture: GUÐNI ÁGÚSTSSON (PP).

Minister of Communications: STURLA BÖÐVARSSON (IP).

Minister of Fisheries: ÁRNI M. MATHIESEN (IP).

Minister of Industry and Commerce and Nordic Co-operation: VALGERÐUR SVERRISDÓTTIR (PP).

Minister of Health and Social Security: JÓN KRISTJÁNSSON (PP).

Minister of Social Affairs: ÁRNI MAGNÚSSON (PP).

Minister of Education, Science and Culture: ÞORGERÐUR KATRÍN GUNNARSDÓTTIR (IP).

Minister of the Environment: SIGRIÐUR ANNA ÞORÐARDÓTTIR (IP).

MINISTRIES

Office of the President: Stadastaður, Soleyjargata 1, 150 Reykjavík; tel. 5404400; fax 5624802; e-mail forseti@forseti.is.

Prime Minister's Office: Stjórnarráðshúsinu v/Lækjargötu, 150 Reykjavík; tel. 5458400; fax 5624014; e-mail postur@for.stjr.is; internet www.stjr.is/for.

Ministry of Agriculture: Sölvhólsgata 7, 150 Reykjavík; tel. 5459750; fax 5521160; e-mail postur@lan.stjr.is; internet www.stjr.is/lan.

Ministry of Communications: Hafnarhúsinu við Tryggvagötu, 150 Reykjavík; tel. 5458200; fax 5621702; e-mail postur@sam.stjr.is; internet www.stjr.is/sam.

Ministry of Education, Science and Culture: Sölvhólsgata 4, 150 Reykjavík; tel. 5459500; fax 5623068; e-mail postur@mrn.stjr.is; internet www.menntamalaraduneyti.is.

Ministry of the Environment: Skuggasundi 1, 150 Reykjavík; tel. 5458600; fax 5624566; e-mail postur@environment.is; internet www.environment.is.

Ministry of Finance: Arnarhváli, 150 Reykjavík; tel. 5459200; fax 5628280; e-mail postur@fjr.stjr.is; internet www.ministryoffinance.is.

Ministry of Fisheries: Skúlagötu 4, 150 Reykjavík; tel. 5458300; fax 5621853; e-mail postur@sjr.stjr.is; internet www.stjr.is/sjr.

Ministry of Foreign Affairs: Raudarárstíg 25, 150 Reykjavík; tel. 5459900; fax 5622373; e-mail external@utn.stjr.is; internet www.mfa.is.

Ministry of Health and Social Security: Vegmúla 3, 150 Reykjavík; tel. 5458700; fax 5519165; e-mail postur@htr.stjr.is; internet www.stjr.is/htr.

Ministry of Industry and Commerce: Arnarhváli, 150 Reykjavík; tel. 5458500; fax 5621289; e-mail postur@ivr.stjr.is; internet www.stjr.is/ivr.

Ministry of Justice and Ecclesiastical Affairs: Skuggasundi, 150 Reykjavík; tel. 5459000; fax 5527340; e-mail postur@dkm.stjr.is; internet www.dkm.is.

Ministry of Social Affairs: Hafnarhúsinu við Tryggvagötu, 150 Reykjavík; tel. 5458100; fax 5524804; e-mail postur@fel.stjr.is; internet felagsmalaraduneyti.is.

President and Legislature

PRESIDENT

Presidential Election, 26 June 2004

	% of votes
Ólafur Ragnar Grímsson	85.6
Baldur Ágústsson	12.3
Ástþór Magnússon	1.9

LEGISLATURE

Althingi
(Alþingi)

v/Austurvöll, 150 Reykjavík; tel. 5630500; fax 5630520; e-mail parlsec@althingi.is; internet www.althingi.is.

Speaker of the Alþingi: HALLDÓR BLÖNDAL.

Secretary-General (Clerk) of the Alþingi: HELGI BERNÓDUSSON.

General Election, 10 May 2003

Party	Votes	% of votes	Seats
Sjálfstæðisflokkurinn (Independence Party)	61,701	33.68	22
Samfylkingin (The Alliance)	56,700	30.95	20
Framsóknarflokkurinn (Progressive Party)	32,484	17.73	12
Vinstrihreyfingin—grænt framboð (Left-Green Movement)	16,129	8.81	5
Frjálslyndi flokkurinn (Liberal Party)	13,523	7.38	4
Nýtt Afl	1,791	0.98	—
Framboð óháðra i Suðurkjördæmi	844	0.46	—
Total	183,172	100.00	63

Political Organizations

Framsóknarflokkurinn (Progressive Party—PP): Hverfisgata 33, POB 453, 121 Reykjavík; tel. 5404300; fax 5404301; e-mail framsokn@framsokn.is; internet www.framsokn.is; f. 1916 with a programme of social liberalism and co-operation; Chair. HALLDÓR ÁSGRÍMSSON; Vice-Chair. GUÐNI ÁGÚSTSSON; Parliamentary Leader HJÁLMAR ÁRNASON.

Frjálslyndi flokkurinn (Liberal Party): c/o v/Austurvöll, 150 Reykjavík; tel. 5630500; fax 5630520; f. by Sverrir Hermannsson, mem. of the IP and former cabinet minister; Leader GUDJÓN A. KRISTJÁNSSON.

Samfylkingin (The Alliance): Austurstræti 14, 101 Reykjavík; tel. 5511600; e-mail samfylking@samfylking.is; internet www.samfylking.is; f. 1999 by merger of Alþýðubandalagið (People's Alliance—PA, f. 1956), Alþýðuflokkurinn (Social Democratic Party—SDP, f. 1916), Samtök um kvennalista (Women's List—WL, f. 1983) and Þjóðvaki—hreyfing fólksins (Awakening of the Nation—People's Movement, f. 1994); Chair. ÖSSUR SKARPHÉÐINSSON; Vice-Chair. MARGRÉT FRÍMANNSDÓTTIR; Parliamentary Leader BRYNDÍS HLÖÐVERSDÓTTIR.

Sjálfstæðisflokkurinn (Independence Party—IP): Háaleitisbraut 1, 105 Reykjavík; tel. 5151700; fax 5151717; e-mail xd@xd.is; internet www.xd.is; f. 1929 by an amalgamation of the Conservative and Liberal Parties; advocates social reform within the framework of private enterprise and the furtherance of national and individual independence; Leader DAVÍÐ ODDSSON; Dep. Leader GEIR H. HAARDE; Parliamentary Leader SIGRÍÐUR ANNA ÞÓRÐARDÓTTIR.

Vinstrihreyfingin—grænt framboð (Left-Green Movement): Hafnarstræti 20, POB 175, 121 Reykjavík; tel. 5528872; e-mail vg@vg.is; internet www.vg.is; f. 1999 by dissident members of the PA, the Women's List, the Greens and independent left-wingers; Leader STEINGRÍMUR J. SIGFÚSSON; Parliamentary Leader ÖGMUNDUR JÓNASSON.

Two new parties, **Nýtt Afl** and **Framboð óháðra i Suðurkjördæmi** (founded by CHRISTIAN PALSSON), were formed to contest the 2003 general election.

Diplomatic Representation

EMBASSIES IN ICELAND

Canada: Túngata 14, 101 Reykjavík; tel. 5756500; fax 5756501; e-mail rkjvk@international.gc.ca; internet www.canada.is; Ambassador RICHARD TÉTU.

China, People's Republic: Víðimelur 29, 107 Reykjavík; tel. 5526751; fax 5626110; e-mail chinaemb@simnet.is; internet www.china-embassy.is; Ambassador JIANG ZHENGYUN.

Denmark: Hverfisgata 29, 101 Reykjavík; tel. 5750300; fax 5750310; e-mail rekamb@rekamb.um.dk; Ambassador LEIF MOGENS REIMANN.

Finland: Túngata 30, 101 Reykjavík; tel. 5100100; fax 5623880; e-mail finamb@finland.is; internet www.finland.is; Ambassador KAI GRANHOLM.

France: Túngata 22, 101 Reykjavík; tel. 5517621; fax 5628177; e-mail amb.fran@itn.is; internet www.ambafrance.is; Ambassador LOUIS BARDOLLET.

Germany: Laufásvegur 31, POB 400, 121 Reykjavík; tel. 5301100; fax 5301101; e-mail embager@li.is; Ambassador JOHANN WENZL.

Japan: Laugavegur 182, 6th Floor, 105 Reykjavík; tel. 5108600; fax 5108605; e-mail japan@int.is; Ambassador FUMIKO SAIGA.

Norway: Fjólugata 17, 101 Reykjavík; tel. 5200700; fax 5529553; e-mail emb.reykjavik@mfa.no; internet www.noregur.is; Ambassador GUTTORM VIK.

Russia: Garðastræti 33, 101 Reykjavík; tel. 5515156; fax 5620633; e-mail russemb@itn.is; Ambassador ALEKSANDER ALEKSANDROVICH RANNIKH.

Sweden: Lagmuli 7, POB 8136, 128 Reykjavík; tel. 5201230; fax 5201235; e-mail sveamb@itn.is; internet www.swedenabroad.com/reykjavik; Ambassador BERTIL G. JOBEUS.

United Kingdom: Laufásvegur 31, 101 Reykjavík; POB 460, 121 Reykjavík; tel. 5505100; fax 5505105; e-mail britemb@centrum.is; internet www.britishembassy.is; Ambassador ALPER MEHMET.

USA: Laufásvegur 21, 101 Reykjavík; tel. 5629100; fax 5629139; e-mail consularreykja@state.gov; internet www.usa.is; Ambassador JAMES I. GADSDEN.

Judicial System

All cases are heard in Ordinary Courts except those specifically within the jurisdiction of Special Courts. The Ordinary Courts include both a lower division of urban and rural district courts presided over by the district magistrates, and the Supreme Court.

Justices of the Supreme Court are appointed by the President and cannot be dismissed except by the decision of a court. The Justices elect the Chief Justice for a period of two years.

Supreme Court

Dómhúsið v. Arnarhól, 150 Reykjavík; tel. 5103030; fax 5623995; e-mail haestirettur@haestirettur.is; internet www.haestirettur.is.

Chief Justice: GUÐRÚN ERLENDSDÓTTIR.

Justices: ÁRNI KOLBEINSSON, GARÐAR GÍSLASON, GUNNLAUGUR CLAESSEN, HARALDUR HENRYSSON, HRAFN BRAGASON, INGIBJÖRG BENEDIKTSDÓTTIR, MARKÚS SIGURBJÖRNSSON, PÉTUR KR. HAFSTEIN.

Religion

CHRISTIANITY

Protestant Churches

Þjóðkirkja Íslands (Evangelical Lutheran Church of Iceland): Biskupsstofa, Laugavegur 31, 150 Reykjavík; tel. 5351500; fax 5513284; e-mail kirkjan@kirkjan.is; internet www.kirkjan.is; the national Church, endowed by the State; about 85.5% of the population are members; Iceland forms one diocese, with two suffragan sees; 280 parishes and 150 pastors; Bishop KARL SIGURBJÖRNSSON.

Fríkirkjan í Reykjavík (The Congregational Church in Reykjavík): POB 1671, 121 Reykjavík; tel. 5527270; fax 5527287; e-mail hjorturm@frikirkjan.is; internet www.frikirkjan.is; f. 1899; Free Lutheran denomination; 5,694 mems; Head HJORTUR M. JOHANNSSON.

Óhádi söfnuðurinn (Independent Congregation): Háteigsvegi 56, 105 Reykjavík; tel. 551099; e-mail afdjoflun@tv.is; internet www .ohadisofnudurinn.is; Free Lutheran denomination; 2,446 mems; Head Rev. PÉTUR ÞORSTEINSSON.

Seventh-day Adventists: Suðurhlið 36, 105 Reykjavík; tel. 5887800; fax 5887808; e-mail sda@mmedia.is; internet www.sda.is; 726 mems.

The Roman Catholic Church

Iceland comprises a single diocese, directly responsible to the Holy See. At 31 December 2003 there were an estimated 5,582 adherents in the country (about 1.9% of the total population).

Bishop of Reykjavík: Most Rev. Dr JOHANNES M. GIJSEN, Biskupsstofa, POB 490, Hávallagata 14, 121 Rekyjavík; tel. 5525388; fax 5623878; e-mail catholica@vortex.is.

The Press

PRINCIPAL DAILIES

DV (Dagblaðið-Vísir): Útgáfufélagið DV ehf, Skaftahlíð 24, POB 5480, 105 Reykjavík; tel. 5505000; fax 5505020; e-mail ritstjorn@dv .is; internet www.strik.is/dv; f. 1981; independent; Editors KRISTJÁN GUY BURGESS, KRISTINN HRAFNSSON; circ. 35,000.

Fréttablaðið (The Newspaper): Útgáfufélagið Frétt ehf, Suðurgata 10, 101 Reykjavík; tel. 5157500; e-mail ristjorn@frettabladid.is; internet www.frettabladid.is; f. 2001; independent; distributed free; Editor GUNNAR SMÁRI EGILSSON; circ. 80,000.

Morgunblaðið (Morning News): Kringlan 1, POB 3040, 103 Reykjavík; tel. 5691100; fax 5691181; e-mail mbl@mbl.is; internet www .mbl.is; f. 1913; independent; Editor-in-Chief STYRMIR GUNNARSSON; circ. 55,000.

WEEKLIES

Andvari: 101 Reykjavík; tel. 5879189; e-mail andvari@andvari.is; internet www.andvari.is; f. 1874; Editor GUNNAR STEFÁNSSON.

Bæjarins besta: Sólgötu 9, 400 Ísafjörður; tel. 4564560; fax 4564564; e-mail bb@bb.is; internet www.bb.is; f. 1984; local; Editor SIGURJÓN J. SIGURÐSSON.

Fiskifréttir: Skaftahlíð 24, 105 Reykjavík; tel. 5116622; e-mail mottaka@vb.is; f. 1983; weekly; for the fishing industry; Editor GUÐJÓN EINARSSON; circ. 6,000.

Séð & Heyrt: Seljavegur 2, 101 Reykjavík; tel. 5155652; fax 5155599; e-mail bjarni@frodi.is; showbusiness and celebrities; Editors BJARNI BRYNJOLFSSON, KRISTJAN THORVALDSSON; circ. 23,000.

Skagablaðið: Skólabraut 21, 300 Akranesi; tel. 4314222; fax 4314122; f. 1984; local newspaper; Editor SIGURDUR SVERRISSON; circ. 1,500.

Skessuhorn: Bjarnarbraut 28, 310 Borgarnes; tel. 4371677; fax 4371678; e-mail gisli@skessuhorn.is; internet www.skessuhorn.is; local; Editor GÍSLI EINARSSON.

Suðurnesjafréttir: Hafnargötu 28, 230 Keflavík; tel. 4213800; fax 4213802; f. 1992; local newspaper; Editors EMIL PÁLL JÓNSSON, HALLDÓR LEVI BJÖRNSSON; circ. 6,500.

Sunnlenska Fréttablaðið: Austurvegi 1, 800 Selfoss; tel. 4823074; fax 4823084; f. 1991; local newspaper; Editor BJARNI HARÐARSON; circ. 6,300.

Vikan: Seljavegur 8, 101 Reykjavík; tel. 5155500; fax 5155592; e-mail johanna@frodi.is; Editors JOHANNA HARDARDOTTIR, HRUND HAUKSDÓTTIR; circ. 13,000–17,000.

Víkurblaðið: Héðinsbraut 1, 640 Húsavík; tel. 4641780; fax 4641399; f. 1979; local newspaper; Editor JÓHANNES SIGURJÓNSSON; circ. 1,300.

Víkurfréttir: Grundarvegur 23, 260 Reykjanesbær; tel. 4214717; fax 4212777; e-mail pket@vf.is; internet www.vf.is; f. 1983; local newspaper; Editor PÁLL KETILSSON; circ. 6,500.

Viðskiptablaðið: Mýrargata 2-8, 101 Reykjavík; tel. 5116622; fax 5116692; e-mail mottaka@vb.is; internet www.vb.is; business weekly in collaboration with the *Financial Times* (United Kingdom); Editor ÖRN VALDIMARSSON.

OTHER PERIODICALS

Atlantica: Borgartún 23, 105 Reykjavík; tel. 5617575; fax 5618646; e-mail heimur@heimur.is; internet www.heimur.is; 6 a year; in-flight magazine of Icelandair; Editor JON KALDAL.

AVS (Arkitektur, verktækni og skipulag): Garðastræti 17, 101 Reykjavík; tel. 5616577; fax 5616571; e-mail skipark@skipark.is; f. 1979; 4 a year; architecture, design, planning and environment; Editor GESTUR ÓLAFSSON; circ. 6,000.

Bændablaðið: POB 7080, 127 Reykjavík; tel. 5630300; fax 5623058; e-mail ath@bi.bondi.is; f. 1995; fortnightly; organ of the Icelandic farmers' union; Editor ÁSKELL THÓRISSON; circ. 6,400.

Billinn: Reykjavík; tel. 5526090; fax 5529490; internet www.billinn .is; f. 1982; 3–4 a year; cars and motoring equipment; Editor LEÓ M. JÓNSSON; circ. 4,000.

Bleikt og Blátt: Seljavegur 2, 101 Reykjavík; tel. 5155500; fax 5155599; e-mail bogb@frodi.is; f. 1989; 6 a year; sex education, communication between men and women; Editor RAGNAR PÉTURSSON; circ. 11,000.

Eiðfaxi: Dugguvogur 10, POB 8133, 128 Reykjavík; tel. 5882525; fax 5882528; e-mail eidfaxi@eidfaxi.is; internet www.eidfaxi.is; f. 1977; monthly (Icelandic edn, English and German edns every two months); horse-breeding and horsemanship; Editor and Publisher JÓNAS KRISTJÁNSSON; circ. 7,000.

Fjármálatíðindi: Kalkofnsvegur 1, 150 Reykjavík; tel. 5699600; fax 5699608; e-mail sedlabanki@sedlabanki.is; internet www .sedlabanki.is; 2 a year; economic journal published by the Central Bank; circ. 1,600.

Freyr, búnaðarblað: Bændahöllin við Hagatorg, 107 Reykjavík; tel. 5630300; fax 5623058; e-mail me@bondi.is; internet www.bondi .is; monthly; agriculture; Editors ASKELL THORISSON, MATTHIAS EGGERTSSON; circ. 1,600.

Frjáls Verslun (Free Trade): Borgartún 23, 105 Reykjavík; tel. 5617575; fax 5618646; e-mail fv@heimur.is; internet www.heimur .is; f. 1939; 10 a year; business magazine; Editor JÓN G. HAUKSSON; circ. 6,000–9,000.

Gestgjafinn: Héðinshúsið, Seljavegur 2, 101 Reykjavík; tel. 5155506; fax 5155599; e-mail gestgjafinn@frodi.is; f. 1981; 12 a year; food and wine; Editor SÓLVEIG BALDURSDÓTTIR; circ. 13,000–16,000.

Hár og Fegurð (Hair and Beauty Magazine): Skúlagata 54, 105 Reykjavík; tel. and fax 5628141; e-mail pmelsted@vortex.is; internet www.vortex.is/fashion; f. 1980; 3 a year; hair, beauty, fashion; Editor PÉTUR MELSTED.

Heilbrigðismál: 105 Reykjavík; tel. 5621414; fax 5621417; f. 1949; quarterly; public health; Editor JÓNAS RAGNARSSON; circ. 6,000.

Heima er Bezt: 108 Reykjavík; tel. 8971385; fax 5155201; e-mail heb@athjgli.is; f. 1951; monthly; general interest; Editor GUÐJÓN BALDVINSSON; circ. 3,000.

Hús og Híbýli: Seljavegur 2, 101 Reykjavík; tel. 5155500; fax 5155599; e-mail hogh@frodi.is; f. 1978; 12 a year; architecture, family and homes; Editor LÓA ALDÍSARDÓTTIR; circ. 13,000–16,000.

Húsfreyjan (The Housewife): Túngata 14, 101 Reykjavík; tel. 5517044; f. 1950; quarterly; the organ of the Federation of Icelandic Women's Societies; Editor HRAFNHILDUR VALGARÐS; circ. 4,000.

Iceland Business: Borgartún 23, 105 Reykjavík; tel. 5617575; fax 5618646; e-mail icelandreview@icelandreview.com; internet www .icelandreview.com; f. 1994; 3 a year; in English; Editor JON KALDAL.

Iceland Review: Borgartún 23, 105 Reykjavík; tel. 5617575; fax 5618646; e-mail icelandreview@icelandreview.com; internet www .icelandreview.com; f. 1963; quarterly, in English; general; Editor JON KALDAL.

Lifandi vísindi: Skipholt 17, 105 Reykjavík; tel. 5708300; fax 5703809; e-mail lifandi@vortex.is; popular science.

Lisin að lifa: 108 Reykjavík; tel. 5356000; fax 5681026; e-mail feb@ islandia.is; f. 1986; 4 a year; for elderly people; Editor ODDNÝ SV. BJÖRGUINS; circ. 13,000–15,000.

Mannlíf: Seljavegur 2, 101 Reykjavík; tel. 5155500; fax 5155599; e-mail mannlif@frodi.is; f. 1984; 10 a year; general interest; Editor GERDUR KRISTNÝ GUÐJÓNSDÓTTIR; circ. 16,000.

Myndbönd mánaðarins (Videos of the Month): Reykjavík; tel. 5811280; fax 5811286; internet nemendur.khi.is/thorsand/myndböö .htm; f. 1993; monthly; Editor GUÐBERGUR ÍSLEIFSSON; circ. 26,000.

Ný menntamál: Lágmúla 7, 108 Reykjavík; tel. 5531117; e-mail hannes@ismennt.is; f. 1983; quarterly; educational issues; Editor HANNES ÍSBERG; circ. 6,500.

NýttLíf: Seljavegur 2, 101 Reykjavík; tel. 5155660; fax 5155599; e-mail nyttlif@frodi.is; f. 1978; 11 a year; fashion; Editor GULLVEIG SÆMUNDSDÓTTIR; circ. 13,000–17,000.

Peningamál: Kalkofnsvegur 1, 150 Reykjavik; tel. 5699600; fax 5699608; e-mail publish@centbk.is; internet www.sedlabanki.is; f. 1999; quarterly bulletin published by the Central Bank; circ. 1,600.

The Reykjavík Grapevine: Hafnarstræti 15, 2nd floor, 101 Reykjavík; tel. 5612323; fax 8452152; e-mail grapevine@grapevine.is; internet www.grapevine.is; f. 2003; in English; Editor VALUR GUNNARSSON.

Skírnir: Síðumúli 21, 108 Reykjavík; tel. 5889060; e-mail hib@islandia.is; internet www.hib.is; f. 1827; Editors YNGVI EGILSSON, SVAVAR HRAFN SVAVARSSON.

Skutull (Harpoon): Fjarðarstræti 2, 400 Isafjörður; tel. 4563948; fax 4565148; e-mail stapi@simnet.is; f. 1923; monthly; organ of the Social Democratic Party; Editor GÍSLI HJARTARSON.

Ský: Borgartún 23, 105 Reykjavík; tel. 5127575; fax 5618646; e-mail tv@heimur.is; internet www.heimur.is; complementary in-flight magazine of Air Iceland.

Stúdentablaðið: Stúdentaheimilinu v/Hringbraut, 101 Reykjavík; tel. 5700850; fax 5700855; e-mail shi@hi.is; internet www.shi.hi.is; f. 1924; 8 issues during the academic year; students' interests; Editor SIGTRYGGUR MAGNASON; circ. 7,500.

Sveitastjórnarmál: Háaleitisbraut 11, 128 Reykjavík; tel. 5813711; fax 5687866; f. 1941; 24 a year; publ. by the Asscn of Icelandic Municipalities; Editor UNNAR STEFÁNSSON; circ. 3,400.

Tölvuheimur (PC World Iceland): Borgartún 23, 105 Reykjavík; tel. 5127575; fax 5618646; e-mail tolvuheimur@heimur.is; internet www.heimur.is; in collaboration with International Data Group; computers; Editor ÓLI KRISTJÁN ÁRMANNSSON.

Uppeldi: Síðumúli 27, 108 Reykjavík; tel. 5709500; fax 5709501; f. 1988; quarterly; children, parenting and family matters; Editor BERGHILDUR ERLA BERNHARÐSDÓTTIR; Dir STEFANÍA JÓNSDÓTTIR; circ. 7,000.

Veiðimaðurinn (The Angler): Borgartún 23, 105 Reykjavík; tel. 5127575; fax 5618646; e-mail heimur@heimur.is; internet www .heimur.is; f. 1984; 3 a year; angling; Editor STEÁN JÓN HAFSTEIN; circ. 5,000–7,000.

Vera: Laugavegi 59, 101 Reykjavík; tel. 5526310; fax 5527560; e-mail vera@vera.is; internet wwww.vera.is; f. 1982; 6 a year; feminist issues; Editor ELÍSABET THORGEIRSDÓTTIR.

Vikan: Seljavegur 2, 101 Reykjavík; tel. 5155500; fax 5155599; e-mail vikan@frodi.is; internet www.vikan.is; f. 1938; 50 a year; family; Editor ELÍN ALBERTSDÓTTIR; circ. 17,000.

Víkingur (Seaman): Borgartún 18, 105 Reykjavík; 10 a year; Editor SIGURJÓN VALDIMARSSON.

Vinnan (Labour): Sætún 1, 105 Reykjavík; tel. 5355600; fax 5355601; e-mail gra@asi.is; internet www.asi.is; 2 a year; f. 1943; publ. by Icelandic Federation of Labour; Editor Dr GUÐMUNDUR RÚNAR ARNASON; circ. 5,000.

Vísbending: Borgartún 23, 105 Reykjavík; tel. 5127575; fax 5618646; e-mail heimur@heimur.is; internet www.heimur.is; f. 1983; business; Editor EYÞÓR ÍVAR JÓNSSON.

Ægir: Hafnarstræti 82, 600 Akureyri; tel. 4615151; fax 4615159; f. 1905; publ. by the Fisheries Association of Iceland in co-operation with Athygli ehf Publishing; monthly; Editor JÓHANN ÓLAFUR HALLDÓRSSON; circ. 2,500.

Æskan og ABC (The Youth and ABC): Eiríksgötu 5, 101 Reykjavík; tel. 5510248; fax 5510248; f. 1897; 9 a year; children's magazine; Editor KARL HELGASON.

NEWS AGENCIES

Foreign Bureaux

Agence France-Presse (AFP): Garðastræti 13, 101 Reykjavík; tel. 5510586; Correspondent GÉRARD LEMARQUIS.

Publishers

Bifröst: Skjaldborg/Birtingur, bokaklubbur, c/o Reynir Johannsson, Grensasvegi 14, 128 Reykjavík; tel. 5882400; fax 5888994; e-mail skjaldborg@skjaldborg.is; f. 1988; spiritual, self-help, new age; Dir BJORN EIRIKSSON.

Bjartur: Bræðraborgarstíg 9, 101 Reykjavík; tel. 5621828; fax 5628360; e-mail snar@itn.is; f. 1989; contemporary fiction; Dir SNÆBJÖRN ARNGRÍMSSON.

Bókaútgáfan Bjartur: Bræðraborgarstígur 9, 101 Reykjavík; tel. 5621826; fax 5628360; f. 1989; contemporary fiction; Man. Dir SNÆBJÖRN ARNGRÍMSSON.

Bókaútgáfan Björk: Birkivöllum 30, 800 Selfoss; tel. 4821394; fax 4823894; f. 1941; children's; Dir ERLENDUR DANIELSSON.

Bókaútgáfan Hólar: Byggðavegi 101B, 600 Akureyri; tel. 4622515; fax 5871180; f. 1995; general; Dir JÓN HJALTASON.

Edda Publishing: Suðurlandsbraut 12, 108 Reykjavík; tel. 5222000; fax 5222026; e-mail edda@edda.is; internet www.edda.is; Man. Dir PÁLL BRAGI KRISTJÓNSSON.

> **Almenna bókafélagið:** Suðurlandsbraut 12, 108 Reykjavík; tel. 5222000; fax 5222022; e-mail edda@edda.is; internet www.edda .is; general, non-fiction; Publ. Dir SIGURÐUR SVAVARSSON.

> **Forlagið:** Suðurlandsbraut 12, 108 Reykjavík; tel. 5222000; fax 5222022; e-mail edda@edda.is; f. 1984; general; Publ. Dir PÁLL VALSSON.

> **Iceland Review, bókadeild:** Suðurlandsbraut 12, 108 Reykjavík; tel. 5222000; fax 5222026; e-mail edda@edda.si; internet www.edda.is; Dir HALLDÓR GUÐMUNDSSON.

> **Mál og menning:** Laugavegi 18, 101 Reykjavík; tel. 5152500; fax 5152505; e-mail info@mm.is; internet www.mm.is; f. 1937; Dir HALLDÓR GUÐMUNDSSON.

> **Vaka-Helgafell:** Suðurlandsbraut 12, 108 Reykjavík; tel. 5222000; fax 5222022; e-mail edda@edda.is; internet www.edda .is; f. 1942; general, fiction, non-fiction; Dir ORÖFN THORISDÓTTIR.

Fjölvi—Vasa: Njörvasundi 15A, 104 Reykjavík; tel. 5688433; fax 5688142; e-mail fjolvi@mmedia.is; f. 1966; general; Dir ÞORSTEINN THORARENSEN.

Fróði Publishing House: Seljavegi 2, 101 Reykjavík; tel. 5155500; fax 5155599; e-mail frodi@frodi.is; internet www.frodi.is; Dir MAGNÚS HREGGVIÐSSON.

> **Fróði Ltd:** Seljavegi 2, 101 Reykjavík; tel. 5155500; fax 5155599; e-mail frodi@frodi.is; internet www.frodi.is; f. 1989; general, magazines; Dir MAGNÚS HREGGVIÐSSON.

> **Iðunn:** Seljavegi 2, 101 Reykjavík; tel. 5155500; fax 5155579; e-mail idunn@idunn.is; internet www.frodi.is; f. 1945; general; Dir JÓN KARLSSON.

Háskólaútgáfan (University of Iceland Press): Háskólabíó v/Hagatorg, 107 Reykjavík; tel. 5254003; fax 5255255; e-mail hu@hi.is; internet www.haskolautgafan.hi.is; f. 1988; non-fiction, science, culture, history; Man. Dir JÖRUNDUR GUÐMUNDSSON.

Hið íslenska bókmenntafélag: Siðumúli 21, 108 Reykjavík; tel. 5889060; fax 5889095; e-mail hib@islandia.is; internet www.hib.is; f. 1816; general; Pres. SIGURÐUR LÍNDAL; Dir SVERRIR KRISTINSSON.

Hið íslenska Fornritafélag: Siðumúli 21, 108 Reykjavík; tel. 5889060; fax 5889095; e-mail hib@islandia.is; internet www.hib.is; f. 1928; Pres. J. NORDAL.

Hörpuútgáfan: Stekkjarholti 8–10, POB 25, 300 Akranes; tel. 4312860; fax 4313309; e-mail bragi@horpuutgafan.is; f. 1960; fiction, general; Dir BRAGI ÞORÐARSON.

Islendingasagnaútgáfan—Muninn: POB 488, 222 Hafnarfjörður; tel. 8985868; fax 5655868; e-mail muninn@isl.is; f. 1945; poetry, fiction, children's, general non-fiction; Dir BENEDIKT KRISTJÁNSSON.

Krydd í tilveruna: Bakkasel 10, 109 Reykjavík; tel. 5575444; fax 5575466; f. 1989; mainly cookery; Dir ANTON ÖRN KJAERNSTED.

Leiðarljós: Sólbrekku, Hellum, 355 Snæfellsbær; tel. 4356810; fax 4356801; e-mail leidar@centrum.is; f. 1995; self-help, spiritual, non-fiction; Dir GUÐRÚN BERGMANN.

Mál og mynd: Bræðraborgarstíg 9, 101 Reykjavík; tel. 5528866; fax 5528870; e-mail malogmynd@centum.is; non-fiction; Dir ÍVAR GISSURARSON.

Námsgagnastofnun (National Centre for Educational Materials): Laugavegí 166, 105 Reykjavík; tel. 5350400; fax 5350401; e-mail simi@nams.is; internet www.nams.is; f. 1979; Dir INGIBJÖRG ÁSGEIRSDÓTTIR.

Ormstunga: Ránargötu 20, 101 Reykjavík; tel. 5610055; fax 5524650; e-mail books@ormstunga.is; internet www.ormstunga.is; f. 1992; Icelandic and foreign fiction and non-fiction; Dir GÍSLI MÁR GÍSLASON.

PP Forlag ehf Ísland: Austurstrond 10, 170 Seltjarnarnes; tel. 5687054; fax 5687053; e-mail info@ppforlag.com; internet www .ppforlag.com; f. 1997; general; Dir SIGRÚN HALLDÓRSDÓTTIR.

Reykholt: Reykjavík; tel. 5888821; fax 5888380; f. 1987; general; Dir REYNIR JÓHANNSSON.

Samhjálp: Hverfisgötu 42, 101 Reykjavík; tel. 5611000; fax 5610050; e-mail samhjalp@samhjalp.is; internet www.samhjalp.is; religious, pentecostal; Dir HEIDAR GUÐNASON.

Setberg: Freyjugötu 14, POB 619, 101 Reykjavík; tel. 5517667; fax 5526640; f. 1950; fiction, cookery, juvenile, picture books, activity books and children's books; Dir ARNBJÖRN KRISTINSSON.

Skálholtsútgáfan: Laugavegi 31, 101 Reykjavík; tel. 5521090; fax 5621595; e-mail kirkbok@ismennt.is; f. 1981; non-fiction, Christian church; Man. Dir EDDA MÖLLER.

Skjaldborg Ltd: Grensásvegi 14, POB 8427, 108 Reykjavík; tel. 5882400; fax 5888994; e-mail skjaldborg@skjaldborg.is; general; Dir BJÖRN EIRÍKSSON.

Sögufélagið: Fischersundi 3, 101 Reykjavík; tel. 5514620; f. 1902; non-fiction, history; Dir RAGNHEIÐUR ÞORLÁKSDÓTTIR.

Stofnun Arna Magnussonar: Arnagarður v/Suðurgotu, 101 Reykjavík; tel. 5254010; fax 5254035; e-mail rosat@hi.is; internet www.am.hi.is; f. 1972; non-fiction; Dir VÉSTEINN ÓLASON.

Útgáfufélagið Heimur: Borgartún 23, 105 Reykjavík; tel. 5127575; fax 5618646; e-mail heimur@heimur.is; internet www.heimur.is; f. 2000; magazines, travel books; Man. Dir BENEDIKT JÓHANNESSON.

Æskan: Stangarhyl 4, 110 Reykjavík; tel. 5305400; fax 5305401; e-mail karl@aeskan.is; internet www.aeskan.is; general, children's books, magazines; Dir KARL HELGASON.

PUBLISHERS' ASSOCIATION

Félag íslenskra bókaútgefenda (Icelandic Publishers' Asscn): Barónsstíg 5, 101 Reykjavík; tel. 5118020; fax 5115020; e-mail baekur@mmedia.is; internet www.bokautgafa.is; f. 1889; Pres. SIGURDUR SVAVARSSON; Man. BENEDIKT KRISTJANSSON.

Broadcasting and Communications

TELECOMMUNICATIONS

The local telecommunications market was deregulated, in accordance with European rules, on 1 January 1998.

Post and Telecom Administration: Smiðjuvegur 68–70, 200 Kópavogur; tel. 5101500; fax 5101509; e-mail pta@pta.is; internet www.pta.is; supervisory authority; Dir HRAFNKELL V. GÍSLASON.

Iceland Telecom Ltd: Austurvöllur, 150 Reykjavík; tel. 5506000; fax 5506009; e-mail siminn@siminn.is; internet www.siminn.is; f. 1998; operation of telecommunications; also operation of Skyggnir, earth station for satellite telecommunications; partially privatized 2001; Pres. and CEO BRYNJÓLFUR BJARNASON.

Lina.Net ehf: Skaftahlíð 24, 105 Reykjavík; tel. 5596000; fax 5596099; e-mail linanet@lina.net; internet www.lina.net; f. 1999; provides infrastructure for data transfer through fibre optic cable system; Man. Dir ERIKUR BRAGASON.

Og Vodafone: Síðumúla 28, 108 Reykjavík; tel. 5999000; fax 5999001; internet www.ogvodafone.is; f. 2003; provides mobile and fixed-line telecommunications; CEO ÓSKAR MAGNÚSSON.

Tal hf: Síðumúli 28, 108 Reykjavík; tel. 5706000; fax 5706001; e-mail tal@tal.is; internet www.tal.is; mobile telephone operator; controlled 30% of mobile calls in 2000; CEO ÓSKAR MAGNÚSSON.

BROADCASTING

Ríkisútvarpið (Icelandic National Broadcasting Service): Broadcasting Centre, Efstaleiti 1, 150 Reykjavík; tel. 5153000; fax 5153010; e-mail isradio@ruv.is; internet www.ruv.is; f. 1930; Dir-Gen. MARKÚS ÖRN ANTONSSON; Chair. of Programme Bd GUNNLAUGUR SÆVAR GUNNLAUGSSON.

Norðurljós hf (Northern Lights Communications Ltd): Lyngháls 5, 110 Reykjavík; tel. 5156000; fax 5156860; internet www.iu.is; f. 1986; privately owned; operates four television channels and four radio stations; Man. Dir SKARPHÉÐINN BERG STEINARSSON.

Radio

Ríkisútvarpið: Radio Division, Efstaleiti 1, 150 Reykjavík; tel. 5153000; fax 5153010; f. 1930; Dir of Radio DORA INGVADOTTIR; Programmes 1 and 2 are broadcast over a network of 89 transmitters each; Programme 1 is broadcast for 112 hours a week, with the remaining hours simulcast with Programme 2; Programme 2 is broadcast 168 hours a week; two long-wave transmitters broadcast the same programme, alternating between Programme 1 and Programme 2.

Akraneskaupstaður: Stillholt 16–18, 300 Akranes; broadcasts only in Akranes; Dir BJÖRN LÁRUSSON.

Bjarni Jónasson: Brekkugata 1, 900 Vestmannaeyjar; tel. 4811534; fax 4813475; broadcasts only in Vestmannaeyjar; Dir BJARNI JÓNASSON.

Búðarhreppur: Hafnargata 12, 750 Fáskrúðsfjörður; broadcasts only in Fáskrúðsfjörður.

Bylgjan: Lyngháls 5, 110 Reykjavík; tel. 5671111; fax 5156900; e-mail bylgjan@bylgjan.is; internet www.bylgjan.is; owned by Íslenska Útvarpfélagið hf.

Evrópsk Fjölmiðlun: Hlaðbæ 11, 110 Reykjavík; tel. 5676111; Dir ERÍKUR SIGURBJÖRNSSON.

Fjölbrautarskóli Norðurlands vestra: 550 Sauðárkrókur; broadcasts only in Sauðárkrókur.

FM 95.7: Lyngháls 5, 110 Reykjavík; owned by Íslenska Útvarpsfélagið hf.

Hallbjörn Hjartarson: Brimnesi, 545 Skagaströnd; tel. 4522960; e-mail hjh@li.is; broadcasts in Skaga-strönd, Blönduós and Sauðárkrókur; Dir HALLBJÖRN HJARTARSON.

Kristilega útvarpsstöðin Lindin: Krókháls 4A, 110 Reykjavík; tel. 5671030; e-mail lindin@lindin.is; Dir MICHAEL E. FITZGERALD.

Létt 96.7: Lyngháls 5, 110 Reykjavík; tel. 5156300; fax 5156830; owned by Íslenska Útvarpsfélagið hf.

Radio X: Lyngháls 5, 110 Reykjavík; tel. 5156060; e-mail xid977@xid977.is; internet www.radiox.is; owned by Íslenska Útvarpfélagið hf.

Útvarp Saga: Lyngháls 5, 110 Reykjavík; tel. 5156945; e-mail saga@utvarpsaga.is; internet www.utvarpsaga.is; owned by Íslenska Útvarpfélagið hf.

Útvarp Vestmannaeyjar: Brekkugata 1, 900 Vestmannaeyjar; tel. 4811534; fax 4813475; broadcasts only in Vestmannaeyjar; Dir BJARNI JÓNASSON.

Vila-Árna Útvarp: Skipholt 6, 355 Ólafsvík; tel. 4361334; fax 4361379; Dir VILHELM ÁRNASON.

Television

Ríkisútvarpið—Sjónvarp (Icelandic National Broadcasting Service—Television): Efstaleiti 1, 150 Reykjavík; tel. 5153000; fax 5153010; e-mail tvnews@ruv.is; internet www.ruv.is; f. 1966; covers 99% of the population; broadcasts daily, total 70 hours a week; Dir-Gen. MARKÚS ÖRN ANTONSSON; Man. Dir BJARNI GUÐMUNDSSON.

Aksjón ehf: Strandgötu 31, 600 Akureyri; tel. 4611050; fax 4612356; e-mail aksjon@nett.is; broadcasts only in Akureyri; Dir GÍSLI GUNNLAUGSSON.

Almiðlun ehf: Trönuhraun 6, 220 Hafnarfjörður; tel. 5651766; fax 5651796; broadcasts only in Hafnarfjörður; Dir HALLDÓR ÁRNI SVEINSSON.

Bíórásin (The Movie Channel): Lyngháls 5, 110 Reykjavík; tel. 5156000; owned by Íslenska Útvarpsfélagið hf.

Fjölsýn: Strandvegur 47, 900 Vestmannaeyjar; tel. 4811300; fax 4812643; e-mail sigit@eyjar.is; broadcasts only in Vestmannaeyjar; Dir OMAR GUÐMUNDSSON.

Íslenska Sjónvarpsfélagið hf: Skipholti 31, 105 Reykjavík; tel. 5956000; e-mail info@sl.is; internet www.sl.is; f. 1999; Dir KRISTINN Þ. GEIRSSON.

Kristniboðskirkjan: Grensásvegur 8, 108 Reykjavík; tel. 5683131; fax 5683741; broadcasts only in the Reykjavík area; religious; Dir EIRÍKUR SIGURBJÖRNSSON.

Popptíví: Lyngháls 5, 110 Reykjavík; tel. 5156000; internet www.popptivi.is; owned by Íslenska Útvarpsfélagið hf; music station.

Stöð 2: Lyngháls 5, 110 Reykjavík; tel. 5156000; fax 5156860; f. 1986; owned by Íslenska Útvarpsfélagið hf; 'pay-TV' station; Pres. SIGURDUR G. GUÐJÓNSSON.

Sýn (Vision): Lyngháls 5, 110 Rekyjavík; tel. 5156000; owned by Íslenska Útvarpsfélagið hf.

Villa Video: Skipholt 6, 335 Ólafsvík; tel. 4361563; fax 4361379; broadcasts only in Ólafsvík; Dir VILHELM ÁRNASON.

The US Navy operates a radio station (24 hours a day), and a cable television service (80 hours a week), on the NATO base at Keflavík.

Finance

(cap. = capital; res = reserves; dep. = deposits; m. = million; kr = krónur; brs = branches)

BANKING

Iceland's banking and finance system has undergone substantial transformation. In 1989–90 the number of commercial banks was reduced from seven to three, by amalgamating four banks to form Íslandsbanki as the only remaining major commercial bank in private ownership. A further restructuring of the banking sector

ICELAND

Directory

commenced in 2000 with the merger of Íslandsbanki with the recently privatized investment bank, FBA. By early 2003 the Icelandic Government had withdrawn completely from the country's commercial banking sector, having sold its controlling stakes in the second and third largest retail banks, Bunarðarbanki Íslands and Landsbanki Íslands. Further consolidation of the banking sector was expected. The 27 savings banks operate a commercial bank, Icebank, which functions as a central banking institution.

Central Bank

Seðlabanki Íslands (Central Bank of Iceland): Kalkofnsvegur 1, 150 Reykjavík; tel. 5699600; fax 5699605; e-mail sedlabanki@sedlabanki.is; internet www.sedlabanki.is; f. 1961; cap. and res 40,217m. kr, dep. 34,174m. kr (Dec. 2003); Chair. of Bd of Govs BIRGIR ÍSLEIFUR GUNNARSSON.

Principal Banks

Icebank Ltd (Sparisjóðabanki Íslands hf): Rauðarárstígur 27, POB 5220, 125 Reykjavík; tel. 5404000; fax 5404001; e-mail icebank@icebank.is; internet www.icebank.is; f. 1986; central bank of the 27 Icelandic savings banks and wholly owned by them; cap. 604m. kr, res 248m. kr, dep. 33,802m. kr (Dec. 2003); Chair. GEIRMUNDUR KRISTINSSON; Man. Dir FINNUR SVEINBJORNSSON.

Íslandsbanki hf: Kirkjusandur, 155 Reykjavík; tel. 4404000; fax 4404001; e-mail isb@isb.is; internet www.isb.is; f. 2000 by merger of Íslandsbanki hf (f. 1990) and FBA; cap. 10,080m. kr, res 3,904m. kr, dep. 135,448m. kr (Dec. 2003); Pres. BJARNI ÁRMANNSSON; Chair. EINAR SVEINSSON; 29 brs.

Kaupþing Búnaðarbanki hf: Borgartun 19, 105 Reykjavík; tel. 4446000; fax 4446009; e-mail info@kbbanki.is; internet www.kbbanki.is; f. 2003 by merger of Búnaðarbanki and Kaupþing Banki hf; cap. 4,384m. kr, res 23,620m. kr, dep. 188,740m. kr (Dec. 2003); Chair. SIGURÐUR EINARSSON; CEOs HREIÐAR MÁR SIGURÐSSON, SOLON R. SIGURÐSSON; 36 brs.

Landsbanki Íslands hf (National Bank of Iceland Ltd): Austurstræti 11, 155 Reykjavík; tel. 5606600; fax 5606000; internet www.landsbanki.is; f. 1885; transferred to the private sector in 2003; cap. 7,500m. kr, res 4,623m. kr, dep. 405,517m. kr (Dec. 2003); Chair. Bd of Dirs BJORGOLFUR GUDMUNDSSON; Group Man. Dir and CEO SIGUJÓN T. ÁRNASON; 54 brs.

STOCK EXCHANGE

Kauphöll Íslands (Iceland Stock Exchange): Laugavegur 182, 105 Reykjavík; tel. 5252800; fax 5252888; e-mail icex@icex.is; internet www.icex.is; f. 1985; part of an alliance (Nordic Exchanges, Norex) with the Copenhagen, Oslo, Stockholm Stock Exchanges, launched June 1999; Pres. and CEO THORDUR FRIDJONSSON; Chair. BJARNI ÁRMANNSSON.

INSURANCE

Tryggingastofnun Ríkisins (State Social-Security Institution): Laugavegi 114, 150 Reykjavík; tel. 5604400; fax 5624535; e-mail tr@tr.is; internet www.tr.is; f. 1936; Man. Dir KARL STEINAR GUÐNASON; Chair. of Tryggingaráð (Social-Security Bd) KRISTINN H. GUNNARSSON.

Private Insurance Companies

Alþjóða líftryggingarfélagið hf: Sóltúni 26, 105 Reykjavík; tel. 5401400; fax 5401401; e-mail alif@alif.is; internet www.alif.is; f. 1966; life insurance.

Íslandstrygging hf: Sætúni 8, 105 Reykjavík; tel. 5141000; fax 5141001; f. 2002; Gen. Man. EINAR BALDVINSSON.

Íslensk Endurtrygging hf (Icelandic Reinsurance Co Ltd): Suðurlandsbraut 6, 108 Reykjavík; tel. 5331200; fax 5331201; f. 1939; Gen. Man. BJARNI THORDARSON.

Líftryggingamiðstöin hf: Aðalstræti 6–8, 101 Reykjavík; tel. 5152000; fax 5152020; f. 2002; Gen. Man. GUNNAR FELIXSON.

Líftryggingafélag Íslands hf: Ármúla 3, 108 Reykjavík; tel. 5605060; fax 5605100; internet www.lif.is.

Sameinaða líftryggingarfélagið hf: Sigtún 42, POB 5180, 125 Reykjavík; tel. 5695400; fax 5815455.

Sjóvá-Almennar tryggingar hf (Marine-General Insurance Co): Kringlan 5, POB 3200, 123 Reykjavík; tel. 5692500; fax 5813718; f. 1988; all branches except life; Chair. BENEDIKT SVEINSSON; Gen. Mans EINAR SVEINSSON, ÓLAFUR B. THORS.

Trygging hf: Aðalstræti 6, 101 Reykjavík; tel. 5152000; fax 5152020.

Tryggingamiðstöðin hf: Aðalstræti 6, 101 Reykjavík; tel. 5152000; fax 5152020; internet www.tmhf.is.

Vátryggingafélag Íslands hf: Ármúla 3, 108 Reykjavík; tel. 5605060; fax 5605100; e-mail info@vis.is; internet www.vis.is; f. 1989; Chair. ÞÓRÓLFUR GÍSLASON; Man. Dir FINNUR INGÓLFSSON.

Vélbátaábyrgðarfélagið Grótta: Síðumúla 29, 108 Reykjavík; tel. 5536800; fax 5536812.

Viðlagatrygging Íslands: Laugavegi 162, 105 Reykjavík; tel. 5529677; fax 5629675.

Vörður—Vátryggingafélag: Skipagötu 9, 600 Akureyri; tel. 4648000; fax 4648001; e-mail oli@vordur.is.

Supervisory Authority

Fjármálaeftirlitið—Financial Supervisory Authority (FME): Suðurlandsbraut 32, 108 Reykjavík; tel. 5252700; fax 5252727; e-mail fme@fme.is; internet www.fme.is; f. 1999 by merger of Insurance Supervisory Authority and Bank Inspectorate of the Central Bank of Iceland; Man. Dir PÁLL GUNNAR PÁLSSON.

Trade and Industry

GOVERNMENT AGENCIES

Orkustofnun (National Energy Authority): Grensásvegi 9, 108 Reykjavík; tel. 5696000; fax 5688896; e-mail os@os.is; internet www.os.is; f. 1967; two main divisions: hydrological research unit and energy administration unit; contracts and supervises energy research projects financed by the national budget, monitors energy consumption and publishes forecasts for energy market; operates United Nations Geothermal Training Programme as independent entity; Dir-Gen. ÞORKELL HELGASON.

Trade Council of Iceland: POB 1000, 121 Reykjavík; tel. 5114000; fax 5114040; e-mail icetrade@icetrade.is; internet www.icetrade.is; provides information on Icelandic exporters and products; Man. Dir JÓN ÁSBERGSSON.

CHAMBER OF COMMERCE

Verslunarrád Íslands (Iceland Chamber of Commerce): Hús verslunarinnar, 103 Reykjavík; tel. 5107100; fax 5686564; e-mail mottaka@chamber.is; internet www.chamber.is; f. 1917; Chair. BOGI PALSSON; Gen. Sec. ÞÓR SIGFÚSSON; 370 mems.

INDUSTRIAL AND TRADE ASSOCIATIONS

Fiskifélag Íslands (Fisheries Assen of Iceland): Glerargata 28, POB 145, 602 Akureyri; tel. 5510500; fax 5527969; e-mail fi@fiskifelag.is; internet www.fiskifelag.is; f. 1911; conducts technical and economic research and services for fishing vessels and for fishing industry; Chair. PETUR BJARNASON.

Landssamband Íslenskra Útvegsmanna (Icelandic Fishing Vessel Owners' Federation): Borgartúni 35, 105 Reykjavík; tel. 5910300; fax 5910301; e-mail fridrik@liu.is; internet www.liu.is; f. 1939; Chair. BJÖRGÓLFUR JÓHANNSSON; Man. FRIÐRIK JÓN ARNGRÍMSSON.

Samtök Iðnaðarins (Federation of Icelandic Industries—FII): Borgartúni 35, POB 1450, 121 Reykjavík; tel. 5910100; fax 5910101; e-mail mottaka@si.is; internet www.si.is; f. 1993 by merger of Federation of Icelandic Industries (f. 1933), Federation of Icelandic Crafts and Industries (f. 1932) and four other employers' orgs; Chair. VILMUNDUR JOSEFSSON; Gen. Man. SVEINN HANNESSON; 2,500 mems.

EMPLOYERS' ORGANIZATION

Samtök atvinnulífsins (Confederation of Icelandic Employers): Borgartúni 35, 105 Reykjavík; tel. 5910000; fax 5910050; e-mail sa@sa.is; f. 1934; Chair. INGIMUNDUR SIGURPÁLSSON; Man. Dir ARI EDWALD.

UTILITIES

Electricity

Hitaveita Suðurnesja (Suðurnes Regional Heating Corpn): Brekkustíg 36, POB 225, 260 Nardvík; f. 1974; produces and distributes hot-water heating and electricity for the Suðurnes region.

Landsvirkjun (National Power Company): Háaleitisbraut 68, 103 Reykjavík; tel. 5159000; fax 5159007; e-mail landsvirkjun@lv.is; internet www.landsvirkjun.com; f. 1965; generates and sells electric power wholesale to public distribution systems and industrial enterprises; Chair. JOHANNES GEIR SIGURGEIRSSON; Man. Dir FRIDRIK SOPHUSSON.

Orkubú Vestfjarda (Vestfjords Power Company): Stakkanesi 1, 400 Isafjördur; f. 1977; produces, distributes and sells electrical energy in the Vestfjords area.

Orkuveita Reykjavíkur: Bærjarháls 1, 110 Reykjavík; tel. 5166000; fax 5166709; e-mail or@or.is; internet www.or.is; f. 1999;

www.europaworld.com

2103

produces and distributes hot-water heating, cold water and electricity for the city of Reykjavík and other regions in south-western Iceland; Chair. ALFRED ÞORSTEINSSON; Man. Dir GUÐMUNDUR ÞÓRODDSSON.

Rafmagnsveitur Ríkisins (RARIK) (Iceland State Electricity): Rauðarárstíg 10, 105 Reykjavík; tel. 5605500; fax 5605600; internet www.rarik.is; f. 1947; produces, procures, distributes and sells electrical energy; also provides consultancy services.

TRADE UNIONS

Althýðusamband Íslands (ASÍ) (Icelandic Federation of Labour): Sætún 1, 105 Reykjavík; tel. 5355600; fax 5355601; e-mail asi@asi.is; internet www.asi.is; f. 1916; affiliated to ICFTU, the European Trade Union Confederation and the Council of Nordic Trade Unions; Chair. GRÉTAR THORSTEINSSON; Gen. Sec. GYLFI ARNBJÖRNSSON; *c.* 80,000 mems.

> **Menningar- og Fræðslusamband Althýðu (MFA)** (Workers' Educational Asscn): Grensásveg 16A, 108 Reykjavík; tel. 5331818; fax 5331819; e-mail ieg@asi.is; internet www.asi.is; Chair. HAUKUR HARDARSON; Gen. Sec. INGIBJORG E. GUÐMUNDSDOTTIR.

Bandalag Háskólamanna (BHM) (Asscn of Academics): Lágmúla 7, 108 Reykjavík; tel. 5812090; fax 5889239; e-mail bhm@bhm.is; internet www.bhm.is; Chair. HALLDÓRA FRIÐJÓNSDÓTTIR; 7,000 mems.

Bandalag Starfsmanna Ríkis og Bæja (BSRB) (Municipal and Government Employees' Asscn): Grettisgötu 89, 105 Reykjavík; tel. 5626688; fax 5629106; e-mail bsrb@tv.is; f. 1942; Chair. ÖGMUNDUR JÓNASSON; 17,506 mems.

Blaðamannafélag Íslands (Union of Icelandic Journalists): Síðumúla 23, Reykjavík; tel. 5539155; fax 5539177; e-mail bi@press .is; internet www.press.is; f. 1897; Chair. RÓBERT MARSHALL; 530 mems.

Transport

RAILWAYS

There are no railways in Iceland.

ROADS

Much of the interior is uninhabited and the main road follows the coastline. Regular motor coach services link the main settlements. At 31 December 2001 Iceland had 12,998 km of roads, of which 4,310 km were main roads. Approximately 75% of the main roads are paved.

Bifreiðastöð Íslands hf (BSÍ) (Iceland Motor Coach Service): Umferðarmiðstöðinni, Vatnsmýrarveg 10, 101 Reykjavík; tel. 5522300; fax 5529973; f. 1936; 45 scheduled bus lines throughout Iceland; also operates sightseeing tours and excursions; Chair. ÓSKAR SIGURJÓNSSON; Man. Dir GUNNAR SVEINSSON.

SHIPPING

Heavy freight is carried by coastal shipping. The principal seaport for international shipping is Reykjavík.

Port Authority

Port of Reykjavík: Harbour Bldg, Tryggvagötu 17, POB 382, 121 Reykjavík; tel. 5258900; fax 5258990; e-mail hofnin@portofreykjavik .is; internet www.portofreykjavik.is; Dir BERGUR THORLEIFSSON.

Principal Companies

Atlantsskip: Vesturvör 29, 200 Kópavogur; tel. 5913000; fax 5913001; e-mail atlantsskip@atlantsskip.is; f. 1998; Chair. and Man. Dir STEFÁN KJÆRNESTED.

Eimskip (Iceland Steamship Co Ltd): Pósthússtræti 2, POB 220, 101 Reykjavík; tel. 5257000; fax 5257009; e-mail info@eimskip.com; internet www.eimskip.com; f. 1914 as Eimskipafélag Íslands; transportation and logistics services incl. ground operation, warehousing,

coastal service, trucking and intermodal transportation between Iceland and the United Kingdom, Scandinavia, the rest of Europe, the USA and Canada; Chair. BENEDIKT JÓHANNESSON; Man. Dir INGIMUNDUR SIGURPÁLSSON.

Nesskip hf: POB 175, 172 Seltjarnarnes; Nesskip's House, Austurstrond 1, 172 Seltjarnarnes; tel. 5625055; fax 5612052; e-mail nesskip@nesskip.is; internet www.nesskip.is; f. 1974; bulk cargo shipping services to the USA, Canada, Russia, Scandinavia, the Baltic countries and other parts of Europe; agency and chartering for vessels in all Icelandic ports; Chair. B. BENEDIKTSSON; Man. Dir G. ÁSGEIRSSON.

Samskip hf: Holtabakki v/Holtaveg, 104 Reykjavík; tel. 5698300; fax 5698327; e-mail samskip@samskip.is; internet www.samskip.is; services to Europe, the USA, and the Far East; Dir ÓLAFUR ÓLAFSSON.

CIVIL AVIATION

Air transport is particularly important to Iceland and is used both for the transport of people and to transport agricultural produce from remote districts. More than 90% of passenger traffic between Iceland and other countries is by air. There are regular air services between Reykjavík and outlying townships. There is an international airport at Keflavík, 47 km from Reykjavík.

Air Atlanta Icelandic: Head Office, Hofdabakki 9, 110 Reykjavík; tel. 5157700; fax 5157716; e-mail admin@atlanta.is; internet www .airatlanta.com; f. 1986; charter international flights; Chair. HAFTHOR HAFSTEINSSON.

Air Iceland: Reykjavík Airport, 101 Reykjavík; tel. 5703000; fax 5703001; e-mail jonkarl@airiceland.is; internet www.airiceland.is; f. 1959; scheduled, regional flights; 96%-owned by Icelandair; Chair. SIGURÐUR HELGASON; Gen. Man. JÓN KARL ÓLAFSSON.

Iceland Express ehf: Suðurlandsbraut 24, 108 Reykjavík; tel. 5500650; fax 5500601; e-mail info@icelandexpress.is; internet www .icelandexpress.com; f. 2002; daily scheduled flights between Iceland, Denmark and the United Kingdom; Chair. SIGURÐUR I. HALLDÓRSSON; Man. Dir JÓHANNES GEORGSSON.

Icelandair (Flugleiðir hf): Reykjavík Airport, 101 Reykjavík; tel. 5050300; fax 5050350; e-mail pr@icelandair.is; internet www .icelandair.net; f. 1973 as the holding company for the two principal Icelandic airlines, Flugfélag Íslands (f. 1937) and Loftleiðir (f. 1944); in 1979 all licences, permits and authorizations previously held by Flugfélag Íslands and Loftleiðir were transferred to it; network centred in Reykjavík, to nine domestic airfields, and scheduled external services to more than 20 international destinations in northern Europe and the USA; Chair. HÖRÐUR SIGURGESTSSON; Pres. and CEO SIGURÐUR HELGASON (resigned on 17 January 2005; to be replaced by Hannes Smárason on 31 May 2005).

Íslandsflug hf: Hlíðasmára 15, 201 Kópavogur; tel. 5708030; fax 5078031; internet www.islandsflug.is; f. 1991 by merger of Eagle Air Domestic and Flugtak; operates scheduled passenger flights to Vestmannaeyja, Hornafjarðar, Sauðárkróks, Bíldudals and Gjögurs; contracted by the Icelandic Government to undertake ambulance flights when needed; Chair. MAGNÚS THORSTEINSSON; Man. Dir ÓMAR BENEDIKTSSON.

Tourism

Iceland's main attraction for tourists lies in the rugged beauty of the interior, with its geysers and thermal springs. In 2000 there were 302,913 tourist arrivals, an increase of more than 40,000 visitors compared with 1998. In 2002 receipts from tourism totalled 37,148m. krónur.

Iceland Tourist Board: Lækjargata 3, 101 Reykjavík; tel. 5355500; fax 5355501; e-mail info@icetourist.is; internet www .icetourist.is; Gen. Man. MAGNÚS ODDSSON.

Höfuðborgarstofa (Reykjavík Complete): Aðalstræti 2, 101 Reykjavík; tel. 5901500; fax 5901501; e-mail info@visitreykjavik.is; internet www.visitreykjavik.is; tourism marketing and events for the city of Reykjavík; Gen. Man. SVANHILDUR KONRÁDSDÓTTIR.

INDIA

Introductory Survey

Location, Climate, Language, Religion, Flag, Capital

The Republic of India forms a natural sub-continent, with the Himalaya mountain range to the north. Two sections of the Indian Ocean—the Arabian Sea and the Bay of Bengal—lie to the west and east, respectively. India's neighbours are Tibet (the Xizang Autonomous Region of the People's Republic of China), Bhutan and Nepal to the north, Pakistan to the north-west and Myanmar (formerly Burma) to the north-east, while Bangladesh is surrounded by Indian territory except for a short frontier with Myanmar in the east. Near India's southern tip, across the Palk Strait, is Sri Lanka. India's climate ranges from temperate to tropical, with an average summer temperature on the plains of approximately 27°C (85°F). Annual rainfall varies widely, but the summer monsoon brings heavy rain over much of the country in June and July. The official language is Hindi, spoken by about 30% of the population. English is used as an associate language for many official purposes. The Indian Constitution also recognizes 17 regional languages, of which the most widely spoken are Telugu, Bengali, Marathi, Tamil, Urdu and Gujarati. In addition, many other local languages are used. According to the 2001 census, about 81% of the population are Hindus and 13% Muslims. There are also Christians, Sikhs, Buddhists, Jains and other minorities. The national flag (proportions 2 by 3) has three equal horizontal stripes, of saffron, white and green, with the Dharma Chakra (Wheel of the Law), in blue, in the centre of the white stripe. The capital is New Delhi.

Recent History

After a prolonged struggle against British colonial rule, India became independent, within the Commonwealth, on 15 August 1947. The United Kingdom's Indian Empire was partitioned, broadly on a religious basis, between India and Pakistan. The principal nationalist movement that had opposed British rule was the Indian National Congress (later known as the Congress Party). At independence the Congress leader, Jawaharlal Nehru, became India's first Prime Minister. Sectarian violence, the movement of 12m. refugees, the integration of the former princely states into the Indian federal structure and a territorial dispute with Pakistan over Kashmir presented major problems to the new Government.

India became independent as a dominion, with the British monarch as Head of State, represented by an appointed Governor-General. In November 1949, however, the Constituent Assembly approved a republican Constitution, providing for a president (with mainly ceremonial functions) as head of state. Accordingly, India became a republic on 26 January 1950, although remaining a member of the Commonwealth. France transferred sovereignty of Chandernagore to India in May 1950, and ceded its four remaining Indian settlements in 1954.

The lack of effective opposition to Congress policies expedited industrialization and social reform. In December 1961 Indian forces overran the Portuguese territories of Goa, Daman and Diu, which were immediately annexed by India. Border disputes with the People's Republic of China escalated into a brief military conflict in 1962. Nehru died in May 1964 and was succeeded by Lal Bahadur Shastri. India and Pakistan fought a second war over Kashmir in 1965. Following mediation by the USSR, Shastri and President Ayub Khan of Pakistan signed a joint declaration, aimed at a peaceful settlement of the Kashmir dispute, on 10 January 1966. Shastri died on the following day, however, and Nehru's daughter, Indira Gandhi, became Prime Minister.

Following the presidential election of August 1969, when two factions of Congress supported different candidates, the success of Indira Gandhi's candidate split the party. The Organization (Opposition) Congress, led by Morarji Desai, emerged in November, but at the next general election to the lower house of the legislature, the Lok Sabha (House of the People), held in March 1971, Indira Gandhi's wing of Congress won 350 of the 515 elective seats.

Border incidents led to a 12-day war with Pakistan in December 1971. The Indian army rapidly occupied East Pakistan, which India recognized as the independent state of Ban-

gladesh. Indira Gandhi and President Zulfikar Ali Bhutto of Pakistan held a summit conference at Shimla in June–July 1972, when the two leaders agreed that their respective forces should respect the cease-fire line in Kashmir, and that India and Pakistan should resolve their differences through bilateral negotiations or other peaceful means. In 1975 the former protectorate of Sikkim became the 22nd state of the Indian Union, leading to tensions in India's relations with Nepal.

A general election to the Lok Sabha was held in March 1977, when the number of elective seats was increased to 542. The election resulted in victory for the Janata (People's) Party, chaired by Morarji Desai, who became Prime Minister. The Janata Party and an allied party, the Congress for Democracy, together won 298 of the 540 seats where polling took place. Congress obtained 153 seats. In January 1978 Indira Gandhi became leader of a new breakaway political group, the Congress (Indira) Party, known as Congress (I).

In 1979 the Government's ineffectual approach to domestic problems provoked a wave of defections by Lok Sabha members of the Janata Party. Many joined Raj Narain, who formed a new party, the Lok Dal, the policies of which were based on secularism. Congress (I) lost its position as official opposition party after defections from its ranks to the then official Congress Party by members who objected to Indira Gandhi's perceived authoritarianism. The resignation of Desai's Government in July was followed by the departure from the Janata Party of Charan Singh, who became the leader of the Lok Dal and, shortly afterwards, Prime Minister in a coalition with both Congress parties. When Congress (I) withdrew its support, Singh's 24-day administration collapsed, and Parliament was dissolved. A general election to the Lok Sabha was held in January 1980. Congress (I) received 42.7% of the total votes and won an overwhelming majority (352) of the elective seats. The Janata Party won only 31 seats, while the Lok Dal secured 41 seats. Indira Gandhi was reinstated as Prime Minister. Presidential rule was imposed in nine states, hitherto governed by opposition parties, in February. At elections to state assemblies in June, Congress (I) won majorities in eight of them.

By-elections in June 1981 for the Lok Sabha and state assemblies were notable because of the overwhelming victory that Rajiv Gandhi, the Prime Minister's son, obtained in the former constituency of his late brother (killed in an air crash in 1980) and because of the failure of the fragmented Janata Party to win any seats. In February 1983 Rajiv Gandhi became a General Secretary of Congress (I).

Indira Gandhi's Government faced serious problems, as inter-communal disturbances in several states (particularly Assam and Meghalaya) continued in 1982–83, with violent protests against the presence of Bengali immigrants. Election defeats in Andhra Pradesh, Karnataka and Tripura represented a series of set-backs for Indira Gandhi. Alleged police corruption and the resurgence of caste violence (notably in Bihar and Gujarat) caused further problems for the Government.

There was also unrest in the Sikh community of the Punjab, despite the election to the Indian presidency in July 1982 of Giani Zail Singh, the first Sikh to hold the position. Demands were made for greater religious recognition, for the settlement of grievances over land and water rights, and over the sharing of the state capital at Chandigarh with Haryana; in addition, a minority called for the creation of a separate Sikh state ('Khalistan'). In October 1983 the state was brought under presidential rule. However, the violence continued, and followers of an extremist Sikh leader, Jarnail Singh Bhindranwale, established a terrorist stronghold inside the Golden Temple (the Sikh holy shrine) at Amritsar. The Government sent in troops to dislodge the terrorists and the assault resulted in the death of Bhindranwale and hundreds of his supporters, and serious damage to sacred buildings. A curfew was imposed, and army personnel blockaded Amritsar.

In October 1984 Indira Gandhi was assassinated by militant Sikh members of her personal guard. Her son, Rajiv Gandhi, was immediately sworn in as Prime Minister, despite his lack of ministerial experience. The widespread communal violence that erupted throughout India, resulting in more than 2,000 deaths, was curbed by prompt government action. Congress (I) achieved a decisive victory in elections to the Lok Sabha in December. Including the results of the January 1985 polling, the party received 49.2% of the total votes and won 403 of the 513 contested seats.

In February 1986 there were mass demonstrations and strikes throughout India in protest at government-imposed increases in the prices of basic commodities. The opposition parties united against Rajiv Gandhi's policies, and Congress (I) suffered considerable reversals in the indirect elections to the upper house of the legislature, the Rajya Sabha (Council of States) in March. In April Rajiv Gandhi attempted to purge Congress (I) of critics calling themselves 'Indira Gandhi loyalists', and, in a major government reorganization, he appointed Sikhs to two senior positions. The Prime Minister survived an assassination attempt by three Sikhs in October.

In June 1986 Laldenga, the leader of the Mizo National Front (MNF), signed a peace agreement with Rajiv Gandhi, thus ending Mizoram's 25 years of rebellion. The accord granted Mizoram limited autonomy in the drafting of local laws, independent trade with neighbouring foreign countries and a general amnesty for all Mizo rebels. Laldenga led an interim coalition government until February 1987, when the MNF won an absolute majority at elections to the state assembly. In that month Mizoram and Arunachal Pradesh were officially admitted as the 23rd and 24th states of India, and in May the Union Territory of Goa became India's 25th state.

During 1987 Congress (I) experienced serious political setbacks. It sustained defeats in a number of state elections, and political tensions were intensified by an open dispute between the Prime Minister and the outgoing President, Giani Zail Singh. Public concern was aroused by various accusations of corruption and financial irregularities made against senior figures in the ruling party. Notable among these scandals was the 'Bofors affair', in which large payments were allegedly made to Indian agents by a Swedish company in connection with its sales of munitions to the Indian Government. The Prime Minister denied any involvement, and a committee of inquiry subsequently exonerated him of any impropriety. Several ministers resigned from the Government, among them the Minister of Defence, Vishwanath Pratap (V. P.) Singh, who was also, with three other senior politicians, expelled from Congress (I) in July for 'anti-party activities'. V. P. Singh soon emerged as the leader of the Congress (I) dissidents, and in October formed a new political group, the Jan Morcha (People's Front), advocating more radical social change.

In 1988 a more confrontational style was adopted by the central administration towards non-Congress (I) state governments, and presidential rule was imposed in states suffering political instability. The opposition forces attained a degree of unity when four major centrist parties, the Indian National Congress (S), the Jan Morcha, the Janata Party and the Lok Dal, and three major regional parties formed a coalition National Front (Rashtriya Morcha), to oppose Congress (I) at the next election. Three of the four centrist parties formed a new political grouping, the Janata Dal (People's Party), which was to work in collaboration with the National Front. V. P. Singh, who was widely regarded as Rajiv Gandhi's closest rival, was elected President of the Janata Dal.

At the general election to the Lok Sabha held in November 1989, Congress (I) lost its overall majority. Of the 525 contested seats, it won 193, the Janata Dal and its electoral allies in the National Front won 141 and three, respectively, and the right-wing Hindu nationalist Bharatiya Janata Party (BJP) won 88. In early December, after the National Front had been promised the support of the communist parties and the BJP, V. P. Singh was sworn in as the new Prime Minister. He appointed Devi Lal, the populist Chief Minister of Haryana and President of Lok Dal (B), as Deputy Prime Minister, and a Kashmiri Muslim, Mufti Mohammed Sayeed, as Minister of Home Affairs. This latter appointment was widely seen as a gesture of reconciliation to the country's Muslims and as reaffirmation of the Government's secular stance. A few weeks later V. P. Singh's Government won a vote of confidence in the Lok Sabha, despite the abstention of all the Congress (I) members. In January 1990 the Government ordered the mass resignation of all the state governors; the President then appointed new ones. In February elections were held to 10 state assemblies, all formerly controlled by Congress (I). Congress (I) lost power in eight of the 10 assemblies and there was a notable increase in support for the BJP.

In July 1990 Devi Lal was dismissed from his post as Deputy Prime Minister, for nepotism, disloyalty and for making unsubstantiated accusations of corruption against ministerial colleagues. In August there were violent demonstrations in many northern Indian states against the Government's populist decision to implement the recommendations of the 10-year-old Mandal Commission and to raise the quota of government and public-sector jobs reserved for deprived sections of the population. In October the Supreme Court directed the Government to halt temporarily the implementation of the quota scheme, in an attempt to curb the caste violence.

In October 1990 the BJP withdrew its support for the National Front, following the arrest of its President, Lal Krishna (L. K.) Advani, as he led a controversial procession of Hindu devotees to the holy town of Ayodhya, in Uttar Pradesh, to begin the construction of a Hindu temple on the site of a disused ancient mosque. V. P. Singh accused the BJP leader of deliberately inciting inter-communal hatred by exhorting Hindu extremists to join him in illegally tearing down the mosque. Paramilitary troops were sent to Ayodhya, and thousands of Hindu activists were arrested, in an attempt to prevent a Muslim–Hindu confrontation. However, following repeated clashes between police and crowds, Hindu extremists stormed and slightly damaged the mosque and laid siege to it for several days.

In November 1990 one of the Prime Minister's leading rivals in the Janata Dal, Chandra Shekhar (with the support of Devi Lal), formed his own dissident faction, known as the Janata Dal (Socialist) or Janata Dal (S) (which merged with the Janata Party in April 1991 to become the Samajwadi Party). The Lok Sabha convened for a special session, at which the Government overwhelmingly lost a vote of confidence. V. P. Singh immediately resigned, and the President invited Rajiv Gandhi, as leader of the party holding the largest number of seats in the Lok Sabha, to form a new government. Rajiv Gandhi refused the offer, in favour of Chandra Shekhar. Although the strength of the Janata Dal (S) in the Lok Sabha comprised only about 60 deputies, Congress (I) had earlier offered it unconditional parliamentary support. On 10 November 1990 Chandra Shekhar was sworn in as Prime Minister. Devi Lal became Deputy Prime Minister and President of the Janata Dal (S). Shekhar won a vote of confidence in the Lok Sabha and a new Council of Ministers was appointed. Although Shekhar succeeded in initiating talks between the two sides in the Ayodhya dispute, violence between Hindus and Muslims increased throughout India in December.

In January 1991 the Prime Minister imposed direct rule in Tamil Nadu, claiming that this was necessitated by the increased activity of Sri Lankan Tamil militants in the state, which had led to the breakdown of law and order. In the resultant riots more than 1,000 arrests were made. The Government suffered a further set-back in February. Five members of the Council of Ministers were forced to resign when they lost their seats in the Lok Sabha for violating India's anti-defection laws: they had left the Janata Dal to join the Janata Dal (S). The fragility of the parliamentary alliance between the Janata Dal (S) and Congress (I) became apparent in March, when the Congress (I) deputies boycotted Parliament, following the revelation that Rajiv Gandhi's house had been kept under police surveillance. In an unexpected counter-move, Chandra Shekhar resigned, but accepted the President's request that he remain as head of an interim Government until the holding of a fresh general election.

As the general election, which was scheduled to take place over three days in late May 1991, approached, it seemed likely that no party would win an outright majority and that the political stalemate would continue. On 21 May, however, after the first day's polling had taken place, Rajiv Gandhi was assassinated, by members of the Tamil separatist group, the Liberation Tigers of Tamil Eelam (LTTE), while campaigning in Tamil Nadu. Consequently, the remaining elections were postponed until mid-June. The final result gave Congress (I) 227 of the 511 seats contested. The BJP, which almost doubled its share of the vote compared with its performance in the 1989 general election, won 119 seats, and the Janata Dal, the popularity of which had considerably declined, gained only 55 seats. P. V. Narasimha Rao, who had been elected as acting President of Congress (which had gradually shed its (I) suffix) following Rajiv Gandhi's assassination, assumed the premiership and appointed a new Council of Ministers. The new Government's main priority on assuming power was to attempt to solve the country's severe economic crisis, caused by an enormous foreign debt, high inflation, a large deficit on the current account of the balance of payments, and an extreme shortage of foreign exchange reserves. The new Minister of Finance, Dr Manmohan Singh (an experienced economist and former Governor of the Reserve Bank of India), launched a far-reaching programme of economic liberalization and reform, including the dismantling of bureaucratic regulations and the encouragement of private and foreign investment. In late September the Government announced the adoption of the recommendations of the Mandal Commission that 27% of government jobs and institutional places be reserved for certain lower castes, in addition to the 22.5% already reserved for 'untouchable' castes and tribal people. (In November 1992 the Supreme Court ruled that non-Hindus, such as Christians and Sikhs, who were socially disadvantaged were also entitled to job reservations.)

After a brief reconciliatory period in the latter half of 1991, Narasimha Rao's Government began to be faced with problems, both from opposition agitation and from within its own ranks. In January 1992 the BJP increased communal tension between Hindus and Muslims by hoisting the national flag on Republic Day in Srinagar, the capital of Kashmir (see below). In mid-1992 efforts were also made by the BJP to use the contentious issue of the Ayodhya site (the Ram Janmabhoomi/Babri Masjid—Hindu temple/Muslim mosque—dispute, see above) to embarrass the Government. In May a major financial scandal involving the Bombay Stock Exchange was uncovered. It was alleged that several members of the Council of Ministers were amongst the beneficiaries, allegations that prompted the resignation of the Minister of State for Commerce. In July, however, the Congress candidate, Dr Shankar Dayal Sharma, was elected, with no serious opposition, to the presidency.

Following the collapse of talks in November 1992 between the Vishwa Hindu Parishad (VHP—World Hindu Council) and the All India Babri Masjid Action Committee regarding the Ayodhya dispute, the VHP and the BJP appealed for volunteers to begin the construction of a Hindu temple on the site of the existing mosque in early December. As thousands of Hindu militants assembled in Ayodhya, thousands of paramilitary troops were dispatched to the town in an attempt to avert any violence. Despite the armed presence, however, the temple/mosque complex was stormed by the Hindu volunteers, who proceeded to tear down the remains of the ancient mosque. This highly inflammatory action provoked widespread communal violence throughout India (Bombay, or Mumbai as it was later renamed, being one of the worst-affected areas), which resulted in more than 1,200 deaths, and prompted world-wide condemnation, notably from the neighbouring Islamic states of Pakistan and Bangladesh, where violent anti-Hindu demonstrations were subsequently held. The central Government also strongly condemned the desecration and demolition of the holy building and pledged to rebuild it. The leaders of the BJP, including L. K. Advani and the party's President, Dr Murli Manohar Joshi, and the leaders of the VHP were arrested, the BJP Chief Minister of Uttar Pradesh resigned, the state legislature was dissolved and Uttar Pradesh was placed under President's rule. The security forces took full control of Ayodhya, including the disputed complex, meeting with little resistance. The Government banned five communal organizations, including the VHP and two Muslim groups, on the grounds that they promoted disharmony among different religious communities. Throughout India stringent measures were taken by the security forces to suppress the Hindu–Muslim violence, which lasted for about one week. In mid-December the Government established a commission of inquiry into the events leading to the demolition of the mosque at Ayodhya. In an attempt to avert any further acts of Hindu militancy, the central Government dismissed the BJP administrations in Madhya Pradesh, Rajasthan and Himachal Pradesh and placed these three states under presidential rule. Narasimha Rao's various actions were given implicit approval later that month when a motion of 'no confidence' presented by the BJP against the Government was soundly defeated. In late December the Government announced plans to acquire all the disputed areas in Ayodhya. The acquired land would be made available to two trusts, which would be responsible for the construction of a new Hindu temple and a new mosque and for the planned development of the site.

There was a resurgence in Hindu–Muslim violence in India's commercial centre, Mumbai, and in Ahmedabad in January 1993, however, necessitating the imposition of curfews and the dispatch of thousands of extra paramilitary troops to curb the serious unrest. Despite a government ban on communal rallies,

thousands of Hindu militants attempted to converge on the centre of New Delhi to attend a mass rally organized by the BJP in late February. In an effort to prevent the proposed rally taking place, thousands of BJP activists were arrested throughout India and the crowds that did gather in the capital were dispersed by the security forces using batons and tear gas. In March there were a number of bomb explosions in Mumbai, resulting in some 250 casualties. Notorious criminals Dawood Ibrahim and Abu Salem, who fled India after the explosions, were suspected of organizing the bomb attacks in retaliation for the nation-wide communal riots provoked by the destruction of the mosque in Ayodhya (see above).

In July 1993 Narasimha Rao narrowly survived a vote of 'no confidence', which was proposed in the Lok Sabha by virtually all the opposition parties. The following month the Prime Minister suffered a blow to his political prestige when the Government was forced to abandon two proposed bills (aimed at the BJP, in particular), which would have banned political parties from using religious appeals in campaigns. However, in November, in the state assembly elections in the four northern states where BJP state administrations had been dismissed by the central Government in December 1992 following the Ayodhya crisis, the BJP regained power in only one state, Rajasthan, while Congress obtained outright majorities in Himachal Pradesh and Madhya Pradesh. These results appeared to highlight a definite decline in the popularity of the BJP. In December 1993 Congress's political standing was strengthened when a small faction of the Janata Dal led by Ajit Singh merged with the ruling party, thus giving the latter a parliamentary majority.

The following year, 1994, was, for the most part, a period of relative political stability. The extensive economic reforms continued to show positive results and Narasimha Rao's premiership appeared fairly secure, with the opposition suffering from fragmentation (particularly the Janata Dal) and with no serious challenges from within Congress itself. In mid-1994, however, the opposition deputies boycotted parliamentary proceedings for three weeks in protest at what they regarded as lack of effective action following an official inquiry into the 1992 securities scandal in order to understate the involvement of Congress ministers. The popularity and strength of the ruling Congress appeared to have declined considerably by the end of 1994, when the party suffered crushing defeats in elections to the state assemblies in Andhra Pradesh and Karnataka (former strongholds of Congress); it was also defeated in state elections in Sikkim. In late December the Government's image was enhanced to some extent when three ministers were finally forced to resign over their alleged roles in corruption scandals (the Prime Minister had earlier been reluctant to dismiss them). Shortly afterwards, the Minister for Human Resource Development, Arjun Singh, who was widely viewed as Narasimha Rao's main rival within Congress, resigned from his post, citing his dissatisfaction and frustration at the Government's perceived incompetence regarding corruption, the Bombay Stock Exchange scandal, the Ayodhya crisis and the investigation into Rajiv Gandhi's assassination. In January 1995, with important state elections rapidly approaching, Narasimha Rao attempted to quell increasing dissent within his Government and party by suspending Arjun Singh from the working committee of Congress for 'anti-party activities'; in the following month the rebel politician was expelled from the party. In May Singh, together with Narain Dutt Tewari, recruited dissident members of Congress in many states and formed a new breakaway party, known as the All India Indira Congress (Tewari); the party merged with Congress, however, in December 1996.

Congress enjoyed mixed results in the state elections held in February–March 1995. In an apparent attempt to bolster his political standing, Narasimha Rao reshuffled and enlarged the Council of Ministers in mid-September. In January 1996, however, accusations of corruption came to the fore in Indian politics when the Central Bureau of Investigation charged seven leading politicians, including L. K. Advani of the BJP, Devi Lal and Arjun Singh, and sought the prosecution of three Union ministers (who subsequently resigned) for allegedly accepting large bribes from a Delhi-based industrialist, Surendra Jain. The sheer scale of the scandal (known as the Hawala—illegal money transfer—case), in terms of the sums involved and the number of people implicated, led to widespread public disillusionment with politicians in general. At the end of January another high-ranking political figure, the President of the Janata Dal, S. R. Bommai, was implicated in the scandal; Bommai subsequently resigned from his post. In February Congress's hopes of retaining power in the forthcoming general election appeared increasingly fragile when three more ministers resigned from the Council of Ministers after their names had been linked to the Hawala case. Meanwhile, the Prime Minister was connected to the prosecution, on charges of cheating and criminal conspiracy, of a flamboyant faith healer and 'godman', Chandraswami, who had been consulted by generations of political leaders, including Narasimha Rao himself.

The results of the general election, which was held over three days at the end of April and early May 1996, gave no party or group an overall majority. The largest party in terms of seats was the BJP, which won 160 seats, and with the support of the Shiv Sena and other smaller allies could count on an overall legislative strength of 194 seats. Congress secured 136 seats. The National Front (comprising the Janata Dal and its allies) and Left Front (representing the two major communist parties) together obtained 179 seats, with the remainder won by minor parties and independents. On 15 May, as soon as the electoral position was clear, the President asked the BJP under its new parliamentary leader, Atal Bihari Vajpayee, to form the new Government and to prove its majority support within two weeks. Given the antagonism felt towards the BJP by the majority of other political parties, the latter task proved impossible, and Vajpayee resigned on 28 May in anticipation of his Government's inevitable defeat in a parliamentary vote of confidence. In the mean time, the National and Left Fronts had merged to form an informal coalition known as the United Front (UF), which comprised a total of 13 parties, with the Janata Dal, the Samajwadi Party, the two communist parties and the regional Dravida Munnetra Kazhagam (DMK) and Telugu Desam as its major components. With Congress prepared to lend external support, the UF was able to form a Government at the end of May. A former Chief Minister of Karnataka, H. D. Deve Gowda, was selected to lead the UF and the new Government.

In September 1996 Narasimha Rao resigned from the leadership of Congress after he was ordered to stand trial for his alleged involvement in the Chandraswami case; the party presidency was assumed by the veteran politician, Sitaram Kesri. Later that month separate charges of forgery and criminal conspiracy (dating back to the former Prime Minister's tenure of the external affairs ministry in the 1980s) were made against the beleaguered Narasimha Rao; he resigned in December 1996 as Congress's parliamentary leader and was replaced in the following month by Kesri.

At the end of March 1997 Deve Gowda was faced with a serious political crisis when Congress threatened to withdraw its parliamentary support for the UF Government. On 11 April the Prime Minister resigned following the defeat of the UF administration in a vote of confidence (by 158 votes to 292). A few days later Inder Kumar Gujral, the Minister of External Affairs in the outgoing Government, was chosen by the UF to replace Deve Gowda as leader of the coalition. On 22 April Gujral was sworn in as Prime Minister and appointed a new Council of Ministers. In May Sonia Gandhi, the widow of the former Prime Minister Rajiv Gandhi, joined Congress as a 'primary member', and in the following month Kesri was re-elected President of the party in Congress's first contested leadership poll since 1977. In June 1997 the ruling coalition was faced with another high-level corruption case when the President of the Janata Dal and Chief Minister of Bihar, Lalu Prasad Yadav, was forced to resign from his posts prior to his arrest on several counts of conspiracy in a corruption scandal involving the supply of animal fodder for non-existent livestock. Yadav subsequently formed a breakaway faction of his party, known as the Rashtriya Janata Dal, and Sharad Yadav was elected as the new President of the Janata Dal. In July Kocheril Raman Narayanan was elected, almost unanimously, as India's new President; this appointment was particularly notable in that Narayanan was the first Indian President to originate from a Dalit (or 'untouchable') background. In September a five-year investigation into the destruction of the mosque at Ayodhya in 1992 led to charges of criminal conspiracy and incitement to riot being filed against senior BJP and religious leaders, including L. K. Advani and the leader of Shiv Sena, Balashaheb 'Bal' Thackeray.

The UF Government looked increasingly insecure in late November 1997 when Congress threatened to withdraw its parliamentary support unless the Tamil Nadu-based DMK, which was alleged to be indirectly implicated in the 1991 assassination of Rajiv Gandhi, was expelled from the coalition. Prime Minister Gujral rejected Congress's demand, and was consequently forced to resign on 28 November when Congress withdrew its support for the Government, as earlier threatened. This constituted the third government collapse in less than two years. In early December President Narayanan dissolved the Lok Sabha following the inability of both Congress and the BJP to form an alternative coalition government. It was announced that Gujral would retain the premiership in an acting capacity pending the holding of a fresh general election in early 1998.

During December 1997 Congress suffered a series of internal splits and defections in at least six states. In an apparent attempt to halt the fragmentation of the ailing party, in late December Sonia Gandhi agreed to campaign on behalf of Congress in the run-up to the general election. After a low-key start Sonia Gandhi gained in confidence and popularity during the campaign and attracted ever-larger crowds; she steadfastly refused, however, to stand for actual parliamentary office. Sonia Gandhi's deceased husband was, once again, in the forefront of political news at the end of January 1998, when 26 Tamil militants implicated in the murder of Rajiv Gandhi were sentenced to death by a court in Chennai (Madras). (In May 1999, however, the Supreme Court in New Delhi acquitted 19 defendants and commuted the sentences of three others.)

In the general election, which was held in February–March 1998, the BJP and its regional allies established themselves as the pre-eminent force in Indian politics. The BJP emerged as the largest party, with 182 of the 545 seats in the Lok Sabha, but failed to win an overall majority. Congress secured 142 seats, and shortly after the election Sonia Gandhi replaced Kesri as the party's President. On 19 March President Narayanan appointed the parliamentary leader of the BJP, Atal Bihari Vajpayee (who had briefly held the premiership in mid-1996), as Prime Minister and asked him to form a stable coalition government and to seek a legislative vote of confidence within the next 10 days. This he did (by 274 votes to 261) on 28 March, with the support of the All-India Anna Dravida Munnetra Kazhagam (AIADMK), the Telugu Desam (which eventually left the UF) and a number of other minor groups. None the less, it was apparent from the very outset that Vajpayee's 14-party coalition Government had a fragile hold on power and that the Prime Minister would be required to use both skill and tact to retain his position.

In May 1998 the Government shocked both India and the rest of the world by ordering the carrying out of a series of underground nuclear test explosions. This provocative action was at first greeted with massive popular enthusiasm, but Pakistan's retaliatory tests and a rapid realization of the negative international consequences (particularly the imposition of economic sanctions by the USA) soon led to a more measured domestic assessment.

In November 1998 Congress showed a strong revival in its popularity at the expense of the BJP when it removed the ruling party from power in state elections to Rajasthan and Delhi (both traditionally BJP strongholds) and unexpectedly retained its majority in the elections to the legislature in Madhya Pradesh. Congress's resurgence was variously ascribed to Sonia Gandhi's rising popularity, a reaction to the BJP's inefficiency and public anger at the soaring prices of basic commodities (notably onions, India's most basic staple after rice).

In early December 1998 tens of thousands of Christians throughout India held a day of protest against alleged Hindu persecution, which, they claimed, had escalated considerably since the assumption of power by the BJP in March. At the end of December a fresh outbreak of violence against Christians by Hindu zealots was reported in Gujarat; further incidents were reported in January 1999.

In early April 1999 Prime Minister Vajpayee rejected demands by the BJP's troublesome coalition partner the AIADMK (whose controversial leader, Jayalalitha Jayaram, was faced with ongoing investigations into corruption allegations) to reinstate the Chief of Staff of the Navy and to dismiss the Minister of Defence, George Fernandes; the following day the two AIADMK ministers resigned from the Government. The President resolved the resultant political stalemate by forcing Vajpayee to seek a parliamentary vote of confidence. The Government narrowly lost the motion (by 270 votes to 269) and the President then invited Sonia Gandhi to assemble a new coalition. Following her failure to do so, the Lok Sabha was dissolved on 26 April and fresh elections were called. Vajpayee and his Government remained in power, in an acting capacity, pending the holding of the polls.

In May 1999 Congress's erstwhile parliamentary leader, Sharad Pawar, who had earlier publicly criticized Sonia Gandhi's foreign (Italian) origins, announced the formation of a breakaway party, entitled the Nationalist Congress Party (NCP); the NCP absorbed the Indian National Congress (S) in the following month. The outbreak of hostilities between Indian and Pakistani troops in the Kargil area of Kashmir in mid-1999 (see below) had a very positive effect on the nationalist BJP's standing and, in particular, on that of Vajpayee, who, as acting Prime Minister, was widely perceived to have responded with dignity, firmness and commendable restraint in the face of Pakistani provocation. The fact that India, in effect, emerged victorious from the Kargil crisis (in forcing a Pakistani retreat) had a major impact on the public's perception of the acting Government.

The BJP contested the general election, held in September–October 1999, at the head of a 24-member alliance, known as the National Democratic Alliance (NDA), which comprised numerous and diverse minor regional and national parties with little shared ideology. The NDA won an outright majority in the Lok Sabha, with 299 of the 545 seats, while Congress and its electoral allies obtained 134 seats. Although Sonia Gandhi won both of the seats that she herself contested in Karnataka and Uttar Pradesh, her lack of political experience, her weak grasp of Hindi and her foreign birth all contributed to Congress's worst electoral defeat since India's independence. Following his appointment as leader of the NDA, Vajpayee was sworn in as Prime Minister for a third term at the head of a large coalition Government.

Despite protests organized by Hindu fundamentalists and threats of sabotage, the head of the Roman Catholic Church, Pope John Paul II, carried out a peaceful state visit to India, amid tight security, in early November 1999. During the pontiff's meetings with senior Indian politicians, he broached the subject of the recent upsurge in anti-Christian persecution and called for greater religious tolerance (while asserting the freedom to proselytize).

In February and March 2000 state elections were held. Overall, regional parties fared better than Congress and the BJP. In mid-November Sonia Gandhi was re-elected President of Congress. In mid-May the Government introduced three items of legislation in the Lok Sabha to establish the states of Chhattisgarh, Jharkhand and Uttaranchal, and amended versions were finally approved by the Lok Sabha and Rajya Sabha in August. The three new states came into being in November.

In July 2000 a threat to arrest the leader of the Shiv Sena, Bal Thackeray, for his alleged role in the 1992–93 communal riots, led to violent conflict on the streets. Although Thackeray was duly arrested, a Mumbai court dismissed the charges on account of the fact that the case was concerned with relatively old events which fell outside the country's statute of limitations. In October the former Prime Minister, P. V. Narasimha Rao, was convicted of corruption. He was sentenced to three years' imprisonment and was fined Rs 100,000. (In March 2002, however, his conviction was overturned by the High Court in New Delhi.) In October 2000 the Central Bureau of Investigation filed charges against three Indian businessmen, the Hinduja brothers, for allegedly accepting bribes in the 'Bofors' affair (see above). In the same month the former Chief Minister of Tamil Nadu, Jayalalitha, was convicted of corruption and sentenced to three years' imprisonment (she successfully appealed against her conviction in December 2001 and was reappointed as Chief Minister following her victory in by-elections in February 2002).

In June 2000 violent attacks against Christians resumed. In an attempt to show that the Government was taking the problem seriously, Vajpayee met a delegation of bishops to discuss the renewed violence. Nevertheless, in July Indian Christians protested across South India, demanding protection against the attacks. In October the leader of the fundamentalist Hindu group Rashtriya Swayamsevak Sangh (RSS—National Volunteer Organization) urged the Government to replace 'foreign' churches with a national church and to expel all Christian missionaries. The RSS campaign caused embarrassment for the Government, in particular Vajpayee, who requested the newly appointed BJP President, Bangaru Laxman, to declare that the views of the RSS did not represent those of the BJP.

In early December 2000 communal tension between Hindus and Muslims increased, following Vajpayee's statement that the construction of the Ram Janmabhoomi, the Hindu temple, in Ayodhya was an expression of 'national sentiment that has yet to be realized' and part of the 'unfinished agenda' of his Govern-

ment. Although the Prime Minister later attempted to diminish his remarks, declaring that he did not support the destruction of the Muslim Babri Masjid mosque, the opposition demanded an immediate apology and forced the abrupt adjournment of the Lok Sabha and Rajya Sabha. Opposition members also called for the resignation of three ministers, including L. K. Advani, who were expected to face charges issued by the Central Bureau of Investigation in a case relating to the demolition of the Babri Masjid. Vajpayee rejected the demand, confirming that the Government would abide by the judgment of the Supreme Court with regard to the three ministers. In February 2001 an Indian high court ruled that nearly 40 people could be brought to trial in connection with the destruction of the mosque in Ayodhya, and that senior BJP leaders would not be among the defendants, owing to certain technicalities. In January plans for a negotiated settlement over the religious site in Ayodhya suffered a set-back when the All India Babri Masjid Action Committee ruled out negotiations with the VHP. VHP leaders convened a religious parliament, the Dharma Sansad, at the Maha Kumbh Mela (the largest ever Hindu gathering) in January–February. The Dharma Sansad stated that all obstacles impeding the construction of the temple should be removed by the relevant organizations by mid-March 2002.

A new series of political and financial scandals exposed continuing corruption at the highest levels of government and commerce, and further undermined popular confidence in the BJP and its moral posturing. In March 2001 an internet news service, tehelka.com, revealed videotaped evidence of senior NDA politicians and army officials accepting bribes from tehelka.com employees posing as facilitators seeking to secure a bogus defence contract. Among those exposed in this way were the President of the BJP, Bangaru Laxman, and the leader of the Samata Party, Jaya Jaitly. Both resigned from their posts following the revelations, as did the Minister of Defence, George Fernandes, who had been implicated in the scandal by Jaitly's use of his official residence as the location for the illicit transaction. (Prime Minister Vajpayee narrowly avoided involvement through implication himself.) The Minister of Railways, Mamata Banerjee of the All India Trinamool Congress, took this opportunity to resign from her cabinet post and withdrew her party from the ruling coalition. Some days later the defence portfolio was assigned to Minister of External Affairs Jaswant Singh, while the railways portfolio was subsequently awarded to the Minister of Agriculture, Nitish Kumar. Although Vajpayee agreed to appoint a commission of inquiry into the affair, his reluctance to agree to the establishment of a joint parliamentary committee to investigate the scandal resulted in (largely successful) opposition attempts to stall proceedings in the lower house during April. Meanwhile, in early March a national financial crisis had been narrowly averted when stocks and shares across the country fluctuated wildly following the resignation of the president of the Bombay Stock Exchange after he was implicated in an investigation by the national stock market regulator into allegations of widespread share price manipulation and insider trading. Moreover, in July the chairman of India's largest investment fund (Unit Trust of India—UTI) was arrested on charges of financial misappropriation. Once again, Vajpayee was alleged to have been loosely connected to the affair.

Elections to four state assemblies and one union territory assembly, conducted in May 2001, resulted in major gains for Congress and its electoral allies (in Kerala and Assam) and significant reversals for the parties of the NDA coalition (most notably in Tamil Nadu where the Secular Front, led by the regional AIADMK, trounced the incumbent DMK—a member of the NDA—by a margin of 160 seats). Mounting political crises in the states of Manipur and Tamil Nadu in May and June (see below) and inconclusive direct negotiations between Vajpayee and President Musharraf of Pakistan in July (see below), all contributed to increasing disillusionment within the NDA. At the end of July Vajpayee offered to resign, exasperated by the factional tensions within the coalition, but was persuaded to retract the offer on the following day, after an expression of consolidated NDA support for his leadership. At the end of August the All India Trinamool Congress and Pattali Makkal Katchi (which had withdrawn from the NDA in February owing to regional party divisions) rejoined the governing coalition. At the beginning of September Vajpayee expanded and reorganized the Council of Ministers, and in October George Fernandes (now the leader of the Samata Party) was reappointed Minister of Defence.

In the aftermath of the devastating terrorist attacks on the US mainland on 11 September 2001, for which the USA held the al-Qa'ida (Base) organization of Osama bin Laden responsible, the Indian Government sought to emphasize its own uncompromising response to the activities of illegal organizations. In late September national security forces clashed with members of the outlawed Students' Islamic Movement of India (SIMI—which was alleged to be linked to both al-Qa'ida and the militant Hizbul Mujahideen, see below) in Lucknow, Uttar Pradesh. Three SIMI supporters were killed during the altercation, after which some 240 SIMI activists were arrested across the country, together with the organization's president. In late October the Government promulgated the Prevention of Terrorism Act 2001 (POTA), which replaced anti-terrorism legislation dating from 1987. The Government claimed that the new Act, which broadened the definitions of terrorist activity and the preventative and retaliatory powers of the Government (to the evident discomfort of the opposition), was necessary to accommodate the recommendations and resolutions of the UN and the international community since 11 September, and to address the recent increase in domestic terrorist activity in India. The new ordinance proscribed indefinitely 23 organizations engaged in principally separatist activities. Meanwhile, the Indian Government was increasingly frustrated by the conciliatory overtures made to the Pakistani Government by the USA in pursuit of full Pakistani co-operation with its activities in neighbouring Afghanistan.

A series of audacious terrorist attacks perpetrated by Kashmiri separatists and suspected Islamist militants severely tested the resolve of the Government in late 2001 and early 2002 (see below), resulting in an unexpected consolidation of popular and political support for the coalition. Some opponents, however, suggested that the Government's uncompromising approach to foreign policy in particular (which had brought the country to the brink of renewed military conflict with Pakistan in December 2001, see below) amounted to little more than irresponsible 'sabre rattling' designed to attract nationalist support ahead of crucial state elections scheduled for early 2002.

In mid-October 2000 the Supreme Court approved the continuation of work on the controversial Sardar Sarovar dam, on the Narmada River in Gujarat. Construction stopped in 1994, when environmental activists, representing the tens of thousands of people whom the dam would displace, lodged a case against the authorities. The World Bank had withdrawn its funding, citing environmental concerns, in 1993. Campaigners against the project claimed that the authorities had failed to provide an acceptable rehabilitation and resettlement programme. In January 2001 a devastating earthquake occurred in Gujarat, the epicentre being in the coastal town of Bhuj. More than 30,000 people were killed and over 1m. people were made homeless. The central Government and the Government of Gujarat were criticized for their tardy reaction to the disaster, a delay that reportedly led to greater loss of life.

In January 2002 Prime Minister Vajpayee resumed efforts to resolve the dispute over a religious site in Ayodhya, Uttar Pradesh. The All India Babri Masjid Action Committee, however, refused to enter negotiations with the uncompromising VHP. In early February the BJP declared in its manifesto for state elections in Uttar Pradesh that it would abide by a court decision or a negotiated settlement between the Hindu and Muslim groups over the disputed site. The BJP had traditionally enjoyed close links with the VHP, but national politics required the governing party to distance itself from the militant Hindu group. As the deadline set by a religious parliament, the Dharma Sansad, to begin building the temple in mid-March approached (see above), hundreds of Hindu activists assembled in Ayodhya to take part in the illegal construction. Despite warnings by the Government that it would enforce the law, a senior VHP leader announced in late February that the movement of building material to the site would begin on 15 March. In late February communal violence broke out in Gujarat after a train carrying members of the VHP returning from Ayodhya was attacked by a suspected group of Muslims in the town of Godhra. The attack, in which 60 Hindu activists were killed, provoked a cycle of communal violence throughout Gujarat that lasted for several weeks and resulted in the deaths of up to 2,000 people, most of whom were Muslims. The Indian army was drafted in to quell the riots. Opposition members demanded the resignation of the Minister of Home Affairs, L. K. Advani, and the Chief Minister of Gujarat, Narendra Modi, for failing to control the riots, amid claims that the Government deliberately

prevented the police from controlling the Hindu activists. In late April the European Union's report on the situation in Gujarat, which corroborated a number of other reports published in the same month, concluded that the riots and killings had been, contrary to the official account, not in reaction to the attack on a train carrying Hindu activists, but in fact an organized massacre of Muslims and that the security forces had been under orders not to intervene. Modi eventually resigned and recommended the dissolution of the state assembly in mid-July; he was requested to continue as leader of an interim administration until state elections were held in December. Meanwhile, in mid-March security forces prevented Hindu nationalists from defying a court order and entering the disputed religious site in Ayodhya. In March 2003 the Allahabad High Court ordered the Archaeological Survey of India to carry out an excavation at the disputed site to ascertain whether a Hindu temple existed beneath the Babri mosque. Meanwhile, the VHP continued its campaign to build a temple at the site.

In the mean time, assembly elections in the states of Manipur, the Punjab, Uttaranchal and Uttar Pradesh took place in late February 2002. The BJP fared badly in all four elections. Congress enjoyed victory in the Punjab and Uttaranchal; Manipur and Uttar Pradesh were left with hung assemblies. Congress formed a coalition government in Manipur in March; Uttar Pradesh was placed under presidential rule until the BJP and Bahujan Samaj Party (BSP) reached a power-sharing agreement in early May. At the end of April the Minister of Coal and Mines resigned and withdrew his Lok Jan Shakti party from the NDA in protest against the Government's handling of the situation in Gujarat. Meanwhile, in late March a constitutional review commission, chaired by former Chief Justice M. N. Venkatachaliah, submitted a report of its two-year review of the country's Constitution. The report recommended about 250 changes in the laws relating to political parties, elections, fundamental rights and judicial and executive accountability. The report, however, did not address the issue of whether a person of foreign origin should hold a constitutional post, a question particularly relevant to Italian-born Sonia Gandhi's position. In mid-May the Lok Sabha elected unopposed Manohar Joshi as its speaker, replacing Mohan Chandra Balayogi, who died in March. At the end of June, the Minister of Home Affairs, L. K. Advani, was assigned the additional portfolio of Deputy Prime Minister, prompting speculation that Advani had been nominated as Vajpayee's eventual successor. In early July a government reorganization took place in which Jaswant Singh and Yashwant Sinha, the Ministers of Foreign Affairs and Finance, respectively, exchanged portfolios. At the same time Venkaiah Naidu was designated President of the BJP, replacing Jana Krishnamurthy, who was appointed Minister of Law and Justice. Later that month a presidential election was held. The Government's candidate, Aavul Pakkiri Jainulabidin Abdul Kalam, a South Indian Muslim who was closely involved in the development of the country's missile and nuclear programme, convincingly won the election. In August the more orthodox Bhairon Singh Shekhawat was elected as Vice-President (his predecessor died two weeks before the scheduled election date). In late August Vajpayee replaced Suresh Prabhu, the widely respected Minister of Power and member of Shiv Sena, with Anant Gangareem Geete, another member of Shiv Sena. Vajpayee had been reportedly under pressure from the leader of Shiv Sena, Bal Thackeray, to carry out the ministerial change, prompting a debate over the Prime Minister's authority with regard to selecting his Council of Ministers. Thackeray had accused Prabhu of not doing enough to serve the financial interests of the militant Hindu party.

In mid-August 2002 the Election Commission rejected interim Chief Minister Narendra Modi's request to conduct early elections to the Gujarat state assembly in October, stating that the situation was not stable enough: many people were still displaced after the riots and communal tensions prevailed in the region. In September Modi launched a controversial 4,800-km Hindu nationalist *gaurav rath yatra* (pride march) around the state of Gujarat in an attempt to garner support for the BJP. Although the Election Commission banned Modi from using the incident in Godhra as an election tool, the symbol of a burning train was displayed on election posters across the state. Communal tensions in the region rose in response to Modi's Hindu nationalist and overtly anti-Muslim election campaign. The elections to the Gujarat state assembly took place on 12 December. The BJP won 51% of the vote, securing 126 of the 182 seats in the state legislature. Congress, criticized for selecting

2110

only five Muslim candidates and for attempting to attract the Hindu nationalist vote (albeit at a lesser level than the BJP), despite being a secular party, won only 51 seats. Modi returned to power as Chief Minister. Meanwhile, in late September two armed assailants forced entry into a Hindu temple in Gujarat and shot dead 29 worshippers and injured 74 people; three commandos were also killed. The gunmen were shot dead by security forces, ending a night-long siege of the temple. It was believed that the perpetrators, reportedly members of a relatively unknown militant Islamist group called Tehrik-i-Kasas (Movement of Revenge), carried out the attack in retaliation for the deaths of Gujarati Muslims in the riots earlier in the year. The Indian Government accused the Pakistani Government of orchestrating the attack, an allegation strongly rejected by the latter. In March 2003 a member of the BJP and former state minister, Haren Pandya, was assassinated in Gujarat. Pandya was a senior member of the RSS and had been accused of participating in the attacks against Gujarati Muslims in 2002. Four men were arrested in April 2003 in connection with Pandya's death. Controversy over the 2002 riots continued as communal tensions persisted; complaints were issued about compensation levels for victims of the riots and the failure to prosecute the perpetrators of the violence. In September 2003 the Supreme Court openly challenged the Government of Gujarat's competence and integrity to pursue any case against alleged rioters. Two months later the Court ordered that 10 high-profile trials of people accused of communal violence in Gujarat in 2002 be halted in response to a petition by the National Human Rights Commission to transfer all such trials to courts outside Gujarat because of witness intimidation and inadequate police investigations. The Government of Gujarat was given two weeks to justify why the trials should not be moved elsewhere. Several days later a court in Gujarat convicted 12 Hindus of killing 14 Muslims during the riots in 2002 and sentenced them to life imprisonment.

In January 2003 Vajpayee carried out an extensive government reorganization, promoting several principal economic reformers to senior cabinet positions in an attempt to boost the economic liberalization programme. The transfer of senior ministers to leading roles within the BJP was regarded as a move to strengthen the party ahead of state elections scheduled for February and the general election due to take place in 2004. In the weeks leading up to the state elections in Himachal Pradesh, Meghalaya, Nagaland and Tripura, Hindu activists representing the BJP and VHP focused on inciting Hindu nationalist sentiment in an attempt to reproduce the victory achieved in Gujarat two months previously. However, the BJP fared badly in all four elections, held on 26 February, losing power in Himachal Pradesh to Congress. Congress formed a coalition government in Meghalaya and lost power in Nagaland to the Democratic Alliance of Nagaland. The Communist Party of India (Marxist) retained power in Tripura. Some attributed the success of Congress to the anti-incumbency factor.

In the mean time, in early January 2003 the Government announced that it had established a Nuclear Command Authority to manage India's nuclear weapons, giving sole authority to launch a nuclear strike to the Prime Minister and his advisers. The Government also stated that it would forego its 'no first use' policy on nuclear weapons if India were the target of a major attack using chemical or biological weapons. A number of bomb explosions occurred in Mumbai in December 2002–January 2003, killing at least two people and injuring almost 90. Another bomb explosion took place in the city in March, killing at least 12 people. No group claimed responsibility for any of the attacks. In August two car-bombs exploded in Mumbai, killing 52 people and injuring 150. In June 2004 five people were charged under the POTA in connection with the bombings.

In March 2003 the Supreme Court declared invalid a provision in the Representation of the People (Amendment) Act and restored an earlier order, thus making it mandatory for electoral candidates to disclose criminal records, educational qualifications and assets when filing their nomination papers. The Court criticized the Government for its 'half-hearted' approach to electoral reform. Earlier that month the Chief Minister of Uttar Pradesh and leader of the BSP, Mayawati, was accused of misappropriating state funds. Meanwhile, relations between the BSP and BJP at the state level deteriorated. In August Mayawati resigned after the coalition state Government disbanded; the President of the Samajwadi Party, Mulayam Singh Yadav, was appointed as the new Chief Minister. Also in August, the

Archaeological Survey of India issued its report on the disputed site in Ayodhya to the Lucknow High Court. The report indicated that there was evidence of a massive temple-like structure existing from the 10th century, supporting claims that a Hindu temple once stood on the site. However, the report was challenged by a group of independent archaeologists and historians, claiming that the Survey had misused or falsified evidence for political reasons, not least because the findings contradicted the Survey's interim report, which was published in June. Meanwhile, in May the Central Bureau of Investigation filed new charges against L. K. Advani and seven other leading politicians in connection with the destruction of the mosque in Ayodhya in December 1992. In September 2003 a special court exonerated L. K. Advani of any role in inciting crowds, provoking the demolition of the mosque and encouraging communal agitation, but sustained the charges against the seven others, including the Minister of Human Resources Development, of Ocean Development and of Science and Technology, Dr Murli Manohar Joshi, who tendered his resignation as a response. In late September a High Court deferred criminal proceedings against Joshi, pending an inquiry into his charges, causing Vajpayee immediately to reject Joshi's resignation.

Meanwhile, in mid-July 2003 the Jammu and Kashmir National Conference announced that it had severed its relationship with the ruling NDA. The leader of the party, Omar Abdullah, claimed that neither the party nor Jammu and Kashmir had benefited from the association. In November the Supreme Court issued a stay on the arrest of six journalists whose 15 days' imprisonment was ordered by Tamil Nadu's state Legislative Assembly. The arrest warrants had been issued in response to an article that criticized the conduct of the Chief Minister of Tamil Nadu, Jayalalitha, published in *The Hindu* and reprinted by *Murasoli*. The editor of *The Hindu* described the court order as a victory for press freedom.

Assembly elections in the states of Chhattisgarh, Madhya Pradesh, Mizoram and Rajasthan and the National Capital Territory of Delhi took place in November–December 2003. The Mizoram National Front retained power in Mizoram, to the surprise of many, while the BJP enjoyed tremendous success in Chhattisgarh, Madhya Pradesh and Rajasthan, at the expense of Congress. The scale of the BJP's victory was attributed to the party's focus on development and governance issues and lack of emphasis on Hindu nationalist themes during its election campaign, and to the anti-incumbency factor. Congress, however, managed to retain power in Delhi, where Sheila Dixit secured a second term as Chief Minister. Vasundhara Raje Scindia, a former minister, became Rajasthan's first female Chief Minister. Scindia and Uma Bharati, the newly appointed Chief Minister of Madhya Pradesh, were also the BJP's first female chief ministers. Encouraged by the BJP's victory at the state elections, and buoyed by a surging economy and an improvement in relations with Pakistan, Vajpayee announced in mid-January 2004 that a general election would be held by the end of April, five months earlier than scheduled. In the mean time, in December 2003 the DMK withdrew its support for the ruling NDA, owing to the BJP's recent support for the AIADMK, the DMK's rival, and to differences over the POTA; the DMK Minister of Environment and Forests, T. R. Baalu, and the DMK Minister of State for Health, A. Raja, resigned as a result. The regional Marumalarchi Dravida Munnetra Kazhagam also withdrew from the NDA; Pattali Makkal Katchi followed suit in January 2004, announcing that it was to form an alliance with the DMK and Congress. The AIADMK, meanwhile, announced that it would form an alliance with the BJP to contest the forthcoming general election. In the same month the NCP split into two factions; the faction led by Sharad Pawar decided to enter an alliance with Congress, while Purno Shangma's group agreed to support the NDA. The Lok Sabha was dissolved on 6 February in preparation for an early general election.

In April–May 2004 the general election was held, taking place over four days for security reasons. In an unprecedented outcome, Congress defeated the NDA, securing, together with its allies, a final total of 222 seats (incorporating the results of voting in several constituencies where polling was postponed until later in that month) in the 545-member Lok Sabha, compared with 186 for the NDA. Congress alone won 145 seats, while the BJP secured only 138. Left Front parties also performed well at the polls, with the Communist Party of India (Marxist) winning 43 seats. Shortly after the election Sonia Gandhi, who had been unanimously endorsed by Congress, its allies and the Left Front (which had offered its support to a

Congress-led Government) as a prime ministerial candidate, announced that she did not intend to stand for the office. She would, however, remain President of Congress, and was elected as Chair of the newly formed Congress-led coalition, the United Progressive Alliance (UPA). The respected Sikh economist Dr Manmohan Singh, a former Minister of Finance and member of the Rajya Sabha, was subsequently appointed as India's first non-Hindu Prime Minister by President Kalam on Gandhi's recommendation, assuming office on 22 May. K. Natwar Singh was appointed Minister of External Affairs in the new UPA Government, while P. Chidambaram was allocated the finance portfolio. Shivraj Patil became Minister of Home Affairs. Following the election, former Prime Minister Vajpayee stood down as parliamentary leader of the BJP; he was replaced by L. K. Advani.

Meanwhile, elections also took place in May 2004 to the state legislative assemblies of Andhra Pradesh, Karnataka, Sikkim and Orissa. In Andhra Pradesh Congress secured a dramatic victory, comprehensively defeating the Telugu Desam, which had previously held a majority in the state. However, in Karnataka the BJP overtook Congress, securing 79 seats in its 224-seat assembly. Despite this, the third-placed party in the state, the Janata Dal (Secular), announced that it would form a coalition with Congress in order to govern. The Biju Janata Dal was victorious in Orissa, while the Sikkim Democratic Front secured 31 seats in the 32-seat Sikkim legislative assembly.

At the first session of the newly elected Lok Sabha, held in June 2004, Somnath Chatterjee, leader of the Communist Party of India (Marxist), was unanimously elected to the role of Speaker. The BJP disrupted the session by protesting against the UPA's appointment of three ministers—all members of the Bihar-based Rashtriya Janata Dal—who had been charged variously with corruption and attempted murder, most notably the new Minister of Railways, Lalu Prasad Yadav, who continued to face corruption charges related to his tenure as Chief Minister of Bihar in 1997. In the following month the Government dismissed the Governors of Goa, Gujarat, Haryana and Uttar Pradesh, owing to their alleged links to the Hindu fundamentalist group RSS. Also in July the Minister of Coal, Shibu Soren, resigned, having fled in order to avoid being arrested on charges that he had incited a mob that had killed 11 tribal settlers in 1975 in what had since become the state of Jharkhand; a fresh warrant for his arrest had been issued in that month following the reopening of the investigation into the case. The BJP-led opposition alliance had refused to conduct any legislative business until Soren had relinquished his cabinet post. Soren was arrested and placed in judicial custody in August. In the same month Uma Bharati, the Chief Minister of Madhya Pradesh, resigned when faced with the possibility that she would be arrested in connection with the part that she had allegedly played in riots in the state of Karnataka 10 years previously; she was replaced by her deputy, Babulal Gaur. Bharati was subsequently arrested but was freed from prison in the following month, when the charges against her were abandoned. Also in September the Cabinet approved the repeal of the controversial POTA and stated its intention to amend the Unlawful Activities (Prevention) Act, 1967, by adding another ordinance in order to incorporate legislative provisions against terrorism. The Rajya Sabha gave its assent to the legislation in December.

Meanwhile, in October 2004 state legislative elections took place in Maharashtra, resulting in another victory for Congress which, together with its allies, secured 141 seats in the 288-member state legislature. Following the BJP's removal from office in the state, its President, Venkaiah Naidu, resigned. L. K. Advani was elected to succeed him. Meanwhile, Congress also secured a majority at legislative elections in the state of Arunachal Pradesh. In November Shibu Soren was restored to the Cabinet as Minister of Coal. In a simultaneous minor cabinet reorganization, K. Chandrasekhar Rao, formerly Minister without Portfolio, was appointed Minister of Labour and Employment, succeeding Sish Ram Ola, who became Minister of Mines. In December Minister of Railways Lalu Prasad Yadav faced charges of alleged bribery after being filmed handing out money to his supporters during a political rally in Bihar. Opposition members in the Lok Sabha demanded his resignation on the grounds of negligence following a fatal train crash in the Punjab in the same month, shortly after Yadav had announced a plan to modernize the railway network.

In February 2005 the BJP-led Government of Goa was dismissed by the Governor, despite its narrow victory in a controversial vote of confidence by the State Assembly. The Goan Chief Minister, Manohar Parrikar of the BJP, was replaced by Pratapsing Rane of Congress as Congress formed a new Government in the state. The BJP subsequently threatened legal action over the controversial assumption of power by Congress, claiming that the Governor's dismissal of the Government was unconstitutional. In March, as a result of the ongoing controversy, Goa was placed under direct presidential rule, despite Rane's victory in a vote of confidence in the State Assembly. In the mean time, elections took place for state legislatures in Bihar, Jharkhand and Haryana. Considerable violence surrounded the elections in Bihar and Jharkhand, as insurgents attempted to disrupt polling. In Haryana Congress secured victory, winning 67 seats in the 90-member legislature. However, in Bihar and Jharkhand results were inconclusive. Despite a hung assembly in Jharkhand, in which the BJP had secured a greater number of seats than Congress, state Governor Sibtey Razi swore in Shibu Soren, of Congress ally the Jharkhand Mukti Morcha, as Chief Minister, generating protests by the opposition in the state. (Soren resigned his federal cabinet portfolio in advance of the appointment.) Controversy over events in Jharkhand contributed to the temporary adjournment of proceedings in the federal Parliament as the BJP protested strongly against the assumption of power in the state by Congress. Partly as a result of the protests, Shibu Soren resigned and Arjun Munda of the BJP was appointed Chief Minister. Shortly afterwards, Munda won a vote of confidence in his appointment in the state legislature. In March direct presidential rule was imposed in Bihar, following the failure of the newly elected Legislative Assembly to form a Government in the state.

Meanwhile, India was one of the countries worst affected by the devastating tsunamis generated by a huge earthquake in the Indian Ocean on 26 December 2004. The states of Tamil Nadu, Kerala and Andhra Pradesh and the Union Territory of Pondicherry on the east coast were all affected, together with the Andaman and Nicobar Islands, which were severely damaged. The disaster resulted in the loss of around 16,000 lives and numerous homes and livelihoods. The Government was able to provide aid to those affected in India without requesting any international assistance, and also provided emergency relief to other countries affected by the disaster, notably Sri Lanka and the Maldives.

Regional issues continue to play an important role in Indian political affairs. In 1986 the Gurkhas (of Nepalese stock) in West Bengal launched a campaign for a separate autonomous homeland in the Darjiling (Darjeeling) region and the recognition of Nepali as an official language. The violent separatist campaign, led by the Gurkha National Liberation Front (GNLF), was prompted by the eviction of about 10,000 Nepalis from the state of Meghalaya, where the native residents feared that they were becoming outnumbered by immigrants. When violent disturbances and a general strike were organized by the GNLF in June 1987, the central Government agreed to hold tripartite talks with the GNLF's leader, Subhas Ghising, and the Chief Minister of West Bengal. The Prime Minister rejected the GNLF's demand for an autonomous Gurkha state, but Ghising agreed to the establishment of a semi-autonomous Darjiling Hill Development Council. Under the formal peace agreement, the GNLF was to cease all agitation and to surrender weapons, while the state Government was to release all GNLF detainees. The Government agreed to grant Indian citizenship to all Gurkhas born or domiciled in India. Elections to the Darjiling Hill Development Council were held in November. The GNLF won 26 of the 28 elective seats (the 14 remaining members of the Council were to be nominated) and Ghising was elected Chairman of the Council. However, the GNLF continued to demand the establishment of a fully autonomous Gurkha state. In 1992 a constitutional amendment providing for the recognition of Nepali as an official language was adopted.

In December 1985 an election for the state assembly in Assam was won by the Asom Gana Parishad (AGP—Assam People's Council), a newly formed regional party. This followed the signing, in August, of an agreement between the central Government and two groups of Hindu activists, concluded after five years of sectarian violence, which limited the voting rights of immigrants (mainly Bangladeshis) to Assam. When the accord was announced, Bangladesh stated that it would not take back Bengali immigrants from Assam and denied that it had allowed illegal refugees to cross its borders into Assam. Another disaffected Indian tribal group, the Bodos of Assam, demanded a separate state of Bodoland within India. In February 1989 the

Bodos, under the leadership of the All Bodo Students' Union (ABSU), intensified their separatist campaign by organizing strikes, bombings and violent demonstrations. The central Government dispatched armed forces to the state. In August the ABSU held peace talks with the state government and central government officials, agreeing to suspend its violent activities, while the Assam Government agreed to suspend emergency security measures. The situation became more complicated in 1989, when a militant Maoist group, the United Liberation Front of Assam (ULFA), re-emerged. The ULFA demanded the outright secession of the whole of Assam from India. In 1990 the ULFA claimed responsibility for about 90 assassinations, abductions and bombings. In November, when the violence began to disrupt the state's tea industry, the central Government placed Assam under direct rule, dispatched troops to the state and outlawed the ULFA. By late December the unrest seemed to have been substantially quelled. In the state elections in 1991 the AGP was defeated, and a Congress (I)—which later became known simply as Congress—ministry took power. In September, following the breakdown of prolonged talks with the ULFA, the Government launched a new offensive against the ULFA guerrillas and declared the entire state a disturbed area. Meanwhile, following the suspension of violence by the ABSU, the Bodo Security Force (BSF) assumed the leading role in the violent campaign for a separate state of Bodoland. The separatist campaign was intensified in 1992 with indiscriminate killings, abductions, bomb explosions and large-scale extortion. The BSF was outlawed by the central Government in November. At a tripartite meeting attended by the Minister of State for Home Affairs, the Chief Minister of Assam and the President of the ABSU in Guwahati in February 1993, a memorandum was signed providing for the establishment of a 40-member Bodoland Autonomous Council, which would be responsible for the socio-economic and cultural affairs of the Bodo people. However, attacks leading to substantial loss of life were made by Bodo and ULFA activists in the second half of the 1990s both on the security forces and on non-tribal groups in the area. In March 2000 the Government and the Bodo Liberation Tigers (BLT—a group that had waged a violent campaign for a separate state for the Bodo people since 1996) agreed to a cease-fire. Peace negotiations were under way, and in September the cease-fire was extended by one year. In February 2002 it was reported that the Assam state assembly had passed a resolution granting a degree of autonomy to the Bodo people through the creation of a territorial council for the Bodos of four western districts of the state. One year later, the Union Government, state Government and BLT signed a pact formally agreeing upon the introduction of a Bodoland Territorial Council. The Council was created in December 2003; the Bodo militants surrendered their weapons to mark the formal disbanding of the BLT. The ULFA continued its violent campaign, however; inter-tribal clashes also occurred in the state. In June 2004 the ULFA was responsible for the bombing of a bus in the north-east of Assam, killing five people. In August an explosion at a parade held to commemorate Independence Day killed 16 people, mainly children, as the violence in the state continued. The ULFA was believed to have perpetrated the attack. In October a spate of violence in Assam and neighbouring Nagaland was attributed to the ULFA and the National Democratic Front of Bodoland (NDFB), one of the militant groups operating in the region. In the same month, however, Assam's state Government and the NDFB announced a six-month cease-fire. Despite this, the violence in the state continued. In February 2005 the ULFA offered to hold conditional peace talks with the Government, having rejected an offer of talks made by the Government in December 2004. However, it was thought that the ULFA's conditions for talks would be unacceptable to the Government, owing to the emphasis that they placed upon discussion of the issue of sovereignty, an issue on which the Government had stated it was not prepared to compromise.

Elsewhere in north-eastern India, violence, both intertribal (particularly against ethnic Bengali settlers) and anti-Government, continued in Tripura, Bihar, Mizoram and Manipur. The Chief Minister of Manipur escaped an assassination attempt by suspected separatists in July 2003. In November the daughter of a Naga state minister in Manipur was kidnapped and killed; no one claimed responsibility. In April 2004 talks between Minister of Home Affairs L. K. Advani and various factions of the militant National Liberation Front of Tripura resulted in the announcement of a six-month cease-fire in Tripura which, it was hoped, would act as a prelude to further peace negotiations. Meanwhile,

however, it was reported that five north-eastern separatist groups, including the ULFA, had rejected an offer by the Prime Minister of unconditional peace talks. In late July 2004 the death of an alleged militant led to a series of violent protests and strikes in Manipur. The protesters demanded the repeal of the Armed Forces Special Powers Act (AFSPA), which they claimed condoned the perpetration of human rights abuses by security forces in the state. In October, in advance of talks between the federal Government and the Apunba Lup, an organization of civil groups leading protests in the state, the Government announced that it was willing to consider lifting the application of the AFSPA in Manipur. In February 2005 the United National Liberation Front (UNLF), another rebel group operating in Manipur, offered to hold peace talks with the Government, stating that it was willing to end conflict in the state if the UN was permitted to mediate in the dispute. However, the condition was expected to be rejected by the Government.

In June 2001 a decision by the Union Government to extend the duration of a cease-fire arrangement with Nagaland separatists, which encompassed territories beyond the state borders, provoked condemnation and concerns about the expansionist ambitions of the rebels in the neighbouring states of Manipur, Assam and Arunachal Pradesh, where there were known to be bases of the National Socialist Council of Nagaland—Isak Muivah (NSCN—IM), a rebel organization that had openly advocated the creation of a 'greater Nagaland'. In Manipur, where the collapse of the governing Samata-led coalition had led to the imposition of President's rule in the previous month, there was consolidated political opposition to the move and fierce popular objection, prompting the dispatch of national paramilitary forces to the region to restore order. In late July the national Government agreed to restrict the cease-fire arrangement to the state of Nagaland, angering local political groups in that state. In November 2002 the central Government lifted its ban on the NSCN—IM and agreed to hold unconditional negotiations on the political status of Nagaland. The move allowed the leaders of the separatist group to travel to India for the first time in 37 years. At the end of talks in January 2003 the Naga leaders declared that the separatist insurgency had ended and both sides declared their commitment to continuing the peace process until a permanent peace settlement was reached. The issue of a 'greater Nagaland', however, was avoided. In state elections in February, Congress lost power to the Democratic Alliance of Nagaland. It was reported that rebels from two branches of the NSCN had kidnapped some 300 political workers, mostly Congress supporters, on the day of the election, to prevent them from voting. None the less, turn-out was estimated at nearly 60% of the electorate. In August 2004 the Goverment extended its cease-fire with the NSCN—IM for another year. In December Prime Minister Manmohan Singh and Minister of Home Affairs Shivraj Patil met with leaders of the NSCN—IM, following which the two sides announced that they would soon begin discussions on substantive issues.

In September 1985 there was a temporary improvement in the unstable situation in the Punjab when an election for the state assembly was held, following an agreement between the central Government and the main Sikh party, the Shiromani Akali Dal (SAD). The election was peaceful and resulted in a victory for the SAD, which assumed power after two years of presidential rule. Part of the 1985 agreement was the proposed transfer of Chandigarh, since 1966 the joint capital of the Punjab and Haryana, to the Punjab alone. In return, Haryana was to benefit from the completion of the Sutlej-Yamuna canal, to bring irrigation water from the Punjab to the dry south of the state, and the transfer of several Hindi-speaking border villages from the Punjab to Haryana. Four commissions were established to organize the transfer, but all failed, and the transfer subsequently appeared to have been suspended indefinitely. In January 1986 Sikh extremists re-established a stronghold inside the Golden Temple complex at Amritsar and Hindu–Sikh violence continued throughout the year. In mid-1986 the extremists separated from the ruling moderate SAD (Longowal) and formed several militant factions. In 1987 Rajiv Gandhi reimposed President's rule in the Punjab. Despite the resumption of discussions between the Government and the moderate Sikh leaders, the violence continued. In November 1991 more than 50,000 extra troops were deployed in the Punjab (bringing the total number of army, paramilitary and police forces in the state to about 200,000) as part of an intensification of operations against Sikh separatists in the run-up to the state elections and parliamentary by-elections, which were held in mid-February 1992.

Congress won 12 of the 13 parliamentary seats in the Punjab and gained an overall majority in the state legislature. The elections, which brought to an end five years of presidential rule, were, however, boycotted by the leading factions of the SAD and attracted an extremely low turn-out. The Congress state Government that was formed under the leadership of Beant Singh, therefore, lacked any real credibility. Despite the continuing violence between the separatists and the security forces, the large turn-out in the municipal elections in September (the first in 13 years) afforded some hope that normality was returning to the Punjab. Local council elections, held in January 1993 (the first in 10 years), also attracted a substantial turn-out. The security situation improved steadily in the course of 1993 and political activity revived. In late August 1995, however, violence erupted in the Punjab again when Beant Singh was killed in a car-bomb exploded by suspected Sikh extremists in Chandigarh. This seemed to have been an isolated act of terrorism. The national elections in April/May 1996 were conducted smoothly in the Punjab, and gave the mainstream SAD a convincing victory in the state's parliamentary constituencies. The incumbent Congress administration was routed by an SAD/BJP electoral alliance in state elections held in February 1997; in contrast to the 1992 state elections, turn-out was high. In both the 1998 and 1999 parliamentary elections the SAD again established an electoral alliance with the BJP, and was awarded representation in Vajpayee's consecutive administrations.

In June 2004 the recently elected Government of Andhra Pradesh agreed a cease-fire with the People's War Group, a faction of the Communist Party of India (Marxist-Leninist), which had been waging a sporadic violent campaign in the state since 1980. The rebels demanded the creation of a communist state comprised of tribal areas in Andhra Pradesh, Maharashtra, Orissa, Bihar and Chhattisgarh. In July the 11-year government ban that had been imposed on the organization was removed ahead of planned peace negotiations. In September the People's War Group merged with another militant separatist group, the Maoist Communist Centre, to become the Communist Party of India (Maoist). The first round of peace negotiations was held in Hyderabad in October, and concluded with both sides deciding to continue the dialogue process. However, in January 2005 the rebels announced that they were breaking off peace negotiations in protest at police killings of their members. They accused the state Government of failing to observe the cease-fire agreed in June 2004.

In 1986 India and Bangladesh signed an agreement on measures to prevent 'cross-border terrorism'. In 1988 the two countries established a joint working committee to examine methods of averting the annual devastating floods in the Ganga (Ganges) delta. In 1992 the Indian Government, under the provisions of an accord signed with Bangladesh in 1974, formally leased the Tin Bigha Corridor (a small strip of land covering an area of only 1.5 ha) to Bangladesh for 999 years. India maintained sovereignty over the Corridor, but the lease gave Bangladesh access to its enclaves of Dahagram and Angarpota. The transfer of the Corridor occasioned protests from right-wing quarters in India, who also made an issue over the presence in Delhi and other cities of illegal immigrants from Bangladesh and claimed that the Bangladeshi Government had done little to protect its Hindu minority. In December 1996 India signed an 'historic' treaty with Bangladesh, which was to be in force for 30 years, regarding the sharing of the Ganga waters. The worst fighting between the two countries since 1976 took place in April 2001 on the Bangladeshi border with the Indian state of Meghalaya. Some 16 members of the Indian Border Security Forces and three members of the Bangladesh Rifles were killed. The situation was brought under control, and the two sides entered border negotiations in June as a result of which two joint working groups were established to review the undemarcated section of the border. Relations between India and Bangladesh deteriorated in November 2002 as a result of accusations by India's Deputy Prime Minister and Minister of Home Affairs, L. K. Advani, that al-Qa'ida had increased its activities in Bangladesh since the BNP-led coalition's assumption of power in October 2001. Advani also claimed that Bangladesh was covertly assisting al-Qa'ida and Pakistan's Inter-Services Intelligence Agency, and was providing refuge for Indian separatist groups. The Bangladeshi Government strongly denied the allegations. In January 2003 the Indian Government announced plans to deport, for reasons of security, some 16m. Bangladeshis who it claimed were working and living in India illegally. The Bangladeshi Government rejected the claim as groundless.

India refused to allow some 213 Bengali-speaking individuals onto its territory in late January, claiming that they were illegal immigrants; Bangladesh, however, alleged that they had been expelled from India as part of the Indian Government's anti-Muslim policy. In mid-February the Bangladeshi Minister of Foreign Affairs visited India to discuss the issue of illegal immigration; India expressed dismay at the outcome of the negotiations. Meanwhile, the number of people stranded between the countries' borders increased. In September 2004 senior Indian and Bangladeshi officials held talks in Dhaka concerning security issues and water sharing. While some agreement was reached on water sharing, and the two countries agreed to co-ordinate their border patrols, Bangladesh continued to deny the existence of Indian separatists inside its borders. Relations remained strained into 2005, and tensions were exacerbated in February by India's decision not to attend a planned summit of the South Asian Association for Regional Co-operation (SAARC, see p. 343) in Bangladesh in February owing to security concerns, forcing the postponement of the meeting.

Relations between India and Nepal deteriorated in 1989, when India decided not to renew two bilateral treaties determining trade and transit, insisting that a common treaty covering both issues be negotiated. Nepal refused, stressing the importance of keeping the treaties separate on the grounds that Indo-Nepalese trade issues are negotiable, whereas the right of transit is a recognized right of land-locked countries. India responded by closing most of the transit points through which Nepal's trade is conducted. The dispute was aggravated by Nepal's acquisition of Chinese-made military equipment, which, according to India, violated the Treaty of Peace and Friendship of 1950. However, in June 1990 India and Nepal signed an agreement restoring trade relations and reopening the transit points. Chandra Shekhar visited Kathmandu in February 1991 (the first official visit to Nepal by an Indian Prime Minister since 1977), shortly after it was announced that the first free elections in Nepal were to be held in May. In June 1997 the Indian Prime Minister, Inder Kumar Gujral, made a visit to Nepal and announced the opening of a transit route through north-east India between Nepal and Bangladesh. Gujral and the Nepalese Prime Minister, Lokendra Bahadur Chand, also agreed that there should be a review of the 1950 treaty between the two countries. In February 2005 relations with Nepal were seriously affected when the Nepalese king orchestrated a coup, dismissing the Government and declaring a state of emergency in the country. It was feared that a significant number of Maoist rebels from Nepal might infiltrate its border with India. India subsequently ceased provision of all military aid to Nepal.

Relations with Pakistan had deteriorated in the late 1970s and early 1980s, owing to Pakistan's potential capability for the development of nuclear weapons and as a result of major US deliveries of armaments to Pakistan. The Indian Government believed that such deliveries would upset the balance of power in the region and precipitate an 'arms race'. Pakistan's President, Gen. Mohammad Zia ul-Haq, visited India in 1985, when he and Rajiv Gandhi announced their mutual commitment not to attack each other's nuclear installations and to negotiate the sovereignty of the disputed Siachen glacier region in Kashmir. Pakistan continued to demand a settlement of the Kashmir problem in accordance with earlier UN resolutions, prescribing a plebiscite under the auspices of the UN in the two parts of the state, now divided between India and Pakistan. India argued that the problem should be settled in accordance with the Shimla Agreement of 1972, which required that all Indo-Pakistani disputes be resolved through bilateral negotiations. The Indian decision to construct a barrage on the River Jhelum in Jammu and Kashmir, in an alleged violation of the 1960 Indus Waters Treaty, also created concern in Pakistan. In December 1988 Rajiv Gandhi visited Islamabad for discussions with Pakistan's Prime Minister, Benazir Bhutto. The resulting agreements included a formal pledge not to attack each other's nuclear installations. Relations reached a crisis in late 1989, when the outlawed Jammu and Kashmir Liberation Front (JKLF) and several other militant Muslim groups intensified their campaigns of civil unrest, strikes and terrorism, demanding an independent Kashmir or unification with Pakistan. The Indian Government dispatched troops to the region and placed the entire Srinagar valley under curfew. Pakistan denied India's claim that the militants were trained and armed in Pakistan-held Kashmir (known as Azad Kashmir). In January 1990 Jammu and Kashmir was placed under Governor's rule, and in July under President's rule. Tension was eased in December, following discussions between the Ministers of External Affairs of both countries. Violence between the Indian security forces and the militant groups, however, continued during 1991–92. Throughout 1993 and in early 1994, the Government's approach to the Kashmir crisis was a combination of a tough military policy and generally fruitless attempts to engage in dialogue. In December 1994 Pakistan was successful in securing the passage of a resolution condemning reported human rights abuses by Indian security forces in Kashmir at a summit meeting of the Organization of the Islamic Conference (OIC, see p. 327). (In the same month Pakistan's decision to close down its consulate in Mumbai, amid claims of Indian support for acts of terrorism in Karachi, provided a further indication of the growing rift between the two countries.) By 1996 the total death toll resulting from the conflict in Jammu and Kashmir, including civilians, security force personnel and militants, was estimated at up to 20,000. The situation in Kashmir improved somewhat, however, when elections for the national parliamentary seats were held in the troubled state shortly after the general election in April–May 1996. Following the successful holding of elections to the Lok Sabha, state elections were conducted in Jammu and Kashmir in September (the first to be held since 1987) and attracted a turn-out of more than 50%, despite being boycotted by the majority of the separatist groups and being dismissed as a sham by the Pakistani Government. The moderate Jammu and Kashmir National Conference, led by Dr Farooq Abdullah, won the majority of seats in the state assembly, and, on assuming power, immediately offered to instigate talks with the separatist leaders.

Meanwhile, in June 1994 the Indian army had begun to deploy a new missile, named the Prithvi, which had the capacity to reach most of Pakistan. While the 'arms race' between the two countries continued, with claims on both sides concerning the other's missile programmes, talks (which had been suspended since 1994) were resumed in March 1997, both at official and at ministerial level. Tension increased in September when a large-scale outbreak of artillery exchanges along the Line of Control (LoC) resulted in about 40 civilian deaths. After a hiatus of more than one year (during which time both countries carried out controversial nuclear test explosions—see above), Indo-Pakistani talks at foreign secretary level regarding Kashmir and other issues were resumed in Islamabad in October 1998. In February 1999 relations appeared to improve considerably when Prime Minister Vajpayee made an historic bus journey (inaugurating the first passenger bus service between India and Pakistan) over the border to Lahore. Following his welcome by the Pakistani Prime Minister, Mohammad Nawaz Sharif, the two leaders held a summit meeting (the first to be conducted in Pakistan for 10 years), at which they signed the Lahore Declaration, which, with its pledges regarding peace and nuclear security, sought to allay world-wide fears of a nuclear 'flash-point' in South Asia, and committed the two sides to working towards better relations and to implementing a range of confidence-building measures. The contentious subject of Jammu and Kashmir was, however, largely avoided.

Despite the apparent *rapprochement* between India and Pakistan, in April 1999 both countries carried out separate tests on their latest missiles, which were capable of carrying nuclear warheads. In early May the situation deteriorated drastically when the Indian army discovered that Islamist guerrilla groups, reinforced by regular Pakistani troops, had occupied strategic positions on the Indian side of the LoC in the Kargil area of Kashmir. Air-strikes launched by the Indian air force at the end of the month failed to dislodge the so-called 'infiltrators', and the army was forced to wage an expensive and lengthy campaign, during which more than 480 Indian soldiers were killed and two Indian military aircraft were shot down. In mid-July, however, Indian military dominance combined with US diplomatic pressure led to a Pakistani withdrawal. In August there was renewed tension when India shot down a Pakistani naval reconnaissance aircraft near Pakistan's border with Gujarat, killing all 16 personnel on board; Pakistan retaliated the following day by opening fire on Indian military aircraft in the same area.

In April 2000 there were indications that the Indian Government was willing to re-establish dialogue with Kashmiri militants. Leaders of the All-Party Hurriyat Conference (APHC), an organization that, to an extent, acted as the political voice for some of the militant groups, were released in April and May. In July one of the main militant groups, the Hizbul Mujahideen, declared a three-month cease-fire. The gesture obtained a quick and positive response from the Indian Government: the Indian

Army suspended all offensive operations against the Kashmiri militants for the first time in 11 years. Other militant groups, however, denounced the cessation of hostilities as a betrayal and continued their violent campaign, in an attempt to disrupt the peace process. The Hizbul Mujahideen ended the cease-fire at the beginning of August because the Indian Government opposed a tripartite discussion including representatives of Pakistan. As a result, Pakistan appeared rather moderate and India somewhat intransigent. Vajpayee accused Pakistan of orchestrating the events, of encouraging divisions among militant leaders and of turning the Kashmir issue into a pan-Islamic movement.

Following the collapse of the cease-fire, violence in the region intensified. In November the Chief Minister of Jammu and Kashmir, Dr Farooq Abdullah, announced the instigation of a judicial inquiry into the killing of 36 unarmed Sikhs in March and the killing of five alleged militants a few days later by Indian security forces. In the same month the Indian Government declared the suspension of combat operations against Kashmiri militants during the Muslim holy month of Ramadan. The unilateral cease-fire began at the end of November (and was subsequently extended, at intervals, until the end of May); Indian security forces were authorized to retaliate if fired upon. The majority of national parties and foreign governments supported the cessation of hostilities, although the Pakistani authorities described the cease-fire as 'meaningless' without simultaneous constructive dialogue. The APHC welcomed the development and offered to enter negotiations with Pakistani authorities in order to prepare for tripartite discussions. The Hizbul Mujahideen and other militant groups, however, rejected the offer and continued their campaign of violence, extending their activities as far as the Red Fort in Old Delhi, where three people were shot dead in December. In the same month Pakistan extended an invitation to the APHC to participate in joint preparations for the establishment of tripartite negotiations. Although Abdul Ghani Lone, a leading member of the APHC, was permitted to make a private visit to Islamabad in November, passport applications for a delegation of leaders were subsequently refused. In mid-January 2001 the Indian High Commissioner to Pakistan visited Gen. Musharraf. This meeting signified the first high-level contact since the military coup in Pakistan in 1999. The two officials urged an early resumption of negotiations on the Kashmir question. At the end of May the Government announced the end of its unilateral cease-fire; more than 1,000 people were estimated to have been killed in violence related to the crisis in the region since the cease-fire was first announced in November 2000.

Relations with Pakistan appeared to improve following the earthquake in Gujarat in January 2001, when Pakistan offered humanitarian relief to India and the leaders of the two countries thus established contact. In May Vajpayee issued an unexpected invitation to Gen. Musharraf to attend bilateral negotiations in Agra in July. However, hopes for a significant breakthrough on the issue of Kashmir were frustrated by the failure of the two leaders to agree to a joint declaration at the conclusion of the dialogue; the divergent views of the two sides on the priority issue in the dispute (cross-border terrorism according to India, and Kashmiri self-determination in the opinion of Pakistan) appeared to be more firmly entrenched than ever. Violence increased in the region following the disappointment engendered by the meeting, and in August the Indian Government extended its official 'disturbed area' designation (invoking the 1990 AFSPA) to cover all districts of the state of Jammu and Kashmir (only Ladakh was unaffected). Tension with Pakistan was heightened considerably following a guerrilla-style attack on the state assembly building in Srinagar on 1 October. An estimated 38 people (including two of the four assailants) were killed and around 70 were wounded in the attack and in the subsequent confrontation with security forces. The Indian Government attributed responsibility for the attack to the Pakistan-based Jaish-e-Mohammed and Lashkar-e-Taiba groups. Tensions were exacerbated later in the month when Gen. Musharraf rejected official Indian requests to ban the activities of the organizations in Pakistan, although he did publicly condemn the attack.

On 13 December 2001 five armed assailants gained access to the grounds of the Union Parliament in New Delhi and attempted to launch an apparent suicide attack on the Parliament building. Although no parliamentary deputies were hurt in the attack, nine people (including a number of policemen, some security officials and a groundsman) were killed and some

25 were injured in the botched assault; the five assailants were also killed in the attack. The Indian authorities again attributed responsibility for the attack to the Jaish-e-Mohammed and Lashkar-e-Taiba groups, and suggested that the five assailants appeared to be of Pakistani origin. Pakistan, which had been among the many countries to express immediate condemnation of the attack (which was popularly described as an assault on democracy), now demanded to see concrete proof to support the allegations made by the Indian Government, while the US Administration urged the Indian authorities to exercise restraint in their response. Tensions between India and Pakistan continued to mount when Mohammed Afzal, a member of Jaish-e-Mohammed arrested in Kashmir on suspicion of complicity in the incident, admitted his involvement and alleged publicly that Pakistani security and intelligence agencies had provided support to those directly responsible for the attack. India recalled its High Commissioner from Islamabad and announced that overground transport services between the two countries would be suspended from 1 January 2002. As positions were reinforced with troops and weapons (including missiles) on both sides of the LoC, there was considerable international concern that such brinkmanship might propel the two countries (each with nuclear capabilities) into renewed armed conflict. Mindful of the potential detriment to security at Pakistan's border with Afghanistan that could result from escalated conflict in Kashmir, the USA applied increased pressure on the beleaguered Pakistani Government (already facing vociferous domestic opposition to its accommodation of US activities in Afghanistan) to adopt a more conciliatory attitude towards India's security concerns, and in late December the Pakistani authorities followed the US Government's lead in 'freezing' the assets of the two groups held responsible for the attack on India. The leaders of the two groups were later detained by the Pakistani authorities (who arrested some 80 suspected militants in the last week of December 2001), but, despite an evident satisfaction at this development, the Indian Government continued to dismiss much of the Pakistani response as superficial and demanded that the two leaders be extradited (together with 20 other named Pakistan-based militants) to stand trial in India. However, in December 2002 Pakistan freed one of the leaders, Maulana Masood Azhar, from house arrest. Later that month a special court established under POTA (see above) convicted three Kashmiri Muslims—Mohammed Afzal, Shaukat Hussain and S. A. R. Geelani—of organizing the attack on the Union Parliament and sentenced them to death. Two of the accused were reportedly members of Jaish-e-Mohammed; the third was a member of the JKLF. Navjot Sandhu, the wife of Shaukat Hussain, was sentenced to five years' imprisonment on charges of criminal conspiracy. (A High Court, however, overturned the convictions of Geelani and Sandhu following an appeal in October 2003.)

It had been hoped that tensions between the two countries might be defused by renewed dialogue between Vajpayee and Musharraf at a SAARC summit meeting convened in Nepal in the first week of January 2002, but contacts between the two men were minimal, and troops on both sides of the LoC continued to exchange gunfire in the days following the conference. However, on 12 January Musharraf yielded to relentless international pressure by publicly condemning the activities of militant extremists based in Pakistan and announcing the introduction of a broad range of measures to combat terrorist activity and religious zealotry, including the proscription of five extremist organizations (among them the Jaish-e-Mohammed and the Lashkar-e-Taiba). Within two days the Pakistani authorities claimed to have closed almost 500 offices used by the five organizations and to have arrested some 1,400 suspected activists, prompting considerable international praise for the initiative. An armed attack by four suspected Islamist militants on a US cultural centre in Kolkata (Calcutta) on 22 January, in which five Indian policeman were killed and more than 20 were injured, placed relations between the two countries under renewed strain when the Indian authorities attempted to link the unidentified assailants (who escaped after the attack) to the Pakistani intelligence services. However, it was hoped that reports published in late January, which indicated that the number of terrorist incidents in Jammu and Kashmir had halved since the introduction of Pakistan's new counter-insurgency measures earlier in the month, would help foster a more substantial improvement in future relations between the two countries. Tensions between the two countries rose again, following a suspected Islamist militant attack on an army camp

in Jammu and Kashmir in mid-May, in which 34 people were killed, including 19 civilians. India identified the gunmen as Pakistani nationals and a few days later requested the withdrawal of Pakistan's High Commissioner to India. The two countries appeared to be on the brink of war again as positions were reinforced with troops and weapons on both sides of the LoC. Exchanges of gunfire across the LoC intensified. Indo-Pakistani relations deteriorated further following the assassination of Abdul Ghani Lone, the leader of the APHC, on 21 May, by suspected Islamist militants. As a result of international efforts to ease tensions between the two neighbours, in June India withdrew five naval ships from patrol of the coast of Pakistan and allowed Pakistani civilian aircraft to enter its airspace, in response to Pakistani pledges to halt cross-border infiltration. In mid-October the Minister of Defence stated that India would withdraw a large number of troops from the international border with Pakistan; the number of troops along the LoC would remain unchanged, however. Pakistan responded by withdrawing a portion of its troops.

Meanwhile, the crisis between India and Pakistan and the related militant activity within Kashmir adversely affected the Indian Government's relations with the APHC. In mid-July the Chief Minister of Jammu and Kashmir announced that scientific tests had shown that five men killed by Indian security forces in March 2000 had been local civilians and not, as maintained at the time, militants responsible for the murder of 36 unarmed Sikhs (see above). In early August 2002 it was announced that state elections would be held in Jammu and Kashmir in four phases, from mid-September. The APHC declared that it would boycott the election, regarding it as meaningless unless a referendum on independence was held first. In September the state Minister of Law and Parliamentary Affairs of Jammu and Kashmir was assassinated by suspected militant Islamists intent on disrupting the election campaign and poll. Violence continued throughout the election period. However, the elections took place in late September–early October; overall, voter turn-out reached 44%. No single party won an outright majority: the Jammu and Kashmir National Conference secured 28 seats, Congress won 20 seats and the regional People's Democratic Party (PDP) won 16 seats. The APHC rejected the result and demanded that a plebiscite be established; the Pakistani Government dismissed the election as a 'sham' and 'farcical'. Violence overshadowed the polls: at least 730 people had reportedly been killed since the announcement of the elections. Congress and the PDP were invited to form a coalition government; however, the national Government had to assume direct control over Jammu and Kashmir after the two parties were unable to come to a power-sharing arrangement by 17 October, the expiry date of the outgoing assembly. Eventually, in late October Congress and the PDP reached a compromise: it was agreed that PDP leader Mufti Mohammed Sayeed would be Chief Minister for the first three years, followed by local Congress president Ghulam Nabi Azad for the next three years. The coalition Government was inaugurated in early November. Kashmiri separatists dismissed Sayeed's policy of reconciliation by continuing their violent campaign. Nevertheless, as promised at the end of October, Sayeed authorized the release of several political prisoners charged with 'non-serious' crimes. The release of Yasin Malik, the leader of the JKLF detained under the POTA in March, was the most significant. The state Government also pledged to disband the Special Operations Group of the police, which had been accused in the past of serious human rights violations. In late November suspected Islamist militants attacked two Hindu temples in Jammu, resulting in the deaths of 14 people. The Indian authorities attributed responsibility for the attack to the Lashkar-e-Taiba group.

Indo-Pakistani relations deteriorated in early 2003. Tensions were exacerbated by India's latest set of 'routine' ballistic-missile tests, the violence in Kashmir and India's new military agreement with Russia (see below). In late January India ordered four officials at Pakistan's High Commission in New Delhi to leave the country for 'indulging in activities incompatible with their official status', a euphemism for spying. Pakistan reacted by expelling four officials at the Indian High Commission in Islamabad. In early February India expelled Pakistan's acting High Commissioner, Jalil Abbas Jilani, accusing him of funding Kashmiri separatist groups; four other Pakistani officials were charged with spying and expelled. Pakistan retaliated by ordering India's acting High Commissioner, Sudhir Vyas, and four colleagues to leave, for allegedly spying. In March separatist violence in Jammu and Kashmir escalated. The killing of 24 Kashmiri Hindus, including women and children, in a remote village south of Srinagar by suspected Islamists at the end of the month, provoked widespread condemnation and was a set-back to Sayeed's reconciliation programme. Tensions between India and Pakistan, meanwhile, increased after Pakistan responded to India's decision to conduct 'routine' missile tests without advance warning by carrying out a set of its own tests. Nevertheless, in mid-April, during a visit to Jammu and Kashmir, Vajpayee offered to enter dialogue with Pakistan; the Pakistani Prime Minister, Zafarullah Khan Jamali, welcomed the decision and formally invited Vajpayee 10 days later to visit Pakistan. Commentators initially attributed Vajpayee's change in tone to diplomatic pressure from the United Kingdom and USA to begin peace negotiations with Pakistan. However, it soon transpired that the USA had not been notified in advance of the Indian Prime Minister's initiative; indeed, Vajpayee had hardly consulted his Cabinet. In early May the Indian and Pakistani premiers agreed to restore diplomatic relations and civil aviation links. Two months later the bus service between the Pakistani city of Lahore and New Delhi was restored. India, however, continued to insist on a complete cessation of cross-border infiltration as a precondition for peace talks.

Meanwhile, violence in Jammu and Kashmir persisted. The security situation worsened in July 2003: militant activity, including suicide attacks, and the exchange of gunfire across the LoC increased. The violence continued during Vajpayee's three-day visit to Srinagar to attend a meeting of the Inter-State Council in late August. The assassination of the militant leader Ghazi Baba at the end of the month provoked a surge in violence in September. In mid-August, meanwhile, Pakistani President Musharraf proposed a cease-fire along the LoC, but wanted India to reciprocate by reducing its armed personnel in the Srinagar valley and by ending the alleged atrocities committed by the Indian armed forces. India refused Musharraf's offer and continued to hold Pakistan-based militants responsible for the rise in attacks. In early September the APHC openly split after the new leadership of Maulvi Abbas Ansari, the first Shi'a Muslim to chair the Hurriyat Conference, was challenged by a significant faction, which proceeded to elect former Chairman Syed Ali Shah Geelani instead. In the mean time, the escalating violence seriously endangered the slight revival in the tourist industry that the state had experienced since May.

In October 2003 the Indian Minister of External Affairs, Yashwant Sinha, announced 12 confidence-building measures to improve and normalize relations with Pakistan, including offers to enter another round of talks to restore civil aviation links, to introduce more transport links (including a bus service between the capitals of the disputed region across the LoC), to resume full sporting contacts and to enter dialogue with separatist politicians in Kashmir. Sinha emphasized, however, that no direct talks on Kashmir between India and Pakistan would take place until the latter ceased cross-border infiltration by Islamist militants. Pakistan issued a cautious welcome to most of the proposals, while declaring that bus travellers in Kashmir would need UN travel documents, but was disappointed that there was no offer of a meeting. On 23 November Pakistani Prime Minister Jamali announced a unilateral cease-fire along the LoC, to begin at midnight two days later (on the Muslim festival of Id). Jamali also responded to Vajpayee's offer to discuss transport links by proposing an additional bus service between the Pakistani city of Lahore and the Indian city of Amritsar. India reciprocated the gesture (but reserved the right to fire at so-called 'infiltrators') and offered to extend the cease-fire across the Actual Ground Position Line in Siachen as well as across the international border. Pakistan agreed to the proposal and at midnight on 25–26 November a cease-fire came into effect. In mid-December the chances of a peace agreement between India and Pakistan improved after President Musharraf declared that Pakistan was prepared to abandon a long-standing demand for a UN-sponsored plebiscite for the Kashmiri people; India welcomed the initiative. At the same time, Indian and Pakistani officials signed a three-year agreement on the restoration from mid-January 2004 of a passenger and freight train service between New Delhi and Lahore. Direct aviation links were resumed on 1 January 2004. In late December 2003 it was reported that, since the implementation of the cease-fire, separatist-related violence in Jammu and Kashmir had declined.

At the ground-breaking SAARC summit meeting in Islamabad in early January 2004, Musharraf assured Vajpayee that he would not permit any territory under Pakistan's control to be used to support terrorism; in return Vajpayee agreed to begin negotiations on all bilateral issues, including Kashmir, in February. A round of 'fruitful' talks between L. K. Advani and a delegation of the APHC took place in New Delhi in January, followed by a second round in March. Meanwhile, however, Islamist militants who were unhappy with what they perceived as a betrayal by Musharraf continued their violent campaign. Indian and Pakistani senior officials opened discussions in Islamabad in mid-February, when a timetable for future dialogue was established. The APHC called for a boycott of the general election, held in April–May, and a series of violent attacks directed at all politicians campaigning in Jammu and Kashmir over the election period resulted in several deaths. In April a grenade attack on a political rally in the town of Uri killed 12 people and injured 25, including two state ministers. Overall electoral turn-out in Kashmir was 35%, although this declined to less than 19% in Srinagar. While many had been deterred from voting by militant intimidation, some claimed that they had been forced to vote by members of the security forces. Following the election the state experienced its worst incidence of violence since April 2003 when a land-mine exploded under a bus carrying Indian soldiers on the Srinagar–Jammu highway, killing at least 33 people, including 18 civilian relatives of the soldiers. The Hizbul Mujahideen claimed responsibility for the attack. In June several rounds of discussions took place between Indian and Pakistani officials in New Delhi. In a joint statement issued at the end of the month both sides stressed their renewed commitment to reaching a negotiated final settlement on the Kashmir issue and agreed to restore their diplomatic missions to full strength and, in principle, to reopen their respective consulates in Mumbai and Karachi. An agreement was also reached that each country would, in future, notify the other of any forthcoming missile tests. In September India and Pakistan held their first, official, ministerial-level talks in over three years in New Delhi. As a result, the two sides agreed to implement a series of confidence-building measures, including the restoration of bilateral transport links.

In November 2004, ahead of his first visit to Kashmir since becoming Prime Minister, Manmohan Singh ordered a 'substantial' reduction in the number of Indian troops deployed in the state, a move welcomed by Pakistan. Later in that month Singh met with his Pakistani counterpart, Shaukat Aziz, in New Delhi. In the following month further high-level talks on the Kashmir issue were held in Islamabad, but with no tangible progress. In January–February 2005 an eight-phase polling process took place in Jammu and Kashmir, as the state held its first municipal elections in 27 years. Meanwhile, tensions resurfaced between India and Pakistan in early 2005, with each side accusing the other of violating the ongoing cease-fire along the LoC. However, in February, following talks between the Indian and Pakistani ministers responsible for foreign affairs, the two countries agreed to open a bus service across the LoC, linking Srinagar with Muzaffarabad. Despite militant threats of disruption, and several attacks on the proposed route, the service opened in early April 2005. Plans were also announced to reopen the consulates in Mumbai and Karachi. In mid-April Musharraf travelled to India for the first time since 2001 and met with Manmohan Singh in New Delhi for further peace talks; the two countries subsequently issued a statement referring to the peace process as 'irreversible' and agreeing to improve trade and transport links over the LoC.

Since 1983 India's relations with Sri Lanka have been dominated by conflicts between the island's Sinhalese and Tamil communities, in which India has sought to arbitrate. In July 1987 Rajiv Gandhi and the Sri Lankan President, Junius Jayewardene, signed an accord aimed at settling the conflict. An Indian Peace-Keeping Force (IPKF) was dispatched to Sri Lanka but encountered considerable resistance from the Tamil separatist guerrillas. Following the gradual implementation of the peace accord, the IPKF troops completed their withdrawal in March 1990. Violence flared up again, however, and the flow of Sri Lankan refugees into Tamil Nadu increased considerably. By late 1991 the number of Sri Lankans living in refugee camps in the southern Indian state was estimated at more than 200,000. The assassination of Rajiv Gandhi in May 1991, by members of the LTTE, completed India's disenchantment with the latter organization. Measures were subsequently taken by the state Government in Tamil Nadu to suppress LTTE activity within the state, and also to begin the process of repatriating refugees. The repatriation programme (allegedly conducted on a voluntary basis) proved a slow and difficult process. In May 1992 the LTTE was officially banned in India. In December 1998 the Indian Prime Minister and Sri Lankan President signed a bilateral free-trade agreement, which finally came into effect in March 2000.

During 1981 there was an improvement in India's relations with the People's Republic of China. Both countries agreed to attempt to find an early solution to their Himalayan border dispute and to seek to normalize relations, and a number of working groups were subsequently established. In February 1991 a major breakthrough occurred when a draft protocol for 1991/92, including the proposed resumption of border trade between the two countries for the first time in three decades, was signed. All six border posts had been closed since the brief border war in 1962. In December 1991 the Chinese Prime Minister, Li Peng, made an official visit to India (the first such visit to India by a Chinese Prime Minister for 31 years), during which a memorandum on the resumption of bilateral border trade was signed. Bilateral border trade was actually resumed between India and China in July 1992. Sino-Indian relations were further strengthened as a result of a three-day visit to India conducted by the Chinese President, Jiang Zemin, in November 1996 (the first visit by a Chinese Head of State to India). Despite the gradual improvement in relations, however, India has frequently indicated that it is unhappy with the nuclear asymmetry between the two countries and with what it perceives as China's willingness to transfer missiles and missile technology to Pakistan. Sino-Indian relations deteriorated following India's 1998 nuclear tests, partly because China believed that India was using a fabricated threat from China to justify its actions. In June 1999 the Indian Minister of External Affairs visited Beijing to restore Sino-Indian dialogue. During border negotiations in November 2000, India and China exchanged detailed maps of the middle sector of the Line of Actual Control: a significant step towards resolving differences. In April 2003 the Indian Minister of Defence paid a week-long visit to Beijing to discuss outstanding bilateral issues, including China's support for Pakistan and Chinese observation posts in the Bay of Bengal. Prime Minister Vajpayee made a state visit to China in June 2003 (the first by an Indian premier in 10 years), during which a number of agreements were signed, the most significant being India's official recognition of Chinese sovereignty over Tibet. China also agreed to trade with the north-eastern Indian state of Sikkim, thus implicitly acknowledging India's control of that area. The two countries appointed special representatives to discuss the border disputes that had led to the 1962 war. In January 2005 India and China held their first-ever strategic dialogue, in New Delhi, agreeing, *inter alia*, to try to resolve their boundary dispute in a fair and mutually satisfactory manner. The dialogue affirmed the ongoing improvement in Sino-Indian relations.

In October 2004 the Chairman of Myanmar's ruling body, the State Peace and Development Council, Field Marshal Than Shwe, paid the first visit to India by a Myanma head of state in 24 years. The visit was illustrative of improving relations between the two countries, necessary if India was to combat successfully the problem of insurgents in north-eastern India establishing bases across the border in Myanmar.

Prior to its disintegration in December 1991, the USSR was a major contributor of economic and military assistance to India. In early 1992 both Russia and Ukraine agreed to maintain arms supplies to India, and in February an Indo-Russian trade and payments protocol was signed. The President of Russia, Boris Yeltsin, made an official visit to India in 1993, during which he signed an Indo-Russian Treaty of Friendship and Co-operation. In October 1996 India and Russia signed a defence co-operation agreement (later extended to 2010), and in December India signed a US $1,800m. contract to purchase 40 fighter aircraft from Russia. In June 1998 Russia defied a Group of Eight (G-8) ban on exporting nuclear technology to India by agreeing to supply the latter with two nuclear reactors. In November 1999 India and Russia signed a defence agreement regarding their joint manufacture of military aircraft and submarines. In October 2000 the newly elected Russian President, Vladimir Putin, visited India. The two countries signed a declaration of 'strategic partnership', which involved co-operation on defence, economic matters and international terrorism issues. India signed a contract to purchase 50 Sukhoi-30 fighter aircraft from Russia, with a licence to manufacture around 150 more. The agreement, reportedly worth more than $3,000m., was finalized in December. In February 2001 India agreed to buy 310 T-90 Russian tanks, at an estimated cost of $700m. In June the two

countries successfully conducted tests of a new, jointly developed supersonic cruise missile; the PJ-10 was thought to be unique in the world. In November it was announced that Russia had been awarded a contract to build a nuclear power plant in Tamil Nadu. At the Conference on Interaction and Confidence-Building Measures in Asia in June 2002 at Almaty, Kazakhstan, Putin attempted to act as a mediator between India and Pakistan, without success. In January 2003 India signed an agreement with Russia to lease four Tu22 long-range nuclear bombers and two nuclear-capable submarines and to pay for the restoration of a Russian aircraft carrier. The contract would significantly improve India's ability to deliver its nuclear warheads.

Following the collapse of the USSR, a long-time ally of India, in December 1991, the Indian Government sought to strengthen its ties with the USA. In January 1992 discussions were held between Indian and US officials regarding military co-operation and ambitious joint defence projects. However, the USA remains concerned about the risks of nuclear proliferation in the South Asia region as a whole, and has yet to achieve a mutual understanding with India on this issue (India has repeatedly refused to sign the Nuclear Non-Proliferation Treaty—NPT). In addition, despite India's recent adoption of a programme of economic liberalization, conflicts over trade and related issues have arisen between the USA and India. During a visit to India by the US Secretary of Defense in January 1995, a 'landmark' agreement on defence and security co-operation was signed by the two countries.

In 1992 India established diplomatic relations with Israel. Relations between India and Israel strengthened following the BJP's rise to power in India in the late 1990s, with both countries embarking on a programme of security and technological co-operation. The USA appeared to sanction the improvement in relations by formally approving the sale of Israel's Phalcon airborne radar system to India in August 2003 (the USA having a veto over the countries to which Israel could sell defence systems based on US technology). The Israeli Prime Minister, Ariel Sharon, made a visit to India in September, the first ever by an Israeli premier. This was followed by a visit by the Israeli Deputy Prime Minister and Minister of Foreign Affairs, Silvan Shalom, in February 2004, during which the two countries discussed further security, political and economic co-operation. Despite the strengthening of relations, however, India frequently expressed its disapproval of Israeli military action against Palestinians. In December 2004 a four-day visit to India by the Israeli Vice-Prime Minister, Ehud Olmert, served to consolidate bilateral relations, following speculation that the assumption of power by Congress following India's general election in mid-2004 would lead to a deterioration in the relationship. In the aftermath of the election Congress's allies, the Left Front, had called for the UPA Government to sever trade and defence ties with Israel.

In mid-1996, in a move that provoked widespread international condemnation, India decided not to be party to the Comprehensive Test Ban Treaty (CTBT), which it had earlier supported, so long as the existing nuclear powers were unwilling to commit themselves to a strict timetable for full nuclear disarmament. In May 1998 India's controversial decision to explode five nuclear test devices and to claim thereby its new status as a nuclear-weapons state, led to a rapid escalation in the 'arms race' with Pakistan (which responded with its own series of nuclear tests). The USA, with limited support from other countries, subsequently imposed economic sanctions on both India and Pakistan until such time as they had signed the NPT and the CTBT and taken steps to reverse their nuclear programmes. Immediately after the tests, India announced a self-imposed moratorium on further testing and launched itself into intense diplomatic activity. During 1998–99 the USA lifted some of the sanctions imposed on India and Pakistan, whilst reiterating its requests that the two countries sign the CTBT and exercise restraint in their respective missile programmes to ensure peace in South Asia. In mid-January 2001 India successfully test-fired its Agni-II intermediate ballistic missile for the second time. Vajpayee declared that the test was necessary for India's national security; however, the move was criticized by Pakistan, Japan and the United Kingdom and caused concern in China.

The US President, Bill Clinton, made an official six-day state visit to India in March 2000 (the first by a US President since 1978), which was widely considered as the opening of a new era in bilateral relations. President Clinton appeared to endorse India's opinion that the Kashmir issue was a local matter and did not directly concern the international community. In September Vajpayee visited the USA. He continued to assert that consensus among Indian ministers had to be reached before a decision on the CTBT could be made. In late September 2001 US President George W. Bush announced an end to the military and economic sanctions imposed against India and Pakistan in 1998. The decision followed the renewal of high-level military contacts between the USA and India in April and May and Pakistan's co-operation with US counter-terrorism initiatives against neighbouring Afghanistan in the aftermath of the terrorist attacks carried out on US mainland targets on 11 September. During a visit to India in November, US Secretary of Defense Donald Rumsfeld discussed further defence co-operation possibilities with the Indian authorities and announced that the US Government was prepared to resume the sale of specific defence materials to India. In July 2003 India declined a request by the USA to contribute peace-keeping troops to the US-led forces in Iraq. In September 2004 the USA agreed to ease its export controls on materials intended for India's nuclear and civilian space programmes. The agreement preceded a meeting between US President Bush and Prime Minister Manmohan Singh in New York, USA.

Government

India is a federal republic. Legislative power is vested in Parliament, consisting of the President and two Houses. The Council of States (Rajya Sabha) has 245 members, most of whom are indirectly elected by the state assemblies for six years (one-third retiring every two years), the remainder being nominated by the President for six years. The House of the People (Lok Sabha) has 543 elected members, serving for five years (subject to dissolution). A small number of members of the Lok Sabha may be nominated by the President to represent the Anglo-Indian community, while the 543 members are directly elected by universal adult suffrage in single-member constituencies. The President is a constitutional Head of State, elected for five years by an electoral college comprising elected members of both Houses of Parliament and the state legislatures. The President exercises executive power on the advice of the Council of Ministers, which is responsible to Parliament. The President appoints the Prime Minister and, on the latter's recommendation, other ministers.

India contains 28 self-governing states, each with a governor (appointed by the President for five years), a legislature (elected for five years) and a council of ministers headed by the chief minister. Bihar, Jammu and Kashmir, Karnataka, Maharashtra and Uttar Pradesh have bicameral legislatures, the other 23 state legislatures being unicameral. Each state has its own legislative, executive and judicial machinery, corresponding to that of the Indian Union. In the event of the failure of constitutional government in a state, presidential rule can be imposed by the Union. There are also six Union Territories and one National Capital Territory, administered by lieutenant-governors or administrators, all of whom are appointed by the President. The territories of Delhi and Pondicherry also have elected chief ministers and state assemblies.

Defence

At 1 August 2004 the total strength of India's armed forces was 1,325,000: an army of 1,100,000, a navy of 55,000 and an air force of 170,000. Active paramilitary forces totalled 1,089,700 men, including the 174,000-strong Border Security Force (based mainly in the troubled state of Jammu and Kashmir). Military service is voluntary, but, under the amended Constitution, it is the fundamental duty of every citizen to perform national service when called upon. The proposed defence budget for 2004/05 was estimated at Rs 891,364m. (equivalent to 18.7% of total expenditure).

Economic Affairs

In 2003, according to estimates by the World Bank, India's gross national income (GNI), measured at average 2001–03 prices, was US $593,482m., equivalent to $530 per head (or $2,880 per head on an international purchasing-power parity basis). During 1990–2003, it was estimated, the population increased at an average annual rate of 1.7%, while gross domestic product (GDP) per head increased, in real terms, by an average of 3.8%. Overall GDP increased, in real terms, at an average annual rate of 5.6% in 1990–2003; the rate of growth was 4.6% in 2002/03 and 8.2% in 2003/04. In 2004/05 GDP growth was 6.9%, according to official sources.

Agriculture (including forestry and fishing) contributed 22.7% of GDP in 2002/03. About 59.2% of the economically active population were employed in agriculture in 2001. The principal

cash crops are cotton (cotton accounted for 3.9% of total export earnings in 2003/04), tea, rice, spices, sugar cane and groundnuts. Coffee and jute production are also important. The average annual growth rate in the output of the agricultural sector was 2.5% in 1990–2003; agricultural GDP contracted by 5.2% in 2002/03, but grew by 6.6% in 2003/04. It was feared that a weak monsoon would have an adverse impact upon growth in the agricultural sector in 2004/05.

Industry (including mining, manufacturing, power and construction) contributed an estimated 26.6% of GDP in 2002/03. According to World Bank estimates, about 12.9% of the working population were employed in the industrial sector in 1995. Industrial GDP increased at an average annual rate of 5.5% in 1990–2003; the rate of growth of the GDP of the industrial sector reached 6.4% in 2002/03 and 5.6% in 2003/04.

Mining contributed an estimated 2.7% of GDP in 2002/03, and employed 0.6% of the working population in 1991. Iron ore and cut diamonds are the major mineral exports. Coal, limestone, zinc and lead are also mined. In 2003 India was the third largest coal producer in the world after the People's Republic of China and the USA. According to the Asian Development Bank (ADB, see p. 159), mining GDP increased at an estimated average annual rate of 4.2% during 1990/91–2003/04.

Manufacturing contributed an estimated 15.6% of GDP in 2002/03, and employed 10.0% of the working population in 1991. The GDP of the manufacturing sector increased at an average annual rate of 5.8% during 1990–2003; manufacturing GDP rose by 6.2% in 2002/03 and by 5.6% in 2003/04. In 1998 the most important branches, measured by gross value of output, were food products (accounting for 16.8% of the total), iron and steel (11.1%), textiles (9.6%) and industrial chemicals (8.5%).

In late 1998 India had a total generating capacity of 81,000 MW. In 2002/03 thermal plants accounted for an estimated 83.6% of total power generation and hydroelectric plants (often dependent on monsoons) for 13.2%; the remaining 3.2% was contributed by nuclear power. Imports of mineral fuels, lubricants, etc. comprised 29.0% of the cost of total imports in 2003/04.

The services sector, which is dominated by the rapidly expanding data-processing business, the growing number of business call centres and the tourism industry, contributed an estimated 50.7% of GDP in 2002/03, and engaged 20.5% of the economically active population in 1991. The GDP of the services sector increased by an average of 7.5% per year in 1990–2003; the rate of growth reached 7.1% in 2002/03 and 7.5% in 2003/04.

In 2002 India recorded a trade deficit of US $12,041m., and there was a surplus of $5,815m. on the current account of the balance of payments. In 2003/04 the principal source of imports (6.4%) and the principal market for exports (18.0%) was the USA. Other major trading partners were the United Kingdom, the United Arab Emirates, the People's Republic of China, Belgium, Hong Kong and Germany. The principal exports in 2003/04 were pearls, precious and semi-precious stones, ready-made garments and mineral fuels and lubricants. The principal imports were mineral fuels and lubricants, pearls, precious and semi-precious stones and nuclear reactors, boilers, machinery and mechanical appliances.

In the financial year ending 31 March 2005 there was a projected budgetary deficit of Rs 1,374,073m., equivalent to 4.5% of GDP. In 2002, according to the UN Development Programme (UNDP), India's total official development assistance stood at US $1,462.7m. India's total external debt was $104,429m. at the end of 2002, of which $88,271m. was long-term public debt. In that year the cost of debt-servicing was equivalent to 14.9% of earnings from the exports of goods and services. The average annual rate of inflation was an estimated 7.8% in 1990–2003; consumer prices rose by 4.1% in 2002 and by 4.0% in 2003. In rural India the number of people wholly unemployed comprised about 6% of the potential labour force for adult males in the early 2000s, but the proportion was around 23% when account was taken of underemployment.

India is a member of the ADB, of the UN Economic and Social Commission for Asia and the Pacific (ESCAP, see p. 31), of the South Asian Association for Regional Co-operation (SAARC, see p. 343) and of the Colombo Plan (see p. 373).

The process of wide-ranging economic reform initiated in 1991, including trade and investment liberalization, industrial deregulation, disinvestment by the Government in public enterprises and their gradual privatization, financial and tax reforms, etc., has continued despite several changes in government. By 2005 a variety of sectors—including power, coal, telecommunications, postal services, tourism, car manufacturing, transport (with the exception of the railways) and insurance—had been opened up to private (domestic and foreign) investment. Restrictions on foreign participation in a number of sectors (including the pharmaceuticals industry) were eased or removed in 2001/02 to encourage greater foreign investment. In January 2004 the Government agreed to raise limits on foreign investment in the petroleum and banking sectors and, in August, limits were also raised on investment in the telecommunications, insurance and civil-aviation industries. In February 2005 the Government announced that, in addition, up to 100% foreign direct investment would be permitted in the construction sector. In 2001/02 India recorded a current-account surplus for the first time in 23 years. The surplus increased in 2002/03, but declined in 2003/04. A substantial recovery in the agricultural sector (assisted by a good monsoon), along with an increase in foreign-exchange reserves, continued growth in industrial production and the services sector, and a rising stock market, contributed to GDP growth of 8.2% in 2003/04. The economic policies of the new, Congress-led Government elected in May 2004, while stressing continued governmental commitment to economic reform, also emphasized increased spending on education and health, public investment in infrastructure and employment creation. In August of that year the Government announced a trade policy intended to encourage exports and double India's share of global trade over the next five years. Among the new measures that were revealed, a level of 100% foreign direct investment was to be permitted in free-trade zones, and incentives were introduced to encourage small-scale industry exports. In November 2004 the Government announced the establishment of an Investment Commission, which was charged with encouraging investment both from overseas and from within India itself. In 2004/05 inflation increased sharply, mainly owing to an increase in domestic food prices, caused by a weak monsoon, and to high global petroleum prices. GDP expanded by 6.9% in 2004, according to official figures, with growth, mainly driven by the industry and services sectors, somewhat depressed by the effect of the disappointing monsoon on the agricultural sector. It was hoped that the relatively localized impact on India of the devastating tsunamis in the Indian Ocean in December 2004 would mitigate against any adverse effect on future national economic performance. The 2005/06 Union budget, announced in February 2005, focused on reducing poverty, increasing spending on primary education and health and allocating funds for the development of rural infrastructure. Ongoing attempts to address India's unwieldy fiscal deficit (traditionally fuelled by the country's modest tax base and cumbersome local government apparatus) have been largely frustrated by the repeated stalling of the divestment programme and the costs associated with natural disasters and volatile foreign relations and internal security concerns; the deficit remains a major cause of concern to potential foreign investors and international donors. The 2004/05 Union budget envisaged a fiscal deficit equivalent to 4.5% of GDP. Further economic reforms were needed to ensure a high level of economic performance in 2005/06 and beyond. Value-added tax was introduced at state level in April 2005, eventually to replace the central sales tax; by November 2004 26 states had agreed to implement the tax. It was hoped that attempts to restore normal relations between India and Pakistan from 2004 and the planned implementation of a South Asia Free Trade Area by 1 January 2006 would lead to an increase in trade between the two neighbours. The late 1990s witnessed India's rapid emergence as a 'software superpower'; in 2000 software

exports constituted the country's single largest export item. The rapidly expanding industry presented increasing employment opportunities. Nevertheless, concern grew over the high number of qualified information technology professionals leaving the country for better-paid work elsewhere. In the early 2000s business call centres had become the fastest growing industry in India, expanding by 70% in 2002. An increasing number of multinational companies were transferring their call centre operations to India, largely owing to cheaper labour costs and low long-distance telephone charges. More than 170,000 people were employed in the outsourcing industry in mid-2003. In 2003/04 software exports reached \$12,500m.; of the total, the outsourcing industry provided \$3,600m. The National Association of Software and Service Companies (Nasscom) forecast that the revenue from call centres would reach \$24,000m. annually by 2008.

Education

Education is primarily the responsibility of the individual state governments. Elementary education for children between the ages of six and 14 years is theoretically compulsory in all states except Nagaland and Himachal Pradesh. There are facilities for free primary education (lower and upper stages) in all the states. Enrolment at lower primary level in 1999/2000 was equivalent to 102% of children aged six to 10 years (111% of boys; 92% of girls). Higher primary and secondary enrolment in 1999/2000 was equivalent to 49% of those aged 11 to 17 (57% of boys; 40% of girls). India had a total of 253 universities and institutions with university status in 2001/02, and some 13,150 university and affiliated colleges. University enrolment was 8.8m. in 2001/02. Budgetary expenditure on education and literacy for 2004/05 was forecast at Rs 110,621m. (2.3% of total spending).

Public Holidays

The public holidays observed in India vary locally. The dates given below apply to Delhi.

2005: 1 January (New Year's Day), 21 January (Id ul-Zuha, Feast of the Sacrifice), 26 January (Republic Day), 10 February (Muharram, Islamic New Year), 8 March (Maha Shivaratri), 25 March (Good Friday), 18 April (Ram Navami), 21 April (Birth of the Prophet), 22 April (Mahavir Jayanti), 24 April (Buddha Purnima), 15 August (Independence Day), 27 August (Janmashtami), 2 October (Mahatma Gandhi's Birthday), 12 October (Dussehra), 2 November (Diwali), 4 November (Id al-Fitr, end of Ramadan), 26 November (Guru Nanak Jayanti), 25 December (Christmas).

2006: 1 January (New Year's Day), 11 January (Id ul-Zuha, Feast of the Sacrifice), 26 January (Republic Day), 31 January (Muharram, Islamic New Year), 26 February (Maha Shivaratri), April (Mahavir Jayanti), 6 April (Ram Navami), 11 April (Birth of the Prophet), 21 April (Good Friday), 13 May (Buddha Purnima), 15 August (Independence Day), 2 September (Dussehra), 5 September (Janmashtami), 2 October (Mahatma Gandhi's Birthday), 21 October (Diwali), 24 October (Id al-Fitr, end of Ramadan), 26 November (Guru Nanak Jayanti), 25 December (Christmas).

Weights and Measures

The metric system has been officially introduced. The imperial system is also still in use, as are traditional Indian weights and measures, including:

1 tola = 11.66 grams;

1 lakh = (1,00,000) = 100,000;

1 crore = (1,00,00,000) = 10,000,000.

Statistical Survey

Source (unless otherwise stated): Central Statistical Organization, Ministry of Statistics and Programme Implementation, Sardar Patel Bhavan, Patel Chowk, New Delhi 110 001; tel. (11) 23742150; fax (11) 23344689; e-mail moscc@bol.net.in; internet mospi.nic.in.

Area and Population

AREA, POPULATION AND DENSITY*

Area (sq km)	3,166,414†
Population (census results)	
1 March 1991‡ §	846,302,688
1 March 2001 ‖	
Males	532,156,772
Females	496,453,556
Total	1,028,610,328
Population (official estimates at mid-year)¶	
2002	1,033,000,000
2003	1,049,000,000
2004	1,086,000,000
Density (per sq km) at mid-2004	343.0

* Including the Indian-held part of Jammu and Kashmir.
† 1,222,559 sq miles.
‡ Excluding adjustment for underenumeration, estimated at 1.5%.
§ Including estimate for the Indian-held part of Jammu and Kashmir.
‖ Including estimates for certain areas in the states of Gujarat and Himachal Pradesh where the census could not be conducted, owing to recent natural disasters.
¶ Source: Central Statistical Organization.

Source: Registrar General of India.

STATES AND TERRITORIES
(population at 2001 census)

	Area (sq km)	Population	Density (per sq km)	Capital
States				
Andhra Pradesh .	275,069	76,210,007	277	Hyderabad
Arunachal Pradesh*	83,743	1,097,968	13	Itanagar
Assam . . .	78,438	26,655,528	340	Dispur
Bihar† . . .	94,163	82,998,509	881	Patna
Chhattisgarh .	135,191	20,833,803	154	Raipur
Goa‡	3,702	1,347,668	364	Panaji
Gujarat . . .	196,022	50,671,017	258	Gandhinagar
Haryana . . .	44,212	21,144,564	478	Chandigarh§
Himachal Pradesh .	55,673	6,077,900	109	Shimla
Jammu and				
Kashmir‖ . .	101,387	10,143,700	100	Srinagar
Jharkhand . .	79,714	26,945,829	338	Ranchi
Karnataka . .	191,791	52,850,562	276	Bangalore
Kerala . . .	38,863	31,841,374	819	Thiruvananthapuram (Trivandrum)
Madhya Pradesh†	308,245	60,348,023	196	Bhopal
Maharashtra .	307,713	96,878,627	314	Mumbai (Bombay)
Manipur . . .	22,327	2,166,788	97	Imphal
Meghalaya . .	22,429	2,318,822	103	Shillong
Mizoram¶ . .	21,081	888,573	42	Aizawl
Nagaland . .	16,579	1,990,036	120	Kohima
Orissa . . .	155,707	36,804,660	236	Bhubaneswar
Punjab . . .	50,362	24,358,999	483	Chandigarh§
Rajasthan . .	342,239	56,507,188	165	Jaipur
Sikkim . . .	7,096	540,851	76	Gangtok
Tamil Nadu . .	130,058	62,405,679	479	Chennai (Madras)
Tripura . . .	10,486	3,199,203	305	Agartala
Uttaranchal† . .	53,483	8,489,349	159	Dehradun
Uttar Pradesh† .	240,928	166,197,921	690	Lucknow
West Bengal .	88,752	80,176,197	903	Kolkata (Calcutta)
Territories				
Andaman and				
Nicobar Islands .	8,249	356,152	43	Port Blair
Chandigarh§ . .	114	900,635	7,900	Chandigarh
Dadra and Nagar				
Haveli . . .	491	220,490	449	Silvassa
Daman and Diu‡ .	112	158,204	1,411	Daman
Delhi	1,483	13,850,507	9,340	Delhi

— *continued*	Area (sq km)	Population	Density (per sq km)	Capital
Lakshadweep . .	32	60,650	1,895	Kavaratti
Pondicherry . . .	480	974,345	2,029	Pondicherry

* Arunachal Pradesh was granted statehood in February 1987.
† Chhattisgarh, Jharkhand and Uttaranchal (formerly parts of Madhya Pradesh, Bihar and Uttar Pradesh, respectively) were granted statehood in November 2000.
‡ Goa was granted statehood in May 1987. Daman and Diu remain a Union Territory.
§ Chandigarh forms a separate Union Territory, not within Haryana or Punjab. As part of a scheme for a transfer of territory between the two states, Chandigarh was due to be incorporated into Punjab on 26 January 1986, but the transfer was postponed.
‖ Figures refer only to the Indian-held part of the territory.
¶ Mizoram was granted statehood in February 1987.

Source: *Census of India*, 2001.

PRINCIPAL TOWNS
(population at 2001 census*)

Greater Mumbai		Hubli-Dharwad . .	786,195
(Bombay) . .	11,978,450	Mysore	755,379
Delhi	10,181,535	Tiruchirapalli . .	752,066
Kolkata (Calcutta) .	4,572,876	Thiruvananthapuram	
Chennai (Madras) .	4,343,645	(Trivandrum) . .	744,983
Bangalore . . .	4,301,326	Bareilly	718,395
Hyderabad . . .	3,612,427	Jalandhar . . .	706,043
Ahmedabad . . .	3,520,085	Navi Mumbai . .	704,002
Kanpur (Cawnpore) .	2,551,337	Salem	696,760
Pune (Poona) . .	2,538,473	Kota	694,316
Surat	2,433,835	Aligarh	669,087
Lucknow	2,185,927	Bhubaneswar . .	648,032
Nagpur	2,052,066	Moradabad . . .	641,583
Jaipur (Jeypore) .	1,870,771	Gorakhpur . . .	622,701
Indore	1,474,968	Raipur	605,747
Bhopal	1,437,354	Bhiwandi . . .	598,741
Ludhiana	1,398,467	Jamshedpur . .	573,096
Patna	1,366,444	Bhilai Nagar . .	556,366
Vadodara (Baroda) .	1,306,227	Amravati . . .	549,510
Agra	1,275,134	Cuttack	534,654
Thane (Thana) . .	1,262,551	Warangal . . .	530,636
Kalyan-Dombivli .	1,193,512	Bikaner	529,690
Varanasi (Banares) .	1,091,918	Mira-Bhayandar .	520,388
Nashik	1,077,236	Guntur	514,461
Meerut	1,068,772	Bhavnagar . . .	511,085
Faridabad Complex .	1,055,938	Kochi (Cochin) . .	504,550
Pimpri-Chinchwad .	1,012,472	Durgapur . . .	493,405
Haora (Howrah) . .	1,007,532	Kolhapur . . .	493,167
Visakhapatnam			
(Vizag) . . .	982,904	Ajmer	485,575
Allahabad . . .	975,393	Asansol	475,439
Ghaziabad . . .	968,256	Ulhasnagar . . .	473,731
Rajkot	967,476	Saharanpur . . .	455,754
Amritsar . . .	966,862	Jamnagar . . .	443,518
Jabalpur			
(Jubbulpore) . .	932,484	Bhatpara . . .	442,385
Coimbatore . . .	930,882	Sangli-Miraj-	
		Kupwad	436,781
Madurai	928,869	Kozhikode (Calicut)	436,556
Srinagar	898,440	Nanded-Waghala .	430,733
Aurangabad . . .	873,311	Ujjain	430,427
Solapur	872,478	Dehradun . . .	426,674
Vijayawada			
(Vijayavada) . .	851,282	Gulbarga . . .	422,569
Jodhpur	851,051	Jaipur	419,778
Ranchi	847,093	Tirunelveli . . .	411,831
Gwalior	827,026	Malegaon . . .	409,403
Guwahati	809,895	Akola	400,520
Chandigarh . . .	808,515		

* Figures refer to the city proper in each case.

Capital: New Delhi, provisional population 294,783 at 2001 census.

Population of principal urban agglomerations at 2001 census: Greater Mumbai 16,434,386; Kolkata 13,205,697; Delhi 12,877,470; Chennai 6,560,242; Hyderabad 5,742,036; Bangalore 5,701,446; Jaipur 5,251,071; Ahmedabad 4,525,013; Pune 3,760,636; Ludhiana 3,032,831; Surat 2,811,614; Kanpur 2,715,555; Lucknow 2,245,509; Faridabad 2,194,586; Nagpur 2,129,500; Patna 1,697,976; Indore 1,516,918; Vadodara 1,491,045; Coimbatore 1,461,139; Bhopal 1,458,416; Kochi 1,355,972; Visakhapatnam 1,345,938; Agra 1,331,339; Varanasi 1,203,961; Madurai 1,203,095; Meerut 1,161,716; Nashik 1,152,326; Jamshedpur 1,104,713; Jabalpur 1,098,000; Asansol 1,067,369; Dhanbad 1,065,327; Allahabad 1,042,229; Vijayawada 1,039,518; Amritsar 1,003,917; Rajkot 1,003,015.

BIRTHS AND DEATHS

(estimates, based on Sample Registration Scheme)

	2000	2001	2002
Birth rate (per 1,000)	25.8	25.4	25.0
Death rate (per 1,000)	8.5	8.4	8.1

Expectation of life (WHO estimates, years at birth): 61.0 (males 60.1; females 62.0) in 2002 (Source: WHO, *World Health Report*).

ECONOMICALLY ACTIVE POPULATION

(persons aged five years and over, 1991 census, excluding Jammu and Kashmir)

	Males	Females	Total
Agriculture, hunting, forestry and fishing	139,361,719	51,979,110	191,340,829
Mining and quarrying	1,536,919	214,356	1,751,275
Manufacturing	23,969,433	4,702,046	28,671,479
Construction	5,122,468	420,737	5,543,205
Trade and commerce	19,862,725	1,433,612	21,296,337
Transport, storage and communications	7,810,126	207,620	8,017,746
Other services	23,995,194	5,316,428	29,311,622
Total employed	221,658,584	64,273,909	285,932,493
Marginal workers	2,705,223	25,493,654	28,198,877
Total labour force	224,363,807	89,767,563	314,131,370

Unemployment (work applicants at 31 December, '000 persons aged 14 years and over): 41,996 (males 31,111; females 10,885) in 2001; 41,171 (males 30,521; females 10,650) in 2002; 41,389 (males 30,636; females 10,752) in 2003 (Source: ILO).

2001 census: Main workers 313,004,983; Marginal workers 89,229,741; Total 402,234,724 (males 275,014,476, females 127,220,248).

Health and Welfare

KEY INDICATORS

Total fertility rate (children per woman, 2002)	3.1
Under-5 mortality rate (per 1,000 live births, 2003)	87
HIV/AIDS (% of persons aged 15–49, 2003)	0.9
Physicians (per 1,000 head, 1999)	0.52
Hospital beds (per 1,000 head, 1999)	0.92
Health expenditure (2001): US $ per head (PPP)	80.0
Health expenditure (2001): % of GDP	5.1
Health expenditure (2001): public (% of total)	17.9
Access to water (% of persons, 2002)	86
Access to sanitation (% of persons, 2002)	30
Human Development Index (2002): ranking	127
Human Development Index (2002): value	0.595

For sources and definitions, see explanatory note on p. vi.

Agriculture

PRINCIPAL CROPS

('000 metric tons, year ending 30 June)

	2001/02	2002/03	2003/04*
Rice (milled)	93,080	72,660	87,000
Sorghum (Jowar)	7,790	7,070	7,320
Cat-tail millet (Bajra)	8,350	4,630	11,790
Maize	13,300	10,300	14,720
Finger millet (Ragi)	2,480	1,450	2,010
Small millets	600	430	550
Wheat	71,810	65,100	72,060
Barley	1,420	1,410	1,370
Total cereals	198,830	163,050	196,820
Chick-peas (Gram)	5,270	4,130	5,770
Pigeon-peas (Tur)	2,300	2,210	2,430
Dry beans, dry peas, lentils and other pulses	5,620	4,800	7,030
Total food grains	212,020	174,190	212,050
Groundnuts (in shell)	7,200	4,363	8,332
Sesame seed	730	434	815
Rapeseed and mustard	5,040	3,918	5,832
Linseed	230	173	179
Castor beans	650	428	804
Total edible oilseeds (incl. others)	20,800	15,058	25,143
Cotton lint†	10,090	8,716	13,788
Jute‡	10,550	10,340	10,265
Kenaf (Mesta)‡	1,090	1,037	932
Tea (made)	841	838	n.a.
Sugar cane: production gur	30,010	28,160	23,620
Sugar cane: production cane	300,100	281,575	236,176
Tobacco (leaves)	345	385	n.a.
Potatoes	23,900	23,200	n.a.

* Provisional figures.
† Production in '000 bales of 170 kg each.
‡ Production in '000 bales of 180 kg each.
Sources: Directorate of Economics and Statistics, Ministry of Agriculture and Ministry of Commerce (for tea).

LIVESTOCK

('000 head, year ending September)

	2001	2002	2003
Cattle	191,218*	189,302*	187,382
Sheep	60,400*	61,100†	61,789
Goats	120,900*	120,500*	120,097
Pigs	13,900*	14,000*	14,142
Horses	800*	800*	788
Asses†	750	750	750
Mules†	300	300	300
Buffaloes	94,382*	95,498*	96,616
Camels	728*	682*	635
Chickens*	377,000	393,000	409,000
Ducks*	32,600	32,800	32,900

* Unofficial figure(s).
† FAO estimate(s).

Source: FAO.

LIVESTOCK PRODUCTS
('000 metric tons)

	2001	2002	2003
Beef and veal*	1,452.3	1,462.6	1,472.9
Buffalo meat*	1,432.7	1,449.7	1,466.7
Mutton and lamb*	230.4	232.8	235.8
Goat meat*	469	470	473
Pig meat*	483.0	486.5	490.0
Chicken meat†	1,250	1,400	1,600
Duck meat*	57.2	59.8	62.4
Cows' milk†	35,600	36,700	38,300
Buffaloes' milk†	46,600	48,000	50,100
Goats' milk†	2,600	2,600	2,700
Butter†	500	530	550
Ghee†	1,750	1,870	1,950
Hen eggs†	1,870.0	2,000.0	2,155.0
Wool: greasy	50.7	51.2*	51.4*
Wool: scoured	34.0†	34.4*	34.5*
Cattle hides (fresh)*	466	470	480
Buffalo hides (fresh)*	510.0	514.2	545.0
Sheepskins (fresh)*	52.4	52.9	53.1
Goatskins (fresh)*	128.9	129.4	129.4

* FAO estimate(s).
† Unofficial figure(s).

Source: FAO.

Forestry

ROUNDWOOD REMOVALS
('000 cubic metres, excl. bark)

	2001	2002	2003
Sawlogs, veneer logs and logs for sleepers*†	18,350	18,350	18,350
Pulpwood	618	306	306
Other industrial wood	331	169	172
Fuel wood*	277,380	300,564	302,199
Total	296,679	319,872	321,027

* FAO estimates.
† Output assumed to be unchanged since 1985.

Source: FAO.

SAWNWOOD PRODUCTION
('000 cubic metres, incl. railway sleepers)

	1999	2000	2001
Coniferous sawnwood	1,200	1,100	1,100
Broadleaved sawnwood . . .	7,200	6,800	6,800
Total	8,400	7,900	7,900

2002–03: Production assumed to be unchanged from 2001 (FAO estimates).

Source: FAO.

Fishing

('000 metric tons, live weight)

	2000	2001	2002
Capture	3,666.4	3,777.1	3,770.9
Bombay-duck (Bummalo) . .	168.7	176.4	135.9
Croakers and drums . . .	268.1	248.4	273.4
Indian oil-sardine (Sardinella) .	327.4	343.1	334.2
Indian mackerel . . .	78.8	46.2	53.1
Giant tiger prawn . . .	204.6	158.0	156.9
Aquaculture	1,942.2	2,119.8	2,191.7
Roho labeo . . .	516.5	378.8	353.1
Mrigal carp . . .	470.5	353.2	321.6
Catla . . .	497.2	373.3	339.9
Total catch	5,608.6	5,896.9	5,962.6

Source: FAO.

Mining

('000 metric tons, unless otherwise indicated)

	2000/01	2001/02	2002/03*
Coal	313,696	327,787	341,248
Lignite	24,247	24,813	26,018
Iron ore†	80,587	86,226	96,962
Manganese ore†	1,595	1,587	1,662
Bauxite	7,993	8,689	9,777
Chalk (Fireclay)	487	494	463
Kaolin (China clay)	873	854	797
Dolomite	3,032	3,201	3,329
Gypsum	2,667	2,859	2,842
Limestone	127,338	130,936	145,552
Crude petroleum	32,426	32,032	33,043
Sea salt‡	13,584	18,496	16,976
Chromium ore†	1,972	1,549	3,066
Phosphorite	1,351	1,239	1,197
Kyanite	5	4	5
Magnesite	318	283	273
Steatite	596	579	676
Copper ore†	3,498	3,418	3,135
Lead concentrates†	54	52	59
Zinc concentrates†	366	399	486
Mica—crude (metric tons) . . .	1,154	2,026	1,217
Gold (kilograms)	2,615	2,810	3,049
Diamonds (carats)	57,407	81,436	84,407
Natural gas (million cu m)§ . .	27,860	28,013	29,969

* Provisional figures.
† Figures refer to gross weight. The estimated metal content is: Iron 63%; Manganese 40%; Chromium 30%; Copper 1.2%; Lead 70%; Zinc 60%.
‡ Unofficial figures.
§ Figures refer to gas utilized.

Source: Indian Bureau of Mines.

Industry

SELECTED PRODUCTS
('000 metric tons, unless otherwise indicated)

	2000/01	2001/02	2002/03
Refined sugar*	19,250	18,496	18,906
Cotton cloth (million sq metres) .	19,718	19,440	19,336
Jute manufactures	1,625	1,400	1,440
Paper and paper board	3,090	4,930	5,170
Soda ash	1,631	1,541	1,610
Fertilizers	14,770	16,964	14,456
Petroleum products	96,600	100,000	104,100
Cement	99,500	106,491	111,778
Pig-iron	3,105	3,836	4,969
Finished steel	29,270	31,100	34,400
Aluminium (metric tons)	620,400	552,100	467,000
Diesel engines—stationary (number)	306,000	219,000	300,000
Sewing machines (number) . .	48,800	76,982	82,697
Television receivers (number) . .	2,335,100	1,990,400	2,186,800
Electric fans (number)	8,080,000	8,940,000	9,220,000
Passenger cars and multipurpose vehicles	632,200	573,146	735,941
Commercial vehicles (number) . .	152,000	146,314	198,827
Motorcycles, mopeds and scooters (number)	3,755,000	4,324,631	5,087,539
Bicycles (number)	14,974,000	12,925,600	11,929,220

* Figures relate to crop year (beginning November) and are in respect of cane sugar only.

Finance

CURRENCY AND EXCHANGE RATES

Monetary Units
100 paise (singular: paisa) = 1 Indian rupee (R).

Sterling, Dollar and Euro Equivalents (31 December 2004)
£1 sterling = Rs 84.17;
US $1 = Rs 43.58;
€1 = Rs 59.36;
1,000 Indian rupees = £11.88 = $22.94 = €16.85.

Average Exchange Rate (rupees per US $)
2002   48.610
2003   46.583
2004   45.317

UNION BUDGET
(Rs million, rounded, year ending 31 March)

Revenue	2002/03*	2003/04†	2004/05‡
Tax revenue (net)	1,594,246	1,875,383	2,339,060
Customs receipts	448,516	493,500	542,500
Union excise duties . . .	823,095	923,790	1,091,990
Corporation tax	461,724	629,860	884,360
Other taxes on income . . .	368,584	402,690	509,290
Other taxes and duties . .	60,743	99,387	149,190
Less States' share of tax revenue	561,221	657,844	822,270
Less Surcharge transferred to National Calamity Contingency Fund . . .	7,194	16,000	16,000
Other current revenue . . .	723,236	754,880	754,157
Interest receipts (net) . .	376,021	359,988	369,500
Dividends and profits . .	212,302	220,808	188,751
Receipts of Union Territories .	5,577	5,785	6,177
External grants	18,682	28,571	35,979
Other receipts (net) . . .	110,653	139,727	153,750
Recoveries of loans (net) . .	341,909	646,250	271,000
Disinvestment of equity in public-sector enterprises	31,507	145,000	40,000
Total	2,690,898	3,421,513	3,404,217

Expenditure	2002/03*	2003/04†	2004/05‡
Central Ministries/Departments .	3,672,821	4,235,649	4,180,961
Agriculture and co-operation (incl. agricultural research and education)	33,484	40,199	47,473
Atomic energy	36,633	37,388	44,700
Defence	663,990	719,973	891,364
Drinking water supply . .	22,429	27,514	33,014
Economic affairs	1,499,628	1,896,736	1,522,956
External affairs	32,511	34,100	36,407
Family welfare	39,865	47,245	55,248
Fertilizers	126,795	122,700	128,282
Food and public distribution .	243,201	254,603	261,416
Health	23,783	25,591	26,876
Home affairs	114,855	121,931	139,876
Education and literacy . . .	90,694	102,870	110,621
Petroleum and natural gas . .	52,324	69,034	35,734
Railways	56,137	69,443	69,190
Road transport and highways .	69,001	71,402	87,690
Rural development . . .	150,907	155,188	114,560
Urban development . . .	32,393	34,430	25,797
State plans	436,240	473,255	562,400
Union territories	32,559	33,643	34,929
Total	4,141,620	4,742,547	4,778,290
Current§	3,396,275	3,628,872	3,854,933
Capital	745,345	1,113,674	923,358

* Provisional figures.
† Estimates.
‡ Forecasts.
§ Including interest payments (Rs million): 1,245,735 in 2002/03 (provisional); 1,284,053 in 2003/04 (estimate); 1,334,999 in 2004/05 (forecast).

Source: Government of India, Union Budget 2003/04.

INTERNATIONAL RESERVES
(US $ million at 31 December)

	2001	2002	2003
Gold*	2,329	2,712	3,323
IMF special drawing rights . .	5	7	3
Reserve position in IMF . .	614	665	1,318
Foreign exchange	45,251	66,994	97,617
Total	48,199	70,377	102,261

* National valuation (Rs 9,756 per troy ounce in 2001; Rs 11,325 per ounce in 2002; Rs 13,176 per ounce in 2003).

Source: IMF, *International Financial Statistics*.

MONEY SUPPLY
(Rs million, last Friday of year ending 31 March)

	2001/02	2002/03	2003/04
Currency with the public . .	2,407,950	2,715,810	3,154,930
Demand deposits with banks . .	1,791,990	1,987,570	2,560,390
Other deposits with Reserve Bank	28,500	32,420	51,190
Total money	4,228,430	4,735,810	5,766,510

Note: Totals may not be equal to sums of components, owing to rounding.

Source: Reserve Bank of India.

COST OF LIVING
(Consumer Price Index for Industrial Workers; base: 2000 = 100)

	2001	2002	2003
Food (incl. beverages) . . .	102.2	104.9	108.4
Fuel and light	109.2	120.5	128.3
Clothing (incl. footwear) . . .	101.3	104.7	106.6
Rent	109.2	120.4	126.5
All items (incl. others)	103.9	108.2	112.5

Source: ILO.

NATIONAL ACCOUNTS
(Rs '000 million at current prices, year ending 31 March)

National Income and Product

	2000/01	2001/02	2002/03
Domestic factor incomes* . .	17,051.03	18,732.03	20,144.50
Consumption of fixed capital .	1,978.95	2,177.54	2,350.43
Gross domestic product at factor cost	19,029.98	20,909.57	22,494.93
Indirect taxes . . . . . } *Less* Subsidies . . . . . }	1,865.01	1,911.86	2,200.71
GDP in purchasers' values .	20,894.99	22,821.43	24,695.64
Factor income from abroad . . } *Less* Factor income paid abroad }	−172.85	−120.86	−192.21
Gross national product . .	20,722.14	22,700.57	24,503.43
Less Consumption of fixed capital	1,978.95	2,177.54	2,350.43
National income in market prices	18,743.19	20,520.03	22,153.00

* Compensation of employees and the operating surplus of enterprises.

Expenditure on the Gross Domestic Product

	2000/01	2001/02	2002/03
Government final consumption expenditure	2,642.4	2,843.1	3,088.3
Private final consumption expenditure	13,600.2	14,940.5	15,911.3
Increase in stocks	138.3	86.5	86.0
Gross fixed capital formation . .	4,597.9	5,004.1	5,552.2
Total domestic expenditure .	20,978.8	22,874.2	24,637.8
Exports of goods and services . .	2,901.8	3,075.8	3,758.7
Less Imports of goods and services	3,060.9	3,218.0	3,852.7
Statistical discrepancy . . .	75.3	89.4	151.8
GDP in purchasers' values . .	20,895.0	22,821.4	24,695.6

Gross Domestic Product by Economic Activity
(at current factor cost)

	2000/01	2001/02	2002/03
Agriculture	4,235.22	4,730.04	4,560.44
Forestry and logging . . .	224.22	243.41	270.13
Fishing	225.35	245.62	268.50
Mining and quarrying . . .	453.99	478.78	616.84
Manufacturing	3,016.28	3,202.16	3,508.48
Electricity, gas and water supply	430.24	444.32	475.64
Construction	1,162.38	1,243.71	1,384.43
Trade, hotels and restaurants . .	2,715.11	2,995.12	3,219.94
Transport, storage and communications . . .	1,408.26	1,573.48	1,733.91
Banking and insurance	1,184.81	1,337.34	1,582.79
Real estate and business services .	1,203.79	1,365.17	1,520.79
Public administration and defence	1,237.21	1,328.61	1,454.06
Other services	1,533.12	1,721.81	1,898.98
Total	19,029.98	20,909.57	22,494.93

BALANCE OF PAYMENTS
(US $ million)

	2000	2001	2002
Exports of goods f.o.b.	43,132	44,612	50,701
Imports of goods f.o.b.	−59,423	−57,358	−62,742
Trade balance	−16,291	−12,746	−12,041
Exports of services	18,181	21,330	23,664
Imports of services	−15,815	−17,765	−16,874
Balance on goods and services	−13,925	−9,180	−5,251
Other income received	2,280	2,524	2,557
Other income paid	−6,156	−5,430	−6,121
Balance on goods, services and income	−17,801	−12,086	−8,814
Current transfers received . . .	13,504	12,346	14,852
Current transfers paid	−51	−83	−222
Current balance	−4,348	177	5,815
Capital account (net)	−542	314	2,563
Direct investment abroad . . .	−254	−788	−488
Direct investment from abroad .	2,496	3,768	3,700
Portfolio investment assets . .	−135	−97	−42
Portfolio investment liabilities .	2,475	2,952	1,064
Other investment assets . . .	−499	1,016	4,780
Other investment liabilities . .	7,152	795	2,040
Net errors and omissions . . .	−267	554	−585
Overall balance	6,077	8,690	18,848

Source: IMF, *International Financial Statistics.*

OFFICIAL DEVELOPMENT ASSISTANCE
(US $ million)

	1998	1999	2000
Bilateral donors	896.4	826.7	638.7
Multilateral donors	713.2	664.6	848.5
Total	1,609.6	1,491.3	1,487.2
Grants	802.6	772.2	775.3
Loans	807.0	719.1	711.9
Per caput assistance (US $) . .	1.7	1.5	1.5

Source: UN, *Statistical Yearbook for Asia and the Pacific.*

External Trade

PRINCIPAL COMMODITIES
(Rs million, year ending 31 March)

Imports c.i.f.	2001/02	2002/03	2003/04
Animal and vegetable oils, fats and waxes	70,800	90,524	118,686
Mineral fuels, mineral oils and products of their distillation . .	752,185	952,449	1,043,111
Organic chemicals	87,951	106,949	143,630
Natural or cultured pearls, precious and semi-precious stones, precious metals and articles thereof; imitation jewellery; coin	445,992	506,957	650,445
Nuclear reactors, boilers, machinery, mechanical appliances and parts thereof .	202,652	248,294	318,575
Electrical machinery and equipment and parts thereof; sound and television apparatus .	151,747	245,231	301,657
Total (incl. others)	2,451,997	2,972,059	3,591,076

Exports f.o.b.	2001/02	2002/03	2003/04
Cereals	46,203	77,468	69,567
Mineral fuels, mineral oils and products of their distillation . .	104,109	131,018	171,598
Organic chemicals	76,739	101,899	129,746
Iron and steel	44,832	92,541	119,068
Cotton	95,100	106,585	113,305
Articles of apparel and clothing accessories, knitted or crocheted	88,898	115,503	124,149
Articles of apparel and clothing accessories, not knitted or crocheted	149,920	162,210	162,731
Natural or cultured pearls, precious and semi-precious stones, precious metals and articles thereof; imitation jewellery; coin	350,056	440,023	494,511
Nuclear reactors, boilers, machinery, mechanical appliances and parts thereof .	74,910	83,175	115,171
Total (incl. others)	2,090,180	2,551,373	2,933,667

Source: Ministry of Commerce and Industry.

PRINCIPAL TRADING PARTNERS
(Rs million, year ending 31 March)

Imports c.i.f.	2001/02	2002/03	2003/04
Australia	62,290	64,694	121,736
Belgium	131,773	179,640	182,699
China, People's Republic . . .	97,119	135,122	186,251
France	40,264	52,953	50,098
Germany	96,724	116,368	134,112
Hong Kong	34,761	47,069	68,591
Indonesia	49,448	66,828	97,512
Italy	33,612	39,296	49,216
Japan	102,368	88,870	122,584
Korea, Republic	54,434	73,658	130,005
Malaysia	54,060	70,919	94,042
Russia	25,539	28,679	44,096
Singapore	62,194	69,438	95,826
South Africa	68,719	101,315	87,271
Switzerland	136,912	112,755	152,225
Taiwan	26,673	32,073	35,334
United Arab Emirates . . .	43,642	46,134	94,653
United Kingdom	122,244	134,394	148,623
USA	150,211	215,048	231,358
Total (incl. others)	2,451,997	2,972,059	3,591,076

Exports f.o.b.	2001/02	2002/03	2003/04
Bangladesh	47,796	56,913	79,990
Belgium	66,321	80,425	82,976
Canada	27,891	33,793	35,070
China, People's Republic . . .	45,400	95,604	135,791
France	45,069	51,981	58,858
Germany	85,290	101,953	116,926
Hong Kong	112,856	126,473	149,885
Indonesia	25,454	39,977	51,797
Iran	12,068	31,686	42,188
Israel	20,413	30,709	33,268
Italy	57,542	65,676	79,469
Japan	72,036	90,210	78,544
Korea, Republic	22,481	31,208	35,146
Malaysia	36,899	36,266	41,024
Nepal	10,228	16,956	30,758
Netherlands	41,200	50,714	59,237
Nigeria	26,857	21,733	25,985
Russia	38,067	34,070	32,798
Saudi Arabia	39,414	45,528	51,618
Singapore	46,371	68,798	97,639
Spain	32,297	39,224	46,070
Sri Lanka	30,088	44,571	60,619
Taiwan	17,174	27,997	24,467
Thailand	30,195	34,419	38,217
United Arab Emirates . . .	118,838	161,034	235,529
United Kingdom	103,056	120,814	138,923
USA	406,018	527,304	527,985
Total (incl. others)	2,090,180	2,551,373	2,933,667

Source: Ministry of Commerce and Industry.

Transport

RAILWAYS
(million, year ending 31 March)

	2001/02	2002/03	2003/04*
Passengers	5,093	4,971	5,112
Passenger-km	490,912	515,044	533,000
Freight (metric tons) . . .	522.2	542.7	557.4
Freight (metric ton-km) . .	336,445	356,027	381,200

* Provisional estimates.
Source: Railway Board, Ministry of Railways.

ROAD TRAFFIC
('000 motor vehicles in use at 31 March)

	2000	2001	2002*
Private cars, jeeps and taxis . .	6,143	7,058	7,571
Buses and coaches	562	634	669
Goods vehicles	2,715	2,948	3,045
Motorcycles and scooters . . .	34,118	38,556	41,478
Others	5,319	5,795	6,100
Total	48,857	54,991	58,863

* Provisional figures.
Source: Ministry of Road Transport and Highways.

SHIPPING
Merchant Fleet
(registered at 31 December)

	2001	2002	2003
Vessels	1,018	1,010	1,028
Displacement ('000 grt)	6,688.2	6,142.1	6,960.6

Source: Lloyd's Register-Fairplay, *World Fleet Statistics*.

International Sea-borne Traffic
(year ending 31 March)

	2000/01	2001/02	2002/03*
Vessels ('000 nrt)†:			
entered	55,466	55,981	n.a.
cleared	38,043	41,716	n.a.
Freight ('000 metric tons)‡:			
loaded	135,331	n.a.	115,534
unloaded	233,007	n.a.	182,229

* Provisional figures.
† Excluding minor and intermediate ports.
‡ Including bunkers.

Sources: Transport Research Division, Ministry of Surface Transport; Department of Shipping, Ministry of Shipping, Road Transport and Highways; Directorate General of Commercial Intelligence and Statistics.

CIVIL AVIATION
(all Indian carriers, traffic on scheduled services)

	2000/01	2001/02	2002/03
Kilometres flown (million) . . .	203	222	250
Passengers carried ('000) . . .	17,540	16,552	18,152
Passenger-km (million)	26,212	24,982	28,667
Freight carried (metric tons) . .	243,373	233,570	258,343
Freight ton-km ('000)	556	513	565
Mail carried (metric tons) . . .	24,646	24,515	24,971
Mail ton-km ('000)	30	35	33

Source: Directorate General of Civil Aviation.

Tourism

FOREIGN VISITORS BY COUNTRY OF ORIGIN*

	2001	2002	2003†
Australia	52,691	44,456	56,083
Canada	88,600	87,440	106,554
CIS	24,831	15,164	38,443
France	102,434	82,044	96,848
Germany	80,011	67,125	74,518
Italy	41,351	32,042	46,238
Japan	80,634	58,721	76,411
Malaysia	57,869	54,943	67,440
Nepal	41,135	46,227	41,153
Netherlands	42,368	32,055	40,047
Singapore	42,824	41,918	44,785
Sri Lanka	112,813	107,729	106,364
United Kingdom	405,472	390,762	427,235
USA	329,147	333,382	400,113
Total (incl. others)	2,053,208	1,899,608	2,750,290

* Figures exclude nationals of Bangladesh and Pakistan. Including these, the total was: 2,537,282 in 2001; 2,361,587 in 2002; n.a. in 2003.
† Provisional estimates.
Source: Ministry of Tourism.

Receipts from tourism (Rs million): 143,440 in 2001; 141,950 in 2002; 164,290 in 2003.

Communications Media

	2000	2001	2002
Television receivers ('000 in use) .	79,000	85,000	n.a.
Telephones ('000 main lines in use)	32,436	38,536	41,420
Mobile cellular telephones ('000 subscribers)	3,577	6,432	12,688
Personal computers ('000 in use)	4,600	6,000	7,500
Internet users ('000)	5,500	7,000	16,580
Daily newspapers	5,364	5,638	n.a.
Non-daily newspapers and other periodicals	43,781	46,322	n.a.

1997: Radio receivers ('000 in use) 116,000; Facsimile machines ('000 in use, year ending 31 March) 100.

2003: Telephones ('000 main lines in use) 48,917; Mobile cellular telephones ('000 subscribers) 26,154; Internet users ('000) 18,481.

Sources: International Telecommunication Union; UN, *Statistical Yearbook*; Register of Newspapers for India, Ministry of Information and Broadcasting.

Education

(2001/02*)

	Institutions	Teachers	Students
Primary	664,041	1,928,075	113,883,060
Middle	219,626	1,467,920	44,828,235
Secondary (high school) . .	91,435	1,018,795	20,053,986
Higher secondary (new pattern) Intermediate/pre-degree/junior college	42,057	758,700	10,453,229

* Provisional figures.

Source: Planning, Monitoring and Statistics Division, Ministry of Human Resource Development.

Adult literacy rate (based on 2001 census): 61.3% (males 69.0%; females 46.4%) in 2002 (Source: UN Development Programme, *Human Development Report*).

Directory

The Constitution

The Constitution of India, adopted by the Constituent Assembly on 26 November 1949, was inaugurated on 26 January 1950. The Preamble declares that the People of India solemnly resolve to constitute a Sovereign Democratic Republic and to secure to all its citizens justice, liberty, equality and fraternity. There are 397 articles and nine schedules, which form a comprehensive document.

UNION OF STATES

The Union of India comprises 28 states, six Union Territories and one National Capital Territory. There are provisions for the formation and admission of new states.

The Constitution confers citizenship on a threefold basis of birth, descent, and residence. Provisions are made for refugees who have migrated from Pakistan and for persons of Indian origin residing abroad.

FUNDAMENTAL RIGHTS AND DIRECTIVE PRINCIPLES

The rights of the citizen contained in Part III of the Constitution are declared fundamental and enforceable in law. 'Untouchability' is abolished and its practice in any form is a punishable offence. The Directive Principles of State Policy provide a code intended to ensure promotion of the economic, social and educational welfare of the State in future legislation.

THE PRESIDENT

The President is the head of the Union, exercising all executive powers on the advice of the Council of Ministers responsible to Parliament. He is elected by an electoral college consisting of elected members of both Houses of Parliament and the Legislatures of the States. The President holds office for a term of five years and is eligible for re-election. He may be impeached for violation of the Constitution. The Vice-President is the *ex officio* Chairman of the Rajya Sabha and is elected by a joint sitting of both Houses of Parliament.

THE PARLIAMENT

The Parliament of the Union consists of the President and two Houses: the Rajya Sabha (Council of States) and the Lok Sabha (House of the People). The Rajya Sabha consists of 245 members, of whom a number are nominated by the President. One-third of its members retire every two years. Elections are indirect, each state's legislative quota being elected by the members of the state's legislative assembly. The Lok Sahba has 543 members elected by adult franchise; not more than 13 represent the Union Territories and National Capital Territory. Two members are nominated by the President to represent the Anglo-Indian community.

GOVERNMENT OF THE STATES

The governmental machinery of states closely resembles that of the Union. Each of these states has a governor at its head appointed by the President for a term of five years to exercise executive power on the advice of a council of ministers. The states' legislatures consist of the Governor and either one house (legislative assembly) or two houses (legislative assembly and legislative council). The term of the assembly is five years, but the council is not subject to dissolution.

LANGUAGE

The Constitution provides that the official language of the Union shall be Hindi. (The English language will continue to be an associate language for many official purposes.)

LEGISLATION—FEDERAL SYSTEM

The Constitution provides that bills, other than money bills, can be introduced in either House. To become law, they must be passed by both Houses and receive the assent of the President. In financial affairs, the authority of the Lower House is final. The various subjects of legislation are enumerated on three lists in the seventh schedule of the Constitution: the Union List, containing nearly 100 entries, including external affairs, defence, communications and atomic energy; the State List, containing 65 entries, including local government, police, public health, education; and the Concurrent List, with over 40 entries, including criminal law, marriage and divorce, labour welfare. The Constitution vests residuary authority in the Centre. All matters not enumerated in the Concurrent or State Lists will be deemed to be included in the Union List, and in the event of conflict between Union and State Law on any subject enumerated in the Concurrent List the Union Law will prevail. In time of emergency Parliament may even exercise powers otherwise exclusively vested in the states. Under Article 356, 'If the President on receipt of a report from the government of a state or otherwise is satisfied that a situation has arisen in which the Government of the state cannot be carried on in accordance with the provisions of this Constitution, the President may by Proclamation: (a) assume to himself all or any of the functions of the government of the state and all or any of the powers of the governor or any body or authority in the state other than the Legislature of the state; (b) declare that the powers of the Legislature of the state shall be exercisable by or under the authority of Parliament; (c) make such incidental provisions as appear to the President to be necessary': provided that none of the powers of a High Court be assumed by the President or suspended in any way. Unless such a Proclamation is approved by both Houses of Parliament, it ceases to operate after two months. A Proclamation so approved ceases to operate after six months, unless renewed by Parliament. Its renewal cannot be extended beyond a total period of three years. An independent judiciary exists to define and interpret the Constitution and to resolve constitutional disputes arising between states, or between a state and the Government of India.

OTHER PROVISIONS

Other Provisions of the Constitution deal with the administration of tribal areas, relations between the Union and states, inter-state trade and finance.

AMENDMENTS

The Constitution is flexible in character, and a simple process of amendment has been adopted. For amendment of provisions concerning the Supreme Courts and the High Courts, the distribution of legislative powers between the Union and the states, the representation of the states in Parliament, etc., the amendment must be passed by both Houses of Parliament and must further be ratified by the legislatures of not less than half the states. In other cases no reference to the state legislatures is necessary.

Numerous amendments were adopted in August 1975, following the declaration of a state of emergency in June. The Constitution (39th Amendment) Bill laid down that the President's reasons for proclaiming an emergency may not be challenged in any court. Under the Constitution (40th Amendment) Bill, 38 existing laws may not be challenged before any court on the ground of violation of fundamental rights. Thus detainees under the Maintenance of Internal Security Act could not be told the grounds of their detention and were forbidden bail and any claim to liberty through natural or common law. The Constitution (41st Amendment) Bill provided that the President, Prime Minister and state Governors should be immune from criminal prosecution for life and from civil prosecution during their term of office.

In November 1976 a 59-clause Constitution (42nd Amendment) Bill was approved by Parliament and came into force in January 1977. Some of the provisions of the Bill are that the Indian Democratic Republic shall be named a 'Democratic Secular and Socialist Republic'; that the President 'shall act in accordance with' the advice given to him by the Prime Minister and the Council of Ministers, and, acting at the Prime Minister's direction, shall be empowered for two years to amend the Constitution by executive order, in any way beneficial to the enforcement of the whole; that the term of the Lok Sabha and of the state assemblies shall be extended from five to six years; that there shall be no limitation on the constituent power of Parliament to amend the Constitution, and that India's Supreme Court shall be barred from hearing petitions challenging constitutional amendments; that strikes shall be forbidden in the public services and the Union Government has the power to deploy police or other forces under its own superintendence and control in any state. Directive Principles are given precedence over Fundamental Rights: 10 basic duties of citizens are listed, including the duty to 'defend the country and render national service when called upon to do so'.

The Janata Party Government, which came into power in March 1977, promised to amend the Constitution during the year, so as to 'restore the balance between the people and Parliament, Parliament and the judiciary, the judiciary and the executive, the states and the centre, and the citizen and the Government that the founding fathers of the Constitution had worked out'. The Constitution (43rd Amendment) Bill, passed by Parliament in December 1977, the Constitution (44th Amendment) Bill, passed by Parliament in December 1977 and later redesignated the 43rd Amendment, and the Constitution (45th Amendment) Bill, passed by Parliament in December 1978 and later redesignated the 44th Amendment, reversed most of the changes enacted by the Constitution (42nd Amendment) Bill. The 44th Amendment is particularly detailed on emergency provisions: an emergency may not be proclaimed unless 'the security of India or any part of its territory was threatened by war or external aggression or by armed rebellion.' Its introduction must be approved by a two-thirds' majority of Parliament within a month, and after six months the emergency may be continued only with the approval of Parliament. Among the provisions left unchanged after these Bills were a section subordinating Fundamental Rights to Directive Principles and a clause empowering the central Government to deploy armed forces under its control in any state without the state government's consent. In May 1980 the Indian Supreme Court repealed sections 4 and 55 of the 42nd Amendment Act, thus curtailing Parliament's power to enforce directive principles and to amend the Constitution. The death penalty was declared constitutionally valid.

The 53rd Amendment to the Constitution, approved by Parliament in August 1986, granted statehood to the Union Territory of Mizoram; the 55th Amendment, approved in December 1986, granted statehood to the Union Territory of Arunachal Pradesh; and the 57th Amendment, approved in May 1987, granted statehood to the Union Territory of Goa (Daman and Diu remains, however, as a Union Territory). The 59th Amendment, approved in March 1988, empowered the Government to impose a state of emergency in the Punjab, on the grounds of internal disturbances. In December 1988 the minimum voting age was lowered from 21 to 18 years. The 69th Amendment, enacted in 1991, declared the Union Territory of Delhi to be the National Capital Territory, and granted it responsible government. The 71st Amendment, approved in August 1992, gave official-language status to Nepali, Konkani and Manipuri. In August 2000 legislation to permit the establishment of three new states, Chhattisgarh, Jharkhand and Uttaranchal, was approved by Parliament. The 93rd amendment, approved in May 2002, ensured free and compulsory education for children from the age of six to 14. The 91st amendment, approved in December 2003, stipulated that the size of the Council of Ministers at the centre and the states should not exceed 15% of the numbers in the Lok Sabha and state legislative assemblies, respectively. The 100th amendment, also approved in December 2003, extended official-language status to Bodo, Santhali, Maithali and Dogri, bringing the total number of official languages in the country to 22.

THE PANCHAYAT RAJ SCHEME

This scheme is designed to decentralize the powers of the Union and state governments. It is based on the Panchayat (Village Council) and the Gram Sabha (Village Parliament) and envisages the gradual transference of local government from state to local authority. Revenue and internal security will remain state responsibilities at present. The 72nd Amendment, approved in late 1992, provided for direct elections to the Panchayats, members of which were to have a tenure of five years.

The Government

President: Aavul Pakkiri Jainulabidin Abdul Kalam (sworn in 25 July 2002).

Vice-President: Bhairon Singh Shekhawat (sworn in 19 August 2002).

COUNCIL OF MINISTERS
(April 2005)

A coalition of the Indian National Congress (Congress), the Nationalist Congress Party (NCP), the Rashtriya Janata Dal (RJD), the Lok Jan Shakti Party (LJSP), Dravida Munnetra Kazhagam (DMK), Telangana Rashtriya Samithi (TRS), Jharkhand Mukti Morcha (JMM), Pattali Makal Katchi (PMK), Marumalarchi Dravida Munnetra Kazhagam (MDMK), the Rashtriya Lok Dal (RLD), the Muslim League Kerala State Committee (MUL), the Republican Party of India—A (RPI—A), the All India Majlis-e-Ittehadul Muslimeen (AIMIM), the People's Democratic Party (PDP) and Kerala Congress.

Prime Minister and Minister-in-charge of Personnel, Public Grievances and Pensions, of Planning, of Coal, of Atomic Energy and of Space: Dr Manmohan Singh (Congress).

Minister of Defence: Pranab Mukherjee (Congress).

Minister of Human Resource Development: Arjun Singh (Congress).

Minister of Agriculture and of Consumer Affairs, Food and Public Distribution: Sharad Pawar (NCP).

Minister of Railways: Lalu Prasad Yadav (RJD).

Minister of Home Affairs: Shivraj V. Patil (Congress).

Minister of Chemicals and Fertilizers and of Steel: Ram Vilas Paswan (LJSP).

Minister of Mines: Sish Ram Ola (Congress).

Minister of Parliamentary Affairs and of Urban Development: Ghulam Nabi Azad (Congress).

Minister of Information and Broadcasting and of Culture: S. Jaipal Reddy (Congress).

Minister of Labour and Employment: K. Chandrasekhar Rao (TRS).

Minister of Finance: P. Chidambaram (Congress).

Minister of Small-scale Industries and of Agro and Rural Industries: Mahavir Prasad (Congress).

Minister of Tribal Affairs and of Development of North Eastern Region: P. R. Kyndiah (Congress).

Minister of Road Transport and Highways and of Shipping: T. R. Baalu (DMK).

Minister of Textiles: Shankarsinh Vaghela (Congress).

Minister of External Affairs: K. Natwar Singh (Congress).

Minister of Commerce and Industry: Kamal Nath (Congress).

Minister of Law and Justice: H. R. Bhardwaj (Congress).

Minister of Power: P. M. Sayeed (Congress).

Minister of Rural Development: Raghubansh Prasad Singh (RJD).

Minister of Water Resources: Priyaranjan Dasmunsi (Congress).

Minister of Petroleum and Natural Gas and of Panchayat Raj: Mani Shankar Aiyar (Congress).

Minister of Youth Affairs and Sports: Sunil Dutt (Congress).

Minister of Social Justice and Empowerment: Meira Kumar (Congress).

Minister of Environment and Forests: A. Raja (DMK).

Minister of Communications and Information Technology: Dayanidhi Maran (DMK).

Minister of Health and Family Welfare: Dr Anbumani Ramdoss (PMK).

Ministers of State with Independent Charge

Minister of State for Heavy Industries and Public Enterprises: Santosh Mohan Dev (Congress).

Minister of State for Overseas Indian Affairs: Jagdish Tytler (Congress).

Minister of State for Statistics and Programme Implementation: Oscar Fernandes (Congress).

Minister of State for Tourism: Renuka Chowdhury (Congress).

Minister of State for Food Processing Industries: Subodh Kant Sahay (Congress).

Minister of State for Science and Technology and Ocean Development: Kapil Sibal (Congress).

Minister of State for Non-Conventional Energy Sources: Vilas Muttemwar (Congress).

Minister of State for Urban Employment and Poverty Alleviation: Kumari Selja (Congress).

Minister of State for Civil Aviation: Praful Patel (NCP).

Minister of State for Company Affairs: Prem Chand Gupta (RJD).

There are, in addition, 28 Ministers of State without independent charge.

MINISTRIES

President's Office: Rashtrapati Bhavan, New Delhi 110 004; tel. (11) 23015321; fax (11) 23017290; internet www.goidirectory.nic.in.

Vice-President's Office: 6 Maulana Azad Rd, New Delhi 110 011; tel. (11) 23016344; fax (11) 23018124.

Prime Minister's Office: South Block, New Delhi 110 011; tel. (11) 23012312; fax (11) 23016857; internet www.pmindia.nic.in.

Ministry of Agriculture: Krishi Bhavan, Dr Rajendra Prasad Rd, New Delhi 110 001; tel. (11) 23383370; fax (11) 23384129.

Ministry of Agro and Rural Industries: Udyog Bhavan, Rafi Marg, New Delhi 110 011; tel. (11) 23012107; fax (11) 23013045; internet ari.nic.in.

Department of Atomic Energy: Anushakti Bhavan, Chatrapathi Shivaji Maharaj Marg, Mumbai 400 001; tel. (22) 22026823; fax (22) 22048476; internet www.dae.gov.in.

Ministry of Chemicals and Fertilizers: Shastri Bhavan, New Delhi 110 001; tel. (11) 23386519; fax (11) 23015477.

Ministry of Civil Aviation: Rajiv Gandhi Bhavan, Safdarjung Airport, New Delhi 110 023; tel. (11) 24613050; fax (11) 24613054; e-mail web@civilav.delhi.nic.in; internet www.civilaviation.nic.in.

Ministry of Coal: Shram Shakti Bhavan, Rafi Marg, New Delhi 110 001; tel. (11) 23384884; fax (11) 23387738; e-mail secy.moc@sb.nic.in.

Ministry of Commerce and Industry: Udyog Bhavan, New Delhi 110 011; tel. (11) 23010008; fax (11) 23019947; internet www.commin.nic.in.

Ministry of Communications and Information Technology: Electronic Niketan, Lodhi Rd, New Delhi 110 003; tel. (11) 24369191; fax (11) 24369179; e-mail ddgir@sancharnet.in; internet www.moc.gov.in.

Ministry of Company Affairs: 'A' Wing, Shastri Bhavan, Rajendra Prasad Rd, New Delhi 110 001; tel. (11) 23073804; fax (11) 23073806; e-mail sardana@nic.in; internet dca.nic.in.

Ministry of Consumer Affairs, Food and Public Distribution: Krishi Bhavan, New Delhi 110 001; tel. (11) 23382349; fax (11) 23388302; internet www.fcamin.nic.in.

Ministry of Culture: Rm 334, 'C' Wing, Shastri Bhavan, New Delhi 110 001; tel. (11) 23386892; fax (11) 23782118; e-mail k_jayakumar@email.com; internet indiaculture.nic.in.

Ministry of Defence: South Block, New Delhi 110 011; tel. (11) 23019030; fax (11) 23015403; internet www.mod.nic.in.

Ministry of Development of North Eastern Region: Vigyan Bhavan Annexe, Maulana Azad Rd, New Delhi 110 011; internet northeast.nic.in.

Ministry of Environment and Forests: Paryavaran Bhavan, CGO Complex Phase II, Lodhi Rd, New Delhi 110 003; tel. (11) 24361727; fax (11) 24362222; e-mail secy@menf.delhi.nic.in; internet www.envfor.nic.in.

Ministry of External Affairs: South Block, New Delhi 110 011; tel. (11) 23011127; fax (11) 23011463; internet meaindia.nic.in.

Ministry of Finance: North Block, New Delhi 110 001; tel. (11) 23092810; fax (11) 23093289; e-mail jsdea@finance.delhi.nic.in; internet www.finmin.nic.in.

Ministry of Food Processing Industries: Panchsheel Bhavan, August Kranti Marg, New Delhi 110 049; tel. (11) 26493889; fax (11) 26493298; internet mofpi.nic.in.

Ministry of Health and Family Welfare: Nirman Bhavan, Maulana Azad Rd, New Delhi 110 011; tel. (11) 23018863; fax (11) 23014252; e-mail secyhlth@mohfw.delhi.nic.in; internet www.mohfw.nic.in.

Ministry of Heavy Industries and Public Enterprises: Udyog Bhavan, New Delhi 110 011; tel. (11) 23011459; fax (11) 23018552.

Ministry of Home Affairs: North Block, Central Secretariat, New Delhi 110 001; tel. (11) 23094221; fax (11) 23093750; e-mail mhaweb@mhant.delhi.nic.in; internet www.mha.nic.in.

Ministry of Human Resource Development: Shastri Bhavan, New Delhi 110 001; tel. (11) 23782698; fax (11) 23382365.

Ministry of Information and Broadcasting: 'A' Wing, Shastri Bhavan, New Delhi 110 001; tel. (11) 23384340; fax (11) 23782118; internet www.mib.nic.in.

Ministry of Labour and Employment: Shram Shakti Bhavan, Rafi Marg, New Delhi 110 001; tel. (11) 23710240; fax (11) 23711708; e-mail labour@lisd.delhi.nic.in; internet www.labour.nic.in.

Ministry of Law and Justice: 'A' Wing, Shastri Bhavan, Dr Rajendra Prasad Rd, New Delhi 110 001; tel. (11) 23384241; fax (11) 23015223; e-mail lawmin@caselaw.delhi.nic.in; internet www.lawmin.nic.in.

Ministry of Non-Conventional Energy Sources: Block 14, CGO Complex, Lodhi Rd, New Delhi 110 003; tel. (11) 24360744; fax (11) 24362554; e-mail secymnes@ren02.nic.in; internet www.mnes.nic.in.

Ministry of Overseas Indian Affairs: South Block, New Delhi 110 011; tel. (11) 23012219; fax (11) 23013386.

Ministry of Parliamentary Affairs: Parliament House, New Delhi 110 001; tel. (11) 23017780; fax (11) 23792341; e-mail parlmin@sansad.nic.in; internet www.mpa.nic.in.

Ministry of Personnel, Public Grievances and Pensions: North Block, New Delhi 110 001; tel. (11) 23094848; fax (11) 23012432; e-mail pgweb@arpg.delhi.nic.in; internet www.persmin.nic.in.

Ministry of Petroleum and Natural Gas: Shastri Bhavan, New Delhi 110 001; tel. (11) 23381462; fax (11) 23386118; e-mail dspdi.png@sb.nic.in; internet www.petroleum.nic.in.

Ministry of Power: Shram Shakti Bhavan, New Delhi 110 001; tel. (11) 23710411; fax (11) 23710065; internet www.powermin.nic.in.

Ministry of Railways: Rail Bhavan, Raisina Rd, New Delhi 110 001; tel. (11) 23386645; fax (11) 23382637; e-mail secyrb@rb.railnet.gov.in; internet www.indianrailways.gov.in.

Ministry of Road Transport and Highways: Parivahan Bhavan, 1 Sansad Marg, New Delhi 110 001; tel. (11) 23710121; fax (11) 23719023; internet morth.nic.in.

Ministry of Rural Development: Krishi Bhavan, New Delhi 110 001; tel. (11) 23383548; fax (11) 23385876; e-mail arunbhat@rural.delhi.nic.in; internet www.rural.nic.in.

Ministry of Science and Technology and Ocean Development: Technology Bhavan, New Mehrauli Rd, New Delhi 110 016; tel. (11) 26524756; fax (11) 26567793; internet www.mst.nic.in.

Ministry of Shipping: Transport Bhavan, 1 Sansad Marg, New Delhi 110 001; tel. (11) 23714938; fax (11) 23313943.

Ministry of Small-scale Industries: Udyog Bhavan, Rafi Marg, New Delhi 110 011; tel. (11) 23011739; fax (11) 23013141; internet ssi.nic.in.

Ministry of Social Justice and Empowerment: Shastri Bhavan, Dr Rajendra Prasad Rd, New Delhi 110 001; tel. (11) 23381390; fax (11) 23321902; e-mail secywel@sb.nic.in; internet www.socialjustice.nic.in.

Ministry of Statistics and Programme Implementation: Sardar Patel Bhavan, Patel Chowk, New Delhi 110 001; tel. (11) 23340884; fax (11) 23340138; e-mail moscc@bol.net.in; internet mospi.nic.in.

Ministry of Steel: Udyog Bhavan, New Delhi 110 011; tel. (11) 23793432; fax (11) 23013236; e-mail dvs@ub.nic.in; internet steel.nic.in.

Ministry of Textiles: Udyog Bhavan, New Delhi 110 011; tel. (11) 23013779; fax (11) 23016575; e-mail textiles@ub.delhi.nic.in; internet www.texmin.nic.in.

Ministry of Tourism: Transport Bhavan, Parliament St, New Delhi 110 001; tel. (11) 23714677; fax (11) 23710518; e-mail contactus@incredibleindia.org; internet incredibleindia.org.

Ministry of Tribal Affairs: Rm 750A, Shastri Bhavan, New Delhi 110 001; tel. (11) 23388482; fax (11) 23381499; e-mail dirit@tribal.nic.in; internet www.tribal.nic.in.

Ministry of Urban Development: Nirman Bhavan, New Delhi 110 011; tel. (11) 23019377; fax (11) 23016179; e-mail secyurban@alpha.nic.in; internet www.urbanindia.nic.in.

Ministry of Urban Employment and Poverty Alleviation: Nirman Bhavan, New Delhi; tel. (11) 23018242; fax (11) 23018780.

Ministry of Water Resources: Shram Shakti Bhavan, Rafi Marg, New Delhi 110 001; tel. (11) 23714663; fax (11) 23710804; internet www.wrmin.nic.in.

Ministry of Youth Affairs and Sports: Shastri Bhavan, Dr Rajendra Prasad Rd, New Delhi 110 001; tel. (11) 23384183; fax (11) 23381898; internet www.yas.nic.in.

Legislature

PARLIAMENT

Rajya Sabha
(Council of States)

Most of the members of the Rajya Sabha are indirectly elected by the State Assemblies for six years, with one-third retiring every two years. The remaining members are nominated by the President.

Chairman: BHAIRON SINGH SHEKHAWAT.

Deputy Chairman: K. RAHMAN KHAN.

Distribution of Seats, July 2004

Party	Seats
Congress*	70
Communist Party of India (Marxist)	14
Telugu Desam	9
Bharatiya Janata Party	49†
Samajwadi Party	12
Rashtriya Janata Dal	9
Dravida Munnetra Kazhagam	2
Shiromani Akali Dal	2
Biju Janata Dal	5
Nationalist Congress Party	4
Samata Party	1
Muslim League	2
All-India Anna Dravida Munnetra Kazhagam	12
Communist Party of India	2
Jammu and Kashmir National Conference	1
Shiv Sena	4
Bahujan Samaj Party	6
Revolutionary Socialist Party	3
Indian National Lok Dal	4
Independents and others	23
Nominated	9
Vacant	2
Total	**245**

* Formerly known as the Indian National Congress (Indira) or Congress (I); name gradually changed to the Indian National Congress or Congress Party in the early to mid-1990s.
† Including three nominated members.

Lok Sabha
(House of the People)

Speaker: SOMNATH CHATTERJEE.

General Election, 20, 22 and 25 April and 5 and 10 May 2004*

Party	Seats
Congress and allies	222
Congress	145
Rashtriya Janata Dal	24
Dravida Munnetra Kazhagam	16
Nationalist Congress Party	9
Pattali Makkal Katchi	6
Telangana Rashtra Samithi	5
Jharkhand Mukti Morcha	5
Lok Jan Shakti Party	4
Marumalarchi Dravida Munnetra Kazhagam	4
All India Majlis-e-Ittehadul Muslimeen	1
Muslim League Kerala State Committee	1
People's Democratic Party	1
Republican Party of India (A)	1
National Democratic Alliance	186
Bharatiya Janata Party	138
Shiv Sena	12
Biju Janata Dal	11
Shiromani Akali Dal	8
Janata Dal (United)	8
Telugu Desam	5
All India Trinamool Congress	2
Mizo National Front	1
Nagaland People's Front	1
Left Front	59
Communist Party of India (Marxist)	43
Communist Party of India	10
All India Forward Bloc	3
Revolutionary Socialist Party	3
Samajwadi Party	36
Bahujan Samaj Party	19
Janata Dal (Secular)	3
Rashtriya Lok Dal	3
Jammu and Kashmir National Conference	2
Asom Gana Parishad	2
Bharatiya Navshakti Party	1
Kerala Congress	1
Sikkim Democratic Front	1
Independents and others	8
Nominated	2†
Total	**545**

* Includes the results of voting in several constituencies where the elections were postponed until 12–31 May, owing to irregularities and technical error.
† Nominated by the President to represent the Anglo-Indian community.

State Governments
(April 2005)

ANDHRA PRADESH
(Capital—Hyderabad)

Governor: SUSHIL KUMAR SHINDE.

Chief Minister: Dr Y. S. RAJASEKHARA REDDY (Congress).

Legislative Assembly: 295 seats (Congress 186, Telugu Desam 44, Telangana Rashtra Samithi 26, Communist Party of India—Marxist 9, Communist Party of India 6, All India Majlis-e-Ittehadul Muslimeen 5, Bharatiya Janata Party 2, Bahujan Samaj Party 1, Samata Party 1, independents and others 13, nominated 1, vacant 1).

ARUNACHAL PRADESH
(Capital—Itanagar)

Governor: S. K. SINGH.

Chief Minister: GEGONG APANG (Congress).

Legislative Assembly: 60 seats (Congress 34, Bharatiya Janata Party 9, Nationalist Congress Party 2, Arunachal Congress 2, independents 13).

ASSAM
(Capital—Dispur)

Governor: Lt-Gen. (retd) AJAY SINGH.

Chief Minister: TARUN GOGOI (Congress).

Legislative Assembly: 126 seats (Congress 70, Asom Gana Parishad 21, Bharatiya Janata Party 8, Nationalist Congress Party 3, All India Trinamool Congress 1, independents and others 23).

BIHAR
(Capital—Patna)

Governor: BUTA SINGH.

Chief Minister: (vacant).

Legislative Assembly: 243 seats (Rashtriya Janata Dal 75, Janata Dal—United 55, Bharatiya Janata Party 37, Jan Shakti 29, Congress 10, Communist Party of India—Marxist-Leninist (Liberation) 7, Samajwadi Party 4, Nationalist Congress Party 3, Communist Party of India—CPI 3, Bahujan Samaj Party 2, Communist Party of India—Marxist 1, independents 17).

Legislative Council: 54 seats.

Direct presidential rule was imposed in Bihar in March 2005 following the failure of the newly elected Legislative Assembly to form a Government in the state.

CHHATTISGARH
(Capital—Raipur)

Governor: Lt-Gen. (retd) KRISHAN MOHAN SETH.

Chief Minister: Dr RAMAN SINGH (Bharatiya Janata Party).

Legislative Assembly: 90 seats (Bharatiya Janata Party 52, Congress 34, Bahujan Samaj Party 3, others 1).

GOA
(Capital—Panaji)

Governor: S. C. JAMIR.

Chief Minister: (vacant).

Legislative Assembly: 40 seats (Bharatiya Janata Party 17, Congress 15, United Goans Democratic Party 1, Maharashtrawadi Gomantak Party 1, National Congress Party 1, independents 1, vacant 4).

Direct presidential rule was imposed in Goa in March 2005.

GUJARAT
(Capital—Gandhinagar)

Governor: NAWAL KISHORE SHARMA.

Chief Minister: NARENDRA DAMODARDAS MODI (Bharatiya Janata Party).

Legislative Assembly: 182 seats (Bharatiya Janata Party 128, Congress 50, Janata Dal—United 2, independents 2).

HARYANA
(Capital—Chandigarh)

Governor: A. R. KIDWAI.

Chief Minister: BHUPINDER SINGH HOODA (Congress).

Legislative Assembly: 90 seats (Congress 67, Indian National Lok Dal 9, Bharatiya Janata Party 2, Bahujan Samaj Party 1, Nationalist Congress Party 1, independents 10).

HIMACHAL PRADESH
(Capital—Shimla)

Governor: VISHNU SADASHIV KOKJE.

Chief Minister: VIRBHADRA SINGH (Congress).

Legislative Assembly: 68 seats (Congress 43, Bharatiya Janata Party 16, Himachal Vikas Congress 1, Himlokantrik Morch 1, Lok Jan Shakti 1, independents 6).

JAMMU AND KASHMIR
(Capitals—(Summer) Srinagar, (Winter) Jammu)

Governor: Lt-Gen. (retd) S. K. SINHA.

Chief Minister: Mufti MOHAMMED SAYEED (People's Democratic Party).

Legislative Assembly: 87 seats (Jammu and Kashmir National Conference 28, Congress 20, People's Democratic Party 16, Panther's Party 4, Communist Party of India—Marxist 2, Ladakh Union Territory Front 2, independents and others 15).

Legislative Council: 36 seats.

JHARKHAND
(Capital—Ranchi)

Governor: SYED SIBTEY RAZI.

Chief Minister: ARJUN MUNDA (Bharatiya Janata Party).

Legislative Assembly: 81 seats (Bharatiya Janata Party 30, Jharkhand Mukti Morcha 17, Congress 9, Rashtriya Janata Dal 7, Janata Dal—United 6, independents and others 12).

KARNATAKA
(Capital—Bangalore)

Governor: T. N. CHATURVEDI.

Chief Minister: N. DHARAM SINGH (Congress).

Legislative Assembly: 225 seats (Bharatiya Janata Party 79, Congress 65, Janata Dal—Secular 58, Janata Dal—United 5, Communist Party of India—Marxist 1, Republican Party of India 1, independents and others 15, nominated 1).

Legislative Council: 75 seats.

KERALA
(Capital—Thiruvananthapuram)

Governor: R. L. BHATIA.

Chief Minister: OOMEN CHANDY (Congress).

Legislative Assembly: 140 seats (Congress 62, Communist—CPI—M 23, Muslim League 17, Kerala Congress (M) 9, Communist—CPI 7, Janata Dal—Secular 3, Nationalist Congress Party 2, Kerala Congress 2, Kerala Congress (Joseph) 2, Revolutionary Socialist Party 2, independents and others 10, vacant 1).

MADHYA PRADESH
(Capital—Bhopal)

Governor: BALRAM JAKHAR.

Chief Minister: BABULAL GAUR (Bharatiya Janata Party).

Legislative Assembly: 230 seats (Bharatiya Janata Party 176, Congress 34, Samajwadi Party 7, Gondwana Gantantra Party 3, Bahujan Samaj Party 2, Rashtriya Samata Dal 2, others 6).

MAHARASHTRA
(Capital—Mumbai)

Governor: S. M. KRISHNA.

Chief Minister: VILASRAO DESHMUKH (Congress).

Legislative Assembly: 288 seats (Nationalist Congress Party 71, Congress 67, Shiv Sena 62, Bharatiya Janata Party 54, Communist—CPI—M 2, independents and others 32).

Legislative Council: 78 seats.

MANIPUR
(Capital—Imphal)

Governor: SHIVINDAR SINGH SIDHU.

Chief Minister: OKRAM IBOBI SINGH (Congress).

Legislative Assembly: 60 seats (Congress 31, Federal Party of Manipur 13, Manipur State Congress Party 2, Communist—CPI 5, Bharatiya Janata Party 4, independents and others 5).

MEGHALAYA
(Capital—Shillong)

Governor: M. M. JACOB.

Chief Minister: D. D. LAPANG (Congress).

Legislative Assembly: 60 seats (Congress 22, United Democratic Party 9, Nationalist Congress Party 14, Meghalaya Democratic Party 4, Bharatiya Janata Party 2, Khun Hynniewtrep National Awakening Movement 2, People's Democratic Movement 2, Hills State People's Democratic Party 2, independents 3).

MIZORAM
(Capital—Aizawl)

Governor: AMOLAK RATTAN KOHLI.

Chief Minister: ZORAMTHANGA (Mizo National Front).

Legislative Assembly: 40 seats (Mizo National Front 21, Congress 12, Mizo People's Conference 3, others 3, vacant 1).

NAGALAND
(Capital—Kohima)

Governor: SHYAMAL DUTTA.

Chief Minister: NEIPHIU RIO (Nagaland People's Front).

Legislative Assembly: 60 seats (Nagaland People's Front 30, Congress 14, Bharatiya Janata Party 7, Janata Dal—United 3, independents and others 6).

ORISSA
(Capital—Bhubaneswar)

Governor: RAMESHWAR THAKUR.

Chief Minister: NAVEEN PATNAIK (Biju Janata Dal).

Legislative Assembly: 147 seats (Biju Janata Dal 61, Congress 38, Bharatiya Janata Party 32, Jharkhand Mukti Morcha 4, Orissa Gana Parishad 2, Communist Party of India 1, Communist Party of India—Marxist 1, independents 8).

THE PUNJAB
(Capital—Chandigarh)

Governor: Gen. S. F. RODRIGUES (retd).

Chief Minister: Capt. AMARINDER SINGH (Congress).

Legislative Assembly: 117 seats (Congress 64, Shiromani Akali Dal 41, Bharatiya Janata Party 3, independents 9).

RAJASTHAN
(Capital—Jaipur)

Governor: PRATIBHA PATIL.

Chief Minister: VASUNDHARA RAJE SCINDIA (Bharatiya Janata Party).

Legislative Assembly: 200 seats (Bharatiya Janata Party 120, Congress 56, Indian National Lok Dal 4, Janata Dal—United 2, Bahujan Samaj Party 2, Communist—CPI—M 1, independents and others 15).

SIKKIM
(Capital—Gangtok)

Governor: V. RAMA RAO.

Chief Minister: PAWAN KUMAR CHAMLING (Sikkim Democratic Front).

Legislative Assembly: 32 seats (Sikkim Democratic Front 31, Congress 1).

TAMIL NADU
(Capital—Chennai)

Governor: SURJIT SINGH BARNALA.

Chief Minister: C. JAYARAM JAYALALITHA (All-India Anna Dravida Munnetra Kazhagam).

Legislative Assembly: 235 seats (All-India Anna Dravida Munnetra Kazhagam 132, Congress 30, Dravida Munnetra Kazhagam 27, Pattali Makkal Katchi 20, Communist—CPI—M 6, Communist—CPI 5, Bharatiya Janata Party 4, All India Forward Bloc 1, independents and others 10).

TRIPURA
(Capital—Agartala)

Governor: D. N. SAHAYA.

Chief Minister: MANIK SARKAR (Communist Party of India—Marxist).

Legislative Assembly: 60 seats (Communist Party of India—Marxist 38, Congress 13, Tripura Upajati Juba Samity 6, others 3).

UTTAR PRADESH
(Capital—Lucknow)

Governor: T. V. RAJESHWAR.

Chief Minister: MULAYAM SINGH YADAV (Samajwadi Party).

Legislative Assembly: 404 seats (Samajwadi Party 142, Bharatiya Janata Party 87, Bahujan Samaj Party 73, Lok Tantrik Bahujan Samaj Party 37, Congress 16, Rashtriya Lok Dal 14, Rashtriya Kranti Party 4, Communist Party of India—Marxist 2, Lok Tantrik Congress 2, independents and others 25, nominated 1, vacant 1).

Legislative Council: 108 seats.

UTTARANCHAL
(Capital—Dehradun)

Governor: SUDARSHAN AGARWAL.

Chief Minister: NARAIN DUTT TIWARI (Congress).

Legislative Assembly: 70 seats (Congress 36, Bharatiya Janata Party 19, Bahujan Samaj Party 7, Uttarakhand Kranti Dal 4, independents and others 4).

WEST BENGAL
(Capital—Kolkata)

Governor: GOPALKRISHNA GANDHI.

Chief Minister: BUDDHADEV BHATTACHARYA (Communist Party of India—Marxist).

Legislative Assembly: 294 seats (Communist—CPI—M 143, All India Trinamool Congress 60, Congress 26, All India Forward Bloc 25, Revolutionary Socialist Party 17, Communist—CPI 7, independents and others 16).

UNION TERRITORIES

Andaman and Nicobar Islands (Headquarters—Port Blair): Lt-Gov. RAMCHANDRA GANESH KAPSE.

Chandigarh (Headquarters—Chandigarh): Administrator Gen. S. F. RODRIGUES (retd).

Chandigarh was to be incorporated into the Punjab state on 26 January 1986, but the transfer was postponed indefinitely.

Dadra and Nagar Haveli (Headquarters—Silvassa): Administrator ARUN MATHUR.

Daman and Diu (Headquarters—Daman): Administrator ARUN MATHUR.

Lakshadweep (Headquarters—Kavaratti): Administrator K. S. MEHRA.

Pondicherry (Capital—Pondicherry): Lt-Gov. M. M. LAKHERA; Chief Minister N. RANGASAMY (Congress).

Assembly: 30 seats (Congress 12, Dravida Munnetra Kazhagam 7, Puduchcheri Makal Congress 4, All-India Anna Dravida Munnetra Kazhagam 2, Tamil Maanila Congress 2, Bharatiya Janata Party 1, independents 2).

NATIONAL CAPITAL TERRITORY

Delhi (Headquarters—Delhi): Lt-Gov. BHANWARI LAL JOSHI; Chief Minister SHEILA DIXIT (Congress).

Assembly: 70 seats (Congress 47, Bharatiya Janata Party 20, Janata Dal—Secular 1, Nationalist Congress Party 1, independent 1).

Political Organizations

MAJOR NATIONAL POLITICAL ORGANIZATIONS

All India Congress Committee: 24 Akbar Rd, New Delhi 110 011; tel. (11) 23019080; fax (11) 23017047; internet www.indiancongress.org; f. 1978 as Indian National Congress (I), as a breakaway group under Indira Gandhi; name of party gradually changed to Indian National Congress or Congress Party in the early to mid-1990s; Pres. SONIA GANDHI; Gen. Secs MUKUL WASNIK, JANARDAN DWIVEDI, SATYAVRAT CHATURVEDI, MARGARET ALVA, AMBIKA SONI, DIGVIJAY SINGH, ASHOK GEHLOT; 35m. mems (1998).

Bahujan Samaj Party (Majority Society Party): c/o Lok Sabha, New Delhi; promotes the rights of the *Harijans* ('Untouchables') of India; Pres. MAYAWATI; Gen. Sec. RASHID ALVI.

Bharatiya Janata Party (BJP) (Indian People's Party): 11 Ashok Rd, New Delhi 110 001; tel. (11) 23382234; fax (11) 23782163; e-mail bjpco@del3.vsnl.net.in; internet www.bjp.org; f. 1980 as a breakaway group from Janata Party; right-wing Hindu party; Pres. Shri L. K. ADVANI; Gen. Secs SHIVRAJ SINGH CHAUHAN, PRAMOD MAHAJAN, RAJNATH SINGH, SANJAY JOSHI, ARUN JAITLEY, ANANT KUMAR; 10.5m. mems.

Communist Party of India (CPI): Ajoy Bhavan, Com. Indrajit Gupta Marg, New Delhi 110 002; tel. (11) 23235546; fax (11) 23235543; e-mail cpi@vsnl.com; internet www.cpofindia.org; f. 1925; advocates the establishment of a socialist society led by the working class, and ultimately of a communist society; nine-mem. central secretariat; Gen. Sec. ARDHENDU BHUSHAN BARDHAN; 486,578 mems (2004).

Communist Party of India—Marxist (CPI—M): A. K. Gopalan Bhavan, 27–29 Bhai Vir Singh Marg, New Delhi 110 001; tel. (11) 23344918; fax (11) 23747483; e-mail cpim@vsnl.com; internet www.cpim.org; f. 1964 as breakaway group from the CPI; maintained an independent position; managed by a central committee of 77 mems and a politburo of 18 mems; Leaders BUDDHADEV BHATTACHARYA, JYOTI BASU, PRAKASH KARAT, SITARAM YECHURY, SOMNATH CHATTERJEE; Gen. Sec. PRAKASH KARAT; 814,408 mems (2002).

Nationalist Congress Party (NCP): 10 Dr Bishambhar Das Marg, New Delhi 110001; tel. (11) 23359218; fax (11) 23352112; f. 1999 as breakaway faction of Congress; split into two factions in Jan. 2004—one headed by Sharad Pawar and another by Purno Shangma; faction led by Sangma merged with the All India Trinamool Congress.

MAJOR REGIONAL POLITICAL ORGANIZATIONS

Akhil Bharat Hindu Mahasabha: Hindu Mahasabha Bhavan, Mandir Marg, New Delhi 110 001; tel. (11) 23342087; fax (11) 23363105; f. 1915; seeks the establishment of a democratic Hindu state; Pres. DINESH CHANDRA TYAGI; Gen. Sec. Dr MADANLAL GOYAL; 525,000 mems.

All-India Anna Dravida Munnetra Kazhagam (AIADMK) (All-India Anna Dravidian Progressive Asscn): Lloyd's Rd, Chennai 600 004; f. 1972; breakaway group from the DMK; Gen. Sec. JAYARAM JAYALALITHA.

All India Forward Bloc: 28 Gurudwara Rakabganj Rd, New Delhi 110 001; tel. and fax (11) 23714131; e-mail dbiswas@sansad.nic.in; f. 1940 by Netaji Subhash Chandra Bose; socialist aims, including nationalization of major industries, land reform and redistribution, and the establishment of a union of socialist republics through revolution; Gen. Sec. DEBABRATA BISWAS; 900,000 mems (1999).

All India Trinamool Congress: 125-D, Parliament House, New Delhi 110 001; tel. (11) 23034355; internet www.trinamool.org; merged with the Sangma faction of the Nationalist Congress Party in 2004; Leader MAMATA BANERJEE; Pres. PANKAJ BANERJEE.

Asom Gana Parishad (AGP) (Assam People's Council): Gopinath Bordoloi Rd, Guwahati 781 001; f. 1985; draws support from the All-Assam Gana Sangram Parishad and the All-Assam Students' Union (Pres. Keshab Mahanta; Gen. Sec. Atul Bora); advocates the unity of India in diversity and a united Assam; Pres. (vacant).

Biju Janata Dal: Naveen Nivas, Aerodrome Gate, Bhubaneswar 751 009; Pres. NAVEEN PATNAIK.

Dravida Munnetra Kazhagam (DMK): Anna Arivalayam, Teynampet, Chennai 600 018; f. 1949; aims at full autonomy for states (primarily Tamil Nadu) within the Union; Pres. MUTHUVEL KARUNANIDHI; Gen. Sec. K. ANBAZHAGAN; more than 4m. mems.

Indian National Lok Dal: 18 Janpath, New Delhi 110 001; tel. (11) 23793409; Leader OM PRAKASH CHAUTALA.

Jammu and Kashmir National Conference (JKNC): Mujahid Manzil, Srinagar 190 002; tel. (194) 271500; fmrly All Jammu and Kashmir National Conference; f. 1931; renamed 1939, reactivated 1975; state-based party campaigning for internal autonomy and responsible self-govt; Pres. OMAR ABDULLAH; Gen. Sec. SHEIKH NAZIR AHMAD; 1m. mems.

Janata Dal—Secular (People's Party—Secular): 5 Safdarjung Lane, New Delhi 110 003; f. 2000 following split of Janata Dal; Pres. H. D. DEVE GOWDA.

Janata Dal—United (People's Party—United): 7 Jantar Mantar Rd, New Delhi 110 001; tel. (11) 23368833; fax (11) 23368138; f. 2000 following split of Janata Dal; merged with Samata Party in 2003; advocates non-alignment, the eradication of poverty, unemployment and wide disparities in wealth, and the protection of minorities; Pres. GEORGE FERNANDES.

Jharkhand Mukti Morcha: Bariatu Rd, Ranchi 834 008; Leader SHIBU SOREN.

Lok Jan Shakti Party (LJSP): New Delhi; left-wing; Pres. RAM VILAS PASWAN.

Pattali Makkal Katchi: Gounder St, Dharamapuri 636 701; tel. (4342) 263275; Leader Dr ANBUMANI RAMDOSS.

Peasants' and Workers' Party of India: Mahatma Phule Rd, Naigaum, Mumbai 400 014; f. 1949; Gen. Sec. DAJIBA DESAI; c. 10,000 mems.

Rashtriya Janata Dal (RJD) (National People's Party): 13 V. P. House, Rafi Marg, New Delhi 110 011; f. 1997 as a breakaway group from Janata Dal; Leader LALU PRASAD YADAV.

Republican Party of India (RPI): Ensa Hutments, I Block, Azad Maidan, Fort, Mumbai 400 001; tel. (22) 22621888; f. 1952; by 2003 the group had split into 10 factions; the three main factions were led by PRAKASH RAO AMBEDKAR, RAMDAS ATHAVALE and R. S. GAVAI, respectively.

Revolutionary Socialist Party: 17 Feroz Shah Rd, New Delhi 110 001; tel. (11) 23782167; fax (11) 23782342; e-mail abani@sansad.nic.in; Leaders DEBABRATA BANDOPADHYAY, ABANI ROY.

Samajwadi Party (Socialist Party): 18 Copernicus Lane, New Delhi; f. 1991; Pres. MULAYAM SINGH YADAV; Gen. Sec. AMAR SINGH.

Shiromani Akali Dal: Baradan Shri Darbar Sahib, Amritsar; f. 1920; Pres. (Shiromani Akali Dal—Badal) PRAKASH SINGH BADAL; Sec.-Gen. GURDEV SINGH DHINDSA.

Shiv Sena (Army of Shiv): Shiv Sena Bhavan, Ram Ganesh Gadkari Chowk, Dadar, Mumbai 400 028; tel. (22) 24309128; e-mail shivalay@shivsena.org; internet www.shivsena.org; f. 1966; militant Hindu group; Working Pres. UDDHAV THACKERAY.

Sikkim Democratic Front: Upper Deorali, Gangtok, East Sikkim; Pres. PAWAN KUMAR CHAMLING.

Telangana Rashtra Samithi: Karimnagar; f. 2001; Pres. K. CHANDRASEKHAR RAO.

Telugu Desam (Telugu Nation): NTR Trust Bhavan, Rd 2, Banjara Hills, Hyderabad 500 033; tel. (40) 23542101; fax (40) 23542108; e-mail tdp@telugudesam.com; internet www.telugudesam.com; f. 1982; state-based party (Andhra Pradesh); Pres. N. CHANDRABABU NAIDU; 8m. mems.

Diplomatic Representation

EMBASSIES AND HIGH COMMISSIONS IN INDIA

Afghanistan: 5/50F Shanti Path, Chanakyapuri, New Delhi 110 021; tel. (11) 26883602; fax (11) 26875439; e-mail afghanembassy@rediffmail.com; Ambassador MASOOD KHALILI.

Algeria: E-6/5 Vasant Vihar, New Delhi 110 057; tel. (11) 26146706; fax (11) 26147033; e-mail abdbelar@yahoo.fr; Ambassador ABDELKRIM BELARBI.

Angola: 5/50F, Nyaya Marg, Chanakyapuri, New Delhi 110 021; tel. (11) 26882680; fax (11) 24673785; e-mail enquiry@angolaembassyindia.com; internet www.angolaembassyindia.com; Ambassador ANA MARIA TELES CARREIRA.

Argentina: B-2, Anand Niketan, New Delhi 110 021; tel. (11) 51661982; fax (11) 51661988; e-mail eindi@mantraonline.com; Ambassador ERNESTO CARLOS ALVAREZ.

Armenia: E-1/20, Vasant Vihar, New Delhi 110 057; tel. (11) 26147328; fax (11) 26147329; e-mail armemb@vsnl.com; Ambassador ARMEN BAIBOURTIAN.

Australia: 1/50-G Shanti Path, Chanakyapuri, New Delhi 110 021; tel. (11) 51399900; fax (11) 26885199; internet www.ausgovindia.com; High Commissioner JOHN MCCARTHY.

Austria: EP–13 Chandragupta Marg, Chanakyapuri, New Delhi 110 021; tel. (11) 26889050; fax (11) 26886929; e-mail new-delhi-ob@bmaa.gv.at; Ambassador Dr JUTTA STEFAN-BASTL.

Azerbaijan: Vasant Marg, Vasant Vihar E-70, New Delhi; tel. (11) 26152228; fax (11) 26152227; e-mail azembassy@touchtelindia.net; Ambassador TAMERLAN GARAYEV.

Bangladesh: EP-39 Dr S. Radhakrishnan Marg, Chanakyapuri, New Delhi 110 021; tel. (11) 24121389; fax (11) 26878953; e-mail bhcdelhi@mantraonline.com; High Commissioner H. ETHEMAYE TUDDIN.

Belarus: 163 Jor Bagh, New Delhi 110 003; tel. (11) 24694518; fax (11) 24697029; e-mail india@belembassy.org; Ambassador OLEG LAPTENOK.

Belgium: 50N, Shanti Path, Chanakyapuri, New Delhi 110 021; tel. (11) 26889851; fax (11) 26885821; e-mail ambabel@del2.vsnl.net.in; internet www.diplomatie.be/newdelhi; Ambassador PATRICK DE BEYTER.

Bhutan: Chandragupta Marg, Chanakyapuri, New Delhi 110 021; tel. (11) 26889807; fax (11) 26876710; e-mail bhutan@vsnl.com; Ambassador: Lyonpo DAGO TSHERING.

Bosnia and Herzegovina: E-9/11 Vasant Vihar, New Delhi 110 057; tel. (11) 26147415; fax (11) 51662481; e-mail bosher@touchtelindia.net; Ambassador ŽELJKO JANJETOVIĆ.

Brazil: 8 Aurangzeb Rd, New Delhi 110 011; tel. (11) 23017301; fax (11) 23793684; e-mail brasindi@vsnl.com; Ambassador L. G. DE MORAES.

Brunei: 4 Poorvi Marg, Vasant Vihar, New Delhi 110 057; tel. (11) 26148340; fax (11) 26142101; e-mail sjtbruneidelhi@starith.net; High Commissioner Dato' PADUKA Haji ABDUL GHAFAR BIN Haji ISMAIL.

Bulgaria: 16/17 Chandragupta Marg, Chanakyapuri, New Delhi 110 021; tel. (11) 26115550; fax (11) 26876190; e-mail bulemb@mantraonline.com; internet www.bulgariaembindia.com; Ambassador DRAGOVEST GORANOV.

Burkina Faso: G-5, Anand Niketan, New Delhi 110 021; tel. (11) 24671678; fax (11) 24671745; e-mail emburnd@bol.net.in; Chargé d'affaires OUSMAN NACAMBO.

Cambodia: N-14 Panchsheel Park, New Delhi 110 017; tel. (11) 26495092; fax (11) 26495093; e-mail camboemb@del2.vsnl.net.in; Ambassador CHEANG ENG NGUON.

Canada: 7/8 Shanti Path, Chanakyapuri, New Delhi 110 021; tel. (11) 51782000; fax (11) 51782020; e-mail delhi@international.gc.ca; internet www.india.gc.ca; High Commissioner LUCIE EDWARDS.

Chile: 146 Jorbagh, New Delhi 110 003; tel. (11) 24617253; fax (11) 24632264; e-mail embchile@vsnl.com; Ambassador JORGE HEINE.

China, People's Republic: 50D Shanti Path, Chanakyapuri, New Delhi 110 021; tel. (11) 26881249; fax (11) 26882024; e-mail chinaemb_in@mfa.gov.cn; internet www.chinaembassyorg.in; Ambassador SUN YUXI.

Colombia: 3 Palam Marg, Vasant Vihar, New Delhi 110 057; tel. (11) 51662103; fax (11) 51662108; Ambassador JAIME INFANTE.

Congo, Democratic Republic: D-6 Anand Niketan, New Delhi 110 021; tel. (11) 51660976; Ambassador BALUMUENE BALU.

Croatia: A-15 West End, New Delhi 110 021; tel. (11) 26876871; fax (11) 26876873; e-mail croemnd@del1.vsnl.net.in; Ambassador DINO DEBELJUH.

Cuba: E-1/9 Vasant Vihar, New Delhi 110 057; tel. (11) 26143849; fax (11) 26143806; e-mail embcuind@ndf.vsnl.net.in; Ambassador JUAN CARRETERO IBÁÑEZ.

Cyprus: 106 Jor Bagh, New Delhi 110 003; tel. (11) 24697503; fax (11) 24628828; e-mail cyprus@del3.vsnl.net.in; internet www.cyprushcdelhi.com; High Commissioner ANDREAS G. SKARPARIS.

Czech Republic: 50M Niti Marg, Chanakyapuri, New Delhi 110 021; tel. (11) 26110205; fax (11) 26886221; e-mail newdelhi@embassy.mzv.cz; internet www.mfa.cz/newdelhi; Ambassador JAROMÍR NOVOTNÝ.

Denmark: 11 Aurangzeb Rd, New Delhi 110 011; tel. (11) 23010900; fax (11) 23792019; e-mail denmark@vsnl.com; internet www.denmarkindia.com; Ambassador MICHAEL STERNBERG.

Egypt: 1/50M Niti Marg, Chanakyapuri, New Delhi 110 021; tel. (11) 26114096; fax (11) 26885355; e-mail egypt@del2.vsnl.net.in; Ambassador KHEIRELDIN ABDEL-LATIF MOHAMMED.

Ethiopia: 7/50G Satya Marg, Chanakyapuri, New Delhi 110 021; tel. (11) 26119513; fax (11) 26875731; e-mail delethem@bol.net.in; Ambassador Dr TEKETEL FORSEDO.

Finland: E-3 Nyaya Marg, Chanakyapuri, New Delhi 110 021; tel. (11) 51497500; fax (11) 51497555; e-mail sanomat.NDE@formin.fi; internet www.finland.org.in; Ambassador GLEN LINDHOLM.

France: 2/50E Shanti Path, Chanakyapuri, New Delhi 110 021; tel. (11) 26118790; fax (11) 26872305; e-mail mef-delhi@tresor-dree.org; internet www.france-in-india.org; Ambassador DOMINIQUE GIRARD.

Germany: 6 Block 50G, Shanti Path, Chanakyapuri, New Delhi 110 021; tel. (11) 26871831; fax (11) 26873117; e-mail germany@vsnl.com; internet www.germanembassy-india.org; Ambassador HEIMO RICHTER.

Ghana: 50-N Satya Marg, Chanakyapuri, New Delhi 110 021; tel. (11) 26883298; fax (11) 26883202; e-mail ghstarin@vsnl.net; internet www.ghanaindia.com; High Commissioner Prof. MIKE OQUAYE.

Greece: 32 Dr S. Radhakrishnan Marg, Chanakyapuri, New Delhi 110 021; tel. (11) 26880700; fax (11) 26888010; e-mail hellemb@id.eth.net; internet www.greeceinindia.com; Ambassador EFSTATHIOS LOZOS.

Guyana: New Delhi.

Holy See: 50C Niti Marg, Chanakyapuri, New Delhi 110 021 (Apostolic Nunciature); tel. (11) 26889184; fax (11) 26874286; e-mail nuntius@starith.net; internet www.apostolicnunciatureindia.com; Nuncio Most Rev. PEDRO LÓPEZ QUINTANA (Titular Archbishop of Agropoli).

Hungary: Plot 2, 50M Niti Marg, Chanakyapuri, New Delhi 110 021; tel. (11) 26114737; fax (11) 26886742; e-mail huembdel2@vsnl.com; Ambassador GYULA PETHÖ.

Indonesia: 50A Chanakyapuri, New Delhi 110 021; tel. (11) 26114100; fax (11) 26885460; e-mail iembassy@giasdl01.vsnl.net.in; Ambassador DONNILO ANWAR.

Iran: 5 Barakhamba Road, New Delhi 110 001; tel. (11) 23329600; fax (11) 23325493; e-mail iranemin@vsnl.com; Ambassador SIYAVASH ZARGAR YAGHOUBI.

Iraq: E-1/24, Vasant Vihar, New Delhi 110 057; tel. (11) 26149085; fax (11) 26149076; Chargé d'affaires a.i. MUAYAD HUSSAIN.

Ireland: 230 Jor Bagh, New Delhi 110 003; tel. (11) 24626733; fax (11) 24697053; e-mail ireland@ndf.vsnl.net.in; Chargé d'affaires a.i. PATRICK SCULLION.

Israel: 3 Aurangzeb Rd, New Delhi 110 011; tel. (11) 23013238; fax (11) 23014298; e-mail israelem@vsnl.com; Ambassador DAVID DANIELI.

Italy: 50E Chandragupta Marg, Chanakyapuri, New Delhi 110 021; tel. (11) 26114355; fax (11) 26873889; e-mail italemb@del3.vsnl.net.in; internet www.italembdelhi.com; Ambassador ANTONIO AMELLINI.

Japan: Plots 4–5, 50G Shanti Path, Chanakyapuri, New Delhi 110 021; tel. (11) 26876581; fax (11) 26885587; Ambassador YASUKUNI ENOKI.

Jordan: 30 Golf Links, New Delhi 110 003; tel. (11) 24653318; fax (11) 24653353; e-mail jordemb@ndf.vsnl.net.in; Ambassador NABIL TALHOUNY.

Kazakhstan: 4 Olof Palme Marg, Vasant Vihar, New Delhi 110 057; tel. (11) 26144779; fax (11) 26144778; e-mail embaskaz@giasdl01.vsnl.net.in; Chargé d'affaires a.i. RUSLAN AKHMET.

Kenya: 34 Paschimi Marg, New Delhi 110 057; tel. (11) 26146537; fax (11) 26146550; e-mail info@kenyamission-delhi.com; internet www.kenyamission-delhi.com; High Commissioner HARRY MUTUMA KATHURIMA.

Korea, Democratic People's Republic: D-14 Maharani Bagh, New Delhi 110 065; tel. (11) 26829644; fax (11) 26829645; Ambassador HAN CHANG ON.

Korea, Republic: 9 Chandragupta Marg, Chanakyapuri, POB 5416, New Delhi 110 021; tel. (11) 26885412; fax (11) 26884840; e-mail embkorea@vsnl.com; Ambassador CHOI JUNG-IL.

Kuwait: 5A Shanti Path, Chanakyapuri, New Delhi 110 021; tel. (11) 24100791; fax (11) 26873516; Ambassador KHALAF ABBAS KHALAF AL-FOUDARI.

Kyrgyzstan: C-93 Anand Niketan, New Delhi 110 021; tel. (11) 24108008; fax (11) 24108009; e-mail kyrghyz@netscape.net; Ambassador BAKTYBEK BESHIMOV.

Laos: A-104/7 Parmanand Estate, Maharani Bagh, New Delhi 110 065; tel. (11) 26933319; fax (11) 26323048; e-mail amlaodl@ndb.vsnl.net.in; Ambassador KHAMPASONG DOUANGSITHI.

Lebanon: 26B Sardar Patel Marg, Chanakyapuri, New Delhi 110 021; tel. (11) 26111919; fax (11) 26111415; e-mail lebemb@vsnl.net.in; Ambassador WALID ADEL NASR.

Libya: 22 Golf Links, New Delhi 110 003; tel. (11) 24697717; fax (11) 24633005; e-mail libya@bol.net.in; Chargé d'affaires a.i. AHMED E. A. ABDURRAHMAN.

Luxembourg: 730 Gadaipur Rd, Branch Post Office, Gadaipur, New Delhi 110 030; tel. (11) 26156663; fax (11) 26801971; e-mail paulsteinmetz@internet.lu; Ambassador PAUL STEINMETZ.

Malaysia: 50M Satya Marg, Chanakyapuri, New Delhi 110 021; tel. (11) 26111291; fax (11) 26881538; e-mail miondelhi@del2.vsnl.net.in; High Commissioner ZULKIFLY IBRAHIM BIN ABDUL RAHMAN.

Mauritius: 41 Jesus and Mary Marg, Chanakyapuri, New Delhi 110 021; tel. (11) 24102161; fax (11) 24102194; e-mail mhcnd@bol.net.in; High Commissioner USHA CHANDNEE DWARKA-CANABADY.

Mexico: 26-D Sardar Patel Marg, New Delhi 110 021; tel. (11) 24107182; fax (11) 24107185; e-mail embamexindia@mantraonline.com; internet www.embamexindia.org; Ambassador ROGELIO GRANGUILLHOME MORFIN.

Mongolia: 34 Archbishop Makarios Marg, New Delhi 110 003; tel. (11) 24631728; fax (11) 24633240; e-mail mongemb@vsnl.net; Ambassador JANTSAN GULGOU.

Morocco: 33 Archbishop Makarios Marg, New Delhi 110 003; tel. (11) 24636920; fax (11) 24636925; e-mail sifamand@giasdl01.vsnl.net.in; internet www.moroccoembindia.com; Chargé d'affaires a.i. MOHAMED EL HIMANI.

Mozambique: B-3/24, Vasant Vihar, New Delhi 110 057; tel. (11) 26156663; fax (11) 26156665; e-mail salvaro64@hotmail.com; High Commissioner CARLOS A. DO ROSARIO.

Myanmar: 3/50F Nyaya Marg, Chanakyapuri, New Delhi 110 021; tel. (11) 26889007; fax (11) 26877942; e-mail myandeli@nda.vsnl.net.in; Ambassador U KYI THEIN.

Namibia: A-2/6 Vasant Vihar, New Delhi 110 057; tel. (11) 26144772; fax (11) 26146120; e-mail nhcdelhi@del2.vsnl.net.in; High Commissioner Maj-Gen. CHARLES-DICKSON NDAXU P. NAMOLOH.

Nepal: Barakhamba Rd, New Delhi 110 001; tel. (11) 23329218; fax (11) 23326857; e-mail ramjanki@del2.vsnl.net.in; Ambassador KARNADHOJ ADHIKARI.

Netherlands: 6/50F Shanti Path, Chanakyapuri, New Delhi 110 021; tel. (11) 26884951; fax (11) 26884956; e-mail nde@minbuza.nl; internet www.holland-in-india.org; Ambassador ERIC F. C. NIEHE.

New Zealand: 50N Nyaya Marg, Chanakyapuri, New Delhi 110 021; tel. (11) 26883170; fax (11) 26883165; e-mail nzhc@ndf.vsnl.net.in; High Commissioner GRAEME WATERS.

Nigeria: Plot No. 4, Chandragupta Marg, Chanakyapuri, New Delhi 110 021; tel. (11) 24122142; fax (11) 24122138; e-mail nhcnder@vsnl.com; internet www.nigeriadelhi.com; High Commissioner ABUBAKAR GARBA ABDULLAHI.

Norway: 50C Shanti Path, Chanakyapuri, New Delhi 110 021; tel. (11) 51779200; fax (11) 26873814; e-mail noramb@vsnl.com; Ambassador JON WESTBORG.

Oman: EP-10/11, Chandragupta Marg, Chankyapuri, New Delhi 110 021; tel. (11) 26885622; fax (11) 26885621; e-mail omandelhi@vsnl.com; Ambassador KHALIFA BIN ALI BIN ESSA AL-HARTHY.

Pakistan: 2/50G Shanti Path, Chanakyapuri, New Delhi 110 021; tel. (11) 26110601; fax (11) 26872339; e-mail pakhc@nda.vsnl.net.in; High Commissioner AZIZ AHMED KHAN.

Panama: C-321, Defence Colony, New Delhi 110 024; tel. (11) 24335627; fax (11) 24335631; e-mail panaind@bol.net.in; Ambassador ALBERTO J. PINZÓN.

Peru: G-15 Maharani Bagh, New Delhi 110 065; tel. (11) 26312610; fax (11) 26312557; e-mail info@embaperuindia.com; internet www.embaperuindia.com; Ambassador BENJAMIN RUIZ SOBERO.

Philippines: 50N Nyaya Marg, Chanakyapuri, New Delhi 110 021; tel. (11) 26889091; fax (11) 26876401; e-mail newdelhipe@vsnl.net.in; Ambassador LAURA QUIAMBAO DEL ROSARIO.

Poland: 50M Shanti Path, Chanakyapuri, New Delhi 110 021; tel. (11) 26889211; fax (11) 26871914; e-mail gorski@del2.vsnl.net.in; internet www.poltradeindia.org; Ambassador Dr KRZYSZTOF MAJKA.

Portugal: 8 Olof Palme Marg, Vasant Vihar, New Delhi 110 057; tel. (11) 26142215; fax (11) 26141343; e-mail embportin@ndf.vsnl.net.in; internet www.embportindia.com; Ambassador JOAQUIM JOSÉ L. F. MARQUES CURTO.

Qatar: G-5 Anand Niketan, New Delhi 110 021; tel. (11) 26117988; fax (11) 26886080; Ambassador YOUSEF H. AS-SAI.

Romania: A-47 Vasant Marg, Vasant Vihar, New Delhi 110 057; tel. (11) 26140447; fax (11) 26140611; e-mail emrond@hotmail.com; Ambassador VASILE SOFINETI.

Russia: Shanti Path, Chanakyapuri, New Delhi 110 021; tel. (11) 26873799; fax (11) 26876823; e-mail indrusem@del2.vsnl.net.in; Ambassador VYACHESLAV TRUBNIKOV.

Rwanda: 41 Paschimi Marg, Vasant Vihar, New Delhi 110 057; tel. (11) 51661604; fax (11) 51661605; e-mail rwandaembassy@yahoo.com; Chargé d'affaires CHARLOTTE MUKANKUSI.

Saudi Arabia: 2 Paschimi Marg, Vasant Vihar, New Delhi 110 057; tel. (11) 26144102; fax (11) 26144244; Ambassador SALEH M. AL-GHAMDI.

Senegal: C-6/11, Vasant Vihar, New Delhi 110 057; tel. (11) 26147687; fax (11) 24103743; Ambassador AMADOU BOCOUM.

Serbia and Montenegro: 3/50G Niti Marg, Chanakyapuri, New Delhi 110 021; tel. (11) 26873661; fax (11) 26885535; e-mail zvezda@del2.vsnl.net.in; Ambassador VUK ZUGIĆ.

Singapore: E-6 Chandragupta Marg, Chanakyapuri, New Delhi 110 021; tel. (11) 26885659; fax (11) 26886798; e-mail singhnd@giasdl01.vsnl.net.in; High Commissioner CHAK MUN SEE.

Slovakia: 50M Niti Marg, Chanakyapuri, New Delhi 110 021; tel. (11) 26889071; fax (11) 26877941; e-mail skdelhi@giasdl01.vsnl.net.in; Ambassador LADISLAV VOLKO.

Slovenia: 46 Poorvi Marg, Vasant Vihar, New Delhi 110 057; tel. (11) 51662891; fax (11) 51662895; e-mail vnd@mzz-dkp.sigov.si; Chargé d'affaires MIKLAVZ BORŠTNIK.

Somalia: A-17, Defence Colony, New Delhi 110 024; tel. (11) 24619559; Ambassador MOHAMED OSMAN OMAR.

South Africa: B-18 Vasant Marg, Vasant Vihar, New Delhi 110 057; tel. (11) 26149411; fax (11) 26143605; e-mail highcommissioner@sahc-india.com; internet www.sahc-india.com; High Commissioner DESMOND MONDE NXIWENI (acting).

Spain: 16 Sunder Nagar, New Delhi 110 003; tel. (11) 24359004; fax (11) 24359040; e-mail embspain@ndb.vsnl.net.in; Ambassador Don RAFAEL CONDE DE SARO.

Sri Lanka: 27 Kautilya Marg, Chanakyapuri, New Delhi 110 021; tel. (11) 23010201; fax (11) 23793604; e-mail lankacom@del2.vsnl.net.in; High Commissioner MANGALA MOONESINGHE.

Sudan: Plot No. 3, Shanti Path, Chanakyapuri, New Delhi 110 021; tel. (11) 26873785; fax (11) 26883758; e-mail sudandel@del3.vsnl.net.in; Ambassador A. ABDALHALEEM MOHAMMED.

Sweden: Nyaya Marg, Chanakyapuri, New Delhi 110 021; tel. (11) 24197100; fax (11) 26885401; e-mail embassy.new.delhi@sida.se; Ambassador INGA ERIKSSON FOGH.

Switzerland: Nyaya Marg, Chanakyapuri, New Delhi 110 021; tel. (11) 26878872; fax (11) 26873093; e-mail swienidel@vsnl.com; Ambassador DOMINIQUE DREYER.

Syria: D-5/8, Vasant Vihar, New Delhi 110 057; tel. (11) 26140233; fax (11) 26143107; Ambassador FAHD SALIM.

Tanzania: F-63, Poorvi Marg, Vasant Vihar, New Delhi 110 057; tel. (11) 26153148; fax (11) 26153289; e-mail tanzrep@del2.vsnl.net.in; High Commissioner EVA LILIAN NZARO.

Thailand: 56N Nyaya Marg, Chanakyapuri, New Delhi 110 021; tel. (11) 26118103; fax (11) 26872029; e-mail thaiemb@nda.vsnl.net.in; Ambassador CHIRASAK THANESNANT.

Trinidad and Tobago: 6/25 Shanti Niketan, New Delhi 110 021; tel. (11) 26888427; fax (11) 26888463; e-mail hcreptt@giasdl01.vsnl.net.in; High Commissioner PUNDIT MANIDEO PERSAD.

Tunisia: A-42 Vasant Marg, Vasant Vihar, New Delhi 110 057; tel. (11) 26145346; fax (11) 26145301; e-mail embtundelhi@dishnetdsl.net; Ambassador ELYES KASRI.

Turkey: 50N Nyaya Marg, Chanakyapuri, New Delhi 110 021; tel. (11) 26889054; fax (11) 26881409; e-mail tembdelhi@mantraonline.com; Ambassador HASAN GOGUS.

Turkmenistan: 1/13 Shanti Niketan, New Delhi 110 021; tel. (11) 26118409; fax (11) 26118332; e-mail turkmind@del3.vsnl.net.in; Chargé d'affaires a.i. Dr CHINAR RUSTAMOVA.

Uganda: B-3/26, Vasant Vihar, New Delhi 110 057; tel. (11) 26144413; fax (11) 26144405; e-mail ughcom@ndb.vsnl.net.in; High Commissioner CHARLES M. P. WALIMBWA.

Ukraine: 46 Paschimi Marg, Vasant Vihar, New Delhi 110 057; tel. (11) 26146041; fax (11) 26146043; e-mail embassy@bol.net.in; internet www.ukraineembassyindia.com; Ambassador OLEH Y. SEMENETS.

United Arab Emirates: EP-12 Chandragupt Marg, New Delhi 110 021; tel. (11) 26872937; fax (11) 26873272; e-mail embassyabudhabi@bol.net.in; Chargé d'affaires ABDULLA JASSIM KASHWANI.

United Kingdom: Shantipath, Chanakyapuri, New Delhi 110 021; tel. (11) 26872161; fax (11) 26872882; e-mail postmaster.newdelhi@fco.gov.uk; internet www.ukinindia.com; High Commissioner Sir MICHAEL ANTHONY ARTHUR.

USA: Shanti Path, Chanakyapuri, New Delhi 110 021; tel. (11) 24198000; fax (11) 24190060; e-mail newdelhi@pd.state.gov; Ambassador DAVID CAMPBELL MULFORD.

Uruguay: A-16/2 Vasant Vihar, New Delhi 110 057; tel. (11) 26151991; fax (11) 26144306; e-mail uruind@del3.vsnl.net.in; Ambassador ENRIQUE ANCHORDOQUI.

Uzbekistan: EP-40 Dr S. Radhakrishnan Marg, Chanakyapuri, New Delhi 110 021; tel. (11) 24670774; fax (11) 24670773; e-mail uzembind@vsnl.com; Ambassador Dr IBRAHIM MAVLANOV.

Venezuela: E-106 Malcha Marg, Chanakyapuri, New Delhi 110 021; tel. (11) 51680218; fax (11) 51750743; e-mail embavene@del2.vsnl.net.in; Ambassador MILENA SANTANA-RAMÍREZ.

Viet Nam: 17 Kautilya Marg, Chanakyapuri, New Delhi 110 021; tel. (11) 23012123; fax (11) 23017714; e-mail sqdelhi@del3.vsnl.net.in; Ambassador TRAN TRONG KHANH.

Yemen: B-3/61, Safdarjung Enclave, New Delhi 110 029; tel. (11) 26179612; fax (11) 26179614; e-mail yemenembnd@yahoo.com; Ambassador Dr MOHAMED SAAD ALI.

Zambia: C-79 Anand Niketan, New Delhi 110 021; tel. (11) 24101289; fax (11) 24101520; e-mail zambiand@sify.com; Chargé d'affaires a.i. CHONGO SHULA.

Zimbabwe: 23 Paschimi Marg, Vasant Vihar, New Delhi 110 057; tel. (11) 26140430; fax (11) 26154316; e-mail zimdelhi@vsnl.net; Ambassador JONATHAN WUTAWUNASHE.

Judicial System

THE SUPREME COURT

The Supreme Court, consisting of a Chief Justice and not more than 25 judges appointed by the President, exercises exclusive jurisdiction in any dispute between the Union and the states (although there are certain restrictions where an acceding state is involved). It has appellate jurisdiction over any judgment, decree or order of the High Court where that Court certifies that either a substantial question of law or the interpretation of the Constitution is involved. The Supreme Court can enforce fundamental rights and issue writs covering habeas corpus, mandamus, prohibition, quo warranto and certiorari. The Supreme Court is a court of record and has the power to punish for its contempt.

Provision is made for the appointment by the Chief Justice of India of judges of High Courts as ad hoc judges at sittings of the Supreme Court for specified periods, and for the attendance of retired judges at sittings of the Supreme Court. The Supreme Court has advisory jurisdiction in respect of questions which may be referred to it by the President for opinion. The Supreme Court is also empowered to hear appeals against a sentence of death passed by a State High Court in reversal of an order of acquittal by a lower court, and in a case in which a High Court has granted a certificate of fitness.

The Supreme Court also hears appeals which are certified by High Courts to be fit for appeal, subject to rules made by the Court. Parliament may, by law, confer on the Supreme Court any further powers of appeal.

The judges hold office until the age of 65 years.

Supreme Court: New Delhi; tel. (11) 23388942; fax (11) 23383792; internet www.caselaw.delhi.nic.in.

Chief Justice of India: RAMESH CHANDRA LAHOTI.

Judges of the Supreme Court: BRIJESH KUMAR, A. K. MATHUR, ASHOK BHAN, P. VENKATARAMA REDDY, C. K. THAKKAR, Y. K. SABHARWAL, HOTOI KHETOHO SEMA, BISHWANATH AGARWAL, RUMA PAL, S. N. VARIAVA, SHIVRAJ V. PATIL, K. G. BALAKRISHNAN, SAROSH HOMI KAPADIA, B. N. SRIKRISHNA, A. R. LAKSHMANAN, SANTOSH HEGDE, S. B. SINHA, GOVIND PRASAD MATHUR, ARIJIT PASSAYAT, BISHESHWAR PRASAD SINGH, ARUN KUMAR, B. M. DHARMADHIKARI, PRAKASH P. NAOLEKAR, TARUN CHATTERJEE, P. K. BALASUBRAMANYAM.

Attorney-General: MILON BANERJEE.

HIGH COURTS

The High Courts are the Courts of Appeal from the lower courts, and their decisions are final except in cases where appeal lies to the Supreme Court.

LOWER COURTS

Provision is made in the Code of Criminal Procedure for the constitution of lower criminal courts called Courts of Session and Courts of Magistrates. The Courts of Session are competent to try all persons duly committed for trial, and inflict any punishment authorized by the law. The President and the local government concerned exercise the prerogative of mercy.

The constitution of inferior civil courts is determined by regulations within each state.

Religion

BUDDHISM

The Buddhists in Ladakh (Jammu and Kashmir) are followers of the Dalai Lama. Head Lama of Ladakh: KAUSHAK SAKULA, Dalgate, Srinagar (Jammu and Kashmir). The Buddhists in Sikkim are also followers of Mahayana Buddhism. In 2001 there were 8.0m. Buddhists in India, representing 0.8% of the population.

Mahabodhi Society of India: 4-A, Bankim Chatterjee St, Kolkata 700 073; tel. and fax (33) 22415214; 11 centres in India, five centres world-wide; Pres. KALASURI M. WIPULASARA MAHA THERO; Gen. Sec. Dr D. REWATHA THERO.

HINDUISM

In 2001 there were 827.6m. Hindus in India, representing 80.5% of the population.

Rashtriya Swayamsevak Sangh (RSS) (National Volunteer Organization): Keshav Kunj, Jhandewala, D. B. Gupta Marg, New Delhi 110 055; tel. (11) 23611372; fax (11) 23611385; e-mail rss@rss.org; internet www.rss.org; f. 1925; 41,000 service centres in rural areas, 50,000 working centres; Pres. K. S. SUDARSHAN; Gen. Sec. MOHAN BHAGWAT.

Sarvadeshik Arya Pratinidhi Sabha: 3/5 Asaf Ali Rd, Near Ram Lila Maidan, New Delhi 110 002; tel. (11) 23274771; e-mail vedicgod@nda.vsnl.net.in; internet www.whereisgod.com; f. 1875 by Maharishi Dayanand Saraswati; the international body for Arya Samaj temples propagating reforms in all fields on the basis of Vedic principles; Pres. Capt. DEV RATNA ARYA; Sec. VIMAL WADHAWAN.

Vishwa Hindu Parishad (VHP) (World Hindu Council): Sankat Mochan Ashram, Ramakrishna Puram VI, New Delhi 110 022; tel. (11) 26178992; fax (11) 26195527; e-mail vhp@vichaar.net; internet www.vhp.org; f. 1964, banned in December 1992–June 1993 for its role in the destruction of the Babri mosque in Ayodhya; Pres. VISHNU HARI DALMIA; Gen. Sec. Dr PRAVEEN TOGADIYA.

ISLAM

Muslims are divided into two main sects, Shi'as and Sunnis. Most of the Indian Muslims are Sunnis. At the 2001 census Islam had 138.2m. adherents (13.4% of the population).

Jamiat Ulama-i-Hind (Assembly of Muslim Religious Leaders of India): 1 Bahadur Shah Zafar Marg, New Delhi 110 002; tel. (11) 23311455; fax (11) 23316173; e-mail info@jamiatulamahind.org; internet www.jamiatulamahind.org; f. 1919; Pres. ASAD MADANI; Gen. Sec. Maulana MAHMOOD MADANI.

SIKHISM

In 2001 there were 19.2m. Sikhs (comprising 1.9% of the population), the majority living in the Punjab.

Sikh Gurdwara Prabandhak Committee: Darbar Sahab, Amritsar 143 001; tel. (183) 2553956; fax (183) 2553919; e-mail sgpc@vsnl.net; internet www.sgpc.net; f. 1925; highest authority in Sikhism; Pres. BIBI JAGIR KAUR; Jathedar Shri Akal Takht Saheb JOGINDER SINGH VEDANTI.

CHRISTIANITY

According to the 2001 census, Christians represented 2.3% of the population in India.

National Council of Churches in India: Christian Council Lodge, Civil Lines, POB 205, Nagpur 440 001; tel. (712) 2531312; fax (712) 2520554; e-mail nccindia_ngp@sancharnet.in; internet www.nccindia.org; f. 1914; mems: 26 reformed and three orthodox churches, 18 regional Christian councils, 14 All-India ecumenical orgs and seven related agencies; represents c. 10m. mems; Pres. Most Rev. GEEVARGHESE MAR COORILOS; Gen. Sec. Rev. Dr IPE JOSEPH.

Orthodox Churches

Malankara Orthodox Syrian Church: Devalokam, Kottayam 686 038; tel. (481) 2578500; fax (481) 2570569; e-mail orthodox@md4.vsnl.net.in; c. 2.5m. mems (1995); 22 bishops, 21 dioceses, 1,340 parishes; Catholicos of the East and Malankara Metropolitan HH BASELIUS MARTHOMA MATHEWS II; Asscn Sec. A. K. THOMAS.

Mar Thoma Syrian Church of Malabar: Mar Thoma Sabha Office, Poolatheen, Tiruvalla 689 101; tel. (473) 2630449; fax (473) 2630327; e-mail sabhaoffice@marthomasyrianchurch.org; internet www.marthomasyrianchurch.org; c. 1m. mems (2001); Metropolitan Most Rev. Dr PHILIPOSE MAR CHRYSOSTOM MAR THOMA; Sec. Rev. Dr CHERIAN THOMAS.

The Malankara Jacobite Syrian Orthodox Church is also represented.

Protestant Churches

Church of North India (CNI): CNI Bhavan, 16 Pandit Pant Marg, New Delhi 110 001; tel. (11) 23716513; fax (11) 23716901; e-mail gscni@ndb.vsnl.net.in; internet www.cnisynod.org; f. 1970 by merger of the Church of India (fmrly known as the Church of India, Pakistan, Burma and Ceylon), the Council of the Baptist Churches in Northern India, the Methodist Church (British and Australasian Conferences), the United Church of Northern India (a union of Presbyterians and Congregationalists, f. 1924), the Church of the Brethren in India, and the Disciples of Christ; comprises 26 dioceses; c. 1.2m. mems (1999); Moderator Most Rev. Z. JAMES TEROM (Bishop of Chotanagpur); Gen. Sec. Rev. ENOS DAS PRADHAN.

Church of South India (CSI): CSI Centre, 5 Whites Rd, Chennai 600 014; tel. (44) 28521566; fax (44) 28523528; e-mail csi@vsnl.com; internet www.churchofsouthindiasynod.com; f. 1947 by merger of the Weslyan Methodist Church in South India, the South India United Church (itself a union of churches in the Congregational and Presbyterian/Reformed traditions) and the four southern dioceses of the (Anglican) Church of India; comprises 22 dioceses (incl. one in Sri Lanka); c. 3m. mems (2003); Moderator Most Rev. Dr B. P. SUGANDHAR (Bishop of Medak); Gen. Sec. Dr PAULINE SATHIAMURTHY.

Methodist Church in India: Methodist Centre, 21 YMCA Rd, Mumbai 400 008; tel. (22) 23094316; fax (22) 23074137; e-mail gensecmci@vsnl.com; f. 1856 as the Methodist Church in Southern Asia; 648,000 mems (2005); Gen. Sec. Rev. Dr ELIA PRADEEP SAMUEL.

Samavesam of Telugu Baptist Churches: A. B. M. Compound, Kavali 524 201; tel. (8626) 241201; fax (8626) 241847; f. 1962; comprises 856 independent Baptist churches; 578,295 mems (1995); Functional Adviser Dr G. DEVADANAM.

United Evangelical Lutheran Churches in India: Martin Luther Bhavan, 95 Purasawalkam High Rd, Kilpauk, Chennai 600 010; tel. (44) 26611364; fax (44) 26430008; e-mail uelci@vsnl.net; internet www.uelci-india.org; f. 1975; 11 constituent denominations: Andhra Evangelical Lutheran Church, Arcot Lutheran Church, Evangelical Lutheran Church in Madhya Pradesh, Evangelical Lutheran Church in the Himalayan States, Gossner Evangelical Lutheran Church in Chotanagpur and Assam, India Evangelical Lutheran Church, Jeypore Evangelical Lutheran Church, Northern Evangelical Lutheran Church, South Andhra Lutheran Church, Good Samaritan Evangelical Lutheran Church and Tamil Evangelical Lutheran Church; c. 1.3m. mems; Pres. Rt Rev. L. G. RAO; Exec. Sec. Rev. CHANDRAN PAUL MARTIN.

Other denominations active in the country include the Assembly of the Presbyterian Church in North East India, the Bengal-Orissa-Bihar Baptist Convention (6,000 mems), the Chaldean Syrian Church of the East, the Convention of the Baptist Churches of Northern Circars, the Council of Baptist Churches of North East

India, the Council of Baptist Churches of Northern India, the Hindustani Convent Church and the Mennonite Church in India.

The Roman Catholic Church

India comprises 28 archdioceses and 122 dioceses. These include four archdioceses and 21 dioceses of the Syro-Malabar rite, and one archdiocese and four dioceses of the Syro-Malankara rite. The archdiocese of Goa and Daman is also the seat of the Patriarch of the East Indies. The remaining archdioceses are metropolitan sees. In December 2002 there were an estimated 17.0m. adherents of the Roman Catholic faith in the country.

Catholic Bishops' Conference of India (CBCI): CBCI Centre, 1 Ashok Place, Goledakkhana, New Delhi 110 001; tel. (11) 23344470; fax (11) 23364615; e-mail cbci@vsnl.com; internet www.cbcisite.com; f. 1944; Pres. Cardinal Telesphore P. Toppo (Archbishop of Ranchi); Sec.-Gen. Most Rev. Percival Joseph Fernandez (Auxiliary Bishop of Bombay (Mumbai)).

Latin Rite

Conference of Catholic Bishops of India (CCBI)

CCBI Centre, 2nd Cross, Hutchins Rd, POB 8490, Bangalore 560 084; tel. (80) 25498282; fax (80) 25498180; e-mail ccbi@touchtelindia.net; internet www.ccbisite.com.

f. 1994; Pres. Cardinal Telesphoro P. Toppo (Archbishop of Ranchi).

Patriarch of the East Indies: Most Rev. Filipe Neri Ferrão (Archbishop of Goa and Daman), Paço Patriarcal, POB 216, Altinho, Panjim, Goa 403 001; tel. (832) 2223353; fax (832) 2224139; e-mail archbp@goatelecom.com.

Archbishop of Agra: Most Rev. Dr Oswald Gracias, Archbishop's House, Wazirpura Rd, Agra 282 003; tel. (562) 2151318; fax (562) 2153939; e-mail abpossie@sancharnet.in.

Archbishop of Bangalore: Most Rev. Bernard Blasius Moras, Archbishop's House, 75 Miller's Rd, POB 2, Bangalore 560 046; tel. (80) 23330438; fax (80) 23330838; e-mail bgarchdi@bgl.vsnl.net.in.

Archbishop of Bhopal: Most Rev. Paschal Topno, Archbishop's House, 33 Ahmedabad Palace Rd, Bhopal 462 001; tel. (755) 2540829; fax (755) 2544737; e-mail adbhopal@vsnl.com; internet cbci.org/bhopal.htm.

Archbishop of Bombay (Mumbai): Cardinal Ivan Dias, Archbishop's House, 21 Nathalal Parekh Marg, Mumbai 400 001; tel. (22) 22021093; fax (22) 22853872; e-mail bombaydiocese@vsnl.com; internet www.archbom.org.

Archbishop of Calcutta (Kolkata): Most Rev. Lucas Sirkar, Archbishop's House, 32 Park St, Kolkata 700 016; tel. (33) 22471960; fax (33) 22474666; e-mail rcacal@giascl01.vsnl.net.in.

Archbishop of Cuttack-Bhubaneswar: Most Rev. Raphael Cheenath, Archbishop's House, Satya Nagar, Bhubaneswar 751 007; tel. (674) 2502234; fax (674) 2501817; e-mail crcdc@mail.com.

Archbishop of Delhi: Most Rev. Vincent M. Concessao, Archbishop's House, 1 Ashok Place, Goledakkhana, New Delhi 110 001; tel. (11) 23343457; fax (11) 23746575; e-mail archbish@vsnl.com.

Archbishop of Gandhinagar: Most Rev. Stanislaus Fernandes, Archbishop's House, Sector 8, Gandhinagar 382 008; tel. (79) 3227541; fax (79) 3221912; e-mail abpstanny@sify.com.

Archbishop of Guwahati: Most Rev. Thomas Menamparampil, Archbishop's House, POB 100, Guwahati 781 001; tel. (361) 2547664; fax (361) 2520588; e-mail menam@sify.com; internet www.peacetoall.com.

Archbishop of Hyderabad: Most Rev. Joji Marampudi, Archbishop's House, Sardar Patel Rd, Secunderabad 500 003; tel. (40) 27805545; fax (40) 27718089; e-mail abphydmjoji@rediffmail.com.

Archbishop of Imphal: Most Rev. Joseph Mittathany, Archbishop's House, POB 35, Imphal 795 001; tel. (385) 2421292; fax (385) 2421293; e-mail jmittathany@hotmail.com.

Archbishop of Madras (Chennai) and Mylapore: (vacant), Archbishop's House, 21 San Thome High Rd, Chennai 600 004; tel. (44) 24941102; fax (44) 24941999; e-mail archmsml@vsnl.com.

Archbishop of Madurai: Most Rev. Peter Fernando, Archbishop's House, Kosakulam Pudur, Madurai 625 007; tel. (452) 2566198; fax (452) 2566630; e-mail secretaryab@yahoo.co.in; internet www.maduraiarchdiocese.org.

Archbishop of Nagpur: Most Rev. Abraham Viruthakulangara, Archbishop's House, 25 Kamptee Rd, Mohan Nagar, Nagpur 440 001; tel. (712) 2533239; fax (712) 2527906; e-mail abpabrah@nagpur.dot.net.in.

Archbishop of Patna: Most Rev. Benedict John Osta, Archbishop's House, Bankipore, Patna 800 004; tel. (612) 2301735; fax (612) 2301816; e-mail archbishop@satyam.net.in.

Archbishop of Pondicherry and Cuddalore: Most Rev. Antony Anandarayar, Archbishop's House, 206 Cathedral St, POB 193, Pondicherry 605 001; tel. (413) 2334748; fax (413) 2339911; e-mail abppondi@satyam.net.in; internet www.pondyarchdiocese.org.in.

Archbishop of Raipur: Most Rev. Joseph Augustine Charanakunnel, Khristbandhu Nivas, Byron Bazar, Raipur 492 001; tel. (771) 423995.

Archbishop of Ranchi: Cardinal Telesphore P. Toppo, Archbishop's House, Purulia Rd, POB 5, Ranchi 834 001; tel. (651) 2204728; fax (651) 2304844; e-mail rca@vitalmail.com; internet www.ranchiarchdiocese.org.

Archbishop of Shillong: Most Rev. Dominic Jala, Archbishop's House, Shillong 793 003; tel. (364) 2223355; fax (364) 2211306; e-mail archbishop@neline.com.

Archbishop of Trivandrum: Most Rev. Maria Callist Soosa Pakiam, Archbishop's House, POB 805, Vellayambalam, Thiruvananthapuram 695 003; tel. (471) 334005; fax (471) 320367.

Archbishop of Verapoly: Most Rev. Daniel Acharuparambil, Latin Archbishop's House, POB 2581, Kochi 682 031; tel. (484) 2372892; fax (484) 2360911; e-mail vpoly@vsnl.com; internet www.verapolyarchdiocese.org.

Archbishop of Visakhapatnam: Most Rev. Mariadas Kagithapu, Archbishop's House, Maharanipeta, Visakhapatnam 530 002; tel. (891) 2706428; fax (891) 2704404; e-mail abphvizag@rediffmail.com.

Syro-Malabar Rite

Major Archbishop of Ernakulam-Angamaly: Cardinal Mar Varkey Vithayathil, Major Archbishop's House, Thrikkakara, POB 2580, Kochi 682 031; tel. (484) 2352629; fax (484) 2355010; e-mail abperang@asianetindia.com; internet www.ernakulamarchdiocese.org.

Archbishop of Changanasserry: Most Rev. Joseph Mar Powathil, Archbishop's House, POB 20, Changanasserry 686 101; tel. (481) 2420040; fax (481) 2422540; e-mail abpchry@sancharnet.in; internet www.archdiocesechanganacherry.org.

Archbishop of Tellicherry: Most Rev. George Valiamattam, Archbishop's House, POB 70, Tellicherry 670 101; tel. (490) 2341058; fax (49) 2341412; e-mail diocese@eth.net.

Archbishop of Trichur: Most Rev. Jacob Thoomkuzhy, Archbishop's House, Trichur 680 005; tel. (487) 2333325; fax (487) 2338204; e-mail carbit@md4.vsnl.net.in; internet archdioceseoftrichur.org.

Syro-Malankara Rite

Archbishop of Trivandrum: Most Rev. Cyril Mar Baselios Malancharuvil, Archbishop's House, Pattom, Thiruvananthapuram 695 004; tel. (471) 2541643; fax (471) 2541635; e-mail archbp03@md3.vsnl.net.in; internet www.malankara.net.

OTHER FAITHS

Jainism: 4.2m. adherents (2001 census), 0.4% of the population.

Zoroastrianism: In 2001 69,601 Parsis practised the Zoroastrian religion, compared with 76,382 in 1991.

Bahá'í Faith

National Spiritual Assembly: Bahá'í House, 6 Shrimant Madhavrao Scindia Rd, POB 19, New Delhi 110 001; tel. (11) 23389326; fax (11) 23782178; e-mail nsaindia@bahaindia.org; internet www.bahaindia.org; c. 2m. mems; Sec.-Gen. Farida Vahedi.

The Press

Freedom of the Press was guaranteed under the 1950 Constitution. In 1979 a Press Council was established (its predecessor was abolished in 1975), the function of which was to uphold the freedom of the press and maintain and improve journalistic standards.

The growth of a thriving press has been inhibited by cultural barriers caused by religious, social and linguistic differences. Consequently the English-language press, with its appeal to the educated middle-class urban readership throughout the states, has retained its dominance. The English-language metropolitan dailies are some of the widest circulating and most influential newspapers. The main Indian language dailies, by paying attention to rural affairs, cater for the increasingly literate non-anglophone provincial population. Most Indian-language papers have a relatively small circulation.

The majority of publications in India are under individual ownership (75% in 2002/03), and they claim a large part of the total circulation (60% in 1999). The most powerful groups, owned by joint stock companies, publish most of the large English dailies and frequently have considerable private commercial and industrial holdings. Four of the major groups are as follows:

Times of India Group: controlled by family of the late ASHOK JAIN; dailies: *The Times of India* (published in 11 regional centres), *Economic Times*, the Hindi *Navbharat Times* and *Sandhya Times*, the Marathi *Maharashtra Times* (Mumbai); periodicals: the English fortnightly *Femina* and monthly *Filmfare*.

Indian Express Group: controlled by the family of the late RAMNATH GOENKA; publishes nine dailies including the *Indian Express*, the Marathi *Lokasatta*, the Tamil *Dinamani*, the Telugu *Andhra Prabha*, the Kannada *Kannada Prabha* and the English *Financial Express*; six periodicals including the English weeklies the *Indian Express* (Sunday edition), *Screen*, the Telugu *Andhra Prabha Illustrated Weekly* and the Tamil *Dinamani Kadir* (weekly).

Hindustan Times Group: controlled by the K. K. BIRLA family; dailies: the *Hindustan Times* (published from 10 regional centres), *Pradeep* (Patna) and the Hindi *Hindustan* (Delhi, Lucknow, Patna and Ranchi); periodicals: the weekly *Overseas Hindustan Times* and the Hindi monthly *Nandan* and *Kadambini* (New Delhi).

Ananda Bazar Patrika Group: controlled by AVEEK SARKAR and family; dailies: the *Ananda Bazar Patrika* (Kolkata) and the English *The Telegraph* (Guwahati, Kolkata and Siliguri); periodicals include: *Business World*, Bengali weekly *Anandamela*, Bengali fortnightly *Desh*, Bengali monthly *Anandalok* and the Bengali monthly *Sananda*.

PRINCIPAL DAILIES

Delhi (incl. New Delhi)

The Asian Age: D-27, South Extension Part II, New Delhi 110 049; tel. (11) 26253137; fax (11) 26251179; internet www.asianage.com; f. 1994; morning; English; also publ. from Ahmedabad, Bangalore, Kolkata, Mumbai and London; Editor-in-Chief M. J. AKBAR.

Business Standard: Pratap Bhavan, 5 Bahadur Shah Zafar Marg, New Delhi 110 002; tel. (11) 23720202; fax (11) 23720201; e-mail editor@business-standard.com; internet www.business-standard.com; morning; English; also publ. from Kolkata, Ahmedabad, Bangalore, Chennai, Hyderabad and Mumbai; Editor T. N. NINAN; combined circ. 61,700.

Daily Milap: 8A Bahadur Shah Zafar Marg, New Delhi 110 002; tel. (11) 23317651; fax (11) 23319166; e-mail info@milap.com; internet www.milap.com; f. 1923; Urdu; nationalist; Man. Editor PUNAM SURI; Chief Editor NAVIN SURI; circ. 31,250.

Daily Pratap: Pratap Bhawan, 5 Bahadur Shah Zafar Marg, New Delhi 110 002; tel. (11) 23317938; fax (11) 51509555; e-mail news@dailypratap.com; internet www.dailypratap.com; f. 1919; Urdu; Chief Editor K. NARENDRA; CEO S. M. AFIF AHSEN; circ. 47,962.

Delhi Mid Day: World Trade Tower, Barakhamba Lane, New Delhi 110 001; tel. (11) 23414224; fax (11) 23412491; e-mail dmd01@rediffmail.com; f. 1989; Editor ANIL SHARMA (acting).

The Economic Times: 7 Bahadur Shah Zafar Marg, New Delhi 110 002; tel. (11) 23492234; fax (11) 23491248; internet www.economictimes.com; f. 1961; English; also publ. from Kolkata, Ahmedabad, Bangalore, Hyderabad, Chennai and Mumbai; Editor (Delhi) RAHUL JOSHI; combined circ. 461,900, circ. (Delhi) 125,800.

Financial Express: Bahadur Shah Zafar Marg, New Delhi 110 002; tel. (11) 23702167; fax (11) 23702164; e-mail editor@financialexpress.com; internet www.financialexpress.com; f. 1961; morning; English; also publ. from Ahmedabad (in Gujarati), Mumbai, Bangalore, Kolkata and Chennai; Editor MYTHILI BHUSNURMATH; combined circ. 50,000.

The Hindu: INS Bldg, Rafi Marg, New Delhi 110 001; tel. (11) 23715426; fax (11) 23718158; f. 1878; morning; English; also publ. from 11 other regional centres; Editor-in-Chief N. RAM; combined circ. 981,600.

Hindustan: 18/20 Kasturba Gandhi Marg, New Delhi 110 001; tel. (11) 23704546; fax (11) 23704645; f. 1936; morning; Hindi; also publ. from Lucknow, Muzaffarpur, Ranchi, Bhagalpur, Varanasi and Patna; Editor MRINAL PANDE; combined circ. 753,500.

Hindustan Times: 18/20 Kasturba Gandhi Marg, New Delhi 110 001; tel. (11) 23704617; fax (11) 23704589; internet www.hindustantimes.com; f. 1923; morning; English; also publ. from nine regional centres; Editor SHEKHAR BHATIA; combined circ. 1,142,600.

Indian Express: Bahadur Shah Zafar Marg, New Delhi 110 002; tel. (11) 26511015; fax (11) 26511615; internet www.indianexpress.com; f. 1953; English; also publ. from seven other towns; Man. Editor VIVEK GOENKA; Editor-in-Chief SHEKHAR GUPTA; combined circ. 688,878, circ. (New Delhi, Jammu and Chandigarh) 138,100.

Janasatta: 9/10 Bahadur Shah Zafar Marg, New Delhi 110 002; tel. (11) 23702100; fax (11) 23702141; f. 1983; Hindi; also publ. from Kolkata; Editor-in-Chief PRABHASH JOSHI; Exec. Editor OM THANVI.

National Herald: Herald House, 5A Bahadur Shah Zafar Marg, New Delhi 110 002; tel. (11) 23315950; fax (11) 23313458; e-mail nationalheralddelhi@rediffmail.com; f. 1938; English; nationalist; Editor T. V. VENKITACHALAM; circ. 33,000.

Navbharat Times: 7 Bahadur Shah Zafar Marg, New Delhi 110 002; tel. (11) 23492041; fax (11) 23492168; f. 1947; Hindi; also publ. from Mumbai; Editor MADHUSUDAN ANAND; combined circ. 398,300, circ. (Delhi) 248,400.

The Pioneer: Link House, 3 Bahadur Shah Zafar Marg, New Delhi 110 002; tel. (11) 23755271; fax (11) 23755275; e-mail pioneer@del2.vsnl.net.in; internet www.dailypioneer.com; f. 1865; also publ. from Lucknow; Editor CHANDAN MITRA; combined circ. 154,000, circ. (Delhi) 78,000.

Punjab Kesari: Romesh Bhavan, 2 Printing Press Complex, nr Wazirpur DTC Depot, Ring Rd, Delhi 110 035; tel. (11) 27194459; fax (11) 27194470; e-mail ashwanik@nda.vsnl.net.in; internet www.punjabkesari.com; Hindi; also publ. from Jalandhar and Ambala; Editor ASHWINI KUMAR; circ. 336,200 (Delhi), combined circ. 829,500.

Rashtriya Sahara: Amba Deep, Kasturba Gandhi Marg, New Delhi 110 001; tel. (11) 23704193; fax (11) 23704113; morning; Hindi; also publ. from Lucknow and Gorakhpur; Resident Editor NISHIT JOSHI; circ. 81,900 (New Delhi), 42,300 (Lucknow), 30,600 (Gorakhpur).

Sandhya Times: 7 Bahadur Shah Zafar Marg, New Delhi 110 002; tel. (11) 23492162; fax (11) 23492047; f. 1979; Hindi; evening; Editor SAT SONI; circ. 44,400.

The Statesman: Statesman House, 148 Barakhamba Rd, New Delhi 110 001; tel. (11) 23315911; fax (11) 23315295; e-mail thestatesman@vsnl.com; internet www.thestatesman.net; f. 1875; English; also publ. from Bhubaneswar, Kolkata and Siliguri; Editor-in-Chief C. R. IRANI; combined circ. 166,300.

The Times of India: 7 Bahadur Shah Zafar Marg, New Delhi 110 002; tel. (11) 23492049; fax (11) 23351606; internet www.timesofindia.com; f. 1838; English; also publ. from 10 other towns; Resident Editor ARINDAM SENGUPTA; combined circ. 2,214,700.

Andhra Pradesh

Hyderabad

Deccan Chronicle: 36 Sarojini Devi Rd, Hyderabad 500 003; tel. (40) 27803930; fax (40) 27805256; f. 1938; English; also publ. from six other regional centres; Editor-in-Chief M. J. AKBAR; Editor A. T. JAYANTI; circ. 342,100.

Eenadu: Somajiguda, Hyderabad 500 082; tel. (40) 23318181; fax (40) 23318555; e-mail feedback@eenadu.net; internet www.eenadu.net; f. 1974; Telugu; also publ. from 22 other towns; Chief Editor RAMOJI RAO; circ. 1,040,000 (weekdays), 1,200,000 (Sunday).

Rahnuma-e-Deccan: 12-2-837/A/3, Asif Nagar, Hyderabad 500 028; tel. (40) 23534943; fax (40) 23534945; e-mail rahnumadeccan@email.com; f. 1949; morning; Urdu; independent; Chief Editor SYED VICARUDDIN; circ. 25,000.

Siasat Daily: Jawaharlal Nehru Rd, Hyderabad 500 001; tel. (40) 24744109; fax (40) 24603188; e-mail info@siasat.com; internet www.siasat.com; f. 1949; morning; Urdu; Editor ZAHID ALI KHAN; circ. 41,600.

Vijayawada

Andhra Jyoti: Andhra Jyoti Bldg, POB 712, Vijayawada 520 010; tel. (866) 2474532; f. 1960; Telugu; also publ. from 13 other regional centres; Editor K. RAMACHANDRA MURTHY; combined circ. 162,400.

Andhra Prabha: 16-1-28, Kolandareddy Rd, Poornanandampet, Vijayawada 520 003; tel. (866) 2571351; internet www.andhraprabha.com; f. 1935; Telugu; also publ. from Bangalore, Hyderabad, Chennai and Visakhapatnam; Editor-in-Chief A. B. K. PRASAD; combined circ. 24,500.

New Indian Express: 16-1-28, Kolandareddy Rd, Poornanandampet, Vijayawada 520 003; tel. (866) 2571351; English; also publ. from Bangalore, Belgaum, Kochi, Kozhikode, Thiruvananthapuram, Madurai, Chennai, Hyderabad, Visakhapatnam, Coimbatore and Bhubaneswar; Man. Editor MANOJ KUMAR SONTHALIA; Editor (Andhra Pradesh) P. S. SUNDARAM; combined circ. 197,400.

Assam

Guwahati

Amar Asom: G. S. Rd, Ulubari, Guwahati 781 007; tel. (361) 2544356; fax (361) 2540664; e-mail glpl@sancharnet.in; f. 1997; Assamese; also publ. from Jorhat; Editor HOMEN BORGOHAIN; circ. 76,500.

Asomiya Pratidin: Maniram Dewan Rd, Guwahati 781 003; tel. (361) 2660420; fax (361) 2666377; e-mail pratidinedi@vsnl.net; morning; Assamese; also published from Dibrugarh, Lakhimpur and Bongaigaon; circ. 121,800.

Assam Tribune: Tribune Bldgs, Maniram Dewan Rd, Chandmari, Guwahati 781 003; tel. (361) 2661357; fax (361) 2666398; e-mail webmaster@assamtribune.com; internet www.assamtribune.com; f. 1939; English; Man. Dir and Editor P. G. BARUAH; circ. 59,200.

Dainik Agradoot: Agradoot Bhavan, Dispur, Guwahati 781 006; tel. (361) 2261923; fax (361) 2260655; e-mail agradoot@sify.com; internet www.dainikagradoot.com; f. 1995; Assamese; Editor K. S. DEKA; circ. 70,973.

Dainik Assam: Tribune Bldgs, Maniram Dewan Rd, Chandmari, Guwahati 781 003; tel. (361) 2541360; fax (361) 2516356; e-mail webmaster@assamtribune.com; internet www.assamtribune.com; f. 1965; Assamese; Editor DHIRENDRA NATH CHAKRAVARTTY; circ. 16,700.

Dainik Jugasankha: Jugasankha Bldg, Green Path, G. S. Rd, Guwahati 781 007; tel. (361) 2547444; fax (361) 2544971; e-mail dainikjugasankha@yahoo.com; f. 1950; Bengali; also publ. from Silchar; Editor ATIN DAS; circ. 52,500.

The North East Daily: Maniram Dewan Rd, Chandmari, Guwahati 781 003; tel. (361) 2524594; fax (361) 2524634; e-mail protidin@gw1.vsnl.net.in; Assamese; circ. 34,891.

The Sentinel: G. S. Rd, Guwahati 781 005; tel. (361) 2529237; fax (361) 2529624; e-mail sentinelghy@sancharnet.in; internet www.sentinelassam.com; f. 1983; English; Editor INDIRA RAJKHEWA; circ. 44,900.

Jorhat

Dainik Janmabhumi: Nehru Park Rd, Jorhat 785 001; tel. (376) 23320033; fax (376) 23321713; e-mail clarionl@sancharnet.in; f. 1972; Assamese; also published from Guwahati; Editor DEVA KR. BORAH; circ. 32,000.

Bihar

Patna

Aryavarta: Mazharul Haque Path, Patna 800 001; tel. (612) 2230716; fax (612) 2222350; e-mail aryavart@dte.vsnl.net.in; morning; Hindi; Editor BHAKTISHWAR JHA.

Hindustan Times: Buddha Marg, Patna 800 001; tel. (612) 2223434; fax (612) 2226120; f. 1918; morning; English; also publ. from nine regional centres; Editor SHEKHAR BHATIA; combined circ. 1,142,600.

Indian Nation: Mazharul Haque Path, Patna 800 001; tel. (612) 2237780; fax (612) 2222350; e-mail aryavart@dte.vsnl.net.in; morning; English; Editor BHAKTISHWAR JHA.

The Times of India: Times House, Fraser Rd, Patna 800 001; tel. (612) 2226301; fax (612) 2233525; also publ. from New Delhi, Mumbai, Ahmedabad, Bangalore and Lucknow; Exec. Editor ARINDAM SENGUPTA; combined circ. 2,214,700.

Chhattisgarh

Raipur

Dainik Bhaskar: Press Complex, Rajbandha Mandan, G. E. Rd, Raipur 492 001; tel. (771) 2535277; fax (771) 2535255; Hindi; morning; also publ. from 18 other regional centres; Editor R. C. AGRAWAL; circ. 109,300.

Deshbandhu: Deshbandhu Complex, Ramsagarpara, Raipur 492 001; tel. (771) 2292011; fax (771) 2534955; e-mail deshbandhu@mantrafreenet.com; internet www.dailydeshbandhu.com; f. 1959; Hindi; also publ. from Jabalpur, Satna, Bilaspur and Bhopal; Chief Editor LALIT SURJAN; circ. 59,904 (Raipur), 19,573 (Satna), 25,650 (Bhopal), 29,505 (Jabalpur), 27,628 (Bilaspur).

Highway Channel: Deshbandhu Complex, Ramsagarpara, Raipur 492 001; tel. (771) 2292011; fax (771) 2534955; e-mail deshbandhu@mantrafreenet.com; internet www.dailydeshbandhu.com; f. 1959; evening; Hindi; also publ. from Bilaspur and Jagdalpur; Chief Editor LALIT SURJAN; circ. 26,727 (Raipur), 17,008 (Bilaspur), 21,323 (Jagdalpur).

Nava Bharat: Nava Bharat Bhavan Press Complex, G. E. Rd, Raipur 492 001; tel. (771) 2535544; fax (771) 2534936; Hindi; also

publ. from six other regional centres; Editor PRAKASH MAHESHWARI; circ. 177,600 (Raipur and Bilaspur).

Goa

Panaji

Gomantak: Gomantak Bhavan, St Inez, Panaji, Goa 403 001; tel. (832) 2422700; fax (832) 2422701; f. 1962; morning; Marathi and English edns; Editor LAXMAN T. JOSHI; circ. 20,700 (Marathi), 6,200 (English).

Navhind Times: Navhind Bhavan, Rua Ismail Gracias, POB 161, Panaji, Goa 403 001; tel. (832) 2224033; fax (832) 2224258; e-mail navhind@navhindtimes.com; internet www.navhindtimes.com; f. 1963; morning; English; Editor ARUN SINHA; circ. 34,426.

Panjim

O Heraldo: Herald Publications Pvt Ltd, Rua St, Tome, Panjim 403 001; tel. (832) 2224202; fax (832) 2225622; e-mail hppltd@goatelecom.com; internet www.oherald.com; f. 1900; English; Editor RAJAN NARAYAN; circ. 36,100.

Gujarat

Ahmedabad

Gujarat Samachar: Gujarat Samachar Bhavan, Khanpur, Ahmedabad 380 001; tel. (79) 5504010; fax (79) 5502000; e-mail editor@gujaratsamachar.com; f. 1930; morning; Gujarati; also publ. from Surat, Rajkot, Vadodara, Mumbai, London and New York; Editor SHANTIBHAI SHAH; combined circ. 1,051,000.

Indian Express: 5th Floor, Sanidhya Bldg, Ashram Rd, Ahmedabad 380 009; tel. (79) 26583023; fax (79) 26575826; e-mail praman@express2.indexp.co.in; f. 1968; English; also publ. in 10 other towns; Man. Editor VIVEK GOENKA; Chief Editor SHEKHAR GUPTA; circ. (Ahmedabad and Vadodara) 28,200.

Lokasatta—Janasatta: Mirzapur Rd, POB 188, Ahmedabad 380 001; tel. (79) 25507307; fax (79) 25507708; f. 1953; morning; Gujarati; also publ. from Rajkot and Vadodara; Man. Editor VIVEK GOENKA; circ. (Ahmedabad) 48,000.

Sandesh: Sandesh Bhavan, Lad Society Rd, Ahmedabad 380 054; tel. (79) 26765480; fax (79) 26754795; e-mail advt@sandesh.com; internet www.sandesh.com; f. 1923; Gujarati; also publ. from Bhavnagar, Vadodara, Rajkot and Surat; Editor FALGUNBHAI C. PATEL; combined circ. 743,200.

The Times of India: 139 Ashram Rd, POB 4046, Ahmedabad 380 009; tel. (79) 26583137; fax (79) 26583758; f. 1968; English; also publ. from Mumbai, Delhi, Bangalore, Patna and Lucknow; Resident Editor KINGSHUK NAG; circ. (Ahmedabad) 129,100.

Western Times: 'Western House', Marutinandan Complex, Madalpur, Ellisbridge, Ahmedabad 380 006; tel. (79) 26576738; fax (79) 26577421; e-mail western@icenet.net; f. 1967; English and Gujarati edns; also publ. (in Gujarati) from eight other towns; Man. Editor NIKUNJ PATEL; Editor RAMU PATEL; circ. (Ahmedabad) 27,183 (English), 43,266 (Gujarati).

Bhuj

Kutchmitra: Kutchmitra Bhavan, nr Indirabai Park, Bhuj 370 001; tel. (2832) 252090; fax (2832) 250271; e-mail kutchmitra@yahoo.com; f. 1947; Gujarati; Propr Saurashtra Trust; Editor KIRTI J. KHATRI; circ. 41,241.

Rajkot

Jai Hind: Jai Hind Press Bldg, Babubhai Shah Rd, POB 59, Rajkot 360 001; tel. (281) 2440511; fax (281) 2448677; e-mail info@jaihinddaily.com; internet www.jaihinddaily.com; f. 1948; morning and evening (in Rajkot as *Sanj Samachar*); Gujarati; also publ. from Ahmedabad; Editor Y. N. SHAH; combined circ. 107,300.

Phulchhab: Phulchhab Bhavan, Phulchhab Chowk, Rajkot 360 001; tel. (281) 2444611; fax (281) 2448751; f. 1950; morning; Gujarati; Propr Saurashtra Trust; Editor DINESH RAJA; circ. 84,500.

Surat

Gujaratmitra and Gujaratdarpan: Gujaratmitra Bhavan, nr Old Civil Hospital, Sonifalia, Surat 395 003; tel. (261) 2478703; fax (261) 2478700; e-mail gujaratmitra@satyam.net.in; f. 1863; morning; Gujarati; Editor B. P. RESHAMWALA; circ. 91,000.

Haryana

Rohtak

Bharat Janani: Sonipat Rd, Rohtak; tel. and fax (1262) 427191; f. 1971; Hindi; morning; Editor Dr R. S. SANTOSHI.

Himachal Pradesh
Shimla

Dainik Himachal Sewa: Hans Kutir, Khalini, Shimla 171 002; tel. (177) 2224119; fax (177) 2260187; f. 1986; Hindi; Editor-in-Chief Dr R. S. SANTOSHI.

Himachal Times: Himachal Times Complex, 64–66, The Mall, Shimla 171 001; tel. (177) 2201057; f. 1949; English; Chief Editor VIJAY PANDHI.

Jammu and Kashmir
Jammu

Daily Excelsior: Excelsior House, Excelsior Lane, Janipura, Jammu Tawi 180 007; tel. (191) 2537055; fax (191) 2537831; e-mail editor@dailyexcelsior.com; internet www.dailyexcelsior.com; f. 1965; English; Editor S. D. ROHMETRA.

Kashmir Times: Residency Rd, Jammu 180 001; tel. (191) 2543676; fax (191) 2542028; e-mail kashmirtimes@rediffmail.com; internet www.kashmirtimes.com; f. 1955; morning; English and Hindi; Editor PRABODH JAMWAL.

Srinagar

Greater Kashmir: 6 Pratap Park, Residency Rd, Srinagar 190 001; tel. (194) 2474339; fax (194) 2477782; e-mail editor@greaterkashmir.com; internet www.greaterkashmir.com; f. 1993; English; Chief Editor FAYAZ AHMED KALOO.

Jharkhand
Ranchi

Aj: Main Rd, Ranchi 834 001; tel. (651) 2311416; fax (651) 2306224; Hindi; morning; also publ. from eight other cities; Editor SHARDUL V. GUPTA; circ. 43,800; combined circ. 930,200.

Hindustan: Circular Court, Circular Rd, Ranchi 834 001; tel. (651) 2205811; Hindi; morning; also publ. from Patna, Delhi, Bhagalpur, Lucknow, Varanasi and Muzaffarpur; Editor MRINAL PANDE; combined circ. 753,500.

Prabhat Khabar: 15-P, Kokar Industrial Area, Kokar, Ranchi 834 001; tel. (651) 2544002; fax (651) 254405; e-mail pkhabar@ushamartin.co.in; internet www.prabhatkhabar.com; f. 1984; Hindi; also publ. from Dhanbad, Kolkata, Jamshedpur and Patna; Chief Editor H. B. N. SINGH; circ. 123,100 (Ranchi).

Ranchi Express: 55 Baralal St, Ranchi 834 001; tel. (651) 2206320; fax (651) 2203466; e-mail rexpress@dte.vsnl.net.in; internet www.ranchiexpress.com; f. 1963; Hindi; morning; Editor AJAY MAROO; circ. 72,400.

Karnataka
Bangalore

Deccan Herald: 75 Mahatma Gandhi Rd, Bangalore 560 001; tel. (80) 25588000; fax (80) 25580523; e-mail ads@deccanherald.co.in; internet www.deccanherald.com; f. 1948; morning; English; also publ. from Hubli-Dharwar, Mangalore and Gulbarga; Editor-in-Chief K. N. SHANTH KUMAR; combined circ. 154,600.

Kannada Prabha: Express Bldgs, 1 Queen's Rd, Bangalore 560 001; tel. (80) 22866893; fax (80) 22866617; e-mail bexpress@bgl.vsnl.net.in; internet www.kannadaprabha.com; f. 1967; morning; Kannada; also publ. from Belgaum and Shimoga; Editor Y. N. KRISHNAMURTHY; circ. 60,700.

New Indian Express: 1 Queen's Rd, Bangalore 560 001; tel. (80) 22256998; fax (80) 22256617; f. 1965; English; also publ. from Kochi, Hyderabad, Chennai, Madurai, Vijayawada and Vizianagaram; Man. Editor MANOJ KUMAR SONTHALIA; combined circ. 197,400.

Prajavani: 75 Mahatma Gandhi Rd, Bangalore 560 001; tel. (80) 25588999; fax (80) 25586443; e-mail ads@deccanherald.co.in; internet www.prajavani.net; f. 1948; morning; Kannada; also publ. from Hubli-Dharwar and Gulbarga; Editor-in-Chief K. N. SHANTH KUMAR; combined circ. 309,500.

Hubli-Dharwar

Samyukta Karnataka: Koppikar Rd, Hubli 580 020; tel. (836) 2364303; fax (836) 2362760; e-mail editorsk@touchtelindia.net; internet www.samyuktakarnataka.com; f. 1933; Kannada; also publ. from Bangalore, Davangere and Gulbarga; Man. Editor K. SHAMA RAO; combined circ. 143,700.

Vijay Karnataka: Giriraj Annexe, Circuit House Rd, Hubli 580 029; tel. (836) 2237556; fax (836) 2253630; e-mail hubli@vkmktg.com; f. 1999; Kannada; also publ. from Bangalore, Gangavati, Gulbarga, Mangalore, Mysore, Bagalkot, Chitradurga and Shimoga; Printer and Publr VIJAY SANKESHWAR; circ. 576,071 (combined).

Manipal

Udayavani: Udayavani Bldg, Press Corner, Manipal 576 104; tel. (820) 2570845; fax (820) 2570563; e-mail udayavani@manipalpress.com; internet www.udayavani.com; f. 1970; Kannada; also publ. from Manipal-Udupi and Mumbai; Editor T. SATISH U. PAI; circ. 189,400.

Kerala
Kottayam

Deepika: POB 7, Kottayam 686 001; tel. (481) 2566706; fax (481) 2567947; e-mail deepika@deepika.com; internet www.deepika.com; f. 1887; Malayalam; independent; also publ. from Kannur, Kochi, Kozhikode, Thiruvananthapuram and Thrissur; Man. Dir JOSE T. PATTARA; Chief Editor JOSE PANTHAPLAMTHOTTIYIL; combined circ. 251,000.

Malayala Manorama: K. K. Rd, POB 26, Kottayam 686 001; tel. (481) 2563646; fax (481) 2562479; e-mail editor@malayalamanorama.com; internet www.manoramaonline.com; f. 1890; Malayalam; also publ. from 12 other regional centres; morning; Man. Dir and Editor MAMMEN MATHEW; Chief Editor K. M. MATHEW; combined circ. 1,296,400.

Kozhikode

Deshabhimani: 11/127 Convent Rd, Kozhikode 673 032; tel. (495) 2365286; fax (495) 2365883; f. 1946; Malayalam; morning; publ. by the CPI—M; also publ. from Kochi, Kottayam, Thrissur and Thiruvananthapuram; Chief Editor S. RAMACHANDRAN PILLAI; combined circ. 266,400.

Mathrubhumi: Mathrubhumi Bldgs, K. P. Kesava Menon Rd, POB 46, Kozhikode 673 001; tel. (495) 2366655; fax (495) 2366656; e-mail mathrelt@md2.vsnl.net.in; internet www.mathrubhumi.com; f. 1923; Malayalam; also publ. from Thiruvananthapuram, Kannur, Thrissur, Kollam, Malappuram, Kottayam, Kochi, Bangalore, Chennai and Mumbai; Editor R. GOPALAKRISHNAN; combined circ. 910,000.

Thiruvananthapuram

Kerala Kaumudi: POB 77, Pettah, Thiruvananthapuram 695 024; tel. (471) 2461010; fax (471) 2461985; e-mail editor@kaumudi.com; internet www.keralakaumudi.com; f. 1911; Malayalam; also publ. from Kollam, Alappuzha, Kochi, Kannur, Kozhikode and Bangalore; Editor-in-Chief M. S. MANI; Man. Editor DEEPU RAVI; combined circ. 147,126.

Madhya Pradesh
Bhopal

Dainik Bhaskar: 6 Dwarka Sadan, Habibganj Rd, Bhopal 462 011; tel. (755) 2551601; fax (755) 2575190; e-mail mp@bhaskarit.com; f. 1958; morning; Hindi; also publ. from 18 other regional centres; Chief Editor R. C. AGARWAL; combined circ. 1,549,800.

Indore

Naidunia: 60/1 Babu Labhchand Chhajlani Marg, Indore 452 009; tel. (731) 2763111; fax (731) 2763120; e-mail editor@naidunia.com; internet www.naidunia.com; f. 1947; morning; Hindi; Editor ABHAY CHHAJLANI; circ. 145,600.

Maharashtra
Kolhapur

Pudhari: 2318, 'C' Ward, Kolhapur 416 002; tel. (231) 222251; fax (231) 222256; f. 1974; Marathi; Editor P. G. JADHAV; circ. 211,200.

Mumbai (Bombay)

Afternoon Courier: 6 Nanabhai Lane, Fort, Mumbai 400 001; tel. (22) 22871616; fax (22) 22870371; e-mail aftnet@bom2.vsnl.net.in; internet www.cybernoon.com; evening; English; Editor MARK MANUEL HUBERT; circ. 65,800.

Bombay Samachar: Red House, Syed Abdulla Brelvi Rd, Fort, Mumbai 400 001; tel. (22) 22045501; fax (22) 22046642; e-mail samachar@vsnl.com; f. 1822; morning and Sunday; Gujarati; political, social and commercial; Editor PINKY DALAL (acting); circ. 107,300.

Dainik Saamana: Sadguru Darshan, Nagu Sayaji Wadi, Dainik Saamana Marg, Prabhadevi, Mumbai 400 028; tel. (22) 24370591; fax (22) 24316590; f. 1989; Marathi; Exec. Editor SANJAY RAUT; circ. 102,900.

The Economic Times: Times of India Bldg, Dr Dadabhai Naoroji Rd, Mumbai 400 001; tel. (22) 22733535; fax (22) 22731344; e-mail etbom@timesgroup.com; internet www.economictimes.com; f. 1961; also publ. from New Delhi, Kolkata, Ahmedabad, Hyderabad,

Chennai and Bangalore; English; Editor (Mumbai) Sudeshna Sen; combined circ. 461,900, circ. (Mumbai) 140,200.

Financial Express: Express Towers, Nariman Point, Mumbai 400 021; tel. (22) 22022627; fax (22) 22022139; e-mail iemumbai@express.indexp.co.in; internet www.financialexpress.com; f. 1961; morning; English; also publ. from New Delhi, Bangalore, Kolkata, Coimbatore, Kochi, Ahmedabad (Gujarati) and Chennai; Man. Editor Vivek Goenka; Editor Mythili Bhusnurmath; combined circ. (English) 50,000.

The Free Press Journal: Free Press House, 215 Free Press Journal Rd, Nariman Point, Mumbai 400 021; tel. (22) 22874566; fax (22) 22874688; e-mail fpj@vsnl.com; f. 1930; English; also publ. from Indore; Man. Editor G. L. Lakhotia; combined circ. 87,000.

Indian Express: 3/50, Lalbaug Industrial Estate, Dr B. Ambedkar Marg, Lalbaug, Mumbai 400 012; tel. (22) 24717600; fax (22) 24717636; f. 1940; English; also publ. from Pune and Nagpur; Man. Editor Vivek Goenka; Chief Editor Shekhar Gupta; combined circ. 191,900.

Inquilab: 156 D. J. Dadajee Rd, Tardeo, Mumbai 400 034; tel. (22) 24942586; fax (22) 24936571; e-mail azizk@mid-day.mailserve.net; internet www.inquilab.com; f. 1938; morning; Urdu; Editor Fuzail Jafferey; circ. 35,600.

Janmabhoomi: Janmabhoomi Bhavan, Janmabhoomi Marg, Fort, POB 62, Mumbai 400 001; tel. (22) 22870831; fax (22) 22874097; e-mail bhoomi@bom3.vsnl.net.in; f. 1934; evening; Gujarati; Propr Saurashtra Trust; Editor Kundan Vyas; circ. 55,395.

Lokasatta: 3/50, Lalbaug Industrial Estate, Dr B. Ambedkar, Lalbaug, Mumbai 400 012; tel. (22) 24717677; fax (22) 24717654; internet www.loksatta.com; f. 1948; morning (incl. Sunday); Marathi; also publ. from Pune, Nagpur and Ahmednagar; Editor Kumar Ketkar; combined circ. 369,400.

Maharashtra Times: Dr Dadabhai Naoroji Rd, POB 213, Mumbai 400 001; tel. (22) 22353535; fax (22) 22731175; f. 1962; Marathi; Editor Bharat Kumar Raut; circ. 247,100.

Mid-Day: 64 Sitaram Mills Compound, N. M. Joshi Marg, Lower Parel, Mumbai 400 011; tel. (22) 23054545; fax (22) 23054861; e-mail mid-day@giasbm01.vsnl.net.in; internet www.mid-day.com; f. 1979; daily and Sunday; English; Editor Akar Patel; circ. 136,000.

Navakal: 13 Shenviwadi, Khadilkar Rd, Girgaun, Mumbai 400 004; tel. (22) 23860978; fax (22) 23860989; f. 1923; Marathi; Editor N. Y. Khadilkar; circ. 139,800.

Navbharat Times: Dr Dadabhai Naoroji Rd, Mumbai 400 001; tel. (22) 22733535; fax (22) 22731144; f. 1950; Hindi; also publ. from New Delhi, Jaipur, Patna and Lucknow; Chief Editor Vishwanath Sachdev; circ. (Mumbai) 142,100.

Navshakti: Free Press House, 215 Nariman Point, Mumbai 400 021; tel. (22) 22874566; fax (22) 22874688; f. 1932; Marathi; Chief Editor Prakash Kulkarni; circ. 65,000.

Sakal: Sakal Bhavan, Plot No. 42-B, Sector No. 11, CBD Belapur, Navi Mumbai 400 614; tel. (22) 27572916; fax (22) 27574280; e-mail sakal@vsnl.in; f. 1970; Marathi; also publ. from Pune, Aurangabad, Nasik, Kolhapur and Solapur; Chief Editor Sanjeev Latkar; combined circ. 667,500.

The Times of India: The Times of India Bldg, Dr Dadabhai Naoroji Rd, Mumbai 400 001; tel. (22) 56353535; fax (22) 22731444; e-mail toieditorial@timesgroup.com; internet www.timesofindia.com; f. 1838; morning; English; also publ. from 10 regional centres; Exec. Editor Arindam Sengupta; circ. (Mumbai) 545,600, combined circ. 2,214,700.

Nagpur

The Hitavada: Pandit Jawaharlal Nehru Marg, POB 201, Nagpur 440 012; tel. (712) 2523155; fax (712) 2535093; e-mail hitavada_ngp@sancharnet.in; f. 1911; morning; English; also publ. from Raipur and Jabalpur; Man. Editor Banwarilal Purohit; Editor V. Phanshikar; circ. 60,700.

Lokmat: Lokmat Bhavan, Wardha Rd, Nagpur 440 012; tel. (712) 2523527; fax (712) 2526923; also publ. from Jalgaon, Pune and Nasik; Marathi; **Lokmat Samachar** (Hindi) publ. from Nagpur, Akola and Aurangabad; **Lokmat Times** (English) publ. from Nagpur and Aurangabad; Editor Vijay Darda; combined circ. (Marathi) 436,800, (Hindi) 62,300.

Nava Bharat: Nava Bharat Bhavan, Cotton Market, Nagpur 440 018; tel. (712) 2726677; fax (712) 2723444; f. 1938; morning; Hindi; also publ. from 10 other cities; Editor-in-Chief R. G. Maheswari; combined circ. 640,400.

Tarun Bharat: 28 Farmland, Ramdaspeth, Nagpur 440 010; tel. (712) 2525052; fax (712) 2531758; e-mail ibharat_ngp@sancharnet.in; internet www.tarunbharat.net; f. 1941; Marathi; independent;

also publ. from Belgaum; Man. Editor Anil Dandekar; Chief Editor Sudhir Pathak; circ. (Nagpur) 58,200.

Pune

Kesari: 568 Narayan Peth, Pune 411 030; tel. (20) 4459250; fax (20) 4451677; f. 1881; Marathi; also publ. from Solapur, Chiplun, Ahmednagar and Sangli; Editor Arvind Vyankatesh Gokhale; circ. (Pune) 42,600.

Sakal: 595 Budhawar Peth, Pune 411 002; tel. (20) 24455500; fax (20) 24450583; e-mail sakal@giaspn01.vsnl.net.in; internet www.esakal.com; f. 1932; daily; Marathi; also publ. from 10 other regional centres; Editor Anant Dixit (Pune); Man. Editor Pratap Pawar; combined circ. 667,500.

Meghalaya

Shillong

The Shillong Times: Rilbong, Shillong 793 004; tel. (364) 2223488; fax (364) 2229488; e-mail shillongtimes@yahoo.com; f. 1945; English; Editor Manas Chaudhuri; circ. 28,700.

Orissa

Bhubaneswar

Dharitri: B-26, Industrial Estate, Bhubaneswar 751 010; tel. (674) 2580101; fax (674) 2580795; e-mail advt@dharitri.com; internet www.dharitri.com; evening and morning; Oriya; Editor Tathagata Satpathy; circ. 175,100.

Pragativadi: 178-B, Mancheswar Industrial Estate, Bhubaneswar 751 010; tel. (674) 2588297; fax (674) 2582709; e-mail pragativadi@yahoo.com; internet www.pragativadi.com; Exec. Editor Samahit Bal; circ. 132,956.

The Samaya: Plot No. 44 and 54, Sector A, Zone D, Mancheswar Industrial Estate, Bhubaneswar 751 017; tel. (674) 2583690; fax (674) 2582565; e-mail samayabbsr@usanet.com; internet www.thesamaya.com; f. 1966; Oriya; Editor Satakadi Hota; circ. 134,400.

Sambad: Eastern Media Ltd, A-62, Nayapalli, Bhubaneswar 751 003; tel. (674) 2561198; fax (674) 2562914; e-mail sambad00@rediffmail.com; internet www.orissasambad.com; f. 1984; Oriya; also publ. from seven other regional centres; Editor S. R. Patnaik; combined circ. 213,600.

Cuttack

Prajatantra: Prajatantra Bldgs, Behari Baug, Cuttack 753 002; tel. (671) 2603071; fax (671) 2603063; f. 1947; Oriya; Editor Bhartruhari Mahtab; circ. 117,300.

Samaj: Gopabandhu Bhavan, Buxibazar, Cuttack 753 001; tel. (671) 2301598; fax (671) 2301384; e-mail samaj@hotmail.com; f. 1919; Oriya; also publ. from Sambalpur; Editor Manorama Mahapatra; circ. 170,700.

The Punjab

Chandigarh

The Tribune: Sector 29c, Chandigarh 160 020; tel. (172) 2655066; fax (172) 2651293; e-mail tribunet@ch1.dot.net.in; internet www.tribuneindia.com; f. 1881; (English edn), f. 1978 (Hindi and Punjabi edns); Editor-in-Chief H. K. Dua; Editor (Hindi edn) Vijay Saighal; Editor (Punjabi edn) G. S. Bhullar; circ. 220,500 (English), 40,300 (Hindi), 66,200 (Punjabi).

Jalandhar

Ajit: Ajit Bhavan, Nehru Garden Rd, Jalandhar 144 001; tel. (181) 22800960; f. 1955; Punjabi; Man. Editor S. Barjinder Singh; circ. 265,500.

Hind Samachar: Civil Lines, Jalandhar 144 001; tel. (181) 2280115; fax (181) 2280113; f. 1948; morning; Hindi; also publ. from Ambala Cantt; Editor-in-Chief Vijay Kumar Chopra; Jt Editor Avinash Chopra; combined circ. 35,565.

Jag Bani: Civil Lines, Jalandhar 144 001; tel. (181) 2280115; fax (181) 2280113; f. 1978; morning; Punjabi; Editor-in-Chief Vijay Kumar Chopra; Jt Editor Avinash Chopra; circ. 264,935.

Punjab Kesari: Civil Lines, Jalandhar 144 001; tel. (181) 2280115; fax (181) 2280113; internet www.punjabkesari.com; f. 1965; morning; Hindi; also publ. from Delhi and Ambala; Editor-in-Chief Vijay Kumar Chopra; Jt Editor Avinash Chopra; combined circ. 829,474.

Rajasthan

Jaipur

Rajasthan Patrika: Kesargarh, Jawaharlal Nehru Marg, Jaipur 302 004; tel. (141) 2561582; fax (141) 2566011; e-mail info@

rajasthanpatrika.com; internet www.rajasthanpatrika.com; f. 1956; Hindi edn also publ. from 16 other towns; Chief Editor GULAB KOTHARI; combined circ. (Hindi) 732,800.

Rashtradoot: M.I. Rd, POB 30, Jaipur 302 001; tel. (141) 2372634; fax (141) 2373513; f. 1951; Hindi; also publ. from Kota, Udaipur, Ajmer and Bikaner; CEO SOMESH SHARMA; Chief Editor RAJESH SHARMA; circ. 368,482 (Jaipur), 76,763 (Kota), 45,250 (Bikaner), 38,023 (Udaipur), 27,514 (Ajmer).

Tamil Nadu

Chennai (Madras)

Daily Thanthi: 46 E.V.K. Sampath Rd, POB 467, Chennai 600 007; tel. (44) 25387731; fax (44) 25381720; f. 1949; Tamil; also publ. from 13 other regional centres; Gen. Man. D. RAJIAH; Editor R. THIRUVADI; combined circ. 714,900.

Dinakaran: 106/107 Kutchery Rd, Mylapore, POB 358, Chennai 600 004; tel. (44) 24941006; fax (44) 24933597; e-mail dinakaran@dinakaran.com; internet www.dinakaran.com; f. 1977; Tamil; also publ. from Madurai, Tiruchirapalli, Vellore, Tirunelveli, Salem and Coimbatore; Man. Dir K. KUMARAN; Editor D. PAULRAJ; combined circ. 351,872.

Dinamalar: 8 Casa Major Rd, Egmore, Chennai 600 008; tel. (44) 28195000; fax (44) 28195003; e-mail demregr@dinamalar.com; internet www.dinamalar.com; f. 1951; Tamil; also publ. from 10 other towns; Editor R. KRISHNAMOORTHY; combined circ. 561,600.

Dinamani: Express Estates, Mount Rd, Chennai 600 002; tel. (44) 8520751; fax (44) 8524500; e-mail express@giasmd01.vsnl.net.in; internet www.dinamani.com; f. 1934; morning; Tamil; also publ. from Madurai, Coimbatore and Bangalore; Editor T. SAMBANDAM; combined circ. 136,300.

Financial Express: Vasanthi Medical Center, 30/20 Pycrofts Garden Rd, Chennai 600 006; tel. (44) 28231112; fax (44) 28231489; internet www.financialexpress.com; f. 1961; morning; English; also publ. from Mumbai, Ahmedabad (in Gujarati), Bangalore, Kochi, Kolkata and New Delhi; Man. Editor VIVEK GOENKA; combined circ. 32,594.

The Hindu: Kasturi Bldgs, 859/860 Anna Salai, Chennai 600 002; tel. (44) 28413344; fax (44) 28415325; e-mail wsvcs@thehindu.co.in; internet www.hinduonnet.com; f. 1878; morning; English; independent; also publ. from 10 other regional centres; Editor-in-Chief N. RAM; combined circ. 981,600.

The Hindu Business Line: Kasturi Bldgs, 859/860 Anna Salai, Chennai 600 002; tel. (44) 28589060; fax (44) 28545703; e-mail wsvcs@thehindu.co.in; internet www.hindubusinessline.com; f. 1994; morning; English; also publ. from 10 other regional centres; Editor-in-Chief N. RAM; combined circ. 56,100.

Murasoli: 93 Kodambakkam High Rd, Chennai 600 034; tel. (44) 28270044; fax (44) 28217515; f. 1960; organ of the DMK; Tamil; Editor S. SELVAM; circ. 54,000.

New Indian Express: Club House Rd, Chennai 600 002; tel. (44) 28461260; fax (44) 28461829; e-mail newexpress@vsnl.com; internet www.newindpress.com; f. 1932 as Indian Express; morning; English; also publ. from 11 other cities; Chair. and Man. Dir MANOJ KUMAR SONTHALIA; combined circ. 197,400.

Tripura

Agartala

Dainik Sambad: 11 Jagannath Bari Rd, POB 2, Agartala 799 001; tel. (381) 2326676; fax (381) 2324845; e-mail dainik2@sanchar.net.in; f. 1966; Bengali; morning; Editor BHUPENDRA CHANDRA DATTA BHAUMIK; circ. 49,000.

Uttaranchal

Dehradun

Amar Ujala: Shed 2, Patel Nagar Industrial Estate, Dehradun 248 003; tel. (135) 2720378; fax (135) 2721776; internet www.amarujala.com; Hindi; morning; also publ. from 10 other cities; Editor AJAY K. AGRAWAL; combined circ. 630,100.

Uttar Pradesh

Agra

Amar Ujala: Sikandra Rd, Agra 282 007; tel. (562) 2321600; fax (562) 2322181; e-mail amarujal@nde.vsnl.net.in; internet www.amarujala.com; f. 1948; Hindi; also publ. from Bareilly, Allahabad, Jhansi, Kanpur, Moradabad, Chandigarh and Meerut; Editor AJAY K. AGRAWAL; combined circ. 630,100.

Allahabad

Amrita Prabhat: 10 Tashkent Marg, Allahabad 211 001; tel. (532) 2600654; fax (532) 2605394; f. 1977; Hindi; CEO S. S. BAGGA; circ. 44,000.

Northern India Patrika: 10 Edmonstone Rd, Allahabad 211 001; tel. (532) 2600654; fax (532) 2605394; f. 1959; English; CEO S. S. BAGGA; circ. 46,000.

Kanpur

Dainik Jagran: Jagran Bldg, 2 Sarvodaya Nagar, Kanpur 208 005; tel. (512) 2216161; fax (512) 2216972; e-mail jpl@jagran.com; internet www.jagran.com; f. 1942; Hindi; also publ. from 25 other cities; Man. Editor MAHENDRA MOHAN GUPTA; Editor SANJAY GUPTA; combined circ. 2,600,000.

Lucknow

National Herald: Lucknow; f. 1938 Lucknow, 1968 Delhi; English; Editor-in-Chief D. V. VENKITACHALAM.

The Pioneer: Sahara Shopping Centre, Faizabad Rd, Lucknow 226 016; tel. (522) 2346444; fax (522) 2345582; f. 1865; English; also publ. from New Delhi; Editor CHANDAN MITRA; combined circ. 136,000.

Swatantra Bharat: 1st Floor, Suraj Deep Complex, 1 Jopling Rd, Lucknow 226 001; tel. (522) 2204306; fax (522) 2208701; e-mail sbharats@satyam.net.in; f. 1947; Hindi; also publ. from Kanpur; Editor K. K. SRIVASTAVA; circ. 80,700 (Lucknow), 65,157 (Kanpur).

Varanasi

Aj: Aj Bhavan, Sant Kabir Rd, Kabirchaura, Varanasi 221 001; tel. (542) 2393981; fax (542) 2393989; f. 1920; Hindi; also publ. from Gorakhpur, Patna, Allahabad, Ranchi, Agra, Bareilly, Lucknow, Jamshedpur, Dhanbad and Kanpur; Editor SHARDUL VIKRAM GUPTA; combined circ. 930,200.

West Bengal

Kolkata (Calcutta)

Aajkaal: 96 Raja Rammohan Sarani, Kolkata 700 009; tel. (33) 23509803; fax (33) 23500877; e-mail aajkaal@cal.vsnl.net.in; f. 1981; morning; Bengali; also publ. from Agartala and Siliguri; Chief Editor PRATAP K. ROY; circ. 140,100.

Ananda Bazar Patrika: 6 Prafulla Sarkar St, Kolkata 700 001; tel. (33) 22374880; fax (33) 22253241; internet www.anandabazar.com; f. 1922; morning; Bengali; also publ. from Baharampore and Siliguri; Editor AVEEK SARKAR; circ. 950,400.

Bartaman: 76A Acharya J.C. Bose Rd, Kolkata 700 014; tel. (33) 22443907; fax (33) 22441215; internet www.bartamanpatrika.com; f. 1984; also publ. from Barddhaman and Siliguri; Editor BARUN SENGUPTA; circ. 427,100.

Business Standard: 4/1 Red Cross Place, Kolkata 700 001; tel. (33) 22101314; fax (33) 22101599; f. 1975; morning; also publ. from New Delhi, Ahmedabad, Hyderabad, Bangalore, Chennai and Mumbai; English; Editor T. N. NINAN; combined circ. 60,000.

The Economic Times: 105/7A, S. N. Banerjee Rd, Kolkata 700 014; tel. (33) 22444243; fax (33) 22453018; English; also publ. from Ahmedabad, Delhi, Bangalore, Chennai, Hyderabad and Mumbai; circ. (Kolkata) 54,300.

Financial Express: 83 B. K. Pal Ave, Kolkata 700 005; morning; English; also publ. from Mumbai, Ahmedabad, Bangalore, Coimbatore, Kochi, Chennai and New Delhi; Man. Editor VIVEK GOENKA; combined circ. 30,800.

Ganashakti: 74A A. J. C. Bose Rd, Kolkata 700 016; tel. (33) 22278950; fax (33) 2278090; e-mail mail@ganashakti.co.in; internet www.ganashakti.com; f. 1967; morning; Bengali; also publ. from Durgapur and Siliguri; Editor NARAYAN DATTA; circ. 165,762.

Sandhya Aajkaal: 96 Raja Rammohan Sarani, Kolkata 700 009; tel. (33) 23509803; fax (33) 23500877; evening; Bengali; Chief Editor PRATAP K. ROY; circ. 17,400.

Sangbad Pratidin: 20 Prafulla Sarkar St, Kolkata 700 072; tel. (33) 22128400; fax (33) 22126031; e-mail pratidin@cal2.vsnl.net.in; internet www.sangbadpratidin.com; morning; Bengali; also publ. from Ranchi and Siliguri; Editor SWAPAN SADHAN BASU; circ. 278,700.

Sanmarg: 160B Chittaranjan Ave, Kolkata 700 007; tel. (33) 22414800; fax (33) 22415087; e-mail sanmarg@satyam.net.in; f. 1948; Hindi; Editor RAMAWATAR GUPTA; circ. 107,700.

The Statesman: Statesman House, 4 Chowringhee Sq., Kolkata 700 001; tel. (33) 22127070; fax (33) 22370054; e-mail thestatesman@vsnl.com; internet www.statesman.net; f. 1875; morning; English; independent; also publ. from New Delhi, Siliguri and Bhubaneswar; Editor-in-Chief C. R. IRANI; combined circ. 166,300.

The Telegraph: 6 Prafulla Sarkar St, Kolkata 700 001; tel. (33) 22374880; fax (33) 22253240; e-mail thetelegraphindia@newscom .com; f. 1982; English; also publ. from Guwahati, Jamshedpur and Siliguri; Editor AVEEK SARKAR; circ. 325,100.

Uttar Banga Sambad: 7 Old Court House St, Kolkata 700 001; tel. (33) 22435663; fax (33) 22435618; e-mail uttarmail@sify.com; internet www.uttarbangasambad.com; f. 1980; Bengali; Editor S. C. TALUKDAR; circ. 133,086.

Vishwamitra: 74 Lenin Sarani, Kolkata 700 013; tel. (33) 22441139; fax (33) 22446393; e-mail vismtra@cal2.vsnl.net.in; f. 1915; morning; Hindi; commercial; Editor PRAKASH CHANDRA AGRAWALLA; circ. 92,533.

SELECTED PERIODICALS

Delhi and New Delhi

Alive: Delhi Press Bldg, E-3 Jhandewala Estate, Rani Jhansi Rd, New Delhi 110 055; tel. (11) 51398888; fax (11) 23625020; e-mail editorial@delhipressgroup.com; internet www.grihshobaindia.com; f. 1940 as Caravan; monthly; English; men's interests; Editor, Publr and Printer PARESH NATH; circ. 10,011.

Bal Bharati: Patiala House, Publications Division, Ministry of Information and Broadcasting, New Delhi; tel. (11) 2387038; f. 1948; monthly; Hindi; for children; Editor SHIV KUMAR; circ. 30,000.

Biswin Sadi: B-1, Nizamuddin West, New Delhi 110 013; tel. (11) 24626556; f. 1937; monthly; Urdu; Editor Z. REHMAN NAYYAR; circ. 32,000.

Business Today: Videocon Towers, E-1 Jhandelwalan Extn, New Delhi 110 055; tel. (11) 23684893; fax (11) 23684819; e-mail btoday@ giasdl01.vsnl.net.in; internet www.business-today.com; fortnightly; English; Editor SANJAY NARAYAN; circ. 124,600.

Catholic India: CBCI Centre, 1 Ashok Place, Goldakkhana, New Delhi 110 001; tel. (11) 23344470; fax (11) 23364615; e-mail cbci@ vsnl.com; internet www.cbcisite.com; quarterly.

Champak: Delhi Press Bldg, E-3 Jhandewala Estate, Rani Jhansi Rd, New Delhi 110 055; tel. (11) 51398888; fax (11) 23625020; e-mail editorial@delhipressgroup.com; internet www.grihshobaindia.com; f. 1968; fortnightly (Hindi, English, Gujarati, Tamil, Telugu, Malayalam and Marathi edns); monthly (Kannada edn); children's; Editor, Publr and Printer PARESH NATH; circ. 73,560 (Hindi), 34,795 (English), 33,043 (Marathi), 16,189 (Gujarati), 10,000 (Malayalam), 3,664 (Telugu), 2,153 (Tamil), 13,823 (Kannada).

Children's World: Nehru House, 4 Bahadur Shah Zafar Marg, New Delhi 110 002; tel. (11) 23316970; fax (11) 23721090; e-mail cbtnd@ vsnl.com; internet www.childrensbooktrust.com; f. 1968; monthly; English; Editor NAVIN MENON; circ. 25,000.

Competition Refresher: 2767, Bright House, Daryaganj, New Delhi 110 002; tel. (11) 23282226; fax (11) 23269227; e-mail psbright@ndf.vsnl.net.in; internet www.brightcareers.com; f. 1984; monthly; English; Chief Editor, Publr and Man. Dir PRITAM SINGH BRIGHT; circ. 175,000.

Competition Success Review: 604 Prabhat Kiran Bldg, Rajendra Place, Delhi 110 008; tel. (11) 25712898; fax (11) 25754647; e-mail csrindia@mantraonline.com; monthly; English; f. 1964; Editor S. K. SACHDEVA; circ. 247,400.

Computers Today: Marina Arcade, G-59 Connaught Circus, New Delhi 110 001; tel. (11) 23736233; fax (11) 23725506; e-mail ctoday@ india-today.com; f. 1984; Editor J. SRIHARI RAJU; circ. 46,300.

Cricket Samrat: L-1, Kanchan House, Najafgarh Rd, Commercial Complex, nr Milan Cinema, New Delhi 110 015; tel. (11) 25191175; fax (11) 25469581; f. 1978; monthly; Hindi; Editor ANAND DEWAN; circ. 64,000.

Employment News: Government of India, East Block IV, Level 5, R. K. Puram, New Delhi 110 066; tel. (11) 26174975; fax (11) 26105875; e-mail empnews@bol.net.in; f. 1976; weekly; Hindi, Urdu and English edns; Gen. Man. and Chief Editor VISHWANATH RAMESH; Editor RANJANA DEV SARMAH; combined circ. 550,000.

Filmi Duniya: 16 Darya Ganj, New Delhi 110 002; tel. (11) 23278087; fax (11) 23279341; f. 1958; monthly; Hindi; Chief Editor NARENDRA KUMAR; circ. 132,100.

Filmi Kaliyan: 4675-B/21 Ansari Rd, New Delhi 110 002; tel. (11) 23272080; f. 1969; monthly; Hindi; cinema; Editor-in-Chief V. S. DEWAN; circ. 82,400.

Global Travel Express: 26F Rajiv Gandhi Chowk (Connaught Place), New Delhi 110 001; tel. (11) 23312329; fax (11) 24621636; e-mail indian_observer@hotmail.com; f. 1993; monthly; English; travel and tourism; Chief Editor HARBHAJAN SINGH; Editor GURINDER SINGH; circ. 28,902.

Grihshobha: Delhi Press Bldg, E-3 Jhandewala Estate, Rani Jhansi Rd, New Delhi 110 055; tel. (11) 51398888; fax (11) 23625020;

e-mail editorial@delhipressgroup.com; internet www .grihshobaindia.com; f. 1979; monthly; Tamil, Telugu, Kannada, Marathi, Hindi, Malayalam and Gujarati edns; women's interests; Editor, Publr and Printer PARESH NATH; circ. 73,857 (Kannada), 48,145 (Gujarati), 104,496 (Marathi), 326,588 (Hindi), 12,641 (Telugu), 17,486 (Tamil), 35,000 (Malayalam).

India Perspectives: Room 149B, 'A' Wing, Shastri Bhavan, New Delhi 110 001; tel. (11) 23389471; f. 1988; Editor BHARAT BHUSHAN.

India Today: F-14/15, Connaught Place, New Delhi 110 001; tel. (11) 23315801; fax (11) 23316180; e-mail letters.editor@intoday.com; internet www.india-today.com; f. 1975; English, Tamil, Telugu, Malayalam and Hindi; weekly; Editor PRABHU CHAWLA; Editor-in-Chief AROON PURIE; circ. 463,800 (English), 353,700 (Hindi), 65,300 (Tamil), 42,900 (Malayalam), 56,800 (Telugu).

Indian Railways: 411 Rail Bhavan, Raisina Rd, New Delhi 110 001; tel. (11) 23383540; fax (11) 23384481; e-mail editorir@rb.railnet .gov.in; f. 1956; monthly; English; publ. by the Ministry of Railways (Railway Board); Editor M. R. KALYANI; circ. 12,000.

Journal of Industry and Trade: Ministry of Commerce, Delhi 110 011; tel. (11) 23016664; f. 1952; monthly; English; Man. Dir A. C. BANERJEE; circ. 2,000.

Junior Science Refresher: 2769, Bright House, Daryaganj, New Delhi 110 002; tel. (11) 23282226; fax (11) 23269227; e-mail psbright@ndf.vsnl.net.in; internet www.brightcareers.com; f. 1987; monthly; English; Chief Editor, Publr and Man. Dir PRITAM SINGH BRIGHT; circ. 118,000.

Kadambini: Hindustan Times House, Kasturba Gandhi Marg, New Delhi 110 001; tel. and fax (11) 23704581; e-mail vnagar@ hindustantimes.com; f. 1960; monthly; Hindi; Editor MRINAL PANDE; Associate Editor VISHNU NAGAR; circ. 31,800.

Krishak Samachar: Bharat Krishak Samaj, Dr Panjabrao Deshmukh Krishak Bhavan, A-1 Nizamuddin West, New Delhi 110 013; tel. (11) 24619508; e-mail ffi@mantraonline.com; f. 1957; monthly; English and Hindi edns; agriculture; Editor Dr KRISHAN BIR CHAUDHARY; circ. (English) 6,000, (Hindi) 17,000.

Kurukshetra: Ministry of Rural Development, Room No. 655/661, 'A' Wing, Nirman Bhavan, New Delhi 110 011; tel. (11) 23015014; fax (11) 23386879; monthly; English; rural development; Editor P. V. RAO; circ. 14,000.

Mainstream: 145/1D Shahpur Jat, 1st Floor, nr Asiad Village, New Delhi 110 049; tel. (11) 26497188; fax (11) 26569352; e-mail mnstrm@nda.vsnl.net.in; internet www.mainstreamweekly.com; English; weekly; politics and current affairs; Editor SUMIT CHAKRAVARTTY.

Mayapuri: A-5, Mayapuri Phase 1, New Delhi 110 064; tel. (11) 28116120; fax (11) 25133120; e-mail mayapuri@hotmail.com; f. 1974; weekly; Hindi; cinema; Editor A. P. BAJAJ; circ. 146,144.

Mukta: Delhi Press Bldg, E-3 Jhandewala Estate, Rani Jhansi Rd, New Delhi 110 055; tel. (11) 51398888; fax (11) 23625020; e-mail editorial@delhipressgroup.com; internet www.grihshobhaindia .com; f. 1961; monthly; Hindi; youth; Editor, Publr and Printer PARESH NATH; circ. 24,396.

Nandan: Hindustan Times House, Kasturba Gandhi Marg, New Delhi 110 001; tel. (11) 23704562; fax (11) 23704600; e-mail jbharti@ hindustantimes.com; f. 1963; monthly; Hindi; Editor JAI PRAKASH BHARTI; circ. 58,400.

New Age Weekly: Ajoy Bhavan, 15 Comrade Indrajeet Gupta Marg, Delhi 110 002; tel. (11) 23230762; fax (11) 23235543; e-mail cpindia@del2.vsnl.net.in; f. 1953; main organ of the Communist Party of India; weekly; English; Editor SHAMEEM FAIZEE; circ. 215,000.

Organiser: Sanskriti Bhavan, D. B. Gupta Rd, Jhandewalan, New Delhi 110 055; tel. (11) 23526097; fax (11) 23516635; e-mail chari_s@ vsnl.com; internet www.organiser.org; f. 1947; weekly; English; Editor R. BALASHANKAR; circ. 44,100.

Outlook: AB-10 Safdarjung Enclave, New Delhi 110 029; tel. (11) 51651471; fax (11) 51651472; e-mail outlook@outlookindia.com; internet www.outlookindia.com; f. 1995; weekly; Hindi and English edns; Editor-in-Chief VINOD MEHTA; circ. 256,300.

Panchjanya: Sanskriti Bhavan, Deshbandhu Gupta Marg, Jhandewala, New Delhi 110 055; tel. (11) 23514244; fax (11) 23558613; e-mail panch@nde.vsnl.net.in; f. 1947; weekly; Hindi; general interest; nationalist; Chair. S. N. BANSAL; Editor TARUN VIJAY; circ. 59,300.

Punjabi Digest: 209 Hemkunt House, 6 Rajendra Place, POB 2549, New Delhi 110 008; tel. (11) 25715225; fax (11) 25761053; f. 1971; literary monthly; Gurmukhi; Chief Editor Sardar S. B. SINGH; circ. 48,600.

Sainik Samachar: Block L-1, Church Rd, New Delhi 110 001; tel. (11) 23094668; f. 1909; pictorial fortnightly for India's armed forces;

English, Hindi, Urdu, Tamil, Punjabi, Telugu, Marathi, Kannada, Gorkhali, Malayalam, Bengali, Assamese and Oriya edns; Editor P. K. Pattayanak; circ. 20,000.

Saras Salil: Delhi Press Bldg, E-3 Jhandewala Estate, Rani Jhansi Rd, New Delhi 110 055; tel. (11) 51398888; fax (11) 23625020; e-mail editorial@delhipressgroup.com; internet www.grihshobhaindia .com; f. 1993; fortnightly; Hindi, Telugu, Tamil, Gujarati and Marathi edns; Editor, Publr and Printer Paresh Nath; circ. 1,019,962 (Hindi), 10,059 (Telugu), 8,223 (Tamil), 5,388 (Gujarati), 13,644 (Marathi).

Sarita: Delhi Press Bldg, E-3 Jhandewala Estate, Rani Jhansi Rd, New Delhi 110 055; tel. (11) 51398888; fax (11) 23625020; e-mail editorial@delhipressgroup.com; internet www.grihshobhaindia .com; f. 1945; fortnightly; Hindi; family magazine; Editor, Publr and Printer Paresh Nath; circ. 102,217.

Shama: 13/14 Asaf Ali Rd, New Delhi 110 002; tel. (11) 23232674; fax (11) 23235167; f. 1939; monthly; Urdu; art and literature; Editors M. Yunus Dehlvi, Idrees Dehlvi, Ilyas Dehlvi; circ. 58,000.

Suman Saurabh: Delhi Press Bldg, E-3 Jhandewala Estate, Rani Jhansi Rd, New Delhi 110 055; tel. (11) 51398888; fax (11) 23625020; e-mail editorial@delhipressgroup.com; internet www .grihshobhaindia.com; f. 1983; monthly; Hindi; youth; Editor, Publr and Printer Paresh Nath; circ. 40,756.

Sushama: 13/14 Asaf Ali Rd, New Delhi 110 002; tel. (11) 23232674; fax (11) 23235167; f. 1959; monthly; Hindi; art and literature; Editors Idrees Dehlvi, Ilyas Dehlvi, Yunus Dehlvi; circ. 30,000.

Vigyan Pragati: NISCAIR (CSIR), Dr K. S. Krishnan Marg, New Delhi 110 012; tel. (11) 25841647; fax (11) 25847062; e-mail vp@ niscair.res.in; f. 1952; monthly; Hindi; popular science; Editor Pradeep Sharma; circ. 40,000.

Woman's Era: Delhi Press Bldg, E-3 Jhandewala Estate, Rani Jhansi Rd, New Delhi 110 055; tel. (11) 51398888; fax (11) 23625020; e-mail editorial@delhipressgroup.com; internet www .grihshobhaindia.com; f. 1973; fortnightly; English; women's interests; Editor, Publr and Printer Paresh Nath; circ. 82,263.

Yojana: Yojana Bhavan, Sansad Marg, New Delhi 110 001; tel. (11) 23710473; e-mail yojana@techpilgrim.com; f. 1957; monthly; English, Tamil, Bengali, Marathi, Gujarati, Assamese, Malayalam, Telugu, Kannada, Punjabi, Urdu, Oriya and Hindi edns; Chief Editor Subhash Setia; circ. 72,000.

Andhra Pradesh

Hyderabad

Andhra Prabha Illustrated Weekly: 591 Lower Tank Bund Rd, Express Centre, Domalaguda, Hyderabad 500 029; tel. (40) 2233586; f. 1952; weekly; Telugu; Editor Potturi Venkateswara Rao; circ. 21,800.

Secunderabad

Andhra Bhoomi Sachitra Masa Patrika: 36 Sarojini Devi Rd, Secunderabad 500 003; tel. (842) 27802346; fax (842) 27805256; f. 1977; fortnightly; Telugu; Editor T. Venkatram Reddy; circ. 25,600.

Vijayawada

Andhra Jyoti Sachitra Vara Patrika: Vijayawada 520 010; tel. (866) 2474532; f. 1967; weekly; Telugu; Editor Puranam Subramanya Sarma; circ. 59,000.

Bala Jyoti: Labbipet, Vijayawada 520 010; tel. (866) 2474532; f. 1980; monthly; Telugu; Assoc. Editor A. Sasikant Satakarni; circ. 12,500.

Jyoti Chitra: Andhra Jyoti Bldgs, Vijayawada 520 010; tel. (866) 2474532; f. 1977; weekly; Telugu; Editor T. Kutumba Rao; circ. 20,100.

Swati Saparivara Patrika: Anil Bldgs, Suryaraopet, POB 339, Vijayawada 520 002; tel. (866) 2431862; fax (866) 2430433; e-mail vjwswati@sancharnet.in; f. 1984; weekly; Telugu; Editor Vemuri Balaram; circ. 252,100.

Vanita Jyoti: Labbipet, POB 712, Vijayawada 520 010; tel. (866) 2474532; f. 1978; monthly; Telugu; Asst Editor J. Satyanarayana; circ. 13,100.

Assam

Guwahati

Agradoot: Agradoot Bhavan, Dispur, Guwahati 781 006; tel. (361) 2261923; fax (361) 2260655; e-mail agradoot@sify.com; f. 1971; bi-weekly; Assamese; Editor K. S. Deka; circ. 29,463.

Asam Bani: Tribune Bldg, Guwahati 781 003; tel. (361) 2661356; fax (361) 2660594; e-mail dileepchandan@yahoo.com; internet www

.assamtribune.com; f. 1955; weekly; Assamese; Editor Dileep Chandan; circ. 14,000.

Sadin: Maniram Dewan Rd, Chandmari, Guwahati 781 003; tel. (361) 2524594; fax (361) 2524634; e-mail protidin@gw1.vsnl.net.in; weekly; Assamese; circ. 39,500.

Bihar

Patna

Anand Digest: Govind Mitra Rd, Patna 800 004; tel. (612) 2656557; fax (612) 2225192; f. 1981; monthly; Hindi; family magazine; Editor Dr S. S. Singh; circ. 44,500.

Balak: Govind Mitra Rd, POB 5, Patna 800 004; tel. (612) 2650341; f. 1926; monthly; Hindi; children's; Editor S. R. Saran; circ. 32,000.

Chhattisgarh

Raipur

Krishak Jagat: A-23, Sector 1, Shankar Nagar, Raipur 492 001; tel. (771) 2420449; e-mail krishjag@sancharnet.in; internet www .krishakjagatindia.com; weekly; Hindi; Chief Editor Vijay Kumar Bondriya; circ. 35,000.

Gujarat

Ahmedabad

Akhand Anand: Anand Bhavan, Relief Rd, POB 123, Ahmedabad 380 001; tel. (79) 2357482; e-mail innitadi@sancharnet.in; f. 1947; monthly; Gujarati; Pres. Anand Amin; Editor Dr Dilavarsinh Jadeja; circ. 10,000.

Chitralok: Gujarat Samachar Bhavan, Khanpur, POB 254, Ahmedabad 380 001; tel. (79) 5504010; fax (79) 5502000; f. 1952; weekly; Gujarati; films; Man. Editor Shreyans S. Shah; circ. 20,000.

Sakhi: Sakhi Publications, Jai Hind Press Bldg, nr Gujarat Chamber, Ashram Rd, Navrangpura, Ahmedabad 380 009; tel. (79) 26581734; fax (79) 26587681; f. 1984; fortnightly; Gujarati; women's; Man. Editor Nita Y. Shah; Editor Y. N. Shah; circ. 10,000.

Shree: Gujarat Samachar Bhavan, Khanpur, Ahmedabad 380 001; tel. (79) 5504010; fax (79) 5502000; f. 1964; weekly; Gujarati; women's; Editor Smrutiben Shah; circ. 20,000.

Stree: Sandesh Bhavan, Lad Society Rd, Ahmedabad 380 054; tel. (79) 26765480; fax (79) 26753587; e-mail stree@sandesh.com; internet www.sandesh.com; f. 1962; weekly; Gujarati; Editor Ritaben Patel; circ. 41,500.

Zagmag: Gujarat Samachar Bhavan, Khanpur, Ahmedabad 380 001; tel. (79) 5508001; f. 1952; weekly; Gujarati; for children; Editor Bahubali S. Shah; circ. 38,000.

Rajkot

Amruta: Jai Hind Publications, Jai Hind Press Bldg, Babubhai Shah Marg, Rajkot 360 001; tel. (281) 2440513; fax (281) 2448677; e-mail info@jaihinddaily.com; f. 1967; weekly; Gujarati; films; Editor Y. N. Shah; circ. 12,500.

Niranjan: Jai Hind Publications, Jai Hind Press Bldg, Babubhai Shah Marg, Rajkot 360 001; tel. (281) 2440517; fax (281) 2448677; e-mail info@jaihinddaily.com; f. 1972; fortnightly; Gujarati; children's; Editor N. R. Shah; circ. 10,500.

Parmarth: Jai Hind Publications, Jai Hind Press Bldg, Babubhai Shah Marg, Rajkot 360 001; tel. (281) 2440511; fax (281) 2448677; e-mail info@jaihinddaily.com; monthly; Gujarati; philosophy and religion; Editor Y. N. Shah; circ. 8,000.

Phulwadi: Jai Hind Publications, Jai Hind Press Bldg, Babubhai Shah Marg, Rajkot 360 001; tel. (281) 2440513; fax (281) 2448677; e-mail info@jaihinddaily.com; f. 1967; weekly; Gujarati; for children; Editor Y. N. Shah; circ. 10,000.

Karnataka

Bangalore

Mayura: 75 Mahatma Gandhi Rd, Bangalore 560 001; tel. (80) 25588999; fax (80) 25587179; e-mail ads@deccanherald.co.in; f. 1968; monthly; Kannada; Editor-in-Chief K. N. Shanth Kumar; circ. 28,600.

Sudha: 75 Mahatma Gandhi Rd, Bangalore 560 001; tel. (80) 25588999; fax (80) 25587179; e-mail ads@deccanherald.co.in; f. 1965; weekly; Kannada; Editor-in-Chief K. N. Hari Kumar; circ. 67,400.

Manipal

Taranga: Udayavani Bldg, Press Corner, Manipal 576 104; tel. (820) 2570845; fax (820) 2570563; e-mail taranga@manipalpress

.com; internet www.udayavani.com; f. 1983; weekly; Kannada; Editor-in-Chief SANDHYA S. PAI; circ. 85,400.

Kerala

Kochi

The Week: Malayala Manorama Buildings, POB 4278, Kochi 682 036; tel. (484) 2316285; fax (484) 2315745; e-mail editor@theweek .com; internet www.the_week.com; f. 1982; weekly; English; current affairs; Chief Editor MAMMEN MATHEW; Editor PHILIP MATHEW; circ. 202,000.

Kottayam

Balarama: MM Publications Ltd, POB 226, Kottayam 686 001; tel. (481) 2563721; fax (481) 2564393; e-mail subscription@ mmpublications.com; f. 1972; children's weekly; Malayalam; Chief Editor BINA MATHEW; Senior Man. V. SAJEEV GEORGE; circ. 276,728.

Malayala Manorama: K. K. Rd, POB 26, Kottayam 686 001; tel. (481) 2563646; fax (481) 2562479; e-mail editor@ malayalamanorama.com; internet www.malayalamanorama.com; f. 1937; weekly; Malayalam; also publ. from Kozhikode; Man. Dir and Editor MAMMEN MATHEW; Chief Editor MAMMEN VARGHESE; combined circ. 1,001,800.

Vanitha: MM Publications Ltd, POB 226, Kottayam 686 001; tel. (481) 2563721; fax (481) 2564393; e-mail vanitha@mmpublications .com; f. 1975; women's fortnightly; Malayalam and Hindi editions; Chief Editor PREMA MAMMEN MATHEW; Gen. Man. V. SAJEEV GEORGE; circ. 543,233 (Malayalam), 134,348 (Hindi).

Kozhikode

Arogya Masika: Mathrubhumi Bldgs, K. P. Kesava Menon Rd, Kozhikode 673 001; tel. (495) 2765381; fax (495) 2760138; e-mail arogyamasika@mat1.mathrubhumi.co.in; monthly; Malayalam; health; Man. Editor P. V. CHANDRAN; circ. 152,702.

Balabhumi: Matrabhumi Bldgs, K. P. Kesava Menon Rd, Kozhikode 673 001; tel. (495) 2366655; fax (495) 2366656; e-mail balabhumi@mpp.co.in; internet www.mathrabhumi.com; f. 1996; weekly; Malayalam; children's; Editor K. K. SREEDHARAN NAIR; circ. 95,500.

Chitrabhumi: Mathrubhumi Bldgs, K. P. Kesava Menon Rd, Kozhikode 673 001; tel. (495) 2366655; fax (495) 2366656; e-mail cinema@mpp.co.in; internet www.mathrubhumi.com; weekly; Malayalam; films; Editor K. K. SREEDHARAN NAIR; circ. 29,589.

Grihalakshmi: Mathrubhumi Bldgs, K. P. Kesava Menon Rd, POB 46, Kozhikode 673 001; tel. (495) 2366655; fax (495) 2366656; e-mail mathrclt@md2.vsnl.net.in; internet www.mathrubhumi.com; f. 1979; monthly; Malayalam; women's; Editor K. K. SREEDHARAN NAIR; circ. 167,800.

Mathrubhumi Illustrated Weekly: Mathrubhumi Bldgs, K. P. Kesava Menon Rd, POB 46, Kozhikode 673 001; tel. (495) 2366655; fax (495) 2356656; f. 1923; weekly; Malayalam; Editor K. K. SREE-DHARAN NAIR; circ. 38,300.

Sports Masika: Mathrubhumi Bldgs, K. P. Kesava Menon Rd, Kozhikode 673 001; tel. (495) 366655; fax (495) 366656; monthly; Malayalam; sport; Editor K. K. SREEDHARAN NAIR; circ. 67,900.

Thozhilvartha: Mathrubhumi Bldgs, K. P. Kesava Menon Rd, Kozhikode 673 001; tel. (495) 2366655; fax (495) 2366656; e-mail mathrclt@md2.vsnl.net.in; internet www.mathrubhumi.com; f. 1992; weekly; Malayalam; employment; Editor K. K. SREEDHARAN NAIR; circ. 172,200.

Quilon

Karala Sabdam: Thevally, Quilon 691 009; tel. (474) 272403; fax (474) 2740710; f. 1962; weekly; Malayalam; Man. Editor B. A. RAJA-KRISHNAN; circ. 66,600.

Thiruvananthapuram

Kalakaumudi: Kaumudi Bldgs, Pettah, Thiruvananthapuram 695 024; tel. (471) 2443531; fax (471) 2442895; e-mail kalakaumudi@ vsnl.com; f. 1975; weekly; Malayalam; Chief Editor M. S. MANI; Editor N. R. S. BABU; circ. 73,000.

Vellinakshatram: Kaumudi Bldgs, Pettah, Thiruvananthapuram 695 024; tel. (471) 2443531; fax (471) 2442895; e-mail kalakaumudi@ vsnl.com; internet www.vellinakshatram.com; f. 1987; film weekly; Malayalam; Editor PRASAD LAKSHMANAN; Man. Editor SUKUMARAN MANI; circ. 55,000.

Madhya Pradesh

Bhopal

Krishak Jagat: 14 Indira Press Complex, M. P. Nagar, POB 37, Bhopal 462 011; tel. (755) 2768452; fax (755) 2760449; e-mail krishjag@sancharnet.in; internet www.krishakjagat.com; f. 1946; weekly; Hindi; agriculture; also published in Jaipur and Raipur; Chief Editor VIJAY KUMAR BONDRIYA; Editor SUNIL GANGRADE; combined circ. 150,000.

Maharashtra

Mumbai (Bombay)

Abhiyaan: Abhiyaan Press and Publications Ltd, 4A/B, Government Industrial Estate, Charkop, Kandivli (W), Mumbai 400 067; tel. (22) 28687515; fax (22) 28680991; f. 1986; weekly; Gujarati; Dir DILIP PATEL; Editor VINOD PANDYA; circ. 74,700.

Arogya Sanjeevani: C-14 Royal Industrial Estate, 5-B Naigaum Cross Rd, Wadala, Mumbai 400 031; tel. (22) 24138723; fax (22) 24133610; e-mail woman@bol.net.in; f. 1990; quarterly; Hindi; Editor RAM KRISHNA SHUKLA; circ. 49,081.

Auto India: Nirmal, Nariman Point, Mumbai 400 021; tel. (22) 22883946; fax (22) 22883940; e-mail editor@auto-india.com; f. 1994; monthly; Editor RAJ WARRIOR; circ. 44,500.

Bhavan's Journal: Bharatiya Vidya Bhavan, Mumbai 400 007; tel. (22) 23634462; fax (22) 23630058; f. 1954; fortnightly; English; literary; Man. Editor J. H. DAVE; Editor S. RAMAKRISHNAN; circ. 25,000.

Bombay Samachar: Red House, Sayed Abdulla Brelvi Rd, Mumbai 400 001; tel. (22) 22045531; fax (22) 22046642; e-mail samachar@ vsnl.com; f. 1822; weekly; Gujarati; Editor P. D. DALAL (acting); circ. 118,213.

Business India: Nirmal, 14th Floor, Nariman Point, Mumbai 400 021; tel. (22) 22883943; fax (22) 22883940; f. 1978; fortnightly; English; Publr ASHOK ADVANI; circ. 75,700.

Business World: 25–28 Atlanta, 2nd Floor, Nariman Point, Mumbai 400 021; tel. (22) 22851352; fax (22) 22870310; f. 1980; weekly; English; Editor TONY JOSEPH; circ. 146,500.

Chitralekha: 62 Vaju Kotak Marg, Fort, Mumbai 400 001; tel. (22) 22614730; fax (22) 22615895; e-mail advertise@chitralekha.com; internet www.chitralekha.com; f. 1950; (Gujarati), f. 1989 (Marathi); weekly; Gujarati and Marathi; Editors BHARAT GHELANI, GYANESH MAHARAO; circ. 240,300 (Gujarati), 95,300 (Marathi).

Cine Blitz Film Monthly: Rifa Publications Pvt Ltd, A/3, Sangam Bhavan, Ground Floor, Brahma Kumaris Rd, nr Strand Cinema, Colaba, Mumbai 400 005; tel. (22) 22830668; fax (22) 22830672; e-mail cbedit@sify.com; f. 1974; English; Editor NISHI PREM; circ. 184,100.

Debonair: Mumbai; e-mail maurya@debonairindia.com; f. 1972; monthly; English; Publr CHAITANYA PRABHU; CEO JOSEPH MASCARE-NHAS; circ. 110,000.

Economic and Political Weekly: Hitkari House, 284 Shahid Bhagatsingh Rd, Mumbai 400 001; tel. (22) 22696073; fax (22) 22696072; e-mail epw@vsnl.com; internet www.epw.org.in; f. 1966; English; Editor C. RAMMANOHAR REDDY; circ. 132,800.

Femina: Times of India Bldg, Dr Dadabhai Naoroji Rd, Mumbai 400 001; tel. and fax (22) 22731385; e-mail femina@timesgroup.com; internet www.feminaindia.com; f. 1959; fortnightly; English; Exec. Editor SHASHI BALIGA; circ. 122,200.

Filmfare: 4th Floor, Times of India Bldg, Dr Dadabhai Naoroji Rd, Mumbai 400 001; tel. (22) 22731187; fax (22) 22731585; e-mail shashi.baliga@wwm.co.in; internet www.filmfare.com; f. 1952; monthly; English; Exec. Editor SHASHI BALIGA; circ. 147,000.

G: 62 Vaju Kotak Marg, Fort, Mumbai 400 001; tel. (22) 22614730; fax (22) 22615895; e-mail advertise@chitralekha.com; internet www .gmagazine.com; f. 1989; monthly; English; Editor MAULIK KOTAK; circ. 65,000.

Gentleman: B-201, Teritex Business Service Centre, Saki Vihar, Mumbai 400 072; tel. (22) 28571490; fax (22) 28572447; e-mail gentleman@vsnl.com; f. 1980; monthly; English; Editor PREMNATH NAIR (acting).

Hi Blitz: Rifa Publications Pvt Ltd, A/3, Sangam Bhavan, Ground Floor, Brahma Kumaris Rd, nr Strand Cinema, Colaba, Mumbai 400 005; tel. (22) 22830668; fax (22) 22830672; e-mail cbedit@sify.com; f. 2002; English; lifestyle; Editor SHALINI SHARMA; 65,000.

Indian PEN: Theosophy Hall, 40 New Marine Lines, Mumbai 400 020; tel. (22) 22032175; e-mail ambika.sirkar@gems.vsnl.net.in; f. 1934; quarterly; organ of Indian Centre of the International PEN; Editor RANJIT HOSKOTE.

Janmabhoomi-Pravasi: Janmabhoomi Bhavan, Janmabhoomi Marg, Fort, POB 62, Mumbai 400 001; tel. (22) 22870831; fax (22) 22874097; e-mail bhoomi@bom3.vsnl.net.in; f. 1939; weekly; Gujarati; Propr Saurashtra Trust; Editor KUNDAN VYAS; circ. 94,100.

JEE: 62 Vaju Kotak Marg, Fort, Mumbai 400 001; tel. (22) 22614730; fax (22) 22615895; e-mail advertise@chitralekha.com;

fortnightly; Gujarati and Marathi; Editor Madhuri Kotak; circ. 92,160 (Gujarati), 30,150 (Marathi).

Meri Saheli: C-14 Royal Industrial Estate, 5-B Naigaum Cross Rd, Wadala, Mumbai 400 031; tel. (22) 24138723; fax (22) 24133610; e-mail woman@bol.net.in; f. 1987; monthly; Hindi; Editor Hema Malini; circ. 334,100.

Movie: Mahalaxmi Chambers, 5th Floor, 22 Bhulabhai Desai Rd, Mumbai 400 026; tel. (22) 24935636; fax (22) 24938406; f. 1981; monthly; English; Editor Dinesh Raheja; circ. 70,700.

New Woman: C-14 Royal Industrial Estate, 5-B Naigaum Cross Rd, Wadala, Mumbai 400 031; tel. (22) 24138723; fax (22) 24133610; e-mail newwoman@newwomanindia.com; f. 1996; monthly; English; Editor Hema Malini; circ. 68,182.

Onlooker: Free Press House, 215 Free Press Journal Marg, Nariman Point, Mumbai 400 021; tel. (22) 22874566; f. 1939; fortnightly; English; news magazine; Exec. Editor K. Srinivasan; circ. 61,000.

Reader's Digest: Orient House, Adi Marzban Path, Ballard Estate, Mumbai 400 001; tel. (22) 22617291; fax (22) 22613347; f. 1954; monthly; English; Publr and Editor Ashok Mahadevan; circ. 389,378.

Savvy: Magna Publishing Co Ltd, Magna House, 100/E Old Prabhadevi Rd, Prabhadevi, Mumbai 400 025; tel. (22) 24362270; fax (22) 24306523; e-mail savvy@magnamags.com; internet www.magnamags.com; f. 1984; monthly; English; Editor Saira Menezes; circ. 99,500.

Screen: Express Tower, Nariman Point, Mumbai 400 021; tel. (22) 22022627; fax (22) 22022139; e-mail iemumbai@expressindia.co.in; f. 1951; film weekly; English; Editor Bhavna Somaya; circ. 90,000.

Society: Magna Publishing Co Ltd, Magna House, 100/E Old Prabhadevi Rd, Prabhadevi, Mumbai 400 025; tel. (22) 24362270; fax (22) 24306523; e-mail magnapub@vsnl.com; internet www.magnamags.com; f. 1979; monthly; English; Editor Priyanka Sinha; circ. 67,200.

Stardust: Magna Publishing Co Ltd, Magna House, 100/E Old Prabhadevi Rd, Prabhadevi, Mumbai 400 025; tel. (22) 24362270; fax (22) 24306523; e-mail magnapub@vsnl.com; internet www.stardustindia.com; f. 1985; monthly; English; Editor Ashwin Varde; circ. 308,000.

Vyapar: Janmabhoomi Bhavan, Janmabhoomi Marg, POB 62, Fort, Mumbai 400 001; tel. (22) 22870831; fax (22) 22874097; e-mail rajeshbhayani@hotmail.com; f. 1949; (Gujarati), 1987 (Hindi); Gujarati (2 a week) and Hindi (weekly); commerce; Propr Saurashtra Trust; Editor Rajesh M. Bhayani; circ. 27,900 (Gujarati), 12,800 (Hindi).

Nagpur

All India Reporter: AIR Ltd, Congress Nagar, POB 209, Nagpur 440 012; tel. (712) 2534321; fax (712) 2526283; e-mail air@allindiareporter.com; internet www.allindiareporter.com; f. 1914; weekly and monthly; English; law journals; Chief Editor V. R. Manohar; circ. 55,500.

Rajasthan

Jaipur

Balhans: Kesargarh, Jawahar Lal Nehru Marg, Jaipur 302 004; tel. (141) 2561582; fax (141) 2566011; e-mail info@rajasthanpatrika.com; internet www.rajasthanpatrika.com; fortnightly; Hindi; circ. 26,700.

Itwari Patrika: Kesargarh, Jawahar Lal Nehru Marg, Jaipur 302 004; tel. (141) 2561582; fax (141) 2566011; weekly; Hindi; circ. 12,000.

Krishak Jagat: F-47, Ghiya Marg, Bani Park, Jaipur 302 016; tel. (141) 2207680; e-mail krishjag@sancharnet.in; internet www.krishakjagatindia.com; Hindi; weekly; Chief Editor Vijay Kumar Bondriya; circ. 32,000.

Rashtradoot Saptahik: HO, M.I. Rd, POB 30, Jaipur 302 001; tel. (141) 2372634; fax (141) 2373513; f. 1983; Hindi; also publ. from Kota and Bikaner; Chief Editor and Man. Editor Rajesh Sharma; CEO Somesh Sharma; combined circ. 167,500.

Tamil Nadu

Chennai (Madras)

Ambulimama: 82 Defence Officers Colony, Ekkatuthangal, Chennai 600 097; tel. (44) 22313637; e-mail chandamama@vsnl.com; f. 1947; children's monthly; Tamil; Editor B. Viswanatha Reddi; circ. 65,000.

Ambuli Ammavan: 82 Defence Officers Colony, Ekkatuthangal, Chennai 600 097; tel. (44) 22313637; e-mail chandamama@vsnl.com; f. 1970; children's monthly; Malayalam; Editor B. Viswanatha Reddi; circ. 12,000.

Ananda Vikatan: 757 Anna Salai, Chennai 600 002; tel. (44) 28524054; fax (44) 28523819; e-mail editor@vikatan.com; internet www.vikatan.com; f. 1924; weekly; Tamil; Editor and Man. Dir S. Balasubramanian; circ. 316,000.

Aval Vikatan: 757 Anna Salai, Chennai 600 002; tel. (44) 28524054; fax (44) 28523819; e-mail editor@vikatan.com; internet www.vikatan.com; f. 1998; fortnightly; Tamil; Editor B. Srinivasan; circ. 100,000.

Chandamama: 82 Defence Officers Colony, Ekkatuthangal, Chennai 600 097; tel. (44) 22313637; e-mail chandamama@vsnl.com; f. 1947; children's monthly; Hindi, Gujarati, Telugu, Kannada, English, Sanskrit, Bengali, Assamese; Editor B. Viswanatha Reddi; combined circ. 420,000.

Chandoba: 82 Defence Officers Colony, Ekkatuthangal, Chennai 600 097; tel. (44) 22313637; e-mail chandamama@vsnl.com; f. 1952; children's monthly; Marathi; Editor B. Viswanatha Reddi; circ. 93,000.

Chutti Vikatan: 757 Anna Salai, Chennai 600 002; tel. (44) 28524054; fax (44) 28523819; e-mail editor@vikatan.com; internet www.chuttivikatan.com; f. 1999; fortnightly; children's; Tamil; Editor B. Srinivasan; Man. Dir S. Balasubramanian; circ. 100,000.

Devi: 727 Anna Salai, Chennai 600 006; tel. (44) 28521428; f. 1979; weekly; Tamil; Editor B. Ramachandra Adityan; circ. 64,800.

Dinamani Kadir: Express Estate, Mount Rd, Chennai 600 002; tel. (44) 28520751; fax (44) 28524500; weekly; Editor G. Kasturi Rangan (acting); circ. 55,000.

Frontline: Kasturi Bldgs, 859/860 Anna Salai, Chennai 600 002; tel. (44) 28413344; fax (44) 28415325; e-mail subs@thehindu.co.in; internet www.flonnet.com; f. 1984; fortnightly; English; current affairs; independent; Publr S. Rangarajan; Editor N. Ram; circ. 62,700.

The Hindu International Edition: Kasturi Bldgs, 859/860 Anna Salai, Chennai 600 002; tel. (44) 28413344; fax (44) 28415325; e-mail subs@thehindu.co.in; f. 1975; weekly; English; independent; Publr S. Rangarajan; Editor N. Ravi; circ. 1,590.

Jahnamamu (Oriya): 82 Defence Officers Colony, Ekkatuthangal, Chennai 600 097; tel. (44) 22313637; e-mail chandamama@vsnl.com; f. 1972; children's monthly; Editor B. Viswanatha Reddi; circ. 111,000.

Junior Vikatan: 757 Anna Salai, Chennai 600 002; tel. (44) 28524054; fax (44) 28523819; e-mail editor@vikatan.com; internet www.vikatan.com; f. 1983; 2 times a week; Tamil; Editor and Man. Dir S. Balasubramanian; circ. 190,300.

Kalai Magal: POB 604, Chennai 600 004; tel. (44) 24983099; f. 1932; monthly; Tamil; literary and cultural; Editor R. Narayanaswamy; circ. 10,200.

Kalki: Kalki Bldgs, 47-NP Jawaharlal Nehru Rd, Ekkatuthangal, Chennai 600 097; tel. (44) 22345622; fax (44) 22345621; e-mail kalki@kalkiweekly.com; internet www.kalkionline.com; f. 1941; weekly; Tamil; literary and cultural; Editor Seetha Ravi; circ. 42,700.

Kumudam: 151 Purasawalkam High Rd, Chennai 600 010; tel. (44) 26422146; fax (44) 26425041; e-mail kumudam@giasmd01.vsnl.net.in; f. 1947; weekly; Tamil; Editor Dr S. A. P. Jawahar Palaniappan; circ. 385,900.

Kungumam: 93A Kodambakkam High Rd, Chennai 600 034; tel. (44) 28268177; f. 1978; weekly; Tamil; Editor Parasakthi; circ. 63,700.

Malaimathi: Chennai; f. 1958; weekly; Tamil; Editor P. S. Elango; circ. 48,100.

Muththaram: 93A Kogambakkam High Rd, Chennai 600 034; tel. (44) 2476306; f. 1980; weekly; Tamil; Editor Parasakthi; circ. 11,800.

Rani Muthu: 86 Periyar E.V.R. High Rd, Chennai 600 007; tel. (44) 25324771; e-mail raniweekly@vsnl.net; f. 1969; fortnightly; Tamil; Editor A. M. Samy; circ. 55,505.

Rani Weekly: 86 Periyar E.V.R. High Rd, Chennai 600 007; tel. (44) 25324771; e-mail raniweekly@vsnl.net; f. 1962; Tamil; Editor A. M. Samy; circ. 201,432.

Sportstar: Kasturi Bldgs, 859/860 Anna Salai, Chennai 600 002; tel. (44) 28413344; fax (44) 28415325; e-mail wsvcs@thehindu.co.in; internet www.tssonnet.com; f. 1978; weekly; English; independent; Publr S. Rangarajan; Editor N. Ram; circ. 48,900.

Thuglak: 46 Greenways Rd, Chennai 600 028; tel. (44) 24936913; fax (44) 24936915; f. 1970; weekly; Tamil; Editor Cho S. Ramaswamy; circ. 78,130.

Uttar Pradesh

Allahabad

Manohar Kahaniyan: 1A, Tagore Town, Hashimpur Rd, Allahabad 211 002; tel. (532) 2415549; fax (532) 2415533; e-mail mayapressalld@rediffmail.com; f. 1940; monthly; Hindi; Editor ASHOK MITRA.

Nutan Kahaniyan: 15 Sheo Charan Lal Rd, Allahabad 211 003; tel. (532) 2400612; f. 1975; Hindi; monthly; Chief Editor K. K. BHARGAVA; circ. 167,500.

Satya Katha: 1A, Tagore Town, Hashimpur Rd, Allahabad 211 002; e-mail mayapressalld@rediffmail.com; f. 1974; monthly; Hindi; Editor ASHOK MITRA.

West Bengal

Kolkata (Calcutta)

All India Appointment Gazette: 7 Old Court House St, Kolkata 700 001; tel. (33) 22435663; fax (33) 22435618; e-mail sambadmail@sify.com; f. 1973; weekly; English; Editor S. C. TALUKDAR; circ. 37,469.

Anandalok: 6 Prafulla Sarkar St, Kolkata 700 001; tel. (33) 22374880; fax (33) 22253240; f. 1975; fortnightly; Bengali; film; Editor DULENDRA BHOWMIK; circ. 98,600.

Anandamela: 6 Prafulla Sarkar St, Kolkata 700 001; tel. (33) 22216600; fax (33) 22253240; f. 1975; weekly; Bengali; juvenile; Editor DEBASHIS BANDOPADHYAY; circ. 41,800.

Contemporary Tea Time: 1/2 Old Court House Corner, POB 14, Kolkata 700 001; tel. (33) 22200099; fax (33) 22435753; e-mail calcutta@ctl.co.in; internet www.ctl.co.in; f. 1988; quarterly; English; tea industry; Exec. Editor GITA NARAYANI; circ. 5,000.

Desh: 6 Prafulla Sarkar St, Kolkata 700 001; tel. (33) 22374880; fax (33) 22253240; f. 1933; fortnightly; Bengali; literary; Editor AVEEK SARKAR; circ. 82,200.

Khela: 96 Raja Rammohan Sarani, Kolkata 700 009; tel. (33) 23509803; f. 1981; weekly; Bengali; sports; Editor ASOKE DASGUPTA; circ. 7,800.

Naba Kallol: 11 Jhamapookur Lane, Kolkata 700 009; tel. (33) 23504294; e-mail devsahityer@caltiger.com; f. 1960; monthly; Bengali; Editor P. K. MAZUMDAR; circ. 37,000.

Prabuddha Bharata (Awakened India): 5 Dehi Entally Rd, Kolkata 700 014; tel. (33) 22440898; fax (33) 22450050; e-mail advaita@vsnl.com; internet www.advaitaonline.com; f. 1896; monthly; art, culture, religion and philosophy; Pubir Swami BODHASARANANDA; Editor Swami SATYASWARUPANANDA; circ. 7,500.

Sananda: 6 Prafulla Sarkar St, Kolkata 700 001; tel. (33) 22374880; fax (33) 22253241; f. 1986; monthly; Bengali; Editor APARNA SEN; circ. 172,500.

Saptahik Bartaman: 76A J. C. Bose Rd, Kolkata 700 014; tel. (33) 22448208; fax (33) 22441215; f. 1988; weekly; Bengali; Editor BARUN SENGUPTA; circ. 111,900.

The Statesman: Statesman House, 4 Chowringhee Sq., Kolkata 700 001; tel. (33) 22127070; fax (33) 22120054; e-mail thestatesman@vsnl.com; internet www.thestatesman.net; f. 1875; overseas weekly; English; Editor-in-Chief C. R. IRANI.

Suktara: 11 Jhamapooker Lane, Kolkata 700 009; tel. (33) 23504294; e-mail devsahityer@caltiger.com; f. 1948; monthly; Bengali; juvenile; Editor M. MAJUMDAR; circ. 44,300.

NEWS AGENCIES

Press Trust of India Ltd: 4 Parliament St, New Delhi 110 001; tel. (11) 23717642; fax (11) 23718714; f. 1947; re-established 1978; Chair. PHILIP MATHEW; Gen. Man. M. K. RAZDAN.

United News of India (UNI): 9 Rafi Marg, New Delhi 110 001; tel. (11) 23710522; fax (11) 23355841; e-mail uninet@uniindia.com; internet www.uniindia.com; f. 1961; Indian language news in Hindi (UNIVARTA) and Urdu; World TV News Service (UNISCAN); photograph service; graphics service; brs in 90 centres in India; Chair. MANOJ KUMAR SONTHALIA; Chief Man. M. K. LAUL.

Foreign Bureaux

Agence France-Presse (AFP): 56 Janpath, 3rd Floor, New Delhi 110 001; tel. (11) 23738700; fax (11) 23311105; e-mail afpdelhi@afp.com; Bureau Chief RENÉ SLAMA.

Agencia EFE (Spain): 94 Jor Bagh, New Delhi 110 003; tel. (11) 24618092; fax (11) 24649114; e-mail efe@nda.vsnl.net.in; internet www.efe.com; South Asia Bureau Chief JOSÉ MARIA ORTIZ REYZÁBAL.

Agenzia Nazionale Stampa Associata (ANSA) (Italy): S-336 Panchsheel Park, New Delhi 110 017; tel. (11) 26016755; fax (11) 26016744; e-mail natale@giasdl01.vsnl.net.in; Bureau Chief ROBERTO SCARIONE.

Associated Press (AP) (USA): 5 Sikandra Rd, New Delhi 110 001; tel. (11) 23074001; fax (11) 23074008; e-mail bbrown@ap.org; Bureau Chief ELIZABETH ANN DUFF BROWN.

Deutsche Presse-Agentur (dpa) (Germany): 114 Jor Bagh, New Delhi 110 003; tel. (11) 24617792; fax (11) 24635772; e-mail dpadelhi@vsnl.com; Chief Rep. CAN MEREY.

Informatsionnoye Telegrafnoye Agentstvo Rossii—Telegrafnoye Agentstvo Suverennykh Stran (ITAR—TASS) (Russia): 3A Vasant Marg, New Delhi 110 057; tel. (11) 26142351; fax (11) 26146292; e-mail tasshind@ndf.vsnl.net.in; Bureau Chief YURI SIDOROV.

Inter Press Service (IPS) (Italy): 49 (F.F.) Defence Colony Market, New Delhi 110 024; tel. (11) 24333489; fax (11) 24333133; e-mail ranjit@ips.org; internet www.ips.org; Correspondent RANJIT DEVRAJ.

Islamic Republic News Agency (IRNA) (Iran): SF-204, Jor Bagh, New Delhi 110 003; tel. (11) 24654911; fax (11) 24643369; e-mail irna@del2.vsnl.net.in; Bureau Chief RAMEZANALI YOUSEFI.

Kyodo News Service (Japan): 308 World Trade Centre, Babar Rd, New Delhi 110 001; tel. (11) 23411954; fax (11) 23414756; e-mail koike.kazumasa@kyodonews.jp; Bureau Chief KAZUMASA KOIKE.

Reuters (United Kingdom): 1 Kautilya Marg, Chanakyapuri, New Delhi 110 021; tel. (11) 23012024; fax (11) 23014043; e-mail del.newsroom@reuters.com; Bureau Chief SIMON COLIN JAMES DENYER.

United Press International (UPI) (USA): 706, Sector 7B, Chandigarh 160 019; tel. (712) 2794017; fax (712) 2790591; e-mail hsnanda@glide.net.in; Bureau Chief HARBAKSH SINGH NANDA.

Xinhua (New China) News Agency (People's Republic of China): A-14/5, Vasant Vihar, New Delhi 110 057; tel. (11) 26142473; fax (11) 26142475; Chief JIANG YACING.

The following agencies are also represented: Associated Press of Pakistan, Bangladesh Sangbad Sangstha, Bloomberg Business News, Dow Jones NewsWires, Korean Central News Agency, Kuwait News Agency, Maghreb Arab Press, Middle East News Agency, Ria Novosti and Viet Nam News Agency.

CO-ORDINATING BODIES

Press Information Bureau: Shastri Bhavan, Dr Rajendra Prasad Rd, New Delhi 110 001; tel. (11) 23383643; fax (11) 23383203; e-mail pio@hub.nic.in; internet www.pib.nic.in; f. 1946 to co-ordinate press affairs for the govt; represents newspaper managements, journalists, news agencies, parliament; has power to examine journalists under oath and may censor objectionable material; Prin. Information Officer Dr SHAKUNTALA MAHAWAL.

Registrar of Newspapers for India: Ministry of Information and Broadcasting, West Block 8, Wing 2, Ramakrishna Puram, New Delhi 110 066; tel. (11) 26108788; fax (11) 26176553; f. 1956 as a statutory body to collect press statistics; maintains a register of all Indian newspapers; Registrar T. G. NALLAMUTHU.

PRESS ASSOCIATIONS

All-India Newspaper Editors' Conference: 36–37 Northend Complex, Rama Krishna Ashram Marg, New Delhi 110 001; tel. (11) 23364519; fax (11) 23317499; f. 1940; c. 370 mems; Pres. VISHWA BANDHU GUPTA; Sec.-Gen. RAMU PATEL.

All India Small and Medium Newspapers' Federation: 26-F Rajiv Gandhi Chowk (Connaught Place), New Delhi 110 001; tel. (11) 23326000; fax (11) 24621636; e-mail indian_observer@hotmail.com; c. 9,000 mems; Pres. HARBHAJAN SINGH; Gen. Secs B. C. GUPTA, B. M. SHARMA.

The Foreign Correspondents' Club of South Asia: AB-19 Mathura Rd, opp. Pragati Maidan Gate 3, New Delhi 110 001; tel. (11) 23385118; fax (11) 23385517; e-mail fcc@fccsouthasia.org; internet www.fccsouthasia.com; f. 1992; 450 mems; Pres. Dr WAIEL S. H. AWWAD; Man. KIRAN KAPUR.

Indian Federation of Working Journalists: A-4/199 Basant Lane, nr Railway Central Hospital, New Delhi 110 001; tel. (11) 23348894; fax (11) 23348871; f. 1950; 27,000 mems; Pres. K. VIKRAM RAO; Sec.-Gen. PARMANAND PANDEY.

Indian Journalists' Association: New Delhi; Pres. VIJAY DUTT; Gen. Sec. A. K. DHAR.

Indian Languages Newspapers' Asscn: Janmabhoomi Bhavan, Janmabhoomi Marg, POB 10029, Fort, Mumbai 400 001; tel. (22) 22870537; f. 1941; 320 mems; Pres. VIJAY KUMAR BONDRIYA; Hon. Gen. Secs PRADEEP G. DESHPANDE, KRISHNA SHEWDKAR, LALIT SHRIMAL.

Indian Newspaper Society: INS Bldg, Rafi Marg, New Delhi 110 001; tel. (11) 23715401; fax (11) 23723800; e-mail indnews@nde.vsnl

.net.in; f. 1939; 685 mems; Pres. M. P. VEERENDRAKUMAR; Sec.-Gen. DEEPAK S. RAJA.

National Union of Journalists (India): 7 Jantar Mantar Rd, 2nd Floor, New Delhi 110 001; tel. (11) 23368610; e-mail nujindia@ndf .vsnl.in; internet www.education.vsnl.com/nujindia; f. 1972; 12,000 mems; Pres. A. N. MISHRA; Sec.-Gen. M. D. GANGWAR.

Press Club of India: 1 Raisina Rd, New Delhi 110 001; tel. (11) 23719844; fax (11) 23357048; f. 1948; 4,500 mems; Pres. (vacant); Sec.-Gen. (vacant).

Press Council of India: Soochna Bhavan, 8 C. G. O Complex, Ground Floor, Lodhi Rd, New Delhi 110 003; tel. (11) 24368723; e-mail pcids@vsnl.net; internet presscouncil.nic.in; established under an Act of Parliament to preserve the freedom of the press and maintain and improve the standards of newspapers and news agencies in India; 28 mems; Chair. Justice K. JAICHANDRA REDDY; Sec. SANGITA DHINGRA SEHGAL.

Press Institute of India: Sapru House Annexe, Barakhamba Rd, New Delhi 110 001; tel. (11) 23318066; fax (11) 23311975; e-mail pii@ndf.vsnl.net.in; internet www.pressinstitute.org; f. 1963; 32 mem. newspapers and other orgs; Chair. N. MURALI; Dir AJIT BHAT-TACHARJEA.

Publishers

DELHI AND NEW DELHI

Affiliated East-West Press (Pvt) Ltd: G-1/16 Ansari Rd, Daryaganj, New Delhi 110 002; tel. (11) 23264180; fax (11) 23260538; e-mail affiliat@vsnl.com; internet www.aewpress.com; textbooks and reference books; also represents scientific societies; Dirs SUNNY MALIK, KAMAL MALIK.

Allied Publishers (Pvt) Ltd: 13/14 Asaf Ali Rd, New Delhi 110 002; tel. (11) 23233002; fax (11) 23235967; e-mail aplnd@del2.vsnl .net.in; academic and general; Man. Dir S. M. SACHDEV.

Amerind Publishing Co (Pvt) Ltd: 66 Janpath, 2nd Floor, New Delhi 110 001; tel. (11) 23324578; fax (11) 23710090; e-mail mohanprimlani@hotmail.com; f. 1970; offices at Kolkata, Mumbai and New York; scientific and technical; Dirs MOHAN PRIMLANI, GULAB PRIMLANI.

Arnold Heinman Publishers (India) Pvt Ltd: New Delhi; f. 1969 as Arnold Publishers (India) Pvt Ltd; literature and general; Man. Dir G. A. VAZIRANI.

Atma Ram and Sons: 1376 Kashmere Gate, POB 1429, Delhi 110 006; tel. (11) 23946466; fax (11) 23973082; e-mail atmaram_books@ hotmail.com; f. 1909; scientific, technical, humanities, medical; Man. Dir S. PURI; Dir Y. PURI.

B.I. Publications Pvt Ltd: 13 Daryaganj, New Delhi 110 002; tel. (11) 23274443; fax (11) 23261290; e-mail bidel@ndb.vsnl.net.in; f. 1959; academic, general and professional; Man. Dir K. S. MANI.

Book Circle: 19A Ansari Rd, Daryaganj, New Delhi 110 002; tel. (11) 23264444; fax (11) 23263050; e-mail bookcircle@vsnl.net; f. 2001; social sciences, art and architecture, technical, medical, scientific; Propr and Dir HIMANSHU CHAWLA.

S. Chand and Co Ltd: 7361 Ram Nagar, Qutab Rd, near New Delhi Railway Station, New Delhi 110 055; tel. (11) 23672080; fax (11) 23677446; e-mail schand@vsnl.com; internet www.schandgroup .com; f. 1917; educational and general in English and Hindi; also book exports and imports; Man. Dir RAVINDRA KUMAR GUPTA.

Children's Book House: A-4 Ring Rd, South Extension Part I, POB 3854, New Delhi 110 049; tel. (11) 24636030; fax (11) 24636011; e-mail neeta@giasdl01.vsnl.net.in; internet www.neetaprakashan .com; f. 1952; educational and general; Dir R. S. GUPTA.

Children's Book Trust: Nehru House, 4 Bahadur Shah Zafar Marg, New Delhi 110 002; tel. (11) 23316970; fax (11) 23721090; e-mail cbtnd@vsnl.com; internet www.childrensbooktrust.com; f. 1957; children's books in English and other Indian languages; Editor C. G. R. KURUP; Gen. Man. RAVI SHANKAR.

Concept Publishing Co: A/15-16, Commercial Block, Mohan Garden, New Delhi 110 059; tel. (11) 25351460; fax (11) 25357103; e-mail publishing@conceptpub.com; f. 1975; Ayurveda, health sciences, communication, mass media, journalism, psychology, community development, management; Man. Editor NITIN MITTAL.

Frank Bros & Co (Publishers) Ltd: 4675A Ansari Rd, 21 Daryaganj, New Delhi 110 002; tel. (11) 23263393; fax (11) 23269032; e-mail connect@frankbros.com; f. 1930; children's, educational and management; Chair. and Man. Dir R. C. GOVIL.

Heritage Publishers: 32 Prakash Apartments, 5 Ansari Rd, Daryaganj, New Delhi 110 002; tel. (11) 23266258; fax (11) 23263050;

e-mail heritage@nda.vsnl.net.in; internet www.meditechbooks.com; f. 1973; social sciences, art and architecture, technical, medical, scientific; Propr and Dir B. R. CHAWLA.

Hindustan Publishing Corpn (India): 4805/24 Bharat Ram Rd, Daryaganj, New Delhi 110 002; tel. (11) 23254401; fax (11) 26193511; e-mail hpc@hpc.cc; internet www.hpc.cc; archaeology, pure and applied sciences, geology, sociology, anthropology, economics; Man. Partner P. C. KUMAR.

Kali for Women: K-36 Hauz Khas Enclave, New Delhi 110 016; tel. (11) 26964947; fax (11) 26496597; e-mail womenunltd@vsnl.net; women's studies, social sciences, humanities, general non-fiction, fiction, etc.; Heads of Organization URVASHI BUTALIA, RITU MENON.

Lalit Kala Akademi: Rabindra Bhavan, New Delhi 110 001; tel. (11) 23387241; fax (11) 23782485; e-mail lka@lalitkala.org.in; internet www.lalitkala.org.in; books on Indian art; CEO Dr SUD-HAKAR SHARMA.

Lancers Books: POB 4236, New Delhi 110 048; tel. (11) 26241617; fax (11) 26992063; e-mail lanbooks@aol.com; f. 1977; politics (with special emphasis on north-east India), defence; Propr S. KUMAR.

Madhuban Educational Books: 576 Masjid Rd, Jangpura, New Delhi 110 014; tel. (11) 24314605; fax (11) 24310879; e-mail info@ madhubunbooks.com; f. 1969; school books, children's books; Dir SAJILI SHIRODKAR.

Motilal Banarsidass Publishers (Pvt) Ltd: 41 U.A. Bungalow Rd, Jawahar Nagar, Delhi 110 007; tel. (11) 23851985; fax (11) 25797221; e-mail mlbd@vsnl.com; internet www.mlbd.com; f. 1903; religion, philosophy, astrology, yoga, linguistic, in English and Sanskrit; offices in Bangalore, Chennai, Kolkata, Mumbai, Patna, Pune and Varanasi; Man. Dir N. P. JAIN.

Munshiram Manoharlal Publishers Pvt Ltd: 54 Rani Jhansi Rd, POB 5715, New Delhi 110 055; tel. (11) 23673650; fax (11) 23612745; e-mail mrml@mantraonline.com; internet www.mrmlbooks.com; f. 1952; Indian art, architecture, archaeology, religion, music, law, medicine, dance, dictionaries, travel, history, politics, numismatics, Buddhism, philosophy, sociology, etc.; Editorial Dir DEVENDRA JAIN; Publishing Dir PANKAJ JAIN.

National Book Trust: A-5 Green Park, New Delhi 110 016; tel. (11) 26564020; fax (11) 26851795; e-mail nbtindia@ndb.vsnl.net.in; internet www.nbtindia.org.in; f. 1957; autonomous organization established by the Ministry of Human Resources Development to produce and encourage the production of good literary works; Chair. BRIJ KISHORE SHARMA; Dir NIRMAL KANTHI BHATACHARJEE.

National Council of Educational Research and Training (NCERT): Sri Aurobindo Marg, New Delhi 110 016; tel. (11) 26562708; fax (11) 26851070; e-mail publica@nda.vsnl.net.in; f. 1961; school textbooks, teachers' guides, research monographs, journals, etc.; CEO PURAN DHAND.

Neeta Prakashan: A-4 Ring Rd, South Extension Part I, POB 3853, New Delhi 110 049; tel. (11) 24636010; fax (11) 24636011; e-mail neetabooks@vsnl.com; internet www.neetaprakashan.com; f. 1960; educational, children's, general; Dir RAJESH GUPTA.

New Age International Pvt Ltd: 4835/24 Ansari Rd, Daryaganj, New Delhi 110 002; tel. (11) 23276802; fax (11) 23267437; e-mail saumya.gupta@newagepublishers.com; internet www .newagepublishers.com; f. 1966; science, engineering, technology, management, humanities, social science; Man. Dir SAUMYA GUPTA.

Oxford and IBH Publishing Co (Pvt) Ltd: 66 Janpath, New Delhi 110 001; tel. (11) 23415896; fax (11) 51517599; e-mail oxford@ vsnl.com; f. 1964; science, technology and reference in English; Man. Dir MOHAN PRIMLANI.

Oxford University Press: YMCA Library Bldg, 1st Floor, 1 Jai Singh Rd, POB 43, New Delhi 110 001; tel. (11) 23747124; fax (11) 23360897; e-mail manzar.khan@oup.com; internet www.oup.com/in; f. 1912; educational, scientific, medical, general, humanities and social science, dictionaries and reference; Man. Dir MANZAR KHAN.

Penguin Books India (Pvt) Ltd: 11 Community Centre, Panchsheel Park, New Delhi 110 017; tel. (11) 26494401; fax (11) 26494403; e-mail penguin@del2.vsnl.net.in; internet www .penguinbooksindia.com; f. 1987; Indian literature and general non-fiction in English; Chair. PETER FIELD; Pres. THOMAS ABRAHAM.

People's Publishing House (Pvt) Ltd: 5E Rani Jhansi Rd, New Delhi 110 055; tel. (11) 27524701; f. 1947; Marxism, Leninism, peasant movt; Dir SHAMEEM FAIZEE.

Pitambar Publishing Co Pvt Ltd: 888 East Park Rd, Karol Bagh, New Delhi 110 005; tel. (11) 23676058; fax (11) 23676058; e-mail pitambar@bol.net.in; academic, children's books, textbooks and general; Man. Dir ANAND BHUSHAN; 5 brs.

Prentice-Hall of India (Pvt) Ltd: M-97 Connaught Circus, New Delhi 110 001; tel. (11) 22143344; fax (11) 23417179; e-mail phi@

phindia.com; internet www.phindia.com; f. 1963; university-level text and reference books; Man. Dir A. K. GHOSH.

Pustak Mahal: J-3/16 Daryaganj, New Delhi 110 002; tel. (11) 23272783; fax (11) 23260518; e-mail info@pustakmahal.com; internet www.pustakmahal.com; children's, general, computers, religious, encyclopaedia; Man. Dir RAM AVTAR GUPTA.

Rajkamal Prakashan (Pvt) Ltd: 1B Netaji Subhas Marg, Daryaganj, New Delhi 110 002; tel. (11) 23274463; fax (11) 23278144; e-mail info@rajkamalprakashan.com; internet www .rajkamalprakashan.com; f. 1947; Hindi; literary; also literary journal and monthly trade journal; Man. Dir ASHOK KUMAR MAHESH-WARI.

Rajpal and Sons: 1590 Madrasa Rd, Kashmere Gate, Delhi 110 006; tel. (11) 23865483; fax (11) 23867791; e-mail orienpbk@ndb.vsnl .net.in; f. 1891; humanities, social sciences, art, juvenile; Hindi; Chair VISHWANATH MALHOTRA.

RIS (Research and Information System) for the Non-Aligned and Other Developing Countries: Zone IV-B, 4th Floor, India Habitat Centre, Lodhi Rd, New Delhi 100 003; tel. (11) 24682177; fax (11) 24682173; e-mail dgoffice@ris.org.in; internet www.ris.org.in; f. 1983; trade and development issues; Dir-Gen. Dr NAGESH KUMAR.

Rupa & Co: 7/16 Ansari Rd, Daryaganj, POB 7017, New Delhi 110 002; tel. (11) 23278586; fax (11) 23277294; e-mail rupa@ndb.vsnl.net .in; internet www.rupaandco.com; f. 1936; Chief Exec. R. K. MEHRA.

Sage Publications India Pvt Ltd: B-42, Panchsheel Enclave, POB 4109, New Delhi 110 017; tel. and fax (11) 26491290; e-mail journalsubs@indiasage.com; internet www.indiasage.com; f. 1981; social science, development studies, business and management studies; Man. Dir TEJESHWAR SINGH.

Sahitya Akademi: Rabindra Bhavan, 35 Ferozeshah Rd, New Delhi 110 001; tel. (11) 23386626; fax (11) 23364207; e-mail secy@ ndb.vsnl.net.in; internet www.sahitya-akademi.org; f. 1956; bibliographies, translations, monographs, encyclopaedias, literary classics, etc.; Pres. Prof. GOPICHAND NARANG; Sec. Dr K. SATCHIDANANDAN.

Scholar Publishing House (P) Ltd: 85 Model Basti, New Delhi 110 005; tel. (11) 23541299; fax (11) 23676565; e-mail scholar@vsnl .com; internet www.scholargroup.com; f. 1968; educational; Man. Dir RAMESH RANADE.

Shiksha Bharati: 1590 Madrasa Rd, Kashmere Gate, Delhi 110 006; tel. (11) 23869812; fax (11) 23867791; e-mail orientpbk@vsnl .com; f. 1955; textbooks, creative literature, popular science and juvenile in Hindi and English; Editor MEERA JOHRI.

Sterling Publishers (Pvt) Ltd: A-59 Okhla Industrial Area, Phase II, New Delhi 110 020; tel. (11) 26387070; fax (11) 26383788; e-mail ghai@nde.vsnl.net.in; internet www.sterlingpublishers.com; f. 1965; academic books on the humanities and social sciences, children's books, computer books, management books, paperbacks; Chair. and Man. Dir S. K. GHAI; Dirs VIKAS GHAI, GAURAV GHAI.

Tata McGraw-Hill Publishing Co Ltd: 7 West Patel Nagar, New Delhi 110 008; tel. (11) 25882743; fax (11) 25885154; e-mail info_india@mcgraw-hill.com; internet www.tatamcgrawhill.com; f. 1970; engineering, computers, sciences, medicine, management, humanities, social sciences; Chair. Dr F. A. MEHTA; Man. Dir Dr N. SUBRAHMANYAM.

Vikas Publishing House (Pvt) Ltd: 576 Masjid Rd, Jangpura, New Delhi 110 014; tel. (11) 24314605; fax (11) 24310879; e-mail helpline@vikaspublishing.com; f. 1969; computers, management, commerce, sciences, engineering textbooks; Dir PIYUSH CHAWLA.

A. H. Wheeler & Co Ltd: 411 Surya Kiran Bldg, 19 K. G. Marg, New Delhi 110 001; tel. (11) 23312629; fax (11) 23357798; e-mail wheelerpub@mantraonline.com; f. 1958; textbooks, reference books, computer science and information technology, electronics, management, telecommunications, social sciences, etc.; Exec. Pres. ALOK BANERJEE.

CHENNAI (MADRAS)

All India Publishers & Distributors: 113 Poonmallee High Rd, Chennai 600 084; tel. (44) 28233004; fax (44) 28204911; e-mail aipdraj@vsnl.com; CEO ARYA RAJENDER.

Emerald Publishers: 15A Casa Major Rd, 1st Floor, Egmore, Chennai 600 008; tel. (44) 28192380; fax (44) 28192380; e-mail olivannan@yahoo.co.in; internet www.emeraldpublishers.com; college and university textbooks in English; CEO G. OLIVANNAN.

Eswar Press: Archana Arcade, 27 Natesan St, T. Nagar, Chennai 600 017; tel. (44) 52030431; fax (44) 24339590; e-mail gempeyes@ md3.vsnl.net.in; science and technology; CEO M. PERIYASAMY.

Higginbothams Ltd: 814 Anna Salai, POB 311, Chennai 600 002; tel. (44) 28520640; fax (44) 28528101; e-mail higginbothams@vsnl .com; f. 1844; general; Dir S. CHANDRASEKHAR.

Minerva Publications: 6 Pycrofts Rd, 1st Floor, Triplicane, Chennai 600 005; tel. (44) 28445674; fax (44) 28445674; e-mail minerva@hathway.com; internet www.minervaa.com; children's books and dictionaries; CEO T. NAZIBUDEEN.

Premier Publishing (Pvt) Ltd: 47 Noor Veerasamy St, Nungambakkam, Chennai 600 034; tel. (44) 28222566; e-mail manahabi2002@hotmail.com; internet www.sambooks.com; business and management, health, religion, culture, etc.; Man. Dir S. HABIBULLAH.

Scitech Publications (India) (Pvt) Ltd: 7/3-C Madley Rd, T. Nagar, Chennai 600 017; tel. (44) 24328737; e-mail scitech@md5 .vsnl.net.in; internet www.scitechpublications.com; science, technology, management, reference, etc.; Man. Dir M. R. PURUSHO-THAMAN.

Sura Books (Pvt) Ltd: 1620 J Block, 16th Main Rd, Anna Nagar, Chennai 600 040; tel. (44) 26161099; fax (44) 26162173; e-mail surabooks@eth.net; children's books, dictionaries, examinations guides, tourist guides, Indology, etc.; Man. Dir V. K. SUBBURAJ.

T. R. Publications Pvt Ltd: PMG Complex, 2nd Floor, 57 South Usman Rd, T. Nagar, Chennai 600 017; tel. (44) 24340765; fax (44) 24348837; e-mail trgeetha@giasmd01.vsnl.net.in; internet www .trpubs.com; Chief Exec. S. GEETHA.

JAIPUR

Aavishkar Publishers and Distributors/Pointer: 807 Vyas Bldg, Chaura Rasta, Jaipur 302 003; tel. (141) 2708286; fax (141) 2568159; e-mail aavishkarbooks@hotmail.com; internet www .pointerpublishers.com; f. 1986; general and reference books on arts, science, agriculture, environmental science, commerce; CEO PREM C. BAKLIWAL.

Mangal Deep Publications: Duggar Bldg, M. I. Rd, Jaipur 302 001; tel. (141) 2365086; fax (141) 5102022; e-mail mdpbk@ sancharnet.net; humanities, social sciences, science, technology; Propr B. K. MANGAL.

Publication Scheme: C 12/13, 1st Floor, Ganga Mandir, Sansar Chandra Rd, Jaipur 302 001; tel. (141) 5104038; fax (141) 2376922; e-mail parampsj@datainfosys.net; internet www.pubscheme.com; social sciences, humanities, Ayurveda, Indology; Propr S. S. NATANI.

Rajasthan Hindi Granth Akademi: Plot No. 1, Jhalana Sansthani Shetra, Jaipur 302 004; tel. (141) 2711129; fax (141) 2710341; e-mail hindigranth@vsnl.net; internet www.rajhga.org; engineering, agriculture, science, social sciences, law, journalism; Dir SHAILENDRA JOSHI.

Shyam Prakashan: Film Colony, Chaura Rasta, Jaipur 302 003; tel. (141) 2317659; fax (141) 2326554; Propr OM PRAKASH AGARWAL.

University Book House (Pvt) Ltd: 79 Chaura Rasta, Jaipur 302 003; tel. (141) 2311466; fax (141) 2313382; e-mail uni_bookhouse@ yahoo.com; commerce, management, home science, history, political science, public administration; Man. Dir CHETAN K. JAIN.

KOLKATA (CALCUTTA)

Academic Publishers: 12/1A Bankim Chatterjee St, POB 12341, Kolkata 700 073; tel. (33) 22414857; fax (33) 22413702; e-mail acabooks@cal.vsnl.net.in; f. 1958; textbooks, management, medical, technical; Man. Partner B. K. DHUR.

Advaita Ashrama: 5 Dehi Entally Rd, Kolkata 700 014; tel. (33) 22164000; fax (33) 22450050; e-mail advaita@vsnl.com; internet www.advaitaonline.com; f. 1899; religion, philosophy, spiritualism, Vedanta; publication centre of Ramakrishna Math and Ramakrishna Mission; Publication Man. Swami MUMUKSHANANDA.

Allied Book Agency: 18A Shyama Charan De St, Kolkata 700 073; general and academic; Dir B. SARKAR.

Ananda Publishers (Pvt) Ltd: 45 Beniatola Lane, Kolkata 700 009; tel. (33) 22414352; fax (33) 22193856; e-mail ananda@cal3.vsnl .net.in; internet www.anandapub.com; literature, general; Dir A. SARKAR; Man. Dir S. MITRA.

Assam Review Publishing Co: 27A Waterloo St, 1st Floor, Kolkata 700 069; tel. (33) 22482251; fax (33) 22482251; f. 1926; publrs of *The Assam Review and Tea News* (monthly) and *The Assam Directory and Tea Areas Handbook* (annually); Chief Exec. GOBIN-DALAL BANERJEE.

Dev Sahitya Kutir: 21 Jhamapukur Lane, Kolkata 700 009; tel. (33) 22417406; children's, general; Dir PRABIR KUMAR MAJUMDAR.

Dey's Publishing: 13 Bankim Chatterjee St, Kolkata 700 073; tel. (33) 22412330; fax (33) 22192041; e-mail deyspublishing@hotmail .com; academic books, religion, philosophy, general; Dir SUDHANGSHU KUMAR DEY.

Eastern Law House (Pvt) Ltd: 54 Ganesh Chunder Ave, Kolkata 700 013; tel. (33) 22374989; fax (33) 22150491; e-mail elh@cal.vsnl

.net.in; internet www.easternlawhouse.com; f. 1918; legal, commercial and accountancy; Dir Asok De; br. in New Delhi.

Firma KLM Private Ltd: 257B B. B. Ganguly St, Kolkata 700 012; tel. (33) 22374391; fax (33) 22217294; e-mail fklm@satyam.net.in; internet www.firmaklm.com; f. 1950; Indology, scholarly in English, Bengali, Sanskrit and Hindi, alternative medicine; Man. Dir S. Mukherji.

Indian Museum: 27 Jawaharlal Nehru Rd, Kolkata 700 016; tel. (33) 22499902; fax (33) 22495696; e-mail imbot@cal12.vsnl.net.in; internet www.indianmuseum-calcutta; social sciences and humanities; Dir S. K. Chakravarti.

Intertrade Publications (India) (Pvt) Ltd: 55 Gariahat Rd, POB 10210, Kolkata 700 019; f. 1954; economics, medicine, law, history and trade directories; Man. Dir Dr K. K. Roy.

A. Mukherjee and Co (Pvt) Ltd: 2 Bankim Chatterjee St, Kolkata 700 073; tel. (33) 22417406; fax (33) 27448172; f. 1940; educational and general in Bengali and English; Man. Dir Rajeev Neogi.

Naya Udyog: 206 Bidhan Sarani, Kolkata 700 006; tel. (33) 22413540; e-mail navudyog@vsnl.net; f. 1992; agriculture, horticulture; Man. Dir Chandan Dutta.

New Age Publishers (Pvt) Ltd: 12B Bankim Chatterjee St, Kolkata 700 073; tel. (33) 22418509; e-mail newagepub@vsnl.net; literature, art, philosophy, history, social and cultural studies; Propr Shiladitya.

Patra's Publication: 2 Shyamacharan Dey St, Kolkata 700 073; tel. (33) 22197297; e-mail manaspatra@vsnl.net; f. 1975; fiction, general; Propr Prafulla Kumar Patra.

Punthi Pustak: 136/4B Bidhan Sarani, Kolkata 700 004; tel. and fax (33) 25555573; e-mail info@punthipustak.com; internet www.punthipustak.com; f. 1956; religion, history, philosophy; Propr P. K. Bhattacharya.

Renaissance Publishers (Pvt) Ltd: 15 Bankim Chatterjee St, Kolkata 700 012; f. 1949; politics, philosophy, history; Man. Dir J. C. Goswami.

Sahitya Sansad: 33 Acharya Prafulla Chandra Rd, Kolkata 700 009; tel. (33) 23507669; fax (33) 23603508; e-mail samsad@cal3.vsnl .net.in; children's, reference, science, literature, philosophy; Man. Dir Debajyoti Dutta.

Saraswati Library: 206 Bidhan Sarani, Kolkata 700 006; f. 1914; history, philosophy, religion, literature; Man. Partner B. Bhattacharjee.

M. C. Sarkar and Sons (Pvt) Ltd: 14 Bankim Chatterjee St, Kolkata 700 073; f. 1910; reference; Dir Samit Sarkar.

Seagull Books (Pvt) Ltd: 26 Circus Ave, Kolkata 700 017; tel. (33) 22403636; fax (33) 22805143; e-mail seagullfoundation@vsnl.com; internet www.seagullindia.com; academic, literary, general; CEO Navin Kishore.

Stree: 16 Southern Ave, Kolkata 700 026; tel. (33) 24660812; fax (33) 24644614; e-mail stree@cal2.vsnl.net.in; internet www .streebooks.com; women's issues and writings in English and Bengali; Propr Mandira Sen.

Visva-Bharati: 6 Acharya Jagadish Bose Rd, Kolkata 700 017; tel. (33) 22479868; f. 1923; literature; Dir Ashoke Mukhopadhyay.

MUMBAI (BOMBAY)

Bharatiya Vidya Bhavan: Munshi Sadan, Kulapati K. M. Munshi Marg, Mumbai 400 007; tel. (22) 24950916; fax (22) 23630058; e-mail brbhavan@bom7.vsnl.net.in; internet www.bhavans.info; f. 1938; art, literature, culture, education, philosophy, religion, history of India; various periodicals in English, Hindi, Sanskrit and other Indian languages; Pres. Pravinchandra V. Gandhi; Dir-Gen. Dhiru Mehta.

Himalaya Publishing House: Dr Bhalerao Marg (Kelewadi), Girgaon, Mumbai 400 004; tel. (22) 23860170; fax (22) 23877178; e-mail himpub@vsnl.com; internet www.himpub.com; f. 1976; textbooks and research work; Publr Meena Pandey; Man. Dir D. P. Pandey.

India Book House (Pvt) Ltd: 412 Tulsiani Chambers, Nariman Point, Mumbai 400 021; tel. (22) 22840165; fax (22) 22835099; e-mail info@ibhworld.com; Man. Dir Deepak Mirchandani.

International Book House (Pvt) Ltd: Indian Mercantile Mansions (Extension), Madame Cama Rd, Mumbai 400 039; tel. (22) 22021634; fax (22) 22851109; e-mail ibh@vsnl.com; internet www .intbh.com; f. 1941; children's, general, educational, scientific, technical, engineering, social sciences, humanities and law; Man. Dir S. K. Gupta; Exec. Dir Sanjeev Gupta.

Jaico Publishing House: 127 Mahatma Gandhi Rd, opp. Mumbai University, Mumbai 400 023; tel. (22) 22676702; fax (22) 22656412; e-mail jaicopub@vsnl.com; f. 1947; general paperbacks, manage-

ment, computer and engineering books, etc.; imports scientific, medical, technical and educational books; Man. Dir Ashwin J. Shah.

Popular Prakashan (Pvt) Ltd: 35C Pandit Madan Mohan Malaviya Marg, Tardeo, opp. Crossroads, Mumbai 400 034; tel. (22) 23265245; fax (22) 24945294; e-mail infor@popularprakashan.com; internet www.popularprakashan.com; f. 1968; sociology, biographies, religion, philosophy, fiction, arts, music, current affairs, medicine, history, politics and administration in English and Marathi; CEO Harsha Bhatkal.

Sheth Publishing House: G-12 Suyog Industrial Estate, nr LBS Marg, Vikhroli (W), Mumbai 400 083; tel. (22) 25773707; fax (22) 25774200; e-mail no.sph@bom5.vsnl.net.in; educational, children's; Propr Nilesh M. Sheth.

Somaiya Publications (Pvt) Ltd: 172 Mumbai Marathi Granthasangrahalaya Marg, Dadar, Mumbai 400 014; tel. (22) 24130230; fax (22) 22047297; e-mail somaiyabooks@rediffmail.com; internet www .somaiya.com; f. 1967; economics, sociology, history, politics, mathematics, sciences, language, literature, education, psychology, religion, philosophy, logic; Chair. Dr S. K. Somaiya.

Taraporevala, Sons and Co (Pvt) Ltd D.B.: 210 Dr Dadabhai Naoroji Rd, Fort, Mumbai 400 001; tel. (22) 22071433; f. 1864; Indian art, culture, history, sociology, scientific, technical and general in English; Chief Exec. R. J. Taraporevala.

N. M. Tripathi (Pvt) Ltd: 164 Shamaldas Gandhi Marg, Mumbai 400 002; tel. (22) 22013651; e-mail mistertripathi@rediffmail.com; f. 1888; general in English and Gujarati; Chair. A. S. Pandya; Man. Dir Kartik R. Tripathi.

K. M. Varghese Co: Hind Rajasthan Bldg, Dada Saheb Phalke Rd, Dadar, Mumbai 400 014; tel. (22) 24149074; fax (22) 24146904; e-mail km@varghese.net; internet www.varghese.net; f. 1960; medicine, pharmacy, nursing, physiotherapy; Propr K. M. Varghese.

Vora Medical Publications: 6 Princess Bldg, E. R. Rd, Mumbai 400 003; tel. (22) 23754161; fax (22) 23704053; e-mail voramedpub@ yahoo.co.in; medicine, nursing, management, spiritualism, general knowledge; Propr R. K. Vora.

OTHER TOWNS

Anada Prakashan (Pvt) Ltd: 1756 Gandhi Rd, Ahmedabad 380 001; tel. (79) 2169956; fax (79) 2139900; e-mail anadaad1@ sancharnet.in; internet www.anada.com; children's, educational, dictionaries; Man. Dir B. R. Anada.

Bharati Bhawan: Thakurbari Rd, Kadamkuan, Patna 800 003; tel. (612) 2671356; fax (612) 2670010; e-mail bbpdpat@sancharnet.in; f. 1942; educational and juvenile; Man. Partner Tarit Kumar Bose.

Bishen Singh Mahendra Pal Singh: 23A New Connaught Place, POB 137, Dehradun 248 001; tel. (135) 2715748; fax (135) 2715107; e-mail bsmps@vsnl.com; internet www.bishensinghbooks.com; f. 1957; botany, forestry, agriculture; Dirs Gajendra Singh Gahlot, Abhimanyu Gahlot.

Books for Change: 139 Richmond Rd, Bangalore 560 025; tel. (80) 25321747; fax (80) 25586284; e-mail bfc@actionaidindia.org; internet www.booksforchange.net; f. 1997; development issues and social sciences; CEO Shoba Ramachandran; Man. Dir Ram Mohan.

Catholic Press: Ranchi 834 001; f. 1928; books and periodicals; Dir William Tigga.

DC Books: POB 214, DC Kizhakemuri Edam, Good Shepherd St, Kottayam 686 001; tel. (481) 2301614; fax (481) 2564758; e-mail ceo@dcbooks.com; internet www.dcbooks.com; f. 1974; fiction, general and reference books in Malayalam; CEO Ravi Deecee.

Hind Pocket Books (Pvt) Ltd: B-13, Sector 81, Phase II, Noida 201305; tel. (120) 3093992; fax (120) 2563983; e-mail gbp@del2.vsnl .net.in; f. 1958; fiction and non-fiction paperbacks in English, Hindi, Punjabi, Malayalam and Urdu; Chair Dina Nath Malhotra; Man. Dir Shekhar Malhotra.

Indica Books: D-40/18 Godowlia, Varanasi 221 001; tel. (542) 2357401; fax (542) 2452258; e-mail indicabooks@satyam.net.in; internet www.indicabooks.com; Indology, philosophy, religion, culture; Propr Dilip Kumar Jaiswal.

Jnan Bichitra: Jogendranagar, Vidyasagar Chowmuhani, Agartala, West Tripura 799 001; tel. (381) 2323781; e-mail jnanbichitra@ rediffmail.com; f. 1976; general, science; Propr Debananda Dam.

Kalyani Publishers: 1/1 Rajinder Nagar, Civil Lines, Ludhiana 141 008; tel. (161) 2745756; fax (161) 2745872; textbooks; Dir Raj Kumar.

Krishna Prakashan Media (P) Ltd: (Unit) Goel Publishing House, 11 Shivaji Rd, Meerut 250 001; tel. (121) 2644766; fax (121) 2645855; e-mail sk_kpm@yahoo.com; textbooks; Man. Dir Satyendra Kumar Rastogi; Dir Anita Rastogi.

Law Publishers: Sardar Patel Marg, Civil Lines, POB 1004, Allahabad 211 001; tel. (532) 2622758; fax (532) 2622781; e-mail lawpub@vsnl.com; internet www.law-publishers.com; f. 1929; legal texts in English; Dir NARESH SAGAR.

Macmillan India Ltd: 315/316 Raheja Chambers, 12 Museum Rd, Bangalore 560 001; tel. (80) 25594120; fax (80) 25588713; e-mail rberi@bgl.vsnl.net.in; internet www.macmillanindia.com; school and university books in English; general; Pres. and Man. Dir RAJIV BERI; Dir (Technical) DEBASHISH BANERJEE.

Mapin Publishing (Pvt) Ltd: 31 Somnath Rd, Usmanpura, Ahmedabad 380 013; tel. (79) 7551833; fax (79) 7550955; e-mail mapin@icenet.net; internet www.mapinpub.com; Indian art, architecture, archaeology, crafts and performing arts; Chair. MALLIKA SARABHAI.

Navajivan Publishing House: PO Navajivan, Ahmedabad 380 014; tel. (79) 7540635; f. 1919; Gandhiana and related social science; in English, Hindi and Gujarati; Man. Trustee JITENDRA DESAI; Sales Man. KAPIL RAWAL.

Neelkamal Publications (Pvt) Ltd: NN Complex, Hyderabad 500 095; tel. (40) 24757140; fax (40) 24757951; e-mail suresh@neelkamalpub.com; internet www.neelkamalpub.com; education, psychology, dictionaries, encyclopaedias; Man. Dir SURESH CHANDRA SHARMA.

Orient Longman (Pvt) Ltd: 3-6-752 Himayat Nagar, Hyderabad 500 029; tel. (40) 27665466; fax (40) 27645046; e-mail hyd2_orlongco@sancharnet.in; f. 1948; educational, technical, general and children's in English and almost all Indian languages; Chair. SHANTA RAMESHWAR RAO; Dirs Dr NANDINI RAO, J. KRISHNADEV RAO.

Parikalpana Prakashan: D-68 Nirala Nagar, Lucknow 226 010; tel. (522) 2786782; e-mail janchetna@rediffmail.com; fiction, poetry, literary criticism, history, political sciences, philosophy; CEO K. L. JOSHI.

Pilgrims Publishing: Pilgrims Book House, B27/98-A-8 Nawabganj Rd, Durga Kund, Varanasi 221 001; tel. (542) 2314060; fax (542) 2314059; e-mail pilgrims@satyam.net.in; internet www.pilgrimsbooks.com; f. 1986; first edition and reprint books on Nepal, Tibet, India and the Himalayas; Senior Editor CHRISTOPHER N. BURCHETT.

Publication Bureau: Panjab University, Chandigarh 160 014; tel. (172) 2541782; f. 1948; textbooks, academic and general; CEO DARSHAN SINGH; Man. H. R. GROVER.

Publication Bureau: Punjabi University, Patiala 147 002; tel. (175) 2282461; university-level text and reference books; CEO Dr B. S. MANGAT.

Ram Prasad and Sons: Hospital Rd, Agra 282 003; tel. (562) 2367904; fax (562) 2360906; e-mail rpsons@sancharnet.in; f. 1905; agricultural, arts, history, commerce, education, general, computing, engineering, pure and applied science, economics, sociology; Dirs R. N, B. N, Y. N, RAVI AGARWAL; Man. S. N. AGARWAL; br. in Bhopal.

Sahitya Bhandar: 50 Chahchand Zero Rd, Allahabad 211 001; tel. (532) 2400787; Hindi literature, children's, science, literary criticism, etc.; Propr SATISH CHANDRA AGGARWAL.

Sahitya Bhawan Publications: Hospital Rd, Agra 282 003; tel. (562) 2151665; fax (562) 2151568; e-mail info@sbpagra.com; internet www.sbpagra.com; social sciences, humanities; Propr RAHUL BANSAL.

Sahitya Sangam: New 100, Lukerganj, Allahabad 211 001; Hindi literature, communication, journalism, political science, art, history, etc.; Propr ALOK CHATURVEDI.

Samvad Prakashan: I-499 Shastri Nagar, Meerut 250 004; tel. (121) 2764866; e-mail samvadindia@vsnl.net; Hindi translations of world literature; biographies, autobiographies, fiction, cinema; Propr NAMITA SRIVASTAVA.

Universities Press (India) (Pvt) Ltd: 3-6-752 Himayat Nagar, Hyderabad 500 029; tel. (40) 27662849; fax (40) 27645046; e-mail hyd2_upilco@sancharnet.in; internet www.universitiespress.com; academic and educational books on science, technology, management; Man. Dir MADHU REDDY.

Vishwavidyalaya Prakashan: CK 56/35, Vishalakshi Bldg, Chowk, Varanasi 221 001; tel. (542) 2353082; fax (542) 2353741; e-mail sales@vvpbooks.com; internet www.vvpbooks.com; f. 1950; literature, Indology, history, spiritualism, journalism, mass communication; Propr PURUSHOTTAM DAS MODI.

GOVERNMENT PUBLISHING HOUSE

Publications Division: Ministry of Information and Broadcasting, Govt of India, Patiala House, New Delhi 110 001; tel. (11) 23386879; fax (11) 23387983; e-mail dpd@sb.nic.in; internet www.publicationdivision.nic.in; f. 1941; culture, art, literature, planning

and development, general; also 21 periodicals in English and 13 Indian languages; Dir UMAKANT MISHRA.

PUBLISHERS' ASSOCIATIONS

Bombay Booksellers' and Publishers' Association: No. 25, 6th Floor, Bldg No. 3, Navjivan Commercial Premises Co-op Society Ltd, Dr Bhadkamkar Marg, Mumbai 400 008; tel. (22) 23088691; e-mail bbpassn@yahoo.co.in; f. 1961; 400 mems; Pres. H. S. KRISHNA PRASAD; Gen. Sec. B. S. FERNANDES.

Delhi State Booksellers' and Publishers' Association: 3026/7-H Shiv Chowk, (South Patel Nagar) Ranjit Nagar, New Delhi 110 008; tel. (11) 25842748; fax (11) 25846769; e-mail rpnbooks@indiatimes.com; f. 1941; 400 mems; Pres. Dr S. K. BHATIA; Sec. K. K. SAXENA.

Federation of Educational Publishers in India: X-39, Institutional Area, Karkardoma, New Delhi 110 092; tel. (11) 22377017; f. 1987; 14 affiliated asscns; 150 life mems; 45 annual mems; Pres. R. K. GUPTA; Sec.-Gen. KAMAL ARORA.

Federation of Indian Publishers: Federation House, 18/1-C Institutional Area, nr JNU, New Delhi 110 067; tel. (11) 26964847; fax (11) 26864054; e-mail fipl@satyam.net.in; internet www.fiponweb.com; 18 affiliated asscns; 190 mems; Pres. ANAND BHUSHAN; Hon. Gen. Sec. SHAKTI MALIK.

Akhil Bharatiya Hindi Prakashak Sangh: 139, Purani Anarkali, Gali No. 4, Delhi 110 051; f. 1954; 400 mems; Pres. KRISHNAN DEV SHARMA; Gen. Sec. ARUN KUMAR SHARMA.

Akhil Bharatiya Marathi Prakashak Sangha: c/o Dilipraj Prakashan (Pvt) Ltd, 251-C, Shaniwar Peth, Pune 411 030; Pres. SHARAD GOGATE.

All Assam Publishers' and Booksellers' Association: Chancellor Bldg, H. B. Rd, Panbazar, Guwahati 781 001; tel. (361) 2634790; fax (361) 2513886; e-mail devchowdhurygp@rediffmail.com; Pres. GIRIPADA DEV CHOWDHURY; Sec. BIDYUT GUHA.

All India Urdu Publishers' and Booksellers' Association: 3243 Kuchatarachand, Daryaganj, New Delhi 110 002; tel. (11) 23257189; fax (11) 23265490; e-mail aakif@del3.vsnl.net.in; internet www.indiamart.com/aakifbooks; f. 1988; 175 mems; Pres. Dr KHALIQ ANJUM; Gen. Sec. S. M. ZAFAR ALI.

All Kerala Publishers' and Booksellers' Association: D. C. Kizhakemuri Edam, Good Shepherd St, Kottayam 686 001; tel. (481) 2563114; fax (481) 2564758; e-mail info@dcbooks.com; Pres. E. N. NANTHAKUMAR.

Booksellers' and Publishers' Association of South India: 8, 2nd Floor, Sun Plaza, G. N. Chetty Rd, Chennai 600 006; 158 mems; Pres. S. CHANDRASEKAR; Sec. RAVI CHOPRA.

Gujarati Publishers' Association: Navajivan Trust, PO Navajivan, Ahmedabad 380 014; tel. (79) 7540635; 125 mems; Pres. JITENDRA DESAI; Sec. K. N. MADRASI.

Karnataka Publishers' Association: c/o Ankita Pustaka, 53 Sham Singh Complex, Gandhi Bazar Main Rd, Bangalore 560 004; tel. (80) 26617100; Pres. Dr RAMAKANT JOSHI.

Orissa Publishers' and Booksellers' Association: Binodbihari, Cuttack 753 002; tel. (671) 2620637; f. 1973–74; 280 mems; Pres. PITAMBAR MISHRA; Sec. SUBHENDU SEKHAR RATHA.

Paschimbanga Prakasak Sabha: 206 Bidhan Sarani, Kolkata 700 006; tel. (33) 23506720; fax (33) 22413852; Pres. BIPLAB BHOWAL; Gen. Sec. SOMENATH MUKHERJEE.

Publishers' Association of West Bengal: 6-B, Ramanath Mazumder St, Kolkata 700 009; tel. (33) 2325580; 164 mems; Pres. MOHIT KUMAR BASU; Gen. Sec. SHANKARI BHUSAN NAYAK.

Publishers' and Booksellers' Association of Bengal: 93 Mahatma Gandhi Rd, Kolkata 700 007; tel. (33) 22411993; f. 1912; 4,500 mems; Pres. KHIMANGSHU BANDYOPADHYAY; Gen. Sec. CHITTA SINGHA ROY.

Punjabi Publishers' Association: Bazar Mai Sewan, Amritsar 143 006; tel. (183) 2545787; fax (183) 2543965; Pres. KULWANT SINGH SURI; Gen. Sec. PARAMJIT SINGH.

Vijayawada Publishers' Association: 27-1-68, Karl Marx Rd, Vijayawada 520 002; tel. (866) 2433353; fax (866) 2426348; 41 mems; Pres. DUPATI VIJAY KUMAR; Sec. U. N. YOGI.

Federation of Publishers' and Booksellers' Associations in India: 2nd Floor, 84 Daryaganj, New Delhi 110 002; tel. (11) 23272845; fax (11) 23281227; e-mail fpbai@vsnl.net; internet www.fpbai.org; 22 affiliated asscns; 507 mems; Pres. SUBHAS CHANDRA SETHI; Hon. Sec. BALDEV VERMA.

Publishers' and Booksellers' Guild: Guild House, 2B Jhamapukur Lane, Kolkata 700 009; tel. (33) 23544417; fax (33) 23604566; e-mail guild@cal2.vsnl.net.in; internet www.kolkatabookfaironline

.com; f. 1975; 37 mems; organizes annual Kolkata Book Fair; Pres. KALYAN SHAH; Sec. TRIDIB CHATTERJEE.

UP Publishers' Association: Bharati Bhavan, Western Kutchery Rd, Meerut 250 001; Pres. RAJENDRA AGARWAL.

Broadcasting and Communications

TELECOMMUNICATIONS

Telecom Regulatory Authority of India (TRAI): 16th Floor, Jawahar Vyapar Bhavan 1, Tolstoy Marg, New Delhi 110 001; tel. (11) 23357815; fax (11) 23738708; e-mail trai@del2.vsnl.net.in; internet www.trai.gov.in; f. 1998; Chair. PRADIP BAIJAL; Vice-Chair. BAL KRISHAN ZUTSHI.

Bharti Telenet Ltd: Indore; f. 1998; India's first privately owned telephone network; Exec. Dir BHAGWAN KHURANA; CEO K. KRISHNAN.

Ericsson India Pvt Ltd: Ericsson Forum, DLF Cyberciti, Sector 25A, 60 Mtr. Sector Rd, Gurgaon 122 002; tel. (124) 2560808; fax (124) 2565454; e-mail marketing-int.communications@eci.ericsson .se; internet www.ericsson.co.in; Man. Dir JAN CAMPBELL.

ITI (Indian Telephone Industries) Ltd: 45/1 Magrath Rd, Bangalore 560 025; tel. (80) 25366116; fax (80) 25593188; e-mail cmd@ itiltd.co.in; internet www.itiltd-india.com; f. 1948; mfrs of all types of telecommunication equipment, incl. telephones, automatic exchanges and long-distance transmission equipment; also produces optical fibre equipment and microwave equipment; will manufacture all ground communication equipment for the 22 earth stations of the Indian National Satellite; in conjunction with the Post and Telegraph Department, a newly designed 2,000-line exchange has been completed; Chair. and Man. Dir Y. K. PANDEY.

Mahanagar Telephone Nigam Ltd (MTNL): Jeevan Bharati Tower 1, 124 Connaught Circus, New Delhi 110 001; tel. (11) 23742212; fax (11) 23314243; e-mail cmd@bol.net.in; internet www .mtnl.net.in; f. 1986; 56% state-owned; owns and operates telecommunications and information technology services in Mumbai and Delhi; Chair. and Man. Dir R. S. P. SINHA.

Videsh Sanchar Nigam Ltd (VSNL): Lok Manya Videsh Sanchar Bhawan, Kasinath Dhuru Marg, Prabhadevi, Mumbai 400 028; tel. (22) 24312700; fax (22) 24365689; e-mail helpdesk@giaspn01.vsnl .net.in; internet www.vsnl.com; f. 1986; 26% state-owned; 45% owned by the Tata Group; Chair. RATAN N. TATA; Man. Dir S. K. GUPTA.

BROADCASTING

Prasar Bharati (Broadcasting Corpn of India): 2nd Floor, PTI Bldg, Sansad Marg, New Delhi 110 001; tel. (11) 23737603; autonomous body; oversees operations of state-owned radio and television services; f. 1997; Chair. M. V. KAMATH; CEO K. S. SARMA.

Radio

All India Radio (AIR): Akashvani Bhavan, Parliament St, New Delhi 110 001; tel. (11) 23715411; fax (11) 23714061; broadcasting is controlled by the Ministry of Information and Broadcasting and is primarily govt-financed; operates a network of 208 stations and 332 transmitters (grouped into four zones— north, south, east and west), covering almost the entire population and over 90% of the total area of the country; Dir-Gen. BRAJESHWAR SINGH.

The News Services Division of AIR, centralized in New Delhi, is one of the largest news organizations in the world. It has 45 regional news units, which broadcast 364 bulletins daily in 24 languages and 38 dialects. Eighty-four bulletins in 19 languages are broadcast in the Home Services, 187 regional bulletins in 65 languages and dialects, and 64 bulletins in 25 languages in the External Services.

Television

Doordarshan India (Television India): Mandi House, Doordarshan Bhavan, Copernicus Marg, New Delhi 110 001; tel. (11) 23385958; fax (11) 23386507; f. 1976; broadcasting is controlled by the Ministry of Information and Broadcasting and is govt-financed; programmes: 280 hours weekly; 5 all-India channels, 11 regional language satellite channels, 5 state networks and 1 international channel; Dir-Gen. NAVEEN KUMAR.

In September 2003 76% of the country's area and 90% of the population were covered by the television network. There were 1,384 transmitters in operation in that month. By 2000 51 programme production centres and nine relay centres had been established.

Finance

(cap. = capital; p.u. = paid up; res = reserves; dep. = deposits; m. = million; brs = branches; amounts in rupees unless otherwise stated)

BANKING

State Banks

Reserve Bank of India: Central Office Bldg, Shahid Bhagat Singh Rd, POB 10007, Mumbai 400 001; tel. (22) 22661602; fax (22) 22658269; e-mail rbiprd@giasbm01.vsnl.net.in; internet www.rbi .org.in; f. 1934; nationalized 1949; sole bank of issue; cap. 50m., res 65,000m., dep. 1,021,962m. (June 2003); Gov. Y. VENUGOPAL REDDY; Dep. Govs V. LEELADHAR, S. GOPINATH, K. JUDESHI; 4 offices and 14 brs.

State Bank of India: Corporate Centre, Madame Cama Rd, POB 10121, Mumbai 400 021; tel. (22) 22022426; fax (22) 22851391; e-mail sbiid@boms.vsnl.net.in; internet www.sbi.co.in; f. 1955; cap. p.u. 5,263m., res and surplus 197,049.8m., dep. 3,186,186.7m. (March 2004); 7 associates, 7 domestic subsidiaries/affiliates, 3 foreign subsidiaries, 4 jt ventures abroad; Chair. A. K. PURWAR; Man. Dirs CHANDAN BHATTACHARYA, ASHOK KINI; 9,593 brs (incl. 51 overseas brs and rep. offices in 31 countries).

State-owned Commercial Banks

Fourteen of India's major commercial banks were nationalized in 1969 and a further six in 1980. They are managed by 15-mem. boards of directors (two directors to be appointed by the central Government, one employee director, one representing employees who are not workmen, one representing depositors, three representing farmers, workers, artisans, etc., five representing persons with special knowledge or experience, one Reserve Bank of India official and one Government of India official). The Department of Banking of the Ministry of Finance controls all banking operations.

There were 66,644 branches of public-sector and other commercial banks in June 2003.

Aggregate deposits of all scheduled commercial banks amounted to Rs 16,557,380m. in January 2005.

Allahabad Bank: 2 Netaji Subhas Rd, Kolkata 700 001; tel. (33) 22208668; fax (33) 22488323; e-mail albfd@giascl01.vsnl.net.in; internet www.allahabadbank.com/; f. 1865; nationalized 1969; cap. p.u. 3,467m., res 12,052.3m., dep. 314,766.5m. (March 2004); Chair. and Man. Dir O. N. SINGH; Exec. Dir SUBODH KUMAR GOEL; 1,935 brs.

Andhra Bank: Andhra Bank Bldgs, Saifabad, 5-9-11 Secretariat Rd, Hyderabad 500 004; tel. (40) 23230001; fax (40) 23211050; e-mail dit@andhrabank.co.in; internet www.andhrabankindia.com; f. 1923; nationalized 1980; cap. p.u. 4,000m., res 10,525.8m., dep. 210,620m. (March 2004); Chair. and Man. Dir T. S. NARAYANASAMI; 1,100 brs and 113 extension counters.

Bank of Baroda: Baroda Corporate Centre, C-26, G-Block, Bandra-Kurla Complex, Bandra (East), Mumbai 400 054; tel. (22) 26985000; fax (22) 22610341; e-mail secbob@bol.net.in; internet www .bankofbaroda.com; f. 1908; nationalized 1969; merged with Benares State Bank in 2002; cap. 2,943.3m., res 40,926.3m., dep. 663,663.7m. (March 2003); Chair. and Man. Dir P. S. SHENOY; Exec. Dir K. RAMAKRISHNAN; 2,641 brs in India, 38 brs overseas.

Bank of India: Star House, C-5, G-Block, Bandra Kurla Complex, Bandra (East), Mumbai 400 051; tel. (22) 56684555; fax (22) 56684558; e-mail boifbd@bom7.vsnl.in; internet www.bankofindia .com; f. 1906; nationalized 1969; cap. 4,881m., res and surplus 35,215m., dep. 710,031m. (March 2004); Chair. and Man. Dir M. VENUGOPALAN; 2,562 brs in India, 19 brs overseas.

Bank of Maharashtra: 'Lokmangal', 1501 Shivajinagar, Pune 411 005; tel. (20) 25532731; fax (20) 25533246; e-mail bomcocmd@vsnl .com; internet www.maharashtrabank.com; f. 1935; nationalized 1969; cap. 4,305.2m., res 10,050.1m., dep. 264,459.3m. (March 2004); Chair. and Man. Dir S. C. BASU; 1,276 brs.

Canara Bank: 112 Jayachamarajendra Rd, POB 6648, Bangalore 560 002; tel. (80) 22223118; fax (80) 22223168; e-mail canbank@blr .vsnl.net.in; internet www.canbankindia.com; f. 1906; nationalized 1969; cap. 4,100m., res 48,416.4m., dep. 863,445.6m. (March 2004); Chair. and Man. Dir V. P. SHETTY; Exec. Dir R. SWAMINATHAN; 2,469 brs.

Central Bank of India: Chandermukhi, Nariman Point, Mumbai 400 021; tel. (22) 22026428; fax (22) 22044336; e-mail cbicpp@b01 .net.in; internet www.centralbankofindia.com; f. 1911; nationalized 1969; cap. 11,241.4m., res and surplus 12,998.2m., dep. 511,651.9m. (March 2003); Chair. and Man. Dir Dr DALBIR SINGH; 3,115 brs.

Corporation Bank: Mangaladevi Temple Rd, POB 88, Mangalore 575 001; tel. (824) 2426416; fax (824) 2444617; e-mail corpho@ corpbank.com; internet www.corpbank.com; f. 1906; nationalized 1980; cap. 1,434.4m., res 22,267.6m., dep. 231,909.3m. (March

2004); Chair. and Man. Dir V. K. CHOPRA; Exec. Dir P. K. GUPTA; 722 brs.

Dena Bank: C-10, G Block, Bandra-Kurla Complex, Bandra (East), Mumbai 400 051; tel. (22) 26545607; fax (22) 26545605; e-mail akk@denabank.co.in; internet www.denabank.com; f. 1938 as Devkaran Nanjee Banking Co Ltd; nationalized 1969; cap. 2,068.2m., res and surplus 7,260.5m., dep. 183,490m. (March 2004); Chair. and Man. Dir A. K. KHANDELWAL; Exec. Dir M. V. NAIR; 1,135 brs.

Indian Bank: 31 Rajaji Salai, POB 1866, Chennai 600 001; tel. (44) 25233231; fax (44) 25231278; e-mail indianbank@vsnl.com; internet www.indian-bank.com; f. 1907; nationalized 1969; cap. 45,739.6m., res 9,638.7m., dep. 304,444m. (March 2004); Chair. and Man. Dir M. B. N. RAO; 1,376 brs.

Indian Overseas Bank: 762 Anna Salai, POB 3765, Chennai 600 002; tel. (44) 28524212; fax (44) 28523595; e-mail iobmail@vsnl.com; internet www.iob.com; f. 1937; nationalized 1969; cap. 5,448m., res 15,362.9m., dep. 414,825.8m. (March 2004); Chair. and Man. Dir S. C. GUPTA; Exec. Dir A. R. NAGAPPAN; 1,457 brs.

Oriental Bank of Commerce: Harsha Bhavan, E Block, Connaught Place, POB 329, New Delhi 110 001; tel. (11) 23323444; fax (11) 23321514; e-mail bdncmd@obcindia.com; internet www.obcindia.com; f. 1943; nationalized 1980; cap. 1,925.4m., res 24,842.6m., dep. 356,740m. (March 2004); Chair. and Man. Dir B. D. NARANG; Exec. Dir H. A. DARUWALA; 533 brs.

Punjab and Sind Bank: Bank House, 21 Rajendra Place, New Delhi 110 008; tel. (11) 25768831; fax (11) 25752501; internet www.psbindia.com; f. 1908; nationalized 1980; cap. 2,430.6m., res 2,235.4m., dep. 136,420.3m. (March 2004); Chair. and Man. Dir P. K. GUPTA; Exec. Dir P. SUBBARAO; 811 brs.

Punjab National Bank: 7 Bhikaiji Cama Place, Africa Ave, New Delhi 110 066; tel. (11) 26102303; fax (11) 26196456; e-mail cmd@pnb.co.in; internet www.pnbindia.com; f. 1895; nationalized 1969; merged with New Bank of India in 1993; cap. 2,653m., res 44,255m., dep. 758,130m. (March 2003); Chair. and Man. Dir S. S. KOHLI; Exec. Dir K. C. CHAKRABORTHY; 4,487 brs.

Syndicate Bank: POB 1, Manipal 576 119; tel. (825) 2571181; fax (825) 2570266; e-mail idcb@syndicatebank.com; internet www.syndicatebank.com; f. 1925 as Canara Industrial and Banking Syndicate Ltd; name changed as above 1964; nationalized 1969; cap. 4,719.4m., res 12,849.6m., dep. 425,850m. (March 2004); Chair. and Man. Dir KANTA KUMAR; 1,948 brs.

UCO Bank: 10 Biplabi Trailokya Maharaj Sarani (Brabourne Rd), POB 2455, Kolkata 700 001; tel. (33) 22254120; fax (33) 22253986; e-mail ucobank@vsnl.net; internet www.ucobank.com; f. 1943 as United Commercial Bank Ltd; nationalized 1969; name changed as above 1985; cap. 7,993.6m., res 9,837.0m., dep. 392,442.6m. (March 2004); Chair. and Man. Dir V. SRIDHAR; Exec. Dir M. M. VAISH; 1,717 brs.

Union Bank of India: Union Bank Bhavan, 239 Vidhan Bhavan Marg, Nariman Point, Mumbai 400 021; tel. (22) 22023060; fax (22) 22025238; e-mail ubihoc@vsnl.net.in; internet www.unionbankofindia.com; f. 1919; nationalized 1969; cap. 4,601.2m., res 26,270m., dep. 505,590m. (March 2004); Chair. and Man. Dir K. CHERIAN VARGHESE; 2,023 brs.

United Bank of India: 16 Old Court House St, Kolkata 700 001; tel. (33) 2487471; fax (33) 2485852; e-mail utbihoc@giascl01.vsnl.net .in; internet www.unitedbankofindia.com; f. 1950; nationalized 1969; cap. 18,108.7m., res 1,508.7m., dep. 210,312.9m. (March 2003); Chair. and Man. Dir PRAKASH SINGH; Exec. Dir G. R. SUNDARAVADIVEL; 1,300 brs.

Vijaya Bank: 41/2 Mahatma Gandhi Rd, Bangalore 560 001; tel. (80) 25584066; fax (80) 25598040; e-mail vijbank@bgl.vsnl.net.in; internet www.vijayabank.com; f. 1931; nationalized 1980; cap. 3,335.2m., res 4,777.5m., dep. 170,198.1m. (March 2003); Chair. and Man. Dir M. S. KAPUR; 858 brs.

Principal Private Banks

The Bank of Rajasthan Ltd: C-3 Sardar Patel Marg, Jaipur 302 001; tel. (141) 2381222; fax (141) 2381123; e-mail borit@jp1.dot.net .in; internet www.bankofrajasthan.com; f. 1943; cap. p.u. 1,059.6m., res 1,792.4m., dep. 52,992.3m. (March 2003); Chair. PRAVIN KUMAR TAYAL; Man. Dir MALLIKARJUN SHARMA; 307 brs.

Bharat Overseas Bank Ltd: Habeeb Towers, 196 Anna Salai, Chennai 600 002; tel. (44) 28522983; fax (44) 28524700; e-mail bobl@md3.vsnl.net.in; internet www.boblonline.com; f. 1973; cap. 157.5m., res 1,564.3m., dep. 24,715.2m. (March 2004); Chair. G. KRISHNAMURTHY; Gen. Man. G. CHANDRAN; 77 brs.

Bombay Mercantile Co-operative Bank Ltd: 78 Mohammed Ali Rd, Mumbai 400 003; tel. (22) 23425961; fax (22) 23433385; e-mail bmcb@bom5.vsnl.net.in; f. 1939; cap. 195m., res 3,714m., dep.

16,117m. (March 2003); Chair. M. RAHMAN; Man. Dir S. U. PATHAN; 53 brs.

The Catholic Syrian Bank Ltd: St Mary's College Rd, POB 502, Trichur 680 020; tel. (487) 2333020; fax (487) 2333435; e-mail csbho@md2.vsnl.net.in; internet www.casybank.com; f. 1920; cap. 105.7m., res 1,294.4m., dep. 38,805m. (March 2004); Chair. and CEO N. R. ACHAN; Gen. Man. JOHN J. ALAPATT; 297 brs.

Centurion Bank Ltd: 1201 Raheja Centre, Free Press Journal Marg, Nariman Point, Mumbai 400 021; tel. (22) 22047234; fax (22) 22845860; e-mail cblho@bom3.vsnl.net.in; internet www.centurionbank.com; f. 1995; cap. 1,524.7m., res 233.5m., dep. 28,347.1m. (March 2003); Chair. and Man. Dir V. JANAKIRAMAN.

City Union Bank Ltd: 149 TSR (Big) St, Kumbakonam 612 001; tel. (435) 2432322; fax (435) 2431746; e-mail cub@vsnl.com; internet www.cityunion.com; f. 1904; cap. 240.0m., res 1,407.7m., dep. 23,173.7m. (March 2003); Chair. S. BALASUBRAMANIAN; Chief Gen. Man. K. VENKATARAMAN; 125 brs.

The Federal Bank Ltd: Federal Towers, POB 103, Alwaye 683 101; tel. (484) 2623620; fax (484) 2621687; e-mail nrihelp@federalbank.co .in; internet www.federal-bank.com; f. 1931; cap. 217.2m., res and surplus 4,997m., dep. 134,760m. (March 2004); Chair. M. VENUGOPALAN; 421 brs.

ICICI Bank Ltd: ICICI Towers, 4th Floor, South Tower, Bandra–Kurla Complex, Bandra (East), Mumbai 400 051; tel. (22) 26531414; fax (22) 26531167; e-mail info@icicibank.com; internet www.icicibank.com; f. 1994; cap. 9,664.0m., res 73,410.7m., dep. 681,085.8m. (March 2004); Man. Dir K. V. KAMATH; Chair. N. VAGHUL; 348 brs.

IndusInd Bank Ltd: IndusInd House, 425 Dadasaheb Bhadkamkar Marg, Lamington Rd, nr Opera House, Mumbai 400 004; tel. (22) 23859901; fax (22) 23859913; e-mail glob@indusind.com; internet www.indusind.com; f. 1994; cap. US $66.4m., res $116.7m., dep. $2,561.8m. (March 2004); Chair. R. J. SAHANEY; Man. Dir BHASKAR GHOSE; 77 brs.

ING Vysya Bank Ltd: 72 St Marks Rd, Bangalore 560 001; tel. (80) 22272021; fax (80) 22272220; e-mail ibdbby.vbl@gnbom.global.net .in; internet www.vysyabank.com; f. 1930; cap. 226.2m., res 6,841m., dep. 91,866m. (March 2003); Chair. G. MALLIKARJUNA RAO; Man. Dir BART HILLEMANS; 490 brs.

Jammu and Kashmir Bank Ltd: Corporate Headquarters, M. A. Rd, Srinagar 190 001; tel. (194) 2481930; fax (194) 2481923; e-mail jkbcosgr@jkbmail.com; internet www.jkbank.org; f. 1938; cap. p.u. 482.0m., res 11,937.9m., dep. 146,748.9m. (March 2003); Chair. and CEO M. Y. KHAN; 454 brs.

The Karnataka Bank Ltd: POB 716, Kodialbail, Mangalore 575 003; tel. (824) 2228222; fax (824) 2225588; e-mail info@ktbank.com; internet www.ktbankltd.com; f. 1924; cap. 404.3m., res 6,577.2m., dep. 94,069.0m. (March 2004); Chair. and CEO Mr ANANTHAKRISHNA; 357 brs.

The Karur Vysya Bank Ltd: Erode Rd, POB 21, Karur 639 002; tel. (4324) 226520; fax (4324) 225700; e-mail kvbcopdd@sancharnet .in; f. 1916; cap. 179.8m., res 6,940.5m., dep. 59,114.8m. (March 2004); Chair. P. T. KUPPUSWAMY; Exec. Dir N. S. VENKATARAMA GUPTA; 222 brs.

Lakshmi Vilas Bank Ltd: Kathaparai, Salem Rd, POB 2, Karur 639 006; tel. (4324) 320051; fax (4324) 220068; e-mail info@lvbank .com; internet www.lvbank.com; f. 1926; cap. 115.1m., res 1,805.8m., dep. 27,705m. (March 2003); Chair. A. KRISHNAMOORTHY; 215 brs.

The Sangli Bank Ltd: Rajwada Chowk, POB 158, Sangli 416 416; tel. (233) 2623611; fax (233) 2620666; e-mail san_sanbank@sancharnet.in; f. 1916; cap. p.u. 204.1m., res 560m., dep. 16,777.6m. (March 2003); Chair. and CEO A. R. BORDE; Gen. Man. S. R. GODBOLE; 178 brs.

The South Indian Bank Ltd: SIB House, Mission Quarters, Thrissur 680 001, Kerala; tel. (487) 2420020; fax (487) 2442021; e-mail head@southindianbank.com; internet www.southindianbank .com; f. 1929; cap. 357.8m., res 3,591.1m., dep. 82,800.3m. (March 2004); Chair. and CEO A. SETHUMADHAVAN; 421 brs.

Tamilnad Mercantile Bank Ltd: 57 Victoria Extension Rd, Tuticorin 628 002; tel. (461) 2321932; fax (461) 2322994; f. 1921 as Nadar Bank, name changed as above 1962; cap. 2.8m., res 3,966m., dep. 44,042.7m. (March 2004); Chair. S. RADHAKRISHNAN; 163 brs.

The United Western Bank Ltd: 172/4 Raviwar Peth, Shivaji Circle, Powai Naka, Satara 415 001; tel. (2162) 231722; fax (2162) 231884; e-mail uwb@uwbankindia.com; internet www.uwbankindia .com; f. 1936; cap. 298.9m., res and surplus 2,490.7m., dep. 53,910.9m. (March 2003); Chair. and Chief Exec. SATISH MARATHE; 230 brs.

Foreign Banks

ABN AMRO Bank NV (Netherlands): 14 Veer Nariman Rd, POB 97, Mumbai 400 023; tel. (22) 22042331; Chief Operating Officer PAUL ABRAHAM; 11 brs.

Abu Dhabi Commercial Bank (United Arab Emirates): Rehmat Manzil, 75-B Veer Nariman Rd, Mumbai 400 020; tel. (22) 22830235; fax (22) 22870686; Chief Exec. KHALIFA MOHAMMAD HUSSEIN; 1 br.

American Express Bank Ltd (USA): Maker Chambers IV, 7th Floor, 211 Nariman Point, Mumbai 400 021; tel. (22) 22833293; fax (22) 22872968; Country Head STEVE MARTIN; 4 brs.

Banca Nazionale del Lavoro Spa (Italy): 61 Maker Chambers VI, Nariman Point, Mumbai 400 021; tel. (22) 22047763; fax (22) 22023482; Rep. L. S. AGARWAL.

Bank Muscat SAOG (Oman): 29 Infantry Rd, Bangalore 560 001; tel. (80) 22867755; fax (80) 22862214; e-mail bmiimgt@bgl.vsnl.net .in; CEO SAMIT GHOSH; 1 br.

Bank of America NA (USA): Express Towers, POB 10080, Nariman Point, Mumbai 400 021; tel. (22) 22852882; fax (22) 22029016; Country Man. VISHWAVIR AHUJA; 5 brs.

Bank of Bahrain and Kuwait BSC: Jolly Maker Chambers II, Ground Floor, POB 11692, 225 Nariman Point, Mumbai 400 021; tel. (22) 22823698; fax (22) 22044458; Gen. Man. and CEO K. S. KRISHNA-KUMAR; 2 brs.

Bank of Ceylon (Sri Lanka): 1090 Poonamallee High Rd, Chennai 600 084; tel. (44) 26420972; fax (44) 25325590; e-mail ceybank@md3 .vsnl.net.in; internet www.bocindia.com; Asst Vice-Pres. B. KARTHIK; Country Man. N. V. MOORTHY.

Bank of Nova Scotia (Canada): Mittal Tower B, Nariman Point, Mumbai 400 021; tel. (22) 22832822; fax (22) 22873125; Sr Vice-Pres. and CEO (India) DENIS VAZ; Vice-Pres. and Man. BHASKAR DESAI; 5 brs.

Bank of Tokyo-Mitsubishi Ltd (Japan): Jeevan Prakash, Sir P. Mehta Rd, Mumbai 400 001; tel. (22) 22660564; fax (22) 22661787; Regional Rep. for India and Gen. Man. KUNIHIKO NISHI-HARA; 4 brs.

Barclays Bank PLC (United Kingdom): 21–23 Maker Chambers VI, 2nd Floor, Nariman Point, Mumbai 400 021; tel. (22) 22044353; fax (22) 22043238; CEO AJAY SONDHI; 2 brs.

BNP Paribas (France): French Bank Bldg, 62 Homji St, Fort, Mumbai 400 001; tel. (22) 22660822; fax (22) 22679709; e-mail Mumbai1.admin@asia.bnpparibas.com; internet www.bnpparibas .co.in; cap. 352m., res 1,700m., dep. 16,300m. (2002); Chief Exec. and Country Man. FREDERIC AMOUNDRU; 9 brs.

Chinatrust Commercial Bank (Taiwan): 21-A Janpath, New Delhi 110 001; tel. (11) 23356001; fax (11) 23731815; e-mail personnel@chinatrustindia.com; internet www.chinatrustindia .com; f. 1996; Gen. Man. and CEO FAN TIEN HSI; 1 br.

Citibank, NA (USA): Citibank Centre, Bandra-Kurla Complex, Bandra (East), Mumbai 400 051; tel. (22) 26535757; fax (22) 26535859; internet www.citibank.com/india; CEO SANJAY NAYAR; 18 brs.

Crédit Agricole Indosuez (France): Ramon House, 169 Backbay Reclamation, Mumbai 400 020; tel. (22) 22045104; fax (22) 22049108; Sr Country Officer ALAIN BUTZBACH; Gen. Man. NIRENDU MAZUMDAR.

Crédit Lyonnais (France): Apeejay House, 3rd Floor, 3 Dinshaw Vachha Rd, Mumbai 400 020; tel. (22) 22330300; fax (22) 22351888; Chief Exec. and Country Man. JEAN-YVES LE PAULMIER; 4 brs.

Deutsche Bank AG (Germany): Kodak House, Dr D.N. Rd, Fort, POB 1142, Mumbai 400 001; tel. (22) 22076191; fax (22) 22073548; CEO DOUGLAS NELSON; 5 brs.

Development Bank of Singapore Ltd: Free Press House, 14th Floor, Nariman Point, Mumbai 400 021; tel. (22) 22388888; fax (22) 22388899; internet www.dbs.com; Country Head SANJAY BHASIN; 1 br.

Hongkong and Shanghai Banking Corpn Ltd (Hong Kong): 52–60 Mahatma Gandhi Rd, POB 128, Mumbai 400 001; tel. (22) 22674921; fax (22) 22658309; e-mail info@hsbc.co.in; internet www .hsbc.co.in; CEO and Country Head NIALL S. K. BOOKER; 30 brs.

ING Bank (Netherlands): Hoechst House, 7th Floor, 193 Backbay Reclamation, Nariman Point, Mumbai 400 005; tel. (22) 22029876; fax (22) 22046134; e-mail atul.sahasrabuddhe@asia.ing.com; Country Head ATUL SAHASRABUDDHE; 2 brs.

JP Morgan Chase Manhattan Bank (USA): Mafatlal Centre, 9/F, Nariman Point, Mumbai 400 021; tel. (22) 22855666; fax (22) 22027772; Man. Dir and Sr Country Officer (India and South Asia) DOMINIC PRICE; 1 br.

Mashreq Bank PSC (United Arab Emirates): 602–604 Tulsiani Chambers, Nariman Point, Mumbai 400 021; tel. (22) 56327200; fax (22) 56301554; e-mail rajivk@india.mashreqbank.com; Country Man. RAJIV N. KAPOOR.

Mizuho Corporate Bank Ltd (Japan): Maker Chambers III, 1st Floor, Jamnalal Bajaj Rd, Nariman Point, Mumbai 400 021; tel. (22) 22886638; fax (22) 22886640; e-mail mhcbmmb@vsnl.com; CEO (India) and Gen. Man. KEN ITO; 1 br.

Oman International Bank SAOG (Oman): 201 Raheja Centre, Free Press Journal Marg, Nariman Point, Mumbai 400 021; tel. (22) 22324848; fax (22) 22875626; e-mail oibind@bom3.vsnl.net.in; Country Man. G. PATTIBIRAMAN; 2 brs.

Société Générale (France): Maker Chambers IV, Bajaj Marg, Nariman Point, POB 11635, Mumbai 400 021; tel. (22) 22870909; fax (22) 22045459; e-mail sg.mumbai@sgcib.com; CEO Dr PAUL H. RUSCH; 2 brs.

Sonali Bank (Bangladesh): Apeejay House, 15 Park St, Kolkata 700 016; tel. (33) 22293788; fax (33) 22457407; e-mail sonalibank@ sancharnet.in; Dep. Gen. Man. A. K. M. ASHRAF UDDIN KHAN; 2 brs.

Standard Chartered Grindlays Bank (United Kingdom): New Excelsior Bldg, 4th Floor, A. K. Naik Marg, POB 1806, Mumbai 400 001; tel. (22) 22075409; fax (22) 22072550; e-mail vkrishn@scbindia .mhs.compuserve.com; Chief Exec. A. CHRISTOPHER M. LOW; 74 brs.

State Bank of Mauritius Ltd: 101 Raheja Centre, 1st Floor, Free Press Journal Marg, Nariman Point, Mumbai 400 021; tel. (22) 22842965; fax (22) 22842966; Gen. Man. and CEO P. THONDRAYEN; 2 brs.

Sumitomo Mitsui Banking Corpn (Japan): 15/F Jolly Maker Chamber No. 2, 225 Nariman Point, Mumbai 400 021; tel. (22) 22880025; fax (22) 22880026; CEO and Gen. Man. KENJI KUWAYAMA.

UFJ Bank Ltd (Japan): Mercantile House, Upper Ground Floor, 15 Kasturba Gandhi Marg, New Delhi 110 001; tel. (11) 23318008; fax (11) 23315162; f. 1933 as Sanwa Bank, name changed to above following merger with Tokai Bank in Jan. 2002; Gen. Man. YOSHIAKI OZAWA.

Banking Organizations

Indian Banks' Association: Unit Nos 1, 2 and 4, 6th Floor, Centre I Bldg, World Trade Centre Complex, Cuffe Parade, Mumbai 400 005; tel. (22) 22844999; fax (22) 22835638; e-mail ibastadium@vsnl .net; internet www.iba.org.in; 154 mems; Chair. V. LEELADHAR; Chief Exec. H. N. SINOR.

Indian Institute of Banking and Finance: 'The Arcade', World Trade Centre, 2nd Floor, East Wing, Cuffe Parade, Mumbai 400 005; tel. (22) 22187003; fax (22) 22185147; e-mail iibgen@bom5.vsnl.net .in; internet www.iibf.org.in; f. 1928; 343,202 mems; Pres. Dr DALBIR SINGH; CEO R. H. SARMA; 4 zonal offices.

National Institute of Bank Management: NIBM Post Office, Kondhwe Khurd, Pune 411 048; tel. (20) 26833080; fax (20) 26834478; e-mail director@nibmindia.org; internet www.nibmindia .org; f. 1969; Chair. Dr Y. V. REDDY; Dir Dr ASHISH SAHA.

DEVELOPMENT FINANCE ORGANIZATIONS

Agricultural Finance Corporation Ltd: Dhanraj Mahal, 1st Floor, Chhatrapati Shivaji Maharaj Marg, Mumbai 400 001; tel. (22) 22028924; fax (22) 22028966; e-mail afcl@vsnl.com; internet www .afcindia.com; f. 1968 by a consortium of 45 public- and private-sector commercial banks including development finance institutions to help increase the flow of investment and credit into agriculture and rural development projects; provides project consultancy services to commercial banks, Union and State govts, public-sector corpns, the World Bank, the ADB, FAO, the International Fund for Agricultural Development and other institutions and to individuals; undertakes techno-economic and investment surveys in agriculture and agro-industries etc.; publishes quarterly journal *Financing Agriculture*; 3 regional offices and 9 br. offices; cap. p.u. 150m., res and surplus 20.5m. (March 2001); Chair. Dr. JAGDISH KAPOOR; Man. Dir A. M. ALAM.

Export-Import Bank of India: Centre One Bldg, Floor 21, World Trade Centre Complex, Cuffe Parade, Mumbai 400 005; tel. (22) 22185272; fax (22) 22182572; e-mail eximcord@vsnl.com; internet www.eximbankindia.com; f. 1982; cap. 6,499.9m., res 14,933m., dep. 20,922.1m. (March 2004); ; Chair. and Man. Dir T. C. VENKAT SUB-RAMANIAN; Exec. Dirs R. M. V. RAMAN, S. SRIDHAR; 14 offices world-wide.

Housing Development Finance Corpn Ltd (HDFC): Ramon House, 169 Backbay Reclamation, Churchgate, Mumbai 400 020; tel. (22) 22836255; fax (22) 22046758; e-mail info@hdfc.com; internet www.hdfc.com; f. 1977; provides loans to individuals and corporate bodies; cap. p.u. 2,466.1m., res 36,471.8m., dep. 93,376.5m. (March

2004); Chair. DEEPAK S. PAREKH; Man. Dir KEKI M. MISTRY; 173 brs (incl. one overseas br).

Industrial Development Bank of India (IDBI): IDBI Tower, World Trade Centre Complex, Cuffe Parade, Mumbai 400 005; tel. (22) 56553355; fax (22) 22181294; internet www.idbi.com; f. 1964; reorg. 1976; 72.1% govt-owned; India's premier financial institution for providing direct finance, refinance of industrial loans and bills, finance to large- and medium-sized industries, and for extending financial services, such as merchant banking and forex services, to the corporate sector; cap. 6,530m., res 51,820m., dep. 38,640m. (Sept. 2004); Chair. and Man. Dir MELEVEETIL DAMODARAN; 5 zonal offices and 36 br. offices.

> **Small Industries Development Bank of India:** 10/10 Madan Mohan Malviya Marg, Lucknow 226 001; tel. (522) 2209517; fax (522) 2209514; e-mail snairan@sidbi.com; internet www.sidbi .com; f. 1990; wholly owned subsidiary of Industrial Development Bank of India; promotes, finances and develops small-scale industries; cap. p.u. 4,500m., res 24,240m. (March 2000); Chair. and Man. Dir N. BALASUBRAMANIAN; 39 offices.

Industrial Finance Corpn of India Ltd: IFCI Tower, 61 Nehru Place, New Delhi 110 019; tel. (11) 26487444; fax (11) 26488471; e-mail ifci@giasd01.vsnl.net.in; internet www.ifciltd.com; f. 1948 to provide medium- and long-term finance to cos and co-operative socs in India, engaged in manufacture, preservation or processing of goods, shipping, mining, hotels and power generation and distribution; promotes industrialization of less developed areas, and sponsors training in management techniques and development banking; cap. p.u. 10,679.5m., res 4,697m. (March 2003); Chair. M. B. MUTHU; Man. Dir V. P. SINGH; 11 regional offices and 6 other offices.

Industrial Investment Bank of India: 19 Netaji Subhas Rd, Kolkata 700 001; tel. (33) 22209941; fax (33) 22208049; e-mail iibiho@vsnl.com; internet www.iibiltd.com; Chair. and Man. Dir Dr B. SAMAL (acting).

National Bank for Agriculture and Rural Development: Plot no. C-24, G Block, Bandra-Kurla Complex, Bandra (East), Mumbai 400 051; tel. (22) 26539060; fax (22) 26539399; e-mail nabrmd@vsnl .net; internet www.nabard.org; f. 1982 to provide credit for agricultural and rural development through commercial, co-operative and regional rural banks; cap. p.u. 20,000m., res 52,910m. (March 2004); held 50% each by the cen. Govt and the Reserve Bank; Man. Dir Y. S. P. THORAT; Chair. RANJANA KUMAR; 28 regional offices, 10 sub-office and 6 training establishments.

STOCK EXCHANGES

There are 23 stock exchanges (with a total of more than 9,985 listed companies) in India, including:

National Stock Exchange of India Ltd: Exchange Plaza, Bandra-Kurla Complex, Bandra (East), Mumbai 400 051; tel. (22) 26598100; fax (22) 26598120; e-mail ignse@nse.co.in; internet www.nseindia .com; f. 1994; Chair. P. P. VORA; Man. Dir RAVI NARAIN.

Ahmedabad Share and Stock Brokers' Association: Kamdhenu Complex, opp. Sahajanand College, Panjarapole, Ambawadi, Ahmedabad 380 015; tel. (79) 26307971; fax (79) 26308877; e-mail ase@ satyam.net.in; f. 1894; 334 mems; Administrator P. K. GHOSH; Exec. Dir RAJIV DESAI.

Bangalore Stock Exchange Ltd: 51 Stock Exchange Towers, 1st Corss, J. C. Rd, Bangalore 560 027; tel. (812) 22995234; fax (80) 22995242; e-mail edbgse@blr.vsnl.net.in; 234 mems; Pres. JAGDISH V. AHUJA; Exec. Dir K. KAMALA.

Bombay Stock Exchange: Phiroze Jeejeebhoy Towers, 25th Floor, Dalal St, Fort, Mumbai 400 001; tel. (22) 22721233; fax (22) 22655720; e-mail info@bseindia.com; internet www.bseindia.com; f. 1875; 711 mems; Chair. RAMESH DAMANI; Exec. Dir. and CEO RAJNI-KANT PATEL; Sec. VISHVESH BHAGAT.

Calcutta Stock Exchange Association Ltd: 7 Lyons Range, Kolkata 700 001; tel. (33) 22206928; fax (33) 22104486; e-mail secretary@cse.india.com; internet www.cse-india.com; f. 1908; 917 mems; Sec. P. K. RAY.

Delhi Stock Exchange Association Ltd: DSE House, 3/1 Asaf Ali Rd, New Delhi 110 002; tel. (11) 23292417; fax (11) 23292181; e-mail dse@vsnl.com; internet www.dseindia.org.in; f. 1947; 379 mems; Exec. Dir P. K. SINGHAL.

Ludhiana Stock Exchange Association Ltd: Feroze Gandhi Market, Ludhiana 141 001; tel. (161) 2412316; fax (161) 2404748; e-mail lse@satyam.net.in; f. 1981; 301 mems; Chair. DINA RATH SHARMA; Gen. Man. H. S. SIDHU.

Madras Stock Exchange Ltd: Exchange Bldg, 11 Second Line Beach, POB 183, Chennai 600 001; tel. (44) 25221085; fax (44) 25244897; e-mail mseed@md3.vsnl.net.in; f. 1760; 171 mems; Pres. D. N. DAS; Exec. Dir P. J. MATHEW.

Mangalore Stock Exchange: Rama Bhavan Complex, 4th Floor, Kodialbail, Mangalore 575 003; tel. (824) 2440581; fax (824) 2440736; 146 mems; Pres. RAMESH RAI; Exec. Dir UMESH P. MASKERI.

Thiruvananthapuram Stock Exchange: Thiruvananthapuram; Dir JOSE JOHN.

Uttar Pradesh Stock Exchange Association Ltd: 14/113 Civil Lines, Kanpur 208 001; tel. (512) 2293174; fax (512) 2293175; e-mail upse@lw1.vsnl.net.in; 520 mems; Pres. R. K. AGARWAL; Exec. Dir Dr J. N. GUPTA.

The other recognized stock exchanges are: Hyderabad, Madhya Pradesh (Indore), Kochi, Pune, Guwahati, Jaipur, Bhubaneswar (Orissa), Coimbatore, Saurashtra, Meerut, Vadodara and Magadh (Patna).

INSURANCE

In January 1973 all Indian and foreign insurance companies were nationalized. The general insurance business in India is now transacted by only four companies, subsidiaries of the General Insurance Corpn of India, formed under the 1972 General Insurance Business Nationalisation Act. The Insurance Regulatory Development Authority Bill, approved by the legislature in December 1999, established a regulatory authority for the insurance sector and henceforth permitted up to 26% investment by foreign companies in new domestic, private-sector insurance companies.

General Insurance Corpn of India (GIC): 'Suraksha', 170 J. Tata Rd, Churchgate, Mumbai 400 020; tel. (22) 22833046; fax (22) 22855423; e-mail pcghosh@gicofindia.com; internet www .gicofindia.com; f. 1973 by the reorg. of 107 private non-life insurance cos (incl. brs of foreign cos operating in the country) as the four subsidiaries listed below; Chair. R. K. JOSHI; Man. Dir P. B. RAM-ANUJAN.

> **National Insurance Co Ltd:** 3 Middleton St, Kolkata 700 071; tel. (33) 22831760; fax (33) 22831712; e-mail hourgent@ nationalinsuranceindia.com; internet www .nationalinsuranceindia.com; Chair. and Man. Dir BIMALENDU CHAKRABARTI; 19 regional offices, 254 divisional offices and 690 branch offices.

> **New India Assurance Co Ltd:** New India Assurance Bldg, 87 Mahatma Gandhi Rd, Fort, Mumbai 400 001; tel. (22) 22674617; fax (22) 22652811; e-mail cmd@niacl.com; internet www.niacl .com; f. 1919; 26 regional offices, 393 divisional offices, 703 branch offices and 37 overseas offices; Chair. and Man. Dir R. BERI.

> **The Oriental Insurance Co Ltd:** Oriental House, A-25/27 Asaf Ali Rd, New Delhi 110 002; tel. (11) 23279221; fax (11) 23263175; e-mail slmohan@oriental.nic.in; internet www.orientalinsurance .nic.in; Chair. and Man. Dir RAMADASS.

> **United India Insurance Co Ltd:** 24 Whites Rd, Chennai 600 014; tel. (44) 28520161; fax (44) 28525280; e-mail knb@united.nic .in; internet www.united.nic.in; Chair. and Man. Dir MAHINDER KUMAR GARG.

Life Insurance Corpn of India (LIC): 'Yogakshema', Jeevan Bima Marg, Mumbai 400 021; tel. (22) 56598701; fax (22) 22880172; e-mail s.mathur@licindia.com; internet www.licindia.com; f. 1956; controls all life insurance business; Chair. R. N. BHARDWAJ; Man. Dirs K. SRIDHAR, A. K. SHUKLA, T. S. VIJAYAN; 100 divisional offices, 2,048 brs and three overseas offices.

Trade and Industry

GOVERNMENT AGENCIES AND DEVELOPMENT ORGANIZATIONS

Coal India Ltd: 10 Netaji Subhas Rd, Kolkata 700 001; tel. (33) 22488099; fax (33) 22435316; internet www.coalindia.nic.in; cen. govt holding co with eight subsidiaries; responsible for almost total (more than 90%) exploration for, planning and production of coal mines; owns 498 coal mines throughout India; marketing of coal and its products; cap. p.u. Rs 72,205.4m., res and surplus Rs 21,324.9m., sales Rs 815.2m. (March 2002); Chair. and Man. Dir SHASHI KUMAR; 515,800 employees (2002).

Cotton Corpn of India Ltd: Plot No. 3A, Sector No. 10, CBD Belapur, Navi Mumbai 400 614; tel. (22) 27579217; fax (22) 27576030; e-mail ccimum@bom7.vsnl.net.in; internet www.cotcorp .com; f. 1970 as an agency in the public sector for the purchase, sale and distribution of home-produced cotton and imported cotton staple fibre; exports long staple cotton; cap. p.u. Rs 250m., res and surplus Rs 2,159.7m., sales Rs 6,280.6m. (March 2002); Chair. and Man. Dir VISHWA NATH.

Export Credit Guarantee Corpn of India Ltd: Express Towers, 10th Floor, Nariman Point, Mumbai 400 021; tel. (22) 22845471; fax (22) 22045253; e-mail ecgcres@bom2.vsnl.net.in; internet www

.ecgcindia.com; f. 1957 to insure for risks involved in exports on credit terms and to supplement credit facilities by issuing guarantees, etc.; cap. Rs 3,900m., res Rs 4,079.3m. (March 2002); Chair. and Man. Dir P. K. Dash; 29 brs.

Fertilizer Corpn of India Ltd: Adil Bhavan, A-14, Sector 1, Noida 201 301; tel. (95120) 2530023; fax (95120) 2537613; e-mail fci@fci .hub.nic.in; f. 1961; fertilizer factories at Sindri (Jharkhand), Gorakhpur (Uttar Pradesh), Talcher (Orissa) and Ramagundam (Andhra Pradesh), producing nitrogenous and some industrial products; cap. Rs 7,547.3m., sales Rs 1,262m. (March 2002); Chair. and Man. Dir Dr Sudhir Krishna.

Food Corpn of India: 16–20 Barakhamba Lane, New Delhi 110 001; tel. (11) 23413871; fax (11) 23413241; e-mail chairman@fci .delhi.nic.in; internet www.fciweb.nic.in; f. 1965 to undertake trading in food grains on a commercial scale but within the framework of an overall govt policy; to provide farmers an assured price for their produce; to supply food grains to the consumer at reasonable prices; also purchases, stores, distributes and sells food grains and other foodstuffs and arranges imports and handling of food grains and fertilizers at the ports; distributes sugar in a number of states and has set up rice mills; cap. p.u. Rs 23,245m., sales Rs 315,562.2m. (March 2002); Chair. and Man. Dir V. K. Malhotra; 59,800 employees (2002).

Handicrafts and Handlooms Exports Corpn of India Ltd: Jawahar Vyapar Bhavan Annexe, 5th Floor, 1 Tolstoy Marg, New Delhi 110 001; tel. (11) 23701086; fax (11) 23701051; e-mail hhecnd@ ndc.vsnl.net.in; internet www.hhecworld.com; f. 1958; govt undertaking dealing in export of handicrafts, handloom goods, ready-to-wear clothes, carpets, jute, leather and precious jewellery, and import of bullion and raw silk; promotes exports and trade development; cap. p.u. Rs 138.2m., res and surplus Rs 91.8m., sales Rs 3,339.4m. (March 2002); Chair. and Man. Dir K. K. Sinha.

Housing and Urban Development Corpn Ltd: HUDCO Bhavan, India Habitat Centre, Lodhi Rd, New Delhi 110 003; tel. (11) 24648160; fax (11) 24625308; e-mail hudco@hudco.org; internet www.hudcoindia.com; f. 1970 to finance and undertake housing and urban development programmes including the establishment of new or satellite towns and building material industries; cap. p.u. Rs 14,080m., res and surplus Rs 8,899.7m., sales Rs 20,757.6m. (March 2002); 21 brs; Chair. and Man. Dir P. S. Rana; Sec. Gopal Krishan.

India Trade Promotion Organisation (ITPO): Pragati Bhavan, Pragati Maidan, Lal Bahadur Shastri Marg, New Delhi 110 001; tel. (11) 23371540; fax (11) 23318142; e-mail itpo@giasdl10.vsnl.net.in; internet www.indiatradepromotion.org; f. 1992 following merger; promotes selective development of exports of high quality products; arranges investment in export-orientated ventures undertaken by India with foreign collaboration; organizes trade fairs; operates Trade Information Centre; cap. p.u. Rs 2.5m., res and surplus Rs 2,311.8m., sales Rs 818.4m. (March 2002); regional offices in Bangalore, Mumbai, Kolkata and Chennai, and international offices in Frankfurt, New York, Moscow, São Paulo and Tokyo; Chair. and Man. Dir N. N. Khanna; Exec. Dir Kanjan Chatterjee.

Jute Corpn of India Ltd: 15-N, Nellie Sengupta Sarani, 7th Floor, Kolkata 700 087; tel. (33) 22166770; fax (33) 22166771; e-mail jutecorp@vsnl.net.in; internet www.jutecorp.com; f. 1971; objects: (i) to undertake price support operations in respect of raw jute; (ii) to ensure remunerative prices to producers through efficient marketing; (iii) to operate a buffer stock to stabilize raw jute prices; (iv) to handle the import and export of raw jute; (v) to promote the export of jute goods; cap. p.u. Rs 50m., sales Rs 576.0m. (March 2002); Chair. and Man. Dir A. K. Khastagir.

Minerals and Metals Trading Corpn of India Ltd (MMTC): Scope Complex, Core-1, 7 Institutional Areas, Lodi Rd, New Delhi 110 003; tel. (11) 24362200; fax (11) 24360724; e-mail cpmr@ mmtclimited.com; internet www.mmtclimited.com; f. 1963; export of iron and manganese ore, ferro-manganese, finished stainless steel products, engineering, agricultural and marine products, textiles, leather items, chemicals and pharmaceuticals, mica, coal and other minor minerals; import of steel, non-ferrous metals, rough diamonds, fertilizers, etc. for supply to industrial units in the country; cap. p.u. Rs 500m., sales Rs 62,546.8m. (March 2003); res Rs 6,348.0m. (March 2004); 9 regional offices and 16 sub-regional offices in India; foreign offices in Japan, the Republic of Korea, Jordan and Romania; Chair. and Man. Dir Shiv Dayal Kapoor; 2,378 employees (2002).

National Co-operative Development Corpn: 4 Siri Institutional Area, Hauz Khas, New Delhi 110 016; tel. (11) 26569246; fax (11) 26962370; e-mail editor@ncdc.stpn.soft.net; internet ncdc.nic.in; f. 1963 to plan, promote and finance country-wide programmes through co-operative societies for the production, processing, marketing, storage, export and import of agricultural produce, foodstuffs and notified commodities; also programmes for the development of poultry, dairy, fish products, coir, handlooms, distribution of

consumer articles in rural areas, industrial and service co-operatives and minor forest produce in the co-operative sector; 18 regional directorates; Pres. Rajnath Singh; Man. Dir Dinesh Rai.

National Industrial Development Corpn Ltd: Chanakya Bhavan, Africa Ave, New Delhi 110 021; tel. (11) 24670153; fax (11) 26876166; e-mail nidc123@del2.vsnl.net.in; internet www .exploreindia.com/nidc; f. 1954; consultative engineering, management and infrastructure services to cen. and state govts, public and private sector enterprises, the UN and overseas investors; cap. p.u. Rs 18.7m. (March 2002); Chair. and Man. Dir Pranab Ghosh.

National Mineral Development Corpn Ltd: Khanij Bhavan, 10-3-311/A Castle Hills, Masab Tank, POB 1352, Hyderabad 500 028; tel. (40) 23538713; fax (40) 23538711; e-mail nmdchyd@hdl.vsnl.net .in; internet www.nmdc-india.com; f. 1958; cen. govt undertaking; to exploit minerals (excluding coal, atomic minerals, lignite, petroleum and natural gas) in public sector; may buy, take on lease or otherwise acquire mines for prospecting, development and exploitation; iron ore mines at Bailadila-11C, Bailadila-14 and Bailadila-5 in Madhya Pradesh, and at Donimalai in Karnataka State; new 5m. metric ton iron ore mine under construction at Bailadila-10/11A; diamond mines at Panna in Madhya Pradesh; research and development laboratories and consultancy services covering all aspects of mineral exploitation at Hyderabad; investigates mineral projects; cap. p.u. Rs 1,321.6m., res and surplus Rs 18,932m., sales Rs 14,536.9m. (March 2004); Chair. and Man. Dir B. Ramesh Kumar.

National Productivity Council: Utpadakta Bhavan, Lodi Rd, New Delhi 110 003; tel. (11) 24690331; fax (11) 24615002; e-mail npc@ren02.nic.in; internet www.npcindia.org; f. 1958 to increase productivity and to improve quality by improved techniques which aim at efficient and proper utilization of available resources; autonomous body representing national orgs of employers and labour, govt ministries, professional orgs, local productivity councils, small-scale industries and other interests; 12 regional directorates, 2 regional offices; 75 mems; Chair. V. Govindarajan; Dir-Gen. S. K. Pachauri.

National Research Development Corpn: 20–22 Zamroodpur Community Centre, Kailash Colony Extension, New Delhi 110 048; tel. (11) 26417821; fax (11) 26460506; e-mail nrdc@giasd101.vsnl.net .in; internet www.nrdcindia.com; f. 1953 to stimulate development and commercial exploitation of new inventions with financial and technical aid; finances development projects to set up demonstration units in collaboration with industry; exports technology; cap. p.u. Rs 44.2m., res and surplus Rs 47.6m. (March 2002); Man. Dir N. K. Sharma.

National Seeds Corpn Ltd: Beej Bhavan, Pusa, New Delhi 110 012; tel. (11) 25842379; fax (11) 25846462; e-mail nsc@vsnl.com; internet www.nscindia.com; f. 1963 to improve and develop the seed industry; cap. p.u. Rs 206.2m., res and surplus Rs 216.1m., sales Rs 658.5m. (March 2002); Chair. and Man. Dir Kumar Bhatia.

The National Small Industries Corpn Ltd: NSIC Bhavan, Okhla Industrial Estate, New Delhi 110 020; tel. (11) 26926067; fax (11) 26926820; e-mail cmd@nsicindia.com; internet www.nsicindia.com; f. 1955 to aid, advise, finance and promote the interests of small industries; establishes and supplies machinery for small industries in other developing countries on turn-key basis; cap. p.u. Rs 1,679.9m., res and surplus Rs 87.2m., sales Rs 1,851m. (March 2002); all shares held by the Govt; Chair. and Man. Dir Rajiv Bhatnagar.

PEC Ltd: 'Hansalaya', 15 Barakhamba Rd, New Delhi 110 001; tel. (11) 23313619; fax (11) 23314797; e-mail pec@pecltd.org; internet www.pecltd.org; f. 1971; export of engineering, industrial and railway equipment; undertakes turn-key and other projects and management consultancy abroad; countertrade, trading in agro-commodities, construction materials (steel, cement, clinkers, etc.) and fertilizers; cap. p.u. Rs 15m., res and surplus Rs 245.6m., sales Rs 22,499.9m. (March 2002); Chair. and Man. Dir A. K. Srivastava.

Rehabilitation Industries Corpn Ltd: 25 Mirza Ghalib St, Kolkata 700 016; tel. (33) 22441185; fax (33) 22451055; f. 1959 to create employment opportunities through multi-product industries, ranging from consumer goods to engineering products and services, for refugees from Bangladesh and migrants from Pakistan, repatriates from Myanmar and Sri Lanka, and other immigrants of Indian extraction; cap. p.u. Rs 47.6m. (March 2000); Chair. and Man. Dir Ashok Basu.

State Farms Corpn of India Ltd: Farm Bhavan, 14–15 Nehru Place, New Delhi 110 019; tel. (11) 26446903; fax (11) 26226898; e-mail sfci@vsnl.net; f. 1969 to administer the central state farms; activities include the production of quality seeds of high-yielding varieties of wheat, paddy, maize, bajra and jowar; advises on soil conservation, reclamation and development of waste and forest land; consultancy services on farm mechanization; auth. cap. Rs 241.9m., res and surplus Rs 371.0m., sales Rs 465.4m. (March 2002); Chair. Bhaskar Barua; Man. Dir Ashish Bahuguna.

State Trading Corpn of India Ltd: Jawahar Vyapar Bhavan, Tolstoy Marg, New Delhi 110 001; tel. (11) 23701100; fax (11) 23701123; e-mail stcindia@vsnl.net; internet www.stcindia.com; f. 1956; govt undertaking dealing in exports and imports; cap. p.u. Rs 300m., res and surplus Rs 2,628m., sales Rs 83,487.5m. (March 2004); 10 regional brs, 5 sub-brs and 1 office overseas; Chair. and Man. Dir Dr ARVIND PANDALAI; 1,069 employees (2002).

Steel Authority of India Ltd (SAIL): Ispat Bhavan, Lodi Rd, POB 3049, New Delhi 110 013; tel. (11) 24367481; fax (11) 24367015; e-mail sail.co@vsnl.com; internet www.sail.co.in; f. 1973 to provide co-ordinated development of the steel industry in the public sector; integrated steel plants at Bhilai, Bokaro, Durgapur, Rourkela; stainless and alloy steel plants at Bhadrawati, Durgapur and Salem; subsidiaries: Bhilai Oxygen Ltd (Chhattisgarh), Indian Iron and Steel Co (West Bengal) and Maharashtra Elektrosmelt Ltd; combined crude steel capacity is 12m. metric tons annually; equity cap. Rs 41,304m., res and surplus Rs 9,072.7m., sales Rs 248,773.1m. (March 2004); Chair. V. S. JAIN; 131,910 employees (March 2004).

Tea Board of India: 14 B. T. M. Sarani (Brabourne Rd), POB 2172, Kolkata 700 001; tel. (33) 22351411; fax (33) 22215715; internet www.teaindia.org; provides financial assistance to tea research stations; sponsors and finances independent research projects in universities and tech. institutions to supplement the work of tea research establishments; also promotes tea production and export; Chair. NABA KRISHNA DAS.

CHAMBERS OF COMMERCE

Associated Chambers of Commerce and Industry of India (ASSOCHAM): 147B, Gautam Nagar, Gulmohar Enclave, New Delhi 110 049; tel. (11) 26512477; fax (11) 26512154; e-mail assocham@sansad.nic.in; internet www.assocham.org; f. 1920; central org. of 350 chambers of commerce and industry and industrial asscns representing more than 130,000 cos throughout India; 6 promoter chambers, 115 ordinary mems, 45 patron mems and 500 corporate associates; Pres. MAHENDRA K. SANGHI; Sec.-Gen. D. S. RAWAT (acting).

Federation of Indian Chambers of Commerce and Industry (FICCI): Federation House, Tansen Marg, New Delhi 110 001; tel. (11) 23738760; fax (11) 23320714; e-mail ficci.bisnet@gems.vsnl.net .in; internet www.bisnetindia.com; f. 1927; 436 ordinary mems, 49 corporate mems, 1,376 assoc. mems; Pres. ONKAR S. KANWAR; Sec.-Gen. Dr AMIT MITRA.

ICC India: Federation House, Tansen Marg, New Delhi 110 001; tel. (11) 23738760; fax (11) 23320714; e-mail iccindia@del2.vsnl.net .in; internet www.iccindiaonline.org; f. 1929; 43 org. mems, 375 corporate mems, 8 patron mems, 113 cttee mems; Pres. SUDHIR JALAN; Exec. Dir M. K. SANGHI.

Associated Chambers of Commerce and Industry of Uttar Pradesh: 2/210 Vikas Khand, Gomti Nagar, Lucknow 226 010; tel. (522) 2301957; fax (522) 2301958; e-mail asochmup@del.sanchar.in; internet www.asochamup.org; 405 mems; Pres. JYOTI MASKARA; Sec.-Gen. R. K. JAIN.

Bengal Chamber of Commerce and Industry: 6 Netaji Subhas Rd, Kolkata 700 001; tel. (33) 22203733; fax (33) 22201289; e-mail bencham@cal3.vsnl.net.in; f. 1853; 210 mems; Pres. BISWADEEP GUPTA; Sec. KHOKAN MOOKERJI.

Bengal National Chamber of Commerce and Industry: BNCCI House, 23 Sir R. N. Mukherjee Rd, Kolkata 700 001; tel. (33) 22482951; fax (33) 22487058; e-mail bncci@bncci.com; internet www .bncci.com; f. 1887; 500 mems, 35 affiliated industrial and trading asscns; Pres. S. K. CHAKRABORTY; Sec. D. P. NAG.

Bharat Chamber of Commerce: 9 Park Mansions, 2nd Floor, 57-A Park Street, Kolkata, 700 016; tel. (33) 22299591; fax (33) 22294947; e-mail bcc@cal2.vsnl.net.in; f. 1900; c. 500 mems; Pres. N. R. GOENKA; Sec. K. SARMA.

Bihar Chamber of Commerce: Khem Chand Chaudhary Marg, POB 71, Patna 800 001; tel. (612) 2670535; fax (612) 2689505; e-mail bcc_chamber@rediffmail.com; f. 1926; 552 ordinary mems; Pres. S. K. CHOUDHARY; Sec.-Gen. RAJA BABU GUPTA.

Bombay Chamber of Commerce and Industry: Mackinnon Mackenzie Bldg, 4 Shoorji Vallabhdas Rd, Ballard Estate, POB 473, Mumbai 400 001; tel. (22) 22614681; fax (22) 22621213; e-mail bcci@ bombaychamber.com; internet www.bombaychamber.com; f. 1836; 935 ordinary mems, 650 assoc. mems, 75 hon. mems; Pres. PRASAD MENON; Exec. Dir L. A. D'SOUZA.

Calcutta Chamber of Commerce: 18H Park St, Stephen Court, Kolkata 700 071; tel. (33) 22298236; fax (33) 22298961; e-mail calchamb@cal3.vsnl.net.in; 300 mems; Pres. PRADEEP SANCHETI; Deputy Sec. Dr T. ROY.

Chamber of Commerce and Industry (Regd): OB 31, Rail Head Complex, Jammu 180 012; tel. (191) 2472266; fax (191) 2472255; 1,069 mems; Pres. RAM SAHAI; Sec.-Gen. RAJENDRA MOTIAL.

Cochin Chamber of Commerce and Industry: Bristow Rd, Willingdon Island, POB 503, Kochi 682 003; tel. (484) 2668349; fax (484) 2668651; e-mail cochinchamber@eth.net; internet www .cochinchamber.org; f. 1857; 200 mems; Pres. A. K. NAIR; Sec. DOMINIC J. MECHERY.

Federation of Andhra Pradesh Chambers of Commerce and Industry: Federation House, 11-6-841, Red Hills, POB 14, Hyderabad 500 004; tel. (40) 23393658; fax (40) 23393712; e-mail info@ fapcci.org; internet www.fapcci.org; f. 1917; 2,510 mems; Pres. O. P. GOENKA RAO; Sec. G. HEMALATA.

Federation of Karnataka Chambers of Commerce and Industry: Kempegowda Rd, Bangalore 560 009; tel. (80) 22262355; fax (80) 22251826; e-mail fkcci@mantraonline.com; internet www .fkcci.net; f. 1916; 2,100 mems; Pres. B. S. ARUN KUMAR; Sec. C. MANOHAR.

Federation of Madhya Pradesh Chambers of Commerce and Industry: Udyog Bhavan, 129A Malviya Nagar, Bhopal 462 003; tel. (755) 2573612; fax (755) 2551451; e-mail fmcci@bom6.vsnl.net.in; f. 1975; 500 ordinary mems, 58 asscn mems; Pres. RANJIT VITHALDAS; Sec.-Gen. PRAFULLA MAHESHWARI.

Goa Chamber of Commerce and Industry: Goa Chamber Bldg, Rua de Ormuz, POB 59, Panjim 403 001; tel. (832) 2223420; fax (832) 2429010; e-mail gcci@goatelecom.com; internet www.goachamber .org; f. 1908; 360 mems; Pres. D. V. SALGAONKAR; Exec. Sec. Air Cmmdre (retd) P. K. PINTO.

Gujarat Chamber of Commerce and Industry: Shri Ambica Mills, Gujarat Chamber Bldg, Ashram Rd, POB 4045, Ahmedabad 380 009; tel. (79) 26582301; fax (79) 26587992; e-mail bis@ gujaratchamber.org; internet www.gujaratchamber.org; f. 1949; 7,713 mems; Pres. SHREYAS V. PANDYA; Sec.-Gen. S. C. SHAH.

Indian Chamber of Commerce: India Exchange, 4 India Exchange Place, India Exchange Bldg, Kolkata 700 001; tel. (33) 22203243; fax (33) 22213377; e-mail info@indianchamber.org; internet www.indianchamber.org; f. 1925; 300 ordinary mems, 42 assoc. mems, 20 corporate group mems, 17 affiliated asscns; Pres. ANUP SINGH; Sec.-Gen. NAZEEB ARIF.

Indian Chamber of Commerce and Industry: 49 Community Centre, New Friends Colony, New Delhi 110 065; tel. (11) 26836468; fax (11) 26840776; e-mail iccind@yahoo.co.in; Pres. LALIT K. MODI; Hon. Sec. R. P. SWAMI.

Indian Merchants' Chamber: IMC Bldg, IMC Marg, Churchgate, Mumbai 400 020; tel. (22) 22046632; fax (22) 22048508; e-mail imc@ imcnet.org; internet www.imcnet.org; f. 1907; 185 asscn mems, 2,915 mem. firms; Pres. NANIK RUPANI; Sec.-Gen. P. N. MOGRE.

Karnataka Chamber of Commerce and Industry: G. Mahadevappa Karnataka Chamber Bldg, Jayachamaraj Nagar, Hubli 580 020; tel. (836) 2218234; fax (836) 2360933; e-mail kccihble@sify.com; internet www.kccihubli.org; f. 1928; 2,500 mems; Pres. SHANKARANNA I. MUNAVALLI; Hon. Sec. MAHENDRA LADHAD.

Madhya Pradesh Chamber of Commerce and Industry: Chamber Bhavan, Sanatan Dharam Mandir Marg, Gwalior 474 009; tel. (751) 2332916; fax (751) 2323844; f. 1906; 1,705 mems; Pres. SATISH AJMERA; Sec. AMBIKA P. BEHERA.

Madras Chamber of Commerce and Industry: Karumuttu Centre, 634 Anna Salai, Chennai 600 035; tel. (44) 24349452; fax (44) 24349164; e-mail mascham@md3.vsnl.net.in; internet www .mascham.com; f. 1836; 267 mem. firms, 48 assoc., 16 affiliated, 11 honorary, 3 others; Pres. MURALI VENKATRAMAN; Sec. R. SUBRAMANIAN.

Maharashtra Chamber of Commerce and Industry: Oricon House, 6th Floor, 12 K. Dubhash Marg, Fort, Mumbai 400 001; tel. (22) 22855259; fax (22) 22855861; e-mail maharashtrachamber@ vsnl.com; f. 1927; 3,000 mems; Pres. EKANATH K. THAKUR; Sec.-Gen. DILIP SALVEKAR.

Mahratta Chamber of Commerce, Industries and Agriculture: Tilak Rd, POB 525, Pune 411 002; tel. (20) 24440371; fax (20) 24447902; e-mail mccipune@vsnl.com; internet www.mcciapune .com; f. 1934; 1,510 mems; Pres. MADHUR BAJAJ; Dir.-Gen. D. K. ABHYANKAR.

Merchants' Chamber of Commerce: 15B Hemanta Basu Sarani, Kolkata 700 001; tel. (33) 22483123; fax (33) 22488657; e-mail mercham@cal.vsnl.net.in; internet www.mercham.org; f. 1901; 600 mems; Pres. ADITYA VARDHAN AGARWAL; Dir-Gen. R. K. SEN.

Merchants' Chamber of Uttar Pradesh: 14/76 Civil Lines, Kanpur 208 001; tel. and fax (512) 2531306; e-mail info@ merchantschamber-up.com; internet merchantschamber-up.com; f. 1932; 180 mems; Pres. M. S. AGARWAL; Sec. A. K. SINHA.

North India Chamber of Commerce and Industry: 9 Gandhi Rd, Dehra Dun; tel. (935) 223479; f. 1967; 105 ordinary mems, 29 asscn mems, 7 mem. firms, 91 assoc. mems; Pres. DEV PANDHI; Hon. Sec. ASHOK K. NARANG.

Oriental Chamber of Commerce: 6A Dr Rajendra Prasad Sarani (Clive Row), Kolkata 700 001; tel. (33) 22202120; fax (33) 22203609; e-mail orientchamb@vsnl.net; f. 1932; 245 ordinary mems, 3 assoc. mems; Pres. IMRAN AHMED; Sec. Kazi ABU ZOBER.

PHD Chamber of Commerce and Industry: PHD House, Thapar Floor, 4/2 Siri Institutional Area, opp. Asian Games Village, POB 130, New Delhi 110 016; tel. (11) 26863801; fax (11) 26863135; e-mail phdcci@del2.vsnl.net.in; internet www.phdcci.org; f. 1905; 1,285 mems, 115 asscn mems; Pres. K. N. MEMANI; Sec. Dr B. P. DHAKA.

Rajasthan Chamber of Commerce and Industry: Rajasthan Chamber Bhavan, M. I. Rd, Jaipur 302 003; tel. (141) 2565163; fax (141) 2561419; e-mail info@rajchamber.com; internet www .rajchamber.com; 575 mems; Pres. MAHENDRA S. DAGA; Hon. Sec.-Gen. Dr K. L. JAIN.

Southern India Chamber of Commerce and Industry: Indian Chamber Bldgs, 6 Esplanade, POB 1208, Chennai 600 108; tel. (44) 25342228; fax (44) 25341876; e-mail sicci@md3.vsnl.net.in; f. 1909; 1,000 mems; Pres. R. VEERAMANI; Sec. S. RAGHAVAN.

Upper India Chamber of Commerce: 113/47, Swaroop Nagar, POB 63, Kanpur 208 002; tel. and fax (512) 2210684; f. 1888; 80 mems; Pres. R. R. MANSINGH; Sec. S. P. SRIVASTAVA.

Utkal Chamber of Commerce and Industry Ltd: Barabati Stadium, Cuttack 753 005; tel. (671) 2301211; fax (671) 2302059; e-mail utkalchamber@yahoo.co.in; f. 1964; 208 mems; Pres. M. U. RAO; Sec. DEBABRATA DAS.

Uttar Pradesh Chamber of Commerce: 15/197 Civil Lines, Kanpur 208 001; tel. 2211696; f. 1914; 200 mems; Pres. Dr B. K. MODI; Sec. AFTAB SAMI.

INDUSTRIAL AND TRADE ASSOCIATIONS

Ahmedabad Textile Mills' Association: Ashram Rd, Navrangpura, POB 4056, Ahmedabad 380 009; tel. (79) 26582273; fax (79) 26588574; e-mail sec_gen@atmaahd.com; f. 1891; 21 mems; Pres. CHINTAN N. PARIKH; Sec.-Gen. ABHINAVA SHUKLA.

All India Federation of Master Printers: 605 Madhuban, 55 Nehru Place, New Delhi 110 019; tel. (11) 26451742; fax (11) 26451743; e-mail aifmp@vsnl.com; f. 1953; 50 affiliates, 800 mems; Pres. SURENDRA B. DHOTE; Hon. Gen. Sec. R. BALA.

All India Manufacturers' Organization (AIMO): Jeevan Sahakar, 4th Floor, Sir P.M. Rd, Fort, Mumbai 400 001; tel. (22) 22661016; fax (22) 22660838; e-mail aimoindia@roltanet.com; f. 1941; 800 mems; Pres. BABULAL B. TODI; Hon. Gen. Sec. JAGDISH P. TODI.

All India Plastics Manufacturers' Association: AIPMA House, A-52, St No. 1, MIDC, Andheri (East), Mumbai 400 093; tel. (22) 28217324; fax (22) 28216390; e-mail aipma@bom2.vsnl.net.in; internet www.aipma.net; f. 1947; 1,800 mems; Chair. SURESH J. ATRE; Hon. Sec. AJAY DESAI.

All India Shippers' Council: Federation House, Tansen Marg, New Delhi 110 001; tel. (11) 23738760; fax (11) 23320714; f. 1967; 82 mems; Chair. RAMU S. DEORA; Sec. M. Y. REDDY.

Association of Man-made Fibre Industry of India: Resham Bhavan, 78 Veer Nariman Rd, Mumbai 400 020; tel. (22) 22040009; fax (22) 22049172; f. 1954; 7 mems; Pres. P. S. SHARMA; Sec. S. K. MARATHE.

Automotive Component Manufacturers' Association of India: 6th Floor, The Capital Court, Olof Parme Marg, Munirka, New Delhi 110 067; tel. (11) 26160315; fax (11) 26160317; e-mail acma@vsnl .com; internet www.acmainfo.com; 486 mems; Pres. DEEP KAPURIA; Exec. Dir VISHNU MATHUR.

Automotive Tyre Manufacturers' Association: PHD House, opp. Asian Games Village, Siri Fort Institutional Area, New Delhi 110 016; tel. (11) 26851187; fax (11) 26864799; e-mail atma@nda .vsnl.net.in; internet www.atmaindia.com; 10 mems; Chair. RAGHUPATI SINGHANIA; Dir-Gen. D. RAVINDRAN.

Bharat Krishak Samaj (Farmers' Forum, India): Dr Panjabrao Deshmukh Krishak Bhavan, A-1 Nizamuddin West, New Delhi 110 013; tel. (11) 24359508; fax (11) 24359509; e-mail ffi@mantraonline .com; f. 1954; national farmers' org.; 5m. ordinary mems, 75,000 life mems; Chair. Dr BAL RAM JAKHAR; Exec. Chair. and Gen. Sec. Dr KRISHAN BIR CHAUDHARY.

Bombay Metal Exchange Ltd: 88/90 Kika St, 1st Floor, Gulalwadi, Mumbai 400 004; tel. (22) 22421964; fax (22) 22422640; e-mail bme@bom8.vsnl.net.in; f. 1950; promotes trade and industry in nonferrous metals; 460 mems; Pres. ROHIT V. SHAH; Sec. T. S. B. IYER.

Bombay Shroffs Association: 233 Sheikh Memon St, Mumbai 400 002; tel. (22) 23425588; f. 1910; 325 mems; Pres. PRANLAL R. SHETH; Hon. Secs KAMLESH C. SHAH, SANJAY I. PARIKH.

Calcutta Flour Mills Association: 25/B Shakespeare Sarani, Kolkata 700 017; tel. (33) 22476723; fax (33) 22475944; e-mail swaika@vsnl.com; f. 1932; 28 mems; Chair. NAVNEET SWAIKA; Hon. Sec. RAVI BHAGAT.

Calcutta Tea Traders' Association: 6 Netaji Subhas Rd, Kolkata 700 001; tel. (33) 22201574; fax (33) 22201289; e-mail ctta@cal3.vsnl .net.in; internet www.cttacal.org; f. 1886; 1,300 mems; Chair. BHAGAT ARYA; Sec. J. KALYANA SUNDARAM.

Cement Manufacturers' Association: CMA Tower, A-2E, Sector 24, Noida 201 301; tel. (95120) 2411955; fax (95120) 2411956; e-mail cmand@vsnl.com; internet cmaindia.org; 54 mems; 126 major cement plants; Pres. N. SRINIVASAN; Sec.-Gen. E. N. MURPHY.

Confederation of Indian Industry (CII): 23 Institutional Area, Lodi Rd, New Delhi 110 003; tel. (11) 24629994; fax (11) 24626149; e-mail cii@ciionline.org; internet www.ciionline.org; f. 1974; 3,800 mem. cos; Pres. SUNIL KANT MUNJAL; Dir-Gen. N. SRINIVASAN.

Consumer Electronics and Television Manufacturers' Association (CETMA): J-13, Jangpura Extension, New Delhi 110 014; tel. (11) 24327777; fax (11) 24321616; e-mail cetma@eth.net; internet www.cetmaindia.org; f. 1978; 85 mems; Pres. RAJIV KARWAL; Sec.-Gen. SURESH KHANNA.

East India Cotton Association: Cotton Exchange Bldg, 2nd Floor, Cotton Green, Mumbai 400 033; tel. (22) 23704401; fax (22) 23700337; e-mail eica@bom8.vsnl.net.in; internet www.eicaindia .org; f. 1921; 415 mems; Pres. K. F. JHUNJHUNWALA; Exec. Dir and Sec.-Gen. S. M. JOSHI.

Electronic Component Industries Association (ELCINA): ELCINA House, 422 Okhla Industrial Estate, New Delhi 110 020; tel. (11) 26928053; fax (11) 26923440; e-mail elcina@vsnl.com; internet www.elcina.com; f. 1967; 255 mems; Pres. R. G. DESHPANDE; Sec.-Gen. RAJOO GOEL.

Federation of Automobile Dealers Associations: 805 Surya Kiran, 19 Kasturba Gandhi Marg, New Delhi 110 001; tel. (11) 23320046; fax (11) 23320093; e-mail fadadelhi@vsnl.net; internet www.fadaweb.com; f. 1964; Pres. JAYENDRA KACHALIA; Sec.-Gen. GULSHAN AHUJA; 1,072 mems.

Federation of Gujarat Industries: Sidcup Tower, 4th Floor, Race Course, Vadodara 390 007; tel. (265) 2311101; fax (265) 2339054; e-mail info@fgibaroda.org; internet www.fgibaroda.org; f. 1918; 350 mems; Pres. RAM DEVIDAYAL; Sec. Dr PARESH RAVAL.

Federation of Hotel and Restaurant Associations of India: B-82 Himalaya House, 23 K. G. Marg, New Delhi 110 001; tel. (11) 23322634; fax (11) 23322645; e-mail fhrai@vsnl.com; internet www .fhrai.com; f. 1955; 2,572 mems; Pres. S. K. KHULLAR; Sec.-Gen. SHYAM SURI.

Federation of Indian Export Organisations: PHD House, 3rd Floor, Siri Institutional Area, Hauz Khas, New Delhi 110 016; tel. (11) 26851310; fax (11) 26863087; e-mail fieo@nda.vsnl.net.in; internet www.fieo.org; f. 1965; 8,000 mems; Pres. O. P. GARG; Dir-Gen. G. BALACHANDHRAN.

The Fertiliser Association of India: 10 Shaheed Jit Singh Marg, New Delhi 110 067; tel. (11) 26567144; fax (11) 26960052; e-mail secy@faidelhi.org; internet www.faidelhi.org; f. 1955; 1,414 mems; Chair. H. C. GROVER; Dir-Gen. B. K. SAHA; Sec. DEEPAK BHANDARI.

Grain, Rice and Oilseeds Merchants' Association: 14-C, Groma House, 2nd Floor, Sector 19, Vashi, Navi Mumbai 400 703; tel. (22) 27897454; fax (22) 27897458; e-mail groma@vsnl.com; internet www .groma.org; f. 1899; 1,200 mems; Pres. SHARADKUMAR D. MARU.

Indian Drug Manufacturers' Association: 102B Poonam Chambers, Dr A. B. Rd, Worli, Mumbai 400 018; tel. (22) 24944624; fax (22) 24950723; e-mail idma@giasbm01.vsnl.net.in; 600 mems; Pres. T. RAVICHANDIRAM; Sec.-Gen. I. A. ALVA.

Indian Electrical and Electronics Manufacturers' Association (IEEMA): 501 Kakad Chambers, 132 Dr Annie Besant Rd, Worli, Mumbai 400 018; tel. (22) 24936528; fax (22) 24932705; e-mail mumbai@ieema.org; internet www.ieema.org; f. 1948; 400 mems; Pres. P. KRISHNAKUMAR; Sec.-Gen. SUNIL P. MORE.

Indian Jute Mills Association: Royal Exchange, 6 Netaji Subhas Rd, Kolkata 700 001; tel. (33) 22209918; fax (33) 22205643; e-mail ijma@cal2.vsnl.net.in; sponsors and operates export promotion, research and product development; regulates labour relations; 36 mems; Chair. A. K. BAJORIA; Sec. SARIT RAY.

Indian Leather Products Association: Suite 6, Chatterjee International Centre, 14th Floor, 33-A, Jawaharlal Nehru Rd, Kolkata 700 071; tel. (33) 22267102; fax (33) 22468339; e-mail ilpa@cal2.vsnl .net.in; 120 mems; Pres. M. V. KULKARNI; Exec. Dir Dr P. K. DEY.

Indian Machine Tool Manufacturers' Association: 17 Nangal Raya Commercial Complex, New Delhi 110 046; tel. (11) 25592814; fax (11) 25599882; e-mail imtma@del2.vsnl.net.in; internet www.imtma.org; 400 mems; Pres. V. S. GOINDI; Sec. A. MUKHERJEE.

Indian Mining Association: 6 Netaji Subhas Rd, Kolkata 700 001; tel. (33) 22203733; f. 1892; 50 mems; Sec. K. MUKERJEE.

Indian Mining Federation: 135 Biplabi Rash Behari Basu Rd, 2nd Floor, Kolkata 700 001; tel. (33) 22428975; f. 1913; 40 mems; Chair. V. K. ARORA; Sec. S. K. GHOSE.

Indian Motion Picture Producers' Association: IMPPA House, Dr Ambedkar Rd, Bandra (West), Mumbai 400 050; tel. (22) 26486344; fax (22) 26480757; e-mail imppa@imppa.net; f. 1938; 2,000 mems; Pres. SUSHMA SHAROVANI; Dir-Gen. DINKAR CHOWDHARY.

Indian National Shipowners' Association: 22 Maker Tower F, Cuffe Parade, Mumbai 400 005; tel. (22) 22182103; fax (22) 22182104; e-mail insa@insa.org.in; internet www.insa.org.in; f. 1929; 29 mems; Pres. P. K. SRIVASTAVA; Sec.-Gen. S. S. KULKARNI.

Indian Oilseeds & Produce Exporters' Association (IOPEA): 78/79 Bajaj Bhavan, Nariman Point, Mumbai 400 021; tel. (22) 22023225; fax (22) 22029236; e-mail iopea@bom3.vsnl.net.in; internet www.iopea.org; f. 1956; 350 mems; Chair. KISHOR TANNA; Sec. A. N. SUBRAMANIAN.

Indian Refractory Makers' Association: 5 Lala Lajpat Rai Sarani, 4th Floor, Kolkata 700 020; tel. (33) 22810868; fax (33) 22814357; e-mail irma@vsnl.com; internet www.irmaindia.org; 85 mems; Chair. U. C. DEVESHWAR; Exec. Dir P. DAS GUPTA.

Indian Soap and Toiletries Makers' Association: 614 Raheja Centre, Free Press Journal Marg, Mumbai 400 021; tel. (22) 22824115; fax (22) 22853649; e-mail istma@bom3.vsnl.net.in; 38 mems; Pres. H. K. PRESS; Sec.-Gen. R. HARIHARAN.

Indian Sugar Mills' Association: Ansal Plaza, C-Block, 2nd Floor, Andrews Ganj, New Delhi 110 049; tel. (11) 26262294; fax (11) 26263231; e-mail sugarmil@nda.vsnl.net.in; internet www.indiansugar.com; f. 1932; 181 mems; Pres. VIVEK M. PITTIE; Dir-Gen. S. L. JAIN.

Indian Tea Association: Royal Exchange, 6 Netaji Subhas Rd, Kolkata 700 001; tel. (33) 22102474; fax (33) 22434301; e-mail ita@cal2.vsnl.net.in; internet www.indiatea.org; f. 1881; 210 mem. cos; 420 tea estates; Chair. C. K. DHANUKA; Sec.-Gen. D. CHAKRABARTI.

Indian Woollen Mills' Federation: Churchgate Chambers, 7th Floor, 5 New Marine Lines, Mumbai 400 020; tel. (22) 22624372; fax (22) 22624675; e-mail iwmf@vsnl.com; f. 1963; 50 mems; Chair. V. K. BHARTIA; Sec.-Gen. A. C. CHAUDHURI.

Industries and Commerce Association: ICO Association Rd, POB 70, Dhanbad 826 001; tel. (326) 2303147; fax (326) 2303787; f. 1933; 70 mems; Pres. B. N. SINGH; Sec. K. R. CHAKRAVARTY.

Jute Balers' Association: 12 India Exchange Place, Kolkata 700 001; tel. (33) 22201491; f. 1909; 300 mems; Chair. NIRMAL KUMAR BHUTORIA; Sec. SUJIT CHOUDHURY.

Maharashtra Motor Parts Dealers' Association: 13 Kala Bhavan, 3 Mathew Rd, Mumbai 400 004; tel. (22) 23614468; 375 mems; Pres. J. C. UNADKAT; Sec. J. R. CHANDAWALLA.

Millowners' Association, Mumbai: Elphinstone Bldg, 10 Veer Nariman Rd, Fort, Mumbai 400 001; tel. (22) 22040411; fax (22) 22832611; f. 1875; 23 mem. cos; Chair. R. K. DALMIA; Sec.-Gen. V. Y. TAMHANE.

Mumbai Motor Merchants' Association Ltd: 304 Sukh Sagar, N. S. Patkar Marg, Mumbai 400 007; tel. (22) 28112769; 409 mems; Pres. S. TARLOCHAN SINGH ANAND; Gen. Sec. S. BHUPINDER SINGH SETHI.

Mumbai Textile Merchants' Mahajan: 250 Sheikh Memon St, Mumbai 400 002; tel. (22) 22411686; fax (22) 22400311; f. 1879; 1,900 mems; Pres. SURENDRA TULSIDAS SAVAI; Hon. Secs DHIRAJ S. KOTHARI, RAJESH B. PATEL.

National Association of Software and Service Companies (NASSCOM): International Youth Centre, Uma Shankar Dixit Marg, Chanakyapuri, New Delhi 110 021; tel. (11) 23010199; fax (11) 23015452; e-mail nasscom@nasscom.org; internet www.nasscom.org; 860 mems; Pres. KIRAN KARNIK; Chair. JERRY RAO.

Organisation of Pharmaceutical Producers of India (OPPI): Peninsular Corporate Park, Peninsular Chambers, Ground Floor, Ganpatrao Kadam Marg, Lower Parel, Mumbai 400 013; tel. (22) 24918123; fax (22) 24915168; e-mail indiaoppi@vsnl.com; internet www.indiaoppi.com; 74 mems; Pres. RANJIT SHAHANI; Dir-Gen. Dr AJIT DANGI.

Society of Indian Automobile Manufacturers: Core 4B, 5th Floor, India Habitat Centre, Lodhi Rd, New Delhi 110 003; tel. (11) 24647810; fax (11) 24648222; e-mail siam@vsnl.com; f. 1960; 36 mems; Pres. JAGDISH KHATTER; Dir-Gen. DILIP CHENOY.

Southern India Mills' Association: 41 Race Course, Coimbatore 641 018; tel. (422) 2211391; fax (422) 2217160; e-mail simacbe@vsnl.com; internet www.simamills.com; f. 1933; 303 mems; Chair. VIJAY VENKATASWAMY; Sec. P. R. SUBRAMANIAN.

Surgical Manufacturers and Traders' Association: 60 Darya Ganj, New Delhi 110 002; tel. (11) 23271027; fax (11) 23258576; e-mail raviawasthi@hotmail.com; Pres. RAKESH SAWHNEY; Sec. RAVI AWASTHI.

Synthetic and Art Silk Mills' Association Ltd: Sasmira Bldg, 3rd Floor, Sasmira Marg, Worli, Mumbai 400 030; tel. (22) 24945372; fax (22) 24938350; e-mail sasma_100@pacific.net.in; f. 1939; 150 mems; Chair. V. S. CHALKE; Sec.-Gen. K. A. SAMUEL.

Telecom Equipment Manufacturers' Association of India (TEMA): PHD House, 4th Floor, R. K. Dalmia Wing, opp. Asian Games Village, New Delhi 110 016; tel. (11) 26859621; fax (11) 26859620; e-mail tema@vsnl.com; internet www.tematelecom.org; Pres. N. K. GOYAL; Exec. Dir. P. BALAJI.

Travel Agents' Association of India: 2D Lawrence and Mayo House, 276 Dr D. N. Rd, Mumbai 400 001; tel. (22) 22074022; fax (22) 22074559; e-mail taai@hathway.com; internet www.taainet.com; 1,692 mems; Pres. S. THOMAS; Hon. Sec.-Gen. BHAGWAN KANUGA.

United Planters' Association of Southern India (UPASI): Glenview, POB 11, Coonoor 643 101; tel. (423) 2230270; fax (423) 2232030; e-mail upasi@vsnl.com; f. 1893; 850 mems; Pres. ANIL BHANDARI; Sec.-Gen. ULLAS MENON.

EMPLOYERS' ORGANIZATIONS

Council of Indian Employers: Federation House, Tansen Marg, New Delhi 110 001; tel. (11) 23316121; fax (11) 23320714; f. 1956; comprises:

All India Organisation of Employers (AIOE): Federation House, Tansen Marg, New Delhi 110 001; tel. (11) 23316121; fax (11) 23320714; f. 1932; 115 mems; Pres. SAROJ KUMAR PODDAR; Sec.-Gen. Dr AMIT MITRA.

Employers' Federation of India (EFI): Army and Navy Bldg, 148 Mahatma Gandhi Rd, Mumbai 400 001; tel. (22) 22844232; fax (22) 22843028; e-mail efisolar@vsnl.com; f. 1933; 28 asscn mems, 182 ordinary mems, 18 hon. mems; Pres. Dr RAM S. TARNEJA; Sec.-Gen. SHARAD S. PATIL.

Standing Conference of Public Enterprises (SCOPE): SCOPE Complex, 1st Floor, Core No. 8, 7 Lodi Rd, New Delhi 110 003; tel. (11) 24360101; fax (11) 24361371; e-mail scope_dg@yahoo.co.in; f. 1973; representative body of all central public enterprises in India; advises the Govt and public enterprises on matters of major policy and co-ordination; trade enquiries, regarding imports and exports of commodities, carried out on behalf of mems; 200 mems; Chair. C. P. JAIN; Sec.-Gen. Dr S. M. DEWAN.

Employers' Association of Northern India: 14/113 Civil Lines, POB 344, Kanpur 208 001; tel. (512) 2210513; f. 1937; 190 mems; Chair. RAJIV KEHR; Sec.-Gen. P. DUBEY.

Employers' Federation of Southern India: Karumuttu Centre, 1st Floor, 634 Anna Salai, Chennai 600 035; tel. (44) 24349452; fax (44) 24349164; e-mail efsi@vsnl.net; f. 1920; 520 mems; Pres. M. SUBRAMANIAM; Sec. T. M. JAWAHARLAL.

UTILITIES

Electricity

Central Electricity Authority (CEA): Sewa Bhavan, R. K. Puram, New Delhi 110 066; tel. (11) 26108476; fax (11) 26105619; e-mail cea-edp@hub.nic.in; internet www.cea.nic.in; responsible for technical co-ordination and supervision of electricity programmes; advises Ministry of Power on all technical, financial and economic issues; Chair. H. L. BAJAJ.

Bangalore Electricity Supply Co Ltd: K. R. Circle, 4th Floor, Bangalore 560 001; tel. (80) 22354939; internet www.bescom.org.

Calcutta Electricity Supply Corpn Ltd (CESC): CESC House, Chouringhee Sq., Kolkata 700 001; tel. (33) 22256040; fax (33) 22256334; f. 1978; generation and supply of electricity; Chair. R. P. GOENKA; Man. Dir SUMANTRA BANERJEE.

Chattisgarh Electricity Co Ltd: Industrial Growth Centre, Siltara, Raipur 493 111; tel. (771) 5093925; Dir P. K. JAIN.

Dabhol Power Co: 611 Midas Sahar Plaza, Mathurdas Vassanji Rd, Andheri (East), Mumbai 400 059; tel. (22) 28239856; fax (22) 28239865; 85% owned jtly by Bechtel Enterprises Inc. (USA) and General Electric Co (USA), 15% owned by the Maharashtra State Electricity Board (MSEB); administered a two-phase project to establish plants with a power-generating capacity of 2,184 MW; first phase completed in 1999, second phase near completion in 2001; supplied electricity to the MSEB on a build-own-operate basis;

production suspended in May 2001, expected to restart in 2006; Man. Dir MOHAN GURUNATH.

Damodar Valley Corpn: DVC Towers, VIP Rd, Kolkata 700 054; tel. (33) 23551935; fax (33) 23551937; e-mail dvchq@wb.nic.in; internet www.dvcindia.org; f. 1948 to administer the first multi-purpose river valley project in India, the Damodar Valley Project, which aims at unified development of irrigation, flood control and power generation in West Bengal and Jharkhand; operates nine power stations, incl. thermal, hydel and gas turbine; power generating capacity 2,761.5 MW (1999); Chair. AJAY SHANKAR.

Essar Power Ltd: Essar House, Mahalaxmi, Mumbai 400 034; tel. (22) 24950606; fax (22) 24950607; e-mail snpuia@essar.com; Chair. S. N. RUIA.

Jaipur Vidyut Vitran Nigam Ltd: Old Power House Premises, Banipark, Jaipur 302 006; tel. (141) 2208098; fax (141) 2202025.

National Hydroelectric Power Corporation: Sector 33, Faridabad 121 003; tel. (129) 2278421; fax (129) 2277941; e-mail webmaster@nhpc.nic.in; internet www.nhpcindia.com; f. 1975; Chair and Man. Dir YOGENDRA PRASAD.

National Thermal Power Corporation Ltd: Core-7, SCOPE Complex, Lodi Rd, New Delhi 110 003; tel. (11) 24360100; fax (11) 24361018; e-mail pr@ntpcn.ernet.in; internet www.ntpc.net; f. 1975; operates 11 coal-fired and five gas-fired power stations throughout India; Chair. and Man. Dir C. P. JAIN; 24,000 employees.

Noida Power Co Ltd: Commercial Complex, H Block, Alpha Sector II, Greater Noida 201 308; tel. (95120) 4326559; fax (95120) 4326448; f. 1922; distribution of electricity; Chair. and Man. Dir USHA CHATRATH; CEO P. NEOGI.

Nuclear Power Corporation of India Ltd: Commerce Center-1, World Trade Centre, Cuffe Parade, Mumbai 400 005; tel. (22) 22182171; fax (22) 22180109; e-mail cswtc@vsnl.com; internet www .npcil.org; Chair. and Man. Dir SHREYANS KUMAR JAIN.

Power Grid Corporation of India Ltd: Saudamani, Plot No. 2, Sector 29, Gurgaon 122 001; tel. (124) 2571700; fax (124) 2571760; internet www.powergridindia.com; f. 1989; responsible for formation of national power grid; Chair. and Man. Dir R. P. SINGH.

Reliance Energy: Nagin Mahal, 6th Floor, 82 Veer Nariman Rd, Mumbai 400 020; tel. (22) 22043287; fax (22) 22041280; internet www.bses.com; f. 1929 as Bombay Suburban Electric Supply Ltd, merged with the Reliance Group in Jan. 2003; has monopoly in supply of electricity to Mumbai; Chair. ANIL AMBANI; Man. Dir S. S. DUA.

Rural Electrification Corpn Ltd: Core-4, SCOPE Complex, 7 Lodhi Rd, New Delhi 110 003; tel. (11) 24365161; fax (11) 24360644; e-mail recorp@recl.nic.in; internet www.recindia.com; Chair. and Man. Dir M. N. PRASAD.

Tata Power Co Ltd: Bombay House, 24 Homi Mody St, Mumbai 400 001; tel. (22) 56658282; fax (22) 56658801; internet www .tatapower.com; generation, transmission and distribution of electrical energy; Chair. RATAN N. TATA; Man. Dir FIRDOSE VANDREWALA.

Thana Electric Supply Co Ltd: Asian Bldg, 1st Floor, 17 Ramji Kamani Marg, Ballard Estate, Mumbai 400 001; tel. (22) 22615444; fax (22) 22611069; e-mail thanaele@bom2.vsnl.net.in; f. 1927; Man. Dir SURESH S. HEMMADY.

Gas

Gas Authority of India Ltd: 16 Bhikaji Cama Place, R. K. Puram, Delhi 110 066; tel. (11) 26172580; fax (11) 26185941; e-mail pbanerjee@gail.com.in; internet www.nic.in/gail; f. 1984; 80% state-owned; transports, processes and markets natural gas; constructing gas-based petrochemical complex; Chair. and Man. Dir PROSHANTO BANERJEE; 1,513 employees.

Gujarat Gas Co Ltd: 2 Shantisadan Society, Ellis Bridge, Ahmedabad 380 006; Chair. HASMUKH SHAH; Man. Dir B. S. SHANTHARAJU.

Indraprastha Gas Ltd: Dr Gopal Das Bhawan, 14th–15th Floors, 28 Barakhamba Rd, New Delhi 110 001.

Water

Brihanmumbai Municipal Corporation (Hydraulic Engineers' Department): Municipal Corporation Offices, Ground Floor, Annex Bldg, Mahapalika Marg, Mumbai 400 001; tel. (22) 22620025; fax (22) 22700532; Head Eng. S. N. TURKAR.

Calcutta Municipal Corporation (Water Supply Department): 5 S. N. Banerjee Rd, Kolkata 700 013; tel. (33) 22444518; fax (33) 22442578; f. 1870; Chief Municipal Eng. DIBYENDU ROY CHOWDHURY.

Chennai Metropolitan Water Supply and Sewerage Board: No. 1 Pumping Station Rd, Chintadripet, Chennai 600 002; tel. (44) 28525717; f. 1978; Chair. and Man. Dir SANTHA SHEELA NAIR.

Delhi Jal Board: Varunalaya Phase II, Karol Bagh, New Delhi 110 005; tel. and fax (11) 23678380; e-mail prodjb@bol.net.in; internet www.delhijalboard.com; f. 1957 as Delhi Water Supply and Sewage Disposal Undertaking, reconstituted as above in 1998; part of the Delhi Municipal Corporation; production and distribution of potable water and treatment and disposal of waste water in Delhi; Chair. SHEILA DIXIT.

Karnataka Rural Water Supply and Sanitation Agency: 2nd Floor, E Block, KHB Complex, Cauvery Bhavan, K. G. Rd, Bangalore 560 009; tel. (80) 22246508; fax (80) 22240509; e-mail jalnirmal@vsnl.net; internet www.jalnirmal.org.

Karnataka Urban Water Supply and Drainage Board: Sir M. Visveswaraya Rd, D. C. Compound, Dharwad 580 001; tel. (836) 2447090; fax (836) 2446890; internet www.kuwsdb.org.

TRADE UNIONS

Indian National Trade Union Congress (INTUC): 4 Bhai Veer Singh Marg, New Delhi 110 001; tel. (11) 23747767; fax (11) 23364244; e-mail intuchq@del3.vsnl.net.in; f. 1947; 4,411 affiliated unions with a total membership of 7.93m.; affiliated to ICFTU; 32 state brs and 29 nat. feds; Pres. G. SANJEEVA REDDY; Gen. Sec. RAJENDRA PRASAD SINGH.

Major affiliated unions:

Indian National Cement Workers' Federation: Mazdoor Karyalaya, Congress House, Mumbai 400 004; tel. (22) 23871809; fax (22) 23870981; 49,000 mems; 38 affiliated unions; Pres. C. L. DHUDHIA; Gen. Sec. N. NANJAPPAN.

Indian National Chemical Workers' Federation: Tel Rasayan Bhavan, Tilak Rd, Dadar, Mumbai 400 014; tel. (22) 24121742; fax (22) 24130950; 35,000 mems; Pres. RAJA KULKARNI; Gen. Sec. R. D. BHARADWAJ.

Indian National Electricity Workers' Federation: 392 Sector 21-B, Faridabad 121 001; tel. (129) 2215089; fax (129) 2215868; e-mail inef@ndf.vsnl.net.in; f. 1950; 187,641 mems; 146 affiliated unions; Pres. D. P. PATHAK; Gen. Sec. S. L. PASSEY.

Indian National Metal Workers' Federation: D-81, Sector 18, Rourkela 769 003; tel. (661) 24646611; Pres. G. SANJEEVA REDDY; Gen. Sec. M. D. N. PANICKER.

Indian National Mineworkers' Federation: CJ 49 Salt Lake, Kolkata 700 091; tel. and fax (33) 23372158; e-mail imme@vsnl .com; f. 1949; 351,454 mems in 139 affiliated unions; Pres. RAJENDRA P. SINGH; Gen. Sec. S. Q. ZAMA.

Indian National Paper Mill Workers' Federation: 6/B, LIGH, Barkatpura, Hyderabad 500 027; tel. (40) 27564706; Pres. G. SANJEEVA REDDY; Gen. Sec. R. CHANDRASEKHARAN.

Indian National Port and Dock Workers' Federation: 15 Coal Dock Rd, Kolkata 700 043; tel. (33) 22455929; f. 1954; 18 affiliated unions; 81,000 mems; Pres. JANAKI MUKHERJEE; Gen. Sec. G. KALAN.

Indian National Sugar Mills Workers' Federation: A-176, Darulsafa Marg, Lucknow 226 001; tel. (522) 2282719; 100 affiliated unions; 40,000 mems; Pres. ASHOK KUMAR SINGH; Gen. Sec. P. K. SHARMA.

Indian National Textile Workers' Federation: 27 Burjorji Bharucha Marg, Mumbai 400 023; tel. (22) 22671577; f. 1948; 400 affiliated unions; 363,790 mems; Pres. SACHIN AHIR; Gen. Sec. P. L. SUBHAIAH.

Indian National Transport Workers' Federation: Bus Mazdoor Karyalaya, L/1, Hathital Colony, Jabalpur 482 001; tel. (761) 2429210; 274 affiliated unions; 364,919 mems; Pres. G. SANJEEVA REDDY; Gen. Sec. K. S. VERMA.

National Federation of Petroleum Workers: Tel Rasayan Bhavan, Tilak Rd, Dadar, Mumbai 400 014; tel. (22) 24181742; fax (22) 24130950; f. 1959; 22,340 mems; Pres. RAJA KULKARNI; Gen. Sec. N. A. KHAN VILKAR.

Bharatiya Mazdoor Sangh: Ram Naresh Bhavan, Tilak Gali, Pahar Ganj, New Delhi 110 055; tel. (11) 23562654; fax (11) 23582648; e-mail bms@indiya.com; f. 1955; 4,700 affiliated unions with a total membership of 8.5m.; 27 state brs; 34 nat. feds; Pres. HASMUKH DAVE; Gen. Sec. UDAY RAO PATWARDHAN.

Major affiliated unions:

Bharatiya Jute Mazdoor Sangh: 10 Kiran Shankar Roy Rd, Kolkata 700 001; tel. (33) 22489210; Pres. RAGHUNATH SINGH; Gen. Sec. TARUN KANTI GHOSE.

Bharatiya Paribahan Mazdoor Mahasangh (Transport Workers' Union): 542 Dr Munje Marg, Congress Nagar, Nagpur 440 012; tel. (712) 2534464; Pres. WAMAN RAO KHEDKAR; Gen. Sec. CHETAN KUMAR DESAI.

Kendriya Karmachari Mahasangh: Ram Naresh Bhawan, Tilak Gali, Paharganj, New Delhi 110 055; tel. (11) 23620654; Pres. K. K. PODDAR; Gen. Sec. CHANDRA MOHAN.

National Organisation of Bank Workers: 542 Dr Munje Marg, Congress Nagar, Nagpur 440 012; tel. (712) 2560808; fax (712) 2542442; Pres. V. B. INDURKAR; Gen. Sec. K. R. POONJA.

National Organisation of Insurance Workers: 3-AB, Hashim Bldg, 40 Veer Nariman Rd, Mumbai 400 023; tel. (22) 22040958; Pres. M. P PATWARDHAN; Gen. Sec. ATUL DESHPANDE.

Centre of Indian Trade Unions: BTR Bhavan, 13-A Rouse Ave, New Delhi 110 002; tel. (11) 23221306; fax (11) 23221284; e-mail citu@vsnl.com; internet www.citu.org.in; f. 1970; 3.37m. mems; 24 state and union territory brs; 4,300 affiliated unions, 12 nat. federations; Pres. M. K. PANDHE; Gen. Sec. CHITTABRATA MAJUMDAR.

Major affiliated unions:

All India Coal Workers' Federation: Koyla Shramik Bhavan, N. S. B. Rd, Raniganj 713 347; Pres. M. K. PANDHE.

All India Road Transport Workers' Federation: 53 Acharya J. C. Bose Rd, Kolkata 700 016; Pres. SHYAMAL CHAKRABORTY.

Steel Workers' Federation of India: 1 Vidyasagar Ave, Durgapur 713 205; Pres. ARDHENDU DHAKI.

Water Transport Workers' Federation of India: 16 Birsa Munda Sarani, Kolkata 700 043; Pres. M. K. PANDHE.

Assam Chah Karmachari Sangha: POB 13, Dibrugarh 786 001; tel. 20870; 13,553 mems; 20 brs; Pres. G. C. SARMAH; Gen. Sec. A. K. BHATTACHARYA.

All-India Trade Union Congress (AITUC): 24 Canning Lane, New Delhi 110 001; tel. (11) 23387320; fax (11) 23386427; e-mail aitucong@bol.net.in; f. 1920; affiliated to WFTU; 4.6m. mems, 2,272 affiliated unions; 28 state brs, 21 national federations; Pres. J. CHITHARANJAN; Gen. Sec. GURUDAS DASGUPTA.

Major affiliated unions:

Annamalai Plantation Workers' Union: Valparai, Via Pollachi, Tamil Nadu; over 21,000 mems.

Zilla Cha Bagan Workers' Union: Mal, Jalpaiguri, West Bengal; 15,000 mems; Pres. NEHAR MUKHERJEE; Gen. Sec. BIMAL DAS GUPTA.

United Trades Union Congress (UTUC): 124-C, Lenin Sarani, Kolkata 700 013; tel. (33) 22461810; f. 1949; 1.2m. mems from 389 affiliated unions; 10 state brs and 6 nat. feds; Pres. SHANKARAN NAIR; Gen. Sec. S. R. SEN GUPTA.

Major affiliated unions:

Bengal Provincial Chatkal Mazdoor Union: Kolkata; textile workers; 28,330 mems.

Dooars Cha Bagan Union: Jalpaiguri; tel. (3564) 255220; 94,532 mems; Pres. SURESH TALUKDAR; Gen. Sec. RANA SEN.

Hind Mazdoor Sabha (HMS): 120 Babar Rd, New Delhi 110 011; tel. (11) 23413519; fax (11) 23411037; e-mail mki@vsnl.com; internet www.mkiindia.org; f. 1948; affiliated to ICFTU; 4.8m. mems from 2,800 affiliated unions; 25 state councils; 18 nat. industrial feds; Pres. THAMPAN THOMAS; Gen. Sec. UMRAOMAL PUROHIT.

Major affiliated unions:

Colliery Mazdoor Congress (Coalminers' Union): Bengal Hotel, 2nd Md Hussain St, Asansol 713 301; tel. (341) 202342; fax (341) 201336; 45,188 mems; Pres. MADHU DANDAVATE; Gen. Sec. JAYANTA PODDER.

Mumbai Port Trust Dock and General Employees' Union: Port Trust Kamgar Sadan, Navab Tank Rd, Mazgaon, Mumbai 400 010; tel. (22) 23776320; fax (22) 23754794; e-mail mbptdgeu@vsnl.net; 7,448 mems; Pres. Dr SHANTI PATEL; Gen. Sec. S. K. SHETYE.

South Central Railway Mazdoor Union: 7c Railway Bldg, Accounts Office Compound, Secunderabad 500 371; tel. (40) 27821351; fax (40) 27821351; e-mail scrmu@hotmail.com; internet www.scrmu.org; f. 1966; 88,900 mems; Pres. C. SANKARA RAO; Gen. Sec. C. H. SANKARRAO; 135 brs.

Transport and Dock Workers' Union: P. D. Mello Bhavan, P. D. Mello Rd, Carnec Bunder, Mumbai 400 038; tel. (22) 22616951; fax (22) 22659087; 25,979 mems; Pres. S. R. KULKARNI; Gen. Sec N. D. KAMBLE.

West Bengal Cha Mazdoor Sabha: Cha Shramik Bhavan, Jalpaiguri 735 101, West Bengal; tel. (3561) 231140; fax (3561) 230349; f. 1947; 55,000 mems; Pres. Prof. SUSHIL ROY; Gen. Sec. SAMIR ROY.

Western Railway Employees' Union: Grant Road Railway Station Bldg, Grant Rd (East), Mumbai 400 007; tel. (22) 23088102; fax (22) 23003185; 150,000 mems; Pres. UMRAOMAL PUROHIT; Gen. Sec. C. S. MENON.

Confederation of Central Government Employees and Workers: 4B/6 Ganga Ram Hospital Marg, New Delhi 110 060; tel. (11) 22587804; 1.2m. mems; Pres. S. MADHUSUDAN; Sec.-Gen. S. K. VYAS.

Affiliated unions:

National Federation of Postal Employees (NFPE): D-7, Postal Staff Quarters, Samru Place, Mandir Marg, New Delhi 110 001; tel. and fax (11) 23364029; e-mail nfpe_hq@hotmail.com; f. 1954 as National Federation of Post and Telegraph Employees, reconstituted as above in 1986; 400,000 mems from seven affiliated unions; Pres. R. N. CHAUDHARY; Sec.-Gen. C. CHANDRAN PILLAI.

National Federation of Telegraph Employees: New Delhi 110 001; f. 1954 as National Federation of Post and Telegraph Employees, reconstituted as above in 1986.

All India Bank Employees' Association (AIBEA): 3B Lall Bazar St, 1st Floor, Kolkata 700 001; tel. (33) 22489371; fax (33) 22486072; e-mail aibea@cal2.vsnl.net.in; internet bankunionaibea.org; 32 state units, 710 affiliated unions, 525,000 mems; Pres. SURESH D. DHOPESWARKAR; Gen. Sec. TARAKESWAR CHAKRABORTI.

All India Defence Employees' Federation (AIDEF): Survey No. 81, Elphinstone Rd, Khadki, Pune 411 003; tel. (20) 25818761; 358 affiliated unions; 200,000 mems; Pres. T. I. MADHAVAN; Gen. Secs S. BHATTACHARYA, C. SRIKUMAR.

All India Port and Dock Workers' Federation: 9 Second Line Beach, Chennai 600 001; tel. (44) 25224222; fax (44) 25225983; f. 1948; 100,000 mems in 34 affiliated unions; Pres. S. R. KULKARNI; Gen. Sec. S. C. C. ANTHONY PILLAI.

All India Railwaymen's Federation (AIRF): 4 State Entry Rd, New Delhi 110 055; tel. (11) 23343493; fax (11) 23363167; e-mail airf@ndb.vsnl.net.in; f. 1924; 1,033,340 mems (2004); 23 affiliated unions; Pres. UMRAOMAL PUROHIT; Gen. Sec. J. P. CHAUBEY.

National Federation of Indian Railwaymen (NFIR): 3 Chelmsford Rd, New Delhi 110 055; tel. (11) 23343305; fax (11) 23744013; e-mail nfir@satyam.net.in; f. 1952; 26 affiliated unions; 925,500 mems (2003); Pres. GUMAN SINGH; Gen. Sec. M. RAGHAVAIAH.

Transport

RAILWAYS

India's railway system is the largest in Asia and the fourth largest in the world. In March 2003 the total length of Indian railways exceeded 63,140 route-km. The network carried 14m. passengers and more than 1m. metric tons of freight traffic per day. The Government exercises direct or indirect control over all railways through the Railway Board. India's largest railway construction project of the 20th century, the 760-km Konkan railway line (which took seven years and almost US $1,000m. to build), was officially opened in January 1998.

A 16.45-km underground railway, which carries more than 1m. people daily, was completed in Kolkata in 1995. The first phase of a partially underground new metro system in New Delhi was completed in late 2004; the final phase was expected to be completed in 2010.

Ministry of Railways (Railway Board): Rail Bhavan, Raisina Rd, New Delhi 110 001; tel. (11) 23384010; fax (11) 23384481; e-mail crb@del2.vsnl.net.in; internet www.indianrailways.gov.in; Chair. RABINDRA KUMAR SINGH.

Zonal Railways

The railways are grouped into 16 zones

Central: Chhatrapati Shivaji Terminus (Victoria Terminus), Mumbai 400 001; tel. (22) 22621230; fax (22) 22624555; e-mail gmcr@bom2.vsnl.net.in; internet www.cr-mumbai.com; Gen. Man. S. B. GHOSH DASTIDAR.

East Central: Hajipur 844 101; tel. (6224) 274728; fax (6224) 274738; f. 1996; Gen. Man. R. S. VARSHNEYA.

East Coast: Rail Vihar, Chandrasekhar Pur, Bhubaneswar 751 023; tel. (674) 230073; fax (674) 2300196; internet www.eastcoastrailway.gov.in; f. 1996; Gen. Man. R. CHOWDHURI.

Eastern: 17 Netaji Subhas Rd, Kolkata 700 001; tel. (33) 22207596; fax (33) 22480370; internet www.easternrailway.gov.in; Gen. Man. SHYAM KUMAR.

North Central: Allahabad 211 001; tel. (532) 2603551; fax (532) 2603900; e-mail secyncr@hotmail.com; f. 1996; Gen Man. I. P. S. ANAND.

North Eastern: Gorakhpur 273 012; tel. (551) 2201041; fax (551) 2201299; e-mail gmner@nda.vsnl.net.in; Gen. Man. OM PRAKASH.

North Western: Jaipur 302 006; tel. (141) 2222695; fax (141) 2222936; Gen. Man. S. S. BHATTACHARYA.

Northeast Frontier: Maligaon, Guwahati 781 011; tel. (361) 2570422; fax (361) 2571124; f. 1958; Gen. Man. A. K. SANWALKA.

Northern: Baroda House, Kasturba Gandhi Marg, New Delhi 110 001; tel. (11) 23387227; fax (11) 23384503; e-mail nragm@vsnl.com; Gen. Man. P. R. JARUHAR.

South Central: Rm 312, 3rd Floor, Rail Nilayam, Secunderabad 500 071; tel. (40) 27822874; fax (40) 27833203; internet www.scrailway.gov.in; Gen. Man. T. STANLEY BABU.

South East Central Railway: R. E. Complex, Bilaspur 495 004; tel. (7752) 47102; Gen. Man. PRAMOD KUMAR.

South Eastern: 11 Garden Reach Rd, Kolkata 700 043; tel. (33) 24393532; fax (33) 24397831; e-mail gm@ser.railnet.gov.in; internet www.serailway.com; Gen. Man. R. R. BHANDARI.

South Western: Hubli 580 023; tel. (836) 2360888; fax (836) 2365809; internet www.southwesternrailway.org; f. 1996; Gen. Man. T. N. PERT.

Southern: Park Town, Chennai 600 003; tel. (44) 25353157; fax (44) 25351439; internet www.srailway.com; Gen. Man. RAMESH CHANDRA.

West Central: Jabalpur 482 001; tel. (761) 2627444; fax (761) 2618233; e-mail osdwcr@yahoo.com; f. 1996; Gen. Man. D. K. GUPTA.

Western: Churchgate, Mumbai 400 020; tel. (22) 22005670; fax (22) 22068545; internet www.westernrailwayindia.com; Gen. Man. M. Z. ANSARI.

ROADS

In December 2002 there were an estimated 3.3m. km of roads in India, 58,112 km of which were national highways. About 50% of the total road network was paved. In March 2004 there were an estimated 65,569 km of national highways. In January 1999 the Government launched the ambitious Rs 500,000m. National Highways Development project, which included plans to build an east–west corridor linking Silchar with Porbandar and a north–south corridor linking Kashmir with Kanyakumari, as well as a circuit of roads linking the four main cities of Mumbai, Chennai, Kolkata and New Delhi.

Ministry of Road Transport and Highways: Parivahan Bhavan, 1 Sansad Marg, New Delhi 110 001; tel. (11) 23710121; fax (11) 23719023; internet morth.nic.in; responsible for the construction and maintenance of India's system of national highways, with a total length of 58,112 km in 2003, connecting the state capitals and major ports and linking with the highway systems of neighbouring countries. This system includes 172 national highways which constitute the main trunk roads of the country.

Border Roads Organisation: f. 1960 to accelerate the economic development of the north and north-eastern border areas; it has constructed 31,061 km and improved 37,077 km of roads, and built permanent bridges totalling a length of 19,544 m in the border areas.

National Highways Authority of India: G-5 and 6, Sector 10, Dwarka, New Delhi 110 045; tel. (11) 25074100; fax (11) 25093507; e-mail nhai@vsnl.com; internet www.nhai.org; f. 1995; planning, designing, construction and maintenance of national highways; under Ministry of Road Transport; Chair. S. NAUTIYAL.

INLAND WATERWAYS

About 14,500 km of rivers are navigable by power-driven craft, and 3,700 km by large country boats. Services are mainly on the Ganga and Brahmaputra and their tributaries, the Godavari, the Mahanadi, the Narmada, the Tapti and the Krishna.

Central Inland Water Transport Corpn Ltd: 4 Fairlie Place, Kolkata 700 001; tel. (33) 22202321; fax (33) 22436164; e-mail ciwtc@cal3.vsnl.net.in; internet www.ciwtc.com; f. 1967; inland water transport services in Bangladesh and the east and north-east Indian states; also shipbuilding and repairing, general engineering, lightering of ships and barge services; Chair. and Man. Dir PRAFUL TAYAL.

SHIPPING

In March 2002 India was 15th in terms of dwt and 19th in terms of gwt on the list of principal merchant fleets of the world. In October 2004 the total fleet had 665 ships, with a total displacement of 7.69m. grt. There were some 102 shipping companies operating in India in January 2000. The major ports are Chennai, Haldia, Jawaharlal Nehru (at Nhava Sheva near Mumbai), Kandla, Kochi, Kolkata, Mormugao, Mumbai, New Mangalore, Paradip (Paradeep), Tuticorin and Visakhapatnam.

Chennai (Madras)

South India Shipping Corpn Ltd: Chennai; Chair. J. H. TARAPORE; Man. Dir F. G. DASTUR.

Kolkata (Calcutta)

India Steamship Co Ltd: 44 Park St, Kolkata 700 016; tel. (33) 22481171; fax (33) 22488133; e-mail india.steamship@gems.vsnl.net.in; f. 1928; cargo services; Chair. K. K. BIRLA; Man. Dir ASHOK KAK; br in Delhi.

Surrendra Overseas Ltd: Apeejay House, 15 Park St, Kolkata 700 016; tel. (33) 22172372; fax (33) 22179596; e-mail solcal@apeejaygroup.com; internet www.apeejaygroup.com; shipowners; Chair. JIT PAUL.

Mumbai (Bombay)

Century Shipping Ltd: Mumbai; tel. (22) 22022734; fax (22) 22027274; Chair. B. K. BIRLA; Pres. N. M. JAIN.

Chowgule & Co (Pvt) Ltd: Bakhtawar, 3rd Floor, Nariman Point, POB 11596, Mumbai 400 021; tel. (22) 22026822; fax (22) 22024845; f. 1963; Chair. VISHWASRAO DATTAJI CHOWGULE; Man. Dir SHIVAJIRAO DATTAJI CHOWGULE.

Essar Shipping Ltd: Essar House, 11 Keshavrao Khadye Marg, Mahalaxmi, Mumbai 400 034; tel. (22) 24950606; fax (22) 24950607; e-mail snruia@essar.com; f. 1975; Chair. S. N. RUIA; Man. Dir SANJAY MEHTA.

The Great Eastern Shipping Co Ltd: Ocean House, 134/A Dr Annie Besant Rd, Worli, Mumbai 400 018; tel. (22) 24922100; fax (22) 24925900; e-mail corp_comm@greatship.com; internet www.greatship.com; f. 1948; cargo services; Exec. Chair. K. M. SHETH; Man. Dirs VIJAY SHETH, BHARAT SHETH; br. in New Delhi.

Shipping Corpn of India Ltd: Shipping House, 245 Madame Cama Rd, Mumbai 400 021; tel. (22) 22026666; fax (22) 22026905; e-mail mail@sci.co.in; internet www.shipindia.com; f. 1961 as a govt undertaking; Chair. and Man. Dir P. K. SRIVASTAVA; brs in Kolkata, New Delhi, Chennai and London.

Tolani Shipping Co Ltd: 10A Bakhtawar, Nariman Point, Mumbai 400 021; tel. (22) 22026878; fax (22) 22870697; e-mail ops@tolanigroup.com; Chair. and Man. Dir Dr N. P. TOLANI.

Varun Shipping Co Ltd: Laxmi Bldg, 3rd Floor, 6 Shoorji Vallabhdas Marg, Ballard Estate, Mumbai 400 001; tel. (22) 22658114; fax (22) 22621723; f. 1971; Chair. and Man. Dir ARUN MEHTA.

CIVIL AVIATION

There are 11 designated international airports and 85 domestic airports and 28 civil enclaves. By 2004 10 airports (in Ahmedabad, Amritsar, Goa, Guwahati, Jaipur, Lucknow, Mangalore, Madurai, Thiruvananthapuram and Udaipur) had been identified for the second round of modernization and restructuring. The process of long-term leasing of Mumbai, Delhi, Chennai and Kolkata airports was under way in 2005.

Airports Authority of India: Rajiv Gandhi Bhavan, Safdarjung Airport, New Delhi 110 003; tel. (11) 24632950; fax (11) 24641088; e-mail aaichmn@vsnl.com; internet www.airportsindia.org.in; manages 124 international and domestic airports; Chair. K. RAMALINGAM.

Air Deccan: 214/33, 7th Cross, Vasanthnagar, Bangalore 560 052; tel. (80) 51148190; fax (80) 2352645; internet www.airdeccan.net; f. 2003; unit of Deccan Aviation Pvt Ltd; low-cost domestic passenger service; Man. Dir Capt. G. R. GOPINATH.

Air-India: Air-India Bldg, 218 Backbay Reclamation, Nariman Point, Mumbai 400 021; tel. (22) 22024142; fax (22) 22023686; e-mail hqpsai@bom3.vsnl.net.in; internet www.airindia.com; f. 1932 as Tata Airlines; renamed Air-India in 1946; in 1953 became a state corpn responsible for international flights; services to 46 online stations (incl. 2 cargo stations) and 84 offline offices throughout the world; Chair.and Man. Dir V. THULASIDAS.

Air Sahara: Dr Gopaldas Bhawan, 3rd Floor, 28 Barakhamba Rd, New Delhi 110 001; tel. (11) 23326851; fax (11) 23755510; internet www.airsahara.net; f. 1991 as Sahara India Airlines; commenced operations 1993; private co; scheduled passenger and cargo services to domestic and regional destinations; Chair. SUBRATA R. SAHARA; Pres. RONO JOY DUTTA.

Airline Allied Services Ltd: Domestic Arrival Terminal, 1st Floor, Indira Gandhi International Airport, Palam, New Delhi 110 037; tel. (11) 25672729; fax (11) 25672006; e-mail aaslmd@del2.net.in; internet www.allianceair-india.com/; f. 1996; 100% owned by Indian Airlines; scheduled passenger services to regional destinations; Man. Dir MANET PAES.

Archana Airways: 41A Friends Colony (East), Mathura Rd, New Delhi 110 065; tel. (11) 26842001; fax (11) 26847762; f. 1991; commenced operations 1993; scheduled and charter passenger services to domestic destinations; Dir/Chair. A. K. BHARTIYA; Man. Dir N. K. BHARTIYA.

Blue Dart Express: 88–89 Old International Terminal, Meenambakkam Airport, Chennai 600027; tel. (44) 22334995; fax (44)

22349067; e-mail bdal@md2.vsnl.net.in; internet www.bluedart .com; f. 1983 as Blue Dart Courier Services; name changed as above in 1990; air express transport co; Chair. Tushar K. Jani; Chief Exec. Niteen Gupte.

Gujarat Airways Ltd: Sapana Shopping Centre, 1st Floor, 20 Vishwas Colony, Alkapuri, Vadodara 390 005; tel. (265) 2330864; fax (265) 2339628; e-mail info@gujaratairways.com; internet www .gujaratairways.com; f. 1994; commenced operations 1995; scheduled services to domestic destinations; Chair. G. N. Patel; Man. Dir R. C. Sharma.

Indian Airlines: Airlines House, 113 Gurudwara Rakabganj Rd, New Delhi 110 001; tel. (11) 23716236; fax (11) 23711730; e-mail ia@ travelindia.com; internet www.indian-airlines.nic.in; f. 1953; state corpn responsible for regional and domestic flights; services to 64 cities throughout India and to 16 destinations in the Middle East and the Far East; Chair. and Man. Dir Sunil Arora.

Jagson Airlines: Vandana Bldg, 3rd Floor, 11 Tolstoy Marg, New Delhi 110 001; tel. (11) 23721594; fax (11) 23324693; e-mail jagson-id@eth.net; f. 1991; scheduled and charter passenger services to domestic destinations; Chair. Jagdish Gupta; Man. Dir Pradeep Gupta.

Jet Airways (India) Ltd: S. M. Centre, 1st Floor, Andheri-Kurla Rd, Andheri (East), Mumbai 400 059; tel. (22) 28505080; fax (22) 28528544; internet www.jetairways.com; f. 1992; commenced operations 1993; private co; scheduled passenger services to domestic and regional destinations; Chair. and Man. Dir Naresh Goyal; CEO Wolfgang Prock Shauer.

TransBharat Aviation Ltd: 201 Laxmi Bhavan, 72 Nehru Place, Delhi 110 019; tel. (11) 26419600; fax (11) 23313353; f. 1990; commenced operations 1991; charter services throughout India.

UP Airways Ltd: Roopali House, A-2 Defence Colony, New Delhi 110 024; tel. (11) 24646290; fax (11) 24646292; e-mail sgsimpex@ del3.vsnl.net.in; private co; charter services to domestic destinations; Chair. and Man. Dir Subhash Gulati; Chief Exec. Capt. H. S. Bedi.

Tourism

The tourist attractions of India include its scenery, its historic forts, palaces and temples, and its rich variety of wild life. Tourist infrastructure has recently been expanded by the provision of more luxury hotels and improved means of transport. In 2003 there were about 2.75m. foreign visitors to India, and revenue from tourism totalled an estimated Rs 164,290m.

Ministry of Tourism: Transport Bhavan, Parliament St, New Delhi 110 001; tel. (11) 23714677; fax (11) 23710518; e-mail contactus@incredibleindia.org; internet www.incredibleindia.org; formulates and administers govt policy for promotion of tourism; plans the organization and development of tourist facilities; operates tourist information offices in India and overseas; Sec. Uma Pillai.

India Tourism Development Corpn Ltd: SCOPE Complex, Core 8, 6th Floor, 7 Lodi Rd, New Delhi 110 003; tel. (11) 24360303; fax (11) 24360185; e-mail itdcscope@usa.net; internet www .theashokgroup.com; f. 1966; operates Ashok Group of hotels (largest hotel chain owner), resort accommodation, tourist transport services, duty-free shops and a travel agency and provides consultancy and management services; Chair. and Man. Dir Amitabh Kant.

INDONESIA

Introductory Survey

Location, Climate, Language, Religion, Flag, Capital

The Republic of Indonesia consists of a group of about 18,108 islands (including rocks, reefs, sandbanks, etc.), lying between the mainland of South-East Asia and Australia. The archipelago is the largest in the world, and it stretches from the Malay peninsula to New Guinea. The principal islands are Java, Sumatra, Kalimantan (comprising more than two-thirds of the island of Borneo), Sulawesi (Celebes), Papua (formerly Irian Jaya, comprising the western part of the island of New Guinea), Maluku (the Moluccas) and West Timor (comprising part of the island of Timor). Indonesia's only land frontiers are with Papua New Guinea, to the east of Papua, with the Malaysian states of Sarawak and Sabah, which occupy northern Borneo, and with Timor-Leste (formerly East Timor), to the east of West Timor. The climate is tropical, with an average annual temperature of 26°C (79°F) and heavy rainfall during most seasons. Rainfall averages 706 mm (28 ins) annually in Indonesia, although there are large variations throughout the archipelago; the heaviest annual rainfall (2,286 mm or 90 ins) is along the equatorial rain belt, which passes through Sumatra, Borneo and Sulawesi. The official language is Bahasa Indonesia (a form of Malay); there are an estimated 583 other languages and dialects spoken in the archipelago, including Javanese, Sundanese, Arabic and Chinese. An estimated 88% of the inhabitants profess adherence to Islam. About 10% of the population are Christians, while most of the remainder are either Hindus or Buddhists. The national flag (proportions 2 by 3) has two equal horizontal stripes, of red and white. The capital is Jakarta, on the island of Java.

Recent History

Indonesia was formerly the Netherlands East Indies (except for the former Portuguese colony of Timor-Leste, see below). Dutch occupation began in the 17th century and gradually extended over the whole archipelago. Nationalist opposition to colonial rule began in the early 20th century. During the Second World War the territory was occupied by Japanese forces from March 1942. On 17 August 1945, three days after the Japanese surrender, a group of nationalists proclaimed the independence of Indonesia. The first President of the self-proclaimed republic was Dr Sukarno, a leader of the nationalist movement since the 1920s. The declaration of independence was not recognized by the Netherlands, which attempted to restore its pre-war control of the islands. After four years of intermittent warfare and negotiations between the Dutch authorities and the nationalists, agreement was reached on a formal transfer of power. On 27 December 1949 the United States of Indonesia became legally independent, with Sukarno continuing as President. Initially, the country had a federal Constitution which gave limited self-government to the 16 constituent regions. In August 1950, however, the federation was dissolved, and the country became the unitary Republic of Indonesia. The 1949 independence agreement excluded West New Guinea (subsequently Irian Jaya and known as Papua from 1 January 2002), which remained under Dutch control until October 1962; following a brief period of UN administration, however, it was transferred to Indonesia in May 1963.

Sukarno followed a policy of extreme nationalism, and his regime became increasingly dictatorial. His foreign policy was sympathetic to the People's Republic of China but, under his rule, Indonesia also played a leading role in the Non-aligned Movement (see p. 384). Inflation and widespread corruption eventually provoked opposition to Sukarno's regime; in September–October 1965 there was an abortive military coup, in which the Partai Komunis Indonesia (PKI—Indonesian Communist Party) was strongly implicated. A mass slaughter of alleged PKI members and supporters ensued. In March 1966 Sukarno was forced to transfer emergency executive powers to military commanders, led by Gen. Suharto, Chief of Staff of the Army, who outlawed the PKI. In February 1967 Sukarno transferred full power to Suharto. In March the Majelis Permusyawaratan Rakyat (MPR—People's Consultative Assembly) removed Sukarno from office and named Suharto acting President. He became Prime Minister in October 1967 and, following

his election by the MPR, he was inaugurated as President in March 1968. In July 1971, in the first general election since 1955, the government-sponsored Sekretariat Bersama Golongan Karya (Joint Secretariat of Functional Groups), known as Golkar, won a majority of seats in the Dewan Perwakilan Rakyat (DPR—House of Representatives). Suharto was re-elected to the presidency in March 1973.

Under Suharto's 'New Order', real power passed from the legislature and the Cabinet to a small group of army officers and to the Operation Command for the Restoration of Order and Security (Kopkamtib), the internal security organization. Left-wing movements were suppressed, and a liberal economic policy adopted. A general election in May 1977 gave Golkar a majority in the legislature, and Suharto was re-elected President (unopposed) in March 1978. Despite criticism of the Government, Golkar won an increased majority in the elections in May 1982. In March 1983 Suharto was re-elected, again unopposed, as President.

During 1984 Suharto's attempt to introduce legislation requiring all political, social and religious organizations to adopt *pancasila*, the five-point state philosophy (belief in a supreme being; humanitarianism; national unity; democracy by consensus; social justice), as their only ideology encountered opposition. Serious rioting and a series of bombings and arson attempts in and around Jakarta were allegedly instigated by Muslim opponents of the proposed legislation, and many Muslims were tried and sentenced to long terms of imprisonment. All the political parties had accepted *pancasila* by July 1985. At the April 1987 general election, despite persistent international allegations of corruption and of abuses of human rights, particularly in East Timor (see below), Golkar won 299 of the 500 seats in the DPR. Moreover, for the first time, the party achieved an overall majority of seats in each of Indonesia's 27 provinces.

In February 1988 new legislation reaffirmed the 'dual (i.e. military and socio-economic) function' of the Indonesian Armed Forces (ABRI). In March Suharto was again re-elected unopposed as President. At the subsequent vice-presidential election, in a departure from previous procedure, Suharto did not recommend a candidate, but encouraged the MPR to choose one. However, Lt-Gen. (retd) Sudharmono, the Chairman of Golkar, and Dr Jailani Naro, the leader of the Partai Persatuan Pembangunan (PPP—United Development Party), were both nominated for the post, and Gen. Suharto was obliged to indicate his preference for Sudharmono. ABRI disapproved of Sudharmono's appointment as, under his chairmanship of Golkar, there had been a shift away from military dominance in the grouping. In October Sudharmono resigned as Chairman of Golkar and was replaced by Gen. (retd) Wahono, who was acceptable to ABRI.

In early 1989 tension arising from land disputes produced social unrest in three areas of Java and on the island of Sumbawa (east of Bali and Lombok), in Nusa Tenggara. The first student demonstrations since 1978 were held to protest against the Government's expropriation of land without sufficient indemnification for those subject to relocation. Meanwhile, speculation over Suharto's successor had begun. In May 1989, however, Suharto warned officials to dismiss the topic of the succession and in September, when the Partai Demokrasi Indonesia (PDI—Indonesian Democratic Party) announced that it would support his candidacy, it appeared likely that he would seek election for a sixth term. In August 1990 a group of 58 prominent Indonesians issued a public demand to Suharto to retire from the presidency at the end of his current term of office and to permit greater democracy in Indonesia.

During 1991, in response to the growing demand for political *keterbukaan* (openness), several new organizations were formed to promote freedom of expression and other democratic values. As labour unrest grew, arrests and the alleged intimidation of political activists were instrumental in curbing expressions of dissent. In an attempt to control student unrest, political campaigns were banned on university campuses. In September Suharto removed several of the most outspoken members of Golkar from the list of candidates to contest the legislative elections, scheduled to take place on 9 June 1992.

The Government had, for some time, been seeking to win the support of the Muslim electorate in preparation for the presidential elections in 1993. In 1989 Suharto promoted legislation whereby decisions by Islamic courts no longer required confirmation by civil courts, and in December 1990 the President opened the symposium of the newly formed Association of Indonesian Muslim Intellectuals (ICMI), an organization which united a broad spectrum of Islamic interests. In 1991 Suharto made his first pilgrimage to Mecca, acceded to Islamic demands for certain educational reforms and supported the establishment of an Islamic bank. ABRI was opposed to the establishment of ICMI because it regarded the polarization of politics by religion as a threat to stability.

During the strictly monitored four-week campaign period leading to elections for the DPR, for local government bodies and for district councils, political parties were prohibited from addressing religious issues, the question of the dominant role of the ethnic Chinese community in the economy, or any subject that might present a threat to national unity. The opposition parties did, however, exploit the increasing public resentment about the rapidly expanding businesses of Suharto's children (some of whom had been awarded monopoly rights). The Forum for the Purification of People's Sovereignty (formed in 1991) urged the voters to boycott the elections, in an effort to elicit reforms from the Government.

On 9 June 1992 90.4% of the electorate participated in the election to the DPR, which resulted in a further victory for Golkar. Golkar secured 282 of the 400 elective seats, while 62 seats were won by the PPP (a gain of one seat compared with 1987) and 56 seats (compared with 40) by the PDI, which had mobilized almost 3m. supporters at a rally in Jakarta in the week prior to the election.

In October 1992 Suharto accepted nominations by Golkar, the PPP, the PDI and ABRI for a sixth term of office as President. His victory in the presidential election, due to take place in March 1993, was thus assured. Attention then focused on the vice-presidency. Owing to increasing public debate over ABRI's active involvement in political affairs and, in particular, concern over whether the appointment of 100 members of ABRI to the DPR remained justifiable, it was deemed important that ABRI consolidate its position through the election to the vice-presidency of its own principal candidate, Sutrisno. Suharto, however, was rumoured to support the prospective candidacy of the Minister of State for Research and Technology, Prof. Dr Ir Bucharuddin Jusuf (B. J.) Habibie, an influential Muslim leader and the then Chairman of ICMI. Sutrisno was subsequently endorsed as a vice-presidential candidate by the PDI, the PPP, ABRI and, finally, Golkar. At a meeting of the MPR on 10 and 11 March Suharto and Sutrisno were duly elected to the posts of President and Vice-President respectively.

Suharto's new 41-member Cabinet, which was announced in mid-March 1993, comprised 22 new appointees. ABRI representation was reduced from 11 to eight members. Those primarily responsible for the country's economic policy since 1988, Prof. Dr Johannes B. Sumarlin, Adrianus Mooy and Radius Prawiro (all western-educated Christians) were replaced, leaving only three Christians in the Cabinet; several members of ICMI were included in the new list, thus advancing the faction led by Habibie, who was unpopular with ABRI. Suharto announced that the new Government would pursue the aim of greater democracy and openness. In mid-1993 Suharto revoked a travel ban on all dissidents and established a National Council on Human Rights.

In October 1993, at the party Congress, the Minister of Information, Harmoko, became the first civilian to be elected to the chairmanship of Golkar. In an unprecedented move, Suharto had openly endorsed Harmoko's candidacy; it was widely speculated that this was to prevent ABRI from supporting its own candidate and effectively denying the President a choice. Also at the Congress, Suharto's family entered active national politics; his son, Bambang Trihatmodjo, and daughter, Siti Hardijanti Rukmana (known as Mbak Tutut), who had both been appointed to the MPR in 1992, were elected to positions of responsibility within Golkar.

In July 1993 the incumbent Chairman of the PDI, Soerjadi, was re-elected to the post at a fractious party Congress. The Government invalidated the election of Soerjadi, who had incurred Suharto's displeasure by campaigning during the 1992 elections for a limited presidential term of office, and appointed a 23-member 'caretaker board' pending new elections. An extraordinary Congress of the PDI ended inconclusively in December owing to the unexpected candidacy for the chairmanship of Megawati Sukarnoputri, the daughter of former President Sukarno. Despite government pressure to elect Budi Hardjono, a senior party official, Megawati received overwhelming support from the participants of the Congress, and the 'caretaker board' prevented a vote from taking place. The Government then ordered the holding of a new PDI Congress, at which Megawati was elected Chairman.

In June 1993 the USA imposed a deadline of February 1994 for Indonesia to improve workers' rights or lose trade privileges under the Generalized System of Preferences. The Government adopted reforms to the only officially recognized trade union, the Serikat Pekerja Seluruh Indonesia (All Indonesia Workers' Union), introduced a substantial increase in the minimum wage and revoked the controversial 1986 Labour Law, which allowed the intervention of the armed forces in labour disputes. Workers subsequently went on strike, accusing employers of failing to pay the new minimum wage and demanding improved working conditions. In February 1994 the independent Serikat Buruh Sejahtera Indonesia (SBSI—Indonesian Prosperous Labour Union), which had had its application for registration formally rejected in June 1993, appealed for a one-hour national work stoppage. Two days prior to the strike the General Secretary of the SBSI, Muchtar Pakpahan, was arrested and charged with inciting hatred against the Government (he was released in the following month). In April 1994 riots broke out in Medan, Sumatra, over workers' demands for improved factory conditions and the implementation of the new minimum wage, and rapidly degenerated into attacks on Chinese property and business executives. The attacks on Chinese companies reflected a widely-held perception that the ethnic Chinese had benefited disproportionately from the country's rapid economic growth. Three members of the SBSI surrendered to the authorities in May and admitted to having organized the protest. Further strikes broke out later in the month in other parts of northern Sumatra. In August Pakpahan was rearrested. He was given a three-year prison sentence in November for inciting labour unrest (which was later extended to four years). By that time, it was estimated that the majority of factories had complied with the provision of the new minimum wage.

In January 1995 it was announced by the armed forces that 300 members of the PDI were to be investigated for links to the 1965 coup attempt, following allegations that many members had relatives or contacts in the banned PKI. This apparent attempt to discredit the opposition grouping was followed in May by a ban on the presence of Megawati at the commemoration, in June, of the 25th anniversary of the death of her father, Sukarno, ostensibly because it might provoke outbreaks of violence.

Throughout 1995 the Indonesian authorities attempted to ascribe social unrest to communist subversion, asserting that a communist revival remained a threat to national security. In September the Chief of Staff of the Armed Forces named several prominent dissidents, including Muchtar Pakpahan (whose conviction for incitement had been overturned by the Supreme Court in that month), as members of 'formless organizations' which, he claimed, had infiltrated pressure groups to promote the resurgence of communism. In November 300 people were arrested in Java as subversives, who were allegedly using the tactics of the PKI.

In July 1995, in response to widespread condemnation of Indonesia's human rights violations, Suharto announced that three prisoners detained for their complicity in the 1965 coup attempt would be released to coincide with the 50th anniversary of independence in August. The administration also subsequently announced that the code ET (which stood for *Eks Tahanan Politik*—former political prisoner) was to be removed from identity papers following the anniversary. The measure affected about 1.3m. citizens, most of whom had been arrested following the 1965 coup attempt, but released without trial; ET status had subjected them to certain restrictions (for example, in employment) and to widespread discrimination. The Government also revoked legislation requiring a permit for political gatherings, although the security forces still had to be notified. This display of liberality was, however, tempered by a new campaign against press freedom and political dissent.

In October 1995 30 members of an extreme right-wing group, the Islamic State of Indonesia, were arrested in western Java for attempting to overthrow 'the unitary state of Indonesia'. There were fears that Suharto's apparent attempt to balance the influence of the armed forces with an emphasis on Islam would

INDONESIA

INDONESIA

create religious disharmony. Critics blamed the ICMI-sponsored newspaper *Republika* and its magazine *Ummat* for fomenting religious passions, leading to outbreaks of violence. Social unrest was also caused, however, by a disparity in living standards; in January 1996 in Bandung, West Java, thousands took part in demonstrations against the disproportionately wealthy ethnic Chinese.

In December 1995 Suharto implemented an unprecedented mid-term cabinet reorganization, in which Prof. Dr Satrio Budiardjo Yudono was dismissed and the Ministry of Trade, over which he had presided, was merged with the Ministry of Industry. This dismissal of one of Habibie's protégés, the day before Habibie's re-election to the chairmanship of the increasingly powerful ICMI, was widely interpreted as a signal from Suharto for Habibie to restrain his political ambitions. The accusations of financial irregularities and nepotism levelled against the Minister of Communications, Haryanto Dhanutirto (also a close associate of Habibie), were similarly interpreted.

In early 1996 there were limited moves to create greater political freedom. In January the Government abolished permit requirements for political meetings (police permission was still necessary for public gatherings and demonstrations). In March a group of political activists established an Independent Election Monitoring Committee, which was immediately declared unconstitutional by the Government. In April the Government restored voting rights to 1,157,820 people who had been associated with the PKI, leaving a further 20,706 still ineligible to vote. The Government's increasing concern over potential opposition to Golkar in the 1997 elections, however, resulted in a return to more authoritarian practices. In May 1996 Sri Bintang Pamungkas, an outspoken member of the PPP expelled from the DPR in March 1995, received a custodial sentence of 34 months for insulting Suharto; he remained free, however, pending an appeal. In the same month Pamungkas formed a new political organization, the Partai Uni Demokrasi Indonesia (PUDI—United Democratic Party of Indonesia), which ABRI and the Government refused to recognize. In December the High Court upheld the verdict against Pamungkas, who subsequently appealed to the Supreme Court.

In June 1996 the Government responded to the increasing popularity of Megawati's leadership of the PDI, and consequent potential threat to Golkar: government supporters within the PDI organized a party congress in the northern Sumatran town of Medan, which removed Megawati as leader of the party, and installed a former Chairman, Soerjadi. PDI members loyal to Megawati organized demonstrations in her support throughout the country during July, and occupied the PDI headquarters in Jakarta. At the end of July members of Soerjadi's PDI faction and the armed forces acted to remove Megawati and her supporters forcibly from the PDI headquarters, prompting mass rioting in Jakarta. Violent clashes ensued between protesters and the security forces, in which five people were killed. The Government declared the minor, Marxist-influenced Partai Rakyat Demokrasi (PRD) to be responsible for the disturbances, and renewed its campaign against communism, claiming that the PRD was the PKI's successor. In September the Government disbanded the PRD, declaring it to be a proscribed organization.

In an attempt to inhibit opposition efforts in the 1997 legislative elections, Suharto, in October 1996, ordered ABRI to suppress all political dissent. The Government's continued lack of commitment to its stated policy of political openness was demonstrated when, in November, it declared that it would take action against non-governmental organizations which violated Indonesian law and the *pancasila* ideology. In December the DPR ratified legislation granting the Government extensive powers to revoke the broadcasting permits of private television and radio stations. In the same month a government decree banned mass rallies during the election campaign. In February 1997 the Government announced that all election campaign speeches, including those broadcast on television and radio, were to be vetted to ensure their adherence to the *pancasila*.

Repressive measures against Megawati's faction of the PDI continued; in September 1996 the Government declared Megawati's new party headquarters in eastern Jakarta to be illegal and it was closed by the military. Candidates nominated by Megawati's faction for the 1997 parliamentary elections were omitted from the final list of candidates in January 1997. In April thousands of supporters of Megawati rallied outside the DPR to demand the right to contest the general election.

Prior to the general election, which was held on 29 May 1997, the Government permitted a campaign period of 25 days during which no two parties were permitted to campaign simultaneously in the same region. Despite this, there was extensive localized pre-election violence. In the worst incident 125 people were killed when a shopping centre was set alight during clashes between supporters of Golkar and the PPP in the provincial capital of Kalimantan, Banjarmasin; more than 150 others were killed in various other incidents across the country. Following the election, riots in Madura, as a result of PPP claims that ballots had not been counted, resulted in an unprecedented repeat of voting at 86 polling stations on 4 June. The final results of the election, which continued to attract allegations of fraud, revealed that Golkar had secured 74.3% of the vote (compared with 68.1% in 1992) giving it control of 325 seats, the PPP had won 89 seats, while Soerjadi's PDI had secured only 11 seats (compared with 56 in 1992).

Social unrest, which had been widespread in 1996, continued throughout 1997, as a result of religious tension, income disparity between social and ethnic groups and the repercussions of the transmigration programme initiated in 1971. The worst violence began in West Kalimantan in December 1996 as indigenous Dayak tribesmen massacred hundreds of Madurese transmigrants following an attack by Muslim youths on local schoolgirls. Despite a peace agreement in February 1997, fighting continued into March and thousands were displaced.

In August 1997 the two principal Muslim leaders, Abdurrahman Wahid and Amien Rais, the leader of the second largest Islamic grouping, Muhammadiyah, were excluded from the list of 500 civilian and military appointees to the MPR. Amien Rais had been forced to resign from a board of experts in ICMI in February for publicly criticizing the controversial Freeport mine in Irian Jaya (now Papua, see below).

Following a massive decline in the value of the Indonesian currency between August and October 1997, Suharto was forced to accept a rescue programme from the IMF to restore confidence in the country's economy. However, Suharto subsequently failed to implement reforms required by the IMF that he feared would provoke social and political unrest and adversely affect his family and friends, who had long benefited from control of lucrative monopolies and tariff protection of their businesses. In December widespread rumours of Suharto's ill health provoked a further crisis of confidence in the Indonesian economy. At the end of the month an unprecedented gathering of Muslim leaders and intellectuals took place, including members of ICMI; the participants rejected Suharto's leadership and rallied around Amien Rais, who had already offered himself as a presidential candidate. Wahid subsequently joined Amien Rais and Megawati (who had entered an informal alliance) in calling for Suharto's resignation. Megawati also, in a largely symbolic gesture since the President had to be a nominee of a party represented in the MPR, presented herself as a presidential candidate. In January 1998 Suharto delivered an unrealistic budget, which failed to comply with IMF stipulations. A further rapid decline of the currency and massive price increases of staple foodstuffs ensued, causing rioting. Following meetings with foreign leaders and IMF representatives, Suharto was forced to announce a second budget. Despite opposition to his candidacy, Suharto declared his acceptance of Golkar's nomination for the presidency (announced in October), thus assuring his victory in the forthcoming election. He indicated that of the 13 contenders for the vice-presidency he would support Habibie's candidacy.

At the presidential election held on 10 March 1998 Suharto was re-elected unopposed. He then endorsed the nomination of Habibie as the new Vice-President, and on 14 March Suharto announced the appointment of a new, 36-member Cabinet, which included a number of members of his immediate circle of friends and family. (Prior to his re-election, Suharto had also appointed his son-in-law, Lt-Gen. Prabowo Subianto, as Commander of Kostrad.) Suharto's appointment of such a Cabinet defied the recommendations of the IMF. Student protests in support of calls for the President's resignation and for fundamental political and economic reforms increased, and on 5 May riots erupted in Jakarta, precipitated by the announcement of a 70% increase in the price of fuel. During the following days violence and unrest spread throughout the archipelago. On 12 May six students were shot dead by military snipers during a student protest at Trisakti University in Jakarta, and violence in the city reached a peak on 14 May. It was initially estimated that during 12–15 May 500 people were killed in the capital, while a further 700 perished elsewhere; however, a report published by Indonesia's leading human rights group in early

June stated that at least 1,188 people had died in Jakarta alone. Indonesia's ethnic-Chinese minority was the target for much of the violence that occurred in May: an uncertain number of Chinese were murdered, numerous Chinese women were raped, and Chinese homes and businesses were looted and burned. On 21 May, following sustained popular and political pressure to step down (including an unprecedented demand for his resignation by Harmoko on 18 May, and the resignation of the 14 economic ministers in the Cabinet), Suharto announced his resignation as President. Vice-President Habibie was sworn in immediately as Suharto's successor, and subsequently appointed a new 'reform Cabinet', which, however, included a number of ministers from the previous administration. The new President also announced the release of a number of political prisoners (including Muchtar Pakpahan and Sri Bintang Pamungkas), encouraged government departments to sever ties with enterprises owned by Suharto's family, and supported Gen. Wiranto in his dismissal of Suharto's son-in-law, Lt-Gen. Prabowo, from his position in Kostrad (it was subsequently announced that Prabowo had been formally dismissed from the army following an investigation into his conduct as Commander of the unit, and was also to face a court martial). Habibie also announced that elections would be held in 1999; new political parties began to be formed in anticipation of fresh electoral laws. On 1 June 1998 an investigation into the assets of former President Suharto and other government officials was announced, and later the same month Habibie expelled 41 members of the MPR, including several close associates of Suharto, on account of alleged corruption, nepotism and collusion. (Seven members of Suharto's family were ousted from their seats in the MPR the following month.) Despite such moves, Habibie was considered by many to be under the control of Suharto, and there were repeated demands from student groups and other opposition organizations for Habibie to relinquish the presidency and for a transitional government to be installed.

Discontent and rioting continued across the archipelago throughout the latter half of 1998, fuelled by dissatisfaction at the pace of change under the new administration and by severe food shortages, as well as by increasing ethnic and religious tension. A four-day special session of the MPR was convened in Jakarta on 10 November, and on 13 November at least 16 people were killed and more than 400 injured when students and civilians clashed with soldiers outside the building where the MPR session was being held. Further riots occurred in Jakarta on 22 November, in which at least another 14 people died during clashes between Muslims and Catholics; churches and Christian schools were also attacked.

In November 1998 a report was published containing the findings of a panel appointed by the Government to investigate the riots in May. The panel found that elements of the military had acted as provocateurs during the riots (with particular suspicion falling on a unit led by Lt-Gen. Prabowo), concluding that the riots had been 'created as part of a political struggle at the level of the élite', and recommended that further investigations be carried out into the causes of the violent unrest. In December former President Suharto faced questioning at the Higher Prosecutor's Office over allegations of corruption; two former cabinet ministers were also summoned for questioning.

In December 1998 it was announced that a legislative election would be held on 7 June 1999; it was further announced that the MPR (including 200 additional delegates) would convene on 29 August to elect a new President. In early December 1998 a large demonstration was held in Jakarta by supporters of Megawati. In January 1999 a number of changes to the electoral laws were announced in advance of the forthcoming election: in accordance with a new electoral system combining both district and proportional voting, seats in the DPR were to be allocated proportionally, but only parties fielding candidates in a substantial number of districts would be permitted to contest the election. It was further announced that civil servants were no longer to be obliged to support Golkar, that the number of seats in the DPR allocated to the military was to be reduced from 75 to 38 and that the membership of the MPR was to be reduced from 1,000 to 700 (500 of whom would comprise the members of the DPR while, of the remainder, 135 were to be elected by the provincial assemblies and 65 appointed by the Komite Pemilihan Umum—General Election Committee).

Violent unrest continued across the archipelago throughout January and February 1999: at least 159 people were killed during clashes between Muslims and Christians on the island of Ambon, in the province of Maluku, while a number of others died

in outbreaks of violence elsewhere. Although the campaigning for the forthcoming legislative election dominated the political agenda during the first half of 1999, the Habibie Government continued to pursue an extensive programme of reform during this period. Amongst new laws passed were several that benefited the provinces, including one providing for the election of district heads (*bupati*) by the district assemblies. In April the Subversion Law, introduced in 1963 and previously applied in the suppression of political dissidents, was repealed by the MPR (although some of the prohibitions covered by the law were retained). In May a presidential decree removed a ban on the use and teaching of the Mandarin Chinese language and also outlawed discrimination on the grounds of ethnic origin. Two significant changes also took place in the armed forces in the first half of 1999: following a reshuffle of military personnel in January, in April the police force—part of the Indonesian military since 1962—was formally separated from the armed forces (although it remained under the control of the Ministry of Defence); and the armed forces resumed their revolutionary-era name, Tentara Nasional Indonesia (TNI—the Indonesian National Defence Forces), in place of the Suharto-era name, ABRI (the Armed Forces of the Republic of Indonesia). The Government remained under considerable public pressure, however, to investigate the accumulation of wealth by the Suharto family.

President Habibie was nominated as the sole presidential candidate of the Golkar party on 14 May 1999, despite concerns expressed by some elements of the party regarding Habibie's close association with former President Suharto. On 18 May the three leading opposition parties—Megawati's Partai Demokrasi Indonesia Perjuangan (PDI—P, Indonesian Democratic Struggle Party), Abdurrahman Wahid's Partai Kebangkitan Bangsa (PKB, National Awakening Party), and Amien Rais's Partai Amanat Nasional (PAN, National Mandate Party)—agreed to form an informal electoral alliance against Golkar; however, the alliance exhibited instability from an early stage. The election campaign was formally opened on 19 May, and proceeded with only minimal incidents of violent disruption, with 48 parties competing for a share of the vote. The election was held as scheduled on 7 June; approximately 118m. people voted (a turn-out of 91%). As expected, Megawati's PDI—P led the polls, winning 34% of the votes cast (154 seats); the second largest share of the vote was unexpectedly won by Golkar, which secured 20% of votes cast (120 seats), performing poorly in the cities but achieving a strong result in the outer islands. Abdurrahman Wahid's PKB secured 59 seats, while Amien Rais's PAN won just 7% of the vote (35 seats). Some 14 other smaller parties also won seats in the MPR. Despite allegations of irregularities in the election process, the results were finally endorsed by President Habibie on 3 August. In the context of the election results, Megawati and Habibie emerged initially as the main candidates for the presidency, which was originally scheduled to be decided in November. On 20 October, however, following the rejection of his presidential record by the MPR in a secret ballot, Habibie withdrew his candidacy just hours before the rescheduled vote was due to be held. Expectations that Megawati would be elected President increased immediately; however, Megawati failed to win the contest, receiving 313 votes compared with the 373 secured by Abdurrahman Wahid, the only other serious candidate, who had received the endorsement of a number of Islamic parties as well as the support of the Golkar party, following the withdrawal of Habibie. The announcement of Wahid's victory provoked outrage among Megawati's supporters, and violent protests ensued in Jakarta and elsewhere on Java, as well as on the island of Bali. On 21 October the MPR voted to appoint Megawati as Vice-President. The new Cabinet was announced on 26 October, and reflected the conciliatory and inclusive approach of the new President: it included both Islamist and nationalist representatives, as well as representatives of non-Javanese groups. Gen. Wiranto, who was appointed Co-ordinating Minister for Political Affairs and Security, was replaced as Minister of Defence by the former Minister of Education and Culture, Yuwono Sudarsono, the first civilian to hold the post. Wiranto was replaced as Commander-in-Chief of the TNI by Adm. Widodo Adi Sutjipto.

In October 1999 the newly appointed Attorney-General, Marzuki Darusman, announced that the investigation into the allegations of corruption made against former President Suharto—which had been closed under the Habibie Government on the alleged grounds of lack of evidence—was to be reopened. The apparent commitment of the new administration to addressing the issue of corruption was further emphasized in November, when Wahid urged the investigation of three government ministers. One of the ministers reportedly implicated, the Co-ordinating Minister for People's Welfare and the Eradication of Poverty and leader of the PPP, Hamzah Haz, resigned from the Cabinet in late November.

In the months following Wahid's election to the presidency, further violent unrest took place across the archipelago. Particularly serious ethnic violence continued on the island of Ambon in Maluku province where, according to official estimates in December 1999, more than 750 people had died and many thousands more had fled the region, since the renewal of violent clashes between Muslims and Christians in the region in January of that year. (Aid agencies, however, estimated the total number of dead to be much higher.) In mid-December President Wahid and Vice-President Megawati (who was subject to harsh criticism for her failure to address the crisis, despite having been charged by Wahid with special responsibility for Maluku) visited the region and urged an end to the conflict. Later in the same month hundreds of additional troops were sent to Ambon to supplement the 2,500 already deployed in Maluku, following a further escalation of the violence and the occurrence of dozens more deaths. Although the predominantly Muslim northern districts of Maluku were formally separated as the new province of North Maluku in late 1999, this failed to dispel the tension, and in December violence flared on other islands in the region, with at least 265 people reported killed in clashes between Christians and Muslims on the island of Halmahera at the end of the month.

On 31 January 2000 Indonesia's National Human Rights Commission released a report containing the results of its investigation into the role of the Indonesian armed forces in human rights abuses in the former Indonesian province of Timor-Leste (see below). Thirty-three military officers, including the former Commander-in-Chief of the armed forces, Gen. Wiranto, were implicated. In response to the Commission's conclusions, President Wahid demanded Wiranto's resignation from his post of Co-ordinating Minister for Political Affairs and Security; Wiranto, however, openly defied Wahid's demands. In mid-February Wahid suspended Wiranto from his position; Wiranto was to maintain his ministerial rank, although his portfolio was allocated to the Minister of Home Affairs, Gen. (retd) Suryadi Sudirja, pending further investigation. Wiranto resigned in mid-May. In January, meanwhile, a reorganization took place within the TNI, in which officers loyal to Wiranto were apparently removed from positions of influence. A second reorganization of senior military personnel was announced in February, in which Maj.-Gen. Agus Wirahadikusumah, who was reportedly committed to Wahid's policy of disengaging the military from Indonesian politics, was appointed as the head of Kostrad. In August doubts concerning the commitment of the Indonesian Government to the trial of military personnel suspected of involvement in gross human rights violations in Timor-Leste were provoked when the MPR introduced a constitutional amendment that excluded military personnel from prosecution for crimes committed prior to the enactment of the relevant legislation. Many international observers feared that this would seriously threaten the possibility of the prosecution of members of the Indonesian military believed responsible for recent human rights abuses in the territory. These doubts were compounded in early September, when Wiranto's name was not included on a list, announced by the Attorney-General's office, of 19 suspects.

In late April 2000 President Wahid dismissed from the Cabinet the Minister of State for Investment and Development of State Enterprises, Laksamana Sukardi of the PDI—P, and the Minister of Trade and Industry, Yusuf Kalla of the pro-Habibie wing of Golkar; Wahid subsequently suggested that both Ministers were guilty of corruption. In July Wahid faced fierce criticism from the DPR when he refused to explain the reasons for his dismissal of the two Ministers. Meanwhile, general misgivings about Wahid's style of government also increased. In August Wahid announced that he was to delegate the daily administration of the Government to Vice-President Megawati, although the President was to retain overall control. It was speculated by many observers that Wahid's announcement had been intended to safeguard his own position during the 12-day session of the MPR held on 7–18 August, in the context of widespread dissatisfaction with the President's record. The announcement of the apparent power-sharing arrangement appeared to placate the MPR. Amendments to the Constitution

passed by the MPR in August, however, included articles defining explicitly the authority of the DPR, particularly in relation to the body's questioning and investigating of government activities; legislation was also passed to extend military representation in the MPR until 2009, four years after the date at which the military had been scheduled to lose its remaining 38 seats in the chamber. On 23 August President Wahid announced the formation of a new 26-member Cabinet. The incoming Cabinet included considerably fewer representatives of Megawati's PDI—P, reportedly resulting in serious tensions between the President and the Vice-President. Two of the most influential cabinet posts were allocated to Wahid loyalists: Gen. (retd) Susilo Bambang Yudhoyono was appointed Co-ordinating Minister for Political Affairs, Security and Social Welfare, while Rizal Ramli was designated Co-ordinating Minister for the Economy, Finance and Industry, replacing Kwik Kian Gie, who had resigned in advance of the reorganization.

In August 2000 former President Suharto was formally charged with corruption arising from his 30 years in power; however, in late September all corruption charges against him were dismissed after an independent team of doctors declared that the former President was mentally and physically unfit to stand trial, thereby provoking violent protests on the streets of Jakarta. (In December 2001, after some vacillation, the Supreme Court stated that it would not pursue the charges, owing to the former President's continued ill health. Although the Government's plans officially to abandon the case against him met with mounting criticism, in August 2002 he was formally declared medically unfit to stand trial.) In mid-September 2000, meanwhile, President Wahid announced that he had ordered the arrest of Suharto's youngest son, Hutomo Mandala Putra, in connection with a series of bomb threats and explosions in Jakarta in August and September. In one attack in mid-September at least 15 people were killed when a bomb exploded at the Jakarta Stock Exchange. In late September Hutomo Mandala Putra was sentenced to 18 months' imprisonment after being convicted on an unrelated charge of fraudulent activity; however, he subsequently evaded arrest and went into hiding.

In July 2001 Justice Syafiuddin Kartasasmita, the judge who had upheld the sentence passed on Hutomo Mandala Putra, was shot by unidentified killers. In August two suspects confessed to the murder, but admitted in custody that Suharto's son had financed them and supplied the weapons used in the attack. Meanwhile, two men were convicted of the bombing of the Jakarta Stock Exchange and sentenced to 20 years' imprisonment each. In October the corruption charge on which Hutomo Mandala Putra had initially been convicted was rejected by the Supreme Court. However, he remained in hiding owing to his suspected involvement in several other cases. In late November police finally arrested the fugitive, and in December the Supreme Court announced that Hutomo Mandala Putra would serve at least 11 months in prison for evading arrest, despite the fact that his original conviction had been overturned. During police questioning Suharto's son claimed that in October 2000 he had given a sum of money to two men close to President Wahid on the understanding that this would secure for him a presidential pardon. (Wahid denied all knowledge of this when questioned early in 2002.) In March 2002, following the conclusion of the police investigation, Hutomo Mandala Putra was charged with murder, illegal possession of weapons and fleeing from justice; his trial began in the same month. Meanwhile, the two men reported to have assassinated Justice Syafiuddin were found guilty of murder and sentenced to life imprisonment. A third man was sentenced to a four-year prison term in a separate trial for his involvement in planning the assassination. In July Hutomo Mandala Putra was found guilty of murder and sentenced to a 15-year prison term; he later announced that he did not intend to appeal against the verdict.

In September 2000 the DPR appointed a committee to investigate two financial scandals with which President Wahid had been linked. The first of the two scandals involved the irregular diversion of US $4.1m. from the funds of the Badan Urusan Logistic (BULOG—the National Logistics Agency), whilst the second concerned a donation of $2m. made by Sultan Hassanal Bolkiah of Brunei. Although, initially, there appeared to be no compelling evidence implicating Wahid in these scandals, the President's refusal to be questioned on either matter provoked intense frustration among legislators. The commission reported the findings of its investigation into President Wahid's involvement in late January 2001, concluding that Wahid 'could be suspected of playing a role' in the theft of BULOG funds by his personal masseur and that the President had been deliberately inconsistent in his explanations of how the donation from Sultan Hassanal Bolkiah (originally intended for social welfare) had been spent; however, the commission failed to present conclusive evidence that Wahid had personally benefited from either situation. In early February the DPR voted by 393 votes to four for the formal censure of Wahid over his alleged involvement in the scandals. According to Indonesian law, Wahid was given three months to respond to the motion of censure and to explain his actions to the DPR. If, three months after the original memorandum of censure, the members of the DPR should remain unsatisfied by the President's response, a further warning could be issued after which Wahid would be given 30 days in which to act before a vote could be held to remove him from office. Following the issue of the original memorandum of censure, however, the President continued to deny any wrongdoing and stated his intention to complete his term of presidential office. Tens of thousands of pro-Wahid demonstrators took to the streets in Surabaya and elsewhere in East Java (President Wahid's home province), and protesters set fire to the regional offices of Golkar, which had supported the vote to censure Wahid. Later in the same month Wahid offered himself for questioning by police investigating the two scandals.

In March 2001 more than 12,000 students held a demonstration in Jakarta to demand the President's resignation. In view of Wahid's unsatisfactory reply to his first censure, on 30 April the DPR voted overwhelmingly to issue a second censure and requested that the MPR convene a special session to begin impeachment proceedings. In May the Attorney-General commented that there was no evidence of the President's involvement in the corruption scandals over which he was being accused. Violent pro-Wahid demonstrations took place in East Java. However, on 30 May the DPR voted by a huge majority to instruct the MPR to begin an impeachment hearing on 1 August. In response, on 1 June the President reorganized his Cabinet, dismissing the Co-ordinating Minister for Political Affairs, Security and Social Welfare, Susilo Bambang Yudhoyono. The Chief of Police, Gen. Surojo Bimantoro, was suspended after efforts to dismiss him were thwarted. A few days later the President initiated a further reallocation of ministerial portfolios. On 9 July the President threatened to declare a state of emergency on 20 July if no compromise had been reached. The next day he reshuffled the Cabinet again and on 20 July he appointed a new Chief of Police without the support of the legislature and moved the deadline for the termination of impeachment efforts to 31 July. A special session of the MPR was convened the next day to which the President was summoned to give an account of his 21 months in power. President Wahid declared the session illegal and refused to attend. The next day he suspended the legislature, declaring a state of civil emergency, and urged that new elections be held in one year's time. However, the military refused to support the declaration, and the MPR declared that the President did not have the constitutional authority to dissolve it.

On 23 July 2001 Abdurrahman Wahid was deposed as President following an immediate impeachment hearing. He was replaced by Vice-President Megawati Sukarnoputri, in a peaceful transition of power. On 26 July legislators elected the leader of the PPP, Hamzah Haz, to act as President Megawati's deputy. On 9 August the new President announced the composition of her first Cabinet. Of its 32 members, only four were ex-military men, in sharp contrast to previous practice. Most of the principal posts went to non-political professionals, including the appointment of Dorodjatun Kuntjoro-Jakti as Co-ordinating Minister for the Economy, Finance and Industry. Susilo Bambang Yudhoyono was reinstated as Co-ordinating Minister for Political Affairs, Security and Social Welfare.

In October 2001 President Megawati gave her assent to a prosecution request to question the Speaker of the DPR, Akbar Tandjung, over the alleged misappropriation of an estimated US $4m. of BULOG funds to finance the Golkar party election campaign in 1999. When questioned, Tandjung admitted that he had handled the money on the orders of President Habibie, but had passed it on to an Islamic charity to fund food supplies for the poor. However, Attorney-General Muhammad Abdul Rachman claimed that investigations showed that such contributions had never taken place. In December 2001 state prosecutors questioned former President Habibie in connection with the scandal, and in January 2002 Akbar Tandjung was formally declared to be a suspect, prompting fears of another political crisis. In March 2002 approximately 1,500 protesters gathered

outside the DPR building to demand Tandjung's resignation and the establishment of an independent inquiry into the allegations that had been made against him; his trial on charges of corruption began one week later. In September Tandjung was convicted of the charges against him and sentenced to a three-year prison term; despite the failure of his first appeal, in February 2004 the Supreme Court overturned his conviction, prompting demonstrations against the verdict in several cities. Meanwhile, in March 2002 the Governor of Bank Indonesia, Dr Syahril Sabirin, was sentenced to three years in prison following his conviction for the theft of bank funds to finance the election campaign of former President Habibie. In August, however, his conviction was overturned by a court of appeal.

In August 2002 a series of constitutional amendments was passed following the annual session of the MPR. These provided for the direct election of both the President and Vice-President at the next national poll, scheduled to be held in 2004, and for the abolition of all seats held by non-elected representatives, effectively terminating military involvement in the legislature five years earlier than originally intended. The legislation also provided for a bicameral legislature through the creation of the Dewan Perwakilan Daerah (DPD—House of Representatives of the Regions) which, together with the DPR, would form the MPR. A total of 14 amendments received legislative assent; these constituted the 'Fourth Amendment' to the Constitution. However, a proposal for the introduction of Islamic *shari'a* law, endorsed by Vice-President Hamzah Haz and the PPP, was rejected. The DPR ratified the amendments into law in 2003.

From 2002 one of the most serious challenges facing the Indonesian Government was the threat posed by terrorist activity, at both a domestic and regional level. In October 2002 the Government's response to this threat came under particularly close scrutiny when two bombs exploded in the tourist resort of Kuta, on the island of Bali. One of these explosions, which occurred outside a night-club, resulted in the deaths of 202 people, many of whom were tourists, mainly Australians. In its first admission that Islamist fundamentalists were operative within Indonesia, the Government initially attributed the attack to the international terrorist network al-Qa'ida, which it believed to have been working in collaboration with local terrorists. The DPR authorized two emergency decrees, bringing into effect several previously delayed anti-terrorism measures, including a law permitting suspects to be detained for up to seven days without charge. Two weeks after the bombings the Muslim cleric Abu Bakar Bashir, commander of the Majelis Mujahidin Indonesia (MMI—Indonesian Mujahideen Council) and alleged to be the spiritual head of the regional Islamist terrorist organization Jemaah Islamiah, was detained for questioning in relation to the attacks. (He had been questioned by police in January of that year over alleged links to al-Qa'ida but had been released without charge.) In the mean time the USA and the UN announced that they had designated Jemaah Islamiah a terrorist entity and 'frozen' its financial assets. The police made several further arrests as the investigation into the bombings proceeded and in November 2002 one of the suspects, Amrozi bin Nurhasyim, confessed to his involvement and to having strong links to Jemaah Islamiah, as well as implicating several others in the attack. Later in the same month Imam Samudra was arrested on suspicion of having organized the attacks. He confessed to being a member of Jemaah Islamiah and to having planned earlier attacks, including the bombing of churches across the archipelago in December 2000 (see below), together with the operational leader of the organization, Riduan Isamuddin, also known as Hambali. In December 2002 Ali Gufron, also known as Mukhlas, who apparently had succeeded Hambali as operational leader, was also arrested and confessed to having helped to plan the Bali attack. The trials of those involved began in Denpasar in May 2003; a total of 34 people had been detained owing to their suspected involvement in the bombings. In July it was reported that another suspect, Idris, also known as Jhoni Hendrawan, had been arrested in the previous month and, in August, the Thai authorities announced that they had finally captured Hambali. He was subsequently taken into custody by the USA. The Indonesian Government was permitted indirect access to Hambali for the first time in February 2004.

In March 2003 the DPR gave its assent to counter-terrorism legislation specifically designating terrorism as a crime and providing for detention without trial for terrorist suspects. The legislation was enacted retrospectively in order to cover the Bali bombing. In April the trial of Abu Bakar Bashir on charges of subversion and involvement in several terrorist attacks, including the bombings carried out on churches in late 2000, began in Jakarta. In August 2003 more than 3,000 Islamist militants attended a demonstration organized by the MMI in the capital to signal their support for Bashir. In the following month Bashir was convicted of the subversion charges against him but, owing to insufficient evidence, was acquitted both of any involvement in terrorist attacks and of the charge that he was the spiritual leader of Jemaah Islamiah. He was sentenced to a four-year prison term. However, in December this was reduced to three years when, following an appeal, a court overturned Bashir's subversion conviction, whilst upholding the remaining charges against him. Bashir's sentence was further reduced to 18 months by the Supreme Court in March 2004. In the following month, immediately after his release from prison, Bashir was rearrested on suspicion of terrorism. Meanwhile, in August 2003 Amrozi became the first person to be convicted in connection with the bombings in Bali; he was sentenced to death for his part in the attack. His appeal against the sentence was later rejected. In the following month Imam Samudra became the second person to be convicted and given a death sentence for his part in the bombings. A further suspect, Ali Imron, was sentenced to life imprisonment, having expressed some remorse for his actions. In October Ali Gufron, generally believed to have been responsible for planning the attacks, was also found guilty of the charges against him and sentenced to death. A further 13 suspects had been sentenced to prison terms for having played minor parts in the bombings. In July 2004 the Constitutional Court declared that the counter-terrorism legislation approved in 2003 and used to convict a number of those responsible for the Bali bombings should not have been applied retroactively. The Minister of Justice and Human Rights Affairs stated that the ruling did not overturn the convictions already secured, but made it impossible to continue using the law in future cases for crimes committed before its enactment.

During 2003 the continued threat posed by terrorist activity in Indonesia was highlighted by a number of bomb attacks on the capital. In April a bomb exploded at the Sukarno-Hatta International Airport, injuring 11 people, and in July an explosion outside the DPR building caused minor damage. In the most serious terrorist incident to have taken place since the Bali bombings of the previous year, in August an explosive device detonated by a suicide bomber outside the Marriott Hotel in Jakarta resulted in the deaths of 12 people. The perpetrator of the attack was later identified as having been a member of Jemaah Islamiah. It was feared that the bombing could have been planned to coincide with the imminent announcement of the first verdict in the Bali bombings. In the aftermath of the bombing the police apprehended a number of suspects, all of whom were believed to be members of Jemaah Islamiah. The first trial in connection with the Marriott bombing began in January 2004. In February Sardono Siliwangi became the first person to be convicted of involvement in the bombing; he was sentenced to a 10-year prison term. A second suspect, Mohammed Rais, was convicted in May and sentenced to seven years in prison. In June two alleged Acehnese separatists were sentenced to prison terms for the bombing of the DPR building in July 2003. In August 2004 Idris was sentenced to 10 years' imprisonment for his part in the hotel bombing, but charges against him in connection with the Bali bombings were withdrawn, owing to the Constitutional Court's July ruling, despite an earlier confession of his involvement. A bomb exploded outside the Australian embassy in Jakarta in September, killing nine people, mostly Indonesians, and injuring more than 180 others. Jemaah Islamiah was held responsible for the attack, and a number of suspects were subsequently detained. In October at least nine people were injured when a bomb exploded outside the Indonesian embassy in Paris, France; no group claimed responsibility. In the same month the trial of Bashir on charges of conspiring and inciting acts of terrorism, including the Bali and Marriott bombings, commenced in Jakarta. He was also again accused of being the spiritual leader of Jemaah Islamiah. In relation to the Bali attacks, Bashir was to be tried under the criminal code. In February 2005, testifying at his ongoing trial, Bashir formally denied any involvement in the Bali and Marriott bombings and any connection with Jemaah Islamiah. In March, however, while being cleared of charges relating to the bombing of the Marriott Hotel, Bashir was found guilty of conspiracy over the Bali attacks and sentenced to a prison term of two-and-a-half years. Australia and the USA

immediately expressed their disappointment at the leniency of the sentence. Bashir was expected to appeal.

Meanwhile, in early 2004 preparations were under way for legislative and local elections scheduled to take place on 5 April, as well as the country's first direct presidential and vice-presidential elections, which were to be held on 5 July. A total of 24 parties had registered to contest the elections. The success of Akbar Tandjung's appeal against his corruption conviction rendered him eligible for the Golkar presidential nomination, which was also being contested by, amongst others, Gen. (retd) Wiranto. The Co-ordinating Minister for Political Affairs, Security and Social Welfare, Gen. (retd) Susilo Bambang Yudhoyono, resigned from the Cabinet in March in advance of declaring his candidacy for the presidential election as the representative of the Partai Demokrat (DP—Democratic Party). The legislative and local elections took place, as planned, on 5 April. The Golkar party secured 128 of the 550 seats in the expanded DPR, while the PDI—P won 109 seats in the legislature. The former thus replaced the PDI—P as the largest parliamentary grouping. Of the smaller parties, the PPP won 58 seats, the DP 57, and the PAN and the PKB each secured 52 seats. An estimated 84% of registered voters participated in the polls. In mid-April the Co-ordinating Minister for People's Welfare, Yusuf Kalla, announced his resignation from the Cabinet to be Yudhoyono's vice-presidential candidate. A few days later Golkar nominated Wiranto as its presidential candidate at its National Convention. In May President Megawati announced that her vice-presidential candidate was to be Ahmad Hasyim, head of the country's largest Muslim organization, Nahdlatul Ulama (NU).

Yudhoyono secured the largest share of the vote in the presidential election on 5 July 2004, receiving 33.6% of the votes cast, followed by Megawati, with 26.6%, and Wiranto, with 22.2%. Amien Rais and Vice-President Hamzah Haz also contested the election on behalf of their respective parties, the PAN and the PPP. As no candidate won more than 50% of the votes, Yudhoyono and Megawati proceeded to a second round of voting, which was held on 20 September. Despite Golkar's declared support for the incumbent, this second poll resulted in a clear victory for Yudhoyono, who secured 60.6% of the votes cast. Estimated voter turn-out in the second round was 75%, compared with 78% in the first. Yudhoyono's election campaign had focused on pledges to stimulate the economy and to combat corruption and terrorism. The new President was inaugurated on 20 October, and on the following day announced the composition of his new Cabinet, which included representatives of several political organizations. Notable new appointees included Adm. (retd) Widodo Adi Sutjipto, a former Commander-in-Chief of the TNI, as Co-ordinating Minister for Political Affairs, Security and Social Welfare, and Aburizal Bakrie, of Golkar, as Co-ordinating Minister for the Economy, Finance and Industry, while Hassan Wirajuda, the Minister of Foreign Affairs, was one of five ministers retained from Megawati's administration.

In September 2004 the DPR approved the proposed creation of a 21-member truth and reconciliation commission to resolve all cases of human rights abuses perpetrated since independence in 1945; the commission was expected to be established by March 2005. In November 2004 it emerged that a leading Indonesian human rights activist who had died on a flight to the Netherlands in September had been poisoned with arsenic. The Indonesian police launched an investigation into Munir's death, and in December President Yudhoyono authorized the formation of an independent team to monitor and assist the police inquiry. Vice-President Yusuf Kalla was elected as Chairman of Golkar in mid-December, defeating the incumbent, Akbar Tandjung. As a result, it was anticipated that Golkar would henceforth broadly support the Government, enabling Yudhoyono to secure legislative approval for his policies. In late December Abdullah Puteh, the Governor of Aceh, became the first person to be prosecuted by the recently formed Corruption Eradication Commission. Puteh, who was suspended from office by Yudhoyono, was charged with corruption in relation to the purchase of a Russian helicopter in 2002.

Indonesia, in particular the province of Aceh, was devastated by a series of tsunamis caused by a massive earthquake in the Indian Ocean on 26 December 2004. The provincial capital, Banda Aceh, was severely damaged, while the town of Meulaboh, 150 km from the epicentre of the earthquake, was completely destroyed; UN officials estimated that 40,000 of the town's 95,000 residents had been killed. Once the scale of the devastation became apparent, the Government accepted humanitarian assistance from foreign troops, notably from the

USA, Australia and Japan. UN agencies and other organizations commenced operations to distribute food, medical supplies and shelter to survivors, although the destruction of many roads and bridges hampered initial relief efforts. Aceh had been under emergency rule prior to the tsunamis and largely closed to foreign agencies and the international media. In early January 2005 an emergency summit meeting of world leaders was convened in Jakarta in response to the disaster, which had also affected 11 other countries in Asia and Africa. Kofi Annan, the UN Secretary-General, appealed for US $977m. in immediate funding for an initial, six-month programme of emergency and recovery assistance. In mid-January the Indonesian Government announced that it hoped that all foreign troops providing disaster relief would have left the country by the end of March, by which time it aimed to be in control of the aid operation. At the same time the Indonesian army ordered all aid workers to register any travel outside Banda Aceh and Meulaboh, stating that it could not guarantee their safety elsewhere in Aceh. At the beginning of February the Government announced that more than 111,000 people were known to have died in Indonesia as a result of the tsunamis, while 127,000 others remained missing and more than 400,000 were homeless.

From 2000 another major challenge facing the Government was the escalation of communal violence across the archipelago, together with separatist tensions in individual regions such as Aceh and Papua (known as Irian Jaya until January 2002—see below). In that year some of the worst such violence again occurred in the provinces of Maluku and North Maluku, arising from the ongoing conflict between the region's Christian and Muslim populations. By mid-2000 more than 4,000 people were reported to have been killed and some 300,000 displaced. In June President Wahid declared a state of civil emergency in the provinces of Maluku and North Maluku. Later the same month it was announced that around 1,400 of the 10,200 members of the armed forces in the region were to be replaced because they had become involved in the conflict, and in the case of at least one outbreak of serious violence it was reported that evidence had emerged of the military's collusion with elements of the militant Muslim paramilitary organization, Laskar Jihad, which had travelled to the region to participate in the campaign of violence, thus supporting the view of many observers that the Indonesian military was allowing Muslim attacks on Christians to take place. In December 18 people were reported to have been killed and more than 80 others injured in a series of bombings of Christian churches in nine towns and cities across Indonesia, including Jakarta, on Christmas Eve. No group claimed initial responsibility for the explosions, which were condemned by President Wahid. (In June 2002 an Iraqi citizen, Omar al-Faruq, who claimed to be the South-East Asian representative of the international terrorist network al-Qa'ida, was arrested and allegedly confessed to having participated in carrying out the bombings. Following the bombings in Bali, a senior operative of Jemaah Islamiah also confessed to involvement in the attacks. In a television broadcast in April 2004 four Malaysians detained in Indonesia admitted involvement in the church bombings and membership of Jemaah Islamiah. However, human rights groups claimed that the statements of the four had been obtained through coercion.) In February 2001 violence also broke out in the province of Central Kalimantan, where fierce resentment of Madurese transmigrants remained rife among the indigenous Dayak tribespeople. At least 428 Madurese were murdered by native Dayaks, and many of the victims were beheaded in accordance with traditional Dayak practices; many thousands more fled their homes. The failure of the armed forces to control the violence—the legacy of a resettlement programme begun under the Suharto Government in the 1970s—and to protect Madurese refugees in their care led to further allegations of the military's complicity in ethnic violence. In February 2002, following negotiations between the warring Muslim and Christian factions in Maluku and North Maluku, a peace treaty—the 'Malino II Agreement'—was signed in an attempt to bring an end to the violence endemic in the region. The agreement urged the expulsion of external groups such as Laskar Jihad from the area; it was criticized by at least one militant group, which claimed that the delegates sent to negotiate terms did not adequately represent its views. Shortly after the treaty was signed a series of bombs exploded in the city of Ambon; the Government condemned the attacks but insisted that they did not signify the failure of the peace agreement. In early April a further bombing took place in Ambon and the residence of the Governor was set alight. Another outbreak of

violence occurred in the same month, following which Alex Manuputty, the leader of the Christian separatist organization the Maluku Sovereignty Front, was arrested and charged with treason for planning to raise a flag to commemorate the 52nd anniversary of the proclamation of the South Maluku Republic. On 25 April the Maluku Sovereignty Front raised flags in Ambon in remembrance of the anniversary, provoking Muslims in the area and prompting the leader of Laskar Jihad, Ja'far Umar Thalib, to urge all Muslims in the region to renew their war against the Christian community. Shortly afterwards violence broke out again in Ambon, resulting in the deaths of 14 Christians. In May Ja'far Umar Thalib was arrested for allegedly inciting the violence that had led to the massacre of the Christians. Thalib was visited by the Vice-President, Hamzah Haz, during his detention, prompting widespread criticism and allegations that the Vice-President was attempting to win the political support of militant Muslims. In August the trial of Alex Manuputty and another Christian leader, Samuel Waileruny, for subversion began; meanwhile, Thalib also went on trial on charges of inciting hatred and rebellion and of defaming the President and Vice-President. In October, following the bombings suspected to have been carried out by the Islamist separatist organization Jemaah Islamiah on the island of Bali, Laskar Jihad disbanded and left the region; Ja'far Umar Thalib claimed that the decision had been taken owing to the group's increasing political involvement and denied that it had any connection to events in Bali. In the same month 14 members of the Maluku Sovereignty Front were sentenced to terms of imprisonment for raising separatist flags in the province in April. In late January 2003 Alex Manuputty and Samuel Waileruny were found guilty of subversion and sentenced *in absentia* to three-year prison terms, later increased to four years. Ja'far Umar Thalib was, however, acquitted of the charges against him. In late 2003, following the rejection of his appeal against his conviction by the Supreme Court, Manuputty fled to the USA in order to evade imprisonment; it was reported later that the Government had requested that the USA deport him to Indonesia.

In April 2003 supporters of the separatist movement in Maluku were again alleged to have flown flags in commemoration of the anniversary of the South Maluku Republic. An estimated 129 such supporters were arrested, and in the following month it was announced that they were to be prosecuted on charges of subversion. However, owing to the relative peace that had been maintained in the province since the signing of the Malino II Agreement, in September it was reported that the Government had revoked the state of civil emergency in Maluku; several battalions of peace-keeping troops would continue to be stationed in the province. The civil emergency status in North Maluku had been revoked in the previous year. In January 2004 nine men were sentenced to prison terms of up to 15 years for membership of the Maluku Sovereignty Front. At least 40 people were killed and around 150 injured in violent clashes in Ambon in late April, following a rally by a predominantly Christian separatist group on the island. More than 1,000 police officers and troops were dispatched to Ambon in an attempt to quell the unrest, which was the worst to have occurred in the area since the signing of the Malino II Agreement. Sporadic violence continued, prompting observers to question the long-term success of the peace treaty, and in late May one person was killed and at least 22 others injured in a series of bomb explosions on Ambon. In late November Moses Tuanakotta, a leader of the Maluku Sovereignty Front, was convicted of subversion and sentenced to nine years in prison for instigating the rally in April.

In late 2001 violence also broke out in the province of Sulawesi, where ongoing religious tensions had caused approximately 1,000 deaths in the previous two years. In the first week of December at least seven people were killed and thousands left homeless following clashes between armed Muslim groups and Christians. The violence was believed to have been precipitated by the recent arrival of members of Laskar Jihad on the island. More than 2,000 police and troop reinforcements were sent to the area in an attempt to bring the situation under control. In late December, following two days of talks, a peace deal was concluded between the parties involved, which, it was hoped, would bring an end to the fighting. However, explosions at four churches in the provincial capital, Palu, during New Year celebrations, highlighted the continuing political instability in the province. Sporadic violence continued to occur in Sulawesi. In June 2002 a bomb exploded on a passenger bus travelling towards Poso, Central Sulawesi, killing four people in the worst outbreak of violence to have occurred in the region since the signing of the peace agreement in the previous year. In December the Government announced that it intended to maintain the existing level of troops in the area, determined for one year under the terms of the peace agreement, for a further six months. In the same month two bombs exploded in Makassar, the capital of South Sulawesi, resulting in the deaths of three people. In October 2003 an estimated 11 people died as a result of an outbreak of sectarian violence in Poso. There was speculation that the renewal of violence in the province had been orchestrated by Jemaah Islamiah to coincide with the anniversary of the bombings in Bali. In the following month three more people died following an outbreak of anti-Christian violence in the city. Further rioting occurred later in that month, resulting in at least one death. In January 2004 a bomb exploded in the town of Palopo, South Sulawesi, killing four people. In October the new province of West Sulawesi, formed from five former regencies of South Sulawesi, was inaugurated. A bomb exploded on a bus in Poso in November, killing six people. The bombing followed a series of other attacks in Central Sulawesi, including the shooting of a Christian bus driver in Poso earlier that month.

On 1 January 2001 new legislation took effect devolving increased financial and administrative control to Indonesia's regional governments. (The central Government was, meanwhile, to retain control over justice, defence, foreign affairs and monetary policy.) The day after the introduction of the new legislation, the Minister of State for State Administrative Reforms, Ryaas Rasyid, resigned from his post, reportedly because of his frustration at the inadequacy of the Government's preparations for the implementation of the new decentralization policy, which was intended to defuse separatist tensions across the archipelago; he was later replaced by Feisal Tamin.

During 1974, meanwhile, several parties emerged within the small Portuguese colony of East Timor (which changed its name to Timor-Leste following its accession to independence on 20 May 2002), with aims ranging from full independence to integration with Indonesia or Australia. Indonesia, which had never presented a claim to East Timor, initially showed little interest in the territory. In 1975 Portuguese forces withdrew from the colony, and the territory's capital, Dili, was occupied by the forces of the left-wing Frente Revolucionária do Timor Leste Independente (Fretilin), which advocated independence for East Timor. To prevent Fretilin from gaining full control of the territory, Indonesian troops intervened and established a provincial government. (In December 2001 the declassification of US state papers relating to the Indonesian occupation revealed that the US Government had endorsed the invasion in the belief that it would curb the spread of communism in the region.) In July 1976 East Timor was declared the 27th province of Indonesia. Human rights organizations subsequently claimed that as many as 200,000 people, from a total population of 650,000, might have been killed by the Indonesian armed forces during the annexation. The Indonesian Government, however, ignored widespread international condemnation of the invasion. The UN meanwhile continued officially to recognize Portugal as the administrative power in East Timor. In February 1983 the UN Commission on Human Rights adopted a resolution affirming East Timor's right to independence and self-determination. In November 1990 the Indonesian Government rejected proposals by the military commander of Fretilin, José Alexandre (Xanana) Gusmão, for unconditional peace negotiations aimed at ending the armed struggle in East Timor. In August 1992 the UN General Assembly adopted its first resolution condemning Indonesia's violations of human rights in East Timor.

The downfall of President Suharto in May 1998 and the subsequent accession to the presidency of Habibie raised hopes, both internationally and within East Timor itself, that independence for the territory might be granted in the near future. In August it was announced that Indonesia and Portugal had agreed to hold discussions on the possibility of 'wide-ranging' autonomy for East Timor. In January 1999, however, the Indonesian Government unexpectedly announced that, if the East Timorese were to vote to reject Indonesia's proposals for autonomy, it would consider granting independence to the province. Although the Government was initially opposed to a referendum on the issue of independence for East Timor, it signed an agreement with Portugal in May, giving its assent to a process of 'popular consultation' to take the form of a UN-supervised poll to determine the territory's future status. The referendum proceeded on 30 August, and resulted in an overwhelming rejection by 78.5% of voters of the Indonesian Government's proposals for

autonomy and in an endorsement of independence for East Timor. Following the announcement of the result of the referendum, which led to a rapid deterioration in the security situation in East Timor, in late September Indonesia and Portugal reiterated their agreement for the transfer of authority in East Timor to the UN. Also in late September the Indonesian armed forces formally relinquished responsibility for security in the territory to the UN peace-keeping force, the International Force for East Timor (Interfet); the last Indonesian troops left East Timor in late October. On 19 October the result of the referendum was ratified by the Indonesian MPR, thus permitting East Timor's accession to independence to proceed. (See the chapter on Timor-Leste.) In September 2000 Indonesia faced outrage from the UN and the international community following the murder of three UN aid workers by pro-Jakarta militias in West Timor. The Indonesian Government came under strong criticism for its failure to control the militia groups, which were believed by many to be receiving the support of the Indonesian military. Indonesia subsequently refused to co-operate with a planned UN investigation into the killings.

In December 2001 10 members of a pro-Indonesia militia became the first individuals to be convicted of crimes against humanity in connection with the violence that had surrounded East Timor's vote for independence in 1999. However, the Indonesian Government continued to obstruct efforts to bring all those culpable to justice, blocking attempts to extradite an 11th man, a special forces officer, to face trial.

In January 2002, after some delay and in response to increasing criticism from the UN and much of Europe, the Government established a special court in Jakarta to try those suspected of contravening human rights, in East Timor and elsewhere. In February 17 pro-Jakarta militiamen and Indonesian soldiers were indicted by international prosecutors for alleged crimes against humanity in East Timor in 1999. Seven people, including the former Governor of East Timor, Abílio Soares, the chief of police, Brig.-Gen. Timbul Silaen, and the former district head, Herman Sedyono, were formally charged with crimes against humanity. Their cases were the first to be submitted to the newly established human rights tribunal in Jakarta; the trials began in March. In June the trial of militia leader Eurico Guterres, head of the youth wing of President Megawati's PDI—P, began. In August Abílio Soares was found guilty of two charges of 'gross rights violations' for his failure to prevent violence involving those subordinate to him and was sentenced to a three-year prison term. The next day the human rights tribunal acquitted Brig.-Gen. Timbul Silaen of charges of failing to control his subordinates; five other police and army officers were also found not guilty. The verdicts provoked widespread international condemnation and led to calls for the UN to establish an international tribunal on Timor-Leste. In November 2002 the tribunal found Eurico Guterres guilty of crimes against humanity; he received a 10-year prison sentence. However, a further four defendants were then acquitted by the tribunal, prompting renewed criticism from human rights activists and legal experts, who claimed that the court was deliberately sparing Indonesian police and military officers; both those convicted thus far were ethnic East Timorese civilians. In late December Lt-Col Soejarwo, Indonesia's military commander in Dili in 1999, became the first Indonesian officer to be found guilty of the charges against him; he was sentenced to a five-year prison term. However, international criticism was reinforced when another Indonesian army officer was acquitted of the charges against him in the same month. In January 2003 Hulman Gultom, a former Indonesian police chief, was found guilty and sentenced to a three-year prison term. In March of that year Brig.-Gen. Noer Muis was sentenced to five years in prison, having been convicted of failing to prevent massacres in the territory in 1999. However, in May 2003 the commander of Indonesian troops in East Timor, Brig.-Gen. Tono Suratman, was acquitted of the charges against him. In August of that year, the most senior military officer to have been charged in relation to the violence, Maj.-Gen. Adam Damiri, was found guilty of having committed crimes against humanity and sentenced to a three-year prison term. His sentence was the final one to be handed down by the tribunal, which continued to draw widespread international criticism for having passed only six guilty verdicts. Meanwhile, in February 2003 a UN-sponsored Special Panel for Serious Crimes (SPSC) that had been established in Dili indicted Gen. (retd) Wiranto, Abílio Soares and six other Indonesian generals for crimes committed in East Timor and, later in the same month, a further 50 indictments were issued;

the Indonesian Government continued to refuse to hand over any of those indicted for trial. The SPSC issued an arrest warrant for Wiranto in May 2004. In July Abílio Soares became the first person convicted by the human rights tribunal in Jakarta to be imprisoned, after the failure of an appeal. In August a court in Jakarta overturned the convictions of Lt-Col Soejarwo, Hulman Gultom, Brig.-Gen. Noer Muis and Maj.-Gen. Adam Damiri, and halved the sentence of Eurico Guterres, who remained free pending an appeal against his conviction; human rights groups condemned the ruling. In November Abílio Soares was also cleared of the charges against him by Indonesia's Supreme Court, leaving only the conviction of Guterres standing. In December Indonesia and Timor-Leste announced the establishment of a joint Commission on Truth and Friendship to investigate human rights violations during the violence in East Timor in 1999. In the previous month the UN Security Council had expressed concern at Indonesia's failure to punish those responsible. Meanwhile, in August 2004 the human rights tribunal acquitted the head of the Kopassus special forces regiment, Maj.-Gen. Sriyanto Muntrasan, who had been accused of human rights violations in connection with the shooting of several Muslim activists near Jakarta's Tanjung Priok port in 1984, despite sentencing Sriyanto's immediate superior, Maj.-Gen. (retd) Rudolf Butar-Butar, to 10 years' imprisonment in April for failing to prevent the shooting; later in August 11 soldiers received prison terms, having been found guilty of systematic attacks against civilians in the same case.

In the mid-1970s dissent re-emerged in Aceh, which, at the end of the war of independence, had held the status of a full province of the Republic of Indonesia but which had subsequently had this status removed before being made a special territory (Daerah Istimewa) with considerable autonomy in religious and educational affairs. The dissent was provoked by the exploitation by the central Government of Aceh's natural resources and the subsequent lack of benefits from these operations received by the region itself. A sense of the erosion of Aceh's autonomy was heightened by the migration and transmigration of other Indonesians into the region and by the increasing power of the central Government, and in 1976 the Gerakan Aceh Merdeka (GAM—Free Aceh Movement) was formed by Hasan di Tiro, who declared independence in 1977. This small rebellion was swiftly suppressed by the armed forces; however, Tiro later established a government-in-exile in Sweden.

In 1989 opposition to the central Government rose again, this time led by the National Liberation Front Acheh Sumatra. The region was made a 'military operations zone' in 1990, thus allowing the armed forces far greater freedom to counter the uprising. By mid-1991 the rebellion had been largely suppressed; however, it was estimated that about 1,000 Acehnese had been killed in the process, as a result of the use of excessive and indiscriminate force by the military. The number of deaths continued to rise in subsequent years, and in 1993 Amnesty International estimated that about 2,000 Acehnese had been killed since 1989, with hundreds of others having 'disappeared'.

Aceh's status as a 'military operations zone' was revoked in June 1998, following the downfall of President Suharto in May, and an apology for past military excesses was made by Gen. Wiranto. The subsequent intended withdrawal of Indonesian troops from the province was suspended, however, following rioting in Aceh in September. Decentralization measures introduced by President Habibie failed to defuse resentment in the province, and public opinion in Aceh became increasingly sympathetic towards the notion of independence. In 1999 the discovery of several mass graves of people killed by the armed forces during security operations further exacerbated tension in the province. Violence continued to escalate following the legislative elections of 9 June as GAM guerrillas intensified their campaign for independence for Aceh.

In early November 1999, following the rejection by legislators in the provincial assembly of demands for the holding of a referendum on self-determination for Aceh, a provincial government building in western Aceh was set on fire during a demonstration by 5,000 protesters. While much of the ongoing widespread violence in the province was attributed to the separatist movement, it was believed by observers that some unrest was initiated by so-called 'provocateurs' acting to destabilize the province and undermine the separatist movement. In November the newly appointed President of Indonesia, Abdurrahman Wahid, confirmed an unexpected statement that the holding of a referendum in Aceh was a possibility. In late November,

however, Wahid made it clear that the suggested poll would not include the option of independence, but would instead offer Aceh a broad degree of autonomy. Wahid's proposals angered the TNI, which, in the wake of the vote in favour of independence in East Timor in August, reportedly feared that, unless brought under control, the separatist movement in Aceh could potentially incite rebellion across the archipelago and contribute to national disintegration. The offer of increased autonomy, rather than independence, also failed to satisfy Acehnese separatists, and violence continued throughout the province. In May 2000 the Indonesian Government and Acehnese rebel negotiators agreed upon a cease-fire, which took effect from 2 June and was subsequently extended for an indefinite period. Violence continued throughout the province, however, and it was estimated by Acehnese human rights groups that more than 1,000 civilians had died in clashes between the Indonesian military and Acehnese rebels during 2000. In December thousands of Acehnese protesters rallied peacefully in Banda Aceh, demanding independence for the province. However, it was reported that at least 34 (and possibly as many as 200, according to human rights groups) unarmed civilians had been killed in the days preceding the rally as the result of military action to target Acehnese en route to the demonstration. On the day after the protest, Acehnese separatists withdrew from peace talks with the Indonesian Government, stating that they would resume negotiations only when the military ceased killing Acehnese civilians. In January 2001 peace talks between the Indonesian Government and Acehnese separatists recommenced.

In March 2001, following talks between GAM and the security forces, 'peace zones' were established in two Aceh districts. These proved to be of limited effectiveness, however, and in April President Wahid signed a decree authorizing the security forces to assist the military in restoring law and order in the province by targeting armed separatist organizations. This brought an end to the uneasy truce prevailing in the region. In July one of President Megawati's first official actions was to sign into law a special autonomy plan for Aceh intended to assuage separatism. However, while generous in its scope, the legislation was criticized for failing to address the problems posed by the continued military presence in the area. Critics' concerns were borne out when an estimated 30 civilians were massacred on an Aceh palm oil plantation in August 2001. According to GAM, the military was responsible, having carried out the attack as retribution for a previous assault on a military post that had left several soldiers dead. In September President Megawati visited the region in an attempt to defuse the tensions there; her visit was met with indifference by many regional groups. On 4 December 2001 Acehnese separatists marked the 25th anniversary of their struggle for independence. Security forces tore down over 100 separatist flags, and there were reports of some clashes between GAM members and the military.

Violence continued in Aceh throughout 2002. In January the commander of GAM, Abdullah Syafei, was killed during a gun battle with security forces on Sumatra; six other GAM members also died. In February talks took place between GAM and government representatives in Geneva, Switzerland, despite an earlier declaration by GAM that it intended to boycott negotiations while mourning the death of Syafei. The talks were adjourned with a statement confirming the right of the people of Aceh to rule themselves peacefully. However, on the same day renewed fighting occurred in the province, prompting the Government to resume a separate military command for Aceh, a move denounced by both GAM and human rights groups as an ill-advised attempt to resolve the region's problems using military means. In the following month fighting between separatists and government troops in the province resulted in the deaths of at least 23 people. In May, following further talks in Geneva, the Government and GAM agreed to work towards a cease-fire, signing an agreement which was to act as a mandate for future negotiations. However, the violence continued, with a GAM commander alleging later in the same month that the armed forces had killed 43 civilians in North Aceh in the preceding 10 days alone. At the end of June 2002 GAM issued a statement in support of the ongoing peace negotiations taking place in Geneva and in July it released 18 hostages whom it had been holding since the previous month, including nine crewmen who had been kidnapped while servicing the offshore petroleum industry near North Aceh. Meanwhile, following a trip to Aceh, the Co-ordinating Minister for Political Affairs, Security and Social Welfare, Susilo Bambang Yudhoyono, declared his support for the regional military commander's request to increase the military presence in the area if GAM did not accept the conditions that had been outlined following the talks that had been held in May and stated that he intended to request the declaration of a state of civil emergency in the province. Aceh's Legal Aid Institute reportedly claimed that, during the first six months of 2002, 771 people had been killed as a result of the conflict in the region. In September a British and a US woman were arrested and charged with having violated their visas while travelling in Aceh; they were believed to have made contact with GAM and stood trial over the allegations in November. In December both women were found guilty of the charges against them and sentenced to short prison terms; they were released in early 2003, having served most of their sentences while in custody.

In early November 2002 GAM announced that it was willing to sign a short-term peace accord with the Government to bring to an end the armed conflict ongoing in the region. On 5 November GAM announced a unilateral truce during the period of the Islamic religious festival of Ramadan, but the truce broke down almost immediately as five people died during an exchange of gunfire in North Aceh. Meanwhile, in the largest military operation to have been carried out in the province for some time, government troops besieged a suspected GAM base in the industrial centre of Lhokseumawe. On 9 December government and GAM representatives finally signed a peace agreement in Geneva. As well as establishing an immediate cease-fire, the deal provided for free elections (to be held in 2004), which would establish an autonomous, although not independent, government. The new provincial government would retain 70% of all fuel revenues. In return all rebels in the province would disarm in designated areas. Following the signing of the peace accord, international peace monitors arrived in the region to observe the disarmament process and ensure adherence to the terms of the agreement.

In February 2003 GAM rebels began surrendering their weapons in compliance with the terms of the peace accord. However, by April of that year the agreement had come close to collapse. Offices occupied by the international monitors for the Joint Security Committee had been attacked and, in one instance, burned down. It was generally believed that the armed forces were responsible for organizing the demonstrations against the monitors. In the same month the Government cancelled a further round of talks that had been scheduled with GAM in Geneva, owing to GAM's attempts to postpone the negotiations. In May peace talks were held in Tokyo, Japan, with the support of Japan, the EU and the USA. However, GAM negotiators were unable to accept the Government's demands that it abandon its goal of independence, accept a special autonomy agreement and immediately begin to disarm its forces. As a consequence, hours after the failure of the talks, President Megawati authorized the imposition of martial law in Aceh, initially for a six-month period, and the commencement of military action against GAM. Owing to the restrictions placed on media reporting of the conflict, little independent information was available as to its progress throughout the succeeding months. However, in June three government soldiers were sentenced to brief prison terms, having been found guilty of committing human rights violations during the military campaign. In November the Government announced that it would extend its military operations in Aceh indefinitely, prompting international criticism. Human rights groups claimed that the conflict had resulted in at least 300 civilian deaths. In December a bomb exploded at a market in the eastern town of Pereulak, killing 10 people. The Government downgraded the status of martial law in Aceh to a state of civil emergency in May 2004, restoring power to the civilian Governor. The security forces, which were to remain in the province, claimed to have killed some 2,000 suspected GAM rebels and arrested a further 3,000 since commencing the military offensive against the separatist movement a year earlier. Human rights groups alleged that many of those killed had been civilians. In June Indonesia welcomed Sweden's decision to arrest two senior GAM leaders who were in exile in that country; GAM's founder, Hasan di Tiro, escaped arrest because of ill health. They were later released, however, owing to insufficient evidence, although investigations were to continue. In November President Yudhoyono extended the state of civil emergency in Aceh by up to six months and, during a visit to the province, offered an amnesty to all GAM rebels who surrendered their arms.

Following the tsunamis that devastated Aceh on 26 December 2004 (see above), the GAM and the Government agreed to an informal cease-fire to facilitate relief efforts. In mid-January 2005, however, the Chief of Staff of the Army, Gen. Ryamizard Ryacudu, announced that in the previous two weeks the security forces had killed 120 GAM rebels who had been stealing aid intended for victims of the tsunamis; GAM dismissed these claims. None the less, the natural disaster in the province appeared to have provided a new impetus for GAM and the Indonesian Government to seek a resolution to their conflict, and in late January formal talks between the two sides were held in Finland. The talks, which were brokered by the former President of Finland, Martti Ahtisaari, ended without a formal agreement, although they were described as 'constructive'; further discussions were expected to take place in late February. At the end of January the Government rejected an offer by GAM to suspend demands for independence in exchange for a referendum on Aceh's future. In early February the army claimed to have killed at least seven GAM rebels.

In May 1977 there was a rebellion in the province of Irian Jaya (now known as Papua), annexed to Indonesia in 1963 (see above). The rebellion was said to have been organized by the Organisasi Papua Merdeka (OPM—Free Papua Movement), which seeks unification with Papua New Guinea. Fighting continued until December 1979, when Indonesia and Papua New Guinea finalized a new border administrative agreement. Frequent border incidents followed, however, and in early 1984 fighting broke out in Jayapura, the capital of Irian Jaya. As a result, about 10,000 refugees fled over the border into Papua New Guinea. In October 1984 Indonesia and Papua New Guinea signed a five-year agreement establishing a joint border security committee; by the end of 1985 Indonesians were continuing to cross into Papua New Guinea, but a limited number of repatriations took place in 1986. There was also concern among native Irian Jayans (who are of Melanesian origin) at the introduction of large numbers of Javanese into the province, under the Government's transmigration scheme. This was interpreted as an attempt to reduce the Melanesians to a minority and thus to stifle opposition. In 1986 it was announced that the Government intended to resettle 65m. people over a 20-year period, in spite of protests from human rights and conservation groups that the scheme would cause ecological damage and interfere with the rights of the native Irian Jayans. Relations with Papua New Guinea improved when the Prime Minister, Paias Wingti, visited Suharto in January 1988. However, a series of cross-border raids by the Indonesian armed forces in October and November, in an attempt to capture Melanesian separatists operating on the border, led to renewed tension between the two countries. In October 1990 the Governments of Indonesia and Papua New Guinea renewed the basic accord on border arrangements, which included an agreement on the formation of a joint defence committee and a formal commitment to share border intelligence. In September 1992 the two countries agreed to facilitate the passage of border trade, and in the following month an Indonesian consulate was established in Vanimo.

In April 1995 the Australian Council for Overseas Aid (ACFOA) alleged that 37 Irian Jayans had been killed by security forces near the Freeport copper and gold mine between June 1994 and February 1995. In August the ACFOA's claims were reiterated by non-governmental organizations, which lodged a complaint with the National Commission on Human Rights in Jakarta about summary executions, arbitrary detentions and torture in the province between mid-1994 and mid-1995. In November 1995 four members of ABRI were arrested in an investigation into the killing in May of 11 unarmed civilians at a prayer meeting. Also in November the Overseas Private Investment Corporation (a US government agency) cancelled political risk insurance valued at US $100m. for Freeport (a subsidiary of a US enterprise), citing environmental concerns. Freeport's perceived responsibility for the situation in Irian Jaya arose from its role as civil administrator in the area of the mine and also because the indigenous inhabitants' campaigns against Freeport's indiscriminate exploitation of natural resources in the area often resulted in their being killed by security forces as suspected members of the OPM.

In December 1995 clashes between Indonesian forces and the OPM intensified, forcing hundreds of refugees to cross into Papua New Guinea. Four people were killed in riots in Jayapura in March 1996. Riots near the Grasberg mine in the same month were the result of problems similar to those experienced by residents in the Freeport area (relating principally to the lack of any benefit from the mining project to the local community and to the potential impact of the project on the local environment). There were also tensions among the local Irianese, Indonesians from other provinces and commercial operators. In April Freeport agreed to allocate 1% of revenue over a period of 10 years to community development programmes for tribal groups living around the mine, and to tighten environmental safeguards.

In July 1998, following the resignation of President Suharto in May and his subsequent replacement by President Habibie, troops clashed with pro-independence demonstrators in Jayapura. Two people were reported to have been killed in the violence, and a further five were reportedly killed during an outbreak of violence on the island of Biak in July. In early October the Government revoked the status of Irian Jaya as a 'military operations zone' following the conclusion of a cease-fire agreement with the OPM in late September; however, the move was not followed by the withdrawal of troops from the region. In February 1999 Irian Jayan tribal leaders raised the issue of independence for the province at a meeting with President Habibie. (A referendum on self-determination for the province had been promised by the Indonesian Government prior to the territory's annexation in 1963; however, whilst a vote was eventually held in 1969, only tribal chiefs selected by Jakarta were allowed to participate and the result was widely discredited.) The independence movement in the province continued to strengthen throughout 1999, and was encouraged by the achievements of the East Timorese independence movement (see above). In early December independence demonstrations took place throughout Irian Jaya. Later the same month a delegation from the DPR visited the province and announced that the administration of the newly elected President Abdurrahman Wahid had agreed to the popular demand that the province's name be changed from Irian Jaya to West Papua, although it was emphasized that this decision should not be construed as implying the Government's approval of any moves towards the province's secession from Indonesia. (It was subsequently reported, however, that the proposed change had failed to receive the requisite approval of the Indonesian legislature.)

In mid-2000 the Papuan People's Congress was held in Jayapura. The Congress concluded with the adoption of a five-point resolution reinstating a declaration of independence for West Papua originally made in 1961, before the province's annexation to Indonesia. The declaration was, however, immediately rebuffed by the Indonesian Government. In early October between 30 and 40 people were killed and many others injured in clashes between police and West Papuan separatists in the town of Wamena when police attempted to remove a Morning Star independence flag being flown by the separatists. Although President Wahid had previously decreed that the flying of the Morning Star flag was allowed, provided that the flag was flown alongside, and slightly lower than, the Indonesian flag, following the violence the Government introduced a ban on the flying of the flag. In November and early December the Indonesian military took severe action against separatists; seven people were shot dead by the armed forces in an outbreak of violence in the town of Merauke, and dozens of separatist sympathizers, including the pro-independence leader, Theys Eluay, were arrested. On 1 December pro-independence supporters rallied in the province to mark the 39th anniversary of the first unilateral declaration of West Papua's independence.

In March 2001 five West Papuan separatist leaders, including Theys Eluay, the leader of the Presidium Dewan Papua (PDP—Papua Presidium Council), were released on bail to await trial on charges of treason. In October the DPR gave its assent to legislation giving greater autonomy to the province, in an effort to defuse the separatist tensions that had given rise to more than 40 years of sporadic violence. As well as giving Irian Jaya more autonomy and a larger share of tax revenues, the legislation also proposed that the region be officially known as Papua and made provision for a bicameral Papua Peoples' Council, intended to safeguard indigenous interests. However, the separatist PDP swiftly rejected the deal as it failed to grant Irian Jaya complete independence. In November 2001 Theys Eluay was found dead in his car. He was believed to have been assassinated; some military involvement was suspected. In late December hundreds of students occupied the parliament building in Jayapura to demand a referendum on independence and to express their anger at the authorities' failure to find the killer of Theys Eluay. The protest came days before the

autonomy reforms came into force on 1 January 2002, when the province officially became known as Papua.

In late August 2002 two US citizens and an Indonesian were killed following an ambush near the Freeport mine; while the Government immediately attributed the attack to the OPM, there was speculation that it could have been carried out by the military in an attempt to discredit local insurgents. In November it was alleged by police that Kopassus soldiers were suspected of involvement in the attack. (In June 2004 the US authorities indicted *in absentia* Anthonius Wamang, an Indonesian, for murdering the two US citizens, describing him as an operational commander for the OPM, although human rights groups reportedly claimed that Wamang had close ties with the Kopassus special forces.) In April 2003 four Kopassus officers and three soldiers were convicted of the abduction, torture and murder of Theys Eluay and sentenced to brief prison terms. However, the trial was criticized both for the leniency of the verdicts delivered and for its failure to investigate the reasons for the murder of Eluay. Meanwhile, the central Government gave its approval in January 2003 to an initiative that would lead to the division of Papua into three smaller provinces—Central Papua, East Papua (or Papua) and West Papua. The proposal angered local leaders, who claimed that such action would threaten the region's autonomy. Following reports that six people had died during fighting in Timika, the designated capital of Central Papua, since the inauguration of the new province in August of that year, the creation of Central Papua was postponed. However, the appointment of a Governor for West Papua was approved in November. In the same month the Government announced provisional plans for the creation of two further provinces in Papua. Meanwhile, it was reported that 10 members of the OPM had been killed in clashes with government troops in East Papua. In December the appointment of Brig.-Gen. Timbul Silaen to the post of regional police commander was criticized by the USA, owing to Silaen's indictment for crimes against humanity in East Timor (see above). In March 2004 it was reported that Leo Warisman, a leader of the OPM, had been killed in a gunfight with security forces in Papua. Another OPM leader, Yance Hembring, was sentenced to 10 years' imprisonment by a court in Jayapura in August for advocating Papua's independence. In December at least five people were injured and 18 arrested during violent clashes between protesters and police at a pro-independence rally in Jayapura.

Indonesia's foreign policy has focused on its leading role in the regional grouping of the Association of South East Asian Nations (ASEAN, see p. 162), which it founded, together with Malaysia, the Philippines, Singapore and Thailand, in 1967. Indonesia supported the organization's opposition to Viet Nam's military presence in Cambodia and played a prominent role in attempts to find a political solution to the situation in Cambodia (q.v.). The Indonesian Minister of Foreign Affairs and his French counterpart were appointed Co-Chairmen of the Paris International Conference on Cambodia, which first met in August 1989. In 1997, following Second Prime Minister Hun Sen's assumption of sole power in Cambodia, Indonesia led ASEAN attempts to resolve the crisis. In August 2001 President Megawati Sukarnoputri embarked on a tour of all ASEAN member states on her first overseas trip since assuming the presidency. The trip duly affirmed Indonesia's close ties with the other ASEAN nations.

In July 1985 Indonesia and the People's Republic of China signed a memorandum of understanding on the resumption of direct trade links, which had been suspended since 1967. In April 1988 the Indonesian Government indicated its readiness to re-establish full diplomatic relations with China, subject to an assurance that the latter would not seek to interfere in Indonesia's internal affairs; previously, Suharto had insisted that China acknowledge its alleged complicity in the 1965 attempted coup. Diplomatic relations were finally restored in August 1990, following an Indonesian undertaking to settle financial debts incurred with China by the Sukarno regime. In November Suharto visited China and Viet Nam (the first Indonesian leader to do so since 1964 and 1975 respectively). In 1995 China extended claims to territorial waters within Indonesia's exclusive economic zone, consequently threatening Indonesia's natural gas resources, in particular those situated in the region of the Natuna Islands.

Bilateral relations between Indonesia and China suffered a reverse in 1998 following the violence perpetrated against ethnic Chinese Indonesians at the time of the fall of Suharto in

May. China issued a strong diplomatic protest at the violence, and gave prominent coverage in the state-controlled media to reports of the rapes, arson and murders. Following his accession to the presidency, President Habibie publicly expressed his sympathy for the plight of the ethnic Chinese victims of violence. Subsequently, in May 1999, as part of an ongoing programme of general reform, Habibie lifted a ban that had existed on the use and teaching of the Mandarin Chinese language within Indonesia. In early December the then-President of Indonesia, Abdurrahman Wahid, made an official visit to China. In November 2001 new President Megawati held discussions with the Chinese Prime Minister, Zhu Rongji, during his visit to the region to strengthen economic ties.

In December 1989 Indonesia and Australia concluded a temporary agreement providing for joint exploration for petroleum and gas in the Timor Gap, which had been a disputed area since 1978. However, no permanent sea boundary was approved. The validity of the Timor Gap agreement was challenged by Portugal, which instituted proceedings at the International Court of Justice (ICJ), on the grounds that the agreement infringed Portuguese sovereignty and interests; however, in June 1995 the ICJ rejected the case on the grounds that it would affect a country that was not represented, as Indonesia did not recognize the ICJ's jurisdiction. In June 1993 the East Timorese resistance began proceedings in the High Court of Australia to overturn legislation confirming the Timor Gap agreement on the grounds that Australia was bound by international law, which did not recognize Indonesia's annexation of East Timor. In April 1990 Indonesia and Australia restored defence co-operation links, following a four-year disruption. In September 1994 Vice-President Sutrisno became the first high-ranking Indonesian official to visit Australia since Suharto's last visit in 1975.

In July 1995 Indonesia withdrew the nomination of Lt-Gen. Herman Mantiri, a former Chief of the General Staff, as ambassador to Australia, owing to widespread protests there concerning his defence of the actions of the Indonesian armed forces in the 1991 Dili massacre. Relations with Australia were also strained by Australia's decision to allow 18 East Timorese refugees to remain in the country following their arrival by boat in May (although they were not granted political asylum), by several incidents involving the burning of the Indonesian flag in Australian cities in protest at Indonesia's occupation of East Timor, and by Australia's decision to investigate claims of new evidence about the killing of six Australia-based journalists during the annexation of East Timor in 1975. The Indonesian Government claimed that the journalists had died in cross-fire, while eyewitnesses stated that they had been executed by Indonesian troops. In June 1996 an Australian government report concluded that the journalists had been killed by the Indonesian army. A report published by the International Commission of Jurists, a human rights organization based in Switzerland, in 1998 concluded that Indonesian troops had killed the journalists in order to conceal Indonesia's invasion of East Timor, and in October of that year it was announced that Australia was to reopen a judicial inquiry into the killings. In late 2000 newly declassified documents provided conclusive evidence that Australian officials had been aware of Indonesia's plans to invade East Timor. Meanwhile, in December 1995 Indonesia signed a treaty with Australia to enhance defence links, committing the two countries to consultation in the event of a threat to security. In October 1996 the Australia-Indonesia Development Area was created to develop economic links between the two countries and in March 1997 Indonesia and Australia signed a treaty defining permanent maritime boundaries between the two countries, whilst retaining the Timor Gap agreement. (Indonesia later ceased to be a party to the Timor Gap agreement when it relinquished control of the territory in October 1999.)

Following the downfall of Suharto in May 1998, relations between Indonesia and Australia continued to be affected by the issue of East Timor. In January 1999 the Indonesian Government expressed its 'deep regret' at Australia's announcement earlier the same month that it was to change its policy on East Timor and actively promote 'self-determination' in the territory. Following the vote in favour of independence held in East Timor in August 1999, Australia committed 4,500 peace-keeping troops to Interfet, which was formed by the UN to restore order in the territory following the violence perpetrated by pro-Jakarta militias after the announcement of the result of the poll. A military co-operation agreement between Indonesia and Australia, which had been signed four years previously, was reported in October to have been cancelled as a result of the

Indonesian Government's displeasure at Australia's leading involvement in the peace-keeping operation. In 2000 relations between Indonesia and Australia continued to be strained. In November the Australian ambassador to Indonesia, John McCarthy, was physically attacked by a pro-Jakarta mob in Makassar, Sulawesi. The Australian Government accepted the Indonesian Government's apology for the incident.

Relations with Australia appeared to be improving in 2001. In June, following several postponements, President Wahid paid an official visit to Australia, the first by an Indonesian head of state for 26 years. The Australian Prime Minister, John Howard, became the first foreign leader to make an official visit to Indonesia following President Megawati's assumption of power when he arrived in Jakarta in August. However, later in the same month relations were strained once again when a cargo ship carrying hundreds of mainly Afghan asylum-seekers became stranded in the international waters between the two countries. Neither country agreed to accept responsibility for the refugees. In early September the Australian Minister for Foreign Affairs, Alexander Downer, arrived in Jakarta for talks with Indonesian Ministers on the problems raised by illegal trafficking of immigrants. In October the pressing nature of the immigrant issue was highlighted when more than 350 refugees, believed to be heading for Australia, drowned when their boat sank off the Indonesian coast. In the same month a missing boat carrying approximately 170 Iraqi and Afghan asylum-seekers was found on the Indonesian island of Wera. Australia co-hosted a regional conference on people-smuggling in February 2002 in an attempt to find a solution to the problem. Earlier in the same month John Howard visited the country again. Both the Speaker of the DPR, Akbar Tandjung, and the Speaker of the MPR, Amien Rais, cancelled scheduled meetings with him and during his stay students protested in response to allegations that Australia was providing funding for separatist groups in Aceh and Papua. Howard denied such charges, claiming that he fully supported Indonesia's territorial integrity, and signed an agreement with President Megawati concerning counter-terrorism measures. Shortly afterwards Australia participated in a trilateral dialogue with Indonesia and East Timor regarding future co-operation issues; the talks were the first ever to be attended by the three countries. In May, following an initiative proposed during Prime Minister Howard's visit, the inaugural Australia-Indonesia dialogue was held in Bogor; Minister of Foreign Affairs Hassan Wirajuda met with his Australian counterpart, Alexander Downer, to discuss bilateral co-operation issues.

In October 2002 relations with Australia were seriously affected by the bomb attacks on the island of Bali, a popular destination for Australian tourists, which resulted in the deaths of almost 90 Australian citizens. While the Australian Government immediately offered its support and assistance to Indonesia in the aftermath of the attacks, as well as participating in the police investigation, a subsequent series of raids on the homes of Indonesian Muslims resident in Australia prompted Vice-President Hamzah Haz to warn that such an offensive could damage bilateral relations. In late November 2002 the Australian Prime Minister, John Howard, threatened Australia's relationship with several South-East Asian countries, including Indonesia, when he stated that Australia was prepared to launch pre-emptive attacks against perceived terrorist threats in other Asian countries. Gen. Endriartono Sutatro, commander-in-chief of the armed forces, commented that such a strike would be interpreted as an act of aggression by the Indonesian Government, as it would infringe the principle of national sovereignty. In February 2003 Howard visited Indonesia again and, in April, Australia co-hosted a second conference on people-smuggling. In February 2004 Australia and Indonesia co-hosted a counter-terrorism conference held on Bali, at which it was announced that a regional counter-terrorism centre would be established in Jakarta. In August, however, the Indonesian Government expressed concern at Australia's stated intention to arm its fighter aircraft with a cruise missile system, and in December relations were further strained by the Australian Government's announcement that it was to create a coastal security zone extending five times as far as its territorial waters. Following the tsunamis that devastated Indonesia in late December, Australia dispatched some 1,000 troops to assist with relief operations in the province of Aceh and pledged US $773m. in aid to be disbursed over a five-year period. Prime Minister John Howard visited Aceh in February 2005.

In October 1996 Indonesia and Malaysia agreed to submit disputed claims to the islands of Ligitan and Sipadan to the ICJ, and in August 1997 the two countries agreed to postpone talks on the issue of the islands, pending a ruling by the Court. In December 2002 the ICJ awarded the islands to Malaysia; both countries had earlier stated that they would abide by the Court's decision, thus bringing an end to the dispute. The forced repatriation in early 1998 of thousands of Indonesian workers from Malaysia as a result of the regional economic crisis placed a strain on relations between the two countries. Relations were further strained in October when the Indonesian Government condemned the treatment received in custody by the former Malaysian Deputy Prime Minister and Minister of Finance, Anwar Ibrahim (see the chapter on Malaysia), breaking with a tradition amongst ASEAN countries of non-interference in the internal affairs of other member countries. In May 2002 Indonesia signed a trilateral security pact with Malaysia and the Philippines, enabling the signatories to exchange intelligence and launch joint police operations in an attempt to combat terrorism in the region; Cambodia and Thailand later also acceded to the agreement. In August relations with Malaysia were also affected by Malaysia's introduction of stringent anti-immigration laws, which resulted in the forced deportation of many illegal immigrants, most of whom were Indonesian, and provoked protests outside the Malaysian embassy in Jakarta. In February 2004 bilateral relations were threatened once again when Indonesia called for a global boycott of Malaysian timber products, following reports that protected trees from Indonesia were being smuggled across the border to Malaysia, laundered and re-exported. In July Indonesia, Malaysia and Singapore commenced co-ordinated patrols of the Strait of Melaka (Malacca), a critical maritime trade route through which 50% of the world's oil passes, in an attempt to curb piracy. At the beginning of February 2005 Malaysia extended an amnesty for illegal immigrants to leave the country before facing legal action in response to a written request from President Susilo Bambang Yudhoyono, who was concerned that a major crackdown in Malaysia would result in an influx of migrants to Indonesia, at a time when the country was still struggling to recover from the December tsunamis.

Meanwhile, in May 2002 President Megawati Sukarnoputri attracted criticism when she attended celebrations in Timor-Leste to mark the territory's official accession to nation status; in February Indonesia and East Timor had agreed to establish full diplomatic relations following independence. In July the newly appointed President of Timor-Leste, Xanana Gusmão, visited Indonesia; during his stay he met with President Megawati, and the two leaders discussed the possibility of compensation for Indonesian assets remaining in Timor-Leste and the extent of Indonesian assistance with which the new country would be provided. In October the first meeting of the Indonesia-Timor-Leste Joint Ministerial Commission for Bilateral Co-operation took place in Jakarta.

In March 1996 the USA ended a ban on military training for members of ABRI, which had been imposed after the Dili massacre in 1991. In early June 1997, however, it was announced that President Suharto had cancelled Indonesia's participation in US military training programmes in response to the recent condemnation by the US House of Representatives of abuses of human rights committed by Indonesian armed forces in East Timor; the planned purchase by Indonesia of a number of US military aircraft was also cancelled. In November 1999 the newly appointed President of Indonesia, Abdurrahman Wahid, made an official visit to the USA. In October 2000, however, relations between Indonesia and the USA deteriorated markedly as the result of a combination of factors, including the perceived 'interference' in Indonesian domestic political affairs of the recently appointed US ambassador to Indonesia, Robert Gelbard, US criticism of Indonesia's failure to control pro-Jakarta militias in West Timor following the murder of three UN workers by militia members in September, and Indonesian perceptions of US bias towards Israel in the Middle East conflict. In late October and early November Muslim groups rallied outside the US embassy in Jakarta, calling for *jihad*, threats were made against US citizens in Indonesia, US companies in the country were attacked and it was reported that the Indonesian Government had requested Gelbard's immediate removal and replacement. In late October the USA closed its embassy in Jakarta for two weeks, and in early November the US Government warned citizens to defer all non-essential travel

to the archipelago. Relations between the two countries remained strained throughout much of 2001.

Following the terrorist attacks of 11 September 2001 on the USA (see the chapter on the USA), in the same month President Megawati became the first leader of a predominantly Muslim country to meet with President George W. Bush. In return for assurances that the US campaign against terror was not one against Islam, she affirmed Indonesia's condemnation of the attacks. However, following the commencement of air strikes against the Taliban regime in Afghanistan in October, fundamentalist Muslims threatened violence if the Indonesian Government did not sever diplomatic relations with the USA. In October the Front Pembela Islam (FPI—Islamic Defenders' Front) warned that if British and US citizens did not leave the country immediately their safety could not be guaranteed. (The FPI disbanded in November 2002, claiming that it did not wish to compound the damage to the reputation of the Islamic religion at what was a violent time for Indonesia. However, it announced in early 2003 that it intended to re-form.) Later in the same month President Megawati, under pressure from Muslim groups and Vice-President Hamzah Haz, indirectly condemned the US attacks for the first time. Protests against the Afghan campaign continued in Jakarta and various regional centres.

In 2002 relations with the USA improved somewhat. In April the two countries held sensitive security talks, during which they discussed measures to combat terrorism and to strengthen civilian control over the armed forces; the talks were perceived to signify an important move towards the renewal of bilateral military ties. In July the US Congress approved legislation awarding US $16m. to the Indonesian police forces; this included $12m. for the establishment of a dedicated anti-terrorism unit and followed a vote by the Senate Appropriations Committee to remove all remaining restrictions on the provision of military training to Indonesia (the vote awaited approval by Congress). The proposed legislation for the resumption of military assistance did, however, include human rights conditions. In August, during a two-day visit to Indonesia, US Secretary of State Colin Powell guaranteed substantial financial aid to the country to fight the terrorist threat within its borders. During his stay Powell also announced the resumption of a training programme for Indonesian army officers at US military schools and US $50m. of funding for Indonesia's police and counter-terrorism units over a three-year period. The bombings in Bali in October were widely perceived to constitute a further justification for the strengthening of military links with the USA. However, in early 2003 bilateral relations were strained when the USA placed Indonesia on a list of countries of which citizens were required to register with the US immigration authorities if they visited the country. The Government stated its intention to file a protest against the decision, claiming that it was discriminatory. In October 2003 President George W. Bush visited Indonesia and announced plans for a US $157m. programme to improve education in the country in an attempt to create a system that discouraged the development of Islamist extremism. In the same month, however, the US Senate approved amendments proposing that funding be withdrawn for the enrolment of Indonesians in US military training programmes and that the restoration of normal military links between the two countries be suspended until the Indonesian Government co-operated fully with the investigation into the murder of two US citizens in Papua in August 2002 (see above). The USA took an active part in relief operations in Indonesia following the tsunamis of December 2004, notably deploying some 13,000 military personnel in the region and providing an aircraft carrier to dispatch helicopters to the province of Aceh, where the destruction of roads and bridges had hindered the distribution of aid to remote areas. In early January 2005 US Secretary of State Colin Powell visited Aceh.

In September 1994 a 220-strong medical detachment from the Indonesian army joined the UN Protection Force in Bosnia and Herzegovina (UNPROFOR), in the first mission of its kind to Europe. Indonesia's international standing was further enhanced when, in January 1995, it replaced Pakistan as the non-permanent Asian representative on the UN Security Council for a period of two years. In October 1997 Indonesia proposed that two permanent seats for the representation of Asia be established on the Council. In October 1994 Indonesia underscored its pivotal regional role through hosting its fifth informal meeting to resolve peacefully the dispute over the conflicting claims of six Asian countries to sovereignty over parts of the South China Sea, particularly the Spratly Islands.

Moreover, in November the Asia-Pacific Economic Co-operation (APEC, see p. 155) summit meeting took place in Bogor. Indonesia had been one of the founding members of APEC, which had been established in 1989.

On 16 November 1994 the UN Convention on the Law of the Sea came into effect and immediately led to recognition of Indonesia's status as an archipelago and the country's sovereignty over all of the waters between its islands. Enforcement of the convention increased Indonesia's territorial waters by more than 3m. sq km.

In August 1995 Queen Beatrix of the Netherlands, the former colonial power in Indonesia, visited Indonesia (the first Dutch monarch to do so for 24 years) and spoke of her regret for the suffering caused by Dutch rule. Bilateral relations were strained from 1992, when Indonesia rejected Dutch aid because it was linked to progress on human rights.

In October 1998 it was reported that Indonesia and Portugal were to open representative offices in each other's capital cities in January 1999. In late December 1999, with the issue of the status of East Timor resolved following a vote in favour of independence at the referendum in August, Indonesia and Portugal formally re-established full diplomatic relations.

In mid-2000 it was reported that President Wahid had expressed his desire to develop Indonesia's relations with Iraq and other Muslim countries. In June of the same year President Wahid made an official visit to Iran, and in October Indonesia and Pakistan signed a memorandum of understanding relating to the promotion of bilateral ties. In January 2001 the Prime Minister of India made a four-day visit to Indonesia, following a visit to India by President Wahid in February 2000.

Government

The highest authority of the State is the Majelis Permusyawaratan Rakyat (MPR—People's Consultative Assembly) which, following a constitutional amendment in 2002 (see below), from 2004 comprised 678 members (reduced from 700) serving for five years. The MPR includes all 550 members of the Dewan Perwakilan Rakyat (DPR—House of Representatives), the country's legislative organ. Executive power rests with the President, elected for five years by the MPR. He or she governs with the assistance of an appointed Cabinet, which is responsible to the President. In August 2002 the MPR approved a series of amendments to the Constitution. These provided for: the direct election of the President and Vice-President; the termination of all non-elected representation in the DPR and MPR; and the creation of the Dewan Perwakilan Daerah (DPD—House of Representatives of the Regions) which, together with the DPR, would comprise the MPR. The changes took effect at the country's next national elections, held in 2004.

There are 33 provinces, and local government is through a three-tier system of provincial, regency and village assemblies. Each province is headed by a Governor, who is elected to a five-year term of office by the Provincial Assembly. Provincial Governors must be confirmed by the President, who also approves the election of the Governor of Jakarta, which is designated as a 'special district', as are Aceh and Yogyakarta.

Defence

In August 2004 the total strength of the armed forces was 302,000 men: army an estimated 233,000, navy 45,000 and air force 24,000. There were also some 280,000 paramilitary forces, including a police 'mobile brigade' of 14,000, 12,000 marine police and an estimated 40,000 trainees of KAMRA (People's Security). Military service is selective and lasts for two years. Defence expenditure for 2004 was budgeted at an estimated Rp. 21,400,000m.

Economic Affairs

In 2003, according to estimates by the World Bank, Indonesia's gross national income (GNI), measured at average 2001–03 prices, was US $199,026m., equivalent to $810 per head (or $3,210 per head on an international purchasing-power parity basis). During 1990–2003, it was estimated, the population increased at an average annual rate of 1.4%, while gross domestic product (GDP) per head increased, in real terms, by an average of 2.6% per year. Overall GDP increased, in real terms, by an average of 4.1% per year in 1990–2003. GDP increased by 3.7% in 2002 and by 4.1% in 2003.

Agriculture, forestry and fishing contributed 16.5% of GDP in 2003, and engaged 44.3% of the employed labour force in 2002. Principal crops for domestic consumption were rice, cassava and maize. Once self-sufficient in rice, Indonesia was obliged to

import supplies from the 1990s onwards, owing to increasing domestic demand. In the early 2000s Indonesia remained a major exporter of rubber and palm oil. Other principal cash crops were coffee, spices, tea, cocoa, tobacco, bananas, coconuts and sugar cane. In 2000 an estimated 58% of Indonesia's land area was covered by tropical rain forests. In January 2003 a report published by the Environmental Investigation Agency (EIA) blamed the corruption endemic in Indonesia for the obstruction of efforts to prevent the widespread environmental damage caused by illegal logging practices. During 1990–2003, according to the Asian Development Bank (ADB), agricultural GDP increased by an estimated average of 2.2% per year. The GDP of the sector expanded by 4.8% in 2003 and by 4.0% in 2004.

Industry (including mining, manufacturing, construction and utilities) engaged 18.8% of the employed labour force in 2002, and provided 43.6% of GDP in 2003. During 1990–2003, according to the ADB, industrial GDP increased by an average of 5.3% per year. The GDP of the sector increased by 3.8% in 2003 and by 3.9% in 2004.

Mining engaged only 0.7% of the employed labour force in 2002, but contributed 10.7% of GDP in 2003. Indonesia's principal mineral resource is petroleum, and the country is a leading exporter of liquefied natural gas. At the end of 2003 proven reserves of petroleum amounted to 4,400m. barrels. In that year production averaged 1.2m. barrels per day. In 2003 natural gas production was 72,600m. cu m, from proven reserves amounting to 256,000m. cu m. In 2002 coal production reached 103.3m. metric tons. With effect from 1 November 2004 Indonesia's petroleum production quota was set by the Organization of the Petroleum Exporting Countries (OPEC, see p. 331) at 1.399m. barrels per day. Indonesia is one of the world's largest producers of tin, output reaching 88,142 metric tons in 2002. Bauxite, nickel, copper, gold, silver and coal are also mined. During 1990–2003, according to the ADB, mining GDP increased by an average of 3.3% per year. The GDP of the sector increased by 2.5% in 2002 and by 0.5% in 2003.

Manufacturing contributed 24.7% of GDP in 2003, and engaged 13.2% of the employed labour force in 2002. Apart from petroleum refineries, the main branches of the sector include food products, textiles, clothing and footwear, transport equipment, electrical machinery and electronic equipment. According to the ADB, manufacturing GDP increased by an estimated average of 6.0% per year in 1990–2003. Manufacturing GDP increased by 3.4% in 2002 and by 3.5% in 2003.

During the 1980s Indonesia broadened the base of its energy supplies to include gas, coal, hydroelectricity and geothermal energy, in addition to the traditional dependence on petroleum. In 2000, of the total 92,821m. kWh of electricity produced, natural gas accounted for 34.3%, coal for 31.1%, petroleum for 21.9% and hydroelectricity for 9.8%. In 2002 imports of petroleum and its products comprised 21.2% of the total value of merchandise imports.

Services (including trade, transport and communications, finance and tourism) provided an estimated 39.9% of GDP in 2003, and engaged 36.9% of the employed labour force in 2002. Tourism is normally one of the principal sources of foreign exchange, but the terrorist attack on the tourist destination of Bali in October 2002 (see Recent History) had a significant impact on the sector. The number of tourists decreased from 5.2m. in 2001 to 5.0m. in 2002 and to fewer than 4.5m. in 2003. Revenue from tourism declined from US $5,396m. in 2001 to $4,306m. in 2002. According to the ADB, the GDP of the services sector expanded by an estimated average of 3.8% per year in 1990–2003. The sector's GDP increased by 6.5% in 2003 and by 6.9% in 2004.

In 2003 Indonesia recorded a visible trade surplus of US $23,990m. In the same year a surplus of $7,534m. was recorded on the current account of the balance of payments. In 2003 the principal source of imports was Japan (13.0%), and in 2002 the principal market for exports (21.1%) was also Japan. Other major suppliers were Singapore (which provided 12.8%), the People's Republic of China and the USA. Other major purchasers were the USA, Singapore and the Republic of Korea. The principal exports in 2002 were petroleum and its products, clothing, textiles, electronic equipment and plywood. In the same year the principal imports were machinery, mechanical appliances and electrical equipment, mineral and chemical products and iron and steel.

The budget for 2001/02 projected a deficit of Rp. 17,340,000m. In 2005 the budget deficit was expected to reach the equivalent of 0.8% of GDP, compared with a target of 1.2% in 2004. Indonesia's total external debt stood at US $132,208m. at the end of 2002, of which $70,011m. was long-term public debt. In that year the cost of debt-servicing was equivalent to 25.0% of revenue from exports of goods and services. The annual rate of inflation averaged 16.0% in 1995–2002. Consumer prices rose by an average of 6.6% in 2003 and by an estimated 6.1% in 2004. In 2003, according to the ADB, 9.5% of the labour force were unemployed. The rate of unemployment was reported to have exceeded 10.0% in 2004 and was expected to increase further in 2005. The level of underemployment also remained very high.

Indonesia is a member of the UN Economic and Social Commission for Asia and the Pacific (ESCAP, see p. 31), the Association of South East Asian Nations (ASEAN, see p. 162), the Asian Development Bank (ADB, see p. 159), the Asia-Pacific Economic Co-operation (APEC, see p. 155) forum, the Colombo Plan (see p. 373) and OPEC (see p. 331). As a member of ASEAN, Indonesia signed an accord in January 1992, pledging to establish a free trade zone, to be known as the ASEAN Free Trade Area (AFTA), within 15 years (subsequently reduced to 10 years), beginning in January 1993. AFTA was formally established on 1 January 2002.

Following its recovery from the regional financial crisis of the late 1990s and the political instability of 2001, the Indonesian economy was badly affected by the terrorist attack on the island of Bali (see Recent History) in October 2002 and by the devastating tsunamis of December 2004. As well as severely affecting the tourism sector, the Bali bombing of 2002 served to exacerbate further the problem of declining foreign investment in the country. Exports also continued to slow, affected by economic deceleration in the country's principal export markets (Japan, the USA and Singapore), as well as by the decline in foreign investment inflows. Meanwhile, the IMF, which had implemented a major programme to assist Indonesia during the economic crisis of the late 1990s, announced that it had reached a new agreement with the Government concerning its ongoing reform programme; the arrangement would allow Indonesia to draw US $450m. of the $1,800m. that remained available to it under the terms of the $5,000m. extended fund facility. In 2003 high levels of consumer spending continued to underpin economic growth. However, there was no significant increase in foreign investment over the course of the year, in part owing to the security concerns prompted by domestic unrest, particularly in the provinces of Aceh and Papua, and to the continued terrorist activity in the country, highlighted by the bombing of the Marriott Hotel in Jakarta in August (see Recent History). Despite the effects of the attack, an overall improvement in the country's economic performance in 2003, largely as a result of the ongoing implementation of reforms, prompted the Government to announce the termination of its involvement with the IMF at the end of the year. In order to ensure that it retained investor confidence, in September 2003 the Government released a plan outlining its intention to continue to implement reforms and to encourage the expansion of investment, employment and exports once it had emerged from the supervision of the IMF. In the first six months of 2004, however, foreign investment approvals reached only $3,000m., a decrease of 34% compared with the first half of 2003. Unemployment continued to rise, and export growth remained weak, largely as a result of a decline in competitiveness. At a meeting of the Consultative Group for Indonesia (CGI—a donor grouping chaired by the World Bank and incorporating IMF representatives) held in December 2003 donors pledged $2,800m. of budgetary support for 2004, $1,000m. of which was dependent upon progress in the area of policy reform. In early 2004 the closure of the agency established in 1998 to supervise the revival of the banking sector—the Indonesian Bank Restructuring Agency (IBRA)—signified further progress in the rehabilitation of the country's banking sector. In March 2004, furthermore, partly as a means of financing the budget deficit, Indonesia released its first global bond since 1996; the issue attracted strong demand from overseas investors and raised a total of $1,000m. in 10-year bonds. Upon taking office in October 2004, President Susilo Bambang

Yudhoyono confirmed his aim to raise the annual rate of GDP growth to 6%–7%, compared with the 4%–5% projected for 2004. Observers identified reforms of the taxation and legal systems, the improvement of the country's infrastructure and greater decentralization as essential if vital foreign investment inflows were to be increased. One of the principal challenges facing the new Government was the need to address the country's persistently high level of unemployment. In mid-2004 it was estimated that two-thirds of those unemployed were in the 15–24 age group. Moreover, new entrants to the labour market were estimated to total 2.5m. annually. Indonesia's hopes of reducing unemployment and of continuing its progress in the area of poverty reduction (the incidence of poverty having decreased from 27% in 1999 to 15% in 2003) were seriously hindered by the tsunamis of late 2004. Preliminary estimates put the total cost of the country's damages and losses at some $4,500m., equivalent to 2.2% of the country's GDP. A total of 1.3m. homes were reported to have been destroyed. The Government estimated that the sum of $150,000m. would be needed over the next five years simply to rebuild damaged roads, communication links and power stations. Of this figure, projects to the value of $22,500m. were to be offered to foreign investors. Meanwhile, a four-year recovery plan was drafted for the devastated province of Aceh, in northern Sumatra. Initially concerned with the immediate provision of food, clothing and temporary shelter for those affected by the disaster, the plan would subsequently redirect its focus to reconstruction work. The effects of the tsunamis were expected to reduce the country's economic growth by as much as 0.4% in 2005. Nevertheless, the Government envisaged that the rate of growth would exceed 5% in the coming year.

Education

Education is mainly under the control of the Ministry of National Education, but the Ministry of Religious Affairs is in charge of Islamic religious schools at the primary level. In 1987 primary education, beginning at seven years of age and lasting for six years, was made compulsory. In 1993 it was announced that compulsory education was to be expanded to nine years. Secondary education begins at 13 years of age and lasts for six years, comprising two cycles of three years each. Primary enrolment in 1994 included 97% of children in the relevant age-group (males 99%; females 95%). In the same year enrolment at secondary level included 42% of the relevant population (males 45%; females 39%). In 1999/2000 there were 1,634 universities. In 1994 enrolment at tertiary level was equivalent to 11.1% of the relevant population (males 13.5%; females 8.6%). In 2000/01, according to provisional data, the Government allocated Rp. 13,433,000m., representing 3.7% of total expenditure, to education.

Public Holidays

2005: 1 January (New Year's Day), 21 January* (Id al-Adha, Feast of the Sacrifice), 9 February (Chinese New Year), 10 February* (Muharram, Islamic New Year), 25 March (Good Friday), 28 March (Easter Monday), 21 April* (Mouloud, Prophet Muhammad's Birthday), 5 May (Ascension Day), 22 May (Vesak Day), 17 August (Independence Day), 2 September* (Ascension of the Prophet Muhammad), 4 November* (Id al-Fitr, end of Ramadan), 25 December (Christmas Day).

2006: 1 January (New Year's Day), 11 January* (Id al-Adha, Feast of the Sacrifice), 29 January (Chinese New Year), 31 January* (Muharram, Islamic New Year), 11 April* (Mouloud, Prophet Muhammad's Birthday), 14 April (Good Friday), 17 April (Easter Monday), 25 May (Ascension Day), May/June (Vesak Day), 17 August (Independence Day), 22 August* (Ascension of the Prophet Muhammad), 24 October* (Id al-Fitr, end of Ramadan), 25 December (Christmas Day).

*These holidays are dependent on the Islamic lunar calendar and may vary by one or two days from the dates given.

Weights and Measures

The metric system is in force.

Statistical Survey

Source (unless otherwise stated): Badan Pusat Statistik (Central Bureau of Statistics/Statistics Indonesia), Jalan Dr Sutomo 6–8, Jakarta 10710; tel. (21) 3507057; fax (21) 3857046; e-mail bpshq@bps.go.id; internet www.bps.go.id.

Note: Unless otherwise stated, figures for East Timor (now Timor-Leste, occupied by Indonesia between July 1976 and October 1999) are not included in the tables.

Area and Population

AREA, POPULATION AND DENSITY

Area (sq km)	1,922,570*
Population (census results)	
31 October 1990	178,631,196
30 June 2000†	
Males	103,417,180
Females	102,847,415
Total	206,264,595
Population (UN estimates at mid-year)‡	
2001	214,356,000
2002	217,131,000
2003	219,883,000
Density (per sq km) at mid-2003	114.4

* 742,308 sq miles.

† Includes non-permanent residents (421,399), estimates for areas where the census could not be carried out (2,317,216), and adjustment for underenumeration (2,283,981).

‡ Source: UN, *World Population Prospects: The 2002 Revision*. Does not take into account the results from the 2000 census.

ISLANDS
(population at 2000 census, including adjustment)*

	Area (sq km)	Population	Density (per sq km)
Jawa (Java) and Madura . . .	127,499	121,352,608	951.8
Sumatera (Sumatra)	482,393	43,309,707	89.8
Sulawesi (Celebes)	191,800	14,946,488	77.9
Kalimantan	547,891	11,331,558	20.7
Nusa Tenggara†	67,502	7,961,540	117.9
Bali	5,633	3,151,162	559.4
Maluku (Moluccas)	77,871	1,990,598	25.6
Papua‡	421,981	2,220,934	5.3
Total	1,922,570	206,264,595	107.3

* Figures refer to provincial divisions, each based on a large island or group of islands but also including adjacent small islands.

† Comprising most of the Lesser Sunda Islands, principally Flores, Lombok, Sumba, Sumbawa and part of Timor.

‡ Formerly Irian Jaya (West Papua).

PRINCIPAL TOWNS
(estimated population at 31 December 1996)

Jakarta (capital)	.	9,341,400	Malang . . .	775,900
Surabaya . . .		2,743,400	Padang . . .	739,500
Bandung . . .		2,429,000	Banjarmasin . . .	544,700
Medan . . .		1,942,000	Surakarta . . .	518,600
Palembang . . .		1,394,300	Pontianak . . .	459,100
Semarang . . .		1,366,500	Yogyakarta	
			(Jogjakarta) . .	421,000
Ujung Pandang				
(Makassar) . .		1,121,300		

Mid-2003 (UN estimates, incl. suburbs): Jakarta 12,295,516; Bandung 3,764,939; Surabaya 2,616,236; Medan 2,009,686; Palembang 1,569,437; Ujung Pandang 1,139,581 (Source: UN, *World Urbanization Prospects: The 2003 Revision*).

BIRTHS AND DEATHS
(UN estimates, annual averages)

	1985–90	1990–95	1995–2000
Birth rate (per 1,000)	28.0	24.9	22.5
Death rate (per 1,000)	9.3	8.3	7.6

Source: UN, *World Population Prospects: The 2002 Revision*.

Expectation of life (WHO estimates, years at birth): 66.4 (males 64.9; females 67.9) in 2002 (Source: WHO, *World Health Report*).

Birth rate (per 1,000): 22.9 in 1997; 22.8 in 1998; 22.4 in 1999 (Source: UN, *Statistical Yearbook for Asia and the Pacific*).

Death rate (per 1,000): 7.5 in 1997; 7.7 in 1998; 7.5 in 1999 (Source: UN, *Statistical Yearbook for Asia and the Pacific*).

ECONOMICALLY ACTIVE POPULATION
(persons aged 15 years and over)

	2000*	2001	2002‡
Agriculture, hunting, forestry and fishing	40,676,713	39,743,908	40,633
Mining and quarrying . . .	n.a.	n.a.	632
Manufacturing	11,641,756	12,086,122	12,110
Electricity, gas and water . .	n.a.	n.a.	178
Construction	3,497,232	3,837,554	4,274
Trade, restaurants and hotels .	18,489,005	17,469,129	17,795
Transport, storage and communications	4,553,855	4,448,279	4,673
Financing, insurance, real estate and business services . .	882,600	1,127,823	992
Public services	9,574,009	11,003,482	10,360
Activities not adequately defined .	522,560†	1,091,120†	—
Total employed	89,837,730	90,807,417	91,647
Unemployed	5,813,231	8,005,031	9,132
Total labour force	95,650,961	98,812,448	100,779

* Excluding Maluku province.

† Includes mining and quarrying and electricity, gas and water.

‡ '000 persons. Source: ILO.

Health and Welfare

KEY INDICATORS

Total fertility rate (children per woman, 2002)	2.4
Under-5 mortality rate (per 1,000 live births, 2002)	41
HIV/AIDS (% of persons aged 15–49, 2003)	0.1
Physicians (per 1,000 head, 1994)	0.16
Hospital beds (per 1,000 head, 1994)	0.66
Health expenditure (2001): US $ per head (PPP)	77
Health expenditure (2001): % of GDP	2.4
Health expenditure (2001): public (% of total)	25.1
Access to water (% of persons, 2002)	78
Access to sanitation (% of persons, 2002)	52
Human Development Index (2002): ranking	111
Human Development Index (2002): value	0.692

For sources and definitions, see explanatory note on p. vi.

Agriculture

PRINCIPAL CROPS

('000 metric tons, incl. East Timor)

	2001	2002	2003
Rice (paddy)	50,461	51,490	52,079
Maize	9,347	9,654	10,910
Potatoes	831	894	851
Sweet potatoes	1,749	1,772	1,998
Cassava (Manioc)	17,055	16,913	18,474
Other roots and tubers* . . .	350	350	350
Sugar cane†	25,185	25,530	24,500
Dry beans	288	335	317
Cashew nuts	86	88	90*
Other nuts	115	118	121*
Soybeans (Soya beans)	827	673	672
Groundnuts (in shell)†	1,245	1,267	1,377
Coconuts†	15,164	16,086	15,630
Oil palm fruit*	40,075	46,400	49,750
Kapok fruit	265†	265*	265*
Cabbages	1,399	1,438	1,551†
Tomatoes	484	574	433
Pumpkins, squash and gourds . .	135	172	103
Cucumbers and gherkins . . .	432	406	514
Aubergines (Eggplants)	244	273	301
Chillies and green peppers . . .	580	635	553
Dry onions	861	767	780
Leeks and other alliacious			
vegetables	283	315	346
Green beans	644	635	770
Carrots	301	282	356
Green corn*	200	200	200
Other vegetables*	516	534	541
Oranges	691	968	1,442
Avocados	142	238	256
Mangoes	923	1,403	731
Pineapples	495	556	677
Bananas	4,300	4,384	4,312
Papayas	501	605	627
Other fruits and berries† . . .	2,907	3,510	4,232
Coffee (green)	575	699	702
Cocoa beans	381	450†	426†
Tea (made)	163	157	159
Peppercorns	67	67	67*
Cinnamon	39	39*	39*
Cloves	81	88	88*
Ginger	150	151*	151*
Tobacco (leaves)	134	143	135†
Natural rubber	1,607	1,630	1,792

* FAO estimate(s).
† Unofficial figure(s).
Source: FAO.

LIVESTOCK

('000 head, incl. East Timor, year ending September)

	2001	2002	2003
Cattle	11,138	11,298	11,396
Sheep	7,401	7,661	8,133
Goats	12,464	12,549	13,276
Pigs	5,867	5,927	6,345
Horses	422	419	453
Buffaloes	2,333	2,403	2,455
Chickens	960,164	1,218,410	1,290,100
Ducks	32,068	46,000	48,119

Source: FAO.

LIVESTOCK PRODUCTS

('000 metric tons, incl. East Timor)

	2001	2002	2003
Beef and veal	338.7	330.3	351.8
Buffalo meat	43.6	42.3	45.3
Mutton and lamb	44.8	68.7	73.5
Goat meat	48.7	58.2	61.3
Pig meat*	463.3	471.4	473.0
Poultry meat	923.5	1,104.9	1,203.3
Cows' milk	479.9	493.4	577.5
Sheep's milk*	88.8	91.9	97.5
Goats' milk*	200	200	212
Hen eggs	692.7	776.1	881.3
Other poultry eggs	157.6	169.7	179.1
Wool: greasy*	22.2	23.0	24.4
Cattle hides (fresh)*	53.5	52.5	56.4
Buffalo hides (fresh)*	6.9	6.9	7.3
Sheepskins (fresh)*	9.9	15.3	16.3
Goatskins (fresh)*	11.2	13.4	14.1

* FAO estimates.
Note: Figures for meat refer to inspected production only, i.e. from animals slaughtered under government supervision.

Source: FAO.

Forestry

ROUNDWOOD REMOVALS

('000 cubic metres, excl. bark)

	2001	2002	2003*
Sawlogs, veneer logs and logs for			
sleepers	20,000	26,500	26,500
Pulpwood*†	3,248	3,248	3,248
Other industrial wood*† . . .	3,249	3,249	3,249
Fuel wood*	85,712	82,556	79,508
Total	112,209	115,553	112,504

* FAO estimates.
† Output assumed to be unchanged since 1999.
Source: FAO.

SAWNWOOD PRODUCTION

('000 cubic metres, incl. railway sleepers)

	2000	2001	2002
Total (all broadleaved)	6,500	6,750	6,500

2003: Production assumed to be the same as for 2002 (FAO estimate).
Source: FAO.

Fishing

('000 metric tons, live weight)

	2000	2001	2002
Capture	4,120.1	4,273.7	4,505.5
Scads	255.4	258.4	267.1
Goldstripe sardinella	172.2	185.9	191.3
'Stolephorus' anchovies . . .	173.9	190.2	197.8
Skipjack tuna	247.5	228.6	238.4
Indian mackerels	207.0	214.4	220.4
Aquaculture	788.5	864.3	914.1
Common carp	180.2	194.9	199.6
Milkfish	217.2	209.5	222.3
Total catch	4,908.6	5,137.9	5,419.5

Note: Figures exclude aquatic plants ('000 metric tons): 247.9 (capture 42.7, aquaculture 205.2) in 2000; 247.0 (capture 34.5, aquaculture 212.5) in 2001; 258.9 (capture 35.8, aquaculture 223.1) in 2002. Also excluded are crocodiles, recorded by number rather than by weight. The number of crocodiles caught was: 10,387 in 2000; 13,402 in 2001; n.a. in 2002.

Source: FAO.

Mining

('000 metric tons, unless otherwise indicated)

	2000	2001	2002
Crude petroleum (million barrels)‡	516.1	489.5	432.0
Natural gas (million cubic metres)	82,334	79,470	90,200
Bauxite	1,151	1,237	1,283
Coal	77,015	92,500	103,329
Nickel*	98.2	102.0	123.0
Copper*	1,012.1	1,048.7	1,171.7
Tin ore (metric tons)*	55,624	61,863	88,142
Gold (kg)†	123,994	162,605	142,238
Silver (kg)†	255,578	269,825	293,520

* Figures refer to the metal content of ores and concentrates.
† Including gold and silver in copper concentrate.
‡ Including condensate.

Source: US Geological Survey.

Industry

SELECTED PRODUCTS

('000 metric tons, unless otherwise indicated)

	1999	2000	2001
Raw sugar (centrifugal)[1]	1,801	1,780	1,836
Refined sugar[1,2]	2,222	2,037	1,910
Palm oil[1]	6,555	7,276	8,080[3]
Cigarettes (million)	254,276	n.a.	n.a.
Veneer sheets ('000 cubic metres)[1]	50	69	94
Plywood ('000 cubic metres)[1]	7,500	8,200	7,300
Newsprint[1]	532	477	511
Other printing and writing paper[1,2]	2,733	2,818	2,697
Other paper and paperboard[1]	3,713	3,682[2]	3,787[2]
Nitrogenous fertilizers[1,4]	2,842[3]	2,853[3]	2,549
Jet fuel	721	2,746	n.a.
Motor spirit (petrol)	8,125	7,997	n.a.
Naphthas	794	1,344	n.a.
Kerosene	7,635	7,494	n.a.
Gas-diesel oil	13,984	14,401	n.a.
Residual fuel oils	11,420	11,421	n.a.
Lubricating oils	332	364	n.a.
Liquefied petroleum gas	1,979	1,762	n.a.
Rubber tyres ('000)[5]	33,089	21,000[2]	20,500[2]
Cement (hydraulic)[6]	23,925	27,789	31,100
Aluminium (unwrought)[2,6,7]	106	160	180
Tin (unwrought, metric tons)[6,7]	49,709	47,129	53,796
Radio receivers ('000)	4,937	n.a.	n.a.
Passenger motor cars ('000)[8]	39	n.a.	n.a.
Electric energy (million kWh)	95,944	99,511	n.a.
Gas from gasworks (terajoules)	27,421	33,380[2]	n.a.

2002: Raw sugar (centrifugal, '000 metric tons) 1,869[1]; Refined sugar ('000 metric tons) 2,000[1,2]; Palm oil ('000 metric tons) 9,350[1,3]; Veneer sheets ('000 cubic metres) 45[1,2]; Plywood ('000 cubic metres) 7,550[1]; Nitrogenous fertilizers ('000 metric tons) 2,868[1,2,4]; Cement (hydraulic, '000 metric tons) 33,000[2,6]; Aluminium (unwrought, '000 metric tons) 160[2,6,7]; Tin (unwrought, metric tons) 67,455[6,7].

2003 ('000 metric tons): Raw sugar (centrifugal, '000 metric tons) 1,730[1,2]; Refined sugar ('000 metric tons) 2,431[1,2]; Palm oil ('000 metric tons) 10,200[1,3].

[1] Source: FAO.
[2] Provisional or estimated production.
[3] Unofficial figure.
[4] Production in terms of nitrogen.
[5] For road motor vehicles, excluding bicycles and motorcycles.
[6] Source: US Geological Survey.
[7] Primary metal production only.
[8] Vehicles assembled from imported parts.

Source (unless otherwise indicated): UN, *Industrial Commodity Statistics Yearbook*.

Finance

CURRENCY AND EXCHANGE RATES

Monetary Units
100 sen = 1 rupiah (Rp.).

Sterling, Dollar and Euro Equivalents (31 December 2004)
£1 sterling = 17,942.7 rupiah;
US $1 = 9,290.0 rupiah;
€1 = 12,653.9 rupiah;
100,000 rupiah = £5.573 = $10.764 = €7.903.

Average Exchange Rate (rupiah per US $)
2002   9,311.2
2003   8,577.1
2004   8,938.9

BUDGET

('000 million rupiah, year ending 31 March)

Revenue	1998/99	1999/2000	2000/01*
Tax revenue	147,600	183,281	196,720
Taxes on income, profits, etc.†	97,313	118,164	94,462
Individual	52,995	15,571	19,146
Corporate‡	41,368	99,638	70,463
Domestic taxes on goods and services	38,750	55,453	78,254
General sales, turnover or VAT	27,803	33,087	55,863
Excises	7,733	10,381	17,394
Taxes on international trade	6,936	5,035	9,568
Import duties	2,306	4,177	9,026
Export duties	4,630	858	542
Non-tax revenue	9,781	15,330	111,121
Entrepreneurial and property income	6,281	10,292	15,834
Other	1,967	3,347	92,787
Total	157,381	198,611	307,841
Capital revenue	31	62	35

Expenditure	1998/99	1999/2000	2000/01*
General public services	16,148	11,425	16,607
Defence	8,955	8,576	10,673
Public order and safety	3,080	4,453	7,400
Education	11,918	14,349	13,433
Health	3,889	5,186	4,542
Social security and welfare	9,220	12,006	30,766
Housing and community amenities	23,435	33,787	4,726
Recreational, cultural and religious affairs	2,992	3,347	2,257
Economic affairs and services	22,164	23,250	12,747
Agriculture, hunting, forestry and fishing	11,511	8,610	4,652
Transportation and communication	6,395	5,580	3,709
Other economic affairs and services	2,481	5,509	858
Other	72,297	109,494	255,886
Interest payments	31,264	42,910	—
Total	174,097	225,874	359,038
Current expenditure	114,412	170,684	n.a.
Capital expenditure	59,686	55,190	n.a.

* Figures are provisional.
† Prior to 1999, tax on income, profits, etc. could not be broken into its components, and almost all income tax was classified as taxes paid by individuals.
‡ Prior to 2000, revenues from natural resources and oil and gas revenue were classified as corporate income tax.

Source: IMF, *Government Finance Statistics Yearbook*.

INTERNATIONAL RESERVES
(US $ million at 31 December)

	2001	2002	2003
Gold*	772	1,077	1,291
IMF special drawing rights . .	16	19	4
Reserve position in IMF . .	183	198	216
Foreign exchange	27,048	30,754	34,742
Total	28,019	32,048	36,253

* Valued at market-related prices.

Source: IMF, *International Financial Statistics*.

MONEY SUPPLY
('000 million rupiah at 31 December)

	2001	2002	2003
Currency outside banks . . .	76,342	80,659	94,539
Demand deposits at deposit money banks	97,746	106,558	125,329
Total money (incl. others) . .	175,110	188,008	220,552

Source: IMF, *International Financial Statistics*.

COST OF LIVING
(Consumer Price Index; base: 1996 = 100)

	2001	2002	2003
Food (incl. beverages)	267.1	296.0	310.0
Non-food	213.4	251.7	270.6
All items	249.2	274.1	279.6

Source: Asian Development Bank, *Key Indicators of Developing Asian and Pacific Countries*.

NATIONAL ACCOUNTS
('000 million rupiah at current prices)

National Income and Product

	1999	2000	2001
Domestic factor incomes* . . .	1,044,745	1,217,917	1,416,425
Consumption of fixed capital . .	54,987	64,101	74,549
Gross domestic product (GDP) at factor cost	1,099,732	1,282,018	1,490,974
Indirect taxes, *less* subsidies . .	—	—	—
GDP in purchasers' values . .	1,099,732	1,282,018	1,490,974
Net factor income from abroad .	−83,765	−92,162	−58,079
Gross national product (GNP) .	1,015,967	1,189,856	1,432,895
Less Consumption of fixed capital	54,987	64,101	74,549
National income in market prices	960,980	1,125,755	1,358,346

* Compensation of employees and the operating surplus of enterprises. The amount is obtained as a residual.

Source: UN, *National Accounts Statistics*.

Expenditure on the Gross Domestic Product

	2001	2002	2003
Government final consumption expenditure	113,416	132,219	163,701
Private final consumption expenditure	972,938	1,120,164	1,238,892
Increase in stocks*	−53,624	−73,876	−67,258
Gross fixed capital formation . .	314,066	326,165	352,361
Total domestic expenditure	1,346,796	1,504,672	1,687,696
Exports of goods and services . .	624,341	577,082	558,091
Less Imports of goods and services	503,482	471,188	459,097
GDP in purchasers' values . .	1,467,655	1,610,565	1,786,691
GDP at constant 1993 prices .	411,752	426,943	444,453

* Figures obtained as a residual.

Source: Asian Development Bank, *Key Indicators of Developing Asian and Pacific Countries*.

Gross Domestic Product by Economic Activity

	2001	2002	2003
Agriculture, forestry and fishing .	244,722	275,271	296,238
Mining and quarrying	193,541	178,197	191,177
Manufacturing	372,916	409,666	440,452
Electricity, gas and water . . .	22,170	30,492	39,665
Construction	85,602	93,966	107,119
Trade, hotels and restaurants . .	235,738	265,535	291,590
Transport, storage and communications	74,247	92,797	111,728
Finance, insurance, real estate and business services	94,819	110,158	123,001
Public administration	81,851	83,294	101,606
Other services	62,049	71,189	84,117
Total	1,467,655	1,610,565	1,786,691

Source: Asian Development Bank, *Key Indicators of Developing Asian and Pacific Countries*.

BALANCE OF PAYMENTS
(US $ million)

	2001	2002	2003
Exports of goods f.o.b.	57,365	59,165	63,252
Imports of goods f.o.b.	−34,668	−35,351	−39,262
Trade balance	22,696	23,814	23,990
Exports of services	5,500	6,663	5,293
Imports of services	−15,880	−17,054	−17,400
Balance on goods and services	12,316	13,432	11,882
Other income received	2,004	1,318	1,054
Other income paid	−8,940	−8,365	−7,272
Balance on goods, services and income	5,381	6,384	5,665
Current transfers received . . .	1,520	2,210	2,053
Current transfers paid	—	−470	−184
Current balance	6,901	8,124	7,534
Direct investment from abroad .	−2,977	145	−597
Portfolio investment liabilities .	−244	1,222	2,251
Other investment assets . . .	−125	−500	−5
Other investment liabilities . .	−4,271	−1,970	−2,599
Net errors and omissions . . .	701	−2,063	−2,937
Overall balance	−15	4,958	3,647

Source: IMF, *International Financial Statistics*.

External Trade

PRINCIPAL COMMODITIES
(distribution by SITC, US $ million)

Imports c.i.f.	2000	2001	2002
Food and live animals	2,781.3	2,496.6	2,851.7
Cereals and cereal preparations	1,100.0	746.0	1,214.6
Crude materials (inedible) except fuels	3,296.6	3,171.3	2,658.9
Textile fibres and waste	1,005.8	1,332.1	914.8
Mineral fuels, lubricants, etc.	6,179.0	5,644.1	6,687.9
Crude petroleum oils, etc.	2,524.9	2,887.5	3,216.9
Refined petroleum products	3,562.5	2,652.9	3,409.3
Gas oils	1,701.3	1,355.2	1,728.4
Chemicals and related products	5,753.6	5,253.0	5,120.4
Organic chemicals	2,476.3	2,188.8	2,005.5
Artificial resins and plastic materials, etc.	1,074.5	984.4	961.4
Basic manufactures	5,152.1	4,345.6	4,333.3
Textile yarn, fabrics, etc.	1,259.0	1,096.1	887.9
Iron and steel	1,684.5	1,300.3	1,458.3
Machinery and transport equipment	9,194.5	9,030.3	8,581.2
Machinery specialized for particular industries	1,610.4	1,546.9	1,340.7
General industrial machinery, equipment and parts	1,950.8	1,941.4	1,926.0
Road vehicles and parts*	1,851.8	1,838.9	1,639.0
Parts and accessories for cars, buses, lorries, etc.*	1,120.9	936.4	829.7
Total (incl. others)	33,514.8	30,962.1	31,288.8

Exports f.o.b.	2000	2001	2002
Food and live animals	3,499.9	3,252.3	3,604.5
Fish, crustaceans and molluscs	1,583.3	1,532.2	1,487.0
Crude materials (inedible) except fuels	4,317.1	4,187.7	4,522.0
Ores and concentrates of non-ferrous base metals	1,943.2	1,987.2	1,889.3
Mineral fuels, lubricants, etc.	15,683.5	14,274.0	13,910.3
Coal, coke and briquettes	1,296.4	1,625.2	1,770.8
Coal, lignite and peat	1,276.1	1,617.7	1,762.4
Petroleum, petroleum products, etc.	7,762.2	6,916.6	6,561.9
Crude petroleum oils, etc.	6,090.1	5,714.7	5,227.6
Petroleum gases, etc., in the liquefied state	6,624.9	5,732.2	5,577.6
Animal and vegetable oils, fats and waxes	1,772.1	1,446.2	2,656.3
Fixed vegetable oils, fluid or solid, crude, refined or purified	1,648.9	1,341.1	2,511.3
Palm oil	1,087.3	1,080.9	2,092.4
Chemicals and related products	3,114.8	2,803.5	2,936.9
Basic manufactures	12,452.5	11,272.4	10,998.7
Wood and cork manufactures (excl. furniture)	3,226.6	2,891.9	2,811.0
Veneers, plywood, etc.	2,286.6	2,073.4	2,023.4
Plywood of wood sheets	1,988.9	1,837.9	1,748.3
Paper, paperboard, etc.	2,300.5	2,048.4	2,118.2
Textile yarn, fabrics, etc.	3,517.3	3,214.4	2,911.2
Machinery and transport equipment	10,740.8	9,079.3	9,766.9
Telecommunications and sound equipment	3,500.1	3,353.7	3,359.4
Miscellaneous manufactured articles	9,913.0	9,271.1	8,171.6
Clothing and accessories (excl. footwear)	4,806.7	4,597.6	4,000.9
Total (incl. others)	62,124.0	56,316.9	57,158.8

* Excluding tyres, engines and electrical parts.

Source: UN, *International Trade Statistics Yearbook.*

PRINCIPAL TRADING PARTNERS
(US $ million)*

Imports c.i.f.	2001	2002	2003
Australia	1,814.1	1,587.2	1,648.4
Canada	356.5	411.9	321.8
China, People's Republic	1,842.7	2,427.4	2,957.5
France	396.9	406.3	453.2
Germany	1,300.5	1,224.3	1,181.2
Hong Kong	257.3	240.7	222.2
Italy	407.5	401.7	323.7
Japan	4,689.5	4,409.3	4,228.3
Korea, Republic	2,209.3	1,646.8	1,527.9
Malaysia	1,005.5	1,037.4	1,138.2
Netherlands	343.8	352.2	369.6
Singapore	3,147.1	4,099.6	4,155.1
Taiwan	1,071.0	1,010.4	877.1
Thailand	986.0	1,190.7	1,701.7
United Kingdom	643.0	656.2	463.7
USA	3,207.5	2,639.9	2,694.8
Total (incl. others)	30,962.1	31,288.9	32,550.7

Exports f.o.b.	2000	2001	2002
Australia	1,519.4	1,844.9	1,924.4
Belgium/Luxembourg	840.6	772.1	793.8
China, People's Republic	2,767.7	2,200.7	2,902.9
France	718.3	662.7	648.9
Germany	1,443.1	1,297.0	1,269.9
Hong Kong	1,554.1	1,290.3	1,242.3
Italy	757.8	621.8	719.8
Japan	14,415.2	13,010.2	12,045.1
Korea, Republic	4,317.9	3,772.5	4,107.2
Malaysia	1,971.8	1,778.6	2,029.9
Netherlands	1,837.4	1,498.2	1,618.4
Philippines	819.5	814.8	778.2
Singapore	6,562.4	5,363.9	5,349.1
Spain	932.2	903.6	996.4
Taiwan	2,378.3	2,188.0	2,067.5
Thailand	1,026.5	1,063.6	1,227.4
United Kingdom	1,507.9	1,383.1	1,252.4
USA	8,475.4	7,748.7	7,558.6
Total (incl. others)	62,124.0	56,320.9	57,158.8

* Imports by country of production; exports by country of consumption. Figures include trade in gold.

Transport

RAILWAYS
(traffic)

	2000	2001	2002
Passengers embarked (million)	192	187	176
Freight loaded ('000 tons)	19,545	18,702	17,099

Source: Indonesian State Railways.

ROAD TRAFFIC
(motor vehicles registered at 31 December)

	1998*	1999	2000†
Passenger cars	2,769,375	2,897,803	3,038,913
Lorries and trucks	1,586,721	1,628,531	1,707,134
Buses and coaches	626,680	644,667	666,280
Motorcycles	12,628,991	13,053,148	13,563,017

* Including East Timor (now Timor-Leste).
† Preliminary figures.

Source: State Police of Indonesia.

SHIPPING

Merchant Fleet
(registered at 31 December)

	2001	2002	2003
Number of vessels	2,528	2,628	2,700
Displacement ('000 grt)	3,613.1	3,723.1	3,840.4

Source: Lloyd's Register-Fairplay, *World Fleet Statistics.*

Sea-borne Freight Traffic
('000 metric tons)

	1999	2000	2001*
International:			
goods loaded	139,340	141,528	143,750
goods unloaded	43,477	45,040	46,659
Domestic:			
goods loaded	113,633	127,740	163,685
goods unloaded	122,368	137,512	138,667

* Preliminary figures.

CIVIL AVIATION
(traffic on scheduled services)

	1999	2000	2001
Kilometres flown (million) . . .	122	138	150
Passengers carried ('000) . . .	8,047	9,916	10,397
Passenger-km (million)	14,544	16,764	16,169
Total ton-km (million)	1,560	1,865	1,978

Source: UN, *Statistical Yearbook.*

Tourism

FOREIGN TOURIST ARRIVALS

Country of residence	2001	2002	2003
Australia	397,982	346,245	268,538
Germany	159,881	142,649	113,895
Japan	611,314	620,722	463,088
Korea, Republic	212,233	210,581	201,741
Malaysia	484,692	475,163	466,811
Netherlands	114,656	110,631	91,446
Singapore	1,477,132	1,447,315	1,469,282
Taiwan	391,696	400,334	381,877
United Kingdom	189,027	160,077	98,916
USA	177,869	160,982	130,276
Total (incl. others)	5,153,620	5,033,400	4,467,021

Receipts from tourism (US $ million): 5,749 in 2000; 5,396 in 2001; 4,306 in 2002 (Source: World Tourism Organization).

Communications Media

	2000	2001	2002
Television receivers ('000 in use)	31,700	n.a.	n.a.
Telephones ('000 main lines in use)	6,662.6	7,218.9	7,750.0
Mobile cellular telephones ('000			
subscribers)	3,669.3	6,520.9	11,700.0
Personal computers ('000 in use) .	2,100	2,300	2,519
Internet users ('000)	2,000	4,000	8,000

Facsimile machines (estimated number in use): 185,000 in 1997.

Radio receivers ('000 in use): 31,500 in 1997 (Source: UN, *Statistical Yearbook*).

Daily newspapers: 172 (average circulation 4,713,000) in 1998 (Source: UN, *Statistical Yearbook*).

Non-daily newspapers: 433 (average circulation 7,838,000) in 1998 (Source: UN, *Statistical Yearbook*).

Source (unless otherwise indicated): International Telecommunication Union.

Education

(2001/02)

	Institutions	Teachers	Pupils and Students
Primary schools	148,516	1,164,808	25,850,849
General junior secondary schools .	20,842	476,827	7,466,458
General senior secondary schools .	7,785	224,149	3,024,176
Vocational senior secondary schools	4,522	139,359	2,027,464
Universities*	1,634	194,828	3,126,307

* Figures from 1999/2000.

Source: Ministry of National Education.

Adult literacy rate (UNESCO estimates): 87.9% (males 92.5%; females 83.4%) in 2002 (Source: UN Development Programme, *Human Development Report*).

Directory

The Constitution

Indonesia had three provisional Constitutions: in August 1945, February 1950 and August 1950. In July 1959 the Constitution of 1945 was re-enacted by presidential decree. The General Elections Law of 1969 supplemented the 1945 Constitution, which has been adopted permanently by the Majelis Permusyawaratan Rakyat (MPR—People's Consultative Assembly). Amendments made to the Constitution in 2001 and 2002 took effect in 2004, when Indonesia held its next general election. The following is a summary of the Constitution's main provisions, with subsequent amendments:

GENERAL PRINCIPLES

The 1945 Constitution consists of 37 articles, four transitional clauses and two additional provisions, and is preceded by a preamble. The preamble contains an indictment of all forms of colonialism, an account of Indonesia's struggle for independence, the declaration of that independence and a statement of fundamental aims and principles. Indonesia's National Independence, according to the text of the preamble, has the state form of a Republic, with

sovereignty residing in the People, and is based upon five fundamental principles, the *pancasila*:

1. Belief in the One Supreme God.
2. Just and Civilized Humanity.
3. The Unity of Indonesia.
4. Democracy led by the wisdom of deliberations (*musyawarah*) and consensus among representatives.
5. Social Justice for all the people of Indonesia.

STATE ORGANS

Majelis Permusyawaratan Rakyat—MPR (People's Consultative Assembly)

Sovereignty is in the hands of the People and is exercised in full by the MPR as the embodiment of the whole Indonesian People. The MPR is the highest authority of the State, and is to be distinguished from the legislative body proper (Dewan Perwakilan Rakyat—DPR, see below), which is incorporated within the MPR. The bicameral MPR, with a total of 678 members (reduced from 700 in 2004), is composed of the 550 members of the DPR and the members of the Dewan Perwakilan Daerah—DPD (see below). Elections to the MPR are held every five years. The MPR sits at least once every five years, and its primary competence is to determine the Constitution and the broad lines of the policy of the State and the Government. It also inaugurates the President and Vice-President, who are responsible for implementing that policy. All decisions are taken unanimously in keeping with the traditions of *musyawarah*.

The President

The highest executive of the Government, the President, holds office for a term of five years and may be re-elected once. As Mandatory of the MPR he/she must execute the policy of the State according to the Decrees determined by the MPR during its Fourth General and Special Sessions. In conducting the administration of the State, authority and responsibility are concentrated in the President. The Ministers of the State are his/her assistants and are responsible only to him/her. The President and Vice-President are to be directly elected on a single ticket (until November 2001 the MPR had exercised the power to elect them). If no candidate succeeds in obtaining more than one-half of the votes cast in a presidential election, a second round of voting shall be held. The President and Vice-President may be dismissed by the MPR on the proposal of the Dewan Perwakilan Rakyat if it is proven that he/she has either violated the law or no longer meets the requirements of his/her office. The President may not freeze or dissolve the Dewan.

Dewan Perwakilan Rakyat—DPR (House of Representatives)

The legislative branch of the State, the Dewan Perwakilan Rakyat, sits at least once a year. Its members are all directly elected. Every statute requires the approval of the Dewan. Members of the Dewan have the right to submit draft bills which require ratification by the President, who has the right of veto. In times of emergency the President may enact ordinances which have the force of law, but such Ordinances must be ratified by the Dewan during the following session or be revoked.

Dewan Perwakilan Daerah—DPD (House of Representatives of the Regions)

The Dewan Perwakilan Daerah is the second chamber of the MPR. Its members are directly elected from every province. Each province has an equal number of members and total membership of the DPD is no more than one-third of the total membership of the DPR. The DPD sits at least once a year. It may propose to the DPR bills relating to regional autonomy, the relationship between central and local government, the formation, expansion and merger of regions, the management of natural and other economic resources, and the financial balance between the centre and the localities. It may also participate in the discussion of such bills and oversee the implementation of regional laws, as well as the state budget, taxation, education and religion.

Dewan Pertimbangan Agung—DPA (Supreme Advisory Council)

The DPA is an advisory body assisting the President, who chooses its members from political parties, functional groups and groups of prominent persons.

Mahkamah Agung (Supreme Court)

The judicial branch of the State, the Supreme Court and the other courts of law (public courts, religious courts, military tribunals, administrative courts and a Constitutional Court) are independent of the Executive in exercising their judicial powers. There is an independent Judicial Commission which is authorized to propose candidates for appointment as justices of the Supreme Court and to ensure the good behaviour of judges. Its members are appointed and dismissed by the President with the approval of the DPR.

Badan Pemeriksa Keuangan (Supreme Audit Board)

Controls the accountability of public finance, enjoys investigatory powers and is independent of the Executive. Its findings are presented to the Dewan.

The Government

HEAD OF STATE

President: SUSILO BAMBANG YUDHOYONO (inaugurated 20 October 2004).

Vice-President: YUSUF KALLA.

CABINET
(April 2005)

Co-ordinating Minister for Political Affairs, Security and Social Welfare: Adm. (retd) WIDODO ADI SUTJIPTO.

Co-ordinating Minister for the Economy, Finance and Industry: ABURIZAL BAKRIE.

Co-ordinating Minister for People's Welfare: ALWI SHIHAB.

Minister of Home Affairs and Regional Autonomy: Lt-Gen. (retd) MUHAMMAD MA'ARUF.

Minister of Foreign Affairs: HASSAN WIRAJUDA.

Minister of Defence: MATORI JUWONO SUDARSONO.

Minister of Justice and Human Rights Affairs: HAMID AWALUDDIN.

Minister of Finance and State Enterprises Development: JUSUF ANWAR.

Minister of Energy and Mineral Resources: Dr Ir PURNOMO YUSGIANTORO.

Minister of Industry: ADUNG NITIMIHARJA.

Minister of Trade: MARI E. PANGESTU.

Minister of Agriculture: ANTON APRIYANTONO.

Minister of Forestry: M. S. KA'BAN.

Minister of Transportation and Telecommunication: HATTA RADJASA.

Minister of Marine Affairs and Fisheries: FREDDY NUMBERI.

Minister of Manpower and Transmigration: FAHMI IDRIS.

Minister of Public Works: JOKO KIRMANTO.

Minister of Health: SITI FADILA SUPARI.

Minister of National Education: BAMBANG SOEDIBYO.

Minister of Social Affairs: BACHTIAR CHAMSYAH.

Minister of Religious Affairs: M. MAFTUH BASYUNI.

Minister of Culture and Tourism: JERO WATJIK.

Minister of State for Research and Technology: KUSMAYANTO KADIMAN.

Minister of State for Co-operatives and Small and Medium-Sized Businesses: SURYADARMA ALI.

Minister of State for the Environment: RACHMAT WITOELAR.

Minister of State for Women's Empowerment: MEUTIA HATTA.

Minister of State for Administrative Reform: TAUFIK EFFENDI.

Minister of State for State Enterprises: SOEGIARTO.

Minister of State for Communications and Information: SOFYAN A. DJALIL.

Minister of State for Acceleration of Development in Backwards Regions: SYAIFULAH YUSUF.

Minister of State for National Development Planning: Sri MULYANI INDRAWATI.

Minister of State for Public Housing: M. JUSUF ANSHARI.

Minister of State for Youth and Sports Affairs: ADYAKSA DAULT.

Officials with the rank of Minister of State:

Attorney-General: MUHAMMAD ABDURRAHMAN SALEH.

State Secretary: YUSRIL IHZA MAHENDRA.

Cabinet Secretary: SUDI SILALAHI.

MINISTRIES

Office of the President: Instant Merdeka, Jakarta; tel. (21) 3840946.

Office of the Vice-President: Jalan Merdeka Selatan 6, Jakarta; tel. (21) 363539.

Office of the Attorney-General: Jalan Sultan Hasanuddin 1, Kebayoran Baru, Jakarta; tel. (21) 7221377; fax (21) 7392576; e-mail kejagung@kejaksaan.go.id; internet www.kejaksaan.go.id.

Office of the Cabinet Secretary: Jalan Veteran 18, Jakarta Pusat; tel. (21) 3810973.

Office of the Co-ordinating Minister for the Economy, Finance and Industry: Jalan Taman Suropati 2, Jakarta 10310; tel. (21) 3849063; fax (21) 334779.

Office of the Co-ordinating Minister for Political Affairs, Security and Social Welfare: Jalan Medan Merdeka Barat 15, Jakarta 10110; tel. (21) 3849453; fax (21) 3450918.

Office of the State Secretary: Jalan Veteran 17, Jakarta 10110; tel. (21) 3849043; fax (21) 3452685; internet www.ri.go.id.

Ministry of Agriculture and Forestry: Jalan Harsono R. M. 3, Gedung D-Lantai 4, Ragunan, Pasar Minggu, Jakarta Selatan 12550; tel. (21) 7805305; fax (21) 7816385; e-mail eko@deptan.go.id; internet www.deptan.go.id.

Ministry of Defence: Jalan Medan Merdeka Barat 13–14, Jakarta Pusat; tel. (21) 3456184; fax (21) 3440023; e-mail postmaster@ dephan.go.id; internet www.dephan.go.id.

Ministry of Energy and Mineral Resources: Jalan Merdeka Selatan 18, Jakarta 10110; tel. (21) 3804242; fax (21) 3847461; e-mail pulahta@setjen.dpe.go.id; internet www.dpe.go.id.

Ministry of Finance and State Enterprises Development: Jalan Lapangan Banteng Timur 2–4, Jakarta 10710; tel. (21) 3814324; fax (21) 353710; internet www.depkeu.go.id.

Ministry of Foreign Affairs: Jalan Taman Pejambon 6, Jakarta 10410; tel. (21) 3441508; fax (21) 3805511; e-mail guestbook@ dfa-deplu.go.id; internet www.deplu.go.id.

Ministry of Health and Social Welfare: Jalan H. R. Rasuna Said, Block X5, Kav. 4–9, Jakarta 12950; tel. (21) 5201587; fax (21) 5203874; e-mail webadmin@depkes.go.id; internet www.depkes.go .id.

Ministry of Home Affairs and Regional Autonomy: Jalan Merdeka Utara 7–8, Gedung Utama Lt. 4, Jakarta Pusat 10110; tel. (21) 3842222; fax (21) 372812; e-mail dpod@indosat.net.id; internet www .depdagri.go.id.

Ministry of Industry and Trade: Jalan Jenderal Gatot Subroto, Kav. 52–53, 2nd Floor, Jakarta Selatan; tel. (21) 5256458; fax (21) 5229592; e-mail men-indag@dprin.go.id; internet www.dprin.go.id.

Ministry of Justice and Human Rights Affairs: Jalan H. R. Rasuna Said, Kav. 6–7, Kuningan, Jakarta Selatan; tel. (21) 5253004; fax (21) 5253095; internet www.depkehham.go.id.

Ministry of Manpower and Transmigration: Jalan Jenderal Gatot Subroto, Kav. 51, Jakarta Selatan 12950; tel. (21) 5255683; fax (21) 515669; internet www.nakertrans.go.id.

Ministry of Marine Affairs and Fisheries: Jalan Harsono R. M. 3, Rangunan, Jakarta 12550; tel. (21) 3522515; fax (21) 3519070; internet www.dkp.go.id.

Ministry of National Education: Jalan Jenderal Sudirman, Senayan, Jakarta Pusat; tel. (21) 5731618; fax (21) 5736870; internet www.depdiknas.go.id.

Ministry of Public Works: Jalan Pattimura 20, Kebayoran Baru, Jakarta 12110; tel. (21) 7392262; internet www.pu.go.id.

Ministry of Religious Affairs: Jalan Lapangan Banteng Barat 3–4, Jakarta Pusat; tel. (21) 3811436; fax (21) 380836; internet www .depag.go.id.

Ministry of Social Affairs: Jakarta; internet www.depsos.go.id.

Ministry of Transportation and Telecommunication: Jalan Merdeka Barat 8, Jakarta 10110; tel. (21) 3811308; fax (21) 3451657; e-mail pusdatin@rad.net.id; internet www.dephub.go.id.

Office of the Minister of State for Co-operatives and Small and Medium-Sized Businesses: Jalan H. R. Rasuna Said, Kav. 3–5, POB 177, Jakarta Selatan 12940; tel. (21) 5204366; fax (21) 5204383; internet www.depkop.go.id.

Office of the Minister of State for the Environment: Jalan D. I. Panjaitan, Kebon Nanas Lt. II, Jakarta 134110; tel. (21) 8580103; fax (21) 8580101; internet www.bapedal.go.id.

Office of the Minister of State for Research and Technology: BPP Teknologi II Bldg, Jalan M. H. Thamrin 8, Jakarta Pusat 10340; tel. (21) 3169166; fax (21) 3101952; e-mail webmstr@ristek.go .id; internet www.ristek.go.id.

Office of the Minister of State for Women's Empowerment: Jalan Medan Merdeka Barat 15, Jakarta 10110; tel. (21) 3805563; fax (21) 3805562; e-mail biroren@menegpp.go.id; internet www .menegpp.go.id.

Office of the Minister of State for Youth and Sports Affairs: Jakarta.

OTHER GOVERNMENT BODY

Badan Pemeriksa Keuangan (BPK) (Supreme Audit Board): Jalan Gatot Subroto 31, Jakarta; tel. (21) 584081; internet www.bpk .go.id; Chair. ANWAR NASUTION; Vice-Chair. ABDULLAH ZAINIE.

President and Legislature

PRESIDENT

Presidential Election, First Ballot, 5 July 2004

Candidate	Votes	% of votes
Gen. (retd) Susilo Bambang Yudhoyono (DP)	39,838,184	33.57
Megawati Sukarnoputri (PDI—P)	31,569,104	26.61
Gen. (retd) Wiranto (Golkar)	26,286,788	22.15
Amien Rais (PAN)	17,392,931	14.66
Hamzah Haz (PPP)	3,569,861	3.01
Total	118,656,868	100.00

Presidential Election, Second Ballot, 20 September 2004

Candidate	Votes	% of votes
Gen. (retd) Susilo Bambang Yudhoyono (DP)	69,266,350	60.62
Megawati Sukarnoputri (PDI—P)	44,990,704	39.38
Total	114,257,054	100.00

LEGISLATURE

Majelis Permusyawaratan Rakyat (MPR)
(People's Consultative Assembly)

Jalan Jendral Gatot Subroto 6, Jakarta 10270; tel. (21) 5715268; fax (21) 5715611; e-mail kotaksurat@mpr.go.id; internet www.mpr.go .id.

In late 2002 the Constitution was amended to provide for the direct election of all members of the Majelis Permusyawaratan Rakyat (MPR—People's Consultative Assembly) at the next general election, held in 2004. The MPR thus became a bicameral institution comprising the Dewan Perwakilan Daerah (DPD—House of Representatives of the Regions) and the Dewan Perwakilan Rakyat (DPR—House of Representatives). The MPR consists of the 550 members of the DPR and 128 regional delegates (subject to confirmation).

Speaker: HIDAYAT NUR WAHID.

	Seats
Members of the Dewan Perwakilan Rakyat	550
Regional representatives	128
Total	678

Dewan Perwakilan Rakyat (DPR)
(House of Representatives)

Jalan Gatot Subroto 16, Jakarta; tel. (21) 586833; e-mail humas-dpr@dpr.go.id; internet www.dpr.go.id.

Speaker: AGUNG LAKSONO.

General Election, 5 April 2004

	Seats
Partai Golongan Karya (Golkar)	128
Partai Demokrasi Indonesia Perjuangan (PDI—P)	109
Partai Persatuan Pembangunan (PPP)	58
Partai Demokrat (DP)	57
Partai Amanat Nasional (PAN)	52
Partai Kebangkitan Bangsa (PKB)	52
Partai Keadilan Sejahtera (PKS)	45
Partai Bintang Reformasi (PBR)	13
Partai Damai Sejahtera (PDS)	12
Partai Bulan Bintang (PBB)	11
Partai Persatuan Demokrasi Kebangsaan (PPDK)	5
Partai Karya Peduli Bangsa (PKPB)	2
Partai Keadilan dan Persatuan Indonesia (PKPI)	1
Others	5
Total	550

Political Organizations

Prior to 1998, electoral legislation permitted only three organizations (Golkar, the PDI and PPP) to contest elections. Following the replacement of President Suharto in May 1998, political restrictions were relaxed and new parties were allowed to form (with the only condition being that all parties must adhere to the *pancasila* and reject communism). A total of 24 parties registered to contest the legislative elections of April 2004.

Barisan Nasional (National Front): Jakarta; f. 1998; committed to ensuring that Indonesia remains a secular state; Sec.-Gen. RACHMAT WITOELAR.

Indonesian National Unity: Jakarta; f. 1995 by fmr mems of Sukarno's National Party; seeks full implementation of 1945 Constitution; Chair. SUPENI.

Indonesian Reform Party (PPI): Jakarta; f. 1998; Gen. Chair. CHANDRA KUWATLI; Sec.-Gen. Dr H. ACE MULYADI.

Islamic Indonesian Party (PII): Jakarta; f. 1998; Pres. SUUD BAJEBER; Sec.-Gen. SYAIFUL MUNIR.

National Brotherhood Foundation: Jakarta; f. 1995; Chair. KHARIS SUHUD.

New Indonesian National Party: Jakarta; f. 1998.

Partai Amanat Nasional (PAN) (National Mandate Party): Jalan H. Nawi 15, Jakarta Selatan 12420; tel. (21) 72794535; fax (21) 7268695; internet www.geocities.com/CapitolHill/Congress/6678; f. 1998; aims to achieve democracy, progress and social justice, to limit the length of the presidential term of office and to increase autonomy in the provinces; Gen. Chair. Dr AMIEN RAIS; Sec.-Gen. HATTA RADJASA.

Partai Bhinneka Tunggal Ika (PBI): c/o Dewan Perwakilan Rakyat, Jalan Gatot Subroto 16, Jakarta.

Partai Bintang Reformasi (PBR) (Reform Star Party): Jalan Radio IV 5, Kramat Pela, Kebayoran Baru, Jakarta; tel. (21) 7211132; fax (21) 7209734; f. 2002 by fmr members of the Partai Persatuan Pembangunan (PPP); Islamic party; Chair. ZAENUDDIN; Sec.-Gen. DJA'FAR BADJEBER.

Partai Bulan Bintang (PBB) (Crescent Moon and Star Party): Jalan Raya Pasar Minggu 1B, Km 18, Jakarta Selatan; tel. (21) 3106739; f. 1998; Leader Dr YUSRIL IHZA MAHENDRA.

Partai Buruh Sosial Demokrat (PBSD) (Socialist Democratic Labour Party): Jalan Kramat Raya 91A, Jakarta Pusat; tel. (21) 3154092; fax (21) 3909834; f. 2002; Chair. MUCHTAR PAKPAHAN; Sec.-Gen. DIAH INDRIASTUTI.

Partai Damai Sejahtera (PDS) (Prosperous Peace Party): Jalan Rukan Artha Gading Niaga 10, Blok B, Kelapa Gading, Jakarta Utara; tel. (21) 45850517; fax (21) 45850518; e-mail berita@partaidamaisejahtera.com; internet www.partaidamaisejahtera.com; f. 2001; Chair. RUYANDI MUSTIKA HUTASOIT; Sec.-Gen. MAGIT LES DENNY TEWU.

Partai Demokrasi Indonesia (PDI) (Indonesian Democratic Party): Jalan Diponegoro 58, Jakarta 10310; tel. (21) 336331; fax (21) 5201630; f. 1973 by merger of five nationalist and Christian parties; Chair. SOERJADI (installed to replace Megawati Sukarnoputri as leader of the party in a government-orchestrated coup in 1996).

Partai Demokrasi Indonesia Perjuangan (PDI—P) (Indonesian Democratic Struggle Party): Jalan Raya Pasar Minggu, Lenteng Agung, Jakarta; established by Megawati Sukarnoputri, fmr leader of the Partai Demokrasi Indonesia (PDI—see above), following her removal from the leadership of the PDI by the Government in 1996; Chair. MEGAWATI SUKARNOPUTRI; Sec.-Gen. SUTJIPTO.

Partai Demokrasi Kasih Bangsa Indonesia (PDKB) (The Nation Compassion Democratic Party of Indonesia): Kompleks Widuri Indah Blok A-4, Jalan Palmerah Barat 353, Jakarta Selatan 12210; tel. and fax (21) 5330973; e-mail info@kasihbangsa.net; internet www.kasihbangsa.net.

Partai Demokrat (DP): Jalan Pemuda 712A, Jakarta; tel. (21) 4755254; fax (21) 4754959; f. 2001; Chair. Dr S. BUDHISANTOSO; Sec.-Gen. Dr UMAR SAID.

Partai Golongan Karya (Golkar) (Functional Group): Jalan Anggrek Nellimurni, Jakarta 11480; tel. (21) 5302222; fax (21) 5303380; f. 1964; reorg. 1971; 23m. mems (1999); Co-ordinator of Advisers Haji HARMOKO; Pres. and Chair. YUSUF KALLA; Sec.-Gen. BUDI HARSONO.

Partai Karya Peduli Bangsa (PKPB) (Concern for the Nation Functional Party): Jalan Cimandiri 30, Raden Saleh Cikini, Jakarta Pusat 13033; tel. (21) 31927421; fax (21) 31937417; f. 2002; Chair. R. HARTONO; Scc. Gcn. H. ARY MARDJONO.

Partai Keadilan (PK) (Justice Party): c/o Dewan Perwakilan Rakyat, Jalan Gatot Subroto 16, Jakarta; e-mail partai@keadilan.or.id; internet www.keadilan.or.id; f. 1998; Islamic; Pres. Dr NUR MAHMUDI ISMA'IL; Sec.-Gen. LUTHFI HASAN ISHAAQ.

Partai Keadilan dan Persatuan Indonesia (PKPI) (Justice and Unity Party): Jalan Cilandak Raya KKO 32, Jakarta 12560; f. 2002; Chair. EDI SUDRADJAT; Sec.-Gen. SEMUEL SAMSON.

Partai Keadilan Sejahtera (PKS) (Prosperous Justice Party): Jalan Mampang Prapatan Raya 98 D–E–F, Jakarta Selatan; tel. (21) 7995425; fax (21) 7995433; e-mail partai@pk-sejahtera.org; internet www.pk-sejahtera.org; f. 2002; Islamic party; Chair. TIFATUL SEMBIRING (acting); Sec.-Gen. ANIS MATTA.

Partai Kebangkitan Bangsa (PKB) (National Awakening Party): Jalan Kalibata Timur 12, Jakarta Selatan 12519; tel. (21) 7974353; fax (21) 7974263; e-mail fahmi201@yahoo.com; internet www.kebangkitanbangsa.org; Islamic; f. 1998; Chair. ALWI ABDURRAHMAN SHIHAB; Sec.-Gen. SAIFULLAH YUSUF.

Partai Kebangkitan Umat (PKU) (Islamic Awakening Party): c/o Dewan Perwakilan Rakyat, Jalan Gatot Subroto 16, Jakarta; f. 1998 by clerics and members of the Nahdlatul Ulama (NU), with the aim of promoting the adoption of Islamic law in Indonesia.

Partai Merdeka (Freedom Party): Jalan Majapahit, Kav. 26, Jakarta Pusat; tel. (21) 3861464; fax (21) 3861465; e-mail info@partaimerdeka.or.id; internet www.partaimerdeka.or.id; f. 2002; Chair. ADI SASONO; Sec.-Gen. DHARMA SETIAWAN.

Partai Nahdlatul Ummah Indonesia (PNUI) (Indonesian Nahdlatul Community Party): Jalan Cipinang Cempedak 4, 1 Jatinegara, Jakarta Timur 13340; tel. and fax (21) 8571736; f. 2003; Islamic party; Chair. SYUKRON MA'MUN; Sec.-Gen. ACHMAD SJATARI.

Partai Nasional Banteng Kemerdekaan (PNBK) (Freedom Bull National Party): Jalan Penjernihan I 50, Jakarta Utara; tel. (21) 5739550; fax (21) 5739519; f. 2002; Chair. EROS DJAROT; Sec.-Gen. SOEHARDI SOEDIRO.

Partai Nasional Indonesia Marhaenisme (PNI Marhaenisme): Jalan Cikoko 15, Pancoran, Jakarta 12770; tel. (21) 8971241; fax (21) 7900489; f. 2002; Chair. SUKMAWATI SUKARNOPUTRI; Sec.-Gen. ACHMAD MARHAEN.

Partai Patriot Pancasila (Pancasila Patriot Party): Gedung Tri Tangguh, 3rd Floor, Jalan Haji Samali 31, Kalibata, Jakarta Selatan; tel. (21) 79198510; fax (21) 79198520; f. 2001; Chair. YAPTO SULISTIO SOERJOSOEMARNO; Sec.-Gen. SOPHAR MARU.

Partai Pelopor (Pioneer Party): Jalan K. H. Syafei A22, Gudang Peluru, Tebet, Jakarta Selatan; tel. (21) 8299112; fax (21) 8301569; internet www.rachmawati.com; f. 2002; Chair. RACHMAWATI SUKARNOPUTRI; Sec.-Gen. EKO SURYO SANTJOJO.

Partai Pembauran (Assimilation Party): Jakarta; f. 1998; Chinese.

Partai Penegak Demokrasi Indonesia (PPDI): Jalan R. E. Martadinata, Kompleks Rukan Permata, Blok E-1, Ancol, Jakarta Utara; tel. (21) 6456215; fax (21) 6456216; f. 2003; Chair. DIMMY HARYANTO; Sec.-Gen. JOSEPH WILLIEM LEA.

Partai Perhimpunan Indonesia Baru (PIB) (New Indonesia Alliance Party): Jalan Teuku Cik Ditiro 31, Jakarta; tel. (21) 3108057; f. 2002; Chair. Dr SYAHRIR; Sec.-Gen. AMIR KARAMOY.

Partai Persatuan Daerah (Regional United Party): Jalan Dr Satrio C-4 18, Jakarta Selatan 12940; tel. (21) 5205764; fax (21) 5273249; f. 2002; Chair. OESMAN SAPTA; Sec.-Gen. H. RONGGO SOENARSO.

Partai Persatuan Demokrasi Kebangsaan (PPDK) (National Democratic Unity Party): Jalan Ampera Raya 99, Jakarta Selatan 12560; tel. (21) 7807432; fax (21) 7817341; f. 2002; Chair. Dr RYAAS RASYID; Sec. Gen. RIVAI PULUNGAN.

Partai Persatuan Pembangunan (PPP) (United Development Party): Jalan Diponegoro 60, Jakarta 10310; tel. (21) 336338; fax (21) 3908070; e-mail dpp@ppp.or.id; internet www.ppp.or.id; f. 1973 by the merger of four Islamic parties; Leader HAMZAH HAZ; Sec.-Gen. YUNUS YOSFIAH.

Partai Rakyat Demokratik (PRD) (People's Democratic Party): Jalan Tebet Barat Dalam VIII Nomor 4, Jakarta Selatan; tel. (21) 8296467; e-mail prd@centrin.net.id; internet www.prd.4-all.org; f. 1996; Chair. BUDIMAN SUJATMIKO.

Partai Reformasi Tionghoa Indonesia (Chinese Indonesian Reform Party): Jakarta; e-mail parti_id@usa.net; f. 1998; Chinese.

Partai Sarikat Indonesia (PSI) (Indonesia Unity Party): Jalan Ampera Raya 65, Cilandak, Jakarta Selatan; tel. (21) 78847138; fax (21) 7800106; e-mail dpppsi@indosat.net.id; internet www.psi.online.or.id; f. 2002; Chair. RAHARDJO TJAKRANINGRAT; Sec.-Gen. MUHAMMAD JUMHUR HIDAYAT.

Partai Uni Demokrasi Indonesia (PUDI) (Democratic Union Party of Indonesia): Jalan Raya Tanjung Barat 81, Jakarta 12530; tel. (21) 7817565; fax (21) 7814765; e-mail pudi@pudi.or.id; internet www.pudi.or.id; f. 1996; Chair. Sri BINTANG PAMUNGKAS; Sec.-Gen. ESA HARUMAN.

Other groups with political influence include:

Ikatan Cendekiawan Muslim Indonesia (ICMI) (Association of Indonesian Muslim Intellectuals): Gedung BPPT, Jalan M. H.

Thamrin 8, Jakarta; tel. (21) 3410382; e-mail nama_anda@icmi.or
.id; internet www.icmi.or.id; f. 1990 with government support;
Chair. ACHMAD TIRTOSUDIRO; Sec.-Gen. ADI SASONO.

Masyumi Baru: Jalan Pangkalan Asem 12, Cempaka Putih Ba,
Jakarta Pusat; tel. (21) 4225774; fax (21) 7353077; Sec.-Gen. RIDWAN
SAIDI.

Muhammadiyah: Jalan Menteng Raya 62, Jakarta Pusat; tel. (21)
3903021; fax (21) 3903024; e-mail ppmuh@indosat.net.id; internet
www.muhammadiyah.or.id; second largest Muslim organization; f.
1912; 28m. mems; Chair. Dr AHMAD SYAFII MAARIF.

Nahdlatul Ulama (NU) (Council of Scholars): Jalan H. Agus Salim
112, Jakarta Pusat; tel. (21) 336250; largest Muslim organization;
30m. mems; Chair. AHMAD HASYIM.

Syarikat Islam: Jalan Taman Amir Hamzah Nomor 2, Jakarta; tel.
(21) 31906037.

The following groups remain in conflict with the Government:

Gerakan Aceh Merdeka (GAM) (Free Aceh Movement): based in
Aceh; f. 1976; seeks independence from Indonesia; Leader HASAN DI
TIRO; Military Commdr MUZZAKIR MANAF.

National Liberation Front Acheh Sumatra: based in Aceh; f.
1989; seeks independence from Indonesia.

Organisasi Papua Merdeka (OPM) (Free Papua Movement):
based in Papua; f. 1963; seeks unification with Papua New Guinea;
Chair. MOZES WEROR; Leader KELLY KWALIK.

Presidium Dewan Papua (PDP) (Papua Presidium Council):
based in Papua; internet www.westpapua.net; seeks independence
from Indonesia; Chair. (vacant); Sec.-Gen. TOM BEANAL.

Diplomatic Representation

EMBASSIES IN INDONESIA

Afghanistan: Jalan Dr Kusuma Atmaja 15, Jakarta Pusat 10310;
tel. (21) 3143169; fax (21) 335390; e-mail afghanembassy_jkk@yahoo
.com; Ambassador ABDUL RAHEEM SAYED JAN.

Algeria: Jalan H. R. Rasuna Said, Kav. 10-1, Kuningan, Jakarta
12950; tel. (21) 5254719; fax (21) 5254654; e-mail ambalyak@rad.net
.id; internet www.algeria-id.org; Ambassador SOUFIANE MIMOUNI.

Argentina: Menara Mulia, Suite 1901, Jalan Jenderal Gatot Subroto, Kav. 9–11, Jakarta 12930; tel. (21) 5265661; fax (21) 5265664;
e-mail embargen@cbn.net.id; Ambassador JOSÉ LUIS MIGNINI.

Australia: Jalan H. R. Rasuna Said, Kav. C15–16, Kuningan,
Jakarta 12940; tel. (21) 25505555; fax (21) 25505467; e-mail
public-affairs-jakt@dfat.gov.au; internet www.austembjak.or.id;
Ambassador DAVID JAMES RITCHIE.

Austria: Jalan Diponegoro 44, Menteng, Jakarta 10310; tel. (21)
31938101; fax (21) 3904927; e-mail jakarta-ob@bmaa.gv.at; internet
www.austrian-embassy.or.id; Ambassador Dr BERNHARD ZIMBURG.

Bangladesh: Jalan Denpasar Raya 3, Block A-13, Kav. 10,
Kuningan, Jakarta 12950; tel. (21) 5221574; fax (21) 5261807; e-mail
bdootjak@dnet.net.id; internet www.bangladeshembassyjakarta.or
.id; Ambassador NASIM FIRDAUS.

Belgium: Deutsche Bank Bldg, 16th Floor, Jalan Imam Bonjol 80,
Jakarta 10310; tel. (21) 3162030; fax (21) 3162035; e-mail jakarta@
diplobel.org; Ambassador HANS-CHRISTIAN KINT.

Bosnia and Herzegovina: Menara Imperium, 11th Floor, Suite D-
2, Metropolitan Kuningan Super Blok, Kav. 1, Jalan H. R. Rasuna
Said, Jakarta 12980; tel. (21) 83703022; fax (21) 83703029; Ambassador ZDRAVKO RAJIĆ.

Brazil: Menara Mulia, Suite 1602, Jalan Jenderal Gatot Subroto,
Kav. 9, Jakarta 12390; tel. (21) 5265656; fax (21) 5265659; e-mail
brasemb@rad.net.id; Ambassador CARLOS EDUARDO SETTE.

Brunei: Jalan Tanjung Karang 7, Jakarta Pusat 10230; tel. (21)
31906080; fax (21) 31905070; e-mail kbjindo@cbn.net.id; Ambassador Dato' Seri Setia Dr Haji MOHAMMAD AMIN BIN PEHI.

Bulgaria: Jalan Imam Bonjol 34–36, Jakarta 10310; tel. (21)
3904048; fax (21) 3904049; e-mail bgemb.jkt@centrin.net.id; Chargé
d'affaires a.i. Dr PANTELEY M. SPASOV.

Cambodia: 33 Jalan Kintamani Raya C-15, Jakarta 12950; tel. (21)
9192895; fax (21) 5202673; e-mail recjkt@cabi.net.id; Ambassador
KHEM BUNNEANG.

Canada: World Trade Centre, 6th Floor, Jalan Jenderal Sudirman,
Kav. 29–31, POB 8324/JKS, Jakarta 12920; tel. (21) 25507800; fax
(21) 25507811; e-mail canadianembassy.jkrta@dfait-maeci.gc.ca;
internet www.dfait-maeci.gc.ca/jakarta/; Ambassador RANDOLPH
MANK.

Chile: Bina Mulia Bldg, 7th Floor, Jalan H. R. Rasuna Said, Kav.
10, Kuningan, Jakarta 12950; tel. (21) 5201131; fax (21) 5201955;
e-mail emchijak@indosat.net.id; Ambassador SINCLAIR MANLEY
JAMES.

China, People's Republic: Jalan Mega Kuningan 2, Karet
Kuningan, Jakarta 12950; tel. (21) 5761038; fax (21) 5761034; e-mail
enbsychn@cbn.net.id; internet www.chinaembassy-indonesia.or.id;
Ambassador LAN LIJUN .

Croatia: Menara Mulia, Suite 2101, Jalan Gatot Subroto, Kav. 9–
11, Jakarta 12930; tel. (21) 5257822; fax (21) 5204073; e-mail
croemb@rad.net.id; internet www.croatemb.or.id; Ambassador ALEK-
SANDAR BROZ.

Cuba: Taman Puri, Jalan Opal, Blok K-1, Permata Hijau, Jakarta
12210; tel. (21) 5304293; fax (21) 53676906; e-mail cubaindo@cbn
.net.id; Ambassador MIGUEL ANGEL RAMÍREZ RAMOS.

Czech Republic: Jalan Gunwarman 2, Kebayoran Baru, Jakarta;
tel. (21) 7231226; fax (21) 7231436; e-mail jakarta@embassy.mzv.cz;
internet www.mfa.cz/jakarta; Ambassador JAROSLAV VESELÝ.

Denmark: Menara Rajawali, 25th Floor, Jalan Mega Kuningan, Lot
5.1, Jakarta 12950; tel. (21) 5761478; fax (21) 5761535; e-mail
jktamb@um.dk; internet www.emb-denmark.or.id; Ambassador
GEERT AAGAARD ANDERSEN.

Egypt: Jalan Denpasar Raya, Blok A12, No. 1, Kuningan Timur,
Setiabudi, Jakarta Selatan 12950; tel. (21) 5204359; fax (21)
5204792; e-mail egypt@indosat.net.id; Ambassador MOHAMED EL
SAYED TAHA.

Finland: Menara Rajawali, 9th Floor, Jalan Mega Kuningan,
Kawasan Mega Kuningan, Jakarta 12950; tel. (21) 5761650; fax (21)
5761631; e-mail sanomat.jak@formin.fi; internet www.finembjak
.com; Ambassador MARKKU NIINIOJA.

France: Jalan M. H. Thamrin 20, Jakarta 10350; tel. (21) 3142807;
fax (21) 3143338; e-mail ambassade@ambafrance-id.org; internet
www.ambafrance-id.org; Ambassador RENAUD VIGNAL.

Germany: Jalan M. H. Thamrin 1, Jakarta 10310; tel. (21) 3901750;
fax (21) 3901757; e-mail germany@rad.net.id; internet www
.deutschebotschaft-jakarta.or.id; Ambassador (vacant).

Greece: Plaza 89, 12th Floor, Suite 1203, Jalan H. R. Rasuna Said,
Kav. X-7 No. 6, Kuningan, Jakarta 12540; tel. (21) 5207776; fax (21)
5207753; e-mail grembas@cbn.net.id; internet www.greekembassy
.or.id; Ambassador ALEXIOS G. CHRISTOPOULOS.

Holy See: Jalan Merdeka Timur 18, POB 4227, Jakarta Pusat
(Apostolic Nunciature); tel. (21) 3841142; fax (21) 3841143; e-mail
vatjak@cbn.net.id; Apostolic Nuncio Most Rev. PATABENDIGE DON
ALBERT MALCOLM RANJITH (Titular Archbishop of Umbriatico).

Hungary: 36 Jalan H. R. Rasuna Said, Kav. X/3, Kuningan, Jakarta
12950; tel. (21) 5203459; fax (21) 5203461; e-mail huembjkt@rad.net
.id; internet www.huembjkt.or.id; Ambassador GYÖRGY BUSZTIN.

India: Jalan H. R. Rasuna Said, Kav. S/1, Kuningan, Jakarta
12950; tel. (21) 5204150; fax (21) 5204160; e-mail eoiisi@indo.net.id;
internet www.eoijakarta.or.id; Ambassador HEMANT KRISHAN SINGH.

Iran: Jalan Hos Cokroaminoto 110, Menteng, Jakarta Pusat 10310;
tel. (21) 331391; fax (21) 3107860; e-mail irembjkt@indo.net.id;
internet www.iranembassy.or.id; Ambassador SHABAN SHAHIDI
MOADAB.

Iraq: Jalan Teuku Umar 38, Jakarta 10350; tel. (21) 3904067; fax
(21) 3904066; e-mail iraqembi@rad.net.id.

Italy: Jalan Diponegoro 45, Jakarta 10310; tel. (21) 337445; fax (21)
337422; e-mail italemba@italambjkt.or.id; internet www.italambjkt
.or.id; Ambassador FRANCESCO MARIA GRECO.

Japan: Menara Thamrin, 7th–10th Floors, Jalan M. H. Thamrin,
Kav. 3, Jakarta 10350; tel. (21) 324308; fax (21) 325460; internet
www.id.emb-japan.go.jp; Ambassador YUTAKA IIMURA.

Jordan: Jalan Denpasar Raya, Blok A XIII, Kav. 1–2, Jakarta
12950; tel. (21) 5204400; fax (21) 5202447; e-mail jordanem@cbn.net
.id; internet www.jordanembassy.or.id; Ambassador MOHAMED ALI
DAHER.

Korea, Democratic People's Republic: Jalan Teluk Betung 1–2,
Jakarta Pusat 12050; tel. (21) 31908425; fax (21) 31908427; Ambassador JANG CHANG-CHON.

Korea, Republic: Jalan Jenderal Gatot Subroto 57, Jakarta
Selatan; tel. (21) 5201915; fax (21) 5254159; e-mail koremb_in@
mofat.go.kr; internet www.mofat.go.kr/indonesia; Ambassador YUN
HAI-JUNG.

Kuwait: Jalan Teuku Umar 51, Menteng, Jakarta 10310; tel. (21)
3919916; fax (21) 3912285; e-mail ami@Kuwait-toplist.com; Ambassador MOHAMMED FADEL KHALAF.

Laos: Jalan Patra Kuningan XIV 1-A, Kuningan, Jakarta 12950; tel. (21) 5229602; fax (21) 5229601; e-mail laoemjktof@hotmail.com; Ambassador LEUANE SOMBOUNKHAN.

Lebanon: Jalan YBR V 82, Kuningan, Jakarta 12950; tel. (21) 5253074; fax (21) 5207121; e-mail lebanon_embassy_jkt@yahoo.com; Ambassador TAUFIK JABER.

Libya: Jalan Pekalongan 24, Jakarta Pusat 10310; tel. (21) 31935308; fax (21) 31935726; e-mail gsplaj@cbn.net.id; Chargé d'affaires a.i. ALI MAMBRUK ASH SHERIQY.

Malaysia: Jalan H. R. Rasuna Said, Kav. X/6, 1–3 Kuningan, Jakarta 12950; tel. (21) 5224947; fax (21) 5224974; e-mail mwjkarta@indosat.net.id; Ambassador Dato' HAMIDON ALI.

Mali: Jalan Mendawai III 18, Kebayoran Baru, Jakarta 12130; tel. (21) 7208472; fax (21) 7229589; e-mail ambamali@indosat.net.id; Ambassador AMADOU N'DIAYE.

Marshall Islands: Jalan Pangeran Jayakarta 115, Blok A-11, Jakarta Pusat 10730; tel. (21) 7248565; fax (21) 7248566; e-mail marshall@idola.net.id; Ambassador CARL L. HEINE.

Mexico: Menara Mulia, Suite 2306, Jalan Jenderal Gatot Subroto, Kav. 9–11, Jakarta Selatan 12930; tel. (21) 5203980; fax (21) 5203978; e-mail embmexic@rad.net.id; Ambassador PEDRO GON-ZÁLES-RUBIO SÁNCHEZ Sr.

Morocco: Suite 512, 5th Floor, South Tower, Kuningan Plaza, Jalan H. R. Rasuna Said C-11–14, Jakarta 12940; tel. (21) 5200773; fax (21) 5200586; e-mail sifamajakar@cbn.net.id; internet www.morocco-embassy.or.id; Ambassador M. ABDERAHMAN DRISSI ALAMI.

Mozambique: Wisma GKBI, 37th Floor, Suite 3709, Jalan Jenderal Sudirman 28, Jakarta 10210; tel. (21) 5740901; fax (21) 5740907; e-mail embamoc@cbn.net.id; Ambassador GERALDO ANTONIO CHIRINZA.

Myanmar: Jalan Haji Agus Salim 109, Jakarta Selatan; tel. (21) 327684; fax (21) 327204; e-mail myanmar@cbn.net.id; Ambassador U KYAW MYINT.

Netherlands: Jalan H. R. Rasuna Said, Kav. S/3, Kuningan, Jakarta 12950; tel. (21) 5251515; fax (21) 5700734; e-mail jak-cdp@minbuza.nl; internet www.netherlandsembassy.or.id; Ambassador RUDOLF JAN TREFFERS.

New Zealand: BRI II Bldg, 23rd Floor, Jalan Jenderal Sudirman, Kav. 44–46, Jakarta; tel. (21) 5709460; fax (21) 5709457; e-mail nzembjak@cbn.net.id; Ambassador CHRIS ELDER.

Nigeria: Jalan Tamam Patra XIV/11–11A, Kuningan Timur, POB 3649, Jakarta Selatan 12950; tel. (21) 5260922; fax (21) 5260924; e-mail embnig@centrin.net.id; Ambassador MUHAMMED BUBA AHMED.

Norway: Menara Rajawali, 25th Floor, Kawasan Mega Kuningan, Jakarta 12950; tel. (21) 5761523; fax (21) 5761537; e-mail emb.jakarta@mfa.no; internet www.norwayemb-indonesia.org; Ambassador BJØRN BLOKHUS.

Pakistan: Jalan Lembang 10, Menteng, Jakarta; tel. (21) 3144008; fax (21) 3103945; e-mail parepjkt@link.net.id; Ambassador Maj.-Gen. (retd) SYED MUSTAFA ANWER HUSAIN.

Panama: World Trade Centre, 8th Floor, Jalan Jenderal Sudirman, Kav. 29–31, Jakarta 12920; tel. (21) 5711867; fax (21) 5711933; e-mail panacon@pacific.net.id; Ambassador VIRGINIA WEDEN DE ACOSTA.

Papua New Guinea: Panin Bank Centre, 6th Floor, Jalan Jenderal Sudirman 1, Jakarta 10270; tel. (21) 7251218; fax (21) 7201012; e-mail kdujkt@cbn.net.id; Ambassador CHRISTOPHER MERO.

Peru: Menara Rajawali, 12th Floor, Jalan Mega Kuningan, Lot 5.1, Kawasan Mega Kuningan, Jakarta 12950; tel. (21) 5761820; fax (21) 5761825; e-mail embaperu@cbn.net.id; Ambassador NILO FIGUEROA CORTAVARRIA.

Philippines: Jalan Imam Bonjol 6–8, Jakarta Pusat 10310; tel. (21) 3100334; fax (21) 3151167; e-mail phjkt@indo.net.id; Ambassador SHULAN O. PRIMAVERA.

Poland: Jalan H. R. Rasuna Said, Kav. X, Blok IV/3, Jakarta Selatan 12950; tel. (21) 2525948; fax (21) 2525958; e-mail plembjkt@net.id; internet www.polandembjak.org; Ambassador KRZYSZTOF SZUMSKI.

Portugal: Bina Mulia Bldg I, 7th Floor, Jalan H. R. Rasuna Said, Kav. X, Kuningan, Jakarta 12950; tel. (21) 5265103; fax (21) 5271981; e-mail porembjak@cbn.net.id; Ambassador JOSÉ MANUEL SANTOS BRAGA.

Qatar: Jalan Taman Ubud I, No. 5, Kuningan Timur, Jakarta 12920; tel. (21) 5277751; fax (21) 5277754; e-mail qataremj@indosat.net.id; Ambassador ABDULLA MOHAMMED TALIB AL-MARRI.

Romania: Jalan Mas Putih 29, Kompleks D, Permata Hijau, Jakarta Selatan; tel. (21) 5305073; fax (21) 5305074; e-mail romind@cbn.net.id; Ambassador GHEORGHE SAVUICA.

Russia: Jalan H. R. Rasuna Said, Kav. X-6, Jakarta; tel. (21) 5222912; e-mail rusembjkt@dnet.net.id; Chargé d'affaires a.i. SERGEI PETLYAKV.

Saudi Arabia: Jalan M. T. Haryono, Kav. 27, Cawang Atas, Jakarta Timur; tel. (21) 8011533; fax (21) 3905864; e-mail idemb@mofa.gov.sa; Ambassador ABDULLAH BIN ABDULRAHMAN A'ALIM.

Serbia and Montenegro: Jalan Hos Cokroaminoto 109, Jakarta 10310; tel. (21) 3143560; fax (21) 3143613; e-mail ambajaka@rad.net.id; Chargé d'affaires a.i. DRAGAN PETROVIĆ.

Singapore: Jalan H. R. Rasuna Said, Blok X/4, Kav. 2, Kuningan, Jakarta 12950; tel. (21) 5201489; fax (21) 5201486; e-mail denpasar@pacific.net.id; internet www.mfa.gov.sg/jkt; Ambassador EDWARD LEE.

Slovakia: Jalan Prof. Mohammed Yamin 29, POB 1368, Jakarta Pusat; tel. (21) 3101068; fax (21) 3101180; e-mail slovemby@indo.net.id; Ambassador PETER HOLASEK.

South Africa: Suite 705, Wisma GKBI, Jalan Jenderal Sudirman 28, Jakarta 10210; tel. (21) 5740660; fax (21) 5740661; e-mail saembhom@mweb.com.id; internet www.saembassy-jakarta.or.id; Ambassador GRIFFITHS MEMELA.

Spain: Jalan H. Agus Salim 61, Jakarta 10350; tel. (21) 3142355; fax (21) 31935134; e-mail emb.yakarta@mae.es; Ambassador DÁMASO DE LARIO RAMÍREZ.

Sri Lanka: Jalan Diponegoro 70, Jakarta 10320; tel. (21) 3161886; fax (21) 3107962; e-mail lankaemb@rad.net.id; Ambassador GRACE NESAMALAR NILIAH.

Sudan: Wisma Bank Dharmala, 7th Floor, Suite 01, Jalan Jenderal Sudirman, Kav. 28, Jakarta 12920; tel. (21) 5212099; fax (21) 5212077; e-mail leen@cbn.net.id; Ambassador SIDIQ YOUSIF ABU-AGLA.

Suriname: Gedung Plaza Central, 16th Floor, Jalan Jenderal Sudirman, Kav. 47, Jakarta 12930; tel. (21) 5742878; fax (21) 5740015; e-mail suramjkt@cbn.net.id; Ambassador SAHIDI RASAM.

Sweden: POB 2824, Jakarta 10001; tel. (21) 55535900; fax (21) 5762691; e-mail ambassaden.jakarta@foreign.ministry.se; internet www.swedenabroad.com/jakarta; Ambassador LENNART LINNÉR.

Switzerland: Jalan H. R. Rasuna Said, Kav. X-3/2, Kuningan, Jakarta Selatan 12950; tel. (21) 5256061; fax (21) 5202289; e-mail vertretung@jak.rep.admin.ch; internet www.eda.admin.ch/jakarta; Ambassador GEORGES MARTIN.

Syria: Jalan Karang Asem I/8, Jakarta 12950; tel. (21) 5255991; fax (21) 5202511; e-mail syrianemb@cbn.net.id; Ambassador Dr BASHAR JAAFARI.

Thailand: Jalan Imam Bonjol 74, Jakarta 10310; tel. (21) 3904052; fax (21) 3107469; e-mail thaijkt@indo.net.id; Ambassador ATCHARA SERIPUTRA.

Timor-Leste: Gedung Surya, 11th Floor, Jalan M. H. Thamrin, Kav. 9, Jakarta; tel. (21) 3902678; fax (21) 3902660; Ambassador Rev. ARLINDO MARÇAL.

Tunisia: Wisma Dharmala Sakti, 11th Floor, Jalan Jenderal Sudirman 32, Jakarta 10220; tel. (21) 5703432; fax (21) 5700016; e-mail atjkt@uninet.net.id; Ambassador MOHAMED MOULDI KEFI.

Turkey: Jalan H. R. Rasuna Said, Kav. 1, Kuningan, Jakarta 12950; tel. (21) 5256250; fax (21) 5226056; e-mail cakartabe@telkom.net; Ambassador FERYAL ÇOTUR.

Ukraine: World Trade Centre, 8th Floor, Jalan Jenderal Sudirman, Kav. 29–31, Jakarta 12920; tel. (21) 5211700; fax (21) 5211710; e-mail uaembas@indo.net.id; Chargé d'affaires a.i. VALERIY KRAV-CENKO.

United Arab Emirates: Jalan Prof. Dr Satrio, Kav. 16–17, Jakarta 12950; tel. (21) 5206518; fax (21) 5206526; e-mail uaeemb@rad.net.id; Ambassador YOUSIF RASHID ALSHRAM.

United Kingdom: Jalan M. H. Thamrin 75, Jakarta 10310; tel. (21) 3156264; fax (21) 3926263; e-mail britem2@ibm.net.id; internet www.britain-in-indonesia.or.id; Ambassador CHARLES HUMFREY.

USA: Jalan Merdeka Selatan 4–5, Jakarta 10110; tel. (21) 34359000; fax (21) 3857189; e-mail jakconsul@state.gov; internet jakarta.usembassy.gov; Ambassador B. LYNN PASCOE (designate).

Uzbekistan: Menara Mulia, 24th Floor, Suite 2401, Jalan Jenderal Gatot Subroto, Kav. 9–11, Jakarta Selatan 12930; tel. (21) 5222581; fax (21) 5222582; e-mail registan@indo.net.id; Ambassador KHAMIS DJABBAROV.

Venezuela: Menara Mulia, 20th Floor, Suite 2005, Jalan Jenderal Gatot Subroto, Kav. 9–11, Jakarta Selatan 12930; tel. (21) 5227547; fax (21) 5227549; e-mail evenjakt@indo.net.id; Ambassador LUIS EDUARDO SOTO.

Viet Nam: Jalan Teuku Umar 25, Jakarta; tel. (21) 3100358; fax (21) 3100359; e-mail embvnam@uninet.net.id; Ambassador NGUYEN DANG QUANG.

Yemen: Jalan Yusuf Adiwinata 29, Menteng, Jakarta 10350; tel. (21) 3108029; fax (21) 3904946; e-mail yemenemb@rad.net.id; internet www.yemenembassyindonesia.com; Ambassador Dr AHMAD SALIM AL-WAHISHI.

Judicial System

There is one codified criminal law for the whole of Indonesia. In December 1989 the Islamic Judicature Bill, giving wider powers to Shari'a courts, was approved by the Dewan Perwakilan Rakyat (House of Representatives). The new law gave Muslim courts authority over civil matters, such as marriage. Muslims may still choose to appear before a secular court. Europeans are subject to the Code of Civil Law published in the State Gazette in 1847. Alien orientals (i.e. Arabs, Indians, etc.) and Chinese are subject to certain parts of the Code of Civil Law and the Code of Commerce. The work of codifying this law has started, but, in view of the great complexity and diversity of customary law, it may be expected to take a considerable time to achieve.

Supreme Court
(Mahkamah Agung)

Jalan Merdeka Utara 9–13, Jakarta 10110; tel. (21) 3843348; fax (21) 3811057; e-mail pansekjen@mari.go.id; internet www.mari.go .id.

The final court of appeal.

Chief Justice: Prof. BAGIR MANAN.

Deputy Chief Justice: H. TAUFIK.

High Courts in Jakarta, Surabaya, Medan, Makassar, Banda Aceh, Padang, Palembang, Bandung, Semarang, Banjarmasin, Menado, Denpasar, Ambon and Jayapura deal with appeals from the District Courts. **District Courts** deal with marriage, divorce and reconciliation.

Religion

All citizens are required to state their religion. According to a survey in 1985, 86.9% of the population were Muslims, while 9.6% were Christians, 1.9% were Hindus, 1.0% were Buddhists and 0.6% professed adherence to tribal religions.

Five national religious councils—representing the Islamic, Catholic, Protestant, Hindu and Buddhist religious traditions—were established to serve as liaison bodies between religious adherents and the Government and to advise the Government on the application of religious principles to various elements of national life.

ISLAM

In 1993 nearly 90% of Indonesians were Muslims. Indonesia has the world's largest Muslim population.

Majelis Ulama Indonesia (MUI) (Indonesian Ulama Council): Komp. Masjid Istiqlal, Jalan Taman Wijaya Kesuma, Jakarta 10710; tel. (21) 3455471; fax (21) 3855412; internet www.mui.or.id; central Muslim organization; Chair. SAHAL MAHFUDZ; Sec.-Gen. DIEN SYAMSUDDIN.

CHRISTIANITY

Persekutuan Gereja-Gereja di Indonesia (Communion of Churches in Indonesia): Jalan Salemba Raya 10, Jakarta 10430; tel. (21) 3908119; fax (21) 3150457; e-mail pgi@bit.net.id; internet www .pgi.or.id; f. 1950; 70 mem. churches; Chair. Rev. Dr SULARSO SOPATER; Gen. Sec. Rev. Dr JOSEPH M. PATTIASINA.

The Roman Catholic Church

Indonesia comprises 10 archdioceses and 26 dioceses. At 31 December 2002 there were an estimated 6,375,984 adherents in Indonesia, representing 3.3% of the population.

Bishops' Conference

Konferensi Waligereja Indonesia (KWI), Jalan Cut Meutia 10, POB 3044, Jakarta 10002; tel. (21) 336422; fax (21) 3918527; e-mail kwi@ parokinet.org.

f. 1973; Pres. Cardinal JULIUS RIYADI DARMAATMADJA (Archbishop of Jakarta).

Archbishop of Ende: Most Rev. ABDON LONGINUS DA CUNHA, Keuskupan Agung, POB 210, Jalan Katedral 5, Ndona-Ende 86312, Flores; tel. (381) 21176; fax (381) 21606; e-mail uskup@ende .parokinet.org.

Archbishop of Jakarta: Cardinal JULIUS RIYADI DARMAATMADJA, Keuskupan Agung, Jalan Katedral 7, Jakarta 10710; tel. (21) 3813345; fax (21) 3855681.

Archbishop of Kupang: Most Rev. PETER TURANG, Keuskupan Agung Kupang, Jalan Thamrin, Oepoi, Kupang 85111, Timor NTT; tel. (380) 826199; fax (380) 833331.

Archbishop of Makassar: Most Rev. JOHANNES LIKU ADA', Keuskupan Agung, Jalan Thamrin 5–7, Makassar 90111, Sulawesi Selatan; tel. (411) 315744; fax (411) 326674; e-mail pseupg@indosat .net.id.

Archbishop of Medan: Most Rev. ALFRED GONTI PIUS DATUBARA, Jalan Imam Bonjol 39, POB 1191, Medan 20152, Sumatra Utara; tel. (61) 4519768; fax (61) 4145745; e-mail mar39@indosat.net.id.

Archbishop of Merauke: Most Rev. NICOLAUS ADI SEPTURA, Keuskupan Agung, Jalan Mandala 30, Merauke 99602, Papua; tel. (971) 321011; fax (971) 321311.

Archbishop of Palembang: Most Rev. ALOYSIUS SUDARSO, Keuskupan Agung, Jalan Tasik 18, Palembang 30135; tel. (711) 350417; fax (711) 314776.

Archbishop of Pontianak: Most Rev. HIERONYMUS HERCULANUS BUMBUN, Keuskupan Agung, Jalan A. R. Hakin 92A, POB 1119, Pontianak 78011, Kalimantan Barat; tel. (561) 732382; fax (561) 738785; e-mail kap@pontianak.wasantara.net.id.

Archbishop of Samarinda: Most Rev. FLORENTINUS SULUI HAJANG HAU, Keuskupan Agung, POB 1062, Jalan Gunung Merbabu 41, Samarinda 75010; tel. (541) 741193; fax (541) 203120.

Archbishop of Semarang: Most Rev. IGNATIUS SUHARYO HARDJOAT-MODJO, Keuskupan Agung, Jalan Pandanaran 13, Semarang 50231; tel. (24) 312276; fax (24) 414741; e-mail uskup@semarang.parokinet .org.

Other Christian Churches

Protestant Church in Indonesia (Gereja Protestan di Indonesia): Jalan Medan Merdeka Timur 10, Jakarta 10110; tel. (21) 3519003; fax (21) 34830224; consists of 10 churches of Calvinistic tradition; 2,789,155 mems, 3,841 congregations, 1,965 pastors (1998); Chair. Rev. Dr D. J. LUMENTA.

Numerous other Protestant communities exist throughout Indonesia, mainly organized on a local basis. The largest of these (1985 memberships) are: the Batak Protestant Christian Church (1,875,143); the Christian Church in Central Sulawesi (100,000); the Christian Evangelical Church in Minahasa (730,000); the Christian Protestant Church in Indonesia (210,924); the East Java Christian Church (123,850); the Evangelical Christian Church in Irian Jaya (Papua—360,000); the Evangelical Christian Church of Sangir-Talaud (190,000); the Indonesian Christian Church/Huria Kristen Indonesia (316,525); the Javanese Christian Churches (121,500); the Kalimantan Evangelical Church (182,217); the Karo Batak Protestant Church (164,288); the Nias Protestant Christian Church (250,000); the Protestant Church in the Moluccas (575,000); the Simalungun Protestant Christian Church (155,000); and the Toraja Church (250,000).

BUDDHISM

All-Indonesia Buddhist Association: Jakarta.

Indonesian Buddhist Council: Jakarta.

HINDUISM

Hindu Dharma Council: Jakarta.

The Press

In August 1990 the Government announced that censorship of both the local and foreign press was to be relaxed and that the authorities would refrain from revoking the licences of newspapers that violated legislation governing the press. In practice, however, there was little change in the Government's policy towards the press. Following the resignation of President Suharto in May 1998, the new Government undertook to allow freedom of expression.

PRINCIPAL DAILIES

Bali

Harian Pagi Umum (Bali Post): Jalan Kepudang 67A, Denpasar 80232; e-mail balipost@indo.net.id; internet www.balipost.co.id; f. 1948; daily (Indonesian edn), weekly (English edn); Editor K. NADHA; circ. 25,000.

Java

Angkatan Bersenjata: Jalan Kramat Raya 94, Jakarta Pusat; tel. (21) 46071; fax (21) 366870.

Bandung Post: Jalan Lodaya 38A, Bandung 40264; tel. (22) 305124; fax (22) 302882; internet www.bandung-post.com; f. 1979; Chief Editor AHMAD SAELAN; Dir AHMAD JUSACC.

Berita Buana: Jalan Tahah Abang Dua 33–35, Jakarta 10110; tel. (21) 5487175; fax (21) 5491555; internet www.beritabuana.net; f. 1970; relaunched 1990; Indonesian; circ. 150,000.

Berita Yudha: Jalan Letjenderal Haryono MT22, Jakarta; tel. (21) 8298331; f. 1971; Indonesian; Editor SUNARDI; circ. 50,000.

Bisnis Indonesia: Wisma Bisnis Indonesia, Jalan Letjenderal S. Parman, Kav. 12, Slipi, Jakarta 11480; tel. (21) 5305869; fax (21) 5305868; e-mail iklana@bisnis.co.id; internet www.bisnis.com; f. 1985; available online; Indonesian; Editor SUKAMDANI S. GITOSARD-JONO; circ. 60,000.

Harian Indonesia (Indonesia Rze Pao): Jalan Toko Tiga Seberang 21, POB 4755, Jakarta 11120; tel. (21) 6295948; fax (21) 6297830; e-mail info@harian-indonesia.com; internet www.harian-indonesia.com; f. 1966; Chinese; Editor W. D. SUKISMAN; Dir HADI WIBOWO; circ. 42,000.

Harian Terbit: Jalan Pulogadung 15, Kawasan Industri Pulogadung, Jakarta 13920; tel. (21) 4602953; fax (21) 4602950; f. 1972; Indonesian; Editor H. R. S. HADIKAMAJAYA; circ. 125,000.

Harian Umum AB: CTC Bldg, 2nd Floor, Kramat Raya 94, Jakarta Pusat; f. 1965; official armed forces journal; Dir GOENARSO; Editor-in-Chief N. SOEPANGAT; circ. 80,000.

The Indonesia Times: Jalan Pulo Lentut 12, Jakarta Timur; tel. (21) 4611280; fax (21) 375012; e-mail info@webpacific.com; internet www.indonesiatimes.com; f. 1974; English; Editor TRIBUANA SAID; circ. 35,000.

Indonesian Observer: Wisma Indovision, 11th Floor, Jalan Raya Panjang Blok Z/III, Green Garden, Jakarta 11520; tel. (21) 5818855; fax (21) 58302414; internet www.indonesian-observer.com; f. 1955; English; independent; Editor TAUFIK DARUSMAN; circ. 25,000.

Jakarta Post: Jalan Palmerah Selatan 15, Jakarta 10270; tel. (21) 5300476; fax (21) 5492685; e-mail editorial@thejakartapost.com; internet www.thejakartapost.com; f. 1983; English; Chief Editor RAYMOND TORUAN; circ. 50,000.

Jawa Pos: Graha Pena Bldg, 4th and 5th Floors, Achmad Yani 88, Surabaya 60234; tel. (31) 8283333; fax (31) 8285555; internet www.jawapos.co.id; f. 1949; Indonesian; CEO DAHLAN ISKAN; circ. 120,000.

Jepara Pos: Jepara; internet www.jeparapos.com; Indonesian.

Kedaulatan Rakyat: Jalan P. Mangkubumi 40–42, Yogyakarta; tel. (274) 65685; fax (274) 63125; internet www.kr.co.id; f. 1945; Indonesian; independent; Editor IMAN SUTRISNO; circ. 50,000.

Kompas: Jalan Palmerah Selatan 26–28, Jakarta; tel. (21) 5483008; fax (21) 5305868; internet www.kompas.com; f. 1965; Indonesian; Editor Drs JAKOB OETAMA; circ. 523,453.

Koran Tempo: Gedung Tempo, Jalan H. R. Rasuna Said, Kav. C-17, Kuningan, Jakarta 10270; tel. (21) 5201022; fax (21) 5200092; internet www.korantempo.com; f. 2001; Indonesian.

Media Indonesia Daily: Jalan Pilar Mas Raya, Kav. A–D, Kedoya Selatan, Kebon Jeruk, Jakarta 11520; tel. (21) 5812088; fax (21) 5812105; e-mail redaksi@mediaindonesia.co.id; internet www.mediaindo.co.id; f. 1989; fmrly Prioritas; Indonesian; Publr SURYA PALOH; Editor DJAFAR H. ASSEGAFF; circ. 2,000.

Merdeka Rakyat: Jalan Raya Kebayoran Lama 17, Jakarta Selatan 12210; tel. (21) 5556059; fax (21) 5556063; f. 1945; Indonesian; independent; Editor KARIM PAPUTUNGAN; circ. 130,000.

Neraca: Jalan Jambrut 2–4, Jakarta; tel. (21) 323969; fax (21) 3101873.

Pelita (Torch): Jalan Jenderal Sudirman 65, Jakarta; f. 1974; Indonesian; Muslim; Editor AKBAR TANDJUNG; circ. 80,000.

Pewarta Surabaya: Jalan Karet 23, POB 85, Surabaya; f. 1905; Indonesian; Editor RADEN DJAROT SOEBIANTORO; circ. 10,000.

Pikiran Rakyat: Jalan Asia-Afrika 77, Bandung 40111; tel. (22) 51216; internet www.pikiran-rakyat.com; f. 1950; Indonesian; independent; Editor BRAM M. DARMAPRAWIRA; circ. 150,000.

Pos Kota: Yayasan Antar Kota, Jalan Gajah Mada 100, Jakarta 10130; tel. (21) 6290874; e-mail iklankilat@poskota.net; internet www.poskota.co.id; f. 1970; Indonesian; Editor H. SOFYAN LUBIS; circ. 500,000.

Republika: Jalan Warung Buncit Raya 37, Jakarta 12510; tel. (21) 7803747; fax (21) 7800420; e-mail kepemimpinan@republika.co.id; internet www.republika.co.id; f. 1993; organ of ICMI; Chief Editor PARNI HADI.

Sinar Pagi: Jalan Letjenderal Haryono MT22, Jakarta Selatan.

Suara Karya: Jalan Bangka II/2, Kebayoran Baru, Jakarta Selatan 12720; tel. (21) 7192656; fax (21) 71790784; internet www.suarakarya-online.com; f. 1971; Indonesian; Editor SYAMSUL BASRI; circ. 100,000.

Suara Merdeka: Jalan Pandanaran 30, Semarang 50241; tel. (24) 412660; fax (24) 411116; internet www.suaramerdeka.com; f. 1950; Indonesian; Publr Ir BUDI SANTOSO; Editor SUWARNO; circ. 200,000.

Suara Pembaruan: Jalan Dewi Sartika 136/D, Cawang, Jakarta 13630; tel. (21) 8013208; fax (21) 8007262; e-mail koransp@suarapembaruan.com; internet www.suarapembaruan.com; f. 1987; licence revoked in 1986 as Sinar Harapan (Ray of Hope); Publr Dr ALBERT HASIBUAN.

Surabaya Post: Jalan Taman Ade Irma Nasution 1, Surayaba; tel. (31) 45394; fax (31) 519585; internet www.surabayapost.co.id; f. 1953; independent; Publr TUTY AZIS; Editor IMAM PUJONO; circ. 115,000.

Kalimantan

Banjarmasin Post: Jalan Haryono MT 54–143, Banjarmasin 70111; tel. (511) 54370; fax (511) 66123; e-mail banjarmasin_post@persda.co.id; internet www.indomedia.com/bpost/; f. 1971; Indonesian; Editor-in-Chief H. PRAMONO; circ. 50,000.

Gawi Manuntung: Jalan Pangeran Samudra 97B, Banjarmasin; f. 1972; Indonesian; Editor M. ALI SRI INDRADJAYA; circ. 5,000.

Harian Umum Akcaya: Pontianak Post Group, Jalan Gajah Mada 2–4, Pontianak; tel. (561) 735071; e-mail redaksi@pontianakpost.com; internet www.pontianakpost.com; Editor B. SALMAN.

Lampung Post: Jalan Pangkal Pinang, Lampung.

Manuntung: Jalan Jenderal Sudirman RT XVI 82, Balikpapan 76144; tel. (542) 35359; internet www.manuntung.co.id; largest newspaper in East Borneo.

Maluku

Ambon Ekspres: Ambon.

Pos Maluku: Jalan Raya Pattimura 19, Ambon; tel. (911) 44614.

Suara Maluku: Komplex Perdagangan Mardikas, Blok D3/11A, Ternate; tel. (911) 44590.

Nusa Tenggara

Pos Kupang: Jalan Kenari 1, Kupang; tel. (380) 833820; fax (380) 831801; e-mail poskupang@persda.co.id; internet www.indomedia.com/poskup.

Papua

Berita Karya: Jayapura.

Cendrawasih Post: Jayapura; Editor RUSTAM MADUBUN.

Teropong: Jalan Halmahera, Jayapura.

Riau

Batam Pos: Jalan Raja Ali Haji, Kompleks Orchid Point, Blok B, No. 9, Batam 29432; tel. (778) 424543; fax (778) 452002; e-mail redaksi@harianbatampos.com; internet www.harianbatampos.com; Editor-in-Chief AMZAR.

Riau Pos: Pekanbaru, Riau; internet www.riaupos.com; circ. 40,000.

Sulawesi

Bulletin Sulut: Jalan Korengkeng 38, Lt. II Manado, 95114, Sulawesi Utara.

Cahaya Siang: Jalan Kembang II 2, Manado, 95114, Sulawesi Utara; tel. (431) 61054; fax (431) 63393.

Fajar (Dawn): Jalan Racing Centre 101, Makassar; tel. (411) 441441; fax (411) 441224; e-mail fajar@fajar.co.id; internet www.fajar.co.id; circ. 35,000.

Manado Post: Manado Post Centre, Jalan Babe Palar 54, Manado; tel. (431) 855558; fax (431) 860398; internet www.mdopost.net.

Pedoman Rakyat: Jalan H. A. Mappanyukki 28, Makassar; f. 1947; independent; Editor M. BASIR; circ. 30,000.

Suluh Merdeka: Jalan R. W. Mongsidi 4/96, POB 1105, Manado, 95110; tel. and fax (431) 866150.

Tegas: Jalan Mappanyukki 28, Makassar; tel. (411) 3960.

Sumatra

Harian Analisa: Jalan Jenderal A. Yani 37–43, Medan; tel. (61) 326655; fax (61) 514031; internet www.analisadaily.com; f. 1972; Indonesian; Editor SOFFYAN; circ. 75,000.

Harian Berita Sore: Jalan Letjen Suprapto 1, Medan; tel. (61) 4158787; fax (61) 4150383; e-mail redaksi@beritasore.com; internet www.beritasore.com; Indonesian; Editor-in-Chief H. Teruna Jasa Said.

Harian Haluan: Jalan Damar 59 C/F, Padang; f. 1948; Editor-in-Chief Rivai Marlaut; circ. 40,000.

Harian Umum Nasional Waspada: Jalan Brigjenderal 1 Katamso, Medan 20151; tel. (61) 4150858; fax (61) 4510025; e-mail waspada@indosat.net.id; internet www.waspada.co.id; f. 1947; Indonesian; Editor-in-Chief H. Prabudi Said.

Mimbar Umum: Merah, Medan; tel. (61) 517807; f. 1947; Indonesian; independent; Editor Mohd Lud Lubis; circ. 55,000.

Serambi Indonesia: Jalan T. Nyak Arief 159, Lampriek, Banda Aceh; e-mail serambi@indomedia.com; internet www.indomedia.com/serambi/.

Sinar Indonesia Baru: Jalan Brigjenderal Katamso 66, Medan 20151; tel. (61) 4512530; fax (61) 438150; e-mail redaksi@hariansib.com; internet www.hariansib.com; f. 1970; Indonesian; Chief Editor G. M. Panggabean; circ. 150,000.

Sriwijaya Post: Jalan Jenderal Basuki Rahmat 1608 B-C-D, Palembang; tel. (711) 310088; fax (711) 312888; e-mail sripo@mdp.net.id; internet www.indomedia.com/sripo; f. 2002.

Suara Rakyat Semesta: Jalan K. H. Ashari 52, Palembang; Indonesian; Editor Djadil Abdullah; circ. 10,000.

Waspada: Jalan Letjen Suprapto, cnr Jalan Brigjen Katamso 1, Medan 20151; tel. (61) 4150868; fax (61) 4510025; e-mail waspada@waspada.co.id; internet www.waspada.co.id; f. 1947; Indonesian; Chief Editors Ani Idrus, Mohammad Said; circ. 60,000 (daily), 55,000 (Sunday).

PRINCIPAL PERIODICALS

Amanah: Jalan Garuda 69, Kemayoran, Jakarta; tel. (21) 410254; fortnightly; Muslim current affairs; Indonesian; Man. Dir Maskun Iskandar; circ. 180,000.

Ayahbunda: Jalan H. R. Rasuna Said, Blok B, Kav. 32–33, Jakarta 12910; tel. (21) 5209370; fax (21) 5209366; e-mail info@femina-online.com; internet www.ayahbunda-online.com; fortnightly; family magazine.

Berita Negara: Jalan Pertjetakan Negara 21, Kotakpos 2111, Jakarta; tel. and fax (21) 4207251; f. 1951; 2 a week; official gazette.

Bobo: PT Gramedia, Jalan Kebahagiaan 4–14, Jakarta 11140; tel. (21) 6297809; fax (21) 6390080; f. 1973; weekly; children's magazine; Editor Tineke Latumeten; circ. 240,000.

Bola: Tunas Bola, Jalan Palmerah Barat 33–37, Jakarta 10270; tel. (21) 53677835; fax (21) 5301952; e-mail redaksi@bolanews.com; internet www.bolanews.com; 2 a week; Tue. and Fri.; sports magazine; Indonesian; Chief Editor Ian Situmorang; circ. 715,000.

Buana Minggu: Jalan Tanah Abang Dua 33, Jakarta Pusat 10110; tel. (21) 364190; weekly; Sunday; Indonesian; Editor Winoto Parartho; circ. 193,450.

Business News: Jalan H. Abdul Muis 70, Jakarta 10160; tel. (21) 3848207; fax (21) 3454280; f. 1956; 3 a week (Indonesian edn), 2 a week (English edn); Chief Editor Sanjoto Sastromihardjo; circ. 15,000.

Cita Cinta: Jalan H. R. Rasuna Said, Blok B, Kav. 32–33, Jakarta 12910; tel. (21) 5209370; fax (21) 5209366; internet www.citacinta.com; f. 2001; teenage lifestyle magazine.

Citra: Gramedia Bldg, Unit 11, 5th Floor, Jalan Palmerah Selatan 24–26, Jakarta 10270; tel. (21) 5483008; fax (21) 5494035; e-mail citra@gramedia-majalah.com; internet www.tabloid-citra.com; f. 1990; weekly; TV and film programmes, music trends and celebrity news; Chief Editor H. Maman Suherman; circ. 239,000.

Depthnews Indonesia: Jalan Jatinegara Barat III/6, Jakarta 13310; tel. (21) 8194994; fax (21) 8195501; f. 1972; weekly; publ. by Press Foundation of Indonesia; Editor Sumono Mustoffa.

Dunia Wanita: Jalan Brigjenderal, Katamso 1, Medan; tel. (61) 4150858; fax (61) 4510025; e-mail waspada@indosat.net.id; f. 1949; fortnightly; Indonesian; women's tabloid; Chief Editor Dr Rayati Syafrin; circ. 10,000.

Economic Review: Bank BNI, Strategic Planning Division, Gedung Bank BNI, Jalan Jenderal Sudirman, Kav. 1, POB 2955, Jakarta 10220; tel. (21) 5728692; fax (21) 5728456; e-mail renkek01@bni.co.id; internet www.bni.co.id; f. 1946; 3 a year; English; economic and business research and analysis; Editor-in-Chief Darwin Suzandi.

Ekonomi Indonesia: Jalan Merdeka, Timur 11–12, Jakarta; tel. (21) 494458; monthly; English; economic journal; Editor Z. Achmad; circ. 20,000.

Eksekutif: Jalan R. S. Fatmawati 20, Jakarta 12430; tel. (21) 7659218; fax (21) 7504018; e-mail eksek@pacific.net.id; internet www.pacific.net.id/eksekutif/.

Femina: Jalan H. R. Rasuna Said, Blok B, Kav. 32–33, Jakarta Selatan 12910; tel. (21) 5209370; fax (21) 5209366; e-mail svida.alisjahbana@feminagroup.com; internet www.femina-online.com; f. 1972; weekly; women's magazine; Publr Svida Alisjahbana; Editor Petty S. Fatimah; circ. 130,000.

Forum: Kebayoran Centre, 12A–14, Jalan Kebayoran Baru, Welbak, Jakarta 12240; tel. (21) 7255625; fax (21) 7255645; internet www.forum.co.id.

Gadis: Jalan H. R. Rasuna Said, Blok B, Kav. 32–33, Jakarta 12910; tel. (21) 5253816; fax (21) 5262131; e-mail gadis@indosat.net.id; internet www.gadis-online.com; f. 1973; every 10 days; Indonesian; teenage lifestyle magazine; Editor-in-Chief Petty S. F.; circ. 100,000.

Gamma: Jakarta; internet www.gamma.co.id; f. 1999 by fmr employees of *Tempo* and *Gatra*.

Gatra: Gedung Gatra, Jalan Kalibata Timur IV/15, Jakarta 12740; tel. (21) 7973535; fax (21) 79196923; e-mail gatra@gatra.com; internet www.gatra.com; f. 1994 by fmr employees of *Tempo* (banned 1994–98); Gen. Man. Beny Suharsono; Editor-in-Chief Iwan Qodar Himawan.

Gugat (Accuse): Surabaya; politics, law and crime; weekly; circ. 250,000.

Hai: Gramedia, Jalan Palmerah Selatan 22, Jakarta 10270; tel. (21) 5483008; fax (21) 6390080; f. 1973; weekly; youth magazine; Editor Arswendo Atmowiloto; circ. 70,000.

Indonesia Business News: Wisma Bisnis Indonesia, Jalan Letjenderal S. Parman, Kav. 12, Slipi, Jakarta 11410; tel. (21) 5304016; fax (21) 5305868; English.

Indonesia Business Weekly: Wisma Bisnis Indonesia, Jalan Letjenderal S. Parman, Kav. 12, Slipi, Jakarta 11410; tel. (21) 5304016; fax (21) 5305868; English; Editor Taufik Darusman.

Indonesia Magazine: 20 Jalan Merdeka Barat, Jakarta; tel. (21) 352015; f. 1969; monthly; English; Chair. G. Dwipayana; Editor-in-Chief Hadely Hasibuan; circ. 15,000.

Intisari (Digest): Jalan Palmerah Selatan 24–26, Gedung Unit II, 5th Floor, Jakarta 10270; tel. (21) 5483008; fax (21) 53696525; e-mail intisari@gramedia-majalah.com; internet www.intisari-online.com; f. 1963; monthly; Indonesian; popular science, health, technology, crime and general interest; Editors Al. Heru Kustara, Irawati; circ. 141,000.

Jakarta Jakarta: Gramedia Bldg, Unit II, 5th Floor, Jalan Palmerah Selatan No. 24–26, Jakarta 10270; tel. (21) 5483008; fax (21) 5494035; f. 1985; weekly; food, fun, fashion and celebrity news; circ. 70,000.

Jurnal Indonesia: Jalan Hos Cokroaminoto 49A, Jakarta 10350; tel. (21) 31901774; fax (21) 3916471; e-mail jurnal@cbn.net.id; internet www.jurnalindonesia.com; monthly; political, economic and business analysis.

Keluarga: Jalan Sangaji 11, Jakarta; fortnightly; women's and family magazine; Editor S. Dahono.

Kontan: Jalan Kebayoran Lama 1119, Jakarta 12210; tel. (21) 5357636; fax (21) 5357633; e-mail red@kontan-online.com; internet www.kontan-online.com; weekly; Indonesian; business newspaper.

Majalah Ekonomis: POB 4195, Jakarta; monthly; English; business; Chief Editor S. Arifin Hutabarat; circ. 20,000.

Majalah Kedokteran Indonesia (Journal of the Indonesian Medical Asscn): Jalan Kesehatan 111/29, Jakarta 11/16; f. 1951; monthly; Indonesian, English.

Manglé: Jalan Lodaya 19–21, 40262 Bandung; tel. (22) 411438; f. 1957; weekly; Sundanese; Chief Editor Drs Oejang Darajatoen; circ. 74,000.

Matra: Grafity Pers, Kompleks Buncit Raya Permai, Kav. 1, Jalan Warung, POB 3476, Jakarta; tel. (21) 515952; f. 1986; monthly; men's magazine; general interest and current affairs; Editor-in-Chief (vacant); circ. 100,000.

Mimbar Kabinet Pembangunan: Jalan Merdeka Barat 7, Jakarta; f. 1966; monthly; Indonesian; publ. by Dept of Information.

Mutiara: Jalan Dewi Sartika 136D, Cawang, Jakarta Timur; general interest; Publr H. G. Rorimpandey.

Nova: PT Gramedia, Gedung Unit II, Lantai V, Jalan Palmerah Selatan No. 24–26, Jakarta 10270; tel. (21) 5483008; fax (21) 5483146; e-mail nova@gramedia-majalah.com; internet www.tabloidnova.com; weekly; Wed.; women's interest; Indonesian; Editor Koes Sabandiyah; circ. 618,267.

Oposisi: Jakarta; weekly; politics; circ. 400,000.

Otomotif: Gramedia Bldg, Unit II, 5th Floor, Jalan Palmerah Selatan 24–26, Jakarta 10270; tel. (21) 5490666; fax (21) 5494035; e-mail iklanmjl@ub.net.id; f. 1990; weekly; automotive specialist tabloid; circ. 215,763.

PC Magazine Indonesia: Jalan H. R. Rasuna Said, Blok B, Kav. 32–33, Jakarta 12910; tel. (21) 5209370; fax (21) 5209366; internet www.pcmag.co.id; computers; Editor-in-Chief SVIDA ALISJAHBANA.

Peraba: Bintaran Kidul 5, Yogyakarta; weekly; Indonesian and Javanese; Roman Catholic; Editor W. KARTOSOEHARSONO.

Pertani PT: Jalan Pasar Minggu, Kalibata, POB 247/KBY, Jakarta Selatan; tel. (21) 793108; f. 1974; monthly; Indonesian; agricultural; Pres. Dir Ir RUSLI YAHYA.

Petisi: Surabaya; weekly; Editor CHOIRUL ANAM.

Rajawali: Jakarta; monthly; Indonesian; civil aviation and tourism; Dir R. A. J. LUMENTA; Man. Editor KARYONO ADHY.

Selecta: Kebon Kacang 29/4, Jakarta; fortnightly; illustrated; Editor SAMSUDIN LUBIS; circ. 80,000.

Simponi: Jakarta; f. 1994 by fmr employees of *DeTik* (banned 1994–98).

Sinar Jaya: Jakarta Selatan; fortnightly; agriculture; Chief Editor Ir SURYONO PROJOPRANOTO.

Swasembada: Gedung Chandra Lt. 2, Jalan M. H. Thamrin 20, Jakarta 10310; tel. (21) 3103316.

Tempo: Gedung Tempo, 8th Floor, Jalan H. R. Rasuna Said, Kav. C-17, Kuningan, Jakarta 12940; tel. (21) 5201022; fax (21) 5200092; internet www.tempointeractive.com; f. 1971; weekly; Editor-in-Chief BAMBANG HARYMURTI.

Tiara: Gramedia Bldg, Unit 11, 5th Floor, Jalan Palmerah Selatan 24–26, Jakarta 10270; tel. (21) 5483008; fax (21) 5494035; f. 1990; fortnightly; lifestyles, features and celebrity news; circ. 47,000.

Ummat: Jakarta; Islamic; sponsored by ICMI.

Wenang Post: Jalan R. W. Mongsidi 4/96, POB 1105, Manado 95115; tel. and fax (431) 866150; weekly.

NEWS AGENCIES

Antara (Indonesian National News Agency): Wisma Antara, 3rd, 19th and 20th Floors, 17 Jalan Merdeka Selatan, POB 1257, Jakarta 10110; tel. (21) 3802383; fax (21) 3840970; e-mail antara@antara.co.id; internet www.antara.co.id; f. 1937; 20 radio, seven television, 96 newspaper, eight foreign newspaper, seven tabloid, seven magazine, two news agency, nine embassy and seven dotcom subscribers in 2001; 26 brs in Indonesia, six overseas brs/correspondents; four bulletins in Indonesian and one in English; monitoring service of stock exchanges world-wide; photo service; Exec. Editor HERU PURWANTO; Man. Dir MOHAMAD SOBARY.

Kantorberita Nasional Indonesia (KNI News Service): Jalan Jatinegara Barat III/6, Jakarta Timur 13310; tel. (21) 811003; fax (21) 8195501; f. 1966; independent national news agency; foreign and domestic news in Indonesian; Dir and Editor-in-Chief Drs SUMONO MUSTOFFA; Exec. Editor HARIM NURROCHADI.

Foreign Bureaux

Agence France-Presse (AFP): Jalan Indramayu 18, Jakarta Pusat 10310; tel. (21) 3336082; fax (21) 3809186; Chief Correspondent PASCAL MALLET.

Agenzia Nazionale Stampa Associata (ANSA) (Italy): Jalan Petogogan 1 Go-2 No, 13 Kompleks RRI, Kebayoran Baru, Jakarta Selatan; tel. (21) 7391996; fax (21) 7392247; Correspondent HERYTNO PUJOWIDAGDO.

Associated Press (AP) (USA): Deutsche Bank Bldg, 14th Floor, No. 1403–1404, Jalan Imam Bonjol 80, Jakarta 10310; tel. (21) 39831269; fax (21) 39831270; e-mail gspencer@ap.org; Chief of Bureau GEOFF SPENCER.

Central News Agency Inc (CNA) (Taiwan): Jalan Gelong Baru Timur 1–13, Jakarta Barat; tel. and fax (21) 5600266; Bureau Chief WU PIN-CHIANG.

Informatsionnoye Telegrafnoye Agentstvo Rossii—Telegrafnoye Agentstvo Suverennykh Stran (ITAR—TASS) (Russia): Jalan Surabaya 7 Menteng, Jakarta Pusat 10310; tel. and fax (21) 3155283; e-mail ab1952@indosat.net.id; Correspondent ANDREY ALEKSANDROVICH BYTCHKOV.

Inter Press Service (IPS) (Italy): Gedung Dewan Pers, 4th Floor, Jalan Kebon Sirih 34, Jakarta 10110; tel. (21) 3453131; fax (21) 3453175; Chief Correspondent ABDUL RAZAK.

Jiji Tsushin (Japan): Jalan Raya Bogor 109B, Jakarta; tel. (21) 8090509; Correspondent MARGA RAHARJA.

Kyodo Tsushin (Japan): Skyline Bldg, 11th Floor, Jalan M. H. Thamrin 9, Jakarta 10310; tel. (21) 345012; Correspondent MASAYUKI KITAMURA.

Reuters (United Kingdom): Wisma Antara, 6th Floor, Jalan Medan Merdeka Selatan 17, Jakarta 10110; tel. (21) 3846364; fax (21) 3448404; e-mail jerry.norton@reuters.com; Bureau Chief JERRY NORTON.

United Press International (UPI) (USA): Wisma Antara, 14th Floor, Jalan Medan Merdeka Selatan 17, Jakarta 10110; tel. (21) 341056; Bureau Chief JOHN HAIL.

Xinhua (New China) News Agency (People's Republic of China): Jakarta.

PRESS ASSOCIATIONS

Aliansi Jurnalis Independen (AJI) (Alliance of Independent Journalists): Jalan PAM Baru Raya 16, Pejompongan, Jakarta Pusat 10210; tel. (21) 9183810; fax (21) 5727018; e-mail jurnalis@idola.net.id; f. 1994; unofficial; aims to promote freedom of the press; Sec.-Gen. AHMAD TAUFIK.

Persatuan Wartawan Indonesia (Indonesian Journalists' Asscn): Gedung Dewan Pers, 4th Floor, Jalan Kebon Sirih 34, Jakarta 10110; tel. (21) 353131; fax (21) 353175; f. 1946; government-controlled; 5,041 mems (April 1991); Chair. TARMAN AGAM; Gen. Sec. H. SOFJAN LUBIS.

Serikat Penerbit Suratkabar (SPS) (Indonesian Newspaper Publishers' Asscn): Gedung Dewan Pers, 6th Floor, Jalan Kebon Sirih 34, Jakarta 10110; tel. (21) 3459671; fax (21) 3862373; e-mail sps-pst@dnet.net.id; internet www.dnet.net.id/sps; f. 1946; Exec. Chair. Drs S. L. BATUBARA; Sec.-Gen. Drs AMIR E. SIREGAR.

Yayasan Pembina Pers Indonesia (Press Foundation of Indonesia): Jalan Jatinegara Barat III/6, Jakarta 13310; tel. (21) 8194994; f. 1967; Chair. SUGIARSO SUROYO, MOCHTAR LUBIS.

Publishers

JAKARTA

Aries Lima/New Aqua Press PT: Jalan Rawagelan II/4, Jakarta Timur; tel. (21) 4897566; general and children's; Pres. TUTI SUNDARI AZMI.

Aya Media Pustaka PT: Wijaya Grand Centre C/2, Jalan Dharmawangsa III, Jakarta 12160; tel. (21) 7206903; fax (21) 7201401; f. 1985; children's; Dir Drs ARIANTO TUGIYO.

PT Balai Pustaka Peraga: Jalan Gunung Sahari Raya 4, Gedung Balai Pustaka, 7th Floor, Jakarta 10710; tel. (21) 3447003; fax (21) 3446555; e-mail bp1917@hotmail.com; internet www.balaiperaga.com; f. 1917; children's, school textbooks, literary, scientific publs and periodicals; Dir R. SISWADI.

Bhratara Niaga Media PT: Jalan Cipinang Bali 17, Jakarta Timur 13420; tel. (21) 8520319; fax (21) 8191858; f. 1986; fmrly Bhratara Karya Aksara; university and educational textbooks; Man. Dir ROBINSON RUSDI.

Bina Rena Pariwara PT: Jalan Pejaten Raya 5-E, Pasar Minggu, Jakarta 12510; tel. (21) 7901931; fax (21) 7901939; e-mail hasanbas@softhome.net; f. 1988; financial, social science, economic, Islamic, children's; Dir Drs HASAN BASRI.

Bulan Bintang PT: Jalan Kramat Kwitang 1/8, Jakarta 10420; tel. (21) 3901651; fax (21) 3107027; f. 1954; Islamic, social science, natural and applied sciences, art; Pres. AMRAN ZAMZAMI; Man. Dir FAUZI AMELZ.

Bumi Aksara PT: Jalan Sawo Raya 18, Rawamanguu, Jakarta 13220; tel. (21) 4717049; fax (21) 4700989; f. 1990; university textbooks; Dir H. AMIR HAMZAH.

Cakrawala Cinta PT: Jalan Minyak I/12B, Duren Tiga, Jakarta 12760; tel. (21) 7990725; fax (21) 7974076; f. 1984; science; Dir Drs M. TORSINA.

Centre for Strategic and International Studies (CSIS): Jalan Tanah Abang III/23–27, Jakarta 10160; tel. (21) 3865532; fax (21) 3847517; e-mail csis@pacific.net.id; internet www.csis.or.id; f. 1971; political and social sciences; Dir Dr DAOED JOESOEF.

Cipta Adi Pustaka: Graha Compaka Mas Blok C 22, Jalan Cempaka Putih Raya, Jakarta Pusat; tel. (21) 4213821; fax (21) 4269315; f. 1986; encyclopedias; Dir BUDI SANTOSO.

Dian Rakyat PT: Jalan Rawagelas I/4, Kaw. Industri Pulo Gadung, Jakarta; tel. (21) 4604444; fax (21) 4609115; f. 1966; general; Dir MARIO ALISJAHBANA.

Djambatan PT: Jalan Wijaya I/39, Jakarta 12170; tel. (21) 7203199; fax (21) 7227989; f. 1954; children's, textbooks, social sciences, fiction; Dir SJARIFUDIN SJAMSUDIN.

Dunia Pustaka Jaya: Jalan Rawa Bambu Rt. 003/07 38, Komp. BATAN, Pasar Minggu, Jakarta Selatan 12520; tel. (21) 7891875; fax (21) 3909320; f. 1971; fiction, religion, essays, poetry, drama, criticism, art, philosophy and children's; Man. A. RIVAI.

EGC Medical Publishers: Jalan Agung Timur 4, No. 39 Blok 0–1, Jakarta 14350; tel. (21) 65306283; fax (21) 6510840; e-mail contact@egc-arcan.com; f. 1978; medical and public health, nursing, dentistry; Dir IMELDA DHARMA.

Elex Media Komputindo: Jalan Palmerah Selatan 22, Kompas–Gramedia Bldg, 6th Floor, Jakarta 10270; tel. (21) 53699059; fax (21) 5326219; e-mail elex@elexmedia.co.id; internet www.elexmedia.co.id; f. 1985; management, computing, software, children's, parenting, self-development and fiction; Dir AL. ADHI MARDHIYONO.

Erlangga PT: Kami Melayani II, Pengetahuan, Jalan H. Baping 100, Ciracas, Jakarta 13740; tel. (21) 8717006; fax (21) 8717011; e-mail erlprom@rad.net.id; internet www.erlangga.com; f. 1952; secondary school and university textbooks; Man. Dir GUNAWAN HUTAURUK.

Gaya Favorit Press: Jalan Rawagelam II/4, Kawasan Industri Pulogadung, Jakarta 13930; tel. (21) 46821321; fax (21) 46821419; f. 1971; fiction, popular science, lifestyle and children's; Vice-Pres. MIRTA KARTOHADIPRODJO; Man. Dir WIDARTI GUNAWAN.

Gema Insani Press: Jalan Kalibata Utara II/84, Jakarta 12740; tel. (21) 7984391; fax (21) 7984388; e-mail gipnet@indosat.net.id; internet www.gemainsani.co.id; f. 1986; Islamic; Dir UMAR BASYARAHIL.

Ghalia Indonesia: Jalan Pramuka Raya 4, Jakarta 13140; tel. (21) 8584330; fax (21) 8502334; f. 1972; children's and general science, textbooks; Man. Dir LUKMAN SAAD.

Gramedia Widyasarana Indonesia: Jalan Palmerah Selatan 22, Lantai IV, POB 615, Jakarta 10270; tel. (21) 5483008; fax (21) 5300545; f. 1973; university textbooks, general non-fiction, children's and magazines; Gen. Man. ALFONS TARYADI.

Gunung Mulia PT: Jalan Kwitang 22–23, Jakarta 10420; tel. (21) 3901208; fax (21) 3901633; e-mail corp.off@bpkgm.com; internet www.bpkgm.com; f. 1951; general, children's, Christian; Pres. Dir STEPHEN Z. SATYAHADI; Dir V. N. LEIMENA.

Hidakarya Agung PT: Jalan Kebon Kosong F/74, Kemayoran, Jakarta Pusat; tel. (21) 4241074; Dir MAHDIARTI MACHMUD.

Ichtiar: Jalan Majapahit 6, Jakarta Pusat; tel. (21) 3841226; f. 1957; textbooks, law, social sciences, economics; Dir JOHN SEMERU.

Indira PT: Jalan Borobudur 20, Jakarta 10320; tel. (21) 882754; f. 1953; general science and children's; Man. Dir BAMBANG P. WAHYUDI.

Kinta CV: Jalan Kemanggisan Ilir V/110, Pal Merah, Jakarta Barat; tel. (21) 5494751; f. 1950; textbooks, social science, general; Man. Drs MOHAMAD SALEH.

Midas Surya Grafindo PT: Jalan Kesehatan 54, Cijantung, Jakarta 13760; tel. (21) 8400414; fax (21) 8400270; f. 1984; children's; Dir Drs FRANS HENDRAWAN.

Mutiara Sumber Widya PT: Jalan Kramat II 55, Jakarta; tel. (21) 3926043; fax (21) 3160313; f. 1951; textbooks, Islamic, social sciences, general and children's; Pres. FADJRAA OEMAR.

Penebar Swadya PT: Jalan Gunung Sahari III/7, Jakarta Pusat; tel. (21) 4204402; fax (21) 4214821; agriculture, animal husbandry, fisheries; Dir Drs ANTHONIUS RIYANTO.

Penerbit Universitas Indonesia: Jalan Salemba Raya 4, Jakarta; tel. (21) 335373; f. 1969; science; Man. S. E. LEGOWO.

Pradnya Paramita PT: Jalan Bunga 8–8A, Matraman, Jakarta 13140; tel. (21) 8504944; e-mail pradnya@centrin.net.id; f. 1973; children's, general, educational, technical and social science; Pres. Dir KONDAR SINAGA.

Pustaka Antara PT: Jalan Taman Kebon Sirih III/13, Jakarta Pusat 10250; tel. (21) 3156994; fax (21) 322745; e-mail nacelod@cbn.net.id; f. 1952; textbooks, political, Islamic, children's and general; Man. Dir AIDA JOESOEF AHMAD.

Pustaka Binaman Pressindo: Bina Manajemen Bldg, Jalan Menteng Raya 9–15, Jakarta 10340; tel. (21) 2300313; fax (21) 2302047; e-mail pustaka@bit.net.id; f. 1981; management; Dir Ir MAKFUDIN WIRYA ATMAJA.

Pustaka LP3ES Indonesia: Jalan Letjen. S. Parman 81, Jakarta 11420; tel. (21) 5663527; fax (21) 56964691; e-mail puslp3es@indo.net.id; f. 1971; general; Dir M. D. MARUTO.

Pustaka Sinar Harapan PT: Jalan Dewi Sartika 136D, Jakarta 13630; tel. (21) 8093208; fax (21) 8091652; f. 1981; general science, fiction, comics, children's; Dir W. M. NAIDEN.

Pustaka Utma Grafiti PT: Jalan Wahid Hasyim Nomor 166A, Jakarta 10250; tel. (21) 31902906; fax (21) 31902435; f. 1981; social sciences, humanities and children's books; Dir ZULKIFLY LUBIS.

Rajagrafindo Persada PT: Jalan Pelepah Hijau IV TN-1 14–15, Kelapa Gading Permai, Jakarta 14240; tel. (21) 4529409; fax (21) 4520951; f. 1980; general science and religion; Dir Drs ZUBAIDI.

Rineka Cipta PT: Blok B/5, Jalan Jenderal Sudirman, Kav. 36A, Bendungan Hilir, Jakarta 10210; tel. (21) 5737646; fax (21) 5711985; f. 1990 by merger of Aksara Baru (f. 1972) and Bina Aksara; general science and university texts; Dir Dr H. SUARDI.

Rosda Jayaputra PT: Jalan Kembang 4, Jakarta 10420; tel. (21) 3904984; fax (21) 3901703; f. 1981; general science; Dir H. ROZALI USMAN.

Sastra Hudaya: Jalan Kalasan 1, Jakarta Pusat; tel. (21) 882321; f. 1967; religious, textbooks, children's and general; Man. ADAM SALEH.

Tintamas Indonesia: Jalan Kramat Raya 60, Jakarta 10420; tel. and fax (21) 3911459; f. 1947; history, modern science and culture, especially Islamic; Man. MARHAMAH DJAMBEK.

Tira Pustaka: Jalan Cemara Raya 1, Kav. 10D, Jaka Permai, Jaka Sampurna, Bekasi 17145; tel. (21) 8841277; fax (21) 8842736; e-mail Tirapus@cbn.net.id; f. 1977; translations, children's; Dir ROBERT B. WIDJAJA.

Toko Buku Walisongo PT: Gedung Idayu, Jalan Kwitang 13, Jakarta 10420; tel. (21) 3154890; fax (21) 3154889; e-mail tokowalisongo@plasa.com; f. 1986; fmrly Masagung Group; general, Muslim religious, textbooks, science; Pres. H. KETUT ABDURRAHMAN MASAGUNG.

Widjaya: Jalan Pecenongan 48C, Jakarta Pusat; tel. (21) 3813446; f. 1950; textbooks, children's, religious and general; Man. DIDI LUTHAN.

Yasaguna: Jalan Minangkabau 44, POB 422, Jakarta Selatan; tel. (21) 8290422; f. 1964; agricultural, children's, handicrafts; Dir HILMAN MADEWA.

Bandung

Alma'arif: Jalan Tamblong 48–50, Bandung; tel. (22) 4264454; fax (22) 4239194; f. 1949; textbooks, religious and general; Man. H. M. BAHARTHAH.

Alumni PT: Jalan Bukit Pakar Timur II/109, Bandung 40197; tel. (22) 2501251; fax (22) 2503044; f. 1968; university and school textbooks; Dir EDDY DAMIAN.

Angkasa: Jalan Merdeka 6, POB 1353 BD, Bandung 40111; tel. (22) 4204795; fax (22) 439183; Dir H. FACHRI SAID.

Armico: Jalan Madurasa Utara 10, Cigereleng, Bandung 40253; tel. (22) 5202234; fax (22) 5201972; f. 1980; school textbooks; Dir Ir ARSIL TANJUNG.

Citra Aditya Bakti PT: Jalan Geusanulun 17, Bandung 40115; tel. (22) 438251; fax (22) 438635; f. 1985; general science; Dir Ir IWAN TANUATMADJA.

Diponegoro Publishing House: Jalan Mohammad Toha 44–46, Bandung 40252; tel. and fax (22) 5201215; e-mail dpnegoro@indosat.net.id; f. 1963; Islamic, textbooks, fiction, non-fiction, general; Dir HADIDJAH DAHLAN.

Epsilon Group: Jalan Marga Asri 3, Margacinta, Bandung 40287; tel. (22) 7567826; f. 1985; school textbooks; Dir Drs BAHRUDIN.

Eresco PT: Jalan Megger Girang 98, Bandung 40254; tel. (22) 5205985; fax (22) 5205984; f. 1957; scientific and general; Man. Drs ARFAN ROZALI.

Ganeca Exact Bandung: Jalan Kiaracondong 167, Pagauban, Bandung 40283; tel. (22) 701519; fax (22) 775329; f. 1982; school textbooks; Dir Ir KETUT SUARDHARA LINGGIH.

Mizan Pustaka PT: Jalan Yodkali 16, Bandung 40124; tel. (22) 7200931; fax (22) 7207038; e-mail info@mizan.com; internet www.mizan.com; f. 1983; Islamic and general books; Pres. Dir HAIDAR BAGIR.

Penerbit ITB: Jalan Ganesa 10, Bandung 40132; tel. and fax (22) 2504257; e-mail itbpress@bdg.centrin.net.id; f. 1971; academic books; Dir EMMY SUPARKA; Chief Editor SOFIA MANSOOR-NIKSOLIHIN.

Putra A. Bardin: Jalan Ganesa 4, Bandung; tel. (22) 2504319; f. 1998; textbooks, scientific and general; Dir NAI A. BARDIN.

Remaja Rosdakarya PT: Jalan Ciateul 34–36, POB 284, Bandung 40252; tel. (22) 5200287; fax (22) 5202529; textbooks and children's fiction; Pres. ROZALI USMAN.

Sarana Panca Karyam PT: Jalan Kopo 633 KM 13/4, Bandung 40014; f. 1986; general; Dir WIMPY S. IBRAHIM.

Tarsito PT: Jalan Guntur 20, Bandung 40262; tel. (22) 304915; fax (22) 314630; academic; Dir T. SITORUS.

Flores

Nusa Indah: Jalan El Tari, Ende 86318, Flores; tel. (0381) 21502; fax (0381) 23974; e-mail namkahu@yahoo.com; f. 1970; religious and general; Dir Lukas Batmomolin.

Kudus

Menara Kudus: Jalan Menara 4, Kudus 59315; tel. (291) 371143; fax (291) 36474; f. 1958; Islamic; Man. Chilman Najib.

Medan

Hasmar: Jalan Letjenderal Haryono M. T. 1, POB 446, Medan 20231; tel. (61) 24181; f. 1962; primary school textbooks; Dir Fauzi Lubis; Man. Amran Said Rangkuti.

Impola: Jalan H. M. Joni 46, Medan 20217; tel. (61) 711415; f. 1984; school textbooks; Dir Pamilang M. Situmorang.

Madju Medan Cipta PT: Jalan Amaliun 37, Medan 20215; tel. (61) 7361990; fax (61) 7367753; e-mail koboi@indosat.net; f. 1950; textbooks, children's and general; Pres. H. Mohamed Arbie; Man. Dir Drs Dino Irsan Arbie.

Masco: Jalan Sisingamangaraja 191, Medan 20218; tel. (61) 713375; f. 1992; school textbooks; Dir P. M. Situmorang.

Monora: Jalan Letjenderal Jamin Ginting 583, Medan 20156; tel. (61) 8212667; fax (61) 8212669; e-mail monora_cv@plasa.com; f. 1962; school textbooks; Dir Chairil Anwar.

Semarang

Aneka Ilmu: Jalan Raya Semarang Demak Km 8.5, Sayung, Demak; tel. (24) 6580335; fax (24) 6582903; e-mail pemasuran@anekailmu.com; internet www.anekailmu.com; f. 1983; general and school textbooks; Dir H. Suwanto.

Effhar COY PT: Jalan Dorang 7, Semarang 50173; tel. (24) 3511172; fax (24) 3551540; e-mail effhar_dahara@yahoo.com; f. 1976; general books; Dir H. Daradjat Harahap.

Intan Pariwara: Jalan Beringin, Klaten Utara, Kotak Pos III, Kotif Klaten, Jawa-Tengah; tel. (272) 22441; fax (272) 22021; school textbooks; Pres. Soetikno.

Mandira PT: Jalan Letjenderal M. T. Haryono 501, Semarang 50241; tel. (24) 316150; fax (24) 415092; f. 1962; Dir Ir A. Hariyanto.

Mandira Jaya Abadi PT: Jalan Letjenderal M. T. Haryono 501, Semarang 50241; tel. (24) 519547; fax (24) 542189; e-mail mjabadi@indosat.net.id; f. 1981; Dir Ir A. Hariyanto.

Solo

Pabelan PT: Jalan Raya Pajang, Kertasura KM 8, Solo 57162; tel. (271) 743975; fax (271) 714775; f. 1983; school textbooks; Dir Agung Sasongko.

Tiga Serangkai PT: Jalan Dr Supomo 23, Solo; tel. (271) 714344; fax (271) 713607; f. 1977; school textbooks; Dir Abdullah.

Surabaya

Airlangga University Press: Kampus C, Jalan Mulyorejo, Surabaya; tel. (31) 5992246; fax (31) 5992248; e-mail aupsby@rad.net.id; academic; Dir Dr Arifaan Razak.

Bina Ilmu PT: Jalan Tunjungan 53e, Surabaya 60275; tel. (31) 5323214; fax (31) 5315421; f. 1973; school textbooks, Islamic; Pres. Ariefin Noor.

Bintang: Jalan Potroagung III/41c, Surabaya; tel. (31) 3770687; fax (31) 3715941; school textbooks; Dir Agus Winarno.

Grip PT: Jalan Rungkut Permai II/C–11, Surabaya; tel. (31) 22564; f. 1958; textbooks and general; Man. Suripto.

Jaya Baya: Jalan Embong Malang 69h, POB 250, Surabaya 60001; tel. (31) 41169; f. 1945; religion, philosophy and ethics; Man. Tadjib Ermadi.

Sinar Wijaya: Jalan Raya Sawo VII/58, Bringin-Lakarsantri, Surabaya; tel. (31) 706615; general; Dir Dulradjak.

Yogyakarta

Andi Publishers: Jalan Beo 38–40, Yogyakarta 55281; tel. (274) 561881; fax (274) 588282; e-mail andi_pub@indo.net.id; f. 1980; Christian, computing, business, management and technical; Dir J. H. Gondowijoyo.

BPFE PT: Jalan Gambiran 37, Yogyakarta 55161; tel. (274) 373760; fax (274) 380819; f. 1984; university textbooks; Dir Drs Indriyo Gitosudarmo.

Centhini Yayasan: Gg. Bekisar UH V/716 E–1, Yogyakarta 55161; tel. (274) 383148; f. 1984; Javanese culture; Chair. H. Karkono Kamajaya.

Gadjah Mada University Press: Jalan Grafika 1, Kampus UGM, Bulaksumur, Yogyakarta 55281; tel. and fax (274) 561037; e-mail gamapress@ugm.ac.id; internet www.gmup.ugm.ac.id; f. 1971; university textbooks; Dir Ana Nadhya Abrar.

Indonesia UP: Gg. Bekisar UH V/716 E–1, Yogyakarta 55161; tel. (274) 383148; f. 1950; general science; Dir H. Karkono Kamajaya.

Kanisius Printing and Publishing: Jalan Cempaka 9, Deresan, POB 1125, Yogyakarta 55281; tel. (274) 588783; fax (274) 563349; e-mail office@kanisiusmedia.com; internet www.kanisiusmedia.com; f. 1922; children's, textbooks, Christian and general; Pres. Dir S. J. Sarwanto.

Kedaulatan Rakyat PT: Jalan P. Mangkubumi 40–42, Yogyakarta; tel. (274) 2163; Dir Drono Hardjusuwongso.

Penerbit Tiara Wacana Yogya: Jalan Kaliurang KM 7, 8 Kopen 16, Banteng, Yogyakarta 55581; tel. and fax (274) 880683; f. 1986; university textbooks and general science; Dir Sitoresmi Prabuningrat.

Government Publishing House

Balai Pustaka PT (Persero) (State Publishing and Printing House): Jalan Gunung Sahari Raya 4, Gedung Balai Pustaka, 7th Floor, Jakarta Pusat 10710; tel. (21) 3447003; fax (21) 3446555; e-mail mail@balaiperaga.com; internet www.balaiperaga.com; history, anthropology, politics, philosophy, medical, arts and literature; Pres. Dir H. R. Siswadi Idris.

PUBLISHERS' ASSOCIATION

Ikatan Penerbit Indonesia (IKAPI) (Asscn of Indonesian Book Publishers): Jalan Kalipasir 32, Jakarta 10330; tel. (21) 3141907; fax (21) 3146050; e-mail sekretariat@ikapi.or.id; internet www.ikapi.or.id; f. 1950; 496 mems (Aug. 2002); Pres. Makfudin Wirya Atmaja; Sec.-Gen. Robinson Rusdi.

Broadcasting and Communications

TELECOMMUNICATIONS

Directorate-General of Posts and Telecommunications (Postel): Gedung Sapta Pesona, Jalan Medan Merdeka Barat 17, Jakarta 10110; tel. (21) 3835912; fax (21) 3860754; e-mail admin@postel.go.id; internet www.postel.go.id; Dir-Gen. Djamhari Sirat.

PT Indosat (Persero) Tbk: Jalan Medan Merdeka Barat 21, POB 2905, Jakarta 10110; tel. (21) 30003001; fax (21) 3804045; e-mail sant@indosat.com; internet www.indosat.com; f. 1967; telecommunications; partially privatized in 1994; 41.94% stake sold to Singapore Technologies Telemedia in 2002; Pres. Dir Widya Purnama.

PT Satelit Palapa Indonesia (SATELINDO): Jalan Daan Mogot Km 11, Jakarta 11710; tel. (21) 5451745; fax (21) 5451748; e-mail webmaster@satelindo.co.id; internet www.satelindo.co.id; f. 1993; telecommunications and satellite services; Pres. Dir Johny Swandi Sjam.

PT Telekomunikasi Indonesia Tbk (TELKOM): Corporate Office, Jalan Japati No. 1, Bandung 40133; tel. (22) 4521510; fax (22) 440313; internet www.telkom.co.id; domestic telecommunications; 24.2% of share capital was transferred to the private sector in 1995; Pres. Dir and CEO Kristiono.

BROADCASTING

Regulatory Authority

Directorate-General of Radio, Television and Film: Jalan Merdeka Barat 4–5, Jakarta 10110; tel. (21) 3849091; fax (21) 3457132; Dir-Gen. Suryanta Saleh.

Radio

Radio Republik Indonesia (RRI): Jalan Medan Merdeka Barat 4–5, Jakarta 10110; tel. (21) 3846817; fax (21) 3457134; e-mail rri@rrionline.com; internet www.rrionline.com; f. 1945; 49 stations; Dir Suryanta Saleh; Dep. Dirs Fachruddin Soekarno (Overseas Service), Abdul Rochim (Programming), Sukri (Programme Development), Sazli Rais (Administration), Chaerul Zen (News).

Voice of Indonesia: Jalan Medan Merdeka Barat 4–5, POB 1157, Jakarta; tel. (21) 3456811; international service provided by Radio Republik Indonesia; daily broadcasts in Arabic, English, French, German, Bahasa Indonesia, Japanese, Bahasa Malaysia, Mandarin, Spanish and Thai.

Television

In March 1989 Indonesia's first private commercial television station began broadcasting to the Jakarta area. In 1996 there were five privately-owned television stations in operation.

PT Cakrawala Andalas Televisi (ANTEVE): Gedung Sentra Mulia, 18th Floor, Jalan H. R. Rasuna Said, Kav. X-6 No. 8, Jakarta 12940; tel. (21) 5222086; fax (21) 5222087; e-mail humas@anteve.co.id; internet www.anteve.co.id; f. 1993; private channel; broadcasting to 10 cities; Pres. Dir H. R. AGUNG LAKSONO; Gen. Man. NENNY SOEMAWINATA.

PT CIPTA TPI: Jalan Pintu II—Taman Mini Indonesia Indah, Pondok Gede, Jakarta Timur 13810; tel. (21) 8412473; fax (21) 8412470; e-mail info@tpi.co.id; internet www.tpi.co.id; f. 1991; private channel funded by commercial advertising; Pres. Dir SITI HARDIJANTI RUKMANA.

PT Rajawali Citra Televisi Indonesia (RCTI): Jalan Raya Pejuangan 3, Kebon Jeruk, Jakarta 11000; tel. (21) 5303540; fax (21) 5493852; e-mail webmaster@rcti.co.id; internet www.rcti.co.id; f. 1989; first private channel; 20-year licence; Pres. Dir M. S. RALIE SIREGAR; Vice-Pres. ALEX KUMARA.

PT Surya Citra Televisi (SCTV): GRHA SCTV, 2nd Floor, Jalan Gatot Subroto, Kav. 21, Jakarta 12930; tel. (21) 5225555; fax (21) 5224777; e-mail pr@sctv.co.id; internet www.sctv.co.id; f. 1990; private channel broadcasting nationally; Pres. Dir Dr Ir AGUS MULYANTO.

Televisi Republik Indonesia (TVRI): TVRI Senayan, Jalan Gerbang Pemuda, Senayan, Jakarta; tel. (21) 5733135; fax (21) 5732408; e-mail info@tvrisby.com; internet www.tvrisby.com; f. 1962; fmrly state-controlled; became independent 2003; Pres. Dir NASIRWAN UYUN.

Finance

(cap. = capital; auth. = authorized; p.u. = paid up; res = reserves; dep. = deposits; m. = million; brs = branches; amounts in rupiah)

BANKING

In December 1996 there were 9,276 banks, with 14,956 branches, in operation in Indonesia, including seven state commercial banks, 27 regional government banks, 164 private national banks and 41 foreign and joint-venture banks. At the end of March 1995 total bank deposits stood at 167,123,000m. rupiah. A programme of extensive reform of the banking sector was ongoing from 1998 onwards, under the auspices of the Indonesian Bank Restructuring Agency (IBRA). Having satisfied its mandate, the IBRA was dissolved in February 2004. However, continued reform of the sector remained a priority for the Government.

Central Bank

Bank Indonesia: Jalan M. H. Thamrin 2, Jakarta Pusat 10002; tel. (21) 2310408; fax (21) 2311058; e-mail humasbi@bi.go.id; internet www.bi.go.id; f. 1828; nationalized as central bank in 1953; cap. 2,948,029m., res 130,820,882m., dep. 341,944,951m. (Dec. 2002); Gov. BURHANUDDIN ABDULLAH; 42 brs.

State Banks

In late December 1997 the Government announced that four of the state-owned banks—Bank Bumi Daya, Bank Dagang Negara, Bank Ekspor Impor Indonesia and Bank Pembangunan Indonesia—were to merge; the four banks subsequently merged into a single new institution, PT Bank Mandiri, which was established in July 1999.

PT Bank Ekspor Indonesia (Persero): Gedung Brs Efek, Menara II, Lt. 8, Jalan Sudirman, Kav. 52–53, Jakarta; tel. (21) 5154638; fax (21) 5154639; e-mail prbei@bexi.co.id; internet www.bexi.co.id; cap. 3,000,000m., res 221,634m., dep. 370,679m. (Dec. 2002); Chair. MANSJURDIN NURDIN; Pres. Dir BAMBANG HENDRAJATIN.

PT Bank Mandiri (Persero): Plaza Mandiri, Jalan Jenderal Gatot Subroto, Kav. 36–38, Jakarta 12190; tel. (21) 5265045; fax (21) 5268246; internet www.bankmandiri.co.id; f. 1999 as a result of the merger of four state-owned banks—PT Bank Bumi Daya, PT Bank Dagang Negara, PT Bank Ekspor Impor Indonesia and PT Bank Pembangunan Indonesia; cap. 10,000,000m., res 7,166,651m., dep. 194,916,764m. (Dec. 2003); Pres. Commr BINHADI; Pres. Dir E. C. W. NELOE.

PT Bank Negara Indonesia (Persero) Tbk: Jalan Jenderal Sudirman, Kav. 1, Jakarta 10220; tel. (21) 2511946; fax (21) 2511221; e-mail hin@bni.co.id; internet www.bni.co.id; f. 1946; commercial bank; specializes in credits to the industrial sector; cap. 7,042,194m., res 2,554,253m., dep. 111,025,247m. (Dec. 2003); Pres. Dir SAIFUDDIEN HASAN; 585 local brs, 5 overseas brs.

PT Bank Rakyat Indonesia (Persero): Jalan Jenderal Sudirman, Kav. 44–46, POB 94, Jakarta 10210; tel. (21) 2510244; fax (21) 2500077; internet www.bri.co.id; f. 1895; present name since 1946; commercial and foreign exchange bank; specializes in agricultural smallholdings and rural development; state-owned; cap. 1,728,000m., res 29,168,432m., dep. 73,435,981m. (Dec. 2002); Pres. Dir RUDJITO; 325 brs.

PT Bank Tabungan Negara (Persero): 10th Floor, Bank BTN Tower, Jalan Gajah Mada 1, Jakarta 10130; tel. (21) 6336789; fax (21) 6336704; e-mail webadmin@btn.co.id; internet www.btn.co.id; f. 1964; commercial bank; state-owned; cap. 1,250,000m., res 13,843,540m., dep. 20,694,532m. (Dec. 2002); Chair. DARMIN NASUTION; 44 brs.

PT BPD Jawa Timur (Bank Jatim): Jalan Basuki Rachmad 98–104, Surabaya; tel. (31) 5310090; fax (31) 5312226; internet www.bankjatim.co.id; f. 1961; cap. and res 196,413m., dep. 4,915,594m. (Dec. 2001); Chair. NANIK KUSMINI.

Commercial Banks

PT ANZ Panin Bank: Panin Bank Centre, Jalan Jenderal Sudirman (Senayan), Jakarta 10270; tel. (21) 5750300; fax (21) 5727447; internet www.anz.com/indonesia; f. 1990 as Westpac Panin Bank; 85%-owned by the Australia and New Zealand Banking Group Ltd; cap. 50,000m., res. 10,000m., dep. 1,112,743m. (Dec. 2002); Pres. Dir SCOTT ARMSTRONG.

PT Bank Artha Graha: Bank Artha Graha Tower, 5th Floor, Jalan Jenderal Sudirman, Kav. 52–53, Jakarta 12920; tel. (21) 5152168; fax (21) 5152162; e-mail agraha@rad.net.id; f. 1967; merged with PT Bank Arta Pratama in 1999; cap. 75,000m., dep. 340,344m. (Dec. 1993); Pres. and Dir ANTON B. S. HUDYANA; Chair. LETJEN; 64 brs.

PT Bank Buana Indonesia Tbk: Jalan Asemka 32–36, Jakarta 11110; tel. (21) 2601015; fax (21) 2601014; e-mail bbitdiv@bankbuanaina.co.id; internet www.bankbuana.com; f. 1956; cap. 744,494m., res 264,530m., dep. 11,802,231m. (Dec. 2002); Chair. R. RACHMAD; Pres. Dir JIMMY KURNJAWAN LAIHAD; 31 brs.

PT Bank Bumiputera Indonesia Tbk: Wisma Bumiputra, 14th Floor, Jalan Jenderal Sudirman, Kav. 75, Jakarta 12910; tel. (21) 5701626; fax (21) 5255244; e-mail bank@bumiputera.co.id; internet www.bumiputera.co.id; f. 1989; cap. 200,000m., res 5,649m., dep. 2,070,454m. (Dec. 2002); Pres. and CEO WINNY ERWINDIA HASSAN.

PT Bank Central Asia Tbk (BCA): Wisma BCA, 5th Floor, Jalan Jenderal Sudirman, Kav. 22–23, Jakarta 12920; tel. (21) 5711250; fax (21) 5701865; e-mail humas@bca.co.id; internet www.klikbca.com; f. 1957; placed under the supervision of the IBRA in May 1998; 51% share sold to Farallon Capital Management (USA) in March 2002; cap. 1,532,784m., res 5,331,095m., dep. 119,308,970m. (Dec. 2003); Pres. Dir D. E. SETIJOSO; 780 local brs, 2 overseas brs.

PT Bank Chinatrust Indonesia: 16th and 17th Floors, Wisma Tamara, Jalan Jenderal Sudirman, Kav. 24, Jakarta 12920; tel. (21) 5207878; fax (21) 5206767; e-mail ctcbjak@rad.net.id; f. 1995; cap. 150,000m., dep. 1,179,015m. (Dec. 2002); Pres. Dir RAY KUO; Chair. JEFFREY L. S. KOO.

PT Bank Danamon Indonesia Tbk: Menara Danamon, Jalan Prof. Dr Satrio 6, Kav. E/4, Mega Kuningan, Jakarta 12930; tel. (21) 57991142; fax (21) 57991008; internet www.danamon.co.id; f. 1956; placed under the supervision of the IBRA in April 1998; merged with PT Bank Tiara Asia, PT Tamara Bank, PT Bank Duta and PT Bank Nusa Nasional in 2000; 51% share sold to consortium led by Singapore's Temasek Holdings in May 2003; cap. 3,562,261m., res 28,524m., dep. 37,017,617m. (Dec. 2002); Pres. Commr SIM KEE BOON; Pres. Dir FRANCIS ANDREW ROZARIO; 737 brs.

PT Bank Internasional Indonesia Tbk (BII): Plaza BII, Jalan M. H. Thamrin 51, Kav. 22, Jakarta 10350; tel. (21) 2300888; fax (21) 2301494; e-mail bii-info@idola.net.id; internet www.bii.co.id; cap. 17,867,731m., res 1,339,320m., dep. 29,743,726m. (Dec. 2003); Chair. SOEDARJONO; Pres. Dir SIGIT PRAMONO; 249 brs; 3 overseas brs.

PT Bank Mayapada Internasional Tbk: Gedung Arthaloka, Ground and 1st Floors, Jalan Jenderal Sudirman, Kav. 2, Jakarta 10220; tel. (21) 2511588; fax (21) 2511539; e-mail mayapada@bankmayapada.com; internet www.bankmayapada.com; f. 1989; cap. 164,145m., dep. 925,394m. (Dec. 2000); Chair. TAHIR; Pres. Dir HARYONO TJAHJARIJADI; 5 brs, 7 sub-brs.

PT Bank Mizuho Indonesia: Plaza B11, 24th Floor, Menara 2, Jalan M. H. Thamrin 51, Jakarta 10350; tel. (21) 3925222; fax (21) 3926354; fmrly PT Bank Fuji International Indonesia; f. 1989; cap. 396,250m., res 11,121m., dep. 4,176,926m. (Dec. 2002); Pres. Dir KEIICHI KOGURE.

PT Bank Muamalat Indonesia (BMI): Arthaloka Bldg, Jalan Jenderal Sudirman 2, Jakarta 10220; tel. (21) 2511414; fax (21) 2511453; internet www.muamalatbank.com; Indonesia's first Islamic bank; cap. 165,593m. (July 2000); Pres. Dir A. RIAWAN AMIN; Chair. ABBAS ADHAR.

PT Bank Niaga Tbk: Graha Niaga, Jalan Jenderal Sudirman, Kav. 58, Jakarta 12190; tel. (21) 2505252; fax (21) 2505205; e-mail caniaga@attglobal.net; internet www.bankniaga.com; f. 1955; cap. 746,907m., res 994,801m., dep. 20,214,100m. (Dec. 2003); Pres. Commr SUKANTO REKSOHADIPRODJO; Pres. Dir PETER B. STOK; 181 brs.

PT Bank NISP Tbk: Jalan Taman Cibeunying Selatan 31, Jakarta 40114; tel. (22) 7234123; fax (22) 7100466; e-mail nisp@banknisp .com; internet www.banknisp.com; f. 1941; cap. 516,747m., res 158,925m., dep. 12,594,401m. (Dec. 2003); Pres. Dir PRAMUKTI SUR-JAUDAJA; Chair. KARMAKA SURJANDAJA; 135 brs.

PT Bank Permata Tbk: PermataBank Tower I, Jalan Jenderal Sudirman, Kav. 27, Jakarta 12920; tel. (21) 5237888; fax (21) 2500702; internet www.permatabank.com; f. 1954 as Bank Persatuan Dagang Indonesia; became PT Bank Bali in 1971 and PT Bank Bali Tbk in 1990; name changed as above Sept. 2002 following merger with PT Bank Prima Express, PT Bank Universal Tbk, PT Arthamedia Bank and PT Bank Patriot; cap. 1,300,534m., res 867,217m., dep. 24,879,795m. (Dec. 2003); Chair. and Pres. Dir AGUS D. W. MARTOWARDOJO; 302 brs.

PT Bank Rabobank International Indonesia: Plaza 89, 9th Floor, Jalan H. R. Rasuna Said, Kav. X-7, Jakarta 12940; tel. (21) 2520876; fax (21) 2520875; internet www.rabobank.com; cap. 350,000m., res 2,741m., dep. 1,010,012m. (Dec. 1999); Pres. and Dir ANTONIO COSTA.

PT Bank Sumitomo Mitsui Indonesia: Summitmas II, 10th Floor, Jalan Jenderal Sudirman, Kav. 61–62, Jakarta 12190; tel. (21) 5227011; fax (21) 5227022; internet www.smbc-jkt.co.id; f. 1989; fmrly PT Bank Sumitomo Indonesia, merged with PT Bank Sakura Swadharma in April 2001; cap. 1,502,441m. (Dec. 2003), res – 517,404m., dep. 3,773,680m. (Dec. 2002); Pres. Dir KIYOZUMI NAKA-MURA; 1 br.

PT Bank UFJ Indonesia: PermataBank Tower I, 4th–5th Floors, Jalan Jenderal Sudirman, Kav. 27, Jakarta 12920; tel. (21) 2500401; fax (21) 2500410; f. 1989 as PT Sanwa Indonesia Bank; fmrly PT Bank Sanwa Indonesia; name changed as above Oct. 2001 following merger with PT Tokai Lippo Bank; cap. 817,449m., res 11,043m., dep. 3,475,818m. (Dec. 2002); Pres. Commr TAKESHI OGASAWARA; Pres. Dir SEIJI OSAKI; 1 br., 6 sub-brs.

PT Bank UOB Indonesia: Menara BCD, 1st–3rd Floors, Jalan Jenderal Sudirman, Kav. 26, Jakarta 12920; tel. (21) 2506330; fax (21) 2506428; e-mail uob.jakarta@uobgroup.com; internet www .uobgroup.com; 99%-owned by United Overseas Bank Ltd, Singapore; cap. 50,000m., res 10,000m., dep. 1,757,128m. (Dec. 2001); Chair. WEE CHO YAW; Pres. Dir CHUA KIM HAY; 7 brs.

PT Hagabank: Jalan Abdul Muis 28, Jakarta 10160; tel. (21) 2312888; fax (21) 2312250; e-mail info@hagabank.com; internet www.hagabank.com; f. 1989; cap. 65,000m., res –170m., dep. 2,277,305m. (Dec. 2002); Pres. DANNY HARTONO; Chair. TIMOTY E. MARNANDUS.

PT Korea Exchange Bank Danamon: Suite 1201, 12th Floor, Wisma GKBI, Jalan Jenderal Sudirman, Kav. 28, Selatan, Jakarta; tel. (21) 5741030; fax (21) 5741032; e-mail kebd@idola.net.id; cap. 150,000m., dep. 1,126,764m. (Dec. 2002); Pres. KANG IN KOO; Chair. KIM KWANG SEOB.

PT Lippo Bank Tbk: Gedung Menara Asia, 20th Floor, Jalan Raya Diponegoro 101, Lippo Karawaci, Tangerang 15810; tel. (21) 5460555; fax (21) 5460816; e-mail info_crc@lippobank.co.id; internet www.lippobank.co.id; f. 1948; cap. 811,494m., res 10,700,381m., dep. 22,080,993m. (Dec. 2002); Pres. Dir Dr JOS LUHUKAY; 379 brs.

PT Pan Indonesia Tbk (Panin Bank): Panin Bank Centre, 11th Floor, Jalan Jenderal Sudirman, Senayan, Jakarta 10270; tel. (21) 2700545; fax (21) 2700340; e-mail jasman@panin.co.id; internet www.panin.co.id; f. 1971; cap. 1,606,543m., res 2,004,564m., dep. 15,085,545m. (Dec. 2004); Chair. ENRIQUE VALDEZ BERNARDO; Pres. H. ROSTIAN SJAMSUDIN; 180 brs, 1 overseas br.

PT Woori Bank Indonesia: Jakarta Stock Exchange Bldg, 16th Floor, Jalan Jenderal Sudirman, Kav. 52–53, Jakarta 12190; tel. (21) 5151919; fax (21) 5151477; e-mail wooridealingroom@yahoo .com; fmrly PT Hanvit Bank Indonesia; cap. 170,000m., res 34,000m., dep. 765,073m. (Dec. 2002); Pres. IN CHUL PARK.

Foreign Banks

ABN AMRO Bank NV (Netherlands): Jalan Ir H. Juanda 23–24, POB 2950, Jakarta 10029; tel. (21) 2312777; fax (21) 2313222; internet www.abnamro.co.id; Country Rep. DOUWE OPPEDIJK; 15 brs.

Bangkok Bank Public Company Ltd (Thailand): POB 4165, Jakarta 11041; tel. (21) 2311008; fax (21) 3853881; f. 1968; Gen. Man. PRASARN TUNTASOOD.

Bank of America NA (USA): Jakarta Stock Exchange Bldg Tower 1, 22nd Floor, Jalan Jenderal Sudirman, Kav. 52–53, Jakarta 12190; tel. (21) 5158000; fax (21) 5158088; e-mail rahul.goswamy@ bankofamerica.com; f. 1968; Man. Dir and Country Man. RAHUL GOSWAMY.

Bank of China (China): Jakarta.

Bank of Tokyo-Mitsubishi Ltd (Japan): Midplaza Bldg, 1st–3rd Floors, Jalan Jenderal Sudirman, Kav. 10–11, POB 2711, Jakarta 10227; tel. (21) 5706185; fax (21) 5731927; e-mail pip@botm.co.id; internet www.btmjkt.com; Gen. Man. HIDEYUKI ABE.

Citibank NA (USA): Citibank Tower, Jalan Jenderal Sudirman, Kav. 54–55, Jakarta 12910; tel. (21) 52962277; fax (21) 52969303; internet www.citibank.co.id; f. 1912; Vice-Pres JAMES F. HUNT, EDWIN GERUNGAN, ROBERT THORNTON.

Deutsche Bank, AG (Germany): POB 1135, Jakarta 10011; tel. (21) 3904792; fax (21) 335252; Gen. Man. HEINZ POEHLSEN.

Hongkong and Shanghai Banking Corpn Ltd (Hong Kong): POB 2307, Jakarta 10023; tel. (21) 5246222; fax (21) 5211103; internet www.hsbc.co.id; CEO P. C. L. HOLBERTON; 6 brs.

JP Morgan Chase Bank, NA (USA): Chase Plaza, 5th Floor, Jalan Jenderal Sudirman, Kav. 21, POB 311/JKT, Jakarta 12920; tel. (21) 5712213; fax (21) 5703690; Vice-Pres. and Sr Officer PETER NICE.

Standard Chartered Bank (United Kingdom): Wisma Standard Chartered Bank, Jalan Jenderal Sudirman, Kav. 33-A, Jakarta 10220; tel. (21) 2513333; fax (21) 5721234; internet www .standardchartered.com/id/index.html; Chief Exec. DAVID HAWKINS; 5 brs.

Banking Association

The Association of Indonesian National Private Commercial Banks (Perhimpunan Bank-Bank Umum Nasional Swasta—PERBANAS): Jalan Perbanas, Karet Kuningan, Setiabudi, Jakarta 12940; tel. (21) 5223038; fax (21) 5223037; e-mail secretariat@ perbanas.web.id; internet www.perbanas.web.id; f. 1952; 94 mems; Chair. GUNARNI SOEWORO; Sec.-Gen. TIMOTY E. MARNANDUS.

STOCK EXCHANGES

At the end of January 2000 278 companies were listed on the Jakarta Stock Exchange, and market capitalization was 410,520,769m. rupiah. At the end of August 2002 there were 287 companies listed on the Jakarta Stock Exchange.

Bursa Paralel: PT Bursa Paralel Indonesia, Gedung Bursa, Jalan Medan Merdeka Selatan 14, Jakarta; tel. (21) 3810963; fax (21) 3810989; f. 1987.

Jakarta Stock Exchange (JSX): PT Bursa Efek Jakarta, Jakarta Stock Exchange Bldg, 4th Floor, Jalan Jenderal Sudirman, Kav. 52–53, Jakarta 12190; tel. (21) 5150515; fax (21) 5150330; e-mail webmaster@jsx.co.id; internet www.jsx.co.id; PT Bursa Efek Jakarta, the managing firm of the JSX, was transferred to the private sector in April 1992; 197 securities houses constitute the members and the shareholders of the exchange, each company owning one share; Pres. Dir ERRY FIRMANSYAH.

Surabaya Stock Exchange: 5th Floor, Gedung Medan Pemuda, Jalan Pemuda 27–31, Surabaya 60271; tel. (31) 5340888; fax (31) 5342888; e-mail helpdesk@bes.co.id; internet www.bes.co.id; f. 1989; Chair. NATAKOESOEMAH.

Regulatory Authority

Badan Pengawas Pasar Modal (BAPEPAM) (Capital Market Supervisory Agency): Jalan Medan Merdeka Selatan 14, Jakarta 10110; tel. (21) 365509; fax (21) 361460; e-mail info@bapepam.go.id; internet www.bapepam.go.id; Chair. HERWIDAYATMO; Exec. Sec. PANDE PUTU RAKA.

INSURANCE

In August 1996 there were 163 insurance companies, comprising 98 non-life companies, 56 life companies, four reinsurance companies and five social insurance companies.

Insurance Supervisory Authority of Indonesia: Directorate of Financial Institutions, Ministry of Finance, Jalan Dr Wahidin, Jakarta 10710; tel. (21) 3451210; fax (21) 3849504; Dir H. FIRDAUS DJAELANI.

Selected Life Insurance Companies

PT Asuransi AIA Indonesia: Gedung Bank Panin Senayan, 7th and 8th Floors, Jalan Jenderal Sudirman, Senayan, Jakarta 10270; tel. (21) 5721388; fax (21) 5721389; e-mail hrd.aiai@aig.com; f. 1975; Pres. Dir HARRY HARMAIN DIAH.

PT Asuransi Allianz Life Indonesia: Gedung Summitmas II, 20th Floor, Jalan Jenderal Sudirman, Kav. 61–62, Jakarta 12190; tel. (21) 52998888; fax (21) 2526953; e-mail general@allianz.co.id; internet www.allianz.co.id; f. 1996; Pres. Dir Dr JENS REISCH.

Asuransi Jiwa Bersama Bumiputera 1912: Wisma Bumiputera, 17th–21st Floors, Jalan Jenderal Sudirman, Kav. 75, Jakarta 12910; tel. (21) 5703812; fax (21) 5712837; e-mail spw@bumiputera .com; internet www.bumiputera.com; Pres. Dir Dr H. Basri Hasanudin.

PT Asuransi Jiwa Central Asia Raya: Wisma Asia, 10th–11th Floors, Jalan S. Parman, Kav. 79, Slipi, Jakarta 11420; tel. (21) 5637901; fax (21) 5637902; e-mail service@car.co.id; internet www .car.co.id; Man. Dir Djonny Wiguna.

PT Asuransi Jiwa 'Panin Putra': Jalan Pintu Besar Selatan 52A, Jakarta 11110; tel. (21) 672586; fax (21) 676354; f. 1974; Pres. Dir Sujono Soepeno; Chair. Nugroho Tjokrowirono.

PT Asuransi Jiwasraya (Persero): Jalan H. Juanda 34, Jakarta 10120; tel. (21) 3845031; fax (21) 3862344; e-mail asuransi@ jiwasraya.co.id; internet www.jiwasraya.co.id; f. 1959; Pres. and CEO Herris B. Simandjuntak.

PT Asuransi Lippo Life: Menara Matahari Lippo Life, Lt. 7, Jalan Bulevar Palem Raya 7, Lippo Karawaci, Tangerang 15811; tel. (21) 5475433; fax (21) 5475401; f. 1983; life insurance, pensions, healthcare.

PT Asuransi Panin Life: Panin Bank Plaza, 5th Floor, Jalan Palmerah Utara 52, Jakarta 11480; tel. (21) 5484870; fax (21) 5484570; Pres. Nugroho Tjokrowirono; Dir Fadjar Gunawan.

Bumi Asih Jaya Life Insurance Co Ltd: Jalan Matraman Raya 165–167, Jakarta 13140; tel. (21) 2800700; fax (21) 8509669; e-mail baj@bajlife.com; internet www.bajlife.co.id; f. 1967; Chair. P. Sitompul; Pres. Virgo Hutagalung.

Koperasi Asuransi Indonesia: Jalan Iskandarsyah I/26, Jakarta; tel. (21) 7207879; fax (21) 7207451; Dir H. J. V. Sugiman.

Selected Non-Life Insurance Companies

PT Asuransi Bina Arta Tbk: Wisma Dharmala Sakti, 8th Floor, Jalan Jenderal Sudirman, Kav. 32, Jakarta 10220; tel. (21) 5708157; fax (21) 5708166; e-mail dharins@uninet.net.id; Pres. Suhanda Wiraatmadja; Vice-Pres. M. Mulyatno.

PT Asuransi Bintang Tbk: Jalan R. S. Fatmawati 32, Jakarta 12430; tel. (21) 7504872; fax (21) 7506197; e-mail bintang@ asuransibintang.com; internet www.asuransibintang.com; f. 1955; general insurance; Pres. Dir Ariyanti Suliyanto.

PT Asuransi Buana Independen: Jalan Pintu Besar Selatan 78, Jakarta 11110; tel. (21) 6904331; fax (21) 6263005; e-mail abipst99@ indosat.net.id; Exec. Vice-Pres. Susanty Purnama.

PT Asuransi Central Asia: Wisma Asia, 12th–15th Floors, Jalan Letjen S. Parman, Kav. 79, Slipi, Jakarta 11420; tel. (21) 5637933; fax (21) 5638029; e-mail cust-aca@aca.co.id; internet www.aca.co.id; Pres. Anthony Salim; Dir Teddy Hailamsah.

PT Asuransi Danamon: Gedung Danamon Asuransi, Jalan H. R. Rasuna Said, Kav. C10, Jakarta 12920; tel. (21) 516512; fax (21) 516832; Chair. Usman Admadjaja; Pres. Dir Otis Wuisan.

PT Asuransi Dayin Mitra: Jalan Raden Saleh Raya, Kav. 1B–1D, Jakarta 10430; tel. (21) 3153577; fax (21) 39129; e-mail nuning@ dayinmitra.co.id; internet www.dayinmitra.co.id; f. 1982; general insurance; Man. Dir Larsoen Haker.

PT Asuransi Indrapura: Jakarta; tel. (21) 5703729; fax (21) 5705000; f. 1954; Pres. Dir Robert Teguh.

PT Asuransi Jasa Indonesia: Jalan Letjenderal M. T. Haryono, Kav. 61, Jakarta 12780; tel. (21) 7994508; e-mail jasindo@jasindo.co .id; internet www.jasindo.co.id; Pres. Dr Ir Bambang Subianto; Dir Amir Imam Poero.

PT Asuransi Parolamas: Komplek Golden Plaza, Blok G 39–42, Jalan R. S. Farmawati 15, Jakarta 12420; tel. (21) 7508983; fax (21) 7506339; internet www.parolamas.co.id; Pres. Tjut Rukma; Dir Drs Syarifuddin Harahap.

PT Asuransi Ramayana: Jalan Kebon Sirih 49, Jakarta 10340; tel. (21) 31937148; fax (21) 31934825; f. 1965; Chair. R. G. Doeriat; Pres. Dir Dr A. Winoto Doeriat.

PT Asuransi Tri Pakarta: Jalan Paletehan I/18, Jakarta 12160; tel. (21) 711850; fax (21) 7394748; Pres. Drs M. Mainggolan; Dir Husni Rustam.

PT Asuransi Wahana Tata: Jalan H. R. Rasuna Said, Kav. C-4, Jakarta 12920; tel. (21) 5203145; fax (21) 5203149; e-mail aswata@ aswata.co.id; internet www.aswata.co.id; Chair. A. R. Ramly; Pres. Rudy Wanandi.

Berdikari Insurance Company: Jalan Merdeka Barat 1, Jakarta 10002; tel. (21) 3841339; fax (21) 3440586; e-mail ho@ berdikari-insurance.com; internet www.berdikari-insurance.com; Pres. Hotbonar Sinaga.

PT Lloyd Indonesia: Jalan Tiang Bendera 34-1, Jakarta 11230; tel. (21) 677195; Dir Johny Basuki.

PT Maskapai Asuransi Indonesia (MAI): Jalan Sultan Hasanuddin 53–54, Kebayoran Baru, Jakarta Selatan 12160; tel. (21) 7204250; fax (21) 7256980; e-mail ptmai@cbn.net.id; Pres. Dir J. Tri Wahono.

PT Maskapai Asuransi Jasa Tania: Gedung Agro Bank, Lt. 4, Jalan Teuku Cik Ditiro 14, Jakarta 10350; tel. (21) 3101912; fax (21) 323089; Pres. H. R. Sutedjio; Dir Drs H. Abellah.

PT Maskapai Asuransi Timur Jauh: Jalan Medan Merdeka Barat 1, Jakarta Pusat; tel. (21) 370266; f. 1954; Pres. Dir Bustanil Arifin; Dirs V. H. Kolondam, Soebakti Harsono.

PT Pan Union Insurance: Panin Bank Plaza, Lt. 6, Jalan Palmerah Utara 52, Jakarta 11480; tel. (21) 5480669; fax (21) 5484047; e-mail paninins@cbn.net.id; Chair. Chandra R. Gunawan; Pres. Nizarwan Harahap.

PT Perusahaan Maskapai Asuransi Murni: Jalan Roa Malaka Selatan 21–23, Jakarta Barat; tel. (21) 679968; f. 1953; Dirs Hasan Day, Hoed Ibrahim, R. Soegiatna Probopinilih.

PT Pool Asuransi Indonesia: Blok A–IV Utara, Jalan Muara Karang Raya 293, Jakarta 14450; tel. (21) 6621946; fax (21) 6678021; f. 1958; Pres. Bambang Gunawan Tanujaya; Dir Tandjung Susanto.

PT Tugu Pratama Indonesia: Wisma Tugu I, Jalan H. R. Rasuna Said, Kav. C8–9, Jakarta 12940; tel. (21) 52961777; fax (21) 52961555; e-mail tpi@tugu.com; internet www.tugu.com; f. 1981; general insurance; Chair. Ainun Na'im; Pres. Bahder Munir Sjamsoeddin.

Joint Ventures

PT Asuransi AIG Lippo Life: Matahari AIG Lippo Cyber Tower, 5th-7th Floors, Jalan Bulevar Palem Raya 7, Lippo Karawaci 1200, Tangerang 15811; tel. (21) 54218888; fax (21) 5475415; e-mail contact@aig-lippo.com; internet www.aig-lippo.com; jt venture between American International Group, Inc, and PT Asuransi Lippo Life; life insurance; Dep. Pres. Dir S. Budisuharto.

PT Asuransi AIU Indonesia: Gedung Bank Panin Senayan, 3rd Floor, Jalan Jenderal Sudirman, Jakarta 10270; tel. (21) 5720888; fax (21) 5703759; Pres. Dir Peter Meyer; Vice-Pres. Dir Swandi Kendy; Dir Gunawan Tjiu.

PT Asuransi Allianz Utama Indonesia: Gedung Summitmas II, 9th Floor, Jalan Jenderal Sudirman, Kav. 61–62, Jakarta Selatan 12190; tel. (21) 2522470; fax (21) 2523246; e-mail general@allianz.co .id; internet www.allianz.co.id; f. 1989; non-life insurance; Pres. Dir Klaus-Dieter Voeste.

PT Asuransi Jayasraya: Jalan M. H. Thamrin 9, Jakarta; tel. (21) 324207; Dirs Supartono, Sadao Suzuki.

PT Asuransi Jiwa EKA Life: Wisma EKA Jiwa, 9th Floor, Jalan Mangga Dua Raya, Jakarta 10730; tel. (21) 6257808; fax (21) 6257837; e-mail cs@ekalife.co.id; internet www.ekalife.co.id; Pres. Dir Henry C. Suryanaga.

PT Asuransi Jiwa John Hancock Indonesia: Plaza DM, 7th Floor, Jalan Jenderal Sudirman, Kav. 25, Jakarta 12920; tel. (21) 5228857; fax (21) 5229730; e-mail info@jhancock.co.id; internet www .jhancock.co.id; f. 1987; life insurance and pension schemes; CEO David W. Cottrell.

PT Asuransi Jiwa Manulife Indonesia: Jalan Pegangsaan Timur 1A, Jakarta 10320; tel. (21) 2303224; fax (21) 2303225; e-mail communication_id@manulife.com; internet www .manulife-indonesia.com; f. 1985; life insurance; Pres. Dir John Harrison.

PT Asuransi Mitsui Marine Indonesia: Menara Thamrin, 14th Floor, Jalan M. H. Thamrin, Kav. 3, Jakarta 10340; tel. (21) 2303432; fax (21) 2302930; internet www.mitsuimarine.co.id; Pres. Dir S. Aoshima; Vice-Pres. Putu Widnyana.

PT Asuransi Royal Indrapura: Jakarta Stock Exchange Bldg, 29th Floor, Jalan Jenderal Sudirman, Kav. 52–53, Jakarta 12190; tel. (21) 5151222; fax (21) 5151771; Pres. Dir Ir Mintarto Halim; Man. Dir Moray B. Martin.

Insurance Association

Asosiasi Asuransi Umum Indonesia (General Insurance Association of Indonesia): Jalan Majapahit 34, Blok V/29, Jakarta 10160; tel. (21) 3454387; fax (21) 354307; e-mail aaui@aaui.or.id; internet www.aaui.or.id; f. 1957 as Dewan Asuransi Indonesia (Insurance Council of Indonesia); name changed as above 2003; Chair. Frans Sahusilawane; Exec. Dir Adrian J. K.

Trade and Industry

GOVERNMENT AGENCIES

Badan Pelaksana Kegiatan Usaha Hulu Minyak dan Gas Bumi (BP Migas): Gedung Patra Jasa, Lantai 1,2,13,14,16,21,22, Jalan Gatot Subroto, Kav. 32–34, Jakarta Selatan; tel. (21) 52900245; fax (21) 52901323; e-mail helpdesk@bpmigas.com; internet www.bpmigas.com; f. 2002; regulates upstream petroleum and natural gas industry; Chair. Ir RACHMAT SUDIBJO.

Badan Pengatur Hilir Minyak dan Gas Bumi: Jakarta; f. 2002; regulates downstream petroleum and gas industry; Chair. TUBAGUS HARYONO.

Badan Pengembangan Industri Strategis (BPIS) (Agency for Strategic Industries): Gedung Arthaloka, 3rd Floor, Jalan Jenderal Sudirman 2, Jakarta 10220; tel. (21) 5705335; fax (21) 3292516; f. 1989; co-ordinates production of capital goods.

Badan Pengkajian dan Penerapan Teknologi (BPPT) (Agency for the Assessment and Application of Technology): Jalan M. H. Thamrin 8, Jakarta 10340; tel. (21) 3162222; e-mail pusyantis@bppt.go.id; internet www.bppt.go.id; Chair. M. HATTA RAJASA.

Badan Tenaga Nuklir Nasional (BATAN) (National Nuclear Energy Agency): Jalan Kuningan Barat, Mampang Prapatan, Jakarta 12710; tel. (21) 5251109; fax (21) 5251110; e-mail humas@batan.go.id; internet www.batan.go.id; Chair. Dr SOEDYARTOMO.

Badan Urusan Logistik (BULOG) (National Logistics Agency): Jalan Jenderal Gatot Subroto, Kav. 49, Jakarta 12950; tel. (21) 5252209; fax (21) 5266482; e-mail rotu03@bulog.go.id; internet www.bulog.go.id; Chair. WIDJANARKO PUSPOYO.

National Agency for Export Development (NAFED): Jalan Gajah Mada 8, Jakarta 10310; tel. (21) 3841082; fax (21) 6338360; e-mail nafed@nafed.go.id; internet www.nafed.go.id.

National Economic Council: Jakarta; f. 1999; 13-member council formed to advise the President on economic policy; Chair. EMIL SALIM; Sec.-Gen. Sri MULYANI INDRAWATI.

DEVELOPMENT ORGANIZATIONS

Badan Koordinasi Penanaman Modal (BKPM) (Investment Co-ordinating Board): Jalan Jenderal Gatot Subroto 3186, POB 3186, Jakarta 12190; tel. (21) 5252008; fax (21) 5254945; e-mail sysadm@bkpm.go.id; internet www.bkpm.go.id; f. 1976; Chair. THEO F. TOEMION.

Badan Perencanaan Pembangunan Nasional (Bappenas) (National Planning Development Board): Jalan Taman Suropati 2, Jakarta 10310; tel. (21) 336207; fax (21) 3145374; e-mail admin@bappenas.go.id; internet www.bappenas.go.id; formulates Indonesia's national economic development plans; Chair. Sri MULYANI INDRAWATI.

Commercial Advisory Foundation in Indonesia (CAFI): Jalan Probolinggo 5, Jakarta 10350; tel. (21) 3156013; fax (21) 3156014; f. 1958; information, economic regulations bulletin, consultancy and translation services; Chair. JOYCE SOSROHADIKOESOEMO; Man. Dir LEILA RIDWAN SOSROHADIKOESOEMO.

CHAMBER OF COMMERCE

Kamar Dagang dan Industri Indonesia (KADIN) (Indonesian Chamber of Commerce and Industry): Chandra Bldg, 3rd–5th Floors, Jalan M. H. Thamrin 20, Jakarta 10350; tel. (21) 324000; fax (21) 3150241; internet www.kadinnet.com; f. 1969; 27 regional offices throughout Indonesia; Chair. Ir ABURIZAL BAKRIE; Sec.-Gen. Ir IMAN SUCIPTO UMAR.

INDUSTRIAL AND TRADE ASSOCIATIONS

Association of Indonesian Automotive Industries (GAIKINDO): Jalan H. O. S. Cokroaminoto 6, Jakarta Pusat 10350; tel. (21) 3157178; fax (21) 3142100; e-mail gaikindo@cbn.net.id.

Association of Indonesian Beverage Industries (ASRIM): Jalan M. Ikhwan Mais 8, Jakarta Pusat; tel. (21) 3841222; fax (21) 3842294.

Association of Indonesian Coal Industries (ABBI): Perum Batu Bara Bldg, Jalan Supomo 10, Jakarta Selatan; tel. (21) 8295608.

Association of Indonesian Coffee Exporters (AICE): Jalan R. P. Soeroso 20, Jakarta 10330; tel. (21) 3106765; fax (21) 3144115; Chair. OESMAN SOEDARGO.

Association of Indonesian Heavy Equipment Industries (HINABI): c/o PT Traktor Nusantara, Jalan Pulogadung 32, Jakarta 13930; tel. (21) 4703932; fax (21) 4713940.

Association of State-Owned Companies: CTC Bldg, Jalan Kramat Raya 94–96, Jakarta; tel. (21) 346071; co-ordinates the activities of state-owned enterprises; Pres. ODANG.

Electric and Electronic Appliance Manufacturers' Association: Jalan Pangeran, Blok 20/A-1D, Jakarta; tel. (21) 6480059.

GINSI (Importers' Asscn of Indonesia): Oil Center Bldg, 1st Floor, Jalan M. H. Thamrin 55, Jakarta 10350; tel. (21) 39837395; fax (21) 39837394; f. 1956; 2,921 mems (1996); Chair. AMIRUDIN SAUD; Sec.-Gen. MUSTAFA KEMAL.

Indonesian Cement Association: Graha Purnayudha, Jalan Jenderal Sudirman, Jakarta; tel. (21) 5207603; fax (21) 5207188.

Indonesian Cocoa Association (AKI): Jalan Brawijaya VII/5, Kebayoran Baru, Jakarta 12160; tel. (21) 771721; fax (21) 7203487.

Indonesian Exporters' Federation: Menara Sudirman, 8th Floor, Jalan Jenderal Sudirman, Kav. 60, Jakarta 12190; tel. (21) 5226522; fax (21) 5203303; Chair. HAMID IBRAHIM GANIE.

Indonesian Footwear Association (APRISINDO): Gedung Adis Dimension Footwear, Jalan Tanah Abang III/18, Jakarta 10160; tel. (21) 3447575; fax (21) 3447572; e-mail aprisindo@vision.net.id; internet www.aprisindo.info; Pres. HARIJANTO; Sec.-Gen. YUDHI KOMARUDIN.

Indonesian Furniture Industry and Handicraft Association (ASMINDO): Jalan Pegambiran 5A, 3rd Floor, Rawamangun Jakarta 13220; tel. (21) 47864028; fax (21) 47864031; e-mail asmindo@indo.net.id; internet www.furniture-indonesia.com/asmindo; Chair. DJALAL KAMAL.

Indonesian Nutmeg Exporters' Association: c/o PT Berdirari (Persero) Trading Division, Jalan Yos Sudarso 1, Jakarta; tel. (21) 4301625; e-mail bnuina@indosat.net.id.

Indonesian Palm Oil Producers' Association: Jalan Pulo Mas IIID/1, Jakarta; tel. (21) 4892635; Chair. NUKMAN NASUTION.

Indonesian Precious Metals Association: Jalan Wahid Hasyim 45, Jakarta; tel. (21) 3841771.

Indonesian Pulp and Paper Association: Jalan Cimandiri 6, Jakarta 10330; tel. (21) 326084; fax (21) 3140168.

Indonesian Tea Association: Wisma 77, 20th Floor, Jalan S. Parman, Kav. 77, Jakarta 11410; tel. (21) 53660366; fax (21) 53660365; e-mail insyaf@hotmail.com; internet www.indotea.org; Chair. INSYAF MALIK.

Indonesian Textile Association (API): Panin Bank Centre, 3rd Floor, Jalan Jenderal Sudirman 1, Jakarta Pusat 10270; tel. (21) 7396094; fax (21) 7396341; f. 1974; Sec.-Gen. DANANG D. JOEDONAGORO.

Indonesian Tobacco Association: Jalan H. Agus Salim 85, Jakarta 10350; tel. (21) 3140627; fax (21) 325181; Pres. H. A. ISMAIL.

Masyarakat Perhutanan Indonesia (MPI) (Indonesian Forestry Community): Gedung Manggala Wanabakti, 9th Floor, Wing B/Blok IV, Jalan Jenderal Gatot Subroto, Jakarta Pusat 10270; tel. (21) 5733010; fax (21) 5732564; f. 1974; nine mems; Pres. M. HASAN.

National Board of Arbitration (BANI): Wahana Graha, 2nd Floor, Jalan Mampang Prapatan 2, Jakarta 12760; tel. (21) 7940542; fax (21) 7940543; e-mail bani-arb@indo.net.id; internet www.bani-arb.org; f. 1977; resolves company disputes; Chair. Prof. H. PRIYATNA ABDURRASYID.

Rubber Association of Indonesia (Gapkindo): Jalan Cideng Barat 62A, Jakarta; tel. (21) 3846813; fax (21) 3846811; e-mail karetind@indosat.net.id; Exec. Dir SUHARTO HONGGOKUSUMO.

Shippers' Council of Indonesia: Jalan Kramat Raya 4–6, Jakarta; Pres. R. S. PARTOKUSUMO.

UTILITIES

Electricity

PT Perusahaan Listrik Negara (Persero) (PLN): Jalan Trunojoyo, Blok M1/135, Kebayoran Baru, Jakarta Selatan 12160; tel. (21) 7261875; fax (21) 7204929; e-mail webmaster@pln.co.id; internet www.pln.co.id; state-owned electricity co; Pres. EDDIE WIDIONO.

Gas

PT Perusahaan Pertambangan Minyak dan Gas Bumi Negara (PERTAMINA): Jalan Medan Merdeka Timur 1A, Jakarta 10110; tel. (21) 3815111; fax (21) 3846865; e-mail mthakky@pertamina.com; internet www.pertamina.com; f. 1968; state-owned petroleum and natural gas mining enterprise; Pres. Dir and CEO WIDYA PURNAMA.

Perusahaan Gas Negara (PGN) (Public Gas Corporation): Jakarta; e-mail webmaster@pgn.co.id; internet www.pgn.co.id;

monopoly of domestic gas distribution; Pres. Dir W. M. P. SIMAND-JUNTAK.

Water

PDAM DKI Jakarta (PAM JAYA): Jalan Penjernihan 11, Pejom-pongan, Jakarta 10210; tel. (21) 5704250; fax (21) 5711796; f. 1977; responsible for the water supply systems of Jakarta; Pres. Dir Ir H. MUZAHIEM MOKHTAR.

PDAM Kodya Dati II Bandung: Jalan Badaksinga 10, Bandung 40132; tel. (22) 2509030; fax (22) 2508063; e-mail pdambdg@elga.net .id; f. 1974; responsible for the water supply and sewerage systems of Bandung; Pres. Dir Ir SOENITIYOSO HADI PRATIKTO.

PDAM Tirtanadi Medan: Jalan Sisingamangaraja 1, Medan 20212; tel. (61) 571666; fax (61) 572771; f. 1979; manages the water supply of Medan and nearby towns and cities; Man. Dir Ir KUMALA SIREGAR.

CO-OPERATIVES

In 1996 there were 48,391 primary and secondary co-operatives in Indonesia; membership of primary co-operatives was 27,006,000 in the same year.

Dewan Koperasi Indonesia (DEKOPIN) (Indonesian Co-oper-ative Council): Jakarta; internet www.dekopin.coop; Pres. Sri EDY SWASONO.

TRADE UNIONS

Serikat Buruh Sejahtera Indonesia (SBSI) (Indonesian Pros-perity Trade Union Central Board): Jakarta; f. 1998; application for official registration rejected in May 1998; 1,228,875 mems in 168 branches in 27 provinces throughout Indonesia; Gen. Chair. MUCHTAR PAKPAHAN; Gen. Sec. SUNARTY.

Federasi Serikat Pekerja Seluruh Indonesia (FSPSI) (Feder-ation of All Indonesian Trades Unions): Jalan Raya Pasar Minggu Km 17 No. 9, Jakarta 12740; tel. (21) 7974359; fax (21) 7974361; f. 1973; renamed 2001; sole officially recognized National Industrial Union; 5.273m. mems in June 2004; Gen. Chair. JACOB NUWA WEA; Gen. Sec. SYUKUR SARTO.

Transport

Directorate General of Land Transport and Inland Water-ways: Ministry of Transportation and Telecommunication, Jalan Medan Merdeka Barat 8, Jakarta 10110; tel. (21) 3502971; fax (21) 3503013; e-mail hubdat@hubdat.go.id; Dir-Gen. SOEJONO.

RAILWAYS

There are railways on Java, Madura and Sumatra, totalling 6,458 km in 1996, of which 125 km were electrified.

In 1995 a memorandum of understanding was signed by a con-sortium of European, Japanese and Indonesian companies for the construction of a 15-km Mass Rapid Transport (MRT) rail system in Jakarta, part of which would be underground. However, in 2004 construction had not yet begun, owing to the Government's inability to fund the project, which was expected to cost US $476m. to implement.

PT Kereta Api (Persero) (PERUMKA): Jalan Perintis Kermede-kaan 1, Bandung 40117; tel. (22) 4230031; fax (22) 4241370; e-mail info@kereta-api.com; internet www.kereta-api.com; six regional offices; transferred to the private sector in 1991; Chief Dir Drs ANWAR SUPRIADI.

ROADS

There is an adequate road network on Java, Sumatra, Sulawesi, Kalimantan, Bali and Madura, but on most of the other islands traffic is by jungle track or river boat. In 1997 the road network in Indonesia totalled 342,700 km; 27,357 km were main roads and 40,490 km were secondary roads. About 158,670 km of the network were paved.

In July 2003 the Government announced that it finally intended to implement a series of infrastructure projects postponed since the Asian financial crisis of 1997. These included the planned con-struction of a series of toll roads around the city of Surabaya, at a cost of Rp. 4,900,000m.

Directorate General of Highways: Ministry of Public Works, Jalan Pattimura 20, Kebayoran Baru, Jakarta Selatan 12110; tel. (21) 7262805; fax (21) 7260769; Dir-Gen. Ir SURYATIN SASTROMIJOYO.

SHIPPING

The Ministry of Communications controls 349 ports and harbours, of which the four main ports of Tanjung Priok (near Jakarta), Tanjung Perak (near Surabaya), Belawan (near Medan) and Makassar (for-merly Ujung Pandang, in South Sulawesi) have been designated gateway ports for nearly all international shipping to deal with Indonesia's exports and are supported by 15 collector ports. Of the ports and harbours, 127 are classified as capable of handling ocean-going shipping.

Directorate General of Sea Communications: Ministry of Com-munications, Jalan Medan Merdeka Barat 8, Jakarta 10110; tel. (21) 3456332; Dir-Gen. SOENTORO.

Indonesian National Ship Owners' Association (INSA): Jalan Gunung Sahari 79, Jakarta Pusat; tel. (21) 414908; fax (21) 416388; Pres. H. HARTOTO HADIKUSUMO.

Shipping Companies

Indonesian Oriental Lines, PT Perusahaan Pelayaran Nusantara: Jalan Raya Pelabuhan Nusantara, POB 2062, Jakarta 10001; tel. (21) 494344; Pres. Dir A. J. SINGH.

PT Jakarta Lloyd: Jalan Agus Salim 28, Jakarta Pusat 10340; tel. (21) 331301; fax (21) 333514; f. 1950; services to USA, Europe, Japan, Australia and the Middle East; Pres. Dir Drs M. MUNTAQA.

PT Karana Line: Jalan Kali Besar Timur 30, POB 1081, Jakarta 11110; tel. (21) 6907381; fax (21) 6908365; Pres. Dir BAMBANG EDIYANTO.

PT Pelayaran Bahtera Adhiguna (Persero): Jalan Kalibesar Timur 10–12, POB 4313, Jakarta 11043; tel. (21) 6912613; fax (21) 6901450; f. 1971; Pres. H. DJAJASUDHARMA.

PT Pelayaran Nasional Indonesia (PELNI): Jalan Gajah Mada 14, Jakarta; tel. (21) 6334342; fax (21) 63854130; internet www.pelni .co.id; state-owned; national shipping co; Pres. Dir ISNOOR HARYANTO.

PT Pelayaran Samudera Admiral Lines: POB 1476, Jakarta 10014; tel. (21) 4247908; fax (21) 4206267; e-mail admiral@uninet .net.id; Pres. Dir DJOKO SOETOPO.

PT (Persero) Pann Multi Finance: Pann Bldg, Jalan Cikini IV 11, POB 3377, Jakarta 10330; tel. (21) 322003; fax (21) 322980; state-controlled; Pres. Dir W. NAYOAN; Dir HAMID HADIJAYA.

PT Pertamina (Persero): Downstream Directorate for Shipping, Jalan Yos Sudarso 32–34, POB 14020, Tanjung Priok, Jakarta; tel. (21) 4301086; fax (21) 4301492; e-mail marketing@ pertaminashipping.com; internet www.pertaminashipping.com; f. 1959; state-owned; maritime business services; Pres. and Chair. Dr IBNU SUTOWO; Senior Vice-Pres. DEDENG WAHYU EDI.

PT Perusahaan Pelayaran Gesuri Lloyd: Gesuri Lloyd Bldg, Jalan Tiang Bendera IV 45, Jakarta 11230; tel. (21) 6904000; fax (21) 6904190; e-mail gesuri@indosat.net.id; internet www.gesuri.co .id; f. 1963; Pres. FRANKIE NURIMBA.

PT Perusahaan Pelayaran 'Nusa Tenggara': Kantor Pusat, Jalan Raya Pelabuhan Benoa, POB 3069, Denpasar 80222, Bali; tel. (361) 723608; fax (361) 722059; e-mail ntship@indo.net.id; Man. Dir KETUT DERESTHA.

PT Perusahaan Pelayaran Samudera 'Samudera Indonesia': Jalan Kali Besar Barat 43, POB 1244, Jakarta; tel. (21) 671093; fax (21) 674242; Chair. and Dir SOEDARPO SASTROSATOMO; Exec. Dir RANDY EFFENDI.

PT Perusahaan Pelayaran Samudera Trikora Lloyd: POB 4076, Jakarta 11001; tel. (21) 6907751; fax (21) 6907757; f. 1964; Pres. Dir GANESHA SOEGIHARTO; Man. Dir P. R. S. VAN HEEREN.

CIVIL AVIATION

The first stage of a new international airport, the Sukarno-Hatta Airport, at Cengkareng, near Jakarta, was opened in 1985, to complement Halim Perdanakusuma Airport, which was to handle charter and general flights only. A new terminal was opened at Sukarno-Hatta in 1991, vastly enlarging airport capacity. Con-struction of an international passenger terminal at the Frans Kai-sepo Airport, in Papua (then Irian Jaya), was completed in 1988. Other international airports include Ngurah Rai Airport at Den-pasar (Bali), Polonia Airport in Medan (North Sumatra), Juanda Airport, near Surabaya (East Java), Sam Ratulangi Airport in Manado (North Sulawesi) and Hasanuddin Airport, near Makassar (formerly Ujung Pandang, South Sulawesi). There are a total of 179 commercial airports, 61 of which are capable of accommodating wide-bodied aircraft. Domestic air services link the major cities, and international services are provided by the state airline, PT Garuda Indonesia, by its subsidiary, PT Merpati Nusantara Airlines, and by numerous foreign airlines. In December 1990 it was announced that private airlines equipped with jet-engined aircraft would be allowed to serve international routes.

In 2000 the Government announced a policy of liberalization for the airline industry. This led to a dramatic increase in the number of airlines operating in Indonesia; by January 2004 Indonesia had 27 domestic airlines (including four that were scheduled to begin oper-ations in 2004), compared with five in 2000.

Directorate-General of Civil Aviation: Jalan Medan Merdeka Barat 8, Jakarta 10110; tel. (21) 3505133; fax (21) 3505139; Dir-Gen. CUCUK SURYO SUPROJO.

Air Paradise International: Jalan Tangkuban Perahu 66, Kerobokan, Kuta Bali 80361; tel. (361) 730088; fax (361) 732332; e-mail flywith@airparadise.co.id; internet www.airparadise.co.id; f. 2002; international services; Man. Dir I. MADE WIRANATHA SITA.

Awair International: Graha Aktiva Bldg, Jalan H. R. Rasuna Said, Jakarta; tel. and fax (21) 5203598; e-mail contact@awairlines .com; internet www.awairlines.com; f. 2000; scheduled domestic passenger services from Jakarta; Pres. YASSIR ISMAIL.

Bayu Indonesia Air (BYU): Jalan Bikatamsu 29E, Jakarta; tel. (21) 4515588; fax (21) 4515777; f. 1975; international services; Man. Dir PERMADI WIRATANUNINGRAT.

PT Bouraq Indonesia Airlines (BOU): Jalan Angkasa 1–3, POB 2965, Kemayoran, Jakarta 10720; tel. (21) 6288815; fax (21) 6008729; e-mail info@bouraq.com; internet www.bouraq.com; f. 1970; private company; scheduled regional and domestic passenger and cargo services linking Jakarta with points in Java, Borneo, Sulawesi, Bali, Timor and Tawau (Malaysia); Pres. Dir DANNY SUMENDAP.

Carstensz Papua Airlines (CPA): Papua; f. 2002; domestic services.

Citilink: Jakarta; internet www.ga-citilink.com; f. 2001; subsidiary of PT Garuda Indonesia; provides shuttle services between domestic destinations.

Deraya Air Taxi (DRY): Terminal Bldg, 1st Floor, Rm 150/HT, Halim Perdanakusuma Airport, Jakarta 13610; tel. (21) 8093627; fax (21) 8095770; e-mail drytech@centrin.net.id; internet www .boedihardjogroup.com; scheduled and charter passenger and cargo services to domestic and regional destinations; Pres. Dir SITI RAHAYU SUMADI.

Dirgantara Air Service (DAS): POB 6154, Terminal Bldg, Halim Perdanakusuma Airport, Rm 231, Jakarta 13610; tel. (21) 8093372; fax (21) 8094348; charter services from Jakarta, Barjarmas and Pontianak to destinations in West Kalimantan; Pres. MAKKI PERDANAKUSUMA.

PT Garuda Indonesia: Garuda Indonesia Bldg, Jalan Merdeka Selatan 13, Jakarta 10110; tel. (21) 2311801; fax (21) 2311962; internet www.garuda.co.id; f. 1949; state airline; operates scheduled domestic, regional and international services to destinations in Europe, the USA, the Middle East, Australasia and the Far East; Pres. and CEO INDRA SETIAWAN.

Indonesia Air Transport (IAT) (IDA): Pondok Cabe Aerodrome, POB 2485, Jakarta; tel. (21) 7490213; fax (21) 7491287; charter passenger and cargo services to domestic, regional and international destinations; f. 1968; Man. Dir AZMAR MUALIM.

Indonesian Airlines: Jakarta; f. 1999; domestic services; Pres. RUDY SETYOPURNOMO.

Lion Mentari Airlines: Gedung Jaya, 7th Floor, Jalan M. H. Thamrin 12, Jakarta 10340; tel. (21) 331838; fax (21) 327808;

internet www.lionairlines.com; f. 1999; domestic and international services; Pres. Dir RUSDI KILANA.

PT Mandala Airlines: Jalan Tomang Raya, Kav. 33–37, Jakarta 11440; tel. (21) 5665434; fax (21) 5663788; e-mail widya@ mandalaair.com; internet www.mandalaair.com; f. 1969; privately-owned; scheduled regional and domestic passenger and cargo services; Pres. and Dir SUHADI.

PT Merpati Nusantara Airlines: Jalan Angkasa, Blok 15, Kav. 2–3, Jakarta 10720; tel. (21) 6546789; fax (21) 6540620; e-mail lt13@ indosat.net.id; internet www.merpati.co.id; f. 1962; subsidiary of PT Garuda Indonesia; scheduled for privatization in 2004; domestic and regional services to Australia and Malaysia; Pres. Dir HOTASI NABABAN.

Pelita Air Service: Jalan Abdul Muls 52–56A, Jakarta 10160; tel. (21) 2312030; fax (21) 2312216; internet www.pelita-air.co.id; f. 1970; domestic services; Pres. Dir SOERATMAN.

Sriwijaya Air: Jakarta; f. 2003; domestic services; Dir CHANDRA LIE.

PT Star Air: Jalan Gunung Sahari Raya 57 A-B, POB 4724, Jakarta Pusat 10610; tel. (21) 4222622; fax (21) 4249538; e-mail starair@cbn .net.id; internet www.starair-online.com; f. 2000; scheduled domestic passenger services; CEO ALE SUGIARTO.

Sumut Airlines: North Sumatra; f. 2002; domestic services.

Tourism

Indonesia's tourist industry is based mainly on the islands of Java, famous for its volcanic scenery and religious temples, and Bali, renowned for its scenery and Hindu-Buddhist temples and religious festivals. Lombok, Sumatra and Sulawesi are also increasingly popular. Domestic tourism within Indonesia has also increased significantly. Following the terrorist attack on Bali in October 2002 (see History) it was feared that the tourist industry would be significantly affected; in 2002 tourist arrivals declined to 5.0m., compared with 5.2m. in 2001. Tourist receipts totalled US $5,411m. in 2001. In 2003 tourist arrivals increased steadily, prompting hopes that the industry might have begun to recover by the end of the year. However, it was feared that the bombing of the Marriott Hotel in Jakarta in August would impact adversely upon this recovery. In early 2004 the Government introduced stringent visa requirements for many foreign nationals wishing to visit Indonesia; it was feared that the regulations would further discourage tourists from visiting the country.

Ministry of Culture and Tourism: Jalan Medan Merdeka Barat 17, Jakarta Pusat 10110; tel. (21) 3838000; fax (21) 3848245; e-mail pusdatin@budpar.go.id; internet www.budpar.go.id; f. 1957; Chair. I. GEDE ARDIKA.

Indonesia Tourism Promotion Board: Wisma Nugra Santana, 9th Floor, Jalan Jenderal Sudirman 7–8, Jakarta 10220; tel. (21) 5704879; fax (21) 5704855; e-mail itpb@cbn.net.id; internet www .goindo.com; private body; promotes national and international tourism; Chair. PONTJO SUTOWO; CEO GATOT SOEMARTONO.

IRAN

Introductory Survey

Location, Climate, Language, Religion, Flag, Capital

The Islamic Republic of Iran lies in western Asia, bordered by Azerbaijan and Turkmenistan to the north, by Turkey and Iraq to the west, by the Persian (Arabian) Gulf and the Gulf of Oman to the south, and by Pakistan and Afghanistan to the east. The climate is one of great extremes. Summer temperatures of more than 55°C (131°F) have been recorded, but in the winter the great altitude of much of the country results in temperatures of −18°C (0°F) and below. The principal language is Farsi (Persian), spoken by about 50% of the population. Turkic-speaking Azerbaijanis form about 27% of the population, and Kurds, Arabs, Balochis and Turkomans form less than 25%. The great majority of Persians and Azerbaijanis are Shi'ite Muslims, while the other ethnic groups are mainly Sunni Muslims. There are also small minorities of Christians (mainly Armenians), Jews and Zoroastrians. The Bahá'í faith, which originated in Iran, has been severely persecuted, being denied rights given to other recognized religious minorities. The national flag (proportions 4 by 7) comprises three unequal horizontal stripes, of green, white and red, with the emblem of the Islamic Republic of Iran (the stylized word Allah) centrally positioned in red, and the inscription 'Allaho Akbar' ('God is Great') written 11 times each in white Kufic script on the red and green stripes. The capital is Tehran.

Recent History

Iran, called Persia until 1935, was formerly a monarchy, ruled by a Shah (Emperor). In 1927 Reza Khan, a Cossack officer, seized power in a military coup, and was subsequently elected Shah, adopting the title Reza Shah Pahlavi. In 1941 British and Soviet forces occupied Iran, and the Shah (who favoured Nazi Germany) was forced to abdicate in favour of his son, Muhammad Reza Pahlavi. British and US forces left Iran in 1945, but Soviet forces remained in the north-west of the country (Azerbaijan province) until 1946. The United Kingdom retained considerable influence through the Anglo-Iranian Oil Co, which controlled much of Iran's extensive petroleum reserves. In March 1951, however, the Majlis (National Consultative Assembly) approved the nationalization of the petroleum industry, despite British and other Western opposition. The leading advocate of nationalization, Dr Muhammad Mussadeq, who became Prime Minister in May 1951, was deposed in August 1953 in a military *coup d'état*, engineered by the US and British intelligence services.

The Shah gradually increased his personal control of government following the coup, assuming dictatorial powers in 1963 with the so-called 'White Revolution'. Large estates were redistributed to small farmers, and women were granted the right to vote in elections, provoking opposition from landlords and the conservative Muslim clergy. In 1965 Prime Minister Hassan Ali Mansur was assassinated, reportedly by a follower of Ayatollah Ruhollah Khomeini, a fundamentalist Shi'ite Muslim leader strongly opposed to the Shah. (Khomeini had been deported in 1964 for his opposition activities, and was living in exile in Iraq.) Amir Abbas Hoveida held the office of Prime Minister until 1977.

Between 1965 and 1977 Iran enjoyed political stability and considerable economic growth, based on substantial petroleum revenues which funded a high level of expenditure on defence equipment and infrastructure projects. From late 1977, however, public opposition to the regime increased dramatically, largely in response to a declining economy and the repressive nature of the Shah's rule. By the end of 1978 anti-Government protests were widespread, involving both left-wing and liberal opponents of the Shah, as well as Islamist activists. The most effective opposition came from supporters of Ayatollah Khomeini, who was now based in France. The growing unrest forced the Shah to leave Iran in January 1979. Khomeini arrived in Tehran on 1 February and effectively took power 10 days later. A 15-member Islamic Revolutionary Council was formed to govern the country, in co-operation with a Provisional Government, and on 1 April Iran was declared an Islamic republic. Supreme authority was vested in the Wali Faqih, a religious leader (initially Khomeini) appointed by the Shi'ite clergy. Executive power was to be vested in a President, to which post Abolhasan Bani-Sadr was elected in January 1980. Elections to a 270-member Majlis (National—later Islamic—Consultative Assembly) took place in two rounds in March and May. The Islamic Republican Party (IRP), which was identified with Khomeini and traditionalist Muslims, won some 60 seats, but subsequently increased its support base.

In November 1979 Iranian students seized 63 hostages at the US embassy in Tehran. The original purpose of the siege was to force the USA (where the Shah was undergoing medical treatment) to return the former monarch to Iran to face trial. The Shah died in Egypt in July 1980, by which time Iran had made other demands, notably for a US undertaking not to interfere in its affairs. Intense diplomatic activity led to the release of the 52 remaining hostages in January 1981, but not before a failed rescue operation by the US military in April 1980 resulted in the deaths of eight US servicemen.

The hostage crisis had forced the resignation of the moderate Provisional Government, and during 1980 it became clear that a rift was developing between President Bani-Sadr and his modernist allies on the one hand, and the IRP and traditionalist elements on the other. In June 1981 clashes between supporters of the two groups escalated into sustained fighting between members of the Mujahidin-e-Khalq (an Islamist guerrilla group which supported Bani-Sadr) and troops of the Revolutionary Guard Corps. The Majlis voted to impeach the President, who was subsequently dismissed by Khomeini. Bani-Sadr fled to France, as did the leader of the Mujahidin, Massoud Rajavi. A presidential election in July resulted in victory for the Prime Minister, Muhammad Ali Rajani, who was himself replaced by Muhammad Javar Bahunar. Meanwhile, conflict between the Mujahidin-e-Khalq and government forces intensified. In August both the President and Prime Minister were killed in a bomb attack attributed to the Mujahidin. A further presidential election, held in October, was won by Hojatoleslam Ali Khamenei. Mir Hussein Moussavi was appointed Prime Minister.

The resignation or dismissal of five ministers, all 'bazaaris' (members of the merchant class), in August 1983 characterized opposition to the policies of nationalization and land reform advocated by technocrats in the Government. Moussavi's attempts to implement such economic reforms were continually obstructed by the predominantly 'conservative', clerical Majlis. Elections to the second Majlis in April and May 1984 resulted in a clear win for the IRP. The elections were boycotted by the sole opposition party to have a degree of official recognition, Nehzat-e Azadi-ye Iran (Liberation Movement of Iran), led by Dr Mehdi Bazargan (who had been Prime Minister of the Provisional Government from February to November 1979), in protest at the allegedly undemocratic conditions prevailing in Iran.

Three candidates, including the incumbent, contested the August 1985 presidential election. The Council of Guardians (responsible for the supervision of elections) had rejected almost 50 others, among them Bazargan, who opposed the continuation of the war with Iraq (see below). Khamenei was elected President for a second four-year term, with 85.7% of the votes cast. Despite some opposition in the Majlis, Hussein Moussavi was reconfirmed as Prime Minister in October.

For most of the 1980s Iran's domestic and foreign policy was dominated by the war with Iraq. In September 1980, ostensibly to assert a claim of sovereignty over the disputed Shatt al-Arab waterway, Iraqi forces invaded Iran along a 500-km front, apparently anticipating a rapid military victory. The Iranian military offered strong resistance, and began a counter-offensive in early 1982; by June Iraq had been forced to withdraw from Iranian territory, and Iranian troops subsequently entered Iraq. A conflict of attrition thus developed, characterized by mutual offensives and targeting of each other's petroleum reserves, installations and transhipment facilities. From 1984 Iraq began attacking tankers using Iran's Kharg Island oil terminal, in the Persian (Arabian) Gulf, and Iran retaliated by targeting Saudi Arabian and Kuwaiti tankers in the Gulf. Despite subsequent efforts by the UN to establish a basis for peace negotiations,

Iran's conditions for peace were the removal from power of the Iraqi President, Saddam Hussain, in conjunction with agreement by Iraq to pay war reparations.

The war had left Iran in virtual diplomatic isolation; however, in late 1986 it emerged that the USA, in contradiction to its active discouragement of arms sales to Iran by other countries, had begun secret negotiations with the country in 1985 and had made shipments of weapons, allegedly in exchange for Iranian assistance in securing the release of US hostages held by Shi'ite groups in Lebanon, and an Iranian undertaking to relinquish involvement in international terrorism. Meanwhile, Iran had begun to attack Kuwaiti shipping, and neutral vessels using Kuwait, in retaliation for Kuwait's support for Iraq. In mid-1987 the USA agreed to re-register 11 Kuwaiti tankers under its own flag, thus entitling them to US naval protection. The United Kingdom, France, the Netherlands, Belgium and Italy subsequently dispatched minesweepers to the Gulf region.

In April 1988 Iraq recaptured the Faw peninsula (which Iran had taken in 1986), forcing the Iranian military to withdraw across the Shatt al-Arab. In June Iraq retook Majnoun Island and the surrounding area (which had been captured by Iran in 1984). In July an Iran Air passenger flight, allegedly mistaken for an attacking fighter jet, was shot down by a US aircraft carrier in the Strait of Hormuz; all 290 passengers and crew were killed. In that month Iraqi troops crossed into Iranian territory for the first time since 1986, and the last Iranian troops on Iraqi territory were dislodged. On 18 July 1988 Iran unexpectedly announced its unconditional acceptance of UN Security Council Resolution 598, adopted one year earlier. This urged an immediate cease-fire, the withdrawal of military forces to international boundaries, and the co-operation of Iran and Iraq in mediation efforts to achieve a peace settlement. More than 1m. people were estimated to have died in the eight-year conflict. A cease-fire came into effect on 20 August, and UN-sponsored peace negotiations began shortly afterwards in Geneva, Switzerland. In the same month a UN Iran-Iraq Military Observer Group (UNIIMOG) was deployed in the region. However, the negotiations soon became deadlocked in disputes regarding the sovereignty of the Shatt al-Arab, the exchange of prisoners of war, and the withdrawal of armed forces to within international boundaries. Hopes of a comprehensive peace settlement were raised by a meeting of the Iranian and Iraqi Ministers of Foreign Affairs in Geneva in July 1990, but were swiftly overshadowed by Iraq's invasion of Kuwait at the beginning of August. Saddam Hussain sought an immediate, formal peace with Iran, accepting all the claims that Iran had pursued since the declaration of a cease-fire (including the reinstatement of the Algiers Agreement of 1975, dividing the Shatt al-Arab waterway), and Iraq immediately began to redeploy troops from its border with Iran to Kuwait. Prisoner exchanges took place, and in September 1990 Iran and Iraq restored diplomatic relations. In February 1991 the withdrawal of all armed forces to internationally recognized boundaries was confirmed by UNIIMOG, whose mandate was terminated shortly afterwards.

Iran denounced Iraq's invasion of Kuwait, and observed the economic sanctions imposed by the UN on Iraq. However, it was unequivocal in its condemnation of the deployment of the US-led multinational force in the Gulf region. Relations between Iran and Iraq deteriorated after the liberation of Kuwait in February 1991. Iran protested strongly against the Baathist regime's suppression of the Shi'a-led rebellion in southern and central Iraq, and the accompanying destruction of Shi'a shrines, and renewed its demand for the resignation of Saddam Hussain. Iraq, in turn, accused Iran of supporting the rebellion. Thus, there was little further progress in implementing the terms of Resolution 598 until late 1993, when high-level bilateral talks recommenced on the exchange of remaining prisoners of war. (See below for further details of Iran's relations with Iraq.)

Elections to the Majlis in April and May 1988 apparently provided a stimulus to 'reformist' elements in the Government (identified with Hashemi Rafsanjani, since 1980 the Speaker of the Majlis, and Prime Minister Moussavi) by producing an assembly strongly representative of their views. (The elections were the Islamic Republic's first not to be contested by the IRP, which had been dissolved in 1987.) In June 1988 Rafsanjani was re-elected as Speaker and Moussavi was overwhelmingly endorsed as Prime Minister. In February 1989, however, Ayatollah Khomeini referred explicitly to a division in the Iranian leadership between 'reformers' (who sought a degree of Western participation in Iran's post-war reconstruction) and 'conservatives' (who opposed such involvement), and declared that he

would never permit the 'reformers' to prevail. His intervention was reportedly prompted by Rafsanjani's decision to contest the presidential election scheduled for mid-1989. A number of prominent 'reformers', among them Ayatollah Ali Hossein Montazeri (who had been designated as successor to Khomeini by the Council of Experts in 1985), subsequently resigned from the Iranian leadership.

Ayatollah Khomeini died on 3 June 1989. In an emergency session on 4 June the Council of Experts elected President Khamenei to succeed Khomeini as Iran's spiritual leader (Wali Faqih). The presidential election, scheduled for mid-August, was brought forward to 28 July, to be held simultaneously with a referendum on proposed amendments to the Constitution. Both 'conservatives' and 'reformers' within the leadership apparently united in support of Rafsanjani's candidacy for the presidency, and Rafsanjani (opposed only by a 'token' candidate) secured an overwhelming victory, with 95.9% of the votes cast. A similar proportion of voters approved the constitutional amendments, the most important of which was the abolition of the post of Prime Minister (and a consequent increase in power for the President).

President Rafsanjani appointed a Government balancing 'conservatives', 'reformers' and technocrats, and its endorsement by the Majlis, in August 1989, was viewed as a mandate for Rafsanjani to conduct a more conciliatory policy towards the West, despite the opposition of certain 'conservative' elements. Large-scale protests against food shortages and high prices in early 1990 demonstrated the urgent need for economic reform. In October, with the co-operation of Ayatollah Khamenei, Rafsanjani was able to prevent the election of many powerful 'conservatives' to the Council of Experts. An estimated 70% of deputies elected to the fourth Majlis in April and May 1992 were, broadly speaking, pro-Rafsanjani. However, economic reform was lowering the living standards of the traditional constituency of the Islamic regime, the urban lower classes, leading to serious rioting in several cities. The extent to which President Rafsanjani had lost popular support became clear when he stood for re-election in June 1993. Competing against three ostensibly 'token' candidates, Rafsanjani received 63.2% of the votes from a low electoral turn-out of 56%. In May 1994 the Government indicated that it would proceed more cautiously with a plan to reduce economic subsidies applied to basic commodities, and in November, after almost a year of debate, its Second Five-Year Development Plan was approved by the Majlis. Meanwhile, in August 1995 it was reported that political parties, associations and groups were free to conduct political activities in Iran on condition that they honoured the country's Constitution, although Nehzat-e Azadi was subsequently refused formal registration as a political party.

Elections to the fifth Majlis in March and April 1996 provided an important measure of the shifting balance of power between 'reformers', or 'liberals', and 'conservatives' in Iranian politics. The first round of voting produced results in some 140 of the total 270 seats; turn-out by voters was put at about 77%. Candidates of the Servants of Iran's Construction, a new pro-Rafsanjani faction, were reported to have won some 70% of the seats. However, the 'conservative' Society of Combatant Clergy, with the unofficial patronage of Ayatollah Khamenei, claimed that its candidates had achieved an equally conclusive victory. After the second round of voting, unofficial sources suggested that the Society of Combatant Clergy would command the loyalty of 110–120 deputies in the new Majlis, and the Servants of Iran's Construction that of 90–100 deputies.

In March 1997 Rafsanjani was appointed Chairman of the Council to Determine the Expediency of the Islamic Order (which arbitrates in disputes between the Majlis and the Council of Guardians) for a further five-year term, indicating that he would continue to play an influential role in political life upon the imminent expiry of his presidential mandate. (Rafsanjani was reappointed as head of the Expediency Council in March 2002.) In early May the Council of Guardians approved four candidatures for that month's presidential election, rejecting 234. It had been widely predicted that Ali Akbar Nateq Nouri, the Majlis Speaker favoured by the Society of Combatant Clergy, would secure an easy victory, but Sayed Muhammad Khatami (a presidential adviser and former Minister of Culture and Islamic Guidance) emerged as a strong contender just prior to the election. Regarded as a 'liberal', Khatami—supported by the Servants of Iran's Construction as well as by intellectuals, professionals, women's and youth groups—took some 69.1% of the total votes cast, ahead of Nateq Nouri, with 24.9%. The rate of participation by voters was more than 88%. (Nateq Nouri was re-elected Speaker of the Majlis in June.)

Taking office in August 1997, President Khatami emphasized his commitment to fostering sustained and balanced growth in the political, economic, cultural and educational spheres, as well as freedom of and respect for the individual and rights of the nation, in the context of the rule of law. In foreign affairs, the President undertook to promote the principle of mutual respect, but pledged that Iran would stand up to any power seeking to subjugate Iranian sovereignty. Notable among the 'moderate' appointees in Khatami's first Council of Ministers were Ata'ollah Mohajerani (a former Vice-President) as Minister of Culture and Islamic Guidance, and Abdollah Nuri as Minister of the Interior (a post he had previously held in 1989–93). Dr Massoumeh Ebtekar, as Vice-President and Head of the Organization for the Protection of the Environment, was the first woman to be appointed to such a senior government post since the Islamic Revolution. In November Khatami appointed a new Committee for Ensuring and Supervising the Implementation of the Constitution.

In the months following his election, President Khatami appeared conciliatory towards the West, and also urged toleration of dissent in Islamic societies among groups who remained 'within the framework of law and order'. Khamenei, meanwhile, continued to denounce the West's military and cultural ambitions, particularly those of the USA and Israel. Western commentators interpreted the divergent messages of Iran's political and spiritual leaders as indicative of conflict between the country's 'moderate' and 'conservative' factions. Within Iran, however, such a rift was denied, and Khamenei denounced reports of tensions within the regime as Western propaganda. Nevertheless, the cases of two leading politicians seemed to illustrate this apparent divergence between the 'moderate' and 'conservative' factions. In April 1998 Gholamhossein Karbaschi, the mayor of Tehran and a popular 'moderate', was arrested on charges of corruption. Karbaschi's detention led to clashes between 'moderate' and 'conservative' students during a rally by his supporters at the University of Tehran, resulting in about 100 arrests. In May the Ministry of the Interior authorized the registration of the Servants of Iran's Construction as a political party (styled the Servants of Construction Party), with Karbaschi as its Secretary-General. However, following a televised trial, Karbaschi was sentenced in July to five years' imprisonment and fined IR 1,000m., having been convicted of embezzlement, squandering state property and mismanagement (but acquitted of bribery charges). The custodial sentence was reduced on appeal to two years, and although Karbaschi began his prison term in May 1999, he eventually received a presidential pardon and was released in January 2000 (shortly before the legislative elections). Meanwhile, in June 1998 the Majlis voted to dismiss Abdollah Nuri as Minister of the Interior, a group of 'conservative' deputies having initiated impeachment on the grounds that he had made provocative statements and was a supporter of Karbaschi. They further maintained that Nuri had permitted dissident rallies and had also failed to counter unrest involving supporters of Ayatollah Montazeri in late 1997. Khatami appointed Abdolvahed Musavi-Lari (also regarded as a relative 'moderate') to the Ministry of the Interior, and later named Nuri as Vice-President in charge of Development and Social Affairs.

During 1998 the Khatami administration moved to formalize its support base, primarily through the registration or establishment of 'reformist' parties such as the Servants of Construction, the Islamic Iran Solidarity Party and the Islamic Iran Participation Front (which counted Vice-President Massoumeh Ebtekar among its leaders). However, at elections to the Council of Experts in October, 'conservatives' retained overwhelming control of the assembly, with an estimated 60% of the 86 seats being won by candidates of the 'radical' right wing; candidates of a 'centrist' grouping apparently associated with ex-President Rafsanjani took about 10% of the seats. Khatami's Government suffered a further setback in February 1999 with the resignation of Qorbanali Dorri Najafabadi, the Minister of Information, after it was admitted that agents of his ministry had (allegedly without his knowledge) been responsible for the murders of several intellectuals and dissident writers (among them Dariush Foruhar, leader of the unauthorized but officially tolerated Iranian People's Party) in late 1998. His successor, Ali Yunesi, had led an investigative commission into the murders.

Iran's first local government elections since the Islamic Revolution took place in February 1999, when some 60% of the electorate voted to elect representatives in 200,000 council seats. The elections resulted in considerable success for 'reformist' candidates, notably in Tehran, Shiraz and Esfahan, while 'conservatives' secured control of councils in their traditional strongholds of Qom and Mashad. Marked successes were recorded by female candidates, who won some 300 seats. In subsequent weeks 'conservative' elements challenged the election of many 'reformist' councillors: among those whose victories were overturned was former Minister of the Interior Abdollah Nuri. Morteza Alviri, an adviser to Khatami, was chosen as the mayor of Tehran in June, following a campaign of obstruction by opponents of the 'reformists'. In April, meanwhile, the Mujahidin-e-Khalq claimed responsibility for the assassination, in Tehran, of the deputy chief of staff of the armed forces, Lt-Gen. Ali Sayyad Shirazi. At the same time Mohsen Kadivar, a prominent 'reformist' cleric, was sentenced to 18 months' imprisonment by the Special Clerical Court, having been found guilty of disseminating false information about the Islamic regime.

The issue of press censorship had, meanwhile, increasingly become a focus of the political rivalries between 'conservatives' and 'reformists'. During 1998 several prominent journals had been closed, and their journalists prosecuted, and Ayatollah Khamenei had personally sought action against publications that he perceived as abusing freedom of speech to weaken Islamic beliefs. Legislation adopted by the Majlis in June 1999 further curbed the activities of 'liberal' publications. In early July the closure of *Salam*, a 'reformist' newspaper with close links to President Khatami, triggered a small demonstration by students at the University of Tehran, which was dispersed with considerable violence by police. This action, in conjuction with a raid on student dormitories by security forces, aided by militant vigilantes of the Ansar-e Hezbollah (in which at least one student was killed), set off five days of rioting in Tehran and other cities, resulting in some 1,400 arrests. Such was the violence with which the police had suppressed the student demonstrations that the Supreme Council for National Security (led by Khatami) was moved to announce the dismissal of two senior police officials; the Chief of Police, Brig.-Gen. Heyedat Loftian, whose removal from office had been sought by the protesters, was reprimanded. Within a year, however, both Lotfian and the Tehran chief of police had been dismissed, while as many as 100 police-officers had been arrested for their role in the campus raid. In July 2000 the former Tehran chief of police and 17 co-defendants were acquitted on charges arising from the police invasion of student dormitories in July 1999, but two police-officers received custodial sentences, having been convicted on relatively minor charges. Of the student demonstrators tried for alleged crimes relating to the unrest, four suspected leaders had their initial death sentences commuted to 15 years' imprisonment in April 2000, 45 were given custodial terms, and another 20 were acquitted.

Meanwhile, in early August 1999 the ban on *Salam* was extended to five years, and the journal's publisher (who had in late July been convicted on charges including defamation and publication of a classified document) was given a suspended 42-month prison sentence, and also fined and banned from publishing for three years. Also in August Muhammad Yazdi was succeeded, upon retirement, as Head of the Judiciary by Ayatollah Mahmoud Hashemi Shahrudi. Yazdi was immediately appointed to the influential Council of Guardians. Abdollah Nuri was brought before the Special Clerical Court in October, accused in his capacity as editor of the 'liberal' *Khordad* daily of insulting Islamic sanctities, publishing reports contrary to religious fundamentals, and refuting the values of Ayatollah Khomeini. Many observers regarded the charges against Nuri as a clear attempt to prevent his standing in the forthcoming elections to the Majlis, where, if elected, he was likely to be a strong contender for the post of Speaker. In November Nuri was convicted on 15 charges and sentenced to five years' imprisonment; he was also fined IR 15m., and the closure of *Khordad* was ordered. An appeal lodged with the Supreme Court was rejected in January 2000, on the grounds that the court had no constitutional authority to overturn a verdict of the Special Clerical Court. However, it was reported in November 2002 that Nuri had been pardoned by Ayatollah Khamenei following the sudden death of his brother, Ali Reza Nuri, a 'reformist' deputy who had achieved success in the 2000 general election (see below).

The process of scrutinizing candidates by the Council of Guardians, in preparation for elections to the Majlis scheduled for February 2000, resulted in the disqualification of many known 'reformist' candidates, on the grounds principally of disloyalty to Islam, to Iran's Constitution or to its spiritual leader. ('Conservative' deputies had in late 1999 introduced legislation giving the Council extensive powers to vet election candidates.) Nevertheless, while there were indications, as lesser-known 'reformist' candidates were approved by the Guardians, that the sixth Majlis might include sufficient numbers of 'liberals' and 'moderates' to present the first real challenge to the 'conservative' majority, the extent of the success achieved by candidates of the Islamic Iran Participation Front and the Servants of Construction was not widely predicted. An estimated 80% of Iran's registered electorate participated in the poll on 18 February 2000. Among those who secured notable victories were Muhammad Reza Khatami (brother of the President and head of the Participation Front's political bureau), Jamileh Kadivar (the wife of Ata'ollah Mohajerani and sister of dissident cleric Mohsen Kadivar) and Ali Reza Nuri. 'Conservative' candidates, meanwhile, were overwhelmingly defeated in Mashad, Esfahan, Shiraz and Tabriz. There was a marked increase in the proportion of Majlis seats won by women, while the number of clerics in the new assembly declined. The Council of Guardians ordered the recount of almost one-third of the votes cast in Tehran, following allegations of irregularities; however, Ayatollah Khamenei intervened to prevent a complete recount of ballots for all 30 of the capital's seats. Principal among those whose election was initially in doubt was former President Rafsanjani; however, Rafsanjani resigned his Tehran seat in late May, thereby relinquishing his ambition to become the new Speaker of the Majlis. Meanwhile, a second round of voting, for 66 undecided seats, proceeded on 5 May. At the end of May the incoming Majlis elected Mahdi Karrubi, the candidate of the Servants of Construction, as Speaker, a post which he had previously held in 1989–92.

The outcome of the first round of legislative voting appeared to exacerbate the struggle for political dominance between 'conservative' and 'reformist' elements. For its part, the judiciary pursued its actions against the 'reformist' press: a new press law, endorsed by the outgoing, 'conservative'-controlled Majlis, made criticism of the Constitution illegal and increased judicial powers to close newspapers. In March 2000 Sayed Hajjarian, a prominent 'reformer', presidential adviser and manager of the daily *Sobh Emruz*, was seriously wounded in a gun attack which some claimed had been perpetrated by forces linked to the intelligence service. In May five men were found guilty of having attempted the assassination and sentenced to terms of imprisonment ranging from three to 15 years; three others were acquitted. By mid-2000 it was estimated that 'reformist' or 'liberal' deputies held some 200 seats in the new Majlis, with the remaining 90 occupied by 'conservatives'. (By-elections were to be held in mid-2001—concurrently with the scheduled presidential election—for 18 seats where the results of earlier voting had been annulled.) However, while 'reformist' deputies acted swiftly to draft legislation to replace the restrictive press law, as well as proposals to curb the powers of the Council of Guardians, Muhammad Reza Khatami, who was elected in June 2000 to the position of First Deputy Speaker of the Majlis, indicated that change would proceed at a moderate pace. At the end of July the Islamic Iran Participation Front elected Muhammad Reza Khatami as its Secretary-General.

In August 2000 Ayatollah Khamenei issued a decree instructing the new Majlis not to debate proposed amendments to the press law (which would make it more difficult for the judiciary to imprison journalists), on the grounds that such reforms would endanger state security and religious faith. This intervention appeared to sanction a more vigorous campaign against the 'liberal' interests in subsequent months. At the end of August a police-officer was killed, and about 100 people were injured, in four days of violent clashes between 'pro-reform' students and Ansar-e Hezbollah militants in the western town of Khorramabad. The confrontations occurred as two 'reformists', including the dissident cleric Mohsen Kadivar, were prevented by the militants from addressing an annual student congress. (Kadivar had been released from prison in July, although he had been informed of the possibility of indictment on further, as yet unknown, political charges.) In November the Council of Guardians rejected for a second time the proposed amendments to the press law, which were thus submitted for jurisdiction by the Council to Determine the Expediency of the Islamic Order. About 30 'pro-reform' publications had reportedly been closed down by the authorities since April, some of which had subsequently reopened under new names. Meanwhile, in September Khamenei dismissed the uncompromising chief of

security police, Brig.-Gen. Muhammad Reza Naqdi, after a number of officers under his command were convicted of torture. In December Khatami accepted the resignation of the Minister of Culture and Islamic Guidance, Ata'ollah Mohajerani, and redesignated him as Chairman of the Organization for the Dialogue of Civilizations.

In November 2000 the trial opened in Tehran of a group of prominent 'reformists', accused of 'acting against national security and propagandizing against the regime' through their attendance at a conference on Iranian political reform, held in Berlin, Germany, in April. The severity of the sentences, pronounced in January 2001, against seven of the defendants, who were given custodial terms of between four and 10 years, was denounced by 'reformist' politicians within Iran. The renowned investigative journalist Akbar Ganji received the maximum prison term, followed by five years' internal exile, having been found guilty of harming national security, propagandizing against the regime, possessing secret documents and committing offences against senior officials. In July an appeal found Ganji guilty of having threatened national security, and he was given a six-year custodial sentence. Appeals had been lodged by all those convicted, resulting in a dramatic reduction in the sentences of five of the prisoners by a Tehran court of appeal in December. Meanwhile, in October 2001 it was reported that a dissident cleric, Hassan Yousefi Eshkevari, had been sentenced to seven years' imprisonment resulting from his participation in the Berlin conference; however, he was released in February 2005. A focus of Ganji's investigations in recent months had been the deaths of dissident intellectuals in late 1998 (see above), which he claimed involved senior 'conservatives', but which the authorities maintained had been instigated by 'rogue' agents of the Ministry of Information. The trial of 18 people, including senior intelligence officers, accused of involvement in the murders began, in camera, before a military court in Tehran in late December 2000. (The court had recently announced that former Minister of Information Najafabadi had no case to answer.) At the end of January 2001 three intelligence agents were condemned to death, having been convicted of perpetrating the killings; five received life sentences, and seven others custodial terms of up to 10 years (the other defendants were acquitted). However, after a retrial was ordered by the Supreme Court, in late January 2003 at least two of the agents had their death sentences commuted to terms of life imprisonment; of those given life sentences, two now received prison terms of 10 years, while seven of the agents were given gaol terms of between two and 10 years. The remaining agents were to have their cases reviewed.

Meanwhile, in January 2001 the trial began of Mustafa Tajzadeh, the 'reformist' Deputy Minister of the Interior whom Khatami had chosen to monitor the forthcoming presidential election; Tajzadeh was accused of vote-rigging in the 2000 Majlis elections and of incitement to violence in Khorramabad in August of that year. More than 150 Majlis deputies signed a letter of protest accusing the judiciary of harassing political and social activists, and insisting that the Majlis must be permitted to exercise its rights of supervision and investigation. In March 2001 Tajzadeh was convicted of involvement in electoral fraud and given a one-year prison sentence (although this was revoked in July); he was banned from supervising elections for six years and from holding a government post for 39 months. In late March and early April 2001 police detained more than 40 leading 'moderates', including relatives and close associates of Mehdi Bazargan—the founder of Nehzat-e Azadi—as well as members of the movement, on charges of conspiring to overthrow the Islamic regime; many deputies condemned the action as illegal, and President Khatami publicly criticized the arrests.

As had been widely predicted, on 8 June 2001 Khatami was re-elected as President, winning some 76.9% of the total votes cast, compared to 15.6% for his closest rival, Ahmed Tavakkoli, a former Minister of Labour and Social Affairs. (The Council of Guardians had endorsed the candidatures of 10 people, several of whom were independent 'conservatives'.) Khatami became the first Iranian President to win a greater number of votes for his second term than for his first, although the rate of participation by voters (at around 67%) was considerably lower than the 88% recorded in 1997. Khatami's victory was seen as a public endorsement of his reform programme, and it appeared initially that he might be assisted in his programme of political and economic reforms by an apparent widening of the divisions between moderate 'conservatives' and their more 'hardline' colleagues. Nevertheless, it soon became apparent that the 'ultra-conservatives' were unwilling to cede control of the Council of Guardians to 'reformist' supporters of Khatami. On 5 August Khatami's scheduled inauguration was postponed after the 'reformist' Majlis refused to approve two of the judiciary's 'conservative' nominees to the Council of Guardians. Ayatollah Khamenei requested, to the strenuous 'reformist' opposition, that the dispute be resolved by the 'conservative'-dominated Council to Determine the Expediency of the Islamic Order. Two days later, however, the Majlis finally endorsed the two candidates, following a ruling that candidates did not require the support of a majority of deputies in order to be elected to the Council of Guardians. Khatami was duly sworn in for a second presidential term on 8 August. In mid-August he presented his 20-member Council of Ministers to the Majlis, which approved the list later in the month. The composition of the new Government was criticized both by 'conservatives' for being too liberal and by 'reformists' for not being sufficiently bold.

The judiciary's campaign against 'pro-reform' activists intensified following Khatami's re-election, including mass arrests, public floggings and even public executions, ordered ostensibly to reduce crime and encourage greater morality. In September 2001 Hossein Loqmanian, a 'reformist' deputy in the Majlis, lost his appeal against a custodial sentence imposed in October 2000 after Loqmanian had condemned in a parliamentary speech the closure by the press court of several 'pro-reform' publications. Sentenced to 10 months' custody, he became the first serving member of the Majlis to be imprisoned since 1979 (under the Constitution deputies are granted parliamentary immunity); meanwhile, four other 'reformist' deputies also appealed against similar sentences, and several others faced charges for speeches they had made to the Majlis. Loqmanian's imprisonment in December 2001 provoked strong protests from his constituents in the western city of Hamedan and, in January 2002, a brief boycott of the Majlis by 'liberal' deputies in a protest led by the Speaker, Mahdi Karrubi. The parliamentary boycott apparently resulted in a rare victory for the 'pro-reform' lobby as Loqmanian was swiftly pardoned by Ayatollah Khamenei and duly released.

In November 2001 trial proceedings, held in camera, began of more than 30 members of the Nehzat-e Azadi movement who had been arrested earlier in the year on charges including acting against national security and plotting to overthrow the Islamic regime. Among the defendants—in what was reported to be the largest political trial in Iran since 1979—were two former ministers and a former mayor of Tehran. Custodial sentences of up to 10 years were handed down to 33 of the activists by the Revolutionary Court in July 2002, and Nehzat-e Azadi was formally banned. Meanwhile, in late November 2001 the Council to Determine the Expediency of the Islamic Order rejected a bill to amend the electoral law that proposed a reduction in the power of the Council of Guardians to vet and disqualify electoral candidates. The new legislation had been proposed by 'reformist' deputies after the Council rejected about 60 of their candidates in the approach to by-elections due to be held in the province of Golestan. Two members of President Khatami's Council of Ministers faced judicial inquiries at the end of 2001. The Minister of Oil, Bijan Namdar-Zangeneh, was asked to answer charges of mismanagement of petroleum revenues and the granting of contract awards to an affiliate of Iran's national oil company, and the Minister of Industries and Mines, Eshaq Jahangiri (along with the Governor of the Central Bank, Dr Mohsen Nourbakhsh) appeared in court on undisclosed charges. In April 2002 Iran's Deputy Foreign Minister for Education and Research, Sadegh Kharrazi, was forced to resign, amid speculation that he had made contact with US officials.

There was a renewed clamp-down on the 'reformist' movement by the judiciary in May 2002, with the closure of two 'liberal' newspapers and a warning from the Tehran judiciary to journalists that publication of any article advocating dialogue between Iranian and US representatives would be regarded as a criminal offence. In early June Mahdi Karrubi was re-elected Speaker of the Majlis for a further 12 months. Behzad Nabavi became First Deputy Speaker of the assembly, replacing Muhammad Reza Khatami, who assumed Nabavi's previous role as Second Deputy Speaker. In July the authorities declared a ban on any rallies and protests organized to commemorate the third anniversary of the violent clashes between students and the security forces in 1999. However, several hundred protesters were reported to have defied the ban in Tehran, resulting in sporadic clashes between protesters demanding political reform on the one side and security forces and 'right-wing' elements on the

other. A prominent 'reformist' cleric in Esfahan, Ayatollah Jalaleddin Taheri, announced his resignation the following day, launching a strong attack against Iran's 'conservative' religious establishment and demanding the release from house arrest of the dissident cleric, Ayatollah Montazeri. In mid-July 2002 the 'left-wing' Participation Front threatened to withdraw its co-operation with the Government and Majlis if 'hardliners' continued to block social and political reforms. In late July Mohsen Mirdamadi, a Majlis deputy and publisher of the Participation Front's *Norouz*, Iran's main 'pro-reform' newspaper, had a six-month gaol term handed down in May for propagandizing against the Islamic regime confirmed by a court of appeal. Mirdamadi was also fined and banned from involvement in press activities for four years, and his publication was closed down for six months. (He had alleged in an article published in *Norouz* to have information that Tehran had held secret talks with the USA.) More than 30 other 'reformists' were also imprisoned during that month. In August and September at least three 'pro-reform' newspapers were banned by the authorities.

During September 2002 President Khatami presented draft legislation to the Majlis which was aimed at reducing the powers of Iran's 'ultra-conservative' establishment in order to accelerate the President's reform programme. The first bill envisaged transferring the rights of the Council of Guardians to approve or disqualify electoral candidates to the Ministry of the Interior. The second bill proposed granting Khatami wider powers to enforce adherence to the terms of the Constitution by the judiciary and other government departments. Both bills required approval by the Majlis and the Council of Guardians prior to becoming law; 'liberal' deputies threatened to resign *en masse* if the Council blocked the reforms. However, the 'pro-reform' movement suffered a setback in early October when Behrouz Geranpayeh, director of a research institute affiliated to the 'reformist'-led Ministry of Culture and Islamic Guidance, was arrested on charges including publishing 'inappropriate' information, acting against national security and passing information to foreign intelligence agencies, and the institute was closed down by the authorities. The action came after a recent poll commissioned by the Majlis and published by Geranpayeh's research institute showed that a large majority of Iranians favoured the resumption of a political dialogue with the USA. During late 2002 a number of other officials, including a 'liberal' parliamentarian and the head of Iran's state news agency, also faced charges in connection with alleged Western influence at Iranian polling institutes. In early November another such organization was closed and its directors were arrested; they included Abbas Abdi, a journalist and leading member of the Islamic Iran Participation Front. Trial proceedings began in Tehran against Geranpayeh, Abdi and another leading Iranian pollster in early December; the defendants were accused of espionage and of fabricating opinion polls. Abdi was sentenced to eight years' imprisonment in early February 2003, having been found guilty of selling information to a US polling institute, while the other researcher received a nine-year term; Geranpayeh awaited a verdict.

Meanwhile, in early November 2002 President Khatami's two reform bills, concerning the vetting of electoral candidates and violations of the Constitution, received preliminary approval by the Majlis. However, at the same time a prominent 'reformist' academic, writer and close ally of the President, Hashem Aghajari, was handed down a death sentence by a court in the western city of Hamedan, having been found guilty of apostasy for a speech he had made to a university audience in June, in which he questioned the divine authority of the Islamic clergy and advocated reform within the religious establishment. (On other charges, Aghajari was sentenced to eight years in prison and 74 lashes, as well as receiving a 10-year teaching ban.) Aghajari had been tried in camera, and the severity of the sentence was widely condemned by academics, 'liberals' and even moderate 'conservatives'; it led to several weeks of student protests—the largest witnessed in Iran since 1999. In mid-November 2002 Ayatollah Khamenei intervened in the worsening crisis by requesting that the judiciary initiate an urgent review of the case. However, this did not prevent further protests by students in Tehran, which resulted in clashes with members of a 'hardline' militia who were calling for Aghajari's execution. In late November four students who had instigated the recent protests were arrested on charges of acting against national security. In early December Aghajari's lawyers filed an appeal against his conviction, while further demonstrations were staged in Tehran by students demanding the release of the academic, some of whom also sought the resignation of the Head of the Judiciary; a number of arrests were made. Later in the month Hussain Mir-Muhammad Sadeghi, the official spokesman for the judiciary, resigned his post, reportedly citing dissatisfaction over the 'politicization' of the judiciary and Aghajari's death sentence. With the divide between 'hardliners' and 'reformists' apparently growing, there was a widespread belief that the 'conservative' establishment was preparing a serious crack-down against the 'liberal' movement, possibly by declaring a state of emergency. In mid-February 2003 the Supreme Court reportedly commuted the death sentence against Aghajari to a prison term of less than four years; however, he was ordered to face a retrial by the court in Hamedan that had issued the initial verdict (see below). Meanwhile, in mid-January Tehran's municipal council was dissolved by the Ministry of the Interior and its mayor, Muhammad Hassan Malek-Madani, was removed from his post and reportedly given a short gaol term, following a series of disagreements between council members. The action, coming only weeks before nation-wide municipal elections, was widely seen as a setback for 'reformists'. At the end of January the dissident cleric, Ayatollah Montazeri, was released from house arrest, following reports that a 'conservative' daily newspaper, *Resalat*, had joined the 'pro-reform' lobby in demanding his release. (Some reports claimed that the authorities feared that the Ayatollah, who was said to be in poor health, could become a focus for the Iranian opposition movement should he die while under house arrest.)

Official results of voting in Iran's second local government elections since the Islamic Revolution, held in late February 2003, indicated a heavy defeat for President Khatami's Islamic Iran Participation Front by candidates of the 'conservative' wing. Electoral turn-out was reported to have been extremely low (at some 39%), as some 'moderate' voters appeared to have boycotted the poll in protest at Khatami's failure to secure vital political reforms. 'Conservative' candidates were said to have secured all 15 seats on the council in Tehran (where electoral turn-out was possibly as low as 10%). Inevitably, however, the results of these elections were overshadowed by events in neighbouring Iraq.

Iran officially opposed the US-led military intervention in Iraq, which commenced in mid-March 2003, despite the not unwelcome removal from power of Saddam Hussain and his Baath regime. This opposition manifested itself in public statements by 'hardline' figures such as Ahmad Jannati, Chairman of the Council of Guardians, and Yahya Rahim-Safavi, Commander of the Revolutionary Guards, as well as in several demonstrations outside the British embassy in Tehran, which became a focal point for protests against the conflict. On several occasions during 2003 the embassy was the target of small arms fire and, in the most serious incident, in March, a fuel-laden truck was driven into the embassy gates, killing the driver. However, Kamal Kharrazi, the Minister of Foreign Affairs, described this last incident as an 'accident'. Moreover, there was a suspicion that three shooting incidents at the British embassy in September might be more closely related to the arrest of the former Iranian ambassador to Argentina by the British authorities (see below) than to events in Iraq.

On the domestic front, the 'conservatives' and 'reformists' continued to clash. Prompted by the refusal of the Council of Guardians to ratify two of President Khatami's reform bills, which had been approved by the Majlis in late 2002, in May 2003 127 'reformist' deputies wrote to Khatami urging him to intervene in the blocked reform process. In March of that year Khatami and the Speaker of the Majlis, Mahdi Karrubi, had reportedly walked out of a meeting of the Council to Determine the Expediency of the Islamic Order in protest at the Council's decision to significantly increase funding to the Council of Guardians for the supervision of the 2004 parliamentary elections. In mid-June 2003 tensions brought about by plans to privatize the Iranian university system erupted into regular clashes between students, the police and pro-Government vigilante groups, and threatened to escalate with plans by student leaders to commemorate the fourth anniversary of the mass demonstrations of July 1999. However, after an appeal by five 'reformist' deputies, the official student demonstrations did not proceed. At the end of July 2003 a group of Sunni Muslim deputies wrote an 'open letter' to the Government complaining about official treatment of the country's Sunni minority.

In August 2003 an independent judge, Javad Esmaili, was appointed to lead an investigation into the death in police custody of an Iranian-born Canadian photojournalist, Zahra

Kazemi, in early July, following her arrest in late June for taking photographs at a notorious prison in Tehran. Kazemi had apparently died as a result of injuries sustained during the police interrogation, and although the Iranian authorities initially claimed that her death was accidental, both Kazemi's family and the Canadian Government exerted pressure on the Iranian authorities to open an investigation into her death. An interrogator from the Ministry of Intelligence and Security was charged with the journalist's 'quasi-intentional murder', but all charges against him were dismissed in late July 2004 because of what was stated to be lack of sufficient evidence, and Kazemi's death was termed an 'accident'. (Canada had withdrawn its ambassador from Iran in protest against the court's decision to bar foreign observers from attending the latter stages of the trial; however, a new ambassador to Iran was appointed in late November.) In August 2003, meanwhile, the Council of Guardians rejected a Majlis-approved bill on women's rights and also a motion condemning the use of torture in interrogation, stating that both cases contradicted Islamic law. In September a group of senior deputies from the Majlis commenced a hunger strike, in protest at the detention and treatment of political prisoners in Iran. In early October the human rights lawyer Shirin Ebadi was awarded the Nobel Peace Prize, becoming both the first Iranian and the first Muslim woman to receive a Nobel prize. (Ebadi was subsequently appointed by the family of Zahra Kazemi to represent them at the trial of the intelligence agent accused of her murder.)

A Ministry of Welfare and Social Security was established in December 2003 as part of new legislation to reform the country's social security provisions. However, the almost complete destruction of the historic city of Bam on 26 December, as a result of a powerful earthquake, dominated the domestic agenda into early 2004. The city, whose historic centre comprises the Arg-e-Bam (Citadel of Bam), was largely constructed of mud and straw, and it was initially believed that more than 40,000 of the city's estimated 100,000 inhabitants had been killed in the earthquake. (At the end of March 2004 the Statistical Centre of Iran stated that 26,271 people had died.) The international community immediately sent emergency teams to assist in the rescue effort, while the USA announced a temporary easing of sanctions to facilitate the transfer of financial aid and essential equipment to Bam.

Meanwhile, a new political crisis was unfolding in early 2004. With elections to the seventh Majlis scheduled for late February, the Council of Guardians announced in early January that, from a preliminary list of around 8,200 candidates, more than 2,000 candidates would be barred from standing in the polls, including 80 current Majlis deputies. ('Reformists' insisted that at least one-half of the proposed candidates would effectively be disqualified.) President Khatami's brother and the leader of the Islamic Iran Participation Front, Muhammad Reza Khatami, was perhaps the most notable of these 'reformist' candidates, along with two other leaders of the party. President Khatami and several of his ministers threatened to resign in protest at the ban, as did all of the country's 27 regional governors, and about 100 deputies staged a 'sit-in' at the Majlis. Although, as a result of two direct interventions by Ayatollah Khamenei, the Council of Guardians reversed its decision in relation to a small number of the barred candidates, in late January the Council vetoed emergency legislation that had been adopted by the Majlis with the intention of weakening the former's control over the election process and thereby reversing the bans on all of the candidates. At the elections to the Majlis, held on 20 February, turn-out by voters was estimated to be as low as 51% (with a recorded rate of only 28% in Tehran); 229 candidates received enough votes to be elected directly to the Majlis, with the remainder of the 290 seats to be filled at a second round of voting, held on 7 May. The 'reformist' Speaker of the outgoing Majlis, Mahdi Karrubi, withdrew his candidacy after failing to secure re-election at the first round. As had been widely predicted, 'conservatives' were confirmed as having secured a majority in the legislature, and in mid-April the First Deputy Speaker of the Majlis, Behzad Nabavi, tendered his resignation in protest at their success in the recent elections. Shortly afterwards the Minister of Labour and Social Affairs, Safdar Hosseni, replaced Tahmasb Mazaheri as Minister of Economic Affairs and Finance; Nasser Khaleqi assumed responsibility for the labour portfolio. Following the second round of voting, the 'conservatives' were estimated to have secured 195 seats in the Majlis and the 'reformists' fewer than 50, with the remainder being held by 'independents'.

In early May 2004 a law banning the use of torture in Iran was approved by the Council of Guardians. In late May the new Majlis took office, nominating the first non-cleric Speaker since the Islamic Revolution, Gholam-Ali Haddad-Adel, who rejected claims that the new legislature would further restrict press freedom and civil rights, and vowed to confront social issues and to persevere with efforts to harmonize relations with the international community. Haddad-Adel was elected to the post in early June, while Muhammad Reza Bahonar and Muhammad Hassan Abu Turabi were named as First and Second Deputy Speakers, respectively. In early June the death sentence imposed on the academic, Hashem Aghajari, for apostasy (see above), which had been reinstated in early May, was revoked by the Supreme Court. In mid-July he was sentenced to a five-year gaol term, two years of which were suspended, and in early August he was released on bail. In early October the Majlis impeached the Minister of Roads and Transport, Ahmad Khorram, for corruption and mismanagement. Muhammad Ramati was appointed as his successor in early February 2005, after Khatami's original nomination for the post was rejected by the Majlis. Also in early October 2004 the Vice-President in charge of Legal and Parliamentary Affairs, Muhammad Ali Abtahi, resigned, citing his frustration with 'conservatives' who were impeding his ability to perform his duties. Majid Ansari was subsequently appointed to the post. It was announced in early January 2005 that the vote to elect President Khatami's successor was to take place on 17 June, simultaneously with by-elections in eight parliamentary constituencies where results of the February 2004 elections were overturned by the Council of Guardians and in the earthquake-devastated city of Bam; one undecided seat in the Tehran constituency was also to be filled.

At the end of May 2004, meanwhile, the Council of Guardians authorized legislation to divide the existing province of Khorasan into three smaller provinces, to be named North Khorasan, South Khorasan and Razavi Khorasan, with provincial capitals at Bojnurd, Birjand and Mashad, respectively; the division took effect in late September.

Relations with the USA since the end of the Iran–Iraq War have continued to be characterized by mutual suspicion. The USA, alleging that Iran is pursuing a programme of military expansion, has expressed particular concern over the nature of nuclear co-operation between the People's Republic of China, Russia and Iran, and has sought to persuade Iran's Western allies to reduce economic and technical assistance to, and direct investment in, the country. Iran maintains that it is not engaged in the development of weapons of mass destruction, while the Chinese and Russian Governments have strenuously denied involvement in non-civilian nuclear projects in Iran. In July 1994 the USA accused Iran of being responsible for bomb attacks against Jewish targets in the United Kingdom and Argentina in an attempt to disrupt the Middle East peace process. (A former Iranian intelligence agent alleged in July 2002 that Iranian agents had plotted and carried out the bombing in Buenos Aires in 1994 with the backing of the Iranian Government, although Iranian officials have persistently denied the claims.)

In April 1995 US efforts to isolate Iran internationally culminated in the announcement that all US companies and their overseas subsidiaries would be banned from investing in, or trading with, Iran (with the subsequent exception of US oil companies in the Caucasus and Central Asia involved in marketing petroleum from the countries of the former USSR). Russia refused to support the embargo, but announced in May that it would henceforth separate the civilian and military components of an agreement to supply Iran with a nuclear reactor, to be constructed at Bushehr, in south-western Iran. In mid-1996 the US Congress approved legislation (termed the Iran-Libya Sanctions Act—ILSA) to penalize companies operating in US markets that were investing US $40m. (subsequently amended to $20m.) or more in energy projects in prescribed countries deemed to be sponsoring terrorism. However, these so-called secondary economic sanctions received little international support. In December Iran and Russia concluded an extensive co-operation agreement. In September 1997, furthermore, a consortium comprising French, Malaysian and Russian energy companies signed a contract with the Iranian National Oil Company to invest some $2,000m. in the development of natural gas reserves in Iranian waters of the Persian Gulf. Threats of sanctions were effectively averted in May 1998, when the US Administration agreed to waive penalties for which the Secretary of State deemed the companies involved to be liable. This decision apparently facilitated further foreign investment in Iran, most notably in hydrocarbons projects.

Khatami's election to the Iranian presidency in mid-1997 prompted speculation regarding prospects for an improvement in relations with the USA and other Western countries. A notable development was the designation by the USA, in October, of the opposition Mujahidin-e-Khalq as one of 30 proscribed terrorist organizations. (The Mujahidin-e-Khalq's parent organization, the National Council of Resistance, also based in France, was proscribed by the USA in October 1999). In December 1997 Khatami expressed his desire to engage in a 'thoughtful dialogue' with the American people. In what was interpreted as a major concession, US President Bill Clinton stated subsequently that the USA would not require Iran (or any other Islamic state) to modify its attitude towards the Middle East peace process. The cautious *rapprochement* continued in January 1998, when Khatami made a widely publicized address, via a US television news network, emphasizing the need for Iran to develop closer cultural links with the USA; his speech was widely interpreted as a compromise between 'moderates' in his administration and the regime's 'conservatives', who continued to oppose any direct political dialogue with the USA.

The announcement, in July 1998, that Iran had successfully test-fired a new ballistic missile, *Shahab-3*, capable of striking targets at a distance of 1,300 km, caused renewed tensions. (The missile could potentially target Israel and also US forces in the Gulf.) US concerns regarding what it perceived as Iran's efforts to acquire weapons of mass destruction remained a principal cause of mutual suspicion, and there was continuing evidence of efforts by the Clinton Administration to block trading agreements deemed to assist Iran's military programme. Nevertheless, earlier in that year Russia, stating that the Bushehr plant conformed with standards prescribed by the International Atomic Energy Agency (IAEA) for the prevention of nuclear weapons' proliferation, declared its willingness to provide equipment for the reactor (which Ukraine had initially offered but later withdrawn under US pressure).

The USA was among countries to condemn the arrest, revealed in mid-1999, of 13 Jews in Shiraz and Esfahan, on charges of espionage on behalf of Israel and the USA. In July 2000, after a closed trial in Shiraz, 10 of the defendants were convicted and given custodial sentences of between four and 13 years; however, in September their sentences were reduced on appeal to terms of between two and nine years. Although it was reported in February 2001 that further appeals had been rejected by the Supreme Court, all the Jews had been released by April 2003. Meanwhile, in September 1999 the US House of Representatives approved non-proliferation legislation requiring the imposition of sanctions against any country aiding Iran in the development of weapons of mass destruction.

Addressing the American-Iranian Council in Washington, DC, in March 2000, US Secretary of State Madeleine Albright announced an end to restrictions on imports from Iran of several non-hydrocarbons items. This substantive step towards the normalization of relations was in recognition of what the US Administration regarded as trends towards democracy under President Khatami. Albright furthermore offered what amounted to an apology for the role played by the USA in the *coup d'état* of 1953, as well as for US support for Iraq in the Iran–Iraq War. Such concessions were, however, accompanied by the assertion that Iran had done little to modify its support for what Albright termed international terrorism and its efforts to develop nuclear weaponry. Hopes of a further *rapprochement* were encouraged by open meetings and other contacts involving Iranian and US officials at the UN Millennium Summit in New York in September 2000. However, relations between Iran and the USA deteriorated in June 2001 after 14 men (13 Saudi Arabians and one Lebanese) were indicted *in absentia* by the US Government, having been charged in connection with the bomb attack at al-Khobar in 1996 (see below). Although no Iranians were among the accused, US officials reiterated allegations that members of the Iranian Government were behind the bombing. Despite early indications that the new Administration of President George W. Bush, inaugurated in January 2001, was reviewing US policy on sanctions, in early August the Bush Administration confirmed that ILSA was to be extended for a further five years. In July 2001 the USA had, for the second time since May, blocked Iran's bid to enter negotiations regarding membership of the World Trade Organization (WTO). Iran's 20th application was vetoed by the USA in December 2004. However, in mid-March 2005 President Bush announced a series of economic incentives, including the removal of the ban on Iran's membership of the WTO, provided that Iran agreed permanently to suspend its nuclear energy programme.

President Khatami was swift to offer his condolences to the American nation following the suicide bombings in New York and Washington, DC, on 11 September 2001. However, as the USA initiated a campaign against the al-Qa'ida (Base) organization of its chief suspect, Osama bin Laden—the Saudi Arabian-born radical Islamist based at that time in Afghanistan—Khatami asserted that the international community should act under the auspices of the UN in order to eradicate terrorism. Although Ayatollah Khamenei also condemned the terrorist attacks, he and Iran's 'conservative' press warned against any large-scale US military offensive targeting the Taliban regime and al-Qa'ida militants in Afghanistan. Iranians strongly condemned the commencement of hostilities in early October, but details subsequently emerged of a secret agreement between Iran and the USA whereby Iran would offer assistance to any US military personnel either shot down or forced to land within its borders, provided that the USA respect Iran's territorial integrity. There were also reports that Iran might be sharing intelligence with the USA. Iranian and US officials held UN-sponsored talks in Geneva in that month to discuss the composition of a future Afghan government. Yet, despite an apparent shift in bilateral relations, Iran continued to head the US Administration's list of states deemed to be 'most active' in sponsoring terrorism.

In 2002 the Iranian administration denied accusations by the USA that it was permitting fleeing al-Qa'ida and Taliban fighters to cross the Afghan border into Iran. Relations deteriorated abruptly at the end of January, when, in his annual State of the Union address, the US President referred to Iran as forming (together with Iraq and the Democratic People's Republic of Korea) an 'axis of evil', explicitly accusing Iran of aggressively pursuing the development of weapons of mass destruction and of 'exporting terror'. Bush's remarks were denounced in the strongest terms by 'moderates' and 'conservatives' in the Iranian leadership, with Khatami accusing his US counterpart of 'warmongering'. The Minister of Foreign Affairs, Kamal Kharrazi, subsequently cancelled a planned visit to New York. In May President Khatami urged 'reformist' deputies in the Majlis not to attempt to hold discussions with US officials. In the same month the US Department of State again designated Iran as the world's 'most active' sponsor of terrorism (as the country was also termed in 2003 and 2004), and US officials reiterated their claims that Russia was assisting Iran in the manufacture of nuclear weapons. In late July the US Administration was angered by Russia's conclusion of a development and co-operation accord with Iran, which reportedly involved the construction of additional reactors at the Bushehr nuclear plant. Meanwhile, President Khatami openly condemned US plans to use military force to bring about 'regime change' in Iraq, warning that such action posed a serious risk to regional stability. At the end of July Iran was reported to have placed its armed forces and Revolutionary Guards on alert in preparation for any US-led military action. In late October Kamal Kharrazi declared that, in the event of 'regime change' in Iraq, Iran strongly opposed any post-war Iraqi government being imposed by the USA. In mid-December Iran again denied allegations made by US officials that they had evidence of Iran's secret involvement in the manufacture of nuclear weapons. Iran has persistently maintained that its nuclear programme is required to meet domestic energy demands rather than for military purposes. However, the USA condemned the announcement made in early February 2003 that Iran was to extract recently discovered deposits of uranium in order to produce nuclear fuel. Inspectors from the IAEA began an assessment of Iran's nuclear programme later in the month (see below), although the dialogue on Iran's nuclear capabilities was temporarily interrupted by the conflict in neighbouring Iraq in early 2003.

Iran had been host to many Iraqi groups-in-exile, most notably the Shi'ite-dominated Supreme Council for the Islamic Revolution in Iraq (SCIRI) and its military wing, the Badr Brigades. Therefore, following the removal from power of Saddam Hussain by the US-led coalition in early April 2003, the US Administration warned Tehran not to get involved in Iraqi affairs, fearing that the Iranian leadership sought a political settlement that would favour the Shi'ite Muslim majority of Iraq and lead to the formation of a Shi'ite bloc in the Middle East antipathetic to US interests. However, in May it became necessary for the USA and Iran to instigate talks in Geneva, Switzer-

land, under the auspices of the UN, to discuss the return of Iraqi exiles and refugees in Iran, as well as the presence in Iraq of the Mujahidin-e-Khalq and its military wing, the National Liberation Army (NLA—see below). The talks collapsed after Ayatollah Khamenei described them as 'tantamount to surrender', and when US officials accused Iran of interfering in Iraqi internal affairs and of sheltering al-Qa'ida militants suspected of masterminding suicide bombings at expatriate compounds in Riyadh, Saudi Arabia, earlier in that month. (Iranian officials subsequently admitted that a group of al-Qa'ida suspects were in Iranian detention and were to stand trial.) When President Bush voiced his support for the student demonstrations in June (see above), President Khatami accused the USA of interference in Iranian affairs. After the Bam earthquake in late December, it appeared that the USA and Iran might be embarking on a process of 'earthquake diplomacy', with the US Administration agreeing to ease financial sanctions and restrictions on the export of technical apparatus to Iran in order to facilitate the reconstruction process. However, at the beginning of 2004 President Bush denied that offers of humanitarian aid to Iran would in any way influence US policy towards Iran. In mid-April Iranian officials denied suggestions that the USA had asked Iran for assistance in its struggle to defeat the insurgency in Iraq or that any Iranian element was supporting the radical Shi'ite movement led by Hojatoleslam Muqtada as-Sadr. An Iranian diplomatic mission, supposedly dispatched upon the request of the United Kingdom to mediate between US troops and as-Sadr's forces around the Iraqi city of Najaf, was withdrawn following the assassination of the first secretary of the Iranian embassy in Baghdad. In late July a further rift in Iranian–US relations developed when the USA declared a group of 3,800 members of the Mujahidin-e-Khalq interned in Iraq to be protected persons under the Geneva Convention. Iran criticized the USA for supporting 'terrorists', and perceived the announcement as evidence that the USA aimed to destroy the bond between the Iraqi and Iranian peoples. The USA emphasized, however, that it would not protect any individuals suspected of carrying out terrorist attacks. The introduction to the US Senate in early August of the Iran Freedom and Support Act of 2004, which was designed to promote 'regime change' in Tehran and to provide US $10m. in support of pro-democracy opposition groups in Iran, was seen as further evidence of the desire of the Bush Administration to use military force against Iran. (A US investigative journalist claimed in mid-January 2005 that US special forces had been conducting surveillance operations in Iran for several months, in preparation for military strikes; however, a spokesman for the US Administration described the allegations as being 'riddled with inaccuracies'.) Meanwhile, Ayatollah Khamenei described US preparations to launch a major assault against militia fighters in Najaf in early August 2004 as 'one of the darkest crimes of humanity'. Despite its vehement opposition to the US-led invasion and occupation of Iraq, the Iranian regime was expected to benefit from closer ties with Iraq following the scheduled formation, by the end of 2005, of an Iraqi government that was likely to be dominated by representatives of the majority Shi'a community.

Following President Khatami's announcement of 9 February 2003 regarding the discovery and successful extraction of uranium, the USA urged the IAEA to declare Iran to be in violation of the nuclear non-proliferation treaty (NPT), and called on Russia to end its collaboration with Iran on the Bushehr plant. In mid-June the Director-General of the IAEA, Muhammad el-Baradei, presented his report on Iran's nuclear capabilities to the IAEA board, in which he called on Iran to open its nuclear programme to a more rigorous system of inspections. Iran responded that it would only comply with this request if it were given access to the nuclear technology it required, thereby increasing the likelihood of censure by the UN and the possible imposition of sanctions. In July it was revealed that Iran had finally brought into service the *Shahab-3* ballistic missile, causing concern in the USA and Israel. Although in early August President Khatami stated that Iran's nuclear programmes were 'entirely peaceful', the USA insisted that Iran was in breach of its nuclear safeguards obligations, and the IAEA (with US support) adopted a resolution on 12 September giving Iran until 31 October to disclose full details of its nuclear programme and to show evidence that it was not developing nuclear weapons. This followed the discovery of enriched uranium at a processing plant south of Tehran. At the beginning of October IAEA officials travelled to Iran in order to re-engage Iran in the nuclear inspections process, as did the foreign ministers of France, Germany and the United Kingdom later in the month. On 21 October it was announced that Iran would accept a more rigorous system of inspections at its nuclear facilities. The IAEA produced a report in late November indicating that there was no evidence that Iran was producing nuclear weapons, although in mid-February 2004 the UN agency reported that it had found evidence of undeclared facilities that could be used for the enrichment of uranium. In mid-March the IAEA adopted a resolution condemning Iran for the secrecy of its nuclear activities; however, it did not threaten the imposition of UN sanctions against Tehran. The resolution angered Iranian officials, who responded by temporarily suspending inspections. In early April Iran and the IAEA were reported to have agreed a new timetable for further inspections of Iran's nuclear facilities. This was followed by the announcement that Iran would voluntarily suspend all centrifuge construction. However, after the IAEA, on 18 June, adopted a resolution criticizing Iran for failing to co-operate with inspections, in late June Iran announced that, although it would adhere to its pledge to suspend actual uranium enrichment, it would resume manufacturing parts for centrifuges and would also recommence the testing and assembly of centrifuges. Iran criticized the United Kingdom, France and Germany for not supplying Iran with the technology and trade they had promised in return for Iran's pledge to freeze its uranium enrichment programme, as part of the October 2003 agreement. In late August 2004 the Iranian authorities announced that they had arrested an unspecified number of spies, mostly from the Mujahidin-e-Khalq, for revealing nuclear secrets to foreign enemies. In mid-October Russia and Iran, to continued protests from the West, completed the construction of the Bushehr nuclear plant. Russia pressed Iran to cease its uranium enrichment programme, apparently fearing that sanctions imposed by the UN Security Council would threaten the Bushehr deal. Iran also tested a long-range satellite-launching rocket, *Shahab-4*, asserting that it would only use its missiles in self-defence. In early November, rejecting UN demands that Iran end all uranium enrichment activities, the Majlis approved a motion urging the Government to continue with efforts to develop a nuclear energy programme. In mid-November, following further talks with French, German and British officials in Paris, France, Iran complied with IAEA demands to temporarily suspend its uranium enrichment programme, averting the possibility of such activities being reported to the UN and the subsequent imposition of sanctions. The USA, however, maintained that Iran was surreptitiously developing weapons-grade uranium. Iran insisted that the suspension was voluntary and was not a legal obligation, and asserted its right to nuclear technologies, emphasizing in late November that the suspension would last for 'months, not years'. In early December Iran asserted that it was under no obligation to permit IAEA inspectors to visit sites believed to be involved in undisclosed nuclear weapons development, but announced that it was prepared to discuss the matter. In mid-March 2005 the US Administration announced a series of economic incentives to Iran (see above) to persuade the country to suspend permanently its uranium enrichment programme, in return for which the United Kingdom, France and Germany agreed to refer Iran to the UN Security Council in the event of its failure to do so; Iran dismissed the offer as insignificant.

The European Union (EU, see p. 217) pursued a policy of 'critical dialogue' with Iran during the 1990s, despite US pressure as well as tensions between Iran and certain EU states. Notably, a lengthy period of strained relations with the United Kingdom developed after Ayatollah Khomeini issued a *fatwa* (edict) in February 1989, imposing a death penalty against a British writer, Salman Rushdie, for material deemed offensive to Islam in his novel *The Satanic Verses*. 'Critical dialogue' was suspended in April 1997, after a German court ruled that the Iranian authorities had ordered the assassination of four prominent members of the dissident Democratic Party of Iranian Kurdistan in Berlin in September 1992. Germany announced the withdrawal of its ambassador to Tehran and expelled four Iranian diplomats, while other EU members similarly withdrew their representatives. In November 1997, following the inauguration of President Khatami and the formation of a new Council of Ministers, a compromise arrangement was finally reached allowing the readmission of all EU ambassadors, and in February 1998 EU ministers responsible for foreign affairs agreed to resume senior-level ministerial contacts with Iran. Despite assurances given to the British Secretary of State for Foreign

and Commonwealth Affairs, Robin Cook, in September by the Iranian Minister of Foreign Affairs that the Iranian Government had no intention of threatening the life of Rushdie or anyone associated with his work, 'conservative' clerics maintained that the *fatwa* issued by Ayatollah Khomeini was irrevocable, and the Qom-based 15 Khordad Foundation subsequently increased its financial reward offered for the writer's murder. President Khatami became the first Iranian Head of State to visit the West since the Islamic Revolution when, in March 1999, he travelled to Italy and the Vatican; in September President Thomas Klestil of Austria made the first visit to Iran by an EU head of state since 1979. Cook's successor, Jack Straw, visited Tehran in late September 2001, following the suicide attacks on the USA in that month; the purpose of Straw's visit was primarily to request Iran's support for a US-led military campaign in Afghanistan (see above). Straw visited Iran again in late November, as part of an official tour of Afghanistan's neighbours aimed at consolidating support for an interim Afghan 'national unity' government, under UN auspices. Meanwhile, during September 2001 the most high-level discussions since 1979 were held between Iranian and EU representatives in Brussels and later Tehran.

Ambassadorial-level relations between Iran and the United Kingdom had been restored in May 1999, but a setback occurred in February 2002, when Iran formally rejected the United Kingdom's nomination for its new British ambassador to Tehran (accusing the diplomat of being an agent of the British intelligence service); the status of Iran's ambassador to Britain was subsequently downgraded to that of chargé d'affaires. However, the dispute was resolved in late September when Tehran accepted the nomination of a new British ambassador. In mid-June 2002 EU ministers of foreign affairs, meeting in Luxembourg, had agreed to initiate negotiations with Iran regarding a trade and co-operation agreement later that year, provided that the accord be linked with consideration of political issues (notably human rights and terrorism); the talks began in Brussels in mid-December. In early October 2002 Jack Straw visited Iran as part of a wider tour of the Middle East which was intended to garner support for a possible US-led military campaign to oust the regime of Saddam Hussain in Iraq. Kamal Kharrazi visited the United Kingdom in early February 2003 for talks with British officials concerning the Iraqi crisis; Kharrazi was reported to have emphasized the desire of the Iranian leadership to avert a war between Iraq and the West. At the end of May, following the US-led campaign in Iraq, Prime Minister Tony Blair echoed statements made by the US Administration that Iran should desist from 'interfering' in Iraq's affairs. In June the French authorities arrested some 160 members of the Mujahidin-e-Khalq in Paris, on the grounds that they were planning terrorist attacks. Among the detainees was Maryam Rajavi, co-leader of the organization, although she was later released without charge. Iranian émigrés in several European cities protested against the arrests. Diplomatic relations between Iran and the United Kingdom deteriorated again in early September, following the refusal of a British court to grant bail to Hadi Soleimanpour, a former Iranian ambassador to Argentina, who had been detained in the United Kingdom in August on charges relating to the bombing of a Jewish cultural centre in Buenos Aires in 1994. Iran recalled its ambassador to London, but Soleimanpour was eventually granted bail in mid-September 2003. In late June 2004 a crisis erupted in relations with the United Kingdom when Iran captured three British patrol craft and detained eight Royal Navy personnel on the Shatt al-Arab waterway dividing Iran from Iraq. Iran asserted that the vessels had entered Iranian territorial waters. The sailors, who were released four days later, alleged that they had been 'forcibly escorted' into Iranian territorial waters.

Relations between Iran and Saudi Arabia were frequently strained after the Islamic Revolution of 1979. A period of particularly hostile relations, following the deaths of 275 Iranian pilgrims as a result of fierce clashes with Saudi security forces in the Islamic holy city of Mecca during the *Hajj* (annual pilgrimage) in July 1987 culminated in the suspension of diplomatic relations in April 1988. Links were restored in March 1991. Allegations of Iranian involvement in the bombing of a US military housing complex at al-Khobar, Saudi Arabia, in June 1996 again strained relations for several months. However, the installation of a new Iranian Government in August 1997 facilitated further *rapprochement*, perhaps reflecting the desire of the two countries, as the region's principal petroleum producers, to co-operate in maintaining world oil prices and in efforts to curtail over-production by members of the Organization of the Petroleum Exporting Countries (OPEC, see p. 331). An Iranian delegation led by former President Rafsanjani began a 10-day visit to Saudi Arabia in February 1998, at the end of which the formation of a joint ministerial committee for bilateral relations was announced, and several co-operation agreements were signed following a visit to Iran by the Saudi Minister of State for Foreign Affairs in May. The signing of a Saudi-Iranian security agreement was announced in April 2001. During the latter part of 2003 Iran countered US accusations that certain suspected al-Qa'ida militants who remained in Iranian custody had been involved in plotting suicide attacks against expatriate compounds in Riyadh in May of that year.

The Khatami administration has also sought improved relations with Saudi Arabia's fellow members of the Co-operation Council for the Arab States of the Gulf (Gulf Co-operation Council—GCC, see p. 193), although a long-standing territorial dispute with the United Arab Emirates (UAE) remains unresolved. In March 1992 Iran occupied those parts of the Abu Musa islands and the Greater and Lesser Tunbs that had remained under the control of the emirate of Sharjah since the original occupation in 1971. In December 1994 the UAE announced its intention to refer the dispute to the International Court of Justice in The Hague, Netherlands. In early 1995 Iran was reported to have deployed air defence systems on Abu Musa and the Greater and Lesser Tunbs, prompting the USA to warn of a potential threat to shipping. In November talks between Iran and the UAE aimed at facilitating ministerial-level negotiations on the disputed islands ended in failure. Relations deteriorated further in the first half of 1996, after Iran opened an airport on Abu Musa and a power station on Greater Tunb. In 1997 the UAE protested that Iran was repeatedly violating the emirates' territorial waters. Talks in March were inconclusive, and in June the UAE protested to Iran and the UN at Iran's construction of a pier on Greater Tunb. Following a meeting with the UAE's Minister of Foreign Affairs during the eighth conference of the Organization of the Islamic Conference (OIC, see p. 327), held in Tehran in December 1997, President Khatami emphasized his willingness to discuss bilateral issues directly with President Zayed bin Sultan an-Nayhan of the UAE. Although the latter was said to be cautious about Iran's attempts at *rapprochement*, in the following month UAE officials expressed willingness to enter into negotiations. None the less, both countries continued to assert their sovereignty over the three areas.

Iran hosts one of the largest refugee populations in the world. At the end of 2003, according to data published by the office of the UN High Commissioner for Refugees (UNHCR), the number of refugees in the country was 984,896, of whom 834,699 were from Afghanistan and 150,196 from Iraq. All of the refugees in Iran were reported to be receiving UNHCR assistance.

Victories achieved by the Sunni fundamentalist Taliban in the Afghan civil war in September 1996 prompted Iran, which supported the Government of President Burhanuddin Rabbani, to express fears for its national security, and to accuse the USA of interference in Afghanistan's internal affairs. In June 1997 the Taliban accused Iran of espionage and ordered the closure of the Iranian embassy in Kabul and the withdrawal of all Iranian diplomats. Iran retaliated by halting all trade across its land border with Afghanistan, prompting Taliban protests that the ban violated international law. In mid-September 1998, as it emerged that nine Iranian diplomats missing since August had been murdered by Taliban militia as they stormed the city of Mazar-i-Sharif, 500,000 Iranian troops were reportedly placed on full military alert in readiness for open conflict with Afghanistan. In an attempt to defuse the crisis, in October the Taliban agreed to free all Iranian prisoners being held in Afghanistan and to punish those responsible for the killing of the nine Iranian diplomats. Following the terrorist attacks on the USA in September 2001, as the USA began preparations for military action against al-Qa'ida and its Taliban hosts, Iran closed its eastern border with Afghanistan and sent a large contingent of troops there in order to prevent a further influx of Afghan refugees. In the following month, however, when the US-led military action began, Iran reportedly agreed to the establishment of eight refugee camps within its borders to provide shelter for some 250,000 Afghan refugees. Although Iran refused to give military assistance to the US-led coalition, it actively supported the Western-backed opposition forces, collectively known as the United National Islamic Front for the Salvation of Afghanistan (the Northern Alliance), and welcomed their swift victory over

the Taliban. A programme allowing for voluntary repatriations of Afghan refugees under UNHCR auspices was inaugurated by the Iranian and Afghan authorities in early April 2002, although UNHCR put the number of 'spontaneous' repatriations prior to that date at 57,000. (More than 1m. Afghan refugees in Iran were estimated by UNHCR to have returned to Afghanistan by mid-September 2004.) In mid-August 2002 President Khatami became the first Iranian Head of State to visit Afghanistan for 40 years. Meanwhile, it was reported in that month that Iran had, in June, extradited 16 Saudis believed to be al-Qa'ida militants who had fled the Afghan conflict. In early November, moreover, Iranian officials declared that the authorities had arrested and extradited some 250 people suspected of having links with al-Qa'ida.

In September 1997 Iraq opened a border crossing with Iran, thereby permitting, for the first time since the Iran–Iraq War, Iranian pilgrims to visit Shi'ite Muslim shrines on its territory. At the end of the month, however, Iranian aircraft violated the air exclusion zone over southern Iraq in order to bomb two bases of the Mujahidin-e-Khalq (prompting Iraqi aircraft also to enter the zone). Vice-President Taha Yassin Ramadan of Iraq, attending December's OIC conference in Tehran, was the most senior Iraqi official to visit Iran since 1979. President Khatami subsequently expressed the hope that problems between the two countries could be resolved 'through negotiation and understanding'. During a visit to Iran by Iraq's Minister of Foreign Affairs in January 1998, it was agreed to establish joint committees with the aim of expediting prisoner exchanges, facilitating pilgrimages for Iranians to Shi'a shrines in Iraq, and addressing other contentious issues. Exchanges of prisoners of war and the remains of troops killed in the 1980–88 conflict were reported at intervals in 1998–2003, despite periodic mutual accusations of failure to comply with obligations in this respect. In October 2000 Kharrazi became the first Iranian Minister of Foreign Affairs to visit Iraq for a decade, and the two countries agreed to reactivate a 1975 border and security agreement that had been in abeyance since 1980. In November 2000 a bilateral transport and communications accord was signed. However, there were unconfirmed reports in October that Iran's Supreme Council for National Security was to suspend all high-level contacts with the Iraqi Government, following a series of mortar attacks on targets in Tehran apparently perpetrated by the Mujahidin-e-Khalq. Tensions between the two sides increased in April 2001 when Iran launched a heavy missile attack against Iraqi military bases used by the organization, apparently in response to repeated attacks by that group on Iranian targets. By early 2002, however, a general thaw in bilateral relations was evident, despite a protest lodged with the UN by Iraq in June stating that Iran was continuing to violate agreements reached at the end of the Iran–Iraq war. It was reported in September that Iran had made preparations for the provision of humanitarian assistance to Iraqi refugees along their joint border in the event of a US-led military campaign to remove the regime of Saddam Hussein. Discussions held between the Iraqi Minister of Foreign Affairs, Naji Sabri, and Kharrazi in Tehran in early February 2003 resulted in demands by several Iranian deputies for the impeachment of Kharrazi; the deputies claimed that many issues of contention between the two sides remained unresolved. Despite gloomy predictions, there was no refugee crisis in Iran during the US-led intervention in Iraq in early 2003; indeed, the movement of refugees was in the other direction as Iraqis-in-exile returned to Iraq following the removal from power of Saddam Hussein's regime. (UNHCR estimated that, by mid-December 2004, an estimated 107,000 Iraqi refugees—more than one-half of the pre-conflict total in Iran—had returned to their homeland.) On the other hand, Tehran was concerned about the status of the armed opposition group, the Mujahidin-e-Khalq, which had been based in Iraq since 1986. After US-led coalition aircraft had launched attacks against training camps of the NLA, in late April 2003 the Mujahidin and its military wing agreed a cease-fire with the occupying forces in Iraq, a move that was condemned by Iran. (For further details regarding Iran and Iraq in the aftermath of the conflict, see above.)

Discussions held in Geneva between President Khatami and President Hosni Mubarak of Egypt in mid-December 2003 represented the first meeting between the two countries' heads of state since diplomatic relations were severed following the Islamic Revolution of 1979. In early January 2004 Egyptian officials refused to confirm reports that Egypt and Iran were planning to restore full diplomatic relations.

Closer relations were developed with Turkey during the 1990s, despite periodic tensions arising particularly from Turkish allegations of Iranian support for the Kurdish separatist Kurdistan Workers' Party (Partiya Karkeren Kurdistan—PKK, now Kurdistan People's Congress—KONGRA-GEL) in its conflict with the armed forces in south-eastern Turkey (q.v.). In 1997 Iran was a founder member of the Istanbul-based Developing Eight (D-8, see p. 373) group of Islamic countries. In early May 2004 Tehran's Imam Khomeini International Airport, which the Turkish-led consortium Tepe-Akfen-Vie was contracted to operate, was closed by the Islamic Revolutionary Guards Corps after only one flight had landed because it was seen as a danger to national security, and apparently owing to Iran's hostility towards Turkey for its links with Israel and the USA. Meanwhile, considerable political and economic advantage has been perceived arising from Iran's potential as a transit route for hydrocarbons from the former Soviet republics of Central Asia, and since the early 1990s Iran has sought to strengthen its position in Central Asia through bilateral economic, security and cultural agreements as well as institutions such as the Tehran-based Economic Co-operation Organization (see p. 210). Relations between Iran and Azerbaijan—already tense owing to disagreement over a contested section of the Caspian Basin—deteriorated in July 2001, when Iran ordered a gunship into the disputed waters in order to prevent foreign companies from undertaking oil exploration there. Subsequent meetings of the five littoral states (Iran, Russia, Azerbaijan, Kazakhstan and Turkmenistan) failed to resolve the dispute regarding the legal status of the Caspian.

In March 2001 Russia pledged to assist Iran with the completion of the nuclear plant at Bushehr (see above). In May Russia reportedly agreed to supply Iran with advanced shipborne cruise missiles. The two countries signed a military co-operation pact in October, believed to amount to annual sales to Iran of Russian weapons worth some US $300m. In July 2002 Russia and Iran concluded a draft 10-year development and co-operation accord, which was reported to include the construction of a further three nuclear reactors at the Bushehr plant. In mid-2003 the USA sought to persuade Russia to withdraw its assistance from the development of the Bushehr plant, particularly the export to Iran of nuclear fuel. President Vladimir Putin of Russia appeared to agree to this request in early June; however, this policy was quickly contradicted in statements made by Alexandr Rumyantsev, the Russian Minister of Atomic Energy, who indicated that Russia would begin reprocessing Iranian nuclear waste in early 2004. Construction of the Bushehr plant was completed in mid-October 2004, although it was not expected to become fully operational until 2006. In late February 2005 Russia agreed to supply Iran with fuel for the plant; however, following international pressure, the deal required that Iran return to Russia spent nuclear fuel rods, which could be used to produce nuclear weapons, from the site.

Government

Legislative power is vested in the Islamic Consultative Assembly (Majlis), with 290 members. The chief executive of the administration is the President. The Majlis and the President are both elected by universal adult suffrage for a term of four years. A 12-member Council of Guardians supervises elections and ensures that legislation is in accordance with the Constitution and with Islamic precepts. The Council to Determine the Expediency of the Islamic Order, created in February 1988 and formally incorporated into the Constitution in July 1989, rules on legal and theological disputes between the Majlis and the Council of Guardians. The executive, legislative and judicial wings of state power are subject to the authority of the Wali Faqih (supreme religious leader).

Iran is divided into 30 provinces, each with an appointed Governor.

Defence

In August 2004 Iran's regular armed forces totalled an estimated 540,000: army 350,000, Revolutionary Guard Corps (Pasdaran Inquilab) some 120,000, navy 18,000, air force around 52,000. There were some 350,000 army reserves. Paramilitary forces comprised an estimated 300,000 volunteers of the Basij and some 40,000 under the command of the Ministry of the Interior. There is an 18-month period of compulsory military service. Defence expenditure for the Iranian year ending 20 March 2004 was budgeted at IR 30,000,000m.

Economic Affairs

In 2003, according to estimates by the World Bank, Iran's gross national income (GNI), measured at average 2001–03 prices, was US $137,687m., equivalent to $2,000, per head (or $7,190 per head on an international purchasing-power parity basis). During 1990–2003, it was estimated, the population increased at an average annual rate of 1.5%, while gross domestic product (GDP) per head increased, in real terms, by an average of 3.0% per year. Overall GDP increased, in real terms, at an average annual rate of 4.6% in 1990–2003; growth was 7.5% in 2002/03 (Iranian year to March) and an estimated 6.7% in 2003/04.

Agriculture (including forestry and fishing) contributed an estimated 11.4% of GDP in 2003/04. About 23.5% of the employed labour force were engaged in agriculture at the time of the 1996 census. The principal cash crops are fresh and dried fruit and nuts, which accounted for some 14.6% of non-petroleum export earnings in 2003/04. The principal subsistence crops are wheat, barley, sugar beet and sugar cane. Imports of cereals comprised some 4.0% of the value of total imports in 2002/03. Agricultural GDP increased by an average of 4.8% per year in 1990–2003; the sector's GDP increased by an estimated 11.4% in 2002/03 and by about 7.1% in 2003/04.

Industry (including mining, manufacturing, construction and power) contributed an estimated 40.3% of GDP in 2003/04, and engaged 31.2% of the employed labour force at the 1996 census. During 1990–2003 industrial GDP increased by an average of 1.3% per year; growth was estimated at 9.3% in 2002/03 and at 9.2% in 2003/04.

Mining (including petroleum refining) contributed an estimated 23.1% of GDP in 2003/04, although the sector engaged only 0.8% of the working population in 1996. Metal ores are the major non-hydrocarbon mineral exports, and coal, magnesite and gypsum are also mined. The sector is dominated by the hydrocarbons sector, which contributed an estimated 22.5% of GDP in 2003/04. At the end of 2003 Iran's proven reserves of petroleum were estimated at 130,700m. barrels, sufficient to maintain the 2003/04 rate of production—averaging 3.74m. barrels per day (b/d)—for almost 93 years. With effect from March 2005, Iran's production quota within the Organization of the Petroleum Exporting Countries (OPEC, see p. 331) was 4.037m. b/d. Iran's reserves of natural gas (26,690,000m. cu m at the end of 2003) are the second largest in the world, after those of Russia. The GDP of the mining sector increased by an average of 0.8% per year in 1991/92–2000/01; mining GDP was estimated to have increased by 12.0% in 2002/03 and by 12.7% in 2003/04.

Manufacturing (excluding petroleum refining) contributed about 11.0% of GDP in 2003/04, and engaged 17.8% of the employed labour force in 1996. The most important sectors, in terms of value added, are textiles, food processing and transport equipment. The sector's GDP increased by an average of 7.0% per year in 1990–2003, with growth estimated at 11.0% in 2002/03 and at 9.9% in 2003/04.

Principal sources of energy are natural gas (providing around 74.9% of total electricity production in 2001) and petroleum (some 21.2% in the same year). Imports of mineral fuels and lubricants comprised 4.8% of the value of total imports in 2002/03. The first phase of Iran's South Pars offshore gasfield (an extension of Qatar's North Field) was brought on stream in June 2004. Gas reserves in the South Pars field are estimated at around 8,000,000m. cu m, with production an estimated 25m. cu m of natural gas a day at the end of 2004.

The services sector contributed an estimated 48.3% of GDP in 2003/04, and engaged 45.3% of the employed labour force in 1996. During 1990–2003 the GDP of the services sector increased by an average of 7.4% per year; the sector's GDP increased by an estimated 5.5% in 2002/03 and by some 5.1% in 2003/04.

According to preliminary figures, in the year ending March 2004 Iran recorded a visible trade surplus of US $4,993m., and there was a surplus of $2,059m. on the current account of the balance of payments. In 2002/03 the principal source of imports was Germany (which supplied 17.0% of total imports); other major suppliers included the United Arab Emirates (UAE), Switzerland, Italy and France. The principal market for exports in 2003 was the UAE (which took 22.5% of total exports); the People's Republic of China, Singapore and Italy were also important markets for Iranian exports. Other than petroleum and natural gas, Iran's principal exports in 2003/04 were chemical products, fruit and nuts, and carpets. Exports of petroleum and gas comprised some 80.0% of the value of total exports in

2003/04. The principal imports in 2002/03 were machinery and transport equipment, basic manufactures, chemicals, and food and live animals.

For the financial year ending 20 March 2004 Iran recorded a budget deficit estimated at IR 29,682,000m., equivalent to 2.7% of GDP. Iran's total external debt was US $9,154m. at the end of 2002, of which $6,578m. was long-term public debt. In that year the cost of debt-servicing was equivalent to 4.1% of the value of exports of goods and services. The annual rate of inflation averaged 24.0% in 1990/91–2000/01. Consumer prices increased by an average of 15.8% in 2002/03 and 15.6% in 2003/04. The rate of unemployment was estimated at 11.2% in 2003/04.

Iran is a member of OPEC, of the Economic Co-operation Organization (ECO, see p. 210), of the Developing Eight (D-8, see p. 373) group of Islamic countries, and was admitted to the Group of 15 developing countries (G-15) in mid-2000.

Notable weaknesses in the Iranian economy include the Government's dependence on revenue from the petroleum sector, high rates of unemployment and inflation, and disparities in the distribution of income. Additional strain has, moreover, been placed on domestic resources by the presence in Iran of large numbers of refugees from Afghanistan and Iraq. The Fourth Five-Year Development Plan (FoFYDP), which took effect in March 2005, emphasized job creation, with a target of some 700,000 new posts annually. Other priorities were the encouragement of competition, privatization, the fostering of a knowledge-based economy, and the attraction of foreign investment. The FoFYDP had initially been rejected by the Council of Guardians in June 2004, but an amended version of the plan, in which a less radical privatization programme was outlined, was eventually approved. In September the Majlis adopted legislation giving 'conservative' deputies the right to veto two contracts with Turkish companies, as part of a crack-down on foreign firms investing in the country, prompting foreign investors to report a significant increase in Iran's risk levels. (A new foreign investment law approved by the Expediency Council in May 2002 had resulted in government approval for the first foreign take-over of an Iranian company.) 'Conservatives' attacked the 'reformist' FoFYDP as being hostile to the constitutional goals of social justice and national independence, asserting that it would lead to wealth concentration among certain interest groups, although in October 2004 the Expediency Council revoked articles in the Constitution advocating a state monopoly of the economy. The Third Five-Year Development Plan (2000–05) had allowed for the private ownership of banks for the first time since the Revolution; by early 2003 four private banks had been authorized to commence operations and the Government declared its intention to privatize all banks except Bank Melli Iran. The country's first private insurance firm was established in February 2003. In addition, a return to international capital markets was achieved, with two Eurobond issues totalling €1,000m. being issued during 2002, while the introduction of a unified exchange rate for the rial was announced in March of that year. In May 2000 the World Bank (despite US objections) resumed lending to Iran for the first time since 1994. Iran received a further World Bank loan in May 2004 to upgrade urban infrastructure and improve water supply and sanitation. Assisted by buoyant oil revenues, real GDP showed sustained growth in 2001/02 and 2002/03, but decelerated slightly in 2003/04. There was, however, an increase in employment creation. The budget for 2004/05 anticipated a rise in both revenue and expenditure, with a significant increase in non-oil revenue expected. Meanwhile, recent developments in the hydrocarbons sector were likely to have a positive impact on the Iranian economy. In mid-February 2004, despite US hostility to the deal, the Iranian Government signed an agreement with a Japanese consortium to develop the Azadegan oilfield (discovered in 1999 and believed to contain 5,000m.–6,000m. barrels of recoverable reserves). In mid-2004 construction of a natural gas pipeline linking Iran to Armenia began, with Iran expected to commence gas deliveries in 2007.

Education

Primary education is officially compulsory, and is provided free of charge, for five years between six and 10 years of age, although this has not been fully implemented in rural areas. Secondary education, from the age of 11, lasts for up to seven years, comprising a first cycle of three years and a second of four years. According to UNESCO estimates, in 1999/2000 primary enrolment included 80% of children in the relevant age-group (81% of boys; 79% of girls), while enrolment at secondary schools was equivalent to 59% of the appropriate age-group in 1996. There are 37 universities, including 16 in Tehran. According to official sources, there were some 809,567 students enrolled at Iran's public colleges and universities in 2002/03, in addition to the 864,190 students enrolled at the Islamic Azad University. Approved budgetary expenditure on education by the central Government in the financial year 2002/03 was IR 34,402,000m. (16.8% of total spending).

Public Holidays

The Iranian year 1384 runs from 21 March 2005 to 20 March 2006, and the year 1385 from 21 March 2006 to 20 March 2007.

2005: 21 January* (Qorban, Feast of the Sacrifice), 29 January* (Qadir-e-Khom), 11 February (Victory of the Islamic Revolution), 19 February* (Ashooray-e-Hosseini) (Tasooay-e-Hosseini), 20 March (Day of Oil Industry Nationalization), 21 March* (Qiyam-e-Khoonin), 21–25 March† (Nowrooz, Iranian New Year), 31 March* (Arbain-e-Hosseini), 1 April (Islamic Republic Day), 2 April (Sizdah-bedar, 13th and final day of Nowrooz celebrations), 8 April* (Flight of Prophet Muhammad), 21 April* (Birth of Prophet Muhammad), 27 April* (Birth of Imam Ali), 4 June (Death of Imam Khomeini), 19 August* (Mabas), 2 September* (Birth of Imam Mahdi), 22 September* (Martyrdom of Imam Ali), 4 November* (Fetr, end of Ramadan), 27 November* (Martyrdom of Imam Sadeq), 23 December* (Birth of Imam Reza).

2006: 11 January* (Qorban, Feast of the Sacrifice), 19 January* (Qadir-e-Khom), 9 February* (Ashooray-e-Hosseini) (Tasooay-e-Hosseini), 11 February (Victory of the Islamic Revolution), 11 March* (Qiyam-e-Khoonin), 20 March (Day of Oil Industry Nationalization), 21 March* (Arbain-e-Hosseini), 21–25 March† (Nowrooz, Iranian New Year), 29 March* (Flight of Prophet Muhammad), 1 April (Islamic Republic Day), 2 April (Sizdah-bedar, 13th and final day of Nowrooz celebrations), 11 April* (Birth of Prophet Muhammad), 17 April* (Birth of Imam Ali), 4 June (Death of Imam Khomeini), 9 August* (Mabas), 22 August* (Birth of Imam Mahdi), 12 September* (Martyrdom of Imam Ali), 24 October* (Fetr, end of Ramadan), 17 November* (Martyrdom of Imam Sadeq), 13 December* (Birth of Imam Reza).

*These holidays are dependent on the Islamic lunar calendar and may vary by one or two days from the dates given.

† This festival begins on the date of the Spring Equinox.

Weights and Measures

The metric system is in force, but some traditional units are still in general use.

Statistical Survey

The Iranian year runs from approximately 21 March to 20 March

Source (except where otherwise stated): Statistical Centre of Iran, POB 14155-6133, Dr Fatemi Ave, Tehran 14144; tel. (21) 8965061; fax (21) 8963451; e-mail sci@sci.org.ir; internet www.sci.org.ir; Bank Markazi Jomhouri Islami Iran (Central Bank), POB 15875-7177, 144 Mirdamad Blvd, Tehran; tel. (21) 29951; fax (21) 3115674; e-mail g.secdept@cbi.ir; internet www.cbi.ir.

Area and Population

AREA, POPULATION AND DENSITY

Area (sq km)	1,648,195*
Population (census results)†	
1 October 1991	55,837,163
25 October 1996	
Males	30,515,159
Females	29,540,329
Total	60,055,488
Population (official estimate at mid-year)	
2002	65,540,224
2003	66,479,838
2004	67,477,500
Density (per sq km) at mid-2004	40.9

* 636,372 sq miles.

† Excluding adjustment for underenumeration.

PROVINCES

(mid-2004)*

Province (Ostan)	Area (sq km)†	Population (estimates)	Density (per sq km)	Provincial capital
Tehran (Teheran) .	19,196	11,931,656	621.6	Tehran (Teheran)
Markazi (Central) .	29,406	1,344,920	45.7	Arak
Gilan	13,952	2,389,195	171.2	Rasht
Mazandaran . . .	23,833	2,796,120	117.3	Sari
Azarbayejan-e-Sharqi (East Azerbaijan) .	45,481	3,482,672	76.6	Tabriz
Azarbayejan-e-Gharbi (West Azerbaijan) .	37,463	2,896,657	77.3	Orumiyeh
Bakhtaran (Kermanshah) . .	24,641	1,921,284	78.0	Bakhtaran
Khuzestan . .	63,213	4,277,998	67.7	Ahvaz
Fars	121,825	4,323,626	35.5	Shiraz
Kerman . . .	181,714	2,380,682	13.1	Kerman
Khorasan . . .	302,966	6,444,320	21.3	Mashhad
Esfahan . . .	107,027	4,395,645	41.1	Esfahan
Sistan and Baluchestan . .	178,431	2,219,393	12.4	Zahedan
Kordestan (Kurdistan) . . .	28,817	1,546,256	53.7	Sanandaj
Hamadan	19,547	1,732,080	88.6	Hamadan
Chaharmahal and Bakhtiyari . .	16,201	832,945	51.4	Shahr-e-Kord
Lorestan . . .	28,392	1,739,644	61.3	Khorramabad
Ilam	20,150	538,877	26.7	Ilam
Kohgiluyeh and Boyerahmad .	15,563	674,113	43.3	Yasuj
Bushehr . . .	23,168	808,482	34.9	Bushehr
Zanjan	21,841	963,434	44.1	Zanjan
Semnan . . .	96,816	578,910	6.0	Semnan
Yazd	73,467	940,802	12.8	Yazd
Hormozgan . . .	71,193	1,284,925	18.0	Bandar Abbas
Ardebil	17,881	1,247,202	7.1	Ardebil

Province (Ostan)—*continued*	Area (sq km)†	Population (estimates)	Density (per sq km)	Provincial capital
Qom	11,237	1,038,424	92.4	Qom
Qazvin . . .	15,491	1,133,547	73.2	Qazvin
Golestan	20,893	1,613,691	77.2	Gorgan
Total	**1,629,807**	**67,477,500**	**41.4†**	**—**

* On 1 January 1997 the legislature approved a law creating a new province, Qazvin (with its capital in the city of Qazvin), by dividing the existing province of Zanjan. In June 1997 the Council of Ministers approved draft legislation to establish another new province, Golestan (with its capital in the city of Gorgan), by dividing the existing province of Mazandaran. On 29 September 2004 legislation was enacted whereby the province of Khorasan was divided into three new provinces: North Khorasan, South Khorasan and Razavi Khorasan (with their respective capitals in the cities of Bojnurd, Birjand and Mashad).

† Excluding inland water.

PRINCIPAL TOWNS

(population at 1996 census)

Tehran (Teheran, the capital) . .	6,758,845	Rasht	417,748
Mashad (Meshed) .	1,887,405	Hamadan . . .	401,281
Esfahan (Isfahan) .	1,266,072	Kerman	384,991
Tabriz	1,191,043	Arak	380,755
Shiraz	1,053,025	Ardabil (Ardebil) .	340,386
Karaj	940,968*	Yazd	326,776
Ahwaz	804,980	Qazvin	291,117
Qom	777,677	Zanjan	286,295
Bakhtaran (Kermanshah) . .	692,986	Sanandaj . . .	277,808
Orumiyeh . . .	435,200	Bandar-e-Abbas . .	273,578
Zahedan . . .	419,518	Khorramabad . .	272,815
		Eslamshahr (Islam Shahr) .	265,450

* Including towns of Rajayishahr and Mehrshahr. Estimated population of Mehrshahr at 1 October 1994 was 413,299 (Source: UN, *Demographic Yearbook*).

Mid-2003 (UN estimate, incl. suburbs): Tehran 7,200,000 (Source: UN, *World Urbanization Prospects: The 2003 Revision*).

BIRTHS, MARRIAGES AND DEATHS

	1985–90	1990–95	1995–2000
Birth rate (per 1,000)	38.9	30.6	19.5
Death rate (per 1,000)	8.3	6.5	5.4

Note: UN estimates of annual averages.

Source: UN, *World Population Prospects: The 2002 Revision*.

Births: 1,095,165 in 2000/01; 1,112,193 in 2001/02; 1,122,104 in 2002/03.

Marriages: 646,498 in 2000/01; 640,710 in 2001/02; 650,960 in 2002/03.

Expectation of life (WHO estimates, years at birth): 68.9 (males 66.5; females 71.7) in 2002 (Source: WHO, *World Health Report*).

ECONOMICALLY ACTIVE POPULATION
(persons aged 10 years and over, excl. armed forces, 1996 census)

	Males	Females	Total
Agriculture, hunting and forestry .	3,024,380	294,156	3,318,536
Fishing	38,418	309	38,727
Mining and quarrying	115,185	4,699	119,884
Manufacturing	1,968,806	583,156	2,551,962
Electricity, gas and water supply .	145,239	5,392	150,631
Construction	1,634,682	15,799	1,650,481
Wholesale and retail trade; repair of motor vehicles, motorcycles and personal and household goods	1,804,143	38,146	1,842,289
Hotels and restaurants	82,293	2,485	84,778
Transport, storage and communications	955,271	17,541	972,792
Financial intermediation . . .	139,286	13,586	152,872
Real estate, renting and business activities	137,039	12,051	149,090
Public administration and defence; compulsory social security . .	1,519,449	98,651	1,618,100
Education	581,597	459,459	1,041,056
Health and social work	184,242	118,897	303,139
Other community, social and personal service activities . .	183,246	41,159	224,405
Private households with employed persons	57,037	4,933	61,970
Extra-territorial organizations and bodies	660	220	880
Central departments and offices .	30,389	2,563	32,952
Activities not adequately defined .	204,808	52,220	257,028
Total employed	12,806,170	1,765,402	14,571,572
Unemployed	1,184,086	271,565	1,455,651
Total labour force	13,990,256	2,036,967	16,027,223

Unemployed (official estimates): 1,598,306 (males 1,005,398, females 592,908) in 2000; 1,633,743 (males 1,318,842, females 314,901) in 2001; 1,687,355 (males 1,117,589, females 569,766) in 2002 (Source: ILO).

Health and Welfare

KEY INDICATORS

Total fertility rate (children per woman, 2002)	2.4
Under-5 mortality rate (per 1,000 live births, 2003) . . .	39
HIV/AIDS (% of persons aged 15–49, 2003)	0.10
Physicians (per 1,000 head, 1996)	0.85
Hospital beds (per 1,000 head, 1996)	1.6
Health expenditure (2001): US $ per head (PPP)	350
Health expenditure (2001): % of GDP	6.3
Health expenditure (2001): public (% of total)	43.5
Access to water (% of persons, 2002)	93
Access to sanitation (% of persons, 2002)	84
Human Development Index (2002): ranking	101
Human Development Index (2002): value	0.732

For sources and definitions, see explanatory note on p. vi.

Agriculture

PRINCIPAL CROPS
('000 metric tons)

	2001	2002	2003
Wheat	9,458	12,450	12,900*
Rice (paddy)	1,990	2,888	3,300*
Barley	2,423	3,085	3,100†
Maize	1,064	1,450†	1,800*
Potatoes	3,485	3,756	3,550†
Sugar cane	3,195	3,712	3,650†
Sugar beet	4,649	6,098	5,300†
Dry beans	144	210	170†
Chick-peas	269	290†	255†
Lentils	104	117	105†
Almonds	97	107	105†
Walnuts	168	178	160†
Pistachios	112	249	310†
Soybeans (Soya beans)	130	135	115†
Cottonseed	225	165*	215†
Cabbages	260	260†	270†
Lettuce	90	90†	90†
Tomatoes	3,009	4,109	3,005†
Pumpkins, squash and gourds . .	455	500	500†
Cucumbers and gherkins . . .	1,233	1,430	1,350†
Aubergines (Eggplants)† . . .	100	120	120
Chillies and green peppers† . .	100	100	100
Dry onions	1,419	1,525	1,500†
Garlic†	70	70	70
Other vegetables	1,720*	1,850†	1,865†
Oranges	1,879	1,880†	1,850†
Tangerines, mandarins, clementines and satsumas . .	710	710†	710†
Lemons and limes	1,039	1,040†	1,040†
Other citrus fruits	103*	102†	103†
Apples	2,353	2,334	2,358†
Pears	191	189	190†
Apricots	283	284†	284†
Cherries	219	220†	220†
Peaches and nectarines† . . .	380	385	385
Plums	143	145†	147†
Grapes	2,517	2,704†	2,525†
Watermelons	1,816	2,170	1,902†
Cantaloupes and other melons . .	1,082	1,218	990†
Figs	71	81	77†
Dates	875	879	875†
Cotton (lint)	125*	99*	120†
Tea (made)	51	52†	52†

* Unofficial figure.
† FAO estimate(s).

Source: FAO.

LIVESTOCK
('000 head)

	2001	2002	2003
Horses*	150	150	150
Mules*	175	175	175
Asses*	1,600	1,600	160
Cattle	8,500	8,738	9,000*
Buffaloes	507	524	550*
Camels	146	146*	146*
Sheep	53,900	53,900	53,900*
Goats	25,757	25,757	26,000
Chickens (million)*	280	270	280

* FAO estimate(s).

Source: FAO.

LIVESTOCK PRODUCTS
('000 metric tons)

	2001	2002	2003
Beef and veal	274.1	284.3	290.0*
Buffalo meat*	11.4	11.8	11.9
Mutton and lamb	332.6	345.0	350.0*
Goat meat	111.1	104.7	105.0*
Chicken meat	885.3	792.4	810.0*
Turkey meat*	15	15	15
Other meat*	18.4	19.4	21.4
Cows' milk	4,865.9	4,975.1	5,000.0*
Buffaloes' milk	221.0	226.0	230.0*
Sheep's milk	560.0*	301.8	350.0*
Goats' milk	365.9	374.2	360.0*
Cheese*	224.0	228.3	227.3
Butter and ghee*	152.4	146.3	148.7
Hen eggs	580.7	580.0	585.0*
Honey	26.6	28.0	29.0*
Wool (greasy)*	75	75	75
Cattle hides*	39.4	40.9	42.3
Sheepskins*	62.4	64.8	64.8
Goatskins*	19.8	18.7	18.8

* FAO estimate(s).

Source: FAO.

Forestry

ROUNDWOOD REMOVALS
(FAO estimates, '000 cubic metres, excl. bark)

	2001	2002	2003
Sawlogs, veneer logs and logs for sleepers	319	319	319
Pulpwood	488	488	488
Other industrial wood	253	253	253
Fuel wood	264	257	251
Total	1,324	1,317	1,311

Source: FAO.

SAWNWOOD PRODUCTION
(FAO estimates, '000 cubic metres, incl. railway sleepers)

	2001	2002	2003
Total (all broadleaved)	106	106	106

Source: FAO.

Fishing

('000 metric tons, live weight)

	2000	2001	2002
Capture	384.0	336.5	324.9
Silver carp	8.8	3.7	4.3
Other cyprinids	10.0	2.7	3.6
Caspian shads	78.0	45.2	26.0
Clupeoids	15.0	17.7	12.9
Skipjack tuna	20.1	26.1	29.9
Longtail tuna	41.4	34.9	29.9
Yellowfin tuna	15.7	20.2	24.0
Aquaculture	40.6	62.6	76.8
Silver carp	17.0	26.3	34.0
Total catch	424.6	399.0	401.7

Source: FAO.

Production of caviar (metric tons, year ending 20 March): 93 in 2000/01; 88 in 2001/02; 68 in 2002/03.

Mining

CRUDE PETROLEUM
('000 barrels per day, year ending 20 March)

	2001/02	2002/03	2003/04
Total production	3,574	3,305	3,736

NATURAL GAS
(million cu metres, year ending 20 March)*

	2000/01	2001/02	2002/03†
Consumption (domestic)‡	62,800	67,200	76,000
Flared	13,800	13,300	10,800
Regional uses and wastes	6,600	5,500	8,000
Gas for export	—	500	1,300
Total production	83,200	86,500	96,100

* Excluding gas reinjected into oil wells (million cu metres): 26,000 in 2000/01; 27,5000 in 2001/02; 26,400 in 2002/03 (estimate).
† Estimates.
‡ Includes gas for household, commercial, industrial, generator and refinery consumption.

Source: IMF, *Islamic Republic of Iran: Statistical Appendix* (September 2003).

OTHER MINERALS
(estimated production, '000 metric tons, unless otherwise indicated, year ending 20 March)

	1999/2000	2000/01	2001/02
Iron ore: gross weight	12,370	10,300	11,300
Iron ore: metal content	6,100	5,100	5,600
Copper concentrates*	125	121	121
Bauxite	400	405	420
Lead concentrates*	15	15	15
Zinc concentrates*	90	120	120
Manganese ore†	105	101	121
Chromium concentrates‡	153	105	80
Molybdenum concentrates (metric tons)*	1,600	1,700	1,700
Silver (metric tons)*	22	22	23
Gold (kilograms)*	765	770	650
Bentonite	70	80	80
Kaolin	850	806	810
Other clays	450	485	
Magnesite	141	143	130
Fluorspar (Fluorite)	20	20	20
Feldspar	156	168	200
Barite (Barytes)	185	218	195
Salt (unrefined)	1,560	1,985	1,970
Gypsum (crude)	10,700	10,890	10,380
Pumice and related materials	150	760	810
Mica (metric tons)	2,000	2,000	2,000
Talc	25	25	25
Turquoise (kilograms)	20,000	20,000	20,000
Coal	1,815	2,002	2,020

* Figures refer to the metal content of ores and concentrates.
† Figures refer to gross weight. The estimated metal content (in '000 metric tons) was: 32 in 1999/2000; 30 in 2000/01; 37 in 2001/02.
‡ Figures refer to gross weight. The estimated chromic oxide content (in '000 metric tons) was: 75 in 1999/2000; 52 in 2000/01; 39 in 2001/02.

Source: US Geological Survey.

Industry

PETROLEUM PRODUCTS
('000 metric tons, year ending 20 March)

	1998/99	1999/2000	2000/01
Liquefied petroleum gas . . .	1,598	1,656	1,624
Naphtha	1,871	1,736	2,055
Motor spirit (petrol)	9,025	9,692	9,877
Aviation gasoline	96	96	108
Kerosene	4,750	4,798	1,272
White spirit	320	300	90
Jet fuel	1,350*	1,377*	114
Gas-diesel (distillate fuel) oil	16,850*	18,100*	21,582
Residual fuel oils*	19,500	2,100	28,415
Lubricating oils*	695	715	448
Petroleum bitumen (asphalt) . .	2,841	2,068	2,879

* Provisional or estimated figure(s).

Source: UN, *Industrial Commodity Statistics Yearbook.*

OTHER PRODUCTS
(year ending 20 March)

	1998/99	1999/2000	2000/01
Refined sugar ('000 metric tons)* .	1,050	923	938
Cigarettes (million)*	14,335	20,143	13,811
Paints ('000 metric tons)* . .	41	44	42
Cement ('000 metric tons) . .	20,049†	22,219*	23,276*
Refrigerators ('000)* . . .	860	798	791
Telephone sets ('000)* . . .	338	192	430
Radio receivers ('000) . . .	127*	114	139
Television receivers ('000) . .	734	860	850
Footwear (million pairs)* . . .	7,156	5,257	4,833
Carpets and rugs ('000 sq m)* . .	80,674	33,965	49,316
Electric energy (million kWh) . .	103,412	117,621	116,327

* Figures refer to production in manufacturing establishments with 10 workers or more.
† Figures refer to production in large-scale manufacturing establishments with 50 workers or more.

Source: UN, *Industrial Commodity Statistics Yearbook.*

2001/02 (year ending 20 March): Refined sugar ('000 metric tons) 1,113; Cigarettes (million) 13,359; Cement ('000 metric tons) 24,755; Radios and recorders ('000) 129; Television receivers ('000) 808; Carpets and rugs ('000 sq m) 51,875.

Finance

CURRENCY AND EXCHANGE RATES

Monetary Units
100 dinars = 1 Iranian rial (IR).

Sterling, Dollar and Euro Equivalents (31 December 2004)
£1 sterling = 16,982.8 rials;
US $1 = 8,793.0 rials;
€1 = 11,977.0 rials;
100,000 Iranian rials = £5.89 = $11.37 = €8.35.

Average Exchange Rate (rials per US $)
2002   6,906.96
2003   8,193.89
2004   8,614.00

Note: In March 1993 the former multiple exchange rate system was unified, and since then the exchange rate of the rial has been market-determined. The foregoing information on average exchange rates refers to the base rate, applicable to receipts from exports of petroleum and gas, payments for imports of essential goods and services, debt-servicing costs and imports related to large national projects. There was also an export rate, set at a mid-point of US $1 = 3,007.5 rials in May 1995, which applied to receipts from non-petroleum exports and to all other official current account transactions not effected at the base rate. In addition, a market rate was determined by transactions on the Tehran Stock Exchange: at 31 January 2002 it was US $1 = 7,924 rials. The weighted average of all exchange rates (rials per US $, year ending 20 December) was: 3,206 in 1997/98; 4,172 in 1998/99; 5,731 in 1999/2000. A new unified exchange rate, based on the market rate, took effect from 21 March 2002.

BUDGET
('000 million rials, year ending 20 March)*

Revenue	2000/01	2001/02	2002/03
Oil and gas revenue	128,205	103,138	149,685
Non-oil revenue	61,784	77,841	98,576
Tax revenue	33,298	41,682	50,533
Taxes on income, profits and capital gains	19,585	22,988	25,653
Domestic taxes on goods and services	5,766	6,853	8,490
Taxes on international trade, transactions . . .	7,948	11,841	16,410
Non-tax revenues	12,004	13,442	15,035
Other non-oil revenues . . .	16,481	22,717	32,988
Total	**189,989**	**180,979**	**248,261**

Expenditure†	2000/01	2001/02	2002/03
Current expenditure	88,068	112,551	148,749
General services	9,947	13,118	18,695
National defence	17,314	20,683	21,248
Social Services	40,160	46,254	65,920
Education	21,640	24,139	34,402
Health and nutrition . . .	4,358	5,099	7,267
Social security and welfare .	11,132	13,093	18,660
Housing	484	589	839
Economic services	2,590	3,641	5,189
Fuel and energy	12	13	19
Transport and communications	377	739	1,053
Agriculture	1,140	1,449	2,065
Water resources	17	21	30
Industry	174	179	255
Commerce	300	517	737
Other current expenditure . .	18,057	28,855	37,697
Capital expenditure	30,115	25,488	56,305
Total	**118,183**	**138,039**	**205,054**

* Figures refer to the consolidated accounts of the central Government, comprising the General Budget, the operations of the Social Security Organization and special (extrabudgetary) revenue and expenditure.
† Excluding lending minus repayments ('000 million rials): 21,710 in 2000/01; 30,948 in 2001/02; 65,567 in 2002/03.

2003/04 ('000 million rials, year ending 20 March, preliminary figures): *Revenue:* Oil and gas revenue 184,535; Non-oil revenue 121,201 (Tax revenue 65,099, Non-tax revenue 15,633, Other non-oil revenue 40,469); Total revenue 305,735. *Expenditure:* Current expenditure 181,600 (Wages and salaries 65,725, Goods and services 26,400, Interest payments 3,344, Subsidies and transfers 39,700, Other 46,432); Capital expenditure 57,772; Total expenditure 239,373 (excl. lending minus repayments 68,148).

Source: IMF, *Islamic Republic of Iran: Statistical Appendix* (September 2004).

INTERNATIONAL RESERVES
(US $ million at 31 December)*

	1993	1994	1995
Gold (national valuation) . . .	229.1	242.2	251.9
IMF special drawing rights . .	144.0	142.9	133.6
Total	**373.1**	**385.1**	**385.5**

* Excluding reserves of foreign exchange, for which no figures have been available since 1982 (when the value of reserves was US $5,287m.).

IMF special drawing rights (US $ million at 31 December): 336 in 2001; 364 in 2002; 399 in 2003.

Source: IMF, *International Financial Statistics.*

MONEY SUPPLY
('000 million rials at 20 December)

	2001	2002	2003
Currency outside banks . . .	21,840	25,945	30,809
Non-financial public enterprises' deposits at Central Bank .	4,552	12,563	6,800
Demand deposits at commercial banks	99,275	123,963	147,018
Total money	**125,667**	**162,471**	**184,627**

Source: IMF, *International Financial Statistics.*

IRAN

COST OF LIVING
(Consumer Price Index in urban areas, year ending 20 March; base: 1997/98 = 100)

	2001/02	2002/03	2003/04
Food, beverages and tobacco	178.5	213.2	246.1
Clothing	127.4	132.6	142.8
Housing, fuel and light	201.8	241.2	285.9
All items (incl. others)	177.9	206.0	238.2

NATIONAL ACCOUNTS
('000 million rials at current prices, year ending 20 March)

National Income and Product

	2001/02	2002/03	2003/04*
Domestic factor incomes†	570,121	793,656	946,229
Consumption of fixed capital	94,500	122,809	149,489
Gross domestic product (GDP) at factor cost	664,620	916,465	1,095,717
Indirect taxes / Less Subsidies	7,116	9,441	12,000
GDP in purchasers' values	671,736	925,906	1,107,717
Factor income from abroad / Less Factor income paid abroad	1,455	-15,932	-22,667
Gross national product (GNP)	673,191	909,974	1,085,051
Less Consumption of fixed capital	94,500	122,809	149,489
National income in market prices	578,692	787,165	935,562

* Provisional figures.
† Compensation of employees and the operating surplus of enterprises.

Expenditure on the Gross Domestic Product

	2001/02	2002/03	2003/04*
Government final consumption expenditure	94,029	118,408	138,176
Private final consumption expenditure	323,314	417,081	500,497
Increase in stocks	48,669	76,691	115,770
Gross fixed capital formation	187,999	261,136	319,296
Statistical discrepancy	6,194	17,292	6,705
Total domestic expenditure	660,205	890,608	1,080,444
Exports of goods and services	137,732	245,868	309,739
Less Imports of goods and services	126,201	210,570	282,466
GDP in purchasers' values	671,736	925,906	1,107,717
GDP at constant 1997/98 prices†	334,104	359,011	383,160

* Provisional figures.
† Including adjustment for changes in terms of trade ('000 million rials): 1,480 in 2001/02; 14,348 in 2002/03; 20,328 in 2003/4 (provisional).

Gross Domestic Product by Economic Activity

	2001/02	2002/03	2003/04*
Agriculture, hunting, forestry and fishing	85,238	107,201	127,578
Oil and gas	100,391	210,085	252,144
Manufacturing and Mining	134,822	171,199	199,943
Mining and quarrying	4,618	5,500	6,491
Manufacturing	88,807	104,799	123,139
Electricity, gas and water	11,294	15,025	18,420
Construction	30,104	45,875	51,892
Services	353,592	444,065	542,185
Trade, restaurants and hotels	90,092	110,242	131,849
Transport, storage and communications	56,590	66,151	83,119
Financial and monetary institutions	12,092	19,218	29,889
Real estate, specialized and professional services	93,919	121,503	145,804
Government services	82,379	102,760	122,496
Other services	18,519	24,191	29,029
Sub-total	674,043	932,550	1,121,850

— continued	2001/02	2002/03	2003/04*
Less Imputed bank service charge	9,423	16,085	26,133
GDP at basic prices	664,620	916,465	1,095,717
Indirect taxes (net)	7,116	9,441	12,000
GDP in purchasers' values	671,736	925,906	1,107,717

* Provisional figures.

BALANCE OF PAYMENTS
(US $ million, year ending 20 March)

	2001/02	2002/03	2003/04*
Exports of goods f.o.b.	23,904	28,237	33,788
Petroleum and gas	19,339	22,966	27,033
Non-petroleum and gas exports	4,565	5,271	6,755
Imports of goods f.o.b.	-18,129	-22,036	-28,795
Trade balance	5,775	6,201	4,993
Exports of services	2,833	4,372	5,782
Imports of services	-3,586	-7,446	9,971
Balance on goods and services	5,022	3,127	804
Other income received	655	653	633
Other income paid	-397	-1,082	-604
Balance on goods, services and income	5,280	2,698	833
Unrequited transfers (net)	705	887	1,226
Current balance	5,985	3585	2,059
Long-term capital (net)	2,361	3,329	1,350
Short-term capital (net)	-1,211	-796	2,665
Net errors and omissions	-2,375	-1,452	-2,553
Overall balance	4,760	4,667	3,521

* Preliminary figures.

External Trade

PRINCIPAL COMMODITIES
(US $ million, year ending 20 March)

Imports c.i.f. (distribution by SITC)	2000/01	2001/02	2002/03
Food and live animals	1,979	2,107	1,522
Cereals and cereal preparations	1,390	1,472	899
Crude materials (inedible) except fuels	707	675	742
Animal and vegetable oils and fats	417	388	488
Vegetable oils and fats	408	382	477
Chemicals	2,027	2,384	2,580
Chemical elements and compounds	460	562	642
Plastic, cellulose and artificial resins	428	579	597
Basic manufactures	3,185	3,319	3,221
Iron and steel	1,819	1,895	1,738
Machinery and transport equipment	5,172	7,565	10,220
Non-electric machinery	2,976	4,051	4,928
Electrical machinery, apparatus, etc.	1,085	1,819	1,808
Transport equipment	1,111	1,696	3,484
Miscellaneous manufactured articles	447	536	716
Total (incl. others)	14,347	17,626	22,275

Exports f.o.b.*	2001/02	2002/03	2003/04†
Agricultural and traditional goods	1,603	1,724	1,987
Carpets	553	514	573
Fruit and nuts (fresh and dried)	666	779	985
Industrial manufactures	2,543	2,852	3,268
Chemical products	1,053	837	1,018
Iron and steel	278	350	318
Processed hydrocarbons (gas)	431	282	371
Total (incl. others)	4,565	5,271	6,755

* Excluding exports of crude petroleum and gas (US $ million): 19,339 in 2001/02; 22,966 in 2002/03; 27,033 in 2003/04 (preliminary figure).
† Preliminary data.
Note: Imports include registration fee, but exclude defence-related imports and imports of refined oil products.
Source: IMF, *Islamic Republic of Iran: Statistical Appendix* (September 2004).

PRINCIPAL TRADING PARTNERS
(US $ million)

Imports c.i.f. (year ending 20 March)	2000/01	2001/02	2002/03
Argentina	304	319	95
Australia	403	455	357
Austria	277	239	252
Belgium	426	440	396
Brazil	538	896	843
Canada	477	353	199
China, People's Republic	565	887	1,046
France	617	1,109	1,318
Germany	1,504	1,807	3,777
India	254	561	717
Indonesia	156	92	103
Italy	856	996	1,389
Japan	684	787	714
Kazakhstan	345	270	262
Korea, Republic	737	958	894
Netherlands	270	346	308
Russia	920	914	874
Singapore	155	159	321
Spain	343	308	300
Sweden	310	377	350
Switzerland	327	435	1,989
Thailand	228	108	123
Turkey	233	291	369
United Arab Emirates	1,154	1,633	2,152
United Kingdom	510	666	769
Total (incl. others)	14,347	17,626	22,275

Exports f.o.b. (year ending 31 December)*	2001	2002	2003
China, People's Republic	2,203	2,133	3,007
France	670	720	1,078
Germany	670	720	1,078
Iceland	879	415	882
Italy	1,920	1,620	1,947
Japan	4,561	4,311	6,764
Korea, Republic	206	620	1,174
New Zealand	752	639	948
Singapore	2,203	2,133	3,007
Spain	752	639	948
Turkey	763	837	1,692
United Kingdom	1,908	1,214	1,472
USA	519	543	686
Total (incl. others)	23,149	21,436	30,001

* Data based on direction of trade reporting by recipient nations.
Source: IMF, *Islamic Republic of Iran: Statistical Appendix* (September 2004).

Transport

RAILWAYS
(traffic, year ending 20 March)

	2000/01	2001/02	2002/03
Passengers carried ('000)	11,707	13,111	n.a.
Passenger-km (million)	7,128	8,043	8,582
Freight ton-km (million)	14,179	14,613	15,842

ROAD TRAFFIC
(registered motor vehicles, year ending 20 March)

	1999/2000	2000/01	2001/02
Passenger cars	181,236	237,462	271,886
Pick-ups and light trucks	42,177	35,894	44,038
Motorcycles	59,553	56,012	124,351

SHIPPING
Merchant Fleet
(registered at 31 December)

	2001	2002	2003
Number of vessels	389	380	382
Displacement ('000 grt)	3,943.6	4,128.4	4,851.9

Source: Lloyd's Register-Fairplay, *World Fleet Statistics*.

International Sea-borne Freight Traffic
('000 metric tons)

	1994	1995	1996
Goods loaded	128,026	132,677	140,581
Crude petroleum and petroleum products	123,457	127,143	134,615
Goods unloaded	20,692	22,604	27,816
Petroleum products	6,949	7,240	7,855

CIVIL AVIATION
(traffic on scheduled services)

	1999	2000	2001
Kilometres flown (million)	63	66	73
Passengers carried ('000)	8,277	8,722	9,533
Passenger-km (million)	7,852	8,202	8,793
Total ton-km (million)	799	801	854

Source: UN, *Statistical Yearbook*.

Tourism

FOREIGN TOURIST ARRIVALS

Country of nationality	1997	1998	1999
Afghanistan	69,728	125,189	146,322
Armenia	17,793	11,758	13,743
Azerbaijan	264,564	383,123	447,797
Bahrain	14,918	14,322	16,740
Kuwait	17,191	26,472	30,941
Pakistan	111,556	115,431	134,917
Russia	34,296	10,191	11,911
Saudi Arabia	16,770	21,093	24,654
Turkey	70,108	160,959	188,130
Total (incl. others)	739,711	1,007,597	1,320,690*

* Including 147,000 of unspecified nationality.

Source: World Tourism Organization, *Yearbook of Tourism Statistics*.

Total arrivals (year ending 20 March): 1,341,762 in 2000/01; 1,402,160 in 2001/02; 1,584,922 in 2002/03.

Tourism receipts (US $ million): 586 in 1999; 671 in 2000; 1,122 in 2001.

Communications Media

	1999	2000	2001
Television receivers ('000 in use) .	10,300	10,400	n.a.
Telephones ('000 main lines in use)	8,371.2	9,486.3	10,896.6
Mobile cellular telephones ('000			
subscribers)	490.5	962.6	2,087.4
Personal computers ('000 in use)	3,500	n.a.	4,500
Internet users ('000)	100	250	1,005
Book production*:			
titles	20,642	23,305	31,660
copies ('000)	105,687	117,785	162,674

* Including pamphlets.

2002: Telephones ('000 main lines in use) 12,200.2; Mobile cellular telephones ('000 subscribers) 2,187.0; personal computers ('000 in use) 4,900; Internet users ('000) 3,168 (Source: International Telecommunication Union).

2003: Telephones ('000 main lines in use) 14,571.1; Mobile cellular telephones ('000 subscribers) 3,376.5; Internet users ('000) 4,300 (Source: International Telecommunication Union).

Radio receivers ('000 in use): 17,400 in 1998.

Facsimile machines (number in use, year ending 20 March 1995): 30,000 in 1994.

Newspapers and periodicals (number): 1,532 in 2000/01.

Education

(2002/03)

	Institu-tions	Teachers	Students			
			Males	Females	Total	
Pre-primary . . .	12,456	4,471	195,487	208,167	403,654	
Primary	68,627	297,711	3,662,507	3,366,417	7,028,924	
Lower secondary	30,630	184,948	2,636,728	2,228,875	4,865,603	
Upper secondary .	18,378	167,570	1,940,924	1,887,600	3,828,524	
Teacher training .	69	970	5,228	4,501	9,729	
Higher	n.a.	84,679	825,474	848,283	1,673,757	

Students ('000, 2003/04): Pre-primary 439; Primary 6,649; Lower secondary 4,679; High schools 3,819; Teacher training 9.

Adult literacy rate (UNESCO estimates): 77.1% (males 83.5%; females 70.4%) in 2002 (Source: UN Development Programme, *Human Development Report*).

Directory

The Constitution

A draft constitution for the Islamic Republic of Iran was published on 18 June 1979. It was submitted to a 'Council of Experts', elected by popular vote on 3 August, to debate the various clauses and to propose amendments. The amended Constitution was approved by a referendum on 2–3 December 1979. A further 45 amendments to the Constitution were approved at a referendum on 28 July 1989.

The Constitution states that the form of government of Iran is that of an Islamic Republic, and that the spirituality and ethics of Islam are to be the basis for political, social and economic relations. Persians, Turks, Kurds, Arabs, Balochis, Turkomans and others will enjoy completely equal rights.

The Constitution provides for a President to act as chief executive. The President is elected by universal adult suffrage for a term of four years. Legislative power is held by the Majlis (Islamic Consultative Assembly), with 290 members (effective from the 2000 election) who are similarly elected for a four-year term. Provision is made for the representation of Zoroastrians, Jews and Christians.

All legislation passed by the Islamic Consultative Assembly must be sent to the Council for the Protection of the Constitution (Article 94), which will ensure that it is in accordance with the Constitution and Islamic legislation. The Council for the Protection of the Constitution consists of six religious lawyers appointed by the Wali Faqih (see below) and six lawyers appointed by the High Council of the Judiciary and approved by the Islamic Consultative Assembly. Articles 19–42 deal with the basic rights of individuals, and provide for equality of men and women before the law and for equal human, political, economic, social and cultural rights for both sexes.

The press is free, except in matters that are contrary to public morality or insult religious belief. The formation of religious, political and professional parties, associations and societies is free, provided they do not negate the principles of independence, freedom, sovereignty and national unity, or the basis of Islam.

The Constitution provides for a Wali Faqih (religious leader) who, in the absence of the Imam Mehdi (the hidden Twelfth Imam), carries the burden of leadership. The amendments to the Constitution that were approved in July 1989 increased the powers of the Presidency by abolishing the post of Prime Minister, formerly the Chief Executive of the Government.

The Government

SUPREME RELIGIOUS LEADER

Wali Faqih: Ayatollah SAYED ALI KHAMENEI.

HEAD OF STATE

President: Hojatoleslam Dr SAYED MUHAMMAD KHATAMI (assumed office 3 August 1997; re-elected 8 June 2001).

First Vice-President: MUHAMMAD REZA AREF.

Vice-President in charge of Legal and Parliamentary Affairs: Hojatoleslam MAJID ANSARI.

Vice-President and Head of the Iranian Atomic Energy Organization: GHOLAMREZA AGHAZADEH.

Vice-President and Head of the Organization for the Protection of the Environment: Dr MASSOUMEH EBTEKAR.

Vice-President and Head of the Physical Education Organization: MOHSEN MEHRALIZADEH.

Vice-President and Head of the Martyrs' and Self-Sacrificers' Affairs Foundation: HOSSEIN DEHGHAAN.

Vice-President and Head of the Cultural Heritage and Tourism Organization: SAYED HOSSEIN MAR'ASHI.

Vice-President and Head of the Presidential Office: SAYED ALI KHATAMI.

COUNCIL OF MINISTERS
(April 2005)

Minister of Foreign Affairs: KAMAL KHARRAZI.

Minister of Education: MORTEZA HAJI.

Minister of Culture and Islamic Guidance: AHMAD MASJED JAME'I.

Minister of Intelligence and Security: Hojatoleslam ALI YUNESI.

Minister of Commerce: MUHAMMAD SHARI'ATMADARI.

Minister of Health and Medical Education: Dr MASSOUD PEZESHKIAN.

Minister of Posts, Telegraphs and Telecommunications: AHMAD MO'TAMEDI.

Minister of Justice: Hojatoleslam MUHAMMAD ISMAÏL SHOUSHTARI.

Minister of Defence and Armed Forces Logistics: Rear-Adm. ALI SHAMKHANI.

Minister of Roads and Transport: MUHAMMAD RAHMATI.

Minister of Science, Research and Technology: Dr JA'FAR TOFIQIDARIAN.

Minister of Industries and Mines: ESHAQ JAHANGIRI.

Minister of Labour and Social Affairs: NASSER KHALEQI.

Minister of the Interior: Hojatoleslam SAYED ABDOLVAHED MUSAVI-LARI.

Directory

Minister of Agricultural Jihad: Mahmud Hojjati.

Minister of Housing and Urban Development: Ali Abd al-Alizadeh.

Minister of Energy: Habibollah Bitaraf.

Minister of Oil: Bijan Namdar Zangeneh.

Minister of Economic Affairs and Finance: Safdar Hosseini.

Minister of Co-operatives: Ali Soufi.

Minister of Welfare and Social Security: Muhammad Hussein Sharifzadegan.

Head of the Management and Planning Organization: Hamid Reza Baradaran Shoraka.

MINISTRIES

Office of the President: Palestine Ave, Azerbaijan Intersection, Tehran; e-mail khatami@president.ir; internet www.president.ir.

Ministry of Agricultural Jihad: 20 Malaei Ave, Vali-e-Asr Sq., Tehran; tel. (21) 8895354; fax (21) 8904357; e-mail webinfo@asid.moa.or.ir; internet www.moa.or.ir.

Ministry of Commerce: Vali-e-Asr Ave, Tehran; tel. (21) 8893620; fax (21) 896504; e-mail minister@irtp.com; internet www.iranministryofcommerce.com.

Ministry of Co-operatives: 16 Bozorgmehr St, Vali-e-Asr Ave, Tehran 14169; tel. (21) 6400938; fax (21) 6498440; e-mail coop_international@icm.gov.ir; internet www.icm.gov.ir.

Ministry of Culture and Islamic Guidance: Baharestan Sq., Tehran; tel. (21) 32411; fax (21) 3117535; e-mail ershad@neda.net; internet www.farhang.gov.ir.

Ministry of Defence and Armed Forces Logistics: Shahid Yousuf Kaboli St, Sayed Khandan Area, Tehran; tel. (21) 21401; fax (21) 864008; e-mail vds@isiran.com; internet www.mod.ir.

Ministry of Economic Affairs and Finance: Sour Esrafil Ave, Nasser Khosrou St, Tehran 11149–43661; tel. (21) 2553401; fax (21) 2581933; e-mail info@mefa.gov.ir; internet mefa.gov.ir.

Ministry of Education: Si-e-Tir St, Emam Khomeini Sq., Tehran; tel. (21) 32421; fax (21) 675503.

Ministry of Energy: North Palestine St, Tehran; tel. (21) 890001; fax (21) 8801995; e-mail webmaster@moe.or.ir; internet www.moe.or.ir.

Ministry of Foreign Affairs: Shahid Abd al-Hamid Mesri St, Ferdowsi Ave, Tehran; tel. (21) 3211; fax (21) 3212763; e-mail matbuat@mfa.gov.ir; internet www.mfa.gov.ir.

Ministry of Health and Medical Education: POB 310, Tehran 11344; tel. (21) 677682; fax (21) 3853947; e-mail webmaster@hbi.dmr.or.ir; internet www.hbi.dmr.or.ir.

Ministry of Housing and Urban Development: Shahid Khoddami St, Vanak Sq., Tehran; tel. (21) 877711; fax (21) 8776634; e-mail minister@icic.gov.ir; internet www.mhud.gov.ir.

Ministry of Industries and Mines: POB 1416, 248 West Somayeh St, Tehran 15996; tel. (21) 8877588; fax (21) 8807817; e-mail mimwebmaster@mim.gov.ir; internet www.mim.gov.ir.

Ministry of Intelligence and Security: POB 16765-1947, Tehran; tel. (21) 233031; fax (21) 23305.

Ministry of the Interior: Jahad Sq., Fatemi St, Tehran; tel. (21) 8967866; fax (21) 8964678; e-mail ravabetomomi@moi.gov.ir; internet www.moi.ir.

Ministry of Justice: Panzdah-e-Khordad Sq., Tehran; tel. (21) 3112001; fax (21) 3113143.

Ministry of Labour and Social Affairs: Azadi Ave, Tehran; tel. (21) 6930031; fax (21) 6931062; e-mail info@irimlsa.org; internet www.irimlsa.org.

Ministry of Oil: Hafez St, Taleghani Ave, Tehran; tel. (21) 6152738; fax (21) 6152823; e-mail webmaster@nioc.org; internet www.nioc.org.

Ministry of Posts, Telegraphs and Telecommunications: POB 16314-145, Dr Shariati Ave, Tehran 163171-3363; tel. (21) 8114315; fax (21) 8429511; internet www.ptt.gov.ir.

Ministry of Roads and Transport: Shahid Dadman Bldg, Africa Ave, Argentina Sq., Tehran; tel. (21) 8878031; fax (21) 8878059; e-mail webmaster@mrt.ir; internet www.mrt.ir.

Ministry of Science, Research and Technology: POB 15875-4375, Central Bldg, Ostad Nejatollahi Ave, Tehran; tel. (21) 8891065; fax (21) 8827234; e-mail oise@msrt.gov.ir; internet www.msrt.gov.ir.

Ministry of Welfare and Social Security: Tehran.

President and Legislature

PRESIDENT

Election, 8 June 2001

Candidates	Votes	%
Sayed Muhammad Khatami	21,656,476	76.9
Ahmed Tavakkoli	4,387,112	15.6
Ali Shamkhani	737,051	2.6
Abdollah Jasbi	259,759	0.9
Mahmoud Kashani	237,660	0.8
Hassan Ghafuri-Fard	129,155	0.5
Mansur Razavi	114,616	0.4
Shahabeddin Sadr	60,546	0.2
Ali Falahian	55,225	0.2
Moustafa Hashemi-Taba	27,949	0.1
Invalid votes	493,740	1.8
Total	28,159,289	100.0

MAJLIS-E-SHURA-E ISLAMI—ISLAMIC CONSULTATIVE ASSEMBLY

Elections to the seventh Majlis took place on 20 February and 7 May 2004. Prior to the elections, the Council of Guardians barred more than 2,000 candidates from standing, including 80 current Majlis deputies. The majority of the barred candidates were recognized as being 'reformists'. At the first round of voting on 20 February, 229 deputies received a sufficient number of votes to be elected directly to the Majlis; at the second round on 7 May, a further 57 deputies were elected. Four seats remained vacant after both rounds: one in Tehran, after election officials postponed the second ballot, citing logistical concerns; and three seats in the earthquake-affected region around Bam were not contested. (It was announced in January 2005 that these seats were to be filled on 17 June, as were other seats where the Council of Guardians had overturned the results of the 2004 polls.) According to official reports, 'conservatives' controlled the seventh Majlis, with 195 seats; 'reformists' secured an estimated 40–50 seats, and the remainder were held by 'independents'.

Speaker: Gholam-Ali Haddad-Adel.

First Deputy Speaker: Muhammad Reza Bahonar.

Second Deputy Speaker: Muhammad Hassan Abu Turabi.

SHURA-YE ALI-YE AMNIYYAT-E MELLI—SUPREME COUNCIL FOR NATIONAL SECURITY

Formed in July 1989 to co-ordinate defence and national security policies, the political programme and intelligence reports, and social, cultural and economic activities related to defence and security. The Council is chaired by the President and includes a representative of the Wali Faqih, the Minister of the Interior, the Speaker of the Majlis, the Head of the Judiciary, the Chief of the Supreme Command Council of the Armed Forces, the Minister of Foreign Affairs, the Head of the Management and Planning Organization and the Minister of Intelligence and Security.

Secretary: Hassan Rohani.

MAJLIS-E KHOBREGAN—COUNCIL OF EXPERTS

Elections were held on 10 December 1982 to appoint a Council of Experts which was to choose an eventual successor to the Wali Faqih (then Ayatollah Khomeini) after his death. The Constitution provides for a three- or five-man body to assume the leadership of the country if there is no recognized successor on the death of the Wali Faqih. The Council comprises 86 clerics. Elections to a third term of the Council were held on 23 October 1998.

Speaker: Ayatollah Ali Meshkini.

First Deputy Speaker: Hojatoleslam Ali Akbar Hashemi Rafsanjani.

Second Deputy Speaker: Ayatollah Ibrahim Amini Najafabadi.

Secretaries: Hojatoleslam Hassan Taheri-Khorramabadi, Ayatollah Qorbanali Dorri Najafabadi.

SHURA-E-NIGAHBAN—COUNCIL OF GUARDIANS

The Council of Guardians, composed of six qualified Muslim jurists appointed by Ayatollah Khomeini and six lay Muslim lawyers, appointed by the Majlis from among candidates nominated by the Head of the Judiciary, was established in 1980 to supervise elections and to examine legislation adopted by the Majlis, ensuring that it accords with the Constitution and with Islamic precepts.

Chairman: Ayatollah Ahmad Jannati.

SHURA-YE TASHKHIS-E MASLAHAT-E NEZAM—COUNCIL TO DETERMINE THE EXPEDIENCY OF THE ISLAMIC ORDER

Formed in February 1988, by order of Ayatollah Khomeini, to arbitrate on legal and theological questions in legislation passed by the Majlis, in the event of a dispute between the latter and the supervisory Council of Guardians. Its permanent members, defined in March 1997, are Heads of the Legislative, Judiciary and Executive Powers, the jurist members of the Council of Guardians and the Minister or head of organization concerned with the pertinent arbitration. Four new members were appointed to the Expediency Council in March 2002, when Rafsanjani was reappointed as Chairman.

Chairman: Hojatoleslam ALI AKBAR HASHEMI RAFSANJANI.

HEY'AT-E PEYGIRI-YE QANUN ASASI VA NEZARAT BAR AN—COMMITTEE FOR ENSURING AND SUPERVISING THE IMPLEMENTATION OF THE CONSTITUTION

Formed by President Khatami in November 1997; members are appointed for a four-year term. Two new members were appointed to the Committee in April 2002.

Members: Dr GUDARZ EFTEKHAR-JAHROMI, MUHAMMAD ISMAÏL SHOUSH-TARI, HASHEM HASHEMZADEH HERISI, Dr HOSSEIN MEHRPUR, Dr MUHAMMAD HOSSEIN HASHEMI, MUHAMMAD ALI ABTAHI.

Political Organizations

Numerous political organizations were registered in the late 1990s, following the election of President Khatami, and have tended to be regarded as either 'conservative' or 'reformist', the principal factions in the legislature. Under the Iranian electoral system, political parties do not field candidates *per se* at elections, but instead back lists of candidates, who are allowed to be members of more than one party. In early 2004 there were estimated to be more than 100 registered political organizations. The following organizations contested elections to the seventh Majlis in February and May 2004:

Association of Technocrats: f. 2003; Sec.-Gen. KHOSRAU NASSIRI-RAD.

Etelaf-e Abadgaran-e Iran-e Islami (Islamic Iran Developers' Council): e-mail info@abadgaran.ir; internet www.abadgaran.ir; f. 2003 to contest municipal elections in February of that year; conservative; Leader GHOLAM-ALI HADDAD-ADEL.

Hezb-e E'tedal va Towse'eh (Moderation and Development Party): first congress held 2002; conservative; Sec.-Gen. MUHAMMAD BAQIR NOBAKHT.

Hezb-e Iran-e Sarfaraz (Proud Iran Party): reformist; Sec.-Gen. RUZBEH MESHKIN.

Hezb-e Islami-ye Kar (Islamic Labour Party): f. 1999 as splinter group of Khaneh-ye Kargar (Workers' House); reformist; Sec.-Gen. ABOLQASEM SARHADIZADEH.

Hezb-e Kargozaran-e Sazandegi (Servants of Construction Party): f. 1996 as Servants of Iran's Construction; authorized as political party in 1998; reformist; Sec.-Gen. GHOLAMHOSSEIN KARBA-SCHI.

Jam'iyat-e Motalefeh-e Islami (Islamic Coalition Party): f. 1963; conservative; Sec.-Gen. MOHAMMAD NABI HABIBI.

Khaneh-ye Kargar (Workers' House): reformist; Sec.-Gen. ALIREZA MAHJUB.

Majma'-e Niruha-ye Khat-e Imam (Assembly of the Followers of the Imam's Line): Sec.-Gen. HADI KHAMENEI.

Majma'-e Ruhaniyun-e Mobarez (Militant Clergy Association): f. 1988 as splinter group of the Jam'-ye Ruhaniyat-e Mobarez-i Tehran (Tehran Militant Clergy Association); reformist; Sec.-Gen. Hojatoleslam MAHDI KARRUBI.

Most of the following are either registered political parties who boycotted the elections to the Majlis in early 2004, or are unregistered organizations or guerrilla groups:

Ansar-e Hezbollah (Helpers of the Party of God): f. 1995; youth movement; conservative.

Daftar-e Tahkim-e Vahdat (Office for Stengthening Unity): national organization of Islamist university students who supported Khatami in the presidential election of 1997 and backed reformist candidates in the Majlis elections of 2000.

Democratic Party of Iranian Kurdistan: POB 102, Paris 75623, France; e-mail pdkiran@club-internet.fr; internet www.pdk-iran.org; f. 1945; seeks a federal system of government in Iran, in order to secure the national rights of the Kurdish people; mem. of the Socialist International; 95,000 mems; Sec.-Gen. MUSTAPHA HIJRI.

Fedayin-e-Khalq (Organization of the Iranian People's Feda-yeen—Majority): Postfach 260268, 50515 Köln, Germany; e-mail info@fadai.org; internet www.fadai.org; f. 1971; Marxist; Spokesman FARRAKH NEGAHDAR.

Fraksion-e Hezbollah: f. 1996 by deputies in the Majlis who had contested the 1996 legislative elections as a loose coalition known as the Society of Combatant Clergy; Leader ALI AKBAR HOSSAINI.

Hezb-e Hambastegi-ye Iran-e Islami (Islamic Iran Solidarity Party): f. 1998; reformist; Sec.-Gen. EBRAHIM ASHGARZADEH.

Hezb-e-Komunist Iran (Communist Party of Iran): POB 70445, 107 25 Stockholm, Sweden; e-mail cpi@cpiran.org; internet www.cpiran.org; f. 1979 by dissident mems of Tudeh Party; Sec.-Gen. 'AZARYUN'.

Jebbeh-ye Masharekat-e Iran-e Islami (Islamic Iran Participation Front): f. 1998; reformist; Leader MUHAMMAD REZA KHATAMI.

Komala: e-mail webmaster_komala@yahoo.se; internet www.komala.org; f. 1969; Kurdish wing of the Communist Party of Iran; Marxist-Leninist; First Sec. IBRAHIM ALIZADEH.

Marze Por-Gohar (Glorious Frontiers Party): POB 111, 1351 Westwood Blvd, Los Angeles, CA 90024, USA; tel. (310) 473-4763; fax (310) 477-8484; e-mail info@marzeporgohar.org; internet www.marzeporgohar.org; f. 1998; nationalist party advocating a secular republic in Iran; Leader ROOZBEH FARAHANIPOUR.

Mujahidin-e-Khalq (Holy Warriors of the People): e-mail mojahed@mojahedin.org; internet www.iran.mojahedin.org; Islamic guerrilla group opposed to clerical regime; since June 1987 comprising the National Liberation Army; mem. of the National Council of Resistance; based in Paris 1981– and in Baghdad 1986–; Leaders MASSOUD RAJAVI, MARYAM RAJAVI.

National Democratic Front: e-mail ndfi@azadi-iran.org; internet www.azadi-iran.org; f. March 1979; Leader HEDAYATOLLAH MATINE-DAFTARI (based in Paris, January 1982–).

National Front (Union of National Front Forces): comprises Iran Nationalist Party, Iranian Party, and Society of Iranian Students; Leader Dr KARIM SANJABI (based in Paris, August 1978–).

Nehzat-e Azadi-ye Iran (Liberation Movement of Iran): e-mail mizan@nehzateazadi.org; internet www.nehzateazadi.org; f. 1961; emphasis on basic human rights as defined by Islam; Gen. Sec. Dr IBRAHIM YAZDI.

Pan-Iranist Party: POB 5921, San José, CA 95150-5921, USA; tel. (510) 468-8279; fax (510) 237-7025; e-mail email@paniranism.org; internet www.paniranism.org; extreme right-wing; calls for a Greater Persia; Leader Dr SORAB AZAM ZANGANEH.

Sazeman-e Mujahidin-e Enqelab-e Islami (Organization of the Mujahidin of the Islamic Revolution): reformist; Sec.-Gen. MUHAMMAD SALAMATI.

Sazmane Peykar dar Rahe Azadieh Tabaqe Kargar (Organization Struggling for the Freedom of the Working Class): Marxist-Leninist.

Tudeh Party (Party of the Masses): POB 100644, 10566 Berlin, Germany; tel. (30) 3241627; e-mail mardom@tudehpartyiran.org; internet www.tudehpartyiran.org; f. 1941; declared illegal 1949; came into open 1979; banned again April 1983; First Sec. Cen. Cttee ALI KHAVARI.

The **National Council of Resistance (NCR)** was formed in Paris in October 1981 by former President Abolhasan Bani-Sadr and the Council's current leader, Massoud Rajavi, the leader of the Mujahidin-e-Khalq in Iran. In 1984 the Council comprised 15 opposition groups, operating either clandestinely in Iran or from exile abroad. Bani-Sadr left the Council in that year because of his objection to Rajavi's growing links with the Iraqi Government. The French Government asked Rajavi to leave Paris in June 1986 and he moved his base of operations to Baghdad, Iraq. On 20 June 1987 Rajavi, Secretary of the NCR, announced the formation of a National Liberation Army (10,000–15,000-strong) as the military wing of the Mujahidin-e-Khalq. However, the status of the Mujahidin was initially uncertain following the invasion of Iraq by the US-led coalition in March 2003 (see the chapter on Iraq) and a crack-down against the activities of the organization by the authorities in Paris, France, in mid-2003. In late July 2004 the USA declared a group of 3,800 members of the Mujahidin-e-Khalq interned in Iraq to have 'protected status' under the Geneva Convention. There is also a National Movement of Iranian Resistance, based in Paris. Dissident members of the Tudeh Party founded the Democratic Party of the Iranian People (internet www.dpip.org) in Paris in February 1988. A new pro-reform party, **Will of the Iranian Nation** (Leader HAKIMI POUR), was founded in February 2001.

Diplomatic Representation

EMBASSIES IN IRAN

Afghanistan: Dr Beheshti Ave, Corner of 4th St, Pakistan St, Tehran; tel. (21) 8737050; fax (21) 8735600; Ambassador (vacant).

Algeria: Tehran; tel. (21) 2420017; fax (21) 2420015; e-mail ambalg_teheran@yahoo.fr; Ambassador (vacant).

Argentina: POB 15875-4335, 3rd and 4th Floor, 7 Argentina Sq., Tehran; tel. (21) 8718294; fax (21) 8712583; e-mail alvarez951@yahoo.com; Chargé d'affaires ERNESTO CARLOS ALVAREZ.

Armenia: 1 Ostad Shahriar St, Razi St, Jomhouri Islami Ave, Tehran 11337; tel. (21) 6704833; fax (21) 6700657; e-mail emarteh@yahoo.com; Ambassador GEGHAM GHARIBJANIAN.

Australia: POB 15875-4334, No. 13, 23rd St, Intifada Ave, Tehran 15138; tel. (21) 8724456; fax (21) 8720484; e-mail dfat-tehran@dfat.gov.au; internet www.iran.embassy.gov.au; Ambassador GREG MORIARTY.

Austria: 3rd Floor, 78 Argentine Sq., Tehran; tel. (21) 8710753; fax (21) 8710778; e-mail teheran-ob@bmaa.gv.at; Ambassador Dr MICHAEL STIGELBAUER.

Azerbaijan: 10 Akdsihi St, Tehran; tel. (21) 2280063; fax (21) 2284929; e-mail azaremb@www.dci.co.ir; Ambassador ABBASALI K. HASANOV.

Bahrain: Intifada Ave, 31st St, No. 16, Tehran; tel. (21) 8773383; fax (21) 8779112; e-mail bahmanama@neda.net; Ambassador KAMAL SALEH AS-SALEH.

Bangladesh: POB 11365-3711, Gandhi Ave, 5th St, Building No. 14, Tehran; tel. (21) 8772979; fax (21) 8778295; e-mail banglaemb@parsonline.net; Ambassador ABDOLLAH AL-HASSAN.

Belarus: 1 Azar St, Aban St, Shahid Taheri St, Zafaranieyeh Ave, Tehran 19887; tel. (21) 2708829; fax (21) 2718682; e-mail iran@belembassy.org; Ambassador LEONID V. RACHKOV.

Belgium: 155–157 Shahid Fayyaz Bakhsh Ave, Shemiran, Elahieh, Tehran 19659; tel. (21) 2041617; fax (21) 2044608; e-mail teheran@diplobel.org; Ambassador JACQUES VERMEULEN.

Bosnia and Herzegovina: No. 485, Aban Alley, 4th St, Iran Zamin Ave, Shahrak-e-Ghods, Tehran; tel. (21) 8092728; Ambassador SENAHID BRISTIĆ.

Brazil: Vanak Sq., 58 Vanak St, Tehran 19964; tel. (21) 8035175; fax (21) 8083348; e-mail emb_brazil@yahoo.com; Ambassador CESARIO MELANTONIO NETO.

Brunei: 60 Babak Bahrami St, Jordan Ave, Tehran 19687; tel. (21) 8784238; fax (21) 8783381; e-mail bneiran@yahoo.com; Ambassador Haji ISHAAQ BIN Haji ABDULLAH.

Bulgaria: POB 11365-7451, Vali-e-Asr Ave, Dr Abbaspour Ave, 82 Nezami-e-Ganjavi St, Tehran; tel. (21) 8775662; fax (21) 8779680; e-mail bulgr.tehr@neda.net; Ambassador DUBROV GEORGIEV.

Burkina Faso: Africa Ave, Ibn Arabi St, No. 25, Tehran; tel. (21) 8785295.

Canada: POB 11365-4647, 57 Shahid Sarafraz St, Ostad Motahhari Ave, Tehran 15868; tel. (21) 8732623; fax (21) 8733202; e-mail teran@dfait-maeci.gc.ca; Ambassador GORDON VENNER.

China, People's Republic: 13 Narenjestan 7th, Pasdaran Ave, Tehran; tel. (21) 2291242; fax (21) 2291243; e-mail emchnir@neda.net; internet www.chinaembassy.ir; Ambassador LIU ZHENTANG.

Croatia: No. 25, 1st Behestan, Pasdaran St, Tehran; tel. (21) 2589923; fax (21) 2549199; e-mail vrh.teheran@mvp.hr; Ambassador MARJAN KOMBOL.

Cuba: Africa Ave, Shahid Azafi Sharqi St, No. 21, Tehran; tel. (21) 2257809; e-mail embacub.iran@apadana.com; Ambassador JOSÉ RAMÓN RODRIGUES.

Cyprus: 328 Shahid Karimi, Dezashib, Tajrish, Tehran; tel. (21) 2219842; fax (21) 2219843; Ambassador STAVROS LOIZIDES.

Czech Republic: POB 11365-4457, No. 199, Lavasani Ave, Cnr of Yas St, Tehran 195376-4358; tel. (21) 2288149; fax (21) 2802079; e-mail teheran@embassy.mzv.cz; internet www.mfa.cz/tehran; Chargé d'affaires a.i. MARTIN KLEPETKO.

Denmark: POB 19395-5358, 18 Dashti St, Dr Shariati Ave, Tehran 19148; tel. (21) 2640009, fax (21) 2640007; e-mail thramb@um.dk; internet www.ambadane.teheran.suite.dk; Ambassador CLAUS JUUL NIELSEN.

Ethiopia: Dar-e-Bad Nur Saadi, Kashanak, No. 38, Tehran; tel. (21) 2289338; Ambassador MOHAMMED HASAN KAHIM.

Finland: No. 4, Shirin Alley, Agha Bozorgi St, Elahiyeh, Tehran; tel. (21) 2230979; fax (21) 2210948; e-mail finlandiran@hotmail.com; Ambassador YRJÖ KARINEN.

France: 85 Neauphle-le-Château Ave, Tehran; tel. (21) 6706005; fax (21) 6706543; e-mail consulaire@ambafrance-ir.org; internet www.ambafrance-ir.org; Ambassador FRANÇOIS NICOULLAUD.

Georgia: POB 19575-379, Elahiyeh, Tehran; tel. (21) 2211470; fax (21) 2206848; e-mail georgia@apadana.com; Ambassador LEVAN ASATIYANI.

Germany: POB 11365-179, 320–324 Ferdowsi Ave, Tehran; tel. (21) 39990000; fax (21) 39991899; e-mail info@tehe.diplo.de; internet www.teheran.diplo.de; Ambassador Baron PAUL VON MALTZAHN.

Greece: POB 11365-8151, Africa Ave, Esfandiar St, No. 43, Tehran; tel. (21) 2050533; fax (21) 2057431; e-mail embgreece1@safineh.net; Ambassador MARCARIOUS KARAFOTIAS.

Guinea: POB 11365-4716, Dr Shariati Ave, Malek St, No. 10, Tehran; tel. (21) 7535744; fax (21) 7535743; e-mail ambaguinee_thr@hotmail.com; Ambassador OLIA KAMARA.

Holy See: Apostolic Nunciature, POB 11365-178, Razi Ave, No. 97, Neauphle-le-Château Ave, Tehran; tel. (21) 6403574; fax (21) 6419442; e-mail apnun-thr@parsonline.net; Apostolic Nuncio Most Rev. ANGELO MOTTOLA (Titular Archbishop of Cercina).

Hungary: POB 6363-19395, Darrous, Hedayat Sq, Shadloo St, No. 16, Tehran; tel. (21) 2550460; fax (21) 2550503; e-mail huembthr@neda.net; Ambassador Dr ISTVÁN VENCZEL.

Iceland: Tehran; Ambassador STEFAN SKJALDARSON.

India: POB 15875-4118, 46 Mir-Emad St, Cnr of 9th St, Dr Beheshti Ave, Tehran; tel. (21) 8755103; fax (21) 8755973; e-mail indmteh@dpimail.net; internet www.indianembassy-tehran.com; Ambassador K. C. SINGH.

Indonesia: POB 11365-4564, Ghaem Magham Farahani Ave, No. 210, Tehran; tel. (21) 8716865; fax (21) 8718822; e-mail kbritehran@safineh.net; internet www.indonesian-embassy.ir; Ambassador BASRI HASANUDDIN.

Iraq: Karamian Alley, No. 17, Pol-e-Roomi, Dr Shariati Ave, Tehran; tel. (21) 2218386; Ambassador MUHAMMAD MIGUID ASH-SHEIKH.

Ireland: Bonbast Nahid St, North Kamranieh Ave, No. 9, Tehran 19369; tel. (21) 2297918; fax (21) 2286933; e-mail irelembteh@padisar.net; Ambassador THOMAS O. BOLSTER.

Italy: POB 11365-7863, 81 Neauphle-le-Château Ave, Tehran; tel. (21) 6726955; fax (21) 6726961; e-mail segreteria.ambteheran@esteri.it; internet sedi.esteri.it/teheran; Ambassador ROBERTO TOSCANO.

Japan: POB 11365-814, Bucharest Ave, Corner of 5th St, Tehran; tel. (21) 8713396; fax (21) 8713515; internet www.ir.emb-japan.go.jp; Ambassador HIDEAKI DOMICHI.

Jordan: POB 14665-835, Shahrak-e-Ghods, Faz 4, Khayaban Flamk, Khayaban 8, Block 1647, Tehran 009821; tel. (21) 8088356; fax (21) 8080496; e-mail jordanemb-teh@hotmail.com; Ambassador AHMAD MOUFLEH.

Kazakhstan: Darrus Ave, Hedayat St, No. 4, Tehran; tel. (21) 2565933; fax (21) 2546400; e-mail kazembir@apadana.com; Ambassador SABIT TAYIROV.

Kenya: POB 19395-4566, 46 Gulshar St, Africa Ave, Tehran; tel. (21) 2059154; fax (21) 2053372; e-mail kenemteh@irtp.com; Ambassador HASSAN MUHAMMAD SALEH BAQA.

Korea, Democratic People's Republic: 349 Shahid Dastjerdi Ave, Africa Ave, Tehran; tel. (21) 8783341; Ambassador KIM CHANG-RYONG.

Korea, Republic: No. 37, Ahmad Ghasir Ave, Tehran; tel. (21) 8711125; fax (21) 8737917; e-mail korth@dpi.net.ir; Ambassador LI SUNG-CHOOL.

Kuwait: Africa Ave, Mahiyar St, No. 15, Tehran; tel. (21) 8785997; Ambassador AHMAD AZ-ZAFIRI.

Lebanon: No. 31, Shahid Kalantari St, Gharani Ave, Tehran; tel. (21) 8908451; fax (21) 8907345; Ambassador ADNAN MANSOUR.

Libya: No. 163, Ostad Motahhari Ave, Shahid Muftahi Ave, Tehran; tel. (21) 8742572; Ambassador ALI MARIA.

Macedonia, former Yugoslav republic: No. 7, 4th Alley, Intifada Ave, Tehran; tel. (21) 8720810, Chargé d'affaires CVETKO SOFKOVSKI.

Malaysia: POB 11365-8518, No. 6, Shahid Akhgan St, Fereshteh Ave, Tehran; tel. (21) 2010016; fax (21) 2010477; e-mail mwtehran@sokhan.com; Ambassador HUSSEIN GHULAN HANIFF.

Mali: Ambassador AMADOU MODY DIALL.

Mexico: No. 41, Golfam St, Africa Ave, Tehran 19156; tel. (21) 2057586; fax (21) 2057589; e-mail embamex@apadana.com; Ambassador LUIS MONASTERIO.

Morocco: 5 Lavasani Ave, Davoud Barati, Tehran; tel. (21) 2206731; fax (21) 2210162; e-mail info@sifamach.com; Ambassador ABDELAZIZ BENNIS.

Netherlands: POB 11365-138, Darrous, Shahrzad Blvd, Kamasaie St, 1st East Lane, No. 33, Tehran 19498; tel. (21) 2567005; fax (21) 2566990; e-mail teh@minbuza.nl; Ambassador HEIN J. DE VRIES.

New Zealand: POB 15875-4313, 34 North Golestan Complex, Cnr of 2nd Park Alley and Sosan St, Aghdasiyeh St, Niavaran, Tehran; tel. (21) 2800289; fax (21) 2831673; e-mail newzealand@mavara .com; Ambassador NIELS HOLM.

Nigeria: No. 9, Intifada Ave, 31st St, Tehran; tel. (21) 8774936; e-mail ngrembtehran@yahoo.com; Ambassador IBRAHIM GANYANA ABUBAKAR.

Norway: POB 19395-5398, Lavasani Ave 201, Tehran; tel. (21) 2291333; fax (21) 2292776; e-mail emb.tehran@mfa.no; internet ud25.mogul.no; Ambassador OLE KRISTIAN HOLTHE.

Oman: No. 12, Tandis Alley, Africa Ave, Tehran; tel. (21) 2056831; fax (21) 2044672; Chargé d'affaires a.i. RASHID BIN MUBARAK BIN RASHID AL-ODWALI.

Pakistan: No. 1, Ahmed Eitmadzadeh Ave, Jamshidabad Shomali, Dr Fatemi Ave, Tehran 14118; tel. (21) 6941388; fax (21) 6944898; e-mail pareptehran@yahoo.com; Ambassador JAVID HUSSEIN.

Philippines: POB 19395-4797, No. 13, Mahyar St, Africa Ave, Tehran; tel. (21) 2047802; fax (21) 2046239; e-mail tehranpe@dfa .gov.ph; Ambassador RODRIGO ARAGON.

Poland: Africa Ave, Piruz St, No. 1/3, Tehran; tel. (21) 8787262; e-mail ambrpri@sokhan.net; Ambassador WITOLD SMIDOWSKI.

Portugal: No. 13, Rouzbeh Alley, Darrous, Hedayat St, Tehran; tel. (21) 2543237; fax (21) 2552668; e-mail portugal@sr.co.ir; Ambassador Dr JOSÉ MANUEL DA COSTA ARSÉNIO.

Qatar: POB 11365-1631, Africa Ave, Golazin Ave, Parke Davar, No. 4, Tehran; tel. (21) 2051255; fax (21) 2056023; e-mail tehran@mofa .gov.qa; Ambassador Dr SALEH IBRAHIM AL-KAWARI.

Romania: Fakhrabad Ave 12, Baharestan Ave, Tehran; tel. (21) 7539041; fax (21) 7535291; e-mail ambrotehran@parsonline.net; internet www.ambrotehran.com; Ambassador NICOLAE STAN.

Russia: 39 Neauphle-le-Château Ave, Tehran; tel. (21) 6701161; fax (21) 6701652; e-mail russembassy@apadana.com; Ambassador (vacant).

Saudi Arabia: No. 1, Niloufar St, Boustan St, Pasdaran Ave, Tehran; tel. (21) 2288543; fax (21) 2294691; e-mail iremb@mofa.gov .sa; Ambassador JAMIL BIN ABDULLAH AL-JISHI.

Senegal: No. 2/48, Waeghsr St, Kabadiyan St, Tehran; tel. (21) 8786688; Ambassador E. MBAKEH.

Serbia and Montenegro: POB 11365–118, Velenjak Ave, 9th St, No. 12, Tehran 19858; tel. (21) 2412569; fax (21) 2402869; e-mail scgambateh@neda.net; Ambassador GORAN OPACIĆ.

Sierra Leone: No. 10, Malek St, off Dr Shariati Ave, Tehran; tel. (21) 7502819.

Somalia: 20 Sohail St, Dr Shariati Ave, Tehran; tel. (21) 8796509.

South Africa: 5 Yekta St, Bagh-e-Ferdows, Vali-e-Asr Ave, Tehran; tel. (21) 2702866; fax (21) 2719516; e-mail info@rsaembassy-tehran .net; internet www.rsaembassy-tehran.net; Ambassador YUSUF SAL-OOJEE.

Spain: 76 Sarv St, Africa Ave, Tehran 19689; tel. (21) 8714575; fax (21) 8727082; e-mail embespir@mail.mae.es; Ambassador ANTONIO PÉREZ-HERNÁNDEZ TORRA.

Sri Lanka: 28 Golazin St, Africa Ave, Tehran; tel. (21) 2052688; fax (21) 2052149; e-mail emblanka@afranet.com; Ambassador OMAR KAMIL.

Sudan: No. 17, Africa Ave, Zafar St, Kuchahi Nur, Tehran; tel. (21) 8781183; fax (21) 8792331; e-mail hamidltinay@yahoo.com; internet www.sudanembassyir.com; Ambassador HAMED ALI MOHAMMAD AT-TINAY.

Sweden: POB 19575-458, 2 Nastaran Ave, Pasdaran Ave, Tehran; tel. (21) 2296802; fax (21) 2296451; e-mail ambassaden.teheran@ foreign.ministry.se; Ambassador CHRISTOFER GYLLENSTIERNA.

Switzerland: POB 19395-4683, 13 Yasaman St, Cnr of Sharifi Manesh Ave, Elahieh, Tehran 19649; tel. (21) 2008333; fax (21) 2006002; e-mail vertretung@teh.rep.admin.ch; Ambassador PHILIPPE WELTI.

Syria: 19 Iraj St, Africa Ave, Tehran; tel. (21) 2052780; e-mail syrambir@www.dci.co.ir; Ambassador Dr HAMED HASSAN.

Thailand: POB 11495-111, 4 Esteghlal Alley, Baharestan Ave, Tehran; tel. (21) 7531433; fax (21) 7532022; e-mail thairan@bkk2000 .org; internet 203.150.20.1/datapr/d_tehran.htm; Ambassador SUWIT SAICHEUA.

Tunisia: No. 12, Shahid Dr Lavasani, Tehran; tel. (21) 2704161; e-mail at-teheran@safineh.net; Ambassador MOLADI AS-SAKERI.

Turkey: POB 11365-8758, 314 Ferdowsi Ave, Africa Ave, Tehran; tel. (21) 3118997; fax (21) 3117928; e-mail tctahranbe@safineh.net; Ambassador HALIT BOZKUR ARAN.

Turkmenistan: No. 9, 5th Golestan St, Pasdaran Ave, Tehran; tel. (21) 2542178; Ambassador MURAT NAZAROV.

Uganda: Tehran; Ambassador MOHAMMAD AHMAD KISSULE.

Ukraine: 101 Vanak St, Vanak Sq., Tehran; tel. (21) 8034119; fax (21) 8007130; e-mail emb_ir@mfa.gov.ua; Ambassador VOLODYMYR BUTYAHA.

United Arab Emirates: POB 19395-4616, No. 355, Vahid Dastjerdi Ave, Vali-e-Asr Ave, Tehran; tel. (21) 8781333; fax (21) 8789084; e-mail uae_emb_thr@universalmail.com; Ambassador KHALIFA SHA-HEEN AL-MERREE.

United Kingdom: POB 11365-4474, 198 Ferdowsi Ave, Tehran 11344; tel. (21) 6705011; fax (21) 6708021; e-mail britishembassytehran@fco.gov.uk; internet www.britishembassy .gov.uk/iran; Ambassador RICHARD DALTON.

Uruguay: 45 Shabnam Alley, Shahid Atefi Shargi St, Africa Ave, Tehran; tel. (21) 2052030; fax (21) 2053322; e-mail uruter@yahoo .com; Ambassador JOSÉ LUIS REMEDI ZUNINI.

Uzbekistan: No. 6, Nastaran Alley, Boustan St, Pasdaran Ave; tel. (21) 2299158; Ambassador ILHAM AKRAMOV.

Venezuela: POB 19395-7137, No. 26, Tandis St, Africa Ave, Tehran; tel. (21) 8715185; fax (21) 2053677; e-mail ileon@embavenez .demon.co.uk; Ambassador VASKO FABRAS.

Viet Nam: 6 East Ordibehesht, Mardani Sharestan, 8th St, Pey Syan St, M. Ardabili Vali-e-Asr Ave, Tehran; tel. (21) 2411670; fax (21) 2416045; e-mail dinh@www.dci.co.ir; Ambassador NGUYEN VAN HAI.

Yemen: Africa Ave, Golestan St, No. 15, Tehran; tel. (21) 2042701; e-mail yem.emb.ir@neda.net; Ambassador ABDOLQAVI AR-RYANI.

Judicial System

In August 1982 the Supreme Court revoked all laws dating from the previous regime which did not conform with Islam; in October all courts set up prior to the Islamic Revolution were abolished. In June 1987 Ayatollah Khomeini ordered the creation of clerical courts to try members of the clergy opposed to government policy. A new system of *qisas* (retribution) was established, placing the emphasis on swift justice. Islamic codes of correction were introduced in 1983, including the dismembering of a hand for theft, flogging for fornication and violations of the strict code of dress for women, and stoning for adultery. In 1984 there were 2,200 judges. The Supreme Court has 16 branches.

Head of the Judiciary: Ayatollah SAYED MAHMOUD HASHEMI SHAH-RUDI.

SUPREME COURT

Chief Justice: Ayatollah HUSSEIN MOFID.

Prosecutor-General: Ayatollah QORBANALI DORI-NAJAFABADI.

Religion

According to the 1979 Constitution, the official religion is Islam of the Ja'fari sect (Shi'ite), but other Islamic sects, including Zeydi, Hanafi, Maleki, Shafe'i and Hanbali, are valid and will be respected. Zoroastrians, Jews and Christians will be recognized as official religious minorities. According to the 1996 census, there were 59,788,791 Muslims, 78,745 Christians (mainly Armenian), 27,920 Zoroastrians and 12,737 Jews in Iran.

ISLAM

The great majority of the Iranian people are Shi'a Muslims, but there is a minority of Sunni Muslims. Persians and Azerbaijanis are mainly Shi'ite, while the other ethnic groups are mainly Sunni.

CHRISTIANITY

The Roman Catholic Church

At 31 December 2002 there were an estimated 24,730 adherents in Iran, comprising 10,000 of the Armenian Rite, 10,000 of the Latin Rite and 4,600 of the Chaldean Rite.

Armenian Rite

Bishop of Esfahan: NECHAN KARAKEHEYAN, Armenian Catholic Bishopric, POB 11365-445, Khiaban Ghazzali 22, Tehran; tel. (21) 6707204; fax (21) 6727533; e-mail arcaveso@yahoo.com.

Chaldean Rite

Archbishop of Ahvaz: HANNA ZORA, POB 61956, Naderi St, Ahvaz; tel. (61) 2224980.

Archbishop of Tehran: RAMZI GARMOU, Archevêché, Enghelab St, Sayyed Abbas Mousavi Ave 91, Tehran 15819; tel. (21) 8823549; fax (21) 8308714.

Archbishop of Urmia (Rezayeh) and Bishop of Salmas (Shahpour): THOMAS MERAM, Khalifagari Kaldani Katholiq, POB 338, Orumiyeh 57135; tel. (441) 2222739; fax (441) 2236031; e-mail thmeram@yahoo.com.

Latin Rite

Archbishop of Esfahan: IGNAZIO BEDINI, Consolata Church, POB 11365-445, 75 Neauphle-le-Château Ave, Tehran; tel. (21) 6703210; fax (21) 6724947; e-mail latin_diocese@parsonline.net.

The Anglican Communion

Anglicans in Iran are adherents of the Episcopal Church in Jerusalem and the Middle East (President and Bishop in Cyprus and the Gulf Most Rev. CLIVE HANDFORD), formally inaugurated in January 1976.

Bishop in Iran: Most Rev. IRAJ KALIMI MOTTAHEDEH, POB 135, 81465 Esfahan; tel. (21) 8801383; fax (21) 8906908; e-mail bishraj@chavoosh.com; diocese founded 1912.

Presbyterian Church

Synod of the Evangelical (Presbyterian) Church in Iran: Assyrian Evangelical Church, Khiaban-i Hanifnejad, Khiaban-i Aramanch, Tehran; Moderator Rev. ADEL NAKHOSTEEN.

ZOROASTRIANS

There are almost 28,000 Zoroastrians, a remnant of a once widespread sect. Their religious leader is MOUBAD.

OTHER COMMUNITIES

Communities of Armenians, and somewhat smaller numbers of Jews, Assyrians, Greek Orthodox Christians, Uniates and Latin Christians are also found as officially recognized faiths. The Bahá'í faith, which originated in Iran, has about 300,000 Iranian adherents, although at least 10,000 are believed to have fled since 1979 in order to escape persecution. The Government banned all Bahá'í institutions in August 1983.

The Press

Tehran dominates the media, as many of the daily papers are published there, and the bi-weekly, weekly and less frequent publications in the provinces generally depend on the major metropolitan dailies as a source of news. A press law announced in August 1979 required all newspapers and magazines to be licensed and imposed penalties of imprisonment for insulting senior religious figures. Offences against the Act will be tried in the criminal courts. Under the Constitution the press is free, except in matters that are contrary to public morality, insult religious belief or slander the honour and reputation of individuals. From the late 1990s the press has been the target of an intense judicial campaign to curb its freedoms: some sources estimate that more than 100 publications have been closed down.

PRINCIPAL DAILIES

Abrar (Rightly Guided): POB 14155-6494, No. 26, Shahid Daneshkian Alley, Vali-e Asr-Sq., Tehran 14158; tel. (21) 8848270; fax (21) 8849200; e-mail info@abrar.ir; internet www.abrar.ir; f. 1985 after closure of *Azadegan* by order of the Prosecutor-General; morning; Farsi; circ. 75,000.

Aftab-e-Yazd (Sun of Yazd): POB 13145-1134, Tehran; tel. (21) 6495833; fax (21) 6495835; e-mail info@aftabdaily.net; internet www.aftabdaily.net; f. 2000; Farsi; pro-reform; Chief Editor MOJTABA VAHEDI; circ. 100,000.

Alik: POB 11365-953, Jomhouri Islami Ave, Alik Alley, Tehran 11357; tel. (21) 8768567; fax 8760994; e-mail alikmail@hyenet.net; internet www.alikonline.com; f. 1931; afternoon; Armenian; political and literary; Propr A. AJEMIAN; circ. 3,400.

Bahar (Spring): Tehran; Man. Dir SAYED POR-AZIZI; publication suspended between 2000–02 and again in 2003.

Entekhab: 12 Noorbakhsh Ave, Vali-e-Asr Ave, Tehran; tel. (21) 8893954; fax (21) 8893951; e-mail public-relations@entekhab-daily.com; internet www.entekhab-daily.com; Farsi; Man. Dir TAHA HASHEMI.

Ettela'at (Information): Ettela'at Bldg, Mirdamad Ave, South Naft St, Tehran 15499; tel. (21) 29999; fax (21) 2258022; e-mail ettelaat@ettelaat.com; internet www.ettelaat.com; f. 1925; evening; Farsi; political and literary; operates under the direct supervision of *wilayat-e-faqih* (religious jurisprudence); Editor SAYED MAHMOUD DO'AYI; circ. 500,000.

Golestan-e Iran: f. 2002; reformist newspaper aimed at Iranian youth; Publr MOHSEN SAZEGARA; publication suspended in Sept. 2002.

Hayat-e No (New Life): 50 North Sohrvardi Ave, Tehran; tel. (21) 8747437; fax (21) 8766373; internet www.hayateno.org; f. 2000; Farsi; pro-reform; Man. Dir SAYED HADI KHAMENEI; publication temporarily suspended in 2003.

Iran News: POB 15875-8551, 41 Lida St, Vali-e-Asr Ave, North of Vanak Sq., Tehran 19697 33811; tel. (21) 8880231; fax (21) 8786475; e-mail info@irannewsdaily.com; internet www.irannewsdaily.com; f. 1994; English; Man. Editor SHIRZAD BOZORGMEHR; circ. 35,000.

Kayhan (Universe): POB 11365-3631, Ferdowsi Ave, Tehran 11444; tel. (21) 3110251; fax (21) 3111120; e-mail kayhan@kayhannews.ir; internet www.kayhannews.ir; f. 1941; evening; Farsi; political; also publishes *Kayhan International* (f. 1959; daily; English; Editor HAMID NAJAFI), *Kayhan Arabic* (f. 1980; daily; Arabic), *Kayhan Persian* (f. 1942; daily; Persian), *Zan-e-Ruz* (Woman Today; f.1964; weekly; Farsi), *Kayhan Varzeshi* (World of Sport; f. 1955; daily and weekly; Farsi), *Kayhan Bacheha* (Children's World; f. 1956; weekly; Farsi), *Kayhan Farhangi* (World of Culture; f. 1984; monthly; Farsi); owned and managed by Mostazafin Foundation from October 1979 until January 1987, when it was placed under the direct supervision of *wilayat-e-faqih* (religious jurisprudence); Man. Dir HOSSEIN SHARIATMADARI; circ. 350,000.

Khorassan: Mashad; Head Office: Khorassan Daily Newspapers, 14 Zohre St, Mobarezan Ave, Tehran; e-mail info@khorasannews.com; internet www.khorasannews.com; f. 1948; Propr MUHAMMAD SADEGH TEHERANIAN; circ. 40,000.

Neshat: Tehran; pro-reform; Man. Dir MASHALLAH SHAMSOLVAEZIN; f. 1998.

Rahnejat: Darvazeh Dowlat, Esfahan; political and social; Propr N. RAHNEJAT.

Ressallat (The Message): POB 11365-777, 53 Ostad Nejatollahi Ave, Tehran; tel. (21) 8902642; fax (21) 8900587; e-mail info@resalat-news.com; internet www.resalat-news.com; f. 1985; organ of right-wing group of the same name; political, economic, social; Propr Ressallat Foundation; Man. Dir SAYED MORTEZA NABAVI; circ. 100,000.

Salam: 2 Shahid Reza Nayebi Alley, South Felestin St, Tehran; tel. (21) 6495831; fax (21) 6495835; f. 1991; Farsi; political, cultural, economic, social; Editor MUHAMMAD MUSAVI KHOIENI; closure ordered in July 1999.

Sobh Emruz: Tehran; pro-reform; Man. SAYED HAJJARIAN; publication suspended in 2000.

Tehran Times: POB 14155–4843, 32 Bimeh Alley, Ostad Nejatollahi Ave, Tehran; tel. (21) 8810293; fax (21) 8808214; e-mail webmaster@tehrantimes.com; internet www.tehrantimes.com; f. 1979; English; independent; Man. Dir PARVIZ ESMAEILI.

PRINCIPAL PERIODICALS

Acta Medica Iranica: Bldg No. 8, Faculty of Medicine, Tehran Medical Sciences Univ., Poursina St, Tehran 14174; tel. and fax (21) 8962510; e-mail acta@sina.tums.ac.ir; internet www.tums.ac.ir/acta; f. 1960; quarterly; English; Editors-in-Chief A. R. DEHPOUR, M. SAMINI; circ. 2,000.

Akhbar-e-Pezeshki: 86 Ghaem Magham Farahani Ave, Tehran; weekly; Farsi; medical; Propr Dr T. FORUZIN.

Ashur: Ostad Motahhari Ave, 11-21 Kuhe Nour Ave, Tehran; tel. (21) 622117; f. 1969; Assyrian; monthly; Founder and Editor Dr W. BET-MANSOUR; circ. 8,000.

Auditor: 77 Ferdowsi Ave North, Tehran; weekly; financial and managerial studies.

Ayandeh: POB 19575-583, Niyavaran, Tehran; tel. (21) 283254; fax (21) 6406426; monthly; Iranian literary, historical and book review journal; Editor Prof. IRAJ AFSHAR.

Bulletin of the National Film Archive of Iran: POB 5158, Baharestan Sq., Tehran 11365; tel. 311242; f. 1989; English periodical; Editor M. H. KHOSHNEVIS.

Daneshmand (The Knowledgeable): POB 15875-3649, No. 106, Villa St, Tehran 15336; tel. (21) 8908757; fax (21) 8908720; e-mail daneshmand_mag@yahoo.com; f. 1963; monthly; Farsi; scientific and technical magazine; Editor-in-Chief A. R. KARIMI.

Daneshkadeh Pezeshki: Faculty of Medicine, Tehran Medical Sciences University; tel. (21) 6112743; fax (21) 6404377; f. 1947; 10 a year; medical magazine; Propr Dr HASSAN AREFI; circ. 1,500.

Donaye Varzesh: Khayyam Ave, Ettela'at Bldg, Tehran; tel. (21) 3281; fax (21) 3115530; weekly; sport; Editor G. H. SHABANI; circ. 200,000.

The Echo of Iran: POB 14155-1168, 4 Hourtab Alley, Hafez Ave, Tehran; tel. (21) 6468114; fax (21) 6464790; e-mail support@echoiran.com; internet www.echoiran.com; f. 1952; monthly; English; news, politics and economics; Editor J. BEHROUZ.

Echo of Islam: POB 14155-3899, Tehran; tel. (21) 8897663; fax (21) 8902725; e-mail echoofislam@itf.org.ir; internet www.itf.org.ir; monthly; English; published by the Islamic Thought Foundation; Man. Dir ALI AKBAR ZIAIE; Editor-in-Chief HAMID TEHRANI.

Economic Echo: POB 14155-1168, 4 Hourtab Alley, Hafez Ave, Tehran; tel. (21) 6468114; fax (21) 6464790; e-mail support@echoiran.com; internet www.echoiran.com; f. 1998; English.

Ettela'at Elmi: 11 Khayyam Ave, Tehran; tel. (21) 3281; fax (21) 3115530; f. 1985; fortnightly; Farsi; sciences; Editor Mrs GHASEMI; circ. 75,000.

Ettela'at Haftegi: 11 Khayyam Ave, Tehran; tel. (21) 311238; fax (21) 3115530; f. 1941; general weekly; Farsi; Editor F. JAVADI; circ. 150,000.

Ettela'at Javanan: POB 15499-51199, Ettela'at Bldg, Mirdamad Ave, South Naft St, Tehran; tel. (21) 29999; fax (21) 2258022; f. 1966; weekly; Farsi; youth; Editor M. J. RAFIZADEH; circ. 120,000.

Farhang-e-Iran Zamin: POB 19575-583, Niyavaran, Tehran; tel. (21) 283254; annual; Farsi; Iranian studies; Editor Prof. IRAJ AFSHAR.

Film International, Iranian Film Quarterly: POB 11365-875, Tehran; tel. (21) 6709373; fax (21) 6719971; e-mail filmmag@apadana.com; f. 1993; quarterly; English; Editor-in-Chief MASSOUD MEHRABI; circ 15,000.

Iran Tribune: POB 111244, Tehran; internet www.irantribune.com; monthly; English.

Iran Who's Who: POB 14155, 4 Hourtab Alley, Hafez Ave, Tehran; tel. (21) 6468114; fax (21) 6464790; e-mail support@echoiran.com; internet www.echoiran.com; annual; English; Editor KARAN BEHROUZ.

Iranian Cinema: POB 5158, Baharestan Sq., Tehran 11365; tel. 311242; f. 1985; annual; English; Editor B. REYPOUR.

JIDA: 94 West Pirozi St, Nasr Place, Tehran 14477; tel. (21) 8269591; fax 8269592; e-mail info@idaweb.org; internet www.idaweb.org; f. 1963; four a year; journal of the Iranian Dental Association; Editor-in-Chief Dr MUHAMMAD MOSHREF.

Kayhan Bacheha (Children's World): Institute Kayhan, Shahid Shahcheraghi Alley, Ferdowsi Ave, Tehran 11444; tel. (21) 3110251; fax (21) 3111120; f. 1956; weekly; Editor AMIR HOSSEIN FARDI; circ. 150,000.

Kayhan Varzeshi (World of Sport): Institute Kayhan, Shahid Shahcheraghi Alley, Ferdowsi Ave, Tehran 11444; tel. (21) 3110246; fax (21) 3114228; f. 1955; weekly; Dir MAHMAD MONSETI; circ. 125,000.

Mahjubah: Tehran; tel. (21) 8000067; fax (21) 8001453; e-mail mahjubah@iran-itf.com; internet www.itf.org.ir; Islamic family magazine; published by the Islamic Thought Foundation; Editor-in-Chief TURAN JAMSHIDIAN.

Music Iran: Tehran; f. 1951; monthly; Editor BAHMAN HIRBOD; circ. 7,000.

Nasim-e Alborz: f. 2003; weekly; politics, economics and society; organ of the opposition Forces of the Islamic Revolution coalition; Publisher DAVUD JA'FARI.

Negin: Vali-e-Asr Ave, Adl St 52, Tehran; monthly; scientific and literary; Propr and Dir M. ENAYAT.

Salamate Fekr: M.20, Kharg St, Tehran; tel. (21) 223034; f. 1958; monthly; organ of the Mental Health Soc.; Editors Prof. E. TCHEHRAZI, ALI REZA SHAFAI.

Soroush: POB 15875-1163, Soroush Bldg, Motahhari Ave, Mofatteh Crossroads, Tehran; tel. and fax and fax (21) 8847602; e-mail cultural@soroushpress.com; internet www.soroushpress.com; f. 1972; one weekly magazine; four monthly magazines, one for women, two for adolescents and one for children; one quarterly review of philosophy; all in Farsi; Editor-in-Chief ALI AKBAR ASHARI.

Vaqt: weekly; Farsi; pro-reform; publication suspended in Sept. 2002.

Zan-e-Ruz (Woman Today): Institute Kayhan, Shahid Shahcheraghi Alley, Ferdowsi Ave, Tehran; tel. (21) 3911575; fax (21) 3911569; e-mail kayhan@istn.irost.com; internet www.irost.com/

kayhan; f. 1964; weekly; women's; circ. over 60,000; closure ordered April 1999.

PRESS ASSOCIATION

Association of Iranian Journalists: No. 87, 7th Alley, Shahid Kabkanian St, Keshavarz Blvd, Tehran; tel. (21) 8954796; fax (21) 8963539; e-mail secretary@aoij.org; internet www.aoij.org; Gen. Sec. MA SOUD HOOSHMAND RAZAVI.

NEWS AGENCIES

Islamic Republic News Agency (IRNA): POB 764, 873 Vali-e-Asr Ave, Tehran; tel. (21) 8902050; fax (21) 8905068; e-mail irna@irna.com; internet www.irna.com; f. 1936; Man. Dir Dr ABDOLLAH NASSERI TAHERI.

Foreign Bureaux

Agence France-Presse (AFP): Bldg 131 (Shiraz), 2nd Floor, Intifada Ave, Tehran 15139; tel. (21) 8723382; fax (21) 8723386; Correspondent CHRISTOPHE DE ROQUEFEUIL.

Agenzia Nazionale Stampa Associata (ANSA) (Italy): Aghadasieh, Golestan Shomali, Yas, 2nd Park 21, Tehran; tel. (21) 2286130; fax (21) 2286574; Chief of Bureau LUCIANO CAUSA.

Anadolu Ajansı (Turkey): Africa Ave, 31 Tur St, Tehran; tel. (21) 2056749; e-mail tahran@anadoluajansi.com.tr.

Informatsionnoye Telegrafnoye Agentstvo Rossii— Telegrafnoye Agentstvo Suverennykh Stran (ITAR—TASS) (Russia): Kehyaban Hamid, Kouche Masoud 73, Tehran.

Kyodo Tsushin (Japan): No. 23, First Floor, Couche Kargozar, Couche Sharsaz Ave, Zafar, Tehran; tel. (21) 220448; Correspondent MASARU IMAI.

Reuters (UK): Tehran; tel. (21) 847700.

Xinhua (New China) News Agency (People's Republic of China): Tehran; tel. (21) 241852; Correspondent CHEN MING.

Publishers

Amir Kabir Book Publishing and Distribution Co: POB 11365-4191, Jomhouri Islami Ave, Esteghlal Sq., Tehran; tel. (21) 6463487; fax (21) 390752; f. 1948; historical, social, literary and children's books; Dir H. ANWARY.

Avayenoor Publications: 31 Roshan Alley, Vali-e-Asr Ave, Tehran; tel. (21) 8899001; fax (21) 8907452; e-mail info@avayenoor.com; internet www.avayenoor.com; f. 1988; sociology, politics and economics; Editor-in-Chief Sayed MOHAMMAD MIRHOSSEINI.

Ebn-e-Sina: No. 2P, Shahid Ekhtari, South Dabirstan St, Hashimi, Tehran; f. 1957; educational publishers and booksellers; Dir EBRAHIM RAMAZANI.

Echo Publishers & Printers: POB 14155-1168, 4 Hourtab Alley, Hafez Ave, Tehran; tel. (21) 6468114; fax (21) 6464790; e-mail support@echoiran.com; internet www.echoiran.com; politics, economics and current affairs.

Eghbal Printing & Publishing Organization: 15 Booshehr St, Dr Shariati Ave, Tehran; tel. (21) 768113; f. 1903; Man. Dir DJAVAD EGHBAL.

Iran Chap Co: Ettela'at Bldg, Mirdamad Ave, South Naft St, Tehran; tel. (21) 29999; fax (21) 2258022; e-mail ettelaat@ettelaat.com; internet www.ettelaat.com; f. 1966; newspapers, books, magazines, book-binding and colour printing; Man. Dir M. DOAEI.

Iran Exports Publication Co Ltd: POB 14335-746, 27 Eftekhar St, Vali-e-Asr Ave, Tehran 15956; tel. (21) 8801800; fax (21) 8900547; f. 1987; business and trade.

Ketab Sara: POB 15745-733, Tehran 15117; tel. (21) 8716104; fax (21) 8712479; e-mail ketab-sara@neda.net.ir; Chair. SADEGH SAMII.

Khayyam: 31 Ishteyani, Daneshgahi, Enghelab St, Tehran; tel. (21) 4394004; Dir MUHAMMAD ALI TARAGHI.

Majlis Press: Ketab-Khane Majlis-e-Showray-e Eslami No. 1 and the Documentation Centre, POB 11365-866, Baharestan Sq., Tehran; Ketab-Khane Majlis-e-Showray-e Eslami No. 2, Imam Khomeini Ave, Tehran 13174; tel. (21) 3130919; fax (21) 3124339; e-mail frelations@majlislib.com; internet www.majlislib.org; tel. (21) 6135335; fax (21) 3124339; f. 1923; f. 1950; library, museum and documentation centre of the Islamic Consultative Assembly; arts, humanities, social sciences, politics, Iranian and Islamic studies; Dir SAYED MUHAMMAD ALI AHMADI ABHARI.

Sahab Geographic and Drafting Institute: POB 11365-617, 30 Somayeh St, Hoquqi Crossroads, Dr Ali Shariati Ave, Tehran 16517; tel. (21) 7535907; fax (21) 7535876; maps, atlases, and books on geography, science, history and Islamic art; Man. Dir MUHAMMAD REZA SAHAB.

Scientific and Cultural Publications Co: Ministry of Science, Research and Technology, Tehran; tel. (21) 8048037; f. 1974; Iranian and Islamic studies and scientific and cultural books; Pres. SAYED JAVAD AZHARS.

Soroush Press: POB 15875-1163, Soroush Bldg, Motahhari Ave, Mofatteh Crossroads, Tehran; tel. and fax (21) 8847602; e-mail cultural@soroushpress.com; internet www.soroushpress.com; part of Soroush Publication Group, the publications dept of Islamic Republic of Iran Broadcasting; publishes books, magazines and multimedia products on a wide range of subjects; Man. Dir ALI AKBAR ASHARI.

Tehran University Press: 16th St, North Karegar St, Tehran; tel. (21) 8012076; fax (21) 8012077; e-mail press@ut.ac.ir; internet press .ut.ac.ir; f. 1944; university textbooks; Man. Dir Dr MOHAMMAD SHEKARCIZADEH.

Broadcasting and Communications

TELECOMMUNICATIONS

In April 2003, as a first step towards the liberalization of the telecommunications sector, the appointment of an independent regulator was announced, with a view to establishing a board initially to oversee the issue of Iran's second GSM (global system for mobile telecommunications) licence. The licence was awarded to Irancell, a consortium led by Turkcell (Turkey), in February 2004 and signed in September. However, it was later announced that Irancell would have to receive the approval of the Majlis before paying a licence fee.

Telecommunications Regulator: Deputy Minister for Telecommunications DAVARI NEJAD.

Telecommunications Company of Iran (TCI): POB 3316–17, Dr Ali Shariati Ave, Tehran; tel. (21) 8429595; fax (21) 8405055; e-mail info@irantelecom.ir; internet www.irantelecom.ir; Chair. and Man. Dir Dr ALIREZA BAHRAMPOUR.

Mobile Company of Iran (MCI): f. 2004.

Irancell: f. 2004; mobile telecommunications; consortium of Turkcell (Turkey—51%), Parman Ertebat (20%), Iranian Electric Development Co (20%) and Telefon AB L.M. Ericsson (Sweden—9%).

BROADCASTING

Islamic Republic of Iran Broadcasting (IRIB): POB 19395-3333, Vali-e-Asr Ave, Jame Jam St, Tehran; tel. (21) 2043036; fax (21) 2044024; e-mail webmaster@irib.ir; internet www.irib.ir; semi-autonomous authority, affiliated with the Ministry of Culture and Islamic Guidance; non-commercial; operates five local television and five national radio channels, as well as local provincial radio stations throughout the country; Pres. SEYYED EZZATOLLAH ZARGHAMI.

Radio

Radio Network 1 (Voice of the Islamic Republic of Iran): there are three national radio channels: Radio Networks 1 and 2 and Radio Quran, which broadcasts recitals of the Quran (Koran) and other programmes related to it; covers whole of Iran and reaches whole of Europe, the Central Asian republics of the CIS, whole of Asia, Africa and part of USA; medium-wave regional broadcasts in local languages; Arabic, Armenian, Assyrian, Azerbaijani, Balochi, Bandari, Dari, Farsi, Kurdish, Mazandarani, Pashtu, Turkoman, Turkish and Urdu; external broadcasts in English, French, German, Spanish, Turkish, Arabic, Kurdish, Urdu, Pashtu, Armenian, Bengali, Russian and special overseas programme in Farsi; Hebrew service introduced in 2002; 53 transmitters.

Television

Television (Vision of the Islamic Republic of Iran): 625-line, System B; Secam colour; two production centres in Tehran producing for two networks and 28 local TV stations.

Finance

(cap. = capital; res = reserves; dep. = deposits; brs = branches; m. = million; amounts in rials)

BANKING

Banks were nationalized in June 1979 and a revised commercial banking system was introduced consisting of nine banks (subsequently expanded to 10). Three banks were reorganized, two (Bank Tejarat and Bank Mellat) resulted from mergers of 22 existing

small banks, three specialize in industry and agriculture and one, the Islamic Bank of Iran (now Islamic Economy Organization), set up in May 1979, was exempt from nationalization. The 10th bank, the Export Development Bank, specializes in the promotion of exports. A change-over to an Islamic banking system, with interest (forbidden under Islamic law) being replaced by a 4% commission on loans, began on 21 March 1984. All short- and medium-term private deposits and all bank loans and advances are subject to Islamic rules. A partial liberalization of the banking sector has been implemented by the Khatami administration, beginning with the establishment of four private banks since 2001.

Although the number of foreign banks operating in Iran has fallen dramatically since the Revolution, some 30 are still represented.

Central Bank

Bank Markazi Jomhouri Islami Iran (Central Bank): POB 15875-7177, 144 Mirdamad Blvd, Tehran; tel. (21) 29951; fax (21) 3115674; e-mail g.secdept@cbi.ir; internet www.cbi.ir; f. 1960; Bank Markazi Iran until Dec. 1983; issuing bank, government banking; cap. 400,000m., res 11,113,896m., dep. 218,075,731m. (March 2003); Gov., Pres. and Chair. EBRAHIM SHEBANI.

Commercial Banks

Bank Keshavarzi (Agricultural Bank): POB 14155-6395, 129 Patrice Lumumba Ave, Jalal al-Ahmad Expressway, Tehran 14454; tel. (21) 8250135; fax (21) 8262313; e-mail info@agri-bank.com; internet www.agri-bank.com; f. 1980 by merger; state-owned; cap. 2,756,210m. (March 2002), res 219,578m., dep. 34,244,851m. (March 2004); Chair. and Man. Dir Dr JALAL RASOULOF; 1,800 brs.

Bank Mellat (Nation's Bank): Head Office Bldg, 327 Taleghani Ave, Tehran 15817; tel. (21) 82962004; fax (21) 82962700; e-mail mellat@mellatbank.com; internet www.bankmellat.ir; f. 1980 by merger of 10 fmr private banks; state-owned; cap. 1,239,000m., res 2,648,469m., dep. 96,810,141m. (March 2003); Chair. and Man. Dir S. MANOUCHEHRI; 1,962 brs in Iran, 6 abroad.

Bank Melli Iran (The National Bank of Iran): POB 11365-171, Ferdowsi Ave, Tehran; tel. (21) 3231; fax (21) 3912813; e-mail inter@bankmelli-iran.com; internet www.bankmelli-iran.com; f. 1928; present name since 1943; state-owned; cap. 2,260,000m., res 6,356,356m., dep. 145,245,068m. (March 2003); Chair. and Man. Dir VALIOLLAH SEIF; 3,061 brs in Iran, 21 abroad.

Bank Refah (Workers' Welfare Bank): POB 15815, 40 Northern Shiraz Ave, Molla Sadra Ave, Tehran 19917; tel. (21) 8042926; fax (21) 8041394; e-mail info@bankrefah.ir; internet www.bankrefah.ir; f. 1960 as Bank Refah Kargaran; name changed as above 1999; state-owned; cap. 895,000m., res 181,589m., dep. 17,274,310m. (March 2003); Chair. and Man. Dir MUHAMMAD TAGHI JAMALIAN; 1,300 brs.

Bank Saderat Iran (The Export Bank of Iran): POB 15745-631, Bank Saderat Tower, 43 Somayeh Ave, Tehran; tel. (21) 8306091; fax (21) 8839539; e-mail saderat@emirates.net.ae; internet www .saderbank.com; f. 1952; state-owned; cap. 1,887,000m., res 4,998,806m., dep. 94,197,647m. (March 2003); Chair. and Man. Dir AHMAD HATAMI YAZD; 3,225 brs in Iran, 23 abroad.

Bank Sepah: POB 9569, Imam Khomeini Sq., Tehran 11364; tel. (21) 3944473; fax (21) 3946770; e-mail info@banksepah.com; internet www.banksepah.com; f. 1925; nationalized in June 1979; cap. 1,052,000m., res 959,310m., dep. 51,791,287m. (March 2003); Chair. and Man. Dir Dr ALIREZA SHIRANI; 1,680 brs in Iran, 3 abroad.

Bank Tejarat (Commercial Bank): POB 11365-5416, 130 Taleghani Ave, Nejatoullahie, Tehran 15994; tel. (21) 81041; fax (21) 8828215; e-mail treasury@tejarat-bank.com; internet www.tejarat-bank.com; f. 1979 by merger of 12 banks; state-owned; cap. and res 2,071,588m., dep. 67,655,336m. (March 2003); Chair. and Man. Dir SAYED ALI MILANI HOSSEINI; 2,022 brs in Iran, 3 abroad.

EN Bank: POB 19395-3796, EN Bank Bldg, Africa Ave, Tehran 196995-4345; tel. (21) 8788960; fax (21) 8880166; e-mail info@bank-en.com; internet www.enbank.net; private bank; granted operating licence in 2001; cap. 250,000m., res 9,010.6m., dep. 606,340.7m. (March 2004); Chair. E. ARABZADEH; CEO N. NAZEM-ZADEH; 20 brs.

Islamic Economy Organization: Ferdowsi Ave, Tehran; f. 1980 as the Islamic Bank of Iran; cap. 2,000m.; provides interest-free loans and investment in small industry.

Karafarin Bank: POB 15875-4659, No. 6, Ahmad Ghasir Ave, Tehran 15137; tel. (21) 8550316; fax (21) 8550291; e-mail info@karafinbank.com; internet www.karafarinbank.com; f. 1999 as Karafarin Credit Institute; converted into private bank in 2001; cap. 200,000m., res 1,818.2m., dep. 360,104.5m. (March 2002); Chair. MOHSEN KHALILI-ARAGHI; Pres. PARVIZ AGHILI; 6 brs.

Parsian Bank: Parsian Bldg, No. 65, Keshavarz Blvd, Tehran; tel. (21) 8979334; fax (21) 8979344; internet www.parsian-bank.com; f.

2002; private bank; cap. 341,000m., res 48,288m., dep. 7,152,501m. (March 2004); Chair. and Pres. ABDOLLAH TALEBI; 14 brs.

Saman Bank: 879 Engelab Ave, Tehran; tel. (21) 6959050; fax (21) 6958935; e-mail info@bankrefah.ir; internet www.sb24.com; f. 2001; private bank; cap. 200,000m., res 7,067m., dep. 732,677m. (March 2003).

Development Banks

Bank of Industry and Mine: POB 15875-4459, 593 Hafiz Ave, Tehran; tel. (21) 8903271; fax (21) 8891671; e-mail pakear@iran-bim.com; internet www.iran-bim.com; f. 1979 as merger of the following: Industrial Credit Bank (ICB), Industrial and Mining Development Bank of Iran (IMDBI), Development and Investment Bank of Iran (DIBI), Iranian Bankers Investment Company (IBICO); cap. 1,613,000m., res 64,000m., total assets 5,264,000m. (2000); Chair. and Man. Dir ABDORAHMAN NADIMI BOUSHEHRI.

Export Development Bank of Iran: POB 151674-7913, 4 Gandhi Ave, Tehran 15167; tel. (21) 8798213; fax (21) 8798259; e-mail kohzadi@edbi-iran.com; internet www.edbi-iran.com; f. 1991; cap. 1,545,000m., res 814,146m., dep. 2,459,308m. (March 2003); Chair. and Man. Dir Dr NOWROOZ KOHZADI; 26 brs.

Housing Bank

Bank Maskan (Housing Bank): POB 11365-5699, 247 Ferdowsi Ave, Tehran; tel. (21) 6706742; fax (21) 6709667; e-mail int-div@bank-maskan.org; internet www.bank-maskan.org; f. 1979; state-owned; cap. 473,333m., dep. 242,943m., dep. 22,760,944m. (March 2002); provides mortgage and housing finance; 630 brs; Pres., Chair. and Gen. Man. AHMAD FARSHCHIAN.

Regulatory Authority

Supreme Council of Banks: Tehran; comprises two bankers and five ministerial appointees; regulates internal affairs of all Iranian banks; Chair. Dr HOSSEIN NEMAZI.

STOCK EXCHANGE

Tehran Stock Exchange: 228 Hafez Ave, Tehran 11389; tel. (21) 6708385; fax (21) 6710111; e-mail info@tase.ir; internet www.tse.ir; f. 1966; Sec.-Gen. and CEO Dr HOSSEIN ABDOH TABRIZI.

INSURANCE

The nationalization of insurance companies was announced in June 1979. However, as part of the reforms to the financial sector undertaken by the Khatami administration, a private insurance firm was established in February 2003.

Bimeh Alborz (Alborz Insurance Co): POB 4489-15875, Alborz Bldg, 234 Sepahboad Garani Ave, Tehran; tel. (21) 8903201; fax (21) 8803771; e-mail asoudeh@alborzins.com; internet www.alborzins.com; f. 1959; state-owned insurance company; all types of insurance; Chair. and Man. Dir MUHAMMAD ASOUDEH; 43 brs.

Bimeh Asia (Asia Insurance Co): POB 15815-1885, Asia Insurance Bldg, 297-299 Taleghani Ave, Tehran; tel. (21) 8800951; fax (21) 8898113; e-mail admin@bimehasia.ir; internet www.bimehasia.com; f. 1959; all types of insurance; Man. Dir MASOUM ZAMIRI; 6 brs.

Bimeh Dana (Dana Insurance Co): 25 Fifteenth St, Ghandi Ave, Tehran 151789-5511; tel. (21) 8770971; fax (21) 8792997; e-mail info@dana-insurance.com; internet www.bimehdana.com; f. 1988; life, personal accident and health insurance; Chair. ABDORREZA GHASEMI.

Bimeh Iran (Iran Insurance Co): POB 14155-6363, Dr Fatemi Ave, No. 107, Tehran; tel. (21) 6704346; fax (21) 6712646; internet info@iraninsurance.org; internet www.iraninsurance.org; f. 1935; all types of insurance; Chair. and Man. Dir Dr SAYED MOHAMMAD ABBASZADEGAN; 246 brs in Iran, 12 brs abroad.

Bimeh Markazi Iran (Central Insurance of Iran): POB 19395-5588, 72 Africa Ave, Tehran 19157; tel. (21) 2050001; fax (21) 2054099; e-mail pr@cent-ir.com; internet www.cent-ir.com; f. 1971; supervises the insurance market and tariffs for new types of insurance cover; the sole state reinsurer for domestic insurance companies, which are obliged to reinsure 50% of their direct business in life insurance and 25% of business in non-life insurance with Bimeh Markazi Iran; Pres. Dr ABDOLNASSER HEMMATI.

Trade and Industry

CHAMBER OF COMMERCE

Iran Chamber of Commerce, Industries and Mines: 254 Taleghani Ave, Tehran 15875-4671; tel. (21) 8830066; fax (21) 8825111;

e-mail info@iccim.org; internet www.iccim.org; supervises the affiliated 32 Chambers in the provinces; Pres. ALI NAGHI KHAMOUSHI.

INDUSTRIAL AND TRADE ASSOCIATIONS

National Iranian Industries Organization (NIIO): POB 15875-1331, No. 11, 13th Alley, Miremad St, Tehran; tel. (21) 8744198; fax (21) 8757126; f. 1979; owns 400 factories in Iran; Man. Dir ALI TOOSI.

National Iranian Industries Organization Export Co (NECO): No. 8, 2nd Alley, Bucharest Ave, Tehran; tel. (21) 4162384; fax (21) 212429.

STATE HYDROCARBONS COMPANIES

Iranian Offshore Oil Co (IOOC): POB 15875-4546, 339 Dr Beheshti Ave, Tehran; tel. (21) 8714102; fax (21) 8717420; wholly owned subsidiary of NIOC; f. 1980; development, exploitation and production of crude petroleum, natural gas and other hydrocarbons in all offshore areas of Iran in the Persian (Arabian) Gulf and the Caspian Sea; Chair. M. AGAZADEH; Dir S. A. JALILIAN.

National Iranian Gas Co (NIGC): 7th Floor, No. 401, Saghitaman, Taleghani Ave, Tehran; tel. (21) 8133347; e-mail pajohesh@nigc.org; internet www.nigc.org; Dir S. H. NAJIBI.

National Iranian Oil Co (NIOC): POB 1863, Taleghani Ave, Tehran; tel. (21) 6152738; fax (21) 6152823; e-mail webmaster@nioc.org; internet www.nioc.org; state organization controlling all 'upstream' activities in the petroleum and natural gas industries; incorporated April 1951 on nationalization of petroleum industry to engage in all phases of petroleum operations; in February 1979 it was announced that, in future, Iran would sell petroleum direct to the petroleum companies, and in September 1979 the Ministry of Oil assumed control of the National Iranian Oil Company; Chair. of Board BIJAN NAMDAR ZANGENEH (Minister of Oil); Man. Dir SAYED MAHDI MIR MOEZI.

National Iranian Oil Refining and Distribution Co (NIORDC): POB 15815-3499, NIORDC Bldg, 140 Ostad Nejatollahi Ave, Tehran 15989; tel. (21) 8801001; fax (21) 6152138; e-mail info@niordc.ws; internet www.prniordc.com; f. 1992 to assume responsibility for refining, pipeline distribution, engineering, construction and research in the petroleum industry from NIOC; Chair. and Man. Dir GHOLAMREZA AQAZADEH.

CO-OPERATIVES

Ministry of Co-operatives: 16 Bozorgmehr St, Vali-e-Asr Ave, Tehran 14169; tel. (21) 6400938; fax (21) 6498440; e-mail coop_international@icm.gov.ir; internet www.icm.gov.ir; f. 1993; 15m. mems in 70,000 co-operative societies.

Central Union of Rural and Agricultural Co-operatives of Iran: 78 North Palestine St, Opposite Ministry of Energy, Tehran; e-mail info@keshavarzonline.com; internet www.keshavarzonline.com; f. 1963; educational, technical, commercial and credit assistance to rural co-operative societies and unions; Chair. and Man. Dir SAYED MUHAMMAD MIRMUHAMMADI.

Transport

RAILWAYS

Iranian Islamic Republic Railways: POB 13185-1498, Shahid Kalantari Bldg, Railway Sq., Tehran 13165; tel. (21) 5641600; fax (21) 5650532; e-mail info@irirw.com; internet www.irirw.com; f. 1934; affiliated with Ministry of Roads and Transport; Pres. and Chair. MOHAMMAD MOSLEHI (acting).

In 2003 the Iranian railway network system was estimated to comprise 7,156 km of mainline track, of which 7,058 km was 1,435 mm standard gauge, 148 km was electrified, and 98 km was wide 1,676 gauge. The system includes the following main routes:

Trans-Iranian Railway: runs 1,392 km from Bandar Turkman on the Caspian Sea in the north, through Tehran, and south to Bandar Imam Khomeini on the Persian (Arabian) Gulf.

Southern Line: links Tehran to Khorramshahr via Qom, Arak, Dorood, Andimeshk and Ahvaz; 937 km.

Northern Line: links Tehran to Gorgan via Garmsar, Firooz Kooh and Sari; 499 km.

Tehran–Kerman Line: via Kashan, Yazd and Zarand; 1,106 km.

Tehran–Tabriz Line: linking with the Azerbaijan Railway; 736 km.

Tabriz–Djulfa Electric Line: 146 km.

Garmsar–Mashad Line: connects Tehran with Mashad via Semnan, Damghan, Shahrud and Nishabur; 812 km. A line is under construction to link Mashad with Sarakhs on the Turkmen border. A 768-km line linking Mashad with Bafq is also under construction.

Qom–Zahedan Line: when completed will be an intercontinental line linking Europe and Turkey, through Iran, with India. Zahedan is situated 91.7 km west of the Baluchistan frontier, and is the end of the Pakistani broad gauge railway. The section at present links Qom to Kerman via Kashan, Sistan, Yazd, Bafq and Zarand; 1,005 km. A branch line from Sistan was opened in 1971 via Esfahan to the steel mill at Zarrin Shahr; 112 km. A broad-gauge (1,976-mm) track connects Zahedan and Mirjaveh, on the border with Pakistan; 94 km.

Zahedan–Quetta (Pakistan) Line: 685 km; not linked to national network.

Ahvaz–Bandar Khomeini Line: connects Bandar Khomeini with the Trans-Iranian railway at Ahvaz; this line is due to be double-tracked; 112 km.

Azerbaijan Railway: extends from Tabriz to Djulfa (146.5 km), meeting the Caucasian railways at the Azerbaijani frontier. Electrification works for this section have been completed and the electrified line was opened in April 1982. A standard gauge railway line (139 km) extends from Tabriz (via Sharaf–Khaneh) to the Turkish frontier at Razi.

Bandar Abbas–Bafq: construction of a 730-km double-track line to link Bandar Abbas and Bafq commenced in 1982. The first phase, linking Bafq to Sirjan (260 km), was opened in May 1990, and the second phase was opened in March 1995. The line provides access to the copper mines at Sarcheshmeh and the iron ore mines at Gole-Gohar.

Bafq–Chadormalou: a 130-km line connecting Bafq to the Chadormalou iron-ore mines is under construction.

Chadormalou–Tabas: a 220-km line is under construction.

Underground Railway

In May 1995 the Tehran Urban and Suburban Railway Co concluded agreements with three Chinese companies for the completion of the Tehran underground railway, on which work had originally commenced in 1977. By 2003 the system consisted of three lines: Line 1, an extension to which was opened in 2002; Line 2, the first 9.3 km of which were opened in 2000 and extended in 2001; and Line 5, a 31-km suburban line, linking Tehran with the satellite city of Karaj, which was inaugurated in February 1999.

Tehran Urban and Suburban Railway Co (Metro): 37 Mir Emad St, Tehran 15878-13113; tel. (21) 8740110; fax (21) 8740114; e-mail info@tehranmetro.com; internet www.tehranmetro.com; Chair. and Man. Dir MOHSEN HASHEMI.

ROADS

In 1998 there were an estimated 167,157 km of roads, including 890 km of motorways, 24,940 km of highways, main or national roads, and 68,238 km of secondary or regional roads. In 2001/02 the Ministry of Roads and Transport was responsible for 80,720 km of roads, including 717 km of motorways, 25,862 km of highways, main or national roads, and 37,363 km of secondary or regional roads. There is a paved highway (A1, 2,089 km) from Bazargan on the Turkish border to the Afghanistan border. The A2 highway runs 2,473 km from the Iraqi border to Mir Javeh on the Pakistan border. A new highway linking the eastern city of Dogharun to Herat in Afghanistan was opened in January 2005.

Ministry of Roads and Transport: see The Government (Ministries), above.

INLAND WATERWAYS

Principal waterways:

Lake Rezaiyeh (Lake Urmia): 80 km west of Tabriz in North-West Iran; and Karun river flowing south through the oilfields into the Shatt al-Arab, thence to the head of the Persian Gulf near Abadan.

Lake Rezaiyeh: From Sharafkhaneh to Golmankhaneh there is a twice-weekly service of tugs and barges for transport of passengers and goods.

Karun River: Regular cargo service is operated by the Mesopotamia-Iran Corpn Ltd. Iranian firms also operate daily motor-boat services for passengers and goods.

SHIPPING

Persian (Arabian) Gulf: The main oil terminal is at Kharg Island. The principal commercial non-oil ports are Bandar Shahid Rajai (which was officially inaugurated in 1983 and handles 9m. of the 12m. tons of cargo passing annually through Iran's Gulf ports), Bandar Khomeini, Bushehr, Bandar Abbas and Chah Bahar. A

project to develop Bandar Abbas port, which predates the Islamic Revolution and was originally to cost IR 1,900,000m., is now in progress. Khorramshahr, Iran's biggest port, was disabled in the war with Iraq, and Bushehr and Bandar Khomeini also sustained war damage, which has restricted their use. In August 1988 it was announced that Iran was to spend US $200m. on the construction of six 'multi-purpose' ports on the Arabian and Caspian Seas, while ports which had been damaged in the war were to be repaired.

Caspian Sea: Principal ports at Bandar Anzali (formerly Bandar Pahlavi) and Bandar Nowshahr.

Ports and Shipping Organization: 751 Enghelab Ave, Tehran; tel. (21) 8809280; fax (21) 8804100; internet www.ir-pso.com; affiliated with Ministry of Roads and Transport; Pres. AHMAD DONYAMALI.

Principal Shipping Companies

Iran Marine Services: 151 Mirdamad Blvd, Tehran 19116; tel. (21) 2222249; fax (21) 2223380; e-mail info@imsiran.com; f. 1981; Chair. and Man. Dir MUHAMMAD HASSAN ASHRAFIAN LAK.

Irano–Hind Shipping Co: POB 15875-4647, 18 Sedaghat St, Vali-e-Asr Ave, Tehran; tel. (21) 2058095; fax (21) 2057739; e-mail administration@iranohind.com; internet www.iranohind.com; f. 1974; joint venture between the Islamic Republic of Iran and the Shipping Corpn of India; Chair. AHAD MUHAMMADI.

Islamic Republic of Iran Shipping Lines (IRISL): POB 19395-1311, Asseman Tower, 37 Shahid Shirazi Sq., Pasdaran Ave, Tehran; tel. (21) 2803232; fax (21) 2813869; e-mail e-pr@irisl.net; internet www.irisl.net; f. 1967; affiliated to the Ministry of Commerce; liner services in the Middle East, Europe, the USA, Far East and Central Asia; Chair. and Man. Dir Eng. ALI ASHRAF AFKHAMI.

National Iranian Tanker Co (NITC): POB 19395-4834, 67–68 Atefis St, Africa Ave, Tehran; tel. (21) 2229093; fax (21) 2228065; e-mail souri@nitc.co.ir; internet www.nitc.co.ir; Chair. and Man. Dir MUHAMMAD SOURI.

CIVIL AVIATION

The two main international airports are Mehrabad (Tehran) and Abadan. An international airport was opened at Esfahan in July 1984 and the first international flight took place in March 1986. Work on a new international airport, 40 km south of Tehran, abandoned in 1979, resumed in the mid-1980s, and work on three others, at Tabas, Ardebil and Ilam was under way by mid-1990. The airports at Urumiyeh, Ahvaz, Bakhtaran, Sanandaz, Abadan, Hamadan and Shiraz were to be modernized and smaller ones constructed at Lar, Lamard, Rajsanjan, Barm, Kashan, Maragheh, Khoy, Sirjan and Abadeh. In early 1995 the Economic Co-operation Organization (ECO) agreed to establish a regional airline (Eco Air), based in Tehran. Construction of the Imam Khomeini International Airport in Tehran, anticipated to be one of the largest airports in the world, began in the late 1990s. The first phase of the project was completed in early 2001, and the first flights landed in February 2003. However, the airport was closed by the Revolutionary Guards Corps in May 2004 (see Economy).

Civil Aviation Organization (CAO): POB 13445-1798, Taleghani Ave, Tehran; fax (21) 4665496; e-mail info@cao.ir; internet www.cao.ir; affiliated with Ministry of Roads and Transport; Pres. HASSAN HAJALIFARD.

Iran Air (Airline of the Islamic Republic of Iran): POB 13185-755, Iran Air Bldg, Mehrabad Airport, Tehran; tel. (21) 9116689; fax (21) 6003248; internet www.iranair.co.ir; f. 1962; serves the Middle East and Persian (Arabian) Gulf area, Europe, Asia and the Far East; scheduled for part-privatization; Chair. and Man. Dir DAVOOD KESHAVARZIAN.

Iran Air Tours: 191 Motahhari Ave, Dr Moffateh Rd, Tehran 15879; tel. (21) 8758390; fax (21) 8755884; e-mail info@iranairtours.com; internet www.iranairtours.com; f. 1992; serves Middle East; Chair. MAHDI SADEGHIL.

Iran Aseman Airlines: POB 141748, Mehrabad Airport, Tehran 13145-1476; tel. (21) 6484198; fax (21) 6404318; internet www.iaa.ir; f. 1980 as result of merger of Air Taxi Co (f. 1958), Pars Air (f. 1969), Air Service Co (f. 1962) and Hoor Asseman; domestic routes and charter services; Man. Dir ALI ABEDZADEH.

Kish Air: POB 19395-4639, 215 Africa Ave, Tehran 19697; tel. (21) 4665639; fax (21) 4665221; internet www.kishairline.com; f. 1989; under the auspices of the Kish Development Organization; serves Persian Gulf area and several European countries; Pres. Capt. YADOLLAH KHALILI.

Mahan Air: POB 14515-411, Mahan Tower, 21 Azadegan St, Tehran; tel. (21) 4076081; fax (21) 4070404; e-mail international@mahanair.ir; internet www.mahanairlines.com; f. 1991; domestic routes and charter services between Europe and the Middle East; Man. Dir HAMID ARABNEJAD.

Saha Airline: POB 13445-956, Karadj Old Rd, Tehran 13873; tel. (21) 6696200; fax (21) 6698016; e-mail saha2@iran-net.com; f. 1990; operates passenger and cargo charter domestic flights and services to Europe, Asia and Africa; Man. Dir Capt. M. NIKUKAR.

Tourism

Tourism was adversely affected by political upheaval following the Revolution. Iran's chief attraction for tourists is its wealth of historical sites, notably Esfahan, Rasht, Tabriz, Susa and Persepolis. Some 1,584,922 international tourist arrivals were recorded in 2002/03 (year ending 20 March), compared with 326,048 in 1994. Receipts from tourism in 2001 totalled US $1,122m. Tourism centres

are currently administered by the State, through the Ministry of Culture and Islamic Guidance, although in late 1997 the ministry indicated its intention to transfer all tourism affairs to the private sector.

Iran Cultural Heritage and Tourism Organization (ICHTO): POB 13445-719, Zanyan Crossroads, Azadi Ave, Tehran; tel. (21) 6035299; fax (21) 6013498; e-mail info@itto.org; internet www.itto .org; f. 2004; Pres. SAYED HOSSEIN MARAASHI; Vice-Pres. SAYED MUHAMMAD BEHESHTI.

Iran Tourist Co (ITC): 257 Motahhari Ave, 15868 Tehran; tel. (21) 8736762; fax (21) 8736158; e-mail info@irantouristco.com; internet www.irantouristco.com; f. 1979; affiliated with Ministry of Culture and Islamic Guidance; Man. Dir ABDOLLAH HOSSEINI.

IRAQ

Introductory Survey

Location, Climate, Language, Religion, Flag, Capital

The Republic of Iraq is an almost land-locked state in western Asia, with a narrow outlet to the sea on the Persian (Arabian) Gulf. Its neighbours are Iran to the east, Turkey to the north, Syria and Jordan to the west, and Saudi Arabia and Kuwait to the south. The climate is extreme, with hot, dry summers, when temperatures may exceed 43°C (109°F), and cold winters, especially in the highlands. Summers are humid near the Persian Gulf. The official language is Arabic, spoken by about 80% of the population; about 15% speak Kurdish, while there is a small Turkoman-speaking minority. Some 95% of the population are Muslims, of whom about 60% belong to the Shi'i sect. However, the Baath regime that was in power during 1968–2003 was dominated by members of the Sunni sect. The national flag (proportions 2 by 3) has three equal horizontal stripes, of red, white and black, with three five-pointed green stars on the central white stripe. The inscription 'Allahu Akhbar' ('God is Great') was added to the flag in January 1991. The capital is Baghdad.

Recent History

Iraq was formerly part of Turkey's Ottoman Empire. During the First World War (1914–18), when Turkey was allied with Germany, the territory was captured by British forces. In 1920 Iraq was placed under a League of Nations mandate, administered by the United Kingdom. In 1921 Amir Faisal ibn Hussain, a member of the Hashimi (Hashemite) dynasty of Arabia, was proclaimed King of Iraq, and his brother, Abdullah, was proclaimed Amir (Emir) of neighbouring Transjordan (later renamed Jordan), also administered by the United Kingdom under a League of Nations mandate. The two new monarchs were sons of Hussain (Hussein) ibn Ali, the Sharif of Mecca, who had proclaimed himself King of the Hedjaz (now part of Saudi Arabia) in 1916. The British decision to nominate Hashemite princes to be rulers of Iraq and Transjordan was a reward for Hussain's co-operation in the wartime campaign against Turkey. After prolonged negotiations, a 25-year Anglo-Iraqi Treaty of Alliance was signed in 1930. The British mandate ended on 3 October 1932, when Iraq became fully independent.

During its early years the new kingdom was faced with Kurdish revolts (1922–32) and with border disputes in the south. The leading personality in Iraqi political life under the monarchy was Gen. Nuri as-Said, who became Prime Minister in 1930 and held the office for seven terms over a period of 28 years. He strongly supported Iraq's close links with the United Kingdom and with the West in general. After the death of King Faisal I in 1933, the Iraqi monarchy remained pro-British in outlook, and in 1955 Iraq signed the Baghdad Pact, a British-inspired agreement on collective regional security. However, following the overthrow of King Faisal II (the grandson of Faisal I) during a military revolution on 14 July 1958, which brought to power a left-wing nationalist regime headed by Brig. (later Lt-Gen.) Abd al-Karim Kassem, the 1925 Constitution was abolished, the legislature was dissolved, and in March 1959 Iraq withdrew from the Baghdad Pact. Kassem, who had maintained a precarious and increasingly isolated position, opposed by pan-Arabists, Kurds and other groups, was assassinated in February 1963 in a coup by members of the armed forces. The new Government of Col (later Field Marshal) Abd as-Salem Muhammad Aref was more pan-Arab in outlook, and sought closer relations with the United Arab Republic (Egypt). Following his death in March 1966, President Aref was succeeded by his brother, Maj.-Gen. Abd ar-Rahman Muhammad Aref, who was ousted on 17 July 1968 by members of the Arab Renaissance (Baath) Socialist Party. Maj.-Gen. (later Field Marshal) Ahmad Hassan al-Bakr, a former Prime Minister, became President and Prime Minister, and supreme authority was vested in the Revolutionary Command Council (RCC), of which President al-Bakr was also Chairman.

On 16 July 1979 the Vice-Chairman of the RCC, Saddam Hussain, who had long exercised real power in Iraq, replaced al-Bakr as RCC Chairman and as President of Iraq. Shortly afterwards several members of the RCC were executed for their alleged part in a coup plot. The suspicion of Syrian involvement in the attempted putsch, exacerbated by the rivalry between the Baathist movements of both countries, resulted in the suspension of discussions concerning political and economic union between Iraq and Syria. During 1979 the Iraqi Communist Party broke away from the National Progressive Front (NPF), an alliance of Baathists, Kurdish groups and Communists, claiming that the Baathists were conducting a 'reign of terror'. In February 1980 Saddam Hussain announced a National Charter, reaffirming the principles of non-alignment. In June elections took place (the first since the 1958 revolution) for a 250-member, legislative National Assembly; these were followed in September by the first elections to a 50-member Kurdish Legislative Council in the Kurdish Autonomous Region (which had been established in 1970).

Saddam Hussain retained his positions as Chairman of the RCC and Regional Secretary of the Baath Party following its Regional Congress in June 1982. A subsequent purge throughout the administration consolidated his control. Kurdish rebels became active in northern Iraq, occasionally supporting Iranian forces in the war with Iraq (see below). Another threat was posed by the Supreme Council of the Islamic Revolution in Iraq (SCIRI), formed in the Iranian capital, Tehran, in November 1982 by the exiled Shi'ite leader Hojatoleslam Muhammad Baqir al-Hakim. None the less, the majority of Iraq's Shi'ite community was not attracted by the fundamentalist Shi'ite doctrine of Ayatollah Khomeini of Iran, remaining loyal to Iraq and its Sunni President, while Iranian-backed militant groups (such as the predominantly Shi'ite Hizb ad-Da'wa al-Islamiya—Voice of Islam Party, which made numerous attempts to assassinate Saddam Hussain) were ineffective.

Relations with Iran, precarious for many years, descended into full-scale war in September 1980. Iraq had become increasingly dissatisfied with the 1975 Algiers Agreement, which had defined the southern border between Iran and Iraq as the mid-point of the Shatt al-Arab waterway, and also sought the withdrawal of Iranian forces from Abu Musa and the Tunb islands, which Iran had occupied in 1971. The Iranian Revolution of 1979 exacerbated these grievances, and conflict soon developed as Iran accused Iraq of encouraging Arab demands for autonomy in Iran's Khuzestan ('Arabistan') region. Tehran's support for the SCIRI and other Iraqi opposition groups increased the fears among Iraq's Sunni leadership that Iran under Ayatollah Khomenei sought to interfere in its internal affairs. In September 1980, following clashes on the border, Iraq abrogated the Algiers Agreement and its forces advanced into Iran. Fierce Iranian resistance led to military deadlock until mid-1982, when Iranian counteroffensives led to the retaking of the port of Khorramshahr and the withdrawal of Iraqi troops from territory occupied in 1980. In July 1982 the Iranian army crossed into Iraq. In 1984 the balance of military power in the war moved in Iraq's favour, and its financial position improved as the USA and the USSR provided aid. (Diplomatic relations between the USA and Iraq were restored in November 1984, having been suspended since the Arab–Israeli War of 1967). By early 1988 Iraqi forces had begun to recapture land occupied by Iran, and in July they crossed into Iran for the first time since 1986. In that month Iran announced its unconditional acceptance of UN Security Council Resolution 598, and by August a UN-monitored cease-fire was in force. However, negotiations on the full implementation of the resolution had made little progress by the time of Iraq's invasion of Kuwait in August 1990 (see below), at which point Saddam Hussain abruptly sought a formal peace agreement with Iran—accepting all the claims that Iran had pursued since the cease-fire, including the reinstatement of the Algiers Agreement of 1975. (For a fuller account of the 1980–88 Iran–Iraq War and of subsequent bilateral relations, see the chapter on Iran.)

In the second half of the 1980s Saddam Hussain consolidated his control over the country and secured the loyalty of Iraq's Shi'ite community. In 1988, as a reward for its role in the war against Iran, the President announced political reforms, including the introduction of a multi-party system, and in January 1989 declared that these would be incorporated into a new permanent constitution. In April 1989 elections took place to the 250-seat National Assembly, in which one-quarter of the candidates were members of the Baath Party and the remainder either independent or members of the NPF. More than 50% of the newly elected deputies were reported to be Baathists. In July the National Assembly approved a new draft Constitution, under the terms of which a 50-member Consultative Assembly was to be established; both institutions would assume the duties of the RCC, which was to be abolished after a presidential election.

During the 1980s representatives of Iraq's 2.5m.–3m. Kurds demanded greater autonomy. Resources were repeatedly diverted from the war with Iran to control Kurdish insurgency in the north-east of the country. Saddam Hussain sought an accommodation with the Kurds, and a series of discussions began in December 1983, after a cease-fire had been agreed with Jalal Talabani, the leader of the Patriotic Union of Kurdistan (PUK). The talks did not, however, include the other main Kurdish group, the Kurdistan Democratic Party (KDP), led by Masoud Barzani. Negotiations collapsed in May 1984, and armed conflict resumed in Kurdistan in January 1985 between PUK guerrillas and government troops, with Kurdish and Iranian forces repeatedly collaborating in raids against Iraqi military and industrial targets. In February 1988 KDP and PUK guerrillas (assisted by Iranian forces) made inroads into government-controlled territory in Iraqi Kurdistan. In March the Iraqi Government retaliated by using chemical weapons against the Kurdish town of Halabja. In May the KDP and the PUK announced the formation of a coalition of six organizations to continue the struggle for Kurdish self-determination and to co-operate militarily with Iran. The cease-fire in the Iran–Iraq War in August allowed Iraq to launch a new offensive to overrun guerrilla bases near the borders with Iran and Turkey, again allegedly employing chemical weapons. Kurdish civilians and fighters fled across the borders, and by mid-September there were reported to be more than 200,000 Kurdish refugees in Iran and Turkey. In that month, with the army effectively in control of the border with Turkey, the Iraqi Government offered a full amnesty to all Iraqi Kurds inside and outside the country, excluding only Jalal Talabani. It also began to evacuate inhabitants of the Kurdish Autonomous Region to the interior of Iraq, as part of a plan to create a 30-km uninhabited 'security zone' along the whole of Iraq's border with Iran and Turkey. By October 1989, despite international censure of the evacuation programme, the 'security zone' was reported to be in place, prompting the PUK to announce a nation-wide urban guerrilla campaign against the Government. In September elections had proceeded to the legislative council of the Kurdish Autonomous Region.

In mid-1990 the Iraqi Government criticized countries (principally Kuwait and the United Arab Emirates—UAE) that had persistently produced petroleum in excess of the quotas imposed by the Organization of the Petroleum Exporting Countries (OPEC, see p. 331). Iraq also accused Kuwait of violating the Iraqi border in order to secure petroleum resources, and demanded that Kuwait waive Iraq's debt repayments. Direct negotiations between Iraq and Kuwait, with the aim of resolving their disputes over territory and Iraq's war debt, failed, and on 2 August Iraqi forces invaded Kuwait, taking control of the country and establishing a provisional 'free government'. On 8 August Iraq announced its formal annexation of Kuwait. The UN Security Council unanimously adopted, on the day of the invasion, Resolution 660, demanding the immediate and unconditional withdrawal of Iraqi forces from Kuwait. Subsequent resolutions imposed mandatory economic sanctions against Iraq and occupied Kuwait (No. 661), and declared Iraq's annexation of Kuwait null and void (No. 662). On 7 August the US Government dispatched troops and aircraft to Saudi Arabia, at the request of King Fahd, in order to secure the country's border with Kuwait against a possible Iraqi attack; other countries quickly lent their support to what was designated 'Operation Desert Shield', and a multinational force was formed to defend Saudi Arabia. At a meeting of the League of Arab States (the Arab League, see p. 290) on the day after the invasion, 14 of the 21 members condemned the invasion and demanded an unconditional withdrawal by Iraq; one week later 12 member states voted to send an Arab deterrent force to the region of the Persian (Arabian) Gulf.

Diplomatic efforts to achieve a peaceful solution to the Gulf crisis all foundered on Iraq's refusal to withdraw its forces from Kuwait. In November 1990 the UN Security Council adopted Resolution 678, authorizing member states to use 'all necessary means' to enforce the withdrawal of Iraqi forces from Kuwait if they had not left by 15 January 1991. 'Operation Desert Storm'—in effect, war with Iraq—began on the night of 16–17 January, with air attacks on Baghdad by the multinational force, and by the end of January the allied force had achieved air supremacy. Although Iraq managed to launch *Scud* missiles against Saudi Arabia and Israel, the latter's refusal to retaliate against this attack by an Arab state was the result of considerable diplomatic pressure aimed at ensuring Arab unity in the coalition. In February Iraq formally severed diplomatic relations with Egypt, France, Italy, Saudi Arabia, Syria, the United Kingdom and the USA. During the night of 23–24 February the multinational force began a ground offensive for the liberation of Kuwait: Iraqi troops were quickly defeated and surrendered in large numbers. A cease-fire was declared by the US Government on 28 February. Iraq agreed to renounce its claim to Kuwait, to release prisoners of war, and to comply with all pertinent UN Security Council resolutions. Resolution 687, adopted in April, provided for the establishment of a commission to demarcate the border between Iraq and Kuwait. The resolution also linked the removal of sanctions imposed on Iraq following its invasion of Kuwait to the elimination of non-conventional weaponry, to be certified by a UN Special Commission (UNSCOM), and also required that Iraq accept proposals for the establishment of a war reparation fund to be derived from Iraqi petroleum reserves.

Within Iraq the war was followed by domestic unrest: in March 1991 rebel forces, including Shi'ite Muslims and disaffected soldiers, were reported to have taken control of Al-Basrah (Basra) and other southern cities, although the rebellion was soon crushed by troops loyal to Saddam Hussain. In the north Kurdish separatists overran a large area of Kurdistan. The various Kurdish factions, allied since 1988 in the Kurdistan Iraqi Front (KIF), claimed that the objective of the northern insurrection was the full implementation of a 15-article peace plan concluded between Kurdish leaders and the Iraqi Government in 1970. Lacking military support from the multinational force, the Kurdish guerrillas were unable to resist the onslaught of the Iraqi armed forces, which were redeployed northwards as soon as they had crushed the uprising in southern Iraq, and an estimated 1m.–2m. Kurds fled before the Iraqi army across the northern mountains into Turkey and Iran. UN Security Council Resolution 688, adopted in April 1991, condemned the repression of Iraqi civilians and provided for the establishment of an international repatriation and relief effort—co-ordinated by a multinational task force, designated 'Operation Provide Comfort', and based in south-east Turkey to provide relief to displaced persons and to secure designated 'safe havens' on Iraqi territory north of latitude 36°N.

A second air exclusion zone, south of latitude 32°N, was established by France, Russia, the United Kingdom and the USA in August 1992, with the aim of protecting the southern Iraqi Shi'ite communities, including the semi-nomadic Ma'dan (Marsh Arabs). Iraqi military excursions into the northern and southern exclusion zones in late 1992 and early 1993 were repelled by Western aircraft. An alleged conspiracy to assassinate former US President George Bush in Kuwait in April provoked a US attack against intelligence headquarters in Baghdad in June. In July Iraqi armed forces were reported to have renewed the Government's offensive against the inhabitants of the marshlands of southern Iraq. In May 1996 government forces launched a major offensive against the Shi'a opposition and tribes in Basra governorate; by the end of the year there were armed clashes between Iraqi security forces and the Shi'a opposition throughout the southern regions. In April 1998 the SCIRI claimed that a renewed offensive against the Shi'a opposition in southern Iraq had resulted in the execution of some 60 Shi'ites during March.

Meanwhile, in April 1991 the PUK leader, Jalal Talabani, announced that President Saddam Hussain had agreed in principle to implement the provisions of the Kurdish peace plan of 1970. However, negotiations subsequently became deadlocked over the Kurdish demand for the inclusion of Kirkuk in the Kurdish Autonomous Region. Therefore, in October the Iraqi Government withdrew all services from the region, effectively subjecting the Kurds to an economic blockade. The KIF proceeded to organize elections, in May 1992, to a 105-member Iraqi Kurdistan National Assembly, and for a paramount Kurdish leader. The outcome of voting, in which virtually the entire electorate (of some 1.1m.) participated, was that the KDP and the PUK were entitled to an almost equal number of seats. None of the smaller Kurdish parties achieved representation, and the KDP and the PUK subsequently agreed to share equally the seats in the new Assembly. The election for an overall Kurdish leader was deemed inconclusive, with Masoud Barzani, the leader of the KDP, receiving 47.5% of the votes cast, and Jalal Talabani 44.9%.

In December 1993 armed conflict broke out between militants of the PUK and the Islamic League of Kurdistan (or Islamic Movement of Iraqi Kurdistan—IMIK). Following mediation by the Iraqi National Congress (INC—a broad coalition of largely foreign-based opposition groups), the two parties signed a peace agreement in February 1994. However, more serious armed conflict between partisans of the PUK and the KDP led, in May, to the division of the northern Kurdish-controlled enclave into two zones. In June 1995 the IMIK withdrew from the INC, and in July there was renewed fighting between PUK and KDP forces, as a result of which scheduled elections to the Iraqi Kurdistan National Assembly were postponed. Peace negotiations under US auspices began in Dublin, Ireland, in August 1995 but collapsed in the following month. Subsequent discussions in the Iranian capital in October led to the signing of an agreement by the KDP and the PUK to hold elections to the Iraqi Kurdistan National Assembly in May 1996.

In early and mid-1995 Turkish armed forces attacked bases of the Kurdistan Workers' Party (Partiya Karkeren Kurdistan—PKK, now People's Congress of Kurdistan—KONGRA-GEL) in the Kurdish enclave of northern Iraq. Turkey's continued support for the KDP in its efforts to expel PKK fighters from the enclave was believed by some observers to have encouraged the PUK to seek support from Iran. The USA and Turkey were concerned at reports in late 1995 that the armed wing of the SCIRI had begun to deploy inside the Kurdish enclave. None the less, in February 1996 Turkey and NATO agreed to continue 'Operation Provide Comfort', which had become controversial in Turkey owing to the presence of PKK bases in the enclave.

In early 1996 the PUK leader, Jalal Talabani, offered to participate in peace negotiations with the KDP, and to take part in new elections to the Iraqi Kurdistan National Assembly. However, hostilities between the two sides escalated in August, as the PUK contested the KDP's monopoly of duties levied on Turkish traders. At the end of the month Iraqi military support for the KDP in the recapture of the PUK-held towns of Irbil (Arbil) and As-Sulaimaniya (Sulaimaniya) in the Kurdish area of northern Iraq provoked a new international crisis. In September the USA unilaterally launched retaliatory 'limited' airstrikes on air defence and communications targets in southern Iraq, and extended the southern air exclusion zone from latitude 32°N to latitude 33°N (thereby incorporating some southern suburbs of Baghdad). Turkey, which had refused to allow the use of its air bases for the US operation, deployed some 20,000 troops to reinforce its border with Iraq. Also in September the KDP gained control of all three Kurdish provinces. The Iraqi Government subsequently announced the restoration of Iraqi sovereignty over Kurdistan, and offered an amnesty to its Kurdish opponents. In late September the KDP formed a KDP-led coalition administration comprising, among others, the IMIK, the Kurdistan Communist Party and representatives of the northern Assyrian and Turkoman communities. In October PUK fighters were reported to have recaptured much of the territory they had ceded to the KDP, and to be approaching the town of Arbil, having regained control of Sulaimaniya and Halabja. The PUK claimed that it would not, however, attempt to recapture Arbil because the town remained under the protection of Iraqi armed forces. Concern that Iran's alleged involvement in the conflict would provoke direct Iraqi intervention in the north prompted renewed diplomatic efforts on the part of the USA and Turkey, and US-sponsored peace talks in Ankara, Turkey, in late October resulted in a truce agreement. Following the termination of 'Operation Provide Comfort', a new air surveillance programme, 'Northern Watch', began in January 1997; the new operation, based in south-east Turkey, was to be conducted by British, Turkish and US forces.

In March 1997 the KDP withdrew from the US-sponsored peace negotiations, and the crisis continued unabated when, in May, as many as 50,000 Turkish troops entered northern Iraq, where, apparently in co-operation with the KDP, they launched a major offensive against PKK bases. Iraq, Iran and Syria all condemned the incursion, and UN Secretary-General Kofi Annan demanded an immediate Turkish withdrawal, fearing an interruption to the supply of humanitarian aid to the Kurdish

enclave. However, Turkish and KDP military operations against PKK bases in northern Iraq resumed in September. As Turkey began to withdraw its armed forces from northern Iraq in mid-October, the PUK launched a massive military offensive against the KDP, targeting several strategic points along the 1996 cease-fire line. The KDP (which subsequently claimed to have regained most of the territory lost to the PUK during the recent hostilities) alleged that the assault had been co-ordinated by Iran and supported by the PKK. By mid-1998 a fragile cease-fire between the PUK and the KDP appeared to be enduring, and the two organizations agreed to exchange prisoners and to seek to co-operate in other areas. In September the USA brokered a formal peace agreement between the two parties: the accord, signed in Washington, DC, by Masoud Barzani on behalf of the KDP and Jalal Talabani for the PUK, provided for Kurdish legislative elections in 1999 (although these did not take place), a unified regional administration, the sharing of local revenues, an end to hostilities and co-operation in implementing the 'oil-for-food' programme (see below) to benefit the Kurdish population. A new Kurdish coalition government was appointed by the Iraqi Kurdistan National Assembly in December 1999.

Since Iraq's defeat by the US-led coalition forces in 1991, Saddam Hussain had strengthened his control over the country by placing family members and close supporters in the most important government positions. In September 1991 Saddam Hussain was re-elected Secretary-General of the Baath Party's powerful Regional Command at its 10th Congress. In May 1994, confronted by a deepening economic crisis, Saddam Hussain personally assumed the post of Prime Minister. Unsuccessful *coups d'état* reportedly took place in January and March 1995; the latter was instigated by the former head of Iraqi military intelligence and supported by Kurdish insurgents in the north and Shi'ite rebels in the south. A new Minister of Defence and a new Chief of the General Staff were appointed in July. In an apparent attempt to re-establish domestic and international recognition of Saddam Hussain's mandate, in September the RCC approved an interim amendment of the Constitution whereby the elected Chairman of the RCC would automatically assume the Presidency of the Republic, subject to the approval by the National Assembly and endorsement by national plebiscite. Saddam Hussain's candidature was duly approved by the Assembly, and the referendum proceeded on 15 October, at which 99.96% of the votes cast endorsed the President's continuing in office. The result of the referendum was declared null and void in a statement issued by nine Iraqi opposition groups. In December 1996 Saddam Hussain's elder son, Uday, sustained serious injuries in an assassination attempt. Both the Sunni Dulaimi clan and Hizb ad-Da'wa al-Islamiya claimed responsibility for the attack, although it was widely reported that the shooting was engineered by a former army officer whose uncle had been executed in 1990 after denouncing the Iraqi regime.

The first elections to the Iraqi National Assembly since 1989 took place in March 1996, when 689 candidates (all of whom had received the prior approval of a government selection committee) contested 220 of the Assembly's 250 seats: the remaining 30 seats were reserved for representatives of the Autonomous Regions of Arbil, D'hok and Sulaimaniya and were filled by presidential decree. An estimated 90% of Iraq's electorate participated in the elections, which were denounced by the INC, based in London, United Kingdom, and other groups opposed to the Government.

Following reports in late 1997 that Saddam Hussain had ordered the execution of a number of senior military officers, Baath Party members and prisoners, internal unrest continued during 1998. The Special Rapporteur of the UN Commission on Human Rights, Max van der Stoel, denounced the assassination of two senior Shi'a religious leaders, Ayatollah Murtada al-Burujirdi and Grand Ayatollah Mirza Ali al-Gharawi, and expressed fears that the murders were part of a systematic attack on the independent leadership of Iraq's Shi'a Muslims. (UN human rights monitors had been banned from Iraq since 1992.) In February 1999 the killing of the leader of Iraq's Shi'a community, Grand Ayatollah Muhammad Sadiq as-Sadr, provoked demonstrations in Baghdad and other cities. Despite claims by the INC that the unrest marked the beginning of an uprising against the Iraqi regime, it was reported that the demonstrations had been brutally suppressed by units of the Sunni-dominated Iraqi Special Republican Guard. In April the Iraqi authorities announced that four men had been executed for the murder of the Grand Ayatollah. Several Western-based Arabic newspapers reported in early 2000 that the Iraqi authorities had foiled a coup attempt, with some sources claiming that about 40 officers of the Republican Guard had been executed for their part in an attempt to assassinate Saddam Hussain. In early May the SCIRI claimed to have perpetrated a rocket attack on presidential offices in Baghdad, where Saddam Hussain had reportedly been scheduled to meet with his sons. In mid-July 2001 the SCIRI again claimed to have launched rocket assaults against a number of official targets in Baghdad, in reprisal for attacks on Shi'a religious leaders: most recently, a leading Shi'a cleric, Grand Ayatollah Sayed Hussain Bahr al-'Ulum, had died in apparently suspicious circumstances in An-Najaf.

Elections took place on 27 March 2000 for 220 seats in the National Assembly. Official results stated that 165 seats had been won by members of the Baath Party, and the remaining 55 elective seats by independent candidates; a further 30 independents were nominated by the Government to fill the seats reserved for representatives of the Kurdish areas of the north, where the Iraqi authorities stated it was impossible to organize elections since the region remained 'occupied' by the USA. Saddam Hussain's elder son, Uday, was elected to the legislature for the first time, having reportedly received the highest number of votes of any candidate. Some 88.6% of the eligible electorate were said to have participated in the polls. The new National Assembly was inaugurated in April, when Sa'adoun Hammadi, who had held the office since 1996, was re-elected as Speaker. In mid-May 2001 Saddam Hussain was re-elected Secretary-General of the Baath Party Command at the organization's 12th Regional Congress, while speculation that the Iraqi leader's son Qusay was being prepared as his successor was further fuelled by his election to the party Command and by his subsequent appointment as a deputy commander of the party's military section. Significant changes to the Council of Ministers were made from April, when Deputy Prime Minister Tareq Aziz assumed the foreign affairs portfolio on an interim basis: the outgoing Minister of Foreign Affairs, Muhammad Saeed as-Sahaf, became Minister of Information. Naji Sabri, formerly Iraq's ambassador to Austria, was appointed to the new position of Minister of State for Foreign Affairs, and was formally promoted to the post of Minister of Foreign Affairs in early August.

Meanwhile, in mid-August 2002 the National Assembly unanimously endorsed the nomination of President Saddam Hussain to face a national referendum on his remaining in office for a further seven-year term. The referendum was duly held on 15 October, at which the President was officially reported to have received 100% of the votes. A general amnesty for prisoners held in Iraqi gaols was subsequently announced by the authorities; however, opposition groups maintained that there were still thousands of political prisoners in Iraq. This proved to be the last major internal political development under the Baath regime prior to the US-led coalition's military campaign of early 2003, which led to the removal of Saddam Hussain's Government, and which was the *de facto* culmination of more than a decade of international diplomatic manoeuvring on the issues of 'oil-for-food' and banned weapons.

Issues of the maintenance of sanctions originally imposed under UN Security Council Resolution 661 and of Iraqi non-compliance with its obligations under Resolution 687 with regard to its weapons capabilities remained inextricably linked in the decade following the Gulf conflict. Security Council Resolution 692, adopted in May 1991, provided for the establishment of the UN Compensation Commission (UNCC) for victims of Iraqi aggression (both governments and individuals), to be financed by a levy (subsequently fixed at 30%) on Iraqi petroleum revenues. In August the Security Council adopted Resolution 706 (subsequently approved in Resolution 712 in September), proposing that Iraq should be allowed to sell petroleum worth up to US $1,600m. over a six-month period, the revenue from which would be paid into an escrow account controlled by the UN. Part of the sum thus realized was to be made available to Iraq for the purchase of food, medicines and supplies for essential civilian needs. Iraq rejected the terms proposed by the UN for the resumption of exports of petroleum, and in February 1992 withdrew from further negotiations, but in October UN Security Council Resolution 778 permitted the confiscation of oil-related Iraqi assets to the value of up to $500m.

UN Security Council Resolution 707, adopted in August 1991, condemned Iraq's failure to comply with UN weapons inspectors, and demanded that Iraq disclose details of all non-conventional weaponry, that it allow members of UNSCOM and of the International Atomic Energy Agency (IAEA) unrestricted access

to necessary areas and records, and that it halt all nuclear activities. Resolution 715, adopted in October, established the terms under which UNSCOM was to inspect Iraq's weapons capabilities. Although by November Iraq had accepted the provisions for long-term weapons-monitoring contained in Resolution 715, neither the Security Council nor the US Administration were willing to allow even a partial easing of sanctions until Iraq had demonstrated a sustained commitment to the dismantling of its weapons systems. In February 1994 it was reported that Iraq had agreed to co-operate with UN weapons inspectors under Resolution 715. Thereafter, the Iraqi Government engaged in a campaign of diplomacy to obtain the removal of economic sanctions, and in July the first signs emerged of a division within the UN Security Council regarding their continuation. Russia, France and the People's Republic of China favoured acknowledging Iraq's increased co-operation with UN agencies, but were unable to obtain the agreement of the other permanent members of the Council—the USA and the United Kingdom. Following a military stand-off between Iraq and the US and British military, prompted by the movement of Iraqi forces towards the south of the country near the border with Kuwait, the Iraqi National Assembly voted in November to recognize Kuwait within the border defined by the UN in April 1992.

Economic sanctions imposed on Iraq were renewed on a 60-day basis in 1995 (and thereafter). In April the Iraqi Government rejected as a violation of its sovereignty a revised UN proposal (contained in Security Council Resolution 986) for the partial resumption of exports of Iraqi petroleum to generate funds for humanitarian supplies under what was designated an 'oil-for-food' programme. However, in May Iraq accepted the UN's terms governing a resumption of crude petroleum sales. At the insistence of the USA and the United Kingdom, it was stipulated that Iraq should not be involved in the distribution to the Kurdish governorates of humanitarian aid purchased with funds realized. The memorandum of understanding signed by Iraq and the UN permitted Iraq to sell some 700,000 barrels per day (b/d) of petroleum over a period of six months, after which the UN would review the situation before deciding whether sales should continue for a further six months. Of every US $1,000m. realized through the sales, $300m. would be paid into the UN reparations fund; $30m.–$50m. would contribute to the costs of UN operations in Iraq; and $130m.–$150m. would go towards funding UN humanitarian operations in Iraq's Kurdish governorates. Remaining revenues would be used for the purchase and distribution, under close UN supervision, of humanitarian goods in Iraq. Iraqi officials heralded the memorandum of understanding as the beginning of the dismantling of the sanctions regime, while the UN emphasized that the embargo on sales of Iraqi petroleum would not be fully revoked until all the country's weapons of mass destruction had been accounted for and destroyed.

In October 1996 UNSCOM rejected Iraq's 'full, final and complete disclosures on its weapons programmes'. The USA was reported at this time to have granted its approval for the opening of an escrow account with the New York branch of the Banque Nationale de Paris, but the implementation of Resolution 986 (which had been postponed in September, in response to the deployment of Iraqi forces inside the Kurdish 'safe haven' in northern Iraq—see above) was now dependent on stability in northern Iraq and the approval by the UN sanctions committee of a formula fixing the value of Iraqi crude petroleum to be sold. In April 1997 the head of UNSCOM, Rolf Ekeus, reiterated concerns that Iraq was not fully co-operating with UNSCOM weapons inspectors. In June the Security Council accused Iraq of obstructing inspection flights over Iraqi territory; Iraq subsequently denied UNSCOM access to three military sites. The UN reported renewed co-operation by Iraq in July, following the inauguration of Richard Butler as the new head of UNSCOM. In October, however, Butler's initial report to the UN Security Council asserted that although some progress had been made in inspecting Iraqi missiles, Iraq had failed to produce a credible account of its biological, chemical and nuclear warfare programmes and was continuing to hinder UNSCOM's work. Subsequently, within the UN Security Council, the USA and the United Kingdom proposed a resolution to prohibit Iraqi officials considered to be responsible for obstructing weapons inspections from leaving the country. France and Russia objected to the draft resolution but approved a revised version whereby a travel ban would be imposed on Iraqi officials in April 1998 should non-co-operation with UNSCOM continue. Meanwhile, Iraq's RCC criticized the high proportion of UNSCOM personnel supplied by the USA, demanding that these should leave the country by 5 November 1997; the deadline was subsequently extended by one week, in order to allow a UN mission to travel to Baghdad to attempt to resolve the dispute. When negotiations failed, the Security Council unanimously adopted a resolution (No. 1137) that immediately activated the travel ban on Iraqi officials.

The confrontation over weapons inspections deepened in January 1998, when Iraq prohibited inspections by an UNSCOM team led by a former US marine officer, Scott Ritter, claiming that Ritter was spying for the US Central Intelligence Agency (CIA). The UN Security Council issued a statement deploring Iraq's failure to provide UNSCOM with 'full, unconditional and immediate access to all sites'. However, the Security Council was essentially divided on the issue of weapons inspections: the USA, supported by the United Kingdom, indicated that it was prepared to respond militarily to Iraq's continued non-co-operation, while China, France and Russia opposed the use of force. Moreover, it became apparent that there was little regional support for military action against Iraq: only Kuwait announced its approval of force if diplomatic efforts should fail; Saudi Arabia and Bahrain refused to authorize military attacks from their territories, while Egypt and Syria notably signalled their disapproval of military strikes against Iraq. In mid-February the five permanent members of the UN Security Council approved a compromise formula whereby a group of diplomats, specially appointed by the UN Secretary-General in consultation with experts from UNSCOM and the IAEA, would be allowed unconditional and unrestricted access to the eight so-called presidential sites. The Secretary-General, Kofi Annan, travelled to Baghdad in order to discuss the compromise, which was accepted by Iraq following a meeting between Annan and Saddam Hussain; a new memorandum of understanding governing inspections was subsequently signed by the Deputy Prime Minister, Tareq Aziz, and Kofi Annan, thus averting the immediate threat of military action. In March the UN Security Council unanimously approved a resolution (No. 1154) endorsing the memorandum of understanding and warning of 'extreme consequences' should Iraq renege on the agreement. Inspection teams returned to Iraq shortly afterwards, and members of the special group began visiting the presidential sites later in the month. In April, in his six-monthly report to the Security Council, the head of UNSCOM concluded that there had been no progress in the disarmament verification process since October 1997, and that the destruction of Iraq's chemical and biological weapons was incomplete. Iraq, however, insisted that all of its weapons of mass destruction had been destroyed and urged the complete and comprehensive removal of sanctions. US and British opposition frustrated Russian attempts to secure a vote on a draft resolution proposing an end to weapons inspections, in view of an IAEA report concluding that it had failed to uncover evidence of a nuclear weapons programme in Iraq, and in late April the UN Security Council, in response to Butler's report, voted not to review the sanctions in force against Iraq. The USA began in May to withdraw military reinforcements deployed in the region at the height of the inspections crisis.

Richard Butler visited Baghdad in June 1998, where during talks with Tareq Aziz significant progress was reportedly made on plans for the verification of Iraqi disarmament and the eventual removal of sanctions. Later in the month the UNSCOM head was said to have informed the UN Security Council that US military tests on weaponry dismantled as part of the inspection process had shown that Iraq had loaded missile warheads with a chemical weapon component prior to the Gulf conflict. The IAEA again reported in July that it had no evidence that Iraq was concealing nuclear weapons, but considered that Iraq lacked 'full transparency' in its disclosures to inspectors. In August negotiations between Butler and Aziz collapsed, Iraq suspended arms inspections, and Saddam Hussain announced new terms and conditions for their resumption, including the establishment of a new executive bureau to supervise UNSCOM's operations. The UN Security Council voted later in August to renew the sanctions regime for a further 60 days, but in September unanimously adopted a resolution (No. 1194) condemning Iraq's action of the previous month, demanding that Iraq co-operate fully with UNSCOM, and suspending indefinitely the review of the sanctions regime. This prompted the Iraqi Government to halt all co-operation with UNSCOM indefinitely. Reporting to the Security Council in October, Richard Butler asserted that while Iraq was close to fulfilling its obliga-

tions with regard to missiles and chemical weapons programmes, UNSCOM remained concerned about the country's capacity for biological warfare. In early November the Security Council unanimously adopted a British-drafted resolution (No. 1205) demanding that Iraq immediately and unconditionally resume co-operation with UNSCOM. US and British military enforcements were again dispatched to the Gulf region to prepare for possible air-strikes against Iraqi targets. Egypt, Saudi Arabia and Syria, while they opposed the threat of force, urged Iraq to resume co-operation. In mid-November Iraq declared that UNSCOM would be permitted unconditionally to resume the weapons inspection programme, and inspectors subsequently returned to Iraq.

However, Iraq's relations with UNSCOM deteriorated once again in early December 1998, after a weapons inspection team conducting a new series of what were termed 'surprise' or 'challenge' inspections was denied access to the Baath Party headquarters in Baghdad. On the night of 16–17 December, following the withdrawal from Iraq of UNSCOM and IAEA personnel, the USA and the United Kingdom commenced a campaign of air-strikes against Iraqi targets; the operation, designated 'Desert Fox' was terminated on 20 December, with US and British forces claiming to have caused significant damage to Iraqi military installations. France, Russia and China contended that the military action had been undertaken without UN Security Council authorization; however, the USA and the United Kingdom maintained that Resolution 1154, adopted in March, provided sufficient legitimacy. In January 1999 US and Iraqi fighter aircraft clashed in the air exclusion zone over southern Iraq, while ground-launched attacks on US aircraft engaged in policing the zone apparently indicated that Iraq was pursuing a more confrontational policy of refusing to recognize the exclusion zone. US and British aircraft continued to attack Iraqi air defence targets between 1999 and early 2001.

The new US Administration of George W. Bush, which assumed office in January 2001, swiftly adopted an uncompromising stance with regard to Iraq. In February US and British fighter aircraft launched their first attack since Operation Desert Fox of December 1998 on air defence targets near Baghdad, in what the US President described as a 'routine mission' to enforce the northern and southern air exclusion zones. Iraq protested that the air-strikes had targeted residential areas of Baghdad, while there were Western media reports that three people had been killed in the initial attacks. In June 2001 Iraq reported that 23 people had been killed by a bomb dropped on a football field outside Al-Mawsil (Mosul—within the northern exclusion zone); the USA and the United Kingdom denied involvement, asserting that any deaths had been caused by Iraqi anti-aircraft shells. US and British military aircraft launched air-strikes against Iraqi air defence installations in the northern and southern exclusion zones during August–November 2001 and in September 2002, in response to what they claimed were continuing Iraqi attacks on allied aircraft patrolling the zones; Iraqi officials reported that a number of civilians had died in the raids.

Meanwhile, the campaign of air-strikes conducted against Iraqi targets in December 1998 was regarded as marking the collapse of UNSCOM's mission. Diplomatic initiatives undertaken by the Netherlands and the United Kingdom from early 1999 with the aim of drafting a proposal—acceptable to all the permanent members of the Security Council—to establish a successor body to UNSCOM culminated, in December, in the adoption by the Security Council of a resolution (No. 1284) that modified the regime in force for monitoring Iraqi weapons systems. Under the new resolution UNSCOM was to be replaced by a UN Monitoring, Verification and Inspection Commission (UNMOVIC). The resolution provided for the suspension of the economic sanctions in force against Iraq for renewable 120-day periods, provided that Iraq co-operated fully with the new weapons inspectorate and the IAEA throughout such periods. The resolution also effectively removed restrictions on the maximum amount of petroleum that Iraq was permitted to sell under the oil-for-food programme. Resolution 1284 was not approved unanimously, with the People's Republic of China, France and Russia, together with Malaysia (a non-permanent member) abstaining. Iraq immediately responded that it would not co-operate with UNMOVIC—although it was notable that the Government did not categorically reject the resolution. In January 2000 the Security Council unanimously endorsed the appointment of Hans Blix, a former Director-General of the IAEA, as head of UNMOVIC. Meanwhile, IAEA personnel undertook the first routine inspection of Iraqi facilities since their withdrawal in December 1998. In his first report to the UN Security Council, submitted in March 2000, Blix emphasized that, should Iraq permit the return of weapons inspectors, UNMOVIC would resume 'challenge' inspections of Iraqi sites. In the same month Iraq's Deputy Prime Minister, Tareq Aziz, decisively rejected the terms of Resolution 1284. In subsequent months the Iraqi Government repeated at frequent intervals that it would never admit UNMOVIC to the country. In March 2001 it was reported that a recent UNMOVIC assessment had concluded that Iraq might still have the ability to build and use biological and chemical weapons, and might possess stocks of mustard gas, biological weapons and anthrax, as well as having the capability to deliver *Scud* missiles.

Exports of Iraqi crude petroleum, under the terms of Resolution 986, recommenced in December 1996, and continued until immediately prior to the US-led military intervention to oust the regime of Saddam Hussain in March 2003 (see below). The first supplies of food purchased with the revenues from these exports arrived in Iraq in March 1997. In February 1998 the UN Security Council raised the maximum permitted revenue from exports of petroleum to US $5,200m. in the six months to the end of July, of which Iraq would be permitted to spend some $3,550m. on humanitarian goods. The remainder would be used to finance reparations and UN operations in the country. However, Iraq stated that without the rehabilitation of its oil sector it would be unable to export more than $4,000m.-worth of oil every six months. In March UN technicians assessed that Iraq was currently able to export oil to the value of only $3,000m. every six months, and that it would only be able to maintain this level of exports if it was allowed to import essential spare parts. Accordingly, the UN Secretary-General requested the Security Council to allow Iraq to divert $300m. of oil revenues in order to carry out repairs to oil production facilities, and to reduce the value of permitted Iraqi exports under the revised agreement to $4,000m. every six months; Iraq was required to submit a new aid distribution programme before the revised agreement could take effect. The new plan, which was approved by the UN Secretary-General at the end of May, provided for oil sales worth $4,500m. over the following six months, of which $3,100m. was to be allocated for humanitarian supplies and urgent infrastructural repairs, while the remainder would finance war reparations. In June the UN Security Council approved a resolution allowing Iraq to purchase spare parts to the value of $300m. for the oil sector. The Security Council renewed the oil-for-food agreement in November, allowing Iraq to sell $5,200m.-worth of oil over six months. In October 1999 the Security Council adopted a resolution permitting Iraq to sell $3,040m.-worth of oil in addition to the quota agreed in May, to compensate for a severe shortfall in oil revenues in the two previous sale periods. In November Iraq rejected a proposal by the Security Council that the oil-for-food programme should be extended for a further two weeks, pending the revision of the programme's terms of reference. Iraq then temporarily suspended its exports of oil, causing world prices to rise to their highest levels since 1990. Nevertheless, the Security Council continued to vote in favour of extending the oil-for-food programme, and under the ninth phase of the programme from December 2000 Iraq was allocated a maximum of US $525m. for the local costs of maintaining the oil industry.

In February 2000 both the UN Humanitarian Co-ordinator in Iraq (responsible for the oil-for-food programme), Hans von Sponeck, and the head of World Food Programme operations in the country, Jutta Burghardt, resigned in protest at the hardship inflicted on the Iraqi people by the continuing sanctions regime. (The previous oil-for-food co-ordinator, Denis Halliday, had resigned in 1998 after similarly denouncing the failure of the sanctions policy). Tun Myat, who became UN Humanitarian Co-ordinator in Baghdad in April 2000, rejected criticism of the oil-for-food programme but undertook to seek to improve its management. The international community became increasingly vocal in its condemnation of the humanitarian consequences of a decade of sanctions. In March, in spite of the objections of the UN sanctions committee, a British parliamentarian led an aid mission by road from the Jordanian capital, Amman, to Baghdad, delivering medicines to the headquarters of the Iraqi Red Crescent Society, and in April a member of the Italian and European parliaments chartered an aircraft from Amman to Baghdad, in direct contravention of the UN embargo on air travel to Iraq. In August President Hugo Chávez Frías of Venezuela became the first democratically

elected head of state to visit Iraq since the Gulf conflict (in his capacity as Chairman of the OPEC Conference), travelling overland from Iran in order to avoid violating the air embargo. Meanwhile, in that month a rail link between Baghdad and Aleppo, Syria, was reopened after an interval of some 20 years. Furthermore, in November Iraq began to transport crude petroleum to Syria, via a pipeline not used since the early 1980s (the oil-for-food agreement permitted oil exports only via two designated outlets).

In September 2000 the UN Security Council approved the payment to Kuwait of US $15,900m. in compensation for lost production and sales of petroleum as a result of the 1990–91 occupation. However, it was agreed to reduce the levy on Iraq's petroleum revenues destined for reparations under the oil-for-food programme from 30% to 25%.

While Saddam Hussain insisted that the sanctions regime was beginning to disintegrate, and the Iraqi leader appeared to be deriving considerable political capital from the increasing international concern at the very evident humanitarian suffering that had resulted from more than a decade of sanctions, in early 2001 the new US Administration under President George W. Bush emphasized its commitment to ensuring the maintenance of the sanctions regime pending the full implementation of Resolution 1284. The new US Secretary of State, Colin Powell, swiftly undertook to secure implementation of a revised sanctions regime, with a view to resolving humanitarian concerns, by means of allowing the direct sale or supply to Iraq of most consumer goods without prior UN approval, while at the same time maintaining strict controls on the supply to Iraq of goods with potential military applications. Supporters of so-called 'smart' sanctions considered that these would have the effect of countering smuggling (of oil out of, and goods into, Iraq), as well as the divisions within the Security Council and delays in approving import contracts at the UN that had severely undermined the credibility of oil-for-food in recent years. The ninth phase of the oil-for-food programme was extended for a further month from the beginning of June 2001, to allow further consideration of a British-drafted initiative on 'smart' sanctions, which had US approval but was opposed by the People's Republic of China, France and Russia. In protest at the 'smart' sanctions scheme, Iraq swiftly suspended exports under oil-for-food, and urged other OPEC members not to increase production to compensate for the shortfall in supply. Intensive diplomatic activity in subsequent weeks resulted in the endorsement by China and France of a compromise list of items that Iraq would be unable to import under the new system. However, Russia maintained its threat to veto the British resolution, after its counter-initiative to defer a decision on 'smart' sanctions for a further six months—whereby Resolution 1284 would be revised to allow a suspension of sanctions if Iraq agreed to readmit UN weapons inspectors—was rejected by other Security Council members. Thus, the United Kingdom withdrew its resolution, and in early July the Security Council unanimously adopted Resolution 1360, extending the oil-for-food regime for a further five months. Iraq resumed oil exports under the UN programme one week later.

In late November 2001, shortly before the end of the 10th phase, Minister of Foreign Affairs Naji Sabri emphasized that Iraq would end participation in oil-for-food if 'smart' sanctions revisions were adopted; he also reiterated that weapons inspectors would not be permitted to return to Iraq. Implementation of 'smart' sanctions was effectively deferred for a further six-month period when, at the end of November, the Security Council unanimously approved Resolution 1382—essentially a compromise whereby Russia agreed to adopt an annexed list of embargoed items with military and civilian purposes before the expiry of the new (11th) phase, while the USA consented to review Resolution 1284. In early 2002 it was reported that the UN's recently imposed policy of assessing the export price for Iraqi oil retroactively, which had deprived Iraq of the opportunity to negotiate prices with brokers, had resulted in a decline in exports from 2.2m. b/d in December 2001 to 1.5m. b/d in January 2002. Meanwhile, Benon Sevan, the Executive Director of the Iraq Programme, expressed what he termed 'grave concern' in early January at an unprecedented surge in delays, amounting in value to almost US $5,000m., at the UN sanctions committee. In mid-May the Security Council adopted Resolution 1409, extending the oil-for-food programme for a further six months (the 12th phase) while implementing a mechanism to accelerate the processing of contracts not subject to inclusion on the Goods Review List. Earlier in May Iraq resumed exports under oil-for-food, which it had suspended a month earlier in protest against the USA's perceived failure to act to end Israel's military offensive against the Palestinian territories. In late November the UN Security Council adopted Resolution 1443, extending the 12th phase of the oil-for-food programme for a further nine days, amid disagreement concerning the issue of the Goods Review List. Resolution 1447 of early December extended the programme for a further six months (the 13th phase), while Resolution 1454, approved at the end of that month, expanded the list of goods subject to review to include certain items with a potential military use. In mid-March 2003, immediately prior to the start of the US-led military campaign in Iraq (see below), the UN announced a temporary suspension of the oil-for-food programme. However, amid a sharp deterioration in the living conditions of Iraqi citizens following the outbreak of hostilities, at the end of March the UN Security Council adopted Resolution 1472, granting the Secretary-General, Kofi Annan, the authority to implement existing contracts and to facilitate the delivery of aid for an initial 45-day period. The Security Council voted in late April to extend the Secretary-General's mandate until the beginning of June. On 22 May the UN Security Council passed Resolution 1483, which removed sanctions against Iraq; the oil-for-food programme was formally discontinued on 21 November.

After the defeat of the Taliban regime in Afghanistan (q.v.) in late 2001, there was considerable speculation that the USA would seek 'regime change' in Iraq as part of its declared 'war on terror'. Iraq had strenuously denied any involvement in the suicide attacks of September 2001 against New York and Washington, DC, highlighting—according to the majority of analysts—the incompatible nature of Iraq's secular regime with the militant Islamism espoused by Osama bin Laden, the Saudia Arabian-born dissident whose al-Qa'ida (Base) network was held responsible for the attacks. In response to demands by George W. Bush that Iraq readmit UN inspectors to prove that it was not developing weapons of mass destruction, or otherwise be 'held accountable', the Iraqi authorities reiterated that UN sanctions should first be ended and the air exclusion zones revoked. Tensions were heightened in late January 2002 when, in his State of the Union address, President Bush assessed Iraq as forming what he termed an 'axis of evil' (with Iran and the Democratic People's Republic of Korea) seeking to develop weapons of mass destruction, specifically accusing Iraq of plotting to develop anthrax, nerve gas and nuclear weapons. The USA reacted with extreme caution to the announcement in early February that the Secretary-General of the Arab League had conveyed to Kofi Annan a message from Saddam Hussain stating Iraq's willingness to resume talks at the UN 'without preconditions', after a one-year hiatus. It was subsequently confirmed that Annan was to meet with Naji Sabri in New York in early March (with the head of UNMOVIC, Hans Blix, also in attendance), for talks focusing on implementation of pertinent Security Council resolutions adopted since 1990, including the return to Iraq of weapons inspectors. The day before the meeting the USA presented new evidence to a committee of the Security Council purportedly showing that Iraq was violating UN sanctions and developing weapons capabilities. Further talks in May and July 2002 ended with no substantive progress regarding the return of weapons inspectors.

In early August 2002 the UN Security Council declined an offer by the Iraqi Government to resume negotiations on the return of weapons inspectors, stating that Iraq should not impose any preconditions on the resumption of inspections. At the same time the USA continued to give clear signals that it intended to intervene to bring about 'regime change' in Baghdad, pursuing attempts to secure a UN resolution that would authorize military action, while indicating that the USA would be prepared to act unilaterally. Both US and British officials greeted with scepticism Iraq's declaration, made on 16 September, of its willingness to readmit weapons inspectors 'without conditions'; however, the People's Republic of China, France and Russia cautiously welcomed the move. In late September the British Government published a dossier outlining its case against the regime of Saddam Hussain and the perceived threat posed by Iraq's 'illicit weapons programmes' to the security of both the West and the Middle East. Shortly afterwards the US Secretary of Defense, Donald Rumsfeld, reiterated US claims that Iraq had provided assistance in the training of al-Qa'ida militants. Talks between Iraqi and UN officials were held in Vienna, Austria, at the end of September. In early October Hans Blix stated that Iraq had agreed to allow inspec-

tors 'unconditional and unrestricted access' to all relevant sites, but that no new agreement had been reached concerning access to Iraq's presidential palaces. (The memorandum of understanding signed by the UN and Iraq in February 1998 placed restrictions on such inspections.) The USA and the United Kingdom were keen for the Security Council to approve a new resolution that would strengthen the mandate under which the UN inspectors were to operate. China, France and Russia all maintained that—in the event of Iraq's failure to comply with the terms of a future resolution concerning Iraqi disarmament—a second UN resolution should be passed prior to any military action being taken against the Iraqi regime. The UN Secretary-General, Kofi Annan, was also said to favour a 'two-step' approach. In mid-October 2002 President Bush signed a resolution adopted by the US Congress authorizing the use of force, if necessary unilaterally, to disarm Saddam Hussain's regime. On 8 November, after a compromise had been reached between the five permanent members, the UN Security Council unanimously adopted Resolution 1441, which demanded, *inter alia*, that Iraq permit weapons inspectors from UNMOVIC and the IAEA unrestricted access to sites suspected of holding illegal weapons (including the presidential palaces) and required the Iraqi leadership to make a full declaration of its chemical, biological, nuclear and ballistic weapons, as well as related materials used in civilian industries, within 30 days. The resolution warned that this represented a 'final opportunity' for Baghdad to comply with its disarmament obligations under previous UN resolutions, affirming that Iraq would face 'serious consequences' in the event of non-compliance with the UN inspectors or of any 'false statements and omissions' in its weapons declaration. Despite an initial rejection of Resolution 1441 by the Iraqi National Assembly on 12 November, on the following day the RCC announced its formal and unconditional acceptance of the terms of the resolution. Iraqi officials, however, repeatedly stated that they did not possess any weapons of mass destruction. Personnel from UNSCOM and the IAEA resumed weapons inspections in Iraq on 27 November.

Iraq presented UNMOVIC officials with a 12,000-page declaration of its weapons programmes on 7 December 2002. In mid-December, however, the USA stated that Iraq was in 'material breach' of UN Resolution 1441 since it had failed to give a complete account of its weapons capabilities, citing in particular Iraq's failure to account for stocks of biological weapons such as anthrax. The United Kingdom also expressed its disappointment at the declaration. Meanwhile, both Hans Blix and the IAEA head, Muhammad el-Baradei, affirmed to the UN Security Council that their inspectors required a greater level of co-operation from Iraqi officials. In early January 2003 Saddam Hussain accused the UN inspectorate of espionage. In mid-January UNMOVIC personnel reported the discovery of several empty chemical warheads to the south of Baghdad; the weapons had reportedly not been included in Iraq's December declaration, although it was unclear as to whether they constituted a significant discovery. Meanwhile, it was reported that some Arab states (including Saudi Arabia and Egypt) were attempting to persuade Saddam Hussain either to stand down or go into exile—suggestions that were immediately dismissed by Iraqi officials. At an emergency summit meeting of the Arab League in Cairo, Egypt, at the beginning of March, the UAE was reported to have presented a plan for the Iraqi President to stand down, and later in the month the King of Bahrain was said to have offered asylum to Saddam Hussain in order to avert an imminent war.

During January 2003 the USA and the United Kingdom ordered a massive deployment of troops to the Gulf region, while asserting that a conflict was not inevitable if Iraq complied with the UN's disarmament terms. Both the French and German Governments, meanwhile, were vociferous in their opposition to military action and advocated an extension of the UN inspectors' mandate. In late January the foreign ministers of Turkey, Syria, Iran, Jordan, Egypt and Saudi Arabia attended a conference in Istanbul, Turkey, at the end of which they issued a joint communiqué urging Iraq to co-operate fully with UN inspectors in order to avoid a new conflict in the region. On 27 January, 60 days after the resumption of UN weapons inspections in Iraq (as stipulated under Resolution 1441), Hans Blix and Muhammad el-Baradei briefed the UN Security Council on the progress of inspections. El-Baradei stated that IAEA inspectors had found no evidence that Iraq had restarted its nuclear weapons programme, but requested more time for the organization to complete its research. Hans Blix, for his part, claimed that there was no evidence that Iraq had destroyed known stocks of illegal chemical and long-range ballistic weapons, and announced that he was sceptical about Baghdad's willingness to disarm. Following the briefing, the British Secretary of State for Foreign and Commonwealth Affairs, Jack Straw, declared Iraq to be in 'material breach' of Resolution 1441. As the likelihood of a US-led military response to the crisis increased, at the end of January eight European countries (including the United Kingdom, Italy and Spain) signed a joint statement expressing support for the USA's stance with regard to Iraq. In February the British Prime Minister, Tony Blair, under pressure from his electorate and members of his own Labour Party, accelerated his efforts to secure a second UN Security Council resolution authorizing a US-led campaign in Iraq should inspectors from UNMOVIC continue to report Baghdad's non-compliance. President Bush asserted that, although he favoured the adoption of a second resolution, Resolution 1441 had given the USA the authority to disarm Iraq, if necessary by military means. The US Secretary of State, Colin Powell, had, on 5 February, presented to the Security Council what the USA claimed to be over-whelming evidence of Iraq's possession of weapons of mass destruction, its attempts to conceal such weapons from the UN inspectorate and its links with international terrorism, including the al-Qa'ida network. Despite signs of progress being reported by Hans Blix in his report on UNMOVIC's inspections to the Security Council on 14 February—Iraqi officials had submitted new documents relating to banned materials, had announced an easing of restrictions governing the questioning by UN inspectors of Iraqi scientists, and had agreed to allow aerial reconnaissance flights over Iraq—the UNMOVIC chief stated that the inspections should continue, in order to determine whether Iraq did possess undeclared weapons of mass destruction.

On 24 February 2003 the USA, the United Kingdom and Spain presented a draft resolution to the UN Security Council effectively authorizing a US-led military campaign against Saddam Hussain's regime, in response to Baghdad's failure to disarm peacefully. The resolution stated that a deadline of 17 March would be set, by which time Iraq should prove that it was disarming; however, no specific mention was made of con-sequent military action in the event of the deadline not being met, apparently in an effort by the US-led coalition to persuade France, Russia and China not to exercise their right of veto. Officials from France, Russia and Germany responded to the draft resolution by presenting an alternative proposal involving an extended timetable of weapons inspections in order to avert a war. At the beginning of March the Turkish parliament voted to allow US military aircraft to use Turkish airspace in the event of a campaign being waged against the Iraqi regime; however, the parliament rejected a plan for US forces to use Turkey's military bases, even for refuelling their aircraft. A few days later the Russian Minister of Foreign Affairs, Igor Ivanov, stated that any US-led military action without UN authorization would constitute a violation of the UN Charter. (France and Russia had by this time pledged to veto a second resolution authorizing the use of force to disarm Saddam Hussain.) On 12 March Tony Blair proposed six new conditions that Iraq must meet in order to prove that it was serious about disarmament: this was seen as an attempt at a compromise that might encourage wavering countries in the Security Council to support an amended reso-lution. The British proposals came a day after President Bush had rejected a suggested 45-day postponement of any decision to go to war by six countries which had the power to influence the Security Council vote. On 15 March, in anticipation of a probable US-led invasion, Iraq's RCC issued a decree dividing the country into four military commands, under the overall leadership of Saddam Hussain. On the following day a summit meeting was held in the Azores, Portugal, between George W. Bush, Tony Blair and the Spanish Prime Minister, José María Aznar. Sev-eral commentators described the Azores summit as a 'council of war'. On 17 March the USA, the United Kingdom and Spain withdrew their draft resolution from the UN, demonstrating that the resolution's co-sponsors had realized the unlikelihood of winning UN support for military action; they stated that they reserved the right to take their own action to ensure Iraqi disarmament. On the same day President Bush issued an ulti-matum giving Saddam Hussain and his two sons 48 hours to leave Baghdad or face military action. The Iraqi National Assembly rejected the ultimatum. UN weapons inspectors, humanitarian aid workers and UNIKOM observers along the Kuwait–Iraq border were subsequently withdrawn from Iraq.

Shortly after the expiry of President Bush's 48-hour deadline, in the early hours of 20 March 2003 US and British armed forces launched a 'broad and concerted campaign' (code-named 'Oper-ation Iraqi Freedom') to oust the regime of Saddam Hussain. An initial wave of air-strikes against a number of sites in the suburbs of Baghdad, apparently aimed at leading members of the Iraqi regime (including the President himself), failed to achieve their principal targets. Meanwhile, US-led coalition forces crossed into Iraq from Kuwait and began a steady advance towards the capital. At the same time a concerted campaign of massive air-strikes was launched against the key symbols of the Iraqi regime in and around Baghdad, including selected military bases, communications sites, government buildings and broadcasting headquarters. US and British forces adopted a simultaneous campaign of distributing leaflets and broadcasting radio messages, in an effort to persuade Iraqi citizens to abandon their support for the Baath regime: their declared intention was that Operation Iraqi Freedom would precipitate the disintegration of the regime 'from within'. British troops were principally engaged in securing towns in southern Iraq, including Iraq's second city of Basra, after the US-led coalition had seized control of the key southern port of Umm Qasr and the Al-Faw Peninsular. It was the intention of the USA and the United Kingdom that the Shi'a Muslim population of Basra would quickly initiate an uprising against the regime of Saddam Hussain, as had occurred following the Gulf War in 1991. Although fighting between US-led troops and Iraqi armed forces was often intense, resistance from the Iraqi army and from a number of *fedayeen* (martyrs) and volunteers from other Arab countries was generally lighter than had been anticipated by the allies. Moreover, there were widespread reports of Iraqi soldiers surrendering to the advancing forces. Shortly after the commencement of Operation Iraqi Freedom, in late March 2003 US forces had opened a second front in the Kurdish-controlled regions of northern Iraq, where Kurdish forces joined US troops in targeting bases of Ansar al-Islam. Fears that Turkey might exploit the situation to stage a mass deployment of its forces proved to be unfounded.

At an emergency summit meeting of Arab League states in Cairo on 24 March 2003, representatives of the 17 member states in attendance (except Kuwait) issued a resolution con-demning the US-led invasion of Iraq and demanding the with-drawal of all foreign forces from Iraqi territory. Although the USA and the United Kingdom persistently maintained that they were seeking to avoid targeting civilian infrastructure, there was considerable anger in the Arab world and elsewhere at the reports of high numbers of civilian casualties as a result of the conflict. By 7 April US armed forces had entered central Baghdad, including its presidential palaces. The expected strong resistance from Saddam Hussain's élite Republican Guard did not materialize, and the disintegration of the Baath regime appeared to be complete on 9 April when crowds of Iraqis staged street demonstrations denouncing Saddam Hussain and destroying images and statues of the Iraqi President. Kurdish *peshmerga* fighters gained control of the northern town of Kirkuk on 10 April, while the town of Mosul was seized by Kurdish and US forces on the following day. Also on 11 April the USA issued a 'most wanted' list of 55 members of the deposed regime whom it sought to arrest: on 25 April the former Deputy Prime Minister, Tareq Aziz, surrendered to US forces, becoming the 12th Iraqi official on the list to be taken into US custody. The seizure by US troops of Saddam Hussain's birthplace and power base, Tikrit (to the north of Baghdad), on 14 April was widely viewed as the last strategic battle of the US-led campaign to remove the Baathist regime. On 1 May President Bush officially declared an end to 'major combat operations' in Iraq.

The US-led coalition initially acted swiftly to fill the political and administrative vacuum that emerged in the aftermath of the removal of the former Baathist regime. On 15 April 2003 a US-sponsored meeting of various Iraqi opposition groups took place in An-Nasiriyah (Nasiriya) in southern Iraq. However, while the participants produced a 13-point resolution detailing proposals for Iraq's future political development, emphasizing their desire for democratic, sovereign government, it became clear that in the interim period the practical day-to-day respon-sibilities of repairing, rebuilding and maintaining the material infrastructure of Iraq, as well as combating guerrilla supporters of the ousted regime and emerging 'resistance' groups, would fall to the US-led coalition. Retired US army general Jay Garner, Director of the USA's Office of Reconstruction and Human-itarian Assistance (ORHA), arrived in the country on 21 April to manage the restoration of basic services to the Iraqi population and to enforce law and order. However, after the ORHA was deemed to have failed in this task, it was subsequently replaced by the Coalition Provisional Authority (CPA), headed by US diplomat L. Paul Bremer, III. Bremer assumed his responsibilities on 12 May, his first act being to outlaw the Baath Party and related organizations, and to demobilize the Iraqi armed forces and security apparatus. The Ministries of Defence, of Information and of Military Affairs were all dissolved.

UN Security Council Resolution 1483, passed on 22 May 2003, recognized the CPA as the legal occupying power in Iraq, and mandated the CPA to establish a temporary Iraqi governing authority. On 13 July the inaugural meeting of the 25-member Iraqi Governing Council was held in Baghdad; members of the Governing Council were appointed by the CPA in direct proportion to the principal ethnic and religious groups in Iraq: 13 Shi'ite Muslims, five Sunni Muslims, five Kurds, one Assyrian Christian and one Turkoman. They were mostly drawn from the main parties who had been in opposition to the former regime of Saddam Hussain, notably Ahmad Chalabi of the INC, Dr Ayad Allawi of the Iraqi National Accord (INA), Jalal Talabani of the PUK, Masoud Barzani of the KDP and Abd al-Aziz al-Hakim of the SCIRI. The Governing Council had no executive powers, but could appoint ministers and diplomatic representatives, set a date for the holding of free elections and formulate a new constitution. At the end of July the Governing Council adopted a system of 'revolving' or 'rotating' presidency, based on the EU model, in which nine members would share the presidency, each serving for one month beginning in September. Under this system Ibrahim al-Ja'fari, previously a spokesman for the Shi'ite Hizb ad-Da'wa al-Islamiya, was chosen as Iraq's first president of the post-Baathist era. In mid-August the UN Security Council passed a resolution 'welcoming', but not formally recognizing, the establishment of the Iraqi Governing Council. On 1 September the Governing Council announced the formation of a 25-member interim Cabinet, also appointed along the same ethnic and religious lines. The interim Cabinet was to administer the country until the holding of legislative elections. Finally, on 15 November a timetable for the transition of power to an elected, sovereign government was published by the CPA and the Governing Council. The plan was threefold: these two authorities were to be dissolved and replaced by an Iraqi Transitional National Assembly by 30 June 2004; a constitutional convention was to take place by mid-2005, after which a popular referendum would be held on the new constitution; and, by the end of 2005, national elections were to be held to select a new Iraqi government. This process of democratic development was subject, however, to the extremely volatile security situation in Iraq since the declared end of major combat operations. Concurrent to the establishment of temporary but stable government, the CPA was overseeing a large-scale programme of economic reconstruction (see Economic Affairs, below).

The *Fedayeen Saddam*, regarded as the most fanatical of the Baathist partisans, were blamed for many of the early attacks against the US-led coalition forces in the aftermath of the war. However, it soon became clear that the arrest or elimination of the main figures of the old regime was not diminishing the level of armed resistance to coalition forces. By early September 2003 a reported 139 US troops had been killed since the end of combat operations was announced on 1 May, exceeding the number killed during the conflict itself. The attacks were not restricted to the occupying forces: the UN, diplomatic missions, Shi'ite clergy, members of the interim Cabinet and NGOs were also targeted. In early August the Jordanian embassy in Baghdad was severely damaged by a car bomb; the 12 Iraqi victims of the attack included at least four police-officers. The militant Islamist group Ansar al-Islam, suspected of having links with al-Qa'ida, was widely held to be responsible. The UN Special Representative for Iraq, Sergio Vieira de Mello, and some 20 others were killed in late August, when a truck laden with explosives was detonated in front of the UN compound in Baghdad. A previously unknown Islamist group, the Armed Vanguards of the Second Muhammad Army, claimed responsibility for the explosion. On 29 August a car bomb exploded in the holy city of Najaf, killing Hojatoleslam Muhammad Bakir al-Hakim and up to 125 of his followers after Friday prayers at which the Shi'ite cleric had presided. The murdered cleric (who had returned to Iraq from exile in mid-2003) was succeeded as leader of the SCIRI by his brother Abd al-Aziz al-Hakim, a member of the Governing Council. Evident Shi'ite discord had already given rise to the suspicion that the various Shi'ite

factions might be attacking each other in order to establish a dominant position among Iraq's majority Shi'ite population. In late September Aquila al-Hashimi, one of only three female members of the Governing Council, was attacked in Baghdad by unidentified gunmen, and died of her wounds a few days later.

At the end of September 2003 the UN announced that it was on the verge of ceasing all operations in Iraq, such was the parlous state of the security situation: a week earlier there had been another, smaller bomb attack on the UN's Baghdad headquarters. A reported 111 coalition troops were killed in Iraq in November—the worst month in terms of casualties since the end of major combat operations had been announced in May. The most serious incident occurred in mid-November when 19 Italian Carabineri were killed in a suicide truck bomb attack on their barracks in Nasiriya. A few days later 18 Iraqi police-officers and civilians were killed in car bomb attacks on police stations in Khan Bani Saad and Baquba, in the so-called 'Sunni Triangle' to the north of Baghdad. In early December 46 *Fedayeen Saddam* were reportedly killed by US troops after they attempted to ambush two coalition convoys in Samarra.

The US-led coalition had initially been unable to apprehend Saddam Hussain and his immediate family after the removal from power of his regime. However, on 22 July 2003, acting on information received from an Iraqi citizen, US special forces shot dead Saddam Hussain's sons, Uday and Qusay, at a house in Mosul where they had apparently been hiding. Finally, Saddam Hussain was captured by US special forces on 13 December following an intense search of the village of Ad-Dawr near the former President's hometown of Tikrit; they were also believed to have acted as the result of information given by an informant. Although Saddam Hussain admitted his identity on being captured, this was later formally confirmed by DNA testing and by members of the Governing Council. He was accorded prisoner-of-war status and was detained in US custody awaiting interrogation by military officials. In early July 2004 Saddam Hussain, along with 11 co-defendants, appeared in front of a special US-appointed court in Baghdad to face seven charges, including the use of chemical weapons against Kurds in Halabja in 1988 and the invasion of Kuwait in 1990. The former Iraqi leader, declaring the proceedings to be illegal, refused to sign the list of charges. In October 2004 US investigators looking for evidence as part of preparations for war crime trials against Saddam Hussain and former senior Iraqi officials found a mass grave in Hatra, near the ancient city of Nineveh, in which they uncovered the bodies of hundreds of Kurds apparently killed in late 1987 or early 1988, when the Iraqi regime was waging a war against the Kurdish resistance movement.

Meanwhile, there appeared to be little sign of the chemical, biological and nuclear weapons which had been the *raison d'être* for the US-led campaign; as early as July 2003 David Kay, the head of the Iraq Survey Group—comprising more than 1,000 experts appointed by the US-led coalition in May to find these banned weapons—told US congressmen that only 'bits of evidence' had been found. In early October 2004 a report issued by the Iraq Survey Group following its 15-month search for weapons of mass destruction concluded that the regime of Saddam Hussain's work with chemical or biological agents prior to the 2003 invasion had been restricted to small quantities of poisons, probably for use in assassinations. According to the report, while no illegal stockpiles of weapons had been found, and there was no evidence of any attempts to recommence Iraq's nuclear weapons programme (the last Iraqi factory capable of producing weapons of mass destruction having been destroyed in 1996), there was evidence to suggest that the Iraqi regime intended to reintroduce its illegal weapons programmes if the UN lifted sanctions against the country. However, subsequent to the release of the report, the IAEA, whose monitors the USA had not allowed into Iraq after the war began in March 2003, announced that buildings used during Iraq's nuclear programme prior to the Gulf War in 1991 had been dismantled, and that specialized equipment and material inside them that could be utilized to produce nuclear weapons had disappeared. The US Administration officially announced the end of the search for weapons of mass destruction on 12 January 2005.

By January 2004 US-led forces had apprehended or killed 42 of the 55 'most wanted' former Baathists. However, during the weekend of 31 January–1 February some 105 people, mostly Kurds, were killed in suicide bomb attacks in Irbil. The attacks were directed against the offices of the principal Kurdish parties, the KDP and the PUK, and coincided with the Muslim festival of Id al-Adha. Iraq's most senior Shi'ite cleric, Ayatollah

Ali as-Sistani, escaped an assassination attempt on 6 February, and on 10–11 February nearly 100 Iraqis were killed in two separate attacks against the Iraqi police and army in Iskandariya and Baghdad, respectively. As with many of the assaults, the identity of the assailants was unclear, but it now appeared that the insurgents regarded as legitimate targets those Iraqis working with or directly for the coalition forces. Fears that the the insurgents sought to provoke sectarian violence in Iraq appeared to be realized on 2 March when a series of bombs exploded among crowds of Shi'ites who had gathered in Baghdad and Karbala to celebrate the festival of Ashoura. More than 180 people were killed and a further 550 injured in the blasts, and although al-Qa'ida purportedly issued a statement denying involvement, Paul Bremer and other key CPA figures claimed that a Jordanian national, Abu Mussab az-Zarqawi, believed to have ties with al-Qa'ida, was responsible for the bombings and was also the mastermind behind the majority of attacks on coalition and civilian targets in Iraq. The bombings had the additional effect of delaying the signing of the interim constitution.

According to the timetable outlining the transferral of power published on 15 November 2003, the Governing Council had been due to agree on an interim constitution (to take effect from 30 June 2004) by 28 February 2004. However, delays in producing the draft constitution were largely ascribed to objections from Shi'ite members of the Governing Council, who argued that Islam should be the only source of law and who were opposed to Kurdish being recognized as an official language. Negotiations on the proposed interim constitution were postponed due to the Ashoura bombings, and after meeting Ayatollah as-Sistani on 7 March the Shi'ite members dropped their opposition to the document. The Transitional Administrative Law (TAL) was signed by the Governing Council on 8 March; most notably, it outlined a new timetable for the establishment of a permanent legislature and sovereign government (see Government, below) which superseded that previously outlined by the agreement of 15 November 2003. This development was interpreted as evidence of as-Sistani's growing influence on the political process: in particular, plans to elect a transitional national assembly by regional caucuses were shelved and replaced by proposals to hold national elections to an interim legislature, probably leading to a political settlement that would favour Iraq's Shi'ite majority. In late May 2004 the Independent Electoral Commission of Iraq was formed by the CPA to organize elections to a 275-member Transitional National Assembly (TNA), to be held by 31 January 2005. Voter registration for the polls began in early November. Despite opposition from leading Sunni politicians, who were concerned that more time was needed to restore order to Iraq's Sunni regions, the election date of 30 January 2005 was announced in late November 2004. Seats within the TNA were to be allocated on the basis of proportional representation. Key functions of the TNA were to be to draft, by 15 August 2005, a permanent constitution, to be submitted to a popular referendum by 15 October; and to elect a President and two Vice-Presidents, together constituting a state Presidency Council, responsible for appointing a Prime Minister and cabinet. Under the timetable for Iraq's political transition, constitutionally elected organs of government were to be installed by 15 December 2005. Voting for the TNA was to be held simultaneously with elections to 18 provincial assemblies and to a new Iraqi Kurdistan National Assembly. A group of 15 primarily Sunni and secular Iraqi political parties, along with the two main Kurdish factions, the PUK and the KDP, subsequently signed a manifesto demanding that the Interim Government hold the elections at least six months later than scheduled, so that it could ensure that they would take place in a secure environment. In early December the two main Kurdish parties further attempted to increase their chances of success in the ballot, when they announced that they had agreed to contest the polls, and to operate in the interim legislature, on a joint list, the Kurdistan Alliance List. Campaigning for the elections began in mid-December, when major Shi'ite groups, backed by as-Sistani, announced that they would also be campaigning on a shared list of 228 candidates, to be known as the United Iraqi Alliance. In late December, after failing to secure a six-month delay in the holding of the ballot, which they claimed would be rendered illegitimate by violence, the Sunni Iraqi Islamic Party withdrew from the campaign, advocating, together with various Sunni clerics and groups, a boycott of the polls.

At the end of March 2004 Bremer announced the re-establishment of the Ministry of Defence, to be headed by Ali Abd al-Amir

Alawi, the Shi'ite Minister of Trade. Meanwhile, the CPA closed down the Baghdad newspaper *Al-Hawza an-Natiqa* for allegedly inciting violence against the coalition. The newspaper was closely associated with Hojatoleslam Muqtada as-Sadr, a Shi'ite cleric whose father had been assassinated by the previous regime in February 1999, and who, a suspect in the murder of a moderate Shi'ite cleric in Najaf in 2003, had become the coalition's most vocal opponent. Several of the cleric's supporters had formed a militia known as the 'Mahdi Army', and protests outside the newsaper offices were the precursor to a nationwide upsurge in violence against coalition forces. After four US private security contractors were killed in an ambush in the Sunni-dominated town of Fallujah, to the west of Baghdad, in early April US forces surrounded and effectively blockaded the town; around 450 Iraqis (including many civilians) and 40 US soldiers died in the ensuing violence. Two members of the interim Cabinet resigned in protest against the coalition's response to the militant violence: they were Abd al-Basit Turki, the Minister of Human Rights, and Nuri al-Badran, the Minister of the Interior. In mid-April a senior Iranian diplomat was killed by unidentified gunmen in Baghdad, while a series of bombings later in that month resulted in a large number of civilian deaths in Basra.

Meanwhile, in late April 2004 the UN Security Council adopted Resolution 1538, beginning an investigation into allegations by the US General Accounting Office that Saddam Hussain had obtained US $4,400m. in bribes and $5,700m. in petroleum smuggled through neighbouring countries during the now discontinued UN oil-for-food programme (see above). In January 2005 an independent investigation commission appointed by the UN Secretary-General estimated the total amount of money involved to be $21,300m. In early February the commission reported that Benon Sevan, the Executive Director of the programme, had negotiated undisclosed oil contracts with Saddam Hussain's regime, failed to tell the truth to investigators and had given no explanation for large cash payments to his personal account. The report also accused the former UN Secretary-General, Boutros Boutros-Ghali, of disregarding UN rules in order to guarantee that a French bank won the contract to oversee oil sales.

Another scandal developed in late April 2004, when pictures taken by US guards of US soldiers coercing Iraqi prisoners into performing degrading sexual acts and other humiliating activities were broadcast world-wide. One soldier received a 10-year gaol sentence in mid-January 2005 in connection with the abuse of prisoners at the Abu Ghraib prison, west of Baghdad, and two others received shorter prison terms in early February. Meanwhile, in mid-January 2005 three British soldiers were accused of abusing Iraqi prisoners (who had been detained for alleged looting offences in Basra in May 2003) when a collection of 22 photographs purportedly constituting evidence of the mistreatment was released. One soldier who had taken the photographs received an 18-month gaol sentence later in the month, while in late February 2005, at a separate trial, the soldiers accused of the abuse (one of whom had pleaded guilty) were discharged from the army and sentenced to prison terms of between five months and two years. In late January 2005 the Interim Government was also accused by the US-based organization Human Rights Watch of human rights abuses relating to the torture of prisoners, the illegal detainment of suspects and politically motivated arrests by Iraqi security forces.

April 2004 also marked the beginning of a series of insurgent kidnappings of foreign workers, some of whom were killed, apparently as part of an attempt to force coalition forces to leave Iraq. In mid-May Sunni insurgents in central Baghdad assassinated the President of the Governing Council, Izzadine Salim, who was replaced by the Sunni Sheikh Ghazi Mashal Ajil al-Yawar.

In late May 2004 the INA Secretary-General, Dr Ayad Allawi, was appointed interim Prime Minister, and in early June it was announced that Ghazi al-Yawar had been appointed President in the Interim Government, to which power was to be transferred from the CPA on 30 June. The post of Deputy Prime Minister and Minister for National Security Affairs in the interim Council of Ministers went to Dr Barham Salih of the PUK. On 8 June the UN Security Council unanimously approved Resolution 1546, which formally recognized the forthcoming transfer of sovereignty from the CPA to the Interim Government on 30 June. However, following an increase in the number of insurgent attacks, and the kidnapping and killing of foreigners, the date for the granting of sovereignty to the

Interim Government was secretly moved forward to 28 June, in order to prevent a major insurgent assault. A low-key ceremony was held in Baghdad, and hours later Paul Bremer left Iraq; the CPA and the Governing Council were both dissolved. Around 140,000 US soldiers remained in Iraq following the handover of power. In mid-August delegates to a national conference in Baghdad declared the appointment of a 100-member transitional national council that was to govern Iraq in conjunction with the Interim Government until the January 2005 elections. The transitional council was given the authority to veto proposed legislation, appoint a new President or Prime Minister in the event of either position becoming vacant, and approve the 2005 budget.

The US military had, in late April 2004, arranged for an Iraqi security force, led by one of Saddam Hussain's ex-generals, to replace the US Marine Corps in Fallujah. Another security development in April was the CPA's decision to re-employ members of the former Baathist security forces. There was a significant decrease in the amount of fighting reported in Fallujah in May. However, throughout that month coalition forces launched major assaults against Muqtada as-Sadr's Mahdi Army, and particularly heavy fighting was reported in Sadr City (a suburb of Baghdad), Karbala, Najaf, and in Kufa, to the east of Najaf. In early June nine of Iraq's political factions, most of whom were represented in the interim Council of Ministers, reached agreement with Dr Allawi to disband their militias by January 2005. According to the agreement, some 100,000 fighters (but excluding members of the Mahdi Army) would join the security forces or return to civilian life. In early June 2004 US forces reached an accommodation with as-Sadr to end his insurgency, without pressuring him to reduce his military, and in July the ban on the newspaper *Al-Hawza an-Natiqa* was lifted. However, a Sunni uprising in Najaf, where the Mahdi Army seized the Imam Ali Mosque, and in other southern cities from early August, led to renewed fighting, with almost 80 people reported killed in a single 24-hour period in late August. Ayatollah as-Sistani ordered Iraqi Shi'ites to descend upon Najaf to end the fighting there. Thousands of people accompanied him as he entered the city, where he negotiated a cease-fire with as-Sadr, including an end to the siege of the mosque. It was reported the same day that almost 100 people had died in a 24-hour period in Najaf and in Kufa, where some 27 Iraqis preparing to march on Najaf were killed. Although the plan stipulated that both Najaf and Kufa were to be designated weapons-free zones and that US troops were to withdraw from both cities, the local and national authorities requested that US forces stay in Najaf. A cease-fire in Sadr City lasted only a week after talks with interim Prime Minister Ayad Allawi failed to negotiate a permanent agreement. Meanwhile, Abu Mussab az-Zarqawi had declared that he had managed a spate of co-ordinated attacks across Iraq in late June, including five car bomb explosions in Mosul which had killed about 100 people. In early July the Interim Government introduced new legislation granting it wider powers to control the insurgency by enabling the Prime Minister to declare a state of emergency for periods of up to 60 days. In early August the death penalty was reintroduced for certain crimes, having been suspended by the CPA following the US-led invasion.

However, there was no evidence in September 2004 that coalition forces, consisting of some 140,000 US troops and 22,000 troops from allied countries, were defeating insurgent forces, of which there were estimated to be between 20,000 and 40,000. There were an estimated 2,300 attacks directed against civilians and military targets in Iraq during the month, culminating in an attack in Baghdad during which 42 people, most of whom were children, were killed by three car bombs.

In early October 2004 US forces in Samarra were reported to have killed almost 100 of the rebels. Meanwhile, in Sadr City as-Sadr's Mahdi Army announced a cease-fire and stated that they would begin to disarm, provided that the Interim Government released all the army's prisoners, and agreed not to arrest or harm any of its supporters. An incident of particular concern for the security of coalition forces in Iraq was the penetration of and attack on Baghdad's 'Green Zone'—a complex with about 10,000 residents where a high level of security is maintained, and which contains the headquarters of the Interim Government and the US and British embassies—in mid-October; at least 10 people, including four US civilians, were killed by two suicide bombers. Az-Zarqawi's group, which had recently named itself the al-Qa'ida Organization for Holy War in Iraq, asserted that it had been the mastermind behind the attack, and also for the

killing in late October of 49 unarmed National Guard soldiers in Diala province near the Iranian border. It was estimated later in the month that 100,000 Iraqi civilians had died in Iraq in the period since the US-led invasion, principally as a result of air-strikes by coalition forces.

In early November 2004 Allawi declared a 60-day state of emergency, closing Baghdad airport and imposing martial law across most of the country as an estimated 15,000 US troops and 3,000 Iraqi troops descended upon Fallujah, which was still dominated by insurgents. Rebels killed at least 37 people across the country as forces prepared for the military assault. One tactic used by insurgents to resist the assault on Fallujah was to attack police stations and police-officers. Meanwhile, in Samarra co-ordinated bomb and mortar attacks killed at least 30 people, many of them police-officers, and there was also a marked increase in insurgent attacks in mid-November in Mosul, where as many as 50 rebels captured 10 police stations in the city centre and police-officers were reported to have supported the insurgents; US and Iraqi forces entered the city and took control of the police stations, but Mosul continued to experience insurgent attacks. However, by mid-November US troops claimed to be in absolute control of Fallujah, having killed an estimated 1,200 insurgents, with losses of a reported 38 US and six Iraqi military. Concern was expressed at the fact that convoys with supplies of humanitarian aid had not been able to enter Fallujah since the beginning of the assault due to the town being effectively blockaded.

Nevertheless, despite the military assault on Fallujah, troops attempting to police the city came under insurgent attacks throughout December 2004; many of the attacks were thought to have been perpetrated by foreigners sympathizing with resistance to the presence of US forces in Iraq. They were also thought to be part of an attempt to disrupt preparations for the forthcoming elections, and to deter citizens from voting. In early December, after a period of relatively little activity by insurgents in Baghdad, around 30 people were killed in the capital when rebels raided a police station and bombed a Shi'a mosque; az-Zarqawi's group declared that it had carried out the attacks. Also in early December it was reported that thus far 1,000 US soldiers had been killed in action in Iraq since the March 2003 invasion. On 15 December 2004, the first day of campaigning for the elections scheduled for January 2005, seven people were killed and 30 people, including a senior aide to as-Sistani, were injured in Karbala in an assassination attempt on the cleric himself. Four days later, suicide car bomb attacks killed at least 62 people in Karbala and Najaf. In late December 22 soldiers were killed at a US military base near Mosul, and around 50 people, about half of whom were police-officers, were killed in a spate of attacks in Sunni areas around Baghdad.

In January 2005 insurgents continued their campaign against the forthcoming elections, killing 18 Iraqi national guardsmen and one Iraqi civilian in a suicide car bomb attack in Balad early in the month. Two days later insurgents assassinated the Governor of Baghdad province. The number of insurgents at this time was estimated at 200,000, more than the number of coalition troops and many more than had previously been estimated, and the state of emergency imposed in November 2004 (see above) was extended for another month. In mid-January 2005 26 people were killed in one day in Baghdad by insurgent attacks, including one on the Australian embassy. Two days later suicide bombers killed 25 people at a Baghdad mosque and at a Shi'ite wedding party, ending a week in which almost 100 people died.

In response to the growing insurgent violence, and, specifically, a militant group's murder of 15 Iraqi soldiers that it had been holding hostage, the Interim Government again closed Baghdad airport and imposed a strict curfew in advance of the elections at the end of January 2005. Az-Zarqawi, who earlier in the month had castigated Shi'ites for assisting the occupying forces, vowed in the week before the poll to launch a violent battle against the elections. Meanwhile, fighters opposed to the US-led occupation and to the elections killed a senior judge and his son, as well as several police-officers, and attacked polling stations and the offices of political organizations. Five days before the scheduled ballot 37 US troops were killed—the highest single death toll for US forces since March 2003. In advance of the elections, over 100,000 Iraqi police and soldiers provided tight security in an attempt to forestall insurgent attacks, and the Interim Government closed Iraq's borders and imposed a vehicle curfew; all voters were subject to searches before being allowed to enter polling stations. Despite appeals for a boycott by some, especially Sunni, political groups, insurgents' threats to attack citizens intending to vote, and the general acceptance (effectively confirmed in an announcement by the Prime Minister) that some areas of the country were too dangerous for secure polls to be held, elections took place as scheduled on 30 January 2005. At least 44 people died in opposition attacks across the country, although the level of violence was in fact lower than had been widely predicted. In the elections to the TNA, the United Iraqi Alliance took 47.6% of the total votes, winning 140 of the 275 seats, the Kurdistan Alliance List won 75 seats (with 25.4% of the votes), and the Iraqi List, a bloc led by Dr Allawi, came third, securing 40 seats (with 13.6% of the votes); nine other parties achieved representation in the interim legislature. The rate of participation was put at some 58% of the registered electorate. Voting for the TNA was held simultaneously with elections to 18 provincial assemblies and to a new Iraqi Kurdistan National Assembly, where the Kurdistan Democratic list won 104 of the 111 seats.

In early February 2005 a prominent association of Iraqi Sunni clerics who had urged a Sunni boycott of the elections declared the results of the polls illegitimate, asserting that the elected Iraqi Transitional Government would not represent the will of the people owing to the boycott of the ballot by a number of different sects and political parties, and that the group would therefore consider the Government's authority, including its power to draft a Constitution, to be restricted.

There was no apparent lessening of resistance to the occupying forces in early February 2005, when at least 21 people were killed in an explosion near an Iraqi army recruitment centre, whilst in Mosul, where Iraqi and US forces were still involved in fighting with rebels, the police chief attempted to put an end to the insurgency by ordering militants to surrender their weapons within two weeks, threatening to 'wipe out' anyone providing them with shelter. However, insurgent attacks in Mosul continued throughout the month. In what was widely conceived to be an attempt to further aggravate the division between Shi'ite and Sunni communities, militants killed over 30 people as Shi'ites celebrated one of their holy days, Ashoura, in mid-February. At the end of the month some 125 people died as the result of a massive suicide bombing in Hillah. Insurgent attacks continued throughout March and April.

On 6 April 2005 the TNA voted to appoint Jalal Talabani, the leader of the PUK, to the post of President. A Sunni, Ghazi al-Yawar (previously the President of the Interim Government), and a Shi'a, Adil Abd al-Mahdi (the Minister of Finance in the interim administration), were appointed Vice-Presidents. The three, together constituting a state Presidency Council, were sworn in on 7 April, whereupon they appointed Ibrahim al-Ja'fari (a leading member of the predominantly Shi'ite Hizb ad-Da'wa al-Islamiya party, and a Vice-President in the Interim Government) to the post of Prime Minister. On 28 April the TNA overwhelmingly approved al-Ja'fari's proposed new Council of Ministers, members of which were sworn in on 3 May. However, in large part owing to disagreements regarding the level of ministerial representation for Sunnis, seven posts remained unallocated, including those of defence (which was to be assumed on an interim basis by al-Ja'fari), oil (temporarily allocated to Deputy Prime Minister Ahmad Chalabi) and human rights (to be adopted by the Minister of the Environment, Narmin Uthman, on an interim basis).

A general improvement was perceived in Iraq's relations with other Arab states from late 2000, although in September Iraq reiterated allegations that Kuwait was stealing Iraqi petroleum by drilling in an area near the Iraq–Kuwait border. Iraq also accused both Kuwait and Saudi Arabia of inflicting (through the maintenance of the sanctions regime) suffering on the Iraqi population, and alleged that Saudi Arabia was appropriating Iraqi petroleum transported under the oil-for-food programme. In October Iraq was represented at a summit meeting of the Arab League for the first time since 1990, as RCC Vice-President Izzat Ibrahim ad-Douri attended the emergency session convened in Cairo, Egypt, to discuss the Israeli–Palestinian crisis that had erupted in September 2000. Saddam Hussain (to whom an invitation had been issued for the first time since the 1990–91 Gulf crisis) was represented by senior officials of the Iraqi Government at the Arab League summit held in Amman, Jordan, in March 2001. The summit was considered as having made the most comprehensive effort hitherto in addressing divisions arising from the Gulf conflict. None the less, a draft resolution presented by the Iraqi delegation urging an end to UN sanctions and a resumption of civilian flights failed to secure adoption, owing to Iraq's unwillingness to accede to a require-

ment of a specific guarantee that Iraq would not repeat the invasion of 1990: Iraq contended that it had already done sufficient to make clear its recognition of Kuwait's territorial integrity.

In the context of a long-standing commitment to establish a regional common market under the auspices of the Council of Arab Economic Unity (see p. 196), plans for a quadripartite free-trade zone encompassing Iraq, Egypt, Libya and Syria were advanced following a meeting of the Council held in Baghdad in June 2001. In the previous month Iraq had participated with Jordanian, Moroccan and Tunisian representatives in a meeting in Agadir, Morocco, at which the four countries agreed to establish a free-trade zone. In August the Syrian Prime Minister, Muhammad Mustafa Mero, leading a ministerial and commercial delegation, became the most senior Syrian official to visit Iraq for two decades; Mero made a further visit in December.

The extent of Iraq's rehabilitation among the majority of Arab states was particularly evident as, from the latter part of 2001, speculation increased regarding potential US-led military action against Iraq. Leaders of influential Arab states, among them Egypt, Jordan and Syria, all expressed particular concern at the likely consequences should the Bush Administration's campaign be directed against any Arab state, warning against exacerbating tensions in a region under great strain because of the Israeli–Palestinian crisis. During talks with a senior representative of the Qatari ruling family in early January 2002, Saddam Hussain issued an appeal to Arab states to set aside their differences, referring specifically to the need to improve relations with Kuwait and Saudi Arabia; later in the month Iraq reportedly announced its preparedness to allow a delegation from Kuwait to visit Iraq to verify that no Kuwaiti prisoners of war were being held (Kuwait continued to assert that Iraq was detaining at least 90 Kuwaiti nationals). At the Arab League summit held in Beirut, Lebanon, in late March it was announced that Kuwait and Iraq had reached agreement on the resolution of outstanding differences (see the chapter on Kuwait). In May Iraq notified the UN of its intention to return to Kuwait the official documents and archives removed during the 1990–91 occupation. Meanwhile, in mid-January 2002 Amr Moussa became the first Secretary-General of the Arab League to visit Baghdad since the Gulf conflict, subsequently conveying to the UN Secretary-General Saddam Hussain's willingness to resume talks (see above). Iraq's relations with Kuwait were significantly affected by the US-led campaign to oust the Baathist regime in March 2003, especially since the coalition forces launched their ground assault from Kuwait. In June 2004, when sovereignty was transferred to the Iraqi Interim Government, Kuwait announced the resumption of diplomatic relations with Iraq.

In early August 2003 the Arab League refused to recognize the Governing Council as the legitimate government of Iraq, stating that it would only recognize an elected sovereign government. However, the new Iraqi Minister of Oil, Ibrahim Bahr al-Ulum, was invited to take Iraq's seat at an OPEC meeting in Vienna in late September. Iraq also attended a summit meeting of the Organization of the Islamic Conference (OIC) in Malaysia during mid-October as a full member.

In October 1998 the US Congress approved the Iraq Liberation Act, permitting the US President to provide up to US $97m. in military assistance to Iraqi opposition groups in exile. In April 1999 11 opposition groups gathered in London, where they undertook to reform the moribund INC and to prepare by July a plan of campaign against Saddam Hussain's regime. Although representatives of the two main Kurdish factions, the KDP and the PUK, attended the meeting, the SCIRI and the Iraqi Communist Party did not participate. Two new organizations were created at the meeting: a collegiate leadership of seven members (six members were nominated, with the remaining place reserved for a representative of the SCIRI), and a five-member committee charged with contacting all opposition groups. In November delegates to a national assembly of the INC, held in New York, USA, elected a 65-member central council and a new, seven-member collegiate leadership. Several INC leaders meanwhile relocated to the USA, with a view to lobbying US support for the Iraqi opposition movement. The USA continued to support Iraqi opposition groups in the build-up to the US-led coalition's military intervention in early 2003, especially since it was clear that following the removal of the regime of Saddam Hussain, not every political or religious group previously opposed to the Baath regime (particularly the Kurdish factions) could be relied upon to act in the interests of the CPA. In May 2004 the USA announced that it had stopped payments to the INC, apparently to facilitate the granting of sovereignty to the Iraqi people, although it was noted that, soon after the announcement of the cessation of payments, the house of one of the INC leaders, Ahmad Chalabi, was raided by US forces and Iraqi police.

From its inauguration, the Iraqi Interim Government repeatedly accused Iran and Syria of supporting insurgents in Iraq, claims which both countries rejected. Nevertheless, the Iranian Government was considered by some to be intent on increasing its influence in Iraq through the predicted rise to power of Shi'ites in the future government. In late February 2005 it was reported that Syria had captured and handed over to Iraqi security forces Sabawi Ibrahim al-Hassan, a half-brother of Saddam Hussein, as a gesture of 'goodwill'; al-Hassan was accused of involvement in the insurgency against coalition forces in Iraq.

Government

Prior to the ousting of the regime of Saddam Hussein by the US-led coalition in early April 2003 (see Recent History), Iraq was divided into 18 governorates (including three Autonomous Regions). In the immediate aftermath of the war in Iraq, a US-led Coalition Provisional Authority (CPA) was established to govern Iraq in the absence of an elected sovereign government. UN Security Council Resolution 1483 of 22 May gave legitimacy to the occupying powers in this task. On 13 July a 25-member interim Governing Council was formed, whose members were selected by the CPA in proportion to the country's main ethnic and religious groups. It had no executive power, but could appoint ministers and diplomatic representatives, draw up a new constitution, and set a date for free elections. The Governing Council decided upon a 'revolving' presidency, commencing in September, with nine members of the council each serving for one month. In the same month, 25 ministers were appointed to serve in an interim Cabinet, also chosen according to ethnicity and creed. On 15 November the CPA and Governing Council jointly published a plan for the creation of a democratically elected, sovereign government and constitution by the end of 2005. However, this plan was superseded by the Transitional Administrative Law (TAL) signed on 8 March 2004. Under the terms of the TAL, an Iraqi Interim Government assumed power on 28 June 2004 (two days earlier than was stipulated), and the CPA and Governing Council were dissolved. The Interim Government was to be replaced by an Iraqi Transitional Government, consisting of a state Presidency Council (comprising a President and two Vice-Presidents) and a Prime Minister and Cabinet to be appointed by the Council, following elections to the 275-member Transitional National Assembly (TNA), which took place on 30 January 2005. (The Presidency Council and Government were appointed in April 2005.) Members of the TNA were required to produce a draft constitution by 15 August 2005, to be approved by national referendum by 15 October 2005. Assuming the approval of the constitution, national elections were to take place by 15 December, and a permanent sovereign government and national legislature was to assume office by 31 December 2005. An alternative timetable was also outlined should the draft constitution be rejected by referendum, a main feature of which was the election of a new National Assembly to prepare a new draft constitution.

Defence

The US-led CPA dissolved the armed forces and security organizations in place under Saddam Hussein's regime on 23 May 2003, following the ousting of the regime in the previous month. On 7 August the CPA promulgated the establishment of the New Iraqi Army (NIA), to which an estimated NID 34,800m. was allocated in the full-year budget for 2004. At 28 June 2004 Iraq's armed forces numbered 9,754, of which 7,116 were active and 2,638 were in training. Those serving in the Iraqi National Guard (which replaced the Iraqi Civil Defence Corps) numbered 37,790 (36,229 active and 1,561 in training), and those in the navy an estimated 410. However, these numbers were far below those required to maintain the country's security in the long term. Personnel were also undergoing training for the Iraqi Police Service, Department of Border Enforcement, Iraqi Coastal Defence Force, Iraqi Riverine Patrol Service, Facilities Protection Service, and an Iraqi air force.

Economic Affairs

In 2002, according to estimates by the UN's Economic and Social Commission for Western Asia (ESCWA), Iraq's gross domestic product (GDP), measured in current prices, was ID 5,924,542m.

In terms of US dollars, GDP was $5,265.9m. ($212 per head) in 2002. Real GDP growth was estimated at 9% in 2001 and 7% in 2002. Over the period 1990–2003 the population increased by an average of 2.4% per year, according to estimates by the World Bank.

Agriculture (including forestry and fishing) contributed 30.0% of GDP in 2002, compared with 15.3% in 1989—i.e. prior to the invasion of Kuwait. An estimated 8.7% of the labour force were employed in agriculture in 2003. Dates are the principal cash crop. Other crops include wheat, barley, potatoes, tomatoes, melons, cucumbers and oranges. Production of eggs, milk and poultry meat is also important. During 1990–2001, according to FAO data, agricultural production declined by an average of 3.8% per year; however, output increased by 8.0% in 2001.

Industry (including mining, manufacturing, construction and power) employed 19.1% of the labour force in 1987; the sector provided 16.2% of GDP in 2002 (compared with 37.9% in 1989).

Mining (including production of crude petroleum and gas) employed 1.3% of the labour force in 1987. The sector contributed less than 0.1% of GDP in 1994 (compared with 17.9% in 1989), and by 1995 its contribution was negative. Iraq had proven reserves of 115,000m. barrels of petroleum at the end of 2003, as well as 3,110,000m. cu m of natural gas. Reserves of phosphates, sulphur, gypsum and salt are also exploited.

Manufacturing employed 7.4% of the labour force in 1987, and contributed 0.7% of GDP in 1995 (compared with 12.3% in 1989). The mining and manufacturing sectors combined accounted for 10.6% of GDP in 2002. Measured by the value of output, chemical, petroleum, coal, rubber and plastic products accounted for 35.2% of manufacturing activity in 1986. Other important branches of the sector in that year were food products (providing 15.8% of manufacturing output), non-metallic mineral products (12.6%) and textiles (6.1%).

Energy is derived principally from petroleum, which accounted for an estimated 98.2% of total electricity generation in 2001.

The services sector employed 67.2% of the labour force in 1987, and contributed 53.8% of GDP in 2002 (compared with 46.7% in 1989).

In 2003, according to the Central Bank, Iraq recorded a trade surplus of US $152.6m., while there was a deficit of $559.5m. on the current account of the balance of payments. Crude petroleum was by far the most important export prior to the imposition of economic sanctions (see below). According to the Central Bank, Iraq's principal exports in 2003 were mineral fuels and lubricants, crude materials, food and live animals, and chemicals. The principal imports in that year were machinery and transport equipment, basic manufactures, food and live animals, and miscellaneous manufactured articles.

Budget proposals for 2004, published in late 2003, forecast expenditure of NID 20,145,100m. and revenue of NID 19,258,800m. The former Iraqi Government estimated that, at 1 January 1991, its total external debt stood at ID 13,118m. (US $42,320m.); and that the servicing of the debt over the period 1991–95 would cost ID 23,388m. ($75,450m.). These estimates did not, however, take into account loans made to Iraq during the Iran–Iraq War by Saudi Arabia and Kuwait. (For details regarding recent estimates of Iraqi debt, see below.) The *Middle East Economic Digest* estimated that in 1996 the average rate of inflation was 450%, compared with inflation averaging 24.4% per year in 1985–89. According to the Central Bank, the annual rate of inflation in Baghdad was 19.3% in 2002 and 33.6% in 2003. Estimates concerning the rate of unemployment in Iraq vary considerably, with some sources claiming in mid-2004 that it might be as high as 70%.

Iraq is a member of the Arab Fund for Economic and Social Development (see p. 151), the Council of Arab Economic Unity (see p. 196), the Organization of Arab Petroleum Exporting Countries (see p. 324), the Organization of the Petroleum Exporting Countries (see p. 331) and the Arab Co-operation Council (see p. 324). Iraq was granted observer status at the World Trade Organization (WTO, see p. 357) in February 2004; in December the WTO agreed to commence membership talks with Iraq.

At the time of the US-led military campaign to oust the regime of Saddam Hussein, Iraq's economy and population were still suffering from the effects of the Gulf crisis of 1990–91 (see above), which left the country's economic infrastructure seriously damaged and resulted in severe food shortages, and from the imposition of economic sanctions in 1990. Following the US-led coalition's success in ousting the Baathist regime in April

2003, attention focused on the cost of rebuilding Iraq and the considerable commercial and government debts accrued by the former regime. The CPA established the Development Fund for Iraq (DFI), to be administered by the Central Bank of Iraq, to fund reconstruction efforts. An initial deposit of US $1,000m. was placed in the fund, comprising receipts from the oil-for-food programme (the remainder of which—approximately $5,600m.—the UN transferred to the DFI by the end of the year), and was to be further supplemented by 95% of future proceeds from oil exports. The US Agency for International Development (USAID) was responsible for awarding contracts for reconstruction work totalling $900m. in eight key areas: seaport administration; personnel support; capital construction; theatre logistics support; public health; primary and secondary education; local government; and airport administration. Estimates for the total cost of the reconstruction of Iraq ranged between $26,000m. and $140,000m. However, Iraq's outstanding debts were estimated at $120,000m., thus precluding the possibility of future proceeds from Iraq's oil exports financing both reconstruction and debt-servicing. Meanwhile, security concerns forced many charities providing aid to operate from outside the country, and in November 2004 the UN Children's Fund (UNICEF) announced the level of acute malnutrition among young Iraqi children was close to twice that at the time of the commencement of military action in March 2003.

International efforts were made to reduce Iraq's external debt from October 2003. The World Bank pledged US $3,000m.–$5,000m. for reconstruction over the next five years following similar offers from the EU ($231m.), Japan ($1,500m.), Spain ($300m.) and the United Kingdom ($835m.). Furthermore, at a conference of international donors convened to discuss Iraqi debt reduction in Madrid, Spain, Japan offered a further $3,500m. in low-interest loans, and Saudi Arabia announced an aid package worth $1,000m. At the beginning of November the US Senate approved an $87,500m. emergency funding package for aid and military operations in Iraq and Afghanistan, of which $20,000m. was earmarked as a non-repayable grant for reconstruction in Iraq. The UAE and Qatar announced in January 2004 that they were prepared to waive most of the $7,000m. they were owed by Iraq following talks with US envoy James Baker, whom President Bush had given the task of leading efforts to reduce Iraq's debt burden. In October the IMF agreed to provide Baghdad with a fund of $436.3m. in the form of loans, in order to provide emergency assistance for reconstruction. In November the 'Paris Club' of international creditor nations agreed to reduce Iraq's $21,000m. of debts owed to them by 80% in a series of stages by 2008, on the condition that Iraq successfully implemented the IMF's emergency assistance programme. In December 2004 the USA cancelled all of the $4,100m. of debt owed to it by Iraq.

The US-led coalition's military campaign to oust Saddam Hussein took place during the 13th phase of the oil-for-food programme, whereby supply and distribution of humanitarian and consumer goods to Iraq and the sale of Iraqi petroleum were monitored by the UN, and the removal from power of the Baathist regime effectively brought to an end the programme and its attendant system of sanctions. In early 2003 industry sources estimated Iraq's oil production capacity to be around 2.8m. b/d; capacity prior to the Gulf crisis of 1990–91 was in the region of 3.5m. b/d. The hiatus in production caused by the recent conflict in Iraq came to an end on 22 April 2003, and the first post-war sales of oil were achieved in mid-June. At the end of 2003 Iraq was producing only 1.3m. b/d, while during the period September to November 2004 production peaked at 2.3m. b/d, although the Ministry of Oil hoped to achieve production levels of 3.0m. b/d by mid-2005. In July 2004 the Interim Government formed a Supreme Board for Reconstruction, the 13 members of which were to supervise all civil reconstruction projects, as well as oversee the US $18,400m. supplementary budget for the Iraq Relief and Reconstruction Fund approved by the US Senate in October 2003; $12,600m. of this fund was set aside for construction projects, with the remaining $5,800m. devoted to restoring Iraqi infrastructure. Another important economic development subsequent to the removal from power of Saddam Hussein was the reunification of Iraq's 13 state-owned oil companies and the fact that the Iraq National Oil Company had once again become the sole body responsible for Iraq's oil and gas resources. In December 2004 the Ministry of Oil awarded Iraq's first post-war oilfield development contracts: one worth $136m. to the Turkish firm Avrasya for the development of the Khurmala Dome oilfield; and the second for the development of the Himrin oilfield to the Canadian firm Ironhorse Oil & Gas Inc. In the mean time, however, insurgent attacks on oil wells and installations during 2004 were estimated to have cost Iraq some $6,000m.

Education

Education is provided free of charge, and primary education, beginning at six years of age and lasting for six years, has been made compulsory in an effort to reduce illiteracy. Enrolment at primary schools of children in the relevant age-group reached 100% in 1978, fell to 76% by 1995, but reportedly rose again, to 93%, in 1999/2000. Secondary education begins at 12 years of age and lasts for up to six years, divided into two cycles of three years each. Enrolment at secondary schools in 1999/2000 was equivalent to 33% of children in the appropriate age-group. There are 43 technical institutes and colleges, two postgraduate commissions and 20 universities. In the 2002/03 academic year there were an estimated 240,000 undergraduates enrolled in courses of higher education. Following the change of regime in Iraq in April 2003, a comprehensive reform of the country's education system was undertaken.

Public Holidays*

2005: 1 January (New Year's Day), 21 January† (Id al-Adha, Feast of the Sacrifice), 10 February† (Islamic New Year), 19 February† (Ashoura), 9 April (National Holiday, commemorating overthrow of the Baath regime), 21 April† (Mouloud, Birth of Muhammad), 2 September† (Leilat al-Meiraj, ascension of Muhammad), 4 November† (Id al-Fitr, end of Ramadan).

2006: 1 January (New Year's Day), 11 January† (Id al-Adha, Feast of the Sacrifice), 31 January† (Islamic New Year), 9 February† (Ashoura), 9 April (National Holiday, commemorating overthrow of the Baath regime), 11 April† (Mouloud, Birth of Muhammad), 22 August† (Leilat al-Meiraj, ascension of Muhammad), 24 October† (Id al-Fitr, end of Ramadan).

* The first act of the now defunct Iraqi Governing Council was to abolish holidays and festivals instituted by the former Baath regime.

† These holidays are dependent on the Islamic lunar calendar and may vary by one or two days from the dates given.

Weights and Measures

The metric system is in force. Local measurements are also used, e.g. 1 meshara or dunum = 2,500 sq m (0.62 acre).

Statistical Survey

Source (unless otherwise indicated): Central Statistical Organization, Ministry of Planning, POB 8001, Karradat Mariam, ash-Shawaf Sq., Baghdad; tel. and fax (1) 885-3653; e-mail mini_of_planning@orha.centcom.mil; Central Bank of Iraq, Ar-Rasheed Street, Baghdad; tel. (1) 816-5170; fax (1) 816-6802; e-mail cbi@cbiraq.org; internet www.cbiraq.org.

Area and Population

AREA, POPULATION AND DENSITY*

Area (sq km)	438,317†
Population (census results)	
17 October 1987	16,335,199
17 October 1997	
Males	10,940,764
Females	11,077,219
Total	22,017,983
Population (UN estimates at mid-year)‡	
2001	23,860,000
2002	24,510,000
2003	25,175,000
Density (per sq km) at mid-2003	57.4

* No account has been taken of the reduction in the area of Iraq as a result of the adjustment to the border with Kuwait that came into force on 15 January 1993.
† 169,235 sq miles. This figure includes 924 sq km (357 sq miles) of territorial waters but excludes the Neutral Zone, of which Iraq's share is 3,522 sq km (1,360 sq miles). The Zone lies between Iraq and Saudi Arabia, and is administered jointly by the two countries. Nomads move freely through it but there are no permanent inhabitants.
‡ Source: UN, *World Population Prospects: The 2002 Revision.*

GOVERNORATES
(population at 1987 census)

	Area* (sq km)	Population	Density (per sq km)
Nineveh	37,698	1,479,430	39.2
Salah ad-Din	29,004	726,138	25.0
At-Ta'meem	10,391	601,219	57.9
Diala	19,292	961,073	49.8
Baghdad	5,159	3,841,268	744.6
Al-Anbar	137,723	820,690	6.0
Babylon	5,258	1,109,574	211.0
Karbala	5,034	469,282	93.2
An-Najaf	27,844	590,078	21.2
Al-Qadisiya	8,507	559,805	65.8
Al-Muthanna	51,029	315,816	6.2
Thi-Qar	13,626	921,066	67.6
Wasit	17,308	564,670	32.6
Maysan	14,103	487,448	34.6
Al-Basrah (Basra)	19,070	872,176	45.7
Autonomous Regions:			
D'hok	6,120	293,304	47.9
Irbil (Arbil)	14,471	770,439	53.2
As-Sulaimaniya (Sulaimaniya)	15,756	951,723	60.4
Total	437,393	16,335,199	37.3

* Excluding territorial waters (924 sq km).

PRINCIPAL TOWNS
(population at 1987 census)

Baghdad (capital) . .	3,841,268	As-Sulaimaniya (Sulaimaniya)	364,096
Al-Mawsil (Mosul) . .	664,221	An-Najaf . .	309,010
Irbil (Arbil) . .	485,968	Karbala	296,705
Kirkuk . . .	418,624	Al-Hillah (Hilla)	268,834
Al-Basrah (Basra) . .	406,296	An-Nasiriyah (Nasiriya) .	265,937

Source: Thomas Brinkhoff, *City Population* (internet www.citypopulation.de).

Mid-2003 (UN estimates, incl. suburbs): Baghdad 5,620,000; Mosul 1,200,000; Basra 1,100,000 (Source: UN, *World Urbanization Prospects: The 2003 Revision*).

BIRTHS AND DEATHS
(UN estimates, annual averages)

	1985–90	1990–95	1995–2000
Birth rate (per 1,000)	40.2	38.8	37.3
Death rate (per 1,000)	6.8	10.1	9.8

Source: UN, *World Population Prospects: The 2002 Revision.*

Registered live births (incomplete registration, 1992): 502,415 (birth rate 27.4 per 1,000).

Registered deaths (incomplete registration, 1990): 76,683 (death rate 4.4 per 1,000).

Expectation of life (WHO estimates, years at birth): 61.0 (males 59.1; females 33.1) in 2002 (Source: WHO, *World Health Report*).

ECONOMICALLY ACTIVE POPULATION*
(persons aged 7 years and over, 1987 census)

	Males	Females	Total
Agriculture, forestry and fishing .	422,265	70,741	493,006
Mining and quarrying	40,439	4,698	45,137
Manufacturing	228,242	38,719	266,961
Electricity, gas and water . . .	31,786	4,450	36,236
Construction	332,645	8,541	341,186
Trade, restaurants and hotels . .	191,116	24,489	215,605
Transport, storage and communications	212,116	12,155	224,271
Financing, insurance, real estate and business services . . .	16,204	10,811	27,015
Community, social and personal services	1,721,748	233,068	1,954,816
Activities not adequately defined .	146,616	18,232	167,848
Total labour force	3,346,177	425,904	3,772,081

* Figures exclude persons seeking work for the first time, totalling 184,264 (males 149,938, females 34,326), but include other unemployed persons.

Source: ILO, *Yearbook of Labour Statistics.*

Mid-2003 (estimates in '000): Agriculture, etc. 618; Total 7,066 (Source: FAO).

Health and Welfare

KEY INDICATORS

Total fertility rate (children per woman, 2002)	4.8
Under-5 mortality rate (per 1,000 live births, 2003) . . .	125
HIV/AIDS (% of persons aged 15–49, 2003)	<0.1
Physicians (per 1,000 head, 1998)	0.55
Hospital beds (per 1,000 head, 1998)	1.45
Health expenditure (2001): US $ per head (PPP)	225
Health expenditure (2001): % of GDP	3.2
Health expenditure (2001): public (% of total)	31.8
Access to water (% of persons, 2002)	81
Access to sanitation (% of persons, 2002)	80
Human Development Index (2000): value	0.567*

* Based on incomplete information.
For sources and definitions, see explanatory note on p. vi.

Agriculture

PRINCIPAL CROPS
('000 metric tons)

	2001	2002	2003
Wheat*	903	1,856	2,553
Rice (paddy)*	128	250	125
Barley*	550	1,032	1,316
Maize*	50	250	125
Potatoes	623	625†	625†
Sugar cane†	65	68	69
Chick-peas*	87	97	104
Sunflower seed	65*	65*	67†
Tomatoes	1,321*	1,200†	1,000†
Cauliflower	32*	35†	30†
Pumpkins, squash and gourds†	35	35	35
Cucumbers and gherkins	361*	400†	350†
Aubergines (Eggplants)†	85	85	85
Dry onions †	160	170	150
Other vegetables†	437	439	437
Watermelons†	380	380	380
Canteloupes and other melons†	195	195	195
Grapes	300*	300†	300†
Oranges†	300	310	310
Tangerines, mandarins, clementines and satsumas†	37	37	37
Apples	70*	75†	75†
Apricots†	22	22	22
Peaches and nectarines†	20	20	20
Plums†	27	27	27
Dates	650*	907*	910†
Other fruits and berries†	95	95	95

* Unofficial figure(s).
† FAO estimate(s).

Source: FAO, *Production Yearbook.*

LIVESTOCK
(FAO estimates, '000 head, year ending September)

	2001	2002	2003
Horses	47	47	47
Mules	11	11	11
Asses	380	380	380
Cattle	1,375	1,400	1,500
Buffaloes	66	67	68
Camels	8	8	8
Sheep	6,100	6,200	6,200
Goats	1,650	1,650	1,650
Poultry	23,000	23,000	23,000

Source: FAO, *Production Yearbook.*

LIVESTOCK PRODUCTS
(FAO estimates, '000 metric tons)

	2001	2002	2003
Beef and veal	46	47	47
Buffalo meat	2	2	2
Mutton and lamb	20	20	20
Goat meat	8	8	8
Poultry meat	41	41	41
Cows' milk	300	300	300
Buffaloes' milk	28	28	28
Sheep's milk	158	158	158
Goats' milk	54	54	54
Cheese	30	30	30
Butter	8	8	8
Hen eggs	14	14	14
Wool: greasy	13	13	13
Wool: scoured	6	6	6
Cattle and buffalo hides	5	5	6
Sheepskins	4	4	4
Goatskins	2	2	2

Source: FAO, *Production Yearbook.*

Forestry

ROUNDWOOD REMOVALS
(FAO estimates, '000 cubic metres, excl. bark)

	2001	2002	2003
Sawlogs, veneer logs and logs for sleepers	25	25	25
Other industrial wood	34	34	34
Fuel wood	52	53	54
Total	111	112	113

Source: FAO.

SAWNWOOD PRODUCTION
('000 cu m, incl. railway sleepers)

	1996	1997	1998
Total (all broadleaved)	8	8	12

1999–2003: Annual production as in 1998 (FAO estimates).
Source: FAO.

Fishing

('000 metric tons, live weight)

	2000	2001*	2002*
Capture	20.8	16.5	13.0
Cyprinids (incl. Comon carp)	4.0	3.8	3.8
Other freshwater fishes	3.4	3.3	3.3
Marine fishes	12.4	8.5	5.0
Aquaculture (Common carp)	1.7	2.0	1.5
Total catch	22.5	18.5	14.5

* FAO estimates.
Source: FAO.

Mining

(estimates, '000 metric tons, unless otherwise indicated)

	2000	2001	2002
Crude petroleum ('000 barrels per day)	937	860	740
Natural gas (million cu m)	7,500	7,000	7,000
Native sulphur	98	98	98
Phosphate rock	200	100	100
Salt (unrefined)	300	300	203

Source: US Geological Survey.

2003 (estimates, '000 metric tons): Phosphate rock 10; Salt (unrefined) 50 (Source: US Geological Survey).

Industry

SELECTED PRODUCTS
(estimates, '000 metric tons, unless otherwise indicated)

	1998	1999	2000
Naphtha	505	487	496
Motor spirit (petrol)	3,066	2,957	3,011
Kerosene	1,023	987	1,005
Jet fuel	567	547	557
Gas-diesel (distillate fuel) oil	6,921	6,676	6,800
Residual fuel oils	7,850	7,572	7,710
Lubricating oils	230	222	226
Paraffin wax	90	87	89
Petroleum bitumen (asphalt)	472	455	463
Liquefied petroleum gas:			
from natural gas plants	498	498	498
from petroleum refineries	1,026*	990	1,008
Cement†	2,000*	2,000*	2,000
Electric energy (million kWh)	30,346	30,491	30,521

* Estimate.
† Source: US Geological Survey.

Cigarettes: 5,794 million in 1992; .

Footwear (excluding rubber): 4,087,000 pairs in 1992.

Source: UN, *Industrial Commodity Statistics Yearbook*.

Cement (estimate, '000 metric tons): 2,000 in 2000–02 (Source: US Geological Survey).

Electric energy (net, million kWh): 36,009 in 2001 (Source: US Energy Information Administration).

Finance

CURRENCY AND EXCHANGE RATES

Monetary Units
  1,000 fils = 20 dirhams = 1 new Iraqi dinar (NID).

Sterling, Dollar and Euro Equivalents (31 December 2004)
  £1 sterling = 2,819.8 fils;
  US $1 = 1,460.0 fils;
  €1 = 1,988.7 fils;
  100,000 Iraqi dinars = £35.46 = $68.49 = €50.28.

Exchange Rate: Following the overthrow of the regime of Saddam Hussain in 2003, the new Coalition Provisional Authority (CPA) established an exchange rate of US $1 = 1,400 dinars. A new dinar currency, known as the new Iraqi dinar (NID) was introduced on 15 October to replace both the 'Swiss' dinar (at NID 1 = 150 'Swiss' dinars), the currency in use in the Kurdish autonomous regions of northern Iraq since 1991, and the 'Saddam' dinar (at par), the official currency of the rest of Iraq. The new currency was to be fully convertible.

BUDGET
(NID '000 million)

Revenue	2004
Oil revenues	18,000.0
Customs duty	450.0
Income tax	45.0
Interest on income tax	15.0
Transfers from state enterprises	562.5
Central bank	75.0
Shopping centres company	75.0
Automobiles company	150.0
Construction materials company	150.0
Agricultural supplies company	105.0
Ar-Rasheed Hotel	7.5
Fees and charges	96.3
Passport fees	0.8
Prescription charges	30.0
Entrance to cultural institutions	0.8
Consultancy charges (Ministry of Planning)	0.2
Sale of statistical publications	0.2
Court fees	7.5
Social security rental incomes	3.0
Vehicle registration	30.0
Course fees for higher education	1.5
Other fees for emergency services	7.5
Flight overpass charges for commercial airlines	15.0
Other taxes	90.0
Excise tax	15.0
Hotel and restaurant service tax	7.5
Land tax	15.0
Other	52.5
Total	**19,258.8**

Expenditure by department*	2004
Ministry of Agriculture	53.2
Ministry of Awqaf (Religious Endowments) and Religious Affairs	10.2
Board of Supreme Audit	4.5
Central Organization of Standards	2.7
Ministry of Communications	9.3
Ministry of Culture	13.8
Ministry of Displacement and Migration	2.4
Ministry of Education	815.9
Electricity Commission	2.2
Office of the Environment	2.4
Ministry of Finance	15,816.7
Ministry of Foreign Affairs	66.6
Governing Council	9.6
Ministry of Health	1,420.5
Ministry of Higher Education and Scientific Research	183.1
Ministry of Housing and Construction	255.3
Ministry of Human Rights	2.4
Ministry of Industry and Minerals	12.0
Ministry of the Interior	187.3
Iraqi Media Network	2.2
Ministry of Justice	207.9
Ministry of Labour and Social Affairs	52.3
Ministry of Municipalities, Utilities and Public Works	309.0
New Iraqi Army	34.8
Ministry of Oil	2.7
Ministry of Planning	67.5
Ministry of Science and Technology	36.4
Ministry of Trade	15.3
Ministry of Transport and Communications	127.2
Ministry of Water Resources	217.5
Ministry of Youth and Sport	22.4
Other expenditures	180.0
Total	**20,145.1**

* Names of departments may have been altered since the publication of the budget proposals in October 2003.

Sources: Ministries of Finance and of Planning; Coalition Provisional Authority.

CENTRAL BANK RESERVES
(ID million at 31 December)

	2001	2002	2003
Gold	0.7	8.0	14.9
Foreign exchange	858.6	2,134.6	41,597.0
Total	859.3	2,142.6	41,611.9

MONEY SUPPLY
(ID '000 million at 31 December)

	2001	2002	2003
Currency outside banks . . .	1,782.7	2,563.7	1,878.5
Demand deposits	376.4	449.9	1,019.7
Total money	2,159.1	3,013.6	2,898.2

COST OF LIVING
(Consumer Price Index for Baghdad; base: 1993 = 100)

	2001	2002	2003
Food	3,289	3,588	4,179
Fuel and light	9,334	9,279	49,011
Clothing	3,019	3,113	3,250
Rent	8,793	14,281	20,234
All items (incl. others)	4,355	5,197	6,943

NATIONAL ACCOUNTS
(UN estimates, ID million at current prices)

National Income and Product

	2000	2001	2002
Compensation of employees . .	1,340,001	1,507,349	1,661,849
Operating surplus	3,150,521	3,478,128	3,837,770
Domestic factor incomes . .	4,490,522	4,985,477	5,499,619
Consumption of fixed capital . .	555,974	613,786	677,252
Gross domestic product (GDP) at factor cost	5,046,496	5,599,264	6,176,871
Indirect taxes	−172,336	−237,687	−252,329
GDP in purchasers' values . .	4,874,160	5,361,576	5,924,542

Source: UN Economic and Social Commission for Western Asia, *National Accounts Studies of the ESCWA Region* (2001).

Expenditure on the Gross Domestic Product

	2000	2001	2002
Government final consumption expenditure	1,043,685	1,150,957	1,273,690
Private final consumption expenditure	3,560,338	3,921,066	4,301,897
Increase in stocks	−131,256	−143,658	−158,023
Gross fixed capital formation . .	421,318	472,068	543,280
Total domestic expenditure .	4,894,085	5,400,433	5,960,844
Exports of goods and services . .	753,482	878,881	1,048,376
Less Imports of goods and services	773,407	917,738	1,084,678
GDP in purchasers' values . .	4,874,160	5,361,576	5,924,542
GDP at constant 1995 prices	2,909,277	3,171,112	3,393,090

Source: UN Economic and Social Commission for Western Asia, *National Accounts Studies of the ESCWA Region* (2001).

Gross Domestic Product by Economic Activity

	2000	2001	2002
Agriculture, hunting, forestry and fishing . .	1,619,150	1,681,536	1,774,856
Mining and quarrying . . . } Manufacturing . . . . . . }	364,993	478,934	628,381
Electricity, gas and water . .	37,171	46,348	55,574
Construction	107,930	170,512	278,326
Trade, restaurants and hotels .	874,070	914,466	975,047
Transport, storage and communications	1,030,775	1,080,814	1,140,611
Finance, insurance and real estate*	483,494	561,583	600,056
Government, community, social and personal services† . . .	356,577	427,383	471,691
GDP in purchasers' values .	4,874,160	5,361,576	5,924,542

* Including imputed rents of owner-occupied dwellings.
† Including private non-profit services to households, domestic services of households and import duties.

Source: UN Economic and Social Commission for Western Asia, *National Accounts Studies of the ESCWA Region* (2001).

BALANCE OF PAYMENTS
(US $ million)

	2002	2003
Exports of goods	10,236.2	10,086.1
Imports of goods	−9,817.3	−9,933.5
Trade balance	418.9	152.6
Exports of services	259.9	470.0
Imports of services	−494.4	−1,809.4
Balance on goods and services	184.4	−1,186.8
Other income (net)	−1,156.5	−361.7
Balance on goods, services and income .	−972.1	−1,548.5
Current transfers received	131.6	2,198.0
Current transfers paid	−1,937.3	−1,209.0
Private transfers (net)	−286.0	—
Current balance	−3,063.8	−559.5
Financial account (net)	−4,188.1	−369.1
Net errors and omissions	1,462.4	−593.5
Overall balance	−5,789.4	−1,522.1

External Trade

PRINCIPAL COMMODITIES
(official estimates, US $ million)

Imports c.i.f.	2003
Food and live animals	506.2
Beverages and tobacco	60.4
Crude materials (inedible) except fuels	24.2
Mineral fuels, lubricants, etc.	10.1
Animal and vegetable oils and fats	80.5
Chemicals	103.7
Basic manufactures	1,620.2
Machinery and transport equipment	7,356.1
Miscellaneous manufactured articles	291.8
Total (incl. others)	10,063.1

Exports c.i.f.	2003
Food and live animals	504.1
Crude materials (inedible) except fuels	806.6
Mineral fuels, lubricants etc.	8,459.1
Animal and vegetable oils and fats	50.4
Chemicals	100.8
Basic manufactures	90.7
Machinery and transport equipment	10.1
Miscellaneous manufactured articles	60.5
Total (incl. others)	10,082.3

PRINCIPAL TRADING PARTNERS
(US $ million)

Imports c.i.f.	1988	1989	1990
Australia	153.4	196.2	108.7
Austria	n.a.	1.1	50.9
Belgium-Luxembourg	57.6	68.2	68.3
Brazil	346.0	416.4	139.5
Canada	169.9	225.1	150.4
China, People's Republic	99.2	148.0	157.9
France	278.0	410.4	278.3
Germany	322.3	459.6	389.4
India	32.3	65.2	57.5
Indonesia	38.9	122.7	104.9
Ireland	150.4	144.9	31.6
Italy	129.6	285.1	194.0
Japan	533.0	621.1	397.2
Jordan	164.3	210.0	220.3
Korea, Republic	98.5	123.9	149.4
Netherlands	111.6	102.6	93.8
Romania	113.3	91.1	30.1
Saudi Arabia	37.2	96.5	62.5
Spain	43.4	129.0	40.5
Sri Lanka	50.1	33.5	52.3
Sweden	63.0	40.6	64.8
Switzerland	65.7	94.4	126.6
Thailand	22.3	59.2	68.9
Turkey	874.7	408.9	196.0
USSR	70.7	75.7	77.9
United Kingdom	394.6	448.5	322.1
USA	979.3	1,001.7	658.4
Yugoslavia	154.5	182.0	123.1
Total (incl. others)	5,960.0	6,956.2	4,833.9

Exports f.o.b.	1988	1989	1990*
Belgium-Luxembourg	147.5	249.6	n.a.
Brazil	1,002.8	1,197.2	n.a.
France	517.4	623.9	0.8
Germany	122.0	76.9	1.7
Greece	192.5	189.4	0.3
India	293.0	438.8	14.7
Italy	687.1	549.7	10.6
Japan	712.1	117.1	0.1
Jordan	28.4	25.2	101.6
Netherlands	152.9	532.3	0.2
Portugal	120.8	125.8	n.a.
Spain	370.0	575.7	0.7
Turkey	1,052.6	1,331.0	83.5
USSR	835.7	1,331.7	8.9
United Kingdom	293.1	167.0	4.4
USA	1,458.9	2,290.8	0.2
Yugoslavia	425.4	342.0	10.4
Total (incl. others)	10,268.3	12,333.7	392.0

* Excluding exports of most petroleum products.

Source: UN, *International Trade Statistics Yearbook*.

Transport

RAILWAYS
(traffic)

	1995*	1996†	1997†
Passenger-km (million)	2,198	1,169	1,169
Freight ton-km (million)	1,120	931	956

* Source: UN, *Statistical Yearbook*.
† Source: Railway Gazette International, *Railway Directory*.

ROAD TRAFFIC
(estimates, '000 motor vehicles in use)

	1995	1996
Passenger cars	770.1	773.0
Buses and coaches	50.9	51.4
Lorries and vans	269.9	272.5
Road tractors	37.2	37.2

Source: IRF, *World Road Statistics*.

SHIPPING
Merchant Fleet
(registered at 31 December)

	2001	2002	2003
Number of vessels	91	88	85
Total displacement ('000 grt)	240.6	188.2	161.0

Source: Lloyd's Register-Fairplay, *World Fleet Statistics*.

CIVIL AVIATION
(revenue traffic on scheduled services)

	1991	1992	1994*
Kilometres flown (million)	0	0	0
Passengers carried ('000)	28	53	31
Passenger-km (million)	17	35	20
Freight ton-km (million)	0	3	2

* Figures for 1993 unavailable.

Source: UN, *Statistical Yearbook*.

Tourism

ARRIVALS AT FRONTIERS OF VISITORS FROM ABROAD*

Country of nationality	1999	2000	2001
India	4,893	3,092	3,714
Iran	20,849	69,155	117,368
Lebanon	780	8	6
Pakistan	2,063	2,985	2,377
Total (incl. others)	30,328	78,457	126,654

* Including same-day visitors.

Tourism receipts (US $ million): 13 in 1998.

Source: World Tourism Organization.

Communications Media

	1997	1998	1999
Radio receivers ('000 in use)	4,850	n.a.	n.a.
Television receivers ('000 in use)	1,750	1,800	1,850
Telephones ('000 main lines in use)	651	650	675*

* Estimate.
Sources: UN, *Statistical Yearbook*; International Telecommunication Union.

Education

(2003/04)

	Institutions	Teachers	Students
Pre-primary	631	2,993	53,499
Primary	11,066	206,953	4,280,602
Secondary:			
academic	2,968	74,681	1,454,775
vocational	158	4,693	62,842
Teacher training	101	2,984	66,139
Higher*	65	14,700	240,000†

* 2002/03.
† Figure for undergraduates only.

Sources: Ministries of Education and Higher Education.

Adult literacy rate (UNESCO estimates): 39.7% (males 55.3%; females 23.7%) in 2001 (Source: UNDP, *Human Development Report*).

Directory

As a result of the US-led military campaign to oust the regime of Saddam Hussain in March–April 2003, buildings occupied by a number of government ministries and other institutions were reported to have been damaged or destroyed.

The Constitution

On 15 November 2003 the Coalition Provisional Authority, established following the overthrow of the regime of Saddam Hussain in April of that year, and the Governing Council, inaugurated in July, agreed on a timetable for the restoration of full Iraqi sovereignty, the creation of a permanent constitution, and the holding of free national elections.The Governing Council signed a Transitional Administrative Law on 8 March 2004, which outlined a new timetable for the establishment of sovereign, elected organs of government. The basic tenets of the Law were to: define the structures of a transitional government and procedures for electing members of the Transitional National Assembly; guarantee basic rights for all Iraqis, including freedom of speech and the press; and respect the Islamic identity of the Iraqi majority, and guarantee religious plurality. The Transitional Administrative Law is scheduled to expire at the end of 2005.

National elections to the 275-member Transitional National Assembly (TNA) were held on 30 January 2005. The elected members of the TNA are required to draw up a constitution by 15 August, to be submitted to the Iraqi people in a national referendum by 15 October. Conditional upon the approval of the new constitution, national elections are scheduled to take place by 15 December, and a permanent sovereign government and national legislature are to assume office by 31 December.

The Government

On 6 April 2005 the Transitional National Assembly (TNA), elected on 30 January, voted to appoint a President and two Vice-Presidents, together constituting a Presidency Council. The members of the Presidency Council were sworn in on 7 April, whereupon they named a Prime Minister. A new Council of Ministers was approved by the TNA on 28 April and sworn in on 3 May. Under the timetable for restoration of sovereign institutions of government, this Iraqi Transitional Government was to be replaced by an elected administration by 31 December 2005.

HEAD OF STATE

President: JALAL TALABANI (assumed office 7 April 2005).

Vice-Presidents: Sheikh GHAZI MASHAL AJIL AL-YAWAR, Dr ADIL ABD AL-MAHDI.

COUNCIL OF MINISTERS
(May 2005)

Prime Minister and acting Minister of Defence: Dr IBRAHIM AL-JA'FARI.

Deputy Prime Minister and acting Minister of Electricity: ROWSCH NURI SHAWAYS.

Deputy Prime Minister and acting Minister of Oil: AHMAD CHALABI.

Minister of Agriculture: ALI AL-BAHADILI.

Minister of Construction and Housing: JASIM MUHAMMAD JA'FAR.

Minister of Culture: NURI FARHAN AR-RAWI.

Minister of Displacement and Migration: SUHAYLAH ABD AL-JA'FAR.

Minister of Education: ABD AL-FALAH HASAN.

Minister of the Environment and acting Minister of Human Rights: NARMIN UTHMAN.

Minister of Finance: ALI ABD AL-AMIR ALLAWI.

Minister of Foreign Affairs: HOSHYAR MAHMOUD MUHAMMAD AZ-ZIBARI.

Minister of Health: ABD AL-MUTTALIB MUHAMMAD ALI.

Minister of Higher Education: SAMI AL-MUZAFFAR.

Minister of Industry and Minerals: MUSLIH KHADR AL-JUBURI (acting).

Minister of the Interior: BAQIR SULAGH JABR.

Minister of Justice: ABD AL-HUSAYN SHANDAL.

Minister of Labour and Social Affairs: IDRIS HADI.

Minister of Municipalities and Public Works: NASREEN MUSTAFA SIDEEQ BARWARI.

Minister of Planning and Development Co-operation: BARHAM SALIH.

Minister of Science and Technology: Dr BASIMAH YOUSUF BUTRUS.

Minister of Telecommunications: JUWAN FU'AD MA'SUM.

Minister of Trade: ABD AL-BASIT KARIM MAWLUD.

Minister of Transport: SALAM AL-MALIKI.

Minister of Water Resources: ABD AL-LATIF JAMAL RASHID.

Minister of Youth and Sports: TALIB AZIZ ZAYNI.

Minister of State for National Security Affairs: ABD AL-KARIM AL-ANZI.

Minister of State for Women's Affairs: AZHAR ABD AL-KARIM ASH-SHAYKHALI.

Minister of State for Governorate Affairs: SA'D NAYIF MUJHIM AL-HARDAN.

Minister of State for Civil Society Affairs: ALA HABIB KAZIM.

Minister of State for Tourism and Antiquities: HASHIM AL-HASHIMI.

Minister of State for National Assembly Affairs: SAFA AD-DIN MUHAMMAD AS-SAFI.

MINISTRIES

Ministry of Agriculture: Khulafa St, Khullani Sq., Baghdad; tel. (1) 887-3251; e-mail min_of_agriculture@orha.centcom.mil.

Ministry of Communications: Baghdad; e-mail moc1@uruklink .net; internet www.uruklink.net/moc.

Ministry of Construction and Housing: Baghdad; e-mail moch@ mochiraq.com; internet www.mochiraq.com.

Ministry of Culture: Baghdad; e-mail min_of_culture@orha .centcom.mil.

Ministry of Defence: Baghdad.

Ministry of Displacement and Migration: Baghdad.

Ministry of Education: Baghdad; internet www.moeiraq.org.

Ministry of Electricity: Baghdad; e-mail min_of_electricity@orha .centcom.mil; internet www.uruklink.net/electric.

Ministry of the Environment: Baghdad.

Ministry of Finance: Khulafa St, nr ar-Russafi Sq., Baghdad; tel. (1) 887-4871.

Ministry of Foreign Affairs: opp. State Org. for Roads and Bridges, Karradat Mariam, Baghdad; tel. (1) 537-0091; e-mail contact@iraqmofa.net; internet www.iraqmofa.net.

Ministry of Health: Baghdad; e-mail info@mohiraq.org; internet www.mohiraq.org.

Ministry of Higher Education: Baghdad; tel. and fax (1) 280-6315; e-mail min_of_higher_edu@orha.centcom.mil; internet www .moheiraq.org.

Ministry of Human Rights: Baghdad.

Ministry of Industry and Minerals: Baghdad; tel. (1) 822-7136; e-mail info@iraqiindustry.com; internet www.iraqiindustry.com.

Ministry of the Interior: Baghdad; e-mail min_of_interior@orha .centcom.mil.

Ministry of Justice: Baghdad; e-mail min_of_justice@orha .centcom.mil.

Ministry of Labour and Social Affairs: Baghdad; e-mail min_of_labo_soci@orha.centcom.mil.

Ministry of National Security Affairs: North Gate, Baghdad; tel. (1) 888-9071; e-mail min_of_defense@orah.centcom.mil.

Ministry of Oil: Oil Complex Bldg, Port Said St, Baghdad; tel. (1) 817-7000; fax (1) 886-9432; e-mail oil@uruklink.net; internet www .uruklink.net/oil.

Ministry of Planning: POB 8001, Karradat Mariam, ash-Shawaf Sq., Baghdad; tel. and fax (1) 885-3653.

Ministry of Public Works: Baghdad; e-mail min_of_public_works@orha.centcom.mil.

Ministry of Science and Technology: Baghdad.

Ministry of Trade: Baghdad; internet www.motiraq.org.

Ministry of Transport: nr Martyr's Monument, Karradat Dakhil, Baghdad; tel. (1) 776-6041; e-mail min_of_trans_comms@orha .centcom.mil; internet www.iraqitransport.com.

Ministry of Water Resources: Baghdad; fax (1) 774-0672; e-mail info@iraqi-mwr.org; internet www.iraqi-mwr.org.

Ministry of Youth and Sport: Baghdad; e-mail min_of_youth@ orha.centcom.mil.

Legislature

TRANSITIONAL NATIONAL ASSEMBLY

Speaker: HAJIM AL-HASSANI.

The Transitional Administrative Law (TAL) of 8 March 2004 outlined the process for the establishment of a new National Assembly. In accordance with this law, elections to a 275-member transitional legislature were held on 30 January 2005. Assuming the approval of a permanent constitution (to be drafted by members of the Transitional National Assembly) by referendum by 15 October 2005, national elections for a permanent legislative assembly were to be held by 15 December 2005.

Election, 30 January 2005

	Valid votes cast	% of valid votes	Seats
United Iraqi Alliance . . .	4,075,295	47.66	140
Kurdistan Alliance List . .	2,175,551	25.44	75
Iraqi List	1,168,943	13.67	40
Iraqis	150,680	1.76	5
Iraqi Turkmen Front . . .	93,480	1.09	3
Independent National Elites and Cadres	69,938	0.82	3
People's Union	69,920	0.82	2
Islamic Group of Kurdistan . .	60,592	0.71	2
Islamic Action Organization . .	43,205	0.51	2
National Democratic Alliance .	36,795	0.43	1
National Rafidain List . . .	36,255	0.42	1
Reconciliation and Liberation Bloc	30,796	0.36	1
Others	539,121	6.31	—
Total	**8,550,571***	**100.00**	**275**

* Excluding 94,305 invalid votes.

Kurdish Autonomous Regions

A 15-article accord signed by the Iraqi Government and Kurdish leaders in 1970 provided for the creation of a unified autonomous area for the Kurdish population, comprising the administrative departments of As-Sulaimaniya (Sulaimaniya), D'hok and Irbil (Arbil), and the Kurdish sector of the city of Kirkuk, and the establishment of a 50-member Kurdish Legislative Council. Following the recapture of Kuwait from Iraqi forces by a multinational military coalition in early 1991, a designated 'safe haven' north of latitude 36°N (encompassing much of the Kurdish-inhabited regions) was imposed by the coalition partners. Renewed negotiations between the Iraqi Government (under Saddam Hussain) and Kurdish groups stalled over the status of Kirkuk, and in October 1991 the central Government withdrew all services from the region, effectively severing all economic and administrative support. In May 1992 the Kurdish Iraqi Front (KIF), an alliance of several Kurdish factions—including the two largest, the Patriotic Union of Kurdistan (PUK) and the Kurdistan Democratic Party (KDP)—established in 1988, organized elections to a new 105-member Iraqi Kurdistan National Assembly (see below). In September 1996, after bitter factional disputes had led to the effective disintegration of the KIF, the Iraqi Government announced the restoration of full Iraqi sovereignty over the Kurdish areas, but the KDP, which, under Masoud Barzani, had established the predominant influence in the region, announced the composition of a coalition administration for the territories (excluding the PUK, with which it was still in open conflict), to be based in Arbil, later in that month. In September 1998 the USA brokered a formal peace agreement between representatives of the PUK and the KDP in Washington, DC, which provided for a unified regional administration, the sharing of local revenues and co-operation in implementing the UN-sponsored 'oil-for-food'

programme. Legislative elections, scheduled to take place in 1999 under the terms of the Washington agreement, were subsequently postponed. In December 1999 the KDP announced the composition of a new 25-member coalition administration (comprising the KDP, the Iraqi Communist Party, the Assyrian Movement, the Independent Workers' Party of Kurdistan, the Islamic Union and independents) for the areas under its control, principally the departments of Arbil and D'hok. Municipal elections (to select 571 officials) were conducted in the KDP-administered region in May 2001; according to official KDP sources, KDP candidates received 81% of votes cast. Negotiations between representatives of the KDP and the PUK for the full implementation of the Washington accord were held during 2002, and resulted in the resumption of a transitional joint session of the Iraqi Kurdistan National Assembly in October (see below). The autonomous regions retained their status following the removal of the regime of Saddam Hussain in early 2003.

IRAQI KURDISTAN NATIONAL ASSEMBLY

In May 1992, negotiations with the Iraqi Government over the full implementation of the 1970 accord on Kurdish regional autonomy having stalled, the KIF organized elections to a 105-member Iraqi Kurdistan National Assembly, in which almost the entire electorate of 1.1m. participated, unilaterally. The KDP and the PUK were the only parties to achieve representation in the new Assembly and subsequently agreed to share seats equally (50 seats each—five having been reserved for two Assyrian Christian parties). The subsequent disintegration of the KIF and prolonged armed conflict between elements of the KDP and the PUK prevented the Assembly from becoming properly instituted, although the KDP attempted to incorporate the legislature into the administration of the territories under its control in the late 1990s and early 2000s, retaining the name of the Assembly and continuing to appoint officials (Jawhar N. Salem and Farsat A. Abdullah were serving as President and Secretary, respectively, in August 2002). Relations between the KDP and the PUK were generally improved following the Washington agreement of September 1998, and on 8 September 2002 representatives of the two parties signed an agreement providing for the inauguration of a transitional joint parliamentary session (with representation based on the results of the May 1992 elections) before the end of the year. On 4 October a joint session of the Iraqi Kurdistan National Assembly was convened for the first time since 1996. Following the removal of the regime of Saddam Hussain by US-led forces in early 2003, elections to a new Iraqi Kurdistan National Assembly took place on 30 January 2005, simultaneously with elections to the Transitional National Assembly. The Kurdistan Democratic List won 104 of the 111 seats, the Islamic Group of Kurdistan six, and the Kurdistan Toilers Party one.

Political Organizations

Following the removal from power of the Baathist regime, restrictions were effectively lifted on opposition political organizations that were either previously declared illegal, forced to operate clandestinely within Iraq, or were based abroad.

Bet-Nahrain Democratic Party (BNDP): e-mail info@bndp.net; internet www.bndp.net; f. 1976; seeks the establishment of an autonomous state for Assyrians in Bet-Nahrain (Iraq); Sec.-Gen. SHIMON KHAMO.

Constitutional Monarchy Movement (CMM): Baghdad; tel. (1) 778-2897; fax (1) 778-0199; e-mail webmaster@iraqcmm.org; internet www.iraqcmm.org; f. 1993; supports the claim to the Iraqi throne of Sharif ALI BIN AL-HUSSAIN, cousin to the late King FAISAL II, as constitutional monarch with an elected government.

Democratic Assyrian Movement (Zowaa): e-mail info@zowaa .org; internet www.zowaa.org; f. 1979; recognition of Assyrian rights within framework of democratic national government; Sec.-Gen. YOUNADAM YOUSUF KANA.

Free Officers and Civilians Movement: Baghdad; f. 1996; formerly Free Officers' Movement; Founder and Leader Brig.-Gen. NAGIB AS-SALIHI.

Hizb ad-Da'wa al-Islamiya (Voice of Islam Party): Baghdad; internet www.daawaparty.com; f. 1958; banned 1980; formerly based in Tehran and London, re-established in Baghdad 2003; mem. of SCIRI; predominantly Shi'ite, but with Sunni members; Leaders Dr IBRAHIM AL-JA'FARI, 'ABD AL-KARIM AL-'ANZI, MUHAMMAD BAKR AN-NASRI, Dr HAYDAR ABBAS (London), ABU BILAL AL-ADIB (Tehran).

Independent Democratic Movement (IDM) (Democratic Centrist Tendency): f. 2003; seeks a secular and democratic government of Iraq; Founder ADNAN PACHACHI (returned from exile in UAE in 2003).

Independent National Elites and Cadres: apparently linked to Shi'ite cleric Muqtada as-Sadr; Leader FATAH ESH-SHEIK.

Iraqi Communist Party: Baghdad; internet www.iraqcp.org; f. 1934; became legally recognized in July 1973 on formation of National Progressive Front; left National Progressive Front March 1979; contested elections of Jan. 2005 on People's Union list; First Sec. HAMID MAJID MOUSSA.

Iraqi Islamic Party (IIP) (al-Hizb al-Islami al-'Iraqi): f. 1960; Sunni; branch of the Muslim Brotherhood; boycotted elections of Jan. 2005; Sec.-Gen. TAREQ AL-HASHIMI.

Iraqi List: secular electoral list formed prior to the Jan. 2005 elections, consisting of a number of political organizations, incl. the IDM; Leader Dr AYAD ALLAWI.

Iraqi National Accord (INA): e-mail wifaq_ina@hotmail.com; internet www.wifaq.com; f. 1990; Founder and Sec.-Gen. Dr AYAD ALLAWI.

Iraqi National Alliance (INA) (at-Tahaluf al-Watani al-Iraqi): f. 1992; frmrly based in Syria; opposed sanctions and US-led invasion of Iraq; supports constitutional multi-party government; Leader ABD AL-JABBAR AL-QUBAYSI.

Iraqi National Congress (INC): internet www.inc.org.uk; f. 1992 in London; multi-party coalition; in November 1999 some 300 delegates to a national assembly, held in New York, USA, elected a 65-member central council and a new, seven-member collegiate leadership; Leaders Dr AYAD ALLAWI (INA), RIYAD AL-YAWAR (Ind.), Sharif ALI BIN AL-HUSSAIN (Constitutional Monarchy Movement), AHMAD CHALABI (Ind.), Sheikh MUHAMMAD MUHAMMAD ALI (ind.), Dr LATIF RASHID (PUK), HOSHYAR AZ-ZIBARI (KDP); following the removal of the regime of Saddam Hussain, many prominent members of the INC returned to Iraq from exile.

Iraqis (Iraqiyun): moderate; includes both Sunnis and Shi'ites; Leader Sheikh GHAZI MASHAL AJIL AL-YAWAR.

Iraqi Turkmen Front: Irbil; e-mail info@turkmenfront.org; internet www.turkmenfront.org; f. 1995; coalition of 26 Turkmen groups; seeks autonomy for Turkmen areas in Iraq, recognition of Turkmen as one of main ethnic groups in Iraq, and supports establishment of multi-party democratic system in Iraq; Leader FARUK ABDULLAH ABD AR-RAHMAN.

Iraqi Women's Organization: Leader SONDUL CHAPOUK.

Islamic Action Organization (Munazzamat al-Amal al-Islami): Karbala; f. 1961; Shi'ite; member of SCIRI, aligned with Hizb ad-Da'wa al-Islamiya; Leaders Sheikh MUHAMMAD TAQI AL-MUDARRISI, HASSAN SHIRAZI, MUHAMMAD HUSSAIN SHIRAZI.

Islamic Group of Kurdistan (Komaleh Islami): Khurmal; f. 2001; splinter group of IMIK; moderate Islamist, aligned with the PUK; Founder and Leader Mullah ALI BAPIR.

Islamic Movement in Iraq: Tehran; Shi'ite; member of SCIRI; Leader Sheikh MUHAMMAD MAHDI AL-KALISI.

Islamic Movement of Iraqi Kurdistan (IMIK): f. 1987; Founder and Leader Sheikh UTHMAN ABD AL-AZIZ.

Jamaat as-Sadr ath-Thani (Sadr II Movement): Najaf; f. 2003; Shi'ite; opposes presence of US-led coalition in Iraq; Leader Hojatoleslam MUQTADA AS-SADR.

Jund al-Imam (Soldiers of the [Twelfth] Imam): f. 1969; Shi'ite; member of SCIRI; Leader SA'D JAWAD QANDIL.

Kurdish Hezbollah (Party of God): f. 1985; splinter group of the KDP; member of SCIRI; Leader Sheikh MUHAMMAD KHALED BARZANI.

Kurdish Socialist Party: splinter group of the PUK; Founder MAHMOUD OSMAN.

Kurdistan Alliance List: f. 2004; coalition of 11 parties, incl. the PUK, the KDP, the Kurdistan Communist Party, Kurdistan Islamic Union and Kurdistan Toilers Party; formed to contest the Jan. 2005 elections.

Kurdistan Communist Party: internet www.kurdistancp.org; f. 1993; branch of the Iraqi Communist Party; Leader KAMAL SHAKIR.

Kurdistan Democratic List: coalition list of seven parties formed to contest the elections to the Iraqi Kurdistan National Assembly in Jan. 2005; includes the KDP, the BNDP and the Assyrian Patriotic Party.

Kurdistan Democratic Party (KDP): European Office (Germany), 10749 Berlin, POB 301516; tel. (30) 79743741; fax (30) 79743746; e-mail kdpeurope@t-online.de; internet www.kdp.pp.se; f. 1946; seeks to protect Kurdish rights and promote Kurdish culture and interests through regional political and legislative autonomy, as part of a federative republic; see also Kurdistan Alliance List and Kurdistan Democratic List; Pres. MASOUD BARZANI; Vice-Pres. ALI ABDULLAH.

Kurdistan Islamic Union: internet kurdiu.org; f. 1991; seeks establishment of Islamic state in Iraq which recognizes the rights of Kurds; branch of the Muslim Brotherhood; Sec.-Gen. SALAHEDDIN BAHAEDDIN.

Kurdistan Socialist Democratic Party (KSDP): Sulaimaniya; f. 1994; splinter group of the KDP, aligned with the PUK; Leader MUHAMMAD HAJI MAHMUD.

Kurdistan Toilers Party (Hizbi Zahmatkeshani Kurdistan): internet www.ktp.nu; f. 1985; advocates a federal Iraq; closely associated with the KSDP; contested Jan. 2005 elections as part of Kurdistan Alliance List; Leader QADIR AZIZ.

National Democratic Alliance: Leader ABED FAISAL AHMAD.

National Democratic Party (al-Hizb al-Watani ad-Dimuqrati): f. 1946; Leaders NASIR KAMAL AL-CHADERCHI, HUDAYB AL-HAJJ MAHMOUD.

National Foundation Congress: Baghdad; f. 2004; multi-party coalition including Nasserites, pre-Saddam Hussain era Baathists, Kurds, Christians, Sunnis and Shi'ites; seeks secular government of national unity; peacefully opposed to presence of US-led coalition in Iraq; led by 25-member secretariat.

National Progressive Front: Former ruling coalition; f. July 1973, when Arab Baath Socialist Party and Iraqi Communist Party signed a joint manifesto agreeing to establish a comprehensive progressive national and nationalistic front. In 1975 representatives of Kurdish parties and organizations and other national and independent forces joined the Front; the Iraqi Communist Party left the National Progressive Front in mid-March 1979; removed from power 2003; Sec.-Gen. NAIM HADDAD (Baath).

> **Arab Baath Socialist Party:** revolutionary Arab socialist movement founded in Damascus in 1947; ruled Iraq 1968–2003; in May 2003 membership of the Baath Party was declared illegal by US forces in Iraq.

> **Kurdistan Revolutionary Party:** f. 1972; succeeded Democratic Kurdistan Party; admitted to National Progressive Front 1974; status uncertain since removal from power of the NPF.

National Rafidain List: f. 2004; Assyrian-Christian list headed by the Assyrian Democratic Movement; Leader YOUNADAM KANA.

Patriotic Union of Kurdistan (PUK): European Office (Germany), 10502 Berlin, POB 210213; tel. (30) 34097850; fax (30) 34097849; e-mail pukoffice@pukq.de; internet www.puk.org; f. 1975; seeks to protect and promote Kurdish rights and interests through self-determination; see also Kurdistan Alliance List; Pres. JALAL TALABANI.

People's Union: largely secular independent list formed prior to Jan. 2005 elections; Iraqi Communist Party contested elections under this name.

Socialist Nasserite Party: f. 2003; merger of Iraqi Socialist Party, Vanguard Socialist Nasserite Party, Unity Socialist Party and one other party; Leader MUBDIR AL-WAYYIS.

Supreme Council for the Islamic Revolution in Iraq (SCIRI): Najaf; internet www.sciri.org; f. 1982; Shi'ite; seeks government based on principle of *wilayat-e-faqih* (guardianship of the jurisprudent); armed faction, the Badr Organization, assisted coalition forces in Iraq after the removal of Saddam Hussain's regime; contested Jan. 2005 elections on United Iraqi Alliance list; Leader ABD AL-AZIZ AL-HAKIM.

Turkoman People's Party (Turkmen Halk Partisi): internet www.angelfire.com/tn/halk; Leader IRFAN KIRKUKLI.

United Iraqi Alliance (UIA): list of 22 mainly Shi'ite parties, incl. Hizb ad-Da'wa al-Islamiya, SCIRI, the Islamic Action Organization and the INC; apparently backed by Iraq's most senior Shi'ite cleric, Ayatollah Ali as-Sistani; Leader ABD AL-AZIZ HAKIM.

United Iraqi Scholars' Group: f. 2004; pan-Iraqi coalition of 35 parties; opposed to presence of US-led coalition in Iraq; Leader Sheikh JAWAD AL-KHALISI.

Worker Communist Party of Iraq (IWCP): Sulaimaniya; internet www.wpiraq.net; f. 1993; opposes presence of US-led coalition in Iraq; Leader REBWAR AHMAD.

Other political, regional, ethnic and military groups based in Iraq, or based abroad and active in Iraq, include: **Free Iraq Council** (f. 1991, following dissolution of the Umma (Nation) Party; London-based; Leader SA'D SALIH JABR); **Iraqi Islamic Forces Union** (f. 2002; splinter group of SCIRI); **Higher Council for National Salvation** (f. 2002; founded by former head of Iraqi Military Intelligence WAFIQ HAMUD AS-SAMARRA'I; offered logistical support to US-led coalition); **Iraqi National Movement** (INM; f. 2001; split from the INC, mainly Sunni military officers; Leader HATEM MUKHLIS); **Kurdistan National Democratic Union** (YNDK; f. 1996; split between factions aligned with either the KDP or the PUK; Leader GHAFUR MAKHMURI); **Action Party for the Independence of Kurdistan** (PKSK–PSKI; based in Irbil; splinter group of Iraqi Communist Party; Leader YUSIF HANNA YUSIF); **Iraqi Turkoman Democratic Party** (f. 2002; supports federal Iraq; Leader AHMET GUNES); **Turkoman Islamic Union** (f. 1991; Leader ABBAS AL-BAYATI); **Assyrian Patriotic Party** (f. 1973; active in northern Iraq; Leaders ALBERT

YELDA, NIMRUD BAITO); **Unified National Movement** (Leader AHMAD AL-KUBAYSI).

Major militant groups which have launched attacks against Iraqis and the US-led coalition include: **Fedayeen Saddam** (Saddam's Martyrs; f. 1995 by members of the former Baathist regime; para-military group); **Ansar al-Islam** (f. 1998; splinter group of IMIK; Islamist; suspected of having links with al-Qa'ida; Leaders MULLAH KREKAR, MUHAMMAD HASSAN); **Hezbollah** (Shi'ite Marsh Arab; Leader ABD AL-KARIM MAHMOUD MOHAMMEDAWI—'ABU HATEM'); **Ansar as-Sunnah** (f. 2003 by members of Ansar al-Islam; Islamist); **Imam al-Mahdi Army** (armed wing of the Jamaat as-Sadr ath-Thaani—Sadr II Movement).

Diplomatic Representation

EMBASSIES IN IRAQ

Algeria: 13/14/613 Hay ad-Daoudi, Baghdad; tel. (1) 543-4137; fax (1) 542-5829; Chargé d'affaires MONCEF BENHADDID.

Australia: 5/5/923 Hay Babel, Baghdad; tel. (1) 778-2210; fax (1) 778-2218; e-mail austemb.baghdad@dfat.gov.au; internet www.dfat.gov.au/iraq; Ambassador HOWARD C. BROWN.

Austria: Baghdad.

Bahrain: 41/6/605, Hay al-Mutanabi, Baghdad; tel. (1) 541-0841; fax (1) 541-2027; Chargé d'affaires HASSAN AL-ANSARI.

Bangladesh: 6/14/929 Hay Babel, Baghdad; tel. (1) 719-0068; fax (1) 718-6045; Ambassador MUHAMMAD FAZLUR RAHMA.

Bulgaria: 12/25/624 al-Ameriya, Baghdad; tel. (1) 556-8197; fax (1) 556-4182; e-mail bulgemb@uruklink.net; Ambassador VALERI RACHEV.

China, People's Republic: POB 15097, 624 New Embassy Area, Hitteen Quarter, Baghdad; tel. (1) 556-2741; fax (1) 556-9721; e-mail chinaemb_iq@mfa.gov.cn; Ambassador YANG HONGLIN.

Czech Republic: POB 27124, 37/11/601 Hay al-Mansour, Baghdad; tel. (1) 360-5952; fax (1) 214-2621; e-mail baghdad@embassy.mzv.cz; Ambassador MARTIN KLEPETKO.

Denmark: Hay al-Jana'a, Karradat Maryam, Baghdad; tel. (790) 190-5752; e-mail dkliaisonbaghdad@yahoo.com; Ambassador TORBEN GETTERMANN.

Egypt: 53A/11/601 al-Mansour, Baghdad; tel. (1) 543-0572; fax (1) 542-5839; e-mail egypt@uruklink.net; Ambassador HUSSEIN AZ-ZUGHBI.

Finland: 86/25/925 Hay Babel, Baghdad; tel. (1) 776-6271; fax (1) 778-0488.

France: POB 118, 7/55/102, Abu Nawas, Baghdad; tel. (1) 790-6061; fax (1) 718-1975; Ambassador BERNARD BAJOLET.

Germany: 16/3/609 Hay al-Mansour, Baghdad; e-mail botschaftbagdad@web.de; Chargé d'affaires BERND ERBEL.

Greece: 63/13/913 Hay Babel, Baghdad; tel. (1) 718-2433; fax (1) 718-8729; e-mail greekembirq@uruklink.net; Ambassador MACRIS PANAYOTIS.

Holy See: POB 2090, Saadoun St, 904/2/46, Baghdad; tel. (1) 222-5410; fax (1) 222-5411; e-mail vatican@uruklink.net; Apostolic Nuncio Most Rev. FERNANDO FILONI (Titular Archbishop of Volturno).

Hungary: POB 2065, 43/4/609 al-Mansour, Hay al-Mutanabi, Baghdad; tel. (1) 543-2956; fax (1) 543-4766; e-mail hunemb@uruklink.net; Chargé d'affaires ANDRÁS NAGY.

India: 6/25/306 Hay al-Maghrib, Baghdad; tel. (1) 422-2014; fax (1) 422-9549; Ambassador R. DAYAKAR.

Iran: POB 39095, Salehiya, Karadeh Maryam, Baghdad; tel. (1) 884-3033; fax (1) 537-5636; Chargé d'affaires HASSAN KAZEMI QOMI.

Italy: Baghdad; Ambassador GIANLUDOVICO DE MARTINO DI MONTE-GIORDANO.

Japan: 50/21/929 Hay Babel, Baghdad; tel. (1) 776-6791; Ambassador TOSHIRO SUZUKI.

Jordan: POB 6314, 145/49/617 Hay al-Andalus, Baghdad; tel. (1) 541-2892; fax (1) 541-2009; e-mail jordan@uruklink.net; Chargé d'affaires DIMAI HADDAD.

Korea, Republic: Baghdad; e-mail kembiraq@mofat.go.kr; Ambassador CHANG KI-HO.

Lebanon: 51/116, Askari St, Al-Liwadiat, Baghdad; tel. (1) 416-7850; fax 416-8092; Chargé d'affaires HASSAN HUJAZI.

Morocco: POB 6039, 27/11/601 al-Mansour, Baghdad; tel. (1) 542-1779; fax (1) 542-3030; Ambassador MUHAMMAD AURAGH.

Netherlands: 10/38/103, Hay an-Nidhal, Baghdad; e-mail bag@minbuza.nl; internet www.netherlands-iraq.ae.

Nigeria: 43/11/601 al-Mansour, Baghdad; tel. (1) 541-3133; fax (1) 543-4513; Ambassador IBRAHIM MOHAMMED.

Pakistan: 14/7/609 al-Mansour, Baghdad; tel. (1) 542-5343; fax (1) 542-8707; Ambassador MUHAMMAD YOUNIS KHAN.

Philippines: POB 3236, 4/22/915 al-Jadriyah, Hay al-Jamiyah, Baghdad; tel. (1) 776-2696; fax 719-3228; e-mail bipe@uruklink.net; Chargé d'affaires a.i. GRACE P. ESCALANTE.

Poland: 22–24/60/904 Hay al-Wihda, Baghdad; tel. (1) 719-0297; fax (1) 719-0296; Ambassador RYSZARD KRYSTOSIK.

Portugal: POB 2123, Alwiya, Baghdad; tel. (1) 541-3376; fax (1) 542-0845; Ambassador FRANCISCO DOMINGOS GARCIA FALÇÃO MACHADO.

Romania: POB 2571, Arassat al-Hindia St, 452A/31/929 Hay Babel, Baghdad; tel. (1) 776-2860; fax (1) 776-7553; e-mail ambrobagd@yahoo.com; Ambassador MIHAI STUPARU.

Russia: 4/5/605 Hay al-Mutanabi, Baghdad; tel. (1) 541-4749; fax (1) 543-4462; Ambassador VLADIMIR TITORENKO.

Serbia and Montenegro: 16/35/923 Hay Babel, Baghdad; tel. (1) 776-7887; fax (1) 717-1069; e-mail embscgb@warkaa.net; Chargé d'affaires a.i. NINO MALJEVIĆ.

Slovakia: 94/28/923 Hay Babel, Baghdad; tel. (1) 776-7367; fax (1) 776-7368; Chargé d'affaires a.i. JOZEF MARÉFKA.

Spain: POB 2072, 1/3/609 al-Mansour, Baghdad; tel. (1) 542-4827; fax (1) 541-9857; Chargé d'affaires (vacant).

Sudan: 32/1/609 al-Mansour, Baghdad; tel. (1) 542-7982; fax (1) 542-5287; e-mail sudan@uruklink.net; Ambassador AHMED TAYES ABDALLAH.

Sweden: Baghdad; Ambassador KARIN ROXMAN.

Tunisia: 1/49/617 Hay al-Andalus, Baghdad; tel. (1) 542-0602; fax (1) 542-8585; Ambassador HADI BEN NASR.

Turkey: 2/8 al-Waziriyah, Baghdad; tel. (1) 422-0022; fax (1) 422-8353; Ambassador AHMET UNAL CEVIKOZ.

Ukraine: Baghdad; Ambassador ANATOLIY OLIYNYK.

United Arab Emirates: 81/34/611 Hay al-Andalus (ad-Daoudi), Baghdad; tel. (1) 543-9174; fax (1) 543-9093; Chargé d'affaires AHMAD ABDULLAH BIN SAYEED.

United Kingdom: c/o Iraq Policy Unit, Foreign and Commonwealth Office, London, SW1A 2AH, United Kingdom; tel. (20) 7008-1500; fax (20) 7008-4119; e-mail britembBaghdad@fco.gov.uk; Ambassador EDWARD CHAPLIN.

USA: APO AE 09316, Baghdad; internet iraq.usembassy.gov; Ambassador Dr ZALMAY KHALILZAD (designate).

Viet Nam: POB 15054, 71/34/611 Hay al-Mansour, Baghdad; tel. (1) 541-3409; fax (1) 541-1388; e-mail vietnam@uruklink.net; Ambassador NGUYEN QUANG KHAI.

Yemen: 4/36/904 Hay al-Wahada, Baghdad; tel. (1) 718-6682; fax (1) 717-2318; Ambassador ABD AL-MALIK SAID ABDO.

Judicial System

Following the ousting of the Baath regime, the judicial system was subject to a process of review and de-Baathification. In June 2003 the Coalition Provisional Authority (CPA) established a **Judicial Review Committee**, whose task was to review and repair the material status of the courts and to assess personnel. In December the Governing Council created the **Iraqi Special Tribunal**, in order to bring to trial those senior members of the former regime accused of war crimes, crimes against humanity and genocide.

In the interim period, a new judicial system was formed. The **Central Criminal Court of Iraq**, consisting of an **Investigative Court** and a **Trial Court**, was created by the CPA in July 2003 as the senior court in Iraq, with jurisdiction over all crimes committed in the country since 19 March 2003. With a few exceptions, the application of justice was to be based upon the 1969 Penal Code of Iraq and the 1971 Criminal Proceedings Code of Iraq.

Prior to the change of regime, courts in Iraq consisted of the following: The Court of Cassation, Courts of Appeal, First Instance Courts, Peace Courts, Courts of Sessions, *Shari'a* Courts and Penal Courts.

The Court of Cassation: This is the highest judicial bench of all the Civil Courts; it sits in Baghdad, and consists of the President and a number of vice-presidents and not fewer than 15 permanent judges, delegated judges and reporters as necessity requires. There are four bodies in the Court of Cassation, these are: (*a*) the General body, (*b*) Civil and Commercial body, (*c*) Personal Status body, (*d*) the Penal body.

Courts of Appeal: The country is divided into five Districts of Appeal: Baghdad, Al-Mawsil (Mosul), Al-Basrah (Basra), Al-Hillah

(Hilla), and Kirkuk, each with its Court of Appeal consisting of a president, vice-presidents and not fewer than three members, who consider the objections against the decisions issued by the First Instance Courts of first grade.

Courts of First Instance: These courts are of two kinds: Limited and Unlimited in jurisdiction.

Limited Courts: deal with Civil and Commercial suits, the value of which is 500 Iraqi dinars and less; and suits, the value of which cannot be defined, and which are subject to fixed fees. Limited Courts consider these suits in the final stage and they are subject to Cassation.

Unlimited Courts: consider the Civil and Commercial suits irrespective of their value, and suits the value of which exceeds 500 Iraqi dinars with first grade subject to appeal.

First Instance Courts consist of one judge in the centre of each *Liwa*, some *Qadhas* and *Nahiyas*, as the Minister of Justice judges necessary.

Courts of Sessions: There is in every District of Appeal a Court of Sessions which consists of three judges under the presidency of the President of the Court of Appeal or one of his vice-presidents. It considers the penal suits prescribed by Penal Proceedings Law and other laws. More than one Court of Sessions may be established in one District of Appeal by notification issued by the Minister of Justice mentioning therein its headquarters, jurisdiction and the manner of its establishment.

Shari'a Courts: A *Shari'a* Court is established wherever there is a First Instance Court; the Muslim judge of the First Instance Court may be a *Qadhi* to the *Shari'a* Court if a special *Qadhi* has not been appointed thereto. The *Shari'a* Court considers matters of personal status and religious matters in accordance with the provisions of the law supplement to the Civil and Commercial Proceedings Law.

Penal Courts: A Penal Court of first grade is established in every First Instance Court. The judge of the First Instance Court is considered as penal judge unless a special judge is appointed thereto. More than one Penal Court may be established to consider the suits prescribed by the Penal Proceedings Law and other laws.

One or more Investigation Court may be established in the centre of each *Liwa* and a judge is appointed thereto. They may be established in the centres of *Qadhas* and *Nahiyas* by order of the Minister of Justice. The judge carries out the investigation in accordance with the provisions of Penal Proceedings Law and the other laws.

There is in every First Instance Court a department for the execution of judgments presided over by the Judge of First Instance if a special president is not appointed thereto. It carries out its duties in accordance with the provisions of Execution Law.

Religion

ISLAM

About 95% of the population are Muslims, some 60% of whom are Shi'ite. The Arabs of northern Iraq, the Bedouins, the Kurds, the Turkomans and some of the inhabitants of Baghdad and Basra are mainly of the Sunni sect, while the remaining Arabs south of the Diyali belong to the Shi'i sect.

CHRISTIANITY

There are Christian communities in all the principal towns of Iraq, but their principal villages lie mostly in the Mosul district. The Christians of Iraq comprise three groups: (*a*) the free Churches, including the Nestorian, Gregorian and Syrian Orthodox; (*b*) the churches known as Uniate, since they are in union with the Roman Catholic Church, including the Armenian Uniates, Syrian Uniates and Chaldeans; (*c*) mixed bodies of Protestant converts, New Chaldeans and Orthodox Armenians. There are estimated to be some 700,000 Christians of various denominations in Iraq.

The Assyrian Church

Assyrian Christians, an ancient sect having sympathies with Nestorian beliefs, were forced to leave their mountainous homeland in northern Kurdistan in the early part of the 20th century. The estimated 550,000 members of the Apostolic Catholic Assyrian Church of the East are now exiles, mainly in Iraq (about 50,000 adherents), Syria, Lebanon and the USA. Their leader is the Catholicos Patriarch, His Holiness MAR DINKHA IV.

The Orthodox Churches

Armenian Apostolic Church: Primate of the Armenian Diocese of Iraq, POB 2280, Younis as-Saba'awi Sq., Baghdad; tel. (1) 815-1853; fax (1) 815-1857; Archbishop AVAK ASADOURIAN; 10 churches (four in Baghdad); 18,000 adherents, mainly in Baghdad.

Syrian Orthodox Church: Archbishop of Baghdad and Basra SEVERIUS HAWA; 12,000 adherents in Iraq.

The Greek Orthodox Church is also represented in Iraq.

The Roman Catholic Church

Armenian Rite

At 31 December 2002 the archdiocese of Baghdad contained an estimated 2,000 adherents.

Archbishop of Baghdad: (vacant), 27/903 Archevêché Arménien Catholique, Karrada Sharkiya, POB 2344, Baghdad; tel. (1) 719-1827; fax (1) 719-1827.

Chaldean Rite

Iraq comprises the patriarchate of Babylon, five archdioceses (including the patriarchal see of Baghdad) and five dioceses (all of which are suffragan to the patriarchate). Altogether, the Patriarch has jurisdiction over 21 archdioceses and dioceses in Iraq, Egypt, Iran, Lebanon, Syria, Turkey and the USA, and the Patriarchal Vicariate of Jerusalem. At 31 December 2002 there were an estimated 209,540 Chaldean Catholics in Iraq (including 140,000 in the archdiocese of Baghdad).

Patriarch of Babylon of the Chaldeans: His Beatitude EMANUEL III DELLY, POB 6112, Patriarcat Chaldéen Catholique, Al-Mansour, Baghdad; tel. (1) 537-9164; fax (1) 537-85-56; e-mail babylonpat@uruklink.net.

Archbishop of Arbil: Most Rev. YACOUB DENHA SCHER, Archevêché Catholique Chaldéen, Ainkawa, Arbil; tel. (665) 2227-4630.

Archbishop of Baghdad: the Patriarch of Babylon (see above).

Archbishop of Basra: Most Rev. DJIBRAIL KASSAB, Archevêché Chaldéen, POB 217, Ashar-Basra; tel. (40) 210323; e-mail archbi.b@warkaa.net.

Archbishop of Kirkuk: Most Rev. LOUIS SAKO, Archevêché Chaldéen, POB 490, Kirkuk; tel. (50) 213978.

Archbishop of Mosul: Most Rev. PAULOS FARAJ RAHHO, Archevêché Chaldéen, POB 757, Mayassa, Mosul; tel. (60) 762022; fax (60) 772460.

Latin Rite

The archdiocese of Baghdad, directly responsible to the Holy See, contained an estimated 2,000 adherents at 31 December 2002.

Archbishop of Baghdad: Most Rev. JEAN BENJAMIN SLEIMAN, Archevêché Latin, Hay al-Wahda—Mahallat 904, rue 8, Imm. 44, POB 35130, 12906 Baghdad; tel. (1) 719-9537; fax (1) 717-2471; e-mail najiblat@uruklink.net.

Melkite Rite

The Greek-Melkite Patriarch of Antioch (GRÉGOIRE III LAHAM) is resident in Damascus, Syria.

Patriarchal Exarchate of Iraq: Exarchat Patriarchal Grec-Melkite, Karradat IN 903/10/50, Baghdad; tel. (1) 719-1082; 100 adherents (31 December 2001); Exarch Patriarchal GEORGES EL-MURR.

Syrian Rite

Iraq comprises two archdioceses and the Patriarchal Exarchate of Basra; there were an estimated 60,000 adherents at 31 December 2002.

Archbishop of Baghdad: Most Rev. ATHANASE MATTI SHABA MATOKA, Archevêché Syrien Catholique, 903/2/1 Baghdad; tel. (1) 719-1850; fax (1) 719-0166.

Archbishop of Mosul: Most Rev. BASILE GEORGES CASMOUSSA, Archevêché Syrien Catholique, Hosh al-Khan, Mosul; tel. (60) 762160; fax (60) 771439; e-mail syrcam.m@warkaa.net.

The Anglican Communion

Within the Episcopal Church in Jerusalem and the Middle East, Iraq forms part of the diocese of Cyprus and the Gulf. Expatriate congregations in Iraq meet at St George's Church, Baghdad (Hon. Sec. GRAHAM SPURGEON). The Bishop in Cyprus and the Gulf is resident in Cyprus.

JUDAISM

A very small Jewish community remains in Baghdad and in the north of Iraq.

OTHERS

About 30,000 Yazidis and a smaller number of Turkomans, Sabians and Shebeks reside in Iraq.

Sabian Community: An-Nasiriyah (Nasiriya); 20,000 adherents; Mandeans, mostly in Nasiriya; Head Sheikh DAKHIL.

Yazidis: Ainsifni; 30,000 adherents; Leader TASHIN SAID BEG.

The Press

Since the overthrow of the regime of Saddam Hussain by US-led coalition forces in early 2003, the number of publications has proliferated—by the end of 2003 an estimated 250 newspapers and periodicals were in circulation. A selection of these is given below.

DAILIES

Baghdad: Baghdad; internet www.wifaq.com/baghdad_arabic .html; organ of the Iraqi National Accord; Publr AYAD ALLAWI.

Al-Bayan (Manifesto): Baghdad; organ of Hizb ad-Da'wa al-Islamiya (Voice of Islam Party); Arabic; Man. Editor SADIQ AR-RIKABI.

Ad-Dustur (Constitution): independent; politics; Arabic; Chair. BASIM ASH-SHAYKH; Man. Editor MUHAMMAD HARUN HASSAN.

Al-Ittihad (Union): Sulaimaniya; Baghdad; published by the PUK; Arabic; Editor ABD AL-HADI; circ. 30,000 (Baghdad).

Al-Jaridah (Newspaper): Arabic; Editor Prof. QAYS AL-AZZAWI.

Al-Mannarah (Minarets): Basra; tel. (40) 620243; internet www .almannarah.com.

As-Sabah (Morning): internet www.alsabaah.com; f. 2003; publ. by the Iraqi Media Network; Arabic and English; Editor-in-Chief ISMAIL ZAYER.

At-Taakhi (Brotherhood): e-mail info@altaakhi.com; internet www .altaakhi.com; f. 2003; organ of the Kurdistan Democratic Party (KDP); Kurdish and Arabic; Editor FALAKEDDIN KAKA'IE; circ. 20,000 (Baghdad).

Tariq ash-Sha'ab (People's Path): as-Sa'adoun St, Baghdad; Arabic; organ of the Iraqi Communist Party; Editor ABD AR-RAZZAK AS-SAFI.

Xebat: e-mail info@xebat.net; internet www.xebat.net; organ of the KDP; Arabic and Kurdish; Editor-in-Chief NAZHAD AZIZ SURME.

Al-Yawm al-Akhar (Other Day): Baghdad; independent; Arabic; Editor FARIS AL-KATIB.

Az-Zaman (Time): internet www.azzaman.com; f. 1997 in the United Kingdom, f. 2003 in Baghdad; Arabic; Editor-in-Chief SAAD AL-BAZZAZ.

WEEKLIES

Al-Ahali (People): Baghdad; e-mail info@ahali-iraq.com; internet www.ahali-iraq.com; politics; Arabic; Editor HAVAL ZAKHOUBI.

Alif Baa: Baghdad; general, social and political affairs; Arabic and English; Chair. of Bd MUHSIN KHUDAYR.

Habazbuz fi Zaman al-Awlamah (Habazbuz in the Age of Globalization): Baghdad; f. 2003; satire; Arabic; Editor ISHTAR AL-YASIRI.

Hawlati: e-mail hawlati@hawlati.com; internet www.hawlati.com; f. 2001; mainly Kurdish politics; Kurdish, Arabic and English.

Iraq Today: Baghdad; internet www.iraq-today.com; f. 2003; current affairs; English; Editor-in-Chief HUSSAIN SINJARI.

Al-Iraq al-Yawm (Iraq Today): e-mail iraqtoday@iraqtoday.net; internet iraqtoday.net; Editor ISRA SHAKIR.

Al-Ittijah al-Akhar (Other Direction): Baghdad; tel. (1) 776-3334; fax (1) 776-3332; e-mail i.h.p@mail.sy; internet www.alitijahalakhar .com; organ of Hizb al-Watan al-Iraqi (Iraqi Homeland Party); Arabic; Chair. and Editor MISHAAN AL-JUBOURI.

Kul al-Iraq (All Iraq): Baghdad; internet www.kululiraq.com; independent; Editor-in-Chief Dr ABBAS AS-SIRAF.

Majallati: POB 8041, Children's Culture House, Baghdad; Arabic; children's newspaper; Editor-in-Chief Dr SHAFIQ AL-MAHDI.

Al-Muajaha (Witness): 6/41/901, Karrada Dakhil, Baghdad; e-mail almuajaha@riseup.net; internet www.almuajaha.com; f. 2003; current affairs; Arabic and English; Editor RAMZI MAJID JARRAR.

Al-Mu'tamar (Congress): Baghdad; published by the Iraqi National Congress; Arabic.

An-Nahda (Renaissance): Basra; f. 2003; Arabic; Editor JALAL AL-MASHTA.

Ar-Rasid (The Monitor): Baghdad; Arabic; general.

Regay Kurdistan: internet www.iraqcp.org/regay; Arabic and Kurdish; organ of the Iraqi and Kurdistan Communist Parties.

As-Sina'i (Industrialist): Baghdad; general; publ. by National Industrialist Coalition; Editor-in-Chief Dr ZAYD ABD AL-MAJID BILAL.

Al-Waqai al-Iraqiya (Official Gazette of Republic of Iraq): Ministry of Justice, Baghdad; f. 1922; Arabic and English; Dir HASHIM N. JAAFER; circ. 5,000.

PERIODICALS

Baghdad Bulletin: 17/718/27, Zayouna, Baghdad; e-mail mark@ baghdadbulletin.com; internet www.baghdadbulletin.com; f. 2003; redevelopment issues; fortnightly; Editor DAVID ENDERS; publication suspended September 2003.

Majallat al-Majma' al-'Ilmi al-'Iraqi (Journal of the Academy of Sciences): POB 4023, Waziriya, Baghdad; tel. (1) 422-1733; fax (1) 425-4523; f. 1950; quarterly; Arabic; scholarly magazine on Arabic Islamic culture; Editor-in-Chief Prof. Dr MAHMOUD HAYAWI-HAMASH.

As-Sa'ah (Hour): Baghdad; 2 a week; organ of the Iraqi Unified National Movement; Publr AHMAD AL-KUBAYSI; Editor NI'MA ABD AR-RAZZAQ.

Sawt at-Talaba (Voice of Students): Baghdad; fortnightly; Arabic; publ. by New Iraq Youth and Students' Organization; Editor MUSTAFA AL-HAYIM.

PRESS ORGANIZATIONS

The General Federation of Journalists: POB 6017, Baghdad; tel. (1) 541-3993.

Iraqi Journalists' Union: POB 14101, Baghdad; tel. (1) 537-0762.

NEWS AGENCIES

Iraqi News Agency (INA): POB 3084, 28 Nissan Complex—Baghdad, Sadoun; tel. (1) 8863024; e-mail ina@uruklink.net; f. 1959; Dir-Gen. UDAI AT-TAIE.

Foreign Bureaux

Anadolu Ajansı (Turkey): Baghdad; tel. (1) 886-1506; e-mail bagdat@anadoluajansi.com.tr.

Associated Press (AP) (USA): Hay al-Khadra 629, Zuqaq No. 23, Baghdad; tel. (1) 555-9041; Correspondent SALAH H. NASRAWI.

Deutsche Presse-Agentur (dpa) (Germany): POB 5699, Baghdad; Correspondent NAJHAT KOTANI.

Informatsionnoye Telegrafnoye Agentstvo Rossii—Telegrafnoye Agentstvo Suverennykh Stran (ITAR—TASS) (Russia): 67 Street 52, Alwiya, Baghdad; Correspondent ANDREI OSTALSKY.

Reuters (UK): House No. 8, Zuqaq 75, Mahalla 903, Hay al-Karada, Baghdad; tel. (1) 719-1843; Correspondent SUBHY HADDAD.

Xinhua (New China) News Agency (People's Republic of China): al-Mansour, Adrus District, 611 Small District, 5 Lane No. 8, Baghdad; tel. (1) 541-8904; Correspondent ZHU SHAOHUA.

Publishers

National House for Publishing, Distribution and Advertising: POB 624, al-Jumhuriyah St, Baghdad; tel. (1) 425-1846; f. 1972; publishes books on politics, economics, education, agriculture, sociology, commerce and science in Arabic and other Middle Eastern languages; Dir-Gen. M. A. ASKAR.

Afaq Arabiya Publishing House: POB 4032, Adamiya, Baghdad; tel. (1) 443-6044; fax (1) 444-8760; publisher of literary monthlies, periodicals and cultural books; Chair. Dr MOHSIN AL-MUSAWI.

Dar al-Ma'mun for Translation and Publishing: POB 24015, Karradat Mariam, Baghdad; tel. (1) 538-3171; publisher of newspapers and magazines.

Al-Hurriyah Printing Establishment: Karantina, Sarrafia, Baghdad; f. 1970.

Al-Jamaheer Press House: POB 491, Sarrafia, Baghdad; tel. (1) 416-9341; fax (1) 416-1875; f. 1963; publisher of a number of newspapers and magazines; Pres. SAAD QASSEM HAMMOUDI.

Al-Ma'arif Ltd: Mutanabi St, Baghdad; f. 1929; publishes periodicals and books in Arabic, Kurdish, Turkish, French and English.

Al-Muthanna Library: Mutanabi St, Baghdad; f. 1936; booksellers and publishers of books in Arabic and oriental languages; Man. ANAS K. AR-RAJAB.

An-Nahdah: Mutanabi St, Baghdad; politics, Arab affairs.

Kurdish Culture Publishing House: Baghdad; f. 1976.

Ath-Thawra Printing and Publishing House: POB 2009, Aqaba bin Nafi's Sq., Baghdad; tel. (1) 719-6161; f. 1970; Chair. (vacant).

Thnayan Printing House: Baghdad.

Broadcasting and Communications

TELECOMMUNICATIONS

Under the former Baathist regime, the Iraqi Telecommunications and Posts Co was the sole provider of telecommunications and postal services. Following the removal from power of Saddam Hussain, the CPA issued three licences for the provision of mobile telephone services to stimulate competition in the telecommunications sector. Asia-Cell, led by the Iraqi Kurdish company Asia-Cell Telcom, was awarded the licence for the northern region; the licence for the central region was won by Orascom Telecom Iraq Corp, led by Orascom Telecom of Egypt; and Atheer Telecom Iraq, led by Mobile Telecommunications Company of Kuwait, won the licence for the southern region.

Iraqi Telecommunications and Posts Co: POB 2450, Karrada Dakhil, Baghdad; tel. (1) 718-0400; fax (1) 718-2125; Dir-Gen. Eng. MEZHER M. HASSAN.

BROADCASTING

Iraqi Communications and Media Commission: Media Development and Regulation, 3rd Floor, Convention Centre, Baghdad; e-mail broadcast-licence@baghdadforum.com; internet www.iraqicmc.org/index.htm; f. 2004; CEO SIYAMEND ZAID OTHMAN.

The **Iraqi Media Network (IMN)** was established by the CPA to replace the Ministry of Information following the ousting of the former regime. The IMN established new television and both FM and AM radio stations. In January 2004 the CPA announced that a consortium led by the US-based Harris Corporation had been awarded the contract to take over from the IMN the control of 18 television channels, two radio stations and the As-Sabah newspaper.

Finance

(cap. = capital; dep. = deposits; res = reserves; brs = branches; m. = million; amounts in Iraqi dinars)

All banks and insurance companies, including all foreign companies, were nationalized in July 1964. The assets of foreign companies were taken over by the State. In May 1991 the Government announced its decision to end the State's monopoly in banking, and during 1992–2000 17 private banks were established; however, they were prohibited by the former regime from conducting international transactions. Following the establishment of the CPA in Iraq in 2003, efforts were made to reform the state-owned Rafidain and Rashid banks, and in October of that year the Central Bank allowed private banks to begin processing international transactions. In January 2004 the Central Bank of Iraq announced that three foreign banks— HSBC and Standard Chartered (both of the United Kingdom), and the National Bank of Kuwait—had been awarded licences to operate in Iraq, the first such licences awarded for 40 years.

BANKING

Central Bank

Central Bank of Iraq: POB 64, Rashid St, Baghdad; tel. (1) 816-5170; fax (1) 816-6802; e-mail cbi@cbiraq.org; internet www.cbiraq.org; f. 1947 as National Bank of Iraq; name changed as above 1956; has the sole right of note issue; cap. and res 125m. (Sept. 1988); Gov. SINAN MUHAMMAD RIDA ASH-SHIBIBI; brs in Mosul and Basra.

Nationalized Commercial Banks

Rafidain Bank: POB 11360, General Administration, Baghdad; tel. (1) 816-0287; fax (1) 816-5035; e-mail user3001@rafidain-bank.org; f. 1941; state-owned; cap. 4,000m., res 9,649.0m., dep. 453,678m., total assets 1,079,418.3m. (Dec. 2001); Pres. DHIA HABIB AL-KHAYYOON; 150 brs in Iraq, 9 brs abroad.

Rashid Bank: Khulafa' St, Baghdad; tel. (1) 885-3411; fax (1) 882-6201; e-mail natbank@uruklink.net; f. 1988; state-owned; cap. 2,000m., res 6,023.8m., dep. 815,521.5m. (Dec. 2001); Chair. and Gen. Man. FAIQ M. AL-OBAIDY; 161 brs.

Private Commercial Banks

Babylon Bank: POB 11032, Bab ash-Sharky, Baghdad; tel. (1) 816-3936; fax babylon-m@uruklink.net.

Bank of Baghdad: POB 3192 Alwiya, Al-Karada St, Baghdad; tel. (1) 717-5007; fax (1) 717-5006; e-mail info@bankofbaghdad.net; internet www.bankofbaghdad.net; f. 1992; cap. 5,280m.; Chair. Dr MUNIB K. AS-SIKOUTI; CEO MUWAFAQ H. MAHMOUD; 5 brs.

Commercial Bank of Iraq SA: POB 5639, 13/14/904 Al-Wahda St, Baghdad; tel. (1) 707-0049; fax (1) 718-4312; e-mail commerce.iraq@hotmail.com; f. 1992; cap. 1,800m.; Chair. MUHAMMAD H. DRAGH.

Credit Bank of Iraq: POB 3420, Alwiya Bldg, Hay as-Saadon, Al-Alwiya, Baghdad; tel. (1) 718-2198; fax (1) 717-5997; e-mail creditbiq@yahoo.com; 1998; cap. 1,250m., res 528m., dep. 16,376.9m. (Dec. 2002); Chair. HIKMET H. KUBBA; Man. Dir FOUAD M. MUSTAFA; 10 brs.

Gulf Commercial Bank: Nr Baghdad Hotel, As-Saadon St, Baghdad; tel. (1) 719-0005; fax (1) 718-9963; e-mail gulfbank1@yahoo.com.

National Bank of Iraq: POB 2568, Al-Karada St, Baghdad; tel. (1) 776-6601; e-mail nationalbankiraq@yahoo.com.

Sumer Commercial Bank: 906/1/87, Al-Walid St, Baghdad; tel. (1) 719-6472; e-mail sumerbank99@hotmail.com.

Specialized Banks

Agricultural Co-operative Bank of Iraq: POB 2421, Rashid St, Baghdad; tel. (1) 886-4768; fax (1) 886-5047; f. 1936; state-owned; cap. 295.7m., res 14m., dep. 10.5m., total assets 351.6m. (Dec. 1988); Dir-Gen. HDIYA H. AL-KHAYOUN; 32 brs.

Al-Baraka Bank for Investment and Financing: POB 3445, 904/14/50, Hay al-Wehda, Baghdad; tel. (1) 717-3201; fax (1) 718-3766; e-mail albaraka@uruklink.net.

Basra Private Bank for Investment: POB 80, AIH Thawra St, Ashar, Basra; tel. (40) 215909.

Dar es-Salaam Investment Bank: 39/1 23/101, Tunis St, Baghdad; e-mail info@daressalam.net; f. 1999; cap. 2,400m., dep. 22,171m.; 14 brs.

Economy Bank for Investment and Financing: POB 55432, 108/54 Al-Khulfa St, Shurgah, Baghdad; tel. (1) 817-6202; fax (1) 885-0018.

Industrial Bank of Iraq: POB 5825, as-Sinak, Baghdad; tel. (1) 887-2181; fax (1) 888-3047; e-mail bank2004@maktoob.com; f. 1940; state-owned; cap. 59.7m., dep. 77.9m. (Dec. 1988); Dir-Gen. BASSIMA ABD AL-HADDI ADH-DHAHIR; 5 brs.

Investment Bank of Iraq: POB 3724, 902/2/27 Hay al-Wahda, Alwiya, Baghdad; tel. (1) 719-2094; fax (1) 719-8505; e-mail investmentiraq@yahoo.com; f. 1993; cap. 11,520,000m. (Jan. 2005); Chair. THAMIR R. SHAIKHLY; Vice-Chair. MUHAMMAD A. HUSSEIN; 20 brs.

Iraqi Islamic Bank for Investment and Development: POB 940, Muathem Al-Kahiay Bldg, Baghdad; tel. (1) 416-4939; fax (1) 414-0697.

Iraqi Middle East Investment Bank: POB 10379, Bldg 65, Hay Babel, 929 Arasat al-Hindiya, Baghdad; tel. (1) 719-2336; e-mail manager@iraqimdlestbank.com; f. 1993; cap. and res 8,500m., dep. 134,000m., total assets 246,000m. (Dec. 2004); Man. Dir M. F. AL-ALOOSI; Exec. Man. SUDAD A. AZIZ; 10 brs.

Mosul Bank for Development and Investment: POB 1292, Senter St, Mosul.

Real Estate Bank of Iraq: POB 8118, 29/222 Haifa St, Baghdad; tel. (1) 885-3212; fax (1) 884-0980; f. 1949; state-owned; gives loans to assist the building industry; cap. 800m., res 11m., total assets 2,593.6m. (Dec. 1988); acquired the Co-operative Bank in 1970; Dir-Gen. ABD AR-RAZZAQ AZIZ; 18 brs.

United Investment Bank: POB 24211, Banks St, Baghdad; tel. (1) 888-112; e-mail united@uruklink.net.

Al-Warka Investment Bank: POB 3559, 902/14/50, Hay al-Wehda, Baghdad; tel. (1) 717-4970; fax (1) 717-9555; e-mail warkabank@hotmail.com.

Trade Bank

Trade Bank of Iraq (TBI): Central Bank Bldg, 4th Floor, Rashid St, Baghdad; e-mail info@tbiraq.com; internet www.tbiraq.com; f. 2003 by the CPA; facilitates export and imports of goods and services; independent of Central Bank of Iraq; cap. US $100m. (CPA $5m., consortium led by JP Morgan Chase & Co $95m.); Chair. HUSSAIN AL-UZRI.

INSURANCE

Iraq Life Insurance Co: POB 989, Aqaba bin Nafi's Sq., Khalid bin al-Waleed St, Baghdad; tel. (1) 719-2184; fax (1) 719-2606; f. 1959; state-owned; Chair. and Gen. Man. WALID SALIH ABD AL-WAHAB.

Iraq Reinsurance Co: POB 297, Aqaba bin Nafi's Sq., Khalid bin al-Waleed St, Baghdad; tel. (1) 719-5131; fax (1) 791497; f. 1960; state-owned; transacts reinsurance business on the international market; total assets 93.2m. (1985); Chair. and Gen. Man. K. M. AL-MUDARIES.

National Insurance Co: POB 248, National Insurance Co Bldg, Al-Khullani St, Baghdad; tel. (1) 885-3026; fax (1) 886-1486; f. 1950; cap. 20m.; all types of general and life insurance, reinsurance and investment; Chair. and Gen. Man. MUHAMMAD HUSSAIN JAAFAR ABBAS.

STOCK EXCHANGE

The last official trading day on the Baghdad Stock Exchange prior to the US-led campaign to oust the regime of Saddam Hussain was 19 March 2003. Following the military campaign, the CPA closed the Stock Exchange, suspended trading, and ordered all listed companies to supply full accounts for audit, as well as checking traders and brokers for evidence of links to the former regime. The new Iraq Stock Exchange recommenced trading in June 2004.

Iraq Stock Exchange: Baghdad; Chair. TALIB AT-TABATABIE.

Trade and Industry

CHAMBERS OF COMMERCE

Federation of Iraqi Chambers of Commerce: POB 3388, Al-Elwiyah Sa'adoun St, Baghdad; tel. (1) 719-9831; fax (1) 719-2479; e-mail ficobaghdad@hotmail.com; f. 1969; all Iraqi Chambers of Commerce are affiliated to the Federation; Chair. ABOUD M. J. AT-TUFAILY; Sec.-Gen. ABD HAFIDH A. S. KADER.

EMPLOYERS' ORGANIZATION

Iraqi Federation of Industries: POB 5665, South Gate Al-Khullani Sq., Baghdad; tel. (1) 818-0091; fax (1) 8180094; f. 1956; 6,000 mems; Pres. HATAM ABD AR-RASHID.

PETROLEUM AND GAS

Ministry of Oil: POB 19244, Zayouna, Baghdad; tel. (1) 817-7000; fax (1) 886-9432; e-mail oil@uruklink.net; internet www.uruklink.net/oil; merged with INOC in 1987; affiliated cos: Oil Marketing Co, Oil Projects Co, Midland Refineries Co, Oil Exploration Co, Oil Products Distribution Co, Gas Filling Co, Pipelines Co, Iraqi Drilling Co, South Oil Co, South Refineries Co, North Oil Co, North Refineries Co, North Gas Co, South Gas Co, Iraqi Oil Tankers Co.

Iraq National Oil Co (INOC): POB 476, al-Khullani Sq., Baghdad; tel. (1) 887-1115; f. in 1964 to operate the petroleum industry at home and abroad; when Iraq nationalized its petroleum industry, structural changes took place in INOC, and it became solely responsible for exploration, production, transportation and marketing of Iraqi crude petroleum and petroleum products. INOC was merged with the Ministry of Oil in 1987, and the functions of some of the organizations under its control were transferred to newly created ministerial departments or to companies responsible to the ministry. Following the US-led campaign to oust Saddam Hussain in March 2003, the INOC remained under the authority of the Ministry of Oil. However, it was reported that the INOC might become an independent company as part of plans for the regeneration of Iraq's economy.

UTILITIES

Electricity

Electricity production in Iraq was greatly diminished as a result of the US-led campaign in Iraq in early 2003, and subsequent looting and sabotage by Baathist loyalists. With ongoing reconstruction of the means of generation, transmission and distribution, however, the Ministry of Electricity expected to achieve peak production levels of 9,000 MW by early 2005.

State Enterprise for Generation and Transmission of Electricity: POB 1098, 4/356 Al-Masbah Bldg, Baghdad; f. 1987 from State Org. for Major Electrical Projects.

TRADE UNIONS

General Federation of Trade Unions of Iraq (GFTU): POB 3049, Tahrir Sq., Rashid St, Baghdad; tel. (1) 887-0810; fax (1) 886-3820; f. 1959; incorporates six vocational trade unions and 18 local trade union federations in the governorates of Iraq; GFTU is a member of the International Confederation of Arab Trade Unions and of the World Federation of Trade Unions; Pres. FADHIL MAHMOUD GHAREB.

Iraqi Federation of Workers' Trade Unions (IFTU): Baghdad; e-mail abdullahmuhsin@iraqitradeunions.org; internet www.iraqitradeunions.org; f. 2003; Pres. RASEM HUSSEIN ABDULLAH; Sec.-Gen. SOBHI ABDULLAH HUSSEIN.

Union of Teachers: Al-Mansour, Baghdad; Pres. Dr ISSA SALMAN HAMID.

Union of Palestinian Workers in Iraq: Baghdad; Sec.-Gen. SAMI ASH-SHAWISH.

There are also unions of doctors, pharmacologists, jurists, artists, and a General Federation of Iraqi Women (Chair. MANAL YOUNIS).

Transport

RAILWAYS

Iraq's railway lines extend over some 2,339 km. A line covers the length of the country, from Rabia, on the Syrian border, via Mosul, to Baghdad (534 km), and from Baghdad to Basra and Umm Qasr (608 km), on the Persian (Arabian) Gulf. A 404-km line links Baghdad, via Radi and Haditha to Husaibah, near the Iraqi–Syrian frontier. Baghdad is linked with Arbil via Khanaqin and Kirkuk, and a 252-km line (designed to serve industrial projects along its route) runs from Kirkuk via Baiji to Haditha. A 638-km line runs from Baghdad, via al-Qaim (on the Syrian border), to Akashat (with a 150-km line linking the Akashat phosphate mines and the fertilizer complex at al-Qaim). As well as the internal service, there is a regular international service between Baghdad and İstanbul, Turkey. Passenger rail services between Mosul and Aleppo, Syria, resumed in August 2000 after an interruption of almost 20 years. The railway system was due to be repaired and upgraded as part of the reconstruction of Iraq following the removal from power of Saddam Hussain's regime in 2003. Eventually, it is planned that the system will be divided, with the infrastructure being kept as a state asset, while operations are to be privatized.

Iraqi Republic Railways: West Station, Baghdad; tel. (1) 537-0011; Dir-Gen. SALAM JABOUR SALOM.

New Railways Implementation Authority: POB 17040, al-Hurriya, Baghdad; tel. (1) 537-0021; responsible for development of railway network; Sec.-Gen. R. A. AL-UMARI.

ROADS

At the end of 1999, according to estimates by the International Road Federation, Iraq's road network extended over 45,550 km, of which approximately 38,400 km were paved.

The most important roads are: Baghdad–Mosul–Tel Kotchuk (Syrian border), 521 km; Baghdad–Kirkuk–Arbil–Mosul-Zakho (border with Turkey), 544 km; Kirkuk–Sulaimaniya, 160 km; Baghdad–Hilla–Diwaniya–Nasiriya–Basra, 586 km; Baghdad-Kut-Nasirya, 186 km; Baghdad–Ramadi–Rurba (border with Syria), 555 km; Baghdad–Kut–Umara–Basra–Safwan (border with Kuwait), 660 km; Baghdad–Baqaba–Kanikien (border with Iran). Most sections of the six-lane 1,264-km international Express Highway, linking Safwan (on the Kuwaiti border) with the Jordanian and Syrian borders, had been completed by June 1990. Studies have been completed for a second, 525-km Express Highway, linking Baghdad and Zakho on the Turkish border. A complex network of roads was constructed behind the war front with Iran in order to facilitate the movement of troops and supplies during the 1980–88 conflict. The road network was included in the US-led coalition's programme of reconstruction following the ousting of the Baathist regime.

Iraqi Land Transport Co: Baghdad; f. 1988 to replace State Organization for Land Transport; fleet of more than 1,000 large trucks; Dir Gen. AYSAR AS-SAFI.

Joint Land Transport Co: Baghdad; joint venture between Iraq and Jordan; operates a fleet of some 750 trucks.

State Enterprise for Implementation of Expressways: f. 1987; Dir-Gen. FAIZ MUHAMMAD SAID.

State Enterprise for Passenger Transport: Dir-Gen. THABIT MAHMUD GHARIB.

State Enterprise for Roads and Bridges: POB 917, Karradat Mariam, Karkh, Baghdad; tel. (1) 32141; responsible for road and bridge construction projects under the Ministry of Construction and Housing.

SHIPPING

The ports of Basra and Umm Qasr are usually the commercial gateway of Iraq. They are connected by various ocean routes with all parts of the world, and constitute the natural distributing centre for overseas supplies. The Iraqi State Enterprise for Maritime Transport maintains a regular service between Basra, the Gulf and north European ports. There is also a port at Khor az-Zubair, which came into use in 1979.

At Basra there is accommodation for 12 vessels at the Maqal Wharves and accommodation for seven vessels at the buoys. There is one silo berth and two berths for petroleum products at Muftia and one berth for fertilizer products at Abu Flus. There is room for eight vessels at Umm Qasr. There are deep-water tanker terminals at Khor al-Amaya and Faw for three and four vessels, respectively. The latter port, however, was abandoned during the early part of the Iran–Iraq War.

For the inland waterways, which are now under the control of the General Establishment for Iraqi Ports, there are 1,036 registered river craft, 48 motor vessels and 105 motor boats.

The port at Umm Qasr was heavily damaged during the early part of the US-led coalition's campaign to oust Saddam Hussain. The contract for subsequent repair work to Umm Qasr was awarded to the US company Stevedore Services of America.

Iraqi Ports Authority (IPA): Basra; Dir-Gen. MAHMOUD SALEH.

State Enterprise for Iraqi Water Transport: POB 23016, Airport St, al-Furat Quarter, Baghdad; f. 1987, when State Org. for Iraqi Water Transport was abolished; responsible for the planning, supervision and control of six nat. water transportation enterprises, incl.:

State Enterprise for Maritime Transport (Iraqi Line): POB 13038, al-Jadiriya al-Hurriya Ave, Baghdad; Basra office: 14 July St, POB 766, Basra; tel. (1) 776-3201; f. 1952; Dir-Gen. JABER Q. HASSAN; Operations Man. M. A. ALI.

Shipping Company

Arab Bridge Maritime Navigation Co: Aqaba, Jordan; tel. (03) 316307; fax (03) 316313; f. 1987; joint venture by Egypt, Iraq and Jordan to improve economic co-operation; an expansion of the company that established a ferry link between the ports of Aqaba, Jordan, and Nuweibeh, Egypt, in 1985; cap. US $6m.; Chair. NABEEH AL-ABWAH.

CIVIL AVIATION

There are international airports at Baghdad, Basra and Mosul. Baghdad's airport, previously named Saddam International Airport, reopened in August 2000, after refurbishment necessitated by damage sustained during the war with the multinational force in 1991. However, international air links were virtually halted by the UN embargo imposed in 1990. Internal flights, connecting Baghdad to Basra and Mosul, recommenced in November 2000. In early April 2003 the capital's airport was renamed Baghdad International Airport by US forces during their military campaign to oust the regime of Saddam Hussain. Following a programme of reconstruction, the airports at Baghdad and Basra were reopened to commercial flights from late 2003.

National Co for Civil Aviation Services: al-Mansour, Baghdad; tel. (1) 551-9443; f. 1987 following the abolition of the State Organization for Civil Aviation; responsible for the provision of aircraft, and for airport and passenger services.

Iraqi Airways Co: Baghdad International Airport; tel. (1) 887-2400; fax (1) 887-5808; f. 1948; Dir-Gen. AYAD ABD AL-KARIM HAMAM.

Tourism

In 2001 some 126,654 tourists visited Iraq. Tourist receipts in 1998 were estimated at US $13m.

Iraq Tourism Board: Baghdad.

IRELAND

Introductory Survey

Location, Climate, Language, Religion, Flag, Capital

The Republic of Ireland consists of 26 of the 32 counties that comprise the island of Ireland. The remaining six counties, in the north-east, form Northern Ireland, which is part of the United Kingdom. Ireland lies in the Atlantic Ocean, about 80 km (50 miles) west of Great Britain. The climate is mild and equable, with temperatures generally between 0°C (32°F) and 21°C (70°F). Irish is the official first language, but its use as a vernacular is now restricted to certain areas, collectively known as the Gaeltacht, mainly in the west of Ireland. English is universally spoken. Official documents are printed in English and Irish. The vast majority of the inhabitants profess Christianity: of these about 95% are Roman Catholics and 5% Protestants. The national flag (proportions 1 by 2) consists of three equal vertical stripes, of green, white and orange. The capital is Dublin.

Recent History

The whole of Ireland was formerly part of the United Kingdom. In 1920 the island was partitioned, the six north-eastern counties remaining part of the United Kingdom, with their own government. In 1922 the 26 southern counties achieved dominion status, under the British Crown, as the Irish Free State. The dissolution of all remaining links with Great Britain culminated in 1937 in the adoption of a new Constitution, which gave the Irish Free State full sovereignty within the Commonwealth. Formal ties with the Commonwealth were ended in 1949, when the 26 southern counties became a republic. The partition of Ireland remained a contentious issue, and in 1969 a clandestine organization, calling itself the Provisional Irish Republican Army (IRA—see Northern Ireland, Vol. II), initiated a violent campaign to achieve reunification.

In the general election of February 1973, the Fianna Fáil party, which had held office, with only two interruptions, since 1932, was defeated. Jack Lynch, who had been Prime Minister since 1966, resigned, and Liam Cosgrave formed a coalition between his own party, Fine Gael, and the Labour Party. The Irish Government remained committed to power-sharing in the six counties, but opposed any British military withdrawal from Northern Ireland (see Northern Ireland, Vol. II).

Following the assassination of the British Ambassador to Ireland by the Provisional IRA in July 1976, the Irish Government introduced stronger measures against terrorism. Fianna Fáil won the general election of June 1977 and Jack Lynch again became Prime Minister. Lynch resigned as Prime Minister in December 1979 and was succeeded by Charles Haughey. In June 1981, following an early general election, Dr Garret FitzGerald became Prime Minister in a coalition Government between his own party, Fine Gael, and the Labour Party. However, the rejection by the Dáil (the lower house of the legislature) of the coalition's budget proposals precipitated a further general election in February 1982. Haughey was returned to power, with the support of three members of the Workers' Party and two independents. The worsening economic situation, however, made the Fianna Fáil Government increasingly unpopular, and in November Haughey lost the support of the independents over proposed reductions in public expenditure. In the subsequent general election Fianna Fáil failed to gain an overall majority, and in December FitzGerald took office as Prime Minister in a coalition with the Labour Party.

During 1986 FitzGerald's coalition lost support, partly due to the formation of a new party, the Progressive Democrats, by disaffected members of Fianna Fáil. In June a controversial government proposal to end a 60-year constitutional ban on divorce was defeated by national referendum, and shortly afterwards, as a result of a series of defections, the coalition lost its parliamentary majority. In January 1987 the Labour Party refused to support Fine Gael's budget proposals and the coalition collapsed. Fianna Fáil, led by Haughey, won 81 of the 166 seats in the Dáil at the general election held in February. Fianna Fáil formed a minority Government, which commenced upon a programme of unprecedented economic austerity.

Prior to the general election of June 1989 Fine Gael and the Progressive Democrats concluded an electoral pact to oppose Fianna Fáil. Although the Haughey administration had achieved significant economic improvements, severe reductions in public expenditure and continuing problems of unemployment and emigration adversely affected Fianna Fáil's electoral support, and it obtained only 77 of the 166 seats in the Dáil, while Fine Gael won 55 seats and the Progressive Democrats six seats.

At the end of June 1989 the Dáil reconvened to elect the Prime Minister. The Progressive Democrats voted in favour of Alan Dukes, the leader of Fine Gael, in accordance with their pre-election pact, and Haughey was defeated by 86 votes to 78. However, Dukes and Dick Spring, the leader of the Labour Party, also failed to be elected and, after nearly four weeks of negotiations, Fianna Fáil formed an 'alliance' with the Progressive Democrats; two of the latter's members were included in a new Cabinet. In mid-July Haughey became Prime Minister in a Fianna Fáil–Progressive Democrats coalition.

In October 1991 the Government defeated a motion of 'no confidence', which had been introduced following a series of financial scandals involving public officials, by 84 votes to 81. Although members of Fianna Fáil were critical of Haughey's management of these affairs, they were reluctant to precipitate a general election, owing to the party's decline in popularity. In November 1991, however, a group of Fianna Fáil deputies proposed a motion demanding Haughey's removal as leader of the party. Albert Reynolds, the Minister for Finance and a former close associate of Haughey, and Padraig Flynn, the Minister for the Environment, announced their intention of supporting the motion, and were immediately dismissed from office. In the event the attempt to depose Haughey was defeated by a substantial majority of the Fianna Fáil parliamentary grouping.

In January 1992 allegations arose that, contrary to his previous denials, Haughey had been aware of the secret monitoring, in 1982, of the telephone conversations of two journalists perceived to be critical of the Government. The Progressive Democrats made their continued support of the Government (without which a general election would have been necessary) conditional on Haughey's resignation. In February 1992 Reynolds was elected as leader of Fianna Fáil and assumed the office of Prime Minister, following Haughey's resignation. Reynolds extensively reshuffled the Cabinet, but retained the two representatives of the Progressive Democrats, in an attempt to preserve the coalition Government.

In June 1992 the leader of the Progressive Democrats, Desmond O'Malley, criticized Reynolds' conduct as Minister for Industry and Commerce in a parliamentary inquiry, which had been established in June 1991 to investigate allegations of fraud and political favouritism in the beef industry during 1987–88. In October 1992, in his testimony to the inquiry, the Prime Minister accused O'Malley of dishonesty. Following Reynolds' refusal to withdraw the allegations, in early November the Progressive Democrats left the coalition, and the Government was defeated on the following day in a motion of 'no confidence', proposed in the Dáil by the Labour Party. It was subsequently announced that a general election was to take place on 25 November, concurrent with three constitutional referendums on abortion. Fianna Fáil suffered a substantial loss of support, securing only 68 of the 166 seats in the Dáil and Fine Gael also obtained a reduced number of seats, taking only 45. In contrast, the Labour Party attracted substantial support, more than doubling its number of seats, to 33, while the Progressive Democrats increased their representation to 10 seats. In the referendums on abortion two of the proposals (on the right to seek an abortion in another member state of the European Community (EC, now European Union, EU, see p. 217) and the right to information on abortion services abroad) were approved by about two-thirds of the votes cast. The third proposal—on the substantive issue of abortion, permitting the operation only in cases where the life (not merely the health) of the mother was threatened—was rejected, also by a two-thirds' majority.

Since no party had secured an overall majority in the general election, an extended period of consultations ensued, during which the four major parties negotiated on the composition of a governing coalition. In January 1993 Fianna Fáil and the Labour Party reached agreement on a joint policy programme and formed a coalition Government, which took office on 12 January. Reynolds retained the premiership, while Spring received the foreign affairs portfolio, as well as the post of Deputy Prime Minister.

In November 1994 serious differences arose within the coalition Government over the insistence by Fianna Fáil that the Attorney-General, Harry Whelehan, be appointed to a senior vacancy that had arisen in the High Court. Although such promotions accorded with past precedent, Whelehan's conservative record on social issues was unacceptable to the Labour Party. However, Reynolds and the Fianna Fáil members of the Cabinet approved the appointment in the absence of the Labour Party ministers. The Labour Party subsequently withdrew from the coalition, and the Government resigned. Reynolds, while remaining as Prime Minister of a 'caretaker' Government, relinquished the Fianna Fáil leadership on 19 November and was succeeded by the Minister for Finance, Bertie Ahern. Whelehan, meanwhile, resigned as President of the High Court.

The desire of all the major political parties to avoid an immediate general election led to protracted efforts to form a new coalition administration. Discussions between Spring and Ahern, however, failed to produce an agreement. Following extensive negotiations between the Labour Party and other parties, a new coalition, led by John Bruton, who had assumed the leadership of Fine Gael in late 1990, and with Spring as the Deputy Prime Minister and Minister for Foreign Affairs, took office on 15 December 1994. A third coalition partner, the Democratic Left, obtained the social welfare portfolio.

In November 1995 a referendum on the termination of the constitutional ban on divorce resulted in a narrow majority (50.3% to 49.7%) in favour of legalizing the dissolution of marriage. The first divorce under the revised constitutional arrangements was granted in January 1997 (although legislation to implement the reform did not come into effect until February).

In November 1996 the Minister for Transport, Energy and Communications, Michael Lowry, resigned following allegations that he had received personal financial gifts from an Irish business executive, Ben Dunne. During 1997 an inquiry into other political donations by Dunne, chaired by Justice Brian McCracken, revealed that payments totalling some IR£1.3m. had been made to the former Irish Prime Minister, Charles Haughey, during his term in office. Haughey later admitted the allegations, although he insisted that he had no knowledge of the donations until he resigned the premiership; however, McCracken's report, published in August, condemned Haughey's earlier misleading evidence given to the tribunal and recommended further legal investigation. The Government, at that time led by Bertie Ahern of Fianna Fáil following a general election (see below), endorsed the results of the inquiry and agreed to establish a new tribunal to investigate further payments made to politicians and the sources of specific 'offshore' bank accounts that had been used by Haughey. In December 1998 it was revealed that a tax liability on some IR£2m. of personal financial gifts received by Haughey, including those made by Dunne, had been cancelled by the Revenue Commission. Opposition criticism of the decision intensified following the disclosure that the tax appeals commissioner responsible for the concession was Ahern's brother-in-law. Ahern, however, denied that he had influenced the decision.

In May 1997 Bruton called a general election, relying on strong economic growth figures and the negative impact of allegations concerning financial donations to Haughey to secure victory for Fine Gael's coalition with the Labour Party and Democratic Left, despite public opinion polls revealing a significant shortfall in support for the Government over the opposition Fianna Fáil. In the election on 6 June none of the main political parties secured an overall majority in the Dáil. Fine Gael increased its representation to 54 seats, having won 27.9% of the first-preference votes cast, while Fianna Fáil secured 77 seats with 39.3% of the votes. Support for the Labour Party, however, declined substantially and the party won just 17 seats. Sinn Féin won its first ever seat in the Dáil at the election. Bruton conceded that he could not form a majority coalition administration, and Ahern, the Fianna Fáil leader, undertook to form a new government, in alliance with the Progressive Democrats, who had won four parliamentary seats, and with the support of independents. A new administration, with Ahern as Prime Minister, was formally approved in the Dáil at the end of June.

In September 1997 the President, Mary Robinson, a liberal human rights lawyer, who had been elected President in November 1990, as an independent candidate with the support of the Labour Party and the Workers' Party, resigned her position in order to assume her new functions as the United Nations High Commissioner for Human Rights. In the ensuing presidential election, conducted on 30 October 1997, the Fianna Fáil candidate, Dr Mary McAleese, won 45.2% of the first-preference votes cast, compared with 29.3% for Mary Banotti of Fine Gael. McAleese was inaugurated on 11 November, and became the country's first President to be from Northern Ireland. In early November Spring resigned as leader of the Labour Party, owing to his party's poor electoral performances; he was replaced by Ruairí Quinn.

During 2000 independent judicial inquiries investigating corruption among politicians implicated many senior political figures. In January at a tribunal chaired by Justice Michael Moriarty, which was continuing the work of the McCracken inquiry, the revelation that Denis Foley, a Fianna Fáil deputy, had held up to IR£100,000 in 'offshore' accounts prompted Foley's eventual resignation from the Fianna Fáil parliamentary party. In late May Foley was suspended from the Dáil for 14 days for breach of parliamentary procedure after admitting he had failed to declare that he held money in such accounts. Meanwhile, in mid-April Frank Dunlop, a political lobbyist and former government press secretary, admitted to an inquiry into planning irregularities in Dublin, headed by Justice Feargus Flood, that in 1991 he had paid a total of IR£112,000 to 15 Dublin county councillors on behalf of a property developer in order to ensure a favourable decision. Dunlop also testified that the Fine Gael leader, Bruton, was aware that a member of Fine Gael had demanded IR£250,000 from Dunlop to secure that member's vote in favour of the decision. Furthermore, Bruton was also accused by Liam Lawlor, a Fianna Fáil deputy, who himself admitted that he had received political contributions from Dunlop for 'legitimate electoral purposes', of benefiting from the decision. Bruton vehemently denied both accusations. In late January 2001 Fine Gael deputies passed a motion of 'no confidence' in Bruton, who resigned as leader of the party with immediate effect. He was replaced the following month by Michael Noonan, a former Minister for Health and Children.

Meanwhile, in late May 2000 the Moriarty tribunal heard that between 1979 and 1996 Haughey had received payments totalling IR£8.5m., a much larger figure than had previously been acknowledged, and it was announced that Haughey would appear before the tribunal as a witness. Haughey duly appeared before the Moriarty tribunal in July and continued to give evidence to the inquiry during late 2000 despite mounting fears regarding his health. In early June Lawlor, who had resigned from the Dáil's Members' Interests Committee in April, resigned from Fianna Fáil following the publication of a report by the party's Standards in Public Life Committee, which described him as 'unco-operative and contradictory' in his dealings with its investigation. In mid-January 2001 Lawlor was sentenced to three months' imprisonment, of which he served just seven days, for failing to comply with a High Court order to give evidence regarding the use of his credit cards to the Flood tribunal.

The inquiries headed by Justices Moriarty and Flood continued to hear evidence during 2001–05. In late March 2001 it was revealed that Lawlor had still not complied fully with the High Court order that he produce comprehensive documents and records of his financial transactions to the Flood tribunal, and was again sentenced to seven days' imprisonment for his ongoing failure satisfactorily to assist the tribunal. Lawlor was also informed that he was required to make a full disclosure of his financial affairs to the Flood tribunal by early September or face further punishment. Lawlor maintained that he had co-operated as fully as possible with the tribunal and appealed against the sentence in the Supreme Court; however, in mid-December the Supreme Court upheld the High Court's verdict and Lawlor was ordered to serve the seven-day prison term. In late January 2002 lawyers for the Flood tribunal informed the High Court of Lawlor's 'very significant and continuing failure' to meet his obligations to the tribunal, and in early February Lawlor was sentenced to one month's imprisonment and also fined €12,500. He announced that he would not appeal against the sentence and again maintained that he had co-operated as fully as possible with the inquiry.

In March 2001 investigations by the Flood tribunal into the financial conduct of Ray Burke, a former Fianna Fáil minister, who had resigned as Minister for Foreign Affairs in October 1997, revealed that Burke had acted illegally by holding money in offshore accounts in the 1980s while a minister, and by transferring money to and from bank accounts held abroad without requesting permission from the Central Bank (as the law stipulated). He also admitted that he had on previous occasions misled the Dáil about his financial affairs. Furthermore, in mid-May 2001 the tribunal heard that Burke made representations to the Chairman of the Revenue Commissioners on behalf of a construction company while he was Minister for Industry and Commerce in 1989. The hearing was adjourned in November, and in February 2002 it was announced that it was unlikely that the tribunal would produce any findings before the general election, which was scheduled to be held on 17 May. In September Justice Flood issued the second interim report into the tribunal's findings thus far in which, most notably, he stated that Burke had received several 'corrupt payments' totalling up to IR£200,000 between 1974 and 1989. A number of prominent figures implicated in the proceedings were criticized for failing to co-operate fully with the tribunal and it was anticipated that criminal proceedings against 15 people, including Burke, would be instigated in 2003. Ahern came under intense political pressure regarding his decision to appoint Burke as Minister for Foreign Affairs in 1997.

The tribunal recommenced hearings in November 2002, when Dunlop alleged that nine Dublin county councillors had received payments totalling IR£25,000 in order to secure the favourable re-zoning of land owned by Jackson Way, a British property company in which Lawlor had a significant stake. All those implicated in the scandal denied any wrongdoing, and in December Jackson Way announced that it would no longer co-operate with the tribunal.

In mid-March 2001 Haughey finished giving evidence to the Moriarty tribunal; however, shortly afterwards he was admitted to hospital having suffered a near-fatal heart attack. It was subsequently announced that it was unlikely he would give any further evidence to the inquiry. In March 2003 Haughey agreed to pay the Irish Revenue Commissioners €5m. in settlement of his outstanding tax liabilities resulting from undisclosed payments made to him between 1979 and 1996, which were subsequently discovered by the Moriarty tribunal.

In May 2003 the Government was reported to be investigating ways of closing down or reforming the nine tribunals currently proceeding, the total costs of which were predicted to amount to more than €500m. by the time of their conclusions. Indeed, it was claimed that the Flood tribunal would continue for another 15 years at its current rate of progress. In June Justice Flood informed the Government that he wished to resign as Chairman of the tribunal, which, by that month, had incurred costs totalling some €26m.; later that month Justice Alan Mahon replaced Flood as the Chairman of the inquiry. In September it was revealed that the Director of Public Prosecutions had yet to decide whether criminal proceedings would be instigated against any of the 15 people identified as having hindered or obstructed the tribunal in its work; however, in December Burke was formally charged with making false tax returns. In September 2004 Mahon rejected Burke's application for assistance with legal costs, estimated to amount to €10m., and in January 2005 Burke was sentenced to six months' imprisonment.

Meanwhile, in 2004 Ahern was implicated in the alleged tax evasion and corruption of another former minister, Pádraig Flynn. In February the British property developer Tom Gilmartin revealed that in 1989, while he was trying to seek approval for the construction of two shopping complexes in Dublin, he had given IR£50,000 to Flynn (then Minister for the Environment) as a donation to Fianna Fáil. It was revealed that this money was never passed on to the party, rather it was personally invested by Flynn in an offshore bank account in order to evade tax. It was alleged that his daughter, Beverley Cooper Flynn, Fianna Fáil MP for Mayo, had assisted him in investing this money. Cooper Flynn dismissed the claims and Ahern (then Minister for Labour) denied any knowledge of the transaction before it became public knowledge. The tribunal commenced hearings in March 2004 to fully investigate Gilmartin's allegations. Again Ahern stated he knew nothing of the events that took place in 1989 and initially denied having attended a meeting between Gilmartin and several other ministers to discuss Gilmartin's intended property developments. However, in April 2004 Ahern conceded that there was a possi-

bility that he had been at this meeting. In May Cooper Flynn was expelled from the party for her part in the affair. The Mahon Tribunal continued into 2005.

Meanwhile, in early June 2001 the removal of all references to the death penalty from the Constitution along with the prohibition of any future legislation allowing capital punishment, and the ratification of the Rome Statute, which provided for the establishment of an International Criminal Court for crimes against humanity, were approved at separate referendums, by 62.1% and 64.2% of the electorate, respectively. However, at a third concurrently-held referendum on the ratification of the Treaty of Nice, which proposed changes to the future size of the European Commission and the European Parliament as well as changes in the number of votes allocated to each member state prior to the enlargement of the EU from 2003, 53.9% of those who voted rejected the endorsement of the treaty, resulting in an embarrassing reverse for the Government, which had urged a vote in favour of the treaty. The referendum was also marred by an extremely low voter participation rate of just 34.8%. The defeat was attributed to fears that ratification of the treaty would result in Irish participation in the EU's proposed rapid reaction force, thus undermining Ireland's neutrality, and concerns that Ireland would receive reduced funding and assistance from the EU.

The Government suffered a further reverse when, at a referendum on abortion held in early March 2002, 50.4% of the electorate voted against proposed changes, which would have removed the constitutional protection accorded by the Supreme Court to the lives of suicidal pregnant women wishing to terminate their pregnancies, and would have made abortion a criminal offence, punishable by 12 years' imprisonment. The rate of voter participation remained low, however, at just 42.9%.

At the general election held on 17 May 2002 Fianna Fáil won 41.5% of the first-preference votes cast, increasing its parliamentary representation to 81 seats (from 77 in 1997), and thus only narrowly failing to achieve an overall majority in the Dáil. Fine Gael suffered a significant loss of support, winning just 31 seats (compared with 54 in 1997) and 22.5% of the votes. The Progressive Democrats and Sinn Féin increased their representation to eight seats (with 4.0% of the votes cast) and five seats (6.5%), respectively, while the Green Party (Comhaontas Glas) obtained six seats (3.8%). The official rate of participation, at 63.0%, was the lowest to be recorded at an Irish general election. Following Fine Gael's poor performance at the election, Michael Noonan announced his resignation as party leader and in early June was succeeded by Enda Kenny. Also in early June Fianna Fáil and the Progressive Democrats successfully concluded their discussions on the formation of a new coalition Government. Ahern was duly re-elected Prime Minister, with Harney continuing as his deputy.

At the EU Heads of State summit meeting held in Seville, Spain, in June 2002 the Irish Government successfully secured support for a declaration which formally stated that Ireland's participation in the rapid reaction force would be limited to those operations with a UN mandate, approved by the Government and sanctioned by the Dáil. For their part, Ireland's EU partners issued a complementary declaration reiterating that neither the Treaty of Nice nor previous EU treaties compromised Ireland's traditional neutrality and that no member state envisaged the rapid reaction force as a future European Army. In September the Irish Government announced that a second constitutional referendum which, as well as providing for the final ratification of the Treaty of Nice, would now explicitly prohibit Irish participation in any future common European defence force, would take place on 19 October. At the referendum 62.9% of those who voted approved the ratification of the Treaty of Nice, with voter turnout recorded at 49.5% of the electorate.

In January 2003 the Irish Supreme Court issued a ruling that declared that non-national parents of Irish-born children and their non-national siblings were not entitled to live in Ireland by virtue of having an Irish-born child. The ruling was passed after appeals were launched by Nigerian and Czech nationals who had been issued with deportation orders, despite having given birth to children in Ireland. The Minister for Justice swiftly allayed fears that this would lead to mass deportations of non-EU immigrant parents of children born in the country; it was officially estimated that some 11,000 applications for residency on the basis of having given birth to a child in Ireland were outstanding. By early 2004 only three families had been deported as a result of the ruling. Following this ruling, a referendum was scheduled for June 2004, to coincide with the elections to the European Parliament, to amend the Constitution so that children born in Ireland would not automatically be entitled to Irish citizenship. The constitutional amendment, which the Government hoped would deter immigrants from exploiting the current position to gain entitlement for their child to residence in any EU state (since Ireland was the only European country with an automatic right to citizenship at birth), was approved by 79.2% of voters; turnout was registered at nearly 60%.

Meanwhile, in March 2003 a government-supported motion to continue to allow US armed forces, which were engaged in military action against the regime of Saddam Hussein in Iraq, to use Shannon Airport and Irish airspace was approved by 77 votes to 60 in the Dáil. A number of deputies, in particular the Fine Gael leader, Kenny, had voiced their vehement opposition to the motion as they feared that Ireland's traditional neutrality would be compromised as a result.

At the elections to the European Parliament on 11 June 2004, Fianna Fáil won four seats in the European Parliament with 29.5% of the votes cast, while Fine Gael secured five with 27.8% of the votes. The Labour Party won one seat and Sinn Féin won one seat in the Republic and one in Northern Ireland. In the local government elections, which took place on the same day, Fianna Fáil received only 32% of the vote—a decrease of 9% compared with the 2002 general election—while Fine Gael received 27% of the vote; Sinn Féin increased its local representation significantly. At the end of September the Prime Minister effected a major cabinet reorganization, in an attempt to restore public confidence in the party, following its poor electoral performance in the European and local elections. The reshuffle was necessitated by the appointment of the Minister for Finance, Charlie McCreevy, who had provoked popular discontent by reneging on a pre-election pledge not to raise taxes or reduce public expenditure, as a member of the European Commission. Three new ministers were appointed, while eight existing ministers were assigned new roles. In December the newly-appointed Minister for Finance, Brian Cowen, announced the budget for 2005, which included a reduction in stamp duty for first-time property buyers and increased spending on social welfare payments and the disabled.

On 1 October 2004 Dr Mary McAleese was deemed to be duly elected as President as she was the only nominee for the post. Two other candidates, the former Member of the European Parliament, Dana Rosemary Scallon, and Eamon Ryan of the Green Party failed to secure the support of the 20 members of parliament or four local authorities required to stand for election. Both Scallon and Ryan criticized the rules governing presidential elections and Scallon accused the establishment parties of conspiring to prevent her from contesting the election by ordering their local councillors not to support her candidacy.

Consultations between the United Kingdom and Ireland on the future of Northern Ireland resulted in November 1985 in the signing of the Anglo-Irish Agreement, which provided for regular participation in Northern Ireland affairs by the Irish Government on political, legal, security and cross-border matters. The involvement of the Government of Ireland was to be through an Intergovernmental Conference. The Agreement maintained that no change in the status of Northern Ireland would be made without the assent of the majority of its population. The terms of the Agreement were approved by both the Irish and the British Parliaments, despite strong opposition by many Protestants in Northern Ireland.

Under the provisions of the Anglo-Irish Agreement, the Irish Government pledged co-operation in the implementation of new measures to improve cross-border security, in order to suppress IRA operations. It also promised to participate in the European Convention on the Suppression of Terrorism, which it signed in February 1986 and ratified in December 1987, when legislation amending the 1965 Extradition Act came into effect. In the same month the Government introduced controversial measures (without consulting the British Government) granting the Irish Attorney-General the right to approve or reject warrants for extradition of suspected IRA terrorists to the United Kingdom. In January 1988, however, the Irish Supreme Court ruled that members of the IRA could not be protected from extradition to Northern Ireland on the grounds that their offences were politically motivated.

Relations between the Irish and British Governments in 1988 were also strained when Irish confidence in the impartiality of the British legal system was severely undermined by proposed legislation to combat terrorism in Northern Ireland and by the decision, in January, not to prosecute members of the Royal Ulster Constabulary (RUC) allegedly implicated in a policy of shooting terrorist suspects, without attempting to apprehend them, in Northern Ireland in 1982. Difficult relations with the United Kingdom did not, however, present a threat to the Anglo-Irish Agreement, and the co-ordination between the Garda Síochána (Irish police force) and the RUC, established under the Agreement, resulted in an unprecedentedly high level of co-operation on cross-border security. In February 1989 a permanent joint consultative assembly, comprising 25 British and 25 Irish MPs, was established. The representatives were selected in October. The assembly's meetings, the first of which began in February 1990, were to take place twice a year, alternately in Dublin and London.

In January 1990 the British Secretary of State for Northern Ireland, Peter Brooke, launched an initiative to convene meetings between representatives from the major political parties in Northern Ireland, and the British and Irish Governments, to discuss devolution in Northern Ireland. In response to demands from Northern Ireland's Unionist parties, the Irish and British Governments publicly stated that they were prepared to consider an alternative to the Anglo-Irish Agreement. In May the Unionists agreed to hold direct discussions with the Irish Government, a concession previously withheld because it lent credence to the Irish claim to a right to be involved in Northern Ireland's affairs. Disagreement remained, however, on the timing and conditions of Ireland's entry to the talks. Following extensive negotiations, discussions between the Northern Ireland parties, which were a prelude to the inclusion of the Irish Government, commenced in June 1991. They were suspended several times but did reach the inclusion of the Irish Government in April and September 1992. The principal point of contention was the Unionists' demand that Ireland hold a referendum on Articles 2 and 3 of its Constitution, which lay claim to the territory of Northern Ireland. Ireland was unwilling to make such a concession except as part of an overall settlement. With no progress made on this question, nor on the subject of Ireland's role in the administration of Northern Ireland, the negotiations formally ended in November, and the Anglo-Irish Conference, which had been temporarily suspended, resumed.

At the end of October 1993 the new Irish Prime Minister, Albert Reynolds, and his British counterpart, John Major, issued a joint statement setting out the principles on which future negotiations were to be based. The statement emphasized the precondition that Sinn Féin permanently renounce violence before being admitted to the negotiations. In December the Prime Ministers made a joint declaration, known as the 'Downing Street Declaration', which provided a specific framework for a peace settlement. The Declaration referred to the possibility of a united Ireland and accepted the legitimacy of self-determination, but insisted on majority consent within Northern Ireland. While Sinn Féin and the Unionist parties considered their response to the Declaration, Reynolds received both groups' conditional support for his proposal to establish a 'Forum for Peace and Reconciliation', which was to encourage both sides to end violent action.

In April 1994 the IRA declared a temporary cease-fire over the Easter period. Despite a subsequent resumption of operations negotiations culminated in an announcement on 31 August by the IRA that it had ceased all military operations. This was followed in October by a similar suspension on the part of its counterpart loyalist organizations. In late 1994 and early 1995 the Irish authorities granted early release to more than 15 prisoners convicted of IRA terrorist offences. Inter-governmental talks were maintained, resulting in the publication, in February 1995, of a 'Joint Framework' document, in which the Irish Government undertook to support the withdrawal of the Republic's constitutional claim to jurisdiction over Northern Ireland. The document's proposals, which included detailed arrangements for cross-border institutions and economic programmes that would operate on an all-island basis, were stated by the British Government to be intended to provide a basis for public discussion and not as a definitive statement of government policy.

During 1995 the Irish Government expressed its increasing concern at the delay in initiating substantive all-party negotiations on the formulation of a permanent settlement of the conflict in Northern Ireland, largely owing to the insistence of the British Government that the IRA decommission its weapons as a precondition to such talks. An international panel, under the chairmanship of George Mitchell (a former US Senator), began work in December to consider the merits of decommissioning in Northern Ireland. Its findings, announced in January 1996, recommended that the decommissioning of arms should take place in parallel with all-party talks, and that their destruction should be monitored by an independent commission. The British and Irish Governments accepted the recommendations of the report, but new controversy arose over proposals by the British Cabinet to hold elections for a Northern Ireland assembly, which was to provide the framework for all-party negotiations. Although broadly acceptable to Unionist interests, this plan was rejected outright by Northern Ireland's Social Democratic and Labour Party (SDLP) and Sinn Féin, and declared unacceptable by the Irish Government.

In February 1996, following a bomb explosion in London, the IRA announced that the cease-fire had been terminated. The British and Irish Governments suspended official contacts with Sinn Féin, pending acceptable assurances that the IRA had discontinued all violence. In May 1997 a meeting of the Irish Prime Minister, Bruton, with the newly elected British premier, Anthony (Tony) Blair, and the new Secretary of State for Northern Ireland, Dr Marjorie Mowlam, generated speculation that significant progress could be achieved in furthering a political agreement. In June the two Governments announced a new initiative to proceed with the decommissioning of paramilitary weapons, on the basis of the Mitchell report, while simultaneously pursuing political negotiations for a constitutional settlement. In early July the newly elected Irish Prime Minister, Bertie Ahern, confirmed his commitment to the peace initiative during a meeting with Blair in London. On 19 July the IRA announced a restoration of its cease-fire. A few days later the Irish and British Governments issued a joint statement that all-party negotiations would commence in mid-September with the participation of Sinn Féin. At the same time, however, the Unionist parties rejected the measures for weapons decommissioning that had been formulated by the two Governments. At the end of July the Irish Government restored official contacts with Sinn Féin and resumed the policy of considering convicted IRA activists for early release from prison.

In September 1997 Sinn Féin endorsed the so-called Mitchell principles, which committed participants in the negotiations to accepting the outcome of the peace process and renouncing violence as a means of punishment or resolving problems, providing for the party's participation in all-party talks when they resumed in the middle of that month. However, the Unionist parties failed to attend the opening session of the talks, owing partly to a statement by the IRA undermining Sinn Féin's endorsement of the Mitchell principles. A procedural agreement to pursue negotiations in parallel with the decommissioning of weapons (which was to be undertaken by a separate commission, the Independent International Commission on Decommissioning—IICD, led by Gen. John de Chastelain of Canada) was signed by all the main parties later in September.

In March 1998 Mitchell set a deadline of 9 April for the conclusion of the peace talks. On 10 April the two Governments and eight political parties involved in the talks signed a comprehensive political accord, the Good Friday (or Belfast) Agreement, at Stormont Castle. Immediately thereafter the two Governments signed a new British-Irish Agreement, replacing the Anglo-Irish Agreement of November 1985, committing them to put the provisions of the multi-party agreement into effect, subject to approval of the Good Friday Agreement by a referendum to be held in the whole of Ireland in May. The peace settlement provided for changes to the Irish Constitution and to British constitutional legislation to enshrine the principle that a united Ireland could be achieved only with the consent of the majority of the people of both Ireland and Northern Ireland. Under the terms of the Good Friday Agreement the new Northern Ireland Assembly was to have devolved legislative powers over areas of social and economic policy, while security, justice, taxation and foreign policy were to remain under the authority of the British Government. Executive authority was to be discharged by an Executive Committee, comprising a First Minister, Deputy First Minister and as many as 10 ministers of government departments. The Assembly, which was to be elected in June, was to operate in transitional mode, without legislative or executive powers, until the establishment of the North/South and British-Irish institutions. In addition, provision was made for the release of paramilitary prisoners affiliated to organizations that established a complete and unequivocal cease-fire. All qualifying prisoners were to be released

within two years of the commencement of the scheme, which was due to begin in June. The decommissioning of paramilitary weapons was to be completed within two years of the approval by referendum of the Good Friday Agreement. On 22 April the Dáil overwhelmingly approved the peace agreement. At referendums held simultaneously on 22 May the people of Ireland and Northern Ireland voted in support of the Good Friday Agreement. In Ireland 94.4% voted in favour of the Agreement, while in Northern Ireland 71.1% voted to approve the accord.

Elections to the 108-member Northern Ireland Assembly were conducted on 25 June 1998; the Assembly convened for the first time in July and elected the leader of the Ulster Unionist Party (UUP), David Trimble, as Northern Ireland's First Minister to head the Executive Committee. The peace process was threatened with disruption by sectarian violence in July and by the detonation of an explosive device in August in Omagh, Northern Ireland; the device was planted by a Republican splinter group, the Real IRA, and caused 29 deaths. Later that month Ahern announced a series of anti-terrorist measures in an effort to facilitate convictions against terrorists based in Ireland. In August 2003 the leader of the Real IRA, Kevin McKevitt, was sentenced to 20 years' imprisonment by the Special Criminal Court in Dublin for directing a terrorist organization.

Progress in the peace process continued to be obstructed throughout late 1998 by a dispute between Unionists and Sinn Féin concerning the decommissioning of paramilitary weapons. As a result of the dispute the deadlines for the formation both of the Executive Committee and the North/South body (specified as 21 October by the Good Friday Agreement), and for the devolution of powers to the new Northern Ireland institutions (envisaged for 10 March 1999) were not met. An 'absolute' deadline for the devolution of powers was set for 30 June 1999, after which date, Blair asserted, he would suspend the Northern Ireland Assembly if agreement had not been reached. On 25 June the two Prime Ministers presented a compromise plan that envisaged the immediate establishment of the Executive Committee prior to the surrender of paramilitary weapons, with the condition that Sinn Féin guarantee that the IRA complete decommissioning by May 2000. Negotiations continued beyond the June deadline but effectively collapsed in mid-July and a review of the peace process, headed by George Mitchell, began in early September. In November, Mitchell succeeded in producing an agreement providing for the devolution of powers to the Executive Committee. The agreement followed a statement by the IRA that it would appoint a representative to enter discussions with the IICD. At a meeting of the ruling council of the UUP held in late November Trimble persuaded his party to vote in favour of the agreement. On 29 November 1999 the Northern Ireland Assembly convened to appoint the 10-member Executive Committee. On 2 December power was officially transferred from Westminster to the new Northern Ireland Executive at Stormont Castle. On the same day, in accordance with the Good Friday Agreement, the Irish Government removed from the Constitution the Republic's territorial claim over Northern Ireland.

In mid-December 1999 the Cabinet of the Republic attended the inaugural meeting, in Armagh, of the North/South Ministerial Council. The British-Irish Council met for the first time later that month. However, in late January 2000 the President of Sinn Féin, Gerry Adams, dismissed the possibility of imminent IRA decommissioning and a report by the IICD confirmed that there had been no disarmament. With the prospect of the collapse of the peace process the British and Irish Governments engaged in intensive negotiations. On 1 February the IRA released a statement giving assurances that its cease-fire would not be broken and expressing support for the peace process. On 4 February the IRA were given until 11 February to begin decommissioning. However, it failed to comply and legislation came into effect on that day suspending the new executive, legislative and co-operative institutions and returning Northern Ireland to direct rule. The IRA subsequently announced its withdrawal from discussions with the IICD, raising serious doubts about the future of its cease-fire. In addition, Adams refused to participate in any further review of the peace process until the suspended institutions had been restored.

Direct talks between the Irish and British Governments and the principal parties resumed in early May 2000 with the British Government pledging to restore the Northern Ireland institutions on 22 May and postpone the deadline for decommissioning until June 2001 subject to a commitment by the IRA on the arms issue. On 6 May 2000 the IRA responded by offering to 'initiate a process that will completely and verifiably put arms beyond use'. On 30 May power was once again transferred from Westminster to the new Northern Ireland institutions. In November the British House of Lords approved legislation which would enable members of the Irish Parliament to stand for election to the Northern Ireland Assembly as well as to the British lower chamber of Parliament, the House of Commons, but prohibited the holding of office in both Northern Ireland and the Republic of Ireland.

The issue of IRA weapons decommissioning continued severely to threaten the peace process during 2001. Prior to the general election held in the United Kingdom in early June, Trimble had announced his intention to resign as First Minister on 1 July, thus precipitating the collapse of the Northern Ireland institutions, if there was no independently confirmed decommissioning of weapons by the IRA by that date. Despite intensive efforts by Ahern and Blair to avert Trimble's resignation, on 1 July Trimble stood down from his post; Sir Reg Empey, the Minister of Enterprise, Trade and Investment assumed the role of acting First Minister. In early August Ahern and Blair announced that they would formulate a package of non-negotiable proposals to be tabled to the pro-Agreement parties, which they expected would bring an end to the impasse. The joint British-Irish proposals did not meet with the approval of the major political parties, and on 10 August the British Government suspended the Northern Ireland Assembly for 24 hours in order to delay the necessity to appoint a new First Minister for a further six weeks. Following the temporary suspension the IRA retracted its earlier offer to put arms 'beyond use', citing the British Government's willingness to suspend the Northern Irish institutions as unacceptable.

The Assembly was again suspended on 22 September 2001 as the deadlock between the major parties continued, and on 8 October, following the defeat of a Unionist motion to exclude Sinn Féin members from the Executive, Trimble announced that he would withdraw the three UUP ministers from the Executive. On 18 October the UUP ministers duly resigned along with two DUP ministers; five days later, however, the IRA announced that it had begun a process of putting arms beyond use in accordance with stipulations of the IICD and later that day the IICD revealed that it had witnessed the 'significant' disposal of IRA weapons. On 24 October Trimble renominated the UUP ministers to the Executive thus preventing the institution's collapse and the following day the two DUP ministers also retook their posts. Trimble subsequently received permission from the UUP executive council to reassume the position of First Minister and was finally re-elected, with Mark Durkan (who replaced John Hume as leader of the SDLP in November) as his deputy.

The alleged IRA involvement in the theft of documents from Special Branch offices in Belfast in March 2002 and the discovery, in June, of an IRA intelligence database listing details of more than 200 judges, politicians and members of the security forces provoked Unionist demands that Sinn Féin ministers be removed from the power-sharing Executive and further 'crisis' meetings between the British and Irish Governments. In mid-July 2002 the IRA issued an apology for the deaths and injuries of 'non-combatants' caused as a result of its actions over the previous 30 years. The sincerity of the apology was questioned by Trimble and senior Unionists were sceptical that the IRA remained committed to the peace process in the light of continued sectarian violence in Belfast, for which the UUP maintained that the IRA was primarily responsible. In early July during talks between the British and Irish Governments and the pro-Agreement parties in Belfast, Trimble had implied that UUP ministers would resign from the Executive by the end of that month if the IRA did not clearly demonstrate its commitment to a 'full transition from violence to democracy'. In September the Ulster Unionist Council (UUC) announced that it would withdraw UUP ministers from the Northern Ireland Executive on 18 January 2003 if the IRA and Sinn Féin had not demonstrated that it had completed its transition to democracy and non-violence.

In early October 2002 Northern Ireland was once again plunged into political crisis after Sinn Féin's offices at the Northern Ireland Assembly were raided by police, who, as part of a major investigation into intelligence-gathering by Republicans, suspected that the IRA had infiltrated the Northern Ireland Office and gained access to large numbers of confidential documents. Among a number of people detained by the police was Sinn Féin's Head of Administration, who was charged with

possession of documents likely to be of assistance to terrorist organizations. Trimble accused Sinn Féin of a 'massive political conspiracy' and threatened to withdraw from the Executive unless the British Government proposed the expulsion of Sinn Féin from the Assembly. Emergency talks between the British and Irish Governments and the Northern Ireland political leaders followed; however, Blair's demands for IRA concessions on the arms issue were not met. On 11 October the two DUP ministers resigned from the Executive, and on 14 October the British Secretary of State for Northern Ireland, John Reid, suspended the Assembly and returned Northern Ireland to direct rule. In a joint statement, Blair and Ahern announced that the devolved institutions would only be restored if Sinn Féin ended its link with paramilitary organizations and Blair subsequently called on the IRA to disband itself. Later that month the IRA announced that it had suspended all contact with the IICD and claimed that the British Government was to blame for the current crisis having failed to honour its commitments under the Good Friday Agreement.

Talks aimed at resolving the impasse continued between the major parties during late 2002 and early 2003; however, relations between Unionists and Nationalists remained strained. In December Trimble walked out of multi-party talks in Belfast in protest at the leaking of a confidential Irish government document which stated that the IRA was still 'actively engaged in training, targeting, recruiting and acquiring small quantities of weapons'. Further talks in January and February 2003 were overshadowed by a severe escalation of the feud between rival loyalist paramilitary organizations in Belfast, in which two senior members of the Ulster Defence Association (UDA) were killed. In March Ahern and Blair announced that the elections to the Northern Ireland Assembly would be postponed until 29 May. In April the US President, George W. Bush, held talks with Ahern and the pro-Agreement parties at which he urged their leaders to 'seize the opportunity for peace'. Despite these efforts, plans to publish proposals for reinstating the Northern Ireland institutions were abandoned just days later after the IRA failed to respond to the British Government's demand for a definitive cessation of paramilitary activities, and in early May Blair postponed the elections until an unspecified date later in 2003.

In early May 2003 Adams stated that the IRA leadership was determined 'that there will be no activities which will undermine in any way the peace process or the Good Friday Agreement'; however, Blair cited the refusal of the IRA to give him 'absolute clarity' that it had ceased all paramilitary activity as the reason for his decision to postpone the elections. Nevertheless, the British and Irish Governments published a Joint Declaration containing their proposals for reinstating the Northern Ireland institutions and Blair and Ahern met in Dublin to discuss the implementation thereof. The Declaration called for a full and permanent cessation of all paramilitary activity, including military attacks, intelligence gathering, weapons procurement and punishment attacks. Both Prime Ministers stressed that political talks would continue to try and break the impasse over the holding of elections, reiterated their commitment to the Good Friday Agreement and pledged that aspects of the Joint Declaration not conditional upon IRA acts of completion would be implemented.

Talks between the British and Irish Governments and the major Northern Irish political parties continued during late 2003, and in September the four members of the International Monitoring Commission (IMC) were appointed. Trimble and Adams met with Ahern and Blair in London in mid-October, and on 21 October it was announced that elections to the Northern Ireland Assembly would take place on 26 November. However, later on 21 October Trimble issued a statement in which he maintained that the acts of decommissioning of IRA weapons witnessed by de Chastelain earlier that day had been lacking in the transparency the UUP required to be convinced of the IRA's genuine desire to commit to a lasting peace. Trimble announced that the peace process would be put on hold pending the convening of the UUC, thus preventing the devolution of powers to the Northern Ireland institutions; however, both Blair and Ahern insisted that the elections would proceed on 26 November as scheduled. The British Government acknowledged in late October that the devolved institutions would not be restored following the elections and that a review of the Good Friday Agreement would take place in early 2004 (although Blair stressed that the fundamental principles of the Agreement were not a matter for negotiation). A statement issued by the IRA on 29 October 2003 maintained that it had honoured its commitments and that there would be no more acts of weapons decommissioning until the UUP agreed to support the restoration of power-sharing to the province.

At elections to the Northern Ireland Assembly, held on 26 November 2003, the anti-Good Friday Agreement DUP secured 30 of the 108 seats, thus becoming the largest party in the province. The election result increased the pressure on Trimble from anti-Agreement factions of the UUP, who again called for him to resign. Furthermore, the DUP demanded a full renegotiation of the Good Friday Agreement. However, both Ahern and Blair reiterated that the principles and values incorporated in the Agreement would not be changed. Talks between the British Secretary of State for Northern Ireland, Paul Murphy, and representatives of the major Northern Irish parties were subsequently held, although it remained unlikely that the Assembly would be reinstated or that a new Executive would be formed in the near future.

In talks with Ahern in January 2004 the leader of the DUP, Rev. Ian Paisley, remained insistent that his party would not conduct direct talks with Sinn Féin until the IRA had disbanded. The review of the Good Friday Agreement commenced in early February; however, in early March Trimble left the talks in protest at the alleged IRA involvement in the kidnapping of a dissident Republican in Belfast. Later that month Ahern and Blair met in Northern Ireland to hold talks with political groups and reiterated their commitment to seeing a power-sharing deal agreed upon. In April the IMC issued its first report in which it highlighted the levels of ongoing paramilitary activity by both Loyalist and Republican groups in Northern Ireland. The British Government subsequently announced that it would impose financial sanctions on Sinn Féin and the Progressive Unionist Party. Blair and Ahern announced in May, following a meeting in Dublin, that they had agreed the basis of a 'road map' to restore the suspended Northern Ireland Assembly and Executive by October.

In September 2004 Blair and Ahern hosted a three-day meeting at Leeds Castle, in southern England, in a further attempt to restore suspended institutions in Northern Ireland. Blair increased the political pressure on the participants by suggesting that if no agreement on power-sharing could be reached in September 'an alternative way' would have to be found, provoking speculation that the devolved institutions could be dissolved. Despite optimism prior to the talks, partly caused by Adams' indication during August that the IRA could disband, no progress towards a power-sharing agreement was made. Although progress was apparently made towards the complete disbandment and disarmament of the IRA, the talks became deadlocked, following a DUP demand for changes to the functioning of the Assembly and the Executive before it would enter a government with Sinn Féin. Disagreements focused notably on the issue of ministerial accountability. In early October 2004 Paisley met Ahern in Dublin, his first formal political meeting with the Taoiseach, to try to break the impasse. In early November, however, the IMC's second report on paramilitary violence reported that the IRA was still recruiting volunteers and gathering intelligence.

In late 2004 the process showed real signs of progressing to a successful conclusion. On 17 November the British and Irish Governments passed their proposals for restoring the power-sharing Executive to the DUP and Sinn Féin for consultation. One week later Paisley met Blair and stated that the disarming of the IRA would only be an acceptable starting point for the peace-sharing deal if photographic evidence were obtained of the event. At the end of the month Adams met the Northern Ireland Chief Constable, Hugh Orde, to discuss the issue of decommissioning, while Paisley met de Chastelain in Belfast to review issues surrounding the destruction of the IRA's weapons.

On 8 December 2004 Blair and Ahern met in Belfast to reveal their final proposals to restore devolution, although neither the DUP nor Sinn Féin had agreed to the terms. The following day an IRA statement was released declaring that photographic proof of decommissioning had never been an option and that although the IRA was committed to the peace process it would not be subjected to a process of humiliation. In early January 2005 Orde placed the blame for a raid on the Belfast headquarters of the Northern Bank in December 2004, in which £26.5m was stolen, on the IRA and was consequently accused by Sinn Féin of jeopardizing the peace process. In early February 2005 Ahern and Blair warned the IRA that its failure to demilitarize was the only obstacle to reaching an agreement on power-sharing; the following day the IRA withdrew its commitment to

decommissioning its weapons. Ahern subsequently announced that little progress in the peace process was likely until after the anticipated British general election, which was subsequently scheduled for May.

Ireland became a member of the EC (now the EU) in 1973. In May 1987 the country affirmed its commitment to the EC when, in a referendum, 69.9% of Irish voters supported adherence to the Single European Act, which provided for closer economic and political co-operation between EC member-states (including the creation of a single Community market by 1993). In December 1991, during the EC summit conference at Maastricht, in the Netherlands, Ireland agreed to the far-reaching Treaty on European Union. Ireland secured a special provision within the Treaty (which was signed by all parties in February 1992), guaranteeing that Ireland's constitutional position on abortion would be unaffected by any future EC legislation. The four major political parties in Ireland united in support of the ratification of the Treaty prior to a referendum on the issue, which took place in June. Despite opposition, from both pro- and anti-abortion campaigners, to the special provision within the Treaty and the threat to Ireland's neutrality inherent in the document's proposals for a common defence policy, ratification of the Treaty was endorsed by 68.7% of the votes cast (57.3% of the electorate participated in the referendum). In a referendum conducted in May 1998, 62% of those who voted endorsed the Amsterdam Treaty, which had been signed by EU ministers in October 1997, amending the Treaty on European Union. The Treaty of Nice, which provided for the impending enlargement of the EU, was approved by 62.9% of those who voted in a national referendum (see above—the Treaty had been rejected by the Irish electorate in an earlier referendum held in June 2001). In January 2004 Ireland assumed the rotating six-month Presidency of the EU, following the failure of the EU Heads of State and of Government to agree to the final text of a draft constitutional treaty for the organization in December 2003. Ahern, in his capacity as President of the Council of the European Union, led intense negotiations through his term of office and proposed a compromise on voting rights in the Council that enabled the leaders of all 25 member states to approve the treaty on 18 June 2004. The constitutional treaty, which was formally signed in October 2004, remained subject to ratification by each member state. Ireland was to hold a referendum on the issue, which was likely to take place in October 2005. In July 2004 Ireland called for Irish to be recognized as an official EU language.

In January 2005 the Irish Minister for Defence announced that for constitutional reasons Ireland would not participate in EU battle groups (13 of which were to be established by 2007 for deployment to international crisis areas). Ireland would find it difficult to comply with the proviso that the battle groups should be deployable in 10 days since a UN mandate was a prerequisite for the deployment of Irish troops, together with approval from the Irish Government and the Irish Parliament. There were also constitutional problems regarding Irish participation in a battle group with other countries and it was not a large enough country to support its own battle group.

Government

Legislative power is vested in the bicameral National Parliament, comprising the Senate (with restricted powers) and the House of Representatives. The Senate (Seanad Éireann) has 60 members, including 11 nominated by the Prime Minister (Taoiseach) and 49 indirectly elected for five years. The House of Representatives (Dáil Éireann) has 166 members (Teachtaí Dála), elected by universal adult suffrage for five years (subject to dissolution) by means of the single transferable vote, a form of proportional representation.

The President (Uachtarán) is the constitutional Head of State, elected by direct popular vote for seven years. Executive power is effectively held by the Cabinet, led by the Prime Minister, who is appointed by the President on the nomination of the Dáil. The President appoints other Ministers on the nomination of the Prime Minister with the previous approval of the Dáil. The Cabinet is responsible to the Dáil.

Defence

At 1 August 2004 the regular armed forces totalled an estimated 10,460. The army comprised 8,500, the navy 1,100 and the air force 860. There was also a reserve of 14,800. Defence was allocated €714.1m. in the 2005 budget. Military service is voluntary.

Economic Affairs

In 2003, according to estimates by the World Bank, Ireland's gross national income (GNI), measured at average 2001–2003 prices, was US $122,990.1m., equivalent to $26,960 per head (or $30,450 on an international purchasing-power parity basis). During 1990–2003, it was estimated, the population increased at an average annual rate of 0.9%, while gross domestic product (GDP) per head increased, in real terms, by an average of 5.7% per year. Overall GDP increased, in real terms, at an average annual rate of 6.6% in 1990–2003; it grew by 6.9% in 2002 and by 1.8% in 2003.

Agriculture (including forestry and fishing) contributed an estimated 2.9% of GDP in 2003. An estimated 6.4% of the working population were employed in the sector in 2004. Beef and dairy production dominate Irish agriculture (in 2001 meat and meat preparations accounted for 18% of total exports while dairy products and birds' eggs accounted for 1.0%). Principal crops include sugar beet, barley, wheat and potatoes. Agricultural GDP declined by an average of 0.3% per year during 1996–2002; it increased by 1.1% in 2001, but declined by 2.4% in 2002.

Industry (comprising mining, manufacturing, construction and utilities) provided 37.4% of GDP in 2003, and employed an estimated 27.6% of the working population in 2004. Industrial GDP increased by an average of 16.3% per year during 1996–2002; it grew by 12.7% in 2002.

Mining (including quarrying and turf production) provided employment to 0.4% of the working population in 1997. Ireland possesses substantial deposits of lead-zinc ore and recoverable peat, both of which are exploited. Natural gas, mainly from the Kinsale field, and small quantities of coal are also extracted. A significant natural gas deposit discovered in 1999 was expected to yield sufficient gas to meet more than one-half of the country's current average demand. Offshore reserves of petroleum have also been located and several licences awarded to foreign-owned enterprises to undertake further exploration.

Manufacturing was estimated to employ 20.3% of the working population in 1997. The manufacturing sector comprises many high-technology, largely foreign-owned, capital-intensive enterprises. During 1992–96 manufacturing production increased by an average of 10.1% per year.

Electricity is derived principally from natural gas, which provided 37.1% of total requirements in 2001, while coal provided 37.6% and petroleum 21.1%. In 2001 imports of mineral fuels were 3.3% (by value) of total merchandise imports.

Service industries (including commerce, finance, transport and communications, and public administration) contributed 59.7% of GDP in 2003, and employed an estimated 66.0% of the working population in 2004. The financial sector is of increasing importance to Ireland. An International Financial Services Centre in Dublin was opened in 1990; by mid-2003 more than 430 companies were participating in the Centre, many of which were foreign concerns attracted by tax concessions offered by the Irish Government. Tourism is one of the principal sources of foreign exchange. Revenue from the tourism and travel sector amounted to an estimated US $3,089m. in 2002. The GDP of the services sector increased by an average of 7.0% per year during 1996–2002, and by an estimated 4.7% in 2002.

In 2003, according to IMF statistics, Ireland recorded a visible trade surplus of US $37,807m. while there was a deficit of $2,105m. on the current account of the balance of payments. In 2003 the principal source of imports (30.9%) was the United Kingdom; other major sources were the USA (15.5%) and Germany (7.2%). The USA was the principal market for exports (20.6%); other major purchasers were the United Kingdom (18.1%), Belgium (12.5%), Germany (8.2%) and France (6.1%). In 2003 principal imports included office equipment and other electrical machinery, chemical products, road vehicles and parts, and other manufactured items. Principal exports included office equipment, chemicals, and food and live animals.

In 2004 there was a budgetary surplus of €33m. (equivalent to 0.9% of GDP). In 2003 Ireland's total national debt was estimated to be €37,611m. The annual rate of inflation averaged 2.9% in 1990–2003. The rate increased to 4.7% in 2002 but declined to 3.5% in 2003. Unemployment stood at 4.2% of the labour force in February 2005.

Ireland is a member of the European Union (EU, see p. 217), and of the EU Exchange Rate Mechanism (ERM, see p. 251).

In the late 1990s the Irish economy enjoyed an unprecedentedly high rate of growth, which was attributed to prudent fiscal and monetary management, an expanding, well-qualified labour force and social partnership agreements between the Government, businesses and trade unions, providing for guaranteed pay rises in return for productivity and 'no strike' agreements. In addition government policies offering financial incentives to foreign-owned enterprises resulted in a substantial increase in direct foreign investment and expansion in the financial services and electronic manufacturing industries. Moreover, Ireland benefited from the low interest rates associated with the launch of the euro in 1999. However, the Irish economy suffered a number of reverses in the early 2000s, experiencing reduced growth and a sharp increase in the rate of inflation as the outbreak of foot-and-mouth disease adversely affected the agriculture and tourism industries and the world-wide economic slowdown reduced levels of foreign investment. Furthermore, the competitiveness of the economy was greatly hampered by the continued strength of the euro as well as by the Government's imprudent fiscal policy during 2000–02. GDP growth of just 1.8% was achieved in 2003, compared with the 11.5% increase recorded in 2000. The economy began to recover at the end of 2003 as inflation started to decline. Both the 2004 and 2005 budgets envisaged a significant rise in expenditure on infrastructural projects following advice made by the Economic and Social Research Institute urging the Government to increase investment in this area in order to prevent the economy from further stagnation. Following strong growth in employment in 2004, conditions in the labour market were expected to remain favourable in 2005. While growth rates comparable with the 'Celtic Tiger' period during the 1990s were highly unlikely, it appeared from early 2005 onwards that Ireland could look forward to a sustained period of growth (of around 5% per year).

Education

The State in Ireland has constitutional responsibility for the national education system. Irish schools are owned, not by the State, but by community groups, traditionally religious groups. It is in general an aided system: the State does not itself operate the schools (with a few minor exceptions) but assists other bodies, usually religious, to do so.

Education in Ireland is compulsory for nine years between six and 15 years of age. Primary education may begin at the age of six and lasts for six years. Aided primary schools account for the education of 98.5% of children in the primary sector, who attend until the age of 12, when they transfer to a post-primary school. Post-primary education lasts for up to six years, comprising a junior cycle of three years and a senior cycle of two or three years. The Junior Certificate examination is taken after three years in post-primary (second-level) education. By 1997 some 92% of 16-year-olds were participating in full-time, post-compulsory education. In 2000/01 there were 16 technical colleges providing a range of craft, technical, professional and other courses. There are four universities: the University of Dublin (Trinity College); the National University of Ireland (comprising the University Colleges of Cork, Dublin and Galway); and the Dublin City University and the University of Limerick (former National Institutes of Higher Education, which obtained university status in 1989).

In the 2005 budget €6,393m. (equivalent to 21.0% of total expenditure) was allocated to education.

Public Holidays

2005: 1 January (New Year), 17 March (St Patrick's Day), 25 March (Good Friday), 28 March (Easter Monday), 2 May (May Day Holiday), 6 June (June Bank Holiday), 1 August (August Bank Holiday), 31 October (October Bank Holiday), 25–26 December (Christmas).

2006: 1 January (New Year), 17 March (St Patrick's Day), 14 April (Good Friday), 17 April (Easter Monday), 8 May (May Day Holiday), 5 June (June Bank Holiday), 7 August (August Bank Holiday), 30 October (October Bank Holiday), 25–26 December (Christmas).

Weights and Measures

The metric system of weights and measures is the primary system in force, but the imperial system is still used in a number of limited activities.

Statistical Survey

Source (unless otherwise stated): Central Statistics Office, Skehard Rd, Cork; tel. (21) 359000; fax (21) 359090; e-mail information@cso.ie; internet www.cso.ie.

Area and Population

AREA, POPULATION AND DENSITY

Area (sq km)	70,182*
Population (census results)	
28 April 1996	3,626,087
28 April 2002	
Males	1,946,164
Females	1,971,039
Total	3,917,203
Population (preliminary estimate at April)	
2003	3,978,900
2004	4,043,800
Density (per sq km) at April 2004	57.6

* 27,097 sq miles.

ADMINISTRATIVE DIVISIONS
(2002 census)

Province/County	Area (sq km)	Population	Density (per sq km)
Connaught	17,713	464,296	26.2
Galway	6,151	209,077	34.0
Galway City	51	65,832	1,290.8
Galway County	6,010	143,245	23.8
Leitrim	1,589	25,799	16.2
Mayo	5,588	117,446	21.0
Roscommon	2,548	53,774	21.1
Sligo	1,837	58,200	31.7
Leinster	19,774	2,105,457	106.5
Carlow	898	46,014	51.2
Dublin	921	1,122,821	1,219.1
Dublin City	118	495,781	4,201.5
Dún Loughaire-Rathdown	127	191,781	1,510.1
Fingal	453	196,413	433.6
South Dublin	223	238,835	1,071.0
Kildare	1,694	163,944	96.8
Kilkenny	2,072	80,339	38.8
Laoighis	1,719	58,774	34.2
Longford	1,091	31,068	28.5
Louth	832	101,812	122.4
Meath	2,335	134,005	57.4
Offaly	1,990	63,663	32.0
Westmeath	1,825	71,858	39.4
Wexford	2,365	116,596	49.3
Wicklow	2,033	114,676	56.4
Munster	24,608	1,100,614	44.7
Clare	3,442	103,277	30.0
Cork	7,508	447,829	59.6
Cork City	40	123,062	3,076.6
Cork County	7,468	324,767	43.5
Kerry	4,735	132,527	28.0
Limerick	2,760	175,304	63.5
Limerick City	20	54,023	2,701.2
Limerick County	2,740	121,281	44.3
Tipperary	4,304	140,131	32.6
Tipperary North	2,046	61,010	29.8
Tipperary South	2,258	79,121	35.0
Waterford	1,859	101,546	54.6
Waterford City	42	44,594	1,061.8
Waterford County	1,817	56,952	31.3
Ulster (part)	8,087	246,714	30.5
Cavan	1,932	56,546	29.3
Donegal	4,860	137,575	28.3
Monaghan	1,296	52,593	40.6
Total	70,182	3,917,203	55.8

PRINCIPAL TOWNS
(population at 2002 census)

Dublin (capital)	495,781	Limerick	54,023
Cork	123,062	Waterford	44,594
Galway	65,832		

BIRTHS, MARRIAGES AND DEATHS

	Registered live births		Registered marriages		Registered deaths	
	Number	Rate (per 1,000)	Number	Rate (per 1,000)	Number	Rate (per 1,000)
1996	50,390	13.9	16,174	4.5	31,514	8.7
1997	52,311	14.3	15,631	4.3	31,605	8.6
1998	53,551	14.5	16,783	4.5	31,352	8.5
1999	53,354	14.2	18,526	4.9	31,683	8.5
2000	54,239	14.3	19,168	5.1	31,115	8.2
2001	57,882	15.1	19,246	5.0	29,812	7.8
2002	60,521	15.4	20,047	5.1	29,348	7.5
2003	61,517	15.5	20,302	5.1	28,823	7.2

Expectation of life (WHO estimates, years at birth): 77.1 (males 74.4; females 79.8) in 2002 (Source: WHO, *World Health Report*).

IMMIGRATION AND EMIGRATION
('000, official estimates, year ending April)

Immigrants

Country of origin	2001/02	2002/03*	2003/04*
United Kingdom	19.1	13.5	13.0
Other EU	11.3	9.7	12.6
USA	6.6	4.7	4.8
Rest of the world	29.9	22.5	19.7
Total	66.9	50.5	50.1

Emigrants

Country of destination	2001/02	2002/03*	2003/04*
United Kingdom	7.4	6.3	4.9
Other EU	4.8	4.3	3.4
USA	4.8	2.5	2.8
Rest of the world	8.5	7.6	7.4
Total	25.6	20.7	18.5

* Preliminary figures.

ECONOMICALLY ACTIVE POPULATION
(estimates, '000 persons, quarterly (March–May) labour force survey)

	2002	2003	2004
Agriculture, forestry and fishing	124.0	116.6	117.0
Mining and quarrying			
Manufacturing	305.0	306.1	300.6
Electricity, gas and water			
Construction	182.2	191.4	206.0
Wholesale and retail trade	246.8	251.6	260.2
Hotels and restaurants	104.2	114.4	107.8
Transport, storage and communications	111.7	112.1	113.2
Financial and other business services	228.9	227.1	237.0
Public administration and defence	90.6	92.4	89.5
Education	111.3	116.1	117.9
Health	159.3	169.9	177.0
Other services	99.8	95.7	110.0
Total employed	1,763.9	1,793.4	1,836.2
Males	1,027.7	1,040.9	1,065.2
Females	736.1	752.5	771.0
Total unemployed	77.0	82.1	84.2
Total labour force	1,840.9	1,875.5	1,920.3

Health and Welfare

KEY INDICATORS

Total fertility rate (children per woman, 2002)	1.9
Under-5 mortality rate (per 1,000 live births, 2003)	6
HIV/AIDS (% of persons aged 15–49, 2003)	0.1
Physicians (per 1,000 head, 2001)	2.4
Hospital beds (per 1,000 head, 1998)	9.7
Health expenditure (2001): US $ per head (PPP)	1,935
Health expenditure (2001): % of GDP	6.5
Health expenditure (2001): public (% of total)	56.0
Human Development Index (2002): ranking	10
Human Development Index (2002): value	0.936

For sources and definitions, see explanatory note on p. vi.

Agriculture

PRINCIPAL CROPS
('000 metric tons)

	2001	2002	2003
Wheat	769	867	794
Oats	119	134	155
Barley	1,277	963	1,198
Potatoes	478	519	488
Sugar beet	1,498	1,313	1,505
Turnips	100	90	95*
Fodder beet	279	250	250*

* FAO estimate.

LIVESTOCK
('000 head at June)

	2001	2002	2003
Cattle	7,050	6,992	6,967
Sheep	5,056	4,807	4,829
Pigs	1,741	1,770	1,713
Poultry	12,603	12,709	12,738

LIVESTOCK PRODUCTS
('000 metric tons)

	2001	2002	2003
Beef and veal	579.0	540.0	568.0
Mutton and lamb	78.1	66.5	64.0*
Pig meat	241.0	231.0	217.2
Poultry meat†	134.3	132.7	132.7
Cows' milk	5,381.8	5,368.0	5,299.0
Butter	139	147	148*
Cheese†	127	127	110.8
Dry milk (excl. whey)†	126.3	129.2	136
Hen eggs	31.4	33.2	31.9
Cattle hides†	65.7	62.4	63
Sheepskins†	15.0	11.5	11.6

* Unofficial figure.
† FAO estimates.

Source: FAO.

Forestry

ROUNDWOOD REMOVALS
('000 cubic metres, excluding bark)

	2001	2002	2003
Sawlogs, veneer logs and logs for sleepers	1,653	1,733	1,893
Pulpwood	770	742	623
Fuel wood	32	34	30
Total	2,455	2,509	2,546

Source: FAO.

SAWNWOOD PRODUCTION
('000 cubic metres, including railway sleepers)

	2001	2002	2003
Coniferous (softwood)	919	807	996
Broadleaved (hardwood)	6	11	9
Total	925	818	1,005

Source: FAO.

Fishing

SEA FISH
(landings in metric tons)

	2000	2001	2002
European plaice	1,029	841	801
Atlantic cod	2,928	2,653	2,503
Haddock	5,812	5,398	3,505
Megrim	3,364	3,703	2,848
Skate and rays	2,077	2,141	2,503
Whiting	6,505	6,581	6,657
Monks and anglers	3,838	3,067	2,523
Dogfish	1,361	1,966	1,871
Orange roughy	3	2,759	4,646
Atlantic herring	42,114	41,979	30,606
Atlantic mackerel	70,183	70,451	71,431
Blue whiting	21,693	29,909	14,268
Horse mackerel	55,438	63,497	34,769
Total fish (incl. others)	243,348	266,760	213,078
Crabs	10,295	11,443	11,527
Norway lobster (Dublin Bay prawn)	4,077	4,901	4,991
Periwinkles	2,634	2,775	2,274
Whelks	4,474	6,363	7,901
Total shellfish (incl. others*)	29,528	31,760	32,087
Total catch	272,875	298,521	245,165

* Excludes oysters, clams and farmed mussels.

INLAND FISH
(catch in metric tons)

	2000	2001	2002
Atlantic salmon	621	792	673
Total catch (incl. others) . . .	881	900	789

Mining

('000 metric tons, unless otherwise indicated)

	2000	2001	2002
Natural gas (million cu m) . . .	2,500*	2,500	2,500*
Lead†	57.8	44.5	32.5*
Zinc†	262.9	225.1	252.7
Peat*‡	5,100	5,100	4,100

* Estimate(s).

† Figures refer to the metal content of ores mined.

‡ Excluding peat for horticultural use ('000 metric tons, estimates): 400 in 2000; 400 in 2001; 250 in 2002.

Source: US Geological Survey.

Industry

SELECTED PRODUCTS
('000 metric tons, unless otherwise indicated)

	1996	1997	1998
Flour	190	195	n.a.
Margarine	54	48	33
Cigarettes (million)	7,500	4,605	6,452
Woven woollen fabrics (sq m) . .	900,000	900,000	800,000
Motor spirit (petrol)	379	452	468
Distillate fuel oils	765	1,000	1,112*
Residual fuel oils	793	1,022	1,099*
Electric energy (million kWh) . .	18,845	19,551	20,485

* Estimate.

Source: mainly UN, *Industrial Commodity Statistics Yearbook*.

1999: Electric energy 21,278 million kWh; Cigarettes (million) 6,176.

2000: Electric energy 22,920 million kWh; Cigarettes (million) 6,855.

2001: Electric energy 24,403 million kWh; Cigarettes (million) 7,918.

Finance

CURRENCY AND EXCHANGE RATES

Monetary Units
100 cent = 1 euro (€).

Sterling and Dollar Equivalents (31 December 2004)
£1 sterling = €1.4180;
US $1 = €0.7341;
€100 = £70.52 = $136.21.

Average Exchange Rate (euros per US $)
2001   1.1175
2002   1.0626
2003   0.8860

Note: The national currency was formerly the Irish pound (or punt). From the introduction of the euro, with Irish participation, on 1 January 1999, a fixed exchange rate of €1 = 78.7564 pence was in operation. Euro notes and coins were introduced on 1 January 2002. The euro and local currency circulated alongside each other until 9 February, after which the euro became the sole legal tender.

BUDGET
(€ million)

Revenue*	2003	2004†	2005‡
Current revenue	41,423	45,995	48,548
Taxes on income and wealth .	14,943	16,758	17,580
Social insurance and health contributions	5,905	6,499	6,909
Taxes on expenditure . . .	17,107	19,267	20,306
Gross trading and investment income	1,415	1,438	1,665
Capital revenue	3,114	3,184	3,242
Taxes on capital	1,650	1,681	1,681
Total	44,537	49,179	51,790

Expenditure§	2003	2004†	2005‡
Current expenditure	38,831	41,257	45,276
Subsidies	831	819	905
National debt interest . . .	1,754	1,741	2,089
Current transfer payments to residents	14,000	15,685	17,055
Current transfer payments to rest of the world	1,245	1,471	1,721
Current expenditure on goods and services (excluding depreciation)	8,077	8,980	9,663
Current expenditure on goods and services by local authorities	11,9230	12,560	13,843
Capital expenditure	6,515	6,574	7,714
Gross fixed capital formation	5,261	5,125	6,189
Total	45,346	47,831	52,990

* Excluding loan repayments and equity sales (€ million): 873 in 2003; 495 in 2004 (provisional); 415 in 2005 (forecast). Also excluding borrowing (€ million): 235 in 2003; −533 in 2004 (provisional); 2,081 in 2005 (forecast).

† Provisional.

‡ Forecast.

§ Excluding debt redemption (€ million): 571 in 2003; 581 in 2004 (provisional); 567 in 2005 (forecast). Also excluding loans and purchase of share capital (€ million): 729 in 2003; 729 in 2004 (provisional); 729 in 2005 (forecast).

Source: Department of Finance.

INTERNATIONAL RESERVES
(US $ million at 31 December)

	2001	2002	2003
Gold*	49	60	73
IMF special drawing rights . .	55	66	79
Reserve position in IMF . . .	336	469	575
Foreign exchange	5,196	4,879	3,425
Total	5,636	5,474	4,152

* Eurosystem valuation.

Source: IMF, *International Financial Statistics*.

MONEY SUPPLY
(€ million at 31 December)

	2001	2002	2003
Currency issued	4,704	4,278*	4,650*
Demand deposits at banking institutions	18,871	19,671	49,721

* Total currency put into circulation by the Central Bank of Ireland was: €6,583m. in 2002; €8,197m. in 2003.

Source: IMF, *International Financial Statistics*.

COST OF LIVING
(Consumer Price Index; base: December 2001 = 100)

	2002	2003	2004
Food and non-alcoholic beverages .	101.7	103.1	102.8
Alcoholic beverages and tobacco .	103.8	114.0	118.0
Clothing and footwear	94.2	90.4	87.2
Housing, water, electricity, gas and other fuel	103.6	103.1	107.5
Furnishings, household equipment and routine household maintenance	99.5	98.8	97.0
Health	105.3	113.4	120.2
Transport	102.9	106.3	110.7
Communications	100.7	102.2	105.0
Recreation and culture	102.7	106.9	108.2
Education	103.9	113.4	120.0
Restaurants and hotels	104.7	111.3	115.7
Miscellaneous goods and services .	104.1	109.0	108.4
All items	102.7	106.3	108.6

NATIONAL ACCOUNTS
(€ million at current prices)

National Income and Product

	2001	2002	2003
Gross domestic product in market prices	115,433	127,992	134,786
Net factor income from abroad .	−18,326	−23,518	−23,115
Gross national product in market prices	97,107	104,474	111,671
Subsidies paid by the EU . . .	1,520	1,896	1,839
Less Taxes paid to the EU . . .	756	488	567
Gross national income in market prices	97,870	105,882	112,943
Net current transfers from abroad (excl. EU subsidies and taxes) .	−569	−699	−832
Gross national disposable income	97,302	105,182	112,111

Expenditure on the Gross Domestic Product

	2001	2002	2003
Government final consumption expenditure	15,474	17,692	19,233
Private final consumption expenditure	54,348	59,019	62,935
Increase in stocks	378	115	499
Gross fixed capital formation . .	27,057	28,983	31,815
Total domestic expenditure .	97,257	105,809	114,482
Exports of goods and services . .	113,642	119,701	112,759
Less Imports of goods and services	96,300	98,508	91,981
Statistical discrepancy	834	990	−474
GDP in market prices . . .	115,433	127,992	134,786
GDP in constant 1995 prices .	88,860	94,310	97,756

Gross Domestic Product by Economic Activity

	2001	2002	2003
Agriculture, forestry and fishing	3,681	3,542	3,577
Mining and quarrying			
Manufacturing			
Electricity, gas and water supply	42,823	47,729	46,259
Construction			
Wholesale and retail trade, repair and hotels and restaurants .			
Transport, storage and communications	16,203	17,899	19,171
Public administration and defence	3,659	3,910	4,205
Other services	41,598	46,317	50,479
Less Financial intermediation services indirectly measured .	3,729	3,870	4,340
Statistical discrepancy . . .	−834	−990	474
Gross value added at factor cost	103,400	114,538	119,825
Taxes (excl. taxes on products) .	977	1,085	1,184
Less Subsidies (excl. subsidies on products)	586	568	527
Gross value added in basic prices	103,791	115,054	120,482
Taxes on products	13,610	15,081	16,479
Less Subsidies on products . .	1,968	2,144	2,175
GDP in market prices . . .	115,433	127,992	134,786

BALANCE OF PAYMENTS
(US $ million)

	2001	2002	2003
Exports of goods f.o.b.	77,623	85,830	87,764
Imports of goods f.o.b.	−50,360	−50,931	−51,451
Trade balance	27,263	34,898	36,313
Exports of services	23,465	28,339	35,892
Imports of services	−35,339	−40,454	−50,234
Balance on goods and services	15,389	22,784	21,971
Other income received	28,850	26,350	31,779
Other income paid	−45,202	−50,819	−57,452
Balance on goods, services and income	−962	−1,730	−3,702
Current transfers received . . .	7,400	7,189	6,833
Current transfers paid	−7,128	−6,384	−6,121
Current balance	−690	−925	−2,990
Capital account (net)	635	575	501
Direct investment abroad . . .	−4,103	−2,963	−1,891
Direct investment from abroad .	9,573	24,698	25,222
Portfolio investment assets . .	−111,347	−106,466	−152,651
Portfolio investment liabilities .	89,085	66,303	105,546
Financial derivatives assets . .	−576	2,183	−2,341
Financial derivatives liabilities .	957	−79	−247
Other investment assets . . .	−21,431	−29,364	−54,989
Other investment liabilities . .	37,859	45,508	81,271
Net errors and omissions . . .	434	240	680
Overall balance	395	−292	−1,890

Source: IMF, *International Financial Statistics.*

External Trade

PRINCIPAL COMMODITIES
(distribution by SITC, € million)

Imports c.i.f.	2001	2002	2003
Food and live animals . . .	3,116.2	3,156.1	3,103.4
Mineral fuels, lubricants, etc. . .	2,218.7	1,841.1	1,800.8
Petroleum and petroleum products	1,729.5	1,477.4	1,466.2
Chemicals and related products	6,340.5	6,861.8	6,848.5
Organic chemicals	1,558.3	1,954.9	1,847.0
Medicinal and pharmaceutical products	1,902.6	2,074.6	2,145.8
Basic manufactures	4,390.7	4,337.2	4,220.0
Machinery and transport equipment	30,224.1	28,301.7	20,725.4
Office machines and automatic data-processing equipment . .	11,269.5	8,442.4	8,018.4
Telecommunications and sound equipment	3,150.2	2,248.2	1,391.2
Other electrical machinery, apparatus, etc.	8,496.0	9,939.2	4,659.9
Road vehicles and parts (excl. tyres, engines and electrical parts) .	3,190.6	3,327.5	2,777.7
Miscellaneous manufactured articles	6,299.7	6,112.4	6,200.8
Total (incl. others)*	57,384.2	55,455.7	47,525.0

* Including transactions not classified by commodity.

Exports f.o.b.	2001	2002	2003
Food and live animals . . .	5,801.1	5,775.1	5,718.5
Chemicals and related products	32,281.4	39,035.8	35,732.4
Organic chemicals	17,117.9	17,383.3	15,365.2
Medical and pharmaceutical products	8,975.1	15,670.2	13,323.9
Essential oils, perfume materials and toilet and cleansing preparations	3,140.9	3,160.5	4,118.7
Machinery and transport equipment	37,606.7	33,137.7	23,400.5
Office machines and automatic data-processing equipment . .	21,034.5	17,309.5	14,795.9
Telecommunications and sound equipment	3,657.6	2,635.8	1,330.3
Electrical machinery, apparatus, etc.	10,164.5	10,559.9	5,127.6
Miscellaneous manufactured articles	8,969.2	8,276.5	9,427.4
Professional, scientific and controlling apparatus . . .	1,881.8	2,061.7	3,268.6
Total (incl. others)*	92,689.9	93,625.6	82,175.5

* Including transactions not classified by commodity.

PRINCIPAL TRADING PARTNERS
(€ million)*

Imports c.i.f.	2001	2002	2003
Belgium	864.4	788.4	742.8
Canada	621.9	423.7	452.0
China, People's Republic . . .	1,085.9	1,493.5	2,214.6
Denmark	725.6	694.1	817.5
Finland	450.1	728.6	261.4
France	2,751.7	2,265.2	1,870.1
Germany	3,520.5	3,564.3	3,439.6
Italy	1,185.4	1,098.6	1,063.6
Japan	1,990.9	1,839.1	2,289.8
Korea, Republic	796.5	889.3	728.1
Malaysia	582.4	674.6	468.4
Netherlands	1,860.0	1,858.8	1,677.6
Norway	942.2	665.9	625.0
Singapore	1,357.0	1,003.5	1,038.7
Spain	645.9	676.9	656.7
Switzerland	530.1	557.5	487.5
Taiwan	1,075.6	997.6	786.0
United Kingdom	20,481.2	20,120.2	14,680.0
USA	8,699.5	8,498.7	7,390.0
Total (incl. others)	57,384.2	55,455.7	47,525.0

Exports f.o.b.	2001	2002	2003
Belgium	4,431.0	13,547.1	10,306.6
France	5,531.5	4,685.4	5,025.4
Germany	11,670.6	6,729.1	6,808.3
Italy	3,309.1	3,597.1	3,738.8
Japan	3,261.1	2,629.3	2,133.6
Malaysia	1,140.3	764.6	577.3
Netherlands	4,236.9	3,597.1	3,738.8
Spain	2,283.3	2,239.7	2,335.2
Sweden	1,354.0	1,202.1	1,184.9
Switzerland	2,705.7	3,115.5	2,662.1
United Kingdom	22,629.8	22,642.9	14,870.2
USA	15,694.4	16,490.1	16,923.8
Total (incl. others)	92,689.9	93,625.6	82,175.5

* Imports by country of origin; exports by country of final destination.

Transport

RAILWAYS
(traffic, '000)

	2001	2002	2003
Passengers carried	34,206	35,370	35,558
Passenger train-km	12,356	n.a.	n.a.
Freight tonnage	2,612	2,246	2,251
Freight train-km	4,133	n.a.	n.a.

ROAD TRAFFIC
(licensed motor vehicles at 31 December)

	1998	1999	2000
Passenger cars	1,196,901	1,269,245	1,319,250
Lorries and vans	170,866	188,814	205,575
Buses and coaches	17,353	19,640	20,594
Motorcycles and mopeds . . .	24,398	26,677	30,638

SHIPPING

Merchant Fleet
(registered at 31 December)

	2001	2002	2003
Number of vessels	193	220	236
Total displacement (grt) . . .	300,289	279,560	471,031

Source: Lloyd's Register-Fairplay, *World Fleet Statistics*.

Sea-borne Freight Traffic
('000 metric tons)*

	2000	2001	2002
Goods loaded	13,594	13,161	12,737
Goods unloaded	31,679	32,634	32,182

* Figures refer to vessels engaged in both international and coastal trade.

CIVIL AVIATION*

	2001	2002	2003
Passengers carried ('000) . . .	18,514	19,313	20,439
Freight (incl. mail) carried (tons) .	202,050	177,685	195,064
Total aircraft movements . . .	284,267	263,653	269,689
Scheduled	182,260	177,656	186,028
Non-scheduled	24,119	25,723	26,292
Cargo	15,702	13,447	12,730

* Figures refer to traffic at Dublin, Cork and Shannon airports.

Tourism

FOREIGN TOURIST ARRIVALS BY ORIGIN
('000)*

	2000	2001	2002
Great Britain	3,893	3,853	4,009
France	283	280	298
Germany	319	285	288
Netherlands	179	182	162
Other continental Europe . . .	655	589	630
USA	958	829	759
Canada	98	74	85
Other areas	261	249	245
Total	6,646	6,353	6,476

* Excluding visitors from Northern Ireland and excursionists.

Tourism receipts (US $ million): 2,608 in 2000; 2,790 in 2001; 3,089 in 2002.

Source: World Tourism Organization.

Communications Media

	2001	2002	2003
Telephone lines ('000 in use) . .	1,860	1,860	1,955
Mobile cellular telephones ('000 subscribers)	2,800	2,969	3,400
Personal computers ('000 in use) .	1,500	1,500	n.a.
Internet users ('000)	895	1,065	1,260
Daily newspapers	6	n.a.	n.a.

1996: Non-daily newspapers 77 (estimated circulation 1,561,000).

1997 (estimates): Radio receivers 2,550,000 in domestic use; Television receivers 1,470,000 in domestic use; Facsimile machines 100,000 (in use).

Source: UNESCO, *Statistical Yearbook,* and International Telecommunication Union.

Education

(2002/03)

	Institutions	Teachers (full-time)	Students (full-time)
National schools* . . .	3,155	24,700	443,720
Secondary schools . . .	410	12,424	189,093
Vocational schools . . .	247	5,685	98,233
Community and comprehensive schools .	89	530	51,905
Teacher (primary and home economics) training colleges	5	56†	1,158
Technology colleges‡ . .	16	3,347†	51,507
Universities and other Higher Education Authority Institutions .	10	3,507†	74,922
Other aided institutions§ .	3	71†	1,696

* National schools are state-aided primary schools.
† 2000/01.
‡ Comprising 14 Institutes of Technology, Tipperary Institute, and the Hotel Training and Catering College, Killybegs, Co Donegal.
§ Refers to the National College of Ireland, Mater Dei Institute and the Pontifical College, Maynooth, Co Kildare.

Source: Department of Education and Science.

Directory

The Constitution

The Constitution took effect on 29 December 1937. Ireland became a republic on 18 April 1949. The following is a summary of the Constitution's main provisions:

TITLE OF THE STATE

The title of the State is Éire or, in the English language, Ireland.

NATIONAL STATUS*

The Constitution declares that Ireland is a sovereign, independent, democratic State. It affirms the inalienable, indefeasible and sovereign right of the Irish nation to choose its own form of government, to determine its relations with other nations, and to develop its life, political, economic and cultural, in accordance with its own genius and traditions.

The Constitution applies to the whole of Ireland, but, pending the reintegration of the national territory, the laws enacted by the Parliament established by the Constitution have the same area and extent of application as those of the Irish Free State.

THE PRESIDENT

At the head of the State is the President, elected by direct suffrage, who holds office for a period of seven years. The President, on the advice of the Government or its head, summons and dissolves Parliament, signs and promulgates laws and appoints judges; on the nomination of the Dáil, the President appoints the Prime Minister (Taoiseach) and, on the nomination of the Prime Minister with the previous approval of the Dáil, the President appoints the other members of the Government. The supreme command of the Defence Forces is vested in the President, its exercise being regulated by law.

In addition, the President has the power to refer certain Bills to the Supreme Court for decision on the question of their constitutionality; and also, at the instance of a prescribed proportion of the members of both Houses of Parliament, to refer certain Bills to the people for decision at a referendum.

The President, in the exercise and performance of certain of his or her constitutional powers and functions, has the aid and advice of a Council of State.

PARLIAMENT

The Oireachtas, or National Parliament, consists of the President and two Houses, viz. a House of Representatives, called Dáil Éireann, and a Senate, called Seanad Éireann. The Dáil consists of 166 members, who are elected for a five-year term by adult suffrage on the system of proportional representation by means of the single, transferable vote. Of the 60 members of the Senate, 11 are nominated by the Prime Minister, six are elected by the universities, and 43 are elected from five panels of candidates established on a vocational basis, representing: national language and culture, literature, art, education and such professional interests as may be defined by law for the purpose of this panel; agriculture and allied interests, and fisheries; labour, whether organized or unorganized; industry and commerce, including banking, finance, accountancy, engineering and architecture; and public administration and social services, including voluntary social activities.

A maximum period of 90 days is afforded to the Senate for the consideration or amendment of Bills sent to that House by the Dáil, but the Senate has no power to veto legislation.

EXECUTIVE

The Executive Power of the State is exercised by the Government, which is responsible to the Dáil and consists of not fewer than seven and not more than 15 members. The head of the Government is the Prime Minister.

FUNDAMENTAL RIGHTS

The State recognizes the family as the natural, primary and fundamental unit group of Society, possessing inalienable and imprescriptible rights antecedent and superior to all positive law. It acknowledges the right to life of the unborn and, with due regard to the equal right to life of the mother, guarantees in its laws to defend and vindicate that right. It acknowledges the right and duty of parents to provide for the education of their children, and, with due regard to that right, undertakes to provide free education. It pledges itself also to guard with special care the institution of marriage.

The Constitution contains special provision for the recognition and protection of the fundamental rights of citizens, such as personal liberty, free expression of opinion, peaceable assembly, and the formation of associations and unions.

Freedom of conscience and the free practice and profession of religion are, subject to public order and morality, guaranteed to every citizen. No religion may be endowed or subjected to discriminatory disability. Since December 1972, when a referendum was taken on the issue, the Catholic Church has no longer enjoyed a special, privileged position.

SOCIAL POLICY

Certain principles of social policy intended for the general guidance of Parliament, but not cognizable by the courts, are set forth in the Constitution. Among their objects are the direction of the policy of the State towards securing the distribution of property so as to subserve the common good, the regulation of credit so as to serve the welfare of the people as a whole, the establishment of families in economic security on the land, and the right to an adequate means of livelihood for all citizens.

The State pledges itself to safeguard the interests, and to contribute where necessary to the support, of the infirm, the widow, the orphan and the aged, and shall endeavour to ensure that citizens shall not be forced by economic necessity to enter occupations unsuited to their sex, age or strength.

AMENDMENT OF THE CONSTITUTION

No amendment to the Constitution can be effected except by the decision of the people given at a referendum.

*Under the terms of the Good Friday Agreement, signed in April 1998 and approved by referendum in May, provision was made for a change to the Constitution to enshrine the principle that a united Ireland could be achieved only with the agreement and consent of the majority of the people of both Ireland and Northern Ireland. Accordingly, Articles 2 and 3 of the Constitution, which lay claim to the territory of Northern Ireland, were removed on 2 December 1999.

The Government

HEAD OF STATE

Uachtarán (President): Dr MARY McALEESE (assumed office 11 November 1997; re-elected unopposed 1 October 2004, inaugurated for second term in office 11 November 2004).

THE CABINET
(April 2005)

A coalition of Fianna Fáil (FF) and the Progressive Democrats (PD).

Taoiseach (Prime Minister): BERTIE AHERN (FF).

Tánaiste (Deputy Prime Minister) and Minister for Health and Children: MARY HARNEY (PD).

Minister for Defence: WILLIE O'DEA (FF).

Minister for Agriculture and Food: MARY COUGHLAN (FF).

Minister for Finance: BRIAN COWEN (FF).

Minister for Foreign Affairs: DERMOT AHERN (FF).

Minister for Education and Science: MARY HANAFIN (FF).

Minister for Communications, Marine and Natural Resources: NOEL DEMPSEY (FF).

Minister for Arts, Sport and Tourism: JOHN O'DONOGHUE (FF).

Minister for Enterprise, Trade and Employment: MICHEÁL MARTIN (FF).

Minister for Transport: MARTIN CULLEN (FF).

Minister for Justice, Equality and Law Reform: MICHAEL McDOWELL (PD).

Minister for the Environment, Heritage and Local Government: DICK ROCHE (FF).

Minister for Community, Rural and Gaeltacht Affairs: ÉAMON Ó CUÍV (FF).

Minister for Social and Family Affairs: SÉAMUS BRENNAN (FF).

In addition there are 17 Ministers of State.

MINISTRIES

Office of the President: Áras an Uachtaráin, Phoenix Park, Dublin 8; tel. (1) 6171000; fax (1) 6171001; e-mail webmaster@aras.irlgov.ie; internet www.irlgov.ie/aras.

Department of the Taoiseach: Government Bldgs, Upper Merrion St, Dublin 2; tel. (1) 6624888; fax (1) 6789791; e-mail webmaster@taoiseach.gov.ie; internet www.taoiseach.gov.ie.

Department of Agriculture and Food: Agriculture House, Kildare St, Dublin 2; tel. (1) 6072000; fax (1) 6616263; e-mail info@agriculture.gov.ie; internet www.agriculture.gov.ie.

Department of Arts, Sports and Tourism: 23 Kildare St, Dublin 2; tel. (1) 6313800; fax (1) 6611201; internet www.arts-sports-tourism.gov.ie.

Department of Communications, Marine and Natural Resources: 29–31 Adelaide Road, Dublin 2; tel. (1) 6782000; fax (1) 6782449; e-mail contact@marine.gov.ie; internet www.marine.gov.ie.

Department of Community, Rural and Gaeltacht Affairs: Dún Aimhirgin, 43–49 Mespil Rd, Dublin 4; tel. (1) 6473000; fax (1) 6670826; e-mail eolas@pobail.ie; internet www.pobail.ie.

Department of Defence: Parkgate, Infirmary Rd, Dublin 7; tel. (1) 8042000; fax (1) 6703399; e-mail webmaster@defence.irlgov.ie; internet www.defence.ie.

Department of Education and Science: Marlborough St, Dublin 1; tel. (1) 8896400; fax (1) 8892367; e-mail info@education.gov.ie; internet www.education.ie.

Department of Enterprise, Trade and Employment: 23 Kildare St, Dublin 2; tel. (1) 6312121; fax (1) 6312827; e-mail info@entemp.ie; internet www.entemp.ie.

Department of the Environment, Heritage and Local Government: Custom House, Dublin 1; tel. (1) 8882000; fax (1) 8882888; e-mail press-office@environ.ie; internet www.environ.ie.

Department of Finance: Government Bldgs, Upper Merrion St, Dublin 2; tel. (1) 6767571; fax (1) 6789936; e-mail webmaster@finance.irlgov.ie; internet www.finance.gov.ie.

Department of Foreign Affairs: 80 St Stephen's Green, Dublin 2; tel. (1) 4780822; fax (1) 4781484; e-mail library1@iveagh.irlgov.ie; internet foreignaffairs.gov.ie.

Department of Health and Children: Hawkins House, Hawkins St, Dublin 2; tel. (1) 6354000; fax (1) 6354001; e-mail info@health.irlgov.ie; internet www.dohc.ie.

Department of Justice, Equality and Law Reform: 94 St Stephen's Green, Dublin 2; tel. (1) 6028202; fax (1) 6615461; e-mail info@justice.ie; internet www.justice.ie.

Department of Social and Family Affairs: Áras Mhic Dhiarmada, Store St, Dublin 1; tel. (1) 7043000; fax (1) 7043870; e-mail press.office@welfare.ie; internet www.welfare.ie.

Department of Transport: 44 Kildare St, Dublin 2; tel. (1) 6707444; fax (1) 6041185; e-mail info@transport.ie; internet www.transport.ie.

Legislature

OIREACHTAS (NATIONAL PARLIAMENT)

Parliament comprises two Houses—Dáil Éireann (House of Representatives), with 166 members (Teachtaí Dála), elected for a five-year term by universal adult suffrage, and Seanad Éireann (Senate), with 60 members serving a five-year term, of whom 11 are nominated by the Taoiseach (Prime Minister) and 49 elected (six by the universities and 43 from specially constituted panels).

Dáil Éireann

Ceann Comhairle (Chairman): Dr RORY O'HANLON (Fianna Fáil).

Leas-Cheann Comhairle (Deputy Chairman): SÉAMUS PATTISON (Labour Party).

General Election, 17 May 2002

Party	Votes*	% of votes*	Seats
Fianna Fáil	770,846	41.49	81
Fine Gael	417,653	22.48	31
Labour Party	200,138	10.77	21
Progressive Democrats . . .	73,628	3.96	8
Green Party	71,480	3.85	6
Sinn Féin	121,039	6.51	5
Others	203,329	10.94	14
Total	1,788,985	100.00	166

*The election was conducted by means of the single transferable vote. Figures refer to first-preference votes.

Seanad Éireann

Cathaoirleach (Chairman): RORY KIELY (Fianna Fáil).

Leas-Chathaoirleach (Deputy Chairman): PADDY BURKE (Fine Gael).

Election, July 2002 (11 non-affiliated members nominated)

Party	Seats at election
Fianna Fáil	30
Fine Gael	15
Independents	5
Labour Party	5
Progressive Democrats	4
Others	1

Political Organizations

Christian Solidarity Party: 14 North Frederick Street, Dublin 1, POB 9646; tel. (1) 8783529; fax (1) 8783529; internet www .comharcriostai.org; Chair. CATHAL LOFTUS; Nat. Sec. MICHAEL F MAGUIRE.

Comhaontas Glas (Green Party): 5A Upper Fownes St, Temple Bar, Dublin 2; tel. (1) 6790012; fax (1) 6797168; e-mail info@greenparty .ie; internet www.greenparty.ie; fmrly The Ecology Party; advocates a humane, ecological society, freedom of information and political decentralization; Pres. JOHN GORMLEY; Leader TREVOR SARGENT.

Communist Party of Ireland: James Connolly House, 43 East Essex St, Dublin 2; tel. and fax (1) 6711943; e-mail cpoi@eircom.net; internet www.communistpartyofireland.ie; f. 1933; advocates a united, socialist, independent Ireland; Chair. JAMES STEWART; Gen. Sec. EUGENE MCCARTAN.

Fianna Fáil (Republican Party): 65–66 Lower Mount St, Dublin 2; tel. (1) 6761551; fax (1) 6785690; e-mail info@fiannafail.ie; internet www.fiannafail.ie; f. 1926; centrist; Pres. and Leader BERTIE AHERN; Gen. Sec. SEÁN DORGAN.

Fine Gael (United Ireland Party): 51 Upper Mount St, Dublin 2; tel. (1) 6198444; fax (1) 6625046; e-mail finegael@finegael.com; internet www.finegael.ie; f. 1933; centrist; Pres. and Leader ENDA KENNY; Gen. Sec. TOM CURRAN.

The Labour Party: 17 Ely Place, Dublin 2; tel. (1) 6784700; fax (1) 6612640; e-mail head_office@labour.ie; internet www.labour.ie; f. 1912; merged with Democratic Left (f. 1992) in 1999; democratic socialist party; affiliated to the Party of European Socialists; Pres. MICHAEL D. HIGGINS; Leader PAT RABBITE; Gen. Sec. MIKE ALLEN.

Muintir na hÉireann Pairti: 58 The Palms, Roebuck Rd, Dublin 14; tel. and fax (1) 2831484; e-mail rnvelgreene@eircom.net; f. 1995; Christian conservative; Leader RICHARD GREENE.

Progressive Democrats: 25 South Frederick St, Dublin 2; tel. (1) 6794399; fax (1) 6794757; e-mail info@progressivedemocrats.ie; internet www.progressivedemocrats.ie; f. 1985 by fmr mems of Fianna Fáil; affiliated to the Liberal parties of Europe; Pres. MICHAEL MCDOWELL; Chair. NOEL GREALISH; Leader MARY HARNEY; Gen. Sec. JOHN HIGGINS.

Sinn Féin (Ourselves Alone): 44 Parnell Sq., Dublin 1; tel. (1) 8726100; fax (1) 8783595; e-mail sfadmin@eircom.net; internet www .sinnfein.ie; f. 1905; advocates the termination of British rule in Northern Ireland; seeks a mandate to establish a democratic socialist republic in a reunified Ireland; Pres. GERRY ADAMS; Chair. MITCHEL MCLAUGHLIN.

The Workers' Party: 23 Hill St, Dublin 1; tel. (1) 8740716; fax (1) 8748702; e-mail wpi@indigo.ie; internet www.workers-party.org; f.

1905; fmrly Sinn Féin The Workers' Party; aims to establish a unitary socialist state on the island of Ireland; Pres. SEAN GARLAND; Gen. Sec. JOHN LOWRY.

Diplomatic Representation

EMBASSIES IN IRELAND

Argentina: 15 Ailesbury Dr., Dublin 4; tel. (1) 2691546; fax (1) 2600404; e-mail argembsy@indigo.ie; Ambassador MARCELO HUERGO.

Australia: Fitzwilton House, 7th Floor, Wilton Terrace, Dublin 2; tel. (1) 6645300; fax (1) 6785185; e-mail austremb.dublin@dfat.gov .au; internet www.australianembassy.ie; Ambassador Dr JOHN HERRON.

Austria: 15 Ailesbury Court, 93 Ailesbury Rd, Dublin 4; tel. (1) 2694577; fax (1) 2830860; e-mail dublin-ob@bmaa.gv.at; Ambassador Dr HARALD MILTNER.

Belgium: 2 Shrewsbury Rd, Dublin 4; tel. (1) 2057100; fax (1) 2057106; e-mail dublin@diplobel.org; internet www.diplomatie.be/ dublin; Ambassador WILFRED GEENS.

Brazil: 5th Floor, HSBC House, Harcourt St, Dublin 2; tel. (1) 4756000; fax (1) 4751341; e-mail brasembdublin@brazil-ie.org; internet www.brazil.ie; Ambassador STÉLIO MARCOS AMARANTE.

Bulgaria: 22 Burlington Rd, Dublin 4; tel. (1) 6603293; fax (1) 6603915; e-mail bgemb@eircom.net; Ambassador BISSERKA BENISHEVA.

Canada: 65–68 St Stephen's Green, Dublin 2; tel. (1) 4174100; fax (1) 4174101; e-mail dubln@dfait-maeci.gc.ca; internet www.canada .ie; Ambassador MARK J. MOHER.

China, People's Republic: 40 Ailesbury Rd, Dublin 4; tel. (1) 2691707; fax (1) 2839938; internet www.chinaembassy.ie; Ambassador SHA HAILIN.

Cyprus: 71 Lower Leeson St, Dublin 2; tel. (1) 6763060; fax (1) 6763099; e-mail embassyofcyprusdub@eircom.net; Ambassador ANDREAS KAKOURIS.

Czech Republic: 57 Northumberland Rd, Ballsbridge, Dublin 4; tel. (1) 6681135; fax (1) 6681660; e-mail dublin@embassy.mzv.cz; internet www.mfa.cz/dublin; Ambassador JOSEF HAVLAS.

Denmark: 121–122 St Stephen's Green, Dublin 2; tel. (1) 4756404; fax (1) 4784536; e-mail dubamb@um.dk; internet www.ambdublin .um.dk; Ambassador K. ERIK TYGESEN.

Egypt: 12 Clyde Rd, Ballsbridge, Dublin 4; tel. (1) 6606566; fax (1) 6683745; e-mail embegypt@indigo.ie; internet www .embegyptireland.ie; Ambassador IBRAHIM KHAIRAT.

Estonia: Riversdale House, St Ann's, Ailsesbury Rd, Dublin 4; tel. (1) 2196730; fax (1) 2196731; e-mail embassy.dublin@mfa.ee; Ambassador SIMMU TIIK.

Finland: Russell House, Stokes Place, St Stephen's Green, Dublin 2; tel. (1) 4781344; fax (1) 4783727; e-mail pekka.oinonen@formin.fi; internet www.finland.ie; Ambassador PEKKA OINONEN.

France: 36 Ailesbury Rd, Ballsbridge, Dublin 4; tel. (1) 2775000; fax (1) 2775001; e-mail chancellerie@ambafrance.ie; internet www .ambafrance.ie; Ambassador FRÉDÉRIC GRASSET.

Germany: 31 Trimleston Ave, Booterstown, Blackrock, Co Dublin; tel. (1) 2693011; fax (1) 2693946; e-mail germany@indigo.ie; internet www.germany.ie; Ambassador Dr GOTTFRIED HAAS.

Greece: 1 Upper Pembroke St, Dublin 2; tel. (1) 6767254; fax (1) 6618892; e-mail embgr@eircom.net; Ambassador STELIOS MALLI-KOURTIS.

Holy See: 183 Navan Rd, Dublin 7 (Apostolic Nunciature); tel. (1) 8380577; fax (1) 8380276; e-mail nuncioirl@eircom.net; Apostolic Nuncio Most Rev. GIUSEPPE LAZZAROTTO (Titular Archbishop of Numana).

Hungary: 2 Fitzwilliam Place, Dublin 2; tel. (1) 6612902; fax (1) 6612880; e-mail Hungarian.embassy@eircom.net; internet www .kum.hu/dublin; Ambassador Dr JÁNOS BALASSA.

India: 6 Leeson Park, Dublin 6; tel. (1) 4970843; fax (1) 4978074; e-mail indembassy@eircom.net; Ambassador SAURABH KUMAR.

Iran: 72 Mount Merrion Ave, Blackrock, Co Dublin; tel. (1) 2880252; fax (1) 2834246; Ambassador SEYED HOSSEIN MIRFAKHAR.

Israel: 122 Pembroke Rd, Dublin 4; tel. (1) 2309400; fax (1) 2309446; e-mail info@dublin.mfa.gov.il; internet www.mfa.gov.il; Ambassador DANIEL MEGIDDO.

Italy: 63–65 Northumberland Rd, Dublin 4; tel. (1) 6601744; fax (1) 6682759; e-mail ambasciata.dublimo@esteri.it; internet www .italianembassy.ie; Ambassador Dr ALBERTO SCHEPISI.

Japan: Nutley Bldg, Merrion Centre, Nutley Lane, Dublin 4; tel. (1) 2028300; fax (1) 2838726; e-mail cultural@embjp.ie; internet www.ie .emb-japan.go.jp; Ambassador TAKESHI KAGAMI.

Korea, Republic: Clyde House, 15 Clyde Rd, Ballsbridge, POB 2101, Dublin 4; tel. (1) 6608800; fax (1) 6608716; Ambassador YANG LEE.

Lithuania: 90 Merrion Road, Ballsbridge, Dublin 4; tel. (1) 6688292; fax (1) 6680004; Ambassador IZOLDA BRIČKOVSKIENE.

Mexico: 43 Ailesbury Rd, Dublin 4; tel. (1) 2600699; fax (1) 2600411; e-mail embasmex@indigo.ie; internet www.sre.gob.mx/irlanda; Ambassador CECILIA JABER BRECEDA.

Morocco: 39 Raglan Rd, Ballsbridge, Dublin 4; tel. (1) 6609449; fax (1) 6609468; e-mail sifamdub@indigo.ie; Chargé d'affaires MINA TOUNSI.

Netherlands: 160 Merrion Rd, Dublin 4; tel. (1) 2693444; fax (1) 2839690; e-mail info@netherlandsembassy.ie; internet www .netherlandsembassy.ie; Ambassador JACOBUS VAN DER VELDEN.

Nigeria: 56 Leeson Park, Dublin 6; tel. (1) 6604366; fax (1) 6604092; Chargé d'affaires a.i. Dr OBIOMA P. OPARAH.

Norway: 34 Molesworth St, Dublin 2; tel. (1) 6621800; fax (1) 6621890; e-mail emb.dublin@mfa.no; internet www.norway.ie; Ambassador TRULS HANEVOLD.

Poland: 5 Ailesbury Rd, Dublin 4; tel. (1) 2830855; fax (1) 2698309; e-mail polembas@iol.ie; internet www.polishembassy.ie; Ambassador WITOLD SOBKÓW.

Portugal: Knocksinna Mews, 7 Willow Park/Westminster Park, Foxrock, Dublin 18; tel. (1) 2894416; fax (1) 2892849; e-mail embpordub@yahoo.co.uk; Ambassador FERNANDO D'OLIVEIRA NEVES.

Romania: 26 Waterloo Rd, Dublin 4; tel. (1) 6681085; fax (1) 6681761; e-mail ambrom@eircom.net; Ambassador SILVIA DAVIDOIU STANCU.

Russia: 186 Orwell Rd, Dublin 14; tel. (1) 4922048; fax (1) 4923525; e-mail russiane@indigo.ie; internet www.ireland.mid.ru; Ambassador VLADIMIR OLEGOVICH RAKHMANIN.

Slovakia: 20 Clyde Rd, Ballsbridge, Dublin 4; tel. (1) 6600012; fax (1) 6600014; e-mail slovak@iol.ie; Ambassador JÁN GÁBOR.

South Africa: Alexandra House, Earlsfort Terrace, Dublin 2; tel. (1) 6615553; fax (1) 6615590; e-mail information@saedublin.com; Ambassador MELANIE VERWOERD.

Spain: 17A Merlyn Park, Dublin 4; tel. (1) 2691640; fax (1) 2691854; e-mail embespie@mail.mae.es; internet www.mae.es/embajadas/ dublin; Ambassador JOSÉ DE CARVAJAL SALIDO.

Sweden: 13–17 Dawson St, Dublin 2; tel. (1) 6715822; fax (1) 6796718; e-mail ambassaden.dublin@foreign.ministry.se; internet www.swedenabroad.com/dublin; Ambassador NILS DAAG.

Switzerland: 6 Ailesbury Rd, Dublin 4; tel. (1) 2186382; fax (1) 2830344; e-mail vertretung@dub.rep.admin.ch; internet www .swissembassy.ie; Ambassador JOSEF DOSWALD.

Turkey: 11 Clyde Rd, Dublin 4; tel. (1) 6685240; fax (1) 6685014; e-mail turkembassy@eircom.net; Ambassador AHMET BERKI DIBEK.

United Kingdom: 29 Merrion Rd, Dublin 4; tel. (1) 2053700; fax (1) 2053885; internet www.britishembassy.ie; Ambassador STEWART ELDON.

USA: 42 Elgin Rd, Ballsbridge, Dublin 4; tel. (1) 6687777; fax (1) 6689946; internet dublin.usembassy.gov; Ambassador JAMES C. KENNY.

Judicial System

Justice is administered in public by judges appointed by the President on the advice of the Government. The judges of all courts are completely independent in the exercise of their judicial functions. The jurisdiction and organization of the courts are dealt with in the Courts (Establishment and Constitution) Act, 1961, and the Courts (Supplemental Provisions) Acts, 1961 to 1981.

Attorney-General: RORY BRADY.

SUPREME COURT

An Chúirt Uachtarach
(The Supreme Court)

Four Courts, Dublin 7; tel. (1) 8886000; fax (1) 8732332; internet www.courts.ie.

Consisting of the Chief Justice and seven other judges, has appellate jurisdiction from all decisions of the High Court. The President of Ireland may, after consultation with the Council of State, refer a bill that has been passed by both Houses of the Oireachtas (other than a money bill or certain others), to the Supreme Court to establish whether it or any other provisions thereof are repugnant to the Constitution. The President of the High Court is *ex officio* a member of the Supreme Court.

Chief Justice: JOHN L. MURRAY.

Judges: SUSAN DENHAM, CATHERINE MCGUINNESS, ADRIAN HARDIMAN, HUGH GEOGHEGAN, NIAL FENNELLY, BRIAN MCCRACKEN, NICHOLAS KEARNS.

COURT OF CRIMINAL APPEAL

The Court of Criminal Appeal, consisting of the Chief Justice or an ordinary judge of the Supreme Court and two judges of the High Court, deals with appeals by persons convicted on indictment, where leave to appeal has been granted. The Court has jurisdiction to review a conviction or sentence on the basis of an alleged miscarriage of justice. The Director of Public Prosecutions may appeal against an unduly lenient sentence. The decision of the Court of Criminal Appeal is final unless the Court or Attorney-General or the Director of Public Prosecutions certifies that a point of law involved should, in the public interest, be taken to the Supreme Court.

HIGH COURT

An Ard-Chúirt
(The High Court)

Four Courts, Dublin 7; tel. (1) 8886000; fax (1) 8725669; internet www.courts.ie.

Consists of the President of the High Court and 28 ordinary judges (this number may be increased to 29 in the case of a serving High Court judge being appointed President of the Law Reform Commission), has full original jurisdiction in, and power to determine, all matters and questions whether of law or fact, civil or criminal. The High Court on circuit acts as an appeal court from the Circuit Court. The Central Criminal Court sits as directed by the President of the High Court to try criminal cases outside the jurisdiction of the Circuit Court. The duty of acting as the Central Criminal Court is assigned, for the time being, to a judge of the High Court. The Chief Justice and the President of the Circuit Court are *ex officio* additional Judges of the High Court.

President: JOSEPH FINNEGAN.

Judges: MELLA CARROLL, RICHARD JOHNSON, VIVIAN LAVAN, PAUL J. P. CARNEY, DECLAN BUDD (also President of the Law Reform Commission), MARY LAFFOY, MICHAEL MORIARTY, PETER KELLY, THOMAS C. SMYTH, DIARMUID B. D. O'DONOVAN, PHILIP O'SULLIVAN, KEVIN C. O'HIGGINS, JOHN QUIRKE, FRANK CLARKE, IARFHLAITH O'NEILL, RODERICK MURPHY, DANIEL HERBERT, PAUL BUTLER, LIAM MCKECHNIE, HENRY ABBOTT, EAMON DE VALERA, MARY FINLAY GEOGHEGAN, MICHAEL PEART, BARRY WHITE, PAUL GILLIGAN, SEAN RYAN, SEÁN O'LEARY, JOHN MACMENAMIN, ELIZABETH DUNNE, MICHAEL HANNA, FIDELMA MACKEN.

Master of the High Court: EDMUND HONOHAN.

CIRCUIT AND DISTRICT COURTS

The civil jurisdiction of the Circuit Court is limited to €100,000 in contract and tort and in actions founded on hire-purchase and credit-sale agreements and to a rateable value of €254 in equity, and in probate and administration, but where the parties consent the jurisdiction is unlimited. In criminal matters the Court has jurisdiction in all cases except murder, rape, treason, piracy and allied offences. One circuit court judge is permanently assigned to each of the circuits outside Dublin with the exception of Cork, which has three judges. Dublin has 10 permanent judges. In addition there are eight permanently unassigned judges. The President of the District Court is *ex officio* an additional Judge of the Circuit Court. The Circuit Court acts as an appeal court from the District Court, which has a summary jurisdiction in a large number of criminal cases where the offence is not of a serious nature. In civil matters the District Court has jurisdiction in contract and tort (except slander, libel, seduction, slander of title, malicious prosecution and false imprisonment) where the claim does not exceed €20,000 and in actions founded on hire-purchase and credit-sale agreements.

All criminal cases, except those dealt with summarily by a judge in the District Court, are tried by a judge and a jury of 12 members. Juries are also used in some civil cases in the High Court. In a criminal case 10 members of the jury may, in certain circumstances, agree on a verdict, and in a civil case the agreement of nine members is sufficient.

President of the Circuit Court: ESMOND SMYTH.

President of the District Court: PETER A. SMITHWICK.

Religion

CHRISTIANITY

The organization of the churches takes no account of the partition of Ireland into two separate political entities; both the Republic of Ireland and Northern Ireland are subject to a unified ecclesiastical jurisdiction. The Roman Catholic Primate of All Ireland and the Church of Ireland (Protestant Episcopalian) Primate of All Ireland have their seats in Northern Ireland, at Armagh, and the headquarters of the Presbyterian Church in Ireland is at Belfast, Northern Ireland.

At 31 December 2002 there were 5,316,812 adherents of the Roman Catholic Church, representing some 77% of the population. In late 2003 there were some 300,000 adherents of the Presbyterian Church and 70,000 of the Methodist Church. In 2004 there were some 350,000 adherents of the Church of Ireland.

Irish Council of Churches: Inter-Church Centre, 48 Elmwood Ave, Belfast, BT9 6AZ, Northern Ireland; tel. (28) 90663145; fax (28) 90664160; e-mail irish.churches@btconnect.com; internet www.irishchurches.org; f. 1922; present name adopted 1966; 14 mem. churches; Pres. Maj. RIK PEARS; Gen. Sec. MICHAEL EARLE.

The Roman Catholic Church

Ireland (including Northern Ireland) comprises four archdioceses and 22 dioceses.

Archbishop of Armagh and Primate of All Ireland: Most Rev. SEÁN B. BRADY, Ara Coeli, Cathedral Rd, Armagh, BT61 7QY, Northern Ireland; tel. (28) 3752-2045; fax (28) 3752-6182; e-mail admin@aracoeli.com; internet www.armagharchdiocese.org.

Archbishop of Cashel and Emly: Most Rev. DERMOT CLIFFORD, Archbishop's House, Thurles, Co Tipperary; tel. (504) 21512; fax (504) 22680; e-mail cashelemly@eircom.net; internet www.cashel-emly.ie.

Archbishop of Dublin and Primate of Ireland: Most Rev. Dr DIARMUID MARTIN, Archbishop's House, Drumcondra, Dublin 9; tel. (1) 8373732; fax (1) 8369796; internet www.dublindiocese.ie.

Archbishop of Tuam: Most Rev. MICHAEL NEARY, Archbishop's House, St Jarlath's, Tuam, Co Galway; tel. (93) 24166; fax (93) 28070; e-mail info@towardsthegoal.com; internet www.towardsthegoal.com.

Numerous Roman Catholic religious orders are strongly established in the country. These play an important role, particularly in the spheres of education, health and social welfare.

Church of Ireland
(The Anglican Communion)

Ireland (including Northern Ireland) comprises two archdioceses and 10 dioceses.

Central Office of the Church of Ireland

Church of Ireland House, Church Ave, Dublin 6; tel. (1) 4978422; fax (1) 4978821; e-mail office@rcbdub.org; internet www.ireland.anglican.org/rcb.html.

346,000 mems (2000); Chief Officer and Sec. to the Representative Church Body D. C. REARDON.

Archbishop of Armagh and Primate of All Ireland and Metropolitan: Most Rev. Lord EAMES, The See House, Cathedral Close, Armagh, BT61 7EE, Northern Ireland; tel. (28) 37527144; fax (28) 37527823; e-mail archbishop@armagh.anglican.org.

Archbishop of Dublin and Primate of Ireland and Metropolitan: Most Rev. Dr JOHN R. W. NEILL, The See House, 17 Temple Rd, Milltown, Dublin 6; tel. (1) 4977849; fax (1) 4976355; e-mail archbishop@dublin.anglian.org.

Orthodox Churches

Greek Orthodox Church in Ireland: Sacred Church of the Annunciation, 46 Arbour Hill, Dublin 7; Pres. Very Rev. Dr IRENEU IOAN CRACIUN.

Russian Orthodox Church (Moscow Patriarchate) in Ireland: Harold's Cross Rd, Dublin 6W; tel. (1) 4969038; e-mail rvgeorge@utvinternet.com; internet stpeterstpaul.net; Priest of Parish Dean Fr MICHAEL GOGOLEFF; Resident Priest Fr GEORGE ZAVERSHINSKY.

Other Christian Churches

Association of Baptist Churches in Ireland: The Baptist Centre, 19 Hillsborough Rd, Moira, BT67 0HG, Northern Ireland; tel. (28) 9261-9267; fax (28) 9261-0150; e-mail abc@thebaptistcentre.org; internet www.baptistireland.org; Pres. J. GRAHAM; Sec. Pastor W. COLVILLE.

Church of Jesus Christ of Latter-day Saints (Mormon): The Willows, Glasnevin, Dublin 11; tel. (1) 8306899; fax (1) 8304638.

Lutheran Church in Ireland: Lutherhaus, 24 Adelaide Rd, Dublin 2; tel. and fax (1) 6766548; e-mail lutheranchurch@eircom.net; Pres. Pastor Rev. FRITZ-GERT MAYER.

Methodist Church in Ireland: 1 Fountainville Ave, Belfast, BT9 6AN, Northern Ireland; tel. (28) 9032-4554; fax (28) 9023-9467; e-mail secretary@irishmethodist.org; internet www.irishmethodist.org; Pres. Rev. DESMOND C. BAIN.

Moravian Church in Ireland: 25 Church Rd, Gracehill, Ballymena, BT42 2NL, Northern Ireland; tel. (28) 2565-3141; f. 1749; Chair. of Conf. Rev. G. I. DAVID.

Non-Subscribing Presbyterian Church of Ireland: Central Hall, 41 Rosemary St, Belfast, Northern Ireland; tel. (28) 9084-3592; Clerk to Gen. Synod Rev. NIGEL PLAYFAIR.

Presbyterian Church in Ireland: Church House, Fisherwick Place, Belfast, BT1 6DW, Northern Ireland; tel. (28) 9032-2284; fax (28) 9041-7301; e-mail info@presbyterianireland.org; internet www.presbyterianireland.org; Moderator of Gen. Assembly Rev. Dr KENNETH NEWELL; Clerk of Assembly and Gen. Sec. Rev. Dr DONALD WATTS.

The Religious Society of Friends: Swanbrook House, Bloomfield Ave, Morehampton Rd, Dublin 4; tel. and fax (1) 6683684; internet www.ipag.com/quakers; Registrar VALERIE O'BRIEN.

Salvation Army: POB 2098, Dublin Central Mission, Lower Abbey St, Dublin 1; tel. (1) 8740987; fax (1) 8747478; Divisional Dir Capt. HOWARD RUSSELL.

BAHÁ'Í FAITH

National Spiritual Assembly: 24 Burlington Rd, Dublin 4; tel. (1) 6683150; fax (1) 6689632; e-mail nsairl@iol.ie; internet www.bahai.ie.

ISLAM

The Muslim population of the Republic of Ireland was enumerated at 3,875 in the 1991 census. The number of adherents was estimated to total 9,000 in 1996, inclusive of Northern Ireland.

Islamic Cultural Centre of Ireland: 19 Roebuck Rd, Clonskeagh, Dublin 14; tel. (1) 2080000; fax (1) 2080001; e-mail info@iccislam.org; internet www.iccislam.org; f. 1996; Dir Dr NOOH AL-KADDO, Imam Sheikh HUSSEIN HALAWA.

Islamic Foundation of Ireland: 163 South Circular Rd, Dublin 8; tel. (1) 4533242; fax (1) 4532785; e-mail ifi@indigo.ie; internet www.islaminireland.com; f. 1959; religious, cultural, educational and social organization; Imam YAHYA MUHAMMAD AL-HUSSEIN.

JUDAISM

The Jewish community was estimated to number 1,200 in 1996.

Chief Rabbi: Dr YAAKOV PEARLMAN, Herzog House, Zion Rd, Rathgar, Dublin 6; tel. (1) 4923751; fax (1) 4924680; e-mail irishcom@iol.ie.

The Press

A significant feature of the Irish press is the number of weekly newspapers published in provincial centres.

DAILIES

Cork

Evening Echo: 1–6 Academy St, Cork; tel. (21) 4272722; fax (21) 4275112; e-mail echo.ed@eecho.ie; internet www.eecho.ie; f. 1892; Editor MAURICE GUBBINS; circ. 28,822.

Irish Examiner: Academy St, POB 21, Cork; tel. (21) 272722; fax (21) 275112; e-mail features@examiner.ie; internet www.examiner.ie; f. 1841; Editor TIM VAUGHAN; circ. 57,000.

Dublin

Evening Herald: Independent House, 90 Middle Abbey St, Dublin 1; tel. (1) 8731666; fax (1) 8731787; e-mail herald.news@independent.ie; f. 1891; Editor GERARD O'REGAN; circ. 115,000.

Irish Independent: Independent House, 90 Middle Abbey St, Dublin 1; tel. (1) 7055333; fax (1) 8720304; internet www.independent.ie; f. 1905; Editor VINCENT DOYLE; circ. 170,000.

The Irish Times: 10–16 D'Olier St, POB 74, Dublin 2; tel. (1) 6792022; fax (1) 6793910; e-mail itemail@irish-times.com; internet www.ireland.com; f. 1859; Editor GERALDINE KENNEDY; circ. 119,252.

The Star: Star House, 62A Terenure Rd North, Dublin 6; tel. (1) 4901228; fax (1) 4902193; Editor GERARD O'REAGAN; circ. 85,000.

PRINCIPAL WEEKLY NEWSPAPERS

An Phoblacht/Republican News: 58 Parnell Sq., Dublin 1; tel. (1) 8733611; fax (1) 8733074; e-mail aprn@eircom.net; internet www .anphoblacht.com; f. 1970; Editor MARTIN SPAIN; circ. 20,000.

Anglo-Celt: Anglo-Celt Pl., Cavan; tel. (49) 4331100; fax (49) 4332280; internet www.unison.ie/anglo_celt; f. 1846; Fri.; Editor J. F. O'HANLON; circ. 16,000.

Argus: Park St, Dundalk, Co Louth; tel. (42) 9331500; fax (42) 9331643; internet www.unison.ie/the_argus; f. 1835; Thurs.; Editor KEVIN MULLIGAN; circ. 11,230.

Clare Champion: Barrack St, Ennis, Co Clare; tel. (65) 6828105; fax (65) 6820374; e-mail editor@clarechampion.ie; internet www .clarechampion.ie; f. 1903; Thurs.; Man. Dir JOHN GALVIN; Editor GERRY COLLISON; circ. 20,000.

Connacht Tribune: 15 Market St, Galway; tel. (91) 536222; fax (91) 567970; e-mail sales@connacht-tribune.ie; internet www .connacht-tribune.ie; f. 1909; Fri.; Editor J. CUNNINGHAM; circ. 28,222.

Connaught Telegraph: Ellison St, Castlebar, Co Mayo; tel. (94) 21711; fax (94) 24007; e-mail conntel@tinet.ie; internet www .con-telegraph.ie; f. 1828; Wed.; Editor TOM GILLESPIE; circ. 16,000.

Donegal Democrat: Pier 1, Quay St, Donegal, Co Donegal; tel. (7497) 40160; fax (7497) 40161; e-mail editorial@donegaldemocrat .com; f. 1919; Tues. and Thurs.; Editor MICHAEL DALY; circ. 15,787 (Tues.); 10,308 (Thurs.).

Drogheda Independent: 9 Shop St, Drogheda, Co Louth; tel. (41) 9838658; fax (41) 9834271; internet www.unison.ie/ drogheda_independent; f. 1884; Thurs.; Editor PAUL MURPHY; circ. 14,000.

Dundalk Democrat: 7C Crowe St, Dundalk, Co Louth; tel. (42) 9334058; fax (42) 9331399; e-mail editor@dundalkdemocrat.ie; f. 1849; Sat.; Editor DOLAN O'HAGAN; circ. 16,000.

Dungarvan Leader and Southern Democrat: 78 O'Connell St, Dungarvan, Co Waterford; tel. (58) 41203; fax (58) 45301; e-mail dungarvanleader@cablesurf.com; Wed.; Editor COLM J. NAGLE; circ. 13,000.

Dungarvan Observer and Munster Industrial Advocate: Shandon, Dungarvan, Co Waterford; tel. (58) 41205; fax (58) 41559; e-mail info@dungarvanobserver.com; Editor JAMES A. LYNCH; circ. 11,000.

Echo and South Leinster Advertiser: Mill Park Rd, Enniscorthy, Co Wexford; tel. (54) 33231; fax (54) 33506; f. 1902; Wed.; Editor JAMES GAHAN; circ. 22,000.

The Guardian: The People Newspapers Ltd, Castle Hill, Enniscorthy, Co Wexford; tel. (54) 33833; fax (54) 35910; e-mail dasherin@ hotmail.com; f. 1881; Wed.; Man. Dir G. WALSH; circ. 36,000.

Ireland on Sunday: 3rd Floor, Embassy House, Herbert Park Lane, Ballsbridge, Dublin 4; tel. (1) 6375800; fax (1) 4179830; e-mail p.drury@irelandonsunday.com; internet www.irelandonsunday .com; acquired by Associated Newspapers in 2001; Chief Exec. JOHN THOMPSON; Editor PAUL DRURY; circ. 148,031 (2004).

Iris Oifigiuil (Official Irish Gazette): 51 St Stephen's Green, Dublin 2; tel. (1) 6476838; fax (1) 6476842; internet www.irisoifigiuil.ie; f. 1922; Editor MICK DUNNE.

The Kerryman/The Corkman: Clash Industrial Estate, Tralee, Co Kerry; tel. (66) 21666; fax (66) 21608; e-mail kerryman@indigo.ie; internet www.unison.ie/corkman; f. 1904; Thurs.; Editor GERARD COLLERAN; circ. 35,000.

Kilkenny People: 34 High St, Kilkenny; tel. (56) 7721015; fax (56) 7721414; e-mail info@kilkennypeople.ie; internet www .kilkennypeople.ie; f. 1892; weekly; Editor THOMAS MOLLOY; circ. 18,105.

Leinster Express: Dublin Rd, Portlaoise, Co Laois; tel. (502) 21666; fax (502) 20491; e-mail lexpress@indigo.ie; internet www.unison.ie/ leinster_express; f. 1831; weekly; Man. Editor TEDDY FENNELLY; circ. 18,500.

Leinster Leader: 19 South Main St, Naas, Co Kildare; tel. (45) 897302; fax (45) 897647; e-mail iain@iol.ie; internet www.unison.ie/ leinster_leader; f. 1880; Wed.; Editor MICHAEL SHEERAN; circ. 15,000.

Leitrim Observer: 3 Hartley Business Park, Carrick-on-Shannon, Co Leitrim, tel. (96) 20025; fax (96) 20112; e-mail editor@ leitrimobserver.ie; internet www.leitrimobserver.ie; f. 1889; Wed.; Editor CLAIRE CASSERLY; circ. 10,000.

Limerick Chronicle: 54 O'Connell St, Limerick; tel. (61) 315233; fax (61) 314804; e-mail lkleader@iol.ie; f. 1766; Tues.; Editor BRENDAN HALLIGAN; circ. 8,500.

Limerick Leader: 54 O'Connell St, Limerick; tel. (61) 214500; fax (61) 314804; e-mail admin@limerick-leader.ie; internet www

.limerick-leader.ie; f. 1889; 4 a week; Editor BRENDAN HALLIGAN; circ. 29,000 (weekend edn).

Limerick Post: Rutland St, Limerick; tel. (61) 413322; fax (61) 417684; e-mail news@limerickpost.ie; internet www.limerickpost.ie; f. 1986; Thurs.; Editor BILLY RYAN; circ. 44,500.

Longford Leader: Leader House, Dublin Rd, Longford; tel. (43) 45241; fax (43) 41489; e-mail newsroom@longford-leader.ie; internet www.longford-leader.ie; f. 1897; Wed.; Editor JOE FLAHERTY; circ. 13,500.

Longford News: Earl St, Longford; tel. (43) 45627; fax (43) 41549; e-mail info@longford-news.iol.ie; internet www.unison.ie/ longford_news; Wed.; Editor PAUL HEALY; circ. 24,000.

Mayo News: The Fairgreen, Westport, Co Mayo; tel. (98) 25311; fax (98) 26108; e-mail mayonews@anu.ie; internet www.mayonews.ie; f. 1892; Wed.; Man. Editor SEÁN STAUNTON; circ. 35,000.

Meath Chronicle and Cavan and Westmeath Herald: 12 Market Sq., Navan, Co Meath; tel. (46) 9079600; fax (46) 9023565; e-mail info@meath-chronicle.ie; internet www.meath-chronicle.ie; f. 1897; Sat.; Editor KEN DAVIS; circ. 18,000.

Midland Tribune: Emmet St, Birr, Co Offaly; tel. (509) 20003; fax (509) 20588; e-mail midtrib@iol.ie; internet www.unison.ie/ midland_tribune; f. 1881; Wed.; Editor JOHN O'CALLAGHAN; circ. 16,000.

The Munster Express: 37 The Quay and 1–3 Hanover St, Waterford; tel. (51) 872141; fax (51) 873452; e-mail munster@iol.ie; internet www.munster-express.ie; f. 1859; 2 a week; Editor K. J. WALSH; circ. 19,000.

The Nationalist: 42 Tullow St, Carlow; tel. (59) 9170100; fax (59) 9131442; e-mail news@carlow-nationalist.ie; internet www.carlow .nationalist.ie; f. 1883; weekly; Editor EDDIE COFFEY; circ. 17,000.

Nationalist Newspaper: Queen St, Clonmel, Co Tipperary; tel. (52) 22211; fax (52) 72528; e-mail ads@nationalist.ie; f. 1890; Thurs.; Editor TOM CORR; circ. 15,461.

The Northern Standard: The Diamond, Monaghan; tel. (47) 81867; fax (47) 72257; e-mail garysmyth@eircom.net; f. 1839; Fri.; Editor MARTIN SMYTH; circ. 15,000.

Offaly Express: Bridge St, Tullamore, Co Offaly; tel. (506) 21744; fax (506) 51930; e-mail lexpress@indigo.ie; internet www.rmbi.ie; weekly; Editor JOHN WHELAN; circ. 18,000 (with Leinster Express).

Roscommon Champion: Abbey St, Roscommon; tel. (903) 25051; fax (903) 25053; e-mail roscommonchampion@tinet.ie; internet homepage.tinet.ie/~roscommonchampion; f. 1927; weekly; Editor PAUL HEALY; circ. 10,000.

Roscommon Herald: Boyle, Co Roscommon; tel. (71) 9662004; fax (71) 9662926; e-mail news@roscommonherald.ie; internet www .roscommonherald.ie; f. 1859; weekly; Editor CHRISTINA MCHUGH; circ. 10,000.

Sligo Champion: Finisklin Rd., Sligo; tel. (71) 9169222; fax (71) 9169040; e-mail info@sligochampion.ie; internet www .sligochampion.com; f. 1836; Wed.; Man. Dir NIALL J. TOWNSEND; Editor SEAMUS FINN; circ. 14,086.

Southern Star: Ilen St, Skibbereen, Co Cork; tel. (28) 21200; fax (28) 21071; e-mail info@southernstar.ie; f. 1889; Sat.; Editor LIAM O'REGAN; circ. 16,000.

Sunday Business Post: 80 Harcourt St, Dublin 2; tel. (1) 6026000; fax (1) 6796496; e-mail sbpost@iol.ie; internet www.thepost.ie; Editor CLIFF TAYLOR; circ. 55,080.

Sunday Independent: Independent House, 90 Middle Abbey St, Dublin 1; tel. (1) 7055333; fax (1) 7055779; e-mail sunday.letters@ independent.ie; internet www.independent.ie; f. 1905; Editor AENGUS FANNING; circ. 334,000.

Sunday Tribune: 15 Lower Baggot St, Dublin 2; tel. (1) 6314300; fax (1) 6615302; e-mail editorial@tribune.ie; internet www.tribune .ie; f. 1980; Editor PADDY MURRAY; circ. 86,000.

Sunday World: Newspaper House, 18 Rathfarnham Rd, Terenure, Dublin 6; tel. (1) 4063500; fax (1) 4901838; e-mail news@ sundayworld.com; internet www.sundayworld.com; f. 1973; Editor COLM MACGINTY; circ. 308,786.

Tipperary Star: Friar St, Thurles, Co Tipperary; tel. (504) 21122; fax (504) 21110; e-mail info@tipperarystar.ie; internet www .tipperarystar.ie; f. 1909; Wed.; Editor MICHAEL DUNDON; circ. 10,000.

Tuam Herald: Dublin Rd, Tuam, Co Galway; tel. (93) 24183; fax (93) 24478; e-mail editor@tuamherald.ie; internet www.unison .ie_tuamherald; f. 1837; Wed.; Editor DAVID BURKE; circ. 11,000.

Tullamore Tribune: Church St, Tullamore, Co Offaly; tel. (506) 21152; fax (506) 21927; e-mail tulltrib@eircom.net; internet www .tullamoretribune.ie; f. 1978; Wed.; Editor G. J. SCULLY; circ. 10,000.

Waterford News & Star: 25 Michael St, Waterford; tel. (51) 874951; fax (51) 855281; e-mail editor@waterford-news.ie; internet www.waterford-news.ie; f. 1848; Thurs.; Editor P. DOYLE; circ. 16,000.

Western People: Francis St, Ballina, Co Mayo; tel. (96) 21188; fax (96) 70208; e-mail info@westernpeople.ie; internet www .westernpeople.ie; f. 1883; Tues.; Editor TERENCE REILLY; circ. 24,000.

Westmeath Examiner: 19 Dominick St, Mullingar, Co Westmeath; tel. (44) 48426; fax (44) 40640; e-mail news@westmeathexaminer.ie; internet www.westmeath-examiner.ie; f. 1882; weekly; Man. Dir MARTIN NALLY; circ. 14,000.

Wicklow Times: 1 Eglinton Rd, Bray, Co Wicklow; tel. (1) 2869111; fax (1) 2869074; e-mail wicklowtimes@tinet.ie; fortnightly; Man. Editor SHAY FITZMAURICE; circ. 30,500.

SELECTED PERIODICALS

Banking Ireland: 50 Fitzwilliam Sq., Dublin 2; tel. (1) 6764587; fax (1) 6619781; f. 1898; quarterly; journal of the Inst. of Bankers in Ireland; Editor GERRY LAWLOR; circ. 15,500.

Books Ireland: 11 Newgrove Ave, Dublin 4; tel. (1) 2692185; e-mail booksi@eircom.net; f. 1976; 9 a year; reviews Irish-interest books; Editor JEREMY ADDIS; circ. 2,350.

Business & Finance: 50 Fitzwilliam Sq., Dublin 2; tel. (1) 6764587; fax (1) 6619781; e-mail belenos@tinet.ie; internet www .businessandfinance.ie; f. 1964; weekly; Man. Editor JOHN MCGEE; circ. 11,000.

History Ireland: POB 695, James's St, Dublin 8; tel. (1) 4535730; fax (1) 4533234; e-mail info@historyireland.com; internet www .historyireland.com; quarterly; Jt Editors HIRAM MORGAN, TOMMY GRAHAM.

Hot Press: 13 Trinity St, Dublin 2; tel. (1) 2411500; fax (1) 2411538; e-mail info@hotpress.ie; internet www.hotpress.com; fortnightly; music, leisure, current affairs; Editor NIALL STOKES; circ. 21,000.

Ireland Afloat: 2 Lower Glenageary Rd, Dún Laoghaire, Co Dublin; tel. (1) 2846161; fax (1) 2846192; e-mail info@afloat.ie; internet www .afloat.ie; monthly; sailing and boating; Man. Editor DAVID O'BRIEN; circ. 10,000.

Ireland's Own: Channing House, Rowe St, Wexford; tel. (53) 40140; fax (53) 40192; e-mail irelands.own@peoplenews.ie; f. 1902; weekly; family interest; Editors PHILIP MURPHY, SEAN NOLAN; circ. 50,000.

The Irish Catholic: 55 Lower Gardiner St, Dublin 1; tel. (1) 8555619; fax (1) 8364805; e-mail news@irishcatholic.ie; internet www.irishcatholic.ie; weekly; Editor GARY O'SULLIVAN; circ. 32,000.

Irish Computer: CPG House, Glenageary Office Park, Dún Laoghaire, Co Dublin; tel. (1) 2847777; fax (1) 2847584; e-mail bskelly@cpg .ie; internet www.irishcomputer.com; f. 1977; monthly; Editor BRIAN SKELLY; circ. 8,000.

Irish Farmers' Journal: Irish Farm Centre, Bluebell, Dublin 12; tel. (1) 4199500; fax (1) 4520876; e-mail editdept@farmersjournal.ie; internet www.farmersjournal.ie; f. 1948; weekly; Editor MATTHEW DEMPSEY; circ. 75,000.

Irish Field: Irish Farm Centre, Bluebell, Dublin 12; tel. (1) 4051100; fax (1) 4554008; e-mail info@irishfield.ie; internet www .irishfield.ie; f. 1870; weekly; horse racing, breeding and equine leisure; Man. Editor LEO POWELL; circ. 14,500.

Irish Historical Studies: c/o Dept of Modern History, Trinity College, Dublin 2; tel. (1) 6081020; e-mail wvaughan@tcd.ie; 2 a year; Editors Dr DAVID HAYTON, Dr JOHN MCCAFFERTY.

Irish Journal of Medical Science: Royal Academy of Medicine in Ireland, International House, 2nd Floor, 20–22 Lower Hatch St, Dublin 2; tel. (1) 6623706; fax (1) 6611684; e-mail journal@rami.ie; internet www.iformix.com; f. 1832; quarterly; organ of the Royal Academy of Medicine; Editor THOMAS N. WALSH.

Irish Law Times: Round Hall Sweet & Maxwell, 43 Fitzwilliam Pl., Dublin 2; tel. (1) 6625301; fax (1) 6625302; e-mail terri.mcdonnell@ roundhall.ie; f. 1983; 20 a year; Editor DAVID BOYLE.

Irish Medical Journal: 10 Fitzwilliam Pl., Dublin 2; tel. (1) 6767273; fax (1) 6612758; e-mail imj@imj.ie; internet www.imj.ie; 10 a year; journal of the Irish Medical Org.; Editor Dr JOHN MURPHY; circ. 8,500.

The Irish Skipper: Taney Hall, Eglinton Terrace, Dublin 14; tel. (1) 2960000; fax (1) 2960383; e-mail skippereditor@iol.ie; internet www.irishskipper.net; f. 1964; monthly; journal of the commercial fishing and aquaculture industries; Editor CORMAC BURKE.

Irish Tatler: 2 Clanwilliam Court, Lower Mount St, Dublin 2; tel. (1) 2405367; fax (1) 6619757; monthly; Editor VANESSA HARRIS.

Irish University Review: Rm J211, School of English, University College Dublin, Belfield, Dublin 4; tel. (1) 7168159; fax (1) 7161174;

e-mail anne.fogarty@ucd.ie; 2 a year; literature, history, fine arts, politics, cultural studies; Editor Dr ANNE FOGARTY.

Modern Woman Nationwide: Market Square, Navan, Co Meath; tel. (46) 9079600; fax (46) 9023565; e-mail info@meath-chronicle.ie; f. 1984; monthly; Editor MARGOT DAVIS.

Motoring Life: Cyndale Enterprises Ltd, 48 North Great George's St, Dublin 1; tel. (1) 8780444; fax (1) 8787740; e-mail info@ motoringlife.ie; internet www.motoringlife.ie; f. 1946; bi-monthly; Editor GERALDINE HERBERT; circ. 15,000.

PC Live!: Prospect House, 3 Prospect Rd, Glasnevin, Dublin 9; tel. (1) 8824444; fax (1) 8300888; e-mail info@scope.ie; internet www .techcentral.ie; monthly; computers and the internet; Editor STEPHEN CAWLEY; circ. 18,000.

Phoenix: 44 Lower Baggot St, Dublin 2; tel. (1) 6611062; fax (1) 6624532; e-mail phoenix@indigo.ie; internet www .phoenix-magazine.com; f. 1983; fortnightly; news and comment; Editor PADDY PRENDIVILLE; circ. 22,000.

Poetry Ireland Review (Éigse Éireann): 120 St Stephen's Green, Dublin 2; tel. (1) 4789974; fax (1) 4780205; e-mail poetry@iol.ie; Editor PETER SIRR.

RTE Guide: Radio Telefís Éireann, Donnybrook, Dublin 4; tel. (1) 2083146; fax (1) 2083085; internet www.rteguide.ie; weekly; programmes of the Irish broadcasting service; Editor RAY WALSH; circ. 145,921.

Studies: 35 Lower Leeson St, Dublin 2; tel. (1) 6766785; fax (1) 6762984; e-mail studies@jesuit.ie; internet www.studiesirishreview .com; f. 1912; quarterly review of letters, history, religious and social questions; Editor Fr FERGUS O'DONOGHUE, S.J.

U Magazine: 2 Clanwilliam Court, Lower Mount St, Dublin 2; tel. (1) 2405300; fax (1) 6619757; e-mail letters@umagazine.ie; f. 1979; monthly; Editor FIONNUALA MCCARTHY; circ. 20,750.

Village Magazine: 44 Westland Row, Dublin 2; tel. (1) 6425050; fax (1) 6425001; e-mail news@villagemagazine.ie; internet www .villagemagazine.ie; f. 2004; weekly; Editor VINCENT BROWNE; circ. 20,000.

The Voice: e-mail editor@thevoice.ie; internet www.thevoice.ie; f. 2004; weekly; Editor SIMON ROWE; circ. 20,000.

Woman's Way: 2 Clanwilliam Court, Lower Mount St, Dublin 2; tel. (1) 6623158; fax (1) 6628719; e-mail ltaylor@smurfit-comms.ie; f. 1963; weekly; Editor LUCY TAYLOR; circ. 67,000.

The Word: Divine Word Missionaries, Maynooth, Co Kildare; tel. (1) 5054467; e-mail wordeditor@eircom.net; internet www.theword .ie; f. 1953; monthly; Catholic general interest; Editor-in-Chief VINCENT TWOMEY; circ. 24,500.

NEWS AGENCIES

Ireland International News Agency: 51 Wellington Quay, Dublin 2; tel. (1) 6712442; fax (1) 6796586; e-mail iina@eircom.net; Man. Dir DIARMAID MACDERMOTT.

Foreign Bureaux

Agenzia Nazionale Stampa Associata (ANSA) (Italy): 56 Greenfield Park, Knocklyon, Dublin 24; tel. (1) 4941389; fax (1) 4941300; e-mail enzo@iol.ie; Bureau Chief ENZO FARINELLA.

Informatsionnoye Telegrafnoye Agentstvo Rossii—Telegrafnoye Agentstvo Suverennykh Stran (ITAR—TASS) (Russia): 59 Glenbrook Park, Dublin; tel. (1) 2885513; Chief of Bureau EVGENY KLESHKOV.

Reuters Ireland: 12–13 Exchange Pl., IFSC, Dublin 12; tel. (1) 5001550; fax (1) 5001501; internet www.reuters.com; Chief Correspondent KEITH WEIR.

Rossiiskoye Informatsionnoye Agentstvo—Novosti (RIA—Novosti) (Russia) is also represented.

PRESS ORGANIZATIONS

National Newspapers of Ireland: Clyde Lodge, 15 Clyde Rd, Dublin 4; tel. (1) 6689099; fax (1) 6689872; e-mail nni@ cullencommunications.ie; internet www.nni.ie; Chair. GAVIN O'REILLY; Co-ordinating Dir FRANK CULLEN.

Regional Newspapers Association of Ireland: Sheridan House, 33 Parkgate St, Dublin 8; tel. (1) 6779049; fax (1) 6779144; e-mail neville@rnan.ie; internet www.rnan.ie; f. 1917; 37 mems; Pres. JOHNNY O'HANLON; CEO NEVILLE GALLOWAY.

Publishers

Anvil Books Ltd: 45 Palmerston Rd, Dublin 6; tel. (1) 4973628; fax (1) 4968263; f. 1964; Irish history and biography, folklore, children's fiction (10 years and above); Dirs R. DARDIS, M. DARDIS.

Attic Press Ltd: Crawford Business Park, Crosses Green, Cork; tel. (21) 4321725; fax (21) 4315329; e-mail corkunip@ucc.ie; internet www.corkuniversitypress.com; imprint of Cork University Press; Dir Prof. DES CLARKE.

Boole Press Ltd: 19 Silchester Rd, Glenageary, Co Dublin; e-mail info@boolepress.com; internet www.boolepress.com; f. 1979; scientific, technical, medical, scholarly; Man. Dir Dr J. MILLER.

Comhairle Bhéaloideas Éireann (Folklore of Ireland Council): c/o Dept of Irish Folklore, University College, Belfield, Dublin 4; tel. (1) 7168216; e-mail cumann@ucd.ie; Editor Prof. SÉAMAS O'CATHÁIN.

Cork University Press: Youngline Industrial Estate, Pouladuff Road, Togher, Cork; tel. (21) 4902980; fax (21) 4315329; e-mail corkuniversitypress@ucc.ie; internet www.corkuniversitypress.com; f. 1925; academic; Man. Dir MIKE COLLINS.

Dominican Publications: 42 Parnell Sq., Dublin 1; tel. (1) 8731355; fax (1) 8731760; e-mail sales@dominicanpublications.com; internet www.dominicanpublications.com; f. 1897; religious affairs in Ireland and the developing world, pastoral-liturgical aids; Man. Rev. BERNARD TREACY.

Dundalgan Press (W. Tempest) Ltd: Francis St, Dundalk, Co Louth; tel. (42) 9334013; fax (42) 9332351; e-mail info@dundalgen.ie; f. 1859; history and biography; Man. Dir GERARD GORMLEY.

C J Fallon: POB 1054, Lucan Rd, Palmerstown, Dublin 20; tel. (1) 6166400; fax (1) 6166499; e-mail info@cjfallon.ie; internet www .cjfallon.ie; f. 1927; educational; Man. Dir H. J. MCNICHOLAS.

Four Courts Press: 7 Malpas St, Dublin 8; tel. (1) 4534668; fax (1) 4534672; e-mail info@four-courts-press.ie; internet www.four .courts-press.ie; f. 1970; philosophy, theology, Celtic and Medieval studies, art, literature, modern history; Dirs MICHAEL ADAMS, MARTIN HEALY, GERARD O'FLAHERTY.

Gallery Press: Loughcrew, Oldcastle, Co Meath; tel. and fax (49) 8541779; e-mail gallery@indigo.ie; internet www.gallerypress.com; f. 1970; poetry, plays, prose by Irish authors; Editor PETER FALLON.

Gill and Macmillan Ltd: Hume Ave, Park West, Dublin 12; tel. (1) 5009500; fax (1) 5009597; e-mail sales@gillmacmillan.ie; internet www.gillmacmillan.ie; f. 1968; literature, biography, history, mind, body and spirit, social sciences, current affairs, popular fiction and textbooks; Man. Dir M. H. GILL.

Goldsmith Press: Newbridge, Co Kildare; tel. (45) 433613; fax (45) 434648; f. 1972; poetry, Irish art, plays, foreign language, general; Dirs DESMOND EGAN, VIVIENNE ABBOTT.

Irish Academic Press: 44 Northumberland Rd, Dublin 4; tel. (1) 6688244; fax (1) 6686769; e-mail info@iap.ie; internet www.iap.ie; f. 1974; academic, mainly history and Irish studies; Dirs FRANK CASS, STEWART CASS; Man. Editor RACHEL MILOTTE.

Lexis Nexis: 24–26 Upper Ormond Quay, Dublin 7; tel. (1) 8728514; fax (1) 8731378; internet www.lexisnexis.ie; taxation and law; Chair. H. MUMFORD.

Liberties Press: 51 Stephens Rd, Inchicore, Dublin 8; tel. (1) 4020805; e-mail info@libertiespress.com; internet www .libertiespress.com; f. 2003; sport, health, food, music, history, religion and politics; Editorial Dir SEAN O'KEEFFE.

Lilliput Press: 62/63 Sitric Rd, Arbour Hill, Dublin 7; tel. (1) 6711647; fax (1) 6711233; e-mail info@lilliputpress.ie; internet www .lilliputpress.ie; f. 1985; ecology and environment, literary criticism, biography, memoirs, fiction, Irish history, general; Publr ANTONY FARRELL; Dirs TERENCE BROWN, KATHY GILFILLAN, VIVIENNE GUINESS.

Mentor Books: 43 Furze Rd, Sandyford Industrial Estate, Dublin 18; tel. (1) 2952112; fax (1) 2952114; e-mail all@mentorbooks.ie; internet www.mentorbooks.ie; adult and children's fiction and non-fiction, educational; Man. Dir DANIEL MCCARTHY.

Mercier Press Ltd: Douglas Village, Cork; tel. (21) 4899858; fax (21) 4899887; e-mail books@mercierpress.ie; internet www .mercierpress.ie; f. 1944; Irish folklore, history, literature, fiction, politics, humour, religious; Chair. GEORGE EATON; Man. Dir JOHN F. SPILLANE.

O'Brien Press Ltd: 20 Victoria Rd, Rathgar, Dublin 6; tel. (1) 4923333; fax (1) 4922777; e-mail books@obrien.ie; internet www .obrien.ie; f. 1974; biography, history, sport, Celtic, politics, travel, crime, children's; Man. Dir MICHAEL O'BRIEN.

Poolbeg Press Ltd: 123 Baldoyle Industrial Estate, Dublin 13; tel. (1) 8321477; fax (1) 8321430; e-mail poolbeg@poolbeg.com; internet www.poolbeg.com; f. 1976; general, poetry, politics, children's; Man. Dir PHILIP MACDERMOTT.

Round Hall Ltd: 43 Fitzwilliam Pl., Dublin 2; tel. (1) 6625301; fax (1) 6625302; e-mail info@roundhall.ie; internet www.roundhall.ie; law books and journals; Dir ELANOR MCGARRY.

Royal Irish Academy (Acadamh Ríoga na hÉireann): 19 Dawson St, Dublin 2; tel. (1) 6762570; fax (1) 6762346; e-mail admin@ria.ie; internet www.ria.ie; f. 1785; humanities and sciences; Pres. M. E. F. RYAN; Exec. Sec. PATRICK BUCKLEY; Editor RACHEL MCNICHOLL.

Sáirséal-Ó Marcaigh: 13 Bóthar Chríoch Mhór, Dublin 11; tel. and fax (1) 8378914; books in Irish; Dirs AINGEAL Ó MARCAIGH, CAOIMHÍN Ó MARCAIGH.

Sporting Books: 4 Sycamore Rd, Mount Merrion, Co Dublin; tel. (1) 2887914; fax (1) 2885779; sports; Publr RAYMOND SMITH.

TownHouse Dublin: Trinity House, Charleston Rd, Ranelagh, Dublin 6; tel. (1) 4972399; fax (1) 4970927; e-mail books@townhouse .ie; internet www.townhouse.ie; fiction, biography, art, environmental, general; jt venture with Simon and Schuster UK Ltd; Dirs TREASA COADY, JIM COADY.

Veritas Publications: 7–8 Lower Abbey St, Dublin 1; tel. (1) 8788177; fax (1) 8786507; e-mail publications@veritas.ie; internet www.veritas.ie; f. 1900; religious and educational; Dir MAURA HYLAND.

Wolfhound Press: 68 Mountjoy Sq., Dublin 1; tel. (1) 8740354; fax (1) 8720207; internet www.wolfhound.ie; f. 1974; literature, biography, art, children's, fiction, history; Publr SÉAMUS CASHMAN.

Woodtown Music Publications Ltd: Teach an Dáma, Stráid an Dáma, Dublin 2; tel. and fax (1) 6793664; f. 1966; original works by Irish composers; Chair. GARECH DE BRÚN.

GOVERNMENT PUBLISHING HOUSE

Stationery Office: Government Publications, 51 St Stephen's Green, Dublin 2; tel. (1) 6476849; fax (1) 6476843.

PUBLISHERS' ASSOCIATION

CLÉ — The Irish Book Publishers' Association: 19 Parnell Sq., Dublin 1; tel. (1) 7756333; e-mail info@publishingireland.com; internet www.publishingireland.com; f. 1970; 54 mems; Pres. FERGAL TOBIN.

Broadcasting and Communications

TELECOMMUNICATIONS

Commission for Communications Regulation (ComReg): Abbey Court, Irish Life Centre, Lower Abbey St, Dublin 1; tel. (1) 8049600; fax (1) 8049680; e-mail patricia.dowling@comreg.ie; internet www.comreg.ie; f. 2002 as the regulatory authority for Ireland's postal and telecommunications sectors; issues licences to service providers; manages the interconnection of tele-communications networks; approves equipment and oversees national telephone numbering; Chair. ISOLDE GOGGIN.

Cable and Wireless Ltd: 1 Airton Rd, Tallaght, Dublin 24; tel. (1) 4346333; fax (1) 4346339; e-mail info@candw.ie; internet www .candw.ie; independent telecommunications services provider; supplies telecommunications equipment including video-conferencing systems and paging devices; Man. Dir EDDIE BRENNAN; Gen. Man. PAT MACGRATH.

eircom plc: St Stephen's Green West, Dublin 2; tel. (1) 6714444; fax (1) 6716916; e-mail press-office@eircom.ie; internet www.eircom.ie; f. 1984; fmrly Telecom Éireann; nationalized body responsible for the provision of national and international telecommunications services, including mobile services; partially privatized in 1999, acquired by Valentia Telecommunications Ltd in September 2001; Chair. Sir ANTHONY O'REILLY; CEO Dr PHILIP NOLAN.

eircom net: Unit B, East Point Business Park, Fairview, Dublin 3; tel. (1) 701000; fax (1) 7010375; e-mail info@eircom.net; internet www.eircom.net; f. 1996 to provide internet services to both business and private customers; Gen. Man. FINTAN LAWLER.

O₂: 76 Lower Baggot St, Dublin 2; tel. (1) 6095000; e-mail customercare@o2.ie; internet www2.o2.ie; f. 1997 as ESAT Digiphone; private telecommunications company; purchased by British Telecommunications PLC in Jan. 2000; renamed as above in May 2002; CEO DANUTA GRAY.

Vodafone: Mountainview, Leopardstown, Dublin 18; tel. (1) 2037777; fax (1) 2037778; e-mail custcare@vodafone.ie; internet www.vodafone.ie; a subsidiary of Vodafone Ltd (UK), providing national mobile telecommunications services; CEO TERESA ELDER.

BROADCASTING

The Radio and Television Act of 1988 provided for the establishment of an independent television station, an independent national radio service and a series of local radio stations (see below).

Broadcasting Commission of Ireland (BCI): Marine House, Clanwilliam Pl., Dublin 2; tel. (1) 6760966; fax (1) 6760948; e-mail info@bci.ie; internet www.bci.ie; f. 1988 as the Independent Radio and Television Commission; renamed as above in 2001 following the introduction of the 2001 Broadcasting Act; established by the Govt to ensure the creation, licensing, development and monitoring of independent broadcasting in Ireland; also responsible for the licensing of new digital, cable, multi-mode digital and satellite television services, as well as the development of codes of programming and advertising standards for television and radio services and the provision of a secretariat to the Broadcasting Complaints Commission; operations are financed by levies paid by franchised stations; Chair. CONOR J. MAGUIRE; CEO MICHAEL O'KEEFFE.

Broadcasting Complaints Commission: 2–5 Warrington Pl., Dublin 2; tel. (1) 6761097; e-mail info@bcc.ie; internet www.bcc.ie; f. 1977; responsible for acting upon complaints relating to material broadcast by RTE and independent broadcasting stations; Chair. OONAH MCCRANN.

Radio

Radio Telefís Éireann (RTÉ): Donnybrook, Dublin 4; tel. (1) 2083111; fax (1) 2083080; e-mail dg@rte.ie; internet www.rte.ie; national public-service broadcasting corpn; f. 1960; financed by net licence revenue and sale of advertising time, which is limited to 10% of transmission time; governed by Authority of nine mems, appointed by the GOA; operates four radio networks, Radio 1 (news, music, drama and variety shows), 2FM (popular music), Lyric FM (music, arts and culture) and Raidió na Gaeltachta (see below); Chair. of Authority PATRICK J. WRIGHT; Dir-Gen. CATHAL GOAN; Man. Dir of Radio ADRIAN MOYNES.

> **Raidió na Gaeltachta:** Casla, Connemara, Co Galway; tel. (91) 506677; fax (91) 506666; e-mail rnag@rte.ie; internet www .rnag,ie; f. 1972; broadcasts 168 hours per week in Irish language; financed by RTE; Controller TOMAS MAC CONIOMAIRE.

100-102 Today FM: Today FM House, 124 Upper Abbey St, Dublin 1; tel. (1) 8049000; fax (1) 8049099; e-mail 100-102@todayfm.com; internet www.todayfm.com; f. 1998; national, independent station; Chair. JOHN MCCOLGAN; CEO WILLIE O'REILLY.

Dublin's 98 FM: The Malt House, Grand Canal Quay, Dublin 2; tel. (1) 6708989; fax (1) 6708969; e-mail info@98fm.ie; internet www .98fm.ie; provides news service to independent local radio stations under contract from the BCI; CEO CIARAN DAVIS; Head of News TEENA GATES.

There are also local radio stations operating under the supervision of the Independent Radio and Television Commission.

Television

Radio Telefís Éireann (RTÉ): see above; operates three television channels: RTÉ 1, RTÉ 2 and TG4—an Irish language television service began transmissions in November 1996; Chair. of Authority PATRICK J. WRIGHT; Dir-Gen. CATHAL GOAN; Man. Dir of Television NOEL CURRAN; Man. Dir of News EDWARD MULHALL; Dir of Digital Media EUGENE MURRAY.

TV3: Westgate Business Park, Ballymount, Dublin 24; tel. (1) 4193333; fax (1) 4193300; e-mail info@tv3; internet www.tv3.ie; f. 1998; first national, commercial, independent television network; Chair. JAMES MORRIS; Man. Dir and CEO RICK HETHERINGTON; Dir of Programming MATTHEW SALWAY; Dir of News ANDREW HANLON.

Finance

(cap. = capital; p.u. = paid up; res = reserves; dep. = deposits; m. = million; brs = branches; amounts in Irish pounds (IR£) or euros (€) unless otherwise stated)

BANKING

Central Bank

Bank Ceannais na hÉireann (Central Bank and Financial Services Authority of Ireland): POB 559, Dame St, Dublin 2; tel. (1) 4344000; fax (1) 6716561; e-mail enquiries@centralbank.ie; internet www.centralbank.ie; f. 1942; bank of issue; cap. and res €1,480.4m., dep. €21,326.1m. (Dec. 2003); Gov. JOHN HURLEY; Dir-Gen. LIAM BARRON.

Principal Banks

ACCBANK PLC: Charlemont Pl., Dublin 2; tel. (1) 4184000; fax (1) 4184444; e-mail info@accbank.ie; internet www.accbank.ie; f. 1927; state-owned; provides banking services to personal customers, small businesses, farmers and corporate entities; total assets €3,065m. (Dec. 1999); Chair. P. O'CONNOR; CEO C. DARLING; 49 brs.

AIB Capital Markets PLC: AIB International Centre, IFSC, Dublin 1; tel. (1) 8740222; fax (1) 6642124; e-mail grouppa@iol.ie; internet www.aib.ie/capitalmarkets; f. 1966; merchant banking and investment management; cap. p.u. IR£8m., dep. IR£1,105m. (Dec. 1997); Man. Dir COLM E. DOHERTY; 7 brs.

AIB Group: POB 452, Bankcentre, Ballsbridge, Dublin 4; tel. (1) 6600311; fax (1) 6604715; e-mail aibtoday@aib.ie; internet www .aibgroup.com; f. 1966; fmrly Allied Irish Banks PLC; cap. €295m., res €2,836m., dep. €66,195m. (Dec. 2003); Chair. DERMOT GLEESON; CEO MICHAEL D. BUCKLEY; over 800 brs and offices.

Anglo Irish Bank Corporation PLC: Stephen Court, 18–21 St Stephen's Green, Dublin 2; tel. (1) 6162000; fax (1) 6162725; e-mail enquiries@angloirishbank.ie; internet www.angloirishbank.com; f. 1964; cap. €105.8m., res €155.6m., dep. €22,425.6m. (Sept. 2003); Chair. PETER MURRAY; Chief Exec. SEAN P. FITZPATRICK; 9 brs.

Ansbacher Bankers Ltd: 18–21 St Stephen's Green, Dublin 2; tel. (1) 6613699; fax (1) 6618408; f. 1950; wholly-owned subsidiary of Anglo Irish Bank Corporation PLC; Chair. SEÁN P. FITZPATRICK.

Bank of Ireland Asset Management: 26 Fitzwilliam Pl., Dublin 2; tel. (1) 6616433; fax (1) 6616688; e-mail biaminfo@biam.boi.ie; internet www.biam.ie; f. 1966; investment management; CEO WILLIAM R. COTTER.

Bank of Ireland Group: Lower Baggot St, Dublin 2; tel. (1) 6615933; fax (1) 6615193; e-mail careline@boimail.com; internet www.bankofireland.ie; f. 1783; cap. €679m., res €1,504m., dep. €84,602m. (March 2004); Gov. LAURENCE CROWLEY; CEO BRIAN GOGGIN; 357 brs.

Bank of Scotland (Ireland) Ltd: Canada House, 65–68 St Stephen's Green, Dublin 2; tel. (1) 4083500; fax (1) 6717797; e-mail info@bankofscotland.ie; internet www.bankofscotland.ie; f. 1965 as Equity Bank Ltd, name changed as above in 2000; cap. and res €105.8m. (Feb. 2001), dep. €10,197.2m. (Dec. 2003); Chair. Sir RON GARRICK; Chief Exec. MARK DUFFY; 2 brs.

Barclays Bank PLC: 47/48 St Stephen's Green, Dublin 2; tel. (1) 6611777; fax (1) 6623141; internet www.barclays.com; total assets €1,376m. (Dec. 2004); Man. Dir TOM MCALEESE.

Bear Stearns Bank PLC: Harcourt Centre, Charlotte Way, Dublin 2; tel. (1) 4026200; fax (1) 4026237; e-mail plambert@bear.com; internet www.bearstearns.com; f. 1996; cap. US $1.0m., res US $104.0m., dep. US $6,858.2m. (Nov. 2003); Chair. PASCAL LAMBERT; Chief Execs NIAMH WALSH, LIAM MACNAMARA.

BNP Paribas Dublin: 5 George's Dock, Dublin 1; tel. (1) 6125000; fax (1) 6125100; e-mail dublin.desk@bnpparibas.com; Chair. J. P. BERNARD; Gen. Man. F. VAN DEN BOSCH.

BW Bank Ireland PLC: POB 4566, 6 George's Dock, IFSC, Dublin 1; tel. (1) 8244500; fax (1) 6701817; e-mail banking@bwbank.ie; internet www.bwbank.ie; f. 1994; cap. €6.7m., res €187.5m., dep. €3,628m. (Dec. 2003); Chair. STEPHEN ZIEGLER; Man. Dir LIAM MILEY.

CIBC World Markets Ireland Ltd: 28 North Wall Quay, IFSC, Dublin 1; tel. (1) 6624400; fax (1) 6624371; f. 1994 as CIBC Wood Grundy Ireland Ltd; cap. US $0.5m., res US $397.5m. (Oct. 2001); Chair. MICHAEL HORROCKS; CEO IAN LETCHFORD.

DePfa-Bank Europe PLC: International House, 3 Harbourmaster Pl., IFSC, Dublin 1; tel. (1) 6071600; fax (1) 8290213; e-mail info@ depfa.com; internet www.depfa.com; cap. €103m., res €437m., dep. €156,025m. (Dec. 2003); Chair. GERHARD E. BRUCKERMANN; Man. Dir DERMOT CAHILLANE.

Dresdner Bank (Ireland) PLC: La Touche House, IFSC, Dublin 1; tel. (1) 8181100; fax (1) 8181500; e-mail dbirl@dresdner-bank.ie; f. 1995; subsidiary of Allianz (AG), Germany; cap. €26.0m., res €229.5m., dep. €1,603.0m. (Dec. 2001); Chair. WOLFGANG BAERTZ; Man. Dirs WERNER SCHWANBERG, THOMAS KIEFER.

DZ Bank Ireland PLC: Guild House, Guild St, IFSC, Dublin 1; tel. (1) 6700715; fax (1) 8290298; e-mail info@dzbank.ie; internet www .dzbank.ie; f. 1994 as SGZ (Ireland) PLC, name changed in 2001; cap. €203.4., dep. €3,185.3m. (Dec. 2003); Man. Dirs THOMAS BUEMSEN, MARK JACOB.

First Active PLC: First Active House, Central Park, Leopardstown, Dublin 18; tel. (1) 2075000; fax (1) 2074900; e-mail info@ firstactive.com; internet www.firstactive.com; f. 1861 as Working Man's Benefit Building Society, name changed as above in 1998; cap. €45.8m., res €4.2m., dep. €7,511.3m. (Dec. 2003); Chair. JOHN CALLAGHAN; Chief Exec. CORMAC MCCARTHY.

Guinness and Mahon (Ireland) Ltd: 56–59 St Stephen's Green, Dublin 2; tel. (1) 7095200; fax (1) 7095210; internet www.gmbank.ie; f. 1836; wholly-owned subsidiary of Irish Life and Permanent PLC; cap. and res IR£5.7m., dep. IR£69.3m. (Dec. 1996); Chair. and Man. Dir BRIAN MCCONNELL.

ICC Bank PLC: 72–74 Harcourt St, Dublin 2; tel. (1) 4155555; fax (1) 6717797; e-mail info@icc.ie; internet www.icc.ie; f. 1933; privatized in 2000; industrial and commercial financing; cap. €46.9m., res €5.7m., dep. €3,508.1m. (Oct. 2000); Chair. PHIL FLYNN; Man. Dir MICHAEL QUINN; 6 brs.

IIB Bank Ltd: 91 Merrion Sq., Dublin 2; tel. (1) 6619744; fax (1) 6785034; e-mail info@iibbank.ie; internet www.iibbank.ie; f. 1973; subsidiary of Kredietbank NV, Belgium; merchant banking; cap. €79.7m., res €271.1m., dep. €9,462m. (Dec. 2003); Chair. PATRICK C. MCEVOY; CEO EDWARD A. MARAH; 1 br.

Intesa Bank Ireland PLC: AIB International Centre, IFSC, Dublin 1; tel. (1) 6115000; fax (1) 6115010; e-mail mail@intesabank.ie; internet www.bancaintesa.it; f. 1994 as Comit Finance (Ireland) PLC; cap. €8m., res €354.9m., dep. €2,256m. (Dec. 2003); Chair. JOHN BROUGHAN; Gen. Man. RICHARD BARKLEY.

Irish Life and Permanent PLC: Lower Abbey St, Dublin 1; tel. (1) 7042000; fax (1) 7041908; internet www.irishlifepermanent.ie; f. 1884 as Irish Temperance Building Society, name changed in 1999; cap. €86.12m., res €2,837.2m., dep. €20,886.8m. (Dec. 2003); Chair. ROY DOUGLAS; CEO DAVID WENT; 94 brs.

Lombard & Ulster Banking Ltd: Ulster Bank Group Centre, George's Quay, Dublin 2; tel. (1) 6085000; fax (1) 6085001; e-mail info@lombard.ie; internet www.lombard.ie; f. 1971; subsidiary of Ulster Bank Ltd; cap. p.u. IR£2.8m. (Dec. 1996); Chair. M. RAFFERTY; CEO B. KINGSTON; 13 brs.

JP Morgan Bank (Ireland) PLC: Chase Manhattan House, IFSC, Dublin 1; tel. (1) 6123000; fax (1) 6123123; internet www.chase.com; f. 1968; cap. US $8.3m., res US $43.8m., dep. US $483.8m. (Dec. 1999); in Sept. 2000 Chase Manhattan and J. P. Morgan agreed to merge to form J. P. Morgan Chase and Co, name changed as above in October 2001; Man. Dir FRANK GAYNOR; 1 br.

National Irish Bank Ltd: 3rd Floor, International House, 3 Harbourmaster Pl., IFSC, Dublin 1; tel. (1) 6385000; fax (1) 6385198; internet www.nib.ie; f. 1986; subsidiary of National Australia Group; cap. €62.6m., res €49.9m., dep. €3,279.1m. (Sep. 2003); Chair. Sir DAVID FELL; CEO DONALD PRICE; 59 brs.

Pfizer International Bank Europe: La Touche House, IFSC, Dublin 1; tel. (1) 4484600; fax (1) 4484698; f. 1985; cap. US $694,000., dep. US $4.8m. (Nov. 2003); Man. Dir CAMILLA UDEN; Financial Dir SUSAN WEBB.

Rabobank Ireland PLC: George's Dock House, IFSC, Dublin 1; tel. (1) 6076100; fax (1) 6701724; e-mail justin.sheridan@rabobank.com; internet www.rabobank.ie; f. 1994; corporate and investment banking; owned by Rabobank Nederland; cap. €7.1m., res €338.9m., dep. €19,618.7m. (Dec. 2003); Chair. WOUTER J. KOLFF; Man. Dir HIDZER KIEWIET DE JONGE.

Sanpaolo IMI Bank Ireland PLC: 3rd Floor, KBC House, 4 George's Dock, IFSC, Custom House Dock, Dublin 1; tel. (1) 6726720; fax (1) 6726727; e-mail sanpaoloirl@sanpaolo.ie; f. 1987; cap. €7.5m., res €505.7m., dep. €600m. (Dec. 2003); Chair. and Pres. DANTE CAMPIONI; Man. Dir PIER CARLO ARENA.

Ulster Bank Ltd: 33 College Green, Dublin 2; tel. (1) 6777623; fax (1) 6775035; subsidiary of National Westminster Bank PLC (United Kingdom); cap. and res IR£115.9m., dep. IR£7,767.2m. (Dec. 1997); Chair. Sir GEORGE QUIGLEY; CEO M. J. WILSON; 205 brs.

Ulster Bank Markets Ltd: Ulster Bank Group Centre, George's Quay, Dublin 2; tel. (1) 6084000; fax (1) 6084288; e-mail admin@ulsterbank.com; internet www.ulsterbank.com; f. 1973; subsidiary of Ulster Bank Ltd; total assets IR£5,061m. (Nov. 1998); Chair. MARTIN RAFFERTY; CEO PATRICK M. MCMAHON.

UniCredito Italiano Bank (Ireland) PLC: La Touche House, IFSC, Dublin 1; tel. (1) 6702000; fax (1) 6702100; e-mail enquiry@unicredito.ie; internet www.unicredito.ie; f. 1996 as Credito Italiano Bank (Ireland) PLC, name changed in 1999; cap. €113.9m., res €510.4m., dep. €10,390.3m. (Dec. 2003); Chair. BRIAN J. HILLERY; Man. Dir FRANCO SCHEPES.

WestLB Ireland PLC: IFSC House, IFSC, Dublin 1; tel. (1) 6127199; fax (1) 6127107; e-mail info@westlb.ie; f. 1978 as Standard Chartered Bank Ireland Ltd, name changed in 1996; cap. €17.7m., res €277.2m., dep €3,386.5m. (Dec. 2003); Chair. F. J. BECKER; Man. Dir K. HEIDLER.

Savings Banks

An Post Savings and Investments: General Post Office, O'Connell St, Dublin 1; tel. (1) 7057000; fax (1) 7057345; internet www

.anpost.ie; f. 1861; dep. €5,000m. (Dec. 2003); Chief Exec. DONAL CURTIN; 1,356 brs.

TSB Bank: TSB Corporate Centre, Blackrock, Co Dublin; tel. (1) 2124000; fax (1) 2124001; e-mail info@tsbbank.ie; internet www .tsbbank.ie; f. 1992; total assets IR£2,028.1m. (Dec. 1999); Chair. FINBARR GOLDEN; CEO HARRY W. LORTON; 80 brs.

Banking Associations

The Institute of Bankers in Ireland: 1 North Wall Quay, Dublin 1; tel. (1) 6116500; fax (1) 6116565; e-mail info@bankers.ie; internet www.bankers.ie; f. 1898; 21,000 mems; Pres. TED MCGOVERN; CEO ANTHONY WALSH.

Irish Bankers' Federation: Nassau House, Nassau St, Dublin 2; tel. (1) 6715311; fax (1) 6796680; e-mail ibf@ibf.ie; internet www.ibis .ie; more than 50 mems; Dir-Gen. JAMES A. BARDON.

STOCK EXCHANGE

The Irish Stock Exchange: 28 Anglesea St, Dublin 2; tel. (1) 6174200; fax (1) 6776045; e-mail info@ise.ie; internet www.ise.ie; f. 1799 as the Dublin Stock Exchange; amalgamated in 1973 with the United Kingdom stock exchanges to form The International Stock Exchange of the United Kingdom and the Republic of Ireland; separated from The International Stock Exchange in 1995; operates independently under the supervision of the Central Bank of Ireland; Chair. D. KINGSTON; CEO TOM HEALY; 99 mems.

SUPERVISORY BODY

In February 2001 the Government announced its intention to establish a single regulatory authority for financial services. Under the umbrella of the Central Bank of Ireland and Financial Services Authority, the Irish Financial Services Regulatory Authority (IFSRA), which was established on 1 May 2003, is responsible for the regulation of banking practices and other financial services in addition to overseeing consumer protection. The Government has also approved the establishment of the Irish Monetary Authority, which will handle the implementation of monetary policy and will report to the European Central Bank.

Irish Financial Services Regulatory Authority: POB 9138, College Green, Dublin 2; tel. (1) 4104000; fax (1) 4104900; e-mail info@ifsra.ie; internet www.ifsra.ie; f. 2003; regulates all financial services firms in Ireland and assists consumers to make informed and responsible decisions on their financial affairs in a safe and fair market; fosters sound and solvent financial institutions which gives depositors and other consumers of financial products confidence that their deposits and investments are safe; Chair. BRIAN PATTERSON; Chief Exec. LIAM O'REILLY.

INSURANCE

Principal Companies

AXA PMPA Insurance Ltd: Wolfe Tone House, Wolfe Tone St, Dublin 1; tel. (1) 8726444; fax (1) 8726536; internet www.axa.ie; f. 1967; Chief Exec. JOHN O'NEILL.

Bank of Ireland Life: Gratton House, Lower Baggot St, Dublin 2; tel. (1) 7039500; fax (1) 6620811; e-mail info@bankofirelandlife.ie; internet www.bankofirelandlife.ie; f. 1987 as Lifetime Assurance Co Ltd, changed name as above in 2003; Chair. JAMES P. GALLIVAN; Man. Dir BRIAN FORRESTER.

Canada Life Assurance (Ireland) Ltd: Canada Life House, Temple Rd, Blackrock, Co Dublin; tel. (1) 2102000; fax (1) 210220; internet www.canadalife.ie; f. 1903; Man. Dir TOM BARRY.

Eagle Star Insurance: Eagle Star House, Ballsbridge Park, Dublin 2; tel. (1) 6770666; fax (1) 6670660; e-mail info@eaglestar.ie; internet www.eaglestar.ie; f. 1919; Man. Dir IAN C. STUART.

Eagle Star Life Assurance Co (Ireland) Ltd: Eagle Star House, Frascati Rd, Blackrock, Co Dublin; tel. (1) 2831301; fax (1) 2831578; e-mail customerservices@eaglestarlife.ie; internet www .eaglestarlife.ie; f. 1950; Man. Dir M. J. BRENNAN.

Hansard Europe Ltd: POB 43, Enterprise House, Frascati Rd, Blackrock, Co Dublin; tel. (1) 2112800; fax (1) 2112850; e-mail enquiries@hansard.com; internet www.hansard.com.

Hibernian Group PLC: Haddington Rd, Dublin 4; tel. (1) 6078000; fax (1) 6608730; internet www.hibernian.ie; f. 1908; life and general; Chair. J. P. CULLITON; CEO BRYAN JENKINS.

Irish Life and Permanent PLC: Irish Life Centre, Lower Abbey St, Dublin 1; tel. (1) 7042000; fax (1) 7041900; e-mail customer .sales@irishlife.ie; internet www.irishlifepermanent.ie; f. 1939; financial services; merger with Lloyds TSB pending; Chair. GILLIAN BOWLER; Chief Exec. DAVID WENT.

New Ireland Assurance Co PLC: 11–12 Dawson St, Dublin 2; tel. (1) 6172000; fax (1) 6172800; e-mail info@newireland.ie; internet www.newireland.ie; f. 1924; Chair. and Man. Dir JOHN F. CASEY.

Royal & SunAlliance: 13–17 Dawson St, Dublin 2; tel. (1) 6771851; fax (1) 6717625; e-mail talktous@royalsunalliance.ie; internet www.royalsunalliance.ie; Gen. Man. PAUL DONALDSON.

Standard Life Assurance Co: 90 St Stephen's Green, Dublin 2; tel. (1) 6397000; fax (1) 6397262; e-mail marketing@standardlife.ie; internet www.standardlife.ie; f. 1834; life assurance, pensions, investments and annuities; Gen. Man. R. O'RIORDAN.

Zurich Insurance Co: Eagle Star House, Ballsbridge Park, Ballsbridge, Dublin 4; tel. (1) 6670666; fax (1) 6670644; internet www.zurich.com; owned by Eagle Star Insurance; property, liability, motor; CEO IAN STUART.

Insurance Associations

Insurance Institute of Ireland: 39 Molesworth St, Dublin 2; tel. (1) 6772582; fax (1) 6772621; e-mail iii@iol.ie; internet www.insurance-institute.ie; f. 1885; Pres. EAMONN DOWNEY; CEO JOHN O'NEIL; Deputy Pres. JOE GROGEN; 7,500 mems.

Irish Brokers' Association: 87 Merrion Sq., Dublin 2; tel. (1) 6613067; fax (1) 6619955; e-mail info@irishbrokers.ie; internet www.irishbrokers.com; Pres. PADRAIG O'SULLIVAN; CEO PAUL LYNCH; 500 mems.

Irish Insurance Federation: Insurance House, 39 Molesworth St, Dublin 2; tel. (1) 6761820; fax (1) 6761943; e-mail fed@iif.ie; internet www.iif.ie; Pres. PAUL DONALDSON; CEO MICHAEL KEMP.

Professional Insurance Brokers' Association (PIBA): 32 Greenmount Office Park, Harolds Cross, Dublin 6W; tel. (1) 4020250; fax (1) 4736920; e-mail info@piba.ie; internet www.piba.ie; CEO DIARMUID KELLY.

Trade and Industry

GOVERNMENT AGENCIES

An Post (The Post Office): General Post Office, Dublin 1; tel. (1) 7057000; fax (1) 8723553; e-mail press-office@anpost.ie; internet www.anpost.ie; f. 1984; provides national postal, savings and agency services through c. 1,600 outlets; Chair. MARGARET MCGINLEY; CEO DONAL CURTIN.

FÁS—Foras Áiseanna Saothair (State Training and Employment Authority): 27–33 Upper Baggot St, Dublin 4; tel. (1) 6070500; fax (1) 6070600; e-mail info@fas.ie; internet www.fas.ie; f. 1988; responsible for the provision of specific skills training, apprenticeships and traineeships, employment programmes provided by a network of 70 nation-wide, local and regional centres; supports co-operative and community enterprise; offers an industrial advisory service; public recruitment service at all levels of occupations; Chair. BRIAN GEOGHEGAN; Dir-Gen. RODY MOLLOY.

Food Safety Authority of Ireland: Abbey Court, Lower Abbey Street, Dublin 1; tel. (1) 8171300; fax (1) 8171301; e-mail info@fsai.ie; internet www.fsai.ie; f. 1998; takes all reasonable steps to ensure that food produced, distributed or marketed in Ireland meets the highest standards of food safety and hygiene reasonably available and to ensure that food complies with legal requirements, or, where appropriate, with recognized codes of good practice; Chair. Dr DANIEL O'HARE; Chief Exec. Dr JOHN O'BRIEN.

FORFÁS: Wilton Park House, Wilton Pl., Dublin 2; tel. (1) 6073000; fax (1) 6073030; e-mail info@forfas.ie; internet www.forfas.ie; f. 1993 to provide advice and to co-ordinate national industrial and technological policy; co-ordinates Enterprise Ireland and IDA Ireland (see below); Chair. PETER CASSELLS; CEO MARTIN CRONIN.

National Economic and Social Council (NESC): 16 Parnell Sq., Dublin 1; tel. (1) 8146300; fax (1) 8146358; e-mail info@nesc.ie; internet www.nesc.ie; f. 1973; analyses and reports on strategic issues relating to the efficient development of the economy and the achievement of social justice; Chair. DERMOT MCCARTHY; Dir Dr RORY O'DONNELL.

DEVELOPMENT ORGANIZATIONS

Enterprise Ireland: Wilton Park House, Wilton Pl., Dublin 2; tel. (1) 8082000; fax (1) 8082020; e-mail client.service@enterprise-ireland.com; internet www.enterprise-ireland.com; f. 1998; combines the activities of the fmr An Bord Tráchtála, Forbairt and the in-company training activities of FÁS (see above); Chair. PATRICK J. MOLLOY; Chief Exec. FRANK RYAN.

IDA Ireland: Wilton Park House, Wilton Pl., Dublin 2; tel. (1) 6034000; fax (1) 6034040; e-mail idaireland@ida.ie; internet www.idaireland.com; f. 1993; government agency with national responsibility for securing new investment from overseas in manufacturing and international services and for encouraging existing foreign enterprises in Ireland to expand their businesses; Chair. JOHN DUNNE; CEO SEAN DORGAN.

Irish Productivity Centre: 4B–5 Blanchardstown Corporate Park, Dublin 15; tel. (1) 8227125; fax (1) 8227116; e-mail ipc@ipc.ie; internet www.ipc.ie; aims to increase industrial productivity in Ireland; its council is composed of representatives from the Irish Business and Employers' Confed. and the Irish Congress of Trade Unions in equal numbers; offers consultancy services and practical assistance to Irish cos; CEO TOM MCGUINNESS.

Sustainable Energy Ireland: Glasnevin, Dublin 9; tel. (1) 8369080; fax (1) 8372848; e-mail info@sei.ie; internet www.sei.ie; promotes and assists environmentally and economically sustainable production, supply and use of energy, in support of government policy, across all sectors of the economy; CEO DAVID TAYLOR.

Teagasc (Agriculture and Food Development Authority): Oak Park, Carlow; tel. (59) 9170200; fax (59) 9142423; e-mail info@hq.teagasc.ie; internet www.teagasc.ie; f. 1988; provides research, educational and training services to agri-food sector and rural communities; Chair. Dr TOM O'DWYER; Nat. Dir JIM FLANAGHAN.

CHAMBERS OF COMMERCE

The Chambers of Commerce of Ireland (CCI): 17 Merrion Sq., Dublin 2; tel. (1) 6612888; fax (1) 6612811; e-mail info@chambersireland.ie; internet www.chambersireland.ie; f. 1923; represents c. 10,000 businesses and 40 direct corporate mems; Pres. ROBIN O'SULLIVAN; Chief Exec. JOHN DUNNE.

Cork Chamber of Commerce: Fitzgerald House, Summerhill North, Cork; tel. (21) 4509044; fax (21) 4508568; e-mail info@corkchamber.ie; internet www.corkchamber.ie; f. 1819; Pres. ROBIN O'SULLIVAN; Chief Exec. MICHAEL GEARY.

Dublin Chamber of Commerce: 7 Clare St, Dublin 2; tel. (1) 6647200; fax (1) 6766043; e-mail info@dubchamber.ie; internet www.dubchamber.ie; f. 1783; Pres. DAVID PIERCE; Chief Exec. SINA QUIN.

INDUSTRIAL AND TRADE ASSOCIATIONS

Construction Industry Federation: Construction House, Canal Rd, Dublin 6; tel. (1) 4066000; fax (1) 4966953; e-mail cif@cif.ie; internet www.cif.ie; 37 asscns representing 3,000 mems; Pres. NORBERT O'REILLY; Dir-Gen. LIAM B. KELLEHER.

Irish Creamery Milk Suppliers' Association (ICMSA): John Feely House, Dublin Rd, Limerick; tel. (61) 314677; fax (61) 315737; e-mail icmsa@eircom.net; f. 1950; Pres. PAT O'ROURKE; Gen. Sec. CIARAN DOLAN.

Irish Farmers' Association (IFA): Irish Farm Centre, Bluebell, Dublin 12; tel. (1) 4500266; fax (1) 4551043; e-mail reception@ifa.ie; internet www.ifa.ie; Pres. JOHN DILLON; Gen. Sec. MICHAEL BERKEREY.

Irish Fishermen's Organisation Ltd: Cumberland House, Fenian St, Dublin 2; tel. (1) 6612400; fax (1) 6612424; e-mail irishfish@eircom.net; f. 1974; representative body for Irish commercial fishermen; Chair. J. V. MADDOCK; Sec.-Gen. J. F. DOYLE.

Irish Grain and Feed Association: 18 Herbert St, Dublin 2; tel. (1) 6760680; fax (1) 6616774; e-mail igfa@cereal.iol.ie; Pres. M. MURPHY; Dir S. A. FUNGE.

EMPLOYERS' ORGANIZATIONS

Irish Business and Employers Confederation (IBEC): Confederation House, 84–86 Lower Baggot St, Dublin 2; tel. (1) 6051500; fax (1) 6381500; e-mail info@ibec.ie; internet www.ibec.ie; f. 1993; represents c. 7,000 cos and orgs; Pres. GARY MCGANN; Dir-Gen. TURLOUGH O'SULLIVAN.

Irish Exporters' Association: 28 Merrion Sq., Dublin 2; tel. (1) 6612182; fax (1) 6612315; e-mail iea@irishexporters.ie; internet www.irishexporters.ie; f. 1951; Pres. MICHAEL COUNAHAN; CEO JOHN WHELAN.

UTILITIES

Electricity

An Coimisiún um Rialáil Leictreachais (Commission for Electricity Regulation—CER): Plaza House, Belgard Rd, Tallaght, Dublin 24; tel. (1) 4000800; fax (1) 4000850; e-mail info@cer.ie; internet www.cer.ie; f. 1999 under the Electricity Regulation Act of 1999; responsible for licensing and regulating the generation and supply of electricity and authorizing construction of new generating plants; Commissioner TOM REEVES.

Electricity Supply Board: Lower Fitzwilliam St, Dublin 2; tel. (1) 6765831; fax (1) 6760727; e-mail service@esb.ie; internet www.esb.ie; f. 1927; reorg. 1988; operates 26 generating stations and manages the transmission and distribution of Ireland's electricity; Chair. TADHG O'DONOGHUE; CEO PADRAIG MCMANUS.

Gas

Bord Gáis Éireann (BGE) (The Irish Gas Board): Gasworks Rd, Co Cork; tel. (21) 4534000; fax (21) 4534001; internet www.bge.ie; f. 1976; natural gas transmission and distribution; Chair. ED O'CONNELL; CEO GERRY WALSH.

Water

Dept of the Environment, Heritage and Local Government: Custom House, Dublin 1; tel. (1) 8882479; fax (1) 8882576; e-mail press-office@environ.irlgov.ie; internet www.environ.ie; responsiblity for water supply.

CO-OPERATIVES

Irish Co-operative Organisation Society Ltd: 84 Merrion Sq., Dublin 2; tel. (1) 6764783; fax (1) 6624502; f. 1894 to co-ordinate the co-operative movement; three operating divisions; offices in Dublin, Cork, Sligo and Brussels, Belgium; Pres. DONAL CASHMAN; Dir-Gen. JOHN TYRRELL; mems: 130 co-operatives representing c. 175,000 farmers.

Irish Dairy Board: Grattan House, Lower Mount St, Dublin 2; tel. (1) 6619599; fax (1) 6612778; e-mail idb@idb.ie; internet www.idb.ie; f. 1961; reorg. 1973 as a famers' co-operative; principal exporter of Irish dairy products; Chair. MICHAEL CRONIN; Man. Dir NOEL CAWLEY.

TRADE UNIONS

Central Organization

Irish Congress of Trade Unions (ICTU): 31–32 Parnell Sq., Dublin 1; tel. (1) 8897777; fax (1) 8872012; e-mail congress@ictu.ie; internet www.ictu.ie; f. 1894; represents 759,360 workers in 64 affiliated unions in the Republic and Northern Ireland (2001); Gen. Sec. DAVID BEGG.

Principal Trade Unions Affiliated to the ICTU

*Amalgamated Transport and General Workers' Union: Transport House, 102 High St, Belfast, BT1 2DL; tel. (28) 9023-2381; fax (28) 9024-0133; internet tgwu.org.uk; Irish Regional Sec. BRENDAN HODGERS; 46,750 mems (2002).

Association of Higher Civil and Public Servants: 4 Warner's Lane, Dartmouth Rd, Dublin 6; tel. (1) 6686077; fax (1) 6686380; e-mail info@ahcps.ie; internet www.ahcps.ie; Chair. BRIGITTA O'DOHERTY; Gen. Sec. SEÁN Ó'RIORDÁIN; 3,200 mems (2004).

*Association of Teachers and Lecturers: 397A Holywood Rd, Belfast; internet www.askatl.org.uk; Irish Rep. E. RODGERS; 2,600 mems (2002).

Building and Allied Trades' Union: Arus Hibernia, 13 Blessington St, Dublin 7; tel. (1) 8301911; fax (1) 8304869; e-mail union@batu.ie; internet www.batu.ie; Pres. MICHAEL MCNALLY; Gen. Sec. PATRICK O'SHAUGHNESSY; 10,020 mems (2002).

Civil, Public & Services Union: 19–20 Adelaide Rd, Dublin 2; tel. (1) 6765394; fax (1) 6762918; e-mail headoffice@cpsu.ie; internet www.cpsu.ie; Pres. BETTY TYRRELL-COLLARD; Gen. Sec. BLAIR HORAN; 13,810 mems (2004).

Communications Workers' Union: Áras Ghaibréil, 575 North Circular Rd, Dublin 1; tel. (1) 8663000; fax (1) 8663099; e-mail info@cwu.ie; internet www.cwu.ie; f. 1922; Gen. Sec. STEVE FITZPATRICK; 19,600 mems (2003).

Electricity Supply Board Officers' Association: 43 East James's Place, Lower Baggot St, Dublin 2; tel. (1) 6767444; fax (1) 6789226; e-mail tonydunne@esboa.ie; f. 1959; Gen. Sec. TONY DUNNE; 2,200 mems (2002).

Federated Union of Government Employees: 32 Parnell Sq., Dublin 1; tel. (1) 8787057; 1,300 mems (2002).

*Graphical, Paper and Media Union: 10 The Anchorage, Charlotte Quay, Dublin 6; tel. (1) 6632048; fax (1) 6632022; e-mail gpmu@eircom.net; internet www.gpmu.org.uk; Irish Rep. E. A. KIRKPATRICK; 7,427 mems (2002).

Guinness Staff Union: 107 James's St, Dublin 8; tel. (1) 4536700; Gen. Sec. S. MACKELL.

Irish Bank Officials' Association: 93 St Stephen's Green, Dublin 2; tel. (1) 4755908; fax (1) 4780567; e-mail iboa@eircom.net; internet www.iboa.ie; Pres. GERRY RYAN; Gen. Sec. LARRY BRODERICK; 13,319 mems (2004).

Irish Federation of University Teachers: 11 Merrion Sq., Dublin 2; tel. (1) 6610910; fax (1) 6610909; e-mail ifut@eircom.net; internet www.ifut.ie; Pres. BREANDÁN Ó'COCHLÁIN; Gen. Sec. DALTÚN Ó'CEALLAIGH; 1,595 mems (2002).

Irish Medical Organization: IMO House, 10 Fitzwilliam Pl., Dublin 2; tel. (1) 6767273; fax (1) 6612758; e-mail imo@imo.ie; internet www.imo.ie; CEO GEORGE MCNEICE; 5,700 mems (2004).

Irish Municipal, Public and Civil Trade Union (IMPACT): Nerney's Court, Dublin 1; tel. (1) 8171500; fax (1) 8171501; e-mail rnolan@impact.ie; internet www.impact.ie; f. 1991; Gen. Sec. PETER MCLOONE; 52,000 mems (2004).

Irish National Teachers' Organization: 35 Parnell Sq., Dublin 1; tel. (1) 8047700; fax (1) 8722462; e-mail info@into.ie; internet www.into.ie; f. 1868; Pres. SHEILA NUNAN; Gen. Sec. JOHN CARR; 30,110 mems (2004).

Irish Nurses' Organization: The Whitworth Bldg, NorthBrunswick St, Dublin 7; tel. (1) 6640600; fax (1) 6610466; e-mail ino@ino.ie; internet www.ino.ie; Pres. ANN MARTIN; Gen. Sec. LIAM DORAN; 28,798 mems (2003).

MANDATE: 9 Cavendish Row, Dublin 1; tel. (1) 8746321; fax (1) 8729581; e-mail mandate@mandate.ie; internet www.mandate.ie; f. 1994; Gen. Sec. OWEN NULTY; 38,386 mems (2002).

*National Union of Journalists (Irish Executive Council): Liberty Hall, 9th Floor, Dublin 1; tel. (1) 8053258; fax (1) 8749250; e-mail liberty.hall@nuj.ie; internet www.nuj.org.uk; Irish Sec. SÉAMUS DOOLEY; Irish Organizer DES FAGAN; 4,713 mems (2002).

Prison Officers' Association: 18 Merrion Sq., Dublin 2; tel. (1) 6625495; Gen. Sec. JOHN CLINTON; 3,250 mems (2002).

Public Service Executive Union: 30 Merrion Sq., Dublin 2; tel. (1) 6767271; fax (1) 6615777; e-mail info@pseu.ie; internet www.pseu.ie; f. 1890; Pres. RHONA MCSWEENEY; Gen. Sec. DAN MURPHY; 9,000 mems (2002).

Services, Industrial, Professional and Technical Union (SIPTU): Liberty Hall, Dublin 1; tel. (1) 8586300; fax (1) 8749466; e-mail info@siptu.ie; internet www.siptu.ie; f. 1990; Gen. Pres. JACK O'CONNOR; Vice-Pres. BRENDAN HAYES; Gen. Sec. JOE O'FLYNN; 206,871 mems (2002).

Teachers' Union of Ireland: 73 Orwell Rd, Rathgar, Dublin 6; tel. (1) 4922588; fax (1) 4922953; e-mail tui@tui.ie; internet www.tui.ie; f. 1955; Pres. DEREK DUNNE; Gen. Sec. JAMES DORNEY; 11,477 mems (2002).

Technical, Engineering and Electrical Union: 5 Cavendish Row, Dublin 1; tel. (1) 8747047; fax (1) 8747048; e-mail info@teeu.ie; internet www.teeu.ie; f. 1992; Gen. Sec. OWEN WILLS; 35,012 mems (2004).

*Transport Salaried Staffs' Association: Nerney's Court, off Temple St, Dublin 1; tel. (1) 8743467; fax (1) 8745662; e-mail enquiries@tssa.ie; internet www.tssa.ie; f. 1897; Sec. RODGER HANNON; 1,944 mems (2004).

*Ulster Teachers' Union: 94 Malone Rd, Belfast, BT9 5HP, Northern Ireland; tel. (28) 9066-2216; e-mail office@utu.edu; internet www.utu.edu; Gen. Sec. RAY CALVIN; 6,045 mems (2002).

*Union of Construction, Allied Trades and Technicians: 56 Parnell Sq. West, Dublin 1; tel. (1) 8731599; internet www.ucatt.org.uk; Regional Sec. JIM MOORE; 14,170 mems (2000).

* These unions have their head office in the United Kingdom. Membership figures relate jointly to the Republic of Ireland and Northern Ireland.

Unions not Affiliated to the ICTU

Association of Secondary Teachers, Ireland (ASTI): ASTI House, Winetavern St, Dublin 8; tel. (1) 6040160; fax (1) 6719280; e-mail info@asti.ie; internet www.asti.ie; Pres. SUSIE HALL; Gen. Sec. JOHN WHITE; 16,500 mems (2004).

Chartered Institute of Journalists (Irish Region): EETPU Section, 5 Whitefriars, Aungier St, Dublin 2; tel. (1) 4784141; fax (1) 4750131; e-mail wims@journalism.com; internet www.cioj.dircon.co.uk; Chair. (Ireland) JAMES WIMS.

National Bus and Rail Union: 54 Parnell Sq., Dublin 1; tel. (1) 8730411; fax (1) 8730137; e-mail nbru@eircom.net; Gen. Sec. LIAM TOBIN.

Transport

Córas Iompair Éireann (CIE) (The Irish Transport Co): Heuston Station, Dublin 8; tel. (1) 6771871; fax (1) 7032276; f. 1945; reorg. 1986; state corpn operating rail and road transport services; three operating cos: Iarnród Éireann (Irish Rail), Bus Éireann (Irish Bus) and Bus Atha Cliath (Dublin Bus); Chair. Dr JOHN LYNCH.

RAILWAYS

In 1999 there were 1,872 km of track, of which 37 km were electrified. Railway services are operated by Iarnród Éireann.

Iarnród Éireann (Irish Rail): Connolly Station, Dublin 1; tel. (1) 8363333; fax (1) 8364760; e-mail info@irishrail.ie; internet www .irishrail.ie; f. 1987; division of CIE; Chair. MICHAEL P. MCDONNELL; Man. Dir JOE MEAGHER.

INLAND WATERWAYS

The Grand and Royal Canals and the canal link into the Barrow Navigation system are controlled by CIE. The Grand Canal and Barrow are open to navigation by pleasure craft, and the rehabilitation and restoration of the Royal Canal is proceeding. The River Shannon, which is navigable from Limerick to Lough Allen, includes stretches of the Boyle, Suck, Camlin, and Inny Rivers, the Erne Navigation, and the Shannon-Erne Waterway. The total length of Irish navigable waterways is about 700 km. A further 10 km of the Suck and Boyle Rivers were opened to navigation in 1998/99.

ROADS

At 31 December 2000 there were an estimated 92,500 km of roads, of which 2,739 km were national primary roads and 2,686 km were national secondary roads. About 94% of all roads were surfaced.

National Roads Authority: St Martin's House, Waterloo Rd, Dublin 4; tel. (1) 6602511; fax (1) 6680009; e-mail info@nra.ie; internet www.nra.ie; f. 1994; responsible for the planning, supervision and maintenance of nat. road network; Chair. PETER MALONE; CEO MICHAEL TOBIN.

SHIPPING

The principal sea ports are Dublin, Dún Laoghaire, Cork, Waterford, Rosslare, Limerick, Foynes, Galway, New Ross, Drogheda, Dundalk, Fenit and Whiddy Island.

Arklow Shipping Ltd: North Quay, Arklow, Co Wicklow; tel. (402) 39901; fax (402) 39902; e-mail chartering@asl.ie; internet www.asl .ie; Man. Dir JAMES S. TYRELL; 9 carriers.

Irish Continental Group PLC: Ferryport, Alexandra Rd, POB 19, Dublin 1; tel. (1) 6075628; fax (1) 8552268; e-mail info@icg.ie; internet www.icg.ie; controls Irish Ferries, operating passenger vehicle and roll-on/roll-off freight ferry services between Ireland, the United Kingdom and continental Europe; Chair. THOMAS TONER; Man. Dir EAMONN ROTHWELL.

Irish Ferries: Ferryport, Alexandra Rd, POB 19, Dublin 1; tel. (1) 8552222; fax (1) 8552272; e-mail info@irishferries.ie; internet www .irishferries.ie; drive-on/drive-off car ferry and roll-on/roll-off freight services between Ireland, the United Kingdom and continental Europe, operating up to 109 sailings weekly; Group Man. Dir E. ROTHWELL.

Stena Line: Ferry Terminal, Dún Laoghaire Harbour, Co Dublin; tel. (1) 2047700; fax (1) 2047620; e-mail info.ie@stenaline.com; internet www.stenaline.com; services between Dún Laoghaire and Dublin Port and Holyhead including high-speed catamaran, Rosslare and Fishguard, Belfast and Stranraer, passengers, drive-on/drive-off car ferry, roll-on/roll-off freight services.

Associations

Irish Chamber of Shipping: Port Centre, Alexandra Rd, Dublin Port, Dublin 1; tel. (1) 8559011; fax (1) 8559022; e-mail bks@iol.ie; Pres. Capt. S. HICKEY; Dir B. W. KERR.

Irish Ship Agents' Association: Ormonde House, 26 Harbour Row, Cobh, Co Cork; tel. (21) 4813180; fax (21) 4811849; e-mail isaal@eircom.net; Pres. MONNIE CLIFFE.

CIVIL AVIATION

There are international airports at Shannon, Dublin, Cork and Knock (Horan International), but only Shannon and Knock are used for transatlantic flights. In 2003 Dublin, Shannon and Cork handled 15.9m., 2.4m., and 2.2m. passengers, respectively. The national airline is Aer Lingus.

Dublin Airport Authority PLC: Dublin Airport, Dublin; tel. (1) 8141111; fax (1) 8415386; internet www.aer-rianta.ie; state-controlled; responsible for the management and development of Dublin,

Shannon and Cork airports; also operates seven hotels in Ireland and manages duty-free retail shops in several overseas locations; Chair. GARY MCGANN; Chief Exec. DECLAN COLLIER.

Commission for Aviation Regulation: 3rd Floor, Alexandra House, Earlsfort Terrace, Dublin 2; tel. (1) 6611700 ; fax (1) 6611269; e-mail info@aviationreg.ie; internet www.aviationreg.ie; f. 2001; sets the maximum level of airport and aviation terminal services charges and is also responsible for licensing the travel trade in Ireland as well as airlines; approves providers of ground handling services under EU regulations; also responsible, under EU legislation, for discharging Ireland's responsibilities for schedule co-ordination/slot allocation and the appointment, where necessary, of a schedules/slot co-ordinator; Commissioner WILLIAM PRASIFKA.

Irish Aviation Authority: Aviation House, Hawkins Street, Dublin 2; tel. (1) 6718655; fax (1) 6792934; e-mail info@iaa.ie; internet www.iaa.ie; f. 1994; provides air traffic management, engineering and communications in airspace controlled by Ireland and related air traffic technological infrastructure; also regulates aircraft airworthiness certification and registration; the licensing of personnel and organizations involved in the maintenance of aircraft, as well as the licensing of pilots and aerodromes; Chair. DONAL J. GEANEY; Chief Exec. EAMONN BRENNAN.

Airlines

Aer Arann: Level 5, The Altrium, Dublin Airport, Dublin 6; tel. (1) 8145240; fax (1) 8145250; e-mail info@aerarran.com; internet www .aerarran.com; Man. Dir PADRAIG O'CEIDIGH.

Aer Lingus Group PLC: Dublin Airport, Dublin; tel. (1) 8862222; fax (1) 8863832; internet www.aerlingus.com; f. 1936; reorg. 1993; state-owned; domestic and international scheduled services; CEO JOHN SHARMAN (acting).

Aer Turas Teoranta: Corballis Park, Dublin Airport, Dublin; tel. (1) 8444131; fax (1) 8446049; e-mail aerturasdublin@tinet.ie; f. 1962; world-wide cargo and passenger charter services; Chair. JOHN J. HARNETT; CEO PATRICK J. COUSINS.

Ryanair: Dublin Airport, Dublin; tel. (1) 8121212; fax (1) 8121213; internet www.ryanair.com; f. 1985; scheduled and charter passenger services to European destinations; Chair. DAVID BONDERMAN; CEO MICHAEL O'LEARY.

Tourism

Intensive marketing campaigns have been undertaken in recent years to develop new markets for Irish tourism. In addition to many sites of historic and cultural interest, the country has numerous areas of natural beauty, notably the Killarney Lakes and the west coast. In 2003 a total of 6.37m. foreign tourists (excluding residents of Northern Ireland and excursionists) visited the Republic.

Dublin Regional Tourism Authority Ltd: Suffolk St, Dublin 2; tel. (1) 6057700; fax (1) 6057757; e-mail reservations@dublintourism .ie; internet www.visitdublin.com; Chair. MICHAEL FLOOD; CEO FRANK MAGEE.

Fáilte Ireland (National Tourism Development Authority): Baggot St Bridge, Dublin 2; tel. (1) 6024000; fax (1) 6024100; e-mail info@ failteireland.ie; internet www.failteireland.ie; f. 1955; Chair. GILLIAN BOWLER; Chief Exec. SHAUN QUINN.

Irish Tourist Industry Confederation: 17 Longford Terrace, Monkstown, Co Dublin; tel. (1) 2844222; fax (1) 2804218; e-mail itic@ eircom.net; internet www.itic.ie; represents all major commercial tourism interests; Chair. CATHERINE REILLY; CEO EAMONN MCKEON.

Irish Travel Agents' Association: Heaton House, 3rd Floor, 32 South William St, Dublin 2; tel. (1) 6794089; fax (1) 6719897; e-mail info@itaa.ie; internet www.itaa.ie; f. 1971; 300 mems; Pres. MICHAEL DOORLEY; CEO (vacant).

Tourism Ireland: f. 2001 to promote jointly the Republic of Ireland and Northern Ireland as a tourist destination; Chair. ANDREW COPPEL; Chief Exec. PAUL O'TOOLE.

ISRAEL

Introductory Survey

Location, Climate, Language, Religion, Flag, Capital

The State of Israel lies in western Asia, occupying a narrow strip of territory on the eastern shore of the Mediterranean Sea. The country also has a narrow outlet to the Red Sea at the northern tip of the Gulf of Aqaba. All of Israel's land frontiers are with Arab countries, the longest being with Egypt to the west and with Jordan to the east. Lebanon lies to the north, and Syria to the north-east. The climate is Mediterranean, with hot, dry summers, when the maximum temperature in Jerusalem is generally between 30°C and 35°C (86°F to 95°F), and mild, rainy winters, with a minimum temperature in the city of about 5°C (41°F). The climate is sub-tropical on the coast but more extreme in the Negev Desert, in the south, and near the shores of the Dead Sea (a lake on the Israeli–Jordanian frontier), where the summer temperature may exceed 50°C (122°F). The official language of Israel is Hebrew, spoken by about two-thirds of the population, including most Jews. About 15% of Israeli residents, including Muslim Arabs, speak Arabic (which is also the language spoken by the inhabitants of the Occupied Territories and the Palestinian Autonomous Areas), while many European languages are also spoken. Some 76.5% of the population profess adherence to Judaism, the officially recognized religion of Israel, while almost 16% are Muslims. The national flag (proportions 8 by 11) has a white background, with a six-pointed blue star composed of two overlapping triangles (the 'Shield of David') between two horizontal blue stripes near the upper and lower edges. Although the Israeli Government has designated the city of Jerusalem (part of which is Jordanian territory annexed by Israel in 1967) as the country's capital, this is not recognized by the UN, and most foreign governments maintain their embassies in Tel-Aviv.

Recent History

The Zionist movement emerged in Europe in the 19th century in response to the growing sense of insecurity felt by Jewish minorities in many European countries as a result of the racial and religious persecution known as anti-semitism. The primary objective of Zionism was defined in 1897 at the Basle Congress, when Dr Theodor Herzl stated that Zionism sought 'to create for the Jewish people a home in Palestine secured by public law'. Zionists aimed to re-establish an autonomous community of Jews in what was their historical homeland.

Palestine was almost entirely populated by Arabs and had become part of the Turkish Ottoman Empire in the early 16th century. During the First World War the empire's Arab subjects launched the so-called Arab Revolt and, following the withdrawal of the Turks, in 1917–18 British troops occupied Palestine. In November 1917 the British Foreign Secretary, Arthur Balfour, declared British support for the establishment of a Jewish national home in Palestine, on condition that the rights of 'the existing non-Jewish communities' there were safeguarded; this became known as the Balfour Declaration and was confirmed by the governments of other countries then at war with Turkey. The British occupation of Palestine continued after the war under the terms of a League of Nations mandate, which also incorporated the Balfour Declaration. (In 1920 Palestine had been formally placed under British administration.) British rule in Palestine was hampered by the conflict between the declared obligations to the Jews and the rival claims of the indigenous Arab majority. In accordance with the mandate, Jewish settlers were admitted to Palestine only on the basis of limited annual quotas. There was serious anti-Jewish rioting by Arabs in 1921 and again in 1929. However, attempts to restrict immigration led to Jewish-sponsored riots in 1933. The extreme persecution of Jews by Nazi Germany caused an increase in the flow of Jewish immigrants, both legal and illegal, which intensified the unrest in Palestine. In 1937 a British proposal to establish separate Jewish and Arab states, while retaining a British-mandated area, was accepted by most Zionists but rejected by the Arabs, and by the end of that year hostilities between the two communities had descended into open conflict. A British scheme offering eventual independence for a bi-communal Palestinian state was postponed because of the Second

World War, during which the Nazis caused the deaths of an estimated 6m. Jews in central and eastern Europe (more than one-third of the world's total Jewish population). The enormity of the Holocaust greatly increased international sympathy for Jewish claims to a homeland in Palestine.

After the war there was strong opposition by Palestinian Jews to continued British occupation. Numerous terrorist attacks were made by Jewish groups against British targets. In November 1947 the UN approved a plan for the partition of Palestine into two states, one Jewish (covering about 56% of the area) and one Arab. The plan was, however, rejected by Arab states and by Palestinian Arab leaders. Meanwhile, the conflict between the two communities in Palestine escalated into full-scale war.

On 14 May 1948 the United Kingdom terminated its Palestine mandate, and Jewish leaders immediately proclaimed the State of Israel, with David Ben-Gurion as Prime Minister. Despite the absence of recognized borders, the new state quickly received international recognition. Neighbouring Arab countries attempted to conquer Israel by military force, and fighting continued until January 1949, when cease-fire agreements left Israel in control of 75% of Palestine, including West Jerusalem. The *de facto* territory of Israel was thus nearly one-third greater than the area assigned to the Jewish State under the original UN partition plan. Jordanian forces controlled most of the remainder of Palestine, the area eventually known as the West Bank (or, to Israelis, as Judea and Samaria) and which was fully incorporated into Jordan in April 1950.

By the end of the British mandate the Jewish population of Palestine was about 650,000 (or 40% of the total). The new State of Israel encouraged further Jewish immigration: the Law of Return, adopted in July 1950, established a right of immigration for all Jews, and resulted in a rapid influx of Jewish settlers. Many former Arab residents of Palestine, meanwhile, had become refugees in neighbouring countries, mainly Jordan and Lebanon. About 400,000 Arabs had evacuated their homes prior to May 1948, and a similar number fled subsequently. In 1964 exiled Palestinian Arabs formed the Palestine Liberation Organization (PLO), with the aim, at that time, of overthrowing Israel.

Israel, together with the United Kingdom and France, launched an attack on Egypt in October 1956 following the nationalization of the Suez Canal by President Nasser; Israel seized the Gaza Strip (part of Palestine occupied by Egypt since 1949) and the Sinai Peninsula. After pressure from the UN and the USA, Israeli forces evacuated these areas in 1957, when a UN Emergency Force (UNEF) was established in Sinai. In 1967 the United Arab Republic (Egypt) secured the withdrawal of UNEF from its territory. Egyptian forces immediately reoccupied the garrison at Sharm esh-Sheikh, near the southern tip of Sinai, and closed the Straits of Tiran to Israeli shipping, effectively (as in 1956) blockading the Israeli port of Eilat. In retaliation, Israeli forces attacked Egypt, Jordan and Syria, swiftly making substantial territorial gains. The so-called Six-Day War left Israel in possession of all Jerusalem, the West Bank area of Jordan, the Sinai Peninsula in Egypt, the Gaza Strip and the Golan Heights in Syria. East Jerusalem was almost immediately integrated into the State of Israel, while the other conquered areas were regarded as Occupied Territories. In November 1967 the UN Security Council passed Resolution 242, calling on Israel to withdraw from all the recently occupied Arab territories.

Ben-Gurion resigned in June 1963 and was succeeded by Levi Eshkol. Three of the parties in the ruling coalition merged to form the Israel Labour Party in 1968. On the death of Eshkol in 1969, Golda Meir was elected Prime Minister. A cease-fire between Egypt and Israel was arranged in August 1970, but other Arab states and Palestinian guerrilla (mainly PLO) groups continued hostilities. Another Arab–Israeli war began on 6 October 1973, as Arab forces invaded Israeli-held territory on Yom Kippur (the Day of Atonement), the holiest day of the Jewish year. Egyptian forces crossed the Suez Canal and reoccupied part of Sinai, while Syrian troops launched an offensive on the Golan Heights. Having successfully repelled these advances, Israel made cease-fire agreements with Egypt and Syria on 24 October. The UN Security Council passed another resolution (No. 338) in that month, urging a cease-fire and reaffirming the principles of Resolution 242.

Gen. Itzhak Rabin succeeded Golda Meir as Prime Minister of a Labour Alignment coalition in 1974. In May 1977 the Labour Alignment was defeated in a general election, and the Likud (Consolidation) bloc, led by Menachem Begin of the Herut (Freedom) Party, formed a Government with the support of minority parties.

In November 1977 the Egyptian President, Anwar Sadat, visited Israel, indicating tacit recognition of the Jewish State. In September 1978 President Jimmy Carter of the USA, President Sadat and Prime Minister Begin met at the US presidential retreat at Camp David, Maryland, and concluded two agreements: a 'framework for peace in the Middle East', providing for autonomy for the West Bank and Gaza Strip after a transitional period of five years; and a 'framework for the conclusion of a peace treaty between Egypt and Israel'. In February 1980 Egypt became the first Arab country to grant diplomatic recognition to Israel. However, approval by the Israeli Knesset (parliament) in that year of legislation stating explicitly that Jerusalem should be forever the undivided capital of Israel, and Israel's formal annexation of the Golan Heights in 1981, subsequently impeded prospects of agreement on Palestinian autonomy.

Israel's phased withdrawal from Sinai was completed in April 1982. In June Israeli forces, under 'Operation Peace for Galilee', advanced through Lebanon and surrounded West Beirut, trapping 6,000 PLO fighters. Egypt withdrew its ambassador from Tel-Aviv in protest. Diplomatic efforts resulted in the evacuation of 14,000–15,000 PLO and Syrian fighters from Beirut to various Arab countries. In September Lebanese Phalangists massacred Palestinian refugees in the Sabra and Chatila camps in Beirut; an official Israeli inquiry found the Israeli leadership to be indirectly responsible through negligence and forced the resignation of Gen. Ariel Sharon as Minister of Defence. In May 1983 Israel and Lebanon concluded a peace agreement, declaring an end to hostilities and envisaging the withdrawal of all foreign forces from Lebanon within three months. Syria's refusal, however, to withdraw some 30,000 troops, and the continued presence of some 7,000 PLO fighters in the Beka'a valley and northern Lebanon, delayed the Israeli withdrawal, although by the end of 1983 only 10,000 Israeli troops (of the original 30,000) remained in Lebanon.

The Government's prestige had been damaged by the Beirut massacre and by a capitulation to wage demands by Israeli doctors. In August 1983 Itzhak Shamir succeeded Begin as leader of the Likud bloc and Prime Minister. However, economic difficulties further undermined the Government, and the Labour Party forced a general election in July 1984. Neither the Labour Alignment nor Likud could form a viable coalition, so President Chaim Herzog invited the Labour leader, Shimon Peres, to form a government of national unity with Likud.

Israel's forces finally completed their withdrawal from Lebanon in June 1985, leaving responsibility for policing the occupied southern area of Lebanon to the Israeli-controlled 'South Lebanon Army' (SLA). During 1986 rocket attacks on settlements in northern Israel were resumed by Palestinian guerrillas. Israel responded with air assaults on Palestinian targets in southern Lebanon. Meanwhile, the Shi'ite fundamentalist Hezbollah intensified attacks on SLA positions within the southern buffer zone. The conflict escalated following the abduction, in July 1989, of a local Shi'a Muslim leader by Israeli agents; and again in February 1992, after the assassination by the Israeli air force of the Hezbollah Secretary-General, Sheikh Abbas Moussawi.

In July 1988 King Hussein abrogated Jordan's legal and administrative responsibilities in the West Bank, and declared that he would no longer represent the Palestinians in any international conference on the Palestinian question, which from 1984 had come to dominate the political landscape of the Middle East. King Hussein's decision strengthened the PLO's negotiating position as the sole legitimate representative of the Palestinian people. Since December 1987 international attention had been focused on the Palestinian cause after the outbreak of an *intifada* (uprising) against Israeli rule in the Occupied Territories and Israeli attempts to suppress the rebellion. In November 1988 the PLO declared an independent Palestinian State (notionally the West Bank and Gaza Strip), and endorsed UN Security Council Resolution 242, thereby implic-

itly granting recognition to Israel. The USA refused to accept PLO proposals for a two-state solution put forward by the Chairman of the PLO, Yasser Arafat, in December, but it did open a dialogue with the organization. However, Prime Minister Itzhak Shamir (the Likud leader had assumed the Israeli premiership in October 1986, in accordance with the 1984 coalition agreement) would not negotiate, distrusting the PLO's undertaking to abandon violence. Instead, he appeared to favour the introduction of limited self-rule for the Palestinians of the West Bank and Gaza, as outlined in the 1978 Camp David accords. At the general election in November 1988 neither Likud nor Labour secured enough seats in the Knesset to form a viable coalition, leading to another Government of national unity being formed under Shamir, with Shimon Peres as Deputy Prime Minister and Minister of Finance.

In April 1989 Shamir presented a peace proposal that would include a reaffirmation by Egypt, Israel and the USA of the Camp David accords, and plans for the holding of free democratic elections in the West Bank and Gaza for Palestinian delegates who could negotiate self-rule under Israeli authority. The proposals, precluding direct talks with the PLO, were unacceptable to the PLO, which did not consider that elections could establish the basis for a political settlement. In September, none the less, President Hosni Mubarak of Egypt invited clarification of Shamir's plans and offered to convene an Israeli-Palestinian meeting in Cairo. This was rejected by Likud ministers, on the grounds that it would entail direct contact with PLO delegates. In November Israel provisionally accepted a proposal by the US Secretary of State, James Baker, for a preliminary meeting to discuss the holding of elections in the West Bank and Gaza, on condition that Israel would not be required to negotiate with the PLO and that the talks would concern only Israel's election proposals. However, the PLO continued to demand a direct role, and the Baker initiative foundered.

The fragile Likud-Labour coalition was endangered in early 1990 by disputes and dismissals, and in March the Knesset adopted a motion of 'no confidence' in Prime Minister Shamir. Shimon Peres was unable to form a new coalition, and in June, after several weeks of political bargaining, Shamir formed a new Government—a narrow, right-wing coalition of Likud and five small parties, with three independent members of the Knesset. In a policy document Shamir emphasized the right of Jews to settle in all parts of 'Greater Israel', his opposition to the creation of an independent Palestinian state, and his refusal to negotiate with the PLO—or with any Palestinians other than those resident in the Occupied Territories (excluding East Jerusalem).

In March 1990 US President George Bush opposed the granting to Israel of a loan of some US $400m. for the housing of Soviet Jewish immigrants, since Israel would not guarantee to refrain from constructing new settlements in the Occupied Territories. Violence erupted throughout Israel and the Occupied Territories in May. The PLO's refusal to condemn the violence caused the USA to suspend its dialogue with the organization and to veto a UN Security Council resolution urging that international observers be dispatched to the Occupied Territories. In June Shamir invited President Hafiz al-Assad of Syria to peace negotiations, and the UN Secretary-General's special envoy also visited Israel for discussions. However, Shamir rejected US proposals for direct talks between Israeli and Palestinian delegations.

Iraq's invasion of Kuwait in August 1990 brought about an improvement in US-Israeli relations: it was imperative, if a coalition of Western and Arab powers opposed to Iraq was to be maintained, that Israel should not become actively involved in the conflict. In October some 17 Palestinians were shot dead by Israeli police, following clashes with Jewish worshippers. International outrage at the shootings resulted in a UN Security Council vote to send an investigative mission, although Israel agreed only to receive a UN emissary. Iraqi missile attacks on Israel in January 1991, shortly after the US-led multinational force had begun its offensive against Iraq, threatened the cohesion of the force. US diplomatic efforts, and the installation in Israel of US air defence systems, averted an immediate Israeli response. Meanwhile, widespread support for Iraq among Palestinians increased the Israeli Government's insistence that Shamir's 1989 peace plan could be the only basis for dialogue.

In March 1991 President Bush identified the resolution of the Arab–Israeli conflict as a priority of his Administration. By August intensive diplomacy by Baker had secured the agreement of the Israeli, Syrian, Egyptian, Jordanian and Lebanese Governments, and of Palestinian representatives, to attend a regional peace conference, the terms of reference for which would be a comprehensive peace settlement based on UN Security Council Resolutions 242 and 338. An initial, 'symbolic' session was held in Madrid, Spain, in October. However, subsequent talks soon became deadlocked over procedural issues. Israel repeatedly questioned the status of the Palestinian-Jordanian delegation and the right of the Palestinian component to participate separately in negotiations; furthermore, Israel's refusal to end construction of new settlements in the Occupied Territories continually jeopardized the peace process. In February 1992, immediately prior to the fourth session of peace talks, to be held in Washington, DC, Baker demanded a complete halt to Israel's settlement-building programme as a precondition for the granting of loan guarantees to the value of US $10,000m. for the housing of Jewish immigrants from the former USSR.

A fifth round of negotiations was held in Washington, DC, in April 1992. Procedural issues were resolved, and, during talks with the Palestinian component of the Palestinian-Jordanian delegation, Israeli representatives presented proposals for the holding of municipal elections in the West Bank and Gaza, and for the transfer of control of health-care provision there to Palestinian authorities. The Palestinian delegation did not reject the proposals outright, although they fell far short of the Palestinians' aim of full legislative control of the Occupied Territories. No progress was made between Israeli and Syrian officials on the issue of the Golan Heights.

In May 1992 the first multilateral negotiations between the parties to the Middle East peace conference commenced; however, the sessions were boycotted by Syria and Lebanon, considering them futile until progress had been made in the bilateral negotiations. Various combinations of delegations in several cities attended discussions concerning regional economic co-operation, arms control, water resources, environmental issues and Palestinian refugees. Israel boycotted the meetings on Palestinian refugees and regional economic development after the USA approved Palestinian proposals to allow exiles (i.e. non-residents of the Occupied Territories) to be included in the Palestinian delegations to these two sessions.

A general election was held in June 1992, following the collapse of Itzhak Shamir's coalition Government in January. The Labour Party won 44 of the 120 seats in the Knesset, and Likud 32. Meretz—an alliance of Ratz, Shinui and the United Workers' Party, which had won 12 seats—confirmed its willingness to form a coalition government with Labour. However, even with the support of the two Arab parties—the Democratic Arab Party and Hadash—which together held five seats in the Knesset, such a coalition would have a majority of only two votes over the so-called 'right bloc' (Likud, Tzomet, Moledet and Tehiya) and the religious parties which had allied themselves with Likud in the previous legislature. The new Chairman of the Labour Party, Itzhak Rabin, was accordingly obliged to solicit support among the religious parties. His Government, presented to the Knesset in July, was an alliance of Labour, Meretz and the ultra-orthodox Shas; the coalition held a total of 62 Knesset seats, and also commanded the unofficial support of the two Arab parties. Most international observers regarded the installation of the Labour-led coalition as having improved the prospects for peace in the Middle East. However, the sixth and seventh rounds of bilateral negotiations between Israeli, Syrian, Lebanese and Palestinian-Jordanian delegations in September–November 1992 failed to achieve any progress.

An eighth round of bilateral negotiations between Israeli and Arab delegations commenced in Washington in December 1992, but were soon overshadowed by events in the Occupied Territories (where there had been violent confrontations between Palestinians and the Israeli security forces), which led to the withdrawal of the Arab participants. In mid-December, in response to the deaths in the Territories of five members of the Israeli security forces, and to the abduction and murder by the Islamic Resistance Movement (Hamas) of an Israeli policeman, the Government ordered the deportation to Lebanon of 413 alleged Palestinian supporters of Hamas. The expulsions provoked international outrage, while the UN Security Council approved Resolution 799 condemning the deportations and demanding the return of the deportees to Israel. Despite threats by the Palestinian delegation to boycott future talks until all of the deportees had been readmitted, in February 1993 the Israeli Government insisted that the majority of the deportees would

have to serve a period of exile. Consequently, the ninth round of bilateral negotiations was formally suspended; although the Security Council welcomed the Israeli Government's decision to permit the return of 100 deportees, Palestinian delegates insisted on full implementation of Resolution 799 as a precondition for resumed discussions. In March, amid a sharp escalation in violence between Palestinians and Israeli security forces in the West Bank and Gaza, Israel sealed off the territories indefinitely.

The suspended ninth round of bilateral negotiations in the Middle East peace process resumed in Washington in April 1993. The Palestinian delegation apparently agreed to attend the sessions following pressure by Arab governments, and after Israel had agreed to allow Faisal Husseini, the nominal leader of the Palestinian delegation and a resident of East Jerusalem, to participate. Israel was also reported to have undertaken to halt punitive deportations, and, with the USA, to have reaffirmed its commitment to Resolutions 242 and 338 as the terms of reference for the peace process. However, no substantive progress was achieved during the talks.

In May 1993 Ezer Weizman was inaugurated as President; Weizman, leader of the Yahad party, had been elected by the Knesset in March. Also in March Binyamin Netanyahu was chosen to replace Shamir as the Likud leader.

At the 10th round of bilateral negotiations, convened in Washington in June 1993, the participants agreed to establish a committee charged with the drafting of a statement of principles concerning Palestinian self-rule in the Occupied Territories—now regarded as the key element in the Middle East peace process. In July Israeli armed forces mounted the most intensive air and artillery attacks on targets in Lebanon since 'Operation Peace for Galilee' in 1982, in retaliation for attacks by Hezbollah fighters on settlements in northern Israel.

On 13 September 1993 Israel and the PLO signed a Declaration of Principles on Palestinian Self-Rule in the Occupied Territories. The agreement, which entailed mutual recognition by Israel and the PLO, had been elaborated during a series of secret negotiations mediated by Norwegian diplomacy (and therefore became known as the Oslo accords). The Declaration of Principles established a detailed timetable for Israel's disengagement from the Occupied Territories, and stipulated that a permanent settlement of the Palestinian question should be in place by December 1998. From 13 October 1993 Palestinian authorities were to assume responsibility for education and culture, health, social welfare, direct taxation and tourism in the Gaza Strip and the Jericho area of the West Bank, and a transitional period of Palestinian self-rule was to begin on 13 December. Although Prime Minister Rabin secured ratification of the Declaration of Principles, and of Israel's recognition of the PLO, by the Knesset on 23 September 1993, there was widespread opposition to it from right-wing Israelis. The PLO Central Council, meeting in the Tunisian capital, approved the accord on 11 October. However, the conclusion of the agreement aggravated divisions in the Palestinian liberation movement, while the reaction by the other Arab states engaged in peace negotiations with Israel was mixed.

Also in September 1993 the resignation of Aryeh Der'i of the ultra-orthodox Shas as Minister of the Interior, following allegations of corruption, provoked the withdrawal from the Government of other Shas ministers, thus reducing the coalition to an alliance between the Labour Party and Meretz (and the Government's majority in the Knesset to only two). Protracted negotiations failed to achieve the return of Shas to the Government and, in July 1994, were superseded by a coalition agreement signed with Yi'ud, a breakaway group from the Tzomet Party.

Itzhak Rabin and Yasser Arafat held their first meeting in the context of the Declaration of Principles in Cairo on 6 October 1993. A joint PLO-Israeli liaison committee subsequently met on 13 October, with delegations headed, respectively, by Mahmud Abbas (Abu Mazen) and Shimon Peres; the committee was to meet frequently to monitor the implementation of the accord. A technical committee also held three meetings during October in the Egyptian resort of Taba: its task was to define the precise details of Israel's military withdrawal from the Gaza Strip and Jericho, scheduled to take place between 13 December 1993 and 13 April 1994. However, it proved impossible satisfactorily to negotiate the details of Israel's withdrawal by December 1993, largely because of a failure to agree on security arrangements for border crossings between the Gaza Strip and Jericho, and Jordan and Egypt.

Following meetings in Damascus between US Secretary of State Warren Christopher and Syria's President Assad and Minister of Foreign Affairs, Farouk ash-Shara', in December 1993, Syria announced its willingness to resume bilateral talks with Israel. In January 1994 Israel appeared to indicate, tentatively, that it might be prepared to execute a full withdrawal from the Golan Heights in return for a comprehensive peace agreement with Syria. Bilateral negotiations between Israeli and Syrian delegations resumed in Washington later that month.

In February 1994 Israel and the PLO reached an agreement to share control of the two future international border crossings. Security arrangements for Jewish settlers in the Gaza Strip had also reportedly been decided, whereby three access routes to settlements were to remain under Israeli control. Talks followed regarding the implementation of the first stage of Palestinian autonomy in the Gaza Strip and Jericho; the size, structure and jurisdiction of a future Palestinian police force; control of sea and air space; and the delineation of the Jericho enclave. Meeting in Cairo, on 4 May the two parties signed an accord detailing arrangements for Palestinian self-rule in the Gaza Strip and Jericho. The accord provided for Israel's military withdrawal from these areas, and for the deployment there of a 9,000-strong Palestinian police force. A nominated Palestinian (National) Authority (PA) was to assume the responsibilities of the Israeli military administration in Gaza and Jericho, although Israeli authorities were to retain control in matters of external security and foreign affairs. Elections for a Palestinian Council, which, under the terms of the Oslo accords, were to have taken place in Gaza and the West Bank in July, were now postponed until October. Israel's military withdrawal from Gaza and Jericho was completed on 13 May, and on 17 May the PLO formally assumed control of the Israeli Civil Administration's departments there. On 26–28 May the PA held its inaugural meeting in Tunis, defining a political programme and distributing ministerial portfolios. Arafat made a symbolic return to Gaza City on 1 July—his first visit for 25 years—and the PA was formally inaugurated in Jericho on 5 July. In August Israel and the PLO signed an agreement extending the authority of the PA to include education, health, tourism, social welfare and taxation.

On 25 July 1994 Israel and Jordan signed a joint declaration formally ending the state of war between them and further defining arrangements for future bilateral negotiations. In September Itzhak Rabin announced details of a plan for a partial withdrawal of Israeli armed forces from the occupied Golan Heights, after which a three-year trial period of Israeli-Syrian 'normalization' would ensue. The proposals were rejected by President Assad; however, the Syrian leader did state his willingness to work towards peace with Israel. In late September Rabin and King Hussein held talks in Aqaba, Jordan, with the aim of devising a timetable for a full Israeli-Jordanian peace treaty. Also in that month Morocco, closely followed by Tunisia, became the second and third Arab states to establish diplomatic ties with Israel, and the six members of the Co-operation Council for the Arab States of the Gulf (the Gulf Co-operation Council, see p. 193) also decided to revoke the subsidiary elements of the Arab economic boycott of Israel. On 26 October Israel and Jordan signed a formal peace treaty, defining their common border and providing for a normalization of relations. The peace treaty was denounced by the Syrian Government, all elements of Palestinian opinion, and by some Islamists in Jordan.

Meanwhile, a World Bank-sponsored conference of international donors, held in Paris in September 1994, collapsed almost immediately, owing to a dispute between Israel and the Palestinians over Palestinian investment plans to fund projects in East Jerusalem. Meeting in Oslo, Norway, shortly afterwards, Arafat and Peres negotiated a 15-point agreement aimed at accelerating economic aid to the PA. Later in September Arafat and Rabin met at the Erez crossing point between Gaza and Israel to discuss the future Palestinian elections in the West Bank and Gaza Strip. The PLO reportedly sought to elect a 100-member Palestinian Council, while Israel insisted that its size should be restricted to 25 members. Israel rejected Arafat's proposal for elections on 1 November as unrealistic; it was, however, agreed to meet again in October to negotiate a compromise. At the same time, Arafat agreed to 'take all measures' to prevent attacks on Israeli targets by opponents of the Oslo process. In late September, however, Rabin approved a plan to build some 1,000 new housing units at a Jewish settlement just

inside the West Bank, in an apparent reversal of the moratorium he had imposed on construction in 1992. The PLO claimed that this contravened the Declaration of Principles. In early October 1994 Hamas claimed responsibility for an attack in Jerusalem in which an Israeli soldier and a Palestinian civilian died. On the same day another Israeli soldier was abducted by Hamas fighters near Tel-Aviv, who subsequently demanded that Israel release the detained Hamas spiritual leader, Sheikh Ahmad Yassin, and other Palestinian prisoners in exchange for his life. Despite Palestinian action to detain some 300 Hamas members in the Gaza Strip, the kidnapped soldier was killed in the West Bank in mid-October. Shortly afterwards an attack by a Hamas suicide bomber in Tel-Aviv, in which 22 people died, prompted Israel to close its borders with the Palestinian territories.

In November 1994 a member of another militant Palestinian organization, Islamic Jihad, was killed in a car bomb attack in Gaza. The attack was blamed on the Israeli security forces by many Palestinians opposed to the Oslo accords. Three Israeli soldiers were subsequently killed in a suicide bombing in the Gaza Strip, for which Islamic Jihad claimed responsibility. It became clear that Israel's security concerns would continue to delay the redeployment of its armed forces in the West Bank and the holding of Palestinian elections, as Rabin stated, in December, that the elections would either have to take place in the continued presence of Israeli forces, or be postponed for a year. In January 1995 a suicide bombing (responsibility for which was again claimed by Islamic Jihad) at Beit Lid, in which 21 Israeli soldiers and civilians died, seriously jeopardized the peace process. The Government again closed Israel's borders with the West Bank and Gaza, and postponed the planned release of some 5,500 Palestinian prisoners. An emergency meeting of the leaders of Egypt, Israel, Jordan and the PLO was convened in Cairo early the following month; the summit's final communiqué condemned acts of terror and violence, and expressed support for the Declaration of Principles and the wider peace process. US President Bill Clinton subsequently held a meeting in Washington involving the Israeli and Egyptian Ministers of Foreign Affairs and the PA Minister of Planning and Economic Co-operation, after which Shimon Peres reportedly stated that any further expansion of Palestinian self-rule in the West Bank was conditional upon real progress by the PA in suppressing terrorism. On 9 February, meanwhile, Israeli armed forces completed their withdrawal from Jordanian territories, in accordance with the bilateral peace treaty concluded in October 1994.

In March 1995 it was announced that Israel and Syria had agreed to resume peace negotiations for the first time since February 1994. In May 1995 Syria and Israel were reported to have concluded a 'framework understanding on security arrangements', intended to facilitate discussions on security issues. Peres subsequently indicated that Israel had proposed that its forces should withdraw from the Golan Heights over a four-year period; Syria, however, had insisted that the withdrawal be effected over 18 months.

Despite intensive negotiations, it proved impossible to conclude an agreement on the expansion of Palestinian self-rule in the West Bank by the target date of 1 July 1995. The principal obstacles remained the question of precisely to where Israeli troops in the West Bank would redeploy, and the exact nature of security arrangements for some 130,000 Jewish settlers who were to remain there. In August Hamas claimed responsibility for a suicide bomb attack on a bus in Jerusalem, which killed six people. (Two suicide bombings in Gaza in April 1995, in which seven Israeli soldiers died, had reportedly led to the arrest by Palestinian police of up to 300 members of Hamas and Islamic Jihad, which claimed responsibility for the attacks.) On 28 September the Israeli-Palestinian Interim Agreement on the West Bank and the Gaza Strip was finally signed by Israel and the PLO. Its main provisions were the withdrawal of Israeli armed forces from a further six West Bank towns (Nablus, Ramallah, Jenin, Tulkaram, Qalqilya and Bethlehem), and a partial redeployment from the town of Hebron; national Palestinian legislative elections to an 82-member Palestinian Council and for a Palestinian Executive President; and the release, in three phases, of Palestinians detained by Israel. In anticipation of a violent reaction against the Interim Agreement by so-called 'rejectionist' groups within the Occupied Territories, Israel immediately sealed its borders with the West Bank and Gaza. Meanwhile, right-wing elements within Israel also denounced the agreement.

On 4 November 1995 Itzhak Rabin was assassinated in Tel-Aviv by a Jewish student opposed to the peace process, in particular the Israeli withdrawal from the West Bank. The assassination caused a further marginalization of those on the extreme right wing of Israeli politics who had advocated violence as a means of halting the Oslo process, and provoked criticism of the opposition Likud, which, it was widely felt, had not sufficiently distanced itself from such extremist elements. The Minister of Foreign Affairs, Shimon Peres, was, with the agreement of Likud, invited to form a new government. The members of the outgoing administration—Labour, Meretz and Yi'ud—subsequently signed a new coalition agreement, and the Cabinet was formally approved by the Knesset in late November. In February 1996 Peres announced that elections to the Knesset and—for the first time—the direct election of the Prime Minister would take place in May 1996.

In spite of Rabin's assassination, Israeli armed forces completed their withdrawal from the West Bank town of Jenin on 13 November 1995, and in December they withdrew from Tulkaram, Nablus, Qalqilya, Bethlehem and Ramallah. With regard to Hebron, Israel and the PA signed an agreement transferring jurisdiction in some 17 areas of civilian affairs from Israel to the PA. At talks with Arafat at Erez in December, Peres confirmed that Israel would release some 1,000 Palestinian prisoners before the impending Palestinian elections.

Peace negotiations between Israel and Syria resumed in December 1995 in Maryland, USA, followed by a second round in January 1996. Also in January King Hussein made a public visit to Tel-Aviv, during which Israel and Jordan signed a number of agreements relating to the normalization of economic and cultural relations.

Palestinian legislative and presidential elections were held in late January 1996, leading in principle to the final stage of the peace process, when Palestinian and Israeli negotiators would address such issues as Jerusalem, the rights of Palestinian refugees, the status of Jewish settlements in the Palestinian territories, and the extent of that autonomy. In February and March, however, more than 50 Israelis died as a result of suicide bomb attacks in Jerusalem, Ashkelon and Tel-Aviv, and talks were suspended. Israel again ordered the indefinite closure of its borders with the Palestinian territories, and demanded that the PA suppress the activities of Hamas and Islamic Jihad in the areas under its control. A hitherto unknown group, the 'Yahya Ayyash Units', claimed responsibility for the attacks, to avenge the assassination—allegedly by Israeli agents—of Ayyash, a leading Hamas activist, in January 1996. Yasser Arafat, now the elected Palestinian President, condemned the bombings, and in late February more than 200 members of Hamas were reported to have been detained by Palestinian security forces. The attacks led Israel to impose even more stringent security measures, notably asserting the right of its armed forces to enter PA-controlled areas when Israeli security was at stake. Furthermore, an agreement to redeploy troops from Hebron by 20 March was rescinded.

The suicide bombings also undermined the talks taking place between Israeli and Syrian representatives in the USA, and in March 1996 the Israeli negotiators returned home. Syria and Lebanon both declined an invitation to attend the so-called 'Summit of Peacemakers', held at the Egyptian resort of Sharm esh-Sheikh in that month, at which some 27 Heads of State expressed their support for the Middle East peace process and pledged to redouble their efforts to combat terrorism. In April Israel and Turkey signed a number of military co-operation agreements, a development condemned by Syria as a threat to its own security and to that of all Arab and Islamic countries.

In April 1996 Israeli armed forces began a sustained campaign of intense air and artillery attacks on alleged Hezbollah positions in southern Lebanon and the southern suburbs of Beirut. The declared aim of the Israeli operation (code-named 'Grapes of Wrath') was to achieve the complete cessation of rocket attacks by Hezbollah on settlements in northern Israel. Some 400,000 Lebanese were displaced northwards, after the Israeli military authorities warned that they would be endangered by the offensive against Hezbollah. Moreover, the shelling by Israeli forces of a base of the UN peace-keeping force at Qana resulted in the deaths of more than 100 Lebanese civilians who had been sheltering there, and of four UN peace-keepers. A cease-fire 'understanding' took effect in late April, which was effectively a compromise confining the conflict to the area of the security zone in southern Lebanon, recognizing both Hezbollah's right to resist Israeli occupation and Israel's right to self-defence; the 'understanding' also envisaged the establishment of an Israel-Lebanon Monitoring Group (ILMG), comprising Israel, Lebanon, Syria, France and the USA, to supervise the cease-fire.

Israel welcomed the decision of the Palestine National Council (PNC) in late April 1996 to amend the Palestinian National Charter (or PLO Covenant), removing all clauses demanding the destruction of Israel: the Israeli Government had demanded that the Covenant be amended as a precondition for participation in the final stage of peace negotiations with the PLO.

No party gained an outright majority of the 120 seats in the elections to the Knesset, held on 19 May 1996, but the Likud leader, Binyamin Netanyahu, achieved a marginal victory over Peres in the direct election for the Prime Minister. Prior to the legislative election a formal alliance between Likud, the Tzomet Party and Gesher had been announced. This alliance secured 32 seats, and Labour 34. The success of the ultra-orthodox Shas and the National Religious Party (NRP), with 10 seats and nine, respectively, was the key factor in determining that the new Government would be formed by Likud. Netanyahu proceeded to sign agreements between the Likud alliance and Shas, the NRP, Israel B'Aliyah, United Torah Judaism and the Third Way, to form a coalition that would command the support of 66 deputies in the Knesset. Moledet also agreed to support the Government, but did not formally enter the coalition. The new Government received the approval of the Knesset in mid-June. Its statement of policy excluded the possibility of granting Palestinian statehood or, with regard to Syria, of relinquishing *de facto* sovereignty of the occupied Golan Heights. Moreover, Netanyahu reportedly postponed further discussion of the withdrawal of Israeli armed forces from the West Bank town of Hebron—where they provided security for some 400 Jewish settlers—and reiterated his refusal to meet the Palestinian President. In late June a summit meeting of all Arab leaders (with the exception of Iraq) was convened in Cairo. The meeting's final communiqué reiterated Israel's withdrawal from all occupied territories (including East Jerusalem) as a basic requirement for a comprehensive Middle East peace settlement. However, in July the likely stance of the new Government was underlined by the incorporation into the Cabinet, as Minister of Infrastructure, of Ariel Sharon—who had played a leading role in the creation and expansion of Jewish settlements in the West Bank. Netanyahu and Arafat did in fact meet in September, at the Erez crossing point, when they confirmed their commitment to the implementation of the Interim Agreement.

In September 1996 it was announced that Israel's Ministry of Defence had approved plans to construct some 1,800 new homes at existing Jewish settlements in the West Bank, causing many observers to conclude that the new Israeli Government had effectively halted the peace process by either abandoning or postponing many of the commitments inherited from its predecessor. Violent confrontations erupted between Palestinian security forces and civilians and the Israeli armed forces, in which at least 50 Palestinians and 18 Israelis were killed and hundreds wounded. The direct cause of the disturbances was attributed to the decision of the Israeli Government to open the north end of the Hasmonean tunnel running beneath the al-Aqsa Mosque in Jerusalem, although it appeared to be the inevitable culmination of Palestinian frustration at Israel's failure to implement agreements previously signed with the PA. The Israeli military authorities declared a state of emergency in the Gaza Strip and the West Bank, and threatened military intervention to suppress the disturbances. A special session of the UN Security Council was convened, and intense international diplomacy facilitated a crisis summit in Washington hosted by US President Clinton and attended by Netanyahu, Arafat and King Hussein of Jordan. In October Israel agreed to resume negotiations on the partial withdrawal of its armed forces from Hebron. Netanyahu subsequently stated that once this issue had been settled Israel would reopen its borders with the West Bank and Gaza—which had remained closed since February—and move quickly towards seeking a final settlement with the Palestinians.

In January 1997 Israel and the PA finally concluded an agreement on the withdrawal of Israeli armed forces from Hebron. The principal terms of the accord were that Israeli forces should withdraw from 80% of the town within 10 days, and that the first of three subsequent redeployments from the West Bank should take place six weeks after the signing of the agreement, and the remaining two by August 1998. With regard to security arrangements for Jewish settlers in central Hebron, Palestinian police patrols would be armed only with pistols in areas close to the Jewish enclaves, while joint Israeli-Palestinian patrols would secure the heights above the enclaves. The 'final status' negotiations on borders, the Jerusalem issue, Jewish settlements and Palestinian refugees were to commence within two months of the signing of the Hebron agreement. As guarantor of the agreement, the USA undertook to obtain the release of Palestinian prisoners, and to ensure that Israel continued to engage in negotiations for a Palestinian airport in the Gaza Strip and on safe passage for Palestinians between the West Bank and Gaza. The USA also undertook to ensure that the PA would continue to combat terrorism, complete the revision of the Palestinian National Charter and consider Israeli requests to extradite Palestinians suspected of involvement in attacks in Israel.

Progress achieved through the agreement on Hebron was severely undermined in February 1997, when Israel announced that it was to proceed with the construction of 6,500 housing units at Har Homa (Jabal Abu Ghunaim in Arabic) in East Jerusalem. Tensions escalated in the following month, after Israel decided unilaterally to withdraw its armed forces from only 9% of the West Bank. Arafat denounced the decision and King Hussein accused Netanyahu of intentionally destroying the peace process. Increasing anti-Israeli sentiment reportedly motivated a Jordanian soldier to murder seven Israeli schoolgirls in Nayarim, an enclave between Israel and Jordan. Israeli intransigence over the Har Homa settlement prompted Palestinians to abandon the 'final status' talks, scheduled to begin on 17 March, and on the following day construction at the site began. Riots among Palestinians erupted immediately, and shortly afterwards Hamas carried out a bomb attack in Tel-Aviv, killing four people. In response, the Israeli Government again ordered the temporary closure of Israel's borders with the West Bank and Gaza Strip. In late March the League of Arab States (the Arab League, see p. 290) voted to resume its economic boycott of Israel, suspend moves to establish diplomatic relations, and withdraw from multilateral peace talks. (Jordan, the PA and Egypt were excluded from the resolution, owing to their binding bilateral agreements with Israel.) Meeting with US President Clinton in Washington in early April, Netanyahu reiterated that he would not suspend the settlement programme. During May the USA's chief Middle East negotiator, Dennis Ross, failed to achieve any progress towards a resumption of peace talks despite a nine-day mediation attempt.

In June 1997 the US House of Representatives voted in favour of recognizing Jerusalem as the undivided capital of Israel and of transferring the US embassy there, from Tel-Aviv. The decision coincided with violent clashes between Palestinian civilians and Israeli troops in both Gaza and Hebron. Meanwhile, Yasser Arafat, fearing Israeli reoccupation of Hebron, assigned 200 police-officers to patrol the area. In the same month Ehud Barak, a former government minister and army chief of staff, was elected to replace Peres as Labour Party Chairman.

In July 1997 the USA brokered an agreement between Israel and the PA to resume peace talks the following month. At the end of July, however, on the eve of a planned visit to Israel by Dennis Ross, two Hamas suicide bombers killed 14 civilians and wounded more than 150 others in Jerusalem. Ross cancelled his visit and Israel suspended payment of tax revenues to the PA and again closed off the Gaza Strip and the West Bank. Netanyahu insisted that the restrictions would remain until the Palestinians demonstrated a commitment to combat terrorism. Israel reopened borders with the West Bank and Gaza in early September, but restrictions were reimposed three days later after suicide bombings in West Jerusalem killed eight people and injured at least 150 others. The security crisis cast doubt on the viability of a planned visit by US Secretary of State Madeleine Albright in mid-September. However, Albright's visit was positively received; Israel released further Palestinian assets (one-third of tax revenues owed to the PA had been released in August), while the Palestinians announced the closure of 17 institutions affiliated to Hamas. In early October Netanyahu and Arafat met for the first time in eight months. Israel announced plans to release further dues to the PA and to reopen the sealed borders. However, Israel failed to participate in a second round of negotiations, scheduled for that month, aimed at accelerating the 'final status' talks, and Netanyahu stated that further redeployments would not take place until Palestinians made further efforts to combat terrorism.

Renewed hostilities erupted in northern Israel in August 1997 after Hezbollah launched a rocket attack on civilians in Kiryat Shmona. The attack, made in retaliation for raids by Israeli commandos in which five Hezbollah members were killed, prompted further air-strikes by Israel in southern Lebanon. Violence escalated, with the shelling by the SLA of the Lebanese port of Sidon resulting in at least six deaths. Domestic pressure for an Israeli withdrawal from southern Lebanon increased after 12 Israeli marines, allegedly on a mission to assassinate Shi'ite leaders, were killed south of Sidon in September. Meanwhile, relations between Jordan and Israel deteriorated in September, after members of the Israeli intelligence force, Mossad, attempted to assassinate Hamas's political leader, Khalid Meshaal, in Amman. Following intensive negotiations between Netanyahu, Crown Prince Hassan of Jordan and US officials, several agreements regarding the release of prisoners ensued: in October Israel freed the Hamas spiritual leader, Sheikh Ahmad Yassin, in return for the release by Jordan of two Mossad agents arrested in connection with the attack on Meshaal; a further 12 Mossad agents were expelled by the Jordanian authorities following the release of 23 Jordanian and 50 Palestinian prisoners by Israel.

Bilateral negotiations between Israel and the PA resumed in November 1997. Israel offered to decelerate its construction of Jewish settlements in return for Palestinian approval of a plan to delay further redeployments of Israeli troops from the West Bank. At the same time, the Israeli Government announced plans to build 900 new housing units in the area. This prompted several Arab states to boycott the Middle East and North Africa economic conference, held in Doha, Qatar, in mid-November, which an Israeli delegation was scheduled to attend. Separate peace talks involving Albright, Netanyahu and Arafat were inconclusive. At the end of November the Israeli Cabinet agreed in principle to a partial withdrawal from the West Bank, but specified neither its timing nor its scale. Conflicting opinions within the Cabinet meant that Netanyahu failed to produce a conclusive redeployment plan to present at talks with Albright in Paris in December; furthermore, the Israeli Government had recently prevented PA officials from conducting a census in East Jerusalem. Israeli and PA officials none the less demonstrated their commitment to peace by signing a security memorandum.

In late 1997 divisions within the coalition Government obliged Netanyahu to grant concessions to right-wing members of the coalition. In January 1998 David Levy, the Gesher leader, withdrew from the Government, citing dissatisfaction with the budget and with the slow rate of progress in the peace talks. Gesher's departure reduced Netanyahu's majority to only two votes, although the budget secured the approval of the Knesset, and Netanyahu subsequently survived a vote of 'no confidence'. Meanwhile, Netanyahu announced that he would not make any further decisions regarding the peace process until the Palestinians had demonstrated further efforts to combat terrorism, reduced their security forces from 40,000 to 24,000 and amended their National Charter to recognize Israel's right to exist. The Israeli premier again failed to present a plan of redeployment in talks with President Clinton in Washington. Netanyahu did express interest in a US proposal to withdraw troops from at least 10% of the land in several stages, but this was decisively rejected by Arafat. At the end of February Arafat also rejected Netanyahu's appeals for a peace summit, stating that he would hold talks only after Israel had agreed to further redeployment and had fully implemented existing agreements.

Addressing the Knesset in March 1998, UN Secretary-General Kofi Annan urged Israel to end 'provocative acts' towards the Palestinians, including the building of Jewish settlements. Meanwhile, the US Special Co-ordinator to the Middle East, Dennis Ross, visited the region, briefing Netanyahu, Arafat and Egypt's President Mubarak on a US peace proposal whereby Israel would redeploy from 13.1% of the West Bank over a 12-week period in exchange for specific security guarantees from the Palestinians. (Israel, however, reportedly agreed only to a phased redeployment from 9% of the territory.) In April Netanyahu and President Mubarak held their first meeting (in Cairo) since May 1997, during which President Mubarak reportedly advised Netanyahu to 'respond positively' to the US peace initiative. However, the Israeli Prime Minister rejected the proposal, which was publicly accepted by Arafat the following day. In May 1998 US Secretary of State Albright conducted separate rounds of talks with Netanyahu and Arafat in London, United Kingdom, with the aim of reviving negotiations on redeployments. The talks were inconclusive, and further meetings held in Washington later that month similarly failed to achieve a breakthrough. Meanwhile, celebrations to commemorate the 50th anniversary of the founding of the State of Israel provoked widespread rioting in the Occupied Territories.

In May 1998 the UN Committee Against Torture ruled for a second successive year that interrogation methods used by the Israeli security service, Shin Bet, were in contravention of the 1984 UN Convention against Torture and Other Cruel, Inhuman or Degrading Treatment or Punishment (which Israel had ratified in 1991). Shortly afterwards proceedings began at the Israeli Supreme Court in an unprecedented appeal case, brought by Palestinian detainees and two human rights groups, questioning the legality of Shin Bet's use of torture.

Details of the US peace plan were published in the Israeli newspaper *Ha'aretz* in June 1998. Although several Jewish settler groups threatened a campaign of civil disobedience in protest at any further redeployments from the West Bank, it became apparent that Netanyahu was under increasing pressure to accept the US initiative. In late June President Weizman (who had been elected for a second presidential term in March) angered Netanyahu by publicly demanding the dissolution of the Knesset and early elections so that Israelis might choose the future direction of peace talks. Meanwhile, further controversy arose when the Cabinet approved Netanyahu's draft plan whereby the municipal boundaries of Jerusalem would be extended to incorporate seven West Bank Jewish settlements— to create a 'Greater Jerusalem' covering six times the current area of the city. Arab leaders accused Netanyahu of seeking formally to annex parts of the West Bank, and the UN Security Council urged Israel to abandon the proposals.

The first substantive senior-level meetings for several months between Israeli and Palestinian negotiators took place in Jerusalem in July 1998. However, Arafat withdrew his delegates in protest at what he described as Israel's 'obscure formulations' on the US peace plan. Israel had reportedly offered a compromise package, proposing redeployment from 10%, and partial redeployment from 3%, of the West Bank. By the end of August there were indications that the so-called '10+3' plan might lead to a revival of peace negotiations, and a US-mediated meeting between Netanyahu and Arafat held in Washington at the end of September resulted in an agreement by the two leaders to attend a peace summit in mid-October, with the aim of finalizing agreement on further Israeli redeployments.

On 23 October 1998, after nine days of intensive talks with President Clinton at the Wye Plantation, Maryland, Netanyahu and Arafat signed an agreement (the Wye River Memorandum) that outlined a three-month timetable for the implementation of the 1995 Interim Agreement and signalled the commencement of 'final status' talks, which should have begun in May 1996. With the mediation of Clinton and King Hussein of Jordan, Israel agreed to redeploy its troops from 13.1% of the West Bank, while the PA agreed to intensify measures to prevent terrorism and to rewrite the Palestinian National Charter. In an effort to reassure Jewish settler groups in the West Bank, who protested against the 'land-for-security' deal, Netanyahu gave assurances that the construction of 1,025 new homes at the Har Homa settlement would proceed. On 11 November, after the postponement of four scheduled meetings (due to a bombing by Islamic Jihad in Jerusalem and Israeli fears of further terrorist attacks), the Israeli Cabinet approved the Wye Memorandum by a majority of eight votes to four. Netanyahu subsequently reiterated that a number of conditions would first have to be met by the Palestinians, and threatened effective Israeli annexation of areas of the West Bank if a Palestinian state were to be declared on 4 May 1999. (Arafat continued to reassert his right to declare a Palestinian state on the expiry date of the interim stage defined in Oslo, an act Netanyahu claimed would fundamentally violate the Oslo accords.) On 17 November the Knesset ratified the Wye Memorandum by 75 votes to 19. Three days later the Israeli Government implemented the first stage of renewed redeployment from the West Bank, also releasing 250 Palestinian prisoners and signing a protocol allowing for the opening of an international airport at Gaza.

During December 1998 it became increasingly evident that divisions within Netanyahu's coalition over implementation of the Wye Memorandum were making government untenable. The administration effectively collapsed when the Minister of Finance, Yaacov Ne'eman, announced his resignation. Shortly afterwards the Knesset voted to hold elections to the legislature and premiership in the spring of 1999. In January 1999 Netanyahu dismissed Itzhak Mordechai as Minister of Defence, appointing Moshe Arens in his place. Speculation that Mordechai had been intending to leave Likud was apparently confirmed when he launched the new Centre Party.

Meanwhile, unrest in the West Bank and Gaza increased prior to a visit by President Clinton in December 1998. Palestinians demonstrated in support of almost 700 prisoners who began a nine-day hunger-strike to protest against Israel's failure to honour commitments made at Wye Plantation to release Palestinians detained on political charges. Clinton attended a session of the PNC, at which the removal from the Palestinian National Charter of all clauses seeking Israel's destruction was reaffirmed. Following a meeting between Clinton, Arafat and Netanyahu at the Erez check-point, Netanyahu reiterated accusations that the Palestinians had not adequately addressed their security commitments and announced that he would not release Palestinian prisoners considered to have 'blood on their hands'. Netanyahu announced that the second phase of Israeli troop deployment envisaged by the Wye Memorandum, scheduled for 18 December, would not be undertaken. The Knesset subsequently voted to suspend implementation of the Wye Memorandum, thereby effectively suspending the peace process. In late December Arafat freed the Hamas spiritual leader, Sheikh Ahmad Yassin, from house arrest, prompting further Israeli claims that agreed anti-terrorism measures were not being implemented. In January 1999 it was reported that the US Secretary of State would refuse to meet Ariel Sharon (redesignated the Minister of Foreign Affairs and National Infrastructure in October 1998), during a visit to the USA, owing to US frustration with Israel's 'freezing' of peace negotiations. The US Administration threatened to withhold US $1,200m. promised to Israel to fund its redeployment in the West Bank unless it complied with the terms of the Wye Memorandum. For several months President Clinton refused to hold a private meeting with Netanyahu, while agreeing to meet Arafat in March to discuss his threatened unilateral declaration of statehood on 4 May; following intense international pressure, the declaration was postponed at the end of April.

In 1998 the conclusion of several bilateral trade agreements indicated an improvement in Israeli-Jordanian relations. In April King Hussein and the Israeli Prime Minister met for the first time since the assassination attempt which had strained relations in 1997. In December 1998 Israel agreed to allow foreign airlines en route to Jordan to use Israeli airspace. There was widespread apprehension about the future of Israel's relations with Jordan following the death, in February 1999, of King Hussein (whose funeral was attended by Netanyahu). Nevertheless, the Israeli Government expected 'continuity' in bilateral relations under Jordan's new King Abdullah. In September Israel commended the Jordanian authorities for their arrest of Khalid Meshaal and two other Hamas leaders. King Abdullah made his first official visit to Israel in April 2000.

Hostilities between Israeli forces and Hezbollah in southern Lebanon persisted throughout 1998. In that year some 23 Israeli soldiers were killed, and there was increasing pressure on Netanyahu, even from some Likud ministers, for a unilateral withdrawal from the territory. On 1 April the Israeli Security Cabinet voted unanimously to adopt UN Resolution 425 (which called for an immediate withdrawal of Israeli troops from all Lebanese territory), provided that the Lebanese army gave security guarantees. However, both Lebanon and Syria demanded an unconditional withdrawal. In June the first Israeli-Lebanese exchange of prisoners and bodies since July 1996 took place. Fighting escalated when, in August 1998, Hezbollah launched rocket attacks on northern Israel in retaliation for an Israeli helicopter attack in which a senior Lebanese military official died. Seven Israeli soldiers died in two attacks in November, leading Netanyahu to curtail a European tour in order to hold an emergency cabinet meeting on a possible withdrawal. In December an Israeli air attack in which eight Lebanese civilians were killed provoked condemnation from the ILMG, which declared it to be a violation of the cease-fire 'understanding' reached in April 1996. Following several Hezbollah attacks, in January 1999 Netanyahu reiterated previous warnings that in the event of further attacks, Israeli troops would target Lebanese infrastructure. In February the commander of the Israeli army unit for liaison with the SLA became the most senior Israeli officer to be killed in southern Lebanon since 1982. Israel responded with its heaviest air raids against Lebanon since the 1996 'Grapes of Wrath' operation, prompting fears of another major conflict.

In July 1998 it had been reported that Israel and Syria might resume talks on the disputed Golan Heights, on the basis of a

French initiative whereby Israel would accept a 'land-for-peace' formula in return for Syrian acceptance of Israel's security needs. However, in late July the Knesset approved preliminary legislation seeking a majority parliamentary vote and a referendum before Israel would withdraw from the territory; the vote was condemned in Syria. Tensions between the two countries increased in September when Israel publicly stated its intention to enter a military alliance with Turkey.

By the time of the general election, held on 17 May 1999, Netanyahu and Ehud Barak were the only remaining candidates for the premiership. Barak was elected Prime Minister with 56.1% of the total votes cast. In the elections to the Knesset, Barak's One Israel alliance (including Gesher and the moderate Meimad) secured 26 seats, while Likud's strength declined from 32 seats to 19. Shas, meanwhile, increased its representation to 17 seats. The new Knesset contained an unprecedented 15 factions. Some 78.8% of the electorate were reported to have voted. Netanyahu subsequently resigned from both the Knesset and the Likud leadership, and in September Ariel Sharon was elected as Likud's new Chairman. Although Barak had received a clear mandate to form a government that would attempt to revive the stalled Middle East peace process, Israel's Prime Minister-elect committed himself only to seek a formula for regional peace. Barak stated that he would observe four 'security red lines' concerning negotiations with the Palestinians: Jerusalem would remain under Israeli sovereignty; there would be no return to the pre-1967 borders; most West Bank settlers would remain in settlements under Israeli sovereignty; and no 'foreign armies' would be based west of the Jordan river. Following complex negotiations, Barak forged a broad coalition of the Centre Party, Shas, Meretz, Israel B'Aliyah and the NRP, which was endorsed by the Knesset in early July 1999. Barak himself took the defence portfolio, while David Levy became the Minister of Foreign Affairs and Shimon Peres the Minister of Regional Co-operation.

In July 1999 the Speaker of the Palestinian Legislative Council became the first senior Palestinian official to address the Knesset. Meanwhile, Barak held a series of summit meetings with Arab and European leaders, culminating in discussions with US President Clinton in mid-July. The first direct talks between the new Israeli premier and Yasser Arafat were held at the Erez check-point in Gaza on 11 July, during which both leaders reaffirmed their commitment to peace. In late July, however, PA negotiators were angered when Barak expressed the desire to combine the Israeli land withdrawals agreed under the terms of the Wye Memorandum with 'final status' negotiations, although Israel later agreed to withdraw its demand to postpone further redeployments.

In early September 1999, during a visit to the region by US Secretary of State Albright, Barak and Arafat travelled to Egypt for talks at Sharm esh-Sheikh. On 4 September the two leaders signed the Sharm esh-Sheikh Memorandum (or Wye Two accords), which outlined a revised timetable for implementation of the outstanding provisions of the original Wye Memorandum in order to facilitate the resumption of 'final status' talks: a new target date—13 September 2000—was set for the conclusion of a comprehensive 'final status' settlement, with a framework agreement to be in place by 13 February. (One important change was the reduction, to 350, of the number of Palestinian prisoners to be released by Israel.) On 8 September the Knesset ratified the Wye Two accords; the following day Israel released some 200 Palestinian prisoners, and on 10 September a further 7% of the West Bank was transferred to Palestinian civilian control. A ceremony marking the launch of 'final status' negotiations between Israel and the PA was held at the Erez check-point on 13 September, and a few days later it was reported that Barak and Arafat had held a secret meeting to discuss an agenda for such talks. Meanwhile, Israel signed an agreement with the USA to purchase 50 F-16 fighter aircraft. A further 151 Palestinian prisoners were released from Israeli custody in mid-October. On 25 October a southern 'safe passage' for Palestinians travelling between Gaza and Hebron was finally opened, under the terms of the Wye Memorandum.

In the autumn of 1999 Barak encountered severe criticism by left-wing groups and Palestinians over his Government's apparent intention to continue to approve the expansion of Jewish settlements in the West Bank. (Since coming to power, the Government had issued tenders for some 2,600 new homes in such settlements.) Barak subsequently angered settler groups with a ruling that several of the 42 'outpost settlements' established in the West Bank under the Likud Government had been built illegally; 12 of the 'outposts' were dismantled in October.

In October 1999 Mauritania became the third member of the Arab League (after Egypt and Jordan) to establish full diplomatic relations with Israel. In early November Arafat, Barak and US President Clinton held talks in Oslo, Norway. Representatives of Israel and the PA commenced talks on 'final status' issues on 8 November in the West Bank city of Ramallah; further rounds of talks were held during November and December. Prior to the discussions, three bombs had exploded in the Israeli town of Netanya, wounding at least 33 people. (Although no group claimed responsibility for the bombings, they followed an alleged warning by the military wing of Hamas of an escalation of violence in protest at Israeli settlement policies.) The redeployment of Israeli armed forces from a further 5% of the West Bank (due on 15 November) was delayed owing to a dispute over which areas were to be transferred. In December Barak and Arafat met on Palestinian territory for the first time. At the end of the month Israel released some 26 Palestinian 'security' prisoners as a 'goodwill' gesture.

On 6–7 January 2000 Israeli troops withdrew from a further 5% of the West Bank. However, Israel subsequently announced the postponement of a third redeployment, agreed under Wye Two (and scheduled for 20 January), until Barak had returned from talks with Syrian representatives in the USA (see below). In early February PA officials suspended peace negotiations with Israel, following the decision by the Israeli Cabinet to withdraw its armed forces from a sparsely populated 6.1% of the West Bank. The redeployment from a further 6.1% of the West Bank took place on 21 March (Israel had on the previous day released 15 Palestinian prisoners), facilitating an official resumption of 'final status' talks. In that month a ruling by Israel's Supreme Court that the allocation of state-owned land on the basis of religion, nationality or ethnicity was illegal allowed Israeli Arabs to purchase land for the first time.

Meanwhile, in May 1999 senior Israeli commanders in southern Lebanon for the first time urged an immediate Israeli withdrawal. (Prime Minister-elect Barak had made a pre-election pledge to recall Israeli troops from Lebanon by July 2000.) In June 1999 the SLA completed a unilateral withdrawal from the Jezzine enclave. Later that month Barak was reportedly angered when the outgoing Netanyahu administration launched a series of air attacks on Lebanon, destroying Beirut's main power station and other infrastructure, in response to Hezbollah rocket attacks on northern Israel. In July Barak confirmed that he would propose to his Cabinet a unilateral withdrawal from Lebanon if no peace accord had been reached (in the context of an agreement with Syria over the Golan Heights) within one year. In December Israel apologized for an attack in which some 18 Lebanese schoolchildren were injured. The incident followed an increase in Hezbollah military action after the announcement of a resumption of Israeli-Syrian peace negotiations (see below). In late December Israel and Syria reached an 'understanding in principle' to limit the fighting in southern Lebanon; the informal cease-fire did not endure, however, and in late January 2000 a senior SLA commander became the first Israeli soldier to be killed there for five months. At the end of January the deaths of another three of its soldiers led Israel to declare that peace talks with Syria would not resume until Syria took action to restrain Hezbollah, but attacks by the militant Shi'ite group continued, and in February Israel retaliated with a massive series of bombing raids on Lebanese infrastructure. Israel announced a unilateral withdrawal from the 1996 'cease-fire' agreement, and there were renewed fears of a major conflict. Following the killing of three Israeli soldiers by Hezbollah in the same month, the Israeli Security Cabinet approved wide powers for the Prime Minister to order immediate retaliatory bombing raids into Lebanon.

In early 2000 two senior political figures were embroiled in scandal. In April the Israeli President, Ezer Weizman, was informed that, owing to insufficient evidence, he would not be prosecuted for accepting some US $450,000 in undeclared donations from a French businessman while serving as a member of the Knesset. However, the police investigation failed completely to exonerate him, and he stated in May that he would resign on 10 July. Meanwhile, in May Itzhak Mordechai, the Deputy Prime Minister and Minister of Transport, was arraigned on three charges of sexual harassment, leading to his resignation as leader of the Centre Party. In March 2001 he was found guilty of committing indecent assault against two women and was awarded an 18-month suspended sentence.

A third round of 'final status' discussions opened in Eilat on 30 April 2000, but maps presented by Israeli officials to the PA in early May, defining Barak's interpretation of a future Palestinian state, were firmly rejected by the Palestinians. Two days later Barak and Arafat held a crisis meeting in Ramallah, at which Barak proposed that Israel transfer to full PA control three Arab villages situated close to Jerusalem, on condition that the third West Bank redeployment (scheduled for June) was postponed until after the conclusion of a final peace settlement. The Knesset approved the transfer in mid-May. In late May Barak ordered an end to 'secret' talks between Israeli and Palestinian officials in Stockholm, Sweden, after an Israeli child was seriously injured in a petrol bomb attack near Jericho. Barak also announced that an Israeli withdrawal from the Arab villages would not be implemented until the PA took appropriate measures to curb unrest in the West Bank, where Palestinians had been protesting in support of gaoled Palestinians on hunger-strike.

In June 2000 the right-wing Shas, One Israel's largest coalition partner, threatened to withdraw from the Government unless its demands regarding the peace process and the funding of its religious schools were met. After Barak capitulated to most of the party's demands, the four Shas ministers withdrew their resignations, thereby averting the collapse of the coalition; however, the return of Shas to the Government led to the departure of the two Meretz ministers, who were both strong supporters of the Oslo peace process. The stability of the Government was again seriously damaged in early July, shortly before Barak and Arafat were due to attend a peace summit at the US presidential retreat at Camp David, in an attempt to reach a framework agreement for a final settlement. The three right-wing parties (Israel B'Aliyah, the NRP and Shas) withdrew from the coalition in protest at what they perceived to be Barak's willingness to concede to PA territorial claims. However, despite the loss of six ministers, Barak survived a 'no confidence' motion in the Knesset.

President Clinton opened the Camp David talks on 11 July 2000, and, although no accord had been reached by their scheduled close on 19 July, he persuaded Israeli and Palestinian negotiators to remain at Camp David. However, despite intensive mediation efforts, the summit ended on 25 July without agreement. Progess had reportedly been made on the issues of the borders of a future Palestinian entity and the status of Palestinian refugees, but the two sides were unable to reach a compromise regarding the future status of Jerusalem. Barak had apparently offered the PA municipal authority over certain parts of East Jerusalem and access to Islamic holy sites in the Old City, although Israel would retain full sovereignty. Arafat, meanwhile, had continued to demand a Palestinian state with East Jerusalem as its capital and sovereignty over the Islamic holy sites. In the summit's final communiqué both sides vowed to continue the pursuit of a 'final status' settlement and to avoid 'unilateral actions'—thereby implying that Arafat would not declare a Palestinian state on 13 September. (Shortly before that date the Palestinian legislature voted to delay such a declaration for an indefinite period.)

In the presidential election held on 31 July 2000, the little-known Moshe Katsav of Likud unexpectedly secured a narrow defeat over Barak's nominee, Shimon Peres. Katsav was duly sworn in as the eighth President of Israel on 1 August, to serve an exceptional seven-year term. Immediately after the election Barak survived another 'no confidence' motion. However, in early August the Minister of Foreign Affairs, David Levy, announced his resignation, citing disagreements with Barak over the peace process. The Minister of Public Security, Shlomo Ben-Ami, was subsequently appointed acting Minister of Foreign Affairs, and was confirmed in the post in November.

In late September 2000 Barak and Arafat met, at the Israeli premier's home, for the first time since the Camp David summit. However, the resumption of contacts was swiftly overshadowed by the escalation of what became known as the al-Aqsa *intifada*, a renewed uprising by Palestinians against Israeli occupation which resulted in the suspension of the Middle East peace process. On 28 September Likud leader Ariel Sharon made a highly controversial visit to the Temple Mount/Haram ash-Sharif compound in Jerusalem (the site of the Dome of the Rock and the al-Aqsa Mosque), provoking protests by stone-throwing Palestinians which in turn triggered violent unrest throughout the Palestinian territories. For the first time Israeli Arabs clashed with security forces within Israel, and the uncompromising response of the Israeli security forces to the uprising

attracted international criticism. On 7 October the UN Security Council issued a resolution condemning the 'excessive use of force' employed by Israeli security forces against Palestinian demonstrators. Israel closed the borders of the Palestinian territories and Gaza airport, and Barak emphasized to Arafat his intention to suspend the peace process if the Palestinian unrest continued, demanding that Arafat re-arrest about 60 militant Islamists who had recently been freed from Palestinian detention. Arafat, for his part, demanded an international inquiry into the causes of the violence. The crisis escalated in mid-October after Israeli forces launched rocket attacks on the headquarters of Arafat's Fatah movement in Ramallah and other PA offices, in response to the murder of two Israeli army reservists by a Palestinian crowd. On 16–17 October an emergency summit meeting between Barak and Arafat was convened by President Clinton and hosted by President Mubarak at Sharm esh-Sheikh, at which the Israelis and Palestinians agreed what the US President termed 'immediate concrete measures' to end the fighting (including the formation of an international fact-finding commission to investigate the causes of the conflict). However, violence intensified, and on 22 October Barak announced that Israel was to take a 'time-out' from the peace process. This declaration came as Barak undertook discussions with Likud on the formation of a 'national unity' government prior to the reconvening of the Knesset for the new parliamentary term; no compromise was reached, however, reportedly owing to Ariel Sharon's demand for a veto on all decisions relating to national security. Barak's decision formally to suspend Israel's participation in the peace process was precipitated by the final communiqué issued by Arab leaders after an emergency summit of the Arab League held in Cairo on 21–22 October, declaring that Israel bore full responsibility for the recent violence. Morocco, Tunisia and Oman announced that they had severed diplomatic relations with Israel, and Qatar broke off ties in November.

A suicide bomb attack perpetrated by Islamic Jihad on an Israeli military target in Gaza at the end of October 2000 apparently signalled a new campaign of violence by militant Palestinian organizations, and led the Israeli army to declare a new strategy of targeting for assassination the leaders of such groups, as well as senior Fatah commanders, whom it held responsible for 'terrorist' actions. (Israeli officials referred to this new policy as 'initiated attacks' or 'targeted killings'.) In early November the Israeli Minister of Regional Co-operation, Shimon Peres, held crisis talks with Arafat in Gaza, at which the two sides were reported to have agreed a fragile 'cease-fire' based on the provisions agreed the previous month at Sharm esh-Sheikh. The truce was broken almost immediately, however, when a car bomb exploded in Jerusalem, killing two Israelis; Islamic Jihad claimed responsibility for the attack, while Barak held the PA responsible through the recent release of dozens of Islamist militants. Arafat, meanwhile, requested US support in his appeal to the UN to provide an international peace-keeping force to protect Palestinians in the Occupied Territories. In mid-November Israel effectively imposed a complete economic blockade of the Palestinian areas, in an effort to overcome increasing concerns over its national security. Later in the month the explosion of a bomb close to a bus carrying Israeli schoolchildren (as a result of which two people died and several children were injured) provoked public outrage and led Israel to launch further air raids against Fatah targets in Gaza. Egypt responded by announcing that it was recalling its ambassador from Tel-Aviv, and in early April 2002 suspended all direct contact with the Israeli Government other than for negotiations aimed at restoring peace in the region. (Egypt did not return an ambassador to Israel until mid-March 2005.)

Meanwhile, in early December 2000 a US-led investigative committee—the Sharm esh-Sheikh Fact-Finding Committee or Mitchell Committee (its chairman was a former US senator, George Mitchell)—began conducting its research into the Israeli–Palestinian violence, which by now increasingly involved fighting between Jewish settlers and Palestinians in the West Bank and Gaza. It was reported at the end of November that the PA had rejected a partial peace plan put forward by Barak, whereby Israel would effect further troop redeployments from the West Bank in exchange for a postponement of discussions concerning the remaining 'final status' issues. Although US-brokered talks between Israeli and Palestinian negotiators resumed in December, in an effort to achieve a framework peace settlement prior to the expiry of Clinton's presidential term in late January 2001, the differences between the two sides remained apparently unbreachable. The outgoing US President had reportedly proposed a far-reaching deal which included granting the PA sovereignty over Islamic holy sites in the Old City of Jerusalem, while the area (also comprising the Temple Mount) would remain under Israeli control. However, the talks stalled in late December 2000 following the deaths of two Israelis in bomb explosions in Tel-Aviv and the Gaza Strip.

At the end of November 2000 Barak had unexpectedly called early prime ministerial elections for 2001, in an apparent attempt to secure his increasingly beleaguered Government. The Likud leader, Ariel Sharon, immediately declared his candidacy for the premiership, as did Netanyahu (although he later withdrew his candidacy). The premiership election, held on 6 February 2001, resulted in an overwhelming victory for Sharon, with 62.4% of the votes cast; the rate of participation was 62.3% of registered voters. Barak had lost the Israeli Arab vote—as the Arab parties had urged their supporters to boycott or abstain in the poll—and his defeat was interpreted as a decisive rejection of the Oslo peace process by the majority of Israelis. Sharon, whose principal election pledge had been the restoration of domestic and regional stability, immediately sought the formation of a broadly-based government of national unity, essentially in an effort to secure a political base in the Knesset (where Likud held only 19 of the 120 seats). Following his defeat, Barak had announced his resignation as Labour leader, leaving the party in disarray. Barak later declared that he would not enter a government of national unity under Sharon and was to withdraw from political life 'for some time'. In late February Labour's Central Committee voted to join a coalition administration, despite objections from prominent members of the party. This enabled Sharon to conclude coalition agreements principally with the religious and right-wing parties, and the 'national unity' Government was approved by the Knesset in early March. The 26-member Cabinet (reportedly the largest in Israel's history) included the ultra-orthodox Shas (whose leader, Eliyahu Yishai, became Deputy Prime Minister and Minister of the Interior), Israel B'Aliyah (Natan Sharansky was named as Deputy Prime Minister and Minister of Construction and Housing) and the extreme right-wing Haichud Haleumi-Israel B'Aitainu bloc.

While Israel's new Minister of Defence, Binyamin Ben-Eliezer of the Labour Party, was known for his uncompromising stance, the appointment of Shimon Peres as Deputy Prime Minister and Minister of Foreign Affairs was a cause for cautious optimism for those who wished to see a revival of the Middle East peace process. However, there was considerable uncertainty regarding the prospects for a continuation of the Oslo process under Ariel Sharon, and without the active involvement of the Administration of Bill Clinton (whose term of office as US President had come to an end in January 2001): the new US Administration under George W. Bush chose initially to disengage itself from Arab–Israeli affairs in terms of its Middle East policy. Following his election victory, Sharon underlined his hardline stance by affirming that he was not prepared to resume negotiations with the PA from their point of suspension in January. In the weeks after the election Hamas and other militant Palestinian groups intensified their campaign against Israeli military and civilian targets. In late February, during an official tour of the Middle East, the new US Secretary of State, Colin Powell, held talks with Prime Minister-elect Sharon, at which Sharon refused Powell's appeal to Israel to end its blockade on the West Bank and Gaza Strip and to deliver overdue tax transfers to the PA. In late March Sharon travelled to Washington for discussions with President Bush. At the end of March Israel responded to the deaths of three settler children by launching military strikes against Palestinian military bases in Gaza City and Ramallah. Also in late March Arab League heads of state, meeting in the Jordanian capital, resolved *inter alia* to reinstate the 'secondary' economic boycott of Israel.

It was announced in early April 2001 that the Israeli Government had issued tenders for the construction of a further 708 Jewish housing units in the West Bank. The al-Aqsa *intifada* intensified in the middle of that month when Israel took unprecedented action in response to a Palestinian mortar attack on the Israeli town of Sderot. Israeli armed forces imposed road blockades which effectively divided the Gaza Strip into three sections, and sent tanks and bulldozers into the Gazan town of Beit Hanun; this was Israel's first armed incursion into territory that it had transferred to PA control under the terms of the Oslo accords. Amid heavy pressure from the US Administration (which described the occupation of Beit Hanun as 'excessive and

disproportionate'), Israel withdrew its forces less than 24 hours later. Hopes of an end to the Israeli–Palestinian conflict and a resumption of the Oslo peace talks were raised in mid-April amid a revival of the so-called 'Egyptian-Jordanian initiative' or Taba plan. The initiative, based on the fragile understanding reached at Sharm esh-Sheikh in October 2000, required that the situation on the ground be restored to that prior to the start of the al-Aqsa *intifada*. It also stipulated that negotiations be resumed from the point at which they stalled in January 2001, and that Israel agree to halt its settlement programme in the Occupied Territories. Sharon stated in late April that Israel would endorse the Taba plan provided that the PA end its demand for a complete 'freeze' on the construction of Jewish settlements, and that all Palestinian violence should cease prior to the resumption of peace talks.

Israeli officials admitted in mid-May 2001 that the killing of five Palestinian police-officers in the West Bank had been 'accidental'. A few days later, following a Hamas suicide bombing in Netanya (in which five Israelis died), Israel deployed US-made F-16 fighter aircraft to shell security targets in the West Bank towns of Nablus and Ramallah, killing a number of Palestinians. In late May the Arab League and the Organization of the Islamic Conference (OIC, see p. 327) both urged member states to suspend all 'political' contacts with Israel. Meanwhile, the Sharm esh-Sheikh Fact-Finding Committee published its recommendations relating to the causes of the Israeli–Palestinian clashes. The so-called Mitchell Report referred to the visit of Ariel Sharon to the Islamic holy sites in September 2000 as 'provocative', but declined to single out for blame either Sharon or the PA leadership (which Israeli officials had accused of having orchestrated the violence). The Mitchell Report also demanded that Arafat undertake further measures to curb Palestinian 'terrorist' attacks, and called on Israel to end its economic blockade of the West Bank and Gaza Strip and to halt its settlement expansion programme. At the beginning of June 21 Israelis were killed, and more than 100 injured, in an attack by a Palestinian suicide bomber at a Tel-Aviv discothèque. As part of diplomatic efforts by the US Administration to revive the Israli-Palestinian dialogue, in early June the Director of the US Central Intelligence Agency (CIA), George Tenet, was dispatched to the region by President Bush. On 12 June proposals for a comprehensive cease-fire, brokered by Tenet, were approved by Israel and the PA; however, although Israel began to implement provisions made under the terms of the cease-fire to pull back troops from PA-controlled towns and to ease the economic blockade, the murder of two West Bank settlers by Palestinian gunmen and the killing of two Israeli soldiers in a suicide bombing in the Gaza Strip again hindered moves towards peace. During discussions in Washington with George W. Bush at the end of June, Sharon reportedly demanded 10 days of 'total calm' before Israel would implement the provisions of the Tenet plan. However, the PA rejected the terms of the US initiative, stating that the agreement favoured Israel.

In early July 2001 Israel's 'inner' Security Cabinet voted to accelerate its strategy of 'targeted killings' of leading Palestinians alleged to have orchestrated 'terrorist' acts against Israeli citizens; some right-wing members of the Sharon Government had even reportedly advocated the assassination of Yasser Arafat. Amid an intensification of reciprocal attacks in the Occupied Territories, Egypt's President Mubarak convened a meeting in Cairo between Arafat and the Israeli Deputy Prime Minister and Minister of Foreign Affairs, Shimon Peres. In mid-July the USA indicated for the first time that it would support the deployment of an international peace-keeping force in the Territories, although Israel continued to oppose such a move. Meanwhile, on several occasions during late 2001 Israel ordered its forces into PA-controlled towns—among them Hebron, Bethlehem, Jenin and Beit Jala—where violent clashes between Israelis and Palestinians were taking place. At the end of the month two leading Hamas members, alleged by Israel to have been involved in the Tel-Aviv nightclub bombing, were killed during an air raid on Hamas media offices in Nablus, prompting the militant Islamist group to threaten the assassination of senior Israeli politicians. In early August the Israeli administration published a 'most wanted' list of seven Palestinians whom it alleged to be prominent in the preparation of 'terrorist' attacks. Only days later at least 15 Israelis (including six children) were killed, and up to 100 injured, by a Palestinian suicide bomber at a Jerusalem restaurant. The Israeli Government responded to the bombing by taking temporary control of

Orient House, the *de facto* headquarters of the PA in East Jerusalem. At the end of August Abu Ali Moustafa, leader of the Popular Front for the Liberation of Palestine (PFLP), was killed by Israeli security forces at the party's offices in Ramallah. In early September the PFLP claimed responsibility for four bomb attacks in Jerusalem, while another suicide bombing was also carried out there.

However, international attention was abruptly distracted from events in Israel and the Palestinian territories following the massive suicide attacks apparently perpetrated by members of the al-Qa'ida group against New York and Washington, DC, on 11 September 2001. The attacks on the USA accelerated US and European Union (EU, see p. 217) efforts to urge Israel and the PA to effect a lasting cease-fire; however, Sharon demanded that he would not meet Arafat until the Palestinian leader could bring about 48 hours of 'complete quiet'. By the time of the first anniversary of the outbreak of the al-Aqsa *intifada* on 28 September, the Israeli–Palestinian violence had led to the deaths of at least 600 Palestinians and more than 160 Israelis. In early October two young Jewish settlers were killed by Hamas militants in Gaza. Israel responded by launching military strikes against Palestinian targets in Gaza City and sending troops into PA-controlled areas of Gaza and the West Bank; moreover, Israeli forces were granted the requisite powers to resume 'initiated attacks' against Palestinians deemed to be involved in 'terrorist' actions. Following further attacks by Palestinian militants within Israel in early October, crisis talks were convened between Shimon Peres and two senior PA officials, Saeb Erakat and Ahmad Quray (Abu Ala).

In mid-October 2001 the right-wing Haichud Haleumi-Israel B'Aitainu bloc withdrew from the governing coalition in protest at the Sharon administration's decision to pull back Israeli armed forces from the West Bank town of Hebron; two ministers thus resigned. Two days later one of these ministers, the hard-line Minister of Tourism, Rechavam Ze'evi, was assassinated at a hotel in Arab East Jerusalem by a PFLP militant, in apparent retaliation for the recent assassination of the group's leader. Following the murder of Ze'evi—who was the first Israeli cabinet minister to be assassinated by an Arab militant—the Haichud Haleumi-Israel B'Aitainu bloc maintained its presence in the Government, with the other minister who had resigned, Minister of National Infrastructure Avigdor Lieberman, retaining his post and Rabbi Binyamin Elon subsequently being named as Ze'evi's successor. Sharon held Arafat personally responsible for the minister's death and suspended all contact with the PA. The Israeli Government also decided to reverse its recent moves to ease the economic restrictions on Palestinians in the West Bank and Gaza, and demanded that the PA immediately extradite the PFLP militants implicated in the assassination. In mid-October Israeli armed forces entered six Palestinian towns in the West Bank (including Ramallah, Jenin, Nablus and Bethlehem) and killed a leading member of Arafat's Fatah movement.

US and European leaders urged restraint from Sharon as the Israeli–Palestinian conflict escalated, and in late October 2001 US officials urged Israel to pull back its troops from PA-controlled areas. Discussions took place between Israeli, Palestinian and US security officials at the end of the month, during which the Israeli representatives declared their terms for a staged withdrawal of troops from the six West Bank towns. Israeli forces duly withdrew from Bethlehem and Beit Jala, despite the continuing violence. However, Sharon announced that the withdrawal from the remaining four towns would not take place until the PA arrested more Islamist militants. In early November Sharon cancelled a scheduled visit to the USA, following an attack on a bus in Jerusalem by a gunman purportedly from Islamic Jihad. It appeared that US officials were set to criticize the Israeli Government for its failure to co-operate in US attempts to ease tensions in the Middle East while the USA pursued its international 'war on terror'.

An EU delegation which visited Israel in mid-November 2001 failed to persuade Sharon to end his demand for a seven-day period without violence prior to the resumption of peace talks with the Palestinians and the redeployment of Israeli armed forces from PA-controlled territory. Later in that month both the UN Committee Against Torture and the human rights group Amnesty International issued warnings to Israel regarding the continuing use of torture by its security forces against Palestinian detainees, and the UN criticized Israel's policy of 'extrajudicial killing'. In late November the USA dispatched its two special envoys to the Middle East, William Burns and Anthony

Zinni, in an attempt to broker a new cease-fire. However, the appointment of a hardline former army general, Meir Dagan, as the chief Israeli negotiator in talks with US and PA representatives diminished any hopes of a diplomatic breakthrough.

Meanwhile, on the domestic front, in mid-November 2001 Sharon was obliged to repay what had been found to be an illegal donation received by his campaign team in the approach to the premiership election. In late December the Minister of Defence, Binyamin Ben-Eliezer, became the new Labour Party leader in a second round of voting after he had won a legal challenge regarding the outcome of the first ballot.

The Israeli–Palestinian crisis escalated in early December 2001 when Palestinian militants launched suicide attacks in Haifa and Jerusalem, in retaliation for the 'targeted killing' of a Hamas leader: in one weekend some 25 Israelis were killed, and scores wounded. Sharon cut short his official visit to the USA, and Israel launched heavy military strikes against Palestinian security targets in the Occupied Territories; two of Arafat's helicopters were destroyed in one Israeli raid. Although the PA was reported to have arrested at least 100 Hamas and Islamic Jihad members in the aftermath of the bloodshed, the US Government still urged Arafat to do more to end the violence. Israel escalated its military operations in the Territories in mid-December after 10 Israelis had died in a bomb attack in the West Bank. The Government demanded 'concrete action' from the PA, despite a recent speech in which Arafat had ordered the Palestinian militant groups to end their armed campaign against Israel. Israeli armed forces staged a 'tactical' withdrawal from areas around Nablus and Ramallah to permit Arafat's security forces to arrest wanted Palestinian militants. However, Arafat remained confined to his headquarters in Ramallah after Israel imposed a travel ban on the Palestinian leader.

Anthony Zinni returned to the Middle East in early January 2002, immediately after the Israeli administration had ordered the partial withdrawal of its forces from some West Bank towns and the easing of certain restrictions against Palestinians there. Meanwhile, it was announced that Israeli forces in the Red Sea had intercepted a freighter ship, the *Karine-A*, which Israel claimed was carrying a large consignment of Iranian-made heavy weaponry destined for the Gaza Strip. Israeli and US officials claimed to have evidence of the PA's involvement in the trafficking of arms into the Occupied Territories, leading Arafat to institute an internal inquiry into the *Karine-A* affair, although he denied any knowledge of the shipment. In mid-January Israeli forces assassinated a leader of the Fatah-affiliated Al-Aqsa Martyrs' Brigades, provoking retaliatory attacks by that organization in Hadera and Jerusalem in which six Israelis died. Israeli forces proceeded to tighten the blockade around Arafat's Ramallah offices. At the end of the month Sharon approved a security plan involving the physical 'separation' of Jerusalem from the West Bank, in order to prevent attacks by Palestinian Islamist groups on Israeli territory.

By February 2002 it was reported that Sharon's popularity among the Israeli electorate was waning; moreover, at least 250 Israeli army reservists signed a petition stating their refusal to serve in the Occupied Territories. The Council for Peace and Security—which included many senior reserve officers—urged the Government to redeploy its forces from most of the West Bank and Gaza. In early February Sharon reportedly rejected new proposals for a peace settlement drafted by Shimon Peres and the Speaker of the Palestinian legislature, Ahmad Quray. Meanwhile, it appeared that Palestinian militants were increasingly targeting their attacks against the Israeli military and Jewish settlers in the Territories. In mid-February six Israeli soldiers died in a Palestinian assault on their West Bank checkpoint—this was the most serious attack on Israeli military forces since the start of the al-Aqsa *intifada*.

In early March 2002 the UN Security Council adopted Resolution 1397, affirming its 'vision' of both Israeli and Palestinian states 'within secure and recognized borders'. Israel rejected a peace initiative put forward by Crown Prince Abdullah of Saudi Arabia at the Arab League summit held in Beirut in late March, due to its objection to the proposal that Israel withdraw from all Arab lands occupied since 1967 in exchange for full recognition of the State of Israel by the Arab states. Towards the end of March 2002 a Hamas suicide bombing at a Passover celebration in Netanya resulted in the deaths of 29 Israelis, while some 140 were injured in the attack. The so-called 'Passover massacre' led the Israeli Government, on 29 March, to initiate a massive campaign of military incursions into West Bank towns—codenamed 'Operation Defensive Shield'—with the declared aim of dismantling the Palestinian 'terrorist infrastructure'. Yasser Arafat's presidential compound at Ramallah was surrounded by Israeli troops, leaving the Palestinian leader isolated. At the end of the month an emergency session of the UN Security Council produced Resolution 1402 expressing 'grave concern' at the escalation of violence in Israel and the Palestinian territories. During the first two weeks of April intense fighting between the Israeli army and Palestinian militias occurred in the Jenin refugee camp—considered by Israel to be a base for Palestinian militants opposed to the Oslo accords. Some 23 Israeli soldiers were reportedly killed in ambushes and gun battles at the Jenin camp, while Palestinian sources claimed that over 100 Palestinians had died in the fighting. Despite subsequent attempts by a UN fact-finding mission to investigate Palestinian allegations of 'war crimes' committed by the Israeli army at Jenin, Israel refused to recognize the composition and mandate of the UN team. In mid-April US Secretary of State Powell arrived in Israel in an attempt to negotiate an Israeli-Palestinian cease-fire, and the Bush Administration repeated demands for Israel to withdraw from PA-controlled towns. There was a subsequent redeployment of Israeli forces from areas of the West Bank, but Israeli troops continued to encircle Arafat's presidential compound in Ramallah, as well as part of Bethlehem. Sharon insisted that the siege in Ramallah would continue until the PA handed over five men suspected of involvement in the assassination of Rechavam Ze'evi, as well as a militant believed to have plotted the shipment of weapons to Gaza aboard the *Karine-A* freighter ship. Arafat was freed by the Israeli authorities at the beginning of May, after the PA agreed to hand over the prisoners: four of the men were convicted of direct involvement in Ze'evi's murder by an *ad hoc* Palestinian court inside the Ramallah compound and sentenced to various terms of imprisonment. (For further details of events in the West Bank and Gaza Strip in March–May 2002, see the chapter on the Palestinian Autonomous Areas.)

The right-wing Haichud Haleumi-Israel B'Aitainu bloc withdrew from the governing coalition in early March 2002, in protest against recent concessions made towards the Palestinians. However, the Government was strengthened a month later by the appointment of David Levy of Gesher and two ministers from the NRP as ministers without portfolio.

The Central Committee of Likud voted in early May 2002 to categorically reject the creation of a Palestinian state; this was interpreted as a reversal for Ariel Sharon, who publicly accepted the possibility of Palestinian independence. In mid-June Israel commenced the construction of an electrified 'security fence', to extend the entire length of its border with the West Bank, with a view to preventing Palestinian militants from infiltrating Israeli territory and perpetrating further attacks. Despite international diplomatic efforts aimed at securing a new round of peace talks between Israel and the PA, and reports of a potential US initiative involving the creation of an 'interim' Palestinian state, there was a marked increase in violence at this time: Israel launched a new offensive, code-named 'Operation Determined Path', ordering troops into several West Bank and Gaza towns, in retaliation for another series of suicide attacks by Palestinian militants. Once again Arafat's headquarters in Ramallah were blockaded by the Israeli military. At the end of June Israeli forces began the removal of a small number of settler 'outposts' deemed to be illegal. Meanwhile, there were reports that a senior commander of Hamas's military wing had been killed by Israeli troops in Nablus; Israel alleged that he was a prominent bomb-maker, who had been responsible for attacks such as the Passover bombing in Netanya. Senior-level talks were resumed between Israel and the PA, while the Quartet group (comprising the USA, Russia, the UN and EU) held discussions in London, United Kingdom, in a bid to re-activate the Oslo peace process.

As new peace talks were being convened by the Quartet group, violence again appeared to be on the increase when several Israelis died in an attack on a bus near a Jewish settlement in the West Bank in mid-July 2002, for which three Palestinian militant groups all claimed responsibility. The Israeli response to the latest assaults included 'freezing' plans to ease some of the restrictions imposed on Palestinians living in the Territories. Human rights organizations criticized plans by Israel to deport a number of relatives of suspected Palestinian militants to the Gaza Strip; however, a ruling by the Israeli Supreme Court in September declared the expulsions to be legitimate. Meanwhile, tensions increased between Israelis and Palestinians in late July, when an Israeli air-strike on a residential building in Gaza

City resulted in the deaths of up to 15 Palestinans (including several children). The Israeli raid had achieved its aim of assassinating a leader of Hamas's military wing. Following international (and especially US) pressure, Israel moved to ease the restrictions in the West Bank and Gaza, and Sharon pledged to release some of the tax revenues owed to the PA. The Gaza air-strike precipitated a new round of violence, however, with four Jewish settlers being killed near Hebron towards the end of July. Israel responded by ordering tanks into the Gaza Strip. However, at the end of the month at least seven Israelis were killed in a suicide bomb attack at the Hebrew University in Jerusalem; Hamas claimed responsibility for the blast. There were at least 15 further Israeli fatalities in early August as a result of attacks by militant Palestinians. The Israeli Government responded by ordering a total ban on freedom of movement for Palestinians in most West Bank cities, and the PA accused Israel of reneging on a recent pledge to pull its troops out of PA-administered towns and villages. The Gaza Strip was the focus of much of Israel's military campaign during late August: a number of leading militants and civilians were killed. Israel and the PA agreed at this time to implement a security plan (termed the 'Gaza, Bethlehem First' plan) whereby Israel would withdraw from the Gaza Strip and Bethlehem, in return for Palestinian security guarantees and a crack-down on militants. Israel began to withdraw its forces from Bethlehem on the following day; however, violence continued throughout the Territories and further talks were cancelled. In early September the Israeli Ministry of the Interior took the unprecedent step of revoking the citizenship of an Arab Israeli who was accused of assisting Palestinian militants in plotting suicide attacks against Israelis. Two suicide bombings in Um al-Fahm and Tel-Aviv in mid-September caused the situation to deteriorate further. Israeli forces began to demolish buildings in Arafat's Ramallah compound, claiming that some 20 Palestinian militants were being sheltered there. Meanwhile, there were reports during October that the USA was assisting Israel with preparations to strengthen its military defences against a possible attack by Iraq, as the prospect of a US-led campaign to oust the regime of Saddam Hussein increased.

Elections to the Knesset were held on 28 January 2003, a few months earlier than scheduled. In October 2002 the Labour Party had withdrawn from Sharon's governing coalition in opposition to provisions in the 2003 budget which allocated funds to Jewish settlements in the West Bank. Sharon and his Likud party won a resounding victory over the left-wing parties at the polls, securing 38 seats in the Knesset; however, the electoral turn-out (at under 68%) was reportedly the lowest in Israel's history. Following lengthy discussions (during which Sharon attempted to persuade the Labour leader, Amram Mitzna, to join a new 'government of national unity' with Likud), a new coalition Government was announced on 28 February 2003. The Cabinet was composed of Likud, the secularist Shinui party, and the right-wing and religious NRP, Haichud Haleumi and Israel B'Aliyah parties. (Mitzna had declared that Labour would only join the Government on the condition that Sharon agreed to close Jewish settlements in the Gaza Strip and to resume peace talks with the PA.) The former Likud premier, Binyamin Netanyahu, was named as Minister of Finance, while the Shinui and NRP leaders were both appointed as Deputy Prime Ministers. Reuven Rivlin became the new Speaker of the Knesset. In early May Amram Mitzna resigned as Labour leader and was subsequently replaced, in an acting capacity, by Shimon Peres.

President Bush announced in mid-April 2003 that he would publish the Quartet-sponsored 'roadmap' for achieving peace in the Middle East once the new Palestinian Prime Minister, Mahmud Abbas—who had been appointed in mid-March—had announced a new Cabinet. On 29 April, the same day that the Palestinian legislature endorsed the new Palestinian administration, two Britons carried out a suicide bombing at a café in Tel-Aviv, killing five people. Nevertheless, on 30 April the USA presented both the Israeli and Palestinian Prime Ministers with copies of the 'roadmap'. This latest peace initiative envisaged the creation of a sovereign Palestinian state by 2005–06 in a process comprising three phases. The first phase dealt largely with Palestinian issues, namely the cessation of militant operations against Israel and the establishment of a civilian and government infrastructure. Israel would be required to withdraw from areas it had occupied since 2000 and to dismantle Jewish settlements constructed since 2001. In phase two, Israel would hold peace talks with Lebanon and Syria regarding Palestinian borders; and the third and final phase would deal with the issues of Jerusalem and refugees. The roadmap emphasized the importance of UN Security Council Resolutions 242, 338 and 1397 in establishing a two-state settlement, and also reiterated that the Arab states must recognize Israel's right to exist. Sharon initially objected to the issue of the 'right to return' of Palestinian refugees and refused to consider the dismantling of Jewish settlements, a requisite of the peace plan. Nevertheless, on 25 May the Israeli Cabinet accepted the terms of the roadmap, and at the end of the month Sharon made the unprecedented admission that Israel was in occupation of the Palestinian areas.

In early June 2003 Ariel Sharon, Mahmud Abbas and President Bush met in Aqaba, Jordan, to discuss the implementation of the roadmap, particularly the contentious issue of Jewish settlements. On 9 June Israeli troops commenced the dismantlement of settlements in the West Bank, but the nascent peace process was subsumed by a resumption of violence. On 10 June Israel attempted to kill a prominent Hamas leader, Abd al-Aziz ar-Rantisi, prompting a retaliatory suicide attack against a bus in Jerusalem, in which 16 people died. Israeli helicopter gunships were subsequently ordered to attack targets in Gaza. In all, 26 people were killed in the renewed hostilities, and the USA condemned Israel's attempt to assassinate ar-Rantisi. However, Israel continued to dismantle the settlements as well as to instigate troop withdrawals from the West Bank and Gaza Strip and release a number of Palestinian prisoners. Though the release of Palestinian prisoners was not a condition of the roadmap, it was regarded as an important expression of support for Abbas. By mid-August more than 400 prisoners had been released, including members of Hamas and Islamic Jihad who had not been involved in planning or executing attacks against Israeli targets. These two militant groups, along with Arafat's Fatah movement, had declared a three-month cease-fire at the end of June. Following these positive first steps, however, the roadmap was threatened by growing international concerns over Israel's construction of a 'security fence' in the West Bank, as well as by a resumption of Israeli–Palestinian hostilities in late August.

Israel had begun construction of the West Bank 'security fence' in mid-2002. It was initially intended to prevent Palestinian militants from covertly crossing into Israel to carry out attacks, but by mid-2003 Israel was being accused of using the barrier to annex Palestinian territory, and it was feared that it would become a permanent border in any future peace settlement. President Bush urged Sharon to remove the 'security fence' when the two leaders met at the end of July, and the US Administration further threatened to withhold nearly US $10,000m. of essential loan guarantees unless construction ceased. Despite international pressure, Israel continued to erect the barrier as well as to maintain its policy of 'targeted attacks' against senior Palestinian militants. On 14 August Israeli forces killed a senior commander of Islamic Jihad in Hebron, and on 19 August a suicide bomber killed 20 Israelis on a bus in Jerusalem, an attack for which both Hamas and Islamic Jihad claimed responsibility. In retaliation, Israel raided militant targets in both the West Bank and Gaza Strip; on 22 August Israel reimposed road-blocks on the main north–south highway in the Gaza Strip, reversing one of the earliest roadmap initiatives.

At the beginning of September 2003 a lengthy Israeli judicial inquiry, led by Justice Theodore Or, released its report on the deaths of 14 Israeli Arabs during protests in October 2000. The report severely criticized the use of 'excessive force' by Israeli security forces during the early days of the al-Aqsa *intifada*, and recommended that neither Shlomo Ben-Avi nor Yehuda Wilk, respectively the Minister of Public Security and the Commissioner of Police at the time of the deaths, should again be allowed to take responsibility for security affairs. Former Prime Minister Ehud Barak was also criticized in the report. On 9 September 2003 13 Israelis were killed in two suicide attacks on targets in Jerusalem and near Tel-Aviv, leading Israel to carry out further strikes against militant targets in Gaza.

In early October 2003 the Israeli Cabinet approved the next phase of the 'security fence'; although this was not contiguous to sections of the barrier already built, it was to completely enclose settlements in the West Bank. Additionally, a tender was issued for the construction of 550 new homes in a Jewish settlement close to Jerusalem. Throughout the month Israeli armed forces carried out operations in the Gaza Strip, including an incursion into the Rafah refugee camp to close down tunnels allegedly used by Palestinian militants to smuggle weapons from Egypt

into Gaza. Towards the end of the month three Israeli soldiers were killed when Palestinian gunmen attacked a settlement in the Gaza Strip; both Hamas and Islamic Jihad claimed responsibility for the attack.

The USA announced at the end of November 2003 that it was cutting US $290m. from a loan package guarantee for Israel as a penalty for renewed settlement construction in the West Bank and Gaza. Israeli troops raided the West Bank town of Ramallah at the beginning of December, arresting 30 suspected Palestinian militants. The raid coincided with a visit by US envoy William Burns, who urged Israel to cease further development of the settlements; however, the request was rebuffed by Sharon, who insisted that the settlements were essential to Israel's security. The issue of the settlements was one raised by the authors of a new peace plan, launched by senior Palestinian and Israeli political figures in Geneva, Switzerland, on 1 December. The Geneva Accords, which did not have the official approval of either the Israeli or Palestinian administrations, outlined a two-state solution to the Israeli–Palestinian issue, including proposals that Palestinians would receive compensation for giving up the right of return; that most settlements in the West Bank and Gaza (except those neighbouring Jerusalem) would be dismantled; and that Jerusalem (to become the capital of two states) would be divided administratively rather than physically. On 8 December the UN General Assembly passed a resolution asking the International Court of Justice (ICJ) in The Hague, Netherlands, to issue a (non-binding) ruling on the legality of Israel's 'security fence'; the hearings began in February 2004. Meanwhile, Ariel Sharon was becoming increasingly embroiled in the investigation, details of which had first prior to the general election in January 2003, into allegations that he had received $1.5m. in illegal campaign contributions. Israel's Supreme Court ordered the Prime Minister's son Gilad to hand over documents relating to a loan from a family friend and South African businessman to repay allegedly illegal donations during the campaign for the leadership of Likud. A secondary matter was the circumstances under which Gilad Sharon had been employed as a consultant on an Israeli-backed development in Greece. Ariel Sharon was able to distract attention from his legal problems when he issued an ultimatum to the Palestinian leadership in mid-December 2003, demanding that unless the PA started disarming and disbanding Palestinian militant groups, Israel would adopt a 'disengagement plan', which would effectively consist of accelerating the construction of the 'security fence' in the West Bank and physically separating Israel from the Palestinian territories. Yet Sharon's speech attracted criticism from right-wing and ultra-Orthodox settler groups when it became clear that the disengagement plan would involve the evacuation of 17 settlements in the Gaza Strip, considered beyond the reach of the 'security fence'. Under the terms of the roadmap, which Sharon stated he was willing to implement if the Palestinians also carried out their obligations, at least 60 settlements in the West Bank and Gaza would have to be dismantled.

At the end of January 2004 an Israeli businessman, David Appel, was formally charged with offering bribes to both Ariel and Gilad Sharon as well as to Deputy Prime Minister Ehud Olmert. In the late 1990s Appel had allegedly offered US $700,000 to Ariel Sharon, who was then Minister of Foreign Affairs, to exert pressure on the Greek authorities to approve the development of an island holiday resort and casino in which Appel had business interests. Although Sharon was not charged, he faced a police investigation in relation to the claims, while the Labour Party tabled a parliamentary motion of 'no confidence' against the Prime Minister. Meanwhile, on 29 January 2004 10 Israelis were killed in a suicide bombing of a bus in Jerusalem; this latest attack by Palestinian militants was regarded as an attempt to stall the Israeli-Lebanese prisoner exchange that was taking place in Cologne, Germany (see below).

Ariel Sharon announced in an interview published in the *Ha'aretz* newspaper in early February 2004 that he had drawn up a plan to evacuate all Jewish settlements in the Gaza Strip. The evacuation would reportedly affect 7,500 settlers in 17 settlements (although details of the plan were subsequently amended—see below). This news was welcomed by the recently appointed Palestinian Prime Minister, Ahmad Quray, and in late February Sharon met officials from the US Administration to discuss his proposed evacuation of the Gaza settlements. However, the proposed withdrawal from Gaza was overshadowed in late March by Israel's most high profile 'targeted killing', namely that of Sheikh Ahmed Yassin, the founder and spiritual leader of Hamas. The decision to kill Yassin was reportedly made by Prime Minister Sharon and his 'inner' Security Cabinet following a double suicide bombing at the southern port of Ashdod on 14 March, in which 10 Israelis died; responsibility for the bombings was claimed jointly by Hamas and the Al-Aqsa Martyrs' Brigades. The 'targeted killing' of the Hamas leader by Israeli helicopter gunships on 22 March, which provoked international condemnation, apparently indicated the start of a campaign by the Israeli Government to eliminate the entire leadership of Hamas. On 26 March the USA vetoed a UN Security Council resolution condemning the Israeli action, reportedly due to the fact that the resolution failed to refer to Hamas as a 'terrorist' organization. Abd al-Aziz ar-Rantisi was appointed leader of Hamas in Gaza after Yassin's death, but his tenure was short-lived as on 17 April he was also killed in a rocket attack by Israeli helicopter gunships. In the aftermath of ar-Rantisi's death, Hamas kept secret the identity of his successor and reportedly adopted a policy of 'collective leadership' in order to prevent future leaders of the organization from being victims of Israeli 'targeted killings'.

In mid-April 2004 Sharon travelled to the USA to discuss the roadmap with President Bush; however, the outcome of the meeting was the endorsement by Bush of Sharon's proposals to 'disengage' from Gaza, which also involved the consolidation of six Jewish settlements in the West Bank. This was regarded as a major diplomatic coup for Sharon, but one which was inimical to the spirit of the roadmap. Sharon suffered a setback in early May, when members of his own Likud party overwhelmingly rejected the disengagement plan at a party ballot. Determined that the disengagement plan be approved, Sharon drew up a slightly modified version of the proposals, and in early June removed Minister of Transport Avigdor Lieberman and Minister of Tourism Binyamin Elon, both from the far-right Haichud Haleumi party and both opposed to an Israeli disengagement from Gaza. A few days later, the NRP Minister of Construction and Housing, Efraim Eitam, resigned after Sharon's proposals were approved in principle by a cabinet vote (he still had to secure support on details of the plan). However, Sharon lost his Knesset majority when Haichud Haleumi's six deputies resigned, and he entered into negotiations with the Labour Party. In mid-June Sharon narrowly survived a parliamentary vote of 'no confidence' prompted by opposition to his disengagement plan.

Also in mid-June 2004 the Attorney-General, Menachem Mazuz, dismissed, on grounds of insufficient evidence, corruption charges against Sharon in connection with his son's, alleged promotion of the business interests of an Israeli property magnate while acting as a consultant on an Israeli-backed development in Greece, closing an investigation that began in December 2003 (see above).

Meanwhile, as attacks by Palestinian militants against Israeli soldiers in the Gaza Strip intensified, with a number of fatalities being reported, in mid-May 2004 Israel launched one of its largest military operations in Gaza for decades. The aims of the offensive, code-named 'Operation Rainbow', were to locate and dismantle tunnels in the Rafah refugee camps through which militants were able to smuggle weapons for use in attacks against Israelis, and to arrest Palestinians wanted for involvement in such attacks. A reported 40 Palestinians, whom Israel claimed to be terrorists, were killed during the operation. In late June, after a petition had been filed by several Palestinian councils, the Israeli Supreme Court ordered the Government to alter the route of part of the 'security fence', including a 30-km section in a Palestinian village, Beit Sourik. In early July the ICJ gave its advisory opinion that the barrier contravened international law and effectively constituted the annexation of Palestinian land, and disrupted thousands of civilians' lives, frustrating Palestinian attempts to achieve self-determination. The ICJ urged Israel to remove parts of the fence and pay compensation to affected Palestinians. Sharon rejected the ruling, which he asserted was politically motivated and detrimental to the 'war on terror'. In mid-July Sharon discharged the Minister of Infrastructure, Joseph Paritzky, of the Shinui party, after Israeli television broadcast evidence that he had planned to discredit fellow party member and Minister of the Interior, Abraham Poraz, during the party's primary elections. In late July the UN General Assembly voted to demand that Israel comply with the ICJ ruling and take down the barrier (the USA voted against the resolution). In mid-August, at a special convention of Sharon's Likud party, members voted against the Prime Minister's proposals to form a coalition with any Zionist

party or Labour. Sharon dismissed the resolutions and vowed to pursue his plans for a coalition government to secure a parliamentary majority for his plan to disengage from Gaza, and to avoid having to call early general elections. Meanwhile, the Supreme Court gave the Government 30 days to produce a statement assessing the implications of the ICJ's findings. Attorney-General Mazuz expressed concern over the possibility of international action being taken against Israel, including the imposition of sanctions, and urged the Government to adopt a new vote for the 'security fence' to show compliance with international law. Also in mid-August Sharon approved the construction of 1,000 new Jewish homes in the West Bank. In January 2005 residents of the Palestinian village, Beit Sourik, protested that the alterations made to the route of the 'security fence' in June 2004 did not conform with the Supreme Court's ruling, nor with that of the ICJ.

In early October 2004 34 people, most of whom were Israelis, were killed by bomb blasts in three resorts in Egypt's Sinai Peninsula; Egypt later blamed the blasts on a Palestinian and three Sinai Bedouins. In mid-October the Israeli army ended a 16-day assault, code-named 'Days of Penitence', in northern and southern Gaza that left 135 Palestinians dead and destroyed an estimated 95 homes, according to UN figures. The attack had been prompted by a Hamas rocket that killed two children in Sderot, close to the Gaza Strip. In late October an Israeli missile strike in Gaza killed a leading Hamas militant. Meanwhile, Egypt pledged to provide 750 border guards to replace Israeli troops along the Egypt–Gaza frontier to attempt to prevent Palestinian arms-smuggling and to stop Hamas and other Palestinian factions from firing rockets into Israel in the event of Israel carrying out its disengagement plan; Israel accepted Egypt's offer in early December, and later in the month Israel released 159 Palestinian prisoners as a gesture of 'goodwill' to Egypt's President Mubarak, after Mubarak had agreed to release an Arab Israeli, Azzam Azzam, who had been serving a sentence in Egypt for espionage. The prisoner release was also interpreted as a 'goodwill' gesture to the newly elected Executive President of the PA, Mahmud Abbas, following the death of Yasser Arafat in November 2004 (for further details, see the chapter on the Palestinian Autonomous Areas). In mid-January 2005, despite initial hopes of negotiations with Abbas, Sharon announced that he refused to meet the new Palestinian leader until he adopted measures to combat Palestinian militant activity. The announcement followed a Palestinian attack that killed six Israelis at the Karni cargo crossing between Gaza and Israel. Sharon ordered the Israeli army to enter several areas of Gaza in order to prevent Palestinian attacks. However, following an announcement from the Central Committee of the PLO to Palestinians to cease all military action against Israel, Sharon called off the offensive in Gaza, while Abbas apparently tried to negotiate a cease-fire with militant groups.

In mid-October 2004 the Knesset voted against a speech by Sharon in which he outlined a timetable to disengage from Gaza; many of the Labour members who voted against the speech supported the Prime Minister's disengagement plan but were opposed to budgetary aspects of his speech. Sharon dismissed demands for an early general election and a national referendum on his plan to disengage from Gaza, and proceeded with his efforts to expand his minority coalition and gain support for the disengagement. Fears of an assassination attempt on Sharon by people opposed to his plan prompted Israel to increase security around him. In late October the Knesset voted to accept Sharon's proposal to dismantle all 21 settlements in Gaza, and four in the northern West Bank. However, the Israeli premier carried out a threat made prior to the vote to discharge any cabinet members who voted against the plan, dismissing Uzi Landau, a Likud minister without portfolio, and a deputy minister. In early November the Cabinet approved a plan to compensate Jewish settlers due to be evacuated from Gaza, and to imprison settlers who resisted evacuation. Also in early November the NRP's six parliamentary members withdrew from the coalition Government in opposition to Sharon's proposals for the Gaza Strip. In early December Sharon dismissed Shinui's five ministers when they voted against the first reading of the 2005 budget because it pledged US $98m. in subsidies to projects backed by United Torah Judaism. (The Cabinet had approved the 2005 budget in mid-August.) Sharon's Likud party was left with only 40 out of the Knesset's 120 seats. After a period of negotiations, Labour agreed in mid-December 2004 to form a coalition with Likud. It was reported at the end of that month that Sharon had agreed a deal with the Labour leader,

Shimon Peres, whereby Peres would become his 'senior deputy', assuming a new title of Vice-Premier. In early January 2005 the Knesset narrowly approved the new coalition Government, to be composed principally of Likud, Labour and United Torah Judaism, thereby restoring Sharon's parliamentary majority. (United Torah Judaism, which subsequently split into its constituent parties of Agudat Israel and Degel Hatora, agreed to join the coalition for a trial period; however, its members did not assume government posts immediately.) In mid-January the new Government narrowly endorsed the 2005 budget proposals.

In mid-February 2005 Attorney-General Menachen Mazuz dismissed charges against Sharon relating to the laundering of illegal campaign funds for his 1999 campaign for the leadership of Likud (see above), citing insufficient evidence. However, Ariel Sharon's son Omri still faced charges, and investigations continued into allegations that Omri Sharon and the premier's other son, Gilad, had used a loan from a family friend and South African businessman to repay illegal donations during the leadership campaign (see above).

Meanwhile, in early February 2005 the Israeli Cabinet approved the withdrawal of Israeli forces from five West Bank towns as well as the release of 500 Palestinian prisoners immediately following a summit meeting that was to be held in Egypt; a further 400 prisoners were to be freed after a three-month period. The summit was duly convened between Sharon, Mahmud Abbas, President Mubarak and King Abdullah of Jordan in Sharm esh-Sheikh on 8 February, amid hopes of a breakthrough in the Middle East peace process following the election of a new Palestinian leadership. Sharon and Abbas shook hands and issued verbal declarations to end hostilities between their two peoples; however, no formal cease-fire was agreed. At the meeting Israel agreed to hand over to PA security control the towns of Jericho, Tulkaram, Bethlehem, Qalqilya and Ramallah in the coming weeks. (Israeli forces duly withdrew from Jericho in mid-March and from Tulkaram later in the month.) However, the militant groups Hamas and Islamic Jihad refused to be bound by the declaration. Shortly after the Sharm esh-Sheikh summit, Israel allowed 56 deported Palestinians to return to the West Bank, and also transferred the bodies of 15 Palestinian bombers to the PA. In late February Israel began the release of 500 Palestinian prisoners as a 'goodwill' gesture. At this time the Israeli Cabinet gave its final approval to the Government's planned disengagement from all settlements in the Gaza Strip and four in the West Bank. Amid hopes for an improvement in Israeli–Arab relations, Jordan returned an ambassador to Israel. However, towards the end of the month a suicide bombing in Tel-Aviv, subsequently claimed by Islamic Jihad, killed four Israelis and wounded about 50 others; it appeared likely that the bombing would deter Israel from carrying out its proposed redeployments from the West Bank. Palestinians, meanwhile, were angered by reports that Israel was planning to construct a further 6,391 homes in existing West Bank settlements during 2005. Nevertheless, amid a general lull in the violence, Israel handed over Tulkaram to Palestinian security control in late March. At a summit meeting of the Arab League held in Algiers, Algeria, during 22–23 March those leaders in attendance adopted a resolution to revive a peace plan put forward by the Saudi Crown Prince in 2002 (see above); however, the Israeli leadership had already rejected the initiative. Towards the end of the month the Knesset voted to reject a bill that would require a national referendum to be held prior to any implementation of Sharon's disengagement plan, and approved the 2005 budget, thus avoiding the need to call general elections and preventing a delay to the Israeli withdrawal from the Gaza Strip, which was scheduled to begin in July 2005.

In early March 2000 the Israeli Cabinet voted unanimously to withdraw its forces from southern Lebanon by 7 July, even in the absence of a peace agreement with Syria. The Lebanese Government responded by demanding that Israel also depart from a small area on the Syrian border known as Shebaa Farms. In mid-April Israel released 13 Lebanese prisoners who had been detained without trial for more than a decade, apparently as 'bargaining chips' for Israeli soldiers missing in Lebanon. Fighting between Israeli troops and Hezbollah intensified in May, and there were fears that further violence might follow an Israeli withdrawal after it was announced that Israel would not disarm the SLA. On 23 May Israel's Security Cabinet voted to accelerate the withdrawal of its remaining troops from southern Lebanon. By this date Hezbollah had taken control of about one-third of the territory following the evacuation by the SLA of outposts transferred to its control by the Israeli army; moreover,

mass defections from the SLA were reported. Meanwhile, Lebanese citizens stormed the al-Khiam prison in the security zone and freed 144 inmates. The rapid departure of all Israeli forces from southern Lebanon was completed on 24 May, nearly six weeks before Barak's original July deadline. Israeli public opinion generally welcomed an end to the occupation, since about 900 Israelis had been killed in southern Lebanon since 1978. After the withdrawal several thousand SLA members and their families fled across the border into northern Israel. In mid-June 2000 the UN Security Council confirmed that Israel had completed its withdrawal from Lebanon in compliance with UN Resolution 425. UNIFIL's mandate was extended for a six-month period at the end of July, by which time UNIFIL personnel were patrolling the area vacated by Israeli forces, monitoring the line of withdrawal and providing humanitarian assistance. Further extensions of UNIFIL's mandate were announced at six-monthly intervals.

Hezbollah reaffirmed in mid-2000 that it would pursue its armed campaign against Israel until Shebaa Farms was returned to Lebanese control. The al-Aqsa *intifada*, which erupted in late September, precipitated renewed operations by Hezbollah against the Israeli army. In early October three Israeli soldiers were kidnapped on the border with Lebanon by Hezbollah militants demanding the release of Arab prisoners held in Israel. One week later an Israeli businessman and army reservist, Elhanan Tannenbaum, was also captured by Hezbollah. Tensions escalated at the end of November when an Israeli soldier was killed by a Hezbollah bomb in Shebaa Farms; Israel responded by launching air raids on suspected Hezbollah targets. Another Israeli soldier was killed in a Hezbollah missile attack near Shebaa Farms in mid-February 2001. In mid-April Israeli helicopter gunships attacked a Syrian radar base in central Lebanon (in which at least one Syrian soldier died), in retaliation for the recent killing by Hezbollah of an Israeli soldier in Shebaa Farms. Israel launched a further raid on a Syrian radar station in eastern Lebanon in early July. In late July the UN announced that it would permit Israeli and Lebanese officials to view a censored copy of a video-cassette made by a UN peace-keeper in Lebanon, which Israel claimed would offer vital information relating to the three soldiers kidnapped by Hezbollah in late 2000. However, at the end of October 2001 Israeli military officials declared that the soldiers were 'almost certainly' dead. In early November 2003 the Israeli Cabinet agreed to release more than 400 Palestinian and Lebanese prisoners in exchange for the remains of the three kidnapped soldiers, as well as the return of Tannenbaum. It was also hoped that information would be received concerning the whereabouts of a missing Israeli pilot, who had been shot down over Lebanon in 1986 and was still believed to be held in captivity. Germany, which had acted as mediator during four years of negotiations between Israel and Hezbollah, agreed to oversee the exchange, and in late January 2004 the first 30 Lebanese and other Arab prisoners to be released by Israel were flown to the airport at Cologne, Germany, where they were exchanged for Tannenbaum and the remains of the Israeli soldiers. The remainder of the Palestinian prisoners, and the remains of 59 Lebanese militants held by Israel, were later released at Israeli border posts. In mid-November Israel threatened retaliation against Lebanon for failing to control its southern border when two *Katyusha* rockets were fired into northern Israel; the attack reportedly caused no damage or casualties.

Syria had welcomed the election of Ehud Barak to the Israeli premiership in May 1999. In July Barak undertook to negotiate a bilateral peace with Syria, based on UN Resolutions 242 and 338: this was interpreted as a signal of his intention to return most of the occupied Golan Heights in exchange for peace and normalized relations. On 20 July Syria ordered a 'cease-fire' with Israel. However, it was not until December that the two sides agreed to a resumption of negotiations from the point at which they had broken off in 1996, reportedly as a result of diplomatic efforts by US President Clinton and secret meetings between Israeli and Syrian officials. The Knesset subsequently approved the decision to resume talks, while Barak reasserted that any agreement concluded with Syria would be put to a national referendum. Clinton inaugurated peace negotiations between Barak and the Syrian Minister of Foreign Affairs, Farouk ash-Shara', in Washington, DC, on 15 December 1999. The talks commenced amid rising tensions in southern Lebanon, and resulted only in an agreement to resume discussions in January 2000. Barak, meanwhile, was encountering growing opposition in Israel to a possible return of the Golan Heights to

Syria. In late December 1999 Israel and Syria agreed an informal 'cease-fire' to curb hostilities in Lebanon. Barak and ash-Shara' attended further discussions (in which President Clinton played an active role) on 3–10 January 2000 in Shepherdstown, West Virginia. As a preliminary to the talks it was agreed that four committees would be established to discuss simultaneously the issues of borders, security, normalization of relations and water sharing. As further discussions proved inconclusive, the US Administration presented a 'draft working document' to both sides, as the basis for a framework agreement. However, Syria announced that it required a commitment from Israel to withdraw from the Golan Heights before negotiations could resume. Israel, meanwhile, demanded the personal involvement of President Hafiz al-Assad in the peace process. In early January a huge demonstration was held in Tel-Aviv by Israelis opposed to any withdrawal from the Golan Heights, while Israel B'Aliyah and the NRP threatened to leave Barak's coalition in any such event. On 17 January talks between Israel and Syria, which had been scheduled to reconvene two days later, were postponed indefinitely. Despite the intensification of the conflict in southern Lebanon (see above), and a Knesset vote in early March to change the majority required in the event of a referendum on an Israeli withdrawal from the Golan Heights from 50% of participants to 50% of the registered electorate, hopes of an imminent breakthrough in the Syrian track of the peace process were raised by the announcement, later in March, that Presidents Clinton and Assad were to meet in Geneva, Switzerland. However, the talks, on 26 March, broke down after only three hours, when it became apparent that the US President had no new Israeli proposals to offer to Syria regarding its demand for a full and unconditional withdrawal from the Golan Heights. In early April Barak declared that the Israeli Government would resume the construction of Jewish settlements in the Golan Heights (following a declared suspension prior to the December 1999 talks).

The prospect of further peace-making initiatives between Israel and Syria was further distanced by the death of President Assad in early June 2000, although Assad's second son, Bashar—who assumed the Syrian presidency in July—promised a continuation of his father's policies towards Israel. The Israeli-Syrian track remained deadlocked following the election of Ariel Sharon as Israel's premier. Despite reports in January 2002 that the Israeli Minister of Defence, Binyamin Ben-Eliezer, had informed the Syrian leadership that Israel would be willing to resume peace negotiations provided that there were no preconditions, by early 2003 the possibility of a swift resumption of talks appeared remote (especially as the USA increasingly referred to Syria as a possible target in President Bush's 'war on terror'). On 5 October Israel launched an air-strike against an alleged training camp for Palestinian militants in Syria. The attack on the Ein Saheb camp, near Damascus, was prompted by a suicide bombing in Haifa a few days previously which killed 19 Israelis. Syria sought a UN Security Council resolution condemning the attack, while both the PFLP and Islamic Jihad denied having used the training camp. In late 2003 and again in early 2004 the Israeli President, Moshe Katsav, issued a proposition to President Bashar al Assad for Syria to start direct negotiations with Israel 'without preconditions'. However, the Syrian leadership dismissed the Israeli offer as being 'not serious'. No agreement on the resumption of talks was reached between Israel and Syria in 2004, and in mid-January 2005 Israel asked Russia to call off negotiations with Syria concerning the proposed sale of Russian missiles, claiming that the deal would disrupt regional stability.

In September 2003 Ariel Sharon led a high-level Israeli delegation to India for a summit meeting, the agenda of which was dominated by the sale of Israeli military technology much sought after by India. In January 2004 Israel and India signed an agreement involving the sale to India of three Phalcon early-warning radar systems worth US $1,100m. In the same month Israel agreed to sell military technology to Turkey in exchange for 50m. cu m of fresh water per year over a 20-year period. In late May the Chairman of the Knesset Foreign Affairs and Defence Committee, Yuval Steinitz, expressed concern that Egypt was building up its store of weapons, many of which were supplied by the USA, asserting that Egypt was simulating a war with Israel. Israel pressed the USA to continue to maintain Israeli military qualitative superiority in the Middle East. In early July, during a visit by the UN's International Atomic Energy Agency (IAEA), Israel maintained its policy of 'strategic ambiguity' by not commenting on whether or not it possessed

nuclear weapons; international experts reported that Israel might have as many as 200 nuclear warheads. Sharon announced his support for the idea of a Middle East free from nuclear weapons, and urged the IAEA Director-General, Muhammad el-Baradei, to exert more pressure on Iran over its suspected uranium enrichment programme. In September the USA agreed to sell Israel $20m.-worth of heavy weaponry, which was apparently intended to serve Israel against a possible military threat from Iran, and which analysts noted could be used to launch strikes against Iran's nuclear facilities.

Government

Supreme authority in Israel rests with the Knesset (Assembly), with 120 members elected by universal suffrage for four years (subject to dissolution), on the basis of proportional representation. The President, a constitutional Head of State, is elected by the Knesset for five years. (Moshe Katsav, who assumed the presidency in August 2000, was exceptionally elected for a seven-year term.) Executive power lies with the Cabinet, led by a directly elected Prime Minister. The Cabinet takes office after receiving a vote of confidence in the Knesset, to which it is responsible. Ministers are usually members of the Knesset, but non-members may be appointed.

The country is divided into six administrative districts. Local authorities are elected at the same time as elections to the Knesset. There are 31 municipalities (including two Arab towns), 115 local councils (46 Arab and Druze) and 49 regional councils (one Arab) comprising representatives of 700 villages.

Defence

The Israel Defence Forces consist of a small nucleus of commissioned and non-commissioned regular officers, a contingent enlisted for national service, and a large reserve. Men are enlisted for 36 months of military service (excluding officers, who serve for 48 months), and women for 24 months. Military service is compulsory for Jews and Druzes, but voluntary for Christians, Circassians and Muslims. Total regular armed forces in August 2004 numbered an estimated 168,000 (including 107,500 conscripts), comprising an army of 125,000, a navy estimated at 8,000 and an air force of 35,000; full mobilization to 576,000 can be quickly achieved with reserves of 408,000. State expenditure on defence in 2004 was estimated at NIS 35,000m.

Economic Affairs

In 2002, according to estimates by the World Bank, Israel's gross national income (GNI), measured at average 2000–02 prices, was US $100,889m., equivalent to $16,020 per head (or $19,000 per head on an international purchasing-power parity basis). During 1990–2003, it was estimated, the population increased at an average annual rate of 2.8%, while gross domestic product (GDP) per head increased, in real terms, by an average of 1.3% per year. Overall GDP increased, in real terms, at an average annual rate of 4.1% in 1990–2003; however, negative growth was recorded in both 2001 and 2002, and growth was only 1.3% in 2003.

Agriculture (including hunting, forestry and fishing) contributed 1.7% of GDP in 2001, and in 2003 engaged 1.9% of the employed labour force. Most agricultural workers live in large co-operatives (*kibbutzim*), of which there were 268 at December 1999, or co-operative smallholder villages (*moshavim*), of which there were 411. Israel is largely self-sufficient in foodstuffs. Citrus fruits constitute the main export crop. Other important crops are vegetables (particularly potatoes, tomatoes and cucumbers), wheat and melons. The export of exotic fruits, winter vegetables and flowers has increased significantly in recent years. Poultry, livestock and fish production are also important. According to FAO data, agricultural output increased at an average annual rate of 1.2% in 1990–2003; production increased by 5.5% in 2002, but declined by 0.4% in 2003.

Industry (comprising mining, manufacturing, construction and power) contributed 23.3% of GDP in 2001, and engaged 22.7% of the employed labour force in 2003. The State plays a major role in all sectors of industry, and there is a significant co-operative sector. Industrial production increased by an average of 5.9% annually in 1988–95.

The mining and manufacturing sectors together contributed 16.6% of GDP in 2001, and engaged 16.5% of the employed labour force in 2002; mining and quarrying employed about 0.2% of the working population in 1997. Israel has small proven reserves of petroleum (of some 3.9m. barrels), from which less than 500 barrels per day are currently produced; however, in

1999 potential new reserves were discovered in central Israel and off the southern coast. Some natural gas is also produced, and significant offshore gas discoveries were made in the south in 1999 and 2000. Phosphates, potash, bromides, magnesium and other salts are mined, and Israel is the world's largest exporter of bromine. Gold, in potentially commercial quantities, was discovered in 1988.

Manufacturing employed 19.3% of the working population in 1997. The principal branches of manufacturing, measured by gross revenue, in 1996 were food products, beverages and tobacco (accounting for 17.4% of the total), chemical, petroleum and coal products (15.0%), electrical machinery (12.1%), metal products (11.1%), scientific, photographic, optical equipment, etc. (8.0%), paper, publishing and printing (6.5%), textiles and clothing (5.6%), non-metallic mineral manufactures (5.4%), rubber and plastic products (5.1%) and non-electrical machinery (5.0%).

Energy is derived principally from coal (accounting for 75.1% of total electricity output in 2001) and imported petroleum (24.8%); however, it is intended that natural gas should eventually become Israel's principal energy source. Imports of mineral fuels comprised 9.6% of the total value of imports in 2003.

Services contributed 75.0% of GDP in 2001, and engaged 75.5% of the employed labour force in 2003. Tourism is an important source of revenue, although the sector has been severely damaged by regional instability and a series of bomb attacks carried out by militant Islamist groups in recent years. The significant upsurge in violence from September 2000 once again deterred many foreign visitors, resulting in hotel closures, redundancies and a reduction in air travel. In 2003 some 1.1m. tourists visited Israel, and receipts from tourism totalled US $1,197m. in 2002; in 2000 the figures were 2.4m. and $3,338m., respectively. Financial services are also important: banking, insurance, real estate and business services together contributed 30.4% of GDP in 2001, and employed 16.4% of the working population in 2003.

In 2003 Israel recorded a visible trade deficit of US $2,560m., and there was a deficit of $174m. on the current account of the balance of payments. Excluding trade with the West Bank and Gaza Strip, in 2003 the principal source of imports was the USA, which supplied 15.6% of imports to Israel; other major suppliers were the Belgo-Luxembourg Economic Union (BLEU), Germany, the United Kingdom and Switzerland. The USA was also the principal market for exports, taking 38.0% of Israeli exports in that year; other important purchasers were the BLEU, Hong Kong, the United Kingdom and Germany. Israel is the world's largest supplier of polished diamonds. The principal exports in 2003 were basic manufactures (chiefly non-metallic mineral manufactures), machinery and transport equipment, chemicals and related products, and miscellaneous manufactured articles. The principal imports in that year were basic manufactures (mainly non-metallic mineral manufactures), machinery and transport equipment, chemicals and related products, mineral fuels and lubricants, and miscellaneous manufactured articles.

In 2001 the overall budgetary deficit (excluding net allocation of credit) rose from the planned NIS 8,400m. (equivalent to some 1.7% of GDP) to NIS 21,300m. (equivalent to about 4.6% of GDP). This was mainly due to increased spending on security provisions prompted by the al-Aqsa *intifada*. Government revenue each year normally includes some US $3,000m. in economic and military aid from the USA. At 31 December 2003 Israel's gross foreign debt amounted to $70,779m., of which $29,733m. was government debt. During 1990–2002 consumer prices rose at an average annual rate of 8.5%. Annual inflation averaged 5.6% in 2002 and 0.7% in 2003. The unemployment rate was reported to be almost 11% in 2003.

The most significant factor affecting the Israeli economy in the 1990s was the mass influx of Jews from the former USSR, which led to a substantial increase in the population, additional flexibility in the labour market and growth in construction. In 1996, however, a period of economic slowdown began, reflecting an end to the demand boom and reduced tourism revenues following an increase in Islamist violence. In May 1998 foreign-exchange restrictions were ended, allowing the shekel to become fully convertible. After the Government of Ehud Barak was elected in mid-1999 and the Middle East peace process was revived, the economy entered a period of recovery, with a significant improvement in business activity and increased foreign investment. Moreover, inflation declined to its lowest level since 1967. The strong rate of economic growth in 2000 was led by the success of Israel's high-technology sector. However, in the fourth quarter of 2000 the economic boom ended as a new *intifada* by Palestinians in the West Bank and Gaza dramatically reduced foreign investment and tourism revenues, while the global economic downturn had a particularly detrimental effect on high-tech companies. The negative growth in the Israeli economy in 2001 was reported to have been the first contraction since 1953; negative growth was also recorded in 2002, and in March 2003 the IMF described the Israeli economy as being 'in the midst of a deep recession'. Following the deregulation of the domestic telecommunications market and the privatization of Bank Hapoalim—Israel's largest bank—in 2000, the Government of Ariel Sharon defined its own privatization programme in May 2001, although structural reforms have generally proceeded slowly. The Knesset approved an austerity budget for 2004, including significant reductions in public expenditure, in January of that year. In February official statistics revealed that the Israeli economy had grown by 1.3% in 2003—the first such rise for three years—but this was considered insufficient to keep pace with the expanding population and the ongoing financial effects of the al-Aqsa *intifada* which, by November 2004 had cost the Israeli economy US $12,000m. Indeed, the potential for Israeli economic growth in the long term will be dependent upon progress towards a comprehensive and enduring regional peace settlement. In December Israel, Egypt and the USA signed a trade agreement allowing Egypt to export goods free of excise duty from three newly established 'qualified industrial zones' to the USA, provided that at least 11.7% of them are manufactured in Israel, and thereby permitting Israel to benefit from the low cost of labour in Egypt. In 2004 it was reported that at least 50,000 Russian *émigrés*, many of them discouraged by Israel's high unemployment and stagnant economy, had returned from Israel between 2001 and 2003, prompting fears that the loss of a large number of skilled workers could be damaging to the economy. At the end of March 2005 the Knesset finally approved the budget for that year, in which some NIS 2,200m. was earmarked for Israel's proposed disengagement from Gaza (see Recent History). In early 2005 it was estimated that the total cost of the disengagement would exceed NIS 5,000m.

Education

Israel has high standards of literacy and advanced educational services. Free, compulsory education is provided for all children between five and 15 years of age; in 1999 legislation was passed allowing for the introduction of free education for pre-primary children. Primary education is provided for all those between five and 10 years of age. There is also secondary, vocational and agricultural education. Post-primary education comprises two cycles of three years. Enrolment at primary and secondary schools in 1995 was equivalent to 93% of children aged six to 17 (primary 98%; secondary 88%). There are six universities, one institute of technology (the Technion) and one institute of science (the Weizmann Institute), which incorporates a graduate school of science. In 2001 budgetary expenditure on education by the central Government was forecast at NIS 31,271m. (13.9% of total spending).

Public Holidays

The Sabbath starts at sunset on Friday and ends at nightfall on Saturday. The Jewish year 5766 begins on 3 October 2005, and the year 5767 on 22 September 2006.

2005: 23–29 April (Pesach, Passover—public holidays on first and last days of festival), 11 May (Yom Ha'atzmaut, Independence Day), 12 June (Shavuot, Feast of Weeks), 3–4 October (Rosh Hashanah, Jewish New Year), 12 October (Yom Kippur, Day of Atonement), 17–23 October (Succot, Feast of the Tabernacles).

2006: 12–18 April (Pesach, Passover—see 2005), 2 May (Yom Ha'atzmaut, Independence Day), 1 June (Shavuot, Feast of Weeks), 22–23 September (Rosh Hashanah, Jewish New Year), 1 October (Yom Kippur, Day of Atonement), 6–12 October (Succot, Feast of the Tabernacles).

(The Jewish festivals and fast days commence in the evening of the dates given.)

Islamic holidays are observed by Muslim Arabs, and Christian holidays by the Christian Arab community.

Weights and Measures

The metric system is in force.
   1 dunum = 1,000 sq metres.

Statistical Survey

Source: Central Bureau of Statistics, POB 13015, Hakirya, Romema, Jerusalem 91130; tel. 2-6592037; fax 2-6521340; e-mail yael@cbs.gov.il; internet www.cbs.gov.il.

Area and Population

AREA, POPULATION AND DENSITY

Area (sq km)

Land	21,671
Inland water	474
Total	22,145*

Population (*de jure*; census results)†

4 June 1983	4,037,620
4 November 1995	
Males	2,738,175
Females	2,810,348
Total	5,548,523

Population (*de jure*; official estimates at 31 December)†

2001	6,508,800
2002	6,631,100
2003	6,748,400
Density (per sq km) at 31 December 2003†	311.4

* 8,550 sq miles. Area includes East Jerusalem, annexed by Israel in June 1967, and the Golan sub-district (1,154 sq km), annexed by Israel in December 1981.
† Including the population of East Jerusalem and Israeli residents in certain other areas under Israeli military occupation since June 1967. Beginning in 1981, figures also include non-Jews in the Golan sub-district, an Israeli-occupied area of Syrian territory. Census results exclude adjustment for underenumeration.

POPULATION BY RELIGION
(31 December 2003)

	Number	%
Jews	5,165,400	76.54
Muslims	1,072,500	15.89
Christians	142,400	2.11
Druze	110,800	1.64
Unclassified	254,600	3.77
Total *	6,748,400	100.00

* Including Lebanese not classified by religion (2,700 at 31 December 2003).

DISTRICTS
(31 December 2003)

	Area (sq km)*	Population (rounded)†	Density (per sq km)
Jerusalem‡	652	812,200	1,245.7
Northern§	4,478	1,148,500	256.5
Haifa	863	846,000	980.3
Central	1,276	1,576,900	1,235.8
Tel-Aviv	171	1,164,300	6,808.8
Southern	14,231	968,600	68.1
Total	21,671	6,516,500	300.7

* Excluding lakes, with a total area of 474 sq km.
† Excluding Israelis residing in Jewish localities in the West Bank and Gaza Strip, totalling some 231,800 at 31 December 2003.
‡ Including East Jerusalem, annexed by Israel in June 1967.
§ Including the Golan sub-district (area 1,154 sq km, population an estimated 37,000 at 31 December 2003), annexed by Israel in December 1981.

PRINCIPAL TOWNS
(estimated population at 31 December 2003)

Jerusalem (capital)*	693,200	Petach-Tikva . .	173,800
Tel-Aviv—Jaffa . .	363,400	Holon	165,800
Haifa	269,400	Netanya	167,100
Rishon LeZiyyon .	214,600	Bene Beraq . . .	139,600
Ashdod	192,000	Bat Yam	131,900
Beersheba . . .	183,000	Ramat Gan . . .	126,500

* The Israeli Government has designated the city of Jerusalem (including East Jerusalem, annexed by Israel in June 1967) as the country's capital, although this is not recognized by the UN.

BIRTHS, MARRIAGES AND DEATHS*

	Registered live births		Registered marriages		Registered deaths	
	Number	Rate (per 1,000)	Number	Rate (per 1,000)	Number	Rate (per 1,000)
1996 .	121,333	21.3	36,081	6.3	34,664	6.1
1997 .	124,478	21.4	37,611	6.5	36,124	6.2
1998 .	130,080	21.8	40,137	6.7	36,955	6.2
1999 .	131,936	21.5	40,236	6.6	37,291	6.1
2000 .	136,390	21.7	38,894	6.4	37,688	6.0
2001 .	136,638	21.2	38,924	6.3	37,181	5.8
2002 .	139,535	21.3	39,718	6.2	38,367	5.8
2003† .	144,936	21.7	25,867	n.a.	38,326	5.7

* Including East Jerusalem.
† Provisional figures.

Expectation of life (WHO estimates, years at birth): 79.4 (males 77.3; females 81.4) in 2002 (Source: WHO, *World Health Report*).

IMMIGRATION*

	2001	2002	2003
Immigrants:			
on immigrant visas	39,571	30,607	20,938
on tourist visas†	3,974	2,947	2,329
Potential immigrants:			
on potential immigrant visas .	6	10	—
on tourist visas†	29	3	1
Total	43,580	33,567	23,268

* Excluding immigrating citizens (2,930 in 2001; 2,358 in 2002; 2,843 in 2003) and Israeli residents returning from abroad.
† Figures refer to tourists who changed their status to immigrants or potential immigrants.

ECONOMICALLY ACTIVE POPULATION

(sample surveys, '000 persons aged 15 years and over, excluding armed forces)*

	2001†	2002	2003
Agriculture, hunting, forestry and fishing	43.0	44.9	43.3
Industry‡	394.2	377.5	377.4
Electricity, gas and water supply	19.5	18.9	18.3
Construction	116.7	118.7	129.8
Wholesale and retail trade; repair of motor vehicles, motorcycles and personal and household goods	299.8	311.8	315.8
Hotels and restaurants . . .	96.8	92.9	93.5
Transport, storage and communications . . .	149.2	146.9	150.0
Financial intermediation . . .	74.7	76.2	78.0
Real estate, renting and business activities	277.2	275.3	301.3
Public administration and defence; compulsory social security . .	126.6	134.3	120.3
Education	283.7	287.5	295.0
Health and social work . . .	225.1	233.6	250.2
Other community, social and personal service activities . .	107.9	110.3	111.4
Private households with employed persons	38.1	34.9	33.4
Extra-territorial organizations and bodies	1.6	2.1	1.8
Not classifiable by economic activity	16.3	18.8	10.6
Total employed	**2,270.5**	**2,284.4**	**2,330.2**
Unemployed	233.1	262.4	280.0
Total labour force	**2,503.3**	**2,546.8**	**2,610.0**
Males	1,357.3	1,376.3	1,400.0
Females	1,146.0	1,170.4	1,210.0

* Figures are estimated independently, so the totals may not be the sum of the component parts.
† Source: ILO.
‡ Comprising mining and quarrying, and manufacturing.

Health and Welfare

KEY INDICATORS

Total fertility rate (children per woman, 2002) . . .	2.7
Under-5 mortality rate (per 1,000 live births, 2003) . . .	6
HIV/AIDS (% of persons aged 15–49, 2003)	0.1
Physicians (per 1,000 head, 2001)	3.75
Hospital beds (per 1,000 head, 2001)	6.16
Health expenditure (2001): US $ per head (PPP)	1,839
Health expenditure (2001 % of GDP	8.7
Health expenditure (2001): public (% of total)	69.2
Access to water (% of persons, 2002)	100
Human Development Index (2002): ranking	22
Human Development Index (2002): value	0.908

For sources and definitions, see explanatory note on p. vi.

Agriculture

PRINCIPAL CROPS

('000 metric tons)

	2001	2002	2003
Wheat	158	177	199
Maize	58*	65*	60†
Potatoes	396	393	418
Olives	26	56	22
Cottonseed	31	30	30*
Cabbages	53	63	58
Lettuce	40	43	40
Tomatoes	349	385	401
Cucumbers and gherkins . .	120	144	147
Aubergines (Eggplants)	46	48	47
Chillies and green peppers . . .	108	116	118
Dry onions	90	98	95
Carrots	89	88	87
Other vegetables	243*	256*	255†
Watermelons	352	366	340
Cantaloupes and other melons .	69	53	49
Bananas	100	96	95
Oranges	231	166	146
Tangerines, mandarins, clementines and satsumas . .	83	58	78*
Grapefruit and pomelo	330	252	256
Apples	112	119	125
Peaches and nectarines . . .	53	66	61
Grapes	122	114	90
Avocados	79	100	59
Other fruits †	151	195	184

* Unofficial figure.
† FAO estimate(s).

Source: FAO.

LIVESTOCK

('000 head, year ending September)

	2001	2002	2003
Cattle	390	390*	400*
Pigs*	155	195	190
Sheep	389	392*	395*
Goats	63	65*	63*
Chickens	29,275	30,000*	30,000*
Geese*	1,400	1,200	1,400
Turkeys*	5,000	5,000	5,000
Ducks*	200	200	200

* FAO estimate(s).

Source: FAO.

LIVESTOCK PRODUCTS

('000 metric tons)

	2001	2002	2003
Beef and veal	62.4	79.9	81.3
Mutton and lamb	5.4*	5.4†	5.4†
Pig meat	15.7	16.5	17.4
Chicken meat	317.6	324.0	334.0
Goose meat	4.0	4.0	5.1†
Turkey meat	125.2	125.0	113.0
Cows' milk	1,229.8	1,262.9	1,300.0†
Sheep's milk	21.2	22.8	23.0†
Goats' milk	11.8	13.1	13.3†
Cheese†	102.1	105.3	104.3
Butter	7.5†	5.4	5.4
Hen eggs	84.7	86.8	89.0†
Honey	3.3	3.5	3.3†
Cattle hides†	5.8	6.0	6.2

* Unofficial figure.
† FAO estimate(s).

Source: FAO.

Forestry

ROUNDWOOD REMOVALS
('000 cubic metres, excl. bark)

	1999*	2000†	2001†
Sawlogs, veneer logs and logs for sleepers	36	28	11
Pulpwood	32	22	7
Other industrial wood	32	22	7
Fuel wood	13	8	2
Total	113	81	27

* FAO estimates.
† Unofficial figures.

2002–03 (FAO estimates): Figures assumed to be unchanged from 2001.

Source: FAO.

Fishing

('000 metric tons, live weight)

	2000	2001	2002
Capture	5,818	5,024	4,880
Carps, barbels, etc.	1,333	994	1,298
Aquaculture	20,098	21,318	22,261
Common carp	6,281	6,208	7,748
Tilapias	7,059	8,217	7,819
Gilthead seabream	2,511	2,688	2,561
Flathead grey mullet	1,661	1,633	1,824
Total catch	25,916	26,342	27,141

Note: Figures exclude crocodiles and alligators, recorded by number rather than weight. The number of American alligators caught was: 233 in 2000; 6 in 2001; 0 in 2002. The number of Nile crocodiles caught was: 1,661 in 2000; 2,289 in 2001; 699 in 2002.

Source: FAO.

Mining

('000 metric tons, unless otherwise indicated)

	2000	2001	2002
Crude petroleum ('000 barrels)	25.0	24.0*	28.0*
Natural gas (million cu m)	9.7	9.6*	8.4*
Kaolin	13.0	n.a	n.a.
Phosphate rock†	4,110	3,511	3,476
Potash salts‡	1,748	1,774	1,918
Salt (unrefined)	526	537*	580*
Gypsum (crude)	130	133	144

* Estimated production.
† Figures refer to beneficiated production. The phosphoric acid content (in '000 metric tons) was: 1,305 in 2000; 1,115 in 2001; 1,110 in 2002.
‡ Figures refer to K_2O content.

Source: US Geological Survey.

Industry

SELECTED PRODUCTS
('000 metric tons, unless otherwise indicated)

	1992	1993	1994
Refined vegetable oils (metric tons)	56,463	57,558	45,447
Margarine	35.1	33.8	24.7
Wine ('000 litres)	12,373	12,733	n.a.
Beer ('000 litres)	51,078	58,681	50,750
Cigarettes (metric tons)	5,742	5,525	5,638
Newsprint (metric tons)	0	247	0
Writing and printing paper (metric tons)	66,334	65,426	65,790
Other paper (metric tons)	32,368	30,446	28,985
Cardboard (metric tons)	92,072	95,108	103,142
Rubber tyres ('000)	892	854	966
Ammonia (metric tons)	41,072	n.a.	n.a.
Ammonium sulphate (metric tons)	12,444	n.a.	n.a.
Sulphuric acid	138	n.a.	n.a.
Chlorine (metric tons)	33,912	35,241	37,555
Caustic soda (metric tons)	29,459	29,851	32,765
Polyethylene (metric tons)	128,739	144,147	126,979
Paints (metric tons)	58,963	57,429	53,260
Cement	3,960	4,536	4,800
Commercial vehicles (number)	852	836	1,260
Electricity (million kWh)	24,731	26,042	28,327

1996 ('000 metric tons, unless otherwise indicated): Cigarettes (metric tons) 4,793; Chlorine 35; Paints 58.0 (Source: UN, *Industrial Commodity Statistics Yearbook*).

1997: Rubber tyres ('000) 792 (Source: UN, *Monthly Bulletin of Statistics*).

2000 ('000 metric tons, unless otherwise indicated): Margarine 29.8; Wine ('000 litres) 7,500 (FAO estimate); Beer ('000 litres) 65,000 (unofficial estimate—Source: FAO); Cement 5,703 (Source: US Geological Survey); Writing and printing paper 95 (FAO estimate); Commercial vehicles (number) 373 (Source: International Road Federation, *World Road Statistics*); Electric energy (million kWh) 41,355.

2001 ('000 metric tons, unless otherwise indicated): Margarine 29.8; Wine ('000 litres) 5,000 (FAO estimate); Beer ('000 litres) 52,000 (unofficial estimate—Source: FAO); Writing and printing paper 95 (FAO estimate); Caustic soda 44.9 (estimate); Cement 4,700 (estimate—Source: US Geological Survey); Electric energy (million kWh) 42,209 .

2002 ('000 metric tons, unless otherwise indicated): Margarine 31.0 (FAO estimate); Wine ('000 litres) 6,000 (FAO estimate); Beer ('000 litres) 55,000 (FAO estimate); Writing and printing paper 95 (FAO estimate); Cement 5,150 (estimate—Source: US Geological Survey); Electric energy (million kWh) 43,867.

2003 ('000 metric tons, unless otherwise indicated): Margarine 32.0 (FAO estimate); Wine ('000 litres) 6,500 (FAO estimate); Beer ('000 litres) 58,000 (FAO estimate).

Finance

CURRENCY AND EXCHANGE RATES

Monetary Units
100 agorot (singular: agora) = 1 new sheqel (plural: sheqalim) or shekel (NIS).

Sterling, Dollar and Euro Equivalents (31 December 2004)
£1 sterling = NIS 8.320;
US $1 = NIS 4.308;
€1 = NIS 5.868;
NIS 100 = £12.02 = $23.21 = €17.42.

Average Exchange Rate (NIS per US $)
2002   4.7378
2003   4.5541
2004   4.4820

STATE BUDGET*
(NIS million)

Revenue and grants	2003	2004†	2005‡
Taxes and compulsory payments	145,285	151,751	163,231
Income and property taxes	76,193	79,700	84,470
Taxes on expenditure	69,091	72,051	78,761
Interest, royalties, etc.	5,592	6,274	5,188
Other income	30,339	30,759	30,135
Total	175,624	182,510	193,366

Expenditure‖	2003	2004†	2005‡
Civilian consumption	41,490	42,960	43,529
Defence consumption	55,845	47,287	46,772
Transfer and support payments .	70,619	68,813	72,816
Direct investment	9,583	8,541	10,754
Interest payments	32,479	35,672	36,507
Other expenditure	4,488	11,822	11,511
Total	214,505	215,095	221,890

* Excluding Bank of Israel.
† Preliminary data.
‡ Forecasts.
§ Revenue excludes grants received from abroad (NIS million): 10,596 in 2003; 11,985 (preliminary) in 2004; 11,873 (forecast) in 2005.
‖ Expenditure excludes the central Government's lending minus repayments (NIS million): –1,878 in 2003; 396 (preliminary) in 2004; –1,698 (forecast) in 2005.

Source: Ministry of Finance, Budget Division.

INTERNATIONAL RESERVES
(US $ million at 31 December, excluding gold)

	2001	2002	2003
IMF special drawing rights . .	1.7	4.6	9.5
Reserve position in IMF . .	197.8	413.3	527.2
Foreign exchange	23,179.1	23,665.0	25,778.4
Total	23,378.6	24,082.9	26,315.1

Source: IMF, *International Financial Statistics*.

MONEY SUPPLY
(NIS million at 31 December)

	2001	2002	2003
Currency outside banks . . .	14,580	15,580	16,184
Demand deposits at deposit money banks	23,053	22,619	26,353
Total money (incl. others) . .	37,796	38,364	42,708

Source: IMF, *International Financial Statistics*.

COST OF LIVING
(Consumer Price Index, annual averages; base: 2000 = 100, unless otherwise indicated)

	2001	2002	2003*
Food (excl. fruit and vegetables) .	102.5	105.1	102.8
Fruit and vegetables	102.7	106.8	103.0
Electricity, fuel and water . . .	100.5	112.8	110.1
Clothing (incl. footwear) . . .	96.2	91.3	96.2
Rent	103.4	115.4	96.5
All items (incl. others)	101.1	106.8	100.7

* Base: 2002 = 100.

NATIONAL ACCOUNTS
(NIS million at current prices)

National Income and Product

	1999	2000	2001
Gross domestic product (GDP) at market prices	446,760	487,013	491,499
Compensation of employees (net) .	–12,170	–12,876	–11,903
Property income (net)	–7,002	–16,042	–8,225
Gross national income (GNI)	427,588	458,095	471,371
Less Consumption of fixed capital	62,667	65,051	69,873
Net national income	364,921	393,044	401,498
Current transfers from abroad .	29,632	30,443	31,729
Less Current transfers paid abroad	3,353	4,127	4,764
Net national disposable income	391,200	419,360	428,463

Source: UN, *National Accounts Statistics*.

Expenditure on the Gross Domestic Product

	2001	2002	2003
Final consumption expenditure .	414,911	444,733	450,672
Private	275,957	291,620	300,160
General government	138,954	153,113	150,513
Gross capital formation	95,435	89,457	76,876
Gross fixed capital formation .	89,136	87,234	84,982
Changes in inventories . .	6,299	2,223	–8,106
Total domestic expenditure	510,346	534,190	527,548
Exports of goods and services . .	168,107	181,962	191,271
Less Imports of goods and services	204,410	224,892	222,633
GDP in market prices . . .	474,043	491,260	496,186
GDP at constant 2000 prices .	463,906	460,222	466,113

Gross Domestic Product by Economic Activity

	1999	2000	2001
Agriculture, hunting, forestry and fishing	7,197	7,043	7,351
Manufacturing, mining and quarrying	70,224	76,007	72,727
Electricity, gas and water supply .	7,414	8,109	8,170
Construction	23,372	22,864	21,321
Wholesale, retail trade, repair of motor vehicles, motorcycles and personal and household goods; hotels and restaurants . .	39,894	43,464	43,038
Transport, storage and communications	31,190	33,614	33,789
Financial intermediation; real estate, renting and business activities	114,233	131,122	132,718
Public administration and defence; compulsory social security . .	32,719	34,381	36,417
Education	32,124	34,720	37,087
Health and social work	22,756	25,045	27,204
Other community, social and personal services	15,330	17,019	18,163
Statistical discrepancy	–1,782	–1,121	–899
Sub-total	394,671	432,267	437,086
Less Financial intermediation services indirectly measured .	5,943	6,534	7,163
Gross value added in basic prices	388,728	425,733	429,923
Taxes on products	60,355	63,516	63,953
Less Subsidies on products . .	2,323	2,236	2,378
GDP in market prices . . .	446,760	487,013	491,498

Source: UN, *National Accounts Statistics*.

BALANCE OF PAYMENTS
(US $ million)

	2001	2002	2003
Exports of goods f.o.b.	27,974	27,653	29,753
Imports of goods f.o.b.	–30,979	–31,212	–32,313
Trade balance	–3,004	–3,559	–2,560
Exports of services	11,950	10,853	12,283
Imports of services	–12,503	–11,470	–11,787
Balance on goods and services	–3,557	–4,176	–2,064
Other income received	2,881	2,852	2,048
Other income paid	–7,509	–6,451	–6,496
Balance on goods, services and income	–8,185	–7,776	–6,512
Current transfers received . .	7,516	7,891	7,458
Current transfers paid	–1,107	–1,342	–1,120
Current balance	–1,776	–1,226	–174
Capital account (net)	519	286	277
Direct investment abroad . . .	–805	–1,232	–1,550
Direct investment from abroad .	3,520	1,649	3,672
Portfolio investment assets . .	–1,099	–2,491	–2,930
Portfolio investment liabilities .	558	449	369
Financial derivatives assets . .	—	—	363

— continued	2001	2002	2003
Other investment assets . . .	−2,710	−1,613	−1,655
Other investment liabilities . .	1,166	1,180	−196
Net errors and omissions . . .	998	2,120	1,266
Overall balance	372	−880	−558

Source: IMF, *International Financial Statistics*.

External Trade

PRINCIPAL COMMODITIES
(US $ million)

Imports c.i.f.	2001	2002	2003
Food and live animals . . .	1,543.8	1,535.4	1,611.7
Mineral fuels, lubricants, etc. .	2,721.6	2,654.4	3,289.8
Petroleum, petroleum products, etc.	2,702.0	2,625.3	3,244.9
Chemicals and related products	3,169.0	3,261.2	3,618.9
Basic manufactures . . .	9,227.6	10,691.4	11,343.7
Non-metallic mineral manufactures	6,056.0	7,646.2	8,153.1
Machinery and transport equipment	11,931.4	10,436.6	9,863.2
General industrial machinery, equipment and parts . . .	1,126.2	1,140.6	1,009.8
Office machines and automatic data-processing machines .	1,410.4	1,279.2	1,290.0
Telecommunications and sound equipment	1,431.6	1,365.2	1,087.9
Other electrical machinery, apparatus, etc.	3,373.0	2,787.2	2,749.1
Road vehicles and parts . . .	2,171.9	1,891.4	1,833.5
Other transport equipment and parts	1,038.7	703.0	382.9
Miscellaneous manufactured articles	3,224.7	2,974.2	2,849.3
Total (incl. others)	33,303.2	33,106.3	34,211.8

Exports f.o.b.	2001	2002	2003
Chemicals and related products	4,159.4	4,547.0	5,135.5
Organic chemicals	990.7	1,130.3	1,295.5
Medical and pharmaceutical products	638.4	927.4	959.3
Basic manufactures . . .	10,513.4	12,072.3	13,444.8
Non-metallic mineral manufactures	8,857.9	10,440.0	11,654.9
Machinery and transport equipment	9,986.9	8,508.6	8,683.7
Telecommunications and sound equipment	3,610.7	2,775.2	2,622.3
Other electrical machinery, apparatus, etc.	3,192.8	2,645.0	2,811.7
Road vehicles and other transport equipment and parts	1,025.0	1,128.4	1,071.5
Miscellaneous manufactured articles	2,948.6	2,768.5	2,826.8
Professional, scientific and controlling instruments, etc. .	921.2	842.8	883.4
Total (incl. others)	29,060.9	29,347.2	31,783.3

PRINCIPAL TRADING PARTNERS
(US $ million)*

Imports (excl. military goods) c.i.f.	2001	2002	2003
Belgium-Luxembourg	2,655.0	3,056.9	3,209.6
Canada	285.4	375.5	233.5
China, People's Republic . . .	737.3	793.3	1,008.1
France	1,254.0	1,186.9	1,182.6
Germany	2,614.8	2,347.8	2,731.1
Hong Kong	805.6	1,194.1	892.7
India	429.5	653.2	888.8
Italy	1,651.3	1,530.5	1,398.2
Japan	1,011.8	782.0	843.7
Korea, Republic	523.7	512.4	579.8
Netherlands	1,353.7	1,177.9	1,196.5
Russia	507.1	519.9	618.2
South Africa	345.9	234.8	288.0
Spain	673.6	637.8	624.5
Sweden	422.6	313.6	313.9
Switzerland-Liechtenstein . . .	1,774.7	2,075.2	2,062.0
Taiwan	430.4	368.6	385.5
Turkey	683.3	813.7	951.5
United Kingdom	2,208.5	2,226.8	2,283.4
USA	6,704.6	6,134.1	5,330.8
Total (incl. others)	33,303.2	33,106.3	34,211.8

Exports	2001	2002	2003
Australia	235.8	267.7	279.1
Belgium-Luxembourg	1,573.9	1,866.7	2,325.2
Brazil	392.1	322.3	364.1
Canada	288.4	297.0	326.5
China, People's Republic . . .	349.6	426.6	612.6
France	712.7	649.0	684.6
Germany	1,288.1	1,026.5	1,123.3
Hong Kong	1,254.4	1,373.2	1,495.4
India	473.5	613.7	717.8
Italy	766.3	693.7	772.5
Japan	800.4	649.8	626.0
Korea, Republic	322.4	317.2	286.9
Malaysia	615.9	289.7	276.8
Netherlands	829.6	909.1	1,085.1
Philippines	245.6	95.5	170.1
Singapore	261.9	272.9	294.0
Spain	506.5	399.7	525.4
Switzerland-Liechtenstein . . .	343.4	384.6	504.9
Taiwan	330.5	331.8	298.0
Thailand	330.8	393.6	458.0
Turkey	316.5	383.1	470.3
United Kingdom	1,219.5	1,164.5	1,224.5
USA	11,111.9	11,712.2	12,088.5
Total (incl. others)	29,060.9	29,347.2	31,783.3

* Imports by country of purchase; exports by country of destination.

Transport

RAILWAYS
(traffic)

	2000	2001	2002
Passengers carried ('000 journeys)	12,698	15,057	17,540
Passenger-km (million)	781	961	1,116
Freight carried ('000 metric tons) .	10,293	8,100	7,889
Freight ton-km (million) . . .	1,173	1,098	1,102

2003: Passengers carried ('000 journeys) 19,826; Freight carried ('000 metric tons) 7,734.

ROAD TRAFFIC
(motor vehicles in use at 31 December)

	2000	2001	2002
Private passenger cars	1,396,947	1,460,851	1,496,878
Taxis	14,806	15,163	15,781
Minibuses	16,476	16,752	16,805
Buses and coaches	11,849	11,897	11,788
Lorries, vans and road tractors .	309,987	326,428	335,778
Special service vehicles . . .	3,993	4,068	4,062
Motorcycles and mopeds . . .	77,472	79,736	78,931

SHIPPING

Merchant Fleet
(registered at 31 December)

	2001	2002	2003
Number of vessels	48	50	52
Displacement ('000 grt)	611.4	765.3	766.0

Source: Lloyd's Register of Shipping, *World Fleet Statistics*.

International Sea-borne Freight Traffic
('000 metric tons)

	2001	2002	2003
Goods loaded	13,287	13,863	15,069
Goods unloaded*	29,695	31,947	31,841

* Including traffic between Israeli ports.

CIVIL AVIATION
(traffic on scheduled services)

	1999	2000	2001
Kilometres flown (million)	86	92	83
Passengers carried ('000)	4,033	4,443	3,989
Passenger-km (million)	13,515	14,507	13,514
Total ton-km (million)	2,259	2,200	2,083

Source: UN, *Statistical Yearbook*.

Tourism

TOURIST ARRIVALS
('000)*

Country of residence	2000	2001	2002†
Canada	55.0	34.2	25.1
France	202.4	129.3	117.9
Germany	176.0	65.5	38.8
Italy	171.4	25.0	16.9
Jordan	77.9	24.6	24.5
Netherlands	91.3	43.3	22.8
Russia	35.9	55.8	36.9
Spain	65.6	11.8	8.6
Ukraine	38.0	33.5	18.4
United Kingdom	201.2	140.2	97.3
USA	488.5	266.2	206.1
Total (incl. others)	2,416.8	1,195.7	861.9

* Excluding arrivals of Israeli nationals residing abroad.
† Provisional figures.

2003 ('000, excl. arrivals of Israeli nationals residing abroad, provisional figure): Total 1,063.

Tourism receipts (US $ million): 3,338 in 2000; 1,570 in 2001; 1,197 in 2002 (Source: World Tourism Organization).

Communications Media

	2000	2001	2002
Television receivers ('000 in use)	2,100	2,150	n.a.
Telephones ('000 main lines in use)	2,974	3,033	n.a.
Mobile cellular telephones ('000 subscribers)	4,400	5,900	6,334
Personal computers ('000 in use)	1,590	1,600	1,610
Internet users ('000)	1,270	1,800	2,000

Radio receivers (1997): 3,070,000 in use.

Facsimile machines (1995): 140,000 in use.

Book production (1998): 2,317 titles.

Daily newspapers (1996): 34 titles (estimated circulation 1,650,000 copies).

Non-daily newspapers (1988): 80 titles.

Other periodicals (1985): 807 titles.

Sources: International Telecommunication Union; UNESCO, *Statistical Yearbook*; UN, *Statistical Yearbook*.

Education

(2003/04)

	Schools	Pupils	Teachers
Jewish			
Kindergarten	n.a.	310,000	n.a.
Primary schools	1,964	567,558	52,274
Special needs	177	8,308	4,573
Intermediate schools	497	189,006	24,284
Secondary schools	1,143	285,520	41,697
Vocational schools	106	113,703	n.a.
Agricultural schools	2	3,015	n.a.
Teacher training colleges	58	31,104	6,004
Arab			
Kindergarten	n.a.	80,000	n.a.
Primary schools	438	208,029	14,625
Special needs	39	2,366	916
Intermediate schools	135	64,999	5,183
Secondary schools	188	62,142	6,607
Vocational schools	21	21,994	n.a.
Agricultural schools	n.a.	118	n.a.
Teacher training colleges	4	3,633	370

Adult literacy rate (UNESCO estimates): 95.3% (males 97.3%; females 93.4%) in 2002 (Source: UN Development Programme, *Human Development Report*).

Directory

The Constitution

There is no written constitution. In June 1950 the Knesset voted to adopt a state constitution by evolution over an unspecified period. A number of laws, including the Law of Return (1950), the Nationality Law (1952), the State President (Tenure) Law (1952), the Education Law (1953) and the 'Yad-va-Shem' Memorial Law (1953), are considered as incorporated into the state Constitution. Other constitutional laws are: The Law and Administration Ordinance (1948), the Knesset Election Law (1951), the Law of Equal Rights for Women (1951), the Judges Act (1953), the National Service and National Insurance Acts (1953), and the Basic Law (The Knesset—1958). The provisions of constitutional legislation that affect the main organs of government are summarized below:

THE PRESIDENT

The President is elected by the Knesset for a maximum of two five-year terms.*

Ten or more Knesset members may propose a candidate for the Presidency.

Voting will be by secret ballot.

The President may not leave the country without the consent of the Government.

The President may resign by submitting his resignation in writing to the Speaker.

The President may be relieved of his duties by the Knesset for misdemeanour.

The Knesset is entitled to decide by a two-thirds' majority that the President is too incapacitated owing to ill health to fulfil his duties permanently.

The Speaker of the Knesset will act for the President when the President leaves the country, or when he cannot perform his duties owing to ill health.

* Moshe Katsav was elected to the presidency on 31 July 2000 for a seven-year term of office.

THE KNESSET

The Knesset is the parliament of the state. There are 120 members.

It is elected by general, national, direct, equal, secret and proportional elections.

Every Israeli national of 18 years or over shall have the right to vote in elections to the Knesset unless a court has deprived him of that right by virtue of any law.

Every Israeli national of 21 and over shall have the right to be elected to the Knesset unless a court has deprived him of that right by virtue of any law.

The following shall not be candidates: the President of the State; the two Chief Rabbis; a judge (shofet) in office; a judge (dayan) of a religious court; the State Comptroller; the Chief of the General Staff of the Defence Army of Israel; rabbis and ministers of other religions in office; senior state employees and senior army officers of such ranks and in such functions as shall be determined by law.

The term of office of the Knesset shall be four years.

The elections to the Knesset shall take place on the third Tuesday of the month of Marcheshvan in the year in which the tenure of the outgoing Knesset ends.

Election day shall be a day of rest, but transport and other public services shall function normally.

Results of the elections shall be published within 14 days.

The Knesset shall elect from among its members a Chairman and Vice-Chairman.

The Knesset shall elect from among its members permanent committees, and may elect committees for specific matters.

The Knesset may appoint commissions of inquiry to investigate matters designated by the Knesset.

The Knesset shall hold two sessions a year; one of them shall open within four weeks after the Feast of the Tabernacles, the other within four weeks after Independence Day; the aggregate duration of the two sessions shall not be less than eight months.

The outgoing Knesset shall continue to hold office until the convening of the incoming Knesset.

The members of the Knesset shall receive a remuneration as provided by law.

THE GOVERNMENT

The Government shall tender its resignation to the President immediately after his election, but shall continue with its duties until the formation of a new government. After consultation with representatives of the parties in the Knesset, the President shall charge one of the members with the formation of a government. The Government shall be composed of a Prime Minister (elected on a party basis from 2003) and a number of ministers from among the Knesset members or from outside the Knesset. After it has been chosen, the Government shall appear before the Knesset and shall be considered as formed after having received a vote of confidence. Within seven days of receiving a vote of confidence, the Prime Minister and the other ministers shall swear allegiance to the State of Israel and its Laws and undertake to carry out the decisions of the Knesset.

The Government

HEAD OF STATE

President: Moshe Katsav (took office 1 August 2000).

THE CABINET
(May 2005)

(Party affiliations in parentheses.)

Prime Minister, Minister of Social Affairs, of Religious Affairs, and of Science and Technology: Ariel Sharon (Likud).

Vice-Prime Minister and Minister of Industry, Trade and Labour: Ehud Olmert (Likud).

Vice-Premier: Shimon Peres (Labour).

Deputy Prime Minister and Minister of Foreign Affairs: Silvan Shalom (Likud).

Minister of Defence: Lt-Gen. Shaul Mofaz.

Minister of the Interior: Ophir Pines-Paz (Labour).

Minister of Health: Dan Naveh (Likud).

Minister of Education, Culture and Sport: Limor Livnat (Likud).

Minister of Finance: Binyamin Netanyahu (Likud).

Minister of Immigrant Absorption and of Justice: Tzipi Livni (Likud).

Minister of the Environment: Shalom Simhon (Labour).

Minister of Construction and Housing: Isaac Herzog (Labour).

Minister of Tourism: Abraham Hirchson (Likud).

Minister of Communications: Dalia Itzik (Labour).

Minister of Agriculture and Rural Development: Yisrael Katz (Likud).

Minister of National Infrastructure: Benjamin Ben-Eliezer (Labour).

Minister of Transport: Meir Sheetrit (Likud).

Minister of Public Security: Gideon Ezra (Likud).

Minister without Portfolio, responsible for Jerusalem, Social and Diaspora Affairs: (vacant).

Ministers without Portfolio: Tzachi Hanegbi (Likud), Haim Ramon (Labour), Matan Vilnai (Labour).

MINISTRIES

Office of the Prime Minister: POB 187, 3 Rehov Kaplan, Kiryat Ben-Gurion, Jerusalem 91919; tel. 2-6705511; fax 2-6512631; e-mail webmaster@pmo.gov.il; internet www.pmo.gov.il.

Ministry of Agriculture and Rural Development: POB 30, Beit Dagan 50250; tel. 3-9485571; fax 3-9485870; e-mail regeva@moag .gov.il; internet www.moag.gov.il.

Ministry of Communications: 23 Jaffa St, Jerusalem 91999; tel. 2-6706320; fax 2-6706372; internet www.moc.gov.il.

Ministry of Construction and Housing: POB 18110, Kiryat Hamemshala (East), Jerusalem 91180; tel. 2-5847654; fax 2-5847250; e-mail webmaster@moch.gov.il; internet www.moch.gov.il.

Ministry of Defence: Kaplan St, Hakirya, Tel-Aviv 67659; tel. 3-5692010; fax 3-6916940; e-mail public@mod.gov.il; internet www .mod.gov.il.

Ministry of Education: POB 292, 34 Shivtei Israel St, Jerusalem 91911; tel. 2-5602222; fax 2-5602752; e-mail info@education.gov.il; internet www.education.gov.il.

Ministry of the Environment: POB 34033, 5 Kanfei Nesharim St, Givat Shaul, Jerusalem 95464; tel. 2-6553745; fax 2-6553752; e-mail ori@sviva.gov.il; internet www.sviva.gov.il.

Ministry of Finance: POB 13191, 1 Rehov Kaplan, Kiryat Ben-Gurion, Jerusalem 91008; tel. 2-5317111; fax 2-5637891; e-mail webmaster@mof.gov.il; internet www.mof.gov.il.

Ministry of Foreign Affairs: Hakirya, Romema, Jerusalem 91950; tel. 2-5303111; fax 2-5303367; e-mail ask@israel-info.gov.il; internet www.mfa.gov.il.

Ministry of Health: POB 1176, 2 Ben-Tabai St, Jerusalem 91010; tel. 2-6705705; fax 2-6796267; e-mail yonit.mor@moh.health.gov.il; internet www.health.gov.il.

Ministry of Immigrant Absorption: 2 Kaplan St, Kiryat Ben-Gurion, Jerusalem 91950; tel. 2-6752691; fax 2-5669244; e-mail ednas@moia.gov.il; internet www.moia.gov.il.

Ministry of Industry, Trade and Labour: POB 299, 30 Rehov Agron, Jerusalem 94190; tel. 2-6220661; fax 2-6222412; e-mail dover@moit.gov.il; internet www.tamas.gov.il.

Ministry of the Interior: POB 6158, 2 Rehov Kaplan, Kiryat Ben-Gurion, Jerusalem 91008; tel. 2-6701411; fax 2-6701628; e-mail pniot@moin.gov.il; internet www.moin.gov.il.

Ministry of Justice: POB 1087, 29 Rehov Salahadin, Jerusalem 91010; tel. 2-6466666; fax 2-6287757; e-mail pniot@justice.gov.il; internet www.justice.gov.il.

Ministry of National Infrastructure: Ala Bldg, 216 Jaffa St, Jerusalem; tel. 2-5006777; fax 2-5006888; e-mail pniot@mmi.gov.il; internet www.mni.gov.il; also responsible for:

> **Israel Lands Administration:** POB 2600, 6 Shamai St, Jerusalem 94631; tel. 2-6208422; fax 2-6234960; e-mail pniot@mmi .gov.il; internet www.mmi.gov.il.

Ministry of Public Security: POB 18182, Bldg 3, Kiryat Hamemshala (East), Jerusalem 91181; tel. 2-5308003; fax 2-5847872; e-mail dover@mops.gov.il; internet www.mops.gov.il.

Ministry of Regional Co-operation: 8 Shaul Hamelech Blvd, Tel-Aviv 64733; tel. 3-6086111; fax 3-6086126; e-mail m_r_c@netvision .net.il; internet www.mrc.gov.il.

Ministry of Religious Affairs: POB 13059, 7 Kanfei Nesharim St, Jerusalem 95464; tel. 2-5311182; fax 2-6513679; e-mail dover@ religions.gov.il; internet www.religions.gov.il.

Ministry of Science and Technology: POB 49100, Kiryat Hamemshala, Hamizrachit, Bldg 3, Jerusalem 91490; tel. 2-5411100; fax 2-5811613; e-mail nps@most.gov.il; internet www.most .gov.il.

Ministry of Social Affairs: POB 915, 2 Rehov Kaplan, Kiryat Ben-Gurion, Jerusalem 91008; tel. 2-6752311; fax 2-6752803; e-mail sar@ molsa.gov.il; internet www.molsa.gov.il.

Ministry of Tourism: POB 1018, 24 Rehov King George, Jerusalem 91009; tel. 2-6754811; fax 2-6253407; e-mail pniot@tourism.gov.il; internet www.tourism.gov.il.

Ministry of Transport: Klal Bldg, 97 Jaffa St, Jerusalem 91000; tel. 2-6228211; fax 2-6228693; e-mail pniot@mot.gov.il; internet www.mot.gov.il.

The Jewish Agency for Israel

POB 92, Jerusalem 91000; tel. 2-6202222; fax 2-6202303; e-mail elibir@jazo.org.il; internet www.jafi.org.il.

Organization: The governing bodies are the Assembly which determines basic policy, the Board of Governors which sets policy for the Agency between Assembly meetings and the Executive responsible for the day-to-day running of the Agency.

Chairman of Executive: SALLAI MERIDOR.

Chairman of Board of Governors: CAROLE SOLOMON.

Director-General: MOSHE VIGDOR.

Treasurer: SHAI HERMESH.

Functions: According to the Agreement of 1971, the Jewish Agency undertakes the immigration and absorption of immigrants in Israel, including absorption in agricultural settlement and immigrant housing; social welfare and health services in connection with immigrants; education, youth care and training; neighbourhood rehabilitation through project renewal.

Budget (2002): US $403m.

Legislature

KNESSET

Speaker: REUVEN RIVLIN.

General Election, 28 January 2003

Party	Valid votes cast	% of valid votes	Seats
Likud	925,279	29.4	38
Labour–Meimad	455,183	14.5	19
Shinui	386,535	12.3	15
Shas	258,879	8.2	11
Haichud Haleumi	173,973	5.5	7
Meretz	164,122	5.2	6
National Religious Party	132,370	4.2	6
United Torah Judaism	135,087	4.3	5
Hadash	93,819	3.0	3
Am Ehad	86,808	2.8	3
Balad	71,299	2.3	3
Israel B'Aliyah	67,719	2.2	2
United Arab List	65,551	2.1	2
Total (incl. others)	3,148,364*	100.0	120

* Excluding 52,409 invalid votes.

Prior to the January 2003 general election, pre-1996 legislation was restored according to which the Prime Minister is not directly elected. As leader of Likud, the incumbent premier, Ariel Sharon, was duly returned as Israel's Prime Minister.

Political Organizations

Agudat Israel: POB 513, Jerusalem; tel. 2-385251; fax 2-385145; orthodox Jewish party; stands for strict observance of Jewish religious law; Leader MENACHEM PORUSH.

Agudat Israel World Organization (AIWO): POB 326, Hacherut Sq., Jerusalem 91002; tel. 2-5384357; fax 2-5383634; f. 1912 at Congress of Orthodox Jewry, Kattowitz, Germany (now Katowice, Poland), to help solve the problems facing Jewish people worldwide; more than 500,000 mems in 25 countries; Chair. Rabbi J. M. ABRAMOWITZ (Jerusalem); Secs Rabbi MOSHE GEWIRTZ, Rabbi CHAIM WEINSTOCK.

Am Ehad (One Nation): tel. 3-6950644; e-mail info@am1.org.il; internet www.am1.org.il; workers' and pensioners' party affiliated to Histadrut trade union federation; Leader AMIR PERETZ.

Balad (National Democratic Alliance): POB 4072, Nazareth; tel. 4-6455071; internet www.balad.org; f. 1999; united Arab party; Leader Dr AZMI BISHARA.

Council for Peace and Security: POB 1320, Ramat Hasharon 47112; internet www.peace-security.org.il; f. 1988; seeks an Israeli withdrawal from the Occupied Territories in return for a peace

treaty with the Arab nations; 1,000 mems; Founders Maj.-Gen. (retd) AHARON YARIV, Maj.-Gen. (retd) ORI ORR, Brig.-Gen. (retd) YORAM AGMON, Brig.-Gen. (retd) EPHRAIM SNEH, MOSHE AMIRAV.

Degel Hatora: 103 Rehov Beit Vegan, Jerusalem; tel. 2-6438106; fax 2-6418967; f. 1988 as breakaway from Agudat Israel; orthodox Western Jews; Chair. AVRAHAM RAVITZ.

Democratic Arab Party (DAP): Nazareth; tel. 6-6560937; fax 6-6560938; e-mail dap@g-ol.com; f. 1988; has the following aims: to unify Arab political forces so as to influence Palestinian and Israeli policy; international recognition of the Palestinian people's right to self-determination; the withdrawal of Israel from all territories occupied in 1967, including East Jerusalem; full civil equality between Arab and Jewish citizens of Israel, and improved social, economic and political conditions for Israel's Arab minority; Dir MUHAMMAD DARAWSHE.

Gush Emunim (Bloc of the Faithful): f. 1967; engaged in unauthorized establishment of Jewish settlements in the Occupied Territories; Leader Rabbi MOSHE LEVINGER.

Hadash (Democratic Front for Peace and Equality—Communist Party of Israel): POB 26205, Tel-Aviv 61261; tel. 3-6293944; fax 3-6297263; e-mail info@hadash.org.il; internet www.hadash.org.il; descended from the Socialist Workers' Party of Palestine (f. 1919); renamed Communist Party of Palestine 1921, Communist Party of Israel (Maki) 1948; pro-Soviet anti-Zionist group formed New Communist Party of Israel (Rakah) 1965; Jewish Arab membership; aims for a socialist system in Israel, a lasting peace between Israel and the Arab countries and the Palestinian Arab people, favours full implementation of UN Security Council Resolutions 242 and 338, Israeli withdrawal from all Arab territories occupied since 1967, formation of a Palestinian Arab state in the West Bank and Gaza Strip (with East Jerusalem as its capital), recognition of national rights of State of Israel and Palestinian people, democratic rights and defence of working class interests, and demands an end to discrimination against Arab minority in Israel and against oriental Jewish communities; Chair. (Hadash) MUHAMMAD BARAKEH; Gen. Sec. (Communist Party) ISSAM MAKHUL.

Haichud Haleumi (National Unity): e-mail info@leumi.org.il; internet www.leumi.org.il; f. 1999 as right-wing coalition comprising Herut, Moledet and Tekuma parties; Israel B'Aitainu joined following withdrawal of Herut in February 2000; Leaders Rabbi BINYAMIN (BENNY) ELON, AVIGDOR LIEBERMAN.

Herut (Freedom): 55 Hamasger St, Tel-Aviv; tel. 3-5621521; fax 3-5618699; e-mail herut@herut.org.il; internet www.herut.org.il; f. 1948; reconstituted 1998; right-wing nationalist party; opposed to further Israeli withdrawal from the Occupied Territories; Leader MICHAEL KLEINER.

Israel B'Aitainu (Israel Is Our Home): e-mail info@beytenu.org.il; internet www.beytenu.org.il; f. 1999; right-wing immigrant party, formed as a rival to Israel B'Aliyah; Leader AVIGDOR LIEBERMAN.

Israel B'Aliyah: f. 1995; campaigns for immigrants' rights; Leader NATAN SHARANSKY.

Israel Labour Party: POB 62033, Tel-Aviv 61620; tel. 3-6899444; fax 3-6899420; e-mail inter@havoda.org.il; internet www.havoda.org.il; f. 1968 as a merger of the three Labour groups, Mapai, Rafi and Achdut Ha'avoda; a Zionist democratic socialist party; Chair. SHIMON PERES.

Kahane Chai (Kahane Lives): 111 Agripas St, Jerusalem; tel. 2-231081; internet www.kahane.org; f. 1977 as 'Kach' (Thus) by Rabbi MEIR KAHANE; right-wing religious nationalist party; advocates creation of a Torah state and expulsion of all Arabs from Israel and the annexation of the Occupied Territories; Leader (vacant).

Likud (Consolidation): 38 Rehov King George, Tel-Aviv 61231; tel. 3-5630666; fax 3-5282901; internet www.likud.org.il; f. September 1973; fmrly a parliamentary bloc of Herut (Freedom) (f. 1948; Leader Itzhak Shamir; Sec.-Gen. Moshe Arens), the Liberal Party of Israel (f. 1961; Chair. Avraham Sharir), Laam (For the Nation) (f. 1976; fmrly led by Yigael Hurwitz, who left the coalition to form his own party, Ometz, before the 1984 general election), Ahdut (a one-man faction—Hillel Seidel), Tami (f. 1981; represents the interests of Sephardic Jews; Leader Aharon Uzan), which joined Likud in June 1987, and an independent faction (f. 1990; Leader Itzhak Modai), which formed the nucleus of a new Party for the Advancement of the Zionist Idea; Herut and the Liberal Party formally merged in August 1988 to form the Likud-National Liberal Movement; aims: territorial integrity (advocates retention of all the territory of post-1922 mandatory Palestine; absorption of newcomers; a social order based on freedom and justice, elimination of poverty and want; development of an economy that will ensure a decent standard of living; improvement of the environment and the quality of life; Leader of Likud ARIEL SHARON.

Meimad: POB 53139, 17 Yad Harutzim St, Jerusalem 91533; tel. 2-6725134; fax 2-6725051; e-mail info@meimad.org.il; internet www

.meimad.org.il; f. 1988; moderate democratic Jewish party; Leader Rabbi MICHAEL MELCHIOR.

Meretz (Vitality): Hamasger 30, Beit Subaru, Tel-Aviv; tel. 3-6360111; fax 3-5375107; e-mail information@meretz.org.il; internet www.meretz.org.il; an alliance of Ratz, Shinui and the United Workers' Party; stands for civil rights, electoral reform, welfarism, Palestinian self-determination, separation of religion from the state and a halt to settlement in the Occupied Territories; Leader ZAHAVA GALON.

Moledet (Homeland): 14 Rehov Yehuda Halevi, Tel-Aviv; tel. 3-654580; e-mail moledet@moledet.org.il; internet www.moledet.org .il; f. 1988; right-wing nationalist party; aims: the expulsion ('transfer') of the 1.5m. Palestinians living in the West Bank and Gaza Strip; united with Tehiya—Zionist Revival Movement in June 1994 as the Moledet—the Eretz Israel Faithful and the Tehiya; Leader Rabbi BINYAMIN (BENNY) ELON.

National Religious Party (NRP): Jerusalem; tel. 2-377277; fax 2-377757; internet www.mafdal.org.il; f. 1902 as the Mizrachi Organization within the Zionist Movement; present name adopted in 1956; stands for strict adherence to Jewish religion and tradition, and strives to achieve the application of religious precepts of Judaism in everyday life; it is also endeavouring to establish a Constitution for Israel based on Jewish religious law (the Torah); 126,000 mems; Leader EFRAIM EITAM; Sec.-Gen. ZEVULUN ORLEV.

Poale Agudat Israel: f. 1924; working-class Orthodox Judaist party; Leader Dr KALMAN KAHANE.

Political Zionist Opposition (Ometz): f. 1982; one-man party; YIGAEL HURWITZ.

Progressive List for Peace: 5 Simtat Lane, Nes Tziona, Tel-Aviv; tel. 3-662457; fax 3-659474; f. 1984; Jewish-Arab; advocates recognition of the PLO and the establishment of a Palestinian state in the West Bank and Gaza Strip; Leader MUHAMMAD MI'ARI.

Ra'am (United Arab List): f. 1996; coalition of Arab parties (Democratic Arab Party, National Unity Front and Islamic Movement); Founder and Leader ABD AL-MALIK DEHAMSHE.

Ratz (Civil Rights and Peace Movement): 21 Tchernihovsky St, Tel-Aviv 63291; tel. 3-5254847; fax 3-5255008; f. 1973; concerned with human and civil rights, opposes discrimination on basis of religion, gender or ethnic identification and advocates a peace settlement with the Arab countries and the Palestinians; Leader Mrs SHULAMIT ALONI.

Shas (Sephardic Torah Guardians): Beit Abodi, Rehov Hahida, Bene Beraq; tel. 3-579776; f. 1984 by splinter groups from Agudat Israel; ultra-orthodox Jewish party; Spiritual Leader Rabbi OVADIA YOSEF; Leader ELIYAHU YISHAI.

Shinui (Change): POB 20533, 100 Ha' Hashmonaim St, Tel-Aviv 67133; tel. 3-5620118; fax 3-5620139; e-mail shinui@shinui.org.il; internet www.shinui.org.il; f. 1974 as a new liberal party; combines an anti-religious coercion policy with a free-market economic philosophy; Leaders YOSEF (TOMMY) LAPID, AVRAHAM PORAZ.

Third Way: f. 1995; opposed to any transfer of the Golan Heights to Syria; Leader AVIGDOR KAHALANI.

Tiqva (Hope): f. 1999; campaigns for rights of new immigrants from former USSR; Leader ALEX TENCHER.

Tzomet (Crossroads): 22 Rehov Huberman, Tel-Aviv; tel. 3-204444; f. 1988; right-wing nationalist party; breakaway group from Tehiya party; Leader (vacant).

United Torah Judaism (Yahadut Hatorah): electoral list of four minor ultra-orthodox parties (Moria, Degel Hatora, Poale Agudat Israel, Agudat Israel) formed, prior to 1992 election, to overcome the increase in election threshold from 1% to 1.5% and help to counter the rising influence of the secular Russian vote; contested 2003 election composed of Degel Hatora and Agudat Israel, into which constituent parties it split in early 2005.

United Workers' Party (Mapam): POB 1777, 2 Homa U'Migdal St, Tel-Aviv; tel. 3-6360111; fax 3-5375107; f. 1948; left-wing socialist-Zionist Jewish-Arab party; grouped in Labour-Mapam Alignment with Israel Labour Party from January 1969 until Sept. 1984 when it withdrew in protest over Labour's formation of a Government with Likud; returned to Labour 1992; member of the Socialist International; 77,000 mems; Chair. CHANAN EREZ; Sec.-Gen. VICTOR BLIT.

Yahad (Together): f. 1984; advocates a peace settlement with the Arab peoples and the Palestinians; joined the Labour Party parliamentary bloc in January 1987.

Yi'ud: f. 1994; breakaway group from the Tzomet Party.

Diplomatic Representation

EMBASSIES IN ISRAEL

Albania: 54/26 Pinkas St, Tel-Aviv 62261; tel. 3-5465866; fax 3-5444545; Chargé d'affaires a.i. TONIN BECI.

Angola: 8 Shaul Hamelech St, Tel-Aviv 64733; tel. 3-6912093; fax 3-6912094; Ambassador JOSÉ JOÃO MANUEL.

Argentina: Apt 3, Medinat Hayeudim 85, Herzliya Business Park, Herzliya Pitauch 46120; tel. 9-9702743; fax 9-9702748; e-mail embarg@netvision.net.il; Ambassador ATLIO NORBERTO MOLTENI.

Australia: Beit Europa, 4th Floor, 37 Shaul Hamelech Blvd, Tel-Aviv 64928; tel. 3-6950451; fax 3-6968404; e-mail info@ australianembassy.org.il; internet www.australianembassy.org.il; Ambassador TIM GEORGE.

Austria: Beit Crystal, 12 Hahilazon, Ramat-Gan, Tel-Aviv 52522; tel. 3-6120924; fax 3-7510716; e-mail tel-aviv-ob@bmaa.gv.at; internet www.austrian-embassy.org.il; Ambassador Dr KURT HENGL.

Belarus: 3 Reines St, Tel-Aviv 64381; tel. 3-5231069; fax 3-5231273; e-mail israel@belembassy.org; Chargé d'affaires a.i. MICHAIL BAN.

Belgium: 12 Hahilazon St, Ramat-Gan, Tel-Aviv 52522; tel. 3-6138130; fax 3-6138160; e-mail telaviv@diplobel.org; Ambassador JEAN-MIGUEL VERANNEMAN DE WATERVLIET.

Bolivia: Toyota Bldg, 65 Rehov Yigal Alon, 13th Floor, Tel-Aviv 67443; tel. 3-5621992; fax 3-5621990; e-mail embolivia-telaviv@emb .co.il; Ambassador Gen. REYNALDO CACERES QUIROGA.

Bosnia and Herzegovina: 13th Floor, 7 Menachim Begin Rd, Ramat Gan 52681; tel. 3-6124499; fax 3-6124488; Ambassador NEDELJKO MASLEŠKA.

Brazil: 2 Rehov Kaplan, Beit Yachin, 8th Floor, Tel-Aviv 64734; tel. 3-6919292; fax 3-6916060; e-mail embrisra@netvision.net.il; internet www.brazilianembassy.org.il; Ambassador SERGIO MOREIRA LIMA.

Bulgaria: 21 Leonardo da Vinci St, Tel-Aviv 64733; tel. 3-6961361; fax 3-6961430; e-mail bgemtlv@netvision.net.il; Chargé d'affaires a.i. SERGEI TASSEV.

Cameroon: Rehov Jabotinsky 50A, Tel-Aviv 62748; tel. 3-5298401; fax 3-5298249; Ambassador HENRI ETOUNDI ESSOMBA.

Canada: 3/5 Nirim St, Tel-Aviv 67060; tel. 3-6363300; fax 3-6363381; e-mail taviv@dfait-maeci.gc.ca; internet www.dfait-maeci .gc.ca/telaviv; Ambassador DONALD SINCLAIR.

Chile: 4 Rehov Kaufman, Tel-Aviv 68012; tel. 3-5102751; fax 3-5100102; e-mail echileil@inter.net.il; internet www.embachile-israel .org.il; Ambassador SALLY BENDERSKY SCHACHNER.

China, People's Republic: POB 6067, 222 Ben Yehuda St, Tel-Aviv 61060; tel. 3–5467277; fax 3–5467311; e-mail chnemb@isdn.net .il; internet www.chinaembassy.org.il; Ambassador CHEN YONGLONG.

Colombia: 6th Floor, Shekel Bldg, 111 Arlozovov St, Tel-Aviv 62068; tel. 3-6953416; fax 3-6957847; e-mail emcolis@netvision.net .il; Ambassador HECTOR FABIO VELASCO CHAVEZ.

Congo, Democratic Republic: Rehov Rachel 1/2, Tel-Aviv 64584; tel. 3-5248306; fax 3-5292623; Chargé d'affaires a.i. KIMBOKO MA MAKENGO.

Congo, Republic: POB 12504, 9 Maskit St, Herzliya Pitauch 46733; tel. 9-9577130; fax 9-9577216; Chargé d'affaires a.i. DAVID MADOUKA.

Costa Rica: 13 Rehov Diskin, Apt 1, Kiryat Wolfson, Jerusalem 92473; tel. 2-5666197; fax 2-5632591; e-mail emcri@netmedia.net.il; Ambassador NOEMÍ JUDITH BARUCH GOLDERG.

Côte d'Ivoire: South Africa Bldg, 12 Menachim Begin St, Ramat-Gan, Tel-Aviv 52521; tel. 3-6126677; fax 3-6126688; e-mail ambacita@netvision.net.il; Ambassador LÉON H. KACOU ADOM.

Croatia: POB 6–7, Canion Ramat Aviv, 40 Einstein St, Tel-Aviv 69101; tel. 3-6438654; fax 3-6438503; e-mail croembis@netvision.net .il; Ambassador IVAN DEL VECHIO.

Cyprus: 14th Floor, Top Tower, Dizengoff Centre, 50 Dizengoff St, Tel-Aviv 64322; tel. 3-5250212; fax 3-6290535; e-mail cyprus@ netvision.net.il; Ambassador GEORGE ZODIATES.

Czech Republic: POB 16361, 23 Rehov Zeitlin, Tel-Aviv 61664; tel. 3-6918282; fax 3-6918286; e-mail telaviv@embassy.mzv.cz; internet www.mfa.cz/telaviv; Ambassador MICHAEL ŽANTOVSKÝ.

Denmark: POB 21080, 23 Rehov Bnei Moshe, Tel-Aviv 61210; tel. 3-5442144; fax 3-5465502; e-mail tlvamb@um.dk; internet www .dk-embassy.org.il; Ambassador A. CARSTEN DAMSGAARD.

Dominican Republic: 19/1 Soutine St, Tel-Aviv 64884; tel. 3-5277073; fax 3-5277074; e-mail embajdom@netvision.net.il; Chargé d'affaires a.i. ALEXANDER DE LA ROSAA.

Ecuador: Asia House, 4 Rehov Weizman, Tel-Aviv 64239; tel. 3-6958764; fax 3-6913604; e-mail mecuaisr@infolink.net.il; Ambassador FRANCISCO RIOFRÍO MALDONADO.

Egypt: 54 Rehov Bazel, Tel-Aviv 62744; tel. 3-5464151; fax 3-5441615; e-mail egypem.ta@zahav.net.il; Ambassador MUHAMMAD ASIM IBRAHIM.

El Salvador: 4/4 Avigail, Abu Tor, Jerusalem; tel. 2-6728411; fax 2-6733641; e-mail embassy@el-salvador.org.il; internet www.el-salvador.org.il; Ambassador SUZANA GUN DE HASENSON.

Ethiopia: 48 Darech Petach Tikva, Tel-Aviv 66184; tel. 3-6397831; fax 3-6397837; e-mail ethembis@netvision.net.il; internet www.ethemb.co.il; Ambassador NEGASH KIBRET.

Finland: Canion Ramat Aviv, 40 Einstein St, Tel-Aviv 69101; tel. 3-7440303; fax 3-7440314; e-mail sanomat.tel@formin.fi; internet www.finemb.org.il; Ambassador KARI VEIJALAINEN.

France: 112 Tayelet Herbert Samuel, Tel-Aviv 63572; tel. 3-5208300; fax 3-5208342; e-mail diplomatie@ambafrance-il.org; internet www.ambafrance-il.org; Ambassador GÉRARD ARAUD.

Georgia: 74/5 Hei Be 'Iyar Kikar, Hamedina, Tel-Aviv 62198; tel. 3-6043232; fax 3-6021542; e-mail geoemba@netvision.net.il; Ambassador REVAZ GACHECHILADZE.

Germany: POB 16038, 19th Floor, 3 Rehov Daniel Frisch, Tel-Aviv 64731; tel. 3-6931313; fax 3-6969217; e-mail ger_emb@netvision.net.il; internet www.germanemb.org.il; Ambassador RUDOLF DRESSLER.

Ghana: 3rd Floor, 12 Hahilazon St, Ramat Gan 52522; tel. 3-7520834; fax 3-7520827; Ambassador Lt-Col LAWRENCE KPABITEY KODJIKU.

Greece: 3 Daniel Frisch St, Tel-Aviv 64731; tel. 3-6953060; fax 3-6951329; e-mail gremil@netvision.net.il; Ambassador PANAYOTIS ZOGRAFOS.

Guatemala: 103 Medinat Hayehudim, Herzliya Pitauch 46766; tel. 9-9577335; fax 9-9518506; e-mail embguate@netvision.net.il; internet www.cyberwebsite.com/embguate; Chargé d'affaires a.i. MYRIAM DE LA ROCA.

Holy See: POB 19199, Jerusalem 91191; tel. 2-6282298; fax 2-6281880; e-mail vatge@netvision.net.il; Apostolic Nuncio Mgr PIETRO SAMBI (Titular Archbishop of Belcastro).

Honduras: 2 Shvil Hasavyon, Kfar Shmaryahu 46910; tel. 9-9577686; fax 9-9577457; e-mail honduras@netvision.net.il; Ambassador FRANCISCO ZEPEDA ANDINO.

Hungary: POB 21095, 18 Pinkas St, Tel-Aviv 62661; tel. 3-5466991; fax 3-5467018; e-mail huembtlv@bezeqint.net; Ambassador Dr ANDRÁS GYENGE.

India: POB 50095, 140 Hayarkon St, Tel-Aviv 63451; tel. 3-5291999; fax 3-5291953; e-mail indemtel@indembassy.co.il; Ambassador ARUN KUMAR SINGH.

Ireland: 17th Floor, The Tower, 3 Daniel Frisch St, Tel-Aviv 64731; tel. 3-6964166; e-mail telaviv@dfa.ie; Ambassador MICHAEL FORBES.

Italy: Trade Tower Bldg, 25 Hamered St, Tel-Aviv 68125; tel. 3-5104004; fax 3-5100235; e-mail italemb@netvision.net.il; internet www.italian-embassy-israel.org; Ambassador SANDRO DE BERNARDIN.

Japan: Asia House, 4 Rehov Weizman, Tel-Aviv 64239; tel. 3-6957292; fax 3-6910516; e-mail ryouji@netvision.net.il; internet www.israel.emb-japan.go.jp; Ambassador JUN YOKOTA.

Jordan: 14 Abba Hillel, Ramat-Gan, Tel-Aviv 52506; tel. 3-7517722; fax 3-7517712; e-mail jordanembassy@barak.net.il; Ambassador Dr MAROUF S. AL-BAKHIT.

Kazakhstan: 270 Rehov Hayarkon, Tel-Aviv 63504; tel. 3-6043349; fax 3-6043364; e-mail kzisrael@netvision.net.il; internet www.kazakhemb.org.il; Ambassador KAIRAT ABDRAKHMANOV.

Kenya: 15 Aba Hillel Silver St, Ramat Gan 52522; tel. 3-5754633; fax 3-5754788; e-mail kenya7@netvision.net.il; Ambassador FELISTAS VUNORO KHAYUMBI.

Korea, Republic: 38 Sderot Chen, Tel-Aviv 64166; tel. 3-6963244; fax 3-6963243; e-mail israel@mofat.go.kr; Ambassador PARK KYUNG-TRAK.

Latvia: 9 Marmorek St, Tel-Aviv 64254; tel. 3-6869544; fax 3-6869543; e-mail latvembi@netvision.net.il; Ambassador KARLIS EIHENBAUMS.

Liberia: 74 Derech Menachim Begin, Tel-Aviv 67215; tel. 3-5611068; fax 3-5610896.

Lithuania: 8 14th Floor, 50 Dizengoff St, Tel-Aviv 64332; tel. 3-6958685; fax 3-6958691; e-mail amb.il@urm.lt; Ambassador ALFONSAS EIDINTAS.

Mauritania: Rehov Arlosoroff 111, Tel-Aviv 62098; tel. 3-6916820; fax 3-6957046; Ambassador AHMAD OULD TEGUEDDI.

Mexico: 25 Hamered St, 5th Floor, Trade Tower, Tel-Aviv 68125; tel. 3-5163938; fax 3-5163711; e-mail embamex@netvision.net.il; internet www.sre.gob.mx/israel; Ambassador CARLOS RICO-FERRAT.

Moldova: 38 Rembrandt St, Tel-Aviv 64045; tel. 3-5231000; fax 3-5233000; Ambassador ARTHUR COZMA.

Myanmar: Textile Centre, 2 Rehov Kaufman, Tel-Aviv 68012; tel. 3-5170760; fax 3-5171440; e-mail teltaman@aquanet.co.il; internet www.metelaviv.co.il; Ambassador U TIN WIN.

Netherlands: Beit Oz, 14 Abba Hillel St, Ramat Gan 52506; tel. 3-7523150; fax 3-7523135; e-mail nigovtel@inter.net.il; internet www.neth-embassy-telaviv.co.il; Ambassador BOB HIENSCH.

Nigeria: 34 Gordon St, Tel-Aviv 63414; tel. 3-5222144; fax 3-5237886; Chargé d'affaires CHRISTIE E. MBONU.

Norway: 13th Floor, 40 Einstein St, Canion Ramat Aviv, Tel-Aviv 69101; tel. 3-7441490; fax 3-7441498; e-mail emb.telaviv@mfa.no; Ambassador HANS J. BJØRN LIAN.

Panama: 10 Rehov Hei Be'Iyar, Kikar Hamedina, Tel-Aviv 62998; tel. 3-6960849; fax 3-6910045; Ambassador Prof. MARIO AROSEMENA QUINTERO.

Peru: Rehov Medinat Hayehudim 60, Herzliya Pituach 46766; tel. 9-9578835; fax 9-9568495; Chargé d'affaires a.i. WALDO ORTEGA MATIAS.

Philippines: 13th Floor, Textile Centre Bldg, 2 Rehov Kaufman, Tel-Aviv 68012; tel. 3-5175263; fax 3-5102229; e-mail filembis@netvision.net.il; Ambassador ANTONIO C. MODENA.

Poland: 16 Soutine St, Tel-Aviv 64684; tel. 3-5240186; fax 3-5237806; e-mail embpol@netvision.net.il; internet www.polemb.org; Ambassador JAN WOJCIECH PIEKARSKI.

Portugal: 12th Floor, 3 Daniel Frisch St, Tel-Aviv 64731; tel. 3-6956373; fax 3-6956366; e-mail eptel@otz.net.il; Ambassador PEDRO NUNO DE ABREU E MELO BÁRTOLO.

Romania: 24 Rehov Adam Hacohen, Tel-Aviv 64585; tel. 3-5230066; fax 3-5247379; e-mail rouembil@netvision.net.il; Ambassador VALERIA MARIANA STOICA.

Russia: 120 Rehov Hayarkon, Tel-Aviv 63573; tel. 3-5226736; fax 3-5226713; e-mail amb_ru@mail.netvision.net.il; internet www.israel.mid.ru; Ambassador GENNADII TARASOV.

Serbia and Montenegro: 10 Bodenheimer St, Tel-Aviv 62008; tel. 3-6045535; fax 3-6049456; e-mail yuamb@netvision.net.il; Ambassador Dr KRINKA VIDAKOVIĆ-PETROV.

Slovakia: POB 6459, 37 Jabotinsky St, Tel-Aviv 61064; tel. 3-5449119; fax 3-5449144; e-mail slovemb1@barak.net.il; Ambassador MILAN DUBČEK.

Slovenia: Top Tower, 50 Dizengoff St, POB 23245, Tel-Aviv 61231; tel. 3-6293563; fax 3-5282214; e-mail vta@mzz-dkp.gov.si; internet www.gov.si/mzz/dkp/vta/eng/index.html; Ambassador IGOR POGAČAR.

South Africa: POB 7138, 16th Floor, Top Tower, 50 Dizengoff St, Tel-Aviv 61071; tel. 3-5252566; fax 3-5253230; e-mail saemtel@isdn.net.il; internet www.safis.co.il; Chargé d'affaires a.i. SAREL JOHANNES KRUGER.

Spain: Dubnov Tower, 3 Rehov Daniel Frisch, 18th Floor, Tel-Aviv 64731; tel. 3-6965218; fax 3-6965217; e-mail embespil@mail.mae.es; Ambassador EUDALDO MIRAPEIX MARTÍNEZ (Baron of Abella).

Sri Lanka: 4 Jean Jaures St, Tel-Aviv 63412; tel. 3-5277638; fax 3-5277634; Ambassador TISSA WIJERATNE.

Sweden: Asia House, 4 Rehov Weizman, Tel-Aviv 64239; tel. 3-6958111; fax 3-6958116; e-mail ambassaden.tel-aviv@foreign.ministry.se; internet www.swedenabroad.com/telaviv; Ambassador ROBERT RYDBERG.

Switzerland: 228 Rehov Hayarkon, Tel-Aviv 63405; tel. 3-5464455; fax 3-5464408; e-mail vertretung@tel.rep.admin.ch; internet www.eda.admin.ch/telaviv; Ambassador ERNST ITEN.

Thailand: 144 Sderot Shaul Hamelech, Tel-Aviv 64367; tel. 3-5244277; fax 3-5244270; Ambassador KASIVAT PARUGGAMANONT.

Turkey: 202 Rehov Hayarkon, Tel-Aviv 63405; tel. 3-5241101; fax 3-5241390; e-mail turqua2@netvision.net.il; internet www.turkishembassy-telaviv.org; Ambassador FERIDUN SINIRLIOGLU.

Ukraine: 50 Yirmiyagu, Tel-Aviv 62594; tel. 3-6040242; fax 3-6042512; e-mail embukr@netvision.net.il; internet www.ukraine-embassy.co.il; Ambassador OLEKSANDR S. SLIPCHENKO.

United Kingdom: 192 Rehov Hayarkon, Tel-Aviv 63405; tel. 3-7251222; fax 3-5243313; e-mail webmaster.telaviv@fco.gov.uk; internet www.britemb.org.il; Ambassador SIMON MCDONALD.

USA: POB 26180, 1 Ben Yahuda St, Tel-Aviv; tel. 3-5103822; fax 3-5103828; e-mail webmaster@usembassy-israel.org.il; internet usembassy-israel.org.il; Ambassador DANIEL C. KURTZER.

Uruguay: POB 12244, G.R.A.P. Bldg, 1st Floor, Industrial Zone, Herzliya Pitauch 46733; tel. 9-9569611; fax 9-9515881; e-mail emrou@netvision.net.il; Ambassador ALFREDO E. CAZES ALVAREZ.

Uzbekistan: 35 Dvora Ha'Nevia St, Tel-Aviv 69350; tel. 3-6447743; fax 3-6447748; e-mail uzecon@barak-onlinr.net; internet www.uzbekistan.org.il; Ambassador OYBEK USMANOV.

Venezuela: Textile Center, 2 Rehov Kaufman, 16th Floor, Tel-Aviv 61500; tel. 3-5176287; fax 3-5176210; e-mail emven@netvision.net.il; Ambassadors ANGEL MACHADO ALMEIDA.

Judicial System

The law of Israel is composed of the enactments of the Knesset and, to a lesser extent, of the acts, orders-in-council and ordinances that remain from the period of the British Mandate in Palestine (1922–48). The pre-1948 law has largely been replaced, amended or reorganized, in the interests of codification, by Israeli legislation. This legislation generally follows a very similar pattern to that operating in England and the USA. However, there is no jury system.

Attorney-General: MENACHEM MAZUZ.

CIVIL COURTS

The Supreme Court

Sha'arei Mishpat St, Kiryat David Ben-Gurion, Jerusalem 91950; tel. 2-6759666; fax 2-6759648; e-mail marcia@supreme.court.gov.il; internet www.court.gov.il.

This is the highest judicial authority in the state. It has jurisdiction as an Appellate Court over appeals from the District Courts in all matters, both civil and criminal (sitting as a Court of Civil Appeal or as a Court of Criminal Appeal). In addition it is a Court of First Instance (sitting as the High Court of Justice) in actions against governmental authorities, and in matters in which it considers it necessary to grant relief in the interests of justice and which are not within the jurisdiction of any other court or tribunal. The High Court's exclusive power to issue orders in the nature of *habeas corpus, mandamus*, prohibition and *certiorari* enables the court to review the legality of and redress grievances against acts of administrative authorities of all kinds.

President of the Supreme Court: AHARON BARAK.

Deputy President of the Supreme Court: MISHAEL CHESHIN.

Justices of the Supreme Court: DORIT BEINISCH, MISHAEL CHESHIN, ASHER D. GRUNIS, MIRIAM NAOR, ELIEZER RIVLIN, EDMOND E. LEVY, AYALA PROCACCIA, EDNA ARBEL, ESTHER HAYUT, ELYAKIM RUBINSTEIN, SALIM JOUBRAN.

Registrars: Justice ODED SHAHAM, YIGAL MERSEL.

The District Courts: There are five District Courts (Jerusalem, Tel-Aviv, Haifa, Beersheba, Nazareth). They have residual jurisdiction as Courts of First Instance over all civil and criminal matters not within the jurisdiction of a Magistrates' Court (e.g. civil claims exceeding NIS 1m.), all matters not within the exclusive jurisdiction of any other tribunal, and matters within the concurrent jurisdiction of any other tribunal so long as such tribunal does not deal with them. In addition, the District Courts have appellate jurisdiction over appeals from judgments and decisions of Magistrates' Courts and judgments of Municipal Courts and various administrative tribunals.

Magistrates' Courts: There are 29 Magistrates' Courts, having criminal jurisdiction to try contraventions, misdemeanours and certain felonies, and civil jurisdiction to try actions concerning possession or use of immovable property, or the partition thereof whatever may be the value of the subject matter of the action, and other civil claims not exceeding one million shekels.

Labour Courts: Established in 1969. Regional Labour Courts in Jerusalem, Tel-Aviv, Haifa, Beersheba and Nazareth, composed of judges and representatives of the public. A National Labour Court in Jerusalem. The Courts have jurisdiction over all matters arising out of the relationship between employer and employee or parties to a collective labour agreement, and matters concerning the National Insurance Law and the Labour Law and Rules.

RELIGIOUS COURTS

The Religious Courts are the courts of the recognized religious communities. They have jurisdiction over certain defined matters of personal status concerning members of their respective communities. Where any action of personal status involves persons of different religious communities the President of the Supreme Court decides which Court will decide the matter. Whenever a question arises as to whether or not a case is one of personal status within the exclusive jurisdiction of a Religious Court, the matter must be referred to a Special Tribunal composed of two Justices of the Supreme Court and the President of the highest court of the religious community concerned in Israel. The judgments of the Religious Courts are executed by the process and offices of the Civil Courts. Neither these Courts nor the Civil Courts have jurisdiction to dissolve the marriage of a foreign subject.

Jewish Rabbinical Courts: These Courts have exclusive jurisdiction over matters of marriage and divorce of Jews in Israel who are Israeli citizens or residents. In all other matters of personal status they have concurrent jurisdiction with the District Courts.

Muslim Religious Courts: These Courts have exclusive jurisdiction over matters of marriage and divorce of Muslims who are not foreigners, or who are foreigners subject by their national law to the jurisdiction of Muslim Religious Courts in such matters. In all other matters of personal status they have concurrent jurisdiction with the District Courts.

Christian Religious Courts: The Courts of the recognized Christian communities have exclusive jurisdiction over matters of marriage and divorce of members of their communities who are not foreigners. In all other matters of personal status they have concurrent jurisdiction with the District Courts.

Druze Courts: These Courts, established in 1963, have exclusive jurisdiction over matters of marriage and divorce of Druze in Israel, who are Israeli citizens or residents, and concurrent jurisdiction with the District Courts over all other matters of personal status of Druze.

Religion

JUDAISM

Judaism, the religion of the Jews, is the faith of the majority of Israel's inhabitants. On 31 December 2003 Judaism's adherents totalled 5,165,400, equivalent to 76.54% of the country's population. Its basis is a belief in an ethical monotheism.

There are two main Jewish communities: the Ashkenazim and the Sephardim. The former are the Jews from Eastern, Central, or Northern Europe, while the latter originate from the Balkan countries, North Africa and the Middle East.

There is also a community of about 10,000 Falashas (Ethiopian Jews) who have been airlifted to Israel at various times since the fall of Emperor Haile Selassie in 1974.

The supreme religious authority is vested in the Chief Rabbinate, which consists of the Ashkenazi and Sephardi Chief Rabbis and the Supreme Rabbinical Council. It makes decisions on interpretation of the Jewish law, and supervises the Rabbinical Courts. There are eight regional Rabbinical Courts, and a Rabbinical Court of Appeal presided over by the two Chief Rabbis.

According to the Rabbinical Courts Jurisdiction Law of 1953, marriage and divorce among Jews in Israel are exclusively within the jurisdiction of the Rabbinical Courts. Provided that all the parties concerned agree, other matters of personal status can also be decided by the Rabbinical Courts.

There are 132 Religious Councils, which maintain religious services and supply religious needs, and about 405 religious committees with similar functions in smaller settlements. Their expenses are borne jointly by the state and the local authorities. The Religious Councils are under the administrative control of the Ministry of Religious Affairs. In all matters of religion, the Religious Councils are subject to the authority of the Chief Rabbinate. There are 365 officially appointed rabbis. The total number of synagogues is about 7,000, most of which are organized within the framework of the Union of Israel Synagogues.

Head of the Ashkenazi Community: The Chief Rabbi YONA METZGER.

Head of the Sephardic Community: Jerusalem; tel. 2-5313131 The Chief Rabbi SHLOMO AMAR.

Two Jewish sects still loyal to their distinctive customs are:

The Karaites: a sect which recognizes only the Jewish written law and not the oral law of the Mishna and Talmud. The community of about 12,000, many of whom live in or near Ramla, has been augmented by immigration from Egypt.

The Samaritans: an ancient sect mentioned in 2 Kings xvii, 24. They recognize only the Torah. The community in Israel numbers about 500; about one-half of this number live in Holon, where a Samaritan synagogue has been built, and the remainder, including the High Priest, live in Nablus, near Mt Gerazim, which is sacred to the Samaritans.

ISLAM

The Muslims in Israel are mainly Sunnis, and are divided among the four rites of the Sunni sect of Islam: the Shafe'i, the Hanbali, the

Hanafi and the Maliki. Before June 1967 they numbered approx. 175,000; in 1971, approx. 343,900. On 31 December 2003 the total Muslim population of Israel was 1,072,500.

Mufti of Jerusalem: POB 19859, Jerusalem; tel. 2-283528; Sheikh IKRIMAH SABRI (also Chair. Supreme Muslim Council for Jerusalem); appointed by the Palestinian (National) Authority (PA).

There was also a total of 110,800 Druzes in Israel at 31 December 2003. The official spiritual leader of the Druze community in Israel is Sheikh MUWAFAK TARIF, but his leadership is not widely recognized.

CHRISTIANITY

The total Christian population of Israel (including East Jerusalem) at 31 December 2003 was 142,400.

United Christian Council in Israel: POB 116, Jerusalem 91000; tel. 2-6714351; fax 2-6721349; e-mail kopp@galanet.net; f. 1956; 28 mems (churches and other bodies); Chair. CHARLES KOPP.

The Roman Catholic Church

Armenian Rite

The Armenian Catholic Patriarch of Cilicia is resident in Beirut, Lebanon.

Patriarchal Exarchate of Jerusalem and Amman: POB 19546, Via Dolorosa 41, Jerusalem 91190; tel. 2-6284262; fax 2-6272123; f. 1885; about 740 adherents (31 December 2002); Exarch Patriarchal KÉVORK KHAZOUMIAN.

Chaldean Rite

The Chaldean Patriarch of Babylon is resident in Baghdad, Iraq.

Patriarchal Exarchate of Jerusalem: Chaldean Patriarchal Vicariate, POB 20108, 7 Chaldean St, Saad and Said Quarter, Jerusalem 91200; tel. 2-6284519; fax 2-6274614; Exarch Patriarchal Mgr PAUL COLLIN.

Latin Rite

The Patriarchate of Jerusalem covers Palestine, Jordan and Cyprus. At 31 December 2002 there were an estimated 77,000 adherents.

Bishops' Conference: Conférence des Evêques Latins dans les Régions Arabes, Notre Dame of Jerusalem Center, POB 20531, Jerusalem 91204; tel. 2-6288554; fax 2-6288555; e-mail evcat@palnet.com; f. 1967; Pres. His Beatitude MICHEL SABBAH (Patriarch of Jerusalem).

Patriarchate of Jerusalem: Patriarcat Latin, POB 14152, Jerusalem 91141; tel. 2-6282323; fax 2-6271652; e-mail chancellery@latinpat.org; internet www.lpj.org; Patriarch His Beatitude MICHEL SABBAH; Vicar-General for Jerusalem KAMAL HANNA BATHISH (Titular Bishop of Jericho); Vicar-General for Israel GIACINTO-BOULOS MAR-CUZZO (Titular Bishop of Emmaus Nicopolis); Vicariat Patriarcal Latin, Street 6191/3, Nazareth 16100; tel. 4-6554075; fax 4-6452416; e-mail latinpat@rannet.com.

Maronite Rite

The Maronite community, under the jurisdiction of the Maronite Patriarch of Antioch (resident in Lebanon), has about 7,000 members.

Patriarchal Exarchate of Jerusalem: Maronite Patriarchal Exarchate, POB 14219, 25 Maronite Convent St, Jaffa Gate, Jerusalem 91141; tel. 2-6282158; fax 2-6272821; about 504 adherents (31 December 2001); Exarch Patriarchal Mgr PAUL NABIL ES-SAYEH (also the Archbishop of Haifa and the Holy Land).

Melkite Rite

The Greek-Melkite Patriarch of Antioch and all the East, of Alexandria and of Jerusalem (Grégoire III Laham) is resident in Damascus, Syria.

Patriarchal Vicariate of Jerusalem
Patriarcat Grec-Melkite Catholique, POB 14130, Porte de Jaffa, Jerusalem 91141; tel. 2-6271968; fax 2-6286652; e-mail gcpjer@p-ol.com.
About 3,300 adherents (31 December 2002); Protosyncellus Archim. MTANIOS HADDAD.

Archbishop of Akka (Acre): (vacant), Archevêché Grec-Catholique, POB 279, 33 Hagefen St, 31002 Haifa; tel. 4-8523114; fax 4-8520798.
67,890 adherents at 31 December 2002.

Syrian Rite

The Syrian Catholic Patriarch of Antioch is resident in Beirut, Lebanon.

Patriarchal Exarchate of Jerusalem: Vicariat Patriarcal Syrien Catholique, POB 19787, 6 Chaldean St, Jerusalem 91191; tel. 2-6282657; fax 2-6284217; e-mail stjossc@l-ol.com; about 1,550 adher-

ents (31 December 2002); Exarch Patriarchal Mgr GRÉGOIRE PIERRE MELKI.

The Armenian Apostolic (Orthodox) Church

Patriarch of Jerusalem: TORKOM MANOOGIAN, Armenian Patriarchate of St James, POB 14235, Jerusalem; tel. 2-6264853; fax 2-6264862; e-mail webmaster@armenian-patriarchate.org; internet www.armenian-patriarchate.org.

The Greek Orthodox Church

The Patriarchate of Jerusalem contains an estimated 260,000 adherents in Israel, the Occupied Territories, Jordan, Kuwait, the United Arab Emirates and Saudi Arabia.

Patriarch of Jerusalem: IRINEOS I, POB 19632-633, Greek Orthodox Patriarchate St, Old City, Jerusalem; tel. 2-6271657; fax 2-6282048; internet www.jerusalem-patriarchate.org.

The Anglican Communion

Episcopal Diocese of Jerusalem and the Middle East: POB 19122, St George's Cathedral Close, Jerusalem 91191; tel. 2-6271670; fax 2-6273847; e-mail ediocese-jer@j-diocese.com; internet www.j-diocese.com; Bishop The Rt Rev. RIAH ABU EL-ASSAL (Anglican Bishop in Jerusalem).

Other Christian Churches

Other denominations include the Coptic Orthodox Church (700 members), the Russian Orthodox Church, the Ethiopian Orthodox Church, the Romanian Orthodox Church, the Baptist Church, the Lutheran Church and the Church of Scotland.

The Press

Tel-Aviv is the main publishing centre. Largely for economic reasons, no local press has developed away from the main cities; hence all papers regard themselves as national. Friday editions, issued on Sabbath eve, are increased to as much as twice the normal size by special weekend supplements, and experience a considerable rise in circulation. No newspapers appear on Saturday.

Most of the daily papers are in Hebrew, and others appear in Arabic, English, French, Polish, Yiddish, Hungarian, Russian and German. The total daily circulation is 500,000–600,000 copies, or 21 papers per hundred people, although most citizens read more than one daily paper.

Most Hebrew morning dailies have strong political or religious affiliations. *Hatzofeh*, for example, is affiliated to the National Religious Party. Most newspapers depend on subsidies from political parties, religious organizations or public funds. The limiting effect on freedom of commentary entailed by this party press system has provoked repeated criticism. There are around 400 other newspapers and magazines including some 50 weekly and 150 fortnightly; over 250 of them are in Hebrew, the remainder in 11 other languages.

The most influential and respected daily, for both quality of news coverage and commentary, is *Ha'aretz*. This is the most widely read of the morning papers, exceeded only by the popular afternoon press, *Ma'ariv* and *Yedioth Aharonoth*. The *Jerusalem Post* gives detailed and sound news coverage in English.

The Israeli Press Council (Chair. Prof. MORDECHAI KREMNITZER), established in 1963, deals with matters of common interest to the Press such as drafting the code of professional ethics which is binding on all journalists.

The Daily Newspaper Publishers' Association represents publishers in negotiations with official and public bodies, negotiates contracts with employees and purchases and distributes newsprint.

DAILIES

Al Anba (The News): Jerusalem Publications Ltd, POB 428, 37 Hillel St, Jerusalem; f. 1968; circ. 10,000.

Globes: POB 5126, Rishon le Zion 75150; tel. 3-9538888; fax 3-9525971; e-mail mailbox@globes.co.il; internet www.globes.co.il; f. 1983; evening; business, economics; CEO AMI EVEN; Editor-in-Chief HAGGAI GOLAN; circ. 45,000.

Ha'aretz (The Land): POB 233, 21 Salman Schocken St, Tel-Aviv 61001; tel. 3-5121110; fax 3-6815859; e-mail iht@haaretz.co.il; internet www.haaretz.co.il; f. 1918; morning; Hebrew; liberal, independent; Editor HANOCH MARMARI; circ. 50,000 (weekdays), 60,000 (weekends).

Hamodia (The Informer): POB 1306, Yehuda Hamackabbi 5, Jerusalem 91012; tel. 2-5389255; fax 2-5389108; e-mail english@hamodia.co.il; morning; Hebrew; also publishes weekly English-language edition; organ of Agudat Israel; Editors M. A. DRUCK, H. M. KNOPF; circ. 35,000.

Hatzofeh (The Watchman): POB 2045, 66 Hamasger St, Tel-Aviv; tel. 3-5622951; fax 3-5621502; e-mail hazofe@zahav.net.il; internet www.hazofe.co.il; f. 1938; morning; Hebrew; organ of the National Religious Party; Editor Gonen Ginat; circ. 60,000.

Israel Nachrichten (News of Israel): POB 28397, 5 Negev St, Tel-Aviv 61283; tel. 3-5372059; fax 3-6877142; internet www.israel-nachrichten.de/israel-nachrichten/aktuell.htm; f. 1974; morning; German; Editor Alice Schwarz-Gardos; circ. 20,000.

Al-Itihad (Unity): POB 104, Haifa; tel. 4-511296; fax 4-511297; f. 1944; Arabic; organ of Hadash; Editor Ahmad Sa'ad; circ. 60,000.

The Jerusalem Post: POB 81, Romema, Jerusalem 91000; tel. 2-5315666; fax 2-5389527; e-mail editors@jpost.com; internet www.jpost.com; f. 1932; morning; English; independent; CEO Mark Ziman; Editor-in-Chief Bret Stephens; circ. 15,000 (weekdays), 40,000 (weekend edition); there is also a weekly international edition, circ. 40,000.

Ma'ariv (Evening Prayer): 2 Carlebach St, Tel-Aviv 61200; tel. 3-5632111; fax 3-5610614; internet www.maariv.co.il; f. 1948; mid-morning; Hebrew; independent; published by Modiin Publishing House; Editor Ya'akov Erez; circ. 150,000 (weekdays), 250,000 (weekends).

Mabat: 8 Toshia St, Tel-Aviv 67218; tel. 3-5627711; fax 3-5627719; f. 1971; morning; Hebrew; economic and social; Editor S. Yarkoni; circ. 7,000.

Nasha Strana (Our Country): 52 Harakeret St, Tel-Aviv 67770; tel. 3-370011; fax 3-5371921; f. 1970; morning; Russian; Editor S. Himmelfarb; circ. 35,000.

Al-Quds (Jerusalem): POB 19788, Jerusalem; tel. 2-6272663; fax 2-6272657; e-mail info@alquds.com; internet www.alquds.com; f. 1968; Arabic; Founder and Publr Mahmoud Abu Zalaf; Gen. Man. Dr Marwan Abu Zalaf; circ. 55,000.

Ash-Shaab (The People): POB 20077, Jerusalem; tel. 2-289881; Arabic.

Shearim (The Gates): POB 11044, 64 Frishman St, Tel-Aviv; tel. 3-242126; organ of the Poale Agudat Israel Party.

Uj Kelet: 49 Tchlenor St, Tel-Aviv; tel. 3-5371395; fax 3-377142; f. 1918; morning; Hungarian; independent; Editor D. Drory; circ. 20,000.

Viata Noastra: 49 Tchlenor St, Tel-Aviv 61351; tel. 3-5372059; fax 3-6877142; e-mail erancourt@shani.co.il; f. 1950; morning; Romanian; Editor George Edri; circ. 30,000.

Yated Ne'eman: POB 328, Bnei Brak; tel. 3-6170800; fax 3-6170801; e-mail let-edit@yatedneman.co.il; f. 1986; morning; religious; Editors Y. Roth, N. Grossman; circ. 25,000.

Yedioth Aharonoth (The Latest News): 2 Yehuda and Noah Mozes St, Tel-Aviv 61000; tel. 3-6972222; fax 3-6082222; internet www.ynet.co.il; f. 1939; evening; Hebrew; independent; Editor-in-Chief Moshe Vardi; circ. 350,000, Friday 600,000.

WEEKLIES AND FORTNIGHTLIES

Akhbar an-Naqab: POB 426, Rahat 85357; tel. (8) 9919202; fax (8) 9917070; e-mail akhbar@akhbarna.com; internet www.akhbarna.com; f. 1988; Arabic; Editor-in-Chief Muhammad Younis.

Aurora: Aurora Ltd, POB 18066, Tel-Aviv 61180; tel. 3-5625216; fax 3-5625082; e-mail aurora@aurora-israel.co.il; internet www.aurora-israel.co.il; f. 1963; weekly; Spanish; for Spanish-speakers in Israel and abroad; Pres. Arie Avidor; circ. 20,000.

Bama'alah: 120 Kibbutz Gabuyot St, Tel-Aviv; tel. 3-6814488; fax 3-6816852; Hebrew; journal of the young Histadrut Movement; Editor Oded Bar-Meir.

Bamahane (In the Camp): Military POB 1013, Tel-Aviv; f. 1948; military, illustrated weekly of the Israel Armed Forces; Hebrew; Editor-in-Chief Yossef Eshkol; circ. 70,000.

Ethgar (The Challenge): 75 Einstein St, Tel-Aviv; twice weekly; Hebrew; Editor Nathan Yalin-Mor.

Harefuah (Medicine): POB 3566, 35 Jabotinsky St, Ramat-Gan 52136; tel. 3-6100444; fax 3-5751616; f. 1920; fortnightly journal of the Israeli Medical Association; Hebrew with English summaries; an English publication, IMAJ, has also been published since 1999; Editor Y. Shoenfeld; circ. 16,000.

InformationWeek: POB 1161, 13 Yad Harutzim St, Tel-Aviv 61116; tel. 3-6385858; fax 3-6889207; e-mail world@pc.co.il; internet www.pc.co.il; weekly; Man. Dirs Dahlia Peled, Peli Peled; Editor-in-Chief Peli Peled.

The Israeli Tourist Guide Magazine: Tourist Guide Communications Ltd, POB 53333, Tel-Aviv 61533; tel. 3-5168282; fax 3-5168284; e-mail ishchori@touristguide.co.il; internet www.touristguide.co.il; f. 1994; weekly; Publisher and Editor Ilan Shchori; circ. 10,000.

Jerusalem Post International Edition: POB 81, Romema, Jerusalem 91000; tel. 2-5315666; fax 2-5389527; e-mail jpedt@jpost.co.il; internet www.jpost.co.il; f. 1959; weekly; English; overseas edition of the Jerusalem Post (q.v.); circ. 70,000 to 106 countries.

Jerusalem Report: POB 1805, Jerusalem 91017; tel. 2-5315440; fax 2-5379489; e-mail jrep@jreport.co.il; internet www.jrep.com; f. 1990; bi-weekly; English; Publr and Editor David Horovitz; published by *Jerusalem Report Publications*; circ. 65,000 worldwide.

The Jerusalem Times: 19 Nablus Rd, East Jerusalem; tel. 2-6264883; fax 2-6264975; e-mail tjt@jerusalem-times.net; internet www.jerusalem-times.net; f. 1994; weekly; English; Editor Hanna Siniora.

Kol Ha'am (Voice of the People): Tel-Aviv; f. 1947; Hebrew; organ of the Communist Party of Israel; Editor B. Balti.

Laisha (For Women): POB 28122, 35 Bnei Brak St, Tel-Aviv 66021; tel. 3-6386977; fax 3-6386933; e-mail laisha@laisha.co.il; f. 1946; Hebrew; women's magazine; Editor Miriam Nofech-Moses; circ. 110,000.

Ma'ariv Lanoar: POB 20020, 2 Carlebach St, Tel-Aviv 67132; tel. 3-5632525; fax 3-5632030; e-mail maariv_lanoar@maariv.co.il; f. 1957; weekly for teenagers; Hebrew; Editor Dana Ben-Naftali; circ. 100,000.

MB (Mitteilungsblatt): POB 1480, Tel-Aviv 61014; tel. 3-5164461; fax 3-5164435; e-mail irgunmb@netvision.net.il; f. 1932; German monthly journal of the Irgun Olei Merkas Europa (The Association of Jews from Central Europe); Editor Micha Limon.

Otiot: Jerusalem; tel. 2-895097; fax 2-895196; f. 1987; weekly for children; English; Editor Uri Auerbach.

Reshumot: Ministry of Justice, POB 1087, 29 Rehov Salahadin, Jerusalem 91010; f. 1948; Hebrew, Arabic and English; official government gazette.

As-Sabar: POB 41199, Ar-Ramiz al-Baridi, Jaffa 61411; e-mail alsabar@netvision.net.il; internet www.hanitzotz.com/alsabar; publ. by the Organization for Democratic Action (ODA); Arabic; Israeli—Palestinian affairs.

Sada at-Tarbia (The Echo of Education): published by the Histadrut and Teachers' Association, POB 2306, Rehovot; f. 1952; fortnightly; Arabic; educational; Editor Tuvia Shamosh.

As-Sinnarah: Nazareth; internet www.asennara.com; twice weekly; for Christian and Muslim Arabs in the region; Arabic; Editor-in-Chief Lufti Mash'ur.

OTHER PERIODICALS

Ariel (The Israel Review of Arts and Letters): Cultural and Scientific Relations Division, Ministry of Foreign Affairs, Jerusalem; Distributor: Youval Tal Ltd, POB 2160, Jerusalem 91021; Editorial Office: POB 7705, Jerusalem 91076; tel. 2-6432147; fax 2-6437502; e-mail debasher@netvision.net.il; internet www.israel-mfa.gov.il; f. 1962; quarterly review of all aspects of culture in Israel; regular edns in English, Spanish, French, German, Arabic and Russian; occasional edns in other languages; Editor Asher Weill; circ. 30,000.

Asakim Vekalkala (Business and Economics): POB 20027, 84 Ha' Hashmonaim St, Tel-Aviv 61200; tel. 3-5631010; fax 3-5612614; monthly; Hebrew; Editor Yosef Shostak; circ. 5,000.

Bitaon Heyl Ha'avir (Israel Air Force Magazine): Military POB 01560, Zahal; tel. 3-5694153; fax 3-5695806; e-mail iaf@inter.net.il; internet www.iaf.org.il; f. 1948; bi-monthly; Hebrew; Dep. Editor U. Etsion; Editor-in-Chief Merav Halperin; circ. 30,000.

Al-Bushra (Good News): POB 6228, Haifa 31061; tel. 4-8385002; fax 4-8371612; f. 1935; monthly; Arabic; organ of the Ahmadiyya movement; Editor Musa Asa'ad O'deh.

Business Diary: Haifa; f. 1947; weekly; English, Hebrew; shipping movements, import licences, stock exchange listings, business failures, etc.; Editor G. Alon.

Challenge: POB 41199, Jaffa 61411; tel. 3-6839145; fax 3-6839148; e-mail oda@netvision.net.il; internet www.hanitzotz.com/challenge; f. 1989; magazine on the Israeli–Palestinian conflict, published by Hanitzotz Publishing House; bi-monthly; English; Editor-in-Chief Roni Ben Efrat; Editor Liz Leyh Levac; circ. 1,000.

Diamond Intelligence Brief: POB 3441, Silver Bldg, 7 Abba Hillel St, Ramat-Gan, Tel-Aviv 52133; tel. 3-5750196; fax 3-5754829; e-mail office@tacy.co.il; internet www.diamondintelligence.com; f. 1985; Publr Chaim Even-Zohar.

Divrei Haknesset: c/o The Knesset, Jerusalem; f. 1949; Hebrew; records of the proceedings of the Knesset; published by the Government Printer, Jerusalem; Editor Dvora Avivi (acting); circ. 350.

Eastern Mediterranean Tourism and Travel: Israel Travel News Ltd, POB 3251, Tel-Aviv 61032; tel. 3-5251646; fax 3-5251605; e-mail travel01@netvision.net.il; f. 1979; monthly; English; Editor GERRY AROHOW; circ. 19,515.

Hamizrah Hehadash (The New East): Israel Oriental Society, The Hebrew University, Mount Scopus, Jerusalem 91905; tel. 2-5883633; e-mail ios49@hotmail.com; f. 1949; annual of the Israel Oriental Society; Middle Eastern, Asian and African Affairs; Hebrew with English summary; Editors HAIM GERBER, ELIE PODEH; circ. 1,500–2,000.

Hamionai (The Hotelier): POB 11586, Tel-Aviv; f. 1962; monthly of the Israel Hotel Asscn; Hebrew and English; Editor Z. PELTZ.

Hapraklit (Law): POB 14152, 8 Wilson St, Tel-Aviv 61141; tel. 3-5614695; fax 3-561476; f. 1943; quarterly; Hebrew; published by the Israel Bar Asscn; Editor-in-Chief A. POLONSKI; Editor ARNAN GAVRIELI; circ. 7,000.

Hassadeh: POB 40044, 8 Shaul Hamelech Blvd, Tel-Aviv 61400; tel. 3-6929018; fax 3-6929979; f. 1920; monthly; review of Israeli agriculture; English and Hebrew; Publr GUY KING; Editor NAAMA DOTAN; circ. 13,000.

Hed Hagan: 8 Ben Saruk St, Tel-Aviv 62969; tel. 3-6922958; f. 1935; quarterly; Hebrew; educational; Editor MIRIAM SNAPIR; circ. 9,000.

Hed Hahinukh: 2 Tashach St, Tel-Aviv 62093; tel. 3-6091819; fax 3-6094521; e-mail hed@itu.org.il; f. 1926; monthly; Hebrew; educational; published by the Israeli Teachers' Union; Editor DALIA LACHMAN; circ. 40,000.

Historia: POB 4179, Jerusalem 91041; tel. 2-5650444; fax 2-6712388; e-mail shazar@shazar.org.il; f. 1998; Hebrew, with English summaries; general history; published by the Historical Society of Israel; Editors Prof. EFRAIM DAVID, Prof. STEVE KAPLAN, Prof. ORA LIMOR, Prof. SHULAMIT VOLKOV.

Internet World (Israel): POB 1161, 13 Yad Harutzim St, Tel-Aviv 61116; tel. 3-6385858; fax 3-6889207; e-mail benrun@netvision.net.il; internet www.people-and-computers.co.il; 24 a year; computers and information technology; Man. Dirs DAHLIA PELED, PELI PELED; Editor-in-Chief PELI PELED.

Israel Agritechnology Focus: 8 Twersky St, Tel-Aviv 61574; tel. 3-5628511; fax 3-5628512; f. 1993; quarterly; farming technology, agricultural company and investment news; Editor NICKY BLACKMAN.

Israel Economist: 6 Hazanowitz St, Jerusalem; tel. 2-234131; fax 2-246569; f. 1945; monthly; English; independent; political and economic; Editor BEN MOLLOV; Publisher ISRAEL KELMAN; also publishes *Keeping Posted* (diplomatic magazine), *Mazel and Brucha* (jewellers' magazine); annuals: *Travel Agents' Manual, Electronics, International Conventions in Israel, Arkia, In Flight*, various hotel magazines.

Israel Environment Bulletin: Ministry of the Environment, POB 34033, 5 Kanfei Nesharim St, Jerusalem 95464; tel. 2-6553777; fax 2-6535937; internet www.environment.gov.il; f. 1973; Editor SHOSHANA GABBAY; circ. 3,500.

Israel Exploration Journal: POB 7041, 5 Avida St, Jerusalem 91070; tel. 2-6257991; fax 2-6247772; e-mail ies@vms.huji.ac.il; internet www.hum.huji.ac.il/ies; f. 1950; bi-annual; English; general and biblical archaeology, ancient history and historical geography of Israel and the Holy Land; Editors S. AHITUV, MIRIAM TADMOR; circ. 2,500.

Israel Export: POB 57500, 8 Twersky St, Tel-Aviv 61574; tel. and fax 3-5628512; f. 1993; annual; Editor NAOYA NAKAMURA.

Israel Export News: POB 50084, 29 Hamered St, Tel-Aviv 68125; tel. 3-5142830; fax 3-5142902; internet www.export.gov.il; f. 1949; bi-monthly; English; commercial and economic; published by Israel Export Institute; Dir of Media Dept DANI BLOCH.

Israel Journal of Chemistry: POB 34299, Jerusalem 91341; tel. 2-6522226; fax 2-6522277; e-mail laserpages@netmedia.net.il; internet www.sciencefromisrael.com; f. 1951; quarterly; published by Science from Israel; Editor Prof. H. LEVANON.

Israel Journal of Earth Sciences: POB 34299, Jerusalem 91341; tel. 2-6522226; fax 2-6522277; e-mail laserpages@netmedia.net.il; internet www.sciencefromisrael.com; f. 1951; quarterly; published by Science from Israel; Editors Prof. ALAN MATTHEWS, Dr AHUUA ALMOGI.

Israel Journal of Mathematics: POB 39099, Jerusalem 91390; tel. 2-6586660; fax 2-5633370; e-mail magnes@vms.huji.ac.il; internet www.ma.huji.ac.il/~ijmath; f. 1951; bi-monthly; published by Magnes Press; Editor Prof. S. MOZES.

Israel Journal of Medical Sciences: Jerusalem; tel. 2-5817727; fax 2-5815722; f. 1965; monthly; Editor-in-Chief Prof. MOSHE PRYWES; circ. 5,500.

Israel Journal of Plant Sciences: POB 34299, Jerusalem 91341; tel. 2-6522226; fax 2-6522277; e-mail laserpages@netmedia.net.il; internet www.sciencefromisrael.com; f. 1951 as *Israel Journal of Botany*; quarterly; published by Science from Israel; Editor Dr DANIEL JOEL.

Israel Journal of Psychiatry and Related Sciences: Gefen Publishing House Ltd, POB 36004, Jerusalem 91360; tel. 2-5380247; fax 2-5388423; e-mail info@gefenpublishing.com; internet www.israelbooks.com; f. 1963; quarterly; Editor-in-Chief Dr DAVID GREENBERG.

Israel Journal of Veterinary Medicine: POB 3076, Rishon Le-Zion 75130; tel. 9-7419929; fax 9-7431778; e-mail ivma@internet-zahav.net; internet www.isrvma.org; f. 1943; formerly *Refuah Veterinarith*; quarterly of the Israel Veterinary Medical Asscn; Editors Z. TRAININ, I. GLAS.

Israel Journal of Zoology: POB 34299, Jerusalem 91341; tel. 2-6522226; fax 2-6522277; e-mail laserpages@netmedia.net.il; internet www.sciencefromisrael.com; f. 1951; quarterly; published by Science from Israel; Editors Prof. ALAN DEGEN, Dr MICHA ILAN.

Israel Law Review: Israel Law Review Association, Faculty of Law, Hebrew University of Jerusalem, Mt Scopus, POB 24100, Jerusalem 91240; tel. 2-5882520; fax 2-5882565; e-mail msilr@mscc.huji.ac.il; internet unixware.mscc.huji.ac.il/~law1/ilr; f. 1966; 3 a year; published by the Israel Law Review Association.

Israel Press Service: POB 33188, Jerusalem 91330; tel. 2-5332825; fax 2-5334081; e-mail junes@netvision.net.il; internet www.israel-press-service.co.il; English; Zionist; Editor JUNE SPITZER.

Israel-South Africa Trade Journal: Tel-Aviv; f. 1973; bi-monthly; English; commercial and economic; published by Israel Publications Corpn Ltd; Man. Dir Z. PELTZ.

Israels Aussenhandel: Tel-Aviv; tel. 3-5280215; f. 1967; monthly; German; commercial; published by Israel Periodicals Co Ltd; Editor PELTZ NOEMI; Man. Dir ZALMAN PELTZ.

Al-Jadid (The New): POB 104, Haifa; f. 1951; literary monthly; Arabic; Editor SALEM JUBRAN; circ. 5,000.

Journal d'Analyse Mathématique: Magnes Press, Hebrew University of Jerusalem , POB 39099, Jerusalem 91390; tel. 2-6586656; fax 2-5633370; e-mail magnes@vms.huji.ac.il; internet www.ma.huji.ac.il/jdm; f. 1955; 2 vols per year; published by Hebrew University of Jerusalem Magnes Press; Editor Prof. L. ZALCMAN.

Leshonenu: Academy of the Hebrew Language, POB 3449, Jerusalem 91034; tel. 2-6493555; fax 2-5617065; e-mail acad2u@vms.huji.ac.il; internet www.hebrew-academy.huji.ac.il; f. 1929; 4 a year; for the study of the Hebrew language and cognate subjects; Editor M. BAR-ASHER.

Leshonenu La'am: Academy of the Hebrew Language, POB 3449, Jerusalem 91034; tel. 2-6493555; fax 2-5617065; e-mail acad2u@vms.huji.ac.il; internet www.hebrew-academy.huji.ac.il; f. 1945; 4 a year; popular Hebrew philology; Editors M. FLORENTIN, D. TALSHIR, Y. OFER.

Lilac: Nazareth; internet www.lilac-m.com; f. 2000; monthly; Arabic; Israel's first magazine for Arab women.

Ma'arachot (Campaigns): POB 7026, Hakirya, 3 Albert Mendler St, Tel-Aviv 61070; tel. 3-5694345; fax 3-5694343; f. 1939; military and political bi-monthly; Hebrew; periodical of Israel Defence Force; Editors HAGGAI GOLAN, EFI MELZER; circ. 20,000.

Magallati (My Magazine): POB 28049, Tel-Aviv; tel. 3-371438; f. 1960; bi-monthly children's magazine; circ. 3,000.

Melaha Vetaassiya (Trade and Industry): Tel-Aviv; f. 1969; bi-monthly review of the Union of Artisans and Small Manufacturers of Israel; Hebrew; Man. Dir Z. PELTZ; circ. 8,500.

M'Lakha V'ta Asiya (Israel Industry): POB 11587, 40 Rembrandt St, Tel-Aviv; monthly; published by Israel Publications Corporation Ltd; circ. 8,500.

Moznaim (Balance): POB 7098, Tel-Aviv; tel. 3-6953256; fax 3-6919681; f. 1929; monthly; Hebrew; literature and culture; Editors ASHER REICH, AZRIEL KAUFMAN; circ. 2,500.

Nekuda: Hebrew; organ of the Jewish settlers of the West Bank and Gaza Strip.

New Outlook: 9 Gordon St, Tel-Aviv 63458; tel. 3-5236496; fax 3-5232252; f. 1957; bi-monthly; Israeli and Middle Eastern Affairs; dedicated to the quest for Arab-Israeli peace; Editor-in-Chief CHAIM SHUR; Senior Editor DAN LEON; circ. 10,000.

News from Within: POB 31417, Jerusalem; tel. 2-6241159; fax 2-6253151; e-mail nfw@alt-info.org; internet www.alternativenews.org; monthly; joint Israeli-Palestinian publication; political, economic, social and cultural; publ. by the Alternative Information Centre.

OTOT: 10 Beit Shamai, Tel-Aviv; tel. 3-5615310; fax 3-5615281; e-mail raya@igud.org.il; f. 1975; monthly; Hebrew; advertising, marketing and communications; Editor Raya Rubin; circ. 4,000.

PC Plus: PC Media, POB 11438, 13 Yad Harutzim St, Tel-Aviv 61114; tel. 3-6385810; fax 3-6889207; e-mail editor@pc.co.il; internet www.pc.co.il; f. 1992; monthly; Hebrew; information on personal computers; Man. Dirs Dahlia Peled, Yehuda Elyada; Editor-in-Chief Yehuda Elyada; circ. 23,000.

Proche-Orient Chrétien: St Anne's Church, POB 19079, Jerusalem 91190; tel. 2-6281992; fax 2-6280764; e-mail mafrpoc@steanne.org; internet www.steanne.org/POC.html; f. 1951; quarterly on churches and religion in the Middle East; circ. 1,000.

Publish Israel: Tel-Aviv; tel. 3-5622744; fax 3-5621808; e-mail olamot@inter.net.il; f. 1998; six times a year; magazine for printers and publishers; Gen. Man. Dan Shekel; circ. 12,000.

The Sea: POB 33706, Hane'emanim 8, Haifa; tel. 4-529818; every six months; published by Israel Maritime League; review of marine problems; Pres. M. Pomrock; Chief Editor M. Litovski; circ. 5,000.

Shituf (Co-operation): POB 7151, 24 Ha'arba St, Tel-Aviv; f. 1948; bi-monthly; Hebrew; economic, social and co-operative problems in Israel; published by the Central Union of Industrial, Transport and Service Co-operative Societies; Editor L. Losh; circ. 12,000.

Shivuk (Marketing): POB 20027, Tel-Aviv 61200; tel. 3-5631010; fax 3-5612614; monthly; Hebrew; publ. by Federation of Israeli Chambers of Commerce; Editor Sara Lipkin.

Sinai: POB 642, Jerusalem 91006; tel. 2-6526231; fax 2-6526968; f. 1937; Hebrew; Torah science and literature; Editor Rabbi Yosef Movshovitz.

As-Sindibad: POB 28049, Tel-Aviv; tel. 3-371438; f. 1970; children's monthly; Arabic; Man. Joseph Eliahou; Editor Walid Hussein; circ. 8,000.

Terra Santa: POB 14038, Jaffa Gate, Jerusalem 91140; tel. 2-6272692; fax 2-6286417; e-mail cicts@netmedia.net.il; f. 1921; every two months; published by the Custody of the Holy Land (the official custodians of the Holy Shrines); Italian, Spanish, French, English and Arabic editions published in Jerusalem, by the Franciscan Printing Press, German edition in Munich, Maltese edition in Valletta.

WIZO Review: Women's International Zionist Organization, 38 Sderot David Hamelech Blvd, Tel-Aviv 64237; tel. 3-6923805; fax 3-6923801; e-mail wreview@wizo.org; internet www.wizo.org; f. 1947; English (quarterly) and Spanish (two a year); Editor Hillel Schenker; circ. 20,000.

World Fellowship of the Israel Medical Assen (Mif'al Haverut Hutz): POB 3604, 2 Twin Towers, 35 Jabotinsky St, Ramat Gan 52136; tel. 3-6100424; fax 3-5751616; e-mail estish@ima.org.il; internet www.ima.org.il/wf; quarterly; English.

The Youth Times: POB 54065, Jerusalem; tel. 2-2343428; fax 2-2343430; e-mail pyalara@pyalara.org; internet www.pyalara.org; f. 1998; monthly; Arabic and English; Editor-in-Chief Hania Bitar.

Zion: POB 4179, Jerusalem 91041; tel. 2-5650444; fax 2-6712388; e-mail shazar@shazar.org.il; f. 1935; quarterly; published by the Historical Society of Israel; Hebrew, with English summaries; research in Jewish history; Editors I. Etkes, Prof. A. Baumgarten, Y. Kaplan; circ. 1,000.

Zraim: POB 40027, 7 Dubnov St, Tel-Aviv; tel. 3-691745; fax 3-6953199; internet www.bneiakiva.org.il/about/zraim; f. 1953; Hebrew; journal of the Bnei Akiva (Youth of Tora Va-avoda) Movement; Editor Uri Auerbach.

Zrakor: Haifa; f. 1947; monthly; Hebrew; news digest, trade, finance, economics, shipping; Editor G. Alon.

PRESS ASSOCIATIONS

Daily Newspaper Publishers' Assen of Israel: POB 51202, 74 Petach Tikva Rd, Tel-Aviv 61200; fax 3-5617938; safeguards professional interests and maintains standards, supplies newsprint to dailies; negotiates with trade unions, etc.; mems all daily papers; affiliated to International Federation of Newspaper Publishers; Pres. Shabtai Himmelfarb; Gen. Sec. Betzalel Eyal.

Foreign Press Assen: Beit Sokolov, 4 Kaplan St, Tel-Aviv; tel. 3-6916143; fax 3-6961548; e-mail fpa@netvision.net.il; internet www.fpa.org.il; Chair. Dan Perry.

Israel Association of the Periodical Press (IAPP): 93 Arlozorof St, Tel-Aviv 62098; tel. 3-6921238; fax 3-6960155; e-mail lavied@arg.huji.ac.il; Chair. (vacant).

Israel Press Assen: Sokolov House, 4 Kaplan St, Tel-Aviv.

NEWS AGENCIES

ITIM (The Israeli News Agency): 10 Tiomkin St, Tel-Aviv; tel. 3-5601011; fax 3-5605190; e-mail noy@itim.co.il; internet www.itim.co.il; f. 1950; jointly owned by main Israeli newspapers, Ha'aretz, Hatzofeh, Jerusalem Post, Ma'ariv, and Yedioth Aharonoth; Editor-in-Chief Haim Noy.

Jerusalem Media and Communication Centre: POB 25047, 7 Nablus Rd, Sheikh Jarrah, Jerusalem; tel. 2-5819777; fax 2-5829543; internet www.jmcc.org; f. 1988 as the Palestine Press Service.

Jewish Telegraphic Agency (JTA): Mideast Bureau, Jerusalem Post Bldg, Romema, Jerusalem 91000; tel. 2-610579; fax 2-536635; internet www.jta.org; Correspondants Leslie Susser (Diplomatic Affairs), Gil Sedan (Arab Affairs).

Foreign Bureaux

Agence France-Presse: POB 1507, 206 Jaffa Rd, Jerusalem 91014; tel. 2-5373243; fax 2-5373873; e-mail afpjer@netvision.net.il; Correspondent Luc de Barochez.

Agencia EFE (Spain): POB 37190, 18 Hilel St, Jerusalem 91371; tel. 2-6242038; fax 2-6242056; e-mail postigocarmen@hotmail.com; Correspondent Carmen Postigo.

Agenzia Nazionale Stampa Associata (ANSA) (Italy): 30 Dizengoff St, Tel-Aviv 64332; 9 Lloyd George St, Jerusalem 93110; tel. 3-6299319; fax 3-5250302; e-mail ansnews@netvision.net.il; Bureau Chief Francesco Cerri; Correspondents Giorgio Raccah, Aldo Baquis.

Anadolu Ajansı (Turkey): Rehov Hanamal 4–1, Tel-Aviv; tel. 3-5460972; e-mail telaviv@anadoluajansi.com.tr.

Associated Press (AP) (USA): POB 34369, 206 Jaffa Rd, Jerusalem 91342; tel. 2-5385577; fax 2-5376083; Chief of Bureau Dan Perry.

Deutsche Presse-Agentur (dpa) (Germany): 30 Ibn Gvirol St, Tel-Aviv 64078; tel. 3-6959007; fax 3-6969594; e-mail dpatlv@trendline.co.il; Correspondents Dr Heinz-Rudolf Othmerding, Jeff Abramovitz.

Jiji Tsushin-Sha (Japan): 9 Schmuel Hanagld, Jerusalem 94592; tel. 2-232553; fax 2-232402; Correspondent Hirokazu Oikawa.

Kyodo News Service (Japan): Tel-Aviv; tel. 3-6958185; fax 3-6917478; Correspondent Hajime Ozaki.

Reuters (UK): 38 Hamasger St, Tel-Aviv 67211; tel. 3-5372211; fax 3-5372045; Jerusalem Capital Studios (JCS) 206 Jaffa Rd, Jerusalem 91131; tel. 2-5370502; fax 2-5374241; e-mail telaviv.newsroom@reuters.com; internet www.reuters.co.il; Chief of Bureau Matthew Tartevin.

United Press International (UPI) (USA): 138 Petach Tikva Rd, Tel-Aviv; Bureau Man. Brooke W. Kroeger; Bureau Man. in Jerusalem Louis Toscano.

Informatsionnoye Telegrafnoye Agentstvo Rossii—Telegrafnoye Agentstvo Suverennykh Stran (ITAR—TASS) (Russia) is also represented.

Publishers

Achiasaf Ltd: POB 8414, Netanya 42504; tel. 9-8851390; fax 9-8851391; e-mail info@achiasaf.co.il; internet www.achiasaf.co.il; f. 1933; general; Man. Dir Matan Achiasaf.

Am Oved Publishers Ltd: POB 470, 22 Mazeh St, Tel-Aviv 61003; tel. 3-6291526; fax 3-6298911; e-mail info@am-oved.co.il; internet www.am-oved.co.il; f. 1942; fiction, non-fiction, reference books, school and university textbooks, children's books, poetry, classics, science fiction; Man. Dir Yaron Sadan.

'Amihai' Publishing House Ltd: POB 8448, 19 Yad Harutzim St, Netanya Darom 42505; tel. 9-8859099; fax 9-8853464; e-mail oron@idc.ac.il; f. 1948; fiction, general science, linguistics, languages, arts; Dir Itzhak Oron.

Arabic Publishing House: 93 Arlozorof St, Tel-Aviv; tel. 3-6921674; f. 1960; established by the Histadrut; periodicals and books; Gen. Man. Gassan Muklashi.

Ariel Publishing House: POB 3328, Jerusalem 91033; tel. 2-6434540; fax 2-6436164; e-mail elysch@netvision.net.il; f. 1976; history, archaeology, religion, geography, folklore; CEO Ely Schiller.

Astrolog Publishing House: POB 11231, Hod Hasharon 45111; tel. 9-7412044; fax 9-7442714; e-mail sarabm@netvision.net.il; f. 1994; general non-fiction, religion, alternative medicine; Man. Dir Sara Ben-Mordechai.

A. Bitan Publishers: POB 22003, Tel-Aviv 61220; tel. 3-6136558; fax 3-6136588; f. 1965; aeronautics, biography, child development, fiction, educational, literature and literary criticism, mysteries, leisure, travel, women's studies, self-help books; Man. A. BITAN.

Carta, The Israel Map and Publishing Co Ltd: POB 2500, 18 Ha'uman St, Industrial Area, Talpiot, Jerusalem 91024; tel. 2-6783355; fax 2-6782373; e-mail cartaben@netvision.net.il; internet www.holyland-jerusalem.com; f. 1958; the principal cartographic publisher; Pres. and CEO SHAY HAUSMAN.

Dvir Publishing Co Ltd: POB 4020, 11 Lev Pesach St, North Industrial Area, Lod 71293; tel. 8-9246565; fax 8-9251770; e-mail info@zmora.co.il; f. 1924; literature, science, art, education; Publr OHAD ZMORA.

Rodney Franklin Agency: POB 37727, 53 Mazeh St, Tel-Aviv 65789; tel. 3-5600724; fax 3-5600479; e-mail rodneyf@netvision.net.il; internet www.rodneyagency.com; f. 1974; exclusive representative of various British, other European, US and Canadian publishers; e-marketing services for academic and professional journal publishers in 15 countries; Dir RODNEY FRANKLIN.

Gefen Publishing House Ltd: POB 36004, 6 Hatzvi St, Jerusalem 91360; tel. 2-5380247; fax 2-5388423; e-mail info@gefenpublishing.com; internet www.israelbooks.com; f. 1981; the largest publisher of English-language books; also publishes wide range of fiction and non-fiction; CEOs ILAN GREENFIELD, DROR GREENFIELD.

Globes Publishers: POB 18041, 127 Igal Alon St, Tel-Aviv 67443; tel. 3-6979797; fax 3-6910334; internet www.globes.co.il.

Gvanim: POB 11138, 29 Bar-Kochba St, Tel-Aviv 61111; tel. 3-5281044; fax 3-5283648; e-mail traklinm@zahav.net.il; f. 1992; poetry, belles lettres, fiction; Man. Dir MARITZA ROSMAN.

Hakibbutz Hameuchad Publishing House Ltd: POB 1432, Bnei Brak, Tel-Aviv 51114; tel. 3-5785810; fax 3-5785811; e-mail bruria@kibutz-poalim.co.il; f. 1940; general; Dir UZI SHAVIT.

Hanitzotz A-Sharara Publishing House: POB 41199, Jaffa 61411; tel. 3-6839145; fax 3-6839148; e-mail oda@netvision.net.il; internet www.hanitzotz.com; 'progressive' booklets and publications in Arabic, Hebrew and English.

Hed Arzi (Ma'ariv) Publishing Ltd: 3A Yoni Netanyahu St, Or-Yehuda, Tel-Aviv 60376; tel. 3-5383333; fax 3-6343205; e-mail shimoni@hed-arzi.co.il; f. 1954 as Sifriat-Ma'ariv Ltd; later known as Ma'ariv Book Guild Ltd; general; Man. Dir ELI SHIMONI.

Hod-Ami—Computer Books Ltd: POB 6108, Herzliya 46160; tel. 9-9564716; fax 9-9571582; e-mail info@hod-ami.co.il; internet www.hod-ami.co.il; f. 1984; information technology, management; CEO ITZHAK AMIHUD.

Intermedia Publishing Enterprises Ltd (IPE): POB 2121, 23 Hataas St, Kefar-Sava 44641; tel. 9-5608501; fax 9-5608513; e-mail freed@inter.net.il; f. 1993; business, education, English as a second language, journalism, health, nutrition, mathematics, medicine, philosophy, self-help; Man. Dir ARIE FRIED.

Israeli Music Publications Ltd: POB 7681, Jerusalem 94188; tel. 2-6251370; fax 2-6241378; e-mail khanukaev@pop.isracom.net.il; f. 1949; books on music, dance and musical works; Dir of Music Publications SERGEI KHANUKAEV.

Jerusalem Center for Public Affairs: 13 Tel Hai St, Jerusalem 92107; tel. 2-5619281; fax 2-5619112; e-mail jcenter@jcpa.org; internet www.jcpa.org; f. 1976; Jewish political tradition; publishes the Jewish Political Studies Review.

The Jerusalem Publishing House Ltd: POB 7147, 39 Tchernechovski St, Jerusalem 91071; tel. 2-5636511; fax 2-5634266; e-mail jphgagi@netvision.net.il; f. 1967; biblical research, history, encyclopedias, archaeology, arts of the Holy Land, cookbooks, guidebooks, economics, politics; Dir SHLOMO S. GAFNI; Man. Editor RACHEL GILON.

The Jewish Agency—Department of Jewish Zionist Education: POB 10615, Jerusalem 91104; tel. 2-6202629; fax 2-6204122; e-mail bookshop@jazo.org.il; f. 1945; education, Jewish philosophy, studies in the Bible, children's books published in Hebrew, English, French, Spanish, German, Swedish and Portuguese, Hebrew teaching material.

Jewish History Publications (Israel 1961) Ltd: POB 1232, 29 Jabotinsky St, Jerusalem 92141; tel. 2-5632310; f. 1961; encyclopedias, World History of the Jewish People series; Chair. ALEXANDER PELI.

Karni Publishers Ltd: POB 4020, 11 Lev Pesach St, North Industrial Area, Lod 71293; tel. 8-9246565; fax 8-9251770; e-mail info@zmora.co.il; f. 1951; biography, fiction, poetry, children's and educational books; Publr OHAD ZMORA.

Keter Publishing House Ltd: POB 7145, Givat Shaul B, Jerusalem 91071; tel. 2-6557822; fax 2-6536811; e-mail info@keter-books.co.il; internet www.keter-books.co.il; f. 1959; original and translated works of fiction, encyclopedias, non-fiction, guidebooks and children's books; publishing imprints: Israel Program for Scientific Translations, Keter Books, Domino, Shikmona, Encyclopedia Judaica; Man. Dir YIPHTACH DEKEL.

Kinneret–ZBU–DVIR Publishing House: 10 Hataasiya St, Or-Yehuda 60212; tel. 3-6344977; fax 3-6340953; e-mail tami@kinneret-zmora.co.il; f. 1980; child development and care, cookery, dance, educational, humour, non-fiction, music, home-care, psychology, psychiatry, travel; Man. Dir YORAM ROS.

Kiryat Sefer: Tel-Aviv 65812; tel. 3-5660188; fax 3-5100227; f. 1933; concordances, dictionaries, textbooks, maps, scientific books; Dir AVRAHAM SIVAN.

LB Publishing Co: POB 32056, Jerusalem 91000; tel. and fax 2-5664637; f. 1993; history, regional issues, religion; Pres. LILI BREZINER.

Magnes Press: The Hebrew University, POB 39099, Jerusalem 91390; tel. 2-6586656; fax 2-5633370; e-mail magnes@vms.huji.ac.il; f. 1929; biblical studies, Judaica, and all academic fields; Dir DAN BENOVICI.

MAP-Mapping and Publishing Ltd (Tel-Aviv Books): POB 56024, 17 Tchernikhovski St, Tel-Aviv 61560; tel. 3-6210500; fax 3-5257725; e-mail info@mapa.co.il; internet www.mapa.co.il; f. 1985; maps, atlases, travel guides, textbooks and reference books; Man. Dir DANI TRACZ; Editor-in-Chief MOULI MELTZER.

Rubin Mass Ltd: POB 990, 7 Ha-Ayin-Het St, Jerusalem 91009; tel. 2-6277863; fax 2-6277864; e-mail rmass@barak.net.il; internet www.rubin-mass.com; f. 1927; Hebraica, Judaica, export of all Israeli books and periodicals; Dir OREN MASS.

Ministry of Defence Publishing House: 107 Ha' Hashmonaim St, Tel-Aviv 67133; tel. 3-5655900; fax 3-5655994; e-mail publish@attmail.com; internet www.modpublishing.co.il; f. 1939; military literature, Judaism, history and geography of Israel; Dir JOSEPH PERLOVITZ.

M. Mizrachi Publishing House Ltd: 67 Levinsky St, Tel-Aviv 66855; tel. 3-6870936; fax 3-6888185; e-mail mizrahi.co@jmail.com; f. 1960; children's books, fiction, history, medicine, science; Dirs MEIR MIZRACHI, ISRAEL MIZRACHI.

Mosad Harav Kook: POB 642, 1 Maimon St, Jerusalem 91006; tel. 2-6526231; fax 2-6526968; f. 1937; editions of classical works, Torah and Jewish studies; Dir Rabbi YOSEF MOVSHOVITZ.

Otsar Hamoreh: c/o Israel Teachers' Union, 8 Ben Saruk, Tel-Aviv 62969; tel. 3-6922983; fax 3-6922988; f. 1951; educational; Man. Dir JOSEPH SALOMAN.

PC Media: POB 11438, 13 Yad Harutzim St, Tel-Aviv 61114; tel. 3-6385810; fax 3-6889207; e-mail pcmedia@pc.co.il; internet www.zdnet.co.il; information technology; Man. Dir DAHLIA PELED.

Alexander Peli Jerusalem Publishing Co Ltd: POB 1232, 29 Jabotinsky St, Jerusalem 92141; tel. 2-5632310; f. 1961; encyclopedias such as the Standard Jewish Encyclopedia, history, the arts, educational material; Chair. ALEXANDER PELI.

Schocken Publishing House Ltd: POB 2316, 24 Nathan Yelin Mor St, Tel-Aviv 67015; tel. 3-5610130; fax 3-5622668; e-mail lind@schocken.co.il; f. 1938; general; Dir Mrs RACHELI EDELMAN.

Science from Israel: POB 34299, Merkaz Sapir 6/36, Givat Shaul, Jerusalem 91341; tel. 2-6522226; fax 2-6522277; e-mail laserpages@netmedia.net.il; internet www.sciencefromisrael.com; fmrly Laser Pages Publishing Ltd; a division of LPP Ltd; scientific journals.

Shalem Press: POB 8787, 13 Yehoshua Bin-Nun St, Jerusalem 93102; tel. 2-5605555; fax 2-5605565; e-mail shalempress@shalem.org.il; internet www.shalem.org.il; f. 1994; economics, political science, history, philosophy, cultural issues.

Shikmona Publishing Co Ltd: POB 7145, Givat Shaul B, Jerusalem 91071; tel. 2-6557822; fax 2-6536811; e-mail info@keter-books.co.il; internet www.keter-books.co.il; f. 1965; Zionism, archaeology, art, guidebooks, fiction and non-fiction; Man. Dir YIPHTACH DEKEL.

Sifriat Poalim: POB 1432, Bnei Brak, Tel-Aviv 51114; tel. 3-5785810; fax 3-5785811; e-mail avram@kibutz-poalim.co.il; internet www.kibutz-poalim.co.il; f. 1939; general literature; Gen. Man. AVRAM KANTOR.

Sinai Publishing: 72 Allenby St, Tel-Aviv 65812; tel. 3-5163672; fax 3-5176783; f. 1853; Hebrew books and religious articles; Dir MOSHE SCHLESINGER.

Steinhart-Katzir: POB 8333, Netanya 42505; tel. 9-8854770; fax 9-8854771; e-mail haolam@haolam.co.il; internet www.haolam.co.il; f. 1991; travel; Man. Dir OHAD SHARAV.

Tcehrikover Publishers Ltd: 12 Hasharon St, Tel-Aviv 66185; tel. 3-6870621; fax 3-6874729; e-mail barkay@inter.net.il; internet www.tcherikover.co.il; education, psychology, economics, psychiatry, literature, literary criticism, essays, history geography, criminology, art, languages, management; Man. Editor S. TCHERIKOVER.

Yachdav United Publishers Co Ltd: POB 20123, 29 Carlebach St, Tel-Aviv 67132; tel. 3-5614121; fax 3-5611996; e-mail info@tbpai .co.il; f. 1960; educational; Chair. EPHRAIM BEN-DOR; Exec. Dir AMNON BEN-SHMUEL.

Yavneh Publishing House Ltd: 4 Mazeh St, Tel-Aviv 65213; tel. 3-6297856; fax 3-6293638; e-mail publishing@yavneh.co.il; internet www.dbook.co.il; f. 1932; general; Man. Dir ELIAV COHEN.

Yeda Lakol Publications Ltd: POB 1232, 29 Jabotinsky St, Jerusalem 92141; tel. 2-5632310; f. 1961; encyclopedias, Judaica, the arts, educational material, children's books; Chair. ALEXANDER PELI.

Yedioth Ahronoth Books: POB 53494, 3 Mikunis St, Tel-Aviv 61534; tel. 3-7683333; fax 3-7683300; e-mail info@ybook.co.il; f. 1952; non-fiction, politics, Jewish religion, health, music, dance, fiction, education; Man. Dir DOV EICHENWALD; Editor-in-Chief ALIZA ZIGLER.

S. Zack and Co: 31 Beit Hadfus St, Jerusalem 95483; tel. 2-6537760; fax 2-6514005; e-mail zackpublishers@bezeqint.net; internet ; www.zack.co.il; f. 1930; fiction, science, philosophy, Judaism, children's books, educational and reference books, dictionaries; Dir MICHAEL ZACK.

PUBLISHERS' ASSOCIATION

The Book Publishers' Association of Israel: POB 20123, 29 Carlebach St, Tel-Aviv 67132; tel. 3-5614121; fax 3-5611996; e-mail info@tbpai.co.il; internet www.tbpai.co.il; f. 1939; mems: 84 publishing firms; Chair. SHAI HAUSMAN; Man. Dir AMNON BEN-SHMUEL.

Broadcasting and Communications

TELECOMMUNICATIONS

Barak I.T.C.: Cibel Industrial Park, 15 Hamelacha St, Rosh Ha'ayin 48091; tel. 3-9001900; fax 3-9001800; e-mail service@ 013barak.net.il; internet www.barak-online.net; f. 1997; Chair. MAIR LAISER; Pres. and CEO AVI PATIR.

Bezeq—The Israel Telecommunication Corpn Ltd: POB 1088, 15 Hazvi St, Jerusalem 91010; tel. 2-5395503; fax 2-5000410; e-mail bzqspk@bezeq.com; internet www.bezeq.co.il; f. 1984; 46.4% state-owned; scheduled for full privatization; launched own cellular network, Pelephone Communications Ltd, in 1986; total assets US $3,674m. (July 2004); Chair. MIRIAM MAZAR; CEO AMNON DICK.

Pelephone Communications Ltd: 33 Hagvura St, Givatayim, Tel-Aviv 53483; tel. 3-5728881; fax 3-5728111; internet www .pelephone.co.il; f. 1986; Chair. BENNY VAKNIN; CEO YAKOV GELBARD.

Cellcom Israel: POB 3164, 3 Hagalim Blvd, Herzliya Pituach, Herzlia B, Netanya 46131; tel. 9-9599599; fax 9-9599700; internet www.cellcom.co.il; f. 1994; mobile telecommunications operator; Chair. S. PIOTRKOWSKY; Pres. and CEO ITZHAK PETERBURG.

ECI Telecom Ltd: POB 3038, 30 Hasivim St, Petach Tikva, Tel-Aviv 49133; tel. 3-9266555; fax 3-9266500; internet www.ecitele .com; Pres. and CEO DORAN INBAR; Chair. SHLOMO DOVRAT.

Partner Communications Co Ltd: POB 435, Rosh Ha'ayin, Tel-Aviv 48103; tel. 3-9054888; fax 3-9054999; internet www.partner.co .il; mobile telecommunications operator; f. 1999; CEO AMIKAM COHEN; Man. Dir E. COHEN.

Vocal Tec: 2 Maskit St, Herzliya 46733; tel. 9-9707777; fax 9-9561867; e-mail info@vocaltec.com; internet www.vocaltec.com; carrier services and telecommunications infrastructure; total assets US$ 51.6m. (Dec. 2001); Chair. and CEO Dr ELON A. GANOR.

BROADCASTING

In 1986 the Government approved the establishment of a commercial radio and television network to be run in competition with the state system.

Radio

Israel Broadcasting Authority (IBA) (Radio): POB 1082, 21 Heleni HaMalka, Jerusalem; tel. 2-5302222; e-mail dover@iba.org.il; internet www.iba.org.il; f. 1948; state-owned station in Jerusalem with additional studios in Tel-Aviv and Haifa. IBA broadcasts six programmes for local and overseas listeners on medium, shortwave and VHF/FM in 16 languages: Hebrew, Arabic, English, Yiddish, Ladino, Romanian, Hungarian, Moghrabi, Persian, French, Russian, Bucharian, Georgian, Portuguese, Spanish and Amharic; Chair. MICHA YINON; Dir-Gen. (vacant); Dir of Radio (vacant); Dir External Services VICTOR GRAJEWSKY.

Galei Zahal: MPOB 01005, Zahal; tel. 3-5126666; fax 3-5126760; e-mail galatz@glz.co.il; internet www.glz.co.il; f. 1950; Israeli

Defence Force broadcasting station, Tel-Aviv, with studios in Jerusalem; broadcasts news, current affairs, music and cultural programmes on medium-wave and FM stereo, 24-hour in Hebrew; Dir ISACK TUNIK.

Kol Israel (The Voice of Israel): POB 1082, 21 Heleni Hamalka, Jerusalem 91010; tel. 2-6248715; fax 2-5383173; internet kolisrael .iba.org.il; broadcasts music, news, and multilingual programmes for immigrants in Hebrew, Arabic, French and English on medium wave and FM stereo; Dir and Prog. Dir AMNON NADAV.

Television

Israel Broadcasting Authority (IBA) (Television): 161 Jaffa Rd, Jerusalem; tel. 2-5301333; fax 2-292944; internet www.iba.org.il; broadcasts began in 1968; station in Jerusalem with additional studios in Tel-Aviv; one colour network (VHF with UHF available in all areas); one satellite channel; broadcasts in Hebrew, Arabic and English; Dir-Gen URI PORAT; Dir of Television YAIR STERN; Dir of Engineering RAFI YEOSHUA.

The Council of Cable TV and Satellite Broadcasting: 23 Jaffa Rd, Jerusalem 91999; tel. 2-6702210; fax 2-6702273; e-mail inbard@ moc.gov.il; Chair. DORIT INBAR.

Israel Educational Television: Ministry of Education, 14 Klausner St, Tel-Aviv; tel. 3-6415270; fax 3-6427091; f. 1966 by Hanadiv (Rothschild Memorial Group) as Instructional Television Trust; began transmission in 1966; school programmes form an integral part of the syllabus in a wide range of subjects; also adult education; Gen. Man. AHUVA FAINMESSE; Dir of Engineering S. KASIF.

Second Channel TV and Radio Administration: 3 Kanfi Nesharim St, POB 34112, Jerusalem 95464; tel. 2-6556222; fax 2-6556287; e-mail channel2@netvision.net.il; internet www.channel2 .co.il; f. 1991; Chair. Prof. GIDEON DORON; Man. Dir NACHMAN SHAI.

Finance

(cap. = capital; dep. = deposits; m. = million; res = reserves;
brs = branches; amounts in shekels)

BANKING

During 1991–98 the Government raised some US $3,995m. through privatization and the issuance of shares and convertible securities in the banking sector.

Central Bank

Bank of Israel: POB 780, Bank of Israel Bldg, Kiryat Ben-Gurion, Jerusalem 91007; tel. 2-6552211; fax 2-6528805; e-mail webmaster@ bankisrael.gov.il; internet www.bankisrael.gov.il; f. 1954 as the Central Bank of the State of Israel; cap. 60m., res –12,795m., dep. 106,647m. (Dec. 2003); Gov. Prof. STANLEY FISCHER; 1 br.

Principal Israeli Banks

Arab-Israel Bank Ltd: POB 207, 48 Bar Yehuda St, Tel Hanan, Nesher 20300; tel. 4-8205201; fax 4-8205233; e-mail aravi@bll.co.il; internet www.bank-aravi-israeli.co.il; total assets 3,023m., dep. 2,660m. (Dec. 2003); subsidiary of Bank Leumi le-Israel BM; Chair. O. HASSON; Gen. Man. B. OSSI.

Bank Hapoalim: 50 Rothschild Blvd, Tel-Aviv 66883; tel. 3-5673333; fax 3-5607028; e-mail international@bnhp.co.il; internet www.bankhapoalim.co.il; f. 1921 as the Workers' Bank, name changed as above 1961; mergers into the above: American-Israel Bank in 1999, Maritime Bank of Israel in 2003, Mishkan-Hapoalim Mortgage Bank and Israel Continental Bank in 2004; privatized in June 2000; total assets 258,855m., dep. 216,778m. (Dec. 2003); Pres. and CEO Z. ZIV; Chair. SHLOMO NEHAMA; 325 brs in Israel and 8 brs abroad.

Bank of Jerusalem Ltd: POB 2255, 2 Herbert Samuel St, Jerusalem 91022; tel. 2-6706211; fax 2-6246793; e-mail webmaster@ bankjerusalem.co.il; internet www.bankjerusalem.co.il; private bank; cap. 128m., res 86m., dep. 5,856m. (Dec. 2002); Chair. DAVID BLUMBERG; Man. Dir and Gen. Man. DAVID BARUCH; 16 brs.

Bank Leumi le-Israel BM: 24–32 Yehuda Halevi St, Tel-Aviv 65546; tel. 3-5148111; fax 3-5661872; e-mail pniot@bll.co.il; internet www.bankleumi.co.il; f. 1902 as Anglo-Palestine Co; renamed Anglo-Palestine Bank 1930; reincorporated as above 1951; 41.73% state-owned; total assets 246,585m., dep. 211,046m. (Dec. 2003); Chair. EITAN RAFF; Pres. and CEO GALIA MAOR; 229 brs in Israel and abroad.

Euro-Trade Bank Ltd: 2 Yavne St, Tel-Aviv/Jaffa 65791; tel. 3-6216806; fax 3-6209062; e-mail info@eurotrade.co.il; internet www .eurotrade.co.il; f. 1953; renamed Israel Building Bank Ltd 1978; name changed as above 1993; total assets 328.2m., dep. 255.4m. (Dec. 2002); Chair. of Bd AMIT BIEL; Man. Dir ISAAC SHVILI.

First International Bank of Israel Ltd: Shalom Mayer Tower, 9 Ahad Ha'am St, Tel-Aviv 62251; tel. 3-5196111; fax 3-5100316; e-mail yuvall@fibimail.co.il; internet www.fibi.co.il; f. 1972 by merger between Foreign Trade Bank Ltd and Export Bank Ltd; total assets 64,585m., dep. 56,961m. (Dec. 2003); Chair. Dr JOSHUA ROSENSWEIG; CEO DAVID GRANOT; 91 brs in Israel and abroad.

Industrial Development Bank of Israel Ltd: POB 33580, 82 Menachem Begin Rd, Tel-Aviv 67138; tel. 3-6972727; fax 3-6272700; internet www.idbi.co.il; f. 1957; 65% state-owned; total assets 12,510m., dep. 11,694.1m. (Dec. 2002); Chair. RA'ANAN COHEN; Gen. Man. URI GALILI.

Investec Bank (Israel) Ltd: POB 677, 38 Rothschild Blvd, Tel-Aviv 61006; tel. 3-5645645; fax 3-5645210; e-mail irroni@igb.co.il; internet www.investec.co.il; f. 1934 as Palestine Credit Utility Bank Ltd, renamed Israel General Bank Ltd 1964; ownership transferred to Investec Bank Ltd (South Africa) in 1996; name changed to Investec Clali Bank Ltd 1999, and as above 2001; total assets 6,307.4m., dep. 5,538.1m. (Dec. 2003); Chair. HUGH SYDNEY HERMAN; Man. Dir and CEO JONATHON IRRONI; 3 brs.

Israel Continental Bank Ltd: POB 37406, 65 Rothschild Blvd, Tel-Aviv 61373; tel. 3-5641616; fax 3-6200399; f. 1973; capital held jointly by Bank Hapoalim BM (63.3%) and SEB AG, Frankfurt am Main (36.7%); total assets 1,982.8m., dep. 1,671.7m. (Dec. 2001); Chair. L. AMIJ; Man. Dir S. WEIZMAN; 3 brs.

Israel Discount Bank Ltd: 27 Yehuda Halevi St, Tel-Aviv 65136; tel. 3-5145555; fax 3-5146954; e-mail contact@discountbank.net; internet www.discountbank.net; f. 1935; 57.9% state-owned; cap. 98m. (June 2003), dep. 125,192m. (Dec. 2003); Chair. ARIE MIENTKAVICH; Pres. and CEO GIORA OFFER; 125 brs in Israel and abroad.

Mercantile Discount Bank Ltd: POB 1292, 103 Allenby Rd, Tel-Aviv 61012; tel. 3-7105550; fax 3-7105532; e-mail fec@mdb.co.il; internet www.mercantile.co.il; f. 1971 as Barclays Discount Bank Ltd; by Barclays Bank International Ltd and Israel Discount Bank Ltd to incorporate Israel brs of Barclays; Israel Discount Bank Ltd became the sole owner in February 1993; name changed as above April 1993; absorbed Mercantile Bank of Israel Ltd in 1997; cap. 50.7m., res 142.5m., dep. 13,466.1m. (Dec. 2003); Chair. ARIE MIENTKAVICH; Gen. Man. Prof. SHALOM JOSEF HOCHMAN; 63 brs.

Union Bank of Israel Ltd: 6–8 Ahuzat Bayit St, Tel-Aviv 65143; tel. 3-5191111; fax 3-5191274; internet www.unionbank.co.il; f. 1951; 18.4% state-owned; total assets 20,335m., dep. 17,482m. (Dec. 2003); Chair. Z. ABELES; CEO and Gen. Man. D. KOTLER; 26 brs in Israel and abroad.

United Mizrahi Bank Ltd: POB 3450, 7 Jabotinsky St, Ramat Gan 52136; tel. 3-7559468; fax 3-7559940; e-mail info@mizrahi.co.il; internet www.mizrahi.co.il; f. 1923 as Mizrahi Bank Ltd; mergers into the above: Hapoel Hamizrahi Bank Ltd and current name adopted in 1969, Finance and Trade Bank Ltd in 1990, Tefahot (Israel Mortgage Bank) in 2004; cap. 3,875m., dep. 72,937m. (Dec. 2003); CEO ELI YUNES; 91 brs.

Mortgage Banks

Discount Mortgage Bank Ltd: POB 2844, 16–18 Simtat Beit Hashoeva, Tel-Aviv 61027; tel. 3-5643311; fax 3-5661704; f. 1959; subsidiary of Israel Discount Bank Ltd; total assets 8,100m. (Sept. 2000); Chair. ARIE MIENTKAVICH; Man. M. ELDAR.

First International Mortgage Bank Ltd: 39 Montefiore St, Tel-Aviv 65201; tel. 3-5643311; fax 3-5643321; internet www.fibi-mashkanta.co.il; f. 1922 as the Mortgage and Savings Bank, name changed as above 1996; subsidiary of First International Bank of Israel Ltd; cap. and res 334m. (Dec. 1996); Chair. SHLOMO PIOTRKOWSKY; Man. Dir P. HAMO; 50 brs.

Leumi Mortgage Bank Ltd: POB 69, 31–37 Montefiore St, Tel-Aviv 65201; tel. 3-5648444; fax 3-5648334; f. 1921 as General Mortgage Bank Ltd; subsidiary of Bank Leumi le-Israel BM; total assets 26,155m., dep. 23,830m. (Dec. 2000); Chair. A. ZELDMAN; Gen. Man. R. ZABAG; 9 brs.

Tefahot, Israel Mortgage Bank Ltd: POB 93, 9 Heleni Hamalka St, Jerusalem 91902; tel. 2-6755222; fax 2-6755344; internet www.tefahot.co.il; f. 1945; subsidiary of United Mizrahi Bank Ltd; total assets 32,514m., cap. and res 1,974m. (Dec. 2002); Chair. REUVEN ADLER; Man. Dir CHAIM FREILICHMAN; 45 brs.

STOCK EXCHANGE

The Tel-Aviv Stock Exchange: 54 Ahad Ha'am St, Tel-Aviv 65202; tel. 3-5677411; fax 3-5105379; e-mail spokesperson@tase.co.il; internet www.tase.co.il; f. 1953; Chair. Prof. YAIR E. ORGLER; Gen. Man. SAUL BRONFELD.

INSURANCE

The Israel Insurance Asscn lists 15 member companies; a selection of these are listed below, as are some non-members.

Ararat Insurance Co Ltd: Ararat House, 13 Montefiore St, Tel-Aviv 65164; tel. 3-640888; f. 1949; became subsidiary of Clal Insurance Enterprise Holdings Ltd in 2000; Co-Chair. AHARON DOVRAT, PHILIP ZUCKERMAN; Gen. Man. PINCHAS COHEN.

Aryeh Insurance Co of Israel Ltd: 9 Ahad Ha'am St, Tel-Aviv 65251; tel. 3-5141777; fax 3-5179339; e-mail rubens@aryeh-ins.co.il; f. 1948; subsidiary of Clal Insurance Enterprise Holdings; Pres. RUBEN SHARONI.

Clal Insurance Co Ltd: POB 326, 46 Petach Tikva Rd, Tel-Aviv 66184; tel. 3-6387777; fax 3-6387676; e-mail avigdork@clal-ins.co.il; internet www.clalbit.co.il; f. 1962; subsidiary of Clal Insurance Enterprises Holdings Ltd; Pres. and CEO AVIGDOR KAPLAN; Man. Dir ELIAHU COHEN.

Eliahu Insurance Co Ltd: 2 Ibn Gvirol St, Tel-Aviv 64077; tel. 3-6920911; fax 3-6956995; e-mail ofer@eliahu.com; Chair. OFER ELIAHU.

Harel Insurance Investments Ltd: internet www.harel-hamishmar.co.il; f. 1935 as Hamishmar Insurance Service; Harel established 1975, became Harel Hamishmar Investment Ltd 1982, current name adopted 1998; Chair. GIDEON HAMBURGER.

Hassneh Insurance Co of Israel Ltd: POB 805, 115 Allenby St, Tel-Aviv 61007; tel. 3-5649111; f. 1924; Man. Dir M. MICHAEL MILLER.

Israel Phoenix Assurance Co Ltd: 30 Levontin St, Tel-Aviv 61020; tel. 3-7141111; fax 3-5666902; e-mail vardab@phoenix.co.il; internet www.phoenix.co.il; f. 1949; CEO BAR-KOCHVA BEN-GERA; Chair. of Bd JOSEPH D. HACKMEY.

Menorah Insurance Co Ltd: Menorah House, 15 Allenby St, Tel-Aviv 65786; tel. 3-7107777; fax 3-7107402; e-mail anat-by@bezeqint.net; f. 1935; Chair. MENACHEM GUREWITZ; Gen. Man. SHABTAI ENGEL.

Migdal Insurance Co Ltd: POB 37633, 26 Sa'adiya Ga'on St, Tel-Aviv 67135; tel. 3-5637637; fax 3-5610220; e-mail sarav@migdal-group.co.il; internet www.migdal.co.il; part of Bank Leumi Group; f. 1934; Chair. AHARON FOGEL; CEO IZZY COHEN.

Samson Insurance Co Ltd: POB 33678, Avgad Bldg, 5 Jabotinsky St, Ramat-Gan, Tel-Aviv 52520; tel. 3-7521616; fax 3-7516644; f. 1933; Chair. E. BEN-AMRAM; Gen. Man. GIORA SAGI.

Sela Insurance Co Ltd: Tel-Aviv; tel. 3-61028; f. 1938; became subsidiary of Migdal in 2000; Man. Dir E. SHANI.

Shiloah Insurance Co Ltd: 3 Abba-Hillel St, Ramat-Gan, Tel-Aviv 52118; tel. 3-7547777; fax 3-7545100; e-mail y_hamburger@harel-hamishmar.co.il; f. 1933; became subsidiary of Harel Insurance Investments Ltd in 2000; Chair. YAIR HAMBURGER; Gen. Man. Dr S. BAMIRAH.

Trade and Industry

CHAMBERS OF COMMERCE

Federation of Bi-National Chambers of Commerce and Industry with and in Israel: POB 50196, 29 Hamered St, Tel-Aviv 61500; tel. 3-5177737; fax 3-5177738; e-mail info@bncc.org; internet www.bncc.org; Chair. G. PROPPER.

Federation of Israeli Chambers of Commerce: POB 20027, 84 Ha'Hashmonaim St, Tel-Aviv 67011; tel. 3-5631010; fax 3-5619025; e-mail chamber@tlv-chamber.org.il; internet www.tlv-chamber.org.il; co-ordinates the Tel-Aviv, Jerusalem, Haifa and Beersheba Chambers of Commerce; Pres. URIEL LYNN.

Chamber of Commerce and Industry of Haifa and the North: POB 33176, 53 Haatzmaut Rd, Haifa 31331; tel. 4-8626364; fax 4-8645428; e-mail main@haifachamber.org.il; internet www.haifachamber.com; f. 1921; 550 mems; Pres. O. FELLER; Man. Dir D. MAROM.

Israel-British Chamber of Commerce: POB 50321, 29 Hamered St, Tel-Aviv 61502; tel. 3-5109424; fax 3-5109540; e-mail isbrit@ibcc.co.il; internet www.ibcc.co.il; f. 1951; 350 mems; Chair. AMNON DOTAN; Exec. Dir FELIX KIPPER.

Jerusalem Chamber of Commerce: POB 2083, Jerusalem 91020; tel. 2-6254333; fax 2-6254335; e-mail jerccom@inter.net.il; internet www.jerccom.co.il; f. 1908; c. 300 mems; Pres. SHMULIK SEMMEL.

Tel-Aviv Chamber of Commerce: POB 20027, 84 Ha'Hashmonaim St, Tel-Aviv 61200; tel. 3-5631010; fax 3-5619025; e-mail chamber@chamber.org.il; internet www.chamber.org.il; f. 1919; 2,500 mems; Pres. URIEL LYNN.

INDUSTRIAL AND TRADE ASSOCIATIONS

Agricultural Export Co (AGREXCO): POB 2061, 121 Ha'Hashmonaim St, Tel-Aviv 61206; tel. 3-5630900; fax 3-5630814; e-mail info@agrexco.com; internet www.agrexco.co.il; state-owned agricultural marketing organization; CEO SHLOMO TIROSH.

The Agricultural Union: Tel-Aviv; consists of more than 50 agricultural settlements and is connected with marketing and supplying organizations, and Bahan Ltd, controllers and auditors.

The Centre for International Agricultural Development Cooperation (CINADCO): POB 30, Beit Dagan 50200; tel. 3-9485760; fax 3-9485761; e-mail cinadco@moag.gov.il; internet www.cinadco.moag.gov.il; shares agricultural experience through the integration of research and project development; runs specialized training courses, advisory missions and feasibility projects in Israel and abroad; co-ordinates advisory missions and feasibility projects in co-operation with developing countries; Dir ZVI HERMAN.

Citrus Marketing Board: POB 54, Beit Dagan 50280; tel. 3-9683811; fax 3-9683838; e-mail info@jaffa.co.il; internet www.jaffa.co.il; f. 1941; the central co-ordinating body of citrus growers and exporters in Israel; represents the citrus industry in international organizations; licenses private exporters; controls the quality of fruit; has responsibility for Jaffa trademarks; mounts advertising and promotion campaigns for Jaffa citrus fruit worldwide; carries out research and development of new varieties of citrus fruit, and 'environmentally friendly' fruit; Chair. D. KRITCHMAN; Gen. Man. M. DAVIDSON.

Farmers' Union of Israel: POB 209, 8 Kaplan St, Tel-Aviv; tel. 3-69502227; fax 3-6918228; f. 1913; membership of 7,000 independent farmers, citrus and winegrape growers; Pres. PESACH GRUPPER; Dir-Gen. SHLOMO REISMAN.

Fruit Board of Israel: POB 20117, 119 Rehov Ha'Hashmonaim, Tel-Aviv 61200; tel. 3-5632929; fax 3-5614672; e-mail fruits@fruit.org.il; internet www.fruit.org.il; Dir-Gen. DANY BRUNER.

General Asscn of Merchants in Israel: Tel-Aviv; the organization of retail traders; has a membership of 30,000 in 60 brs.

Israel Cotton Production and Marketing Board Ltd: POB 384, Herzlia B 46103; tel. 9-9509493; fax 9-9509159; e-mail mali@cotton.co.il.

Israel Diamond Exchange Ltd: POB 3222, Ramat-Gan, Tel-Aviv; tel. 3-5760211; fax 3-5750652; e-mail judi@isde.co.il; f. 1937; production, export, import and finance facilities; exports: polished diamonds US $6,333m., rough diamonds US $2,920m. (2004); Pres. SHMUEL SCHNITZER.

Israel Export Institute: POB 50084, 29 Hamered St, Tel-Aviv 68125; tel. 3-5142830; fax 3-5142902; e-mail library@export.gov.il; internet www.export.gov.il; Dir-Gen. YECHIEL ASSIA.

Israel Journalists' Asscn: 4 Kaplan St, Tel-Aviv 64734; tel. 3-6956141; Man. Dir TUVIA SAAR.

Kibbutz Industries' Asscn: POB 40012, 13 Leonardo da Vinci St, Tel-Aviv 61400; tel. 3-6955413; fax 3-6951464; e-mail uri@kia.co.il; internet www.kia.co.il; liaison office for marketing and export of the goods produced by Israel's kibbutzim; Chair. URI ESHKOLI; Man. Dir AMOS RABIN.

Manufacturers' Asscn of Israel: POB 50022, Industry House, 29 Hamered St, Tel-Aviv 61500; tel. 3-5198787; fax 3-5162026; e-mail gendiv@industry.org.il; internet www.industry.org.il; 1,700 mem. enterprises employing nearly 85% of industrial workers in Israel; Pres. ODED TYRAH.

National Federation of Israeli Journalists: POB 7009, 4 Kaplan St, Tel-Aviv 64734; tel. 3-6956141; fax 3-6951438.

Plants Production and Marketing Board: 46 Derech Ha'macabim, Rishon le Zion 75359; tel. 3-9595695; fax 3-9502211; e-mail fruchter@fbi.org.il; internet www.plants.org.il.

UTILITIES

Israel Electric Corporation Ltd (IEC): POB 8810, 2 Ha'Haganah St, Haifa 31086; tel. 4-8548148; fax 4-8538149; internet www.israel-electric.co.il; state-owned; total assets US $10,832m. (Dec. 1997); Chair. ELI LANDAU.

Mekorot (Israel National Water Co): 9 Lincoln St Development, Tel-Aviv 61201; tel. 3-6230806; fax 3-6230598; e-mail akanarek@mekorot.co.il; internet www.mekorot.co.il; state-owned; total assets US $1,978m. (Dec. 1997); Chair. URI SAGIE.

The Histadrut

Histadrut (General Federation of Labour in Israel): 93 Arlozorof St, Tel-Aviv 62098; tel. 3-6921513; fax 3-6921512; e-mail histint@netvision.net.il; internet www.histadrut.org.il; f. 1920.

The General Federation of Labour in Israel, the Histadrut, is the largest labour organization in Israel. It strives to ensure the social security, welfare and rights of workers, and to assist in their professional advancement, while endeavouring to reduce the divisions in Israeli society. Membership of the Histadrut is voluntary, and open to all men and women of 18 years of age and above who live on the earnings of their own labour without exploiting the work of others. These include the self-employed and professionals, as well as housewives, students, pensioners and the unemployed. Workers' interests are protected through a number of occupational and professional unions affiliated to the Histadrut (see below). The organization operates courses for trade unionists and new immigrants, as well as apprenticeship classes. It maintains an Institute for Social and Economic Issues and the International Institute, one of the largest centres of leadership training in Israel, for students from Africa, Asia, Latin America and Eastern Europe, which includes the Levinson Centre for Adult Education and the Jewish-Arab Institute for Regional Co-operation. Attached to the Histadrut is Na'amat, a women's organization which promotes changes in legislation, operates a network of legal service bureaux and vocational training courses, and runs counselling centres for the treatment and prevention of domestic violence.

Chair.: AMIR PERETZ.

Secretary-General: HAIM RAMON.

ORGANIZATION

In 1989 the Histadrut had a membership of 1,630,000. In addition some 110,000 young people under 18 years of age belong to the Organization of Working and Student Youth, a direct affiliate of the Histadrut.

All members take part in elections to the Histadrut Convention (Veida), which elects the General Council (Moetsa) and the Executive Committee (Vaad Hapoel). The latter elects the 41-member Executive Bureau (Vaada Merakezet), which is responsible for day-to-day implementation of policy. The Executive Committee also elects the Secretary-General, who acts as its chairman as well as head of the organization as a whole and chairman of the Executive Bureau. Nearly all political parties are represented on the Histadrut Executive Committee.

The Executive Committee has the following departments: Trade Union, Organization and Labour Councils, Education and Culture, Social Security, Industrial Democracy, Students, Youth and Sports, Consumer Protection, Administration, Finance and International.

TRADE UNION ACTIVITIES

Collective agreements with employers fix wage scales, which are linked with the retail price index; provide for social benefits, including paid sick leave and employers' contributions to sick and pension and provident funds; and regulate dismissals. Dismissal compensation is regulated by law. The Histadrut actively promotes productivity through labour management boards and the National Productivity Institute, and supports incentive pay schemes.

There are unions for the following groups: clerical workers, building workers, teachers, engineers, agricultural workers, technicians, textile workers, printing workers, diamond workers, metal workers, food and bakery workers, wood workers, government employees, seamen, nurses, civilian employees of the armed forces, actors, musicians and variety artists, social workers, watchmen, cinema technicians, institutional and school staffs, pharmacy employees, medical laboratory workers, X-ray technicians, physiotherapists, social scientists, microbiologists, psychologists, salaried lawyers, pharmacists, physicians, occupational therapists, truck and taxi drivers, hotel and restaurant workers, workers in Histadrut-owned industry, garment, shoe and leather workers, plastic and rubber workers, editors of periodicals, painters and sculptors and industrial workers.

Histadrut Trade Union Department: Dir SHLOMO SHANI.

ECONOMIC ACTIVITIES AND SOCIAL SERVICES

These include Hevrat Haovdim (employing 260,000 workers in 1983), Kupat Holim (the Sick Fund, covering almost 77% of Israel's population), seven pension funds, and Na'amat (see above).

Other Trade Unions

Histadrut Haovdim Haleumit (National Labour Federation): 23 Sprintzak St, Tel-Aviv 64738; tel. 3-6958351; fax 3-6961753; e-mail nol@netvision.net.il; f. 1934; 220,000 mems; CEO ITZHAK RUSSO.

Histadrut Hapoel Hamizrahi (National Religious Workers' Party): 166 Ibn Gvirol St, Tel-Aviv 62023; tel. 3-5442151; fax 3-5468942; 150,000 mems in 85 settlements and 15 kibbutzim; Sec.-Gen. ELIEZER ABTABI.

Histadrut Poale Agudat Israel (Agudat Israel Workers' Organization): POB 11044, 64 Frishman St, Tel-Aviv; tel. 3-5242126; fax 3-5230689; has 33,000 members in 16 settlements and 8 educational insts.

Transport

RAILWAYS

Freight traffic consists mainly of grain, phosphates, potash, containers, petroleum and building materials. Rail service serves Haifa and Ashdod ports on the Mediterranean Sea, while a combined rail-road service extends to Eilat port on the Red Sea. Passenger services operate between the main towns: Nahariya, Haifa, Tel-Aviv and Jerusalem. In 1988 the National Ports Authority assumed responsibility for the rail system, creating the Ports and Railways Authority. It was decided in 1996 that Israel Railways should become a separate state concern, although this has not yet occurred. A US $1,400m. light railway network in Jerusalem was expected to begin operating in 2008.

Israel Railways (IR): POB 18085, Central Station, Tel-Aviv 61180; tel. 3-6937530; fax 3-6958176; e-mail pniyot@rail.org.il; internet www.israrail.org.il; in 2003 the total length of railway line was 610 km; Gen. Man. YOSSI SNIR.

Underground Railway

Haifa Underground Funicular Railway: 122 Hanassi Ave, Haifa 34633; tel. 4-8376861; fax 4-8376875; e-mail funicular@netvision .net.il; opened 1959; 2 km in operation; Man. AVI TELLEM.

ROADS

In 2003 there were 17,202 km of paved roads, of which 9,593 km were urban roads, 6,036 km were non-urban roads and 1,573 km were access roads.

Ministry of Transport: Public Works Dept, Klal Bldg, 97 Jaffa St, Jerusalem 91000; tel. 2-6228211; fax 2-6228693; e-mail pniot@mot .gov.il; internet www.mot.gov.il.

SHIPPING

At 31 December 2003 Israel's merchant fleet consisted of 52 vessels amounting to 766,004 grt.

Haifa and Ashdod are the main ports in Israel. The former is a natural harbour, enclosed by two main breakwaters and dredged to 45 ft below mean sea-level. In 1965 the deep water port was completed at Ashdod which had a capacity of about 8.6m. tons in 1988.

The port of Eilat is Israel's gateway to the Red Sea. It is a natural harbour, operated from a wharf. Another port, to the south of the original one, started operating in 1965.

Israel Ports Authority (PRA): POB 20121, 74 Menachem Begin Rd, Tel-Aviv 61201; tel. 3-5657000; fax 3-5617142; e-mail dovf@ israports.org.il; internet www.israports.org.il; f. 1961; merged with Israel Railways in 1988; separated from Israel Railways in 2003; plans, builds, develops, maintains and operates the commercial ports of Haifa, Ashdod and Eilat. A contract to expand Ashdod port was awarded in mid-2000, involving 1,900 m of new cargo and container quays, a breakwater extension and hinterland development; in early 2005 the first berth at the new Hayovel terminal was ready for operations, but labour relations issues were preventing container operations at the terminal from commencing. In early 2005 the tender for the construction of a new terminal called the Hacarmel terminal at Haifa port was being conducted. Cargo traffic in 2003 amounted to 35m. tons; Chair. GAD YAACOBI; Dir-Gen. AMOS RON.

Ofer (Ships Holding) Ltd: POB 1755, 2 Hanamal St, Haifa 31016; tel. 4-8610610; fax 4-8675666; e-mail contact@oferbrothers.com; internet www.oferbrothers.com; runs cargo and container services; operates some 30 vessels; Chair. Y. OFER; CEO E. ANGEL.

ZIM Israel Navigation Co Ltd: POB 1723, 7–9 Pal-Yam Ave, Haifa 31000; tel. 4-8652111; fax 4-8652956; e-mail zimpress@zim.co .il; internet www.zim.co.il; f. 1945; international integrated transportation system providing door-to-door services around the world; operates about 80 vessels; estimated total cargo carried: 1,500,000 TEUs in 2002; Chair. U. ANGEL; Pres. and CEO Dr YORAM SEBBA.

CIVIL AVIATION

Israel Airports Authority: Ben-Gurion International Airport, Tel-Aviv; tel. 3-9710101; fax 3-9712436; e-mail avia@iaa.gov.il; internet www.ben-gurion-airport.co.il; Chair. TSVI SHALOM; Dir-Gen. GABRIEL OFFIR.

El Al Israel Airlines Ltd: POB 41, Ben-Gurion International Airport, Tel-Aviv 70100; tel. 3-9716111; fax 3-9716040; internet www.elal.com; f. 1948; 100% state-owned, but scheduled for gradual privatization from early 2004; total assets US $980m. (Dec. 1997); daily services to most capitals of Europe; over 20 flights weekly to New York; services to the USA, Canada, China, Egypt, India, Kenya, South Africa, Thailand and Turkey; Chair. MICHAEL LEVY; Pres. HAIM ROMANO.

Arkia Israeli Airlines Ltd: POB 39301, Dov Airport, Tel-Aviv 61392; tel. 3-6902222; fax 3-6991512; e-mail income@arkia.co.il; internet www.arkia.co.il; f. 1980 by merger of Kanaf-Arkia Airlines and Aviation Services; scheduled passenger services linking Tel-Aviv, Jerusalem, Haifa, Eilat, Rosh Pina, Kiryat Shmona and Yotveta; charter services to European destinations; Chair. YIGAL ARNON; Pres. and CEO Prof. ISRAEL BOROVICH.

Tourism

In 2003 an estimated 1,063,400 tourists visited Israel, compared with some 861,900 in 2002. Tourist receipts in 2002 totalled US $1,197m.

Ministry of Tourism: POB 1018, 5 Bank of Israel St, Jerusalem 91009; tel. 2-6664200; fax 2-6664416; e-mail pniot@tourism.gov.il; internet www.tourism.gov.il; Dir-Gen. EL COHEN.

OCCUPIED TERRITORIES

THE GOLAN HEIGHTS

LOCATION, CLIMATE

The Golan Heights, a mountainous plateau that formed most of Syria's Quneitra Province (1,710 sq km) and parts of Dera'a Province, was occupied by Israel after the Arab–Israeli War of June 1967. Following the Disengagement Agreement of 1974, Israel continued to occupy some 70% of the territory (1,176 sq km), valued for its strategic position and abundant water resources (the headwaters of the Jordan river have their source on the slopes of Mount Hermon). The average height of the Golan is approximately 1,200 m above sea level in the northern region and about 300 m above sea level in the southern region, near Lake Tiberias (the Sea of Galilee). Rainfall ranges from about 1,000 mm per year in the north to less than 600 mm per year in the southern region.

ADMINISTRATION

Prior to the Israeli occupation, the Golan Heights were incorporated by Syria into a provincial administration of which the city of Quneitra, with a population at the time of 27,378, was capital. The disengagement agreement that was mediated by US Secretary of State Henry Kissinger in 1974 (after the 1973 Arab–Israeli War) provided for the withdrawal of Israeli forces from Quneitra. Before they withdrew, however, Israeli army engineers destroyed the city. In December 1981 the Israeli Knesset enacted the Golan Annexation Law, whereby Israeli civilian legislation was extended to the territory of Golan, now under the administrative jurisdiction of the Commissioner for the Northern District of Israel. The Arab-Druze community of the Golan responded immediately by declaring a strike and appealed to the UN Secretary-General to force Israel to rescind the annexation decision. At the seventh round of multilateral talks between Israeli and Arab delegations in Washington, DC, USA, in August 1992, the Israeli Government of Itzhak Rabin for the first time accepted that UN Security Council Resolution 242, adopted in 1967, applied to the Golan Heights. In January 1999 the Knesset passed legislation which stated that any transfer of land under Israeli sovereignty (referring to the Golan Heights and East Jerusalem) was conditional on the approval of at least 61 of the 120 Knesset members and of the Israeli electorate in a subsequent national referendum. Following the election of Ehud Barak as Israel's Prime Minister in May 1999, peace negotiations between Israel and Syria were resumed in mid-December. However, in January 2000 the talks were postponed indefinitely after Syria demanded a written commitment from Israel to withdraw from the Golan Heights. In July 2001 Israel's recently elected premier, Ariel Sharon, stated that he would be prepared to resume peace talks with Syria; however, Sharon also declared that the Israeli occupation of the Golan was 'irreversible'. The withdrawal of Israel from the disputed territory is one of Syria's primary objectives in any future peace agreement with Israel. Peace negotiations between Israel and Syria had not resumed by early 2005.

DEMOGRAPHY AND ECONOMIC AFFAIRS

As a consequence of the Israeli occupation, an estimated 93% of the ethnically diverse Syrian population of 147,613, distributed across 163 villages and towns and 108 individual farms, was expelled. The majority were Arab Sunni Muslims, but the population also included Alawite and Druze minorities and some Circassians, Turcomen, Armenians and Kurds. Approximately 9,000 Palestinian refugees from the 1948 Arab–Israeli War also inhabited the area. At the time of the occupation, the Golan was a predominantly agricultural province, 64% of the labour force being employed in agriculture. Only one-fifth of the population resided in the administrative centres. By 1991 the Golan Heights had a Jewish population of about 12,000 living in 21 Jewish settlements (four new settlements had been created by the end of 1992), and a predominantly Druze population of some 16,000 living in the only six remaining villages, of which Majd ash-Shams is by far the largest. According to official figures, at the end of 2003 the Golan Heights had a total population of 37,000 (comprising Jews, Druze and Muslims). The Golan Heights have remained largely an agricultural area, and although many Druze now work in Israeli industry in Eilat, Tel-Aviv and Jerusalem, the indigenous economy relies almost solely on the cultivation of apples, for which the area is famous. The apple orchards benefit from a unique combination of fertile soils, abundance of water and a conducive climate.

EAST JERUSALEM

LOCATION

Greater Jerusalem includes Israeli West Jerusalem (99% Jewish), the Old City and Mount of Olives, East Jerusalem (the Palestinian residential and commercial centre), Arab villages declared to be part of Jerusalem by Israel in 1967 and Jewish neighbourhoods constructed since 1967, either on land expropriated from Arab villages or in areas requisitioned as 'government land'. Although the area of the Greater Jerusalem district is 627 sq km, the Old City of Jerusalem covers just 1 sq km.

ADMINISTRATION

Until the 1967 Arab–Israeli War, Jerusalem had been divided into the new city of West Jerusalem—captured by Jewish forces in 1948—and the old city, East Jerusalem, which was part of Jordan. Israel's victory in 1967, however, reunited the city under Israeli control. Two weeks after the fighting had ended, on 28 June, Israeli law was applied to East Jerusalem and the municipal boundaries were extended by 45 km (28 miles). Jerusalem had effectively been annexed. Israeli officials, however, still refer to the 'reunification' of Jerusalem.

DEMOGRAPHY AND ECONOMIC AFFAIRS

In June 1993 the Deputy Mayor of Jerusalem, Avraham Kahila, declared that the city now had 'a majority of Jews', based on population forecasts which estimated the Jewish population at 158,000 and the Arab population at 155,000. For the Israeli administration this signified the achievement of a long-term objective. Immediately prior to the 1967 Arab–Israeli War, East Jerusalem and its Arab environs had an Arab population of approximately 70,000, and a small Jewish population in the old Jewish quarter of the city. By contrast, Israeli West Jerusalem had a Jewish population of 196,000. As a result of this imbalance, in the Greater Jerusalem district as a whole the Jewish population was in the majority even prior to the occupation of the whole city in 1967. Israeli policy following the occupation of East Jerusalem and the West Bank consisted of encircling the eastern sector of the city with Jewish settlements. In contrast to the more politically sensitive siting of Jewish settlements in the old Arab quarter of Jerusalem, the Government of Itzhak Rabin concentrated on the outer circle of settlement building. Official statistics for the end of 1998 reported that Greater Jerusalem had a total population of 633,700, of whom 433,600 (68%) were Jews. At the end of 2003 the city's population was 693,200. The Jerusalem Institute for Israel Studies estimates that the Arab population of Greater Jerusalem is increasing at a rate three times greater than the Jewish population.

The Old City, within the walls of which are found the ancient quarters of the Jews, Christians, Muslims and Armenians, has a population of approximately 25,500 Arabs and 2,600 Jews. In addition, there are some 600 recent Jewish settlers in the Arab quarter.

Many imaginative plans have been submitted with the aim of finding a solution to the problem of sharing Jerusalem between Arabs and Jews, including the proposal that the city be placed under international trusteeship, under UN auspices. However, to make the implementation of such plans an administrative as well as a political quagmire, the Israeli administration, after occupying the whole city in June 1967, began creating 'facts on the ground'. Immediately following the occupation, all electricity, water and telephone grids in West Jerusalem were extended to the east. Roads were widened and cleared, and the Arab population immediately in front of the

'Wailing Wall' was forcibly evicted. Arabs living in East Jerusalem became 'permanent residents' and could apply for Israeli citizenship if they wished (in contrast to Arabs in the West Bank and Gaza Strip). However, few chose to do so. None the less, issued with identity cards (excluding the estimated 25,000 Arabs from the West Bank and Gaza living illegally in the city), the Arab residents were taxed by the Israeli authorities, and their businesses and banks became subject to Israeli laws and business regulations. Now controlling approximately one-half of all land in East Jerusalem and the surrounding Palestinian villages (previously communally, or privately, owned by Palestinians), the Israeli authorities allowed Arabs to construct buildings on only 10%–15% of the land in the city; and East Jerusalem's commercial district has been limited to three streets.

Since the 1993 signing of the Declaration of Principles on Palestinian Self-Rule, the future status of Jerusalem and the continuing expansion of Jewish settlements in East Jerusalem have emerged as two of the most crucial issues affecting the peace process. In May 1999 the Israeli Government announced its refusal to grant Israeli citizenship to several hundred Arabs living in East Jerusalem, regardless of their compliance with the conditions stipulated under the Citizenship Law. In October, however, Israel ended its policy of revoking the right of Palestinians to reside in Jerusalem if they had spent more than seven years outside the city. Moreover, the Israeli Government announced in March 2000 that Palestinian residents of Jerusalem who had had their identity cards revoked could apply for their restoration.

At the Camp David talks held between Israel and the Palestinian (National) Authority (PA) in July 2000, the issue of who would have sovereignty over East Jerusalem in a future 'permanent status' agreement proved to be the principal obstacle to the achievement of a peace deal. It was reported in late July that the Israeli Government had offered the PA municipal autonomy over certain areas of East Jerusalem (including access to the Islamic holy sites), although sovereignty would remain in Israeli hands; the proposals were rejected by Yasser Arafat. In late September the holy sites of East Jerusalem were the initial focal point of a renewed uprising by Palestinians against the Israeli authorities, which became known as the al-Aqsa *intifada* and which continued into early 2005. Although the publication of the internationally sponsored 'roadmap' peace plan at the end of April 2003 offered directions for discussions on the Jerusalem issue, the resumption of attacks by Palestinian militants against Israeli citizens in mid-2003 and Israeli counter-strikes against Palestinian targets, made any such discussions untenable *pro tempore.*

ITALY

Introductory Survey

Location, Climate, Language, Religion, Flag, Capital

The Italian Republic comprises a peninsula, extending from southern Europe into the Mediterranean Sea, and a number of adjacent islands. The two principal islands are Sicily, to the south-west, and Sardinia, to the west. The Alps form a natural boundary to the north, where the bordering countries are France to the north-west, Switzerland and Austria to the north and Slovenia to the north-east. The climate is temperate in the north and Mediterranean in the south, with mild winters and long, dry summers. The average temperature in Rome is 7.4°C (45.3°F) in January and 25.7°C (78.3°F) in July. The principal language is Italian. German and Ladin are spoken in the Alto Adige region on the Austrian border, and French in the Valle d'Aosta region (bordering France and Switzerland), while in southern Italy there are Greek-speaking and Albanian minorities. A language related to Catalan is spoken in north-western Sardinia. Almost all of the inhabitants profess Christianity: more than 90% are adherents of the Roman Catholic Church. There is freedom of expression for other Christian denominations and for non-Christian religions. The national flag (proportions 2 by 3) has three equal vertical stripes, of green, white and red. The capital is Rome.

Recent History

The Kingdom of Italy, under the House of Savoy, was proclaimed in 1861 and the country was unified in 1870. Italy subsequently acquired an overseas empire, comprising the African colonies of Eritrea, Italian Somaliland and Libya. Benito Mussolini, leader of the Fascist Party, became Prime Minister in October 1922 and assumed dictatorial powers in 1925–26. Relations between the Italian State and the Roman Catholic Church, a subject of bitter controversy since Italy's unification, were codified in 1929 by a series of agreements, including the Lateran Pact, which recognized the sovereignty of the State of the Vatican City (q.v.), a small enclave within the city of Rome, under the jurisdiction of the Pope. Under Mussolini, Italian forces occupied Ethiopia in 1935–36 and Albania in 1939. Italy supported the fascist forces in the Spanish Civil War of 1936–39, and from June 1940 supported Nazi Germany in the Second World War. In 1943, however, as forces from the allied powers invaded Italy, the fascist regime collapsed. In July of that year King Victor Emmanuel III dismissed Mussolini, and the Fascist Party was dissolved.

In April 1945 German forces in Italy surrendered and Mussolini was killed. In June 1946, following a referendum, the monarchy was abolished and Italy became a republic. Until 1963 the Partito della Democrazia Cristiana (DC—Christian Democratic Party) held power unchallenged, while industry expanded rapidly, supported by capital from the USA. By the early 1960s, however, public discontent was increasing, largely owing to low wage rates and a lack of social reform. In the general election of 1963 the Partito Comunista Italiano (PCI—Italian Communist Party), together with other parties of the extreme right and left, made considerable gains at the expense of the DC. During the next decade there was a rapid succession of mainly coalition Governments, involving the DC and one or more of the other major non-communist parties.

Aldo Moro's coalition Government of the DC and the Partito Repubblicano Italiano (PRI—Italian Republican Party), formed in November 1974, resigned in January 1976, following the withdrawal of support by the Partito Socialista Italiano (PSI—Italian Socialist Party). After the failure of a minority DC administration, general elections to both legislative chambers took place in June, at which the PCI won 228 seats in the 630-member Camera dei Deputati (Chamber of Deputies). The DC remained the largest party, but could no longer govern against PCI opposition in the legislature. However, the DC continued to insist on excluding the PCI from power, and in July formed a minority Government, with Giulio Andreotti as Prime Minister. He relied on the continuing abstention of PCI deputies to introduce severe austerity measures in response to the economic crisis. In January 1978 the minority Government was forced to resign under pressure from the PCI, which wanted more active participation in government (the PCI had for several months been allowed to participate in policy-making but had no direct role in government), although Andreotti subsequently formed a new, almost identical Government, with PCI support. In May of the same year Aldo Moro was murdered by the Brigate Rosse (Red Brigades) terrorist group. In July Alessandro Pertini was inaugurated as Italy's first socialist head of state, succeeding Giovanni Leone, who had resigned as President in the previous month in response to allegations of corruption.

The Andreotti administration collapsed in January 1979, when the PCI withdrew from the official parliamentary majority. A new coalition Government, formed by Andreotti in March, lasted only 10 days before being defeated on a vote of 'no confidence'. Following elections in June, at which its representation in the Camera dei Deputati declined to 201 seats, the PCI returned to the role of opposition. In August Francesco Cossiga, a former Minister of the Interior, formed a minority 'government of truce', composed of the DC, the Partito Liberale Italiano (PLI—Italian Liberal Party) and the Partito Socialista Democratico Italiano (PSDI—Italian Social Democratic Party), relying on the abstention of the PSI to remain in office. However, the new Government was continually thwarted by obstructionism in Parliament. In April 1980 Cossiga formed a majority coalition, comprising members of the DC, the PRI and the PSI. The exclusion of the PCI prompted a concerted effort on the part of its deputies in the legislature to defeat the new Government, and in September the Government resigned after losing a vote on its economic programme. A four-party coalition Government assembled by Arnaldo Forlani, the Chairman of the DC, was beset with allegations of corruption, and in turn was forced to resign in May 1981, after it became known that more than 1,000 of Italy's foremost establishment figures belonged to a secret masonic lodge, P-2 ('Propaganda Due'), which had extensive criminal connections both in Italy and abroad. The lodge was linked with many political and financial scandals and with right-wing terrorism, culminating in 1982 with the collapse of one of Italy's leading banks, Banco Ambrosiano, and the death (later deemed to be murder) of its President, Roberto Calvi. Calvi's death was initially classified as suicide but in February 2003 a judicial inquiry found that he had been murdered. The decision to initiate prosecution proceedings was formalized in July and the trial of four suspects was scheduled to begin in October 2005. In April 1992 Carlo De Benedetti, formerly one of Italy's most prominent financiers, and Licio Gelli, the former head of P-2, were convicted (along with more than 30 other defendants) on charges relating to the Banco Ambrosiano scandal. (Six years later De Benedetti was cleared on appeal of the fraud charges, while Gelli's 12-year prison sentence was confirmed by the Supreme Court.)

In June 1981 Senator Giovanni Spadolini, leader of the PRI, formed a five-party coalition Government, thus becoming the first non-DC Prime Minister since 1946. Spadolini resigned in November 1982, following a dispute over economic policy. Amintore Fanfani, a former DC Prime Minister, formed a new, four-party coalition in December. This administration lasted until the PSI withdrew its support in April 1983. A general election was held in June, at which the DC lost considerable support, winning only 32.9% of the votes for the Camera dei Deputati. The PSI increased its share of the votes to 11.4%, and its leader, Bettino Craxi, was subsequently appointed Italy's first socialist Prime Minister, at the head of a five-party coalition. This Government lost a vote of confidence in the Camera dei Deputati in June 1986, thus bringing to an end Italy's longest administration (1,060 days) since the Second World War. Craxi resigned, and President Francesco Cossiga (who had succeeded Alessandro Pertini as head of state in July 1985) nominated the former DC Prime Minister, Giulio Andreotti, to attempt to form a new government. However, the refusal of other parties to support Andreotti led to Craxi's return to power in July, on condition that he transfer the premiership to a DC member in March 1987. Craxi accordingly submitted his resignation, and that of his Government, at that time. After several unsuccessful attempts to form a coalition, a general election was held in June, at which the DC obtained 34.3% of the votes cast and the PSI increased its share to 14.3%. With 26.6% of the votes, the PCI suffered its worst post-war electoral result, and lost 21 seats in the Camera dei Deputati. Giovanni Goria, a DC member and the former Minister of the Treasury, became Prime Minister of a five-party coalition Government. By the end of the year, however, the Government had lost considerable support. Goria offered his resignation in November (following the withdrawal of the PLI from the coalition) and again in February 1988, but it was rejected both times by President Cossiga; Goria finally resigned in March. Ciriaco De Mita, the Secretary-General of the DC, formed a coalition with the same five parties that had served in Goria's administration. In May the Government's decision to grant a measure of autonomy to the Alto Adige region (Südtirol), on the north-eastern border with Austria, prompted a series of bombings, perpetrated by German-speaking extremists in the region.

Severe criticism by Craxi of De Mita's premiership led to the collapse of the coalition Government in May 1989. In June President Cossiga nominated De Mita to form a new government, but he was unsuccessful and it was not until late July that the coalition partners of the outgoing Government agreed to form a new administration, with Andreotti as Prime Minister. De Mita resigned from the presidency of the DC in February 1990, following an internal party dispute. His supporters, who together constituted a left-wing alliance within the DC, also withdrew from party posts, but pledged their continued support for the Government. Andreotti resigned the premiership in March 1991, accused by the PSI of failing to implement effectively policies on key issues. President Cossiga none the less nominated Andreotti to form a new government (Italy's 50th since the Second World War). The new Government comprised the same coalition partners as the outgoing administration, other than the PRI (whose members had rejected the portfolios they had been allocated).

From late 1989, meanwhile, the PCI, which had suffered a recent series of electoral reverses, began a process of transforming itself from a communist into a mass social democratic party. In early 1991 the party was renamed the Partito Democratico della Sinistra (PDS—Democratic Party of the Left). A minority of members of the former PCI refused to join the PDS, and in May they formed the Partito della Rifondazione Comunista (PRC—Party of Reconstructed Communism).

In September 1991, apparently in response to widespread nationalist fervour in parts of Eastern Europe, German-speaking separatists from the Alto Adige region made demands for greater autonomy from Italy. In the same month the Union Valdôtaine, the nationalist party governing the Aosta Valley (on the borders of France and Switzerland), announced that it was planning a referendum on secession. In January 1992 the Italian Government, in an attempt to end a long-standing dispute with Austria over the Alto Adige area, agreed to grant further autonomy to the region. Demands for greater autonomy were also made in Sardinia, following a resurgence of activism by militant separatists there.

In February 1992 President Cossiga dissolved the legislature and announced that a general election would take place on 5 April. The election campaign was marred by the murder of Salvatore Lima, an associate of Andreotti (see below). At the election, support for the DC was reduced to less than 30% of votes cast. The PDS won 16.1% of votes cast for the Camera dei Deputati, while the PSI received 13.6%. The Lega Nord (Northern League), an increasingly vocal grouping of regionalist parties which denounced the 'southern hegemony' of the central Government, led by Umberto Bossi, performed well in northern Italy, as did a new anti-Mafia political party, La Rete per il Partito Democratico (Democratic Network Party), in the south. Andreotti announced his resignation following the election, as did Cossiga (whose mandate was not due to expire until July). In May Cossiga was succeeded by Oscar Luigi Scalfaro, the newly elected President of the Camera dei Deputati. In the following month Giuliano Amato, of the PSI, was appointed Prime Minister. The new Council of Ministers comprised mainly members of the PSI and DC, with the remaining portfolios being allocated to the PSDI, PLI and non-party politicians.

A corruption scandal uncovered in Milan in 1992 assumed wider implications in subsequent months. It was alleged that politicians (mainly of the PSI and DC) and government officials had accepted bribes in exchange for the awarding of large public contracts. Among those accused of corruption was senior PSI official Gianni De Michelis, a former Minister of Foreign Affairs.

The Amato Government's credibility was seriously undermined in February 1993 when the Minister of Justice, Claudio Martelli of the PSI, was obliged to resign, after being placed under formal investigation for alleged complicity in the 1982 collapse of Banco Ambrosiano. Shortly afterwards Craxi resigned as Secretary-General of the PSI, although he continued to deny accusations of fraud. The Prime Minister's difficulties were compounded by the resignation of four senior ministers in February and March 1993. Also in March, five DC politicians, including Andreotti, were placed under investigation over their alleged links with the Mafia. The Government's position became increasingly untenable, but President Scalfaro prevailed upon Amato to remain in office until impending referendums on constitutional reform had taken place.

Nation-wide referendums proceeded in April 1993 on a number of proposed changes to the Constitution, including an amendment providing for the election by majority vote of 75% of the 315 elective seats in the upper legislative chamber, the Senato (Senate), while the remainder would be elected under a system of proportional representation, and the end of state funding of political parties. These amendments, intended to prevent electoral malpractice and, in particular, interference by organized crime, were overwhelmingly approved. (In August Parliament approved a similar system for elections to the Camera dei Deputati.)

Amato resigned as Prime Minister shortly after the referendums, and Carlo Azeglio Ciampi was invited by President Scalfaro to form a new government. Ciampi, hitherto Governor of the Bank of Italy, was the first non-parliamentarian to be appointed to the premiership. His proposed coalition comprised the four parties of the outgoing administration, but also included the PDS, the PRI and the Federazione dei Verdi (Green Party). The PDS and the Federazione dei Verdi immediately withdrew their ministers from the coalition, in protest at the new administration's refusal to revoke Craxi's parliamentary immunity from prosecution, although both continued to support Ciampi's Government. In May 1993 the Camera dei Deputati voted overwhelmingly to abolish parliamentary immunity in cases of corruption and serious crime; while the Senato approved the removal of Andreotti's parliamentary immunity, to allow investigations into his alleged association with the Mafia, although his arrest remained prohibited. In the same month the PLI elected Raffaele Costa, the Minister of Transport, to succeed Renato Altissimo as party Secretary-General, following Altissimo's arrest on corruption charges in March. Meanwhile, investigations began in April into the activities of former DC Prime Minister Arnaldo Forlani. The investigations were subsequently extended to encompass politicians of the PDS and PRI, as arrests of leading political and business figures multiplied. In August the Camera dei Deputati voted to allow Craxi to be investigated by magistrates on four charges of corruption. In the following month Diego Curto, head of Milan's commercial court, became the first member of the judiciary to be investigated in connection with the corruption scandals. At the end of the month Andreotti was charged with having provided the Sicilian Mafia (Cosa Nostra) with political protection in exchange for votes in Sicily, and with complicity in the murder of an investigative journalist who had allegedly discovered evidence linking Andreotti with the Mafia (see below).

Ciampi resigned in January 1994, in response to parliamentary divisions over the timing of a general election. Scalfaro dissolved the legislature, but requested that Ciampi remain in office until the forthcoming elections in March. In January Silvio Berlusconi, the principal shareholder in and former manager of the media-based Fininvest, Italy's third largest private business group, announced the formation of a right-wing organization, Forza Italia (Come on, Italy!), to contest the elections. The liberal wing of the DC, whose mainstream was now discredited by corruption scandals, relaunched itself as the centrist Partito Popolare Italiano (PPI—Italian People's Party). In subsequent weeks, parties of the left, right and centre sought to form alliances capable of securing a majority in the Camera dei Deputati; seven parties—including the PDS, the PRC, the Federazione dei Verdi and La Rete—formed I Progressisti (the Progressives); the Polo per le Libertà e del Buon Governo (hereafter referred to as the Polo per le Libertà—known in English as the Freedom Alliance) was formed by the Lega Nord, Forza Italia and the Alleanza Nazionale (AN—National Alliance, a new party led by Gianfranco Fini and incorporating members of the neo-fascist Movimento Sociale Italiano-Destra Nazionale—MSI-DN—Italian Social Movement-National

Right), under the leadership of Berlusconi; the centre-right Patto per l'Italia (Pact for Italy), comprised Mario Segni's Patto Segni and the PPI. The election campaign intensified against a background of judicial investigations and mutual accusations of media bias and malpractice, while Berlusconi's popularity increased markedly—despite the arrest of a number of senior Fininvest executives on suspicion of financial malpractice. The Polo per le Libertà alliance won an outright majority in the Camera dei Deputati, obtaining 366 of the 630 seats, and was only three seats short of an outright majority in the elections to the Senato, winning 156 of the 315 seats. The Progressisti took 213 seats in the Camera dei Deputati and 122 seats in the Senato, while the Patto per l'Italia won only 46 and 31 seats respectively. In spite of the success of the right-wing alliance, major differences divided its constituent parties. Berlusconi selected his own candidates for the usually non-partisan posts of President of the Camera dei Deputati and President of the Senato. In April Berlusconi was invited by President Scalfaro to form a government. The new Council of Ministers, announced in May, included five members of the AN, including Roberto Maroni of the Lega Nord as Minister of the Interior and two members of the neo-fascist MSI-DN. Forza Italia won 30.6% of the votes at elections to the European Parliament held in June. The PDS won only 19.1% of the votes, and its leader, Achille Occhetto, resigned and was replaced by Massimo D'Alema in July.

In July 1994 Bettino Craxi and the former Deputy Prime Minister and Minister of Justice, Claudio Martelli, were both sentenced for fraudulent bankruptcy in relation to the collapse of Banco Ambrosiano in 1982. Craxi, who claimed to be too ill to return from his residence in Tunisia, was sentenced *in absentia*. (In July 1995 he was formally declared a fugitive from justice.) Also in July 1994 two Fininvest employees were arrested on charges of bribing the finance police (Guardi di Finanza). In conjunction with the ongoing controversy regarding the extent of the Prime Minister's media holdings, this fuelled concern about Berlusconi's continued involvement in Fininvest. In November Berlusconi was placed under investigation for bribery. In the following month Antonio Di Pietro, the most high-profile magistrate in Milan and one of the most popular public figures in Italy, resigned in protest at increasing government interference in the work of the Milanese judiciary. The failure of the Prime Minister to resolve his conflict of business and political interests, together with the growing tension between the Government and the judiciary, undermined the integrity of the Government and precipitated the disintegration of the coalition and Berlusconi's resignation. In January 1995 Lamberto Dini, the Minister of the Treasury and a former Director-General of the Bank of Italy, was invited to form an interim government. Dini appointed a Council of Ministers comprised of technocrats, and pledged to hold elections once he had implemented a programme to improve public finances, reform the state pension system, introduce new regional electoral laws, and establish controls on media ownership and its use during electoral campaigns. In March it was announced that Berlusconi was to be subject to further investigation on charges of financial irregularities. Moreover, his Polo per le Libertà was defeated by the centre-left parties in nine of the 15 regional elections held in April.

New political alliances emerged during 1995 in preparation for legislative elections. In January the MSI-DN was officially disbanded and most of its members were absorbed in the AN. The AN leader, Gianfranco Fini, distanced the party from its neo-fascist past in an attempt to widen support. The PSI had been dissolved in November 1994 and reformed as the Socialisti Italiani (Italian Socialists), under the leadership of Enrico Bosselli. Divisions within the Lega Nord led to the formation of a breakaway group in February 1995 under the leadership of Roberto Maroni. In the same month Romano Prodi, a respected business executive, offered to lead the centre-left parties to challenge Berlusconi in the forthcoming elections. In March the PPI rejected a proposed alliance with Berlusconi, deposing its leader, Rocco Buttiglione, in favour of Gerardo Bianco; Buttiglione subsequently founded a new centre-right party, the Cristiani Democratici Uniti (CDU—United Christian Democrats). In July the PDS formally endorsed Prodi as leader of the centre-left electoral alliance, subsequently named L'Ulivo (The Olive Tree).

In June 1995 12 referendums were held on issues including media ownership, trade union and electoral reform and crime. Significantly, the majority of the voters who participated in the

referendums on media ownership approved the retention of laws permitting an individual to own more than one commercial television channel and preserving the existing monopoly on television advertising. Furthermore, the majority of voters supported the partial privatization of the state-owned RAI broadcasting company, control of which had become increasingly contentious since the resignation of its directorate in mid-1994 in protest at increased government control over appointments. Another important outcome was the endorsement of proposed restrictions on trade unions' powers of representation, effectively reducing the dominance of the three largest trade union federations.

In October 1995 the Minister of Justice, Filippo Mancuso, refused to resign from the Council of Ministers despite a successful motion of 'no confidence' in him, which had been prompted by his allegedly ruthless vendetta against anti-corruption magistrates in Milan. Scalfaro revoked Mancuso's mandate, appointing Dini as interim Minister of Justice. Dini's administration remained precarious, however, and shortly afterwards Berlusconi allied himself with Mancuso and proposed a motion of 'no confidence' in the Government, claiming the support of the PRC. The Government narrowly defeated the motion, after having forged an agreement whereby PRC deputies abstained from the vote on condition that Dini resign as Prime Minister by the end of the year. Dini's resignation, submitted in late December, was, however, rejected by President Scalfaro, who asked the Prime Minister to remain in office pending a parliamentary debate to resolve the political crisis. In January 1996 the AN tabled a resolution demanding Dini's resignation, which it was expected to win with the support of parties of the extreme left. Scalfaro was thus obliged to accept Dini's resignation, which he submitted prior to the vote. In February Scalfaro dissolved Parliament and asked Dini to remain as interim Prime Minister until a general election in April. In October 1995, meanwhile, all 22 defendants were convicted in a trial concerning illegal funding of political parties. Among those convicted were former Prime Ministers Craxi, who was sentenced *in absentia* to four years' imprisonment, and Forlani, sentenced to 28 months' custody; Umberto Bossi of the Lega Nord received a suspended sentence.

At the legislative elections, held in April 1996, Romano Prodi's L'Ulivo alliance (dominated by the PDS, but also including the PPI and Dini's newly formed, centrist Rinnovamento Italiano, RI—Italian Renewal) narrowly defeated the Polo per le Libertà, securing 284 of the 630 seats in the Camera dei Deputati and 157 of the 315 elective seats in the Senato. President Scalfaro invited Prodi to form a government; Prodi announced his intention to introduce educational and constitutional reforms, reduce unemployment, address the contentious issue of media ownership and persevere with a policy of economic austerity. Massimo D'Alema, the influential General Secretary of the PDS, elected not to serve in the new Council of Ministers; however, his second-in-command, Walter Veltroni, was appointed Deputy Prime Minister. Prodi's Government was endorsed by votes of confidence in the Camera dei Deputati and in the Senato in May. Although the PRC agreed to support the Government in the vote of confidence in the Camera dei Deputati, its Secretary-General, Fausto Bertinotti, emphasized that his party could express only 'conditional confidence' in the new administration, and on several occasions in subsequent months the Government was obliged to accede to PRC demands in return for that party providing crucial parliamentary support.

In May 1996 Umberto Bossi of the Lega Nord announced the formation of an 11-member 'Government of the Independent Republic of Padania' (a territory comprising the regions of Liguria, Emilia-Romagna, Lombardy, Piedmont and the Veneto). The Lega Nord fared relatively poorly in key northern cities at local elections in June, however, and in September Bossi's credibility was damaged further by the expulsion from the party of Irene Pivetti (a highly-regarded Lega Nord member and former President of the Camera dei Deputati) for publicly supporting a less extreme policy of local autonomy. In addition, a well-publicized rally in Venice to mark the formal independence of 'Padania' was poorly attended.

Meanwhile, former magistrate Antonio Di Pietro was alleged to have abused his position within the judiciary to extort favours and to have attempted to discredit Berlusconi to further his own political ambitions. In March 1996, after a court in Brescia dismissed charges against Di Pietro, Berlusconi's brother, Paolo, and Cesare Previti, a former Minister of Defence and a lawyer for Fininvest, were placed under investigation for allegedly attempting to discredit him. Although Di Pietro had been appointed Minister of Public Works in May, by November he had resigned from the post, in protest at renewed investigations into his affairs. In December the Court of Review ruled that raids on Di Pietro's home and offices by the finance police (suspected of seeking vengeance on Di Pietro for his earlier investigations into their affairs) were 'unjustified and illegitimate'. Paolo Berlusconi and Previti were acquitted in January 1997. In November 1996 Romano Prodi was himself placed under investigation for alleged abuse of office while head of the state holding company Istituto per la Ricostruzione Industriale (Iri) during 1993–94; the Prime Minister dismissed the allegations and pledged to co-operate fully with the inquiry.

In July 1996 the Government had presented draft legislation on media reform that would allow Berlusconi's Mediaset organization to convert one of its three television channels to cable or satellite (or else reduce its share of the terrestrial audience) rather than to divest it. The draft legislation also envisaged the establishment of a telecommunications and media regulator, while the RAI broadcasting group would be obliged to convert one of its channels to a regional network. However, the reforms failed to receive parliamentary approval prior to the deadline set by the Constitutional Court, and the Court ruled that its recommendation to reduce the proportion of television companies held by any one group from 25% to 20% would take effect. It consequently announced that it would block the transmission of one of Mediaset's channels as of 22 December. In early December Massimo D'Alema, who had increasingly been acknowledged as the principal strategist in the Government, secured the postponement of the Constitutional Court's decision to enforce its broadcasting ruling and indicated that the Government might support the introduction of judicial reforms that could result in extensive plea-bargaining in corruption cases—thereby successfully exploiting Berlusconi's vulnerability with regard to both media legislation and to judicial investigations into his affairs (see below). In return, Berlusconi agreed to co-operate with the Government and support the rapid conversion of numerous decrees into law. In January 1997 the co-operation of the Polo per le Libertà enabled the Senato to approve the creation of a bicameral commission on constitutional reform. In June the commission presented its recommendations, which included a directly-elected President, a reduction in the size of the Camera dei Deputati and the Senato, and greater regional financial autonomy.

In October 1997 the PRC announced that it would oppose the 1998 budget, thus leaving the Government without a legislative majority. Following the failure of negotiations, Prodi offered his resignation to Scalfaro. He remained as caretaker Prime Minister, and a one-year political pact was subsequently announced. Scalfaro thereupon formally rejected Prodi's resignation, and the Prime Minister won a parliamentary vote of confidence.

In December 1997 Berlusconi and four associates were convicted on charges of false accounting with regard to the purchase of a film group in 1988. Later in December 1997 Berlusconi and Previti were ordered to stand trial on charges relating to allegations that they had accumulated funds with the intention of bribing judges. In two separate trials in July 1998 Berlusconi was convicted of bribing tax inspectors involved in Fininvest audits and of making illicit payments to Craxi and the PSI in 1991. The prescribed custodial sentences were not, however, to be enforced as the former Prime Minister (who was awaiting trial on several further charges) was protected by parliamentary immunity. In the same month warrants were issued for the arrest of 113 people on corruption charges, among them local administration officials and members of the finance police. Further allegations against Berlusconi were uncovered in August when a witness in an unrelated corruption trial accused him of money-laundering on behalf of the Mafia; Berlusconi strenuously denied the charge.

In May 1997 the Lega Nord organized a referendum to determine the level of popular support for 'Padania'. Despite media reports that participation levels had been low, Umberto Bossi claimed that 5m. people had voted, of whom 99% supported an independent 'Republic of Padania'. In local elections in April the Lega Nord had suffered a sharp decline in support. In October elections to a 200-seat constituent assembly in the 'Republic of Padania', organized by the Lega Nord, were contested by 63 parties. In January 1998 Bossi received a one-year suspended prison sentence for inciting criminal acts during a Lega Nord meeting in 1995; in July 1998 he received a second sentence, of

seven months, for resistance to authority and offensive behaviour.

In June 1998 the Camera dei Deputati approved legislation endorsing the admission to the North Atlantic Treaty Organization (NATO, see p. 301) of Hungary, Poland and the Czech Republic. The vote, which had become an issue of confidence in the Prodi Government as the PRC (on which the coalition relied in parliamentary votes) opposed the eastward expansion of the alliance and thus withdrew its support, was carried with the support of the new, centrist Unione Democratica per la Repubblica (UDR—Democratic Union for the Republic, led by former President Francesco Cossiga) and with the abstention of Forza Italia. Inter-party talks on the proposed constitutional reforms collapsed earlier that month without any agreement, the principal area of contention being the issue of presidential powers. Berlusconi, in particular, opposed any alteration of the presidential mandate and demanded greater reform of the judiciary, including a curb on the power of the magistrates. There was a further political crisis in October, when the PRC again withdrew its support for the Government on the issue of the 1999 budget. The Government lost an ensuing confidence motion by one vote, and Prodi was forced to resign. The leader of the Democratici di Sinistra (DS, as the PDS had been renamed), Massimo D'Alema, was asked to assume the premiership. D'Alema announced the formation of a coalition Government, composed of members of the DS, the Federazione dei Verdi, the Partito dei Comunisti Italiani, the UDR, the PPI, the Socialisti Democratici Italiani (SDI—Italian Democratic Socialists) and RI.

In March 1999 Berlusconi was acquitted on charges of tax fraud; his 1998 conviction for making illicit payments to Craxi and the PSI was overturned in October 1999. In the following month, however, Berlusconi was ordered to stand trial in two cases involving charges of bribery and false accounting; in one of the cases the former Minister of Defence, Cesare Previti, was also to stand trial on a charge of perverting the course of justice. Meanwhile, in June a new trial had been ordered against Craxi on charges of illegal party financing; however, in January 2000 Craxi died in exile in Tunisia.

In May 1999 the former Prime Minister, Ciampi, was elected to succeed Scalfaro as President of the Republic. In that month, Massimo D'Antona, an adviser to the Minister of Employment and Social Welfare, Antonio Bassolino, was shot dead. Responsibility was claimed by the Brigate Rosse (the terrorist grouping had been believed inactive since the late 1980s), which cited D'Antona's involvement in formulating a series of liberalizing labour reforms, together with Italy's involvement in the NATO action in Kosovo (see below). Municipal and provincial elections in June resulted in a number of defeats for the governing coalition, most notably in the leftist stronghold of Bologna, where a right-wing candidate was elected Mayor for the first time since 1945; elections to the European Parliament also showed increased support for right-wing parties.

D'Alema tendered his resignation as Prime Minister in December 1999, following several months of tension within the governing coalition which had culminated in the withdrawal of support by an alliance of parties including the SDI and the UDR. D'Alema was asked by Ciampi to form a new government, and forged a new coalition of parties of the left and centre, including I Democratici per l'Ulivo (The Democrats for the Olive Tree), founded earlier in the year by Romano Prodi, and the Unione Democratici per l'Europa (UDEUR—Union of Democrats for Europe). At regional elections held in April 2000, however, the new centre-left coalition was defeated by a centre-right alliance composed of Berlusconi's Forza Italia and Bossi's Lega Nord. In an attempt to avert a general election, which would follow his predicted defeat in a parliamentary confidence motion, D'Alema resigned. The Minister of Treasury and the Budget, former Prime Minister Giuliano Amato, was appointed in his place, and in late April a new, eight-party centre-left Government was sworn in.

In May 2000, at a first appeal, Berlusconi was acquitted of one charge of bribing tax inspectors involved in Fininvest audits on which he had been convicted in 1998; the appeals court also invoked the statute of limitations to overturn his convictions on three similar counts. In June 2000 Berlusconi was further acquitted at a pre-trial hearing of bribery charges relating to his acquisition of the Mondadori publishing company in 1991.

In September 2000 Amato announced that he would stand down as leader of the centre-left alliance in advance of the next parliamentary elections, scheduled to take place in May 2001, in favour of the Mayor of Rome, Francesco Rutelli of I Democratici per l'Ulivo. Rutelli was endorsed as the centre-left's official candidate for Prime Minister in October. In late 2000 the Regional Councils of Lombardy, Piedmont and the Veneto announced their intention of holding referendums on possible devolution. However, the Government asserted in November that referendums could be declared only by central Government.

Berlusconi's Casa delle Libertà (House of Freedoms) alliance won a decisive victory over the L'Ulivo alliance at the general election, held on 13 May 2001, securing majorities in both legislative chambers. The Casa delle Libertà won 177 seats in the Senato (compared with the 128 held by L'Ulivo), and 368 in the Camera dei Deputati (compared with 242 for L'Ulivo). In the elections to the lower house the Casa delle Libertà took 49.4% of the total votes cast for the seats allocated by proportional representation. Berlusconi's Forza Italia won the largest share of the vote by a single party, with 29.4%; within L'Ulivo, the DS obtained 16.6% of votes cast, thus remaining the second largest party in Parliament, and Rutelli's Margherita alliance (including I Democratici per l'Ulivo, the PPI, UDEUR and RI) 14.5%. The AN secured 12.0% of the vote, but Bossi's Lega Nord did not perform as well as expected, winning just 3.9% of votes cast, compared with 10.1% in the 1996 legislative elections. Berlusconi was appointed Prime Minister by President Ciampi, and his coalition Government—composed of Forza Italia, the AN, the Lega Nord, the CDU, the Centro Cristiano Democratico (Christian Democratic Centre—CCD) and independents, was named in June. The AN leader, Gianfranco Fini, became Deputy Prime Minister. The appointment of Bossi as Minister without Portfolio, with responsibility for Reforms and Devolution, and of two other reputedly extremist Lega Nord members (Roberto Castelli as Minister of Justice and Roberto Maroni as Minister of Labour and Welfare) was condemned by opposition parties on the grounds that this gave the Lega Nord responsibility for the sensitive issue of immigration. Berlusconi's new Government was endorsed in confidence votes in both chambers of Parliament later in June. Meanwhile, despite its defeat in the general election, at mayoral elections in May L'Ulivo retained control of the cities of Rome, Naples and Turin.

The issue of apparent conflict of interest between Berlusconi's political role and business interests was heightened by the general election. Berlusconi's new position as Prime Minister placed him in effective control of the state broadcasting company, RAI, and this, coupled with his ownership of the media company Fininvest (which operates Italy's principal private television concern, Mediaset), potentially gave him control over the majority of the Italian television network. Prior to the May 2001 election Berlusconi had apparently contradicted earlier indications that, should he become premier, he would relinquish a significant proportion of his media interests—stating that he had no intention of selling any part of Fininvest but that he would introduce legislation addressing conflict of interest.

A parliamentary inquiry into alleged police brutality was ordered by the Government in late July 2001 after serious rioting in Genoa earlier that month around the summit meeting of the Group of Eight (G-8) industrialized nations. One person was shot dead by a police officer during clashes between anti-capitalist protesters and security forces, and an estimated 300 (among them some 70 members of the security forces) were injured. Italy's chief of police later admitted that he believed excessive violence had been used during the riots, and three senior police commanders were subsequently dismissed from their posts. The official report into the G-8 riots, published in September, effectively absolved the security forces of any wrong-doing, and asserted that the protester's death and the wide-spread violence and material damage arising from the incidents in Genoa had not prevented the G-8 summit's success. However, the trial of 28 police officers on charges of inflicting injuries and abuse of office began in April 2005; the case against a further police officer was suspended, owing to his involvement in a car accident. The trial was, however, subsequently postponed.

In August 2001 a bomb was detonated at a court building in Venice, prior to a visit later that day by Berlusconi and the Minister of Infrastructure and Transport, Pietro Lunardi. Later that month another bomb explosion occurred at the offices of the Lega Nord near Padua. Responsibility for the bombings was claimed by a number of extremist groups, including one purporting to be associated with the Brigate Rosse. Also in that month legislation to decriminalize fraud associated with false accounting was approved by the Camera dei Deputati despite opposition claims that Berlusconi was personally motivated.

Furthermore, in October legislation was adopted by the Senato which altered regulations governing the use of evidence in criminal cases. Opposition parties protested that Berlusconi would directly benefit from the new regulations, which were likely to invalidate legal proceedings against himself and Previti in respect of allegations that they had bribed judges in return for a favourable court judgment over the sale of a state-owned food company, SME Meridionale. Prior to the trial's commencement, in January 2002, an attempt by the Minister of Justice, Roberto Castelli, to remove one of the three judges on the case caused public and judicial consternation. In October 2001 Italy's Supreme Court of Appeal overturned Berlusconi's 1998 conviction on charges of bribing tax inspectors in exchange for favourable audits of Fininvest.

At a referendum held in October 2001 a proposal to devolve certain powers to Regional Councils was overwhelmingly approved, although the electoral turn-out was only 34%; the constitutional amendment would grant greater legislative powers to the regions, increasing local control over areas including taxation, education, health and agriculture, while the central Government would remain in charge of the national police forces, defence, treasury and foreign policy.

Berlusconi's continued popularity was apparently confirmed in November 2001 when the Forza Italia candidate at Palermo's mayoral election won 56.1% of votes cast, compared with only 23.3% won by the candidate for L'Ulivo. However, the resignation of the Minister of Foreign Affairs, Renato Ruggiero, in January 2002 exposed severe divisions within the Government over European policy. Ruggiero's resignation was prompted by comments made by three other ministers expressing their disapproval of the new European currency. As an independent, Ruggiero failed to receive the support of Berlusconi, who stated that he himself was responsible for Italy's foreign policy; Berlusconi subsequently assumed the foreign affairs portfolio on an interim basis and reiterated Italy's commitment to full participation in Economic and Monetary Union (EMU).

In February 2002 Berlusconi announced his intention to transfer to private ownership two of the three state-owned RAI television channels. The planned privatization was heavily criticized by opposition members as well as by the outgoing President of RAI, Roberto Zaccaria. In April a 'conflict of interest' bill was passed in the Camera dei Deputati, following a 'walk-out' by all of the L'Ulivo deputies. The legislation prohibited a figure in public office from actively running a company, but did not forbid ownership, thus permitting Berlusconi's continued possession of Mediaset. (The bill finally became law in July 2004.)

In March 2002 Marco Biagi, an adviser to the Minister of Labour and Welfare, Roberto Maroni, was shot dead. Responsibility for the assassination was claimed by a faction of the Brigate Rosse, which cited Biagi's key role in the drafting of controversial new labour legislation as the motive for the shooting. Nation-wide protests against the proposed legislation, which would ease employers' restrictions on the employment and dismissal of workers, led to a general strike in April. A Patto per l'Italia (Pact for Italy), was signed in July between the Government and two major trade unions, the Confederazione Italiana Sindacati Lavoratori (CISL) and the Unione Italiana del Lavoro (UIL), which agreed to increase the flexibility of the labour market while allowing for the reintroduction of consultation. The accord, however, caused a split in the trade union movement (and consequently the affiliations of the political left), through the exclusion of the Confederazione Generale Italiana del Lavoro (CGIL), Italy's largest trade union. Protests against the labour-market reform, led by the CGIL, continued.

Meanwhile, prior to local elections in mid-2002 the PPI, RI and I Democratici per l'Ulivo merged into a single electoral coalition within L'Ulivo, entitled Democrazia è Libertà—La Margherita (Democracy is Freedom—The Daisy Party), without UDEUR. The first round of local elections in May seemed to confirm the strength of the centre-right coalition, comprising Forza Italia, the AN, the Lega Nord and Marco Follini's Unione dei Democratici Cristiani e di Centro (UDC—Christian Democratic and Centrist Union, a coalition of the CDU and the CCD). However, the second round in early June saw the coalition suffer unexpected defeats in nine out of 11 major cities, following a concerted effort by L'Ulivo, in alliance with Fausto Bertinotti's PRC and Antonio Di Pietro's Italia dei Valori (Italy of Values). The defeats were widely viewed as a statement of general public uncertainty about Berlusconi's Government one year after its election.

Following the rejection of an appeal by Berlusconi in May 2002 to have his bribery trial moved from Milan, several bills proposing judicial reform provoked controversy in the legislature and the judiciary. Proposed reforms, including the nomination of magistrates by the Minister of Justice rather than by an independent body, precipitated a judges' strike in late June. A Trial Bill, which would allow a process to be rescheduled and relocated if there was 'legitimate suspicion' of prosecutorial bias on the part of the judge, aroused concern that Berlusconi would make use of the new legislation in a corruption trial involving himself and the former Minister for Defence, Cesare Previti. Nevertheless, the bill was passed by the Senato in August amid 'walk-outs' by the opposition; members of the centre-right coalition were alleged to have voted electronically for absent colleagues, which elicited large-scale street protests in September against Berlusconi's judicial policies. The bill was subsequently passed by the Camera dei Deputati in November, again amid widespread opposition protest.

Meanwhile, further concerns about Berlusconi's influence over the news media were engendered in August 2002 by the dismissal of a television journalist at RAI accused of bias by Berlusconi; this followed an attempt in May to pass legislation forcing four allegedly 'one-sided' television programmes off the air. Berlusconi's actions aroused anger from the opposition and journalists' organizations, who accused the Prime Minister of threatening freedom of speech and of acting with political motivation. (Berlusconi's problems were compounded in November by the resignation of three RAI directors in protest at government interference.) In March 2003 Lucia Annunziata became the first female President of RAI following the resignation of both Baldassare and his potential successor, Paoli Mieli, who had refused to assume the position, when his requests for control over the appointment and dismissal of directors and the reinstatement of two journalists who had opposed the Government, were rejected.

On 15 October 2002 a constitutional amendment was approved allowing Italy's long-exiled royal family to return to the country. Also in October, a second general strike, led by the CGIL, was staged in protest at the Government's budget proposals for 2003, which, it was estimated, could lead to 260,000 job losses. During November 2002 a devolution bill, which would allow regional control over education, the health service and the police, was put forward by Umberto Bossi of the Lega Nord; although the opposition tabled 1,600 amendments in an effort to derail the bill, Berlusconi threatened a vote of confidence if the bill was not passed. Bossi created splits in the ruling coalition, however, when he attacked President Ciampi for seeking assurances that the bill would not threaten national unity. Bossi's determination to withdraw the Lega Nord from the coalition if the bill was blocked coincided with a similar threat from the UDC, which cited its lack of influence within the alliance. The devolution bill was passed in December. In November Franco Frattini was appointed Minister of Foreign Affairs, ending 10 months of interim control of that portfolio by Berlusconi.

In November 2002 an appeals court in Palermo overturned the acquittal of Giulio Andreotti on charges of conspiracy to murder a journalist in 1979, and sentenced the former Prime Minister to 24 years' imprisonment; the sentence aroused widespread condemnation of the judicial system by politicians, including Berlusconi. The Court of Cassation overturned this ruling, acquitting Andreotti of the murder in October 2003. In May an appeal court upheld a 1999 ruling exonerating Andreotti of charges of association with the Mafia; the judicial report, which was published in July 2003, observed that although Andreotti's relations with the Mafia were close until 1980, the legislation proscribing association with the Mafia did not come into effect until 1982. (In October 2004 Andreotti was aquitted by the Supreme Court of Cassation of collusion with the Mafia while in office.)

In January 2003, after a further bid to relocate his bribery trial was rejected by the Supreme Court, Berlusconi announced the possible reintroduction of immunity from prosecution for MPs (removed after the corruption scandal of 1992), which aroused opposition protest. He also confirmed that he would complete his mandate as Prime Minister even if found guilty. In that month a UN report accused Berlusconi of attempting to undermine the judiciary. In April Berlusconi's trial opened in Milan and he reiterated his claims that the local judiciary was biased against him. Later that month Berlusconi's associate, Previti, was sentenced to 11 years' imprisonment for bribing judges to influence two corporate takeovers in the 1990s. (In

November Previti was convicted of corruption charges in Milan and sentenced to five years' imprisonment, although he was acquitted of a further charge of bribing judges.) In May it was announced that Berlusconi would be tried separately from his co-defendants. However, in June the trial was halted, following the adoption of a bill granting immunity while in office to Italy's five most senior politicians (the President, the Prime Minister, the head of the Constitutional Court and the leaders of the two chambers of Parliament). This legislation removed the possibility of the potential conviction of Berlusconi during Italy's presidency of the EU, which was to begin on 1 July, but also rendered unlikely the probability of the trial reaching its conclusion, as Berlusconi's term of office extended until 2006, by which time the statute of limitations would prevent the resumption of legal proceedings against him (on the grounds that too much time had elapsed since the perpetration of the crimes). In September 2003 Antonio Di Pietro delivered a petition containing 900,000 signatures to the Court of Cassation which condemned the immunity legislation and called for a referendum on the issue (a referendum requires only 500,000 authenticated signatures).

In the local elections of late May and early June 2003 the centre-left made significant gains against the centre-right coalition, partly because of the failure of the latter to present a united front; owing to its coalition partners' lack of support for devolution, the Lega Nord presented its candidates separately in several northern cities. The poor electoral performance of the ruling coalition heightened tension between Bossi and Berlusconi, with Bossi demanding the enactment of legislation on devolution and immigration (23,000 immigrants arrived in Italy in 2002) to prevent his resignation. Later in June the Lega Nord threatened to leave the coalition if no further progress were achieved. The arrival in Italy of 3,500 immigrants in that month precipitated a government decree enabling the navy to board ships carrying illegal immigrants and divert them away from the Italian coast. The measure was condemned as inadequate by Bossi. In July 2003 the Government experienced further problems, when the UDC threatened to withdraw from the ruling coalition, owing to an attempt by the Minister of Justice, Castelli, to prevent a judicial investigation into allegations of tax fraud and false accounting in 1994–96 in Berlusconi's media company, Mediaset. Castelli invoked the immunity legislation adopted in June, which the UDC claimed protected Berlusconi from prosecution but not from investigation. The UDC threatened to support a planned opposition motion of no confidence in Castelli; the motion was withdrawn, however, following Castelli's announcement that the investigation would be allowed to proceed unhindered.

In July 2003 a group comprising members of all four coalition parties was established to draft legislation for constitutional reform. The reform plan called for, amongst other things, an increase in prime ministerial powers and a decrease in the presidential mandate, more regional autonomy, and a separation of the roles of the upper and lower chambers. In July 2003 Scajola, the former Minister of Internal Affairs, was appointed to the newly created post of Minister without Portfolio for the Implementation of Government Programmes in what was widely regarded as an attempt by Berlusconi to consolidate control over the coalition following a number of internal disputes.

In October 2003 a police operation led to the arrest of six Brigate Rosse members, who were thought to be implicated in the murders of D'Antona in 1999 and Biagi in 2002; information leading to the arrests had emerged during the interrogation of another member of the Brigate Rosse, Nadia Lioce, who had been arrested in March, following an armed struggle in which a further suspect and a police-officer were killed. Lioce's intelligence also led to the arrests in January 2004 of the brothers, Maurizio and Fabio Viscido and of Rita Algranati, who had previously been convicted in absentia of the murder of former Prime Minister Aldo Moro in 1978. On 1 March 2005 two members of the Brigate Rosse, Laura Proietti and Cinzia Banelli, were given prison sentences for their part in D'Antona's murder. A further 15 members of the group were awaiting trial on charges relating to the murder.

In November 2003 Romano Prodi, who had been the President of the European Commission since 1999, issued a document on European foreign policy that was implicitly critical of Berlusconi's policies. This was widely regarded as the start of Prodi's return to Italian politics, and in mid-February 2004 Prodi announced that he would resume his involvement in Italian politics at the end of his term at the EU, in October 2004. It was later announced that Prodi would lead the L'Ulivo coalition in the 2006 election. Prodi was criticized by some EU officials for compromising the neutrality of the EU Commission through his focus on domestic Italian politics. Also in November 2003, Alessandra Mussolini, the grand-daughter of Benito Mussolini, left the AN, after its leader Fini dissociated the party from its traditional ties with fascism on an official visit to Israel, in which he described Mussolini's fascist regime as evil; Alessandra Mussolini subsequently formed her own party, Libertà di Azione.

In December 2003 President Ciampi refused to sign into law the media regulation bill, known as the Gasparri Bill, which had been adopted by the two chambers of Parliament earlier in the month. The controversial legislation was designed to reduce restrictions on media ownership, and raise current advertisement limits, ostensibly to promote the expansion of digital broadcasting. The bill would overturn the High Court's decision requiring Berlusconi to transfer one of his three terrestrial channels (Rete 4) to a satellite channel by 1 January 2004 and would also lift a ban on a single company owning a licence to broadcast television and to publish a newspaper. Opponents of the bill maintained that it would allow Berlusconi to expand his media holdings and thereby reduce freedom of the press. Through his indirect influence on the state broadcaster RAI (four of the five board members were associated with the ruling coalition), and his own company, Mediaset, Berlusconi already controlled more than 90% of television media. Ciampi returned the bill to Parliament for further consideration, and published his opinion that the bill was contrary to constitutional court rulings regarding the plurality of the media. In late December the Government issued an emergency decree allowing Rete 4 to continue broadcasting as a terrestrial channel until May 2004. In early February 2004 discussion of the bill in the lower house was suspended when it became apparent that members of the ruling coalition had voted against amendments proposed by the Government. The bill was approved later that month by the Camera dei Deputati, as the Government linked the vote to a motion of confidence, a method that had been used to gain approval for the 2004 budget in October 2003. The bill received final approval in the Senato at the end of April 2004 and President Ciampi was constitutionally obliged to sign it into law in early May. The President of RAI, Annunziata, who had threatened to leave her job should the bill become law, duly resigned. During the previous week a leading television journalist, Lilli Grüber, had also resigned from RAI in protest at the corporation's alleged bias in favour of the Government.

In late October 2003 the three biggest trade unions, CGIL, CISL and UIL, staged a half-day strike to protest against the Government's proposed reform of the pension system. Further protests took place in early December, and in February 2004 concessions by the Government paved the way for a possible agreement with the unions. Meanwhile, in December 2003 and January 2004 a series of strikes were staged across the country by transport workers demanding higher wage increases. In February there were further strikes as hospital workers and pilots protested at a reduction in the health-care budget and salary freezes.

In January 2004 the Constitutional Court announced that the legislation passed in June 2003 granting immunity from prosecution to, among others, the Prime Minister, was illegal. This paved the way for the resumption in April 2004 of Berlusconi's trial on charges of corruption. Berlusconi was acquitted on one charge in December; the court ruled that the statute of limitations had expired on the second.

In July 2004, following poor results in regional and local elections the previous month, divisions began to appear within the governing coalition. The AN, which did not support Berlusconi's plan to reduce income tax, threatened to leave the coalition unless Giulio Tremonti resigned as Minister of Economy and Finance. Tremonti subsequently resigned in early July, and his portfolio was temporarily assumed by Berlusconi until the appointment later that month of Domenico Siniscalco, a non-aligned technocrat. In mid-July, citing health problems, Umberto Bossi resigned from his post as Minister without Portfolio for Reforms and Devolution. The UDC, which opposed the constitutional reform advocated by the Lega Nord, also threatened to leave the coalition, and in mid-July voted with the opposition—which contended that Berlusconi exercised too much control over the media—to dismiss the board of RAI. In July controversial legislation regulating conflict of interests was approved by the Camera dei Deputati, having already been endorsed by the Senato. Later in the month the legislation concerning pension reform was passed by the Camera dei Deputati.

In September 2004 plans were announced for the controversial partial privatization of RAI. Berlusconi stated that 20% of the shares in the broadcasting company would be divested in early 2005; however, the sale of the shares was subsequently postponed until late 2005. The UDC and the opposition both opposed these plans.

In mid-October 2004 the Camera dei Deputati approved the first reading of a constitutional reform bill which would extend the executive powers of the President and Prime Minister and devolve some authority over health, education and policing to Italy's regions. The proposals were severely criticized by the opposition. Under existing Italian law, the Prime Minister is appointed by the President and is not competent to appoint or dismiss government ministers. The proposed new legislation provided for the election of the Prime Minister by popular vote and conferred increased powers on the office to form and disband the Council of Ministers. The Lega Nord had earlier threatened to leave the coalition unless the measures were passed. In September President Ciampi, alarmed by the proposed reforms, had appealed to the Government to preserve the power of the legislature. Also in mid-October a bill allowing for an amnesty on illegal construction in supposedly protected areas was passed by the Senato, in conjunction with a vote of confidence in the Government. The bill was criticized by the opposition as an attempt to legitimize improvements, allegedly made without planning permission, to Berlusconi's villa in Sardinia.

In late October 2004 Romano Prodi's term as President of the European Commission ended and he returned to domestic politics. Earlier that month he had announced the creation of a broad left-wing alliance, the Grande Alleanza Democratica, later restyled L'Unione, incorporating members of L'Ulivo coalition and the PRC. Also in late October the centre-left won elections to seven seats in the Camera dei Deputati, including the seat vacated by Umberto Bossi, who had been elected to the European Parliament in June.

In November 2004 Berlusconi's nominee for the European Commission, who was to assume responsibility for justice, freedom and security, Rocco Buttiglione, an outspoken Roman Catholic, was forced to withdraw from the proposed Commission after controversy arose over his views on homosexuality. The erstwhile Minister of Foreign Affairs, Franco Frattini, was subsequently appointed to the EU post. Gianfranco Fini replaced Frattini as the Minister of Foreign Affairs, while retaining his post as Deputy Prime Minister; this appointment was widely viewed as further proof of the increasing respectability of the AN, once seen as the political heir of Italian fascism, within Italian politics. The AN and the CDU, however, continued to disagree with Berlusconi over proposed tax reductions amounting to €6,500m., which were to be included in the 2005 budget. The EU expressed concern over the proposed cuts, stating that they might result in Italy's budget deficit rising above the agreed threshold of 3% of gross domestic product. Berlusconi threatened to call an early general election if the tax reductions were not approved by the Government, and in late November the ruling coalition finally agreed to reductions of €6,000m. in income tax (although, as a concession, Berlusconi agreed that the cuts would not be implemented until 2006). In the same month a series of strikes were organized in protest against proposed reductions in public expenditure, culminating in the holding of a general strike on 30 November.

In late November 2004 employees in the legal profession organized a strike to protest against planned judicial reform which, it was claimed, would reduce the independence of the judiciary, increase the power of the Ministry of Justice, and reduce the power of the legal professionals to prosecute politicians for corruption. Although the legislation was passed by both houses of Parliament, on 16 December President Ciampi (for the second time in two years) refused to sign the legislation and returned it to Parliament, stating that it was unconstitutional. On the same day the Camera dei Deputati passed a bill reducing the statute of limitations for business-related crimes, including fraud and corruption. The bill was criticized as being designed to halt the prosecution of Cesare Previti.

At regional elections held on 3–4 April 2005 the ruling coalition won only two of the 13 regions, while the centre-left won 11; the Government had previously controlled eight of the regions. The centre-left retained a further region in elections held later in the month, giving it control of 16 of the 20 regions. The coalition's poor electoral performance precipitated the withdrawal of four ministers from the UDC from the governing coalition and a threat from the AN to do likewise. The UDC and the AN believed that policy decisions were biased in favour of the prosperous north represented by the Lega Nord and demanded changes in policy including more state aid to the poorer southern regions. Berlusconi resigned on 20 April in order to form a new Government, which was duly inaugurated on 23 April. The new Government comprised representatives of the four parties in the previous Government, the PRI, the Nuovo Partito Socialista Italiano (New Italian Socialist Party—Nuovo PSI) and independents. Although responsibility for the principal portfolios remained unchanged, new ministers were appointed to oversee industry and communication, and the AN and UDC each gained an additional portfolio, being awarded health and culture respectively. Berlusconi's close associate, the former Minister of Economy and Finance, Tremonti, rejoined the Council of Ministers as a Deputy Prime Minister.

Despite mass trials of Mafia suspects in the late 1980s, the Italian Government continued to experience problems in dealing with organized crime. In 1992 the murders of Salvatore Lima, a Sicilian politician and member of the European Parliament, Giovanni Falcone, a prominent anti-Mafia judge, and that of his colleague, Paolo Borsellino, provoked renewed public outrage, and later that year, following an increase in the powers of the police and the judiciary, hundreds of suspects were detained. In January 1993 the capture of Salvatore Riina, the alleged head of the Sicilian Mafia, was regarded as a significant success in the Government's campaign against organized crime. In 1993 the judiciary mounted a campaign to seize Mafia funds, and in the course of the year several suspects, alleged to be leading figures in the world of organized crime, were arrested. Among these were Paolo Benedetto, regarded as the leader of the Mafia in Catania, Giuseppe Pulvirenti, alleged to be another principal figure of the Mafia in Eastern Sicily, and Michele Zaza, the alleged head of the Camorra, based in Naples. In the second half of the 1990s numerous alleged mafiosi were arrested, including Leoluca Bagarella, the alleged head of the Sicilian Mafia in 1995. In November of that year Francesco Musotto, a senior politician in Palermo and an ally of Berlusconi, was arrested and charged with assisting high-ranking members of the Sicilian Mafia to evade capture over a four-year period. In July 1997 troops were dispatched to Naples to assist the security forces, owing to violent territorial disputes between rival Mafia groups. In September 24 influential members of the Mafia, including Salvatore Riina, were sentenced to life imprisonment for their part in the murder of Giovanni Falcone. Several senior Mafia figures were arrested in 1998, including Vito Vitale, the alleged head of the Mafia in Trapani, Sicily, and Francesco Schiavone, the leader of the Camorra. In July 18 people, including Salvatore Riina, were convicted of complicity in the murder of Salvatore Lima in 1992; this constituted Riina's 13th sentence of life imprisonment. In April 1999 an official of the treasury ministry was arrested on charges of external complicity with the Mafia; he was the first serving government member to be taken into preventive detention. In December 17 Mafia members were sentenced to life imprisonment for the murder of Borsellino. In January 2000 Riina was sentenced to life imprisonment for, amongst other charges, the bombing of the Uffizi Gallery in Florence in May 1993 in which six people were killed. Emergency measures were decreed in November 2000 in an attempt to prevent the early release from prison of those accused of Mafia-related crimes. The laws followed the discharge, on technical grounds, of 10 detainees accused of involvement in murders attributed to the Mafia. Magistrates were granted greater powers in determining the length of preventive detention for suspects and a ban on plea-bargaining was introduced. In February 2001 Vincenzo Virga, the financial head of the Sicilian Mafia, who had been in hiding since 1994, was arrested. Benedetto Spera, reputedly the closest colleague of the head of the Sicilian Mafia, Bernardo Provenzano, had also been arrested at the end of January; Spera had been convicted *in absentia* for his role in the 1992 murders of Giovanni Falcone and Paolo Borsellino. In April 2001 Riina, along with six others, was sentenced to 30 years' imprisonment for the murder, in 1979, of a journalist, Mario Francese. Organized crime continued to be problematic during Berlusconi's second tenure of the premiership. In July 2002 a member of Forza Italia was arrested at a Cosa Nostra summit meeting in Sicily. Meanwhile, although a murder charge was dropped against Berlusconi in May, the trial of his

close friend, and one of the founders of Forza Italia, Marcello dell'Utri, on charges of Mafia collusion resulted in the imposition of a nine-year prison sentence in December 2004. Further allegations about Berlusconi's links with the Mafia emerged during dell'Utri's trial in January 2003, when it was alleged by a Mafia informer that the Mafia had transferred its allegiance in the 1990s from the DC, which was engulfed in scandal, to Berlusconi's Forza Italia. Bernardo Provenzano's closest accomplice, Antonino Giuffre, was arrested in April 2002 near Palermo. In December Giuffre directly implicated Berlusconi in the bribing of the Mafia for votes in Sicily in 1993. In March 2003 a Mafia leader, Salvatore Rinella, was arrested in Palermo; he had escaped from prison in 1994, where he had been serving a life sentence for a murder committed in 1979. In October 2003 Salvatore Sciarrabba, alleged to be a close associate of Bernardo Provenzano, was arrested. In August 2004 Pasquale Tegano, allegedly one of the heads of the Mafia was arrested; a warrant had been out for his arrest for 10 years. In September an investigation into the President of Sicily, Salvatore Cuffaro, concluded that he had aided the Mafia; his trial was due to commence in February 2005. In late September 2004 more than 100 people were arrested in an anti-Mafia operation launched in Calabria, and in December 52 people were arrested in another operation in Naples; 46 people were later arrested in Sicily, including Francesco Pastoia, reported to have been a close associate of Provenzano, who subsequently committed suicide in prison. During 2004 more than 100 people were killed in the Naples area in attacks which were suspected to be Mafia related.

Italy's foreign policy has traditionally been governed by its firm commitment to Europe, notably through its membership of the European Community (EC—now EU) and NATO.

In July 1991, following the escalation of hostilities in the neighbouring Yugoslav republic of Slovenia, the Italian Government temporarily deployed military personnel in the north-east of Italy and reinforced border posts in the region. Italy gave firm support to the EC's efforts to find a peaceful solution to the Yugoslav crisis. In May 1992 the Italian Government was obliged to declare a state of emergency, following an influx of thousands of refugees from Bosnia and Herzegovina. The victory of Berlusconi's right-wing alliance in the general election in March 1994 was met with unease by the European Parliament due to the neo-fascist element of the grouping. In May Italy was refused a place on the international 'Contact Group' formed to facilitate a cease-fire in Bosnia and Herzegovina, following alleged statements by AN members reviving claims to territories of the former Yugoslavia. In July relations between Italy and Slovenia deteriorated, following a threat by the Italian Government to veto Slovenian membership of the EU if some form of non-monetary compensation were not given to the ethnic Italians who were dispossessed when Slovenia (then part of the former Yugoslavia) was awarded the Italian territory of Istria under the post-1945 peace settlement. Slovenia subsequently conceded that legislation would be amended to allow foreign nationals to acquire property in Slovenia, and in March 1995 the Italian Government withdrew its veto on Slovenian negotiations to become a member of the EU. In February 1998 Italy and Slovenia agreed a set of compensation measures for those Italians expelled from Slovenia at the end of the Second World War.

Following Italy's accession to the EU's Schengen Agreement on cross-border travel in late October 1997, large numbers of refugees, mainly Turkish and Iraqi Kurds, began arriving in southern Italy, provoking concern from Italy's EU partners. These concerns were partially alleviated by the initial approval, in November, of a bill designed to facilitate the deportation of illegal immigrants. However, the concerns resurfaced in January 1998, following comments by President Scalfaro, who proclaimed that Italy had an 'open arms' policy towards refugees. On 1 April 1998 the Schengen Agreement, which had previously only been applicable to air travel between Italy and the other EU member states, was fully implemented, opening the borders with Austria and France. In order to comply with the terms of the agreement, a new law had been promulgated in February, providing for the detention, prior to forcible repatriation, of illegal immigrants; previously they had been given unenforced expulsion orders and released. In August the discovery of ambiguities in the new immigration law led to renewed fears of a 'flood' of immigrants. In February 1999 legislation was approved allowing for the detention of illegal immigrants arriving in Italy without making an asylum application. In March 2002 a state of emergency was declared following the arrival of 1,000 Kurdish refugees in Sicily; conflict arose within the Government between the Minister of the Interior, Claudio Scajola, who was prepared to offer asylum and Umberto Bossi, who wanted the refugees ejected and demanded stricter immigration controls. Berlusconi voiced concern over the rise in the level of immigration into Italy, and in early June legislation was passed allowing for the fingerprinting of non-EU nationals and requiring residence permits to be renewed every two years. Further increases in arrivals of immigrants prompted a government decree in June 2003, enabling the Italian navy to board ships carrying illegal immigrants and divert them away from the Italian coast. In July 2004 the captain of a German ship, the *Cap Anamur*, carrying 37 African immigrants who had been rescued after their boat capsized, was arrested (but later released) after landing the immigrants in Sicily. The immigrants were subsequently deported, provoking international criticism from, among others, the United Nations High Commissioner for Refugees (see p. 59) and the European Court of Human Rights (see p. 199). In the same month the Constitutional Court ruled that legislation on immigration, which had come into force in August 2002, was unconstitutional. In August 2004 an agreement was reached with Libya on controlling immigration through that country, and in early October the Italian Government commenced returning would-be immigrants to Libya by aircraft.

In March 1999, as the conflict in the Serbian province of Kosovo deepened (see the chapter on Serbia and Montenegro), Italian bases were used for NATO bombing raids on Yugoslavia. However, political opinion within Italy was strongly in favour of a diplomatic solution, and the Camera dei Deputati overwhelmingly endorsed a motion urging the reopening of negotiations and an immediate suspension of the bombing. D'Alema averted a crisis in May by proposing a compromise resolution seeking the suspension of the bombing raids only if a UN Security Council resolution to end the conflict was achieved with Russian and Chinese backing. In April the Senato had approved the deployment of 2,000 Italian troops in Albania to aid the humanitarian mission; by mid-1999 some 5,500 Italians had been deployed in Kosovo as part of a NATO contingent. In March Italy had launched a programme of humanitarian aid for Kosovan refugees in Albania, and a large number of Kosovan refugees arrived in Italy. However, in July Italy announced that as the conflict in Kosovo had ended, those arriving from the region would no longer be accorded refugee status.

The deployment of some 2,700 Italian troops to assist military efforts as part of the US-led 'campaign against terror', following the September 2001 suicide attacks on New York and Washington, DC, was approved by the Italian Parliament in November. An investigation into the existence of terrorist cells possibly connected with the al-Qa'ida (Base) organization headed by the Saudi-born dissident Osama bin Laden led to a number of arrests in Italy in 2002–03. Berlusconi's increasing political allegiance with the so-called 'coalition of the willing' (the group of powers, including the USA, the United Kingdom and Spain, which was in favour of military action against the regime of Saddam Hussein in Iraq), gave rise to massive nation-wide protests on 15 February 2003. Official estimates numbered the marchers in Rome at 650,000; however, other sources placed the figure at up to 3m. Similar large-scale protests were staged in Milan. At the onset of armed conflict in Iraq in March, the anti-war movement in Italy gained momentum, with the trade unions organizing a general strike on 20 March, and protests in Rome continuing on a daily basis. The Italian Government offered the USA the use of Italy's bases and airspace for logistical purposes. In addition, following a request by the US authorities, Italy was the first EU country to expel a number of Iraqi diplomatic staff. Discontent at Berlusconi's stance on the conflict in Iraq deepened following the discovery of a large munitions dump at the US Army's Camp Darby near Livorno and the deployment in northern Iraq of 1,000 US troops that had been stationed in Italy. In April the Government decided to provide humanitarian support for Iraq; however, by November Italy had approximately 2,400 troops stationed in Iraq. In that month a suicide bombing took place at an Italian base in Nasiriyah, killing 19 Italian soldiers; this led to renewed calls from the centre-left for Italy to withdraw from Iraq. In January 2005 the Government announced that Italian peace-keeping missions overseas, including the 3,000 troops in Iraq, would remain in place until June 2005.

In July 2003 Italy took over the rotating EU presidency for six months. In the following months talks relating to a new EU constitution failed to result in an agreement, and in December an EU summit collapsed over the issue of voting rights. The draft EU constitutional treaty was eventually agreed upon by the Heads of State and of Governmnet of the EU in mid-2004. The Camera dei Deputati approved the document in January, but the endorsement of the Senato was required before Italy could ratify the controversial treaty.

Government

Under the 1948 Constitution, legislative power was held by the bicameral Parliament, elected by universal suffrage for five years (subject to dissolution) on the basis of proportional representation. A referendum held in April 1993 supported the amendment of the Constitution to provide for the election of 75% of the members of the Senato (Senate) by a simple plurality and the remainder under a system of proportional representation, and provided for further electoral reform. In August the Parlamento (Parliament) approved a similar system for elections to the Camera dei Deputati (Chamber of Deputies). The Senato has 315 elected members (seats allocated on a regional basis) and 10 life Senators. The Camera dei Deputati has 630 members. The minimum voting age is 25 years for the Senato and 18 years for the Camera dei Deputati. The two houses have equal power.

The President of the Republic is a constitutional Head of State elected for seven years by an electoral college comprising both Houses of Parliament and 58 regional representatives. Executive power is exercised by the Council of Ministers. The Head of State appoints the President of the Council (Prime Minister) and, on the latter's recommendation, other ministers. The Council is responsible to Parliament.

The country is divided into 20 regions, of which five (Sicily, Sardinia, Trentino-Alto Adige, Friuli-Venezia Giulia and Valle d'Aosta) enjoy a special status. There is a large degree of regional autonomy. Each region has a Regional Council elected every five years by universal suffrage and a Giunta regionale responsible to the regional council. The Regional Council is a legislative assembly, while the Giunta holds executive power. The regions are subdivided into a total of 95 provinces.

Defence

Italy has been a member of the North Atlantic Treaty Organization (NATO, see p. 301) since 1949. In August 2004 it maintained armed forces totalling 194,000 (conscripts numbered an estimated 11,000), comprising an army of 116,000, a navy of 34,000 and an air force of 48,000. There were also paramilitary forces numbering 254,300 men (including 111,800 Carabinieri). Military service lasts 10 months in all the services. However, in 1999 the Government approved a draft law phasing out military conscription by 2006 and introducing women soldiers. The law, which would replace the current defence force with a professional army of some 190,000, was approved by the legislature in June 2000. Conscription was actually phased out by December 2004. The 2004 state budget allocated €14,100m. to defence.

Economic Affairs

In 2003, according to estimates by the World Bank, Italy's gross national income (GNI), measured at average 2001–03 prices, was US $1,450,119.5m., equivalent to $21,560 per head (or $26,760 per head on an international purchasing-power parity basis). During 1990–2003, it was estimated, the population increased at an average rate of 0.2% per year, while Italy's gross domestic product (GDP) per head increased, in real terms, by an average of 2.6% per year. Overall GDP increased, in real terms, at an average annual rate of 2.9% in 1990–2003; growth in 2003 was 0.3%.

Agriculture (including forestry and fishing) contributed 2.4% of GDP in 2003 and engaged 4.9% of the employed labour force. The principal crops are sugar beet, maize, grapes, wheat and tomatoes. Italy is a leading producer and exporter of wine. According to the World Bank, during 1990–2002 the real GDP of the agricultural sector increased at an average rate of 1.3% per year. Real agricultural GDP declined by 0.7% in 2001, and by 2.5% in 2002.

Industry (including mining, manufacturing, construction and power) contributed 24.9% of GDP in 2003, and engaged 31.4% of the employed labour force. In 1990–2002 industrial GDP increased, in real terms, at an average annual rate of 1.0% per year. Real industrial GDP increased by 1.5% in 2001 and remained stable in 2002.

The mining sector contributed just 0.5% of GDP in 2000, and engaged only 0.3% of the employed labour force in 2003. The major product of the mining sector is petroleum (reserves of which were estimated at 620m. barrels in 2002), followed by rock salt, talc, fluorspar and barytes. Italy also has reserves of lignite, lead and zinc. Reserves of epithermal gold in Sardinia were discovered in 1996. In 2002 mining contributed 1.1% to total industrial output, measured by production value at factor cost. Average annual growth in the GDP of the mining sector was negligible in 1990–2000; mining GDP declined by 1.1% in 1999 and by 4.6% in 2000.

Manufacturing contributed 17.6% of GDP in 2003 and engaged 22.5% of the employed labour force. In 2001 the most important branches of manufacturing, measured by production value at factor cost, were metals and metal products (12.1% of total industrial output), non-electric machinery (10.7%), food (9.1%), electric machinery (7.7%), and chemical products (7.2%). In 1990–2002 the GDP of the manufacturing sector increased, in real terms, at an average annual rate of 1.1%, according to the World Bank. Manufacturing GDP increased by 0.8% in 2001 and decreased by 0.7% in 2002.

More than 80% of energy requirements are imported. According to World Bank figures, in 2001 natural gas-fired stations provided 38.3% of electricity production, petroleum provided 27.6%, coal-fired electricity generating stations provided 13.5%, and hydroelectric power stations provided 17.2%. In 1987 Italy's four nuclear power stations ceased production following a referendum on the use of nuclear power, although Prime Minister Silvio Berlusconi announced in early 2005 that the country should reconsider its use of nuclear power stations. In October 2004 Libya began delivering natural gas to Sicily through a pipeline financed by Ente Nazionale Idrocarburi (Eni) and its Libyan counterpart. In 2003 fuel and water imports accounted for 0.7% of the value of total merchandise imports.

Services engaged 63.4% of the employed labour force and accounted for 66.4% of GDP in 2003. Tourism is an important source of income, and in 2003 an estimated 34.7m. foreigners visited Italy. Tourism receipts totalled an estimated €27,620m. in that year. The combined GDP of the services sector increased, in real terms, at an estimated average rate of 1.7% per year in 1990–2002. Services GDP increased by 2.1% in 2001 and by 0.9% in 2002.

In 2003 Italy recorded a visible trade surplus of US $10,201m., and a deficit of $20,556m. on the current account of the balance of payments. However, in 2004 Italy's first trade deficit, totalling €393m., since 1992 was recorded. In 2002 the principal source of imports (17.8%) was Germany; other major suppliers were France (11.3%), the Netherlands (5.9%) and the United Kingdom (5.0%). Germany was also the principal market for exports (13.7%); other major purchasers in that year were France (12.2%), the USA (9.7%), the United Kingdom (6.9%) and Spain (6.3%). In 2002 Italy's fellow members of the European Union (EU, see p. 217) purchased 38.6% of its exports. The principal exports in 2002 were machinery and transport equipment, basic manufactures, chemicals and related products, and clothing and footwear. The principal imports were machinery and transport equipment, basic manufactures, chemicals and related products, and food and live animals.

The budgetary deficit for 2004 was equivalent to 4.0% of annual GDP. At the end of 2004 Italy's total accumulated government debt was equivalent to 105.8% of annual GDP. The annual rate of inflation averaged 3.5% in 1990–2002; consumer prices increased by an annual average of 2.7% in 2003 and 2.2% in 2004. As a percentage of the total labour force, unemployment was 8.6% in 2003.

Italy is a member of the EU, the Organisation for Economic Co-operation and Development (OECD, see p. 307), and the Central European Initiative (see p. 383).

Italy has long-term structural problems, principally the underdevelopment of the southern part of the country, a low level of agricultural productivity, and heavy dependence on imported energy supplies. Despite a continuing high level of public debt, Italy was among the first countries to adopt the single European currency, the euro, in January 1999. In 2002–03 sales of government stakes in, among others, gas and electricity companies, earned an estimated €16,600m. This sum helped reduce public debt, which, nevertheless, remained the highest in the EU. In 2003 two of Italy's largest companies, Cirio and Parmalat, were found to be in serious financial difficulties (Parmalat had an unacknowledged deficit of €14,300m.), and in February 2004 the Government unveiled plans for the creation of a new financial regulatory authority. However, the passage of proposed legislation to increase market regulation was delayed in Parliament later in the year and was only resumed in Febuary 2005. The

trial of former Parmalat officials and of institutions connected to the company was expected to take place in Milan later that year. In July 2004 Berlusconi, who had temporarily assumed control of the economy and finance portfolio following the resignation of Giulio Tremonti, came under pressure from the EU to prevent Italy's budget deficit exceeding the limit of 3% of GDP imposed under the EU's Stability and Growth Pact. An EU-approved plan to reduce the deficit in 2004 was passed by the Camera dei Deputati in mid-July 2004, and at the end of the month an economic programme for 2005–08 was approved by the Government. This aimed to reduce the budget deficit to 2.7% of GDP by 2005 and to 1.2% by 2008. The public debt was also to be lowered from 106% of GDP in 2004 to 98.1% in 2008. A privatization programme reportedly worth €100,000m. was also planned. In October 2004 the Government sold 20% of its stake in the power company Enel. In early 2005 plans had been initiated to privatize the troubled national airline carrier, Alitalia. (In January 2005 the EU launched an investigation into whether the Government's guarantee of an emergency loan of €400m. to Alitalia was illegal.) In February 2005 the Minister of Economy and Finance, Domenico Siniscalco, confirmed that the proposed privatization of the broadcasting company RAI (see Recent History) would take place within the year. He announced that Poste Italiane would also be partially privatized. In the same month the Government approved a decree for the privatization of Snam Rete Gas, the gas distributor. Meanwhile, in July 2004 reforms to the pension system, a principal element of the Government's economic policy, given Italy's ageing population, was passed by the Camera dei Deputati. It was anticipated that the reforms would reduce expenditure on pensions by the equivalent of 0.7% of GDP annually. In December the Parliament approved the 2005 budget, which was tied to a vote of confidence in the Government, following disputes within the ruling coalition over the inclusion of tax cuts worth €6,500m. The budget aimed to reduce the budget deficit to 2.7% of GDP; however, concerns were expressed about the one-off nature of measures to reduce the deficit. The Government also pledged a €29,000m. reduction in public expenditure in 2005. The economic disparity between the north and the south persists, with unemployment levels in southern regions at 17.7% in 2003, compared with a national average of 8.6%. Furthermore, the enlargement of the EU in May 2004 to include countries of central and eastern Europe was expected to be to the detriment of those regions in Italy benefiting from special regional development status within the Union, since income per head in much of the southern parts of the country now exceeded 75% of the EU average, the key criterion.

Education

Education is free and compulsory between the ages of six and 15 years, comprising five years of primary education, three years of lower secondary education and one year of higher secondary education. The curricula of all Italian schools are standardized by the Ministry of Education, Universities and Scientific Research. After primary school, for children aged six to 11 years, the pupil enters the lower secondary school (scuola media unificata). An examination at the end of three years leads to a lower secondary school certificate (Diploma di Licenza della Scuola Media), which gives access to all higher secondary schools, of which only the first year is compulsory. Pupils wishing to enter a classical lycée (liceo classico) must also pass an examination in Latin.

Higher secondary education is provided by classical, artistic, linguistic and scientific lycées, training schools for elementary teachers and technical and vocational institutes (industrial, commercial, nautical, etc.). After five years at a lycée, the student sits an examination for the higher secondary school certificate (Diploma di Esame di Stato), which allows automatic entry into any university or non-university institute of higher education. Special four-year courses are provided at the teachers' training schools and the diploma obtained permits entry to a special university faculty of education, the magistero, and a few other faculties. The technical institutes provide practical courses that prepare students for a specialized university faculty.

Following the approval of educational reforms in March 2003, an eight-year first cycle, comprising five years of primary education (scuola primaria) and three years of secondary education (scuola secondaria di I grado), was to culminate in a diploma (Esame di Stato); this was to qualify the student for entrance to a four-year second cycle at either a lycée or vocational instution, concluding in a fifth year specifically directed towards higher education. A further Esame di Stato would then lead to either university or non-university higher education.

In 2000/2001 the total enrolment at primary schools was 100% of all children in the relevant age-group, while the comparable ratio for secondary enrolment, according to UNESCO estimates, was 91% (females 91%; males 90%). In 2004/05 2.5m. children were enrolled in primary education, and 4.2m. were enrolled in secondary education.

In 2000 65.2% of students taking school-leaving examinations enrolled at university, 25% of whom left their courses during their first year. In 2004/5 there were 2.03m. students in higher education in Italy; the largest universities were La Sapienza in Rome (with around 170,000 students) and Bologna (more than 100,000 students). In 2001/02 there were 776 university instutions, including 52 state universities. Following the introduction of university reforms, courses last for a three-year cycle, followed by a two-year specialized cycle. Study allowances are awarded to students according to their means and merit; however, 90% of parents pay fees. In 2002 government expenditure

on education (including higher education) was €61,550m. (equivalent to 10.4% of total government expenditure).

Public Holidays

2005: 1 January (New Year's Day), 6 January (Epiphany), 28 March (Easter Monday), 25 April (Liberation Day), 1 May (Labour Day), 2 June (Republic Day), 15 August (Assumption), 1 November (All Saints' Day), 8 December (Immaculate Conception), 25 December (Christmas Day), 26 December (St Stephen).

2006: 1 January (New Year's Day), 6 January (Epiphany), 17 April (Easter Monday), 25 April (Liberation Day), 1 May (Labour Day), 2 June (Republic Day), 15 August (Assumption), 1 November (All Saints' Day), 8 December (Immaculate Conception), 25 December (Christmas Day), 26 December (St Stephen).

There are also numerous local public holidays, held on the feast day of the patron saint of each town.

Weights and Measures

The metric system is in force.

Statistical Survey

Source (unless otherwise stated): Istituto Nazionale di Statistica, Via Cesare Balbo 16, 00184 Roma; tel. (06) 46731; fax (06) 46733101; e-mail dipdiff@istat.it; internet www.istat.it.

Area and Population

AREA, POPULATION AND DENSITY

Area (sq km)	301,338*
Population (census results)†	
20 October 1991	56,778,031
21 October 2001	
Males	27,586,982
Females	29,408,762
Total	56,995,744
Population (official estimates at 1 January)†	
2002	56,993,742
2003	57,321,070
2004	57,888,245
Density (per sq km) at 1 January 2004	192.1

* 116,346 sq miles.

† Census figures are *de jure*, and official estimates are based on this data. The *de facto* population in 2001 was 57,110,144 (males 27,617,335, females 29,492,809).

REGIONS

(at census of 21 October 2001*)

Region	Area (sq km)	Population	Density (per sq km)	Regional capital(s)
Abruzzo . . .	10,798	1,262,392	116.9	L'Aquila
Basilicata . .	9,992	597,768	59.8	Potenza
Calabria . .	15,080	2,011,466	133.4	Catanzaro
Campania . .	13,595	5,701,931	419.4	Napoli (Naples)
Emilia-Romagna . .	22,124	3,983,346	180.0	Bologna
Friuli-Venezia Giulia . . .	7,855	1,183,764	150.7	Trieste
Lazio . . .	17,207	5,112,413	297.1	Roma (Rome)
Liguria . . .	5,421	1,571,783	289.9	Genova (Genoa)
Lombardia (Lombardy) .	23,861	9,032,554	378.5	Milano (Milan)
Marche . . .	9,694	1,470,581	151.7	Ancona
Molise . . .	4,438	320,601	72.2	Campobasso
Piemonte (Piedmont) .	25,399	4,214,677	165.9	Torino (Turin)
Puglia . . .	19,362	4,020,707	207.7	Bari
Sardegna (Sardinia) .	24,090	1,631,880	67.7	Cagliari
Sicilia (Sicily) .	25,708	4,968,991	193.3	Palermo
Toscana (Tuscany) .	22,997	3,497,806	152.1	Firenze (Florence)

Region— *continued*	Area (sq km)	Population	Density (per sq km)	Regional capital(s)
Trentino-Alto Adige . . .	13,607	940,016	69.1	Bolzano (Bozen), Trento (Trent, Trient)†
Umbria . . .	8,456	825,826	97.7	Perugia
Valle d'Aosta .	3,263	119,548	36.6	Aosta
Veneto . . .	18,392	4,527,694	246.2	Venezia (Venice)

* Population is *de jure*.

† Joint regional capitals.

PRINCIPAL TOWNS

(population at census of 21 October 2001, measured by *comune**)

Roma (Rome, the capital) . . .	2,546,804	Foggia	155,203
Milano (Milan) . .	1,256,211	Perugia	149,125
Napoli (Naples) . .	1,004,500	Reggio nell' Emilia .	141,877
Torino (Turin) . .	865,263	Salerno	138,188
Palermo	686,722	Ravenna	134,631
Genova (Genoa) . .	610,307	Ferrara	130,992
Bologna	371,217	Rimini	128,656
Firenze (Florence) .	356,118	Siracusa (Syracuse) .	123,657
Bari	316,532	Sassari	120,729
Catania	313,110	Monza	120,204
Venezia (Venice) .	271,073	Pescara	116,286
Verona	253,208	Bergamo	113,143
Messina	252,026	Forlí	108,335
Trieste	211,184	Latina	107,898
Padova (Padua) . .	204,870	Vicenza	107,223
Taranto	202,033	Terni	105,018
Brescia	187,567	Trento (Trent, Trient)	104,946
Reggio di Calabria .	180,353	Novara	101,910
Modena	175,502	Ancona	100,507
Prato	172,499	Piacenza	95,594
Cagliari	164,249	Catanzaro . . .	95,251
Parma	163,457	Udine	95,030
Livorno (Leghorn) .	156,274	Bolzano (Bozen) . .	94,989

* Population is *de jure*.

BIRTHS, MARRIAGES AND DEATHS

	Registered live births		Registered marriages		Registered deaths	
	Number	Rate (per 1,000)	Number	Rate (per 1,000)	Number	Rate (per 1,000)
1996	528,103	9.2	278,611	4.9	554,576	9.7
1997	528,901*	9.2	277,738	4.8	561,207	9.6
1998	515,439	9.0	276,570	4.8	574,231	10.0
1999	523,463	9.1	275,250	4.9	565,838	9.8
2000*	538,999	9.3	280,488	4.9	560,121	9.7
2001*	531,880	9.2	260,904	4.6	555,247	9.6
2002*	535,538	9.4	265,635	4.6	558,270	9.8
2003†	542,629	9.4	258,580	4.5	594,118	10.3

* Provisional figure(s).
† Estimates.

Expectation of life (WHO estimates, years at birth): 79.7 (males 76.8; females 82.5) in 2002 (Source: WHO, *World Health Report*).

IMMIGRATION AND EMIGRATION

Immigrants

Origin*	1997	1998
European Union (EU)	19,911	19,235
Non-EU European	51,341	60,298
Albania	13,724	12,463
Russia	—	10,731
former Yugoslavia	6,745	13,079
Africa	13,021	19,493
Morocco	5,185	8,325
Middle East and Asia	15,116	27,666
India	2,061	3,267
Sri Lanka	1,563	3,066
North America	7,310	6,616
USA	6,754	5,954
Central and South America	14,849	16,426
Brazil	4,015	4,055
Oceania	910	982
Total (incl. others)	123,824	153,353

* Refers to country of immigrants' last permanent residence.

Source: Ministry of Internal Affairs.

Emigrants:

Destination	1994	1995	1996
Belgium	3,845	2,177	1,870
France	5,181	3,371	3,448
Germany	21,407	10,816	10,805
Switzerland	10,449	4,560	5,149
United Kingdom	3,515	2,787	3,666
Other European countries	6,380	6,780	8,049
Argentina	1,936	1,592	1,478
Brazil	636	641	770
Canada	1,082	693	706
USA	4,135	3,043	3,939
Venezuela	632	433	484
Oceania	866	692	656
Other countries	5,484	5,718	6,590
Total	65,548	43,303	47,610

2002: Total immigrants 222,801; Total emigrants 49,383.

ECONOMICALLY ACTIVE POPULATION
(annual averages, '000 persons aged 15 years and over)

	2001	2002	2003
Agriculture, hunting and forestry	1,084	1,057	1,038
Fishing	42	39	37
Mining and quarrying	64	63	59
Manufacturing	4,907	4,962	4,990
Electricity, gas and water supply	162	159	161
Construction	1,707	1,748	1,809
Wholesale and retail trade; repair of motor vehicles, motorcycles and personal and household goods	3,416	3,456	3,530
Hotels and restaurants	880	907	953

— continued	2001	2002	2003
Transport, storage and communications	1,180	1,167	1,162
Financial intermediation	659	663	665
Real estate, renting and business activities	1,550	1,675	1,728
Public administration and defence; compulsory social security	1,987	1,982	1,934
Education	1,520	1,531	1,532
Health and social work	1,321	1,329	1,331
Other community, social and personal service activities	939	970	985
Private households with employed persons	193	198	202
Extra-territorial organizations and bodies	20	16	17
Total employed	21,634	21,922	22,133
Unemployed	2,267	2,163	2,096
Total labour force	23,901	24,085	24,229
Males	14,640	14,701	14,765
Females	9,261	9,383	9,465

Source: ILO.

Health and Welfare

KEY INDICATORS

Total fertility rate (children per woman, 2002)	1.2
Under-5 mortality rate (per 1,000 live births, 2003)	4
HIV/AIDS (% of persons aged 15–49, 2003)	0.5
Physicians (per 1,000 head, 2001)	4.3
Hospital beds (per 1,000 head, 1999)	4.9
Health expenditure (2001): US $ per head (PPP)	2,204
Health expenditure (2001): % of GDP	8.4
Health expenditure (2001): public (% of total)	75.3
Human Development Index (2002): ranking	21
Human Development Index (2002): value	0.920

For sources and definitions, see explanatory note on p. vi.

Agriculture

PRINCIPAL CROPS
('000 metric tons)

	2001	2002	2003
Wheat	6,510	7,529	6,243
Rice (paddy)	1,273	1,371	1,360
Barley	1,134	1,190	1,026
Maize	10,554	10,824	8,978
Oats	315	329	308
Sorghum	215	215	158
Potatoes	2,010	2,075	1,951
Sugar beet	11,107	12,726	9,726
Almonds (in the shell)	113	105	91
Hazelnuts (Filberts)	119	119	87
Soybeans (Soya beans)	895	566	424
Olives	2,894	3,231	3,150
Sunflower seed	425	358	239
Other oil seed crops*	143	128	122
Cabbages	579	422	456
Artichokes	505	456	392
Lettuce	966	916	914
Tomatoes	6,529	5,748	6,634
Cauliflowers	490	452	504
Pumpkins, squash and gourds	424	410	466
Aubergines (Eggplants)	358	332	377
Chillies and green peppers	392	326	358
Dry onions	426	412	355
Green beans	219	205	178
Carrots	591	561	578
Other vegetables*	2,891	2,886	2,861
Watermelons	507	545	528
Cantaloupes and other melons	443	506	580
Oranges	1,857	1,724	1,962
Tangerines, mandarins, clementines and satsumas	613	548	562
Lemons and limes	574	486	549

— *continued*	2001	2002	2003
Apples	2,341	2,199	1,945
Pears	963	923	822
Apricots	194	200	109
Cherries†	117	126	101
Peaches and nectarines	1,708	1,587	1,357
Plums	177	168	127
Strawberries	184	151	155
Grapes	8,988	7,394	7,484
Kiwi fruit	382	379	364
Tobacco	130	122	106†

* FAO estimates.
† Unofficial figure(s).
Source: FAO.

LIVESTOCK
('000 head, year ending September)

	2001	2002	2003
Horses*	285	285	290
Mules*	10	10	10
Asses*	23	23	23
Cattle	6,739	6,510	6,504
Buffaloes	194	185	223
Pigs	8,877	9,166	9,157
Sheep	8,311	8,138	7,952
Goats	924	1,025	988
Chickens*	100,000	100,000	100,000
Turkeys*	25,000	25,000	25,000
Rabbits*	67,000	67,000	67,000

* FAO estimates.
Source: FAO.

LIVESTOCK PRODUCTS
('000 metric tons)

	2001	2002	2003
Beef and veal	1,133.0	1,133.8	1,126.9
Mutton and lamb	62.1	58.4	58.1
Pig meat	1,509.6	1,535.9	1,588.7
Horse meat	63.0	45.5	45.0*
Poultry meat	1,135.0†	1,069.0	1,022.8
Rabbit meat*	222	222	222
Cows' milk	11,275.1	11,335.0	11,153.0
Buffaloes' milk	153.8	142.5	127.3
Sheep's milk	788.1	819.5	790.0*
Goats' milk	112.4	107.6	112.0*
Butter	128.4	130.6	122.0†
Cheese	1,083.6	1,134.2	1,131.4
Hen eggs	656.8	692.6	672.0
Cattle hides (fresh)*	130	132	132

* FAO estimate(s).
† Unofficial figure.
Source: FAO.

Forestry

ROUNDWOOD REMOVALS
('000 cubic metres, excl. bark)

	2001	2002	2003
Sawlogs, veneer logs and logs for sleepers	1,597	1,618	1,632
Pulpwood	555	652	594
Other industrial wood	797	358	413
Fuel wood	5,150	4,883	5,580
Total	**8,099**	**7,511**	**8,219**

SAWNWOOD PRODUCTION
('000 cubic metres, incl. railway sleepers)

	2001	2002	2003
Coniferous (softwood)	700	715	710
Broadleaved (hardwood) . . .	900	890	880
Total	**1,600**	**1,605**	**1,590**

Source: FAO.

Fishing

('000 metric tons, live weight)

	2000	2001	2002
Capture	302.1	310.4	269.8
European hake	9.2	9.2	9.9
European pilchard . . .	25.8	24.0	18.0
European anchovy . . .	50.7	53.0	42.1
Mediterranean mussel . . .	44.2*	44.2*	46.0
Striped venus	34.2	34.9	26.0
Aquaculture	213.5	218.3	184.0
Rainbow trout	44.5	44.0	33.8
Mediterranean mussel . . .	94.0	94.0	92.2
Clams	53.0	55.0	41.1
Total catch	**515.6***	**528.7***	**453.8**

* FAO estimate.
Note: Figures exclude aquatic plants ('000 metric tons): 5.0 (capture 2.0; aquaculture 3.0) in 2000; n.a. in 2001; 2.0 (all capture) in 2002.
Source: FAO.

Mining

('000 metric tons, unless otherwise indicated)

	2001	2002	2003
Crude petroleum	4,122.1	5,394.2	5,529.9
Natural methane gas (million cu m)	15,560.5	14,941.5	13,735.1
Manganese (metric tons) . . .	803	867	763
Lead (metric tons)*	4,016	4,709	4,017
Gold (kilograms)*†	503	500‡	500‡
Fluorspar (Fluorite)	70.2	53.3	26.4
Barite (Barytes)	10.8	10.2	12.2
Feldspar	3,240.5	3,159.6	2,972.2
Bentonite	579.0	463.2	474.5
Kaolin	295.3	175.0	224.8
Salt: Marine†‡§	600	600	600
Salt (rock)	3,301.2	3,343.0	2,923.3
Loam (rock)	13,973.9	13,561.3	14,090.5
Gypsum	1,545.3	1,531.5	1,783.9
Pumice†‡‖	600	600	600
Pozzolan†‡	4,000	4,000	4,000
Talc and steatite	126.9	125.0	122.8

* Metal content of ores and concentrates.
† Source: US Geological Survey.
‡ Estimates.
§ Excluding production from Sardinia and Sicily, estimated at 200,000 metric tons per year.
‖ Including pumiceous lapilli.

Industry

SELECTED PRODUCTS
('000 metric tons, unless otherwise indicated)

	2001	2002	2003
Wine (thousand hectolitres)* . .	52,293.0	44,604.1	44,086.1
Cotton yarn	249.2	231.8	212.0
Cotton woven fabrics . . .	214.7	209.8	197.1
Wood pulp, mechanical . . .	276.7	309.2	341.4
Newsprint	917.6	955.1	1,012.1
Other printing and writing paper .	2,032.9	2,104.5	2,091.2
Sulphuric acid at 50° Bé . . .	1,581.2	n.a.	n.a.
Nitric acid at 36° Bé	996.1	n.a.	n.a.
Washing powders and detergents .	2,048.9	1,982.0	2,123.8
Jet fuels	2,607.8	2,458.8	2,626.8
Benzene	20,890.3	20,999.1	20,759.4
Motor gasoline	36,755.9	37,297.0	38,349.5
Naphthas	3,165.2	3,243.3	4,287.7
Gas-diesel oil	13,492.1	12,286.3	12,166.5
Bitumen	2,925.2	2,942.3	3,274.8
Coke	4,738.5	3,973.9	3,663.1
Tyres for road motor vehicles . .	253.1	258.6	265.4
Glass bottles and other containers of common glass	2,914.5	2,939.8	3,139.5
Cement	40,190.6	41,722.3	43,580.0
Pig iron	10,562.4	n.a.	n.a.
Steel	26,526.2	26,301.4	26,832.1
Rolled iron	23,854.7	24,165.6	25,608.6
Other iron and steel-finished manufactures	3,109.8	3,260.2	3,133.9
Refrigerators for household use ('000 units)	6,935.8	7,088.8	6,715.3
Washing machines for household use ('000 units)	8,507.4	8,884.0	9,666.8
Passenger motor cars ('000 units) .	1,271.8	1,125.8	1,026.5
Lorries (Trucks) ('000 units) . .	280.7	266.4	267.4
Motorcycles, scooters, etc. ('000 units)	635.1	588.9	572.5
Bicycles ('000 units)	711.8	597.7	581.6
Hydroelectric power (million kWh)†	53.9	47.3	n.a.
Thermoelectric power (million kWh)†	219.4	231.1	n.a.

* Provisional data.
† Net production.

Finance

CURRENCY AND EXCHANGE RATES

Monetary Units
100 cent = 1 euro (€).

Sterling, Dollar and Euro Equivalents (31 December 2004)
£1 sterling = 1.4180 euros;
US $1 = 0.7342 euros;
100 euros = £70.52 = $136.21.

Average Exchange Rate (euros per US $)
2002   1.0626
2003   0.8860
2004   0.8054

Note: The national currency was formerly the Italian lira (plural: lire). From the introduction of the euro, with Italian participation, on 1 January 1999, a fixed exchange rate of €1 = 1,936.27 lire was in operation. Euro notes and coins were introduced on 1 January 2002. The euro and local currency circulated alongside each other until 28 February, after which the euro became the sole legal tender.

STATE BUDGET
(€ million, consolidated account)

Revenue	2001	2002	2003
Direct taxation	182,690	178,964	177,370
Indirect taxation	176,492	185,116	188,522
Social security contributions . .	153,905	161,325	171,028
Other current revenue	40,090	40,613	41,345
Capital revenue	3,402	5,586	24,498
Total	556,579	571,604	602,763

Expenditure	2001	2002	2003
General public services	118,102	115,675	117,794
Defence	14,747	16,288	18,146
Public order and safety	24,207	25,274	27,767
Economic affairs	53,346	53,118	54,732
Environmental protection . . .	5,558	6,148	6,481
Housing and community amenities .	8,782	853	9,622
Health	77,422	81,256	83,769
Recreation, culture and religion .	9,816	10,072	10,724
Education	61,215	63,416	67,628
Social protection	215,646	227,907	237,932
Total	588,841	600,007	634,595

INTERNATIONAL RESERVES
(US $ million at 31 December)*

	2001	2002	2003
Gold†	21,796	27,019	32,891
IMF special drawing rights . .	297	108	156
Reserve position in IMF . .	3,217	3,907	4,154
Foreign exchange	20,905	24,588	26,056
Total	46,215	55,622	63,185

* Excluding deposits made with the European Monetary Institute (now the European Central Bank).
† Valued at market-related prices.

Source: IMF, *International Financial Statistics*.

MONEY SUPPLY
(€ '000 million at 31 December)

	2001	2002	2003
Currency issued	65.89	65.49*	76.09*
Demand deposits at banking institutions	449.75	492.52	519.67

* Currency put into circulation by the Banca d'Italia was (€ '000 million): 71.23 in 2002; 81.78 in 2003.

Source: IMF, *International Financial Statistics*.

COST OF LIVING
(Consumer Price Index; base: 1995 = 100)

	2002	2003	2004
Food (incl. non-alcoholic beverages)	116.0	119.6	122.2
Alcohol and tobacco	125.2	133.8	144.5
Rent and utilities	123.0	127.1	129.6
Clothing (incl. footwear) . . .	120.8	124.4	127.2
Household goods	115.9	118.3	120.6
Health services	121.3	121.7	123.2
Transport	118.4	121.4	125.2
Communications	92.4	90.8	85.0
Recreation, entertainment and culture	114.2	115.9	117.9
Education	119.5	122.9	125.7
Hotels, restaurants and public services	126.8	131.8	136.0
All items (incl. others)	118.8	122.0	124.7

NATIONAL ACCOUNTS
(€ million at current prices)
National Income and Product

	2001	2002	2003
Compensation of employees . .	499,512	521,283	543,817
Operating surplus and mixed income (net)	395,569	399,809	408,418
Domestic factor incomes . .	895,081	921,092	952,235
Consumption of fixed capital . .	160,445	168,857	176,015
Gross domestic product (GDP) at factor cost	1,055,526	1,089,949	1,128,250
Taxes on production and imports .	183,011	189,803	192,563
Less Subsidies	20,001	19,324	19,886
GDP in market prices . . .	1,218,535	1,260,428	1,300,926
Net primary income received from abroad	−8,786	−9,605	−14,030
Gross national product . . .	1,209,749	1,250,823	1,286,896
Less Consumption of fixed capital	160,445	168,857	176,015
Net national income	1,049,304	1,081,966	1,110,881
Net current transfers from abroad.	−5,340	−6,630	−8,416
Net national disposable income	1,043,964	1,075,336	1,102,465

Expenditure on the Gross Domestic Product

	2001	2002	2003
Government final consumption expenditure*	234,887	244,465	259,182
Private final consumption expenditure	725,968	751,847	780,436
Changes in inventories	−416	2,626	5,654
Gross fixed capital formation . .	240,564	249,263	248,770
Total domestic expenditure .	1,201,003	1,248,201	1,294,042
Exports of goods and services . .	345,943	340,158	330,202
Less Imports of goods and services	328,412	327,930	323,318
GDP in market prices . . .	1,218,535	1,260,428	1,300,926
GDP at constant 1995 prices .	1,032,985	1,036,701	1,039,367

* Including non-profit institutions serving households.

Gross Domestic Product by Economic Activity

	2001	2002	2003
Agriculture, forestry and fishing .	30,881	30,522	30,882
Manufacturing	226,606	229,426	228,973
Electricity, gas and water supply .	31,887	31,226	34,104
Construction	55,155	58,351	61,437
Commerce, hotels and public commercial concerns . . .	188,551	193,431	199,355
Transport and communications .	84,169	85,402	87,457
Financial intermediation, insurance, real estate, renting and business activities* . . .	300,211	318,139	333,082
Public administration and defence; compulsory social security . .	61,426	65,217	68,972
Other community, social and personal service activities . .	160,373	166,593	174,565
Sub-total	1,139,259	1,178,307	1,218,828
Less Financial intermediation services indirectly measured .	48,041	50,298	51,714
Gross value added in basic prices	1,091,218	1,128,009	1,167,114
Net taxes on products	127,316	132,419	133,812
GDP in purchasers' values . .	1,218,535	1,260,428	1,300,926

* Including imputed rents of owner-occupied dwellings.

BALANCE OF PAYMENTS
(US $ million)

	2001	2002	2003
Exports of goods f.o.b.	244,931	252,618	293,122
Imports of goods f.o.b.	−229,392	−239,206	−282,922
Trade balance	15,540	13,412	10,201
Exports of services	57,676	60,439	71,217
Imports of services	−57,753	−63,166	−74,543
Balance on goods and services	15,463	10,685	6,874
Other income received	38,574	43,303	53,519
Other income paid	−48,911	−57,854	−72,837
Balance on goods, services and income	5,127	−3,865	−12,444
Current transfers received . . .	16,136	20,871	20,637
Current transfers paid	−21,915	−26,375	−28,749
Current balance	−652	−9,369	−20,556
Capital account (net)	846	−80	2,893
Direct investment abroad . . .	−21,758	−17,247	−8,986
Direct investment from abroad .	14,874	14,699	16,538
Portfolio investment assets . .	−36,167	−15,265	−57,404
Portfolio investment liabilities .	29,329	32,924	60,150
Financial derivatives assets . .	−2,277	−6,137	−10,284
Financial derivatives liabilities .	1,839	3,431	4,809
Other investment assets . . .	2,032	6,229	−21,150
Other investment liabilities . .	8,560	−7,412	36,200
Net errors and omissions . . .	2,787	1,395	−1,096
Overall balance	−588	3,169	1,115

Source: IMF, *International Financial Statistics*.

External Trade

Note: Figures refer to the trade of Italy, San Marino and the Vatican City.

PRINCIPAL COMMODITIES
(distribution by SITC, US $ million)

Imports c.i.f.	2000	2001	2002
Food and live animals . . .	16,617	16,761	17,475
Crude materials (inedible) except fuels	13,076	12,130	11,539
Mineral fuels, lubricants, etc. .	23,157	21,778	22,042
Petroleum, petroleum products, etc.	21,590	18,575	18,661
Crude petroleum oils, etc. . .	17,071	14,790	14,357
Chemicals and related products	28,463	28,467	30,855
Organic chemicals	7,012	6,616	6,932
Basic manufactures	38,083	37,211	36,970
Textile yarn, fabrics, etc. . . .	6,476	6,402	6,330
Iron and steel	8,631	8,145	8,222
Machinery and transport equipment	79,168	78,217	80,674
General industrial machinery, equipment and parts	8,889	8,723	8,931
Office machines and automatic data-processing equipment . .	8,473	7,785	7,740
Telecommunications and sound equipment	8,116	7,520	7,436
Other electrical machinery, apparatus, etc.	12,175	11,449	10,871
Road vehicles and parts* . . .	25,919	26,906	29,601
Passenger motor cars (excl. buses)	17,371	18,564	20,566
Miscellaneous manufactured articles	23,471	24,233	25,953
Clothing and accessories (excl. footwear)	6,113	6,700	7,538
Total (incl. others)	238,257	236,066	242,744

Exports f.o.b.	2000	2001	2002
Food and live animals . . .	10,408	11,069	11,920
Chemicals and related products	21,683	22,666	25,036
Basic manufactures	50,803	51,319	51,925
Textile yarn, fabrics, etc. . . .	12,100	12,190	12,105
Non-metallic mineral manufactures	8,185	8,065	8,259
Machinery and transport equipment . . .	92,037	91,992	93,991
Machinery specialized for particular industries	15,310	15,653	15,082
General industrial machinery and equipment	20,679	21,055	22,129
Electrical machinery, apparatus, etc.	14,620	14,306	14,724
Road vehicles and parts* . . .	19,445	18,764	19,297
Passenger motor cars (excl. buses)	7,252	6,650	6,656
Miscellaneous manufactured articles	50,739	51,519	52,290
Furniture and parts	8,631	8,674	8,846
Clothing and accessories (excl. footwear)	13,631	14,207	14,494
Total (incl. others)	240,516	244,181	251,003

* Data on parts exclude tyres, engines and electrical parts.
Source: UN, *International Trade Statistics Yearbook*.

PRINCIPAL TRADING PARTNERS
(US $ million)*

Imports c.i.f.	2000	2001	2002
Austria	5,536	5,786	6,05
Belgium	9,601	10,293	10,483
China, People's Repub.	6,466	6,674	7,840
France	26,837	26,493	27,309
Germany	41,806	42,062	42,782
Ireland	3,234	3,215	3,355
Japan	5,915	5,617	5,026
Libya	5,884	4,892	4,637
Netherlands	13,531	13,927	13,461
Romania	2,363	3,015	3,594
Russia	4,841	4,630	4,725
Spain	9,926	10,010	11,109
Sweden	3,517	151	3,251
Switzerland	7,063	8,649	9,252
Turkey	2,035	2,708	2,775
United Kingdom	13,058	12,111	12,143
USA	12,434	11,450	11,747
Total (incl. others)	238,257	236,066	242,744

Exports f.o.b.	2000	2001	2002
Austria	5,316	5,267	5,458
Belgium	6,541	7,301	7,568
China, People's Repub.	2,160	2,900	3,757
China, Hong Kong	3,008	2,920	2,909
France	30,161	29,883	30,249
Germany	36,305	35,655	34,132
Greece	4,962	4,787	5,169
Hungary	2,232	2,659	2,567
Japan	3,976	4,172	4,222
Netherlands	6,377	6,493	6,381
Poland	3,526	3,774	4,024
Portugal	3,312	3,243	3,066
Romania	2,448	2,996	3,406
Russia	2,322	3,155	3,582
Spain	15,308	15,095	15,785
Sweden	2,416	2,259	2,385
Switzerland	7,910	8,792	8,875
Turkey	4,185	3,421	3,744
United Kingdom	16,557	16,434	17,232
USA	24,551	23,396	24,381
Total (incl. others)	240,516	244,191	251,003

* Imports by country of production; exports by country of consumption.
Source: UN, *International Trade Statistics Yearbook*.

Transport

STATE RAILWAYS
(traffic)

	2001	2002	2003
Passenger journeys (million) . .	482.8	491.9	497.9
Passenger-km (million)	46,752	45,956	45,221
Freight carried ('000 metric tons) .	86,479	83,209	82,107
Freight ton-km (million) . . .	24,352	23,060	22,457

ROAD TRAFFIC
(vehicles in use at 31 December)

	2001	2002	2003
Passenger motor cars	33,239,029	33,706,153	34,310,446
Buses and coaches	89,858	91,716	92,701
Trucks (lorries)	3,541,545	3,751,699	3,933,930
Tractors	124,149	132,622	139,402
Motorcycles (incl. sidecars) . . .	4,114,455	4,405,867	4,746,698

SHIPPING

Merchant Fleet
(registered at 31 December)

	2001	2002	2003
Number of vessels	1,476	1,486	1,504
Displacement ('000 grt)	9,655	9,596	10,246

Source: Lloyd's Register-Fairplay, *World Fleet Statistics*.

International Sea-borne Traffic

	2000	2001	2002
Goods loaded ('000 metric tons) .	71,765	69,252	73,402
Goods unloaded ('000 metric tons)	255,619	260,741	260,986
Passengers embarked ('000) . .	3,239	2,834	2,841
Passengers disembarked ('000) .	3,236	2,832	2,873

CIVIL AVIATION
(traffic on scheduled services)

	2000	2001	2002*
Passengers carried ('000):			
domestic	45,237	43,725	45,222
international	44,729	44,686	45,777
Freight carried ('000 metric tons):†			
domestic	148.1	158.4	165.5
international	504.7	555.8	570.2

* Provisional figures.
† Includes mail.

Tourism

TOURIST ARRIVALS BY COUNTRY OF ORIGIN
(arrivals in registered accommodation establishments)

	2001	2002	2003*
Austria	1,893,993	1,810,603	1,708,112
Belgium	797,769	815,030	806,659
France	2,860,712	2,746,459	2,811,159
Germany	9,800,706	9,332,069	8,660,593
Japan	1,543,477	1,815,520	1,593,382
Netherlands	1,376,190	1,352,650	1,325,212
Spain	1,085,832	1,198,375	1,230,927
Switzerland-Liechtenstein . .	1,482,603	1,510,859	1,529,606
United Kingdom	2,459,550	2,625,672	2,759,980
USA	3,719,477	3,470,134	3,254,428
Total (incl. others)	35,767,981	36,355,046	34,741,548

* Provisional figures.

Tourism receipts (€ million): 28,962 in 2001; 28,207 in 2002; 27,620 in 2003 (provisional).

Communications Media

	2001	2002	2003
Telephones ('000 main lines in use)	27,133	27,452	26,596
Mobile cellular telephones ('000 in use)	48,698	52,316	55,918
Personal computers ('000 in use) .	11,300	13,025	n.a.
Internet users ('000)	16,000	17,000	18,500
Book production (number of titles)*	32,298	32,781	n.a.

* First editions only.

Facsimile machines ('000 in use): 1,800 in 1997.

Television receivers ('000 in use): 28,300 in 2000.

Radio receivers ('000 in use): 50,500 in 1997.

Daily newspapers (1996): Titles 78; Average circulation 5,960,000.

Non-daily newspapers (1995): Titles 274; Average circulation 2,132,000.

Sources: mainly UNESCO, *Statistical Yearbook*; International Telecommunication Union.

Education

(state education, 2004/05 unless otherwise indicated)

	Schools	Teachers*	Students
Pre-primary	13,572	75,593	972,250
Primary	16,174	235,948	2,523,240
Secondary:			
Scuola Media	7,025	166,562	1,708,599
Scuola Secondaria Superiore .	4,934	226,437†	2,465,416
of which:			
Technical	1,758	89,195	908,235
Professional	1,384	48,913	545,966
Art Licei and institutes . .	154	10,084	96,854
Classical, linguistic and			
scientific Licei	1,538	66,003	914,361
Higher‡	74	56,480	2,036,525

* Full-time teaching staff.
† Includes 12,242 teachers not assigned to a specific type of institution.
‡ Includes private institutions.
Source: mainly Ufficio di Statistica, Ministero dell'Istruzione, dell'Università e della Ricerca.

Adult literacy rate (UNESCO estimates): 98.5% (males 98.9%; females 98.1%) in 2001 (Source: UN Development Programme, *Human Development Report*).

Directory

The Constitution

The Constitution of the Italian Republic was approved by the Constituent Assembly on 22 December 1947 and came into force on 1 January 1948 (and was amended in April 1993). The fundamental principles are declared in Articles 1–12, as follows:

Italy is a democratic republic based on the labour of the people.

The Republic recognizes and guarantees as inviolable the rights of its citizens, either as individuals or in a community, and it expects, in return, devotion to duty and the fulfilment of political, economic and social obligations.

All citizens shall enjoy equal status and shall be regarded as equal before the law, without distinction of sex, race, language or religion, and without regard to the political opinions which they may hold or their personal or social standing.

It shall be the function of the Republic to remove the economic and social inequalities which, by restricting the liberty of the individual, impede the full development of the human personality, thereby reducing the effective participation of the citizen in the political, economic and social life of the country.

The Republic recognizes the right of all citizens to work and shall do all in its power to give effect to this right.

The Republic, while remaining one and indivisible, shall recognize and promote local autonomy, fostering the greatest possible decentralization in those services which are administered by the State, and subordinating legislative methods and principles to the exigencies of decentralized and autonomous areas.

The State and the Catholic Church shall be sovereign and independent, each in its own sphere. Their relations shall be governed by the Lateran Pact (Patti Lateranensi), and any modification in the pact agreed upon by both parties shall not necessitate any revision of the Constitution.

All religious denominations shall have equal liberty before the law, denominations other than the Catholic having the right to worship according to their beliefs, in so far as they do not conflict with the common law of the country.

The Republic shall do all in its power to promote the development of culture and scientific and technical research. It shall also protect and preserve the countryside and the historical and artistic monuments which are the inheritance of the nation.

The juridical system of the Italian Republic shall be in conformity with the generally recognized practice of international law. The legal rights of foreigners in the country shall be regulated by law in accordance with international practice.

Any citizen of a foreign country who is deprived of democratic liberty such as is guaranteed under the Italian Constitution, has the right of asylum within the territory of the Republic in accordance with the terms of the law, and his extradition for political offences will not be granted.

Italy repudiates war as an instrument of offence against the liberty of other nations and as a means of resolving international disputes. Italy accepts, under parity with other nations, the limitations of sovereignty necessary for the preservation of peace and justice between nations. To that end, it will support and promote international organizations.

The Constitution is further divided into Parts I and II, in which are set forth respectively the rights and responsibilities of the citizen and the administration of the Republic.

PART I

Civic Clauses

Section I (Articles 13–28). The liberty of the individual is inviolable and no form of detention, restriction or inspection is permitted unless it be for juridical purposes and in accordance with the provisions of the law. The domicile of a person is likewise inviolable and shall be immune from forced inspection or sequestration, except according to the provisions of the law. Furthermore, all citizens shall be free to move wheresoever they will throughout the country, and may leave it and return to it without let or hindrance. Right of public meeting, if peaceful and without arms, is guaranteed. Secret organizations of a directly or indirectly political or military nature are, however, prohibited.

Freedom in the practice of religious faith is guaranteed.

The Constitution further guarantees complete freedom of thought, speech and writing, and lays down that the Press shall be entirely free from all control or censorship. No person may be deprived of civic or legal rights on political grounds.

The death penalty is not allowed under the Constitution except in case of martial law. The accused shall be considered 'not guilty' until he is otherwise proven. All punishment shall be consistent with humanitarian practice and shall be directed towards the re-education of the criminal.

Ethical and Social Clauses

Section II (Articles 29–34). The Republic regards the family as the fundamental basis of society and considers the parents to be responsible for the maintenance, instruction and education of the children. The Republic shall provide economic assistance for the family, with special regard to large families, and shall make provision for maternity, infancy and youth, subject always to the liberty and freedom of choice of the individuals as envisaged under the law.

Education, the arts and science shall be free, the function of the State being merely to indicate the general lines of instruction. Private entities and individuals shall have the right to conduct educational institutions without assistance from the State, but such non-state institutions must ensure to their pupils liberty and instruction equal to that in the state schools. Institutions of higher culture, universities and academies shall be autonomous within the limitations prescribed by the law.

Education is available to all and is free and obligatory for at least eight years. Higher education for students of proven merit shall be aided by scholarships and other allowances made by the Republic.

Economic Clauses

Section III (Articles 35–47). The Republic shall safeguard the right to work in all its aspects, and shall promote agreement and co-operation with international organizations in matters pertaining to the regulation of labour and the rights of workers. The rights of Italian workers abroad shall be protected.

All workers shall be entitled to remuneration proportionate to the quantity and quality of their work, and in any case shall be ensured of sufficient to provide freedom and a dignified standard of life for themselves and their families.

The maximum working hours shall be fixed by law, and the worker shall be entitled to a weekly day of rest and an annual holiday of nine days with pay.

Women shall have the same rights and, for equal work, the same remuneration as men. Conditions of work shall be regulated by their special family requirements and the needs of mother and child. The work of minors shall be specially protected.

All citizens have the right to sickness, unemployment and disability maintenance.

Liberty to organize in trade unions is guaranteed and any union may register as a legal entity, provided it is organized on a democratic basis. The right to strike is admitted within the limitations of the relevant legislation.

Private enterprise is permitted in so far as it does not run counter to the well-being of society nor constitute a danger to security, freedom and human dignity.

Ownership of private property is permitted and guaranteed within the limitations laid down by the law regarding the acquisition, extent and enjoyment of private property. Inheritance and testamentary bequests shall be regulated by law.

Limitation is placed by law on private ownership of land and on its use, with a view to its best exploitation for the benefit of the community.

The Republic recognizes the value of mutual co-operation and the right of the workers to participate in management.

The Republic shall encourage all forms of saving, by house purchase, by co-operative ownership and by investment in the public utility undertakings of the country.

Political Clauses

Section IV (Articles 48–54). The electorate comprises all citizens, both men and women, who have attained their majority. Voting is free, equal and secret, and its exercise is a civic duty. All citizens have the right to associate freely together in political parties, and may also petition the Chambers to legislate as may be deemed necessary.

All citizens of both sexes may hold public office on equal terms.

Defence of one's country is a sacred duty of the citizen, and military service is obligatory within the limits prescribed by law. Its fulfilment shall in no way prejudice the position of the worker nor hinder the exercise of political rights. The organization of the armed forces shall be imbued with the spirit of democracy.

All citizens must contribute to the public expenditure, in proportion to their capacity.

All citizens must be loyal to the Republic and observe the terms of the law and the Constitution.

PART II

Sections I, II and III (Articles 55–100). These sections are devoted to a detailed exposition of the Legislature and legislative procedure of the Republic.

Parliament shall comprise two Chambers, namely the Camera dei Deputati (Chamber of Deputies) and the Senato (Senate of the Republic).

The Camera dei Deputati is elected by direct universal suffrage, the number of Deputies being 630. All voters who on the day of the elections are 25 years of age may be elected Deputies.

Three-quarters of the seats are allocated on the basis of a simple plurality and the remaining one-quarter by proportional representation.

The Senato is elected on a regional basis, the number of eligible Senators being 315. No region shall have fewer than seven Senators. Valle d'Aosta has only one Senator.

Three-quarters of the seats are allocated on the basis of a simple plurality and the remaining one-quarter by proportional representation.

The Camera dei Deputati and the Senato are elected for five years. The term of each House cannot be extended except by law and only in the case of war.

Members of Parliament shall receive remuneration fixed by law.

The President of the Republic must be a citizen of at least 50 years of age and in full enjoyment of all civic and political rights. The person shall be elected for a period of seven years (Articles 84–85).

The Government shall consist of the President of the Council and the Ministers (Consiglio dei Ministri) who themselves shall form the Council. The President of the Council, or Prime Minister, shall be nominated by the President of the Republic, who shall also appoint the ministers on the recommendation of the Prime Minister (Article 92).

Section IV (Articles 101–113). Sets forth the judicial system and procedure.

Section V (Articles 114–133). Deals with the division of the Republic into regions, provinces and communes, and sets forth the limits and extent of autonomy enjoyed by the regions. Under Article 131 the regions are enumerated as follows:

Piemonte (Piedmont)	Marche
Lombardia (Lombardy)	Lazio
Veneto	Abruzzo
Liguria	Molise
Emilia-Romagna	Campania
Toscana (Tuscany)	Puglia
Umbria	Basilicata
Calabria	Trentino-Alto Adige*
Sicilia (Sicily)*	Friuli-Venezia Giulia*
Sardegna (Sardinia)*	Valle d'Aosta*

*These five regions have a wider form of autonomy, based on constitutional legislation specially adapted to their regional characteristics (Article 116). Each region shall be administered by a Regional Council, in which is vested the legislative power and which may make suggestions for legislation to the Chambers, and the Giunta regionale, which holds the executive power (Article 121).

The final articles provide for the establishment of the Corte Costituzionale to deal with constitutional questions and any revisions that may be found necessary after the Constitution has come into operation.

The Government

HEAD OF STATE

President of the Republic: Carlo Azeglio Ciampi (inaugurated 18 May 1999).

COUNCIL OF MINISTERS
(April 2005)

A coalition of Forza Italia (FI), Alleanza Nazionale (AN), Lega Nord (LN), Unione dei Democratici Cristiani e di Centro (UDC), Nuovo Partito Socialista Italiano (Nuovo PSI), Partito Repubblicano Italiano (PRI) and Independents (Ind.).

Prime Minister: Silvio Berlusconi (FI).

Deputy Prime Minister and Minister of Foreign Affairs: Gianfranco Fini (AN).

Deputy Prime Minister: Giulio Tremonti (FI).

Minister of Economy and Finance: Domenico Siniscalco (Ind.).

Minister of Internal Affairs: Giuseppe Pisanu (FI).

Minister of Justice: Roberto Castelli (LN).

Minister of Productive Activities: Claudio Scajola (FI).

Minister of Education, Universities and Scientific Research: Letizia Moratti (Ind.).

Minister of Labour and Social Affairs: Roberto Maroni (LN).

Minister of Defence: Antonio Martino (FI).

Minister of Agriculture and Forestry: Giovanni Alemanno (AN).

Minister of the Environment and Land Management: Altero Matteoli (AN).

Minister of Infrastructure and Transport: Pietro Lunardi (Ind.).

Minister of Health: Francesco Storace (AN).

Minister of Cultural Assets and Activities: Rocco Buttiglione (UDC).

Minister of Communications: Mario Landolfi (AN).

Ministers without Portfolio:

Public Function: Mario Baccini (UDC).

Implementation of Government Programmes: Stefano Caldoro (Nuovo PSI).

European Union Affairs: Giorgio La Malfa (PRI).

Technology and Innovation: Lucio Stanca (Ind.).

Regional Affairs: Enrico La Loggia (FI).

Equal Opportunities: Stefania Prestigiacomo (FI).

Italians in the World: Mirko Tremaglia (AN).

Institutional Reforms and Devolution: Roberto Calderoli (LN).

Relations with Parliament: Carlo Giovanardi (UDC).

Development and Territorial Cohesion: Gianfranco Miccichè (FI).

MINISTRIES

Office of the President: Palazzo del Quirinale, 00187 Roma; tel. (06) 46991; fax (06) 46993125; e-mail presidenza.repubblica@ quirinale.it; internet www.quirinale.it.

Office of the Prime Minister: Palazzo Chigi, Piazza Colonna 370, 00186 Roma; tel. (06) 67791; fax (06) 67793169; e-mail redazione .web@governo.it; internet www.palazzochigi.it.

Ministry of Agriculture and Forestry: Via XX Settembre 20, 00187 Roma; tel. (06) 46651; fax (06) 4742314; e-mail ministro.staff@ politicheagricole.it; internet www.politicheagricole.it.

Ministry of Communications: Viale America 201, 00144 Roma; tel. (06) 54441; fax (06) 5407728; e-mail ufficio.stampa@ comunicazioni.it; internet www.comunicazioni.it.

Ministry of Cultural Assets and Activities: Via del Collegio Romano 27, 00186 Roma; tel. (06) 67231; e-mail ufficiostampa@ beniculturali.it; internet www.beniculturali.it.

Ministry of Defence: Palazzo Baracchini, Via XX Settembre 8, 00187 Roma; tel. (06) 46911; fax (06) 4747775; e-mail spi .ufficiostampa@difesa.it; internet www.difesa.it.

Ministry of Economy and Finance: Via XX Settembre 99, 00187 Roma; tel. (06) 47611; fax (06) 5910993; e-mail dpt.comist@finanze .it; internet www.mef.gov.it.

Ministry of Education, Universities and Scientific Research: Viale Trastevere 76A, 00153 Roma; tel. (06) 58491; fax (06) 5803381; e-mail comunicazione.uff2@istruzione.it; internet www.istruzione .it.

Ministry of the Environment and Land Management: Via Cristoforo Colombo 44, 00147 Roma; tel. (06) 57221; fax (06) 5728513; e-mail segreteria.ministro@minambiente.it; internet www .minambiente.it.

Ministry of Foreign Affairs: Piazzale della Farnesina 1, 00194 Roma; tel. (06) 36911; fax (06) 36918899; e-mail relazioni.pubblico@ esteri.it; internet www.esteri.it.

Ministry of Health: Eur, Piazzale dell'Industria 20, 00144 Roma; tel. (06) 59941; fax (06) 59647749; e-mail ufficiostampa@sanita.it; internet www.ministerosalute.it.

Ministry of Infrastructure and Transport: Piazza Porta Pia 1, 00161 Roma; tel. (06) 44121; fax (06) 8415693; e-mail ufficio .stampa@infrastrutturetrasporti.it; internet www .infrastrutturetrasporti.it.

Ministry of Internal Affairs: Piazzale del Viminale, Via Agostino Depretis 7, 00184 Roma; tel. (06) 4651; fax (06) 4741717; e-mail redazionetecnica@mininterno.it; internet www.mininterno.it.

Ministry of Justice: Via Arenula 71, 00186 Roma; tel. (06) 68851; fax (06) 6875419; e-mail staff@giustizia.it; internet www.giustizia.it.

Ministry of Labour and Social Affairs: Via Flavia 6, 00187 Roma; tel. (06) 46831; fax (06) 48161441; e-mail uffstampa@ minwelfare.it; internet www.welfare.gov.it.

Ministry of Productive Activities: International Trade: Viale Boston 25, 00144 Roma; tel. (06) 59931; e-mail info@mincomes.it; internet www.mincomes.it; Industry: Via Molise 2, 00187 Roma; tel. (06) 47051; e-mail ufficio.stampa@minindustria.it; internet www .minindustria.it.

Legislature

PARLAMENTO
(Parliament)

Senato
(Senate)

President: Marcello Pera.

General Election, 13 May 2001

Parties/Alliances	% of votes for seats elected by proportional representation*	Total seats
Casa delle Libertà†	42.5	177
L'Ulivo and Südtiroler Volkspartei (SVP)‡	38.7	128
Rifondazione Comunista	5.0	3
Democrazia Europea	3.2	2
Lista Di Pietro	3.4	1
Lista Bonino	2.0	—
Movimento Sociale—Fiamma Tricolore	1.0	—
Others	4.2	4
Total§	100.0	315

* Figures refer to seats elected by proportional representation (25% of the total); percentages for the remaining 75% of seats, elected by majority vote, are not available.

† Centre-right grouping including Forza Italia (FI), the Alleanza Nazionale (AN), the Centro Cristiano Democratico (CCD), the Cristiani Democratici Uniti (CDU), the Lega Nord per l'Indipendenza della Padania, and the Nuovo Partito Socialista Italiano.

‡ Centre-left alliance comprising the Democratici di Sinistra (DS), the Partito Popolare Italiano (PPI), the Rinnovamento Italiano (RI), the Federazione dei Verdi (FV), the Partito dei Comunisti Italiani (PdCI), the Democratici per l'Ulivo, the Socialisti Democratici Italiani (SDI) and the Unione Democratici per l'Europa (UDEUR).

§ In addition to the 315 elected members, there are 10 life members.

Camera dei Deputati
(Chamber of Deputies)

President: Pier Ferdinando Casini.

General Election, 13 May 2001

Parties/Alliances	% of votes for seats elected by proportional representation*	Total seats
Casa delle Libertà	49.4	368
Forza Italia (FI)	29.4	
Alleanza Nazionale (AN)	12.0	
Lega Nord	3.9	
Biancofiore†	3.2	
Nuovo Partito Socialista Italiano	0.9	
L'Ulivo	35.0	242
Democratici di Sinistra (DS)	16.6	
Partito dei Comunisti Italiani (PdCI)	1.7	
Margherita‡	14.5	
Girasole§	2.2	
Rifondazione Comunista	5.0	11
Lista Di Pietro	3.9	—
Democrazia Europea	2.4	—
Lista Bonino	2.3	—
Movimento Sociale—Fiamma Tricolore	0.4	—
Others	1.6	1
L'Ulivo and Südtiroler Volkspartei (SVP)	—	8
Total	100.0	630

* Figures refer to seats elected by proportional representation (25% of the total); percentages for the remaining 75% of seats, elected by majority vote, are not available.

† Coalition of the Cristiani Democratici Uniti (CDU) and the Centro Cristiano Democratico (CCD).

‡ Coalition of the Partito Popolare Italiano (PPI), the Unione Democratici per l'Europa (UDEUR) and Rinnovamento Italiano.

§ Coalition of the Federazione dei Verdi and the Socialisti Democratici Italiani (SDI).

Political Organizations

Alleanza Nazionale (AN) (National Alliance): Via della Scrofa 39, 00186 Roma; tel. (06) 68817300; fax (06) 6892953; e-mail internet@ alleanzanazionale.it; internet www.alleanzanazionale.it; f. 1994; in early 1995 absorbed the neo-fascist Movimento Sociale Italiano-Destra Nazionale (MSI-DN, f. 1946); Sec.-Gen. Gianfranco Fini; 400,000 mems.

Associazione Riformatori per l'Europa (Association of Reformists for Europe): Largo A. Sarti 4, 00196 Roma; tel. (06) 36001070; fax (06) 36001231; Spokesman GIORGIO BENVENUTO.

Cattolici Liberali (Liberal Catholics): Piazza San Salvatore in Lauro 15, 00186 Roma; tel. (06) 68805651; fax (06) 68805706; Pres. ALBERTO MICHELINI.

Il Centro-Unione Popolare Democratica (The Popular Democratic Centre-Union): Piazza C. Battisti 30, 38100 Trento; tel. and fax (0461) 260416; f. 1998; Pres. RENZO GUBERT.

Coalizione Cristiana (Christian Coalition): Via U. Bassi 20, 00152 Roma; tel. (06) 58340843; fax (06) 58179926; e-mail consorzio .esteuropa@flashnet.it; Gen. Sec. DEMETRIO ERRIGO.

Cristiano Democratici Europei (CDE) (European Christian Democrats): Via Cicerone 28, 00193 Roma; fax (06) 3223927; internet www.cristianodemocraticieuropei.it; Pres. ALESSANDRO MELUZZI; Gen. Sec. STEFANO PEDICA.

I Democratici per l'Ulivo (The Democrats for the Olive Tree): Piazza SS Apostoli 73, Roma; tel. (06) 695191; fax (06) 69781764; e-mail info@democraticiperlulivo.it; internet www .democraticiperlulivo.it; f. 1999; Pres. ARTURO PARISI.

Democratici di Sinistra (DS) (Democrats of the Left): Via Nazionale 75, 00184 Roma; tel. (06) 67111; fax (06) 6711596; e-mail posta@democraticidisinistra.it; internet www.dsonline.it; f. 1921 as the Partito Comunista Italiano (PCI) (Italian Communist Party); name changed to Partito Democratico della Sinistra 1991; name changed as above 1998; advocates a democratic and libertarian society; Pres. MASSIMO D'ALEMA; Gen. Sec. PIERO FASSINO; approx. 1.4m. mems.

Democrazia Europea (European Democracy): Corso Vitorio Emanuele 326, 00186, Roma; tel. (06) 6872545; fax (06) 6872543; e-mail info@sergiodantoni.it; internet www.democraziaeuropea.it; f. 2001; Sec.-Gen. SERGIO D'ANTONI.

Democrazia è Libertà—La Margherita (Democracy is Liberty—The Margherita): Via Sant'Andrea delle Fratte 16, 00187 Roma; tel. (06) 695321; fax (06) 6953253; e-mail sedeargheritaonline.it; internet www.margheritaonline.it; f. 2002 as sub-coalition of L'Ulivo; comprising I Democratici per l'Ulivo, the Partito Popolare Italiano and Rinnovamento Italiano; Pres. FRANCESCO RUTELLI; Vice-Pres. ARTURO PARISI.

Federalisti (The Federalists): Via P. Micca 4, 21047 Saronno; tel. and fax (02) 96700677; Pres. DACIRIO GHIDORZI GHIZZI.

Federazione dei Liberali Italiani (Federation of Italian Liberals): Via Laurina 20, 00187 Roma; tel. and fax (06) 32110200; e-mail info@liberali.it; internet www.liberali.it; Pres. VALERIO ZANONE; Gen. Sec. RAFAELLO MORELLI.

Federazione dei Verdi (Verdi) (Green Party): Via Antonio Salandra 6, 00187 Roma; tel. (06) 4203061; fax (06) 42004600; e-mail federazione@verdi.it; internet www.verdi.it; f. 1986; advocates environmentalist and anti-nuclear policies; branch of the European Green movement; Pres. ALFONSO PECORARO SCANIO; Hon. Pres. GRAZIA FRANCESCATO.

Forza Italia (FI) (Come on, Italy!): Via dell'Umiltà 36, 00187 Roma; tel. (06) 67311; fax (06) 6788255; e-mail lettere@forza-italia.it; internet www.forza-italia.it; f. 1993; advocates principles of market economy; Leader SILVIO BERLUSCONI.

Italia dei Valori—Lista Di Pietro (Italy of Values—Di Pietro List): Via dei Prefetti 17, 00186 Roma; tel. (06) 6840721; fax (06) 68132711; e-mail italiadeivalori@antoniodipietro.it; internet www .antoniodipietro.it; Pres. ANTONIO DI PIETRO.

L'Italia Democratica (Democratic Italy): Viale Col di Lana 12, 20136 Milano; tel. (02) 8392338; fax (02) 8356459; e-mail italiademocratica@virgilio.it; internet www.litaliademocratica.it; Gen. Sec. NANDO DELLA CHIESA.

Lega Nord per l'Indipendenza della Padania (Northern League for the Independence of Padania): Via C. Bellerio 41, 20161 Milano; tel. (02) 66234236; fax (02) 66234402; e-mail webmaster@leganord .org; internet www.leganord.org; f. 1991; advocates federalism and transfer of control of resources to regional govts; in 1996 declared the 'Independent Republic of Padania'; opposes immigration; Pres. LUCIANO GASPERINI; Sec. UMBERTO BOSSI.

Libertà di Azione: Viale Regina Margherita 239, 00198, Roma; tel. (06) 44251916; fax (06) 45442757; e-mail info@libertadazione.it; internet www.libertadiazione.net; f. 2003; founded by Alessandra Mussolini after split from the Alleanza Nazionale; Pres. ALESSANDRA MUSSOLINI.

Movimento Cristiano-Sociali (Christian-Social Movement): Piazza Adriana 5, 00193 Roma; tel. (06) 68300537; fax (06) 68300539; e-mail movcs@tin.it; internet www.cristianosociali.it; Pres. DOMENICO LUCÀ; National Co-ordinator MIMMO LUCÀ.

Movimento Federalista (Federalist Movement): Via Soperga 39, 20127 Milano; tel. (02) 26826465; fax (02) 26826788; e-mail federalisti@movimentofederalista.it; internet www .movimentofederalista.it; f. 1993; Sec. UMBERTO GIOVINE.

Movimento Italiano Democratico (Italian Democratic Movement): Via del Tritone 61, 00187 Roma; tel. (06) 6796912; fax (06) 6796915; Pres. SERGIO BERLINGUER; Gen. Sec. CARMELO PUJIA.

Movimento Nordest: Via Rossarol 22, 30175 Marghera; tel. (041) 5381399; fax (041) 925884; e-mail venetonordest@hotmail.com; fmrly Lega Autonoma Veneta (League for the Autonomy of the Veneto); Contact PIERO CADEI.

Movimento Sociale—Fiamma Tricolore (Social Movement of the Tricolour Flame): Via Simon de Saint Bon 89, 00195 Roma; tel. (06) 3701756; fax (06) 3720376; e-mail fiamma@msifiammatric.it; internet www.msifiammatric.it; f. 1996; electoral alliance incorporating fmr mems of neo-fascist Movimento Sociale Italiano-Destra Nazionale; Nat. Sec. LUCA ROMAGNOLI.

Movimento per l'Ulivo (Movement for the Olive Tree alliance): Piazza S. Apostoli 73, Roma; tel. (06) 695191; fax (06) 69781764; e-mail scrivi@perlulivo.it; internet www.perlulivo.it; Gen. Sec. MARINA MAGISTRELLI.

Movimento Unitario Pensionati—Uomini Vivi (Unitary Pensioners Movement—Living Men): Via Boezio 17, 00193 Roma; tel. (06) 6878628; fax (06) 6878697; Pres. GIUSEPPE POLINI; Sec. BALILLA TATA.

Nuovo Partito Socialista Italiano (New Italian Socialist Party): Via di Torre Argentina 47, 00186 Roma; tel. (06) 68892583; fax (06) 6892000; e-mail segretario@nuovopsi.com; internet www.nuovopsi .com; f. 1994 following dissolution of the Partito Socialista Italiano (PSI); Sec. GIANNI DE MICHELIS.

Partito Autonomista Trentino Tirolese (PATT) (Autonomist Party of Trent and the Tyrol): Piazza Silvio Pellico 5, 38100, Trento; tel. (0461) 986633; fax (0461) 986417; e-mail info@patt.tn.it; internet www.patt.tn.it; Pres. RUDI OSS.

Partito dei Comunisti Italiani (PdCI) (Party of Italian Communists): Piazza Augusto Imperatore 32, 00186 Roma; tel. (06) 686271; fax (06) 68627230; e-mail direzionenazionale@comunisti-italiani.it; internet www.comunisti-italiani.it; f. 1998; Chair. ARMANDO COSSUTTA.

Partito Liberal (Liberal Party): Via del Corso 117, 00187 Roma; tel. (06) 69549041; fax (06) 69549043; e-mail info@partitoliberale.it; internet www.partitoliberale.it; Pres. Prof. CARLA MARTINO; Sec. STEFANO DE LUCA.

Partito Popolare Italiano (PPI) (Italian People's Party): Piazza del Gesù 46, 00186 Roma; tel. (06) 699591; fax (06) 69959324; e-mail uffstampa@pronet.it; internet www.popolari.it; f. 1994 as the successor to the Partito della Democrazia Cristiana (DC) (Christian Democrat Party, f. 1943); while extending its appeal to voters of all classes, the party attempts to maintain a centre position; Sec.-Gen. PIERLUIGI CASTAGNETTI.

Partito Repubblicano Italiano (PRI) (Italian Republican Party): Corso Vittorio Emanuele 326, 00186 Roma; tel. (06) 6865044; fax (06) 6893002; e-mail nucarapri@libero.it; internet www.pri.it; f. 1897; followers of the principles of Mazzini (social justice in a modern free society) and modern liberalism; Pres. GIORGIO LA MALFA; Gen. Sec. FRANCESCO NUCARA; 110,000 mems.

Partito della Rifondazione Comunista (PRC) (Reconstructed Communism): Viale del Policlinico 131, 00161 Roma; tel. (06) 441821; fax (06) 44182282; e-mail ufficiostampa.prc@rifondazione .it; internet www.rifondazione.it; f. 1991 by former members of the Partito Comunista Italiano (Italian Communist Party); Sec.-Gen. FAUSTO BERTINOTTI.

Partitu Sardu—Partito Sardo d'Azione (Sardinian Action Party): Via Roma 231, 09123 Cagliari; tel. (070) 657599; fax (070) 657779; internet www.psdaz-ichnos.com; Pres. LORENZO PALERMO; Sec. GIACOMO SANNA.

Patto Segni Liberaldemocratici (Segni's Pact—Liberal Democrats): Via Vittorio Jenetto 169, 00187 Roma; tel. (06) 4744916; fax (06) 47821834; e-mail info@mariosegni.it; internet www.mariosegni .it; f. 1993; liberal party, advocating institutional reform; Leader MARIO SEGNI.

Popolari—UDEUR (Alleanza Popolare—Unione Democratici per l'Europa) (Union of Democrats for Europe): Largo Arenula 34, 00186 Roma; tel. (06) 684241; fax (06) 68210615; e-mail info@ popolariudcur.it; internet www.popolariudeur.it; f. 1999; Pres. MINO MARTINAZZOLI; Sec. CLEMENTE MASTELLA.

Pour la Vallée d'Aoste (For the Aosta Valley): Via Festaz 47, 11100 Aosta; tel. and fax (0165) 41055; Pres. CESARE DUJANY; Sec. ILARJO LANIVI.

Radicali Italiani: Roma; e-mail d.capezzone@radicali.it; internet www.radicali.it; f. 2001 as il Partito Radicale; Pres. LUCA COSCIONI; Gen. Sec. DANIELE CAPEZZONE.

Riforme e Libertà (Reforms and Freedom): Via del Corso 117, 00186 Roma; tel. (06) 67609416; fax (06) 67609416; e-mail liberta@pobox.com; Pres. GIULIO SAVELLI.

Rinnovamento Italiano (Italian Renewal): Via di Ripetta 142, 00186 Roma; tel. (06) 68808380; fax (06) 68808480; e-mail informa@rinnovamento.it; internet www.rinnovamento.it; f. 1996; centrist; Leader Prof. LAMBERTO DINI.

Socialisti Democratici Italiani (SDI) (Italian Democratic Socialists): Piazza S. Lorenzo in Lucina 26, 00186 Roma; tel. (06) 68307666; fax (06) 68307659; e-mail socialisti@socialisti.org; internet www.socialisti.org; f. 1892 as Partito Socialista Italiano (PSI); in 1966 merged with the Social Democratic Party to form the United Socialist Party, but in 1969 the Social Democrats broke away; name changed to Socialisti Italiani in 1994; in 1998 re-merged with Social Democratic Party, name changed as above; centre-left; it adheres to the Socialist International and believes that socialism is inseparable from democracy and individual freedom; Pres. ENRICO BOSSELLI.

Socialisti Riformisti Sicilia: Via XX Settembre 62, 90141 Palermo; tel. (380) 7173055; fax (02) 700425897; e-mail info@psi2000.it; internet www.psi2000.it; f. 2001; left-wing Sicilian party; Pres. ANTONIO MATASSO.

Südtiroler Volkspartei (SVP) (South Tyrol People's Party): Brennerstrasse 7A, 39100 Bozen/Bolzano; tel. (0471) 304000; fax (0471) 981473; e-mail info@svpartei.org; internet www.svpartei.org; regional party of the German and Ladin-speaking people in the South Tyrol; Pres. ELMAR PICHLER ROLLE; Gen. Sec. ALEXANDER MITTERMAIR.

L'Ulivo (The Olive Tree): Piazza SS. Apostoli 55, 00187 Roma; tel. (06) 696881; fax (06) 69380442; e-mail info@ulivo.it; internet www.ulivo.it; f. 1995; centre-left alliance comprising the Democratici di Sinistra (formerly the Partito Democratico della Sinistra), the Partito Popolare Italiano, the Südtiroler Volkspartei, the Unione Democratica, the Lista Romano Prodi, the Rinnovamento Italiano, the Margherita coalition, the Federazione dei Verdi and the Movimento Repubblicani Europei; Leader FRANCESCO RUTELLI.

Union Autonomista Ladina (Autonomist Ladin Movement): Via Pilat 8, 38039 Vigo di Fassa; tel. (0462) 763396; fax (0462) 763407; Pres. GINO FONTANA; Sec. GIUSEPPE DETOMAS.

Union Valdôtaine (Aosta Valley Union): Ave des Maquisards 27/29, 11100 Aosta; tel. (0165) 235181; fax (0165) 364289; internet www.unionvaldotaine.org; Pres. AUGUSTE ROLLANDIN.

L'Unione: f. 2005; broad centre-left/left-wing coalition comprising members of L'Ulivo coalition and the Partito della Rifondazione Comunista; Leader ROMANO PRODI.

Unione dei Democratici Cristiani e di Centro (UDC) (Union of the Democratic Christians of the Centre): Via dei Due Macelli 66, 00182 Roma; tel. (06) 69791001; fax (06) 6791574; e-mail info@udc-italia.it; internet www.udc-italia.it; f. 2002 by merger of following parties; Pres. ROCCO BUTTIGLIONE; Sec. MARCO FOLLINI.

  Centro Cristiano Democratico (CCD) (Christian-Democratic Centre): Via dei Due Macelli 66, 00187 Roma; tel. (06) 69190700; fax (06) 6795940; e-mail amministrazione1@ccd.it; internet www.ccd.it; f. 1994; Pres. MARCO FOLLINI; Pres. of National Council SANDRO FONTANA.

  Cristiani Democratici Uniti (CDU) (United Christian Democrats): Piazza del Gesù 46, 00186 Roma; tel. (06) 6775204; fax (06) 6785956; e-mail buttiglione@cdu.it; internet www.cdu.it; f. 1995 after split with Partito Popolare Italiano; advocates centre-right policies; Sec.-Gen. ROCCO BUTTIGLIONE.

Unione per la Repubblica (Union for the Republic): Via Cicerone 44, 00193 Roma; tel. (06) 36003745; fax (06) 32609549; Sec. ANGELO SANZA; Pres. FRANCESCO COSSIGA.

Veneti d'Europa (Inhabitants of the Veneto region for Europe): Via Catania 11, 37138 Verona; tel. and fax (045) 566433; e-mail info@ligafronteveneto.org; internet www.ligafronteveneto.org; Pres. FABRIZIO COMENCINI; Gen. Sec. ETTORE BEGGIATO.

Diplomatic Representation

EMBASSIES IN ITALY

Afghanistan: Via Nomentana 120, 00161 Roma; tel. (06) 8611009; fax (06) 86322939; e-mail afghanembassy.rome@flashnet.it; Ambassador MOSTAPHA ZAHIR.

Albania: Via Asmara 3–5, 00199 Roma; tel. (06) 86224120; fax (06) 86216005; internet www.mfa.gov.al; Ambassador PAVLI ZERI.

Algeria: Via Barnaba Oriani 26, 00197 Roma; tel. (06) 80687620; fax (06) 8083436; Ambassador MOKHTAR REGUIEG.

Angola: Via Filippo Bernardini 21, 00165 Roma; tel. (06) 39366902; fax (06) 3938821; e-mail ambasciatangola@libero.it; Ambassador MANUEL PEDRO PACAVIRA.

Argentina: Piazza dell'Esquilino 2, 2°, 00185 Roma; tel. (06) 4742551; fax (06) 4819787; e-mail ambasciata.argentina@diginet.it; internet www.ambasciata.argentina.it; Ambassador VICTORIO MARÍA JOSÉ TACCETTI.

Armenia: Via dei Colli della Farnesina 174, 00194 Roma; tel. (06) 3296638; fax (06) 3297763; e-mail embarmit@tin.it; internet www.embarmit.it; Ambassador GAGHIK BAGHDASSARIAN.

Australia: Via A. Bosio 5, 00161 Roma; tel. (06) 852721; fax (06) 85272300; e-mail info-rpme@dfat.gov.au; internet www.italy.embassy.au; Ambassador PETER RICHARD WOOLCOTT.

Austria: Via G. B. Pergolesi 3, 00198 Roma; tel. (06) 8440141; fax (06) 8543286; e-mail rom-ob@bmaa.gv.at; internet www.austria.it; Ambassador ALFONS KLOSS.

Azerbaijan: Via Savoia 78, A/7, Piano 3, Roma; tel. (06) 85237235; fax (06) 85237246; e-mail azerb.roma@azembassy.it; internet www.azembassy.it; Ambassador EMIL ZULFGAR OĞLU KARIMOV.

Bangladesh: Via Antonio Bertoloni 14, 00197 Roma; tel. (06) 8078541; fax (06) 8084853; e-mail embangrm@mclink.it; Ambassador ANWARUL BAR CHOWDHURY.

Belarus: Via delle Alpi Apuane 16, 00141 Roma; tel. (06) 8208141; fax (06) 82084099; e-mail italy@belembassy.org; Ambassador ALEKSEI SKRIPKO.

Belgium: Via dei Monti Parioli 49, 00197 Roma; tel. (06) 3609511; fax (06) 3226935; e-mail ambelrom@tin.it; internet www.diplomatie.be/romeit; Ambassador JEAN DE RUYT.

Belize: Piazza di Spagna 81, 00187 Roma; tel. (06) 69190776; fax (06) 69925794; Ambassador NUNZIO ALFREDO D'ANGIERI.

Bolivia: Via Brenta 2A, int. 18, 00198 Roma; tel. and fax (06) 8841001; e-mail embolivia-roma@rree.gov.bo; Ambassador MOIRA PAZ ESTENSSORO CORTEZ.

Bosnia and Herzegovina: Piazzale Clodio 12, int. 17/18, 00195 Roma; tel. (06) 39742817; fax (06) 39030567; e-mail ambasciata@ambiti.191.it; Ambassador LUKSA SOLJAN.

Brazil: Palazzo Pamphili, Piazza Navona 14, 00186 Roma; tel. (06) 683981; fax (06) 6867858; e-mail info@ambrasile.it; internet www.ambasciatadelbrasile.it; Ambassador ITAMAR AUGUSTO CAUTIERO FRANCO.

Bulgaria: Via Pietro Paolo Rubens 21, 00197 Roma; tel. (06) 3224640; fax (06) 3226122; e-mail bgamb.roma@tin.it; Ambassador NIKOLA IVANOV KALOUDOV.

Burkina Faso: Via XX Settembre 86, 00185 Roma; tel. (06) 42013335; fax (06) 42391063; e-mail ambabf.roma@tin.it; Ambassador MAMADOU SISSOKO.

Burundi: Corso Francia 221, 00919 Roma; tel. and fax (06) 36381511; Ambassador FAUSTIN NDISABIYE.

Cameroon: Via Siracusa 4–6, 00161 Roma; tel. (06) 44291285; fax (06) 44291323; internet www.cameroonembassy.it; Ambassador MICHAEL TABONG KIMA.

Canada: Via G. B. de Rossi 27, 00161 Roma; tel. (06) 445981; fax (06) 445983760; e-mail rome@dfait-maeci.gc.ca; internet www.canada.it; Ambassador ROBERT R. FOWLER.

Cape Verde: Via Giosuè Carducci 4, 1°, 00187 Roma; tel. (06) 4744678; fax (06) 4744643; Ambassador JORGE MARIA CUSTODIO SANTOS.

Chile: Via Po 23, 00198 Roma; tel. (06) 844091; fax (06) 8841452; e-mail echileit@flashnet.it; internet www.target.it./cile; Chargé d'affaires a.i. GUSTAVO NELSON AYARES OSSANDON.

China, People's Republic: Via Bruxelles 56, 00198 Roma; tel. (06) 8413458; fax (06) 85352891; Ambassador CHENG WENDONG.

Colombia: Via Giuseppe Pisanelli 4, 00196 Roma; tel. (06) 3612131; fax (06) 3225798; e-mail eroma@minrelext.gov.co; Ambassador FABIO VALENCIA COSSIO.

Congo, Democratic Republic: Via Barberini 3, 00187 Roma; tel. (06) 42010779; fax (06) 42010779; Ambassador EDOUARD UMBA ILUNGA.

Congo, Republic: Via Ombrone 8–10, 00198 Roma; tel. and fax (06) 8417422; Ambassador MAMADOU KAMARA DEKAMO.

Costa Rica: Viale Liegi 2, int 8, 00198 Roma; tel. (06) 84242853; fax (06) 85355956; e-mail embcosta@tiscalinet.it; internet www.mix.it/utenti/embcosta; Ambassador MANUEL HERNÁNDEZ GUTIÉRREZ.

Côte d'Ivoire: Via Guglielmo Saliceto 6–10, 00161 Roma; tel. (06) 44231129; fax (06) 44292531; Ambassador RICHARD GBAKA ZADY.

Croatia: Via Luigi Bodio 74–76, 00191 Roma; tel. (06) 36307650; fax (06) 36303405; e-mail vhrim@mvp.hr; Ambassador DRAGO KRALJEVIĆ.

Cuba: Via Licinia 7, 00153 Roma; tel. (06) 5717241; fax (06) 5745445; e-mail embajada@ecuitalia.it; internet www .ambasciatacuba.com; Ambassador MARÍA DE LOS ANGELES FLÓREZ PRIDA.

Cyprus: Via Francesco Denza 15, 00197 Roma; tel. (06) 8088365; fax (06) 8088338; e-mail emb.rome@flashnet.it; Ambassador ALEXANDROS N. ZENON.

Czech Republic: Via dei Gracchi 322, 00192 Roma; tel. (06) 3244459; fax (06) 3244466; e-mail rome@embassy.mzv.cz; Ambassador LIBOR ŠECKA.

Denmark: Via dei Monti Parioli 50, 00197 Roma; tel. (06) 9774831; fax (06) 97748399; e-mail romamb@um.dk; internet www.ambrom .um.dk; Ambassador POUL SKYTTE CHRISTOFFERSEN.

Dominican Republic: Via Pisanelli 1, int. 8, 00196 Roma; tel. (06) 36004377; fax (06) 36004380; e-mail embajadadominicana@yahoo.it; Chargé d'affaires a.i. CAMILO DE JESÚS GARCÍA RIVAS.

Ecuador: Via Antonio Bertoloni 8, 00197 Roma; tel. (06) 45439007; fax (06) 8076271; e-mail mecuroma@flashnet.it; Ambassador EMILIO IZQUIERDO MIÑO.

Egypt: Villa Savoia, Via Salaria 267, 00199 Roma; tel. (06) 8440191; fax (06) 8554424; e-mail amb.egi@pronet.it; Ambassador HELMY ABDELHAMID SALEH BEDEIR.

El Salvador: Via G. Castellini 13, 00197 Roma; tel. (06) 8076605; fax (06) 8079726; e-mail embasalvaroma@iol.it; internet www .embasalvaroma.com; Chargé d'affaires a.i. MARÍA EULALIA JIMÉNEZ ZEPEDA.

Eritrea: Via Boncompagni 16, Int. 6, 00187 Roma; tel. (06) 42741293; fax (06) 42741514; e-mail segretaria@embassyoferitrea .it; Ambassador ZEMEDE TEKLE WOLDETATIOS.

Estonia: Viale Liegi 28, int. 5, 00198 Roma; tel. (06) 8440751; fax (06) 844075119; e-mail saatkond@estemb.it; internet www.estemb .it; Ambassador JURI SEILENTHAL.

Ethiopia: Via Andrea Vesalio 16–18, 00161 Roma; tel. (06) 4416161; fax (06) 4403676; Ambassador Dr MENGISTU HULLUKA DEYAS.

Finland: Via Lisbona 3, 00198 Roma; tel. (06) 852231; fax (06) 8540362; e-mail sanomat.roo@formin.fi; internet www.finland.it; Ambassador ALEC AALTO.

France: Piazza Farnese 67, 00186 Roma; tel. (06) 686011; fax (06) 68601260; internet www.france-italia.it; Ambassador LOÏC HENNE-KINE.

Gabon: Via San Marino 36A, 00198 Roma; tel. (06) 85358970; fax (06) 8417278; e-mail ambagabon@tiscali.net; Ambassador VINCENT BOULÉ.

Georgia: Palazzo Pierret, Piazza di Spagna 20, 00187 Roma; tel. (06) 69941972; fax (06) 69941942; e-mail amgeorgia@pronet.it; Ambassador ZAAL GOGSADZE.

Germany: Via San Martino della Battaglia 4, 00185 Roma; tel. (06) 492131; fax (06) 4452672; e-mail mail@deutschebotschaft-rom.it; internet www.ambgermania.it; Ambassador MICHAEL GERDTS.

Ghana: Via Ostriana 4, 00199 Roma; tel. (06) 86217191; fax (06) 86325762; e-mail ghembrom@rdn.it; Ambassador DR KOFI DSANE-SELBY.

Greece: Viale G. Rossini 4, 00198 Roma; tel. (06) 8537551; fax (06) 8415927; e-mail gremroma@tin.it; internet www.greekembassy.it; Ambassador ANASTASSIS MITSIALIS.

Guatemala: Via dei Colli della Farnesina 128, 00194 Roma; tel. (06) 36381143; fax (06) 3291639; e-mail embaguate.italia@tin.it; Ambassador FRANCISCO EDUARDO BONIFAZ RODRÍGUEZ.

Guinea: Via Adelaide Ristori, 9B 13, 00197 Roma; tel. (06) 8078989; fax (06) 8077588; e-mail ambaguineerome1@virgilio.it; Ambassador El Hadj THIERNO MAMADOU CELLOU DIALLO.

Haiti: Via di Villa Patrizi 7/7A, 00161 Roma; tel. (06) 44254106; fax (06) 44254208; e-mail amb.haiti@tiscali.it; Chargé d'affaires a.i. EUCHER-LUC JOSEPH.

Holy See: Via Po 27–29, 00198 Roma; tel. (06) 8546287; fax (06) 8549725; e-mail nunzital@tin.it; Apostolic Nuncio Most Rev. PAOLO ROMEO (Titular Archbishop of Vulturia).

Honduras: Via Giambattista Vico 40, int. 8, 00197 Roma; tel. (06) 3207236; fax (06) 3207973; e-mail embhon@tin.it; Ambassador LUIS ARMANDO BOTAZZI SUÁREZ.

Hungary: Via dei Villini 12–16, 00161 Roma; tel. (06) 4402032; fax (06) 4403270; e-mail titkarsag2@huembrom.it; internet www .huembit.it; Ambassador ISTVAN KOVACS.

India: Via XX Settembre 5, 00187 Roma; tel. (06) 4884642; fax (06) 4819539; e-mail admin.wing@indianembassy.it; internet www .indianembassy.it; Ambassador HIMACHAL SOM.

Indonesia: Via Campania 55, 00187 Roma; tel. (06) 4200911; fax (06) 4880280; e-mail indorom@uni.net; internet www .indonesianembassy.it; Ambassador FREDDY NUMBERI.

Iran: Via Nomentana 361, 00162 Roma; tel. (06) 86328485; fax (06) 86328492; e-mail info@iranembassy.it; Ambassador BAHRAM GHA-SEMI.

Iraq: Via della Camilluccia, 355, 00135 Roma; tel. (06) 3014508; fax (06) 3014445; e-mail alyacoubi@tiscalinet.it; Ambassador MOHAMMED MAHMOUD AL AMILI.

Ireland: Piazza di Campitelli 3, 00186 Roma; tel. (06) 6979121; fax (06) 6792354; e-mail irish.embassy@esteri.it; Ambassador JOHN F. COGAN.

Israel: Via Michele Mercati 12, 00197 Roma; tel. (06) 36198500; fax (06) 36198555; e-mail adm-sec@roma.mfa.gov.il; internet www .israel.amb.it; Ambassador EHUD GOL.

Japan: Via Quintino Sella 60, 00187 Roma; tel. (06) 487991; fax (06) 4873316; internet www.it.emb-japan.go.jp; Ambassador NOBUKO MATSUBARA.

Jordan: Via G. Marchi 1B, 00161 Roma; tel. (06) 86205303; fax (06) 8606122; e-mail embroma@jordanembassy.it; Ambassador RAMEZ GOUSSOUS.

Kazakhstan: Piazza Farnese 101, int. 3, 00186 Roma; tel. (06) 68808640; fax (06) 68891360; e-mail kazakhstan.emb@agora.stm.it; internet www.embkaz.it; Ambassador ALMAZ N. KHAMZAYEV.

Kenya: Via Archimede 164, 00197 Roma; tel. (06) 8082717; fax (06) 8082707; e-mail kenroma@rdn.it; internet www.embassyofkenya.it; Ambassador BRUCE MISOGA MADETE.

Korea, Democratic People's Republic: Via dell'Esperanto 26, 00144 Roma; tel. (06) 54220749; fax (06) 54210090; e-mail permerepun@hotmail.com; Ambassador CHOE THAEK SAN.

Korea, Republic: Via Barnaba Oriani 30, 00197 Roma; tel. (06) 802461; fax (06) 802462259; Ambassador YOUNG JAE CHO.

Kuwait: Via Archimede 124–126, 00197 Roma; tel. (06) 8078415; fax (06) 8076651; Ambassador ABDULA AS SULEIMAN AL-GANAIE.

Latvia: Viale Liegi 42, 00198 Roma; tel. (06) 8841227; fax (06) 8841239; e-mail embassy.italy@mfa.gov.lv; Ambassador JĀNIS LŪSIS.

Lebanon: Via Giacomino Carissimi 38, 00198 Roma; tel. (06) 8537211; fax (06) 8411794; e-mail liban@tiscali.it; internet www .liban.it; Ambassador MELHEM NASRI MISTOU.

Lesotho: Via Serchio 8, 00198 Roma; tel. (06) 8542496; fax (06) 8542527; e-mail les.rome@flashnet.it; Chargé d'affaires a.i. KABELO GILBERT MAFURA.

Liberia: Piazzale delle Medaglie d'Oro 7, 00136 Roma; tel. (06) 35453399; fax (06) 35344729; e-mail liberiaembassy@hotmail.com; Ambassador LILY BEHNA.

Libya: Via Nomentana 365, 00162 Roma; tel. (06) 86320951; fax (06) 86205473; e-mail allibyaroma@libero.it; Chargé d'affaires a.i. ABDUL-HAMID ZOUBI.

Lithuania: Viale di Villa Grazioli 9, 00198 Roma; tel. (06) 8559052; fax (06) 8559053; e-mail info@ltemb.it; Ambassador (vacant).

Luxembourg: Via S. Croce in Gerusalemme 90, 00185 Roma; tel. (06) 77201177; fax (06) 77201055; e-mail rome.amb@mae.etat.lu; Ambassador JEAN FALTZ.

Macedonia, former Yugoslav republic: Viale Bruxelles 73–75, 00198 Roma; tel. (06) 84241109; fax (06) 84241131; e-mail rmacedonia@amb-rm.it; Ambassador MIRIE RUSANI.

Madagascar: Via Riccardo Zandonai 84A, 00194 Roma; tel. (06) 36307797; fax (06) 3294306; e-mail ambamad@hotmail.com; Ambassador AUGUSTE RICHARD PARAINA.

Malaysia: Via Nomentana 297, 00162 Roma; tel. (06) 8415764; fax (06) 8555040; e-mail mw.rome@flashnet.it; Ambassador LILY ZACHARIAH.

Mali: Via Antonio Bosio 2, 00161 Roma; tel. (06) 44254068; fax (06) 44254029; e-mail amb.malirome@tiscalinet.it; Ambassador IBRAHIM BOCAR DAGA.

Malta: Lungotevere Marzio 12, 00186 Roma; tel. (06) 6879990; fax (06) 6892687; e-mail maltaembassy.rome@gov.mt; Ambassador EDWARD MELILLO.

Mauritania: Via Giovanni Paisiello 26, 00198 Roma; tel. (06) 85351530; fax (06) 85351441; Ambassador YAHYA NGAM.

Mexico: Via Lazzaro Spallanzani 16, 00161 Roma; tel. (06) 441151; fax (06) 4403876; e-mail emexpart@tin.it; internet www.target.it/ messico; Ambassador RAFAEL TOVAR Y DE TERESA.

Moldova: Via Montebello 8, 00185 Roma; tel. (06) 4740210; fax (06) 47881092; e-mail ada.mol@flashnet.it; internet www.ambasada.it; Ambassador NICOLAE DUDAU.

Monaco: Via Antonio Bertoloni 36, 00197 Roma; tel. (06) 8083361; fax (06) 8077692; e-mail monaco@ambasciatadimonaco.it; Ambassador HENRI FISSORE.

Morocco: Via Lazzaro Spallanzani 8, 00161 Roma; tel. (06) 4402524; fax (06) 4402695; e-mail sifaroma@ambasciatadelmarocco.it; internet www.ambasciatadelmarocco.it; Ambassador TAJEDDINE BADDOU.

Mozambique: Via Filippo Corridoni 14, 00195 Roma; tel. (06) 37514852; fax (06) 37514699; e-mail segretaria@ambasciatamozambico.it; Ambassador FRANCISCO ELIAS PAULO CIGARRO.

Myanmar: Via della Camilluccia 551, 00135 Roma; tel. (06) 36304056; fax (06) 36298566; e-mail meroma@tiscali.it; Ambassador U KHIN MAUNG AYE.

Netherlands: Via Michele Mercati 8, 00197 Roma; tel. (06) 3221141; fax (06) 3221440; e-mail rom-az@minbuza.nl; internet www.olanda.it; Ambassador RONALD HENRY LOUDON.

New Zealand: Via Zara 28, 00198 Roma; tel. (06) 4417171; fax (06) 4402984; e-mail nzemb.rom@flashnet.it; internet www.nzembassy.com/italy; Ambassador JULIE CLAIRE MACKENZIE.

Nicaragua: Via Brescia 16, 00198 Roma; tel. (06) 8413471; fax (06) 85304079; Ambassador JOSÉ CUADRA CHAMORRO.

Niger: Via Antonio Baiamonti 10, 00195 Roma; tel. (06) 3720164; fax (06) 3729013; Ambassador FATOUMA MIREILLE AUSSEIL.

Nigeria: Via Orazio 14–18, 00193 Roma; tel. (06) 6896243; fax (06) 6832528; e-mail embassy@nigerian.it; Ambassador WILLY STEPHEN WABARA.

Norway: Via delle Terme Deciane 7, 00153 Roma; tel. (06) 5717031; fax (06) 57170326; e-mail emb.rome@mfa.no; internet www.amb-norvegia.it; Ambassador EVA BUGGE.

Oman: Via della Camilluccia 625, 00135 Roma; tel. (06) 36300517; fax (06) 3296802; e-mail omanembassy@tin.it; Ambassador YAHYA BIN ABDULLAH BIN SALIM AL-IRAIMY.

Pakistan: Via della Camilluccia 682, 00135 Roma; tel. (06) 36301775; fax (06) 36301936; e-mail pareprom@linet.it; Ambassador MIRZA QAMAR BEG.

Panama: Viale Regina Margherita 239, 00198 Roma; tel. (06) 44252173; fax (06) 44252237; Ambassador (vacant).

Paraguay: Viale Castro Pretorio 116, 00185 Roma; tel. (06) 44704684; fax (06) 4465517; e-mail ambaparoman@tiscali.it; Ambassador JORGE FIGUEREDO FRATTA.

Peru: Via Siacci 4, 00197 Roma; tel. (06) 80691510; fax (06) 80691777; e-mail emb.peru@aambasciataperu2.191.it; Ambassador HAROLD FORSYTH.

Philippines: Viale delle Medaglie d'Oro 112–114, 00136 Roma; tel. (06) 39746621; fax (06) 39740872; e-mail romepe@agora.it; Ambassador PHILIPPE J. LHUILLIER.

Poland: Via Pietro Paolo Rubens 20, 00197 Roma; tel. (06) 36204200; fax (06) 3217895; e-mail ufficio.stampa@ambasciatapolonia.it; internet www.ambasciatapolonia.it; Ambassador MICHAŁ RADLICKI.

Portugal: Viale Liegi 21–23, 00198 Roma; tel. (06) 844801; fax (06) 8417404; e-mail embptroma@virgilio.it; Ambassador VASCO TAVEIRA DA CUNHA VALENTE.

Qatar: Via Antonio Bosio 14, 00161 Roma; tel. (06) 44249450; fax (06) 44245273; e-mail info@qatarembassy.it; internet www.qatarembassy.it; Ambassador ALI FAHAD ASH-SHAHAWANI AL-HAJERI.

Romania: Via Nicolò Tartaglia 36, 00197 Roma; tel. (06) 8078807; fax (06) 8084995; e-mail amdiroma@roembit.org; internet www.roembit.org; Ambassador CRISTIAN VALENTIN COLTEANU.

Russia: Via Gaeta 5, 00144 Roma; tel. (06) 4941680; fax (06) 491031; e-mail ambrus@ambrussia.it; internet www.ambrussia.it; Ambassador ALEXEI MESHKOV.

San Marino: Via Eleonora Duse 35, 00197 Roma; tel. (06) 8072511; fax (06) 8070072; e-mail ambasciatasanmarino@tin.it; Ambassador BARBARA PARA.

Saudi Arabia: Via G. B. Pergolesi 9, 00198 Roma; tel. (06) 844851; fax (06) 8551781; e-mail ambasciata@arabia-saudita.it; internet www.arabia-saudita.it; Ambassador MUHAMMAD BIN NAWAF BIN ABDU-LAZIZ AL-SAUD.

Senegal: Via Giulia 66, 00186 Roma; tel. (06) 6872381; fax (06) 68219294; e-mail ambasenequiri@tiscali.it; Ambassador MOMAR GUEYE.

Serbia and Montenegro: Via dei Monti Parioli 20, 00197 Roma; tel. (06) 3200805; fax (06) 3200868; e-mail amb.jug@flashnet.it; Ambassador BRANKO LUKOVAC.

Slovakia: Via dei Colli della Farnesina 144, 00194 Roma; tel. (06) 367151; fax (06) 36715265; e-mail amb.slovac@virgilio.it; Ambassador JOZEF MIKLOŠKO.

Slovenia: Via Leonardo Pisano 10, 00197 Roma; tel. (06) 80914310; fax (06) 8081471; e-mail vri@mzz-dkp.gov.si; Ambassador VOJKO VOLK.

South Africa: Via Tanaro 14, 00198 Roma; tel. (06) 852541; fax (06) 85254300; e-mail sae2@sudafrica.it; internet www.sudafrica.it; Ambassador LENIN MAGIGWANE SHOPE.

Spain: Palazzo Borghese, Largo Fontanella Borghese 19, 00186 Roma; tel. (06) 6840401; fax (06) 6872256; e-mail ambespit@mail.mae.es; internet www.amba.spagna.com; Ambassador JOSÉ DE CARVAJAL SALIDO.

Sri Lanka: Via Adige 2, 00198 Roma; tel. (06) 8554560; fax (06) 84241670; e-mail slembassy@tiscali.it; Ambassador ELUPITTI RODNEY MUDIYANSELAGE PERERA.

Sudan: Via Lazzaro Spallanzani 24, 00161 Roma; tel. (06) 4403071; fax (06) 4402358; Ambassador RABIE HASSAN AHMED.

Sweden: Piazza Rio de Janeiro 3, 00161 Roma; tel. (06) 441941; fax (06) 44194760; e-mail ambassaden.rom@foreign.ministry.se; Ambassador STAFFAN WRIGSTAD.

Switzerland: Via Barnaba Oriani 61, 00197 Roma; tel. (06) 809571; fax (06) 8088510; e-mail vertretung@rom.rep.admin.ch; Ambassador BRUNO MAX SPINNER.

Syria: Piazza dell'Ara Coeli, 00186 Roma; tel. (06) 6749801; fax (06) 6794989; e-mail syria@email.it; Ambassador SAMIR NASER AL QASIR.

Tanzania: Viale Cortina d'Ampezzo 185, 00135 Roma; tel. (06) 33485801; fax (06) 33485828; e-mail info@embassyoftanzania.it; internet www.tanzania-gov.it; Ambassador COSTA RICKY MAHALU.

Thailand: Via Nomentana 132, 00162 Roma; tel. (06) 86202051; fax (06) 86220555; e-mail thai.em.rome@wind.it.net; Ambassador VARA-POJ SNIDVONGS.

Tunisia: Via Asmara 7, 00199 Roma; tel. (06) 8603060; fax (06) 86218204; e-mail at.roma@tiscali.it; Ambassador HABIB MANSOUR.

Turkey: Via Palestro 28, 00185 Roma; tel. (06) 445941; fax (06) 4941526; e-mail roma.be@libero.it; internet www.ambasciataditurchia.it; Ambassador UGUR ZIYAL.

Uganda: Lungotevere dei Mellini 44, 1°, Scala Valadier int. B, 00193 Roma; tel. (06) 3225220; fax (06) 3213688; Chargé d'affaires a.i. NASSER ABDU KABUNGA.

Ukraine: Via Guido d'Arezzo 9, 00198 Roma; tel. (06) 8412630; fax (06) 8547539; e-mail posta@amb-ucraina.com; Ambassador ANATOLII OREL.

United Arab Emirates: Via della Camilluccia 492, 00135 Roma; tel. (06) 36306100; fax (06) 36306155; e-mail uaeroma@tin.it; Ambassador ABDEL AL HAMID ABD AL FATTAH KAZEM ABD AL FATTAH.

United Kingdom: Via XX Settembre 80A, 00187 Roma; tel. (06) 42200001; fax (06) 42202333; e-mail romepoliticalsection@fco.gov.uk; internet www.britain.it; Ambassador IVOR ANTHONY ROBERTS.

USA: Palazzo Margherita, Via Vittorio Veneto 119A, 00187 Roma; tel. (06) 46741; fax (06) 46742217; internet www.usis.it; Ambassador MELVIN FLOYD SEMBLER.

Uruguay: Via Vittorio Veneto 183, 5°, 00187 Roma; tel. (06) 4821776; fax (06) 4823695; e-mail uruguay@tuttopmi.it; Ambassador CARLOS ALEJANDRO BARROS OREIRO.

Uzbekistan: Via Tolmino 12, 00198 Roma; tel. (06) 8542456; fax (06) 8541020; e-mail uzbembass@libero.it; Chargé d'affaires a.i. KHURSHID M. BABASHEV.

Venezuela: Via Nicolò Tartaglia 11, 00197 Roma; tel. (06) 8079797; fax (06) 8084410; e-mail embaveit@iol.it; internet users.libero.it/embaveit; Ambassador RODRIGO OSWALDO CHÁVES SAMUDIO.

Viet Nam: Via Clitunno 34–36, 00198 Roma; tel. (06) 8543223; fax (06) 8548501; e-mail suquanvn@tin.it; Ambassador LE VINH THU.

Yemen: Via Antonio Bosio 10, 00161 Roma; tel. (06) 44231679; fax (06) 44234763; Ambassador MUHAMMAD SALEH AHMED AL-HELALY.

Zambia: Via Ennio Quirino Visconti 8, 00193 Roma; fax (06) 97613035; Ambassador LUCY M. MUNGOMA.

Zimbabwe: Via Virgilio 8, 00193 Roma; tel. (06) 68308282; fax (06) 68308324; e-mail zimrome.wolit@tiscalinet.it; Ambassador MARY MARGARET MUCHADA.

Judicial System

The Constitutional Court was established in 1956 and is an autonomous constitutional body, standing apart from the judicial system. Its most important function is to pronounce on the constitutionality of legislation both subsequent and prior to the present Constitution of 1948. It also judges accusations brought against the President of the Republic or ministers.

At the base of the system of penal jurisdiction are the Preture (District Courts), where offences carrying a sentence of up to four years' imprisonment are tried. Above the Preture are the Tribunali (Tribunals) and the Corti di Assise presso i Tribunali (Assize Courts attached to the Tribunals), where graver offences are dealt with. From these courts appeal lies to the Corti d'Appello (Courts of Appeal) and the parallel Corti di Assise d'Appello (Assize Courts of Appeal). Final appeal may be made, on juridical grounds only, to the Corte Suprema di Cassazione.

Civil cases may be taken in the first instance to the Giudici Conciliatori (Justices of the Peace), Preture or Tribunali, according to the economic value of the case. Appeal from the Giudici Conciliatori lies to the Preture, from the Preture to the Tribunali, from the Tribunali to the Corti d'Appello, and finally, as in penal justice, to the Corte Suprema di Cassazione on juridical grounds only.

Special divisions for cases concerning labour relations are attached to civil courts. Cases concerned with the public service and its employees are tried by Tribunali Amministrativi Regionali and the Consiglio di Stato. Juvenile courts have criminal and civil jurisdiction.

A new penal code was introduced in late 1989.

Consiglio Superiore della Magistratura (CSM)

Piazza dell'Indipendenza 6, 00185 Roma; tel. (06) 444911; internet www.csm.it.

f. 1958; supervisory body of judicial system; 27 mems.

President: The President of the Republic.

CONSTITUTIONAL COURT

Corte Costituzionale

Palazzo della Consulta, Piazza del Quirinale 41, 00187 Roma; tel. (06) 4698560; fax (06) 4698915; e-mail segreteria.generale@ cortecostituzionale.it; internet www.cortecostituzionale.it.

Consists of 15 judges, one-third appointed by the President of the Republic, one-third elected by Parliament in joint session, and one-third by the ordinary and administrative supreme courts.

President: Prof. PIERO ALBERTO CAPOTOSTI.

ADMINISTRATIVE COURTS

Consiglio di Stato

Palazzo Spada, Piazza Capo di Ferro 13, 00186 Roma; tel. (06) 68212743; fax (06) 68272501; e-mail urp.cds@ giustizia-amministrativa.it; internet www.giustizia-amministrativa .it.

Established in accordance with Article 10 of the Constitution; has both consultative and judicial functions.

President: ALBERTO DE ROBERTO.

Corte dei Conti

Via Antonio Baiamonti 25, 00195 Roma; and Via Barberini 38, Roma; tel. (06) 38761; fax (06) 38763477; e-mail uric@corteconti.it; internet www.corteconti.it.

Functions as the court of public auditors for the State.

President: FRANCESCO STADERINI.

SUPREME COURT OF APPEAL

Corte Suprema di Cassazione

Palazzo di Giustizia, 00193 Roma; tel. (06) 68831; fax (06) 6883420. Supreme court of civil and criminal appeal.

First President: NICOLA MARVULLI.

Religion

More than 90% of the population of Italy are adherents of the Roman Catholic Church. Under the terms of the Concordat formally ratified in June 1985, Roman Catholicism was no longer to be the state religion, compulsory religious instruction in schools was abolished and state financial contributions reduced. The Vatican City's sovereign rights as an independent state, under the terms of the Lateran Pact of 1929, were not affected.

Several Protestant churches also exist in Italy, with a total membership of about 50,000. There is a small Jewish community, and in 1987 an agreement between the State and Jewish representatives recognized certain rights for the Jewish community, including the right to observe religious festivals on Saturdays by not attending

school or work. In March 2000 Jehovah's Witnesses and Buddhism were officially recognized as religions by the Italian legislature.

CHRISTIANITY

The Roman Catholic Church

For ecclesiastical purposes, Italy comprises the Papal See of Rome, the Patriarchate of Venice, 60 archdioceses (including three directly responsible to the Holy See), 2 eparchies, 156 dioceses (including seven within the jurisdiction of the Pope, as Archbishop of the Roman Province, and 11 directly responsible to the Holy See), two territorial prelatures and seven territorial abbacies (including four directly responsible to the Holy See). Almost all adherents follow the Latin rite, but there are two dioceses and one abbacy (all directly responsible to the Holy See) for Catholics of the Italo-Albanian (Byzantine) rite.

Bishops' Conference

Conferenza Episcopale Italiana, Circonvallazione Aurelia 50, 00165 Roma; tel. (06) 663981; fax (06) 6623037; e-mail segrgen@ chiesacattolica.it; internet www.chiesacattolica.it.

f. 1965; Pres. Cardinal CAMILLO RUINI (Vicar-General of Rome); Sec.-Gen. Mgr GIUSEPPE BETORI.

Primate of Italy, Archbishop and Metropolitan of the Roman Province and Bishop of Rome: His Holiness Pope BENEDICT XVI.

Patriarch of Venice: Cardinal ANGELO SCOLA.

Archbishops

Acerenza: Most Rev. MICHELE SCANDIFFIO.

Agrigento: Most Rev. CARMELO FERRARO.

Amalfi-Cava de'Tirreni: Most Rev. ORAZIO SORICELLI.

Ancona-Osimo: Most Rev. EDOARDO MENICHELLI.

Bari-Bitonto: Most Rev. FRANCESCO CACUCCI.

Benevento: Most Rev. SERAFINO SPROVIERI.

Bologna: Most Rev. CARLO CAFFARRA.

Brindisi-Otsuni: Most Rev. ROCCO TALUCCI.

Cagliari: Most Rev. GIUSEPPE MANI.

Camerino-San Severino Marche: Most Rev. ANGELO FAGIANI.

Campobasso-Boiano: Most Rev. ARMANDO DINI.

Capua: Most Rev. BRUNO SCHETTINO.

Catania: Most Rev. SALVATORE GRISTINA.

Catanzaro-Squillace: Most Rev. ANTONIO CILIBERTI.

Chieti-Vasto: Most Rev. BRUNO FORTE.

Cosenza-Bisignano: Most Rev. SALVATORE NUNNARI.

Crotone-Santa Severina: Most Rev. ANDREA MUGIONE.

Fermo: Most Rev. GENNARO FRANCESCHETTI.

Ferrara-Comacchio: Most Rev. PAOLO RABITTI.

Florence (Firenze): Cardinal EMILIO ANTONELLI.

Foggia-Bovino: Most Rev. FRANCESCO PIO TAMBURRINO.

Gaeta: Most Rev. PIER LUIGI MAZZONI.

Genoa: Cardinal TARCISIO BERTONE.

Gorizia: Most Rev. DINO DE ANTONI.

Lanciano-Ortona: Most Rev. CARLO GHIDELLI.

L'Aquila: Most Rev. GIUSEPPE MOLINARI.

Lecce: Most Rev. COSMO FRANCESCO RUPPI.

Lucca: Most Rev. BRUNO TOMMASI.

Manfredonia-Vieste-San Giovanni Rotondo: Most Rev. DOMENICO UMBERTO D'AMBROSIO.

Matera-Irsina: (vacant).

Messina-Lipari-Sant Lucia del Mela: Most Rev. GIOVANNI MARRA.

Milan (Milano): Cardinal DIONIGI TETTAMANZI.

Modena-Nonantola: Most Rev. BENITO COCCHI.

Monreale: Most Rev. CATALDO NARO.

Naples (Napoli): Cardinal MICHELE GIORDANO.

Oristano: Most Rev. PIER GIULIANO TIDDIA.

Otranto: Most Rev. DONATO NEGRO.

Palermo: Cardinal SALVATORE DE GIORGI.

Perugia-Città della Pieve: Most Rev. GIUSEPPE CHIARETTI.

Pesaro: (vacant).

Pescara-Penne: Most Rev. FRANCESCO CUCCARESE.

Pisa: Most Rev. ALESSANDRO PLOTTI.

Potenza-Muro Lucano-Marsico Nuovo: Most Rev. AGOSTINO SUPERBO.

Ravenna-Cervia: Most Rev. GIUSEPPE VERUCCHI.

Reggio Calabria-Bova: Most Rev. VITTORIO LUIGI MONDELLO.

Rossano-Cariati: Most Rev. ANDREA CASSONE.

Salerno-Campagna-Acerno: Most Rev. GERARDO PIERRO.

Sant'Angelo dei Lombardi-Conza-Nusco-Bisaccia: Most Rev. SALVATORE NUNNARI.

Sassari: Most Rev. PAOLO MARIO VIRGILIO ATZEI.

Siena-Colle di Val d'Elsa-Montalcino: Most Rev. ANTONIO BUON-CRISTIANI.

Sorrento-Castellamare di Stabia: Most Rev. FELICE CECE.

Spoleto-Norcia: Most Rev. RICCARDO FONTANA.

Syracuse: Most Rev. GIUSEPPE COSTANZO.

Taranto: Most Rev. BENIGNO LUIGI PAPA.

Trani-Barletta-Bisceglie: Most Rev. GIOVANNI BATTISTA PICHIERRI.

Trent (Trento): Most Rev. LUIGI BRESSAN.

Turin (Torino): Cardinal SEVERINO POLETTO.

Udine: Most Rev. PIETRO BROLLO.

Urbino-Urbania-Sant'Angelo in Vado: Most Rev. FRANCESCO MARINELLI.

Vercelli: Most Rev. ENRICO MASSERONI.

Protestant Churches

Federazione delle Chiese Evangeliche in Italia (Federation of the Protestant Churches in Italy): Via Firenze 38, 00184 Roma; tel. (06) 4825120; fax (06) 4828728; e-mail nev@fcei.it; internet www.fedevangelica.it; f. 1967; total mems 65,000; Pres. Dott. GIANNI LONG; Sec. Dr RENATO MAIOCCHI; includes the following organizations:

Chiesa Evangelica Luterana in Italia (Lutheran Church): Via Toscana 7, 00187 Roma; tel. (06) 4880394; fax (06) 4874506; e-mail decanato@elki-celi.org; internet www.elki-celi.org; Dean JÜRGEN ASTFALK; 7,000 mems.

Esercito della Salvezza (Salvation Army): Via degli Apuli 39, 00185 Roma; tel. (06) 4463912; fax (06) 490078; e-mail pascalads@hotmail.com; internet www.esercitodellasalvezza.org; Officer Commanding for Italy Maj. MASSIMO PAONE; 19 regional centres.

Opera per le Chiese Evangeliche Metodiste in Italia (Board of the Evangelical Methodist Churches in Italy): Via Firenze 38, 00184 Roma; tel. (06) 4743695; fax (06) 47885308; e-mail metodismo@chiesavaldese.org; f. 1861; merged with Waldensian Church 2002; Pres. Pastor MASSIMO AQUILANTE; 4,000 mems.

Tavola Valdese (Waldensian Church): Via Firenze 38, 00184 Roma; tel. (06) 4745537; fax (06) 47885308; e-mail moderatore@chiesavaldese.org; internet www.chiesavaldese.org; Moderator GIANNI GENRE; Sec.-Treas. ROSELLA PANZIRONI; 27,465 mems.

Unione Cristiana Evangelica Battista d'Italia (Italian Baptist Union): Piazza San Lorenzo in Lucina 35, 00186 Roma; tel. (06) 6876124; fax (06) 6876185; e-mail ucebit@tin.it; f. 1873; Pres. ANNA MAFFEI; 5,000 mems.

Associated Organization

Seventh-day Adventists: Lungotevere Michelangelo 7, 00192 Roma; tel. (06) 3609591; fax (06) 36095952; e-mail uicca@avventisti.it; internet www.avventisti.it; f. 1929; represents 90 communities in Italy and Malta; Supt LUCIO ALTIN; Sec. IGNAZIO BARBUSCIA.

ISLAM

Associazione Musulmani Italiani (AMI) (Italian Muslim Association): Roma, CP 7167; tel. and fax (06) 44360619; e-mail info@amimuslims.org; internet www.amimuslims.org; f. 1982; Pres. OMAR DANILO SPERANZA.

Unione delle Comunità ed Organizzazioni Islamiche in Italia (UCOII): tel. (0183) 767601; fax (0183) 764735; e-mail ucoii@uno.it; internet www.islam-ucoii.it; f. 1990; Pres. MOHAMED NOUR DACHAN; Sec. HAMZA PICCARDO.

JUDAISM

The number of Jews in Italy was estimated at 30,000 in 1997.

Union of Italian Jewish Communities: Lungotevere Sanzio 9, 00153 Roma; tel. (06) 5803667; fax (06) 5899569; f. 1930; represents 21 Jewish communities in Italy; Pres. AMOS LUZZATTO; Chief Rabbi of Rome Dott. RICCARDO DI SEGNI.

Rabbinical Council: Chief Rabbi Prof. GIUSEPPE LARAS (Via Guastalla 19, Milano), Rabbi SHALOM BACHBOUT (c/o UCEI, Lungotevere Sanzio 9, Roma); Chief Rabbi ALBERTO SOMEKH (Ptta. Primo Levi 12, Torino).

BAHÁ'Í FAITH

Assemblea Spirituale Nazionale: Via Stoppani 10, 00197 Roma; tel. (06) 8079647; fax (06) 8070184; e-mail segreteria@bahai.it; internet www.bahai.it; mems resident in 420 localities.

The Press

Relative to the size of Italy's population, the number of daily newspapers is rather small. Rome and Milan are the main press centres. The most important national dailies are *Corriere della Sera* in Milan and Rome and *La Repubblica* in Rome, followed by Turin's *La Stampa*, *Il Sole 24 Ore* in Milan, the economic and financial newspaper with the highest circulation in Europe, *Il Messaggero* in Rome, *Il Resto del Carlino* in Bologna, *La Nazione* in Florence, and *Il Giornale* and *Il Giorno*, which circulate mainly in the north.

Many illustrated weekly papers and magazines maintain very high levels of circulation, with *TV Sorrisi e Canzoni* and *Famiglia Cristiana* enjoying the highest figures. Other very popular general-interest weeklies are *Gente* and *Oggi*. Among the serious and influential magazines are *Panorama* and *L'Espresso*.

PRINCIPAL DAILIES

Ancona

Il Corriere Adriatico: Via Berti 20, 60126 Ancona; tel. (071) 4581; fax (071) 42980; e-mail info@corriereadriaticonline.it; internet www.corriereadriaticonline.it; f. 1860; Pres. FRANCESCO SENSI; Editorial Dir PAOLO TRAINI; circ. 29,349.

Bari

La Gazzetta del Mezzogiorno: Viale Scipione l'Africano 264, 70124 Bari; tel. (080) 5470200; fax (080) 5470488; internet www.gdmland.it; f. 1887; independent; Man. Dir PASQUALE PATRUNO; circ. 82,398.

Il Quotidiano di Bari: Piazza Aldo Moro 31, 70121 Bari; tel. (080) 5240473; fax (080) 5245486; e-mail redazione@quotidianodibari.it; internet www.quotidianodibari.it; Dir LUCIANO VENTURA.

Bergamo

L'Eco di Bergamo: Viale Papa Giovanni XXIII 118, 24121 Bergamo; tel. (035) 386111; fax (035) 386217; e-mail redazione@eco.bg.it; internet www.eco.bg.it; f. 1880; Catholic; Man. Dr ETTORE ONGIS; circ. 59,114.

Il Nuovo Giornale di Bergamo: Vis S. Bernardino 120, 24126 Bergamo; tel. (035) 4243161; fax (035) 4243160; Dir SERGIO CARRARO; circ 15,000.

Bologna

Il Resto del Carlino: Via Enrico Mattei 106, 40138 Bologna; tel. (051) 6006111; fax (051) 536111; internet www.ilrestodelcarlino.it; f. 1885; independent; Dir MARCO LEONELLI; circ. 250,000.

Bolzano/Bozen

Dolomiten: Via del Vigneto/Weinbergweg 7, 39100 Bozen; tel. (0471) 925111; fax (0471) 925440; e-mail dolomiten@athesia.it; internet www.dolomiten.it; internet www.stol.it; f. 1882; independent; German language; Dir Dr TONI EBNER; circ. 56,623.

Brescia

Bresciaoggi Nuovo: Via Eritrea 20A, 25126 Brescia; tel. (030) 2294260; fax (030) 2294229; internet www.bresciaoggi.it; f. 1974; Dir MAURIZIO CATTANEO; circ. 19,000.

Il Giornale di Brescia: Via Solferino 22, 25121 Brescia; tel. (030) 37901; fax (030) 292226; internet www.giornaledibrescia.it; f. 1945; Dir/Editor GIAN BATTISTA LANZANI; circ. 70,000.

Cagliari

L'Unione Sarda: Viale Regina Elena 12, 9100 Cagliari; tel. (070) 60131; fax (070) 6013306; e-mail unione@unionesarda.it; internet www.unionesarda.it; f. 1889; independent; Man. ANTONANGELO LIORI; circ. 97,000.

Catania

La Sicilia: Viale Odorico da Pordenone 50, 95126 Catania; tel. (095) 330544; fax (095) 336466; e-mail teee-lasicilia@ctonline.it; internet www.lasicilia.it; f. 1945; independent; Man. Dott. MARIO CIANCIO SANFILIPPO; circ. 80,000.

Como

Corriere di Como: Via Vittorio Emanuele II 115, 22100 Como; tel. (031) 337788; fax (031) 3377823; e-mail redazione@corrierecomo.it; internet www.corrieredicomo.it; Dir MARIO RAPISARDA.

La Provincia di Como: Via Pasquale Paoli 21, 22100 Como; tel. (031) 582211; fax (031) 526450; e-mail laprovincia@laprovincia.it; internet www.laprovinciadicomo.it; f. 1892; independent; Dir MICHELE BRAMBILLA; circ. 56,000.

Cremona

La Provincia di Cremona: Via delle Industrie 2, 26100 Cremona; tel. (0372) 4981; fax (0372) 28487; internet www.cremonaonline.it; f. 1947; independent; Pres. MARIO MAESTRONI; Man. Dir ENRICO PIRONDINI; circ. 23,826.

Ferrara

La Nuova Ferrara: Via Baruffaldi 22, 44100 Ferrara; tel. (0532) 214211; fax (0532) 247689; internet www.lanuovaferrara.it; f. 1989; independent; Man. Dir VALENTINO PESCI; circ. 18,788.

Foggia

Foggia Sera: Corso Roma 204B, 71100 Foggia; tel. (0881) 632259; fax (0881) 661534; Dir MATTEO TATTARELLA.

Quotidiano di Foggia: Corso Roma 204B, 71100 Foggia; tel. (0881) 721259; fax (0881) 639368; internet www.quotidianodifoggia.it; Dir MATTEO TATTARELLA.

Florence/Firenze

La Nazione: Viale Giovase Italia 17, 50121 Firenze; tel. (055) 249511; fax (055) 2478207; internet www.lanazione.it; f. 1859; independent; Dir FRANCESCO GARRASS; circ. 200,000.

Genoa/Genova

L'Avvisatore Marittimo: Piazza Piccapietra 21, 16121 Genova; tel. (010) 545341; fax (010) 5453436; e-mail avvmar@tin.it; internet www.avvmar.it; f. 1919; shipping and financial; Editor SANDRO GRIMALDI; circ. 5,000.

Corriere Mercantile: Via Archimede 169/R, 16142 Genova; tel. (010) 53691; fax (010) 504148; f. 1824; political and financial; independent; Editor MIMMO ANGELI; circ. 16,000.

Il Secolo XIX: Piazza Piccapietra 21, 16122 Genova; tel. (010) 53881; fax (010) 5388388; e-mail amministrazione@ilsecoloxix.it; internet www.ilsecoloXIX.it; f. 1886; independent; Dir ANTONIO DI ROSA; circ. 179,360.

Lecce

Quotidiano di Lecce, Brindisi e Taranto: Via dei Mocenigo 25–29, 73100 Lecce; tel. (0832) 3382000; fax (0832) 338244; e-mail quotidiano@caltanet.it; f. 1979; Dir GIANCARLO MINICUCCI; circ. 28,527.

Leghorn/Livorno

Il Tirreno: Viale Alfieri 9, 57124 Livorno; tel. (0586) 220111; fax (0586) 220717; e-mail iltirreno@petrurianet.it; internet www.iltirreno.it; f. 1978; independent; Dir SANDRA BONSANTI; circ. 91,595.

Lodi

Il Cittadino: Via Paolo Gorini 34, 26900, Lodi; tel. (0371) 544200; fax (0371) 544201; e-mail redazione@ilcittadino.it; internet www.ilcittadino.it; f. 1890; Dir FERRUCCIO PALLAVERA; circ. 14,200.

Mantua

Gazzetta di Mantova: Via Fratelli Bandiera 32, 46100 Mantova; tel. (0376) 3031; fax (0376) 303263; internet www.gazzettadimantova.it; f. 1664; independent; Man. SERGIO VARALDI; circ. 45,000.

Messina

Gazzetta del Sud: Uberto Bonino 15C, 98124 Messina; tel. (090) 2261; fax (090) 2936359; internet www.gazzettadelsud.it; f. 1952; independent; Dir NINO CALARCO; circ. 70,000.

Milan/Milano

Avvenire: Piazza Carbonari 3, 20125 Milano; tel. (02) 67801; fax (02) 6780208; internet www.avvenire.it; f. 1968; Catholic; Man. Dir DINO BOFFO; circ. 148,000.

Corriere della Sera: Via Solferino 28, 20121 Milano; tel. (02) 6339; fax (02) 29009668; internet www.corriere.it; f. 1876; independent; contains weekly supplement, *Sette*; Dir (vacant); circ. 886,832.

Il Foglio Quotidiano: Largo Corsua dei Servi 3, 20122 Milano; tel. (02) 7712951; fax (02) 781378; e-mail lettere@ilfoglio.it; internet www.ilfoglio.it; Dir GIULIANO FERRARA.

La Gazzetta dello Sport: RCS Editoriale Quotidiani SpA, Via Solferino 28, 20121 Milano; tel. (02) 6339; fax (02) 29009668; e-mail gasport@rcs.it; internet www.gazzetta.it; f. 1896; sport; Dir CANDIDO CANNAVÒ; circ. 426,000.

Il Giornale: Via Gaetano Negri 4, 20123 Milano; tel. (02) 85661; fax (02) 72023859; e-mail segreteria@ilgiornale.it; f. 1974; independent, controlled by staff; Editor MAURIZIO BELPIETRO; circ. 350,000.

Il Giorno: Via Stradivari 4, 20131 Milano; tel. (02) 277991; fax (02) 27799537; e-mail ilgiorno@ilgiorno.it; internet www.ilgiorno.it; Chief Editor GABRIELE CANE; circ. 255,377.

Italia Oggi: Classe Editori, Via M. Burigozzo 5, 20122 Milano; tel. (02) 58219256; e-mail italiaoggi@class.it; internet www.italiaoggi.it; economic daily.

MF (Milano Finanza): Classe Editori, Via M. Burigozzo 5, 20122 Milano; internet www.milanofinanza.it; economic daily.

Il Sole 24 Ore: Via Paolo Lomazzo 52, 20154 Milano; tel. (02) 30221; fax (02) 312055; internet www.ilsole24ore.com; f. 1865; financial, political, economic; Dir GUIDO GENTILI; circ. 417,153.

Modena

Nuova Gazzetta di Modena: Via Ricci 56, 41100 Modena; tel. (059) 247311; fax (059) 226533; internet www.nuovagazzettadimodena.it; Dir ANTONIO MASCOLO; circ. 16,500.

Naples/Napoli

Corriere del Mezzogiorno: Vico II san Nicola alla dogana 9, 80133 Napoli; tel. (081) 7602001; fax (081) 5802779; internet www.corrieredelmezzogiorno.it; Dir MARCO DEMARCO.

Il Denaro: Piazza dei Martiri 58, 80121 Napoli; tel. (081) 421900; fax (081) 422212; e-mail denaro@denaro.it; internet www.denaro.it; economic daily; Dir ALFONSO RUFFO.

Il Giornale di Napoli: Piazzetta Matilde Serao 19, 80133 Napoli; tel. (081) 497200; fax (081) 497227; e-mail gdn@itb.it; internet dns .itb.it/gdn/; f. 1985; Editor ROBERTO TUMBARELLO; circ. 11,000.

Il Mattino: Soc Ed Edime Spa, Via Chiatamone 65, 80121 Napoli; tel. (081) 7947111; fax (081) 7947288; internet www.ilmattino.it; f. 1892; reformed 1950; independent; Dir PAOLO GRALDI; Editor MARINO LONGONI; circ. 200,000.

Padua/Padova

Il Mattino di Padova: Via Pelizzo 3, 35128 Padua; tel. (049) 8083411; fax (049) 8079067; internet www.mattinopadova.it; f. 1978; Dir ALBERTO STATERA; circ. 30,082.

Palermo

Giornale di Sicilia: Via Lincoln 21, 90122 Palermo; tel. (091) 6627111; fax (091) 6627280; e-mail gds@gestelnet.it; internet www.gds.it; f. 1860; independent; Dir ANTONIO ARDIZZONE; circ. 87,189.

Parma

Gazzetta di Parma: Via Mantova 68, 43100 Parma; tel. (0521) 2251; fax (0521) 285522; e-mail gazzetta@gazzettadiparma.net; internet www.gazzettadiparma.it; f. 1735; Dir GIULIANO MOLOSSI; circ. 56,000.

Pavia

La Provincia Pavese: Viale Canton Ticino 16–18, 27100 Pavia; tel. (0382) 434511; fax (0382) 473875; e-mail info@laprovincia.pv.it; internet www.laprovinciapavese.it; f. 1879; independent; Dir ROBERTO GALLI; circ. 25,000.

Perugia

Corriere dell'Umbria: Via Pievaiola km 5700, 06100 Perugia; tel. (075) 52731; fax (075) 5273259; internet www.corr.it; f. 1983; independent; Editor FEDERICO FIORAVANTI; circ. 23,000.

Pescara

Il Centro: Corso Vittorio Emanuele 372, 65100 Pescara; tel. (085) 20521; fax (085) 4212460; e-mail ilcentro@micso.it; internet www.ilcentro.it; f. 1986; independent; Dir ANTONIO DEL GIUDICE; circ. 30,000.

Piacenza

Libertà: Via Benedettine 68, 29100 Piacenza; tel. (0523) 393939; fax (0523) 393962; e-mail area.prestampa@liberta; internet www .liberta.it; f. 1883; Dir GAETANO RIZZUTO; circ. 40,000.

Reggio Emilia

Gazzetta di Reggio: Via Isonzo 72/A-B, 42100 Reggio Emilia; tel. (0552) 501511; fax (0522) 517301; internet www.gazzettadireggio.it; f. 1860; Man. LUIGI CARLETTI; circ. 19,563.

Rimini

Corriere di Romagna: Piazza Tre Martiri 43A, 47900 Rimini; tel. (0541) 354111; fax (0541) 351499; e-mail lega@corriereromagna.it; internet www.corrieromagna.it; also distributed in San Marino; Dir MARIA PATRIZIA LANZETTI; Editor CLAUDIO CASALI.

Rome

Conquiste del Lavoro: Via Po 21, 00198 Roma; tel. (06) 84731; fax (06) 8413782; e-mail conquiste_lavoro@cisl.it; internet www .conquistedellavoro.it; owned by Confederazione Italiana Sindacati Lavoratori (CISL); circ. 50,000.

Il Corriere dello Sport: Piazza Indipendenza 11B, 00185 Roma; tel. (06) 49921; fax (06) 4992690; internet www.corsport.it; f. 1924; Editor MARIO SCONCERTI; circ. 239,249.

Europa Quotidiano: Via di Ripetta 142, 00186 Roma; tel. (06) 45401010; fax (06) 45401041; internet www.europaquotidiano.it; f. 2003; organ of the Margherita coalition, replacing Il Popolo, which ceased operations Jan. 2003; Dir NINO RIZZO NERVO.

Il Giornale d'Italia: Società Editrice Esedra Srl, Via Parigli 11, 00185 Roma; tel. (06) 474901; fax (06) 4883435; e-mail g.italia@ tiscalinet.it; f. 1901; Man. PAOLO FRAIOLI; Editor MATTIAS MAINIERO; circ. 70,000.

Liberazione: Viale del Policlinico 131, 00161 Roma; tel. (06) 441831; fax (06) 44183247; e-mail posta@liberazione.it; internet www.liberazione.it; organ of the Partito della Rifondazione Comunista; Dir ALESSANDRO CURZI; circ. 41,897.

Il Manifesto: Via Tomacelli 146, 00186 Roma; tel. (06) 687191; fax (06) 68719573; e-mail redazione@ilmanifesto.it; internet www .ilmanifesto.it; f. 1971; splinter communist; Dir RICCARDO BARENGHI; circ. 55,000.

Il Messaggero: Via del Tritone 152, 00187 Roma; tel. (06) 47201; fax (06) 4720300; e-mail posta@ilmessaggero.it; internet www .ilmessaggero.it; f. 1878; independent; Dir PAOLO GAMBESCIA; Editor F. G. CALTAGIRONE; circ. 369,000.

L'Opinione: Via del Corso 117, 00186 Roma; tel. (06) 69200880; fax (06) 6787573; internet www.opinione.it; f. 1977; independent; Man. Editor ARTURO DIACONALE; circ. 5,000.

La Repubblica: Gruppo Editoriale L'Espresso Div. La, Piazza dell'Indipendenza 11B, 00185 Roma; tel. (06) 49821; fax (06) 49822923; e-mail larepubblica@repubblica.it; internet www .repubblica.it; f. 1976; left-wing; Editor EZIO MAURO; circ. 616,700.

Secolo d'Italia: Via della Scrofa 43, 00186 Roma; tel. (06) 68899221; fax (06) 6861598; internet www.alleanzanazionale.it/ secolo/; f. 1951; organ of the AN; Editor GENNARO MALGIERI; circ. 15,000.

Il Tempo: L'Editrice Romana SpA, Piazza Colonna 366, 00187 Roma; tel. (06) 675881; fax (06) 6758869; internet www.iltempo.it; f. 1944; right-wing; Editor GIAN PAOLO CRESCI; circ. 85,000.

L'Unità: Via dei Due Macelli 23/13, 00187 Roma; tel. (06) 699961; fax (06) 69996359; e-mail unitaedi@unita.it; internet www.unita.it; f. 1924; Dir FURIO COLOMBO; circ. 100,000.

Salerno

La Città: Corso Garibaldi 215, 84100 Salerno; tel. (089) 245111; fax (089) 245236; internet www.lacittadisalerno.it; Dir MAURIZIO DE LUCA.

Sassari

La Nuova Sardegna: Via Porcellana 9, 7100 Sassari; tel. (079) 222400; fax (079) 236293; internet www.lanuovasardegna.it; f. 1891; independent; Editor LIVIO LIUZZI; circ. 78,000.

Taranto

Corriere del Giorno di Puglia e Lucania: Piazza Maria Immacolata 30, 74100 Taranto; tel. (099) 4553111; fax (099) 4538322; e-mail cdg@corgiorno.it; internet www.corgiorno.it; f. 1947; Dir ANTONIO BIELLA; circ. 12,000.

Trent/Trento/Trient

l'Adige: Via Missioni Africane 17, 38100 Trento; tel. (0461) 886111; fax (0461) 886264; internet www.ladige.it; f. 1946; independent; Dir Dott. PAOLO GHEZZI; circ. 30,308.

Treviso

La Tribuna di Treviso: Corso del Popolo 42, 31100 Treviso; tel. (0422) 417611; fax (0422) 579212; internet www.tribunatreviso.it; f. 1978; independent; Editor Dr ALBERTO STATERA; circ. 20,000.

Trieste

Il Piccolo (Giornale di Trieste): Via Guido Reni 1, 34123 Trieste; tel. (040) 3733111; fax (040) 3733283; e-mail piccolo@ilpiccolo.it; internet www.ilpiccolo.it; f. 1881; independent; Man. Dr MARIO QUAIA; circ. 60,000.

Primorski Dnevnik: Via dei Montecchi 6, 34137 Trieste; tel. (040) 7786300; fax (040) 772418; e-mail redakcija@primorski.it; internet www.primorski.it; f. 1945; Slovene; Editor-in-Chief BOJAN BREZIGAR; circ. 11,282.

Turin/Torino

La Stampa: Via Marenco 32, 10126 Torino; tel. (011) 656811; fax (011) 655306; e-mail lettere@lastampa.it; internet www.lastampa.it; f. 1867; independent; Dir MARCELLO SORGI; circ. 410,000.

Udine

Il Messaggero Veneto: Viale Palmanova 290, 33100 Udine; tel. (0432) 5271; fax (0432) 523072; e-mail direzione@messaggeroveneto .it; internet www.messaggeroveneto.it; f. 1946; Dir SERGIO BARALDI; circ. 60,000.

Varese

La Prealpina: Viale Tamagno 13, 21100 Varese; tel. (0332) 275700; fax (0332) 275701; e-mail prealpina@betanet.it; internet www .laprealpinagiorn.it; f. 1888; Dir SANDRO MOSER; circ. 40,000.

Venice/Venezia

Il Gazzettino: Via Torino 110, 30172 Venezia-Mestre; tel. (041) 665111; fax (041) 665386; internet www.gazzettino.it; f. 1887; independent; Dir LUIGI BACIALLI; circ. 152,789.

La Nuova Venezia: Castello 5620, Campo San Lio, 30122 Venezia; tel. (041) 5074611; fax (041) 958856; e-mail nuova@nuovavenezia.it; internet www.nuovavenezia.it; Dir ALBERTO STATERA; circ. 11,000.

Verona

L'Arena: Viale del Lavoro 11, 37036, San Martino Buon Albergo, Verona; tel. (045) 8094899; fax (045) 597966; e-mail redazione@ larena.it; internet www.larena.it; f. 1866; independent; Editor-in-Chief MAURIZIO CATTANEO; Man. Dir Ing. ALESSANDRO ZELGER; circ. 68,000.

Vicenza

Il Giornale di Vicenza: Viale S. Lazzaro 89, 36100 Vicenza; tel. (0444) 396311; fax (0444) 396333; internet www.ilgiornaledivicenza .it; f. 1945; Editor NINO ALLIONE; circ. 50,000.

SELECTED PERIODICALS

Fine Arts, etc.

Abitare: Via Ventura 5, 20134 Milano; tel. (02) 210581; fax (02) 21058316; e-mail redazione@abitare.it; internet www.abitare.it; f. 1962; monthly; architecture and design; in Italian and English; Editor RENATO MINETTO; Dir ITALO LUPI.

Casabella: Via Trentacoste 7, 20134 Milano; tel. (02) 215631; fax (02) 21563260; e-mail casabella@mondadori.it; f. 1938; 10 a year; architecture and interior design; Editor FRANCESCO DAL CO; circ. 43,000.

Domus: Via Achille Grandi 5/7, 20089 Rozzano, Milano; tel. (02) 824721; fax (02) 82472386; e-mail domus@edidomus.it; internet www.edidomus.it; f. 1928; 11 a year; architecture, interior design and art; Editor Dott. G. MAZZOCCHI; circ. 53,000.

Graphicus: Casa Editrice ProFashion, Viale Espinasse 141, 20156 Milano; tel. (02) 3024121; fax (02) 30039400; internet www .eurographicus.com; f. 1911; 10 a year; printing and graphic arts; circ. 7,200.

Interni: Via D. Trentacoste 7, 20134 Milano; tel. (02) 215631; fax (02) 26410847; e-mail interni@mondadori.it; internet www .internimagazine.it; monthly; interior decoration and design; Editor GILDA BOJARDI; circ. 40,000.

Lotus International: Via Santa Marta 19A, 20123 Milano; tel. (02) 45475745; fax (02) 45475746; e-mail lotus@editorialelotus.it; f. 1963; quarterly; architecture, town-planning; Editor PIERLUIGI NICOLIN.

Rivista Italiana di Musicologia: Leo S. Olschki, Viuzzo del Pozzetto, 50126 Firenze; tel. (055) 6530684; fax (055) 6530214; e-mail sara.ciccarelli@tin.it; internet www.olschki.it/riviste/rivmusic.htm; f. 1966; twice a year; musicology; Editor ENRICO FUBINI.

Il Saggiatore Musicale: Leo S. Olschki, Viuzzo del Pozzetto, 50126 Firenze; tel. (055) 6530684; fax (055) 6530214; e-mail saggmus@muspe.unibo.it; internet www.muspe.unibo.it/period/saggmus; f. 1994; twice a year; musicology; Dir GIUSEPPINA LA FACE BIANCONI.

Storia dell'Arte: CAM Editrice, Srl, Via Capodiferro 4, 00186 Roma; tel. and fax (06) 68300889; e-mail info@cameditrice.com; internet www.cameditrice.com; f. 1969; quarterly; art history; Dirs MAURIZIO CALVESI, ORESTE FERRARI, ANGIOLA M. ROMANINI; circ. 1,200.

Studi Musicali: Leo S. Olschki, Viuzzo del Pozzetto, 50126 Firenze; tel. (055) 6530684; fax (055) 6530214; e-mail tmgialdroni@libero.it; internet www.olschki.it/riviste/stmusic.htm; f. 1972; twice a year; musicology; Editor AGOSTINO ZIINO.

General, Literary and Political

Archivio Storico Italiano: Leo S. Olschki, Viuzzo del Pozzetto, 50126 Firenze; tel. (055) 6530684; fax (055) 6530214; e-mail celso@olschki.it; internet www.storia.unifi.it/_pim/asi-dspt; f. 1842; quarterly; history; Editor GIULIANO PINTO.

Belfagor: Leo S. Olschki, Viuzzo del Pozzetto, 50126 Firenze; tel. (055) 6530684; fax (055) 6530214; e-mail celso@olschki.it; internet www.olschki.it/riviste/belfagor.htm; f. 1946; every 2 months; historical and literary criticism; Editor CARLO FERDINANDO RUSSO; circ. 2,500.

La Bibliofilia: Leo S. Olschki, Viuzzo del Pozzetto, 50126 Firenze; tel. (055) 6530684; fax (055) 6530214; e-mail celso@olschki.it; internet www.olschki.it/riviste/bibliof.htm; f. 1899; every 4 months; bibliography, history of printing; Editor LUIGI BALSAMO.

Diario: Via Melzo 9, 20129 Milano; tel. (02) 2771181; fax (02) 2046261; e-mail redazione@diario.it; internet www.diario.it; f. 1996; weekly; general interest; Dir ENRICO DEAGLIO.

Economy: Via Mondadori 1, 20090 Segrate (Milano); tel. (02) 75421; fax (02) 75422302; e-mail economy@mondadori.it; internet www.mondadori.com; f. 2003; weekly; economics and finance; Dir GIORGIO MULÉ; circ. 92,000.

L'Espresso: Via Po 12, 00198 Roma; tel. (06) 84781; fax (06) 8550246; e-mail segred@espresso.it; internet www.espressoedit.it; weekly; independent left; political; illustrated; Dir DANIELA HAMAUI; circ. 450,000.

Famiglia Cristiana: Via Giotto 36, 20145 Milano; tel. (02) 48071; fax (02) 48008247; e-mail famigliacristiana@stpauls.it; internet www.famigliacristiana.it; f. 1931; weekly; Catholic; illustrated; Dir ANTONIO SCIORTINO; circ. 862,600.

Francofonia: Leo S. Olschki, Viuzzo del Pozzetto, 50126 Firenze; tel. (055) 6530684; fax (055) 6530214; e-mail francofonia@lingue.unibo.it; internet www.olschki.it/riviste/francof.htm; f. 1981; twice a year; French language; Editor CARMINELLA BIONDI.

Gazzetta del Lunedì: Via Archimede 169/R, 16142 Genova; tel. (010) 53691; fax (010) 504148; f. 1946; weekly; political; Dir GEROLAMO ANGELI; circ. 83,315.

Gente: Viale Sarca 235, 20126 Milano; tel. (02) 27751; f. 1957; weekly; illustrated political, cultural and current events; Editor Dott. RENDINI; circ. 758,440.

Giornale della Libreria: Via Bergonzoli 1/5, 20127 Milano; tel. (02) 28315996; fax (02) 28315906; e-mail bibliografica@bibliografica.it; f. 1888; monthly; organ of the Associazione Italiana Editori; bibliographical; Editor FEDERICO MOTTA; circ. 5,000.

Lettere Italiane: Leo S. Olschki, POB 66, 50100 Firenze; tel. (055) 6530684; fax (055) 6530214; e-mail celso@olschki.it; internet www.olschki.it/riviste/lettital.htm; f. 1949; quarterly; literary; Dir CARLO OSSOLA.

Mondo Economico: Via Paolo Lomazzo 51, 20154 Milano; tel. (02) 3492451; fax (02) 316905; f. 1946; weekly; economics, business, finance; Editor ENRICO SASSOON; circ. 85,752.

Il Mulino: Strada Maggiore 37, 40125 Bologna; tel. (051) 222419; fax (051) 6486014; e-mail ilmulino@mulino.it; internet www.mulino.it/ilmulino; f. 1951; every 2 months; culture and politics; Dir EDMONDO BERCELLI; Editor-in-Chief EDMONDO BERSELLI.

Oggi: Via Angelo Rizzoli 2, 20132 Milano; tel. (02) 25841; fax (02) 27201485; f. 1945; weekly; topical, literary; illustrated; Dir PAOLO OCCHIPINTI; circ. 760,038.

Panorama: Arnoldo Mondadori Editore SpA, Via Marconi 27, 20090 Segrate, Milano; tel. (02) 75421; fax (02) 75422769; e-mail panorama@mondadori.it; internet www.mondadori.com/panorama; f. 1962; weekly; current affairs; Dir CARLO ROSSELLA; circ. 200,000.

Il Pensiero Politico: Leo S. Olschki, Viuzzo del Pozzetto, 50126 Firenze; tel. (055) 6530684; fax (055) 6530214; e-mail penspol@unipg.it; internet www.olschki.it/riviste/penspol.htm; f. 1968; every 4 months; political and social history; Editor VITTOR IVO COMPARATO.

Rassegna Storica Toscana: Leo S. Olschki, Viuzzo del Pozzetto, 50126 Firenze; tel. (055) 6530684; fax (055) 6530214; e-mail rogari@unifi.it; internet www.olschki.it/riviste/rasstor.htm; f. 1955; twice a year; Tuscan history; Editors FRANCESCO ADORNO, SANDRO ROGARI.

Rivista di Storia della Filosofia: Via de Togni 7, 20123 Milano; tel. (02) 8052538; fax (02) 8053948; e-mail riviste@francoangeli.it; internet www.francoangeli.it/riviste; f. 1946; quarterly; philosophy.

Scuola e Didattica: Via Luigi Cadorna 11, 25124 Brescia; tel. (030) 2993245; e-mail sdid@lascuola.it; internet www.lascuola.it; f. 1955; 19 a year; education; Editor GIUSEPPE VICO; circ. 40,000.

Selezione dal Reader's Digest: Via Lorenzini 4, 20139 Milano; tel. 800 351090; fax (02) 61293497; e-mail readerd@tin.it; internet www.selezionerd.it; monthly; Editor-in-Chief CLAUDIO PINA (acting); circ. 521,432.

Visto: Via Rizzoli 4, 20132 Milano; tel. (02) 25843961; fax (02) 25843907; f. 1989; illustrated weekly review; Editor-in-Chief PINO BELLERI; circ. 342,850.

Zett-Die Zeitung am Sonntag: Weinbergweg 7, 39100 Bozen; tel. (0471) 925500; fax (0471) 200462; e-mail zett@athesia.it; f. 1989; Sundays; German language; circ. 34,000.

Religion

Città di Vita: Piazza Santa Croce 16, 50122 Firenze; tel. and fax (055) 242783; e-mail info@cittadivita.org; internet www.cittadivita.org; f. 1946; every 2 months; cultural review of religious research in theology, art and science; Dir P. M. GIUSEPPE ROSITO; circ. 2,000.

La Civiltà Cattolica: Via di Porta Pinciana 1, 00187 Roma; tel. (06) 6979201; fax (06) 69792022; e-mail civcatt@laciviltacattolica.it; internet www.laciviltacattolica.it; f. 1850; fortnightly; Catholic; Editor GIAN PAOLO SALVINI; circ. 17,000.

Humanitas: Via G. Rosa 71, 25121 Brescia; tel. (030) 46451; fax (030) 2400605; e-mail redazione@morcelliana.it; f. 1946; every 2 months; religion, philosophy, science, politics, history, sociology, literature, etc.; Dir ILARIO BERTOLETTI.

Protestantesimo: Via Pietro Cossa 42, 00193 Roma; tel. (06) 3207055; fax (06) 3201040; e-mail fvt.protest@chiesavaldese.org; internet www.chiesavaldese.org/facolta/protestantesimo; f. 1946; quarterly; theology and current problems, book reviews; Dir Prof. FULVIO FERRARIO.

La Rivista del Clero Italiano: Largo Gemelli 1, 20123 Milano; tel. (02) 72342335; fax (02) 72342260; e-mail redazione.vp@unicatt.it; internet www.vitaepensiero.it; f. 1920; monthly; Dir BRUNO MAGGIONI; circ. 4,300.

Rivista di Storia della Chiesa in Italia: Piazza San Giovanni in Laterano 4, 00184 Roma; tel. and fax (06) 69886176; e-mail rsci@pul.it; internet www.vitaepensiero.it; f. 1947; twice a year; Editor AGOSTINO PARAVICINI BAGLIANI.

Rivista di Storia e Letteratura Religiosa: Leo S. Olschki, Viuzzo del Pozzetto, 50126 Firenze; tel. (055) 6530684; fax (055) 6530214; e-mail celso@olschki.it; internet www.olschki.it; f. 1965; every 4 months; religious history and literature; Dir MARIO ROSA.

Science and Technology

L'Automobile: Viale Regina Margherita 290, 00198 Roma; tel. (06) 441121; fax (06) 44231160; e-mail lea.srl@iol.it; f. 1945; monthly; motor mechanics, tourism; Dir PAOLO BASILI; circ. 1,083,210.

Gazzetta Medica Italiana Archivio per le Scienze Mediche: Edizioni Minerva Medica, Corso Bramante 83–85, 10126 Torino; tel. (011) 678282; fax (011) 674502; e-mail minervamedica@minervamedica.it; internet www.minervamedica.it; 6 a year; medical science; Dir ALBERTO OLIARO; circ. 2,900.

Il Nuovo Medico d'Italia: Via Monte Oliveto 2, 00141 Roma; tel. (06) 87185017; fax (06) 87185017; e-mail numedi@tiscalinet.it; internet www.numedi.it; monthly; medical science; Editor-in-Chief Dott. MARIO BERNARDINI.

Minerva Medica: Corso Bramante 83–85, 10126 Torino; tel. (011) 678282; fax (011) 674502; e-mail minervamedica@minervamedica.it; internet www.minervamedica.it; 10 a year; medical science; Dir ALBERTO OLIARO; circ. 4,900.

Monti e Boschi: Via Goito 13, 40126 Bologna; tel. (051) 65751; e-mail mb@gce.it; internet www.gce.it; f. 1949; every 2 months; ecology and forestry; Publr Edagricole; Editor UMBERTO BAGNARESI; circ. 16,700.

Motor: Piazza Antonio Mancini 4G, 00196 Roma; tel. (06) 3233195; fax (06) 3233309; e-mail info@rivistamotor.com; internet www .rivistamotor.com; f. 1940; monthly; motor mechanics; Dir S. FAVIA DEL CORE; circ. 35,500.

Newton: Via Vitruvio 43 20124, Milano; tel. (02) 675781; e-mail special.newton@editingsrl.it; internet www.newton.rcs.it; f. 1997; monthly; popular science; Dir GIORGIO RIVIECCIO; circ. 138,555.

Nuncius: Leo S. Olschki, Viuzzo del Pozzetto, 50126 Firenze; tel. (055) 6530684; fax (055) 6530214; e-mail ciardi@imss.fi.it; internet galileo.imss.firenze.it/pubblic/inuncius.html; f. 1976; twice a year; history of science; Dir PAOLO GALLUZZI.

Physis: Leo S. Olschki, Viuzzo del Pozzetto, 50126 Firenze; tel. (055) 6530684; fax (055) 6530214; e-mail guido.cimino@uniroma1.it; internet www.olschki.it/riviste/physis.htm; f. 1959; twice a year; history of science; Editors GUIDO CIMINO, VINCENZO CAPPELLETTI.

Rivista Geografica Italiana: Via S. Gallo 10, 50129 Firenze; tel. (055) 2757956; fax (055) 2757956; e-mail info@societastudigeografici .it; f. 1894; quarterly geographical review; Editors PAOLO DOCCIOLI, LEONARDO ROMBAI, BRUNO VECCHIO.

Women's Publications

Amica: Via Angelo Rizzoli 2, 20132 Milano; tel. (02) 2588; f. 1962; monthly; Dirs MARIA LAURA RODOTA, EMANUELA TESTORI; circ. 292,269.

Anna: Via Civitavecchia 102, Milano; tel. (02) 25843213; f. 1932; weekly; Editor M. VENTURI; circ. 291,784.

Confidenze: Arnoldo Mondadori Editore SpA, Via Mondadori 1, 20090 Segrate, Milano; tel. (02) 75421; fax (02) 75422806; e-mail bnaeeif@mondadori.it; f. 1946; weekly; Dir CHRISTINA MAGMASCHI; circ. 229,825.

Cosmopolitan Italia: Arnoldo Mondadori Editore SpA, Via Marconi 27, 20090 Segrate, Milano; internet home.mondadori.com/ cosmopolitan; monthly; Dir CINZIA FELICETTI.

Donna Moderna: Arnoldo Mondadori Editore SpA, Via Marconi 27, 20090 Segrate, Milano; internet www.donnamoderna.com; monthly; Dir PATRIZIA AVOLEDO.

Gioia: Viale Sarca 235, 20126 Milano; tel. (02) 66191; fax (02) 66192717; e-mail gioia@rusconi.it; f. 1937; weekly; Dir VERA MONTANARI; circ. 297,516.

Grazia: Arnoldo Mondadori Editore SpA, Via Mondadori 1, 20090 Segrate, Milano; tel. (02) 75422390; fax (02) 75422515; e-mail grazia@mondadori; f. 1938; weekly; Dir CARLA VANNI; circ. 379,820.

Intimità della Famiglia: Piazza Aspromonte 13, 20131 Milano; tel. (02) 706421; fax (02) 70642306; e-mail intimita@quadratum.it; internet www.quadratum.it; weekly; published by Quadratum; Dir ANNA GIUSTI; circ. 424,946.

Vogue Italia: Piazza Castello 27, 20121 Milano; tel. (02) 85611; fax (02) 8055716; internet www.vogue.com; monthly; Editor FRANCA SOZZANI; circ. 102,123.

Miscellaneous

Annali della Classe di Lettere e Filosofia: Scuola Normale Superiore, Piazza dei Cavalieri 7, 56100 Pisa; tel. (050) 509111; fax (050) 563513; e-mail publ_lettere@sns.it; internet www.sns.it; f. 1873; quarterly; archaeology, art history, philosophy, philology, history, literature; Editor ENRICO CASTELNUOVO; circ. 1,200.

Capital: Via Angelo Rizzoli 2, 20132, Milano; f. 1979; monthly; men's lifestyle, economics, technology; Dir GIOVANNI IOZZIA; circ. 90,199.

Cooperazione Educativa: Edizioni Junior, Via dei Piceni 16, 00185 Roma; tel. (06) 4457228; fax (06) 4460386; f. 1952; monthly; education; Dir MIRELLA GRIEG.

Dove: Via Angelo Rizzoli 2, 20132, Milano; f. 1991; monthly; lifestyle and travel; Dir VALERIA TEGAMI; circ. 106,807.

Gambero Rosso: GRH SpA, Via Angelo Bargoni 8, 00153, Roma; tel. (06) 5852121; fax (06) 58310170; e-mail gambero@gamberorosso .it; internet www.gamberorosso.it; f. 1986; monthly; food and wine; Dir STEFANO BONILLI.

Lares: Leo S. Olschki, Viuzzo del Pozzetto, 50126 Firenze; tel. (055) 6530684; fax (055) 6530214; e-mail clementep@unifi.it.it; internet www.olschki.it/riviste/lares.htm; f. 1912; every four months; folk-lore; Editor PIETRO CLEMENTE.

Il Maestro: Clivo di Monte del Gallo 48, 00165 Roma; tel. (06) 634651; fax (06) 39375903; e-mail a.i.m.c@flashnet.it; internet www .aimc.it; f. 1945; monthly; Catholic teachers' magazine; Dir GIUSEPPE DESIDERI; circ. 40,000.

Max: Via Angelo Rizzoli 2, 20132, Milano; internet www.max.rcs.it; f. 1985; monthly; men's lifestyle; Dir GIUSEPPE DI PIAZZA; circ. 147,836.

Quattroruote: Via Gianni Mazzocchi 1/3, 20089 Rozzano, Milano; tel. (02) 824721; fax (02) 57500416; e-mail redazione@quattroruote .it; internet www.quattroruote.it; f. 1956; motoring; monthly; Editor MAURO TEDESCHINI; circ. 650,000.

NEWS AGENCIES

AdnKronos: Via Ripetta 73, 00186 Roma; tel. (06) 324961; fax (06) 32002204; internet www.adnkronos.it; Dir-Gen. MARIA ROSARIA BELLIZZI DE MARCO.

Agenzia Giornalistica Italia (AGI): Via Cristoforo Colombo 98, 00147 Roma; tel. (06) 519961; fax (06) 51996201; e-mail info@agi.it; internet www.agi.it; Gen. Man. NICOLA LAINÉ.

Agenzia Nazionale Stampa Associata (ANSA): Via della Dataria 94, 00187 Roma; tel. (06) 67741; fax (06) 69797383; e-mail webmaster@ansa.it; internet www.ansa.it; f. 1945; 22 regional offices in Italy and 90 brs all over the world; service in Italian, Spanish, French, English; Pres. BORIS BIANCHERI; CEO and Man. Dir GIUSEPPE CERBONE; Gen. Man. PIERLUIGI MAGNASCHI.

Asca: Via Due Macelli 23, 00187 Roma; tel. (06) 69792911; fax (06) 6783535; e-mail segreteria@asca.it; internet www.asca.it; Dir CLAUDIO SONZOGNO.

Documentazioni Informazioni Resoconti (Dire): Via Abruzzi 3, 00187 Roma; tel. (06) 4203811; fax (06) 42012689; e-mail dire@dire .it; internet www.dire.it; Dir ADRIANO PANICCIA.

Inter Press Service International Association (IPS): Via Panisperna 207, 00184 Roma; tel. (06) 485692; fax (06) 4827112; e-mail romaser@ips.org; internet www.ips.org; f. 1964; international daily news agency; Dir-Gen. PATRICIA A. MADE.

Foreign Bureaux

Agencia EFE (Spain): Via dei Canestrari 5, 00186 Roma; tel. (06) 6834087; fax (06) 6874918; e-mail eferoma@efe.it; Bureau Chief JAIME ANTONIO CASTILLO ARROYO.

Anadolu Agency (A.A.) (Turkey): Stampa Estera, Via della Mercede 55, 00187 Rome; tel. (06) 7591251; fax (06) 4819729; e-mail roma@anadoluajansi.com.tr; Correspondent SENHAN BOLELLI.

Agence France-Presse (AFP): Piazza Santi Apostoli 66, 00187 Roma; tel. (06) 6793588; fax (06) 6793623; e-mail afp-rome@afp.com; internet www.afp.com; Bureau Chief PATRICK CRAMPONT.

Associated Press (AP) (USA): Piazza Grazioli 5, 00186 Roma; tel. (06) 6798382; fax (06) 6790103; internet www.ap.org/italia; Bureau Chief DENNIS F. REDMONT.

Česká tisková kancelář (ČTK) (Czech Republic): Via di Vigna Stelluti 150/13, 00191 Roma; tel. (06) 3270777.

Deutsche Presse-Agentur (dpa) (Germany): Via Vespasiano 12, int. 12C 5°, 00192 Roma; tel. (06) 89927213; fax (06) 89927215; Bureau Chief PEER W. MEINERT.

Informatsionnoye Telegrafnoye Agentstvo Rossii (ITAR—TASS) (Russia): Viale dell'Umanesimo 172, 00144 Roma; tel. (06) 5912882; fax (06) 5926800; e-mail romatass@mail.com; Correspondents OLEG OSSIPOV, ALEXEI BULGAKOV.

Kyodo Tsushin (Japan): Via Toscana 30, 00187 Roma; tel. (06) 42012289; fax (06) 42014066; internet home.kyodo.co.jp; Bureau Chief KATSUO UEDA.

Maghreb Arabe Presse: Corso Trieste 10, 00198 Roma; tel. (06) 4402431; fax (06) 4403431; Correspondent AMIR NOUREDDINE.

Reuters Italia SpA (United Kingdom): Viale Fulvio Testi 280, 20126 Milano; tel. (02) 661291; fax (02) 66118167; e-mail milan .newsroom@reuters.com; internet www.reuters.it; second office in Rome; Editor NELSON GRAVES.

United Press International (UPI) (USA): Via della Mercede 55, 00187 Roma; tel. (06) 6795747; fax (06) 6781540; Correspondent CHARLES RIDLEY.

Xinhua (New China) News Agency (People's Republic of China): Via Bruxelles 59, 00198 Roma; tel. (06) 865028; fax (06) 8450575; Bureau Chief HUANG CHANGRUI.

CNA (Taiwan), Jiji Tsushin (Japan), Kuwait News Agency, Agencija Roma (Croatia), Magyar Távirati Iroda (Hungary), Norsk Telegrambyrå (Norway), Polska Agencja Prasowa (Poland), Syrian Arab News Agency, Notimex (Mexico), Bulgarska Telegrafna Agentsiya (Bulgaria), RIA Novosti (Russia), Austria Presse Agentur, Tanjug (Serbia and Montenegro) and Algemeen Nederlands Persbureau (Netherlands) are also represented.

PRESS ASSOCIATIONS

Associazione della Stampa Estera in Italia: Via della Umiltà 83C, 00187 Roma; tel. (06) 675911; fax (06) 67591262; e-mail segreteria@stampa-estera.it; internet www.stampa-estera.it; foreign correspondents' asscn; Pres. ANTONIO PELAYO; Sec. MAARTEN SAM AALDEREN.

Federazione Italiana Editori Giornali (FIEG): Via Piemonte 64, 00187 Roma; tel. (06) 4881683; fax (06) 4871109; e-mail fiegroma@iol.it; internet www.fieg.it; f. 1950; association of newspaper publishers; Pres. LUCA CORDERO DI MONTEZEMOLO; 268 mems.

Federazione Nazionale della Stampa Italiana: Corso Vittorio Emanuele II 349, 00186 Roma; tel. (06) 6833879; fax (06) 6871444; internet www.fnsi.it; f. 1877; 19 affiliated unions; Pres. FRANCO SIDDI; Sec.-Gen. PAOLO SERVENTI LONGHI; 16,000 mems.

Unione Stampa Periodica Italiana (USPI): Viale Bardanzellu 95, 00155 Roma; tel. (06) 4071388; fax (06) 4066859; e-mail uspi@uspi.it; internet www.uspi.it; Pres. MARIO NEGRI; Gen. Sec. FRANCESCO SAVERIO VETERE; 4,500 mems.

Publishers

There are more than 300 major publishing houses and many smaller ones.

BOLOGNA

Gruppo Calderini Edagricole: Via Goito 13, 40126 Bologna; tel. (051) 65751; fax (051) 6575800; e-mail sede@gce.it; internet www.gce.it; group includes Calderini (f. 1960; art, sport, electronics, mechanics, university and school textbooks, travel guides, nursing, architecture) and Edagricole (f. 1935; agriculture, veterinary science, gardening, biology, textbooks); Pres. Prof. GIORGIO AMADEI; Man. Dir GIOVANNA VILLANI PERDISA.

Nuova Casa Editrice Licinio Cappelli GEM SrL: Via Farini 14, 40124 Bologna; tel. (051) 239060; fax (051) 239286; f. 1848; medical science, history, politics, literature, textbooks; Chair. and Man. Dir MARIO MUSSO.

Editrice CLUEB: Via Marsala 31, 40126 Bologna; tel. (051) 220736; fax (051) 237758; e-mail clueb@clueb.com; internet www.clueb.com; f. 1959; education, arts, business, history, literature; Man. Dir LUIGI GUARDIGLI.

Società Editrice Il Mulino: Strada Maggiore 37, 40125 Bologna; tel. (051) 256011; fax (051) 256034; e-mail info@mulino.it; internet www.mulino.it; f. 1954; politics, history, philosophy, social sciences, linguistics, literary criticism, law, psychology, economics, journals; Gen. Man. GIOVANNI EVANGELISTI.

Zanichelli Editore SpA: Via Irnerio 34, 40126 Bologna; tel. (051) 293111; fax (051) 249782; e-mail zanichelli@zanichelli.it; internet www.zanichelli.it; f. 1859; educational, history, literature, philosophy, mathematics, science, technical books, law, psychology, architecture, reference books, dictionaries, atlases, earth sciences, linguistics, medicine, economics, etc.; Chair. and Gen. Man. FEDERICO ENRIQUES; Vice-Chair. and Man. Dir LORENZO ENRIQUES.

BRESCIA

Editrice La Scuola SpA: Via Cadorna 11, Brescia; tel. (030) 29931; fax (030) 2993299; e-mail lascuola@tin.it; internet www.lascuola.it; f. 1904; educational magazines, educational textbooks, audiovisual aids and toys; Chairs Dott. Ing. LUCIANO SILVERI, Dott. Ing. GIORGIO RACCIS; Man. Dir Rag. GIUSEPPE COVONE.

FLORENCE

Casa Editrice Bonechi: Via dei Cairoli 18B, 50131 Firenze; tel. (055) 576841; fax (055) 5000766; e-mail bonechi@bonechi.it; internet www.bonechi.com; f. 1973; art, travel, cooking, CD-Rom; Pres. GIAMPAOLO BONECHI.

Cremonese: Borgo Santa Croce 17, 50122 Firenze; tel. (055) 2476371; fax (055) 2476372; e-mail cremonese@ed-cremonese.it; internet www.ed-cremonese.it; f. 1929; history, reference, engineering, science, textbooks, architecture, mathematics, aviation; Chair. ALBERTO STIANTI.

Giunti Gruppo Editoriale: Via Bolognese 165, 50139 Firenze; tel. (055) 5062376; fax (055) 5062397; e-mail informazioni@giunti.it; internet www.giunti.it; f. 1839; art, psychology, literature, science, law; Man. Dir MARCINO MONTANARINI.

Casa Editrice Edumond-Le Monnier SpA: Via A. Meucci 2, 50015 Grassina, Firenze; tel. (055) 64910; fax (055) 6491310; e-mail lemonnier@lemonnier.it; internet www.lemonnier.it; f. 1837; from 1999, part of Gruppo Mondadori; academic and cultural books, textbooks, dictionaries; Pres. GIUSEPPE DE RITA.

La Nuova Italia Editrice SpA: Via Ernesto Codignola 1, 50018 Firenze; tel. (055) 75901; fax (055) 7590208; internet www.lanuovaitalia.it; f. 1926; part of RCS Scuola; biography, psychology, philosophy, philology, education, history, politics, belles-lettres, art,

music and science; Man. Dirs FEDERICO CODIGNOLA, CARMELO SAMBUGAR.

Casa Editrice Leo S. Olschki: CP 66, 50100 Firenze; tel. (055) 6530684; fax (055) 6530214; e-mail celso@olschki.it; internet www.olschki.it; f. 1886; reference, periodicals, textbooks, humanities; Man. ALESSANDRO OLSCHKI.

Vallecchi Editore SpA: Via Maragliano 6 int., 50144 Firenze; tel. (055) 324761; e-mail dire@vallecchi.it; internet www.vallecchi.it; f. 1903; art, fiction, literature, essays, media; Editor-in-Chief LAURA CATTANEO.

GENOA

Casa Editrice Marietti SpA: Via Piandilucco, 16155 Genova; tel. (010) 6984226; fax (010) 667092; e-mail marietti1820@split.it; internet mall.shopla.it/marietti/index.html; f. 1820; liturgy, theology, fiction, history, politics, literature, philosophy, art, children's books; Editor CARLA VILLATA.

MILAN

Adelphi Edizioni SpA: Via S. Giovanni sul Muro 14, 20121 Milano; tel. (02) 725731; fax (02) 89010337; e-mail info@adelphi.it; internet www.adelphi.it; f. 1962; classics, philosophy, biography, music, art, psychology, religion and fiction; Pres. ROBERTO CALASSO.

Editrice Ancora: Via G. B. Niccolini 8, 20154 Milano; tel. (02) 3456081; fax (02) 34560866; e-mail editrice@ancoralibri.it; internet www.ancoralibri.it; f. 1934; religious, educational; Dir GILBERTO ZINI.

Franco Angeli Editore Srl: Viale Monza 106, CP 17175, 20127 Milano; tel. (02) 2837141; fax (02) 26144793; e-mail redazione@francoangeli.it; internet www.francoangeli.it; f. 1956; general nonfiction; Man. Dir FRANCO ANGELI.

Bramante Editrice: Viale Bianca Maria 19, 20122 Milano; tel. (02) 760759; fax (02) 780904; f. 1958; art, history, encyclopaedias, natural sciences, interior decoration, arms and armour, music; Chair. Dott. GUIDO CERIOTTI.

Giangiacomo Feltrinelli Editore SpA: Via Andegari 6, 20121 Milano; tel. (02) 725721; fax (02) 72572500; e-mail scrivimi@feltrinelli.it; internet www.feltrinelli.it; f. 1954; fiction, juvenile, science, technology, history, literature, political science, philosophy; Chair. INGE FELTRINELLI; Publr CARLO FELTRINELLI.

Garzanti Libri SpA: Via Gasparotto 1, 20124 Milano; tel. (02) 674171; fax (02) 67417260; internet www.garzantilibri.it; f. 1938; literature, poetry, science, art, history, politics, encyclopaedias; Chair. STEFANO MAURI; Gen. Dir RENZO GUIDIERI.

Hachette Rusconi SpA: Viale Sarca 235, 20126 Milano; tel. (02) 66191; fax (02) 66192758; e-mail info@rusconi.it; internet www.rusconi.it; f. 1969 as Rusconi Libri Srl; magazines; Pres. ALBERTO RUSCONI.

Ulrico Hoepli Casa Editrice Libraria SpA: Via Hoepli 5, 20121 Milano; tel. (02) 864871; fax (02) 864322; e-mail hoepli@hoepli.it; internet www.hoepli.it; f. 1870; grammars, art, technical, scientific and school books, encyclopaedias; Chair. Dott. ULRICO HOEPLI; Man. Dir GIANNI HOEPLI.

Longanesi e C. SpA: Via Gherardini 10, 20145 Milano; tel. (02) 34537620; fax (02) 34537212; e-mail info@longanesi.it; internet www.longanesi.it; f. 1946; art, history, philosophy, fiction; Pres. STEFANO PASSIGLI; Man. Dir STEFANO MAURI.

Massimo: Viale Bacchiglione 20A, 20139 Milano; tel. (02) 55210800; fax (02) 55211315; f. 1950; fiction, biography, history, social science, philosophy, pedagogy, theology, school texts; Chair. CESARE CRESPI.

Arnoldo Mondadori Editore SpA: Via Mondadori 1, 20090 Segrate, Milano; tel. (02) 75421; fax (02) 75422302; e-mail infolibri@mondadori.it; internet www.librimondadori.it; f. 1907; books, magazines and online publishing; Pres. MARINA BERLUSCONI.

Gruppo Ugo Mursia Editore SpA: Via M. Gioia 45, 20124 Milano; tel. (02) 67378500; fax (02) 67378605; e-mail info@mursia.com; internet www.mursia.com; f. 1955; general fiction and non-fiction, reference, art, history, nautical books, philosophy, biography, sports, children's books; Gen. Man. FIORENZA MURSIA.

Paravia Bruno Mondadori Editori (PBM Editori): Via Archimede 23, 20129 Milano; tel. (02) 748231; fax (02) 74823278; internet www.pbmeditori.it; f. 1946 as Edizioni Bruno Mondadori; merged with G.B.Paravia di Torino in 2000 and name changed as above; school and university textbooks.

RCS Libri SpA: Via Mecenate 91, 20138 Milano; tel. (02) 50951; fax (02) 5065361; internet www.rcslibri.it; f. 1947; juveniles, education, textbooks, reference, literature, art books; Chair. NICOLÒ NEFRI; CEO FERRUCCIO DE BORTOLI; Gen. Man. GIULIO LATTANZI.

Bompiani: internet www.rcs.it/rcslibri/bompiani; f. 1929; modern literature, biographies, theatre, science, art, history, classics, dictionaries, pocket books; Dir MARIO ANDREOSE.

Etas Srl: e-mail etaslab@rcs.it; internet www.etaslab.it; finance, economics, management, business; Man. Dir Dott. GIORGIO ORSI.

Fabbri: internet www.rcs.it.rcslibri/fabbri; children's.

Rizzoli: internet www.rcs.it/rcslibri/rizzoli; f. 1929; newspapers, magazines and books; Dir-Gen. GIOVANNI UNGARELLI; Man. Dir GIORGIO FATTORI.

Sonzogno: internet www.rcs.it/rcslibri/sonzogno; f. 1861; fiction, non-fiction, illustrated, manuals; Dir MARIO ANDREOSE.

Riccardo Ricciardi Editore SpA: c/o Arnoldo Mondadori Editore, Via Mondadori 1, 20090 Segrate, Milano; tel. (02) 75421; f. 1907; classics, philology, history, literature; Gen. Man. GIAN ARTURO FERRARI.

Casa Ricordi SpA: Via Berchet 2, 20121 Milano; tel. (02) 88811; fax (02) 88812212; internet www.ricordi.it; f. 1808; academic, art, sheet music; Chair. GIANNI BABINI; Man. Dir Dott. TINO GENNAMO.

Gruppo Editoriale il Saggiatore: Via Melzo 9, 20129 Milano; tel. (02) 201301; fax (02) 29513061; e-mail carra@saggiatore.it; internet www.saggiatore.it; art, fiction, social sciences, history, travel, current affairs, popular science; Pres. LUCA FORMENTON.

Adriano Salani Editore SpA: Via Gherardini 10, 20145 Milano; tel. (02) 34597624; fax (02) 34597206; e-mail info@salani.it; internet www.salani.it; f. 1988; fiction, children's books; Editor MARIAGRAZIA MAZZITELLI.

Edizioni San Paolo: Piazza Soncino 5, 20092 Cinisello Balsamo—Milano; tel. (02) 660751; fax (02) 66075211; e-mail sanpaoloedizioni@stpauls.it; internet www.sanpaolo.org.it; f. 1914; religious; Gen. Man. VINCENZO SANTARCANGELO.

SEDES SpA-Ghisetti e Corvi Editori: Corso Concordia 7, 20129 Milano; tel. (02) 76006232; fax (02) 76009468; e-mail sedes.spa@gpa.it; internet www.sedes.gpa.it; f. 1937; educational textbooks.

Selezione dal Reader's Digest: Camuzzi Editoriale, SpA, Via Lorenzini 4, 20139 Milano; fax (02) 61293497; e-mail reader@tin.it; internet www.selezionerd.it; f. 1948; Reader's Digest, educational, reference, general interest; Man. Dir CHARLES J. LOBKOWICZ.

Sugarco Edizioni Srl: Via Fermi 9, 21040 Camago (VA); tel. (0331) 985511; fax (0331) 985385; f. 1957; fiction, biography, history, philosophy, guidebooks, Italian classics; Chair. Prof. SERGIO CIGADA; Gen. Man. OLIVIERO CIGADA.

Casa Editrice Luigi Trevisini: Via Tito Livio 12, 20137 Milano; tel. (02) 5450704; fax (02) 55195782; e-mail trevisini@trevisini.it; internet www.trevisini.it; f. 1849; school textbooks; Dirs LUIGI TREVISINI, GIUSEPPINA TREVISINI.

Vita e Pensiero: Largo A. Gemelli 1, 20123 Milano; tel. (02) 72342335; fax (02) 72342260; e-mail editrice.vp@unicatt.it; internet www.vitaepensiero.it; f. 1918; publisher to the Catholic University of the Sacred Heart; philosophy, literature, social science, theology, history; Dir LORENZO ORNAGHI.

NAPLES

Idelson Gnocchi Editore Srl: Via Michele Pietrasalle 85, 80131 Napoli; tel. (081) 5453443; fax (081) 5464991; e-mail info@idelson-gnocchi.com; internet www.idelson-gnocchi.com; f. 1908; botany, medicine, radiology, psychology, anatomy, biology, chemistry, physics, nursing; CEO GUIDO GNOCCHI.

Liguori Editore Srl: Via Posillipo 394, 80123 Napoli; tel. (081) 7206111; fax (081) 7206244; e-mail guido@liguori.it; internet www.liguori.it; f. 1949; linguistics, mathematics, engineering, economics, law, history, philosophy, sociology; Man. Dir Dott. GUIDO LIGUORI.

Edizioni Scientifiche Italiane SpA: Via Chiatamone 7, 80121 Napoli; tel. (081) 7645443; fax (081) 7646477; e-mail info@esispa.com; internet www.esispa.com; f. 1945; law, economics, literature, arts, history, science; Pres. PIETRO PERLINGIERI.

NOVARA

De Agostini Editore: Via Giovanni da Verrazano 15, 28100 Novara; tel. (0321) 4241; fax (0321) 471286; e-mail ufficio.stampa@deagostini.it; internet www.deagostini.it; f. 1901; geography, maps, encyclopaedias, dictionaries, art, literature, textbooks, science; CEO STEFANO BELLA.

PADUA

CEDAM (Casa Editrice Dr A. Milani): Via Jappelli 5/6, 35121 Padua; tel. (049) 8239111; fax (049) 8752900; e-mail info@cedam.com; internet www.cedam.com; f. 1903; law, economics, political and social sciences, engineering, science, medicine, literature, philos-

ophy, textbooks; Dirs ANTONIO MILANI, CARLO PORTA, FRANCESCO GIORDANO.

Libreria Editrice Gregoriana: Via Roma 82, 35122 Padua; tel. (049) 8758455; e-mail l.gregoriana@mclink.it; f. 1922; *Lexicon Totius Latinitatis*, religion, philosophy, psychology, social studies; Dir DON GIANCARLO MINOZZI.

Piccin Nuova Libraria SpA: Via Altinate 107, 35121 Padua; tel. (049) 655566; fax (049) 8750693; e-mail info@piccinonline.com; internet www.piccinonline.com; f. 1980; scientific and medical textbooks and journals; Man. Dir Dott. MASSIMO PICCIN.

PALERMO

Editrice Ciranna: Via G. Besio 143, 90145 Palermo; tel. (091) 224499; fax (091) 311064; e-mail info@ciranna.it; internet www.ciranna.it; f. 1940; school textbooks; Man. Dir LIDIA FABIANO.

ROME

Armando Armando Srl: Viale Trastevere 236, 00153 Roma; tel. (06) 5806420; fax (06) 5818564; e-mail armando@palomar.it; internet www.armando.it; f. 1950; philosophy, psychology, social sciences, languages, ecology, education; Man. Dir ENRICO JACOMETTI.

Caltagirone Editore: Via Montello, 00195 Roma; tel. (06) 374921; fax (06) 3728546; e-mail investor.relations@caltagironeeditore.com; internet www.caltagironeeditore.com; f. 1999; news publisher.

Edizioni d'Arte di Carlo E. Bestetti & C. Sas: Via di San Giacomo 18, 00187 Roma; tel. (06) 6790174; f. 1947; art, architecture, industry; Man. Dir CARLO BESTETTI.

AVE (Anonima Veritas Editrice): Via Aurelia 481, 00165 Roma; tel. (06) 6631545; fax (06) 6620207; f. 1935; theology, sociology, pedagogy, psychology, essays, learned journals, religious textbooks; Pres. ARMANDO OBERTI.

Edizioni Borla Srl: Via delle Fornaci 50, 00165 Roma; tel. (06) 39376728; fax (06) 39376620; e-mail borla@edizioni-borla.it; internet www.edizioni-borla.it; f. 1863; religion, philosophy, psychoanalysis, ethnology, literature; Man. Dir VINCENZO D'AGOSTINO.

Bulzoni Editore—Le edizioni universitarie d'Italia: Via dei Liburni 14, 00185 Roma; tel. (06) 4455207; fax (06) 4450355; e-mail bulzoni@bulzoni.it; internet www.bulzoni.it; f. 1969; science, arts, fiction, textbooks; Man. Dir IVANA BULZONI.

Edizioni Europa: Via G. B. Martini 6, 00198 Roma; tel. (06) 8449124; f. 1944; essays, literature, art, history, politics, music, economics; Chair. Prof. PIER FAUSTO PALUMBO.

Jandi Sapi Editori Srl: Via Crescenzio 62, 00193 Roma; tel. (06) 68805515; fax (06) 6832612; e-mail info@jandisapi.com; internet www.jandisapi.com; f. 1941; industrial and legal publications, art books.

Editori Laterza: Via di Villa Sacchetti 17, 00197 Roma; tel. (06) 3218393; fax (06) 3223853; e-mail laterza@laterza.it; internet www.laterza.it; f. 1885; belles-lettres, biography, reference, religion, art, classics, history, economics, philosophy, social science; Editorial Dirs ALESSANDRO LATERZA, GIUSEPPE LATERZA.

Edizioni Lavoro: Via G. M. Lancisi 25, 00161 Roma; tel. (06) 44251174; fax (06) 44251177; e-mail info@edizionilavoro.it; f. 1982; history, politics, political philosophy, sociology, religion, Islamic, African, Arab and Caribbean literature; Chair. PIETRO GELARDI; Man. Dir LIONELLA CARPITA.

Edizioni Mediterranee Srl: Via Flaminia 109, 00196 Roma; tel. (06) 3201656; fax (06) 3236277; e-mail info@ediz-mediterranee.com; internet www.edizionimediterranee.it; f. 1953; alchemy, astrology, esoterism, meditation, natural medicine, parapsychology, hobbies, martial arts, zen.

Guida Monaci SpA: Via Salaria 1319, 00138 Roma; tel. (06) 8887777; fax (06) 8889996; e-mail guida.monaci@italybygm.it; internet www.italybygm.it; f. 1870; commercial and industrial, financial, administrative and medical directories; Dir Ing. GIANCARLO ZAPPONINI.

Fratelli Palombi Srl: Via dei Gracchi 181–185, 00192 Roma; tel. (06) 3214150; fax (06) 3214752; e-mail flli.palombi@mail.sth.it; f. 1914; history, art, etc,. of Rome; Man. Dir MARIO PALOMBI.

Società Editrice Dante Alighieri Srl: Via Timavo 3, 00195 Roma; tel. (06) 3725870; fax (06) 37514807; e-mail seda@dantealighierisrl.191.it; internet www.nuovarivistastorica.it; f. 1928; school textbooks, science and general culture; Pres. and Man. MAURO SPINELLI.

Edizioni Studium: Via Cassiodoro 14, 00193 Roma; tel. (06) 6865846; fax (06) 6875456; e-mail edizionistudium@libero.it; f. 1927; philosophy, literature, sociology, pedagogy, religion, economics, law, science, history, psychology; periodical *Studium*.

STRESA

Edizioni Rosminiane Sodalitas Sas: Centro Internazionale di Studi Rosminiani, Corso Umberto I 15, 28838 Stresa; tel. (0323) 30091; fax (0323) 31623; e-mail edizioni@rosmini.it; internet www .rosmini.it; f. 1925; philosophy, theology, *Rivista Rosminiana* (quarterly); Dir Prof. PIER PAOLO OTTONELLO.

TURIN

Bollati Boringhieri Editore: Corso Vittorio Emanuele II 86, 10121 Torino; tel. (011) 5591711; fax (011) 543024; e-mail info@ bollatiboringhieri.it; internet www.bollatiboringhieri.it; f. 1957; history, economics, natural sciences, psychology, social and human sciences, fiction and literary criticism; Chair. ROMILDA BOLLATI.

Giulio Einaudi Editore SpA: Via Umberto Biancamano 2, CP 245, 10121 Torino; tel. (011) 56561; fax (011) 542903; internet www .einaudi.it; f. 1933; fiction, classics, general; Chair. ROBERTO CERATI; Gen. Man. VITTORIO BO.

G. Giappichelli Editore Srl: Via Po 21, 10124 Torino; tel. (011) 8153511; fax (011) 8125100; e-mail editoriale@giappichelli.com; internet www.giappichelli.it; f. 1921; university publications on law, economics, politics and sociology.

S. Lattes e C. Editori SpA: Via Confienza 6, 10121 Torino; tel. (011) 5625335; fax (011) 5625070; internet www.latteseditori.it; f. 1893; technical, textbooks; Pres. CATERINA BOTTARI LATTES; Man. Dir RENATA LATTES.

Levrotto e Bella, Libreria Editrice Universitaria: Via Pigafetta Antonio 2/E, 10129 Torino; tel. (011) 5097367; fax (011) 504025; e-mail info@levrotto-bella.net; internet shop.levrotto-bella.net; f. 1911; university textbooks; Man. Dir Dott. ELISABETTA GUALINI.

Loescher Editore: Via Vittorio Amedeo II 18, 10121 Torino; tel. (011) 5654111; fax (011) 5625822; e-mail mail@loescher.it; internet www.loescher.it; f. 1867; school textbooks, general literature, academic books; Chair. LORENZO ENRIQUES.

Edizioni Minerva Medica: Corso Bramante 83–85, 10126 Torino; tel. (011) 678282; fax (011) 674502; e-mail minmed@tin.it; internet www.minervamedica.it; medical books and journals; Pres. ALBERTO OLIARO.

Petrini Editore: Strada del Portone 179, 10095 Grugliasco, Torino; tel. (011) 2098768; fax (011) 2098710; e-mail petrini@petrini.it; internet www.petrini.it; f. 1872; school textbooks.

Rosenberg & Sellier: Via Andrea Doria 14, 10123 Torino; tel. (011) 8127808; fax (011) 8127820; e-mail info@rosenbergesellier.it; internet www.rosenbergesellier.it; f. 1883; economics, history, gender studies, social sciences, philosophy, linguistics, Latin, dictionaries, scientific journals; Chair. and Man. Dir UGO GIANNI ROSENBERG.

Società Editrice Internazionale SpA (SEI): Corso Regina Margherita 176, 10152 Torino; tel. (011) 52271; fax (011) 5211320; e-mail sei@seieditrice.com; internet www.seieditrice.com; f. 1908; textbooks, religion, history, education, multimedia; Head of Editorial Dept ULISSE JACOMUZZI.

Unione Tipografico-Editrice Torinese (UTET): Corso Raffaello 28, 10125 Torino; tel. (011) 2099111; fax (011) 2099394; internet www.utet.it; f. 1791; university and specialized editions on history, geography, art, literature, economics, sciences, encyclopaedias, dictionaries, etc.; Pres. ANTONIO BELLONI.

VENICE

Alfieri Edizioni d'Arte: San Marco 1991, 30124 Venezia; tel. (041) 23323; f. 1939; modern art, Venetian art, architecture, periodicals; Chair. GIORGIO FANTONI; Gen. Man. MASSIMO VITTA ZELMAN.

Marsilio Editori: Marittima, Fabbricato 205, 30135 Venezia; tel. (041) 2406511; fax (041) 5238352; e-mail info@marsilioeditori.it; internet www.marsilioeditori.it; f. 1961; fiction, non-fiction, history of art, catalogues, cartography; Man. Dirs Dott. EMANUELA BASSETTI, Prof. CESARE DE MICHELIS.

VERONA

Giorgio Bertani Editore Srl: Verona; tel. (045) 8011345; fax (045) 8350402; f. 1973; politics, literature, anthropology, sociology, theatre, cinema, geography, humanities, history of Verona and Veneto, psychology, cultural journals; Man. Dir MARIO QUARANTA; Editorial Dir GIORGIO BERTANI.

VICENZA

Neri Pozza Editore SpA: Contrà Oratorio dei Servi 21, 36100 Vicenza; tel. (0444) 320787; fax (0444) 324613; e-mail info@ neripozza.it; internet www.neripozza.it; f. 1946; art, fiction, history, politics; Pres. SILVIO FORTUNA; Dir GIUSEPPE RUSSO.

GOVERNMENT PUBLISHING HOUSE

Istituto Poligrafico e Zecca dello Stato: Piazza Verdi 10, 00198 Roma; tel. (06) 85082391; fax (06) 85084135; e-mail editoriale@ipzs .it; internet www.ipzs.it; f. 1928; art, literary, scientific, technical books and reproductions; Chair. Dott. MICHELE TEDESCHI; Man. Dir Dott. LAMBERTO GABRIELLI.

PUBLISHERS' ASSOCIATION

Associazione Italiana Editori (AIE): Via delle Erbe 2, 20121 Milano; tel. (02) 86463091; fax (02) 89010863; e-mail aie@aie.it; internet www.aie.it; f. 1869; Pres. FEDERICO MOTTA; Dir IVAN CECCHINI.

Broadcasting and Communications

REGULATORY AUTHORITY

L'Autorità per le Garanzie nelle Communicazioni (AGCOM): Centro Direzionale, Isola B5, Torre Francesco, 80143 Napoli; tel. (081) 7507111; fax (081) 7507616; e-mail info@agcom.it; internet www.agcom.it; regulatory authority with responsibility for telecommunications, broadcasting and publishing; also has representation in Rome; Pres. ENZO CHELI; Sec.-Gen. ALESSANDRO BOTTO.

TELECOMMUNICATIONS

Telecom Italia SpA: Piazza Affari 2, 20123 Milano; internet www .telecomitalia.it; Italy's leading telecommunications operator; merged with Società Finanziaria Telefonica SpA in 1997; controlling stake owned by Pirelli SpA; Chair. MARCO TRONCHETTI PROVERA; co-CEOs ENRICO BONDI, CARLO BUORA.

Telecom Italia Mobile SpA (TIM): Via Luigi Rizzo 22, 00136 Roma; tel. (06) 39001; internet www.tim.it; f. 1995 after split from Telecom Italia SpA; repurchased by Telecom Italia in 2004; Italy's leading mobile telecommunications operator; Chair. ENRICO BONDI.

Tiscali Italia SpA: Viale Trento 39, 09123 Cagliari; tel. (070) 46011; fax (070) 4601400; internet www.tiscali.it; f. 1998; internet service provider; Chair. and CEO RENATO SORU.

Vodafone Omnitel SpA.: Via Caboto 15, 20094 Milano; tel. (02) 41431; internet www.omnitel.it; f. 1995; operates mobile network; Chief Exec. PIETRO GUINDANI.

WIND Telecomunicazioni SpA: Via Cesare Giulio Viola 48, 00148 Roma; tel. (06) 83111; internet www.wind.it; f. 1997; Chair. JEAN-YVES GOUIFFES; CEO TOMMASO POMPEI.

BROADCASTING

Radio

In April 1975 legislation was adopted to ensure the political independence of Radiotelevisione Italiana (RAI). The state monopoly on broadcasting was abolished in 1976.

Rai, Radiotelevisione Italiana, SpA (RAI): Viale Mazzini 14, 00195 Roma; tel. (06) 38781; fax (06) 3725680; e-mail webmaster@ rai.it; internet www.radio.rai.it; f. 1924; name changed in 2004, when RAI merged with RAI Holding, SpA; a public share capital company; undergoing 20% privatization; programmes comprise the national programme (general), Second Programme (recreational), Third Programme (educational); there are also regional programmes in Italian and in the languages of ethnic minorities; the foreign and overseas service (Radio Roma) broadcasts in 27 languages; Interim Pres. FRANCESCO ALBERONI; Dir-Gen. FLAVIO CATTANEO.

Rundfunk Anstalt Südtirol (RAS): Europaallee 164A, 39100 Bozen; tel. (0471) 546666; fax (0471) 200378; e-mail info@ras.bz.it; internet www.ras.bz.it; f. 1975; relays television and radio broadcasts from Germany, Austria and Switzerland to the population of South Tyrol; Pres. HELMUTH HENDRICH; Man. Dir GEORG PLATTNER.

Television

Gruppo Mediaset: Piazza SS. Giovanni e Paolo 8, 00184 Roma; tel. (06) 770801; or Palazzo Cigni, Milano 2, 20090 Segrate, Milano; tel. (02) 21021; f. 1993; operates the TV channels Canale 5, Italia 1 and Retequattro; and the telecommunications company Albacom, SpA; owned by Fininvest; Pres. FEDELE CONFALONIERI; Vice-Pres. SILVIO BERLUSCONI.

Gruppo Telepiù: Via Piranesi 46, Milano; tel. (02) 700271; fax (02) 70027201; internet www.telepiu.it; f. 1991; operates pay digital channels Tele+Bianco, Tele+Nero, Tele+Grigio, Tele+ 16/9 and Tele+ 30; 80.1% owned by News Corpn, 19.9% owned by Telecom Italia following purchase from Vivendi in 2002; expected to be merged with Stream and renamed Sky Italia; Pres. EMANUEL GOUT.

Rai, Radiotelevisione Italiana (RAI): Viale Mazzini 14, 00195 Roma; tel. (06) 38781; fax (06) 3226070; e-mail rai-tv@rai.it; internet www.rai.it; f. 1924; operates three channels, RAI Uno, RAI Due and RAI Tre; also broadcasts local programmes in Italian and in German for the Alto Adige; Pres. (vacant); Dir-Gen. FLAVIO CATTANEO.

Rundfunk Anstalt Südtirol (RAS): see Radio.

Finance

(cap. = capital; res = reserves; dep. = deposits; m. = million; brs = branches; amounts in euros (€), unless otherwise stated)

The number of Italian banks fell during the 1990s, from 1,156 in 1990 to 788 in 2003, owing to an increasing number of mergers. In 1990 a programme of privatization of state-controlled banks was initiated and in November 1999 the last state-controlled bank was divested. There are 82 banking groups, with a total of 305 members. There are more than 100 private banks, 445 co-operative banks, and a large number of savings banks (*banche popolari, casse di risparmio, casse rurali*) of widely ranging size and importance. In addition, there are some 90 specialized credit institutions which provide medium- and long-term finance, together with other services outside the scope of the banks. In 2003 there were 61 foreign banks operating in Italy.

BANKING

Central Bank

Banca d'Italia: Via Nazionale 91, 00184 Roma; tel. (06) 47921; fax (06) 47922983; internet www.bancaditalia.it; f. 1893; cap. 0.2m., res 13,665.8m., dep. 23,622.3m. (Dec. 2003); since 1926 the Bank has had the sole right to issue notes in Italy; Gov. ANTONIO FAZIO; Dir-Gen. VINCENZO DESARIO; 99 brs.

Major Commercial Banks

Banca Agricola Mantovana SpA: Corso Vittorio Emanuele 30, 46100 Mantua; tel. (0376) 3111; fax (0376) 313566; e-mail intl.rel@bam.it; internet www.bam.it; f. 1871; cap. 780.0m., res 401.0m., dep. 8,560.7m. (Dec. 2003); Chair. PIERMARIA PACCHIONI; Gen. Man. GIUSEPPE MENZI; 287 brs.

Banca Antonveneta SpA: Piazzetta Turati 2, 35131 Padua; tel. (049) 6991111; fax (049) 6991605; e-mail servizio.estero.pd@antonveneta.it; internet www.antonveneta.it; f. 1893 as Antoniana; July 1996 merged with Banca Popolare di Veneta Scarl; name changed September 2001; cap. 864.8m., res 2,425.1m., dep. 31,060.3m. (Dec. 2003); CEO PIERO MONTANI; Gen. Man. ENRICO PERNICE; 1,049 brs.

Banca Carige SpA (Cassa di Risparmio di Genova e Imperia): Via Cassa di Risparmio 15, 16123 Genova; tel. (010) 5791; fax (010) 5794000; e-mail carige@carige.it; internet www.gruppocarige.it; f. 1846; cap. 1,113.3m., res 492.7m., dep. 11,165.0m. (Dec. 2003); Chair. Dott. GIOVANNI BERNESCHI; Gen. Man. Dott. ALFREDO SANGUINETTO; 245 brs.

Banca Carime SpA: Viale Crati, 87100 Cosenza; tel. (0984) 8011; fax (0984) 806988; internet www.carime.it; f. 1998 as a result of merger of Carical, Carisal and Caripuglia savings banks; cap. 1,411.7m., res 2.7m. dep., 8,739.7m. (Dec. 2003); Man. Dir MARCELLO CALBIANI; Gen. Man. RICCARDO SORA; 344 brs.

Banca CR Firenze SpA: Via Bufalini 4/6, 50122 Firenze; tel. (055) 26121; fax (055) 2613872; e-mail estero@carifirenze.it; internet www.carfirenze.it; f. 1829; cap. 620.1m., res 222.5m., dep. 9,451.5m. (Dec. 2003); Chair. and Pres. AURELIANO BENEDETTI; Gen. Man. and CEO LINO MOSCATELLI; 270 brs and agencies.

Banca Fideuram: Corso di Porta Romana 16, 20122 Milano; tel. (02) 85181; fax (02) 85185235; internet www.fideuram.it; f. 1913; cap. 254.9m., res 643.5m., dep. 3,854.7m. (Dec. 2003); Chair. MARIO CUCCIA; Gen. Man. UGO RUFFOLO; 53 brs.

Banca d'Intermediazione Mobiliare IMI SpA: Corso Matteotti 6, 20121 Milano; tel. (02) 77511; fax (02) 77512030; e-mail bancaimi@bancaimi.it; internet www.bancaimi.it; f. 1974 as Imisigeco Sim SpA; name changed as above 1998; cap. 180.0m., res 169.3m., dep. 15,784.1m. (Dec. 2003); Chair. LUIGI MARANZANA; Man. Dir MASSIMO MATTERA.

Banca Intesa SpA: Via Monte de Pietà 8, 20121 Milan; tel. (02) 87911; e-mail info@bancaintesa.it; internet www.bancaintesa.it; f. 2001 by merger of Banca Commerciale Italiana with Banco Ambrosiano Veneto and Cariplo; cap. 3,561.0m., res 10,193.0m., dep. 193,408.0m. (Dec. 2003); Chair. GIOVANNI BAZOLI; CEO CORRADO PASSERA; 3,206 brs.

Banca Lombarda e Piemontese SpA: Via Cefalonia 62, 25175 Brescia; tel. (030) 24731; fax (030) 2473509; e-mail call.center@bancalombarda.com; internet www.bancalombarda.it; f. 1998 by merger of Banca San Paolo di Brescia SpA into CAB SpA; cap. 316.6m., res 1,481.6m., dep. 25,199.0m. (Dec. 2003); Chair. GINO TROMBI; Gen. Man. VICTOR MASSIAH.

Banca delle Marche SpA: Via Alessandro Ghislieri 6, 60035 Jesi; tel. (0731) 5391; fax (0731) 539695; e-mail info@bancamarche.it; internet www.bancamarche.it; f. 1994; cap. 386.5m., res 290.5m., dep. 9,420.8m. (Dec. 2003); Chair. TONINO PERINI; Gen. Man. MASSIMO Bianconi; 216 brs.

Banca Monte dei Paschi di Siena SpA: Piazza Salimbeni 3, 53100 Siena; tel. (0577) 294111; fax (0577) 294313; e-mail international@banca.mps.it; internet www.mps.it; f. 1472; joint stock company; cap. 3,958.7m., res 4,052.7m., dep. 66,670.9m. (June 2004); Chair. PIER LUIGI FABRIZI; CEO EMILIO TONINI; 1,080 brs.

Banca Nazionale del Lavoro SpA: Via Vittorio Veneto 119, 00187 Roma; tel. (06) 47021; fax (06) 47026646; e-mail webmaster.bnl@bnl.it; internet www.bnl.it; f. 1913; cap. 1,005,8m., res 2,752.6m., dep. 63,969.5m. (Dec. 2003); Chair. Dr LUIGI ABETE; Gen. Man. MARIO GIROTTI; 701 brs.

Banca Popolare Commercio e Industria SpA: POB 10167, Via della Moscova 33, 20121 Milano; tel. (02) 62751; fax (02) 62755640; e-mail intbkg@bpci.it; internet www.bpci.it; f. 1888; cap. €650.0m., dep. €8,300.7m. (Dec. 2003); Chair. GIUSEPPE VIGORELLI; Man. Dir CARLO PORCARI; 171 brs.

Banca Popolare di Bergamo: Piazza Vittorio Veneto 8, 24122 Bergamo; tel. (035) 392111; fax (035) 392910; e-mail info@bpb.it; internet www.bpb.it; f. 1869; co-operative bank; cap. 1,256.3m., dep. 18,499.1m. (Dec. 2003); Chair. EMILIO ZANETTI; Man. Dir GUIDO LUPINI; 648 brs.

Banca Popolare dell'Emilia Romagna Scarl: Via San Carlo 8/20, I–41100 Modena; tel. (059) 2021111; fax (059) 220537; e-mail relest@bper.it; internet www.bper.it; f. 1867; cap. 220.8m., res 1,101.7m., dep. 15,784.2m. (Dec. 2003); Chair. Prof. GIOVANNI MARANI; Man. Dir Dott. GUIDO LEONI; 249 brs.

Banca Popolare di Lodi Scarl: Bipielle City, Via Polenghi Lombardo 13, 26900 Lodi; tel. (0371) 580111; fax (0371) 580762; e-mail v.manzoni@bpl.bipielle.it; internet www.bipielle.it; f. 1864; cap. 862.2m., res 2,009.8m., dep. 22,271.5m. (Dec. 2003); Chair. GIOVANNI BENEVENTO; CEO GIANPIERO FIORANI; 393 brs.

Banca Popolare di Milano Scarl: Piazza F. Meda 4, 20121 Milano; tel. (02) 77001; fax (02) 77002993; e-mail bipiemme@bpm.it; internet www.bpm.it; f. 1865; cap. 1,158.0m., res 1,190.5m., dep. 22,682.7m. (Dec. 2003); Pres. Dott. ROBERTO MAZZOTTA; Gen. Man. Dott. ERNESTO PAOLILLO; 495 brs.

Banca Popolare di Sondrio Scarl: Piazza Garibaldi 16, 23100 Sondrio; tel. (0342) 528111; fax (0342) 528204; internet www.popso.it; f. 1871; cap. 412.7m., res 321.3m., dep. 9,139.5m. (Dec. 2003); Chair. and CEO PIERO MELAZZINI; Gen. Man. MARIO ALBERTO PEDRANZINI; 184 brs.

Banca Popolare di Vicenza Scparl: Via Battaglione Framarin 18, I–36100 Vicenza; tel. (0444) 339111; fax (0444) 329364; e-mail info@popvi.it; internet www.popolarevicenza.it; f. 1866; cap. 154.3m., res 1,403.9m., dep. 8,753.9m. (Dec. 2003); Chair. GIANNI ZONIN; Gen. Man. DIVO GRONCHI; 332 brs.

Banca Regionale Europea Spa: Via Monte di Pietà 7, 20121 Milano; tel. (02) 721211; fax (02) 865413; e-mail banca.regionale.europea@bancalombarda.it; internet www.brebanca.it; cap. 442.0m., res 431.3m., dep. 5,812.8m. (Dec. 2003); Chair. PIERO BERTOLOTTO; Gen. Man. ARGANTE DEL MONTE; 260 brs.

Banca di Roma: Viale Umberto Tupini 180, 00144 Roma; tel. (06) 54451; fax (06) 54453154; e-mail webmaster@bancaroma.it; internet www.bancaroma.it; f. 2002 as result of reorganization of Capitalia; cap. 2,000.0m., res 3,010.6m., dep. 45,908.2m. (Dec. 2003); Chair. BERARDINO LIBONATI; Man. Dir CESARE CALETTI; 1,123 brs.

Banca Toscana SpA: Via Leone Pancaldo 4, 50127 Firenze; tel. (055) 43911; fax (055) 4360061; e-mail international.dept@bancatoscana.it; internet www.bancatoscana.it; f. 1904; cap. 1,000.0m., res 20.0m., dep. 13,078.1m. (Dec. 2003); Pres. PAOLO MOTTURA; Gen. Man. and CEO PIERO FARRONI; 415 brs.

Banco di Brescia San Paolo Cab SpA: Corso Martiri della Libertà 13, 25171 Brescia; tel. (030) 29921; fax (030) 2992470; e-mail info@bancodibrescia.com; internet www.bancodibrescia.com; f. 1999; cap. 453.7m., res 337.2m., dep. 13,052.3m. (Dec. 2003); Chair. GINO TROMBI; Gen. Man. COSTANTINO VITALI; 374 brs.

Banco Popolare di Verona e Novara Scrl: Piazza Nogara 2, POB 509, 37100 Verona; tel. (045) 8675111; fax (045) 8675474; e-mail relaxest@bpv.it; internet www.bpv.it; f. 2002 by merger of Banco Popolare di Verona—Banco S. Geminiano e S. Prospero and Banco Popolare di Novara; cap. 1,332.8m., res 1,592.5m., dep. 22,266.3m. (Dec. 2003); Pres. Prof. CARLO FRATTA PASINI; Man. Dir FABIO INNOCENZI; 372 brs.

Banco di Sardegna SpA: Viale Umberto 36, 07100 Sassari; tel. (079) 226000; fax (079) 226015; internet www.bancosardegna.it; f. 1953; cap. 147.4m., res 639.8m., dep. 10,528.6m. (Dec. 2003); Chair. Prof. ANTONIO SASSU; Gen. Man. NATALINO OGGIANO; 391 brs.

Banco di Sicilia SpA: Via Generale Magliocco 1, 90141 Palermo; tel. (091) 6081111; fax (091) 6085124; internet www.bancodisicilia.it; f. 1860; cap. 500.0m., res 976.5m., dep. 19,371.3m. (Dec. 2002); Chair. and Pres. SABINO CASSESE; Man. Dir BENIAMINO ANSELMI; 507 brs.

BIPOP-CARIRE SpA: Via Leonardo da Vinci 74, 25122 Brescia; tel. (030) 39931; fax (030) 396313; e-mail info@bipop.it; internet www.bipop.it; f. 1999 by merger of Banca Popolare di Brescia and Cassa di Risparmio di Reggio Emilia; owned by Capitalia SpA; due to merge with Banca di Roma in 2003; cap. 855.2m., res 0.1m., dep. 8,020.3m. (Dec. 2003); Chair. FRANCESCO SPINELLI; Gen. Man. VITTORIO DE STASIO; 69 brs.

Cassa di Risparmio di Padova e Rovigo SpA: POB 1088, Corso Garibaldi 22/26, 35122 Padua; tel. (049) 8368111; fax (049) 8368540; e-mail direzione.generale@caripardo.it; internet www.cariparo.it; f. 1822; cap. 500.0m., res 126.5m., dep. 9,954m. (Dec. 2002); Pres. ORAZIO ROSSI; Man. Dir PIO BUSSOLOTTO; 269 brs.

Cassa di Risparmio di Parma e Piacenza SpA: Via Università l, I–43100 Parma; tel. (0521) 912111; fax (0521) 912976; e-mail crprpc@cariprpc.it; internet www.cariprpc.it; f. 1860; cap. 500.0m., res 227.6m., dep. 11,739.7m. (Dec. 2002); Chair. GIANCARLO FOREST-IERI; Gen. Man. GUIDO CORRADI; 300 brs.

Cassa di Risparmio in Bologna SpA (CARISBO): Via Farini 22, 40124 Bologna; tel. (051) 6454111; fax (051) 6454366; internet www .carisbo.it; f. 1837; cap. 450m., res 107.6m., dep. 8,232.1m. (Dec. 2002); Pres. and Chair. EMILIO RUBBI; Gen. Man. PAOLO LELLI; 184 brs.

Credito Bergamasco SpA: Largo Porta Nuova 2, 24122 Bergamo; tel. (035) 393111; fax (035) 393144; e-mail ufficio.estero@creberg.it; internet www.creberg.it; f. 1891; cap. 185.2m., res 470.8m., dep. 9,621.9m. (Dec. 2003); Pres. CESARE ZONCA; Gen. Man. FRANCO MENINI; 223 brs.

Credito Emiliano SpA (CREDEM): Via Emilia S. Pietro 4, 42100 Reggio-Emilia; tel. (0522) 582111; fax (0522) 433969; e-mail intmil@ credem.it; internet www.credem.it; f. 1910; cap. 274.3m., res 403.2m., dep. 12,013.9m. (Dec. 2003); Pres. GIORGIO FERRARI; Gen. Man. ADOLFO BIZZOCCHI; 429 brs.

Credito Valtellinese Scarl: Piazza Quadrivio 8, 23100 Sondrio; tel. (0342) 522111; fax (0342) 522700; e-mail creval@creval.it; internet www.creval.it; f. 1908; cap. 163.7m., res 263.3m., dep. 4,356.8m. (Dec. 2003); Chair. GIOVANNI DE CENSI; Man. Dir RENATO BARTESAGHI; 85 brs.

MCC SpA: Via Piemonte 51, 00187 Roma; tel. (06) 47911; fax (06) 47912219; e-mail mcc@mcc.it; internet www.mcc.it; f. 1952 as Medi-ocredito Centrale; changed name as above in 2002; owned by Capi-talia banking group; cap. 475.1m., res 151.7m., dep. 6,444.5m. (Dec. 2002); Chair. FRANCO CARRARO; CEO MATTEO ARPE.

SANPAOLO IMI SpA: Piazza San Carlo 156, 10121 Torino; tel. (011) 5551; fax (011) 5552404; e-mail investor.relation@sanpaoloimi .com; internet www.sanpaoloimi.com; f. 1563 as a foundation; merged with Istituto Mobiliare Italiano SpA 1998; name changed as above in 1999; cap. 5,144.1m., res 4,377.7m., dep. 97,430.9m. (Dec. 2003); Chair. ENRICO SALZA; Man. Dir ALFONSO IOZZO; 3,158 brs.

UniCredito Italiano SpA: Piazza Cordusio, 20123 Milano; tel. (02) 88621; fax (02) 88623034; e-mail info@unicredito.it; internet www .unicredito.it; f. 1870; cap. 3,158.2m., res 7,760.6m., dep. 179,352.8m. (Dec. 2003); Chair. CARLO SALVATORI; CEO ALESSANDRO PROFUMO; 973 brs.

FINANCIAL INSTITUTIONS

CENTROBANCA—Banca di Credito Finanziario e Mobiliare SpA: Corso Europa 16, 20122 Milano; tel. (02) 77811; fax (02) 77814509; e-mail comunica@centrobanca.it; internet www .centrobanca.it; f. 1946; central organization for medium- and long-term operations of Banche Popolari (co-operative banks) throughout Italy; cap. 336.0m., res 190.4m., dep. 6,429.1m. (Dec. 2002); Pres. TANCREDI BIANCHI; Man. Dir SALVATORE BRIGANTINI.

Dexia Crediop SpA: Via XX Settembre 30, 00187 Rome; tel. (06) 47711; fax (06) 47715952; e-mail contact@dexia-crediop.it; internet www.dexia-crediop.it; f. 1919; newly incorporated 1996; name changed from Crediop SpA in May 2001; cap. 450.2m., res 34.2m., dep. 18,865.9m. (Dec. 2003); Man. Dir GÉRARD BAYOL; Sec.-Gen. ALBERTO MARI.

EFIBANCA SpA (Ente Finanziario Interbancario SpA): Via Bon-compagni 71, 00187 Roma; tel. (06) 422981; fax (06) 42298923; internet www.bipielle.it; f. 1939; cap. 89.3m., res 616.9m., dep. 5,255.2m. (Dec. 2003); Chair. PIETRO RASTELLI; Man. Dir ENRICO MARIA LUIGI FAGIOLI MARZOCCHI; 8 brs.

ICCRI Banca Federale Europea SpA: Via Boncompagni 71H, 00187 Roma; tel. (06) 47151; fax (06) 47153579; internet www.iccri .it; f. 1919 as Istituto di Credito delle Casse di Risparmio Italiane, name changed in 1999; cap. 1,040,468.8m. lire, res 281,073.4m. lire, dep. 10,501,599.8m. lire (Dec. 2000); Chair. Prof. DINO PIERO GIARDA; Gen. Man. Dr MARCO BELLINZONI.

INTERBANCA SpA: Corso Venezia 56, 20121 Milano; tel. (02) 77311; fax (02) 784321; internet www.interbanca.it; f. 1961; cap. 180.9m., res 456.6m., dep. 8,657.4m. (Dec. 2003); Chair. FRANCESCO SPINELLI; Man. Dir GIORGIO CIRLA; Gen. Man. MAURO GAMBARO; 11 brs.

Istituto Centrale delle Banche di Credito Cooperativo (ICCREA SpA): Via Torino 146, 00184 Roma; tel. (06) 47161; fax (06) 47887706; f. 1963; cap. 6216.9m., res 66.3m., dep. 5,382.0m. (Dec. 2003); Pres. GIORGIO CLEMENTI; Gen. Man. LUCIANO GIORGIO GORNATI; 6 brs.

Mediobanca—Banca di Credito Finanziario SpA: Piazzetta Enrico Cuccia 1, 20121 Milano; tel. (02) 88291; fax (02) 8829367; e-mail info@mediobanca.it; internet www.mediobanca.it; f. 1946; cap. 389.3m., res 3,189.2m., dep. 21,631.6m. (June 2003); Chair. GABRIELE GALATERI DI GENOLA; Man. Dir ALBERT NAGEL.

BANKERS' ORGANIZATIONS

Associazione Bancaria Italiana: Palazzo Altieri, Piazza del Gesù 49, 00186 Roma; tel. (06) 67671; fax (06) 6767457; e-mail abi@abi.it; internet www.abi.it; f. 1919; advocates the common interests of the banking industry; Pres. MAURIZIO SELLA; Gen. Man. Dott. GIUSEPPE ZADRA; membership (1,003 mems) is comprised of the following institutions: banks authorized to gather savings from the general public and exercise credit business as well as to perform other financial activities; brs and representative offices of foreign banks; asscns of banks or financial intermediaries; financial intermediaries engaging in one or more of the activities subject to mutual recognition under the Second Banking Directive or other financial activities subject to public prudential supervision.

Associazione tra Banche per la Finanza d'Impresa: Piazza della Marina 1, 00196 Roma; tel. (06) 888557; fax (06) 888601; Pres. Prof. ANGELO CALOIA; Gen. Man. Dott. ANTONIO DE VITO.

Associazione fra le Casse di Risparmio Italiane: POB 7221, Viale di Villa Grazioli 23, 00198 Roma; tel. (06) 855621; fax (06) 8540192; internet www.acri.it; f. 1912; Chair. Dott. GIUSEPPE GUZ-ZETTI; Gen. Man. STEFANO MARCHETTINI.

Associazione Italiana per il Factoring: Via Cerva 9, 20122 Milano; tel. (02) 76020127; fax (02) 76020159; e-mail assifact@ assifact.it; internet www.assifact.it; Pres. Dott. FRANCO ROSSO; Sec.-Gen. Prof. ALESSANDRO CARRETTA.

Associazione Italiana Leasing (ASSILEA): Piazza di Priscilla 4, 00199 Roma; tel. (06) 8622531; fax (06) 86211214; e-mail info@ assilea.it; internet www.assilea.it; Pres. Dott. ROSARIO CORSO; Dir-Gen. Ing. FABRIZIO MARAFINI.

Associazione Italiana delle Società ed Enti di Gestione Mobiliare ed Immobiliare: Via in Lucina 17, 00186 Roma; tel. (06) 6840591; fax (06) 6893262; e-mail info.roma@assogestioni.it; internet www.assogestioni.it; f. 1984; Pres. Prof. GUIDO CAMMARANO; Sec.-Gen. FABIO GALLI.

Associazione Nazionale fra le Banche Popolari: Piazza Venezia 11, 00187 Roma; tel. (06) 695351; Pres. Prof. SIRO LOMBARDINI; Dir-Gen. Dott. GIORGIO CARDUCCI.

Associazione Nazionale Banche Private (ASSBANK): Via Cosimo del Fante 7, 20122 Milano; tel. (02) 5821261; fax (02) 58212650; e-mail assbank@assbank.it; internet www.assbank.it; Pres. Dott. Prof. TANCREDI BIANCHI.

Associazione Nazionale fra gli Istituti di Credito Agrario (ANICA): Roma; tel. (06) 8077506; fax (06) 8077506; f. 1946; Pres. Prof. GIUSEPPE GUERRIERI; Sec.-Gen. Dott. ERNESTO DE MEDIO.

STOCK EXCHANGES

Commissione Nazionale per le Società e la Borsa (CONSOB) (Commission for Companies and the Stock Exchange): Via G. B. Martini 3, 00198 Roma; tel. (06) 84771; fax (06) 8417707; e-mail consob@consob.it; internet www.consob.it; f. 1974; regulatory control over cos quoted on stock exchanges, convertible bonds, unlisted securities, insider trading, all forms of public saving except bank deposits and mutual funds; Pres. LAMBERTO CARDIA; the following is a list of the most important stock exchanges:

  Genoa: Borsa Valori, Via G. Boccardo 1, Genova; tel. (010) 590920; f. 1855; Pres. LUCIANO GAMBAROTTA.

  Borsa Italiana (Italian Stock Exchange): Piazza degli Affari 6, 20123 Milano; tel. (02) 724261; fax (02) 72004333; e-mail info@ borsaitaliana.it; internet www.borsaitalia.it; Pres. ANGELO TANTAZZI; Dir-Gen. MASSIMO CAPUANO; 5 mems, 140 listed cos.

Naples: Borsa Valori, Palazzo Borsa, Piazza Bovio, Napoli; tel. (081) 269151; Pres. GIORGIO FOCAS.

Rome: Borsa Valori, Via dei Burro 147, 00186 Roma; tel. (06) 6792701; f. 1821; Pres. ALBERTO BORTI.

INSURANCE

In 2003 there were 240 insurance and reinsurance companies operating in Italy, of which 189 were Italian and 51 were foreign.

Alleanza Assicurazioni SpA: Viale Luigi Sturzo 35, 20154 Milano; tel. (02) 62961; fax (02) 653718; e-mail comunicazione@mailalleanzaassicurazioni.it; internet www.alleanzaassicurazioni.it; f. 1898; life insurance; subsidiary of Assicurazioni Generali (q.v.); cap. 423.1m. (Dec. 1999); Chair. Dott. SANDRO SALVATI.

Allianz Subalpina SpA: Via Alfieri 22, 10121 Torino; tel. (011) 5161111; fax (011) 5161255; e-mail info@azs.it; internet www.allianzsubalpina.it; f. 1928; part of Gruppo Ras; cap. 21.3m. (Dec. 2004); CEO Dott. MASSIMO ARRIGHI.

Assicuratrice Edile SpA: Via A. De Togni 2, 20123 Milano; tel. (02) 480411; fax (02) 48041292; e-mail cauzioni@assedile.it; internet www.assedile.it; f. 1960; cap. 16,000m. lire (Jan. 2000); Chair. CHRISTIAN HUOT; Man. Dir ANTOINE NINU.

Assicurazioni Generali SpA: Piazza Duca degli Abruzzi 2, 34132 Trieste; tel. (040) 671111; fax (040) 671600; internet www.generali.com; f. 1831; cap. 1,275.7m. (2002); Chair. ANTOINE BERNHEIM; Gen. Man. SERGIO BALBINOT.

Le Assicurazioni d'Italia (ASSITALIA) SpA: Corso d'Italia 33, 00198 Roma; tel. (06) 84831; fax (06) 84833142; internet www.assitalia-assicurazioni.it; f. 1923; joined Gruppo Generali in 2000; cap. 91m. (2002); Pres. FRANCESCO PROCACCINI; Dir-Gen. GIUSEPPE ROSNATI.

Axa Assicurazioni: Via Leopardi 15, 20123 Milano; tel. (02) 480841; fax (02) 48084331; internet www.axa-italia.it; f. 1956 as UAP Italiana SpA; cap. 8,211m. lire (Dec. 1990); Chair. and Man. Dir MASSIMO MICHAUD.

Carige Assicurazioni: Viale Certosa 222, 20156 Milano; tel. (02) 30761; fax (02) 3086125; internet www.levantenorditalia.it; f. 1963 as Levante Norditalia Assicurazioni; cap. 102.5m. (Dec. 2000); Pres. Dott. GIOVANNI BERNESCHI; Man. Dir Dr FERDINANDO MENCONI.

Compagnia di Assicurazioni di Milano SpA: Strada 6, Pal. A13, Assago Milanofiori, 20090 Milano; tel. (02) 82291; fax (02) 82295389; f. 1825; cap. 175,333m. lire (Dec. 1996); Pres. Dott. AMATO MOLINARI; Dir-Gen. Ing. LUCIANO PASQUALI.

FATA (Fondo Assicurativo Tra Agricoltori) SpA: Via Urbana 169/A, 00184 Roma; tel. (06) 47651; fax (06) 4871187; e-mail info@fata-assicurazioni.it; internet www.fata-assicurazioni.it; f. 1927; total assets 79.6m. (Dec. 2001); Pres. GIUSEPPE PERISSINOTTO; Man. Dir GIUSEPPE VECCHIONE.

La Fiduciaria Vita: Via A. Finelli 8, 40126 Bologna; tel. (051) 6307011; fax (051) 243030; internet www.mmiweb.it/fiduciaria; f. 1972; cap. 5.2m. (2002); owned by Mutuelles du Mans Assurances (France); Chair. JEAN PAUL GALBRUN; Man. Dir Dott. Ing. SERGIO BEDINI.

Fondiaria—Sai SpA: Piazza della Libertà 6, 50129 Firenze; tel. (055) 47941; fax (055) 476026; internet www.fondiaria.it; internet www.sai.it; internet www.fondiaria-sai.it; f. 1879 as La Fondiaria; merged with SAI SpA in 2002 and name changed as above.

HDI Assicurazioni SpA: Via Abruzzi 10, 00187 Roma; tel. (06) 421031; fax (06) 42103500; e-mail hdi.assicurazioni@hdia.it; internet www.hdia.it; f. 1927 as BNC Assicurazioni SpA; 70% acquired by Hilft Dir Immer (HDI), Germany, in 1997 and renamed as above; cap. 141.8m. (Dec. 2002).

Istituto Nazionale delle Assicurazioni SpA (INA): Via Sallustiana 51, 00187 Roma; tel. (06) 47221; fax (06) 47224559; internet www.gruppoina.it; f. 1912; Chair. Dott. SERGIO SIGLIENTI; Man. Dir LINO BENASSI.

ITAS, Istituto Trentino-Alto Adige per Assicurazioni: Via Mantova 67, 38100 Trento; tel. (0461) 891702; fax (0461) 980297; e-mail itas.direzione@gruppoitas.it; internet www.gruppoitas.it; f. 1821; cap. 40m. (Dec. 2001); Chair. Dott. EDO BENEDETTI; Gen. Man. Dott. ETTORE LOMBARDO.

Italiana Assicurazioni SpA: Via Marco Ulpio Traiano 18, 20149 Milano; tel. (02) 397161; fax (02) 3271270; internet www.italiana.it; f. 1898 as Cooperativa Italiana Incendia; changed name as above in 1995; merged with Universo Assicurazione in 2000.

Lloyd Adriatico SpA: Largo Ugo Irneri 1, 34123 Trieste; tel. (040) 77811; fax (040) 7781311; e-mail info@lloydadriatico.it; internet www.lloydadriatico.it; f. 1936; part of Allianz Group; cap. 60m. (Dec. 2002); Pres. and Man. Dir Dott. ENRICO TOMASO CUCCHIANI; Vice-Pres. Dott. GIOVANNI GABRIELLI.

Lloyd Italico: Via Fieschi 9, 16121 Genova; tel. (010) 53801; fax (010) 592856; internet www.lloyditalico.it; f. 1917; part of Gruppo Toro; total assets 195.6m. (Dec. 2002); Pres. EDUARDO RICCIO; Man. Dir GIORVANNI PANSOYA DI BORIO.

Mediolanum Vita SpA: Palazzo Meucci, Via Francesco Sforza 15, 20080 Basiglio; tel. (02) 90491; fax (02) 90492427; f. 1972; cap. 170,000m. lire (Dec. 1996); Pres. Dott. ALFREDO MESSINA.

Meieaurora Assicurazioni SpA: Corso di Porta Vigentina 9, 20122 Milano; tel. (02) 59922205; fax (02) 59922561; e-mail marketing@meieaurora.it; internet www.meieaurora.it; f. 2001 by merger of Meie Assicurazioni SpA and Aurora Assicurazioni SpA; cap. 2,595m., res 2,438m. (Sept. 2002); Gen. Man. Dott. GIAMPIERO GELMI.

MMI Assicurazioni SpA: Via Egidio Galbani 68, 00156 Roma; tel. (06) 682801; fax (06) 820041163; internet www.mmiweb.it/nationale.htm; f. 1962; owned by Mutuelles du Mans Assurances (France); cap. 25m. (2002); Pres. PASCAL GUENOIT; Dir-Gen. SALVATORE PASSARO.

Nuova Tirrena SpA: Via Massimi 158, 00136 Roma; tel. (06) 30181; fax (06) 30183382; internet www.nuovatirrena.it; f. 1929; cap. 142.6m. (Dec. 2002); became part of Gruppo Toro in 1996; Pres. FRANCESCO TORRI; Dir-Gen. Dott. LUCIANO BECCHIO.

Ras, SpA (Riunione Adriatica di Sicurtà): Corso Italia 23, 20122 Milano; tel. (02) 72161; internet www.ras.it; f. 1838; merged with Lavoro & Sicurtà, SpA, in 1999; 55.55% owned by Allianz; cap. 437.8m.; Chair. Dott. GIUSEPPE VITA; Man. Dir Dott. MARIO GRECO.

SARA Assicurazioni SpA: Via Po 20, 00198 Roma; tel. (06) 84751; fax (06) 8475223; internet www.sara.it; f. 1924; Chair. ROSARIO ALESSI; Gen. Man. Dott. MARCO ROCCA.

Società Cattolica di Assicurazione Cooperativa a. r.l.: Lungadige Cangrande 16, 37126 Verona; tel. (045) 8391111; fax (045) 8391112; e-mail investor.relations@cattolicaassicurazioni.it; internet www.cattolicaassicurazioni.it; f. 1896; total assets 966m. (Dec. 2001); Gen. Man. Dott. EZIO PAOLO REGGIA.

Società Italiana Cauzioni SpA (SIC): Via Crescenzio 12, 00193 Roma; tel. (06) 688121; fax (06) 6874418; e-mail sic.dirgen@atradius.it; internet www.atradius.it; f. 1948; cap. 15m. (Dec. 2003); Chair. PETER INGENLATH; Man. Dir ARNOLD VAN DEN ESSCHERT.

Società Reale Mutua di Assicurazioni: Via Corte d'Appello 11, 10122 Torino; tel. (011) 431111; fax (011) 4350966; e-mail webmaster@realmutua.it; internet www.realmutua.it; f. 1828; total assets 8,195,584m. lire (1998); Chair. CARLO ALBANI CASTELBARCO VISCONTI; Gen. Man. Dott. PIERO CASTELLI.

Swiss Re Italia SpA: Via dei Giuochi Istmici 40, 00194 Roma; tel. (06) 323931; fax (06) 36303398; e-mail srit-communicazione@swissre.com; internet www.swissre.com; f. 1922; cap. 100m. (Dec. 2001); Chair. Avv. BERARDINO LIBONATI; Man. Dir ANTONIO SOLARI.

Toro Assicurazioni SpA: Via Mazzini 53, 10123 Torino; tel. (011) 0029111; fax (011) 837554; internet www.toroassicurazioni.it; f. 1833; total assets 1,165m. (Dec. 2002); Pres. ANTONIO BELLONI; Man. Dir FRANCESCO TORRI.

Unipol Assicurazioni SpA: Via Stalingrado 45, 40128 Bologna; tel. (051) 6097111; fax (051) 375349; internet www.unipolonline.it; f. 1963; cap. 261,680m. lire (Sept. 1999); Chair. GIOVANNI CONSORTE; Vice-Chair. IVANO SACCHETTI.

Vittoria Assicurazioni SpA: Via Caldera 21, 20153 Milano; tel. (02) 482191; fax (02) 48203693; e-mail direzione@vittoriaassicurazioni.it; internet www.vittoriaassicurazioni.com; f. 1921; cap. 30m. (Dec. 2003); Chair. Prof. LUIGI GUATRI; Man. Dir Rag. ROBERTO GUARENA.

Winterthur Assicurazioni SpA: Piazza Missori 2, 20122 Milano; tel. (02) 85471; fax (02) 8547701; internet www.winterthur.it; f. 1919; acquired by Unipol Assicurazioni SpA in 2003; cap. 223,000m. lire (Dec. 1996); Pres. and Man. Dir FABRIZIO RINDI.

REGULATORY AUTHORITY

Istituto per la Vigilanza sulle Assicurazioni Private e di Interesse Collettivo (ISVAP): Roma; internet www.isvap.it; supervises private insurance cos; Pres. and Dir-Gen. GIANNCARLO GIANNINI.

INSURANCE ASSOCIATION

Associazione Nazionale fra le Imprese Assicuratrici (ANIA): Piazza S. Babila 1, 20122 Milano; tel. (02) 77641; fax (02) 780870; e-mail info@ania.it; internet www.ania.it; f. 1944; Pres. Dott. FABIO CERCHIAI; Dir-Gen. Dott. GIAMPAOLO GALLI; 210 mems.

Trade and Industry

GOVERNMENT AGENCIES

Autorità Garante della Concorrenza e del Mercato (Regulatory Authority for Competition and Markets): Piazza Verdi 6/A, 00198 Roma; tel. (06) 858211; fax (06) 85821256; e-mail antitrust@agcm.it; internet www.agcm.it; Pres. GIUSEPPE TESAURO; Sec.-Gen. RITA CICCONE.

Cassa depositi e prestiti (CDP SpA): Via Goito 4, Roma 00185; tel. (06) 42211; internet www.cassaddpp.it; govt agency for the management of government and public resources; authorized to grant loans to government and public bodies; Chair. SALVATORE REBECCHINI; Man. Dir ANTONINO TURICCHI.

Istituto Nazionale per il Commercio Estero (ICE) (National Institute for Foreign Trade): Via Liszt 21, 00144 Roma; tel. (06) 59921; fax (06) 59926899; e-mail ice@ice.it; internet www.ice.it; f. 1919; govt agency for the promotion of foreign trade; Chair. and CEO Prof. BENIAMINO QUINTIERI.

CHAMBERS OF COMMERCE

Unione Italiana delle Camere di Commercio, Industria, Artigianato e Agricoltura (Italian Union of Chambers of Commerce, Industry, Crafts and Agriculture): Piazza Sallustio 21, 00187 Roma; tel. (06) 47041; fax (06) 4704240; e-mail segretaria.generale@unioncamere.it; internet www.unioncamere.it; f. 1954 to promote the development of chambers of commerce, industry, trade and agriculture; Pres. CARLO SANGALLI; Sec.-Gen. GIUSEPPE TRIPOLI.

INDUSTRIAL AND TRADE ASSOCIATIONS

Confederazione Generale dell'Industria Italiana (Confindustria) (General Confederation of Italian Industry): Viale dell'Astronomia 30, 00144 Roma; tel. (06) 59031; fax (06) 5919615; e-mail confindustria@confindustria.it; internet www.confindustria.it; f. 1910; re-established 1944; mems: 107 territorial asscns and 110 branch asscns, totalling 111,000 firms and 4.5m. employees; office in Brussels; Pres. LUCA CORDERO DE MONTEZEMOLO; Dir-Gen. MAURIZIO BERETTA.

Principal Affiliated Organizations

Associazione degli Industriali della Birra e del Malto (Brewers): Viale di Val Fiorita 90, 00144 Roma; tel. (06) 543932; fax (06) 5912910; e-mail birra.viva@assobirra.it; internet www.assobirra.it; f. 1946; Pres. Dott. HARALD FUCHS; Dir Dott. FILIPPO TERZAGHI.

Associazione Industrie per l'Aerospazio, i Sistemi e la Difesa (AIAD) (Aerospace, Systems and Defence Industries): Via Nazionale 54, 00184 Roma; tel. (06) 4880247; fax (06) 4827476; e-mail aiad@aiad.it; internet www.aiad.it; f. 1947; Pres. Dott. GIORGIO ZAPPA; Sec.-Gen. CARLO FESTUCCI.

Associazione Italiana delle Industrie della Filiera Tessile Abbigliamento (SISTEMA MODA ITALIA) (Clothing and Knitwear Manufacturers): Viale Sarca 223, 20123 Milano; tel. (02) 66103391; fax (02) 66103670; e-mail info@sistemamodaitalia.it; internet www.sistemamodaitalia.it; f. 1945; produces weekly, fortnightly and annual periodicals; Pres. Dott. VITTORIO GIULINI; Dir Dott. PIERO COSTA.

Associazione Italiana Industrie Prodotti Alimentari (AIIPA) (Food Manufacturers): Corso di Porta Nuova 34, 20121 Milano; tel. (02) 654184; fax (02) 654822; e-mail aiipa@aiipa.it; internet www.aiipa.it; f. 1946; Pres. Dott. ALESSANDRO AMBROSOLI; Dir Dott. GIOVANNI FRANCO CRIPPA; 300 mems.

Associazione Italiana Tecnico Economica del Cemento (AITEC) (Cement): Piazza G. Marconi 25, 00144 Roma; tel. (06) 54210237; fax (06) 5915408; e-mail aitec@aitecweb.com; internet www.aitecweb.com; f. 1959; Pres. GIACOMO MARAZZI; Dir Dott. Ing. FRANCESCO CURCIO.

Associazione Mineraria Italiana (ASSOMINERARIA) (Italian Oil and Mining Industry): Via delle Tre Madonne 20, 00197 Roma; tel. (06) 8073045; fax (06) 8073385; e-mail info@assomineraria.org; internet www.assomineraria.org; f. 1944; Pres. Dott. Ing. STEFANO CAO; Dir-Gen. Dott. ANDREA KETOFF; 100 mems.

Associazione Nazionale Costruttori Edili (ANCE) (Builders): Via Guattani 16, 00161 Roma; tel. (06) 845671; fax (06) 44232832; e-mail info@ance.it; internet www.ance.it; f. 1946; Pres. Dott. Ing. CLAUDIO DE ALBERTIS; Man. Dir CARLO FERRONI; mems: 19,000 firms in 101 provincial and 20 regional asscns.

Associazione Nazionale dell'Industria Farmaceutica (FARMINDUSTRIA) (Pharmaceutical Industry): Largo del Nazareno 3/8, 00187 Roma; tel. (06) 675801; fax (06) 6786494; e-mail farmindustria@farmindustria.it; internet www.farmindustria.it; f. 1978; Pres. Dott. FEDERICO NAZZARI; 221 mem. firms (2005).

Associazione Nazionale fra Industrie Automobilistiche (ANFIA) (Motor Vehicle Industries): Corso Galileo Ferraris 61, 10128 Torino; tel. (011) 5546511; fax (011) 545986; e-mail anfia@anfia.it; internet www.anfia.it; f. 1912; Pres. Dott. CARLO SINCERI; 260 mems.

Associazione Nazionale Italiana Industrie Grafiche, Cartotecniche e Trasformatrici (ASSOGRAFICI) (Printing and Paper-Converting Industries): Piazza Conciliazione 1, 20123 Milano; tel. (02) 4981051; fax (02) 4816947; e-mail assografici@assografici.it; internet www.assografici.it; f. 1946; Pres. MARCO SPADA; Gen. Dir Dott. CLAUDIO COVINI; 1,200 mems.

Federazione delle Associazioni Nazionali dell'Industria Meccanica Varia ed Affine (ANIMA) (Federation of the Italian Associations of Mechanical and Engineering Industries): Via L. Battistotti Sassi 11/B, 20133 Milano; tel. (02) 73971; fax (02) 7397316; e-mail anima@anima-it.com; internet www.anima-it.com; f. 1945; Pres. Dott. Ing. SAVINO RIZZIO; Dir Dott. Ing. ENRICO MALCOVATI; 1,500 mems.

Federazione Italiana Industriali Produttori Esportatori ed Importatori di Vini, Acquaviti, Liquori, Sciroppi, Aceti ed Affini (FEDERVINI) (Producers, Importers and Exporters of Wines, Brandies, Liqueurs, Syrups, Vinegars and Allied Products): Via Mentana 2B, 00185 Roma; tel. (06) 4941630; fax (06) 4941566; e-mail federvini@federvini.it; internet www.federvini.it; f. 1917; Pres. PIERO MASTROBERARDINO; Dir-Gen. OTTAVIO CAGIANO DE AZEVEDO.

Federazione Nazionale Fonderie (ASSOFOND) (Foundries): Via Copernico 54, 20090 Trezzano Sul Naviglio; tel. (02) 48400967; fax (02) 48401282; e-mail info@assofond.it; internet www.assofond.it; f. 1948; Pres. EMILIO CREMONA; Dir PAOLO PONZINI.

Federazione Nazionale dell'Industria Chimica (FEDERCHIMICA) (Chemical Industry): Via Giovanni da Procida 11, 20149 Milano; tel. (02) 345651; fax (02) 34565310; e-mail federchimica@federchimica.it; internet www.federchimica.it; f. 1945; Pres. DIANA BRACCO; Dir Dott. CLAUDIO BENEDETTI.

Federazione Nazionale Imprese Elettrotecniche ed Elettroniche (ANIE) (Electrotechnic and Electronic Companies): Via Gattamelata 34, 20149 Milano; tel. (02) 32641; fax (02) 3264212; e-mail info@anie.it; internet www.anie.it; Pres. Dott. Ing. RENZO TANI; Dir ROBERTO TARANTO.

Unione Industriali Pastai Italiani (UNIPI) (Pasta Manufacturers): Via Po 102, 00198 Roma; tel. (06) 8543291; fax (06) 8415132; e-mail unipi@unipi-pasta.it; internet www.unipi-pasta.it; f. 1968; Pres. Dott. MARIO RUMMO; Dir RAFFAELLO RAGAGLINI.

Unione Nazionale Cantieri e Industrie Nautiche ed Affini (UCINA) (Italian Marine Industry Association): Piazzale Kennedy 1, 16129 Genova; tel. (010) 5769811; fax (010) 5531801; e-mail ucina@ucina.it; internet www.ucina.it; Pres. Dott. PAOLO VITELLI; Sec.-Gen. Dott. Ing. LORENZO POLLICARDO.

Unione Petrolifera (Petroleum Industries): Via Giorgione 129, 00147 Roma; tel. (06) 5423651; fax (06) 59602925; e-mail info@unionepetrolifera.it; internet www.unionepetrolifera.it; f. 1948; Pres. Dott. PASQUALE DE VITA; Dir-Gen. Dott. PIETRO DE SIMONE; 28 mems.

Others

Associazione Nazionale Comuni Italiani (ANCI): Via dei Prefetti 46, 00186 Roma; tel. (06) 680091; fax (06) 68009202; e-mail baroni@anci.it; internet www.anci.it; Pres. Dott. LEONARDO DOMENICI; Dir-Gen. Dott. FABIO MELILLI.

Associazione Nazionale fra i Concessionari del Servizio di Riscossione dei Tributi (ASCOTRIBUTI) (Services relating to Collection of Payments): Via Parigi 11, 00185 Roma; tel. (06) 4870330; fax (06) 4740422; e-mail segretariadirezione@ascotributi.it; internet www.ascotributi.it; Pres. RICCARDO TRIGLIA; Dir-Gen. Dott. GERARDO CHIRO.

Associazione Nazionale delle Imprese Elettriche (ASSOELETTRICA): Via Benozzo Gozzoli 24, 00142 Roma; tel. (06) 8537281; fax (06) 85356431; e-mail info@assoelettrica.it; internet www.assoelettrica.it; f. 1946; represents the interests of electricity producers; Pres. Dott. Ing. GIORDANO SERENA; Dir-Gen. FRANCESCO DE LUCA; c. 170 mem. cos.

Associazione fra le Società Italiane per Azioni (ASSONIME) (Limited Cos): Piazza Venezia 11, 00187 Roma; tel. (06) 695291; fax (06) 6790487; e-mail assonime@assonime.it; internet www.assonime.it; f. 1911; Pres. Dott. VITTORIO MERLONI; Dir-Gen. Prof. STEFANO MICOSSI.

Confederazione Generale della Agricoltura Italiana (CONFAGRICOLTURA) (General Agricultural): Corso Vittorio Emanuele II 101, 00186 Roma; tel. (06) 68521; fax (06) 68308578; e-mail immco@mail.confagricoltura.it; internet www.confagricoltura.it; f. 1945; Pres. Dott. AUGUSTO BOCCHINI; Dir-Gen. VITO BIANCO.

Confederazione Generale Italiana del Commercio, del Turismo, dei Servizi e delle Piccole e Medie Industrie (CONFCOMMERCIO) (Commerce, Tourism, Services and Small and Medium-sized Industry): Piazza G.G. Belli 2, 00153 Roma; tel. (06) 58661; fax (06) 5809425; e-mail confcommercio@confcommercio.it; internet www.confcommercio.it; f. 1946; Pres. Dott. SERGIO BILLÈ; Sec.-Gen. Dott. GIUSEPPE CERRONI.

Confederazione Italiana della Piccola e Media Industria Privata (CONFAPI) (Small and Medium-sized Private Industry): Via della Colonna Antonina 52, 00186 Roma; tel. (06) 690151; fax (06) 6791488; e-mail mail@confapi.org; internet www.confapi.org; f. 1947; Pres. Dott. DANILO BROGGI; Dir-Gen. Dott. SANDRO NACCARELLI; 55,000 mems.

Confederazione Italiana della Proprietà Edilizia (CONFEDILIZIA) (Property and Building): Via Borgognona 47, 00187 Roma; tel. (06) 6793489; fax (06) 6793447; e-mail roma@confedilizia.it; internet www.confedilizia.it; Pres. Avv. CORRADO SFORZA FOGLIANI; Sec.-Gen. Avv. GIORGIO SPAZIANI TESTA.

Federazione delle Associazioni Italiane Alberghi e Turismo (FEDERALBERGHI) (Hotels and Tourism): Via Toscana 1, 00187 Roma; tel. (06) 42741151; fax (06) 42871197; e-mail info@federalberghi.it; internet www.federalberghi.it; f. 1950; Pres. BERNABO BOCCA; Gen. Man. ALESSANDRO CIANELLA; 30,000 mems.

UTILITIES

In 2004 there were 550 local power companies in Italy.

Autorità per l'Energia Elettrica e il Gas: Piazza Cavour 5, 20121 Milano; tel. (02) 655651; fax (02) 65565260; e-mail info@autorita .energia.it; internet www.autorita.energia.it; regulatory authority; Pres. ALESSANDRO ORTIS.

Electricity

AEM, SpA: Corso di Porta Vittoria 4, 20122 Milano; tel. (02) 77201; fax (02) 77303920; e-mail aem@aem.it; internet www.aem.it; power manufacture and distribution.

Edison, SpA: Foro Buonaparte 31, 20121 Milano; tel. (02) 62221; e-mail infoweb@edison.it; internet www.edison.it; f. 1884 as Società Generale Italiana di Elettricità Sistema Edison; upon privatization in electricity industry in 1963 merged with Montecatini; changed name as above in 1991; electricity and natural gas; 62% owned by Italenergia; Chair. UMBERTO QUADRINO; CEO GIULIO DEL NINNO.

Enel, Spa: Via le Regina Margherita 137, 00198 Roma; tel. (06) 85091; fax (06) 85092162; internet www.enel.it; f. 1962; 60% state-owned; partially privatized in 2003; generates electrical power and natural gas in Italy; Chair. PIERO GNUDI; CEO PAULO SACRONI.

Gestore dalla Rete di Trasmissione Nazionale SpA (GRTN): Viale Maresciallo Pilsudski 92, 00197 Roma; tel. (06) 81651; fax (06) 81654392; e-mail info@grtn.it; internet www.grtn.it; f. 2000 as part of energy liberalization; owned by the Ministry of Economy and Finance; manages electricity transmission and co-ordinates the power network; Chair. CARLO ANDREA BOLLINO; CEO LUCA D'AGNESE.

Trasmissione Elettricità Rete Nazionale SpA (Terna): Viale Regina Margherita 125, Roma; tel. (06) 85094905; e-mail info .terna@enel.it; internet www.enel.it/it/terna; f. 1999; owned by Enel; electricity transmission co; owns 90% of electricity transmission grid; Pres. F. CONTI; CEO S. MOBILI.

Gas

In 2002 the Governnment's stake in the gas sector was sold in order to comply with European Union regulations.

Edison, SpA: see Electricity.

Ente Nazionale Idrocarburi (Eni): Piazzale Mattei 1, 00144 Rome; tel. (06) 5982; fax (06) 59822141; e-mail segreteriasocietaria .azionisti@eni.it; internet www.eni.it; f. 1953; natural gas exploration, oil and gas power; fmrly state-owned entity, privatized in 1995; Pres. ROBERTO POLI; Dir-Gen. STEFANO CAO.

Snam Rete Gas: Piazza Vanoni 1, 20097 San Donato Milanese; tel. (02) 5201; fax (02) 52043226; internet www.snamretegas.it; subsidiary of Ente Nazionale Idrocarburi (Eni), fmrly Rete Gas Italia, fmrly Snam; transports natural gas; Pres. and CEO SALVATORE RUSSO.

Italgas, SpA: Via XX Settembre 41, 10121, Torino; internet www .italgas.it; 40.9% owned by Snam; supplies 6.7m. customers; Pres. ALBERTO MEOMARTINI; Vice-Pres. and Man. Dir GIACOMO VITALI.

Linde Gas Italia, Srl: Via Guido Rossa 3, 20010 Arluno, Milano; tel. (02) 903731; fax (02) 90373500; internet www.linde-gas.it.

Plurigas: Corso di Porta Vittoria 4, 20122 Milano; tel. (02) 77203033; fax (02) 77203255; e-mail info@plurigas.it; internet www

.plurigas.it; f. 2001; gas distribution; 40% owned by AEM Milano; Chair. ROBERTO CAPRA; Man. Dir RICCARDO PASETTO.

TRADE UNIONS

There are three main federations of Italian trade unions, the Confederazione Generale Italiana del Lavoro (CGIL), the Confederazione Italiana Sindacati Lavoratori (CISL) and the Unione Italiana del Lavoro (UIL), all of which have close ties with political parties. The CGIL was formerly dominated by the Partito Comunista Italiano (Italian Communist Party, now the Democratici di Sinistra—Democrats of the Left), the CISL has links with the Partito Popolare Italiano (Italian Popular Party, formerly Partito della Democrazia Cristiana—Christian Democrat Party) and the UIL is associated with the socialists.

National Federations

Confederazione Autonoma Italiana del Lavoro (CONFAIL): Viale Abruzzi 38, 20131 Milano; tel. (02) 29404554; fax (02) 29525692; e-mail info@confail.org; Gen. Sec. EVANGELISTA ZACCARIA.

Confederazione Autonoma Sindacati Artigiani (CASARTIGIANI): Via Flaminio Ponzio 2, 00153 Roma; tel. (06) 5758081; fax (06) 5755036; e-mail casartigiani@tiscalinet; internet www .casartigiani.org; f. 1958; federation of artisans' unions and regional and provincial asscns; Pres. GIACOMO BASSO.

Confederazione Generale Italiana dell'Artigianato (CONFARTIGIANATO) (Artisans): Via di S. Giovanni in Laterano 152, 00184 Roma; tel. (06) 703741; fax (06) 70452188; e-mail confartigianato@confartigianato.it; internet www.confartigianato .it; f. 1945; independent; 20 regional feds, 121 provincial asscns; 521,000 associate enterprises; Pres. LUCIANO PETRACCHI.

Confederazione Generale Italiana del Lavoro (CGIL) (General Confederation of Italian Labour): Corso d'Italia 25, 00198 Roma; tel. (06) 84761; fax (06) 8845683; e-mail conf.segreteria@mail.cgil.it; internet www.cgil.it; f. 1944; federation of 15 federations; Sec.-Gen. GUGLIELMO EPIFANI; 5,402,408 mems.

Confederazione Generale dei Sindacati Autonomi dei Lavoratori (CONFSAL): Viale Trasevere 60, 00153 Roma; tel. (06) 5852071; fax (06) 5818218; e-mail info@confsal.it; internet www .confsal.it; f. 1979; Sec.-Gen. Prof. MARCO PAOLO NIGI.

Confederazione Italiana Dirigenti e Alte Professionalità (CIDA): Via Nazionale 75, 00184 Roma; tel. (06) 4888241; fax (06) 4873994; e-mail dirigenti@tin.it; internet www.cida.it; federation of eight managers' unions; Pres. Prof. GIORGIO REMBADO; Sec.-Gen. Dott. GIOVANNI CARDEGNA.

Confederazione Italiana Lavoratori Liberi (CONFIL): Via di Campo Marzio 46, 00186 Roma; tel. (06) 6872508; fax (06) 6872509; Gen. Sec. FRANCESCO BRUNETTI.

Confederazione Italiana dei Professionisti ed Artisti (CIPA) (Artists and the Liberal Professions).

Confederazione Italiana Sindacati Addetti ai Servizi (CISAS): Via Sapri 6, 00185 Roma; tel. (06) 4466618; fax (06) 4466617; internet www.cisas.org; Gen. Sec. ONOFRIO DANIELLO.

Confederazione Italiana Sindacati Lavoratori (CISL): Via Po 21, 00198 Roma; tel. (06) 84731; fax (06) 8413782; e-mail cisl@cisl.it; internet www.cisl.it; 8413782; f. 1950; affiliated to the International Confederation of Free Trade Unions and the European Trade Union Confederation; federation of 14 unions; publishes *Conquiste del Lavoro* (see Press); Sec.-Gen. SAVINO PEZZOTTA; 4,200,000 mems.

Confederazione Nazionale dell'Artigianato e delle Piccole Imprese (CNA): Via G. A. Guattani 13, 00161 Roma; tel. (06) 441881; fax (06) 44249513; e-mail cna@cna.it; internet www.cna.it; provincial asscns; Pres. IVAN MALAVDSI; Gen. Sec. Dott. GIAN CARLO SANGALLI.

Confederazione Generale dei Sindacati Autonomi dei Lavoratori (CONFSAL): Viale Trasevere 60, 00153 Roma; tel. (06) 5852071; fax (06) 5818218; e-mail info@confsal.it; internet www .confsal.it; f. 1979; Sec.-Gen. Prof. MARCO PAOLO NIGI.

Confederazione Unitaria Quadri (CUQ): Via XX Settembre 58, 10121 Torino; tel. (011) 5612042; fax (011) 5620362; e-mail confquadri@tin.it; f. 1995; Pres. CARLO CAPELLARO.

Confederazione Unitaria Sindacati Autonomi Lavoratori (CUSAL): Via di Campo Marzio 46, 00186 Roma; tel. (06) 6872508; fax (06) 6872509; Pres. DOMENICO MANNO; Gen. Sec. FRANCESCO BRUNETTI.

Sindacato Nazionale dei Funzionari Direttivi, Dirigenti e delle Alte Professionalità della Pubblicha Amminstrazione (DIRSTAT): Via Ezio 12, 00192 Roma; tel. (06) 3211535; fax (06) 3212690; e-mail dirstat@dirstat.it; internet www.dirstat.it; f. 1948; federation of 33 unions and asscns of civil-service executives and officers; Sec.-Gen. ARCANGELO D'AMBROSIO; Treas. Dott. SERGIO DI DONNA.

Unione Generale del Lavoro (UGL): Via Margutta 19, 00187 Roma; tel. (06) 324821; fax (06) 324820; e-mail ugl@ugl.it; internet www.ugl.it; f. 1950 as CISNAL, name changed as above 1995; upholds traditions of national syndicalism; federation of 64 unions, 77 provincial unions; Gen. Sec. STEFANO CETICA; 2,137,979 mems.

Unione Italiana del Lavoro (UIL): Via Lucullo 6, 00187 Roma; tel. (06) 4753210; fax (06) 4753295; e-mail segretariagenerale@uil.it; internet www.uil.it; f. 1950; socialist, social democrat and republican; affiliated to the International Confederation of Free Trade Unions and European Trade Union Confederation; 18 national trade union federations and 108 provincial union councils; Gen. Sec. LUIGI ANGELETTI; 1,758,729 mems.

Principal Unions

Banking and Insurance

Federazione Autonoma Bancari Italiana (FABI) (Bank, Tax and Finance Workers): Via Tevere 46, 00198 Roma; tel. (06) 8415751; fax (06) 8559220; internet www.fabi.it; f. 1948; independent; Pres. ENZO SCOLA; Sec.-Gen. CARLO GIORGETTI; 69,000 mems.

Federazione Autonoma Lavoratori del Credito e del Risparmio Italiani (FALCRI) (Savings Banks Workers): Viale Liegi 48B, 00198 Roma; tel. (06) 8416336; fax (06) 8416343; e-mail segretaria@falcri.it; internet www.falcri.it; f. 1950; Sec.-Gen. MARIA FRANCESCA FURFARO.

Federazione Italiana Bancari e Assicuratori (FIBA): Via Modena 5, 00184 Roma; tel. (06) 4741245; fax (06) 4746136; e-mail fiba@fiba.it; internet www.fiba.it; affiliated to the CISL; Sec.-Gen. GIUSEPPE GALLO; 58,980 mems.

Federazione Italiana Sindacale Lavoratori Assicurazioni Credito (Employees of Credit Institutions): Via Vicenza 5A, 00184 Roma; tel. (06) 448841; fax (06) 4457356; e-mail fisac@fisac.it; internet www.fisac.it; affiliated to the CGIL; Sec.-Gen. MARCELLO TOCCO; 60,000 mems.

Federazione Nazionale Assicuratori (FNA) (Insurance Workers): Via Vincenzo Monti 25, Milano; Via Val Montebello 104, 00185 Roma; e-mail fnami@fnaitalia.org; internet www.fnaitalia.org; f. 1947; independent; Pres. LUIGI PERAZZI; Sec.-Gen. TEODORO SYLOS.

Unione Italiana Lavoratori Credito, Esattorie e Assicurazioni (UILCA) (Credit and Assurance Workers and Tax Collectors): Via Lombardia 30, 00187 Roma; tel. (06) 4872132; fax (06) 484704; internet www.uilca.it; affiliated to the UIL; Sec.-Gen. ELIO PORINO; 37,453 mems.

Building and Building Materials

Federazione Autonoma Italiana Lavoratori Edili e Affini (FAILEA) (Workers in Construction and Allied Trades): Via della Rosa 91, 00171 Roma; affiliated to the CISAL; Sec. RAUL VIOZZI.

Federazione Italiana Lavoratori Costruzioni e Affini (FILCA) (Building Industries' Workers): Via del Viminale 43, 00184 Roma; tel. (06) 4870634; fax (06) 4818884; e-mail federazione_filca@cisl.it; internet www.filca.cisl.it; f. 1955; affiliated to the CISL; Sec.-Gen. DOMENICO PESENTI; 215,990 mems.

Federazione Italiana Lavoratori del Legno, dell'Edilizia, delle Industrie Affini (FILLEA) (Wood-workers, Construction Workers and Allied Trades): Via G. B. Morgagni 27, 00161 Roma; tel. (06) 441141; fax (06) 44235849; e-mail fillea@mail.cgil.it; internet www.filleacgil.it; affiliated to the CGIL; Sec.-Gen. FRANCO MARTINI; 434,154 mems.

Federazione Nazionale Costruzioni (Construction): Lungotevere Sanzio 5, Roma; tel. (06) 585511; fax (06) 5815184; affiliated to the UGL; Sec. EGIDIO SANGUE.

Federazione Nazionale Lavoratori Edili Affini e del Legno (FENEAL) (Builders and Woodworkers): Via Alessandria 171, 00198 Roma; tel. (06) 8547393; fax (06) 8547423; e-mail fineal-uil@feneal-uil.it; internet www.feneal-uil.it; f. 1951; affiliated to the UIL; Sec.-Gen. FRANCESCO MARABOTTINI; 106,698 mems.

Chemical, Mining and Allied Industries

Federazione Energia, Moda, Chimica e Settori Affini (FEMCA) (Energy, Fashion, Chemicals and Allied Workers): Via Bolzano 16, 00198 Roma; tel. (06) 83034422; fax (06) 83034414; e-mail femca.nazionale@cisl.it; internet www.femcacisl.it; affiliated to the CISL; Sec.-Gen. SERGIO GIGLI.

Federazione Nazionale Chimici (Chemicals): Via Daniele Manin 53, Roma; tel. (06) 4818313; fax (06) 4820554; e-mail uglchimicnazionale@tiscali.net; internet www.ugl.it/confederazione/chimici/index.htm; affiliated to the UGL; Sec. DOMENICO SCOPELLITI.

Unione Italiana Lavoratori Chimici, Energia e Manufatturiero (UILCEM) (Chemicals, Energy and Manufacturing Workers): Via Bolzano 16, 00198 Roma; tel. (06) 83034305; fax (06) 83034307;

e-mail segretaria@uilcem-nazionale.it; internet www.uilcem.it; affiliated to the UIL; Sec.-Gen. ROMANO BELLISSIMA; 84,649 mems.

Clothing and Textiles

Federazione Italiana Lavoratori Tessili, Abbigliamento, Cuoio e Calzature (FILTEA) (Textile, Clothing, Leather and Footwear Workers): Via Leopoldo Serra 31, 00153 Roma; tel. (06) 5836828; fax (06) 5803182; e-mail filtea@mail.cgil.it; internet www.filtea.cgil.it; f. 1966; affiliated to the CGIL; Gen. Sec. VALERIA FEDELI; 150,000 mems.

Unione Italiana Lavoratori Tessili e Abbigliamento (UILTA): Via del Viminale 43, 00184 Roma; tel. (06) 4883486; fax (06) 4819421; e-mail uilta.roma@libero.it; internet www.uil.it/uilta/; affiliated to the UIL; Sec.-Gen. PASQUALE ROSSETTI.

Engineering and Metallurgy

Federazione Impiegati Operai Metallurgici (FIOM-CGIL) (Metalworkers): Corso Trieste 36, 00198 Roma; tel. (06) 852621; fax (06) 85303079; e-mail organizzazione@fiom.cgil.it; internet www.fiom.cgil.it; f. 1901; affiliated to the CGIL; Sec. GIANNI RINALDINI; 400,000 mems.

Federazione Italiana Metalmeccanici (FIM-CISL) (Metal Mechanic Workers): Corso Trieste 36, 00198 Roma; tel. (06) 852621; fax (06) 85262464; internet www.cisl.it/fim; f. 1951; affiliated to the CISL; Sec.-Gen. GIORGIO CAPRIOLI; 190,000 mems.

Federazione Nazionale Metalmeccanici: Via Amadeo 23, Roma; tel. (06) 4741808; fax (06) 4881236; affiliated to the UGL; Sec. DOMENICO FRESILLI.

Federazione Sindacale dell'Industria Metalmeccanica Italiana (Federmeccanica): Piazzale B. Juarez 14, 00144 Roma; tel. (06) 5925446; fax (06) 5911913; e-mail mail.roma@federmeccanica.it; internet www.federmeccanica.it; f. 1971; Pres. ALBERTO BOMBASSEI.

Sindacato Nazionale Ingegneri Liberi Professionisti Italiana (SNILPI) (Liberal Professionals-Engineers): Via Salaria 292, 00199 Roma; tel. (06) 8549796; fax (06) 85830308; e-mail info@snilpi.it; internet www.snilpi.it; Pres. Dott. Ing. LUIGI LUCHERINI; Sec.-Gen. Dott. Ing. GIUSEPPE MILONE.

Unione Italiana Lavoratori Metalmeccanici (UILM) (Metal-workers): Corso Trieste 36, 00198 Roma; tel. (06) 85262201; fax (06) 85262203; e-mail uilm@uil.it; internet www.uil.it/uilm/; f. 1950; affiliated to the UIL; Sec.-Gen. ANTONINO REGAZZI; 100,534 mems.

Food and Agriculture

Confederazione Italiana Agricoltori (CIA) (Farmers): Via Mariano Fortuny 20, 00196 Roma; tel. (06) 32687302; fax (06) 32687308; e-mail segreteriacentrale@cia.it; internet www.cia.it; independent; Pres. MASSIMO PACETTI; Vice-Pres. MASSIMO BELLOTTI.

Confederazione Italiana Dirigenti, Quadri e Impiegati dell' Agricoltura (CONFEDERDIA): Viale Beethoven 48, 00144 Roma; tel. (06) 5912808; fax (06) 5915014; e-mail confederdia@confederdia.it; internet www.confederdia.it; Pres. LUCIANO BOZZATO; Gen. Sec. TOMMASO BRANDONI.

Confederazione Nazionale Coltivatori Diretti (COLDIRETTI) (Small-holders): Via XXIV Maggio 43, 00187 Roma; tel. (06) 46821; fax (06) 4682305; e-mail coldiretti@coldiretti.it; internet www.coldiretti.it; independent; Pres. PAOLO BEDONI; Sec.-Gen. Dott. FRANCO PASQUALI; mems: 18 regional federations, 98 provincial federations.

Federazione Agricola Alimentare Ambientale Industriale (FAI-CISL) (Agriculture, Food and Environment Industries): Via Tevere 20, 00198 Roma; tel. (06) 845691; fax (06) 8840652; e-mail federazione_fai@cisl.it; internet www.fai.cisl.it; f. 1997 by merger of FISBA and FAT.

Federazione Lavoratori Agro Industria (FLAI-CGIL) (Workers in Agro-industry): Via Leopoldo Serra 31, 00153 Roma; tel. (06) 585611; fax (06) 58561334; e-mail flai-nazionale@flai.it; internet www.flai.it; f. 1988; affiliated to the CGIL; Sec.-Gen. FRANCO CHIRIACO; 309,524 mems.

Unione Coltivatori Italiana (UCI) (Farmers): Via in Lucina 10, 00186 Roma; tel. (06) 6871043; Pres. VINCENZO PANDOVINO.

Unione Generale Coltivatori (UGC): Via Tevere 44, 00198 Roma; tel. (06) 8552383; fax (06) 8553891; affiliated to the CISL; Pres. GAVINO DERUDA; 151,625 mems.

Unione Italiana Lavoratori Agroalimentari (UILA-UIL) (Food Workers): Via Savoia 80, 00198 Roma; tel. (06) 85301610; fax (06) 85303253; e-mail uilanazionale@uila.it; internet www.uila.it; affiliated to the UIL; Sec. STEFANO MANTEGAZZA.

Unione Italiana Mezzadri e Coltivatori Diretti (UIMEC) (Land Workers): Via Reno 30, 00198 Rome; tel. (06) 85304428; fax (06)

85357571; e-mail uimec@uil.it; affiliated to the UIL; Pres. GIO-VANBATTISTA AIUTO; 100,000 mems.

Medical

Confederazione Unitaria Medici Italiani—Associazione dei Medici Specialisti e Specializzandi (CUMI—AISS) (Doctors—Association of Medical Specialists): Via Livorno 36, 00162 Roma; tel. (06) 44254168; fax (06) 44254160; e-mail info@cumiaiss.it; internet www.cumiaiss.it; f. 2000 by fusion of CUMI and AISS; Pres. COSMO DE MATTEIS; Sec.-Gen. SALVO CALÌ.

Federazione Italiana Servizi Territoriali (FIST) (Hospital and Regional Municipal Workers' Unions): Via Lancisi 25, 00161 Roma; tel. (06) 4425981; fax (06) 44230114; e-mail fist@cisl.it; internet www.mclink.it/com/fist; affiliated to the CISL; Sec.-Gen. ERMENE-GILDO BONFANTI; 250,000 mems.

Federazione Nazionale Medici (Doctors): Via Amendola 7, Roma; tel. (06) 4870444; fax (06) 4874323; e-mail federmed@flashnet.it; affiliated to the UGL; Sec.-Gen. GIOVANNI PALOMBI.

Public Services

Confederazione dei Quadri Direttivi e Dirigenti della Funzione Pubblica (CONFEDIR) (Public Office Managers): Arco dei Banchi 8, 00186 Roma; tel. and fax (06) 68803688; Gen. Sec. ROBERTO CONFALONIERI.

Federazione Italiana Lavoratori Organi Costituzionali (Employees of Constitutional Bodies): Via del Parlamento 9, 00187 Roma; tel. (06) 67609118; fax (06) 67604890; e-mail uiloocc@uil.it; internet www.uilorganicostituzionali.it; affiliated to the UIL; Sec.-Gen. Dott. SILVANO SGREVI.

Federazione Lavoratori Aziende Elettriche Italiane (FLAEI) (Workers in Italian Electrical Undertakings): Via Salaria 83, 00198 Roma; tel. (06) 8440421; fax (06) 8548458; e-mail nazionale@flaei.org; internet www.flaei.org; f. 1948; affiliated to the CISL; Sec. ARSENIO CAROSI; 32,000 mems.

Federazione Lavoratori Pubblici e dei Servizi (FPI) (Public-Sector and Services Workers): Via Lancisi 25, 00161 Roma; tel. (06) 440071; fax (06) 44007512; e-mail fps@cisl.it; internet www.fps.cisl.it; affiliated to the CISL.

Federazione Nazionale Energia (Energy): Via Filiberto 125, Roma; tel. (06) 7005935; fax (06) 7003451; affiliated to the UGL; Sec. LUIGI DE NARDIS.

Federazione Nazionale Enti Locali (Employees of Local Authorities): Via Amendola 5, 00185 Roma; tel. (06) 4743418; fax (06) 4743853; e-mail quesiti@uglentilocali.it; internet www.uglentilocali.it; affiliated to the UGL; Sec. GIUSEPPE VIGLIANESI.

Federazione Nazionale Dipendenti Enti Pubblici UGL (UGL-FEDEP) (Public Employees): Via del Corea 13, Roma; tel. (06) 3233363; fax (06) 3226052; e-mail info@uglfedep.org; internet www.uglfedep.org; f. 1962; affiliated to the UGL; Gen. Sec. GIUSEPPE MARO.

Federazione Nazionale Lavoratori Funzione Pubblica: Via Leopoldo Serra 31, 00153 Roma; tel. (06) 585441; fax (06) 5836970; e-mail posta@fpcgil.it; internet www.fpcgil.it; f. 1980; affiliated to the CGIL, Public Services International, and European Public Services Union (EPSU); Gen. Sec. CARLO PODDA; 390,000 mems.

Federazione Nazionale Lavoratori Energia (Gas, Water and Electricity): Via Piemonte 32, 00187 Roma; tel. (06) 4620091; fax (06) 4824246; e-mail fnle@mail.cgil.it; internet www.cgil.it/fnle; f. 1977; affiliated to the CGIL; Sec. GIACOMO BERNI; 36,728 mems.

Federazione Nazionale Sanità (Sanitary Workers): Via Farini 16, Roma; tel. (06) 4814678; fax (06) 4814651; affiliated to the UGL; Sec. SALVATORE GALIZIA.

Unione Italiana Lavoratori Federazione Poteri Locali (UIL FPL) (Local Authority Employees): Via di tor Fiorenza 35, 00199 Roma; tel. (06) 865081; fax (06) 86508235; e-mail info@uilfpl.it; internet www.uilfpl.it; affiliated to the UIL; Gen. Sec. CARLO FIORDA-LISO; 89,179 mems.

Unione Italiana Lavoratori Pubblico Amministrazione (UILPA) (Public Office Workers): Via Emilio Lepido 46, 00175 Roma; tel. (06) 71588888; fax (06) 71582046; e-mail uilpa@uilpa.it; internet www.uilpa.it; affiliated to the UIL; Sec.-Gen. SALVATORE BOSCO; 67,702 mems.

Unione Italiana Lavoratori Sanità (UIL Sanità) (Sanitary Workers): Via di Tor Fiorenza 35, 00199 Roma; tel. (06) 865081; fax (06) 86508235; e-mail info@uilfpl.it; internet www.uilfpl.it; affiliated to the UIL; Sec.-Gen. CARLO FIORDALISO; 98,669 mems.

Teachers

Cisl-Scuola (School Teachers): Via Bargoni 8, 00153 Roma; tel. (06) 583111; fax (06) 5881713; internet www.cislscuola.it; f. 1997; affiliated to the CISL; Sec.-Gen. DANIELA COLTURANI; 185,173 mems.

Cisl-Università (University Teachers): Via Rovereto 11, 00198 Roma; tel. (06) 8840772; fax (06) 8844977; e-mail info@cisluniversita.it; internet www.cisluniversita.it; affiliated to the CISL; Sec.-Gen. ANTONIO MARSILIA.

Sindacato Nazionale Scuola (School Teachers): Via Leopoldo Serra 31, Roma; tel. (06) 585480; e-mail mail@cgilscuola.it; internet www.cgilscuola.it; affiliated to the CGIL; 97,149 mems (1997).

Sindacato Nazionale Università Ricerca (SNUR-CGIL): Via Leopoldo Serra 31, 00153 Roma; tel. (06) 5883383; fax (06) 5883926; e-mail comren@snur-cgil.it; internet www.snur-cgil.it.

UGL-Federazione Nazionale Università (University Teachers): Lungotevere Rio Sanzio 5, Roma; tel. (06) 58551; fax (06) 58551223; e-mail ugluniversita@mclink.it; internet www.ugl.it/confederazione/newuniversita/index.htm; affiliated to the UGL; Dir CLARA VALLI.

Unione Italiana Lavoratori Scuola (UIL Scuola) (School Workers): Via Marino Laziale 44, 00179 Roma; tel. (06) 7846941; fax (06) 7842858; e-mail uilscuola@uil.it; internet www.uil.it/uilscuola; affiliated to the UIL; Sec.-Gen. MASSIMO DI MENNA; 59,402 mems.

Tourism and Entertainment

Federazione Informazione Spettacolo e Telecomunicazioni (FISTEL) (Actors, Artists and Media Workers): Via Palestro 30, 00185 Roma; tel. (06) 492171; fax (06) 4457330; affiliated to the CISL; Sec.-Gen. FULVIO GIACOMASSI; 43,388 mems.

Federazione Italiana Lavoratori Commercio, Turismo e Servizi (FILCAMS) (Hotel and Catering Workers): Via Leopoldo Serra 31, 00153 Roma; tel. (06) 5885102; fax (06) 5885323; e-mail post@filcams.cgil.it; internet www.filcams.cgil.it; f. 1960; affiliated to the CGIL; Sec.-Gen. IVANO CORRAINI; 189,000 mems.

Federazione Italiana Sindacati Addetti Servizi Commerciali Affini e del Turismo (FISASCAT-CISL) (Commercial and Tourist Unions): Via Livenza 7, 00198 Roma; tel. (06) 8541042; fax (06) 8558057; internet www.fisascat.it; Sec.-Gen. GIANNI BARATTA; 153,900 mems.

Federazione Nazionale Informazione e Spettacolo (Actors, Artists and Media Workers): Via Margutta 19, Roma; tel. (06) 324821; fax (06) 323420; affiliated to the UGL; Sec. GIANNI IMPROTA.

Sindacato Attori Italiani (SAI) (Actors): Via Ofanto 18, 00198 Roma; tel. (06) 8411288; fax (06) 8546780; e-mail sai-slc@cgil.it; internet www.cgil.it/sai-slc; affiliated to the CGIL; Pres. MASSIMO GHINI; Sec.-Gen. MASSIMO CESTARO.

Unione Italiana Lavoratori Turismo Commercio e Servizi (UILTuCS): Via Nizza 154, 00198 Roma; tel. (06) 84242268; fax (06) 84242292; e-mail info@uiltucs.it; internet www.uiltucs.it; f. 1977; affiliated to the UIL; Gen. Sec. BRUNO BOCO; 75,042 mems.

Transport and Telecommunications

Federazione Italiana Lavoratori Postelegrafonici (Filpt) (Postal, Telegraph and Telephone Workers): Piazza Verdi 5, Ferrara; tel. (05) 32783111; affiliated to the CGIL; division of Sindacato Lavoratori Comunicazione; Sec. GIUSEPPE MASTRACCHI; 35,000 mems.

Federazione Italiana Lavoratori dei Trasporti (FILT-CGIL): Via G. B. Morgagni 27, 00161 Roma; tel. (06) 442961; fax (06) 44293313; e-mail filt@mail.cgil.it; affiliated to the CGIL; Sec. GUIDO ABBADESSA.

Federazione Italiana Trasporti (FIT-CISL): Via A. Musa 4, 00161 Roma; tel. (06) 442861; fax (06) 44266336; e-mail federazione_fit@cisl.it; internet www.fit.cisl.it; f. 1950; affiliated to the CISL; Sec.-Gen. CLAUDIO CLAUDIANI; 40,000 mems.

Federazione Nazionale Comunicazioni (UGL-Comunicazioni) (Communications): Via Volturno 40, Roma; tel. (06) 4464649; fax (06) 49384693; e-mail comunicazione@ugl.it; internet www.ugl.it/confederazione/fedcomun/nuovahome.htm; f. 1997; affiliated to the UGL; Sec. SERAFINO CABRAS.

Federazione Nazionale Trasporti (Transport): Via Margutta 19, Roma; tel. (06) 324821; fax (06) 3232420; affiliated to the UGL; Sec. PAOLO SEGARELLI.

Sindacato Lavoratori Comunicazione (SLC) (Communications Workers): Piazza Sallustio 24, 00187 Roma; tel. (06) 421071; fax (06) 4824325; e-mail segreteria.nazionale@slc.cgil.it; internet www.cgil.it/slc; affiliated to the CGIL; Gen. Sec. FULVIO FAMMONI.

SLP—Federazione Lavoratori Poste e Appalti (Postal Workers): Via dell'Esquilino 38, 00185 Roma; internet www.slp-cisl.it; affiliated to the CISL; Sec.-Gen. ANTONINO SORGI.

Unione Italiana Lavoratori Trasporti (UILTRASPORTI) (Transport Workers): Via Salaria 44, 00198 Roma; tel. (06) 852511; fax (06) 85350502; e-mail uiltrasporti@uil.it; internet www.uil.it/uiltrasporti/; affiliated to the UIL; Sec. SANDRO DEGNI; 103,687 mems.

Unione Italiana Lavoratori della Comunicazione (UILCOM) (Media and Telecommunications): Via Belisario 7, 00187 Roma; tel.

(06) 4204021; fax (06) 42744897; e-mail uilcom@uilcom.it; internet www.uilcom.it; affiliated to the UIL; Sec.-Gen. Bruno Di Cola.

Unione Italiana Lavoratori Postelegrafonici (UILPOST) (Post, Telegraph and Telephone Workers): Via Sallustiana 15, 00187 Roma; tel. (06) 4883222; fax (06) 4814403; e-mail uilpost@uil.it; internet www.uilpost.it; affiliated to the UIL; Sec.-Gen. Ciro Amicone; 30,853 mems.

Miscellaneous

Federazione Nazionale Pensionati (FNP) (Pensioners): Via Castelfidardo 47, 00185 Roma; tel. (06) 448811; fax (06) 4452608; e-mail andrea.pellicari@fnp.cisl.it; internet fnp.cisl.it; f. 1952; affiliated to the CISL; Sec. Carmelo Muscolimo; 1,180,000 mems.

Federazione Nazionale Pensionati dell'Unione Generale del Lavoro (Pensioners): Via Margutta 19, 00187 Roma; tel. (06) 32482248; fax (06) 3612027; internet www.pensionatiugl.it; affiliated to the UGL; Sec. Corrado Mannucci.

Federazione Nazionale Terziario (Service Sector Workers): Via Farini 62, 00185 Roma; tel. (06) 4820754; fax (06) 4820702; affiliated to the UGL; Sec. Renata Polverini.

Sindacato Pensionati Italiani SPI-Cgil (Pensioners): Via Frentani 4A, 00185 Roma; tel. (06) 444811; fax (06) 4440941; e-mail spi@mail.cgil.it; f. 1948; affiliated to the CGIL; Sec.-Gen. Elisabetta Leone; 2,757,010 mems.

Unione Italiana Lavoratori Pensionati (UILP) (Pensioners): Via Po 162, 00198 Roma; tel. (06) 852591; fax (06) 8548632; e-mail segreteria@uilpensionati.it; internet www.uilpensionati.it; affiliated to the UIL; Sec.-Gen. Silvano Miniati; 682,000 mems.

Co-operative Unions

Associazione Generale delle Cooperative Italiane (AGCI): Via A. Bargoni, 00153 Roma; tel. (06) 583271; fax (06) 58327210; e-mail info@agci.it; internet www.agci.it; f. 1952; Pres. Maurizio Zaffi.

Confederazione Cooperative Italiane (CONFCOOPERATIVE): Borgo S. Spirito 78, 00193 Roma; tel. (06) 680041; fax (06) 68134236; e-mail confcooperative@confcooperative.it; internet www.confcooperative.it; f. 1919; confederation of co-operative unions; Pres. Luigi Marino; Dir Guiseppe Maggi; Sec.-Gen. Vincenzo Mannino.

Lega Nazionale delle Cooperative e Mutue (National League of Co-operative and Friendly Societies): Via Guattani 9, 00161 Roma; tel. (06) 84439391; fax (06) 84439370; e-mail presidenza@legacoop.it; internet www.legacoop.it; f. 1886; nine affiliated unions; Pres. Ivano Barberini.

Unione Nazionale Cooperative Italiane: Via San Sotero 32, 00165 Roma; tel. (06) 39366729; fax (06) 39375080; e-mail uncinazionale@mclink.it; internet www.uncinazionale.it; Pres. Luciano D'Ulizia.

Transport

Direzione Generale della Motorizzazione Civile e dei Trasporti in Concessione: Via Giuseppe Caraci 36, 00157 Roma; tel. (06) 41581; fax (06) 41582211; controls road transport and traffic, and public transport services (railways operated by private cos, motor-buses, trolley-buses, funicular railways and inland waterways); Dir-Gen. Dott. Giorgio Berruti.

RAILWAYS

The majority of Italian lines are controlled by an independent state-owned corporation. In 2004 the total length of the network was 16,200 km, of which two-thirds were electrified. In that year there were 2,700 passenger stations and 479 goods stations. Apart from the state railway system there are 24 local and municipal railway companies, many of whose lines are narrow gauge. There are metro systems in Rome, Milan and Naples; a metro system is also planned for Turin. A high-speed service is planned on the following routes: Rome–Milan–Turin, Naples–Rome, Milan–Genoa and Milan–Venice. In 1991 TAV, a semi-private company for the creation of a high-speed train network, was established; from 1998 it was wholly-owned by Ferrovie dello Stato. Work on the following lines was to be completed by 2006: Naples–Rome and Rome–Milan. In 2004 an agreement was reached between Italy and France to construct a high-speed rail link between Lyons and Turin. A 52-km rail tunnel under the Alps was to be built as part of this new link.

Ferrovie dello Stato SpA: Piazza della Croce Rossa 1, 00161 Roma; tel. (06) 84903758; fax (06) 84905186; e-mail redazioneweb@ferroviedellostato.it; internet www.fs-on-line.it; controls 9 subsidiaries; Pres. and CEO Elio Catania.

ROADS

In 2003 there were an estimated 172,178 km of roads in Italy, including 6,487 km of motorway, 45,696 km of major roads and 119,644 km of secondary roads. All the *autostrade* (motorways) are toll roads except for the one between Salerno and Reggio Calabria and motorways in Sicily. Plans were approved in 2001 for the construction of a 3.89-km bridge linking Sicily to the Italian mainland; the bridge was to be completed over a seven-year period starting in 2005.

ANAS SpA: Via Monzambano 10, 00185 Roma; tel. (06) 44461; fax (06) 4456224; e-mail urp@stradeanas.it; internet www.stradeanas.it; f. 1928 as Azienda Autonoma Statale della Strada (AASS); joint-stock co supervised by Ministry of Infrastructure and Transport; owned by Ministry of Economy and Finance; responsible for the administration of state roads and their improvement and extension; Pres. Ing. Vincenzo Pozzi.

Autostrade SpA: Via Alberto Berganini 50, 00159 Roma; tel. (06) 43631; fax (06) 43634090; e-mail info@autostrade.it; internet www.autostrade.it; maintenance and management of motorway network; CEOs Vito Gamberale, GianMaria Gros Pietro.

SHIPPING

In 2003 the Italian merchant fleet (1,504 vessels) had a combined aggregate displacement of 10,246,000 grt. In that year there were 66 ports in Italy.

Direzione Generale della Marina Mercantile: Via dell'Arte 16, 00144 Roma.

Genoa

Costa Crociere SpA: Via XII Ottobre 2, 16121 Genova; tel. (010) 54831; fax (010) 5483290; e-mail info@costa.it; internet www.costa.it; passenger and cargo service; Mediterranean, Northern Europe, Central and South America; Caribbean cruises; Chair. Nicola Costa.

'Garibaldi' Società Cooperativa di Navigazione Srl: Piazza Dante 8, 16121 Genova; tel. (010) 581635; fax (010) 5702386; f. 1918; tanker and cargo services; Pres. Gian Franco Viale.

'Italia di Navigazione' SpA: Torre WTC, Via de Marini 1, Genova; tel. (010) 24021; fax (010) 2402386; e-mail bo@italialine.it; internet www.italialine.it; f. 1932; freight services to Mediterranean, and North, South and Central America; Chair. Antonio d'Amico; CEO Cesare d'Amico.

Messina, Ignazio and C. SpA: Via G. d'Annunzio 91, 16121 Genova; tel. (010) 53961; fax (010) 5396264; e-mail info@messinaline.it; internet www.messinaline.it; services to Arabian Gulf, India, Pakistan, Nigeria, North, East, South and West Africa, Libya and Near East, Red Sea, Malta, Europe; Chair. Gianfranco Messina.

Naples

Grimaldi Group: Via Fieschi 17/17A, 16121 Genova; tel. (010) 55091; fax (010) 5509333; internet www1.grimaldi.it; f. 1947; passenger, cargo, containers and tramp to Europe, Middle East, North and West Africa, South, Central and North America; Dirs M. Grimaldi, G. Grimaldi, A. Grimaldi, U. Grimaldi.

Tirrenia di Navigazione SpA: Head Office: Palazzo Sirignano, Rione Sirignano 2, 80121 Napoli; tel. (081) 7201111; fax (081) 7201441; internet www.tirrenia.it; ferry services to Sardinia, Sicily, North Africa; part of Gruppo Tirrenia di Navigazione; Man. Dir and Dir-Gen. Franco Pecorini.

Palermo

Sicilia Regionale Marittima SpA (SIREMAR): Calata Marinai d'Italia, Porto, Palermo; tel. (091) 6021111; fax (091) 6021221; e-mail siremar@infovoce24.it; internet www.siremar.it; owned by Gruppo Tirrenia di Navigazione; ferry services; Pres. Dott Giuseppe Ravera; Man. Dir Carlo Costa.

Sicula Oceanicas SA (SIOSA): Via dei Cartari 18, 90139 Palermo; tel. (091) 217939; f. 1941; cruises, passenger and cargo; Italy to North Europe, South, Central, North America; Dir G. Grimaldi.

Rome

D'Amico Fratelli, SpA: Via Liguria 36, 00187 Roma; tel. (06) 4671; fax (06) 4871914; e-mail damiship@damicofratelli.it; internet www.damicofratelli.it; dry cargo and tankers; Pres. Giuseppe d'Amico; Gen. Man. Carlo Cameli.

Trieste

Fratelli Cosulich SpA: Piazza S. Antonio 4, 34122 Trieste; tel. (040) 6797111; fax (040) 6797777; internet www.cosulich.it; f. 1854; shipowners and shipping agents; domestic network and cargo to Near East, Red Sea, Hong Kong, Singapore, New York and Zürich; Chair. and Man. Dir Gerolimich Cosulich.

Lloyd Triestino di Navigazione SpA: Palazzo della Marineria, Passeggio S. Andrea 4, 34123 Trieste; tel. (040) 3180111; fax (040) 3180296; e-mail headoffice@ts.lloydtriestino.it; internet www .lloydtriestino.it; f. 1836; cargo services by container to South Africa, Australasia and Far East, plus trans-Pacific services; privatized 1998; Pres. PIER LUIGI MANESCHI; Vice-Pres. GEORGE HSU; Man. Dir BRONSON HSIEH.

Navigazione Montanari SpA: Corso Italia 31, 34122 Trieste; fax (0721) 830430; e-mail giovanip@navmont.com; internet www .navmont.com; f. 1889; cargo services to Mediterranean, Northern Europe, USA and Far East.

Venice

Adriatica di Navigazione SpA: Zattere 1411, CP 705, 30123 Venezia; tel. (041) 781861; fax (041) 781818; e-mail adrnav@ interbusiness.it; internet www.adriatica.it; f. 1937; owned by Gruppo Tirrenia di Navigazione; passenger services from Italy, Albania, Croatia and Serbia and Montenegro; Pres. GIORGIO GROSSO; Man. Dir ANTONIO CACUCCI.

SHIPPING ASSOCIATION

Confederazione Italiana Armatori (CONFITARMA): Piazza SS. Apostoli 66, 00187 Roma; tel. (06) 674811; fax (06) 69783726; e-mail confitarma@confitarma.it; internet www.confitarma.it; f. 1901; shipowners' asscn; Pres. GIOVANNI MONTANARI; Dir-Gen. LUIGI PERISSICH; 140 mems.

CIVIL AVIATION

In 2002 there were 41 commercial airports in Italy.

Civil Aviation Authority

Ente Nazionale per l'Aviazione Civile (ENAC) (Italian Civil Aviation Authority): Viale del Castro Pretorio 118, 00185 Roma; tel. (06) 44596; internet www.enac-italia.it; Pres. VITO RIGGIO; Dir-Gen. SILVANO MANERA.

National Airline

Alitalia (Linee Aeree Italiane): Viale Alessandro Marchetti 111, 00148 Roma; tel. (06) 65621; fax (06) 7093065; internet www.alitalia .com; f. 1946; state-owned; domestic and international services throughout Europe and to Africa, North and South America, the Middle East, the Far East and Australia; Chair. and CEO GIANCARLO CIMOLI.

Other Airlines

Air Dolomiti: Via Senatore Augusto Tambarin 36, 34077 Ronchi dei Legionari; tel. (0481) 477711; fax (0481) 474540; internet www .airdolomiti.it; f. 1989; main regional airline in northern Italy; Pres. and CEO ALCIDE LEALI.

Air Europe: Via Carlo Noè 3, 21013 Gallarate, Varese; tel. (0331) 713111; fax (0331) 713850; e-mail marketing@aireurope.it; internet www.aireurope.it; f. 1988; international charter flights; Chair. LUPO RATTAZZI; Man. Dir ISABELLA ANTONELLO.

Air One: Via Sardegna 14, 00187 Roma; tel. (06) 478761; fax (06) 4820399; internet www.flyairone.it; f. 1983 as Aliadriatica, adopted

current name in 1995; private co; domestic flights; Chair. GIOVANNI SEBASTIANI; Pres. CARLO TOTO.

Air Sicilia: Via G. La Rosa 21, 95041 Caltagirone; tel. (0993) 26714; fax (0916) 25510; internet www.airsicilia.it; f. 1994; operates domestic and international scheduled services throughout Europe; Chair. ARMANDO CRISPINO.

Alpi Eagles: c/o Valecenter, Via Enrico Mattei 1/98, 30020 Marcon; tel. (041) 5997777; fax (041) 5997707; e-mail info@alpieagles.com; internet www.alpieagles.com; f. 1979; privately-owned regional carrier operating scheduled passenger services within Italy and to some European destinations; Pres. PAOLO SINIGAGLIA.

Azzurra Air: Via Pietro Paleocapa 3D, 24122 Bergamo; tel. (035) 4160311; fax (035) 4160300; e-mail info@azzurraair.it; internet www .azzurraair.it; f. 1995; scheduled and chartered European flights; CEO DOMINIC R. ATTARD.

Gandalfair: Via Aeroporto 13, Orio al Serio, 24050 Bergamo; tel. (035) 4595011; fax (035) 4595083; e-mail info@gandalfair.it; internet www.gandalfair.it; f. 1998; private airline operating scheduled services aimed at business travellers; Chair. CARLO PERETTI.

Meridiana SpA: Aeroporto Costa Smeralda, Olbia, 07026 Sardinia; tel. (0789) 52821; fax (0789) 52972; e-mail relazioni.clienti@ meridiana.it; internet www.meridiana.it; f. 1963 as Alisarda, renamed 1991; scheduled and charter services throughout Italy and Europe; Chair. FRANCO TRIVI; CEO GIOVANNI SEBASTIANI.

Volare: Milano; e-mail info@volareweb.com; internet www .volareweb.com; low cost airline; suspended flights in late 2004 due to insolvency, and was put under government administration; Commissioner CARLO RINALDINI; Dir-Gen. COSIMO GIULIO DE METRIO.

Tourism

A great number of tourists are attracted to Italy by its Alpine and Mediterranean scenery, sunny climate, Roman archaeological remains, medieval and Baroque churches, Renaissance towns and palaces, paintings and sculpture and famous opera houses. Each of the 95 provinces has a Board of Tourism; there are also about 300 Aziende Autonome di Cura, Soggiorno e Turismo, with information about tourist accommodation and health treatment, and about 2,000 Pro Loco Associations concerned with local amenities. In 2004 there were 39 UNESCO World Heritage Sites in Italy. In 2003 an estimated 34.7m. foreign visitors (including excursionists) arrived in Italy; tourist receipts totalled an estimated €27,620m. in that year.

Compagnia Italiana Turismo: Via Nazionale 196, 00184 Roma; tel. (06) 48787252; fax (06) 4819120; internet www.citonline.it.

Direzione Generale per il Turismo: Ministero della Attività Produttive, Via della Ferratella in Laterano 51, 00184 Roma; tel. (06) 7732431; fax (06) 77209808; e-mail a.m.guzzardi@virgilio.it; Dir-Gen. Ing. FRANCO VITALE.

Ente Nazionale Italiano per il Turismo (ENIT) (Italian State Tourist Board): Via Marghera 2, 00185 Roma; tel. (06) 49711; fax (06) 4463379; e-mail sedecentrale@enit.it; internet www.enit.it; f. 1919; Chair. AMEDEO OTTAVIANI; Dir-Gen. PIERGIORGIO TOGNI.

JAMAICA

Introductory Survey

Location, Climate, Language, Religion, Flag, Capital

Jamaica is the third largest island in the Caribbean Sea, lying 145 km (90 miles) to the south of Cuba and 160 km (100 miles) to the south-west of Haiti. The climate varies with altitude, being tropical at sea-level and temperate in the mountain areas. The average annual temperature is 27°C (80°F) and mean annual rainfall is 198 cm (78 ins). The official language is English, although a local patois is widely spoken. The majority of the population belong to Christian denominations, the Church of God being the most numerous. The national flag (proportions 1 by 2) consists of a diagonal yellow cross on a background of black (hoist and fly) and green (above and below). The capital is Kingston.

Recent History

Jamaica, a British colony from 1655, was granted internal self-government in 1959, and full independence, within the Commonwealth, was achieved on 6 August 1962. Jamaica formed part of the West Indies Federation between 1958 and 1961, when it seceded, following a referendum. The Federation was dissolved in May 1962. The two dominant political figures after the Second World War were the late Sir Alexander Bustamante, leader of the Jamaica Labour Party (JLP), who retired as Prime Minister in 1967, and Norman Manley, a former Premier and leader of the People's National Party (PNP), who died in 1969. The JLP won the elections of 1962 and 1967 but, under the premiership of Hugh Shearer, it lost the elections of February 1972 to the PNP, led by Michael Manley, the son of Norman Manley. Michael Manley advocated democratic socialism and his Government put great emphasis on social reform and economic independence.

The early 1970s were marked by escalating street violence and crime, with gang warfare rife in the deprived areas of Kingston. More than 160 people were killed in the first half of 1976, and in June the Government declared a state of emergency (which remained in force until June 1977). Despite the unrest, high unemployment and severe economic stagnation, the PNP was returned to power in December 1976 with an increased majority. By January 1979, however, there was again widespread political unrest, and violent demonstrations signalled growing discontent with the Manley administration. In February 1980, in the context of a worsening economic crisis, Manley rejected the stipulation of the IMF that economic austerity measures be undertaken, as a condition of its making further loans to Jamaica. He called a general election to seek support for his economic policies and his decision to end dependence on the IMF. The electoral campaign was one of the most violent in Jamaica's history. In the October election the JLP received about 57% of the total votes and won 51 of the 60 seats in the House of Representatives. Edward Seaga, the leader of the JLP, became Prime Minister; he supported closer political and economic links with the USA and the promotion of free enterprise. Seaga severed diplomatic relations with Cuba in October 1981, and secured valuable US financial support for the economy. Negotiations on IMF assistance were resumed.

In November 1983, before the completion of a new electoral roll, Seaga announced that an election would take place in mid-December. Only four days were allowed for the nomination of candidates, and the PNP, unable to present candidates at such short notice, refused to participate and declared the elections void. The JLP, opposed in only six constituencies (by independent candidates), won all 60 seats in the House of Representatives and formed a one-party legislature.

Devaluations of the Jamaican dollar and the withdrawal of food subsidies provoked demonstrations and sporadic violence in 1984, as the prices of foodstuffs and energy increased by between 50% and 100%. Despite government attempts to offset the effects of these economic austerity measures, imposed at the instigation of the IMF, unemployment, together with the consequences of illicit trading in drugs, contributed to a rise in the incidence of crime and violence, especially in Kingston. In 1985 another increase in fuel prices precipitated further violent demonstrations in the capital and industrial unrest in the public sector. In May 1986 Seaga defied recommendations by the IMF and other aid agencies, and introduced an expansionary budget for 1986/87, in an attempt to stimulate economic growth.

A significant increase in drugs-related violence in 1987 prompted the Government to announce more severe punishments for drugs-related offences.

In September 1988 Jamaica was struck by 'Hurricane Gilbert', the most damaging storm in the country's recorded history. More than 100,000 homes were destroyed, while the economy, particularly the agriculture sector, was severely disrupted. Seaga's successful efforts to secure international aid won him some initial support, but this soon declined, particularly following controversy over the alleged preferential allocation of relief resources to JLP supporters.

After a brief, and relatively peaceful, campaign, a general election took place in February 1989. The PNP received about 56% of the votes cast, thereby securing 45 of the 60 seats in the House of Representatives. Manley, who had developed a more moderate image during his years in opposition, again became Prime Minister. The Government conceded the necessity for a devaluation of the Jamaican dollar, which was announced in October. Unusually for Jamaican politics, the two main parties achieved a limited consensus on the pursuit of an economic policy of austerity, despite its unpopularity. There was also agreement that further action should be taken against the drugs trade. The Government was particularly anxious to prevent the use of Jamaican shipping and aviation for the smuggling of illegal drugs, and demanded increased security measures, despite the consequent impediment to normal trade movements.

New economic adjustment measures (including a further devaluation of the Jamaican dollar) were adopted in January 1990, in order to secure another IMF stand-by arrangement. In June a five-year economic development plan was announced, as part of the Government's programme of deregulation and reform. However, the cost of living continued to rise, prompting industrial unrest in late 1991.

In December 1991 controversy surrounding the waiving of taxes worth some US $30m. that were owed to Jamaica by an international petroleum company, Shell, resulted in the resignation of Horace Clarke, the Minister of Mining and Energy, and Percival Patterson, the Deputy Prime Minister, amid opposition allegations of corruption and misconduct. Patterson requested not to be included in the new Cabinet (which was reorganized following the scandal), but remained as Chairman of the PNP. In March 1992 Manley announced his resignation, owing to ill health, from the premiership and from the presidency of the PNP. Patterson was elected as Manley's successor by members of the PNP, and was appointed Prime Minister at the end of the month.

At a general election in March 1993 Patterson's PNP secured 52 of the 60 seats in the House of Representatives. The scale of the PNP victory was widely attributed to the success of Patterson's populist overtures to the island's majority population of African origin, and a perceived shift in political influence away from the capital, traditionally a power base of the JLP (which won the remaining eight seats). In April Patterson announced plans to reform and modernize the electoral system. However, allegations of electoral malpractice and demands by the JLP for an official inquiry into suspected procedural abuses were rejected by the PNP, prompting the JLP to boycott the official opening of Parliament later in the month. By February 1994 attempts at electoral reform had been undermined by the resignation of the Chairman of the Electoral Advisory Committee (EAC), and by the failure of the EAC to appoint a new Director of Elections. Demands for constitutional and electoral reform continued, and the JLP repeatedly accused the Government of seeking to delay progress towards any such reforms. Proposals drafted in late 1994 recommended the establishment of a permanent electoral commission to supervise elections, the publication of a revised register of voters every six months, and rules governing political campaigning and the nomination of candidates. An electronic voter registration system was installed in 1996 and new electoral rolls were completed in late 1997.

Industrial relations deteriorated in 1994, and there was further industrial unrest in 1995, as workers in both the public and private sectors argued for large pay increases to compensate for high rates of inflation. Meanwhile, the country's poor economic performance (particularly its high inflation rate and increasing trade deficit) and an increase in violent crime in Kingston compounded widespread dissatisfaction with the Government.

In early 1995 widespread dissatisfaction with the leadership of Edward Seaga of the JLP was reported among party members. However, Seaga survived an attempt to remove him as leader of the party in March, and in September the party leadership dismissed the main critics of Seaga as prospective parliamentary candidates for the JLP. In October Bruce Golding, who had resigned as Chairman of the JLP in February after disagreements with Seaga, announced the formation of a political party, the National Democratic Movement (NDM). The NDM, which aimed to achieve constitutional reform, including the introduction of an elected, executive president, gathered support from former members of both the JLP and the PNP.

In an effort to stabilize the economy, and, in particular, to address the problem of continuing industrial unrest, in 1996 the Government sought the agreement of a 'social contract' with trade unions and the private sector. In return for a commitment to increase its efforts to reduce inflation, the Government hoped to secure an undertaking from the labour organizations to moderate their wage demands. In July the Government implemented a 60% increase in the minimum wage. However, efforts to establish a 'social contract' continued to be frustrated during 1997 owing to trade union intransigence concerning demands for salary increases.

A general election was held in December 1997, at which the PNP won 56% of the votes cast and 50 of the 60 seats in the House of Representatives. The JLP obtained 39% of the votes and secured 10 seats, but the NDM, which won 5% of the votes, failed to gain parliamentary representation. It was estimated that 67% of the electorate participated. Patterson, who was subsequently sworn in as Prime Minister for a third consecutive term, appointed a new Cabinet in January 1998 and announced plans for Jamaica to become a republic within five years.

Local elections, which had been repeatedly postponed since 1993 following allegations of electoral malpractice, finally took place in September 1998. The PDP secured control of all 13 local councils, one of which had previously been controlled by the JLP. The NDM, which had called for the introduction of further electoral reforms in order to prevent procedural abuses, did not contest the elections, while Seaga resigned from the JLP leadership for three months in protest at the party's decision to contest the elections; Seaga opposed the decision on the grounds of possible electoral malpractice.

In 1998 and 1999 there were many public protests against police actions and the deepening economic crisis, several of which resulted in riots. There was further unrest in April 1999 following the announcement made in the 1999/2000 budget proposals of a significant increase in the price of diesel. The JLP and NDM, while initially helping to organize the protests, dissociated themselves from the subsequent violence, in which eight people were killed and many businesses were set alight or looted. The Government later agreed to reduce the proposed increase. In July the authorities announced that army personnel were to be deployed on patrols in greater Kingston in an attempt to combat the high incidence of criminal activity, the majority of which was reportedly related to drugs-trafficking. In October the British Government announced that it would contribute £2.9m. in grant assistance towards a programme to reform and modernize the Jamaican police force. In early September 2000 the Jamaican Government announced the establishment of a specialized police unit to combat organized crime. In October 2000 an investigation was initiated in response to widespread allegations of corruption in the police force, which included involvement in drugs-trafficking and the illicit recording of ministerial telephone conversations.

In July 1999 the JLP's central executive voted to suspend the party's deputy leader, Mike Henry. Henry, who was replaced by Dwight Nelson, had been accused of publicly criticizing Seaga earlier in the year. In November a recently established pressure group, Citizens for Civil Society (CCS), organized a demonstration to protest at what it termed Seaga's 'ineffective' leadership of the opposition and to demand his resignation. In the same month the CCS staged a protest march to demand the dismissal of the Minister of National Security and Justice, Keith (K. D.) Knight, whom the CCS held responsible for the country's

high crime rate, and that of the Minister of Finance and Planning, Dr Omar Davies, whom the CCS accused of mishandling the economy.

Despite the measures implemented by the Government in the previous year, confrontations between the police and various sectors of the community continued in 2001. In March the killing of seven young men in the Kingston suburb of Braeton during a police raid provoked accusations of excessive brutality by the police force. The human rights organization Amnesty International claimed that the Jamaican police force had the one of the highest records for the execution of its own citizens in the world. In 2000 the police had shot dead 140 suspected criminals. Furthermore, in July conflict broke out between police and rival PNP and JLP factions in Kingston, reportedly caused by an exchange of gunfire between police and a group of civilians during a weapons patrol. Following three days of fighting, in which 25 people were reported to have been killed, units of the Jamaica Defence Force were deployed to restore order. Seaga alleged that the violence had been deliberately instigated by the PNP in suburbs where the JLP had influence, in an attempt to damage the credibility of his party.

A Commission of Inquiry into the July disturbances opened in September 2001, chaired by a Canadian former chief justice, Julius Alexander Isaac. The Commission was to investigate the conduct of the security forces during the unrest and to consider evidence of criminal activity in the area in the months preceding the violence, specifically the significance of drugs- and weapons-trafficking. The Commission was also to make proposals on ways of preventing further civil unrest. Seaga and the JLP's team of lawyers refused to co-operate with the Commission of Inquiry on several occasions. Meanwhile, the sporadic outbreaks of violence in the Kingston suburbs continued: in October 2001 the Government was forced to deploy army, air and coast-guard units to suppress unrest; and in January 2002 seven people were shot dead by as many as 30 gunmen in a suburb known to be a traditional stronghold of the PNP, leading to accusations that the killings were politically motivated. In July 2002 the Commission of Inquiry cleared the security forces of any misconduct, concluding that there was no evidence to suggest that either soldiers or police had used excessive brutality to quell the unrest.

The social unrest and the perceived decline in popularity of the PNP prompted the Prime Minister to reorganize the Government in October 2001. K. D. Knight, Minister of National Security and Justice for the previous 13 years, was appointed Minister of Foreign Affairs and Foreign Trade. The previous Minister of Foreign Affairs, Paul Robertson, had resigned in order to co-ordinate the PNP's election campaign. Dr Peter Phillips, hitherto Minister of Transportation and Works, was appointed Minister of National Security and given the task of thoroughly reviewing the country's security systems. One of Phillips' first acts as Minister of National Security was to propose legislation that would give the police the power to intercept the telephone calls of individuals thought to be involved in the illegal trafficking of drugs and weapons. The legislation was approved by Parliament in late January 2002. Other proposed measures to reduce crime included the extension of the death penalty to crimes that involved drugs-trafficking.

In October 2001 record levels of torrential rain and high winds caused by 'Hurricane Michelle' caused severe damage, estimated at US $30m., to eastern Jamaica. The Government subsequently announced a relief programme worth US $23.9m. for the region. In February 2002, in an attempt to improve the transparency of the financial sector, the Government amended the 1964 Money Laundering Act to include money transfer and remittance companies in the clause relating to financial institutions. Henceforth, financial institutions would be required to report all suspicious transactions exceeding US $50,000.

In May 2002 the Minister of Water and Housing, Karl Blythe, was forced to resign following the results of an inquiry into his ministry's land redistribution programme, which had revealed poor budget management, fraud and cronyism. Similar accusations of mismanagement had been directed at Ministry of Industry, Commerce and Technology in March, although the minister, Philip Paulwell, retained his post.

Parliament was dissolved in September 2002, in advance of legislative elections scheduled for 16 October. Although the two main parties vowed to work together to halt the rise in violence, some 11 murders were committed during the months preceding the ballot. The PNP was re-elected for a fourth consecutive term, receiving 52.2% of votes cast, although its majority in the House of Representatives was reduced, by 14 seats, to 34. The JLP won the remaining 26 seats, with 47.2% of the votes cast. The rate of participation by voters was, at some, 51.2%, was particularly low. Voting was deemed to have been fair and democratic by an international delegation, led by former US President Jimmy Carter, which oversaw the process.

At his inauguration, on 23 October 2002, Patterson became the first Jamaican Prime Minister to swear allegiance to the people and Constitution of Jamaica, rather than to the British monarch, in accordance with new legislation introduced in August. He subsequently formed a new Cabinet, retaining most of the members of the previous administration. At a subsequent meeting with Patterson Seaga outlined a number of proposals for reform, including the appointment of an independent Governor-General for Jamaica and a restructuring of the police force.

In December 2002 the armed forces and police began a joint offensive on crime. The Government also revived a previously debated proposal to extend capital punishment to drugs-related crimes and to replace the Privy Council in London with a Caribbean Court of Justice (CCJ, see below) as the final court of appeal, thereby removing the Privy Council's ability to commute death sentences to life imprisonment. More than 1,000 murders were reported in 2002 and extended use of capital punishment gained increasing popular support. Some units of the police force and human rights organizations, however, demanded the dismissal of Renato Adams, the head of the Crime Management Unit (CMU) amid allegations of human rights abuses by his staff. The CMU had been established in 2000 in response to the rising rate of violent crime; however, it was repeatedly criticized for its excessive use of force. In June 2003, following the shooting of four people during a police raid, Adams was suspended and the CMU disbanded and replaced by an Organised Crime Investigation Division. Nevertheless, the crime rate continued to increase. In 2003 the number of murders totalled 975, and in 2004 the rate reached a record 1,445 homicides; this rise was largely attributed to gang-related conflicts.

Local elections were held on 19 June 2003. The ruling PNP performed badly, losing control of 12 of the 13 parish councils (including Kingston and St Andrew) to the JLP. The results were seen as an indication of the electorate's growing dissatisfaction with the Government, particularly its economic management.

In October 2003 the police force was further criticized after two elderly men were accidentally shot during a confrontation between police and an armed gang. The killings prompted a protest, involving some 2,000 people, against alleged police and army tactics. In the same month a report on alleged extra-judicial executions by the Jamaican police force was published by the UN Special Rapporteur, Asma Jahangir. The report condemned the Government and state security forces for the misuse of force and for failing properly to investigate those accused of extra-judicial executions. In its 2004 annual report, Amnesty International asserted that at least 114 people had been killed by police in Jamaica in 2003, many in circumstances suggesting extra-judicial executions. The degree of impunity enjoyed by the police was highlighted by the dismissal of a case in early 2004 against an officer charged with killing a 13-year-old girl in April 2000, after evidence for the prosecution went missing. In mid-2004 the Prime Minister announced the launch of a National Investigative Authority to investigation allegations against the police. In April 2004 Adams and five former colleagues at the CMU were charged with murder in connection with the deaths of the seven men in Kingston in March 2001; their trial began in January 2005.

In July 2004 the Privy Council had abolished Jamaica's mandatory death sentence for convicted murderers. Legislative amendments to this effect were approved by the Senate in November. However, at the same time, amendments were also passed increasing the minimum period a convicted murderer must serve before being granted parole from seven to 20 years.

On 16 September 2004 'Hurricane Ivan' caused 18 deaths and significant loss of crops. However, overall damage was less than anticipated; the important tourism and bauxite sectors escaped relatively unscathed. Reconstruction costs were estimated at J $5,200m.

On 19 January 2005, after more than 30 years in the post, Seaga retired as leader of the JLP and as a member of Parliament. He was succeeded as party leader in the following month by Orrett Bruce Golding, following a bitterly fought leadership contest with Pearnel Charles. In 2005 a contest was also under way to succeed Patterson as leader of the PNP in September. The principal contenders to lead the PNP into the next general election, due by 2007, were Minister of National Security Peter Phillips, local government minister Portia Simpson-Miller, Minister of Finance and Planning Omar Davies, Robert Pickersgill, the PNP Chairman and Minister of Transport and Works, and Karl Blythe, first Vice-President of the PNP.

A decision in November 1993 by the Judicial Committee of the Privy Council in the United Kingdom (in its capacity as the final court of appeal for the Jamaican legal system) to commute to life imprisonment the death sentences imposed on two Jamaicans in 1979, in recognition of their prolonged suffering in anticipation of execution, threw doubt on the legal position of many similarly sentenced prisoners in Jamaica and other Caribbean Commonwealth countries, given the recommendation of the Judicial Committee that all executions not effected within five years of sentencing should be subject to review, with a recommendation for commutation. In January 1998 Jamaica withdrew from a UN treaty that had hitherto allowed prisoners sentenced to death to appeal for a review by the UN Commission on Human Rights and later that year it also withdrew from the Inter-American Court of Human Rights (see p. 320) of the Organization of American States. In February 2001, following legislative approval in November 2000, Patterson and 10 other Caribbean leaders signed an agreement to establish a CCJ, to be based in Trinidad and Tobago. The Court was to replace the Privy Council as the final court of appeal, and would allow for the executions of convicted criminals. The JLP opposed the move, and demanded that a referendum be held on the issue. Despite opposition from the JLP and from the Jamaica Bar Association, in late July 2004 Parliament approved legislation replacing the Privy Council with the CCJ as Jamaica's final court of appeal. The Jamaican Bar Association and opposition groupings appealed to the Privy Council itself that the legislation should be annuled because it had been passed without the approval of the electorate in a referendum. In February 2005 the Privy Council upheld the appeal. In response, the Government proposed inaugurating the CCJ to have jurisdiction only in matters relating to the Caribbean Community and Common Market (CARICOM, see p. 172).

Relations between Jamaica and the USA have been hampered by persistent demands by the USA for the eradication of Jamaica's marijuana crop. In May 1997, after months of negotiation, the two countries concluded a counter-narcotics agreement, permitting officials of the US Drug Enforcement Agency to pursue suspected drugs-traffickers in Jamaican airspace and territorial waters. In August 1999 a Jamaican delegation visited the USA to discuss the prospect of increasing US assistance in measures aimed at combating crime.

Government

The Head of State is the British monarch, who is represented locally by the Governor-General, who is appointed on the recommendation of the Prime Minister in consultation with the Leader of the Opposition. The Governor-General acts, in almost all matters, on the advice of the Cabinet.

Legislative power is vested in the bicameral Parliament: the Senate, with 21 appointed members, and the House of Representatives, with 60 elected members. Thirteen members of the Senate are appointed by the Governor-General on the advice of the Prime Minister and eight on the advice of the Leader of the Opposition. Members of the House are elected by universal adult suffrage for five years (subject to dissolution). Executive power lies with the Cabinet. The Prime Minister is appointed from the House of Representatives by the Governor-General, and is the leader of the party that holds the majority of seats in the House of Representatives. The Cabinet is responsible to Parliament. Jamaica is divided into 13 parishes.

Defence

In August 2004 the Jamaica Defence Force consisted of 2,830 men on active service, including an army of 2,500, a coastguard of 190 and an air wing of 140 men. There are reserves of some 953. The defence budget for 2004 was estimated at J $3,000m.

Economic Affairs

In 2003, according to estimates by the World Bank, Jamaica's gross national income (GNI), measured at average 2001–03 prices, was US $7,086.9m., equivalent to US $2,760 per head (or US $3,790 per head on an international purchasing-power parity basis). During 1990–2003, it was estimated, the population increased at an average rate of 0.8% per year, while gross domestic product (GDP) per head was estimated to have increased, in real terms, by an average of 0.2% per year. Overall GDP increased, in real terms, at an average annual rate of 0.9% in 1990–2003; growth was 1.1% in 2002 and 2.3% in 2003.

Agriculture (including forestry and fishing) contributed an estimated 5.3% of GDP in 2003, and engaged an estimated 19.4% of the economically active population in 2002. The principal cash crops are sugar cane (sugar accounted for an estimated 5.0% of total export earnings in 2002), bananas, coffee, citrus fruit and cocoa. The cultivation of vegetables, fruit and rice is being encouraged, in an attempt to reduce imports and diversify agricultural exports. According to the World Bank, agricultural GDP increased at an average annual rate of 0.4% in 1990–2003; the sector decreased by 7.0% in 2002, but increased by 2.1% in 2003.

Industry (including mining, manufacturing, public utilities and construction) contributed an estimated 30.5% of GDP in 2003 and engaged an estimated 17.5% of the economically active population in 2002. According to the World Bank, industrial GDP declined at an average rate of 0.3% per year in 1990–2003; however, the sector grew by 1.4% in 2002 and by 3.2% in 2003.

Mining and quarrying contributed an estimated 4.4% of GDP in 2003, but engaged only 0.4% of the active labour force in the previous year. Mining is the principal productive sector of the economy, and in 2002 bauxite and its derivative, alumina (aluminium oxide), accounted for an estimated 65.6% of total export earnings. Bauxite, of which Jamaica is one of the world's leading producers, is the major mineral mined, but there are also reserves of marble, gypsum, limestone, silica and clay. The Alumina Partners of Jamaica (of which the US-owned Kaiser Aluminium was the principal owner) re-opened its bauxite refinery in late 2000, and in 2004 the state-owned Jamalco (Alcoa Minerals of Jamaica, Inc) invested US $115m. in its bauxite plant to increase capacity by 25% by 2007. The mining of gold began in March 2001; however, in December 2003 the depletion of reserves, as well as industrial unrest, resulted in the temporary closure of Jamaica's only gold mine.

Manufacturing contributed an estimated 12.8% of GDP in 2003 and engaged some 6.9% of the active labour force in 2002. Much of the activity in the sector is dependent upon the processing of sugar and bauxite. The export of garments, mainly to the USA, became increasingly important in the late 20th century, providing an estimated 11.4% of total value of export earnings in 2000. According to the World Bank, manufacturing GDP decreased at an average annual rate of 1.7% during 1990–2003; the sector decreased by 0.7% in 2002 and by a further estimated 0.1% in 2003.

Energy is derived almost completely from imported hydrocarbon fuels. Most of Jamaica's petroleum requirements are fulfilled by imports from Venezuela and Mexico. In 2003 imports of mineral fuels and lubricants accounted for 22.6% of the total value of merchandise imports. In 2002 the Government announced plans to replace fuel oil as the country's main source of fuel with liquified natural gas (LNG) by 2005/06. In November 2004 the Government signed a memorandum of understanding with Trinidad and Tobago for the annual purchase of 1.1m. metric tons of LNG over a period of 20 years. In January 2004 the state-owned Petroleum Corporation of Jamaica announced plans to develop the its wind-generated power capacity to 21 MW per year.

The services sector contributed an estimated 64.3% of GDP in 2003 and engaged some 62.8% of the active labour force in 2002. The principal earner of foreign exchange is tourism. Visitor arrivals (excluding cruise-ship passengers) stood at an estimated 1.4m. in 2002. The largest proportion of tourists is from the USA (70.4% in 2004). Expenditure by tourists totalled an estimated US $1,209m. in 2002. According to the World Bank, the GDP of the services sector increased at an average annual rate of 1.8% in 1990–2003; the sector increased by 1.9% in 2002 and by 1.5% in 2003.

In 2003 Jamaica recorded a visible trade deficit of US $1,943.8m., and there was a deficit of US $761.4m. on the current account of the balance of payments. In 2003 the principal source of imports (44.4%) was the USA. Other major suppliers in that year were Trinidad and Tobago, Japan and Venezuela. In that year the USA was also the principal market for exports (28.8%), while the United Kingdom, Canada and Norway were among other important purchasers. The principal

exports in 2003 were bauxite and alumina. Foods, including sugar and bananas, were also important export commodities, as well as garments. The principal imports in 2003 were machinery and transport equipment, and mineral fuels and lubricants. The illegal production of hemp (marijuana) is also believed to generate significant export revenue.

In the financial year ending 31 March 2001 Jamaica's overall budget deficit was estimated at J $9,282m., equivalent to 2.6% of GDP. Total external debt in 2002 was US $5,477m., of which US $4,678m. was long-term public debt. In that year the cost of debt-servicing was equivalent to 18.4% of earnings from exports of goods and services. The average annual rate of inflation was 20.7% in 1990–2003; consumer prices rose by 7.1% in 2002 and by 10.3% in 2003. Some 12.8% of the labour force were unemployed in 2003/04.

Jamaica is a founding member of the Caribbean Community and Common Market (CARICOM, see p. 172) and of the Inter-American Development Bank (IDB, see p. 268).

The Jamaican economy was impeded in recent years by persistent fiscal imbalances and a high rate of inflation. Bauxite and alumina production rose significantly in the 1990s, although weak international market prices meant that the sector's improved productivity did not create increased revenue. The sugar and coffee industries were both affected by aberrant climatic conditions and a lack of investment. Despite the adverse conditions, the Government's stringent monetary policy succeeded in reducing the annual rate of increase in consumer prices from 31% in 1995/96 to 10.3% in 2003. However, GDP grew by just 1.1% in 2002 and by 2.3% in 2003. The main reasons for the lack of significant growth were thought to be the continuing social unrest, the reduction in the number of tourists to the island following the suicide attacks in the USA in September 2001, and the damage to crops and infrastructure caused by 'Hurricane Michelle' in the following month. Furthermore, increased expenditure on national security and a growing problem of tax evasion contributed to a widening of the fiscal deficit, to 10.8% of GDP, in 2002/03. In an attempt to reduce the budget deficit, in 2003 the Government imposed a 'freeze' on public-sector employment, which accounted for one-third of government expenditure. According to preliminary estimates for 2003/04, the deficit was reduced to 8.7% of GDP. In 2003 tourist arrivals recovered to pre-2001 levels, but high levels of violent crime remained a deterrent to growth in the industry. In November 2003 a 10-year development plan for the tourism sector was implemented and strong sectoral growth continued in 2004 despite the impact of 'Hurricane Ivan'. However, the agricultural sector was affected by the hurricane, which destroyed some 60% of the coffee crop. Furthermore, a steep rise in international fuel prices contributed to an estimated annual inflation rate of 16.8% in the year as a whole. According to preliminary estimates, real GDP growth in 2004 was 2.0%. Following the hurricane, the Government's economic objectives for 2004/05 were subsequently revised; the forecast for GDP growth was reduced from 2.5% to 1.5%, and the budget deficit target was increased from 3.5% to 4.6% of GDP. None the less, the Minister of Finance and Planning, Omar Davies, maintained that the Government would return a balanced budget by 2006.

Education

Primary education is compulsory in certain districts, and free education is ensured. The education system (which begins at six years of age) consists of a primary cycle of six years, followed by two secondary cycles of three and four years, respectively. In 2002 enrolment at primary schools included 95.2% of children in the relevant age-group (males 95.1%; females 95.3%), while enrolment at secondary schools was equivalent to only 74.9% of children in the appropriate age-group (males 73.5%; females 76.4%). Higher education is provided by technical colleges and by the University of the West Indies, which has five faculties situated at its Mona campus in Kingston. Government expenditure on education during the financial year 2000/01 was estimated to be some J $21,628m., representing 16.0% of total budgetary expenditure.

Public Holidays

2005: 1 January (New Year's Day), 9 February (Ash Wednesday), 25 March (Good Friday), 28 March (Easter Monday), 23 May (Labour Day), 1 August (Emancipation Day), 6 August (Independence Day), 17 October (National Heroes Day), 25 December (Christmas Day), 26 December (Boxing Day).

2006: 1 January (New Year's Day), 1 March (Ash Wednesday), 14 April (Good Friday), 17 April (Easter Monday), 23 May (Labour Day), 1 August (Emancipation Day), 6 August (Inde-

pendence Day), 16 October (National Heroes' Day), 25 December (Christmas Day), 26 December (Boxing Day).

Weights and Measures

Both the imperial and the metric systems are in use.

Statistical Survey

Sources (unless otherwise stated): Statistical Institute of Jamaica, 7 Cecelio Ave, Kingston 10, Jamaica; tel. 926-5311; fax 926-1138; e-mail info@statinja .com; internet www.statinja.com; Jamaica Information Service, 58a Half Way Tree Rd, POB 2222, Kingston 10, Jamaica; tel. 926-3740; fax 926-6715; e-mail jis@jis.gov.jm; internet www.jis.gov.jm; Bank of Jamaica, Nethersole Pl., POB 621, Kingston, Jamaica; tel. 922-0752; fax 922-0854; e-mail info@boj .org.jm; internet www.boj.org.jm.

Area and Population

AREA, POPULATION AND DENSITY

Area (sq km)	10,991*
Population (census results)	
7 April 1991	2,314,479
10 September 2001	
Males	1,283,547
Females	1,324,085
Total	2,607,632
Population (official estimates at 31 December)	
2001	2,612,500
2002	2,624,700
2003	2,641,600
Density (per sq km) at 31 December 2003	240.3

* 4,243.6 sq miles.

PARISHES

	Area (sq km)	Population (census of 2001)	Parish capitals (with population at 1991 census)
Kingston . .	22 ⎫	651,880	Kingston M.A. (587,798)
St Andrew . .	431 ⎭		
St Thomas . .	743	91,604	Morant Bay (9,185)
Portland . .	814	80,205	Port Antonio (13,246)
St Mary . .	611	111,466	Port Maria (7,651)
St Ann . . .	1,213	166,762	St Ann's Bay (10,518)
Trelawny . .	875	73,066	Falmouth (7,245)
St James . .	595	175,127	Montego Bay (83,446)
Hanover . . .	450	67,037	Lucea (6,002)
Westmoreland .	807	138,947	Savanna La Mar (16,553)
St Elizabeth .	1,212	146,404	Black River (3,675)
Manchester . .	830	185,801	Mandeville (39,430)
Clarendon . .	1,196	237,024	May Pen (46,785)
St Catherine .	1,192	482,308	Spanish Town (92,383)
Total . . .	10,991	2,607,632	—

PRINCIPAL TOWNS

(population at census of 7 April 1991)

Kingston (capital) .	587,798		Montego Bay . . .	83,446
Spanish Town . .	92,383		May Pen . . .	46,785
Portmore	90,138		Mandeville . . .	39,430

Source: Thomas Brinkhoff, *City Population* (internet www.citypopulation.de).

Mid-2003 (UN estimate, incl. suburbs): Kingston 575,105 (Source: UN, *World Urbanization Prospects: The 2003 Revision*).

BIRTHS, MARRIAGES AND DEATHS*

	Registered live births		Registered marriages		Registered deaths	
	Number	Rate (per 1,000)	Number	Rate (per 1,000)	Number	Rate (per 1,000)
1992	56,276	23.5	13,042	5.6	13,225	5.5
1993	58,627	24.0	14,352	5.9	13,927	5.7
1994	57,404	23.2	15,171	6.1	13,503	5.5
1995	57,607	23.0	16,515	6.6	12,776	5.1
1996	59,194	23.4	19,170	7.6	16,926	6.7
1997	59,385	23.3	21,502	8.4	15,087	5.9
1998	56,937	22.1	24,131	9.4	15,967	6.2
1999	56,911	22.0	26,871	10.4	17,353	6.7

2000: Birth rate 20.9 per 1,000; Death rate 6.3 per 1,000.

2001: Birth rate 20.6 per 1,000; Death rate 6.2 per 1,000.

2002: Birth rate 20.0 per 1,000; Death rate 6.5 per 1,000.

2003: Birth rate 19.3 per 1,000; Death rate 6.4 per 1,000.

* Data are tabulated by year of registration rather than by year of occurrence, and 1992–99 figures have not been revised to take account of 2001 census results.

Source: partly UN, *Demographic Yearbook*.

Expectation of life (WHO estimates, years at birth): 72.8 (males 71.1; females 74.6) in 2002 (Source: WHO, *World Health Report*.

ECONOMICALLY ACTIVE POPULATION

('000 persons aged 14 years and over)

	2000	2001	2002
Agriculture, forestry and fishing .	194.5	195.2	182.4
Mining and quarrying	4.7	5.2	3.9
Manufacturing	65.8	69.1	64.6
Electricity, gas and water . . .	5.6	6.4	6.3
Construction	82.4	80.5	90.4
Trade, restaurants and hotels . .	204.8	214.7	209.0
Transport, storage and communications	57.6	60.6	62.9
Financing, insurance, real estate and business services . . .	55.9	46.4	60.4
Community, social and personal services	261.4	261.9	259.1
Activities not adequately defined .	2.9	2.3	3.3
Total employed	935.6	942.3	942.3
Males	552.5	556.6	546.3
Females	383.1	385.7	396.0

Source: ILO.

Health and Welfare

KEY INDICATORS

Total fertility rate (children per woman, 2002)	2.4
Under-5 mortality rate (per 1,000 live births, 2003) . . .	20
HIV/AIDS (% of persons aged 15–49, 2003)	1.2
Physicians (per 1,000 head, 1996)	1.40
Hospital beds (per 1,000 head, 1996)	2.12
Health expenditure (2001): US $ per head (PPP)	253
Health expenditure (2001): % of GDP	6.8
Health expenditure (2001): public (% of total)	42.1
Access to water (% of persons, 2002)	93
Access to sanitation (% of persons, 2002)	80
Human Development Index (2002): ranking	79
Human Development Index (2002): value	0.764

For sources and definitions, see explanatory note on p. vi.

Agriculture

PRINCIPAL CROPS
('000 metric tons)

	2001	2002	2003
Sweet potatoes	25	20	25
Yams	158	148	151
Other roots and tubers	42	40*	42*
Sugar cane	2,231	1,966	1,776
Coconuts	170*	170*	170
Cabbages	22	19	29
Tomatoes	24	19	19*
Pumpkins, squash and gourds . .	36	36*	36*
Carrots	20	19	19*
Other vegetables (incl. melons)* .	94	92	93
Bananas*	130	130	130
Plantains	25	21	20
Oranges*	140	140	140
Lemons and limes*	24	24	24
Grapefruit and pomelos* . . .	42	42	42
Pineapples	20	21	21*
Other fruit*	90	90	90
Pimento, allspice*	10	10	10

* FAO estimate(s).

Source: FAO.

LIVESTOCK
(FAO estimates, '000 head, year ending September)

	2001	2002	2003
Horses	4	4	4
Mules	10	10	10
Asses	23	23	23
Cattle	400	400	430
Pigs	180	150	180
Sheep	1	1	1
Goats	440	440	440
Poultry	13,000	13,000	11,000

Source: FAO.

LIVESTOCK PRODUCTS
('000 metric tons)

	2001	2002	2003
Beef and veal	13.4	14.3	14.5*
Goat meat*	1.7	1.6	1.6
Pig meat	6.4	5.5	5.5*
Poultry meat	83.0†	83.8	81.3
Cows' milk*	28.5	28.5	28.5
Hen eggs	7.9*	7.9*	5.8
Honey*	1	1	1
Cattle hides*	1.3	1.4	1.4

* FAO estimate(s).
† Unofficial figure.

Source: FAO.

Forestry

ROUNDWOOD REMOVALS
(FAO estimates, '000 cubic metres, excl. bark)

	2001	2002	2003
Sawlogs, veneer logs and logs for			
sleepers	132	132	132
Other industrial wood	150	150	150
Fuel wood	591	584	577
Total	874	867	860

Source: FAO.

SAWNWOOD PRODUCTION
('000 cubic metres, incl. railway sleepers)

	1996	1997	1998
Coniferous (softwood) . . .	3	3	3
Broadleaved (hardwood) . . .	61	62	63
Total	64	65	66

1999–2003: Annual production as in 1998 (FAO estimates).

Source: FAO.

Fishing

('000 metric tons, live weight)

	2000	2001*	2002
Capture	5.7	5.7	5.7*
Marine fishes	4.6	4.7	4.7*
Caribbean spiny lobster . . .	0.5	0.5	0.5*
Aquaculture	4.5	4.5	6.2
Nile tilapia	4.5	4.5	6.0
Total catch*	10.2	10.2	11.8

* FAO estimate(s).

Source: FAO.

Mining

('000 metric tons)

	2001	2002	2003
Bauxite*	12,139	13,139	13,443
Alumina	3,542	3,630	3,844
Crude gypsum	320	165	162
Salt	19.1	19.0†	n.a.

* Dried equivalent of crude ore.
† Estimate.

Source: partly US Geological Survey.

Industry

SELECTED PRODUCTS

	2001	2002	2003
Sugar (metric tons)	205,128	174,949	153,542
Molasses (metric tons)	86,983	79,653	72,631
Rum ('000 litres)	23,705	24,727	25,519
Beer and stout ('000 litres) . . .	78,566	77,551	75,189
Fuel oil ('000 litres)	576,736	671,826	511,900
Gasoline (petrol) ('000 litres) . .	181,045	271,215	130,229
Kerosene, turbo and jet fuel ('000			
litres)	94,105	122,488	81,902
Auto diesel oil ('000 litres) . . .	231,451	302,497	172,340
Cement ('000 metric tons) . . .	596,248	621,831	607,682
Concrete ('000 cu metres) . . .	86,820	140,314	176,815

Electrical energy (million kWh): 6,609 in 1999; 6,631 in 2000 (Source: UN, *Industrial Commodity Statistics Yearbook*).

Finance

CURRENCY AND EXCHANGE RATES

Monetary Units
100 cents = 1 Jamaican dollar (J $).

Sterling, US Dollar and Euro Equivalents (31 December 2004)
£1 sterling = J $118.685;
US $1 = J $61.450;
€1 = J $83.701;
J $1,000 = £8.43 = US $16.27 = €11.95.

Average Exchange Rate (J $ per US $)
2002   48.416
2003   57.741
2004   61.197

BUDGET*
(J $ million, year ending 31 March)

Revenue†	1999	2000	2001
Tax revenue	74,634	84,659	90,985
Taxes on income, profits and capital gains	32,185	35,456	35,495
Individual	16,681	16,386	19,750
Corporate	9,051	8,825	6,680
Domestic taxes on goods and services	29,451	34,285	38,561
General sales, turnover or value-added taxes	26,392	30,717	34,625
Taxes on international trade	6,919	7,503	8,501
Other current revenue	22,777	29,260	27,423
Entrepreneurial and property income	8,626	9,875	9,954
Administrative fees, non-industrial and incidental sales	6,606	8,260	9,365
Fines and forfeits	2,590	2,891	2,808
Capital revenue	601	5,063	4,595
Total	98,012	118,982	123,004

Expenditure	1999	2000	2001
General public services	11,164	26,992	13,698
Defence	1,802	1,896	2,212
Public order and safety	8,143	8,677	10,693
Education	17,470	4,877	21,628
Health	7,048	3,743	8,222
Social security and welfare	1,182	1,697	1,295
Housing and community amenities	2,565	2,572	2,741
Recreational, cultural and religious affairs and services	167	260	276
Economic affairs and services	10,689	11,969	11,258
Agriculture, forestry, fishing and hunting	2,327	2,048	2,291
Transport and communications	3,383	3,576	3,577
Other purposes	52,278	60,245	63,500
Total expenditure	112,506	122,929	135,523
Current‡	97,945	105,461	120,192
Capital	14,561	17,468	15,331

* Figures refer to consolidated accounts of the central Government.
† Excluding grants received (J $ million): 797 in 1999; 3,236 in 2001.
‡ Including interest payments (J $ million): 41,911 in 1999; 43,335 in 2000; 51,550 in 2001.

Source: IMF, *Government Finance Statistics Yearbook*.

INTERNATIONAL RESERVES
(US $ million, at 31 December)

	2001	2002	2003
IMF special drawing rights	1.5	0.9	0.1
Foreign exchange	1,899.0	1,644.2	1,194.8
Total	1,900.5	1,645.1	1,194.9

Source: IMF, *International Financial Statistics*.

MONEY SUPPLY
(J $ million at 31 December)

	2001	2002	2003
Currency outside banks	18,783	20,399	23,186
Demand deposits at commercial banks	35,359	39,020	39,871
Total money	54,142	59,419	63,057

Source: IMF, *International Financial Statistics*.

COST OF LIVING
(Consumer Price Index; base: 2000 = 100)

	2001	2002	2003
Food (incl. beverages)	103.4	109.7	120.2
Fuel and power	110.7	114.9	129.9
Clothing and footwear	104.2	107.2	112.9
Rent	129.9	145.5	157.1
All items (incl. others)	107.0	114.6	126.4

Source: ILO.

NATIONAL ACCOUNTS
(J $ million at current prices)

Expenditure on the Gross Domestic Product

	2001	2002	2003
Government final consumption expenditure	59,146	66,734	71,015
Private final consumption expenditure	266,035	293,869	345,412
Increase in stocks	408	664	769
Gross fixed capital formation	108,323	129,497	140,427
Total domestic expenditure	433,913	490,764	557,623
Exports of goods and services	144,614	147,948	191,473
Less Imports of goods and services	205,484	229,947	278,656
GDP in purchasers' values	373,042	408,765	470,440
GDP at constant 1996 prices	227,070	229,536	234,730

Source: IMF, *International Financial Statistics*.

Gross Domestic Product by Economic Activity

	2001	2002	2003
Agriculture, forestry and fishing	22,892.1	22,678.9	24,250.5
Mining and quarrying	14,820.1	15,689.5	20,153.6
Manufacturing	48,250.0	51,279.2	59,105.4
Electricity and water	12,489.9	13,577.6	17,191.9
Construction	35,013.7	38,590.2	43,766.0
Wholesale and retail trade	72,426.8	78,605.2	88,496.3
Transport, storage and communication	43,408.2	51,093.7	56,539.3
Finance and insurance services	23,275.6	22,177.2	35,501.7
Real estate and business services	21,529.6	24,292.0	27,200.3
Producers of government services	43,694.8	49,593.3	54,643.4
Household and private non-profit services	2,100.2	2,261.5	2,326.3
Other services	24,936.5	26,510.5	31,289.2
Sub-total	364,837.4	396,348.9	460,463.9
Value-added tax	23,337.3	26,590.3	33,866.7
Less Imputed bank service charge	15,132.2	14,173.9	23,890.4
GDP in purchasers' values	373,042.6	408,765.3	470,440.2

BALANCE OF PAYMENTS
(US $ million)

	2001	2002	2003
Exports of goods f.o.b.	1,454.4	1,309.1	1,385.6
Imports of goods f.o.b.	–3,072.6	–3,179.6	–3,329.4
Trade balance	–1,618.2	–1,870.5	–1,943.8
Exports of services	1,897.0	1,912.2	2,131.6
Imports of services	–1,513.9	–1,597.5	–1,566.9
Balance on goods and services	–1,235.1	–1,555.8	–1,379.1
Other income received . . .	218.2	221.0	217.6
Other income paid	–656.0	–826.3	–789.0
Balance on goods, services and income	–1,672.9	–2,161.1	–1,950.5
Current transfers received . . .	1,090.7	1,337.9	1,523.5
Current transfers paid	–176.6	–251.0	–334.4
Current balance	–758.8	–1,074.2	–761.4
Capital account (net)	–22.3	–16.9	0.1
Direct investment abroad . .	–89.0	–73.9	–116.3
Direct investment from abroad .	613.9	481.1	720.7
Portfolio investment assets . .	–39.3	–351.3	–1,105.2
Portfolio investment liabilities .	69.7	155.8	819.6
Other investment assets . . .	–215.5	–164.9	–308.8
Other investment liabilities . .	1,320.7	859.6	302.1
Net errors and omissions . . .	–14.4	–55.1	14.1
Overall balance	865.0	–239.8	–435.1

Source: IMF, *International Financial Statistics*.

External Trade

PRINCIPAL COMMODITIES
(US $ million)

Imports c.i.f.	2001	2002	2003
Foods	476.8	480.1	487.4
Mineral fuels and lubricants . .	615.5	636.8	830.1
Chemicals	383.5	375.4	444.1
Manufactured goods . . .	467.0	459.5	486.4
Machinery and transport equipment	883.3	1,036.9	878.9
Misc. manufactured articles . .	394.5	399.4	384.0
Total (incl. others)	3,402.6	3,570.5	3,678.9

Exports f.o.b.	2001	2002	2003
Foods	224.9	206.3	219.6
Beverages and tobacco	48.4	56.2	53.9
Crude materials (excl. fuels) . .	742.7	716.1	785.6
Chemicals	68.5	59.4	57.7
Misc. manufactured articles . .	98.1	30.4	22.3
Total (incl. others)	1,223.1	1,117.3	1,196.0

PRINCIPAL TRADING PARTNERS
(US $ million)

Imports c.i.f.	2001	2002	2003
Canada	97.6	112.6	97.9
CARICOM*	433.0	398.6	469.3
Latin America	361.0	447.8	388.8
United Kingdom	102.5	93.1	149.6
Other European Union (EU) . .	214.3	281.5	235.2
USA	1,525.8	1,546.6	1,632.0
Total (incl. others)	3,402.6	3,570.5	3,678.9

Exports f.o.b.	2001	2002	2003
Canada	191.1	157.1	192.1
CARICOM*	50.6	48.7	50.9
Latin America	12.0	14.7	6.8
United Kingdom	157.1	134.3	153.2
Other European Union (EU) . .	202.7	213.9	205.2
Norway	91.6	93.5	44.4
USA	380.2	313.4	344.4
Total (incl. others)	1,223.1	1,117.3	1,196.0

* Caribbean Community and Common Market.

Transport

RAILWAYS
(traffic)

	1988	1989	1990
Passenger-km ('000)	36,146	37,995	n.a.
Freight ton-km ('000)	115,076	28,609	1,931

Source: Jamaica Railway Corporation.

ROAD TRAFFIC
('000 motor vehicles in use)

	1999	2000	2001
Passenger cars	140.4	129.4	129.4
Commercial vehicles . . .	56.6	57.6	65.2

Source: UN, *Statistical Yearbook*.

SHIPPING

Merchant Fleet
(registered at 31 December)

	2001	2002	2003
Number of vessels	7	11	16
Total displacement ('000 grt) . .	23.1	75.4	56.8

Source: Lloyd's Register-Fairplay, *World Fleet Statistics*.

International Sea-borne Freight Traffic
(estimates, '000 metric tons)

	1989	1990	1991
Goods loaded	7,711	8,354	8,802
Goods unloaded	5,167	5,380	5,285

Source: Port Authority of Jamaica.

CIVIL AVIATION
(traffic on scheduled services)

	1999	2000	2001
Kilometres flown (million) . . .	35	32	46
Passengers carried ('000) . . .	1,670	1,922	1,946
Passenger-km (million)	3,495	4,087	4,412
Total ton-km (million)	377	400	471

Source: UN, *Statistical Yearbook*.

Tourism

VISITOR ARRIVALS BY COUNTRY OF ORIGIN

	2002	2003	2004
Canada	89,570	87,908	105,623
Europe	173,412	211,011	241,925
USA	859,347	904,666	996,131
Total (incl. others)	1,266,366	1,350,284	1,414,786

Visitor expenditure (US $ million): 1,333 in 2000; 1,232 in 2001; 1,209 in 2002.

Sources: partly World Tourism Organization.

Communications Media

	2000	2001	2002
Television receivers ('000 in use)	500	510	n.a.
Telephones ('000 main lines in use)	429	376	367
Mobile cellular telephones ('000 subscribers)	367	700	1,400
Personal computers ('000 in use)	110*	130*	141
Internet users ('000)	60*	100	600

Radio receivers ('000 in use): 1,215 in 1997.

Facsimile machines (number in use): 1,567 in 1992†.

Daily newspapers: 3 in 1996 (circulation 158,000).

* Estimate.
† Year ending 1 April.

Sources: International Telecommunication Union; UN, *Statistical Yearbook*; UNESCO, *Statistical Yearbook*.

Education

	Institutions	Teachers	Students
Pre-primary*	1,681	4,158†	133,687†
Primary‡	—	9,512†	293,863†
Secondary§	—	10,931	235,071
Tertiary‖	1	418	8,191

* Figures for 1990/91.
† Public sector only.
‡ Figures for 1996/97.
§ Figures for 1992/93.
‖ Figures for 1995/96.

Source: UNESCO, *Statistical Yearbook*.

2002 ('000 students): Primary 332.9; Secondary 226.5; Tertiary 12.5; University 20.7 (Source: Planning Institute of Jamaica).

Adult literacy rate (UNESCO estimates): 87.6% (males 83.9%; females 91.4%) in 2002 (Source: UN Development Programme, *Human Development Report*).

Directory

The Constitution

The Constitution came into force at the independence of Jamaica on 6 August 1962. Amendments to the Constitution are enacted by Parliament, but certain entrenched provisions require ratification by a two-thirds' majority in both chambers of the legislature, and some (such as a change of the head of state) require the additional approval of a national referendum.

HEAD OF STATE

The Head of State is the British monarch, who is locally represented by a Governor-General, appointed by the British monarch, on the recommendation of the Jamaican Prime Minister in consultation with the Leader of the Opposition party.

THE LEGISLATURE

The Senate or Upper House consists of 21 Senators, of whom 13 will be appointed by the Governor-General on the advice of the Prime Minister and eight by the Governor-General on the advice of the Leader of the Opposition. (Legislation enacted in 1984 provided for eight independent Senators to be appointed, after consultations with the Prime Minister, in the eventuality of there being no Leader of the Opposition.)

The House of Representatives or Lower House consists of 60 elected members called Members of Parliament.

A person is qualified for appointment to the Senate or for election to the House of Representatives if he or she is a citizen of Jamaica or other Commonwealth country, of the age of 21 or more and has been ordinarily resident in Jamaica for the immediately preceding 12 months.

THE PRIVY COUNCIL

The Privy Council consists of six members appointed by the Governor-General after consultation with the Prime Minister, of whom at least two are persons who hold or who have held public office. The functions of the Council are to advise the Governor-General on the exercise of the Prerogative of Mercy and on appeals on disciplinary matters from the three Service Commissions.

THE EXECUTIVE

The Prime Minister is appointed from the House of Representatives by the Governor-General, and is the leader of the party that holds the majority of seats in the House of Representatives. The Leader of the party is voted in by the members of that party. The Leader of the Opposition is voted in by the members of the Opposition party.

The Cabinet consists of the Prime Minister and not fewer than 11 other ministers, not more than four of whom may sit in the Senate. The members of the Cabinet are appointed by the Governor-General on the advice of the Prime Minister.

THE JUDICATURE

The Judicature consists of a Supreme Court, a Court of Appeal and minor courts. Judicial matters, notably advice to the Governor-General on appointments, are considered by a Judicial Service Commission, the Chairman of which is the Chief Justice, members being the President of the Court of Appeal, the Chairman of the Public Service Commission and three others.

CITIZENSHIP

All persons born in Jamaica after independence automatically acquire Jamaican citizenship and there is also provision for the acquisition of citizenship by persons born outside Jamaica of Jamaican parents. Persons born in Jamaica (or persons born outside Jamaica of Jamaican parents) before independence who immediately prior to independence were citizens of the United Kingdom and colonies also automatically become citizens of Jamaica.

Appropriate provision is made which permits persons who do not automatically become citizens of Jamaica to be registered as such.

FUNDAMENTAL RIGHTS AND FREEDOMS

The Constitution includes provisions safeguarding the fundamental freedoms of the individual, irrespective of race, place of origin, political opinions, colour, creed or sex, subject only to respect for the rights and freedoms of others and for the public interest. The fundamental freedoms include the rights of life, liberty, security of the person and protection from arbitrary arrest or restriction of movement, the enjoyment of property and the protection of the law, freedom of conscience, of expression and of peaceful assembly and association, and respect for private and family life.

The Government

HEAD OF STATE

Monarch: HM Queen ELIZABETH II (succeeded to the throne 6 February 1952).

Governor-General: Sir HOWARD FELIX HANLAN COOKE (appointed 1 August 1991).

PRIVY COUNCIL OF JAMAICA

KENNETH SMITH, DONALD MILLS, DENNIS LALOR, JAMES KERR, ELSA LEO RHYNIE, HEADLEY CUNNINGHAM.

CABINET
(April 2005)

Prime Minister and Minister of Defence: PERCIVAL JAMES PATTERSON.

Minister of Finance and Planning: Dr OMAR DAVIES.

Minister of Labour and Social Security: HORACE DALLEY.

Minister of Industry and Tourism: ALOUN N'DOMBET-ASSAMBA.

Minister of Local Government, Community Development and Sport: PORTIA SIMPSON-MILLER.

Minister of National Security and Leader of Government Business in the House of Representatives: Dr PETER PHILLIPS.

Minister of Justice and Attorney-General: ARNOLD J. NICHOLSON.

Minister of Agriculture: ROGER CLARKE.

Minister of Foreign Affairs and Foreign Trade: Keith (K. D.) Knight.

Minister of Health: John Junor.

Minister of Education, Youth and Culture: Maxine Henry-Wilson.

Minister of Transport and Works: Robert Pickersgill.

Minister of Water and Housing: Donald Buchanan.

Minister of Commerce, Science and Technology: Phillip Paulwell.

Minister of Land and Environment: Dean Peart.

Minister of Information and Leader of Government Business in the Senate: Burchell Whiteman.

Minister of Development: Paul Robertson.

MINISTRIES

Office of the Governor-General: King's House, Hope Rd, Kingston 10; tel. 927-6424; fax 978-6025; e-mail kingshouse@cwjamica.com.

Office of the Prime Minister: Jamaica House, 1 Devon Rd, POB 272, Kingston 6; tel. 927-9941; fax 929-0005; e-mail pmo@opm.gov.jm.

Ministry of Agriculture: Hope Gardens, POB 480, Kingston 6; tel. 927-1731; fax 927-1904; e-mail psoffice@moa.gov.jm; internet www.moa.gov.jm.

Ministry of Commerce, Science and Technology: PCJ Bldg, 36 Trafalgar Rd, Kingston 10; tel. 929-8990; fax 960-1623; e-mail admin@mct.gov.jm; internet www.mct.gov.jm.

Ministry of Development: Cabinet Office, 1 Devon Rd, POB 272, Kingston 6; tel. 927-9941; fax 929-8405; e-mail info@cabinet.gov.jm; internet www.cabinet.gov.jm.

Ministry of Education, Youth and Culture: 2a National Heroes Circle, Kingston 4; tel. 922-1400; fax 922-1837; internet www.moec.gov.jm.

Ministry of Finance and Planning: 30 National Heroes Circle, Kingston 4; tel. 922-8600; fax 922-7097; e-mail info@mof.gov.jm; internet www.mof.gov.jm.

Ministry of Foreign Affairs and Foreign Trade: 21 Dominica Dr., POB 624, Kingston 5; tel. 926-4220; fax 929-6733; e-mail mfaftjam@cwjamaica.com; internet www.mfaft.gov.jm.

Ministry of Health: Oceana Hotel Complex, 2–4 King St, Kingston; tel. 967-1092; fax 967-7293; e-mail junorj@moh.gov.jm; internet www.moh.gov.jm.

Ministry of Industry and Tourism: 64 Knutsford Blvd, Kingston 5; tel. 920-4924; fax 920-4944; e-mail mts@cwjamaica.com.

Ministry of Information: Kingston.

Ministry of Justice and Attorney-General's Department: 2 Oxford Rd, Kingston 5; tel. 906-2414; fax 922-5109; internet www.moj.gov.jm.

Ministry of Labour and Social Security: 1F North St, POB 10, Kingston; tel. 922-8000; fax 922-6902; e-mail mlss@netcomm-jm.com; internet www.minlab.gov.jm.

Ministry of Land and Environment: 16A Halfway Tree Rd, Kingston 5; tel. 920-3273; fax 929-7349; e-mail mehsys@hotmail.com.

Ministry of Local Government, Community Development and Sport: 85 Hagley Park Rd, Kingston 10; tel. 754-0994; fax 754-0210; e-mail communications@mlgcd.gov.jm; internet www.mlgycd.gov.jm.

Ministry of National Security: Mutual Life Bldg, North Tower, 2 Oxford Rd, Kingston 5; tel. 906-4908; fax 906-1724; e-mail enquiries@mns.gov.jm; internet www.mns.gov.jm.

Ministry of Transport and Works: 1c Pawsey Rd, Kingston 5; tel. 754-1900; fax 927-8763; e-mail ps@mtw.gov.jm; internet www.mtw.gov.jm.

Ministry of Water and Housing: 25 Dominica Dr., Kingston 5; tel. 754-0973; fax 754-2853; e-mail genefa@cwjamaica.com; internet www.mwh.gov.jm.

Legislature

PARLIAMENT

Houses of Parliament: Gordon House, 81 Duke St, POB 636, Kingston; tel. 922-0200; e-mail slewis@mail.infochan.com.

Senate

President: Syringa Marshall-Burnett.
Vice-President: Navel Foster Clarke.
The Senate has 19 other members.

House of Representatives

Speaker: Michael Peart.
Deputy Speaker: Onel T. Williams.
General Election, 16 October 2002

	% of votes cast	Seats
People's National Party (PNP)	52.2	34
Jamaica Labour Party (JLP)	47.2	26
Total (incl. others)	100.0	60

Political Organizations

Jamaica Labour Party (JLP): 20 Belmont Rd, Kingston 5; tel. 929-1183; fax 968-0873; e-mail info@thejlp.com; internet www.thejlp.org; f. 1943; supports free enterprise in a mixed economy and close co-operation with the USA; Leader Orrett Bruce Golding; Chair. Robert Pickersgill; Gen. Sec. Karl Samuda.

Jamaican Alliance for National Unity (JANU): Kingston; f. 2002; mem. of the New Jamaica Alliance; Chair. Rev. Al Miller.

Jamaica Alliance Movement (JAM): Kingston; f. 2001; Rastafarian; Pres. Astor Black.

National Democratic Movement (NDM): 72 Half Way Tree Rd, Kingston 10; e-mail ndmjamaica@yahoo.com; internet www.ndm4jamaica.org; f. 1995; advocates a clear separation of powers between the central executive and elected representatives; supports private investment and a market economy; mem. of the New Jamaica Alliance; Gen. Sec. Michael Williams; Chair. Peter Townsend (acting).

Natural Law Party: c/o 21st Century Integrated Medical Centre, Shop OF3, Overton Plaza, 49 Union St, Montego Bay; tel. 971-9107; fax 971-9109; e-mail nlp@cwjamaica.com; f. 1996; Leader Dr Leo Campbell.

People's National Party (PNP): 89 Old Hope Rd, Kingston 5; tel. 978-1337; fax 927-4389; e-mail information@pnpjamaica.com; internet www.pnpjamaica.com; f. 1938; socialist principles; affiliated with the National Workers' Union; Leader Percival J. Patterson; Gen. Sec. Burchell Whiteman; First Vice-Pres. Peter Phillips.

Republican Party of Jamaica (RPJ): Kingston; mem. of the New Jamaica Alliance; Leader Denzil Taylor.

United People's Party (UPP): 6 Trinidad Terrace, Kingston 5; tel. 929-6429; fax 968-4615; e-mail uppjam@cwjamaica.com; f. 2001; Pres. Antoinette Haughton Cardenas; Gen. Sec. Horace Matthews.

Diplomatic Representation

EMBASSIES AND HIGH COMMISSIONS IN JAMAICA

Argentina: Dyoll Life Bldg, 6th Floor, 40 Knutsford Blvd, Kingston 5; tel. 926-5588; fax 926-0580; e-mail embargen@kasnet.com; Ambassador Gonzalo Fernández Medrano.

Brazil: First Life Bldg, 3rd Floor, 64 Knutsford Blvd, Kingston 5; tel. 929-8607; fax 929-1259; e-mail brasking@infochan.com; Ambassador Cézar Augusto de Souza Lima Amaral.

Canada: 3 West Kings House Rd, POB 1500, Kingston 10; tel. 926-1500; fax 511-3491; e-mail kngtn@dfait-maeci.gc.ca; internet www.kingston.gc.ca; High Commissioner Claudio Valle.

Chile: Island Life Centre, 5th Floor, South Sixth St, Lucia Ave, Kingston 5; tel. 968-0260; fax 968-0265; e-mail chilejam@cwjamaica.com; Ambassador Oscar Alfonso Silva Navarro.

China, People's Republic: 8 Seaview Ave, POB 232, Kingston 6; tel. 927-3871; fax 927-6920; e-mail chinaemba@cwjamaica.com; Ambassador Zhao Zhenyu.

Colombia: Victoria Mutual Bldg, 3rd Floor, 53 Knutsford Blvd, Kingston 5; tel. 929-1701; fax 968-0577; Ambassador Dr Francis James Kent.

Costa Rica: Belvedere House, Beverly Dr., Kingston 6; tel. 927-5988; fax 978-3946; e-mail cr_emb_jam14@hotmail.com; Ambassador JOYCELYN SAWYERS ROYAL.

Cuba: 9 Trafalgar Rd, Kingston 10; tel. 978-0931; fax 978-5372; e-mail embacubajam@cwjamaica.com; Ambassador GISELA GARCÍA RIVERA.

Dominican Republic: 32 Earls Court, Kingston 8; tel. 755-4155; fax 755-4156; e-mail domemb@cwjamaica.com; Ambassador ARSENIO JIMENEZ-POLANCO.

France: 13 Hillcrest Ave, POB 93, Kingston 6; tel. 978-0210; fax 927-4998; e-mail frenchembassy@cwjamaica.com; internet ambafrance-jm.org; Ambassador FRANCIS HURTUT.

Germany: 10 Waterloo Rd, POB 444, Kingston 10; tel. 926-6728; fax 929-8282; e-mail germanemb@cwjamaica.com; Ambassador Dr CHRISTIAN HAUSMANN.

Haiti: 2 Munroe Rd, Kingston 6; tel. 927-7595; fax 978-7638; Ambassador JEAN-GABRIEL AUGUSTIN.

Honduras: 7 Lady Kay Dr., Norbrook, Kingston 8; tel. 931-5248; fax 941-6470; e-mail emhonjam@kasnet.com; Ambassador CARLOS AUGUSTO MATUTE RIVERA.

India: 27 Seymour Ave, POB 446, Kingston 6; tel. 927-3114; fax 978-2801; e-mail hicomindkin@cwjamaica.com; High Commissioner INDER VIR CHOPRA.

Japan: Mutual Life Centre, North Tower, 6th Floor, 2 Oxford Rd, POB 8104, Kingston 5; tel. 929-3338; fax 968-1373; Ambassador HIROSHI SAKURAI.

Mexico: PCJ Bldg, 36 Trafalgar Rd, Kingston 10; tel. 926-6891; fax 929-7995; e-mail mexicoj@kasnet.com; Ambassador BENITO ANDIÓN.

Nigeria: 5 Waterloo Rd, POB 94, Kingston 10; tel. 926-6400; fax 968-7371; High Commissioner F. A. UKONGA.

Panama: 1 St Lucia Ave, Spanish Court, Suite 26, Kingston 5; tel. 968-2928; fax 960-1618; Ambassador FRANKLIN ANTONIO BARRETT TAIT.

Peru: 23 Barbados Ave, Kingston 5; tel. 920-5027; fax 920-4360; e-mail embaperu-kingston@rree.gob.pe; Ambassador LUIS SÁNDIGA CABRERA .

Russia: 22 Norbrook Dr., Kingston 8; tel. 924-1048; fax 925-8290; e-mail Rusembja@colis.com; Ambassador EDUARD MALAYAN.

Saint Christopher and Nevis: 11A Opal Ave, POB 157, Golden Acres, Kingston 7; tel. 944-3861; fax 945-0105; High Commissioner CEDRIC HARPER.

South Africa: First Life Bldg, 7th Floor, 60 Knutsford Blvd, Kingston 5; tel. 960-3750; fax 929-0240; High Commissioner THANDYISE CHILIZA.

Spain: The Towers, 9th Floor, 25 Dominica Dr., Kingston 5; tel. 929-6710; fax 929-8965; e-mail jamesp@jamweb.net; Ambassador RAFAEL ADOLFO JOVER Y DE MORA FIGUEROA.

Trinidad and Tobago: First Life Bldg, 3rd Floor, 60 Knutsford Blvd, Kingston 5; tel. 926-5730; fax 926-5801; e-mail t&thckgn@infochan.com; High Commissioner DENNIS FRANCIS.

United Kingdom: 28 Trafalgar Rd, POB 575, Kingston 10; tel. 510-0700; fax 511-5303; e-mail bhckingston@cwjamaica.com; internet www.britishhighcommission.gov.uk/jamaica; High Commissioner PETER J. MATHERS.

USA: Mutual Life Centre, 2 Oxford Rd, Kingston 5; tel. 929-4850; fax 935-6019; e-mail opakgn@state.gov; internet kingston.usembassy.gov; Ambassador SUE McCOURT COBB.

Venezuela: PCJ Bldg, 3rd Floor, 36 Trafalgar Rd, Kingston 10; tel. 926-5510; fax 926-7442; Ambassador ROCIO MANEIRO GONZÁLEZ.

Judicial System

The judicial system is based on English common law and practice. Final appeal is to the Judicial Committee of the Privy Council in the United Kingdom, although in 2001 the Jamaican Government signed an agreement to establish a Caribbean Court of Justice to fulfil this function.

Justice is administered by the Privy Council, Court of Appeal, Supreme Court (which includes the Revenue Court and the Gun Court), Resident Magistrates' Court (which includes the Traffic Court), two Family Courts and the Courts of Petty Sessions.

Judicial Service Commission: Office of the Services Commissions, 63–67 Knutsford Blvd, Kingston 5; advises the Governor-General on judicial appointments, etc.; chaired by the Chief Justice.

Attorney-General: ARNOLD J. NICHOLSON.

SUPREME COURT
(Public Bldg E, 134 Tower St, POB 491, Kingston; tel. 922-8300; fax. 967-0669; e-mail webmaster@sc.gov.jm; internet www.sc.gov.jm)

Chief Justice: LENSLEY H. WOLFE.

Senior Puisne Judge: H. F. COOKE.

Master: CHRISTINE McDONALD.

Registrar: AUDRE LINDO.

COURT OF APPEAL
(POB 629, Kingston; tel. 922-8300)

President: I. X. FORTE.

Registrar: G. P. LEVERS.

Religion

CHRISTIANITY

There are more than 100 Christian denominations active in Jamaica. According to the 2001 census, the largest religious bodies were the Church of God (whose members represented 24% of the population), Seventh-day Adventists (11% of the population), Pentecostalist (10%), Baptists (7%) and Anglicans (4%). Other denominations include Jehovah's Witnesses, the Methodist and Congregational Churches, United Church, the Church of the Brethren, the Ethiopian Orthodox Church, the Disciples of Christ, the Moravian Church, the Salvation Army and the Society of Friends (Quakers).

Jamaica Council of Churches: 14 South Ave, Kingston 10; tel. and fax 926-0974; e-mail jchurch@cwjamaica.com; f. 1941; 10 member churches and three agencies; Gen. Sec. HARRIS CUNNINGHAM.

The Anglican Communion

Anglicans in Jamaica are adherents of the Church in the Province of the West Indies, comprising eight dioceses. The Archbishop of the Province is the Bishop of the North East Caribbean and Aruba. The Bishop of Jamaica, whose jurisdiction also includes Grand Cayman (in the Cayman Islands), is assisted by three suffragan Bishops (of Kingston, Mandeville and Montego Bay). The 2001 census recorded that some 4% of the population were Anglicans.

Bishop of Jamaica: Rt Rev. ALFRED C. REID, Church House, 2 Caledonia Ave, Kingston 5; tel. 952-4963; fax 952-2933.

The Roman Catholic Church

Jamaica comprises the archdiocese of Kingston in Jamaica (also including the Cayman Islands), and the dioceses of Montego Bay and Mandeville. At 31 December 2002 the estimated total of adherents in Jamaica was 30,989, representing about 2% of the total population. The Archbishop and Bishops participate in the Antilles Episcopal Conference (currently based in Port of Spain, Trinidad and Tobago).

Archbishop of Kingston in Jamaica: Most Rev. EDGERTON ROLAND CLARKE, Archbishop's Residence, 21 Hopefield Ave, POB 43, Kingston 6; tel. 927-9915; fax 927-4487; e-mail rcabkgn@cwjamaica.com.

Other Christian Churches

Assembly of God: Evangel Temple, 3 Friendship Park Rd, Kingston 3; tel. 928-2995; Sec. Pastor WILSON.

Baptist Union: 6 Hope Rd, Kingston 10; tel. 926-7820; fax 968-7832; e-mail info@jbu.org.jm; internet www.jbu.org.jm; Pres. Rev. JONATHAN HEMMINGS; Gen. Sec. Rev. KARL JOHNSON; mems 40,000.

Church of God in Jamaica: 35 Hope Rd, Kingston 10; tel. 927-5990.

First Church of Christ, Scientist: 17 National Heroes Circle, Kingston 4; tel. 967-3814.

Methodist Church (Jamaica District): 143 Constant Spring Rd, POB 892, Kingston 8; tel. and fax 925-6768; e-mail jamaicamethodist@cwjamaica.com; f. 1789; 15,820 mems; Pres. Rev. Dr BYRON CHAMBERS; Synod Sec. Rev. CATHERINE GALE.

Moravian Church in Jamaica: 3 Hector St, POB 8369, Kingston 5; tel. 928-1861; fax 928-8336; e-mail moravianchja@colis.com; f. 1754; 30,000 mems; Pres. Rev. Dr LIVINGSTONE THOMPSON.

Seventh-day Adventist Church: 56 James St, Kingston; tel. 922-7440; f. 1901; 205,000; Pres. Dr PATRICK ALLEN.

United Church in Jamaica and the Cayman Islands: 12 Carlton Cres., POB 359, Kingston 10; tel. 926-6059; fax 929-0826; e-mail churchunited@hotmail.com; internet www.ucjci.netfirms.com; f. 1965 by merger of the Congregational Union of Jamaica (f. 1877); and the Presbyterian Church of Jamaica and Grand Cayman to become United Church of Jamaica and Grand Cayman; merged with Disciples of Christ in Jamaica in 1992 when name changed as above; 20,000 mems; Moderator Roderick Hewitt; Gen. Sec. Rev. Maitland Evans.

RASTAFARIANISM

Rastafarianism is an important influence in Jamaican culture. The cult is derived from Christianity and a belief in the divinity of Ras (Prince) Tafari Makonnen (later Emperor Haile Selassie) of Ethiopia. It advocates racial equality and non-violence, but causes controversy in its use of 'ganja' (marijuana) as a sacrament. The 2001 census recorded 24,020 Rastafarians (0.9% of the total population). Although the religion is largely unorganized, there are some denominations.

Haile Selassie Rastafari Royal Ethiopian Judah Coptic Church: Balcombe Dr., Waterhouse, Kingston; not officially incorporated, on account of its alleged use of marijuana; Leader Abuna Bongo Blackheart.

BAHÁ'Í FAITH

National Spiritual Assembly: 208 Mountain View Ave, Kingston 6; tel. 927-7051; fax 978-2344; incorporated in 1970.

ISLAM

At the 2001 census there were an estimated 5,000 Muslims.

JUDAISM

The 2001 census recorded some 350 Jews.

United Congregation of Israelites: Shaare Shalom Synagogue, POB 540, Kingston 6; tel. 927-7948; fax 978-6240; internet www.ujcl.org; f. 1655; c. 250 mems; Leader Tony Lindo.

The Press

DAILIES

Daily Gleaner: 7 North St, POB 40, Kingston; tel. 922-3400; fax 922-6223; e-mail feedback@jamaica-gleaner.com; internet www.jamaica-gleaner.com; f. 1834; morning; independent; Chair. and Man. Dir Oliver Clarke; Editor-in-Chief Garfield Grandison; circ. 50,000.

Daily Star: 7 North St, POB 40, Kingston; tel. 922-3400; fax 922-6223; e-mail feedback@jamaica-gleaner.com; internet www.jamaica-gleaner.com; f. 1951; evening; Editor-in-Chief Garfield Grandison; Editor Claire Clarke-Grant; circ. 45,000.

Jamaica Herald: 86 Hagley Park Rd, Kingston 10; tel. 937-7304; Man. Editor Franklin McKnight.

Jamaica Observer: 40 Beechwood Ave, Kingston 5; tel. 920-8136; fax 926-7655; e-mail feedback@jamaicaobserver.com; internet www.jamaicaobserver.com; f. 1993; Chair. Gordon 'Butch' Stewart.

PERIODICALS

Catholic Opinion: Roman Catholic Chancery Office, 21 Hopefield Ave, POB 43, Kingston 6; tel. 927-9915; fax 927-4487; e-mail rcabkgn@cwjamaica.com; 6 a year; religious; circulated in the Sunday Gleaner; Editor Very Rev. Fr Michael Lewis; circ. over 500,000.

Children's Own: 7 North St, POB 40, Kingston; tel. 922-3400; fax 922-6223; e-mail feedback@jamaica-gleaner.com; internet www.jamaica-gleaner.com; weekly during term time; Editor-in-Chief Garfield Grandison; circ. 120,000.

Jamaica Churchman: 2 Caledonia Ave, Kingston 5; tel. 926-6608; quarterly; Editor Barbara Gloudon; circ. 7,000.

Jamaica Journal: 12 East St, Kingston; tel. 929-0620; fax 926-1147; e-mail ioj.jam@mail.infochan.com; internet www.instituteofjamaica.org.jm; f. 1967; 3 a year; literary, historical and cultural review; publ. by Instit. of Jamaica Publs Ltd; Chair. of Editorial Cttee Barbara Gloudon.

Mandeville Weekly: 31 Ward Ave, Mandeville, Manchester; tel. 961-0118; fax 961-0119; internet www.eyegrid.com/mandevilleweekly; Chief Editor Anthony Freckleton.

Sunday Gleaner: 7 North St, POB 40, Kingston; tel. 922-3400; fax 922-6223; e-mail feedback@jamaica-gleaner.com; internet www.jamaica-gleaner.com; weekly; Editor-in-Chief Garfield Grandison; circ. 100,000.

Sunday Herald: 17 Norwood Ave, Kingston 5; tel. 906-7572; fax 908-4044; e-mail mainsection@sundayheraldjamaica.com; internet www.sundayheraldjamaica.com; f. 1997; weekly; Consulting Editor Franklin McKnight; Exec. Editor R. Christine King.

Sunday Observer: 2 Fagan Ave, Kingston 8; tel. 920-8136; fax 926-7655; internet www.jamaicaobserver.com; weekly; Chair. Gordon 'Butch' Stewart.

Teen Herald: 86 Hagley Park Rd, Kingston 10; tel. 758-5275; fax 901-9335; e-mail teenherald@yahoo.com.

Weekend Star: 7 North St, POB 40, Kingston; tel. 922-3400; fax 922-6223; e-mail feedback@jamaica-gleaner.com; internet www.jamaica-gleaner.com; f. 1951; weekly; Editor-in-Chief Garfield Grandison; Editor Claire Clarke-Grant; circ. 80,000.

The Western Mirror: 4 Cottage Rd, POB 1258, Montego Bay; tel. 952-5253; fax 952-6513; e-mail westernmirror@mail.infochan.com; internet www.westernmirror.com; f. 1980; 2 a week; Man. Dir and Editor Lloyd B. Smith; circ. 20,000.

West Indian Medical Journal: Faculty of Medical Sciences, University of the West Indies, Kingston 7; tel. 927-1214; fax 927-1846; e-mail wimj@uwimona.edu.jm; f. 1951; quarterly; Editor Everard N. Barton; circ. 2,000.

X-News Jamaica: 86 Hagley Park Rd, Kingston 10; tel. 937-7304; fax 901-7667; e-mail comments@xnewsjamaica.com; internet www.xnewsjamaica.com; f. 1993; weekly.

PRESS ASSOCIATION

Press Association of Jamaica (PAJ): 5 East Ave, Kingston 8; tel. 925-7836; f. 1943; Pres. Donna Ortega.

Foreign Bureaux

Associated Press (USA), Caribbean Media Corpn and Inter Press Service (Italy) are represented in Jamaica.

Publishers

Jamaica Publishing House Ltd: 97 Church St, Kingston; tel. 967-3866; fax 922-5412; e-mail jph@mail.infochan.com; f. 1969; wholly-owned subsidiary of Jamaica Teachers' Asscn; educational, English language and literature, mathematics, history, geography, social sciences, music; Chair. Woodburn Miller; Man. Elaine R. Stennett.

Kingston Publishers Ltd: 7 Norman Rd, Suite 10, LOJ Industrial Complex, Kingston CSO; tel. 938-0005; fax 759-8752; e-mail lmhbookpublishing@cwjamaica.com; internet lmhpublishingjamaica.com; f. 1970; educational textbooks, general, travel, fiction, non-fiction, children's books; Chair. L. Michael Henry.

Western Publishers Ltd: 4 Cottage Rd, POB 1258, Montego Bay; tel. 952-5253; fax 952-6513; e-mail westernmirror@mail.infochan.com; f. 1980; Man. Dir and Editor-in-Chief Lloyd B. Smith.

GOVERNMENT PUBLISHING HOUSE

Jamaica Printing Services: 77 Duke St, Kingston; tel. 967-2250; internet www.jps1992.com; Chair. Evadne Sterling; Man. Ralph Bell.

Broadcasting and Communications

TELECOMMUNICATIONS

The telecommunications sector became fully liberalized on 1 March 2003. The sector was regulated by the Office of Utilities Regulation (see Utilities).

Cable & Wireless Jamaica Ltd: 7 Cecilio Ave, Kingston 10; tel. 926-9450; fax 929-9530; f. 1989; in 1995 merged with Jamaica Telephone Co Ltd and Jamaica International Telecommunications Ltd, name changed as above 1995; 79% owned by Cable & Wireless (United Kingdom); Pres. Gary Barrow.

Cellular One Caribbean: Kingston; mobile cellular telephone operator; licence granted Dec. 1999.

Digicel: Kingston; internet www.digiceljamaica.com; mobile cellular telephone operator; owned by Irish consortium, Mossel (Jamaica) Ltd; f. 2001; Chair. Denis O'Brien; CEO (Jamaica) David Hall.

Mossel (Jamaica) Ltd: Kingston; mobile cellular telephone operator consortium, operates the Digicel network.

Oceanic Digital Jamaica: Kingston; e-mail dkcastaldi@oceanicdigital.com; internet www.oceanicdigital.com; mobile cellular telephone operator; formerly Centennial Digital; Oceannic Digital, 49% stockholder, bought remaining 51% in August 2002.

BROADCASTING

Radio

Educational Broadcasting Service: Multi-Media Centre, 37 Arnold Rd, Kingston 4; tel. 922-9370; f. 1964; radio broadcasts during school term; Pres. OUIDA HYLTON-TOMLINSON.

Independent Radio: 6 Bradley Ave, Kingston 10; tel. 968-4880; fax 968-9165; commercial radio station; broadcasts 24 hrs a day on FM; Gen. Man. NEWTON JAMES.

IRIE FM: 1B Derrymore Rd, Kingston 10; tel. 968-5013; fax 968-8332; e-mail iriefmmarket@cwjamaica.com; internet www.iriefm.net; f. 1991; commercial radio station owned by Grove Broadcasting Co.; plays only reggae music.

Island Broadcasting Services Ltd: 41B Half Way Tree Rd, Kingston 5; tel. 968-8115; fax 929-1345; commercial; broadcasts 24 hrs a day on FM; Exec. Chair. NEVILLE JAMES.

KLAS-FM 89: 81 Knutsford Blvd, Kingston 5; tel. 929-1344; f. 1991; commercial radio station.

Love FM: 12 Carlton Cres., Kingston 10; tel. 968-9596; f. 1997; commercial radio station, broadcasts religious programming on FM; owned by Religious Media Ltd.

Radio Jamaica Ltd (RJR): Broadcasting House, 32 Lyndhurst Rd, POB 23, Kingston 5; tel. 926-1100; fax 929-7467; e-mail rjr@radiojamaica.com; internet www.radiojamaica.com; f. 1947; commercial, public service; 3 channels.

   FAME FM: internet www.famefm.fm; broadcasts on FM, island-wide 24 hrs a day; Exec. Producer FRANCOIS ST. JUSTE.

   Radio 2 FM: broadcasts on FM, island-wide 24 hrs a day; Media Services Man. DONALD TOPPING.

   RJR 94 FM: internet www.rjr94fm.com; broadcasts on AM and FM, island-wide 24 hrs a day; Exec. Producer NORMA BROWN-BELL.

ZIP 103 FM: 1B Derrymore Rd, Kingston 10, Jamaica; tel. 929-6233; fax 960-0523; e-mail zip103fm@cwjamaica.com; internet www.ZIPFM.net; f. 2002; commercial radio station.

Other stations broadcasting include Hot 102 FM, Power 106 FM, Roots FM and TBC FM.

Television

CVM Television: 69 Constant Sprint Rd, Kingston 10; tel. 931-9400; fax 931-9417; e-mail wsmith@cvmtv.com; internet www.cvmtv.com.

Love Television: Kingston; f. 1997; religious programming; owned by Religious Media Ltd.

Television Jamaica Limited (TVJ): 5–9 South Odeon Ave, POB 100, Kingston 10; tel. 926-5620; fax 929-1029; e-mail tvjadmin@cwjamaica.com; internet www.televisionjamaica.com; f. 1959 as Jamaica Broadcasting Corporation; privatized 1997, name changed as above; island-wide VHF transmission 24 hrs a day; Gen. Man. MARCIA FORBES.

Finance

(cap. = capital; p.u. = paid up; res = reserves; dep. = deposits; m. = million; brs = branches; amounts in Jamaican dollars)

BANKING

Central Bank

Bank of Jamaica: Nethersole Pl., POB 621, Kingston; tel. 922-0750; fax 922-0828; e-mail info@boj-org.jm; internet www.boj.org.jm; f. 1960; cap. 4.0m., res 2,396.4m., dep. 112,307.9m. (Dec. 2003); Gov. DERICK MILTON LATIBEAUDIÈRE.

Commercial Banks

Bank of Nova Scotia Jamaica Ltd (Canada): Scotiabank Centre Bldg, cnr Duke and Port Royal Sts, POB 709, Kingston; tel. 922-1000; fax 924-9294; f. 1967; cap. 1,463.6m., res 9,612.6m., dep. 91,314.6m. (Oct. 2003); Chair. R. H. PITFIELD; Man. Dir WILLIAM E. CLARKE; 35 brs.

Citibank, NA (USA): 63–67 Knutsford Blvd, POB 286, Kingston 5; tel. 926-3270; fax 929-3745; internet www.citibank.com/jamaica; Vice-Pres. PETER MOSES.

FirstCaribbean International Bank Ltd (Canada/United Kingdom): 23–27 Knutsford Blvd, POB 762, Kingston 5; tel. 929-9310; fax 960-2837; internet www.firstcaribbeanbank.com; 51% owned by Canadian Imperial Bank of Commerce and Barclays Bank

PLC; cap. 96.7m., res 1,025.2m., dep. 16,058.5m. (Oct. 2003); Chair. MICHAEL MANSOOR; Man. RAYMOND CAMPBELL; 12 brs.

National Commercial Bank Jamaica Ltd: 'The Atrium', 32 Trafalgar Rd, POB 88, Kingston 10; tel. 929-9050; fax 929-8399; internet www.jncb.com; f. 1977; merged with Mutual Security Bank in 1996; cap. 2,466.8m., res 6,552.6m., dep. 121,525.6m. (Sept. 2003); Chair. MICHAEL LEE-CHIN; Man. Dir AUBYN HILL; 37 brs.

RBTT Bank Jamaica Ltd: 17 Dominica Dr., Kingston 5; tel. 960-2340; fax 960-2332; internet www.rbtt.com; f. 1993 as Jamaica Citizens Bank Ltd; name changed to Union Bank of Jamaica Ltd; acquired by Royal Bank of Trinidad and Tobago in 2001 and name changed as above; Chair. Dr OWEN JEFFERSON; Man. Dir MICHAEL E. A. WRIGHT; 614 brs.

Development Banks

Development Bank of Jamaica Ltd: 11A–15 Oxford Rd, POB 466, Kingston 5; tel. 929-6124-7; fax 929-6055; e-mail dbank@cwjamaica.com; replaced Jamaica Development Bank; f. 1969; provides funds for medium- and long-term devt-orientated projects in the agricultural, tourism, industrial, manufacturing and services sectors through financial intermediaries; Man. Dir KINGSLEY THOMAS.

Jamaica Mortgage Bank: 33 Tobago Ave, POB 950, Kingston 5; tel. 929-6350; fax 968-5428; e-mail jmb@cwjamaica.com; internet www.jamaicamortgagebank.com; f. 1971 by the Jamaican Govt and the US Agency for Int. Devt; govt-owned statutory org. since 1973; intended to function primarily as a secondary market facility for home mortgages and to mobilize long-term funds for housing devts in Jamaica; also insures home mortgage loans made by approved financial institutions, thus transferring risk of default on a loan to the Govt; Man. Dir PETER THOMAS; Gen. Man. EVERTON HANSON.

Pan Caribbean Financial Services: 60 Knutsford Blvd, Kingston 5; tel. 929-5583-4; fax 926-4385; e-mail options@gopancaribbean.com; internet www.gopancaribbean.com; fmrly Trafalgar Development Bank, name changed as above in December 2002; Chair. RICHARD O. BYLES; Pres. DONOVAN H. PERKINS.

Other Banks

National Export-Import Bank of Jamaica Ltd: 48 Duke St, POB 3, Kingston; tel. 922-9690; fax 922-9184; e-mail eximjam@cwjamaica.com; internet www.eximbankja.com; replaced Jamaica Export Credit Insurance Corpn; finances import and export of goods and services; Chair. Dr OWEN JEFFERSON; Deputy Chair. PAUL THOMAS.

National Investment Bank of Jamaica Ltd: 11 Oxford Rd, POB 889, Kingston 5; tel. 960-9691; fax 920-0379; e-mail nibj@infochan.com; internet www.nibj.com; Chair. DAVID COORE; Pres. REX JAMES.

Banking Association

Jamaica Bankers' Association: 39 Hope Rd, POB 1079, Kingston 10; tel. 927-6238; fax 927-5137; e-mail jbainfo@jba.org.jm; internet www.jba.org.jm; f. 1973; Pres. WILLIAM CLARKE.

Financial Sector Adjustment Company

FINSAC Ltd: 76 Knutsford Blvd, POB 54, Kingston 5; tel. 906-1809; fax 906-1822; e-mail info@finsac.com; internet www.finsac.com; f. 1997; state-owned; intervenes in the banking and insurance sectors to restore stability in the financial sector; Chair. KENNETH RATTRAY.

STOCK EXCHANGE

Jamaica Stock Exchange Ltd: 40 Harbour St, Kingston; tel. 967-3271; fax 922-6966; internet www.jamstockex.com; f. 1968; 32 listed cos (2004); Chair. ROY JOHNSON.

INSURANCE

Office of the Superintendent of Insurance: 51 St Lucia Ave, POB 800, Kingston 5; tel. 926-1790; fax 968-4346; f. 1972; regulatory body; Supt ERROL MCLEAN (acting).

Jamaica Association of General Insurance Companies: 3-3A Richmond Ave, Kingston 10; tel. 929-8404; e-mail jagic@cwjamaica.com; internet www.jagonline.com; Man. GLORIA M. GRANT; Chair. LESLIE CHUNG.

Principal Companies

British Caribbean Insurance Co Ltd: 36 Duke St, POB 170, Kingston; tel. 922-1260; fax 922-4475; e-mail bricar@cwjamaica.com; internet www.bciconline.com; f. 1962; general insurance; Man. Dir LESLIE W. CHUNG.

First Life Insurance Group: 60 Knutsford Blvd, Kingston 5; tel. 926-3700; fax 929-8523; e-mail info@firstlife.com.jm; internet www.firstlife.com.jm; division of the Pan-Jamaican Investment Trust Group; all branches.

General Accident Insurance Co Jamaica Ltd: 58 Half Way Tree Rd, Kingston 10; tel. 929-8451; fax 929-1074; e-mail genac@cwjamaica.com; internet www.genac.com; f. 1981; Gen. Man. SHARON E. DONALDSON.

Globe Insurance Co of the West Indies Ltd: 19 Dominica Dr., POB 401, Kingston 5; tel. 926-3720; fax 929-2727; e-mail admin@globeins.com; internet www.globeins.com; f. 1962; Man. Dir EVAN THWAITES.

Guardian Life: 12 Trafalgar Rd, Kingston 5; tel. 978-8815; fax 978-4225; internet www.guardianholdings.com; pension and life policies; Chair. ARTHUR LOK JACK; Pres. and CEO DOUGLAS CAMACHO.

Insurance Co of the West Indies Ltd (ICWI): 2 St Lucia Ave, POB 306, Kingston 5; tel. 926-9182; fax 929-6641; Chair. DENNIS LALOR; CEO KENNETH BLAKELEY.

Island Life Insurance Co: 6 St Lucia Ave, Kingston 5; tel. 968-6874; e-mail ceo@islandlife-ja-com.jm; 64% owned by Barbados Mutual Life Assurance Co; 26.5% owned by FINSAC with Life of Jamaica Ltd in 2001.

Jamaica General Insurance Co Ltd: 9 Duke St, POB 408, Kingston; tel. 922-6420; fax 922-2073; Man. Dir A. C. LEVY.

Life of Jamaica Ltd: 28–48 Barbados Ave, Kingston 5; tel. 960-8705; fax 929-4730; f. 1970; life and health insurance, pensions; 76% owned by Barbados Mutual Life Assurance Co merged with Island Life Insurance Co in 2001; Pres. R. D. WILLIAMS.

NEM Insurance Co (Jamaica) Ltd: NEM House, 9 King St, Kingston; tel. 922-1460; fax 922-4045; e-mail info@nemjam.com; internet www.nemjam.com; fmrly the National Employers' Mutual General Insurance Assen; Man. Dir ERROL ZIADIE.

Trade and Industry

GOVERNMENT AGENCIES

Jamaica Commodity Trading Co Ltd: 107 Constant Spring Rd, Kingston 10; tel. 969-0883; fax 925-6513; f. 1981 as successor to State Trading Corpn; oversees all importing on behalf of state; Chair. MICHAEL VACCIANA; Man. Dir ANDREE NEMBHARD.

Jamaica Information Service (JIS): 58a Half Way Tree Rd, POB 2222, Kingston 10; tel. 926-3741; fax 920-7427; e-mail jis@jis.gov.jm; internet www.jis.gov.jm; f. 1963; information agency for govt policies and programmes, ministries and public sector agencies; CEO CARMEN E. TIPLING.

DEVELOPMENT ORGANIZATIONS

Agricultural Development Corpn (ADC) Group of Companies: Mais House, Hope Rd, POB 552, Kingston; tel. 977-4412; fax 977-4411; f. 1989; manages and develops breeds of cattle, provides warehousing, cold storage, offices and information for exporters and distributors of non-traditional crops and ensures the proper utilization of agricultural lands under its control; Chair. Dr ASTON WOOD; Gen. Man. DUDLEY IRVING.

Coffee Industry Development Co: Marcus Garvey Dr., Kingston 15; tel. 923-5645; fax 923-7587; e-mail cofeboard-jam@cwjamaica.com; f. 1981 to implement coffee devt and rehabilitation programmes financed by international aid agencies; Sec. JOYCE CHANG.

Jamaica Promotions Corpn (JAMPRO): 18 Trafalgar Rd, Kingston 10; tel. 978-7755; fax 946-0090; e-mail jampro@investjamaica.com; internet www.investjamaica.com; f. 1988 by merger of Jamaica Industrial Development Corpn, Jamaica National Export Corpn and Jamaica Investment Promotion Ltd; trade and investment promotion agency; Pres. PATRICIA FRANCIS; Chair. JOSEPH A. MATALON.

National Development Agency Ltd: Kingston; tel. 922-5445; Exec. Dir ROBERT GREGORY.

Planning Institute of Jamaica: 10–16 Grenada Way, Kingston 5; tel. 906-4463; fax 906-5011; e-mail doccen@mail.colis.com; internet www.pioj.gov.jm; f. 1955 as the Central Planning Unit; adopted current name in 1984; formulates policy on and monitors performance in the fields of the economy and and social, environmental and trade issues; publishing and analysis of social and economic performance data; Dir-Gen. WESLEY HUGHES.

Urban Development Corpn: The Office Centre, 8th Floor, 12 Ocean Blvd, Kingston; tel. 922-8310; fax 922-9326; e-mail info@udcja.com; internet www.udcja.com; f. 1968; responsibility for urban renewal and devt within designated areas; Chair. Dr VINCENT LAWRENCE; Gen. Man. MARJORIE CAMPBELL.

CHAMBERS OF COMMERCE

Associated Chambers of Commerce of Jamaica: 7–8 East Parade, POB 172, Kingston; tel. 922-0150; f. 1974; 12 associated Chambers of Commerce; Pres. RAY CAMPBELL.

Jamaica Chamber of Commerce: 7–8 East Parade, POB 172, Kingston; tel. 922-0150; fax 924-9056; e-mail jamcham@cwjamaica.com; internet www.jcc.org.jm; f. 1779; 450 mems.

INDUSTRIAL AND TRADE ASSOCIATIONS

Cocoa Industry Board: Marcus Garvey Dr., POB 1039, Kingston 15; tel. 923-6411; fax 923-5837; e-mail cocoajam@cwjamaica.com; f. 1957; has statutory powers to regulate and develop the industry; owns and operates four central fermentaries; Chair. JOSEPH SUAH; Man. and Sec. NABURN NELSON.

Coconut Industry Board: 18 Waterloo Rd, Half Way Tree, Kingston 10; tel. 926-1770; fax 968-1360; f. 1945; 9 mems; Chair. Dr RICHARD JONES; Gen. Man. JAMES S. JOYLES.

Coffee Industry Board: Marcus Garvey Dr., POB 508, Kingston 15; tel. 923-5850; fax 923-7587; e-mail coffeeboard@jamaicancoffee.gov.jm; internet www.jamaicancoffee.gov.jm; f. 1950; 9 mems; has wide statutory powers to regulate and develop the industry; Chair. RICHARD DOWNER.

Jamaica Bauxite Institute: Hope Gardens, POB 355, Kingston 6; tel. 927-2073; fax 927-1159; f. 1975; adviser to the Govt in the negotiation of agreements, consultancy services to clients in the bauxite/alumina and related industries, laboratory services for mineral and soil-related services, Pilot Plant services for materials and equipment testing, research and development; Chair. CARLTON DAVIS; Gen. Man. PARRIS LYEW-AYEE.

Jamaica Export Trading Co Ltd (JETCO): 188 Spanish Town Rd, AMC Complex, Kingston 11; tel. 937-1798; fax 937-6547; e-mail jetcoja@mail.infochan.com; internet www.exportjamaica.org; f. 1977; export trading in non-traditional products, incl. spices, fresh produce, furniture, garments, processed foods, minerals, etc.; Man. Dir HERNAL HAMILTON.

Sugar Industry Authority: 5 Trevennion Park Rd, POB 127, Kingston 5; tel. 926-5930; fax 926-6149; e-mail sia@cwjamaica.com; internet www.jamaicasugar.org; f. 1970; statutory body under portfolio of Ministry of Agriculture; responsible for regulation and control of sugar industry and sugar marketing; conducts research through Sugar Industry Research Institute; Exec. Chair. DERICK HEAVEN.

Trade Board: 107 Constant Spring Rd, Kingston 8; tel. 969-0478; fax 969-6513; e-mail tboard@colis.com; Admin. JEAN MORGAN.

EMPLOYERS' ORGANIZATIONS

All-Island Banana Growers' Association Ltd: Banana Industry Bldg, 10 South Ave, Kingston 4; tel. 922-5492; fax 922-5497; f. 1946; 1,500 mems (1997); Chair. A. A. POTTINGER; Sec. I. CHANG.

All-Island Jamaica Cane Farmers' Association: 4 North Ave, Kingston Gardens, Kingston 4; tel. 922-3010; fax 922-2077; e-mail allcane@cwjamaica.com; f. 1941; registered cane farmers; 27,000 mems; Chair. ABIJAH B. BUCHANAN; Man. ADITER MILLER.

Banana Export Co (BECO): 1A Braemar Ave, Kingston 10; tel. 978-8762; fax 978-6096; f. 1985 to replace Banana Co of Jamaica; oversees the devt of the banana industry; Chair. Dr MARSHALL HALL.

Citrus Growers' Association Ltd: Bog Walk, Linstead; tel. 922-8230; f. 1944; 13,000 mems; Chair. C. L. BENT.

Jamaica Association of Sugar Technologists: c/o Sugar Industry Research Institute, Kendal Rd, Mandeville; tel. 962-2241; fax 962-1288; f. 1936; 275 mems; Chair. KARL JAMES; Pres. GILBERT THORNE.

Jamaica Exporters' Association (JEA): 39 Hope Rd, Kingston 10; tel. 927-6238; fax 927-5137; e-mail jea@cwjamaica.com; internet www.exportjamaica.org; Pres. KARL JAMES; Exec. Dir PAULINE GRAY.

Jamaica Livestock Association: Newport East, POB 36, Kingston; tel. 922-7130; fax 923-5046; e-mail jlapurch@cwjamaica.com; internet www.jlatd.com; f. 1941; 7,584 mems; Chair. Dr JOHN MASTERTON; Man. Dir and CEO HENRY J. RAINFORD.

Jamaica Manufacturers' Association Ltd: 85a Duke St, Kingston; tel. 922-8880; fax 922-9205; e-mail jma@toj.com; internet www.jma.com.jm; f. 1947; 400 mems; Pres. CLARENCE CLARK.

Jamaica Producers' Group Ltd: 6A Oxford Rd, POB 237, Kingston 5; tel. 926-3503; fax 929-3636; e-mail cosecretary@jpjamaica.com; f. 1929; fmrly Jamaica Banana Producers' Assen; Chair. C. H. JOHNSTON; Man. Dir Dr MARSHALL HALL.

Private Sector Organization of Jamaica (PSOJ): 39 Hope Rd, POB 236, Kingston 10; tel. 927-6238; fax 927-5137; e-mail psojinfo@psoj.org; internet www.psoj.org; federative body of private business individuals, cos and asscns; Pres. Hon. OLIVER F. CLARK; Exec. Dir GRETA BOGUES.

Small Businesses' Association of Jamaica (SBAJ): 2 Trafalgar Rd, Kingston 5; tel. 927-7071; fax 978-2738; e-mail sbaj@anbell.net; internet www.sbaj.org.jm; Chair. ADOLPH BROWN; Man ALBERT HUIE.

Sugar Manufacturing Corpn of Jamaica Ltd: 5 Trevennion Park Rd, Kingston 5; tel. 926-5930; fax 926-6149; established to represent the sugar manufacturers in Jamaica; deals with all aspects of the sugar industry and its by-products; provides liaison between the Govt, the Sugar Industry Authority and the All-Island Jamaica Cane Farmers' Asscn; 9 mems; Chair. CHRISTOPHER BOVELL; Gen. Man. DERYCK T. BROWN.

UTILITIES

Regulatory Authority

Office of Utilities Regulation (OUR): PCJ Resource Centre, 3rd Floor, 36 Trafalgar Rd, Kingston 10; tel. 929-6672; fax 929-3635; e-mail office@our.org.jm; internet www.our.org.jm; f. 1995; regulates provision of services in the following sectors: water, electricity, telecommunications, public passenger transportation, sewerage; Dir-Gen. J. PAUL MORGAN.

Electricity

Jamaica Public Service Co (JPSCo): Dominion Life Bldg, 6 Knutsford Blvd, POB 54, Kingston 5; tel. 926-3190; fax 968-5341; e-mail media@jpsco.com; internet www.jpsco.com; responsible for the generation and supply of electricity to the island; 80% sold to Mirant Corpn (USA) in March 2001; Pres. and CEO CHARLES MATTHEWS.

Water

National Water Commission: 4A Marescaux Rd, Kingston 5; tel. 929-3540; internet www.nwcjamaica.com; f. 1980; statutory body; provides potable water and waste water services; Chair. RICHARD BYLES.

Water Resources Authority: Hope Gardens, POB 91, Kingston 7; tel. 927-0077; fax 977-0179; e-mail commander@cwjamaica.com; internet www.wra-ja.org; f. 1996; manages, protects and controls allocation and use of water supplies; Man. Dir BASIL FERNANDEZ.

TRADE UNIONS

Bustamante Industrial Trade Union (BITU): 98 Duke St, Kingston; tel. 922-2443; fax 967-0120; e-mail bitu@cwjamaica.com; f. 1938; HUGH SHEARER; Gen. Sec. GEORGE FYFFE; 60,000 mems.

Jamaica Confederation of Trade Unions (JCTU): 1A Hope Blvd, Kingston 6; tel. 977-5170; fax 977-4575; e-mail jctu@cwjamaica.com; Sec.-Gen. LLOYD GOODLEIGH.

National Workers' Union of Jamaica (NWU): 130–132 East St, POB 344, Kingston 16; tel. 922-1150; e-mail nwyou@cwjamaica.com; f. 1952; affiliated to the International Confederation of Free Trade Unions, etc.; Pres. CLIVE DOBSON; Gen. Sec. LLOYD GOODLEIGH; 10,000 mems.

Trades Union Congress of Jamaica: 25 Sutton St, POB 19, Kingston; tel. 922-5313; fax 922-5468; affiliated to the Caribbean Congress of Labour and the International Confederation of Free Trade Unions; Pres. E. SMITH; Gen. Sec. HOPETON CRAVEN; 20,000 mems.

Principal Independent Unions

Caribbean Union of Teachers: 97 Church St, Kingston; tel. 922-1385; fax 922-3257; e-mail jta@cwjamaica.com; Pres. BYRON FARQUHARSON; Gen. Sec. ADOLPH CAMERON.

Jamaica Association of Local Government Officers: 15A Old Hope Rd, Kingston 5; tel. 929-5123; fax 960-4403; e-mail jalgo@cwjamaica.com; Pres. STANLEY THOMAS.

Jamaica Civil Service Association: 2 Caledonia Ave, Kingston 5; tel. 968-7087; fax 926-2042; e-mail jacisera@cwjamaica.com; Pres. WAYNE JONES.

Jamaica Federation of Musicians: 5 Balmoral Ave, Kingston 10; tel. 926-8029; fax 929-0485; e-mail jafedmusic@cwjamaica.com; internet jafedmusic.tripod.com; f. 1958; Pres. HEDLEY H. G. JONES; Sec. CARL AYTON; 2,000 mems.

Jamaica Teachers' Association: 97 Church St, Kingston; tel. 922-1385-7; fax 922-3257; e-mail jta@cwjamaica.com; Gen. Sec. Dr ADOLPH CAMERON.

Jamaica Union of Public Officers and Public Employees: 4 Northend Pl., Kingston 10; tel. 929-1354; Pres. FITZROY BRYAN; Gen. Sec. NICKELLOH MARTIN.

Jamaica Workers' Union: 3 West Ave, Kingston 4; tel. 922-3222; fax 967-3128; Pres. CLIFTON BROWN; Gen. Sec. MICHAEL NEWTON.

Union of Schools, Agricultural and Allied Workers (USAAW): 2 Wildman St, Kingston; tel. 967-2970; f. 1978; Pres. DWAYNE BARNETT.

Union of Technical, Administrative and Supervisory Personnel: 108 Church St, Kingston; tel. 922-2086; Pres. ANTHONY DAWKINS; Gen. Sec. REG ENNIS.

United Portworkers' and Seamen's Union (UPWU): Kingston.

United Union of Jamaica: 35A Lynhurst Rd, Kingston; tel. 960-4206; Pres. JAMES FRANCIS; Gen. Sec. WILLIAM HASFAL.

University and Allied Workers' Union (UAWU): 50 Lady Musgrave Rd, Kingston; tel. 927-7968; fax 927-9931; e-mail jacisera@cwjamaica.com; affiliated to the WPJ; Pres. Prof. TREVOR MUNROE.

There are also some 30 associations registered as trade unions.

Transport

RAILWAYS

There are about 272 km (169 miles) of railway, all standard gauge, in Jamaica. The government-subsidized Jamaica Railway Corpn operated 207 km of the track until freight and passenger services were suspended in 1992 owing to falling revenues not meeting maintenance costs. Negotiations towards the privatization of the Jamaica Railway Corpn between the Government and the Indian/Canadian consortium Railtech broke down in late 2003. In early 2005 the Government signed a memorandum of understanding with China National Machinery and Equipment Corpn for the reconstruction of the railway system, including the provision of passengers coaches and engines.

Jamaica Railway Corpn (JRC): 142 Barry St, POB 489, Kingston; tel. 922-6620; fax 922-4539; f. 1845 as Jamaica Railway Co, the earliest British colonial railway; transferred to JRC in 1960; govt-owned, but autonomous, statutory corpn until 1990, when it was partly leased to Alcan Jamaica Co Ltd (subsequently West Indies Alumina Co) as the first stage of a privatization scheme; 207 km of railway; Chair. W. TAYLOR; Gen. Man. OWEN CROOKS.

Alcoa Railroads: Alcoa Minerals of Jamaica Inc, May Pen PO; tel. 986-2561; fax 986-2026; 43 km of standard-gauge railway; transport of bauxite; Supt RICHARD HECTOR; Man. FITZ CARTY (Railroad Operations and Maintenance).

Kaiser Jamaica Bauxite Co Railway: Discovery Bay PO, St Ann; tel. 973-2221; 25 km of standard-gauge railway; transport of bauxite; Gen. Man. TIM DAMON.

ROADS

Jamaica has a good network of tar-surfaced and metalled motoring roads. According to estimates by the International Road Federation, there were 18,700 km of roads in 2004, of which 70.1% were paved. In 2001 a consortium of two British companies, Kier International and Mabey & Johnson, was awarded a contract to supply the materials for and construct six road bridges in Kingston and Montego Bay, and a further 20 bridges in rural areas. In the same year the Inter-American Development Bank approved a US $24.5m. loan to improve road maintenance. In March 2002 construction of the first part of a 230 km highway system linking major cities was scheduled to begin.

SHIPPING

The principal ports are Kingston, Montego Bay and Port Antonio. The port at Kingston has four container berths, and is a major transhipment terminal for the Caribbean area. Jamaica has interests in the multinational shipping line WISCO (West Indies Shipping Corpn—based in Trinidad and Tobago). Services are also provided by most major foreign lines serving the region. In January 2004 a US $35m. plan to expand Kingston's container-handling capacity by 25% was announced.

Port Authority of Jamaica: 15–17 Duke St, Kingston; tel. 922-0290; fax 924-9437; e-mail pajmktg@infochan.com; internet www.seaportsofjamaica.com; f. 1966; Govt's principal maritime agency; responsible for monitoring and regulating the navigation of all vessels berthing at Jamaican ports, for regulating the tariffs on public wharves, and for the devt of industrial Free Zones in Jamaica; Pres. and Chair. NOEL HYLTON.

Kingston Free Zone Co Ltd: 27 Shannon Dr., POB 1025, Kingston 15; tel. 923-5274; fax 923-6023; e-mail kfzclsvc@infochan.com; internet www.seaportsofjamaica.com; f. 1976; subsidiary of Port Authority of Jamaica; management and promotion of an export-orientated industrial free trade zone for cos from various countries; Gen. Man. CLAUDE FLETCHER.

Montego Bay Free Zone: POB 1377, Montego Bay; tel. 979-8696-8; fax 979-8088; e-mail clients-mbfz@jadigiport.com; internet www.seaportsofjamaica.com; Gen. Man. CLAUDE FLETCHER.

Shipping Association of Jamaica: 4 Fourth Ave, Newport West, POB 1050, Kingston 15; tel. 923-3491; fax 923-3421; e-mail jfs@jashipco.com; internet www.seaportsofjamaica.com; f. 1939; 63 mems; an employers' trade union which regulates the supply and management of stevedoring labour in Kingston; represents members in negotiations with govt and trade bodies; Pres. GRANTLEY STEPHENSON; Gen. Man. PAULINE GRAY.

Principal Shipping Companies

Jamaica Freight and Shipping Co Ltd (JFS): 80–82 Second St, Port Bustamante, POB 167, Kingston 13; tel. 923-9271; fax 923-4091; e-mail cshaw@toj.com; cargo services to and from the USA, Caribbean, Central and South America, the United Kingdom, Japan and Canada; Exec. Chair. CHARLES JOHNSTON; Man. Dir GRANTLEY STEPHENSON.

Portcold Ltd: 122 Third St, Newport West, Kingston 13; tel. 923-7425; fax 923-5713; Chair. and Man. Dir ISHMAEL E. ROBERTSON.

CIVIL AVIATION

There are two international airports linking Jamaica with North America, Europe, and other Caribbean islands. The Norman Manley International Airport is situated 22.5 km (14 miles) outside Kingston. The Donald Sangster International Airport is 5 km (3 miles) from Montego Bay. A J $800m. programme to expand and improve the latter was under consideration.

Airports Authority of Jamaica: Victoria Mutual Bldg, 53 Knutsford Blvd, POB 567, Kingston 5; tel. 926-1622; fax 929-8171; e-mail aaj@aaj.com.jm; internet www.aaj.com.jm; Chair. DENNIS MORRISON; Pres. EARL RICHARDS.

Civil Aviation Authority: 4 Winchester Rd, POB 8998, Kingston 10; tel. 960-3948; fax 920-0194; e-mail jcivav@jcaa.gov.jm; internet www.jcaa.gov.jm.

Air Jamaica Ltd: 72–76 Harbour St, Kingston; tel. 922-3460; fax 922-0107; internet www.airjamaica.com; f. 1968; privatized in 1994, Govt reacquired 45% in 2001 and the remaining 55% in 2005; services within the Caribbean and to Canada (in asscn with Air Canada), the USA and the United Kingdom; CEO CHRISTOPHER ZACCA.

Air Jamaica Express: Tinson Pen Aerodrome, Kingston 11; tel. 923-6664; fax 937-3807; internet www.airjamaica.com/express; previously known as Trans-Jamaican Airlines; internal services between Kingston, Montego Bay, Negril, Ocho Rios and Port Antonio and services to the Cayman Islands, the Bahamas, the Dominican Republic and Cuba; Man. Dir PAULO MOREIRA.

Air Negril: Montego Bay; tel. 940-7741; fax 940-6491; e-mail negriljeff@yahoo.com; internet caribbean-travel.com/airnegril; domestic charter services.

Tourism

Tourists, mainly from the USA, visit Jamaica for its beaches, mountains, historic buildings and cultural heritage. In 2004 there were an estimated 1,414,786 visitors (excluding cruise-ship passengers). Tourist receipts were estimated to be US $1,209m. in 2002. In 2001 there were some 24,007 rooms in all forms of tourist accommodation.

Jamaica Tourist Board (JTB): 64 Knutsford Blvd, Kingston 5; tel. 929-9200; fax 929-9375; e-mail info@visitjamaica.com; internet www.visitjamaica.com; f. 1955; a statutory body set up by the Govt to promote all aspects of the tourist industry; Chair. DENNIS MORRISON; Dir of Tourism PAUL PENNICOOK.

Jamaica Hotel and Tourist Association (JHTA): 2 Ardenne Rd, Kingston 10; tel. 926-3635; fax 929-1054; e-mail info@jhta.org; internet www.jhta.org; f. 1961; trade asscn for hoteliers and other cos involved in Jamaican tourism; Pres. GODFREY DYER; Exec. Dir CAMILLE NEEDHAM.

JAPAN

Introductory Survey

Location, Climate, Language, Religion, Flag, Capital

Japan lies in eastern Asia and comprises a curved chain of more than 3,000 islands. Four large islands, named (from north to south) Hokkaido, Honshu, Shikoku and Kyushu, account for about 98% of the land area. Hokkaido lies just to the south of Sakhalin, a large Russian island, and about 1,300 km (800 miles) east of Russia's mainland port of Vladivostok. Southern Japan is about 150 km (93 miles) east of the Republic of Korea (South Korea). Although summers are temperate everywhere, the climate in winter varies sharply from cold in the north to mild in the south. Temperatures in Tokyo range from –6°C (21°F) to 30°C (86°F). Typhoons and heavy rains are common in summer. The language is Japanese. The major religions are Shintoism and Buddhism, and there is a Christian minority. The national flag (proportions 7 by 10) is white, with a red disc (a sun without rays) in the centre. The capital is Tokyo.

Recent History

Following Japan's defeat in the Second World War, Japanese forces surrendered in August 1945. Japan signed an armistice in September, and the country was placed under US military occupation. A new democratic constitution, which took effect from May 1947, renounced war and abandoned the doctrine of the Emperor's divinity. Following the peace treaty of September 1951, Japan regained its independence on 28 April 1952, although it was not until 1972 that the last of the US-administered outer islands were returned to Japanese sovereignty.

In November 1955 rival conservative groups merged to form the Liberal-Democratic Party (LDP). Nobusuke Kishi, who became Prime Minister in February 1957, was succeeded by Hayato Ikeda in July 1960. Ikeda was replaced by Eisaku Sato in November 1964. Sato remained in office until July 1972, when he was succeeded by Kakuei Tanaka.

Tanaka's premiership was beset by problems, leading to his replacement by Takeo Miki in December 1974. Tanaka was subsequently accused of accepting bribes from the Marubeni Corporation, and he was arrested in July 1976. The LDP lost its overall majority in the House of Representatives (the lower house of the Diet) at a general election held in December 1976. Miki resigned and was succeeded by Takeo Fukuda. However, Masayoshi Ohira defeated Fukuda in the LDP presidential election of November 1978, and replaced him as Prime Minister in December. Ohira was unable to win a majority in the lower house at elections in October 1979. In May 1980 the Government was defeated in a motion of 'no confidence', forcing the dissolution of the lower house. Ohira died before the elections in June, when the LDP won 284 of the 511 seats, despite obtaining only a minority of the votes cast. In July Zenko Suzuki, a relatively little-known compromise candidate, was elected President of the LDP, and subsequently appointed Prime Minister. In November 1981 Suzuki reorganized the Cabinet, distributing major posts among the five feuding LDP factions. The growing factionalism of the LDP and the worsening economic crisis prompted Suzuki's resignation as Prime Minister and LDP President in October 1982. He was succeeded by Yasuhiro Nakasone.

At elections in June 1983 for one-half of the seats in the House of Councillors (the upper house of the Diet), a new electoral system was used. Of the 126 contested seats, 50 were filled on the basis of proportional representation. As a result, two small parties entered the House of Councillors for the first time. The LDP increased its strength from 134 to 137 members in the 252-seat chamber. This result was seen as an endorsement of Nakasone's policies of increased expenditure on defence, closer ties with the USA and greater Japanese involvement in international affairs.

In October 1983 the former Prime Minister, Kakuei Tanaka, was found guilty of accepting bribes. However, Tanaka refused to relinquish his legislative seat (he had already resigned from the LDP). The opposition parties therefore led a boycott of the Diet, forcing Nakasone to call a premature general election in December 1983. The Komeito (Clean Government Party), the Democratic Socialist Party (DSP) and the Japan Socialist Party

(JSP) gained seats, at the expense of the Communists and the New Liberal Club (NLC). The LDP, which had performed badly in the election, formed a coalition with the NLC (which had split from the LDP over the Tanaka affair in 1976) and several independents. Nakasone remained President of the LDP, after promising to reduce Tanaka's influence. Following the trial of Tanaka, reforms were introduced, whereby cabinet members were required to disclose the extent of their personal assets.

Nakasone called another premature general election for July 1986, which coincided with elections for one-half of the seats in the House of Councillors. In the election to the House of Representatives, the LDP obtained its highest level of electoral support since 1963, and won a record 304 of the 512 seats. The increased LDP majority was achieved largely at the expense of the JSP and the DSP, thus enabling the LDP to dispense with its coalition partner, the NLC (which disbanded in August and rejoined the LDP). In September the leaders of the LDP agreed to alter by-laws to allow party presidents one-year extensions beyond the normal limit of two terms of two years each. Nakasone was thus able to retain the posts of President of the LDP and Prime Minister until October 1987.

In July 1987 the Secretary-General of the LDP, Noboru Takeshita, left the Tanaka faction, with 113 other members, and announced the formation of a major new grouping within the ruling party. In the same month Tanaka's political influence was further weakened when the Tokyo High Court upheld the decision, taken in 1983, declaring him guilty of accepting bribes. (In February 1995 this ruling was upheld by the Supreme Court.)

In October 1987 Nakasone nominated Takeshita as his successor. The Diet was convened and Takeshita was formally elected as Prime Minister in November. In the new Cabinet, Takeshita maintained a balance among the five major factions of the LDP, retaining only two members of Nakasone's previous Cabinet, but appointing four members of the Nakasone faction to senior ministerial posts (including Nakasone's staunch ally, Sosuke Uno, as Minister of Foreign Affairs).

The implementation of a programme of tax reforms was one of the most important issues confronting Takeshita's Government. In June 1988 the proposed introduction of a new indirect tax (a general consumption tax, or a form of value-added tax) aroused widespread opposition. In the same month the Prime Minister and the LDP suffered a serious set-back when several leading figures in the party, including Nakasone, Shintaro Abe, Kiichi Miyazawa and Takeshita himself, were alleged to have been indirectly involved in share-trading irregularities with the Recruit Cosmos Company. In November, shortly after the LDP had agreed to establish a committee to investigate the Recruit scandal, the House of Representatives approved proposals for tax reform (which constituted the most wide-ranging revision of the tax system for 40 years). Three cabinet ministers and the Chairman of the DSP were subsequently forced to resign, owing to their alleged involvement in the Recruit affair.

In January 1989 Emperor Hirohito, who had reigned since 1926, died after a long illness, thus ending the Showa era. He was succeeded by his son, Akihito, and the new era was named Heisei ('achievement of universal peace').

In April 1989, as the allegations against politicians widened to include charges of bribery and malpractice, Takeshita announced his resignation. He was subsequently found to have accepted donations worth more than 150m. yen from the Recruit organization. Takeshita nominated Sosuke Uno as his successor. Uno was elected Prime Minister by the Diet on 2 June; a new Cabinet was appointed on the same day. Uno thus became the first Japanese Prime Minister since the foundation of the LDP not to command his own political faction. In May, following an eight-month investigation undertaken by the LDP's special committee, public prosecutors indicted 13 people. Nakasone resigned from his faction and from the LDP, assuming responsibility for the Recruit affair, but did not relinquish his seat in the Diet.

Within a few days of Uno's assumption of office, a Japanese magazine published allegations of sexual impropriety involving the Prime Minister, which precipitated demands for his resignation. Serious losses suffered by the LDP in Tokyo's municipal elections in July 1989 further discredited Uno. As a result of a considerable increase in support for the JSP, led by Takako Doi, the LDP lost its majority in the upper house for the first time in its history. Uno's offer to resign was accepted by the LDP, which in August chose the relatively unknown Toshiki Kaifu, a former Minister of Education, to replace Uno as the party's President and as the new Prime Minister. Although the House of Councillors' ballot rejected Kaifu as the new Prime Minister in favour of Takako Doi, the decision of the lower house was adopted, in accordance with stipulations embodied in the Constitution. This was the first time in 41 years that the two houses of the Diet had disagreed over the choice of Prime Minister. In October Kaifu was re-elected as President of the LDP for a further two-year term.

At a general election held in February 1990, the LDP was returned to power with an unexpectedly large measure of support, securing 275 of the 512 seats in the lower house. In December Toshiyuki Inamura, a former cabinet minister, resigned from the LDP after charges of large-scale tax evasion and complicity in a new stock-manipulation scandal were brought against him. A prison sentence with hard labour, which he received in November 1991, was regarded as a deterrent to other politicians from engaging in financial corruption. In January 1991 the JSP changed its English name to the Social Democratic Party of Japan (SDPJ) and Makato Tanabe later replaced Takako Doi as Chairman of the party. In September senior LDP officials forced Kaifu to abandon proposals for electoral reform and the Takeshita faction of the LDP subsequently withdrew its support for the Prime Minister. Sponsored by the faction, the former Minister of Finance, Kiichi Miyazawa, was elected President of the LDP in October, and in November the Diet endorsed his appointment as Prime Minister. New allegations of involvement in the Recruit affair, publicized by the SDPJ in December 1991, seriously undermined Miyazawa's position.

In early 1992 public disgust at official corruption was registered at two prefectural by-elections to the upper house, when the LDP lost seats, which had previously been considered secure, to Rengo-no-kai (the political arm of RENGO, the trade union confederation). However, the anti-Government alliance, which had supported Rengo-no-kai, disintegrated in May over the issue of the authorization of Japanese involvement in UN peace-keeping operations. Members of the SDPJ attempted to obstruct the vote in the lower house by submitting their resignations *en masse*. The Speaker, however, ruled that these could not be accepted during the current Diet session. The successful passage through the Diet of the legislation on international peace-keeping improved the Government's standing, and in elections to the upper house in July the LDP won 69 of the 127 seats contested. The SDPJ, by contrast, lost 25 of its 46 seats; the Komeito increased its total strength from 20 to 24 seats, but Rengo-no-kai failed to win any seats, owing to the dissolution of the informal coalition it had facilitated between the SDPJ and the DSP. The Japan New Party (JNP), founded only two months prior to the election by LDP dissidents, secured four seats. A formal split within the Takeshita faction took place in December 1992. The new faction was to be led nominally by Tsutomu Hata, the Minister of Finance, although it was widely recognized that Ichiro Ozawa held the real power in the grouping.

Electoral reform was a major political issue in the first half of 1993. While the LDP favoured a single-member constituency system, the opposition parties proposed various forms of proportional representation. The LDP's lack of a majority in the upper house rendered it unable to enforce any reforms without the agreement of the opposition parties. Within the LDP itself there was conflict over whether or not to compromise with opposition parties. In June the lower house adopted a motion of 'no confidence' against the Government, after the LDP refused to modify its reform proposals to meet opposition demands. Numerous LDP members opposed the Government or abstained. The Ozawa-Hata group, comprising 44 former LDP members, immediately established a new party, the Shinseito (Japan Renewal Party, JRP), in order to contest the forthcoming general election. Another new party, the New Party Sakigake, was also formed by LDP Diet members. In the election to the House of Representatives, held in July, the LDP won 223 of the 511 seats, and was thus 33 seats short of a majority. Miyazawa resigned as Prime Minister and a coalition Government was formed. On 6 August Morihiro Hosokawa, the leader of the JNP,

was elected Prime Minister, defeating the new President of the LDP, Yohei Kono.

In late 1993 three senior politicians, Noboru Takeshita, Ichiro Ozawa and Kishiro Nakamura (a former Minister of Construction), were implicated in a scandal involving payments from construction companies in return for awarding building contracts. Ozawa claimed that the payments were legal, since none had exceeded 1.5m. yen. In January 1994 the Public Prosecutor's office began investigations into bribery allegations against Nakamura and Hideo Watanabe, the former Minister of Posts and Telecommunications.

In November 1993 four items of electoral reform legislation were passed by a majority of 270 to 226 votes in the House of Representatives (they were opposed by the LDP). In January 1994, however, the reform bills were defeated in the upper house, but Hosokawa (who had threatened to resign if the legislation were not passed) subsequently reached agreement with the LDP on modifications to the reform bills (see below).

Hosokawa resigned as Prime Minister in April 1994. Tsutomu Hata was subsequently appointed Prime Minister, at the head of a minority Government that excluded the SDPJ and the New Party Sakigake. Hata was obliged to resign in June, however, owing to his continued failure to command a viable majority in the Diet, and a new coalition of the SDPJ, the LDP and the New Party Sakigake took office. Tomiichi Murayama, the leader of the SDPJ, became Prime Minister, and Kono was appointed Deputy Prime Minister and Minister of Foreign Affairs.

In July 1994 Murayama recognized the constitutional right to the existence of Japan's Self-Defence Forces (SDF, the armed forces), thereby effectively contradicting official SDPJ policy on the issue. (The SDPJ amended its policy to accord with Murayama's statement in September.) In December nine opposition parties, including the JNP, the JRP, the DSP and the Komeito, amalgamated to form a new political party, the Shinshinto (New Frontier Party, NFP). A faction of Komeito remained outside the new party and was renamed Komei. Kaifu, the former LDP Prime Minister, was elected leader of the NFP; Ozawa was appointed Secretary-General.

The creation of the NFP was widely perceived to be a response to the approval by the Diet in November 1994 of the electoral reform bills first proposed in 1993, which appeared to favour larger political parties. Under the terms of the new law, the House of Representatives was to be reduced to 500 seats, comprising 300 single-seat constituencies and 200 seats determined by proportional representation; the proportional-representation base was to be divided into 11 regions, and a party would qualify for a proportional-representation seat if it received a minimum of 2% of the vote; donations amounting to 500,000 yen annually per private sector corporation to individual politicians were permitted, but this was to be phased out after five years; restrictions on corporate donations would be subsidized by the State; door-to-door campaigning was to be permitted and an independent body would draw up new electoral boundaries. In June 1995 the first distribution of public money to political parties took place.

In January 1995 a massive earthquake in the Kobe region caused thousands of deaths and serious infrastructural damage. The Government was severely criticized for the poor co-ordination of the relief operation. In March a poisonous gas, sarin, was released into the Tokyo underground railway system, killing 12 people and injuring more than 5,000. A religious sect, Aum Shinrikyo, was accused of perpetrating the attack. Following a further gas attack in Yokohama in April, a number of sect members were detained by the authorities. In June Shoko Asahara, the leader of Aum Shinrikyo, was indicted on a charge of murder. The trial of Asahara opened in April 1996. In September Asahara and two other members of the sect were instructed to pay some US $7.3m. in compensation to victims of the Tokyo incident.

Participation in the elections to the House of Councillors, held in July 1995, was low. With one-half of the 252 seats being contested, the LDP won only 49 seats, the SDPJ 16 and the New Party Sakigake three, whereas the NFP, benefiting from the support of the Soka Gakkai religious organization, won 40 seats. In September Ryutaro Hashimoto, the Minister of International Trade and Industry, was elected leader of the LDP, after Yohei Kono announced that he would not seek re-election.

Conflict in the Diet escalated between February and June 1995 over government plans, announced in June 1994, to issue a resolution to commemorate the 50th anniversary of the ending of the Second World War. The resolution was to constitute an apology to countries whose citizens had suffered from the actions of the Japanese army during the war. The New Party Sakigake threatened to withdraw from the coalition if an apology were not made, while a group of 160 LDP Diet members, led by Seisuke Okuno, objected to the definition of Japan as an aggressor. A resolution was finally passed in June 1995, despite a boycott of the vote by the NFP.

In December 1995 Toshiki Kaifu was succeeded by Ichiro Ozawa as leader of the NFP. In January 1996 Tomiichi Murayama resigned as Prime Minister; he was, however, re-elected Chairman of the SDPJ. The LDP leader, Ryutaro Hashimoto, was elected Prime Minister on 11 January. A coalition Cabinet, largely dominated by the LDP, was formed.

In March 1996 the New Socialist Party (NSP) was formed by left-wing defectors from the SDPJ. Osamu Yatabe was elected Chairman of the NSP and Tetsuo Yamaguchi was appointed Secretary-General. In mid-1996, in an attempt to strengthen their electoral bases, particularly in the new single-member districts, there was a further realignment of political parties. In August Shoichi Ide and Hiroyuki Sonoda were elected Leader and Secretary-General, respectively, of the New Party Sakigake following the resignations of Masayoshi Takemura and Yukio Hatoyama. Hatoyama left the party and founded the Democratic Party of Japan (DPJ), with other dissident members of the New Party Sakigake and individual members of the SDPJ and NFP.

A general election was held in October 1996. The LDP won 239 of the 500 seats in the House of Representatives, while the NFP secured 156, the DPJ 52, the Japan Communist Party (JCP) 26, the SDPJ 15, and the New Party Sakigake two seats. Four deputies, who were elected as independents, subsequently formed a new party called the 21st Century. In November Ryutaro Hashimoto was re-elected Prime Minister, and formed the first single-party Cabinet since 1993.

Soon after the election several government ministers and party leaders were implicated in various official corruption scandals. In December 1996 the former Prime Minister, Tsutomu Hata, left the NFP and formed a new party, called Taiyoto (Sun Party), together with 12 other dissident NFP members. In late December Takako Doi was formally appointed Chairwoman of the SDPJ (she had been acting Chairwoman since the dissolution of the House of Representatives in September).

In early 1997 the Government established several commissions, charged with devising a comprehensive programme of administrative and economic reforms. A reduction in government bureaucracy and public expenditure was envisaged, and details of a series of financial deregulation measures were announced in February, including the transfer of the Ministry of Finance's supervisory role to an independent agency in mid-1998. The Government's management of the nuclear programme was comprehensively reviewed, following two accidents at plants in December 1995 and March 1997. Allegations that a further 11 unreported radiation leaks had occurred over the previous three years heightened public disquiet.

In mid-1997 Hosokawa resigned from the NFP, reportedly owing to dissatisfaction with Ozawa's leadership. (In December Hosokawa formed a new party—From Five.) In addition, the NFP lost all of its seats in elections to the Tokyo Metropolitan Assembly, held in July. The LDP and the JCP, by contrast, increased their representation in the Assembly. By September the LDP had regained its majority in the House of Representatives, following a series of defections by members of the NFP. In December a much-reduced NFP was dissolved. Six new parties were founded by former NFP members, Ozawa and his supporters forming the Liberal Party (LP), and a significant political realignment thus took place. In January 1998 six opposition parties, including the DPJ, formed a parliamentary group, Minyuren, which constituted the largest opposition bloc in the Diet. In March the parties comprising Minyuren agreed on their integration into the DPJ, formally establishing a new DPJ, with Naoto Kan as its President, in the following month.

Meanwhile, during 1997 various circumstances, including continuing financial corruption, an increase in the rate of the unpopular consumption tax, a decrease in public expenditure and the collapse of several prominent financial institutions, together with the threat of further bankruptcies, contributed to the development of an economic crisis. The Government announced a series of measures designed to encourage economic growth, including a reduction in taxes and, in a major reversal of policy, the use of public funds to support the banking system. In January 1998 the Diet reconvened earlier than scheduled, in order to approve the budget for 1998/99, as well as supple-

mentary budget proposals incorporating the tax reductions. In late January 1998 two senior officials from the Ministry of Finance were arrested on suspicion of accepting bribes from banks. The Minister of Finance, Hiroshi Mitsuzuka, resigned, accepting full moral responsibility for the affair. As more banks and other financial institutions became implicated in the bribery scandal, the central bank initiated an internal investigation into its own operations. In March the Governor resigned after a senior bank executive was arrested amid further allegations of bribery. Trials of those implicated in the financial scandals took place in 1998 and 1999. A number of financial deregulation measures took effect on 1 April 1998, as part of Japan's 'Big Bang' reform process. The economy continued to stagnate, however, and Hashimoto's administration was widely criticized for its slow reaction to the crisis. In June the SDPJ and the New Party Sakigake withdrew from their alliance with the ruling LDP.

The LDP performed poorly in elections for one-half of the seats in the House of Councillors in July 1998, retaining only 44 of its 61 seats contested, while the DPJ won 27 seats, increasing its representation to 47 seats, and the JCP became the third-largest party in the upper house, taking 15 seats. Hashimoto resigned as Prime Minister and President of the LDP and was succeeded by Keizo Obuchi, hitherto Minister for Foreign Affairs. Obuchi was elected Prime Minister on 30 July.

Although Obuchi's Government was designated an 'economic reconstruction' Cabinet, doubts arose about its commitment to comprehensive reform. Kiichi Miyazawa, the former Prime Minister, was appointed Minister of Finance. In his inaugural policy speech, Obuchi announced the establishment of an Economic Strategy Council and promised substantial tax cuts. As Japan's economic situation worsened, political disputes over banking reform dominated the following months, with the Government reluctant to commit itself to the closure of failing banks. Following weeks of negotiations, in October 1998 the Diet approved banking legislation that included provisions for the nationalization of failing banks, as demanded by the opposition.

Shinto Heiwa and Komei merged in November 1998 to form New Komeito, which thus became the second-largest opposition party. Also in that month Fukushiro Nukaga, the Director-General of the Defence Agency, resigned from the Government to assume responsibility for a procurement scandal involving his agency. In mid-November the LDP and the Liberal Party (LP) reached a basic accord on the formation of a coalition, which would still remain short of a majority in the upper house. In January 1999 agreement was reached on coalition policies, including measures to reduce the influence of bureaucrats on the legislative process. The Cabinet was reorganized to include the LP, the leader of which, Ichiro Ozawa, had refused a cabinet position. At the end of January the Government adopted an administrative reform plan, which aimed to reduce further the number of cabinet ministers and public servants and to establish an economic and fiscal policy committee. Draft legislation on the implementation of the plan was introduced in the Diet in April.

At local elections in April 1999, 11 of the 12 governorships contested were won by the incumbents, all standing as independents. At the gubernatorial election for Tokyo, the convincing victory of Shintaro Ishihara, a nationalist writer and a former Minister of Transport under the LDP (although now unaffiliated), was regarded as an embarrassment for the ruling party. Ishihara immediately provoked controversy, making inflammatory comments about the 1937 Nanjing massacre and criticizing the Chinese Government, which responded angrily, prompting the Japanese Government to distance itself publicly from the new Governor's remarks. In November the Chinese Government also expressed its concern regarding an unofficial visit by Ishihara to Taiwan, which had recently suffered a major earthquake. Ishihara also angered the People's Republic of China by visiting Taiwan in May 2000 for the inauguration of the latter's new President, Chen Shui-bian, despite having refused an invitation to visit China as part of celebrations to mark the anniversary of the establishment of relations between Beijing and Tokyo.

In June 1999 the Government voted to grant official legal status to the *de facto* national flag (*Hinomaru*) and anthem (*Kimigayo*), despite considerable opposition owing to their association with Japan's militaristic past. The necessary legislation became effective in mid-August, following approval by the Diet. Meanwhile, in July New Komeito agreed to join the ruling LDP-LP coalition, giving the Government a new majority in the upper house and expanding its control in the lower house to more than 70% of the seats. Negotiations on policy initiatives proved difficult, however, owing to differences over a number of contentious issues such as constitutional revision and New Komeito's opposition to a reduction in the number of seats in the lower house, as favoured by the LP. Obuchi was re-elected President of the LDP in September. Naoto Kan was replaced as President of the DPJ by Yukio Hatoyama, hitherto Secretary-General of the party.

At the end of September 1999 a serious accident at a uranium-processing plant at Tokaimura severely undermined public confidence in the safety of Japan's nuclear industry. Furthermore, in November it was revealed that 15 of 17 nuclear facilities recently inspected by government officials had failed to meet legal health and safety standards. In December the Diet enacted legislation aimed at preventing accidents and improving procedures. In February 2000 the Government announced that 439 people had been exposed to radiation in the Tokaimura accident, far more than the 69 recorded in the initial report. Two workers from the plant subsequently died from radiation exposure. In September 2000 compensation was agreed for the victims of the accident. Former staff at the plant were arrested in October and charged with negligence resulting in death. In November 2000 the plant was authorized to be reopened.

A new Cabinet was appointed in October 1999. Notably, Michio Ochi was appointed Chairman of the Financial Reconstruction Commission. The LP and New Komeito each received one cabinet post. A basic accord on coalition policy included an agreement to seek a reduction in the number of seats in the House of Representatives, initially by 20 and subsequently by a further 30. A Vice-Minister at the Defence Agency resigned shortly after being appointed, following widespread criticism of his suggestion that Japan should arm itself with nuclear weapons. Obuchi, whose judgement in the affair was questioned, subsequently apologized to the nation in a speech to the Diet.

Trials continued in 1997–99 of members of Aum Shinrikyo, the cult accused of perpetrating the sarin gas attack on the Tokyo underground railway system in March 1995. In September 1999 Masato Yokoyama, a leading member of the cult, became the first of those accused to receive the death sentence. In late 1999 Aum Shinrikyo issued a series of statements in an apparent attempt to avert any restriction on the cult or seizure of its assets. The leaders of the cult announced a suspension of all external activities from October, and in December acknowledged its culpability for a number of crimes, including the 1995 gas attack. Moreover, in January 2000 the cult announced that it was changing its name to Aleph and renouncing its leader, Shoko Asahara, who was still being tried for his part in the gas attack. In February, following a police raid on Aum Shinrikyo premises, it was revealed that a number of major companies and government agencies had placed orders for computer software with a firm believed to be major source of revenue for the cult; the Defence Agency subsequently announced that it was to abandon software purchased from the company for use by the SDF.

In December 1999 a political crisis was averted when Ozawa was persuaded not to withdraw the LP from the ruling coalition, as he had threatened, over a delay in the proposal of legislation to reduce the number of seats in the lower house. The ruling parties had earlier agreed also to postpone the consideration of a proposal to expand Japan's participation in UN peace-keeping activities. In early 2000 the ruling coalition approved the controversial legislation on the reduction in seats through the Diet, despite an opposition boycott, which continued for some two weeks. Multi-party committees were established in both houses in January, which were to review the Constitution over a period of five years. In late February Michio Ochi was forced to resign from the Cabinet over remarks that suggested he would be lenient on banking reform.

Discord within the coalition increased, and in April 2000 the LP withdrew from the Government; 26 members of the LP formed the New Conservative Party—NCP (Hoshuto). Keizo Obuchi, however, suffered a stroke and went into a coma from which he never regained consciousness. The Government was criticized for not releasing the news of Obuchi's condition (it was not reported in the media for at least 24 hours) even though the country had effectively been without a premier. Chief Cabinet Secretary Mikio Aoki became Acting Prime Minister, claiming that Obuchi had specifically asked him to fulfil the role, but the LDP elected Yoshiro Mori, the Secretary-General, as party

President; he was subsequently elected Prime Minister by both houses of the Diet. Mori immediately affirmed his commitment to the economic and political reform initiatives of his predecessor and formed a coalition with New Komeito and the NCP. All ministers from the Obuchi administration were retained. Both Seiroku Kajiyama (a former Chief Cabinet Secretary) and Noboru Takeshita, the former Prime Minister, announced their retirement from politics and from the LDP; both men died shortly afterwards. Former Prime Minister Ryutaro Hashimoto was appointed head of the Takeshita faction of the LDP, which had been led by Obuchi.

Following his appointment as Prime Minister, Mori made a number of controversial public statements, expressing imperialist views. Although forced to issue apologies, he did not retract his remarks. In the general election held on 25 June 2000 the number of seats in the House of Representatives was reduced from 500 to 480. The LDP won the most seats, although its representation was reduced to 233 and many of its key political figures, including current and former cabinet ministers, lost their seats, particularly in metropolitan areas. The DPJ increased its representation to 127 seats, New Komeito won 31 seats, the LP 22 seats, the NCP 20 seats and the SDPJ 19 seats. The LDP benefited from the electoral system, which gave rural areas (where the LDP had strong support) disproportionately high representation. Tradition and family connections remained important, with two candidates (the brother of Noboru Takeshita and the daughter of Keizo Obuchi) winning seats despite their lack of political experience. The participation rate was 62.5%. Although remaining in power, the LDP faced serious problems, among the most prominent of which related to the suitability of its leadership, Mori having made numerous political gaffes and public errors of protocol. Nevertheless, Mori was returned as Prime Minister and announced the composition of his new Cabinet in July.

Meanwhile, in February 2000 Governor Ishihara of Tokyo proposed that a tax be levied on major banks based on the size of their business rather than their profits; he was criticized by the central Government, which had previously been the only body able to introduce taxes. Ishihara attracted criticism from the foreign residents of Tokyo, and from neighbouring countries, in April when, in an address to members of the SDF, he blamed foreign residents for a number of serious crimes and referred to them as *sangokujin*, a derogatory wartime term for people from Taiwan and Korea.

In October 2000 an amendment to the voting system, under which electors would choose to vote either for a party or for an individual candidate, was proposed by the governing coalition. The opposition strongly criticized the proposed changes and, following the Government's insistence that they be passed through the Diet, commenced a boycott of proceedings. The bill was approved in the House of Representatives despite the boycott, which lasted 18 days and ended following an agreement between the Government and the opposition to debate the proposed legislation in the House of Representatives. It was enacted in late October. Meanwhile, Juro Saito resigned as President of the House of Councillors, owing to his failure successfully to mediate in the dispute. He was replaced by the former Minister of Education, Yutaka Inoue.

Corruption was a major issue throughout 2000, particularly the taking of bribes, revelations of which resulted in several resignations. Among the most serious incidents was a 'cash for questions' scandal involving an insurance company. One LDP member resigned and another was arrested in connection with the affair in November, and in January 2001 Fukushiro Nukaga, the Minister of State for Economy, Industry and Information Technology, resigned, having earlier admitted that he had accepted bribes from the firm. An LDP ally of Yoshiro Mori, Masakuni Murakami, was implicated in the case and arrested in March. In October 2000 Hidenao Nakagawa, Minister of State, Chief Cabinet Secretary, Director-General of the Okinawa Development Agency and Minister in Charge of Information Technology, resigned after it was alleged, *inter alia*, that he had links to a right-wing activist. In the following month the former Minister of Construction, Eiichi Nakao, acknowledged in court that he had taken bribes in 1996 in exchange for the allocation of public works contracts.

The high incidence of corruption further undermined Mori, and during October 2000 the Prime Minister came under increasing pressure to resign after it was alleged in a magazine that some years previously he had been arrested for violation of an anti-prostitution law. Mori denied the allegation and sued the publication for libel. Later that month, during a meeting with Tony Blair, the British Prime Minister, Mori reportedly suggested that the Democratic People's Republic of Korea (DPRK—North Korea) could release Japanese hostages (see below) to a third country in order to avoid any admission of their existence. Harsh criticism ensued, and subsequent attempts to mitigate the situation, by claiming that the remarks referred to an episode from the past, proved unsuccessful. In mid-November the opposition launched a motion of 'no confidence' in the Prime Minister. Furthermore, LDP member Koichi Kato publicly criticized Mori and declared himself ready to form a government. The Prime Minister won the vote, however, following threats by the party leadership that rebels voting against Mori would be expelled from the LDP. In early December, Mori suffered a set-back when his strong ally, Hiromu Nonaka, resigned as Secretary-General of the LDP and retired from politics. His nominated successor, Makoto Koga, subsequently assumed the role.

Meanwhile, in November 2000 Fusako Shigenobu, the founder of the extremist left-wing Japanese Red Army which had been responsible for a number of terrorist attacks during the 1970s, was arrested in Tokyo. She was detained on suspicion of the seizure of the French embassy in The Hague, the Netherlands, in 1974 and subsequently indicted on various related charges. A number of other members had been repatriated from several countries since 1995, and now faced trials for terrorism. Japan hoped to obtain the extradition from the DPRK, in return for economic aid, of more Red Army members, who had hijacked a Japanese aircraft and forced it to fly to Pyongyang in 1970, later being granted political asylum there. (In October 2004 the wife of one of these members, Tamiko Uomoto, was sentenced to a term of imprisonment after refusing to submit her passport.)

A major cabinet reorganization was effected in December 2000, and substantial changes were made to the government structure. The number of ministries was to be reduced from 23 to 13, mainly through mergers, and various state agencies were absorbed into the newly created Cabinet Office. (Legislation providing for these changes had been approved in June 1998.) The new structure was not fully implemented until January 2001, following an administrative reform. Notable appointments to the new Cabinet included the leader of the largest LDP faction and former Prime Minister, Ryutaro Hashimoto, and Hakuo Yanagisawa, the former Director-General of the Financial Reconstruction Commission. The former was appointed Minister of State for the Development of Okinawa and the Settlement of the Northern Territories, and the latter became Minister of State for Financial Affairs. Both men were well-respected and enjoyed considerable political support, and their appointment was seen as an attempt by Mori to strengthen his position. During December 2000, however, photographs showing the Prime Minister in the company of an alleged gangster and convicted murderer were published. In the same month, and again in January 2001, senior officials of the party were implicated in a bribery scandal (see above), resulting in the resignations of the Minister of State for the Economy, Industry and Information Technology, Fukushiro Nukaga, and the LDP leader in the House of Councillors, Masakuni Murakami, amongst others. Mori won another vote of confidence in March, but in early April announced his intention to resign.

In late April 2001 Junichiro Koizumi, a former Minister of Health and Welfare, unexpectedly defeated two other candidates, including Ryutaro Hashimoto, to secure the presidency of the ruling LDP and thus the post of Prime Minister. Koizumi owed his victory to a change in party election rules that allowed a greater influence of local and ordinary party members in selecting the President. He subsequently reorganized the Cabinet, largely ignoring LDP factional politics, and appointed a number of reformists, including Makiko Tanaka, daughter of former Prime Minister Kakuei Tanaka, as Japan's first woman Minister of Foreign Affairs; Heizo Takenaka, an economics professor, as Minister of State for Economy, Industry and Information Technology; and Nobuteru Ishihara as Minister of State for Administrative Reform. However, there were concerns that the relatively unknown new Minister of Finance, Masajuro Shiokawa, lacked the authority necessary to bring about economic and financial reforms. At the same time, Koizumi also reshuffled the LDP's senior leadership, appointing his ally Taku Yamasaki as Secretary-General, and Taro Aso as Chairman of the Policy Research Council. Immediately after taking office, Koizumi attained a record popularity rating of above 80%, leading to hopes that he would use his popularity to secure the

passage of difficult economic reforms against the wishes of his more reluctant party. In addition to according priority to economic reform, Koizumi also sought to introduce direct elections for the post of Prime Minister, and upgrade the status of the SDF into that of a full army, a move that would involve changing Article 9 of the Constitution, whereby Japan renounces the use of war. This, coupled with his stated intention to pay an official visit in August to the Yasukuni Shrine, a controversial war memorial, led to fears in neighbouring countries of a growth of nationalism in Japan. In May 2001 the Government issued an apology and agreed to pay compensation to 127 leprosy victims (who had been forcibly isolated for years) following a ruling by a provincial court. Koizumi's refusal to challenge the ruling was seen as a sign of greater political openness. The Government also approved the construction of a new nuclear power plant for the first time since the Tokaimura accident in September 1999, thereby ending a hiatus in the country's nuclear programme.

In June 2001 the Government finally announced an economic reform programme, drafted by Minister for Economy Takenaka. The plan consisted of the privatization of special public institutions, a review of regulatory economic laws, the strengthening of insurance functions, improving human resources, including assistance to business entrepreneurs, revitalizing urban areas, promoting regional autonomy and a reduction of public-works projects. Despite his warnings of economic hardship ahead, Koizumi's high popularity was a major factor behind the LDP's gains in the Tokyo assembly elections in late June. Veteran members of the LDP, particularly the Hashimoto faction, however, remained opposed to Koizumi's reforms. By early July, Koizumi had already retreated from his earlier long-held plan to privatize the post office savings system.

Elections to the House of Councillors were held on 29 July 2001, and Koizumi's personal popularity enabled the LDP to make gains. Of the 121 seats being contested, the LDP won 64, bringing its total in the upper chamber to 110, a net gain of eight seats. The opposition DPJ won 26 seats, raising its strength to 60 seats, a net gain of 13 seats, while New Komeito won 23 seats, a net gain of one seat. The elections were widely seen as a test for Koizumi's reformist agenda and as a victory for the LDP after years of declining popularity. Koizumi was re-elected unopposed for a further two-year term as LDP President in early August.

Koizumi aroused controversy in mid-August 2001 when he made an official visit to the Yasukuni Shrine to honour Japan's war dead. He sought to diminish the controversy by visiting two days before the anniversary of Japan's surrender in the Second World War, but nevertheless drew both domestic and international criticism. Left-wingers opposed the visit on principle, while right-wingers denounced Koizumi for bringing forward his visit to placate critics.

In September 2001 the terrorist attacks on the USA again raised the subject of the role of Japan's military, with Koizumi apparently using the USA's war against the Taliban regime of Afghanistan to expand the role of the SDF. The Diet in late October approved new legislation for the overseas deployment of the SDF in a non-combat support role, and in late November Japan deployed warships to the Indian Ocean, in the biggest such deployment since the Second World War (see below). The Japanese people strongly supported logistical assistance to the USA, but there remained considerable public opposition to any amendment to Article 9. Amid the worsening economic situation, meanwhile, the Government in September introduced emergency stimulus measures to counter rising unemployment, the deteriorating situation in the corporate sector and the banking crisis. Also in September, the Government confirmed the country's first case of BSE-infected cattle, giving rise to widespread public concern and a decline in beef consumption. In late October the Government proclaimed Japanese beef to be safe for consumption; however, a second infected cow was discovered in late November.

By November 2001 Koizumi was in dispute with Minister of Foreign Affairs Tanaka over bureaucratic reform in her ministry, her occasional failure to meet visiting foreign dignitaries and her absence from two major international forums. Koizumi had meanwhile formed a new 'foreign policy taskforce' to deal more efficiently with international affairs. There was increasing speculation about a cabinet reorganization, with members of the LDP's Hashimoto faction keen to modify reforms and regain ministerial posts. Koizumi had in previous months indicated his willingness to work with the opposition DPJ if the LDP continued to block his reforms; later in the month more than 50 LDP legislators formed a group aimed at stalling them.

Also in November 2001, hundreds of people filed lawsuits against Koizumi over his visit to the Yasukuni Shrine, claiming that he had violated the constitutional separation of religion and state. In early December Princess Masako, wife of Crown Prince Naruhito, finally gave birth to her first child, Princess Aiko. However, the Constitution forbade females from succeeding to the 'Chrysanthemum Throne', leading to calls for an amendment to the rules at a future date, a suggestion that was strongly supported by the public. The last female ruler had been Empress Gosakuramachi in the late 1700s.

In mid-December 2001 the Government agreed to abolish 17 public corporations and transfer 45 others (of a total of 163) to the private sector; it also showed signs of addressing the problems of the banking sector. Koizumi's major reform of privatizing the postal savings system, however, was further delayed. Meanwhile, the opposition DPJ itself experienced divisions, between those who favoured co-operation with Koizumi and his reforms (including the President of the DPJ, Yukio Hatoyama), and those who favoured greater co-operation with other opposition parties. The latter group was led by DPJ Deputy President Takahiro Yokomichi, who in late November held meetings with the Liberal Party leader, Ichiro Ozawa, and the SDPJ leader, Takako Doi. The DPJ had failed to make a significant impact against the LDP during the ongoing economic crisis.

By the beginning of 2002 Koizumi had failed to deliver tangible economic results, and there was considerable uncertainty regarding his ability to do so. Shizuka Kamei, a senior LDP official, accused Koizumi of damaging the economy in order to push through his reform agenda, highlighting the stiff resistance within the LDP. In the first week of January Koizumi appointed two members of the Hashimoto faction as vice-ministers, in a bid to placate his main opponents. At the end of the month Koizumi dismissed his Minister of Foreign Affairs, Makiko Tanaka, following months of disputes over reform within the ministry, which had delayed the passage of a supplementary budget through the Diet. Tanaka had been one of the most popular politicians in the country, and her dismissal was regarded as a victory for LDP veterans and as a set-back for reform. She was replaced by Yoriko Kawaguchi, hitherto Minister of the Environment, after former UN High Commissioner for Refugees Sadako Ogata turned down the post. In March the LDP suffered a reverse as one Diet member, Muneo Suzuki, was accused of exerting pressure on officials of the Ministry of Foreign Affairs to limit bids for a construction project to companies from within his own parliamentary constituency, and Saburo Sato, a former aide to LDP faction leader Koichi Kato, was arrested on suspicion of tax evasion. Suzuki resigned in disgrace from the LDP in mid-March, as did Kato, who also resigned from his seat in the Diet in early April. In March former Prime Minister Ryutaro Hashimoto, one of the most influential men in the LDP, underwent heart surgery, forcing him to halt temporarily his political activities

The LDP suffered further set-backs in April 2002 when its candidates lost the election for the mayoralty of Yokohama, and a by-election in Niigata Prefecture. In Yokohama, an independent young reformist, Hiroshi Nakada, defeated the incumbent Hidenobu Takahide, who had the support of both the LDP and opposition parties. The electoral defeats, and Koizumi's unscheduled visit to the Yasukuni Shrine in late April, led to renewed criticism of the Prime Minister. In early May Yutaka Inoue, a former President of the House of Councillors and a member of the LDP, resigned from the party owing to allegations of bribery. At the same time, opponents of Koizumi within the LDP were increasingly holding discussions with Shintaro Ishihara, the Governor of Tokyo, with a view to replacing the Prime Minister with the latter.

In June 2002 the LDP suspended Makiko Tanaka from the party for a two-year period owing to her failure to co-operate with an investigation into the misuse of state funds at the Ministry of Foreign Affairs. Tanaka relinquished her seat in the Diet in early August. Also in June Muneo Suzuki was arrested on bribery charges. Meanwhile, the sitting session of the Diet was extended until July in order for Koizumi to draft legislation for reforms to the postal service, as well as health, and defence and security sectors, which were opposed by considerable elements within the LDP. In July Koizumi was forced to accept a compromise with anti-reformist LDP elements over his plans to reform the postal service—a key promise that he had made when seeking the position of Prime Minister a year earlier. Meanwhile, in the middle of that month the Governor of Nagano Prefecture, Yasuo Tanaka, was ousted by the prefectural

assembly owing to his policies of reducing major public works projects, which were often used by local politicians to generate political support. Tanaka, a former novelist, was one of an increasing number of independent, reformist candidates who had been elected to prefectural governorships as a protest against traditional political parties. However, he was overwhelmingly re-elected to the post of Governor in September 2002, in what was seen as a victory for reformist forces.

In August 2002 the Government introduced a controversial new database that stored personal data of all citizens. Civil liberty groups immediately opposed the scheme on the grounds that it inveighed on personal privacy. Thousands of people protested against the system, and several municipalities refused to join the scheme.

In late September Koizumi implemented a long-expected cabinet reorganization, dismissing the Minister of State for the Financial Services Agency, Hakuo Yanagisawa, and appointing the Minister of State for Economic and Fiscal Policy, Heizo Takenaka, to concurrently hold that post. The portfolios for agriculture, defence, disaster management, environment, food safety, and Okinawa and the Northern Territories, were also replaced. It was widely believed that the reallocation of portfolios came in support of a plan by the Governor of the Bank of Japan, Masaru Hayami, to shore up the ailing banking sector by buying poorly-performing shares owned by commercial banks— a proposal opposed by Yanagisawa. Plans to reform the banking sector also created tensions between the LDP and its two coalition partners, New Komeito and the NCP. At the end of October a tripartite committee of the ruling coalition published a banking-sector reform plan that was far less radical than that sought by Takenaka, who had urged the nationalization of major banks to prevent their collapse. The political wrangling over how to revive Japan's economy and reform the banking system continued throughout the remainder of 2002. Despite the political tensions, the LDP in late October won five out of seven by-elections, strengthening the reputation of Prime Minister Koizumi following his visit to the DPRK in September. At the same time Japan witnessed its first political assassination since 1960, when a member of the DPJ, Koki Ishii, a known campaigner against corruption, was stabbed to death. (In June 2004 Hakusui Ito, a right-wing extremist, was sentenced to life imprisonment for his murder.)

In early December 2002 the opposition DPJ elected Naoto Kan as its President, replacing Yukio Hatoyama, who had himself been re-elected to a third term as party President in late September. Hatoyama was forced to resign after the failure of secret attempts to merge the party with the smaller opposition LP, led by Ichiro Ozawa. Katsuya Okada, Kan's main rival for the DPJ presidency, was appointed secretary-general. Kan had previously led the DPJ during 1997–99, and although his leadership was expected to strengthen the opposition, analysts noted that the DPJ had hitherto failed to make a significant impact against the ruling LDP. Four DPJ members of the Diet, led by former party Vice-President Hiroshi Kumagai, resigned from the party in late December and joined the ruling coalition's NCP; the President of that party, Takeshi Noda, resigned in favour of Kumagai.

In mid-January 2003 Junichiro Koizumi visited the Yasukuni Shrine for the third time since becoming Prime Minister, once again prompting criticism within Japan as well as in the region. Also at that time Emperor Akihito underwent surgery for prostate cancer, his duties being temporarily transferred to Crown Prince Naruhito. In late February Toshihiko Fukui, a long-serving official at the Bank of Japan, was appointed Governor. His conservative background, however, raised concerns that he would not bring about radical reforms to the banking sector.

In early March 2003 the Governor of Tokyo, Shintaro Ishihara, announced that he would seek re-election in April, ending months of speculation that he might form a new political party in order to challenge Koizumi. Ishihara's announcement was welcomed by Koizumi, since the Governor had been seen as the Prime Minister's most serious rival, and had been holding discussions with Shizuka Kamei, an LDP faction leader who was Koizumi's main opponent within the party. However, the LDP was, in early March, embarrassed by the arrest of one of its Diet members over the illicit management of political donations. At the end of the month the Minister of Agriculture, Forestry and Fisheries, Tadamori Oshima, resigned over a series of financial scandals concerning his aides—the wife of one having committed suicide days earlier. Oshima was the first minister in Koizumi's Cabinet to resign over a funding scandal, and further

weakened public faith in party politics. He was replaced by Yoshiyuki Kamei.

The 15th unified quadrennial local elections, comprising gubernatorial elections in 11 prefectures (including Tokyo), one city mayoral election, and local assembly elections in 44 prefectures and 12 cities, were held in mid-April 2003. In Tokyo, Governor Ishihara was overwhelmingly re-elected, and pledged to use his position to campaign for reform in the country as a whole. Three other incumbent governors were also re-elected, and it was noted that independent candidates performed strongly or won posts in several prefectures, at the expense of traditional political parties. Turn-out in the gubernatorial elections was a record low of 52.6%, however. The LDP won 1,309 of 2,634 local seats contested, an improvement on the 1,288 seats it had won four years earlier. By-elections for three seats in the House of Representatives and one seat in the House of Councillors were held in late April; the LDP won three seats and the DPJ one seat.

In late April 2003 the LDP announced that it aimed to amend the Constitution explicitly to state the legitimacy of the SDF and to expand its role in international peace-keeping and collective self-defence. In mid-May the House of Representatives approved new legislation granting the Government and the SDF greater powers to act in the event of an attack on Japan. In June the new legislation, outlining the circumstances in which the Government would be able to authorize military action by the SDF, was approved by the House of Councillors. The legislation was supported by the DPJ as well as by the ruling coalition. However, the SDP, the JCP and the Liberal Party opposed the legislation on the grounds that it violated the pacifist principle of Japan's Constitution. Also in June, Koizumi declared his support for Heizo Takenaka, Minister of State responsible for the Financial Services Agency, following criticism of Takenaka's decision to use public funds to finance a rescue programme for the failed bank Resona.

In July 2003 the House of Councillors approved, by 136 votes to 102, proposals to send peace-keeping forces to Iraq, thereby allowing the largest deployment of Japanese troops abroad since the Second World War and representing a political success for Koizumi. Opposition to the proposals was vehement, involving physical violence among parliamentary representatives. Although troops were to engage in humanitarian work only, critics argued that the deployment would violate Japan's pacifist Constitution, as in practice troops would be unable to avoid conflict areas.

In September 2003 Koizumi was re-elected as leader of the LDP, winning 399 of the 657 votes cast and thus defeating the three rival candidates (Shizuka Kamei, Masahiko Komura and Takao Fujii) for the leadership. Following his success in the leadership election, Koizumi made appointments to a new Cabinet, which included the reappointment of Heizo Takenaka as Minister of State responsible for the Financial Services Agency, despite criticism of his banking reform policies (see above). Also in September, a merger agreement between the DPJ and the Liberal Party, originally agreed in July, was signed, with the aim of creating an opposition movement capable of presenting a strong challenge to the LDP at the forthcoming general election. In October the House of Representatives was dissolved. Also in October, the House of Councillors voted to extend legislation, first approved in 2001, allowing the Japanese SDF to provide logistical support to the USA in its 'war on terror' (see below).

At the general election, held on 9 November 2003, the LDP won 237 seats, thus losing 10 of its previous 247 seats in the House of Representatives. The party's strength increased to 245 following the recruitment of four independent candidates and the absorption of the New Conservative Party, one of the LDP's two coalition partners, which had won four seats. The LDP's other coalition partner, the New Komeito party, secured 34 seats. Naoto Kan's DPJ (incorporating the former Liberal Party) won 177 seats, thereby increasing its number of seats by 40 and representing a serious challenge to the LDP's hold on power. A further potential threat to the LDP was the success of the former Minister of Foreign Affairs, Makiko Tanaka, in securing a seat as an independent candidate. Tanaka had been suspended from the LDP in 2002 following allegations of misappropriation of funds (see above), but was able to stand in the 2003 election after the charges against her were abandoned. Tanaka, who had become increasingly critical of the Koizumi administration, joined a DPJ-led Diet group following her re-election to the House of Representatives.

In December 2003 plans were announced for an SDF deployment to Iraq, following the approval of the requisite legislation on the issue in July (see above). The plans were strongly criticized by DPJ leader Naoto Kan, and popular protests against the Iraq mission took place in mid-December. Opposition within Japan to the deployment had been strengthened by the deaths of two Japanese diplomats in Iraq in November. Also in December, the Government outlined proposals to expand Japan's defence capacity with the development of a ballistic missile defence system in co-operation with the USA. The project was to cost an estimated 500,000m. yen by 2007. In January 2004 the first Japanese troops departed for Iraq, amid further popular protests in Tokyo. In the same month it was announced that legislation on the reform of Japan's Constitution, including an amendment to Article 9, would be submitted in 2005. Also in January 2004 Koizumi made a fourth visit to the Yasukuni Shrine, again prompting criticism. In February Shoko Asahara, leader of the Aum Shinrikyo sect, which had released poisonous gas into the Tokyo underground system in 1995, was sentenced to death for his role in the attack. Public support for Koizumi was tested in April, when three Japanese civilians were taken hostage in Iraq. Their captors threatened to kill them by burning them alive if Japanese troops were not withdrawn. Despite the Government's steadfast refusal to comply with the Iraqi militants' demands, the hostages were released unharmed a week later. Media polls indicated that the majority of the population approved of Koizumi's handling of the hostage crisis, despite widespread initial public resistance to Japan's involvement in Iraq.

In May 2004 a scandal over pension contributions prompted resignations by senior officials from the LDP as well as the opposition DPJ. Chief Cabinet Secretary Yasuo Fukuda of the LDP resigned after admitting that he not made the required payments to the compulsory state pension programme. DPJ Chairman Naoto Kan resigned shortly afterwards on similar grounds. Kan was replaced by Katsuya Okada, who had hitherto been General Secretary of the DPJ. In the same month a government proposal for pension reform, involving increased premiums and reduced benefits, was approved by the House of Representatives. The reform plan was approved by the House of Councillors in June despite strong opposition from the DPJ. In July 2004 nation-wide voting took place to elect one-half of the members of the House of Councillors. Of the 121 seats contested, Prime Minister Koizumi's LDP won 49, while the DPJ won 50 (thus increasing its overall representation in the chamber from 60 seats to 82). Although the LDP and its coalition partner New Komeito, with a combined total of 139 seats, retained a majority in the 242-member House, the outcome was generally interpreted as reflecting a decline in the popularity of Koizumi's administration. In September Koizumi effected a major reorganization and reallocation of cabinet portfolios. Among notable new appointments was that of Nobutaka Machimura as Minister of Foreign Affairs. The Minister of Economic and Fiscal Policy, Heizo Takenaka, was given responsibility for a portfolio for privatization of the postal services, while Sadakazu Tanigaki remained Minister of Finance. From October 2004 there were renewed protests against Japanese support for military operations in Iraq following the beheading of a 24-year-old Japanese tourist, Shosei Koda, who had been taken hostage by a militant group. None the less, in December the LDP announced that the term of the SDF mission in Iraq was to be extended by one year. In the same month a revision of Japanese defence policy was announced. Whilst reaffirming Japan's commitment not to engage in offensive military action against other nations, the new policy eased some restrictions on weapons exports. Also in December a group of Tokyo teachers initiated legal action against the nationalistic Governor of Tokyo, Shintaro Ishihara, in protest against the latter's policy that school pupils and teachers should be required daily to sing the national anthem.

Japan's bilateral security arrangements with the USA, concluded by treaty in 1951, together with trade issues, continued to be the focus of Japanese-US relations. The treaty granted the use of military bases in Japan to the USA, in return for a US commitment to provide military support to Japan in the event of external aggression. From 1982 Japan remained under pressure from the USA to increase its defence expenditure and to assume greater responsibility for security in the Western Pacific area. In December 1990 the Government announced a new five-year programme to develop the country's defence capability. The new programme also envisaged that Japan would assume a greater share of the cost of maintaining the US troops stationed in

Japan. In January 1992, the 'Tokyo declaration on the US-Japan global partnership' was issued, whereby the two countries undertook to co-operate in promoting international security and prosperity. In February 1993 Japan and the USA reaffirmed their security relationship, with the USA agreeing to protect Japan from the threat posed by potential nuclear proliferation around the world. In November 1995 the Cabinet approved a new national defence programme, which envisaged a 20% reduction in troops and confirmed Japan's security co-operation with the USA. In September 1997 revised Guidelines for Japan-US Defense Co-operation (first compiled in 1978) were issued. The Guidelines envisaged enhanced military co-operation between the USA and Japan, not only on Japanese territory, but also in situations in unspecified areas around Japan. In April 1998 the LDP Government approved legislation on the implementation of the revised Guidelines, which was enacted in May 1999, prompting criticism from China and Russia. Its approval was ensured by an agreement concluded by the LDP, the LP and New Komeito to exclude a clause that would have allowed the inspection of unidentified foreign ships by the SDF, with the aim of enforcing economic sanctions. In August 1999 the Japanese Government formally approved a memorandum of understanding with the USA stipulating details of joint technical research on the development of a theatre missile defence system, which aims to detect and shoot down incoming ballistic missiles within a 3,000-km radius.

From the mid-1990s Japan's growing trade surplus with the USA became a matter of increasing concern for the US authorities. In October 1994 trade agreements in three of the four main areas under bilateral discussion were signed. Negotiations concerning the automobile trade resulted in the signing of an agreement with the USA in June 1995. However, an increase in the export of Japanese vehicles to the USA in 1997, and a concomitant rise in the US trade deficit with Japan, caused growing tension between the two countries. Negotiations in April and June focused on trade issues. In September an agreement to reform Japanese port operations was concluded shortly after the USA imposed large fines on Japanese companies for employing restrictive harbour practices. Negotiations on increased access to airline routes were successfully concluded in January 1998. However, relations were again strained by trade disputes in 1998, with Japan's high tariffs on rice, in the forestry and fisheries sectors, and low-priced steel exports being of particular concern to the USA. Tension also arose over the USA's repeated criticism that Japan was not doing enough to stimulate its own economy and alleviate the Asian economic crisis. During a visit to Japan in November 1998, President Clinton urged the Government rapidly to implement measures to encourage domestic demand, reform the banking sector and liberalize its markets. Meanwhile, Japan's trade surplus with the USA continued to increase, and in 1998 reached its highest level since 1987. In May 1999, during a visit by Prime Minister Obuchi to the USA (the first such official state visit in 12 years), Clinton praised Obuchi's efforts to promote economic recovery and welcomed Japanese plans for further deregulation in several sectors. Meanwhile, a dispute over Japanese steel exports had escalated. A ruling, in April 1999, by the US Department of Commerce that Japan had 'dumped' hot-rolled steel into the US market was endorsed, in June, by the US International Trade Commission, and punitive duties were subsequently imposed. In November Japan announced its intention to bring a complaint before the World Trade Organization (WTO) against the US ruling. Relations between the two countries deteriorated in mid-2000, following the expansion by Japan of its hunting of whales as part of a 'scientific research' programme. The USA subsequently banned Japan from future access to its territorial waters and threatened to impose sanctions on Japanese food imports. Japan warned that if any such sanctions were imposed, it would take the dispute to the WTO. The International Whaling Commission refused a bid by Japan to hold its next meeting in the country.

The presence of US forces in Japan continued to provoke much debate. In November 1995 three US servicemen were arrested and subsequently imprisoned for the rape of a schoolgirl in Okinawa. Considerable civil unrest ensued and legal proceedings were initiated against the Governor of Okinawa, Masahide Ota, following his refusal to renew the leases for US military installations in the region. Protracted negotiations between the two countries resulted in the USA agreeing, in December 1996, to release 21% of the land used for US military purposes in Okinawa, and to build a floating offshore helicopter base to replace the air base at Futenma. In April 1997 it was proposed to relocate several of the US bases to other prefectures. In December, in a non-binding referendum held in Nago, Okinawa, to assess public opinion concerning the construction of the offshore helicopter base, the majority of voters rejected the proposal, prompting the resignation of the Mayor of Nago. Governor Ota stated his opposition to the proposed base, a position also adopted by the new Mayor, elected in February 1998. In November 1998 Keiichi Inamine defeated Ota in the Okinawa gubernatorial elections. Inamine, who had been supported by the LDP, presented an alternative solution, proposing that a military-commercial airport be built in northern Okinawa and leased to the USA for a period of 15 years. In December 1998 a US military site was the first of the 11 bases to be returned under the 1996 agreement. In December 1999 Inamine's proposal for the relocation of the Futenma air base was approved by both the local authorities and the Japanese Government, with the Henoko district of Nago chosen as the site for the new airport; at the same time funding was allocated for a 10-year development plan for northern Okinawa. Negotiations with the US Government, which opposed any time limit on its use of the airport, took place in October 2000; no progress was made.

In November 2000 the Japanese House of Representatives approved a five-year agreement, to commence in April 2001, to reduce host nation spending for US forces stationed in Japan. Although the administration of US President George W. Bush favoured stronger links with Japan than its predecessor, relations between Japan and the USA briefly deteriorated in February 2001 when a Japanese trawler sank, killing the entire crew, following a collision with a US submarine, the *Greenville*, off Hawaii. The revelation that a civilian had been at the controls of the submarine at the time caused fury in Japan, as did reports that Yoshiro Mori had insisted on finishing a game of golf before dealing with the situation. The USA subsequently appointed the navy's second-in-command as a special envoy to Japan, who travelled to Tokyo at the end of the month to apologize in person and to brief the Japanese Prime Minister on the progress of investigations into the accident. The captain of the submarine also apologized to the families of those who had died. In April the USA announced that the captain would not be court-martialled. Also in that month, Japan banned US nuclear submarines from visiting its ports after the US Navy failed to give prior notification of such a visit, as required. The Japanese victims of the submarine collision, and their relatives, accepted US $13m. in compensation from the US Navy in November 2002.

In May 2001 US Deputy Secretary of State Richard Armitage urged even stronger relations with Japan and greater Japanese participation in regional security, a view shared by Koizumi. In June Minister of Foreign Affairs Tanaka stated that Japan needed to become more independent of the USA. Tanaka also expressed doubts about the USA's planned 'national missile defense' (NMD) system, and the Director-General of the Defence Agency, Gen Nakatani, stated that any Japanese missile defence programme would be separate from the USA's plan. Koizumi held talks with President Bush at Camp David, USA, in late June–early July, but the summit meeting was marred by the news that a woman in Okinawa had allegedly been raped by a US serviceman; he was later surrendered to the Japanese authorities. Meanwhile, Japan and the USA disagreed over how to reduce global 'greenhouse gas' emissions, following the USA's withdrawal of support for the Kyoto Treaty in early 2001. The disagreements threatened to nullify the treaty.

Following the terrorist attacks on the USA in September 2001, Japan immediately pledged co-operation with the USA's 'war on terror', including military support within the framework of Japan's Constitution. Koizumi visited Washington, DC, later that month and announced that Japan would assist in the gathering of intelligence, the delivery of supplies and of medical and humanitarian relief. The requisite legislation was approved by the Diet, and in November Japan deployed several warships and 1,500 personnel to the Indian Ocean in this capacity; however, Japanese forces were still forbidden to participate in combat activities. At this time, several Japanese companies signed a deal with a US firm to build air-defence systems for Japan's military.

President Bush visited Japan in February 2002 and praised Koizumi, urging him to reform the country's economy. Disagreements remained, however, over the USA's description of North Korea as part of an 'axis of evil' and over measures to reduce global warming. Japan pursued a policy of engagement with the

DPRK, while the USA adopted a more sceptical attitude to that country. None the less, Japan, along with the Republic of Korea, sought to encourage the USA to support Koizumi's visit to the North in September 2002 (see below). However, the USA adopted a harder line towards the DPRK after it allegedly admitted to pursuing a secret nuclear-weapons programme, in October 2002. In early November 2002 the Japanese Government extended the deployment of its Maritime Self-Defense Force vessels in the Indian Ocean in support of the USA's 'war on terror'. In mid-December, at the request of the USA, Japan dispatched an advanced *Aegis* destroyer to the region, its highest-profile deployment to date. Meanwhile, in November Keiichi Inamine was re-elected Governor of Okinawa, having strongly campaigned in preceding months for a significant reduction in US troops stationed on the island.

There were signs in 2002 that Japan was gradually moving to reduce its dependency on the USA for its security. During that year Japan launched four H-IIA rockets as part of its civilian space programme, but analysts noted that the rocket could be put to military use. In addition, several politicians indicated that Japan could eventually develop nuclear weapons if the country felt threatened.

In mid-December 2002 Japan and the USA held a meeting of ministers of defence and foreign affairs in Tokyo on outstanding security issues. In addition to seeking an early resolution of the crisis over the North Korean nuclear weapons programme, the two countries moved closer to agreement on the deployment of a joint missile shield (see below). In February 2003 the Japanese Government stated that the two countries would conduct joint training of ballistic missile interception off the coast of Hawaii for a period of two years, beginning in 2004. Also in February 2003, the Defence Agency revealed that it had considered the possibility of developing nuclear weapons in 1995, but decided against such a move. In March 2003 Japan launched its first spy satellites, aiming to improve its independent intelligence-gathering capabilities.

Koizumi gave President Bush his full support for the USA's military offensive against Iraq, which commenced in late March 2003, despite strong opposition from the Japanese public. However, Japan refused to close the Iraqi embassy in Tokyo, despite requests from the USA. Following the approval of legislation to permit the dispatch of Japanese troops to Iraq in a peace-keeping capacity, in early 2004 the first Japanese soldiers were deployed. Prime Minister Koizumi's reappointment of Yoriko Kawaguchi as Minister of Foreign Affairs in a cabinet reshuffle in September 2003 indicated continued support for the Bush Administration's policy on Iraq. On economic matters, in October 2003 President Bush urged Japan to abandon its policy of manipulating the yen's exchange rate against the dollar by means of market intervention (see Economic Affairs). In December 2003 plans were announced by the Japanese Government for the development of a ballistic missile defence system in co-operation with the USA, reportedly intended to protect Japan in the event of an attack by the DPRK.

In 2004 there was renewed public resentment at the US military presence on Okinawa following the crash of a US military helicopter in the grounds of a university in August. At a meeting in December it was agreed that Japan would resume air traffic control over Okinawa within three years. Following a meeting of Japanese and US defence officials in February 2005, in a development likely adversely to affect relations with the People's Republic of China, Japan and the USA issued a joint statement claiming that security in the Taiwan Straits was a 'common strategic objective'.

Despite the signing of a treaty of peace and friendship with the People's Republic of China in 1978, relations deteriorated in the late 1980s after China expressed concern at Japan's increased defence expenditure and its more assertive military stance. Japanese aid to China was suspended in June 1989, following the Tiananmen Square massacre in Beijing, and was not resumed until November 1990. Relations between the two countries were strengthened by the visits to China by Emperor Akihito in October 1992, the first-ever Japanese imperial visit to China, and by Prime Minister Hosokawa in March 1994. However, in August of that year Japan announced the suspension of economic aid to China, following renewed nuclear testing by the Chinese Government. The provision of economic aid was resumed in early 1997, following the declaration of a moratorium on Chinese nuclear testing.

In July 1996 Japan's relations with both China and Taiwan were strained when a group of nationalists, the Japan Youth

Federation, constructed a lighthouse and war memorial on the Senkaku Islands (or Diaoyu Islands in Chinese), a group of uninhabited islands situated in the East China Sea, to which China, Japan and Taiwan all laid claim. The situation was further aggravated in September by the accidental drowning of a Hong Kong citizen during a protest near the islands against Japan's claim. In October a flotilla of small boats, operated by activists from Taiwan, Hong Kong and Macao, raised the flags of China and Taiwan on the disputed islands. The Japanese Government sought to defuse tensions with China and Taiwan by withholding official recognition of the lighthouse; it did not, however, condemn those who had constructed the controversial buildings. In May 1997 China expressed serious concern, when a member of the Japanese Diet landed on one of the disputed islands. The Japanese Government distanced itself from the action.

In September 1997 Hashimoto visited China to commemorate the 25th anniversary of the normalization of relations between the two countries. China expressed concern at the revised US-Japanese security arrangements, following a statement by a senior Japanese minister that the area around Taiwan might be covered under the new guidelines. Procedures for the removal of chemical weapons, deployed in China by Japanese forces during the Second World War, were also discussed. During a visit to Japan by the Chinese Premier, Li Peng, in November, a bilateral fisheries agreement was signed. In November 1998, during a six-day state visit by President Jiang Zemin, Obuchi and Jiang issued (but declined to sign) a joint declaration on friendship and co-operation, in which Japan expressed deep remorse for past aggression against China. China, however, was reported to be displeased by the lack of a written apology, and remained concerned by the implications of US-Japanese defence arrangements regarding Taiwan. A subsequent US-Japanese agreement to initiate joint technical research on the development of a theatre missile defence system, followed by the Japanese Diet's approval, in May 1999, of legislation on the implementation of the revised US-Japanese defence guidelines (see above), provoked severe criticism from China, despite Japan's insistence that military co-operation with the USA was purely defensive. In July a meeting in Beijing between Obuchi and the Chinese Premier, Zhu Rongji, resulted in the formalization of a bilateral agreement on China's entry to the WTO, following several months of intense negotiations on the liberalization of trade in services. In August 2000 China withdrew permission for the Japanese Minister of Transport, Hajime Morita, to visit the People's Republic in September, owing to scheduling difficulties with Chinese officials. The Japanese media, however, attributed the Chinese change of attitude to a recent visit by Morita to a shrine honouring Japan's war dead, including those convicted of war crimes. Zhu Rongji visited Japan in October, and admitted that his failure to demand an apology for the host country's wartime conduct had attracted criticism in China.

In April 2001 a trade dispute broke out between China and Japan after the latter, seeking to protect its domestic manufacturers, imposed tariffs on imports of Chinese mushrooms, leeks and rushes. China responded by introducing tariffs on Japanese consumer goods, leading to further disputes, which persisted throughout the rest of 2001. China was further angered by Japan's decision to allow former Taiwanese President Lee Teng-hui to visit the country in May. These disagreements led to a postponement of a visit to Japan by former Chinese Premier Li Peng. Meanwhile, China reacted angrily to Koizumi's visit to the Yasukuni Shrine, and a senior official of the Chinese Ministry of Foreign Affairs urged Japan to take 'visible action' to renounce its militaristic past. Koizumi travelled to China in early October, when he visited the Marco Polo Bridge (the site of a clash between China and Japan that led to full-scale war in 1937) and apologized for Japan's past crimes in China. The visit was also aimed at reassuring Beijing about Japan's support for the USA's 'war on terror', and bilateral relations subsequently improved, although Chinese concerns about Tokyo's military deployment remained. In November China and Japan, along with the Republic of Korea, agreed to hold regular meetings of their ministers of finance and of foreign affairs in order to foster closer co-operation. However, in late December 2001 a state-supported Chinese newspaper criticized Japan for allowing the yen to depreciate, a move that might curb Chinese exports.

In March 2002 Makiko Tanaka, the former Minister of Foreign Affairs, visited China to mark 30 years of diplomatic relations between the two countries. (Her father, Kakuei

Tanaka, had overseen the restoration of relations in 1972.) Li Peng visited Japan in early April, stating that he was optimistic about improving bilateral relations. However, Koizumi's second visit to the Yasukuni Shrine in late April was condemned by China, as was a third visit to the shrine in January 2003. Tensions remained in Japan's relations with China. In April 2002 the leader of the opposition Liberal Party, Ichiro Ozawa, warned that Japan was capable of developing thousands of nuclear warheads in response to China's military build-up, if necessary. In May Japan strongly protested against the entry by Chinese security forces into the Japanese consulate in Shenyang, China, to remove several North Koreans who had sought refuge there. China responded that Japanese officials had consented to the move. The dispute was resolved when both sides allowed the North Koreans to travel to the Republic of Korea via a third country. The confrontation raised mutual suspicions, although in June China allowed Japan to salvage an alleged North Korean spy vessel from its territorial waters.

Although China had, in October 2001, invited Japanese Crown Prince Naruhito and Crown Princess Masako to visit China to mark the occasion of the 30th anniversary, in September 2002, of the establishment of diplomatic relations, the royal couple did not attend the ceremonies. None the less, in late 2002 Japan and China were increasingly seeking to forge a tripartite free-trade agreement with the Republic of Korea, and Koizumi held discussions with Jiang Zemin in Mexico at the summit meeting of Asia-Pacific Economic Co-operation (APEC, see p. 155) in October. Tokyo hoped that Beijing would use its influence with the DPRK to bring about a peaceful resolution to the diplomatic crisis surrounding the latter's nuclear weapons programme. In February 2003 China agreed to allow a Japanese escapee from the DPRK to travel to Japan after she sought asylum at the Japanese consulate in Shenyang. Several other such cases were subsequently reported.

In May 2003 a Japanese court rejected compensation claims from five residents of China's Heilongjiang Province who had been injured by chemical weapons left in China by the Japanese army at the end of the Second World War. However, in August the Japanese Government apologized to China following a similar incident in which 29 people were injured by weapons abandoned by the Japanese army. In September a Tokyo court ordered the Japanese Government to pay compensation to 13 Chinese people injured by dumped Japanese weapons. There were tensions between China and Japan over the disputed Senkaku Islands in June 2003, when a boat carrying Chinese activists entered Japanese waters in the vicinity of the islands. Further tensions in Sino-Japanese relations in 2003 arose over an incident in September in which a group of Japanese men reportedly took part in an orgy in Guangdong involving Chinese prostitutes. China was especially offended by the timing of the alleged event, coinciding as it did with a sensitive Second World War anniversary. Despite these problems, China and Japan, with the Republic of Korea, agreed to increase co-operation in various areas, including security and technology, on the occasion of a summit meeting of the Association of South East Asian Nations (ASEAN, see p. 162) in Bali in October 2003 (see below). However, no agreement was reached on the establishment of a free-trade area.

In early 2004 there were renewed disputes over the Senkaku Islands, with two Chinese boats being sighted in Japanese waters in January, and the arrest in March by Japanese police of seven Chinese activists who had landed on one of the islands. In January there was a fourth visit by Prime Minister Koizumi to the Yasukuni Shrine. In March, in an unprecedented ruling, a Japanese District Court required the Government to pay compensation to former Chinese slave labourers who had been forced to work in a Japanese harbour transport company during the Second World War.

Sino-Japanese relations deteriorated further in late 2004 following an incident in early November in which a Chinese submarine reportedly intruded on Japanese waters. Later in the month Prime Minister Koizumi and Chinese President Hu Jintao held talks at an APEC summit meeting in Chile. During the meeting Koizumi admonished Hu over the submarine intrusion, whereas Hu expressed China's strong opposition to Koizumi's repeated visits to the Yasukuni shrine. In December China was further angered when a revision of Japanese defence policy identified China as a potential security threat. Other factors influencing the Sino-Japanese relationship were competing claims to petroleum exploration fields in the East China Sea, as well as competition over an oil pipeline project with Russia (see below). Despite political tensions, observers noted that exports to China had been a major factor in promoting Japan's economic recovery during 2003 and 2004. China was angered in February 2005 by the joint statement made by Japan and the USA on Taiwan (see above). In April 2005 violent anti-Japanese protests took place across China, following Japan's introduction of new school textbooks that reportedly omitted any references to Japanese war crimes in China.

In January 1993, meanwhile, Prime Minister Miyazawa toured four member countries of ASEAN, during which he advocated an expansion of political and economic co-operation in the region. A visit by Prime Minister Hashimoto to ASEAN countries in January 1997 aimed to strengthen economic and security relations with the member countries. During 1998 Japan was widely criticized for its slow response to the Asian economic crisis. Japan's proposals for an 'Asian Monetary Fund' to stabilize the region were rejected by the USA and IMF, fearing a loss of influence in debtor countries. The weakness of the Japanese currency adversely affected financial markets throughout Asia, undermining efforts to stimulate regional economic recovery. As a result of increasing international pressure, in October the Japanese Government announced a US $30,000m. aid 'package' for Asian countries. In November the USA and Japan presented a joint initiative for growth and economic recovery in Asia, and in the following month Japan pledged further aid, to be disbursed over a three-year period. In January 2000 Prime Minister Obuchi visited Cambodia, Laos and Thailand. In April Japan proposed that its coast guard participate in joint anti-piracy patrols in the Melaka (Malacca) Straits (lying between Indonesia and Malaysia) with other regional navies, but was prevented from doing so following Chinese objections. In May Japan provided Myanmar with a substantial aid programme, aimed at building closer bilateral ties. Also in May, Singapore agreed to allow Japan to use its military bases for evacuating its citizens from crisis locations, and for regional peace-keeping missions, the first agreement of its kind between Japan and another country. In April 2001 Japan provided another aid programme for Myanmar, despite a *de facto* international moratorium on such aid owing to the repressive nature of the country's ruling military junta. In October Japan reached a comprehensive free-trade agreement with Singapore, and in January 2002 Prime Minister Koizumi visited Indonesia, Malaysia, the Philippines, Singapore and Thailand. Japan's influence in South-East Asia largely depended on its aid and investment programmes, both of which were being curtailed owing to Japan's economic problems. In April 2002 Koizumi also visited Viet Nam, East Timor (now Timor-Leste), Australia and New Zealand, and in November he attended the ASEAN summit meeting in Phnom-Penh, Cambodia, where he signed an agreement to develop a comprehensive economic partnership with ASEAN members within 10 years—including the possible formation of a Japan-ASEAN free-trade area. In November Japan's free-trade agreement with Singapore took effect. In February 2003 the Secretary-General of ASEAN urged Japan to develop political, security, and cultural co-operation with the organization. In June 2003 Japan announced that financial aid to Myanmar would be suspended in protest at the detention of the country's opposition leader, Aung San Suu Kyi. In December Japan hosted an ASEAN summit meeting at which Japan offered US $3,000m. in financial aid to ASEAN countries. At the Tokyo summit meeting it was also announced that Japan would begin negotiations on free-trade agreements with Thailand, Malaysia and the Philippines. These developments followed agreement between China and ASEAN in November 2002 to establish a China-ASEAN free-trade area by 2010.

Attempts to establish full diplomatic relations with the DPRK in early 1991 were hindered by North Korean demands for financial reparations for the Japanese colonization of the country during 1910–45 and by the DPRK's refusal to allow International Atomic Energy Agency inspectors access to its nuclear facilities. Relations improved in 1995 and 1996 after Japan provided emergency aid to the DPRK when serious food shortages were reported. Concerns that the DPRK had developed a missile capable of reaching Japanese territory resulted in the suspension of food aid in mid-1996, but, following bilateral negotiations in August 1997, at which it was agreed to reopen discussions aimed at restoring full diplomatic relations, provision of food aid resumed in October. Agreement was also reached concerning the issue of visits to relatives in Japan by the estimated 1,800 Japanese nationals resident in the DPRK. The first such visits took place in November. However, food aid and normalization talks were suspended in mid-1998, following the testing by the DPRK of a suspected missile over Japanese territory. Tensions were exacerbated in March 1999, when two suspected North Korean spy ships, which had infiltrated Japanese waters, were pursued and fired on by Japanese naval forces. In mid-1999 it was reported that Japanese components had been used by the DPRK for the construction of weapons and other military equipment. Relations improved following the DPRK's agreement with the USA, in September, to suspend its reported plans to test a new long-range missile. In October, following unofficial talks between Japanese and North Korean government officials in Singapore, Japan lifted a ban on charter flights to the DPRK. In December the Japanese Government announced that it would resume the provision of food aid. Later that month intergovernmental preparatory talks on re-establishing diplomatic relations were held in Beijing, after Japanese and North Korean Red Cross officials reached an agreement on humanitarian issues. Most notably, the Red Cross organization of the DPRK promised to urge its Government to co-operate in an investigation into the fate of some 10 missing Japanese nationals, believed by the Japanese Government to have been abducted by North Korean agents in the 1970s and 1980s. Full negotiations on the establishment of diplomatic relations were held in April 2000, and several further rounds of talks took place during the year, despite an announcement by Japan in September that normal bilateral relations would not be restored until the cases of Japanese citizens allegedly abducted by North Korean agents had been solved. In October, however, a further round of negotiations took place in Beijing, China. Meanwhile, in September the long-delayed third series of visits to their homeland by the Japanese wives of North Korean men took place. In February 2001 Pyongyang again reiterated the need for compensation from Japan. In early May Japan expelled Kim Jong Nam, the son of North Korean leader Kim Jong Il, and Jong Nam's wife, son and a second woman, when they attempted to enter the country on false passports. The DPRK was one of several Asian countries that condemned Junichiro Koizumi's visit to the Yasukuni Shrine in August. In November Japanese police arrested Kan Young Kwan, an executive of the Japan-based, pro-North Korean organization, *Chongryon*, on charges of misappropriating funds through local credit unions. The incident highlighted the sometimes-illegal activities of the North Korean community in Japan.

In late December 2001 Japan's coast guard sank a suspected North Korean spy vessel after it had been expelled from Japan's exclusive economic zone. The DPRK condemned the incident, but denied any involvement. Japanese coast guard forces searched the sunken vessel in May 2002, and raised it in September of that year. Japan's concerns had been heightened in early 2002 when US President Bush referred to North Korea as one of three countries forming an 'axis of evil', comments that Japan viewed as inconsistent with aims of reducing regional tensions.

In an unexpected diplomatic move, Junichiro Koizumi visited Pyongyang in mid-September 2002, becoming the first incumbent Japanese Prime Minister to do so. His one-day visit, during which he held discussions with Kim Jong Il, was dominated by the latter's admission that North Korean agents had abducted 12 Japanese citizens in the 1970s and 1980s, of whom five were still alive. The remainder were said to have died of natural causes, although suspicions remained that they might have been executed, after Pyongyang failed to locate their graves. Kim apologized for the incidents, but attributed them to rogue elements within the security services. The admission led to a hardening of attitudes against the DPRK among the Japanese public, with some sources indicating that the total number of Japanese abductees might be as high as 100. The surviving captives were temporarily allowed to return to Japan in mid-October, although they had to leave behind any spouses or children. The Japanese authorities, however, refused to allow them to return to the DPRK after the visit. Despite this, representatives from the two countries held the first round of resumed discussions on the restoration of normal diplomatic relations in Malaysia at the end of October, but failed to make any progress.

Japan became alarmed in October 2002 after North Korean representatives allegedly admitted to visiting US officials that Pyongyang was pursuing a secret nuclear weapons programme. Koizumi announced that Japan would halt further economic co-operation with the DPRK until the issues of the abducted

Japanese citizens and the nuclear programme were resolved. Pyongyang's admission led to increased co-operation between Japan and the USA over how to resolve the crisis, with Japan moving closer to participating in a missile shield with the USA (see above). Pyongyang warned Japan that it would abandon its moratorium on missile-testing if normalization talks failed to make any progress. In separate incidents in late February and early March 2003 the DPRK test-launched two short-range ground-to-ship missiles in the Sea of Japan, and in early April tested a third missile in the Yellow Sea. However, it refrained from testing longer-range ballistic missiles, which Tokyo considered a threat to its security. The director-general of Japan's Defence Agency warned the DPRK that Japan could conduct a pre-emptive strike on North Korean missile facilities if necessary. In June 2003 Japan detained two North Korean cargo ships on safety grounds, following US pressure to increase inspections of North Korean shipping; the DPRK denounced the detentions as sanctions. Japan took part in six-party talks held in Beijing in August to discuss the DPRK's nuclear weapons programme; however, the talks ended inconclusively. A further two rounds of discussions took place in 2004; however, a fourth round, scheduled for September 2004, was cancelled after the DPRK refused to participate in the talks.

In January 2004, meanwhile, the House of Representatives approved legislation allowing Japan to impose economic sanctions on the DPRK. In April the House of Councillors approved legislation requiring all ships entering Japanese ports from March 2005 to be insured against oil damage. This in practice amounted to a ban on entry by North Korean ships. Following a further visit by Koizumi to Pyongyang in May 2004, five children of the abductees who had returned to Japan in 2002 (see above) were permitted to fly to Tokyo. Their release had been secured in return for pledges of food aid and medical supplies. However, suspicions remained over the fate of other missing Japanese nationals. In November the DPRK handed over human remains which it claimed were those of Megumi Yokota, who had been kidnapped by the DPRK in 1977. Pyongyang claimed that she had committed suicide. However, subsequent DNA tests indicated that the remains were not those of Megumi Yokota.

Relations with the Republic of Korea were strained during 1996–98 for various reasons, principally concerning territorial and fishing disputes. Relations improved, however, during a four-day state visit by the South Korean President, Kim Dae-Jung, to Japan in October 1998, when a joint declaration was signed, in which Japan apologized for the suffering inflicted on the Korean people during Japanese colonial rule. Japan also pledged substantial aid to the Republic of Korea to stimulate economic recovery. In November the two countries concluded negotiations on the renewal of their bilateral fisheries agreement, which came into effect in January 1999. An agreement to modify some of the terms of the accord was reached in March 1999, following a series of differences over its implementation. Increased co-operation was emphasized during a visit by Obuchi to the Republic of Korea later that month, when both countries agreed to strengthen bilateral economic relations, and Japan pledged further aid. In August Japan and the Republic of Korea held their first joint military exercises since the Second World War, in the Tsushima Straits. Prime Minister Mori visited Seoul in May 2000, where he advocated closer bilateral ties and pledged support for the inter-Korean summit meeting held in June.

Relations between Japan and the Republic of Korea deteriorated in 2001, however, following Tokyo's official endorsement of a new history school textbook, which minimized the suffering of Chinese and Koreans during Japanese occupation. In early April the Republic of Korea recalled its ambassador, cancelled planned exchanges in protest and demanded 35 revisions to the text. In July Japan stated that there would be no revisions, further inflaming public opinion in Korea. This anger was exacerbated in August when Prime Minister Koizumi visited the Yasukuni Shrine, leading to many protests. In October Koizumi visited Seoul and apologized for past crimes and suffering under Japanese rule; however, he was forced to cancel a visit to the National Assembly, owing to hostility against him there. In November Japan and the Republic of Korea, along with China, agreed to establish regular contacts between their ministers of finance and foreign affairs. In late March 2002 Koizumi again visited the Republic of Korea and discussed the possibility of establishing a free-trade pact, as well as Japan's policy towards the DPRK.

Along with China and the DPRK, the Republic of Korea condemned Koizumi's visits to the Yasukuni Shrine in late April 2002 and mid-January 2003. However, Koizumi and Kim Dae-Jung in late March agreed to begin discussions on a possible bilateral free-trade agreement, and at the end of May Koizumi attended the opening ceremony of the 2002 football World Cup in Seoul. Also in attendance was Prince Takamado (who died in November 2002) and his wife, who were making the first official visit to the Republic of Korea by a member of the Imperial family. The football tournament, a major source of prestige to both countries, passed by without incident. Any remaining mutual hostility between the two countries was overshadowed in 2002 by the need for co-operation in engaging with the North. In December 2002 Koizumi and South Korean President-elect Roh Moo-Hyun agreed to form a united front when dealing with the North. Koizumi subsequently attended Roh's inauguration in late February 2003, and the two were expected to continue efforts towards reaching a free-trade agreement. In June President Roh made his first state visit to Japan, in the course of which he held talks with Koizumi on the issue of the DPRK's nuclear weapons programme. Although both leaders agreed that North Korean nuclear proliferation should not be tolerated, Koizumi advocated strict policies towards the DPRK, such as inspections and blockades of goods transport, whereas Roh stressed the need for dialogue with Pyongyang. On the occasion of an ASEAN summit meeting in Bali in October 2003, the Republic of Korea and Japan agreed, with China, to increased co-operation in various spheres, but did not reach agreement on the establishment of a free-trade area. Later in that month, however, Japan and the Republic of Korea confirmed at an APEC meeting in Bangkok that they would continue negotiations towards a free-trade agreement. In January 2004 the Republic of Korea criticized a fourth visit by Prime Minister Koizumi to the Yasukuni Shrine.

The actions of the Japanese army in the Second World War proved to be a contentious issue from the mid-1990s, both domestically and in Japan's relations with neighbouring Asian countries, in the context of the 50th anniversary, in August 1995, of the surrender of Japanese forces. In November 1994 an international ruling that Asian women, used for sexual purposes by the Japanese army during the Second World War ('comfort women'), should receive compensation was rejected by the Japanese Government, which insisted that the issue of reparation payments to individuals had been fully covered under the terms of the peace treaty of 1951. Japan also applied this policy to claims for compensation made by former prisoners of war belonging to the Allied forces. In February 1995 Prime Minister Murayama publicly acknowledged that Japan was responsible, in part, for the post-war division of the Korean peninsula. He was forced to retract the statement, however, following bitter controversy in the Diet. In June a resolution was passed apologizing for Japanese actions in the war, despite considerable disagreement in the Diet. However, countries whose citizens had been prisoners of the Japanese army criticized the resolution as being insufficiently explicit. In August 1996 the first compensation payments, accompanied by a letter of apology from Prime Minister Hashimoto, were made from a private fund to four Philippine victims, who had been used as 'comfort women' during the war. The majority of groups representing South Korean victims refused to accept payment from the fund, demanding that compensation be forthcoming from official, rather than private, sources. In April 1998, however, a Japanese district court ordered the Government to pay compensation to three former 'comfort women' from the Republic of Korea. Another group of South Korean 'comfort women' was refused the right to compensation by the Japanese High Court in November 2000.

In late 1999 a lawsuit was filed in the US state of California against several large Japanese corporations on behalf of former prisoners of war and civilians from various countries, who alleged that the companies had profited from their forced labour during the Second World War. In November 2000 one of these corporations agreed to pay compensation to Chinese forced labourers used during the War. There were fears among Japan's neighbours that the emergence of Junichiro Koizumi as Prime Minister marked the emergence of a more nationalistic Japan. Tokyo's endorsement of a high school textbook that played down Japan's atrocities in Asia during the 1930s and 1940s, and Koizumi's regular visits to the Yasukuni Shrine from 2001 were widely condemned in the region, especially in China and the Koreas (see above). In July 2002 a court in Hiroshima rejected a compensation claim by five Chinese labourers who had been brought to Japan during the Second World War, but acknowledged that the men had been forcibly brought to the country. At the same time Koizumi and his Cabinet agreed to donate 10% of their annual salary to a fund designed to compensate former 'comfort women'. In August a Tokyo court rejected a compensation claim by 180 Chinese for damages inflicted in biological warfare during the 1930s and 1940s, but acknowledged that Japan had, in fact, waged such warfare in China at that time. This was corroborated by a former member of Japan's biological warfare division, who testified to such crimes at the trial. Historians estimated that 300,000 Chinese had been killed by Japanese biological warfare schemes. In September 2003 compensation was granted to 13 Chinese people injured by Second World War weapons left behind by the Japanese army, and in March 2004 former Chinese slave labourers were granted compensation from the Japanese Government (see above). Koizumi stated in early 2005 that he would not visit the Yasukuni Shrine during the New Year period, as he had done in 2004; however, it was believed that he would make a visit later in the year.

Japan's relations with Russia have been dominated by the issue of the Northern Territories, four small islands situated close to Hokkaido, which were annexed in 1945 by the USSR. Both countries claim sovereignty over the islands, and there has been no substantial progress towards resolving the situation since 1956, when Japan and the USSR resumed diplomatic relations. In February 1992 a joint Japanese-Russian working group began discussions about a prospective peace treaty (formally ending the Second World War), and meetings on the issue took place in 1992 and 1993. However, relations between the two countries deteriorated, following the disposal of nuclear waste in Japanese waters by Russian ships in November, and Russia's decision, in August 1994, to open fire on Japanese vessels, that were alleged to have been fishing in Russian waters. Bilateral negotiations over the status of the disputed territory opened in March 1995. In November 1996 Japan indicated that it was prepared to resume the disbursement of an aid 'package', withheld since 1991, and in May 1997 the Japanese Government abandoned its opposition to Russia's proposed membership of the G-7 group. Russian plans for joint development of the mineral and fishing resources of the disputed territory were followed, in July, by an outline agreement on the jurisdiction of the islands. Later in that month a new diplomatic policy was forged, based on 'trust, mutual benefit and long-term prospects'. At an informal summit meeting in November, the two parties agreed to work towards the conclusion of a formal peace treaty by the year 2000. Negotiations resulted in the conclusion of a framework fisheries agreement in December 1997. The Japanese Government offered considerable financial aid to Russia during a visit by President Yeltsin to Japan in April 1998, and agreement was reached on the expansion of economic co-operation. In November Prime Minister Obuchi and Yeltsin signed a joint declaration on bilateral relations in Moscow. During Obuchi's visit Yeltsin reportedly submitted proposals on the resolution of the territorial dispute, in response to suggestions made by Hashimoto in April. Although it had been agreed that the contents of the proposals should not be made public, it was widely reported that both countries still claimed sovereignty over the islands, with Japan advocating a transitional period of Russian administrative control. Agreement was reached on the establishment of subcommissions to examine issues of border delimitation and joint economic activity on the disputed islands. However, little progress was achieved by the subcommissions during 1999. In September Japan agreed to resume lending to Russia, which had been suspended since the Russian Government had effectively devalued the rouble and defaulted on some of its debts in mid-1998. At the same time an accord was concluded on improved access to the disputed islands for former Japanese inhabitants. Negotiations achieved little progress during 2000, a major obstacle being the issue of how many of the islands should be returned. Despite Russian President Vladimir Putin's repudiation of Japan's claim to any of the islands during his first official visit to Tokyo in September, Russia subsequently offered to abide by a 1956 declaration that it would relinquish two of the islands after the signature of a peace treaty, but Japan initially rejected this partial solution. Meanwhile, in November 2000 a former Japanese naval officer on trial in Tokyo admitted spying for Russia. There was outrage in Japan at the fact that the crime carried possible punishments that were perceived as being extremely lenient in relation to the severity of the offence.

In March 2001 Prime Minister Mori met President Putin in Irkutsk, Russia, and discussed the future of the islands; however, no new agreements were reached. Nevertheless, in April Japanese and Russian military leaders agreed to improve bilateral military co-operation. In May Prime Minister Koizumi adopted a harder stance than his predecessor, and demanded that all four islands be relinquished, a position rejected by Russia. Prime Minister Koizumi met Putin at the Group of Eight summit meeting in July, amid Japanese anger that Russia had permitted South Korean vessels to fish off the islands. The ongoing disputes meant that no agreement was reached on developing a Japan-Russia-Europe transport corridor, and in August Koizumi warned of serious damage to relations with Russia if the fishing dispute were not resolved. Japanese officials met their Russian counterparts on the margins of the G-8 summit meeting and the Asian security summit in Brunei in mid-2002, and both sides expressed a willingness to expand relations in all fields.

By late 2002 Koizumi was increasingly seeking Russia's assistance in persuading the DPRK to abandon its nuclear weapons programme. In early January 2003 Koizumi visited Moscow and held a summit meeting with Putin, during which the two agreed to engage the DPRK. Koizumi also visited the Russian Far East, where he met regional leaders. Both Japan and Russia were keen to build a 3,800-km pipeline that would transport petroleum from Angarsk, in Siberia, to Nakhodka on Russia's Pacific coast, from where it could be shipped to Japan. The cost, estimated at US $5,000m., was considered a prohibitive factor, but the scheme would reduce Japan's dependency on Middle Eastern supplies (see Economic Affairs). Talks on the pipeline took place amid competition from China, which was negotiating for the pipeline to be built to the Chinese city of Daqing instead. In late 2004 Russia announced its decision to build a pipeline to Nakhodka. There were suggestions by Russia that it would still be possible to transport oil to China as well as to Japan. Meanwhile Japan and Russia both attended three rounds of six-party talks in Beijing on the North Korean nuclear weapons programme in 2003 and 2004 (see above). Tensions over the disputed Northern Territories islands (see above) were exacerbated in September 2004 when Prime Minister Koizumi embarked on a boat trip within sight of the islands. Hopes for 'two-track' negotiations (dealing with two of the four islands separately from the other two) were in doubt following a statement by Japan in November that it would be not be satisfied with the return of only two of the four disputed islands.

The Japanese Government criticized India and Pakistan for conducting nuclear tests in mid-1998, and in response suspended grants of non-humanitarian aid and loans to both countries. A series of missile tests carried out by India and Pakistan in April 1999 again provoked criticism from Japan. Following a visit to India by the Japanese Prime Minister in August 2000, differences over nuclear testing were set aside in favour of enhanced security, defence and research co-operation between Japan and India, which continued during 2001. Indian Prime Minister Vajpayee visited Japan in December, the first such visit since 1992. In addition to security issues, the two countries discussed closer co-operation in their software and computer industries.

In November 2000 the Peruvian President, Alberto Fujimori, arrived in Tokyo from where he submitted his resignation by fax, following increasing allegations of domestic corruption. In December Japan announced that Fujimori possessed dual nationality as his father had been a Japanese citizen, and that he was therefore entitled to remain indefinitely in the country. In March 2001, however, the Peruvian authorities charged Fujimori with criminal abuse of power and requested his extradition. Japan refused, despite Peruvian warnings of serious consequences if the former President did not return. Fujimori remained in Japan throughout 2002, refusing to co-operate with members of a Peruvian Truth and Reconciliation Commission who visited Japan. In March 2003 Japan refused to extradite Fujimori, despite Interpol's issue of a warrant for his arrest. In August 2003 the Peruvian ambassador to Japan, Luis Macchiavello, issued a formal request for Fujimori's extradition; however, the Japanese Ministry of Foreign Affairs indicated that Japan was likely to reject the request.

Japan's urgent need for new oil supplies prompted the visit to the country in October 2000 of the Iranian President, Muhammad Khatami, the first by an Iranian Head of State since the revolution of 1979. The trip culminated in Japan's acquisition of negotiation rights over the world's largest unde-veloped oilfield, Azadegan field, in Iran. In July 2001 the Minister of Economy, Trade and Industry visited Iran, Kuwait, Saudi Arabia and the United Arab Emirates, in order to promote Japan's oil interests in the Middle East. In February 2004 an agreement was signed granting Japan exploitation rights in Iran's Azadegan oil field, despite US concerns relating to development of nuclear weapons in Iran.

In January 2002 Japan hosted an international conference on the reconstruction of Afghanistan, and emerged as the largest single donor, pledging some US $500m. over two-and-a-half years. During 2002 and early 2003 Japan also sought to bring a lasting peace settlement to Sri Lanka, and pledged to continue overseas development assistance to the war-ravaged island.

In September 1990, meanwhile, Japan contributed to the international effort to force an unconditional Iraqi withdrawal from Kuwait. A controversial LDP-sponsored Peace Co-operation Bill, which provided for the dispatch to the Persian (Arabian) Gulf area of some 2,000 non-combatant personnel, was withdrawn in November after it encountered severe political opposition. In January 1991, following repeated US demands for a greater financial commitment to the resolution of the Gulf crisis (and a swifter disbursement of moneys already pledged), the Japanese Government announced plans substantially to increase its contribution and to provide aircraft for the transport of refugees in the region. Opposition to the proposal was again vociferous. The Government secured the support of several centrist parties, by pledging that any financial aid from Japan would be employed in a 'non-lethal' capacity, and legislation to approve the new contribution was adopted by the Diet in March. In June 1992 controversial legislation to permit the SDF to participate in UN peace-keeping operations was approved. Their role, however, was to be confined to logistical and humanitarian tasks, unless a special dispensation from the Diet were granted. In September members of the SDF were dispatched to serve in the UN Transitional Authority in Cambodia (UNTAC). Japanese troops participated in further UN peace-keeping operations in Mozambique, in 1993, and, under Japanese command, on the Rwandan–Zairean border, in 1994. Legislation was approved in November 1994 to enable Japanese forces to be deployed overseas if the Government believed the lives of Japanese citizens to be at risk. In September Japan reiterated its desire to be a permanent member of the UN Security Council, particularly in view of its status as the world's largest donor of development aid and the second largest contributor (after the USA) to the UN budget. In October 1996 the UN General Assembly voted to allocate to Japan a non-permanent seat on the Security Council, to be held for a two-year period from January 1997. In the late 1990s and early 2000s the Japanese Government continued its campaign to obtain a permanent seat on the UN Security Council. In a speech to the UN General Assembly in September 2004 Koizumi stated that Japan's role in supporting reconstruction in Afghanistan and Iraq, as well as the Japanese contributions to negotiations with the DPRK on its nuclear programme, entitled Japan to a permanent seat.

In November 2001 Japan announced plans to send 700 SDF members to East Timor as part of the international peace-keeping force. The force consisted mostly of engineers, and the first contingent arrived in March 2002. In February 2002 the Japanese Government planned to revise the 1992 law on peace-keeping missions, in order to allow the dispatch of the SDF without the consent of those in conflict, following a UN request. SDF personnel were also to be equipped with more powerful weapons, rather than purely defensive ones.

Following the commencement of US military action in Iraq in March 2003, the House of Councillors approved legislation to allow SDF forces to be dispatched to Iraq in a peace-keeping capacity. There were also increasing suggestion from 2003 of a revision of Japan's Constitution to give the SDF the status of a conventional army (see above). In mid-January 2004 an advance group of 30 SDF troops was dispatched, and by mid-April there were some 550 Japanese troops stationed in Iraq. In June 2004 Koizumi informed US President George W. Bush that Japanese troops would remain in Iraq after the transfer of sovereignty to an interim government at the end of that month. In December 2004 it was announced that the term of SDF involvement in Iraq would be extended by one year to aid reconstruction of the country.

In 2004 Japan concluded a free-trade agreement with Mexico, which was expected to take effect from April 2005.

Government

Under the Constitution of 1947, the Emperor is Head of State but has no governing power. Legislative power is vested in the bicameral Diet, comprising the House of Representatives (lower house), whose members are elected for a four-year term, and the House of Councillors (upper house), members of which are elected for six years, one-half being elected every three years. The House of Representatives comprises 480 seats—300 single-seat constituencies and 180 determined by proportional representation—and there are 242 seats in the House of Councillors. The number of seats in the House of Representatives was reduced from 500 for the 2000 elections; the reduction was in the number of seats determined by proportional representation. There is universal suffrage for all adults from 20 years of age. Executive power is vested in the Cabinet, which is responsible to the Diet. The Emperor appoints the Prime Minister (on designation by the Diet), who appoints the other Ministers in the Cabinet.

Japan has 47 prefectures, each administered by an elected Governor.

Defence

Although the Constitution renounces war and the use of force, the right of self-defence is not excluded. Japan maintains ground, maritime and air self-defence forces. Military service is voluntary. The USA provides equipment and training staff and also maintains bases in Japan. US forces in Japan totalled 43,550 at 1 August 2004. The total strength of the Japanese Self-Defence Forces at 1 August 2004 was some 239,900: army 148,200, navy 44,400, air force 45,600 and central staff 1,700. The defence budget for 2004 was 4,900,000m. yen.

Economic Affairs

In 2003, according to estimates by the World Bank, Japan's gross national income (GNI), measured at average 2001–03 prices, was US $4,397,524m., equivalent to $34,510 per head (or $28,620 per head on an international purchasing-power parity basis). During 1990–2003, it was estimated, the population increased by an average annual of 0.2%, while gross domestic product (GDP) per head increased, in real terms, by an average of 1.1% per year. According to World Bank figures, overall GDP increased, in real terms, by an average annual rate of 1.4% in 1990–2003. According to official sources, compared with the previous year GDP contractedby more than 0.3% in 2002 but was estimated to have increased by 2.5% in 2003.

Agriculture (including forestry and fishing) contributed 1.2% of GDP, and engaged 4.6% of the employed labour force, in 2003. The principal crops are rice, potatoes, cabbages, sugar beets, and citrus fruits. During 1990–2003, according to official sources, agricultural GDP declined, in real terms, at an average rate of 3.2% annually. Compared with the previous year, the sector's GDP declined by 8.9% in 2003.

Industry (including mining, manufacturing, construction and utilities) contributed 29.1% of GDP, and engaged 28.8% of the employed labour force, in 2003. During 1990–2003, according to official sources, industrial GDP decreased at an average annual rate of 0.3%. In 2003 the industrial sector's GDP increased by 6.3%.

Mining and quarrying contributed 0.1% of GDP and engaged less than 0.1% of the employed labour force in 2003. While the domestic output of limestone and sulphur is sufficient to meet domestic demand, all of Japan's requirements of bauxite, crude petroleum and iron ore, and a high percentage of its requirements of copper ore and coking coal are met by imports.

In 2003 manufacturing contributed 20.0% of GDP, and in that year 18.7% of the employed labour force were engaged in the sector. Manufacturing GDP increased by an average of 1.1% per year in 1990–2003. Manufacturing GDP declined for the second successive year in 2002, when it contracted by more than 2.0%; however, in 2003 the sector's GDP increased by 9.6%. The most important branches of manufacturing are machinery and transport equipment, electrical and electronic equipment, and iron and steel.

Japan imports most of its energy requirements, with imports of crude and partly refined petroleum comprising 12.0% of the value of total imports in 2003. Thermal energy accounted for 61% of electricity output in 2001, nuclear power for 30% and hydropower for 9%. There are proposals to construct a further 20 nuclear reactors by 2010. Following an accident at a nuclear power plant at Mihama in 2004, in which four people were killed, a number of reactors owned by Kansai Electric Power were temporarily shut down. In October 2000, meanwhile,

Japan secured negotiation rights over the world's largest undeveloped oilfield, in Iran. In February 2004 a deal worth US $2,000m. was signed granting Japan rights to exploit Iran's Azadegan oil field. From 2003 Japan also held negotiations with Russia on proposals to import petroleum from Siberia via a pipeline to Nakhodka, Russia's closest port to Japan (see above).

The services sector contributed 69.6% of GDP, and engaged 66.6% of the employed labour force, in 2003. The GDP of the services sector increased by an average of 2.2% annually in 1990–2003, expanding by 0.1% in 2003 compared with the previous year. Tourist receipts, totalling US $3,499m. in 2002, are an important source of revenue. The number of tourist arrivals, however, declined from 5,238,963 to 5,211,725 in 2003.

In 2003 Japan recorded a visible trade surplus of US $10,640m., and there was a surplus of $136,220m. on the current account of the balance of payments. In 2003 the principal market for exports was the USA (24.6%), which was also a major source of imports (15.4%). The principal source of imports in that year was the People's Republic of China (19.7%), which was also a major market for exports (12.2%). Other major suppliers in 2003 were Australia, Indonesia, the Republic of Korea, the United Arab Emirates and Taiwan, and other leading purchasers of Japanese exports were the Republic of Korea, Taiwan and Hong Kong. In 2004, for the first time, the value of Japan's total trade with China was larger than that of Japan's total trade with the USA. The principal imports and exports in 2003 were machinery and transport equipment.

The budget for the financial year ending March 2005 projected expenditure of 82,111,000m. yen, an increase of 0.4% compared with the previous year. The budget for 2005/06 envisaged expenditure of 82,183,000m. yen. The increase in expenditure, despite reductions in spending on public works, was due largely to plans for higher expenditure on social security to support the ageing population. According to World Bank figures, the annual rate of inflation averaged 0.6% in 1990–2002. Consumer prices declined by 0.9% in 2002. According to official figures, the rate of deflation was 0.3% in 2003, and in 2004 consumer prices continued to decline for the sixth consecutive year. The rate of unemployment stood at 4.4% of the labour force in December 2004. Unofficial forecasts predicted that unemployment would remain at around 4.5% of the labour force in 2005.

Japan is a member of the UN Economic and Social Commission for Asia and the Pacific (ESCAP, see p. 31), the Asia-Pacific Economic Co-operation (APEC, see p. 155) forum, the Asian Development Bank (ADB, see p. 159), the Organisation for Economic Co-operation and Development (OECD, see p. 307), the Colombo Plan (see p. 373) and the World Trade Organization (WTO, see p. 357).

Following a period of rapid economic expansion in the 1980s, Japan underwent a period of prolonged economic stagnation, including several recessions, during the 1990s and re-entered recession in 2001. On becoming Prime Minister in April 2001, Junichiro Koizumi pledged to introduce major structural reforms, to address the problem of the country's debt burden, to compel the closure of businesses with excessive bad debts and to transfer the state-managed postal savings system to the private sector. However, he faced immense opposition to such plans from elements within his own party, which had strong links with vested interest groups. By December 2001 the unemployment rate had reached its highest level since the Second World War. Furthermore, the economic deceleration in the USA from 2001 limited Japan's ability to implement an export-led recovery, and also had an indirect adverse effect on Japan's regional trade, as other Asian countries reliant on extensive export revenue from the USA found their purchasing power for Japanese goods reduced. In the financial sector, the process of consolidation became widespread from 2000, and bankruptcies of high-profile organizations continued. The banking system remained troubled by bad loans, with non-performing loans (NPLs) amounting to 8.4% of lending by major banks in March 2002. The Government committed itself to halving the ratio of NPLs by March 2005. By September 2004 the ratio of NPLs was reported to have been reduced to 4.7% of total lending. Despite the decrease in NPLs, major banks continued to rely on government funds, amounting to an estimated 10,000,000m. yen in early 2005. In August 2004 plans were announced for a merger between UFJ Holdings and Mitsubishi Tokyo Financial Group which, upon completion, was expected to create the world's largest bank. Meanwhile, political instability and a lack of confidence in the Government's commitment to reform contributed to a decline of the Japanese stock market in the period to March 2003, when the benchmark Nikkei 225 index declined to its lowest level for more than 20 years, falling to below 8,000 points—a decrease of 80% compared with its peak of December 1989. Stronger economic performance was evident from 2003, following improvements in the export sector in particular, with increases in exports to China being especially pronounced. Official reports indicated that in September 2004 the value of exports was greater than at any time in the last 50 years; however, exports decreased again later in the year. The unemployment rate began to stabilize, standing at an estimated 4.7% in 2004. However, unemployment amongst young people remained high in 2004, at around 10% of those in the 15–24 age group. Unofficial sources estimated that GDP growth in 2004 had been 2.6% and predicted a growth rate of 2.1% for 2005. However, the economy was believed to have re-entered recession in late 2004, with a decrease in GDP of 0.1% in the fourth quarter of the year. Japan faced international pressure to combat the problem of continuing deflation, which remained a potential threat to the economy, as consumer prices reportedly continued to decrease in 2004. In October 2004, however, the Bank of Japan predicted a return to inflation for the fiscal year beginning in April 2005. Another problem affecting the Japanese economy in 2004 was the persistence of a high level of public debt, which was reported to have reached the equivalent of 160% of GDP. The fiscal deficit also remained high in 2004 at an estimated 5% of GDP. Meanwhile, the yen appreciated by 7.5% against the US dollar during 2003, owing primarily to the weakening of the US currency. The appreciation of the yen against the dollar was curbed by the Japanese Government's intervention in the currency market, with a record 20,057,000m. yen being spent on supporting the yen in 2003. Currency intervention was halted in March 2004. The yen continued to appreciate, rising in value by 6.7% against the US dollar in 2004. In the long term the proposed privatization of Japan's postal service was a highly significant reform project. Japan Post included substantial savings and life insurance assets, and the organization was reported to constitute the world's largest financial body. The transfer of assets to the private sector was expected to begin in 2007, and was to involve reorganization of the postal service into four separate companies for postal savings, postal life insurance, mail delivery and post office management. The reform process was expected to be completed by 2017.

Education

A kindergarten (*yochien*) system provides education for children aged between three and five years of age, although the majority of kindergartens are privately controlled. Education is compulsory between the ages of six and 15. Elementary education, which begins at six years of age, lasts for six years. Lower secondary education lasts for a further three years. In 2000 more than 11.4m. children aged six to 15 were enrolled in compulsory education, while 4.2m. of those aged 15 to 18 received upper secondary education. Upper secondary schools provide a three-year course in general topics, or a vocational course in subjects such as agriculture, commerce, fine art and technical studies. There are four types of institution for higher education. Universities (*daigaku*) offer a four-year degree course, as well as postgraduate courses. In 2003 there were 702 graduate schools and universities in Japan. Junior colleges (*tanki-daigaku*) provide less specialized two- to three-year courses. In 2003 there were 525 junior colleges in Japan. Both universities and junior colleges offer facilities for teacher-training. Colleges of technology (*koto-senmon-gakko*), of which there were 63 in 2003, offer a five-year specialized training. Since 1991 colleges of technology have been able to offer short-term advanced courses. Special training colleges (*senshu-gakko*) offer advanced courses in technical and vocational subjects, lasting for at least one year. Fiscal expenditure on education in 2000 was 24,300,000m. yen (equivalent to 15.9% of expenditure of national and local governments).

Public Holidays

2005: 1 January (New Year's Day), 15 January (Coming of Age Day), 11 February (National Foundation Day), 20 March (Vernal Equinox Day), 29 April (Greenery Day), 3 May (Constitution Memorial Day), 5 May (Children's Day), 20 July (Marine Day), 15 September (Respect for the Aged Day), 23 September (Autumnal Equinox), 14 October (Sports Day), 3 November (Culture Day), 23 November (Labour Thanksgiving Day), 23 December (Emperor's Birthday).

2006: 1 January (New Year's Day), 15 January (Coming of Age Day), 11 February (National Foundation Day), 21 March (Vernal Equinox Day), 29 April (Greenery Day), 3 May (Constitution Memorial Day), 5 May (Children's Day), 20 July (Marine Day), 15 September (Respect for the Aged Day), 23 September (Autumnal Equinox), 14 October (Sports Day), 3 November (Culture Day), 23 November (Labour Thanksgiving Day), 23 December (Emperor's Birthday).

Weights and Measures

The metric system is in force.

Statistical Survey

Source (unless otherwise stated): Statistics Bureau and Statistics Center, Ministry of Public Management, Home Affairs, Posts and Telecommunications, 2-1-2, Kasumigaseki, Chiyoda-ku, Tokyo 100-8926; tel. (3) 5253-5111; fax (3) 3504-0265; e-mail webmaster@stat.go.jp; internet www.stat.go.jp.

Area and Population

AREA, POPULATION AND DENSITY

Area (sq km)	377,864*
Population (census results)†	
1 October 1995	125,570,246
1 October 2000	
Males	62,110,764
Females	64,815,079
Total	126,925,843
Population (official estimates at 1 October)	
2001	127,291,000
2002	127,435,000
2003	127,619,000
Density (per sq km) at 1 October 2003	337.7

* 145,894 sq miles.
† Excluding foreign military and diplomatic personnel and their dependants.

BIRTHS, MARRIAGES AND DEATHS*

	Registered live births		Registered marriages†		Registered deaths	
	Number	Rate (per 1,000)	Number	Rate (per 1,000)	Number	Rate (per 1,000)
1996 . .	1,206,555	9.7	795,080	6.4	896,211	7.2
1997 . .	1,191,665	9.5	775,651	6.2	913,402	7.3
1998 . .	1,203,147	9.6	784,595	6.3	936,484	7.5
1999 . .	1,177,669	9.4	762,011	6.1	982,031	7.8
2000 . .	1,190,547	9.5	798,138	6.4	961,653	7.7
2001 . .	1,170,662	9.3	799,999	6.4	970,331	7.7
2002 . .	1,153,900	9.2	757,300	6.0	982,400	7.8
2003 . .	1,123,800	8.9	740,220	5.9	1,015,000	8.0

* Figures relate only to Japanese nationals in Japan.
† Data are tabulated by year of registration rather than by year of occurrence.

Expectation of life (WHO estimates, years at birth): 81.9 (males 78.4; females 85.3) in 2002 (Source: WHO, *World Health Report*).

PRINCIPAL CITIES
(population at census of 1 October 2000)*

Tokyo (capital)† . .	8,130,408		Utsunomiya . . .	443,787
Yokohama . . .	3,426,506		Nishinomiya . . .	438,129
Osaka	2,598,589		Oita	436,490
Nagoya	2,171,378		Kurashiki . . .	430,239
Sapporo . . .	1,822,300		Yokosuka	428,836
Kobe	1,493,595		Nagasaki . . .	423,163
Kyoto	1,467,705		Gifu	402,748
Fukuoka	1,341,489		Hirakata . . .	402,586
Kawasaki . . .	1,249,851		Toyonaka . . .	391,732
Hiroshima . . .	1,126,282		Wakayama . . .	386,501
Kitakyushu‡ . . .	1,011,491		Fujisawa . . .	379,151
Sendai	1,008,024		Fukuyama . . .	378,793
Chiba	887,163		Machida	377,546
Sakai	792,034		Nara	366,196
Kumamoto . . .	662,123		Toyohashi . . .	364,868
Okayama	626,534		Iwaki	360,143
Sagamihara . . .	605,555		Nagano	360,117
Hamamatsu . . .	582,120		Asahikawa . . .	359,526
Kagoshima . . .	552,099		Takatsuki . . .	357,440
Funabashi . . .	550,079		Toyota	351,068
Hachioji . . .	536,000		Suita	347,938
Higashiosaka . .	515,055		Okazaki	336,570
Niigata	501,378		Koriyama . . .	334,845
Urawa	484,834		Takamatsu . . .	332,866
Himeji	478,312		Kawagoe . . .	330,737
Matsuyama . . .	473,397		Kochi	330,613
Shizuoka	469,679		Tokorozawa . . .	330,152
Amagasaki . . .	466,161		Kashiwa	327,868
Matsudo . . .	464,836		Toyama	325,693
Kawaguchi . . .	459,952		Akita	317,563
Kanazawa . . .	456,434		Koshigaya . . .	308,277
Omiya	456,164		Miyazaki	305,777
Ichikawa	448,553		Naha	301,107

* Except for Tokyo, the data for each city refer to an urban county (*shi*), an administrative division which may include some scattered or rural population as well as an urban centre.

† The figure refers to the 23 wards (*ku*) of the old city. The population of Tokyo-to (Tokyo Prefecture) was 12,059,237.

‡ Including Kokura, Moji, Tobata, Wakamatsu and Yahata (Yawata).

Source: UN, *Demographic Yearbook*.

ECONOMICALLY ACTIVE POPULATION*
(annual averages, '000 persons aged 15 years and over)

	2001	2002	2003
Agriculture and forestry . . .	2,860	2,680	2,660
Fishing and aquaculture . . .	270	280	270
Mining and quarrying	50	50	50
Manufacturing	12,840	12,220	11,780
Electricity, gas and water . . .	340	340	320
Construction	6,320	6,180	6,040
Wholesale and retail trade, restaurants and hotels . . .	14,730	14,380	14,830
Transport, storage and communications	4,070	4,010	4,960
Financing, insurance, real estate and business services . . .	2,400	2,410	2,320
Community, social and personal services	17,680	18,040	17,050
Government (not elsewhere classified)	2,110	2,170	2,270
Activities not adequately defined .	450	540	610
Total employed	64,120	63,300	63,160
Unemployed	3,400	3,590	3,500
Total labour force	67,520	66,890	66,660
Males	39,920	39,560	39,340
Females	27,600	27,330	27,320

* Figures are rounded to the nearest 10,000 persons.

Health and Welfare

KEY INDICATORS

Total fertility rate (children per woman, 2002)	1.3
Under-5 mortality rate (per 1,000 live births, 2003) . . .	4
HIV/AIDS (% of persons aged 15–49, 2003)	<0.1
Physicians (per 1,000 head, 2000)	1.9
Hospital beds (per 1,000 head, 2000)	16.5
Health expenditure (2001): US $ per head (PPP)	2,131
Health expenditure (2001): % of GDP	8.0
Health expenditure (2001): public (% of total)	77.9
Access to water (% of persons, 2002)	100
Access to sanitation (% of persons, 2002)	100
Human Development Index (2002): ranking	9
Human Development Index (2002): value	0.938

For sources and definitions, see explanatory note on p. vi.

Agriculture

PRINCIPAL CROPS
('000 metric tons)

	2001	2002	2003
Wheat	699.9	827.8	855.2
Rice (paddy)	11,320.0	11,111.0	9,740.0
Barley	206.4	217.2	198.5
Potatoes	2,959.0	3,069.0	3,200.0*
Sweet potatoes	1,063.0	1,030.0	941.1
Taro (Coco yam)	217.8	209.2	210.0*
Yams	182.4	181.7	180.0*
Other roots and tubers	75.3	75.3*	75.3*
Sugar cane	1,499.0	1,328.0	1,400.0†
Sugar beets	3,796.0	4,098.0	4,161.0
Dry beans	94.6	99.9	81.8
Soybeans (Soya beans)	290.6	270.2	231.2
Cabbages	2,473.0	2,392.0	2,400.0*
Lettuce	554.2	561.6	570.0*
Spinach	319.3	311.6	313.0*
Tomatoes	797.6	784.5	780.0*
Cauliflowers	120.9	124.6	130.0*
Pumpkins, squash and gourds . .	227.5	219.5	215.0
Cucumbers and gherkins . . .	735.0	728.9	720.0*
Aubergines (Eggplants)	448.0	432.4	420.0*
Chillies and green peppers . . .	159.4	161.0	160.0*
Green onions and shallots . . .	526.9	518.7	515.0*
Dry onions	1,259.0	1,274.0	1,260.0*
Green beans	62.1	58.8	58.0*
Carrots	691.3	644.5	630.0*
Green corn*	290.0	290.0	290.0
Mushrooms	67.2	67.0*	67.0*
Other vegetables†	2,800.0	2,800.0	2,700.0
Watermelons	573.3	526.9	520.0*
Cantaloupes and other melons .	307.4	286.7	285.0*
Grapes	225.4	231.7	220.8
Apples	930.7	925.8	891.7
Pears	396.4	406.7	365.8
Peaches and nectarines	175.6	175.1	157.0
Plums	123.7	112.7	115.0*
Oranges	104.4	105.0†	108.0*
Tangerines, mandarins, clementines and satsumas . .	1,281.0	1,131.0	1,147.0
Other citrus fruit	246.0	202.0	200.0*
Persimmons	281.8	269.3	280.0*
Strawberries	208.6	210.5	208.0†
Other fruits and berries* . . .	87.3	90.4	88.8
Tea (made)	85.0	84.0	92.0†
Tobacco (leaves)	61.0	58.0	60.0†

* FAO estimate(s).
† Unofficial figure(s).

Source: FAO.

LIVESTOCK
('000 head at 30 September)

	2001	2002	2003
Horses*	21	20	20
Cattle	4,531	4,564	5,523
Pigs	9,788	9,612	9,725
Sheep*	10	11	11
Goats*	35	35	34
Poultry	292,437	287,404	283,955

* FAO estimates.

Source: FAO.

LIVESTOCK PRODUCTS
('000 metric tons)

	2001	2002	2003
Beef and veal	458.0	535.1	505.0*
Pig meat	1,231.6	1,244.1	1,258.8
Poultry meat	1,216.4	1,229.1	1,218.0
Cows' milk	8,301.0	8,385.3	8,360.0*
Butter	79.5	82.7	83.0*
Cheese	123.4	122.8	121.0†
Hen eggs	2,514.2	2,513.7	2,500.0†
Cattle hides (fresh)†	28.5	33.2	32.4

* Unofficial figure.
† FAO estimate(s).

Source: FAO.

Forestry

ROUNDWOOD REMOVALS
('000 cubic metres, excl. bark)

	2001	2002	2003
Sawlogs, veneer logs and logs for sleepers	11,948	11,421	11,421*
Pulpwood	3,826	3,671	3,671*
Other industrial wood	0	0	0
Fuel wood*	129	124	119
Total	15,903	15,216	15,211

* FAO estimate(s).

Source: FAO.

SAWNWOOD PRODUCTION
('000 cubic metres, incl. railway sleepers)

	2000	2001	2002
Coniferous (softwood)	16,479	14,974	13,970
Broadleaved (hardwood)	615	511	432
Total	17,094	15,485	14,402

2003: Figures assumed to be unchanged from 2002 (FAO estimates).

Source: FAO.

Fishing

('000 metric tons, live weight)

	2000	2001	2002
Capture	4,984.8	4,713.0	4,443.0
Chum salmon (Keta or Dog salmon)	163.5	217.4	211.7
Alaska (Walleye) pollock	300.0	241.9	213.3
Atka mackerel	165.1	161.2	154.7
Pacific saury (Skipper)	216.5	269.8	205.3
Japanese jack mackerel	246.0	214.4	196.0
Japanese pilchard (sardine)	149.6	178.4	50.3
Japanese anchovy	381.0	301.2	443.2
Skipjack tuna (Oceanic skipjack)	341.4	276.7	276.1
Chub mackerel	346.2	375.3	279.0
Yesso scallop	304.3	291.0	306.7
Japanese flying squid	337.3	298.2	273.6
Aquaculture	762.8	801.9	828.4
Pacific cupped oyster	221.3	231.5	221.4
Yesso scallop	210.7	235.6	272.0
Total catch	5,747.6	5,515.0	5,271.4

Note: Figures exclude aquatic plants ('000 metric tons): 647.9 (capture 119.0, aquaculture 528.9) in 2000; 633.9 (capture 122.1, aquaculture 511.8) in 2001; 686.1 (capture 127.9, aquaculture 558.2) in 2002. Also excluded are aquatic mammals (generally recorded by number rather than by weight), pearls, corals and sponges. The number of whales caught was: 923 in 2000; 1,131 in 2001; 796 in 2002. The catch of other aquatic mammals (in '000 metric tons) was: 1.8 in 2000; 1.9 in 2001; 2.0 in 2002. For the remaining categories, catches (in kilograms) were: Pearls 29.9 in 2000; 34.5 in 2001; 31.9 in 2002; Corals (including FAO estimates) 8.9 in 2000; 3.5 in 2001; 4.2 in 2002; Sponges (FAO estimate) 4.0 in 2000; n.a. in 2001 and 2002.

Source: FAO.

Mining

('000 metric tons, unless otherwise indicated)

	2000	2001	2002*
Hard coal	3,126	3,198	1,367
Zinc ore†	64	45	43
Iron ore‡	1.5	0.8	0.7
Silica stone	15,578	14,213	13,571
Limestone	185,569	182,255	171,948
Copper ore (metric tons)†	1,211	744	n.a.
Lead ore (metric tons)†	8,835	4,997	5,723
Gold ore (kg)†	8,400	7,815	8,615
Crude petroleum ('000 barrels)	4,656	4,782	4,548
Natural gas (million cu m)	2,453	2,521	2,571

* Provisional figures.
† Figures refer to the metal content of ores.
‡ Figures refer to gross weight. The estimated iron content is 54%.

Source: US Geological Survey.

Industry

SELECTED PRODUCTS
('000 metric tons, unless otherwise indicated)

	1999	2000	2001
Refined sugar*	2,242	2,281	2,257
Cotton yarn—pure	157.9[1]	144.5[1]	125.8
Cotton yarn—mixed	13.1[1]	14.3[1]	13.7
Woven cotton fabrics—pure and mixed (million sq m)	774	664	603
Flax, ramie and hemp yarn	1.0	0.9	0.5
Linen fabrics (million sq m)	4.0	3.9	3.2
Woven silk fabrics—pure and mixed ('000 sq m)	34,564	33,444	30,837
Wool yarn—pure and mixed	42.0	33.7	29.6
Woven woollen fabrics—pure and mixed (million sq m)	199.1[2]	98.2[2]	94.9
Rayon continuous filaments	34	30	18
Acetate continuous filaments	24	25	23

— continued	1999	2000	2001
Rayon discontinuous fibres . .	77	72	66
Acetate discontinuous fibres[3] . .	81	84	89
Woven rayon fabrics—pure and			
mixed (million sq m)[2]	325	241	213
Woven acetate fabrics—pure and			
mixed (million sq m)[2]	27	32	28
Non-cellulosic continuous			
filaments (metric tons) . . .	664	669	640
Non-cellulosic discontinuous fibres	754	764	727
Woven synthetic fabrics (million sq			
m)[2, 4]	1,581	1,573	1,484
Leather footwear ('000 pairs) . .	37,546	35,961	34,667
Mechanical wood pulp	1,474	1,405	1,394
Chemical wood pulp[5]	9,497	9,968	9,398
Newsprint	3,295	3,419	3,464
Other printing and writing paper .	11,330	11,740	11,163
Other paper	3,769	3,877	3,758
Paperboard	12,238	21,791	12,332
Synthetic rubber	1,577	1,590	1,465
Road motor vehicle tyres ('000) .	163,705	166,709	165,063
Rubber footwear ('000 pairs) . .	15,480	12,421	10,999
Ethylene—Ethene	7,087	7,614	7,361
Propylene—Propene	5,520	5,453	5,342
Benzene—Benzol	4,459	4,426	4,261
Toluene—Toluol	1,488	1,489	1,423
Xylenes—Xylol	5,520	4,681	4,798
Ethyl alcohol—95% (kilolitres) .	263,633	n.a.	n.a.
Sulphuric acid—100%	6,493	7,059	6,727
Caustic soda—Sodium hydroxide .	4,215	4,337	4,162
Soda ash—Sodium carbonate . .	722	669	680
Ammonia	1,685	1,715	1,604
Nitrogenous fertilizers	751	756	683
Phosphate fertilizers	399	369	334
Liquefied petroleum gas . . .	4,885	4,946	n.a.
Naphtha	13,251	13,234	n.a.
Motor spirit—gasoline[6]	41,448	41,776	n.a.
Kerosene	21,709	22,699	n.a.
Jet fuel	8,187	8,323	n.a.
Gas–diesel oil	60,904	60,032	n.a.
Residual fuel oil	37,432	35,668	n.a.
Lubricating oil	2,399	2,363	n.a.
Petroleum bitumen—Asphalt . .	5,597	5,504	n.a.
Coke-oven coke	36,473	39,954	n.a.
Cement	80,120	81,097	76,550
Pig-iron	74,520	81,071	78,836
Ferro-alloys[7]	984	1,049	1,056
Crude steel	94,192	106,444	102,866
Aluminium—unwrought . . .	1,158	1,214	1,171
Refined copper—unwrought . .	1,342	1,437	1,426
Refined lead—unwrought . . .	227.1	239.4	236.0
Electrolytic, distilled and rectified			
zinc—unwrought	633.4	654.4	644.4
Calculating machines ('000) . .	2,402	1,841	1,301
Still cameras ('000)	10,326	9,743	7,907
DVD players ('000)	4,524	4,517	2,832
Television receivers ('000) . . .	4,386	3,382	2,862
Cellular telephones ('000) . . .	43,350	55,272	53,652
Personal computers (incl. servers,			
'000)	9,254	12,149	11,350
Passenger motor cars ('000) . .	8,100	8,363	8,118
Lorries and trucks ('000) . . .	1,742	1,720	1,596
Motorcycles, scooters and mopeds			
('000)	2,252	2,415	2,328
Watches	531,289	554,130	515,302
Construction: new dwellings			
started ('000)	1,215	1,230	1,174
Electric energy (million kWh)*	1,066,130	1,091,499	1,075,890

* Twelve months beginning 1 April of the year stated.
[1] Including condenser cotton yarn.
[2] Including finished fabrics.
[3] Including cigarette filtration tow.
[4] Including blankets made of synthetic fibres.
[5] Including pulp prepared by semi-chemical processes.
[6] Not including aviation gasoline.
[7] Including silico-chromium.

Source: UN, *Industrial Commodity Statistics Yearbook*.

Finance

CURRENCY AND EXCHANGE RATES

Monetary Units
100 sen = 1 yen.

Sterling, Dollar and Euro Equivalents (31 December 2004)
£1 sterling = 201.10 yen;
US $1 = 104.12 yen;
€1 = 141.82 yen;
1,000 yen = £4.97 = $9.60 = €7.05.

Average Exchange Rate (yen per US $)
2002   125.39
2003   115.93
2004   108.19

BUDGET
('000 million yen, year ending 31 March)*

Revenue†	2003/04	2004/05	2005/06
Tax and stamp revenues . . .	41,786	41,747	44,007
Individual income tax . . .	13,810	13,778	n.a.
Corporation tax	9,114	9,407	n.a.
Consumption tax	9,489	9,563	n.a.
Liquor tax	1,733	1,588	n.a.
Stamp revenue	1,129	1,148	n.a.
Government bond issues . . .	36,445	36,590	34,390
Total (incl. others)	81,789	82,111	82,183

Expenditure†	2003/04	2004/05	2005/06
Defence	4,953	4,903	4,856
Social security	18,991	19,797	20,381
Public works	8,097	7,816	7,531
Servicing of national debt‡ . . .	16,798	17,569	18,442
Transfer of local allocation tax to			
local governments	17,399	16,494	16,089
Total (incl. others)	81,789	82,111	82,183

* Figures refer only to the operations of the General Account budget. Data exclude transactions of other accounts controlled by the central Government: two mutual aid associations and four special accounts (including other social security funds).
† Initial forecasts.
‡ Including the repayment of debt principal and administrative costs.

Source: Ministry of Finance, Tokyo.

INTERNATIONAL RESERVES
(US $ million at 31 December)

	2001	2002	2003
Gold*	1,082	1,171	1,280
IMF special drawing rights . .	2,377	2,524	2,766
Reserve position in IMF . . .	5,051	7,203	7,733
Foreign exchange	387,727	451,458	652,790
Total	396,237	462,357	664,569

* Valued at SDR 35 per troy ounce.

Source: IMF, *International Financial Statistics*.

MONEY SUPPLY
('000 million yen at 31 December)

	2001	2002	2003
Currency outside banks . . .	66,676	71,328	72,455
Demand deposits at deposit money			
banks	215,109	276,651	291,144
Total money	281,785	347,979	363,599

Source: IMF, *International Financial Statistics*.

COST OF LIVING
(Consumer Price Index; average of monthly figures; base: 2000 = 100)

	2001	2002	2003
Food (incl. beverages) . . .	99.4	98.6	98.4
Housing	100.2	100.1	100.0
Rent	100.4	100.4	100.4
Fuel, light and water charges . .	100.6	99.4	98.9
Clothing and footwear	97.8	95.6	93.8
Miscellaneous	99.8	100.0	100.9
All items	**99.3**	**98.4**	**98.1**

NATIONAL ACCOUNTS
('000 million yen at current prices, year ending 31 December)

National Income and Product

	2001	2002	2003
Compensation of employees .	273,372.8	266,793.1	265,484.8
Operating surplus and mixed income	87,045.4	88,819.9	90,285.1
Domestic primary incomes .	**360,418.2**	**355,613.0**	**355,769.9**
Consumption of fixed capital . .	99,380.4	98,554.2	101,301.0
Statistical discrepancy	7,213.6	6,049.9	3,851.5
Gross domestic product (GDP) at factor cost	**467,012.2**	**460,217.1**	**460,922.4**
Indirect taxes	42,911.7	41,464.1	41,019.6
Less Subsidies	4,076.8	3,784.4	4,457.2
GDP in purchasers' values . .	**505,847.1**	**497,896.8**	**497,485.0**
Primary incomes received from abroad	13,783.4	12,791.9	12,574.9
Less Primary incomes paid abroad	5,462.7	4,598.5	4,050.8
Gross national income (GNI) .	**514,167.8**	**506,090.2**	**506,009.1**

Expenditure on the Gross Domestic Product

	2001	2002	2003
Government final consumption expenditure	86,418.5	88,002.6	87,956.8
Private final consumption expenditure	285,965.5	284,153.5	282,702.1
Changes in stocks	−21.8	−1,136.3	−257.2
Gross fixed capital formation .	130,310.9	120,465.2	119,107.8
Total domestic expenditure .	**502,673.1**	**491,485.0**	**489,509.5**
Exports of goods and services . .	52,567.0	55,829.1	58,882.4
Less Imports of goods and services	49,392.8	49,417.2	50,906.9
GDP in purchasers' values .	**505,847.1**	**497,896.8**	**497,485.0**
GDP at constant 2000 prices .	**512,608.5**	**511,056.0**	**517,727.3**

Gross Domestic Product by Economic Activity

	2001	2002	2003
Agriculture, hunting, forestry and fishing	6,780.9	6,691.4	6,485.4
Mining and quarrying	683.5	605.7	635.0
Manufacturing	105,220.9	101,793.6	103,626.2
Electricity, gas and water . . .	14,505.7	14,134.6	13,697.6
Construction	36,268.0	34,259.8	33,697.4
Wholesale and retail trade . . .	69,275.2	67,623.2	66,071.2
Transport, storage and communications	32,651.1	31,870.9	31,786.4
Finance and insurance	33,210.0	34,024.7	34,815.3
Real estate*	67,383.8	68,398.8	69,151.1
Public administration	26,879.2	27,237.3	27,052.4
Other government services . . .	18,466.3	18,754.3	18,571.1
Other business, community, social and personal services . . .	103,840.8	103,344.1	104,016.6
Private non-profit services to households	9,433.2	9,801.8	9,774.5
Sub-total	**524,598.6**	**518,540.1**	**519,380.0**
Import duties	3,242.9	3,157.3	3,278.5
Less Imputed bank service charge	25,777.8	26,817.7	25,856.4
Less Consumption taxes for gross capital formation	3,430.3	3,032.9	3,168.7

— *continued*	2001	2002	2003
Statistical discrepancy	7,214.0	6,050.0	3,851.7
GDP in purchasers' values . .	**505,847.4**	**497,896.8**	**497,485.0**

* Including imputed rents of owner-occupied dwellings.
Source: Economic and Social Research Institute, Tokyo.

BALANCE OF PAYMENTS
(US $ million)*

	2001	2002	2003
Exports of goods f.o.b.	383,600	395,580	449,120
Imports of goods f.o.b.	−313,380	−301,750	−342,720
Trade balance	**70,210**	**93,830**	**10,640**
Exports of services	64,520	65,710	77,620
Imports of services	−108,250	−107,940	−111,530
Balance on goods and services	**26,480**	**51,600**	**72,490**
Other income received	103,090	91,480	95,210
Other income paid	−33,870	−25,710	−23,970
Balance on goods, services and income	**95,700**	**117,370**	**143,730**
Current transfers received . . .	6,150	10,040	6,510
Current transfers paid	−14,060	−14,960	−14,020
Current balance	**87,790**	**112,450**	**136,220**
Capital account (net)	−2,870	−3,320	−4,000
Direct investment abroad . . .	−38,500	−32,020	−28,770
Direct investment from abroad . .	6,190	9,090	6,240
Portfolio investment assets .	−106,790	−85,930	−176,290
Portfolio investment liabilities .	60,500	−20,040	81,180
Financial derivatives assets .	102,790	77,250	64,960
Financial derivatives liabilities .	−101,400	−74,770	−59,380
Other investment assets .	46,590	36,410	149,890
Other investment liabilities .	−17,550	26,630	34,100
Net errors and omissions . . .	3,720	390	−16,990
Overall balance	**40,490**	**46,130**	**187,150**

* Figures are rounded to the nearest US $10m.

Source: IMF, *International Financial Statistics.*

JAPANESE DEVELOPMENT ASSISTANCE
(net disbursement basis, US $ million)

	2000	2001	2002
Official:			
Bilateral assistance:			
Grants	5,813	4,849	4,473
Grant assistance . . .	2,109	1,907	1,718
Technical assistance . . .	3,705	2,943	2,754
Loans	3,827	2,603	2,253
Total	**9,640**	**7,452**	**6,726**
Contributions to multilateral institutions	3,779	2,448	2,633
Total	**13,419**	**9,900**	**9,359**
Other official flows:			
Export credits	−1,552	−495	−469
Equities and other bilateral assets, etc.	−3,052	−1,328	−2,360
Transfers to multilateral institutions	−252	−875	−2,512
Total	**−4,855**	**−2,698**	**−5,341**
Total official	**8,564**	**7,202**	**4,018**
Private flows:			
Export credits	−358	593	−1,078
Direct investment and others .	6,191	12,127	12,108
Bilateral investment in securities, etc.	478	−4,133	−3,413
Transfers to multilateral institutions	−52	−355	−2,804
Grants from private voluntary agencies	231	235	157
Total private	**6,490**	**8,467**	**4,970**
Grand total	**15,053**	**15,669**	**8,989**

External Trade

PRINCIPAL COMMODITIES
(million yen)

Imports c.i.f.	2001	2002	2003
Food and live animals . . .	5,250,600	5,282,300	5,104,600
Fish and fish preparations* . .	1,626,474	1,658,025	1,475,463
Crude materials (inedible) except fuels	2,586,100	2,522,000	2,659,000
Mineral fuels, lubricants, etc. .	8,523,700	8,173,900	9,350,000
Crude and partly refined petroleum	4,718,360	4,573,000	5,328,000
Liquefied natural gas	1,594,000	1,492,000	1,695,000
Chemicals	3,101,100	3,239,000	3,458,000
Machinery and transport equipment	13,215,900	13,434,000	13,974,000
Office machines	2,764,027	2,698,000	2,745,000
Thermionic valves, tubes, etc. .	1,909,535	1,910,000	2,015,000
Textiles	2,890,000	2,752,000	2,819,000
Clothing (excl. footwear) . .	2,318,293	2,189,000	2,241,000
Total (incl. others)†	42,415,533	42,227,500	44,362,000

* Including crustacea and molluscs.
† Including re-imports not classified according to kind.

Exports f.o.b.	2001	2002	2003
Chemicals	3,738,800	4,173,700	4,525,000
Metals and metal products .	2,889,100	3,227,400	3,388,500
Iron and steel	1,649,543	1,939,592	2,066,009
Machinery and transport equipment	32,895,700	35,523,000	37,143,000
Non-electric machinery . . .	10,229,500	10,599,000	11,025,000
Power-generating machinery .	1,720,000	1,748,000	1,730,000
Office machines	2,820,710	3,005,000	2,619,000
Electrical machinery, apparatus, etc.	11,533,300	11,924,000	12,857,000
Thermionic valves, tubes, etc. .	3,647,382	3,867,000	4,074,000
Transport equipment . . .	11,132,900	13,000,000	13,261,000
Road motor vehicles . . .	7,210,812	8,775,000	8,895,000
Road motor vehicle parts . .	1,880,380	2,117,000	2,300,000
Precision instruments . .	2,629,101	2,019,000	2,154,000
Scientific instruments and photographic equipment . .	2,504,480	1,897,000	2,038,000
Total (incl. others)*	48,979,244	52,109,000	54,548,000

* Including re-exports not classified according to kind.

PRINCIPAL TRADING PARTNERS
(million yen)*

Imports c.i.f.	2001	2002	2003
Australia	1,755,871	1,753,000	1,744,000
Canada	941,469	895,000	871,000
China, People's Republic . .	7,026,677	7,727,793	8,731,000
France	750,358	817,000	837,000
Germany	1,505,798	1,553,000	1,644,000
Indonesia	1,805,632	1,774,000	1,905,000
Iran	609,819	593,000	862,000
Ireland	441,373	401,000	411,000
Italy	654,978	679,000	707,000
Korea, Republic	2,088,356	1,936,787	2,071,000
Kuwait	538,096	526,000	529,000
Malaysia	1,561,324	1,401,350	1,458,000
Philippines	778,879	818,000	815,000
Qatar	731,801	657,000	755,000
Russia	468,419	410,000	490,000
Saudi Arabia	1,496,299	1,455,000	1,689,000
Singapore	653,684	626,767	629,000
Switzerland	399,000	413,000	447,000
Taiwan	1,722,643	1,698,926	1,656,000
Thailand	1,260,472	1,314,594	1,376,000
United Arab Emirates . . .	1,559,855	1,450,000	1,663,000
United Kingdom	729,016	677,000	676,000
USA	7,671,481	7,237,000	6,825,000
Total (incl. others)	42,415,533	42,228,000	44,362,000

Exports f.o.b.	2001	2002	2003
Australia	933,178	1,039,000	1,147,000
Belgium	555,798	575,000	668,000
Canada	797,113	918,000	855,000
China, People's Republic . . .	3,763,723	4,979,796	6,635,000
France	758,786	768,000	818,000
Germany	1,896,740	1,766,000	1,898,000
Hong Kong	2,826,044	3,176,000	3,455,000
Indonesia	777,704	780,000	830,000
Italy	584,615	562,000	636,000
Korea, Republic	3,071,871	3,572,439	4,022,000
Malaysia	1,337,217	1,377,609	1,302,000
Mexico	496,995	472,000	421,000
Netherlands	1,393,132	1,323,000	1,361,000
Panama	586,630	579,000	632,000
Philippines	995,303	1,058,000	1,042,000
Singapore	1,786,059	1,775,000	1,716,000
Taiwan	2,942,227	3,281,188	3,610,000
Thailand	1,442,488	1,648,577	1,854,000
United Kingdom	1,474,989	1,498,000	1,529,000
USA	14,711,055	14,873,000	13,412,000
Total (incl. others)	48,979,244	52,109,000	54,548,000

* Imports by country of production; exports by country of last consignment.

Transport

RAILWAYS
(traffic, year ending 31 March)

	2000	2001	2002
National railways:			
Passengers (million) . . .	8,670	8,650	8,590
Passenger-km (million) . .	240,659	241,133	239,240
Freight ('000 tons) . . .	39,620	39,026	38,200
Freight ton-km (million) . .	21,855	21,907	21,860
Private railways:			
Passengers (million) . . .	12,980	13,070	12,980
Passenger-km (million) . .	384,442	144,288	142,990
Freight ('000 tons) . . .	19,654	19,642	18,400
Freight ton-km (million) . .	280	286	270
Total:			
Passengers (million) . . .	21,646	21,720	21,560
Passenger-km (million) . .	384,441	385,421	382,240
Freight ('000 tons) . . .	59,274	58,668	56,600
Freight ton-km (million) . .	22,135	22,193	22,130

ROAD TRAFFIC
('000 motor vehicles owned, year ending 31 March)

	2000	2001	2002
Passenger cars	42,365	42,528	42,655
Buses and coaches	236	234	233
Trucks, incl. trailers	8,106	7,907	7,666
Special use vehicles	1,754	1,754	1,720
Heavy use vehicles	323	325	n.a.
Light two-wheeled vehicles . .	1,308	1,334	1,352
Light motor vehicles . . .	21,755	22,513	23,266
Total	75,525	76,271	76,893

SHIPPING

Merchant Fleet
(registered at 31 December)

	2001	2002	2003
Number of vessels	7,924	7,458	7,151
Total displacement ('000 grt) . .	16,653	13,918	13,562

Source: Lloyd's Register-Fairplay, *World Fleet Statistics*.

International Sea-borne Traffic
('000 metric tons)

	2000	2001	2002
Goods loaded	101,727	106,986	119,385
Goods unloaded	787,987	772,996	762,329

CIVIL AVIATION
(traffic on scheduled services)

	2000	2001	2002
Kilometres flown (million) . . .	942	929	n.a.
Passengers carried ('000) . . .	112,177	111,690	114,590
Passenger-km (million)	176,628	165,618	156,770
Total ton-km (million)	8,728	7,630	8,150

Tourism

FOREIGN VISITOR ARRIVALS
(excl. Japanese nationals resident abroad)

Country of nationality	2001	2002	2003
Australia	149,621	164,896	172,134
Canada	125,570	131,542	126,065
China, People's Republic . . .	391,384	452,520	448,782
Germany	87,740	93,936	93,571
Hong Kong	262,229	290,624	260,214
Korea, Republic	1,133,971	1,271,835	1,459,333
Philippines	124,072	129,914	137,584
Taiwan	807,202	877,709	785,379
United Kingdom	197,965	219,271	200,543
USA	692,192	731,900	655,821
Total (incl. others)	**4,771,555**	**5,238,963**	**5,211,725**

Source: Japan National Tourist Organization.

Receipts from tourism (US $ million): 3,374 in 2000; 3,301 in 2001; 3,499 in 2002.

Communications Media

	2000	2001	2002
Television receivers ('000 in use) .	92,000	n.a.	n.a.
Telephones ('000 main lines in use)	74,343.6	73,325.0	71,149.0
Mobile telephones ('000			
subscribers)	56,845.6	66,784.4	74,819.0
Personal computers ('000 in use) .	40,000	44,400	48,700
Internet users ('000)	47,080	48,900	57,200
Book production:			
titles	65,065	71,073	74,259
copies (million)	1,420	1,390	n.a.
Daily newspapers:			
number	122	124	n.a.
circulation ('000 copies) . . .	n.a.	53,681	n.a.

Radio receivers ('000 in use): 120,500 in 1997.

Facsimile machines ('000 in use): 16,000 in 1997.

2003: Mobile telephones ('000 subscribers) 86,658.6; Internet users ('000) 61,600.

Sources: Foreign Press Center, *Facts and Figures of Japan*; UNESCO, *Statistical Yearbook*; UN, *Statistical Yearbook*; International Telecommunication Union.

Education

(2003)

	Institutions	Teachers	Students
Elementary schools	23,633	414,000	7,227,000
Lower secondary schools . . .	11,134	252,000	3,748,000
Upper secondary schools . . .	5,450	259,000	3,810,000
Colleges of technology	63	4,000	58,000
Junior colleges	525	14,000	250,000
Graduate schools and universities	702	156,000	2,804,000

Directory

The Constitution

The Constitution of Japan was promulgated on 3 November 1946 and came into force on 3 May 1947. The following is a summary of its major provisions, with subsequent amendments:

THE EMPEROR

Articles 1–8. The Emperor derives his position from the will of the people. In the performance of any state act as defined in the Constitution, he must seek the advice and approval of the Cabinet, though he may delegate the exercise of his functions, which include: (i) the appointment of the Prime Minister and the Chief Justice of the Supreme Court; (ii) promulgation of laws, cabinet orders, treaties and constitutional amendments; (iii) the convocation of the Diet, dissolution of the House of Representatives and proclamation of elections to the Diet; (iv) the appointment and dismissal of Ministers of State, the granting of amnesties, reprieves and pardons, and the ratification of treaties, conventions or protocols; (v) the awarding of honours and performance of ceremonial functions.

RENUNCIATION OF WAR

Article 9. Japan renounces for ever the use of war as a means of settling international disputes.

Articles 10–40 refer to the legal and human rights of individuals guaranteed by the Constitution.

THE DIET

Articles 41–64. The Diet is convened once a year, is the highest organ of state power and has exclusive legislative authority. It comprises the House of Representatives (480 seats—300 single-seat constituencies and 180 determined by proportional representation) and the House of Councillors (242 seats). The members of the former are elected for four years whilst those of the latter are elected for six years and election for approximately one-half of the members takes place every three years. If the House of Representatives is dissolved, a general election must take place within 40 days and the Diet must be convoked within 30 days of the date of the election. Extraordinary sessions of the Diet may be convened by the Cabinet when one-quarter or more of the members of either House request it. Emergency sessions of the House of Councillors may also be held. A quorum of at least one-third of the Diet members is needed to carry out parliamentary business. Any decision arising therefrom must be passed by a majority vote of those present. A bill becomes law having passed both Houses, except as provided by the Constitution. If the House of Councillors either vetoes or fails to take action within 60 days upon a bill already passed by the House of Representatives, the bill becomes law when passed a second time by the House of Representatives, by at least a two-thirds' majority of those members present.

The Budget must first be submitted to the House of Representatives. If, when it is approved by the House of Representatives, the House of Councillors votes against it or fails to take action on it within 30 days, or failing agreement being reached by a joint committee of both Houses, a decision of the House of Representatives shall be the decision of the Diet. The above procedure also applies in respect of the conclusion of treaties.

THE EXECUTIVE

Articles 65–75. Executive power is vested in the Cabinet, consisting of a Prime Minister and such other Ministers as may be appointed. The Cabinet is collectively responsible to the Diet. The Prime Minister is designated from among members of the Diet by a resolution thereof.

If the House of Representatives and the House of Councillors disagree on the designation of the Prime Minister, and if no agreement can be reached even through a joint committee of both Houses, provided for by law, or if the House of Councillors fails to make designation within 10 days, exclusive of the period of recess, after the House of Representatives has made designation, the decision of the House of Representatives shall be the decision of the Diet.

The Prime Minister appoints and may remove other Ministers, a majority of whom must be from the Diet. If the House of Representatives passes a no-confidence motion or rejects a confidence motion, the whole Cabinet resigns, unless the House of Representatives is dissolved within 10 days. When there is a vacancy in the post of Prime Minister, or upon the first convocation of the Diet after a general election of members of the House of Representatives, the whole Cabinet resigns.

The Prime Minister submits bills, reports on national affairs and foreign relations to the Diet. He exercises control and supervision over various administrative branches of the Government. The Cabinet's primary functions (in addition to administrative ones) are to: (a) administer the law faithfully; (b) conduct State affairs; (c) conclude treaties subject to prior (or subsequent) Diet approval; (d) administer the civil service in accordance with law; (e) prepare and present the budget to the Diet; (f) enact Cabinet orders in order to make effective legal and constitutional provisions; (g) decide on amnesties, reprieves or pardons. All laws and Cabinet orders are signed by the competent Minister of State and countersigned by the Prime Minister. The Ministers of State, during their tenure of office, are not subject to legal action without the consent of the Prime Minister. However, the right to take that action is not impaired.

Articles 76–95. Relate to the Judiciary, Finance and Local Government.

AMENDMENTS

Article 96. Amendments to the Constitution are initiated by the Diet, through a concurring vote of two-thirds or more of all the members of each House, and are submitted to the people for ratification, which requires the affirmative vote of a majority of all votes cast at a special referendum or at such election as the Diet may specify.

Amendments when so ratified must immediately be promulgated by the Emperor in the name of the people, as an integral part of the Constitution.

Articles 97–99 outline the Supreme Law, while Articles 100–103 consist of Supplementary Provisions.

The Government

HEAD OF STATE

His Imperial Majesty AKIHITO, Emperor of Japan (succeeded to the throne 7 January 1989).

THE CABINET
(April 2005)

A coalition of the Liberal-Democratic Party (LDP) and New Komeito; the New Conservative Party, previously a coalition partner, was absorbed into the LDP in November 2003.

Prime Minister: JUNICHIRO KOIZUMI.

Minister of Internal Affairs and Communications: TARO ASO.

Minister of Justice and Minister of State for Youth Affairs and Measures for Declining Birthrate: CHIEKO NOHNO.

Minister of Foreign Affairs: NOBUTAKA MACHIMURA.

Minister of Finance: SADAKAZU TANIGAKI.

Minister of Education, Culture, Sports, Science and Technology: NARIAKI NAKAYAMA.

Minister of Health, Labour and Welfare: HIDEHISA OTSUJI.

Minister of Agriculture, Forestry and Fisheries: YOSHINOBU SHIMAMURA.

Minister of Economy, Trade and Industry: SHOICHI NAKAGAWA.

Minister of Land, Infrastructure and Transport: KAZUO KITAGAWA.

Minister of the Environment and Minister of State for Okinawa and Northern Territories Affairs: YURIKO KOIKE.

Chairman of the National Public Safety Commission and Minister of State for Disaster Management and for National Emergency Legislation: YOSHITAKA MURATA.

Chief Cabinet Secretary and Minister of State for Gender Equality: HIROYUKI HOSODA.

Minister of State for Defence: YOSHINORI OHNO.

Minister of State for Financial Services: TATSUYA ITO.

Minister of State for Economic and Fiscal Policy and for Privatization of the Postal Services: HEIZO TAKENAKA.

Minister of State (Administrative Reform, Regulatory Reform): SEIICHIRO MURAKAMI.

Minister of State (Science and Technology Policy, Food Safety, Information Technology): YASUFUMI TANAHASHI.

MINISTRIES

Imperial Household Agency: 1-1, Chiyoda, Chiyoda-ku, Tokyo 100-8111; tel. (3) 3213-1111; fax (3) 3282-1407; e-mail information@ kunaicho.go.jp; internet www.kunaicho.go.jp.

Prime Minister's Office: 1-6-1, Nagata-cho, Chiyoda-ku, Tokyo 100-8968; tel. (3) 3581-2361; fax (3) 3581-1910; internet www.kantei .go.jp.

Cabinet Office: 1-6-1, Nagata-cho, Chiyoda-ku, Tokyo 100-8914; tel. (3) 5253-2111; internet www.cao.go.jp.

Ministry of Agriculture, Forestry and Fisheries: 1-2-1, Kasumigaseki, Chiyoda-ku, Tokyo 100-8950; tel. (3) 3502-8111; fax (3) 3592-7697; internet www.maff.go.jp.

Ministry of Economy, Trade and Industry: 1-3-1, Kasumigaseki, Chiyoda-ku, Tokyo 100-8901; tel. (3) 3501-1511; fax (3) 3501-6942; e-mail webmail@meti.go.jp; internet www.meti.go.jp.

Ministry of Education, Culture, Sports, Science and Technology: 3-2-2, Kasumigaseki, Chiyoda-ku, Tokyo 100-8959; tel. (3) 5253-4111; fax (3) 3595-2017; internet www.mext.go.jp.

Ministry of the Environment: 1-2-2, Kasumigaseki, Chiyoda-ku, Tokyo 100-8975; tel. (3) 3581-3351; fax (3) 3502-0308; e-mail moe@ eanet.go.jp; internet www.env.go.jp.

Ministry of Finance: 3-1-1, Kasumigaseki, Chiyoda-ku, Tokyo 100-8940; tel. (3) 3581-4111; fax (3) 5251-2667; e-mail info@mof.go .jp; internet www.mof.go.jp.

Ministry of Foreign Affairs: 2-11-1, Shiba-Koen, Minato-ku, Tokyo 105-8519; tel. (3) 3580-3311; fax (3) 3581-2667; e-mail webmaster@mofa.go.jp; internet www.mofa.go.jp.

Ministry of Health, Labour and Welfare: 1-2-2, Kasumigaseki, Chiyoda-ku, Tokyo 100-8916; tel. (3) 5253-1111; fax (3) 3501-2532; internet www.mhlw.go.jp.

Ministry of Internal Affairs and Communications: 2-1-2, Kasumigaseki, Chiyoda-ku, Tokyo 100-8926; tel. (3) 5253-5111; fax (3) 3504-0265; internet www.soumu.go.jp.

Ministry of Justice: 1-1-1, Kasumigaseki, Chiyoda-ku, Tokyo 100-8977; tel. (3) 3580-4111; fax (3) 3592-7011; e-mail webmaster@moj .go.jp; internet www.moj.go.jp.

Ministry of Land, Infrastructure and Transport: 2-1-3, Kasumigaseki, Chiyoda-ku, Tokyo 100-8918; tel. (3) 5253-8111; fax (3) 3580-7982; e-mail webmaster@mlit.go.jp; internet www.mlit.go.jp.

Defence Agency: 5-1 Ichigaya, Honmura-cho, Shinjuku-ku, Tokyo 162-8801; tel. (3) 3268-3111; e-mail info@jda.go.jp; internet www.jda .go.jp.

Financial Services Agency: 3-1-1 Kasumigaseki, Chiyoda-ku, Tokyo 100-8967; tel. (3) 3506-6000; internet www.fsa.go.jp.

National Public Safety Commission: 2-1-2, Kasumigaseki, Chiyoda-ku, Tokyo 100-8974; tel. (3) 3581-0141; internet www.npsc .go.jp.

Legislature

KOKKAI
(Diet)

The Diet consists of two Chambers: the House of Councillors (upper house) and the House of Representatives (lower house). The members of the House of Representatives are elected for a period of four years (subject to dissolution). Following the enactment of reform legislation in December 1994, the number of members in the House of Representatives was reduced to 500 (from 511) at the general election of October 1996. Further legislation was enacted in February 2000, reducing the number of members in the House of Representatives to 480, comprising 300 single-seat constituencies and 180 seats determined by proportional representation. For the House of Councillors, which has 242 members (reduced from 247 at the 2004 election), the term of office is six years, with approximately one-half of the members elected every three years.

House of Councillors

Speaker: CHIKAGE OGI.

Party	Seats after elections*	
	29 July 2001	11 July 2004
Liberal-Democratic Party	110	115
Democratic Party of Japan . . .	60	82
New Komeito	23	24
Japanese Communist Party . . .	20	9
Social Democratic Party of Japan	8	5
Liberal Party†	8	—
New Conservative Party‡	5	—
Independents	8	7
Other parties	5	—
Total	247	242

* Approximately one-half of the seats are renewable every three years. At the 2004 election 48 of the 121 seats were allocated on the basis of proportional representation.
† Absorbed by the Democratic Party of Japan in September 2003.
‡ Absorbed by the Liberal-Democratic Party in November 2003.

House of Representatives

Speaker: YOHEI KONO.

General Election, 9 November 2003

Party	Seats
Liberal-Democratic Party	241*
Democratic Party of Japan	177
New Komeito	34
Japanese Communist Party	9
Social Democratic Party of Japan	6
New Conservative Party†	4
Independents and others	9
Total	480

* Including four independents who joined the party after the election.
† The New Conservative Party was subsequently absorbed by the Liberal-Democratic Party.

Political Organizations

The Political Funds Regulation Law provides that any organization wishing to support a candidate for an elective public office must be registered as a political party. There are more than 10,000 registered parties in the country, mostly of local or regional significance.

Dai-Niin Club: Rm 531, Sangiin Kaikan, 2-1-1, Nagata-cho, Chiyoda-ku, Tokyo 100-0014; tel. (3) 3508-8531; e-mail info@niinkuraba.gr.jp; successor to the Green Wind Club (Ryukufukai), which originated in the House of Councillors in 1946–47.

Democratic Party of Japan (DPJ): 1-11-1, Nagata-cho, Chiyoda-ku, Tokyo 100-0014; tel. (3) 3595-9960; fax (3) 3595-7318; e-mail dpjenews@dpj.or.jp; internet www.dpj.or.jp; f. 1998 by the integration into the original DPJ (f. 1996) of the Democratic Reform League, Minseito and Shinto Yuai; advocates a cabinet formed and controlled by the people; absorbed Party Sakigake in March 2001; absorbed Liberal Party in Sept. 2003; Pres. KATSUYA OKADA; Acting Pres. HIROHISA FUJII; Sec.-Gen. TATSUO KAWABATA.

Japanese Communist Party (JCP): 4-26-7, Sendagaya, Shibuya-ku, Tokyo 151-8586; tel. (3) 3403-6111; fax (3) 3746-0767; e-mail intl@jcp.jp; internet www.jcp.or.jp; f. 1922; 400,000 mems (2004); Chair. of Cen. Cttee TETSUZO FUWA; Chair. of Exec. Cttee KAZUO SHII.

Liberal-Democratic Party—LDP (Jiyu-Minshuto): 1-11-23, Nagata-cho, Chiyoda-ku, Tokyo 100-8910; tel. (3) 3581-6211; e-mail koho@ldp.jimin.or.jp; internet www.jimin.jp; f. 1955; advocates the establishment of a welfare state, the promotion of industrial development, the improvement of educational and cultural facilities and constitutional reform as needed; absorbed New Conservative Party in Nov. 2003; 2,369,252 mems (2001); Pres. JUNICHIRO KOIZUMI; Sec.-Gen. TSUTOMU TAKEBE; Acting Sec.-Gen. SHINZO ABE; Chair. of Gen. Council FUMIO KYUMA.

New Komeito: 17, Minami-Motomachi, Shinjuku-ku, Tokyo 160-0012; tel. (3) 3353-0111; internet www.komei.or.jp/; f. 1964 as Komeito, renamed as Komei 1994 following defection of a number of mems to the New Frontier Party (Shinshinto, dissolved Dec. 1997); absorbed Reimei Club Jan. 1998; renamed as above Nov. 1998 following merger of Komei and Shinto Heiwa; advocates political moderation, humanism and globalism, and policies respecting 'dignity of human life'; 400,000 mems (2003); Chief Representative TAKENORI KANZAKI; Sec.-Gen. TETSUZO FUYUSHIBA.

New Socialist Party: Sanken Bldg, 6th Floor, 4-3-7, Hatchobori, Chuo-ku, Tokyo 104-0032; tel. (3) 3551-3980; e-mail honbu@sinsyakai.or.jp; internet www.sinsyakai.or.jp; f. 1996 by left-wing defectors from SDPJ; opposed to US military bases on Okinawa and to introduction in 1996 of new electoral system; seeks to establish an ecological socio-economic system; Chair. TATSUKUNI KOMORI; Sec.-Gen. KEN-ICHI UENO.

Social Democratic Party of Japan—SDPJ (Shakai Minshuto): 1-8-1, Nagata-cho, Chiyoda-ku, Tokyo 100-0014; tel. (3) 3580-1171; fax (3) 3580-0691; e-mail sdpjmail@omnics.co.jp; internet www.sdp.or.jp; f. 1945 as the Japan Socialist Party (JSP); adopted present name in 1996; seeks the establishment of collective non-aggression and a mutual security system, including Japan, the USA, the CIS and the People's Republic of China; 115,000 mems (1994); Chair. MIZUHO FUKUSHIMA; Sec.-Gen. SADAO FUCHIGAMI.

Diplomatic Representation

EMBASSIES IN JAPAN

Afghanistan: Matsumoto International House (MIH), 37-8 Nishihara 3-chome, Shibuya-ku, Tokyo 151-0066; tel. (3) 5465-1219; fax (3) 5465-1229; e-mail info@afghanembassyjp.com; internet www.afghanembassyjp.com; Ambassador HARON AMIN.

Algeria: 2-10-67, Mita, Meguro-ku, Tokyo 153-0062; tel. (3) 3711-2661; fax (3) 3710-6534; Ambassador AMAR BENDJAMA.

Angola: 2-10-24 Daizawa, Setagaya-ku, Tokyo 155-0032; tel. (3) 5430-7879; fax (3) 5712-7481; e-mail embassy@angola.or.jp; internet www.angola.or.jp; Ambassador VICTOR MANUEL RITA DA FONSECA LIMA.

Argentina: 2-14-14, Moto Azabu, Minato-ku, Tokyo 106-0046; tel. (3) 5420-7101; fax (3) 5420-7109; internet www.embargentina.or.jp; Ambassador ALFREDO VICENTE CHIARADIA.

Australia: 2-1-14, Mita, Minato-ku, Tokyo 108-8361; tel. (3) 5232-4111; fax (3) 5232-4149; internet www.australia.or.jp; Ambassador MURRAY MCLEAN.

Austria: 1-1-20, Moto Azabu, Minato-ku, Tokyo 106-0046; tel. (3) 3451-8281; fax (3) 3451-8283; e-mail austria@gol.com; internet www.austria.or.jp; Ambassador HANS DIETMAR SCHWEISGUT.

Bangladesh: 4-15-15, Meguro, Meguro-ku, Tokyo 153-0063; tel. (3) 5704-0216; fax (3) 5704-1696; Ambassador S. M. RASHED AHMED.

Belarus: 4-14-12, Shirogane K House, Shirogane, Minato-ku, Tokyo 108-0072; tel. (3) 3448-1623; fax (3) 3448-1624; e-mail belarus@japan.co.jp; Ambassador PETR K. KRAVCHANKA.

Belgium: 5, Niban-cho, Chiyoda-ku, Tokyo 102-0084; tel. (3) 3262-0191; fax (3) 3262-0651; e-mail tokyo@diplobel.org; internet www.diplomatie.be/tokyo; Ambassador JEAN-FRANÇOIS BRANDERS.

Benin: Sougo Nagatacho Bldg 2F N-3, 1-11-28 Nagata-cho, Chiyoda-ku, Tokyo 100-0014; tel. (3) 3591-6565; Ambassador BANTOLE YABA.

Bolivia: Kowa Bldg, No. 38, Room 804, 4-12-24, Nishi Azabu, Minato-ku, Tokyo 106-0031; tel. (3) 3499-5441; fax (3) 3499-5443; e-mail emboltk@interlink.or.jp; Ambassador EUDORO GALINDO ANZE.

Bosnia and Herzegovina: 3–4 Rokuban-cho, Chiyoda-ku, Tokyo 102-0085; tel. (3) 3556-4151; Ambassador VLADIMIR RASPUDIĆ.

Brazil: 2-11-12, Kita Aoyama, Minato-ku, Tokyo 107-0061; tel. (3) 3404-5211; fax (3) 3405-5846; internet www.brasemb.or.jp; Ambassador FERNANDO GUIMARÃES REIS.

Brunei: 6-5-2, Kita Shinagawa, Shinagawa-ku, Tokyo 141-0001; tel. (3) 3447-7997; fax (3) 3447-9260; Ambassador P. S. N. YUSUF.

Bulgaria: 5-36-3, Yoyogi, Shibuya-ku, Tokyo 151-0053; tel. (3) 3465-1021; fax (3) 3465-1031; e-mail bulemb@gol.com; Ambassador Prof. BLAGOVEST SENDOV.

Burkina Faso: Apt 301, Hiroo Glisten Hills, 3-1-17, Hiroo, Shibuya-ku, Tokyo 150-0012; tel. (3) 3400-7919; fax (3) 3400-6945; Chargé d'affaires a.i. PATRICE KAFANDO.

Burundi: 3-27-16, Nozawa, Setagaya-ku 154, Kita-Shinagawa, Shinagawa-ku, Tokyo 141; tel. (3) 3443-7321; fax (3) 3443-7720; Ambassador GABRIEL NDIHOKUBWAYO.

Cambodia: 8-6-9, Akasaka, Minato-ku, Tokyo 107-0052; tel. (3) 5412-8521; fax (3) 5412-8526; e-mail aap33850@hkg.odn.ne.jp; Ambassador ING KIETH.

Cameroon: 3-27-16, Nozawa, Setagaya-ku, Tokyo 154-0003; tel. (3) 5430-4381; fax (3) 5430-6489; e-mail ambacamtokyo@gol.com; Chargé d'affaires a.i. MBELLA MBELLA LEJEUNE.

Canada: 7-3-38, Akasaka, Minato-ku, Tokyo 107-8503; tel. (3) 5412-6200; fax (3) 5412-6249; internet www.canadanet.or.jp; Ambassador ROBERT G. WRIGHT.

Chile: Nihon Seimei Akabanebashi Bldg, 8th Floor, 3-1-14, Shiba, Minato-ku, Tokyo 105-0014; tel. (3) 3452-7561; fax (3) 3452-4457; e-mail embajada@chile.or.jp; internet www.chile.or.jp; Ambassador DANIEL CARVALLO.

China, People's Republic: 3-4-33, Moto Azabu, Minato-ku, Tokyo 106-0046; tel. (3) 3403-3380; fax (3) 3403-3345; internet www.china-embassy.or.jp; Ambassador WANG YI.

Colombia: 3-10-53, Kami Osaki, Shinagawa-ku, Tokyo 141-0021; tel. (3) 3440-6451; fax (3) 3440-6724; e-mail embajada@emcoltokyo.or.jp; internet www.colombianembassy.org; Ambassador FRANCISCO J. SIERRA.

Congo, Democratic Republic: Harajuku Green Heights, Room 701, 3-53-17, Sendagaya, Shibuya-ku, Tokyo 151-0051; tel. (3) 3423-3981; fax (3) 3423-3984; Chargé d'affaires NGAMBANI ZI-MIZELE.

Costa Rica: Kowa Bldg, No. 38, Room 901, 4-12-24, Nishi Azabu, Minato-ku, Tokyo 106-0031; tel. (3) 3486-1812; fax (3) 3486-1813; Chargé d'affaires a.i. ANA LUCÍA NASSAR SOTO.

Côte d'Ivoire: 2-19-12, Uehara, Shibuya-ku, Tokyo 151-0064; tel. (3) 5454-1401; fax (3) 5454-1405; e-mail ambacijn@yahoo.fr; Ambassador S. E. M. KOUADIO FRY.

Croatia: 3-3-100, Hiroo, Shibuya-ku, Tokyo 150-0012; tel. (3) 5469-3014; fax (3) 5469-3015; e-mail veltok@hpo.net; Ambassador DRAGO BOVAČ.

Cuba: 1-28-4 Higashi-Azabu, Minato-ku, Tokyo 106-0044; tel. (3) 5570-3182; internet www.cyborg.ne.jp/~embcubaj; Ambassador ERNESTO MELÉNDEZ BACHS.

Czech Republic: 2-16-14, Hiroo, Shibuya-ku, Tokyo 150-0012; tel. (3) 3400-8122; fax (3) 3400-8124; e-mail tokyo@embassy.mzv.cz; internet www.mzv.cz/tokyo; Ambassador KAREL ŽEBRAKOVSKÝ.

Denmark: 29-6, Sarugaku-cho, Shibuya-ku, Tokyo 150-0033; tel. (3) 3496-3001; fax (3) 3496-3440; e-mail embassy.tokyo@denmark.or.jp; internet www.denmark.or.jp; Ambassador POUL HOINESS.

Djibouti: 5-18-10, Shimo Meguro, Meguro-ku, Tokyo 153-0064; tel. (3) 5704-0682; fax (3) 5725-8305; Ambassador (vacant); Chargé d'Affaires a.i. YACIN HOUSSEIN DOUALE.

Dominican Republic: Kowa Bldg, No. 38, Room 904, 4-12-24, Nishi Azabu, Minato-ku, Tokyo 106-0031; tel. (3) 3499-6020; fax (3) 3499-2627.

Ecuador: Kowa Bldg, No. 38, Room 806, 4-12-24, Nishi Azabu, Minato-ku, Tokyo 106-0031; tel. (3) 3499-2800; fax (3) 3499-4400; internet www.embassy-avenue.or.jp/ecuador/index-j.htm; Ambassador MARCELO AVILA.

Egypt: 1-5-4, Aobadai, Meguro-ku, Tokyo 153-0042; tel. (3) 3770-8022; fax (3) 3770-8021; internet embassy.kcom.ne.jp/egypt/index.html; Ambassador Dr MAHMOUD KAREM.

El Salvador: Kowa Bldg, No. 38, 8th Floor, 4-12-24, Nishi Azabu, Minato-ku, Tokyo 106-0031; tel. (3) 3499-4461; fax (3) 3486-7022; e-mail embesal@gol.com; Ambassador RICARDO PAREDES-OSORIO.

Estonia: 2-6-15, Jingu-mae, Shibuya-ku 150-0001; tel. (3) 5412-7281; fax (3) 5412-7282; e-mail embassy.tokyo@mfa.ee; internet www.estemb.or.jp; Chargé d'affaires a.i. ARGO KANGRO.

Ethiopia: 3-4-1, Takanawa, Minato-ku, Tokyo 108-0074; tel. (3) 5420-6860; fax (3) 5420-6866; e-mail ethioemb@gol.com; Ambassador Dr KOANG TUTAM DUNG.

Fiji: Noa Bldg, 14th Floor, 2-3-5, Azabudai, Minato-ku, Tokyo 106-0041; tel. (3) 3587-2038; fax (3) 3587-2563; e-mail fijiemb@hotmail.com; Ambassador Ratu TEVITA MOMOEDONU.

Finland: 3-5-39, Minami Azabu, Minato-ku, Tokyo 106-8561; tel. (3) 5447-6000; fax (3) 5447-6042; e-mail sanomat.tok@formin.fi; internet www.finland.or.jp; Ambassador EERO KALEVI SALOVAARA.

France: 4-11-44, Minami Azabu, Minato-ku, Tokyo 106-8514; tel. (3) 5420-8800; fax (3) 5420-8917; e-mail ambafrance.tokyo@diplomatie.fr; internet www.ambafrance-jp.org; Ambassador BERNARD DE MONTFERRAND.

Gabon: 1-34-11, Higashigaoka, Meguro-ku, Tokyo 152-0021; tel. (3) 5430-9171; fax (3) 5430-9175; e-mail info@gabonembassy-tokyo.org; Ambassador JEAN-CHRISTIAN OBAME.

Germany: 4-5-10, Minami Azabu, Minato-ku, Tokyo 106-0047; tel. (3) 5791-7700; fax (3) 3473-4243; e-mail germtoky@ma.rosenet.ne.jp; internet www.tokyo.diplo.de; Ambassador HENRIK SCHMIEGELOW.

Ghana: 1-5-21, Nishi Azabu, Minato-ku, Tokyo 106-0031; tel. (3) 5410-8631; fax (3) 5410-8635; e-mail mission@ghanaembassy.or.jp; internet www.ghanaembassy.or.jp; Ambassador Dr BARFUOR ADJEI-BARWUAH.

Greece: 3-16-30, Nishi Azabu, Minato-ku, Tokyo 106-0031; tel. (3) 3403-0871; fax (3) 3402-4642; e-mail greekemb@gol.com; Ambassador KYRIAKOS RODOUSSAKIS.

Guatemala: Kowa Bldg, No. 38, Room 905, 4-12-24, Nishi Azabu, Minato-ku, Tokyo 106-0031; tel. (3) 3400-1830; fax (3) 3400-1820; e-mail embguate@twics.com; Ambassador ANTONIO ROBERTO CASTELLANOS LÓPEZ.

Guinea: 12-9, Hachiyama-cho, Shibuya-ku, Tokyo 150-0035; tel. (3) 3770-4640; fax (3) 3770-4643; e-mail ambagui-tokyo@gol.com; Ambassador OUSMANE TOLO THIAM.

Haiti: Kowa Bldg, No. 38, Room 906, 4-12-24, Nishi Azabu, Minato-ku, Tokyo 106; tel. (3) 3486-7096; fax (3) 3486-7070; Ambassador MARCEL DURET.

Holy See: Apostolic Nunciature, 9-2, Sanban-cho, Chiyoda-ku, Tokyo 102-0075; tel. (3) 3263-6851; fax (3) 3263-6060; Apostolic Nuncio Emeritus Most Rev. WILLIAM AQUIN CAREW (Titular Archbishop of Telde).

Honduras: Kowa Bldg, No. 38, Room 802, 8th Floor, 4-12-24, Nishi Azabu, Minato-ku, Tokyo 106-0031; tel. (3) 3409-1150; fax (3) 3409-0305; e-mail honduras@interlink.or.jp; Ambassador CARLOS MANUEL ZERÓN.

Hungary: 2-17-14, Mita, Minato-ku, Tokyo 108-0073; tel. (3) 3798-8801; fax (3) 3798-8812; e-mail huembtio@gol.com; internet www.hungary.or.jp; Ambassador Dr GYULA DABRÓNAKI.

Iceland: 4-18-26, Takanawa, Minato-ku, Tokyo 108-0074; tel. (3) 3447-1944; fax (3) 3447-1945; e-mail icemb.tokyo@utn.stjr.is; internet www.iceland.org/jp; Ambassador THORDUR AEGIR OSKARSSON.

India: 2-2-11, Kudan Minami, Chiyoda-ku, Tokyo 102-0074; tel. (3) 3262-2391; fax (3) 3234-4866; internet embassy.kcom.ne.jp/embnet/india.html; Ambassador SIDDHARTH SINGH.

Indonesia: 5-2-9, Higashi Gotanda, Shinagawa-ku, Tokyo 141-0022; tel. (3) 3441-4201; fax (3) 3447-1697; Ambassador SOEMADI D. M. BROTODININGRAT.

Iran: 3-10-32, Minami Azabu, Minato-ku, Tokyo 106-0047; tel. (3) 3446-8011; fax (3) 3446-9002; internet www2.gol.com/users/sjei/indexjapanese.html; Ambassador ALI MAJEDI.

Iraq: 8-4-7, Akasaka, Minato-ku, Tokyo 107-0052; tel. (3) 3423-1727; fax (3) 3402-8636.

Ireland: Ireland House, 2-10-7, Kojimachi, Chiyoda-ku, Tokyo 102-0083; tel. (3) 3263-0695; fax (3) 3265-2275; internet www.embassy-avenue.jp/ireland/; Ambassador PÁDRAIG MURPHY.

Israel: 3, Niban-cho, Chiyoda-ku, Tokyo 102-0084; tel. (3) 3264-0911; fax (3) 3264-0791; e-mail consular@tky.mfa.gov.il; internet tokyo.mfa.gov.il; Ambassador ELI COHEN.

Italy: 2-5-4, Mita, Minato-ku, Tokyo 108-8302; tel. (3) 3453-5291; fax (3) 3456-2319; internet www.embitaly.jp; Ambassador MARIO BOVA.

Jamaica: Toranomon Yatsuka Bldg, 2nd Floor, 1-1-11, Atago, Minato-ku, Tokyo 105-0002; tel. (3) 3435-1861; fax (3) 3435-1864; e-mail secrat@jamaicaemb.or.jp; Ambassador PAUL ANTHONY ROBOTHAM.

Jordan: Chiyoda House, 4th Floor, 2-17-8, Nagata-cho, Chiyoda-ku, Tokyo 100-0014; tel. (3) 3580-5856; fax (3) 3593-9385; internet www2.giganet.net/private/users/emb-jord; Ambassador SAMIR NAOURI.

Kazakhstan: 5-9-8 Himonya, Meguro-ku, Tokyo 152-0003; tel. (3) 3791-5273; fax (3) 3791-5279; e-mail embkazjp@gol.com; internet www.embkazjp.org; Ambassador BOLAT NURGALIYEV.

Kenya: 3-24-3, Yakumo, Meguro-ku, Tokyo 152-0023; tel. (3) 3723-4006; fax (3) 3723-4488; e-mail info@kenrep-jp.com; internet www.kenyarep-jp.com; Ambassador DENNIS N.O. AWORI.

Korea, Republic: 1-2-5, Minami Azabu, Minato-ku, Tokyo 106-0047; tel. (3) 3452-7611; fax (3) 5232-6911; internet www.mofat.go.kr/japan; Ambassador RA JONG-YIL.

Kuwait: 4-13-12, Mita, Minato-ku, Tokyo 108-0073; tel. (3) 3455-0361; fax (3) 3456-6290; internet kuwait-embassy.or.jp; Ambassador Sheikh AZZAM MUBARAK SABAH AL-SABAH.

Kyrgyzstan: 9-8 Himonya 5-chome, Meguro-ku, Tokyo 152-003; tel. (3) 3791-5273; fax (3) 3791-5279; e-mail embkazjp@gol.com; Ambassador ASKAR KUTANOV.

Laos: 3-3-22, Nishi Azabu, Minato-ku, Tokyo 106-0031; tel. (3) 5411-2291; fax (3) 5411-2293; Ambassador SOUKTHAVONE KEOLA.

Lebanon: Chiyoda House, 5th Floor, 2-17-8, Nagata-cho, Chiyoda-ku, Tokyo 100-0014; tel. (3) 3580-1227; fax (3) 3580-2281; e-mail ambaliba@cronos.ocn.ne.jp; Ambassador JAAFAR MOAWI.

Liberia: Sugi Terrace 201, 3-13-11, Okusawa, Setagaya-ku, Tokyo 158; tel. (3) 3726-5711; fax (3) 3726-5712; Chargé d'affaires a.i. HARRY TAH FREEMAN.

Libya: 10-14, Daikanyama-cho, Shibuya-ku, Tokyo 150-0034; tel. (3) 3477-0701; fax (3) 3464-0420; Secretary of the People's Bureau SULAIMAN ABU BAKER BADI (acting).

Lithuania: 2-11-25 Oyamadai, Setagaya-ku, Tokyo 158-0086; tel. (3) 3703-6000; fax (3) 5758-8281; e-mail lithemb@gol.com; internet www2.gol.com/users/lithemb; Ambassador Dr ALGIRDAS KUDZYS.

Luxembourg: 1/F Luxembourg House, 1st Floor, 8–9, Yonban-cho, Chiyoda-ku, 102-0081; tel. (3) 3265-9621; fax (3) 3265-9624; internet www.luxembourg.or.jp; Ambassador MICHÈLE PRANCHÈRE-TOMASSINI.

Madagascar: 2-3-23, Moto Azabu, Minato-ku, Tokyo 106-0046; tel. (3) 3446-7252; fax (3) 3446-7078; Ambassador JOCELYN B. RADIFERA.

Malawi: Takanawa-Kaisei Bldg, 7th Floor, 3-4-1, Takanawa, Minato-ku, Tokyo 108-0074; tel. (3) 3449-3010; fax (3) 3449-3220; e-mail malawi@mx1.ttcn.ne.jp; internet embassy.kcom.ne.jp/malawi; Ambassador BRIGHT S. M. MANGULAMA.

Malaysia: 20-16, Nanpeidai-cho, Shibuya-ku, Tokyo 150-0036; tel. (3) 3476-3840; fax (3) 3476-4971; e-mail maltokyo@kln.gov.my; Ambassador Dato' MARZUKI MOHAMMAD NOOR.

Mali: 15-15 Sikazawa, 5-chome, Sitagaya-ku, Tokyo; tel. (3) 3705-3433; fax (3) 3705-3489.

Marshall Islands: Meiji Park Heights 101, 9-9, Minamimoto-machi, Shinjuku-ku, Tokyo 106; tel. (3) 5379-1701; fax (3) 5379-1810; Ambassador AMATLAIN ELIZABETH KABUA.

Mauritania: 5-17-5, Kita Shinagawa, Shinagawa-ku, Tokyo 141-0001; tel. (3) 3449-3810; fax (3) 3449-3822; Ambassador (vacant).

Mexico: 2-15-1, Nagata-cho, Chiyoda-ku, Tokyo 100-0014; tel. (3) 3581-1131; fax (3) 3581-4058; e-mail embamex@mexicoembassy.jp; internet www.sre.gob.mx/japon; Ambassador MIGUEL RUIZ-CABAÑAS IZQUIERDO.

Micronesia: Reinanzaka Bldg, 2nd Floor, 1-14-2, Akasaka, Minato-ku, Tokyo 107-0052; tel. (3) 3585-5456; fax (3) 3585-5348; e-mail fsmemb@fsmemb.or.jp; Ambassador KASIO MIDA.

Mongolia: Pine Crest Mansion, 21-4, Kamiyama-cho, Shibuya-ku, Tokyo 150-0047; tel. (3) 3469-2088; fax (3) 3469-2216; e-mail embmong@gol.com; internet www.embassy-avenue.jp/mongolia/index.htm; Ambassador ZAMBA BATJARGAL.

Morocco: Silva Kingdom Bldg, 5th–6th Floors, 3-16-3, Sendagaya, Shibuya-ku, Tokyo 151-0051; tel. (3) 3478-3271; fax (3) 3402-0898; Ambassador SAAD EDDIN TAIB.

Mozambique: Shiba Amerex Bldg, 6th Floor, 3-12-17 Mita, Minato-ku, Tokyo 108-0073; tel. (3) 5419-0973; fax (3) 5442-0556; internet home.att.ne.jp/kiwi/mozambique; Ambassador DANIEL ANTÓNIO.

Myanmar: 4-8-26, Kita Shinagawa, Shinagawa-ku, Tokyo 140-0001; tel. (3) 3441-9291; fax (3) 3447-7394; Ambassador U SAW LLA MIN.

Nepal: 7-14-9, Todoroki, Setagaya-ku, Tokyo 158-0082; tel. (3) 3705-5558; fax (3) 3705-8264; e-mail nepembjp@big.or.jp; internet www.nepal.co.jp/embassy.html; Ambassador KEDAR BHAKTA MATHEMA.

Netherlands: 3-6-3, Shiba Koen, Minato-ku, Tokyo 105-0011; tel. (3) 5401-0411; fax (3) 5401-0420; e-mail nlgovtok@oranda.or.jp; internet www.oranda.or.jp; Ambassador EGBERT F. JACOBS.

New Zealand: 20-40, Kamiyama-cho, Shibuya-ku, Tokyo 150-0047; tel. (3) 3467-2271; fax (3) 3467-2278; e-mail nzemb.tky@mail.com; internet www.nzembassy.com/japan; Ambassador JOHN MCARTHUR (designate).

Nicaragua: Kowa Bldg, No. 38, Room 903, 9th Floor, 4-12-24, Nishi Azabu, Minato-ku, Tokyo 106; tel. (3) 3499-0400; fax (3) 3499-3800; Ambassador Dr HARRY BODÁN-SHIELDS.

Nigeria: 5-11-17, Shimo-Meguro, Meguro-ku, Tokyo 153-0064; tel. (3) 5721-5391; fax (3) 5721-5342; internet www.crisscross.com/users/nigeriaemb/home.htm; Ambassador ADAMU ALIYU.

Norway: 5-12-2, Minami Azabu, Minato-ku, Tokyo 106-0047; tel. (3) 3440-2611; fax (3) 3440-2620; e-mail emb.tokyo@mfa.no; internet www.norway.or.jp; Ambassador ÅGE BERNHARD GRUTLE.

Oman: 2-28-11, Sendagaya, Shibuya-ku, Tokyo 151-0051; tel. (3) 3402-0877; fax (3) 3404-1334; e-mail omanemb@gol.com; Ambassador MOHAMMED ALI AL-KHUSAIBY.

Pakistan: 2-14-9, Moto Azabu, Minato-ku, Tokyo 106-0046; tel. (3) 3454-4861; fax (3) 3457-0341; e-mail pakemb@gol.com; Ambassador TOUQIR HUSSAIN.

Palau: Rm 201, 1-1, Katamachi, Shinjuku-ku, Tokyo 160-0001; tel. (3) 3354-5500; Ambassador SANTOS OLIKONG.

Panama: Kowa Bldg, No. 38, Room 902, 4-12-24, Nishi Azabu, Minato-ku, Tokyo 106-0031; tel. (3) 3499-3741; fax (3) 5485-3548; e-mail panaemb@gol.com; internet www.embassy-avenue.jp/panama/index-j.html; Ambassador JOSÉ A. SOSA.

Papua New Guinea: Mita Kokusai Bldg, Room 313, 3rd Floor, 1-4-28, Mita, Minato-ku, Tokyo 108; tel. (3) 3454-7801; fax (3) 3454-7275; Ambassador AIWA OLMI.

Paraguay: 3-12-9, Kami-Osaki, Shinagawa-ku, Tokyo 141-0021; tel. (3) 5485-3101; fax (3) 5485-3103; e-mail embapar@gol.com; internet www.embassy-avenue.jp/paraguay/index-j.htm; Ambassador ISAO TAOKA.

Peru: 4-4-27, Higashi, Shibuya-ku, Tokyo 150-0011; tel. (3) 3406-4243; fax (3) 3409-7589; e-mail 1-tokio@ma.kcom.ne.jp; Ambassador LUIS MACHIAVELLO.

Philippines: 5-15-5, Roppongi, Minato-ku, Tokyo 106-8537; tel. (3) 5562-1600; e-mail phpjp@gol.com; internet www.rptokyo.org; Ambassador ROMEO ABELARDO ARGUELLES.

Poland: 2-13-5, Mita, Meguro-ku, Tokyo 153-0062; internet www.poland.or.jp; tel. (3) 5794-7020; Ambassador MARCIN RYBICKI.

Portugal: Kamiura-Kojimachi Bldg, 5th Floor, 3-10-3, Kojimachi, Chiyoda-ku, Tokyo 102-0083; tel. (3) 5212-7322; fax (3) 5226-0616; e-mail tokyo.delegation@portugal.or.jp; internet www.portugal.or.jp; Ambassador MANUEL GERVÁSIO DE ALMEIDA LEITE.

Qatar: 2-3-28, Moto-Azabu, Minato-ku, Tokyo 106-0046; tel. (3) 5475-0611; Ambassador REYAD ALI AL-ANSARI.

Romania: 3-16-19, Nishi Azabu, Minato-ku, Tokyo 106-0031; tel. (3) 3479-0311; fax (3) 3479-0312; e-mail romembjp@gol.com; internet www2.gol.com/users/romembjp/; Ambassador ION PASCU.

Russia: 2-1-1, Azabu-dai, Minato-ku, Tokyo 106-0041; tel. (3) 3583-4224; fax (3) 3505-0593; internet www.embassy.jp/russia/index-j.html; e-mail rosconsl@ma.kcom.ne.jp; Ambassador ALEKSANDR LOSYUKOV.

Rwanda: Kowa Bldg, No. 38, 4-12-24, Nishi Azabu, Minato-ku, Tokyo 106; tel. (3) 3486-7801; fax (3) 3409-2334; Ambassador MATANGUHA ZEPHYR.

Saudi Arabia: 1-8-4, Roppongi, Minato-ku, Tokyo 106-0032; tel. (3) 3589-5241; fax (3) 3589-5200; Ambassador MOHAMED BASHIR KURDI.

Senegal: 1-3-4, Aobadai, Meguro-ku, Tokyo 153-0042; tel. (3) 3464-8451; fax (3) 3464-8452; e-mail senegal@senegal.jp; Ambassador GABRIEL ALEXANDRE SAR.

Serbia and Montenegro: 4-7-24, Kita-Shinagawa, Shinagawa-ku, Tokyo 140-0001; tel. (3) 3447-3571; fax (3) 3447-3573; e-mail embassy@embassy-serbia-montenegro.jp; internet www.embassy-serbia-montenegro.jp; Ambassador Dr PREDRAG FILIPOV.

Singapore: 5-12-3, Roppongi, Minato-ku, Tokyo 106-0032; tel. (3) 3586-9111; fax (3) 3582-1085; Ambassador LIM CHIN BENG.

Slovakia: POB 35, 2-16-14, Hiroo, Shibuya-ku, Tokyo 150-8691; tel. (3) 3400-8122; fax (3) 3406-6215; e-mail zutokio@twics.com; internet www.embassy-avenue.jp/slovakia/index-j.html; Ambassador JÚLIUS HAUSER.

Slovenia: 7-5-15, Akasaka, Minato-ku, Tokyo 107-0052; tel. (3) 5570-6275; fax (3) 5570-6075; e-mail vto@mzz-dkp.gov.si; Ambassador ROBERT BASEJ.

South Africa: 414 Zenkyoren Bldg, 4th Floor, 2-7-9, Hirakawa-cho, Chiyoda-ku, Tokyo 102-0093; tel. (3) 3265-3366; fax (3) 3265-1108; e-mail sajapan@rsatk.com; internet www.rsatk.com; Ambassador KARAMCHUND MACKERDHUJ.

Spain: 1-3-29, Roppongi, Minato-ku, Tokyo 106-0032; tel. (3) 3583-8531; fax (3) 3582-8627; e-mail embspjp@mail.mae.es; Ambassador FRANCISCO JAVIER CONDE DE SARO.

Sri Lanka: 2-1-54, Takanawa, Minato-ku, Tokyo 108-0074; tel. (3) 3440-6911; fax (3) 3440-6914; e-mail lankaemb@sphere.ne.jp; internet www.embassy-avenue.jp/srilanka/index.html; Ambassador KARUNATILAKA AMUNUGAMA.

Sudan: 2-7-11, Shirogane, Minato-ku, Tokyo 108-0072; tel. (3) 3280-3161; Ambassador Dr AWAD MURSI TAHA.

Sweden: 1-10-3-100, Roppongi, Minato-ku, Tokyo 106-0032; tel. (3) 5562-5050; fax (3) 5562-9095; e-mail ambassaden.tokyo@foreign.ministry.se; internet www.sweden.or.jp; Ambassador MIKAEL LINDSTROM.

Switzerland: 5-9-12, Minami Azabu, Minato-ku, Tokyo 106-8589; tel. (3) 3473-0121; fax (3) 3473-6090; e-mail vertretung@tok.rep.admin.ch; internet www.eda.admin.ch/Tokyo; Ambassador JACQUES REVERDIN.

Syria: Homat Jade, 6-19-45, Akasaka, Minato-ku, Tokyo 107-0052; tel. (3) 3586-8977; fax (3) 3586-8979; Chargé d'affaires a.i. HAMZAH HAMZAH.

Tanzania: 4-21-9, Kami Yoga, Setagaya-ku, Tokyo 158-0098; tel. (3) 3425-4531; fax (3) 3425-7844; e-mail tzrepjp@gol.com; Ambassador ELLY E. E. MTANGO.

Thailand: 3-14-6, Kami Osaki, Shinagawa-ku, Tokyo 141-0021; tel. (3) 3447-2247; fax (3) 3442-6750; e-mail thaitke@crisscross.com; Ambassador CHAWAT ARTHAYUKTI.

Tunisia: 3-6-6, Kudan-Minami, Chiyoda-ku, Tokyo 102-0074; tel. (3) 3511-6622; fax (3) 3511-6600; Ambassador SALAH HANNACHI.

Turkey: 2-33-6, Jingumae, Shibuya-ku, Tokyo 150-0001; tel. (3) 3470-5131; fax (3) 3470-5136; e-mail embassy@turkey.jp; internet www.turkey.jp; Ambassador YAMAN BAŞKUT.

Uganda: 4-15-3, Shimomeguro, Meguro-ku, Tokyo 153-0064; tel. (3) 5773-0481; fax (3) 5725-3720; e-mail ugabassy@hpo.net; internet www.ugandaembassy.jp; Ambassador JAMES B. BABA.

Ukraine: 3-15-6, Nishi Azabu, Minato-ku, Tokyo 106-0046; tel. (3) 5474-9770; fax (3) 5474-9772; e-mail ukremb@rose.ocn.ne.jp; internet ukremb-japan.gov.ua; Ambassador YURIY KOSTENKO.

United Arab Emirates: 9–10, Nanpeidai-cho, Shibuya-ku, Tokyo 150-0036; tel. (3) 5489-0804; fax (3) 5489-0813; e-mail info@uaeembassy.jp; internet www.uaeembassy.jp; Ambassador AHMED ALI HAMAD ALMUALLA.

United Kingdom: 1, Ichiban-cho, Chiyoda-ku, Tokyo 102-8381; tel. (3) 5211-1203; fax (3) 5211-1111; e-mail embassy.tokyo@fco.gov.uk; internet www.uknow.or.jp; Ambassador GRAHAM FRY.

USA: 1-10-5, Akasaka, Minato-ku, Tokyo 107-8420; tel. (3) 3224-5000; internet tokyo.usembassy.gov; Ambassador THOMAS SCHIEFFER.

Uruguay: Kowa Bldg, No. 38, Room 908, 4-12-24, Nishi Azabu, Minato-ku, Tokyo 106-0031; tel. (3) 3486-1888; fax (3) 3486-9872; e-mail urujap@luck.ocn.ne.jp; Ambassador CARLOS CLULOW.

Uzbekistan: 5-11-8, Shimo-Meguro, Meguro-ku, Tokyo 153-0064; tel. (3) 3760-5625.

Venezuela: Kowa Bldg, No. 38, Room 703, 4-12-24, Nishi Azabu, Minato-ku, Tokyo 106-0031; tel. (3) 3409-1501; fax (3) 3409-1505; e-mail embavene@interlink.or.jp; internet sunsite.sut.ac.jp/embassy/venemb/embvenez.html; Ambassador Dr CARLOS ENRIQUE NONES.

Viet Nam: 50-11, Moto Yoyogi-cho, Shibuya-ku, Tokyo 151-0062; tel. (3) 3466-3313; fax (3) 3466-3391; Ambassador NGUYEN TAM CHIEN.

Yemen: Kowa Bldg, No. 38, Room 807, 4-12-24, Nishi Azabu, Minato-ku, Tokyo 106-0031; tel. (3) 3499-7151; fax (3) 3499-4577; Chargé d'affaires a.i. ABDULRAHMAN M. AL-HOTHI.

Zambia: 1-10-2, Ebara, Shinagawa-ku, Tokyo 142-0063; tel. (3) 3491-0121; fax (3) 3491-0123; e-mail emb@zambia.or.jp; Ambassador GODFREY S. SIMASIKU.

Zimbabwe: 5-9-10, Shiroganedai, Minato-ku, Tokyo 108; tel. (3) 3280-0331; fax (3) 3280-0466; e-mail zimtokyo@chive.ocn.ne.jp; Ambassador STUART H. COMBERBACH.

Judicial System

The basic principles of the legal system are set forth in the Constitution, which lays down that judicial power is vested in the Supreme Court and in such inferior courts as are established by law, and enunciates the principle that no organ or agency of the Executive shall be given final judicial power. Judges are to be independent in the exercise of their conscience, and may not be removed except by public impeachment, unless judicially declared mentally or physically incompetent to perform official duties. The justices of the Supreme Court are appointed by the Cabinet, the sole exception being the Chief Justice, who is appointed by the Emperor after designation by the Cabinet.

The Court Organization Law, which came into force on 3 May 1947, decreed the constitution of the Supreme Court and the establishment of four types of lower court—High, District, Family (established 1 January 1949) and Summary Courts. The constitution and functions of the courts are as follows:

Supreme Court

4-2, Hayabusa-cho, Chiyoda-ku, Tokyo 102-8651; tel. (3) 3264-8111; fax (3) 3221-8975; internet www.courts.go.jp.

This court is the highest legal authority in the land, and consists of a Chief Justice and 14 associate justices. It has jurisdiction over Jokoku (Jokoku appeals) and Kokoku (Kokoku appeals), prescribed in codes of procedure. It conducts its hearings and renders decisions through a Grand Bench or three Petty Benches. Both are collegiate bodies, the former consisting of all justices of the Court, and the latter of five justices. A Supreme Court Rule prescribes which cases are to be handled by the respective Benches. It is, however, laid down by law that the Petty Bench cannot make decisions as to the constitutionality of a statute, ordinance, regulation, or disposition, or as to cases in which an opinion concerning the interpretation and application of the Constitution, or of any laws or ordinances, is at variance with a previous decision of the Supreme Court.

Chief Justice: AKIRA MACHIDA.

Secretary-General: HIRONOBU TAKESAKI.

LOWER COURTS

High Court

A High Court conducts its hearings and renders decisions through a collegiate body, consisting of three judges, though for cases of insurrection the number of judges must be five. The Court has jurisdiction over the following matters:

Koso appeals from judgments in the first instance rendered by District Courts, from judgments rendered by Family Courts, and from judgments concerning criminal cases rendered by Summary Courts.

Kokoku appeals against rulings and orders rendered by District Courts and Family Courts, and against rulings and orders concerning criminal cases rendered by Summary Courts, except those coming within the jurisdiction of the Supreme Court.

Jokoku appeals from judgments in the second instance rendered by District Courts and from judgments rendered by Summary Courts, except those concerning criminal cases.

Actions in the first instance relating to cases of insurrection.

Presidents: TOKUJI IZUMI (Tokyo), YOSHIO OKADA (Osaka), REISUKE SHIMADA (Nagoya), TOYOZO UEDA (Hiroshima), TOSHIMARO KOJO (Fukuoka), FUMIYA SATO (Sendai), KAZUO KATO (Sapporo), FUMIO ARAI (Takamatsu).

District Court

A District Court conducts hearings and renders decisions through a single judge or, for certain types of cases, through a collegiate body of three judges. It has jurisdiction over the following matters:

Actions in the first instance, except offences relating to insurrection, claims where the subject matter of the action does not exceed 900,000 yen, and offences liable to a fine or lesser penalty.

Koso appeals from judgments rendered by Summary Courts, except those concerning criminal cases.

Kokoku appeals against rulings and orders rendered by Summary Courts, except those coming within the jurisdiction of the Supreme Court and High Courts.

Family Court

A Family Court handles cases through a single judge in case of rendering judgments or decisions. However, in accordance with the provisions of other statutes, it conducts its hearings and renders decisions through a collegiate body of three judges. A conciliation is effected through a collegiate body consisting of a judge and two or more members of the conciliation committee selected from among citizens.

It has jurisdiction over the following matters:

Judgment and conciliation with regard to cases relating to family as provided for by the Law for Adjudgment of Domestic Relations.

Judgment with regard to the matters of protection of juveniles as provided for by the Juvenile Law.

Actions in the first instance relating to adult criminal cases of violation of the Labour Standard Law, the Law for Prohibiting Liquors to Minors, or other laws especially enacted for protection of juveniles.

Summary Court

A Summary Court handles cases through a single judge, and has jurisdiction in the first instance over the following matters:

Claims where the value of the subject matter does not exceed 900,000 yen (excluding claims for cancellation or change of administrative dispositions).

Actions which relate to offences liable to a fine or lesser penalty, offences liable to a fine as an optional penalty, and certain specified offences such as habitual gambling and larceny.

A Summary Court cannot impose imprisonment or a graver penalty. When it deems proper the imposition of a sentence of imprisonment or a graver penalty, it must transfer such cases to a District Court, but it can impose imprisonment with labour not exceeding three years for certain specified offences.

Religion

The traditional religions of Japan are Shintoism and Buddhism. Neither is exclusive, and many Japanese subscribe at least nominally to both. Since 1945 a number of new religions (Shinko Shukyo) have evolved, based on a fusion of Shinto, Buddhist, Daoist, Confucian and Christian beliefs. In 1995 there were some 184,000 religious organizations registered in Japan, according to the Ministry of Education.

SHINTOISM

Shintoism is an indigenous religious system embracing the worship of ancestors and of nature. It is divided into two cults: national Shintoism, which is represented by the shrines; and sectarian Shintoism, which developed during the second half of the 19th century. In 1868 Shinto was designated a national religion and all Shinto shrines acquired the privileged status of a national institution. Complete freedom of religion was introduced in 1947, and state support of Shinto was prohibited. In the mid-1990s there were 81,307 shrines, 90,309 priests and 106.6m. adherents.

BUDDHISM

World Buddhist Fellowship: Hozenji Buddhist Temple, 3-24-2, Akabane-dai, Kita-ku, Tokyo; Rev. FUJI NAKAYAMA.

CHRISTIANITY

In 1993 the Christian population was estimated at 1,050,938.

National Christian Council in Japan: Japan Christian Centre, 2-3-18-24, Nishi Waseda, Shinjuku-ku, Tokyo 169-0051; tel. (3) 3203-0372; fax (3) 3204-9495; e-mail ncc-j@jca.apc.org; internet www.jca.apc.org/ncc-j; f. 1923; 14 mems (churches and other bodies), 18 assoc. mems; Chair. REIKO SUZUKI; Gen. Sec. Rev. TOSHIMASA YAMAMOTO.

The Anglican Communion

Anglican Church in Japan (Nippon Sei Ko Kai): 65, Yarai-cho, Shinjuku-ku, Tokyo 162-0805; tel. (3) 5228-3171; fax (3) 5228-3175; e-mail general-sec.po@nskk.org; internet www.nskk.org; f. 1887; 11 dioceses; Primate of Japan Rt Rev. JAMES TORU UNO (Bishop of Osaka); Gen. Sec. LAURENCE Y. MINABE; 57,003 mems (2004).

The Orthodox Church

Japanese Orthodox Church (Nippon Haristosu Seikyoukai): Holy Resurrection Cathedral (Nicolai-Do), 4-1-3, Kanda Surugadai, Chiyoda-ku, Tokyo 101; tel. (3) 3291-1885; fax (3) 3291-1886; e-mail ocj@gol.com; three dioceses; Archbishop of Tokyo, Primate and Metropolitan of All Japan Most Rev. DANIEL; 24,821 mems.

Protestant Church

United Church of Christ in Japan (Nihon Kirisuto Kyodan): Japan Christian Center, Room 31, 2-3-18, Nishi Waseda, Shinjuku-ku, Tokyo 169-0051; tel. (3) 3202-0541; fax (3) 3207-3918; e-mail ecumeni-c@uccj.org; f. 1941; union of 34 Congregational, Methodist, Presbyterian, Reformed and other Protestant denominations; Moderator Rev. NOBUHISHA YAMAKITA; Gen. Sec. Rev. NOBORU TAKEMAE; 196,044 mems (2002).

The Roman Catholic Church

Japan comprises three archdioceses and 13 dioceses, and the Apostolic Prefecture of Karafuto. There were an estimated 516,176 adherents at 31 December 2002.

Catholic Bishops' Conference of Japan (Chuo Kyogikai)

2-10-10, Shiomi, Koto-ku, Tokyo 135-8585; tel. (3) 5632-4411; fax (3) 5632-4457; e-mail info@cbcj.catholic.jp; internet www.cbcj.catholic.jp.

Pres. Most Rev. AUGUSTINE JUN-ICHI NOMURA (Bishop of Nagoya).

Archbishop of Nagasaki: JOSEPH MITSUAKI TAKAMI, Catholic Center, 10–34 Uenomachi, Nagasaki-shi 852-8113; tel. (95) 846-4246; fax (95) 848-8310.

Archbishop of Osaka: Most Rev. LEO JUN IKENAGA, Archbishop's House, 2-24-22, Tamatsukuri, Chuo-ku, Osaka 540-0004; tel. (6) 6941-9700; fax (6) 6946-1345.

Archbishop of Tokyo: Most Rev. PETER TAKEO OKADA, Archbishop's House, 3-16-15, Sekiguchi, Bunkyo-ku, Tokyo 112-0014; tel. (3) 3943-2301; fax (3) 3944-8511; e-mail peter2000@nifty.com.

Other Christian Churches

Japan Baptist Convention: 1-2-4, Minami Urawa, Minami-ku-Saitama-shi, Saitama 336-0017; tel. (48) 883-1091; fax (48) 883-1092; f. 1947; Gen. Sec. Rev. MAKOTO KATO; 33,734 mems (March 2003).

Japan Baptist Union: 2-3-18, Nishi Waseda, Shinjuku-ku, Tokyo 169-0051; tel. (3) 3202-0053; fax (3) 3202-0054; e-mail gs@jbu.or.jp; f. 1958; Moderator YOSHIHISA SAWANO; Gen. Sec. KAZUO OYA; 4,600 mems.

Japan Evangelical Lutheran Church: 1-1, Sadohara-cho, Ichigaya-shi, Shinjuku-ku, Tokyo 162-0842; tel. (3) 3260-8631; fax (3) 3268-3589; e-mail s-matsuoka@jelc.or.jp; internet www.jelc.or.jp; f. 1893; Moderator Rev. MASATOSHI YAMANOUCHI; Gen. Sec. Rev. SHU-NICHIRO MATSUOKA; 21,967 mems (2000).

Korean Christian Church in Japan: Room 52, Japan Christian Center, 2-3-18, Nishi Waseda, Shinjuku-ku, Tokyo 169-0051; tel. (3) 3202-5398; fax (3) 3202-4977; e-mail kccj@kb3.so-net.ne.jp; f. 1909;

Moderator CHOI JUNG-KANG; Gen. Sec. PARK SOO-KIL; 7,119 mems (2002).

Among other denominations active in Japan are the Christian Catholic Church, the German Evangelical Church and the Tokyo Union Church.

OTHER COMMUNITIES

Bahá'í Faith

The National Spiritual Assembly of the Bahá'ís of Japan: 7-2-13, Shinjuku, Shinjuku-ku, Tokyo 160-0022; tel. (3) 3209-7521; fax (3) 3204-0773; e-mail nsajp@bahaijp.org; internet www.bahaijp.org.

Judaism

Jewish Community of Japan: 3-8-8 Hiro-o, Shibuya-ku, Tokyo 150-0012; tel. (3) 3400-2559; fax (3) 3400-1827; e-mail office@jccjapan.or.jp; internet www.jccjapan.or.jp; Man. LIOR JACOBI; Leader Rabbi HENRI NOACH.

Islam

Islam has been active in Japan since the late 19th century. There is a small Muslim community, maintaining several mosques, including those at Kobe, Nagoya, Chiba and Isesaki, the Arabic Islamic Institute and the Islamic Center in Tokyo. The construction of Tokyo Central mosque was completed in 2000.

Islamic Center, Japan: 1-16-11, Ohara, Setagaya-ku, Tokyo 156-0041; tel. (3) 3460-6169; fax (3) 3460-6105; e-mail islamcpj@islamcenter.or.jp; internet www.islamcenter.or.jp; f. 1965; Chair. Dr SALIH M. SAMARRAI.

The New Religions

Many new cults have emerged in Japan since the end of the Second World War. Collectively these are known as the New Religions (Shinko Shukyo), among the most important of which are Tenrikyo, Omotokyo, Soka Gakkai, Rissho Kosei-kai, Kofuku-no-Kagaku, Agonshu and Aum Shinrikyo. (Following the indictment on charges of murder of several members of Aum Shinrikyo, including its leader, Shoko Asahara, the cult lost its legal status as a religious organization in 1996. In January 2000 the cult announced its intention to change its name to Aleph. At that time it named a new leader, TATSUKO MURAOKA.)

Kofuku-no-Kagaku (Institute for Research in Human Happiness): Tokyo; tel. (3) 5750-0771; fax (3) 5750-0782; internet www.irhpress.co.jp; e-mail web-office@irhpress.co.jp; f. 1986; believes its founder to be reincarnation of Buddha; 8.25m. mems; Leader RYUHO OKAWA.

Rissho Kosei-kai: 2-11-1 Wada, Suginami-ku, Tokyo 166-8537; tel. (3) 3383-1111; fax (3) 3381-9792; e-mail info@rk-world.org; internet www.kosei-kai.or.jp; internet www.rk-world.org; f. 1938; Buddhist lay organization based on the teaching of the Lotus Sutra, active inter-faith co-operation towards peace; Pres. Rev. Dr NICHIKO NIWANO; 6.3m. mems with 245 brs world-wide (2000).

Soka Gakkai: 32, Shinano-machi, Shinjuku-ku, Tokyo 160-8583; tel. (3) 5360-9830; fax (3) 5360-9885; e-mail webmaster@sokagakkai.info; internet sokagakkai.info; f. 1930; society of lay practitioners of the Buddhism of Nichiren; membership of 8.21m. households (2000); group promotes activities in education, international cultural exchange and consensus-building towards peace, based on the humanist world view of Buddhism; Hon. Pres. DAISAKU IKEDA; Pres. EINOSUKE AKIYA.

The Press

In December 2000 there were 122 daily newspapers in Japan. Their average circulation was the highest in the world, and the circulation per head of population was also among the highest, at 573 copies per 1,000 inhabitants in 1999. The large number of weekly news journals is a notable feature of the Japanese press. At December 1998 a total of 2,763 periodicals were produced, 85 of which were weekly publications. Technically the Japanese press is highly advanced, and the major newspapers are issued in simultaneous editions in the main centres.

The two newspapers with the largest circulations are the *Yomiuri Shimbun* and *Asahi Shimbun*. Other influential papers include *Mainichi Shimbun, Nihon Keizai Shimbun, Chunichi Shimbun* and *Sankei Shimbun*.

NATIONAL DAILIES

Asahi Shimbun: 5-3-2, Tsukiji, Chuo-ku, Tokyo 104-8011; tel. (3) 3545-0131; fax (3) 3545-0358; internet www.asahi.com; f. 1879; also published by Osaka, Seibu and Nagoya head offices and Hokkaido branch office; Pres. SHINICHI HAKOSHIMA; Dir and Exec. Editor MASAO KIMIWADA; circ. morning 8.3m., evening 4.1m.

Mainichi Shimbun: 1-1-1, Hitotsubashi, Chiyoda-ku, Tokyo 100-8051; tel. (3) 3212-0321; fax (3) 3211-3598; internet www.mainichi .co.jp; f. 1882; also published by Osaka, Seibu and Chubu head offices, and Hokkaido branch office; Pres. MASATOU KITAMURA; Man. Dir and Editor-in-Chief TATSUAKI HASHIMOTO; circ. morning 4.0m., evening 1.7m.

Nihon Keizai Shimbun: 1-9-5, Otemachi, Chiyoda-ku, Tokyo 100-8066; tel. (3) 3270-0251; fax (3) 5255-2661; internet www.nikkei.co .jp; f. 1876; also published by Osaka head office and Sapporo, Nagoya and Seibu branch offices; Pres. TAKUHIKO TSURUTA; Dir and Man. Editor YASUO HIRATA; circ. morning 3.0m., evening 1.7m.

Sankei Shimbun: 1-7-2, Otemachi, Chiyoda-ku, Tokyo 100-8077; tel. (3) 3231-7111; internet www.sankei.co.jp; f. 1933; also published by Osaka head office; Man. Dir and Editor NAGAYOSHI SUMIDA; circ. morning 2.0m., evening 905,771.

Yomiuri Shimbun: 1-7-1, Otemachi, Chiyoda-ku, Tokyo 100-8055; tel. (3) 3242-1111; e-mail webmaster@yomiuri.co.jp; internet www .yomiuri.co.jp; f. 1874; also published by Osaka, Seibu and Chubu head offices, and Hokkaido and Hokuriku branch offices; Pres. and Editor-in-Chief TSUNEO WATANABE; circ. morning 10.2m., evening 4.3m.

PRINCIPAL LOCAL DAILIES

Tokyo

Daily Sports: 1-20-3, Osaki, Shinagawa-ku, Tokyo 141-8585; tel. (3) 5434-1752; f. 1948; morning; Man. Dir HIROHISA KARUO; circ. 400,254.

The Daily Yomiuri: 1-7-1, Otemachi, Chiyoda-ku, Tokyo 100-8055; tel. (3) 3242-1111; f. 1955; morning; Man. Editor TSUTOMU YAMAGUCHI; circ. 51,421.

Dempa Shimbun: 1-11-15, Higashi Gotanda, Shinagawa-ku, Tokyo 141-8790; tel. (3) 3445-6111; fax (3) 3444-7515; f. 1950; morning; Pres. TETSUO HIRAYAMA; Man. Editor TOSHIO KASUYA; circ. 298,000.

Hochi Shimbun: 4-6-49, Kohnan, Minato-ku, Tokyo 108-8485; tel. (3) 5479-1111; internet www.yomiuri.co.jp/hochi/home.htm; f. 1872; morning; Pres. MASARU FUSHIMI; Man. Editor TATSUE AOKI; circ. 755,670.

The Japan Times: 4-5-4, Shibaura, Minato-ku, Tokyo 108-8071; tel. (3) 3453-5312; internet www.japantimes.co.jp; f. 1897; morning; English; Chair. and Pres. TOSHIAKI OGASAWARA; Dir and Editor-in-Chief YUTAKA MATAEBARA; circ. 61,929.

The Mainichi Daily News: 1-1-1, Hitotsubashi, Chiyoda-ku, Tokyo 100-8051; tel. (3) 3212-0321; f. 1922; morning; English; also publ. from Osaka; Man. Editor TETSUO TOKIZAWA; combined circ. 49,200.

Naigai Times: 1-1-15, Ariake, Koto-ku, Tokyo 135-0063; tel. (3) 5564-7021; fax (3) 5564-1022; e-mail info@naigai-times.co.jp; f. 1949; evening; Pres. MITSUGU ONDA; Vice-Pres. and Editor-in-Chief KENICHIRO KURIHARA; circ. 410,000.

Nihon Kaiji Shimbun (Japan Maritime Daily): 5-19-2, Shimbashi, Minato-ku, Tokyo 105-0004; tel. (3) 3436-3221; internet www.jmd.co .jp; f. 1942; morning; Man. Editor OSAMI ENDO; circ. 55,000.

Nihon Kogyo Shimbun: 1-7-2, Otemachi, Chiyoda-ku, Tokyo 100-8125; tel. (3) 3231-7111; internet www.jij.co.jp; f. 1933; morning; industrial, business and financial; Man. Editor YOSHIMI KURA; circ. 408,444.

Nihon Nogyo Shimbun (Agriculture): 2–3, Akihabara, Taito-ku, Tokyo 110-8722; tel. (3) 5295-7411; fax (3) 3253-0980; f. 1928; morning; Man. Editor YASUNORI INOUE; circ. 423,840.

Nihon Sen-i Shimbun (Textile and Fashion): 13-10, Nihombashi-kobunacho, Chuo-ku, Tokyo 103-0024; tel. (3) 5649-8711; f. 1943; morning; Man. Editor KIYOSHIGE SEIRYU; circ. 116,000.

Nikkan Kogyo Shimbun (Industrial Daily News): 1-8-10, Kudan-kita, Chiyoda-ku, Tokyo 102-8181; tel. (3) 3222-7111; fax (3) 3262-6031; internet www.nikkan.co.jp; f. 1915; morning; Man. Editor HIDEO WATANABE; circ. 533,145.

Nikkan Sports News: 3-5-10, Tsukiji, Chuo-ku, Tokyo 104-8055; tel. (3) 5550-8888; fax (3) 5550-8901; internet www.nikkansports .com; f. 1946; morning; Man. Editor YUKIHIRO MORI; circ. 993,240.

Sankei Sports: 1-7-2, Otemachi, Chiyoda-ku, Tokyo 100-8077; tel. (3) 3231-7111; internet www.xusxus.com; f. 1963; morning; Man. Editor YUKIO INADA; circ. 809,245.

Shipping and Trade News: Tokyo News Service Ltd, Tsukiji Hamarikyu Bldg, 5-3-3, Tsukiji, Chuo-ku, Tokyo 104-8004; tel. (3) 3542-6511; fax (3) 3542-5086; internet www.tvguide.or.jp; f. 1949; English; Man. Editor TAKASHI INOUE; circ. 15,000.

Sports Nippon: 2-1-30, Etchujima, Koto-ku, Tokyo 135-8735; tel. (3) 3820-0700; internet www.mainichi.co.jp/suponichi; f. 1949; morning; Man. Editor SUSUMU KOMURO; circ. 929,421.

Suisan Keizai Shimbun (Fisheries): 6-8-19, Roppongi, Minato-ku, Tokyo 106-0032; tel. (3) 3404-6531; fax (3) 3404-0863; f. 1948; morning; Man. Editor KOSHI TORINOUMI; circ. 61,000.

Tokyo Chunichi Sports: 2-3-13, Kohnan, Minato-ku, Tokyo 108-8010; tel. (3) 3471-2211; f. 1956; evening; Head Officer TETSUO TANAKA; circ. 330,431.

Tokyo Shimbun: 2-3-13, Kohnan, Minato-ku, Tokyo 108-8010; tel. (3) 3471-2211; fax (3) 3471-1851; internet www.tokyo-np.co.jp; f. 1942; Man. Editor KATSUHIKO SAKAI; circ. morning 655,970, evening 354,191.

Tokyo Sports: 2-1-30, Etchujima, Koto-ku, Tokyo 135-8721; tel. (3) 3820-0801; f. 1959; evening; Man. Editor YASUO SAKURAI; circ. 1,321,250.

Yukan Fuji: 1-7-2, Otemachi, Chiyoda-ku, Tokyo 100-8077; tel. (3) 3231-7111; fax (3) 3246-0377; internet www.zakzak.co.jp; f. 1969; evening; Man. Editor MASAMI KATO; circ. 268,984.

Osaka District

Daily Sports: 1-18-11, Edobori, Nishi-ku, Osaka 550-0002; tel. (6) 6443-0421; f. 1948; morning; Man. Editor TOSHIAKI MITANI; circ. 562,715.

The Mainichi Daily News: 3-4-5, Umeda, Kita-ku, Osaka 530-8251; tel. (6) 6345-1551; f. 1922; morning; English; Man. Editor KATSUYA FUKUNAGA.

Nikkan Sports: 5-92-1, Hattori-kotobuki-cho, Toyonaka 561-8585; tel. (6) 6867-2811; internet www.nikkansports.com/osaka; f. 1950; morning; Man. Editor KATSUO FURUKAWA; circ. 513,498.

Osaka Shimbun: 2-4-9, Umeda, Kita-ku, Osaka 530-8279; tel. (6) 6343-1221; internet www.osakanews.com; f. 1922; evening; Man. Editor KAORU YURA; circ. 88,887.

Osaka Sports: Osaka Ekimae Daiichi Bldg, 4th Floor, 1-3-1-400, Umeda, Kita-ku, Osaka 530-0001; tel. (6) 6345-7657; f. 1968; evening; Head Officer KAZUOMI TANAKA; circ. 470,660.

Sankei Sports: 2-4-9, Umeda, Kita-ku, Osaka 530-8277; tel. (6) 6343-1221; f. 1955; morning; Man. Editor MASAKI YOSHIDA; circ. 552,519.

Sports Nippon: 3-4-5, Umeda, Kita-ku, Osaka 530-8278; tel. (6) 6346-8500; f. 1949; morning; Man. Editor HIDETOSHI ISHIHARA; circ. 477,300.

Kanto District

Chiba Nippo (Chiba Daily News): 4-14-10, Chuo, Chuo-ku, Chiba 260-0013; tel. (43) 222-9211; internet www.chibanippo.co.jp; f. 1957; morning; Man. Editor NOBORU HAYASHI; circ. 190,187.

Ibaraki Shimbun: 2-15, Kitami-cho, Mito 310-8686; tel. (292) 21-3121; internet www.ibaraki-np.co.jp; f. 1891; morning; Pres. and Editor-in-Chief TADANORI TOMOSUE; circ. 117,240.

Jomo Shimbun: 1-50-21, Furuichi-machi, Maebashi 371-8666; tel. (272) 54-9911; internet www.jomo-news.co.jp; f. 1887; morning; Man. Editor MUTSUO ODAGIRI; circ. 296,111.

Joyo Shimbun: 2-7-6, Manabe, Tsuchiura 300-0051; tel. (298) 21-1780; internet www.tsukuba.com; f. 1948; morning; Pres. MINEO IWANAMI; Man. Editor AKIRA SAITO; circ. 88,700.

Kanagawa Shimbun: 6-145, Hanasaki-cho, Nishi-ku, Yokohama 220-8588; tel. (45) 411-2222; internet www.kanagawa-np.co.jp; f. 1890; morning; Man. Editor NOBUYUKI CHIBA; circ. 238,203.

Saitama Shimbun: 6-12-11, Kishi-cho, Urawa 336-8686; tel. (48) 862-3371; internet www.saitama-np.co.jp; f. 1944; morning; Man. Editor YOTARO NUMATA; circ. 162,071.

Shimotsuke Shimbun: 1-8-11, Showa, Utsunomiya 320-8686; tel. (286) 25-1111; internet www.shimotsuke.co.jp; f. 1884; morning; Man. Dir and Editor-in-Chief EISUKE TODA; circ. 306,072.

Tohoku District
(North-east Honshu)

Akita Sakigake Shimpo: 1-1, San-no-rinkai-machi, Akita 010-8601; tel. (18) 888-1800; fax (188) 23-1780; internet www.sakigake .co.jp; f. 1874; Man. Editor SHIGEAKI MAEKAWA; circ. 263,246.

Daily Tohoku: 1-3-12, Shiroshita, Hachinohe 031-8601; tel. (178) 44-5111; f. 1945; morning; Man. Editor TOKOJU YOSHIDA; circ. 104,935.

Fukushima Mimpo: 13-17, Ota-machi, Fukushima 960-8602; tel. (245) 31-4111; internet www.fukushima-minpo.co.jp; f. 1892; Pres. and Editor-in-Chief TSUTOMU HANADA; circ. morning 308,353, evening 9,489.

Fukushima Minyu: 4-29, Yanagi-machi, Fukushima 960-8648; tel. (245) 23-1191; internet www.minyu-net.com; f. 1895; Man. Editor KENJI KANNO; circ. morning 201,414, evening 6,066.

Hokuu Shimpo: 3-2, Nishi-dori-machi, Noshiro 016-0891. (185) 54-3150; f. 1895; morning; Chair. KOICHI YAMAKI; circ. 31,490.

Ishinomaki Shimbun: 2-1-28, Sumiyoshi-machi, Ishinomaki 986; tel. (225) 22-3201; f. 1946; evening; Man. Editor MASATOSHI SATO; circ. 13,050.

Iwate Nichi-nichi Shimbun: 60, Minamishin-machi, Ichinoseki 021-8686; tel. (191) 26-5114; internet www.isop.ne.jp/iwanichi; f. 1923; morning; Pres. TAKESHI YAMAGISHI; Man. Editor SEIICHI WATANABE; circ. 59,850.

Iwate Nippo: 3-7, Uchimaru, Morioka 020-8622; tel. (196) 53-4111; internet www.iwate-np.co.jp; f. 1876; Man. Editor TOKUO MIYAZAWA; circ. morning 230,073, evening 229,815.

Kahoku Shimpo: 1-2-28, Itsutsubashi, Aoba-ku, Sendai 980-8660; tel. (22) 211-1111; fax (22) 224-7947; internet www.kahoku.co.jp; f. 1897; Exec. Dir and Man. Editor MASAHIKO ICHIRIKI; circ. morning 503,318, evening 133,855.

Mutsu Shimpo: 2-1, Shimo-shirogane-cho, Hirosaki 036-8356; tel. (172) 34-3111; f. 1946; morning; Man. Editor YUJI SATO; circ. 53,500.

Shonai Nippo: 8-29, Baba-cho, Tsuruoka 997-8691; tel. (235) 22-1480; f. 1946; morning; Pres. TAKAO SATO; Man. Editor MASAYUKI HASHIMOTO; circ. 19,100.

To-o Nippo: 78, Kanbayashi, Yatsuyaku, Aomori 030-0180; tel. (177) 39-1111; internet www.toonippo.co.jp; f. 1888; Exec. Dir YOSHIO WAJIMA; Man. Editor TAKAO SHIOKOSHI; circ. morning 262,532, evening 258,590.

Yamagata Shimbun: 2-5-12, Hatagomachi, Yamagata 990-8550; tel. (236) 22-5271; internet www.yamagata-np.co.jp; f. 1876; Man. Editor TOSHINOBU SHIONO; circ. morning 213,057, evening 213,008.

Yonezawa Shimbun: 3-3-7, Monto-cho, Yonezawa 992-0039; tel. (238) 22-4411; f. 1879; morning; Man. Dir and Editor-in-Chief MAKOTO SATO; circ. 13,750.

Chubu District
(Central Honshu)

Chubu Keizai Shimbun: 4-4-12, Meieki, Nakamura-ku, Nagoya 450-8561; tel. (52) 561-5215; f. 1946; morning; Man. Editor NORIMITSU INAGAKI; circ. 97,000.

Chukyo Sports: Chunichi Kosoku Offset Insatsu Bldg, 4-3-9, Kinjo, Naka-ku, Nagoya 460-0847; tel. (52) 982-1911; f. 1968; evening; circ. 289,430; Head Officer OSAMU SUETSUGU.

Chunichi Shimbun: 1-6-1, San-no-maru, Naka-ku, Nagoya 460-8511; tel. (52) 201-8811; internet www.chunichi.ne.jp; f. 1942; Man. Editor NOBUAKI KOIDE; circ. morning 2.7m., evening 748,635.

Chunichi Sports: 1-6-1, San-no-maru, Naka-ku, Nagoya 460-8511; tel. (52) 201-8811; f. 1954; evening; Head Officer YASUHIKO AIBA; circ. 631,429.

Gifu Shimbun: 10, Imakomachi, Gifu 500-8577; tel. (582) 64-1151; internet www.jic-gifu.or.jp/np; f. 1881; Exec. Dir and Man. Editor TADASHI TANAKA; circ. morning 170,176, evening 31,775.

Higashi-Aichi Shimbun: 62, Torinawate, Shinsakae-machi, Toyohashi 441-8666; tel. (532) 32-3111; f. 1957; morning; Man. Editor YOSHIYUKI SUZUKI; circ. 52,300.

Nagano Nippo: 3-1323-1, Takashima, Suwa 392-8611; tel. (266) 52-2000; f. 1901; morning; Man. Editor ETSUO KOIZUMI; circ. 73,000.

Nagoya Times: 1-3-10, Marunouchi, Naka-ku, Nagoya 460-8530; tel. (52) 231-1331; f. 1946; evening; Man. Editor NAOKI KITO; circ. 146,137.

Shinano Mainichi Shimbun: 657, Minamiagata-machi, Nagano 380-8546; tel. (26) 236-3000; fax (26) 236-3197; internet www.shinmai.co.jp; f. 1873; Man. Editor SEIICHI INOMATA; circ. morning 469,801, evening 55,625.

Shizuoka Shimbun: 3-1-1, Toro, Shizuoka 422-8033; tel. (54) 284-8900; internet www.sbs-np.co.jp; f. 1941; Man. Editor HISAO ISHIHARA; circ. morning 730,746, evening 730,782.

Yamanashi Nichi-Nichi Shimbun: 2-6-10, Kitaguchi, Kofu 400-8515; tel. (552) 31-3000; internet www.sannichi.co.jp; f. 1872; morning; Man. Editor KATSUHITO NISHIKAWA; circ. 205,758.

Hokuriku District
(North Coastal Honshu)

Fukui Shimbun: 1-1-14, Haruyama, Fukui 910-8552; tel. (776) 23-5111; internet www.fukuishimbun.co.jp; f. 1899; morning; Man. Editor KAZUO UCHIDA; circ. 202,280.

Hokkoku Shimbun: 2-5-1, Korinbo, Kanazawa 920-8588; tel. (762) 63-2111; internet www.hokkoku.co.jp; f. 1893; Man. Editor WATARU INAGAKI; circ. morning 328,532, evening 97,051.

Hokuriku Chunichi Shimbun: 2-7-15, Korinbo, Kanazawa 920-8573; tel. (762) 61-3111; internet www.hokuriku.chunichi.co.jp; f. 1960; Man. Editor KANJI KOMIYA; circ. morning 116,719, evening 12,820.

Kitanippon Shimbun: 2-14, Azumi-cho, Toyama 930-8680; tel. (764) 45-3300; internet www.kitanippon.co.jp; f. 1884; Dir and Man. Editor MINORU KAWATA; circ. morning 223,033, evening 29,959.

Niigata Nippo: 772-2, Zenku, Niigata 950-1189; tel. (25) 378-9111; internet www.niigata-nippo.co.jp; f. 1942; Dir and Man. Editor MICHIEI TAKAHASHI; circ. morning 496,567, evening 66,836.

Toyama Shimbun: 5-1, Ote-machi, Toyama 930-8520; tel. (764) 91-8111; internet www.toyama.hokkoku.co.jp; f. 1923; morning; Man. Editor SACHIO MIYAMOTO; circ. 42,988.

Kinki District
(West Central Honshu)

Daily Sports: 1-5-7, Higashikawasaki-cho, Chuo-ku, Kobe 650-0044; tel. (78) 362-7100; morning; Man. Editor TAKASHI HIRAI.

Ise Shimbun: 34-6, Honmachi, Tsu 514-0831; tel. (592) 24-0003; internet www.isenp.co.jp; f. 1878; morning; Man. Editor FUJIO YAMAMOTO; circ. 100,550.

Kii Minpo: 100, Akizucho, Tanabe 646-8660; tel. (739) 22-7171; internet www.agara.co.jp; f. 1911; evening; Man. Editor KAZUSADA TANIGAMI; circ. 38,165.

Kobe Shimbun: 1-5-7, Higashikawasaki-cho, Chuo-ku, Kobe 650-8571; tel. (78) 362-7100; internet www.kobe-np.co.jp; f. 1898; Man. Editor MASAO MAEKAWA; circ. morning 545,854, evening 268,787.

Kyoto Shimbun: 239, Shoshoi-machi, Ebisugawa-agaru, Karasuma-dori, Nakagyo-ku, Kyoto 604-8577; tel. (75) 241-5430; internet www.kyoto-np.co.jp; f. 1879; Man. Editor OSAMU SAITO; circ. morning 505,723, evening 319,313.

Nara Shimbun: 606, Sanjo-machi, Nara 630-8686; tel. (742) 26-1331; internet www.nara-shimbun.com; f. 1946; morning; Dir and Man. Editor HISAMI SAKAMOTO; circ. 118,064.

Chugoku District
(Western Honshu)

Chugoku Shimbun: 7-1, Dobashi-cho, Naka-ku, Hiroshima 730-8677; tel. (82) 236-2111; fax (82) 236-2321; e-mail denshi@hiroshima-cdas.or.jp; internet www.chugoku-np.co.jp; f. 1892; Man. Editor NOBUYUKI AOKI; circ. morning 734,589, evening 85,089.

Nihonkai Shimbun: 2-137, Tomiyasu, Tottori 680-8678; tel. (857) 21-2888; internet www.nnn.co.jp; f. 1976; morning; Man. Editor KOTARO TAMURA; circ. 101,768.

Okayama Nichi-Nichi Shimbun: 6-30, Hon-cho, Okayama 700-8678; tel. (86) 231-4211; f. 1946; evening; Man. Dir and Man. Editor TAKASHI ANDO; circ. 45,000.

San-In Chuo Shimpo: 383, Tono-machi, Matsue 690-8668; tel. (852) 32-3440; f. 1882; morning; Man. Editor MASAMI MOCHIDA; circ. 172,605.

Sanyo Shimbun: 2-1-23, Yanagi-machi, Okayama 700-8634; tel. (86) 231-2210; internet www.sanyo.oni.co.jp; f. 1879; Man. Dir and Man. Editor TAKAMASA KOSHIMUNE; circ. morning 454,263, evening 71,200.

Ube Jiho: 3-6-1, Kotobuki-cho, Ube 755-8557; tel. (836) 31-1511; f. 1912; evening; Exec. Dir and Man. Editor KAZUYA WAKI; circ. 42,550.

Yamaguchi Shimbun: 1-1-7, Higashi-Yamato-cho, Shimonoseki 750-8506; tel. (832) 66-3211; internet www.minato-yamaguchi.co.jp; f. 1946; morning; Man. Editor SHOICHI SASAKI; circ. 84,000.

Shikoku Island

Ehime Shimbun: 1-12-1, Otemachi, Matsuyama 790-8511; tel. (899) 35-2111; internet www.ehime-np.co.jp; f. 1876; morning; Man. Editor RYOJI YANO; circ. 319,522.

Kochi Shimbun: 3-2-15, Honmachi, Kochi 780-8572; tel. (888) 22-2111; internet www.kochinews.co.jp; f. 1904; Dir and Man. Editor KENGO FUJITO; circ. morning 233,319, evening 146,276.

Shikoku Shimbun: 15-1, Nakano-cho, Takamatsu 760-8572; tel. (878) 33-1111; internet www.shikoku-np.co.jp; f. 1889; morning; Man. Editor JUNJI YAMASHITA; circ. 208,816.

Tokushima Shimbun: 2-5-2, Naka-Tokushima-cho, Tokushima 770-8572; tel. (886) 55-7373; fax (866) 54-0165; internet www.topics.or.jp; f. 1944; Dir and Man. Editor HIROSHI MATSUMURA; circ. morning 253,184, evening 52,203.

Hokkaido Island

Doshin Sports: 3-6, Odori-nishi, Chuo-ku, Sapporo 060-8711; tel. (11) 241-1230; internet douspo.aurora-net.or.jp; f. 1982; morning; Pres. KOSUKE SAKAI; circ. 139,178.

Hokkai Times: 10-6, Nishi, Minami-Ichijo, Chuo-ku, Sapporo 060; tel. (11) 231-0131; f. 1946; Man. Editor KOKI ITO; circ. morning 120,736.

Hokkaido Shimbun: 3-6, Odori-nishi, Chuo-ku, Sapporo 060-8711; tel. (11) 221-2111; internet www.aurora-net.or.jp; f. 1942; Man. Editor RYOZO ODAGIRI; circ. morning 1.2m., evening 740,264.

Kushiro Shimbun: 7-3, Kurogane-cho, Kushiro 085-8650; tel. (154) 22-1111; internet www.hokkai.or.jp/senshin/index.html; f. 1946; morning; Man. Editor YUTAKA ITO; circ. 55,686.

Muroran Mimpo: 1-3-16, Hon-cho, Muroran 051-8550; tel. (143) 22-5121; internet www.muromin.mnw.jp; f. 1945; Man. Editor TSU-TOMO KUDO; circ. morning 60,300, evening 52,500.

Nikkan Sports: 3-1-30, Higashi, Kita-3 jo, Chuo-ku, Sapporo 060-0033; tel. (11) 242-3900; fax (11) 231-5470; internet www.kita-nikkan.co.jp; f. 1962; morning; Pres. SATOSHI KATO; circ. 160,355.

Tokachi Mainichi Shimbun: 8-2, Minami, Higashi-Ichijo, Obihiro 080-8688; tel. (155) 22-2121; fax (155) 25-2700; internet www.tokachi.co.jp; f. 1919; evening; Dir and Man. Editor TOSHIAKI NAKA-HASHI; circ. 89,264.

Tomakomai Mimpo: 3-1-8, Wakakusa-cho, Tomakomai 053-8611; tel. (144) 32-5311; internet www.tomamin.co.jp; f. 1950; evening; Dir and Man. Editor RYUICHI KUDO; circ. 60,676.

Yomiuri Shimbun: 4-1, Nishi, Kita-4 jo, Chuo-ku, Sapporo 060-8656; tel. (11) 242-3111; f. 1959; Head Officer TSUTOMO IKEDA; circ. morning 261,747, evening 81,283.

Kyushu Island

Kagoshima Shimpo: 7-28, Jonan-cho, Kagoshima 892-8551; tel. (99) 226-2100; internet www.kagoshimashimpo.com; f. 1959; morning; Dir and Man. Editor JUNSUKE KINOSHITA; circ. 39,330.

Kumamoto Nichi-Nichi Shimbun: 172, Yoyasu-machi, Kumamoto 860-8506; tel. (96) 361-3111; internet www.kumanichi.co.jp; f. 1942; Man. Editor HIROSHI KAWARABATA; circ. morning 389,528, evening 101,795.

Kyushu Sports: Fukuoka Tenjin Center Bldg, 2-14-8, Tenjin-cho, Chuo-ku, Fukuoka 810-0001; tel. (92) 781-7401; f. 1966; morning; Head Officer HIROSHI MITOMI; circ. 449,850.

Minami Nippon Shimbun: 1-9-33, Yojirou, Kagoshima 890-8603; tel. (99) 813-5001; fax (99) 813-5016; e-mail tuusin@po.minc.ne.jp; internet www.minaminippon.co.jp; f. 1881; Man. Editor YASUSHI MOMIKI; circ. morning 401,938, evening 27,959.

Miyazaki Nichi-Nichi Shimbun: 1-1-33, Takachihodori, Miyazaki 880-8570; tel. (985) 26-9315; internet www.the-miyanichi.co.jp; f. 1940; morning; Man. Editor MASAAKI MINAMIMURA; circ. 236,083.

Nagasaki Shimbun: 3-1, Mori-machi, Nagasaki 852-8601; tel. (958) 44-2111; internet www.nagasaki-np.co.jp; f. 1889; Dir and Man. Editor SADAKATSU HONDA; circ. morning 200,128.

Nankai Nichi-Nichi Shimbun: 10-3, Nagahama-cho, Naze 894-8601; tel. (997) 53-2121; internet www.amami.or.jp/nankai; f. 1946; morning; Man. Editor TERUMI MATSUI; circ. 24,038.

Nishi Nippon Shimbun: 1-4-1, Tenjin, Chuo-ku, Fukuoka 810-8721; tel. (92) 711-5555; internet www.nishinippon.co.jp; f. 1877; Exec. Dir and Man. Editor TAKAMICHI TAMAGAWA; circ. morning 834,800, evening 188,444.

Nishi Nippon Sports: 1-4-1, Tenjin, Chuo-ku, Fukuoka 810; tel. (92) 711-5555; f. 1954; Man. Editor KENJI ISHIZAKI; circ. 184,119.

Oita Godo Shimbun: 3-9-15, Funai-machi, Oita 870-8605; tel. (975) 36-2121; internet www.oita-press.co.jp; f. 1886; Dir and Man. Editor MASAKATSU TANABE; circ. morning 245,257, evening 245,227.

Okinawa Times: 2-2-2, Kumoji, Naha 900-8678; tel. (98) 860-3000; internet www.okinawatimes.co.jp; f. 1948; Dir and Man. Editor MASAO KISHIMOTO; circ. morning 204,420, evening 204,420.

Ryukyu Shimpo: 1-10-3, Izumizaki, Naha 900-8525; tel. (98) 865-5111; internet www.ryukyushimpo.co.jp; f. 1893; Man. Editor TOMO-KAZU TAKAMINE; circ. 200,936.

Saga Shimbun: 3-2-23, Tenjin, Saga 840-8585; tel. (952) 28-2111; fax (952) 29-4829; internet www.saga-s.co.jp; f. 1884; morning; Man. Editor TERUHIKO WASHIZAKI; circ. 138,079.

Yaeyama Mainichi Shimbun: 614, Tonoshiro, Ishigaki 907-0004; tel. (9808) 2-2121; internet www.cosmos.ne.jp/~mainichi; f. 1950; morning; Exec. Dir and Man. Editor YOSHIO UECHI; circ. 14,500.

WEEKLIES

An-An: Magazine House, 3-13-10, Ginza, Chuo-ku, Tokyo 104-03; tel. (3) 3545-7050; fax (3) 3546-0034; f. 1970; fashion; Editor MIYOKO YODOGAWA; circ. 650,000.

Asahi Graphic: Asahi Shimbun Publishing Dept, 5-3-2, Tsukiji, Chuo-ku, Tokyo 104-11; tel. (3) 3545-0131; f. 1923; pictorial review; Editor KIYOKAZU TANNO; circ. 120,000.

Diamond Weekly: Diamond Inc, 1-4-2, Kasumigaseki, Chiyoda-ku, Tokyo 100; tel. (3) 3504-6250; f. 1913; economics; Editor YUTAKA IWASA; circ. 78,000.

Focus: Shincho-Sha, 71, Yaraicho, Shinjuku-ku, Tokyo 162; tel. (3) 3266-5271; fax (3) 3266-5390; politics, economics, sport; Editor KAZU-MASA TAJIMA; circ. 850,000.

Friday: Kodan-Sha Co Ltd, 2-12-21, Otowa, Bunkyo-ku, Tokyo 112; tel. (3) 5395-3440; fax (3) 3943-8582; current affairs; Editor-in-Chief TETSU SUZUKI; circ. 1m.

Hanako: Magazine House, 3-13-10, Ginza, Chuo-ku, Tokyo 104-03; tel. (3) 3545-7070; fax (3) 3545-7281; f. 1988; consumer guide; Editor AYAKO OTA; circ. 350,000.

Nikkei Business: Nikkei Business Publications Inc, 2-7-6, Hirakawa-cho, Chiyoda-ku, Tokyo 102-8622; tel. (3) 5210-8101; fax (3) 5210-8520; internet www.nikkeibp.co.jp; f. 1969; Editor-in-Chief HIROTOMO NOMURA; circ. 350,000.

Shukan Asahi: Asahi Shimbun Publishing Dept, 5-3-2, Tsukiji, Chuo-ku, Tokyo 104-8011; tel. (3) 3545-0131; f. 1922; general interest; Editor-in-Chief AKIRA KATO; circ. 482,000.

Shukan Bunshun: Bungei-Shunju Ltd, 3-23, Kioicho, Chiyoda-ku, Tokyo 102-8008; tel. (3) 3265-1211; fax (3) 3234-3964; e-mail kawabe@bunshun.co.jp; internet www.bunshun.co.jp; general interest; Editor YOJI SUZUKI; circ. 800,000.

Shukan Gendai: Kodan-Sha Co Ltd, 2-12-21, Otowa, Bunkyo-ku, Tokyo 112; tel. (3) 5395-3438; fax (3) 3943-7815; f. 1959; general; Editor-in-Chief TETSU SUZUKI; circ. 930,000.

Shukan Josei: Shufu-To-Seikatsu Sha Ltd, 3-5-7, Kyobashi, Chuo-ku, Tokyo 104; tel. (3) 3563-5130; fax (3) 3563-2073; f. 1957; women's interest; Editor HIDEO KIKUCHI; circ. 638,000.

Shukan Post: Shogakukan Publishing Co Ltd, 2-3-1, Hitotsubashi, Chiyoda-ku, Tokyo 101-01; tel. (3) 3230-5951; f. 1969; general; Editor NORIMICHI OKANARI; circ. 696,000.

Shukan Shincho: Shincho-Sha, 71, Yarai-cho, Shinjuku-ku, Tokyo 162-8711; tel. (3) 3266-5311; fax (3) 3266-5622; f. 1956; general interest; Editor HIROSHI MATSUDA; circ. 521,000.

Shukan SPA: Fuso-Sha Co, 1-15-1, Kaigan, Minato-ku, Tokyo 105; tel. (3) 5403-8875; f. 1952; general interest; Editor-in-Chief TOSHI-HIKO SATO; circ. 400,000.

Shukan ST: Japan Times Ltd, 4-5-4, Shibaura, Minato-ku, Tokyo 108-0023; tel. (3) 3452-4077; fax (3) 3452-3303; e-mail shukanst@japantimes.co.jp; f. 1951; English and Japanese; Editor MITSURU TANAKA; circ. 150,000.

Shukan Yomiuri: Yomiuri Shimbun Publication Dept, 1-2-1, Kiyosumi, Koto-ku, Tokyo 135; tel. (3) 5245-7001; e-mail yw@yomiuri.com; internet www.yomiuri.co.jp; f. 1938; general interest; Editor SHINI KAGEYAMA; circ. 453,000.

Sunday Mainichi: Mainichi Newspapers Publishing Dept, 1-1-1, Hitotsubashi, Chiyoda-ku, Tokyo 100-51; tel. (3) 3212-0321; fax (3) 3212-0769; f. 1922; general interest; Editor KENJI MIKI; circ. 237,000.

Tenji Mainichi: Mainichi Newspapers Publishing Dept, 3-4-5, Umeda, Osaka; tel. (6) 6346-8386; fax (6) 6346-8385; f. 1922; in Japanese braille; Editor TADAMITSU MORIOKA; circ. 12,000.

Weekly Economist: Mainichi Newspapers Publishing Dept, 1-1-1, Hitotsubashi, Chiyoda-ku, Tokyo 100-51; tel. (3) 3212-0321; f. 1923; Editorial Chief NOBUHIRO SHUDO; circ. 120,000.

Weekly Toyo Keizai: Toyo Keizai Inc, 1-2-1, Hongoku-cho, Nihombashi, Chuo-ku, Tokyo 103-8345; tel. (3) 3246-5655; fax (3) 3270-0159; e-mail sub@toyokeizai.co.jp; internet www.toyokeizai.co.jp; f. 1895; business, economics, finance, and corporate information; Editor TOSHIKI OTA; circ. 62,000.

PERIODICALS

All Yomimono: Bungei-Shunju Ltd, 3-23, Kioicho, Chiyoda-ku, Tokyo 102; tel. (3) 3265-1211; fax (3) 3239-5481; f. 1930; monthly; popular fiction; Editor KOICHI SASAMOTO; circ. 95,796.

Any: 1-3-14, Hirakawa-cho, Chiyoda-ku, Tokyo 102; tel. (3) 5276-2200; fax (3) 5276-2209; f. 1989; every 2 weeks; women's interest; Editor YUKIO MIWA; circ. 380,000.

Asahi Camera: Asahi Shimbun Publishing Dept, 5-3-2, Tsukiji, Chuo-ku, Tokyo 104-8011; tel. (3) 3545-0131; fax (3) 5565-3286; f. 1926; monthly; photography; Editor HIROSHI HIROSE; circ. 90,000.

Balloon: Shufunotomo Co Ltd, 2-9, Kanda Surugadai, Chiyoda-ku, Tokyo 101; tel. (3) 3294-1132; fax (3) 3291-5093; f. 1986; monthly; expectant mothers; Dir MARIKO HOSODA; circ. 250,000.

Brutus: Magazine House, 3-13-10, Ginza, Chuo-ku, Tokyo 104-03; tel. (3) 3545-7000; fax (3) 3546-0034; f. 1980; every 2 weeks; men's interest; Editor KOICHI TETSUKA; circ. 250,000.

Bungei-Shunju: Bungei-Shunju Ltd, 3-23, Kioicho, Chiyoda-ku, Tokyo 102-8008; tel. (3) 3265-1211; fax (3) 3221-6623; internet bunshun.topica.ne.jp; f. 1923; monthly; general; Pres. MASARU SHIR-AISHI; Editor KIYONDO MATSUI; circ. 656,000.

Business Tokyo: Keizaikai Bldg, 2-13-18, Minami-Aoyama, Minato-ku, Tokyo 105; tel. (3) 3423-8500; fax (3) 3423-8505; f. 1987; monthly; Dir TAKUO IDA; Editor ANTHONY PAUL; circ. 125,000.

Chuokoron: Chuokoron-Shinsha Inc, 2-8-7, Kyobashi, Chuo-ku, Tokyo 104-8320; tel. (3) 3563-2751; fax (3) 3561-5929; internet www .chuko.co.jp; f. 1887; monthly; general interest; Chief Editor JUN MAYIMA; circ. 90,000.

Croissant: Magazine House, 3-13-10, Ginza, Chuo-ku, Tokyo 104-03; tel. (3) 3545-7111; fax (3) 3546-0034; f. 1977; every 2 weeks; home; Editor MASAAKI TAKEUCHI; circ. 600,000.

Fujinkoron: Chuokoron-Sha Inc, 2-8-7, Kyobashi, Chuo-ku, Tokyo 104; tel. (3) 3563-1866; fax (3) 3561-5920; f. 1916; women's literary monthly; Editor YUKIKO YUKAWA; circ. 185,341.

Geijutsu Shincho: Shincho-Sha, 71, Yarai-cho, Shinjuku-ku, Tokyo 162-8711; tel. (3) 3266-5381; fax (3) 3266-5387; e-mail geishin@shinchosha.co.jp; f. 1950; monthly; fine arts, music, architecture, films, drama and design; Editor-in-Chief KAZUHIRO NAGAI; circ. 50,000.

Gendai: Kodan-Sha Ltd, 2-12-21, Otowa, Bunkyo-ku, Tokyo 112; tel. (3) 5395-3517; fax (3) 3945-9128; f. 1966; monthly; cultural and political; Editor SHUNKICHI YABUKI; circ. 250,000.

Ginza: Magazine House, 3-13-10, Ginza, Chuo-ku, Tokyo 104-8003; tel. (3) 3545-7080; fax (3) 3542-6375; internet webmaster.magazine .co.jp; f. 1997; monthly; women's interest; Editor MIYOKO YODOGAWA; circ. 250,000.

Hot-Dog Press: Kodan-Sha Ltd, 2-12-21, Otowa, Bunkyo-ku, Tokyo 112-01; tel. (3) 5395-3473; fax (3) 3945-9128; every 2 weeks; men's interest; Editor ATSUHIDE KOKUBO; circ. 650,000.

Ie-no-Hikari (Light of Home): Ie-no-Hikari Asscn, 11, Ichigaya Funagawaramachi, Shinjuku-ku, Tokyo 162-8448; tel. (3) 3266-9013; fax (3) 3266-9052; e-mail hikari@mxd.meshnet.or.jp; internet www.mediagalaxy.co.jp/ienohikarinet; f. 1925; monthly; rural and general interest; Pres. SHUZO SUZUKI; Editor KAZUO NAKANO; circ. 928,000.

Japan Company Handbook: Toyo Keizai Inc, 1-2-1, Nihombashi Hongoku-cho, Chuo-ku, Tokyo 103-8345; tel. (3) 3246-5621; fax (3) 3246-5473; e-mail sub@toyokeizai.co.jp; internet www.toyokeizai.co .jp; f. 1974; quarterly; English; Editor MASAKI HARA; total circ. 100,000.

Jitsugyo No Nihon: Jitsugyo No Nihon-Sha Ltd, 1-3-9, Ginza, Chuo-ku, Tokyo 104; tel. (3) 3562-1967; fax (3) 2564-2382; f. 1897; monthly; economics and business; Editor TOSHIO KAWAJIRI; circ. 60,000.

Junon: Shufu-To-Seikatsu Sha Ltd, 3-5-7, Kyobashi, Chuo-ku, Tokyo 104; tel. (3) 3563-5132; fax (3) 5250-7081; f. 1973; monthly; television and entertainment; circ. 560,000.

Kagaku (Science): Iwanami Shoten Publishers, 2-5-5, Hitotsubashi, Chiyoda-ku, Tokyo 102; tel. (3) 5210-4070; fax (3) 5210-4073; f. 1931; Editor NOBUAKI MIYABE; circ. 29,000.

Kagaku Asahi: Asahi Shimbun Publishing Dept, 5-3-2, Tsukiji, Chuo-ku, Tokyo 104-8011; tel. (3) 5540-7810; fax (3) 3546-2404; f. 1941; monthly; scientific; Editor TOSHIHIRO SASAKI; circ. 105,000.

Keizaijin: Kansai Economic Federation, Nakanoshima Center Bldg, 6-2-27, Nakanoshima, Kita-ku, Osaka 530-6691; tel. (6) 6441-0101; fax (6) 6443-5347; internet www.kankeiren.or.jp; f. 1947; monthly; economics; Editor M. YASUTAKE; circ. 2,600.

Lettuce Club: SS Communications, 11-2, Ban-cho, Chiyoda-ku, Tokyo 102; tel. (3) 5276-2151; fax (3) 5276-2229; f. 1987; every 2 weeks; cookery; Editor MITSURU NAKAYA; circ. 800,000.

Money Japan: SS Communications, 11-2, Ban-cho, Chiyoda-ku, Tokyo 102; tel. (3) 5276-2220; fax (3) 5276-2229; internet www.sscom .co.jp/money; f. 1985; monthly; finance; Editor TOSHIO KOBAYASHI; circ. 500,000.

Popeye: Magazine House, 3-13-10, Ginza, Chuo-ku, Tokyo 104-8003; tel. (3) 3545-7160; fax (3) 3545-9026; f. 1976; every 2 weeks; fashion, youth interest; Editor KATSUMI NAMAIZAWA; circ. 320,000.

President: President Inc, Bridgestone Hirakawacho Bldg, 2-13-12, Hirakawa-cho, Chiyoda-ku, Tokyo 102; tel. (3) 3237-3737; fax (3) 3237-3748; internet www.president.co.jp; f. 1963; monthly; business; Editor KAYOKO ABE; circ. 263,308.

Ray: Shufunotomo Co Ltd, 2-9, Kanda Surugadai, Chiyoda-ku, Tokyo 101; tel. (3) 3294-1163; fax (3) 3291-5093; f. 1988; monthly; women's interest; Editor TATSURO NAKANISHI; circ. 450,000.

Ryoko Yomiuri: Ryoko Yomiuri Publications Inc, 2-2-15, Ginza, Chuo-ku, Tokyo 104; tel. (3) 3561-8911; fax (3) 3561-8950; f. 1966; monthly; travel; Editor TETSUO KINUGAWA; circ. 470,000.

Sekai: Iwanami Shoten Publishers, 2-5-5, Hitotsubashi, Chiyoda-ku, Tokyo 101–8002; tel. (3) 5210-4141; fax (3) 5210-4144; e-mail sekai@iwanami.co.jp; internet www.iwanami.co.jp/sekai; f. 1946; monthly; review of world and domestic affairs; Editor ATSUSHI OKA-MOTO; circ. 120,000.

Shinkenchiku: Shinkenchiku-Sha Co Ltd, 2-31-2, Yushima, Bunkyo-ku, Tokyo 113-8501; tel. (3) 3811-7101; fax (3) 3812-8229; e-mail ja-business@japan-architect.co.jp; internet www .japan-architect.co.jp; f. 1925; monthly; architecture; Editor AKIHIKO OMORI; circ. 87,000.

Shiso (Thought): Iwanami Shoten Publishers, 2-5-5, Hitotsubashi, Chiyoda-ku, Tokyo 101-8002; tel. (3) 5210-4055; fax (3) 5210-4037; e-mail shiso@iwanami.co.jp; internet www.iwanami.co.jp/shiso; f. 1921; monthly; philosophy, social sciences and humanities; Editor KIYOSHI KOJIMA; circ. 20,000.

Shosetsu Shincho: Shincho-Sha, 71, Yarai-cho, Shinjuku-ku, Tokyo 162-8711; tel. (3) 3266-5241; fax (3) 3266-5412; internet www .shincho.net/magazines/shosetsushincho; f. 1947; monthly; literature; Editor-in-Chief TSUYOSHI MENJO; circ. 80,000.

Shufunotomo: Shufunotomo Co Ltd, 2-9, Kanda Surugadai, Chiyoda-ku, Tokyo 101; tel. (3) 5280-7531; fax (3) 5280-7431; f. 1917; monthly; home and lifestyle; Editor KYOKO FURUTO; circ. 450,000.

So-en: Bunka Publishing Bureau, c/o Bunka Fashion College, 3-22-1, Yoyogi, Shibuya-ku, Tokyo,151-8522; tel. (3) 3299-2531; fax (3) 3370-3712; internet books.bunka.ac.jp; e-mail info-bpb@bunka.ac .jp; f. 1936; fashion monthly; Editor KEIKO SASAKI; circ. 270,000.

NEWS AGENCIES

Jiji Tsushin (Jiji Press Ltd): 5-15-8 Ginza, Chuo-ku, Tokyo 104-8178; tel. (3) 3591-1111; e-mail info@jiji.co.jp; internet www.jiji.com; f. 1945; Pres. JUN SAKAKIBARA; Man. Dir and Man. Editor HIROYUKI YAMAKI.

Kyodo Tsushin (Kyodo News): 2-2-5, Toranomon, Minato-ku, Tokyo 105-8474; tel. (3) 5573-8081; fax (3) 5573-2268; e-mail kokusai@kyodonews.jp; internet home.kyodo.co.jp; f. 1945; Pres. TOYOHIKO YAMANOUCHI; Man. Editor TOSHIEI KOKUBU.

Radiopress Inc: R-Bldg Shinjuku, 5F, 33-8, Wakamatsu-cho, Shinjuku-ku, Tokyo 162-0056; tel. (3) 5273-2171; fax (3) 5273-2180; e-mail rptokyo@oak.ocn.ne.jp; f. 1945; provides news from China, the former USSR, Democratic People's Repub. of Korea, Viet Nam and elsewhere to the press and govt offices; Pres. AKIO IJUIN.

Sun Telephoto: Palaceside Bldg, 1-1-1, Hitotsubashi, Chiyoda-ku, Tokyo 100-0003; tel. (3) 3213-6771; e-mail photo@suntelephoto.com; internet www.suntelephoto.com; e-mail shimazaki@suntelephoto .com; f. 1952; Pres. KOZO TAKINO; Man. Editor GORO SHIMAZAKI.

Foreign Bureaux

Agence France-Presse (AFP): Asahi Shimbun Bldg, 11th Floor, 5-3-2, Tsukiji, Chuo-ku, Tokyo 104-0045; tel. (3) 3545-3061; fax (3) 3546-2594; Bureau Chief PHILIPPE RIES.

Agencia EFE (Spain): Kyodo Tsushin Bldg, 2nd Floor, 2-2-5, Toranomon, Minato-ku, Tokyo 105-0001; tel. (3) 3585-8940; fax (3) 3585-8948; Bureau Chief JUAN ANTONIO SANZ.

Agenzia Nazionale Stampa Associata (ANSA) (Italy): Kyodo Tsushin Bldg, 9th Floor, 2-2-5, Toranomon, Minato-ku, Tokyo 105-0001; tel. (3) 3584-6667; fax (3) 3584-5114; Bureau Chief ALBERTO ZANCONATO.

Antara (Indonesia): Kyodo Tsushin Bldg, 9th Floor, 2-2-5, Toranomon, Minato-ku, Tokyo 105-0001; tel. (3) 3584-4234; fax (3) 3584-4591; Correspondent MARIA ANDRIANA.

Associated Press (AP) (USA): Shiodome Media Tower, 7/F, 1-7-1 Higashi-Shimbashi, Minato-ku, Tokyo 105-7207; tel. (3) 6215-8930; fax (3) 6215-8949; internet www.ap.org; Gen. Man. KAZUO ABIKO.

Central News Agency (Taiwan): 3-7-3-302, Shimo-meguro, Meguro-ku, Tokyo 153-0064; tel. (3) 3495-2046; fax (3) 3495-2066; Bureau Chief CHANG FANG MIN.

Deutsche Presse-Agentur (dpa) (Germany): Nippon Press Center, 3rd Floor, 2-2-1, Uchisaiwai-cho, Chiyoda-ku, Tokyo 100-

0011; tel. (3) 3580-6629; fax (3) 3593-7888; Bureau Chief LARS NICOLAYSEN.

Informatsionnoye Telegrafnoye Agentstvo Rossii—Telegrafnoye Agentstvo Suverennykh Stran (ITAR—TASS) (Russia): 1-5-1, Hon-cho, Shibuya-ku, Tokyo 151-0071; tel. (3) 3377-0380; fax (3) 3378-0606; Bureau Chief VASILII GOLOVNIN.

Inter Press Service (IPS) (Italy): 1-15-19, Ishikawa-machi, Ota-ku, Tokyo 145-0061; tel. (3) 3726-7944; fax (3) 3726-7896; Correspondent SUVENDRINI KAKUCHI.

Magyar Távirati Iroda (MTI) (Hungary): 1-3-4-306, Okamoto, Setagaya-ku, Tokyo 157-0076; tel. (3) 3708-3093; fax (3) 3708-2703; Bureau Chief JÁNOS MARTON.

Reuters (UK): Shuwa Kamiya-cho Bldg, 5th Floor, 4-3-13, Toranomon, Minato-ku, Tokyo 105-0001; tel. (3) 3432-4141; fax (3) 3433-2921; Editor WILLIAM SPOSATO.

Rossiiskoye Informatsionnoye Agentstvo—Novosti (RIA—Novosti) (Russia): 3-9-13 Higashi-gotanda, Shinagawa-ku, Tokyo 141-0022; tel. (3) 3441-9241; fax (3) 3447-8443; e-mail riatokyo@ma.kcom.ne.jp; Bureau Chief VYACHESLAV BANTIN.

United Press International (UPI) (USA): AH 1-Bldg, 8/F, 1-9-14 Azabudai, Minato-ku Tokyo 106-0041; tel. (3) 3586-2370; fax (3) 3586-2373; Bureau Chief RUTH YOUNGBLOOD.

Xinhua (New China) News Agency (People's Republic of China): 3-35-23, Ebisu, Shibuya-ku, Tokyo 150-0013; tel. (3) 3441-3766; fax (3) 3446-3995; Bureau Chief WANG DAJUN.

Yonhap (United) News Agency (Republic of Korea): Kyodo Tsushin Bldg, 2-2-5, Toranomon, Minato-ku, Tokyo 105-0001; tel. (3) 3584-4681; fax (3) 3584-4021; f. 1945; Bureau Chief MOON YOUNG SHIK.

PRESS ASSOCIATIONS

Foreign Correspondents' Club of Japan: 20th Floor, 1-7-1, Yuraku-cho, Chiyoda-ku, Tokyo 100-0006; tel. (3) 3211-3161; fax (3) 3211-3168; e-mail yoda@fccj.or.jp; internet www.fccj.or.jp; f. 1945; 193 companies; Pres. ANTHONY ROWLEY; Man. SEISHI YODA.

Foreign Press Center: Nippon Press Center Bldg, 6th Floor, 2-2-1, Uchisaiwai-cho, Chiyoda-ku, Tokyo 100-0011; tel. (3) 3501-3401; fax (3) 3501-3622; e-mail rr@fpcjpn.or.jp; internet www.fpcj.jp; f. 1976; est. by the Japan Newspaper Publrs' and Editors' Asscn and the Japan Fed. of Economic Orgs; provides services to the foreign press; Pres. TERUSUKE TERADA.

Nihon Shinbun Kyokai (The Japan Newspaper Publishers and Editors Asscn): Nippon Press Center Bldg, 2-2-1, Uchisaiwai-cho, Chiyoda-ku, Tokyo 100-8543; tel. (3) 3591-3462; fax (3) 3591-6149; e-mail s_intl@pressnet.or.jp; internet www.pressnet.or.jp; f. 1946; mems include 151 companies (111 daily newspapers, 4 news agencies and 36 radio and TV companies); Chair. SHIN-ICHI HAKOSHIMA; Man. Dir SHIGEMI MURAKAMI.

Nihon Zasshi Kyokai (Japan Magazine Publishers Asscn): 1-7, Kanda Surugadai, Chiyoda-ku, Tokyo 101-0062; tel. (3) 3291-0775; fax (3) 3293-6239; f. 1956; 85 mems; Pres. HARUHIKO ISHIKAWA; Sec. GENYA INUI.

Publishers

Akane Shobo Co Ltd: 3-2-1, Nishikanda, Chiyoda-ku, Tokyo 101-0065; tel. (3) 3263-0641; fax (3) 3263-5440; f. 1949; juvenile; Pres. MASAHARU OKAMOTO.

Akita Publishing Co Ltd: 2-10-8, Iidabashi, Chiyoda-ku, Tokyo 102-8101; tel. (3) 3264-7011; fax (3) 3265-5906; f. 1948; social sciences, history, juvenile; Chair. SADAO AKITA; Pres. SADAMI AKITA.

ALC Press Inc: 2-54-12, Eifuku, Suginami-ku, Tokyo 168-0064; tel. (3) 3323-1101; fax (3) 3327-1022; e-mail menet@alc.co.jp; internet www.alc.co.jp; f. 1969; linguistics, educational materials, dictionary, juvenile; Pres. TERUMARO HIRAMOTO.

Asahi Shimbun Publications Division: 5-3-2, Tsukiji, Chuo-ku, Tokyo 104-8011; tel. (3) 3545-0131; fax (3) 5540-7682; f. 1879; general; Pres. MUNEYUKI MATSUSHITA; Dir of Publications HISAO KUWASHIMA.

Asakura Publishing Co Ltd: 6-29, Shin Ogawa-machi, Shinjuku-ku, Tokyo 162-8707; tel. (3) 3260-0141; fax (3) 3260-0180; e-mail edit@asakura.co.jp; internet www.asakura.co.jp; f. 1929; natural science, medicine, social sciences; Pres. KUNIZO ASAKURA.

Baifukan Co Ltd: 4-3-12, Kudan Minami, Chiyoda-ku, Tokyo 102-8260; tel. (3) 3262-5256; fax (3) 3262-5276; f. 1924; engineering, natural and social sciences, psychology; Pres. ITARU YAMAMOTO.

Baseball Magazine-Sha: 3-10-10, Misaki-cho, Chiyoda-ku, Tokyo 101-8381; tel. (3) 3238-0081; fax (3) 3238-0106; internet www.bbm-japan.com; f. 1946; sports, physical education, recreation, travel; Pres. TETSUO IKEDA.

Bijutsu Shuppan-Sha Ltd: Inaoka Kudan Bldg, 6th Floor, 2-36, Kanda Jimbo-cho, Chiyoda-ku, Tokyo 101-8417; tel. (3) 3234-2151; fax (3) 3234-9451; f. 1905; fine arts, graphic design; Pres. ATSUSHI OSHITA.

Bonjinsha Co Ltd: 1-3-13, Hirakawa-cho, Chiyoda-ku, Tokyo 102-0093; tel. (3) 3263-3959; fax (3) 3263-3116; f. 1973; Japanese language teaching materials; Pres. HISAMITSU TANAKA.

Bungeishunju Ltd: 3-23, Kioi-cho, Chiyoda-ku, Tokyo 102-8008; tel. (3) 3265-1211; fax (3) 3239-5482; internet www.bunshun.co.jp; f. 1923; fiction, general literature, recreation, economics, sociology; Dir MASARU SHIRAISHI.

Chikuma Shobo: Chikumashobo Bldg, 2-5-3, Kuramae, Taito-ku, Tokyo 111-8755; tel. (3) 5687-2671; fax (3) 5687-1585; e-mail webinfo@chikumashobo.co.jp; internet www.chikumashobo.co.jp; f. 1940; general literature, fiction, history, juvenile, fine arts; Pres. AKIO KIKUCHI.

Child-Honsha Co Ltd: 5-24-21, Koishikawa, Bunkyo-ku, Tokyo 112-8512; tel. (3) 3813-3785; fax (3) 3813-3765; e-mail ehon@childbook.co.jp; internet www.childbook.co.jp; f. 1930; juvenile; Pres. YOSHIAKI SHIMAZAKI.

Chuokoron-Shinsha Inc: 2-8-7, Kyobashi, Chuo-ku, Tokyo 104-8320; tel. (3) 3563-1261; fax (3) 3561-5920; internet www.chuko.co.jp; f. 1886; philosophy, history, sociology, general literature; Pres. JUNICHI HAYAKAWA.

Corona Publishing Co Ltd: 4-46-10, Sengoku, Bunkyo-ku, Tokyo 112-0011; tel. (3) 3941-3131; fax (3) 3941-3137; e-mail info@coronasha.co.jp; internet www.coronasha.co.jp; f. 1927; electronics business publs; Pres. TATSUMI GORAI.

Dempa Publications Inc: 1-11-15, Higashi Gotanda, Shinagawa-ku, Tokyo 141-8755; tel. (3) 3445-6111; fax (3) 3447-4666; f. 1950; electronics, personal computer software, juvenile, trade newspapers, English and Japanese language publications; Pres. TETSUO HIRAYAMA.

Diamond Inc: 6-12-17, Jingumae, Shibuya-ku, Tokyo 150-8409; tel. (3) 5778-7203; fax (3) 5778-6612; e-mail mitachi@diamond.co.jp; internet www.diamond.co.jp; f. 1913; business, management, economics, financial; Pres. YUTAKA IWASA.

Dohosha Ltd: TAS Bldg, 2-5-2, Nishikanda, Chiyoda-ku, Tokyo 101-0065; tel. (3) 5276-0831; fax (3) 5276-0840; e-mail intl@dohosha.co.jp; internet www.dohosha.co.jp; f. 1997; general works, architecture, art, Buddhism, business, children's education, cooking, flower arranging, gardening, medicine.

Froebel-Kan Co Ltd: 6-14-9, Honkomagome, Bunkyo-ku, Tokyo 113-8611; tel. (3) 5395-6614; fax (3) 5395-6639; e-mail info-e@froebel-kan.co.jp; internet www.froebel-kan.co.jp; f. 1907; juvenile, educational; Pres. MAMORU KITABAYASHI; Dir MITSUHIRO TADA.

Fukuinkan Shoten Publishers Inc: 6-6-3, Honkomagome, Bunkyo-ku, Tokyo 113-8686; tel. (3) 3942-2151; fax (3) 3942-1401; f. 1952; juvenile; Pres. SHIRO TOKITA; Chair. KATSUMI SATO.

Gakken Co Ltd: 4-40-5, Kamiikedai, Ota-ku, Tokyo 145-8502; tel. (3) 3726-8111; fax (3) 3493-3338; f. 1946; juvenile, educational, art, encyclopaedias, dictionaries; Pres. KAZUHIKO SAWADA.

Graphic-sha Publishing Co Ltd: 1-9-12, Kudan Kita, Chiyoda-ku, Tokyo 102-0073; tel. (3) 3263-4318; fax (3) 3263-5297; e-mail info@graphicsha.co.jp; internet www.graphicsha.co.jp; f. 1963; art, design, architecture, manga techniques, hobbies; Pres. SEIICHI SUGAYA.

Gyosei Corpn: 4-30-16, Ogikubo, Suginami-ku, Tokyo 167-8088; tel. (3) 5349-6666; fax (3) 5349-6677; e-mail business@gyosei.co.jp; internet www.gyosei.co.jp; f. 1893; law, education, science, politics, business, art, language, literature, juvenile; Pres. MOTOO FUJISAWA.

Hakusui-Sha Co Ltd: 3-24, Kanda Ogawa-machi, Chiyoda-ku, Tokyo 101-0052; tel. (3) 3291-7821; fax (3) 3291-7810; f. 1915; general literature, science and languages; Pres. KAZUAKI FUJIWARA.

Hayakawa Publishing Inc: 2-2, Kanda-Tacho, Chiyoda-ku, Tokyo 101-0046; tel. (3) 3252-3111; fax (3) 3258-0250; e-mail hirohaya@giganet.net; f. 1945; wine books, children's books, coffee-table books, drama, comic books, monthly magazines; Pres. HIROSHI HAYAKAWA.

Heibonsha Ltd: 2-29-4 Hakusan, Bunkyo-ku, Tokyo 112-0001; tel. (3) 3818-0641; fax (3) 3818-0754; internet www.heibonsha.co.jp; f. 1914; encyclopaedias, art, history, geography, literature, science; Pres. NAOTO SHIMONAKA.

Hirokawa Publishing Co: 3-27-14, Hongo, Bunkyo-ku, Tokyo 113-0033; tel. (3) 3815-3651; fax (3) 5684-7030; f. 1925; natural sciences, medicine, pharmacy, nursing, chemistry; Pres. SETSUO HIROKAWA.

Hoikusha Publishing Co: 1-6-12, Kawamata, Higashi, Osaka 577-0063; tel. (6) 6788-4470; fax (6) 6788-4970; internet www.hoikusha

.co.jp; f. 1947; natural science, juvenile, fine arts, geography; Pres. YUKI IMAI.

Hokuryukan Co Ltd: 3-8-14, Takanawa, Minato-ku, Tokyo 108-0074; tel. (3) 5449-4591; fax (3) 5449-4950; e-mail hk-ns@mk1 .macnet.or.jp; internet www.macnet.or.jp/co/hk-ns; f. 1891; natural science, medical science, juvenile, dictionaries; Pres. HISAKO FUKUDA.

The Hokuseido Press: 3-32-4, Honkomagome, Bunkyo-ku, Tokyo 113-0021; tel. (3) 3827-0511; fax (3) 3827-0567; e-mail info@ hokuseido.com; f. 1914; regional non-fiction, dictionaries, textbooks; Pres. MASAZO YAMAMOTO.

Ie-No-Hikari Association: 11, Funagawara-cho, Ichigaya, Shinjuku-ku, Tokyo 162-8448; tel. (3) 3266-9000; fax (3) 3266-9048; e-mail hikari@mxd.mesh.ne.jp; internet www.ienohikari.or.jp; f. 1925; social science, agriculture, cooking; Exec. Man. MASAYUKI YAMAMOTO; Pres. HARUTO SATO.

Igaku-Shoin Ltd: 5-24-3, Hongo, Bunkyo-ku, Tokyo 113-8719; tel. (3) 3817-5610; fax (3) 3815-4114; e-mail info@igaku-shoin.co; internet www.igaku-shoin.co.jp; f. 1944; medicine, nursing; Pres. YU KANEHARA.

Institute for Financial Affairs Inc (KINZAI): 19, Minami-Motomachi, Shinjuku-ku, Tokyo 160-8519; tel. (3) 3358-1161; fax (3) 3359-7947; e-mail JDI04072@nifty.ne.jp; internet www.kinzai.or.jp; f. 1950; finance and economics, banking laws and regulations, accounting; Pres. MASATERU YOSHIDA.

Ishiyaku Publishers Inc: 1-7-10, Honkomagome, Bunkyo-ku, Tokyo 113-8612; tel. (3) 5395-7600; fax (3) 5395-7606; internet www .ishiyaku.co.jp; f. 1921; medicine, dentistry, rehabilitation, nursing, nutrition and pharmaceutics; Pres. KATSUJI FUJITA.

Iwanami Shoten, Publishers: 2-5-5, Hitotsubashi, Chiyoda-ku, Tokyo 101-8002; tel. (3) 5210-4000; fax (3) 5210-4039; e-mail rights@ iwanami.co.jp; internet www.iwanami.co.jp; f. 1913; natural and social sciences, humanities, literature, fine arts, juvenile, dictionaries; Pres. AKIO YAMAGUCHI.

Japan Broadcast Publishing Co Ltd: 41-1, Udagawa-cho, Shibuya-ku, Tokyo 150-8081; tel. (3) 3464-7311; fax (3) 3780-3353; e-mail kikaka@nhk-book.co.jp; internet www.nhk-book.co.jp; f. 1931; foreign language textbooks, gardening, home economics, sociology, education, art, juvenile; Pres. TAKESHI MATSUO.

Japan External Trade Organization (JETRO): 2-2-5, Toranomon, Minato-ku, Tokyo 105-8466; tel. (3) 3582-5511; fax (3) 3587-2485; internet www.jetro.go.jp; f. 1958; trade, economics, investment.

Japan Publications Trading Co Ltd: 1-2-1, Sarugaku-cho, Chiyoda-ku, Tokyo 101-0064; tel. (3) 3292-3751; fax (3) 3292-0410; e-mail jpt@po.iijnet.or.jp; internet www.jptco.co.jp; f. 1942; general works, art, health, sports; Pres. SATOMI NAKABAYASHI.

The Japan Times Ltd: 4-5-4, Shibaura, Minato-ku, Tokyo 108-0023; tel. (3) 3453-2013; fax (3) 3453-8023; e-mail jt-books@kt.rim.or .jp; internet bookclub.japantimes.co.jp; f. 1897; linguistics, culture, business; Pres. TOSHIAKI OGASAWARA.

Japan Travel Bureau Inc: JTB Bldg, 2-3-11 Higashi-Shinagawa, Shinagawa-ku, Tokyo; tel. (3) 3477-9521; fax (3) 3477-9538; internet www.jtb.co.jp; f. 1912; travel, geography, history, fine arts, languages; Vice-Pres. MITSUMASA IWATA.

Jimbun Shoin: 9, Nishiuchihata-cho, Takeda, Fushimi-ku, Kyoto 612-8447; tel. (75) 603-1344; fax (75) 603-1814; e-mail edjimbun@ mbox.kyoto-inet.or.jp; internet www.jimbunshoin.co.jp; f. 1922; general literature, philosophy, fiction, social science, religion, fine arts; Pres. MUTSUHISA WATANABE.

Kadokawa Shoten Publishing Co Ltd: 2-13-3, Fujimi, Chiyoda-ku, Tokyo 102-0071; tel. (3) 3238-8611; fax (3) 3238-8612; f. 1945; literature, history, dictionaries, religion, fine arts, books on tape, compact discs, CD-ROM, comics, animation, video cassettes, computer games; Pres. TSUGUHIKO KADOKAWA.

Kaibundo Publishing Co Ltd: 2-5-4, Suido, Bunkyo-ku, Tokyo 112-0005; tel. (3) 5684-6289; fax (3) 3815-3953; e-mail okadayo@ kaibundo.jp; internet www.kaibundo.jp; f. 1914; marine affairs, natural science, engineering, industry; Pres. YOSHIHIRO OKADA.

Kaiseisha Publishing Co Ltd: 3–5, Ichigaya Sadohara-cho, Shinjuku-ku, Tokyo 162-8450; tel. (3) 3260-3229; fax (3) 3260-3540; e-mail foreign@kaiseisha.co.jp; internet www.kaiseisha.co.jp; f. 1936; juvenile; Pres. MASAKI IMAMURA.

Kanehara & Co Ltd: 2-31-14, Yushima, Bunkyo-ku, Tokyo 113-8687; tel. (3) 3811-7185; fax (3) 3813-0288; f. 1875; medical, agricultural, engineering and scientific; Pres. SABURO KOMURO.

Kenkyusha Ltd: 2-11-3, Fujimi, Chiyoda-ku, Tokyo 102-8152; tel. (3) 3288-7711; fax (3) 3288-7821; e-mail hanbai@kenkyusha.co.jp; internet www.kenkyusha.co.jp; f. 1907; bilingual dictionaries, books on languages; Pres. KUNIKATSU ARAKI.

Kinokuniya Co Ltd: 13-11, Higashi 3-chome, Shibuya-ku, Tokyo 150-8513; tel. (3) 5469-5919; fax (3) 5469-5959; e-mail publish@ kinokuniya.co.jp; internet www.kinokuniya.co.jp; f. 1927; humanities, social science, natural science; Pres. OSAMU MATSUBARA.

Kodansha International Ltd: 1-17-14, Otowa, Bunkyo-ku, Tokyo 112-8652; tel. (3) 3944-6492; fax (3) 3944-6323; e-mail sales@ kodansha-intl.co.jp; f. 1963; art, business, cookery, crafts, gardening, language, literature, martial arts; Pres. SAWAKO NOMA.

Kodansha Ltd: 2-12-21, Otowa, Bunkyo-ku, Tokyo 112-8001; tel. (3) 5395-3574; fax (3) 3944-9915; f. 1909; fine arts, fiction, literature, juvenile, comics, dictionaries; Pres. SAWAKO NOMA.

Kosei Publishing Co Ltd: 2-7-1, Wada, Suginami-ku, Tokyo 166-8535; tel. (3) 5385-2319; fax (3) 5385-2331; e-mail dharmaworld@ kosei-shuppan.co.jp; internet www.kosei-shuppan.co.jp; f. 1966; general works, philosophy, religion, history, pedagogy, social science, art, juvenile; Pres. YUKIO YOKOTA.

Kyoritsu Shuppan Co Ltd: 4-6-19, Kohinata, Bunkyo-ku, Tokyo 112-8700; tel. (3) 3947-2511; fax (3) 3947-2539; e-mail general@ kyoritsu-pub.co.jp; internet www.kyoritsu-pub.co.jp; f. 1926; scientific and technical; Pres. MITSUAKI NANJO.

Maruzen Co Ltd: 3-9-2, Nihombashi, Chuo-ku, Tokyo 103-8244; tel. (3) 3272-0521; fax (3) 3272-0693; internet www.maruzen.co.jp; f. 1869; general works; Pres. SEISHIRO MURATA.

Medical Friend Co Ltd: 3-2-4, Kudan Kita, Chiyoda-ku, Tokyo 102-0073; tel. (3) 3264-6611; fax (3) 3261-6602; f. 1947; medical and allied science, nursing; Pres. KAZUHARU OGURA.

Minerva Shobo: 1, Tsutsumi dani-cho, Hinooka, Yamashina-ku, Kyoto 607-8494; tel. (75) 581-5191; fax (75) 581-0589; e-mail info@ minervashobo.co.jp; internet www.minervashobo.co.jp; f. 1948; general non-fiction and reference; Pres. KEIZO SUGITA.

Misuzu Shobo Ltd: 5-32-21, Hongo, Bunkyo-ku, Tokyo 113-0033; tel. (3) 3815-9181; fax (3) 3818-8497; e-mail info@msz.co.jp; internet www.msz.co.jp; f. 1947; general, philosophy, history, psychiatry, literature, science, art; Pres. TAKASHI ARAI.

Morikita Shuppan Co Ltd: 1-4-11, Fujimi, Chiyoda-ku, Tokyo 102-0071; tel. (3) 3265-8341; fax (3) 3264-8709; e-mail info@morikita .co.jp; internet www.morikita.co.jp; f. 1950; natural science, engineering; Pres. HAJIME MORIKITA.

Nakayama-Shoten Co Ltd: 1-25-14, Hakusan, Bunkyo-ku, Tokyo 113-8666; tel. (3) 3813-1100; fax (3) 3816-1015; e-mail eigyo@ nakayamashoten.co.jp; internet www.nakayamashoten.co.jp; f. 1948; medicine, biology, zoology; Pres. TADASHI HIRATA.

Nanzando Co Ltd: 4-1-11, Yushima, Bunkyo-ku, Tokyo; tel. (3) 5689-7868; fax (3) 5689-7869; e-mail info@nanzando.com; internet www.nanzando.com; medical reference, paperbacks; Pres. HAJIME SUZUKI.

Nigensha Publishing Co Ltd: 2-2, Kanda Jimbo-cho, Chiyoda-ku, Tokyo 101-8419; tel. (3) 5210-4733; fax (3) 5210-4723; e-mail sales@ nigensha.co.jp; internet www.nigensha.co.jp; f. 1953; calligraphy, fine arts, art reproductions, cars, watches; Pres. TAKAO WATANABE.

Nihon Keizai Shimbun Inc, Publications Bureau: 1-9-5, Otemachi, Chiyoda-ku, Tokyo 100-0004; tel. (3) 3270-0251; fax (3) 5255-2864; f. 1876; economics, business, politics, fine arts, video cassettes, CD-ROM; Pres. TOYOHIKO KOBAYASHI.

Nihon Vogue Co Ltd: 3-23, Ichigaya Honmura-cho, Shinjuku-ku, Tokyo 162-8705; tel. (3) 5261-5139; fax (3) 3269-8726; e-mail asai@ tezukuritown.com; internet www.tezukuritown.com; f. 1954; quilt, needlecraft, handicraft, knitting, decorative painting, pressed flowers; Pres. NOBUAKI SETO.

Nippon Jitsugyo Publishing Co Ltd: 3-2-12, Hongo, Bunkyo-ku, Tokyo 113-0033; tel. (3) 3814-5651; fax (3) 3818-2723; e-mail int@njg .co.jp; internet www.njg.co.jp; f. 1950; business, management, finance and accounting, sales and marketing; Chair. and CEO YOICHIRO NAKAMURA.

Obunsha Co Ltd: 78, Yarai-cho, Shinjuku-ku, Tokyo 162-0805; tel. (3) 3266-6000; fax (3) 3266-6291; internet www.obunsha.co.jp; f. 1931; textbooks, reference, general science and fiction, magazines, encyclopaedias, dictionaries; software; audio-visual aids; CEO FUMIO AKAO.

Ohmsha Ltd: 3-1, Kanda Nishiki-cho, Chiyoda-ku, Tokyo 101-8460; tel. (3) 3233-0641; fax (3) 3233-2426; e-mail kaigaika@ohmsha.co.jp; internet http://www.ohmsha.co.jp/index_e.htm; f. 1914; engineering, technical and scientific; Pres. SEIJI SATO; Dirs M. MORI, O. TAKEO.

Ondorisha Publishers Ltd: 11-11, Nishigoken-cho, Shinjuku-ku, Tokyo 162-8708; tel. (3) 3268-3101; fax (3) 3235-3530; f. 1945; knitting, embroidery, patchwork, handicraft books; Pres. HIDEAKI TAKEUCHI.

Ongaku No Tomo Sha Corpn (ONT): 6-30, Kagurazaka, Shinjuku-ku, Tokyo 162-0825; tel. (3) 3235-2111; fax (3) 3235-2119;

internet www.ongakunotomo.co.jp; f. 1941; compact discs, videograms, music magazines, music books, music data, music textbooks; Pres. JUN MEGURO.

PHP Institute Inc: 11, Kitanouchi-cho, Nishikujo, Minami-ku, Kyoto 601-8411; tel. (75) 681-4431; fax (75) 681-9921; internet www .php.co.jp; f. 1946; social science; Pres. MASAHARU MATSUSHITA.

Poplar Publishing Co Ltd: 5, Suga-cho, Shinjuku-ku, Tokyo 160-8565; tel. (3) 3357-2216; fax (3) 3351-0736; e-mail henshu@poplar.co .jp; internet www.poplar.co.jp; f. 1947; children's; Pres. HARUO TANAKA.

Sanseido Co Ltd: 2-22-14, Misaki-cho, Chiyoda-ku, Tokyo 101-8371; tel. (3) 3230-9411; fax (3) 3230-9547; f. 1881; dictionaries, educational, languages, social and natural science; Chair. HISANORI UENO; Pres. TOSHIO GOMI.

Sanshusha Publishing Co Ltd: 1-5-34, Shitaya, Taito-ku, Tokyo 110-0004; tel. (3) 3842-1711; fax (3) 3845-3965; e-mail maeda_k@ sanshusha.co.jp; internet www.sanshusha.co.jp; f. 1938; languages, dictionaries, philosophy, sociology, electronic publishing (CD-ROM); Pres. KANJI MAEDA.

Seibundo-Shinkosha Co Ltd: 3-3-1, Hongo, Bunkyo-ku, Tokyo 113-0033; tel. (3) 5800-5775; fax (3) 5800-5773; f. 1912; technical, scientific, design, general non-fiction; Pres. MINORU TAKITA.

Sekai Bunka Publishing Inc: 4-2-29, Kudan-Kita, Chiyoda-ku, Tokyo 102-8187; tel. (3) 3262-5111; fax (3) 3221-6843; internet www .sekaibunka.com; f. 1946; history, natural science, geography, education, art, literature, juvenile; Pres. TSUTOMU SUZUKI.

Shincho-Sha Co Ltd: 71, Yarai-cho, Shinjuku-ku, Tokyo 162-8711; tel. (3) 3266-5411; fax (3) 3266-5534; e-mail shuppans@shinchosha .co.jp; internet www.shinchosha.co.jp; f. 1896; general literature, fiction, non-fiction, fine arts, philosophy; Pres. TAKANOBU SATO.

Shinkenchiku-Sha Co Ltd: 2-31-2, Yushima, Bunkyo-ku, Tokyo 113-8501; tel. (3) 3811-7101; fax (3) 3812-8229; e-mail ja-business@ japan-architect.co.jp; internet www.japan-architect.co.jp; f. 1925; architecture; Pres. AKIHIKO OMORI.

Shogakukan Inc: 2-3-1, Hitotsubashi, Chiyoda-ku, Tokyo 101-8001; tel. (3) 3230-5526; fax (3) 3288-9653; internet www .shogakukan.co.jp; f. 1922; juvenile, education, geography, history, encyclopaedias, dictionaries; Pres. MASAHIRO OHGA.

Shokabo Publishing Co Ltd: 8-1, Yomban-cho, Chiyoda-ku, Tokyo 102-0081; tel. (3) 3262-9166; fax (3) 3262-7257; e-mail info@ shokabo.co.jp; internet www.shokabo.co.jp; f. 1895; natural science, engineering; Pres. TATSUJI YOSHINO.

Shokokusha Publishing Co Ltd: 25, Saka-machi, Shinjuku-ku, Tokyo 160-0002; tel. (3) 3359-3231; fax (3) 3357-3961; e-mail eigyo@ shokokusha.co.jp; f. 1932; architectural, technical and fine arts; Pres. TAKESHI GOTO.

Shueisha Inc: 2-5-10, Hitotsubashi, Chiyoda-ku, Tokyo 101-8050; tel. (3) 3230-6320; fax (3) 3262-1309; f. 1925; literature, fine arts, language, juvenile, comics; Pres. and CEO TAMIO KOJIMA.

Shufunotomo Co Ltd: 2-9, Kanda Surugadai, Chiyoda-ku, Tokyo 101-8911; tel. (3) 5280-7567; fax (3) 5280-7568; e-mail international@shufunotomo.co.jp; internet www.shufunotomo.co.jp; f. 1916; domestic science, fine arts, gardening, handicraft, cookery and magazines; Pres. KUNIHIKO MURAMATSU.

Shunju-Sha: 2-18-6, Soto-Kanda, Chiyoda-ku, Tokyo 101-0021; tel. (3) 3255-9614; fax (3) 3255-9370; f. 1918; philosophy, religion, literature, economics, music; Pres. AKIRA KANDA; Man. RYUTARO SUZUKI.

Taishukan Publishing Co Ltd: 3-24, Kanda-Nishiki-cho, Chiyoda-ku, Tokyo 101-8466; tel. (3) 3294-2221; fax (3) 3295-4107; internet www.taishukan.co.jp; f. 1918; reference, Japanese and foreign languages, sports, dictionaries, audio-visual aids; Pres. KAZUYUKI SUZUKI.

Tankosha Publishing Co Ltd: 19-1, Miyanishi-cho Murasakino, Kita-ku, Kyoto 603-8691; tel. (75) 432-5151; fax (75) 432-0273; e-mail tankosha@magical.egg.or.jp; internet tankosha.topica.ne.jp; f. 1949; tea ceremony, fine arts, history; Pres. YOSHITO NAYA.

Teikoku-Shoin Co Ltd: 3-29, Kanda Jimbo-cho, Chiyoda-ku, Tokyo 101-0051; tel. (3) 3262-0834; fax (3) 3262-7770; e-mail kenkyu@teikokushoin.co.jp; f. 1926; geography, atlases, maps, textbooks, history, civil studies; Pres. MISAO MORIYA.

Tokai University Press: 2-28-4, Tomigaya, Shibuya-ku, Tokyo 151-8677; tel. (3) 5478-0891; fax (3) 5478-0870; f. 1962; social science, cultural science, natural science, engineering, art; Pres. TATSURO MATSUMAE.

Tokuma Shoten Publishing Co Ltd: 1-1-16, Higashi Shimbashi, Minato-ku, Tokyo 105-8055; tel. (3) 3573-0111; fax (3) 3573-8788; e-mail info@tokuma.com; internet www.tokuma.com; f. 1954; Japanese classics, history, fiction, juvenile; Pres. YASUYOSHI TOKUMA.

Tokyo News Service Ltd: Tsukiji Hamarikyu Bldg, 5-3-3, Tsukiji, Chuo-ku, Tokyo 104; tel. (3) 3542-6511; fax (3) 3545-3628; f. 1947; shipping, trade and television guides; Pres. T. OKUYAMA.

Tokyo Shoseki Co Ltd: 2-17-1, Horifune, Kita-ku, Tokyo 114-8524; tel. (3) 5390-7513; fax (3) 5390-7409; internet www.tokyo-shoseki.co .jp; f. 1909; textbooks, reference books, cultural and educational books; Pres. YOSHIKATSU KAWAUCHI.

Tokyo Sogen-Sha Co Ltd: 1-5, Shin-Ogawa-machi, Shinjuku-ku, Tokyo 162-0814; tel. (3) 3268-8201; fax (3) 3268-8230; f. 1954; mystery and detective stories, science fiction, literature; Pres. YASUNOBU TOGAWA.

Tuttle Publishing Co Inc: RK Bldg, 2nd Floor, 2-12-10 Shimo-Meguro, Meguro-ku, Tokyo, 153 Japan; tel. (3) 5437-0171; fax (44) 5437-0755; e-mail info@tuttlepublishing.com; internet www .tuttlepublishing.com; f. 1948; books on Japanese and Asian religion, history, social science, arts, languages, literature, juvenile, cookery; Pres. ERIC OEY.

United Nations University Press: 5-53-70, Jingumae, Shibuya-ku, Tokyo 150-8925; tel. (3) 3499-2811; fax (3) 3499-2828; e-mail sales@hq.unu.edu; internet www.unu.edu/unupress; f. 1975; social sciences, humanities, pure and applied natural sciences; Rector HANS J. H. VAN GINKEL.

University of Tokyo Press: 7-3-1, Hongo, Bunkyo-ku, Tokyo 113-8654; tel. (3) 3811-0964; fax (3) 3815-1426; e-mail info@utp.or.jp; f. 1951; natural and social sciences, humanities; Japanese and English; Chair. MASARU NISHIO; Man. Dir TADASHI YAMASHITA.

Weekly Toyo Keizai: 1-2-1, Nihombashi, Hongoku-cho, Chuo-ku, Tokyo 103-8345; tel. (3) 3246-5655; fax (3) 3231-0906; e-mail sub@ toyokeizai.co.jp; internet www.toyokeizai.co.jp; f. 1895; economics, business, finance and corporate, information; Pres. HIROSHI TAKAHASHI.

Yama-Kei Publishers Co Ltd: 1-1-33, Shiba-Daimon, Minato-ku, Tokyo 105-0012; tel. (3) 3436-4021; fax (3) 3438-1949; f. 1930; natural science, geography, mountaineering; Pres. YOSHIMITSU KAWASAKI.

Yohan (New Yohan): 32-8, Ikebukuro 4-chome, Toshima-ku, Tokyo 171-004; tel. (3) 3984-0084; fax (3) 3984-0170; e-mail webinfo@yohan .co.jp; internet www.yohan.co.jp; f. 1963; social science, language, art, juvenile, dictionary; merged with Tuttle Shokai in 2003; Pres. MASANORI WATANABE.

Yuhikaku Publishing Co Ltd: 2-17, Kanda Jimbo-cho, Chiyoda-ku, Tokyo 101-0051; tel. (3) 3264-1312; fax (3) 3264-5030; f. 1877; social sciences, law, economics; Pres. TADATAKA EGUSA.

Yuzankaku Shuppan: 2-6-9, Fujimi, Chiyoda-ku, Tokyo 102; tel. (3) 3262-3231; fax (3) 3262-6938; e-mail yuzan@cf.mbn.or.jp; internet www.nepto.co.jp/yuzankaku; f. 1916; history, fine arts, religion, archaeology; Pres. KEIKO NAGASAKA.

Zoshindo Juken Kenkyusha Co Ltd: 2-19-15, Shinmachi, Nishi-ku, Osaka 550-0013; tel. (6) 6532-1581; fax (6) 6532-1588; e-mail zoshindo@mbox.inet-osaka.or.jp; internet www.zoshindo.co.jp; f. 1890; educational, juvenile; Pres. AKITAKA OKAMATO.

GOVERNMENT PUBLISHING HOUSE

Government Publications' Service Centre: 1-2-1, Kasumigaseki, Chiyoda-ku, Tokyo 100-0013; tel. (3) 3504-3885; fax (3) 3504-3889.

PUBLISHERS' ASSOCIATIONS

Japan Book Publishers Association: 6, Fukuro-machi, Shinjuku-ku, Tokyo 162-0828; tel. (3) 3268-1301; fax (3) 3268-1196; internet www.jbpa.or.jp; f. 1957; 499 mems; Pres. TAKAO WATANABE; Exec. Dir TOSHIKAZU GOMI.

Publishers' Association for Cultural Exchange, Japan: 1-2-1, Sarugaku-cho, Chiyoda-ku, Tokyo 101-0064; tel. (3) 3291-5685; fax (3) 3233-3645; e-mail office@pace.or.jp; internet www.pace.or.jp; f. 1953; 135 mems; Pres. Dr TATSURO MATSUMAE; Man. Dir YASUKO KORENAGA.

Broadcasting and Communications

TELECOMMUNICATIONS

International Digital Communications: 5-20-8, Asakusabashi, Taito-ku, Tokyo 111; tel. (3) 5820-5080; fax (3) 5820-5363; f. 1985; 53% owned by Cable and Wireless Communications (UK); Pres. SIMON CUNNINGHAM.

Japan Telecom Co Ltd: 4-7-1, Hatchobori, Chuo-ku, Tokyo 104-8508; tel. (3) 5540-8417; fax (3) 5540-8485; internet www .japan-telecom.co.jp; fixed-line business acquired by Ripplewood

Holdings Aug. 2003; acquired by Softbank Corpn in 2004; Chair. Haruo Murakami; Pres. Hideki Kurashige.

KDDI Corpn: KDDI Bldg, 2-3-2, Nishi Shinjuku, Shinjuku-ku, Tokyo 163-03; tel. (3) 3347-7111; fax (3) 3347-6470; internet www .kddi.com; f. 2000 by merger of DDI Corpn, Kokusai Denshin Denwa Corpn (KDD) and Nippon Idou Tsushin Corpn (IDO); major international telecommunications carrier; Pres. Tadashi Onodera.

Livedoor Co Ltd: Roppongi Hills Mori Tower 38th Floor, 6-10-1 Roppongi, Minato-ku, Tokyo; e-mail info@livedoor.jp; internet www .livedoor.co.jp; internet corp.livedoor.com/en; f. 1996; internet portal; Pres. and CEO Takafumi Horie.

Nippon Telegraph and Telephone Corpn (NTT): 2-3-1, Otemachi, Chiyoda-ku, Tokyo 100-0004; tel. (3) 5359-2122; internet www.ntt.co.jp; operates local, long-distance and international services; largest telecommunications co in Japan; Pres.and CEO Norio Wada.

NTT DoCoMo: 2-11-1 Nagatacho, Chiyoda-ku, Tokyo 100-6150; tel. (3) 5156-1111; fax (3) 5156-0271; internet www.nttdocomo.com; f. 1991; operates mobile phone network; Pres. Masao Nakamura.

Tokyo Telecommunication Network Co Inc: 4-9-25, Shibaura, Minato-ku, Tokyo 108; tel. (3) 5476-0091; fax (3) 5476-7625.

KDDI, Digital Phone and Digital TU-KA also operate mobile telecommunication services in Japan.

BROADCASTING

NHK (Japan Broadcasting Corporation): 2-2-1, Jinnan, Shibuya, Tokyo 150-8001; tel. (3) 3465-1111; fax (3) 3469-8110; e-mail webmaster@www.nhk.or.jp; internet www.nhk.or.jp; f. 1925; fmrly Nippon Hose Kyokai, NHK (Japan Broadcasting Corpn); Japan's sole public broadcaster; operates five TV channels (incl. two terrestrial services—general TV and educational TV, two digital satellite services—BS-1 and BS-2 and a digital Hi-Vision service—HDTV), three radio channels, Radio 1, Radio 2, and FM Radio, and three worldwide services, NHK World TV, NHK World Premium and NHK World Radio Japan; headquarters in Tokyo, regional headquarters in Osaka, Nagoya, Hiroshima, Fukuoka, Sendai, Sapporo and Matsuyama; Pres. (vacant).

National Association of Commercial Broadcasters in Japan (NAB-J): 3-23, Kioi-cho, Chiyoda-ku, Tokyo 102-8577; tel. (3) 5213-7727; fax (3) 5213-7730; internet www.nab.or.jp; f. 1951; asscn of 201 companies (133 TV cos, 110 radio cos). Among these companies, 42 operate both radio and TV, with 664 radio stations and 8,315 TV stations (incl. relay stations); Pres. Seiichiro Ujiie; Exec. Dir Akira Sakai.

In June 2000 there were a total of 99 commercial radio broadcasting companies and 127 commercial television companies operating in Japan.

Some of the most important companies are:

Asahi Hoso—Asahi Broadcasting Corpn: 2-2-48, Ohyodominami, Kita-ku, Osaka 531-8501; tel. (6) 6458-5321; fax (6) 6458-3672; internet www.asahi.co.jp; Pres. Toshiharu Shibata.

Asahi National Broadcasting Co Ltd—TV Asahi: 6-9-1, Roppongi, Minato-ku, Tokyo 106-8001; tel. (3) 6406-1275; fax (3) 3405-3714; internet www.tv-asahi.co.jp; f. 1957; Pres. Michisada Hirose.

Bunka Hoso—Nippon Cultural Broadcasting, Inc: 1-5, Wakaba, Shinjuku-ku, Tokyo 160-8002; tel. (3) 3357-1111; fax (3) 3357-1140; internet www.joqr.co.jp; f. 1952; Pres. Shigeki Sato.

Chubu-Nippon Broadcasting Co Ltd: 1-2-8, Shinsakae, Naka-ku, Nagoya 460-8405; tel. (052) 241-8111; internet hicbc.com.co.jp; Pres. Ken-ichi Yokoyama.

Fuji Television Network, Inc: 2-4-8, Daiba, Minato-ku, Tokyo 137-8088; tel. (3) 5500-8888; fax (3) 5500-8027; internet www.fujitv .co.jp; f. 1959; 22.5% stake owned by Nippon Broadcasting; Pres. Hisashi Hieda.

Kansai TV Hoso (KTV)—Kansai: 2-1-7, Ogimachi, Kita-ku, Osaka 530-8408; tel. (6) 6314-8888; internet www.ktv.co.jp; Pres. Michio Izuma.

Mainichi Hoso (MBS)—Mainichi Broadcasting System, Inc: 17-1, Chayamachi, Kita-ku, Osaka 530-8304; tel. (6) 6359-1123; fax (6) 6359-3503; internet mbs.co.jp; Pres. Masahiro Yamamoto.

Nippon Hoso—Nippon Broadcasting System, Inc: 2-4-8, Daiba, Minato-ku, Tokyo 137-8686; tel. (3) 5500-1234; internet www.1242 .com; f. 1954; 49.8% stake owned by Livedoor Co Ltd; Pres. Michiyasu Kawauchi.

Nippon TV Hoso-MO (NTV)—Nippon Television Network Corpn: 1-6-1 Higashi Shimbashi, Minato-ku, Tokyo 105-7444; tel. (3) 6215-3156; fax (3) 6215-3157; internet www.ntv.co.jp; f. 1953; Pres. Seiichiro Ujiie.

Okinawa TV Hoso (OTV)—Okinawa Television Broadcasting Co Ltd: 1-2-20, Kumoji, Naha 900-8588; tel. (988) 63-2111; fax (988) 61-0193; internet www.otv.co.jp; f. 1959; Pres. Bunki Toma.

Radio Tampa—Nihon Short-Wave Broadcasting Co: 1-9-15, Akasaka, Minato-ku, Tokyo 107-8373; tel. (3) 3583-8151; fax (3) 3583-7441; internet www.tampa.co.jp; f. 1954; Pres. Tamio Ikeda.

Ryukyu Hoso (RBC)—Ryukyu Broadcasting Co: 2-3-1, Kumoji, Naha 900-8711; tel. (98) 867-2151; fax (98) 864-5732; internet www .rbc-ryukyu.co.jp; f. 1954; Pres. Yoshio Ishigake.

TV Osaka (TVO)—Television Osaka, Inc: 1-2-18, Otemae, Chuo-ku, Osaka 540-8519; tel. (6) 6947-0019; fax (6) 6946-9796; internet www.tv-osaka.co.jp; f. 1982; Pres. Makoto Fukagawa.

TV Tokyo (TX)—Television Tokyo Channel 12 Ltd: 4-3-12, Toranomon, Minato-ku, Tokyo 105-8012; tel. (3) 3432-1212; fax (3) 5473-3447; internet www.tv-tokyo.co.jp; f. 1964; Pres. Yutaka Ichiki.

Tokyo –Hoso (TBS)—Tokyo Broadcasting System, Inc: 5-3-6, Akasaka, Minato-ku, Tokyo 107-8006; tel. (3) 3746-1111; fax (3) 3588-6378; internet www.tbs.co.jp/index.html; f. 1951; Chair. Hiroshi Shiho; Pres. Yukio Sunahara.

Yomiuri TV Hoso (YTV)—Yomiuri Telecasting Corporation: 2-2-33, Shiromi, Chuo-ku, Osaka 540-8510; tel. (6) 6947-2111; internet www.ytv.co.jp; f. 1958; 20 hrs colour broadcasting daily; Pres. Tomonari Doi.

Satellite, Cable and Digital Television

In addition to the two broadcast satellite services that NHK introduced in 1989, a number of commercial satellite stations are in operation. Cable television is available in many urban areas, and in 1996/97 there were some 12.6m. subscribers to cable services in Japan. Satellite digital television services, which first became available in 1996, are provided by Japan Digital Broadcasting Services (f. 1998 by the merger of PerfecTV and JSkyB—now Sky Perfect Communications Inc) and DirecTV. Terrestrial digital broadcasting was launched in Japan in December 2003.

Finance

(cap. = capital; p.u. = paid up; res = reserves; dep. = deposits; m. = million; brs = branches; amounts in yen)

BANKING

Japan's central bank and bank of issue is the Bank of Japan. More than one-half of the credit business of the country is handled by 131 private commercial banks, 32 trust banks and three long-term credit banks, collectively designated 'All Banks'.

Of the private commercial banks, the most important are the eight city banks, some of which have a long and distinguished history, originating in the time of the *zaibatsu*, the private entrepreneurial organizations on which Japan's capital wealth was built before the Second World War. Although the *zaibatsu* were abolished as integral industrial and commercial enterprises during the Allied Occupation, the several businesses and industries that bear the former *zaibatsu* names, such as Mitsubishi, Mitsui and Sumitomo, continue to operate and to give each other mutual assistance through their respective banks and trust corporations.

Among the commercial banks, the Bank of Tokyo-Mitsubishi specializes in foreign-exchange business, while the Industrial Bank of Japan (now part of Mizuho Bank Ltd) finances capital investment by industry. Shinsei Bank and Nippon Credit Bank (now Aozora Bank) also specialize in industrial finance; the work of these three privately-owned banks is supplemented by the government-controlled Development Bank of Japan.

The Government has established a number of other specialized institutions to provide services that are not offered by the private banks. Thus the Japan Bank for International Cooperation advances credit for the export of heavy industrial products and the import of raw materials in bulk. A Housing Loan Corporation assists firms in building housing for their employees, while the Agriculture, Forestry and Fisheries Finance Corporation provides loans to the named industries for equipment purchases. Similar services are provided for small enterprises by the Japanese Finance Corporation for Small Business (now the Japanese Finance Corporation for Small and Medium Enterprise).

An important financial role is played by co-operatives and by the many small enterprise institutions. Each prefecture has its own federation of co-operatives, with the Central Co-operative Bank of Agriculture and Forestry as the common central financial institution. This bank also acts as an agent for the government-controlled Agriculture, Forestry and Fisheries Finance Corporation.

There are also two types of private financial institutions for small business. There were 277 Credit Co-operatives, with total assets of

22,000,000m. yen, and 369 Shinkin Banks (credit associations), which lend only to members. The latter also receive deposits.

The most common form of savings is through the government-operated Postal Savings System, which collects small savings from the public by means of the post office network. Total deposits amounted to 248,000,000m. yen in November 1998. The funds thus made available are used as loan funds by government financial institutions, through the Ministry of Finance's Trust Fund Bureau. In 2004 plans were announced for privatization of Japan Post, which was expected to be split into four companies by April 2007.

In June 1998 the Financial Supervisory Agency (now the Financial Services Agency) was established to regulate Japan's financial institutions.

Central Bank

Nippon Ginko (Bank of Japan): 2-1-1, Hongoku-cho, Nihombashi, Chuo-ku, Tokyo 100-8630; tel. (3) 3279-1111; fax (3) 5200-2256; e-mail prd@info.boj.or.jp; internet www.boj.or.jp; f. 1882; cap. 100m., res 2,493,915m., dep. 72,609,780m. (2004); Gov. Toshihiko Fukui; Dep. Govs Toshiro Muto, Kazumasa Iwata; 32 brs.

Principal Commercial Banks

Ashikaga Bank Ltd: 4-1-25, Sakura, Utsunomiya, Tochigi 320-8610; tel. (286) 22-0111; e-mail ashigin@ssctnet.or.jp; internet www.ashikagabank.co.jp; f. 1895; nationalized Nov. 2003 owing to insolvency; cap. 147,429m., res 1,859m., dep. 5,055,042m. (March 2003); Pres. Norito Ikeda; 140 brs.

Bank of Fukuoka Ltd: 2-13-1, Tenjin, Chuo-ku, Fukuoka 810-8727; tel. (92) 723-2591; fax (92) 711-1746; f. 1945; cap. 58,658m., res 245,835m., dep. 6,411,752m. (March 2003); Chair. Kiyoshi Teramoto; Pres. Ryoji Tsukuda.

Bank of Tokyo-Mitsubishi Ltd: 2-7-1, Marunouchi, Chiyoda-ku, Tokyo 100-8388; tel. (3) 93240-1111; fax (3) 93240-4197; internet www.btm.co.jp; subsidiary of Mitsubishi Tokyo Financial Group; f. 1996 as a result of merger between Bank of Tokyo Ltd (f. 1946) and Mitsubishi Bank Ltd (f. 1880); specializes in international banking and financial business; agreement signed in Aug. 2004 for merger of Mitsubishi Tokyo Financial Group with UFJ Holdings by Oct. 2005; cap. 871,973m., res 819,583m., dep. 64,347,975m. (March 2003); Chair. Satoru Kishi; Pres. Shigemitsu Miki; 805 brs.

Bank of Yokohama Ltd: 3-1-1, Minatomirai, Nishi-ku, Yokohama, Kanagawa 220-8611; tel. (45) 225-1111; fax (45) 225-1160; e-mail iroffice@hamagin.co.jp; internet www.boy.co.jp; f. 1920; cap. 188,223m., res 305,307m., dep. 9,202,366m. (March 2004); Pres. and CEO Sadaaki Hirasawa; 184 brs.

Chiba Bank Ltd: 1–2, Chiba-minato, Chuo-ku, Chiba 260-8720; tel. (43) 245-1111; e-mail int@chibabank.co.jp; internet www.chibabank.co.jp; f. 1943; cap. 121,019m., res 189,524m., dep. 7,463,569m. (March 2003); Dir Kenji Yasui; Pres. Tsuneo Hayakawa; 163 brs.

Hachijuni Bank: 178-8 Okada, Nagano-shi, Nagano 380-8682; tel. (26) 227-1182; fax (26) 226-5077; internet www.82bank.co.jp; f. 1931; cap. 52,243m., res 108,365m., dep. 5,197,137m. (March 2004); Pres. Kazuyuki Narusawa.

Hokuriku Bank Ltd: 1-2-26, Tsutsumichodori, Toyama 930-8637; tel. (764) 237-111; fax (764) 915-908; e-mail kokusaibu@hokugin.co.jp; internet www.hokugin.co.jp; f. 1877; cap. 140,409m., res 14,667m., dep. 5,245,753m. (March 2003); Pres. Shigeo Takagi; 191 brs.

Japan Net Bank: internet www.japannetbank.co.jp; f. 2000; Japan's first internet-only bank.

Joyo Bank Ltd: 2-5-5, Minami-machi, Mito-shi, Ibaraki 310-0021; tel. (29) 231-2151; fax (29) 255-6522; e-mail joyointl@po.net-ibaraki.ne.jp; internet www.joyobank.co.jp; f. 1935; cap. 85,113m., res 263,511m., dep. 6,203,315m. (March 2003); Chair. Toranosuke Nishino; Pres. Isao Shibuya; 175 brs.

Mizuho Bank Ltd: 1-5 Uchisaiwai-cho, 1-chrome, Chiyodu-ku, Tokyo 100-0011; tel. (3) 3596-1111; fax (3) 3596-2179; internet www.mizuhobank.co.jp; f. 1971 as Dai-Ichi Kangyo Bank; merged with Fuji Bank and Industrial Bank of Japan to form above in 2002; cap. 650,000m., res 909,757m., dep. 64,672,802m. (March 2004); Pres. and CEO Katsuyuki Sugita; 334 brs.

North Pacific Bank (Hokuyo Bank): 3-11 Odori Nishi, Sapporo 060-8661; tel. (11) 261-1416; fax (11) 232-6921; internet www.hokuyobank.co.jp; f. 1917 as Hokuyo Sogo Bank Ltd; assumed present name in 1989; cap. 54,993m., res 64,646m., dep. 5,404,646m. (March 2003); Chair. Masanao Takei; Pres. Iwao Takamuki.

Resona Bank Ltd: 2-2-1, Bingo-machi, Chuo-ku, Osaka 540-8610; tel. (6) 6271-1221; internet www.resona-gr.co.jp; f. 1918; merged with Asahi Bank in 2002 and changed name as above; cap. 279,928m., res 538,853m., dep. 25,289,367m. (March 2004); Chair. Eiji Hosoya; Pres. Masaaki Nomura; 367 brs.

Shizuoka Bank Ltd: 1-10, Gofuku-cho, Shizuoka 420-8760; tel. (54) 261-3131; fax (54) 344-0090; internet www.shizuokabank.co.jp; f. 1943; cap. 90,845m., res 69,975m., dep. 7,259,476m. (March 2003); Chair. Soichiro Kamiya; Pres. Yasuo Matsuura; 199 brs.

Sumitomo Mitsui Banking Corpn: 1-2 Yuraku-cho, Chiyoda-ku, Tokyo 100-0006; tel. (3) 3230-8811; fax (3) 3239-4170; internet www.smbc.co.jp; f. 1895; merged with Sakura Bank Ltd in April 2001 and assumed present name; wholly-owned subsidiary of Sumitomo Mitsui Financial Group (SMFG—established Dec. 2002); plans for merger between SMFG and Daiwa Securities announced Feb. 2005; cap. 559,985m., res 1,642,823m., dep. 84,195,075m. (March 2004); Chair. Akishige Okada; Pres. Yoshifumi Nishikawa; 351 brs.

Tokyo Star Bank: 1-6-16 Akasaka, Minato-ku, Tokyo; tel. (3) 3586-3111; fax (3) 3582-8949; internet www.tokyostarbank.co.jp; f. 1950 as Tokyo Sogo Bank, name changed as above in 2001; cap. 21,000m., res 19,080m., dep. 1,093,419m. (March 2003); Chair. Shoichi Osada; Pres. Todd Budge; 100 brs.

UFJ Bank Ltd: 3-5-6, Fushimi-machi, Chuo-ku, Osaka-shi, Osaka 541-8530; tel. (6) 6206-8111; fax (6) 6299-1066; internet www.ufj.co.jp; subsidiary of UFJ Holdings, Inc.; f. April 2001 following merger of Sanwa Bank, Tokai Bank, and Toyo Trust and Banking; agreement signed in Aug. 2004 for merger of UFJ Holdings with Mitsubishi Tokyo Financial Group by Oct. 2005; cap. 843,582m., res 1,469,757m., dep. 61,028,460m. (March 2003); Pres.and CEO Takamune Okihara.

Principal Trust Banks

Chuo Mitsui Trust and Banking Co Ltd: 3-33-1, Shiba, Minato-ku, Chuo-ku, Tokyo 105-8574; tel. (3) 5232-3331; fax (3) 5232-8879; internet www.chuomitsui.co.jp; f. 1962 as Chuo Trust and Banking Co Ltd, name changed as above in 2000, following merger with Mitsui Trust and Banking Co Ltd; cap. 356,264m., res 77,299m., dep. 10,156,148m. (March 2004); Pres. Kazuo Tanabe; 169 brs.

Mitsubishi Trust and Banking Corporation: 1-4-5 Marunouchi, Chiyoda-ku, Tokyo 100-8212; tel. (3) 3212-1211; fax (3) 3514-6660; internet www.mitsubishi-trust.co.jp; subsidiary of Mitsubishi Tokyo Financial Group; f. 1927; absorbed Nippon Trust Bank Ltd and Tokyo Trust Bank Ltd in Oct. 2001; agreement signed in Aug. 2004 for merger of Mitsubishi Tokyo Financial Group with UFJ Holdings by Oct. 2005; cap. 324,279m., res 264,428m., dep. 16,848,004m. (March 2003); Chair. Toyoshi Nakano; Pres. Akio Utsumi; 54 brs.

Mizuho Trust and Banking Co Ltd: 1-2-1, Yaesu, Chuo-ku, Tokyo 103-8670; tel. (3) 3278-8111; fax (3) 3281-6947; internet www.mizuho-tb.co.jp; fmrly Yasuda Trust and Banking Co Ltd; f. 1925; cap. 247,231m., res 118,487m., dep. 4,200,412m. (March 2003); Chair. Takahiko Kiminami; Pres. and CEO Hiroaki Etoh; 50 brs.

Sumitomo Trust and Banking Co Ltd: 4-5-33, Kitahama, Chuo-ku, Osaka 540-8639; tel. (6) 6220-2121; fax (6) 6220-2043; e-mail ipda@sumitomotrust.co.jp; internet www.sumitomotrust.co.jp; f. 1925; cap. 287,015m., res 373,155m., dep. 12,053,917m. (March 2004); Chair. Hitoshi Murakami; Pres. Atsushi Takahashi; 57 brs.

UFJ Trust Bank: 1-4-3, Marunouchi, Chiyoda-ku, Tokyo 100-0005; tel. (3) 3287-2211; fax (3) 3201-1448; internet www.ufjtrustbank.co.jp; subsidiary of UFJ Holdings, Inc; f. 1959 as Toyo Trust and Banking; merged with Sanwa Bank Ltd and Tokai Bank Ltd in April 2001 (see above); agreement signed in Aug. 2004 for merger of UFJ Holdings with Mitsubishi Tokyo Financial Group by Oct. 2005; cap. 280,536m., res 19,966m., dep. 4,270,193m. (March 2003); Pres. Shintaro Yasuda; 56 brs.

Long-Term Credit Banks

Aozora Bank: 3-1, Kudan-minami, Chiyoda-ku, Tokyo 102-8660; tel. (3) 3263-1111; fax (3) 3265-7024; e-mail sora@aozora.co.jp; internet www.aozorabank.co.jp; f. 1957; nationalized Dec. 1998, sold to consortium led by Softbank Corpn in Aug. 2000; fmrly The Nippon Credit Bank, name changed as above 2001; 62% owned by Cerberus Group; cap. 419,781m., res 36,731m., dep. 4,413,509m. (March 2004); Pres. and CEO Hiroshi Maruyama; 17 brs.

Mizuho Corporate Bank Ltd (The Industrial Bank of Japan Ltd): 3-3, Marunouchi, Chiyoda-ku, Tokyo 100-8210; tel. (3) 3214-1111; fax (3) 3201-7643; internet www.mizuhocbk.co.jp; f. 1902; renamed as above in 2002 following merger of the Dai-Ichi Kangyo Bank, the Fuji Bank and the Industrial Bank of Japan; medium- and long-term financing; cap. 1,070,965m., res 672,400m., dep. 51,643,176m. (March 2004); Pres. and CEO Hiroshi Saito; 23 domestic brs, 20 overseas brs.

Shinsei Bank Ltd: 2-1-8, Uchisaiwai-cho, Chiyoda-ku, Tokyo 100-8501; tel. (3) 5511-5111; fax (3) 5511-5505; internet www.shinseibank.co.jp; f. 1952 as The Long-Term Credit Bank of Japan; nationalized Oct. 1998, sold to Ripplewood Holdings (USA), renamed as above June 2000; cap. 180,853m., res 300,941m., dep. 4,818,547m. (March 2004); Pres. Thierry Porte; 23 brs.

Co-operative Bank

Shinkin Central Bank: 3-8-1, Kyobashi, Chuo-ku, Tokyo 104-0031; tel. (3) 3563-4111; fax (3) 3563-7553; internet www.shinkin.co.jp; f. 1950; cap. 290,998m., res 494,202m. (March 2001), dep. 25,505,148m. (March 2004); Chair. YUKIHIKO NAGANO; Pres. YASUTAKA MIYAMOTO; 17 brs.

Principal Government Credit Institutions

Agriculture, Forestry and Fisheries Finance Corporation: Koko Bldg, 1-9-3, Otemachi, Chiyoda-ku, Tokyo 100-0004; tel. (3) 3270-2261; e-mail intl@afc.go.jp; internet www.afc.go.jp; f. 1953; finances mainly plant and equipment investment; Gov. TOSHIHIKO TSURUOKA; Dep. Gov. SHIGEO OHARA; 22 brs.

Development Bank of Japan: 1-9-1, Otemachi, Chiyoda-ku, Tokyo 100-0004; tel. (3) 3244-1770; fax (3) 3245-1938; e-mail safukas@dbj.go.jp; internet www.dbj.go.jp; f. 1951 as the Japan Development Bank; renamed Oct. 1999 following consolidation with the Hokkaido and Tohoku Development Finance Public Corpn; provides long-term loans; subscribes for corporate bonds; guarantees corporate obligations; invests in specific projects; borrows funds from Govt and abroad; issues external bonds and notes; provides market information and consulting services for prospective entrants to Japanese market; cap. 1,182,286m., res 1,000,908m., dep. 1,596,630m. (March 2003); Gov. TAKESHI KOMURA; Dep. Govs NORITADA TERASAWA, KIMIO YAMAGUCHI; 10 domestic brs, 6 overseas brs.

Housing Loan Corporation: 1-4-10, Koraku, Bunkyo-ku, Tokyo 112-8570; tel. (3) 3812-1111; fax (3) 5800-8257; internet www.jyukou.go.jp; f. 1950 to provide long-term capital for the construction of housing at low interest rates; cap. 97,200m. (1994); plans announced by Japanese Government to abolish the Housing Loan Corporation in 2006; Pres. SUSUMU TAKAHASHI; Vice-Pres. HIROYUKI ITOU; 12 brs.

Japan Bank for International Cooperation (JBIC): 1-4-1, Otemachi, Chiyoda-ku, Tokyo 100-8144; tel. (3) 5218-3101; fax (3) 5218-3955; internet www.jbic.go.jp; f. 1999 by merger of The Export-Import Bank of Japan (f. 1950) and The Overseas Economic Co-operation Fund (f. 1961); governmental financial institution, responsible for Japan's external economic policy and co-operation activities; cap. 7,489,844m., res 889,055m., dep. 1,589,084m. (March 2003); Gov. KYOSUKE SHINOZAWA.

Japan Finance Corporation for Small and Medium Enterprise: 9-3, Otemachi 1–chome, Chiyoda-ku, Tokyo 100-0004; tel. (3) 3270-0505; fax (3) 3279-5910; internet www.jasme.go.jp; f. 1953 to promote long-term growth and development of small businesses by providing the necessary funds and information on their use in accordance with national policy; cap. 433,715m. (Jan. 2002); wholly subscribed by Govt; Gov. TOMIO TSUTSUMI; Vice-Gov. SOHEI HIDAKA; 58 brs.

National Life Finance Corporation: Koko Bldg, 1-9-3, Otemachi, Chiyoda-ku, Tokyo 100-0004; tel. (3) 3270-1361; internet www.kokukin.go.jp; f. 1999 following consolidation of The People's Finance Corpn (f. 1949 to provide business funds, particularly to small enterprises unable to obtain loans from banks and other private financial institutions) and the Environmental Sanitation Business Finance Corpn (f. 1967 to improve sanitary facilities); cap. 347,971m. (July 2003); Gov. NOBUAKI USUI; 152 brs.

Norinchukin Bank (Central Co-operative Bank for Agriculture, Forestry and Fisheries): 1-13-2, Yuraku-cho, Chiyoda-ku, Tokyo 100; tel. (3) 3279-0111; fax (3) 3218-5177; internet www.nochubank.or.jp; f. 1923; main banker to agricultural, forestry and fisheries co-operatives; receives deposits from individual co-operatives, federations and agricultural enterprises; extends loans to these and to local govt authorities and public corpns; adjusts excess and shortage of funds within co-operative system; issues debentures, invests funds and engages in other regular banking business; cap. 1,224,999m., res 1,107,766m., dep. 55,535,904m. (March 2004); Pres. HIROFUMI UENO; 39 brs.

Shoko Chukin Bank (Central Co-operative Bank for Commerce and Industry): 2-10-17, Yaesu, Chuo-ku, Tokyo 104-0028; tel. (3) 3272-6111; fax (3) 3272-6169; e-mail JDK06560@nifty.ne.jp; internet www.shokochukin.go.jp; f. 1936 to provide general banking services to facilitate finance for smaller enterprise co-operatives and other organizations formed mainly by small- and medium-sized enterprises; issues debentures; cap. 514,265m., res 110,334m., dep. 10,732,690m. (March 2004); Pres. TADASHI EZAKI; Dep. Pres. SHIGENORI SHIODA; 99 brs.

Other government financial institutions include the Japan Finance Corpn for Municipal Enterprises, the Small Business Credit Insurance Corpn and the Okinawa Development Finance Corpn.

Principal Foreign Banks

In 2004 there were 84 foreign banks operating in Japan.

ABN AMRO Bank NV (Netherlands): Atago Green Hills MORI Tower, 32nd Floor, 2-5-1, Atago, Minato-ku, Tokyo 105-6231; tel. (3) 5405-6500; fax (3) 5405-6900; Br. Man. ATSUSHI WATANABE.

Bangkok Bank Public Co Ltd (Thailand): Bangkok Bank Bldg, 2-8-10, Nishi Shinbashi, Minato-ku, Tokyo 105-0003; tel. (3) 3503-3333; fax (3) 3502-6420; Senior Vice-Pres. and Gen. Man. (Japan) THAWEE PHUANGKETKEOW; br. in Osaka.

Bank of America NA: Sanno Park Tower, 15th Floor, 2-11-1, Nagatacho, Chiyoda-ku, Tokyo 100-6115; tel. (3) 3508-5800; fax (3) 3508-5811.

Bank of India: Mitsubishi Denki Bldg, 2-2-3, Marunouchi, Chiyoda-ku, Tokyo 100-0005; tel. (3) 3212-0911; fax (3) 3214-8667; e-mail boitok@gol.com; CEO (Japan) P. SIVARAMAN; br. in Osaka.

Bank Negara Indonesia (Persero): Rm 117-18, Kokusai Bldg, 3-1-1, Marunouchi, Chiyoda-ku, Tokyo 100-0005; tel. (3) 3214-5621; fax (3) 3201-2633; e-mail tky-br@ptbni.co.jp; Gen. Man. SURYO DANISWORO.

Bank One NA (USA): Hibiya Central Bldg, 7th Floor, 1-2-9, Nishi Shimbashi, Minato-ku, Tokyo 105; tel. (3) 3596-8700; fax (3) 3596-8744; Sr Vice-Pres. and Gen. Man. YOSHIO KITAZAWA.

Barclays Bank PLC (UK): Urbannet Otemachi Bldg, 15th Floor, 2-2-2, Otemachi, Chiyoda-ku, Tokyo 100-0004; tel. (3) 3276-5100; fax (3) 3276-5085; CEO ANDY SIMMONDS.

Bayerische Hypo- und Vereinsbank AG (Germany): Otemachi 1st Sq. East Tower, 17th Floor, 1-5-1, Otemachi, Chiyoda-ku, Tokyo 100-0004; tel. (3) 3284-1341; fax (3) 3284-1370; Exec. Dirs Prof. PETER BARON, KENJI AKAGI.

BNP Paribas (France): Tokyo Sankei Bldg, 22rd Floor, 1-7-2, Otemachi, Chiyoda-ku, Tokyo 100-0004; tel. (3) 5290-1000; fax (3) 5290-1111; internet www.bnpparibas.co.jp; CEO (Japan) ERIC MARTIN; Representative in Japan HIROAKI INOUE; br. in Osaka.

Commerzbank AG (Germany): Tokio Marine Bldg, Shinkan 9/F 1-2-1, Marunouchi, Chiyoda-ku, Tokyo 100-0005; tel. (3) 3286-4989; fax (3) 3286-4987; Gen. Man. NORIO YATOMI.

Crédit Agricole Indosuez (France): Indosuez Bldg, 3-29-1, Kanda Jimbo-cho, Chiyoda-ku, Tokyo 101; tel. (3) 3261-3001; fax (3) 3261-0426; Sr Country Exec. FRANÇOIS BEYER.

Deutsche Bank AG (Germany): Sanno Park Tower, 2-11-1 Nagatacho, Chiyoda-ku, Tokyo 100-6170; tel. (3) 5156-4000; fax (3) 5156-6070; internet www.japan.db.com; CEO and Chief Country Officer JOHN MACFARLANE.

The Hongkong and Shanghai Banking Corpn Ltd (Hong Kong): HSBC Bldg, 3-11-1, Nihombashi, Chuo-ku, Tokyo 103-0027; tel. (3) 5203-3000; fax (3) 5203-3108; CEO NORMAN A. WILSON; br. in Osaka.

International Commercial Bank of China (Taiwan): Togin Bldg, 1-4-2, Marunouchi, Chiyoda-ku, Tokyo 100; tel. (3) 3211-2501; fax (3) 3216-5686; Sr Vice-Pres. and Gen. Man. SHIOW-SHYONG LAI; br. in Osaka.

JP Morgan Chase Bank (USA): Akasaka Park Bldg, 11th–13th Floors, 5-2-20, Akasaka, Minato-ku, Tokyo 107; tel. (3) 5570-7500; fax (3) 5570-7960; Man. Dir and Gen. Man. NORMAN J. T. SCOTT; br. in Osaka.

Korea Exchange Bank (Republic of Korea): Shin Kokusai Bldg, 3-4-1, Marunouchi, Chiyoda-ku, Tokyo 100; tel. (3) 3216-3561; fax (3) 3214-4491; f. 1967; Acting Gen. Man. CHO YOUNG-HYO; brs in Osaka and Fukuoka.

Lloyds TSB Bank PLC (UK): Akasaka Twin Tower, New Tower 5th Floor, 11-7, Akasaka 2-chome, Minato-ku, Tokyo 107-0052; tel. (3) 3589-7700; fax (3) 3589-7722; e-mail tokyo@lloydstsb.co.jp; internet www.lloydstsb.co.jp; Principal Man. (Japan) KAH HIN LIM.

Morgan Guaranty Trust Co of New York (USA): Akasaka Park Bldg, 5-2-20, Akasaka, Minato-ku, Tokyo 107-6151; tel. (3) 5573-1100; Man. Dir TAKESHI FUJIMAKI.

National Bank of Pakistan: S. K. Bldg, 3rd Floor, 2-7-4, Nishi Shimbashi, Minato-ku, Tokyo 105; tel. (3) 3502-0331; fax (3) 3502-0359; f. 1949; Gen. Man. ZIAULLAH KHAN.

Oversea-Chinese Banking Corpn Ltd (Singapore): Akasaka Twin Tower, 15th Floor, 2-17-22, Akasaka, Minato-ku, Tokyo 107-0052; tel. (3) 5570-3421; fax (3) 5570-3426; Gen. Man. ONG SING YIK.

Société Générale (France): Ark Mori Bldg, 1-12-32, Akasaka, Minato-ku, Tokyo 107-6014; tel. (3) 5549-5800; fax (3) 5549-5809; Chief Operating Officer SHOZO NURISHI; br. in Osaka.

Standard Chartered Bank (UK): 21st Floor, Sanno Park Tower, 2-11-1, Nagata-cho, Chiyoda-ku, Tokyo 100-6155; tel. (3) 5511-1200; fax (3) 5511-9333; Chief Exec. (Japan) JULIAN WYNTER.

State Bank of India: 352 South Tower, Yuraku-cho Denki Bldg, 1-7-1, Yuraku-cho, Chiyoda-ku, Tokyo 100-0006; tel. (3) 3284-0085; fax (3) 3201-5750; e-mail sbitok@gol.com; internet www.sbijapan.com; CEO J. K. SINHA; br. in Osaka.

UBS AG: East Tower, Otemachi First Square, 5-1 Otemachi 1-chome, Chiyoda-ku, Tokyo 100-0004; tel. (3) 5293-3500; fax (3) 5293-3620; Man. Mitsuru Tsunemi.

Union de Banques Arabes et Françaises (UBAF) (France): Sumitomo Jimbocho Bldg, 8th Floor, 3-25, Kanda Jimbocho, Chiyoda-ku, Tokyo 101-0051; tel. (3) 3263-8821; fax (3) 3263-8820; e-mail antoine.homsy@ubaf.fr; Gen. Man. (Japan) Antoine R. Homsy; br. in Osaka.

WestLB AG (Germany): Fukoku Seimei Bldg, 2-2-2, Uchisaiwaicho, Chiyoda-ku, Tokyo 100-0011; tel. (3) 5510-6200; fax (3) 5510-6299; internet www.westlb.co.jp; Man. Dir and Gen. Man. Michael Kramer.

Bankers' Associations

Japanese Bankers Association: 1-3-1, Marunouchi, Chiyoda-ku, Tokyo 100-8216; tel. (3) 3216-3761; fax (3) 3201-5608; internet www.zenginkyo.or.jp; f. 1945; fmrly Federation of Bankers Associations of Japan; 132 full mems, 48 associate mems, 65 special mems, 3 bank holding company mems; Chair. Terunobu Maeda (designate).

Tokyo Bankers Association, Inc: 1-3-1, Marunouchi, Chiyoda-ku, Tokyo 100-8216; tel. (3) 3216-3761; fax (3) 3201-5608; f. 1945; 108 mem. banks; conducts the above Association's administrative business; Chair. Terunobu Maeda (designate).

National Association of Labour Banks: 2-5-15, Kanda Suru-gadai, Chiyoda-ku, Tokyo 101-0062; tel. (3) 3295-6721; fax (3) 3295-6752; Pres. Tetsuei Tokugawa.

Regional Banks Association of Japan: 3-1-2, Uchikanda, Chiyoda-ku, Tokyo 101-0047; tel. (3) 3252-5171; fax (3) 3254-8664; f. 1936; 64 mem. banks; Chair. Sadaaki Hirosawa.

Second Association of Regional Banks: 5, Sanban-cho, Chiyoda-ku, Tokyo 102-0075; tel. (3) 3262-2181; fax (3) 3262-2339; f. 1989; fmrly National Asscn of Sogo Banks; 65 commercial banks; Chair. Masanao Takei.

STOCK EXCHANGES

Jasdaq Market: 1-14-8 Nihombashi-Ningyocho, Chuo-ku, Tokyo 103-0013; tel. (3) 5641-1818; internet www.jasdaq.co.jp.

Nagoya Stock Exchange: 3-3-17, Sakae, Naka-ku, Nagoya 460-0008; tel. (52) 262-3172; fax (52) 241-1527; e-mail kikaku@nse.or.jp; internet www.nse.or.jp; f. 1949; Pres. Hiroshi Fujita; Sr Exec. Dir Kazunori Ishimoto.

Osaka Securities Exchange: 1-8-16, Kitahama, Chuo-ku, Osaka 541-0041; tel. (6) 4706-0875; fax (6) 6231-2639; e-mail koho@ose.or.jp; internet www.ose.or.jp/e; f. 1949; 83 regular transaction partners, 5 transaction partners in futures and options trading, 2 IPO transaction partners; Pres.and CEO Michio Yoneda.

Sapporo Securities Exchange: 5-14-1, Nishi, Minami Ichijo, Chuo-ku, Sapporo 060-0061; tel. (11) 241-6171; Pres. Yoshiro Itoh.

Tokyo Stock Exchange, Inc: 2-1, Nihombashi-kabuto-cho, Chuo-ku, Tokyo 103-8220; tel. (3) 3666-0141; fax (3) 3662-0547; internet www.tse.or.jp; f. 1949; 107 general trading participants, 79 bond futures trading participants, 2 stock index futures trading participants (Nov. 2003); Pres. and CEO Masaaki Tsuchida; Sr Man. Dir and CFO Sadao Yoshino.

Supervisory Body

The Securities and Exchange Surveillance Commission: 3-1-1, Kasumigaseki, Chiyoda-ku, Tokyo 100; tel. (3) 3581-7868; fax (3) 5251-2136; f. 1992 for the surveillance of securities and financial futures transactions; Chair. Toshihiro Mizuhara.

INSURANCE

Principal Life Companies

Aetna Heiwa Life Insurance Co Ltd: 3-2-16, Ginza, Chuo-ku, Tokyo 104-8119; tel. (3) 3563-8111; fax 3374-7114; f. 1907; Pres. Barry S. Halpern.

American Family Life Assurance Co of Columbus AFLAC Japan: Shinjuku Mitsui Bldg, 12th Floor, 2-1-1, Nishishinjuku, Shinjuku-ku, Tokyo 163-0456; tel. (3) 3344-2701; fax (3) 0424-41-3001; f. 1974; Chair. Yoshiki Otake; Pres. Hidefumi Matsui.

American Life Insurance Co (Japan): 1-1-3, Marunouchi, Chiyoda-ku, Tokyo 100-0005; tel. (3) 3284-4111; fax (3) 3284-3874; f. 1972; Pres. Tomio Miyamoto.

Aoba Life Insurance Co Ltd: 3-6-30, Aobadai, Meguro-ku, Tokyo 153-8523; tel. (3) 3462-0007; fax (3) 3780-8169; Pres. Takashi Kasagami.

Asahi Mutual Life Insurance Co: 1-7-3, Nishishinjuku, Shinjuku-ku, Tokyo 163-8611; tel. (3) 3342-3111; fax (3) 3346-9397; internet www.asahi-life.co.jp; f. 1888; Pres. Yuzuru Fujita.

AXA Japan Holding Co Ltd: 1-2-19 Higashi, Shibuya-ku, Tokyo 150-8020; tel. (3) 3407-6210; internet www.axa.co.jp; Pres. and CEO Philippe Donnet.

Cardif Assurance Vie: 9/F Infoss Tower, 20-1 Sakuragaoka-cho, Shibuya-ku, Tokyo 150-0031; f. 2000; Pres. Atsushi Sakauchi.

Chiyodakasai EBISU Life Insurance Co Ltd: Ebisu MF Bldg, 6th Floor, 4-6-1, Ebisu Shibuya-ku, Tokyo 150-0013; tel. (3) 5420-8282; fax (3) 5420-8273; f. 1996; Pres. Shigeji Minoshima.

Dai-ichi Mutual Life Insurance Co: 1-13-1, Yuraku-cho, Chiyoda-ku, Tokyo 100-8411; tel. (3) 3216-1211; fax (3) 5221-8139; f. 1902; Chair. Takahide Sakurai; Pres. Tomijiro Morita.

Dai-Tokyo Happy Life Insurance Co Ltd: Shinjuku Square Tower, 17th Floor, 6-22-1, Nishishinjuku, Shinjuku-ku, Tokyo 163-1131; tel. (3) 5323-6411; fax (3) 5323-6419; f. 1996; Pres. Hitoshi Hasunuma.

DIY Life Insurance Co Ltd: 5-68-2, Nakano, Nakano-ku, Tokyo 164-0001; tel. (3) 5345-7603; fax (3) 5345-7608; f. 1999; Pres. Hitoshi Kase.

Fuji Life Insurance Co Ltd: 1-18-17, Minamisenba, Chuo-ku, Osaka-shi 542-0081; tel. (6) 6261-0284; fax (6) 6261-0113; f. 1996; Pres. Yoshiaki Yonemura.

Fukoku Mutual Life Insurance Co: 2-2-2, Uchisaiwai-cho, Chiyoda-ku, Tokyo 100-0011; tel. (3) 3508-1101; fax (3) 3597-0383; f. 1923; Chair. Takashi Kobayashi; Pres. Tomofumi Akiyama.

GE Edison Life Insurance Co: Shibuya Markcity, 1-12-1, Dogen-zaka, Shibuya-ku, Tokyo 150-8674; tel. (3) 5457-8100; fax (3) 5457-8017; acquired by American International Group (AIG) August 2003; Chair. Michael D. Fraizer; Pres. and CEO K. Rone Baldwin.

Gibraltar Life Insurance Co Ltd: 4-4-1, Nihombashi, Hongoku-cho, Chuo-ku, Tokyo 103-0021; tel. (3) 3270-8511; fax (3) 3231-8276; internet www.gib-life.co.jp; f. 1947; fmrly Kyoei Life Insurance Co Ltd, declared bankrupt Oct. 2000; Pres. Kazuo Maeda.

ING Life Insurance Co Ltd: 26th Floor, New Otani Garden Court, 4-1, Kioi-cho, Chiyoda-ku, Tokyo 102-0094; tel. (3) 5210-0300; fax (3) 5210-0430; f. 1985; Pres. Makoto Chiba.

Koa Life Insurance Co Ltd: 3-7-3, Kasumigaseki, Chiyoda-ku, Tokyo 100-0013; tel. (3) 3593-3111; fax (3) 5512-6651; internet www.koa.co.jp; f. 1996; Pres. Akio Okada.

Kyoei Kasai Shinrai Life Insurance Co Ltd: J. City Bldg, 5-8-20, Takamatsu, Nerima-ku, Tokyo 179-0075; tel. (3) 5372-2100; fax (3) 5372-7701; f. 1996; Pres. Yoshihiro Tokumitsu.

Manulife Life Insurance Co: 4-34-1, Kokuryo-cho, Chofu-shi, Tokyo 182-8621; tel. (3) 2442-7120; fax (3) 2442-7977; e-mail geoff_crickmay@manulife.com; internet www.manulife.co.jp; f. 1999; fmrly Manulife Century Life Insurance Co; Pres. and CEO Geoff Crickmay.

Meiji Life Insurance Co: 2-1-1, Marunouchi, Chiyoda-ku, Tokyo 100-0005; tel. (3) 3283-8111; fax (3) 3215-5219; internet www.meiji-life.co.jp; f. 1881; merged with Yasuda Mutual Life Insurance Co in 2004; Chair. Kenjiro Hata; Pres. Ryotaro Kaneko.

Mitsui Mutual Life Insurance Co: 1-2-3, Otemachi, Chiyoda-ku, Tokyo 100-8123; tel. (3) 3211-6111; fax (3) 5252-7265; internet www.mitsui-seimei.co.jp; f. 1927; Chair. Koshiro Sakata; Pres. Akira Miyake.

NICOS Life Insurance Co Ltd: Hongo MK Bldg, 1-28-34, Hongo, Bunkyo-ku, Tokyo 113-8414; tel. (3) 5803-3111; fax (3) 5803-3199; internet www.nicos-life.co.jp; f. 1986; Pres. Rene Muller.

Nippon Fire Partner Life Insurance Co Ltd: 3-4-2, Tsukiji, Chuo-ku, Tokyo 104-8407; tel. (3) 5565-8080; fax (3) 5565-8365; f. 1996; Pres. Hironobu Hara.

Nippon Life Insurance Co (Nissay): 3-5-12, Imabashi, Chuo-ku, Osaka 541-8501; tel. (6) 6209-4500; e-mail hosokawa15560@nissay.co.jp; internet www.nissay.co.jp; f. 1889; Chair. Josei Itoh; Pres. Ikuo Uno.

ORIX Life Insurance Corpn: Shinjuku Chuo Bldg, 5-17-5, Shinjuku, Shinjuku-ku, Tokyo 160-0022; tel. (3) 5272-2700; fax (3) 5272-2720; f. 1991; Chair. Shogo Kajinishi; Pres. Shinobu Shiraishi.

Prudential Life Insurance Co Ltd: 1-7, Kojimachi, Chiyoda-ku, Tokyo 102-0083; tel. (3) 3221-0961; fax (3) 3221-2305; f. 1987; Chair. Kiyofumi Sakaguchi; Pres. Ichiro Kono.

Saison Life Insurance Co Ltd: Sunshine Sixty Bldg, 39th Floor, 3-1-1, Higashi Ikebukuro, Toshima-ku, Tokyo 170-6067; tel. (3) 3983-6666; fax (3) 2980-0598; internet www.saison-life.co.jp; f. 1975; Chair. and Pres. Toshio Takeuchi.

Skandia Life Insurance Co (Japan) Ltd: 5-6-6, Hiroo, Shibuya-ku, Tokyo 150-0012; tel. (3) 5488-1500; fax (3) 5488-1501; f. 1996; Pres. and CEO IAIN MESSENGER.

Sony Life Insurance Co Ltd: 1-1-1, Minami-Aoyama, Minato-ku, Tokyo 107-8585; tel. (3) 3475-8811; fax (3) 3475-8914; Chair. TSUNAO HASHIMOTO; Pres. KEN IWAKI.

Sumitomo Life Insurance Co: 7-18-24, Tsukiji, Chuo-ku, Tokyo 104-8430; tel. (3) 5550-1100; fax (3) 5550-1160; f. 1907; Pres. SHINICHI YOKOYAMA.

T & D Holdings Inc.: 2-7-9 Nihonbashi, Chuo-ku, Tokyo 103-0027; tel. (3) 3231-8685; fax (3) 3231-8893; internet www.td-holdings.co.jp; f. 1895; fmrly Tokyo Mutual Life Insurance Co; T&D Financial Life Insurance Co Holdings company formed in April 2004 through merger of T&D Financial Life Insurance Co, Taiyo Mutual Life Insurance Co and Daido Life Insurance Co.; Pres. NAOTERU MIYATO.

Tokio Marine & Nichido Life Insurance Co Ltd: 5-3-16, Ginza, Chuo-ku, Tokyo 106-0041; tel. (3) 5223-2111; fax (3) 5223-2165; internet www.tmn-anshin.co.jp; Pres. SUKEAKI OHTA.

Yamato Mutual Life Insurance Co: 1-1-7, Uchisaiwai-cho, Chiyoda-ku, Tokyo 100-0011; tel. (3) 3508-3111; fax (3) 3508-3118; f. 1911; Pres. KEIJI NONOMIYA.

Yasuda Kasai Himawari Life Insurance Co Ltd: 2-1-1, Nishi-Shinjuku, Shinjuku-ku, Tokyo 163-0434; tel. (3) 3348-7011; fax (3) 3346-9415; f. 1981; fmrly INA Himawari Life Insurance Co Ltd; Chair. (vacant); Pres. MAKOTO YOSHIDA.

Yasuda Mutual Life Insurance Co: 1-9-1, Nishi-Shinjuku, Shin-juku-ku, Tokyo 169-8701; tel. (3) 3342-7111; fax (3) 3349-8104; f. 1880; merged with Meiji Life Insurance Co in 2004; Chair. YUJI OSHIMA; Pres. MIKIHIKO MIYAMOTO.

Zurich Life Insurance Co Ltd: Shinanomachi Rengakan, 35, Shinanomachi, Shinjuku-ku, Tokyo 160-0016; tel. (3) 5361-2700; fax (3) 5361-2728; f. 1996; Pres. KENICHI NOGAMI.

Principal Non-Life Companies

ACE Insurance: Arco Tower, 1-8-1, Shimomeguro, Meguro-ku, Tokyo 153-0064; tel. (3) 5740-0600; fax (3) 5740-0608; internet www.ace-insurance.co.jp; f. 1999; Chair. FUMIO TOKUHIRA; Pres. TAKASHI IMAI.

Allianz Fire and Marine Insurance Japan Ltd: MITA N. N. Bldg, 4th Floor, 4-1-23, Shiba, Minato-ku, Tokyo 108-0014; tel. (3) 5442-6500; fax (3) 5442-6509; e-mail admin@allianz.co.jp; internet www.allianz.co.jp; f. 1990; Chair. HEINZ DOLLBERG; Pres. ALEXANDER ANKEL.

The Asahi Fire and Marine Insurance Co Ltd: 2-6-2, Kaji-cho, Chiyoda-ku, Tokyo 101-8655; tel. (3) 3254-2211; fax (3) 3254-2296; e-mail asahifmi@blue.ocn.ne.jp; f. 1951; Pres. MORIYA NOGUCHI.

AXA Non-Life Insurance Co Ltd: Ariake Frontier Bldg, Tower A, 3-1-25, Ariake Koto-ku, Tokyo 135-0063; tel. (3) 3570-8900; fax (3) 3570-8911; f. 1998; Pres. GUY MARCILLAT.

The Chiyoda Fire and Marine Insurance Co Ltd: 1-28-1, Ebisu, Shibuya-ku, Tokyo 150-8488; tel. (3) 5424-9288; fax (3) 5424-9382; bought by Dai-Tokyo Fire and Marine Insurance Co in 2000, to combine in April 2001; f. 1897; Pres. KOJI FUKUDA.

The Daido Fire and Marine Insurance Co Ltd: 1-12-1, Kumoji, Naha-shi, Okinawa 900-8586; tel. (98) 867-1161; fax (98) 862-8362; f. 1971; Pres. MUNEMASA URA.

The Dai-ichi Property and Casualty Insurance Co Ltd: 1-2-10, Hirakawa-cho, Chiyoda-ku, Tokyo 102-0093; tel. (3) 5213-3124; fax (3) 5213-3306; f. 1996; Pres. TSUYOSHI SHINOHARA.

The Dai-Tokyo Fire and Marine Insurance Co Ltd: 3-25-3, Yoyogi, Shibuya-ku, Tokyo 151-8530; tel. (3) 5371-6122; fax (3) 5371-6248; internet www.daitokyo.index.or.jp; f. 1918; bought Chiyoda Fire and Marine Insurance Co in 2000; Chair. HAJIME OZAWA; Pres. AKIRA SESHIMO.

The Fuji Fire and Marine Insurance Co Ltd: 1-18-11, Minami-senba, Chuo-ku, Osaka 542-8567; tel. (6) 6271-2741; fax (6) 6266-7115; internet www.fujikasai.co.jp; f. 1918; Pres. YASUO ODA.

The Japan Earthquake Reinsurance Co Ltd: Kobuna-cho, Fuji Plaza, 4th Floor, 8-1, Nihombashi, Kobuna-cho, Chuo-ku, Tokyo 103-0024; tel. (3) 3664-6107; fax (3) 3664-6169; e-mail kanri@nihonjishin.co.jp; f. 1966; Pres. KAZUMOTO ADACHI.

JI Accident & Fire Insurance Co Ltd: A1 Bldg, 20-5, Ichiban-cho, Chiyoda-ku, Tokyo 102-0082; tel. (3) 3237-2045; fax (3) 3237-2250; internet www.jihoken.co.jp; f. 1989; Pres. TSUKASA IMURA.

The Kyoei Mutual Fire and Marine Insurance Co: 1-18-6, Shimbashi, Minato-ku, Tokyo 105-8604; tel. (3) 3504-2335; fax (3) 3508-7680; e-mail reins.intl@kyoeikasai.co.jp; internet www.kyoeikasai.co.jp; f. 1942; Pres. WATARU OZAWA.

Meiji General Insurance Co Ltd: 2-11-1, Kanda-tsukasa-cho, Chiyoda-ku, Tokyo 101-0048; tel. (3) 3257-3141; fax (3) 3257-3295; e-mail uwredept@meiji-sonpo.co.jp; internet meiji-general.aaapc.co.jp; f. 1996; Pres. SEISUKE ADACHI.

Mitsui Seimei General Insurance Co Ltd: 2-1-1, Toranomon, Minato-ku, Tokyo 105-0001; tel. (3) 3224-2830; fax (3) 3224-2677; internet www.mitsui-seimei.co.jp; f. 1996; Pres. KIYOSHI MATSUOKA.

Mitsui Sumitomo Insurance Co Ltd: 27-2, Shinkawa 2-chome, Chuo-ku, Tokyo 104-8252; tel. (3) 3297-1111; internet www.ms-ins.com; f. 2001; formed by merger of Mitsui Marine and Fire Insurance and Sumitomo Marine and Fire Insurance; Pres. and CEO HIROYUKI UEMURA; Chair. TAKEO INOKUCHI.

The Nichido Fire and Marine Insurance Co Ltd: 5-3-16, Ginza, Chuo-ku, Tokyo 104-0061; tel. (3) 3289-1066; fax (3) 3574-0646; e-mail nichido@mu2.so-net.ne.jp; internet www.mediagalaxy.co.jp/nichido; f. 1914; Chair. IKUO EGASHIRA; Pres. TAKASHI AIHARA.

The Nipponkoa Insurance Co Ltd: 3-7-3, Kasumigaseki, Chiyoda-ku, Tokyo 100-8965; tel. (3) 3593-3111; fax (3) 3593-5388; internet www.nipponkoa.co.jp; f. 1892; fmrly The Nippon Fire and Marine Insurance Co Ltd before merging with The Koa Fire and Marine Insurance Co Ltd; acquired Taiyo Fire and Marine Insurance Co Ltd in 2002; Pres. and CEO KEN MATSUZAWA.

Nissay Dowa General Insurance Co Ltd: St Luke's Tower, 8-1, Akashi-cho, Chuo-ku, Tokyo 104-8556; tel. (3) 3542-5511; fax (3) 5550-0318; internet www.nissaydowa.co.jp; f. 2001; formed by merger of Nissay General Insurance Co Ltd and Dowa Fire and Marine Insurance Co Ltd; Pres. SHUICHIRO SUDO; Chair. MASAO OKAZAKI.

The Nisshin Fire and Marine Insurance Co Ltd: 2-3 Kanda Surugadai, Chiyoda-ku, Tokyo 100-8329; tel. (3) 5282-5534; fax (3) 5282-5582; e-mail nisshin@mb.infoweb.ne.jp; internet www.nisshinfire.co.jp; f. 1908; Pres. MICHIO NODA.

Saison Automobile and Fire Insurance Co Ltd: Sunshine 60 Bldg, 3-1-1, Higashi Ikebukuro, Toshima-ku, Tokyo 170-6068; tel. (3) 3988-2572; fax (3) 3980-7367; internet www.ins-saison.co.jp; f. 1982; Pres. TOMONORI KANAI.

Secom General Insurance Co Ltd: 2-6-2, Hirakawa-cho, Chiyoda-ku, Tokyo 103-8645; tel. (3) 5216-6129; fax (3) 5216-6149; internet www.secom-sonpo.co.jp; Pres. SEIJI YAMANAKA.

Sompo Japan Insurance Inc: 26-1, Nishi-Shinjuku 1-chome, Shinjuku-ku, Tokyo 160-8338; tel. (3) 3349-3111; fax (3) 3349-4697; internet www.sompo-japan.co.jp; Pres. HIROSHI HIRANO; formed by merger of Yasuda Fire and Marine Insurance and Nissan Fire and Marine Insurance 2002.

Sony Assurance Inc.: Aromia Square 11/F, 5-37-1, Kamata, Ota-ku, Tokyo 144-8721; tel. (3) 5744-0300; fax (3) 5744-0480; internet www.sonysonpo.co.jp; f. 1999; Pres. SHINIEH YAMAMOTO.

The Sumi-Sei General Insurance Co Ltd: Sumitomo Life Yot-suya Bldg, 8-2, Honshio-cho, Shinjuku-ku, Tokyo 160-0003; tel. (3) 5360-6229; fax (3) 5360-6991; internet www.sumisei-sonpo.com; f. 1996; Chair. HIDEO NISHIMOTO; Pres. HIDEKI ISHII.

The Toa Reinsurance Co Ltd: 3-6, Kanda Surugadai, Chiyoda-ku, Tokyo 101-8703; tel. (3) 3253-3177; fax (3) 3253-5298; f. 1940; Dir TAKAYA IMASHIMIZU.

The Tokio Marine and Fire Insurance Co Ltd (Tokio Kaiji): 1-2-1, Marunouchi, Chiyoda-ku, Tokyo 100-8050; tel. (3) 3285-1900; fax (3) 5223-3040; internet www.tokiomarine.co.jp; f. 1879; Chair. SHUNJI KONO; Pres. KOUKEI HIGUCHI.

The Yasuda General Insurance Co Ltd: Shinjuku MAYNDS Tower, 29th Floor, 2-1-1, Yoyogi, Shibuya-ku, Tokyo 151-0053; tel. (3) 5352-8129; fax (3) 5352-8213; e-mail uwdept@mx7.mesh.ne.jp; f. 1996; Chair. SHIGEO FUJINO; Pres. IEJI YOSHIOKA.

The Post Office also operates life insurance and annuity plans.

Insurance Associations

The General Insurance Association of Japan Inc (Nihon Songai Hoken Kyokai): Non-Life Insurance Bldg, 2-9, Kanda Awaji-cho, Chiyoda-ku, Tokyo 101-8335; tel. (3) 3255-1437; fax (3) 3255-1234; e-mail kokusai@sonpo.or.jp; internet www.sonpo.or.jp; f. 1946; 23 mems (Nov. 2003); Chair. KEN MATSUZAWA; Exec. Dir EIJI NISHIURA.

Japan Trade and Investment Insurance Organization (Boeki Hoken Kiko): 6th Floor, 2-8-6, Nishi-Shinjuku, Minato-ku, Tokyo 105-0003; tel. (3) 3580-0321; internet www.jtio.or.jp; Pres. YUKIO OTSU.

The Life Insurance Association of Japan (Seimei Hoken Kyokai): Shin Kokusai Bldg 3-4-1, Marunouchi, Chiyoda-ku, Tokyo 100-0005; tel. (3) 3286-2652; fax (3) 3286-2630; internet www.seiho.or.jp; f. 1908; 39 mem. cos; Chair. IKUO UNO; Senior Man. Dir SHIGERU SUWA.

Non-Life Insurance Rating Organization of Japan: 1-9, Kanda-nishikicho, Chiyoda-ku, Tokyo 101-0054; tel. (3) 3233-4762; fax (3) 3295-9301; e-mail service@grp.nliro.or.jp; internet www.nliro .or.jp; f. 1964; 39 mems (July 2004); Chair. AKIO MORISHIMA; Senior Exec. Dir MASAHIRO ISHII.

Trade and Industry

CHAMBERS OF COMMERCE AND INDUSTRY

The Japan Chamber of Commerce and Industry (Nippon Shoko Kaigi-sho): 3-2-2, Marunouchi, Chiyoda-ku, Tokyo 100-0005; tel. (3) 3283-7851; fax (3) 3216-6497; e-mail info@jcci.or.jp; internet www.jcci.or.jp/home-e.html; f. 1922; the cen. org. of all chambers of commerce and industry in Japan; mems 524 local chambers of commerce and industry; Chair. YOBUO YAMAGUCHI; Pres. SATOSHI UEMATSU.

Principal chambers include:

Kobe Chamber of Commerce and Industry: 6-1, Minatojima-nakamachi, Chuo-ku, Kobe 650-8543; tel. (78) 303-5806; fax (78) 306-2348; e-mail info@kobe-cci.or.jp; internet www2.kobe-cci.or.jp/index.e.htm; f. 1878; 12,000 mems; Chair. KOSHI MIZUKOSHI; Pres. HITOSHI NAKANISHI.

Kyoto Chamber of Commerce and Industry: 240, Shoshoi-cho, Ebisugawa-agaru, Karasumadori, Nakakyo-ku, Kyoto 604-0862; tel. (75) 212-6450; fax (75) 251-0743; e-mail kyoto@kyo.or.jp; f. 1882; 13,008 mems; Chair. KAZUO INAMORI; Pres. OSAMU KOBORI.

Nagoya Chamber of Commerce and Industry: 2-10-19, Sakae, Naka-ku, Nagoya, Aichi 460-8422; tel. (52) 223-5722; fax (52) 232-5751; f. 1881; 20,622 mems; Chair. SEITARO TANIGUCHI; Pres. YOSHIKI KOBAYASHI.

Naha Chamber of Commerce and Industry: 2-2-10, Kume Naha, Okinawa; tel. (98) 868-3758; fax (98) 866-9834; e-mail cci-naha@cosmos.ne.jp; f. 1927; 4,874 mems; Chair. AKIRA SAKIMA; Pres. KOSEI YONEMURA.

Osaka Chamber of Commerce and Industry: 2-8, Hommachi-bashi, Chuo-ku, Osaka 540-0029; tel. (6) 6944-6400; fax (6) 6944-6248; e-mail intl@osaka.cci.or.jp; internet www.osaka.cci.or.jp; f. 1878; 35,069 mems; Chair. WA TASHIRO; Pres. TAKAO OHNO.

Tokyo Chamber of Commerce and Industry: 3-2-2, Marunouchi, Chiyoda-ku, Tokyo 100-0005; tel. (3) 3283-7523; fax (3) 3216-6497; e-mail kokusai@tokyo-cci.or.jp; f. 1878; 118,642 mems; Chair. NOBUO YAMAGUCHI; Pres. SATOSHI UEMATSU.

Yokohama Chamber of Commerce and Industry: Sangyo Boueki Center Bldg, 8th Floor, Yamashita-cho, Naka-ku, Yokohama 231-8524; tel. (45) 671-7400; fax (45) 671-7410; e-mail info@yokohama-cci.or.jp; f. 1880; 14,965 mems; Chair. MASAYOSHI TAKANASHI; Pres. NAMIO OBA.

INDUSTRIAL AND TRADE ASSOCIATIONS

General

The Association for the Promotion of International Trade, Japan (JAPIT): 1-26-5, Toranomon, Minato-ku, Tokyo; tel. (3) 3506-8261; fax (3) 3506-8260; f. 1954 to promote trade with the People's Repub. of China; 700 mems; Chair. YOSHIO NAKATA; Pres. YOSHIO SAKURAUCHI.

Industry Club of Japan: 1-4-6, Marunouchi, Chiyoda-ku, Tokyo; tel. (3) 3281-1711; f. 1917 to develop closer relations between industrialists at home and abroad and promote expansion of Japanese business activities; c. 1,600 mems; Pres. GAISHI HIRAIWA; Exec. Dir KOUICHIROU SHINNO.

Japan Commercial Arbitration Association: Taishoseimei Hibiya Bldg, 1-9-1, Yurakucho, Chiyoda-ku, Tokyo 100-1006; tel. (3) 3287-3061; fax (3) 3287-3064; e-mail info@jcaa.or.jp; internet www .jcaa.or.jp; f. 1950; 1,012 mems; provides facilities for mediation, conciliation and arbitration in international trade disputes; Pres. NOBUO YAMAGUCHI.

Japan External Trade Organization (JETRO): 2-2-5, Toranomon, Minato-ku, Tokyo 105-8466; tel. (3) 3582-5511; fax (3) 3582-5662; e-mail seh@jetro.go.jp; internet www.jetro.go.jp; f. 1958; information for international trade, investment, import promotion, exhibitions of foreign products; Chair. and CEO OSAMU WATANABE; Pres. HIROSHI TSUKAMOTO.

Japan Federation of Smaller Enterprise Organizations (JFSEO) (Nippon Chusokigyo Dantai Renmei): 2-8-4, Nihombashi, Kayaba-cho, Chuo-ku, Tokyo 103-0025; tel. (3) 3669-6862; f. 1948; 18 mems and c. 1,000 co-operative socs; Pres. MASATAKA TOYODA; Chair. of Int. Affairs SEIICHI ONO.

Japan General Merchandise Exporters' Association: 2-4-1, Hamamatsu-cho, Minato-ku, Tokyo; tel. (3) 3435-3471; fax (3) 3434-6739; f. 1953; 40 mems; Pres. TADAYOSHI NAKAZAWA.

Japan Productivity Center for Socio-Economic Development (JPC-SED) (Shakai Keizai Seisansei Honbu): 3-1-1, Shibuya, Shibuya-ku, Tokyo 150-8307; tel. (3) 3409-1112; fax (3) 3409-1986; f. 1994 following merger between Japan Productivity Center and Social Economic Congress of Japan; 10,000 mems; concerned with management problems and research into productivity; Chair. SUGII-CHIRO WATARI; (acting); Pres. YASUO SAWAMA.

Keizai Doyukai (Japan Association of Corporate Executives): 1-4-6, Marunouchi, Chiyoda-ku, Tokyo 100-0005; tel. (3) 3211-1271; fax (3) 3212-3774; e-mail contact@doyukai.or.jp; internet www.doyukai .or.jp; f. 1946; mems: c. 1,400; corporate executives concerned with national and international economic and social policies; Chair. KAKU-TARO KITASHIRO.

Nihon Boeki-Kai (Japan Foreign Trade Council, Inc): World Trade Center Bldg, 6th Floor, 2-4-1, Hamamatsu-cho, Minato-ku, Tokyo 105-6106; tel. (3) 3435-5952; fax (3) 3435-5969; e-mail mail@jftc.or .jp; internet www.jftc.or.jp; f. 1947; 192 mems; Chair. KENJI MIYA-HARA; Exec. Man. Dir KEISUKE TAKANASHI; Man. Dir HISAO IKEGAMI.

Chemicals

Federation of Pharmaceutical Manufacturers' Associations of Japan: Tokyo Yakugyo Bldg, 2-1-5, Nihombashi Honcho, Chuo-ku, Tokyo 103-0023; tel. (3) 3270-0581; fax (3) 3241-2090; Pres. TADASHI SUZUKI.

Japan Chemical Industry Association: Sumitomo Fudosan Rokko Bldg, 4-1 Shinkawa 1-chome, Chuo-ku, Tokyo 104-0033; tel. (3) 3297-2576; fax (3) 3297-2606; e-mail chemical@jcia-net.or.jp; internet www.nikkakyo.org; f. 1948; 266 mems; Pres. Dr MITSUO OHASHI.

Japan Cosmetic Industry Association: Hatsumei Bldg, 2-9-14, Toranomon, Minato-ku, Tokyo 105-0001; tel. (3) 3502-0576; fax (3) 3502-0829; f. 1959; 687 mem. cos; Chair. REIJIRO KOBAYASHI.

Japan Gas Association: 1-15-12, Toranomon, Minato-ku, Tokyo 105-0001; tel. (3) 3502-0116; fax (3) 3502-3676; f. 1947; Chair. SHINICHIRO RYOKI; Vice-Chair. and Sr Man. Dir KOSHIRO GODA.

Japan Perfumery and Flavouring Association: Saeki No. 3 Bldg, 3rd Floor, 37 Kandakonya-cho, Chiyoda-ku, Tokyo 101-0035; tel. and fax (3) 3526-7855; f. 1947; Chair. YONEJIRO KORAYASHI.

Photo-Sensitized Materials Manufacturers' Association: JCII Bldg, 25, Ichiban-cho, Chiyoda-ku, Tokyo 102-0082; tel. (3) 5276-3561; fax (3) 5276-3563; f. 1948; Pres. MASAYUKI MUNEYUKI.

Fishing and Pearl Cultivation

Japan Fisheries Association (Dainippon Suisankai): Sankaido Bldg, 1-9-13, Akasaka, Minato-ku, Tokyo 107-0052; tel. (3) 3585-6683; fax (3) 3582-2337; internet www.suisankai.or.jp; Pres. HIROYA SANO.

Japan Pearl Export and Processing Co-operative Association: 3-7, Kyobashi, Chuo-ko, Tokyo; f. 1951; 130 mems.

Japan Pearl Exporters' Association: 122, Higashi-machi, Chuo-ku, Kobe; tel. (78) 331-4031; fax (78) 331-4345; e-mail jpeakobe@lime .ocn.ne.jp; internet www.japan-pearl.com; f. 1954; 56 mems; Pres. YOSHIHIRO SHIMIZU.

Paper and Printing

Japan Federation of Printing Industries: 1-16-8, Shintomi, Chuo-ku, Tokyo 104; tel. (3) 3553-6051; fax (3) 3553-6079; Pres. HIROMICHI FUJITA.

Japan Paper Association: Kami Parupu Bldg, 3-9-11, Ginza, Chuo-ku, Tokyo 104-8139; tel. (3) 3248-4801; fax (3) 3248-4826; internet www.jpa.gr.jp; f. 1946; 54 mems; Chair. MASAO KOBAYASHI; Pres. KIYOSHI SAKAI.

Japan Paper Exporters' Association: Kami Parupu Bldg, 3-9-11, Ginza, Chuo-ku, Tokyo 104-8139; tel. (3) 3248-4831; fax (3) 3248-4834; e-mail japex@green.an.egg.or.jp; f. 1952; 37 mems; Chair. IWAO NAKAJIMA.

Japan Paper Importers' Association: Kami Parupu Bldg, 3-9-11, Ginza, Chuo-ku, Tokyo 104-8139; tel. (3) 3248-4832; fax (3) 3248-4834; e-mail japim@yacht.ocn.ne.jp; f. 1981; 27 mems; Chair. KYOUICHI HIRATO.

Japan Paper Products Manufacturers' Association: 4-2-6, Kotobuki, Taito-ku, Tokyo; tel. (3) 3543-2411; f. 1949; Exec. Dir KIYOSHI SATOH.

Mining and Petroleum

Asbestos Cement Products Association: Takahashi Bldg, 7-10-8, Ginza, Chuo-ku, Tokyo; tel. (3) 3571-1359; f. 1937; Chair. KOSHIRO SHIMIZU.

Japan Cement Association: Shuwa-sakurabashi Bldg, 4-5-4, Hatchobori, Chuo-ku, Tokyo 104-0032; tel. (3) 3523-2704; fax (3) 3523-2700; e-mail international@jcassoc.or.jp; internet www.jcassoc.or.jp; f. 1948; 20 mem. cos; Chair. FUMIO SAMESHIMA.

Japan Coal Energy Center (JCOAL): Meiji-Seimei Bldg 9/F, 3-14-10 Mita, Minato-ku, ,Tokyo 108-0073; tel. (3) 6400-5191; fax (3) 6400-5206; e-mail info@jcoal.or.jp; internet www.jcoal.or.jp; formed in 1997 by merger of the Japan Coal Association, Coal Mining Research Centre, and the Japan Technical Cooperation Center for Coal Resources Development; Chair. MASAYA FUJIMURA.

Japan Mining Industry Association: Shuwa Toranomon Bldg, No. 3, 1-21-8 Toranomon, Minato-ku, Tokyo 105-0001; tel. (3) 3502-7451; fax (3) 3591-9841; f. 1948; 53 mem. cos; Chair. HIROSHI MAKIHARA; Pres. HIROE TAKAHARA; Dir-Gen. HIROE TAKAHARA.

Japan Petrochemical Industry Association: 2nd Floor, 2-1-1, Uchisaiwai-cho, Chiyoda-ku, Tokyo 100-0011; tel. (3) 3501-2151; internet www.jpca.or.jp; Chair. MITSUO OHASHI.

Japan Petroleum Development Association: Keidanren Bldg, 1-9-4, Otemachi, Chiyoda-ku, Tokyo 100; tel. (3) 3279-5841; fax (3) 3279-5844; f. 1961; Chair. TAMOTSU SHOYA.

Metals

Japan Aluminium Association (JAA): Tsukamoto-Sozan Bldg, 4-2-15, Ginza, Chuo-ku, Tokyo 104-0061; tel. (3) 3538-0221; fax (3) 3538-0233; f. 1999 by merger of Japan Aluminium Federation and Japan Light Metal Association; Chair. AKIKUNI NOZOE.

Japan Brass Makers' Association: 1-12-22, Tsukiji, Chuo-ku, Tokyo 104-0045; tel. (3) 3542-6551; fax (3) 3542-6556; e-mail jbmajwcc@copper-brass.gr.jp; internet www.copper-brass.gr.jp; f. 1948; 62 mems; Pres. S. SATO; Man. Dir J. HATANO.

The Japan Iron and Steel Federation: Tekko Kaikan Bldg, 3-2-10, Nihombashi Kayaba-cho, Chuo-ku, Tokyo 103-0025; tel. (3) 3669-4818; fax (3) 3661-0798; internet www.jisf.or.jp; f. 1948; mems 64 mfrs, 67 dealers; Chair. AKIO MIMURA.

Japan Stainless Steel Association: Tekko Bldg, 3-2-10, Nihombashi Kayaba-cho, Chuo-ku, Tokyo 103; tel. (3) 3669-4431; fax (3) 3669-4431; e-mail yabe@jssa.gr.jp; internet www.jssa.gr.jp; Pres. MIKIO KATOH; Exec. Dir TAKEO YABE.

The Kozai Club: Tekko Bldg, 3-2-10, Nihombashi Kayaba-cho, Chuo-ku, Tokyo 103-0025; tel. (3) 3669-4815; fax (3) 3667-0245; f. 1947; mems 39 mfrs, 69 dealers; Chair. AKIRA CHIHAYA.

Steel Castings and Forgings Association of Japan (JSCFA): Shikoku Bldg Bekkan, 1-14-4, Uchikannda, Chiyoda-ku, Tokyo 101-0047; tel. (3) 5283-1611; fax (3) 5283-1613; e-mail cf@jscfa.gr.jp; f. 1972; mems 42 cos, 44 plants; Exec. Dir TOMOO TAKENOUCHI.

Machinery and Precision Equipment

Electronic Industries Association of Japan: 3-2-2, Marunouchi, Chiyoda-ku, Tokyo 100-0005; tel. (3) 3213-5861; fax (3) 3213-5863; e-mail pao@eiaj.or.jp; internet www.eiaj.or.jp; f. 1948; 540 mems; Chair. FUMIO SATO.

Japan Camera Industry Association: JCII Bldg, 25, Ichibancho, Chiyoda-ku, Tokyo 102-0082; tel. (3) 5276-3891; fax (3) 5276-3893; internet www.photo-jcia.gr.jp; f. 1954; Pres. MASATOSHI KISHIMOTO.

Japan Clock and Watch Association: Kudan Sky Bldg, 1-12-11, Kudan-kita, Chiyoda-ku, Tokyo 102-0073; tel. (3) 5276-3411; fax (3) 5276-3414; internet www.jcwa.or.jp; Chair. HIROSHI HARUTA.

Japan Electric Association: 1-7-1, Yuraku-cho, Chiyoda-ku, Tokyo 100-0006; tel. (3) 3216-0551; fax (3) 3214-6005; f. 1921; 4,610 mems; Pres. TATSUO KAWAI.

Japan Electric Measuring Instruments Manufacturers' Association (JEMIMA): 1-9-10, Toranomon, Minato-ku, Tokyo 105-0001; tel. (3) 3502-0601; fax (3) 3502-0600; e-mail o-mitani@jemima.or.jp; internet www.jemima.or.jp; 117 mems; Gen. Man. OSAMU MITANI.

Japan Electrical Manufacturers' Association: 2-4-15, Nagata-cho, Chiyoda-ku, Tokyo 100-0014; tel. (3) 3581-4841; fax (3) 3593-3198; internet www.jema-net.or.jp; f. 1948; 245 mems; Chair. TAIZO NISHIMURO.

Japan Energy Association: Houwa Mita Tsunasaka Bldg, 2-7-7, Mita, Minato-ku, Tokyo 108-0073; tel. (3) 3451-1651; fax (3) 3451-1360; e-mail common@jea-wec.or.jp; internet www.jea-wec.or.jp; f. 1950; 133 mems; Chair. SHIGE-ETSU MIYAHARA; Exec. Dir HAJIME MURATA.

Japan Machine Tool Builders' Association: Kikai Shinko Bldg, 3-5-8, Shiba Koen, Minato-ku, Tokyo 105-0011; tel. (3) 3434-3961; fax (3) 3434-3763; f. 1951; 112 mems; Chair. TOYO KATO; Exec. Dir S. ABE.

Japan Machinery Center for Trade and Investment (JMC): Kikai Shinko Bldg, 3-5-8, Shiba Koen, Minato-ku, Tokyo 105-0011; tel. (3) 3431-9507; fax (3) 3436-6455; Pres. ISAO YONEKURA.

The Japan Machinery Federation: Kikai Shinko Bldg, 3-5-8, Shiba Koen, Minato-ku, Tokyo 105-0011; tel. (3) 3434-5381; fax (3) 3434-2666; f. 1952; Pres. SHOICHI SADA; Exec. Vice-Pres. SHINICHI NAKANISHI.

Japan Machinery Importers' Association: Koyo Bldg, 8th Floor, 1-2-11, Toranomon, Minato-ku, Tokyo 105-0001; tel. (3) 3503-9736; fax (3) 3503-9779; f. 1957; 94 mems; Pres. ISAO YONEKURA.

Japan Microscope Manufacturers' Association: c/o Olympus Optical Co Ltd, 2-43-2, Hatagaya, Shibuya-ku, Tokyo 151-0072; tel. (3) 3377-2139; fax (3) 3377-2139; e-mail jmma@olympus.co.jp; f. 1954; 31 mems; Chair. T. SHIMOYAMA.

Japan Motion Picture Equipment Industrial Association: Kikai Shinko Bldg, 3-5-8, Shiba Koen, Minato-ku, Tokyo 105; tel. (3) 3434-3911; fax (3) 3434-3912; Pres. MASAO SHIKATA; Gen. Sec. TERUHIRO KATO.

Japan Optical Industry Association: Kikai Shinko Bldg, 3-5-8, Shiba Koen, Minato-ku, Tokyo 105-0011; tel. (3) 3431-7073; f. 1946; 7 mems; Chair. SHOICHIRO YOSHIDA; Exec. Sec. SHIRO IWAHASHI.

The Japan Society of Industrial Machinery Manufacturers: Kikai Shinko Bldg, 3-5-8, Shiba Koen, Minato-ku, Tokyo 105-0011; tel. (3) 3434-6821; fax (3) 3434-4767; e-mail obd@jsim.or.jp; internet www.jsim.or.jp; f. 1948; 213 mems; Exec. Man. Dir KOJI FUJISAKI; Pres. KENTARO AIKAWA.

Japan Textile Machinery Association: Kikai Shinko Bldg, Room 310, 3-5-8, Shiba Koen, Minato-ku, Tokyo 105; tel. (3) 3434-3821; fax (3) 3434-3043; f. 1951; Pres. JUNICHI MURATA.

Textiles

Central Raw Silk Association of Japan: 1-9-4, Yuraku-cho, Chiyoda-ku, Tokyo; tel. (3) 3214-5777; fax (3) 3214-5778.

Japan Chemical Fibers Association: Seni Kaikan, 3-1-11, Nihombashi-Honcho, Chuo-ku, Tokyo 103-0023; tel. (3) 3241-2311; fax (3) 3246-0823; internet www.fcc.co.jp/JCFA; f. 1948; 41 mems, 9 assoc. mems; Pres. KATSUHIKO HIRAI; Dir-Gen. KUNIO YAGI.

Japan Cotton and Staple Fibre Weavers' Association: 1-8-7, Nishi-Azabu, Minato-ku, Tokyo; tel. (3) 3403-9671.

Japan Silk Spinners' Association: f. 1948; 95 mem. firms; Chair. ICHIJI OHTANI.

Japan Spinners' Association: Mengyo Kaikan Bldg, 2-5-8, Bingo-machi, Chuo-ku, Osaka 541-0051; tel. (6) 6231-8431; fax (6) 6229-1590; e-mail spinas@cotton.or.jp; internet www.jsa-jp.org; f. 1948; Exec. Dir HARUTA MUTO.

Transport Machinery

Japan Association of Rolling Stock Industries: Awajicho Suny Bldg, 1-2, Kanda-Sudacho, Chiyoda-ku, Tokyo 101-0041; tel. (3) 3257-1901.

Japan Auto Parts Industries Association: 1-16-15, Takanawa, Minato-ku, Tokyo 108-0074; tel. (3) 3445-4211; fax (3) 3447-5372; e-mail japiaint@green.am.egg.or.jp; f. 1948; 530 mem. firms; Chair. TSUNEO ISHIMARU; Exec. Dir K. SHIBASAKI.

Japan Automobile Manufacturers Association, Inc (JAMA): Jidosha Kaikan, 1-1-30, Shiba Daimaon, Minato-ku, Tokyo 105-0012; tel. (3) 5405-6126; fax (3) 5405-6136; e-mail kaigai_tky@mta.jama.or.jp; internet www.jama.or.jp; f. 1967; 14 mem. firms; Chair. YOSHIHIDE MUNEKUNI; Pres. TAKAO SUZUKI.

Japan Bicycle Manufacturers' Association: 1-9-3, Akasaka, Minato-ku, Tokyo 107; tel. (3) 3583-3123; fax (3) 3589-3125; f. 1955.

Japan Ship Exporters' Association: Nippon-Zaidan Bldg, 1-15-16, Toranomon, Minato-ku, Tokyo 105-0001; tel. (3) 3502-2094; fax (3) 3508-2058; e-mail postmaster@jsea.or.jp; 38 mems; Exec. Man. Dir YUICHI WATANABE.

Japanese Marine Equipment Association: Kaiyo Senpaku Bldg, 15-16, Toranomon, Minato-ku, Tokyo 105-0001; tel. (3) 3502-2041; fax (3) 3591-2206; e-mail info@jsmea.or.jp; internet www.jsmea.or.jp; f. 1956; 240 mems; Pres. TADAO YAMAOKA.

Japanese Shipowners' Association: Kaiun Bldg, 2-6-4, Hirakawa-cho, Chiyoda-ku, Tokyo 102-0093; tel. (3) 3264-7171; fax (3) 3262-4760; Pres. KENTARO KAWAMURA.

Shipbuilders' Association of Japan: 1-15-16, Toranomon, Minato-ku, Tokyo 105-0001; tel. (3) 3502-2010; fax (3) 3502-2816; internet www.sajn.or.jp; f. 1947; 21 mems; Chair. MOTOTSUGU ITO.

Society of Japanese Aerospace Companies Inc (SJAC): Toshin-Tameike Bldg, 2nd Floor, 1-1-14, Akasaka, Minato-ku, Tokyo 107-0052; tel. (3) 3585-0511; fax (3) 3585-0541; e-mail miwa-shuichi@sjac.or.jp; internet www.sjac.or.jp; f. 1952; reorg. 1974; 117 mems, 41 assoc. mems; Chair. MASAMOTO TAZAKI; Pres. TAKATOSHI HOSOYA.

Miscellaneous

Communications Industry Association of Japan (CIA-J): Sankei Bldg, 1-7-2, Otemachi, Chiyoda-ku, Tokyo 100-0004; tel. (3) 3231-3005; fax (3) 3231-3110; e-mail admin@ciaj.or.jp; internet www.ciaj.or.jp; f. 1948; non-profit org. of telecommunications equipment mfrs; 236 mems; Chair. TADASHI SEKIZAWA; Pres. YUTAKA HAYASHI.

Japan Canners' Association: Yurakucho Denki Bldg, 1-7-1, Yuraku-cho, Chiyoda-ku, Tokyo 100-0006; tel. (3) 3213-4751; fax (3) 3211-1430; Pres. KEINOSUKE HISAI.

Japan Hardwood Exporters' Association: Matsuda Bldg, 1-9-1, Ironai, Otaru, Hokkaido 047; tel. (134) 23-8411; fax (134) 22-7150; 7 mems.

Japan Lumber Importers' Association: Yushi Kogyo Bldg, 3-13-11, Nihombashi, Chuo-ku, Tokyo 103; tel. (3) 3271-0926; fax (3) 3271-0928; f. 1950; 130 mems; Pres. SHOICHI TANAKA.

Japan Plastics Industry Federation: Kaseihin-Kaikan, 5-8-17, Roppongi, Minato-ku, Tokyo 106-0032; tel. (3) 3586-9761; fax (3) 3586-9760; internet www.jpif.gr.jp; Chair. AKIO SATO.

Japan Plywood Manufacturers' Association: Meisan Bldg, 1-18-17, Nishi-Shimbashi, Minato-ku, Tokyo 105; tel. (3) 3591-9246; fax (3) 3591-9240; f. 1965; 92 mems; Pres. KOICHI MATAGA.

Japan Pottery Manufacturers' Federation: Toto Bldg, 1-1-28, Toranomon, Minato-ku, Tokyo; tel. (3) 3503-6761.

The Japan Rubber Manufacturers' Association: Tobu Bldg, 1-5-26, Moto Akasaka, Minato-ku, Tokyo 107-0051; tel. (3) 3408-7101; fax (3) 3408-7106; f. 1950; 125 mems; Pres. YASUO TOMINAGA.

Japan Spirits and Liquors Makers' Association: Koura Dai-ichi Bldg, 7th Floor, 1-1-6, Nihombashi-Kayaba-cho, Chuo-ku, Tokyo 103; tel. (3) 3668-4621.

Japan Sugar Import and Export Council: Oshima Bldg 1-3, Nihonbashi Koamicho, Chuo-ku, Tokyo; tel. (3) 3571-2362; fax (3) 3571-2363; 16 mems.

Japan Sugar Refiners' Association: 5-7, Sanban-cho, Chiyoda-ku, Tokyo 102; tel. (3) 3288-1151; fax (3) 3288-3399; f. 1949; 17 mems; Sr Man. Dir KATSUYUKI SUZUKI.

Japan Tea Exporters' Association: 17, Kitaban-cho, Shizuoka, Shizuoka Prefecture 420-0005; tel. (54) 271-3428; fax (54) 271-2177; e-mail japantea@sound.jp; 44 mems.

Japan Toy Association: 4-22-4, Higashi-Komagata, Sumida-ku, Tokyo 130; tel. (3) 3829-2513; fax (3) 3829-2549; Chair. MAKOTO YAMASHINA.

Motion Picture Producers' Association of Japan, Inc: Tokyu Ginza Bldg, 2-15-2, Ginza, Chuo-ku, Tokyo 104-0061; tel. (3) 3547-1800; fax (3) 3547-0909; e-mail eiren@mc.neweb.ne.jp; internet www.eiren.org; Pres. ISAO MATSUOKA.

EMPLOYERS' ORGANIZATION

Japan Business Federation (JBF) (Keidanren Kaikan): 1-9-4, Otemachi, Chiyoda-ku, Tokyo 100-8188; tel. (3) 5204-1920; fax (3) 5204-1943; e-mail intlab@keidanren.or.jp; internet www.keidanren.or.jp; f. 2002 by merger of Keidanren (f. 1946) and Nikkeiren (f. 1948); 1,540 mem. asscns; Chair. HIROSHI OKUDA; Dir-Gen. RYUKOH WADA.

UTILITIES

Electricity

Chubu Electric Power Co Inc: 1, Higashi-Shincho, Higashi-ku, Nagoya 461-8680; tel. (52) 951-8211; fax (52) 962-4624; internet www.chuden.co.jp; Chair. KOHEI ABE; Pres. HIROJI OTA.

Chugoku Electric Power Co Inc: 4-33, Komachi, Naka-ku, Hiroshima 730-8701; tel. (82) 241-0211; fax (82) 523-6185; e-mail angel@inet.energia.co.jp; internet www.energia.co.jp; f. 1951; Chair. SHITOMI TAKASU; Pres. SHIGEO SHIRAKURA.

Hokkaido Electric Power Co Inc: internet www.hepco.co.jp; Chair. KAZUO TODA; Pres. SEIJI IZUMI.

Hokuriku Electric Power Co Inc: internet www.rikuden.co.jp.

Kansai Electric Power Co Inc: 3-3-22, Nakanoshima, Kita-ku, Osaka 530-8270; tel. (6) 6441-8821; fax (6) 6441-8598; e-mail postmaster@kepco.co.jp; internet www.kepco.co.jp; Chair. YOSHIHISA AKIYAMA; Pres. Y. FUJI.

Kyushu Electric Power Co Inc: 2-1-82, Watanabe-dori, Chuo-ku, Fukuoka 810-8726; tel. (92) 726-1649; fax (92) 731-8719; internet www.kyuden.co.jp; Chair. MICHISADA KAMATA.

Shikoku Electric Power Co Inc: 2-5, Marunouchi, Takamatsu 760-8573; tel. (878) 21-5061; fax (878) 26-1250; e-mail postmaster@yonden.co.jp; internet www.yonden.co.jp; Chair. HIROSHI YAMAMOTO; Pres. KOZO KONDO.

Tohoku Electric Power Co Inc: 7-1, 1-chome, Aoba-ku, Sendai 980-8550; tel. (22) 225-2111; fax (22) 223-6224; e-mail webmaster@tohoku-epco.co.jp; internet www.tohoku-epco.co.jp; Chair. TOSHIAKI YASHIMA; Pres. KEIICHI MAKUTA.

Tokyo Electric Power Co Inc: 1-1-3, Uchisaiwai-cho, Chiyoda-ku, Tokyo 100; tel. (3) 3501-8111; fax (3) 3592-1795; internet www.tepco.co.jp; Chair. SHOH NASU; Pres. N. MINAMI.

Gas

Osaka Gas Co Ltd: e-mail intlstaff@osakagas.co.jp; internet www.osakagas.co.jp.

Toho Gas Co Ltd: 19-18, Sakurada-cho, Atsuta-ko, Nagoya 456; tel. (52) 871-3511; internet www.tohogas.co.jp; f. 1922; Chair. SUSUMU OGAWA; Pres. SADAHIKO SIMIZU.

Tokyo Gas Co Inc: 1-5-20, Kaigan, Minato-ku, Tokyo 105; tel. (3) 3433-2111; fax (3) 5472-5385; internet www.tokyo-gas.co.jp; f. 1885; Chair. HIROSHI WATANABE; Pres. H. UEHARA.

CO-OPERATIVE ORGANIZATION

Nikkenkyo (Council of Japan Construction Industry Employees' Unions): Moriyama Bldg, 1-31-16, Takadanobaba, Shinjuku-ku, Tokyo 169; tel. (3) 5285-3870; fax (3) 5285-3879; Pres. NOBORU SEKIGUCHI.

TRADE UNIONS

A feature of Japan's trade union movement is that the unions are usually based on single enterprises, embracing workers of different occupations in that enterprise. In June 1994 there were 32,581 unions; union membership stood at 12.5m. workers in 1996. In November 1989 the two largest confederations, SOHYO and RENGO, merged to form the Japan Trade Union Confederation (JTUC—RENGO).

Japanese Trade Union Confederation (JTUC–RENGO): 3-2-11, Kanda Surugadai, Chiyoda-ku, Tokyo 101-0062; tel. (3) 5295-0526; fax (3) 5295-0548; e-mail jtuc-kokusai@sv.rengo-net.or.jp; internet www.jtuc-rengo.org; f. 1989; 6.6m. mems; Pres. KIYOSHI SASAMORI.

Principal Affiliated Unions

Ceramics Rengo (All-Japan Federation of Ceramics Industry Workers): 3-11, Heigocho, Mizuho-ku, Nagoya-shi, Aichi 467; tel. (52) 882-4562; fax (52) 882-9960; 30,083 mems; Pres. TSUNEYOSHI HAYAKAWA.

Chain Rokyo (Chain-store Labour Unions' Council): 3rd Floor, 2-29-8, Higashi-ikebukuro, Toshima-ku, Tokyo 170; tel. (3) 5951-1031; fax (3) 5951-1051; 40,015 mems; Pres. TOSHIFUMI HIRANO.

Denki Rengo (Japanese Electrical, Electronic & Information Union): Denkirengo Bldg, 1-10-3, Mita, Minato-ku, Tokyo 108-8326; tel. (3) 3455-6911; fax (3) 3452-5406; internet www.jeiu.or.jp; f. 1953; 688,436 mems; Pres. NOBUAKI KOGA.

Denryoku Soren (Federation of Electric Power Related Industry Workers' Unions of Japan): TDS Mita 7-13, 3rd Floor, Mita 2-Chome, Minato-ku, Tokyo 108-0073; tel. (3) 3454-0231; fax (3) 3798-1470; e-mail info@denryokusoren.or.jp; internet www.denryokusoren.or.jp; 255,278 mems; Pres. NORIO TSUMAKI.

Dokiro (Hokkaido Seasonal Workers' Union): Hokuro Bldg, Kita 4, Nishi 12, Chuo-ku, Sapporo, Hokkaido 060; tel. (11) 261-5775; fax (11) 272-2255; 19,063 mems; Pres. YOSHIZO ODAWARA.

Food Rengo: Hiroo Office Bldg 8/F, 1-3-18 Hiroo, Shibuya-ku, Tokyo; tel. (3) 3446-2082; fax (3) 3446-6779; internet www.ny.airnet.ne.jp/jfu; f. 2000 by merger of Shokuhin Rengo and Shokuhin Rokyo to form Shokuhin Renmei, renamed as above 2002; 111,599 mems.

Gomu Rengo (Japanese Rubber Workers' Union Confederation): 2-3-3, Mejiro, Toshima-ku, Tokyo 171; tel. (3) 3984-3343; fax (3) 3984-5862; 60,070 mems; Pres. YASUO FURUKAWA.

Hitetsu Rengo (Japanese Metal Mine Workers' Union): Gotanda Metalion Bldg, 5-21-15, Higashi-gotanda, Shinagawa-ku, Tokyo 141; tel. (3) 5420-1881; fax (3) 5420-1880; 23,500 mems; Pres. SHOUZOU HIMENO.

Insatsu Roren (Federation of Printing Information Media Workers' Unions): Yuai-kaikan, 7th Floor, 2-20-12, Shiba, Minato-ku, Tokyo 105-0014; tel. (3) 5442-0191; fax (3) 5442-0219; 22,303 mems; Pres. HIROFUMI NAKABAYASHI.

JA Rengo (All-Japan Agriculture Co-operative Staff Members' Union): 964-1, Toyotomicho-mikage, Himeji-shi, Hyogo 679-21; tel. and fax (792) 64-3618; 2,772 mems; Pres. YUTAKA OKADA.

Japan Federation of Service and Distributive Workers' Unions: New State Manor Bldg, 3rd Floor, 2-23-1, Yoyogi, Shibuya-ku, Tokyo 151-0053; tel. (3) 3370-4121; fax (3) 3370-1640; e-mail honda@jsd-union.org; internet www.jsd-union.org; 170,000 mems; Pres. TAKAAKI SAKURADA.

Jichi Roren (National Federation of Prefectural and Municipal Workers' Unions): 1-15-22, Oji-honcho, Kita-ku, Tokyo 114; tel. and fax (3) 3907-1584; 5,728 mems; Pres. NOBUO UENO.

Jichiro (All-Japan Prefectural and Municipal Workers' Union): Jichiro Bldg, 1, Rokubancho, Chiyoda-ku, Tokyo 102-0085; tel. (3) 3263-0263; fax (3) 5210-7422; internet www.jichiro.gr.jp; f. 1951; 1,004,000 mems; Pres. MORISHIGE GOTO.

Jidosha Soren (Confederation of Japan Automobile Workers' Unions): U-Life Center, 1-4-26, Kaigan, Minato-ku, Tokyo 105-8523; tel. (3) 3434-7641; fax (3) 3434-7428; internet www.jaw.or.jp; f. 1972; 700,000 mems; Pres. YUJI KATO.

Jiunro (Japan Automobile Drivers' Union): 2-3-12, Nakameguro, Meguro-ku, Tokyo 153; tel. (3) 3711-9387; fax (3) 3719-2624; 1,958 mems; Pres. SADAO KANEZUKA.

JR-Rengo (Japan Railway Trade Unions Confederation): TOKO Bldg, 9th Floor, 1-8-10, Nihonbashi-muromachi, Chuo-ku, Tokyo 103; tel. (3) 3270-4590; fax (3) 3270-4429; 78,418 mems; Pres. KAZUAKI KUZUNO.

JRU Soren (Japan Confederation of Railway Workers' Unions): Meguro-satsuki Bldg, 3-2-13, Nishi-gotanda, Shinagawa-ku, Tokyo 141-0031; tel. (3) 3491-7191; fax (3) 3491-7192; internet www.jru7.net; 87,000 mems; Pres. YUJI ODA.

Jyoho Roren (Japan Federation of Telecommunications, Electronic Information and Allied Workers): Zendentsu-rodo Bldg, 3-6, Kanda Surugadai, Chiyoda-ku, Tokyo 101-0062; tel. (3) 3219-2231; fax (3) 3253-3268; 265,132 mems; Pres. KAZUO SASAMORI.

Kagaku League 21 (Japanese Federation of Chemistry Workers' Unions): Senbai Bldg, 5-26-30, Shiba, Minato-ku, Tokyo 108-8389; tel. (3) 3452-5591; fax (3) 3454-7462; internet www.jec-u.com; formed by merger of Goka Roren and Zenkoku Kagaku; 104,000 mems; Pres. KATUTOSHI KATO.

Kagaku Soren (Japanese Federation of Chemical Workers' Unions): Kyodo Bldg, 7th Floor, 2-4-10, Higashi-shimbashi, Minato-ku, Tokyo 105; tel. (3) 5401-2268; fax (3) 5401-2263; Pres. HIROKAZU IWASAKI.

Kaiin Kumiai (All-Japan Seamen's Union): 7-15-26, Roppongi, Minato-ku, Tokyo 106-0032; tel. (3) 5410-8330; fax (3) 5410-8336; internet www.jsu.or.jp; 35,000 mems; Pres. SAKAE IDEMOTO.

Kamipa Rengo (Japanese Federation of Pulp and Paper Workers' Unions): 2-12-4, Kita Aoyama, Minato-ku, Tokyo 107-0061; tel. (3) 3402-7656; fax (3) 3402-7659; 50,858 mems; Pres. TUNEO MUKAI.

Kensetsu Rengo (Japan Construction Trade Union Confederation): Yuai Bldg, 7th Floor, 2-20-12, Shiba, Minato-ku, Tokyo 105; tel. (3) 3454-0951; fax (3) 3453-0582; 13,199 mems; Pres. MASAYASU TERASAWA.

Kinzoku Kikai (National Metal and Machinery Workers' Unions of Japan): 6-2, Sakuraokacho, Shibuya-ku, Tokyo 150-0031; tel. (3) 3463-4231; fax (3) 3463-7391; f. 1989; 205,082 mems; Pres. MASAOKI KITAURA.

Kokko Soren (Japan General Federation of National Public Service Employees' Unions): 1-2-1, Kasumigaseki, Chiyoda-ku, Tokyo 100; tel. (3) 3508-4990; fax (3) 5512-7555; 40,370 mems; Pres. MARUYAMA KENZO.

Koku Domei (Japanese Confederation of Aviation Labour): Nikko-kiso Bldg, 2nd Floor, 1-6-3, Haneda-kuko, Ota-ku, Tokyo 144; tel. (3) 3747-7642; fax (3) 3747-7647; 16,310 mems; Pres. KATSUMI UTAGAWA.

Kokuzei Roso (Japanese Confederation of National Tax Unions): R154, Okurasho Bldg, 3-1-1, Kasumigaseki, Chiyoda-ku, Tokyo 100; tel. (3) 3581-2573; fax (3) 3581-3843; 40,128 mems; Pres. TATSUO SASAKI.

Kotsu Roren (Japan Federation of Transport Workers' Unions): Yuai Bldg, 3rd Floor, 2-20-12, Shiba, Minato-ku 105-0014; tel. (3) 3451-7243; fax (3) 3454-7393; 97,239 mems; Pres. SHIGEO MAKI.

Koun-Domei (Japanese Confederation of Port and Transport Workers' Unions): 5-10-2, Kamata, Ota-ku, Tokyo 144-0052; tel. (3) 3733-5285; fax (3) 3733-5280; f. 1987; 1,638 mems; Pres. SAKAE IDEMOTO.

Leisure Service Rengo (Japan Federation of Leisure Service Industries Workers' Unions): Zosen Bldg, 4th Floor, 3-5-6, Misaki-cho, Chiyoda-ku, Tokyo 101-0061; tel. (3) 3230-1724; fax (3) 3239-1553; 47,601 mems; Pres. HIROSHI SAWADA.

NHK Roren (Federation of All-NHK Labour Unions): NHK, 2-2-1, Jinnan, Shibuya-ku, Tokyo 150; tel. (3) 3485-6007; fax (3) 3469-9271; 12,526 mems; Pres. YASUZO SUDO.

Nichirinro (National Forest Workers' Union of Japan): 1-2-1, Kasumigaseki, Chiyoda-ku, Tokyo 100; tel. (3) 3580-8891; fax (3) 3580-1596; Pres. KOH IKEGAMI.

Nikkyoso (Japan Teachers' Union): Japan Education Hall, 2-6-2, Hitotsubashi, Chiyoda-ku, Tokyo 101-0003; tel. (3) 3265-2171; fax (3) 3230-0172; internet www.jtu-net.or.jp; f. 1947; 400,000 mems; Pres. NAGAKAZU SAKAKIBARA.

Rosai Roren (National Federation of Zenrosai Workers' Unions): 2-12-10, Yoyogi, Shibuya-ku, Tokyo 151; tel. (3) 3299-0161; fax (3) 3299-0126; 2,091 mems; Pres. TADASHI TAKACHI.

Seiho Roren (National Federation of Life Insurance Workers' Unions): Tanaka Bldg, 3-19-5, Yushima, Bunkyo-ku, Tokyo 113-0034; tel. (3) 3837-2031; fax (3) 3837-2037; 414,021 mems; Pres. YOHTARU KOHNO.

Seiroren (Labour Federation of Government-Related Organizations): Hasaka Bldg, 4th–6th Floors, 1-10-3, Kanda-ogawacho, Chiyoda-ku, Tokyo 101; tel. (3) 5295-6360; fax (3) 5295-6362; Chair. MITSURU WATANABE.

Sekiyu Roren (Japan Confederation of Petroleum Industry Workers' Union): NKK Bldg, 7th Floor, 2-18-2, Nishi-shinbashi, Minato-ku, Tokyo 105–0003; tel. (3) 3578-1315; fax (3) 3578-3455; 28,807 mems; Pres. HIROSHI MOCHIMARU.

Shigen Roren (Federation of Japanese Metal Resources Workers' Unions): Roppongi Azeria Bldg, 1-3-8, Nishi-azabu, Minato-ku, Tokyo 106; tel. (3) 3402-6666; fax (3) 3402-6667; Pres. MINORU TAKAHASHI.

Shin Unten (F10-Drivers' Craft Union): 4th Floor, 3-25-6, Negishi, Taito-ku, Tokyo 110; tel. (3) 5603-1015; fax (3) 5603-5351; 4,435 mems; Pres. SHOHEI SHINOZAKI.

Shinkagaku (National Organization of All Chemical Workers): MF Bldg, 2nd Floor, 2-3-3, Fujimi, Chiyoda-ku, Tokyo 102-0071; e-mail skagaku@sepia.ocn.ne.jp; tel. (3) 3239-2933; fax (3) 3239-2932; 8,400 mems; Pres. SHIN'ICHI IWANAGA   .

Shinrin Roren (Japanese Federation of Forest and Wood Workers' Unions): 3-28-7, Otsuka, Bunkyo-ku, Tokyo 112; tel. (3) 3945-6385; fax (3) 3945-6477; 13,928 mems; Pres. ISAO SASAKI.

Shitetsu Soren (General Federation of Private Railway Workers' Unions): 4-3-5, Takanawa, Minato-ku, Tokyo 108-0074; tel. (3) 3473-0166; fax (3) 3447-3927; f. 1947; 160,000 mems; Pres. RYOICHI IKE-MURA.

Sonpo Roren (Federation of Non-Life Insurance Workers' Unions of Japan): Kanda MS Bldg, 4th Floor, 27, Kanda-higashimatsushi-tacho, Chiyoda-ku, Tokyo 101; tel. (3) 5295-0071; fax (3) 5295-0073; Pres. KUNIO MATSUMOTO.

Tanro (Japan Coal Miners' Union): 5-2-23 Okotsu, Kushiro-shi, Hokkaido 085-0811 ; tel. (15) 491-6112; fax (15) 491-9253; 1,051 mems; Pres. TAKASHI CHIBA.

Tanshokukyo (Association of Japan Coal Mining Staff Unions): 2-30, Nishiminatomachi, Omuta-shi, Fukuoka 836; tel. (944) 52-3883; fax (944) 52-3853; Pres. KEIZO UMEKI.

Tekko Roren (Japan Federation of Steel Workers' Unions): I&S Riverside Bldg, 4th Floor, 1-23-4, Shinkawa, Chuo-ku, Tokyo 104-0033; tel. (3) 3555-0401; fax (3) 3555-0407; internet www.tekko-roren.or.jp; 135,000 mems; Pres. TAKESHI OGINO.

Tokei Roso (Statistics Labour Union Management and Co-ordination Agency): 19-1, Somucho, Wakamatsucho, Shinjuku-ku, Tokyo 162; tel. (3) 3202-1111; fax (3) 3205-3850; Pres. TOSHIAKI MAGARA.

Toshiko (The All-Japan Municipal Transport Workers' Union): 3-1-35, Shibaura, Minato-ku, Tokyo 108; tel. (3) 3451-5221; fax (3) 3452-2977; 43,612 mems; Pres. SHUNICHI SUZUKI.

Ui Zensen Domei (Japanese Federation of Textile, Chemical, Food, Commercial, Service and General Workers' Unions): 4-8-16, Kudan-minami, Chiyoda-ku, Tokyo 102-0074; tel. (3) 3288-3723; fax (3) 3288-3728; e-mail kokusai@uizensen.or.jp; internet www.uizensen.or.jp; f. 2002 by merger of CSG Rengo, Zensen Domei and Sen'i Seikatsu Roren; 1,986 affiliates; 790,289 mems (Jan. 2003); Pres. TSUYOSHI TAKAGI.

Unyu Roren (All-Japan Federation of Transport Workers' Union): Zennittsu Kasumigaseki Bldg, 5th Floor, 3-3-3, Kasumigaseki, Chiyoda-ku, Tokyo 100-0013; tel. (3) 3503-2171; fax (3) 3503-2176; f. 1968; 143,084 mems; Pres. KAZUMARO SUZUKI.

Zeikan Roren (Federation of Japanese Customs Personnel Labour Unions): 3-1-1, Kasumigaseki, Chiyoda-ku, Tokyo 100; tel. and fax (3) 3593-1788; Pres. RIKIO SUDO.

Zen Insatsu (All-Printing Agency Workers' Union): 3-59-12, Nishigahara, Kita-ku, Tokyo 114; tel. (3) 3910-7131; fax (3) 3910-7155; 5,431 mems; Chair. TOSHIO KATAKURA.

Zen Yusei (All-Japan Postal Labour Union): 1-20-6, Sendagaya, Shibuya-ku, Tokyo 151; tel. (3) 3478-7101; fax (3) 5474-7085; 77,573 mems; Pres. NOBUAKI IZAWA.

Zenchuro (All-Japan Garrison Forces Labour Union): 3-41-8, Shiba, Minato-ku, Tokyo 105; tel. (3) 3455-5971; fax (3) 3455-5973; Pres. EIBUN MEDORUMA.

Zendensen (All-Japan Electric Wire Labour Union): 1-11-6, Hatanodai, Shinagawa-ku, Tokyo 142; tel. (3) 3785-2991; fax (3) 3785-2995; Pres. NAOKI TOKUNAGA.

Zen-eien (National Cinema and Theatre Workers' Union): Hibiya Park Bldg, 1-8-1, Yurakucho, Chiyoda-ku, Tokyo 100; tel. (3) 3201-4476; fax (3) 3214-0597; Pres. SADAHIRO MATSUURA.

Zengin Rengo (All-Japan Federative Council of Bank Labour Unions): 1-14-12 Higashi-kanda, Chiyoda-ku, Tokyo 101-0031; tel. (3) 5687-5155; fax (3) 5687-5156; internet www.zengin.jp; 16,474 mems; Pres. YOSHIHIRO KONO.

Zenjiko Roren (National Federation of Automobile Transport Workers' Unions): 3-7-9, Sendagaya, Shibuya-ku, Tokyo 151; tel. (3) 3408-0875; fax (3) 3497-0107; Pres. OSAMU MIMASHI.

Zenkairen (All-Japan Shipping Labour Union): Shinbashi Ekimae Bldg, No. 1, 8th Floor, 2-20-15, Shimbashi, Minato-ku, Tokyo 105; tel. (3) 3573-2401; fax (3) 3573-2404; Chair. MASAHIKO SATO.

Zenkin Rengo (Japanese Federation of Metal Industry Unions): Yuai Bldg, 5th Floor, 2-20-12, Shiba, Minato-ku, Tokyo 105-0014; tel. (3) 3451-2141; fax (3) 3452-0239; f. 1989; 310,818 mems; Pres. MITSURO HATTORI.

Zenkoku Gas (Federation of Gas Workers' Unions of Japan): 5-11-1, Omori-nishi, Ota-ku, Tokyo 143; tel. (3) 5493-8381; fax (3) 5493-8216; 31,499 mems; Pres. AKIO HAMAUZU.

Zenkoku Keiba Rengo (National Federation of Horse-racing Workers): 2500, Mikoma, Miho-mura, Inashiki-gun, Ibaragi 300-04; tel. (298) 85-0402; fax (298) 85-0416; Pres. TOYOHIKO OKUMURA.

Zenkoku Nodanro (National Federation of Agricultural, Forestry and Fishery Corporations' Workers' Unions): 1-5-8, Hamamatsu-cho, Minato-ku, Tokyo 105; tel. (3) 3437-0931; fax (3) 3437-0681; 26,010 mems; Pres. SHIN-ICHIRO OKADA.

Zenkoku Semento (National Federation of Cement Workers' Unions of Japan): 5-29-2, Shimbashi, Minato-ku, Tokyo 105; tel. (3) 3436-3666; fax (3) 3436-3668; Pres. KIYONORI URAKAWA.

Zenkoku-Ippan (National Council of General Amalgamated Workers' Unions): Zosen Bldg, 5th Floor, 3-5-6, Misakicho, Chiyoda-ku, Tokyo 101-0061; tel. (3) 3230-4071; fax (3) 3230-4360; 54,708 mems; Pres. YASUHIKO MATSUI.

Zenkyoro (National Race Workers' Union): Nihon Kyoiku Kaikan, 7th Floor, 2-6-2, Hitotsubashi, Chiyoda-ku, Tokyo 101-0003; e-mail zenkoro-honbu@nifty.com; internet homepage2.nifty.com/zenkyoro; tel. (3) 5210-5156; fax (3) 5210-5157; 24,720 mems; Pres. TAKESHI KAWASHIMA.

Zennitto (Japan Painting Workers' Union): Shin-osaka Communication Plaza, 1st Floor, 1-6-36, Nishi-miyahara, Yodogawa-ku, Osaka-shi, Osaka 532; tel. (6) 6393-8677; fax (6) 6393-8533; Pres. SEIICHI UOZA.

Zenrokin (Federation of Labour Bank Workers' Unions of Japan): Nakano Bldg, 3rd Floor, 1-11, Kanda-Awajicho, Chiyoda-ku, Tokyo 101; tel. (3) 3256-1015; fax (3) 3256-1045; Pres. EIICHI KAKU.

Zensuido (All-Japan Water Supply Workers' Union): 1-4-1, Hongo, Bunkyo-ku, Tokyo 113; tel. (3) 3816-4132; fax (3) 3818-1430; 33,522 mems; Pres. KAZUMASA KATO.

Zentanko (National Union of Coal Mine Workers): 1162, Ikeshima, Sotome-cho, Nishi-Sonogi-gun, Nagasaki 857-0071; tel. (9) 5926-0004; fax (9) 5926-1000; Pres. NOBORU TAGAWA.

Zentei (Japan Postal Workers' Union): 1-2-7, Koraku, Bunkyo-ku, Tokyo 112-0004; tel. (3) 3812-4260; fax (3) 5684-7201; internet www.zentei.or.jp; 156,784 mems; Pres. MASAYUKI ISHIKAWA.

Zenzohei (All-Mint Labour Union): 1-1-79, Temma, Kita-ku, Osaka-shi, Osaka 530; tel. and fax (6) 6354-2389; Pres. CHIKASHI HIGUCHI.

Zenzosen-kikai (All-Japan Shipbuilding and Engineering Union): Zosen Bldg, 6th Floor, 3-5-6, Misakicho, Chiyoda-ku, Tokyo 101; tel. (3) 3265-1921; fax (3) 3265-1870; Pres. YOSHIMI FUNATSU.

Zosen Juki Roren (Japan Confederation of Shipbuilding and Engineering Workers' Unions): Yuai Kaikan Bldg, 4th Floor, 2-20-12, Shiba, Minato-ku, Tokyo 105-0014; tel. (3) 3451-6783; fax (3) 3451-6935; e-mail zosenjuki@mth.biglobe.ne.jp; 111,405 mems; Pres. MASAYUKI YOSHII.

Transport

RAILWAYS

Japan Railways (JR) Group: 1-6-5, Marunouchi, Chiyoda-ku, Tokyo 100-0005; tel. (3) 3215-9649; fax (3) 3213-5291; internet www.japanrail.com; fmrly the state-controlled Japanese National Railways (JNR); reorg. and transferred to private-sector control in 1987; the high-speed Shinkansen rail network consists of the Tokaido line (Tokyo to Shin-Osaka, 552.6 km), the Sanyo line (Shin-Osaka to Hakata, 623.3 km), the Tohoku line (Tokyo to Morioka, 535.3 km) and the Joetsu line (Omiya to Niigata, 303.6 km). The 4-km link between Ueno and Tokyo stations was opened in June 1991. The Yamagata Shinkansen (Fukushima to Yamagata, 87 km) was converted in 1992 from a conventional railway line. It is operated as a branch of the Tohoku Shinkansen with through trains from Tokyo, though not at full Shinkansen speeds. In 1997 the total railway route length was about 36,634 km. In 2003–04 magnetically levitated (Maglev) trains were being tested for use in commercial service.

Central Japan Railway Co: Yaesu Center Bldg, 1-6-6, Yaesu, Chuo-ku, Tokyo 103-8288; tel. (3) 3274-9727; fax (3) 5255-6780; internet www.jr-central.co.jp; f. 1987; also operates travel agency services, etc.; Chair. HIROSHI SUDA; Pres. YOSHIYUKI KASAI.

East Japan Railway Co: 2-2-2, Yoyogi, Shibuya-ku, Tokyo 151-8578; tel. (3) 5334-1151; fax (3) 5334-1110; internet www.jreast.co.jp; privatized in 1987; Pres. MUTSUTAKE OTSUKA.

Hokkaido Railway Co: West 15-chome, Kita 11-jo, Chuo-ku, Sapporo 060-8644; tel. (11) 700-5717; fax (11) 700-5719; e-mail keieki@jrhokkaido.co.jp; internet www.jrhokkaido.co.jp; Chair. YOSHIHIRO OHMORI; Pres. SHINICHI SAKAMOTO.

Japan Freight Railway Co: 3-13-1 Iidabashi, Chiyoda-ku, Tokyo; internet www.jrfreight.co.jp; Pres. NAOHIKO ITOH.

Kyushu Railway Co: 3-25-21, Hakataekimae, Hakata-ku, Fukuoka 812-8566; tel. (92) 474-2501; fax (92) 474-9745; internet www.jrkyushu.co.jp; Chair. K. TANAKA; Pres. S. ISHIHARA.

Shikoku Railway Co: 8-33, Hamano-cho, Takamatsu, Kagawa 760-8580; tel. (87) 825-1622; fax (87) 825-1623; internet www.jr-shikoku.co.jp; Chair. HIROATSU ITO; Pres. TOSHIYUKI UMEHARA.

West Japan Railway Co: 2-4-24, Shibata, Kita-ku, Osaka 530-8341; tel. (6) 6375-8981; fax (6) 6375-8919; e-mail wjr01020@mxy.meshnet.or.jp; internet www.westjr.co.jp; scheduled for privatization in 2001; Chair. MASATAKA IDE; Pres. SHOJIRO NANYA.

Other Principal Private Companies

Hankyu Corpn: 1-16-1, Shibata, Kita-ku, Osaka 530-8389; tel. (6) 6373-5092; fax (6) 6373-5670; e-mail koho@hankyu.co.jp; internet www.hankyu.co.jp; f. 1907; links Osaka, Kyoto, Kobe and Takarazuka; Chair. KOHEI KOBAYASHI; Pres. T. OHASHI.

Hanshin Electric Railway Co Ltd: 1-1-24, Ebie, Fukushima-ku, Osaka 553; tel. (6) 6457-2123; f. 1899; Chair. S. KUMA; Pres. M. TEZUKA.

Keihan Electric Railway Co Ltd: 1-2-27, Shiromi, Chuo-ku, Osaka 540; tel. (6) 6944-2521; fax (6) 6944-2501; internet www.keihan.co.jp; f. 1906; Chair. MINORU MIYASHITA; Pres. A. KIMBA.

Keihin Express Electric Railway Co Ltd: 2-20-20, Takanawa, Minato-ku, Tokyo 108-8625; tel. (3) 3280-9120; fax (3) 3280-9199; internet www.keikyu.co.jp; f. 1899; Chair. ICHIRO HIRAMATSU; Pres. M. KOTANI.

Keio Electric Railway Co Ltd: 1-9-1, Sekido, Tama City, Tokyo 206-8052; tel. (42) 337-3106; fax (42) 374-9322; internet www.keio.co.jp; f. 1913; Chair. K. KUWAYAMA; Pres. H. NISHIYAMA.

Keisei Electric Railway Co Ltd: 1-10-3, Oshiage, Sumida-ku, Tokyo 131; tel. (3) 3621-2242; fax (3) 3621-2233; internet www.keisei.co.jp; f. 1909; Chair. (vacant); Pres. M. SATO.

Kinki Nippon Railway Co Ltd: 6-1-55, Uehommachi, Tennoji-ku, Osaka 543-8585; tel. (6) 6775-3444; fax (6) 6775-3468; internet www.kintetsu.co.jp; f. 1910; Chair. WA TASHIRO; Pres. AKIO TSUJII.

Nagoya Railroad Co Ltd: 1-2-4, Meieki, Nakamura-ku, Nagoya-shi 450; tel. (52) 571-2111; fax (52) 581-6060; e-mail info@meitetsu.co.jp; internet www.meitetsu.co.jp; Chair. S. TANIGUCHI; Pres. S. MINOURA.

Nankai Electric Railway Co Ltd: 5-1-60, Namba, Chuo-ku, Osaka 542; tel. (6) 6644-7121; internet www.nankai.co.jp; Pres. SHIGERU YOSHIMURA; Vice-Pres. K. OKAMOTO.

Nishi-Nippon Railroad Co Ltd: 1-11-17, Tenjin-cho, Chuo-ku, Fukuoka 810; tel. (92) 761-6631; fax (92) 722-1405; internet www.nnr.co.jp; serves northern Kyushu; Chair. H. YOSHIMOTO; Pres. G. KIMOTO.

Odakyu Electric Railway Co Ltd: 1-8-3, Nishi Shinjuku, Shinjuku-ku, Tokyo 160-8309; tel. (3) 3349-2526; fax (3) 3349-2447; e-mail ir@odakyu-dentetsu.co.jp; internet www.odakyu-group.co.jp; f. 1948; Chair. TATSUZO TOSHIMITSU; Pres. M. KITANAKA.

Sanyo Electric Railway Co Ltd: 3-1-1, Oyashiki-dori, Nagata-ku, Kobe 653; tel. (78) 611-2211; Pres. T. WATANABE.

Seibu Railway Co Ltd: 1-11-1, Kasunokidai, Tokorozawa-shi, Saitama 359; tel. (429) 26-2035; fax (429) 26-2237; internet www .seibu-group.co.jp/railways; f. 1894; Pres. YOSHIAKI TSUTSUMI.

Tobu Railway Co Ltd: 1-1-2, Oshiage, Sumida-ku, Tokyo 131-8522; tel. (3) 3621-5057; internet www.tobu.co.jp; f. 1897; Chair. KAICHIRO NEZU; Pres. TAKASHIGE UCHIDA.

Tokyo Express Electric Railway (Tokyu) Co Ltd : 5-6, Nanpeidai-cho, Shibuya-ku, Tokyo 150; tel. (3) 3477-6111; fax (3) 3496-2965; e-mail public@tokyu.co.jp; internet www.tokyu.co.jp; f. 1922; Pres. S. SHIMUZU.

Principal Subways, Monorails and Tunnels

Subway services operate in Tokyo, Osaka, Kobe, Nagoya, Sapporo, Yokohama, Kyoto, Sendai and Fukuoka. A subway was being planned for Kawasaki by 2010. Most subway lines operate reciprocal through-services with existing private railway lines which connect the cities with suburban areas.

The first commercial monorail system was introduced in 1964 with straddle-type cars between central Tokyo and Tokyo International Airport, a distance of 13 km. Monorails also operate in other cities, including Chiba, Hiroshima, and Kitakyushu.

In 1985 the 54-km Seikan Tunnel (the world's longest undersea tunnel), linking the islands of Honshu and Hokkaido, was completed. Electric rail services through the tunnel began operating in March 1988.

Fukuoka City Subway: Fukuoka Municipal Transportation Bureau, 2-5-31, Daimyo, Chuo-ku, Fukuoka 810-0041; tel. (92) 732-4107; fax (92) 721-0754; internet subway.city.fukuoka.jp; 2 lines of 17.8 km open; Dir KENNICHIROU NISHI.

Kobe Rapid Transit: 6-5-1, Kanocho, Chuo-ku, Kobe 650; tel. (78) 331-8181; 22.7 km open; Dir YASUO MAENO.

Kyoto Rapid Transit: 48, Bojocho Mibu, Nakakyo-ku, Kyoto 604; tel. (75) 822-9115; fax (75) 822-9240; 26.4 km open; Chair. T. TANABE.

Nagoya Subway: Transportation Bureau City of Nagoya, Nagoya City Hall, 3-1-1, Sannomaru, Naka-ku, Nagoya 460-8508; tel. (52) 972-3824; fax (52) 972-3938; internet www.kotsu.city.nagoya.jp; 89.1 km open (2004); Dir-Gen. NOBUO YOSHII.

Osaka Monorail: 5-1-1, Higashi-machi, Shin-Senri, Toyonakashi, Osaka 565; tel. (6) 871-8280; fax (6) 871-8284; 113.5 km open; Gen. Man. S. OKA.

Osaka Underground Railway: Osaka Municipal Transportation Bureau, 1-11-53, Kujominami, Nishi-ku, Osaka 550; tel. (6) 6582-1101; fax (6) 6582-7997; f. 1933; 120 km open in 1998; the 6.6 km computer-controlled 'New Tram' service began between Suminoe-koen and Nakafuto in 1981; a seventh line between Kyobashi and Tsurumi-ryokuchi was opened in 1990; Gen. Man. HARUMI SAKAI.

Sapporo Transportation Bureau: Higashi, 2-4-1, Oyachi, Atsubetsu-ku, Sapporo 004; tel. (11) 896-2708; fax (11) 896-2790; f. 1971; 3 lines of 48 km open in 1993/94; Dir T. IKEGAMI.

Sendai City Subway: Sendai City Transportation Bureau, 1-4-15, Kimachidori, Aoba-ku, Sendai-shi, Miyagi-ken 980-0801; tel. (22) 224-5502; fax (22) 224-6839; internet www.comminet.or.jp/~kotsu-s; 15.4 km open; Dir T. IWAMA.

Tokyo Metro Co Ltd: 3-19-6, Higashi Ueno, Taito-ku, Tokyo 110-8614; tel. (3) 3837-7046; fax (3) 3837-7219; internet www .tokyometro.jp; f. 2004; operates eight lines; 183.2 km open (March 2003); Pres. HISASHI UMEZAKI.

Tokyo Metropolitan Government (TOEI) Underground Railway: Bureau of Transportation, Tokyo Metropolitan Government, 2-8-1 Nishi-Shinjuku, Tokyo 163-8001; tel. (3) 5320-6026; internet www.kotsu.metro.tokyo.jp; operates four underground lines, totalling 105 km.

Yokohama Rapid Transit: Municipal Transportation Bureau, 1-1, Minato-cho, Naka-ku, Yokohama 231-80; tel. (45) 671-3201; fax (45) 664-3266; 40.4 km open; Dir-Gen. MICHINORI KISHIDA.

ROADS

In December 2000 Japan's road network extended to an estimated 1,166,340 km, including 6,617 km of motorways and 53,777 km of highways. In May 1999 work was completed on a 29-year project to construct three routes, consisting of a total of 19 bridges, between the islands of Honshu and Shikoku across the Seto inland sea, at a cost of some US $25,000m.

There is a national omnibus service, 60 publicly-operated services and 298 privately-operated services.

Japan Highway Public Corpn: 3-3-2, Kasumigaseki, Chiyoda-ku, Tokyo 100-8979; tel. (3) 3506-0111; privatization plans announced in March 2004.

SHIPPING

Shipping in Japan is subject to the supervision of the Ministry of Transport. At 31 December 2003 the Japanese merchant fleet (7,151 vessels) had a total displacement of 13,561,521 grt. The main ports are Tokyo, Yokohama, Nagoya and Osaka.

Principal Companies

Daiichi Chuo Kisen Kaisha: Dowa Bldg, 3-7-13, Toyoi, Koto-ku, Tokyo 103-8271; tel. (3) 5634-2276; fax (3) 5634-2262; f. 1960; liner and tramp services; Pres. MAHIKO SAOTOME.

Iino Kaiun Kaisha Ltd: Iino Bldg, 2-1-1, Uchisaiwai-cho, Chiyoda-ku, Tokyo 100; tel. (3) 3506-3037; fax (3) 3508-4121; f. 1918; cargo and tanker services; Chair. T. CHIBA; Pres. A. KARINO.

Kansai Kisen KK: Osaka Bldg, 3-6-32, Nakanoshima, Kita-ku, Osaka 552; tel. (6) 6574-9131; fax (6) 6574-9149; f. 1942; domestic passenger services; Pres. TOSHIKAZU EGUCHI.

Kawasaki Kisen Kaisha Ltd (K Line): 1-2-9, Nishi Shimbashi, Minato-ku, Tokyo 105-8421; tel. (3) 3595-5082; fax (3) 3595-5001; e-mail otaki@email.kline.co.jp; internet www.kline.co.jp; f. 1919; containers, cars, LNG, LPG and oil tankers, bulk carriers; Chair. of Bd I. SHINTANI; Exec. Vice-Pres. Z. WAKABAYASHI.

Nippon Yusen Kaisha (NYK) Line: 2-3-2, Marunouchi, Chiyoda-ku, Tokyo 100-0005; tel. (3) 3284-5151; fax (3) 3284-6361; e-mail prteam@jp.nykline.com; internet www.nykline.com; f. 1885; merged with Showa Line Ltd in 1998; world-wide container, cargo, pure car and truck carriers, tanker and bulk carrying services; Chair. JIRO NEMOTO; Pres. KENTARO KAWAMURA.

Nissho Shipping Co Ltd: 33, Mori Bldg, 7th Floor, 3-8-21, Toranomon, Minato-ku, Tokyo 105; tel. (3) 3438-3511; fax (3) 3438-3566; f. 1943; Pres. MINORU IKEDA.

OSK Mitsui Ltd: Shosen Mitsui Bldg, 2-1-1, Toranomon, Minato-ku, Tokyo 105-91; tel. (3) 3587-7092; fax (3) 3587-7734; f. 1942; merged with Navix Line Ltd in 1999; world-wide container, liner, tramp, and specialized carrier and tanker services; Chair. SUSUMU TEMPORIN; Pres. MASAHURU IKUTA.

Ryukyu Kaiun KK: 1-24-11, Nishi-machi, Naha, Okinawa 900; tel. (98) 868-8161; fax (98) 868-8561; cargo and passenger services on domestic routes; Pres. M. AZAMA.

Taiheiyo Kaiun Co Ltd: Mitakokusai Bldg, 23rd Floor, 1-4-28, Minato-ku, Tokyo 100; tel. (3) 5445-5805; fax (3) 5445-5806; f. 1951; cargo and tanker services; Pres. SANROKURO YAMAJI.

CIVIL AVIATION

There are international airports at Tokyo (Haneda and Narita), Osaka, Nagoya and Fukuoka. In 1991 the Government approved a plan to build five new airports, and to expand 17 existing ones. In September 1994 the world's first offshore international airport (Kansai International Airport) was opened in Osaka Bay, and a second runway at that airport was due for completion in 2007. In April 2002 a second runway was opened at Narita. In December 2001 plans were approved for a fourth runway at Haneda, scheduled for completion by 2009. Narita airport was privatized in 2004. A further international offshore airport opened at Chubu in February 2005. An international airport at Shizuoka was scheduled to open in 2006.

Air Central: c/o Central Japan International Airport, 1-1, Centrair, Tokoname, Aichi 479-0881; tel. (569) 389302; fax (569) 381562; internet www.nals.co.jp; f. 1988; fmrly Nakanihon Airlines, name changed as above Feb. 2005; regional and domestic services; Pres. AKIRA HIRABAYASHI.

Air Do (Hokkaido International Airlines Co Ltd): 1, Nishi, Kita 2, 9-chome, Chuo-ku, Sapporo; tel. (11) 252-5533; fax (11) 252-5580; e-mail postbear@airdo.co.jp; internet www.airdo.co.jp; f. 1996; domestic service between Tokyo and Sapporo; Pres. AKIRA NAKAMURA.

Air Nippon: 3-5-10, Haneda Airport, Ota-ku, Tokyo 144-0041; tel. (3) 5756-4710; fax (3) 5756-4788; internet www.air-nippon.co.jp; f. 1974; fmrly Nihon Kinkyori Airways; international and domestic passenger services; Pres. and CEO YUZURU MASUMOTO.

All Nippon Airways (ANA): Shiodome City Center, 1-5-2 Higashi-Shimbashi, Minato-ku, Tokyo 105-7133; tel. (3) 6735-1111; fax (3) 6735-1115; internet www.ana.co.jp; f. 1952; operates domestic passenger and freight services; scheduled international services to the Far East, the USA and Europe; charter services world-wide; Pres. and CEO YOJI OHASHI.

Hokkaido Air System: New Chitose Airport, Bibi Chitose City, Hokkaido 066-0055; tel. (123) 46-5533; fax (123) 46-5534; internet www.hac-air.co.jp; f. 1997; domestic services on Hokkaido; Pres. YASAYUKI BABA.

JALways Co Ltd: Sphere Tower Tennoz 23 F. 2-8, Higashi-Shinagawa 2-chome, Shinagawa-ku, Tokyo, Japan 140-0002; tel. (3) 5460-6830; fax (3) 5460-8660; e-mail jazgz.jaz@jal.com; internet www.jalways.co.jp; f. 1990; subsidiary of JAL; domestic and international scheduled and charter services; Chair. KAZUNARI YASHIRO; Pres. KATSUMI CHIYO.

Japan Air Commuter: 8-2-2, Fumoto, Mizobe-cho, Aira-gun, Kagoshima 899-64; tel. (995) 582151; fax (995) 582673; e-mail info@jac.co.jp; internet www.jac.co.jp; f. 1983; subsidiary of Japan Air System; domestic services; Chair. YOSHITOMI ONO.

Japan Airlines Domestic: 4-11, Higashi-shinagawa 2-chome, Shinagawa-ku, Tokyo 140-8637; internet www.jal.co.jp; fmrly Japan Air System; affiliated to Japan Airlines Corpn (fmrly Japan Airlines System); Chair. ISAO KANEKO; CEO MITSUO KOMATSUBARA.

Japan Airlines International: 4-11, Higashi-shinagawa 2-chome, Shinagawa-ku, Tokyo 140-8637; internet www.jal.co.jp; fmrly Japan Airlines Co Ltd; affiliated to Japan Airlines Corpn (fmrly Japan Airlines System); Chair. ISAO KANEKO; Pres. KATSUO HANEDA.

Japan Asia Airways Co: JAL Bldg, 19th Floor, 2-4-11. Higashi-shinagawa, Shinagawa-ku, Tokyo 140-0002; tel. (3) 5460-7285; fax (3) 5460-7286; e-mail jaabz@jaa.jalgroup.or.jp; internet www.japanasia.co.jp; f. 1975; subsidiary of JAL; international services from Tokyo, Osaka, Nagoya and Okinawa to Hong Kong and Taiwan; Chair. TEIICHI KURIBAYASHI; Pres. OSAMU IGARASHI.

Japan Transocean Air: 3-24, Yamashita-cho, Naha-shi, Okinawa 9000027; tel. (98) 857-2112; fax (98) 857-9396; internet www.jal.co.jp/jta; f. 1967; present name since 1993; subsidiary of JAL; domestic passenger services; 8 brs; Chair. KEIICHI INAMINE; Pres. TAKESHI IOHINOSAWA.

Skymark Airlines: World Trade Center, Bldg 3F, 2-4-1, Hamamatsucho, Minato-ku, Tokyo 105-6103; tel. (3) 5402-6767; fax (3) 5402-6770; e-mail info@skymark.co.jp; internet www.skymark.co.jp; f. 1997; domestic services; Chair. HIDEO SAWADA; Pres MASAYUKI INOUE.

Tourism

The ancient capital of Kyoto, pagodas and temples, forests and mountains, traditional festivals and the classical Kabuki theatre are some of the many tourist attractions of Japan. The number of foreign visitors to Japan declined from 5,238,963 in 2002 to 5,211,725 in 2003. Receipts from tourism in 2002 totalled US $3,499m.

Department of Tourism: 2-1-3, Kasumigaseki, Chiyoda-ku, Tokyo 100; tel. (3) 3580-4488; fax (3) 3580-7901; f. 1946; a dept of the Ministry of Transport; Dir-Gen. KIMITAKA FUJINO.

Japan National Tourist Organization: Tokyo Kotsu Kaikan Bldg, 2-10-1, Yuraku-cho, Chiyoda-ku, Tokyo 100-0006; tel. (3) 3216-1901; fax (3) 3216-1846; internet www.jnto.go.jp; Pres. MINORU NAKAMURA.

Japan Travel Bureau Inc: JTB Bldg, 2-3-11 Higashi-Shinagawa, Shinagawa-ku, Tokyo; tel. (3) 3284-7028; internet www.jtb.co.jp; f. 1912; 10,297 mems; Chair. RYUJI FUNAYAMA; Pres. TAKASHI SASAKI.

JORDAN

Introductory Survey

Location, Climate, Language, Religion, Flag, Capital

The Hashemite Kingdom of Jordan is an almost land-locked state in western Asia. It is bordered by Israel and the Palestinian Autonomous Areas to the west, by Syria to the north, by Iraq to the east and by Saudi Arabia to the south. The port of Al-Aqabah (Aqaba), in the far south, gives Jordan a narrow outlet to the Red Sea. The climate is hot and dry. The average annual temperature is about 15°C (60°F) but there are wide diurnal variations. Temperatures in Amman are generally between –1°C (30°F) and 32°C (90°F). More extreme conditions are found in the valley of the River Jordan and on the shores of the Dead Sea (a lake on the Israeli–Jordanian frontier), where the temperature may exceed 50°C (122°F) in summer. The official language is Arabic. More than 90% of the population are Sunni Muslims, while there are small communities of Christians and Shi'i Muslims. The national flag (proportions 1 by 2) has three equal horizontal stripes, of black, white and green, with a red triangle, containing a seven-pointed white star, at the hoist. The capital is Amman.

Recent History

Palestine (including the present-day West Bank of Jordan) and Transjordan (the East Bank) were formerly parts of Turkey's Ottoman Empire. During the First World War (1914–18), when Turkey was allied with Germany, the Arabs under Ottoman rule rebelled. British forces, with Arab support, occupied Palestine and Transjordan in 1917–18, when the Turks withdrew. British occupation continued after the war, when the Ottoman Empire was dissolved. In 1920 Palestine and Transjordan were formally placed under British administration by a League of Nations mandate. In 1921 Abdullah ibn Hussein, a member of the Hashimi (Hashemite) dynasty of Arabia, was proclaimed Amir (Emir) of Transjordan. In the same year his brother, Faisal, became King of neighbouring Iraq. The two new monarchs were sons of Hussein ibn Ali, the Sharif of Mecca, who had proclaimed himself King of the Hedjaz (now part of Saudi Arabia) in 1916. The British decision to nominate Hashemite princes as rulers of Iraq and Transjordan was a reward for Hussein's co-operation in the wartime campaign against Turkey.

Under the British mandate Transjordan (formally separated from Palestine in 1923) gained increasing autonomy. In 1928 the United Kingdom acknowledged the nominal independence of Transjordan, while retaining certain financial and military powers. Amir Abdullah followed a generally pro-British policy and supported the Allied cause in the Second World War (1939–45). The mandate was terminated on 22 March 1946, when Transjordan attained full independence. On 25 May Abdullah was proclaimed King, and a new Constitution took effect.

When the British Government terminated its mandate in Palestine in May 1948, Jewish leaders there proclaimed the State of Israel. Palestinian Arabs, however, with military support from Arab states, opposed Israeli claims and hostilities continued until July. Transjordan's forces occupied about 5,900 sq km of Palestine, including East Jerusalem, and this was confirmed by the armistice with Israel in April 1949. In June the country was renamed Jordan, and in April 1950, following a referendum, King Abdullah formally annexed the West Bank territory, which contained many Arab refugees from Israeli-held areas.

In July 1951 King Abdullah was assassinated in Jerusalem by a Palestinian belonging to an extremist Islamist organization. Abdullah was succeeded by his eldest son, Talal ibn Abdullah, hitherto Crown Prince. However, in August 1952, because of Talal's mental incapacity, the crown passed to his son, Hussein ibn Talal, then 16 years of age. King Hussein formally came to power in May 1953.

In March 1956, responding to Arab nationalist sentiment, King Hussein dismissed the British army officer who had been Chief of Staff of the British-equipped and -financed Arab Legion (the Jordanian armed forces) since 1939. Jordan's treaty relationship with the United Kingdom was ended in March 1957, and British troops completed their withdrawal from Jordan in July.

The refugee camps in the West Bank became the centre of Palestinian resistance to Israel, and during the 1950s there were numerous attacks on Israeli territory by groups of Palestinian *fedayeen* ('martyrs'). In September 1963 the creation of a unified 'Palestinian entity' was approved by the Council of the League of Arab States (the Arab League, see p. 290), and the first Palestinian congress was held in the Jordanian sector of Jerusalem in May–June 1964, at which it was agreed to form the Palestine Liberation Organization (PLO), which would be financed by the Arab League and would recruit military units to form a Palestine Liberation Army (PLA). The principal Palestinian guerrilla organization within the PLO was the Palestine National Liberation Movement, known as Fatah ('Conquest'), led from 1968 by Yasser Arafat. However, King Hussein regarded the establishment of the PLO as a threat to Jordanian sovereignty, and from the outset refused to allow the PLA to train in Jordan or the PLO to levy taxes from Palestinian refugees residing in his country.

In April 1965 Hussein nominated his brother Hassan ibn Talal to be Crown Prince. During the Six-Day War of June 1967 Israel made substantial military gains, including possession of the whole of Jerusalem (which was incorporated into Israel) and the West Bank; the latter became an Israeli 'administered territory'. The influx of Palestinian refugees into the East Bank bolstered the strength of the PLO, whose continued armed raids on the Israeli-administered territories challenged the personal authority of King Hussein and the sovereignty of the Jordanian Government. King Hussein responded by expelling the guerrilla groups, after a civil war which lasted from September 1970 to July 1971. Aid to Jordan from Kuwait and other wealthy Arab states, suspended after the expulsion of the Palestinian fighters, was only restored following Jordan's military support for Syria during the Arab–Israeli War of October 1973. At an Arab summit meeting in Rabat, Morocco, in October 1974 King Hussein supported a unanimous resolution recognizing the PLO as the 'sole legitimate representative of the Palestinian people' and granting the organization the right to establish an independent national authority on any piece of Palestinian land to be liberated.

In November 1974, as a response to this resolution, both chambers of the Jordanian National Assembly (which had equal representation for the East and West Banks) approved constitutional amendments that empowered the King to dissolve the Assembly and to postpone elections for up to 12 months. The Assembly was dissolved later that month, although it was briefly reconvened in February 1976, when it approved a constitutional amendment giving the King power to postpone elections indefinitely and to convene the Assembly as required. A royal decree of April 1978 provided for the creation of a National Consultative Council, with 60 members appointed for a two-year term by the King, on the Prime Minister's recommendation, to debate proposed legislation.

A proposal put forward by US President Ronald Reagan in September 1982 for an autonomous Palestinian authority on the West Bank, in association with Jordan, was rejected by Yasser Arafat following talks with King Hussein. In January 1984, however, the King responded by dissolving the National Consultative Council and recalling the National Assembly for the first time since 1967—in effect creating the kind of Palestinian forum envisaged by the Reagan initiative. Israel allowed the surviving West Bank deputies to attend the Assembly, which approved constitutional amendments enabling elections to be held in the East Bank, while West Bank deputies would be chosen by the Assembly itself. After discussions with the PLO leader in January 1984 on a joint Palestinian-Jordanian peace initiative, King Hussein's proposals for negotiations, based on UN Security Council Resolution 242 (the resolution, adopted in November 1967, sought to return the region's territorial boundaries to the pre-Six-Day War status, but incorporated implicit recognition of an Israeli state), met with a non-committal response from the Palestine National Council (PNC), which convened in Amman in November 1984. President Hosni Mubarak of Egypt gave his support to Hussein's proposals, following the resumption of diplomatic relations between the two countries in September. In February 1985 King Hussein and Yasser Arafat announced the terms of a Jordanian-Palestinian agreement, proposing a confederated state of Jordan and Palestine to be reached through the convening of a conference of all concerned parties in the Middle East, including the PLO.

In July 1985 Israel rejected a list of seven Palestinians, five of whom were members of the PLO or had links with the PNC, whom King Hussein had presented to the USA as candidates for a joint Jordanian-Palestinian delegation to preliminary peace talks. Further progress was hampered by a series of terrorist incidents in which the PLO was implicated, thereby giving Israel further cause to reject the PLO as a credible partner in peace negotiations. King Hussein came under increasing pressure to advance the peace process, if necessary without PLO participation. In September President Reagan revived his 1984 plan to sell military equipment to the value of some US $1,900m. to Jordan. The proposal was approved by the US Congress on the condition that Jordan enter into direct talks with Israel before 1 March 1986. However, such talks were obstructed by a gradual *rapprochement* between Jordan and Syria, both of which supported a Middle East peace settlement through an international conference, having recently rejected 'partial and unilateral' solutions.

Frustrated by the lack of co-operation from Yasser Arafat in advancing the aims of the Jordanian-PLO peace initiative, King Hussein publicly severed political links with the PLO on 19 February 1986. Arafat was subsequently ordered to close his main PLO offices in Jordan by 1 April. The PLO's activities were henceforth to be restricted even further, and a number of Fatah officers loyal to Arafat were expelled. In July the Jordanian authorities closed all 25 Fatah offices in Amman; only 12 bureaux belonging to the PLO remained.

Despite the termination of political co-ordination with the PLO, Jordan continued to reject Israeli requests for direct peace talks that excluded a form of PLO representation. However, Jordan's subsequent efforts to strengthen its influence in the Israeli-occupied territories (Occupied Territories), and to foster a Palestinian constituency there independent of Arafat's PLO, coincided with Israeli measures to grant limited autonomy to Palestinians in the West Bank. In March 1986 the Jordanian House of Representatives approved a draft law increasing the number of seats in the House from 60 to 142 (71 seats each for the East and West Banks), thereby providing for greater representation for West Bank Palestinians in the National Assembly. In August, with Israeli support, Jordan announced a five-year development plan, valued at US $1,300m., for the West Bank and Gaza Strip; the plan was condemned by Arafat and West Bank Palestinians as representing a normalization of relations with Israel. Support for Arafat among Palestinians in the Occupied Territories, and in Jordan, was consolidated as he re-established himself at the head of a reunified PLO at the 18th session of the PNC in April 1987 (when the Jordanian-PLO accord of 1985 was formally abrogated).

In May 1987, following secret meetings with King Hussein, the Israeli Minister of Foreign Affairs, Shimon Peres, claimed to have made significant progress on the crucial issue of Palestinian representation at a Middle East peace conference, and to have the consent of Egypt, Jordan and the USA to convene a conference involving the five permanent members of the UN Security Council and a delegation of Palestinians who rejected terrorism and accepted Security Council Resolutions 242 and 338 (the latter defined the terms of immediate peace following the 1973 Arab–Israeli War) as the basis for negotiations. The Jordanian Prime Minister, Zaid ar-Rifai, confirmed his country's willingness to participate in a joint Jordanian-Palestinian delegation including the PLO, provided that the organization complied with the stated conditions. However, Israel's Prime Minister, Itzhak Shamir, reiterated his alternative proposal of direct regional talks excluding the PLO, and Peres failed to secure the support of a majority of the Israeli Cabinet for his proposals.

At the first full meeting of the Arab League for eight years, convened in Amman in November 1987, King Hussein pursued an agenda of greater Arab unity in support of Iraq in its war with Iran. Prior to the summit, Jordan restored full diplomatic relations with Libya (severed in 1984), which had modified its support for Iran. However, King Hussein's appeal for Egypt to be restored to membership of the League (suspended following the peace treaty with Israel in 1979) was resisted by Libya and Syria, although 11 Arab states subsequently re-established

diplomatic relations. Jordan also announced the resumption of co-operation with the PLO.

These achievements were soon overshadowed by the Palestinian *intifada* (uprising), which erupted in the West Bank and Gaza Strip in December 1987, in protest at the continued Israeli occupation and the seemingly indifferent attitude of Arab League states to the Palestinians' plight. The *intifada*, and the increasingly violent Israeli response, increased international support for the PLO and Palestinian national rights. At an extraordinary meeting of the Arab League held in the Algerian capital in June 1988, King Hussein gave the *intifada* his unconditional support and insisted that the PLO must represent the Palestinians at any future peace conference. Furthermore, in accordance with agreements reached at the meeting, Jordan cancelled the West Bank development plan and severed its legal and administrative links with the territory. Jordan's disengagement from the West Bank effectively rendered a proposal put forward earlier in the year by the US Secretary of State, George Shultz, for an international peace conference excluding the PLO or a joint Jordanian-Palestinian delegation, redundant.

On 15 November 1988 the PNC, meeting in Algiers, proclaimed the establishment of an independent State of Palestine and, for the first time, endorsed UN Security Council Resolution 242 as a basis for a Middle East peace settlement, thus implicitly recognizing Israel. Jordan and 60 other countries recognized the new state. Addressing a special session of the UN General Assembly in Geneva, Switzerland, in December, Arafat renounced violence on behalf of the PLO. The USA subsequently opened a dialogue with the PLO, making it more probable that Israel would have to do likewise.

In April 1989 there was rioting in several cities, after the Jordanian Government imposed sizeable price increases on basic goods and services. The riots led to the resignation of Prime Minister ar-Rifai and his Cabinet. Field Marshal Sharif Zaid ibn Shaker, a cousin of the King who had been Commander-in-Chief of the Jordanian Armed Forces in 1976–88, was appointed to head a new Government. While King Hussein refused to make any concessions regarding the price increases, he announced that a general election would be held for the first time since 1967. The election to the 80-seat House of Representatives, which proceeded in November 1989, was contested by 647 candidates, mostly independents, as the ban on political parties (in force since 1963) remained. However, the Muslim Brotherhood was able to present candidates for election, owing to its legal status as a charity. At the election the Muslim Brotherhood won 20 seats, while as many as 14 seats were won by independent Islamist candidates who supported the Brotherhood. The strength of support for opposition candidates was unexpected, especially since a disproportionately large number of seats had been assigned to rural areas from which the Government had traditionally drawn most support. In December King Hussein appointed former premier Mudar Badran as Prime Minister. The Muslim Brotherhood declined participation in the new Cabinet after its demand for the education portfolio was rejected. However, the Government included three independent Muslim deputies and three 'leftists', all of whom were regarded as members of the opposition. In January 1990 Badran pledged to abolish martial law (which had been suspended in December 1989) within four to six months, and to liberalize the judicial system; he also announced the abolition of the anti-communism law (in force since 1954). In April King Hussein appointed a 60-member commission, under the chairmanship of former premier Ahmad Ubeidat, to devise a national charter that would legalize political parties. The commission's draft national charter was approved by the King in January 1991, and further endorsed by Hussein and leading political figures in June. Also in January the Cabinet was reorganized to include five members of the Muslim Brotherhood.

Iraq's invasion of Kuwait in August 1990, and the consequent imposition of economic sanctions by the UN against Iraq, had a profound impact on Jordan: Iraq was its principal trading partner, and Jordan relied on supplies of Iraqi petroleum. Although King Hussein condemned the Iraqi invasion, he was slow to do so, and advocated an 'Arab solution' to the crisis. There was considerable support for the Iraqi President, Saddam Hussain, among the Jordanian population, particularly among Palestinians. King Hussein was critical of the US-led deployment of multinational military forces in Saudi Arabia and the Persian (Arabian) Gulf, and in the closing months of 1990 he visited numerous Middle East and other capitals in an attempt to avert a war. Jordan's response to the Gulf crisis prompted the

USA to review its military and economic assistance to Jordan and led to a deterioration in Jordan's relations with Egypt and Saudi Arabia, both of which contributed to the US-led force. However, diplomatic relations between Jordan and Iran were re-established (having been severed in 1981).

In the early stages of the Gulf crisis Jordan experienced the additional problem of a large-scale influx of refugees from Iraq and Kuwait, many of whom were seeking passage through Jordan in order to return to the Indian sub-continent and South East Asia. Large numbers of Jordanian nationals also returned from the Gulf region. Some 300,000 of these expatriates remained in Jordan after the liberation of Kuwait in February 1991, fearing reprisals in Kuwait, where most Jordanian and Palestinian residents were regarded by the authorities as collaborators with the Iraqi occupation forces.

In the months following the Gulf War Jordan concentrated on attempts to revive its shattered economy and on improving relations with its Arab neighbours, particularly Saudi Arabia. In response to Jordanian co-operation in the arrest of a Saudi dissident in Amman, Saudi Arabia revoked a ban on the entry of Jordanian transport vehicles into its territory, and trade between Jordan and Saudi Arabia was resumed. However, high-level ministerial contacts were not renewed until mid-1995.

Meanwhile, Jordan secured the approval of the USA by agreeing to join with a Palestinian delegation at the Middle East peace conference which opened in Madrid, Spain, in October 1991. Subsequent talks in Washington, DC, and Moscow, Russia, between the Israeli and the joint Jordanian-Palestinian delegations remained deadlocked with regard to substantive issues until September 1993, when Israel and the PLO agreed to a declaration of principles regarding Palestinian self-rule in the Occupied Territories. On the signing of the Declaration of Principles, which King Hussein welcomed, the Jordanian-Palestinian delegation was disbanded, and Jordan and Israel concluded an agreement that defined the agenda for subsequent bilateral negotiations within the context of the Middle East peace conference. The talks were to address the following issues: refugees and displaced persons; security; water resources; the demarcation of the border between Jordan and Israel; and future bilateral co-operation.

In 1991 Jordan and the PLO had agreed on the principle of confederation between Jordan and whatever Palestinian entity ultimately emerged from the Middle East peace process; and in July 1993 Jordan and the PLO agreed to form six committees to discuss relations between Jordan and the Occupied Territories during a period of transitional Palestinian self-rule. Within the terms of the Declaration of Principles, however, Jordan was formally excluded from the discussion of some of the issues—henceforth to be dealt with bilaterally by Israeli and Palestinian authorities—which the committees had already begun to address. Jordan was also to be invited to participate in a joint Israeli-Palestinian Liaison Committee to determine procedures for the return of Palestinians displaced from the West Bank and Gaza in 1967. However, Jordan stated its unwillingness to join such a committee, since it had not been consulted about its establishment. In January 1994, after King Hussein had twice warned that Jordan might otherwise pursue its own agenda in the ongoing peace talks with Israel, the PLO agreed to sign a comprehensive economic co-operation agreement with Jordan, and to establish a joint committee to co-ordinate financial policy in the Palestinian territories. In the same month Jordan signed a draft security accord with the PLO. Yasser Arafat visited Amman immediately following the signing of the Cairo Agreement on the Gaza Strip and Jericho by Israel and the PLO in May (see the chapter on Israel), but King Hussein reportedly remained disappointed at the PLO's failure to liaise fully with Jordan in the peace process.

On 25 July 1994 King Hussein and the Israeli Prime Minister, Itzhak Rabin, meeting in the US capital, signed the Washington Declaration, which formally ended the state of war that had existed between Jordan and Israel since 1948. In October 1994 the two countries signed a full peace treaty settling outstanding issues of contention between them and providing, *inter alia*, for the establishment of diplomatic relations and for talks on economic and security co-operation. The official normalization of relations between Jordan and Israel had been completed by 18 January 1996. In Jordan the peace treaty was opposed by Islamist militants, and it was also criticized by Syria. The PLO leadership complained that the treaty undermined Palestinian claims to sovereignty over Jerusalem. None the less, in January 1995 the PLO and Jordan signed an agreement regulating

relations between Jordan and the Palestinian Autonomous Areas with regard to economic affairs, finance, banking, education, transport, telecommunications, information and administration. At the same time, the PLO acknowledged Jordan's custodianship of the Muslim holy places in Jerusalem for as long as Jordan recognized and supported Palestinian claims to sovereignty over East Jerusalem.

Meanwhile, in June 1991 Taher al-Masri was appointed to replace Mudar Badran as Prime Minister. However, in the period preceding the opening of the National Assembly in December, it became clear that al-Masri could not command majority support in the legislature; he was forced to resign in November, whereupon Sharif Zaid ibn Shaker again assumed the premiership. In July 1992 the House of Representatives adopted legislation whereby, subject to certain conditions, political parties were formally legalized. In May 1993 King Hussein appointed Abd as-Salam al-Majali, the head of the Jordanian delegation to the Middle East peace conference, to the premiership; his Government was regarded as a transitional administration pending legislative elections to be held before November of that year.

In August 1993 King Hussein unexpectedly dissolved the House of Representatives, provoking criticism from some politicians who had expected the House to debate proposed amendments to Jordan's electoral law. Changes in voting procedures at the general election were announced by the King in that month: voters were to be allowed to cast one vote only, rather than multiple votes equal to the number of candidates contesting a given constituency. Some 68% of the electorate were reported to have participated in Jordan's first multi-party general election, held on 8 November. By far the largest number of deputies returned to the House of Representatives were independent centrists loyal to the King. The Islamic Action Front (IAF, the political wing of the Muslim Brotherhood), which emerged as the second largest party in the legislature, maintained that the new electoral law had prevented it from winning more seats. A new Senate (House of Notables) was appointed by the King on 18 November, and a new Cabinet, led by al-Majali, was announced in December. Al-Majali was dismissed in January 1995, whereupon Sharif Zaid ibn Shaker once again assumed the premiership at the head of an extensively reorganized Cabinet. Islamist and left-wing groups failed to win significant popular support at municipal elections held in July, most elected candidates being largely pro-Government or independent. The IAF attributed its poor performance to a low level of voter participation, and to official harassment of its members during the campaign.

King Hussein implemented a further extensive cabinet reshuffle in February 1996, appointing Abd al-Karim al-Kabariti, hitherto Minister of Foreign Affairs, as Prime Minister. (Kabariti retained the foreign affairs portfolio, and also assumed responsibility for defence.) In August rioting erupted in southern Jordan after the Government imposed a sharp increase on the price of bread. The unrest quickly spread to other parts of the country, including impoverished areas of the capital, and was regarded as the greatest challenge to the King's rule since the rioting over fuel prices in 1989. King Hussein responded by suspending the legislature and deploying the army in order to suppress the worst disturbances. In December 1996 the Government announced its commitment to certain reforms of electoral legislation before the next general election. Kabariti was unexpectedly dismissed by Hussein in March 1997, reportedly as a result of disagreement over issues relating to Jordan's policies towards Israel. Abd as-Salam al-Majali again assumed the premiership, taking the defence portfolio in the new Cabinet.

In July 1997 the IAF announced its intention to boycott the forthcoming parliamentary elections, in protest at what it regarded as the Government's overly concessionary policies towards Israel and at recent restrictive amendments to press legislation. Several other parties also boycotted the polls. Many of the 524 candidates at the elections, which took place on 4 November, were independents or tribal leaders campaigning on local issues. In all, 62 of the 80 seats in the new House of Representatives were won by pro-Government candidates (including two members of the recently formed National Constitutional Party); 10 seats were secured by nationalist and left-wing candidates, and eight by independent Islamists. The overall level of voter participation was reported to have been 54.6%, and was declared by the Government to be an endorsement of the country's electoral system and of the policies of King Hussein. However, there were reports that the level of turn-out was only 20% in some districts of Amman, and that the majority of Jordan's Palestinians had not voted. A new Senate was appointed by the King on 22 November. The Government was reorganized in February 1998. In July widespread public discontent arising from severe water shortages and the contamination of water supplies in Amman prompted the resignation of the Minister of Water and Irrigation. In August Fayez at-Tarawneh was appointed Prime Minister, in place of al-Majali (who had also been criticized with regard to the water crisis); a new Cabinet was subsequently named.

Meanwhile, in July 1998 King Hussein began to undergo treatment for cancer in the USA. In August he issued a royal decree transferring responsibility for certain executive duties to his brother, Crown Prince Hassan. On King Hussein's return to Jordan in January 1999, amid official assurances that his health had been restored, the King prompted renewed speculation about the royal succession by appointing Crown Prince Hassan as his 'deputy'. On 24 January King Hussein issued a royal decree naming his eldest son, Abdullah, as Crown Prince of Jordan. Although Hassan had been regent since 1965, King Hussein was said to have been dissatisfied with his brother's handling of Jordanian affairs during his absence, in particular his attempts to intervene in military matters. King Hussein had also accused his brother's supporters of slandering his immediate family, fuelling rumours that serious divisions had emerged within the royal family. Two days later the King left Jordan for emergency treatment in the USA, following a rapid deterioration in his health. King Hussein returned to Amman on 5 February 1999 and was pronounced dead on 7 February. The Crown Prince was sworn in, as King Abdullah ibn al-Hussein of Jordan, on the same day. Prince Hamzeh ibn al-Hussein, the late King's youngest son, became the new Crown Prince.

In March 1999 King Abdullah announced the formation of a new Cabinet. Abd ar-Raouf ar-Rawabdeh, a former Deputy Prime Minister and mayor of Amman, replaced Fayez at-Tarawneh as Prime Minister and Minister of Defence; Abd al-Karim al-Kabariti was appointed Chief of the Royal Court. Ar-Rawabdeh's Cabinet retained eight ministers from the outgoing administration, including those responsible for the key portfolios of the interior, finance and foreign affairs, although several ministers regarded as loyal to Prince Hassan were replaced. King Abdullah charged ar-Rawabdeh with implementing what he termed 'fundamental reforms', including a strengthening of the rule of law and further democratization, as well as economic reforms to address the serious problems of poverty and unemployment in Jordan. Opposition groups expressed cautious loyalty to the new King. The Muslim Brotherhood urged an open dialogue with the Government, and its political wing, the IAF, indicated that it would participate in municipal elections scheduled for July. However, the IAF declined to join the Popular Participation Bloc, a new grouping of 13 leftist, Baathist and pan-Arab parties subsequently formed to contest the elections, owing to a disagreement regarding each party's quota of candidates.

Although in March 1999 King Abdullah had, under a recent amnesty law, released almost 500 prisoners, in April the Arab Human Rights Organization in Jordan criticized the Government for an increase in human rights violations, including arrests of journalists and harsh treatment of prisoners held in detention centres. Nevertheless, censorship of the foreign press was revoked in that month, and in June the Government agreed to amend part of the controversial Press and Publications Law in order to ease certain restrictions on journalists.

The final results of municipal elections held in July 1999 indicated that independent and tribal candidates had secured the most seats. Islamists too were successful in their traditional urban strongholds: the IAF, which notably increased its presence on the Amman municipal council, announced subsequently that it would contest the general election scheduled for late 2001 if the electoral law was amended. The overall level of voter participation was around 59%; voting in some areas was marred by violence, in which two people died. In September the Government agreed in principle to some of the opposition's demands regarding electoral reform; these included an increase in the number of seats in the House of Representatives from 80 to 120, and the division of the country into 80 electoral districts.

In January 2000 Abd al-Karim al-Kabariti, a long-standing rival of ar-Rawabdeh, resigned as Chief of the Royal Court for unspecified reasons. He was replaced by former premier Fayez at-Tarawneh. A reorganization of the Government followed shortly afterwards: the new Cabinet was dominated by techno-crats and supporters of the Prime Minister, and the key ministries remained unchanged. In February the Deputy Prime Minister and Minister of Planning, Dr Rima Khalaf al-Hunaidi, announced her resignation, owing to alleged differences with the Government regarding economic reforms; Dr Taleb ar-Rifai was appointed to succeed her in May. Also in February, meanwhile, a parliamentary committee charged with investigating allegations of corruption made against ar-Rawabdeh and his son Issam (both had been accused of having sought a US $20m. bribe from a Gulf businessman in return for securing approval to build a tourism complex in Jordan) cleared both the Prime Minister and his son of any wrongdoing. Later that month a majority of deputies in the House of Representatives submitted a petition to the Speaker, Abd al-Hadi al-Majali, demanding the implementation of *Shari'a* (Islamic) law in order to reduce corruption and nepotism in public office.

In April 2000 a group of deputies in the House of Representatives, among them al-Majali and the Chairman of the Economic and Finance Committee, Ali Abu ar-Ragheb, urged King Abdullah to dismiss the ar-Rawabdeh Government for its failure to implement reforms and safeguard public freedoms, and demanded the establishment of a 'parliamentary government' of deputies. At the same time opposition groups accused the Government of using excessive force in controlling public dissent. Although the King responded by expressing his confidence in the Prime Minister, in June Abdullah dismissed ar-Rawabdeh, appointing the more liberal ar-Ragheb in his place; a new Cabinet was duly appointed. A leading member of the IAF, Abd ar-Rahim al-Akour, was named as Minister of Municipal, Rural and Environmental Affairs, which led the IAF to suspend his party membership. King Abdullah stated that the priorities of the new Government were to end corruption, to introduce electoral legislation prior to the next parliamentary elections, and to accelerate the economic reform programme. In August the King was said to have called for the formation of a royal committee whose task would be to implement a 'drastic review' of the country's judicial system. In March–April 2001 King Abdullah convened a National Economic Forum, with the participation of both public- and private-sector organizations; delegates at the conference concluded that task forces should be created to reform agriculture, education, administration and financial services.

On 23 April 2001 King Abdullah exercised his constitutional right to extend the current term of the House of Representatives by two years. There was some speculation that the King's decision to postpone legislative elections—scheduled for November—had been taken in an attempt to prevent Islamist opposition parties (which were highly critical of the Government's policies towards Israel) from presenting a serious challenge to his leadership. On 16 June the King ordered the dissolution of the House, which had been sitting in extraordinary session since April, and effected a cabinet reshuffle involving 11 new ministerial appointments (but excluding the key portfolios). The following day King Abdullah set the Government the task of drafting amendments to the electoral law within one month. On 22 July the King approved the new electoral legislation, which provided for the redrawing of electoral boundaries (the number of constituencies was to rise from 21 to 44) in order to increase the number of seats in the House of Representatives from 80 to 104, and a reduction of the age of eligibility to vote from 19 years to 18. The Muslim Brotherhood threatened to boycott the forthcoming parliamentary elections, in view of the Government's failure to meet its demand for the reintroduction of an 'electoral list' system. Critics of the amendments also complained that they failed to address the issue of under-representation in the legislature of Jordanians of Palestinian origin. Nevertheless, the new law did provide for the formation of special committees whose task would be to monitor the electoral process. Shortly afterwards it was reported that the November elections were to be postponed until late 2002 for technical reasons. At the end of August 2001 legislation was enacted imposing a ban on public gatherings and demonstrations. In early October, following the suicide attacks on the USA (see below), King Abdullah issued a royal decree amending Jordan's penal code in order to strengthen counter-terrorism measures; he also imposed tougher penalties on those found guilty of 'publication crimes'. Later that month, at the King's request, Prime Minister ar-Ragheb effected a minor reorganization of the Cabinet. On 23 November King Abdullah appointed a new 40-member Senate upon the expiry of its term.

In mid-January 2002 Prime Minister ar-Ragheb again submitted the resignation of his Government, but was asked by King Abdullah to form a new administration capable of initiating economic and social reforms prior to parliamentary elections (now expected by November). A new Cabinet was named shortly afterwards; seven new ministers joined the Government, including Marwan al-Muashar as Minister of Foreign Affairs and Qaftan al-Majali as Minister of the Interior. In late January the King suffered one of the most serious challenges to his rule when two days of violent clashes, in which one policeman died, erupted between protesters and security forces in Ma'an, following the death of a local youth in police custody, whom demonstrators alleged had been the victim of police brutality. The Government later announced that two investigations had been launched to determine the causes of both the adolescent's death and the subsequent riots.

King Abdullah announced in mid-August 2002 that legislative elections would be postponed until 2003, owing to the continuing instability in the region. A limited reorganization of the Cabinet was effected in late September 2002: the most significant change was the promotion of the Minister of Justice, Faris an-Nabulsi, to a new post of Deputy Prime Minister. In early November security forces in Ma'an carried out a large-scale operation aimed at detaining a local Islamist cleric, Muhammad Shalabi (or 'Abu Sayyaf') and his supporters, whom the Government claimed had played an important role in January's riots. Many observers believed that the security operation was linked to the recent assassination of a US diplomat (see below). At least three civilians and two police-officers were reportedly killed during the week-long campaign; however, despite the security forces making a large number of arrests, Abu Sayyaf apparently evaded capture. Renewed clashes between police and local gunmen later in November resulted in another civilian death in Ma'an. At the end of the month the Government announced that it would henceforth have the authority to disband any trade union-affiliated committee opposed to the normalization of relations with Israel.

A limited reshuffle of the Cabinet took place in early January 2003. King Abdullah approved amendments to draft electoral legislation on 9 February: the amendments, which were to take effect from the next general election, increased the number of seats in the House of Representatives from 104 to 110, in order to provide a quota of six seats for female legislators. At the end of February Prime Minister ar-Ragheb announced that elections to the House of Representatives would be held on 17 June. In early March the King effected several changes to the composition of the Royal Court, including the appointment of a former army general and minister of state, Yousuf ad-Dalabeeh, as Chief of the Royal Court, in place of Fayez at-Tarawneh. The King also appointed Faisal al-Fayez to the new government post of Minister of the Royal Court.

Popular opposition to the US-led military campaign in Iraq (see the chapter on Iraq) manifested itself in Government-approved rallies in Amman in February 2003, and in mid-March 14 opposition parties coalesced to protest against the presence of US troops in eastern Jordan. At the end of March 95 prominent establishment figures, including former premiers and security officials, petitioned the King demanding that Jordan refuse to recognize the legality of the conflict in Iraq. A further attempt by 99 prominent Jordanians to petition the King occurred in mid-April, following the capture of Baghdad by US forces on 9 April. At the same time, the IAF issued a *fatwa* (Islamic edict) declaring that it was a 'great sin' to allow US-led forces to use Jordanian territory. The war in Iraq generally had little impact on Jordan's domestic affairs; however, when up to 12 people were killed by unknown assailants in the bombing of the Jordanian embassy in Baghdad on 7 August, it was widely interpreted as a 'revenge' attack for Jordan's official stance during the conflict.

At the parliamentary elections held on 17 June 2003 tribal representatives and Hashemite loyalists won 80 of the 110 seats to the House of Representatives, while the IAF, the largest opposition party, won 17 seats. Under the legislation approved in February, six seats were reserved for female candidates. Therefore, the new parliament was regarded as largely pro-Government, with some representation for Islamists and those opposed to Jordan's peace treaty with Israel. On 21 July a new 28-member Cabinet was announced, including eight new ministers. Those who retained their portfolios from the previous administration included Faris an-Nabulsi as Deputy Prime Minister and Minister of Justice, Dr Marwan al-Muasher as

Minister of Foreign Affairs, and Dr Michel Marto as Minister of Finance. New appointments included Dr Muhammad al-Halaiqa as Deputy Prime Minister and Minister of Administrative Development, and Samir Habashneh as Minister of the Interior. The composition of the new Cabinet was believed to reflect the increased Islamist presence in the newly elected House of Representatives, which at the beginning of August notably rejected a law granting Jordanian women the right to file for divorce.

The new administration of ar-Ragheb proved to be short-lived, however; following considerable criticism of the Government over the slow pace of reform and accusations of corruption, the Prime Minister resigned on 21 October 2003. On 25 October King Abdullah inaugurated a new, reduced 21-member Cabinet under Prime Minister Faisal al-Fayez, who had served as Minister of the Royal Court in the previous administration. Al-Fayez was also named as the Minister of Defence, while Dr Marwan al-Muasher and Samir Habashneh retained their posts as the Ministers of Foreign Affairs and of the Interior, respectively. The previous Minister of Industry and Commerce, Muhammad Abu Hammur, was named as the new Minister of Finance, while Salah ed-Din al-Bashir replaced Faris an-Nabulsi as the Minister of Justice; al-Bashir was also named as the Minister of State for Cabinet Affairs. The appointment of three female ministers preceded that of an expanded 55-member Senate on 17 November, in accordance with constitutional guidelines that membership of the Senate must be no larger than one-half that of the House of Representatives.

In April 2004 it was revealed that Jordanian security forces had made a number of arrests which had possibly averted a major terrorist attack in the kingdom. It was alleged that militant Islamists closely linked to the al-Qa'ida (Base) network under the command of Saudi-born Osama bin Laden had laden trucks with huge quantities of explosives and planned to detonate them against the Office of the Prime Minister and the Ministry of the Interior. One of the arrested militants reportedly confessed that the instigator of the plot was Abu Mussab az-Zarqawi, the Jordanian national whom US officials believed was directing attacks against the US-led coalition in Iraq. In late December the State Security Court cleared 10 Jordanians and three Saudi fugitives of charges of planning attacks against the US embassy in Jordan and military bases near the Iraqi border, where US troops were believed to be stationed. However, 11 of the men were given prison terms ranging from six to 15 years for possessing explosives; the other two were acquitted owing to a lack of evidence.

Meanwhile, in late September 2004 King Abdullah announced his decision to postpone the reopening of the House of Representatives from 1 October to 1 December, apparently in anticipation of an expected government reshuffle. In mid-October 11 small political parties merged to form the centrist, pro-Government Jordanian National Movement, which sought to encourage national unity and respect for the Constitution and state institutions. In late October Prime Minister Faisal al-Fayez carried out a reorganization of the Cabinet: Dr Marwan al-Muasher assumed the role of Deputy Prime Minister from Dr Muhammad al-Halaiqa, and was also named as Minister of State for Prime Ministry Affairs and Government Performance. Jordan's ambassador to Egypt, Hani Mulki, became the new Minister of Foreign Affairs, al-Muasher's previous role. Dr Salah ed-Din al-Bashir retained the justice portfolio, but lost the title of Minister of State for Cabinet Affairs. Munther Shara became Minister of Political Development. In late November King Abdullah took away the title of Crown Prince from his half-brother, Hamzeh ibn al-Hussein, citing the wish to give him more freedom to undertake tasks that this 'symbolic' position did not permit. According to the Constitution, Abdullah's 10-year-old son, Hussein, became heir to the throne; although the position of Crown Prince remained vacant, many commentators expected the King to give the title to his son in the future.

On 5 April 2005 King Abdullah accepted the resignation of al-Fayez's Government and appointed Adnan Badran (a former Minister of Education) Prime Minister. Two days later a new Government, apparently considered more 'reformist' than the previous one, was sworn in. Faruq Kasrawi adopted the foreign affairs portfolio, Bassem Awadallah became Minister of Finance, and Awni Yervas was named Minister of the Interior. Badran, like his predecessor, also assumed responsibility for defence. Abdullah had criticized al-Fayez's administration at a summit of Arab countries in the previous month and the change of Government was considered part of an attempt by the King to accelerate political reform.

In September 1997 relations with Israel were severely undermined when the head of the political bureau of the Palestinian Islamist group Hamas, Khalid Meshaal, survived an assassination attempt in Amman by agents of the Israeli intelligence service, Mossad. Intensive negotiations involving Crown Prince Hassan, Israeli Prime Minister Binyamin Netanyahu and US officials resulted in an agreement in October whereby Israel freed the Hamas spiritual leader, Sheikh Ahmad Yassin, in return for Jordan's release of two Mossad agents arrested in connection with the attack on Meshaal. A further 12 Mossad agents were expelled from Jordan following the release from Israeli custody of 23 Jordanian and 50 Palestinian detainees. Israel and Jordan signed several bilateral trade agreements in March 1998, and in the following month King Hussein met with Netanyahu for the first time since the attempt on Meshaal's life. King Hussein's mediation at the US-brokered peace summit held between Israel and the Palestinian (National) Authority (PA) in October was crucial to the signing of the Wye Memorandum (see the chapter on Israel). In December Israel agreed to open its airspace to foreign airlines *en route* for Jordan.

Upon his accession in February 1999 King Abdullah assured Israel that he would pursue his father's commitment to the Middle East peace process. None the less, Netanyahu's first official visit to Amman, in late February, was largely overshadowed by recent comments made by the Israeli premier to the effect that Jordan intended to strengthen its links with Iraq at the expense of improving relations with Israel. In July Abdullah held talks with the new Israeli Prime Minister, Ehud Barak; discussions reportedly focused on ways to revive the peace process. The King welcomed the reactivation of the stalled Wye Memorandum by the signing (to which he was a witness) of the Sharm esh-Sheikh Memorandum (Wye Two—see the chapter on Israel) by Barak and Arafat in September.

There was considerable speculation at the time of the Wye Two agreement that recent efforts to bring an end to Hamas's political activities in Jordan had been motivated by a consensus among the Jordanian, Palestinian, Israeli and US authorities on the need to contain potential Islamist opposition to a revival of the peace process. In August 1999 the Jordanian security forces closed down Hamas offices in Amman, on the grounds that these were being used by foreign groups for illegal political activities. The home of Khalid Meshaal was also raided, while some 15 Hamas officials were detained and arrest warrants issued for a further five of the organization's leaders. In September three of the five (including Meshaal and the Hamas spokesman, Ibrahim Ghosheh) were arrested on their return to Amman from Iran, on charges of involvement in illicit political activities and the illegal possession of firearms. Further charges were brought against Meshaal and Ghosheh in October. In November another senior Hamas official was arrested, amid reports that the organization had rejected an offer by the Jordanian Government to release the detained activists provided that they agreed to cease all political activity and that their leaders left the country. Later in the month the Jordanian authorities released some 24 Hamas officials, including four leaders (among them Meshaal and Ghosheh) who were immediately flown to Qatar. An appeal against this effective deportation, lodged by the four men at Jordan's Higher Court of Justice in January 2000, was rejected in June. In November, during talks with Khalid Meshaal in Qatar, Jordan's Prime Minister, Ali Abu ar-Ragheb, reportedly reiterated the conditions under which the Hamas leaders would be allowed to return to Jordan. The Jordanian authorities granted permission for Ibrahim Ghosheh to enter the country in June 2001, after he had agreed to end his involvement with Hamas.

Meanwhile, in December 1999 16 people, all of whom were alleged to belong to the al-Qa'ida network, were arrested on charges of plotting attacks against US and Israeli tourist targets in Jordan. Trial proceedings began against the detainees in Amman in May 2000, while 12 further alleged militants were tried *in absentia*. In September six of the defendants were sentenced to death, having been convicted of charges including membership of al-Qa'ida and the manufacture of explosives; 16 were condemned to various terms of imprisonment, while six defendants were acquitted. The Jordanian authorities arrested a number of suspected Islamist extremists in July 2000, apparently in response to a warning that the US embassy in Amman was vulnerable to attacks by militant groups; in September four of the defendants received the death sentence. In February 2002 a Jordanian-US national, Raed Hijazi, was sentenced to death, having been found guilty of several charges relating to the

alleged terrorist plot in late 1999; however, he was cleared of any involvement with al-Qa'ida. (After an appeals court ordered a retrial of Hijazi's case in early October 2002, claiming that there had been insufficient evidence to convict him, the death sentence was upheld by the State Security Court in early January 2003.) At the end of February 2002 at least two people were killed in an attack in Amman on a car belonging to the wife of a senior anti-terrorism police-officer who had played a prominent role in the original trial of the 28 al-Qa'ida suspects.

King Abdullah postponed his first visit to Israel in February 2000, apparently in protest at recent Israeli bombing raids against infrastructure targets in Lebanon (although Jordanian officials cited the lack of progress in the Middle East peace process). Abdullah finally visited Israel in April, when he held brief discussions with Ehud Barak regarding the peace process, as well as water management and other bilateral issues. In advance of the Israeli-Palestinian peace talks held at the US presidential retreat at Camp David, Maryland, in July, Prime Minister ar-Ragheb emphasized that the Jordanian Government would not accept any more Palestinian refugees and that it supported their right of return to their homeland. (Recent reports had implied that Jordan was being considered as a possible home for those displaced persons currently in refugee camps in Lebanon.) In June 2004 there were 1,758,274 Palestinian refugees in Jordan and a further 675,670 in the West Bank registered with the UN Relief and Works Agency for Palestine Refugees in the Near East (UNRWA, see p. 80). Meanwhile, in August 2000 King Abdullah reiterated that Jordan would not accept Israeli or international sovereignty over the Islamic holy sites in East Jerusalem, an issue that had been a major obstacle to progress at Camp David.

King Abdullah participated in the intense diplomatic efforts aimed at restoring peace in the region following the outbreak of violence in the West Bank and Gaza in late September 2000 (see the chapters on Israel and the Palestinian Autonomous Areas). In mid-October the King attended a US-brokered summit meeting between Ehud Barak and Yasser Arafat in Sharm esh-Sheikh, Egypt. As violence between Palestinians and Israeli security forces escalated, Jordan came under growing pressure from other Arab states to sever diplomatic ties with Israel, while large-scale public demonstrations against Israeli and US policies towards the new Palestinian uprising (often termed the al-Aqsa *intifada*) were held in Amman and at Jordan's refugee camps. One 'anti-normalization' protest held in early October resulted in violent confrontations between protesters and police; the Government subsequently issued a ban on public demonstrations. Meanwhile, Jordan delayed the dispatch of its new ambassador to Israel, in response to the deteriorating situation in the West Bank and Gaza; also in October 30 parliamentary deputies signed a petition demanding the expulsion of the Israeli ambassador in Amman. In late October Jordanian police used tear gas and water cannons to disperse thousands of protesters who had gathered on Jordan's border with the West Bank in support of the right of return for Palestinian refugees. In November the Israeli Vice-Consul in Amman was injured in a gun attack by militant Islamists; another Israeli diplomat was wounded in a similar attack in December. In late November, meanwhile, King Abdullah appealed to the USA to intervene in order to halt 'Israeli aggressive practices' which threatened to destroy the prospects for achieving peace in the Middle East. Abdullah expressed his hope that the peace process would continue following the election of the uncompromising Ariel Sharon as Israeli Prime Minister in early February 2001, and appealed to the new US Administration under President George W. Bush to engage actively in efforts to bring an end to the violence.

The convening of a summit meeting of Arab League heads of state in Amman in late March 2001 reflected Jordan's prominent role in diplomatic efforts to resolve the Israeli–Palestinian conflict. At the summit Arab leaders pledged to transfer funds to the PA as part of a US $1,000m. fund established in late 2000. Jordan and Egypt both refused to return their ambassadors to Tel-Aviv in protest at Israeli military actions against the Palestinians, although they did not proceed to a formal suspension of diplomatic relations. (Egypt did, however, downgrade its relations with Israel in April 2002.) The summit's final communiqué—termed the Amman Declaration—repeated demands for Israel to withdraw its armed forces from all occupied territory. It was reported at the end of March 2001 that a joint Egyptian-Jordanian initiative for Middle East peace had been submitted to European Union (EU) and US officials in an attempt to encourage Israel and the PA to revive negotiations. However, fears among Jordanians that the violence in the Occupied Territories might spread to Jordan were heightened in August when an Israeli businessman in Amman was murdered by a militant Islamist.

Further mass demonstrations were held in Jordanian cities and Palestinian refugee camps during late March and April 2002, after public anger had been fuelled by Israel's reoccupation of Palestinian-controlled towns in the West Bank. Jordanian anti-riot police responded forcefully to many unlicensed rallies, at which several protesters demanded that Jordan sever diplomatic ties with Israel. In early April Jordan was reported to be considering the expulsion of Israel's ambassador to Amman, in protest against continuing Israeli military action in the Palestinian territories. In mid-April the Jordanian Minister of Foreign Affairs, Marwan al-Muasher, held talks with Yasser Arafat at his besieged compound in Ramallah, in an apparent demonstration of solidarity with the Palestinian leader. Moreover, in that month the Jordanian authorities began to deliver large consignments of humanitarian aid from Jordan and other Arab states to the West Bank.

On 4 June 2003 King Abdullah hosted a summit meeting between US President George W. Bush, Israeli premier Ariel Sharon and the newly appointed Palestinian Prime Minister, Mahmud Abbas (Abu Mazen). The aim of the summit was to begin the implementation of the 'roadmap' peace plan, an initiative which had been drawn up in late 2002 by the 'Quartet' group (comprising the USA, the UN, Russia and the EU) and unveiled by President Bush at the end of April 2003, following the US-led invasion of Iraq and the removal from power of the Iraqi leader, Saddam Hussein. In mid-September the Governor of the Central Bank of Jordan circulated a letter among the members of the Jordanian Banks Association urging them to suspend transactions involving members of Hamas and also those of five Palestinian non-militant organizations.

In late February 2004 a Jordanian delegation travelled to the International Court of Justice (ICJ) in The Hague, Netherlands, to present a 100-page document condemning Israel's construction of a 'security fence' in the West Bank (see the chapters on Israel and the Palestinian Autonomous Areas). The ICJ had been asked by the UN General Assembly to rule on the legality of the barrier, and Jordan was one of 14 countries to present evidence against its construction. It was reported in late March that King Abdullah and Ariel Sharon had held secret talks in southern Israel regarding the controversial barrier. In mid-May, following discussions held on the sidelines of the World Economic Forum in Amman, Israel and Jordan agreed to upgrade their bilateral trade agreement, which had been signed months after the 1994 peace treaty. In early February 2005 King Abdullah attended the summit meeting which took place in Sharm esh-Sheikh, Egypt, between Sharon and Mahmud Abbas—recently elected as Executive President of the PA following the death of Yasser Arafat in November 2004—at which the two leaders issued verbal declarations that Israel and the PA would cease all acts of violence against each other (although no formal cease-fire agreement was signed). In late February 2005 Jordan returned an ambassador to Tel-Aviv.

Jordan's relations with the USA in the early 1990s were frequently strained by US allegations of Jordanian assistance to Iraq in circumventing the UN trade embargo, as well as Jordan's vocal criticism of US-led policies towards Iraq. In July 1993 the USA reportedly informed Jordan that it must make payments to the UN Compensation Fund for Kuwait if it continued to receive deliveries of petroleum from Iraq. In September, however, US President Bill Clinton announced that some US $30m. in economic and military aid to Jordan was to be released in recognition of the country's enforcement of sanctions against Iraq and of its role in the Middle East peace process. In early 1994 renewed tensions emerged with the USA over the Jerusalem issue and the US-led naval blockade of Jordan's only port at Aqaba. In August 1995, as King Hussein formally severed political ties with Iraq (see below), Clinton promised to support Jordan in the event of any threat to its security; however, the USA failed to persuade Jordan to sever all economic links with Iraq. In January 1996 the USA offered Jordan $300m. in military assistance, and an expansion of bilateral military co-operation was announced in March. In June 1997 the USA pledged $100m. in economic aid to Jordan, reportedly in recognition of Jordan's contributions to the regional peace process; an assistance fund was established in August. In the same month Jordan signed a debt-rescheduling agreement with the USA, in

accordance with a deal reached in May by members of the 'Paris Club' of Western official creditors to reschedule approximately $400m. of Jordanian debt. During a visit to Washington, DC, in March 1998 King Hussein reiterated demands that the USA exert pressure on Israel to make concessions over the West Bank; Hussein also proposed that Jordan participate in future negotiations between US and Iraqi officials.

In May 1999 King Abdullah began a three-week tour of the USA and several European capitals. Prior to the visit, the King had announced that, in anticipation of a summit of leaders of the Group of Eight (G-8) industrialized countries, due to be held in Germany in June, he would be seeking US support for an agreement by Western countries to write off as much as 50% of Jordan's debt. He achieved some success when, in late May (two days after a meeting with President Clinton) the 'Paris Club' agreed to reschedule about US $800m. of Jordanian debt; in June the G-8 leaders recommended arrangements for debt-reduction for Jordan. In mid-2000 King Abdullah held a series of meetings with President Clinton and senior US officials to discuss the Middle East peace process and bilateral trade. During a visit by the King to Washington, DC, in late October, Jordan and the USA signed a free-trade agreement involving the reciprocal removal of all customs duties by 2010. The deal was fully implemented in early December 2001.

King Abdullah strongly condemned the September 2001 suicide attacks against New York and Washington, DC, for which the USA held Osama bin Laden's al-Qa'ida network principally responsible, and the King swiftly affirmed Jordan's commitment to the proposed US-led 'war on terror'. Jordanian armed forces joined US and European forces when, from early October, they launched military strikes against al-Qa'ida bases and the Sunni fundamentalist Taliban regime in Afghanistan (which was believed to be harbouring bin Laden). However, Abdullah emphasized that the international community must simultaneously renew efforts to resolve the Israeli–Palestinian conflict. He also warned persistently that any extension of the US-led military action to target any Arab country, such as Iraq, would undermine the international campaign. In April 2002 certain sections of Jordan's business community called on the Government to boycott US products, in protest against perceived US support for Israeli aggression in the West Bank (see above). In July King Abdullah warned that Jordan would not allow its territory to be used by US troops to launch a military attack aimed at ousting the regime of Saddam Hussein in Iraq, and Jordanian officials denied reports in late September that the Government had agreed to allow US forces to use Jordanian military bases in return for a guaranteed supply of cheap oil during a potential disruption to Iraq's oil supplies. In early October the USA was said to have pledged a further US $85m. to Jordan, apparently in an effort to secure the country's support during a possible US-led military campaign in Iraq and to enable the Jordanian economy to withstand the consequences of a war.

At the end of October 2002 a senior US diplomat, Laurence Foley, became the first Western official to be assassinated in Jordan. The Jordanian security forces detained a large number of suspected Islamic militants following the assassination. In mid-December two alleged members of al-Qa'ida—one Jordanian and the other Libyan—were arrested on suspicion of involvement in Foley's murder. The trial of 11 suspects charged with involvement in the murder began in early July 2003 and concluded in April 2004. Of the 11 defendants, six were tried in absentia, including Abu Mussab az-Zarqawi (see above). Ten of the defendants were convicted of charges relating to the murder of Foley, with eight being sentenced to death (among them az-Zarqawi) and two being given terms of imprisonment; the eleventh defendant was acquitted. In early February 2003, meanwhile, Jordanian officials confirmed that the USA was to provide an anti-missile defence system to Jordan in the event of a conflict in Iraq; the kingdom had received six F-16 fighter aircraft from the US military in late January. King Abdullah met President Bush at Camp David in mid-September. The two leaders discussed issues such as smuggling from Iraq, progress relating to the implementation of the 'roadmap' peace plan, and Palestinian militant funds held in Jordan. In December King Abdullah met President Bush in Washington, DC, and also held talks with British Prime Minister Tony Blair in London. Discussions concerning Iraq and the stalled Israeli-Palestinian peace process reportedly dominated both meetings. King Abdullah visited the USA in mid-April 2004, but a meeting with President Bush was cancelled in protest at US support for

Israel, particularly following Israel's recent 'targeted killings' of Hamas leaders Sheikh Ahmad Yassin and Abd al-Aziz ar-Rantisi and Bush's endorsement of Sharon's plan for an Israeli 'disengagement' from Gaza (see the chapter on Israel). The rescheduled meeting took place in Washington, DC, in early May.

After August 1995, when Jordan granted political asylum to the two sons-in-law of the Iraqi President, Saddam Hussain, and their wives (see the chapter on Iraq), King Hussein became more openly critical of the Iraqi regime, although Jordan continued to provide Iraq with a crucial external economic link. In December 1997 Jordan recalled its chargé d'affaires in Baghdad and expelled a number of Iraqi diplomats from Jordan, in protest at the execution of four Jordanians by the Iraqi authorities. Later in that month, however, the two countries signed an agreement whereby Iraq was to supply 4.8m. metric tons of crude petroleum and refined petroleum products to Jordan in 1998. In January of that year more than 50 Jordanian detainees were released by Iraq.

In response to critical confrontations between Iraq and the UN during 1998 over the issue of weapons inspections, Jordan indicated that it would not allow its territory or airspace to be used for air-strikes against Iraq. King Hussein consistently advocated a resolution of the crises by diplomatic means, whilst urging Iraq to comply with all pertinent UN resolutions. This position allowed Jordan to improve its relations with some Arab states, notably Egypt. Jordan strongly condemned the air-strikes carried out against Iraq by US and British forces in December, and in early 1999 the Jordanian National Assembly voted in favour of an end to the UN embargo against Iraq.

King Abdullah made attempts to improve Jordan's relations with Iraq following his accession in February 1999. However, in June 2000 Jordan condemned the execution by Iraq of a Jordanian national charged with spying for the US Central Intelligence Agency (CIA). Tensions were eased somewhat following a visit to Amman in mid-July by Iraqi Vice-President Taha Yassin Ramadan. In November Prime Minister ar-Ragheb undertook an official visit to Iraq—the first visit by a Jordanian premier since 1991—and the two states agreed to increase the value of their trade agreement from US $300m. in 2000 to $450m. in 2001. Jordan condemned the air-strikes launched on Baghdad by US and British forces in February 2001. By mid-2001 Jordan was increasingly concerned that the proposed imposition of so-called 'smart' sanctions against Iraq (the initiative, supported principally by the USA and United Kingdom, was under debate at the UN Security Council—see the chapter on Iraq) would result in the loss of its oil supply from Iraq, in addition to its main regional export market. However, although Jordanian officials declared publicly their opposition to 'smart' sanctions, they were said to have privately assured Western governments that they accepted the policy. The Iraqi leadership, meanwhile, threatened to halt trade with any government that assisted in the implementation of the sanctions regime. In June Royal Jordanian Airline resumed scheduled flights to Iraq for the first time since 1990. At senior-level discussions held in Amman in early January 2002, Iraq and Jordan renewed their oil protocol and also agreed to the creation of a free-trade zone.

Following discussions held in London, United Kingdom, between the British Prime Minister, Tony Blair, and King Abdullah in late February 2003, the two leaders issued a joint statement calling on the Iraqi regime to comply with the terms of UN Security Council Resolution 1441 (see the chapter on Iraq), but stating that both Jordan and the United Kingdom favoured a peaceful solution to the crisis regarding Iraqi disarmament. King Abdullah had asserted in early February that the dispute regarding Iraq's alleged non-compliance with UN weapons inspectors should only be resolved under the umbrella of the UN. During early 2003 Jordan was said to be taking measures to prevent an influx of Iraqi refugees into the kingdom in the event of a US-led military campaign to remove Saddam Hussain from power. Following the outbreak of hostilities in Iraq in mid-March, it was reported in early April that two Iraqi terrorist squads had recently been detained in Jordan, after allegedly plotting to poison a reservoir used by US troops and to bomb a hotel frequented by Western journalists and military officials; three Iraqi diplomats were expelled from Jordan in late March after being implicated in the alleged poisoning plot. In early June the establishment was announced of a joint Jordanian-Iraqi business council to facilitate business relations between the two countries following the ousting of Saddam Hussain's regime and to aid the recovery of the Iraqi economy.

At the end of July it was revealed that two daughters of the former Iraqi President had fled to Jordan via the United Arab Emirates. (In 1995 the women's husbands had been granted asylum in Jordan, but later returned to Iraq where they were executed on the orders of Saddam Hussain.) Official Jordanian sources stated that the two women and their children were being allowed to stay in Jordan for 'humanitarian reasons'. In early July 2004 King Abdullah offered to send troops to Iraq if the recently appointed Iraqi interim President or Prime Minister requested them to assist in restoring security to the country. In late November the King held talks in Jordan with Iraq's interim Prime Minister, Dr Ayad Allawi, and Iraqi exiles, in an attempt to win support for elections to a transitional Iraqi legislature, scheduled to be held at the end of January 2005. In early January 2005 Amman hosted a meeting of five of the six countries neighbouring Iraq to discuss the forthcoming elections. The Iranian Minister of Foreign Affairs, Kamal Kharrazi, boycotted the meeting after Jordanian officials accused Iran of seeking to influence Iraqi voting in order to encourage the formation of a Shi'ite-dominated government, which would give largely Shi'ite Iran greater influence in the country. The conference emphasized the need to warn countries against external efforts to influence the outcome of the elections in Iraq.

President Hafiz al-Assad of Syria led a high-level Syrian delegation at King Hussein's funeral in February 1999, since when Jordan's relations with Syria have improved significantly. It was announced in May that Syria would supply Jordan with water in order to ease the summer drought. In June Jordan refused to participate in joint Turkish-Israeli naval exercises, scheduled for the following month; similar exercises in 1998 had provoked a diplomatic crisis with Syria. In August 1999 the first senior Syrian delegation for almost a decade visited Amman for a session of the Jordanian-Syrian Higher Committee; the meeting resulted in an accord that officials hoped might double the volume of bilateral trade. Later in the month Syria reportedly agreed to end the ban (imposed in 1994) on the free circulation of Jordanian newspapers and publications. King Abdullah made an unscheduled visit to Syria in July 1999, amid Jordanian concerns that any peace agreement concluded by Israel and Syria could damage the Palestinians' position and effectively isolate them in future negotiations. None the less, following the brief resumption of Israeli-Syrian peace talks in December, Abdullah urged Israel to make concessions to Syria in order to increase the likelihood of a bilateral settlement being reached. The King attended the funeral of President Assad in June 2000, and acted swiftly to forge close relations with the new Syrian President, Bashar al-Assad. In November Syria confirmed that it had upgraded its diplomatic representation in Amman to ambassadorial status, and the Syrian state airline resumed regular flights to Amman after a hiatus of more than 20 years. The Syrian authorities declared in January 2001 that all Jordanian prisoners held in Syria would soon be released. In late August 2002 Jordan and Syria signed an agreement under which Syria was to provide Jordan with water to ease Jordan's water shortages.

Meanwhile, King Abdullah sought to strengthen relations with other Arab states. His first major foreign visit was to Egypt for talks with President Mubarak in March 1999. (Jordan and Egypt had signed an agreement in December 1998 providing for the establishment of a free-trade zone by 2005.) During April 1999 the new King visited a number of Middle Eastern countries, including Kuwait. Jordan's embassy there had been re-opened in March of that year, following the restoration of full diplomatic relations between the two countries (which had been severed in 1990), and in September 1999 the *rapprochement* was apparently confirmed as King Abdullah again visited Kuwait. Kuwait subsequently announced an end to a nine-year ban on the sale of Jordanian newspapers. In October Kuwait returned an ambassador to Amman, the post having been vacant since the Gulf crisis. Abdullah became the first Jordanian monarch to visit Lebanon for more than 30 years when, in September 1999, he held discussions with senior Lebanese officials regarding the Middle East peace process and bilateral issues (including a planned free-trade agreement). Jordan's relations with Qatar deteriorated in early August 2002, after the Jordanian authorities announced a ban on broadcasts in Jordan by the Qatar-based Al-Jazeera television station following criticism of the Government's foreign policy. The Jordanian authorities responded by summoning the Qatari ambassador and later withdrawing its ambassador to Qatar. In late October a Jordanian journalist employed by Qatari state television received a death sentence from a court in Qatar, having been convicted of espionage.

Arab relations were strained as a result of the US-led military campaign in Iraq in early 2003. In mid-March King Abdullah met with President Mubarak to discuss the divisions within the Arab League. Jordan arranged to import oil from Saudi Arabia, Kuwait and the UAE, reportedly at no cost, to circumvent shortages induced by the conflict in Iraq, and in mid-May it was revealed that Jordan was conducting negotiations with the USA and the UN to seek a solution to the problem of interrupted oil supplies from Iraq. In late November Minister of Foreign Affairs Dr Marwan al-Muasher visited Iran, primarily to discuss the status of some 1,000 members of the dissident Iranian guerrilla group, the Mujahidin-e-Khalq, who were formerly based in Iraq but who were now being held under Jordanian supervision in the border area between Iraq and Jordan.

Government

Jordan is a constitutional monarchy. Legislative power is vested in a bicameral National Assembly: the Senate (House of Notables) has 55 members, appointed by the King for eight years (one-half of the members retiring every four years), while the House of Representatives (House of Deputies) has 110 members, elected by universal adult suffrage for four years. Executive power is vested in the King, who governs with the assistance of an appointed Council of Ministers, responsible to the Assembly.

There are eight administrative provinces, of which three have been occupied by Israel since June 1967.

Defence

The total strength of the Jordanian armed forces in August 2004 was 100,500. The army had 85,000 men, the air force 15,000 and the navy (coastguard) an estimated 500. Reserve forces numbered 35,000 (30,000 in the army). Paramilitary forces numbered an estimated 45,000 men, comprising a Civil Militia of some 35,000 and a Public Security Force of an estimated 10,000. Military service is based on selective conscription. Budgeted defence expenditure for 2004 was estimated at JD 653m.

Economic Affairs

In 2003, according to estimates by the World Bank, the East Bank of Jordan's gross national income (GNI), measured at average 2001–03 prices, was US $9,784m., equivalent to $1,850 per head (or $4,290 per head on an international purchasing-power parity basis). During 1990–2003, it was estimated, the population increased at an average annual rate of 4.0%, while the East Bank's gross domestic product (GDP) per head increased, in real terms, by an average of 0.8% per year. Overall GDP increased, in real terms, by an average annual rate of 4.9% in 1990–2003; growth was reported to be 4.8% in 2002 and 3.2% in 2003.

Agriculture (including hunting, forestry and fishing) contributed about 2.3% of Jordan's GDP in 2003. The sector accounted for an estimated 3.6% of the country's employed labour force in 2004. The principal cash crops are vegetables, fruit and nuts, which accounted for about 6.6% of export earnings in 2003. Wheat production is also important. During 1990–2003 the sector's GDP increased at an average annual rate of 0.1%. Agricultural GDP increased by 13.4% in 2002 and by 1.0% in 2003.

Industry (including mining, manufacturing, construction and power) provided an estimated 25.6% of GDP in 2003; about 22.7% of the country's active labour force were employed in the sector in 2004. During 1990–2003 industrial GDP increased by an average of 5.4% per year. The sector's GDP increased by 9.1% in 2002 and by 5.0% in 2003.

Mining and quarrying contributed an estimated 3.0% of GDP in 2003. The sector accounted for about 1.2% of the employed labour force in 2004. Phosphates and potash are the principal mineral exports, together accounting for around 14.1% of total export earnings in 2003. Jordan also has reserves of oil-bearing shale, but exploitation of this resource is at present undeveloped. The GDP of the mining sector declined by an estimated 5.9% in 1998.

Manufacturing provided an estimated 15.6% of GDP in 2003, and engaged some 12.7% of the employed labour force in 2004. In 1997 the most important branches of manufacturing, measured by gross value of output, were food, beverages and tobacco (accounting for 25.3% of the total), refined petroleum products (17.4%), chemicals (11.0%), non-metallic mineral products (9.1%) and metal products (7.2%). Manufacturing GDP in-

creased by an average of 5.6% per year in 1990–2003; the sector recorded growth of 10.6% in 2002 and 3.5% in 2003.

Energy is derived principally from imported petroleum, but attempts are being made to develop alternative sources of power, including wind and solar power. In 2001 petroleum provided 89.2% of total electricity production, while natural gas accounted for 10.2%. Imports of mineral fuels comprised some 16.5% of the total value of imports in 2003. Following an agreement signed in mid-2001, Egypt commenced exports of gas to Jordan via a high-capacity pipeline in mid-2003.

Services accounted for some 72.1% of Jordan's GDP in 2003. In 2004 an estimated 73.8% of the total employed labour force were engaged in the service sector. During 1990–2003 the GDP of the service sector increased by an average of 4.5% per year. Services GDP increased by 3.0% in 2002 and by 2.5% in 2003.

In 2003 Jordan recorded a visible trade deficit of US $1,996.3m., and there was a surplus of $962.8m. on the current account of the balance of payments. In 2003 the People's Republic of China was the main source of imports (with 8.0% of the total), while the USA was the principal market for exports (with 28.0% of the total). Other major trading partners in that year were Germany, Saudi Arabia and Iraq. The principal exports in 2003 were miscellaneous manufactured articles, chemicals and minerals, while the principal imports were machinery and transport equipment, basic manufactures, and mineral fuels and lubricants.

In 2004 there was an estimated budget deficit of JD 845m. Jordan's external debt totalled US $8,094m. at the end of 2002, of which US $7,076m. was long-term public debt. In that year the cost of debt-servicing was equivalent to 8.7% of the value of exports of goods and services. The annual rate of inflation averaged 3.2% in 1990–2002. Consumer prices increased by an annual average of 2.3% in 2003 and 3.4% in 2004. Unemployment was officially put at 14.5% of the labour force in 2003, but unofficially estimated to be 20%–30%.

Jordan is a member of the Council of Arab Economic Unity (see p. 196), the Arab Monetary Fund (see p. 153) and the World Trade Organization (WTO, see p. 357). In September 1999 the Jordanian parliament ratified the Jordanian-European Partnership Agreement (signed with the EU in November 1997), which provides for the creation of a duty-free zone and the abolition of import duties by 2010.

Since the early 1990s the Jordanian economy has been constrained by a heavy burden of foreign debt and, until the conflict in Iraq in 2003, by the loss, owing to the imposition of UN sanctions, of its vital Iraqi market. Nevertheless, the conclusion of a peace treaty with Israel in 1994, as well as the recent improvement in relations with other Arab states, has created new opportunities in tourism, transport, banking and trade. Moreover, exports from Jordan to the USA rose considerably following the conclusion of a bilateral free-trade agreement which took effect in late 2001. Jordan has implemented an IMF-supported adjustment and reform programme with the aim of reducing state intervention in industry and, through privatization, raising funds to support the repayment of foreign debt. In order to encourage foreign investment, all foreign-exchange restrictions were revoked in June 1997. By early 2001 the restructuring of a number of state enterprises was under way, notably in the utilities, transport and telecommunications sectors. Jordan is deemed to have brought its external debt under control, a process facilitated by a series of debt-relief measures by Western creditors in the late 1990s and early part of this century; however, the IMF has recommended a faster pace of structural reform and the introduction of new banking legislation. It was reported in early 2003 that a two-year social and economic programme introduced by the Government in November 2001 had already achieved considerable success; the programme involved large-scale industrial privatization, the receipts from which were to be used to fund vital education, health and development projects. Meanwhile, a value-added tax was introduced in 2001, while in January 2002 a new income tax law reduced the tax burden on private companies in an effort to encourage competition. In December of that year the WTO agreed to exempt Jordanian exports from income tax for a five-year period. In January 2001 the Aqaba region was accorded the status of a Special Economic Zone, which was officially inaugurated in May, in an attempt to attract foreign investment and create jobs. However, Jordan's economic growth rate was deemed to be insufficient to reduce unemployment and raise living standards. Since the outbreak of the al-Aqsa *intifada* in September 2000, the impact on regional security of the Israeli–

Palestinian conflict has hampered efforts by the Jordanian Government to attract foreign investment, and has had a particularly detrimental effect on Jordan's tourist and banking sectors. The conflict in Iraq, Jordan's vital trading partner, during March–April 2003 was especially damaging to the Jordanian economy. However, in September 2004 the IMF reported that Jordan had achieved substantial economic growth in the aftermath of the war, driven by export growth and increased domestic demand, although it noted the problems still posed by Jordan's high debt burden, dependence on external grants and higher international oil prices. In response to the IMF report, the Jordanian Government announced plans to end fuel subsidies by the end of 2006 and to expand its privatization programme, forecasting proceeds of JD 300m. from privatization in 2004. The privatization of the Jordan Petroleum Refinery Company was approved in early December as part of an extensive, long-term plan to modernize Jordan's energy sector, at an estimated cost of US $3,000m. In mid-December the Government signed an official memorandum of understanding with Sonoran Energy to assess the exploration potential of an oilfield to the east of Amman.

Education

Primary education, beginning at six years of age, is free and compulsory. This 10-year preparatory cycle is followed by a two-year secondary cycle. UNRWA provides schooling for Palestinian refugees. In 2001, at the primary level, there were 50,562 teachers and 1,173,314 pupils. At the secondary level (including both general and vocational education) there were 14,280 teachers and 173,755 pupils in that year. There were 6,036 teachers and 153,965 pupils engaged in higher education in 2001. Education in Jordan was provided at 4,999 schools and 22 institutions of higher education in that year. Budgetary expenditure on education by the central Government in 2003 accounted for 11.6% of total spending.

Public Holidays

2005: 15 January (Arbor Day), 21 January* (Id al-Adha, Feast of the Sacrifice), 30 January (King Abdullah's Birthday), 10 February* (Muharram, Islamic New Year), 22 March (Arab League Day), 21 April* (Mouloud, Birth of Muhammad), 25 May (Independence Day), 9 June (King Abdullah's Accession), 2 September* (Leilat al-Meiraj, Ascension of Muhammad), 4 November* (Id al-Fitr, end of Ramadan), 14 November (the late King Hussein's Birthday).

2006: 11 January* (Id al-Adha, Feast of the Sacrifice), 15 January (Arbor Day), 30 January (King Abdullah's Birthday), 31 January* (Muharram, Islamic New Year), 22 March (Arab League Day), 11 April* (Mouloud, Birth of Muhammad), 25 May (Independence Day), 9 June (King Abdullah's Accession), 22 August* (Leilat al-Meiraj, Ascension of Muhammad), 24 October* (Id al-Fitr, end of Ramadan), 14 November (the late King Hussein's Birthday).

*These holidays are dependent on the Islamic lunar calendar and may vary by one or two days from the dates given.

Weights and Measures

The metric system is in force. In Jordan the dunum is 1,000 sq m (0.247 acre).

Statistical Survey

Source: Department of Statistics, POB 2015, Amman; tel. (6) 5300700; fax (6) 5300710; e-mail stat@dos.gov.jo; internet www.dos.gov.jo.

Area and Population

AREA, POPULATION AND DENSITY
(East Bank only)

Area (sq km)	88,778*
Population (census results)	
10–11 November 1979	2,100,019
10 December 1994	
Males	2,160,725
Females	1,978,733
Total	4,139,458
Population (official estimates at 31 December)	
2001	5,182,000
2002	5,329,000
2003	5,480,000
Density (per sq km) at 31 December 2003	61.7

* 34,277 sq miles.

GOVERNORATES
(East Bank only; estimated population at 31 December 2003)

	Area (sq km)	Population	Density (per sq km)
Amman	7,579	2,085,140	275.1
Irbid	1,572	977,635	621.0
Az-Zarqa (Zarqa)	4,761	862,000	181.1
Al-Balqa	1,119	359,485	321.3
Al-Mafraq	26,541	252,625	9.5
Al-Karak (Kerak)	3,495	220,295	63.0
Jarash (Jerash)	410	161,115	393.0
Madaba	940	139,740	148.7
Ajloun	420	121,660	289.7
Al-Aqabah (Aqaba)	6,900	110,150	16.0
Ma'an	32,832	106,860	3.3
At-Tafilah	2,209	83,295	37.7
Total	**88,778**	**5,480,000**	**61.7**

PRINCIPAL TOWNS
(population at 1994 census)

Amman (capital) .	969,598	Al-Baqa'a	58,592
Az-Zarqa (Zarqa) .	350,849	As-Salt	56,458
Irbid	208,329	Madaba	55,749
Ar-Rusayfah (Russeifa) . . .	137,247	Ar-Ramtha . . .	55,022
Wadi as-Sir . . .	89,104	Suwaylih	53,250
Al-Aqabah (Aqaba) .	62,773		

Source: Thomas Brinkhoff, *City Population* (internet www.citypopulation.de).

Population at 31 December 2003 (including suburbs): Amman 1,864,809; Zarqa 472,830; Irbid 272,681; Russeifa 240,630.

BIRTHS, MARRIAGES AND DEATHS
(East Bank only)*

	Registered live births		Registered marriages		Registered deaths	
	Number	Rate (per 1,000)	Number	Rate (per 1,000)	Number	Rate (per 1,000)
1996 . .	142,404	32.6	34,425	7.9	13,302	3.0
1997 . .	130,633	28.4	37,278	8.1	13,190	2.9
1998 . .	133,714	28.0	39,376	8.3	13,552	5.0
1999 . .	135,300†	28.0	39,443†	8.0	13,900†	5.0
2000 . .	143,800†	28.0	45,600†	9.0	14,600†	5.0
2001 . .	143,000†	28.0	49,800†	9.7	16,200†	5.0
2002 . .	146,100†	29.0	46,900†	8.8	17,000†	5.0
2003 . .	148,294	27.1	48,784	8.9	16,937	3.1

* Data are tabulated by year of registration rather than by year of occurrence. Registration of births and marriages is reported to be complete, but death registration is incomplete. Figures exclude foreigners, but include registered Palestinian refugees.
† Figures are rounded.

Expectation of life (years at birth): 70.8 (males 68.6; females 73.3) in 2002 (Source: WHO, *World Health Report*).

ECONOMICALLY ACTIVE POPULATION
(Jordanians only)

	1990	1991	1992
Agriculture	38,266	40,848	44,400
Mining and manufacturing	53,468	56,856	61,800
Electricity and water	6,815	7,176	6,600
Construction	51,895	54,096	60,000
Trade	52,944	56,856	63,000
Transport and communications	44,557	48,576	52,200
Financial and insurance services	16,774	17,664	19,800
Social and administrative services	259,478	269,928	292,200
Total employed	524,197	552,000	600,000
Unemployed	106,000	128,000	106,000
Total civilian labour force	630,197	680,000	706,000

Source: Ministry of Labour, *Annual Report.*

2004 (Jordanians aged 15 and over, % of total): Agriculture 3.6; Mining and quarrying 1.2; Manufacturing 12.7; Electricity, gas and water supply 1.7; Construction 7.1; Wholesale and retail trade 18.0; Hotels and restaurants 2.2; Transport, storage and communications 9.6; Financial intermediation 1.6; Real estate, renting and business activities 3.8; Public administration 16.6; Education 11.0; Health and social work 5.0; Other community activities 5.4; Private households with employed persons 0.3; Extra-territorial organizations and bodies 0.3.

Health and Welfare

KEY INDICATORS

Total fertility rate (children per woman, 2002)	3.6
Under-5 mortality rate (per 1,000 live births, 2003)	28
HIV/AIDS (% of persons aged 15–49, 2003)	<0.1
Physicians (per 1,000 head, 1997)	1.66
Hospital beds (per 1,000 head, 1997)	1.80
Health expenditure (2001): US $ per head (PPP)	412
Health expenditure (2001): % of GDP	9.5
Health expenditure (2001): Public (% of total)	47.0
Access to water (% of persons, 2002)	91
Access to sanitation (% of persons, 2002)	93
Human Development Index (2002): Ranking	90
Human Development Index (2002): Value	0.750

For sources and definitions, see explanatory note on p. vi.

Agriculture

PRINCIPAL CROPS
(East Bank only; '000 metric tons)

	2001	2002	2003
Wheat	19.3	43.7	42.5
Barley	17.3	56.8	25.8
Maize	10.4	13.8	10.7
Potatoes	101.3	105.3	122.4
Olives	65.7	180.9	85.0
Cabbages	11.3	29.1	14.0
Lettuce	10.9	19.7	32.7
Tomatoes	310.2	359.8	415.0
Cauliflowers	18.7	59.1	53.8
Pumpkins, squash and gourds	57.5	47.7	49.0
Cucumbers and gherkins	78.1	120.3	122.0†
Aubergines (Eggplants)	36.7	59.4	60.0†
Chillies and green peppers	21.3	33.2	28.1
Green onions and shallots	10.6	44.4	45.0†
Dry onions	23.5	33.7	28.8
Green beans	13.1	18.4	13.6
Green broad beans	13.9	18.2	8.7
Other vegetables	53.7	113.1	107.6†
Watermelons	34.2	71.8	64.6
Cantaloupes and other melons	51.6*	36.5*	35.0†
Bananas	24.3	47.4	50.4
Oranges	32.5	34.2	42.8
Tangerines, mandarins, clementines and satsumas	61.5	50.9	72.1
Lemons and limes	34.7	32.0	44.5

— *continued*	2001	2002	2003
Apples	37.1	39.2	53.0
Peaches and nectarines	8.1	14.0	25.0
Grapes	27.0	34.8	34.0
Other fruits†	31.7	50.0	49.7

* Unofficial estimate.
† FAO estimate(s).

Source: FAO.

LIVESTOCK
(East Bank only; '000 head, year ending September)

	2001	2002	2003
Horses*	4	4	4
Mules*	3	3	27
Asses*	18	18	18
Cattle	67	68	67
Camels*	18	18	18
Sheep	1,484	1,458	1,476
Goats	426	557	547
Chickens	24	24,000	24,000*

* FAO estimate(s).

Source: FAO.

LIVESTOCK PRODUCTS
(East Bank only; '000 metric tons)

	2001	2002	2003
Beef and veal	3.6	2.8	3.0*
Mutton and lamb	4.8	3.9	3.8*
Goat meat	1.6	1.4	1.6*
Poultry meat	117.3	110.1	114.3
Cows' milk	162.8	176.9	158.1
Sheep's milk	23.1	22.7	64.6
Goats' milk	12.4	11.3	28.5
Cheese*	2.6	2.5	7.3
Hen eggs	54.5	58.9	34.1
Wool: greasy	1.8	1.9	2.1*
Sheepskins*	74.4	59.7	58.0
Goatskins*	18.4	16.6	18.2

* FAO estimate(s).

Source: FAO.

Forestry

ROUNDWOOD REMOVALS
(estimates, '000 cubic metres, excluding bark)

	2001	2002	2003
Industrial wood	4	4	4
Fuel wood	230	237	245
Total	234	241	249

Source: FAO.

Fishing

(metric tons, live weight)

	2000	2001	2002
Capture	550	520	526
Freshwater fishes	400	350	350
Tunas	90	110	105
Aquaculture	569	540	515
Tilapias	563	540	515
Total catch	1,119	1,060	1,041

Source: FAO.

Mining

('000 metric tons, unless otherwise indicated)

	2000	2001	2002
Crude petroleum ('000 barrels) .	14.6	14.6	14.6
Phosphate rock	5,526	5,843	7,179
Potash salts*	1,162	1,178	1,174
Salt (unrefined)	311.2	321.0†	347.0

* Figures refer to the K_2O content.
† Estimate.

Source: US Geological Survey.

Industry

SELECTED PRODUCTS
('000 barrels, unless otherwise indicated)

	2000	2001	2002
Liquefied petroleum gas . .	1,684	1,750*	1,720*
Motor spirit (petrol) . . .	4,957	5,160*	5,070*
Kerosene	1,991	2,070*	2,030*
Jet fuels	1,950	2,030*	2,000*
Distillate fuel oils . . .	10,001	10,400*	10,200*
Asphalt	688	690*	680*
Phosphate fertilizers ('000 metric tons) . .	409.1	435.0*	459.0*
Cement ('000 metric tons) . .	2,640	3,173	3,455
Electricity (million kWh) . .	7,056	7,200	8,127

* Estimate.

Sources: Ministry of Energy and Mineral Resources, Amman; US Geological Survey.

Finance

CURRENCY AND EXCHANGE RATES

Monetary Units
1,000 fils = 1 Jordanian dinar (JD).

Sterling, Dollar and Euro Equivalents (31 December 2004)
£1 sterling = JD 1.369;
US $1 = 709 fils;
€1 = 966 fils;
JD 100 = £73.03 = $141.04 = €103.55.

Exchange Rate: An official mid-point rate of US $1 = 709 fils (JD1 = $1.4104) has been maintained since October 1995.

BUDGET
(East Bank only; JD million)*

Revenue†	2002‡	2003§	2004§
Taxation	1,000.3	1,083.2	1,186.0
Taxes on income and profits .	196.2	195.4	212.0
Corporations	120.9	128.3	141.0
Individuals	36.4	38.6	45.0
Taxes on domestic transactions	564.5	657.2	761.5
General sales tax . . .	510.7	596.3	700.0
Taxes on foreign trade . . .	219.8	209.4	190.0
Customs duties	214.4	202.2	184.0
Other revenue	570.5	571.5	600.0
Licences	31.9	32.1	34.5
Fees	225.0	249.1	241.5
Interest and profits	136.6	121.0	90.2
Repayment	73.3	43.9	39.0
Total	**1,644.1**	**1,698.6**	**1,825.0**

Expenditure	2002‡	2003§	2004§
Current	1,899.9	2,145.9	2,133.0
Wages and salaries . . .	401.6	418.5	453.0
Purchases of goods and services	80.6	93.7	115.5
Interest payments . . .	251.4	270.3	260.6
Other transfers	519.3	581.9	576.6
Pensions	320.2	345.7	370.1
Decentralized agencies .	91.8	97.1	98.3
University and municipalities	44.0	44.0	46.0
Defence and security	551.3	629.3	653.0
Other current	53.7	63.5	74.3
Capital‖	438.8	485.4	537.0
Total	**2,338.7**	**2,631.3**	**2,670.0**

* Figures represent a consolidation of the Current, Capital and Development Plan Budgets of the central Government. The data exclude the operations of the Health Security Fund and of other government agencies with individual budgets.
† Excluding foreign grants received (JD million): 418.7 in 2002; 771.3 in 2003; 472.0 in 2004.
‡ Revised figures.
§ Preliminary figures.
‖ Includes overdue settlements and arrears on public sector.

Source: Ministry of Finance, Amman.

INTERNATIONAL RESERVES
(US $ million at 31 December)

	2001	2002	2003
Gold*	112.2	141.2	171.3
IMF special drawing rights . .	1.2	0.9	1.1
Foreign exchange	3,061.0	3,975.0	5,193.1
Total	**3,174.4**	**4,117.1**	**5,365.6**

* National valuation.

Source: IMF, *International Financial Statistics*.

MONEY SUPPLY
(JD million at 31 December)

	2001	2002	2003
Currency outside banks . . .	1,202.4	1,252.7	1,443.7
Demand deposits at commercial banks	888.4	1,019.2	1,382.1
Total money (incl. others) . .	**2,094.8**	**2,273.2**	**2,827.0**

Source: IMF, *International Financial Statistics*.

COST OF LIVING
(Consumer Price Index; base: 1997 = 100)

	2002	2003	2004
Food (incl. beverages) . . .	102.9	104.8	109.6
Clothing (incl. footwear) . . .	110.6	106.2	103.6
Housing	108.3	110.9	112.8
Other goods and services . . .	118.5	124.4	130.1
All items	**108.2**	**110.7**	**114.5**

NATIONAL ACCOUNTS
(East Bank only; JD million at current prices)

National Income and Product

	2000	2001	2002
Gross domestic product (GDP) in purchasers' values . . .	5,989	6,339	6,699
Compensation of employees from abroad (net)	114	126	135
Property income from abroad (net)	−19	6	−56
Gross national income (GNI) .	6,085	6,471	6,778
Less Consumption of fixed capital	671	691	721
Net national income	5,414	5,780	6,057
Current transfers from abroad .	1,851	1,656	1,790
Less Current transfers paid abroad	303	196	185
National disposable income .	**6,962**	**7,240**	**7,662**

Expenditure on the Gross Domestic Product

	2000	2001	2002
Government final consumption expenditure	1,422	1,458	1,542
Private final consumption expenditure	4,843	5,158	5,198
Changes in stocks	64	79	52
Gross fixed capital formation . .	1,263	1,239	1,294
Total domestic expenditure .	7,592	7,934	8,086
Exports of goods and services .	2,507	2,677	3,036
Less Imports of goods and services	4,110	4,273	4,424
GDP in purchasers' values .	5,989	6,338	6,698
GDP at constant 1994 prices .	5,393	5,658	5,931

Gross Domestic Product by Economic Activity

	2001	2002	2003
Agriculture, hunting, forestry and fishing	124.3	134.6	145.6
Mining and quarrying	176.4	188.7	188.1
Manufacturing	836.9	922.3	990.2
Electricity and water	140.6	156.6	163.4
Construction	231.0	251.7	279.3
Trade, restaurants and hotels . .	618.6	635.0	680.9
Transport, storage and communications	907.2	934.9	1,025.7
Finance, insurance, real estate and business services	1,135.6	1,235.7	1,297.8
Social and personal services . .	250.8	283.5	308.1
Public administration and defence; compulsory social security . .	1,077.1	1,135.5	1,178.6
Producers of private non-profit services for households . . .	58.2	63.0	67.6
Private households with employed persons	11.5	12.5	12.9
Sub-total	5,568.2	5,954.0	6,338.2
Less Imputed bank service charge	123.0	199.8	225.8
Gross value added in basic prices	5,445.2	5,754.2	6,112.4
Taxes on products (net) . . .	893.8	944.6	943.8
GDP in purchasers' values .	6,339.0	6,698.8	7,056.2

BALANCE OF PAYMENTS
(US $ million)

	2001	2002	2003
Exports of goods f.o.b.	2,294.4	2,770.0	3,081.6
Imports of goods f.o.b.	−4,301.5	−4,500.7	−5,077.9
Trade balance	−2,007.0	−1,730.8	−1,996.3
Exports of services	1,482.5	1,512.8	1,493.1
Imports of services	−1,725.9	−1,796.6	−1,763.1
Balance on goods and services	−2,250.4	−2,014.6	−2,266.3
Other income received . . .	648.7	484.1	492.7
Other income paid	−461.2	−372.3	−370.2
Balance on goods, services and income	−2,062.9	−1,902.8	−2,143.9
Current transfers received . . .	2,365.8	2,524.3	3,371.2
Current transfers paid . . .	−306.9	−260.1	−264.5
Current balance	−4.1	361.4	962.9
Capital account (net)	21.6	68.8	93.5
Direct investment abroad . . .	−5.6	—	—
Direct investment from abroad .	96.5	30.6	376.2
Portfolio investment assets . .	−227.1	−191.8	−118.9
Portfolio investment liabilities .	−171.7	−52.2	−349.1
Other investment assets . . .	−615.1	11.4	283.1
Other investment liabilities . .	580.3	643.3	−438.6
Net errors and omissions . . .	81.4	58.8	539.2
Overall balance	−243.9	930.3	1,348.2

Source: IMF, *International Financial Statistics*.

External Trade

PRINCIPAL COMMODITIES
(distribution by SITC, JD '000)

Imports c.i.f.	2001	2002	2003
Food and live animals	524,323	489,979	566,416
Crude materials (inedible) except fuels	106,101	106,311	98,770
Mineral fuels, lubricants, etc. . .	495,376	540,290	661,421
Crude petroleum	385,871	404,631	467,970
Chemicals	379,414	402,384	445,237
Basic manufactures	666,575	689,814	802,698
Machinery and transport equipment	938,668	890,610	920,445
Miscellaneous manufactured articles	204,985	247,197	247,458
Total (incl. others)	3,453,729	3,558,960	4,008,085

Exports f.o.b.	2001	2002	2003
Food and live animals	135,530	141,316	156,641
Vegetables, fruit and nuts . .	94,393	107,040	110,988
Crude materials (inedible) except fuels	250,165	252,324	258,607
Phosphates	90,485	96,446	90,810
Potash	138,334	136,744	144,832
Animal and vegetable oils and fats	42,735	67,819	41,775
Chemicals	345,135	391,855	389,664
Phosphoric acid	37,012	61,709	n.a.
Medical and pharmaceutical products	129,716	142,791	130,971
Polishing and cleaning preparations and perfume materials	33,490	52,264	47,354
Fertilizers	61,099	63,952	73,661
Basic manufactures	168,795	159,721	132,218
Paper and cardboard . . .	50,084	37,316	30,634
Machinery and transport equipment	122,826	101,175	77,083
Miscellaneous manufactured articles	264,262	412,111	567,514
Clothing	203,851	357,697	479,087
Total (incl. others)	1,352,371	1,556,748	1,675,075

PRINCIPAL TRADING PARTNERS
(countries of consignment, JD million)

Imports c.i.f.	2001	2002	2003
Argentina	73.0	69.6	89.6
Australia	52.9	42.1	44.6
Belgium-Luxembourg	31.1	45.6	41.4
China, People's Republic . .	168.6	236.9	322.4
Egypt	36.6	53.9	83.6
France	131.8	147.8	127.8
Germany	317.1	329.7	310.1
India	52.1	58.3	60.3
Indonesia	42.3	55.8	61.1
Iraq	485.6	532.4	265.6
Italy	114.0	126.1	153.2
Japan	124.1	112.4	141.5
Korea, Republic	99.6	93.6	102.0
Malaysia	34.1	37.0	48.9
Netherlands	47.8	68.4	59.3
Russia	42.5	22.2	32.5
Saudi Arabia	110.9	102.5	459.4
Spain	59.7	45.0	45.7
Sweden	56.6	34.3	36.6
Switzerland	40.1	38.5	53.2
Syria	47.1	68.7	108.6
Taiwan	60.2	78.2	97.6
Turkey	86.4	87.4	98.7
United Arab Emirates	41.7	55.6	102.1
United Kingdom	124.3	132.7	140.3
USA	280.7	258.3	255.9
Total (incl. others)	3,453.7	3,559.0	4,008.1

Exports f.o.b.		2001	2002	2003
China, People's Republic	. . .	29.5	32.4	25.5
Egypt	. . . .	14.9	11.3	17.0
Germany	. . . .	16.8	7.8	7.9
India	. . . .	145.3	159.7	141.1
Indonesia	. . . .	21.0	14.8	19.2
Iraq	. . . .	299.4	311.8	224.0
Israel	. . . .	72.9	87.1	68.5
Kuwait	. . . .	24.8	24.7	26.6
Lebanon	. . . .	27.7	34.7	32.6
Malaysia	. . . .	16.7	12.2	13.6
Pakistan	. . . .	18.1	21.9	16.1
Qatar	. . . .	17.8	18.6	17.5
Saudi Arabia	. . . . . .	95.6	105.3	109.4
Syria	. . . .	25.6	46.7	63.9
United Arab Emirates	. . .	58.9	56.6	65.7
United Kingdom	. . . . .	14.8	6.4	5.8
USA	. . . .	164.6	304.4	468.7
Total (incl. others)	. . . . .	1,352.4	1,556.7	1,675.1

Transport

RAILWAYS
(traffic)

	2000	2001	2002
Passenger-km (million)	2.1	2.6	2.1
Freight ton-km (million) . . .	348	371	531

ROAD TRAFFIC
(motor vehicles in use at 31 December)

	2000	2001	2002
Passenger cars	245,357	323,560	346,866
Buses and coaches	9,839	13,852	14,553
Lorries and vans	102,531	152,831	144,931

Motorcycles and mopeds ('000 in use): 271 in 1998; 311 in 1999; 273 in 2000.

SHIPPING
Merchant Fleet
(registered at 31 December)

	2001	2002	2003
Number of vessels	10	14	15
Displacement ('000 grt) . . .	42.1	68.7	224.2

Source: Lloyd's Register-Fairplay, *World Fleet Statistics*.

International Sea-borne Freight Traffic
('000 metric tons)

	2000	2001	2002
Goods loaded	7,188	7,791	8,972
Goods unloaded	5,364	5,251	5,286

CIVIL AVIATION
(traffic on scheduled services)

	1999	2000	2001
Kilometres flown (million) . . .	36	37	36
Passengers carried ('000) . . .	1,252	1,282	1,178
Passenger-km (million)	4,195	4,207	3,848
Total ton-km (million)	579	591	530

Source: UN, *Statistical Yearbook*.

Passengers carried ('000): 1,343.4 in 2000; 1,236.3 in 2001.

Tourism

ARRIVALS BY NATIONALITY
('000)*

	2001	2002	2003
Egypt	325.1	354.8	410.3
Iraq	417.3	391.6	370.7
Saudi Arabia	602.7	687.4	680.6
Syria	1,127.2	1,364.0	1,352.6
Turkey	70.6	104.1	107.1
United Kingdom	36.7	35.1	35.1
USA	59.3	58.3	72.7
Total (incl. others)	3,511.7	3,916.0	3,897.4

*Including pilgrims and excursionists (same-day visitors).

Tourism receipts (JD million): 564.0 in 1999; 512.4 (preliminary figure) in 2000; 496.1 (preliminary figure) in 2001.

Source: Central Bank of Jordan.

Communications Media

(East Bank only)

	2000	2001	2002
Telephones ('000 main lines in use)	602.0	660.0	629.0
Mobile cellular telephones ('000 subscribers)	388.9	866.0	1,219.0
Personal computers ('000 in use)	150	170	170
Internet users ('000)	127.3	212.0	234.0

1996: Book production (titles) 511.

1997: Radio receivers ('000 in use) 1,660.

1998: Facsimile machines ('000 in use) 51.6; Daily newspapers (titles) 8, (average circulation) 352,000 copies; Non-daily newspapers (titles) 13; Periodicals (titles) 270, (average circulation) 148,000 copies.

Television receivers ('000 in use): 560 in 2000.

Sources: partly International Telecommunication Union; UNESCO, *Statistical Yearbook*; UN, *Statistical Yearbook*.

Education

(East Bank, 2001, unless otherwise indicated)

	Schools	Teachers	Pupils
Pre-primary	1,165	3,878	83,777
Primary	2,708	50,562	1,173,314
Secondary: general	912	11,254	129,894
Secondary: vocational	214	3,026	43,861
Higher	22	6,036	153,965
of which universities* . . .	n.a.	3,982	89,010

* 1996/97 figures.

Adult literacy rate (UNESCO estimates): 90.9% (males 95.5%; females 85.9%) in 2002 (Source: UN Development Programme, *Human Development Report*).

Directory

The Constitution

The revised Constitution was approved by King Talal I on 1 January 1952.

The Hashemite Kingdom of Jordan is an independent, indivisible sovereign state. Its official religion is Islam; its official language Arabic.

RIGHTS OF THE INDIVIDUAL

There is to be no discrimination between Jordanians on account of race, religion or language. Work, education and equal opportunities shall be afforded to all as far as is possible. The freedom of the individual is guaranteed, as are his dwelling and property. No Jordanian shall be exiled. Labour shall be made compulsory only in a national emergency, or as a result of a conviction; conditions, hours worked and allowances are under the protection of the state.

The Press, and all opinions, are free, except under martial law. Societies can be formed, within the law. Schools may be established freely, but they must follow a recognized curriculum and educational policy. Elementary education is free and compulsory. All religions are tolerated. Every Jordanian is eligible for public office, and choices are to be made by merit only. Power belongs to the people.

THE LEGISLATIVE POWER

Legislative power is vested in the National Assembly and the King. The National Assembly consists of two houses: the Senate and the House of Representatives.

THE SENATE

The number of Senators is one-half of the number of members of the House of Representatives. Senators must be unrelated to the King, over 40, and are chosen from present and past Prime Ministers and Ministers, past Ambassadors or Ministers Plenipotentiary, past Presidents of the House of Representatives, past Presidents and members of the Court of Cassation and of the Civil and *Shari'a* Courts of Appeal, retired officers of the rank of General and above, former members of the House of Representatives who have been elected twice to that House, etc... They may not hold public office. Senators are appointed for four years. They may be reappointed. The President of the Senate is appointed for two years.

THE HOUSE OF REPRESENTATIVES

The members of the House of Representatives are elected by secret ballot in a general direct election and retain their mandate for four years. General elections take place during the four months preceding the end of the term. The President of the House is elected by secret ballot each year by the Representatives. Representatives must be Jordanians of over 30, they must have a clean record, no active business interests, and are debarred from public office. Close relatives of the King are not eligible. If the House of Representatives is dissolved, the new House shall assemble in extraordinary session not more than four months after the date of dissolution. The new House cannot be dissolved for the same reason as the last.

GENERAL PROVISIONS FOR THE NATIONAL ASSEMBLY

The King summons the National Assembly to its ordinary session on 1 November each year. This date can be postponed by the King for two months, or he can dissolve the Assembly before the end of its three months' session. Alternatively, he can extend the session up to a total period of six months. Each session is opened by a speech from the throne.

Decisions in the House of Representatives and the Senate are made by a majority vote. The quorum is two-thirds of the total number of members in each House. When the voting concerns the Constitution, or confidence in the Council of Ministers, 'the votes shall be taken by calling the members by name in a loud voice'. Sessions are public, though secret sessions can be held at the request of the Government or of five members. Complete freedom of speech, within the rules of either House, is allowed.

The Prime Minister places proposals before the House of Representatives; if accepted there, they are referred to the Senate and finally sent to the King for confirmation. If one house rejects a law while the other accepts it, a joint session of the House of Representatives and the Senate is called, and a decision made by a two-thirds majority. If the King withholds his approval from a law, he returns it to the Assembly within six months with the reasons for his dissent; a joint session of the Houses then makes a decision, and if the law is accepted by this decision it is promulgated. The Budget is submitted to the National Assembly one month before the beginning of the financial year.

THE KING

The throne of the Hashemite Kingdom devolves by male descent in the dynasty of King Abdullah ibn al-Hussein. The King attains his majority on his eighteenth lunar year; if the throne is inherited by a minor, the powers of the King are exercised by a Regent or a Council of Regency. If the King, through illness or absence, cannot perform his duties, his powers are given to a Deputy, or to a Council of the Throne. This Deputy, or Council, may be appointed by Iradas (decrees) by the King, or, if he is incapable, by the Council of Ministers.

On his accession, the King takes the oath to respect and observe the provisions of the Constitution and to be loyal to the nation. As Head of State he is immune from all liability or responsibility. He approves laws and promulgates them. He declares war, concludes peace and signs treaties; treaties, however, must be approved by the National Assembly. The King is Commander-in-Chief of the navy, the army and the air force. He orders the holding of elections; convenes, inaugurates, adjourns and prorogues the House of Representatives. The Prime Minister is appointed by him, as are the President and members of the Senate. Military and civil ranks are also granted, or withdrawn, by the King. No death sentence is carried out until he has confirmed it.

MINISTERS

The Council of Ministers consists of the Prime Minister, President of the Council, and of his ministers. Ministers are forbidden to become members of any company, to receive a salary from any company, or to participate in any financial act of trade. The Council of Ministers is entrusted with the conduct of all affairs of state, internal and external.

The Council of Ministers is responsible to the House of Representatives for matters of general policy. Ministers may speak in either House, and, if they are members of one House, they may also vote in that House. Votes of confidence in the Council are cast in the House of Representatives, and decided by a two-thirds' majority. If a vote of 'no confidence' is returned, the ministers are bound to resign. Every newly formed Council of Ministers must present its programme to the House of Representatives and ask for a vote of confidence. The House of Representatives can impeach ministers, as it impeaches its own members.

AMENDMENTS

Two amendments were passed in November 1974 giving the King the right to dissolve the Senate or to take away membership from any of its members, and to postpone general elections for a period not to exceed a year, if there are circumstances in which the Council of Ministers feels that it is impossible to hold elections. A further amendment in February 1976 enabled the King to postpone elections indefinitely. In January 1984 two amendments were passed, allowing elections 'in any part of the country where it is possible to hold them' (effectively, only the East Bank) and empowering the National Assembly to elect deputies from the Israeli-held West Bank. In February 2003 the King ratified legislation according to which six seats in the House of Representatives were, from the next general election, to be reserved for women.

The Government

HEAD OF STATE

King: King ABDULLAH IBN AL-HUSSEIN (succeeded to the throne on 7 February 1999).

CABINET
(April 2005)

Prime Minister and Minister of Defence: ADNAN BADRAN.

Deputy Prime Minister and Minister of Political Development and Parliamentary Affairs: HISHAM AT-TAL.

Minister of Foreign Affairs: FARUQ KASRAWI.

Minister of Justice: MUHAMMAD ALAWNEH.

Minister of the Interior: AWNI YERVAS.

Minister of Awqaf (Religious Endowments), Islamic Affairs and Holy Places: ABD ES-SALAM ABBADI.

Minister of Government Performance: Dr SALAH ED-DIN AL-BASHIR.

Minister of Health: SAEED DARWAZEH.

Minister of Finance: Dr BASSEM AWADALLAH.

Minister of Industry and Trade: SHERIF AZ-ZOHBI.

Minister of Labour: BASSEM AS-SALEM.

Minister of Public Reforms: Dr TAYSEER SMADI.

Minister of Public Works and Housing: YOUSUF HIYASSAT.

Minister of Energy and Mineral Resources: AZMI KHREISAT.

Minister of Education: Dr KHALID TOUQAN.

Minister of Municipal and Rural Affairs: TAWFIQ KREISHAN.

Minister of Water and Irrigation: RAED ABU SAUD.

Minister of Planning: SUHAIR ALI.

Minister of Agriculture: YOUSUF ASH-SHURAIKI.

Minister of Social Development: ABDULLAH OWEIDAT.

Minister of Information and Communications Technology: Dr NADIA SAEED.

Minister of the Environment: KHALID IRANI.

Minister of Transport: SOUD NSAIRAT.

Minister of Tourism and Antiquities: Dr ALIA HATTOUGH-BOURAN.

Minister of Culture and Government Spokesperson: ASMA KHADER.

Minister of State for Legal Affairs: ABED ASH-SHAKHANBEH.

Note: The Head of Intelligence and the Governor of the Central Bank also have full ministerial status.

MINISTRIES

Office of the Prime Minister: POB 80, Amman; tel. (6) 4641211; fax (6) 4642520; e-mail pmic@pm.gov.jo; internet www.pm.gov.jo.

Ministry of Administrative Development: Amman.

Ministry of Agriculture: POB 2099, Amman; tel. (6) 5686151; fax (6) 5686310; e-mail falah-a@moa.gov.jo; internet www.moa.gov.jo.

Ministry of Awqaf (Religious Endowments), Islamic Affairs and Holy Places: POB 659, Amman; tel. (6) 5666141; fax (6) 5602254; e-mail info@awqaf.gov.jo; internet www.awqaf.gov.jo.

Ministry of Culture: POB 6140, Amman; tel. (6) 5696218; fax (6) 5696598; e-mail info@culture.gov.jo; internet www.culture.gov.jo.

Ministry of Defence: POB 80, Amman; tel. (6) 4641211; fax (6) 4642520; e-mail info@jaf.mil.jo; internet www.jaf.mil.jo.

Ministry of Education: POB 1646, Amman 11118; tel. (6) 5607181; fax (6) 5666019; e-mail moe@amra.nic.gov.jo; internet www.moe.gov.jo.

Ministry of Energy and Mineral Resources: POB 2310, Amman; tel. (6) 5863326; fax (6) 5818336; e-mail memr@memr.gov.jo; internet www.memr.gov.jo.

Ministry of the Environment: Amman; internet www.moenv.gov.jo.

Ministry of Finance: POB 85, Amman 11118; tel. (6) 4636321; fax (6) 4643132; e-mail webmaster@mof.gov.jo; internet www.mof.gov.jo.

Ministry of Foreign Affairs: POB 35217, Amman 11180; tel. (6) 5735150; fax (6) 5735163; e-mail inquiry@mfa.gov.jo; internet www.mfa.gov.jo.

Ministry of Health: POB 86, Amman; tel. (6) 5665131; fax (6) 5665232; e-mail info@moh.gov.jo; internet www.moh.gov.jo.

Ministry of Higher Education and Scientific Research: POB 35262, Amman; tel. (6) 5347671; fax (6) 5337616; internet www.mohe.gov.jo.

Ministry of Industry and Trade: POB 2019, Amman; tel. (6) 5607191; fax (6) 5603721; e-mail info@mit.gov.jo; internet www.mit.gov.jo.

Ministry of Information and Communications Technology: POB 9903, Amman 11191; tel. (6) 5859001; fax (6) 5825262; e-mail cio@moict.gov.jo; internet www.moict.gov.jo.

Ministry of the Interior: POB 100, Amman; tel. (6) 4638849; fax (6) 5606908; e-mail info@moi.gov.jo; internet www.moi.gov.jo.

Ministry of Justice: POB 6040, Amman; tel. (6) 4653533; fax (6) 4643197; e-mail moj@nic.net.jo; internet amon.nic.gov.jo/justice.

Ministry of Labour: POB 8160, Amman; tel. (6) 5629130; fax (6) 5667193; e-mail info@mol.gov.jo; internet www.mol.gov.jo.

Ministry of Municipal and Rural Affairs: POB 1799, Amman; tel. (6) 4641393; fax (6) 4640404.

Ministry of Planning and International Co-operation: POB 555, Amman 11118; tel. (6) 4641460; fax (6) 4649341; e-mail mop@mop.gov.jo; internet www.mop.gov.jo.

Ministry of Public Works and Housing: POB 1220, Amman; tel. (6) 5850470; fax (6) 5857590; e-mail mhpw@nic.net.jo; internet www.mpwh.gov.jo.

Ministry of Social Development: POB 6720, Amman; tel. (6) 5931391; fax (6) 5932645; e-mail mosd@mosd.gov.jo; internet www.mosd.gov.jo.

Ministry of Tourism and Antiquities: POB 224, Amman 11118; tel. (6) 4642311; fax (6) 4648465; e-mail tourism@mota.gov.jo; internet www.mota.gov.jo.

Ministry of Transport: POB 35214, Amman 11180; tel. (6) 5518111; fax (6) 5527233; e-mail info@mot.gov.jo; internet mot.gov.jo.

Ministry of Water and Irrigation: POB 2412, Amman 5012; tel. (6) 5680100; fax (6) 5680075; e-mail info@mwi.gov.jo; internet www.mwi.gov.jo.

Legislature

MAJLIS AL-UMMA
(National Assembly)

Senate

Speaker: ZAID AR-RIFAI.

The Senate (House of Notables) consists of 55 members, appointed by the King. A new Senate was appointed by the King on 17 November 2003.

House of Representatives

Speaker: ABD AL-HADI AL-MAJALI.

General Election, 17 June 2003

Party/Group	Seats
Independents and tribal representatives	80
Islamic Action Front (IAF)	17
Independent Islamists	5
Leftist Democratic Party	2
Total	110*

* Including female representatives elected in accordance with legislation ratified by King Abdullah in February 2003, whereby six seats were reserved for women.

Political Organizations

With the exception of the officially sanctioned Jordanian National Union (1971–76), political parties were effectively banned for most of the reign of King Hussein. However, a royal commission was appointed in April 1990 to draft a National Charter, one feature of which was the legalization of political parties. In January 1991 King Hussein approved the National Charter, which was formally endorsed in June. In August 1992 legislation allowing the formation of political parties was approved by royal decree, and by March 1993 nine political parties had received official recognition.

Arab Democratic Front: f. 2003; Leaders AHMAD UBEIDAT, TAHER AL-MASRI.

Islamic Action Front (IAF): POB 925310, Abdali, Amman; tel. (6) 5696985; fax (6) 5696987; e-mail info@jabha.net; internet www.jabha.net; f. 1992; seeks implementation of *Shari'a* (Islamic law) and preservation of the *Umma* (Islamic community); Sec.-Gen. HAMZEH MANSOUR.

Jordan People's Democratic Party (HASHID): PIB 9966, Luweibdeh, Amman; tel. (6) 5691451; fax (6) 5686857; f. 1993; seeks to establish legal and institutional processes to protect the people, instigate economic, social, democratic and agricultural reform, and organize, unify and protect the working classes; supports the Palestinian cause; Sec.-Gen. SALEM NAHHAS.

Jordan Rafah (Welfare) Party: f. 2001; Leader MUHAMMAD RIJJAL SHUMALI.

Jordanian Arab New Dawn Party: 7th Bldg, Abd al-Rahman Gharib St, Sweifiyeh, Amman; tel. (6) 5822667; fax (6) 5822667; f. 1999; supports the nation's constitution and legal structures; Arab nationalist; pro-Palestinian; Sec.-Gen. MUHAHHAM DARWISH SHAHWAN.

Jordanian Arab Socialist Baath Party: POB 8383, Amman; tel. (6) 4658618; fax (6) 4658617; f. 1993; promotes Pan-Arabism; Sec.-Gen. Tayseer Salameh al-Homsi.

Jordanian People's Committees Movement: f. 2001; moderate; Sec.-Gen. Khalid Shubaki.

Leftist Democratic Party (Jordanian Democratic Left Party): POB 84545, Abdali, Amman; tel. (7) 9524708; fax (6) 5538614; f. 1994; supports the National Charter; pro-Palestinian; Sec.-Gen. Moussa al-Ma'aitah.

Muslim Centrist Party: Haswa Bldg, 3rd Floor, Amman; tel. (6) 5066866; fax (6) 5353966; f. 2001 by former members of IAF and Muslim Brotherhood; Pres. Muhammad Alawneh; Sec.-Gen. Marwan Fa'ouri.

Al-Mustuqbal (Future) Party: Shmeisani, Al-Maqdisi St, Amman; tel. (6) 5690911; fax (6) 5690805; f. 1992; development of legal, state and social institutions; promotion of democracy; pro-Palestinian; Sec.-Gen. Suleiman Arar.

National Constitutional Party (NCP): POB 1825237, Amman 11118; tel. (6) 5696256; fax (6) 5686248; f. 1997; merger of nine parties; Pres. Abd al-Hadi al-Majali; Sec.-Gen. Ahmad Shunnaq.

Diplomatic Representation

EMBASSIES IN JORDAN

Australia: POB 35201, Amman 11180; tel. (6) 5807000; fax (6) 5807001; e-mail ausemb@nets.com.jo; Ambassador John A. Tilemann.

Austria: POB 830795, Jabal Amman, Amman 11183; tel. (6) 4601101; fax (6) 4612725; e-mail amman-ob@bmaa.gv.at; internet www.bmaa.gv.at; Ambassador Dr Heinrich Querner.

Bahrain: POB 5220, Amman 11183; tel. (6) 5664148; fax (6) 5664190; Ambassador Muhammad Seif Jaber al-Msallam.

Bangladesh: POB 5685, Amman 11183; tel. (6) 5529192; fax (6) 5529194; e-mail embangl@wanadoo.jo; Ambassador Masood Aziz.

Belgium: POB 942, Amman 11118; tel. (6) 5932683; fax (6) 5930487; e-mail belgica@accessme.com; Ambassador Marc de Schoutheete de Tervarent.

Bosnia and Herzegovina: POB 850836, Amman 11185; tel. (6) 5856921; fax (6) 5856923; e-mail ambamman@wanadoo.jo; Ambassador Vasilj Krunoslav.

Brazil: POB 5497, Amman 11183; tel. (6) 4642183; fax (6) 4641328; e-mail jorbrem@wanadoo.jo; Ambassador Antônio Carlos Coelho da Rocha.

Brunei: POB 851752, Amman 11185; tel. (6) 5928021; fax (6) 5928024; e-mail kbnbdjor@cyberia.jo; Ambassador Pehin Dato Harimaupadang.

Bulgaria: POB 950578, Amman 11195; tel. (6) 5529391; fax (6) 5539393; e-mail bulembjord@joinnet.com.jo; Ambassador Nikolay Nikolov.

Canada: POB 815403, Amman 11180; tel. (6) 5666124; fax (6) 5689227; e-mail amman@dfait-maeci.gc.ca; Ambassador John Holmes.

Chile: POB 830663, 28 Hussein Abu Ragheb St, Abdoun, Amman 11183; tel. (6) 5923360; fax (6) 5924263; e-mail echilejo@go.com.jo; Ambassador Ovid Alejandro Harasich Miserda.

China, People's Republic: POB 423, Amman 111183; tel. (6) 5516194; fax (6) 5537417; e-mail poli@index.com.jo; Ambassador Luo Xingwu.

Czech Republic: POB 2213, Amman 11181; tel. (6) 5927051; fax (6) 5927053; e-mail amman@embassy.mzv.cz; internet www.mzv.cz/amman; Ambassador Tomas Lane.

Egypt: POB 35178, Amman 11180; tel. (6) 5605175; fax (6) 5604082; e-mail egyptemb@joinnet.com.jo; Ambassador Muhammad Hijazi.

France: POB 35287, Amman 11183; tel. (6) 4641273; fax (6) 4642879; e-mail ambafr@joinnet.com.jo; internet www.ambafrance.org.jo; Ambassador Jean-Michel Casa.

Georgia: Amman; Ambassador Ekaterine Mikadze.

Germany: 25 Benghazi St, Jabal Amman 11118; tel. (6) 5930351; fax (6) 5929413; e-mail germaemb@go.com.jo; internet www.diplo.de; Ambassador Dr Klaus Burkhardt.

Greece: POB 35069, Amman 11180; tel. (6) 5672331; fax (6) 5696591.

Holy See: POB 142916, Amman 11814; tel. (6) 5929934; fax (6) 5929931; e-mail nuntius@nol.com.jo; Apostolic Nuncio Most Rev. Fernando Filoni.

Honduras: POB 840526, Amman 33384; tel. (6) 5856414; fax (6) 5853501; Chargé d'affaires a.i. Faiz Roberto Elmadi.

Hungary: POB 3441, Amman 11181; tel. (6) 5925614; fax (6) 5930836; e-mail huembamm@nol.com.jo; Ambassador Balazs Bokor.

India: POB 2168, Amman 11181; tel. (6) 4622098; fax (6) 4659540; e-mail indambjo@nets.com.jo; Ambassador B. A. Roy.

Indonesia: POB 811784, Amman 11181; tel. (6) 5538911; fax (6) 5528380; e-mail amman96@go.com.jo; Ambassador Ribhan Abdul Wahab.

Iran: POB 173, Amman 11118; tel. (6) 4641281; fax (6) 4641383; e-mail iran110@go.com.jo; Ambassador Muhammad Irani.

Iraq: POB 2025, 1st Circle, Jabal Amman; tel. (6) 4623175; fax (6) 4619172; e-mail baghdad@nets.com.jo; Ambassador Atah Abd al-Wahab Abd ar-Razak.

Israel: 47 Maysaloon St, Dahiat al-Rabieh, Amman; tel. (6) 5525408; fax (6) 5521971; e-mail isrem@go.com.jo.

Italy: POB 9800, Jabal Luweibdeh, Amman 11191; tel. (6) 4638185; fax (6) 4659730; e-mail italemb1@go.com.jo; internet www.italembamman.org; Ambassador Stefano Jedrkiewicz.

Japan: POB 2835, Amman 11181; tel. (6) 5932005; fax (6) 5931006; e-mail mail@embjapan.org.jo; Ambassador Koichi Obata.

Korea, Democratic People's Republic: POB 799, Amman; tel. (6) 4417614; fax (6) 4424735; e-mail dprk-embv@scs-net.org; Ambassador Kim Hyong Jun.

Korea, Republic: POB 3060, Amman 11181; tel. (6) 5930745; fax (6) 5930280; e-mail jordan@mofat.go.kr; Ambassador Kim Kyung-Keun.

Kuwait: POB 2107, Amman 11181; tel. (6) 5675135; fax (6) 5681971; e-mail kwtemb@cyberia.jo; Ambassador Youssuf Abdullah al-Onaizi.

Lebanon: POB 811779, Amman 11181; tel. and fax (6) 5929111; Ambassador Adib Alam ed-Din.

Libya: POB 2987, Amman; tel. (6) 5693101; fax (6) 5693404; Chargé d'affaires Muhammad Amer Sulh.

Malaysia: POB 5351, Amman 11183; tel. (6) 5902400; fax (6) 5934343; e-mail mwamman@go.com.jo; Ambassador Dato Syed Sultan bin Seni Pakir.

Mauritania: POB 851594, Amman 11185; tel. (6) 5855146; fax (6) 5855148; Ambassador Ahmad ben Khalifeh ben Jado.

Morocco: POB 2175, Amman 11183; tel. (6) 5921771; fax (6) 5925185; e-mail ambmaroc@nets.com.jo; Ambassador Abdelkader Zaoui.

Netherlands: 22 Ibrahim Ayoub St, 4th Circle, Amman 11194; tel. (6) 5902200; fax (6) 5930214; e-mail nlgovamm@index.com.jo; internet www.netherlandsembassy.com.jo; Ambassador H. G. Scheltema.

Norway: POB 830510, Amman 11183; tel. (6) 5931646; fax (6) 5931650; e-mail emb.amman@mfa.no; Ambassador Sverre Stub.

Oman: POB 926024, Amman 11110; tel. (6) 5686155; fax (6) 5689404; Ambassador Hamad bin Hilal al-Ma'mari.

Pakistan: POB 1232, Amman 11118; tel. (6) 4622787; fax (6) 4611633; e-mail pakembjo@go.com.jo; Ambassador Dr Arif Kamal.

Philippines: POB 925207, Amman 11190; tel. (6) 5923748; fax (6) 5923744; e-mail ammanpe@index.com.jo; Ambassador Ruperto M. Dizon.

Poland: POB 942050, Amman 11194; tel. (6) 5512593; fax (6) 5512595; e-mail polemb@nol.com.jo; Ambassador Andrzej Biera.

Qatar: POB 831222, Amman 11183; tel. (6) 4659724; fax (6) 4659723; e-mail qataremb@index.com.jo; Ambassador Mana Abd al-Hadi al-Hajri.

Romania: POB 2869, 33 Madina Munawwara St, Amman; tel. (6) 5813423; fax (6) 5812521; e-mail romania@accessme.com; Ambassador Radu Onofrei.

Russia: POB 2224, Amman 11181; tel. (6) 4625607; fax (6) 4644698; e-mail russjo@nets.com.jo; Ambassador Dr Aleksandr Shein.

Saudi Arabia: POB 2133, 5th Circle, Jabal Amman; tel. (6) 5924154; fax (6) 4659853; e-mail joemb@mofa.gov.sa; Ambassador Abd ar-Rahman N. al-Ohaly.

South Africa: POB 851508, Sweifiyeh 11185, Amman; tel. (6) 5921194; fax (6) 5920080; e-mail saembjor@index.com.jo; Ambassador Boy Geldenhuys.

Spain: Zahran St, POB 454, Amman 11118; tel. (6) 4621369; fax (6) 4614173; e-mail embespjo@mail.mae.es; Ambassador Antonio López Martínez.

Sri Lanka: POB 830731, Amman 11183; tel. (6) 5820611; fax (6) 5820615; e-mail lankaemb@go.com.jo; Ambassador Kathan Marimuttu.

Sudan: POB 3305, Amman 11181; tel. (6) 5854500; fax (6) 5854501; e-mail sudani@firstnet.com.jo; Ambassador MOHAMMAD AHMOUD ABU SEN.

Sweden: POB 830536, 4th Circle, Amman 11183; tel. (6) 5931177; fax (6) 5930179; e-mail info@swe-embamman.org; internet www.swe-embamman.org; Ambassador KLAS GIEROW.

Switzerland: POB 5341, 19 Ibrahim Ayoub St, 4th Circle, Amman 11183; tel. (6) 5931416; fax (6) 5930685; e-mail vertretung@amm.rep.admin.ch; Ambassador PAUL WIDMER.

Syria: POB 1733, Amman 11118; tel. (6) 4641935; fax (6) 4651945; Ambassador ABD al-FATTAH AMMOURAH.

Thailand: POB144329, Amman 11814; tel. (6) 5925410; fax (6) 5926109; e-mail thaibgw@mfa.go.th; Ambassador WIBOON KHUSAKUL.

Tunisia: POB 945600, ash-Shumaysani, nr Atta Ali, Amman; tel. (6) 5674307; fax (6) 5605790; Ambassador MUHAMMAD al-BASATI.

Turkey: POB 2062, Amman 11181; tel. (6) 4641251; fax (6) 4612353; e-mail ammanbe@nets.com.jo; Ambassador HUSEYIN DIRIOZ.

Ukraine: POB 33944, 115 Hani Rifai St, S. Abdoun, Amman; tel. (6) 5922402; fax (6) 5922405; e-mail ukremb@nets.com.jo; Ambassador Dr VIKTOR NAGAICHUK.

United Arab Emirates: POB 2623, Amman 11181; tel. (6) 5934780; fax (6) 5932666; Ambassador RAHMA HUSSAIN R. az-ZA'ABI.

United Kingdom: POB 87, Abdoun, Amman 11118; tel. (6) 5923100; fax (6) 5923759; e-mail info@britain.org.jo; internet www.britain.org.jo; Ambassador CHRISTOPHER PRENTICE.

USA: POB 354, Amman 11118; tel. (6) 5920101; fax (6) 5920163; e-mail administration@usembassy-amman.org.jo; internet www.usembassy-amman.org.jo; Ambassador EDWARD WILLIAM GNEHM, Jr.

Yemen: POB 3085, Amman 11181; tel. (6) 5923771; fax (6) 5923773; Ambassador Dr IBRAHIM S. al-ADOOFI.

Judicial System

With the exception of matters of purely personal nature concerning members of non-Muslim communities, the law of Jordan was based on Islamic Law for both civil and criminal matters. During the days of the Ottoman Empire, certain aspects of Continental law, especially French commercial law and civil and criminal procedure, were introduced. Due to British occupation of Palestine and Transjordan from 1917 to 1948, the Palestine territory has adopted, either by statute or case law, much of the English common law. Since the annexation of the non-occupied part of Palestine and the formation of the Hashemite Kingdom of Jordan, there has been a continuous effort to unify the law.

Court of Cassation (Supreme Court): The Court of Cassation consists of seven judges, who sit in full panel for exceptionally important cases. In most appeals, however, only five members sit to hear the case. All cases involving amounts of more than JD 100 may be reviewed by this Court, as well as cases involving lesser amounts and cases which cannot be monetarily valued. However, for the latter types of cases, review is available only by leave of the Court of Appeal, or, upon refusal by the Court of Appeal, by leave of the President of the Court of Cassation. In addition to these functions as final and Supreme Court of Appeal, the Court of Cassation also sits as High Court of Justice to hear applications in the nature of habeas corpus, mandamus and certiorari dealing with complaints of a citizen against abuse of governmental authority.

President of the Court of Cassation (Supreme Court): AHMAD TARAWMEH.

Courts of Appeal: There are three Courts of Appeal, each of which is composed of three judges, whether for hearing of appeals or for dealing with Magistrates Courts' judgments in chambers. Jurisdiction of the three Courts is geographical, with one each in Amman, Irbid and Ma'an. Appellate review of the Courts of Appeal extends to judgments rendered in the Courts of First Instance, the Magistrates' Courts, and Religious Courts.

Courts of First Instance: The Courts of First Instance are courts of general jurisdiction in all matters civil and criminal except those specifically allocated to the Magistrates' Courts. Three judges sit in all felony trials, while only two judges sit for misdemeanour and civil cases. Each of the 11 Courts of First Instance also exercises appellate jurisdiction in cases involving judgments of less than JD 20 and fines of less than JD 10, rendered by the Magistrates' Courts.

Magistrates' Courts: There are 17 Magistrates' Courts, which exercise jurisdiction in civil cases involving no more than JD 250 and in criminal cases involving maximum fines of JD 100 or maximum imprisonment of one year.

Religious Courts: There are two types of religious court: the *Shari'a* Courts (Muslims); and the Ecclesiastical Courts (Eastern Orthodox, Greek Melkite, Roman Catholic and Protestant). Jurisdiction extends to personal (family) matters, such as marriage, divorce, alimony, inheritance, guardianship, wills, interdiction and, for the Muslim community, the constitution of Waqfs (Religious Endowments). When a dispute involves persons of different religious communities, the Civil Courts have jurisdiction in the matter unless the parties agree to submit to the jurisdiction of one or the other of the Religious Courts involved.

Each *Shari'a* (Muslim) Court consists of one judge (*Qadi*), while most of the Ecclesiastical (Christian) Courts are normally composed of three judges, who are usually clerics. *Shari'a* Courts apply the doctrines of Islamic Law, based on the Koran and the *Hadith* (Precepts of Muhammad), while the Ecclesiastical Courts base their law on various aspects of Canon Law. In the event of conflict between any two Religious Courts or between a Religious Court and a Civil Court, a Special Tribunal of three judges is appointed by the President of the Court of Cassation, to decide which court shall have jurisdiction. Upon the advice of experts on the law of the various communities, this Special Tribunal decides on the venue for the case at hand.

Religion

Over 90% of the population are Sunni Muslims, and the King can trace unbroken descent from the Prophet Muhammad. There is a Christian minority, living mainly in the towns, and there are smaller numbers of non-Sunni Muslims.

ISLAM

Chief Justice and President of the Supreme Muslim Secular Council: Sheikh IZZEDIN al-KHATIB at-TAMIMI.

Director of Shari'a Courts: Sheikh ISSAM ABD ar-RAZZAQ ARABIYYAT.

Mufti of the Hashemite Kingdom of Jordan: Sheikh MUHAMMAD ABDO HASHEM.

CHRISTIANITY

The Roman Catholic Church

Latin Rite

Jordan forms part of the Patriarchate of Jerusalem (see the chapter on Israel).

Vicar-General for Transjordan: Mgr SELIM SAYEGH (Titular Bishop of Aquae in Proconsulari), Latin Vicariate, POB 851379, Sweifiyeh, Amman 11185; tel. (6) 5929546; fax (6) 5920548; e-mail regina-pacis2000@yahoo.com.

Melkite Rite

The Greek-Melkite archdiocese of Petra (Wadi Musa) and Philadelphia (Amman) contained 31,300 adherents at 31 December 2002.

Archbishop of Petra and Philadelphia: Most Rev. GEORGES el-MURR, Archevêché Grec-Melkite Catholique, POB 2435, Jabal Amman 11181; tel. (6) 4624757; fax (6) 4628560.

Syrian Rite

The Syrian Catholic Patriarch of Antioch is resident in Beirut, Lebanon.

Patriarchal Exarchate of Jerusalem (Palestine and Jordan): Mont Achrafieh, POB 510393, Rue Barto, Amman; e-mail stjossc@p-ol.com; Exarch Patriarchal Mgr GRÉGOIRE PIERRE MELKI (Titular Bishop of Batne of the Syrians).

The Anglican Communion

Within the Episcopal Church in Jerusalem and the Middle East, Jordan forms part of the diocese of Jerusalem. The President Bishop of the Church is the Bishop in Cyprus and the Gulf (see the chapter on Cyprus).

Other Christian Churches

The Coptic Orthodox Church, the Greek Orthodox Church (Patriarchate of Jerusalem) and the Evangelical Lutheran Church in Jordan are also active.

The Press

Jordan Press Association (JPA): POB 6788, Abbas Mahmoud al-Aqqad St, Jabal Amman, 2nd Circle, Amman; tel. (6) 5600800; fax (6) 5696183; e-mail jotimes@jpf.com.jo; f. 1953; Chair. KHALID WAZANI; Dir-Gen. NADER HORANI.

DAILIES

Al-Akhbar (News): POB 62420, Amman; f. 1976; Arabic; publ. by the Arab Press Co; Editor RACAN EL-MAJALI; circ. 15,000.

Arab Daily: Amman; internet www.arabdaily.com.jo; f. 1999; English.

Al-Arab al-Yawm: POB 962198, Queen Rania St, Amman 11196; tel. (6) 5683333; fax (6) 5620552; internet www.alarab-alyawm.com .jo; Chief Editor TAHER AL-ODWAN.

Al-Aswaq (Markets): POB 11117, Queen Rania St, Amman 11123; tel. (6) 5157690; fax (6) 5154390; e-mail alaswaq@nets.com.jo; f. 1992; Arabic; business; Man. Editor YAHYA MAHMOUD; Editor-in-Chief MUSTAFA ABU LIBDEH; circ. 40,000.

Ad-Dustour (The Constitution): POB 591, Amman 11118; tel. (6) 5608000; fax (6) 5667170; e-mail dustour@addustour.com.jo; internet www.addustour.com; f. 1967; Arabic; publ. by the Jordan Press and Publishing Co Ltd; owns commercial printing facilities; Chair. KAMEL ASH-SHARIF; Editor OSAMA ASH-SHARIF; Man. Dir SAIF ASH-SHARIF; circ. 70,000.

The Jordan Times: POB 6710, Amman 11118; tel. (6) 5600800; fax (6) 5696183; e-mail jotimes@jpf.com.jo; internet www.jordantimes .com; f. 1975; English; publ. by Jordan Press Foundation; Editor-in-Chief JENNIFER HAMARNEH; circ. 10,000.

Al-Mithaq (The Covenant): Amman; f. 1993; Arabic.

Ar-Rai (Opinion): POB 6710, Queen Rania St, Amman 11118; tel. (6) 5667171; fax (6) 5676581; e-mail alrai@jpf.com.jo; internet www .alrai.com; f. 1971; morning; Arabic; independent; publ. by Jordan Press Foundation; Chair. AHMAD ABD AL-FATTAH; Editor-in-Chief GEORGE HAWATMEH; circ. 100,000.

Sawt ash-Shaab (Voice of the People): POB 3037, Amman; tel. (6) 5667101; fax (6) 5667993; f. 1983; Arabic; Editor-in-Chief HASHEM KHAISAT; circ. 30,000.

WEEKLIES

Al-Ahali (The People): POB 9966, Amman; tel. (6) 691452; fax (6) 5686857; e-mail ahali@go.com.jo; internet www.hashd-ahali.org.jo; f. 1990; Arabic; publ. by the Jordan People's Democratic Party; Editor-in-Chief SALEM NAHHAS; circ. 5,000.

Akhbar al-Usbou (News of the Week): POB 605, Amman; tel. (6) 5677881; fax (6) 5677882; f. 1959; Arabic; economic, social, political; Chief Editor and Publr ABD AL-HAFIZ MUHAMMAD; circ. 50,000.

Al-Liwa' (The Standard): POB 3067, 2nd Circle, Jabal Amman 11181; tel. (6) 5642770; fax (6) 5656324; e-mail info@al-liwa.com; internet www.al-liwa.com; f. 1972; Arabic; Editor-in-Chief HASSAN AT-TAL; circ. 15,000.

Al-Majd (The Glory): POB 926856, Amman 11190; tel. (6) 5530553; fax (6) 5530352; e-mail almajd@almajd.net; internet www.almajd .net; f. 1994; Arabic; political; Editor-in-Chief FAHID NIMER; circ. 8,000.

As-Sabah (The Morning): POB 2396, Amman; Arabic; circ. 6,000.

Shihan: POB 96-654, Amman; tel. (6) 5603585; fax (6) 5696183; e-mail shihan@go.com.jo; internet www.alarab-alyawm.com.jo/ shihan; Arabic; Editor-in-Chief JIHAD MONANI; circ. 60,000.

The Star: POB 591, University St, Amman 11118; tel. (6) 5664153; fax (6) 5667170; e-mail star@addustour.com.jo; internet star.arabia .com; f. 1966 as *The Jerusalem Star*; resumed publication in Jordan in 1990; English and French; political, economic and cultural; publ. by the Jordan Press and Publishing Co; Publr and Editor-in-Chief OSAMA ASH-SHERIF; circ. 12,000.

Wihda: 6th Floor, Ramallah Bldg, Jamal Abd an-Nasir, Amman; tel. (6) 5655433; fax (6) 5655434; e-mail wihda@nets.com.jo; f. 2002; independent leftist and nationalist; Chair. MOHAMMAD EL-BASHIR; Chief Editor OSAMA RANTISI.

PERIODICALS

Al-Ghad al-Iqtisadi: Media Services International, POB 9313, Amman 11191; tel. (6) 5645380; fax (6) 5648298; fortnightly; English; economic; Chief Editor RIAD AL-KHOURI.

Huda El-Islam (The Right Way of Islam): POB 659, Amman; tel. (6) 5666141; f. 1956; monthly; Arabic; scientific and literary; published by the Ministry of Awqaf and Islamic Affairs; Editor Dr AHMAD MUHAMMAD HULAYYEL.

Jordan: POB 224, Amman; f. 1969; published quarterly by Jordan Information Bureau, Washington; circ. 100,000.

Jordan Today: Media Services International, POB 9313, Amman 11191; tel. (6) 652380; fax (6) 648298; e-mail star@arabia.com; internet www.jordantoday.com.jo; f. 1995; monthly; English; tourism, culture and entertainment; Editor-in-Chief ZEID NASSER; circ. 10,000.

Military Magazine: Army Headquarters, Amman; f. 1955; quarterly; dealing with military and literary subjects; published by Armed Forces.

Royal Wings: POB 341018 Amman 11134; tel. (6) 4875201; fax (6) 4875656; e-mail info@royalwings.com.jo; internet www.royalwings .com.jo; bi-monthly; Arabic and English; magazine for Royal Jordanian Airline; Man. Dir AHID QUNTAR; circ. 40,000.

Shari'a: POB 585, Amman; f. 1959; fortnightly; Islamic affairs; published by Shari'a College; circ. 5,000.

World Travel Gazette (WTG): POB 658, Amman; tel. (6) 5665091; fax (6) 5667933; Arabic; Editor A. S. SHREIM.

NEWS AGENCIES

Jordan News Agency (PETRA): POB 6845, Amman; tel. (6) 5644455; e-mail petra@petranews.gov.jo; internet www.petra.gov.jo; f. 1965; government-controlled; Dir-Gen. ABDULLAH AL-UTUM.

Foreign News Bureaux

Agence France-Presse (AFP): POB 3340, Amman 11181; tel. (6) 4644978; fax (6) 4654680; e-mail afp@globalone.com.jo; Bureau Man. Mrs RANDA HABIB.

Associated Press (AP) (USA): POB 35111, Amman 11180; tel. (6) 4614660; fax (6) 4614661; e-mail jhalaby@ap.org; Correspondent JAMAL HALABY.

Deutsche Presse Agentur (dpa) (Germany): POB 35111, Amman; tel. (6) 5623907.

Reuters (UK): POB 667, Amman; tel. (6) 5623776; fax (6) 5619231; Bureau Chief JACK REDDEN.

Central News Agency (Taiwan), Iraqi News Agency, Kuwait News Agency (KUNA), Middle East News Agency (Egypt), Qatar News Agency, Saudi Press Agency and UPI (USA) also maintain bureaux in Amman.

Publishers

Alfaris Publishing and Distribution Co: POB 9157, Amman 11191; tel. (6) 5605432; fax (6) 5685501; e-mail mkayyali@nets.com .jo; Dir MAHER SAID KAYYALI.

Aram Studies Publishing and Distribution House: POB 997, Amman 11941; tel. (6) 835015; fax (6) 835079; art, finance, health, management, science, business; Gen. Dir SALEH ABOUSBA.

Jordan Book Centre Co Ltd: POB 301, Al-Jubeiha, Amman 11941; tel. (6) 5151882; fax (6) 5152016; e-mail jbc@go.com.jo; f. 1982; fiction, business, economics, computer science, medicine, engineering, general non-fiction; Man. Dir J. J. SHARBAIN.

Jordan Distribution Agency: POB 3371, Amman 11181; tel. (6) 5358855; fax (6) 5337733; e-mail jda@aramex.com; f. 1951; history; subsidiary of Aramex; Chair. FADI GHANDOUR; Gen. Man. WADIE SAYEGH.

Jordan House for Publication: POB 1121, Basman St, Amman; tel. (6) 24224; fax (6) 51062; f. 1952; medicine, nursing, dentistry; Man. Dir MURSI EL-ASHKAR.

Jordan Press and Publishing Co Ltd: POB 591, Amman 11118; tel. (6) 5664153; fax (6) 5667170; e-mail dustour@go.com.jo; f. 1967 by *Al-Manar* and *Falastin* dailies; publishes *Ad-Dustour* (daily), *Ad-Dustour Sport* (weekly) and *The Star* (English weekly); Chair. KAMEL ASH-SHARIF; Dir-Gen. SAIF ASH-SHARIF.

Jordan Press Foundation: POB 6710, Amman 11118; tel. (6) 5667171; fax (6) 5661242; e-mail alrai@jpf.com.jo; internet www .alrai.com.jo; f. 1971; publishes *Ar-Rai* (daily), the *Jordan Times* (daily) and *Hatem* (monthly for children); Chair. AHMAD ABD AL-FATAH; Gen. Dir NADER HORANI.

El-Nafa'es: POB 927511, Al-Abdali, Amman 11190; tel. (6) 5693940; fax (6) 5693941; e-mail alnafaes@hotmail.com; f. 1990; education, Islamic; CEO SUFYAN OMAR AL-ASHQR.

At-Tanwir al-Ilmi (Scientific Enlightenment Publishing House): POB 4237, Al-Mahatta, Amman 11131; tel. and fax (6) 4899619; e-mail taisir@yahoo.com; education, engineering, philosophy, science, sociology; Owner DR TAISIR SUBHI MAHMOUD.

Other publishers in Amman include: Dairat al-Ihsaat al-Amman, George N. Kawar, Al-Matbaat al-Hashmiya and The National Press.

Broadcasting and Communications

TELECOMMUNICATIONS

Telecommunications Regulatory Commission (TRC): POB 850967, Amman 11185; tel. (6) 5862020; fax (6) 5863641; e-mail webmaster@trc.gov.jo; internet www.trc.gov.jo; f. 1995; Dir-Gen. MAMOUN BALQAR.

Jordan Mobile Telephone Services Company (JMTS—Fastlink): POB 940821, 8th Circle, King Abdullah II St, Amman 11194; tel. (6) 5828100; fax (6) 5828200; e-mail info@fastlink.com.jo; internet www.fastlink.com.jo; f. 1994; private co; since 1995 operates Jordan's first mobile telecommunications network; Pres. and CEO MUHAMMAD SAQER.

Jordan Telecom: POB 1689, Amman 11118; tel. (6) 4606666; fax (6) 4606111; e-mail info@jtc.com.jo; internet www.jordantelecom.jo; f. 1971; formerly Jordan Telecommunications Corpn and then Jordan Telecommunications Co; 41.5% govt-owned; 58.5% privately-owned; Chair. Dr SHABIB AMMARI; CEO LAURENT MIALET.

MobileCom: POB 851114, Amman 11185; tel. (7) 7700177; internet www.mobilecom.jo; f. 1999; launched cellular telecommunications service in 2000; subsidiary of Jordan Telecom; CEO MICHAEL GHOSSEIN.

Umniah Telecommunications and Technology Co: Amman; awarded contract for Jordan's third GSM licence in 2004; subsidiary of Alghanim Group (Kuwait); CEO and Man. Dir MICHAEL DAGHER.

BROADCASTING

Radio and Television

Jordan Radio and Television Corporation (JRTV): POB 1041, Amman; tel. (6) 773111; fax (6) 751503; e-mail general@jrtv.gov.jo; internet www.jrtv.com; f. 1968; government TV station; broadcasts for 90 hours weekly in Arabic and English; in colour; advertising accepted; Dir-Gen. IHSAN RAMZI SHIKIM; Dir of Television NASSER JUDEH; Dir of Radio HASHIM KHURAYSAT.

Finance

(cap. = capital; dep. = deposits; m. = million; res = reserves; brs = branches; JD = Jordanian dinars)

BANKING

Central Bank

Central Bank of Jordan: POB 37, King Hussein St, Amman 11118; tel. (6) 4630301; fax (6) 4638889; e-mail info@cbj.gov.jo; internet www.cbj.gov.jo; f. 1964; cap. JD 18m., res JD 142.8m., dep. JD 4,191.1m. (Dec. 2004); Gov. and Chair. Dr UMMAYA TOUKAN; 2 brs.

National Banks

Arab Bank PLC: POB 950545, Shmeisani, Amman 11195; tel. (6) 5607231; fax (6) 5606793; e-mail international@arabbank.com.jo; internet www.arabbank.com; f. 1930; cap. US $146.9m., res US $2,691.7m., dep. US $20,930.1m. (Dec. 2003); Chair. ABD AL-MAJID SHOMAN; CEO and Dep. Chair. ABD AL-HAMID SHOMAN; 84 brs in Jordan, 99 brs abroad.

Bank of Jordan PLC: POB 2140, Shmeisani, Amman 11181; tel. (6) 5696277; fax (6) 5696291; e-mail boj@go.com.jo; internet www.bankofjordan.com; f. 1960; cap. JD 36.5m., dep. JD 807.0m. res JD 17.6m. (Dec. 2003); Chair. TAWFIK SHAKER FAKHOURI; 77 brs and offices.

Cairo Amman Bank: POB 950661, Cairo Amman Bank Bldg, Wadi Saqra St, Amman 11195; tel. (6) 4616910; fax (6) 4642890; e-mail cainfo@ca-bank.com.jo; internet www.ca-bank.com; f. 1960; cap. JD 20m., res JD 12.4m., dep. JD 779.8m. (Dec. 2003); Chair. KHALED AL-MASRI; Gen. Man. YAZID AL-MUFTI; 48 brs in Jordan, 19 brs in the West Bank.

Export and Finance Bank: POB 941283, Issam Ajlouni St, Amman 11194; tel. (6) 5694250; fax (6) 5624874; e-mail info@efbank.com.jo; internet www.efbank.com.jo; f. 1995; cap. JD 34.5m., res JD 6.3m., dep. JD 182.4m. (Dec. 2003); Chair. and CEO MUHAMMAD ALI AL-HUSARI; Gen. Man. HAKOUB BANNAYAN (acting).

Jordan Commercial Bank: POB 9989, Yakoub Sarrouf St, Shmeisani, Amman; tel. (6) 5603931; fax (6) 5603989; e-mail tareq.nasser@jgbank.com.jo; f. 2004; dep. JD 127m., total assets JD 209m. (Oct. 2004); Chair. MICHEL AS-SAYEGH; CEO JAWAD HADID.

Jordan Gulf Bank: POB 9989, Shmeisani-Al Burj Area, Amman 11191; tel. (6) 5603931; fax (6) 5664110; e-mail jgb@jgbank.com.jo; f.

1977; cap JD 33m., res JD –0.1m., dep. JD 253.8m. (Dec. 1999); Chair. NABEEL YOUSUF BARAKAT; Gen. Man. FAYEZ R. ABUL-ENEIN; 33 brs.

Jordan Islamic Bank for Finance and Investment: POB 926225, Shmeisani, Amman 11190; tel. (6) 5677377; fax (6) 5666326; e-mail jib@islamicbank.com.jo; internet www.jordanislamicbank.com; f. 1978; cap. JD 40m., res JD 15.5m., dep. JD 881.5m. (Dec. 2003); Chair. MAHMOUD J. HASSOUBEH; Vice-Chair. and Gen. Man. MUSA ABD AL-AZIZ SHIHADEH; 52 brs.

Jordan Kuwait Bank: POB 9776, Abdali, Amman 11191; tel. (6) 5629000; fax (6) 5687452; e-mail webmaster@jkbank.com.jo; internet www.jordan-kuwait-bank.com; f. 1976; cap. US $35.3m., res US $46.7m., dep. US $720.3m. (Dec. 2003); Chair. and CEO ABD AL-KARIM AL-KABARITI; 28 brs.

Jordan National Bank PLC: POB 3103, Queen Noor St, Shmeisani, Amman 11181; tel. (6) 5622283; fax (6) 5622281; e-mail info@jnb.com.jo; internet www.ahli.com; f. 1955; cap. JD 49.4m., res JD 25.0m., dep. JD 1,203m. (Dec. 2003); Chair. Dr RAJAI MOUASHER; Deputy CEO RASHID DAOUDI; 41 brs in Jordan, 6 brs abroad.

Société Générale de Banque-Jordanie: POB 560, 30 Prince Shaker bin Zeid St, Shmeisani, Amman 11118; tel. (6) 5695470; fax (6) 5693410; e-mail sgbj@sgbj.com.jo; internet www.sgbj.com.jo; f. 1981; fmrly Middle East Investment Bank; part of the Société Générale Group; cap. JD 15.9m., res JD 0.9m., dep. JD 42.2m. (Dec. 2003); Chair. HASSAN MANGO; Gen. Man. ELIANE TANNOUS; 14 brs.

Foreign Banks

Arab Banking Corpn: POB 926691, ABC Bldg, Al-Malekah Noor St, Shmeisani, Amman 11190; tel. (6) 5664183; fax (6) 5686291; e-mail info@arabbanking.com.jo; internet www.arabbanking.com.jo; f. 1990; cap. JD 20m., res JD 8.0m., dep. US $257m., dep. US $23,159m. (Dec. 2002); Chair. GHAZI M. ABD AL-JAWAD; CEO Dr ZIAD FARIZ; 16 brs.

Citibank NA (USA): POB 5055, Amman 11183; tel. (6) 5675100; fax (6) 5674888; internet www.citibank.com/jordan; f. 1974; cap. JD 5m., dep. JD 56.2m., total assets JD 75.4m. (Dec. 1992); Gen. Man. SUHEIR AL-ALI; 2 brs.

Egyptian Arab Land Bank: POB 6729, 94 Queen Noor St, Shmeisani, Amman 11118; tel. (6) 5650180; fax (6) 5677574; e-mail ealb@arakari.com.jo; internet www.arakari.com.jo; f. 1976; wholly-owned by Government of Egypt; cap. JD 10m., dep. JD 103.3m., res JD 5.5m., total assets JD 136.1m. (Dec. 1997); Chair. ALAA AL-OUSSIYA; Gen. Man. SAMIR MAHDI; 19 brs in Jordan, 32 brs in Egypt and the Palestinian Autonomous Areas.

HSBC Bank Middle East (United Kingdom): POB 922376, Khalid Bin Walid St, Jebel Hussein, Amman 11193; tel. (6) 5607471; fax (6) 5682047; internet www.jordan.hsbc.com; f. 1889; cap. JD 5m., dep. JD 150m., total assets JD 169m. (Dec. 1994); Chair. Sir JOHN BOND; Services Man. NICHOLAS BAHOU; 3 brs.

Islamic International Arab Bank: POB 925802, Amman 11190; tel. (6) 5694901; fax (6) 5694914; internet www.iiabank.com.jo; f. 1997; subsidiary of Arab Bank plc; *Shari'a* banking; cap. JD 40m., dep. JD 214.0m., res JD 9.6m. (Dec. 2004); Chair. ABD AL-HAMID SHOMAN; Gen. Man. GHASSAN BUNDUQJI; 11 brs.

Rafidain Bank (Iraq): POB 1194, Amman 11118; tel. (6) 4624076; fax (6) 4658698; f. 1941; cap. JD 5m., res JD 2.1m., dep. JD 31.4m. (Dec. 1992); Pres. and Chair. DHIA HABEEB AL-KHAYOON; Regional Man. MUHSEN ABD AL-HASSAN; 4 brs.

Standard Chartered Bank: POB 9997, Shmeisani, Amman 11191; tel. (6) 5607201; fax (6) 5624106; e-mail muntaser.dawwas@jo.standardchartered.com; internet www.standardchartered.com/jo; cap. JD 13m., dep. JD 200m., total assets JD 240m. (Dec. 2002); CEO ZAHID RAHIM; 7 brs.

Bank Al-Mashrek (Lebanon) also has a branch in Amman.

Specialized Credit Institutions

Agricultural Credit Corporation: POB 684, Amman 11118; tel. (6) 5661105; fax (6) 5668365; e-mail agri-cc@nets.com.jo; internet www.acc.gov.jo; f. 1959; cap. JD 24m., res JD 12.4m., total assets JD 125.1m. (Dec. 2000); Chair. HASHIM ASH-SHBOUL; Vice-Chair. and Dir-Gen. NIMER AN-NABULSI; 20 brs.

Arab Jordan Investment Bank: POB 8797, Arab Jordan Investment Bank Bldg, Shmeisani Commercial Area, Amman 11121; tel. (6) 5607126; fax (6) 5681482; e-mail info@ajib.com; internet www.ajib.com; f. 1978; cap. JD 20m., res JD 17.6m., dep. JD 332.4m. (Dec. 2003); Chair. and CEO ABD AL-KADER AL-QADI; 15 brs and offices in Jordan, 1 br. abroad.

Housing Bank for Trade and Finance: POB 7693, Parliament St, Amman 11118; tel. (6) 4625877; fax (6) 4616234; e-mail mqasem@hbtf.com.jo; internet www.the-housingbank.com.jo; f. 1973; cap. JD 100m., res JD 154.5m., dep. JD 1,410.4m. (Dec. 2002), total assets JD 2,500m. (Dec. 2004); Chair. Dr MICHEL MARTO; CEO AHMAD ABD AL- FATTAH; 97 brs.

Industrial Development Bank: POB 1982, Zahran St, Amman 11118; tel. (6) 4642216; fax (6) 4647821; e-mail idb@indevbank.com .jo; internet www.indevbank.com.jo; f. 1965; cap. JD 24m., res JD 16.3m., dep. JD 38.1m. (Dec. 2002); Chair. MOFLEH AKEL; Gen. Man. MARAW AWAD; 3 brs.

Jordan Co-operative Organization: POB 1343, Amman; tel. (6) 5665171; fax (6) 5695803; f. 1968; cap. JD 5.2m., dep. JD 11.5m., res JD 6.8m. (Nov. 1992); Man. Dir HASSAN AN-NABULSI.

Jordan Investment and Finance Bank (JIFBANK): POB 950601, Amman 11195; tel. (6) 5665145; fax (6) 5681410; e-mail souha@jifbank.com; internet www.jifbank.com; f. 1982 as Jordan Investment and Finance Corpn, name changed 1989; cap. JD 20m., res JD 4.8m., dep. JD 363.9m. (Dec. 2001); Chair. NIZAR JARDANEH; Man. Dir BASIL JARDANEH; 5 brs.

Jordan Investment Board (JIB): POB 893, Amman 11821; tel. (6) 5608400; fax (6) 5608416; e-mail info@jib.com.jo; internet www .jordaninvestment.com; f. 1995; Dir-Gen. REEM BADRAN.

Jordan Investment Corporation (JIC): Amman; state-owned; Dir-Gen. (vacant).

Rural and Urban Development Bank: POB 1572, Amman 11118; tel. (6) 5668150; fax (6) 5668153; e-mail cvdb100@hotmail.com; f. 1979; 30% state-owned; cap. US $37.7m. (Dec. 2002); Chair. ABD AR-RAZZAQ TBEISHAT; Gen. Man. MUHAMMAD SHINNAR; 4 brs.

Social Security Corporation: POB 9260, Amman 11110; tel. (6) 4643000; fax (6) 4610014; e-mail sscpd@nic.net.jo; internet www.ssc .gov.jo; f. 1978; Dir-Gen. AHMAD ABD AL-FATAH.

Union Bank for Savings and Investment: POB 35104, Amman 11180; tel. (6) 5607011; fax (6) 5666149; e-mail info@unionbankjo .com; internet www.unionbankjo.com; f. 1978 as Arab Finance Corpn, name changed 1991; cap. JD 20m., res 11.7m., dep. 333.6m. (Dec. 2002); Chair. and Gen. Man. ISAM AS-SALFITI; Dep. Gen. Man. AMMAR HADADDIN; 13 brs.

STOCK EXCHANGE

Amman Stock Exchange (ASE): POB 212466, Arjan, nr Ministry of the Interior, Amman 11121; tel. (6) 5664109; fax (6) 5664071; e-mail info@ase.com.jo; internet www.ase.com.jo; f. 1978 as Amman Financial Market; name changed March 1999; Chair. MUHAMMAD SALHEH HOURANI; Exec. Man. JALIL TARIF.

INSURANCE

Jordan Insurance Co Ltd: POB 279, Company's Bldg, 3rd Circle, Jabal Amman, Amman 11118; tel. (6) 4634161; fax (6) 4637905; e-mail jicjo@go.com.jo; internet www.jicjo.com; f. 1951; cap. JD 9.9m.; Chair. KHALDUN ABU HASSAN; 6 brs (3 in Saudi Arabia, 3 in the United Arab Emirates).

Middle East Insurance Co Ltd: POB 1802, Al Kindy St, Um Uthaina 5th Circle, Jabal Amman, Amman; tel. (6) 5527100; fax (6) 5527801; e-mail meico@go.com.jo; internet www.meico.com.jo; f. 1963; cap. US $5.0m.; Chair. SAMIR KAWAR; 1 br. in Saudi Arabia.

National Ahlia Insurance Co: POB 6156-2938, Sayed Qotub St, Shmeisani, Amman 11118; tel. (6) 5671169; fax (6) 5684900; e-mail natinsur@go.com.jo; internet www.nationalahlia.com; f. 1965; cap. JD 2m.; Chair. MUSTAFA ABU-GOURA; Gen. Man. GHALEB ABU-GOURA.

United Insurance Co Ltd: POB 7521, United Insurance Bldg, King Hussein St, Amman; tel. (6) 4648513; fax (6) 4629417; e-mail uic@united.com.jo; internet www.1stjordan.net/united-insurance; f. 1972; all types of insurance; cap. JD 2m.; Gen. Man. TAISIR MASHAL.

There are 17 local and one foreign insurance company operating in Jordan.

Trade and Industry

DEVELOPMENT ORGANIZATIONS

Amman Development Corporation: POB 926621, Amman; tel. (6) 5629471; f. 1979; development of services in the Amman municipality by constructing and running real estate; industrial and other complexes; Dir Gen. SAMI AR-RASHID.

Jordan Valley Authority (JVA): POB 2769, Amman; tel. (6) 5689400; fax (6) 5689916; e-mail jvadewan2@mwi.gov.jo; internet www.mwi.gov.jo/NewJVA/jva-master.htm; f. 1977 as a governmental organization responsible for the integrated social and economic development of the Jordan Valley. Projects in Stage I of the Jordan Valley Development Plan were completed in 1979. In 1988 the JVA was incorporated into the Ministry of Water and Irrigation. By late 2000 completed infrastructure projects included 2,205 km of

roads, 2,223 housing units, 90 schools, 15 health centres, 16 local government buildings, 4 marketing centres, 2 tomato paste factories, 1 cold storage facility and several workshops. Electricity is now provided to all towns and villages in the valley from the national network and potable water is supplied to them from tube wells. Many of the Stage II irrigation projects are now completed. These include the construction of the King Talal, Wadi Arab, Kafrein and Karamah dams; the extension of the King Abdullah Canal to total 110.5 km in length; the construction of major municipal water projects in Amman and Irbid; the construction and conversion of a surface irrigation system into a pressurized pipe system covering an irrigated area of 25,000 ha; the development of groundwater resources and subsurface drainage systems. Projects under way include the construction of the Al-Wehdeh, Tanour and Wala dams, as well as the Mujeb dam and diversion weir. Future developments in tourist and industrial infrastructure will include the development of the Dead Sea East shore, Christ's baptism site on the Jordan river, and industrial free zones; Sec.-Gen. AVEDIS SERPEKIAN.

CHAMBERS OF COMMERCE AND INDUSTRY

Amman Chamber of Commerce: POB 1800, Amman 11118; tel. (6) 5666151; fax 5666155; e-mail info@ammanchamber.org.jo; internet www.ammanchamber.org.jo; f. 1923; Chair. HAIDER MURAD; Sec.-Gen. MUHAMMAD AL-MUHTASSEB.

Amman Chamber of Industry: POB 1800, Amman 11118; tel. (6) 5643001; fax (6) 5647852; e-mail aci@aci.org.jo; internet www.aci .org.jo; f. 1962; 7,500 industrial companies registered (1999); Pres. KHALDUN ABU HASSAN; Dir-Gen. Dr MUHAMMAD SMADI.

Federation of the Jordanian Chambers of Commerce: POB 7029, Amman 11118; e-mail fjcc@nets.com.jo; internet www.fjcc .com; tel. (6) 5665492; fax (6) 5685997; f. 1955; Chair. HAIDAR MURAD; Sec.-Gen. AMIN HUSSEINI.

Professional Associations Council (PAC): Professional Associations Complex, Amman; Pres. HASHIM GHARAIBEH.

UTILITIES

Electricity

Central Electricity Generating Company (CEGCO): POB 2564, Amman 11953; tel. (6) 5356989; fax (6) 5357210; e-mail chairman@cegco.com.jo; internet www.cegco.com.jo; electricity generation; govt-owned; scheduled for privatization; Chair. Eng. ALI YOUSUF ENSOUR.

Electricity Distribution Company (EDCO): POB 2310, Orthodox St, 7th Circle, Jabal Amman; tel. (6) 5858615; fax (6) 5818336; e-mail info@nepco.com.jo; internet www.edco.com.jo; electricity distribution; govt-owned; scheduled for privatization.

Jordanian Electric Power Company (JEPCO): POB 618, Amman 11118; tel. (6) 4636381; fax (6) 4648482; e-mail jepco@go .com.jo; internet www.jepco.jo; privately-owned; Chair. ISSAM BDEIR; Gen. Man. MARWAN BUSHNAQ.

National Electric Power Company (NEPCO): POB 2310, Amman 11118; tel. (6) 5858615; fax (6) 5818336; e-mail info@nepco .com.jo; internet www.nepco.com.jo; f. 1996; formerly Jordan Electricity Authority; electricity transmission; govt-owned; scheduled for privatization; Chair. WAE'L SABRI; Gen. Man. MUHAMMAD AZZAM.

Water

Water Authority of Jordan (WAJ): POB 241, Amman; govt-owned; scheduled for privatization; Sec.-Gen. Eng. MUNTHIR KHULIFAT.

TRADE UNIONS

The General Federation of Jordanian Trade Unions: POB 1065, Amman; tel. (6) 5675533; fax (6) 5687911; f. 1954; 33,000 mems; member of Arab Trade Unions Confederation; Pres. MAZEN MA'AYTEH.

There are also a number of independent unions, including:

Jordan Engineers' Association (JEA): POB 940188, Professional Associations Center, Shmeisani, Amman; tel. (6) 5607616; fax (6) 5676933; e-mail info@jea.org.jo; internet www.jea.org.jo; f. 1958; Pres. WAEL SAQQA; Sec.-Gen. ALI ABU AS-SUKKAR.

General Trade Union of Petroleum and Chemical Employees: POB 305, As-Sa'ada St, Zarqa; tel. (5) 398330; fax (5) 393874; f. 1963; Pres. KHALID ZEYOUD.

Transport

RAILWAYS

Aqaba Railways Corporation (ARC): POB 50, Ma'an; tel. (3) 2132114; fax (3) 2131861; f. 1975; length of track 292 km (1,050-mm gauge); privately-owned; Dir-Gen. HUSSEIN KRISHAN.

Formerly a division of the Hedjaz–Jordan Railway (see below), the Aqaba Railway was established as a separate entity in 1972; it retains close links with the Hedjaz but there is no regular through traffic between Aqaba and Amman. It comprises 292 km of 1,050–mm gauge track, consisting in the main of the 169-km line south of Menzil (leased from the Hedjaz–Jordan Railway) and the 115-km extension to Aqaba, opened in October 1975, which serves phosphate mines at el-Hasa and Wadi el-Abyad.

Hedjaz–Jordan Railway: POB 4448, Amman; tel. (6) 4895414; fax (6) 4894117; e-mail hji@nets.com.jo; f. 1902; administered by the Ministry of Transport; length of track 496 km (1,050-mm gauge); Chair. NADER DAHABI; Dir-Gen. A. ABULAL-FEILAT.

This was formerly a section of the Hedjaz Railway (Damascus to Medina) for Muslim pilgrims to Medina and Mecca. It crosses the Syrian border and enters Jordanian territory south of Dera'a, and runs for approximately 366 km to Naqb Ishtar, passing through Az-Zarqa, Amman, Qatrana and Ma'an. Some 844 km of the line, from Ma'an to Medina in Saudi Arabia, were abandoned for more than 60 years. Reconstruction of the Medina line, begun in 1965, was scheduled to be completed in 1971 at a cost of £15m., divided equally between Jordan, Saudi Arabia and Syria. However, the reconstruction work was suspended at the request of the Arab states concerned, pending further studies on costs. The line between Ma'an and Saudi Arabia (114 km) is now completed, as well as 15 km in Saudi Arabia as far as Halet Ammar Station. A new 115-km extension to Aqaba (owned by the Aqaba Railway Corporation (see above) was opened in 1975. In 1987 a study conducted by Dorsch Consult (Federal Republic of Germany) into the feasibility of reconstructing the Hedjaz Railway to high international specifications to connect Saudi Arabia, Jordan and Syria concluded that the reopening of the Hedjaz line would be viable only if it were to be connected with European rail networks. In August 1999 an express rail link between Amman and the Syrian capital, Damascus, was inaugurated.

ROADS

Amman is linked by road with all parts of the kingdom and with neighbouring countries. All cities and most towns are connected by a two-lane paved road system. In addition, several thousand km of tracks make all villages accessible to motor transport. According to official estimates, in 2001 there were 2,911 km of main roads and 2,062 km of rural roads; in 2002 there were 2,954 km of side roads.

Iraqi-Jordanian Joint Land Transport Co: Amman; joint venture of Govts of Jordan and Iraq; operates 294 trucks.

Jordanian-Syrian Land Transport Co: POB 20686, Amman; tel. (6) 5661134; fax (6) 5669645; internet www.josyco.com.jo; f. 1976; transports goods between ports in Jordan and Syria; operates 390 trucks; Chair. and Gen. Man. HAMDI AL-HABASHNEH.

SHIPPING

The port of Aqaba is Jordan's only outlet to the sea and consists of a main port, container port (540 m in length) and industrial port, with 25 modern and specialized berths. The port has 761,300 sq m of open and contained storage area, and is used for Jordan's international trade and regional transit trade (mainly with Iraq). There is a ferry link between Aqaba and the Egyptian port of Nuweibeh.

Ports Corporation of Aqaba: POB 115, Aqaba 77110; tel. (3) 2014031; fax (3) 2016204; e-mail ports@amra.nic.gov.jo; internet www.nis.gov.jo/portscorp/main.html; Dir-Gen. Capt. MUHAMMAD ED-DALABIEH.

Amman Shipping & Trading Co: POB 213083, 5th Floor, Al-Aqqad Trading Centre, Gardens St, Amman; tel. (6) 5514620; fax (6) 5532324; e-mail admin@astco.jo; internet www.astco.com.jo.

Arab Bridge Maritime Co: POB 989, Aqaba; tel. (3)2016305; fax (3) 2016312; e-mail bridge1@abm.index.com.jo; internet www .arabbridge.com.jo; f. 1988; joint venture by Egypt, Iraq and Jordan to improve economic co-operation; an extension of the company that established a ferry link between Aqaba and the Egyptian port of Nuweibeh in 1985; Chair. Eng. MUHAMMAD N. ALKOUSI; Dir Capt. BASSAM AL-KINJI.

Arrow Trans Shipping SA: POB 213083, 5th Floor, Aqad Complex Bldg, Wasfi at-Tal St, Amman 11121; tel. (6) 5512621; fax (6) 5532324; e-mail arrow@albitar.com; f. 1990; Gen. Man. MARWAN JAMAL ED-DIN BITAR.

Assaf Shipping Co SA: POB 2637, Irbid 21110; tel. (2) 7279117; fax (2) 7261329; e-mail reefer_assaf@yahoo.com.

Tawfiq Gargour & Fils: POB 419, 4th Floor, Da'ssan Commercial Centre, Wasfi at-Tal St, Amman; tel. (6) 5524142; fax (6) 5530512; e-mail tgf@tgf.com.jo; f. 1928; shipping agents and owners; Chair. JOHN GARGOUR; Man. Dir NADIM GARGOUR.

Hijazi & Ghosheh Co: POB 183292, Amman; tel. (6) 4886166; fax (6) 4886211.

International Ship Management Co Ltd (ISM): POB 941430, 2nd Floor, Noor Centre, Islam Abad St, Ar-Rabeiah, Amman 11194; tel. (6) 5512607; fax (6) 5532083; e-mail ism@go.com.jo; Gen. Man. MOUSTAFA MASSAD.

Jordan National Shipping Lines Co Ltd: POB 5406, Nasir Ben Jameel St, Wadi Saqra, Amman 11183; POB 557, Aqaba; tel. (6) 5511500; fax (6) 5515119; e-mail jnl@go.com.jo; internet www.jnsl-jo .com; 75% govt-owned; service from Antwerp, Bremen and Tilbury to Aqaba; daily passenger ferry service to Egypt; land transportation to destinations in Iraq and elsewhere in the region; Chair. MUHAMMAD SMADI; Gen. Man. Eng. AKEF ABU TAYEH.

Amin Kawar & Sons Co WLL: POB 222, 24 Abd al-Hamid Sharaf St, Shmeisani, Amman 11118; tel. (6) 5603703; fax (6) 5672170; e-mail kawar@kawar.com.jo; internet www.kawar.com.jo; chartering, forwarding and shipping line agents; Chair. TAWFIQ A. KAWAR; CEO RUDAIN T. KAWAR; Gen. Man. GHASSOUB F. KAWAR.

Al-Mansour Marine Transportation and Trading Co: POB 960359, Amman; tel. (6) 697958; fax (6) 702352.

Orient Shipping Co Ltd: POB 207, Amman 11118; tel. (6) 5641695; fax (6) 5651567.

Petra Navigation and International Trading Co Ltd: POB 8362, White Star Bldg, King Hussein St, Amman 11121; tel. (6) 5607021; fax (6) 5601362; e-mail petra@armoush.com.jo; internet www.petranav.com.jo; general cargo, ro/ro and passenger ferries; Chair. MAJED ARMOUSH.

Red Sea Shipping Agency Co: POB 1248, 24 Sharif Abd al-Hamid Sharaf St, Shmeisani, Amman 11118; tel. (6) 5609501; fax (6) 5688241; e-mail rss@rssa.com.jo; internet www.aqabashipping.com .jo; f. 1955.

Salam International Transport and Trading Co: King Hussein St, Abdali, Amman 11121; tel. (6) 5607021.

Syrian-Jordanian Shipping Co: POB 148, rue Port Said, Latakia, Syria; tel. (41) 471635; fax (41) 470250; Chair. OSMAN LEBBADI.

PIPELINES

Two oil pipelines cross Jordan. The former Iraq Petroleum Co pipeline, carrying petroleum from the oilfields in Iraq to Haifa, has not operated since 1967. The 1,717-km (1,067-mile) pipeline, known as the Trans-Arabian Pipeline (Tapline), carries petroleum from the oilfields of Dhahran in Saudi Arabia to Sidon on the Mediterranean seaboard in Lebanon. Tapline traverses Jordan for a distance of 177 km (110 miles) and has frequently been cut by hostile action. Tapline stopped pumping to Syria and Lebanon at the end of 1983, when it was first due to close. It was later scheduled to close in 1985, but in September 1984 Jordan renewed an agreement to receive Saudi Arabian crude oil through Tapline. The agreement can be cancelled by either party at two years' notice.

CIVIL AVIATION

There are international airports at Amman and Aqaba. The Queen Alia International Airport at Zizya, 40 km south of Amman, was opened in 1983.

Jordan Civil Aviation Authority (JCAA): POB 7547, Amman; tel. (6) 4891401; fax (6) 4892065; e-mail info@jcaa.gov.jo; internet www.jcaa.gov.jo; f. 1950; Dir-Gen. HANNA NAJJAR.

Royal Jordanian Airline: Head Office: POB 302, Housing Bank Commercial Centre, Shmeisani, Amman 11118; tel. (6) 5607300; fax (6) 5672527; e-mail rj@go.com.jo; internet www.rja.com.jo; f. 1963; privatized in 2001; scheduled and charter services to Middle East, North Africa, Europe, USA and Far East; Chair. WALID ASFOUR; Pres. and CEO SAMER MAJALI.

Arab Wings Co Ltd: POB 341018, Amman 11134; tel. (6) 4893901; fax (6) 4893158; e-mail info@arabwings.com.jo; internet www .arabwings.com.jo; f. 1975; subsidiary of Royal Jordanian; executive jet charter service, air ambulances, priority cargo; Man. Dir AHED QUNTAR.

Royal Wings Co Ltd: POB 314018, Amman 11134; tel. (6) 4875206; fax (6) 4875656; e-mail info@royalwings.com.jo; internet www

.royalwings.com.jo; f. 1996; subsidiary of Royal Jordanian; operates scheduled and charter regional and domestic services; Man. Dir AHED QUNTAR.

Tourism

The ancient cities of Jarash (Jerash) and Petra, and Jordan's proximity to biblical sites, have encouraged tourism. The development of Jordan's Dead Sea coast is currently under way; owing to the Sea's mineral-rich waters, the growth of curative tourism is anticipated. The Red Sea port of Aqaba is also undergoing a major programme of development, with a view to becoming a centre for diving holidays. In 2003 Jordan received some 3.9m. visitors (including pilgrims and excursionists). Income from tourism in 2001 was estimated at JD $496.1m.

Ministry of Tourism and Antiquities: POB 224, Amman 11118; tel. (6) 4642311; fax (6) 4648465; e-mail tourism@mota.gov.jo; internet www.mota.gov.jo; f. 1952; Minister of Tourism and Antiquities and of the Environment Dr ALIA HATTOUGH-BOURAN; Sec.-Gen. SULTAN ABU JABER.

Jordan Tourism Board: POB 830688, Amman 11183; tel. (6) 5678294; fax (6) 5678295; e-mail jtb@nets.com.jo; internet www.see-jordan.com; f. 1997; Gen. Man. MARWAN KHOURY.

INDEX OF INTERNATIONAL ORGANIZATIONS

(Main reference only)

J

The Europa Biographical Reference Series

WHO'S WHO IN INTERNATIONAL AFFAIRS 2005

Invaluable biographical details of the thousands of major figures involved in all aspects of international affairs.

- Over 6,000 entries
- Includes an A-Z guide to international organizations and the officials working in them
- Covers diplomats, politicians, government ministers, heads of state, academics, journalists and writers who are prominent in the world of international affairs.

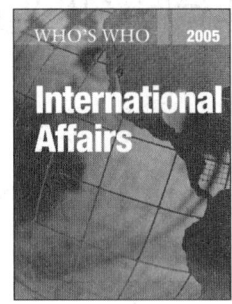

INTERNATIONAL WHO'S WHO OF WOMEN 2006

The most influential and distinguished women throughout the world are brought together in this unique publication.

- Lists recognized personalities as well as those women who are rising to prominence
- Some 6,000 entries are listed
- Easy to use, this one-stop reference source for information on the world's leading women is also indexed by profession.

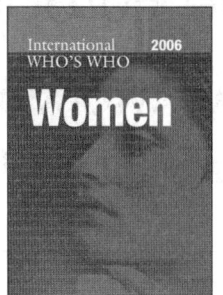

INTERNATIONAL WHO'S WHO IN CLASSICAL MUSIC 2005

An invaluable and practical source of biographical information on classical musicians, composers and conductors and the organizations behind them.

- Over 8,000 detailed biographical entries cover the Classical and Light Classical fields
- Entries include details of career, repertoire, recordings and compositions.

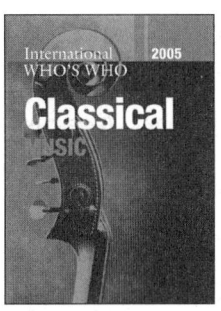

INTERNATIONAL WHO'S WHO IN POETRY 2005

Profiles the careers of leading and emerging poets.

- Over 4,000 biographical entries
- Each entry provides full career history and publication details
- Contact details are provided for poetry organizations, poetry publishers and for organizations that chair poetry awards and prizes.

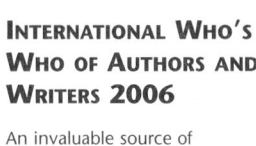

INTERNATIONAL WHO'S WHO IN POPULAR MUSIC 2005

Comprehensive biographical information covering the leading names in all aspects of popular music.

- Over 5,000 entries
- Profiles pop, rock, folk, jazz, dance, world and country artists
- Provides full biographical information: major career details, concerts, recordings and compositions, honours and contact address
- Includes full contact details for companies and organizations throughout the popular music industry.

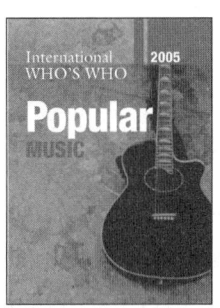

INTERNATIONAL WHO'S WHO OF AUTHORS AND WRITERS 2006

An invaluable source of information on the personalities and organizations of the literary world.

- Over 8,000 entries
- Provides concise biographical information on novelists, authors, playwrights, columnists, journalists, editors and critics
- Each entry details career, works published, literary awards and prizes, membership and contact addresses where available.

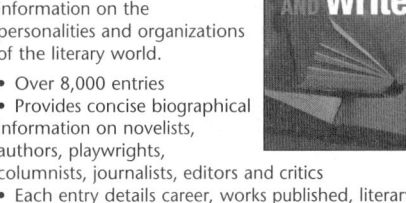

For further information on any of the above titles contact our marketing department on:
tel: + 44 (0) 20 7017 6649
fax: + 44 (0) 20 7017 6720
e-mail: info.europa@tandf.co.uk
web: www.europapublications.com

Routledge
Taylor & Francis Group

The Europa World of Learning ONLINE

www.worldoflearning.com
Available Now